THE NEW STRONG'S EXHAUSTIVE CONCORDANCE OF THE BIBLE

THE NEW STRONG'S EXHAUSTIVE CONCORDANCE OF THE BIBLE

with

—MAIN CONCORDANCE
—APPENDIX TO THE MAIN CONCORDANCE
—TOPICAL INDEX TO THE BIBLE
—DICTIONARY OF THE HEBREW BIBLE
—DICTIONARY OF THE GREEK TESTAMENT

JAMES STRONG, LL.D., S.T.D.

THOMAS NELSON PUBLISHERS
Nashville • Camden • Kansas City

Published in Nashville, Tennessee, by Thomas Nelson, Inc., Publishers and distributed in Canada by Lawson Falle, Ltd., Cambridge, Ontario.

Library of Congress Cataloging in Publication Data

Strong, James, 1822–1894.
New Strong's exhaustive concordance of the Bible.

1. Bible—Concordances, English. 2. Hebrew language—Dictionaries—English. 3. Greek language, Biblical—Dictionaries—English. I. Bible. II. Title III. Title: New exhaustive concordance of the Bible.
BS425.S8 1984 220.5'2033 84-16562
ISBN 0-8407-6750-1

Printed in the United States of America
5 6 7 8 9 10 — 95 94 93

PUBLISHER'S PREFACE

In 1890 Dr. James Strong, Professor of Exegetical Theology at Drew Theological Seminary, published his monumental concordance to the Holy Scriptures. The fruit of 35 years labor by Dr. Strong and more than 100 colleagues, his volume has since become the most widely used concordance ever compiled from the King James Version of the Bible, still the standard English version of the Bible. Assembled without the aid of computers or other electronic devices, *Strong's* has stood the test of time and has confirmed Professor Strong's vision for a complete, simple, and accurate concordance that would become "a permanent standard for purposes of reference."*

The New Strong's Exhaustive Concordance of the Bible improves upon the original volume in a number of significant ways. An entirely new computer-generated typesetting provides an easy-to-read text set in modern type, insures even greater completeness and accuracy than the original edition, gives an opportunity to correct errors that remain to this day in all other editions, and allows for a number of improvements in design and format. Scripture references are placed between the context line and reference number to the Hebrew or Greek Dictionary, making it easier to use all the features of the concordance.

Variant spellings of proper names from modern versions have been cross-referenced into the body of the concordance. This is done so that readers of these versions might be able to use *Strong's* while searching for references to words that do not appear in the King James Version. Thus, the person who uses the Revised Standard Version, the New International Version, or the New American Standard Bible, for instance, and looks up the word *Abronah*—which appears in these versions—will be directed to *Ebronah*—the King James Version spelling.

To further aid the Bible student, entry words that refer to more than one person or place (such as the entry "Joseph," which refers to twelve separate individuals) have been defined, and the content lines have been arranged in biblical order under the proper sub-entry. Furthermore, the Appendix to the Main Concordance has been reset in a new format that allowed for corrections to be made and considerable space to be saved, thus insuring greater accuracy and reduced cost to the student. Finally, over 200 pages of supplemental materials have been added to help the Bible student. These include "The Laws of the Bible," "Teachings and Illustrations of Christ," the comprehensive "Universal Subject Guide to the Bible," a "Harmony of the Gospels," and much more. The dictionaries to the Hebrew and Greek texts have been presented as originally published. No section from the original *Strong's* has been eliminated; new materials have been added and existing materials have been updated and improved.

*from the General Preface to the 1890 Edition

INSTRUCTIONS TO THE READER

The New Strong's Exhaustive Concordance of the Bible enables the reader to locate any Scripture passage in the King James Version, as well as every Hebrew or Greek word behind the English words. The most direct way of using these features is as follows:

1. Beginning with the word you are researching, find that word in the Main Concordance, which lists every occurrence of every word in the Bible. If you are looking for a specific occurrence of that word, you should read the context lines until you find the reference.

2. Each context line has three segments. From left to right, they are: The text of the Scripture in which the reference word appears; the reference to the book, chapter and verse where it may be found; and a reference number to the Hebrew and Greek dictionaries at the back of the concordance. If the reference number is set in Italic type (such as this: *2614*) you should look for it in the Greek Dictionary. If no number appears, the word may have been supplied by the translators to clarify the meaning, even though no specific Hebrew or Greek word was used to express it. In other instances more than one word in the original language was included in the English translations.

ABBREVIATIONS

Old Testament

Gen . . . . Genesis
Ex . . . . Exodus
Lev . . . . Leviticus
Num . . . . Numbers
Deut . . . . Deuteronomy
Josh . . . . Joshua
Judg . . . . Judges
Ruth . . . . Ruth
1Sa . . . . 1 Samuel
2Sa . . . . 2 Samuel
1Kin . . . . 1 Kings
2Kin . . . . 2 Kings
1Chr . . . . 1 Chronicles
2Chr . . . . 2 Chronicles
Ezr . . . . Ezra
Neh . . . . Nehemiah
Est . . . . Esther
Job . . . . Job
Ps . . . . Psalms
Prov . . . . Proverbs
Eccl . . . . Ecclesiastes
Song . . . . Song of Solomon
Is . . . . Isaiah
Jer . . . . Jeremiah
Lam . . . . Lamentations
Eze . . . . Ezekiel
Dan . . . . Daniel
Hos . . . . Hosea
Joel . . . . Joel
Amos . . . . Amos
Obad . . . . Obadiah
Jonah . . . . Jonah
Mic . . . . Micah
Nah . . . . Nahum
Hab . . . . Habakkuk
Zeph . . . . Zephaniah
Hag . . . . Haggai
Zec . . . . Zechariah
Mal . . . . Malachi

New Testament

Mt . . . . Matthew
Mk . . . . Mark
Lk . . . . Luke
Jn . . . . John
Acts . . . . Acts
Rom . . . . Romans
1Cor . . . . 1 Corinthians
2Cor . . . . 2 Corinthians
Gal . . . . Galatians
Eph . . . . Ephesians
Phil . . . . Philippians
Col . . . . Colossians
1Th . . . . 1 Thessalonians
2Th . . . . 2 Thessalonians
1Ti . . . . 1 Timothy
2Ti . . . . 2 Timothy
Titus . . . . Titus
Philem . . . . Philemon
Heb . . . . Hebrews
Jas . . . . James
1Pet . . . . 1 Peter
2Pet . . . . 2 Peter
1Jn . . . . 1 John
2Jn . . . . 2 John
3Jn . . . . 3 John
Jude . . . . Jude
Rev . . . . Revelation

MAIN CONCORDANCE

MAIN CONCORDANCE

A

A See PREFACE.

AARON (*a'-ur-un*) See AARON'S, AARONITES.
First high priest of Israel; brother of Moses.

Is not *A* the Levite thy brother	Ex 4:14	175
And the LORD said to *A*, Go into	Ex 4:27	175
Moses told *A* all the words of the	Ex 4:28	175
A went and gathered together all	Ex 4:29	175
A spake all the words which the	Ex 4:30	175
A went in, and told Pharaoh, Thus	Ex 5:1	175
them, Wherefore do ye, Moses and *A*	Ex 5:4	175
And they met Moses and *A*	Ex 5:20	175
LORD spake unto Moses and unto *A*	Ex 6:13	175
and she bare him *A* and Moses	Ex 6:20	175
A took him Elisheba, daughter of	Ex 6:23	175
These are that *A* and Moses, to	Ex 6:26	175
these are that Moses and *A*	Ex 6:27	175
A thy brother shall be thy	Ex 7:1	175
A thy brother shall speak unto	Ex 7:2	175
A did as the LORD commanded them,	Ex 7:6	175
A fourscore and three years old,	Ex 7:7	175
LORD spake unto Moses and unto *A*	Ex 7:8	175
then thou shalt say unto *A*	Ex 7:9	175
A went in unto Pharaoh, and they	Ex 7:10	175
A cast down his rod before	Ex 7:10	175
LORD spake unto Moses, Say unto *A*	Ex 7:19	175
A did so, as the LORD commanded	Ex 7:20	175
LORD spake unto Moses, Say unto *A*	Ex 8:5	175
A stretched out his hand over the	Ex 8:6	175
Pharaoh called for Moses and *A*	Ex 8:8	175
Moses and *A* went out from Pharaoh	Ex 8:12	175
LORD said unto Moses, Say unto *A*	Ex 8:16	175
for *A* stretched out his hand with	Ex 8:17	175
Pharaoh called for Moses and for *A*	Ex 8:25	175
LORD said unto Moses and unto *A*	Ex 9:8	175
sent, and called for Moses and *A*	Ex 9:27	175
A came in unto Pharaoh, and said	Ex 10:3	175
A were brought again unto Pharaoh	Ex 10:8	175
called for Moses and *A* in haste	Ex 10:16	175
A did all these wonders before	Ex 11:10	175
A in the land of Egypt, saying,	Ex 12:1	175
had commanded Moses and *A*	Ex 12:28	175
A by night, and said, Rise up, and	Ex 12:31	175
And the LORD said unto Moses and *A*	Ex 12:43	175
as the LORD commanded Moses and *A*	Ex 12:50	175
the prophetess, the sister of *A*	Ex 15:20	175
Moses and *A* in the wilderness	Ex 16:2	175
A said unto all the children of	Ex 16:6	175
And Moses spake unto *A*, Say unto	Ex 16:9	175
as *A* spake unto the whole	Ex 16:10	175
And Moses said unto *A*, Take a pot,	Ex 16:33	175
so *A* laid it up before the	Ex 16:34	175
and Moses, *A*, and Hur went up to	Ex 17:10	175
and *A* and Hur stayed up his hands,	Ex 17:12	175
A came, and all the elders of	Ex 18:12	175
come up, thou, and *A* with thee	Ex 19:24	175
Come up unto the LORD, thou, and *A*	Ex 24:1	175
Then went up Moses, and *A*, Nadab,	Ex 24:9	175
and, behold, *A* and Hur are with you	Ex 24:14	175
which is before the testimony, *A*	Ex 27:21	175
take thou unto thee *A* thy brother	Ex 28:1	175
me in the priest's office, even *A*	Ex 28:1	175
for *A* thy brother for glory	Ex 28:2	175
holy garments for *A* thy brother	Ex 28:4	175
A shall bear their names before	Ex 28:12	175
A shall bear the names of the	Ex 28:29	175
A shall bear the judgment of the	Ex 28:30	175
And it shall be upon *A* to minister	Ex 28:35	175
that *A* may bear the iniquity of	Ex 28:38	175
shalt put them upon *A* thy brother	Ex 28:41	175
And they shall be upon *A*, and upon	Ex 28:43	175
And *A* and his sons thou shalt bring	Ex 29:4	175
garments, and put upon *A* the coat	Ex 29:5	175
shalt gird them with girdles, *A*	Ex 29:9	175
and thou shalt consecrate *A*	Ex 29:9	175
and *A* and his sons shall put their	Ex 29:10	175
and *A* and his sons shall put their	Ex 29:15	175
and *A* and his sons shall put their	Ex 29:19	175
the tip of the right ear of *A*	Ex 29:20	175
oil, and sprinkle it upon *A*	Ex 29:21	175
shalt put all in the hands of *A*	Ex 29:24	175
even of that which is for *A*	Ex 29:27	175
the holy garments of *A* shall be	Ex 29:29	175
And *A* and his sons shall eat the	Ex 29:32	175
And thus shalt thou do unto *A*	Ex 29:35	175
I will sanctify also both *A*	Ex 29:44	175
A shall burn thereon sweet	Ex 30:7	175
when *A* lighteth the lamps at even	Ex 30:8	175
A shall make an atonement upon	Ex 30:10	175
For *A* and his sons shall wash	Ex 30:19	175
And thou shalt anoint *A* and his	Ex 30:30	175
holy garments for *A* the priest	Ex 31:10	175
themselves together unto *A*	Ex 32:1	175
A said unto them, Break off the	Ex 32:2	175
ears, and brought them unto *A*	Ex 32:3	175
when *A* saw it, he built an altar	Ex 32:5	175
A made proclamation, and said, To	Ex 32:5	175
And Moses said unto *A*, What did	Ex 32:21	175
A said, Let not the anger of my	Ex 32:22	175
(for *A* had made them naked unto	Ex 32:25	175
they made the calf, which *A* made	Ex 32:35	175
And when *A* and all the children of	Ex 34:30	175
and *A* and all the rulers of the	Ex 34:31	175
holy garments for *A* the priest	Ex 35:19	175
of Ithamar, son to *A* the priest	Ex 38:21	175
and made the holy garments for *A*	Ex 39:1	175
of fine linen of woven work for *A*	Ex 39:27	175
holy garments for *A* the priest	Ex 39:41	175
And thou shalt bring *A* and his sons	Ex 40:12	175
put upon *A* the holy garments	Ex 40:13	175
And Moses and *A* and his sons	Ex 40:31	175
the sons of *A* the priest shall	Lev 1:7	175
the sons of *A* shall sprinkle the	Lev 3:13	175
Command *A* and his sons, saying,	Lev 6:9	175
the sons of *A* shall offer it	Lev 6:14	175
And the remainder thereof shall *A*	Lev 6:16	175
the children of *A* shall eat of it	Lev 6:18	175
This is the offering of *A*	Lev 6:20	175
Speak unto *A* and to his sons,	Lev 6:25	175
dry, shall all the sons of *A* have	Lev 7:10	175
He among the sons of *A*, that	Lev 7:33	175
have given them unto *A* the priest	Lev 7:34	175
the portion of the anointing of *A*	Lev 7:35	175
Take *A* and his sons with him, and	Lev 8:2	175
And Moses brought *A* and his sons,	Lev 8:6	175
and *A* and his sons laid their hands	Lev 8:14	175
and *A* and his sons laid their hands	Lev 8:18	175
and *A* and his sons laid their hands	Lev 8:22	175
the altar, and sprinkled it upon *A*	Lev 8:30	175
and sanctified *A*, and his garments,	Lev 8:30	175
And Moses said unto *A* and to his	Lev 8:31	175
as I commanded, saying, *A*	Lev 8:31	175
So *A* and his sons did all things	Lev 8:36	175
eighth day, that Moses called *A*	Lev 9:1	175
And he said unto *A*, Take thee a	Lev 9:2	175
And Moses said unto *A*, Go unto the	Lev 9:7	175
A therefore went unto the altar,	Lev 9:8	175
the sons of *A* brought the blood	Lev 9:9	175
the right shoulder *A* waved for a	Lev 9:21	175
A lifted up his hand toward the	Lev 9:22	175
A went into the tabernacle of the	Lev 9:23	175
And Nadab and Abihu, the sons of *A*	Lev 10:1	175
Then Moses said unto *A*, This is	Lev 10:3	175
And *A* held his peace	Lev 10:3	175
the sons of Uzziel the uncle of *A*	Lev 10:4	175
And Moses said unto *A*, and unto	Lev 10:6	175
And the LORD spake unto *A*, saying,	Lev 10:8	175
And Moses spake unto *A*, and unto	Lev 10:12	175
the sons of *A* which were left	Lev 10:16	175
A said unto Moses, Behold, this	Lev 10:19	175
the LORD spake unto Moses and to *A*	Lev 11:1	175
LORD spake unto Moses and *A*	Lev 13:1	175
be brought unto *A* the priest	Lev 13:2	175
LORD spake unto Moses and unto *A*	Lev 14:33	175
the LORD spake unto Moses and to *A*	Lev 15:1	175
the death of the two sons of *A*	Lev 16:1	175
Speak unto *A* thy brother, that he	Lev 16:2	175
Thus shall *A* come into the holy	Lev 16:3	175
A shall offer his bullock of the	Lev 16:6	175
A shall cast lots upon the two	Lev 16:8	175
A shall bring the goat upon which	Lev 16:9	175
A shall bring the bullock of the	Lev 16:11	175
A shall lay both his hands upon	Lev 16:21	175
A shall come into the tabernacle	Lev 16:23	175
Speak unto *A*, and unto his sons,	Lev 17:2	175
unto the priests the sons of *A*	Lev 21:1	175
Speak unto *A*, saying, Whosoever	Lev 21:17	175
A the priest shall come nigh to	Lev 21:21	175
And Moses told it unto *A*, and to	Lev 21:24	175
Speak unto *A* and to his sons, that	Lev 22:2	175
of the seed of *A* is a leper	Lev 22:4	175
Speak unto *A*, and to his sons, and	Lev 22:18	175
shall *A* order it from the evening	Lev 24:3	175
A shall number them by their	Num 1:3	175
A took these men which are	Num 1:17	175
A numbered, and the princes of	Num 1:44	175
LORD spake unto Moses and unto *A*	Num 2:1	175
also are the generations of *A*	Num 3:1	175
are the names of the sons of *A*	Num 3:2	175
are the names of the sons of *A*	Num 3:3	175
in the sight of *A* their father	Num 3:4	175
present them before *A* the priest	Num 3:6	175
shalt give the Levites unto *A*	Num 3:9	175
And thou shalt appoint *A* and his	Num 3:10	175
Eleazar the son of *A* the priest	Num 3:32	175
eastward, shall be Moses, and *A*	Num 3:38	175
A numbered at the commandment of	Num 3:39	175
of them is to be redeemed, unto *A*	Num 3:48	175
of them that were redeemed unto *A*	Num 3:51	175
LORD spake unto Moses and unto *A*	Num 4:1	175
A shall come, and his sons, and	Num 4:5	175
And when *A* and his sons have made	Num 4:15	175
office of Eleazar the son of *A*	Num 4:16	175
LORD spake unto Moses and unto *A*	Num 4:17	175
A and his sons shall go in, and	Num 4:19	175
At the appointment of *A* and his	Num 4:27	175
Ithamar the son of *A* the priest	Num 4:28	175
Ithamar the son of *A* the priest	Num 4:33	175
And Moses and *A* and the chief of the	Num 4:34	175
A did number according to the	Num 4:37	175
A did number according to the	Num 4:41	175
A numbered according to the word	Num 4:45	175
of the Levites, whom Moses and *A*	Num 4:46	175
Speak unto *A* and unto his sons,	Num 6:23	175
Ithamar the son of *A* the priest	Num 7:8	175
Speak unto *A*, and say unto him,	Num 8:2	175
And *A* did so	Num 8:3	175
A shall offer the Levites before	Num 8:11	175
shalt set the Levites before *A*	Num 8:13	175
given the Levites as a gift to *A*	Num 8:19	175
And Moses, and *A*, and all the	Num 8:20	175
A offered them as an offering	Num 8:21	175
A made an atonement for them to	Num 8:21	175
of the congregation before *A*	Num 8:22	175
Moses and before *A* on that day	Num 9:6	175
And the sons of *A*, the priests,	Num 10:8	175
A spake against Moses because of	Num 12:1	175
suddenly unto Moses, and unto *A*	Num 12:4	175
of the tabernacle, and called *A*	Num 12:5	175
A looked upon Miriam, and, behold,	Num 12:10	175
A said unto Moses, Alas, my lord,	Num 12:11	175
went and came to Moses, and to *A*	Num 13:26	175
against Moses and against *A*	Num 14:2	175
A fell on their faces before all	Num 14:5	175
LORD spake unto Moses and unto *A*	Num 14:26	175
brought him unto Moses and *A*	Num 15:33	175
against Moses and against *A*	Num 16:3	175
and what is *A*, that ye murmur	Num 16:11	175
the LORD, thou, and they, and *A*	Num 16:16	175
thou also, and *A*, each of you his	Num 16:17	175
the congregation with Moses and *A*	Num 16:18	175
LORD spake unto Moses and unto *A*	Num 16:20	175
Eleazar the son of *A* the priest	Num 16:37	175
which is not of the seed of *A*	Num 16:40	175
against Moses and against *A*	Num 16:41	175
against Moses and against *A*	Num 16:42	175
A came before the tabernacle of	Num 16:43	175
And Moses said unto *A*, Take a	Num 16:46	175
A took as Moses commanded, and ran	Num 16:47	175
A returned unto Moses unto the	Num 16:50	175
the rod of *A* was among their rods	Num 17:6	175
the rod of *A* for the house of	Num 17:8	175
And the LORD said unto *A*, Thou and	Num 18:1	175
And the LORD spake unto *A*, Behold,	Num 18:8	175
And the LORD spake unto *A*, Thou	Num 18:20	175
heave offering to *A* the priest	Num 18:28	175
LORD spake unto Moses and unto *A*	Num 19:1	175
against Moses and against *A*	Num 20:2	175
A went from the presence of the	Num 20:6	175
A thy brother, and speak ye unto	Num 20:8	175
A gathered the congregation	Num 20:10	175
LORD spake unto Moses and *A*	Num 20:12	175
A in mount Hor, by the coast of	Num 20:23	175
A shall be gathered unto his	Num 20:24	175
Take *A* and Eleazar his son, and	Num 20:25	175
strip *A* of his garments, and put	Num 20:26	175
A shall be gathered unto his	Num 20:26	175
Moses stripped *A* of his garments,	Num 20:28	175
A died there in the top of the	Num 20:28	175
congregation saw that *A* was dead	Num 20:29	175
they mourned for *A* thirty days	Num 20:29	175
Eleazar, the son of *A* the priest	Num 25:7	175
Eleazar, the son of *A* the priest	Num 25:11	175
Eleazar the son of *A* the priest	Num 26:1	175
against *A* in the company of Korah	Num 26:9	175
bare unto Amram *A* and Moses	Num 26:59	175
unto *A* was born Nadab, and Abihu,	Num 26:60	175
A the priest numbered, when they	Num 26:64	175
as *A* thy brother was gathered	Num 27:13	175
under the hand of Moses and *A*	Num 33:1	175
A the priest went up into mount	Num 33:38	175
A was an hundred and twenty and	Num 33:39	175
with *A* to have destroyed him	Deut 9:20	175
I prayed for *A* also the same time	Deut 9:20	175
there *A* died, and there he was	Deut 10:6	175
as *A* thy brother died in mount	Deut 32:50	175
and the children of *A* the priest	Josh 21:4	175
Which the children of *A*, being of	Josh 21:10	175
of *A* the priest Hebron with her	Josh 21:13	175
the cities of the children of *A*	Josh 21:19	175
I sent Moses also and *A*, and I	Josh 24:5	175
And Eleazar the son of *A* died	Josh 24:33	175
the son of Eleazar, the son of *A*	Judg 20:28	175
the LORD that advanced Moses and *A*	1Sa 12:6	175
then the LORD sent Moses and *A*	1Sa 12:8	175
A, and Moses, and Miriam	1Chr 6:3	175
The sons also of *A*	1Chr 6:3	175
But *A* and his sons offered upon	1Chr 6:49	175

And these are the sons of *A* ... 1Chr 6:50 175
in their coasts, of the sons of *A* ... 1Chr 6:54 175
to the sons of *A* they gave the ... 1Chr 6:57 175
David assembled the children of *A* ... 1Chr 15:4 175
sons of Amram; *A* and Moses ... 1Chr 23:13 175
A was separated, that he should ... 1Chr 23:13 175
was to wait on the sons of *A* for ... 1Chr 23:28 175
of the sons of *A* their brethren ... 1Chr 23:32 175
the divisions of the sons of *A* ... 1Chr 24:1 175
The sons of *A*; Nadab, and Abihu ... 1Chr 24:1 175
under *A* their father, as the LORD ... 1Chr 24:19 175
their brethren the sons of *A* in ... 1Chr 24:31 175
of the LORD, the sons of *A* ... 2Chr 13:9 175
unto the LORD, are the sons of *A* ... 2Chr 13:10 175
but to the priests the sons of *A* ... 2Chr 26:18 175
the priests the sons of *A* to ... 2Chr 29:21 175
Also of the sons of *A* the priests ... 2Chr 31:19 175
of *A* were busied in offering of ... 2Chr 35:14 175
and for the priests the sons of *A* ... 2Chr 35:14 175
the son of *A* the chief priest ... Ezr 7:5 175
the priest the son of *A* shall be ... Neh 10:38 175
them unto the children of *A* ... Neh 12:47 175
a flock by the hand of Moses and *A* ... Ps 77:20 175
A among his priests, and Samuel ... Ps 99:6 175
and *A* whom he had chosen ... Ps 105:26 175
camp, and *A* the saint of the LORD ... Ps 106:16 175
O house of *A*, trust in the LORD ... Ps 115:10 175
he will bless the house of *A* ... Ps 115:12 175
Let the house of *A* now say ... Ps 118:3 175
bless the LORD, O house of *A* ... Ps 135:19 175
and I sent before thee Moses, *A* ... Mic 6:4 175
wife was of the daughters of *A* ... Lk 1:5 2
Saying unto *A*, Make us gods to go ... Acts 7:40 2
that is called of God, as was *A* ... Heb 5:4 2
be called after the order of *A* ... Heb 7:11 2

AARONITES (*a'-ur-un-ites*) *Priests; Aaron's descendants.*
Jehoiada was the leader of the *A* ... 1Chr 12:27 175
of the *A*, Zadok ... 1Chr 27:17 175

AARON'S (*a'-ur-uns*)
Eleazar *A* son took him one of the ... Ex 6:25 175
but *A* rod swallowed up their rods ... Ex 7:12 175
Abihu, Eleazar and Ithamar, *A* sons ... Ex 28:1 175
that they may make *A* garments to ... Ex 28:3 175
and they shall be upon *A* heart ... Ex 28:30 175
And it shall be upon *A* forehead ... Ex 28:38 175
for *A* sons thou shalt make coats ... Ex 28:40 175
of the ram of *A* consecration ... Ex 29:26 175
And it shall be *A* and his sons' by ... Ex 29:28 175
A sons, shall bring the blood, and ... Lev 1:5 175
A sons, shall lay the parts, the ... Lev 1:8 175
A sons, shall sprinkle his blood ... Lev 1:11 175
bring it to *A* sons the priests ... Lev 2:2 175
of the meat offerings shall be *A* ... Lev 2:3 175
of the meat offering shall be *A* ... Lev 2:10 175
A sons the priests shall sprinkle ... Lev 3:2 175
A sons shall burn it on the altar ... Lev 3:5 175
A sons shall sprinkle the blood ... Lev 3:8 175
but the breast shall be *A* ... Lev 7:31 175
of the anointing oil upon *A* head ... Lev 8:12 175
And Moses brought *A* sons, and put ... Lev 8:13 175
it upon the tip of *A* right ear ... Lev 8:23 175
And he brought *A* sons, and Moses ... Lev 8:24 175
And he put all upon *A* hands ... Lev 8:27 175
A sons presented unto him the ... Lev 9:12 175
A sons presented unto him the ... Lev 9:18 175
And it shall be *A* and his sons' ... Lev 24:9 175
thou shalt write *A* name upon the ... Num 17:3 175
Bring *A* rod again before the ... Num 17:10 175
down upon the beard, even *A* beard ... Ps 133:2 175
A rod that budded, and the tables ... Heb 9:4 2

ABADDON (*ab ad' dun*) *Angel of the Abyss.*
name in the Hebrew tongue is *A* ... Rev 9:11 *3*

ABAGTHA (*ab-ag'-thah*) *Servant of King Ahasuerus.*
Biztha, Harbona, Bigtha, and *A* ... Est 1:10 5

ABANA (*ab-ay'-nah*) *A river in Syria.*
Are not *A* and Pharpar, rivers of ... 2Kin 5:12 71

ABANAH See ABANA.

ABARIM (*ab'-ar-im*) See IJE-ABARIM. *A mountain range in Moab.*
Get thee up into this mount *A* ... Num 27:12 5682
and pitched in the mountains of *A* ... Num 33:47 5682
departed from the mountains of *A* ... Num 33:48 5682
Get thee up into this mountain *A* ... Deut 32:49 5682

ABASE
every one that is proud, and *a* him ... Job 40:11 8213
nor *a* himself for the noise of ... Is 31:4 6031
is low, and *a* him that is high ... Eze 21:26 8213
walk in pride he is able to *a* ... Dan 4:37 8214

ABASED
shall exalt himself shall be *a* ... Mt 23:12 *5013*
exalteth himself shall be *a* ... Lk 14:11 *5013*
that exalteth himself shall be *a* ... Lk 18:14 *5013*
I know both how to be *a*, and I ... Phil 4:12 *5013*

ABASING
Have I committed an offence in *a* ... 2Cor 11:7 *5013*

ABATED
and fifty days the waters were *a* ... Gen 8:3 2637
to see if the waters were *a* from ... Gen 8:8 7043
waters were *a* from off the earth ... Gen 8:11 7043
it shall be *a* from thy estimation ... Lev 27:18 1639
not dim, nor his natural force *a* ... Deut 34:7 5127
Then their anger was *a* toward him ... Judg 8:3 7503

ABBA (*ab'-bah*) *Aramaic for "Father."*
And he said, *A*, Father, all things ... Mk 14:36 5
of adoption, whereby we cry, *A* ... Rom 8:15 5
Son into your hearts, crying, *A* ... Gal 4:6 5

ABDA (*ab'-dah*)
1. Father of Adoniram.
Adoniram the son of *A* was over ... 1Kin 4:6 5653
2. A chief Levite after the exile.
A the son of Shammua, the son of ... Neh 11:17 5653

ABDEEL (*ab'-de-el*) *Father of Shelemiah.*
Azriel, and Shelemiah the son of *A* ... Jer 36:26 5655

ABDI (*ab'-di*)
1. Levite grandfather of Ethan.
the son of Kishi, the son of *A* ... 1Chr 6:44 5660
sons of Merari, Kish the son of *A* ... 2Chr 29:12 5660
2. Married a foreigner while in exile.
Zechariah, and Jehiel, and *A* ... Ezr 10:26 5660

ABDIEL (*ab'-de-el*) *Son of Guni.*
Ahi the son of *A*, the son of Guni ... 1Chr 5:15 5661

ABDON (*ab'-dun*)
1. Levitical city in Asher.
her suburbs, *A* with her suburbs, ... Josh 21:30 5658
suburbs, and *A* with her suburbs, ... 1Chr 6:74 5658
2. A judge of Israel.
after him *A* the son of Hillel, a ... Judg 12:13 5658
And *A* the son of Hillel the ... Judg 12:15 5658
3. A Benjamite in Jerusalem.
And *A*, and Zichri, and Hanan, ... 1Chr 8:23 5658
4. Son of Jehiel.
And his firstborn son *A*, and Zur, ... 1Chr 8:30 5658
And his firstborn son *A*, then Zur, ... 1Chr 9:36 5658
5. Son of Micah.
A the son of Micah, and Shaphan ... 2Chr 34:20 5658

ABED-NEGO (*ab-ed'-ne-go*) *A companion of Daniel in captivity.*
and to Azariah, of *A* ... Dan 1:7 5664
and he set Shadrach, Meshach, and *A* . Dan 2:49 5665
Babylon, Shadrach, Meshach, and *A* ... Dan 3:12 5665
to bring Shadrach, Meshach, and *A* ... Dan 3:13 5665
true, O Shadrach, Meshach, and *A* ... Dan 3:14 5665
Shadrach, Meshach, and *A*, answered .. Dan 3:16 5665
against Shadrach, Meshach, and *A* ... Dan 3:19 5665
to bind Shadrach, Meshach, and *A* ... Dan 3:20 5665
took up Shadrach, Meshach, and *A* ... Dan 3:22 5665
men, Shadrach, Meshach, and *A* ... Dan 3:23 5665
and said, Shadrach, Meshach, and *A* ... Dan 3:26 5665
Then Shadrach, Meshach, and *A* ... Dan 3:26 5665
God of Shadrach, Meshach, and *A* ... Dan 3:28 5665
God of Shadrach, Meshach, and *A* ... Dan 3:29 5665
promoted Shadrach, Meshach, and *A* ... Dan 3:30 5665

ABEL (*a'-bel*)
1. Second son of Adam.
And she again bare his brother *A* ... Gen 4:2 1893
A was a keeper of sheep, but Cain ... Gen 4:2 1893
And *A*, he also brought of the ... Gen 4:4 1893
And the LORD had respect unto *A* ... Gen 4:4 1893
And Cain talked with *A* his brother ... Gen 4:8 1893
rose up against *A* his brother ... Gen 4:8 1893
unto Cain, Where is *A* thy brother ... Gen 4:9 1893
me another seed instead of *A* ... Gen 4:25 1893
from the blood of righteous *A* ... Mt 23:35 *6*
From the blood of *A* unto the ... Lk 11:51 *6*
By faith *A* offered unto God a ... Heb 11:4 *6*
better things than that of *A* ... Heb 12:24 *6*
2. Great stone near Beth-shemesh.
even unto the great stone of *A* ... 1Sa 6:18 59
3. A city in Naphtali.
all the tribes of Israel unto *A* ... 2Sa 20:14 62
besieged him in *A* of Beth-maachah ... 2Sa 20:15 62
shall surely ask counsel at *A* ... 2Sa 20:18 59

ABEL ACACIA GROVE See ABEL-SHITTIM.

ABEL BETH MAACAH See BETH-MAACHAH.

ABEL-BETH-MAACHAH (*a'-bel-beth-ma'-a-kah*) *A city in northern Israel.*
and smote Ijon, and Dan, and *A* ... 1Kin 15:20 62
of Assyria, and took Ijon, and *A* ... 2Kin 15:29 62

ABEL-MAIM (*a'-bel-ma'-im*) *Another name for Abel-beth-maachah.*
and they smote Ijon, and Dan, and *A* .. 2Chr 16:4 66

ABEL-MEHOLAH (*a'-bel-me-ho'-lah*) *A city in Issachar.*
Zererath, and to the border of *A* ... Judg 7:22 65
Jezreel, from Beth-shean to *A* ... 1Kin 4:12 65
Elisha the son of Shaphat of *A* ... 1Kin 19:16 65

ABEL-MIZRAIM (*a'-bel-miz'-ra-im*) *A place east of the Jordan River.*
the name of it was called *A* ... Gen 50:11 67

ABEL-SHITTIM (*a'-bel-shit'-tim*) *A place in Moab.*
even unto *A* in the plains of Moab ... Num 33:49 63

ABEZ (*a'-bez*) *A place in Issachar.*
And Rabbith, and Kishion, and *A* ... Josh 19:20 77

ABHOR
and my soul shall not *a* you ... Lev 26:11 1602
or if your soul *a* my judgments ... Lev 26:15 1602
idols, and my soul shall *a* you ... Lev 26:30 1602
them away, neither will I *a* them ... Lev 26:44 1602
it, and thou shalt utterly *a* it ... Deut 7:26 8581
Thou shalt not *a* an Edomite ... Deut 23:7 8581
thou shalt not *a* an Egyptian ... Deut 23:7 8581
people Israel utterly to *a* him ... 1Sa 27:12 887
and mine own clothes shall *a* me ... Job 9:31 8581
They *a* me, they flee far from me, ... Job 30:10 8581
Wherefore I *a* myself, and repent ... Job 42:6 3988
the LORD will *a* the bloody ... Ps 5:6 8581
I hate and *a* lying ... Ps 119:163 8581
people curse, nations shall *a* him ... Prov 24:24 2194
Do not *a* us, for thy name's sake, ... Jer 14:21 5006
gate, and they *a* him that speaketh ... Amos 5:10 8581
I *a* the excellency of Jacob, and ... Amos 6:8 8374
that *a* judgment, and pervert all ... Mic 3:9 8581
A that which is evil ... Rom 12:9 *655*

ABHORRED
to be *a* in the eyes of Pharaoh ... Ex 5:21 887
things, and therefore I *a* them ... Lev 20:23 6973
because their soul *a* my statutes ... Lev 26:43 1602
he *a* them, because of the ... Deut 32:19 5006
for men *a* the offering of the ... 1Sa 2:17 5006
that thou art *a* of thy father ... 2Sa 16:21 887
he *a* Israel, and reigned over ... 1Kin 11:25 6973
All my inward friends *a* me ... Job 19:19 8581
For he hath not despised nor *a* ... Ps 22:24 8262
he was wroth, and greatly *a* Israel ... Ps 78:59 3988
But thou hast cast off and *a* ... Ps 89:38 3988
insomuch that he *a* his own ... Ps 106:40 8581
he that is *a* of the LORD shall ... Prov 22:14 2194
he hath *a* his sanctuary, he hath ... Lam 2:7 5010
and hast made thy beauty to be *a* ... Eze 16:25 8581
them, and their soul also *a* me ... Zec 11:8 973

ABHORREST
the land that thou *a* shall be ... Is 7:16 6973
thou that *a* idols, dost thou ... Rom 2:22 948

ABHORRETH
So that his life *a* bread, and his ... Job 33:20 2092
the covetous, whom the LORD *a* ... Ps 10:3 5006
he *a* not evil ... Ps 36:4 3988
Their soul *a* all manner of meat ... Ps 107:18 8581
to him whom the nation *a* ... Is 49:7 8581

ABHORRING
they shall be an *a* unto all flesh ... Is 66:24 1860

ABI (*a'-bi*) See ABI-ABLON, ABI-EZER. *Mother of King Hezekiah.*
His mother's name also was *A* ... 2Kin 18:2 21

ABIA (*ab-i'-ah*) See ABIAH, ABIJAH, ABIJAM.
1. A son of Rehoboam.
Rehoboam, *A* his son, Asa his son, ... 1Chr 3:10 29
and Roboam begat *A* ... Mt 1:7 7
and *A* begat Asa ... Mt 1:7 7
2. A priest.
Zacharias, of the course of *A* ... Lk 1:5 7

ABIAH (*ab-i'-ah*) See ABIA.
1. A son of Samuel.
and the name of his second, *A* ... 1Sa 8:2 29
the firstborn Vashni, and *A* ... 1Chr 6:28 29
2. Mother of Ashur.
then *A* Hezron's wife bare him ... 1Chr 2:24 29
3. Son of Becher.
and Omri, and Jerimoth, and *A* ... 1Chr 7:8 29

ABI-ALBON (*ab'-i-al'-bun*) *A "mighty man" of David.*
A the Arbathite, Azmaveth the ... 2Sa 23:31 45

ABIASAPH (*ab-i'-as-af*) See EBI-ASAPH. *A son of Korah.*
Assir, and Elkanah, and *A* ... Ex 6:24 23

ABIATHAR (*ab-i'-uth-ur*) See ABITHAR'S. *High priest during David's reign.*
the son of Ahitub, named *A* ... 1Sa 22:20 54
A shewed David that Saul had ... 1Sa 22:21 54
And David said unto *A*, I knew it ... 1Sa 22:22 54
when *A* the son of Ahimelech fled ... 1Sa 23:6 54
and he said to *A* the priest ... 1Sa 23:9 54
And David said to *A* the priest ... 1Sa 30:7 54
A brought thither the ephod to ... 1Sa 30:7 54
Ahitub, and Ahimelech the son of *A* ... 2Sa 8:17 54
A went up, until all the people ... 2Sa 15:24 54
thy son, and Jonathan the son of *A* ... 2Sa 15:27 54
A carried the ark of God again to ... 2Sa 15:29 54
with thee Zadok and *A* the priests ... 2Sa 15:35 54
tell it to Zadok and *A* the priests ... 2Sa 15:35 54
to *A* the priests, Thus and thus ... 2Sa 17:15 54
to *A* the priests, saying, Speak ... 2Sa 19:11 54
and Zadok and *A* were the priests ... 2Sa 20:25 54
of Zeruiah, and with *A* the priest ... 1Kin 1:7 54
A the priest, and Joab the captain ... 1Kin 1:19 54
of the host, and *A* the priest ... 1Kin 1:25 54
the son of *A* the priest came ... 1Kin 1:42 54
for *A* the priest, and for Joab the ... 1Kin 2:22 54
unto *A* the priest said the king, ... 1Kin 2:26 54
So Solomon thrust out *A* from ... 1Kin 2:27 54
did the king put in the room of *A* ... 1Kin 2:35 54
and Zadok and *A* were the priests ... 1Kin 4:4 54
A the priests, and for the Levites ... 1Chr 15:11 54
Ahitub, and Abimelech the son of *A* ... 1Chr 18:16 54
priest, and Ahimelech the son of *A* ... 1Chr 24:6 54
Jehoiada the son of Benaiah, and *A* ... 1Chr 27:34 54
in the days of *A* the high priest ... Mk 2:26 *8*

ABIATHAR'S (*ab-i'-uth-urs*)
Zadok's son, and Jonathan *A* son ... 2Sa 15:36 54

ABIB (*a'-bib*) See TEL-ABIB. *First month of the Hebrew year.*
day came ye out in the month *A* ... Ex 13:4 24
the time appointed of the month *A* ... Ex 23:15 24
thee, in the time of the month *A* ... Ex 34:18 24
for in the month *A* thou camest ... Ex 34:18 24
Observe the month of *A*, and keep ... Deut 16:1 24
for in the month of *A* the LORD ... Deut 16:1 24

ABIDA (*ab'-id-ah*) See ABIDAH. *A son of Midian.*
Ephah, and Epher, and Henoch, and *A* 1Chr 1:33 28

ABIDAH (*ab'-id-ah*) See ABIDA. *Same as Abida.*
Ephah, and Epher, and Hanoch, and *A* Gen 25:4 28

ABIDAN (*ab'-id-an*) *Son of Gideoni.*
A the son of Gideoni ... Num 1:11 27
shall be *A* the son of Gideoni ... Num 2:22 27
On the ninth day *A* the son of ... Num 7:60 27
offering of *A* the son of Gideoni ... Num 7:65 27
Benjamin was *A* the son of Gideoni ... Num 10:24 27

ABIDE

but we will *a* in the street all	Gen 19:2	3885
young men, *A* ye here with the ass	Gen 22:5	3427
Let the damsel *a* with us a few	Gen 24:55	3427
a with me	Gen 29:19	3427
let thy servant *a* instead of the	Gen 44:33	3427
a ye every man in his place, let	Ex 16:29	3427
Therefore shall ye *a* at the door	Lev 8:35	3427
a with thee all night until the	Lev 19:13	3885
earth, and they *a* over against me	Num 22:5	3427
do ye *a* without the camp seven	Num 31:19	2583
Every thing that may *a* the fire	Num 31:23	935
he shall *a* in it unto the death	Num 35:25	3427
shall *a* in your cities which I	Deut 3:19	3427
Judah shall *a* in their coast on	Josh 18:5	5975
the house of Joseph shall *a* in	Josh 18:5	5975
but *a* here fast by my maidens	Ruth 2:8	1692
the LORD, and there *a* for ever	1Sa 1:22	3427
God of Israel shall not *a* with us	1Sa 5:7	3427
a in a secret place, and hide	1Sa 19:2	3427
unto David, *A* not in the hold	1Sa 22:5	3427
A thou with me, fear not	1Sa 22:23	3427
made also to *a* at the brook Besor	1Sa 30:21	3427
and Israel, and Judah, *a* in tents	2Sa 11:11	3427
to thy place, and *a* with the king	2Sa 15:19	3427
will I be, and with him will I *a*	2Sa 16:18	3427
place for thee to *a* in for ever	1Kin 8:13	3427
a now at home	2Chr 25:19	3427
that ye *a* in the siege in	2Chr 32:10	3427
nor *a* in the paths thereof	Job 24:13	3427
a in the covert to lie in wait	Job 38:40	3427
to serve thee, or *a* by thy crib	Job 39:9	3885
who shall *a* in thy tabernacle	Ps 15:1	1481
I will *a* in thy tabernacle for	Ps 61:4	1481
He shall *a* before God for ever	Ps 61:7	3427
shall *a* under the shadow of the	Ps 91:1	3885
her feet *a* not in her house	Prov 7:11	7937
he that hath it shall *a* satisfied	Prov 19:23	3885
for that shall *a* with him of his	Eccl 8:15	3867
not be able to *a* his indignation	Jer 10:10	3557
If ye will still *a* in this land	Jer 42:10	3427
the LORD, no man shall *a* there	Jer 49:18	3427
there shall no man *a* there	Jer 49:33	3427
so shall no man *a* there, neither	Jer 50:40	3427
Thou shalt *a* for me many days	Hos 3:3	3427
shall *a* many days without a king	Hos 3:4	3427
the sword shall *a* on his cities	Hos 11:6	2342
and who can *a* it	Joel 2:11	3557
and they shall *a*	Mic 5:4	3427
who can *a* in the fierceness of	Nah 1:6	6965
But who may *a* the day of his	Mal 3:2	3557
there *a* till ye go thence	Mt 10:11	*3306*
there *a* till ye depart from that	Mk 6:10	*3306*
house ye enter into, there *a*	Lk 9:4	*3306*
for to day I must *a* at thy house	Lk 19:5	*3306*
him, saying, *A* with us	Lk 24:29	*3306*
on me should not *a* in darkness	Jn 12:46	*3306*
that he may *a* with you for ever	Jn 14:16	*3306*
A in me, and I in you	Jn 15:4	*3306*
itself, except it *a* in the vine	Jn 15:4	*3306*
no more can ye, except ye *a* in me	Jn 15:4	*3306*
If a man *a* not in me, he is cast	Jn 15:6	*3306*
If ye *a* in me, and my words *a*	Jn 15:7	*3306*
a in me, and my words *a* in you	Jn 15:7	*3306*
ye shall *a* in my love	Jn 15:10	*3306*
commandments, and *a* in his love	Jn 15:10	*3306*
it pleased Silas to *a* there still	Acts 15:34	*1961*
come into my house, and *a* there	Acts 16:15	*3306*
that bonds and afflictions *a* me	Acts 20:23	*3306*
Except these *a* in the ship	Acts 27:31	*3306*
if they *a* not still in unbelief,	Rom 11:23	*1961*
If any man's work *a* which he hath	1Cor 3:14	*3306*
good for them if they *a* even as I	1Cor 7:8	*3306*
Let every man *a* in the same	1Cor 7:20	*3306*
he is called, therein *a* with God	1Cor 7:24	*3306*
But she is happier if she so *a*	1Cor 7:40	*3306*
And it may be that I will *a*	1Cor 16:6	*3887*
Nevertheless to *a* in the flesh is	Phil 1:24	*1961*
confidence, I know that I shall *a*	Phil 1:25	*3306*
thee to *a* still at Ephesus	1Ti 1:3	*4357*
Let that therefore *a* in you	1Jn 2:24	*3306*
taught you, ye shall *a* in him	1Jn 2:27	*3306*
And now, little children, *a* in him	1Jn 2:28	*3306*

ABIDETH

all that *a* not the fire ye shall	Num 31:23	935
king, Behold, he *a* at Jerusalem	2Sa 16:3	3427
a on the rock, upon the crag of	Job 39:28	3885
man being in honour *a* not	Ps 49:12	3885
them, even he that *a* of old	Ps 55:19	3427
established the earth, and it *a*	Ps 119:90	5975
cannot be removed, but *a* for ever	Ps 125:1	3427
reproof of life *a* among the wise	Prov 15:31	3885
but the earth *a* for ever	Eccl 1:4	5975
He that *a* in this city shall die	Jer 21:9	3427
but the wrath of God *a* on him	Jn 3:36	*3306*
the servant *a* not in the house	Jn 8:35	*3306*
but the Son *a* ever	Jn 8:35	*3306*
the ground and die, it *a* alone	Jn 12:24	*3306*
of the law that Christ *a* for ever	Jn 12:34	*3306*
He that *a* in me, and I in him, the	Jn 15:5	*3306*
now *a* faith, hope, charity, these	1Cor 13:13	*3306*
we believe not, yet he *a* faithful	2Ti 2:13	*3306*
a a priest continually	Heb 7:3	*3306*
God, which liveth and *a* for ever	1Pet 1:23	*3306*
He that saith he *a* in him ought	1Jn 2:6	*3306*
loveth his brother *a* in the light	1Jn 2:10	*3306*
and the word of God *a* in you	1Jn 2:14	*3306*
doeth the will of God *a* for ever	1Jn 2:17	*3306*
ye have received of him *a* in you	1Jn 2:27	*3306*
Whosoever *a* in him sinneth not	1Jn 3:6	*3306*
loveth not his brother *a* in death	1Jn 3:14	*3306*
And hereby we know that he *a* in us	1Jn 3:24	*3306*
a not in the doctrine of Christ,	2Jn 9	*3306*
He that *a* in the doctrine of	2Jn 9	*3306*

ABIDING

he saw Israel *a* in his tents	Num 24:2	7931
a with her in the chamber	Judg 16:9	3427
liers in wait *a* in the chamber	Judg 16:12	3427
driven me out this day from *a* in	1Sa 26:19	5596
as a shadow, and there is none *a*	1Chr 29:15	4723
country shepherds *a* in the field	Lk 2:8	*63*
And ye have not his word *a* in you	Jn 5:38	*3306*
were in that city *a* certain days	Acts 16:12	*1304*
hath eternal life *a* in him	1Jn 3:15	*3306*

ABIEL (*a'-be-el*)

1. Grandfather of King Saul.

whose name was Kish, the son of *A*	1Sa 9:1	22
father of Abner was the son of *A*	1Sa 14:51	22

2. A "mighty man" of David.

brooks of Gaash, *A* the Arbathite,	1Chr 11:32	22

ABI-EZER (*ab-i-e'-zur*) See ABIEZRITE, JEEZER.

1. A descendant of Manasseh.

and *A* was gathered after him	Judg 6:34	44
better than the vintage of *A*	Judg 8:2	44

ABIEZER

for the children of *A*, and for the	Josh 17:2	44
A the Anethothite, Mebunnai the	2Sa 23:27	44
Hammoleketh bare Ishod, and *A*	1Chr 7:18	44
the Tekoite, *A* the Antothite,	1Chr 11:28	44
ninth month was *A* the Anetothite	1Chr 27:12	44

ABI-EZRITE (*ab-i-ez'-rite*) See ABI-EZRITES. *A descendant of Abiezer.*

that pertained unto Joash the *A*	Judg 6:11	33

ABI-EZRITES (*ab-i-ez'-rites*)

day it is yet in Ophrah of the *A*	Judg 6:24	33
his father, in Ophrah of the *A*	Judg 8:32	33

ABIGAIL (*ab'-e-gul*)

1. A wife of David.

and the name of his wife *A*	1Sa 25:3	26
But one of the young men told *A*	1Sa 25:14	26
Then *A* made haste, and took two	1Sa 25:18	26
when *A* saw David, she hasted, and	1Sa 25:23	26
And David said to *A*, Blessed be	1Sa 25:32	26
And *A* came to Nabal	1Sa 25:36	26
David sent and communed with *A*	1Sa 25:39	26
of David were come to *A* to Carmel	1Sa 25:40	26
A hasted, and arose, and rode upon	1Sa 25:42	26
A the Carmelitess, Nabal's wife	1Sa 27:3	26
A the wife of Nabal the Carmelite	1Sa 30:5	26
A Nabal's wife the Carmelite	2Sa 2:2	26
of *A* the wife of Nabal the	2Sa 3:3	26
Daniel, of *A* the Carmelitess	1Chr 3:1	26

2. Mother of Amasa.

that went in to *A* the daughter of	2Sa 17:25	26
Whose sisters were Zeruiah, and *A*	1Chr 2:16	26
And *A* bare Amasa	1Chr 2:17	26

ABIHAIL (*ab-e-ha'-il*)

1. Head of Levital family of Merari.

of Merari was Zuriel the son of *A*	Num 3:35	32

2. Wife of Abishur.

name of the wife of Abishur was *A*	1Chr 2:29	32

3. Chief of a family of Gad.

the children of *A* the son of Huri	1Chr 5:14	32

4. Descendant of Eliab.

A the daughter of Eliab the son	2Chr 11:18	32

5. Father of Esther.

the daughter of *A* the uncle of	Est 2:15	32
the queen, the daughter of *A*	Est 9:29	32

ABIHU (*a-bi'-hew*) *A son of Aaron.*

and she bare him Nadab, and *A*	Ex 6:23	30
LORD, thou, and Aaron, Nadab, and *A*	Ex 24:1	30
up Moses, and Aaron, Nadab, and *A*	Ex 24:9	30
office, even Aaron, Nadab and *A*	Ex 28:1	30
And Nadab and *A*, the sons of Aaron,	Lev 10:1	30
Nadab the firstborn, and *A*	Num 3:2	30
A died before the LORD, when they	Num 3:4	30
unto Aaron was born Nadab, and *A*	Num 26:60	30
A died, when they offered strange	Num 26:61	30
Nadab, and *A*, Eleazar, and Ithamar	1Chr 6:3	30
Nadab, and *A*, Eleazar, and Ithamar	1Chr 24:1	30
A died before their father, and	1Chr 24:2	30

ABIHUD (*a-bi'-hud*) *A son of Bela.*

Bela were, Addar, and Gera, and *A*	1Chr 8:3	31

ABIJAH (*a-bi'-jah*) See ABIA, ABIJAM.

1. A son of Jeroboam I.

At that time *A* the son of	1Kin 14:1	29

2. A priest during David's reign.

to Hakkoz, the eighth to *A*	1Chr 24:10	29

3. A son of Rehoboam.

which bare him *A*, and Attai, and	2Chr 11:20	29
Rehoboam made *A* the son of	2Chr 11:22	29
A his son reigned in his stead	2Chr 12:16	29
began *A* to reign over Judah	2Chr 13:1	29
And there was war between *A*	2Chr 13:2	29
A set the battle in array with an	2Chr 13:3	29
A stood up upon mount Zemaraim,	2Chr 13:4	29
Jeroboam and all Israel before *A*	2Chr 13:15	29
And *A* and his people slew them with	2Chr 13:17	29
A pursued after Jeroboam, and took	2Chr 13:19	29
strength again in the days of *A*	2Chr 13:20	29
But *A* waxed mighty, and married	2Chr 13:21	29
And the rest of the acts of *A*	2Chr 13:22	29
So *A* slept with his fathers, and	2Chr 14:1	29

4. Mother of King Hezekiah.

And his mother's name was *A*	2Chr 29:1	29

5. A priest in Nehemiah's time.

Meshullam, *A*, Mijamin,	Neh 10:7	29

6. A priest who returned from exile under Zerubbabel.

Iddo, Ginnetho, *A*,	Neh 12:4	29
Of *A*, Zichri	Neh 12:17	29

ABIJAM (*a-bi'-jum*) *Son and successor of King Rehoboam.*

A his son reigned in his stead	1Kin 14:31	38
son of Nebat reigned *A* over Judah	1Kin 15:1	38
Now the rest of the acts of *A*	1Kin 15:7	38
And there was war between *A*	1Kin 15:7	38
And *A* slept with his fathers	1Kin 15:8	38

ABILENE (*ab-i-le'-ne*) *A Roman tetrarchy in northern Palestine.*

and Lysanias the tetrarch of *A*	Lk 3:1	*9*

ABILITY

according to his *a* that vowed	Lev 27:8	5381
They gave after their *a* unto the	Ezr 2:69	3581
We after our *a* have redeemed our	Neh 5:8	1767
such as had *a* in them to stand in	Dan 1:4	3581
man according to his several *a*	Mt 25:15	*1411*
every man according to his *a*	Acts 11:29	*2141*
it as of the *a* which God giveth	1Pet 4:11	*2479*

ABIMAEL (*a-bim'-ah-el*) *A son of Joktan in Arabia.*

And Obal, and *A*, and Sheba,	Gen 10:28	39
And Ebal, and *A*, and Sheba,	1Chr 1:22	39

ABIMELECH (*a-bim'-e-lek*) See ABIMELECH'S.

1. Philistine king in Abraham's time.

A king of Gerar sent, and took	Gen 20:2	40
But God came to *A* in a dream by	Gen 20:3	40
But *A* had not come near her	Gen 20:4	40
Therefore *A* rose early in the	Gen 20:8	40
Then *A* called Abraham, and said	Gen 20:9	40
A said unto Abraham, What sawest	Gen 20:10	40
A took sheep, and oxen, and	Gen 20:14	40
A said, Behold, my land is before	Gen 20:15	40
and God healed *A*, and his wife, and	Gen 20:17	40
all the wombs of the house of *A*	Gen 20:18	40
came to pass at that time, that *A*	Gen 21:22	40
Abraham reproved *A* because of a	Gen 21:25	40
A said, I wot not who hath done	Gen 21:26	40
and oxen, and gave them unto *A*	Gen 21:27	40
A said unto Abraham, What mean	Gen 21:29	40
then *A* rose up, and Phichol the	Gen 21:32	40
Isaac went unto *A* king of the	Gen 26:1	40
that *A* king of the Philistines	Gen 26:8	40
A called Isaac, and said, Behold,	Gen 26:9	40
A said, What is this thou hast	Gen 26:10	40
A charged all his people, saying,	Gen 26:11	40
A said unto Isaac, Go from us	Gen 26:16	40
Then *A* went to him from Gerar, and	Gen 26:26	40

2. Son of Gideon.

him a son, whose name he called *A*	Judg 8:31	40
A the son of Jerubbaal went to	Judg 9:1	40
their hearts inclined to follow *A*	Judg 9:3	40
wherewith *A* hired vain and light	Judg 9:4	40
of Millo, and went, and made *A* king	Judg 9:6	40
in that ye have made *A* king	Judg 9:16	40
upon one stone, and have made *A*	Judg 9:18	40
this day, then rejoice ye in *A*	Judg 9:19	40
if not, let fire come out from *A*	Judg 9:20	40
the house of Millo, and devour *A*	Judg 9:20	40
there, for fear of *A* his brother	Judg 9:21	40
When *A* had reigned three years	Judg 9:22	40
God sent an evil spirit between *A*	Judg 9:23	40
dealt treacherously with *A*	Judg 9:23	40
be laid upon *A* their brother	Judg 9:24	40
and it was told *A*	Judg 9:25	40
and did eat and drink, and cursed *A*	Judg 9:27	40
the son of Ebed said, Who is *A*	Judg 9:28	40
then would I remove *A*	Judg 9:29	40
And he said to *A*, Increase thine	Judg 9:29	40
he sent messengers unto *A* privily	Judg 9:31	40
A rose up, and all the people that	Judg 9:34	40
A rose up, and the people that	Judg 9:35	40
wherewith thou saidst, Who is *A*	Judg 9:38	40
men of Shechem, and fought with *A*	Judg 9:39	40
A chased him, and he fled before	Judg 9:40	40
And *A* dwelt at Arumah	Judg 9:41	40
and they told *A*	Judg 9:42	40
And *A*, and the company that was	Judg 9:44	40
A fought against the city all	Judg 9:45	40
And it was told *A*, that all the	Judg 9:47	40
A gat him up to mount Zalmon, he	Judg 9:48	40
A took an axe in his hand, and cut	Judg 9:48	40
man his bough, and followed *A*	Judg 9:49	40
Then went *A* to Thebez, and	Judg 9:50	40
A came unto the tower, and fought	Judg 9:52	40
men of Israel saw that *A* was dead	Judg 9:55	40
God rendered the wickedness of *A*	Judg 9:56	40
after *A* there arose to defend	Judg 10:1	40
Who smote *A* the son of	2Sa 11:21	40

3. Son of Abiathar the High Priest.

A the son of Abiathar, were the	1Chr 18:16	40

4. Used in title of Psalm 34.

he changed his behaviour before *A*	Ps 34:t	40

ABIMELECH'S (*a-bim'-e-leks*)

which *A* servants had violently	Gen 21:25	40
piece of a millstone upon *A* head	Judg 9:53	40

ABINADAB (*a-bin'-ah-dab*)

1. A Levite of Kirjath-jearim.

into the house of *A* in the hill	1Sa 7:1	41
the house of *A* that was in Gibeah	2Sa 6:3	41
and Uzzah and Ahio, the sons of *A*	2Sa 6:3	41
house of *A* which was at Gibeah	2Sa 6:4	41
a new cart out of the house of *A*	1Chr 13:7	41

2. A brother of David.

Then Jesse called *A*, and made him	1Sa 16:8	41
first born, and next unto him *A*	1Sa 17:13	41
A the second, and Shimma the third	1Chr 2:13	41

3. A son of King Saul.

Philistines slew Jonathan, and *A*	1Sa 31:2	41
Jonathan, and Malchi-shua, and *A*	1Chr 8:33	41
Jonathan, and Malchi-shua, and *A*	1Chr 9:39	41
Philistines slew Jonathan, and *A*	1Chr 10:2	41

4. Father of an officer of Solomon.
The son of A, in all the region ... 1Kin 4:11 41

ABINOAM (*a-bin'-o-am*) *Father of Barak.*
son of A out of Kedesh-naphtali ... Judg 4:6 42
of A was gone up to mount Tabor ... Judg 4:12 42
and Barak the son of A on that day ... Judg 5:1 42
captivity captive, thou son of A ... Judg 5:12 42

ABIRAM (*a-bi'-rum*)
1. A conspirator against Moses.
the son of Levi, and Dathan and A ... Num 16:1 48
And Moses sent to call Dathan and A ... Num 16:12 48
tabernacle of Korah, Dathan, and A ... Num 16:24 48
rose up and went unto Dathan and A ... Num 16:25 48
tabernacle of Korah, Dathan, and A ... Num 16:27 48
A came out, and stood in the door ... Num 16:27 48
Nemuel, and Dathan, and A ... Num 26:9 48
This is that Dathan and A, which ... Num 26:9 48
And what he did unto Dathan and A ... Deut 11:6 48
and covered the company of A ... Ps 106:17 48
2. Son of Hiel the Bethelite.
thereof in A his firstborn ... 1Kin 16:34 48

ABISHAG (*ab'-e-shag*) *An attendant of David.*
found A a Shunammite, and brought ... 1Kin 1:3 49
A the Shunammite ministered unto ... 1Kin 1:15 49
that he give me A the Shunammite ... 1Kin 2:17 49
Let A the Shunammite be given to ... 1Kin 2:21 49
And why dost thou ask A the ... 1Kin 2:22 49

ABISHAI (*ab'-e-shahee*) *David's nephew.*
to A the son of Zeruiah, brother ... 1Sa 26:6 52
A said, I will go down with thee ... 1Sa 26:6 52
A came to the people by night ... 1Sa 26:7 52
Then said A to David, God hath ... 1Sa 26:8 52
And David said to A, Destroy him ... 1Sa 26:9 52
sons of Zeruiah there, Joab, and A ... 2Sa 2:18 52
also and A pursued after Abner ... 2Sa 2:24 52
A his brother slew Abner, because ... 2Sa 3:30 52
into the hand of A his brother ... 2Sa 10:10 52
then fled they also before A ... 2Sa 10:14 52
Then said A the son of Zeruiah ... 2Sa 16:9 52
And David said to A, and to all his ... 2Sa 16:11 52
the hand of A the son of Zeruiah ... 2Sa 18:2 52
And the king commanded Joab and A ... 2Sa 18:5 52
the king charged thee and A ... 2Sa 18:12 52
But A the son of Zeruiah answered ... 2Sa 19:21 52
And David said to A, Now shall ... 2Sa 20:6 52
A his brother pursued after Sheba ... 2Sa 20:10 52
But A the son of Zeruiah ... 2Sa 21:17 52
And A, the brother of Joab, the ... 2Sa 23:18 52
A, and Joab, and Asahel, three ... 1Chr 2:16 52
A the brother of Joab, he was ... 1Chr 11:20 52
A the son Zeruiah slew of the ... 1Chr 18:12 52
unto the hand of A his brother ... 1Chr 19:11 52
fled before A his brother ... 1Chr 19:15 52

ABISHALOM (*a-bish'-ah-lum*) See ABSALOM.
Father of Maachah.
was Maachah, the daughter of A ... 1Kin 15:2 53
was Maachah, the daughter of A ... 1Kin 15:10 53

ABISHUA (*a-bish'-u-ah*)
Son of Phinehas.
begat Phinehas, Phinehas begat A ... 1Chr 6:4 50
A begat Bukki, and Bukki begat ... 1Chr 6:5 50
son, Phinehas his son, A his son ... 1Chr 6:50 50
The son of A, the son of Phinehas ... Ezr 7:5 50
And A, and Naaman, and Ahoah ... 1Chr 8:4 50

ABISHUR (*ab'-e-shur*) *A son of Shammai.*
Nadab, and A ... 1Chr 2:28 51
name of the wife of A was Abihail ... 1Chr 2:29 51

ABITAL (*ab'-e-tal*) *A wife of David.*
fifth, Shephatiah the son of A ... 2Sa 3:4 37
The fifth, Shephatiah of A ... 1Chr 3:3 37

ABITUB (*ab'-e-tub*) *Son of Shahareim.*
And of Hushim he begat A, and ... 1Chr 8:11 36

ABIUD (*a-bi'-ud*) *A descendant of Zerubbabel; ancestor of Jesus.*
And Zorobabel begat A ... Mt 1:13 *10*
and A begat Eliakim ... Mt 1:13 *10*

ABJECTS
the a gathered themselves ... Ps 35:15 5222

ABLE
the land was not a to bear them ... Gen 13:6 5375
if thou be a to number them ... Gen 15:5 3201
me and the children be a to endure ... Gen 33:14 7272
one cannot be a to see the earth ... Ex 10:5 3201
thou art not a to perform it ... Ex 18:18 3201
out of all the people a men ... Ex 18:21 2428
then thou shalt be a to endure ... Ex 18:23 3201
Moses chose a men out of all ... Ex 18:25 2428
Moses was not a to enter into the ... Ex 40:35 3201
if he be not a to bring a lamb ... Lev 5:7
But if he be not a to bring two ... Lev 5:11 5381
if she be not a to bring a lamb ... Lev 12:8
pigeons, such as he is a to get ... Lev 14:22 5381
Even such as he is a to get ... Lev 14:31 5381
whose hand is not a to get that ... Lev 14:32 5381
himself be a to redeem it ... Lev 25:26 5381
But if he be not a to restore it ... Lev 25:28
or if he be a, he may redeem ... Lev 25:49 5381
all that are a to go forth to war ... Num 1:3 3318
all that were a to go forth to ... Num 1:20 3318
all that were a to go forth to ... Num 1:22 3318
all that were a to go forth to ... Num 1:24 3318
all that were a to go forth to ... Num 1:26 3318
all that were a to go forth to ... Num 1:28 3318
all that were a to go forth to ... Num 1:30 3318
all that were a to go forth to ... Num 1:32 3318
all that were a to go forth to ... Num 1:34 3318
all that were a to go forth to ... Num 1:36 3318
all that were a to go forth to ... Num 1:38 3318
all that were a to go forth to ... Num 1:40 3318
all that were a to go forth to ... Num 1:42 3318
all that were a to go forth to ... Num 1:45 3318
I am not a to bear all this ... Num 11:14 3201
for we are well a to overcome it ... Num 13:30 3201
We be not a to go up against the ... Num 13:31 3201
Because the LORD was not a to ... Num 14:16 3201
I shall be a to overcome them ... Num 22:11 3201
am I not a indeed to promote thee ... Num 22:37 3201
all that are a to go to war in ... Num 26:2 3318
I am not a to bear you myself ... Deut 1:9 3201
no man be a to stand before thee ... Deut 7:24 3320
Because the LORD was not a to ... Deut 9:28 3201
no man be a to stand before you ... Deut 11:25 3320
that thou art not a to carry it ... Deut 14:24 3201
Every man shall give as he is a ... Deut 16:17
There shall not any man be a to ... Josh 1:5 3320
then I shall be a to drive them ... Josh 14:12
no man hath been a to stand ... Josh 23:9 5975
what was I a to do in comparison ... Judg 8:3 3201
Who is a to stand before this ... 1Sa 6:20 3201
If he be a to fight with me, and ... 1Sa 17:9 3201
Thou art not a to go against this ... 1Sa 17:33 3201
for who is a to judge this thy so ... 1Kin 3:9 3201
were not a utterly to destroy ... 1Kin 9:21 3201
all that were a to put on armour ... 2Kin 3:21 2296
if thou be a on thy part to set ... 2Kin 18:23 3201
for he shall not be a to deliver ... 2Kin 18:29 3201
men a to bear buckler and sword ... 1Chr 5:18 5375
very a men for the work of the ... 1Chr 9:13 2428
a men for strength for the ... 1Chr 26:8 2428
that we should be a to offer so ... 1Chr 29:14
But who is a to build him an ... 2Chr 2:6
a to receive the burnt offerings ... 2Chr 7:7 3201
so that none is a to withstand ... 2Chr 20:6
they were not a to go to Tarshish ... 2Chr 20:37 6113
a to go forth to war, that could ... 2Chr 25:5
The LORD is a to give thee much ... 2Chr 25:9
a to deliver their lands out of ... 2Chr 32:13 3201
that your God should be a to ... 2Chr 32:14 3201
a to deliver his people out of ... 2Chr 32:15 3201
we are not a to stand without ... Ezr 10:13 3581
we are not a to build the wall ... Neh 4:10 3201
who then is a to stand before me ... Job 41:10
them that they were not a to rise ... Ps 18:38 3201
which they are not a to perform ... Ps 21:11 3201
down, and shall not be a to rise ... Ps 36:12 3201
me, so that I am not a to look up ... Ps 40:12 3201
but who is a to stand before envy ... Prov 27:4
yet shall he not be a to find it ... Eccl 8:17 3201
if thou be a on thy part to set ... Is 36:8 3201
he shall not be a to deliver you ... Is 36:14 3201
thou shalt not be a to put it off ... Is 47:11 3201
so be thou shalt be a to profit ... Is 47:12 3201
not be a to abide his indignation ... Jer 10:10 3201
they shall not be a to escape ... Jer 11:11 3201
he shall not be a to hide himself ... Jer 49:10 3201
from whom I am not a to rise up ... Lam 1:14 3201
their gold shall not be a to ... Eze 7:19 3201
a to live for his righteousness ... Eze 33:12 3201
lambs as he shall be a to give ... Eze 46:5
to the lambs as he is a to give ... Eze 46:11
Art thou a to make known unto me ... Dan 2:26 3546
our God whom we serve is a to ... Dan 3:17 3202
not a to make known unto me the ... Dan 4:18 3202
but thou art a ... Dan 4:18 3546
walk in pride he is a to abase ... Dan 4:37 3202
a to deliver thee from the lions ... Dan 6:20 3202
the land is not a to bear all his ... Amos 7:10 3201
a to deliver them in the day of ... Zeph 1:18 3201
that God is a of these stones to ... Mt 3:9 *1410*
Believe ye that I am a to do this ... Mt 9:28 *1410*
but are not a to kill the soul ... Mt 10:28 *1410*
which is a to destroy both soul ... Mt 10:28 *1410*
He that is a to receive it, let ... Mt 19:12 *1410*
Are ye a to drink of the cup that ... Mt 20:22 *1410*
They say unto him, We are a ... Mt 20:22 *1410*
no man was a to answer him a word ... Mt 22:46 *1410*
I am a to destroy the temple of ... Mt 26:61 *1410*
them, as they were a to hear it ... Mk 4:33 *1410*
not a to speak, until the day ... Lk 1:20 *1410*
That God is a of these stones to ... Lk 3:8 *1410*
If ye then be not a to do that ... Lk 12:26 *1410*
to enter in, and shall not be a ... Lk 13:24 *2480*
is not a to finish it, all that ... Lk 14:29 *2480*
to build, and was not a to finish ... Lk 14:30 *2480*
consulteth whether he be a with ... Lk 14:31 *1415*
not be a to gainsay nor resist ... Lk 21:15 *1410*
no man is a to pluck them out of ... Jn 10:29 *1410*
now they were not a to draw it ... Jn 21:6 *2480*
they were not a to resist the ... Acts 6:10 *2480*
our fathers nor we were a to bear ... Acts 15:10 *2480*
which is a to build you up, and to ... Acts 20:32 *1410*
said he, which among you are a ... Acts 25:5 *1415*
he was a also to perform ... Rom 4:21 *1415*
shall be a to separate us from ... Rom 8:39 *1410*
for God is a to graff them in ... Rom 11:23 *1415*
for God is a to make him stand ... Rom 14:4 *1415*
a also to admonish one another ... Rom 15:14 *1410*
hitherto ye were not a to bear it ... 1Cor 3:2 *1410*
neither yet now are ye a ... 1Cor 3:2 *1410*
not one that shall be a to judge ... 1Cor 6:5 *1410*
to be tempted above that ye are a ... 1Cor 10:13 *1410*
that ye may be a to bear it ... 1Cor 10:13 *1410*
that we may be a to comfort them ... 2Cor 1:4 *1410*
Who also hath made us a ministers ... 2Cor 3:6 *2427*
God is a to make all grace abound ... 2Cor 9:8 *1415*
May be a to comprehend with all ... Eph 3:18 *1840*
Now unto him that is a to do ... Eph 3:20 *1410*
that ye may be a to stand against ... Eph 6:11 *1410*
that ye may be a to withstand in ... Eph 6:13 *1410*
wherewith ye shall be a to quench ... Eph 6:16 *1410*
to the working whereby he is a ... Phil 3:21 *1410*
am persuaded that he is a to keep ... 2Ti 1:12 *1415*
who shall be a to teach others ... 2Ti 2:2 *2425*
never a to come to the knowledge ... 2Ti 3:7 *1410*
which are a to make thee wise ... 2Ti 3:15 *1410*
that he may be a by sound ... Titus 1:9 *1415*
he is a to succour them that are ... Heb 2:18 *1410*
that was a to save him from death ... Heb 5:7 *1410*
Wherefore he is a also to save ... Heb 7:25 *1410*
that God was a to raise him up ... Heb 11:19 *1415*
which is a to save your souls ... Jas 1:21 *1410*
a also to bridle the whole body ... Jas 3:2 *1415*
who is a to save and to destroy ... Jas 4:12 *1410*
a after my decease to have these ... 2Pet 1:15 *2192*
Now unto him that is a to keep ... Jude 24 *1410*
was a to open the book, neither ... Rev 5:3 *1410*
and who shall be a to stand ... Rev 6:17 *1410*
who is a to make war with him ... Rev 13:4 *1410*
no man was a to enter into the ... Rev 15:8 *1410*

ABNER (*ab'-nur*) See ABNER'S. *King Saul's military commander.*
of the captain of his host was A ... 1Sa 14:50 74
Ner the father of A was the son ... 1Sa 14:51 74
the Philistine, he said unto A ... 1Sa 17:55 74
the captain of the host, A ... 1Sa 17:55 74
A said, As thy soul liveth, O ... 1Sa 17:55 74
A took him, and brought him before ... 1Sa 17:57 74
A sat by Saul's side, and David's ... 1Sa 20:25 74
A the son of Ner, the captain of ... 1Sa 26:5 74
but A and the people lay round ... 1Sa 26:7 74
to A the son of Ner, saying ... 1Sa 26:14 74
Answerest thou not, A ... 1Sa 26:14 74
Then A answered and said, Who art ... 1Sa 26:14 74
And David said to A, Art not thou ... 1Sa 26:15 74
But A the son of Ner, captain of ... 2Sa 2:8 74
A the son of Ner, and the servants ... 2Sa 2:12 74
A said to Joab, Let the young men ... 2Sa 2:14 74
A was beaten, and the men of ... 2Sa 2:17 74
And Asahel pursued after A ... 2Sa 2:19 74
nor to the left from following A ... 2Sa 2:19 74
Then A looked behind him, and said ... 2Sa 2:20 74
A said to him, Turn thee aside to ... 2Sa 2:21 74
A said again to Asahel, Turn thee ... 2Sa 2:22 74
wherefore A with the hinder end ... 2Sa 2:23 74
also and Abishai pursued after A ... 2Sa 2:24 74
themselves together after A ... 2Sa 2:25 74
Then A called to Joab, and said ... 2Sa 2:26 74
And A and his men walked all that ... 2Sa 2:29 74
And Joab returned from following A ... 2Sa 2:30 74
that A made himself strong for ... 2Sa 3:6 74
and Ish-bosheth said to A ... 2Sa 3:7 74
Then was A very wroth for the ... 2Sa 3:8 74
So do God to A, and more also ... 2Sa 3:9 74
could not answer A a word again ... 2Sa 3:11 74
A sent messengers to David on his ... 2Sa 3:12 74
Then said A unto him, Go, return ... 2Sa 3:16 74
A had communication with the ... 2Sa 3:17 74
A also spake in the ears of ... 2Sa 3:19 74
A went also to speak in the ears ... 2Sa 3:19 74
So A came to David to Hebron, and ... 2Sa 3:20 74
And David made A and the men that ... 2Sa 3:20 74
A said unto David, I will arise ... 2Sa 3:21 74
And David sent A away ... 2Sa 3:21 74
but A was not with David in ... 2Sa 3:22 74
A the son of Ner came to the king ... 2Sa 3:23 74
behold, A came unto thee ... 2Sa 3:24 74
Thou knowest A the son of Ner ... 2Sa 3:25 74
David, he sent messengers after A ... 2Sa 3:26 74
when A was returned to Hebron ... 2Sa 3:27 74
the blood of A the son of Ner ... 2Sa 3:28 74
and Abishai his brother slew A ... 2Sa 3:30 74
with sackcloth, and mourn before A ... 2Sa 3:31 74
And they buried A in Hebron ... 2Sa 3:32 74
voice, and wept at the grave of A ... 2Sa 3:32 74
And the king lamented over A ... 2Sa 3:33 74
and said, Died A as a fool dieth ... 2Sa 3:33 74
the king to slay A the son of Ner ... 2Sa 3:37 74
heard that A was dead in Hebron ... 2Sa 4:1 74
in the sepulchre of A in Hebron ... 2Sa 4:12 74
unto A the son of Ner, and unto ... 1Kin 2:5 74
A the son of Ner, captain of the ... 1Kin 2:32 74
A the son of Ner, and Joab the son ... 1Chr 26:28 74
of Benjamin, Jaasiel the son of A ... 1Chr 27:21 74

ABNER'S (*ab'-nurs*)
of A men, so that three hundred ... 2Sa 2:31 74

ABOARD
over unto Phenicia, we went a ... Acts 21:2 *1910*

ABODE
he a with him the space of a ... Gen 29:14 3427
But his bow a in strength ... Gen 49:24 3427
of the LORD a upon mount Sinai ... Ex 24:16 7931
because the cloud a thereon ... Ex 40:35 7931
and in the place where the cloud a ... Num 9:17 7931
as long as the cloud a upon the ... Num 9:18 7931
of the LORD they a in their tents ... Num 9:20 2583
when the cloud a from even unto ... Num 9:21 1961
of Israel a in their tents ... Num 9:22 2583
and a at Hazeroth ... Num 11:35 1961
and the people a in Kadesh ... Num 20:1 3427
the princes of Moab a with Balaam ... Num 22:8 3427
Israel a in Shittim, and the ... Num 25:1 3427
So ye a in Kadesh many days ... Deut 1:46 3427
unto the days that ye a there ... Deut 1:46 3427
So we a in the valley over ... Deut 3:29 3427
then I a in the mount forty days ... Deut 9:9 3427
a there three days, until the ... Josh 2:22 3427
that they a in their places in ... Josh 5:8 3427
a between Beth-el and Ai, on the ... Josh 8:9 3427
Gilead a beyond Jordan ... Judg 5:17 7931
sea shore, and a in his breaches ... Judg 5:17 7931
and Israel a in Kadesh ... Judg 11:17 3427
and he a with him three days ... Judg 19:4 3427
a in the rock Rimmon four months ... Judg 20:47 3427
a there till even before God, and ... Judg 21:2 3427

So the woman *a*, and gave her son 1Sa 1:23 3427
while the ark *a* in Kirjath-jearim 1Sa 7:2 3427
them, *a* in Gibeah of Benjamin 1Sa 13:16 3427
(now Saul *a* in Gibeah under a 1Sa 22:6 3427
David *a* in the wilderness in 1Sa 23:14 3427
David *a* in the wood, and Jonathan 1Sa 23:18 3427
a in the wilderness of Maon 1Sa 23:25 3427
two hundred *a* by the stuff 1Sa 25:13 3427
But David *a* in the wilderness, and 1Sa 26:3 3427
for two hundred *a* behind, which 1Sa 30:10 5975
David had *a* two days in Ziklag 2Sa 1:1 3427
So Uriah *a* in Jerusalem that day, 2Sa 11:12 3427
vow while I *a* at Geshur in Syria 2Sa 15:8 3427
him up into a loft, where he *a* 1Kin 17:19 3427
But I know thy *a*, and thy going 2Kin 19:27 3427
there *a* we in tents three days Ezr 8:15 2583
Jerusalem, and *a* there three days Ezr 8:32 3427
But I know thy *a*, and thy going Is 37:28 3427
So Jeremiah *a* in the court of the Jer 38:28 3427
And while they *a* in Galilee Mt 17:22 *390*
Mary *a* with her about three Lk 1:56 *3306*
neither *a* in any house, but in Lk 8:27 *3306*
a in the mount that is called the Lk 21:37 *835*
like a dove, and it *a* upon him Jn 1:32 *3306*
he dwelt, and *a* with him that day Jn 1:39 *3306*
and he *a* there two days Jn 4:40 *3306*
unto them, he *a* still in Galilee Jn 7:9 *3306*
a not in the truth, because there Jn 8:44 *2476*
and there he *a* Jn 10:40 *3306*
he *a* two days still in the same Jn 11:6 *3306*
unto him, and make our *a* with him Jn 14:23 *3438*
where *a* both Peter, and James, and Acts 1:13 *2650*
Judaea to Caesarea, and there *a* Acts 12:19 *1304*
Long time therefore *a* they Acts 14:3 *1304*
there they *a* long time with the Acts 14:28 *1304*
Silas and Timotheus *a* there still Acts 17:14 *5278*
he *a* with them, and wrought Acts 18:3 *3306*
And there *a* three months Acts 20:3 *4160*
where we *a* seven days Acts 20:6 *1304*
brethren, and *a* with them one day Acts 21:7 *3306*
of the seven; and *a* with him Acts 21:8 *3306*
Peter, and *a* with him fifteen days Gal 1:18 *1961*
Erastus *a* at Corinth 2Ti 4:20 *3306*

ABODEST
Why *a* thou among the sheepfolds, Judg 5:16 3427

ABOLISH
And the idols he shall utterly *a* Is 2:18 2498

ABOLISHED
my righteousness shall not be *a* Is 51:6 2865
cut down, and your works may be *a* Eze 6:6 4229
to the end of that which is *a* 2Cor 3:13 *2673*
Having *a* in his flesh the enmity, Eph 2:15 *2673*
Jesus Christ, who hath *a* death 2Ti 1:10 *2673*

ABOMINABLE
or any *a* unclean thing, and eat of Lev 7:21 8263
a with any creeping thing that Lev 11:43 8262
not any one of these *a* customs Lev 18:30 8441
at all on the third day, it is *a* Lev 19:7 6292
not make your souls *a* by beast Lev 20:25 8262
Thou shalt not eat any *a* thing Deut 14:3 8441
for the king's word was *a* to Joab 1Chr 21:6 8581
put away the *a* idols out of all 2Chr 15:8 8251
How much more *a* and filthy is man, Job 15:16 8581
corrupt, they have done *a* works Ps 14:1 8581
are they, and have done *a* iniquity Ps 53:1 8581
out of thy grave like an *a* branch Is 14:19 8581
broth of *a* things is in their Is 65:4 6292
of their detestable and *a* things Jer 16:18 8441
do not this *a* thing that I hate Jer 44:4 8441
neither came there *a* flesh into Eze 4:14 6292
a beasts, and all the idols of the Eze 8:10 8263
hast committed more *a* than they Eze 16:52 8581
and the scant measure that is *a* Mic 6:10 2194
I will cast *a* filth upon thee, and Nah 3:6 8251
in works they deny him, being *a* Titus 1:16 *947*
banquetings, and *a* idolatries 1Pet 4:3 *111*
fearful, and unbelieving, and the *a* Rev 21:8 *948*

ABOMINABLY
he did very *a* in following idols, 1Kin 21:26 8581

ABOMINATION
for that is an *a* unto the Gen 43:32 8441
is an *a* unto the Egyptians Gen 46:34 8441
for we shall sacrifice the *a* of Ex 8:26 8441
shall we sacrifice the *a* of the Ex 8:26 8441
it shall be an *a*, and the soul Lev 7:18 6292
they shall be an *a* unto you Lev 11:10 8263
They shall be even an *a* unto you Lev 11:11 8263
ye shall have their carcases in *a* Lev 11:11 8262
that shall be an *a* unto you Lev 11:12 8263
shall have in *a* among the fowls Lev 11:13 8262
shall not be eaten, they are an *a* Lev 11:13 8263
all four, shall be an *a* unto you Lev 11:20 8263
four feet, shall be an *a* unto you Lev 11:23 8263
upon the earth shall be an *a* Lev 11:41 8263
for they are an *a* Lev 11:42 8263
with womankind: it is *a* Lev 18:22 8441
both of them have committed an *a* Lev 20:13 8441
for it is an *a* to the LORD thy Deut 7:25 8441
thou bring an *a* into thine house Deut 7:26 8441
for every *a* to the LORD, which he Deut 12:31 8441
that such *a* is wrought among you Deut 13:14 8441
for that is an *a* unto the LORD Deut 17:1 8441
that such *a* is wrought in Israel Deut 17:4 8441
things are an *a* unto the LORD Deut 18:12 8441
do so are *a* unto the LORD thy God Deut 22:5 8441
these are *a* unto the LORD thy God Deut 23:18 8441
for that is *a* before the LORD Deut 24:4 8441
are an *a* unto the LORD thy God Deut 25:16 8441
an *a* unto the LORD, the work of Deut 27:15 8441
was had in *a* with the Philistines 1Sa 13:4 887
Milcom the *a* of the Ammonites 1Kin 11:5 8251
the *a* of Moab, in the hill that 1Kin 11:7 8251
the *a* of the children of Ammon 1Kin 11:7 8251
Ashtoreth the *a* of the Zidonians 2Kin 23:13 8251
for Chemosh the *a* of the Moabites 2Kin 23:13 8251
for Milcom the *a* of the children 2Kin 23:13 8441
thou hast made me an *a* unto them Ps 88:8 8441
For the froward is *a* to the LORD Prov 3:32 8441
yea, seven are an *a* unto him Prov 6:16 8441
and wickedness is an *a* to my lips Prov 8:7 8441
A false balance is *a* to the LORD Prov 11:1 8441
a froward heart are *a* to the LORD Prov 11:20 8441
Lying lips are *a* to the LORD Prov 12:22 8441
but it is *a* to fools to depart Prov 13:19 8441
of the wicked is an *a* to the LORD Prov 15:8 8441
the wicked is an *a* unto the LORD Prov 15:9 8441
the wicked are an *a* to the LORD Prov 15:26 8441
in heart is an *a* to the LORD Prov 16:5 8441
It is an *a* to kings to commit Prov 16:12 8441
even they both are *a* to the LORD Prov 17:15 8441
of them are alike *a* to the LORD Prov 20:10 8441
weights are an *a* unto the LORD Prov 20:23 8441
The sacrifice of the wicked is *a* Prov 21:27 8441
and the scorner is an *a* to men Prov 24:9 8441
law, even his prayer shall be *a* Prov 28:9 8441
An unjust man is an *a* to the just Prov 29:27 8441
in the way is *a* to the wicked Prov 29:27 8441
incense is an *a* unto me Is 1:13 8441
an *a* is he that chooseth you Is 41:24 8441
I make the residue thereof an *a* Is 44:19 8441
eating swine's flesh, and the *a* Is 66:17 8263
land, and made mine heritage an *a* Jer 2:7 8441
ashamed when they had committed *a* Jer 6:15 8441
ashamed when they had committed *a* Jer 8:12 8441
mind, that they should do this *a* Jer 32:35 8441
haughty, and committed *a* before me Eze 16:50 8441
to the idols, hath committed *a* Eze 18:12 8441
one hath committed *a* with his Eze 22:11 8441
stand upon your sword, ye work *a* Eze 33:26 8441
place the *a* that maketh desolate Dan 11:31 8251
the *a* that maketh desolate set up Dan 12:11 8251
an *a* is committed in Israel and in Mal 2:11 8441
shall see the *a* of desolation Mt 24:15 *946*
ye shall see the *a* of desolation Mk 13:14 *946*
men is *a* in the sight of God Lk 16:15 *946*
neither whatsoever worketh *a* Rev 21:27 *946*

ABOMINATIONS
shall not commit any of these *a* Lev 18:26 8441
(For all these *a* have the men of Lev 18:27 8441
shall commit any of these *a* Lev 18:29 8441
do after the *a* of those nations Deut 18:9 8441
because of these *a* the LORD thy Deut 18:12 8441
you not to do after all their *a* Deut 20:18 8441
And ye have seen their *a*, and their Deut 29:17 8251
with *a* provoked they him to anger Deut 32:16 8441
a of the nations which the LORD 1Kin 14:24 8441
according to the *a* of the heathen 2Kin 16:3 8441
after the *a* of the heathen, whom 2Kin 21:2 8441
king of Judah hath done these *a* 2Kin 21:11 8441
all the *a* that were spied in the 2Kin 23:24 8251
after the *a* of the heathen whom 2Chr 28:3 8441
like unto the *a* of the heathen, 2Chr 33:2 8441
Josiah took away all the *a* out of 2Chr 34:33 8441
his *a* which he did, and that which 2Chr 36:8 8441
after all the *a* of the heathen 2Chr 36:14 8441
lands, doing according to their *a* Ezr 9:1 8441
people of the lands, with their *a* Ezr 9:11 8441
with the people of these *a* Ezr 9:14 8441
there are seven *a* in his heart Prov 26:25 8441
their soul delighteth in their *a* Is 66:3 8251
put away thine *a* out of my sight Jer 4:1 8251
are delivered to do all these *a* Jer 7:10 8441
they have set their *a* in the Jer 7:30 8251
thine *a* on the hills in the Jer 13:27 8251
But they set their *a* in the house Jer 32:34 8251
because of the *a* which ye have Jer 44:22 8441
the like, because of all thine *a* Eze 5:9 8441
things, and with all thine *a* Eze 5:11 8441
have committed in all their *a* Eze 6:9 8441
Alas for all the evil *a* of the Eze 6:11 8441
recompense upon thee all thine *a* Eze 7:3 8441
thine *a* shall be in the midst of Eze 7:4 8441
recompense thee for all thine *a* Eze 7:8 8441
thine *a* that are in the midst of Eze 7:9 8441
they made the images of their *a* Eze 7:20 8441
even the great *a* that the house Eze 8:6 8441
and thou shalt see greater *a* Eze 8:6 8441
the wicked *a* that they do here Eze 8:9 8441
shalt see greater *a* that they do Eze 8:13 8441
shalt see greater *a* than these Eze 8:15 8441
the *a* which they commit here Eze 8:17 8441
that cry for all the *a* that be Eze 9:4 8441
all the *a* thereof from thence Eze 11:18 8441
detestable things and their *a* Eze 11:21 8441
a among the heathen whither they Eze 12:16 8441
away your faces from all your *a* Eze 14:6 8441
cause Jerusalem to know her *a* Eze 16:2 8441
And in all thine *a* and thy Eze 16:22 8441
and with all the idols of thy *a* Eze 16:36 8441
this lewdness above all thine *a* Eze 16:43 8441
ways, nor done after their *a* Eze 16:47 8441
multiplied thine *a* more than they Eze 16:51 8441
all thine *a* which thou hast done Eze 16:51 8441
borne thy lewdness and thine *a* Eze 16:58 8441
he hath done all these *a* Eze 18:13 8441
the *a* that the wicked man doeth Eze 18:24 8441
to know the *a* of their fathers Eze 20:4 8441
away every man the *a* of his eyes Eze 20:7 8251
man cast away the *a* of their eyes Eze 20:8 8251
commit ye whoredom after their *a* Eze 20:30 8251
thou shalt shew her all her *a* Eze 22:2 8441
yea, declare unto them their *a* Eze 23:36 8441
their *a* which they have committed Eze 33:29 8441
for your iniquities and for your *a* Eze 36:31 8441
their *a* that they have committed Eze 43:8 8441
let it suffice you of all your *a* Eze 44:6 8441
my covenant because of all your *a* Eze 44:7 8441
their *a* which they have committed Eze 44:13 8441
for the overspreading of *a* he Dan 9:27 8251
their *a* were according as they Hos 9:10 8251
his *a* from between his teeth Zec 9:7 8251
golden cup in her hand full of *a* Rev 17:4 *946*
AND A OF THE EARTH Rev 17:5 *946*

ABOUND
man shall *a* with blessings Prov 28:20 7227
And because iniquity shall *a* Mt 24:12 *4129*
entered, that the offence might *a* Rom 5:20 *4121*
abounded, grace did much more *a* Rom 5:20 *5248*
continue in sin, that grace may *a* Rom 6:1 *4121*
believing, that ye may *a* in hope Rom 15:13 *4052*
the sufferings of Christ *a* in us 2Cor 1:5 *4052*
as ye *a* in every thing, in faith, 2Cor 8:7 *4052*
see that ye *a* in this grace also 2Cor 8:7 *4052*
to make all grace *a* toward you 2Cor 9:8 *4052*
things, may *a* to every good work 2Cor 9:8 *4052*
that your love may *a* yet more Phil 1:9 *4052*
to be abased, and I know how to *a* Phil 4:12 *4052*
full and to be hungry, both to *a* Phil 4:12 *4052*
fruit that may *a* to your account Phil 4:17 *4121*
But I have all, and *a* Phil 4:18 *4052*
a in love one toward another, and 1Th 3:12 *4052*
to please God, so ye would *a* more 1Th 4:1 *4052*
if these things be in you, and *a* 2Pet 1:8 *4121*

ABOUNDED
a through my lie unto his glory Rom 3:7 *4052*
Jesus Christ, hath *a* unto many Rom 5:15 *4052*
But where sin *a*, grace did much Rom 5:20 *4121*
their deep poverty *a* unto the 2Cor 8:2 *4052*
Wherein he hath *a* toward us in Eph 1:8 *4052*

ABOUNDETH
a furious man *a* in transgression Prov 29:22 7227
our consolation also *a* by Christ 2Cor 1:5 *4052*
of you all toward each other *a* 2Th 1:3 *4121*

ABOUNDING
were no fountains *a* with water Prov 8:24 3513
always *a* in the work of the Lord, 1Cor 15:58 *4052*
a therein with thanksgiving Col 2:7 *4052*

ABOUT
were in all the borders round *a* Gen 23:17
the cities that were round *a* them Gen 35:5
your sheaves stood round *a* Gen 37:7
it came to pass *a* three months Gen 38:24
And it came to pass *a* this time Gen 39:11
shewed Pharaoh what he is *a* to do Gen 41:25
What God is *a* to do he sheweth Gen 41:28
and put a gold chain *a* his neck Gen 41:42 5921
which was round *a* every city Gen 41:48
And he turned himself *a* from them Gen 42:24
been *a* cattle from our youth even Gen 46:34
a the river for water to drink Ex 7:24
to morrow *a* this time I will Ex 9:18
A midnight will I go out into the Ex 11:4
a six hundred thousand on foot Ex 12:37
But God led the people *a*, through Ex 13:18 5437
the dew lay round *a* the host Ex 16:13
bounds unto the people round *a* Ex 19:12
saying, Set bounds *a* the mount Ex 19:23 854
upon it a crown of gold round *a* Ex 25:11
thereto a crown of gold round *a* Ex 25:24
border of an hand breadth round *a* Ex 25:25
to the border thereof round *a* Ex 25:25
All the pillars round *a* the court Ex 27:17
woven work round *a* the hole of it Ex 28:32
scarlet, round *a* the hem thereof Ex 28:33
of gold between them round *a* Ex 28:33
upon the hem of the robe round *a* Ex 28:34
it round *a* upon the altar Ex 29:16
the blood upon the altar round *a* Ex 29:20
and the sides thereof round *a* Ex 30:3
unto it a crown of gold round *a* Ex 30:3
that day *a* three thousand men Ex 32:28
a crown of gold to it round *a* Ex 37:2
thereunto a crown of gold round *a* Ex 37:11
border of an handbreadth round *a* Ex 37:12
for the border thereof round *a* Ex 37:12
it, and the sides thereof round *a* Ex 37:26
unto it a crown of gold round *a* Ex 37:26
round *a* were of fine twined linen Ex 38:16
and of the court round *a*, were of Ex 38:20
the sockets of the court round *a* Ex 38:31
all the pins of the court round *a* Ex 38:31
with a band round *a* the hole Ex 39:23
round *a* between the pomegranates Ex 39:25
round *a* the hem of the robe to Ex 39:26
shalt set up the court round *a* Ex 40:8
the court round *a* the tabernacle Ex 40:33
sprinkle the blood round *a* upon Lev 1:5
his blood round *a* upon the altar Lev 1:11
the blood upon the altar round *a* Lev 3:2
thereof round *a* upon the altar Lev 3:8
thereof upon the altar round *a* Lev 3:13
Or all that *a* which he hath sworn Lev 6:5 5921
sprinkle round *a* upon the altar Lev 7:2
the altar round *a* with his finger Lev 8:15
the blood upon the altar round *a* Lev 8:19
the blood upon the altar round *a* Lev 8:24
sprinkled round *a* upon the altar Lev 9:12
sprinkled upon the altar round *a* Lev 9:18
to be scraped within round *a* Lev 14:41
the horns of the altar round *a* Lev 16:18
which have no wall round *a* them Lev 25:31
the heathen that are round *a* you Lev 25:44
encamp round *a* the tabernacle Num 1:50
a the tabernacle of testimony Num 1:53
far off *a* the tabernacle of the Num 2:2 5439

and by the altar round *a*, and the Num 3:26
the pillars of the court round *a* Num 3:37
a the most holy things Num 4:4
wherewith they minister *a* it Num 4:14 5921
and by the altar round *a*, and their Num 4:26
the pillars of the court round *a* Num 4:32
And the people went *a*, and gathered Num 11:8 7751
set them round *a* the tabernacle Num 11:24
round *a* the camp, and as it were Num 11:31
for themselves round *a* the camp Num 11:32
Get you up from *a* the tabernacle Num 16:24 5439
all Israel that were round *a* them Num 16:34
that died *a* the matter of Korah Num 16:49 5921
lick up all that are round *a* us Num 22:4
the cities of the country round *a* Num 32:33
with the coasts thereof round *a* Num 34:12
for the cities round *a* them Num 35:2
outward a thousand cubits round *a* Num 35:4
the people which are round *a* you Deut 6:14
from all your enemies round *a* Deut 12:10
the people which are round *a* you Deut 13:7
as all the nations that are *a* me Deut 17:14 5439
are round *a* him that is slain Deut 21:2
from all thine enemies round *a* Deut 25:19
their imagination which they go *a* Deut 31:21 6213
he led him *a*, he instructed him, Deut 32:10 5437
it came to pass *a* the time of Josh 2:5
a two thousand cubits by measure Josh 3:4
A forty thousand prepared for war Josh 4:13
war, and go round *a* the city once Josh 6:3
the city, going *a* it once Josh 6:11 5362
that they rose early *a* the Josh 6:15
but let *a* two or three thousand Josh 7:3
the people *a* three thousand men Josh 7:4
men of Ai smote of them *a* thirty Josh 7:5
he took *a* five thousand men, and Josh 8:12
not to go down *a* a whole day Josh 10:13
for to morrow *a* this time will I Josh 11:6
a according to their families Josh 15:12
the border went *a* eastward unto Josh 16:6 5437
by the coasts thereof round *a* Josh 18:20
a these cities to Baalath-beer Josh 19:8
the suburbs thereof round *a* it Josh 21:11
with their suburbs round *a* them Josh 21:42
the LORD gave them rest round *a* Josh 21:44
from all their enemies round *a* Josh 23:1
the people that were round *a* them Judg 2:12
hands of their enemies round *a* Judg 2:14
at that time *a* ten thousand men Judg 3:29
man in his place round *a* the camp Judg 7:21
a fifteen thousand men, all that Judg 8:10
that were *a* their camels' necks Judg 8:26
a a thousand men and women Judg 9:49
the roof *a* three thousand men Judg 16:27
a which thou cursedst, and spakest Judg 17:2
Belial, beset the house round *a* Judg 19:22
house round *a* upon me by night Judg 20:5
set liers in wait round *a* Gibeah Judg 20:29
the field, *a* thirty men of Israel Judg 20:31
men of Israel *a* thirty persons Judg 20:39
inclosed the Benjamites round *a* Judg 20:43 3803
and they dwelled there *a* ten years Ruth 1:4
all the city was moved *a* them Ruth 1:19 5921
it was *a* an ephah of barley Ruth 2:17
when the time was come *a* after 1Sa 1:20
in the field *a* four thousand men 1Sa 4:2
a the time of her death the women 1Sa 4:20
of Israel be carried *a* unto Gath 1Sa 5:8 5437
of the God of Israel *a* thither 1Sa 5:8 5437
that, after they had carried it *a* 1Sa 5:9 5437
They have brought *a* the ark of 1Sa 5:10 5437
for *a* this time ye shall find him 1Sa 9:13
To morrow *a* this time I will send 1Sa 9:16
which were *a* thirty persons 1Sa 9:22
it came to pass *a* the spring of 1Sa 9:26
with him, *a* six hundred men 1Sa 13:15
with him were *a* six hundred men 1Sa 14:2
was *a* twenty men, within as it 1Sa 14:14
the camp from the country round *a* 1Sa 14:21
set him up a place, and is gone *a* 1Sa 15:12 5437
And as Samuel turned *a* to go away 1Sa 15:27 5437
And when the Philistine looked *a* 1Sa 17:42 5027
my father *a* to morrow any time 1Sa 20:12
kept from us *a* these three days 1Sa 21:5
were with him *a* four hundred men 1Sa 22:2
his servants were standing *a* him 1Sa 22:6 5921
his servants that stood *a* him 1Sa 22:7 5921
unto the footmen that stood *a* him 1Sa 22:17 5921
which were *a* six hundred, arose 1Sa 23:13
and his men round *a* to take them 1Sa 23:26
up after David *a* four hundred men 1Sa 25:13
it came to pass *a* ten days after 1Sa 25:38
and the people pitched round *a* him 1Sa 26:5
and the people lay round *a* him 1Sa 26:7
land of the Philistines round *a* 1Sa 31:9
to bring *a* all Israel unto thee 2Sa 3:12 5437
came *a* the heat of the day to the 2Sa 4:5
And David built round *a* from Millo 2Sa 5:9
rest round *a* from all his enemies 2Sa 7:1
To fetch *a* this form of speech 2Sa 14:20 5437
bare Joab's armour compassed *a* 2Sa 18:15 5437
Jairite was a chief ruler *a* David 2Sa 20:26
sorrows of hell compassed me *a* 2Sa 22:6 5437
darkness pavilions round *a* him 2Sa 22:12
came to Dan-jaan, and *a* to Zidon, 2Sa 24:6 5439
his girdle that was *a* his loins 1Kin 2:5
howbeit the kingdom is turned *a* 1Kin 2:15 5437
and the wall of Jerusalem round *a* 1Kin 3:1
peace on all sides round *a* him 1Kin 4:24
fame was in all nations round *a* 1Kin 4:31
which were *a* him on every side 1Kin 5:3 5437
house he built chambers round *a* 1Kin 6:5
the walls of the house round *a* 1Kin 6:5
and he made chambers round *a* 1Kin 6:5
he made narrowed rests round *a* 1Kin 6:6
round *a* with carved figures of 1Kin 6:29 4524
the great court round *a* was with 1Kin 7:12
did compass either of them *a* 1Kin 7:15 5437
two rows round *a* upon the one 1Kin 7:18
round *a* upon the other chapiter 1Kin 7:20
it was round all *a*, and his height 1Kin 7:23
cubits did compass it round *a* 1Kin 7:23
under the brim of it round *a* 1Kin 7:24
cubit, compassing the sea round *a* 1Kin 7:24
every one, and additions round *a* 1Kin 7:36
And the king turned his face *a* 1Kin 8:14
and he made a trench *a* the altar 1Kin 18:32 5439
the water ran round *a* the altar 1Kin 18:35
of them by to morrow *a* this time 1Kin 19:2
unto thee to morrow *a* this time 1Kin 20:6
a four hundred men, and said unto 1Kin 22:6
throughout the host *a* the going 1Kin 22:36
a girdle of leather *a* his loins 2Kin 1:8
howbeit the slingers went *a* it 2Kin 3:25 5437
A this season, according to the 2Kin 4:16
by night, and compassed the city *a* 2Kin 6:14 5362
chariots of fire round *a* Elisha 2Kin 6:17
To morrow *a* this time shall a 2Kin 7:1
shall be to morrow *a* this time in 2Kin 7:18
Edomites which compassed him *a* 2Kin 8:21 413
the house of the LORD *a* the king 2Kin 11:7 413
ye shall compass the king round *a* 2Kin 11:8
round *a* the king, from the right 2Kin 11:11 5921
heathen that were round *a* them 2Kin 17:15
in the places round *a* Jerusalem 2Kin 23:5
built forts against it round *a* 2Kin 25:1
were against the city round *a* 2Kin 25:4
the walls of Jerusalem round *a* 2Kin 25:10
upon the chapiter round *a* 2Kin 25:17
that were round *a* the same cities 1Chr 4:33
and the suburbs thereof round *a* it 1Chr 6:55
lodged round *a* the house of God 1Chr 9:27
land of the Philistines round *a* 1Chr 10:9
And he built the city round *a* 1Chr 11:8
even from Millo round *a* 1Chr 11:8
he instructed *a* the song, because 1Chr 15:22
of David were chief *a* the king 1Chr 18:17
rest from all his enemies round *a* 1Chr 22:9
and of all the chambers round *a* 1Chr 28:12
for the house which I am *a* to 2Chr 2:9
cubits did compass it round *a* 2Chr 4:2
which did compass it round *a* 2Chr 4:3
cubit, compassing the sea round *a* 2Chr 4:3
ambushment to come *a* behind them 2Chr 13:13 5437
make *a* them walls, and towers, 2Chr 14:7 5437
all the cities round *a* Gerar 2Chr 14:14
the LORD gave them rest round *a* 2Chr 15:15
went *a* throughout all the cities 2Chr 17:9 5437
the lands that were round *a* Judah 2Chr 17:10
they compassed *a* him to fight 2Chr 18:31
a the time of the sun going down 2Chr 18:34
for his God gave him rest round *a* 2Chr 20:30
And they went *a* in Judah, and 2Chr 23:2 5437
shall compass the king round *a* 2Chr 23:7
the temple, by the king round *a* 2Chr 23:10
Ashdod, and built cities *a* Ashdod 2Chr 26:6
fish gate, and compassed *a* Ophel 2Chr 33:14
with their mattocks round *a* 2Chr 34:6
all they that were *a* them Ezr 1:6 5439
were employed *a* this matter Ezr 10:15 5921
among the heathen that are *a* us Neh 5:17
that were *a* us saw these things Neh 6:16
plain country round *a* Jerusalem Neh 12:28
them villages round *a* Jerusalem Neh 12:29
them, Why lodge ye *a* the wall Neh 13:21 5048
of their feasting were gone *a* Job 1:5 5362
Hast not thou made an hedge *a* him Job 1:10 1157
a his house, and *a* all that he Job 1:10 1157
His roots are wrapped *a* the heap Job 8:17 5440
and fashioned me together round *a* Job 10:8
yea, thou shalt dig *a* thee Job 11:18 5439
His archers compass me round *a* Job 16:13
encamp round *a* my tabernacle Job 19:12
When he is *a* to fill his belly, Job 20:23
Therefore snares are round *a* thee Job 22:10
me, when my children were *a* me Job 29:5 5439
it bindeth me *a* as the collar of Job 30:18 247
is turned round *a* by his counsels Job 37:12
of the brook compass him *a* Job 40:22
his teeth are terrible round *a* Job 41:14
set themselves against me round *a* Ps 3:6
of the people compass thee *a* Ps 7:7
deadly enemies, who compass me *a* Ps 17:9
sorrows of hell compassed me *a* Ps 18:5
his pavilion round *a* him were Ps 18:11
up above mine enemies round *a* me Ps 27:6
thou shalt compass me *a* with Ps 32:7
LORD, mercy shall compass him *a* Ps 32:10
round *a* them that fear him Ps 34:7
evils have compassed me *a* Ps 40:12
to them that are round *a* us Ps 44:13
Walk *a* Zion, and go round *a* Ps 48:12 5439
of my heels shall compass me *a* Ps 49:5
be very tempestuous round *a* him Ps 50:3
night they go *a* it upon the walls Ps 55:10 5437
a dog, and go round *a* the city Ps 59:6
a dog, and go round *a* the city Ps 59:14
compasseth them *a* as a chain Ps 73:6
let all that be round *a* him bring Ps 76:11
round *a* their habitations Ps 78:28
shed like water round *a* Jerusalem Ps 79:3
to them that are round *a* us Ps 79:4
They came round *a* me daily like Ps 88:17
they compassed me *a* together Ps 88:17
of all them that are *a* him Ps 89:7 5439
to thy faithfulness round *a* thee Ps 89:8
and darkness are round *a* him Ps 97:2
and burneth up his enemies round *a* Ps 97:3
They compassed me *a* also with Ps 109:3
All nations compassed me *a* Ps 118:10
They compassed me *a* Ps 118:11
yea, they compassed me *a* Ps 118:11
They compassed me *a* like bees Ps 118:12
mountains are round *a* Jerusalem Ps 125:2
so the LORD is round *a* his people Ps 125:2
olive plants round *a* thy table Ps 128:3
the night shall be light *a* me Ps 139:11 1157
head of those that compass me *a* Ps 140:9
the righteous shall compass me *a* Ps 142:7
thy head, and chains *a* thy neck Prov 1:9
bind them *a* thy neck Prov 3:3 5921
heart, and tie them *a* thy neck Prov 6:21 5921
He that goeth *a* as a talebearer Prov 20:19 1980
and turneth *a* unto the north Eccl 1:6
it whirleth *a* continually Eccl 1:6
Therefore I went *a* to cause my Eccl 2:20 5437
and the mourners go *a* the streets Eccl 12:5 5437
go *a* the city in the streets, and Song 3:2 5437
that go *a* the city found me Song 3:3 5437
threescore valiant men are *a* it Song 3:7 5439
that went *a* the city found me Song 5:7 5437
heap of wheat set *a* with lilies Song 7:2 5473
tinkling ornaments *a* their feet Is 3:18
gone round *a* the borders of Moab Is 15:8
go *a* the city, thou harlot that Is 23:16 5437
and shut thy doors *a* thee Is 26:20 1157
wheel turned *a* upon the cummin Is 28:27
I will camp against thee round *a* Is 29:3
it hath set him on fire round *a* Is 42:25
Lift up thine eyes round *a* Is 49:18
compass yourselves *a* with sparks Is 50:11
Lift up thine eyes round *a* Is 60:4
all the walls thereof round *a* Jer 1:15
Why gaddest thou *a* so much to Jer 2:36 235
are they against her round *a* Jer 4:17
their tents against her round *a* Jer 6:3
the birds round *a* are against her Jer 12:9
the priest go *a* into a land that Jer 14:18 5503
and from the places *a* Jerusalem Jer 17:26 5439
devour all things round *a* it Jer 21:14
against all these nations round *a* Jer 25:9
How long wilt thou go *a*, O thou Jer 31:22 2559
and shall compass *a* to Goath Jer 31:39
and in the places *a* Jerusalem Jer 32:44 5439
and in the places *a* Jerusalem Jer 33:13 5439
away captive from Mizpah cast *a* Jer 41:14 5437
for fear was round *a*, saith the Jer 46:5
sword shall devour round *a* thee Jer 46:14
All ye that are *a* him, bemoan him Jer 48:17 5439
and a dismaying to all them *a* him Jer 48:39 5439
from all those that be *a* thee Jer 49:5 5439
in array against Babylon round *a* Jer 50:14
Shout against her round *a* Jer 50:15
the bow, camp against it round *a* Jer 50:29
it shall devour all round *a* him Jer 50:32
they shall be against her round *a* Jer 51:2
and built forts against it round *a* Jer 52:4
were by the city round *a* Jer 52:7
the walls of Jerusalem round *a* Jer 52:14
upon the chapiters round *a* Jer 52:22
network were an hundred round *a* Jer 52:23
adversaries should be round *a* him Lam 1:17
fire, which devoureth round *a* Lam 2:3
a solemn day my terrors round *a* Lam 2:22
He hath hedged me *a*, that I Lam 3:7 1157
itself, and a brightness was *a* it Eze 1:4 5439
full of eyes round *a* them four Eze 1:18
of fire round *a* within it Eze 1:27
and it had brightness round *a* Eze 1:27
of the brightness round *a* Eze 1:28
battering rams against it round *a* Eze 4:2
part, and smite *a* it with a knife Eze 5:2 5439
and countries that are round *a* her Eze 5:5
countries that are round *a* her Eze 5:6
the nations that are round *a* you Eze 5:7
the nations that are round *a* you Eze 5:7
fall by the sword round *a* thee Eze 5:12
the nations that are round *a* thee Eze 5:14
the nations that are round *a* thee Eze 5:15
your bones round *a* your altars Eze 6:5
their idols round *a* their altars Eze 6:13
pourtrayed upon the wall round *a* Eze 8:10
porch and the altar, were *a* five Eze 8:16
wheels, were full of eyes round *a* Eze 10:12
the heathen that are round *a* you Eze 11:12
all that are *a* him to help him Eze 12:14 5439
I girded thee *a* with fine linen, Eze 16:10
gather them round *a* against thee Eze 16:37
and all that are round *a* her Eze 16:57
which despise thee round *a* Eze 16:57
and shield and helmet round *a* Eze 23:24
army were upon thy walls round *a* Eze 27:11
shields upon thy walls round *a* Eze 27:11
of all that are round *a* them Eze 28:24
that despise them round *a* them Eze 28:26
rivers running round *a* his plants Eze 31:4
his graves are *a* him Eze 32:22 5439
her company is round *a* her grave Eze 32:23
her multitude round *a* her grave Eze 32:24
her graves are round *a* him Eze 32:25
her graves are round *a* him Eze 32:26
the places round *a* my hill *a* Eze 34:26
of the heathen that are round *a* Eze 36:4
Surely the heathen that are *a* you Eze 36:7 5439
a you shall know that I the LORD Eze 36:36
caused me to pass by them round *a* Eze 37:2
the outside of the house round *a* Eze 40:5
of the court round *a* the gate Eze 40:14
posts within the gate round *a* Eze 40:16
and windows were round *a* inward Eze 40:16
made for the court round *a* Eze 40:17
and in the arches thereof round *a* Eze 40:25

and in the arches thereof round *a* Eze 40:29
And the arches round *a* were five Eze 40:30
and in the arches thereof round *a* Eze 40:33
and the windows to it round *a* Eze 40:36
an hand broad, fastened round *a* Eze 40:43
round *a* the house on every side Eze 41:5
for the side chambers round *a* Eze 41:6
a winding *a* still upward to the Eze 41:7
for the winding *a* of the house Eze 41:7
still upward round *a* the house Eze 41:7
the height of the house round *a* Eze 41:8
round *a* the house on every side Eze 41:10
was left was five cubits round *a* Eze 41:11
was five cubits thick round *a* Eze 41:12
the galleries round *a* on their Eze 41:16
door, cieled with wood round *a* Eze 41:16
and by all the wall round *a* within Eze 41:17
through all the house round *a* Eze 41:19
the east, and measured it round *a* Eze 42:15
with the measuring reed round *a* Eze 42:16
with the measuring reed round *a* Eze 42:17
He turned *a* to the west side, and Eze 42:19
it had a wall round *a*, five Eze 42:20
round *a* shall be most holy Eze 43:12
thereof round *a* shall be a span Eze 43:13
the border *a* it shall be half a Eze 43:17 5439
bottom thereof shall be a cubit *a* Eze 43:17 5439
and upon the border round *a* Eze 43:20
all the borders thereof round *a* Eze 45:1
in breadth, square round *a* Eze 45:2
fifty cubits round *a* for the Eze 45:2
a row of building round *a* in them Eze 46:23
round *a* them four, and it was made Eze 46:23
places under the rows round *a* Eze 46:23
led me *a* the way without unto the Eze 47:2 5437
It was round *a* eighteen thousand Eze 48:35
have a chain of gold *a* his neck Dan 5:7 5922
have a chain of gold *a* thy neck Dan 5:16 5922
and put a chain of gold *a* his neck Dan 5:29 5922
being *a* threescore and two years Dan 5:31
a reproach to all that are *a* us Dan 9:16 5439
touched me *a* the time of the Dan 9:21
own doings have beset them *a* Hos 7:2 5437
Ephraim compasseth me *a* with lies Hos 11:12
yourselves together round *a* Joel 3:11
to judge all the heathen round *a* Joel 3:12
shall be even round *a* the land Amos 3:11
and the floods compassed me *a* Jonah 2:3
The waters compassed me *a* Jonah 2:5
the depth closed me round *a* Jonah 2:5
the weeds were wrapped *a* my head Jonah 2:5
with her bars was *a* me for ever Jonah 2:6 1157
that had the waters round *a* it Nah 3:8
doth compass *a* the righteous Hab 1:4
unto her a wall of fire round *a* Zec 2:5
and the cities thereof round *a* her Zec 7:7
I will encamp *a* mine house Zec 9:8
unto all the people round *a* Zec 12:2
devour all the people round *a* Zec 12:6 1157
a shall be gathered together Zec 14:14 1157
a the time they were carried away Mt 1:11 1909
and a leathern girdle *a* his loins Mt 3:4 4012
and all the region round *a* Jordan Mt 3:5 4066
Jesus went *a* all Galilee, Mt 4:23 4013
Jesus saw great multitudes *a* him Mt 8:18 4012
But Jesus turned him *a*, and when Mt 9:22 1994
Jesus went *a* all the cities and Mt 9:35 4013
eaten were *a* five thousand men Mt 14:21 5616
out into all that country round *a* Mt 14:35 4066
millstone were hanged *a* his neck Mt 18:6 1909
he went out *a* the third hour, and Mt 20:3 4012
Again he went out *a* the sixth Mt 20:5 4012
a the eleventh hour he went out, Mt 20:6 4012
were hired *a* the eleventh hour Mt 20:9 4012
a vineyard, and hedged it round *a* Mt 21:33 4060
a the ninth hour Jesus cried with Mt 27:46 4012
a girdle of a skin *a* his loins Mk 1:6 4012
all the region round *a* Galilee Mk 1:28 4066
no, not so much as *a* the door Mk 2:2 4314
looked round *a* on them with anger Mk 3:5 4017
and they *a* Tyre and Sidon, a great Mk 3:8 4012
And the multitude sat *a* him Mk 3:32 4012
a on them which sat *a* him Mk 3:34 4012
they that were *a* him with the Mk 4:10 4012
(they were *a* two thousand Mk 5:13 5613
turned him *a* in the press, and Mk 5:30 1994
he looked round *a* to see her that Mk 5:32 4017
And he went round *a* the villages Mk 6:6 2945
may go into the country round *a* Mk 6:36 2945
loaves were *a* five thousand men Mk 6:44 5616
a the fourth watch of the night Mk 6:48 4012
through that whole region round *a* Mk 6:55 4066
began to carry *a* in beds those Mk 6:55 4064
had eaten were *a* four thousand Mk 8:9 5613
But when he had turned *a* and Mk 8:33 1994
when they had looked round *a* Mk 9:8 4017
he saw a great multitude *a* them Mk 9:14 4012
millstone were hanged *a* his neck Mk 9:42 4012
And Jesus looked round *a*, and saith Mk 10:23 4017
looked round *a* upon all things Mk 11:11 4017
a vineyard, and set an hedge *a* it Mk 12:1 5418
linen cloth cast *a* his naked body Mk 14:51 1909
of thorns, and put it *a* his head, Mk 15:17 4060
abode with her *a* three months Lk 1:56 5616
on all that dwelt round *a* them Lk 1:65 4037
of the Lord shone round *a* them Lk 2:9 4034
And she was a widow of *a* fourscore Lk 2:37 5613
I must be *a* my Father's business Lk 2:49 1722
into all the country *a* Jordan Lk 3:3 4066
began to be *a* thirty years of age Lk 3:23 5616
through all the region round *a* Lk 4:14 4066
place of the country round *a* Lk 4:37 4066
And looking round *a* upon them all Lk 6:10 4017
marvelled at him, and turned him *a* Lk 7:9 4762
throughout all the region round *a* Lk 7:17 4066
a besought him to depart from Lk 8:37 4066
a twelve years of age, and she lay Lk 8:42 5613
into the towns and country round *a* Lk 9:12 2945
For they were *a* five thousand men Lk 9:14 5616
it came to pass *a* an eight days Lk 9:28 5616
was cumbered *a* much serving Lk 10:40 4012
careful and troubled *a* many things Lk 10:41 4012
Let your loins be girded *a* Lk 12:35 4024
year also, till I shall dig *a* it Lk 13:8 4012
millstone were hanged *a* his neck Lk 17:2 4012
shall cast a trench *a* thee Lk 19:43 4016
from them *a* a stone's cast Lk 22:41 5616
When they which were *a* him saw Lk 22:49 4012
a the space of one hour after Lk 22:59 5616
it was *a* the sixth hour, and there Lk 23:44 5616
Jerusalem *a* threescore furlongs Lk 24:13
for it was *a* the tenth hour Jn 1:39 5613
disciples and the Jews *a* purifying Jn 3:25 4012
and it was *a* the sixth hour Jn 4:6 5616
in number *a* five thousand Jn 6:10 5616
So when they had rowed *a* five Jn 6:19 5613
Now *a* the midst of the feast Jn 7:14
Why go ye *a* to kill me Jn 7:19 2212
who goeth *a* to kill thee Jn 7:20 2212
Then came the Jews round *a* him Jn 10:24 2944
Jerusalem, *a* fifteen furlongs off Jn 11:18 5613
face was bound *a* with a napkin Jn 11:44 4019
the passover, and *a* the sixth hour Jn 19:14 5616
a an hundred pound weight Jn 19:39 5616
the napkin, that was *a* his head Jn 20:7 1909
Then Peter, turning *a*, seeth the Jn 21:20 1994
names together were *a* an hundred Acts 1:15 5613
and in the parts of Libya *a* Cyrene Acts 2:10 2596
unto them *a* three thousand souls Acts 2:41 5616
John *a* to go into the temple Acts 3:3 3195
of the men was *a* five thousand Acts 4:4 5616
it was *a* the space of three hours Acts 5:7 5613
the cities round *a* unto Jerusalem Acts 5:16 4038
a four hundred, joined themselves Acts 5:36 5616
round *a* him a light from heaven Acts 9:3 4015
but they went *a* to slay him Acts 9:29 2021
a the ninth hour of the day an Acts 10:3 5616
housetop to pray *a* the sixth hour Acts 10:9 4012
who went *a* doing good, and healing Acts 10:38 1330
a Stephen travelled as far as Acts 11:19 1909
Now *a* that time Herod the king Acts 12:1 2596
unto him, Cast thy garment *a* thee Acts 12:8 4016
he went *a* seeking some to lead Acts 13:11 4013
a the time of forty years Acts 13:18 5613
a the space of four hundred Acts 13:20 5613
the region that lieth round *a* Acts 14:6 4066
the disciples stood round *a* him Acts 14:20 2944
and elders *a* this question Acts 15:2 4012
Paul was now *a* to open his mouth Acts 18:14 3195
And all the men were *a* twelve Acts 19:7 5616
arose no small stir *a* that way Acts 19:23 4012
all with one voice *a* the space of Acts 19:34 5613
as he was *a* to sail into Syria, Acts 20:3 3195
And as they went *a* to kill him Acts 21:31 2212
come nigh unto Damascus *a* noon Acts 22:6 4012
heaven a great light round *a* me Acts 22:6 4012
Who also hath gone *a* to profane Acts 24:6 3985
down from Jerusalem stood round *a* Acts 25:7 3936
A whom, when I was at Jerusalem, Acts 25:15 4012
a whom all the multitude of the Acts 25:24 4012
of the sun, shining round *a* me Acts 26:13 4034
the temple, and went *a* to kill me Acts 26:21 3985
a midnight the shipmen deemed Acts 27:27 2596
as the shipmen were *a* to flee out Acts 27:30 2212
when he was *a* an hundred years Rom 4:19 4225
going *a* to establish their own Rom 10:3 2212
round *a* unto Illyricum, I have Rom 15:19 2945
we not power to lead *a* a sister 1Cor 9:5 4013
know that they which minister *a* 1Cor 9:13
Always bearing *a* in the body the 2Cor 4:10 4064
carried *a* with every wind of Eph 4:14 4064
your loins girt *a* with truth Eph 6:14 4024
wandering *a* from house to house 1Ti 5:13 4022
nothing, but doting *a* questions 1Ti 6:4 4012
strive not *a* words to no profit 2Ti 2:14
and strivings *a* the law Titus 3:9 3163
he was *a* to make the tabernacle Heb 8:5 3195
overlaid round *a* with gold Heb 9:4 3840
they were compassed *a* seven days Heb 11:30 2944
they wandered *a* in sheepskins Heb 11:37 4022
a with so great a cloud of Heb 12:1 4029
Be not carried *a* with divers Heb 13:9 4064
we turn *a* their whole body Jas 3:3 3329
yet are they turned *a* with a very Jas 3:4 3329
as a roaring lion, walketh *a* 1Pet 5:8 4043
the cities *a* them in like manner, Jude 7 4012
he disputed *a* the body of Moses Jude 9 4012
without water, carried *a* of winds Jude 12 4064
girt *a* the paps with a golden Rev 1:13 4024
was a rainbow round *a* the throne Rev 4:3 2943
round *a* the throne were four and Rev 4:4 2943
round *a* the throne, were four Rev 4:6 2943
had each of them six wings *a* him Rev 4:8 2943
of many angels round *a* the throne Rev 5:11 2943
angels stood round *a* the throne Rev 7:11 2943
a the elders and the four beasts, Rev 7:11 2943
a the space of half an hour Rev 8:1 5613
their voices, I was *a* to write Rev 10:4 3195
every stone *a* the weight of a Rev 16:21 5613
the camp of the saints *a*, and the Rev 20:9 2944

ABOVE

waters which were *a* the firmament Gen 1:7 5921
fowl that may fly *a* the earth in Gen 1:20 5921
thou art cursed *a* all cattle Gen 3:14
a every beast of the field Gen 3:14
in a cubit shalt thou finish it *a* Gen 6:16 4605
and it was lift up *a* the earth Gen 7:17 5921
and of the dew of heaven from *a* Gen 27:39 5921
And, behold, the LORD stood *a* it Gen 28:13 5921
thee one portion *a* thy brethren Gen 48:22 5921
thee with blessings of heaven *a* Gen 49:25 5921
of thy father have prevailed *a* Gen 49:26 5921
they dealt proudly he was *a* them Ex 18:11 5921
treasure unto me *a* all people Ex 19:5
of any thing that is in heaven *a* Ex 20:4 4605
put the mercy seat *a* upon the ark Ex 25:21 4605
with thee from *a* the mercy seat Ex 25:22 5921
a covering *a* of badgers' skins Ex 26:14 4605
a the head of it unto one ring Ex 26:24 5921
a the curious girdle of the ephod Ex 28:27 4605
that it may be *a* the curious Ex 28:28 4605
and the caul that is *a* the liver Ex 29:13 5921
the caul *a* the liver, and the two Ex 29:22
from twenty years old and *a* Ex 30:14 4605
covering of badgers' skins *a* that Ex 36:19 4605
a the curious girdle of the ephod Ex 39:20 4605
that it might be *a* the curious Ex 39:21 5921
covering of the tent *a* upon it Ex 40:19 4605
put the mercy seat *a* upon the ark Ex 40:20 4605
the caul *a* the liver, with the Lev 3:4 5921
the caul *a* the liver, with the Lev 3:10 5921
the caul *a* the liver, with the Lev 3:15 5921
the caul *a* the liver, with the Lev 4:9 5921
and the caul that is *a* the liver Lev 7:4 5921
the caul *a* the liver, and the two Lev 8:16
the caul *a* the liver, and the two Lev 8:25
the caul *a* the liver of the sin Lev 9:10 4480
kidneys, and the caul *a* the liver Lev 9:19 5921
which have legs *a* their feet Lev 11:21 4605
it be from sixty years old and *a* Lev 27:7 4605
a them that were redeemed by the Num 3:49 5921
badgers' skins that is *a* upon it Num 4:25 4605
a all the men which were upon the Num 12:3
then lift ye up yourselves *a* the Num 16:3 5921
the LORD he is God in heaven *a* Deut 4:39 4605
of any thing that is in heaven *a* Deut 5:8 4605
a all people that are upon the Deut 7:6
shalt be blessed *a* all people Deut 7:14
even you *a* all people, as it is Deut 10:15
a all the nations that are upon Deut 14:2
be not lifted up *a* his brethren Deut 17:20
beat him *a* these with many Deut 25:3 5921
to make thee high *a* all nations Deut 26:19 5921
high *a* all nations of the earth Deut 28:1 5921
and thou shalt be *a* only, and thou Deut 28:13 4605
shall get up *a* thee very high Deut 28:43 5921
and multiply thee *a* thy fathers Deut 30:5
your God, he is God in heaven *a* Josh 2:11 4605
the waters that come down from *a* Josh 3:13 4605
which came down from *a* stood Josh 3:16 4605
Blessed *a* women shall Jael the Judg 5:24
shall she be *a* women in the tent Judg 5:24
and honourest thy sons *a* me 1Sa 2:29
He sent from *a*, he took me 2Sa 22:17 4791
a them that rose up against me 2Sa 22:49
with cedar *a* upon the beams 1Kin 7:3 4605
a were costly stones, after the 1Kin 7:11 4605
pillars had pomegranates also *a* 1Kin 7:20 4605
and the sea was set *a* upon them 1Kin 7:25 4605
the ledges there was a base *a* 1Kin 7:29 4605
the chapiter and *a* was a cubit 1Kin 7:31 4605
the ark and the staves thereof *a* 1Kin 8:7 4605
is no God like thee, in heaven *a* 1Kin 8:23 4605
But hast done evil *a* all that 1Kin 14:9
a all that their fathers had done 1Kin 14:22
LORD *a* all that were before him 1Kin 16:30
hath done wickedly *a* all that the 2Kin 21:11
set his throne *a* the throne of 2Kin 25:28 5921
Judah prevailed *a* his brethren 1Chr 5:2
also is to be feared *a* all gods 1Chr 16:25 5921
from twenty years old and *a* 1Chr 23:27 4605
among the thirty, and *a* the thirty 1Chr 27:6 5921
a all that I have prepared for 1Chr 29:3 4605
and thou art exalted as head *a* all 1Chr 29:11
for great is our God *a* all gods 2Chr 2:5
and the sea was set *a* upon them 2Chr 4:4 4605
the ark and the staves thereof *a* 2Chr 5:8 4605
of Absalom *a* all his wives 2Chr 11:21
priest, which stood *a* the people 2Chr 24:20
them from twenty years old and *a* 2Chr 25:5 4605
images, that were on high *a* them 2Chr 34:4 5921
From *a* the horse gate repaired Neh 3:28
man, and feared God *a* many Neh 7:2
(for he was *a* all the people Neh 8:5 5921
which is exalted *a* all blessing Neh 9:5 5921
a the house of David, even unto Neh 12:37 5921
from *a* the gate of Ephraim, and Neh 12:39 5921
a the old gate, and *a* the fish Neh 12:39 5921
king loved Esther *a* all the women Est 2:17
set his seat *a* all the princes Est 3:1 5921
he had advanced him *a* the princes Est 5:11 5921
let not God regard it from *a* Job 3:4 4605
a shall his branch be cut off Job 18:16 4605
the price of wisdom is *a* rubies Job 28:18
portion of God is there from *a* Job 31:2 4605
have denied the God that is *a* Job 31:28 4605
hast set thy glory *a* the heavens Ps 8:1 5921
are far *a* out of his sight Ps 10:5 4791
He sent from *a*, he took me, he Ps 18:16 4791
thou liftest me up *a* those that Ps 18:48
up *a* mine enemies round about me Ps 27:6 5921
the oil of gladness *a* thy fellows Ps 45:7
shall call to the heavens from *a* Ps 50:4 5921
exalted, O God, *a* the heavens Ps 57:5 5921
let thy glory be *a* all the earth Ps 57:5 5921
exalted, O God, *a* the heavens Ps 57:11 5921
let thy glory be *a* all the earth Ps 57:11 5921
had commanded the clouds from *a* Ps 78:23 4605
God, and a great King *a* all gods Ps 95:3 5921
he is to be feared *a* all gods Ps 96:4 5921
LORD, art high *a* all the earth Ps 97:9 5921

thou art exalted far *a* all gods	Ps 97:9	5921
he is high *a* all the people	Ps 99:2	5921
as the heaven is high *a* the earth	Ps 103:11	5921
the waters stood *a* the mountains	Ps 104:6	5921
thy mercy is great *a* the heavens	Ps 108:4	5921
exalted, O God, *a* the heavens	Ps 108:5	5921
thy glory *a* all the earth	Ps 108:5	5921
The LORD is high *a* all nations	Ps 113:4	5921
and his glory *a* the heavens	Ps 113:4	5921
I love thy commandments *a* gold	Ps 119:127	
yea, *a* fine gold	Ps 119:127	
and that our Lord is *a* all gods	Ps 135:5	
out the earth *a* the waters	Ps 136:6	5921
not Jerusalem *a* my chief joy	Ps 137:6	5921
magnified thy word *a* all thy name	Ps 138:2	5921
Send thine hand from *a*	Ps 144:7	4791
ye waters that be *a* the heavens	Ps 148:4	4791
his glory is *a* the earth and	Ps 148:13	4791
When he established the clouds *a*	Prov 8:28	4605
The way of life is *a* to the wise	Prov 15:24	4605
for her price is far *a* rubies	Prov 31:10	
small cattle *a* all that were in	Eccl 2:7	
man hath no preeminence *a* a beast	Eccl 3:19	4480
and shall be exalted *a* the hills	Is 2:2	
A it stood the seraphims	Is 6:2	4605
in the depth, or in the height *a*	Is 7:11	4605
my throne *a* the stars of God	Is 14:13	4605
I will ascend *a* the heights of	Is 14:14	5921
Drop down, ye heavens, from *a*	Is 45:8	4605
mourn, and the heavens *a* be black	Jer 4:28	4605
to me *a* the sand of the seas	Jer 15:8	
heart is deceitful *a* all things	Jer 17:9	
If heaven *a* can be measured, and	Jer 31:37	4605
which was *a* the chamber of	Jer 35:4	4605
set his throne *a* the throne of	Jer 52:32	4605
From *a* hath he sent fire into my	Lam 1:13	4791
forth over their heads *a*	Eze 1:22	4605
a the firmament that was over	Eze 1:26	4605
the appearance of a man *a* upon it	Eze 1:26	4605
in the firmament that was *a* the	Eze 10:1	5921
the God of Israel was over them *a*	Eze 10:19	4605
the God of Israel was over them *a*	Eze 11:22	4605
lewdness *a* all thine abominations	Eze 16:43	5921
itself any more *a* the nations	Eze 29:15	5921
his height was exalted *a* all the	Eze 31:5	
them, and the skin covered them *a*	Eze 37:8	4605
To that *a* the door, even unto the	Eze 41:17	5921
From the ground unto *a* the door	Eze 41:20	5921
was preferred *a* the presidents	Dan 6:3	5922
and he shall be strong *a* him	Dan 11:5	5921
and magnify himself *a* every god	Dan 11:36	5921
he shall magnify himself *a* all	Dan 11:37	5921
yet I destroyed his fruit from *a*	Amos 2:9	4605
it shall be exalted *a* the hills	Mic 4:1	
merchants *a* the stars of heaven	Nah 3:16	
The disciple is not *a* his master	Mt 10:24	5228
nor the servant *a* his lord	Mt 10:24	5228
Added yet this *a* all, that he	Lk 3:20	1909
The disciple is not *a* his master	Lk 6:40	5228
were sinners *a* all the Galilaeans	Lk 13:2	3844
a all men that dwelt in Jerusalem	Lk 13:4	3844
that cometh from *a* is *a* all	Jn 3:31	509
that cometh from *a* is *a* all	Jn 3:31	1883
that cometh from heaven is *a* all	Jn 3:31	5228
a unto them that had eaten	Jn 6:13	
I am from *a*	Jn 8:23	507
except it were given thee from *a*	Jn 19:11	509
I will shew wonders in heaven *a*	Acts 2:19	507
For the man was *a* forty years old	Acts 4:22	4117
a the brightness of the sun,	Acts 26:13	5228
is, to bring Christ down from *a*	Rom 10:6	
man esteemeth one day *a* another	Rom 14:5	3844
of men *a* that which is written	1Cor 4:6	5228
to be tempted *a* that ye are able	1Cor 10:13	5228
he was seen of *a* five hundred	1Cor 15:6	1883
a strength, insomuch that we	2Cor 1:8	5228
abundant, in stripes *a* measure	2Cor 11:23	4253
in Christ *a* fourteen years ago	2Cor 12:2	4253
me *a* that which he seeth me to be	2Cor 12:6	5228
lest I should be exalted *a*	2Cor 12:7	
I should be exalted *a* measure	2Cor 12:7	
a many my equals in mine own	Gal 1:14	5228
But Jerusalem which is *a* is free	Gal 4:26	507
Far *a* all principality, and power,	Eph 1:21	5231
a all that we ask or think	Eph 3:20	5228
and Father of all, who is *a* all	Eph 4:6	1909
ascended up far *a* all heavens	Eph 4:10	5231
A all, taking the shield of faith	Eph 6:16	1909
him a name which is *a* every name	Phil 2:9	5228
seek those things which are *a*	Col 3:1	507
Set your affection on things *a*	Col 3:2	507
a all these things put on charity	Col 3:14	1909
exalteth himself *a* all that is	2Th 2:4	1909
but *a* a servant, a brother	Philem 16	5228
the oil of gladness *a* thy fellows	Heb 1:9	3844
A when he said, Sacrifice and	Heb 10:8	511
and every perfect gift is from *a*	Jas 1:17	509
This wisdom descendeth not from *a*	Jas 3:15	509
that is from *a* is first pure	Jas 3:17	509
But *a* all things, my brethren,	Jas 5:12	4253
a all things have fervent charity	1Pet 4:8	4253
I wish *a* all things that thou	3Jn 2	4012

ABRAHAM (*a'-bra-ham*) See ABRAHAM'S, ABRAM. *Father of the nation of Israel.*

Abram, but thy name shall be *A*	Gen 17:5	85
And God said unto *A*, Thou shalt	Gen 17:9	85
And God said unto *A*, As for Sarai	Gen 17:15	85
Then *A* fell upon his face, and	Gen 17:17	85
A said unto God, O that Ishmael	Gen 17:18	85
with him, and God went up from *A*	Gen 17:22	85
A took Ishmael his son, and all	Gen 17:23	85
A was ninety years old and nine,	Gen 17:24	85
selfsame day was *A* circumcised	Gen 17:26	85
A hastened into the tent unto	Gen 18:6	85
A ran unto the herd, and fetcht a	Gen 18:7	85
Now *A* and Sarah were old and well	Gen 18:11	85
And the LORD said unto *A*,	Gen 18:13	85
A went with them to bring them on	Gen 18:16	85
Shall I hide from *A* that thing	Gen 18:17	85
Seeing that *A* shall surely become	Gen 18:18	85
A that which he hath spoken of	Gen 18:19	85
but *A* stood yet before the LORD	Gen 18:22	85
A drew near, and said, Wilt thou	Gen 18:23	85
A answered and said, Behold now, I	Gen 18:27	85
as he had left communing with *A*	Gen 18:33	85
A returned unto his place	Gen 18:33	85
A gat up early in the morning to	Gen 19:27	85
the plain, that God remembered *A*	Gen 19:29	85
A journeyed from thence toward	Gen 20:1	85
A said of Sarah his wife, She is	Gen 20:2	85
Then Abimelech called *A*, and said	Gen 20:9	85
And Abimelech said unto *A*, What	Gen 20:10	85
A said, Because I thought, Surely	Gen 20:11	85
and gave them unto *A*, and restored	Gen 20:14	85
So *A* prayed unto God	Gen 20:17	85
bare *A* a son in his old age, at	Gen 21:2	85
A called the name of his son that	Gen 21:3	85
A circumcised his son Isaac being	Gen 21:4	85
A was an hundred years old, when	Gen 21:5	85
said, Who would have said unto *A*	Gen 21:7	85
A made a great feast the same day	Gen 21:8	85
which she had born unto *A*	Gen 21:9	85
Wherefore she said unto *A*	Gen 21:10	85
And God said unto *A*, Let it not be	Gen 21:12	85
A rose up early in the morning,	Gen 21:14	85
captain of his host spake unto *A*	Gen 21:22	85
And *A* said, I will swear	Gen 21:24	85
A reproved Abimelech because of a	Gen 21:25	85
A took sheep and oxen, and gave	Gen 21:27	85
A set seven ewe lambs of the	Gen 21:28	85
And Abimelech said unto *A*, What	Gen 21:29	85
A planted a grove in Beer-sheba,	Gen 21:33	
A sojourned in the Philistines'	Gen 21:34	85
things, that God did tempt *A*	Gen 22:1	85
and said unto him, *A*	Gen 22:1	85
A rose up early in the morning,	Gen 22:3	85
third day *A* lifted up his eyes	Gen 22:4	85
A said unto his young men, Abide	Gen 22:5	85
A took the wood of the burnt	Gen 22:6	85
And Isaac spake unto *A* his father	Gen 22:7	85
A said, My son, God will provide	Gen 22:8	85
A built an altar there, and laid	Gen 22:9	85
A stretched forth his hand, and	Gen 22:10	85
of heaven, and said, *A*, *A*	Gen 22:11	85
A lifted up his eyes, and looked,	Gen 22:13	85
A went and took the ram, and	Gen 22:13	85
A called the name of that place	Gen 22:14	85
A out of heaven the second time	Gen 22:15	85
So *A* returned unto his young men,	Gen 22:19	85
and *A* dwelt at Beer-sheba	Gen 22:19	85
these things, that it was told *A*	Gen 22:20	85
A came to mourn for Sarah, and to	Gen 23:2	85
A stood up from before his dead,	Gen 23:3	85
the children of Heth answered *A*	Gen 23:5	85
A stood up, and bowed himself to	Gen 23:7	85
Ephron the Hittite answered *A* in	Gen 23:10	85
A bowed down himself before the	Gen 23:12	85
And Ephron answered *A*, saying unto	Gen 23:14	85
And *A* hearkened unto Ephron	Gen 23:16	85
A weighed to Ephron the silver,	Gen 23:16	
Unto *A* for a possession in the	Gen 23:18	85
A buried Sarah his wife in the	Gen 23:19	85
were made sure unto *A* for a	Gen 23:20	85
A was old, and well stricken in	Gen 24:1	85
LORD had blessed *A* in all things	Gen 24:1	85
A said unto his eldest servant of	Gen 24:2	85
A said unto him, Beware thou that	Gen 24:6	85
under the thigh of *A* his master	Gen 24:9	85
said, O LORD God of my master *A*	Gen 24:12	85
and shew kindness unto my master *A*	Gen 24:12	85
be the LORD God of my master *A*	Gen 24:27	85
said, O LORD God of my master *A*	Gen 24:42	85
the LORD God of my master *A*	Gen 24:48	85
Then again *A* took a wife, and her	Gen 25:1	85
A gave all that he had unto Isaac	Gen 25:5	85
of the concubines, which *A* had	Gen 25:6	85
A gave gifts, and sent them away	Gen 25:6	85
Then *A* gave up the ghost, and died	Gen 25:8	85
The field which *A* purchased of	Gen 25:10	85
there was *A* buried, and Sarah his	Gen 25:10	85
came to pass after the death of *A*	Gen 25:11	85
Sarah's handmaid, bare unto *A*	Gen 25:12	85
A begat Isaac	Gen 25:19	85
famine that was in the days of *A*	Gen 26:1	85
which I sware unto *A* thy father	Gen 26:3	85
Because that *A* obeyed my voice,	Gen 26:5	85
in the days of *A* his father	Gen 26:15	85
in the days of *A* his father	Gen 26:18	85
stopped them after the death of *A*	Gen 26:18	85
I am the God of *A* thy father	Gen 26:24	85
And give thee the blessing of *A*	Gen 28:4	85
a stranger, which God gave unto *A*	Gen 28:4	85
I am the LORD God of *A* thy father	Gen 28:13	85
God of my father, the God of *A*	Gen 31:42	85
The God of *A*, and the God of Nahor	Gen 31:53	85
Jacob said, O God of my father *A*	Gen 32:9	85
And the land which I gave *A*	Gen 35:12	85
Arbah, which is Hebron, where *A*	Gen 35:27	85
God, before whom my fathers *A*	Gen 48:15	85
them, and the name of my fathers *A*	Gen 48:16	85
which *A* bought with the field of	Gen 49:30	85
There they buried *A* and Sarah his	Gen 49:31	85
which *A* bought with the field for	Gen 50:13	85
unto the land which he sware to *A*	Gen 50:24	85
remembered his covenant with *A*	Ex 2:24	85
God of thy father, the God of *A*	Ex 3:6	85
God of your fathers, the God of *A*	Ex 3:15	85
God of your fathers, the God of *A*	Ex 3:16	85
of their fathers, the God of *A*	Ex 4:5	85
And I appeared unto *A*, unto Isaac,	Ex 6:3	85
which I did swear to give it to *A*	Ex 6:8	85
Remember *A*, Isaac, and Israel, thy	Ex 32:13	85
the land which I sware unto *A*	Ex 33:1	85
covenant with *A* will I remember	Lev 26:42	85
see the land which I sware unto *A*	Num 32:11	85
LORD sware unto your fathers, *A*	Deut 1:8	85
he sware unto thy fathers, to *A*	Deut 6:10	85
LORD sware unto thy fathers, *A*	Deut 9:5	85
Remember thy servants, *A*, Isaac,	Deut 9:27	85
hath sworn unto thy fathers, to *A*	Deut 29:13	85
LORD sware unto thy fathers, to *A*	Deut 30:20	85
is the land which I sware unto *A*	Deut 34:4	85
time, even Terah, the father of *A*	Josh 24:2	85
I took your father *A* from the	Josh 24:3	85
came near, and said, LORD God of *A*	1Kin 18:36	85
because of his covenant with *A*	2Kin 13:23	85
Abram; the same is *A*	1Chr 1:27	85
The sons of *A*; Isaac, and	1Chr 1:28	85
And *A* begat Isaac	1Chr 1:34	85
the covenant which he made with *A*	1Chr 16:16	85
O LORD God of *A*, Isaac, and of	1Chr 29:18	85
the seed of *A* thy friend for ever	2Chr 20:7	85
turn again unto the LORD God of *A*	2Chr 30:6	85
and gavest him the name of *A*	Neh 9:7	85
even the people of the God of *A*	Ps 47:9	85
O ye seed of *A* his servant	Ps 105:6	85
Which covenant he made with *A*	Ps 105:9	85
holy promise, and *A* his servant	Ps 105:42	85
saith the LORD, who redeemed *A*	Is 29:22	85
chosen, the seed of *A* my friend	Is 41:8	85
Look unto *A* your father, and unto	Is 51:2	85
though *A* be ignorant of us, and	Is 63:16	85
to be rulers over the seed of *A*	Jer 33:26	85
A was one, and he inherited the	Eze 33:24	85
truth to Jacob, and the mercy to *A*	Mic 7:20	85
the son of David, the son of *A*	Mt 1:1	11
A begat Isaac	Mt 1:2	11
from *A* to David are fourteen	Mt 1:17	11
We have *A* to our father	Mt 3:9	11
to raise up children unto *A*	Mt 3:9	11
and west, and shall sit down with *A*	Mt 8:11	11
I am the God of *A*, and the God of	Mt 22:32	11
him, saying, I am the God of *A*	Mk 12:26	11
As he spake to our fathers, to *A*	Lk 1:55	11
which he sware to our father *A*	Lk 1:73	11
We have *A* to our father	Lk 3:8	11
to raise up children unto *A*	Lk 3:8	11
of Isaac, which was the son of *A*	Lk 3:34	11
this woman, being a daughter of *A*	Lk 13:16	11
of teeth, when ye shall see *A*	Lk 13:28	11
seeth *A* afar off, and Lazarus in	Lk 16:23	11
And he cried and said, Father *A*	Lk 16:24	11
But *A* said, Son, remember that	Lk 16:25	11
A saith unto him, They have Moses	Lk 16:29	11
And he said, Nay, father *A*	Lk 16:30	11
as he also is a son of *A*	Lk 19:9	11
he calleth the Lord the God of *A*	Lk 20:37	11
and said unto him, *A* is our father	Jn 8:39	11
ye would do the works of *A*	Jn 8:39	11
of God: this did not *A*	Jn 8:40	11
A is dead, and the prophets	Jn 8:52	11
thou greater than our father *A*	Jn 8:53	11
Your father *A* rejoiced to see my	Jn 8:56	11
years old, and hast thou seen *A*	Jn 8:57	11
I say unto you, Before *A* was	Jn 8:58	11
The God of *A*, and of Isaac, and of	Acts 3:13	11
with our fathers, saying unto *A*	Acts 3:25	11
glory appeared unto our father *A*	Acts 7:2	11
so *A* begat Isaac, and circumcised	Acts 7:8	
laid in the sepulchre that *A*	Acts 7:16	11
nigh, which God had sworn to *A*	Acts 7:17	11
God of thy fathers, the God of *A*	Acts 7:32	11
children of the stock of *A*	Acts 13:26	11
we say then that *A* our father	Rom 4:1	11
For if *A* were justified by works,	Rom 4:2	11
A believed God, and it was counted	Rom 4:3	11
reckoned to *A* for righteousness	Rom 4:9	11
of that faith of our father *A*	Rom 4:12	11
heir of the world, was not to *A*	Rom 4:13	11
also which is of the faith of *A*	Rom 4:16	11
because they are the seed of *A*	Rom 9:7	11
am an Israelite, of the seed of *A*	Rom 11:1	11
Are they the seed of *A*	2Cor 11:22	11
Even as *A* believed God, and it was	Gal 3:6	11
the same are the children of *A*	Gal 3:7	11
preached before the gospel unto *A*	Gal 3:8	11
faith are blessed with faithful *A*	Gal 3:9	11
That the blessing of *A* might come	Gal 3:14	11
Now to *A* and his seed were the	Gal 3:16	11
but God gave it to *A* by promise	Gal 3:18	11
that *A* had two sons, the one by a	Gal 4:22	11
but he took on him the seed of *A*	Heb 2:16	11
For when God made promise to *A*	Heb 6:13	11
who met *A* returning from the	Heb 7:1	11
To whom also *A* gave a tenth part	Heb 7:2	11
A gave the tenth of the spoils	Heb 7:4	11
they come out of the loins of *A*	Heb 7:5	11
from them received tithes of *A*	Heb 7:6	11
tithes, payed tithes in *A*	Heb 7:9	11
By faith *A*, when he was called to	Heb 11:8	11
By faith *A*, when he was tried,	Heb 11:17	11
Was not *A* our father justified by	Jas 2:21	11
A believed God, and it was imputed	Jas 2:23	11
Even as Sarah obeyed *A*, calling	1Pet 3:6	11

ABRAHAM'S (*a'-bra-hams*)

male among the men of *A* house	Gen 17:23	85
because of Sarah *A* wife	Gen 20:18	85
in *A* sight because of his son	Gen 21:11	85
did bear to Nahor, *A* brother	Gen 22:23	85
A brother, with her pitcher upon	Gen 24:15	85

And he said, I am *A* servant Gen 24:34 85
when *A* servant heard their words, Gen 24:52 85
nurse, and *A* servant, and his men Gen 24:59 85
years of *A* life which he lived Gen 25:7 85
A son, whom Hagar the Egyptian, Gen 25:12 85
the generations of Isaac, *A* son Gen 25:19 85
thy seed for my servant *A* sake Gen 26:24 85
the daughter of Ishmael *A* son Gen 28:9 85
the sons of Keturah, *A* concubine 1Chr 1:32 85
by the angels into *A* bosom Lk 16:22 *11*
They answered him, We be *A* seed Jn 8:33 *11*
I know that ye are *A* seed Jn 8:37 *11*
unto them, If ye were *A* children Jn 8:39 *11*
be Christ's, then are ye *A* seed Gal 3:29 *11*

ABRAM (*a'-brum*) See ABRAHAM, ABRAM'S.
Abraham's original name.
lived seventy years, and begat *A* Gen 11:26 87
Terah begat *A*, Nahor, and Haran Gen 11:27 87
And *A* and Nahor took them wives Gen 11:29 87
And Terah took *A* his son, and Lot Gen 11:31 87
Now the LORD had said unto *A* Gen 12:1 87
So *A* departed, as the LORD had Gen 12:4 87
A was seventy and five years old Gen 12:4 87
A took Sarai his wife, and Lot his Gen 12:5 87
A passed through the land unto Gen 12:6 87
And the LORD appeared unto *A* Gen 12:7 87
A journeyed, going on still Gen 12:9 87
A went down into Egypt to sojourn Gen 12:10 87
when *A* was come into Egypt, the Gen 12:14 87
he entreated *A* well for her sake Gen 12:16 87
And Pharaoh called *A*, and said, Gen 12:18 87
A went up out of Egypt, he, and Gen 13:1 87
A was very rich in cattle, in Gen 13:2 87
there *A* called on the name of the Gen 13:4 87
And Lot also, which went with *A* Gen 13:5 87
A said unto Lot, Let there be no Gen 13:8 87
A dwelled in the land of Canaan, Gen 13:12 87
And the LORD said unto *A*, after Gen 13:14 87
Then *A* removed his tent, and came Gen 13:18 87
had escaped, and told *A* the Hebrew Gen 14:13 87
and these were confederate with *A* Gen 14:13 87
when *A* heard that his brother was Gen 14:14 87
Blessed be *A* of the most high God Gen 14:19 87
And the king of Sodom said unto *A* Gen 14:21 87
A said to the king of Sodom, I Gen 14:22 87
shouldest say, I have made *A* rich Gen 14:23 87
the LORD came unto *A* in a vision Gen 15:1 87
in a vision, saying, Fear not, *A* Gen 15:1 87
A said, Lord GOD, what wilt thou Gen 15:2 87
A said, Behold, to me thou hast Gen 15:3 87
the carcases, *A* drove them away Gen 15:11 87
down, a deep sleep fell upon *A* Gen 15:12 87
And he said unto *A*, Know of a Gen 15:13 87
the LORD made a covenant with *A* Gen 15:18 87
And Sarai said unto *A*, Behold now, Gen 16:2 87
A hearkened to the voice of Sarai Gen 16:2 87
after *A* had dwelt ten years in Gen 16:3 87
to her husband *A* to be his wife Gen 16:3 87
And Sarai said unto *A*, My wrong be Gen 16:5 87
But *A* said unto Sarai, Behold, Gen 16:6 87
And Hagar bare *A* a son Gen 16:15 87
A called his son's name, which Gen 16:15 87
A was fourscore and six years old, Gen 16:16 87
old, when Hagar bare Ishmael to *A* Gen 16:16 87
when *A* was ninety years old and Gen 17:1 87
and nine, the LORD appeared to *A* Gen 17:1 87
And *A* fell on his face Gen 17:3 87
thy name any more be called *A* Gen 17:5 87
A; the same is Abraham 1Chr 1:27 87
LORD the God, who didst choose *A* Neh 9:7 87

ABRAM'S (*a'-brums*)
the name of *A* wife was Sarai Gen 11:29 87
daughter in law, his son *A* wife Gen 11:31 87
plagues because of Sarai *A* wife Gen 12:17 87
between the herdmen of *A* cattle Gen 13:7 87
A brother's son, who dwelt in Gen 14:12 87
Now Sarai *A* wife bare him no Gen 16:1 87
Sarai *A* wife took Hagar her maid Gen 16:3 87

ABROAD
of the Canaanites spread *a* Gen 10:18 5310
lest we be scattered *a* upon the Gen 11:4 6527
So the LORD scattered them *a* from Gen 11:8 6527
did the LORD scatter them *a* upon Gen 11:9 6527
And he brought him forth *a* Gen 15:5 2351
they had brought them forth *a* Gen 19:17 2351
thou shalt spread *a* to the west Gen 28:14 6555
a throughout all the land of Ex 5:12 6527
I will spread *a* my hands unto the Ex 9:29 6566
spread *a* his hands unto the LORD Ex 9:33 6566
of the flesh *a* out of the house Ex 12:46 2351
walk *a* upon his staff, then shall Ex 21:19 2351
he spread *a* the tent over the Ex 40:19 6566
scab spread much *a* in the skin Lev 13:7 6581
a leprosy break out *a* in the skin Lev 13:12 6524
if it spread much *a* in the skin Lev 13:22 6581
it be spread much *a* in the skin Lev 13:27 6581
shall tarry *a* out of his tent Lev 14:8 2351
she be born at home, or born *a* Lev 18:9 2351
they spread them all *a* for Num 11:32 7849
shall he go *a* out of the camp Deut 23:10 2351
whither thou shalt go forth *a* Deut 23:12 2351
be, when thou wilt ease thyself *a* Deut 23:13 2351
Thou shalt stand *a*, and the man to Deut 24:11 2351
bring out the pledge *a* unto thee Deut 24:11 2351
her young, spreadeth *a* her wings Deut 32:11 6566
thirty daughters, whom he sent *a* Judg 12:9 2351
daughters from *a* for his sons Judg 12:9 2351
out both of them, he and Samuel, *a* 1Sa 9:26 2351
they were spread *a* upon all the 1Sa 30:16 5203
the street, and did spread them *a* 2Sa 22:43 7554
walkest *a* any whither, that thou 1Kin 2:42
borrow thee vessels *a* of all thy 2Kin 4:3 2351
let us send *a* unto our brethren 1Chr 13:2 6555
spread themselves *a* in the valley 1Chr 14:13 6584
his name spread *a* even to the 2Chr 26:8
And his name spread far *a* 2Chr 26:15 7350
to carry it out *a* into the brook 2Chr 29:16 2351
as soon as the commandment came *a* 2Chr 31:5 6555
scatter you *a* among the nations Neh 1:8 6327
queen shall come *a* unto all women Est 1:17 3318
is a certain people scattered *a* Est 3:8 6340
lion's whelps are scattered *a* Job 4:11 6504
He wandereth *a* for bread, saying, Job 15:23 5074
Cast *a* the rage of thy wrath Job 40:11 6327
when he goeth *a*, he telleth it Ps 41:6 2351
thine arrows also went *a* Ps 77:17 1980
Let thy fountains be dispersed *a* Prov 5:16 2351
scattereth *a* the inhabitants Is 24:1 6327
doth he not cast *a* the fitches Is 28:25 6327
that spreadeth *a* the earth by Is 44:24 7554
pour it out upon the children *a* Jer 6:11 2351
a the sword bereaveth, at home Lam 1:20 2351
till ye have scattered them *a* Eze 34:21 2351
prosperity shall yet be spread *a* Zec 1:17 6527
for I have spread you *a* as the Zec 2:6 6566
hereof went *a* into all that land Mt 9:26 *1831*
spread *a* his fame in all that Mt 9:31 *1310*
they fainted, and were scattered *a* Mt 9:36 *4496*
not with me scattereth *a* Mt 12:30 *4650*
of the flock shall be scattered *a* Mt 26:31 *1287*
immediately his fame spread *a* Mk 1:28 *1831*
to blaze *a* the matter, insomuch Mk 1:45 *1310*
secret, but that it should come *a* Mk 4:22
(for his name was spread *a* Mk 6:14
all these sayings were noised *a* Lk 1:65 *1255*
they made known *a* the saying Lk 2:17 *1232*
more went there a fame *a* of him Lk 5:15 *1330*
that shall not be known and come *a* Lk 8:17
of God that were scattered *a* Jn 11:52 *1287*
this saying *a* among the brethren Jn 21:23 *1831*
Now when this was noised *a* Acts 2:6
they were all scattered *a* Acts 8:1 *1289*
they that were scattered *a* went Acts 8:4 *1289*
Now they which were scattered *a* Acts 11:19 *1289*
a in our hearts by the Holy Ghost Rom 5:5 *1632*
obedience is come *a* unto all men Rom 16:19 *864*
is written, He hath dispersed *a* 2Cor 9:9 *4650*
faith to God-ward is spread *a* 1Th 1:8 *1831*
tribes which are scattered *a* Jas 1:1 *1290*

ABRONAH See EBRONAH.

ABSALOM (*ab'-sal-um*) *A son of David.*
A the son of Maachah the daughter 2Sa 3:3 53
that *A* the son of David had a 2Sa 13:1 53
A her brother said unto her, Hath 2Sa 13:20 53
A spake unto his brother Amnon 2Sa 13:22 53
for *A* hated Amnon, because he had 2Sa 13:22 53
that *A* had sheepshearers in 2Sa 13:23 53
A invited all the king's sons 2Sa 13:23 53
A came to the king, and said, 2Sa 13:24 53
And the king said to *A*, Nay, my 2Sa 13:25 53
Then said *A*, If not, I pray thee, 2Sa 13:26 53
But *A* pressed him, that he let 2Sa 13:27 53
Now *A* had commanded his servants, 2Sa 13:28 53
the servants of *A* did unto Amnon 2Sa 13:29 53
did unto Amnon as *A* had commanded 2Sa 13:29 53
A hath slain all the king's sons, 2Sa 13:30 53
for by the appointment of *A* this 2Sa 13:32 53
But *A* fled 2Sa 13:34 53
But *A* fled, and went to Talmai, 2Sa 13:37 53
So *A* fled, and went to Geshur, and 2Sa 13:38 53
David longed to go forth unto *A* 2Sa 13:39 53
the king's heart was toward *A* 2Sa 14:1 53
bring the young man *A* again 2Sa 14:21 53
Geshur, and brought *A* to Jerusalem 2Sa 14:23 53
So *A* returned to his own house, 2Sa 14:24 53
much praised as *A* for his beauty 2Sa 14:25 53
unto *A* there were born three sons 2Sa 14:27 53
So *A* dwelt two full years in 2Sa 14:28 53
Therefore *A* sent for Joab, to 2Sa 14:29 53
came to *A* unto his house, and said 2Sa 14:31 53
A answered Joab, Behold, I sent 2Sa 14:32 53
and when he had called for *A* 2Sa 14:33 53
and the king kissed *A* 2Sa 14:33 53
that *A* prepared him chariots and 2Sa 15:1 53
A rose up early, and stood beside 2Sa 15:2 53
then *A* called unto him, and said, 2Sa 15:2 53
A said unto him, See, thy matters 2Sa 15:3 53
A said moreover, Oh that I were 2Sa 15:4 53
on this manner did *A* to all 2Sa 15:6 53
so *A* stole the hearts of the men 2Sa 15:6 53
that *A* said unto the king, I pray 2Sa 15:7 53
But *A* sent spies throughout all 2Sa 15:10 53
shall say, *A* reigneth in Hebron 2Sa 15:10 53
with *A* went two hundred men out 2Sa 15:11 53
A sent for Ahithophel the 2Sa 15:12 53
increased continually with *A* 2Sa 15:12 53
of the men of Israel are after *A* 2Sa 15:13 53
we shall not else escape from *A* 2Sa 15:14 53
is among the conspirators with *A* 2Sa 15:31 53
return to the city, and say unto *A* 2Sa 15:34 53
city, and *A* came into Jerusalem 2Sa 15:37 53
into the hand of *A* thy son 2Sa 16:8 53
And *A*, and all the people the men 2Sa 16:15 53
David's friend, was come unto *A* 2Sa 16:16 53
A, that Hushai said unto *A* 2Sa 16:16 53
A said to Hushai, Is this thy 2Sa 16:17 53
And Hushai said unto *A*, Nay 2Sa 16:18 53
Then said *A* to Ahithophel, Give 2Sa 16:20 53
And Ahithophel said unto *A* 2Sa 16:21 53
So they spread *A* a tent upon the 2Sa 16:22 53
A went in unto his father's 2Sa 16:22 53
both with David and with *A* 2Sa 16:23 53
Moreover Ahithophel said unto *A* 2Sa 17:1 53
And the saying pleased *A* well 2Sa 17:4 53
Then said *A*, Call now Hushai the 2Sa 17:5 53
And when Hushai was come to *A* 2Sa 17:6 53
A spake unto him, saying, 2Sa 17:6 53
And Hushai said unto *A*, The 2Sa 17:7 53
among the people that follow *A* 2Sa 17:9 53
And *A* and all the men of Israel 2Sa 17:14 53
the LORD might bring evil upon *A* 2Sa 17:14 53
and thus did Ahithophel counsel *A* 2Sa 17:15 53
a lad saw them, and told *A* 2Sa 17:18 53
A passed over Jordan, he and all 2Sa 17:24 53
A made Amasa captain of the host 2Sa 17:25 53
A pitched in the land of Gilead 2Sa 17:26 53
with the young man, even with *A* 2Sa 18:5 53
the captains charge concerning *A* 2Sa 18:5 53
A met the servants of David 2Sa 18:9 53
A rode upon a mule, and the mule 2Sa 18:9 53
Behold, I saw *A* hanged in an oak 2Sa 18:10 53
that none touch the young man *A* 2Sa 18:12 53
them through the heart of *A* 2Sa 18:14 53
armour compassed about and smote *A* 2Sa 18:15 53
And they took *A*, and cast him into 2Sa 18:17 53
Now *A* in his lifetime had taken 2Sa 18:18 53
said, Is the young man *A* safe 2Sa 18:29 53
Cushi, Is the young man *A* safe 2Sa 18:32 53
my son *A*, my son, my son *A* 2Sa 18:33 53
God I had died for thee, O *A* 2Sa 18:33 53
king weepeth and mourneth for *A* 2Sa 19:1 53
loud voice, O my son *A*, O *A* 2Sa 19:4 53
that if *A* had lived, and all we 2Sa 19:6 53
he is fled out of the land for *A* 2Sa 19:9 53
And *A*, whom we anointed over us, 2Sa 19:10 53
Bichri do us more harm than did *A* 2Sa 20:6 53
and his mother bare him after *A* 1Kin 1:6 53
I fled because of *A* thy brother 1Kin 2:7 53
though he turned not after *A* 1Kin 2:28 53
A the son of Maachah the daughter 1Chr 3:2 53
he took Maachah the daughter of *A* 2Chr 11:20 53
daughter of *A* above all his wives 2Chr 11:21 53
when he fled from *A* his son Ps 3:*t*

ABSALOM'S (*ab'-sal-ums*)
I love Tamar, my brother *A* sister 2Sa 13:4 53
desolate in her brother *A* house 2Sa 13:20 53
A servants set the field on fire 2Sa 14:30 53
when *A* servants came to the woman 2Sa 17:20 53
is called unto this day, *A* place 2Sa 18:18 53

ABSENCE
them in the *a* of the multitude Lk 22:6 *817*
only, but now much more in my *a* Phil 2:12 *666*

ABSENT
when we are *a* one from another Gen 31:49 5641
as *a* in body, but present in 1Cor 5:3 *548*
the body, we are *a* from the Lord 2Cor 5:6 *553*
rather to be *a* from the body 2Cor 5:8 *553*
that, whether present or *a* 2Cor 5:9 *553*
but being *a* am bold toward you 2Cor 10:1 *548*
in word by letters when we are *a* 2Cor 10:11 *548*
being *a* now I write to them which 2Cor 13:2 *548*
I write these things being *a* 2Cor 13:10 *548*
I come and see you, or else be *a* Phil 1:27 *548*
For though I be *a* in the flesh Col 2:5 *548*

ABSTAIN
that they *a* from pollutions of Acts 15:20 *567*
That ye *a* from meats offered to Acts 15:29 *567*
that ye should *a* from fornication 1Th 4:3 *567*
A from all appearance of evil 1Th 5:22 *567*
and commanding to *a* from meats 1Ti 4:3 *567*
a from fleshly lusts, which war 1Pet 2:11 *567*

ABSTINENCE
But after long *a* Paul stood forth Acts 27:21 *776*

ABUNDANCE
of heart, for the *a* of all things Deut 28:47 7230
shall suck of the *a* of the seas Deut 33:19 8228
for out of the *a* of my complaint 1Sa 1:16 7230
the spoil of the city in great *a* 2Sa 12:30 7235
oxen and fat cattle and sheep in *a* 1Kin 1:19 7230
oxen and fat cattle and sheep in *a* 1Kin 1:25 7230
there came no more such *a* of 1Kin 10:10 7230
trees that are in the vale, for *a* 1Kin 10:27 7230
for there is a sound of *a* of rain 1Kin 18:41 1995
David prepared iron in *a* for the 1Chr 22:3 7230
brass in *a* without weight 1Chr 22:3 7230
Also cedar trees in *a* 1Chr 22:4
for it is in *a* 1Chr 22:14 7230
there are workmen with thee in *a* 1Chr 22:15 7230
stones, and marble stones in *a* 1Chr 29:2 7230
sacrifices in *a* for all Israel 1Chr 29:21 7230
trees that are in the vale for *a* 2Chr 1:15 7230
Even to prepare me timber in *a* 2Chr 2:9 7230
made all these vessels in great *a* 2Chr 4:18 7230
that bare spices, and gold in *a* 2Chr 9:1 7230
of gold, and of spices great *a* 2Chr 9:9 7230
that are in the low plains in *a* 2Chr 9:27 7230
and he gave them victual in *a* 2Chr 11:23 7230
carried away sheep and camels in *a* 2Chr 14:15 7230
fell to him out of Israel in *a* 2Chr 15:9 7230
and he had riches and honour in *a* 2Chr 17:5 7230
had riches and honour in *a* 2Chr 18:1 7230
killed sheep and oxen for him in *a* 2Chr 18:2 7230
they found among them in *a* both 2Chr 20:25 7230
by day, and gathered money in *a* 2Chr 24:11 7230
the burnt offerings were in *a* 2Chr 29:35 7230
in *a* the firstfruits of corn 2Chr 31:5 7235
and made darts and shields in *a* 2Chr 32:5 7230
of flocks and herds in *a* 2Chr 32:29 7230
oliveyards, and fruit trees in *a* Neh 9:25 7230
from another,) and royal wine in *a* Est 1:7 7227
and *a* of waters cover thee Job 22:11 8229
he giveth meat in *a* Job 36:31 4342
that *a* of waters may cover thee Job 38:34 8229
themselves in the *a* of peace Ps 37:11 7230
trusted in the *a* of his riches Ps 52:7 7230
a of peace so long as the moon Ps 72:7 7230

- land brought forth frogs in *a* — Ps 105:30 — 8317
- he that loveth *a* with increase — Eccl 5:10 — 1995
- but the *a* of the rich will not — Eccl 5:12 — 7647
- for the *a* of milk that they shall — Is 7:22 — 7230
- Therefore the *a* they have gotten, — Is 15:7 — 3502
- and for the great *a* of thine — Is 47:9 — 6109
- because the *a* of the sea shall be — Is 60:5 — 1995
- delighted with the *a* of her glory — Is 66:11 — 2123
- reveal unto them the *a* of peace — Jer 33:6 — 6283
- *a* of idleness was in her and in — Eze 16:49 — 7962
- By reason of the *a* of his horses — Eze 26:10 — 8229
- and silver, and apparel, in great *a* — Zec 14:14 — 7230
- for out of the *a* of the heart the — Mt 12:34 — 4051
- be given, and he shall have more *a* — Mt 13:12 — 4052
- be given, and he shall have *a* — Mt 25:29 — 4052
- all they did cast in of their *a* — Mk 12:44 — 4052
- for of the *a* of the heart his — Lk 6:45 — 4051
- in the *a* of the things which he — Lk 12:15 — 4052
- For all these have of their *a* — Lk 21:4 — 4052
- they which receive *a* of grace — Rom 5:17 — 4050
- of affliction the *a* of their joy — 2Cor 8:2 — 4050
- that now at this time your *a* may — 2Cor 8:14 — 4051
- that their *a* also may be a supply — 2Cor 8:14 — 4051
- *a* which is administered by us — 2Cor 8:20 — 100
- through the *a* of the revelations — 2Cor 12:7 — 5236
- through the *a* of her delicacies — Rev 18:3 — 1411

ABUNDANT
- and *a* in goodness and truth, — Ex 34:6 — 7227
- be as this day, and much more *a* — Is 56:12 — 1419
- *a* in treasures, thine end is come — Jer 51:13 — 7227
- these we bestow more *a* honour — 1Cor 12:23 — 4055
- parts have more *a* comeliness — 1Cor 12:23 — 4055
- having given more *a* honour to — 1Cor 12:24 — 4055
- that the *a* grace might through — 2Cor 4:15 — 4121
- affection is more *a* toward you — 2Cor 7:15 — 4056
- the saints, but is *a* also by many — 2Cor 9:12 — 4052
- in labours more *a*, in stripes — 2Cor 11:23 — 4056
- *a* in Jesus Christ for me by my — Phil 1:26 — 4052
- Lord was exceeding *a* with faith — 1Ti 1:14 — 5250
- which according to his *a* mercy — 1Pet 1:3 — 4183

ABUNDANTLY
- Let the waters bring forth *a* the — Gen 1:20 — 8317
- which the waters brought forth *a* — Gen 1:21 — 8317
- they may breed *a* in the earth — Gen 8:17 — 8317
- bring forth *a* in the earth, and — Gen 9:7 — 8317
- were fruitful, and increased *a* — Ex 1:7 — 8317
- river shall bring forth frogs *a* — Ex 8:3 — 8317
- and the water came out *a*, and the — Num 20:11 — 7227
- wine, and oil, and oxen, and sheep *a* — 1Chr 12:40 — 7230
- David prepared *a* before his death — 1Chr 22:5 — 7230
- saying, Thou hast shed blood *a* — 1Chr 22:8 — 7230
- of all things brought they in *a* — 2Chr 31:5 — 7230
- into whose hand God bringeth *a* — Job 12:6
- do drop and distil upon man *a* — Job 36:28 — 7227
- They shall be *a* satisfied with — Ps 36:8 — 7301
- waterest the ridges thereof *a* — Ps 65:10 — 7301
- I will *a* bless her provision — Ps 132:15 — 1288
- They shall *a* utter the memory of — Ps 145:7 — 5042
- drink, yea, drink *a*, O beloved — Song 5:1 — 7937
- every one shall howl, weeping *a* — Is 15:3 — 3381
- It shall blossom *a*, and rejoice — Is 35:2 — 6524
- to our God, for he will *a* pardon — Is 55:7 — 7235
- and that they might have it more *a* — Jn 10:10 — 4053
- I laboured more *a* than they all — 1Cor 15:10 — 4054
- the world, and more *a* to you-ward — 2Cor 1:12 — 4056
- love which I have more *a* unto you — 2Cor 2:4 — 4056
- by you according to our rule *a* — 2Cor 10:15
- though the more *a* I love you — 2Cor 12:15 — 4056
- that is able to do exceeding *a* — Eph 3:20
- endeavoured the more *a* to see — 1Th 2:17 — 4056
- Which he shed on us *a* through — Titus 3:6 — 4146
- willing more *a* to shew unto the — Heb 6:17 — 4054
- shall be ministered unto you *a* — 2Pet 1:11 — 4146

ABUSE
- and thrust me through, and *a* me — 1Sa 31:4 — 5953
- these uncircumcised come and *a* me — 1Chr 10:4 — 5953
- that I *a* not my power in the — 1Cor 9:18 — 2710

ABUSED
- *a* her all the night until the — Judg 19:25 — 5953

ABUSERS
- nor *a* of themselves with mankind, — 1Cor 6:9 — 733

ABUSING
- that use this world, as not *a* it — 1Cor 7:31 — 2710

ACBOR See ACHBOR.

ACCAD (*ak'-kad*) *A city of Shinar.*
- kingdom was Babel, and Erech, and *A*. — Gen 10:10 — 390

ACCEPT
- peradventure he will *a* of me — Gen 32:20 — 5375
- the owner of it shall *a* thereof — Ex 22:11 — 3947
- they then *a* of the punishment of — Lev 26:41 — 7521
- they shall *a* of the punishment of — Lev 26:43 — 7521
- and *a* the work of his hands — Deut 33:11 — 7521
- against me, let him *a* an offering — 1Sa 26:19 — 7306
- the king, The LORD thy God *a* thee — 2Sa 24:23 — 7521
- Will ye *a* his person — Job 13:8 — 5375
- you, if ye do secretly *a* persons — Job 13:10 — 5375
- *a* any man's person, neither let — Job 32:21 — 5375
- for him will I *a* — Job 42:8 — 5375
- and *a* thy burnt sacrifice — Ps 20:3 — 1878
- *a* the persons of the wicked — Ps 82:2 — 5375
- *A*, I beseech thee, the freewill — Ps 119:108 — 7521
- It is not good to *a* the person of — Prov 18:5 — 5375
- the LORD doth not *a* them — Jer 14:10 — 7521
- and an oblation, I will not *a* them — Jer 14:12 — 7521
- there will I *a* them, and there — Eze 20:40 — 7521
- I will *a* you with your sweet — Eze 20:41 — 7521
- and I will *a* you, saith the Lord — Eze 43:27 — 7521
- meat offerings, I will not *a* them — Amos 5:22 — 7521
- with thee, or *a* thy person — Mal 1:8 — 5375
- neither will I *a* an offering at — Mal 1:10 — 7521
- should I *a* this of your hand — Mal 1:13 — 7521
- We *a* it always, and in all places, — Acts 24:3 — 588

ACCEPTABLE
- for it shall not be *a* for you — Lev 22:20 — 7522
- let him be *a* to his brethren, and — Deut 33:24 — 7522
- be *a* in thy sight, O LORD, my — Ps 19:14 — 7522
- unto thee, O LORD, in an *a* time — Ps 69:13 — 7522
- of the righteous know what is *a* — Prov 10:32 — 7522
- judgment is more *a* to the LORD — Prov 21:3 — 977
- sought to find out *a* words — Eccl 12:10 — 2656
- In an *a* time have I heard thee, — Is 49:8 — 7522
- a fast, and an *a* day to the LORD — Is 58:5 — 7522
- To proclaim the *a* year of the — Is 61:2 — 7522
- your burnt offerings are not *a* — Jer 6:20 — 7522
- let my counsel be *a* unto thee — Dan 4:27 — 8232
- To preach the *a* year of the Lord — Lk 4:19 — 1184
- *a* unto God, which is your — Rom 12:1 — 2101
- may prove what is that good, and *a* — Rom 12:2 — 2101
- things serveth Christ is *a* to God — Rom 14:18 — 2101
- up of the Gentiles might be *a* — Rom 15:16 — 2144
- Proving what is *a* unto the Lord — Eph 5:10 — 2101
- of a sweet smell, a sacrifice *a* — Phil 4:18 — 1184
- *a* in the sight of God our Saviour — 1Ti 2:3 — 587
- for that is good and *a* before God — 1Ti 5:4 — 587
- *a* to God by Jesus Christ — 1Pet 2:5 — 2144
- it patiently, this is *a* with God — 1Pet 2:20 — 5285

ACCEPTABLY
- we may serve God *a* with reverence — Heb 12:28 — 2102

ACCEPTANCE
- come up with *a* on mine altar — Is 60:7 — 7522

ACCEPTATION
- saying, and worthy of all *a* — 1Ti 1:15 — 594
- saying and worthy of all *a* — 1Ti 4:9 — 594

ACCEPTED
- doest well, shalt thou not be *a* — Gen 4:7 — 7613
- I have *a* thee concerning this — Gen 19:21 — 5375
- they may be *a* before the LORD — Ex 28:38 — 7522
- it shall be *a* for him to make — Lev 1:4 — 7521
- the third day, it shall not be *a* — Lev 7:18 — 7521
- should it have been *a* in the — Lev 10:19 — 3190
- it shall not be *a* — Lev 19:7 — 7521
- it shall be perfect to be *a* — Lev 22:21 — 7522
- but for a vow it shall not be *a* — Lev 22:23 — 7521
- they shall not be *a* for you — Lev 22:25 — 7521
- thenceforth it shall be *a* for an — Lev 22:27 — 7521
- before the LORD, to be *a* for you — Lev 23:11 — 7522
- he was *a* in the sight of all the — 1Sa 18:5 — 3190
- thy voice, and have *a* thy person — 1Sa 25:35 — 5375
- *a* of the multitude of his — Est 10:3 — 7521
- the LORD also *a* Job — Job 42:9 — 5375
- shall be *a* upon mine altar — Is 56:7 — 7522
- I pray thee, be *a* before thee — Jer 37:20 — 5307
- our supplication be *a* before thee — Jer 42:2 — 5307
- No prophet is *a* in his own — Lk 4:24 — 1184
- righteousness, is *a* with him — Acts 10:35 — 1184
- Jerusalem may be *a* of the saints — Rom 15:31 — 2144
- or absent, we may be *a* of him — 2Cor 5:9 — 2101
- I have heard thee in a time *a* — 2Cor 6:2 — 1184
- behold, now is the *a* time — 2Cor 6:2 — 2144
- it is *a* according to that a man — 2Cor 8:12 — 2144
- For indeed he *a* the exhortation — 2Cor 8:17 — 1209
- gospel, which ye have not *a* — 2Cor 11:4 — 1209
- he hath made us *a* in the beloved — Eph 1:6 — 5487

ACCEPTEST
- neither *a* thou the person of any, — Lk 20:21 — 2983

ACCEPTETH
- How much less to him that *a* not — Job 34:19 — 5375
- for God now *a* thy works — Eccl 9:7 — 7521
- but the LORD *a* them not — Hos 8:13 — 7521
- God *a* no man's person — Gal 2:6 — 2983

ACCEPTING
- were tortured, not *a* deliverance — Heb 11:35 — 4327

ACCESS
- By whom also we have *a* by faith — Rom 5:2 — 4318
- For through him we both have *a* by — Eph 2:18 — 4318
- *a* with confidence by the faith of — Eph 3:12 — 4318

ACCHO (*ak'-ko*) *A coastal city in Asher.*
- drive out the inhabitants of *A* — Judg 1:31 — 5910

ACCO See ACCHO.

ACCOMPANIED
- certain brethren from Joppa *a* him — Acts 10:23 — 4905
- Moreover these six brethren *a* me — Acts 11:12 — 4862
- there *a* him into Asia Sopater of — Acts 20:4 — 4902
- And they *a* him unto the ship — Acts 20:38 — 4311

ACCOMPANY
- you, and things that *a* salvation — Heb 6:9 — 2192

ACCOMPANYING
- was at Gibeah, *a* the ark of God — 2Sa 6:4 — 5973

ACCOMPLISH
- unto the LORD to *a* his vow — Lev 22:21 — 6381
- and thou shalt *a* my desire — 1Kin 5:9 — 6213
- that he may rest, till he shall *a* — Job 14:6 — 7521
- they *a* a diligent search — Ps 64:6 — 8552
- but it shall *a* that which I — Is 55:11 — 6213
- ye will surely *a* your vows — Jer 44:25 — 6965
- thus will I *a* my fury upon them — Eze 6:12 — 3615
- thee, and *a* mine anger upon thee — Eze 7:8 — 3615
- Thus will I *a* my wrath upon the — Eze 13:15 — 3615
- to *a* my anger against them in the — Eze 20:8 — 3615
- to *a* my anger against them in the — Eze 20:21 — 3615
- that he would *a* seventy years in — Dan 9:2 — 4390
- which he should *a* at Jerusalem — Lk 9:31 — 4137

ACCOMPLISHED
- the mouth of Jeremiah might be *a* — 2Chr 36:22 — 3615
- the days of their purifications *a* — Est 2:12 — 4390
- It shall be *a* before his time, and — Job 15:32 — 4390
- The desire *a* is sweet to the soul — Prov 13:19 — 1961
- unto her, that her warfare is *a* — Is 40:2 — 4390
- to pass, when seventy years are *a* — Jer 25:12 — 4390
- and of your dispersions are *a* — Jer 25:34 — 4390
- be *a* at Babylon I will visit you — Jer 29:10 — 4390
- they shall be *a* in that day — Jer 39:16
- The LORD hath *a* his fury — Lam 4:11 — 3615
- punishment of thine iniquity is *a* — Lam 4:22 — 8552
- And when thou hast *a* them, lie — Eze 4:6 — 3615
- Thus shall mine anger be *a* — Eze 5:13 — 3615
- when I have *a* my fury in them — Eze 5:13 — 3615
- prosper till the indignation be *a* — Dan 11:36 — 3615
- when he shall have *a* to scatter — Dan 12:7 — 3615
- days of his ministration were *a* — Lk 1:23 — 4130
- the days were *a* that she should — Lk 2:6 — 4130
- when eight days were *a* for the — Lk 2:21 — 4130
- to the law of Moses were *a* — Lk 2:22 — 4130
- how am I straitened till it be *a* — Lk 12:50 — 5055
- the Son of man shall be *a* — Lk 18:31 — 5055
- is written must yet be *a* in me — Lk 22:37 — 5055
- that all things were now *a* — Jn 19:28 — 5055
- And when we had *a* those days — Acts 21:5 — 1822
- *a* in your brethren that are in — 1Pet 5:9 — 2005

ACCOMPLISHING
- tabernacle, *a* the service of God — Heb 9:6 — 2005

ACCOMPLISHMENT
- to signify the *a* of the days of — Acts 21:26 — 1604

ACCORD
- *a* of thy harvest thou shalt not — Lev 25:5 — 5599
- Joshua and with Israel, with one *a* — Josh 9:2 — 6310
- continued with one *a* in prayer — Acts 1:14 — 3661
- were all with one *a* in one place — Acts 2:1 — 3661
- daily with one *a* in the temple — Acts 2:46 — 3661
- up their voice to God with one *a* — Acts 4:24 — 3661
- all with one *a* in Solomon's porch — Acts 5:12 — 3661
- ears, and ran upon him with one *a* — Acts 7:57 — 3661
- the people with one *a* gave heed — Acts 8:6 — 3661
- which opened to them of his own *a* — Acts 12:10 — 844
- but they came with one *a* to him — Acts 12:20 — 3661
- us, being assembled with one *a* — Acts 15:25 — 3661
- with one *a* against Paul, and — Acts 18:12 — 3661
- with one *a* into the theatre — Acts 19:29 — 3661
- of his own *a* he went unto you — 2Cor 8:17 — 830
- the same love, being of one *a* — Phil 2:2 — 4861

ACCORDING
- *a* to all that God commanded him, — Gen 6:22
- Noah did *a* unto all that the LORD — Gen 7:5
- unto thee *a* to the time of life — Gen 18:10
- *a* to the time of life, and Sarah — Gen 18:14
- altogether *a* to the cry of it — Gen 18:21
- but *a* to the kindness that I have — Gen 21:23
- names, *a* to their generations — Gen 25:13
- twelve princes *a* to their nations — Gen 25:16
- obey my voice *a* to that which I — Gen 27:8
- I have done *a* as thou badest me — Gen 27:19
- I would it might be *a* to thy word — Gen 30:34
- *a* as the cattle that goeth before — Gen 33:14 — 7272
- I will give *a* as ye shall say — Gen 34:12
- *a* to their families, after their — Gen 36:40
- *a* to their habitations in the — Gen 36:43
- spake unto him *a* to these words — Gen 39:17
- each man *a* to the interpretation — Gen 40:5
- we dreamed each man *a* to the — Gen 41:11
- to each man *a* to his dream he did — Gen 41:12
- *a* unto thy word shall all my — Gen 41:40 — 5921
- to come, *a* as Joseph had said — Gen 41:54
- we told him *a* to the tenor of — Gen 43:7 — 5921
- the firstborn *a* to his birthright — Gen 43:33
- and the youngest *a* to his youth — Gen 43:33
- he did *a* to the word that Joseph — Gen 44:2
- should do *a* to this thing — Gen 44:7
- also let it be *a* unto your words — Gen 44:10
- *a* to the commandment of Pharaoh, — Gen 45:21 — 5921
- with bread, *a* to their families — Gen 47:12 — 6310
- every one *a* to his blessing he — Gen 49:28 — 834
- father, *a* as he made them swear — Gen 50:6
- unto him *a* as he commanded them — Gen 50:12 — 3651
- of Levi *a* to their generations — Ex 6:16
- and Shimi, *a* to their families — Ex 6:17
- of Levi *a* to their generations — Ex 6:19
- the Levites *a* to their families — Ex 6:25
- land of Egypt *a* to their armies — Ex 6:26
- And he said, Be it *a* to thy word — Ex 8:10
- the LORD did *a* to the word of — Ex 8:13
- the LORD did *a* to the word of — Ex 8:31
- *a* to the house of their fathers, — Ex 12:3
- it *a* to the number of the souls — Ex 12:4
- every man *a* to his eating shall — Ex 12:4 — 6310
- take you a lamb *a* to your — Ex 12:21
- *a* as he hath promised, that ye — Ex 12:25
- Israel did *a* to the word of Moses — Ex 12:35
- of it every man *a* to his eating — Ex 16:16 — 6310
- *a* to the number of your persons — Ex 16:16
- every man *a* to his eating — Ex 16:18 — 6310
- every man *a* to his eating — Ex 16:21 — 6310
- *a* to the commandment of the LORD, — Ex 17:1 — 5921
- *a* as the woman's husband will lay — Ex 21:22
- *a* to this judgment shall it be — Ex 21:31
- he shall pay money *a* to the dowry — Ex 22:17
- *a* to the twelve tribes of Israel — Ex 24:4
- *A* to all that I shew thee, after — Ex 25:9
- *a* to the six branches that — Ex 25:35
- *a* to the fashion thereof which — Ex 26:30
- the same, *a* to the work thereof — Ex 28:8
- the other stone, *a* to their birth — Ex 28:10
- *a* to their names, like the — Ex 28:21 — 5921
- they be *a* to the twelve tribes — Ex 28:21
- *a* to all things which I have — Ex 29:35
- shalt do thereto *a* to the meat — Ex 29:41
- *a* to the drink offering thereof, — Ex 29:41
- *a* to the composition thereof — Ex 30:37

a to all that I have commanded Ex 31:11
Levi did *a* to the word of Moses Ex 32:28
a to all that the LORD had Ex 36:1
a to the six branches going out Ex 37:21
a to the work of the apothecary Ex 37:29
a to the commandment of Moses, Ex 38:21 5921
the same, *a* to the work thereof Ex 39:5
the stones were *a* to the names of Ex 39:14 5921
a to their names, like the Ex 39:14 5921
his name, *a* to the twelve tribes Ex 39:14 5921
the children of Israel did *a* to Ex 39:32
A to all that the LORD commanded Ex 39:42
a to all that the LORD commanded Ex 40:16
do sin *a* to the sin of the people Lev 4:3
a to the offerings made by fire Lev 4:35 5921
a burnt offering, *a* to the manner Lev 5:10
a to the offerings made by fire Lev 5:12
offered it *a* to the manner Lev 9:16
they did *a* to the word of Moses Lev 10:7
a to the days of the separation Lev 12:2
A to the number of years after Lev 25:15
a unto the number of years of the Lev 25:15
A to the multitude of years thou Lev 25:16 6310
a to the fewness of years thou Lev 25:16 6310
for *a* to the number of the years Lev 25:16
be *a* unto the number of years Lev 25:50
a to the time of an hired servant Lev 25:50
a unto them he shall give again Lev 25:51 6310
a unto his years shall he give Lev 25:52 6310
plagues upon you *a* to your sins Lev 26:21 5921
a to his ability that vowed shall Lev 27:8
shall be *a* to the seed thereof Lev 27:16 6310
a to thy estimation it shall Lev 27:17
money *a* to the years that remain Lev 27:18
all thy estimations shall be *a* to Lev 27:25
redeem it *a* to thine estimation Lev 27:27
shall be sold *a* to thy estimation Lev 27:27
a to the number of the names, Num 1:18
a to the number of the names, by Num 1:20
a to the number of the names, by Num 1:22
a to the number of the names, Num 1:24
a to the number of the names, Num 1:26
a to the number of the names, Num 1:28
a to the number of the names, Num 1:30
a to the number of the names, Num 1:32
a to the number of the names, Num 1:34
a to the number of the names, Num 1:36
a to the number of the names, Num 1:38
a to the number of the names, Num 1:40
a to the number of the names, Num 1:42
the children of Israel did *a* to Num 1:54
camp of Reuben *a* to their armies Num 2:10
camp of Ephraim *a* to their armies Num 2:18
the children of Israel did *a* to Num 2:34
a to the house of their fathers Num 2:34 5921
Moses numbered them *a* to the word Num 3:16 5921
a to the house of their fathers Num 3:20
a to the number of all the males, Num 3:22
a to the number of all the males, Num 3:34
a to the word of the LORD, as the Num 3:51 5921
a to all their service in the Num 4:31
a to all their service, in the Num 4:33
Aaron did number *a* to the Num 4:37 5921
Aaron did number *a* to the Num 4:41 5921
Aaron numbered *a* to the word of Num 4:45 5921
A to the commandment of the LORD Num 4:49 5921
every one *a* to his service, and Num 4:49 5921
his service, and *a* to his burden Num 4:49 5921
a to the vow which he vowed, so Num 6:21 6310
to every man *a* to his service Num 7:5 6310
of Gershon, *a* to their service Num 7:7 6310
a unto their service, under the Num 7:8 6310
a unto the pattern which the LORD Num 8:4
did to the Levites *a* unto all Num 8:20
a to all the rites of it, and Num 9:3
a to all the ceremonies thereof, Num 9:3
a to all that the LORD commanded Num 9:5
a to all the ordinances of the Num 9:12
a to the ordinance of the Num 9:14
a to the manner thereof, so shall Num 9:14
a to the commandment of the LORD Num 9:20 5921
a to the commandment of the LORD Num 9:20 5921
they first took their journey *a* Num 10:13 5921
of Judah *a* to their armies Num 10:14
set forward *a* to their armies Num 10:18
set forward *a* to their armies Num 10:22
of Israel *a* to their armies Num 10:28
a as thou hast spoken, saying, Num 14:17
the iniquity of this people *a* Num 14:19
I have pardoned *a* to thy word Num 14:20
a to your whole number, from Num 14:29
A to the number that ye shall Num 15:12
do to every one *a* to their number Num 15:12
a to the manner, and one kid of Num 15:24
a to the house of their fathers Num 17:2
of all their princes *a* to the Num 17:2
a to their fathers' houses, even Num 17:6
a to thine estimation, for the Num 18:16
a to this time it shall be said Num 23:23
in his tents *a* to their tribes Num 24:2
a to those that were numbered of Num 26:18
a to those that were numbered of Num 26:22
are the families of Issachar *a* to Num 26:25
a to those that were numbered of Num 26:27
a to those that were numbered of Num 26:37
a to those that were numbered of Num 26:43
families of the sons of Asher *a* Num 26:47
of Naphtali *a* to their families Num 26:50
a to the number of names Num 26:53
a to those that were numbered of Num 26:54 6310
a to the names of the tribes of Num 26:55
A to the lot shall the possession Num 26:56
a unto their manner, for a sweet Num 29:6
shall be *a* to their number, after Num 29:18
shall be *a* to their number, after Num 29:21
shall be *a* to their number, after Num 29:24
shall be *a* to their number, after Num 29:27
shall be *a* to their number, after Num 29:30
shall be *a* to their number, after Num 29:33
shall be *a* to their number, after Num 29:37
told the children of Israel *a* to Num 29:40
he shall do *a* to all that Num 30:2
out *a* to their journeys by the Num 33:2
journeys *a* to their goings out Num 33:2
a to the tribes of your fathers Num 33:54
a to the house of their fathers Num 34:14
tribe of the children of Gad *a* to Num 34:14
a to his inheritance which he Num 35:8 6310
of blood *a* to these judgments Num 35:24 5921
the children of Israel *a* to the Num 36:5 5921
a unto all that the LORD had Deut 1:3
a to all that he did for you in Deut 1:30
a to all that the LORD our God Deut 1:41
a unto the days that ye abode Deut 1:46
a to thy works, and *a* to thy might Deut 3:24
a to all that the LORD your God Deut 4:34
was written *a* to all the words Deut 9:10
a to the first writing, the ten Deut 10:4
a as the LORD thy God promised Deut 10:9
a to the first time, forty days Deut 10:10
a to the blessing of the LORD thy Deut 12:15
a as the LORD thy God hath Deut 16:10
a to the blessing of the LORD thy Deut 16:17
thou shalt do *a* to the sentence, Deut 17:10
thou shalt observe to do *a* to all Deut 17:10
A to the sentence of the law Deut 17:11 5921
a to the judgment which they Deut 17:11 5921
A to all that thou desiredst of Deut 18:16
a as thou hast vowed unto the Deut 23:23
do *a* to all that the priests the Deut 24:8
a to his fault, by a certain Deut 25:2 1767
a to all thy commandments which Deut 26:13
have done *a* to all that thou hast Deut 26:14
a to all the curses of the Deut 29:21
shalt obey his voice *a* to all Deut 30:2
that ye may do unto them *a* unto Deut 31:5
a to the number of the children Deut 32:8
a to the word of the LORD Deut 34:5 5921
observe to do *a* to all the law Josh 1:7
a to all that is written therein Josh 1:8
A as we hearkened unto Moses in Josh 1:17
A unto your words, so be it Josh 2:21
a unto the number of the tribes Josh 4:5
a to the number of the tribes of Josh 4:8
a to all that Moses commanded Josh 4:10
shall be brought *a* to your tribes Josh 7:14
come *a* to the families thereof Josh 7:14
a to the commandment of the LORD Josh 8:8
a unto the word of the LORD which Josh 8:27
a to all that is written in the Josh 8:34
a to all that he had done to Josh 10:32
a to all that he had done to Josh 10:35
a to all that he had done to Josh 10:37
a to all that the LORD said unto Josh 11:23
a to their divisions by their Josh 11:23
a possession *a* to their divisions Josh 12:7
inheritance *a* to their families Josh 13:15
children of Gad *a* their families Josh 13:24
round about *a* to their families Josh 15:12
a to the commandment of the LORD Josh 15:13 413
of Judah *a* to their families Josh 15:20
a to their families was thus Josh 16:5
Therefore *a* to the commandment of Josh 17:4 413
describe it *a* to the inheritance Josh 18:4 6310
of Israel *a* to their divisions Josh 18:10
came up *a* to their families Josh 18:11
round about, *a* to their families Josh 18:20
of the children of Benjamin *a* to Josh 18:21
of Benjamin *a* to their families Josh 18:28
of Simeon *a* to their families Josh 19:1
of Simeon *a* to their families Josh 19:8
of Zebulun *a* to their families Josh 19:10
of Zebulun *a* to their families Josh 19:16
of Issachar *a* to their families Josh 19:17
of Issachar *a* to their families Josh 19:23
of Asher *a* to their families Josh 19:24
of Asher *a* to their families Josh 19:31
of Naphtali *a* to their families Josh 19:32
of Naphtali *a* to their families Josh 19:39
of Dan *a* to their families Josh 19:40
of Dan *a* to their families Josh 19:48
A to the word of the LORD they Josh 19:50 5921
the cities of the Gershonites *a* Josh 21:33
a to all that he sware unto their Josh 21:44
a to the word of the LORD by the Josh 22:9 5921
a to that which I did among them Josh 24:5
a to all the goodness which he Judg 8:35
have done unto him *a* to the Judg 9:16
if we do not so *a* to thy words Judg 11:10
do to me *a* to that which hath Judg 11:36
who did with her *a* to his vow Judg 11:39
a to all the folly that they have Judg 20:10
a to their number, of them that Judg 21:23
did *a* to all that her mother in Ruth 3:6
that shall do *a* to that which is 1Sa 2:35
a to the number of the lords of 1Sa 6:4
a to the number of all the cities 1Sa 6:18
A to all the works which they 1Sa 8:8
a to the set time that Samuel had 1Sa 13:8
I am with thee *a* to thy heart 1Sa 14:7
spake *a* to the same words 1Sa 17:23
come down *a* to all the desire of 1Sa 23:20
they spake to Nabal *a* to all 1Sa 25:9
a to all the good that he hath 1Sa 25:30
doer of evil *a* to his wickedness 2Sa 3:39
A to all these words, and 2Sa 7:17
a to all this vision, so did 2Sa 7:17
a to thine own heart, hast thou 2Sa 7:21
a to all that we have heard with 2Sa 7:22
A to all that my lord the king 2Sa 9:11
a to the wisdom of an angel of 2Sa 14:20
rewarded me *a* to my righteousness 2Sa 22:21
a to the cleanness of my hands 2Sa 22:21
me *a* to my righteousness 2Sa 22:25
a to my cleanness in his eye 2Sa 22:25
a to the saying of Gad, went up 2Sa 24:19
Do therefore *a* to thy wisdom, and 1Kin 2:6
a as he walked before thee in 1Kin 3:6
I have done *a* to thy words 1Kin 3:12
every man *a* to his charge 1Kin 4:28
I give hire for thy servants *a* to 1Kin 5:6
fir trees *a* to all his desire 1Kin 5:10
a to the breadth of the house 1Kin 6:3
a to all the fashion of it 1Kin 6:38 5921
a to the measures of hewed stones 1Kin 7:9
a to the proportion of every one, 1Kin 7:36
righteous, to give him *a* to his 1Kin 8:32
give to every man *a* to his ways 1Kin 8:39 3605
do *a* to all that the stranger 1Kin 8:43
a to all that he promised 1Kin 8:56
to do *a* to all that I have 1Kin 9:4
a to all his desire,) that then 1Kin 9:11
thou shalt reign *a* to all that 1Kin 11:37
a to the word of the LORD 1Kin 12:24
a to the sign which the man of 1Kin 13:5
a to the word of the LORD, which 1Kin 13:26
a to the word of the LORD, which 1Kin 14:18
and they did *a* to all the 1Kin 14:24
a unto the saying of the LORD, 1Kin 15:29
a to the word of the LORD, which 1Kin 16:12
a to the word of the LORD, which 1Kin 16:34
these years, but *a* to my word 1Kin 17:1 6310
did *a* unto the word of the LORD 1Kin 17:5
did *a* to the saying of Elijah 1Kin 17:15
a to the word of the LORD, which 1Kin 17:16
a to the number of the tribes of 1Kin 18:31
a to thy saying, I am thine, and 1Kin 20:4
a to all things as did the 1Kin 21:26
a unto the word of the LORD which 1Kin 22:38
a to all that his father had done 1Kin 22:53
So he died *a* to the word of the 2Kin 1:17
a to the saying of Elisha which 2Kin 2:22
a to the time of life, thou shalt 2Kin 4:16
unto her, *a* to the time of life 2Kin 4:17
a to the word of the LORD 2Kin 4:44
a to the saying of the man of God 2Kin 5:14
blindness *a* to the word of Elisha 2Kin 6:18
a to the word of the LORD 2Kin 7:16
a to the word of the LORD 2Kin 9:26
a to the saying of the LORD, 2Kin 10:17
done unto the house of Ahab *a* to 2Kin 10:30
captains over the hundreds did *a* 2Kin 11:9
he did *a* to all things as Joash 2Kin 14:3
a unto that which is written in 2Kin 14:6
a to the word of the LORD God of 2Kin 14:25
a to all that his father Amaziah 2Kin 15:3
he did *a* to all that his father 2Kin 15:34
a to the abominations of the 2Kin 16:3
a to all the workmanship thereof 2Kin 16:10
the priest built an altar *a* to 2Kin 16:11
a to all that king Ahaz commanded 2Kin 16:16
a to all the law which I 2Kin 17:13
a to all that David his father 2Kin 18:3
do *a* to all that I have commanded 2Kin 21:8
a to all the law that my servant 2Kin 21:8
to do *a* unto all that which is 2Kin 22:13
a to the word of the LORD which 2Kin 23:16
did to them *a* to all the acts 2Kin 23:19
a to all the law of Moses 2Kin 23:25
a to all that his fathers had 2Kin 23:32
the land to give the money *a* to 2Kin 23:35 5921
of every one *a* to his taxation, 2Kin 23:35
a to all that his fathers had 2Kin 23:37
a to the word of the LORD, which 2Kin 24:2
of Manasseh, *a* to all that he did 2Kin 24:3
a to all that his father had done 2Kin 24:9
a to all that Jehoiakim had done 2Kin 24:19
of the Levites *a* to their fathers 1Chr 6:19
on their office *a* to their order 1Chr 6:32
a to all that Moses the servant 1Chr 6:49
a to their generations, nine 1Chr 9:9
a to the word of the LORD by 1Chr 11:3
a to the word of the LORD 1Chr 11:10
a to the word of the LORD 1Chr 12:23
as Moses commanded *a* to the word 1Chr 15:15
to do *a* to all that is written in 1Chr 16:40
A to all these words, and 1Chr 17:15
a to all this vision, so did 1Chr 17:15
hast regarded me *a* to the estate 1Chr 17:17
a to thine own heart, hast thou 1Chr 17:19
a to all that we have heard with 1Chr 17:20
a to their father's house 1Chr 23:11
a to the order commanded unto 1Chr 23:31
a to their offices in their 1Chr 24:3
a to the house of their fathers 1Chr 24:4
a to their manner, under Aaron 1Chr 24:19
workmen *a* to their service was 1Chr 25:1
which prophesied *a* to the order 1Chr 25:2 5921
a to the king's order to Asaph, 1Chr 25:6 5921
a to the house of their fathers, 1Chr 26:13
a to the generations of his 1Chr 26:31
a to the use of every candlestick 1Chr 28:15
the length of it was *a* to the 2Chr 3:4 5921
the length whereof was *a* to the 2Chr 3:8 5921
of gold *a* to their form, and set 2Chr 4:7
righteous, by giving him *a* to his 2Chr 6:23
every man *a* unto all his ways 2Chr 6:30
do *a* to all that the stranger 2Chr 6:33
do *a* to all that I have commanded 2Chr 7:17
a as I have covenanted with David 2Chr 7:18
offering *a* to the commandment of 2Chr 8:13
a to the order of David his 2Chr 8:14

a to the house of their fathers	2Chr 17:14	
all Judah did *a* to all things	2Chr 23:8	
a to the commandment of Moses the	2Chr 24:6	
a to the houses of their fathers,	2Chr 25:5	
a to all that his father Amaziah	2Chr 26:4	
a to the number of their account	2Chr 26:11	
a to all that his father Uzziah	2Chr 27:2	
a to all that David his father	2Chr 29:2	
a to the commandment of the king,	2Chr 29:15	
a to the commandment of David, and	2Chr 29:25	
a to the commandment of the king,	2Chr 30:6	
a to the law of Moses the man of	2Chr 30:16	
though he be not cleansed *a* to	2Chr 30:19	
every man *a* to his service, the	2Chr 31:2	6310
their charges *a* to their courses	2Chr 31:16	
a to the benefit done unto him	2Chr 32:25	
a to the whole law and the	2Chr 33:8	
did *a* to the covenant of God	2Chr 34:32	
a to the writing of David king of	2Chr 35:4	
a to the writing of Solomon his	2Chr 35:4	
place *a* to the divisions of the	2Chr 35:5	
that they may do *a* to the word of	2Chr 35:6	
a to the king's commandment	2Chr 35:10	
that they might give *a* to the	2Chr 35:12	
with fire *a* to the ordinance	2Chr 35:13	
a to the commandment of David, and	2Chr 35:15	
a to the commandment of king	2Chr 35:16	
a to that which was written in	2Chr 35:26	
a to the custom, as the duty of	Ezr 3:4	
a to the grant that they had of	Ezr 3:7	
a to the appointment of the	Ezr 6:9	
a to that which Darius the king	Ezr 6:13	6903
a to the commandment of the God	Ezr 6:14	4481
a to the commandment of Cyrus, and	Ezr 6:14	
a to the number of the tribes of	Ezr 6:17	
a to the hand of the LORD his God	Ezr 7:6	
a to the good hand of his God	Ezr 7:9	
a to the law of thy God which is	Ezr 7:14	
doing *a* to their abominations,	Ezr 9:1	
a to the counsel of my lord, and	Ezr 10:3	
and let it be done *a* to the law	Ezr 10:3	
they should do *a* to this word	Ezr 10:5	
a to the counsel of the princes	Ezr 10:8	
a to the good hand of my God upon	Neh 2:8	
they should do *a* to this promise	Neh 5:12	
the people did *a* to this promise	Neh 5:13	
a to all that I have done for	Neh 5:19	
be their king, *a* to these words	Neh 6:6	
to the king *a* to these words	Neh 6:7	
Sanballat *a* to these their works,	Neh 6:14	
assembly, *a* unto the manner	Neh 8:18	
a to thy manifold mercies thou	Neh 9:27	
deliver them *a* to thy mercies	Neh 9:28	
a to the commandment of David the	Neh 12:24	
a to the commandment of David, and	Neh 12:45	
spare me *a* to the greatness of	Neh 13:22	
but *a* to the language of each	Neh 13:24	
a to the state of the king	Est 1:7	
And the drinking was *a* to the law	Est 1:8	
that they should do *a* to every	Est 1:8	
do unto the queen Vashti *a* to law	Est 1:15	
the king did *a* to the word of	Est 1:21	
into every province *a* to the	Est 1:22	
that it should be published *a* to	Est 1:22	
a to the manner of the women	Est 2:12	
a to the state of the king	Est 2:18	
there was written *a* to all that	Est 3:12	
province *a* to the writing thereof	Est 3:12	
king, which is not *a* to the law	Est 4:16	
did *a* to all that Esther had	Est 4:17	
it was written *a* to all that	Est 8:9	
unto every province *a* to the	Est 8:9	
to the Jews *a* to their writing,	Est 8:9	
and *a* to their language	Est 8:9	
also *a* unto this day's decree	Est 9:13	
these two days *a* to their writing	Est 9:27	
a to their appointed time every	Est 9:27	
a as Mordecai the Jew and Esther	Est 9:31	
offered burnt offerings *a* to the	Job 1:5	
a to his substance shall the	Job 20:18	
I am *a* to thy wish in God's stead	Job 33:6	
every man to find *a* to his ways	Job 34:11	
Should it be *a* to thy mind	Job 34:33	
they pour down rain *a* to the	Job 36:27	
did *a* as the LORD commanded them	Job 42:9	
a to my righteousness, and	Ps 7:8	
a to mine integrity that is in me	Ps 7:8	
the LORD *a* to his righteousness	Ps 7:17	
rewarded me *a* to my righteousness	Ps 18:20	
a to the cleanness of my hands	Ps 18:20	
me *a* to my righteousness,	Ps 18:24	
a to the cleanness of my hands in	Ps 18:24	
Grant thee *a* to thine own heart,	Ps 20:4	
a to thy mercy remember thou me	Ps 25:7	
Give them *a* to their deeds, and	Ps 28:4	
a to the wickedness of their	Ps 28:4	
be upon us, *a* as we hope in thee	Ps 33:22	
my God, *a* to thy righteousness	Ps 35:24	
A to thy name, O God, so is thy	Ps 48:10	
O God, *a* to thy lovingkindness	Ps 51:1	
a unto the multitude of thy	Ps 51:1	
to every man *a* to his work	Ps 62:12	
turn unto me *a* to the multitude	Ps 69:16	
A man was famous *a* as he had	Ps 74:5	
So he fed them *a* to the integrity	Ps 78:72	
a to the greatness of thy power	Ps 79:11	
even *a* to thy fear, so is thy	Ps 90:11	
Make us glad *a* to the days	Ps 90:15	
nor rewarded us *a* to our	Ps 103:10	
repented *a* to the multitude of	Ps 106:45	
O save me *a* to thy mercy	Ps 109:26	
taking heed thereto *a* to thy word	Ps 119:9	
quicken thou me *a* to thy word	Ps 119:25	
thou me *a* unto thy word	Ps 119:28	
even thy salvation, *a* to thy word	Ps 119:41	
be merciful unto me *a* to thy word	Ps 119:58	
servant, O LORD, *a* unto thy word	Ps 119:65	
a to thy word unto thy servant	Ps 119:76	
this day *a* to thine ordinances	Ps 119:91	
me, O LORD, *a* unto thy word	Ps 119:107	
Uphold me *a* unto thy word, that I	Ps 119:116	
with thy servant *a* unto thy mercy	Ps 119:124	
Hear my voice *a* unto thy	Ps 119:149	
quicken me *a* to thy judgment	Ps 119:149	
quicken me *a* to thy word	Ps 119:154	
quicken me *a* to thy judgments	Ps 119:156	
O LORD, *a* to thy lovingkindness	Ps 119:159	
me understanding *a* to thy word	Ps 119:169	
deliver me *a* to thy word	Ps 119:170	
praise him *a* to his excellent	Ps 150:2	
be commended *a* to his wisdom	Prov 12:8	6310
to every man *a* to his works	Prov 24:12	
render to the man *a* to his work	Prov 24:29	
Answer not a fool *a* to his folly	Prov 26:4	
Answer a fool *a* to his folly	Prov 26:5	
returneth again *a* to his circuits	Eccl 1:6	5921
unto whom it happeneth *a* to the	Eccl 8:14	
to whom it happeneth *a* to the	Eccl 8:14	
if they speak not *a* to this word	Is 8:20	
they joy before thee *a* to the joy	Is 9:3	
a to the slaughter of Midian at	Is 10:26	
a to the years of an hireling, and	Is 21:16	
a to the days of one king	Is 23:15	
or is he slain *a* to the slaughter	Is 27:7	
a man, *a* to the beauty of a man	Is 44:13	
A to their deeds, accordingly he	Is 59:18	5921
a to all that the LORD hath	Is 63:7	5921
bestowed on them *a* to his mercies	Is 63:7	
a to the multitude of his	Is 63:7	
for *a* to the number of thy cities	Jer 2:28	
give you pastors *a* to mine heart	Jer 3:15	
a to all which I command you	Jer 11:4	
For *a* to the number of thy cities	Jer 11:13	
a to the number of the streets of	Jer 11:13	
So I got a girdle *a* to the word	Jer 13:2	
to give every man *a* to his ways	Jer 17:10	
a to the fruit of his doings	Jer 17:10	
us *a* to all his wondrous works	Jer 21:2	
But I will punish you *a* to the	Jer 21:14	
recompense them *a* to their deeds	Jer 25:14	
a to the works of their own hands	Jer 25:14	
against this land *a* to all the	Jer 26:20	
of Judah *a* to all these words	Jer 27:12	
Not *a* to the covenant that I made	Jer 31:32	
prison *a* to the word of the LORD	Jer 32:8	
which was sealed *a* to the law	Jer 32:11	
to give every one *a* to his ways	Jer 32:19	
a to the fruit of his doings	Jer 32:19	
done *a* to all that Jonadab our	Jer 35:10	
done *a* unto all that he hath	Jer 35:18	
did *a* to all that Jeremiah the	Jer 36:8	
he told them *a* to all these words	Jer 38:27	
it, and done *a* as he hath said	Jer 40:3	
the LORD your God *a* to your words	Jer 42:4	
if we do not even *a* to all things	Jer 42:5	
a unto all that the LORD our God	Jer 42:20	
do *a* to all that I have commanded	Jer 50:21	
recompense her *a* to her work	Jer 50:29	
a to all that she hath done, do	Jer 50:29	
a to all that Jehoiakim had done	Jer 52:2	
yet will he have compassion *a* to	Lam 3:32	
a to the work of their hands	Lam 3:64	
a to the number of the days that	Eze 4:4	
a to the number of the days,	Eze 4:5	
a to the number of the days that	Eze 4:9	
neither have done *a* to the	Eze 5:7	
and will judge thee *a* to thy ways	Eze 7:3	
I will judge thee *a* to thy ways	Eze 7:8	
recompense thee *a* to thy ways	Eze 7:9	
a to their deserts will I judge	Eze 7:27	
a to the vision that I saw in the	Eze 8:4	
will answer him that cometh *a* to	Eze 14:4	
doeth *a* to all the abominations	Eze 18:24	
every one *a* to his ways, saith	Eze 18:30	
not *a* to your wicked ways	Eze 20:44	
nor *a* to your corrupt doings, O	Eze 20:44	
judge thee *a* to their judgments	Eze 23:24	
a to thy ways, and *a* to	Eze 24:14	
a to all that he hath done shall	Eze 24:24	
a to mine anger and *a* to my fury	Eze 25:14	
I will even do *a* to thine anger	Eze 35:11	
a to thine envy which thou hast	Eze 35:11	
a to their way and *a* to	Eze 36:19	
A to their uncleanness and	Eze 39:24	
a to their transgressions have I	Eze 39:24	
thereof *a* to these measures	Eze 40:24	
south gate *a* to these measures	Eze 40:28	
thereof, *a* to these measures	Eze 40:29	
the gate *a* to these measures	Eze 40:32	
thereof, were *a* to these measures	Eze 40:33	
measured it *a* to these measures	Eze 40:35	
out were both *a* to their fashions	Eze 42:11	
and *a* to their doors	Eze 42:11	
a to the doors of the chambers	Eze 42:12	
it was *a* to the appearance of the	Eze 43:3	
even *a* to the vision that I saw	Eze 43:3	
shall judge it *a* to my judgments	Eze 44:24	
house of Israel *a* to their tribes	Eze 45:8	
a to the sin offering	Eze 45:25	
a to the burnt offering, and	Eze 45:25	
a to the meat offering, and	Eze 45:25	
meat offering, and *a* to the oil	Eze 45:25	
for the lambs *a* as his hand shall	Eze 46:7	
fish shall be *a* to their kinds	Eze 47:10	
forth new fruit *a* to his months	Eze 47:12	
ye shall inherit the land *a* to	Eze 47:13	
you *a* to the tribes of Israel	Eze 47:21	
a to the name of my god, and in	Dan 4:8	
he doeth *a* to his will in the	Dan 4:35	
a to the law of the Medes and	Dan 6:8	
a to the law of the Medes and	Dan 6:12	
but he did *a* to his will, and	Dan 8:4	
a to all thy righteousness, I	Dan 9:16	
dominion, and do *a* to his will	Dan 11:3	
nor *a* to his dominion which he	Dan 11:4	
him shall do *a* to his own will	Dan 11:16	
the king shall do *a* to his will	Dan 11:36	
a to the love of the LORD toward	Hos 3:1	
abominations were *a* as they loved	Hos 9:10	
a to the multitude of his fruit	Hos 10:1	
a to the goodness of his land	Hos 10:1	
will punish Jacob *a* to his ways	Hos 12:2	
a to his doings will he	Hos 12:2	
silver, and idols *a* to their own	Hos 13:2	
A to their pasture, so were they	Hos 13:6	
a to the word of the LORD	Jonah 3:3	
A to the days of thy coming out	Mic 7:15	
a to the oaths of the tribes,	Hab 3:9	
A to the word that I covenanted	Hag 2:5	
a to our ways, and *a* to	Zec 1:6	
cut off as on this side *a* to it	Zec 5:3	3644
cut off as on that side *a* to it	Zec 5:3	3644
a as ye have not kept my ways,	Mal 2:9	6310
a to the time which he had	Mt 2:16	*2596*
A to your faith be it unto you	Mt 9:29	*2596*
reward every man *a* to his works	Mt 16:27	*2596*
to every man *a* to his several	Mt 25:15	*2596*
Why walk not thy disciples *a* to	Mk 7:5	*2596*
A to the custom of the priest's	Lk 1:9	*2596*
be it unto me *a* to thy word	Lk 1:38	*2596*
a to the law of Moses were	Lk 2:22	*2596*
to offer a sacrifice *a* to that	Lk 2:24	*2596*
depart in peace, *a* to thy word	Lk 2:29	*2596*
things *a* to the law of the Lord	Lk 2:39	*2596*
a as Moses commanded, for a	Lk 5:14	
neither did *a* to his will	Lk 12:47	*4314*
sabbath day *a* to the commandment	Lk 23:56	*2596*
Judge not *a* to the appearance,	Jn 7:24	*2596*
him, and judge him *a* to your law	Jn 18:31	*2596*
a to the flesh, he would raise up	Acts 2:30	*2596*
unto every man *a* as he had need	Acts 4:35	*2530*
that he should make it *a* to the	Acts 7:44	*2596*
every man *a* to his ability,	Acts 11:29	*2531*
God *a* to his promise raised unto	Acts 13:23	*2596*
taught *a* to the perfect manner of	Acts 22:3	*2596*
a devout man *a* to the law	Acts 22:12	*2596*
and would have judged *a* to our law	Acts 24:6	*2596*
the seed of David *a* to the flesh	Rom 1:3	*2596*
a to the spirit of holiness, by	Rom 1:4	*2596*
is *a* to truth against them which	Rom 2:2	*2596*
to every man *a* to his deeds	Rom 2:6	*2596*
by Jesus Christ *a* to my gospel	Rom 2:16	*2596*
a to that which was spoken, So	Rom 4:18	*2596*
the saints *a* to the will of God	Rom 8:27	*2596*
are the called *a* to his purpose	Rom 8:28	*2596*
my kinsmen *a* to the flesh	Rom 9:3	*2596*
of God *a* to election might stand	Rom 9:11	*2596*
of God, but not *a* to knowledge	Rom 10:2	*2596*
a to the election of grace	Rom 11:5	*2596*
(*A* as it is written, God hath	Rom 11:8	*2531*
a as God hath dealt to every man	Rom 12:3	
Having then gifts differing *a* to	Rom 12:6	*2596*
let us prophesy *a* to the	Rom 12:6	*2596*
toward another *a* to Christ Jesus	Rom 15:5	*2596*
to stablish you *a* to my gospel	Rom 16:25	*2596*
a to the revelation of the	Rom 16:25	*2596*
a to the commandment of the	Rom 16:26	*2596*
a as it is written, He that	1Cor 1:31	*2531*
own reward *a* to his own labour	1Cor 3:8	*2596*
A to the grace of God which is	1Cor 3:10	*2596*
for our sins *a* to the scriptures	1Cor 15:3	*2596*
the third day *a* to the scriptures	1Cor 15:4	*2596*
do I purpose *a* to the flesh	2Cor 1:17	*2596*
a as it is written, I believed,	2Cor 4:13	*2596*
a to that he hath done, whether	2Cor 5:10	*4314*
it is accepted *a* to that a man	2Cor 8:12	*2526*
not *a* to that he hath not	2Cor 8:12	*2526*
Every man *a* as he purposeth in	2Cor 9:7	*2531*
us as if we walked *a* to the flesh	2Cor 10:2	*2596*
but *a* to the measure of the rule	2Cor 10:13	*2596*
by you *a* to our rule abundantly	2Cor 10:15	*2596*
end shall be *a* to their works	2Cor 11:15	*2596*
a to the power which the Lord	2Cor 13:10	*2596*
a to the will of God and our	Gal 1:4	*2596*
a to the truth of the gospel	Gal 2:14	*4314*
seed, and heirs *a* to the promise	Gal 3:29	*2596*
And as many as walk *a* to this rule	Gal 6:16	
A as he hath chosen us in him	Eph 1:4	*2531*
a to the good pleasure of his	Eph 1:5	*2596*
a to the riches of his grace	Eph 1:7	*2596*
a to his good pleasure which he	Eph 1:9	*2596*
being predestinated *a* to the	Eph 1:11	*2596*
a to the working of his mighty	Eph 1:19	*2596*
a to the course of this world	Eph 2:2	*2596*
a to the prince of the power of	Eph 2:2	*2596*
a to the gift of the grace of God	Eph 3:7	*2596*
A to the eternal purpose which he	Eph 3:11	*2596*
a to the riches of his glory, to	Eph 3:16	*2596*
a to the power that worketh in us	Eph 3:20	*2596*
a to the measure of the gift of	Eph 4:7	*2596*
a to the effectual working in the	Eph 4:16	*2596*
which is corrupt *a* to the	Eph 4:22	*2596*
are your masters *a* to the flesh	Eph 6:5	*2596*
A to my earnest expectation and my	Phil 1:20	*2596*
a to the working whereby he is	Phil 3:21	*2596*
need *a* to his riches in glory by	Phil 4:19	*2596*
a to his glorious power, unto all	Col 1:11	*2596*
a to the dispensation of God	Col 1:25	*2596*
striving *a* to his working, which	Col 1:29	*2596*
your masters *a* to the flesh	Col 3:22	*2596*
a to the grace of our God and the	2Th 1:12	*2596*
A to the glorious gospel of the	1Ti 1:11	*2596*

a to the prophecies which went 1Ti 1:18 2596
doctrine which is a to godliness 1Ti 6:3 2596
a to the promise of life which is 2Ti 1:1 2596
the gospel a to the power of God 2Ti 1:8 2596
not a to our works
but a to his own purpose and grace 2Ti 1:9 2596
from the dead a to my gospel 2Ti 2:8 2596
Lord reward him a to his works 2Ti 4:14 2596
a to the faith of God's elect, and Titus 1:1 2596
which is committed unto me a to Titus 1:3 2596
but a to his mercy he saved us, Titus 3:5 2596
we should be made heirs a to the Titus 3:7 2596
the Holy Ghost, a to his own will Heb 2:4 2596
tithes of the people a to the law Heb 7:5 2596
that offer gifts a to the law Heb 8:4 2596
that thou make all things a to Heb 8:5 2596
Not a to the covenant that I made Heb 8:9 2596
to all the people a to the law Heb 9:19 2596
the royal law a to the scripture Jas 2:8 2596
Elect a to the foreknowledge of 1Pet 1:2 2596
which a to his abundant mercy 1Pet 1:3 2596
not fashioning yourselves a to 1Pet 1:14 2596
judgeth a to every man's work 1Pet 1:17 2596
dwell with them a to knowledge 1Pet 3:7 2596
be judged a to men in the flesh 1Pet 4:6 2596
but live a to God in the spirit 1Pet 4:6 2596
a to the will of God commit the 1Pet 4:19 2596
A as his divine power hath given 2Pet 1:3 5613
unto them a to the true proverb 2Pet 2:22
a to his promise, look for new 2Pet 3:13 2596
a to the wisdom given unto him 2Pet 3:15 2596
if we ask any thing a to his will 1Jn 5:14 2596
every one of you a to your works Rev 2:23 2596
unto her double a to her works Rev 18:6 2596
in the books, a to their works Rev 20:12 2596
judged every man a to their works Rev 20:13 2596
a to the measure of a man, that Rev 21:17
to give every man a as his work Rev 22:12 5613

ACCORDINGLY
a he will repay, fury to his Is 59:18 5922

ACCOUNT
of every one that passeth the a 2Kin 12:4
was the number put in the a of 1Chr 27:24 4557
to the number of their a by the 2Chr 26:11 6486
for he giveth not a of any of his Job 33:13 6030
of man, that thou makest a of him Ps 144:3 2803
one by one, to find out the a Eccl 7:27 2808
they shall give a thereof in the Mt 12:36 3056
would take a of his servants Mt 18:23 3056
give an a of thy stewardship Lk 16:2 3056
may give an a of this concourse Acts 19:40 3056
us shall give a of himself to God Rom 14:12 3056
Let a man so a of us, as of the 1Cor 4:1 3049
fruit that may abound to your a Phil 4:17 3056
thee ought, put that on mine a Philem 18 1677
souls, as they that must give a Heb 13:17 3056
Who shall give a to him that is 1Pet 4:5 3056
a that the longsuffering of our 2Pet 3:15 2233

ACCOUNTED
Which also were a giants, as the Deut 2:11 2803
(That also was a a land of giants Deut 2:20 2803
it was nothing a of in the days 1Kin 10:21 2803
it was not any thing a of in the 2Chr 9:20 2803
it shall be a to the Lord for a Ps 22:30 5608
for wherein is he to be a of Is 2:22 2803
are a to rule over the Gentiles Mk 10:42 1380
But they which shall be a worthy Lk 20:35 2661
that ye may be a worthy to escape Lk 21:36 2661
of them should be a the greatest Lk 22:24 1380
we are a as sheep for the Rom 8:36 3049
it was a to him for righteousness Gal 3:6 3049

ACCOUNTING
A that God was able to raise him Heb 11:19 3049

ACCOUNTS
princes might give a unto them Dan 6:2 2941

ACCURSED
for he that is hanged is a of God Deut 21:23 7045
And the city shall be a, even it, Josh 6:17 2764
keep yourselves from the a thing Josh 6:18 2764
lest ye make yourselves a Josh 6:18 2763
when ye take of the a thing Josh 6:18 2764
a trespass in the a thing Josh 7:1 2764
of Judah, took of the a thing Josh 7:1 2764
have even taken of the a thing Josh 7:11 2764
enemies, because they were a Josh 7:12 2764
ye destroy the a from among you Josh 7:12 2764
There is an a thing in the midst Josh 7:13 2764
away the a thing from among you Josh 7:13 2764
a thing shall be burnt with fire Josh 7:15 2764
commit a trespass in the a thing Josh 22:20 2764
who transgressed in the thing a 1Chr 2:7 2764
an hundred years old shall be a Is 65:20 7043
a from Christ for my brethren Rom 9:3 331
the Spirit of God calleth Jesus a 1Cor 12:3 331
preached unto you, let him be a Gal 1:8 331
ye have received, let him be a Gal 1:9 331

ACCUSATION
wrote they unto him an a against Ezr 4:6 7855
up over his head his a written Mt 27:37 156
of his a was written over Mk 15:26 156
they might find an a against him Lk 6:7 2724
any thing from any man by false a Lk 19:8 4811
What a bring ye against this man Jn 18:29 2724
they brought none a of such Acts 25:18 156
Against an elder receive not an a 1Ti 5:19 2724
bring not railing a against them 2Pet 2:11 2920
not bring against him a railing a Jude 9 2920

ACCUSE
A not a servant unto his master, Prov 30:10 3960
that they might a him Mt 12:10 2723
that they might a him Mk 3:2 2723
to no man, neither a any falsely Lk 3:14 4811
his mouth, that they might a him Lk 11:54 2722
And they began to a him, saying, Lk 23:2 2722
those things whereof ye a him Lk 23:14 2722
that I will a you to the Father Jn 5:45 2722
that they might have to a him Jn 8:6 2722
forth, Tertullus began to a him Acts 24:2 2722
these things, whereof we a him Acts 24:8 2722
the things whereof they now a me Acts 24:13 2722
a this man, if there be any Acts 25:5 2722
these things whereof these a me Acts 25:11 2722
I had ought to a my nation of Acts 28:19 2722
a your good conversation in 1Pet 3:16 1908

ACCUSED
came near, and a the Jews Dan 3:8 7170
those men which had a Daniel Dan 6:24 7170
when he was a of the chief Mt 27:12 2723
the chief priests a him of many Mk 15:3 2723
the same was a unto him that he Lk 16:1 1225
scribes stood and vehemently a him Lk 23:10 2722
wherefore he was a of the Jews Acts 22:30 2722
the cause wherefore they a him Acts 23:28 1458
Whom I perceived to be a of Acts 23:29 1458
before that he which is a have Acts 25:16 2722
things whereof I am a of the Jews Acts 26:2 1458
king Agrippa, I am a of the Jews Acts 26:7 1458
children not a of riot or unruly Titus 1:6
which a them before our God day Rev 12:10 2722

ACCUSER
for the a of our brethren is cast Rev 12:10 2723

ACCUSERS
Woman, where are those thine a Jn 8:10 2723
gave commandment to his a also to Acts 23:30 2723
when thine a are also come Acts 23:35 2723
Commanding his a to come unto Acts 24:8 2723
accused have the a face to face Acts 25:16 2723
Against whom when the a stood up Acts 25:18 2723
affection, trucebreakers, false a 2Ti 3:3 1228
as becometh holiness, not false a Titus 2:3 1228

ACCUSETH
there is one that a you, even Jn 5:45 2723

ACCUSING
a or else excusing one another Rom 2:15 2722

ACCUSTOMED
do good, that are a to do evil Jer 13:23 3928

ACELDAMA (as-el'-dam-ah) *A burial ground bought with Judas' betrayal money.*
called in their proper tongue, A Acts 1:19 184

ACHAIA (ak-ah'-yah) *Roman province in Greece.*
when Gallio was the deputy of A Acts 18:12 882
he was disposed to pass into A Acts 18:27 882
had passed through Macedonia and A Acts 19:21 882
A to make a certain contribution Rom 15:26 882
the firstfruits of A unto Christ Rom 16:5 882
that it is the firstfruits of A 1Cor 16:15 882
all the saints which are in all A 2Cor 1:1 882
that A was ready a year ago 2Cor 9:2 882
this boasting in the regions of A 2Cor 11:10 882
that believe in Macedonia and A 1Th 1:7 882
Lord not only in Macedonia and A 1Th 1:8 882

ACHAICUS (ak-ah'-yah-cus) *A Corinthian who visited Paul in Philippi.*
of Stephanas and Fortunatus and A 1Cor 16:17 883
by Stephanus, and Fortunatus, and A 1Cor s

ACHAN (a'-kan) See ACHAR. *Soldier under Joshua executed for disobedience.*
for A, the son of Carmi, the son Josh 7:1 5912
and A, the son of Carmi, the son Josh 7:18 5912
And Joshua said unto A, My son, Josh 7:19 5912
A answered Joshua, and said, Josh 7:20 5912
took A the son of Zerah, and the Josh 7:24 5912
Did not A the son of Zerah commit Josh 22:20 5912

ACHAR (a'-kar) See ACHAN. *A form of Achan.*
A, the troubler of Israel, who 1Chr 2:7 5917

ACHAZ (a'-kaz) See AHAZ. *The Greek form of Ahaz.*
and Joatham begat A Mt 1:9 881
and A begat Ezekias Mt 1:9 881

ACHBOR (ak'-bor)
1. Father of an Edomite king.
the son of A reigned in his stead Gen 36:38 5907
And Baal-hanan the son of A died Gen 36:39 5907
the son of A reigned in his stead 1Chr 1:49 5907
2. A messenger of Josiah to Huldah.
A the son of Michaiah, and Shaphan 2Kin 22:12 5907
the priest, and Ahikam, and A 2Kin 22:14 5907
3. Father of Elnathan.
namely, Elnathan the son of A Jer 26:22 5907
and Elnathan the son of A Jer 36:12 5907

ACHIM (a'-kim) *Son of Sadoc; ancestor of Jesus.*
and Sadoc begat A Mt 1:14 885
and A begat Eliud Mt 1:14 885

ACHISH (a'-kish)
1. A king of Gath who aided David.
went to A the king of Gath 1Sa 21:10 397
the servants of A said unto him 1Sa 21:11 397
sore afraid of A the king of Gath 1Sa 21:12 397
Then said A unto his servants, Lo 1Sa 21:14 397
men that were with him unto A 1Sa 27:2 397
And David dwelt with A at Gath 1Sa 27:3 397
And David said unto A, If I have 1Sa 27:5 397
Then A gave him Ziklag that day 1Sa 27:6 397
and returned, and came to A 1Sa 27:9 397
A said, Whither have ye made a 1Sa 27:10 397
A believed David, saying, He hath 1Sa 27:12 397
A said unto David, Know thou 1Sa 28:1 397
And David said to A, Surely thou 1Sa 28:2 397
A said to David, Therefore will I 1Sa 28:2 397
passed on in the rereward with A 1Sa 29:2 397
A said unto the princes of the 1Sa 29:3 397
Then A called David, and said unto 1Sa 29:6 397
And David said unto A, But what 1Sa 29:8 397
A answered and said to David, I 1Sa 29:9 397
2. A king of Gath during Solomon's reign.
of Shimei ran away unto A son of 1Kin 2:39 397
went to Gath to A to seek his 1Kin 2:40 397

ACHMETHA (ak'-meth-ah) *A city in Media.*
And there was found at A, in the Ezr 6:2 307

ACHOR (a'-kor) *A valley near Jericho.*
brought them unto the valley of A Josh 7:24 5911
place was called, The valley of A Josh 7:26 5911
toward Debir from the valley of A Josh 15:7 5911
the valley of A a place for the Is 65:10 5911
the valley of A for a door of Hos 2:15 5911

ACHSA (ak'-sah) See ACHSAH. *Daughter of Caleb.*
and the daughter of Caleb was A 1Chr 2:49 5915

ACHSAH (ak'-sah) See ACHSA. *A form of Achsa.*
to him will I give A my daughter Josh 15:16 5915
he gave him A his daughter to Josh 15:17 5915
to him will I give A my daughter Judg 1:12 5919
he gave him A his daughter to Judg 1:13 5919

ACHSHAPH (ak'-shaf) *A Phoenician city in Asher.*
of Shimron, and to the king of A Josh 11:1 407
the king of A, one Josh 12:20 407
Helkath, and Hali, and Beten, and A Josh 19:25 407

ACHZIB (ak'-zib) See CHEZIB.
1. A town in western Judah.
And Keilah, and A, and Mareshah Josh 15:44 392
the houses of A shall be a lie to Mic 1:14 392
2. A coastal city in Asher.
at the sea from the coast to A Josh 19:29 392
of Zidon, nor of Ahlab, nor of A Judg 1:31 392

ACKNOWLEDGE
But he shall a the son of the Deut 21:17 5234
neither did he a his brethren Deut 33:9 5234
For I a my transgressions Ps 51:3 3045
In all thy ways a him, and he Prov 3:6 3045
and, ye that are near, a my might Is 33:13 3045
all that see them shall a them Is 61:9 5234
of us, and Israel a us not Is 63:16 5234
Only a thine iniquity, that thou Jer 3:13 3045
We a, O LORD, our wickedness, and Jer 14:20 3045
so will I a them that are carried Jer 24:5 5234
a strange god, whom he shall a Dan 11:39 5234
till they a their offence, and Hos 5:15
let him a that the things that I 1Cor 14:37 1921
therefore a ye them that are such 1Cor 16:18 1921
unto you, than what ye read or a 2Cor 1:13 1921
trust ye shall a even to the end 2Cor 1:13 1921

ACKNOWLEDGED
And Judah a them, and said, She Gen 38:26 5234
I a my sin unto thee, and mine Ps 32:5 3045
As also ye have a us in part 2Cor 1:14 1922

ACKNOWLEDGEMENT
to the a of the mystery of God, Col 2:2 1922

ACKNOWLEDGETH
[but] he that a the Son hath 1Jn 2:23

ACKNOWLEDGING
repentance to the a of the truth 2Ti 2:25 1922
the a of the truth which is after Titus 1:1 1922
may become effectual by the a of Philem 6 1922

ACQUAINT
A now thyself with him, and be at Job 22:21 5532

ACQUAINTANCE
it to them, every man of his a 2Kin 12:5 4378
receive no more money of your a 2Kin 12:7 4378
mine a are verily estranged from Job 19:13 3045
that had been of his a before Job 42:11 3045
neighbours, and a fear to mine a Ps 31:11 3045
mine equal, my guide, and mine a Ps 55:13 3045
hast put away mine a far from me Ps 88:8 3045
from me, and mine a into darkness Ps 88:18 3045
him among their kinsfolk and a Lk 2:44 1110
And all his a, and the women that Lk 23:49 1110
a to minister or come unto him Acts 24:23 2398

ACQUAINTED
down, and art a with all my ways Ps 139:3 5532
a man of sorrows, and a with grief Is 53:3 3045

ACQUAINTING
yet a mine heart with wisdom Eccl 2:3 5090

ACQUIT
thou wilt not a me from mine Job 10:14 5352
and will not at all a the wicked Nah 1:3 5352

ACRE
as it were an half a of land 1Sa 14:14 4618

ACRES
ten a of vineyard shall yield one Is 5:10 6776

ACSAH See ACHSA.

ACSHAPH See ACHSHAPH.

ACT
to pass his a, his strange a Is 28:21 5556
the a of violence is in their Is 59:6 6467
taken in adultery, in the very a Jn 8:4 1888

ACTIONS
and by him *a* are weighed 1Sa 2:3 5949

ACTIVITY
knowest any men of *a* among them Gen 47:6 2428

ACTS
And his miracles, and his *a* Deut 11:3 4640
great *a* of the LORD which he did Deut 11:7 4640
the righteous *a* of the LORD Judg 5:11
even the righteous *a* toward the Judg 5:11
all the righteous *a* of the LORD 1Sa 12:7
of Kabzeel, who had done many *a* 2Sa 23:20 6467
I heard in mine own land of thy *a* 1Kin 10:6 1697
And the rest of the *a* of Solomon 1Kin 11:41 1697
in the book of the *a* of Solomon 1Kin 11:41 1697
And the rest of the *a* of Jeroboam 1Kin 14:19 1697
Now the rest of the *a* of Rehoboam 1Kin 14:29 1697
Now the rest of the *a* of Abijam 1Kin 15:7 1697
The rest of all the *a* of Asa 1Kin 15:23 1697
Now the rest of the *a* of Nadab 1Kin 15:31 1697
Now the rest of the *a* of Baasha 1Kin 16:5 1697
Now the rest of the *a* of Elah 1Kin 16:14 1697
Now the rest of the *a* of Zimri 1Kin 16:20 1697
Now the rest of the *a* of Omri 1Kin 16:27 1697
Now the rest of the *a* of Ahab 1Kin 22:39 1697
the rest of the *a* of Jehoshaphat 1Kin 22:45 1697
Now the rest of the *a* of Ahaziah 2Kin 1:18 1697
And the rest of the *a* of Joram 2Kin 8:23 1697
Now the rest of the *a* of Jehu 2Kin 10:34 1697
And the rest of the *a* of Joash 2Kin 12:19 1697
Now the rest of the *a* of Jehoahaz 2Kin 13:8 1697
And the rest of the *a* of Joash 2Kin 13:12 1697
Now the rest of the *a* of Jehoash 2Kin 14:15 1697
And the rest of the *a* of Amaziah 2Kin 14:18 1697
Now the rest of the *a* of Jeroboam 2Kin 14:28 1697
And the rest of the *a* of Azariah 2Kin 15:6 1697
And the rest of the *a* of Zachariah 2Kin 15:11 1697
And the rest of the *a* of Shallum 2Kin 15:15 1697
And the rest of the *a* of Menahem 2Kin 15:21 1697
And the rest of the *a* of Pekahiah 2Kin 15:26 1697
And the rest of the *a* of Pekah 2Kin 15:31 1697
Now the rest of the *a* of Jotham 2Kin 15:36 1697
Now the rest of the *a* of Ahaz 2Kin 16:19 1697
And the rest of the *a* of Hezekiah 2Kin 20:20 1697
Now the rest of the *a* of Manasseh 2Kin 21:17 1697
Now the rest of the *a* of Amon 2Kin 21:25 1697
the *a* that he had done in Beth-el 2Kin 23:19 4640
Now the rest of the *a* of Josiah 2Kin 23:28 1697
the rest of the *a* of Jehoiakim 2Kin 24:5 1697
of Kabzeel, who had done many *a* 1Chr 11:22 6467
Now the *a* of David the king, 1Chr 29:29 1697
heard in mine own land of thine *a* 2Chr 9:5 1697
Now the rest of the *a* of Solomon 2Chr 9:29 1697
Now the *a* of Rehoboam, first and 2Chr 12:15 1697
And the rest of the *a* of Abijah 2Chr 13:22 1697
the *a* of Asa, first and last, lo, 2Chr 16:11 1697
the rest of the *a* of Jehoshaphat 2Chr 20:34 1697
Now the rest of the *a* of Amaziah 2Chr 25:26 1697
Now the rest of the *a* of Uzziah 2Chr 26:22 1697
Now the rest of the *a* of Jotham 2Chr 27:7 1697
Now the rest of his *a* and of all 2Chr 28:26 1697
Now the rest of the *a* of Hezekiah 2Chr 32:32 1697
Now the rest of the *a* of Manasseh 2Chr 33:18 1697
Now the rest of the *a* of Josiah 2Chr 35:26 1697
the rest of the *a* of Jehoiakim 2Chr 36:8 1697
all the *a* of his power and of his Est 10:2 4640
his *a* unto the children of Israel Ps 103:7 5949
utter the mighty *a* of the LORD Ps 106:2
and shall declare thy mighty *a* Ps 145:4
of the might of thy terrible *a* Ps 145:6
to the sons of men his mighty *a* Ps 145:12
Praise him for his mighty *a* Ps 150:2

ACZIB See ACHZIB.

ADADAH (*ad'-ad-ah*) *A city in southern Judah.*
And Kinah, and Dimonah, and *A* Josh 15:22 5735

ADAH (*a'-dah*)
1. A wife of Lemech.
the name of the one was *A* Gen 4:19 5711
And *A* bare Jabal Gen 4:20 5711
And Lamech said unto his wives, *A* Gen 4:23 5711
2. A wife of Esau.
A the daughter of Elon the Gen 36:2 5711
And *A* bare to Esau Eliphaz Gen 36:4 5711
the son of *A* the wife of Esau Gen 36:10 5711
were the sons of *A* Esau's wife Gen 36:12 5711
these were the sons of *A* Gen 36:16 5711

ADAIAH (*ad-a-i'-yah*)
1. Grandfather of King Josiah.
the daughter of *A* of Boscath 2Kin 22:1 5718
2. A Levite descendant of Gershon.
the son of Zerah, the son of *A* 1Chr 6:41 5718
3. A son of Shimhi.
And *A*, and Beraiah, and Shimrath, 1Chr 8:21 5718
4. A Levite of Jerusalem.
A the son of Jeroham, the son of 1Chr 9:12 5718
5. Father of Maaseiah.
of Obed, and Maaseiah the son of *A* 2Chr 23:1 5718
6. Married a foreign wife in exile.
Meshullam, Malluch, and *A*, Jashub, Ezr 10:29 5718
7. Married a foreign wife in exile.
And Shelemiah, and Nathan, and *A* Ezr 10:39 5718
8. A descendant of Pharez.
the son of Hazaiah, the son of *A* Neh 11:5 5718
9. An Aaronite Levite.
A the son of Jeroham, the son of Neh 11:12 5718

ADALIA (*ad-al-i'-yah*) *A son of Haman.*
And Poratha, and *A*, and Aridatha, Est 9:8 118

ADAM (*ad'-um*) See ADAM'S.
1. First man created by God.
brought them unto *A* to see what Gen 2:19 120
whatsoever *A* called every living Gen 2:19 120
A gave names to all cattle, and to Gen 2:20 120
but for *A* there was not found an Gen 2:20 120
a deep sleep to fall upon *A* Gen 2:21 121
A said, This is now bone of my Gen 2:23 120
and *A* and his wife hid themselves Gen 3:8 120
And the LORD God called unto *A* Gen 3:9 120
unto *A* he said, Because thou hast Gen 3:17 121
A called his wife's name Eve Gen 3:20 120
Unto *A* also and to his wife did Gen 3:21 120
And *A* knew Eve his wife Gen 4:1 120
And *A* knew his wife again Gen 4:25 120
the book of the generations of *A* Gen 5:1 120
them, and called their name *A* Gen 5:2 120
A lived an hundred and thirty Gen 5:3 121
the days of *A* after he had Gen 5:4 121
all the days that *A* lived were Gen 5:5 121
when he separated the sons of *A* Deut 32:8 120
A, Sheth, Enosh, 1Chr 1:1 121
I covered my transgressions as *A* Job 31:33 121
of Seth, which was the son of *A* Lk 3:38 *76*
death reigned from *A* to Moses Rom 5:14 *76*
For as in *A* all die, even so in 1Cor 15:22 *76*
The first man *A* was made a living 1Cor 15:45 *76*
the last *A* was made a quickening 1Cor 15:45 *76*
For *A* was first formed, then Eve 1Ti 2:13 *76*
A was not deceived, but the woman 1Ti 2:14 *76*
And Enoch also, the seventh from *A* Jude 14 *76*
2. A town in Manasseh.
an heap very far from the city *A* Josh 3:16 121

ADAMAH (*ad'-am-ah*) *A walled city in Naphtali.*
And *A*, and Ramah, and Hazor, Josh 19:36 128

ADAMANT
As an *a* harder than flint have I Eze 3:9 8068
made their hearts as an *a* stone Zec 7:12 8068

ADAMI (*ad'-am-i*) *A variant of Adamah.*
from Allon to Zaanannim, and *A* Josh 19:33 129

ADAMI NEKEB See NEKEB.

ADAM'S (*ad'-ums*)
the similitude of *A* transgression Rom 5:14 *76*

ADAR (*a'-dar*) See ADDAR, ATABOTH-ADAR.
1. A city in southern Judah.
along to Hezron, and went up to *A* Josh 15:3 146
2. Twelfth month of the Hebrew year.
on the third day of the month *A* Ezr 6:15 144
month, that is, the month *A* Est 3:7 143
month, which is the month *A* Est 3:13 143
month, which is the month *A* Est 8:12 143
month, that is, the month *A* Est 9:1 143
day also of the month *A*, and slew Est 9:15 143
the thirteenth day of the month *A* Est 9:17 143
of the month *A* a day of gladness Est 9:19 143
the fourteenth day of the month *A* Est 9:21 143

ADBEEL (*ad'-be-el*) *Son of Ishmael.*
and Kedar, and *A*, and Mibsam, Gen 25:13 110
then Kedar, and *A*, and Mibsam, 1Chr 1:29 110

ADD
The LORD shall *a* to me another Gen 30:24 3254
shall *a* the fifth part thereto, Lev 5:16 3254
shall *a* the fifth part more Lev 6:5 3254
then he shall *a* a fifth part Lev 27:13 3254
then he shall *a* the fifth part of Lev 27:15 3254
then he shall *a* the fifth part of Lev 27:19 3254
shall *a* a fifth part of it Lev 27:27 3254
he shall *a* thereto the fifth part Lev 27:31 3254
a unto it the fifth part thereof, Num 5:7 3254
and to them ye shall *a* forty Num 35:6 5414
Ye shall not *a* unto the word Deut 4:2 3254
thou shalt not *a* thereto, nor Deut 12:32 3254
then shalt thou *a* three cities Deut 19:9 3254
to *a* drunkenness to thirst Deut 29:19 5595
LORD thy God *a* unto the people 2Sa 24:3 3254
heavy yoke, I will *a* to your yoke 1Kin 12:11 3254
heavy, and I will *a* to your yoke 1Kin 12:14 3254
I will *a* unto thy days fifteen 2Kin 20:6 3254
and thou mayest *a* thereto 1Chr 22:14 3254
yoke heavy, but I will *a* thereto 2Chr 10:14 3254
ye intend to *a* more to our sins 2Chr 28:13 3254
A iniquity unto their iniquity Ps 69:27 5414
and peace, shall they *a* to thee Prov 3:2 3254
A thou not unto his words, lest Prov 30:6 3254
a ye year to year Is 29:1 5595
that they may *a* sin to sin Is 30:1 5595
I will *a* unto thy days fifteen Is 38:5 3254
can *a* one cubit unto his stature Mt 6:27 *4369*
can *a* to his stature one cubit Lk 12:25 *4369*
supposing to *a* affliction to my Phil 1:16 *2018*
diligence, *a* to your faith virtue 2Pet 1:5 *2023*
If any man shall *a* unto these Rev 22:18 *2007*
God shall *a* unto him the plagues Rev 22:18 *2007*

ADDAN (*ad'-dan*) *Home of some exiles in Babylon.*
Tel-melah, Tel-harsa, Cherub, *A* Ezr 2:59 135

ADDAR (*ad'-dar*) See ADAR, ATAROTH-ADDAR.
Son of Bela.
And the sons of Bela were, *A* 1Chr 8:3 146

ADDED
and he *a* no more Deut 5:22 3254
for we have *a* unto all our sins 1Sa 12:19 3254
there were *a* besides unto them Jer 36:32 3254
for the LORD hath *a* grief to my Jer 45:3 3254
excellent majesty was *a* unto me Dan 4:36 3255
these things shall be *a* unto you Mt 6:33 *4369*
A yet this above all, that he Lk 3:20 *4369*
these things shall be *a* unto you Lk 12:31 *4369*
as they heard these things, he *a* Lk 19:11 *4369*
the same day there were *a* unto Acts 2:41 *4369*
the Lord *a* to the church daily Acts 2:47 *4369*
were the more *a* to the Lord Acts 5:14 *4369*
much people was *a* unto the Lord Acts 11:24 *4369*
in conference *a* nothing to me Gal 2:6 *4323*
It was *a* because of Gal 3:19 *4369*

ADDER
an *a* in the path, that biteth the Gen 49:17 8207
the deaf *a* that stoppeth her ear Ps 58:4 6620
shalt tread upon the lion and *a* Ps 91:13 6620
a serpent, and stingeth like an *a* Prov 23:32 6848

ADDERS'
a poison is under their lips Ps 140:3 5919

ADDETH
For he *a* rebellion unto his sin, Job 34:37 3254
rich, and he *a* no sorrow with it Prov 10:22 3254
mouth, and *a* learning to his lips Prov 16:23 3254
no man disannulleth, or *a* thereto Gal 3:15 *1928*

ADDI (*ad'-di*) *Son of Cozam; ancestor of Jesus.*
of Melchi, which was the son of *A* Lk 3:28 *78*

ADDICTED
that they have *a* themselves to 1Cor 16:15 *5021*

ADDITION
molten, at the side of every *a* 1Kin 7:30 3914

ADDITIONS
were certain *a* made of thin work 1Kin 7:29 3914
of every one, and *a* round about 1Kin 7:36 3914

ADDON (*ad'-don*) *A form of Addan.*
Tel-melah, Tel-haresha, Cherub, *A* Neh 7:61 114

ADER (*a'-dur*) *A son of Beriah.*
And Zebadiah, and Arad, and *A* 1Chr 8:15 5738

ADIEL (*a'-de-el*)
1. A descendant of Simeon.
and Jeshohaiah, and Asaiah, and *A* 1Chr 4:36 5717
2. Father of Massiai.
and Maasiai the son of *A*, the son 1Chr 9:12 5717
3. Father of Azmaveth.
was Azmaveth the son of *A* 1Chr 27:25 5717

ADIN (*a'-din*)
1. Family who returned from exile.
The children of *A*, four hundred Ezr 2:15 5720
The children of *A*, six hundred Neh 7:20 5720
2. Family who sealed the covenant with Nehemiah.
Adonijah, Bigvai, *A*, Neh 10:16 5720
3. An exilic family with Ezra.
Of the sons also of *A* Ezr 8:6 5720

ADINA (*ad'-in-ah*) *A "mighty man" of David.*
A the son of Shiza the Reubenite, 1Chr 11:42 5721

ADINO (*ad'-in-o*) *A "mighty man" of David.*
the same was *A* the Eznite 2Sa 23:8 5722

ADITHAIM (*ad-ith-a'-im*) *A city in the plain of Judah.*
And Sharaim, and *A*, and Josh 15:36 5723

ADJURE
How many times shall I *a* thee 1Kin 22:16 7650
How many times shall I *a* thee 2Chr 18:15 7650
I *a* thee by the living God, that Mt 26:63 *1844*
I *a* thee by God, that thou Mk 5:7 *3726*
We *a* you by Jesus whom Paul Acts 19:13 *3726*

ADJURED
Joshua *a* them at that time, Josh 6:26 7650
for Saul had *a* the people 1Sa 14:24 422

ADLAI (*ad'-la-i*) *Father of Shapat.*
valleys was Shaphat the son of *A* 1Chr 27:29 5724

ADMAH (*ad'-mah*) *A city destroyed with Sodom and Gomorrah.*
unto Sodom, and Gomorrah, and *A* Gen 10:19 126
of Gomorrah, Shinab king of *A* Gen 14:2 126
of Gomorrah, and the king of *A* Gen 14:8 126
of Sodom, and Gomorrah, *A*, and Deut 29:23 126
how shall I make thee as *A* Hos 11:8 126

ADMATHA (*ad'-math-ah*) *A prince of Persia.*
unto him was Carshena, Shethar, *A* Est 1:14 133

ADMINISTERED
which is *a* by us to the glory of 2Cor 8:19 *1247*
this abundance which is *a* by us 2Cor 8:20 *1247*

ADMINISTRATION
For the *a* of this service not 2Cor 9:12 *1248*

ADMINISTRATIONS
And there are differences of *a* 1Cor 12:5 *1248*

ADMIRATION
persons in *a* because of advantage Jude 16 *2296*
saw her, I wondered with great *a* Rev 17:6 *2295*

ADMIRED
to be *a* in all them that believe 2Th 1:10 *2296*

ADMONISH
able also to *a* one another Rom 15:14 *3560*
over you in the Lord, and *a* you 1Th 5:12 *3560*
an enemy, but *a* him as a brother 2Th 3:15 *3560*

ADMONISHED
king, who will no more be *a* Eccl 4:13 2094
further, by these, my son, be *a* Eccl 12:12 2094
that I have *a* you this day Jer 42:19 5749
was now already past, Paul *a* them Acts 27:9 *3867*
as Moses was *a* of God when he was Heb 8:5 *5537*

ADMONISHING
a one another in psalms and hymns Col 3:16 *3560*

ADMONITION
and they are written for our *a* 1Cor 10:11 *3559*
in the nurture and *a* of the Lord Eph 6:4 *3559*
the first and second *a* reject Titus 3:10 *3559*

ADNA (ad'-nah) See ADNAH.
1. Married a foreigner while in exile.
A, and Chelal, Benaiah, Maaseiah, ... Ezr 10:30 5733
2. A priest during Joiakim's reign.
Of Harim, A ... Neh 12:15 5733

ADNAH (ad'-nah) See ADNA.
1. A captain in David's army.
there fell to him of Manasseh, A ... 1Chr 12:20 5734
2. A commander in Jehoshaphat's army.
A the chief, and with him mighty ... 2Chr 17:14 5734

ADO
unto them, Why make ye this a ... Mk 5:39 *2350*

ADONI-BEZEK (ad'-on-i-be'-zek) *A lord of a Canaanite city.*
And they found A in Bezek ... Judg 1:5 137
But A fled ... Judg 1:6 137
A said, Threescore and ten kings, ... Judg 1:7 137

ADONIJAH (ad-on-i'-jah) See TOB-ADONIJAH.
1. A son of David.
the fourth, A the son of Haggith ... 2Sa 3:4 138
Then A the son of Haggith exalted ... 1Kin 1:5 138
and they following A helped him ... 1Kin 1:7 138
to David, were not with A ... 1Kin 1:8 138
A slew sheep and oxen and fat ... 1Kin 1:9 138
Hast thou not heard that A the ... 1Kin 1:11 138
why then doth A reign ... 1Kin 1:13 138
And now, behold, A reigneth ... 1Kin 1:18 138
A shall reign after me, and he ... 1Kin 1:24 138
him, and say, God save king A ... 1Kin 1:25 138
And A and all the guests that were ... 1Kin 1:41 138
and A said unto him, Come in ... 1Kin 1:42 138
And Jonathan answered and said to A 1Kin 1:43 138
that were with A were afraid ... 1Kin 1:49 138
A feared because of Solomon, and ... 1Kin 1:50 138
Behold, A feareth king Solomon ... 1Kin 1:51 138
A the son of Haggith came to ... 1Kin 2:13 138
Solomon, to speak unto him for A ... 1Kin 2:19 138
be given to A thy brother to wife ... 1Kin 2:21 138
ask Abishag the Shunammite for A ... 1Kin 2:22 138
if A have not spoken this word ... 1Kin 2:23 138
A shall be put to death this day ... 1Kin 2:24 138
for Joab had turned after A ... 1Kin 2:28 138
the fourth, A the son of Haggith ... 1Chr 3:2 138
2. A Levite under King Jehoshaphat.
Shemiramoth, and Jehonathan, and A. 2Chr 17:8 138
3. A clan leader who sealed the covenant with Nehemiah.
A, Bigvai, Adin, ... Neh 10:16 138

ADONIKAM (ad-on-i'-kam) *A family in exile.*
The children of A, six hundred ... Ezr 2:13 140
And of the last sons of A, whose ... Ezr 8:13 140
The children of A, six hundred ... Neh 7:18 140

ADONIRAM (ad-on-i'-ram) See ADORAM. *A tribute officer under Solomon.*
A the son of Abda was over the ... 1Kin 4:6 141
and A was over the levy ... 1Kin 5:14 141

ADONI-ZEDEK (ad'-on-i-ze'-dek) *Canaanite king slain by Joshua.*
when A king of Jerusalem had ... Josh 10:1 139
Wherefore A king of Jerusalem ... Josh 10:3 139

ADOPTION
ye have received the Spirit of a ... Rom 8:15 *5206*
ourselves, waiting for the a ... Rom 8:23 *5206*
to whom pertaineth the a, and the ... Rom 9:4 *5206*
we might receive the a of sons ... Gal 4:5 *5206*
predestinated us unto the a of ... Eph 1:5 *5206*

ADORAIM (ad-o-ra'-im) *A city built by Rehoboam.*
And A, and Lachish, and Azekah, ... 2Chr 11:9 115

ADORAM (ad-o'-ram) See ADONIRAM.
1. A tribute officer under David.
And A was over the tribute ... 2Sa 20:24 151
2. A tribute officer under Solomon.
Then king Rehoboam sent A ... 1Kin 12:18 151

ADORN
that women a themselves in modest ... 1Ti 2:9 *2885*
that they may a the doctrine of ... Titus 2:10 *2885*

ADORNED
shalt again be a with thy tabrets ... Jer 31:4 5710
how it was a with goodly stones ... Lk 21:5 *2885*
a themselves, being in subjection ... 1Pet 3:5 *2885*
as a bride a for her husband ... Rev 21:2 *2885*

ADORNETH
as a bride a herself with her ... Is 61:10 5710

ADORNING
Whose a let it not be that ... 1Pet 3:3 *2889*
outward a of plaiting the hair ... 1Pet 3:3 *2889*

ADRAMMELECH (a-dram'-mel-ek)
1. A god of the Avites.
burnt their children in fire to A ... 2Kin 17:31 152
2. A son of Sennacherib.
house of Nisroch his god, that A ... 2Kin 19:37 152
house of Nisroch his god, that A ... Is 37:38 152

ADRAMYTTIAN See ADRAMYTTIUM.

ADRAMYTTIUM (a-dram-mit'-te-um) *A seaport of Mysia in Asia Minor.*
And entering into a ship of A ... Acts 27:2 *98*

ADRIA (a'-dre-ah) *The Adriatic Sea.*
as we were driven up and down in A ... Acts 27:27 *99*

ADRIATIC See ADRIA.

ADRIEL (a'-dre-el) *Husband of Merab, Saul's daughter.*
unto A the Meholathite to wife ... 1Sa 18:19 5741
whom she brought up for A the son ... 2Sa 21:8 5741

ADULLAM (a-dul'-lam) See ADULLAMITE.
1. A city south of Jerusalem.
the king of A, one ... Josh 12:15 5725
Jarmuth, and A, Socoh, and Azekah, ... Josh 15:35 5725
And Beth-zur, and Shoco, and A ... 2Chr 11:7 5725
Zanoah, A, and in their villages, ... Neh 11:30 5725
he shall come unto A the glory of ... Mic 1:15 5725
2. A large cave near the city of Adullam.
thence, and escaped to the cave A ... 1Sa 22:1 5725
harvest time unto the cave of A ... 2Sa 23:13 5725
rock to David, into the cave of A ... 1Chr 11:15 5725

ADULLAMITE (a-dul'-lam-ite) *A native of Adullam.*
and turned in to a certain A ... Gen 38:1 5726
he and his friend Hirah the A ... Gen 38:12 5726
by the hand of his friend the A ... Gen 38:20 5726

ADULTERER
with his neighbour's wife, the a ... Lev 20:10 5003
The eye also of the a waiteth for ... Job 24:15 5003
the sorceress, the seed of the a ... Is 57:3 5003

ADULTERERS
him, and hast been partaker with a ... Ps 50:18 5003
for they be all a, an assembly of ... Jer 9:2 5003
For the land is full of a ... Jer 23:10 5003
They are all a, as an oven heated ... Hos 7:4 5003
the sorcerers, and against the a ... Mal 3:5 5003
men are, extortioners, unjust, a ... Lk 18:11 *3432*
fornicators, nor idolaters, nor a ... 1Cor 6:9 *3432*
whoremongers and a God will judge ... Heb 13:4 *3432*
Ye a and adulteresses, know ye not ... Jas 4:4 *3432*

ADULTERESS
the a shall surely be put to ... Lev 20:10 5003
the a will hunt for the precious ... Prov 6:26
beloved of her friend, yet an a ... Hos 3:1 5003
man, she shall be called an a ... Rom 7:3 *3428*
so that she is no a, though she ... Rom 7:3 *3428*

ADULTERESSES
judge them after the manner of a ... Eze 23:45 5003
because they are a, and blood is ... Eze 23:45 5003
Ye adulterers and a, know ye not ... Jas 4:4 *3428*

ADULTERIES
I have seen thine a, and thy ... Jer 13:27 5004
said I unto her that was old in a ... Eze 23:43 5004
her a from between her breasts ... Hos 2:2 5005
proceed evil thoughts, murders, a ... Mt 15:19 *3430*
of men, proceed evil thoughts, a ... Mk 7:21 *3430*

ADULTEROUS
Such is the way of an a woman ... Prov 30:20 5003
a generation seeketh after a sign ... Mt 12:39 *3428*
a generation seeketh after a sign ... Mt 16:4 *3428*
of me and of my words in this a ... Mk 8:38 *3428*

ADULTERY
Thou shalt not commit a ... Ex 20:14 5003
a with another man's wife ... Lev 20:10 5003
even he that committeth a with ... Lev 20:10 5003
Neither shalt thou commit a ... Deut 5:18 5003
committeth a with a woman lacketh ... Prov 6:32 5003
committed a I had put her away ... Jer 3:8 5003
committed a with stones and with ... Jer 3:9 5003
the full, they then committed a ... Jer 5:7 5003
ye steal, murder, and commit a ... Jer 7:9 5003
they commit a, and walk in lies ... Jer 23:14 5003
have committed a with their ... Jer 29:23 5003
But as a wife that committeth a ... Eze 16:32 5003
That they have committed a ... Eze 23:37 5003
their idols have they committed a ... Eze 23:37 5003
and stealing, and committing a ... Hos 4:2 5003
and your spouses shall commit a ... Hos 4:13 5003
your spouses when they commit a ... Hos 4:14 5003
old time, Thou shalt not commit a ... Mt 5:27 *3431*
a with her already in his heart ... Mt 5:28 *3431*
causeth her to commit a ... Mt 5:32 *3429*
her that is divorced committeth a ... Mt 5:32 *3429*
shall marry another, committeth a ... Mt 19:9 *3429*
which is put away doth commit a ... Mt 19:9 *3429*
murder, Thou shalt not commit a ... Mt 19:18 *3431*
another, committeth a against her ... Mk 10:11 *3429*
to another, she committeth a ... Mk 10:12 *3429*
the commandments, Do not commit a. Mk 10:19 *3431*
and marrieth another, committeth a ... Lk 16:18 *3431*
from her husband committeth a ... Lk 16:18 *3431*
the commandments, Do not commit a. Lk 18:20 *3431*
unto him a woman taken in a ... Jn 8:3 *3430*
Master, this woman was taken in a ... Jn 8:4 *3431*
sayest a man should not commit a ... Rom 2:22 *3431*
dost thou commit a? ... Rom 2:22 *3431*
For this, Thou shalt not commit a ... Rom 13:9 *3431*
A, fornication, uncleanness, ... Gal 5:19 *3430*
For he that said, Do not commit a ... Jas 2:11 *3431*
Now if thou commit no a, yet if ... Jas 2:11 *3431*
Having eyes full of a, and that ... 2Pet 2:14 *3428*
them that commit a with her into ... Rev 2:22 *3431*

ADUMMIM (a-dum'-mim)
that is before the going up to A ... Josh 15:7 131
is over against the going up of A ... Josh 18:17 131

ADVANCED
It is the LORD that a Moses ... 1Sa 12:6 6213
a him, and set his seat above all ... Est 3:1 5375
how he had a him above the ... Est 5:11 5375
whereunto the king a him ... Est 10:2 1431

ADVANTAGE
What a will it be unto thee ... Job 35:3 5532
What a then hath the Jew ... Rom 3:1 *4053*
Lest Satan should get an a of us ... 2Cor 2:11 *4122*
in admiration because of a ... Jude 16 *5622*

ADVANTAGED
For what is a man a, if he gain ... Lk 9:25 *5623*

ADVANTAGETH
what a it me, if the dead rise ... 1Cor 15:32 *3786*

ADVENTURE
which would not a to set the sole ... Deut 28:56 5254
not a himself into the theatre ... Acts 19:31 *1325*

ADVENTURED
a his life far, and delivered you ... Judg 9:17 7993

ADVERSARIES
and an adversary unto thine a ... Ex 23:22 6696
lest their a should behave ... Deut 32:27 6862
and will render vengeance to his a ... Deut 32:43 6862
Art thou for us, or for our a ... Josh 5:13 6862
The a of the LORD shall be broken ... 1Sa 2:10 7378
ye should this day be a unto me ... 2Sa 19:22 7854
Now when the a of Judah and ... Ezr 4:1 6862
our a said, They shall not know, ... Neh 4:11 6862
render evil for good are mine a ... Ps 38:20 7853
mine a are all before thee ... Ps 69:19 6887
and consumed that are a to my soul ... Ps 71:13 7853
and turned my hand against their a ... Ps 81:14 6862
set up the right hand of his a ... Ps 89:42 6862
For my love they are my a ... Ps 109:4 7853
reward of mine a from the LORD ... Ps 109:20 7853
Let mine a be clothed with shame, ... Ps 109:29 7853
Ah, I will ease me of mine a ... Is 1:24 6862
set up the a of Rezin against him ... Is 9:11 6862
the a of Judah shall be cut off ... Is 11:13 6887
he will repay, fury to his a ... Is 59:18 6862
our a have trodden down thy ... Is 63:18 6862
to make thy name known to thine a ... Is 64:2 6862
and all thine a, every one of them ... Jer 30:16 6862
that he may avenge him of his a ... Jer 46:10 6862
and their a said, We offend not, ... Jer 50:7 6862
Her a are the chief, her enemies ... Lam 1:5 6862
the a saw her, and did mock at her ... Lam 1:7 6862
that his a should be round about ... Lam 1:17 6862
hath set up the horn of thine a ... Lam 2:17 6862
shall be lifted up upon thine a ... Mic 5:9 6862
LORD will take vengeance on his a ... Nah 1:2 6862
things, all his a were ashamed ... Lk 13:17 *480*
which all your a shall not be ... Lk 21:15 *480*
unto me, and there are many a ... 1Cor 16:9 *480*
And in nothing terrified by your a ... Phil 1:28 *480*
which shall devour the a ... Heb 10:27 *5227*

ADVERSARY
an a unto thine adversaries ... Ex 23:22 6887
in the way for an a against him ... Num 22:22 7854
her a also provoked her sore, for ... 1Sa 1:6 6869
in the battle he be an a to us ... 1Sa 29:4 7854
is neither a nor evil occurrent ... 1Kin 5:4 7854
LORD stirred up an a unto Solomon ... 1Kin 11:14 7854
And God stirred him up another a ... 1Kin 11:23 7854
he was an a to Israel all the ... 1Kin 11:25 7854
And Esther said, The a and enemy is ... Est 7:6 6862
that mine a had written a book ... Job 31:35
how long shall the a reproach ... Ps 74:10 6862
who is mine a? ... Is 50:8
The a hath spread out his hand ... Lam 1:10 6862
stood with his right hand as an a ... Lam 2:4 6862
not have believed that the a ... Lam 4:12 6862
An a there shall be even round ... Amos 3:11 6862
Agree with thine a quickly ... Mt 5:25 *476*
lest at any time the a deliver ... Mt 5:25 *476*
with thine a to the magistrate ... Lk 12:58 *476*
him, saying, Avenge me of mine a ... Lk 18:3 *476*
to the a to speak reproachfully ... 1Ti 5:14 *480*
because your a the devil, as a ... 1Pet 5:8 *476*

ADVERSITIES
saved you out of all your a ... 1Sa 10:19 7451
thou hast known my soul in a ... Ps 31:7 6869

ADVERSITY
redeemed my soul out of all a ... 2Sa 4:9 6869
for God did vex them with all a ... 2Chr 15:6 6869
for I shall never be in a ... Ps 10:6 7451
But in mine a they rejoiced, and ... Ps 35:15 6761
give him rest from the days of a ... Ps 94:13 7451
times, and a brother is born for a ... Prov 17:17 6869
If thou faint in the day of a ... Prov 24:10 6869
but in the day of a consider ... Eccl 7:14 7451
the Lord give you the bread of a ... Is 30:20 6862
and them which suffer a, as being ... Heb 13:3 *2558*

ADVERTISE
I will a thee what this people ... Num 24:14 3289
And I thought to a thee, saying, ... Ruth 4:4

ADVICE
consider of it, take a, and speak ... Judg 19:30 5779
give here your a and counsel ... Judg 20:7 1697
And blessed be thy a, and blessed ... 1Sa 25:33 2940
that our a should not be first ... 2Sa 19:43 1697
What a give ye that we may return ... 2Chr 10:9 3289
them after the a of the young men ... 2Chr 10:14 6098
Then Amaziah king of Judah took a ... 2Chr 25:17 3289
and with good a make war ... Prov 20:18 8458
And herein I give my a ... 2Cor 8:10 *1106*

ADVISE
now a, and see what answer I shall ... 2Sa 24:13 3045
How do ye a that I may answer ... 1Kin 12:6 3289
Now therefore a thyself what word ... 1Chr 21:12 7200

ADVISED
but with the well a is wisdom ... Prov 13:10 3289
the more part a to depart thence ... Acts 27:12

ADVISEMENT
Philistines upon a sent him away.......... 1Chr 12:19 6098

ADVOCATE
we have an a with the Father,.............. 1Jn 2:1 3875

AENEAS (*e'-ne-as*) *A paralytic healed by Peter.*
he found a certain man named A.......... Acts 9:33 132
And Peter said unto him, A .... Acts 9:34 132

AENON (*e'-non*) *A place in the valley of Shechem.*
was baptizing in A near to Salim .... Jn 3:23 137

AFAR
his eyes, and saw the place a off.............. Gen 22:4 7350
And when they saw him a off................ Gen 37:18 7350
And his sister stood a off....................... Ex 2:4 7350
it, they removed, and stood a off............ Ex 20:18 7350
And the people stood a off.................... Ex 20:21 7350
and worship ye a off.............................. Ex 24:1 7350
a off from the camp, and called it......... Ex 33:7 7368
body, or be in a journey a off............... Num 9:10 7350
stood on the top of an hill a off............ 1Sa 26:13 7350
went, and stood to view a off............... 2Kin 2:7 7350
when the man of God saw her a off...... 2Kin 4:25 7350
and the noise was heard a off............... Ezr 3:13 7350
of Jerusalem was heard even a off......... Neh 12:43 7350
they lifted up their eyes a off................ Job 2:12 7350
I will fetch my knowledge from a........... Job 36:3 7350
man may behold it a off........................ Job 36:25 7350
and he smelleth the battle a off............ Job 39:25 7350
prey, and her eyes behold a off............. Job 39:29 7350
Why standest thou a off, O LORD.......... Ps 10:1 7350
and my kinsmen stand a off.................... Ps 38:11 7350
them that are a off upon the sea............ Ps 65:5 7350
but the proud he knoweth a off.............. Ps 138:6 4801
understandest my thought a off.............. Ps 139:2 7350
she bringeth her food from a................... Prov 31:14 4801
shall carry her a off to sojourn.............. Is 23:7 7350
and justice standeth a off...................... Is 59:14 7350
and Javan, to the isles a off................... Is 66:19 7350
the LORD, and not a God a off............... Jer 23:23 7350
for, lo, I will save thee from a................ Jer 30:10 7350
and declare it in the isles a off.............. Jer 31:10 4801
I will save thee from a off..................... Jer 46:27 7350
remember the LORD a off, and let........... Jer 51:50 7350
and rebuke strong nations a off.............. Mic 4:3 7350
But Peter followed him a off unto........... Mt 26:58 3113
women were there beholding a off......... Mt 27:55 3113
But when he saw Jesus a off.................. Mk 5:6 3113
a fig tree a off having leaves................. Mk 11:13 3113
And Peter followed him a off................. Mk 14:54 3113
were also women looking on a off.......... Mk 15:40 3113
torments, and seeth Abraham a off......... Lk 16:23 3113
were lepers, which stood a off............... Lk 17:12 4207
And the publican, standing a off............ Lk 18:13 3113
And Peter followed a off....................... Lk 22:54 3113
him from Galilee, stood a off................ Lk 23:49 3113
and to all that are a off........................ Acts 2:39 3112
peace to you which were a off............... Eph 2:17 3112
but having seen them a off.................... Heb 11:13 4207
is blind, and cannot see a off................ 2Pet 1:9 3467
Standing a off for the fear of................ Rev 18:10 3113
shall stand a off for the fear of............. Rev 18:15 3113
many as trade by sea, stood a off.......... Rev 18:17 3113

AFFAIRS
to God, and a of the king....................... 1Chr 26:32 1697
will guide his a with discretion.............. Ps 112:5 1697
over the a of the province of.................. Dan 2:49 5673
the a of the province of Babylon............. Dan 3:12 5673
But that ye also may know my a.............. Eph 6:21 2596
purpose, that ye might know our a......... Eph 6:22 4012
be absent, I may hear of your a............. Phil 1:27 4012
himself with the a of this life................ 2Ti 2:4 4230

AFFECT
They zealously a you, but not................. Gal 4:17 2206
exclude you, that ye might a them.......... Gal 4:17 2206

AFFECTED
minds evil a against the brethren.......... Acts 14:2 2559
a always in a good thing, and not.......... Gal 4:18 2206

AFFECTETH
Mine eye a mine heart because of.......... Lam 3:51 5953

AFFECTION
because I have set my a to the............... 1Chr 29:3 7521
without natural a, implacable,................ Rom 1:31 794
his inward a is more abundant................ 2Cor 7:15 4698
Set your a on things above, not .... Col 3:2 5426
uncleanness, inordinate a .... Col 3:5 3806
Without natural a, trucebreakers,........... 2Ti 3:3 794

AFFECTIONATELY
So being a desirous of you, we 1Th 2:8 2442

AFFECTIONED
Be kindly a one to another with............. Rom 12:10 5387

AFFECTIONS
God gave them up unto vile a................. Rom 1:26 3806
crucified the flesh with the a................. Gal 5:24 3804

AFFINITY
Solomon made a with Pharaoh king 1Kin 3:1 2859
abundance, and joined a with Ahab 2Chr 18:1 2859
join in a with the people of.................... Ezr 9:14 2859

AFFIRM
as some a that we say,) Let us do.......... Rom 3:8 5346
what they say, nor whereof they a.......... 1Ti 1:7 1226
I will that thou a constantly................... Titus 3:8 1226

AFFIRMED
hour after another confidently a .... Lk 22:59 1340
But she constantly a that it was............ Acts 12:15 1340
was dead, whom Paul a to be alive........ Acts 25:19 5335

AFFLICT
they shall a them four hundred............... Gen 15:13 6031
If thou shalt a my daughters.................. Gen 31:50 6031
to a them with their burdens .... Ex 1:11 6031
Ye shall not a any widow, or.................. Ex 22:22 6031
If thou a them in any wise, and .... Ex 22:23 6031
ye shall a your souls, and do no .... Lev 16:29 6031
ye shall a your souls, by a.................... Lev 16:31 6031
ye shall a your souls, and offer............ Lev 23:27 6031
of rest, and ye shall a your souls......... Lev 23:32 6031
a Asshur, and shall a Eber .... Num 24:24 6031
and ye shall a your souls...................... Num 29:7 6031
every binding oath to a the soul............ Num 30:13 6031
that we may bind him to a him.............. Judg 16:5 6031
thou mightest be bound to a thee.......... Judg 16:6 6031
and she began to a him, and his........... Judg 16:19 6031
of wickedness a them any more 2Sa 7:10 6031
I will for this a the seed of................... 1Kin 11:39 6031
their sin, when thou dost a them 2Chr 6:26 6031
that we might a ourselves before .... Ezr 8:21 6031
he will not a.. Job 37:23 6031
how thou didst a the people.................. Ps 44:2 7489
a them, even he that abideth of............. Ps 55:19 6031
nor the son of wickedness a him............. Ps 89:22 6031
O LORD, and a thine heritage .... Ps 94:5 6031
destroy all them that a my soul.............. Ps 143:12 6887
a her by the way of the sea .... Is 9:1 3513
into the hand of them that a thee.......... Is 51:23 3013
a day for a man to a his soul................. Is 58:5 6031
hold thy peace, and a us very sore .... Is 64:12 6031
down, and to destroy, and to a .... Jer 31:28 7489
For he doth not a willingly nor............. Lam 3:33 6031
they a the just, they take a .... Amos 5:12 6887
they shall a you from the...................... Amos 6:14 3905
thee, I will a thee no more.................... Nah 1:12 6031
time I will undo all that a thee............. Zeph 3:19 6031

AFFLICTED
But the more they a them, the............... Ex 1:12 6031
shall not be a in that same day............. Lev 23:29 6031
Wherefore hast thou a thy servant......... Num 11:11 7489
a us, and laid upon us hard................... Deut 26:6 6031
me, and the Almighty hath a me............. Ruth 1:21 7489
the a people thou wilt save.................... 2Sa 22:28 6041
because thou hast been a in all.............. 1Kin 2:26 6031
in all wherein my father was a 1Kin 2:26 6031
a them, and delivered them into............ 2Kin 17:20 6031
To him that is a pity should be.............. Job 6:14 4523
a me, they have also let loose .... Job 30:11 6031
and he heareth the cry of the a............. Job 34:28 6041
For thou wilt save the a people............. Ps 18:27 6041
abhorred the affliction of the a .... Ps 22:24 6041
for I am desolate and a......................... Ps 25:16 6041
do justice to the a and needy................ Ps 82:3 6041
thou hast a me with all thy waves......... Ps 88:7 6031
I am a and ready to die from my .... Ps 88:15 6041
the days wherein thou hast a us .... Ps 90:15 6031
A Prayer of the a, when he is................ Ps 102:t 6041
of their iniquities, are a....................... Ps 107:17 6031
I was greatly a .... Ps 116:10 6031
Before I was a I went astray................. Ps 119:67 6031
is good for me that I have been a......... Ps 119:71 6031
thou in faithfulness hast a me.............. Ps 119:75 6031
I am a very much.................................. Ps 119:107 6031
time have they a me from my youth....... Ps 129:1 6887
time have they a me from my youth....... Ps 129:2 6887
will maintain the cause of the a............ Ps 140:12 6041
All the days of the a are evil................ Prov 15:15 6041
neither oppress the a in the gate........... Prov 22:22 6041
hateth those that are a by it................. Prov 26:28 1790
the judgment of any of the a .... Prov 31:5 6040
he lightly a the land of Zebulun........... Is 9:1 7043
and will have mercy upon his a............. Is 49:13 6041
Therefore hear now this, thou a............. Is 51:21 6041
stricken, smitten of God, and a.............. Is 53:4 6031
He was oppressed, and he was a .... Is 53:7 6031
O thou a, tossed with tempest, and .... Is 54:11 6041
wherefore have we a our soul................ Is 58:3 6031
the hungry, and satisfy the a soul......... Is 58:10 6031
The sons also of them that a thee......... Is 60:14 6031
In all their affliction he was a.............. Is 63:9 6862
priests sigh, her virgins are a............... Lam 1:4 3013
for the LORD hath a her for the............. Lam 1:5 3013
wherewith the LORD hath a me in .... Lam 1:12 3013
driven out, and her that I have a .... Mic 4:6 7489
Though I have a thee, I will................. Nah 1:12 6031
leave in the midst of thee an a .... Zeph 3:12 6041
shall they deliver you up to be a........... Mt 24:9 2347
And whether we be a, it is for 2Cor 1:6 2346
feet, if she have relieved the a 1Ti 5:10 2346
being destitute, a, tormented................ Heb 11:37 2346
Be a, and mourn, and weep .... Jas 4:9 5003
Is any among you a............................... Jas 5:13 2553

AFFLICTEST
from their sin, when thou a them 1Kin 8:35 6031

AFFLICTION
because the LORD hath heard thy a......... Gen 16:11 6040
the LORD hath looked upon my a........... Gen 29:32 6040
God hath seen mine a and the............... Gen 31:42 6040
be fruitful in the land of my a............... Gen 41:52 6040
I have surely seen the a of my............... Ex 3:7 6040
a of Egypt unto the land of the............. Ex 3:17 6040
that he had looked upon their a............. Ex 4:31 6040
therewith, even the bread of a.............. Deut 16:3 6040
our voice, and looked on our a.............. Deut 26:7 6040
look on the a of thine handmaid............ 1Sa 1:11 6040
that the LORD will look on mine a 2Sa 16:12 6040
bread of a and with water of a 1Kin 22:27 3905
For the LORD saw the a of Israel........... 2Kin 14:26 6040
bread of a and with water of a 2Chr 18:26 3905
house,) and cry unto thee in our a 2Chr 20:9 6869
And when he was in a, he besought....... 2Chr 33:12 6887
in the province are in great a............... Neh 1:3 7451
didst see the a of our fathers in............ Neh 9:9 6040
Although a cometh not forth of.............. Job 5:6 205
therefore see thou mine a..................... Job 10:15 6040
the days of a have taken hold............... Job 30:16 6040
the days of a prevented me.................. Job 30:27 6040
and be holden in cords of a.................. Job 36:8 6040
He delivereth the poor in his a .... Job 36:15 6040
hast thou chosen rather than a .... Job 36:21 6040
abhorred the a of the afflicted............... Ps 22:24 6039
Look upon mine a and my pain.............. Ps 25:18 6040
thy face, and forgettest our a................ Ps 44:24 6040
thou laidst a upon our loins................... Ps 66:11 4157
Mine eye mourneth by reason of a.......... Ps 88:9 6040
Nevertheless he regarded their a............ Ps 106:44 6862
shadow of death, being bound in a......... Ps 107:10 6040
brought low through oppression, a......... Ps 107:39 7451
he the poor on high from a.................... Ps 107:41 6040
This is my comfort in my a.................... Ps 119:50 6040
then have perished in mine a................ Ps 119:92 6040
Consider mine a, and deliver me .... Ps 119:153 6040
of adversity, and the water of a............ Is 30:20 3905
chosen thee in the furnace of a............. Is 48:10 6040
In all their a he was afflicted,............... Is 63:9 6869
publisheth a from mount Ephraim.......... Jer 4:15 205
time of evil and in the time of a............ Jer 15:11 6869
and my refuge in the day of a............... Jer 16:19 6869
Why criest thou for thine a................... Jer 30:15 7667
to come, and his a hasteth fast............. Jer 48:16 7451
gone into captivity because of a............. Lam 1:3 6040
remembered in the days of her a............ Lam 1:7 6040
O LORD, behold my a............................ Lam 1:9 6040
seen a by the rod of his wrath.............. Lam 3:1 6040
Remembering mine a and my misery,.. Lam 3:19 6040
in their a they will seek me.................. Hos 5:15 6862
not grieved for the a of Joseph.............. Amos 6:6 7667
not have looked on their a in the.......... Obad 13 7451
by reason of mine a unto the LORD .... Jonah 2:2 6869
a shall not rise up the second.............. Nah 1:9 6869
I saw the tents of Cushan in a............... Hab 3:7 205
and they helped forward the a............... Zec 1:15 7451
out or came in because of the a............ Zec 8:10 6862
shall pass through the sea with a.......... Zec 10:11 6869
when a or persecution ariseth for......... Mk 4:17 2347
For in those days shall be a.................. Mk 13:19 2347
of Egypt and Chanaan, and great a......... Acts 7:11 2347
I have seen the a of my people............. Acts 7:34 2561
For out of much a and anguish of.......... 2Cor 2:4 2347
For our light a, which is but for............ 2Cor 4:17 2347
of a the abundance of their joy 2Cor 8:2 2347
supposing to add a to my bonds............ Phil 1:16 2347
that ye did communicate with my a........ Phil 4:14 2347
received the word in much a................. 1Th 1:6 2347
comforted over you in all our a............. 1Th 3:7 2347
suffer a with the people of God .... Heb 11:25 4797
fatherless and widows in their a........... Jas 1:27 2347
for an example of suffering a .... Jas 5:10 2552

AFFLICTIONS
Many are the a of the righteous............ Ps 34:19 7451
remember David, and all his a .... Ps 132:1 6031
And delivered him out of all his a......... Acts 7:10 2347
saying that bonds and a abide me.......... Acts 20:23 2347
of God, in much patience, in a.............. 2Cor 6:4 2347
a of Christ in my flesh for his.............. Col 1:24 2347
no man should be moved by these a....... 1Th 3:3 2347
but be thou partaker of the a of........... 2Ti 1:8 4777
Persecutions, a, which came unto........... 2Ti 3:11 3804
thou in all things, endure a.................. 2Ti 4:5 2553
ye endured a great fight of a............... Heb 10:32 3804
both by reproaches and a..................... Heb 10:33 2347
knowing that the same a are................. 1Pet 5:9 3804

AFFORDING
be full, a all manner of store .... Ps 144:13 6329

AFFRIGHT
to a them, and to trouble them............. 2Chr 32:18 3372

AFFRIGHTED
Thou shalt not be a at them.................. Deut 7:21 6206
as they that went before were a............ Job 18:20
He mocketh at fear, and is not a.......... Job 39:22 2865
My heart panted, fearfulness a me......... Is 21:4 1204
fire, and the men of war are a.............. Jer 51:32 926
and they were a.................................... Mk 16:5 1568
And he saith unto them, Be not a......... Mk 16:6 1568
But they were terrified and a .... Lk 24:37 1719
and the remnant were a, and gave .... Rev 11:13 1719

AFOOT
ran a thither out of all cities,............... Mk 6:33 3979
minding himself to go a........................ Acts 20:13 3978

AFORE
a Isaiah was gone out into the 2Kin 20:4 3808
which withereth a it groweth up............ Ps 129:6 6924
For a the harvest, when the bud........... Is 18:5 6440
a he that was escaped came.................. Eze 33:22 6440
(Which he had promised a by his.......... Rom 1:2 4279
which he had a prepared unto.............. Rom 9:23 4282
(as I wrote a in few words,................... Eph 3:3 4270

AFOREHAND
she is come a to anoint my body........... Mk 14:8 4301

AFORETIME
where a they laid the meat.................... Neh 13:5 6440
and a I was as a tabret........................ Job 17:6 6440
My people went down a into Egypt......... Is 52:4 7223
Their children also shall be as a .... Jer 30:20 6924
before his God, as he did a.................. Dan 6:10
Pharisees him that a was blind............. Jn 9:13 4218
a were written for our learning............ Rom 15:4 4270

AFRAID
voice in the garden, and I was a .... Gen 3:10 3372
for she was a....................................... Gen 18:15 3372
and the men were sore a....................... Gen 20:8 3372

And he was *a*, and said, How	Gen 28:17	3372
and said to Laban, Because I was *a*	Gen 31:31	3372
Then Jacob was greatly *a* and	Gen 32:7	3372
heart failed them, and they were *a*	Gen 42:28	2729
the bundles of money, they were *a*	Gen 42:35	3372
And the men were *a*, because they	Gen 43:18	3372
for he was *a* to look upon God	Ex 3:6	3372
and they were sore *a*	Ex 14:10	3372
The people shall hear, and be *a*	Ex 15:14	7264
they were *a* to come nigh him	Ex 34:30	3372
down, and none shall make you *a*	Lev 26:6	2729
wherefore then were ye not *a* to	Num 12:8	3372
And Moab was sore *a* of the people	Num 22:3	1481
ye shall not be *a* of the face of	Deut 1:17	1481
Dread not, neither be *a* of them	Deut 1:29	3372
and they shall be *a* of you	Deut 2:4	3372
for ye were *a* by reason of the	Deut 5:5	3372
Thou shalt not be *a* of them	Deut 7:18	3372
all the people of whom thou art *a*	Deut 7:19	3373
For I was *a* of the anger and hot	Deut 9:19	3025
thou shalt not be *a* of him	Deut 18:22	1481
more than thou, be not *a* of them	Deut 20:1	3372
and they shall be *a* of thee	Deut 28:10	3372
of Egypt, which thou wast *a* of	Deut 28:60	3025
fear not, nor be *a* of them	Deut 31:6	6206
be not *a*, neither be thou	Josh 1:9	6206
therefore we were sore *a* of our	Josh 9:24	3372
Joshua, Be not *a* because of them	Josh 11:6	3372
saying, Whosoever is fearful and *a*	Judg 7:3	2730
at midnight, that the man was *a*	Ruth 3:8	2729
And the Philistines were *a*	1Sa 4:7	3372
they were *a* of the Philistines	1Sa 7:7	3372
they were dismayed, and greatly *a*	1Sa 17:11	3372
fled from him, and were sore *a*	1Sa 17:24	3372
And Saul was *a* of David, because	1Sa 18:12	3372
very wisely, he was *a* of him	1Sa 18:15	1481
Saul was yet the more *a* of David	1Sa 18:29	3372
Ahimelech was *a* at the meeting of	1Sa 21:1	2729
was sore *a* of Achish the king of	1Sa 21:12	3372
Behold, we be *a* here in Judah	1Sa 23:3	3373
host of the Philistines, he was *a*	1Sa 28:5	3372
the king said unto her, Be not *a*	1Sa 28:13	3372
along on the earth, and was sore *a*	1Sa 28:20	3372
for he was sore *a*	1Sa 31:4	3372
How wast thou not *a* to stretch	2Sa 1:14	3372
David was *a* of the LORD that day,	2Sa 6:9	3372
because the people have made me *a*	2Sa 14:15	3372
weak handed, and will make him *a*	2Sa 17:2	2729
floods of ungodly men made me *a*	2Sa 22:5	1204
they shall be *a* out of their	2Sa 22:46	2296
that were with Adonijah were *a*	1Kin 1:49	2729
be not *a* of him	2Kin 1:15	3372
But they were exceedingly *a*	2Kin 10:4	3372
Be not *a* of the words which thou	2Kin 19:6	3372
for they were *a* of the Chaldees	2Kin 25:26	3372
for he was sore *a*	1Chr 10:4	3372
David was *a* of God that day	1Chr 13:12	3372
for he was *a* because of the sword	1Chr 21:30	1204
Be not *a* nor dismayed by reason	2Chr 20:15	3372
be not *a* nor dismayed for the	2Chr 32:7	3372
Then I was very sore *a*,	Neh 2:2	3372
the people, Be not ye *a* of them	Neh 4:14	3372
For they all made us *a*, saying,	Neh 6:9	3372
was he hired, that I should be *a*	Neh 6:13	3372
Then Haman was *a* before the king	Est 7:6	1204
that which I was *a* of is come	Job 3:25	3025
neither shalt thou be *a* of	Job 5:21	3372
neither shalt thou be *a* of the	Job 5:22	3372
ye see my casting down, and are *a*	Job 6:21	3372
I am *a* of all my sorrows, I know	Job 9:28	3025
down, and none shall make thee *a*	Job 11:19	2729
not his excellency make you *a*	Job 13:11	1204
and let not thy dread make me *a*	Job 13:21	1204
and anguish shall make him *a*	Job 15:24	1204
shall make him *a* on every side	Job 18:11	1204
Be ye *a* of the sword	Job 19:29	1481
Even when I remember I am *a*	Job 21:6	926
when I consider, I am *a* of him	Job 23:15	6342
wherefore I was *a*, and durst not	Job 32:6	2119
my terror shall not make thee *a*	Job 33:7	1204
thou make him *a* as a grasshopper	Job 39:20	7493
up himself, the mighty are *a*	Job 41:25	1481
I will not be *a* of ten thousands	Ps 3:6	3372
floods of ungodly men made me *a*	Ps 18:4	1204
be *a* out of their close places	Ps 18:45	2727
of whom shall I be *a*	Ps 27:1	6342
Be not thou *a* when one is made	Ps 49:16	3372
What time I am *a*, I will trust in	Ps 56:3	3372
I will not be *a* what man can do	Ps 56:11	3372
parts are *a* at thy tokens	Ps 65:8	3372
they were *a*	Ps 77:16	2342
make them *a* with thy storm	Ps 83:15	926
Thou shalt not be *a* for the	Ps 91:5	3372
He shall not be *a* of evil tidings	Ps 112:7	3372
is established, he shall not be *a*	Ps 112:8	3372
and I am *a* of thy judgments	Ps 119:120	3372
liest down, thou shalt not be *a*	Prov 3:24	6342
Be not *a* of sudden fear, neither	Prov 3:25	3372
She is not *a* of the snow for her	Prov 31:21	3372
shall be *a* of that which is high	Eccl 12:5	3372
fear ye their fear, nor be *a*	Is 8:12	6206
in Zion, be not *a* of the Assyrian	Is 10:24	3372
Ramah is *a*	Is 10:29	2729
I will trust, and not be *a*	Is 12:2	6342
And they shall be *a*	Is 13:8	926
down, and none shall make them *a*	Is 17:2	2729
and it shall be *a* and fear because	Is 19:16	2729
thereof shall be *a* in himself	Is 19:17	6342
And they shall be *a* and ashamed of	Is 20:5	2865
he will not be *a* of their voice	Is 31:4	2865
princes shall be *a* of the ensign	Is 31:9	2865
The sinners in Zion are *a*	Is 33:14	6342
Be not *a* of the words that thou	Is 37:6	3372
lift it up, be not *a*	Is 40:9	3372
the ends of the earth were *a*	Is 41:5	2729
Fear ye not, neither be *a*	Is 44:8	7297
of men, neither be ye *a* of their	Is 51:7	2865
that thou shouldest be *a* of a man	Is 51:12	3372
whom hast thou been *a* or feared	Is 57:11	1672
Be not *a* of their faces	Jer 1:8	3372
at this, and be horribly *a*	Jer 2:12	8175
Be not *a* of them	Jer 10:5	3372
when Urijah heard it, he was *a*	Jer 26:21	3372
quiet, and none shall make him *a*	Jer 30:10	2729
the words, they were *a* both one	Jer 36:16	6342
Yet they were not *a*, nor rent	Jer 36:24	6342
I am *a* of the Jews that are	Jer 38:19	1672
of the men of whom thou art *a*	Jer 39:17	3025
for they were *a* of them, because	Jer 41:18	3372
Be not *a* of the king of Babylon,	Jer 42:11	3372
of whom ye are *a*	Jer 42:11	3373
be not *a* of him, saith the LORD	Jer 42:11	3372
and the famine, whereof ye were *a*	Jer 42:16	1672
at ease, and none shall make him *a*	Jer 46:27	2729
be not *a* of them	Eze 2:6	3372
neither be *a* of their words,	Eze 2:6	3372
be not *a* of their words, nor be	Eze 2:6	3372
and their kings shall be sore *a*	Eze 27:35	8175
to make the careless Ethiopians *a*	Eze 30:9	2729
shall be horribly *a* for thee	Eze 32:10	8175
safely, and none shall make them *a*	Eze 34:28	2729
their land, and none made them *a*	Eze 39:26	2729
I saw a dream which made me *a*	Dan 4:5	1763
and when he came, I was *a*, and fell	Dan 8:17	1204
Be not *a*, ye beasts of the field	Joel 2:22	3372
the city, and the people not be *a*	Amos 3:6	2729
Then the mariners were *a*, and	Jonah 1:5	3372
Then were the men exceedingly *a*	Jonah 1:10	3372
and none shall make them *a*	Mic 4:4	2729
they shall be *a* of the LORD our	Mic 7:17	6342
lion's whelp, and none made them *a*	Nah 2:11	2729
of beasts, which made them *a*	Hab 2:17	2865
I have heard thy speech, and was *a*	Hab 3:2	3372
down, and none shall make them *a*	Zeph 3:13	2729
me, and was *a* before my name	Mal 2:5	2865
Herod, he was *a* to go thither	Mt 2:22	5399
be not *a*	Mt 14:27	5399
saw the wind boisterous, he was *a*	Mt 14:30	5399
on their face, and were sore *a*	Mt 17:6	5399
them, and said, Arise, and be not *a*	Mt 17:7	5399
And I was *a*, and went and hid thy	Mt 25:25	5399
said Jesus unto them, Be not *a*	Mt 28:10	5399
and they were *a*	Mk 5:15	5399
ruler of the synagogue, Be not *a*	Mk 5:36	5399
be not *a*	Mk 6:50	5399
for they were sore *a*	Mk 9:6	1630
that saying, and were *a* to ask him	Mk 9:32	5399
and as they followed, they were *a*	Mk 10:32	5399
thing to any man for they were *a*	Mk 16:8	5399
and they were sore *a*	Lk 2:9	5399
And they being *a* wondered, saying	Lk 8:25	5399
and they were *a*	Lk 8:35	5399
Be not *a* of them that kill the	Lk 12:4	5399
And as they were *a*, and bowed down	Lk 24:5	1719
and they were *a*	Jn 6:19	5399
be not *a*	Jn 6:20	5399
be troubled, neither let it be *a*	Jn 14:27	1168
that saying, he was the more *a*	Jn 19:8	5399
but they were all *a* of him	Acts 9:26	5399
when he looked on him, he was *a*	Acts 10:4	1719
the night by a vision, Be not *a*	Acts 18:9	5399
saw indeed the light, and were *a*	Acts 22:9	1719
and the chief captain also was *a*	Acts 22:29	5399
thou then not be *a* of the power	Rom 13:3	5399
thou do that which is evil, be *a*	Rom 13:4	5399
I am *a* of you, lest I have	Gal 4:11	5399
they were not *a* of the king's	Heb 11:23	5399
are not *a* with any amazement	1Pet 3:6	5399
be not *a* of their terror, neither	1Pet 3:14	5399
they are not *a* to speak evil of	2Pet 2:10	5141

AFRESH

to themselves the Son of God *a*	Heb 6:6	388

AFTER

tree yielding fruit *a* his kind	Gen 1:11	
and herb yielding seed *a* his kind	Gen 1:12	
seed was in itself, *a* his kind	Gen 1:12	
brought forth abundantly, *a* their kind	Gen 1:21	
and every winged fowl *a* his kind	Gen 1:21	
the living creature *a* his kind	Gen 1:24	
and beast of the earth *a* his kind	Gen 1:24	
the beast of the earth *a* his kind	Gen 1:25	
cattle *a* their kind, and every	Gen 1:25	
upon the earth *a* his kind	Gen 1:25	
man in our image, *a* our likeness	Gen 1:26	
a the name of his son, Enoch	Gen 4:17	
in his own likeness, *a* his image	Gen 5:3	
the days of Adam *a* he had	Gen 5:4	310
Seth lived *a* he begat Enos eight	Gen 5:7	310
Enos lived *a* he begat Cainan	Gen 5:10	310
And Cainan lived *a* he begat	Gen 5:13	310
Mahalaleel lived *a* he begat Jared	Gen 5:16	310
Jared lived *a* he begat Enoch	Gen 5:19	310
Enoch walked with God *a* he begat	Gen 5:22	310
Methuselah lived *a* he begat	Gen 5:26	310
Lamech lived *a* he begat Noah five	Gen 5:30	310
and also *a* that, when the sons of	Gen 6:4	310
Of fowls *a* their kind, and of	Gen 6:20	
of cattle *a* their kind, of every	Gen 6:20	
thing of the earth *a* his kind	Gen 6:20	
And it came to pass *a* seven days	Gen 7:10	
They, and every beast *a* his kind	Gen 7:14	
and all the cattle *a* their kind	Gen 7:14	
upon the earth *a* his kind	Gen 7:14	
and every fowl *a* his kind	Gen 7:14	
a the end of the hundred and fifty	Gen 8:3	
a their kinds, went forth out of	Gen 8:19	
with you, and with your seed *a* you	Gen 9:9	310
Noah lived *a* the flood three	Gen 9:28	310
them were sons born *a* the flood	Gen 10:1	310
every one *a* his tongue	Gen 10:5	
a their families, in their	Gen 10:5	
a their families, *a* their	Gen 10:20	
a their families, *a* their	Gen 10:31	
in their lands, *a* their nations	Gen 10:31	
a their generations, in their	Gen 10:32	
divided in the earth *a* the flood	Gen 10:32	310
Arphaxad two years *a* the flood	Gen 11:10	310
Shem lived *a* he begat Arphaxad	Gen 11:11	310
Arphaxad lived *a* he begat Salah	Gen 11:13	310
Salah lived *a* he begat Eber four	Gen 11:15	310
Eber lived *a* he begat Peleg four	Gen 11:17	310
Peleg lived *a* he begat Reu two	Gen 11:19	310
Reu lived *a* he begat Serug two	Gen 11:21	310
Serug lived *a* he begat Nahor two	Gen 11:23	310
Nahor lived *a* he begat Terah an	Gen 11:25	310
a that Lot was separated from him	Gen 13:14	310
a his return from the slaughter	Gen 14:17	310
A these things the word of the	Gen 15:1	310
a Abram had dwelt ten years in	Gen 16:3	7093
here looked *a* him that seeth me	Gen 16:13	310
thee and thy seed *a* thee in their	Gen 17:7	310
unto thee, and to thy seed *a* thee	Gen 17:7	310
unto thee, and to thy seed *a* thee	Gen 17:8	310
thou, and thy seed *a* thee in their	Gen 17:9	310
me and you and thy seed *a* thee	Gen 17:10	310
covenant, and with his seed *a* him	Gen 17:19	310
a that ye shall pass on	Gen 18:5	310
with Sarah *a* the manner of women	Gen 18:11	
A I am waxed old shall I have	Gen 18:12	310
children and his household *a* him	Gen 18:19	310
far from thee to do *a* this manner	Gen 18:25	
unto them, and shut the door *a* him	Gen 19:6	310
us *a* the manner of all the earth	Gen 19:31	
And it came to pass *a* these things	Gen 22:1	310
And it came to pass *a* these things	Gen 22:20	310
a this, Abraham buried Sarah his	Gen 23:19	310
a that she shall go	Gen 24:55	310
comforted *a* his mother's death	Gen 24:67	310
it came to pass *a* the death of	Gen 25:11	310
a that came his brother out, and	Gen 25:26	310
them *a* the death of Abraham	Gen 26:18	310
he called their names *a* the names	Gen 26:18	
pursued *a* him seven days' journey	Gen 31:23	310
longedst *a* thy father's house	Gen 31:30	
thou hast so hotly pursued *a* me	Gen 31:36	310
it that thou dost ask *a* my name	Gen 32:29	
and Leah and her children *a*	Gen 33:2	314
a came Joseph near and Rachel, and	Gen 33:7	310
not pursue *a* the sons of Jacob	Gen 35:5	310
to thy seed *a* thee will I give	Gen 35:12	310
a their places, by their names	Gen 36:40	
Joseph went *a* his brethren, and	Gen 37:17	310
came to pass about three months *a*	Gen 38:24	
And it came to pass *a* these things	Gen 39:7	310
A this manner did thy servant to	Gen 39:19	
And it came to pass *a* these things	Gen 40:1	310
a the former manner when thou	Gen 40:13	
came up *a* them out of the river	Gen 41:3	310
the east wind sprung up *a* them	Gen 41:6	310
seven other kine came up *a* them	Gen 41:19	310
the east wind, sprung up *a* them	Gen 41:23	310
came up *a* them are seven years	Gen 41:27	310
there shall arise *a* them seven	Gen 41:30	310
his steward, Up, follow *a* the men	Gen 44:4	310
a that his brethren talked with	Gen 45:15	310
his father he sent *a* this manner	Gen 45:23	
And it came to pass *a* these things	Gen 48:1	310
seed *a* thee for an everlasting	Gen 48:4	310
which thou begettest *a* them	Gen 48:6	310
shall be called *a* the name of	Gen 48:6	5921
a he had buried his father	Gen 50:14	310
a that he will let you go	Ex 3:20	310
a it was said, Ye shall not	Ex 5:19	
a that the LORD had smitten the	Ex 7:25	310
neither *a* them shall be such	Ex 10:14	310
and *a* that I will go out	Ex 11:8	310
that he shall follow *a* them	Ex 14:4	310
he pursued *a* the children of	Ex 14:8	310
But the Egyptians pursued *a* them	Ex 14:9	310
the Egyptians marched *a* them	Ex 14:10	310
went in *a* them to the midst of	Ex 14:23	310
that came into the sea *a* them	Ex 14:28	310
went out *a* her with timbrels	Ex 15:20	310
day of the second month *a* their	Ex 16:1	
a their journeys, according to	Ex 17:1	
wife, *a* he had sent her back,	Ex 18:2	310
he shall deal with her *a* the	Ex 21:9	
decline *a* many to wrest judgment	Ex 23:2	310
serve them, nor do *a* their works	Ex 23:24	
a the pattern of the tabernacle,	Ex 25:9	
thou make them *a* their pattern	Ex 25:40	
a the work of the ephod thou	Ex 28:15	
ever unto him and his seed *a* him	Ex 28:43	310
of Aaron shall be his sons' *a* him	Ex 29:29	310
children of Israel *a* their number	Ex 30:12	
half a shekel *a* the shekel of the	Ex 30:13	
a the shekel of the sanctuary, and	Ex 30:24	
an ointment compound *a* the art of	Ex 30:25	
like it, *a* the composition of it	Ex 30:32	
a confection *a* the art of the	Ex 30:35	
a he had made it a molten calf	Ex 32:4	
his tent door, and looked *a* Moses	Ex 33:8	310
and they go a whoring *a* their gods	Ex 34:15	310
go a whoring *a* their gods	Ex 34:16	310
sons go a whoring *a* their gods	Ex 34:16	310
for *a* the tenor of these words I	Ex 34:27	5921
Three bowls made *a* the fashion of	Ex 37:19	
a the shekel of the sanctuary	Ex 38:24	
a the shekel of the sanctuary	Ex 38:25	
a the shekel of the sanctuary,	Ex 38:26	
a the shekel of the sanctuary,	Lev 5:15	

vulture, and the kite *a* his kind Lev 11:14
Every raven *a* his kind Lev 11:15
cuckow, and the hawk *a* his kind Lev 11:16
the stork, the heron *a* her kind Lev 11:19
the locust *a* his kind Lev 11:22
and the bald locust *a* his kind Lev 11:22
and the beetle *a* his kind Lev 11:22
and the grasshopper *a* his kind Lev 11:22
mouse, and the tortoise *a* his kind Lev 11:29
a that he hath been seen of the Lev 13:7 310
much in the skin *a* his cleansing Lev 13:35 310
the plague, *a* that it is washed Lev 13:55 310
somewhat dark *a* the washing of it Lev 13:56 310
a that he shall come into the Lev 14:8 310
a that he hath taken away the Lev 14:43 310
a he hath scraped the house Lev 14:43 310
and *a* it is plaistered Lev 14:43 310
a the house was plaistered Lev 14:48 310
a that she shall be clean Lev 15:28 310
the LORD spake unto Moses *a* the Lev 16:1 310
a whom they have gone a whoring Lev 17:7 310
A the doings of the land of Egypt Lev 18:3
a the doings of the land of Lev 18:3
spirits, neither seek *a* wizards Lev 19:31 413
and all that go a whoring *a* him Lev 20:5 310
the soul that turneth *a* such as Lev 20:6 413
a wizards, to go a whoring *a* Lev 20:6 310
on the morrow *a* the sabbath the Lev 23:11
you from the morrow *a* the sabbath Lev 23:15
Even unto the morrow *a* the Lev 23:16
to the number of years *a* the Lev 25:15 310
within a whole year *a* it is sold Lev 25:29
for your children *a* you, to Lev 25:46 310
A that he is sold he may be Lev 25:48 310
and will draw out a sword *a* you Lev 26:33 310
a the shekel of the sanctuary Lev 27:3
sanctify his field *a* the jubile Lev 27:18 310
in the second year *a* they were Num 1:1
a their families, by the house of Num 1:2
their pedigrees *a* their families Num 1:18
a their families, by the house of Num 1:20
a their families, by the house of Num 1:22
a their families, by the house of Num 1:24
a their families, by the house of Num 1:26
a their families, by the house of Num 1:28
a their families, by the house of Num 1:30
a their families, by the house of Num 1:32
a their families, by the house of Num 1:34
a their families, by the house of Num 1:36
a their families, by the house of Num 1:38
a their families, by the house of Num 1:40
a their families, by the house of Num 1:42
But the Levites *a* the tribe of Num 1:47
every one *a* their families, Num 2:34
Levi *a* the house of their fathers Num 3:15
a the shekel of the sanctuary Num 3:47
a the shekel of the sanctuary Num 3:50
a their families, by the house of Num 4:2
a that, the sons of Kohath shall Num 4:15 310
number them *a* their families Num 4:29
the Kohathites *a* their families Num 4:34
a the house of their fathers, Num 4:34
numbered of them *a* their families Num 4:44
a their families, and *a* the Num 4:46
a the hair of his separation is Num 6:19 310
a that the Nazarite may drink Num 6:20 310
so he must do *a* the law of his Num 6:21 5921
a the shekel of the sanctuary Num 7:13
a the shekel of the sanctuary Num 7:19
a the shekel of the sanctuary Num 7:25
a the shekel of the sanctuary Num 7:31
a the shekel of the sanctuary Num 7:37
a the shekel of the sanctuary Num 7:40
a the shekel of the sanctuary Num 7:49
a the shekel of the sanctuary Num 7:55
a the shekel of the sanctuary Num 7:61
a the shekel of the sanctuary Num 7:67
a the shekel of the sanctuary Num 7:73
a the shekel of the sanctuary Num 7:79
a the shekel of the sanctuary Num 7:85
a the shekel of the sanctuary Num 7:86
the altar, *a* that it was anointed Num 7:88 310
a that shall the Levites go in to Num 8:15 310
a that went the Levites in to do Num 8:22 310
a they were come out of the land Num 9:1
then *a* that the children of Num 9:17 310
a that let her be received in Num 12:14 310
of the land *a* forty days Num 13:25 7093
A the number of the days in which Num 14:34
do these things *a* this manner Num 15:13 3602
that ye seek not *a* your own heart Num 15:39 310
a which ye use to go a whoring Num 15:39 310
or if they be visited *a* the Num 16:29
a the shekel of the sanctuary, Num 18:16
he went *a* the man of Israel into Num 25:8 310
shall have it, and his seed *a* him Num 25:13 310
And it came to pass *a* the plague Num 26:1 310
sons of Simeon *a* their families Num 26:12
children of Gad *a* their families Num 26:15
the sons of Judah *a* their Num 26:20
sons of Issachar *a* their families Num 26:23
sons of Zebulun *a* their families Num 26:26
The sons of Joseph *a* their Num 26:28
sons of Ephraim *a* their families Num 26:35
sons of Joseph *a* their families Num 26:37
sons of Benjamin *a* their families Num 26:38
sons of Benjamin *a* their families Num 26:41
the sons of Dan *a* their families Num 26:42
families of Dan *a* their families Num 26:42
of Asher *a* their families Num 26:44
sons of Naphtali *a* their families Num 26:48
of the Levites *a* their families Num 26:57
who shall ask counsel for him *a* Num 27:21
A this manner ye shall offer Num 28:24

a your weeks be out, ye shall Num 28:26
to their number, *a* the manner Num 29:18
to their number, *a* the manner Num 29:21
to their number, *a* the manner Num 29:24
to their number, *a* the manner Num 29:27
to their number, *a* the manner Num 29:30
to their number, *a* the manner Num 29:33
to their number, *a* the manner Num 29:37
void *a* that he hath heard them Num 30:15 310
For if ye turn away from *a* him Num 32:15 310
called it Nobah, *a* his own name Num 32:42
on the morrow *a* the passover the Num 33:3
in the fortieth year *a* the Num 33:38
but *a* the death of the high Num 35:28 310
A he had slain Sihon the king of Deut 1:4 310
unto them and to their seed *a* them Deut 1:8 310
of it, *a* the cubit of a man Deut 3:11
called them *a* his own name, Deut 3:14 5921
he chose their seed *a* them Deut 4:37 310
thee, and with thy children *a* thee Deut 4:40 310
a they came forth out of Egypt, Deut 4:45
a they were come forth out of Deut 4:46
Ye shall not go *a* other gods Deut 6:14 310
walk *a* other gods, and serve them, Deut 8:19 310
a that the LORD thy God hath cast Deut 9:4
and he chose their seed *a* them Deut 10:15 310
them as they pursued *a* you Deut 11:4 310
to go *a* other gods, which ye have Deut 11:28 310
Ye shall not do *a* all the things Deut 12:8
whatsoever thy soul lusteth *a* Deut 12:15
whatsoever thy soul lusteth *a* Deut 12:20
whatsoever thy soul lusteth *a* Deut 12:21
thee, and with thy children *a* thee Deut 12:25 310
with thy children *a* thee for ever Deut 12:28 310
a that they be destroyed from Deut 12:30 310
thou enquire not *a* their gods Deut 12:30
Let us go *a* other gods, which Deut 13:2 310
Ye shall walk *a* the LORD your God Deut 13:4 310
kite, and the vulture *a* his kind Deut 14:13
And every raven *a* his kind Deut 14:14
cuckow, and the hawk *a* his kind Deut 14:15
stork, and the heron *a* her kind Deut 14:18
for whatsoever thy soul lusteth *a* Deut 14:26
a that thou hast gathered in thy Deut 16:13
to do *a* the abominations of those Deut 18:9
to do *a* all their abominations Deut 20:18
a that thou shalt go in unto her, Deut 21:13 310
thee until thy brother seek *a* it Deut 22:2
his wife, *a* that she is defiled Deut 24:4 310
a that ye were come forth out of Deut 24:9
to go *a* other gods to serve them Deut 28:14 310
children that shall rise up *a* you Deut 29:22 310
go a whoring *a* the gods of the Deut 31:16 310
and how much more *a* my death Deut 31:27 310
For I know that *a* my death ye Deut 31:29 310
Now *a* the death of Moses the Josh 1:1 310
pursue *a* them quickly Josh 2:5 310
the men pursued *a* them the way to Josh 2:7 310
pursued *a* them were gone out Josh 2:7 310
And it came to pass *a* three days Josh 3:2 7097
from your place, and go *a* it Josh 3:3 310
the way, *a* they came out of Egypt Josh 5:4
land on the morrow *a* the passover Josh 5:11
a they had eaten of the old corn Josh 5:12
and the rereward came *a* the ark Josh 6:9 310
came *a* the ark of the LORD Josh 6:13 310
compassed the city *a* the same Josh 6:15
a they had stoned them with Josh 7:25
(For they will come out *a* us) Josh 8:6 310
called together to pursue *a* them Josh 8:16 310
and they pursued *a* Joshua, and were Josh 8:16 310
that went not out *a* Israel Josh 8:17 310
city open, and pursued *a* Israel Josh 8:17
a they had made a league with Josh 9:16 310
day like that before it or *a* it Josh 10:14 310
but pursue *a* your enemies, and Josh 10:19 310
of Reuben *a* their families Josh 13:23
children of Gad *a* their families Josh 13:28
a the name of Dan their father Josh 19:47
the avenger of blood pursue *a* him Josh 20:5 310
and you, and our generations *a* us Josh 22:27 310
it came to pass a long time *a* Josh 23:1 310
the Egyptians pursued *a* your Josh 24:6 310
a that he hath done you good Josh 24:20 310
And it came to pass *a* these things Josh 24:29 310
Now *a* the death of Joshua it came Judg 1:1 310
and they pursued *a* him, and caught Judg 1:6 310
arose another generation *a* them Judg 2:10 310
they went a whoring *a* other gods Judg 2:17 310
the haft also went in *a* the blade Judg 3:22 310
And he said unto them, Follow *a* me Judg 3:28 310
And they went down *a* him, and took Judg 3:28 310
a him was Shamgar the son of Judg 3:31 310
Tabor, and ten thousand men *a* him Judg 4:14 310
But Barak pursued *a* the chariots Judg 4:16 310
a the host, unto Harosheth of the Judg 4:16 310
a thee, Benjamin, among thy Judg 5:14 310
and Abi-ezer was gathered *a* him Judg 6:34 310
who also was gathered *a* him Judg 6:35 310
and pursued *a* the Midianites Judg 7:23 310
faint, and I am pursuing *a* Zebah Judg 8:5 310
Zalmunna fled, he pursued *a* them Judg 8:12 310
went thither a whoring *a* it Judg 8:27 310
again, and went a whoring *a* Baalim Judg 8:33 310
a Abimelech there arose to defend Judg 10:1 310
a him arose Jair, a Gileadite, and Judg 10:3 310
a him Ibzan of Beth-lehem judged Judg 12:8 310
a him Elon, a Zebulonite, judged Judg 12:11 310
a him Abdon the son of Hillel, a Judg 12:13 310
went *a* his wife, and came to the Judg 13:11 310
Why askest thou thus *a* my name Judg 13:18
a a time he returned to take her, Judg 14:8
it came to pass within a while *a* Judg 15:1
of you, and *a* that I will cease Judg 15:7 310

to grow again *a* he was shaven Judg 16:22 834
a the manner of the Zidonians, Judg 18:7
a the name of Dan their father, Judg 18:29
her husband arose, and went *a* her Judg 19:3 310
pursued hard *a* them unto Gidom, Judg 20:45 310
return thou *a* thy sister in law Ruth 1:15 310
to return from following *a* thee Ruth 1:16 310
glean ears of corn *a* him in whose Ruth 2:2 310
in the field *a* the reapers Ruth 2:3 310
gather *a* the reapers among the Ruth 2:7 310
they do reap, and go thou *a* them Ruth 2:9 310
had reserved *a* she was sufficed Ruth 2:18
and I am *a* thee Ruth 4:4 310
So Hannah rose up *a* they had 1Sa 1:9 310
in Shiloh, and *a* they had drunk 1Sa 1:9 310
come about *a* Hannah had conceived 1Sa 1:20
a they had carried it about, the 1Sa 5:9 310
went *a* them unto the border of 1Sa 6:12 310
of Israel lamented *a* the LORD 1Sa 7:2 310
ways, but turned aside *a* lucre 1Sa 8:3 310
A that thou shalt come to the 1Sa 10:5 310
Saul came *a* the herd out of the 1Sa 11:5 310
Whosoever cometh not forth *a* Saul 1Sa 11:7 310
a Samuel, so shall it be done 1Sa 11:7 310
then should ye go *a* vain things 1Sa 12:21 310
called together *a* Saul to Gilgal 1Sa 13:4 310
sought him a man *a* his own heart 1Sa 13:14
his armourbearer, Come up *a* me 1Sa 14:12 310
feet, and his armourbearer *a* him 1Sa 14:13 310
and his armourbearer slew *a* him 1Sa 14:13 310
hard *a* them in the battle 1Sa 14:22 310
Let us go down *a* the Philistines 1Sa 14:36 310
Shall I go down *a* the Philistines 1Sa 14:37 310
So Samuel turned again *a* Saul 1Sa 15:31 310
people answered him *a* this manner 1Sa 17:27
and spake *a* the same manner 1Sa 17:30
him again *a* the former manner 1Sa 17:30
And I went out *a* him, and smote him 1Sa 17:35 310
from chasing *a* the Philistines 1Sa 17:53 310
a they went forth, that David 1Sa 18:30 167
shot, Jonathan cried *a* the lad 1Sa 20:37 311
And Jonathan cried *a* the lad 1Sa 20:38 311
escaped, and fled *a* David 1Sa 22:20 310
he pursued *a* David in the 1Sa 23:25 310
returned from pursuing *a* David 1Sa 23:28 310
out of the cave, and cried *a* Saul 1Sa 24:8 310
A whom is the king of Israel come 1Sa 24:14 310
a whom dost thou pursue 1Sa 24:14 310
a a dead dog, *a* a flea 1Sa 24:14 310
wilt not cut off my seed *a* me 1Sa 24:21 310
there went up *a* David about four 1Sa 25:13 310
behold, I come *a* you 1Sa 25:19 310
it came to pass about ten days *a* 1Sa 25:38
damsels of hers that went *a* her 1Sa 25:42 7272
she went *a* the messengers of 1Sa 25:42 310
he saw that Saul came *a* him into 1Sa 26:3 310
my lord thus pursue *a* his servant 1Sa 26:18 310
Shall I pursue *a* this troop 1Sa 30:8 310
came to pass *a* the death of Saul 2Sa 1:1 310
and horsemen followed hard *a* him 2Sa 1:6
not live *a* that he was fallen 2Sa 1:10 310
And it came to pass *a* this 2Sa 2:1 310
And Asahel pursued *a* Abner 2Sa 2:19 310
also and Abishai pursued *a* Abner 2Sa 2:24 310
themselves together *a* Abner 2Sa 2:25 310
pursued *a* Israel no more, neither 2Sa 2:28 310
David, he sent messengers *a* Abner 2Sa 3:26 310
a he was come from Hebron 2Sa 5:13 310
I will set up thy seed *a* thee 2Sa 7:12 310
a this it came to pass, that 2Sa 8:1 310
And it came to pass *a* this 2Sa 10:1 310
a the year was expired, at the 2Sa 11:1
sent and enquired *a* the woman 2Sa 11:3
city, and it be called *a* my name 2Sa 12:28 5921
And it came to pass *a* this 2Sa 13:1 310
from me, and bolt the door *a* her 2Sa 13:17 310
her out, and bolted the door *a* her 2Sa 13:18 310
it came to pass *a* two full years 2Sa 13:23
shekels *a* the king's weight 2Sa 14:26
And it came to pass *a* this 2Sa 15:1 310
And it came to pass *a* forty years 2Sa 15:7 7093
the men of Israel are *a* Absalom 2Sa 15:13 310
forth, and all his household *a* him 2Sa 15:16 7272
forth, and all the people *a* him 2Sa 15:17 7272
men which came *a* him from Gath 2Sa 15:18 7272
pursue *a* David this night 2Sa 17:1 310
hath spoken *a* this manner 2Sa 17:6
shall we do *a* his saying 2Sa 17:6
a they were departed, that they 2Sa 17:21 310
returned from pursuing *a* Israel 2Sa 18:16 310
called the pillar *a* his own name 2Sa 18:18 5921
me, I pray thee, also run *a* Cushi 2Sa 18:22 310
of Israel went up from *a* David 2Sa 20:2 310
lord's servants, and pursue *a* him 2Sa 20:6 310
there went out *a* him Joab's men 2Sa 20:7 310
to pursue *a* Sheba the son of 2Sa 20:7 310
pursued *a* Sheba the son of Bichri 2Sa 20:10 310
is for David, let him go *a* Joab 2Sa 20:11 310
all the people went on *a* Joab 2Sa 20:13 310
to pursue *a* Sheba the son of 2Sa 20:13 310
together, and went also *a* him 2Sa 20:14 310
of David three years, year *a* year 2Sa 21:1 310
a that God was intreated for the 2Sa 21:14 310
And it came to pass *a* this 2Sa 21:18 310
the earth by clear shining *a* rain 2Sa 23:4
a him was Eleazar the son of Dodo 2Sa 23:9 310
returned *a* him only to spoil 2Sa 23:10 310
a him was Shammah the son of Agee 2Sa 23:11 310
David's heart smote him *a* that he 2Sa 24:10 310
and his mother bare him *a* Absalom 1Kin 1:6 310
Solomon thy son shall reign *a* me 1Kin 1:13 310
king, I also will come in *a* thee 1Kin 1:14 310
Solomon thy son shall reign *a* me 1Kin 1:17 310
throne of my lord the king *a* him 1Kin 1:20 310

said, Adonijah shall reign *a* me 1Kin 1:24 310
throne of my lord the king *a* him 1Kin 1:27 310
Solomon thy son shall reign *a* me 1Kin 1:30 310
Then ye shall come up *a* him 1Kin 1:35 310
And all the people came up *a* him 1Kin 1:40 310
for Joab had turned *a* Adonijah 1Kin 2:28 310
though he turned not *a* Absalom 1Kin 2:28 310
neither *a* thee shall any arise 1Kin 3:12 310
third day *a* that I was delivered 1Kin 3:18
eightieth year *a* the children of 1Kin 6:1
a the measures of hewed stones, 1Kin 7:11
was round *a* the work of the base 1Kin 7:31
A this manner he made the ten 1Kin 7:37
that were left *a* them in the land 1Kin 9:21 310
turn away your heart *a* their gods 1Kin 11:2 310
away his heart *a* other gods 1Kin 11:4 310
For Solomon went *a* Ashtoreth the 1Kin 11:5 310
a Milcom the abomination of the 1Kin 11:5 310
and went not fully *a* the LORD 1Kin 11:6 310
he should not go *a* other gods 1Kin 11:10 310
a he had smitten every male in 1Kin 11:15
spake to them *a* the counsel of 1Kin 12:14
went *a* the man of God, and found 1Kin 13:14 310
a he had eaten bread, and *a* he 1Kin 13:23 310
a he had buried him, that he 1Kin 13:31 310
A this thing Jeroboam returned 1Kin 13:33 310
to set up his son *a* him, and to 1Kin 15:4 310
a the name of Shemer, owner of 1Kin 16:24 5921
And it came to pass *a* a while 1Kin 17:7 7093
a make for thee and for thy son 1Kin 17:13 314
And it came to pass *a* these things 1Kin 17:17 310
And it came to pass *a* many days 1Kin 18:1
cut themselves *a* their manner 1Kin 18:28
and *a* the wind an earthquake 1Kin 19:11 310
And *a* the earthquake a fire 1Kin 19:12 310
a the fire a still small voice 1Kin 19:12 310
ran *a* Elijah, and said, Let me, I 1Kin 19:20 310
went *a* Elijah, and ministered unto 1Kin 19:21 310
a them he numbered all the people 1Kin 20:15 310
And it came to pass *a* these things 1Kin 21:1 310
Israel *a* the death of Ahab 2Kin 1:1 310
the LORD liveth, I will run *a* him 2Kin 5:20 310
So Gehazi followed *a* Naaman 2Kin 5:21 310
when Naaman saw him running *a* him 2Kin 5:21 310
And it came to pass *a* this 2Kin 6:24 310
the king sent *a* the host of the 2Kin 7:14 310
they went *a* them unto Jordan 2Kin 7:15 310
did *a* the saying of the man of 2Kin 8:2
rode together *a* Ahab his father 2Kin 9:25 310
And Jehu followed *a* him, and said, 2Kin 9:27 310
Jehu departed not from *a* them 2Kin 10:29 310
a the death of Jehoash son of 2Kin 14:17 310
but they sent *a* him to Lachish, 2Kin 14:19 310
a that the king slept with his 2Kin 14:22 310
went *a* the heathen that were 2Kin 17:15 310
a the manner of the nations whom 2Kin 17:33
day they do *a* the former manners 2Kin 17:34
neither do they *a* their statutes 2Kin 17:34
or *a* their ordinances 2Kin 17:34
or *a* the law and commandment 2Kin 17:34 310
but they did *a* their former 2Kin 17:40
so that *a* him was none like him 2Kin 18:5 310
a the abominations of the heathen 2Kin 21:2
to walk *a* the LORD, and to keep 2Kin 23:3 310
neither *a* him arose there any 2Kin 23:25 310
the Chaldees pursued *a* the king 2Kin 25:5 310
a that Hezron was dead in 1Chr 2:24 310
to be reckoned *a* the birthright 1Chr 5:1
went a whoring *a* the gods of the 1Chr 5:25 310
the LORD, *a* that the ark had rest 1Chr 6:31
a the house of their fathers, 1Chr 7:4
a their genealogy by their 1Chr 7:9
of Moab, *a* he had sent them away 1Chr 8:8 4480
were to come *a* seven days from 1Chr 9:25
hard *a* Saul, and *a* his sons 1Chr 10:2 310
a him was Eleazar the son of Dodo 1Chr 11:12 310
said unto him, Go not up *a* them 1Chr 14:14 310
we sought him not *a* the due order 1Chr 15:13
I will raise up thy seed *a* thee 1Chr 17:11 310
Now *a* this it came to pass, that 1Chr 18:1 310
Now it came to pass *a* this 1Chr 19:1 310
that *a* the year was expired, at 1Chr 20:1 6256
And it came to pass *a* this 1Chr 20:4 310
Levi *a* the house of their fathers 1Chr 23:24
a the house of their fathers 1Chr 24:30
children of Israel *a* their number 1Chr 27:1
Joab, and Zebadiah his son *a* him 1Chr 27:7 310
a Ahithophel was Jehoiada the son 1Chr 27:34 310
for your children *a* you for ever 1Chr 28:8 310
to offer so willingly *a* this sort 1Chr 29:14
LORD, on the morrow *a* that day 1Chr 29:21
there any *a* thee have the like 2Chr 1:12 310
a the numbering wherewith David 2Chr 2:17 310
The length by cubits *a* the first 2Chr 3:3
that they should burn *a* the 2Chr 4:20
who were left *a* them in the land, 2Chr 8:8 310
Even *a* a certain rate every day, 2Chr 8:13
Come again unto me *a* three days 2Chr 10:5
answered them *a* the advice of the 2Chr 10:14
a them out of all the tribes of 2Chr 11:16 310
a her he took Maachah the 2Chr 11:20 310
have made you priests *a* the 2Chr 13:9
And Abijah pursued *a* Jeroboam 2Chr 13:19 310
not *a* the doings of Israel 2Chr 17:4 310
a certain years he went down to 2Chr 18:2 7093
And one spake saying *a* this manner 2Chr 18:19 3602
and another saying *a* that manner 2Chr 18:19 3602
It came to pass *a* this also 2Chr 20:1 310
a this did Jehoshaphat king of 2Chr 20:35 310
a all this the LORD smote him in 2Chr 21:18 310
a the end of two years, his 2Chr 21:19
for they were his counsellors *a* 2Chr 22:4 310
He walked also *a* their counsel 2Chr 22:5
a that they had slain Athaliah 2Chr 23:21

And it came to pass *a* this 2Chr 24:4 310
Now *a* the death of Jehoiada came 2Chr 24:17 310
a that Amaziah was come from the 2Chr 25:14 310
Why hast thou sought *a* the gods 2Chr 25:15
they sought *a* the gods of Edom 2Chr 25:20
lived *a* the death of Joash son of 2Chr 25:25 310
Now *a* the time that Amaziah did 2Chr 25:27
but they sent to Lachish *a* him 2Chr 25:27 310
a that the king slept with his 2Chr 26:2 310
Azariah the priest went in *a* him 2Chr 26:17 310
a the abominations of the heathen 2Chr 28:3
in their place *a* their manner 2Chr 30:16
the Levites *a* their courses, 2Chr 31:2 5921
A these things, and the 2Chr 32:1 310
A this did Sennacherib king of 2Chr 32:9 310
Now *a* this he built a wall 2Chr 33:14 310
he began to seek *a* the God of 2Chr 34:3
to do *a* all that is written in 2Chr 34:21
to walk *a* the LORD, and to keep 2Chr 34:31 310
a your courses, according to the 2Chr 35:4
a the division of the families of 2Chr 35:5
A all this, when Josiah had 2Chr 35:20 310
transgressed very much *a* all the 2Chr 36:14
and was called *a* their name Ezr 2:61 5921
They gave *a* their ability unto Ezr 2:69
a the ordinance of David king of Ezr 3:10 5921
said we unto them *a* this manner Ezr 5:4 310
But *a* that our fathers had Ezr 5:12 4481
Now *a* these things, in the reign Ezr 7:1 310
that do *a* the will of your God Ezr 7:18
a the wisdom of thy God, that is Ezr 7:25
our God, what shall we say *a* this Ezr 9:10 310
a all that is come upon us for Ezr 9:13 310
a the house of their fathers, and Ezr 10:16
A him repaired Nehemiah the son Neh 3:16 310
A him repaired the Levites, Rehum Neh 3:17 310
A him repaired their brethren, Neh 3:18 310
A him Baruch the son of Zabbai Neh 3:20 310
A him repaired Meremoth the son Neh 3:21 310
a him repaired the priests, the Neh 3:22 310
A him repaired Benjamin and Hashub Neh 3:23 310
A him repaired Azariah the son of Neh 3:23 310
A him repaired Binnui the son of Neh 3:24 310
A him Pedaiah the son of Parosh Neh 3:25 310
A them the Tekoites repaired Neh 3:27 310
A them repaired Zadok the son of Neh 3:29 310
A him repaired also Shemaiah the Neh 3:29 310
A him repaired Hananiah the son Neh 3:30 310
A him repaired Meshullam the son Neh 3:30 310
A him repaired Malchiah the Neh 3:31 310
I even set the people *a* their Neh 4:13
We *a* our ability have redeemed Neh 5:8 1767
unto me four times *a* this sort Neh 6:4
I answered them *a* the same manner Neh 6:4
wife, and was called *a* their name Neh 7:63 5921
But *a* they had rest, they did Neh 9:28
a the houses of our fathers, at Neh 10:34 310
a him Gabbai, Sallai, nine Neh 11:8 310
a them went Hoshaiah, and half of Neh 12:32 310
I *a* them, and the half of the Neh 12:38 310
a certain days obtained I leave Neh 13:6 7093
not be opened till *a* the sabbath Neh 13:19 310
to every people *a* their language Est 1:22
A these things, when the wrath of Est 2:1 310
a that she had been twelve months Est 2:12 7093
A these things did king Ahasuerus Est 3:1 310
to every people *a* their language Est 3:12
every people *a* their language Est 8:9
days Purim *a* the name of Pur Est 9:26 5921
A this opened Job his mouth, and Job 3:1 310
thou enquirest *a* mine iniquity Job 10:6 310
and searchest *a* my sin Job 10:6 310
They that come *a* him shall be Job 18:20 314
though *a* my skin worms destroy Job 19:26 310
a that I have spoken, mock on Job 21:3 310
hath he in his house *a* him Job 21:21 310
and every man shall draw *a* him Job 21:33 310
A my words they spake not again Job 29:22 310
(they cried *a* them as *a* a Job 30:5 5921
and mine heart walked *a* mine eyes Job 31:7 310
A it a voice roareth Job 37:4 310
he searcheth *a* every green thing Job 39:8 310
will he harrow the valleys *a* thee Job 39:10 310
He maketh a path to shine *a* him Job 41:32 310
a that the LORD had spoken these Job 42:7 310
lest I deal with you *a* your folly Job 42:8 310
A this lived Job an hundred and Job 42:16 310
ye love vanity, and seek *a* leasing Ps 4:2
countenance, will not seek *a* God Ps 10:4
that hasten *a* another god Ps 16:4
of the LORD, that will I seek *a* Ps 27:4
give them *a* the work of their Ps 28:4
put to shame that seek *a* my soul Ps 35:4
They also that seek *a* my life lay Ps 38:12
that seek *a* my soul to destroy it Ps 40:14
hart panteth *a* the water brooks Ps 42:1 5921
brooks, so panteth my soul *a* thee Ps 42:1 413
their lands *a* their own names Ps 49:11
his glory shall not descend *a* him Ps 49:17 310
a he had gone in to Bath-sheba Ps 51:t 834
me, and oppressors seek *a* my soul Ps 54:3
My soul followeth hard *a* thee Ps 63:8 310
players on instruments followed *a* Ps 68:25 310
and confounded that seek *a* my soul Ps 70:2
returned and enquired early *a* God Ps 78:34
violent men have sought *a* my soul Ps 86:14
hath not dealt with us *a* our sins Ps 103:10
The young lions roar *a* their prey Ps 104:21
ever *a* the order of Melchizedek Ps 110:4 5921
I have longed *a* thy precepts Ps 119:40
for me, which are not *a* thy law Ps 119:85
Quicken me *a* thy lovingkindness Ps 119:88
draw nigh that follow *a* mischief Ps 119:150
my soul thirsteth *a* thee, as a Ps 143:6

polished *a* the similitude of a Ps 144:12
Yea, if thou criest *a* knowledge Prov 2:3
Lust not *a* her beauty in thine Prov 6:25
He goeth *a* her straightway, as an Prov 7:22 310
that followeth *a* righteousness Prov 15:9
his children are blessed *a* him Prov 20:7 310
holy, and *a* vows to make enquiry Prov 20:25 310
He that followeth *a* righteousness Prov 21:21
but he that followeth *a* vain Prov 28:19
come with those that shall come *a* Eccl 1:11 314
the man do that cometh *a* the king Eccl 2:12 310
unto the man that shall be *a* me Eccl 2:18 310
him to see what shall be *a* him Eccl 3:22 310
they also that come *a* shall not Eccl 4:16 314
what shall be *a* him under the sun Eccl 6:12 310
man should find nothing *a* him Eccl 7:14 310
a that they go to the dead Eccl 9:3 310
and what shall be *a* him, who can Eccl 10:14 310
thou shalt find it *a* many days Eccl 11:1
nor the clouds return *a* the rain Eccl 12:2 310
Draw me, we will run *a* thee Song 1:4 310
gifts, and followeth *a* rewards Is 1:23
the lambs feed *a* their manner Is 5:17
thee, *a* the manner of Egypt Is 10:24
lift it up *a* the manner of Egypt Is 10:26
he shall not judge *a* the sight of Is 11:3
neither reprove *a* the hearing of Is 11:3 310
a the end of seventy years shall Is 23:15
it shall come to pass *a* the end Is 23:17
a many days shall they be visited Is 24:22
neither shall there be *a* me Is 43:10 310
maketh it *a* the figure of a man, Is 44:13
they shall come *a* thee Is 45:14 310
a thou hast lost the other, shall Is 49:20
ye that follow *a* righteousness Is 51:1 310
not good, *a* their own thoughts Is 65:2 310
when thou wentest *a* me in the Jer 2:2 310
from me, and have walked *a* vanity Jer 2:5 310
walked *a* things that do not Jer 2:8 310
I have not gone *a* Baalim Jer 2:23 310
strangers, and *a* them will I go Jer 2:25 310
I said *a* she had done all these Jer 3:7 310
shall they walk any more *a* the Jer 3:17 310
every one neighed *a* his Jer 5:8 413
neither walk *a* other gods to your Jer 7:6 310
walk *a* other gods whom ye know Jer 7:9 310
a whom they have walked, and whom Jer 8:2 310
But have walked *a* the imagination Jer 9:14 310
a Baalim, which their fathers Jer 9:14 310
and I will send a sword *a* them Jer 9:16 310
as the handful *a* the harvestman Jer 9:22 310
they went *a* other gods to serve Jer 11:10 310
have called a multitude *a* thee Jer 12:6 310
a that I have plucked them out I Jer 12:15 310
And it came to pass *a* many days Jer 13:6 7093
A this manner will I mar the Jer 13:9 3602
walk *a* other gods, to serve them, Jer 13:10 310
LORD, and have walked *a* other gods Jer 16:11 310
behold, ye walk every one *a* the Jer 16:12 310
a will I send for many hunters, Jer 16:16 310
we will walk *a* our own devices Jer 18:12 310
a the imagination of his own Jer 23:17
a that Nebuchadrezzar king of Jer 24:1 310
go not *a* other gods to serve them Jer 25:6 310
of Sheshach shall drink *a* them Jer 25:26 310
a that Hananiah the prophet had Jer 28:12 310
(*A* that Jeconiah the king, and the Jer 29:2 310
the LORD, That *a* seventy years be Jer 29:10 6310
is Zion, whom no man seeketh *a* Jer 30:17 310
shall remain *a* the manner thereof Jer 30:18 5921
Surely *a* that I was turned, I Jer 31:19 310
a that I was instructed, I smote Jer 31:19 310
A those days, saith the LORD, I Jer 31:33 310
bosom of their children *a* them Jer 32:18 310
them, and of their children *a* them Jer 32:39 310
a that the king Zedekiah had made Jer 34:8 310
go not *a* other gods to serve them Jer 35:15 310
a that the king had burned the Jer 36:27 310
Chaldeans' army pursued *a* them Jer 39:5 310
a that Nebuzar-adan the captain Jer 40:1 310
day *a* he had slain Gedaliah Jer 41:4
a that he had slain Gedaliah the Jer 41:16 310
And it came to pass *a* ten days Jer 42:7 7093
follow close *a* you there in Egypt Jer 42:16 310
and I will send the sword *a* them Jer 49:37 310
waste and utterly destroy *a* them Jer 50:21 310
a that in another year shall come Jer 51:46 310
the Chaldeans pursued *a* the king Jer 52:8 310
and I will draw out a sword *a* them Eze 5:2 310
and I will draw out a sword *a* them Eze 5:12 310
which go a whoring *a* their idols Eze 6:9 310
I will do unto them *a* their way Eze 7:27
Go ye *a* him through the city, and Eze 9:5 310
but have done *a* the manners of Eze 11:12
a the heart of their detestable Eze 11:21
I will draw out the sword *a* them Eze 12:14 310
it came to pass *a* all thy Eze 16:23 310
hast thou not walked *a* their ways Eze 16:47
nor done *a* their abominations Eze 16:47
their heart went *a* their idols Eze 20:16 310
their eyes were *a* their fathers' Eze 20:24 310
Are ye polluted *a* the manner of Eze 20:30
ye whoredom *a* their abominations Eze 20:30 310
a the manner of the Babylonians Eze 23:15
hast gone a whoring *a* the heathen Eze 23:30 310
they shall judge them *a* the Eze 23:45
a the manner of women that shed Eze 23:45
taught not to do *a* your lewdness Eze 23:48 310
when they shall look *a* them Eze 29:16 310
judge you every one *a* his ways Eze 33:20
heart goeth *a* their covetousness Eze 33:31 310
and none did search or seek *a* them Eze 34:6
settle you *a* your old estates Eze 36:11
A many days thou shalt be visited Eze 38:8

a the end of seven months shall ... Eze 39:14
A that they have borne their ... Eze 39:26
in the fourteenth year a that the ... Eze 40:1 310
the arches thereof were a the ... Eze 40:21
were a the measure of the gate ... Eze 40:22
A that he brought me toward the ... Eze 40:24
A he measured the wall of the ... Eze 41:5
of the altar a the cubits ... Eze 43:13
astray away from me a their idols ... Eze 44:10 310
a he is cleansed, they shall ... Eze 44:26 310
thereof shall be a the homer ... Eze 45:11
a his going forth one shall shut ... Eze 46:12 310
a, it shall return to the prince ... Eze 46:17
A he brought me through the entry ... Eze 46:19
be a the names of the tribes of ... Eze 48:31 5921
a thee shall arise another ... Dan 2:39 870
God that can deliver a this sort ... Dan 3:29 1863
a that thou shalt have known that ... Dan 4:26 1767
A this I beheld, and lo another, ... Dan 7:6 870
A this I saw in the night visions ... Dan 7:7 870
and another shall rise a them ... Dan 7:24 311
a that which appeared unto me at ... Dan 8:1 310
a threescore and two weeks shall ... Dan 9:26 310
shall certainly come a certain ... Dan 11:13 7093
A this shall he turn his face ... Dan 11:18
a the league made with him he ... Dan 11:23
she said, I will go a my lovers ... Hos 2:5 310
And she shall follow a her lovers ... Hos 2:7 310
she went a her lovers, and forgat ... Hos 2:13 310
at Beth-aven, a thee, O Benjamin ... Hos 5:8 310
walked a the commandment ... Hos 5:11 310
A two days will he revive us ... Hos 6:2
who ceaseth from raising a he ... Hos 7:4
They shall walk a the LORD ... Hos 11:10 310
followeth a the east wind ... Hos 12:1
neither shall be any more a it ... Joel 2:2 310
a the which their fathers have ... Amos 2:4 310
That pant a the dust of the earth ... Amos 2:7 5921
and your tithes a three years ... Amos 4:4
pestilence a the manner of Egypt ... Amos 4:10
growth a the king's mowings ... Amos 7:1 310
A the glory hath he sent me unto ... Zec 2:8 310
and the white go forth a them ... Zec 6:6 310
Thus the land was desolate a them ... Zec 7:14 310
a they were brought to Babylon, ... Mt 1:12 3326
but he that cometh a me is ... Mt 3:11 3694
hunger and thirst a righteousness ... Mt 5:6
looketh on a woman to lust a her ... Mt 5:28
A this manner therefore pray ye ... Mt 6:9 3779
(For a all these things do the ... Mt 6:32 1934
not his cross, and followeth a me ... Mt 10:38 3694
generation seeketh a a sign ... Mt 12:39 3326
a they heard this saying ... Mt 15:12
for she crieth a us ... Mt 15:23 3693
generation seeketh a a sign ... Mt 16:4 1934
If any man will come a me ... Mt 16:24 3694
a six days Jesus taketh Peter, ... Mt 17:1 3326
a that he had called him, said ... Mt 18:32
but do not ye a their works ... Mt 23:3 2596
Immediately a the tribulation of ... Mt 24:29 3326
A a long time the lord of those ... Mt 25:19 3326
Ye know that a two days is the ... Mt 26:2 3326
But a I am risen again, I will go ... Mt 26:32 3326
a a while came unto him they that ... Mt 26:73 3326
a that they had mocked him, they ... Mt 27:31 3753
of the graves a his resurrection ... Mt 27:53 3326
A three days I will rise again ... Mt 27:63 3326
cometh one mightier than I a me ... Mk 1:7 3694
Now a that John was put in prison ... Mk 1:14 3326
said unto them, Come ye a me ... Mk 1:17 3694
the hired servants, and went a him ... Mk 1:20 3694
that were with him followed a him ... Mk 1:36 2614
into Capernaum a some days ... Mk 2:1 1223
a that the full corn in the ear ... Mk 4:28 1534
this generation seek a a sign ... Mk 8:12 1934
A that he put his hands again ... Mk 8:25 1534
and a three days rise again ... Mk 8:31 3326
them, Whosoever will come a me ... Mk 8:34 3694
a six days Jesus taketh with him ... Mk 9:2 3326
a that he is killed, he shall ... Mk 9:31 3326
no man a that durst ask him any ... Mk 12:34 3765
a that tribulation, the sun shall ... Mk 13:24 3326
A two days was the feast of the ... Mk 14:1 3326
But a that I am risen, I will go ... Mk 14:28 3326
And a little a, they that stood by ... Mk 14:70 3326
A that he appeared in another ... Mk 16:12 3326
which had seen him a he was risen ... Mk 16:14
So then a the Lord had spoken ... Mk 16:19 3326
a those days his wife Elisabeth ... Lk 1:24 3326
a the name of his father ... Lk 1:59 1909
to do for him a the custom of the ... Lk 2:27 2596
a the custom of the feast ... Lk 2:42 2596
that a three days they found him ... Lk 2:46 3326
a these things he went forth, and ... Lk 5:27 3326
on the second sabbath a the first ... Lk 6:1 1207
And it came to pass the day a ... Lk 7:11 1836
all, If any man will come a me ... Lk 9:23 3694
an eight days a these sayings ... Lk 9:28 3326
A these things the Lord appointed ... Lk 10:1 3326
a that have no more that they can ... Lk 12:4 3326
which a he hath killed hath power ... Lk 12:5 3326
the nations of the world seek a ... Lk 12:30 1934
then a that thou shalt cut it ... Lk 13:9
not bear his cross, and come a me ... Lk 14:27 3694
a he hath laid the foundation, and ... Lk 14:29
go a that which is lost, until he ... Lk 15:4 1909
not many days a the younger son ... Lk 15:13 3326
go not a them, nor follow them ... Lk 17:23
him, and sent a message a him ... Lk 19:14 3694
a that they durst not ask him any ... Lk 20:40 2089
go ye not therefore a them ... Lk 21:8 3694
for looking a those things which ... Lk 21:26 4329
Likewise also the cup a supper ... Lk 22:20 3326
a a little while another saw him, ... Lk 22:58 3326
about the space of one hour a ... Lk 22:59
that he might bear it a Jesus ... Lk 23:26 3693
with him from Galilee, followed a ... Lk 23:55 2628
He that cometh a me is preferred ... Jn 1:15 3694
who coming a me is preferred ... Jn 1:27 3694
A me cometh a man which is ... Jn 1:30 3694
Again the next day a John stood ... Jn 1:35 1887
a the manner of the purifying of ... Jn 2:6 2596
A this he went down to Capernaum, ... Jn 2:12 3326
A these things came Jesus and his ... Jn 3:22 3326
Now a two days he departed thence ... Jn 4:43 3326
A this there was a feast of the ... Jn 5:1 3326
whosoever then first a the ... Jn 5:4 3326
A these things Jesus went over ... Jn 6:1 3326
a that the Lord had given thanks ... Jn 6:23
A these things Jesus walked in ... Jn 7:1 3326
Ye judge a the flesh ... Jn 8:15 2596
Then a that saith he to his ... Jn 11:7 3326
a that he saith unto them, Our ... Jn 11:11 3326
behold, the world is gone a him ... Jn 12:19 3694
A that he poureth water into a ... Jn 13:5 1534
So a he had washed their feet, and ... Jn 13:12 3753
a the sop Satan entered into him ... Jn 13:27 3326
A this, Jesus knowing that all ... Jn 19:28 3326
a this Joseph of Arimathaea, ... Jn 19:38 3326
a eight days again his disciples ... Jn 20:26 3326
A these things Jesus shewed ... Jn 21:1 3326
a that he was risen from the dead ... Jn 21:14
a that he through the Holy Ghost ... Acts 1:2
also he shewed himself alive a ... Acts 1:3 3326
a that the Holy Ghost is come ... Acts 1:8
Samuel and those that follow a ... Acts 3:24 2517
a it was sold, was it not in ... Acts 5:4
about the space of three hours a ... Acts 5:7
A this man rose up Judas of ... Acts 5:37 3326
and drew away much people a him ... Acts 5:37 3694
possession, and to his seed a him ... Acts 7:5 3326
a that shall they come forth, and ... Acts 7:7 3326
a that he had shewed wonders and ... Acts 7:36
also our fathers that came a ... Acts 7:45 3326
a that many days were fulfilled, ... Acts 9:23 5618
the morrow a they entered into ... Acts 10:24 3326
a the baptism which John preached ... Acts 10:37 3326
drink with him a he rose from the ... Acts 10:41 3326
intending a Easter to bring him ... Acts 12:4 3326
a the reading of the law and the ... Acts 13:15 3326
a that he gave unto them judges ... Acts 13:20 3326
a man a mine own heart, which ... Acts 13:22 2596
behold, there cometh one a me ... Acts 13:25 3326
David, a he had served his own ... Acts 13:36
a they had passed throughout ... Acts 14:24
circumcised a the manner of Moses ... Acts 15:1
a they had held their peace, ... Acts 15:13 3326
A this I will return, and will ... Acts 15:16 3326
of men might seek a the Lord ... Acts 15:17 1567
letters by them a this manner ... Acts 15:23
a they had tarried there a space, ... Acts 15:33
some days a Paul said unto ... Acts 15:36 3326
A they were come to Mysia, they ... Acts 16:7
a he had seen the vision, ... Acts 16:10 5613
if haply they might feel a him ... Acts 17:27
A these things Paul departed from ... Acts 18:1 3326
Paul a this tarried there yet a ... Acts 18:18 3326
a he had spent some time there, ... Acts 18:23 3326
on him which should come a him ... Acts 19:4 3326
A these things were ended, Paul ... Acts 19:21 5613
A I have been there, I must also ... Acts 19:21 3326
a the uproar was ceased, Paul ... Acts 20:1 3326
a the days of unleavened bread ... Acts 20:6 3326
a what manner I have been with ... Acts 20:18 4459
that a my departing shall ... Acts 20:29 3326
to draw away disciples a them ... Acts 20:30 3694
that a we were gotten from them, ... Acts 21:1 5613
a those days we took up our ... Acts 21:15 3326
neither to walk a the customs ... Acts 21:21
of the people followed a, crying, ... Acts 21:36
a he knew that he was a Roman, and ... Acts 22:29
thou to judge me a the law ... Acts 23:3 2596
he wrote a letter a this manner ... Acts 23:25 4023
a five days Ananias the high ... Acts 24:1 3326
a that the governor had beckoned ... Acts 24:10
that a the way which they call ... Acts 24:14 2596
Now a many years I came to bring ... Acts 24:17 1223
a certain days, when Felix came ... Acts 24:24 3326
But a two years Porcius Festus ... Acts 24:27 4137
a three days he ascended from ... Acts 25:1 3326
a certain days king Agrippa and ... Acts 25:13 1230
a examination had, I might have ... Acts 25:26
that a the most straitest sect of ... Acts 26:5 2596
But not long a there arose ... Acts 27:14
But a long abstinence Paul stood ... Acts 27:21 5225
but a they had looked a great ... Acts 28:6
a three months we departed in a ... Acts 28:11 3326
a one day the south wind blew, and ... Acts 28:13 3326
that a three days Paul called the ... Acts 28:17 3326
a that Paul had spoken one word, ... Acts 28:25
But a thy hardness and impenitent ... Rom 2:5 2596
there is none that seeketh a God ... Rom 3:11 1567
sinned a the similitude of Adam's ... Rom 5:14 1909
I speak a the manner of men ... Rom 6:19
the law of God a the inward man ... Rom 7:22 2596
a the flesh, but a the Spirit ... Rom 8:1 2596
a the flesh, but a the Spirit ... Rom 8:4 3326
For they that are a the flesh do ... Rom 8:5 2596
but they that are a the Spirit ... Rom 8:5 2596
to the flesh, to live a the flesh ... Rom 8:12 2596
For if ye live a the flesh ... Rom 8:13 2596
followed not a righteousness ... Rom 9:30
which followed a the law of ... Rom 9:31
unto them that asked not a me ... Rom 10:20 1905
Let us therefore follow a the ... Rom 14:19 1377
For a that in the wisdom of God ... 1Cor 1:21 1894
sign, and the Greeks seek a wisdom ... 1Cor 1:22
not many wise men a the flesh ... 1Cor 1:26 2596
one a this manner, and another a ... 1Cor 7:7 3326
if she so abide, a my judgment ... 1Cor 7:40 2596
we should not lust a evil things ... 1Cor 10:6 1938
Behold Israel a the flesh ... 1Cor 10:18 2596
A the same manner also he took ... 1Cor 11:25 5615
a that miracles, then gifts of ... 1Cor 12:28 1899
Follow a charity, and desire ... 1Cor 14:1
A that, he was seen of above five ... 1Cor 15:6 1899
A that, he was seen of James ... 1Cor 15:7 3326
If a the manner of men I have ... 1Cor 15:32 2596
know we no man a the flesh ... 2Cor 5:16 2596
we have known Christ a the flesh ... 2Cor 5:16 2596
were made sorry a a godly manner ... 2Cor 7:9 2596
that ye sorrowed a a godly sort ... 2Cor 7:11 2596
for you, which long a you for the ... 2Cor 9:14 1971
flesh, we do not war a the flesh ... 2Cor 10:3 2596
Do ye look on things a the ... 2Cor 10:7 2596
speak, I speak it not a the Lord ... 2Cor 11:17 2596
that many glory a the flesh ... 2Cor 11:18 2596
was preached of me is not a man ... Gal 1:11 2596
Then a three years I went up to ... Gal 1:18 2596
Then fourteen years a I went up ... Gal 2:1 1223
livest a the manner of Gentiles, ... Gal 2:14
I speak a the manner of men ... Gal 3:15 2596
four hundred and thirty years a ... Gal 3:17 3326
But a that faith is come, we are ... Gal 3:25
a that ye have known God, or ... Gal 4:9
bondwoman was born a the flesh ... Gal 4:23 2596
But as then he that was born a ... Gal 4:29 2596
him that was born a the Spirit ... Gal 4:29 2596
a the counsel of his own will ... Eph 1:11 2596
a that ye heard the word of truth ... Eph 1:13
in whom also a that ye believed, ... Eph 1:13
a I heard of your faith in the ... Eph 1:15
which a God is created in ... Eph 4:24 2596
how greatly I long a you all in ... Phil 1:8 1971
For he longed a you all, and was ... Phil 2:26 1971
but I follow a, if that I may ... Phil 3:12
a the tradition of men, a the ... Col 2:8 2596
of the world, and not a Christ ... Col 2:8 2596
a the commandments and doctrines ... Col 2:22 2596
a the image of him that created ... Col 3:10 2596
But even a that we had suffered ... 1Th 2:2
whose coming is a the working of ... 2Th 2:9 2596
not a the tradition which he ... 2Th 3:6 2596
are already turned aside a Satan ... 1Ti 5:15 3694
and some men they follow a ... 1Ti 5:24 1872
which while some coveted a ... 1Ti 6:10
follow a righteousness, godliness ... 1Ti 6:11
but a their own lusts shall they ... 2Ti 4:3 2596
of the truth which is a godliness ... Titus 1:1 2596
mine own son a the common faith ... Titus 1:4 2596
But a that the kindness and love ... Titus 3:4 3753
that is an heretick a the first ... Titus 3:10 3326
things which were to be spoken a ... Heb 3:5
David, To day, a so long a time ... Heb 4:7 3326
lest any man fall a the same ... Heb 4:11 1722
ever a the order of Melchisedec ... Heb 5:6 2569
priest a the order of Melchisedec ... Heb 5:10 2569
a he had patiently endured, he ... Heb 6:15
ever a the order of Melchisedec ... Heb 6:20 2569
a that also King of Salem, which ... Heb 7:2 1899
rise a the order of Melchisedec ... Heb 7:11 2596
not be called a the order of ... Heb 7:11 2596
for that a the similitude of ... Heb 7:15 2596
not a the law of a carnal ... Heb 7:16 2596
but a the power of an endless ... Heb 7:16 2596
ever a the order of Melchisedec ... Heb 7:17 2596
ever a the order of Melchisedec ... Heb 7:21 2596
the house of Israel a those days ... Heb 8:10 3326
a the second veil, the tabernacle ... Heb 9:3 3326
is of force a men are dead ... Heb 9:17
to die, but a this the judgment ... Heb 9:27 3326
a he had offered one sacrifice ... Heb 10:12
for a that he had said before, ... Heb 10:15 3326
will make with them a those days ... Heb 10:16 3326
For if we sin wilfully a that we ... Heb 10:26 3326
a ye were illuminated, ye endured ... Heb 10:32
a ye have done the will of God, ... Heb 10:36
a receive for an inheritance ... Heb 11:8 3195
a they were compassed about seven ... Heb 11:30
chastened us a their own pleasure ... Heb 12:10 2596
which are made a the similitude ... Jas 3:9 2596
For a this manner in the old time ... 1Pet 3:5 3779
a that ye have suffered a while, ... 1Pet 5:10
endeavour that ye may be able a ... 2Pet 1:15 3326
those that a should live ungodly ... 2Pet 2:6 3195
walk a the flesh in the lust of ... 2Pet 2:10 3694
For if a they have escaped the ... 2Pet 2:20 3326
a they have known it, to turn ... 2Pet 2:21
walking a their own lusts, ... 2Pet 3:3 2596
that we walk a his commandments ... 2Jn 6 2596
on their journey a a godly sort ... 3Jn 6 516
going a strange flesh, are set ... Jude 7 3694
ran greedily a the error of ... Jude 11
walking a their own lusts ... Jude 16 2596
who should walk a their own ... Jude 18 2596
A this I looked, and, behold, a ... Rev 4:1 3326
a these things I saw four angels ... Rev 7:1 3326
A this I beheld, and, lo, a great ... Rev 7:9 3326
a three days and an half the ... Rev 11:11 3326
water as a flood a the woman ... Rev 12:15 3694
the world wondered a the beast ... Rev 13:3 3694
a that I looked, and, behold, the ... Rev 15:5 3326
a these things I saw another ... Rev 18:1 3326
lusted a are departed from thee ... Rev 18:14
a these things I heard a great ... Rev 19:1 3326
a that he must be loosed a little ... Rev 20:3 3326

AFTERNOON

And they tarried until a, and they ... Judg 19:8

AFTERWARD

a were the families of the ... Gen 10:18 310
a shall they come out with great ... Gen 15:14

me, and a I will see his face Gen 32:20
a came out his brother, that had Gen 38:30 310
a Moses and Aaron went in, and told Ex 5:1 310
a all the children of Israel came Ex 34:32
a he shall kill the burnt Lev 14:19 310
a the priest shall go in to see Lev 14:36
in water, and a come into the camp Lev 16:26
a he shall come into the camp Lev 16:28
shall a eat of the holy things Lev 22:7 310
a shall cause the woman to drink Num 5:26 310
a the people removed from Num 12:16 310
a he shall come into the camp, and Num 19:7 310
a shalt thou be gathered unto thy Num 31:2 310
a ye shall come into the camp Num 31:24 310
then a ye shall return, and be Num 32:22 310
a the hands of all the people Deut 17:7 314
thou shalt not glean it a Deut 24:21 310
and a may ye go your way Josh 2:16 310
a he read all the words of the Josh 8:34
a Joshua smote them, and slew them Josh 10:26
and a I brought you out Josh 24:5 310
a the children of Judah went down Judg 1:9 310
and a shall thine hands be Judg 7:11 310
And it came to pass a, that he Judg 16:4
morsel of bread, and a go your way Judg 19:5 310
And it came to pass a, that 1Sa 24:5
David also arose a, and went out 1Sa 24:8
a when David heard it, he said, I 2Sa 3:28
a Hezron went in to the daughter 1Chr 2:21 310
a they made ready for themselves, 2Chr 35:14 310
a offered the continual burnt Ezr 3:5
A I came unto the house of Neh 6:10
counsel, and a receive me to glory Ps 73:24 310
a thou shalt be called, The city Is 1:26
a did more grievously afflict her Is 9:1 314
And a, saith the LORD, I will Jer 21:7
But a they turned, and caused the Jer 34:11
a it shall be inhabited, as in Jer 46:26
And a I will bring again the Jer 49:6
A he brought me to the temple, and Eze 41:1
A he brought me to the gate, even Eze 43:1
A he brought me again unto the Eze 47:1
A he measured a thousand Eze 47:5
a I rose up, and did the king's Dan 8:27
A shall the children of Israel Hos 3:5 310
And it shall come to pass a Joel 2:28
forty nights, he was a an hungred Mt 4:2 5305
but a he repented, and went Mt 21:29 5305
ye had seen it, repented not a Mt 21:32 5305
A came also the other virgins, Mt 25:11 5305
a, when affliction or persecution Mk 4:17 1534
A he appeared unto the eleven as Mk 16:14 5305
they were ended, he a hungered Lk 4:2 5305
And it came to pass a, that he Lk 8:1 2517
a thou shalt eat and drink Lk 17:8
but a he said within himself, Lk 18:4
A Jesus findeth him in the temple Jn 5:14
And a they desired a king Acts 13:21 2547
a they that are Christ's at his 1Cor 15:23 1899
a that which is spiritual 1Cor 15:46 1899
then would he not a have spoken Heb 4:8
nevertheless a it yieldeth the Heb 12:11 5305
For ye know how that a, when he Heb 12:17 3347
a destroyed them that believed Jude 5 1208

AFTERWARDS

a she bare a daughter, and called Gen 30:21 310
a he will let you go hence Ex 11:1
a the hand of all the people Deut 13:9 314
a they eat that be bidden 1Sa 9:13
mark, and a we will speak Job 18:2 310
but a his mouth shall be filled Prov 20:17 310
and a build thine house Prov 24:27 310
He that rebuketh a man a shall Prov 28:23 310
a wise man keepeth it in till a Prov 29:11 268
A the spirit took me up, and Eze 11:24
but thou shalt follow me a Jn 13:36 5305
A I came into the regions of Gal 1:21 1899
faith which should a be revealed Gal 3:23

AGABUS (*ag'-ab-us*) *A Christian prophet.*

stood up one of them named A Acts 11:28 13
Judaea a certain prophet, named A Acts 21:10 13

AGAG (*a'-gag*) See AGAGITE. *A king of Amalek during Exodus.*

his king shall be higher than A Num 24:7 90
he took A the king of the 1Sa 15:8 90
But Saul and the people spared A 1Sa 15:9 90
have brought A the king of Amalek 1Sa 15:20 90
Bring ye hither to me A the king 1Sa 15:32 90
A came unto him delicately 1Sa 15:32 90
A said, Surely the bitterness of 1Sa 15:32 90
Samuel hewed A in pieces before 1Sa 15:33 90

AGAGITE (*ag'-ag-ite*) *A member of an Amalekite tribe.*

Haman the son of Hammedatha the A Est 3:1 91
Haman the son of Hammedatha the A Est 3:10 91
away the mischief of Haman the A Est 8:3 91
Haman the son of Hammedatha the A Est 8:5 91
the son of Hammedatha, the A Est 9:24 91

AGAIN

she a bare his brother Abel Gen 4:2 3254
And Adam knew his wife a Gen 4:25 5750
a he sent forth the dove out of Gen 8:10 3254
returned not a unto him any more Gen 8:12 3254
I will not a curse the ground any Gen 8:21 3254
neither will I a smite any more Gen 8:21 3254
also brought a his brother Lot, Gen 14:16 7725
they shall come hither a Gen 15:16 7725
And he spake unto him yet a Gen 18:29 3254
And they said a, This one fellow Gen 19:9
and worship, and come a to you Gen 22:5 7725
must I needs bring thy son a unto Gen 24:5 7725
thou bring not my son thither a Gen 24:6 7725
only bring not my son thither a Gen 24:8 7725
ran a unto the well to draw water Gen 24:20 5750
Then a Abraham took a wife, and Gen 25:1 3254
Isaac digged a the wells of water Gen 26:18 7725
will bring thee a into this land Gen 28:15 7725
So that I come a to my father's Gen 28:21 7725
put the stone a upon the well's Gen 29:3 7725
And she conceived a, and bare a son Gen 29:33 5750
And she conceived a, and bare a son Gen 29:34 5750
And she conceived a, and bare a son Gen 29:35 5750
Bilhah Rachel's maid conceived a Gen 30:7 5750
And Leah conceived a, and bare Gen 30:19 5750
this thing for me, I will a feed Gen 30:31 7725
And God appeared unto Jacob a Gen 35:9 5750
and bring me word a Gen 37:14 7725
to deliver him to his father a Gen 37:22 7725
And she conceived a, and bare a son Gen 38:4 5750
she yet a conceived, and bare a Gen 38:5 5750
And he knew her a no more Gen 38:26 3254
butler unto his butlership a Gen 40:21 7725
and returned to them a, and Gen 42:24 7725
and I will bring him to thee a Gen 42:37 7725
their father said unto them, Go a Gen 43:2 7725
a in the mouth of your sacks Gen 43:12 7725
carry it a in your hand Gen 43:12 7725
and arise, go a unto the man Gen 43:13 7725
we have brought it a in our hand Gen 43:21 7725
we brought a unto thee out of the Gen 44:8 7725
And our father said, Go a, and buy Gen 44:25 7725
will also surely bring thee up a Gen 46:4
bring you a unto the land of your Gen 48:21 7725
bury my father, and I will come a Gen 50:5 7725
Put thine hand into thy bosom a Ex 4:7 7725
he put his hand into his bosom a Ex 4:7 7725
it was turned a as his other Ex 4:7 7725
Aaron were brought a unto Pharaoh Ex 10:8 7725
I will see thy face a no more Ex 10:29 3254
shall see them a no more for ever Ex 14:13 3254
may come a upon the Egyptians Ex 14:26 7725
the LORD brought a the waters of Ex 15:19 7725
If he rise a, and walk abroad upon Ex 21:19
surely bring it back to him a Ex 23:4 7725
for us, until we come a unto you Ex 24:14 7725
he turned a into the camp Ex 33:11 7725
put the vail upon his face a Ex 34:35 7725
look on him a the seventh day Lev 13:6 8145
he shall be seen of the priest a Lev 13:7 8145
Or if the raw flesh turn a Lev 13:16 7725
shall come a the seventh day Lev 14:39 7725
And if the plague come a, and break Lev 14:43 7725
A, thou shalt say to the children Lev 20:2
man, so shall it be done to him a Lev 24:20
he is sold he may be redeemed a Lev 25:48
unto them he shall give a the Lev 25:51 7725
him a the price of his redemption Lev 25:52 7725
you your bread a by weight Lev 26:26 7725
children of Israel also wept a Num 11:4 7725
that let her be received in a Num 12:14
not till Miriam was brought in a Num 12:15 7725
Bring Aaron's rod a before the Num 17:10 7725
night, and I will bring you word a Num 22:8 7725
And Balak sent yet a princes Num 22:15 3254
and he smote her a Num 22:25 3254
thee, I will get me back a Num 22:34 7725
Go a unto Balak, and say thus Num 23:16 7725
he will yet a leave them in the Num 32:15 3254
turned a unto Pi-hahiroth, which Num 33:7 7725
that he should come a to dwell in Num 35:32 7725
bring us word a by what way we Deut 1:22 7725
unto us, and brought us word a Deut 1:25 7725
them, Get you into your tents a Deut 5:30 7725
it shall not be built a Deut 13:16 5750
foreigner thou mayest exact it a Deut 15:3
Let me not hear a the voice of Deut 18:16 3254
bring them a unto thy brother Deut 22:1 7725
and thou shalt restore it to him a Deut 22:2 7725
surely help him to lift them up a Deut 22:4
he shall come into the camp a Deut 23:11
may not take her a to be his wife Deut 24:4 7725
pledge a when the sun goeth down Deut 24:13 7725
thou shalt not go a to fetch it Deut 24:19 7725
shalt not go over the boughs a Deut 24:20 310
thee into Egypt a with ships Deut 28:68 7725
thee, Thou shalt see it no more a Deut 28:68 3254
for the LORD will a rejoice over Deut 30:9 7725
hate him, that they rise not a Deut 33:11
circumcise a the children of Josh 5:2 7725
city ascended, then they turned a Josh 8:21 7725
I brought him word a as it was in Josh 14:7 7725
and they shall come a to me Josh 18:4
come a to me, that I may here Josh 18:8 7725
came a to Joshua to the host at Josh 18:9
time to come, that we may say a Josh 22:28
of Israel, and brought them word a Josh 22:32 7725
evil a in the sight of the LORD Judg 3:12 3254
But he himself turned a from the Judg 3:19 7725
the children of Israel a did evil Judg 4:1 3254
A he said unto her, Stand in the Judg 4:20
I will tarry until thou come a Judg 6:18 7725
saying, When I come a in peace Judg 8:9 7725
the children of Israel turned a Judg 8:33 7725
And Gaal spake a and said, See Judg 9:37
evil a in the sight of the LORD Judg 10:6 3254
Therefore we turn a to thee now Judg 11:8 7725
If ye bring me home a to fight Judg 11:9 7725
restore those lands a peaceably Judg 11:13 7725
Jephthah sent messengers a unto Judg 11:14
evil a in the sight of the LORD Judg 13:1 3254
thou didst send come a unto us Judg 13:8 5750
the angel of God came a unto the Judg 13:9 5750
he had drunk, his spirit came a Judg 15:19 7725
to grow a after he was shaven Judg 16:22
unto her, and to bring her a Judg 19:3 7725
therefore he lodged there a Judg 19:7 7725
set their battle a in array in Judg 20:22 3254
Shall I go up a to battle against Judg 20:23 3254
of Israel a eighteen thousand men Judg 20:25 5750
Shall I yet a go out to battle Judg 20:28 3254
when the men of Israel turned a Judg 20:41
the men of Israel turned a upon Judg 20:48 7725
And Benjamin came a at that time Judg 21:14 7725
And Naomi said, Turn a, my Ruth 1:11 7725
Turn a, my daughters, go your way Ruth 1:12 7725
lifted up their voice, and wept a Ruth 1:14 5750
LORD hath brought me home a empty Ruth 1:21 7725
that is come a out of the country Ruth 4:3 7725
lie down a 1Sa 3:5 7725
And the LORD called yet a, Samuel 1Sa 3:6 3254
lie down a 1Sa 3:6 7725
called Samuel a the third time 1Sa 3:8 3254
And the LORD appeared a in Shiloh 1Sa 3:21 3254
shout, so that the earth rang a 1Sa 4:5
Dagon, and set him in his place a 1Sa 5:3 7725
let it go a to his own place, 1Sa 5:11 7725
brought a the ark of the LORD 1Sa 6:21 7725
And the servant answered Saul a 1Sa 9:8 3254
turn a with me, that I may 1Sa 15:25 7725
turn a with me, that I may 1Sa 15:30 7725
So Samuel turned a after Saul 1Sa 15:31 7725
A, Jesse made seven of his sons 1Sa 16:10
him a after the former manner 1Sa 17:30 7725
And there was war a 1Sa 19:8 3254
the messengers a to see David 1Sa 19:15
sent messengers a the third time 1Sa 19:21 3254
Jonathan caused David to swear a 1Sa 20:17 3254
David enquired of the LORD yet a 1Sa 23:4 3254
and come ye a to me with the 1Sa 23:23 7725
men turned their way, and went a 1Sa 25:12 7725
and he sought no more a for him 1Sa 27:4 3254
that he may go a to his place 1Sa 29:4 7725
eaten, his spirit came a to him 1Sa 30:12 7725
He said unto me a, Stand, I pray 2Sa 1:9
And Abner said a to Asahel 2Sa 2:22
could not answer Abner a word a 2Sa 3:11 5750
which brought him a from the well 2Sa 3:26 5750
And all the people wept a over him 2Sa 3:34 3254
And the Philistines came up yet a 2Sa 5:22 3254
A, David gathered together all 2Sa 6:1 5750
can I bring him back a 2Sa 12:23 5750
not fetch home a his banished 2Sa 14:13 7725
which cannot be gathered up a 2Sa 14:14
bring the young man Absalom a 2Sa 14:21 7725
when he sent a the second time, 2Sa 14:29 5750
bring me a indeed to Jerusalem 2Sa 15:8 7725
of the LORD, he will bring me a 2Sa 15:25 7725
the ark of God a to Jerusalem 2Sa 15:29 7725
And a, whom should I serve 2Sa 16:19 8145
the son of Zadok yet a to Joab 2Sa 18:22 3254
until the day he came a in peace 2Sa 19:24
a in peace unto his own house 2Sa 19:30 7725
servant, I pray thee, turn back a 2Sa 19:37 7725
the ground, and struck him not a 2Sa 20:10 8138
had yet war a with Israel 2Sa 21:15 5750
that there was a a battle with 2Sa 21:18 5750
there was a a battle in Gob with 2Sa 21:19 5750
turned not a until I had consumed 2Sa 22:38 7725
a the anger of the LORD was 2Sa 24:1 3254
so that the city rang a 1Kin 1:45
Benaiah brought the king word a 1Kin 2:30 7725
Jerusalem to Gath, and was come a 1Kin 2:41 7725
thee, and shall turn a to thee 1Kin 8:33 7725
bring them a unto the land which 1Kin 8:34 7725
for three days, then come a to me 1Kin 12:5 7725
Come to me a the third day 1Kin 12:12 7725
heard that Jeroboam was come a 1Kin 12:20 7725
to bring the kingdom a to 1Kin 12:21 7725
people turn a unto their lord 1Kin 12:27 7725
go a to Rehoboam king of Judah 1Kin 12:27 7725
he could not pull it in a to him 1Kin 13:4 7725
that my hand may be restored me a 1Kin 13:6 7725
king's hand was restored him a 1Kin 13:6 7725
nor turn a by the same way that 1Kin 13:9 7725
nor turn a to go by the way that 1Kin 13:17 7725
but made a of the lowest of the 1Kin 13:33 7725
this child's soul come into him a 1Kin 17:21 7725
soul of the child came into him a 1Kin 17:22 7725
hast turned their heart back a 1Kin 18:37 322
And he said, Go a seven times 1Kin 18:43 7725
eat and drink, and laid him down a 1Kin 19:6 7725
the LORD came a the second time 1Kin 19:7 7725
And he said unto him, Go back a 1Kin 19:20 7725
And the messengers came a, and said 1Kin 20:5 7725
departed, and brought him word a 1Kin 20:9 7725
turn a unto the king that sent 2Kin 1:6 7725
A also he sent unto him another 2Kin 1:11 7725
he sent a a captain of the third 2Kin 1:13 7725
And when they came a to him 2Kin 2:18 7725
run to the man of God, and come a 2Kin 4:22 7725
any salute thee, answer him not a 2Kin 4:29
Wherefore he went a to meet him 2Kin 4:31 7725
And Elisha came a to Gilgal 2Kin 4:38 7725
He said a, Give the people, that 2Kin 4:43
and thy flesh shall come a to thee 2Kin 5:10 7725
his flesh came a like unto the 2Kin 5:14 7725
when the man turned a from his 2Kin 5:26
and came a, and entered into 2Kin 7:8 7725
came to them, but he cometh not a 2Kin 9:18 7725
even unto them, and cometh not a 2Kin 9:20 7725
Wherefore they came a, and told 2Kin 9:36 7725
the son of Jehoahaz took a out of 2Kin 13:25 7725
sent messengers a unto Hezekiah 2Kin 19:9 7725
shall yet a take root downward 2Kin 19:30 3254
Turn a, and tell Hezekiah the 2Kin 20:5 7725
For he built up a the high places 2Kin 21:3 7725
king, and brought the king word a 2Kin 22:9 7725
And they brought the king word a 2Kin 22:20 7725
not a any more out of his land 2Kin 24:7 3254

let us bring *a* the ark of our God	1Chr 13:3	5437
the Philistines yet *a* spread	1Chr 14:13	3254
Therefore David enquired *a* of God	1Chr 14:14	5750
And there was war *a* with the	1Chr 20:5	5750
yet *a* there was war at Gath,	1Chr 20:6	5750
shall bring *a* to him that sent me	1Chr 21:12	7725
he put up his sword *a* into the	1Chr 21:27	7725
bring them *a* unto the land which	2Chr 6:25	7725
Come *a* unto me after three days	2Chr 10:5	7725
Come *a* to me on the third day	2Chr 10:12	7725
bring the kingdom *a* to Rehoboam	2Chr 11:1	7725
brought them *a* into the guard	2Chr 12:11	7725
strength *a* in the days of Abijah	2Chr 13:20	5750
A he said, Therefore hear the	2Chr 18:18	
they turned back *a* from pursuing	2Chr 18:32	7725
he went out *a* through the people	2Chr 19:4	7725
to go *a* to Jerusalem with joy	2Chr 20:27	7725
it, and carried it to his place *a*	2Chr 24:11	7725
to bring them *a* unto the LORD	2Chr 24:19	7725
him out of Ephraim, to go home *a*	2Chr 25:10	
and deliver the captives *a*	2Chr 28:11	
For *a* the Edomites had come and	2Chr 28:17	5750
turn *a* unto the LORD God of	2Chr 30:6	7725
For if ye turn *a* unto the LORD	2Chr 30:9	7725
they shall come *a* into this land	2Chr 30:9	7725
But Hezekiah rendered not *a*	2Chr 32:25	7725
For he built *a* the high places	2Chr 33:3	7725
brought him *a* to Jerusalem into	2Chr 33:13	7725
and brought the king word back *a*	2Chr 34:16	5750
So they brought the king word *a*	2Chr 34:28	7725
came *a* unto Jerusalem and Judah,	Ezr 2:1	7725
be builded, and the walls set up *a*	Ezr 4:13	
that, if this city be builded *a*	Ezr 4:16	
brought *a* unto the temple which	Ezr 6:5	1946
Israel, which were come *a* out of	Ezr 6:21	7725
Should we *a* break thy	Ezr 9:14	7725
came *a* to Jerusalem and to Judah,	Neh 7:6	7725
of them that were come *a* out of	Neh 8:17	7725
rest, they did evil *a* before thee	Neh 9:28	7725
bring them *a* unto thy law	Neh 9:29	7725
thither brought I *a* the vessels	Neh 13:9	7725
if ye do so *a*, I will lay hands	Neh 13:21	3138
A Esther spake unto Hatach, and	Est 4:10	
Mordecai came *a* to the king's	Est 6:12	7725
the king said *a* unto Esther on	Est 7:2	1571
spake yet *a* before the king	Est 8:3	3254
A there was a day when the sons	Job 2:1	
yea, return *a*, my righteousness	Job 6:29	5750
and wilt thou bring me into dust *a*	Job 10:9	7725
a thou shewest thyself marvellous	Job 10:16	7725
down, and it cannot be built *a*	Job 12:14	
nations, and straiteneth them *a*	Job 12:23	
cut down, that it will sprout *a*	Job 14:7	5750
If a man die, shall he live *a*	Job 14:14	
and he shall vomit them up *a*	Job 20:15	
After my words they spake not *a*	Job 29:22	3138
and man shall turn *a* unto dust	Job 34:15	7725
neither did I turn *a* till they	Ps 18:37	7725
wicked borroweth, and payeth not *a*	Ps 37:21	7999
O turn thyself to us *a*	Ps 60:1	7725
said, I will bring *a* from Bashan	Ps 68:22	7725
I will bring my people *a* from the	Ps 68:22	7725
sore troubles, shalt quicken me *a*	Ps 71:20	7725
shalt bring me up *a* from the	Ps 71:20	7725
passeth away, and cometh not *a*	Ps 78:39	7725
Turn us *a*, O God, and cause thy	Ps 80:3	7725
Turn us *a*, O God of hosts, and	Ps 80:7	7725
Turn us *a*, O LORD God of hosts,	Ps 80:19	7725
Wilt thou not revive us *a*	Ps 85:6	7725
but let them not turn *a* to folly	Ps 85:8	7725
turn not *a* to cover the earth	Ps 104:9	7725
they go down *a* to the depths	Ps 107:26	
A, they are minished and brought	Ps 107:39	
When the LORD turned *a* the	Ps 126:1	
Turn *a* our captivity, O LORD, as	Ps 126:4	7725
doubtless come *a* with rejoicing	Ps 126:6	
pits, that they rise not up *a*	Ps 140:10	
None that go unto her return *a*	Prov 2:19	7725
unto thy neighbour, Go, and come *a*	Prov 3:28	7725
he hath given will he pay him *a*	Prov 19:17	7999
him, yet thou must do it *a*	Prov 19:19	3254
much as bring it to his mouth *a*	Prov 19:24	7725
I will seek it yet *a*	Prov 23:35	5750
seven times, and riseth up *a*	Prov 24:16	
him to bring it *a* to his mouth	Prov 26:15	7725
the wind returneth *a* according to	Eccl 1:6	7725
come, thither they return *a*	Eccl 1:7	7725
the dust, and all turn to dust *a*	Eccl 3:20	7725
A, I considered all travail, and	Eccl 4:4	
A, if two lie together, then they	Eccl 4:11	1571
a, there be wicked men, to whom	Eccl 8:14	
the LORD spake *a* unto Ahaz	Is 7:10	3254
The LORD spake also unto me *a*	Is 8:5	3254
shall no more *a* stay upon him	Is 10:20	3254
the Lord shall set his hand *a* the	Is 11:11	3254
and it shall fall, and not rise *a*	Is 24:20	3254
Judah shall *a* take root downward	Is 37:31	
I will bring *a* the shadow of the	Is 38:8	7725
bring it *a* to mind, O ye	Is 46:8	7725
servant, to bring Jacob *a* to him	Is 49:5	7725
shall say *a* in thine ears, The	Is 49:20	5750
thou shalt no more drink it *a*	Is 51:22	5750
when the LORD shall bring *a* Zion	Is 52:8	7725
man's, shall he return unto her *a*	Jer 3:1	5750
yet return *a* to me, saith the	Jer 3:1	
on them, and will bring them *a*	Jer 12:15	7725
return, then will I bring thee *a*	Jer 15:19	7725
I will bring them *a* into their	Jer 16:15	7725
so he made it *a* another vessel,	Jer 18:4	7725
that cannot be made whole *a*	Jer 19:11	5750
will bring them *a* to their folds	Jer 23:3	7725
A the word of the LORD came unto	Jer 24:4	
I will bring them *a* to this land	Jer 24:6	7725
Turn ye *a* now every one from his	Jer 25:5	7725
shortly be brought *a* from Babylon	Jer 27:16	7725
two full years will I bring *a*	Jer 28:3	7725
I will bring *a* to this place	Jer 28:4	7725
to bring *a* the vessels of the	Jer 28:6	7725
I will bring you *a* into the place	Jer 29:14	7725
that I will bring *a* the captivity	Jer 30:3	7725
I will bring *a* the captivity of	Jer 30:18	7725
A I will build thee, and thou	Jer 31:4	5750
thou shalt *a* be adorned with thy	Jer 31:4	5750
they shall come *a* from the land	Jer 31:16	7725
shall come *a* to their own border	Jer 31:17	7725
turn *a*, O virgin of Israel	Jer 31:21	7725
turn *a* to these thy cities	Jer 31:21	7725
I shall bring *a* their captivity	Jer 31:23	7725
shall be possessed *a* in this land	Jer 32:15	5750
will bring them *a* unto this place	Jer 32:37	7725
A there shall be heard in this	Jer 33:10	5750
A in this place, which is	Jer 33:12	5750
shall the flocks pass *a* under the	Jer 33:13	5750
Take thee *a* another roll, and	Jer 36:28	7725
And the Chaldeans shall come *a*	Jer 37:8	7725
whom he had brought *a* from Gibeon	Jer 41:16	7725
let us go *a* to our own people, and	Jer 46:16	7725
Yet will I bring *a* the captivity	Jer 48:47	7725
afterward I will bring *a* the	Jer 49:6	7725
that I will bring *a* the captivity	Jer 49:39	7725
bring Israel *a* to his habitation	Jer 50:19	7725
our ways, and turn *a* to the LORD	Lam 3:40	7725
A, When a righteous man doth turn	Eze 3:20	7725
lie *a* on thy right side, and thou	Eze 4:6	8145
Then take of them *a*, and cast them	Eze 5:4	5750
the sounding *a* of the mountains	Eze 7:7	1906
but turn thee yet *a*, and thou	Eze 8:6	5750
also unto me, Turn thee yet *a*	Eze 8:13	5750
turn thee yet *a*, and thou shalt	Eze 8:15	5750
A the word of the LORD came unto	Eze 11:14	
A the word of the LORD came to me	Eze 12:26	
The word of the LORD came *a* to me	Eze 14:12	
A the word of the LORD came unto	Eze 16:1	
I shall bring *a* their captivity	Eze 16:53	7725
then will I bring *a* the captivity	Eze 16:53	
word of the LORD came unto me *a*	Eze 18:1	
A, when the wicked man turneth	Eze 18:27	
A the word of the LORD came unto	Eze 21:8	
word of the LORD came unto me *a*	Eze 21:18	
word of the LORD came *a* unto me	Eze 23:1	
A in the ninth year, in the tenth	Eze 24:1	
word of the LORD came *a* unto me	Eze 25:1	
yet shalt thou never be found *a*	Eze 26:21	5750
word of the LORD came *a* unto me	Eze 27:1	
word of the LORD came *a* unto me	Eze 28:1	
A the word of the LORD came unto	Eze 28:20	
I will bring *a* the captivity of	Eze 29:14	7725
word of the LORD came *a* unto me	Eze 30:1	
A the word of the LORD came unto	Eze 33:1	
A, when I say unto the wicked,	Eze 33:14	
give *a* that he had robbed, walk	Eze 33:15	7999
neither have ye brought *a* that	Eze 34:4	7725
bring *a* that which was driven	Eze 34:16	7725
A he said unto me, Prophesy upon	Eze 37:4	
word of the LORD came *a* unto me	Eze 37:15	
Now will I bring *a* the captivity	Eze 39:25	7725
brought them *a* from the people	Eze 39:27	7725
Afterward he brought me *a* unto	Eze 47:1	7725
A he measured a thousand, and	Eze 47:4	
A he measured a thousand, and	Eze 47:4	
They answered *a* and said, Let the	Dan 2:7	8579
the street shall be built *a*	Dan 9:25	7725
Then there came *a* and touched me	Dan 10:18	3284
And she conceived *a*, and bare a	Hos 1:6	5750
time, when I shall bring *a* the	Joel 3:1	7725
I will not *a* pass by them any	Amos 7:8	3254
But prophesy not *a* any more at	Amos 7:13	3254
I will not *a* pass by them any	Amos 8:2	3254
shall fall, and never rise up *a*	Amos 8:14	5750
I will bring *a* the captivity of	Amos 9:14	7725
yet I will look *a* toward thy holy	Jonah 2:4	3254
He will turn *a*, he will have	Mic 7:19	7725
At that time will I bring you *a*	Zeph 3:20	
a the word of the LORD came unto	Hag 2:20	8145
I lifted up mine eyes *a*, and	Zec 2:1	
land, and shall choose Jerusalem *a*	Zec 2:12	5750
angel that talked with me came *a*	Zec 4:1	7725
And I answered *a*, and said unto him	Zec 4:12	8145
A the word of the LORD of hosts	Zec 8:1	
So *a* have I thought in these days	Zec 8:15	7725
I will bring them *a* to place them	Zec 10:6	7725
with their children, and turn *a*	Zec 10:9	7725
I will bring them *a* also out of	Zec 10:10	7725
be inhabited *a* in her own place	Zec 12:6	5750
And this have ye done *a*, covering	Mal 2:13	8145
have found him, bring me word *a*	Mt 2:8	518
said unto him, It is written *a*	Mt 4:7	3825
A, the devil taketh him up into	Mt 4:8	3825
A, ye have heard that it hath	Mt 5:33	3825
it shall be measured to you *a*	Mt 7:2	488
them under their feet, and turn *a*	Mt 7:6	4762
shew John *a* those things which ye	Mt 11:4	518
A, the kingdom of heaven is like	Mt 13:44	3825
A, the kingdom of heaven is like	Mt 13:45	3825
A, the kingdom of heaven is like	Mt 13:47	3825
be raised *a* the third day	Mt 16:21	1453
of man be risen *a* from the dead	Mt 17:9	450
third day he shall be raised *a*	Mt 17:23	1453
A I say unto you, That if two of	Mt 18:19	3825
a I say unto you, It is easier	Mt 19:24	3825
A he went out about the sixth and	Mt 20:5	3825
and the third day he shall rise *a*	Mt 20:19	450
A, he sent other servants more	Mt 21:36	3825
and spake unto them *a* by parables	Mt 22:1	3825
A, he sent forth other servants,	Mt 22:4	3825
But after I am risen *a*, I will go	Mt 26:32	1453
He went away *a* the second time,	Mt 26:42	3825
And he came and found them asleep *a*	Mt 26:43	3825
And he left them, and went away *a*	Mt 26:44	3825
Put up *a* thy sword into his place	Mt 26:52	654
a he denied with an oath, I do	Mt 26:72	3825
brought *a* the thirty pieces of	Mt 27:3	654
he had cried *a* with a loud voice	Mt 27:50	3825
After three days I will rise *a*	Mt 27:63	1453
a he entered into Capernaum after	Mk 2:1	3825
he went forth *a* by the sea side	Mk 2:13	3825
he entered *a* into the synagogue	Mk 3:1	3825
the multitude cometh together *a*	Mk 3:20	3825
he began *a* to teach by the sea	Mk 4:1	3825
when Jesus was passed over *a* by	Mk 5:21	3825
And *a*, departing from the coasts	Mk 7:31	3825
entering into the ship *a* departed	Mk 8:13	3825
he put his hands *a* upon his eyes	Mk 8:25	3825
and after three days rise *a*	Mk 8:31	450
and the people resort unto him *a*	Mk 10:1	3825
as he was wont, he taught them *a*	Mk 10:1	3825
asked him *a* of the same matter	Mk 10:10	3825
But Jesus answereth *a*, and saith	Mk 10:24	3825
he took *a* the twelve, and began to	Mk 10:32	3825
and the third day he shall rise *a*	Mk 10:34	450
And they come *a* to Jerusalem	Mk 11:27	3825
a he sent unto them another	Mk 12:4	3825
And *a* he sent another	Mk 12:5	3825
back *a* for to take up his garment	Mk 13:16	1994
a he went away, and prayed, and	Mk 14:39	3825
returned, he found them asleep *a*	Mk 14:40	3825
A the high priest asked him, and	Mk 14:61	3825
And a maid saw him *a*, and began to	Mk 14:69	3825
And he denied it *a*	Mk 14:70	3825
that stood by said *a* to Peter	Mk 14:70	3825
And Pilate asked him *a*, saying,	Mk 15:4	3825
said *a* unto them, What will ye	Mk 15:12	3825
And they cried out *a*, Crucify him	Mk 15:13	3825
rising *a* of many in Israel	Lk 2:34	386
they turned back *a* to Jerusalem	Lk 2:45	5290
he gave it *a* to the minister, and	Lk 4:20	591
away thy goods ask them not *a*	Lk 6:30	523
to sinners, to receive as much *a*	Lk 6:34	618
and lend, hoping for nothing *a*	Lk 6:35	560
it shall be measured to you *a*	Lk 6:38	488
into the ship, and returned back *a*	Lk 8:37	5290
And her spirit came *a*, and she	Lk 8:55	1994
of the old prophets was risen *a*	Lk 9:8	450
of the old prophets is risen *a*	Lk 9:19	450
it teareth him that he foameth *a*	Lk 9:39	3326
and delivered him *a* to his father	Lk 9:42	591
if not, it shall turn to you *a*	Lk 10:6	344
the seventy returned *a* with joy	Lk 10:17	5290
thou spendest more, when I come *a*	Lk 10:35	1880
a he said, Whereunto shall I	Lk 13:20	3825
not answer him *a* to these things	Lk 14:6	470
lest they also bid thee *a*	Lk 14:12	479
my son was dead, and is alive *a*	Lk 15:24	326
brother was dead, and is alive *a*	Lk 15:32	326
times in a day turn *a* to thee	Lk 17:4	1994
and the third day he shall rise *a*	Lk 18:33	450
a he sent another servant	Lk 20:11	4388
And *a* he sent a third	Lk 20:12	4388
robe, and sent him *a* to Pilate	Lk 23:11	375
to release Jesus, spake *a* to them	Lk 23:20	3825
and the third day rise *a*	Lk 24:7	450
A the next day after John stood,	Jn 1:35	3825
unto thee, Except a man be born *a*	Jn 3:3	509
said unto thee, Ye must be born *a*	Jn 3:7	509
and departed *a* into Galilee	Jn 4:3	3825
of this water shall thirst *a*	Jn 4:13	3825
So Jesus came *a* into Cana of	Jn 4:46	3825
This is *a* the second miracle that	Jn 4:54	3825
he departed *a* into a mountain	Jn 6:15	3825
raise it up *a* at the last day	Jn 6:39	450
morning he came *a* into the temple	Jn 8:2	3825
a he stooped down, and wrote on	Jn 8:8	3825
Then spake Jesus *a* unto them	Jn 8:12	3825
Then said Jesus *a* unto them	Jn 8:21	3825
Then *a* the Pharisees also asked	Jn 9:15	3825
They say unto the blind man *a*	Jn 9:17	3825
Then *a* called they the man that	Jn 9:24	1208
Then said they to him *a*, What did	Jn 9:26	3825
wherefore would ye hear it *a*	Jn 9:27	3825
Then said Jesus unto them *a*	Jn 10:7	3825
my life, that I might take it *a*	Jn 10:17	3825
and I have power to take it *a*	Jn 10:18	3825
a among the Jews for these	Jn 10:19	3825
took up stones *a* to stone him	Jn 10:31	3825
they sought *a* to take him	Jn 10:39	3825
went away *a* beyond Jordan into	Jn 10:40	3825
Let us go into Judaea *a*	Jn 11:7	3825
and goest thou thither *a*	Jn 11:8	3825
her, Thy brother shall rise *a*	Jn 11:23	450
I know that he shall rise *a* in	Jn 11:24	450
Jesus therefore *a* groaning in	Jn 11:38	3825
a Andrew and Philip tell Jesus	Jn 12:22	3825
it, and will glorify it *a*	Jn 12:28	3825
because that Esaias said *a*	Jn 12:39	3825
his garments, and was set down *a*	Jn 13:12	3825
a place for you, I will come *a*	Jn 14:3	3825
I go away, and come *a* unto you	Jn 14:28	
and *a*, a little while, and ye shall	Jn 16:16	3825
and *a*, a little while, and ye shall	Jn 16:17	3825
and *a*, a little while, and ye shall	Jn 16:19	3825
but I will see you *a*, and your	Jn 16:22	3825
a, I leave the world, and go to	Jn 16:28	3825
Then asked he them *a*, Whom seek	Jn 18:7	3825
Peter then denied *a*	Jn 18:27	3825
entered into the judgment hall *a*	Jn 18:33	3825
he went out *a* unto the Jews, and	Jn 18:38	3825
Then cried they all *a*, saying,	Jn 18:40	3825
Pilate therefore went forth *a*	Jn 19:4	3825
went *a* into the judgment hall, and	Jn 19:9	3825
a another scripture saith, They	Jn 19:37	3825
that he must rise *a* from the dead	Jn 20:9	450
went away *a* unto their own home	Jn 20:10	3825

Then said Jesus to them *a*	Jn 20:21	*3825*
after eight days *a* his disciples	Jn 20:26	*3825*
things Jesus shewed himself *a* to	Jn 21:1	*3825*
He saith to him *a* the second time	Jn 21:16	*3825*
restore *a* the kingdom to Israel	Acts 1:6	*600*
and would have set them at one *a*	Acts 7:26	*1515*
hearts turned back *a* into Egypt	Acts 7:39	*4762*
spake unto him *a* the second time	Acts 10:15	*3825*
was received up *a* into heaven	Acts 10:16	*3825*
voice answered me *a* from heaven	Acts 11:9	*1208*
all were drawn up *a* into heaven	Acts 11:10	*3825*
in that he hath raised up Jesus *a*	Acts 13:33	*450*
But he, whom God raised *a*	Acts 13:37	*1458*
many, they returned *a* to Lystra	Acts 14:21	*5290*
will build *a* the tabernacle of	Acts 15:16	*456*
I will build *a* the ruins thereof,	Acts 15:16	*456*
said unto Barnabas, Let us go *a*	Acts 15:36	*1994*
and risen *a* from the dead	Acts 17:3	*450*
will hear thee *a* of this matter	Acts 17:32	*3825*
but I will return *a* unto you	Acts 18:21	*3825*
When he therefore was come up *a*	Acts 20:11	
and they returned home *a*	Acts 21:6	*5290*
when I was come *a* to Jerusalem	Acts 22:17	*5290*
a little further, they sounded *a*	Acts 27:28	*3825*
offences, and was raised *a* for our	Rom 4:25	*1453*
the spirit of bondage *a* to fear	Rom 8:15	*3825*
died, yea rather, that is risen *a*	Rom 8:34	*1453*
bring up Christ *a* from the dead	Rom 10:7	*321*
God is able to graff them in *a*	Rom 11:23	*3825*
shall be recompensed unto him *a*	Rom 11:35	*467*
a he saith, Rejoice, ye Gentiles,	Rom 15:10	*3825*
And *a*, Praise the Lord, all ye	Rom 15:11	*3825*
And *a*, Esaias saith, There shall	Rom 15:12	*3825*
And *a*, The Lord knoweth the	1Cor 3:20	*3825*
and come together *a*, that Satan	1Cor 7:5	*3825*
nor *a* the head to the feet, I	1Cor 12:21	*3825*
that he rose *a* the third day	1Cor 15:4	*1453*
to come *a* out of Macedonia unto	2Cor 1:16	*3825*
not come *a* to you in heaviness	2Cor 2:1	*3825*
Do we begin *a* to commend	2Cor 3:1	*3825*
commend not ourselves *a* unto you	2Cor 5:12	*3825*
which died for them, and rose *a*	2Cor 5:15	*1453*
let him of himself think this *a*	2Cor 10:7	*3825*
I say *a*, Let no man think me a	2Cor 11:16	*3825*
A, think ye that we excuse	2Cor 12:19	*3825*
And lest, when I come *a*, my God	2Cor 12:21	*3825*
to all other, that, if I come *a*	2Cor 13:2	*3825*
As we said before, so say I now *a*	Gal 1:9	*3825*
and returned *a* unto Damascus	Gal 1:17	*3825*
up *a* to Jerusalem with Barnabas	Gal 2:1	*3825*
For if I build *a* the things which	Gal 2:18	*3825*
of God, how turn ye *a* to the weak	Gal 4:9	*3825*
ye desire *a* to be in bondage	Gal 4:9	
of whom I travail in birth *a*	Gal 4:19	*3825*
be not entangled *a* with the yoke	Gal 5:1	*3825*
For I testify *a* to every man that	Gal 5:3	*3825*
for me by my coming to you *a*	Phil 1:26	*3825*
that, when ye see him *a*, ye may	Phil 2:28	*3825*
and *a* I say, Rejoice	Phil 4:4	*3825*
your care of me hath flourished *a*	Phil 4:10	*330*
sent once and *a* unto my necessity	Phil 4:16	*1364*
unto you, even I Paul, once and *a*	1Th 2:18	*1364*
can we render to God *a* for you	1Th 3:9	*467*
believe that Jesus died and rose *a*	1Th 4:14	*450*
not answering *a*	Titus 2:9	*483*
Whom I have sent *a*	Philem 12	*375*
And *a*, I will be to him a Father,	Heb 1:5	*3825*
And *a*, when he bringeth in the	Heb 1:6	*3825*
And *a*, I will put my trust in him	Heb 2:13	*3825*
And *a*, Behold I and the children	Heb 2:13	*3825*
And in this place *a*, If they shall	Heb 4:5	*3825*
A, he limiteth a certain day,	Heb 4:7	*3825*
a which be the first principles	Heb 5:12	*3825*
not laying *a* the foundation of	Heb 6:1	*3825*
to renew them *a* unto repentance	Heb 6:6	*3825*
there is a remembrance *a* made of	Heb 10:3	*364*
And *a*, The Lord shall judge his	Heb 10:30	*3825*
their dead raised to life *a*	Heb 11:35	*386*
that brought *a* from the dead our	Heb 13:20	*321*
And he prayed *a*, and the heaven	Jas 5:18	*3825*
us *a* unto a lively hope by the	1Pet 1:3	*313*
Being born *a*, not of corruptible	1Pet 1:23	*313*
he was reviled, reviled not *a*	1Pet 2:23	*486*
they are *a* entangled therein, and	2Pet 2:20	*3825*
dog is turned to his own vomit *a*	2Pet 2:22	*1994*
A, a new commandment I write unto	1Jn 2:8	*3825*
heard from heaven spake unto me *a*	Rev 10:8	*3825*
Thou must prophesy *a* before many	Rev 10:11	*3825*
And *a* they said, Alleluia	Rev 19:3	*1208*
a until the thousand years were	Rev 20:5	*326*

AGAINST

Cain rose up *a* Abel his brother	Gen 4:8	413
And he divided himself *a* them	Gen 14:15	5921
and laid each piece one *a* another	Gen 15:10	7125
his hand will be *a* every man	Gen 16:12	
and every man's hand *a* him	Gen 16:12	
withheld thee from sinning *a* me	Gen 20:6	
sat her down over *a* him a good	Gen 21:16	5048
And she sat over *a* him, and lift up	Gen 21:16	5048
anger was kindled *a* Rachel	Gen 30:2	
saw that he prevailed not *a* him	Gen 32:25	
gather themselves together *a* me	Gen 34:30	5921
they conspired *a* him to slay him	Gen 37:18	834
great wickedness, and sin *a* God	Gen 39:9	
Pharaoh was wroth *a* two of his	Gen 40:2	5921
a the chief of the butlers, and	Gen 40:2	5921
a the chief of the bakers	Gen 40:2	5921
land *a* the seven years of famine	Gen 41:36	
saying, Do not sin *a* the child	Gen 42:22	
all these things are *a* me	Gen 42:36	5921
that he may seek occasion *a* us	Gen 43:18	5921
the present *a* Joseph came at noon	Gen 43:25	5704
thine anger burn *a* thy servant	Gen 44:18	
as for you, ye thought evil *a* me	Gen 50:20	5921
unto our enemies, and fight *a* us	Ex 1:10	
of the LORD was kindled *a* Moses	Ex 4:14	
by the river's brink *a* he come	Ex 7:15	7125
which he had brought *a* Pharaoh	Ex 8:12	
exaltest thou thyself *a* my people	Ex 9:17	5921
a the LORD your God, and *a* you	Ex 10:16	
But *a* any of the children of	Ex 11:7	
move his tongue, *a* man or beast	Ex 11:7	
a all the gods of Egypt I will	Ex 12:12	
and the sea, over *a* Baal-zephon	Ex 14:2	6440
servants was turned *a* the people	Ex 14:5	413
fighteth for them *a* the Egyptians	Ex 14:25	
and the Egyptians fled *a* it	Ex 14:27	7125
them that rose up *a* thee	Ex 15:7	6965
And the people murmured *a* Moses	Ex 15:24	5921
of Israel murmured *a* Moses	Ex 16:2	5921
your murmurings *a* the LORD	Ex 16:7	5921
what are we, that ye murmur *a* us	Ex 16:7	5921
murmurings which ye murmur *a* him	Ex 16:8	5921
not *a* us, but *a* the LORD	Ex 16:8	5921
and the people murmured *a* Moses	Ex 17:3	5921
And be ready *a* the third day	Ex 19:11	
people, Be ready *a* the third day	Ex 19:15	
false witness *a* thy neighbour	Ex 20:16	
of the field multiply *a* thee	Ex 23:29	5921
lest they make thee sin *a* me	Ex 23:33	
Over *a* the border shall the rings	Ex 25:27	5980
they may give light over *a* it	Ex 25:37	
board, set in order one *a* another	Ex 26:17	413
the candlestick over *a* the table	Ex 26:35	5227
over *a* the other coupling thereof	Ex 28:27	5980
that my wrath may wax hot *a* them	Ex 32:10	
thy wrath wax hot *a* thy people	Ex 32:11	
repent of this evil *a* thy people	Ex 32:12	
Moses, Whosoever hath sinned *a* me	Ex 32:33	
Over *a* the border were the rings,	Ex 37:14	5980
over *a* the other coupling thereof	Ex 39:20	5980
over *a* the table, on the side of	Ex 40:24	5227
shall sin through ignorance *a* any	Lev 4:2	
done, and shall do *a* any of them	Lev 4:2	
they have done somewhat *a* any of	Lev 4:13	
sin, which they have sinned *a* it	Lev 4:14	5921
a any of the commandments of the	Lev 4:22	
while he doeth somewhat *a* any of	Lev 4:27	
certainly trespassed *a* the LORD	Lev 5:19	
and commit a trespass *a* the LORD	Lev 6:2	
I will even set my face *a* that	Lev 17:10	
neither shalt thou stand *a* the	Lev 19:16	5921
nor bear any grudge *a* the	Lev 19:18	
And I will set my face *a* that man	Lev 20:3	
I will set my face *a* that man	Lev 20:5	
a his family, and will cut him off	Lev 20:5	
will even set my face *a* that soul	Lev 20:6	
And I will set my face *a* you	Lev 26:17	
which they trespassed *a* me	Lev 26:40	
to do a trespass *a* the LORD	Num 5:6	
give it unto him *a* whom he hath	Num 5:7	
aside, and commit a trespass *a* him	Num 5:12	
and there be no witness *a* her	Num 5:13	
have done trespass *a* her husband	Num 5:27	
give light over *a* the candlestick	Num 8:2	
thereof over *a* the candlestick	Num 8:3	
if ye go to war in your land *a*	Num 10:9	5921
set up the tabernacle *a* they came	Num 10:21	5704
Sanctify yourselves *a* to morrow	Num 11:18	
the LORD was kindled *a* the people	Num 11:33	
Aaron spake *a* Moses because of	Num 12:1	
to speak *a* my servant Moses	Num 12:8	
of the LORD was kindled *a* them	Num 12:9	
be not able to go up *a* the people	Num 13:31	431
murmured *a* Moses and *a* Aaron	Num 14:2	5921
Only rebel not ye *a* the LORD	Num 14:9	
congregation, which murmur *a* me	Num 14:27	5921
of Israel, which they murmur *a* me	Num 14:27	5921
upward, which have murmured *a* me	Num 14:29	5921
that are gathered together *a* me	Num 14:35	5921
the congregation to murmur *a* him	Num 14:36	5921
themselves together *a* Moses	Num 16:3	5921
a Aaron, and said unto them, Ye	Num 16:3	5921
are gathered together *a* the LORD	Num 16:11	5921
is Aaron, that ye murmur *a* him	Num 16:11	5921
a them unto the door of the	Num 16:19	5921
these sinners *a* their own souls	Num 16:38	
of Israel murmured *a* Moses	Num 16:41	5921
a Aaron, saying, Ye have killed	Num 16:41	5921
congregation was gathered *a* Moses	Num 16:42	5921
a Aaron, that they looked toward	Num 16:42	5921
Israel, whereby they murmur *a* you	Num 17:5	5921
be kept for a token *a* the rebels	Num 17:10	
together *a* Moses and *a* Aaron	Num 20:2	5921
lest I come out *a* thee with the	Num 20:18	7125
Edom came out *a* him with much	Num 20:20	7125
because ye rebelled *a* my word at	Num 20:24	4775
then he fought *a* Israel, and took	Num 21:1	
And the people spake *a* God	Num 21:5	
a Moses, Wherefore have ye	Num 21:5	
a the LORD, and *a* thee	Num 21:7	
went out *a* Israel into the	Num 21:23	7125
came to Jahaz, and fought *a* Israel	Num 21:23	
who had fought *a* the former king	Num 21:26	
king of Bashan went out *a* them	Num 21:33	7125
earth, and they abide over *a* me	Num 22:5	4136
in the way for an adversary *a* him	Num 22:22	
crushed Balaam's foot *a* the wall	Num 22:25	413
thou stoodest in the way *a* me	Num 22:34	7125
there is no enchantment *a* Jacob	Num 23:23	
is there any divination *a* Israel	Num 23:23	
anger was kindled *a* Balaam	Num 24:10	413
of the LORD was kindled *a* Israel	Num 25:3	
them up before the LORD *a* the sun	Num 25:4	5048
congregation, who strove *a* Moses	Num 26:9	5921
a Aaron in the company of Korah,	Num 26:9	5921
when they strove *a* the LORD	Num 26:9	5921
a the LORD in the company of	Num 27:3	5921
For ye rebelled *a* my commandment	Num 27:14	
their souls, shall stand *a* her	Num 30:9	5921
let them go *a* the Midianites, and	Num 31:3	5921
they warred *a* the Midianites, as	Num 31:7	5921
to commit trespass *a* the LORD in	Num 31:16	
LORD's anger was kindled *a* Israel	Num 32:13	
behold, ye have sinned *a* the LORD	Num 32:23	
one witness shall not testify *a*	Num 35:30	
in the plain over *a* the Red sea	Deut 1:1	4136
but rebelled *a* the commandment of	Deut 1:26	
me, We have sinned *a* the LORD	Deut 1:41	
but rebelled *a* the commandment of	Deut 1:43	
in that mountain, came out *a* you	Deut 1:44	7125
the hand of the LORD was *a* them	Deut 2:15	
nigh over *a* the children of Ammon	Deut 2:19	4136
Then Sihon came out *a* us, he and	Deut 2:32	7125
the king of Bashan came out *a* us	Deut 3:1	7125
in the valley over *a* Beth-peor	Deut 3:29	4136
earth to witness *a* you this day	Deut 4:26	
in the valley over *a* Beth-peor	Deut 4:46	4136
false witness *a* thy neighbour	Deut 5:20	
LORD thy God be kindled *a* thee	Deut 6:15	
of the LORD be kindled *a* you	Deut 7:4	
I testify *a* you this day that ye	Deut 8:19	
have been rebellious *a* the LORD	Deut 9:7	5973
ye had sinned *a* the LORD your God	Deut 9:16	
was wroth *a* you to destroy you	Deut 9:19	5921
then ye rebelled *a* the	Deut 9:23	
Ye have been rebellious *a* the	Deut 9:24	5973
the LORD's wrath be kindled *a* you	Deut 11:17	
in the champaign over *a* Gilgal	Deut 11:30	4136
eye be evil *a* thy poor brother	Deut 15:9	
and he cry unto the LORD *a* thee	Deut 15:9	5921
in wait for him, and rise up *a* him	Deut 19:11	5921
rise up *a* a man for any iniquity	Deut 19:15	
If a false witness rise up *a* any	Deut 19:16	
testify *a* him that which is wrong	Deut 19:16	
testified falsely *a* his brother	Deut 19:18	
out to battle *a* thine enemies	Deut 20:1	5921
day unto battle *a* your enemies	Deut 20:3	5921
to fight for you *a* your enemies	Deut 20:4	5973
nigh unto a city to fight *a* it	Deut 20:10	5921
thee, but will make war *a* thee	Deut 20:12	5973
so should ye sin *a* the LORD your	Deut 20:18	
in making war *a* it to take it	Deut 20:19	5921
thereof by forcing an ax *a* them	Deut 20:19	5921
thou shalt build bulwarks *a* the	Deut 20:20	5921
forth to war *a* thine enemies	Deut 21:10	5921
And give occasions of speech *a* her	Deut 22:14	
given occasions of speech *a* her	Deut 22:17	
when a man riseth *a* his neighbour	Deut 22:26	5921
because they hired *a* thee Balaam	Deut 23:4	5921
host goeth forth *a* thine enemies	Deut 23:9	5921
lest he cry *a* thee unto the LORD,	Deut 24:15	5921
thine enemies that rise up *a* thee	Deut 28:7	5921
shall come out *a* thee one way	Deut 28:7	413
thou shalt go out one way *a* them	Deut 28:25	413
which the LORD shall send *a* thee	Deut 28:48	
bring a nation *a* thee from far	Deut 28:49	5921
came out *a* us unto battle, and we	Deut 29:7	7125
jealousy shall smoke *a* that man	Deut 29:20	
the LORD was kindled *a* this land	Deut 29:27	
and earth to record this day *a* you	Deut 30:19	
be kindled *a* them in that day	Deut 31:17	
for me *a* the children of Israel	Deut 31:19	
shall testify *a* them as a witness	Deut 31:21	6440
may be there for a witness *a* thee	Deut 31:26	
have been rebellious *a* the LORD	Deut 31:27	5973
heaven and earth to record *a* them	Deut 31:28	
of Moab, that is over *a* Jericho	Deut 32:49	6440
Because ye trespassed *a* me among	Deut 32:51	
the loins of them that rise *a* him	Deut 33:11	
of Pisgah, that is over *a* Jericho	Deut 34:1	6440
land of Moab, over *a* Beth-peor	Deut 34:6	4136
that doth rebel *a* thy commandment	Josh 1:18	
passed over right *a* Jericho	Josh 3:16	5048
there stood a man over *a* him with	Josh 5:13	5048
kindled *a* the children of Israel	Josh 7:1	
Sanctify yourselves *a* to morrow	Josh 7:13	
Indeed I have sinned *a* the LORD	Josh 7:20	
the people of war, to go up *a* Ai	Josh 8:3	
ye shall lie in wait *a* the city	Josh 8:4	
to pass, when they come out *a* us	Josh 8:5	7125
city went out *a* Israel to battle	Josh 8:14	7125
in ambush *a* him behind the city	Josh 8:14	
issued out of the city *a* them	Josh 8:22	7125
half of them over *a* mount Gerizim	Josh 8:33	4136
and half of them over *a* mount Ebal	Josh 8:33	4136
of the great sea over *a* Lebanon	Josh 9:1	4136
murmured *a* the princes	Josh 9:18	5921
before Gibeon, and made war *a* it	Josh 10:5	5921
are gathered together *a* us	Josh 10:6	413
none moved his tongue *a* any of	Josh 10:21	
all your enemies *a* whom ye fight	Josh 10:25	
unto Libnah, and fought *a* Libnah	Josh 10:29	5973
and encamped *a* it, and fought *a* it	Josh 10:31	5921
encamped *a* it, and fought *a* it	Josh 10:34	5921
a it, and fought *a* it	Josh 10:34	
and they fought *a* it	Josh 10:36	5921
and fought *a* it	Josh 10:38	5921
of Merom, to fight *a* Israel	Josh 11:5	5973
a them by the waters of Merom	Josh 11:7	5921
should come *a* Israel in battle	Josh 11:20	7125
which is over *a* the going up of	Josh 18:17	5227
the side over *a* Arabah northward	Josh 18:18	4136
of Dan went up to fight *a* Leshem	Josh 19:47	5973
altar over *a* the land of Canaan	Josh 22:11	4136
at Shiloh, to go up to war *a* them	Josh 22:12	5921
committed *a* the God of Israel	Josh 22:16	
might rebel this day *a* the LORD	Josh 22:16	
seeing ye rebel to day *a* the LORD	Josh 22:18	
a the LORD, nor rebel *a* us	Josh 22:19	
or if in transgression *a* the LORD	Josh 22:22	

that we should rebel *a* the LORD ... Josh 22:29
this trespass *a* the LORD ... Josh 22:31
intend to go up *a* them in battle ... Josh 22:33 5921
of the LORD be kindled *a* you ... Josh 23:16
of Moab, arose and warred *a* Israel ... Josh 24:9
the men of Jericho fought *a* you ... Josh 24:11
Ye are witnesses *a* yourselves ... Josh 24:22
Who shall go up for us *a* ... Judg 1:1
Canaanites first, to fight *a* them ... Judg 1:1
we may fight *a* the Canaanites ... Judg 1:3
and they fought *a* him, and they ... Judg 1:5
of Judah had fought *a* Jerusalem ... Judg 1:8
down to fight *a* the Canaanites ... Judg 1:9
Judah went *a* the Canaanites that ... Judg 1:10 413
from thence he went *a* the ... Judg 1:11 413
they also went up *a* Beth-el ... Judg 1:22
of the LORD was hot *a* Israel ... Judg 2:14
of the LORD was *a* them for evil ... Judg 2:15
of the LORD was hot *a* Israel ... Judg 2:20
of the LORD was hot *a* Israel ... Judg 3:8
prevailed *a* Chushan-rishathaim ... Judg 3:10 5921
Eglon the king of Moab *a* Israel ... Judg 3:12 5921
prevailed *a* Jabin the king of ... Judg 4:24 5921
was there a root of them *a* Amalek ... Judg 5:14
in their courses fought *a* Sisera ... Judg 5:20 5973
the help of the LORD *a* the mighty ... Judg 5:23
hand of Midian prevailed *a* Israel ... Judg 6:2 5921
east, even they came up *a* them ... Judg 6:3 5921
And they encamped *a* them, and ... Judg 6:4 5921
said unto all that stood *a* him ... Judg 6:31 5921
saying, Let Baal plead *a* him ... Judg 6:32
Let not thine anger be hot *a* me ... Judg 6:39
lest Israel vaunt themselves *a* me ... Judg 7:2 5921
every man's sword *a* his fellow ... Judg 7:22
Come down *a* the Midianites, and ... Judg 7:24 7125
ye are risen up *a* my father's ... Judg 9:18 5921
they fortify the city *a* thee ... Judg 9:31 5921
that is with him come out *a* thee ... Judg 9:33 413
they laid wait *a* Shechem in four ... Judg 9:34 5921
and he rose up *a* them, and smote ... Judg 9:43 5921
Abimelech fought *a* the city all ... Judg 9:45
to Thebez, and encamped *a* Thebez ... Judg 9:50 413
unto the tower, and fought *a* it ... Judg 9:52
of the LORD was hot *a* Israel ... Judg 10:7
over Jordan to fight also *a* Judah ... Judg 10:9
a Benjamin, and *a* the house ... Judg 10:9
saying, We have sinned *a* thee ... Judg 10:10
to fight *a* the children of Ammon ... Judg 10:18
of Ammon made war *a* Israel ... Judg 11:4 5973
of Ammon made war *a* Israel ... Judg 11:5 5973
fight *a* the children of Ammon, and ... Judg 11:8
to fight *a* the children of Ammon ... Judg 11:9
that thou art come *a* me to fight ... Judg 11:12 413
in Jahaz, and fought *a* Israel ... Judg 11:20 5973
did he ever strive *a* Israel ... Judg 11:25 5973
or did he ever fight *a* them ... Judg 11:25 5973
I have not sinned *a* thee, but ... Judg 11:27
thou doest me wrong to war *a* me ... Judg 11:27
children of Ammon to fight *a* them ... Judg 11:32
to fight *a* the children of Ammon ... Judg 12:1
passed over *a* the children of ... Judg 12:3 413
unto me this day, to fight *a* me ... Judg 12:3
an occasion *a* the Philistines ... Judg 14:4
behold, a young lion roared *a* him ... Judg 14:5 7125
said, Why are ye come up *a* us ... Judg 15:10 5921
the Philistines shouted *a* him ... Judg 15:14 7125
what means we may prevail *a* him ... Judg 16:5
Arise, that we may go up *a* them ... Judg 18:9 5921
concubine played the whore *a* him ... Judg 19:2 5921
and departed, and came over *a* Jebus ... Judg 19:10 5227
And the men of Gibeah rose *a* me ... Judg 20:5 5921
we will go up by lot *a* it ... Judg 20:9 5921
Israel were gathered *a* the city ... Judg 20:11 413
to go out to battle *a* the ... Judg 20:14 5973
battle *a* the children of Benjamin ... Judg 20:18 5973
the morning, and encamped *a* Gibeah ... Judg 20:19 5921
went out to battle *a* Benjamin ... Judg 20:20 5973
array to fight *a* them at Gibeah ... Judg 20:20
a the children of Benjamin my ... Judg 20:23 5973
And the LORD said, Go up *a* him ... Judg 20:23 413
a the children of Benjamin the ... Judg 20:24 413
Benjamin went forth *a* them out of ... Judg 20:25 7125
a the children of Benjamin my ... Judg 20:28 5973
the children of Israel went up *a* ... Judg 20:30 413
put themselves in array *a* Gibeah ... Judg 20:30 413
of Benjamin went out *a* the people ... Judg 20:31 7125
there came *a* Gibeah ten thousand ... Judg 20:34 5048
a Gibeah toward the sunrising ... Judg 20:43 5227
hand of the LORD is gone out *a* me ... Ruth 1:13
the LORD hath testified *a* me ... Ruth 1:21
If one man sin *a* another, the ... 1Sa 2:25
but if a man sin *a* the LORD ... 1Sa 2:25
In that day I will perform *a* Eli ... 1Sa 3:12 413
Now Israel went out *a* the ... 1Sa 4:1 7125
put themselves in array *a* Israel ... 1Sa 4:2 7125
the hand of the LORD was *a* the ... 1Sa 5:9
there, We have sinned *a* the LORD ... 1Sa 7:6
the Philistines went up *a* Israel ... 1Sa 7:7 413
drew near to battle *a* Israel ... 1Sa 7:10
the hand of the LORD was *a* the ... 1Sa 7:13
behold, Samuel came out *a* them ... 1Sa 9:14 7125
up, and encamped *a* Jabesh-gilead ... 1Sa 11:1 5921
witness *a* me before the LORD, and ... 1Sa 12:3
them, The LORD is witness *a* you ... 1Sa 12:5
of Moab, and they fought *a* them ... 1Sa 12:9
the children of Ammon came *a* you ... 1Sa 12:12 5921
not rebel *a* the commandment of ... 1Sa 12:14
but rebel *a* the commandment of ... 1Sa 12:15
the hand of the LORD be *a* you ... 1Sa 12:15
you, as it was *a* your fathers ... 1Sa 12:15
God forbid that I should sin *a* ... 1Sa 12:23
situate northward over *a* Michmash ... 1Sa 14:5 4136
the other southward over *a* Gibeah ... 1Sa 14:5 4136
man's sword was *a* his fellow ... 1Sa 14:20
Behold, the people sin *a* the LORD ... 1Sa 14:33
sin not *a* the LORD in eating with ... 1Sa 14:34
fought *a* all his enemies on every ... 1Sa 14:47
a Moab, and *a* the children ... 1Sa 14:47
a Edom, and *a* the kings of ... 1Sa 14:47
a the kings of Zobah, and *a* ... 1Sa 14:47
And there was sore war *a* the ... 1Sa 14:52 5921
to Shur, that is over *a* Egypt ... 1Sa 15:7 6440
fight *a* them until they be ... 1Sa 15:18
battle in array *a* the Philistines ... 1Sa 17:2 7125
but if I prevail *a* him, and kill ... 1Sa 17:9
the battle in array, army *a* army ... 1Sa 17:21 7125
Eliab's anger was kindled *a* David ... 1Sa 17:28
Thou art not able to go *a* this ... 1Sa 17:33 413
and when he arose *a* me, I caught ... 1Sa 17:35 5921
David go forth *a* the Philistine ... 1Sa 17:55 7125
of the Philistines may be *a* him ... 1Sa 18:21
sin *a* his servant, *a* David ... 1Sa 19:4
because he hath not sinned *a* thee ... 1Sa 19:4
wilt thou sin *a* innocent blood ... 1Sa 19:5
anger was kindled *a* Jonathan ... 1Sa 20:30
all of you have conspired *a* me ... 1Sa 22:8 5921
hath stirred up my servant *a* me ... 1Sa 22:8 5921
him, Why have ye conspired *a* me ... 1Sa 22:13 5921
for him, that he should rise *a* me ... 1Sa 22:13 413
the Philistines fight *a* Keilah ... 1Sa 23:1
a the armies of the Philistines ... 1Sa 23:3 413
secretly practised mischief *a* him ... 1Sa 23:9 5921
David, and went *a* the Philistines ... 1Sa 23:28 7125
to stretch forth mine hand *a* him ... 1Sa 24:6
suffered them not to rise *a* Saul ... 1Sa 24:7 413
not put forth mine hand *a* my lord ... 1Sa 24:10
hand, and I have not sinned *a* thee ... 1Sa 24:11
evil is determined *a* our master ... 1Sa 25:17 413
master, and *a* all his household ... 1Sa 25:17 5921
David and his men came down *a* her ... 1Sa 25:20 7125
light any that pisseth *a* the wall ... 1Sa 25:22
light any that pisseth *a* the wall ... 1Sa 25:34
his hand *a* the LORD's anointed ... 1Sa 26:9
mine hand *a* the LORD's anointed ... 1Sa 26:11
LORD have stirred thee up *a* me ... 1Sa 26:19
mine hand *a* the LORD's anointed ... 1Sa 26:23
A the south of Judah, and *a* ... 1Sa 27:10 5921
a the south of the Kenites ... 1Sa 27:10 413
for the Philistines make war *a* me ... 1Sa 28:15
that I may not go fight *a* the ... 1Sa 29:8
that came *a* us into our hand ... 1Sa 30:23 5921
the Philistines fought *a* Israel ... 1Sa 31:1
And the battle went sore *a* Saul ... 1Sa 31:3 413
thy mouth hath testified *a* thee ... 2Sa 1:16
which *a* Judah do shew kindness ... 2Sa 3:8
them over *a* the mulberry trees ... 2Sa 5:23 4136
of the LORD was kindled *a* Uzzah ... 2Sa 6:7
because he had fought *a* Hadadezer ... 2Sa 8:10
of the battle was *a* him before ... 2Sa 10:9 413
put them in array *a* the Syrians ... 2Sa 10:9 7125
in array *a* the children of Ammon ... 2Sa 10:10 7125
unto the battle *a* the Syrians ... 2Sa 10:13
set themselves in array *a* David ... 2Sa 10:17 7125
Surely the men prevailed *a* us ... 2Sa 11:23 5921
thy battle more strong *a* the city ... 2Sa 11:25 413
was greatly kindled *a* the man ... 2Sa 12:5
I will raise up evil *a* thee out ... 2Sa 12:11 5921
Nathan, I have sinned *a* the LORD ... 2Sa 12:13
Joab fought *a* Rabbah of the ... 2Sa 12:26
and said, I have fought *a* Rabbah ... 2Sa 12:27
encamp *a* the city, and take it ... 2Sa 12:28 5921
and went to Rabbah, and fought *a* it ... 2Sa 12:29
family is risen *a* thine handmaid ... 2Sa 14:7 5921
such a thing *a* the people of God ... 2Sa 14:13 5921
on the hill's side over *a* him ... 2Sa 16:13 5980
hath Ahithophel counselled *a* you ... 2Sa 17:21 5921
went out into the field *a* Israel ... 2Sa 18:6 7125
forth mine hand *a* the king's son ... 2Sa 18:12 413
wrought falsehood *a* mine own life ... 2Sa 18:13
wouldest have set thyself *a* me ... 2Sa 18:13 5048
up their hand *a* my lord the king ... 2Sa 18:28
of all them that rose up *a* thee ... 2Sa 18:31 5921
all that rise *a* thee to do thee ... 2Sa 18:32 5921
and they cast up a bank *a* the city ... 2Sa 20:15 413
a the king, even *a* David ... 2Sa 20:21
that devised *a* us that we should ... 2Sa 21:5
him, and fought *a* the Philistines ... 2Sa 21:15
them that rose up *a* me hast thou ... 2Sa 22:40
high above them that rose up *a* me ... 2Sa 22:49
lift up his spear *a* eight hundred ... 2Sa 23:8 5921
up his spear *a* three hundred ... 2Sa 23:18 5921
of the LORD was kindled *a* Israel ... 2Sa 24:1
and he moved David *a* them to say ... 2Sa 24:1
the king's word prevailed *a* Joab ... 2Sa 24:4 413
a the captains of the host ... 2Sa 24:4 5921
thine hand, I pray thee, be *a* me ... 2Sa 24:17
and *a* my father's house ... 2Sa 24:17
spoken this word *a* his own life ... 1Kin 2:23
a the wall of the house he built ... 1Kin 6:5 5921
a the walls of the house round ... 1Kin 6:5
he built chambers *a* all the house ... 1Kin 6:10 5921
light was *a* light in three ranks ... 1Kin 7:4 413
light was *a* light in three ranks ... 1Kin 7:5
over *a* the belly which was by the ... 1Kin 7:20 5980
house eastward over *a* the south ... 1Kin 7:39 4136
any man trespass *a* his neighbour ... 1Kin 8:31
because they have sinned *a* thee ... 1Kin 8:33
because they have sinned *a* thee ... 1Kin 8:35
go out to battle *a* their enemy ... 1Kin 8:44 5921
If they sin *a* thee, (for there is ... 1Kin 8:46
people that have sinned *a* thee ... 1Kin 8:50
they have transgressed *a* thee ... 1Kin 8:50
he lifted up his hand *a* the king ... 1Kin 11:26
he lifted up his hand *a* the king ... 1Kin 11:27
So Israel rebelled *a* the house of ... 1Kin 12:19
to fight *a* the house of Israel, ... 1Kin 12:21 5973
nor fight *a* your brethren the ... 1Kin 12:24 5973
he cried *a* the altar in the word ... 1Kin 13:2 5921
which had cried *a* the altar in ... 1Kin 13:4 5921
hand, which he put forth *a* him ... 1Kin 13:4 5921
the LORD *a* the altar in Beth-el ... 1Kin 13:32 5921
a all the houses of the high ... 1Kin 13:32 5921
him that pisseth *a* the wall ... 1Kin 14:10
king of Egypt came up *a* Jerusalem ... 1Kin 14:25 5921
king of Israel went up *a* Judah ... 1Kin 15:17 5921
he had *a* the cities of Israel ... 1Kin 15:20 5921
of Issachar, conspired *a* him ... 1Kin 15:27 5921
Jehu the son of Hanani *a* Baasha ... 1Kin 16:1 5921
the word of the LORD *a* Baasha ... 1Kin 16:7 413
a his house, even for all the ... 1Kin 16:7 413
his chariots, conspired *a* him ... 1Kin 16:9 5921
him not one that pisseth *a* a wall ... 1Kin 16:11
which he spake *a* Baasha by Jehu ... 1Kin 16:12 413
people were encamped *a* Gibbethon ... 1Kin 16:15 5921
that followed Omri prevailed *a* ... 1Kin 16:22
besieged Samaria, and warred *a* it ... 1Kin 20:1
themselves in array *a* the city ... 1Kin 20:12 5921
king of Syria will come up *a* thee ... 1Kin 20:22 5921
but let us fight *a* them in the ... 1Kin 20:23
we will fight *a* them in the plain ... 1Kin 20:25
up to Aphek, to fight *a* Israel ... 1Kin 20:26 5973
were all present, and went *a* them ... 1Kin 20:27 7125
one over *a* the other seven days ... 1Kin 20:29 5227
before him, to bear witness *a* him ... 1Kin 21:10
the men of Belial witnessed *a* him ... 1Kin 21:13
even *a* Naboth, in the presence of ... 1Kin 21:13
Ahab him that pisseth *a* the wall ... 1Kin 21:21
Shall I go *a* Ramoth-gilead to ... 1Kin 22:6 5921
shall we go *a* Ramoth-gilead to ... 1Kin 22:15 413
they turned aside to fight *a* him ... 1Kin 22:32 5921
up in his chariot *a* the Syrians ... 1Kin 22:35 5227
Then Moab rebelled *a* Israel after ... 2Kin 1:1
rebelled *a* the king of Israel ... 2Kin 3:5
king of Moab hath rebelled *a* me ... 2Kin 3:7
thou go with me *a* Moab to battle ... 2Kin 3:7 413
were come up to fight *a* them ... 2Kin 3:21
was great indignation *a* Israel ... 2Kin 3:27 5921
see how he seeketh a quarrel *a* me ... 2Kin 5:7
the king of Syria warred *a* Israel ... 2Kin 6:8
a us the kings of the Hittites ... 2Kin 7:6 5921
the war *a* Hazael king of Syria in ... 2Kin 8:28 5973
when he fought *a* Hazael king of ... 2Kin 8:29
Ahab him that pisseth *a* the wall ... 2Kin 9:8
son of Nimshi conspired *a* Joram ... 2Kin 9:14 413
chariot, and they went out *a* Jehu ... 2Kin 9:21 7125
behold, I conspired *a* my master ... 2Kin 10:9 5921
Syria went up, and fought *a* Gath ... 2Kin 12:17 5921
of the LORD was kindled *a* Israel ... 2Kin 13:3
he fought *a* Amaziah king of Judah ... 2Kin 13:12 5973
a conspiracy *a* him in Jerusalem ... 2Kin 14:19 5921
the son of Jabesh conspired *a* him ... 2Kin 15:10 5921
king of Assyria came *a* the land ... 2Kin 15:19 5921
a captain of his, conspired *a* him ... 2Kin 15:25 5921
a Pekah the son of Remaliah ... 2Kin 15:30 5921
days the LORD began to send *a* ... 2Kin 15:37
of Israel, which rise up *a* me ... 2Kin 16:7 5921
of Assyria went up *a* Damascus ... 2Kin 16:9 413
it *a* king Ahaz came from Damascus ... 2Kin 16:11 5704
A him came up Shalmaneser king of ... 2Kin 17:3 5921
had sinned *a* the LORD their God ... 2Kin 17:7
not right *a* the LORD their God ... 2Kin 17:9 5921
Yet the LORD testified *a* Israel ... 2Kin 17:13
a Judah, by all the prophets, and ... 2Kin 17:13
which he testified *a* them ... 2Kin 17:15
he rebelled *a* the king of Assyria ... 2Kin 18:7
king of Assyria came up *a* Samaria ... 2Kin 18:9 5921
king of Assyria come up *a* all the ... 2Kin 18:13 5921
with a great host *a* Jerusalem ... 2Kin 18:17
trust, that thou rebellest *a* me ... 2Kin 18:20
LORD *a* this place to destroy it ... 2Kin 18:25 5921
Go up *a* this land, and destroy it ... 2Kin 18:25 5921
king of Assyria warring *a* Libnah ... 2Kin 19:8 5921
he is come out to fight *a* thee ... 2Kin 19:9
which thou hast prayed to me *a* ... 2Kin 19:20 413
a whom hast thou exalted thy ... 2Kin 19:22 5921
even *a* the Holy One of Israel ... 2Kin 19:22 5921
thy coming in, and thy rage *a* me ... 2Kin 19:27 413
Because thy rage *a* me and thy ... 2Kin 19:28 413
with shield, nor cast a bank *a* it ... 2Kin 19:32 5921
servants of Amon conspired *a* him ... 2Kin 21:23 5921
that had conspired *a* king Amon ... 2Kin 21:24 5921
of the LORD that is kindled *a* us ... 2Kin 22:13
shall be kindled *a* this place ... 2Kin 22:17
what I spake *a* this place ... 2Kin 22:19 5921
a the inhabitants thereof, that ... 2Kin 22:19 5921
hast done *a* the altar of Beth-el ... 2Kin 23:17 5921
his anger was kindled *a* Judah ... 2Kin 23:26
king of Egypt went up *a* the king ... 2Kin 23:29 5921
and king Josiah went *a* him ... 2Kin 23:29 7125
then he turned and rebelled *a* him ... 2Kin 24:1
the LORD sent *a* him bands of the ... 2Kin 24:2
sent them *a* Judah to destroy it, ... 2Kin 24:2
of Babylon came up *a* Jerusalem ... 2Kin 24:10
king of Babylon came *a* the city ... 2Kin 24:11 5921
rebelled *a* the king of Babylon ... 2Kin 24:20
a Jerusalem, and pitched *a* ... 2Kin 25:1 5921
they built forts *a* it round about ... 2Kin 25:1 5921
were *a* the city round about ... 2Kin 25:4 5921
children of Gad dwelt over *a* them ... 1Chr 5:11 5048
And they were helped *a* them ... 1Chr 5:20 5921
they transgressed *a* the God of ... 1Chr 5:25
in Jerusalem, over *a* them ... 1Chr 8:32 5048
Jerusalem, over *a* their brethren ... 1Chr 9:38 5048
the Philistines fought *a* Israel ... 1Chr 10:1 5921
And the battle went sore *a* Saul ... 1Chr 10:3 5921
which he committed *a* the LORD ... 1Chr 10:13
even *a* the word of the LORD, ... 1Chr 10:13 5921
he lifted up his spear *a* three ... 1Chr 11:11 5921
up his spear *a* three hundred ... 1Chr 11:20 5921
the Philistines *a* Saul to battle ... 1Chr 12:19 5921
they helped David *a* the band of ... 1Chr 12:21 5921
of the LORD was kindled *a* Uzza ... 1Chr 13:10

heard of it, and went out *a* them 1Chr 14:8 6640
Shall I go up *a* the Philistines 1Chr 14:10 5921
them over *a* the mulberry trees 1Chr 14:14 4136
because he had fought *a* Hadarezer 1Chr 18:10
the battle was set *a* him before 1Chr 19:10 413
put them in array *a* the Syrians 1Chr 19:10 7125
in array *a* the children of Ammon 1Chr 19:11 7125
and set the battle in array *a* them 1Chr 19:17 413
the battle in array *a* the Syrians 1Chr 19:17 7125
And Satan stood up *a* Israel 1Chr 21:1 5921
the king's word prevailed *a* Joab 1Chr 21:4 5921
over *a* their brethren the sons of 1Chr 24:31 5984
over *a* their younger brethren 1Chr 24:31 5984
And they cast lots, ward *a* ward 1Chr 25:8 5984
men, having wards one *a* another 1Chr 26:12 5984
of the going up, ward *a* ward 1Chr 26:16 5984
there fell wrath for it *a* Israel 1Chr 27:24 5921
of the east end, over *a* the south 2Chr 4:10 4136
If a man sin *a* his neighbour, and 2Chr 6:22
because they have sinned *a* thee 2Chr 6:24
because they have sinned *a* thee 2Chr 6:26
If thy people go out to war *a* 2Chr 6:34 5921
If they sin *a* thee, (for there is 2Chr 6:36
people which have sinned *a* thee 2Chr 6:39
Hamath-zobah, and prevailed *a* it 2Chr 8:3 5921
seer *a* Jeroboam the son of Nebat 2Chr 9:29 5921
Israel rebelled *a* the house of 2Chr 10:19
were warriors, to fight *a* Israel 2Chr 11:1 5973
nor fight *a* your brethren 2Chr 11:4 5973
and returned from going *a* Jeroboam 2Chr 11:4 413
king of Egypt came up *a* Jerusalem 2Chr 12:2 5921
they had transgressed *a* the LORD 2Chr 12:2
king of Egypt came up *a* Jerusalem 2Chr 12:9 5921
also set the battle in array *a* 2Chr 13:3 5971
up, and hath rebelled *a* his lord 2Chr 13:6 5921
a Rehoboam the son of Solomon 2Chr 13:7 5921
trumpets to cry alarm *a* you 2Chr 13:12 5921
fight ye not *a* the LORD God of 2Chr 13:12 5973
there came out *a* them Zerah the 2Chr 14:9 413
Then Asa went out *a* him, and they 2Chr 14:10 6440
thy name we go *a* this multitude 2Chr 14:11 5921
let not man prevail *a* thee 2Chr 14:11 5973
king of Israel came up *a* Judah 2Chr 16:1 5921
his armies *a* the cities of Israel 2Chr 16:4 413
and strengthened himself *a* Israel 2Chr 17:1 5921
they made no war *a* Jehoshaphat 2Chr 17:10 5973
the LORD hath spoken evil *a* thee 2Chr 18:22 5921
himself up in his chariot *a* the 2Chr 18:34 5227
that they trespass not *a* the LORD 2Chr 19:10
came *a* Jehoshaphat to battle 2Chr 20:1 5921
a thee from beyond the sea on 2Chr 20:2 5921
for we have no might *a* this great 2Chr 20:12 6440
great company that cometh *a* us 2Chr 20:12 5921
To morrow go ye down *a* them 2Chr 20:16 5921
to morrow go out *a* them 2Chr 20:17 6440
a the children of Ammon, Moab, and 2Chr 20:22 5921
Seir, which were come *a* Judah 2Chr 20:22
Moab stood up *a* the inhabitants 2Chr 20:23 5921
fought *a* the enemies of Israel 2Chr 20:29 5973
Mareshah prophesied *a* Jehoshaphat 2Chr 20:37 5921
up *a* Jehoram the spirit of the 2Chr 21:16 5921
to war *a* Hazael king of Syria at 2Chr 22:5 5921
Jehoram *a* Jehu the son of Nimshi 2Chr 22:7 413
and they testified *a* them 2Chr 24:19
And they conspired *a* him, and 2Chr 24:21 5921
the host of Syria came up *a* him 2Chr 24:23 5921
So they executed judgment *a* Joash 2Chr 24:24
his own servants conspired *a* him 2Chr 24:25 5921
are they that conspired *a* him 2Chr 24:26 5921
anger was greatly kindled *a* Judah 2Chr 25:10
of the LORD was kindled *a* Amaziah 2Chr 25:15
a conspiracy *a* him in Jerusalem 2Chr 25:27 5921
warred *a* the Philistines, and 2Chr 26:6
God helped him *a* the Philistines, 2Chr 26:7 5921
a the Arabians that dwelt in 2Chr 26:7 5921
to help the king *a* the enemy 2Chr 26:13 5921
transgressed *a* the LORD his God 2Chr 26:16
Ammonites, and prevailed *a* them 2Chr 27:5 5921
you, sins *a* the LORD your God 2Chr 28:10
stood up *a* them that came from 2Chr 28:12 5921
have offended *a* the LORD already 2Chr 28:13
and there is fierce wrath *a* Israel 2Chr 28:13 5921
and transgressed sore *a* the LORD 2Chr 28:19
he trespass yet more *a* the LORD 2Chr 28:22
which trespassed *a* the LORD God 2Chr 30:7
encamped *a* the fenced cities, and 2Chr 32:1 5921
was purposed to fight *a* Jerusalem 2Chr 32:2 5921
he himself laid siege *a* Lachish 2Chr 32:9 5921
spake yet more *a* the LORD God 2Chr 32:16 5921
and *a* his servant Hezekiah 2Chr 32:16 5921
God of Israel, and to speak *a* him 2Chr 32:17 5921
they spake *a* the God of Jerusalem 2Chr 32:19 413
as *a* the gods of the people of 2Chr 32:19 5921
And his servants conspired *a* him 2Chr 33:24 5921
that had conspired *a* king Amon 2Chr 33:25 5921
heardest his words *a* this place 2Chr 34:27 5921
a the inhabitants thereof, and 2Chr 34:27 5921
fight *a* Charchemish by Euphrates 2Chr 35:20
and Josiah went out *a* him 2Chr 35:20 7125
I come not *a* thee this day 2Chr 35:21 5921
but *a* the house wherewith I have 2Chr 35:21 413
A him came up Nebuchadnezzar king 2Chr 36:6 5921
And he also rebelled *a* king 2Chr 36:13
of the LORD arose *a* his people 2Chr 36:16
And hired counsellors *a* them Ezr 4:5 5921
a the inhabitants of Judah Ezr 4:6 5921
the scribe wrote a letter *a* Ezr 4:8 5922
hath made insurrection *a* kings Ezr 4:19 5922
be wrath *a* the realm of the king Ezr 7:23 5922
horsemen to help us *a* the enemy Ezr 8:22
his wrath is *a* all them that Ezr 8:22 5921
We have trespassed *a* our God Ezr 10:2
which we have sinned *a* thee Neh 1:6
have dealt very corruptly *a* thee Neh 1:7
will ye rebel *a* the king Neh 2:19 5921
Harumaph, even over *a* his house Neh 3:10 5048
unto the place over *a* the Neh 3:16 5048
another piece over *a* the going up Neh 3:19 5048
and Hashub over *a* their house Neh 3:23 5048
over *a* the turning of the wall, Neh 3:25 5048
unto the place over *a* the water Neh 3:26 5048
over *a* the great tower that lieth Neh 3:27 5048
every one over *a* his house Neh 3:28 5048
the son of Immer over *a* his house Neh 3:29 5048
of Berechiah over *a* his chamber Neh 3:30 5048
over *a* the gate Miphkad, and to Neh 3:31 5921
to fight *a* Jerusalem, and to Neh 4:8
God, and set a watch *a* them day Neh 4:9 5921
of their wives *a* their brethren Neh 5:1 413
And I set a great assembly *a* them Neh 5:7 5921
he pronounced this prophecy *a* me Neh 6:12 5921
every one to be over *a* his house Neh 7:3 5048
that they dealt proudly *a* them Neh 9:10 5921
disobedient, and rebelled *a* thee Neh 9:26
a them to turn them to thee Neh 9:26
And testifiedst *a* them, that thou Neh 9:29
but sinned *a* thy judgments, Neh 9:29
testifiedst *a* them by thy spirit Neh 9:30
thou didst testify *a* them Neh 9:34
were over *a* them in the watches Neh 12:9 5048
with their brethren over *a* them Neh 12:24 5048
the man of God, ward over *a* ward Neh 12:24 5980
gate, which was over *a* them Neh 12:37 5048
that gave thanks went over *a* them Neh 12:38 4136
water, but hired Balaam *a* them Neh 13:2 5921
I testified *a* them in the day Neh 13:15
Then I testified *a* them, and said Neh 13:21
to transgress *a* our God in Neh 13:27
done, and what was decreed *a* her Est 2:1 5921
they should be ready *a* that day Est 3:14
house, over *a* the king's house Est 5:1 5227
over *a* the gate of the house Est 5:1 5227
full of indignation *a* Mordecai Est 5:9 5921
thou shalt not prevail *a* him Est 6:13
evil determined *a* him by the king Est 7:7 413
that he had devised *a* the Jews Est 8:3 5921
a that day to avenge themselves Est 8:13
had devised *a* the Jews to destroy Est 9:24 5921
which he devised *a* the Jews Est 9:25 5921
although thou movedst me *a* him Job 2:3
do set themselves in array *a* me Job 6:4
hast thou set me as a mark *a* thee Job 7:20
If thy children have sinned *a* him Job 8:4
who hath hardened himself *a* him Job 9:4 413
Thou renewest thy witnesses *a* me Job 10:17 5048
changes and war are *a* me Job 10:17 5973
speak, and open his lips *a* thee Job 11:5 5973
thou writest bitter things *a* me Job 13:26 5921
Thou prevailest for ever *a* him Job 14:20
thine own lips testify *a* thee Job 15:6
thou turnest thy spirit *a* God Job 15:13 413
they shall prevail *a* him, as a Job 15:24
he stretcheth out his hand *a* God Job 15:25 413
himself *a* the Almighty Job 15:25 413
I could heap up words *a* you Job 16:4 5921
wrinkles, which is a witness *a* me Job 16:8
gathered themselves together *a* me Job 16:10 5921
stir up himself *a* the hypocrite Job 17:8 5921
and the robber shall prevail *a* him Job 18:9 5921
ye will magnify yourselves *a* me Job 19:5 5921
and plead *a* me my reproach Job 19:5 5921
hath also kindled his wrath *a* me Job 19:11 5921
and raise up their way *a* me Job 19:12 5921
I arose, and they spake *a* me Job 19:18
they whom I loved are turned *a* me Job 19:19
and the earth shall rise up *a* him Job 20:27
which ye wrongfully imagine *a* me Job 21:27 5921
Will he plead *a* me with his great Job 23:6 5978
of those that rebel *a* the light Job 24:13
he that riseth up *a* me as the Job 27:7
they raise up *a* me the ways of Job 30:12 5921
hand thou opposest thyself *a* me Job 30:21
up my hand *a* the fatherless Job 31:21 5921
If my land cry *a* me, or that the Job 31:38 5921
a Job was his wrath kindled, Job 32:2
Also *a* his three friends was his Job 32:3
hath not directed his words *a* me Job 32:14 413
Behold, he findeth occasions *a* me Job 33:10 5921
Why dost thou strive *a* him Job 33:13 413
Should I lie *a* my right Job 34:6 5921
a a nation, or *a* a man only Job 34:29 5921
and multiplieth his words *a* God Job 34:37
sinnest, what doest thou *a* him Job 35:6
reserved *a* the time of trouble Job 38:23
a the day of battle and war Job 38:23
She is hardened *a* her young ones Job 39:16
The quiver rattleth *a* him Job 39:23 5921
My wrath is kindled *a* thee Job 42:7
thee, and *a* thy two friends Job 42:7
a the LORD, and *a* his Ps 2:2 5921
many are they that rise up *a* me Ps 3:1 5921
set themselves *a* me round about Ps 3:6 5921
for they have rebelled *a* thee Ps 5:10
his arrows *a* the persecutors Ps 7:13
eyes are privily set *a* the poor Ps 10:8
enemy say, I have prevailed *a* him Ps 13:4
up a reproach *a* his neighbour Ps 15:3 5921
nor taketh reward *a* the innocent Ps 15:5 5921
from those that rise up *a* them Ps 17:7
under me those that rose up *a* me Ps 18:39
up above those that rise up *a* me Ps 18:48
For they intended evil *a* thee Ps 21:11 5921
thy strings *a* the face of them Ps 21:12 5921
Though an host should encamp *a* me Ps 27:3 5921
though war should rise *a* me Ps 27:3 5921
false witnesses are risen up *a* me Ps 27:12
they took counsel together *a* me Ps 31:13 5921
and contemptuously *a* the righteous Ps 31:18 5921
the LORD is *a* them that do evil Ps 34:16
a them that fight *a* me Ps 35:1
and stop the way *a* them that Ps 35:3 7125
gathered themselves together *a* me Ps 35:15 5921
they devise deceitful matters *a* Ps 35:20 5921
they opened their mouth wide *a* me Ps 35:21 5921
that magnify themselves *a* me Ps 35:26 5921
not the foot of pride come *a* me Ps 36:11
envious *a* the workers of iniquity Ps 37:1
The wicked plotteth *a* the just Ps 37:12
they magnify themselves *a* me Ps 38:16 5921
for I have sinned *a* thee Ps 41:4
hate me whisper together *a* me Ps 41:7 5921
a me do they devise my hurt Ps 41:7 5921
hath lifted up his heel *a* me Ps 41:9 5921
plead my cause *a* an ungodly Ps 43:1
them under that rise up *a* us Ps 44:5
Israel, and I will testify *a* thee Ps 50:7
sittest and speakest *a* thy brother Ps 50:20
A thee, thee only, have I sinned, Ps 51:4
of him that encampeth *a* thee Ps 53:5
For strangers are risen up *a* me Ps 54:3 5921
me that did magnify himself *a* me Ps 55:12 5921
from the battle that was *a* me Ps 55:18
He hath put forth his hands *a* Ps 55:20
for they be many that fight *a* me Ps 56:2
their thoughts are *a* me for evil Ps 56:5 5921
me from them that rise up *a* me Ps 59:1
the mighty are gathered *a* me Ps 59:3 5921
will ye imagine mischief *a* a man Ps 62:3 5921
Iniquities prevail *a* me Ps 65:3
that sit in the gate speak *a* me Ps 69:12
For mine enemies speak *a* me Ps 71:10
set their mouth *a* the heavens Ps 73:9
I should offend *a* the generation Ps 73:15
smoke *a* the sheep of thy pasture Ps 74:1
up *a* thee increaseth continually Ps 74:23
they sinned yet more *a* him by Ps 78:17
Yea, they spake *a* God Ps 78:19
so a fire was kindled *a* Jacob Ps 78:21
and anger also came up *a* Israel Ps 78:21
O remember not *a* us former Ps 79:8
angry *a* the prayer of thy people Ps 80:4
and turned my hand *a* their Ps 81:14 5921
taken crafty counsel *a* thy people Ps 83:3 5921
consulted *a* thy hidden ones Ps 83:3 5921
they are confederate *a* thee Ps 83:5 5921
O God, the proud are risen *a* me Ps 86:14 5921
lest thou dash thy foot *a* a stone Ps 91:12
of the wicked that rise up *a* me Ps 92:11 5921
rise up for me *a* the evildoers Ps 94:16 5973
for me *a* the workers of iniquity Ps 94:16 5973
a the soul of the righteous Ps 94:21 5921
are mad *a* me are sworn *a* me Ps 102:8
and they rebelled not *a* his word Ps 105:28
he lifted up his hand *a* them Ps 106:26
of the LORD kindled *a* his people Ps 106:40
they rebelled *a* the words of God Ps 107:11
of the deceitful are opened *a* me Ps 109:2 5921
they have spoken *a* me with a Ps 109:2
fought *a* me without a cause Ps 109:3
of them that speak evil *a* my soul Ps 109:20 5921
that I might not sin *a* thee Ps 119:11
also did sit and speak *a* me Ps 119:23
The proud have forged a lie *a* me Ps 119:69 5921
our side, when men rose up *a* us Ps 124:2 5921
when their wrath was kindled *a* us Ps 124:3
yet they have not prevailed *a* me Ps 129:2
thy little ones *a* the stones Ps 137:9 413
hand *a* the wrath of mine enemies Ps 138:7 5921
For they speak *a* thee wickedly Ps 139:20
with those that rise up *a* thee Ps 139:21
Devise not evil *a* thy neighbour Prov 3:29 5921
But he that sinneth *a* me wrongeth Prov 8:36
but his wrath is *a* him that Prov 14:35
messenger shall be sent *a* him Prov 17:11
and his heart fretteth *a* the LORD Prov 19:3 5921
to anger sinneth *a* his own soul Prov 20:2
nor counsel *a* the LORD Prov 21:30 5048
is prepared *a* the day of battle Prov 21:31
Be not thou envious *a* evil men Prov 24:1
a the dwelling of the righteous Prov 24:15
Be not a witness *a* thy neighbour Prov 24:28
witness *a* his neighbour is a maul Prov 25:18
a whom there is no rising up Prov 30:31 5973
And if one prevail *a* him, two Eccl 4:12
hath set the one over *a* the other Eccl 7:14 5980
Because sentence *a* an evil work Eccl 8:11
and there came a great king *a* it Eccl 9:14 413
it, and built great bulwarks *a* it Eccl 9:14 5921
of the ruler rise up *a* thee Eccl 10:4 5921
and they have rebelled *a* me Is 1:2
shall not lift up sword *a* nation Is 2:4 413
himself proudly *a* the ancient Is 3:5
the base *a* the honourable Is 3:5
and their doings are *a* the LORD Is 3:8 413
countenance doth witness *a* them Is 3:9
of the LORD kindled *a* his people Is 5:25
stretched forth his hand *a* them Is 5:25 5921
in that day they shall roar *a* Is 5:30 5921
up toward Jerusalem to war *a* it Is 7:1 5921
but could not prevail *a* it Is 7:1 5921
have taken evil counsel *a* thee Is 7:5 5921
Let us go up *a* Judah, and vex it, Is 7:6
up the adversaries of Rezin *a* him Is 9:11 5921
and they together shall be *a* Judah Is 9:21 5921
I will send him *a* an hypocritical Is 10:6
a the people of my wrath will I Is 10:6 5921
a him that heweth therewith Is 10:15 5921
itself *a* him that shaketh it Is 10:15 5921
itself *a* them that lift it up Is 10:15
and shall lift up his staff *a* thee Is 10:24 5921
he shall shake his hand *a* the Is 10:32
I will stir up the Medes *a* them Is 13:17 5921

proverb *a* the king of Babylon	Is 14:4	5921
down, no feller is come up *a* us	Is 14:8	5921
For I will rise up *a* them	Is 14:22	5921
set the Egyptians *a* the Egyptians	Is 19:2	
fight every one *a* his brother	Is 19:2	
every one *a* his neighbour	Is 19:2	
city *a* city, and kingdom *a*	Is 19:2	
which he hath determined *a* it	Is 19:17	5921
sent him,) and fought *a* Ashdod	Is 20:1	
hath taken this counsel *a* Tyre	Is 23:8	5921
a commandment *a* the merchant city	Is 23:11	413
ones is as a storm *a* the wall	Is 25:4	
briers and thorns *a* me in battle	Is 27:4	
I will camp *a* thee round about,	Is 29:3	5921
will lay siege *a* thee with a	Is 29:3	5921
and I will raise forts *a* thee	Is 29:3	5921
the nations that fight *a* Ariel	Is 29:7	5921
even all that fight *a* her	Is 29:7	
be, that fight *a* mount Zion	Is 29:8	5921
but will arise *a* the house of the	Is 31:2	5921
a the help of them that work	Is 31:2	5921
shepherds is called forth *a* him	Is 31:4	5921
and to utter error *a* the LORD	Is 32:6	413
king of Assyria came up *a* all the	Is 36:1	5921
trust, that thou rebellest *a* me	Is 36:5	
LORD *a* this land to destroy it	Is 36:10	5921
Go up *a* this land, and destroy it	Is 36:10	413
king of Assyria warring *a* Libnah	Is 37:8	5921
me *a* Sennacherib king of Assyria	Is 37:21	413
a whom hast thou exalted thy	Is 37:23	5921
even *a* the Holy One of Israel	Is 37:23	413
thy coming in, and thy rage *a* me	Is 37:28	413
Because thy rage *a* me, and thy	Is 37:29	413
shields, nor cast a bank *a* it	Is 37:33	5921
incensed *a* thee shall be ashamed	Is 41:11	
they that war *a* thee shall be as	Is 41:12	
he shall prevail *a* his enemies	Is 42:13	5921
LORD, he *a* whom we have sinned	Is 42:24	
teachers have transgressed *a* me	Is 43:27	
incensed *a* him shall be ashamed	Is 45:24	
a thee shall fall for thy sake	Is 54:15	5921
is formed *a* thee shall prosper	Is 54:17	5921
a thee in judgment thou shalt	Is 54:17	
A whom do ye sport yourselves	Is 57:4	5921
a whom make ye a wide mouth, and	Is 57:4	5921
thee, and our sins testify *a* us	Is 59:12	
lying *a* the LORD, and departing	Is 59:13	
shall lift up a standard *a* him	Is 59:19	
their enemy, and he fought *a* them	Is 63:10	
men that have transgressed *a* me	Is 66:24	
a all the walls thereof round	Jer 1:15	5921
a all the cities of Judah	Jer 1:15	5921
a them touching all their	Jer 1:16	5921
brasen walls *a* the whole land,	Jer 1:18	5921
a the kings of Judah, *a* the	Jer 1:18	
a the priests thereof, and *a*	Jer 1:18	
And they shall fight *a* thee	Jer 1:19	413
but they shall not prevail *a* thee	Jer 1:19	
pastors also transgressed *a* me	Jer 2:8	
ye all have transgressed *a* me	Jer 2:29	
transgressed *a* the LORD thy God	Jer 3:13	
we have sinned *a* the LORD our God	Jer 3:25	
also will I give sentence *a* them	Jer 4:12	
publish *a* Jerusalem, that	Jer 4:16	5921
their voice *a* the cities of Judah	Jer 4:16	5921
are they *a* her round about	Jer 4:17	5921
she hath been rebellious *a* me	Jer 4:17	
dealt very treacherously *a* me	Jer 5:11	
their tents *a* her round about	Jer 6:3	5921
Prepare ye war *a* her	Jer 6:4	5921
and cast a mount *a* Jerusalem	Jer 6:6	5921
in array as men for war *a* thee	Jer 6:23	5921
because we have sinned *a* the LORD	Jer 8:14	
I would comfort myself *a* sorrow	Jer 8:18	
thee, hath pronounced evil *a* thee	Jer 11:17	5921
which they have done *a* themselves	Jer 11:17	
they had devised devices *a* me	Jer 11:19	5921
it crieth out *a* me	Jer 12:8	5921
the birds round about are *a* her	Jer 12:9	5921
Thus saith the LORD *a* all mine	Jer 12:14	5921
And I will dash them one *a* another	Jer 13:14	413
our iniquities testify *a* us	Jer 14:7	
we have sinned *a* thee	Jer 14:7	
for we have sinned *a* thee	Jer 14:20	
will I stretch out my hand *a* thee	Jer 15:6	5921
I have brought upon them *a* the	Jer 15:8	5921
and they shall fight *a* thee	Jer 15:20	413
but they shall not prevail *a* thee	Jer 15:20	
all this great evil *a* us	Jer 16:10	5921
have committed *a* the LORD our God	Jer 16:10	
a whom I have pronounced, turn	Jer 18:8	5921
Behold, I frame evil *a* you	Jer 18:11	5921
and devise a device *a* you	Jer 18:11	5921
let us devise devices *a* Jeremiah	Jer 18:18	5921
all their counsel *a* me to slay me	Jer 18:23	5921
evil that I have pronounced *a* it	Jer 19:15	5921
and we shall prevail *a* him	Jer 20:10	
king of Babylon maketh war *a* us	Jer 21:2	5921
wherewith ye fight *a* the king of	Jer 21:4	
a the Chaldeans, which besiege	Jer 21:4	
I myself will fight *a* you with an	Jer 21:5	
set my face *a* this city for evil	Jer 21:10	
Behold, I am *a* thee, O inhabitant	Jer 21:13	413
say, Who shall come down *a* us	Jer 21:13	5921
I will prepare destroyers *a* thee	Jer 22:7	5921
saith the LORD God of Israel *a*	Jer 23:2	5921
I am *a* the prophets, saith the	Jer 23:30	5921
I am *a* the prophets, saith the	Jer 23:31	5921
I am *a* them that prophesy false	Jer 23:32	5921
and will bring them *a* this land	Jer 25:9	5921
a the inhabitants thereof, and	Jer 25:9	5921
a all these nations round about,	Jer 25:9	5921
which I have pronounced *a* it	Jer 25:13	5921
hath prophesied *a* all the nations	Jer 25:13	5921
thou *a* them all these words	Jer 25:30	413
a all the inhabitants of the	Jer 25:30	413
a Jeremiah in the house of the	Jer 26:9	413
he hath prophesied *a* this city	Jer 26:11	413
sent me to prophesy *a* this house	Jer 26:12	413
a this city all the words that ye	Jer 26:12	413
that he hath pronounced *a* you	Jer 26:13	5921
which he had pronounced *a* them	Jer 26:19	5921
we procure great evil *a* our souls	Jer 26:19	5921
who prophesied *a* this city	Jer 26:20	5921
a this land according to all the	Jer 26:20	5921
as the LORD hath spoken *a* the	Jer 27:13	413
prophesied both *a* many countries	Jer 28:8	413
a great kingdoms, of war, and of	Jer 28:8	5921
hast taught rebellion *a* the LORD	Jer 28:16	413
hath taught rebellion *a* the LORD	Jer 29:32	5921
for since I spake *a* him, I do	Jer 31:20	
over *a* it upon the hill Gareb	Jer 31:39	5048
of the Chaldeans, that fight *a* it	Jer 32:24	5921
Chaldeans, that fight *a* this city	Jer 32:29	5921
whereby they have sinned *a* me	Jer 33:8	
they have transgressed *a* me	Jer 33:8	
fought *a* Jerusalem, and *a*	Jer 34:1	5921
Babylon's army fought *a* Jerusalem	Jer 34:7	5921
a all the cities of Judah that	Jer 34:7	5921
a Lachish, and *a* Azekah	Jer 34:7	413
and they shall fight *a* it, and	Jer 34:22	5921
that I have pronounced *a* them	Jer 35:17	5921
I have spoken unto thee *a* Israel	Jer 36:2	5921
a Judah, and *a* all the nations	Jer 36:2	5921
hath pronounced *a* this people	Jer 36:7	413
that I have pronounced *a* them	Jer 36:31	413
fight *a* this city, and take it, and	Jer 37:8	5921
of the Chaldeans that fight *a* you	Jer 37:10	
What have I offended *a* thee	Jer 37:18	
or *a* thy servants, or *a*	Jer 37:18	
come *a* you, nor *a* this land	Jer 37:19	5921
he that can do any thing *a* you	Jer 38:5	
thee on, and have prevailed *a* thee	Jer 38:22	
and all his army *a* Jerusalem	Jer 39:1	413
because ye have sinned *a* the LORD	Jer 40:3	
of Neriah setteth thee on *a* us	Jer 43:3	
ye this great evil *a* your souls	Jer 44:7	413
I will set my face *a* you for evil	Jer 44:11	
because ye have sinned *a* the LORD	Jer 44:23	
shall surely stand *a* you for evil	Jer 44:29	5921
the prophet *a* the Gentiles	Jer 46:1	5921
A Egypt, *a* the army of	Jer 46:2	
man hath stumbled *a* the mighty	Jer 46:12	
come *a* her with axes, as hewers	Jer 46:22	
the prophet *a* the Philistines	Jer 47:1	413
a Ashkelon, and *a* the sea shore	Jer 47:7	413
A Moab thus saith the LORD of	Jer 48:1	
they have devised evil *a* it	Jer 48:2	5921
he magnified himself *a* the LORD	Jer 48:26	5921
hath magnified himself *a* the LORD	Jer 48:42	5921
Gather ye together, and come *a* her	Jer 49:14	5921
from the swelling of Jordan *a* the	Jer 49:19	413
LORD, that he hath taken *a* Edom	Jer 49:20	413
that he hath purposed *a* the	Jer 49:20	413
Babylon hath taken counsel *a* you	Jer 49:30	5921
and hath conceived a purpose *a* you	Jer 49:30	5921
a Elam in the beginning of the	Jer 49:34	413
that the LORD spake *a* Babylon	Jer 50:1	413
a the land of the Chaldeans by	Jer 50:1	413
there cometh up a nation *a* her	Jer 50:3	5921
they have sinned *a* the LORD	Jer 50:7	
cause to come up *a* Babylon an	Jer 50:9	5921
set themselves in array *a* her	Jer 50:9	
in array *a* Babylon round about	Jer 50:14	5921
for she hath sinned *a* the LORD	Jer 50:14	
Shout *a* her round about	Jer 50:15	5921
Go up *a* the land of Merathaim,	Jer 50:21	5921
the land of Merathaim, even *a* it	Jer 50:21	5921
a the inhabitants of Pekod	Jer 50:21	413
thou hast striven *a* the LORD	Jer 50:24	
Come *a* her from the utmost border	Jer 50:26	
together the archers *a* Babylon	Jer 50:29	413
the bow, camp *a* it round about	Jer 50:29	5921
she hath been proud *a* the LORD	Jer 50:29	413
a the Holy One of Israel	Jer 50:29	413
Behold, I am *a* thee, O thou most	Jer 50:31	413
a thee, O daughter of Babylon	Jer 50:42	5921
that he hath taken *a* Babylon	Jer 50:45	413
that he hath purposed *a* the land	Jer 50:45	413
Behold, I will raise up *a* Babylon	Jer 51:1	5921
a them that dwell in the midst of	Jer 51:1	413
midst of them that rise up *a* me	Jer 51:1	
they shall be *a* her round about	Jer 51:2	5921
A him that bendeth let the archer	Jer 51:3	413
a him that lifteth himself up in	Jer 51:3	413
with sin *a* the Holy One of Israel	Jer 51:5	
for his device is *a* Babylon	Jer 51:11	5921
done that which he spake *a* the	Jer 51:12	413
they shall lift up a shout *a* thee	Jer 51:14	5921
Behold, I am *a* thee, O destroying	Jer 51:25	413
prepare the nations *a* her	Jer 51:27	5921
call together *a* her the kingdoms	Jer 51:27	5921
appoint a captain *a* her	Jer 51:27	5921
Prepare *a* her the nations with	Jer 51:28	5921
LORD shall be performed *a* Babylon	Jer 51:29	5921
in the land, ruler *a* ruler	Jer 51:46	5921
words that are written *a* Babylon	Jer 51:60	413
thou hast spoken *a* this place	Jer 51:62	413
rebelled *a* the king of Babylon	Jer 52:3	
a Jerusalem, and pitched *a*	Jer 52:4	5921
built forts *a* it round about	Jer 52:4	5921
my bones, and it prevaileth *a* them	Lam 1:13	
a me to crush my young men	Lam 1:15	5921
I have rebelled *a* his commandment	Lam 1:18	
he burned *a* Jacob like a flaming	Lam 2:3	
have opened their mouth *a* thee	Lam 2:16	5921
Surely *a* me is he turned	Lam 3:3	
turneth his hand *a* me all the day	Lam 3:3	
He hath builded *a* me, and	Lam 3:5	5921
have opened their mouths *a* us	Lam 3:46	5921
and all their imaginations *a* me	Lam 3:60	
and all their imaginations *a* me	Lam 3:61	5921
lips of those that rose up *a* me	Lam 3:62	
their device *a* me all the day	Lam 3:62	5921
thou art very wroth *a* us	Lam 5:22	5921
wheels were lifted up over *a* them	Eze 1:20	5980
wheels were lifted up over *a* them	Eze 1:21	5980
nation that hath rebelled *a* me	Eze 2:3	
fathers have transgressed *a* me	Eze 2:3	
thy face strong *a* their faces	Eze 3:8	5980
forehead strong *a* their foreheads	Eze 3:8	5980
noise of the wheels over *a* them	Eze 3:13	5980
And lay siege *a* it, and build a	Eze 4:2	5921
a it, and cast a mount *a* it	Eze 4:2	5921
set the camp also *a* it, and set	Eze 4:2	5921
battering rams *a* it round about	Eze 4:2	5921
and set thy face *a* it, and it shall	Eze 4:3	413
and thou shalt lay siege *a* it	Eze 4:3	5921
and thou shalt prophesy *a* it	Eze 4:7	5921
am *a* thee, and will execute	Eze 5:8	5921
of Israel, and prophesy *a* them	Eze 6:2	413
Therefore prophesy *a* them	Eze 11:4	5921
prophesy *a* the prophets of Israel	Eze 13:2	413
therefore, behold, I am *a* you	Eze 13:8	413
set thy face *a* the daughters of	Eze 13:17	413
and prophesy thou *a* them,	Eze 13:17	5921
I am *a* your pillows, wherewith ye	Eze 13:20	413
And I will set my face *a* that man	Eze 14:8	
when the land sinneth *a* me by	Eze 14:13	
And I will set my face *a* them	Eze 15:7	
LORD, when I set my face *a* them	Eze 15:7	
gather them round about *a* thee	Eze 16:37	5921
also bring up a company *a* thee	Eze 16:40	5921
shall use this proverb *a* thee	Eze 16:44	5921
But he rebelled *a* him in sending	Eze 17:15	
that he hath trespassed *a* me	Eze 17:20	
Then the nations set *a* him on	Eze 19:8	5921
But they rebelled *a* me, and would	Eze 20:8	
to accomplish my anger *a* them in	Eze 20:8	
rebelled *a* me in the wilderness	Eze 20:13	
the children rebelled *a* me	Eze 20:21	
my anger *a* them in the wilderness	Eze 20:21	
have committed a trespass *a* me	Eze 20:27	
and them that transgress *a* me	Eze 20:38	
prophesy *a* the forest of the	Eze 20:46	413
prophesy *a* the land of Israel,	Eze 21:2	413
Behold, I am *a* thee, and will draw	Eze 21:3	413
go forth out of his sheath *a* all	Eze 21:4	413
of the sword *a* all their gates	Eze 21:15	5921
battering rams *a* the gates	Eze 21:22	5921
I will blow *a* thee in the fire of	Eze 21:31	5921
maketh idols *a* herself to defile	Eze 22:3	5921
I will raise up thy lovers *a* thee	Eze 23:22	5921
I will bring them *a* thee on every	Eze 23:22	5921
they shall come *a* thee with	Eze 23:24	5921
which shall set *a* thee buckler	Eze 23:24	5921
And I will set my jealousy *a* thee	Eze 23:25	
himself *a* Jerusalem this same day	Eze 24:2	413
set thy face *a* the Ammonites, and	Eze 25:2	413
the Ammonites, and prophesy *a* them	Eze 25:2	5921
a my sanctuary, when it was	Eze 25:3	413
a the land of Israel, when it was	Eze 25:3	413
a the house of Judah, when they	Eze 25:3	413
thy despite *a* the land of Israel	Eze 25:6	413
a the house of Judah by taking	Eze 25:12	
that Tyrus hath said *a* Jerusalem	Eze 26:2	5921
Behold, I am *a* thee, O Tyrus, and	Eze 26:3	5921
many nations to come up *a* thee	Eze 26:3	5921
and he shall make a fort *a* thee	Eze 26:8	5921
and cast a mount *a* thee	Eze 26:8	5921
and lift up the buckler *a* thee	Eze 26:8	5921
set engines of war *a* thy walls	Eze 26:9	
their voice to be heard *a* thee	Eze 27:30	5921
swords *a* the beauty of thy wisdom	Eze 28:7	5921
a Zidon, and prophesy *a* it	Eze 28:21	5921
Behold, I am *a* thee, O Zidon	Eze 28:22	5921
set thy face *a* Pharaoh king of	Eze 29:2	5921
a him, and *a* all Egypt	Eze 29:2	5921
Behold, I am *a* thee, Pharaoh king	Eze 29:3	5921
Behold, therefore I am *a* thee	Eze 29:10	413
a thy rivers, and I will make the	Eze 29:10	413
to serve a great service *a* Tyrus	Eze 29:18	413
service that he had served *a* it	Eze 29:18	5921
labour wherewith he served *a* it	Eze 29:20	
shall draw their swords *a* Egypt	Eze 30:11	5921
I am *a* Pharaoh king of Egypt, and	Eze 30:22	413
are talking *a* thee by the walls	Eze 33:30	
prophesy *a* the shepherds of	Eze 34:2	5921
Behold, I am *a* the shepherds	Eze 34:10	413
of man, set thy face *a* mount Seir	Eze 35:2	5921
mount Seir, and prophesy *a* it	Eze 35:2	5921
Behold, O mount Seir, I am *a* thee	Eze 35:3	413
will stretch out mine hand *a* thee	Eze 35:3	5921
used out of thy hatred *a* them	Eze 35:11	
which thou hast spoken *a* the	Eze 35:12	5921
your mouth ye have boasted *a* me	Eze 35:13	5921
have multiplied your words *a* me	Eze 35:13	5921
Because the enemy hath said *a* you	Eze 36:2	5921
a the residue of the heathen	Eze 36:5	5921
and *a* all Idumea, which have	Eze 36:5	5921
Son of man, set thy face *a* Gog	Eze 38:2	413
and Tubal, and prophesy *a* him	Eze 38:2	5921
Behold, I am *a* thee, O Gog, the	Eze 38:3	413
a the mountains of Israel, which	Eze 38:8	5921
thou shalt come up *a* my people of	Eze 38:16	5921
and I will bring thee *a* my land	Eze 38:16	5921
that I would bring thee *a* them	Eze 38:17	5921
shall come *a* the land of Israel	Eze 38:18	5921
I will call for a sword *a* him	Eze 38:21	5921
sword shall be *a* his brother	Eze 38:21	
And I will plead *a* him with	Eze 38:22	
thou son of man, prophesy *a* Gog	Eze 39:1	5921

Behold, I am *a* thee, O Gog, the	Eze 39:1	413
because they trespassed *a* me	Eze 39:23	
whereby they have trespassed *a* me	Eze 39:26	
and twenty cubits, door *a* door	Eze 40:13	5048
by the side of the gates over *a*	Eze 40:18	5980
over *a* the gate toward the north	Eze 40:23	5048
a the separate place which was	Eze 41:15	6440
over *a* the door, cieled with wood	Eze 41:16	5048
was over *a* the separate place	Eze 42:1	5048
Over *a* the twenty cubits which	Eze 42:3	5048
over *a* the pavement which was for	Eze 42:3	5048
was gallery *a* gallery in three	Eze 42:3	
was without over *a* the chambers	Eze 42:7	5980
over *a* the separate place	Eze 42:10	6440
and over *a* the building	Eze 42:10	6440
have I lifted up mine hand *a* them	Eze 44:12	5921
over *a* the oblation of the holy	Eze 45:6	5980
be over *a* one of the portions	Eze 45:7	5980
in, but shall go forth over *a* it	Eze 46:9	5227
till a man come over *a* Hamath	Eze 47:20	
over *a* the border of the priests	Eze 48:13	5980
in the breadth over *a* the five	Eze 48:15	
over *a* the oblation of the holy	Eze 48:18	5980
it shall be over *a* the oblation	Eze 48:18	5980
over *a* the five and twenty	Eze 48:21	
and westward over *a* the five	Eze 48:21	
over *a* the portions for the	Eze 48:21	5980
his visage was changed *a* Shadrach	Dan 3:19	5922
thing amiss *a* the God of Shadrach	Dan 3:29	5922
wrote over *a* the candlestick upon	Dan 5:5	6903
and his knees smote one *a* another	Dan 5:6	
up thyself *a* the Lord of heaven	Dan 5:23	5922
a Daniel concerning the kingdom	Dan 6:4	
find any occasion *a* this Daniel	Dan 6:5	5922
except we find it *a* him	Dan 6:5	
the saints, and prevailed *a* them	Dan 7:21	
speak great words *a* the most High	Dan 7:25	6655
and he was moved with choler *a* him	Dan 8:7	413
an host was given him *a* the daily	Dan 8:12	5921
stand up *a* the Prince of princes	Dan 8:25	5921
that they have trespassed *a* thee	Dan 9:7	
because we have sinned *a* thee	Dan 9:8	
though we have rebelled *a* him	Dan 9:9	
God, because we have sinned *a* him	Dan 9:11	
his words, which he spake *a* us	Dan 9:12	5921
a our judges that judged us, by	Dan 9:12	5921
stir up all *a* the realm of Grecia	Dan 11:2	
the north, and shall deal *a* them	Dan 11:7	
stand up *a* the king of the south	Dan 11:14	5921
But he that cometh *a* him shall do	Dan 11:16	413
his devices *a* the strong holds	Dan 11:24	5921
his courage *a* the king of the	Dan 11:25	5921
they shall forecast devices *a* him	Dan 11:25	5921
shall be *a* the holy covenant	Dan 11:28	5921
ships of Chittim shall come *a* him	Dan 11:30	
have indignation *a* the holy	Dan 11:30	5921
such as do wickedly *a* the	Dan 11:32	
things *a* the God of gods, and	Dan 11:36	5921
shall come *a* him like a whirlwind	Dan 11:40	5921
increased, so they sinned *a* me	Hos 4:7	
dealt treacherously *a* the LORD	Hos 5:7	
they dealt treacherously *a* me	Hos 6:7	
they have transgressed *a* me	Hos 7:13	
yet they have spoken lies *a* me	Hos 7:13	5921
corn and wine, and they rebel *a* me	Hos 7:14	
yet do they imagine mischief *a* me	Hos 7:15	413
an eagle *a* the house of the LORD	Hos 8:1	5921
covenant, and trespassed *a* my law	Hos 8:1	5921
mine anger is kindled *a* them	Hos 8:5	
the battle in Gibeah *a* the	Hos 10:9	5921
people shall be gathered *a* them	Hos 10:10	5921
for she hath rebelled *a* her God	Hos 13:16	
for the violence *a* the children	Joel 3:19	
and I will turn mine hand *a* Ekron	Amos 1:8	5921
that the LORD hath spoken *a* you	Amos 3:1	5921
a the whole family which I	Amos 3:1	5921
this word which I take up *a* you	Amos 5:1	5921
the spoiled *a* the strong, so that	Amos 5:9	5921
spoiled shall come *a* the fortress	Amos 5:9	5921
I will raise up *a* you a nation	Amos 6:14	5921
I will rise *a* the house of	Amos 7:9	5921
Amos hath conspired *a* thee in the	Amos 7:10	5921
sayest, Prophesy not *a* Israel	Amos 7:16	5921
drop not thy word *a* the house of	Amos 7:16	5921
and let us rise up *a* her in battle	Obad 1	5921
thee, and prevailed *a* thee	Obad 7	
For thy violence *a* thy brother	Obad 10	
that great city, and cry *a* it	Jonah 1:2	5921
and was tempestuous *a* them	Jonah 1:13	5921
let the Lord GOD be witness *a* you	Mic 1:2	
a this family do I devise an evil	Mic 2:3	5921
shall one take up a parable *a* you	Mic 2:4	5921
they even prepare war *a* him	Mic 3:5	5921
not lift up a sword *a* nation	Mic 4:3	413
many nations are gathered *a* thee	Mic 4:11	5921
he hath laid siege *a* us	Mic 5:1	5921
we raise *a* him seven shepherds	Mic 5:5	5921
testify *a* me	Mic 6:3	
daughter riseth up *a* her mother	Mic 7:6	
in law *a* her mother in law	Mic 7:6	
Rejoice not *a* me, O mine enemy	Mic 7:8	
LORD, because I have sinned *a* him	Mic 7:9	
What do ye imagine *a* the LORD	Nah 1:9	413
that imagineth evil *a* the LORD	Nah 1:11	5921
they shall justle one *a* another	Nah 2:4	
Behold, I am *a* thee, saith the	Nah 2:13	413
Behold, I am *a* thee, saith the	Nah 3:5	413
all these take up a parable *a* him	Hab 2:6	5921
and a taunting proverb *a*	Hab 2:6	
people, and hast sinned *a* thy soul	Hab 2:10	
the LORD displeased *a* the rivers	Hab 3:8	
was thine anger *a* the rivers	Hab 3:8	
was thy wrath *a* the sea, that	Hab 3:8	
alarm *a* the fenced cities	Zeph 1:16	5921
and *a* the high towers	Zeph 1:16	5921
they have sinned *a* the LORD	Zeph 1:17	
the word of the LORD is *a* you	Zeph 2:5	5921
themselves *a* their border	Zeph 2:8	5921
magnified themselves *a* the people	Zeph 2:10	5921
stretch out his hand *a* the north	Zeph 2:13	5921
thou hast transgressed *a* me	Zeph 3:11	
a which thou hast had indignation	Zec 1:12	
evil *a* his brother in your heart	Zec 7:10	
all men every one *a* his neighbour	Zec 8:10	
in your hearts *a* his neighbour	Zec 8:17	
a thy sons, O Greece, and made	Zec 9:13	5921
anger was kindled *a* the shepherds	Zec 10:3	5921
both *a* Judah and *a* Jerusalem	Zec 12:2	5921
earth be gathered together *a* it	Zec 12:3	5921
do not magnify themselves *a* Judah	Zec 12:7	5921
the nations that come *a* Jerusalem	Zec 12:9	5921
a my shepherd, and *a* the man	Zec 13:7	5921
all nations *a* Jerusalem to battle	Zec 14:2	413
fight *a* those nations, as when he	Zec 14:3	
that have fought *a* Jerusalem	Zec 14:12	5921
his hand shall rise up *a* the hand	Zec 14:13	5921
of all the nations which came *a*	Zec 14:16	5921
The people *a* whom the LORD hath	Mal 1:4	
every man *a* his brother, by	Mal 2:10	
thy youth, *a* whom thou hast dealt	Mal 2:14	
a the wife of his youth	Mal 2:15	
a swift witness *a* the sorcerers	Mal 3:5	
a the adulterers, and *a*	Mal 3:5	
a those that oppress the hireling	Mal 3:5	
Your words have been stout *a* me	Mal 3:13	5921
have we spoken so much *a* thee	Mal 3:13	5921
time thou dash thy foot *a* a stone	Mt 4:6	4314
all manner of evil *a* you falsely	Mt 5:11	2596
thy brother hath ought *a* thee	Mt 5:23	2596
gave them power *a* unclean spirits	Mt 10:1	
my sake, for a testimony *a* them	Mt 10:18	
shall rise up *a* their parents	Mt 10:21	1909
a man at variance *a* his father	Mt 10:35	2596
and the daughter *a* her mother	Mt 10:35	2596
in law *a* her mother in law	Mt 10:35	2596
went out, and held a council *a* him	Mt 12:14	2596
Every kingdom divided *a* itself is	Mt 12:25	2596
divided *a* itself shall not stand	Mt 12:25	2596
Satan, he is divided *a* himself	Mt 12:26	1909
He that is not with me is *a* me	Mt 12:30	2596
but the blasphemy *a* the Holy	Mt 12:31	
speaketh a word *a* the Son of man	Mt 12:32	2596
speaketh *a* the Holy Ghost	Mt 12:32	2596
of hell shall not prevail *a* it	Mt 16:18	2729
thy brother shall trespass *a* thee	Mt 18:15	1519
how oft shall my brother sin *a* me	Mt 18:21	1519
they murmured *a* the goodman of	Mt 20:11	2596
indignation *a* the two brethren	Mt 20:24	4012
Go into the village over *a* you	Mt 21:2	561
up the kingdom of heaven *a* men	Mt 23:13	1715
For nation shall rise *a* nation	Mt 24:7	1909
and kingdom *a* kingdom	Mt 24:7	1909
Are ye come out as *a* a thief with	Mt 26:55	1909
sought false witness *a* Jesus	Mt 26:59	2596
is it which these witness *a* thee	Mt 26:62	2649
a Jesus to put him to death	Mt 27:1	2596
many things they witness *a* thee	Mt 27:13	
sitting over *a* the sepulchre	Mt 27:61	561
counsel with the Herodians *a* him	Mk 3:6	2596
if a kingdom be divided *a* itself	Mk 3:24	1909
And if a house be divided *a* itself	Mk 3:25	1909
And if Satan rise up *a* himself	Mk 3:26	1909
a the Holy Ghost hath never	Mk 3:29	1519
your feet for a testimony *a* them	Mk 6:11	
Herodias had a quarrel *a* him	Mk 6:19	
that is not *a* us is on our part	Mk 9:40	2596
committeth adultery *a* her	Mk 10:11	1909
way into the village over *a* you	Mk 11:2	2713
forgive, if ye have ought *a* any	Mk 11:25	2596
he had spoken the parable *a* them	Mk 12:12	4314
And Jesus sat over *a* the treasury	Mk 12:41	2713
mount of Olives over *a* the temple	Mk 13:3	2713
For nation shall rise *a* nation	Mk 13:8	1909
and kingdom *a* kingdom	Mk 13:8	1909
my sake, for a testimony *a* them	Mk 13:9	
shall rise up *a* their parents	Mk 13:12	1909
And they murmured *a* her	Mk 14:5	1690
as *a* a thief, with swords and with	Mk 14:48	1909
a Jesus to put him to death	Mk 14:55	2596
For many bare false witness *a* him	Mk 14:56	2596
and bare false witness *a* him	Mk 14:57	2596
is it which these witness *a* thee	Mk 14:60	
many things they witness *a* thee	Mk 15:4	
centurion, which stood over *a* him	Mk 15:39	
a sign which shall be spoken *a*	Lk 2:34	483
time thou dash thy foot *a* a stone	Lk 4:11	4314
murmured *a* his disciples, saying,	Lk 5:30	4314
might find an accusation *a* him	Lk 6:7	
a which the stream did beat	Lk 6:49	4366
the counsel of God *a* themselves	Lk 7:30	1519
which is over *a* Galilee	Lk 8:26	495
your feet for a testimony *a* them	Lk 9:5	1909
for he that is not *a* us is for us	Lk 9:50	2596
on us, we do wipe off *a* you	Lk 10:11	
Every kingdom divided *a* itself is	Lk 11:17	1909
a house divided *a* a house falleth	Lk 11:17	1909
Satan also be divided *a* himself	Lk 11:18	1909
He that is not with me is *a* me	Lk 11:23	2596
speak a word *a* the Son of man	Lk 12:10	1519
but unto him that blasphemeth *a*	Lk 12:10	1519
three *a* two, and two *a* three	Lk 12:52	1909
father shall be divided *a* the son	Lk 12:53	1909
and the son *a* the father	Lk 12:53	1909
the mother *a* the daughter	Lk 12:53	1909
and the daughter *a* the mother	Lk 12:53	1909
the mother in law *a* her daughter	Lk 12:53	1909
in law *a* her mother in law	Lk 12:53	1909
going to make war *a* another king	Lk 14:31	
to meet him that cometh *a* him	Lk 14:31	1909
Father, I have sinned *a* heaven	Lk 15:18	1519
Father, I have sinned *a* heaven	Lk 15:21	1519
If thy brother trespass *a* thee	Lk 17:3	1519
if he trespass *a* thee seven times	Lk 17:4	1519
Go ye into the village over *a* you	Lk 19:30	2713
he had spoken this parable *a* them	Lk 20:19	4314
them, Nation shall rise *a* nation	Lk 21:10	1909
and kingdom *a* kingdom	Lk 21:10	1909
as *a* a thief, with swords and	Lk 22:52	1909
ye stretched forth no hands *a* me	Lk 22:53	1909
blasphemously spake they *a* him	Lk 22:65	1519
a the day of my burying hath she	Jn 12:7	1519
me hath lifted up his heel *a* me	Jn 13:18	1519
that we have need of *a* the feast	Jn 13:29	
accusation bring ye *a* this man	Jn 18:29	2596
have no power at all *a* me	Jn 19:11	2596
himself a king speaketh *a* Caesar	Jn 19:12	483
them, they could say nothing *a* it	Acts 4:14	471
a the Lord, and *a* his Christ	Acts 4:26	2596
For of a truth *a* thy holy child	Acts 4:27	1909
ye be found even to fight *a* God	Acts 5:39	
of the Grecians *a* the Hebrews	Acts 6:1	4314
words *a* Moses, and *a* God	Acts 6:11	
words *a* this holy place, and the	Acts 6:13	2596
a the church which was at	Acts 8:1	1909
slaughter *a* the disciples of the	Acts 9:1	1519
for thee to kick *a* the pricks	Acts 9:5	4314
Jesus, and disputed *a* the Grecians	Acts 9:29	4314
spake *a* those things which were	Acts 13:45	483
and raised persecution *a* Paul	Acts 13:50	1909
off the dust of their feet *a* them	Acts 13:51	1909
evil affected *a* the brethren	Acts 14:2	2596
multitude rose up together *a* them	Acts 16:22	2596
with one accord *a* Paul, and	Acts 18:12	
them, and prevailed *a* them	Acts 19:16	2596
these things cannot be spoken *a*	Acts 19:36	368
with him, have a matter *a* any man	Acts 19:38	4314
and came the next day over *a* Chios	Acts 20:15	481
all men every where *a* the people	Acts 21:28	2596
wherefore they cried so *a* him	Acts 22:24	2019
to him, let us not fight *a* God	Acts 23:9	
before thee what they had *a* him	Acts 23:30	4314
who informed the governor *a* Paul	Acts 24:1	2596
and object, if they had ought *a* me	Acts 24:19	4314
of the Jews informed him *a* Paul	Acts 25:2	2596
And desired favour *a* him, that he	Acts 25:3	2596
and grievous complaints *a* Paul	Acts 25:7	2596
Neither *a* the law of the Jews,	Acts 25:8	1519
a the temple, nor yet *a* Caesar	Acts 25:8	1519
desiring to have judgment *a* him	Acts 25:15	2596
concerning the crime laid *a* him	Acts 25:16	
A whom when the accusers stood up	Acts 25:18	4012
But had certain questions *a* him	Acts 25:19	4314
to signify the crimes laid *a* him	Acts 25:27	2596
to death, I gave my voice *a* them	Acts 26:10	2702
and being exceedingly mad *a* them	Acts 26:11	1693
for thee to kick *a* the pricks	Acts 26:14	4314
and scarce were come over *a* Cnidus	Acts 27:7	2596
under Crete, over *a* Salmone	Acts 27:7	2596
arose *a* it a tempestuous wind	Acts 27:14	2596
committed nothing *a* the people	Acts 28:17	1727
But when the Jews spake *a* it	Acts 28:19	483
that every where it is spoken *a*	Acts 28:22	483
from heaven *a* all ungodliness	Rom 1:18	1909
use into that which is *a* nature	Rom 1:26	3844
of God is according to truth *a*	Rom 2:2	1909
thyself wrath *a* the day of wrath	Rom 2:5	1722
Who *a* hope believed in hope, that	Rom 4:18	3844
warring *a* the law of my mind, and	Rom 7:23	497
the carnal mind is enmity *a* God	Rom 8:7	1519
If God be for us, who can be *a* us	Rom 8:31	2596
who art thou that repliest *a* God	Rom 9:20	470
intercession to God *a* Israel	Rom 11:2	2596
Boast not *a* the branches	Rom 11:18	2620
be puffed up for one *a* another	1Cor 4:6	2596
of you, having a matter *a* another	1Cor 6:1	4314
sinneth *a* his own body	1Cor 6:18	1519
But when ye sin so *a* the brethren	1Cor 8:12	1519
weak conscience, ye sin *a* Christ	1Cor 8:12	1519
but if *a* my will, a dispensation	1Cor 9:17	210
I think to be bold *a* some	2Cor 10:2	1909
itself *a* the knowledge of God	2Cor 10:5	2596
For we can do nothing *a* the truth	2Cor 13:8	2596
Is the law then *a* the promises of	Gal 3:21	2596
the flesh lusteth *a* the Spirit	Gal 5:17	2596
and the Spirit *a* the flesh	Gal 5:17	2596
a such there is no law	Gal 5:23	2596
to stand *a* the wiles of the devil	Eph 6:11	4314
For we wrestle not *a* flesh	Eph 6:12	4314
but *a* principalities, *a* powers	Eph 6:12	4314
a the rulers of the darkness of	Eph 6:12	4314
a spiritual wickedness in high	Eph 6:12	4314
of ordinances that was *a* us	Col 2:14	2596
if any man have a quarrel *a* any	Col 3:13	4314
wives, and be not bitter *a* them	Col 3:19	4314
have begun to wax wanton *a* Christ	1Ti 5:11	2691
A an elder receive not an	1Ti 5:19	2596
foundation *a* the time to come	1Ti 6:19	1519
committed unto him *a* that day	2Ti 1:12	1519
of sinners *a* himself, lest ye be	Heb 12:3	1519
unto blood, striving *a* sin	Heb 12:4	4314
and mercy rejoiceth *a* judgment	Jas 2:13	2620
glory not, and lie not *a* the truth	Jas 3:14	2596
of them shall be a witness *a* you	Jas 5:3	
Grudge not one *a* another,	Jas 5:9	2596
lusts, which war *a* the soul	1Pet 2:11	2596
they speak *a* you as evildoers	1Pet 2:12	1909
the Lord is *a* them that do evil	1Pet 3:12	1909
accusation *a* them before the Lord	2Pet 2:11	2596
reserved unto fire *a* the day of	2Pet 3:7	1519
prating *a* us with malicious words	3Jn 10	5396
durst not bring *a* him a railing	Jude 9	2018
ungodly sinners have spoken *a* him	Jude 15	2596

I have somewhat *a* thee, because Rev 2:4 2596
But I have a few things *a* thee Rev 2:14 2596
will fight *a* them with the sword Rev 2:16 3326
I have a few things *a* thee Rev 2:20 2596
pit shall make war *a* them Rev 11:7 3326
and his angels fought *a* the dragon Rev 12:7 2596
his mouth in blasphemy *a* God Rev 13:6 4314
war *a* him that sat on the horse Rev 19:19 3326
sat on the horse, and *a* his army Rev 19:19 3326

AGAR (*a'-gar*) See HAGAR. *Greek form of Hagar.*
gendereth to bondage, which is *A* Gal 4:24 28
For this *A* is mount Sinai in Gal 4:25 28

AGATE
And the third row a ligure, an *a* Ex 28:19 7618
And the third row, a ligure, an *a* Ex 39:12 7618
and fine linen, and coral, and *a* Eze 27:16 3539

AGATES
And I will make thy windows of *a* Is 54:12 3539

AGE
shalt be buried in a good old *a* Gen 15:15 7872
were old and well stricken in *a* Gen 18:11 3117
bare Abraham a son in his old *a* Gen 21:2
have born him a son in his old *a* Gen 21:7
was old, and well stricken in *a* Gen 24:1 3117
ghost, and died in a good old *a* Gen 25:8 7872
he was the son of his old *a* Gen 37:3
old man, and a child of his old *a* Gen 44:20
so the whole *a* of Jacob was an Gen 47:28 3117
the eyes of Israel were dim for *a* Gen 48:10 2207
from the *a* of fifty years they Num 8:25 1121
Joshua waxed old and stricken in *a* Josh 23:1 3117
them, I am old and stricken in *a* Josh 23:2 3117
son of Joash died in a good old *a* Judg 8:32 7872
and a nourisher of thine old *a* Ruth 4:15 7872
die in the flower of their *a* 1Sa 2:33 582
eyes were set by reason of his *a* 1Kin 14:4 7869
in the time of his old *a* he was 1Kin 15:23
from the *a* of thirty years 1Chr 23:3 1121
from the *a* of twenty years and 1Chr 23:24 1121
And he died in a good old *a* 1Chr 29:28 7872
man, or him that stooped for *a* 2Chr 36:17 3485
come to thy grave in a full *a* Job 5:26 3624
I pray thee, of the former *a* Job 8:8 1755
thine *a* shall be clearer than the Job 11:17 2465
in whom old *a* was perished Job 30:2 3624
mine *a* is as nothing before thee Ps 39:5 2465
me not off in the time of old *a* Ps 71:9
still bring forth fruit in old *a* Ps 92:14 7872
Mine *a* is departed, and is removed Is 38:12 1755
And even to your old *a* I am he Is 46:4 2209
his staff in his hand for very *a* Zec 8:4 3117
she was of the *a* of twelve years Mk 5:42
also conceived a son in her old *a* Lk 1:36
she was of a great *a*, and had Lk 2:36 2250
to be about thirty years of *a* Lk 3:23
daughter, about twelve years of *a* Lk 8:42 2244
he is of *a* Jn 9:21 2244
said his parents, He is of *a* Jn 9:23 2244
if she pass the flower of her *a* 1Cor 7:36 5230
to them that are of full *a* Heb 5:14 5046
of a child when she was past *a* Heb 11:11 2244

AGED
Now Barzillai was a very *a* man 2Sa 19:32 2204
away the understanding of the *a* Job 12:20 2205
both the grayheaded and very *a* men Job 15:10 3453
and the *a* arose, and stood up Job 29:8 2205
neither do the *a* understand Job 32:9 2205
the *a* with him that is full of Jer 6:11 2205
That the *a* men be sober, grave, Titus 2:2 4246
The *a* women likewise, that they Titus 2:3 4247
being such an one as Paul the *a* Philem 9 4246

AGEE (*ag'-ee*) *Father of a "mighty man" of David.*
Shammah the son of *A* the Hararite 2Sa 23:11 89

AGES
That in the *a* to come he might Eph 2:7 165
Which in other *a* was not made Eph 3:5 1074
by Christ Jesus throughout all *a* Eph 3:21 1074
which hath been hid from *a* Col 1:26 165

AGO
asses that were lost three days *a* 1Sa 9:20 3117
heard long *a* how I have done it 2Kin 19:25 7350
was builded these many years *a* Ezr 5:11 6928
unto him that fashioned it long *a* Is 22:11 7350
Hast thou not heard long *a* Is 37:26 7350
have repented long *a* in sackcloth Mt 11:21 3819
How long is it *a* since this came Mk 9:21
they had a great while *a* repented Lk 10:13 3819
Four days *a* I was fasting until Acts 10:30 575
while *a* God made choice among us Acts 15:7 575
but also to be forward a year *a* 2Cor 8:10 575
that Achaia was ready a year *a* 2Cor 9:2 575
in Christ above fourteen years *a* 2Cor 12:2 4253

AGONE
because three days *a* I fell sick 1Sa 30:13

AGONY
being in an *a* he prayed more Lk 22:44 74

AGREE
A with thine adversary quickly, Mt 5:25 2132
That if two of you shall *a* on Mt 18:19 4856
didst not thou *a* with me for a Mt 20:13 4856
so did their witness *a* together Mk 14:59 2470
to this *a* the words of the Acts 15:15 4856
and these three *a* in one 1Jn 5:8 1526
to fulfil his will, and to *a* Rev 17:17

AGREED
walk together, except they be *a* Amos 3:3 3259
when he had *a* with the labourers Mt 20:2 4856
but their witness *a* not together Mk 14:56 2470
for the Jews had *a* already Jn 9:22 4934
How is it that ye have *a* together Acts 5:9 4856
And to him they *a* Acts 5:40 3982
The Jews have *a* to desire thee Acts 23:20 4934
when they *a* not among themselves, Acts 28:25 800

AGREEMENT
Make an *a* with me by a present, 2Kin 18:31
death, and with hell are we at *a* Is 28:15 2374
your *a* with hell shall not stand Is 28:18 2380
Make an *a* with me by a present, Is 36:16
king of the north to make an *a* Dan 11:6 4339
what *a* hath the temple of God 2Cor 6:16 4783

AGREETH
and thy speech *a* thereto Mk 14:70 3662
out of the new *a* not with the old Lk 5:36 4856

AGRIPPA (*ag-rip'-pah*) *Great-grandson of Herod the Great.*
And after certain days king *A* Acts 25:13 67
Then *A* said unto Festus, I would Acts 25:22 67
when *A* was come, and Bernice, with Acts 25:23 67
And Festus said, King *A*, and all Acts 25:24 67
specially before thee, O king *A* Acts 25:26 67
Then *A* said unto Paul, Thou art Acts 26:1 67
I think myself happy, king *A* Acts 26:2 67
For which hope's sake, king *A* Acts 26:7 67
Whereupon, O king *A*, I was not Acts 26:19 67
King *A*, believest thou the Acts 26:27 67
Then *A* said unto Paul, Almost Acts 26:28 67
Then said *A* unto Festus, This man Acts 26:32 67

AGROUND
two seas met, they ran the ship *a* Acts 27:41 2027

AGUE
consumption, and the burning *a* Lev 26:16 6920

AGUR (*a'-gur*) *Son of Jakeh.*
The words of *A* the son of Jakeh, Prov 30:1 94

AH
them not say in their hearts, *A* Ps 35:25 253
A sinful nation, a people laden Is 1:4 1945
the mighty One of Israel, *A* Is 1:24 1945
Then said I, *A*, Lord GOD Jer 1:6 162
Then said I, *A*, Lord GOD Jer 4:10 162
Then said I, *A*, Lord GOD Jer 14:13 162
for him, saying, *A* my brother Jer 22:18 1945
or, *A* sister Jer 22:18 1945
lament for him, saying, *A* lord Jer 22:18 1945
or, *A* his glory Jer 22:18 1945
A Lord GOD Jer 32:17 162
will lament thee, saying, *A* lord Jer 34:5 1945
Then said I, *A* Lord GOD Eze 4:14 162
and cried, and said, *A* Lord GOD Eze 9:8 162
a loud voice, and said, *A* Lord GOD Eze 11:13 162
Then said I, *A* Lord GOD Eze 20:49 162
a! it is made bright Eze 21:15 253
wagging their heads, and saying, *A* Mk 15:29 3758

AHA
wide against me, and said, *A*, *a* Ps 35:21 253
shame that say unto me, *A*, *a* Ps 40:15 253
of their shame that say, *A*, *a* Ps 70:3 253
he warmeth himself, and saith, *A* Is 44:16 253
Because thou saidst, *A*, against Eze 25:3 253
hath said against Jerusalem, *A* Eze 26:2 253
enemy hath said against you, *A* Eze 36:2 253

AHAB (*a'-hab*) See AHAB'S.
1. A king of Israel.
A his son reigned in his stead 1Kin 16:28 256
A the son of Omri to reign over 1Kin 16:29 256
A the son of Omri reigned over 1Kin 16:29 256
A the son of Omri did evil in the 1Kin 16:30 256
And *A* made a grove 1Kin 16:33 256
A did more to provoke the LORD 1Kin 16:33 256
of Gilead, said unto *A*, As the 1Kin 17:1 256
saying, Go, shew thyself unto *A* 1Kin 18:1 256
went to shew himself unto *A* 1Kin 18:2 256
A called Obadiah, which was the 1Kin 18:3 256
A said unto Obadiah, Go into the 1Kin 18:5 256
A went one way by himself, and 1Kin 18:6 256
thy servant into the hand of *A* 1Kin 18:9 256
and so when I come and tell *A* 1Kin 18:12 256
So Obadiah went to meet *A* 1Kin 18:16 256
and *A* went to meet Elijah 1Kin 18:16 256
when *A* saw Elijah, that *A* said 1Kin 18:17 256
So *A* sent unto all the children 1Kin 18:20 256
And Elijah said unto *A*, Get thee 1Kin 18:41 256
So *A* went up to eat and to drink 1Kin 18:42 256
And he said, Go up, say unto *A* 1Kin 18:44 256
A rode, and went to Jezreel 1Kin 18:45 256
ran before *A* to the entrance of 1Kin 18:46 256
A told Jezebel all that Elijah 1Kin 19:1 256
he sent messengers to *A* king of 1Kin 20:2 256
a prophet unto *A* king of Israel 1Kin 20:13 256
And *A* said, By whom 1Kin 20:14 256
Then said *A*, I will send thee 1Kin 20:34
the palace of *A* king of Samaria 1Kin 21:1 256
A spake unto Naboth, saying, Give 1Kin 21:2 256
And Naboth said to *A*, The LORD 1Kin 21:3 256
A came into his house heavy and 1Kin 21:4 256
was dead, that Jezebel said to *A* 1Kin 21:15 256
when *A* heard that Naboth was dead 1Kin 21:16 256
that *A* rose up to go down to the 1Kin 21:16 256
go down to meet *A* king of Israel 1Kin 21:18 256
A said to Elijah, Hast thou found 1Kin 21:20 256
will cut off from *A* him that 1Kin 21:21 256
Him that dieth of *A* in the city 1Kin 21:24 256
But there was none like unto *A* 1Kin 21:25 256
when *A* heard those words, that he 1Kin 21:27 256
Seest thou how *A* humbleth himself 1Kin 21:29 256
LORD said, Who shall persuade *A* 1Kin 22:20 256
Now the rest of the acts of *A* 1Kin 22:39 256
So *A* slept with his fathers 1Kin 22:40 256
fourth year of *A* king of Israel 1Kin 22:41 256
the son of *A* unto Jehoshaphat 1Kin 22:49 256
Ahaziah the son of *A* began to 1Kin 22:51 256
Israel after the death of *A* 2Kin 1:1 256
Now Jehoram the son of *A* began to 2Kin 3:1 256
when *A* was dead, that the king of 2Kin 3:5 256
Joram the son of *A* king of Israel 2Kin 8:16 256
of Israel, as did the house of *A* 2Kin 8:18 256
the daughter of *A* was his wife 2Kin 8:18 256
year of Joram the son of *A* king 2Kin 8:25 256
in the way of the house of *A* 2Kin 8:27 256
the LORD, as did the house of *A* 2Kin 8:27 256
the son in law of the house of *A* 2Kin 8:27 256
he went with Joram the son of *A* 2Kin 8:28 256
see Joram the son of *A* in Jezreel 2Kin 8:29 256
smite the house of *A* thy master 2Kin 9:7 256
the whole house of *A* shall perish 2Kin 9:8 256
I will cut off from *A* him that 2Kin 9:8 256
I will make the house of *A* like 2Kin 9:9 256
rode together after *A* his father 2Kin 9:25 256
year of Joram the son of *A* began 2Kin 9:29 256
A had seventy sons in Samaria 2Kin 10:1 256
spake concerning the house of *A* 2Kin 10:10 256
of the house of *A* in Jezreel 2Kin 10:11 256
that remained unto *A* in Samaria 2Kin 10:17 256
unto them, *A* served Baal a little 2Kin 10:18 256
hast done unto the house of *A* 2Kin 10:30 256
a grove, as did *A* king of Israel 2Kin 21:3 256
and the plummet of the house of *A* 2Kin 21:13 256
and joined affinity with *A* 2Chr 18:1 256
he went down to *A* to Samaria 2Chr 18:2 256
A killed sheep and oxen for him in 2Chr 18:2 256
A king of Israel said unto 2Chr 18:3 256
Who shall entice *A* king of Israel 2Chr 18:19 256
like as did the house of *A* 2Chr 21:6 256
he had the daughter of *A* to wife 2Chr 21:6 256
the whoredoms of the house of *A* 2Chr 21:13 256
in the ways of the house of *A* 2Chr 22:3 256
of the LORD like the house of *A* 2Chr 22:4 256
went with Jehoram the son of *A* 2Chr 22:5 256
Jehoram the son of *A* at Jezreel 2Chr 22:6 256
to cut off the house of *A* 2Chr 22:7 256
judgment upon the house of *A* 2Chr 22:8 256
all the works of the house of *A* Mic 6:16 256
2. A false prophet during the Exile.
of *A* the son of Kolaiah, and of Jer 29:21 256
make thee like Zedekiah and like *A* Jer 29:22 256

AHAB'S (*a'-habs*)
So she wrote letters in *A* name 1Kin 21:8 256
them that brought up *A* children 2Kin 10:1 256

AHARAH (*a-har'-ah*) See AHER, AHIRAM, EHI. *Third son of Benjamin.*
the second, and *A* the third, 1Chr 8:1 315

AHARHEL (*a-har'-hel*) *A descendant of Judah.*
the families of *A* the son of 1Chr 4:8 316

AHASAI (*a-ha'-sa-i*) *Family of returned exiles.*
the son of Azareel, the son of *A* Neh 11:13 273

AHASBAI (*a-has'-ba-i*) *Father of a "mighty man" of David.*
Eliphelet the son of *A*, the son 2Sa 23:34 308

AHASUERUS (*a-has-u-e'-rus*) See AHASUERUS'.
1. A Persian king, Cambyses.
And in the reign of *A*, in the Ezr 4:6 325
2. Father of Darius the Mede.
first year of Darius the son of *A* Dan 9:1 325
3. A king of Persia, Xerxes.
it came to pass in the days of *A* Est 1:1 325
(this is *A* which reigned from Est 1:1 325
when the king *A* sat on the throne Est 1:2 325
house which belonged to king *A* Est 1:9 325
in the presence of *A* the king Est 1:10 325
of the king *A* by the chamberlains Est 1:15 325
all the provinces of the king *A* Est 1:16 325
The king *A* commanded Vashti the Est 1:17 325
Vashti come no more before king *A* Est 1:19 325
the wrath of king *A* was appeased Est 2:1 325
turn was come to go in to king *A* Est 2:12 325
A into his house royal in the Est 2:16 325
sought to lay hand on the king *A* Est 2:21 325
king *A* promote Haman the son of Est 3:1 325
throughout the whole kingdom of *A* Est 3:6 325
in the twelfth year of king *A* Est 3:7 325
And Haman said unto king *A* Est 3:8 325
the name of king *A* was it written Est 3:12 325
sought to lay hand on the king *A* Est 6:2 325
Then the king *A* answered and said Est 7:5 325
On that day did the king *A* give Est 8:1 325
Then the king *A* said unto Esther Est 8:7 325
in all the provinces of king *A* Est 8:12 325
all the provinces of the king *A* Est 9:2 325
all the provinces of the king *A* Est 9:20 325
provinces of the kingdom of *A* Est 9:30 325
the king *A* laid a tribute upon Est 10:1 325
the Jew was next unto king *A* Est 10:3 325

AHASUERUS' (*a-has-u-e'-rus*) *Refers to Ahasuerus 3.*
And he wrote in the king *A* name Est 8:10 325

AHAVA (*a-ha'-vah*) See IVA. *A river of Babylon.*
to the river that runneth to *A* Ezr 8:15 163
a fast there, at the river of *A* Ezr 8:21 163
we departed from the river of *A* Ezr 8:31 163

AHAZ (*a'-haz*) See ACHAZ.
1. A king of Judah.
A his son reigned in his stead 2Kin 15:38 271

of Pekah the son of Remaliah A 2Kin 16:1 271
Twenty years old was A when he 2Kin 16:2 271
and they besieged A, but could not 2Kin 16:5 271
So A sent messengers to 2Kin 16:7 271
A took the silver and gold that 2Kin 16:8 271
king A went to Damascus to meet 2Kin 16:10 271
king A sent to Urijah the priest 2Kin 16:10 271
king A had sent from Damascus 2Kin 16:11 271
against king A came from Damascus 2Kin 16:11 271
king A commanded Urijah the 2Kin 16:15 271
to all that king A commanded 2Kin 16:16 271
king A cut off the borders of the 2Kin 16:17 271
of the acts of A which he did 2Kin 16:19 271
A slept with his fathers, and was 2Kin 16:20 271
In the twelfth year of A king of 2Kin 17:1 271
that Hezekiah the son of A king 2Kin 18:1 271
it had gone down in the dial of A 2Kin 20:11 271
the top of the upper chamber of A 2Kin 23:12 271
A his son, Hezekiah his son, 1Chr 3:13 271
A his son reigned in his stead 2Chr 27:9 271
A was twenty years old when he 2Chr 28:1 271
At that time did king A send unto 2Chr 28:16 271
low because of A king of Israel 2Chr 28:19 271
For A took away a portion out of 2Chr 28:21 271
this is that king A 2Chr 28:22 271
A gathered together the vessels 2Chr 28:24 271
A slept with his fathers, and they 2Chr 28:27 271
which king A in his reign did 2Chr 29:19 271
in the days of Uzziah, Jotham, A Is 1:1 271
the days of A the son of Jotham Is 7:1 271
Isaiah, Go forth now to meet A Is 7:3 271
the LORD spake again unto A Is 7:10 271
But A said, I will not ask, Is 7:12 271
that king A died was this burden Is 14:28 271
is gone down in the sun dial of A Is 38:8 271
in the days of Uzziah, Jotham, A Hos 1:1 271
in the days of Jotham, A, and Mic 1:1 271
2. A Benjaminite and relative of Saul.
Pithon, and Melech, and Tarea, and A. 1Chr 8:35 271
And A begat Jehoadah 1Chr 8:36 271
and Melech, and Tahrea, and A 1Chr 9:41
And A begat Jarah 1Chr 9:42 271

AHAZIAH (*a-haz-i'-ah*) See AZARIAH, JEHOAHAZ.
1. A king of Israel.
A his son reigned in his stead 1Kin 22:40 274
Then said A the son of Ahab unto 1Kin 22:49 274
A the son of Ahab began to reign 1Kin 22:51 274
A fell down through a lattice in 2Kin 1:2 274
of the acts of A which he did 2Kin 1:18 274
A his son, Joash his son, 1Chr 3:11 274
himself with A king of Israel 2Chr 20:35 274
thou hast joined thyself with A 2Chr 20:37 274
2. Son and successor of King Jehoram of Judah.
A his son reigned in his stead 2Kin 8:24 274
did A the son of Jehoram king of 2Kin 8:25 274
twenty years old was A when he 2Kin 8:26 274
A the son of Jehoram king of 2Kin 8:29 274
A king of Judah was come down to 2Kin 9:16 274
A king of Judah went out, each in 2Kin 9:21 274
his hands, and fled, and said to A 2Kin 9:23 274
There is treachery, O A 2Kin 9:23 274
But when A the king of Judah saw 2Kin 9:27 274
Ahab began A to reign over Judah 2Kin 9:29 274
the brethren of A king of Judah 2Kin 10:13 274
We are the brethren of A 2Kin 10:13 274
of A saw that her son was dead 2Kin 11:1 274
of king Joram, sister of A 2Kin 11:2 274
took Joash the son of A 2Kin 11:2 274
Jehoshaphat, and Jehoram, and A 2Kin 12:18 274
year of Joash the son of A king 2Kin 13:1 274
the son of Jehoash the son of A 2Kin 14:13 274
A his youngest son king in his 2Chr 22:1 274
So A the son of Jehoram king of 2Chr 22:1 274
two years old was A when he began 2Chr 22:2 274
the destruction of A was of God 2Chr 22:7 274
and the sons of the brethren of A 2Chr 22:8 274
that ministered to A 2Chr 22:8 274
And he sought A 2Chr 22:9 274
So the house of A had no power to 2Chr 22:9 274
of A saw that her son was dead 2Chr 22:10 274
the king, took Joash the son of A 2Chr 22:11 274
(for she was the sister of A 2Chr 22:11 274

AHBAN (*ah'-ban*) *A descendant of Pharez.*
was Abihail, and she bare him A 1Chr 2:29 257

AHER (*a'-hur*) See AHARAH. *A descendant of Benjamin.*
of Ir, and Hushim, the sons of A 1Chr 7:12 313

AHI (*a'-hi*)
1. A son of Abdiel.
A the son of Abdiel, the son of 1Chr 5:15 277
2. A chief of the Asherites.
A, and Rohgah, Jehubbah, and Aram 1Chr 7:34 277

AHIAH (*a-hi'-ah*) See AHIJAH.
1. Grandson of Phinehas.
And A, the son of Ahitub, 1Sa 14:3 281
And Saul said unto A, Bring hither 1Sa 14:18 281
2. A scribe of Solomon.
Elihoreph and A, the sons of 1Kin 4:3 281
3. A descendant of Benjamin.
And Naaman, and A, and Gera, he 1Chr 8:7 281

AHIAM (*a-hi'-am*) *Son of Shahar.*
A the son of Sharar the Hararite, 2Sa 23:33 279
A the son of Sacar the Hararite, 1Chr 11:35 279

AHIAN (*a-hi'-an*)
And the sons of Shemidah were, A 1Chr 7:19 291

AHIEZER (*a-hi-e'-zer*)
1. One who numbered the people.
A the son of Ammishaddai Num 1:12 295
shall be A the son of Ammishaddai Num 2:25 295
On the tenth day A the son of Num 7:66 295
of A the son of Ammishaddai Num 7:71 295
over his host was A the son of Num 10:25 295
2. A chief of the Benjamites.
The chief was A, then Joash, the 1Chr 12:3 295

AHIHUD (*a-hi'-hud*)
1. A prince of Asher.
of Asher, A the son of Shelomi Num 34:27 282
2. A Benjamite of the Ehud family.
removed them, and begat Uzza, and A 1Chr 8:7 284

AHIJAH (*a-hi'-jah*) See AHIAH, AHIMELECH.
1. A prophet during the reigns of Solomon and Rehoboam.
that the prophet A the Shilonite 1Kin 11:29 281
A caught the new garment that was 1Kin 11:30 281
which the LORD spake by A the 1Kin 12:15 281
there is A the prophet, which 1Kin 14:2 281
Shiloh, and came to the house of A 1Kin 14:4 281
But A could not see 1Kin 14:4 281
And the LORD said unto A, Behold, 1Kin 14:5 281
when A heard the sound of her 1Kin 14:6 281
hand of his servant A the prophet 1Kin 14:18 281
by his servant A the Shilonite 1Kin 15:29 281
the prophecy of A the Shilonite 2Chr 9:29 281
A the Shilonite to Jeroboam the 2Chr 10:15 281
2. Father of Baasha.
And Baasha the son of A, of the 1Kin 15:27 281
of A to reign over all Israel in 1Kin 15:33 281
the house of Baasha the son of A 1Kin 21:22 281
the house of Baasha the son of A 2Kin 9:9 281
3. Son of Jerahmeel.
and Oren, and Ozem, and A 1Chr 2:25 281
4. A "mighty man" of David.
the Mecherathite, A the Pelonite, 1Chr 11:36 281
5. A treasury official under David.
A was over the treasures of the 1Chr 26:20 281
6. A Levite who renewed the covenant.
And A, Hanan, Anan, Neh 10:26 281

AHIKAM (*a-hi'-kam*) *An officer in Josiah's court.*
A the son of Shaphan, and Achbor 2Kin 22:12 296
So Hilkiah the priest, and A 2Kin 22:14 296
he made Gedaliah the son of A 2Kin 25:22 296
A the son of Shaphan, and Abdon 2Chr 34:20 296
Nevertheless the hand of A the Jer 26:24 296
the son of A the son of Shaphan Jer 39:14 296
the son of A the son of Shaphan Jer 40:5 296
Gedaliah the son of A to Mizpah Jer 40:6 296
the son of A governor in the land Jer 40:7 296
Gedaliah the son of A the son of Jer 40:9 296
the son of A the son of Shaphan Jer 40:11 296
the son of A believed them not Jer 40:14 296
But Gedaliah the son of A said Jer 40:16 296
Gedaliah the son of A to Mizpah Jer 41:1 296
smote Gedaliah the son of A the Jer 41:2 296
Come to Gedaliah the son of A Jer 41:6 296
to Gedaliah the son of A Jer 41:10 296
had slain Gedaliah the son of A Jer 41:16 296
had slain Gedaliah the son of A Jer 41:18 296
the son of A the son of Shaphan Jer 43:6 296

AHILUD (*a-hi'-lud*) *Father of a recorder under David and Solomon.*
the son of A was recorder 2Sa 8:16 286
the son of A was recorder 2Sa 20:24 286
Jehoshaphat the son of A, the 1Kin 4:3 286
Baana the son of A 1Kin 4:12 286
and Jehoshaphat the son of A 1Chr 18:15 286

AHIMAAZ (*a-him'-a-az*)
1. Father of Ahinoam.
was Ahinoam, the daughter of A 1Sa 14:50 290
2. Son of Zadok.
A thy son, and Jonathan the son of 2Sa 15:27 290
A Zadok's son, and Jonathan 2Sa 15:36 290
Jonathan and A stayed by En-rogel 2Sa 17:17 290
the house, they said, Where is A 2Sa 17:20 290
Then said A the son of Zadok, Let 2Sa 18:19 290
Then said A the son of Zadok yet 2Sa 18:22 290
Then A ran by the way of the 2Sa 18:23 290
the running of A the son of Zadok 2Sa 18:27 290
A called, and said unto the king, 2Sa 18:28 290
A answered, When Joab sent the 2Sa 18:29 290
begat Zadok, and Zadok begat A 1Chr 6:8 290
A begat Azariah, and Azariah begat 1Chr 6:9 290
Zadok his son, A his son 1Chr 6:53 290
3. An officer of Solomon.
A was in Naphtali 1Kin 4:15 290

AHIMAN (*a-hi'-man*)
1. A giant of Anak.
where A, Sheshai, and Talmai, the Num 13:22 289
three sons of Anak, Sheshai, and A Josh 15:14 289
and they slew Sheshai, and A Judg 1:10 289
2. A Levite Temple servant.
and Akkub, and Talmon, and A 1Chr 9:17 289

AHIMELECH (*a-him'-el-ek*)
1. A priest.
came David to Nob to A the priest 1Sa 21:1 288
A was afraid at the meeting of 1Sa 21:1 288
And David said unto A the priest 1Sa 21:2 288
And David said unto A, And is there 1Sa 21:8 288
to Nob, to A the son of Ahitub 1Sa 22:9 288
king sent to call A the priest 1Sa 22:11 288
Then A answered the king, and said 1Sa 22:14 288
said, Thou shalt surely die, A 1Sa 22:16 288
the sons of A the son of Ahitub 1Sa 22:20 288
son of A fled to David to Keilah 1Sa 23:6 288
A the son of Abiathar, were the 2Sa 8:17 288
A of the sons of Ithamar, 1Chr 24:3 288
A the son of Abiathar, and before 1Chr 24:6 288
of David the king, and Zadok, and A 1Chr 24:31 288
David is come to the house of A Ps 52:*t* 288
2. A Hittite officer.
said to A the Hittite, and to 1Sa 26:6 288

AHIMELECH'S (*a-him'-el-eks*) *Refers to Ahimelech 1.*
A son, I pray thee, bring me 1Sa 30:7 288

AHIMOTH
Amasai, and A 1Chr 6:25 287

AHINADAB (*a-hin'-ad-ab*) *A son of Iddo.*
A the son of Iddo had Mahanaim 1Kin 4:14 292

AHINOAM (*a-hin'-o-am*)
1. A wife of King Saul.
And the name of Saul's wife was A 1Sa 14:50 293
2. A wife of David.
David also took A of Jezreel 1Sa 25:43 293
A the Jezreelitess, and Abigail 1Sa 27:3 293
A the Jezreelitess, and Abigail 1Sa 30:5 293
A the Jezreelitess, and Abigail 2Sa 2:2 293
was Amnon, of A the Jezreelitess 2Sa 3:2 293
Amnon, of A the Jezreelitess 1Chr 3:1 293

AHIO (*a-hi'-o*)
1. A son of Abinadab.
and Uzzah and A, the sons of 2Sa 6:3 283
and A went before the ark 2Sa 6:4 283
and Uzza and A drave the cart 1Chr 13:7 283
2. A son of Beriah the Benjamite.
And A, Shashak, and Jeremoth, 1Chr 8:14 283
3. A son of Jehiel.
And Gedor, and A, and Zacher 1Chr 8:31 283
Gedor, and A, and Zechariah 1Chr 9:37 283

AHIRA (*a-hi'-rah*) *A chief of Naphtali.*
A the son of Enan Num 1:15 299
shall be A the son of Enan Num 2:29 299
the twelfth day A the son of Enan Num 7:78 299
the offering of A the son of Enan Num 7:83 299
of Naphtali was A the son of Enan Num 10:27 299

AHIRAM (*a-hi'-rum*) See AHARAH, AHIRAMITES. *A descendant of Benjamin.*
of A, the family of the Num 26:38 297

AHIRAMITES (*a-hi'-rum-ites*) *Desendants of Ahiram.*
of Ahiram, the family of the A Num 26:38 298

AHISAMACH (*a-his'-am-ak*) *Father of Aholiab.*
with him Aholiab, the son of A Ex 31:6 294
both he, and Aholiab, the son of A Ex 35:34 294
And with him was Aholiab, son of A Ex 38:23 294

AHISHAHAR (*a-hish'-a-har*) *A son of Bilhan.*
and Zethan, and Tharshish, and A 1Chr 7:10 300

AHISHAR (*a-hi'-shar*) *Governor of the palace under Solomon.*
And A was over the household 1Kin 4:6 301

AHITHOPHEL (*a-hith'-o-fel*) *A counsellor of David.*
Absalom sent for A the Gilonite 2Sa 15:12 302
A is among the conspirators with 2Sa 15:31 302
the counsel of A into foolishness 2Sa 15:31 302
for me defeat the counsel of A 2Sa 15:34 302
came to Jerusalem, and A with him 2Sa 16:15 302
Then said Absalom to A, Give 2Sa 16:20 302
A said unto Absalom, Go in unto 2Sa 16:21 302
And the counsel of A, which he 2Sa 16:23 302
the counsel of A both with David 2Sa 16:23 302
Moreover A said unto Absalom, Let 2Sa 17:1 302
A hath spoken after this manner 2Sa 17:6 302
The counsel that A hath given is 2Sa 17:7 302
is better than the counsel of A 2Sa 17:14 302
to defeat the good counsel of A 2Sa 17:14 302
thus did A counsel Absalom and the 2Sa 17:15 302
for thus hath A counselled 2Sa 17:21 302
when A saw that his counsel was 2Sa 17:23 302
Eliam the son of A the Gilonite 2Sa 23:34 302
A was the king's counsellor 1Chr 27:33 302
after A was Jehoiada the son of 1Chr 27:34 302

AHITUB (*a-hi'-tub*)
1. The son of Phinehas.
And Ahiah, the son of A, 1Sa 14:3 285
to Nob, to Ahimelech the son of A 1Sa 22:9 285
the priest, the son of A, and all 1Sa 22:11 285
said, Hear now, thou son of A 1Sa 22:12 285
sons of Ahimelech the son of A 1Sa 22:20 285
2. Father of the high priest during David's reign.
And Zadok the son of A, and 2Sa 8:17 285
begat Amariah, and Amariah begat A 1Chr 6:7 285
A begat Zadok, and Zadok begat 1Chr 6:8 285
son, Amariah his son, A his son, 1Chr 6:52 285
And Zadok the son of A, and 1Chr 18:16 285
the son of Zadok, the son of A Ezr 7:2 285
3. A priest seven generations later than Ahitub 2.
begat Amariah, and Amariah begat A 1Chr 6:11 285
A begat Zadok, and Zadok begat 1Chr 6:12 285
4. A priest in Nehemiah's time.
the son of Meraioth, the son of A 1Chr 9:11 285
the son of Meraioth, the son of A Neh 11:11 285

AHLAB (*ah'-lab*) *A city of Asher.*
inhabitants of Zidon, nor of A Judg 1:31 303

AHLAI (*ah'-lahee*)
1. A daughter of Sheshan.
And the children of Sheshan; A 1Chr 2:31 304
2. Father of a "mighty man" of David.
the Hittite, Zabad the son of A 1Chr 11:41 304

AHOAH (*a-ho'-ah*) See AHOHITE. *The son of Bela.*
And Abishua, and Naaman, and A 1Chr 8:4 265

AHOHITE (*a-ho'-hite*)
1. A descendant of Ahoah.
Zalmon the A, Maharai the ... 2Sa 23:28 266
Eleazar the son of Dodo, the A ... 1Chr 11:12 266
the Hushathite, Ilai the A ... 1Chr 11:29 266
the second month was Dodai an A ... 1Chr 27:4 266
2. A rendering of "son of Ahohi."
was Eleazar the son of Dodo the A ... 2Sa 23:9

AHOLAH (*a-ho'-lah*) *A name for Samaria and the Ten Tribes.*
names of them were A the elder ... Eze 23:4 170
Samaria is A, and Jerusalem ... Eze 23:4 170
A played the harlot when she was ... Eze 23:5 170
Son of man, wilt thou judge A ... Eze 23:36 170
so went they in unto A and unto ... Eze 23:44 170

AHOLIAB (*a-ho'-lee-ab*) *A Danite craftsman.*
behold, I have given with him A ... Ex 31:6 171
that he may teach, both he, and A ... Ex 35:34 171
Then wrought Bezaleel and A ... Ex 36:1 171
And Moses called Bezaleel and A ... Ex 36:2 171
And with him was A, son of ... Ex 38:23 171

AHOLIBAH (*a-hol'-ib-ah*) *A name for Jerusalem and Judah.*
Aholah the elder, and A her sister ... Eze 23:4 172
Samaria is Aholah, and Jerusalem A ... Eze 23:4 172
And when her sister A saw this ... Eze 23:11 172
Therefore, O A, thus saith the ... Eze 23:22 172
man, wilt thou judge Aholah and A ... Eze 23:36 172
they in unto Aholah and unto A ... Eze 23:44 172

AHOLIBAMAH (*a-hol'-ib-a'-mah*)
1. A wife of Esau.
A the daughter of Anah the ... Gen 36:2 173
A bare Jeush, and Jaalam, and Korah .. Gen 36:5 173
And these were the sons of A ... Gen 36:14 173
are the sons of A Esau's wife ... Gen 36:18 173
came of A the daughter of Anah ... Gen 36:18 173
Dishon, and A the daughter of Anah ... Gen 36:25 173
2. A chief from Esau.
Duke A, duke Elah, duke Pinon, ... Gen 36:41 173
Duke A, duke Elah, duke Pinon, ... 1Chr 1:52 173

AHUMAI (*a-hoo'-mahee*) *Grandson of Shobal.*
and Jahath begat A, and Lahad ... 1Chr 4:2 267

AHUZAM (*a-hoo'-zam*) *A son of Ashur.*
And Naarah bare him A, and Hepher, .. 1Chr 4:6 275

AHUZZAM See AHUZAM.

AHUZZATH (*a-huz'-zath*) *A friend of Ahimilech the Philistine king.*
A one of his friends, and Phichol ... Gen 26:26 276

AHZAI See AHASAI.

AI (*a'-i*) See AIATH, AIJA, HAI. *A city near Bethel in Benjamin.*
Joshua sent men from Jericho to A ... Josh 7:2 5857
And the men went up and viewed A ... Josh 7:2 5857
thousand men go up and smite A ... Josh 7:3 5857
and they fled before the men of A ... Josh 7:4 5857
the men of A smote of them about ... Josh 7:5 5857
with thee, and arise, go up to A ... Josh 8:1 5857
given into thy hand the king of A ... Josh 8:1 5857
And thou shalt do to A and her king ... Josh 8:2 5857
people of war, to go up against A ... Josh 8:3 5857
and A, on the west side of A ... Josh 8:9 5857
of Israel, before the people to A ... Josh 8:10 5857
and pitched on the north side of A ... Josh 8:11 5857
was a valley between them and A ... Josh 8:11 5857
in ambush between Beth-el and A ... Josh 8:12 5857
pass, when the king of A saw it ... Josh 8:14 5857
all the people that were in A ... Josh 8:16 5892
not a man left in A or Beth-el ... Josh 8:17 5857
that is in thy hand toward A ... Josh 8:18 5857
when the men of A looked behind ... Josh 8:20 5857
again, and slew the men of A ... Josh 8:21 5857
the king of A they took alive, and ... Josh 8:23 5857
the inhabitants of A in the field ... Josh 8:24 5857
the Israelites returned unto A ... Josh 8:24 5857
thousand, even all the men of A ... Josh 8:25 5857
all the inhabitants of A ... Josh 8:26 5857
And Joshua burnt A, and made it an ... Josh 8:28 5857
the king of A he hanged on a tree ... Josh 8:29 5857
had done unto Jericho and to A ... Josh 9:3 5857
had heard how Joshua had taken A ... Josh 10:1 5857
and her king, so he had done to A ... Josh 10:1 5857
and because it was greater than A ... Josh 10:2 5857
the king of A, which is beside ... Josh 12:9 5857
The men of Beth-el and A, two ... Ezr 2:28 5857
The men of Beth-el and A, an ... Neh 7:32 5857
Howl, O Heshbon, for A is spoiled ... Jer 49:3 5857

AIAH (*a-i'-ah*) See AJAH.
1. A son of Zibeon the Horite.
A, and Anah ... 1Chr 1:40 345
2. The father of Saul's concubine.
was Rizpah, the daughter of A ... 2Sa 3:7 345
sons of Rizpah the daughter of A ... 2Sa 21:8 345
the daughter of A took sackcloth ... 2Sa 21:10 345
what Rizpah the daughter of A ... 2Sa 21:11 345

AIATH (*a-i'-ath*) See AI. *A form of Ai.*
He is come to A, he is passed to ... Is 10:28 5857

AIDED
which *a* him in the killing of his ... Judg 9:24

AIJA (*a-i'-jah*) See AI. *A form of Ai.*
from Geba dwelt at Michmash, and A . Neh 11:31 5857

AIJALON (*a-ij'-el-on*) See AJALON.
1. A Levitical city in Dan.
A with her suburbs, Gath-rimmon ... Josh 21:24 357
would dwell in mount Heres in A ... Judg 1:35 357
2. A place in Zebulun.
was buried in A in the country of ... Judg 12:12 357
3. A town between Benjamin and Judah.
that day from Michmash to A ... 1Sa 14:31 357
fathers of the inhabitants of A ... 1Chr 8:13 357
And Zorah, and A, and Hebron, which 2Chr 11:10 357
4. A Levitical city in Ephraim.
And A with her suburbs, and ... 1Chr 6:69 357

AIJELETH (*a-ij'-el-eth*) *A musical notation.*
the chief Musician upon A Shahar ... Ps 22:t 365

AILED
What *a* thee, O thou sea, that ... Ps 114:5

AILETH
and said unto her, What *a* thee ... Gen 21:17
and said unto Micah, What *a* thee ... Judg 18:23
that ye say unto me, What *a* thee ... Judg 18:24
What *a* the people that they weep ... 1Sa 11:5
king said unto her, What *a* thee ... 2Sa 14:5
king said unto her, What *a* thee ... 2Kin 6:28
What *a* thee now, that thou art ... Is 22:1

AIN (*ah'-yin*) See EN.
1. A place between Riblah and the Sea of Chinnereth.
to Riblah, on the east side of A ... Num 34:11 5871
2. A Levitical city in Simeon.
And Lebaoth, and Shilhim, and A ... Josh 15:32 5871
A, Remmon, and Ether, and Ashan ... Josh 19:7 5871
A with her suburbs, and Juttah ... Josh 21:16 5871
their villages were, Etam, and A ... 1Chr 4:32 5871

AIR
sea, and over the fowl of the *a* ... Gen 1:26 8064
sea, and over the fowl of the *a* ... Gen 1:28 8064
earth, and to every fowl of the *a* ... Gen 1:30 8064
the field, and every fowl of the *a* ... Gen 2:19 8064
cattle, and to the fowl of the *a* ... Gen 2:20 8064
thing, and the fowls of the *a* ... Gen 6:7 8064
Of fowls also of the *a* by sevens ... Gen 7:3 8064
and upon every fowl of the *a* ... Gen 9:2 8064
winged fowl that flieth in the *a* ... Deut 4:17 8064
be meat unto all fowls of the *a* ... Deut 28:26 8064
thy flesh unto the fowls of the *a* ... 1Sa 17:44 8064
this day unto the fowls of the *a* ... 1Sa 17:46 8064
of the *a* to rest on them by day ... 2Sa 21:10 8064
shall the fowls of the *a* eat ... 1Kin 14:11 8064
shall the fowls of the *a* eat ... 1Kin 16:4 8064
shall the fowls of the *a* eat ... 1Kin 21:24 8064
and the fowls of the *a*, and they ... Job 12:7 8064
close from the fowls of the *a* ... Job 28:21 8064
that no *a* can come between them ... Job 41:16 7307
The fowl of the *a*, and the fish of ... Ps 8:8 8064
The way of an eagle in the *a* ... Prov 30:19 8064
for a bird of the *a* shall carry ... Eccl 10:20 8064
Behold the fowls of the *a* ... Mt 6:26 3772
and the birds of the *a* have nests ... Mt 8:20 3772
so that the birds of the *a* come ... Mt 13:32 3772
side, and the fowls of the *a* came ... Mk 4:4 3772
so that the fowls of the *a* may ... Mk 4:32 3772
and the fowls of the *a* devoured it ... Lk 8:5 3772
and birds of the *a* have nests ... Lk 9:58 3772
the fowls of the *a* lodged in the ... Lk 13:19 3772
things, and fowls of the *a* ... Acts 10:12 3772
things, and fowls of the *a* ... Acts 11:6 3772
clothes, and threw dust into the *a* ... Acts 22:23 109
I, not as one that beateth the *a* ... 1Cor 9:26 109
for ye shall speak into the *a* ... 1Cor 14:9 109
the prince of the power of the *a* ... Eph 2:2 109
clouds, to meet the Lord in the *a* ... 1Th 4:17 109
the *a* were darkened by reason of ... Rev 9:2 109
poured out his vial into the *a* ... Rev 16:17 109

AJAH (*a'-jah*) See AIAH. *A son of Zibeon the Horite.*
both A, and Anah ... Gen 36:24 345

AJALON (*aj'-a-lon*) See AIJALON.
1. A valley of Dan.
and thou, Moon, in the valley of A ... Josh 10:12 357
2. A Levitical city in Dan.
And Shaalabbin, and A, and Jethlah ... Josh 19:42 357
3. A town between Benjamin and Judah.
and had taken Beth-shemesh, and A ... 2Chr 28:18 357

AKAN (*a'-kan*) See JAAKAN, JAKAN. *A son of Ezer.*
Bilhan, and Zaavan, and A ... Gen 36:27 6130

AKEL DAMA See ACELDAMA.

AKKAD See ACCAD.

AKKUB (*ak'-kub*)
1. A descendant of David.
and Eliashib, and Pelaiah, and A ... 1Chr 3:24 6126
2. A Levitical gatekeeper.
the porters were, Shallum, and A ... 1Chr 9:17 6126
Moreover the porters, A, Talmon, ... Neh 11:19 6126
Obadiah, Meshullam, Talmon, A ... Neh 12:25 6126
3. A family of Levitical porters.
of Talmon, the children of A ... Ezr 2:42 6126
of Talmon, the children of A ... Neh 7:45 6126
4. A family of returned exiles.
of Hagabah, the children of A ... Ezr 2:45 6126
5. A priest in Ezra's time.
and Bani, and Sherebiah, Jamin, A ... Neh 8:7 6126

AKRABBIM (*ac-rab'-bim*) See MAALE-ACRABBIM. *An ascent south of the Dead Sea.*
from the south to the ascent of A ... Num 34:4 6137
was from the going up to A ... Judg 1:36 6137

ALABASTER
a box of very precious ointment ... Mt 26:7 211
an *a* box of ointment of spikenard ... Mk 14:3 211
brought an *a* box of ointment, ... Lk 7:37 211

ALAMETH (*al'-am-eth*) *A son of Becher.*
and Abiah, and Anathoth, and A ... 1Chr 7:8 5964

ALAMMELECH (*a-lam'-mel-ek*) *A town in Asher.*
And A, and Amad, and Misheal ... Josh 19:26 487

ALAMOTH (*al'-am-oth*) *A musical notation.*
and Benaiah, with psalteries on A ... 1Chr 15:20 5961
the sons of Korah, A Song upon A ... Ps 46:t 5961

ALARM
When ye blow an *a*, then the camps ... Num 10:5 8643
When ye blow an *a* the second time ... Num 10:6 8643
blow an *a* for their journeys ... Num 10:6 8643
blow, but ye shall not sound an *a* ... Num 10:7 7321
shall blow an *a* with the trumpets ... Num 10:9 7321
trumpets to cry *a* against you ... 2Chr 13:12 7321
of the trumpet, the *a* of war ... Jer 4:19 8643
that I will cause an *a* of war to ... Jer 49:2 8643
sound an *a* in my holy mountain ... Joel 2:1 7321
a against the fenced cities, and ... Zeph 1:16 8643

ALAS
And Aaron said unto Moses, A ... Num 12:11 994
took up his parable, and said, A ... Num 24:23 188
And Joshua said, A, O Lord GOD, ... Josh 7:7 160
angel of the LORD, Gideon said, A ... Judg 6:22 160
he rent his clothes, and said, A ... Judg 11:35 160
they mourned over him, saying, A ... 1Kin 13:30 1945
And the king of Israel said, A ... 2Kin 3:10 160
and he cried, and said, A, master ... 2Kin 6:5 160
And his servant said unto him, A ... 2Kin 6:15 160
A! for that day is great ... Jer 30:7 1945
A for all the evil abominations ... Eze 6:11 253
A for the day ... Joel 1:15 160
say in all the highways, A! *a*! ... Amos 5:16 1930
fear of her torment, saying, A ... Rev 18:10 3758
a that great city Babylon, that ... Rev 18:10 3758
And saying, A, *a* that great ... Rev 18:16 3758
weeping and wailing, saying, A ... Rev 18:19 3758
a that great city, wherein were ... Rev 18:19 3758

ALBEIT
a I have not spoken ... Eze 13:7
a I do not say to thee how thou ... Philem 19 2443

ALEMETH (*al-e'-meth*)
1. A Levitical city in Benjamin.
A with her suburbs, and Anathoth ... 1Chr 6:60 5964
2. A descendant of Jonathan.
and Jehoadah begat A, and Azmaveth, 1Chr 8:36 5964
Jarah begat A, and Azmaveth ... 1Chr 9:42 5964

ALEXANDER (*al-ex-an'-dur*)
1. Son of Simeon who bore Jesus'cross.
of the country, the father of A ... Mk 15:21 223
2. A Christian leader in Jerusalem.
and Caiaphas, and John, and A ... Acts 4:6 223
3. A participant in the Ephesian riot.
they drew A out of the multitude, ... Acts 19:33 223
A beckoned with the hand, and ... Acts 19:33 223
4. An opponent of Paul.
Of whom is Hymenaeus and A ... 1Ti 1:20
A the coppersmith did me much ... 2Ti 4:14 223

ALEXANDRIA (*al-ex-an'-dree-ah*) See ALEXANDRIANS. *A city in Egypt.*
Jew named Apollos, born at A ... Acts 18:24 221
a ship of A sailing into Italy ... Acts 27:6 221
months we departed in a ship of A ... Acts 28:11 221

ALEXANDRIAN See ALEXANDRIA.

ALEXANDRIANS (*al-ex-an'-dree-uns*) *Residents of Alexandria.*
Libertines, and Cyrenians, and A ... Acts 6:9 221

ALGUM
trees, and *a* trees, out of Lebanon ... 2Chr 2:8 418
gold from Ophir, brought *a* trees ... 2Chr 9:10 418
the king made of the *a* trees ... 2Chr 9:11 418

ALIAH (*a-li'-ah*) See ALVAH. *A chief of Edom.*
duke Timnah, duke A, duke Jetheth ... 1Chr 1:51 5933

ALIAN (*a-li'-un*) See ALVAN. *A son of Shobal.*
A, and Manahath, and Ebal, Shephi, ... 1Chr 1:40 5935

ALIEN
I have been an *a* in a strange ... Ex 18:3 1616
or thou mayest sell it unto an *a* ... Deut 14:21 5237
I am an *a* in their sight ... Job 19:15 5237
an *a* unto my mother's children ... Ps 69:8 5237
the sons of the *a* shall be your ... Is 61:5 5236

ALIENATE
nor *a* the firstfruits of the land ... Eze 48:14 5674

ALIENATED
them, and her mind was *a* from them .. Eze 23:17 3363
then my mind was *a* from her ... Eze 23:18 3363
as my mind was *a* from her sister ... Eze 23:18 5361
thee, from whom thy mind is *a* ... Eze 23:22 5361
of them from whom thy mind is *a* ... Eze 23:28 5361
being *a* from the life of God ... Eph 4:18 526
And you, that were sometime *a* ... Col 1:21 526

ALIENS
to strangers, our houses to *a* ... Lam 5:2 5237
being *a* from the commonwealth of ... Eph 2:12 526
to flight the armies of the *a* ... Heb 11:34 245

ALIKE
and the clean shall eat of them *a* ... Deut 12:22 3162
the clean person shall eat it *a* ... Deut 15:22 3162
they shall part *a* ... 1Sa 30:24 3162
They shall lie down *a* in the dust ... Job 21:26 3162
He fashioneth their hearts *a* ... Ps 33:15 3162
and the light are both *a* to thee ... Ps 139:12
both of them are *a* abomination to ... Prov 20:10 1571
day and a contentious woman are *a* ... Prov 27:15 7737
All things come *a* to all ... Eccl 9:2 834

whether they both shall be *a* good Eccl 11:6 259
another esteemeth every day *a* Rom 14:5

ALIVE
the ark, to keep them *a* with thee Gen 6:19 2421
come unto thee, to keep them *a* Gen 6:20 2421
to keep seed *a* upon the face of Gen 7:3 2421
and Noah only remained *a*, and they ... Gen 7:23
me, but they will save thee *a* Gen 12:12 2421
saying, Is your father yet *a* Gen 43:7 2416
Is he yet *a* Gen 43:27 2416
is in good health, he is yet *a* Gen 43:28 2416
told him, saying, Joseph is yet *a* Gen 45:26 2416
Joseph my son is yet *a* Gen 45:28 2416
thy face, because thou art yet *a* Gen 46:30 2416
this day, to save much people *a* Gen 50:20 2421
but saved the men children *a* Ex 1:17 2421
and have saved the men children *a* Ex 1:18 2421
and every daughter ye shall save *a* Ex 1:22 2421
and see whether they be yet *a* Ex 4:18 2416
be certainly found in his hand *a* Ex 22:4
sons of Aaron which were left *a* Lev 10:16
is to be cleansed two birds *a* Lev 14:4 2416
be presented *a* before the LORD Lev 16:10 2416
upon them that are left *a* of you Lev 26:36
went down *a* into the pit, and the Num 16:33 2416
until there was none left him *a* Num 21:35 8300
I had slain thee, and saved her *a* Num 22:33 2421
Have ye saved all the women *a* Num 31:15 2421
with him, keep *a* for yourselves Num 31:18 2421
are *a* every one of you this day Deut 4:4 2416
who are all of us here *a* this day Deut 5:3 2416
that he might preserve us *a* Deut 6:24 2421
thou shalt save *a* nothing that Deut 20:16 2421
while I am yet *a* with you this Deut 31:27 2416
I kill, and I make *a* Deut 32:39 2421
And that ye will save *a* my father Josh 2:13 2421
Joshua saved Rahab the harlot *a* Josh 6:25 2421
And the king of Ai they took *a* Josh 8:23 2416
behold, the LORD hath kept me *a* Josh 14:10 2421
liveth, if ye had saved them *a* Judg 8:19 2421
a of the women of Jabesh-gilead Judg 21:14 2421
The LORD killeth, and maketh *a* 1Sa 2:6 2421
Agag the king of the Amalekites *a* 1Sa 15:8 2416
and left neither man nor woman *a* 1Sa 27:9 2421
saved neither man nor woman *a* 1Sa 27:11 2421
and with one full line to keep *a* 2Sa 8:2 2421
Behold, while the child was yet *a* 2Sa 12:18 2416
for the child, while it was *a* 2Sa 12:21 2416
said, While the child was yet *a* 2Sa 12:22 2416
while he was yet *a* in the midst 2Sa 18:14 2416
to save the horses and mules *a* 1Kin 18:5 2421
come out for peace, take them *a* 1Kin 20:18 2416
be come out for war, take them *a* 1Kin 20:18 2416
And he said, Is he yet *a* 1Kin 20:32 2416
for Naboth is not *a*, but dead 1Kin 21:15 2416
Am I God, to kill and to make *a* 2Kin 5:7 2421
if they save us *a*, we shall live 2Kin 7:4 2421
the city, we shall catch them *a* 2Kin 7:12 2416
And he said, Take them *a* 2Kin 10:14 2416
And they took them *a*, and slew them. 2Kin 10:14 2416
other ten thousand left *a* did the 2Chr 25:12 2416
and none can keep *a* his own soul Ps 22:29 2421
thou hast kept me *a*, that I Ps 30:3 2421
and to keep them *a* in famine Ps 33:19 2421
will preserve him, and keep him *a* Ps 41:2 2421
us swallow them up *a* as the grave Prov 1:12 2416
than the living which are yet *a* Eccl 4:2 2416
children, I will preserve them *a* Jer 49:11 2421
is sold, although they were yet *a* Eze 7:13 2416
the souls *a* that come unto you Eze 13:18 2421
to save the souls *a* that should Eze 13:19 2421
right, he shall save his soul *a* Eze 18:27 2421
and whom he would he kept *a* Dan 5:19 2418
deceiver said, while he was yet *a* Mt 27:63 *2198*
when they had heard that he was *a* Mk 16:11 *2198*
my son was dead, and is *a* again Lk 15:24 *326*
brother was dead, and is *a* again Lk 15:32 *326*
angels, which said that he was *a* Lk 24:23 *2198*
a after his passion by many Acts 1:3 *2198*
saints and widows, presented her *a* Acts 9:41 *2198*
And they brought the young man *a* Acts 20:12 *2198*
dead, whom Paul affirmed to be *a* Acts 25:19 *2198*
but *a* unto God through Jesus Rom 6:11 *2198*
as those that are *a* from the dead Rom 6:13 *2198*
For I was *a* without the law once Rom 7:9 *2198*
so in Christ shall all be made *a* 1Cor 15:22 *2227*
of the Lord, that we which are *a* 1Th 4:15 *2198*
Then we which are *a* and remain 1Th 4:17 *2198*
I am *a* for evermore, Amen Rev 1:18 *2198*
the last, which was dead, and is *a* Rev 2:8 *2198*
These both were cast *a* into a Rev 19:20 *2198*

ALL
over *a* the earth, and over every Gen 1:26 3605
is upon the face of *a* the earth Gen 1:29 3605
finished, and *a* the host of them Gen 2:1 3605
from *a* his work which he had made Gen 2:2 3605
from *a* his work which God created Gen 2:3 3605
And Adam gave names to *a* cattle Gen 2:20 3605
thou art cursed above *a* cattle Gen 3:14 3605
dust shalt thou eat *a* the days of Gen 3:14 3605
eat of it *a* the days of thy life Gen 3:17 3605
she was the mother of *a* living Gen 3:20 3605
he was the father of *a* such as Gen 4:21 3605
a the days that Adam lived were Gen 5:5 3605
a the days of Seth were nine Gen 5:8 3605
a the days of Enos were nine Gen 5:11 3605
a the days of Cainan were nine Gen 5:14 3605
a the days of Mahalaleel were Gen 5:17 3605
a the days of Jared were nine Gen 5:20 3605
a the days of Enoch were three Gen 5:23 3605
a the days of Methuselah were Gen 5:27 3605
a the days of Lamech were seven Gen 5:31 3605
them wives of *a* which they chose Gen 6:2 3605
for *a* flesh had corrupted his way Gen 6:12 3605
The end of *a* flesh is come before Gen 6:13 3605
the earth, to destroy *a* flesh Gen 6:17 3605
of every living thing of *a* flesh Gen 6:19 3605
unto thee of *a* food that is eaten Gen 6:21 3605
according to *a* that God commanded Gen 6:22 3605
thou and *a* thy house into the ark Gen 7:1 3605
upon the face of *a* the earth Gen 7:3 3605
Noah did according unto *a* that Gen 7:5 3605
the same day were *a* the fountains Gen 7:11 3605
a the cattle after their kind, and Gen 7:14 3605
the ark, two and two of *a* flesh Gen 7:15 3605
went in male and female of *a* flesh Gen 7:16 3605
a the high hills, that were under Gen 7:19 3605
a flesh died that moved upon the Gen 7:21 3605
A in whose nostrils was the Gen 7:22 3605
of *a* that was in the dry land, Gen 7:22 3605
a the cattle that was with him in Gen 8:1 3605
of *a* flesh, both of fowl, and of Gen 8:17 3605
upon *a* that moveth upon the earth Gen 9:2 3605
upon *a* the fishes of the sea Gen 9:2 3605
herb have I given you *a* things Gen 9:3 3605
from *a* that go out of the ark, to Gen 9:10 3605
neither shall *a* flesh be cut off Gen 9:11 3605
every living creature of *a* flesh Gen 9:15 3605
become a flood to destroy *a* flesh Gen 9:15 3605
every living creature of *a* flesh Gen 9:16 3605
a flesh that is upon the earth Gen 9:17 3605
a the days of Noah were nine Gen 9:29 3605
the father of *a* the children of Gen 10:21 3605
a these were the sons of Joktan Gen 10:29 3605
one, and they have *a* one language Gen 11:6 3605
upon the face of *a* the earth Gen 11:8 3605
the language of *a* the earth Gen 11:9 3605
upon the face of *a* the earth Gen 11:9 3605
in thee shall *a* families of the Gen 12:3 3605
a their substance that they had Gen 12:5 3605
and his wife, and *a* that he had Gen 12:20 3605
a that he had, and Lot with him, Gen 13:1 3605
beheld *a* the plain of Jordan, Gen 13:10 3605
Then Lot chose him *a* the plain of Gen 13:11 3605
For *a* the land which thou seest, Gen 13:15 3605
A these were joined together in Gen 14:3 3605
smote *a* the country of the Gen 14:7 3605
they took *a* the goods of Sodom and ... Gen 14:11 3605
a their victuals, and went their Gen 14:11 3605
And he brought back *a* the goods Gen 14:16 3605
And he gave him tithes of *a* Gen 14:20 3605
And he took unto him *a* these Gen 15:10 3605
in the presence of *a* his brethren Gen 16:12 3605
a the land of Canaan, for an Gen 17:8 3605
a that were born in his house, and Gen 17:23 3605
a that were bought with his money Gen 17:23 3605
a the men of his house, born in Gen 17:27 3605
a the nations of the earth shall Gen 18:18 3605
the Judge of *a* the earth do right Gen 18:25 3605
then I will spare *a* the place for Gen 18:26 3605
wilt thou destroy *a* the city for Gen 18:28 3605
servant's house, and tarry *a* night Gen 19:2 3885
will abide in the street *a* night Gen 19:2 3885
a the people from every quarter Gen 19:4 3605
neither stay thou in *a* the plain Gen 19:17 3605
and *a* the plain, and *a* the Gen 19:25 3605
toward *a* the land of the plain, Gen 19:28 3605
after the manner of *a* the earth Gen 19:31 3605
die, thou, and *a* that are thine Gen 20:7 3605
called *a* his servants Gen 20:8 3605
told *a* these things in their ears Gen 20:8 3605
unto *a* that are with thee, and Gen 20:16 3605
are with thee, and with *a* other Gen 20:16 3605
up *a* the wombs of the house of Gen 20:18 3605
so that *a* that hear will laugh Gen 21:6 3605
in *a* that Sarah hath said unto Gen 21:12 3605
is with thee in *a* that thou doest Gen 21:22 3605
in thy seed shall *a* the nations Gen 22:18 3605
even of *a* that went in at the Gen 23:10 3605
a the trees that were in the Gen 23:17 3605
that were in *a* the borders round Gen 23:17 3605
before *a* that went in at the gate Gen 23:18 3605
had blessed Abraham in *a* things Gen 24:1 3605
that ruled over *a* that he had Gen 24:2 3605
for *a* the goods of his master Gen 24:10 3605
water, and drew for *a* his camels Gen 24:20 3605
him hath he given *a* that he hath Gen 24:36 3605
were with him, and tarried *a* night Gen 24:54 3885
the servant told Isaac *a* things Gen 24:66 3605
A these were the children of Gen 25:4 3605
Abraham gave *a* that he had unto Gen 25:5 3605
in the presence of *a* his brethren Gen 25:18 3605
a over like an hairy garment Gen 25:25 3605
I will give *a* these countries, and Gen 26:3 3605
unto thy seed *a* these countries Gen 26:4 3605
in thy seed shall *a* the nations Gen 26:4 3605
And Abimelech charged *a* his people ... Gen 26:11 3605
For *a* the wells which his Gen 26:15 3605
I have eaten of *a* before thou Gen 27:33 3605
a his brethren have I given to Gen 27:37 3605
place, and tarried there *a* night Gen 28:11 3885
in thy seed shall *a* the families Gen 28:14 3605
will keep thee in *a* places Gen 28:15 3605
of *a* that thou shalt give me I Gen 28:22 3605
thither were *a* the flocks Gen 29:3 3605
until *a* the flocks be gathered Gen 29:8 3605
And he told Laban *a* these things Gen 29:13 3605
together *a* the men of the place Gen 29:22 3605
pass through *a* thy flock to day Gen 30:32 3605
from thence *a* the speckled Gen 30:32 3605
a the brown cattle among the Gen 30:32 3605
a the she goats that were Gen 30:35 3605
a the brown among the sheep, and Gen 30:35 3605
a the brown in the flock of Laban Gen 30:40 3605
away *a* that was our father's Gen 31:1 3605
hath he gotten *a* this glory Gen 31:1 3605
ye know that with *a* my power I Gen 31:6 3605
then *a* the cattle bare speckled Gen 31:8 3605
then bare *a* the cattle Gen 31:8 3605
a the rams which leap upon the Gen 31:12 3605
for I have seen *a* that Laban Gen 31:12 3605
For *a* the riches which God hath Gen 31:16 3605
And he carried away *a* his cattle Gen 31:18 3605
a his goods which he had gotten, Gen 31:18 3605
So he fled with *a* that he had Gen 31:21 3605
And Laban searched *a* the tent Gen 31:34 3605
thou hast searched *a* my stuff Gen 31:37 3605
found of *a* thy household stuff Gen 31:37 3605
a that thou seest is mine Gen 31:43 3605
tarried *a* night in the mount Gen 31:54 3885
of the least of *a* the mercies Gen 32:10 3605
of *a* the truth, which thou hast Gen 32:10 3605
a that followed the droves, Gen 32:19 3605
What meanest thou by *a* this drove Gen 33:8 3605
one day, *a* the flock will die Gen 33:13 3605
than *a* the house of his father Gen 34:19 3605
a that went out of the gate of Gen 34:24 3605
a that went out of the gate of Gen 34:24 3605
city boldly, and slew *a* the males Gen 34:25 3605
a their wealth, and *a* their Gen 34:29 3605
spoiled even *a* that was in the Gen 34:29 3605
to *a* that were with him, Put away Gen 35:2 3605
they gave unto Jacob *a* the Gen 35:4 3605
a their earrings which were in Gen 35:4
a the people that were with him Gen 35:6 3605
a the persons of his house, and Gen 36:6 3605
and *a* his beasts, and *a* his Gen 36:6 3605
Joseph more than *a* his children Gen 37:3 3605
him more than *a* his brethren Gen 37:4 3605
a his sons and *a* his daughters Gen 37:35 3605
that the LORD made *a* that he did Gen 39:3 3605
a that he had he put into his Gen 39:4 3605
over *a* that he had, that the LORD Gen 39:5 3605
upon *a* that he had in the house Gen 39:5 3605
he left *a* that he had in Joseph's Gen 39:6 3605
he hath committed *a* that he hath Gen 39:8 3605
committed to Joseph's hand *a* the Gen 39:22 3605
uppermost basket there was of *a* Gen 40:17 3605
made a feast unto *a* his servants Gen 40:20 3605
called for *a* the magicians of Gen 41:8 3605
Egypt, and *a* the wise men thereof Gen 41:8 3605
such as I never saw in *a* the land Gen 41:19 3605
throughout *a* the land of Egypt Gen 41:29 3605
a the plenty shall be forgotten Gen 41:30 3605
let them gather *a* the food of Gen 41:35 3605
and in the eyes of *a* his servants Gen 41:37 3605
as God hath shewed thee *a* this Gen 41:39 3605
word shall *a* my people be ruled Gen 41:40 3605
set thee over *a* the land of Egypt Gen 41:41 3605
ruler over *a* the land of Egypt Gen 41:43 3605
or foot in *a* the land of Egypt Gen 41:44 3605
went out over *a* the land of Egypt Gen 41:45
went throughout *a* the land of Gen 41:46 3605
he gathered up *a* the food of the Gen 41:48 3605
a my toil, and *a* my father's house Gen 41:51 3605
and the dearth was in *a* lands Gen 41:54 3605
but in *a* the land of Egypt there Gen 41:54 3605
when *a* the land of Egypt was Gen 41:55 3605
Pharaoh said unto *a* the Egyptians Gen 41:55 3605
the famine was over *a* the face of Gen 41:56 3605
Joseph opened *a* the storehouses, Gen 41:56 3605
a countries came into Egypt to Gen 41:57 3605
the famine was so sore in *a* lands Gen 41:57 3605
sold to *a* the people of the land Gen 42:6 3605
We are *a* one man's sons Gen 42:11 3605
he put them *a* together into ward Gen 42:17 622
told him *a* that befell unto them Gen 42:29 3605
a these things are against me Gen 42:36 3605
before *a* them that stood by him Gen 45:1 3605
lord of *a* his house, and a ruler Gen 45:8 3605
throughout *a* the land of Egypt Gen 45:8 3605
God hath made me lord of *a* Egypt Gen 45:9 3605
and thy herds, and *a* that thou hast Gen 45:10 3605
a that thou hast, come to poverty Gen 45:11 3605
my father of *a* my glory in Egypt Gen 45:13 3605
and of *a* that ye have seen Gen 45:13 3605
Moreover he kissed *a* his brethren Gen 45:15 3605
for the good of *a* the land of Gen 45:20 3605
To *a* of them he gave each man Gen 45:22 3605
governor over *a* the land of Egypt Gen 45:26 3605
they told him *a* the words of Gen 45:27 3605
his journey with *a* that he had Gen 46:1 3605
Jacob, and *a* his seed with him Gen 46:6 3605
a his seed brought he with him Gen 46:7 3605
a the souls of his sons and his Gen 46:15 3605
a the souls were fourteen Gen 46:22 3605
a the souls were seven Gen 46:25 3605
A the souls that came with Jacob Gen 46:26 3605
a the souls were threescore and Gen 46:26 3605
a the souls of the house of Jacob Gen 46:27 3605
their herds, and *a* that they have Gen 46:32 3605
a that they have, are come out of Gen 47:1 3605
a his father's household, with Gen 47:12 3605
there was no bread in *a* the land Gen 47:13 3605
a the land of Canaan fainted by Gen 47:13
Joseph gathered up *a* the money Gen 47:14 3605
a the Egyptians came unto Joseph, Gen 47:15 3605
for *a* their cattle for that year Gen 47:17 3605
Joseph bought *a* the land of Egypt Gen 47:20 3605
the God which fed me *a* my life Gen 48:15
which redeemed me from *a* evil Gen 48:16 3605
A these are the twelve tribes of Gen 49:28 3605
with him went up *a* the servants Gen 50:7 3605
a the elders of the land of Egypt Gen 50:7 3605
a the house of Joseph, and his Gen 50:8 3605
a that went up with him to bury Gen 50:14 3605
will certainly requite us *a* the Gen 50:15 3605
a the souls that came out of the Ex 1:5 3605
a his brethren, and *a* that Ex 1:6 3605
in *a* manner of service in the Ex 1:14 3605
a their service, wherein they Ex 1:14 3605

And Pharaoh charged *a* his people	Ex 1:22	3605
is my memorial unto *a* generations	Ex 3:15	
smite Egypt with *a* my wonders	Ex 3:20	3605
for *a* the men are dead which	Ex 4:19	3605
see that thou do *a* those wonders	Ex 4:21	3605
Moses told Aaron *a* the words of	Ex 4:28	3605
him, and *a* the signs which he had	Ex 4:28	3605
gathered together *a* the elders of	Ex 4:29	3605
Aaron spake *a* the words which the	Ex 4:30	3605
a the land of Egypt to gather	Ex 5:12	3605
thou delivered thy people at *a*	Ex 5:23	
of Egypt *a* that I say unto thee	Ex 6:29	3605
Thou shalt speak *a* that I command	Ex 7:2	3605
upon *a* their pools of water, that	Ex 7:19	3605
throughout *a* the land of Egypt	Ex 7:19	3605
a the waters that were in the	Ex 7:20	3605
throughout *a* the land of Egypt	Ex 7:21	3605
a the Egyptians digged round	Ex 7:24	3605
I will smite *a* thy borders with	Ex 8:2	3605
people, and upon *a* thy servants	Ex 8:4	3605
throughout *a* the land of Egypt	Ex 8:16	3605
a the dust of the land became	Ex 8:17	3605
throughout *a* the land of Egypt	Ex 8:17	3605
and into *a* the land of Egypt	Ex 8:24	3605
of *a* that is the children's of	Ex 9:4	3605
a the cattle of Egypt died	Ex 9:6	3605
small dust in *a* the land of Egypt	Ex 9:9	3605
throughout *a* the land of Egypt	Ex 9:9	3605
and upon *a* the Egyptians	Ex 9:11	3605
a my plagues upon thine heart	Ex 9:14	3605
is none like me in *a* the earth	Ex 9:14	3605
declared throughout *a* the earth	Ex 9:16	3605
a that thou hast in the field	Ex 9:19	3605
be hail in *a* the land of Egypt	Ex 9:22	3605
in *a* the land of Egypt since it	Ex 9:24	3605
the hail smote throughout *a* the	Ex 9:25	3605
of Egypt *a* that was in the field	Ex 9:25	3605
and the houses of *a* thy servants	Ex 10:6	3605
and the houses of *a* the Egyptians	Ex 10:6	3605
even *a* that the hail hath left	Ex 10:12	3605
a that day, and *a* that night	Ex 10:13	3605
went up over *a* the land of Egypt	Ex 10:14	3605
rested in *a* the coasts of Egypt	Ex 10:14	3605
a the fruit of the trees which	Ex 10:15	3605
through *a* the land of Egypt	Ex 10:15	3605
locust in *a* the coasts of Egypt	Ex 10:19	3605
in *a* the land of Egypt three days	Ex 10:22	3605
but *a* the children of Israel had	Ex 10:23	3605
a the firstborn in the land of	Ex 11:5	3605
a the firstborn of beasts	Ex 11:5	3605
throughout *a* the land of Egypt	Ex 11:6	3605
a these thy servants shall come	Ex 11:8	3605
a the people that follow thee	Ex 11:8	3605
Aaron did *a* these wonders before	Ex 11:10	3605
Speak ye unto *a* the congregation	Ex 12:3	3605
raw, nor sodden at *a* with water	Ex 12:9	
will smite *a* the firstborn in the	Ex 12:12	3605
against *a* the gods of Egypt I	Ex 12:12	3605
in *a* your habitations shall ye	Ex 12:20	3605
called for *a* the elders of Israel	Ex 12:21	3605
a the firstborn in the land of	Ex 12:29	3605
a the firstborn of cattle	Ex 12:29	3605
a his servants, and *a* the	Ex 12:30	3605
his servants, and *a* the Egyptians	Ex 12:30	3605
for they said, We be *a* dead men	Ex 12:33	3605
that *a* the hosts of the LORD went	Ex 12:41	3605
of the LORD to be observed of *a*	Ex 12:42	3605
A the congregation of Israel	Ex 12:47	3605
let *a* his males be circumcised,	Ex 12:48	3605
Thus did *a* the children of Israel	Ex 12:50	3605
Sanctify unto me *a* the firstborn	Ex 13:2	3605
seen with thee in *a* thy quarters	Ex 13:7	3605
LORD *a* that openeth the matrix	Ex 13:12	3605
a the firstborn of man among thy	Ex 13:13	3605
us go, that the LORD slew *a* the	Ex 13:15	3605
LORD *a* that openeth the matrix	Ex 13:15	3605
but *a* the firstborn of my	Ex 13:15	3605
upon Pharaoh, and upon *a* his host	Ex 14:4	3605
a the chariots of Egypt, and	Ex 14:7	3605
a the horses and chariots of	Ex 14:9	3605
upon *a* his host, upon his	Ex 14:17	3605
not near the other *a* the night	Ex 14:20	3605
a strong east wind *a* that night	Ex 14:21	3605
even *a* Pharaoh's horses, his	Ex 14:23	3605
a the host of Pharaoh that came	Ex 14:28	3605
a the inhabitants of Canaan shall	Ex 15:15	3605
a the women went out after her	Ex 15:20	3605
keep *a* his statutes, I will put	Ex 15:26	3605
a the congregation of the	Ex 16:1	3605
Aaron said unto *a* the children of	Ex 16:6	3605
Say unto *a* the congregation of	Ex 16:9	3605
a the rulers of the congregation	Ex 16:22	3605
a the congregation of the	Ex 17:1	3605
heard of *a* that God had done for	Ex 18:1	3605
law *a* that the LORD had done unto	Ex 18:8	3605
a the travail that had come upon	Ex 18:8	3605
Jethro rejoiced for *a* the	Ex 18:9	3605
the LORD is greater than *a* gods	Ex 18:11	3605
a the elders of Israel, to eat	Ex 18:12	3605
saw *a* that he did to the people	Ex 18:14	3605
a the people stand by thee from	Ex 18:14	3605
out of *a* the people able men	Ex 18:21	3605
judge the people at *a* seasons	Ex 18:22	3605
a this people shall also go to	Ex 18:23	3605
in law, and did *a* that he had said	Ex 18:24	3605
chose able men out of *a* Israel	Ex 18:25	3605
judged the people at *a* seasons	Ex 18:26	3605
treasure unto me above *a* people	Ex 19:5	3605
for *a* the earth is mine	Ex 19:5	3605
laid before their faces *a* these	Ex 19:7	3605
a the people answered together,	Ex 19:8	3605
A that the LORD hath spoken we	Ex 19:8	3605
of *a* the people upon mount Sinai	Ex 19:11	3605
so that *a* the people that was in	Ex 19:16	3605
God spake *a* these words, saying,	Ex 20:1	3605
thou labour, and do *a* thy work	Ex 20:9	3605
a that in them is, and rested the	Ex 20:11	3605
a the people saw the thunderings,	Ex 20:18	3605
in *a* places where I record my	Ex 20:24	3605
For *a* manner of trespass, whether	Ex 22:9	3605
wise, and they cry at *a* unto me	Ex 22:23	
If thou at *a* take thy neighbour's	Ex 22:26	
in *a* things that I have said unto	Ex 23:13	3605
Three times in the year *a* thy	Ex 23:17	3605
his voice, and do *a* that I speak	Ex 23:22	3605
will destroy *a* the people to whom	Ex 23:27	3605
I will make *a* thine enemies turn	Ex 23:27	3605
told the people *a* the words of	Ex 24:3	3605
of the LORD, and *a* the judgments	Ex 24:3	3605
a the people answered with one	Ex 24:3	3605
A the words which the LORD hath	Ex 24:3	3605
Moses wrote *a* the words of the	Ex 24:4	3605
A that the LORD hath said will we	Ex 24:7	3605
with you concerning *a* these words	Ex 24:8	3605
According to *a* that I shew thee,	Ex 25:9	3605
the pattern of *a* the instruments	Ex 25:9	3605
of *a* things which I will give	Ex 25:22	3605
a it shall be one beaten work of	Ex 25:36	3605
he make it, with *a* these vessels	Ex 25:39	3605
shall be *a* of one measure	Ex 26:8	
thus shalt thou make for *a* the	Ex 26:17	3605
a the vessels thereof thou shalt	Ex 27:3	3605
A the pillars round about the	Ex 27:17	3605
A the vessels of the tabernacle	Ex 27:19	3605
in *a* the service thereof, and *a*	Ex 27:19	3605
a the pins of the court, shall be	Ex 27:19	3605
unto *a* that are wise hearted	Ex 28:3	3605
the robe of the ephod *a* of blue	Ex 28:31	3632
hallow in *a* their holy gifts	Ex 28:38	3605
pour *a* the blood beside the	Ex 29:12	3605
thou shalt take *a* the fat that	Ex 29:13	3605
thou shalt put *a* in the hands of	Ex 29:24	3605
according to *a* things which I	Ex 29:35	3605
a his vessels, and the candlestick	Ex 30:27	3605
burnt offering with *a* his vessels	Ex 30:28	3605
in *a* manner of workmanship,	Ex 31:3	3605
of timber, to work in *a* manner of	Ex 31:5	3605
in the hearts of *a* that are wise	Ex 31:6	3605
that they may make *a* that I have	Ex 31:6	3605
a the furniture of the tabernacle	Ex 31:7	3605
candlestick with *a* his furniture	Ex 31:8	3605
offering with *a* his furniture	Ex 31:9	3605
according to *a* that I have	Ex 31:11	3605
a the people brake off the golden	Ex 32:3	3605
a this land that I have spoken of	Ex 32:13	3605
a the sons of Levi gathered	Ex 32:26	3605
that *a* the people rose up, and	Ex 33:8	3605
a the people saw the cloudy	Ex 33:10	3605
and *a* the people rose up and	Ex 33:10	3605
from *a* the people that are upon	Ex 33:16	3605
I will make *a* my goodness pass	Ex 33:19	3605
be seen throughout *a* the mount	Ex 34:3	3605
before *a* thy people I will do	Ex 34:10	3605
have not been done in *a* the earth	Ex 34:10	3605
a the people among which thou art	Ex 34:10	3605
A that openeth the matrix is mine	Ex 34:19	3605
A the firstborn of thy sons thou	Ex 34:20	3605
Thrice in the year shall *a* your	Ex 34:23	3605
a the children of Israel saw	Ex 34:30	3605
a the rulers of the congregation	Ex 34:31	3605
afterward *a* the children of	Ex 34:32	3605
he gave them in commandment *a*	Ex 34:32	3605
Moses gathered *a* the congregation	Ex 35:1	3605
And Moses spake unto *a* the	Ex 35:4	3605
make *a* that the LORD hath	Ex 35:10	3605
a his vessels, and the shewbread,	Ex 35:13	3605
a his vessels, the laver and his	Ex 35:16	3605
a the congregation of the	Ex 35:20	3605
for *a* his service, and for the	Ex 35:21	3605
and tablets, *a* jewels of gold	Ex 35:22	3605
a the women that were wise	Ex 35:25	3605
a the women whose heart stirred	Ex 35:26	3605
to bring for *a* manner of work	Ex 35:29	3605
in *a* manner of workmanship	Ex 35:31	3605
to work *a* manner of work, of the	Ex 35:35	3605
to know how to work *a* manner of	Ex 36:1	3605
according to *a* that the LORD had	Ex 36:1	3605
received of Moses *a* the offering	Ex 36:3	3605
a the wise men, that wrought *a*	Ex 36:4	3605
for *a* the work to make it	Ex 36:7	3605
the curtains were of *a* one size	Ex 36:9	3605
thus did he make for *a* the boards	Ex 36:22	3605
a of it was one beaten work of	Ex 37:22	3605
he it, and *a* the vessels thereof	Ex 37:24	3605
he made *a* the vessels of the	Ex 38:3	3605
a the vessels thereof made he of	Ex 38:3	3605
A the hangings of the court round	Ex 38:16	3605
a the pillars of the court were	Ex 38:17	3605
a the pins of the tabernacle, and	Ex 38:20	3605
made *a* that the LORD commanded	Ex 38:22	3605
A the gold that was occupied for	Ex 38:24	3605
in *a* the work of the holy place	Ex 38:24	3605
a the vessels of the altar,	Ex 38:30	3605
a the pins of the tabernacle, and	Ex 38:31	3605
a the pins of the court round	Ex 38:31	3605
ephod of woven work, *a* of blue	Ex 39:22	3632
Thus was *a* the work of the	Ex 39:32	3605
of Israel did according to *a* that	Ex 39:32	3605
a his furniture, his taches, his	Ex 39:33	3605
a the vessels thereof, and the	Ex 39:36	3605
a the vessels thereof, and the oil	Ex 39:37	3605
a his vessels, the laver and his	Ex 39:39	3605
a the vessels of the service of	Ex 39:40	3605
According to *a* that the LORD	Ex 39:42	3605
of Israel made *a* the work	Ex 39:42	3605
And Moses did look upon *a* the work	Ex 39:43	3605
a that is therein, and shalt	Ex 40:9	3605
it, and *a* the vessels thereof	Ex 40:9	3605
a his vessels, and sanctify the	Ex 40:10	3605
according to *a* that the LORD	Ex 40:16	3605
went onward in *a* their journeys	Ex 40:36	3605
in the sight of *a* the house of	Ex 40:38	3605
throughout *a* their journeys	Ex 40:38	3605
priest shall burn *a* on the altar	Lev 1:9	3605
and the priest shall bring it *a*	Lev 1:13	3605
with *a* the frankincense thereof	Lev 2:2	3605
with *a* thine offerings thou shalt	Lev 2:13	3605
with *a* the frankincense thereof	Lev 2:16	3605
a the fat that is upon the	Lev 3:3	3605
a the fat that is upon the	Lev 3:9	3605
a the fat that is upon the	Lev 3:14	3605
a the fat is the LORD's	Lev 3:16	3605
throughout *a* your dwellings	Lev 3:17	3605
shall pour *a* the blood of the	Lev 4:7	3605
he shall take off from it *a* the	Lev 4:8	3605
a the fat that is upon the	Lev 4:8	3605
a his flesh, with his head, and	Lev 4:11	3605
shall pour out *a* the blood at the	Lev 4:18	3605
he shall take *a* his fat from him,	Lev 4:19	3605
he shall burn *a* his fat upon the	Lev 4:26	3605
shall pour out *a* the blood	Lev 4:30	3605
shall take away *a* the fat thereof	Lev 4:31	3605
shall pour out *a* the blood	Lev 4:34	3605
shall take away *a* the fat thereof	Lev 4:35	3605
in any of *a* these that a man	Lev 6:3	3605
Or *a* that about which he hath	Lev 6:5	3605
thing of *a* that he hath done in	Lev 6:7	3605
altar *a* night unto the morning	Lev 6:9	3605
a the frankincense which is upon	Lev 6:15	3605
A the males among the children of	Lev 6:18	3605
A the males among the priests	Lev 6:29	3605
offer of it *a* the fat thereof	Lev 7:3	3605
a the meat offering that is baken	Lev 7:9	3605
oven, and *a* that is dressed in the	Lev 7:9	3605
shall *a* the sons of Aaron have,	Lev 7:10	3605
be eaten at *a* on the third day	Lev 7:18	
a that be clean shall eat thereof	Lev 7:19	3605
gather thou *a* the congregation	Lev 8:3	3605
a that was therein, and sanctified	Lev 8:10	3605
a his vessels, both the laver and	Lev 8:11	3605
he took *a* the fat that was upon	Lev 8:16	3605
a the fat that was upon the	Lev 8:25	3605
he put *a* upon Aaron's hands, and	Lev 8:27	3605
his sons did *a* things which the	Lev 8:36	3605
a the congregation drew near and	Lev 9:5	3605
LORD appeared unto *a* the people	Lev 9:23	3605
which when *a* the people saw, they	Lev 9:24	3605
before *a* the people I will be	Lev 10:3	3605
lest wrath come upon *a* the people	Lev 10:6	3605
a the statutes which the LORD	Lev 10:11	3605
a the beasts that are on the	Lev 11:2	3605
These shall ye eat of *a* that are	Lev 11:9	3605
a that have not fins and scales in	Lev 11:10	3605
of *a* that move in the waters, and	Lev 11:10	3605
A fowls that creep, going upon *a*	Lev 11:20	3605
thing that goeth upon *a* four	Lev 11:21	
But *a* other flying creeping	Lev 11:23	3605
a manner of beasts that go on *a*	Lev 11:27	3605
unclean to you among *a* that creep	Lev 11:31	3605
Of *a* meat which may be eaten,	Lev 11:34	3605
a drink that may be drunk in	Lev 11:34	3605
and whatsoever goeth upon *a* four	Lev 11:42	
a creeping things that creep upon	Lev 11:42	3605
the leprosy cover *a* the skin of	Lev 13:12	3605
leprosy have covered *a* his flesh	Lev 13:13	3605
it is *a* turned white	Lev 13:13	3605
A the days wherein the plague	Lev 13:46	3605
clothes, and shave off *a* his hair	Lev 14:8	3605
that he shall shave *a* his hair	Lev 14:9	3605
even *a* his hair he shall shave	Lev 14:9	3605
that *a* that is in the house be	Lev 14:36	3605
a the morter of the house	Lev 14:45	3605
a the while that it is shut up	Lev 14:46	3605
This is the law for *a* manner of	Lev 14:54	3605
shall wash *a* his flesh in water	Lev 15:16	3605
And if any man lie with her at *a*	Lev 15:24	
a the bed whereon he lieth shall	Lev 15:24	3605
a the days of the issue of her	Lev 15:25	3605
Every bed whereon she lieth *a* the	Lev 15:26	3605
that he come not at *a* times into	Lev 16:2	3605
transgressions in *a* their sins	Lev 16:16	3605
for *a* the congregation of Israel	Lev 16:17	3605
confess over him *a* the iniquities	Lev 16:21	3605
a their transgressions in *a*	Lev 16:21	3605
a their iniquities unto a land	Lev 16:22	3605
your souls, and do no work at *a*	Lev 16:29	3605
from *a* your sins before the LORD	Lev 16:30	3605
and for *a* the people of the	Lev 16:33	3605
for *a* their sins once a year	Lev 16:34	3605
unto *a* the children of Israel, and	Lev 17:2	3605
For it is the life of *a* flesh	Lev 17:14	3605
for the life of *a* flesh is the	Lev 17:14	3605
for in *a* these the nations are	Lev 18:24	3605
(For *a* these abominations have	Lev 18:27	3605
Speak unto *a* the congregation of	Lev 19:2	3605
it be eaten at *a* on the third day	Lev 19:7	
thee *a* night until the morning	Lev 19:13	
not at *a* redeemed, nor freedom	Lev 19:20	
shall have planted *a* manner of	Lev 19:23	3605
But in the fourth year *a* the	Lev 19:24	3605
shall ye observe *a* my statutes	Lev 19:37	3605
a my judgments, and do them	Lev 19:37	3605
a that go a whoring after him, to	Lev 20:5	3605
therefore keep *a* my statutes	Lev 20:22	3605
a my judgments, and do them	Lev 20:22	3605
for they committed *a* these things	Lev 20:23	3605
unto *a* the children of Israel	Lev 21:24	3605
Whosoever he be of *a* your seed	Lev 22:3	3605
unto *a* the children of Israel, and	Lev 22:18	3605
offer his oblation for *a* his vows	Lev 22:18	3605
for *a* his freewill offerings,	Lev 22:18	3605
of the LORD in *a* your dwellings	Lev 23:3	3605

generations in *a* your dwellings	Lev 23:14	3605
a your dwellings throughout your	Lev 23:21	3605
generations in *a* your dwellings	Lev 23:31	3605
beside *a* your vows, and beside *a*	Lev 23:38	3605
a that are Israelites born shall	Lev 23:42	3605
let *a* that heard him lay their	Lev 24:14	3605
let *a* the congregation stone him	Lev 24:14	3605
and *a* the congregation shall	Lev 24:16	3605
shall *a* the increase thereof be	Lev 25:7	3605
sound throughout *a* your land	Lev 25:9	3605
a the land unto *a* the	Lev 25:10	3605
in *a* the land of your possession	Lev 25:24	3605
will not do *a* these commandments	Lev 26:14	3605
ye will not do *a* my commandments	Lev 26:15	3605
yet for *a* this hearken unto me	Lev 26:18	
if ye will not for *a* this hearken	Lev 26:27	
And yet for *a* that, when they be	Lev 26:44	1571
a that any man giveth of such	Lev 27:9	3605
if he shall at *a* change beast for	Lev 27:10	
But if he will at *a* redeem it	Lev 27:13	
a thy estimations shall be	Lev 27:25	3605
unto the LORD of *a* that he hath	Lev 27:28	3605
a the tithe of the land, whether	Lev 27:30	3605
if a man will at *a* redeem ought	Lev 27:31	
and if he change it at *a*, then	Lev 27:33	
Take ye the sum of *a* the	Num 1:2	3605
a that are able to go forth to	Num 1:3	3605
they assembled *a* the congregation	Num 1:18	3605
a that were able to go forth to	Num 1:20	3605
a that were able to go forth to	Num 1:22	3605
a that were able to go forth to	Num 1:24	3605
a that were able to go forth to	Num 1:26	3605
a that were able to go forth to	Num 1:28	3605
a that were able to go forth to	Num 1:30	3605
a that were able to go forth to	Num 1:32	3605
a that were able to go forth to	Num 1:34	3605
a that were able to go forth to	Num 1:36	3605
a that were able to go forth to	Num 1:38	3605
a that were able to go forth to	Num 1:40	3605
a that were able to go forth to	Num 1:42	3605
So were *a* those that were	Num 1:45	3605
a that were able to go forth to	Num 1:45	3605
Even *a* they that were numbered	Num 1:46	3605
over *a* the vessels thereof, and	Num 1:50	3605
over *a* things that belong to it	Num 1:50	3605
and *a* the vessels thereof	Num 1:50	3605
of Israel did according to *a* that	Num 1:54	3605
A that were numbered in the camp	Num 2:9	3605
A that were numbered in the camp	Num 2:16	3605
A that were numbered of the camp	Num 2:24	3605
A they that were numbered in the	Num 2:31	3605
a those that were numbered of the	Num 2:32	3605
of Israel did according to *a* that	Num 2:34	3605
they shall keep *a* the instruments	Num 3:8	3605
children of Israel instead of *a*	Num 3:12	3605
Because *a* the firstborn are mine	Num 3:13	3605
for on the day that I smote *a* the	Num 3:13	3605
unto me *a* the firstborn in Israel	Num 3:13	3605
to the number of *a* the males	Num 3:22	3605
of it for *a* the service thereof	Num 3:26	3605
In the number of *a* the males	Num 3:28	3605
hanging, and *a* the service thereof	Num 3:31	3605
to the number of *a* the males	Num 3:34	3605
a the vessels thereof, and *a*	Num 3:36	3605
A that were numbered of the	Num 3:39	3605
a the males from a month old and	Num 3:39	3605
Number *a* the firstborn of the	Num 3:40	3605
of *a* the firstborn among the	Num 3:41	3605
of the Levites instead of *a* the	Num 3:41	3605
a the firstborn among the	Num 3:42	3605
a the firstborn males by the	Num 3:43	3605
of *a* the firstborn among the	Num 3:45	3605
a that enter into the host, to do	Num 4:3	3605
a the oil vessels thereof,	Num 4:9	3605
a the vessels thereof within a	Num 4:10	3605
they shall take *a* the instruments	Num 4:12	3605
put upon it *a* the vessels thereof	Num 4:14	3605
a the vessels of the altar	Num 4:14	3605
a the vessels of the sanctuary,	Num 4:15	3605
the oversight of *a* the tabernacle	Num 4:16	3605
of *a* that therein is, in the	Num 4:16	3605
a that enter in to perform the	Num 4:23	3605
a the instruments of their	Num 4:26	3605
and *a* that is made for them	Num 4:26	3605
his sons shall be *a* the service	Num 4:27	3605
in *a* their burdens, and in *a*	Num 4:27	3605
them in charge *a* their burdens	Num 4:27	3605
according to *a* their service in	Num 4:31	3605
with *a* their instruments	Num 4:32	3605
and with *a* their service	Num 4:32	3605
according to *a* their service, in	Num 4:33	3605
a that might do service in the	Num 4:37	3605
of *a* that might do service in the	Num 4:41	3605
A those that were numbered of the	Num 4:46	3605
every offering of *a* the holy	Num 5:9	3605
shall execute upon her *a* this law	Num 5:30	3605
A the days of his separation	Num 6:4	3605
A the days of the vow of his	Num 6:5	3605
A the days that he separateth	Num 6:6	3605
A the days of his separation he	Num 6:8	3605
a the instruments thereof, both	Num 7:1	3605
a the vessels thereof, and had	Num 7:1	3605
a the silver vessels weighed two	Num 7:85	3605
a the gold of the spoons was an	Num 7:86	3605
A the oxen for the burnt offering	Num 7:87	3605
a the oxen for the sacrifice of	Num 7:88	3605
and let them shave *a* their flesh	Num 8:7	3605
of *a* the children of Israel	Num 8:16	3605
For *a* the firstborn of the	Num 8:17	3605
I have taken the Levites for *a*	Num 8:18	3605
a the congregation of the	Num 8:20	3605
a that the LORD commanded Moses	Num 8:20	3605
according to *a* the rites of it,	Num 9:3	3605
according to *a* the ceremonies	Num 9:3	3605
according to *a* that the LORD	Num 9:5	3605
according to *a* the ordinances of	Num 9:12	3605
a the assembly shall assemble	Num 10:3	3605
which was the rereward of *a* the	Num 10:25	3605
there is nothing at *a*, beside	Num 11:6	3605
burden of *a* this people upon me	Num 11:11	3605
Have I conceived *a* this people	Num 11:12	3605
flesh to give unto *a* this people	Num 11:13	3605
able to bear *a* this people alone	Num 11:14	3605
or shall *a* the fish of the sea be	Num 11:22	3605
would God that *a* the LORD'S	Num 11:29	3605
And the people stood up *a* that day	Num 11:32	3605
a that night, and *a* the next day	Num 11:32	3605
they spread them *a* abroad for	Num 11:32	3605
above *a* the men which were upon	Num 12:3	
who is faithful in *a* mine house	Num 12:7	3605
a those men were heads of the	Num 13:3	3605
to *a* the congregation of the	Num 13:26	3605
unto *a* the congregation, and	Num 13:26	3605
a the people that we saw in it	Num 13:32	3605
a the congregation lifted up	Num 14:1	3605
a the children of Israel murmured	Num 14:2	3605
before *a* the assembly of the	Num 14:5	3605
they spake unto *a* the company of	Num 14:7	3605
But *a* the congregation bade stone	Num 14:10	3605
before *a* the children of Israel	Num 14:10	3605
for *a* the signs which I have	Num 14:11	3605
kill *a* this people as one man	Num 14:15	
a the earth shall be filled with	Num 14:21	3605
Because *a* those men which have	Num 14:22	3605
a that were numbered of you,	Num 14:29	3605
it unto *a* this evil congregation	Num 14:35	3605
made *a* the congregation to murmur	Num 14:36	3605
unto *a* the children of Israel	Num 14:39	3605
A that are born of the country	Num 15:13	3605
not observed *a* these commandments	Num 15:22	3605
Even *a* that the LORD hath	Num 15:23	3605
that *a* the congregation shall	Num 15:24	3605
for *a* the congregation of the	Num 15:25	3605
it shall be forgiven *a* the	Num 15:26	3605
seeing *a* the people were in	Num 15:26	3605
Aaron, and unto *a* the congregation	Num 15:33	3605
a the congregation shall stone	Num 15:35	3605
a the congregation brought him	Num 15:36	3605
remember *a* the commandments of	Num 15:39	3605
do *a* my commandments, and be holy	Num 15:40	3605
seeing *a* the congregation are	Num 16:3	3605
unto *a* his company, saying, Even	Num 16:5	3605
censers, Korah, and *a* his company	Num 16:6	3605
a thy brethren the sons of Levi	Num 16:10	3605
a thy company are gathered	Num 16:11	3605
a thy company before the LORD,	Num 16:16	3605
Korah gathered *a* the congregation	Num 16:19	3605
appeared unto *a* the congregation	Num 16:19	3605
the God of the spirits of *a* flesh	Num 16:22	3605
be wroth with *a* the congregation	Num 16:22	3605
ye be consumed in *a* their sins	Num 16:26	3605
hath sent me to do *a* these works	Num 16:28	3605
men die the common death of *a* men	Num 16:29	3605
after the visitation of *a* men	Num 16:29	3605
with *a* that appertain unto them,	Num 16:30	3605
an end of speaking *a* these words	Num 16:31	3605
a the men that appertained unto	Num 16:32	3605
unto Korah, and *a* their goods	Num 16:32	3605
a that appertained to them, went	Num 16:33	3605
a Israel that were round about	Num 16:34	3605
But on the morrow *a* the	Num 16:41	3605
of *a* their princes according to	Num 17:2	3605
Moses brought out *a* the rods from	Num 17:9	3605
unto *a* the children of Israel	Num 17:9	3605
we die, we perish, we *a* perish	Num 17:12	3605
the charge of *a* the tabernacle	Num 18:3	3605
for *a* the service of the	Num 18:4	3605
of *a* the hallowed things of the	Num 18:8	3605
with *a* the wave offerings of the	Num 18:11	3605
A the best of the oil, and *a* the	Num 18:12	3605
openeth the matrix in *a* flesh	Num 18:15	3605
A the heave offerings of the holy	Num 18:19	3605
Levi *a* the tenth in Israel for an	Num 18:21	3605
unto the LORD of *a* your tithes	Num 18:28	3605
Out of *a* your gifts ye shall	Num 18:29	3605
of *a* the best thereof, even the	Num 18:29	3605
a that come into the tent, and *a*	Num 19:14	3605
upon *a* the vessels, and upon the	Num 19:18	3605
Thou knowest *a* the travel that	Num 20:14	3605
the sight of *a* the congregation	Num 20:27	3605
when *a* the congregation saw that	Num 20:29	3605
even *a* the house of Israel	Num 20:29	3605
but Sihon gathered *a* his people	Num 21:23	3605
Israel took *a* these cities	Num 21:25	3605
Israel dwelt in *a* the cities of	Num 21:25	3605
in *a* the villages thereof	Num 21:25	3605
taken *a* his land out of his hand,	Num 21:26	3605
a his people, to the battle at	Num 21:33	3605
a his people, and his land	Num 21:34	3605
a his people, until there was	Num 21:35	3605
saw *a* that Israel had done to the	Num 22:2	3605
lick up *a* that are round about us	Num 22:4	3605
any power at *a* to say any thing	Num 22:38	
he, and *a* the princes of Moab	Num 23:6	3605
of them, and shalt not see them *a*	Num 23:13	3605
them at *a*, nor bless them at *a*	Num 23:25	
A that the LORD speaketh, that I	Num 23:26	3605
destroy *a* the children of Sheth	Num 24:17	3605
Take *a* the heads of the people,	Num 25:4	3605
Moses, and in the sight of *a* the	Num 25:6	3605
Take the sum of *a* the	Num 26:2	3605
a that are able to go to war in	Num 26:2	3605
A the families of the Shuhamites,	Num 26:43	3605
a males from a month old and	Num 26:62	3605
a the congregation, by the door	Num 27:2	3605
the God of the spirits of *a* flesh	Num 27:16	3605
before *a* the congregation	Num 27:19	3605
that *a* the congregation of the	Num 27:20	3605
a the children of Israel with him	Num 27:21	3605
with him, even *a* the congregation	Num 27:21	3605
before *a* the congregation	Num 27:22	3605
a that the LORD commanded Moses	Num 29:40	3605
he shall do according to *a* that	Num 30:2	3605
then *a* her vows shall stand, and	Num 30:4	3605
And if she had at *a* an husband	Num 30:6	
then *a* her vows shall stand, and	Num 30:11	3605
then he establisheth *a* her vows	Num 30:14	3605
or *a* her bonds, which are upon	Num 30:14	3605
throughout *a* the tribes of Israel	Num 31:4	3605
and they slew *a* the males	Num 31:7	3605
the children of Israel took *a* the	Num 31:9	
took the spoil of *a* their cattle	Num 31:9	3605
a their flocks, and *a* their	Num 31:9	3605
they burnt *a* their cities wherein	Num 31:10	3605
a their goodly castles, with fire	Num 31:10	3605
And they took *a* the spoil, and *a*	Num 31:11	3605
a the princes of the congregation	Num 31:13	3605
Have ye saved *a* the women alive	Num 31:15	3605
But *a* the women children, that	Num 31:18	3605
purify *a* your raiment, and *a*	Num 31:20	3605
a work of goats' hair, and *a*	Num 31:20	3605
a that abideth not the fire ye	Num 31:23	3605
between *a* the congregation	Num 31:27	3605
of *a* manner of beasts, and give	Num 31:30	3605
and two thousand persons in *a*	Num 31:35	3605
of them, even *a* wrought jewels	Num 31:51	3605
a the gold of the offering that	Num 31:52	3605
until *a* the generation, that had	Num 32:13	3605
and ye shall destroy *a* this people	Num 32:15	3605
will go *a* of you armed over	Num 32:21	3605
a our cattle, shall be there in	Num 32:26	3605
in the sight of *a* the Egyptians	Num 33:3	3605
buried *a* their firstborn, which	Num 33:4	3605
Then ye shall drive out *a* the	Num 33:52	3605
destroy *a* their pictures, and	Num 33:52	3605
destroy *a* their molten images, and	Num 33:52	3605
quite pluck down *a* their high	Num 33:52	3605
goods, and for *a* their beasts	Num 35:3	3605
So *a* the cities which ye shall	Num 35:7	3605
generations in *a* your dwellings	Num 35:29	3605
words which Moses spake unto *a*	Deut 1:1	3605
according unto *a* that the LORD	Deut 1:3	3605
unto *a* the places nigh thereunto,	Deut 1:7	3605
I commanded you at that time *a*	Deut 1:18	3605
we went through *a* that great	Deut 1:19	3605
according to *a* that he did for	Deut 1:30	3605
in *a* the way that ye went, until	Deut 1:31	3605
according to *a* that the LORD our	Deut 1:41	3605
thee in *a* the works of thy hand	Deut 2:7	3605
until *a* the generation of the men	Deut 2:14	3605
when *a* the men of war were	Deut 2:16	3605
a his people, to fight at Jahaz	Deut 2:32	3605
him, and his sons, and *a* his people	Deut 2:33	3605
we took *a* his cities at that time	Deut 2:34	3605
LORD our God delivered *a* unto us	Deut 2:36	3605
a his people, to battle at Edrei	Deut 3:1	3605
a his people, and his land, into	Deut 3:2	3605
king of Bashan, and *a* his people	Deut 3:3	3605
we took *a* his cities at that time	Deut 3:4	3605
a the region of Argob, the	Deut 3:4	3605
A these cities were fenced with	Deut 3:5	3605
But *a* the cattle, and the spoil of	Deut 3:7	3605
A the cities of the plain, and *a*	Deut 3:10	3605
a Bashan, unto Salchah and Edrei,	Deut 3:10	3605
a Bashan, being the kingdom of Og	Deut 3:13	3605
a the region of Argob, with *a*	Deut 3:13	3605
a the country of Argob unto the	Deut 3:14	3605
a that are meet for the war	Deut 3:18	3605
Thine eyes have seen *a* that the	Deut 3:21	3605
unto *a* the kingdoms whither thou	Deut 3:21	3605
for *a* the men that followed	Deut 4:3	3605
which shall hear *a* these statutes	Deut 4:6	3605
as the LORD our God is in *a*	Deut 4:7	3605
so righteous as *a* this law	Deut 4:8	3605
thy heart *a* the days of thy life	Deut 4:9	3605
a the days that they shall live	Deut 4:10	3605
even *a* the host of heaven,	Deut 4:19	3605
a nations under the whole heaven	Deut 4:19	3605
a thy heart and with *a* thy soul	Deut 4:29	3605
a these things are come upon thee	Deut 4:30	3605
according to *a* that the LORD your	Deut 4:34	3605
a the plain on this side Jordan	Deut 4:49	3605
And Moses called *a* Israel, and said	Deut 5:1	3605
who are *a* of us here alive this	Deut 5:3	3605
shalt labour, and do *a* thy work	Deut 5:13	3605
a your assembly in the mount out	Deut 5:22	3605
even *a* the heads of your tribes,	Deut 5:23	3605
For who is there of *a* flesh	Deut 5:26	3605
hear *a* that the LORD our God	Deut 5:27	3605
speak thou unto us *a* that the	Deut 5:27	3605
they have well said *a* that they	Deut 5:28	3605
keep *a* my commandments always,	Deut 5:29	3605
unto thee *a* the commandments	Deut 5:31	3605
Ye shall walk in *a* the ways which	Deut 5:33	3605
to keep *a* his statutes and his	Deut 6:2	3605
son's son, *a* the days of thy life	Deut 6:2	3605
LORD thy God with *a* thine heart	Deut 6:5	3605
a thy soul, and with *a* thy might	Deut 6:5	3605
And houses full of *a* good things	Deut 6:11	3605
To cast out *a* thine enemies from	Deut 6:19	3605
upon *a* his household, before our	Deut 6:22	3605
us to do *a* these statutes	Deut 6:24	3605
if we observe to do *a* these	Deut 6:25	3605
above *a* people that are upon the	Deut 7:6	3605
ye were the fewest of *a* people	Deut 7:7	3605
shalt be blessed above *a* people	Deut 7:14	3605
take away from thee *a* sickness	Deut 7:15	3605
them upon *a* them that hate thee	Deut 7:15	3605
thou shalt consume *a* the people	Deut 7:16	3605
did unto Pharaoh, and unto *a* Egypt	Deut 7:18	3605
a the people of whom thou art	Deut 7:19	3605
A the commandments which I	Deut 8:1	3605

thou shalt remember *a* the way	Deut 8:2	3605
a that thou hast is multiplied	Deut 8:13	3605
if thou do at *a* forget the LORD	Deut 8:19	
written according to *a* the words	Deut 9:10	3605
because of *a* your sins which ye	Deut 9:18	3605
thy God, to walk in *a* his ways	Deut 10:12	3605
a thy heart and with *a* thy soul,	Deut 10:12	3605
also, with *a* that therein is	Deut 10:14	3605
them, even you above *a* people	Deut 10:15	3605
king of Egypt, and unto *a* his land	Deut 11:3	3605
a the substance that was in their	Deut 11:6	3605
in the midst of *a* Israel	Deut 11:6	3605
But your eyes have seen *a* the	Deut 11:7	3605
Therefore shall ye keep *a* the	Deut 11:8	3605
a your heart and with *a* your soul	Deut 11:13	3605
keep *a* these commandments which I	Deut 11:22	3605
your God, to walk in *a* his ways	Deut 11:22	3605
Then will the LORD drive out *a*	Deut 11:23	3605
the dread of you upon *a* the land	Deut 11:25	3605
observe to do *a* the statutes	Deut 11:32	3605
a the days that ye live upon the	Deut 12:1	3605
utterly destroy *a* the places	Deut 12:2	3605
of *a* your tribes to put his name	Deut 12:5	3605
ye shall rejoice in *a* that ye put	Deut 12:7	3605
Ye shall not do after *a* the	Deut 12:8	3605
from *a* your enemies round about	Deut 12:10	3605
ye bring *a* that I command you	Deut 12:11	3605
a your choice vows which ye vow	Deut 12:11	3605
shalt do *a* that I command thee	Deut 12:14	3605
kill and eat flesh in *a* thy gates	Deut 12:15	3605
before the LORD thy God in *a* that	Deut 12:18	3605
hear *a* these words which I	Deut 12:28	3605
a your heart and with *a* your soul	Deut 13:3	3605
the hand of *a* the people	Deut 13:9	3605
a Israel shall hear, and fear, and	Deut 13:11	3605
a that is therein, and the cattle	Deut 13:15	3605
thou shalt gather *a* the spoil of	Deut 13:16	3605
a the spoil thereof every whit,	Deut 13:16	3605
to keep *a* his commandments which	Deut 13:18	3605
above *a* the nations that are upon	Deut 14:2	3605
These ye shall eat of *a* that are	Deut 14:9	3605
a that have fins and scales shall	Deut 14:9	3605
Of *a* clean birds ye shall eat	Deut 14:11	3605
But of *a* clean fowls ye may eat	Deut 14:20	3605
Thou shalt truly tithe *a* the	Deut 14:22	3605
years thou shalt bring forth *a*	Deut 14:28	3605
in *a* the work of thine hand which	Deut 14:29	3605
thy God, to observe to do *a* these	Deut 15:5	3605
shall bless thee in *a* thy works	Deut 15:10	3605
in *a* that thou puttest thine hand	Deut 15:10	3605
bless thee in *a* that thou doest	Deut 15:18	3605
A the firstling males that come	Deut 15:19	3605
of Egypt *a* the days of thy life	Deut 16:3	3605
thee in *a* thy coast seven days	Deut 16:4	3605
remain *a* night until the morning	Deut 16:4	3885
bless thee in *a* thine increase	Deut 16:15	3605
in *a* the works of thine hands,	Deut 16:15	3605
a thy males appear before the	Deut 16:16	3605
thou make thee in *a* thy gates	Deut 16:18	3605
the hands of *a* the people	Deut 17:7	3605
to *a* that they inform thee	Deut 17:10	3605
a the people shall hear, and fear,	Deut 17:13	3605
like as *a* the nations that are	Deut 17:14	3605
therein *a* the days of his life	Deut 17:19	3605
to keep *a* the words of this law	Deut 17:19	3605
a the tribe of Levi, shall have	Deut 18:1	3605
chosen him out of *a* thy tribes	Deut 18:5	3605
any of thy gates out of *a* Israel	Deut 18:6	3605
come with *a* the desire of his	Deut 18:6	3605
as *a* his brethren the Levites do,	Deut 18:7	3605
For *a* that do these things are an	Deut 18:12	3605
According to *a* that thou	Deut 18:16	3605
them *a* that I shall command him	Deut 18:18	3605
give thee *a* the land which he	Deut 19:8	3605
If thou shalt keep *a* these	Deut 19:9	3605
that *a* the people that is found	Deut 20:11	3605
a that is in the city, even *a*	Deut 20:14	3605
Thus shalt thou do unto *a* the	Deut 20:15	3605
to do after *a* their abominations	Deut 20:18	3605
a the elders of that city, that	Deut 21:6	3605
shalt not sell her at *a* for money	Deut 21:14	
double portion of *a* that he hath	Deut 21:17	3605
a the men of his city shall stone	Deut 21:21	3605
a Israel shall hear, and fear	Deut 21:21	3605
not remain *a* night upon the tree	Deut 21:23	3885
with *a* lost things of thy	Deut 22:3	3605
for *a* that do so are abomination	Deut 22:5	3605
may not put her away *a* his days	Deut 22:19	3605
may not put her away *a* his days	Deut 22:29	3605
prosperity *a* thy days for ever	Deut 23:6	3605
LORD thy God may bless thee in *a*	Deut 23:20	3605
do according to *a* that the	Deut 24:8	3605
thee in *a* the work of thine hands	Deut 24:19	3605
For *a* that do such things, and *a*	Deut 25:16	3605
even *a* that were feeble behind	Deut 25:18	3605
from *a* thine enemies round about	Deut 25:19	3605
first of *a* the fruit of the earth	Deut 26:2	3605
hast made an end of tithing *a* the	Deut 26:12	3605
according to *a* thy commandments	Deut 26:13	3605
have done according to *a* that	Deut 26:14	3605
and do them with *a* thine heart	Deut 26:16	3605
thine heart, and with *a* thy soul	Deut 26:16	3605
shouldest keep *a* his commandments	Deut 26:18	3605
to make thee high above *a* nations	Deut 26:19	3605
Keep *a* the commandments which I	Deut 27:1	3605
upon them *a* the words of this law	Deut 27:3	3605
a the words of this law very	Deut 27:8	3605
the Levites spake unto *a* Israel	Deut 27:9	3605
say unto *a* the men of Israel with	Deut 27:14	3605
a the people shall answer and say,	Deut 27:15	3605
a the people shall say, Amen	Deut 27:16	3605
a the people shall say, Amen	Deut 27:17	3605
a the people shall say, Amen	Deut 27:18	3605
a the people shall say, Amen	Deut 27:19	3605
a the people shall say, Amen	Deut 27:20	3605
a the people shall say, Amen	Deut 27:21	3605
a the people shall say, Amen	Deut 27:22	3605
a the people shall say, Amen	Deut 27:23	3605
a the people shall say, Amen	Deut 27:24	3605
a the people shall say, Amen	Deut 27:25	3605
be he that confirmeth not *a* the	Deut 27:26	
a the people shall say, Amen	Deut 27:26	3605
to do *a* his commandments which I	Deut 28:1	3605
high above *a* nations of the earth	Deut 28:1	3605
a these blessings shall come on	Deut 28:2	3605
in *a* that thou settest thine hand	Deut 28:8	3605
a people of the earth shall see	Deut 28:10	3605
to bless *a* the work of thine hand	Deut 28:12	3605
observe to do *a* his commandments	Deut 28:15	3605
that *a* these curses shall come	Deut 28:15	3605
in *a* that thou settest thine hand	Deut 28:20	3605
shalt be removed into *a* the	Deut 28:25	3605
be meat unto *a* fowls of the air	Deut 28:26	3605
longing for them *a* the day long	Deut 28:32	3605
a thy labours, shall a nation	Deut 28:33	3605
among *a* nations whither the LORD	Deut 28:37	3605
trees throughout *a* thy coasts	Deut 28:40	3605
A thy trees and fruit of thy land	Deut 28:42	3605
Moreover *a* these curses shall	Deut 28:45	3605
for the abundance of *a* things	Deut 28:47	3605
nakedness, and in want of *a* things	Deut 28:48	3605
shall besiege thee in *a* thy gates	Deut 28:52	3605
trustedst, throughout *a* thy land	Deut 28:52	3605
he shall besiege thee in *a* thy	Deut 28:52	3605
thy gates throughout *a* thy land	Deut 28:52	3605
distress thee in *a* thy gates	Deut 28:55	3605
of *a* things secretly in the siege	Deut 28:57	3605
a the words of this law that are	Deut 28:58	3605
upon thee *a* the diseases of Egypt	Deut 28:60	3605
shall scatter thee among *a* people	Deut 28:64	3605
And Moses called unto *a* Israel	Deut 29:2	3605
Ye have seen *a* that the LORD did	Deut 29:2	3605
unto *a* his servants, and unto *a*	Deut 29:2	3605
ye may prosper in *a* that ye do	Deut 29:9	3605
Ye stand this day *a* of you before	Deut 29:10	3605
with *a* the men of Israel,	Deut 29:10	3605
a the curses that are written in	Deut 29:20	3605
out of *a* the tribes of Israel	Deut 29:21	3605
according to *a* the curses of the	Deut 29:21	3605
Even *a* nations shall say,	Deut 29:24	3605
to bring upon it *a* the curses	Deut 29:27	3605
that we may do *a* the words of	Deut 29:29	3605
when *a* these things are come upon	Deut 30:1	3605
them to mind among *a* the nations	Deut 30:1	3605
obey his voice according to *a*	Deut 30:2	3605
with *a* thine heart, and with *a*	Deut 30:2	3605
and gather thee from *a* the nations	Deut 30:3	3605
LORD thy God with *a* thine heart	Deut 30:6	3605
with *a* thy soul, that thou mayest	Deut 30:6	3605
the LORD thy God will put *a* these	Deut 30:7	3605
do *a* his commandments which I	Deut 30:8	3605
a thine heart, and with *a* thy soul	Deut 30:10	3605
spake these words unto *a* Israel	Deut 31:1	3605
a the commandments which I have	Deut 31:5	3605
unto him in the sight of *a* Israel	Deut 31:7	3605
unto *a* the elders of Israel	Deut 31:9	3605
When *a* Israel is come to appear	Deut 31:11	3605
before *a* Israel in their hearing	Deut 31:11	3605
observe to do *a* the words of this	Deut 31:12	3605
hide my face in that day for *a*	Deut 31:18	3605
Gather unto me *a* the elders of	Deut 31:28	3605
Moses spake in the ears of *a* the	Deut 31:30	3605
for *a* his ways are judgment	Deut 32:4	3605
and the LORD hath not done *a* this	Deut 32:27	3605
spake *a* the words of this song in	Deut 32:44	3605
a these words to *a* Israel	Deut 32:45	3605
Set your hearts unto *a* the words	Deut 32:46	3605
to do, *a* the words of this law	Deut 32:46	3605
a his saints are in thy hand	Deut 33:3	3605
shall cover him *a* the day long	Deut 33:12	3605
shewed him *a* the land of Gilead	Deut 34:1	3605
a Naphtali, and the land of	Deut 34:2	3605
a the land of Judah, unto the	Deut 34:2	3605
In *a* the signs and the wonders,	Deut 34:11	3605
to *a* his servants, and to *a* his	Deut 34:11	3605
in *a* that mighty hand, and in *a*	Deut 34:12	3605
shewed in the sight of *a* Israel	Deut 34:12	3605
a this people, unto the land	Josh 1:2	3605
a the land of the Hittites, and	Josh 1:4	3605
thee *a* the days of thy life	Josh 1:5	3605
to do according to *a* the law	Josh 1:7	3605
to *a* that is written therein	Josh 1:8	3605
a the mighty men of valour, and	Josh 1:14	3605
A that thou commandest us we will	Josh 1:16	3605
hearkened unto Moses in *a* things	Josh 1:17	3605
in *a* that thou commandest him	Josh 1:18	3605
come to search out *a* the country	Josh 2:3	3605
that *a* the inhabitants of the	Josh 2:9	3605
a that they have, and deliver our	Josh 2:13	3605
a thy father's household, home	Josh 2:18	3605
sought them throughout *a* the way	Josh 2:22	3605
told him *a* things that befell	Josh 2:23	3605
into our hands *a* the land	Josh 2:24	3605
for even *a* the inhabitants of the	Josh 2:24	3605
a the children of Israel, and	Josh 3:1	3605
thee in the sight of *a* Israel	Josh 3:7	3605
a the earth passeth over before	Josh 3:11	3605
the LORD, the Lord of *a* the earth	Josh 3:13	3605
(for Jordan overfloweth *a* his	Josh 3:15	3605
his banks *a* the time of harvest	Josh 3:15	3605
a the Israelites passed over on	Josh 3:17	3605
until *a* the people were passed	Josh 3:17	3605
when *a* the people were clean	Josh 4:1	3605
according to *a* that Moses	Josh 4:10	3605
when *a* the people were clean	Josh 4:11	3605
Joshua in the sight of *a* Israel	Josh 4:14	3605
Moses, *a* the days of his life	Josh 4:14	3605
place, and flowed over *a* his banks	Josh 4:18	3605
That *a* the people of the earth	Josh 4:24	3605
when *a* the kings of the Amorites,	Josh 5:1	3605
a the kings of the Canaanites,	Josh 5:1	3605
A the people that came out of	Josh 5:4	3605
even *a* the men of war, died in	Josh 5:4	3605
Now *a* the people that came out	Josh 5:5	3605
but *a* the people that were born	Josh 5:5	3605
till *a* the people that were men	Josh 5:6	3605
done circumcising *a* the people	Josh 5:8	3605
a ye men of war, and go round	Josh 6:3	3605
a the people shall shout with a	Josh 6:5	3605
a that are therein, to the LORD	Josh 6:17	3605
a that are with her in the house,	Josh 6:17	3605
But *a* the silver, and gold, and	Josh 6:19	3605
destroyed *a* that was in the city	Josh 6:21	3605
a that she hath, as ye sware unto	Josh 6:22	3605
her brethren, and *a* that she had	Josh 6:23	3605
and they brought out *a* her kindred	Josh 6:23	3605
with fire, and *a* that was therein	Josh 6:24	3605
household, and *a* that she had	Josh 6:25	3605
noised throughout *a* the country	Josh 6:27	3605
Let not *a* the people go up	Josh 7:3	3605
make not *a* the people to labour	Josh 7:3	3605
wherefore hast thou at *a* brought	Josh 7:7	
a the inhabitants of the land	Josh 7:9	3605
with fire, he and *a* that he hath	Josh 7:15	3605
unto *a* the children of Israel, and	Josh 7:23	3605
a Israel with him, took Achan the	Josh 7:24	3605
and his tent, and *a* that he had	Josh 7:24	3605
a Israel stoned him with stones,	Josh 7:25	3605
take *a* the people of war with	Josh 8:1	3605
a the people of war, to go up	Josh 8:3	3605
from the city, but be ye *a* ready	Josh 8:4	3605
a the people that are with me,	Josh 8:5	3605
a the people, even the people of	Josh 8:11	3605
even *a* the host that was on the	Josh 8:13	3605
a his people, at a time appointed	Josh 8:14	3605
a Israel made as if they were	Josh 8:15	3605
a the people that were in Ai were	Josh 8:16	3605
a Israel saw that the ambush had	Josh 8:21	3605
had made an end of slaying *a* the	Josh 8:24	3605
when they were *a* fallen on the	Josh 8:24	3605
that *a* the Israelites returned	Josh 8:24	3605
that *a* that fell that day, both	Josh 8:25	3605
thousand, even *a* the men of Ai	Josh 8:25	3605
destroyed *a* the inhabitants of Ai	Josh 8:26	3605
a Israel, and their elders, and	Josh 8:33	3605
afterward he read *a* the words of	Josh 8:34	3605
according to *a* that is written in	Josh 8:34	3605
a word of *a* that Moses commanded	Josh 8:35	3605
a the congregation of Israel	Josh 8:35	3605
when *a* the kings which were on	Josh 9:1	3605
in *a* the coasts of the great sea	Josh 9:1	3605
a the bread of their provision	Josh 9:5	3605
him, and *a* that he did in Egypt,	Josh 9:9	3605
a that he did to the two kings of	Josh 9:10	3605
a the inhabitants of our country	Josh 9:11	3605
a the congregation murmured	Josh 9:18	3605
But *a* the princes said unto *a*	Josh 9:19	3605
of water unto *a* the congregation	Josh 9:21	3605
Moses to give you *a* the land	Josh 9:24	3605
to destroy *a* the inhabitants of	Josh 9:24	3605
a the men thereof were mighty	Josh 10:2	3605
a their hosts, and encamped before	Josh 10:5	3605
for *a* the kings of the Amorites	Josh 10:6	
a the people of war with him, and	Josh 10:7	3605
a the mighty men of valour	Josh 10:7	3605
and went up from Gilgal *a* night	Josh 10:9	3605
a Israel with him, unto the camp	Josh 10:15	3605
a the people returned to the camp	Josh 10:21	3605
called for *a* the men of Israel	Josh 10:24	3605
to *a* your enemies against whom ye	Josh 10:25	3605
a the souls that were therein	Josh 10:28	3605
a Israel with him, unto Libnah,	Josh 10:29	3605
a the souls that were therein	Josh 10:30	3605
a Israel with him, unto Lachish,	Josh 10:31	3605
a the souls that were therein,	Josh 10:32	3605
according to *a* that he had done	Josh 10:32	3605
unto Eglon, and *a* Israel with him	Josh 10:34	3605
a the souls that were therein he	Josh 10:35	3605
according to *a* that he had done	Josh 10:35	3605
a Israel with him, unto Hebron	Josh 10:36	3605
a the cities thereof, and *a* the	Josh 10:37	3605
according to *a* that he had done	Josh 10:37	3605
a the souls that were therein	Josh 10:37	3605
a Israel with him, to Debir	Josh 10:38	3605
thereof, and *a* the cities thereof	Josh 10:39	3605
utterly destroyed *a* the souls	Josh 10:39	3605
So Joshua smote *a* the country of	Josh 10:40	3605
of the springs, and *a* their kings	Josh 10:40	3605
utterly destroyed *a* that breathed	Josh 10:40	3605
a the country of Goshen, even	Josh 10:41	3605
a these kings and their land did	Josh 10:42	3605
a Israel with him, unto the camp	Josh 10:43	3605
a their hosts with them, much	Josh 11:4	3605
when *a* these kings were met	Josh 11:5	3605
them up *a* slain before Israel	Josh 11:6	3605
a the people of war with him,	Josh 11:7	3605
was the head of *a* those kingdoms	Josh 11:10	3605
they smote *a* the souls that were	Josh 11:11	3605
a the cities of those kings, and	Josh 11:12	3605
a the kings of them, did Joshua	Josh 11:12	3605
a the spoil of these cities, and	Josh 11:14	3605
he left nothing undone of *a* that	Josh 11:15	3605
So Joshua took *a* that land	Josh 11:16	3605
a the south country, and *a* the	Josh 11:16	3605
a their kings he took, and smote	Josh 11:17	3605
a long time with *a* those kings	Josh 11:18	3605
a other they took in battle	Josh 11:19	3605
from *a* the mountains of Judah, and	Josh 11:21	3605
from *a* the mountains of Israel	Josh 11:21	3605
according to *a* that the LORD said	Josh 11:23	3605
and *a* the plain on the east	Josh 12:1	3605
in *a* Bashan, unto the border of	Josh 12:5	3605

Context	Reference	Strong's
a the kings thirty and one	Josh 12:24	3605
a the borders of the Philistines,	Josh 13:2	3605
of the Philistines, and *a* Geshuri,	Josh 13:2	3605
a the land of the Canaanites, and	Josh 13:4	3605
a Lebanon, toward the sunrising,	Josh 13:5	3605
A the inhabitants of the hill	Josh 13:6	3605
a the Sidonians, them will I	Josh 13:6	3605
a the plain of Medeba unto Dibon	Josh 13:9	3605
a the cities of Sihon king of the	Josh 13:10	3605
a mount Hermon, and *a* Bashan	Josh 13:11	3605
A the kingdom of Og in Bashan,	Josh 13:12	3605
river, and *a* the plain by Medeba	Josh 13:16	3605
a her cities that are in the	Josh 13:17	3605
a the cities of the plain, and *a*	Josh 13:21	3605
a the cities of Gilead, and half	Josh 13:25	3605
a Bashan, *a* the kingdom of Og	Josh 13:30	3605
a the towns of Jair, which are in	Josh 13:30	3605
a the cities are twenty and nine,	Josh 15:32	3605
a that lay near Ashdod, with	Josh 15:46	3605
a the cities with their villages	Josh 16:9	3605
a the Canaanites that dwell in	Josh 17:16	3605
a the villages that were round	Josh 19:8	3605
for *a* the children of Israel	Josh 20:9	3605
A the cities of the children of	Josh 21:19	3605
A the cities were ten with their	Josh 21:26	3605
A the cities of the Gershonites	Josh 21:33	3605
four cities in *a*	Josh 21:39	3605
So *a* the cities for the children	Josh 21:40	3605
A the cities of the Levites	Josh 21:41	3605
thus were *a* these cities	Josh 21:42	3605
the LORD gave unto Israel *a* the	Josh 21:43	3605
according to *a* that he sware unto	Josh 21:44	3605
there stood not a man of *a* their	Josh 21:44	3605
the LORD delivered *a* their	Josh 21:44	3605
a came to pass	Josh 21:45	3605
Ye have kept *a* that Moses the	Josh 22:2	3605
voice in *a* that I commanded you	Josh 22:2	3605
God, and to walk in *a* his ways	Josh 22:5	3605
a your heart and with *a* your soul	Josh 22:5	3605
throughout *a* the tribes of Israel	Josh 22:14	3605
wrath fell on *a* the congregation	Josh 22:20	3605
from *a* their enemies round about	Josh 23:1	3605
And Joshua called for *a* Israel	Josh 23:2	3605
ye have seen *a* that the LORD your	Josh 23:3	3605
a these nations because of you	Josh 23:3	3605
with *a* the nations that I have	Josh 23:4	3605
to do *a* that is written in the	Josh 23:6	3605
I am going the way of *a* the earth	Josh 23:14	3605
ye know in *a* your hearts and in	Josh 23:14	3605
in *a* your souls, that not one	Josh 23:14	3605
not one thing hath failed of *a*	Josh 23:14	3605
a are come to pass unto you, and	Josh 23:14	3605
that as *a* good things are come	Josh 23:15	3605
LORD bring upon you *a* evil things	Josh 23:15	3605
Joshua gathered *a* the tribes of	Josh 24:1	3605
And Joshua said unto *a* the people	Josh 24:2	3605
throughout *a* the land of Canaan	Josh 24:3	3605
preserved us in *a* the way wherein	Josh 24:17	3605
among *a* the people through whom	Josh 24:17	3605
out from before us *a* the people	Josh 24:18	3605
And Joshua said unto *a* the people	Josh 24:27	3605
for it hath heard *a* the words of	Josh 24:27	3605
the LORD *a* the days of Joshua	Josh 24:31	3605
a the days of the elders that	Josh 24:31	3605
which had known *a* the works of	Josh 24:31	3605
let go the man and *a* his family	Judg 1:25	3605
unto *a* the children of Israel	Judg 2:4	3605
the LORD *a* the days of Joshua	Judg 2:7	3605
a the days of the elders that	Judg 2:7	3605
who had seen *a* the great works of	Judg 2:7	3605
also *a* that generation were	Judg 2:10	3605
enemies *a* the days of the judge	Judg 2:18	3605
not known *a* the wars of Canaan	Judg 3:1	3605
and *a* the Canaanites, and the	Judg 3:3	3605
a that stood by him went out from	Judg 3:19	3605
a lusty, and *a* men of valour	Judg 3:29	3605
gathered together *a* his chariots	Judg 4:13	3605
a the people that were with him,	Judg 4:13	3605
a his chariots, and *a* his host,	Judg 4:15	3605
a the host of Sisera fell upon	Judg 4:16	3605
So let *a* thine enemies perish, O	Judg 5:31	3605
the hand of *a* that oppressed you	Judg 6:9	3605
why then is *a* this befallen us	Judg 6:13	3605
where be *a* his miracles which our	Judg 6:13	3605
Joash said unto *a* that stood	Judg 6:31	3605
Then *a* the Midianites and the	Judg 6:33	3605
messengers throughout *a* Manasseh	Judg 6:35	3605
it be dry upon *a* the earth beside	Judg 6:37	3605
upon *a* the ground let there be	Judg 6:39	3605
and there was dew on *a* the ground	Judg 6:40	3605
a the people that were with him,	Judg 7:1	3605
but *a* the rest of the people	Judg 7:6	3605
let *a* the other people go every	Judg 7:7	3605
he sent *a* the rest of Israel	Judg 7:8	3605
a the children of the east lay	Judg 7:12	3605
delivered Midian, and *a* the host	Judg 7:14	3605
a that are with me, then blow ye	Judg 7:18	3605
also on every side of *a* the camp	Judg 7:18	3605
a the host ran, and cried, and fled	Judg 7:21	3605
even throughout *a* the host	Judg 7:22	3605
out of *a* Manasseh, and pursued	Judg 7:23	3605
throughout *a* mount Ephraim	Judg 7:24	3605
Then *a* the men of Ephraim	Judg 7:24	3605
a that were left of *a* the hosts	Judg 8:10	3605
and discomfited *a* the host	Judg 8:12	3605
a Israel went thither a whoring	Judg 8:27	3605
them out of the hands of *a* their	Judg 8:34	3605
according to *a* the goodness which	Judg 8:35	3605
with *a* the family of the house of	Judg 9:1	3605
in the ears of *a* the men of	Judg 9:2	3605
either that *a* the sons of	Judg 9:2	3605
spake of him in the ears of *a* the	Judg 9:3	3605
the men of Shechem *a* these words	Judg 9:3	3605
a the men of Shechem gathered	Judg 9:6	3605
a the house of Millo, and went, and	Judg 9:6	3605
Then said *a* the trees unto the	Judg 9:14	3605
they robbed *a* that came along	Judg 9:25	3605
a the people that were with him,	Judg 9:34	3605
a the people that were in the	Judg 9:44	3605
against the city *a* that day	Judg 9:45	3605
when *a* the men of the tower of	Judg 9:46	3605
that *a* the men of the tower of	Judg 9:47	3605
a the people that were with him	Judg 9:48	3605
a the people likewise cut down	Judg 9:49	3605
so that *a* the men of the tower of	Judg 9:49	3605
city, and thither fled *a* the men	Judg 9:51	3605
a they of the city, and shut it to	Judg 9:51	3605
head, and *a* to brake his skull	Judg 9:53	
a the evil of the men of Shechem	Judg 9:57	3605
a the children of Israel that	Judg 10:8	3605
he shall be head over *a* the	Judg 10:18	3605
Ammon, and be our head over *a* the	Judg 11:8	3605
Jephthah uttered *a* his words	Judg 11:11	3605
but Sihon gathered *a* his people	Judg 11:20	3605
a his people into the hand of	Judg 11:21	3605
so Israel possessed *a* the land of	Judg 11:21	3605
they possessed *a* the coasts of	Judg 11:22	3605
in *a* the cities that be along by	Judg 11:26	3605
together *a* the men of Gilead	Judg 12:4	3605
Of *a* that I said unto the woman	Judg 13:13	3605
a that I commanded her let her	Judg 13:14	3605
he have shewed us *a* these things	Judg 13:23	3605
or among *a* my people, that thou	Judg 14:3	3605
laid wait for him *a* night in the	Judg 16:2	3605
city, and were quiet *a* the night	Judg 16:2	3605
and went away with them, bar and *a*	Judg 16:3	5973
That he told her *a* his heart	Judg 16:17	3605
that he had told her *a* his heart	Judg 16:18	3605
for he hath shewed me *a* his heart	Judg 16:18	3605
a the lords of the Philistines	Judg 16:27	3605
he bowed himself with *a* his might	Judg 16:30	
upon *a* the people that were	Judg 16:30	3605
a the house of his father came	Judg 16:31	3605
for unto that day *a* their	Judg 18:1	
a the time that the house of God	Judg 18:31	3605
I pray thee, and tarry *a* night	Judg 19:6	3885
evening, I pray you tarry *a* night	Judg 19:9	3885
of these places to lodge *a* night	Judg 19:13	3885
howsoever let *a* thy wants lie	Judg 19:20	3605
abused her *a* the night until the	Judg 19:25	3605
sent her into *a* the coasts of	Judg 19:29	3605
that *a* that saw it said, There	Judg 19:30	3605
Then *a* the children of Israel	Judg 20:1	3605
And the chief of *a* the people	Judg 20:2	3605
even of *a* the tribes of Israel,	Judg 20:2	3605
sent her throughout *a* the country	Judg 20:6	3605
ye are *a* children of Israel	Judg 20:7	3605
a the people arose as one man,	Judg 20:8	3605
throughout *a* the tribes of Israel	Judg 20:10	3605
according to *a* the folly that	Judg 20:10	3605
So *a* the men of Israel were	Judg 20:11	3605
through *a* the tribe of Benjamin	Judg 20:12	3605
Among *a* this people there were	Judg 20:16	3605
a these were men of war	Judg 20:17	3605
a these drew the sword	Judg 20:25	3605
Then *a* the children of Israel, and	Judg 20:26	3605
a the people, went up, and came	Judg 20:26	3605
a the men of Israel rose up out	Judg 20:33	3605
chosen men out of *a* Israel	Judg 20:34	3605
a these drew the sword	Judg 20:35	3605
smote *a* the city with the edge of	Judg 20:37	3605
a these were men of valour	Judg 20:44	3605
So that *a* which fell that day of	Judg 20:46	3605
a these were men of valour	Judg 20:46	3605
the beast, and *a* that came to hand	Judg 20:48	3605
also they set on fire *a* the	Judg 20:48	3605
Who is there among *a* the tribes	Judg 21:5	3605
that *a* the city was moved about	Ruth 1:19	3605
a that thou hast done unto thy	Ruth 2:11	3605
they have ended *a* my harvest	Ruth 2:21	3605
A that thou sayest unto me I will	Ruth 3:5	3605
did according to *a* that her	Ruth 3:6	3605
I will do to thee *a* that thou	Ruth 3:11	3605
for *a* the city of my people doth	Ruth 3:11	3605
she told her *a* that the man had	Ruth 3:16	3605
changing, for to confirm *a* things	Ruth 4:7	3605
unto *a* the people, Ye are	Ruth 4:9	3605
that I have bought *a* that was	Ruth 4:9	3605
a that was Chilion's and Mahlon's,	Ruth 4:9	3605
a the people that were in the	Ruth 4:11	3605
to *a* her sons and her daughters,	1Sa 1:4	3605
the LORD *a* the days of his life	1Sa 1:11	3605
a his house, went up to offer	1Sa 1:21	3605
a that the fleshhook brought up	1Sa 2:14	3605
unto *a* the Israelites that came	1Sa 2:14	3605
a that his sons did unto *a* Israel	1Sa 2:22	3605
evil dealings by *a* this people	1Sa 2:23	3605
did I choose him out of *a* the	1Sa 2:28	3605
unto the house of thy father *a*	1Sa 2:28	3605
fat with the chiefest of *a* the	1Sa 2:29	3605
in *a* the wealth which God shall	1Sa 2:32	3605
a the increase of thine house	1Sa 2:33	3605
Eli *a* things which I have spoken	1Sa 3:12	3605
of *a* the things that he said unto	1Sa 3:17	3605
a Israel from Dan even to	1Sa 3:20	3605
word of Samuel came to *a* Israel	1Sa 4:1	3605
a Israel shouted with a great	1Sa 4:5	3605
a the plagues in the wilderness	1Sa 4:8	3605
and told it, *a* the city cried out	1Sa 4:13	3605
gathered *a* the lords of the	1Sa 5:8	3605
gathered together *a* the lords of	1Sa 5:11	3605
destruction throughout *a* the city	1Sa 5:11	3605
for one plague was on you *a*	1Sa 6:4	3605
according to the number of *a* the	1Sa 6:18	3605
a the house of Israel lamented	1Sa 7:2	3605
Samuel spake unto *a* the house of	1Sa 7:3	3605
unto the LORD with *a* your hearts	1Sa 7:3	3605
Gather *a* Israel to Mizpeh, and I	1Sa 7:5	3605
Philistines *a* the days of Samuel	1Sa 7:13	3605
Israel *a* the days of his life	1Sa 7:15	3605
judged Israel in *a* those places	1Sa 7:16	3605
Then *a* the elders of Israel	1Sa 8:4	3605
to judge us like *a* the nations	1Sa 8:5	3605
in *a* that they say unto thee	1Sa 8:7	3605
According to *a* the works which	1Sa 8:8	3605
Samuel told *a* the words of the	1Sa 8:10	3605
we also may be like *a* the nations	1Sa 8:20	3605
Samuel heard *a* the words of the	1Sa 8:21	3605
a that he saith cometh surely to	1Sa 9:6	3605
will tell thee *a* that is in thine	1Sa 9:19	3605
on whom is *a* the desire of Israel	1Sa 9:20	3605
thee, and on *a* thy father's house	1Sa 9:20	3605
my family the least of *a* the	1Sa 9:21	3605
a those signs came to pass that	1Sa 10:9	3605
when *a* that knew him beforetime	1Sa 10:11	3605
and out of the hand of *a* kingdoms	1Sa 10:18	3605
you out of *a* your adversities	1Sa 10:19	3605
when Samuel had caused *a* the	1Sa 10:20	3605
And Samuel said to *a* the people	1Sa 10:24	3605
none like him among *a* the people	1Sa 10:24	3605
a the people shouted, and said,	1Sa 10:24	3605
Samuel sent *a* the people away,	1Sa 10:25	3605
a the men of Jabesh said unto	1Sa 11:1	3605
may thrust out *a* your right eyes	1Sa 11:2	3605
it for a reproach upon *a* Israel	1Sa 11:2	3605
unto *a* the coasts of Israel	1Sa 11:3	3605
a the people lifted up their	1Sa 11:4	3605
sent them throughout *a* the coasts	1Sa 11:7	3605
ye shall do with us *a* that	1Sa 11:10	3605
a the people went to Gilgal	1Sa 11:15	3605
a the men of Israel rejoiced	1Sa 11:15	3605
And Samuel said unto *a* Israel	1Sa 12:1	3605
voice in *a* that ye said unto me	1Sa 12:1	3605
with you before the LORD of *a* the	1Sa 12:7	3605
a the people greatly feared the	1Sa 12:18	3605
a the people said unto Samuel,	1Sa 12:19	3605
added unto *a* our sins this evil	1Sa 12:19	3605
ye have done *a* this wickedness	1Sa 12:20	3605
serve the LORD with *a* your heart	1Sa 12:20	3605
him in truth with *a* your heart	1Sa 12:24	3605
the trumpet throughout *a* the land	1Sa 13:3	3605
a Israel heard say that Saul had	1Sa 13:4	3605
a the people followed him	1Sa 13:7	3605
throughout *a* the land of Israel	1Sa 13:19	3605
But *a* the Israelites went down to	1Sa 13:20	3605
Do *a* that is in thine heart	1Sa 14:7	3605
the field, and among *a* the people	1Sa 14:15	3605
a the people that were with him	1Sa 14:20	3605
Likewise *a* the men of Israel	1Sa 14:22	3605
a they of the land came to a wood	1Sa 14:25	3605
a the people brought every man	1Sa 14:34	3605
a the chief of the people	1Sa 14:38	3605
a the people that answered him	1Sa 14:39	3605
Then said he unto *a* Israel	1Sa 14:40	3605
fought against *a* his enemies on	1Sa 14:47	3605
Philistines *a* the days of Saul	1Sa 14:52	3605
utterly destroy *a* that they have	1Sa 15:3	3605
to *a* the children of Israel	1Sa 15:6	3605
utterly destroyed *a* the people	1Sa 15:8	3605
a that was good, and would not	1Sa 15:9	3605
and he cried unto the LORD *a* night	1Sa 15:11	3605
Jesse, Are here *a* thy children	1Sa 16:11	8552
a Israel heard those words of the	1Sa 17:11	3605
a the men of Israel, were in the	1Sa 17:19	3605
a the men of Israel, when they	1Sa 17:24	3605
that *a* the earth may know that	1Sa 17:46	3605
a this assembly shall know that	1Sa 17:47	3605
in the sight of *a* the people	1Sa 18:5	3605
came out of *a* cities of Israel	1Sa 18:6	3605
himself wisely in *a* his ways	1Sa 18:14	3605
But *a* Israel and Judah loved David	1Sa 18:16	3605
thee, and *a* his servants love thee	1Sa 18:22	3605
than *a* the servants of Saul	1Sa 18:30	3605
to *a* his servants, that they	1Sa 19:1	3605
a great salvation for *a* Israel	1Sa 19:5	3605
shewed him *a* those things	1Sa 19:7	3605
told him *a* that Saul had done to	1Sa 19:18	3605
a that day and *a* that night	1Sa 19:24	3605
If thy father at *a* miss me	1Sa 20:6	
sacrifice there for *a* the family	1Sa 20:6	3605
a his father's house heard it,	1Sa 22:1	3605
they dwelt with him *a* the while	1Sa 22:4	3605
a his servants were standing	1Sa 22:6	3605
make you *a* captains of thousands,	1Sa 22:7	3605
That *a* of you have conspired	1Sa 22:8	3605
a his father's house, the priests	1Sa 22:11	3605
they came *a* of them to the king	1Sa 22:11	3605
among *a* thy servants as David	1Sa 22:14	3605
nor to *a* the house of my father	1Sa 22:15	3605
servant knew nothing of *a* this	1Sa 22:15	3605
thou, and *a* thy father's house	1Sa 22:16	3605
of *a* the persons of thy father's	1Sa 22:22	3605
Saul called *a* the people together	1Sa 23:8	3605
come down according to *a* the	1Sa 23:20	3605
take knowledge of *a* the lurking	1Sa 23:23	3605
a the thousands of Judah	1Sa 23:23	3605
chosen men out of *a* Israel	1Sa 24:2	3605
a the Israelites were gathered	1Sa 25:1	3605
peace be unto *a* that thou hast	1Sa 25:6	3605
a the while they were in Carmel	1Sa 25:7	3605
to *a* those words in the name of	1Sa 25:9	3605
came and told him *a* those sayings	1Sa 25:12	3605
a the while we were with them	1Sa 25:16	3605
and against *a* his household	1Sa 25:17	3605
Surely in vain have I kept *a* that	1Sa 25:21	3605
of *a* that pertained unto him	1Sa 25:21	3605
if I leave of *a* that pertain to	1Sa 25:22	3605
not been found in thee *a* thy days	1Sa 25:28	
to *a* the good that he hath spoken	1Sa 25:30	3605
for they were *a* asleep	1Sa 26:12	3605
deliver me out of *a* tribulation	1Sa 26:24	3605
so will be his manner *a* the while	1Sa 27:11	3605

a Israel had lamented him, and ... 1Sa 28:3 3605
Saul gathered *a* Israel together, ... 1Sa 28:4 3605
straightway *a* along on the earth ... 1Sa 28:20 4393
a the day, nor *a* the night ... 1Sa 28:20 3605
together *a* their armies to Aphek ... 1Sa 29:1 3605
because the soul of *a* the people ... 1Sa 30:6 3605
them, and without fail recover *a* ... 1Sa 30:8 3605
spread abroad upon *a* the earth ... 1Sa 30:16 3605
because of *a* the great spoil that ... 1Sa 30:16 3605
David recovered *a* that the ... 1Sa 30:18 3605
David recovered *a* ... 1Sa 30:19 3605
And David took *a* the flocks ... 1Sa 30:20 3605
Then answered *a* the wicked men and. 1Sa 30:22 3605
to *a* the places where David ... 1Sa 30:31 3605
a his men, that same day together ... 1Sa 31:6 3605
A the valiant men arose, and went ... 1Sa 31:12 3605
went *a* night, and took the body of ... 1Sa 31:12 3605
likewise *a* the men that were with ... 2Sa 1:11 3605
over Benjamin, and over *a* Israel ... 2Sa 2:9 3605
a the people stood still, and ... 2Sa 2:28 3605
his men walked *a* that night ... 2Sa 2:29 3605
Jordan, and went through *a* Bithron ... 2Sa 2:29 3605
gathered *a* the people together ... 2Sa 2:30 3605
And Joab and his men went *a* night ... 2Sa 2:32 3605
to bring about *a* Israel unto thee ... 2Sa 3:12 3605
of the hand of *a* their enemies ... 2Sa 3:18 3605
a that seemed good to Israel ... 2Sa 3:19 3605
will gather *a* Israel unto my lord ... 2Sa 3:21 3605
over *a* that thine heart desireth ... 2Sa 3:21 3605
a the host that was with him were ... 2Sa 3:23 3605
to know *a* that thou doest ... 2Sa 3:25 3605
Joab, and on *a* his father's house ... 2Sa 3:29 3605
to *a* the people that were with ... 2Sa 3:31 3605
and *a* the people wept ... 2Sa 3:32 3605
a the people wept again over him ... 2Sa 3:34 3605
when *a* the people came to cause ... 2Sa 3:35 3605
a the people took notice of it, ... 2Sa 3:36 3605
the king did pleased *a* the people ... 2Sa 3:36 3605
For *a* the people and *a* Israel ... 2Sa 3:37 3605
a the Israelites were troubled ... 2Sa 4:1 3605
away through the plain *a* night ... 2Sa 4:7 3605
my soul out of *a* adversity ... 2Sa 4:9 3605
Then came *a* the tribes of Israel ... 2Sa 5:1 3605
So *a* the elders of Israel came to ... 2Sa 5:3 3605
and three years over *a* Israel ... 2Sa 5:5 3605
a the Philistines came up to seek ... 2Sa 5:17 3605
David gathered together *a* the ... 2Sa 6:1 3605
went with *a* the people that were ... 2Sa 6:2 3605
a the house of Israel played ... 2Sa 6:5 3605
played before the LORD on *a* ... 2Sa 6:5 3605
Obed-edom, and *a* his household ... 2Sa 6:11 3605
a that pertaineth unto him, ... 2Sa 6:12 3605
before the LORD with *a* his might ... 2Sa 6:14 3605
a the house of Israel brought up ... 2Sa 6:15 3605
And he dealt among *a* the people ... 2Sa 6:19 3605
So *a* the people departed every ... 2Sa 6:19 3605
before *a* his house, to appoint me ... 2Sa 6:21 3605
round about from *a* his enemies ... 2Sa 7:1 3605
do *a* that is in thine heart ... 2Sa 7:3 3605
In *a* the places wherein I have ... 2Sa 7:7 3605
walked with *a* the children of ... 2Sa 7:7 3605
have cut off *a* thine enemies out ... 2Sa 7:9 3605
thee to rest from *a* thine enemies ... 2Sa 7:11 3605
According to *a* these words ... 2Sa 7:17 3605
and according to *a* this vision ... 2Sa 7:17 3605
hast thou done *a* these great ... 2Sa 7:21 3605
according to *a* that we have heard ... 2Sa 7:22 3605
David houghed *a* the chariot ... 2Sa 8:4 3605
smitten *a* the host of Hadadezer ... 2Sa 8:9 3605
of *a* nations which he subdued ... 2Sa 8:11 3605
throughout *a* Edom put he ... 2Sa 8:14 3605
a they of Edom became David's ... 2Sa 8:14 3605
And David reigned over *a* Israel ... 2Sa 8:15 3605
and justice unto *a* his people ... 2Sa 8:15 3605
will restore thee *a* the land of ... 2Sa 9:7 3605
son *a* that pertained to Saul ... 2Sa 9:9 3605
to Saul and to *a* his house ... 2Sa 9:9 3605
According to *a* that my lord the ... 2Sa 9:11 3605
a that dwelt in the house of Ziba ... 2Sa 9:12 3605
a the host of the mighty men ... 2Sa 10:7 3605
he chose of *a* the choice men of ... 2Sa 10:9 3605
he gathered *a* Israel together, and ... 2Sa 10:17 3605
when *a* the kings that were ... 2Sa 10:19 3605
servants with him, and *a* Israel ... 2Sa 11:1 3605
with *a* the servants of his lord ... 2Sa 11:9 3605
sent and told David *a* the things ... 2Sa 11:18 3605
shewed David *a* that Joab had sent ... 2Sa 11:22 3605
do this thing before *a* Israel ... 2Sa 12:12 3605
lay *a* night upon the earth ... 2Sa 12:16 3885
David gathered *a* the people ... 2Sa 12:29 3605
thus did he unto *a* the cities of ... 2Sa 12:31 3605
a the people returned unto ... 2Sa 12:31 3605
said, Have out *a* men from me ... 2Sa 13:9 3605
David heard of *a* these things ... 2Sa 13:21 3605
Absalom invited *a* the king's sons ... 2Sa 13:23 3605
Nay, my son, let us not *a* now go ... 2Sa 13:25 3605
a the king's sons go with him ... 2Sa 13:27 3605
Then *a* the king's sons arose, and ... 2Sa 13:29 3605
hath slain *a* the king's sons ... 2Sa 13:30 3605
a his servants stood by with ... 2Sa 13:31 3605
suppose that they have slain *a* ... 2Sa 13:32 3605
to think that *a* the king's sons ... 2Sa 13:33 3605
a his servants wept very sore ... 2Sa 13:36 3605
hand of Joab with thee in *a* this ... 2Sa 14:19 3605
he put *a* these words in the mouth ... 2Sa 14:19 3605
to know *a* things that are in the ... 2Sa 14:20 3605
But in *a* Israel there was none to ... 2Sa 14:25 3605
to *a* Israel that came to the king ... 2Sa 15:6 3605
throughout *a* the tribes of Israel ... 2Sa 15:10 3605
David said unto *a* his servants ... 2Sa 15:14 3605
a his household after him ... 2Sa 15:16 3605
a the people after him, and ... 2Sa 15:17 3605
a his servants passed on beside ... 2Sa 15:18 3605
a the Cherethites, and *a* the ... 2Sa 15:18 3605
a the Gittites, six hundred men ... 2Sa 15:18 3605
a his men, and *a* the little ones ... 2Sa 15:22 3605
a the country wept with a loud ... 2Sa 15:23 3605
and *a* the people passed over ... 2Sa 15:23 3605
a the people passed over, toward ... 2Sa 15:23 3605
a the Levites were with him, ... 2Sa 15:24 3605
until *a* the people had done ... 2Sa 15:24 3605
a the people that was with him ... 2Sa 15:30 3605
thine are *a* that pertained unto ... 2Sa 16:4 3605
at *a* the servants of king David ... 2Sa 16:6 3605
a the people and *a* the mighty ... 2Sa 16:6 3605
LORD hath returned upon thee *a* ... 2Sa 16:8 3605
to *a* his servants, Behold, my son ... 2Sa 16:11 3605
a the people that were with him, ... 2Sa 16:14 3605
a the people the men of Israel, ... 2Sa 16:15 3605
a the men of Israel, choose, his ... 2Sa 16:18 3605
a Israel shall hear that thou art ... 2Sa 16:21 3605
then shall the hands of *a* that ... 2Sa 16:21 3605
in the sight of *a* Israel ... 2Sa 16:22 3605
so was *a* the counsel of ... 2Sa 16:23 3605
a the people that are with him ... 2Sa 17:2 3605
I will bring back *a* the people ... 2Sa 17:3 3605
thou seekest is as if *a* returned ... 2Sa 17:3 3605
so *a* the people shall be in peace ... 2Sa 17:3 3605
well, and *a* the elders of Israel ... 2Sa 17:4 3605
for *a* Israel knoweth that thy ... 2Sa 17:10 3605
Therefore I counsel that *a* Israel ... 2Sa 17:11 3605
of *a* the men that are with him ... 2Sa 17:12 3605
then shall *a* Israel bring ropes ... 2Sa 17:13 3605
a the men of Israel said, The ... 2Sa 17:14 3605
a the people that are with him ... 2Sa 17:16 3605
a the people that were with him, ... 2Sa 17:22 3605
a the men of Israel with him ... 2Sa 17:24 3605
a the people came out by hundreds ... 2Sa 18:4 3605
a the people heard when the king ... 2Sa 18:5 3605
a the captains charge concerning ... 2Sa 18:5 3605
over the face of *a* the country ... 2Sa 18:8 3605
a Israel fled every one to his ... 2Sa 18:17 3605
and said unto the king, *A* is well ... 2Sa 18:28
hath avenged thee this day of *a* ... 2Sa 18:31 3605
a that rise against thee to do ... 2Sa 18:32 3605
into mourning unto *a* the people ... 2Sa 19:2 3605
day the faces of *a* thy servants ... 2Sa 19:5 3605
a we had died this day, then it ... 2Sa 19:6 3605
will be worse unto thee than *a* ... 2Sa 19:7 3605
And they told unto *a* the people ... 2Sa 19:8 3605
a the people came before the king ... 2Sa 19:8 3605
a the people were at strife ... 2Sa 19:9 3605
throughout *a* the tribes of Israel ... 2Sa 19:9 3605
seeing the speech of *a* Israel is ... 2Sa 19:11 3605
the heart of *a* the men of Judah ... 2Sa 19:14 3605
Return thou, and *a* thy servants ... 2Sa 19:14 3605
a the house of Joseph to go down ... 2Sa 19:20 3605
For *a* of my father's house were ... 2Sa 19:28 3605
the king, Yea, let him take *a* ... 2Sa 19:30 3605
a the people went over Jordan ... 2Sa 19:39 3605
a the people of Judah conducted ... 2Sa 19:40 3605
a the men of Israel came to the ... 2Sa 19:41 3605
a David's men with him, over ... 2Sa 19:41 3605
a the men of Judah answered the ... 2Sa 19:42 3605
have we eaten at *a* of the king's ... 2Sa 19:42 3605
Pelethites, and *a* the mighty men ... 2Sa 20:7 3605
when the man saw that *a* the ... 2Sa 20:12 3605
a the people went on after Joab, ... 2Sa 20:13 3605
he went through *a* the tribes of ... 2Sa 20:14 3605
to Beth-maachah, and *a* the Berites ... 2Sa 20:14 3605
a the people that were with Joab ... 2Sa 20:15 3605
unto *a* the people in her wisdom ... 2Sa 20:22 3605
Now Joab was over *a* the host of ... 2Sa 20:23 3605
they fell *a* seven together, and ... 2Sa 21:9 3605
they performed *a* that the king ... 2Sa 21:14 3605
out of the hand of *a* his enemies ... 2Sa 22:1 3605
For *a* his judgments were before ... 2Sa 22:23 3605
he is a buckler to *a* them that ... 2Sa 22:31 3605
covenant, ordered in *a* things ... 2Sa 23:5 3605
for this is *a* my salvation, and ... 2Sa 23:5 3605
a my desire, although he make it ... 2Sa 23:5 3605
a of them as thorns thrust away ... 2Sa 23:6 3605
thirty and seven in *a* ... 2Sa 23:39 3605
Go now through *a* the tribes of ... 2Sa 24:2 3605
to *a* the cities of the Hivites, ... 2Sa 24:7 3605
they had gone through *a* the land ... 2Sa 24:8 3605
A these things did Araunah, as a ... 2Sa 24:23 3605
throughout *a* the coasts of Israel ... 1Kin 1:3 3605
called *a* his brethren the king's ... 1Kin 1:9 3605
a the men of Judah the king's ... 1Kin 1:9 3605
hath called *a* the sons of the ... 1Kin 1:19 3605
the eyes of *a* Israel are upon ... 1Kin 1:20 3605
hath called *a* the king's sons, and ... 1Kin 1:25 3605
my soul out of *a* distress ... 1Kin 1:29 3605
a the people said, God save king ... 1Kin 1:39 3605
a the people came up after him, ... 1Kin 1:40 3605
a the guests that were with him ... 1Kin 1:41 3605
a the guests that were with ... 1Kin 1:49 3605
I go the way of *a* the earth ... 1Kin 2:2 3605
prosper in *a* that thou doest ... 1Kin 2:3 3605
me in truth with *a* their heart ... 1Kin 2:4 3605
with *a* their soul, there shall ... 1Kin 2:4 3605
that *a* Israel set their faces on ... 1Kin 2:15 3605
thou hast been afflicted in *a* ... 1Kin 2:26 3605
Thou knowest *a* the wickedness ... 1Kin 2:44 3605
kings like unto thee *a* thy days ... 1Kin 3:13 3605
and made a feast to *a* his servants ... 1Kin 3:15 3605
a Israel heard of the judgment ... 1Kin 3:28 3605
Solomon was king over *a* Israel ... 1Kin 4:1 3605
had twelve officers over *a* Israel ... 1Kin 4:7 3605
Sochoh, and *a* the land of Hepher ... 1Kin 4:10 3605
Abinadab, in *a* the region of Dor ... 1Kin 4:11 3605
a Beth-shean, which is by ... 1Kin 4:12 3605
Solomon reigned over *a* kingdoms ... 1Kin 4:21 3605
served Solomon *a* the days of his ... 1Kin 4:21 3605
For he had dominion over *a* the ... 1Kin 4:24 3605
over *a* the kings on this side the ... 1Kin 4:24 3605
he had peace on *a* sides round ... 1Kin 4:24 3605
Beer-sheba, *a* the days of Solomon ... 1Kin 4:25 3605
for *a* that came unto king ... 1Kin 4:27 3605
of *a* the children of the east ... 1Kin 4:30 3605
country, and *a* the wisdom of Egypt ... 1Kin 4:30 3605
For he was wiser than *a* men ... 1Kin 4:31 3605
his fame was in *a* nations round ... 1Kin 4:31 3605
there came of *a* people to hear ... 1Kin 4:34 3605
from *a* kings of the earth, which ... 1Kin 4:34 3605
to *a* that thou shalt appoint ... 1Kin 5:6 3605
I will do *a* thy desire concerning ... 1Kin 5:8 3605
trees according to *a* his desire ... 1Kin 5:10 3605
raised a levy out of *a* Israel ... 1Kin 5:13 3605
chambers against *a* the house ... 1Kin 6:10 3605
keep *a* my commandments to walk in. 1Kin 6:12 3605
a was cedar ... 1Kin 6:18 3605
until he had finished *a* the house ... 1Kin 6:22 3605
he carved *a* the walls of the ... 1Kin 6:29 3605
throughout *a* the parts thereof ... 1Kin 6:38 3605
according to *a* the fashion of it ... 1Kin 6:38 3605
years, and he finished *a* his house ... 1Kin 7:1 3605
a the doors and posts were square, ... 1Kin 7:5 3605
A these were of costly stones, ... 1Kin 7:9 3605
cunning to work *a* works in brass ... 1Kin 7:14 3605
Solomon, and wrought *a* his work ... 1Kin 7:14 3605
it was round *a* about, and his ... 1Kin 7:23
a their hinder parts were inward ... 1Kin 7:25 3605
and their spokes, were *a* molten ... 1Kin 7:33 3605
a of them had one casting, one ... 1Kin 7:37 3605
a the work that he made king ... 1Kin 7:40 3605
a these vessels, which Hiram made ... 1Kin 7:45 3605
Solomon left *a* the vessels ... 1Kin 7:47 3605
Solomon made *a* the vessels that ... 1Kin 7:48 3605
So was ended *a* the work that king ... 1Kin 7:51 3605
a the heads of the tribes, the ... 1Kin 8:1 3605
a the men of Israel assembled ... 1Kin 8:2 3605
a the elders of Israel came, and ... 1Kin 8:3 3605
a the holy vessels that were in ... 1Kin 8:4 3605
a the congregation of Israel, ... 1Kin 8:5 3605
blessed *a* the congregation of ... 1Kin 8:14 3605
a the congregation of Israel ... 1Kin 8:14 3605
I chose no city out of *a* the ... 1Kin 8:16 3605
of *a* the congregation of Israel ... 1Kin 8:22 3605
before thee with *a* their heart ... 1Kin 8:23 3605
or by *a* thy people Israel, which ... 1Kin 8:38 3605
hearts of *a* the children of men ... 1Kin 8:39 3605
That they may fear thee *a* the ... 1Kin 8:40 3605
do according to *a* that the ... 1Kin 8:43 3605
that *a* people of the earth may ... 1Kin 8:43 3605
unto thee with *a* their heart ... 1Kin 8:48 3605
with *a* their soul, in the land of ... 1Kin 8:48 3605
a their transgressions wherein ... 1Kin 8:50 3605
to hearken unto them in *a* that ... 1Kin 8:52 3605
among *a* the people of the earth ... 1Kin 8:53 3605
an end of praying *a* this prayer ... 1Kin 8:54 3605
blessed *a* the congregation of ... 1Kin 8:55 3605
according to *a* that he promised ... 1Kin 8:56 3605
one word of *a* his good promise ... 1Kin 8:56 3605
unto him, to walk in *a* his ways ... 1Kin 8:58 3605
of his people Israel at *a* times ... 1Kin 8:59
That *a* the people of the earth ... 1Kin 8:60 3605
a Israel with him, offered ... 1Kin 8:62 3605
king and *a* the children of Israel ... 1Kin 8:63 3605
a Israel with him, a great ... 1Kin 8:65 3605
glad of heart for *a* the goodness ... 1Kin 8:66 3605
a Solomon's desire which he was ... 1Kin 9:1 3605
to do according to *a* that I have ... 1Kin 9:4 3605
But if ye shall at *a* turn from ... 1Kin 9:6
and a byword among *a* people ... 1Kin 9:7 3605
brought upon them *a* this evil ... 1Kin 9:9 3605
gold, according to *a* his desire ... 1Kin 9:11 3605
a the cities of store that ... 1Kin 9:19 3605
in *a* the land of his dominion ... 1Kin 9:19 3605
a the people that were left of ... 1Kin 9:20 3605
him of *a* that was in her heart ... 1Kin 10:2 3605
Solomon told her *a* her questions ... 1Kin 10:3 3605
Sheba had seen *a* Solomon's wisdom ... 1Kin 10:4 3605
the queen of Sheba *a* her desire ... 1Kin 10:13 3605
of *a* the kings of Arabia, and of ... 1Kin 10:15 3605
a king Solomon's drinking vessels ... 1Kin 10:21 3605
a the vessels of the house of the ... 1Kin 10:21 3605
So king Solomon exceeded *a* the ... 1Kin 10:23 3605
a the earth sought to Solomon, to ... 1Kin 10:24 3605
so for *a* the kings of the ... 1Kin 10:29 3605
did he for *a* his strange wives ... 1Kin 11:8 3605
will not rend away *a* the kingdom ... 1Kin 11:13 3605
Joab remain there with *a* Israel ... 1Kin 11:16 3605
to Israel *a* the days of Solomon ... 1Kin 11:25 3605
he made him ruler over *a* the ... 1Kin 11:28 3605
out of *a* the tribes of Israel ... 1Kin 11:32 3605
but I will make him prince *a* the ... 1Kin 11:34 3605
to *a* that thy soul desireth ... 1Kin 11:37 3605
unto *a* that I command thee ... 1Kin 11:38 3605
a that he did, and his wisdom, are ... 1Kin 11:41 3605
over *a* Israel was forty years ... 1Kin 11:42 3605
for *a* Israel were come to Shechem ... 1Kin 12:1 3605
a the congregation of Israel came ... 1Kin 12:3 3605
a the people came to Rehoboam the ... 1Kin 12:12 3605
So when *a* Israel saw that the ... 1Kin 12:16 3605
a Israel stoned him with stones, ... 1Kin 12:18 3605
when *a* Israel heard that Jeroboam ... 1Kin 12:20 3605
and made him king over *a* Israel ... 1Kin 12:20 3605
he assembled *a* the house of Judah ... 1Kin 12:21 3605
unto *a* the house of Judah and ... 1Kin 12:23 3605
told him *a* the works that the man ... 1Kin 13:11 3605
against *a* the houses of the high ... 1Kin 13:32 3605
who followed me with *a* his heart ... 1Kin 14:8 3605
above *a* that were before thee ... 1Kin 14:9 3605
away dung, till it be *a* gone ... 1Kin 14:10 8552
a Israel shall mourn for him, and ... 1Kin 14:13 3605
a Israel mourned for him, ... 1Kin 14:18 3605
out of *a* the tribes of Israel ... 1Kin 14:21 3605
above *a* that their fathers had ... 1Kin 14:22 3605
they did according to *a* the ... 1Kin 14:24 3605
he even took away *a* ... 1Kin 14:26 3605

he took away *a* the shields of ... 1Kin 14:26 3605
a that he did, are they not ... 1Kin 14:29 3605
Rehoboam and Jeroboam *a* their days. 1Kin 14:30 3605
he walked in *a* the sins of his ... 1Kin 15:3 3605
him *a* the days of his life ... 1Kin 15:5 3605
Jeroboam *a* the days of his life ... 1Kin 15:6 3605
a that he did, are they not ... 1Kin 15:7 3605
removed *a* the idols that his ... 1Kin 15:12 3605
perfect with the LORD *a* his days ... 1Kin 15:14 3605
king of Israel *a* their days ... 1Kin 15:16 3605
Then Asa took *a* the silver ... 1Kin 15:18 3605
a Cinneroth, with *a* the land of ... 1Kin 15:20 3605
a proclamation throughout *a* Judah ... 1Kin 15:22 3605
The rest of *a* the acts of Asa, and ... 1Kin 15:23 3605
a his might, and *a* that he did, ... 1Kin 15:23 3605
a Israel laid siege to Gibbethon ... 1Kin 15:27 3605
that he smote *a* the house of ... 1Kin 15:29 3605
a that he did, are they not ... 1Kin 15:31 3605
king of Israel *a* their days ... 1Kin 15:32 3605
to reign over *a* Israel in Tirzah ... 1Kin 15:33 3605
even for *a* the evil that he did ... 1Kin 16:7 3605
that he slew *a* the house of ... 1Kin 16:11 3605
destroy *a* the house of Baasha ... 1Kin 16:12 3605
For *a* the sins of Baasha, and the ... 1Kin 16:13 3605
a that he did, are they not ... 1Kin 16:14 3605
wherefore *a* Israel made Omri, the ... 1Kin 16:16 3605
a Israel with him, and they ... 1Kin 16:17 3605
did worse than *a* that were before ... 1Kin 16:25 3605
For he walked in *a* the way of ... 1Kin 16:26 3605
LORD above *a* that were before him ... 1Kin 16:30 3605
God of Israel to anger than *a* the ... 1Kin 16:33 3605
unto *a* fountains of water, and ... 1Kin 18:5 3605
and unto *a* brooks: peradventure ... 1Kin 18:5
that we lose not *a* the beasts ... 1Kin 18:5 3605
gather to me *a* Israel unto mount ... 1Kin 18:19 3605
So Ahab sent unto *a* the children ... 1Kin 18:20 3605
And Elijah came unto *a* the people ... 1Kin 18:21 3605
a the people answered and said, It ... 1Kin 18:24 3605
And Elijah said unto *a* the people ... 1Kin 18:30 3605
a the people came near unto him ... 1Kin 18:30 3605
that I have done *a* these things ... 1Kin 18:36 3605
when *a* the people saw it, they ... 1Kin 18:39 3605
Ahab told Jezebel *a* that Elijah ... 1Kin 19:1 3605
withal how he had slain *a* the ... 1Kin 19:1 3605
a the knees which have not bowed ... 1Kin 19:18 3605
gathered *a* his host together ... 1Kin 20:1 3605
I am thine, and *a* that I have ... 1Kin 20:4 3605
called *a* the elders of the land ... 1Kin 20:7 3605
a the elders and *a* the people ... 1Kin 20:8 3605
A that thou didst send for to thy ... 1Kin 20:9 3605
for *a* the people that follow me ... 1Kin 20:10 3605
Hast thou seen *a* this great ... 1Kin 20:13 3605
them he numbered *a* the people ... 1Kin 20:15 3605
even *a* the children of Israel, ... 1Kin 20:15 3605
were *a* present, and went against ... 1Kin 20:27
therefore will I deliver *a* this ... 1Kin 20:28 3605
according to *a* things as did the ... 1Kin 21:26 3605
a the prophets prophesied before ... 1Kin 22:10 3605
a the prophets prophesied so, ... 1Kin 22:12 3605
I saw *a* Israel scattered upon the ... 1Kin 22:17 3605
a the host of heaven standing by ... 1Kin 22:19 3605
in the mouth of *a* his prophets ... 1Kin 22:22 3605
the mouth of *a* these thy prophets ... 1Kin 22:23 3605
If thou return at *a* in peace ... 1Kin 22:28
a that he did, and the ivory house ... 1Kin 22:39 3605
a the cities that he built, are ... 1Kin 22:39 3605
he walked in *a* the ways of Asa ... 1Kin 22:43 3605
according to *a* that his father ... 1Kin 22:53 3605
same time, and numbered *a* Israel ... 2Kin 3:6 3605
stop *a* wells of water, and mar ... 2Kin 3:19 3605
when *a* the Moabites heard that ... 2Kin 3:21 3605
they gathered *a* that were able to ... 2Kin 3:21 3605
they stopped *a* the wells of water ... 2Kin 3:25 3605
and felled *a* the good trees ... 2Kin 3:25 3605
abroad of *a* thy neighbours ... 2Kin 4:3 3605
pour out into *a* those vessels ... 2Kin 4:4 3605
careful for us with *a* this care ... 2Kin 4:13 3605
better than *a* the waters of ... 2Kin 5:12 3605
a his company, and came, and stood ... 2Kin 5:15 3605
there is no God in *a* the earth ... 2Kin 5:15 3605
to meet him, and said, Is *a* well ... 2Kin 5:21
And he said, *A* is well ... 2Kin 5:22
king of Syria gathered *a* his host ... 2Kin 6:24 3605
they are as *a* the multitude of ... 2Kin 7:13 3605
they are even as *a* the multitude ... 2Kin 7:13 3605
a the way was full of garments and ... 2Kin 7:15 3605
a the great things that Elisha ... 2Kin 8:4 3605
Restore *a* that was hers, and *a* ... 2Kin 8:6 3605
Zair, and *a* the chariots with him ... 2Kin 8:21 3605
a that he did, are they not ... 2Kin 8:23 3605
And Jehu said, Unto which of *a* us ... 2Kin 9:5 3605
the blood of *a* the servants of ... 2Kin 9:7 3605
and one said unto him, Is *a* well ... 2Kin 9:11
a Israel, because of Hazael king ... 2Kin 9:14 3605
will do *a* that thou shalt bid us ... 2Kin 10:5 3605
said to *a* the people, Ye be ... 2Kin 10:9 3605
but who slew *a* these ... 2Kin 10:9 3605
So Jehu slew *a* that remained of ... 2Kin 10:11 3605
a his great men, and his kinsfolks ... 2Kin 10:11 3605
he slew *a* that remained unto Ahab ... 2Kin 10:17 3605
Jehu gathered *a* the people ... 2Kin 10:18 3605
unto me *a* the prophets of Baal ... 2Kin 10:19 3605
a his servants, and *a* his ... 2Kin 10:19 3605
And Jehu sent through *a* Israel ... 2Kin 10:21 3605
a the worshippers of Baal came, ... 2Kin 10:21 3605
for *a* the worshippers of Baal ... 2Kin 10:22 3605
to *a* that was in mine heart ... 2Kin 10:30 3605
God of Israel with *a* his heart ... 2Kin 10:31 3605
them in *a* the coasts of Israel ... 2Kin 10:32 3605
a the land of Gilead, the Gadites ... 2Kin 10:33 3605
a that he did, and *a* his might, ... 2Kin 10:34 3605
destroyed *a* the seed royal ... 2Kin 11:1 3605
two parts of *a* you that go forth ... 2Kin 11:7 3605
the hundreds did according to *a* ... 2Kin 11:9 3605
a the people of the land rejoiced ... 2Kin 11:14 3605
a the people of the land went ... 2Kin 11:18 3605
and *a* the people of the land ... 2Kin 11:19 3605
a the people of the land rejoiced ... 2Kin 11:20 3605
a his days wherein Jehoiada the ... 2Kin 12:2 3605
A the money of the dedicated ... 2Kin 12:4 3605
a the money that cometh into any ... 2Kin 12:4 3605
that kept the door put therein *a* ... 2Kin 12:9 3605
for *a* that was laid out for the ... 2Kin 12:12 3605
took *a* the hallowed things that ... 2Kin 12:18 3605
a the gold that was found in the ... 2Kin 12:18 3605
a that he did, are they not ... 2Kin 12:19 3605
the son of Hazael, *a* their days ... 2Kin 13:3 3605
a that he did, and his might, are ... 2Kin 13:8 3605
he departed not from *a* the sins ... 2Kin 13:11 3605
a that he did, and his might ... 2Kin 13:12 3605
Israel *a* the days of Jehoahaz ... 2Kin 13:22 3605
he did according to *a* things as ... 2Kin 14:3 3605
he took *a* the gold and silver, and ... 2Kin 14:14 3605
a the vessels that were found in ... 2Kin 14:14 3605
a the people of Judah took ... 2Kin 14:21 3605
he departed not from *a* the sins ... 2Kin 14:24 3605
a that he did, and his might, how ... 2Kin 14:28 3605
according to *a* that his father ... 2Kin 15:3 3605
a that he did, are they not ... 2Kin 15:6 3605
a that were therein, and the ... 2Kin 15:16 3605
a the women therein that were ... 2Kin 15:16 3605
he departed not *a* his days from ... 2Kin 15:18 3605
even of *a* the mighty men of ... 2Kin 15:20 3605
a that he did, are they not ... 2Kin 15:21 3605
a that he did, behold, they are ... 2Kin 15:26 3605
a the land of Naphtali, and ... 2Kin 15:29 3605
a that he did, behold, they are ... 2Kin 15:31 3605
he did according to *a* that his ... 2Kin 15:34 3605
a that he did, are they not ... 2Kin 15:36 3605
according to *a* the workmanship ... 2Kin 16:10 3605
built an altar according to *a* ... 2Kin 16:11 3605
of *a* the people of the land ... 2Kin 16:15 3605
sprinkle upon it *a* the blood of ... 2Kin 16:15 3605
a the blood of the sacrifice ... 2Kin 16:15 3605
according to *a* that king Ahaz ... 2Kin 16:16 3605
came up throughout *a* the land ... 2Kin 17:5 3605
high places in *a* their cities ... 2Kin 17:9 3605
incense in *a* the high places ... 2Kin 17:11 3605
by *a* the prophets, and by *a* the ... 2Kin 17:13 3605
according to *a* the law which I ... 2Kin 17:13 3605
they left *a* the commandments of ... 2Kin 17:16 3605
worshipped *a* the host of heaven, ... 2Kin 17:16 3605
the LORD rejected *a* the seed of ... 2Kin 17:20 3605
children of Israel walked in *a* ... 2Kin 17:22 3605
as he had said by *a* his servants ... 2Kin 17:23 3605
out of the hand of *a* your enemies ... 2Kin 17:39 3605
according to *a* that David his ... 2Kin 18:3 3605
him among *a* the kings of Judah ... 2Kin 18:5 3605
a that Moses the servant of the ... 2Kin 18:12 3605
a the fenced cities of Judah ... 2Kin 18:13 3605
Hezekiah gave him *a* the silver ... 2Kin 18:15 3605
of Egypt unto *a* that trust on him ... 2Kin 18:21 3605
of the nations delivered at *a* his ... 2Kin 18:33
Who are they among *a* the gods of ... 2Kin 18:35 3605
hear *a* the words of Rab-shakeh ... 2Kin 19:4 3605
of Assyria have done to *a* lands ... 2Kin 19:11 3605
of *a* the kingdoms of the earth ... 2Kin 19:15 3605
that *a* the kingdoms of the earth ... 2Kin 19:19 3605
a the rivers of besieged places ... 2Kin 19:24 3605
behold, they were *a* dead corpses ... 2Kin 19:35 3605
shewed them *a* the house of his ... 2Kin 20:13 3605
a the house of his armour ... 2Kin 20:13 3605
a that was found in his treasures ... 2Kin 20:13 3605
nor in *a* his dominion, that ... 2Kin 20:13 3605
A the things that are in mine ... 2Kin 20:15 3605
that *a* that is in thine house, and ... 2Kin 20:17 3605
a his might, and how he made a ... 2Kin 20:20 3605
worshipped *a* the host of heaven, ... 2Kin 21:3 3605
he built altars for *a* the host of ... 2Kin 21:5 3605
chosen out of *a* tribes of Israel ... 2Kin 21:7 3605
to *a* that I have commanded them ... 2Kin 21:8 3605
according to *a* the law that my ... 2Kin 21:8 3605
above *a* that the Amorites did ... 2Kin 21:11 3605
a spoil to *a* their enemies ... 2Kin 21:14 3605
a that he did, and his sin that he ... 2Kin 21:17 3605
he walked in *a* the way that his ... 2Kin 21:21 3605
the people of the land slew *a* ... 2Kin 21:24 3605
walked in *a* the way of David his ... 2Kin 22:2 3605
for *a* Judah, concerning the words ... 2Kin 22:13 3605
to do according unto *a* that which ... 2Kin 22:13 3605
even *a* the words of the book ... 2Kin 22:16 3605
with *a* the works of their hands ... 2Kin 22:17 3605
thine eyes shall not see *a* the ... 2Kin 22:20 3605
unto him *a* the elders of Judah ... 2Kin 23:1 3605
a the men of Judah and *a* the ... 2Kin 23:2 3605
a the people, both small and great ... 2Kin 23:2 3605
he read in their ears *a* the words ... 2Kin 23:2 3605
his statutes with *a* their heart ... 2Kin 23:3 3605
a their soul, to perform the ... 2Kin 23:3 3605
a the people stood to the ... 2Kin 23:3 3605
out of the temple of the LORD *a* ... 2Kin 23:4 3605
and for *a* the host of heaven ... 2Kin 23:4 3605
and to *a* the host of heaven ... 2Kin 23:5 3605
he brought *a* the priests out of ... 2Kin 23:8 3605
a the houses also of the high ... 2Kin 23:19 3605
did to them according to *a* the ... 2Kin 23:19 3605
he slew *a* the priests of the high ... 2Kin 23:20 3605
the king commanded *a* the people ... 2Kin 23:21 3605
nor in *a* the days of the kings of ... 2Kin 23:22 3605
a the abominations that were ... 2Kin 23:24 3605
to the LORD with *a* his heart ... 2Kin 23:25 3605
with *a* his soul, and with *a* his ... 2Kin 23:25 3605
according to *a* the law of Moses ... 2Kin 23:25 3605
because of *a* the provocations ... 2Kin 23:26 3605
a that he did, are they not ... 2Kin 23:28 3605
according to *a* that his fathers ... 2Kin 23:32 3605
according to *a* that his fathers ... 2Kin 23:37 3605
according to *a* that he did ... 2Kin 24:3 3605
a that he did, are they not ... 2Kin 24:5 3605
a that pertained to the king of ... 2Kin 24:7 3605
according to *a* that his father ... 2Kin 24:9 3605
he carried out thence *a* the ... 2Kin 24:13 3605
cut in pieces *a* the vessels of ... 2Kin 24:13 3605
And he carried away *a* Jerusalem ... 2Kin 24:14 3605
a the princes, and *a* the mighty ... 2Kin 24:14 3605
a the craftsmen and smiths ... 2Kin 24:14 3605
a the men of might, even seven ... 2Kin 24:16 3605
a that were strong and apt for war ... 2Kin 24:16 3605
according to *a* that Jehoiakim had ... 2Kin 24:19 3605
a his host, against Jerusalem, and ... 2Kin 25:1 3605
a the men of war fled by night by ... 2Kin 25:4 3605
a his army were scattered from ... 2Kin 25:5 3605
a the houses of Jerusalem, and ... 2Kin 25:9 3605
a the army of the Chaldees, that ... 2Kin 25:10 3605
a the vessels of brass wherewith ... 2Kin 25:14 3605
the brass of *a* these vessels was ... 2Kin 25:16 3605
chapiter round about, *a* of brass ... 2Kin 25:17 3605
when *a* the captains of the armies ... 2Kin 25:23 3605
a the people, both small and great ... 2Kin 25:26 3605
before him *a* the days of his life ... 2Kin 25:29 3605
every day, *a* the days of his life ... 2Kin 25:30 3605
A these were the sons of Joktan ... 1Chr 1:23 3605
A these are the sons of Keturah ... 1Chr 1:33 3605
A the sons of Judah were five ... 1Chr 2:4 3605
five of them in *a* ... 1Chr 2:6 3605
A these belonged to the sons of ... 1Chr 2:23 3605
These were *a* the sons of David, ... 1Chr 3:9 3605
neither did *a* their family ... 1Chr 4:27 3605
a their villages that were round ... 1Chr 4:33 3605
a the east land of Gilead ... 1Chr 5:10 3605
in *a* the suburbs of Sharon, upon ... 1Chr 5:16 3605
A these were reckoned by ... 1Chr 5:17 3605
hand, and *a* that were with them ... 1Chr 5:20 3605
unto *a* manner of service of the ... 1Chr 6:48 3605
were appointed for *a* the work of ... 1Chr 6:49 3605
according to *a* that Moses the ... 1Chr 6:49 3605
A their cities throughout their ... 1Chr 6:60 3605
a of them chief men ... 1Chr 7:3 3605
their brethren among *a* the ... 1Chr 7:5 3605
of might, reckoned in *a* by their ... 1Chr 7:5 3605
A these are the sons of Becher ... 1Chr 7:8 3605
A these the sons of Jediael, by ... 1Chr 7:11 3605
A these were the children of ... 1Chr 7:40 3605
A these were the sons of Azel ... 1Chr 8:38 3605
A these are of the sons of ... 1Chr 8:40 3605
So *a* Israel were reckoned by ... 1Chr 9:1 3605
A these men were chief of the ... 1Chr 9:9 3605
A these which were chosen to be ... 1Chr 9:22 3605
and *a* the instruments of the ... 1Chr 9:29 3605
a his house died together ... 1Chr 10:6 3605
when *a* the men of Israel that ... 1Chr 10:7 3605
when *a* Jabesh-gilead heard *a* ... 1Chr 10:11 3605
a the valiant men, and took away ... 1Chr 10:12 3605
Then *a* Israel gathered themselves ... 1Chr 11:1 3605
Therefore came *a* the elders of ... 1Chr 11:3 3605
a Israel went to Jerusalem, which ... 1Chr 11:4 3605
with *a* Israel, to make him king, ... 1Chr 11:10 3605
when it had overflown *a* his banks ... 1Chr 12:15 3605
they put to flight *a* them of the ... 1Chr 12:15 3605
for they were *a* mighty men of ... 1Chr 12:21 3605
a their brethren were at their ... 1Chr 12:32 3605
with *a* instruments of war, fifty ... 1Chr 12:33 3605
with *a* manner of instruments of ... 1Chr 12:37 3605
A these men of war, that could ... 1Chr 12:38 3605
to make David king over *a* Israel ... 1Chr 12:38 3605
a the rest also of Israel were of ... 1Chr 12:38 3605
And David said unto *a* the ... 1Chr 13:2 3605
that are left in *a* the land of ... 1Chr 13:2 3605
a the congregation said that they ... 1Chr 13:4 3605
right in the eyes of *a* the people ... 1Chr 13:4 3605
David gathered *a* Israel together ... 1Chr 13:5 3605
a Israel, to Baalah, that is, to ... 1Chr 13:6 3605
a Israel played before God with ... 1Chr 13:8 3605
of Obed-edom, and *a* that he had ... 1Chr 13:14 3605
was anointed king over *a* Israel ... 1Chr 14:8 3605
a the Philistines went up to seek ... 1Chr 14:8 3605
of David went out into *a* lands ... 1Chr 14:17 3605
the fear of him upon *a* nations ... 1Chr 14:17 3605
David gathered *a* Israel together ... 1Chr 15:3 3605
a the Levites that bare the ark, ... 1Chr 15:27 3605
Thus *a* Israel brought up the ark ... 1Chr 15:28 3605
talk ye of *a* his wondrous works ... 1Chr 16:9 3605
his judgments are in *a* the earth ... 1Chr 16:14 3605
Sing unto the LORD, *a* the earth ... 1Chr 16:23 3605
marvellous works among *a* nations ... 1Chr 16:24 3605
also is to be feared above *a* gods ... 1Chr 16:25 3605
For *a* the gods of the people are ... 1Chr 16:26 3605
Fear before him, *a* the earth ... 1Chr 16:30 3605
rejoice, and *a* that is therein ... 1Chr 16:32 3605
a the people said, Amen, and ... 1Chr 16:36 3605
to do according to *a* that is ... 1Chr 16:40 3605
a the people departed every man ... 1Chr 16:43 3605
Do *a* that is in thine heart ... 1Chr 17:2 3605
I have walked with *a* Israel ... 1Chr 17:6 3605
have cut off *a* thine enemies from ... 1Chr 17:8 3605
I will subdue *a* thine enemies ... 1Chr 17:10 3605
According to *a* these words ... 1Chr 17:15 3605
and according to *a* this vision ... 1Chr 17:15 3605
hast thou done *a* this greatness ... 1Chr 17:19 3605
in making known *a* these great ... 1Chr 17:19 3605
according to *a* that we have heard ... 1Chr 17:20 3605
also houghed *a* the chariot horses ... 1Chr 18:4 3605
heard how David had smitten *a* the ... 1Chr 18:9 3605
with him *a* manner of vessels of ... 1Chr 18:10 3605
he brought from *a* these nations ... 1Chr 18:11 3605
a the Edomites became David's ... 1Chr 18:13 3605
So David reigned over *a* Israel ... 1Chr 18:14 3605
and justice among *a* his people ... 1Chr 18:14 3605
a the host of the mighty men ... 1Chr 19:8 3605
he chose out of *a* the choice of ... 1Chr 19:10 3605
and he gathered *a* Israel, and ... 1Chr 19:17 3605
Even so dealt David with *a* the ... 1Chr 20:3 3605

David and *a* the people returned to 1Chr 20:3 3605
are they not *a* my lord's servants 1Chr 21:3 3605
and went throughout *a* Israel 1Chr 21:4 3605
a they of Israel were a thousand 1Chr 21:5 3605
throughout *a* the coasts of Israel 1Chr 21:12 3605
I give it *a* 1Chr 21:23 3605
of glory throughout *a* countries 1Chr 22:5 3605
from *a* his enemies round about 1Chr 22:9 3605
a manner of cunning men for every 1Chr 22:15 3605
David also commanded *a* the 1Chr 22:17 3605
he gathered together *a* the 1Chr 23:2 3605
in the purifying of *a* holy things 1Chr 23:28 3605
for *a* manner of measure and size 1Chr 23:29 3605
to offer *a* burnt sacrifices unto 1Chr 23:31 3605
A these were the sons of Heman 1Chr 25:5 3605
A these were under the hands of 1Chr 25:6 3605
even *a* that were cunning, was two 1Chr 25:7 3605
A these of the sons of Obed-edom 1Chr 26:8 3605
a the sons and brethren of Hosah 1Chr 26:11 3605
his brethren were over *a* the 1Chr 26:26 3605
a that Samuel the seer, and Saul 1Chr 26:28 3605
in *a* the business of the LORD 1Chr 26:30 3605
a the months of the year, of 1Chr 27:1 3605
of Perez was the chief of *a* the 1Chr 27:3 3605
A these were the rulers of the 1Chr 27:31 3605
David assembled *a* the princes of 1Chr 28:1 3605
the stewards over *a* the substance 1Chr 28:1 3605
with *a* the valiant men, unto 1Chr 28:1 3605
a the house of my father to be 1Chr 28:4 3605
me to make me king over *a* Israel 1Chr 28:4 3605
of *a* my sons, (for the LORD hath 1Chr 28:5 3605
in the sight of *a* Israel the 1Chr 28:8 3605
seek for *a* the commandments of 1Chr 28:8 3605
for the LORD searcheth *a* hearts 1Chr 28:9 3605
understandeth *a* the imaginations 1Chr 28:9 3605
the pattern of *a* that he had by 1Chr 28:12 3605
of *a* the chambers round about, of 1Chr 28:12 3605
for *a* the work of the service of 1Chr 28:13 3605
for *a* the vessels of service in 1Chr 28:13 3605
for *a* instruments of *a* manner 1Chr 28:14 3605
silver also for *a* instruments of 1Chr 28:14 3605
for *a* instruments of every kind 1Chr 28:14 3605
A this, said David, the LORD made 1Chr 28:19 3605
even *a* the works of this pattern 1Chr 28:19 3605
until thou hast finished *a* the 1Chr 28:20 3605
they shall be with thee for *a* the 1Chr 28:21 3605
for *a* manner of workmanship every 1Chr 28:21 3605
a the people will be wholly at 1Chr 28:21 3605
king said unto *a* the congregation 1Chr 29:1 3605
Now I have prepared with *a* my 1Chr 29:2 3605
a manner of precious stones, and 1Chr 29:2 3605
above *a* that I have prepared for 1Chr 29:3 3605
for *a* manner of work to be made 1Chr 29:5 3605
LORD before *a* the congregation 1Chr 29:10 3605
for *a* that is in the heaven and in 1Chr 29:11 3605
thou art exalted as head above *a* 1Chr 29:11 3605
of thee, and thou reignest over *a* 1Chr 29:12 3605
great, and to give strength unto *a* 1Chr 29:12 3605
for *a* things come of thee, and of 1Chr 29:14 3605
sojourners, as were *a* our fathers 1Chr 29:15 3605
a this store that we have 1Chr 29:16 3605
of thine hand, and is *a* thine own 1Chr 29:16 3605
willingly offered *a* these things 1Chr 29:17 3605
to do *a* these things, and to build 1Chr 29:19 3605
David said to *a* the congregation, 1Chr 29:20 3605
a the congregation blessed the 1Chr 29:20 3605
in abundance for *a* Israel 1Chr 29:21 3605
and *a* Israel obeyed him 1Chr 29:23 3605
a the princes, and the mighty men, 1Chr 29:24 3605
a the sons likewise of king David 1Chr 29:24 3605
in the sight of *a* Israel, and 1Chr 29:25 3605
of Jesse reigned over *a* Israel 1Chr 29:26 3605
With *a* his reign and his might, and 1Chr 29:30 3605
over *a* the kingdoms of the 1Chr 29:30 3605
Then Solomon spake unto *a* Israel 2Chr 1:2 3605
and to every governor in *a* Israel 2Chr 1:2 3605
a the congregation with him, went 2Chr 1:3 3605
for *a* the kings of the Hittites 2Chr 1:17 3605
for great is our God above *a* gods 2Chr 2:5 3605
Solomon numbered *a* the strangers 2Chr 2:17 3605
a their hinder parts were inward 2Chr 4:4 3605
a their instruments, did Huram 2Chr 4:16 3605
Thus Solomon made *a* these vessels 2Chr 4:18 3605
Solomon made *a* the vessels that 2Chr 4:19 3605
Thus *a* the work that Solomon made 2Chr 5:1
Solomon brought in *a* the things 2Chr 5:1 3605
a the instruments, put he among 2Chr 5:1 3605
a the heads of the tribes, the 2Chr 5:2 3605
Wherefore *a* the men of Israel 2Chr 5:3 3605
a the elders of Israel came 2Chr 5:4 3605
a the holy vessels that were in 2Chr 5:5 3605
a the congregation of Israel that 2Chr 5:6 3605
(for *a* the priests that were 2Chr 5:11 3605
a of them of Asaph, of Heman, of 2Chr 5:12 3605
a the congregation of Israel 2Chr 6:3 3605
a the tribes of Israel to build 2Chr 6:5 3605
of *a* the congregation of Israel 2Chr 6:12 3605
a the congregation of Israel 2Chr 6:13 3605
before thee with *a* their hearts 2Chr 6:14 3605
or of *a* thy people Israel, when 2Chr 6:29 3605
man according unto *a* his ways 2Chr 6:30 3605
do according to *a* that the 2Chr 6:33 3605
that *a* people of the earth may 2Chr 6:33 3605
return to thee with *a* their heart 2Chr 6:38 3605
with *a* their soul in the land of 2Chr 6:38 3605
when *a* the children of Israel saw 2Chr 7:3 3605
a the people offered sacrifices 2Chr 7:4 3605
a the people dedicated the house 2Chr 7:5 3605
before them, and *a* Israel stood 2Chr 7:6 3605
a Israel with him, a very great 2Chr 7:8 3605
a that came into Solomon's heart 2Chr 7:11 3605
do according to *a* that I have 2Chr 7:17 3605
and a byword among *a* nations 2Chr 7:20 3605
he brought *a* this evil upon them 2Chr 7:22 3605

a the store cities, which he 2Chr 8:4 3605
a the store cities that Solomon 2Chr 8:6 3605
a the chariot cities, and the 2Chr 8:6 3605
a that Solomon desired to build 2Chr 8:6 3605
throughout *a* the land of his 2Chr 8:6 3605
As for *a* the people that were 2Chr 8:7 3605
Now *a* the work of Solomon was 2Chr 8:16 3605
him of *a* that was in her heart 2Chr 9:1 3605
Solomon told her *a* her questions 2Chr 9:2 3605
the queen of Sheba *a* her desire 2Chr 9:12 3605
And *a* the kings of Arabia and 2Chr 9:14 3605
a the drinking vessels of king 2Chr 9:20 3605
a the vessels of the house of the 2Chr 9:20 3605
king Solomon passed *a* the kings 2Chr 9:22 3605
a the kings of the earth sought 2Chr 9:23 3605
he reigned over *a* the kings from 2Chr 9:26 3605
out of Egypt, and out of *a* lands 2Chr 9:28 3605
over *a* Israel forty years 2Chr 9:30 3605
for to Shechem were *a* Israel come 2Chr 10:1 3605
a Israel came and spake to 2Chr 10:3 3605
a the people came to Rehoboam on 2Chr 10:12 3605
when *a* Israel saw that the king 2Chr 10:16 3605
So *a* Israel went to their tents 2Chr 10:16 3605
to *a* Israel in Judah and Benjamin, 2Chr 11:3 3605
the Levites that were in *a* Israel 2Chr 11:13 3605
to him out of *a* their coasts 2Chr 11:13 3605
after them out of *a* the tribes of 2Chr 11:16 3605
of Absalom above *a* his wives 2Chr 11:21 3605
dispersed of *a* his children 2Chr 11:23 3605
a the countries of Judah and 2Chr 11:23 3605
of the LORD, and *a* Israel with him 2Chr 12:1 3605
he took *a*: he carried away 2Chr 12:9 3605
out of *a* the tribes of Israel 2Chr 12:13 3605
me, thou Jeroboam, and *a* Israel 2Chr 13:4 3605
a Israel before Abijah and Judah 2Chr 13:15 3605
Also he took away out of *a* the 2Chr 14:5 3605
a these were mighty men of valour 2Chr 14:8 3605
they smote *a* the cities round 2Chr 14:14 3605
and they spoiled *a* the cities 2Chr 14:14 3605
me, Asa, and *a* Judah and Benjamin 2Chr 15:2 3605
upon *a* the inhabitants of the 2Chr 15:5 3605
God did vex them with *a* adversity 2Chr 15:6 3605
idols out of *a* the land of Judah 2Chr 15:8 3605
And he gathered *a* Judah and 2Chr 15:9 3605
their fathers with *a* their heart 2Chr 15:12 3605
their heart and with *a* their soul 2Chr 15:12 3605
a Judah rejoiced at the oath 2Chr 15:15 3605
they had sworn with *a* their heart 2Chr 15:15 3605
of Asa was perfect *a* his days 2Chr 15:17 3605
a the store cities of Naphtali 2Chr 16:4 3605
Then Asa the king took *a* Judah 2Chr 16:6 3605
he placed forces in *a* the fenced 2Chr 17:2 3605
a Judah brought to Jehoshaphat 2Chr 17:5 3605
throughout *a* the cities of Judah 2Chr 17:9 3605
a the kingdoms of the lands that 2Chr 17:10 3605
fenced cities throughout *a* Judah 2Chr 17:19 3605
a the prophets prophesied before 2Chr 18:9 3605
a the prophets prophesied so, 2Chr 18:11 3605
I did see *a* Israel scattered upon 2Chr 18:16 3605
a the host of heaven standing on 2Chr 18:18 3605
in the mouth of *a* his prophets 2Chr 18:21 3605
And he said, Hearken, *a* ye people 2Chr 18:27 3605
a the fenced cities of Judah 2Chr 19:5 3605
over you in *a* matters of the LORD 2Chr 19:11 3605
Judah, for *a* the king's matters 2Chr 19:11 3605
a fast throughout *a* Judah 2Chr 20:3 3605
even out of *a* the cities of Judah 2Chr 20:4 3605
rulest not thou over *a* the 2Chr 20:6
a Judah stood before the LORD, 2Chr 20:13 3605
a Judah, and ye inhabitants of 2Chr 20:15 3605
a Judah and the inhabitants of 2Chr 20:18 3605
the fear of God was on *a* the 2Chr 20:29 3605
a these were the sons of 2Chr 21:2 3605
slew *a* his brethren with the 2Chr 21:4 3605
and *a* his chariots with him 2Chr 21:9 3605
and thy wives, and *a* thy goods 2Chr 21:14 3605
carried away *a* the substance that 2Chr 21:17 3605
after *a* this the LORD smote him 2Chr 21:18 3605
the camp had slain *a* the eldest 2Chr 22:1 3605
sought the LORD with *a* his heart 2Chr 22:9 3605
destroyed *a* the seed royal of the 2Chr 22:10 3605
out of *a* the cities of Judah 2Chr 23:2 3605
a the congregation made a 2Chr 23:3 3605
a the people shall be in the 2Chr 23:5 3605
but *a* the people shall keep the 2Chr 23:6 3605
a Judah did according to *a* 2Chr 23:8 3605
he set *a* the people, every man 2Chr 23:10 3605
a the people of the land rejoiced 2Chr 23:13 3605
between *a* the people, and between 2Chr 23:16 3605
Then *a* the people went to the 2Chr 23:17 3605
a the people of the land, and 2Chr 23:20 3605
a the people of the land rejoiced 2Chr 23:21 3605
right in the sight of the LORD *a* 2Chr 24:2 3605
gather of *a* Israel money to 2Chr 24:5 3605
also *a* the dedicated things of 2Chr 24:7 3605
a the princes and *a* the people 2Chr 24:10 3605
a the days of Jehoiada 2Chr 24:14 3605
destroyed *a* the princes of the 2Chr 24:23 3605
sent *a* the spoil of them unto the 2Chr 24:23 3605
their fathers, throughout *a* Judah 2Chr 25:5 3605
with *a* the children of Ephraim 2Chr 25:7 3605
that they *a* were broken in pieces 2Chr 25:12 3605
he took *a* the gold and the silver, 2Chr 25:24 3605
a the vessels that were found in 2Chr 25:24 3605
Then *a* the people of Judah took 2Chr 26:1 3605
according to *a* that his father 2Chr 26:4 3605
throughout *a* the host shields 2Chr 26:14 3605
a the priests, looked upon him, 2Chr 26:20 3605
according to *a* that his father 2Chr 27:2 3605
a his wars, and his ways, lo, they 2Chr 27:7 3605
one day, which were *a* valiant men 2Chr 28:6 3605
the princes and *a* the congregation 2Chr 28:14 3605
with the spoil clothed *a* that 2Chr 28:15 3605
carried *a* the feeble of them upon 2Chr 28:15 3605

the ruin of him, and of *a* Israel 2Chr 28:23 3605
of *a* his ways, first and last, 2Chr 28:26 3605
according to *a* that David his 2Chr 29:2 3605
brought out *a* the uncleanness 2Chr 29:16 3605
We have cleansed *a* the house of 2Chr 29:18 3605
with *a* the vessels thereof, and 2Chr 29:18 3605
with *a* the vessels thereof 2Chr 29:18 3605
Moreover *a* the vessels, which 2Chr 29:19 3605
to make an atonement for *a* Israel 2Chr 29:24 3605
should be made for *a* Israel 2Chr 29:24 3605
a the congregation worshipped, and 2Chr 29:28 3605
a this continued until the burnt 2Chr 29:28 3605
a that were present with him 2Chr 29:29 3605
a these were for a burnt offering 2Chr 29:32 3605
not flay *a* the burnt offerings 2Chr 29:34 3605
a the people, that God had 2Chr 29:36 3605
And Hezekiah sent to *a* Israel 2Chr 30:1 3605
a the congregation in Jerusalem, 2Chr 30:2 3605
the king and *a* the congregation 2Chr 30:4 3605
proclamation throughout *a* Israel 2Chr 30:5 3605
his princes throughout *a* Israel 2Chr 30:6 3605
a the altars for incense took 2Chr 30:14 3605
a the Levites that taught the 2Chr 30:22 3605
a the congregation of Judah, with 2Chr 30:25 3605
a the congregation that came out 2Chr 30:25 3605
Now when *a* this was finished, *a* 2Chr 31:1 3605
and the altars out of *a* Judah 2Chr 31:1 3605
they had utterly destroyed them *a* 2Chr 31:1
Then *a* the children of Israel 2Chr 31:1 3605
of *a* the increase of the field 2Chr 31:5 3605
the tithe of *a* things brought 2Chr 31:5 3605
genealogy of *a* their little ones 2Chr 31:18 3605
through *a* the congregation 2Chr 31:18 3605
to give portions to *a* the males 2Chr 31:19 3605
to *a* that were reckoned by 2Chr 31:19 3605
did Hezekiah throughout *a* Judah 2Chr 31:20 3605
God, he did it with *a* his heart 2Chr 31:21 3605
who stopped *a* the fountains, and 2Chr 32:4 3605
built up *a* the wall that was 2Chr 32:5 3605
nor for *a* the multitude that is 2Chr 32:7 3605
a his power with him,) unto 2Chr 32:9 3605
unto *a* Judah that were at 2Chr 32:9 3605
unto *a* the people of other lands 2Chr 32:13 3605
Who was there among *a* the gods of 2Chr 32:14 3605
which cut off *a* the mighty men of 2Chr 32:21 3605
and from the hand of *a* other 2Chr 32:22 3605
of *a* nations from thenceforth 2Chr 32:23 3605
for *a* manner of pleasant jewels 2Chr 32:27 3605
stalls for *a* manner of beasts, and 2Chr 32:28 3605
Hezekiah prospered in *a* his works 2Chr 32:30 3605
that he might know *a* that was in 2Chr 32:31 3605
a Judah and the inhabitants of 2Chr 32:33 3605
worshipped *a* the host of heaven, 2Chr 33:3 3605
he built altars for *a* the host of 2Chr 33:5 3605
before *a* the tribes of Israel 2Chr 33:7 3605
do *a* that I have commanded them 2Chr 33:8 3605
put captains of war in *a* the 2Chr 33:14 3605
a the altars that he had built in 2Chr 33:15 3605
a his sin, and his trespass, and 2Chr 33:19 3605
unto *a* the carved images which 2Chr 33:22 3605
a them that had conspired against 2Chr 33:25 3605
cut down *a* the idols throughout 2Chr 34:7 3605
throughout *a* the land of Israel 2Chr 34:7 3605
of *a* the remnant of Israel 2Chr 34:9 3605
and of *a* Judah and Benjamin 2Chr 34:9 3605
a that could skill of instruments 2Chr 34:12 3605
were overseers of *a* that wrought 2Chr 34:13 3605
A that was committed to thy 2Chr 34:16 3605
to do after *a* that is written in 2Chr 34:21 3605
even *a* the curses that are 2Chr 34:24 3605
with *a* the works of their hands 2Chr 34:25 3605
neither shall thine eyes see *a* 2Chr 34:28 3605
gathered together *a* the elders of 2Chr 34:29 3605
a the men of Judah, and the 2Chr 34:30 3605
a the people, great and small 2Chr 34:30 3605
he read in their ears *a* the words 2Chr 34:30 3605
with *a* his heart, and with *a* his 2Chr 34:31 3605
he caused *a* that were present in 2Chr 34:32 3605
a the abominations out of *a* the 2Chr 34:33 3605
made *a* that were present in 2Chr 34:33 3605
a his days they departed not from 2Chr 34:33 3605
the Levites that taught *a* Israel 2Chr 35:3 3605
a for the passover offerings 2Chr 35:7 3605
for *a* that were present, to the 2Chr 35:7 3605
them speedily among *a* the people 2Chr 35:13 3605
So *a* the service of the LORD was 2Chr 35:16 3605
neither did *a* the kings of Israel 2Chr 35:18 3605
a Judah and Israel that were 2Chr 35:18 3605
After *a* this, when Josiah had 2Chr 35:20 3605
a Judah and Jerusalem mourned for 2Chr 35:24 3605
a the singing men and the singing 2Chr 35:25 3605
Moreover *a* the chief of the 2Chr 36:14 3605
transgressed very much after *a* 2Chr 36:14 3605
he gave them *a* into his hand 2Chr 36:17 3605
a the vessels of the house of God 2Chr 36:18 3605
a these he brought to Babylon 2Chr 36:18 3605
burnt *a* the palaces thereof with 2Chr 36:19 3605
destroyed *a* the goodly vessels 2Chr 36:19 3605
throughout *a* his kingdom, and put 2Chr 36:22 3605
A the kingdoms of the earth hath 2Chr 36:23 3605
there among you of *a* his people 2Chr 36:23 3605
throughout *a* his kingdom, and put Ezr 1:1 3605
me *a* the kingdoms of the earth Ezr 1:2 3605
there among you of *a* his people Ezr 1:3 3605
with *a* them whose spirit God had Ezr 1:5 3605
a they that were about them Ezr 1:6 3605
beside *a* that was willingly Ezr 1:6 3605
A the vessels of gold and of Ezr 1:11 3605
A these did Sheshbazzar bring up Ezr 1:11 3605
in *a* an hundred thirty and nine Ezr 2:42 3605
A the Nethinims, and the children Ezr 2:58 3605
and *a* Israel in their cities Ezr 2:70 3605
of *a* the set feasts of the LORD Ezr 3:5 3605
a they that were come out of the Ezr 3:8 3605

a the people shouted with a great Ezr 3:11 3605
a the days of Cyrus king of Ezr 4:5 3605
which have ruled over *a* countries Ezr 4:20 3606
Unto Darius the king, *a* peace Ezr 5:7 3606
to dwell there destroy *a* kings Ezr 6:12 3606
for a sin offering for *a* Israel Ezr 6:17 3606
a of them were pure Ezr 6:20 3605
killed the passover for *a* the Ezr 6:20 3605
and *a* such as had separated Ezr 6:21 3605
king granted him *a* his request Ezr 7:6 3605
that *a* they of the people of Ezr 7:13 3606
a the silver and gold that thou Ezr 7:16 3606
find in *a* the province of Babylon Ezr 7:16 3606
do make a decree to *a* the Ezr 7:21 3606
which may judge *a* the people that Ezr 7:25 3606
a such as know the laws of thy Ezr 7:25 3606
before *a* the king's mighty Ezr 7:28 3605
a of them were expressed by name Ezr 8:20 3605
ones, and for *a* our substance Ezr 8:21 3605
a them for good that seek him Ezr 8:22 3605
his wrath is against *a* them that Ezr 8:22 3605
a Israel there present, had Ezr 8:25 3605
a the weight was written at that Ezr 8:34 3605
twelve bullocks for *a* Israel Ezr 8:35 3605
a this was a burnt offering unto Ezr 8:35 3605
after *a* that is come upon us for Ezr 9:13 3605
our God to put away *a* the wives Ezr 10:3 3605
a Israel, to swear that they Ezr 10:5 3605
Jerusalem unto *a* the children of Ezr 10:7 3605
a his substance should be Ezr 10:8 3605
Then *a* the men of Judah and Ezr 10:9 3605
a the people sat in the street of Ezr 10:9 3605
Then *a* the congregation answered Ezr 10:12 3605
Let now our rulers of *a* the Ezr 10:14 3605
let *a* them which have taken Ezr 10:14 3605
a of them by their names, were Ezr 10:16 3605
they made an end with *a* the men Ezr 10:17 3605
A these had taken strange wives Ezr 10:44 3605
a the wall was joined together Neh 4:6 3605
conspired *a* of them together to Neh 4:8 3605
From *a* places whence ye shall Neh 4:12 3605
that we returned *a* of us to the Neh 4:15 3605
were behind *a* the house of Judah Neh 4:16 3605
a the congregation said, Amen, and Neh 5:13 3605
a my servants were gathered Neh 5:16 3605
ten days store of *a* sorts of wine Neh 5:18 3605
yet for *a* this required not I the Neh 5:18 5973
according to *a* that I have done Neh 5:19 3605
For they *a* made us afraid, saying Neh 6:9 3605
that when *a* our enemies heard Neh 6:16 3605
a the heathen that were about us Neh 6:16 3605
A the Nethinims, and the children Neh 7:60 3605
a Israel, dwelt in their cities Neh 7:73 3605
a the people gathered themselves Neh 8:1 3605
women, and *a* that could hear with Neh 8:2 3605
the ears of *a* the people were Neh 8:3 3605
the book in the sight of *a* people Neh 8:5 3605
(for he was above *a* the people Neh 8:5 3605
opened it, *a* the people stood up Neh 8:5 3605
a the people answered, Amen, Amen Neh 8:6 3605
said unto *a* the people, This day Neh 8:9 3605
For *a* the people wept, when they Neh 8:9 3605
the Levites stilled *a* the people Neh 8:11 3605
a the people went their way to Neh 8:12 3605
of the fathers of *a* the people Neh 8:13 3605
proclaim in *a* their cities, and in Neh 8:15 3605
a the congregation of them that Neh 8:17 3605
themselves from *a* strangers Neh 9:2 3605
which is exalted above *a* blessing Neh 9:5 3605
with *a* their host, the earth, and Neh 9:6 3605
a things that are therein, the Neh 9:6 3605
a that is therein Neh 9:6 3605
and thou preservest them *a* Neh 9:6 3605
on *a* his servants, and on *a* the Neh 9:10 3605
possessed houses full of *a* goods Neh 9:25 3605
let not *a* the trouble seem little Neh 9:32 3605
on *a* thy people, since the time Neh 9:32 3605
just in *a* that is brought upon us Neh 9:33 3605
because of *a* this we make a sure Neh 9:38 3605
a they that had separated Neh 10:28 3605
do *a* the commandments of the LORD Neh 10:29 3605
for *a* the work of the house of Neh 10:33 3605
of *a* fruit of *a* trees, year by Neh 10:35 3605
the fruit of *a* manner of trees, Neh 10:37 3605
might have the tithes in *a* the Neh 10:37 3605
And the people blessed *a* the men Neh 11:2 3605
A the sons of Perez that dwelt at Neh 11:6 3605
A the Levites in the holy city Neh 11:18 3605
were in *a* the cities of Judah, Neh 11:20 3605
was at the king's hand in *a* Neh 11:24 3605
the Levites out of *a* their places Neh 12:27 3605
And *a* Israel in the days of Neh 12:47 3605
from Israel *a* the mixed multitude Neh 13:3 3605
But in *a* this time was not I at Neh 13:6 3605
therefore I cast forth *a* the Neh 13:8 3605
Then brought *a* Judah the tithe of Neh 13:12 3605
a manner of burdens, which they Neh 13:15 3605
a manner of ware, and sold on the Neh 13:16 3605
our God bring *a* this evil upon us Neh 13:18 3605
sellers of *a* kind of ware lodged Neh 13:20 3605
God made him king over *a* Israel Neh 13:26 3605
unto you to do *a* this great evil Neh 13:27 3605
cleansed I them from *a* strangers Neh 13:30 3605
made a feast unto *a* his princes Est 1:3 3605
the king made a feast unto *a* the Est 1:5 3605
to *a* the officers of his house Est 1:8 3605
manner toward *a* that knew law Est 1:13 3605
only, but also to *a* the princes Est 1:16 3605
to *a* the people that are in *a* Est 1:16 3605
shall come abroad unto *a* women Est 1:17 3605
day unto *a* the king's princes Est 1:18 3605
published throughout *a* his empire Est 1:20 3605
a the wives shall give to their Est 1:20 3605
into *a* the king's provinces Est 1:22 3605
in *a* the provinces of his kingdom Est 2:3 3605
a the fair young virgins unto Est 2:3 3605
of *a* them that looked upon her Est 2:15 3605
loved Esther above *a* the women Est 2:17 3605
his sight more than *a* the virgins Est 2:17 3605
a great feast unto *a* his princes Est 2:18 3605
set his seat above *a* the princes Est 3:1 3605
a the king's servants, that were Est 3:2 3605
Haman sought to destroy *a* the Est 3:6 3605
in *a* the provinces of thy kingdom Est 3:8 3605
laws are diverse from *a* people Est 3:8 3605
a that Haman had commanded unto Est 3:12 3605
posts into *a* the king's provinces Est 3:13 3605
a Jews, both young and old, little Est 3:13 3605
was published unto *a* people Est 3:14 3605
perceived *a* that was done Est 4:1 3605
Mordecai told him of *a* that had Est 4:7 3605
A the king's servants, and the Est 4:11 3605
house, more than *a* the Jews Est 4:13 3605
gather together *a* the Jews that Est 4:16 3605
did according to *a* that Esther Est 4:17 3605
a the things wherein the king had Est 5:11 3605
Yet *a* this availeth me nothing, Est 5:13 3605
a his friends unto him, Let a Est 5:14 3605
let nothing fail of *a* that thou Est 6:10 3605
a his friends every thing that Est 6:13 3605
are in *a* the king's provinces Est 8:5 3605
it was written according to *a* Est 8:9 3605
a the power of the people and Est 8:11 3605
Upon one day in *a* the provinces Est 8:12 3605
was published unto *a* people Est 8:13 3605
a the provinces of the king Est 9:2 3605
fear of them fell upon *a* people Est 9:2 3605
a the rulers of the provinces, and Est 9:3 3605
out throughout *a* the provinces Est 9:4 3605
Thus the Jews smote *a* their Est 9:5 3605
sent letters unto *a* the Jews that Est 9:20 3605
in *a* the provinces of the king Est 9:20 3605
Agagite, the enemy of *a* the Jews Est 9:24 3605
Therefore for *a* the words of this Est 9:26 3605
upon *a* such as joined themselves Est 9:27 3605
the Jew, wrote with *a* authority Est 9:29 3605
sent the letters unto *a* the Jews Est 9:30 3605
a the acts of his power and of his Est 10:2 3605
and speaking peace to *a* his seed Est 10:3 3605
greatest of *a* the men of the east Job 1:3 3605
according to the number of them *a* Job 1:5 3605
about *a* that he hath on every Job 1:10 3605
touch *a* that he hath, and he will Job 1:11 3605
a that he hath is in thy power Job 1:12 3605
In *a* this Job sinned not, nor Job 1:22 3605
a that a man hath will he give Job 2:4 3605
In *a* this did not Job sin with Job 2:10 3605
of *a* this evil that was come upon Job 2:11 3605
which made *a* my bones to shake Job 4:14 7230
the paths of *a* that forget God Job 8:13 3605
I am afraid of *a* my sorrows Job 9:28 3605
Who knoweth not in *a* these that Job 12:9 3605
thing, and the breath of *a* mankind Job 12:10 3605
Lo, mine eye hath seen *a* this Job 13:1 3605
ye are *a* physicians of no value Job 13:4 3605
lookest narrowly unto *a* my paths Job 13:27 3605
a the days of my appointed time Job 14:14 3605
travaileth with pain *a* his days Job 15:20 3605
miserable comforters are ye *a* Job 16:2 3605
hast made desolate *a* my company Job 16:7 3605
a my members are as a shadow Job 17:7 3605
But as for you *a*, do ye return, Job 17:10 3605
A my inward friends abhorred me Job 19:19 3605
A darkness shall be hid in his Job 20:26 3605
taken out of the way as *a* other Job 24:24 3605
A the while my breath is in me, Job 27:3 3605
a ye yourselves have seen it Job 27:12 3605
and searcheth out *a* perfection Job 28:3 3605
is hid from the eyes of *a* living Job 28:21 3605
the dew lay *a* night upon my Job 29:19 3885
the house appointed for *a* living Job 30:23 3605
see my ways, and count *a* my steps Job 31:4 3605
and would root out *a* mine increase Job 31:12 3605
and hearken to *a* my words Job 33:1 3605
the stocks, he marketh *a* my paths Job 33:11 3605
a these things worketh God Job 33:29 3605
A flesh shall perish together, and Job 34:15 3605
for they *a* are the work of his Job 34:19 3605
of man, and he seeth *a* his goings Job 34:21 3605
nor *a* the forces of strength Job 36:19 3605
that *a* men may know his work Job 37:7 3605
a the sons of God shouted for joy Job 38:7 3605
declare if thou knowest it *a* Job 38:18 3605
where *a* the beasts of the field Job 40:20 3605
He beholdeth *a* high things Job 41:34 3605
he is a king over *a* the children Job 41:34 3605
there unto him *a* his brethren Job 42:11 3605
a his sisters, and *a* they that Job 42:11 3605
comforted him over *a* the evil Job 42:11 3605
in *a* the land were no women found Job 42:15 3605
Blessed are *a* they that put their Ps 2:12 3605
for thou hast smitten *a* mine Ps 3:7 3605
thou hatest *a* workers of iniquity Ps 5:5 3605
But let *a* those that put their Ps 5:11 3605
a the night make I my bed to swim Ps 6:6 3605
old because of *a* mine enemies Ps 6:7 3605
from me, *a* ye workers of iniquity Ps 6:8 3605
Let *a* mine enemies be ashamed and Ps 6:10 3605
save me from *a* them that Ps 7:1 3605
is thy name in *a* the earth Ps 8:1 3605
thou hast put *a* things under his Ps 8:6 3605
A sheep and oxen, yea, and the Ps 8:7 3605
is thy name in *a* the earth Ps 8:9 3605
I will shew forth *a* thy Ps 9:1 3605
That I may shew forth *a* thy Ps 9:14 3605
a the nations that forget God Ps 9:17 3605
God is not in *a* his thoughts Ps 10:4 3605
as for *a* his enemies, he puffeth Ps 10:5 3605
shall cut off *a* flattering lips Ps 12:3 3605
They are *a* gone aside Ps 14:3 3605
they are *a* together become filthy Ps 14:3
Have *a* the workers of iniquity no Ps 14:4 3605
in whom is *a* my delight Ps 16:3 3605
from the hand of *a* his enemies Ps 18:t 3605
For *a* his judgments were before Ps 18:22 3605
he is a buckler to *a* those that Ps 18:30 3605
is gone out through *a* the earth Ps 19:4 3605
Remember *a* thy offerings, and Ps 20:3 3605
heart, and fulfil *a* thy counsel Ps 20:4 3605
the LORD fulfil *a* thy petitions Ps 20:5 3605
shall find out *a* thine enemies Ps 21:8 3605
A they that see me laugh me to Ps 22:7 3605
a my bones are out of joint Ps 22:14 3605
I may tell *a* my bones Ps 22:17 3605
a ye the seed of Jacob, glorify Ps 22:23 3605
fear him, *a* ye the seed of Israel Ps 22:23 3605
A the ends of the world shall Ps 22:27 3605
a the kindreds of the nations Ps 22:27 3605
A they that be fat upon earth Ps 22:29 3605
a they that go down to the dust Ps 22:29 3605
follow me *a* the days of my life Ps 23:6 3605
on thee do I wait *a* the day Ps 25:5 3605
A the paths of the LORD are mercy Ps 25:10 3605
and forgive *a* my sins Ps 25:18 3605
O God, out of *a* his troubles Ps 25:22 3605
tell of *a* thy wondrous works Ps 26:7 3605
of the LORD *a* the days of my life Ps 27:4 3605
a reproach among *a* mine enemies Ps 31:11 3605
O love the LORD, *a* ye his saints Ps 31:23 3605
a ye that hope in the LORD Ps 31:24 3605
through my roaring *a* the day long Ps 32:3 3605
a ye that are upright in heart Ps 32:11 3605
a his works are done in truth Ps 33:4 3605
a the host of them by the breath Ps 33:6 3605
Let *a* the earth fear the LORD Ps 33:8 3605
let *a* the inhabitants of the Ps 33:8 3605
of his heart to *a* generations Ps 33:11
he beholdeth *a* the sons of men Ps 33:13 3605
a the inhabitants of the earth Ps 33:14 3605
he considereth *a* their works Ps 33:15 3605
I will bless the LORD at *a* times Ps 34:1 3605
and delivered me from *a* my fears Ps 34:4 3605
saved him out of *a* his troubles Ps 34:6 3605
them out of *a* their troubles Ps 34:17 3605
LORD delivereth him out of them *a* Ps 34:19 3605
He keepeth *a* his bones Ps 34:20 3605
A my bones shall say, LORD, who Ps 35:10 3605
and of thy praise *a* the day long Ps 35:28 3605
I go mourning *a* the day long Ps 38:6 3605
a my desire is before thee Ps 38:9 3605
and imagine deceits *a* the day long Ps 38:12 3605
Deliver me from *a* my Ps 39:8 3605
a sojourner, as *a* my fathers were Ps 39:12 3605
Let *a* those that seek thee Ps 40:16 3605
thou wilt make *a* his bed in his Ps 41:3 3605
A that hate me whisper together Ps 41:7 3605
a thy waves and thy billows are Ps 42:7 3605
In God we boast *a* the day long Ps 44:8 3605
A this is come upon us Ps 44:17 3605
sake are we killed *a* the day long Ps 44:22 3605
A thy garments smell of myrrh, and Ps 45:8 3605
daughter is *a* glorious within Ps 45:13 3605
make princes in *a* the earth Ps 45:16 3605
to be remembered in *a* generations Ps 45:17 3605
O clap your hands, *a* ye people Ps 47:1 3605
is a great King over *a* the earth Ps 47:2 3605
God is the King of *a* the earth Ps 47:7 3605
Hear this, *a* ye people Ps 49:1 3605
a ye inhabitants of the world Ps 49:1 3605
dwelling places to *a* generations Ps 49:11
I know *a* the fowls of the Ps 50:11 3605
blot out *a* mine iniquities Ps 51:9 3605
Thou lovest *a* devouring words, O Ps 52:4 3605
delivered me out of *a* trouble Ps 54:7 3605
a their thoughts are against me Ps 56:5 3605
that performeth *a* things for me Ps 57:2
thy glory be above *a* the earth Ps 57:5 3605
thy glory be above *a* the earth Ps 57:11 3605
awake to visit *a* the heathen Ps 59:5 3605
thou shalt have *a* the heathen in Ps 59:8 3605
ye shall be slain *a* of you Ps 62:3 3605
Trust in him at *a* times Ps 62:8 3605
a that see them shall flee away Ps 64:8 3605
a men shall fear, and shall Ps 64:9 3605
a the upright in heart shall Ps 64:10 3605
unto thee shall *a* flesh come Ps 65:2 3605
of *a* the ends of the earth Ps 65:5 3605
joyful noise unto God, *a* ye lands Ps 66:1 3605
A the earth shall worship thee, Ps 66:4 3605
a ye that fear God, and I will Ps 66:16 3605
thy saving health among *a* nations Ps 67:2 3605
let *a* the people praise thee Ps 67:3 3605
let *a* the people praise thee Ps 67:5 3605
a the ends of the earth shall Ps 67:7 3605
adversaries are *a* before thee Ps 69:19 3605
Let *a* those that seek thee Ps 70:4 3605
and with thy honour *a* the day Ps 71:8 3605
and thy salvation *a* the day Ps 71:15 3605
thy righteousness *a* the day long Ps 71:24 3605
endure, throughout *a* generations Ps 72:5
a kings shall fall down before Ps 72:11 3605
a nations shall serve him Ps 72:11 3605
a nations shall call him blessed Ps 72:17 3605
For *a* the day long have I been Ps 73:14 3605
thou hast destroyed *a* them that Ps 73:27 3605
that I may declare *a* thy works Ps 73:28 3605
even *a* that the enemy hath done Ps 74:3 3605
they have burned up *a* the Ps 74:8 3605
Thou hast set *a* the borders of Ps 74:17 3605
a the inhabitants thereof are Ps 75:3 3605
a the wicked of the earth shall Ps 75:8 3605
A the horns of the wicked also Ps 75:10 3605

to save *a* the meek of the earth Ps 76:9 3605
let *a* that be round about him Ps 76:11 3605
will meditate also of *a* thy work Ps 77:12 3605
a the night with a light of fire Ps 78:14 3605
For *a* this they sinned still, and Ps 78:32 3605
and did not stir up *a* his wrath Ps 78:38 3605
smote *a* the firstborn in Egypt Ps 78:51 3605
forth thy praise to *a* generations Ps 79:13
so that *a* they which pass by the Ps 80:12 3605
a the foundations of the earth Ps 82:5
a of you are children of the most Ps 82:6 3605
for thou shalt inherit *a* nations Ps 82:8 3605
a their princes as Zebah, and as Ps 83:11 3605
the most high over *a* the earth Ps 83:18 3605
thou hast covered *a* their sin Ps 85:2 3605
Thou hast taken away *a* thy wrath Ps 85:3 3605
out thine anger to *a* generations Ps 85:5 3605
plenteous in mercy unto *a* them Ps 86:5 3605
A nations whom thou hast made Ps 86:9 3605
O Lord my God, with *a* my heart Ps 86:12 3605
than *a* the dwellings of Jacob Ps 87:2 3605
a my springs are in thee Ps 87:7 3605
afflicted me with *a* thy waves Ps 88:7 3605
thy faithfulness to *a* generations Ps 89:1
up thy throne to *a* generations Ps 89:4
of *a* them that are about him Ps 89:7 3605
name shall they rejoice *a* the day Ps 89:16 3605
hast broken down *a* his hedges Ps 89:40 3605
A that pass by the way spoil him Ps 89:41 3605
thou hast made *a* his enemies to Ps 89:42 3605
hast thou made *a* men in vain Ps 89:47 3605
reproach of *a* the mighty people Ps 89:50 3605
dwelling place in *a* generations Ps 90:1
For *a* our days are passed away in Ps 90:9 3605
may rejoice and be glad *a* our days Ps 90:14 3605
thee, to keep thee in *a* thy ways Ps 91:11 3605
when *a* the workers of iniquity do Ps 92:7 3605
a the workers of iniquity shall Ps 92:9 3605
a the workers of iniquity boast Ps 94:4 3605
a the upright in heart shall Ps 94:15 3605
God, and a great King above *a* gods Ps 95:3 3605
sing unto the LORD, *a* the earth Ps 96:1 3605
his wonders among *a* people Ps 96:3 3605
he is to be feared above *a* gods Ps 96:4 3605
For *a* the gods of the nations are Ps 96:5 3605
fear before him, *a* the earth Ps 96:9 3605
be joyful, and *a* that is therein Ps 96:12 3605
then shall *a* the trees of the Ps 96:12 3605
a the people see his glory Ps 97:6 3605
Confounded be *a* they that serve Ps 97:7 3605
worship him, *a* ye gods Ps 97:7 3605
LORD, art high above *a* the earth Ps 97:9 3605
thou art exalted far above *a* gods Ps 97:9 3605
a the ends of the earth have seen Ps 98:3 3605
noise unto the LORD, *a* the earth Ps 98:4 3605
and he is high above *a* the people Ps 99:2 3605
noise unto the LORD, *a* ye lands Ps 100:1 3605
truth endureth to *a* generations Ps 100:5
I will early destroy *a* the wicked Ps 101:8 3605
that I may cut off *a* wicked doers Ps 101:8 3605
enemies reproach me *a* the day Ps 102:8 3605
remembrance unto *a* generations Ps 102:12
a the kings of the earth thy Ps 102:15 3605
are throughout *a* generations Ps 102:24
a of them shall wax old like a Ps 102:26 3605
a that is within me, bless his Ps 103:1 3605
forget not *a* his benefits Ps 103:2 3605
Who forgiveth *a* thine iniquities Ps 103:3 3605
who healeth *a* thy diseases Ps 103:3 3605
judgment for *a* that are oppressed Ps 103:6 3605
and his kingdom ruleth over *a* Ps 103:19 3605
Bless ye the LORD, *a* ye his hosts Ps 103:21 3605
a his works in *a* places of his Ps 103:22 3605
wherein *a* the beasts of the Ps 104:20 3605
In wisdom hast thou made them *a* Ps 104:24 3605
These wait *a* upon thee Ps 104:27 3605
talk ye of *a* his wondrous works Ps 105:2 3605
his judgments are in *a* the earth Ps 105:7 3605
and ruler of *a* his substance Ps 105:21 3605
flies, and lice in *a* their coasts Ps 105:31 3605
did eat up *a* the herbs in their Ps 105:35 3605
He smote also *a* the firstborn in Ps 105:36 3605
the chief of *a* their strength Ps 105:36 3605
who can shew forth *a* his praise Ps 106:2 3605
doeth righteousness at *a* times Ps 106:3 3605
unto *a* generations for evermore Ps 106:31
of *a* those that carried them Ps 106:46 3605
let *a* the people say, Amen Ps 106:48 3605
soul abhorreth *a* manner of meat Ps 107:18 3605
a iniquity shall stop her mouth Ps 107:42 3605
and thy glory above *a* the earth Ps 108:5 3605
extortioner catch *a* that he hath Ps 109:11 3605
sought out of *a* them that have Ps 111:2 3605
a his commandments are sure Ps 111:7 3605
a good understanding have *a* they Ps 111:10 3605
The LORD is high above *a* nations Ps 113:4 3605
said in my haste, *A* men are liars Ps 116:11 3605
LORD for *a* his benefits toward me Ps 116:12 3605
in the presence of *a* his people Ps 116:14 3605
in the presence of *a* his people Ps 116:18 3605
O praise the LORD, *a* ye nations Ps 117:1 3605
praise him, *a* ye people Ps 117:1 3605
A nations compassed me about Ps 118:10 3605
respect unto *a* thy commandments Ps 119:6 3605
a the judgments of thy mouth Ps 119:13 3605
as much as in *a* riches Ps 119:14 3605
unto thy judgments at *a* times Ps 119:20 3605
of *a* them that fear thee, and of Ps 119:63 3605
A thy commandments are faithful Ps 119:86 3605
is unto *a* generations Ps 119:90
for *a* are thy servants Ps 119:91 3605
have seen an end of *a* perfection Ps 119:96 3605
it is my meditation *a* the day Ps 119:97 3605
understanding than *a* my teachers Ps 119:99 3605

Thou hast trodden down *a* them Ps 119:118 3605
Thou puttest away *a* the wicked of Ps 119:119 3605
Therefore I esteem *a* thy precepts Ps 119:128 3605
concerning *a* things to be right Ps 119:128 3605
a thy commandments are truth Ps 119:151 3605
for *a* my ways are before thee Ps 119:168 3605
for *a* thy commandments are Ps 119:172 3605
shall preserve thee from *a* evil Ps 121:7
Jerusalem *a* the days of thy life Ps 128:5
Let them *a* be confounded and Ps 129:5
Israel from *a* his iniquities Ps 130:8 3605
David, and *a* his afflictions Ps 132:1 3605
a ye servants of the LORD, which Ps 134:1 3605
and that our Lord is above *a* gods Ps 135:5 3605
in the seas, and *a* deep places Ps 135:6 3605
Pharaoh, and upon *a* his servants Ps 135:9 3605
and *a* the kingdoms of Canaan Ps 135:11 3605
O LORD, throughout *a* generations Ps 135:13
Who giveth food to *a* flesh Ps 136:25 3605
thy word above *a* thy name Ps 138:2 3605
A the kings of the earth shall Ps 138:4 3605
and art acquainted with *a* my ways Ps 139:3 3605
in thy book *a* my members were Ps 139:16 3605
I meditate on *a* thy works Ps 143:5
destroy *a* them that afflict my Ps 143:12 3605
affording *a* manner of store Ps 144:13
The LORD is good to *a* Ps 145:9 3605
mercies are over *a* his works Ps 145:9 3605
A thy works shall praise thee, O Ps 145:10 3605
endureth throughout *a* generations Ps 145:13
The LORD upholdeth *a* that fall Ps 145:14 3605
raiseth up *a* those that be bowed Ps 145:14 3605
The eyes of *a* wait upon thee Ps 145:15 3605
LORD is righteous in *a* his ways Ps 145:17 3605
his ways, and holy in *a* his works Ps 145:17 3605
The LORD is nigh unto *a* them that Ps 145:18 3605
to *a* that call upon him in truth Ps 145:18 3605
preserveth *a* them that love him Ps 145:20 3605
but *a* the wicked will he destroy Ps 145:20 3605
let *a* flesh bless his holy name Ps 145:21 3605
the sea, and *a* that therein is Ps 146:6 3605
God, O Zion, unto *a* generations Ps 146:10
he calleth them *a* by their names Ps 147:4 3605
Praise ye him, *a* his angels Ps 148:2 3605
praise ye him, *a* his hosts Ps 148:2 3605
praise him, *a* ye stars of light Ps 148:3 3605
the earth, ye dragons, and *a* deeps Ps 148:7 3605
Mountains, and *a* hills Ps 148:9 3605
fruitful trees, and *a* cedars Ps 148:9 3605
Beasts, and *a* cattle Ps 148:10 3605
Kings of the earth, and *a* people Ps 148:11 3605
princes, and *a* judges of the earth Ps 148:11 3605
the praise of *a* his saints Ps 148:14 3605
this honour have *a* his saints Ps 149:9 3605
We shall find *a* precious Prov 1:13 3605
let us *a* have one purse Prov 1:14 3605
have set at nought *a* my counsel Prov 1:25 3605
they despised *a* my reproof Prov 1:30 3605
in the LORD with *a* thine heart Prov 3:5 3605
In *a* thy ways acknowledge him, and Prov 3:6 3605
firstfruits of *a* thine increase Prov 3:9 3605
a the things thou canst desire Prov 3:15 3605
and *a* her paths are peace Prov 3:17 3605
and with *a* thy getting get Prov 4:7 3605
them, and health to *a* their flesh Prov 4:22 3605
Keep thy heart with *a* diligence Prov 4:23 3605
let *a* thy ways be established Prov 4:26 3605
I was almost in *a* evil in the Prov 5:14 3605
breasts satisfy thee at *a* times Prov 5:19 3605
and he pondereth *a* his goings Prov 5:21 3605
he shall give *a* the substance of Prov 6:31 3605
A the words of my mouth are in Prov 8:8 3605
They are *a* plain to him that Prov 8:9 3605
a the things that may be desired Prov 8:11 3605
even *a* the judges of the earth Prov 8:16 3605
a they that hate me love death Prov 8:36 3605
but love covereth *a* sins Prov 10:12 3605
In *a* labour there is profit Prov 14:23 3605
A the days of the afflicted are Prov 15:15 3605
A the ways of a man are clean in Prov 16:2 3605
hath made *a* things for himself Prov 16:4 3605
a the weights of the bag are his Prov 16:11 3605
A friend loveth at *a* times Prov 17:17 3605
and intermeddleth with *a* wisdom Prov 18:1 3605
A the brethren of the poor do Prov 19:7 3605
away *a* evil with his eyes Prov 20:8 3605
searching *a* the inward parts of Prov 20:27 3605
coveteth greedily *a* the day long Prov 21:26 3605
the LORD is the maker of them *a* Prov 22:2 3605
fear of the LORD *a* the day long Prov 23:17 3605
be filled with *a* precious Prov 24:4 3605
it was *a* grown over with thorns, Prov 24:31 3605
The great God that formed *a* Prov 26:10 3605
seek the LORD understand *a* things Prov 28:5 3605
A fool uttereth *a* his mind Prov 29:11 3605
a his servants are wicked Prov 29:12 3605
who hath established *a* the ends Prov 30:4 3605
go they forth *a* of them by bands Prov 30:27 3605
of *a* such as are appointed to Prov 31:8 3605
not evil *a* the days of her life Prov 31:12 3605
for *a* her household are clothed Prov 31:21 3605
but thou excellest them *a* Prov 31:29 3605
a is vanity Eccl 1:2 3605
What profit hath a man of *a* his Eccl 1:3 3605
A the rivers run into the sea Eccl 1:7 3605
A things are full of labour Eccl 1:8 3605
a things that are done under Eccl 1:13 3605
I have seen *a* the works that are Eccl 1:14 3605
a is vanity and vexation of spirit Eccl 1:14 3605
have gotten more wisdom than *a* Eccl 1:16 3605
heaven *a* the days of their life Eccl 2:3 4557
trees in them of *a* kind of fruits Eccl 2:5 3605
small cattle above *a* that were in Eccl 2:7 3605
instruments, and that of *a* sorts Eccl 2:8 3605

increased more than *a* that were Eccl 2:9 3605
my heart rejoiced in *a* my labour Eccl 2:10 3605
was my portion of *a* my labour Eccl 2:10 3605
Then I looked on *a* the works that Eccl 2:11 3605
a was vanity and vexation of Eccl 2:11 3605
one event happeneth to them *a* Eccl 2:14 3605
days to come shall *a* be forgotten Eccl 2:16 3605
for *a* is vanity and vexation of Eccl 2:17 3605
I hated *a* my labour which I had Eccl 2:18 3605
over *a* my labour wherein I have Eccl 2:19 3605
a the labour which I took under Eccl 2:20 3605
For what hath man of *a* his labour Eccl 2:22 3605
For *a* his days are sorrows, and Eccl 2:23 3605
and enjoy the good of *a* his labour Eccl 3:13 3605
yea, they have *a* one breath Eccl 3:19 3605
for *a* is vanity Eccl 3:19 3605
A go unto one place Eccl 3:20 3605
a are of the dust, and *a* turn to Eccl 3:20 3605
considered *a* the oppressions that Eccl 4:1 3605
Again, I considered *a* travail Eccl 4:4 3605
is there no end of *a* his labour Eccl 4:8 3605
I considered *a* the living which Eccl 4:15 3605
There is no end of *a* the people Eccl 4:16 3605
even of *a* that have been before Eccl 4:16 3605
the profit of the earth is for *a* Eccl 5:9 3605
that in *a* points as he came, so Eccl 5:16 3605
A his days also he eateth in Eccl 5:17 3605
to enjoy the good of *a* his labour Eccl 5:18 3605
the sun *a* the days of his life Eccl 5:18 4557
his soul of *a* that he desireth Eccl 6:2 3605
do not *a* go to one place Eccl 6:6 3605
A the labour of man is for his Eccl 6:7 3605
a the days of his vain life which Eccl 6:12 4557
for that is the end of *a* men Eccl 7:2 3605
A things have I seen in the days Eccl 7:15 3605
God shall come forth of them *a* Eccl 7:18 3605
heed unto *a* words that are spoken Eccl 7:21 3605
A this have I proved by wisdom Eccl 7:23 3605
but a woman among *a* those have I Eccl 7:28 3605
A this have I seen, and applied my Eccl 8:9 3605
Then I beheld *a* the work of God, Eccl 8:17 3605
For *a* this I considered in my Eccl 9:1 3605
my heart even to declare *a* this Eccl 9:1 3605
hatred by *a* that is before them Eccl 9:1 3605
A things come alike to *a* Eccl 9:2 3605
This is an evil among *a* things Eccl 9:3 3605
that there is one event unto *a* Eccl 9:3 3605
to *a* the living there is hope Eccl 9:4 3605
a the days of the life of thy Eccl 9:9 3605
the sun, *a* the days of thy vanity Eccl 9:9 3605
and chance happeneth to them *a* Eccl 9:11 3605
but money answereth *a* things Eccl 10:19 3605
not the works of God who maketh *a* Eccl 11:5 3605
many years, and rejoice in them *a* Eccl 11:8 3605
A that cometh is vanity Eccl 11:8 3605
that for *a* these things God will Eccl 11:9 3605
a the daughters of musick shall Eccl 12:4 3605
a is vanity Eccl 12:8 3605
he shall lie *a* night betwixt my Song 1:13 3885
with *a* powders of the merchant Song 3:6 3605
They *a* hold swords, being expert Song 3:8 3605
bucklers, *a* shields of mighty men Song 4:4 3605
Thou art *a* fair, my love Song 4:7 3605
of thine ointments than *a* spices Song 4:10 3605
with *a* trees of frankincense Song 4:14 3605
and aloes, with *a* the chief spices Song 4:14 3605
at our gates are *a* manner of Song 7:13 3605
if a man would give *a* the Song 8:7 3605
thy dross, and take away *a* thy tin Is 1:25 3605
a nations shall flow unto it Is 2:2 3605
upon *a* the cedars of Lebanon, Is 2:13 3605
upon *a* the oaks of Bashan, Is 2:13 3605
upon *a* the high mountains, and Is 2:14 3605
upon *a* the hills that are lifted Is 2:14 3605
upon *a* the ships of Tarshish Is 2:16 3605
and upon *a* pleasant pictures Is 2:16 3605
for upon *a* the glory shall be a Is 4:5 3605
For *a* this his anger is not Is 5:25 3605
a their bows bent, their horses' Is 5:28 3605
shall rest *a* of them in the Is 7:19 3605
upon *a* thorns, and upon *a* bushes Is 7:19 3605
because *a* the land shall become Is 7:24 3605
on *a* hills that shall be digged Is 7:25 3605
king of Assyria, and *a* his glory Is 8:7 3605
shall come up over *a* his channels Is 8:7 3605
and go over *a* his banks Is 8:7 3605
give ear, *a* ye of far countries Is 8:9 3605
to *a* them to whom this people Is 8:12 3605
a the people shall know, even Is 9:9 3605
For *a* this his anger is not Is 9:12 3605
For *a* this his anger is not Is 9:17 3605
For *a* this his anger is not Is 9:21 3605
For *a* this his anger is not Is 10:4 3605
left, have I gathered *a* the earth Is 10:14 3605
in the midst of *a* the land Is 10:23 3605
nor destroy in *a* my holy mountain Is 11:9 3605
this is known in *a* the earth Is 12:5 3605
Therefore shall *a* hands be faint Is 13:7 3605
even *a* the chief ones of the Is 14:9 3605
a the kings of the nations Is 14:9 3605
A they shall speak and say unto Is 14:10 3605
A the kings of the nations Is 14:18 3605
even *a* of them, lie in glory, Is 14:18 3605
stretched out upon *a* the nations Is 14:26 3605
on *a* their heads shall be Is 15:2 3605
with *a* that great multitude Is 16:14 3605
A ye inhabitants of the world, and Is 18:3 3605
a the beasts of the earth shall Is 18:6 3605
a they that cast angle into the Is 19:8 3605
a that make sluices and ponds for Is 19:10 3605
a the sighing thereof have I made Is 21:2 3605
a the graven images of her gods Is 21:9 3605
a the glory of Kedar shall fail Is 21:16 3605
A thy rulers are fled together, Is 22:3 3605

a that are found in thee are Is 22:3 3605
they shall hang upon him *a* the Is 22:24 3605
a vessels of small quantity, from Is 22:24 3605
even to *a* the vessels of flagons Is 22:24 3605
it, to stain the pride of *a* glory Is 23:9 3605
to bring into contempt *a* the Is 23:9 3605
shall commit fornication with *a* Is 23:17 3605
a the merryhearted do sigh Is 24:7 3605
a joy is darkened, the mirth of Is 24:11 3605
the LORD of hosts make unto *a* Is 25:6 3605
the covering cast over *a* people Is 25:7 3605
that is spread over *a* nations Is 25:7 3605
wipe away tears from off *a* faces Is 25:8 3605
he take away from off *a* the earth Is 25:8 3605
hast wrought *a* our works in us Is 26:12 3605
made *a* their memory to perish Is 26:14 3605
far unto *a* the ends of the earth Is 26:15 3605
this is *a* the fruit to take away Is 27:9 3605
when he maketh *a* the stones of Is 27:9 3605
For *a* tables are full of vomit and Is 28:8 3605
the plowman plow *a* day to sow Is 28:24 3605
the multitude of *a* the nations Is 29:7 3605
even *a* that fight against her and Is 29:7 3605
the multitude of *a* the nations be Is 29:8 3605
the vision of *a* is become unto Is 29:11 3605
a that watch for iniquity are cut Is 29:20 3605
They were *a* ashamed of a people Is 30:5 3605
blessed are *a* they that wait for Is 30:18 3605
they *a* shall fail together Is 31:3 3605
upon *a* the houses of joy in the Is 32:13 3605
are ye that sow beside *a* waters Is 32:20 3605
earth hear, and *a* that is therein Is 34:1 4393
a things that come forth of it Is 34:1 3605
of the LORD is upon *a* nations Is 34:2 3605
and his fury upon *a* their armies Is 34:2 3605
a the host of heaven shall be Is 34:4 3605
a their host shall fall down, as Is 34:4 3605
a her princes shall be nothing Is 34:12 3605
a the defenced cities of Judah Is 36:1 3605
of Egypt to *a* that trust in him Is 36:6 3605
Who are they among *a* the gods of Is 36:20 3605
to *a* lands by destroying them Is 37:11 3605
of *a* the kingdoms of the earth Is 37:16 3605
hear *a* the words of Sennacherib, Is 37:17 3605
have laid waste *a* the nations Is 37:18 3605
that *a* the kingdoms of the earth Is 37:20 3605
up *a* the rivers of the besieged Is 37:25 3605
behold, they were *a* dead corpses Is 37:36 3605
lion, so will he break *a* my bones Is 38:13 3605
I shall go softly *a* my years in Is 38:15 3605
in *a* these things is the life of Is 38:16 3605
for thou hast cast *a* my sins Is 38:17 3605
a the days of our life in the Is 38:20 3605
a the house of his armour, and *a* Is 39:2 3605
nor in *a* his dominion, that Is 39:2 3605
A that is in mine house have they Is 39:4 3605
that *a* that is in thine house, and Is 39:6 3605
LORD's hand double for *a* her sins Is 40:2 3605
a flesh shall see it together Is 40:5 3605
A flesh is grass, and *a* the Is 40:6 3605
A nations before him are as Is 40:17 3605
he calleth them *a* by names by the Is 40:26 3605
a they that were incensed against Is 41:11 3605
Behold, they are *a* vanity Is 41:29 3605
to the sea, and *a* that is therein Is 42:10 4393
and hills, and dry up *a* their herbs Is 42:15 3605
they are *a* of them snared in Is 42:22 3605
Let *a* the nations be gathered Is 43:9 3605
have brought down *a* their nobles Is 43:14 3605
graven image are *a* of them vanity Is 44:9 3605
a his fellows shall be ashamed Is 44:11 3605
let them *a* be gathered together, Is 44:11 3605
am the LORD that maketh *a* things Is 44:24 3605
and shall perform *a* my pleasure Is 44:28 3605
I the LORD do *a* these things Is 45:7
a their host have I commanded Is 45:12 3605
and I will direct *a* his ways Is 45:13 3605
and also confounded, *a* of them Is 45:16 3605
ye saved, *a* the ends of the earth Is 45:22
a that are incensed against him Is 45:24 3605
In the LORD shall *a* the seed of Is 45:25 3605
a the remnant of the house of Is 46:3 3605
stand, and I will do *a* my pleasure Is 46:10 3605
Thou hast heard, see *a* this Is 48:6 3605
A ye, assemble yourselves, and Is 48:14 3605
shall be in *a* high places Is 49:9 3605
I will make *a* my mountains a way, Is 49:11 3605
a these gather themselves Is 49:18 3605
surely clothe thee with them *a* Is 49:18 3605
a flesh shall know that I the Is 49:26 3605
Is my hand shortened at *a* Is 50:2
they *a* shall wax old as a garment Is 50:9 3605
a ye that kindle a fire, that Is 50:11 3605
he will comfort *a* her waste Is 51:3 3605
is none to guide her among *a* the Is 51:18 3605
a the sons that she hath brought Is 51:18 3605
lie at the head of *a* the streets Is 51:20 3605
arm in the eyes of *a* the nations Is 52:10 3605
a the ends of the earth shall see Is 52:10 3605
A we like sheep have gone astray Is 53:6 3605
laid on him the iniquity of us *a* Is 53:6 3605
a thy borders of pleasant stones Is 54:12 3605
a thy children shall be taught of Is 54:13 3605
a the trees of the field shall Is 55:12 3605
an house of prayer for *a* people Is 56:7 3605
A ye beasts of the field, come to Is 56:9 3605
a ye beasts in the forest Is 56:9 3605
they are *a* ignorant, they are *a* Is 56:10 3605
they *a* look to their own way, Is 56:11 3605
the wind shall carry them *a* away Is 57:13 3605
pleasure, and exact *a* your labours Is 58:3 3605
We roar *a* like bears, and mourn Is 59:11 3605
a they gather themselves together Is 60:4 3605
a they from Sheba shall come Is 60:6 3605
A the flocks of Kedar shall be Is 60:7 3605
a they that despised thee shall Is 60:14 3605
people also shall be *a* righteous Is 60:21 3605
to comfort *a* that mourn Is 61:2 3605
a that see them shall acknowledge Is 61:9 3605
spring forth before *a* the nations Is 61:11 3605
and *a* kings thy glory Is 62:2 3605
and I will stain *a* my raiment Is 63:3 3605
according to *a* that the LORD hath Is 63:7 3605
In *a* their affliction he was Is 63:9 3605
carried them *a* the days of old Is 63:9 3605
But we are *a* as an unclean thing, Is 64:6 3605
a our righteousnesses are as Is 64:6 3605
and we *a* do fade as a leaf Is 64:6 3605
we *a* are the work of thy hand Is 64:8 3605
beseech thee, we are *a* thy people Is 64:9 3605
a our pleasant things are laid Is 64:11 3605
hands *a* the day unto a rebellious Is 65:2 3605
a fire that burneth *a* the day Is 65:5 3605
that I may not destroy them *a* Is 65:8 3605
ye shall *a* bow down to the Is 65:12 3605
nor destroy in *a* my holy mountain Is 65:25 3605
For *a* those things hath mine hand Is 66:2 3605
a those things have been, saith Is 66:2 3605
glad with her, *a* ye that love her Is 66:10 3605
with her, *a* ye that mourn for her Is 66:10 3605
will the LORD plead with *a* flesh Is 66:16 3605
that I will gather *a* nations Is 66:18 3605
they shall bring *a* your brethren Is 66:20 3605
LORD out of *a* nations upon horses Is 66:20 3605
shall *a* flesh come to worship Is 66:23 3605
be an abhorring unto *a* flesh Is 66:24 3605
for thou shalt go to *a* that I Jer 1:7 3605
a the inhabitants of the land Jer 1:14 3605
I will call *a* the families of the Jer 1:15 3605
against *a* the walls thereof round Jer 1:15 3605
against *a* the cities of Judah Jer 1:15 3605
them touching *a* their wickedness Jer 1:16 3605
speak unto them *a* that I command Jer 1:17 3605
a that devour him shall offend Jer 2:3 3605
a the families of the house of Jer 2:4 3605
a they that seek her will not Jer 2:24 3605
ye *a* have transgressed against me Jer 2:29 3605
secret search, but upon *a* these Jer 2:34 3605
after she had done *a* these things Jer 3:7 3605
when for *a* the causes whereby Jer 3:8 3605
yet for *a* this her treacherous Jer 3:10 3605
a the nations shall be gathered Jer 3:17 3605
a the hills moved lightly Jer 4:24 3605
a the birds of the heavens were Jer 4:25 3605
a the cities thereof were broken Jer 4:26 3605
sepulchre, they are *a* mighty men Jer 5:16 3605
our God *a* these things unto us Jer 5:19 3605
nay, they were not at *a* ashamed Jer 6:15
They are *a* grievous revolters, Jer 6:28 3605
they are *a* corrupters Jer 6:28 3605
a ye of Judah, that enter in at Jer 7:2 3605
to do *a* these abominations Jer 7:10 3605
ye have done *a* these works Jer 7:13 3605
I have cast out *a* your brethren Jer 7:15 3605
walk ye in *a* the ways that I have Jer 7:23 3605
you *a* my servants the prophets Jer 7:25 3605
speak *a* these words unto them Jer 7:27 3605
a the host of heaven, whom they Jer 8:2 3605
be chosen rather than life by *a* Jer 8:3 3605
which remain in *a* the places Jer 8:3 3605
nay, they were not at *a* ashamed Jer 8:12
the land, and *a* that is in it Jer 8:16 4393
for they be *a* adulterers, an Jer 9:2 3605
that I will punish *a* them which Jer 9:25 3605
a that are in the utmost corners, Jer 9:26 3605
for *a* these nations are Jer 9:26 3605
a the house of Israel are Jer 9:26 3605
forasmuch as among *a* the wise men Jer 10:7 3605
in *a* their kingdoms, there is Jer 10:7 3605
they are *a* the work of cunning Jer 10:9 3605
for he is the former of *a* things Jer 10:16 3605
spoiled, and *a* my cords are broken Jer 10:20 3605
a their flocks shall be scattered Jer 10:21 3605
according to *a* which I command Jer 11:4 3605
Proclaim *a* these words in the Jer 11:6 3605
I will bring upon them *a* the Jer 11:8 3605
at *a* in the time of their trouble Jer 11:12
wherefore are *a* they happy that Jer 12:1 3605
assemble *a* the beasts of the Jer 12:9 3605
upon *a* high places through the Jer 12:12 3605
against *a* mine evil neighbours Jer 12:14 3605
I will fill *a* the inhabitants of Jer 13:13 3605
a the inhabitants of Jerusalem, Jer 13:13 3605
be carried away captive *a* of it Jer 13:19 3605
for thou hast made *a* these things Jer 14:22 3605
into *a* kingdoms of the earth Jer 15:4 3605
price, and that for *a* thy sins Jer 15:13 3605
even in *a* thy borders Jer 15:13 3605
shew this people *a* these words Jer 16:10 3605
hath the LORD pronounced *a* this Jer 16:10 3605
from *a* the lands whither he had Jer 16:15 3605
mine eyes are upon *a* their ways Jer 16:17 3605
a thy treasures to the spoil, and Jer 17:3 3605
for sin, throughout *a* thy borders Jer 17:3 3605
heart is deceitful above *a* things Jer 17:9 3605
a that forsake thee shall be Jer 17:13 3605
in *a* the gates of Jerusalem Jer 17:19 3605
a Judah, and *a* the inhabitants Jer 17:20 3605
thou knowest *a* their counsel Jer 18:23 3605
hiss because of *a* the plagues Jer 19:8 3605
because of *a* the houses upon Jer 19:13 3605
incense unto *a* the host of heaven Jer 19:13 3605
and said to *a* the people, Jer 19:14 3605
upon *a* her towns *a* the evil Jer 19:15 3605
to thyself, and to *a* thy friends Jer 20:4 3605
I will give *a* Judah into the hand Jer 20:4 3605
Moreover I will deliver *a* the Jer 20:5 3605
a the labours thereof, and *a* the Jer 20:5 3605
a the treasures of the kings of Jer 20:5 3605
a that dwell in thine house shall Jer 20:6 3605
a thy friends, to whom thou hast Jer 20:6 3605
A my familiars watched for my Jer 20:10 3605
according to *a* his wondrous works Jer 21:2 3605
it shall devour *a* things round Jer 21:14 3605
for *a* thy lovers are destroyed Jer 22:20 3605
wind shall eat up *a* thy pastors Jer 22:22 3605
confounded for *a* thy wickedness Jer 22:22 3605
the remnant of my flock out of *a* Jer 23:3 3605
from *a* countries whither I had Jer 23:8 3605
a my bones shake Jer 23:9 3605
they are *a* of them unto me as Jer 23:14 3605
gone forth into *a* the land Jer 23:15 3605
shall not profit this people at *a* Jer 23:32
a the kingdoms of the earth for Jer 24:9 3605
in *a* places whither I shall drive Jer 24:9 3605
a the people of Judah in the Jer 25:1 3605
spake unto *a* the people of Judah Jer 25:2 3605
to *a* the inhabitants of Jerusalem Jer 25:2 3605
you *a* his servants the prophets Jer 25:4 3605
take *a* the families of the north, Jer 25:9 3605
against *a* these nations round Jer 25:9 3605
that land *a* my words which I have Jer 25:13 3605
even *a* that is written in this Jer 25:13 3605
prophesied against *a* the nations Jer 25:13 3605
cause *a* the nations, to whom I Jer 25:15 3605
made *a* the nations to drink, unto Jer 25:17 3605
and his princes, and *a* his people Jer 25:19 3605
a the mingled people, and *a* the Jer 25:20 3605
a the kings of the land of the Jer 25:20 3605
a the kings of Tyrus, and *a* the Jer 25:22 3605
a that are in the utmost corners, Jer 25:23 3605
a the kings of Arabia, and *a* the Jer 25:24 3605
a the kings of Zimri, and *a* the Jer 25:25 3605
a the kings of the Medes, Jer 25:25 3605
a the kings of the north, far and Jer 25:26 3605
a the kingdoms of the world, Jer 25:26 3605
a the inhabitants of the earth Jer 25:29 3605
thou against them *a* these words Jer 25:30 3605
against *a* the inhabitants of the Jer 25:30 3605
he will plead with *a* flesh Jer 25:31 3605
speak unto *a* the cities of Judah, Jer 26:2 3605
a the words that I command thee Jer 26:2 3605
to *a* the nations of the earth Jer 26:6 3605
a the people heard Jeremiah Jer 26:7 3605
had made an end of speaking *a* Jer 26:8 3605
him to speak unto *a* the people Jer 26:8 3605
a the people took him, saying, Jer 26:8 3605
a the people were gathered Jer 26:9 3605
to *a* the people, saying, This man Jer 26:11 3605
spake Jeremiah unto *a* the princes Jer 26:12 3605
to *a* the people, saying, The LORD Jer 26:12 3605
against this city *a* the words Jer 26:12 3605
speak *a* these words in your ears Jer 26:15 3605
a the people unto the priests and Jer 26:16 3605
spake to *a* the assembly of the Jer 26:17 3605
spake to *a* the people of Judah, Jer 26:18 3605
a Judah put him at *a* to death Jer 26:19 3605
to *a* the words of Jeremiah Jer 26:20 3605
with *a* his mighty men, and *a* the Jer 26:21 3605
now have I given *a* these lands Jer 27:6 3605
a nations shall serve him, and his Jer 27:7 3605
Judah according to *a* these words Jer 27:12 3605
to *a* this people, saying, Thus Jer 27:16 3605
and *a* the nobles of Judah and Jer 27:20 3605
and of *a* the people, saying, Jer 28:1 3605
I bring again into this place *a* Jer 28:3 3605
with *a* the captives of Judah, Jer 28:4 3605
in the presence of *a* the people Jer 28:5 3605
a that is carried away captive, Jer 28:6 3605
and in the ears of *a* the people Jer 28:7 3605
in the presence of *a* the people Jer 28:11 3605
of Babylon from the neck of *a* Jer 28:11 3605
upon the neck of *a* these nations Jer 28:14 3605
prophets, and to *a* the people whom Jer 29:1 3605
unto *a* that are carried away Jer 29:4 3605
search for me with *a* your heart Jer 29:13 3605
gather you from *a* the nations Jer 29:14 3605
from *a* the places whither I have Jer 29:14 3605
of *a* the people that dwelleth in Jer 29:16 3605
to *a* the kingdoms of the earth Jer 29:18 3605
among *a* the nations whither I Jer 29:18 3605
a ye of the captivity, whom I Jer 29:20 3605
by *a* the captivity of Judah which Jer 29:22 3605
unto *a* the people that are at Jer 29:25 3605
to *a* the priests, saying, Jer 29:25 3605
Send to *a* them of the captivity, Jer 29:31 3605
Write thee *a* the words that I Jer 30:2 3605
a faces are turned into paleness Jer 30:6 3605
end of *a* nations whither I have Jer 30:11 3605
A thy lovers have forgotten thee Jer 30:14 3605
Therefore *a* they that devour thee Jer 30:16 3605
a thine adversaries, every one of Jer 30:16 3605
a that prey upon thee will I give Jer 30:16 3605
I will punish *a* that oppress them Jer 30:20 3605
will I be the God of *a* the Jer 31:1 3605
shall not sorrow any more at *a* Jer 31:12
in *a* the cities thereof together, Jer 31:24 3605
for they shall *a* know me, from Jer 31:34 3605
I will also cast off *a* the seed Jer 31:37 3605
Israel for *a* that they have done Jer 31:37 3605
a the fields unto the brook of Jer 31:40 3605
before *a* the Jews that sat in the Jer 32:12 3605
a the ways of the sons of men Jer 32:19 3605
they have done nothing of *a* that Jer 32:23 3605
therefore thou hast caused *a* this Jer 32:23 3605
I am the LORD, the God of *a* flesh Jer 32:27 3605
Because of *a* the evil of the Jer 32:32 3605
gather them out of *a* countries Jer 32:37 3605
Like as I have brought *a* this Jer 32:42 3605
so will I bring upon them *a* the Jer 32:42 3605
for *a* whose wickedness I have hid Jer 33:5 3605
them from *a* their iniquity Jer 33:8 3605

I will pardon *a* their iniquities,	Jer 33:8	3605
an honour before *a* the nations of	Jer 33:9	3605
which shall hear *a* the good that	Jer 33:9	3605
tremble for *a* the goodness and for	Jer 33:9	3605
for *a* the prosperity that I	Jer 33:9	3605
in *a* the cities thereof, shall be	Jer 33:12	3605
a his army, and *a* the kingdoms	Jer 34:1	3605
a the people, fought against	Jer 34:1	3605
against *a* the cities thereof,	Jer 34:1	3605
a these words unto Zedekiah king	Jer 34:6	3605
against *a* the cities of Judah	Jer 34:7	3605
with *a* the people which were at	Jer 34:8	3605
Now when *a* the princes, and *a*	Jer 34:10	3605
a the people, which had entered	Jer 34:10	3605
into *a* the kingdoms of the earth	Jer 34:17	3605
a the people of the land, which	Jer 34:19	3605
a his sons, and the whole house of	Jer 35:3	3605
but *a* your days ye shall dwell in	Jer 35:7	3605
in *a* that he hath charged us	Jer 35:8	3605
to drink no wine *a* our days	Jer 35:8	3605
done according to *a* that Jonadab	Jer 35:10	3605
you *a* my servants the prophets	Jer 35:15	3605
a the inhabitants of Jerusalem *a*	Jer 35:17	3605
kept *a* his precepts	Jer 35:18	3605
done according unto *a* that he	Jer 35:18	3605
write therein *a* the words that I	Jer 36:2	3605
against *a* the nations, from the	Jer 36:2	3605
the house of Judah will hear *a*	Jer 36:3	3605
Jeremiah *a* the words of the LORD	Jer 36:4	3605
of *a* Judah that come out of their	Jer 36:6	3605
to *a* that Jeremiah the prophet	Jer 36:8	3605
LORD to *a* the people in Jerusalem	Jer 36:9	3605
to *a* the people that came from	Jer 36:9	3605
in the ears of *a* the people	Jer 36:10	3605
the book *a* the words of the LORD	Jer 36:11	3605
a the princes sat there, even	Jer 36:12	3605
son of Hananiah, and *a* the princes	Jer 36:12	3605
a the words that he had heard	Jer 36:13	3605
Therefore *a* the princes sent	Jer 36:14	3605
when they had heard *a* the words	Jer 36:16	3605
tell the king of *a* these words	Jer 36:16	3605
How didst thou write *a* these	Jer 36:17	3605
He pronounced *a* these words unto	Jer 36:18	3605
told *a* the words in the ears of	Jer 36:20	3605
in the ears of *a* the princes	Jer 36:21	3605
until *a* the roll was consumed in	Jer 36:23	3605
servants that heard *a* these words	Jer 36:24	3605
write in it *a* the former words	Jer 36:28	3605
a the evil that I have pronounced	Jer 36:31	3605
from the mouth of Jeremiah *a* the	Jer 36:32	3605
until *a* the bread in the city	Jer 37:21	3605
had spoken unto *a* the people	Jer 38:1	3605
and the hands of *a* the people	Jer 38:4	3605
these men have done evil in *a*	Jer 38:9	3605
a the women that are left in the	Jer 38:22	3605
they shall bring out *a* thy wives	Jer 38:23	3605
Then came *a* the princes unto	Jer 38:27	3605
he told them according to *a* these	Jer 38:27	3605
a his army against Jerusalem, and	Jer 39:1	3605
a the princes of the king of	Jer 39:3	3605
with *a* the residue of the princes	Jer 39:3	3605
a the men of war, then they fled,	Jer 39:4	3605
slew *a* the nobles of Judah	Jer 39:6	3605
a the king of Babylon's princes	Jer 39:13	3605
a that were carried away captive	Jer 40:1	3605
a the land is before thee	Jer 40:4	3605
Now when *a* the captains of the	Jer 40:7	3605
Likewise when *a* the Jews that	Jer 40:11	3605
that were in *a* the countries,	Jer 40:11	3605
a the Jews returned out of *a*	Jer 40:12	3605
a the captains of the forces that	Jer 40:13	3605
that *a* the Jews which are	Jer 40:15	3605
Ishmael also slew *a* the Jews that	Jer 41:3	3605
weeping *a* along as he went	Jer 41:6	
cast *a* the dead bodies of the men	Jer 41:9	3605
Ishmael carried away captive *a*	Jer 41:10	3605
a the people that remained in	Jer 41:10	3605
a the captains of the forces that	Jer 41:11	3605
heard of *a* the evil that Ishmael	Jer 41:11	3605
Then they took *a* the men, and went	Jer 41:12	3605
that when *a* the people which were	Jer 41:13	3605
a the captains of the forces that	Jer 41:13	3605
So *a* the people that Ishmael had	Jer 41:14	3605
a the captains of the forces that	Jer 41:16	3605
a the remnant of the people whom	Jer 41:16	3605
Then *a* the captains of the forces	Jer 42:1	3605
a the people from the least even	Jer 42:1	3605
thy God, even for *a* this remnant	Jer 42:2	3605
a things for the which the LORD	Jer 42:5	3605
a the captains of the forces	Jer 42:8	3605
a the people from the least even	Jer 42:8	3605
So shall it be with *a* the men	Jer 42:17	3605
according unto *a* that the LORD	Jer 42:20	3605
made an end of speaking unto *a*	Jer 43:1	3605
a the words of the LORD their God	Jer 43:1	3605
him to them, even *a* these words,	Jer 43:1	3605
a the proud men, saying unto	Jer 43:2	3605
a the captains of the forces, and	Jer 43:4	3605
a the people, obeyed not the	Jer 43:4	3605
a the captains of the forces,	Jer 43:5	3605
took *a* the remnant of Judah	Jer 43:5	3605
that were returned from *a* nations	Jer 43:5	3605
a the Jews which dwell in the	Jer 44:1	3605
Ye have seen *a* the evil that I	Jer 44:2	3605
upon *a* the cities of Judah	Jer 44:2	3605
Howbeit I sent unto you *a* my	Jer 44:4	3605
a reproach among *a* the nations of	Jer 44:8	3605
for evil, and to cut off *a* Judah	Jer 44:11	3605
they shall *a* be consumed, and fall	Jer 44:12	3605
Then *a* the men which knew that	Jer 44:15	3605
a the women that stood by, *a*	Jer 44:15	3605
even *a* the people that dwelt in	Jer 44:15	3605
unto her, we have wanted *a* things	Jer 44:18	3605
Jeremiah said unto *a* the people	Jer 44:20	3605
to *a* the people which had given	Jer 44:20	3605
Jeremiah said unto *a* the people	Jer 44:24	3605
to *a* the women, Hear the word of	Jer 44:24	3605
a Judah that are in the land of	Jer 44:24	3605
a Judah that dwell in the land of	Jer 44:26	3605
of Judah in *a* the land of Egypt	Jer 44:26	3605
a the men of Judah that are in	Jer 44:27	3605
a the remnant of Judah, that are	Jer 44:28	3605
I will bring evil upon *a* flesh	Jer 45:5	3605
in *a* places whither thou goest	Jer 45:5	3605
and *a* them that trust in him	Jer 46:25	
of *a* the nations whither I have	Jer 46:28	3605
the land, and *a* that is therein	Jer 47:2	4393
a the inhabitants of the land	Jer 47:2	3605
cometh to spoil *a* the Philistines	Jer 47:4	3605
A ye that are about him, bemoan	Jer 48:17	3605
a ye that know his name, say, How	Jer 48:17	3605
upon *a* the cities of the land of	Jer 48:24	3605
and I will cry out for *a* Moab	Jer 48:31	3605
upon *a* the hands shall be	Jer 48:37	3605
upon *a* the housetops of Moab	Jer 48:38	3605
a dismaying to *a* them about him	Jer 48:39	3605
from *a* those that be about thee	Jer 49:5	3605
a the cities thereof shall be	Jer 49:13	3605
shall hiss at *a* the plagues	Jer 49:17	3605
a the men of war shall be cut off	Jer 49:26	3605
a their vessels, and their camels	Jer 49:29	3605
I will scatter into *a* winds them	Jer 49:32	3605
calamity from *a* sides thereof	Jer 49:32	3605
scatter them toward *a* those winds	Jer 49:36	3605
A that found them have devoured	Jer 50:7	3605
a that spoil her shall be	Jer 50:10	3605
and hiss at *a* her plagues	Jer 50:13	3605
a ye that bend the bow, shoot at	Jer 50:14	3605
do according to *a* that I have	Jer 50:21	3605
Slay *a* her bullocks	Jer 50:27	3605
a ye that bend the bow, camp	Jer 50:29	3605
according to *a* that she hath done	Jer 50:29	3605
a her men of war shall be cut off	Jer 50:30	3605
it shall devour *a* round about him	Jer 50:32	3605
a that took them captives held	Jer 50:33	3605
upon *a* the mingled people that	Jer 50:37	3605
destroy ye utterly *a* her host	Jer 51:3	3605
that made *a* the earth drunken	Jer 51:7	3605
for he is the former of *a* things	Jer 51:19	3605
to *a* the inhabitants of Chaldea	Jer 51:24	3605
a their evil that they have done	Jer 51:24	3605
which destroyest *a* the earth	Jer 51:25	3605
a the rulers thereof, and *a* the	Jer 51:28	3605
a her slain shall fall in the	Jer 51:47	3605
a that is therein, shall sing for	Jer 51:48	3605
fall the slain of *a* the earth	Jer 51:49	3605
through *a* her land the wounded	Jer 51:52	3605
So Jeremiah wrote in a book *a* the	Jer 51:60	3605
even *a* these words that are	Jer 51:60	3605
see, and shalt read *a* these words	Jer 51:61	3605
according to *a* that Jehoiakim had	Jer 52:2	3605
a his army, against Jerusalem, and	Jer 52:4	3605
a the men of war fled, and went	Jer 52:7	3605
a his army was scattered from him	Jer 52:8	3605
he slew also *a* the princes of	Jer 52:10	3605
a the houses of Jerusalem, and *a*	Jer 52:13	3605
a the army of the Chaldeans, that	Jer 52:14	3605
brake down *a* the walls of	Jer 52:14	3605
carried *a* the brass of them to	Jer 52:17	3605
a the vessels of brass wherewith	Jer 52:18	3605
the brass of *a* these vessels was	Jer 52:20	3605
chapiters round about, *a* of brass	Jer 52:22	3605
a the pomegranates upon the	Jer 52:23	3605
a the persons were four thousand	Jer 52:30	3605
before him *a* the days of his life	Jer 52:33	3605
his death, *a* the days of his life	Jer 52:34	3605
among *a* her lovers she hath none	Lam 1:2	3605
a her friends have dealt	Lam 1:2	3605
a her persecutors overtook her	Lam 1:3	3605
a her gates are desolate	Lam 1:4	3605
of Zion *a* her beauty is departed	Lam 1:6	3605
of her miseries *a* her pleasant	Lam 1:7	3605
a that honoured her despise her,	Lam 1:8	3605
hand upon *a* her pleasant things	Lam 1:10	3605
A her people sigh, they seek	Lam 1:11	3605
nothing to you, *a* ye that pass by	Lam 1:12	3605
me desolate and faint *a* the day	Lam 1:13	3605
Lord hath trodden under foot *a* my	Lam 1:15	3605
a people, and behold my sorrow	Lam 1:18	3605
a mine enemies have heard of my	Lam 1:21	3605
Let *a* their wickedness come	Lam 1:22	3605
unto me for *a* my transgressions	Lam 1:22	3605
up *a* the habitations of Jacob	Lam 2:2	3605
fierce anger *a* the horn of Israel	Lam 2:3	3605
slew *a* that were pleasant to the	Lam 2:4	3605
hath swallowed up *a* her palaces	Lam 2:5	3605
A that pass by clap their hands	Lam 2:15	3605
A thine enemies have opened their	Lam 2:16	3605
his hand against me *a* the day	Lam 3:3	3605
I was a derision to *a* my people	Lam 3:14	3605
and their song *a* the day	Lam 3:14	3605
To crush under his feet *a* the	Lam 3:34	3605
A our enemies have opened their	Lam 3:46	3605
of *a* the daughters of my city	Lam 3:51	3605
Thou hast seen *a* their vengeance	Lam 3:60	3605
a their imaginations against me	Lam 3:60	3605
a their imaginations against me	Lam 3:61	3605
their device against me *a* the day	Lam 3:62	3605
a the inhabitants of the world,	Lam 4:12	3605
for *a* the house of Israel are	Eze 3:7	3605
a my words that I shall speak	Eze 3:10	3605
forth into *a* the house of Israel	Eze 5:4	3605
because of *a* thine abominations	Eze 5:9	3605
will I scatter into *a* the winds	Eze 5:10	3605
with *a* thy detestable things	Eze 5:11	3605
with *a* thine abominations,	Eze 5:11	3605
a third part into *a* the winds	Eze 5:12	3605
in the sight of *a* that pass by	Eze 5:14	3605
In *a* your dwellingplaces the	Eze 6:6	3605
committed in *a* their abominations	Eze 6:9	3605
Alas for *a* the evil abominations	Eze 6:11	3605
in *a* the tops of the mountains,	Eze 6:13	3605
sweet savour to *a* their idols	Eze 6:13	3605
Diblath, in *a* their habitations	Eze 6:14	3605
upon thee *a* thine abominations	Eze 7:3	3605
thee for *a* thine abominations	Eze 7:8	3605
for wrath is upon *a* the multitude	Eze 7:12	3605
the trumpet, even to make *a* ready	Eze 7:14	3605
for my wrath is upon *a* the	Eze 7:14	3605
a of them mourning, every one for	Eze 7:16	3605
A hands shall be feeble, and *a*	Eze 7:17	3605
and shame shall be upon *a* faces	Eze 7:18	3605
and baldness upon *a* their heads	Eze 7:18	3605
a the idols of the house of	Eze 8:10	3605
that cry for *a* the abominations	Eze 9:4	3605
wilt thou destroy *a* the residue	Eze 9:8	3605
a the house of Israel wholly, are	Eze 11:15	3605
they shall take away *a* the	Eze 11:18	3605
a the abominations thereof from	Eze 11:18	3605
unto them of the captivity *a* the	Eze 11:25	3605
a the house of Israel that are	Eze 12:10	3605
a that are about him to help him	Eze 12:14	3605
him to help him, and *a* his bands	Eze 12:14	3605
that they may declare *a* their	Eze 12:16	3605
desolate from *a* that is therein	Eze 12:19	4393
of *a* them that dwell therein	Eze 12:19	3605
that sew pillows to *a* armholes	Eze 13:18	3605
I be enquired of at *a* by them	Eze 14:3	
because they are *a* estranged from	Eze 14:5	3605
faces from *a* your abominations	Eze 14:6	3605
more with *a* their transgressions	Eze 14:11	3605
even concerning *a* that I have	Eze 14:22	3605
cause *a* that I have done in it	Eze 14:23	3605
salted at *a*, nor swaddled at *a*	Eze 16:4	
in *a* thine abominations and thy	Eze 16:22	3605
to pass after *a* thy wickedness	Eze 16:23	3605
seeing thou doest *a* these things	Eze 16:30	3605
They give gifts to *a* whores	Eze 16:33	3605
givest thy gifts to *a* thy lovers	Eze 16:33	3605
and with *a* the idols of thy	Eze 16:36	3605
I will gather *a* thy lovers	Eze 16:37	3605
a them that thou hast loved	Eze 16:37	3605
with *a* them that thou hast hated	Eze 16:37	3605
that they may see *a* thy nakedness	Eze 16:37	3605
hast fretted me in *a* these things	Eze 16:43	3605
above *a* thine abominations	Eze 16:43	3605
more than they in *a* thy ways	Eze 16:47	3605
a thine abominations which thou	Eze 16:51	3605
in *a* that thou hast done, in that	Eze 16:54	3605
a that are round about her, the	Eze 16:57	3605
thee for *a* that thou hast done	Eze 16:63	3605
it shall wither in *a* the leaves	Eze 17:9	3605
hath done *a* these things, he	Eze 17:18	3605
a his fugitives with *a* his	Eze 17:21	3605
shall be scattered toward *a* winds	Eze 17:21	3605
shall dwell *a* fowl of every wing	Eze 17:23	3605
a the trees of the field shall	Eze 17:24	3605
Behold, *a* souls are mine	Eze 18:4	3605
he hath done *a* these abominations	Eze 18:13	3605
that seeth *a* his father's sins	Eze 18:14	3605
hath kept *a* my statutes, and hath	Eze 18:19	3605
if the wicked will turn from *a*	Eze 18:21	3605
keep *a* my statutes, and do that	Eze 18:21	3605
A his transgressions that he hath	Eze 18:22	3605
Have I any pleasure at *a* that the	Eze 18:23	
and doeth according to *a* the	Eze 18:24	3605
A his righteousness that he hath	Eze 18:24	3605
and turneth away from *a* his	Eze 18:28	3605
from *a* your transgressions	Eze 18:30	3605
Cast away from you *a* your	Eze 18:31	3605
which is the glory of *a* lands	Eze 20:6	3605
which is the glory of *a* lands	Eze 20:15	3605
the fire *a* that openeth the womb	Eze 20:26	3605
a the thick trees, and they	Eze 20:28	3605
yourselves with *a* your idols	Eze 20:31	3605
into your mind shall not be at *a*	Eze 20:32	
there shall *a* the house of Israel	Eze 20:40	3605
a of them in the land, serve me	Eze 20:40	3605
with *a* your holy things	Eze 20:40	3605
a your doings, wherein ye have	Eze 20:43	3605
in your own sight for *a* your	Eze 20:43	3605
a faces from the south to the	Eze 20:47	3605
a flesh shall see that I the LORD	Eze 20:48	3605
a flesh from the south to the	Eze 21:4	3605
That *a* flesh may know that I the	Eze 21:5	3605
a hands shall be feeble, and every	Eze 21:7	3605
a knees shall be weak as water	Eze 21:7	3605
it shall be upon *a* the princes of	Eze 21:12	3605
the sword against *a* their gates	Eze 21:15	3605
so that in *a* your doings your	Eze 21:24	3605
shalt shew her *a* her abominations	Eze 22:2	3605
and a mocking to *a* countries	Eze 22:4	3605
a they are brass, and tin, and iron	Eze 22:18	3605
Because ye are *a* become dross	Eze 22:19	3605
a of them desirable young men,	Eze 23:6	3605
with *a* them that were the chosen	Eze 23:7	
and with *a* on whom she doted	Eze 23:7	3605
with *a* their idols she defiled	Eze 23:7	3605
a of them desirable young men	Eze 23:12	3605
a of them princes to look to,	Eze 23:15	3605
a the Chaldeans, Pekod, and Shoa,	Eze 23:23	3605
a the Assyrians with them	Eze 23:23	3605
a of them desirable young men,	Eze 23:23	3605
a of them riding upon horses	Eze 23:23	3605
and shall take away *a* thy labour	Eze 23:29	3605
that *a* women may be taught not to	Eze 23:48	3605
according to *a* that he hath done	Eze 24:24	3605
rejoiced in heart with *a* thy	Eze 25:6	3605
Judah is like unto *a* the heathen	Eze 25:8	3605
shall he tread down *a* thy streets	Eze 26:11	3605
Then *a* the princes of the sea	Eze 26:16	3605
terror to be on *a* that haunt it	Eze 26:17	3605

They have made *a* thy ship boards	Eze 27:5	3605
a the ships of the sea with their	Eze 27:9	3605
the multitude of *a* kind of riches	Eze 27:12	3605
for the multitude of *a* riches	Eze 27:18	3605
a the princes of Kedar, they	Eze 27:21	3605
thy fairs with chief of *a* spices	Eze 27:22	3605
with *a* precious stones, and gold	Eze 27:22	3605
merchants in *a* sorts of things	Eze 27:24	3605
a thy men of war, that are in	Eze 27:27	3605
in *a* thy company which is in the	Eze 27:27	3605
a that handle the oar, the	Eze 27:29	3605
a the pilots of the sea, shall	Eze 27:29	3605
a thy company in the midst of	Eze 27:34	3605
A the inhabitants of the isles	Eze 27:35	3605
sight of *a* them that behold thee	Eze 28:18	3605
A they that know thee among the	Eze 28:19	3605
of *a* that are round about them	Eze 28:24	3605
a those that despise them round	Eze 28:26	3605
against him, and against *a* Egypt	Eze 29:2	3605
a the fish of thy rivers shall	Eze 29:4	3605
thee and *a* the fish of thy rivers	Eze 29:5	3605
a the inhabitants of Egypt shall	Eze 29:6	3605
break, and rend *a* their shoulder	Eze 29:7	3605
madest *a* their loins to be at *a*	Eze 29:7	3605
a the mingled people, and Chub, and	Eze 30:5	3605
when *a* her helpers shall be	Eze 30:8	3605
a that is therein, by the hand of	Eze 30:12	4393
unto *a* the trees of the field	Eze 31:4	3605
above *a* the trees of the field	Eze 31:5	3605
A the fowls of heaven made their	Eze 31:6	3605
under his branches did *a* the	Eze 31:6	3605
his shadow dwelt *a* great nations	Eze 31:6	3605
so that *a* the trees of Eden, that	Eze 31:9	3605
in *a* the valleys his branches are	Eze 31:12	3605
by *a* the rivers of the land	Eze 31:12	3605
a the people of the earth are	Eze 31:12	3605
Upon his ruin shall *a* the fowls	Eze 31:13	3605
a the beasts of the field shall	Eze 31:13	3605
To the end that none of *a* the	Eze 31:14	3605
their height, *a* that drink water	Eze 31:14	3605
for they are *a* delivered unto	Eze 31:14	3605
a the trees of the field fainted	Eze 31:15	3605
a the trees of Eden, the choice	Eze 31:16	3605
a that drink water, shall be	Eze 31:16	3605
a his multitude, saith the Lord	Eze 31:18	3605
will cause *a* the fowls of the	Eze 32:4	3605
A the bright lights of heaven	Eze 32:8	3605
of the nations, *a* of them	Eze 32:12	3605
a the multitude thereof shall be	Eze 32:12	3605
I will destroy also *a* the beasts	Eze 32:13	3605
when I shall smite *a* them that	Eze 32:15	3605
for *a* her multitude, saith the	Eze 32:16	3605
draw her and *a* her multitudes	Eze 32:20	3605
Asshur is there and *a* her company	Eze 32:22	3605
a of them slain, fallen by the	Eze 32:22	3605
a of them slain, fallen by the	Eze 32:23	3605
a her multitude round about her	Eze 32:24	3605
a of them slain, fallen by the	Eze 32:24	3605
of the slain with *a* her multitude	Eze 32:25	3605
a of them uncircumcised, slain by	Eze 32:25	3605
Tubal, and *a* her multitude	Eze 32:26	3605
a of them uncircumcised, slain by	Eze 32:26	3605
a her princes, which with their	Eze 32:29	3605
a of them, and *a* the Zidonians,	Eze 32:30	3605
be comforted over *a* his multitude	Eze 32:31	3605
a his army slain by the sword,	Eze 32:31	3605
a his multitude, saith the Lord	Eze 32:32	3605
a his righteousnesses shall not	Eze 33:13	3605
a their abominations which they	Eze 33:29	3605
they became meat to *a* the beasts	Eze 34:5	3605
wandered through *a* the mountains	Eze 34:6	3605
upon *a* the face of the earth	Eze 34:6	3605
will deliver them out of *a* places	Eze 34:12	3605
in *a* the inhabited places of the	Eze 34:13	3605
pushed *a* the diseased with your	Eze 34:21	3605
in *a* thy rivers, shall they fall	Eze 35:8	3605
LORD, and that I have heard *a* thy	Eze 35:12	3605
Seir, and *a* Idumea, even *a* of it	Eze 35:15	3605
the heathen, and against *a* Idumea	Eze 36:5	3605
with the joy of *a* their heart	Eze 36:5	3605
a the house of Israel, even *a*	Eze 36:10	3605
and gather you out of *a* countries	Eze 36:24	3605
from *a* your filthiness, and from	Eze 36:25	3605
from *a* your idols, will I cleanse	Eze 36:25	3605
you from *a* your uncleannesses	Eze 36:29	3605
a your iniquities I will also	Eze 36:33	3605
in the sight of *a* that passed by	Eze 36:34	3605
for *a* the house of Israel his	Eze 37:16	3605
one king shall be king to them *a*	Eze 37:22	3605
into two kingdoms any more at *a*	Eze 37:22	
out of *a* their dwellingplaces	Eze 37:23	3605
they *a* shall have one shepherd	Eze 37:24	3605
a thine army, horses and horsemen,	Eze 38:4	3605
a of them clothed with *a* sorts	Eze 38:4	3605
a of them handling swords	Eze 38:4	3605
a of them with shield and helmet	Eze 38:5	3605
Gomer, and *a* his bands	Eze 38:6	3605
north quarters, and *a* his bands	Eze 38:6	3605
a thy company that are assembled	Eze 38:7	3605
they shall dwell safely *a* of them	Eze 38:8	3605
a thy bands, and many people with	Eze 38:9	3605
a of them dwelling without walls,	Eze 38:11	3605
with *a* the young lions thereof,	Eze 38:13	3605
a of them riding upon horses, *a*	Eze 38:15	3605
a creeping things that creep upon	Eze 38:20	3605
a the men that are upon the face	Eze 38:20	3605
him throughout *a* my mountains	Eze 38:21	3605
a thy bands, and the people that	Eze 39:4	3605
they bury Gog and *a* his multitude	Eze 39:11	3605
a the people of the land shall	Eze 39:13	3605
a of them fatlings of Bashan	Eze 39:18	3605
with *a* men of war, saith the Lord	Eze 39:20	3605
a the heathen shall see my	Eze 39:21	3605
so fell they *a* by the sword	Eze 39:23	3605
a their trespasses whereby they	Eze 39:26	3605
set thine heart upon *a* that I	Eze 40:4	3605
declare *a* that thou seest to the	Eze 40:4	3605
by *a* the wall round about within	Eze 41:17	3605
it was made through *a* the house	Eze 41:19	3605
a their goings out were both	Eze 42:11	3605
ashamed of *a* that they have done	Eze 43:11	3605
a the forms thereof, and *a* the	Eze 43:11	3605
a the forms thereof, and *a* the	Eze 43:11	3605
a the ordinances thereof, and do	Eze 43:11	3605
hear with thine ears *a* that I say	Eze 44:5	3605
a the ordinances of the house of	Eze 44:5	3605
the LORD, and *a* the laws thereof	Eze 44:5	3605
you of *a* your abominations	Eze 44:6	3605
because of *a* your abominations	Eze 44:7	3605
for *a* the service thereof	Eze 44:14	3605
for *a* that shall be done therein	Eze 44:14	3605
my statutes in *a* mine assemblies	Eze 44:24	3605
a the firstfruits of *a* things	Eze 44:30	3605
and every oblation of *a*	Eze 44:30	3605
This shall be holy in *a* the	Eze 45:1	3605
A the people of the land shall	Eze 45:16	3605
in *a* solemnities of the house of	Eze 45:17	3605
for *a* the people of the land *a*	Eze 45:22	3605
shall grow *a* trees for meat,	Eze 47:12	3605
a the length shall be five and	Eze 48:13	3605
it out of *a* the tribes of Israel	Eze 48:19	3605
A the oblation shall be five and	Eze 48:20	3605
favoured, and skilful in *a* wisdom	Dan 1:4	3605
fatter in flesh than *a* the	Dan 1:15	3605
knowledge and skill in *a* learning	Dan 1:17	3605
had understanding in *a* visions	Dan 1:17	3605
among them *a* was found none like	Dan 1:19	3605
in *a* matters of wisdom and	Dan 1:20	3605
times better than *a* the magicians	Dan 1:20	3605
that were in *a* his realm	Dan 1:20	3605
commanded to destroy *a* the wise	Dan 2:12	3606
hath made thee ruler over them *a*	Dan 2:38	3606
shall bear rule over *a* the earth	Dan 2:39	3606
in pieces and subdueth *a* things	Dan 2:40	3606
and as iron that breaketh *a* these	Dan 2:40	3606
consume *a* these kingdoms, and it	Dan 2:44	3606
over *a* the wise men of Babylon	Dan 2:48	3606
a the rulers of the provinces, to	Dan 3:2	3606
a the rulers of the provinces,	Dan 3:3	3606
a kinds of musick, ye fall down	Dan 3:5	3606
when *a* the people heard the sound	Dan 3:7	3606
a kinds of musick, *a* the people	Dan 3:7	3606
a kinds of musick, shall fall	Dan 3:10	3606
a kinds of musick, ye fall down	Dan 3:15	3606
unto *a* people, nations, and	Dan 4:1	3606
that dwell in *a* the earth	Dan 4:1	3606
made I a decree to bring in *a* the	Dan 4:6	3606
thereof to the end of *a* the earth	Dan 4:11	3606
much, and in it was meat for *a*	Dan 4:12	3606
thereof, and *a* flesh was fed of it	Dan 4:12	3606
forasmuch as *a* the wise men of my	Dan 4:18	3606
the sight thereof to *a* the earth	Dan 4:20	3606
much, and in it was meat for *a*	Dan 4:21	3606
A this came upon the king	Dan 4:28	3606
a the inhabitants of the earth	Dan 4:35	3606
a whose works are truth, and his	Dan 4:37	3606
Then came in *a* the king's wise	Dan 5:8	3606
a people, nations, and languages,	Dan 5:19	3606
heart, though thou knewest *a* this	Dan 5:22	3606
is, and whose are *a* thy ways	Dan 5:23	3606
A the presidents of the kingdom,	Dan 6:7	3606
brake *a* their bones in pieces or	Dan 6:24	3606
king Darius wrote unto *a* people	Dan 6:25	3606
that dwell in *a* the earth	Dan 6:25	3606
it was diverse from *a* the beasts	Dan 7:7	3606
that *a* people, nations, and	Dan 7:14	3606
and asked him the truth of *a* this	Dan 7:16	3606
was diverse from *a* the others	Dan 7:19	3606
shall be diverse from *a* kingdoms	Dan 7:23	3606
a dominions shall serve and obey	Dan 7:27	3606
to *a* the people of the land	Dan 9:6	3605
unto *a* Israel, that are near, and	Dan 9:7	3605
through *a* the countries whither	Dan 9:7	3605
a Israel have transgressed thy	Dan 9:11	3605
a this evil is come upon us	Dan 9:13	3605
in *a* his works which he doeth	Dan 9:14	3605
according to *a* thy righteousness,	Dan 9:16	3605
a reproach to *a* that are about us	Dan 9:16	3605
neither did I anoint myself at *a*	Dan 10:3	
shall be far richer than they *a*	Dan 11:2	3605
up *a* against the realm of Grecia	Dan 11:2	3605
he shall magnify himself above *a*	Dan 11:37	3605
over *a* the precious things of	Dan 11:43	3605
a these things shall be finished	Dan 12:7	3605
I will also cause *a* her mirth to	Hos 2:11	3605
sabbaths, and *a* her solemn feasts	Hos 2:11	3605
I have been a rebuker of them *a*	Hos 5:2	3605
I remember *a* their wickedness	Hos 7:2	3605
They are *a* adulterers, as an oven	Hos 7:4	3605
their baker sleepeth *a* the night	Hos 7:6	3605
They are *a* hot as an oven, and	Hos 7:7	3605
a their kings are fallen	Hos 7:7	3605
God, nor seek him for *a* this	Hos 7:10	3605
a that eat thereof shall be	Hos 9:4	3605
a snare of a fowler in *a* his ways	Hos 9:8	3605
A their wickedness is in Gilgal	Hos 9:15	3605
a their princes are revolters	Hos 9:15	3605
a thy fortresses shall be spoiled	Hos 10:14	3605
none at *a* would exalt him	Hos 11:7	3162
in *a* my labours they shall find	Hos 12:8	3605
a of it the work of the craftsmen	Hos 13:2	3605
may save thee in *a* thy cities	Hos 13:10	3605
treasure of *a* pleasant vessels	Hos 13:15	3605
unto him, Take away *a* iniquity	Hos 14:2	3605
a ye inhabitants of the land	Joel 1:2	3605
a ye drinkers of wine, because of	Joel 1:5	3605
even *a* the trees of the field,	Joel 1:12	3605
lie *a* night in sackcloth, ye	Joel 1:13	3885
a the inhabitants of the land	Joel 1:14	3605
the flame hath burned *a* the trees	Joel 1:19	3605
let *a* the inhabitants of the land	Joel 2:1	3605
a faces shall gather blackness	Joel 2:6	3605
ye even to me with *a* your heart	Joel 2:12	3605
pour out my spirit upon *a* flesh	Joel 2:28	3605
I will also gather *a* nations	Joel 3:2	3605
a the coasts of Palestine	Joel 3:4	3605
let *a* the men of war draw near	Joel 3:9	3605
and come, *a* ye heathen, and gather	Joel 3:11	3605
judge *a* the heathen round about	Joel 3:12	3605
a the rivers of Judah shall flow	Joel 3:18	3605
the sword, and did cast off *a* pity	Amos 1:11	
will slay *a* the princes thereof	Amos 2:3	3605
You only have I known of *a* the	Amos 3:2	3605
punish you for *a* your iniquities	Amos 3:2	3605
earth, and have taken nothing at *a*	Amos 3:5	
of teeth in *a* your cities	Amos 4:6	3605
and want of bread in *a* your places	Amos 4:6	3605
Wailing shall be in *a* streets	Amos 5:16	3605
they shall say in *a* the highways	Amos 5:16	3605
in *a* vineyards shall be wailing	Amos 5:17	3605
the city with *a* that is therein	Amos 6:8	4393
is not able to bear *a* his words	Amos 7:10	3605
a your songs into lamentation	Amos 8:10	3605
bring up sackcloth upon *a* loins	Amos 8:10	3605
cut them in the head, *a* of them	Amos 9:1	3605
a that dwell therein shall mourn	Amos 9:5	3605
house of Israel among *a* nations	Amos 9:9	3605
A the sinners of my people shall	Amos 9:10	3605
of *a* the heathen, which are	Amos 9:12	3605
wine, and *a* the hills shall melt	Amos 9:13	3605
A the men of thy confederacy have	Obad 7	3605
LORD is near upon *a* the heathen	Obad 15	3605
so shall *a* the heathen drink	Obad 16	3605
a thy billows and thy waves passed	Jonah 2:3	3605
Hear, *a* ye people	Mic 1:2	3605
O earth, and *a* that therein is	Mic 1:2	4393
transgression of Jacob is *a* this	Mic 1:5	3605
a the graven images thereof shall	Mic 1:7	3605
a the hires thereof shall be	Mic 1:7	3605
a the idols thereof will I lay	Mic 1:7	3605
it not at Gath, weep ye not at *a*	Mic 1:10	
assemble, O Jacob, *a* of thee	Mic 2:12	3605
they shall *a* cover their lips	Mic 3:7	3605
judgment, and pervert *a* equity	Mic 3:9	3605
For *a* people will walk every one	Mic 4:5	3605
a thine enemies shall be cut off	Mic 5:9	
throw down *a* thy strong holds	Mic 5:11	3605
a the works of the house of Ahab,	Mic 6:16	3605
they *a* lie in wait for blood	Mic 7:2	3605
and be confounded at *a* their might	Mic 7:16	3605
thou wilt cast *a* their sins into	Mic 7:19	3605
will not at *a* acquit the wicked	Nah 1:3	
it dry, and drieth up *a* the rivers	Nah 1:4	3605
world, and *a* that dwell therein	Nah 1:5	3605
glory out of *a* the pleasant	Nah 2:9	3605
and much pain is in *a* loins	Nah 2:10	3605
faces of them *a* gather blackness	Nah 2:10	3605
it is *a* full of lies and robbery	Nah 3:1	3605
that *a* they that look upon thee	Nah 3:7	3605
at the top of *a* the streets	Nah 3:10	3605
a her great men were bound in	Nah 3:10	3605
A thy strong holds shall be like	Nah 3:12	3605
a that hear the bruit of thee	Nah 3:19	3605
They shall come *a* for violence	Hab 1:9	3605
They take up *a* of them with the	Hab 1:15	3605
but gathereth unto him *a* nations	Hab 2:5	3605
and heapeth unto him *a* people	Hab 2:5	3605
Shall not *a* these take up a	Hab 2:6	3605
a the remnant of the people shall	Hab 2:8	3605
city, and of *a* that dwell therein	Hab 2:8	3605
city, and of *a* that dwell therein	Hab 2:17	3605
no breath at *a* in the midst of it	Hab 2:19	3605
let *a* the earth keep silence	Hab 2:20	3605
I will utterly consume *a* things	Zeph 1:2	3605
upon *a* the inhabitants of	Zeph 1:4	3605
a such as are clothed with	Zeph 1:8	3605
I punish *a* those that leap on the	Zeph 1:9	3605
for *a* the merchant people are cut	Zeph 1:11	3605
a they that bear silver are cut	Zeph 1:11	3605
of *a* them that dwell in the land	Zeph 1:18	3605
a ye meek of the earth, which	Zeph 2:3	3605
for he will famish *a* the gods of	Zeph 2:11	3605
even *a* the isles of the heathen	Zeph 2:11	3605
a the beasts of the nations	Zeph 2:14	3605
and corrupted *a* their doings	Zeph 3:7	3605
even *a* my fierce anger	Zeph 3:8	3605
for *a* the earth shall be devoured	Zeph 3:8	3605
that they may *a* call upon the	Zeph 3:9	3605
not be ashamed for *a* thy doings	Zeph 3:11	3605
glad and rejoice with *a* the heart	Zeph 3:14	3605
I will undo *a* that afflict thee	Zeph 3:19	3605
a praise among *a* people of the	Zeph 3:20	3605
upon *a* the labour of the hands	Hag 1:11	3605
with *a* the remnant of the people,	Hag 1:12	3605
the spirit of *a* the remnant of	Hag 1:14	3605
a ye people of the land, saith	Hag 2:4	3605
And I will shake *a* nations	Hag 2:7	3605
the desire of *a* nations shall	Hag 2:7	3605
with hail in *a* the labours of	Hag 2:17	3605
a the earth sitteth still, and is	Zec 1:11	3605
O *a* flesh, before the LORD	Zec 2:13	3605
and behold a candlestick *a* of gold	Zec 4:2	3605
resemblance through *a* the earth	Zec 5:6	3605
before the Lord of *a* the earth	Zec 6:5	3605
Speak unto *a* the people of the	Zec 7:5	3605
did ye at *a* fast unto me, even to	Zec 7:5	
them with a whirlwind among *a* the	Zec 7:14	3605
for I set *a* men every one against	Zec 8:10	3605
people to possess *a* these things	Zec 8:12	3605
for *a* these are things that I	Zec 8:17	3605
out of *a* languages of the nations	Zec 8:23	3605
as of *a* the tribes of Israel,	Zec 9:1	3605

Context	Reference	Number
a the deeps of the river shall	Zec 10:11	3605
I had made with *a* the people	Zec 11:10	3605
unto *a* the people round about	Zec 12:2	3605
a burdensome stone for *a* people	Zec 12:3	3605
a that burden themselves with it	Zec 12:3	3605
though *a* the people of the earth	Zec 12:3	3605
they shall devour *a* the people	Zec 12:6	3605
that I will seek to destroy *a* the	Zec 12:9	3605
A the families that remain, every	Zec 12:14	3605
that in *a* the land, saith the	Zec 13:8	3605
For I will gather *a* nations	Zec 14:2	3605
come, and *a* the saints with thee	Zec 14:5	3605
shall be king over *a* the earth	Zec 14:9	3605
A the land shall be turned as a	Zec 14:10	3605
a the people that have fought	Zec 14:12	3605
the wealth of *a* the heathen round	Zec 14:14	3605
of *a* the beasts that shall be in	Zec 14:15	3605
a the nations which came against	Zec 14:16	3605
a the families of the earth unto	Zec 14:17	
the punishment of *a* nations that	Zec 14:19	3605
a they that sacrifice shall come	Zec 14:21	3605
and base before *a* the people	Mal 2:9	3605
Have we not *a* one father	Mal 2:10	3605
Bring ye *a* the tithes into the	Mal 3:10	3605
a nations shall call you blessed	Mal 3:12	3605
a the proud, yea, and *a* that do	Mal 4:1	3605
unto him in Horeb for *a* Israel	Mal 4:4	3605
So *a* the generations from Abraham	Mt 1:17	3956
Now *a* this was done, that it	Mt 1:22	3650
troubled, and *a* Jerusalem with him	Mt 2:3	3956
had gathered *a* the chief priests	Mt 2:4	3956
slew *a* the children that were in	Mt 2:16	3956
in *a* the coasts thereof, from two	Mt 2:16	3956
a Judaea, and *a* the region round	Mt 3:5	3956
us to fulfil *a* righteousness	Mt 3:15	3956
sheweth him *a* the kingdoms of the	Mt 4:8	3956
A these things will I give thee,	Mt 4:9	3956
And Jesus went about *a* Galilee	Mt 4:23	3650
healing *a* manner of sickness and	Mt 4:23	3956
a manner of disease among the	Mt 4:23	3956
his fame went throughout *a* Syria	Mt 4:24	3650
they brought unto him *a* sick	Mt 4:24	3956
shall say *a* manner of evil	Mt 5:11	3956
it giveth light unto *a* that are	Mt 5:15	3956
from the law, till *a* be fulfilled	Mt 5:18	3956
I say unto you, Swear not at *a*	Mt 5:34	3654
That even Solomon in *a* his glory	Mt 6:29	3956
(For after *a* these things do the	Mt 6:32	537
ye have need of *a* these things	Mt 6:32	3956
a these things shall be added	Mt 6:33	3956
Therefore *a* things whatsoever ye	Mt 7:12	3956
word, and healed *a* that were sick	Mt 8:16	3956
went abroad into *a* that land	Mt 9:26	3650
abroad his fame in *a* that country	Mt 9:31	3650
And Jesus went about *a* the cities	Mt 9:35	3956
to heal *a* manner of sickness and	Mt 10:1	3956
sickness and *a* manner of disease	Mt 10:1	3956
ye shall be hated of *a* men for my	Mt 10:22	3956
hairs of your head are *a* numbered	Mt 10:30	3956
For *a* the prophets and the law	Mt 11:13	3956
A things are delivered unto me of	Mt 11:27	3956
a ye that labour and are heavy	Mt 11:28	3956
followed him, and he healed them *a*	Mt 12:15	3956
a the people were amazed, and said	Mt 12:23	3956
A manner of sin and blasphemy	Mt 12:31	3956
indeed is the least of *a* seeds	Mt 13:32	3956
A these things spake Jesus unto	Mt 13:34	3956
his kingdom *a* things that offend	Mt 13:41	3956
selleth *a* that he hath, and buyeth	Mt 13:44	3956
sold *a* that he had, and bought it	Mt 13:46	3956
Have ye understood *a* these things	Mt 13:51	3956
sisters, are they not *a* with us	Mt 13:56	3956
then hath this man *a* these things	Mt 13:56	3956
And they did *a* eat, and were filled	Mt 14:20	3956
they sent out into *a* that country	Mt 14:35	3650
brought unto him *a* that were	Mt 14:35	3956
And they did *a* eat, and were filled	Mt 15:37	3956
first come, and restore *a* things	Mt 17:11	3956
a that he had, and payment to be	Mt 18:25	3956
with me, and I will pay thee *a*	Mt 18:26	3956
with me, and I will pay thee *a*	Mt 18:29	3956
unto their lord *a* that was done	Mt 18:31	3956
I forgave thee *a* that debt	Mt 18:32	3956
till he should pay *a* that was due	Mt 18:34	3956
A men cannot receive this saying,	Mt 19:11	3956
A these things have I kept from	Mt 19:20	3956
but with God *a* things are	Mt 19:26	3956
him, Behold, we have forsaken *a*	Mt 19:27	3956
Why stand ye here *a* the day idle	Mt 20:6	3650
A this was done, that it might be	Mt 21:4	3650
a the city was moved, saying, Who	Mt 21:10	3956
cast out *a* them that sold and	Mt 21:12	3956
a things, whatsoever ye shall ask	Mt 21:22	3956
for *a* hold John as a prophet	Mt 21:26	3956
But last of *a* he sent unto them	Mt 21:37	
are killed, and *a* things are ready	Mt 22:4	3956
gathered together *a* as many as	Mt 22:10	3956
last of *a* the woman died also	Mt 22:27	3956
for they *a* had her	Mt 22:28	3956
the Lord thy God with *a* thy heart	Mt 22:37	3650
a thy soul, and with *a* thy mind	Mt 22:37	3650
two commandments hang *a* the law	Mt 22:40	3650
A therefore whatsoever they bid	Mt 23:3	3956
But *a* their works they do for to	Mt 23:5	3956
and *a* ye are brethren	Mt 23:8	3956
by it, and by *a* things thereon	Mt 23:20	3956
men's bones, and of *a* uncleanness	Mt 23:27	3956
That upon you may come *a* the	Mt 23:35	3956
A these things shall come upon	Mt 23:36	3956
See ye not *a* these things	Mt 24:2	3956
for *a* these things must come to	Mt 24:6	3956
A these are the beginning of	Mt 24:8	3956
ye shall be hated of *a* nations	Mt 24:9	3956
in *a* the world for a witness unto	Mt 24:14	3650
for a witness unto *a* nations	Mt 24:14	3956
then shall *a* the tribes of the	Mt 24:30	3956
when ye shall see *a* these things	Mt 24:33	3956
till *a* these things be fulfilled	Mt 24:34	3956
flood came, and took them *a* away	Mt 24:39	537
make him ruler over *a* his goods	Mt 24:47	3956
they *a* slumbered and slept	Mt 25:5	3956
Then *a* those virgins arose, and	Mt 25:7	3956
a the holy angels with him, then	Mt 25:31	3956
him shall be gathered *a* nations	Mt 25:32	3956
had finished *a* these sayings	Mt 26:1	3956
to them, saying, Drink ye *a* of it	Mt 26:27	3956
A ye shall be offended because of	Mt 26:31	3956
Though *a* men shall be offended	Mt 26:33	3956
also said *a* the disciples	Mt 26:35	3956
for *a* they that take the sword	Mt 26:52	3956
But *a* this was done, that the	Mt 26:56	3650
Then *a* the disciples forsook him,	Mt 26:56	3956
a the council, sought false	Mt 26:59	3650
But he denied before them *a*	Mt 26:70	3956
a the chief priests and elders of	Mt 27:1	3956
They *a* say unto him, Let him be	Mt 27:22	3956
Then answered *a* the people	Mt 27:25	3956
a the land unto the ninth hour	Mt 27:45	3956
Jesus met them, saying, *A* hail	Mt 28:9	
a the things that were done	Mt 28:11	537
A power is given unto me in	Mt 28:18	3956
teach *a* nations, baptizing them	Mt 28:19	3956
a things whatsoever I have	Mt 28:20	3956
out unto him *a* the land of Judaea	Mk 1:5	3956
were *a* baptized of him in the	Mk 1:5	3956
And they were *a* amazed, insomuch	Mk 1:27	3956
fame spread abroad throughout *a*	Mk 1:28	3650
unto him *a* that were diseased	Mk 1:32	3956
a the city was gathered together	Mk 1:33	3650
unto him, *A* men seek for thee	Mk 1:37	3956
synagogues throughout *a* Galilee	Mk 1:39	3650
bed, and went forth before them *a*	Mk 2:12	3956
insomuch that they were *a* amazed	Mk 2:12	3956
a the multitude resorted unto him	Mk 2:13	3956
A sins shall be forgiven unto the	Mk 3:28	3956
a these things are done in	Mk 4:11	3956
how then will ye know *a* parables	Mk 4:13	3956
is less than *a* the seeds that be	Mk 4:31	3956
and becometh greater than *a* herbs	Mk 4:32	3956
he expounded *a* things to his	Mk 4:34	3956
a the devils besought him, saying	Mk 5:12	3956
and *a* men did marvel	Mk 5:20	3956
had spent *a* that she had, and was	Mk 5:26	3956
him, and told him *a* the truth	Mk 5:33	3956
But when he had put them *a* out	Mk 5:40	537
unto Jesus, and told him *a* things	Mk 6:30	3956
ran afoot thither out of *a* cities	Mk 6:33	3956
he commanded them to make *a* sit	Mk 6:39	3956
fishes divided he among them *a*	Mk 6:41	3956
And they did *a* eat, and were filled	Mk 6:42	3956
For they *a* saw him, and were	Mk 6:50	3956
a the Jews, except they wash	Mk 7:3	3956
when he had called *a* the people	Mk 7:14	3956
into the draught, purging *a* meats	Mk 7:19	3956
A these evil things come from	Mk 7:23	3956
He hath done *a* things well	Mk 7:37	3956
first, and restoreth *a* things	Mk 9:12	3956
And straightway *a* the people	Mk 9:15	3956
a things are possible to him that	Mk 9:23	3956
be last of *a*, and servant of *a*	Mk 9:35	3956
a these have I observed from my	Mk 10:20	3956
for with God *a* things are	Mk 10:27	3956
say unto him, Lo, we have left *a*	Mk 10:28	3956
chiefest, shall be servant of *a*	Mk 10:44	3956
looked round about upon *a* things	Mk 11:11	3956
of *a* nations the house of prayer	Mk 11:17	3956
him, because *a* the people was	Mk 11:18	3956
for *a* men counted John, that he	Mk 11:32	537
last of *a* the woman died also	Mk 12:22	3956
is the first commandment of *a*	Mk 12:28	3956
The first of *a* the commandments	Mk 12:29	3956
the Lord thy God with *a* thy heart	Mk 12:30	3650
with *a* thy soul, and with *a* thy	Mk 12:30	3650
thy mind, and with *a* thy strength	Mk 12:30	3650
And to love him with *a* the heart	Mk 12:33	3650
with *a* the understanding, and with	Mk 12:33	3650
with *a* the soul, and with *a* the	Mk 12:33	3650
is more than *a* whole burnt	Mk 12:33	3956
than *a* they which have cast into	Mk 12:43	3956
For *a* they did cast in of their	Mk 12:44	3956
did cast in *a* that she had	Mk 12:44	3956
that she had, even *a* her living	Mk 12:44	3650
what shall be the sign when *a*	Mk 13:4	3956
be published among *a* nations	Mk 13:10	3956
ye shall be hated of *a* men for my	Mk 13:13	3956
I have foretold you *a* things	Mk 13:23	3956
till *a* these things be done	Mk 13:30	3956
what I say unto you I say unto *a*	Mk 13:37	3956
and they *a* drank of it	Mk 14:23	3956
A ye shall be offended because of	Mk 14:27	3956
Although *a* shall be offended, yet	Mk 14:29	3956
Likewise also said they *a*	Mk 14:31	3956
a things are possible unto thee	Mk 14:36	3956
they *a* forsook him, and fled	Mk 14:50	3956
assembled *a* the chief priests	Mk 14:53	3956
a the council sought for witness	Mk 14:55	3650
they *a* condemned him to be guilty	Mk 14:64	3956
unto them, Go ye into *a* the world	Mk 16:15	537
of *a* things from the very first	Lk 1:3	3956
walking in *a* the commandments and	Lk 1:6	3956
from henceforth *a* generations	Lk 1:48	3956
And they marvelled *a*	Lk 1:63	3956
fear came on *a* that dwelt round	Lk 1:65	3956
a these sayings were noised	Lk 1:65	3956
a the hill country of Judaea	Lk 1:65	3650
a they that heard them laid them	Lk 1:66	3956
from the hand of *a* that hate us	Lk 1:71	3956
him, *a* the days of our life	Lk 1:75	3956
that *a* the world should be taxed	Lk 2:1	3956
a went to be taxed, every one	Lk 2:3	3956
joy, which shall be to *a* people	Lk 2:10	3956
a they that heard it wondered at	Lk 2:18	3956
But Mary kept *a* these things	Lk 2:19	3956
praising God for *a* the things	Lk 2:20	3956
before the face of *a* people	Lk 2:31	3956
spake of him to *a* them that	Lk 2:38	3956
when they had performed *a* things	Lk 2:39	537
a that heard him were astonished	Lk 2:47	3956
but his mother kept *a* these	Lk 2:51	3956
he came into *a* the country about	Lk 3:3	3956
a flesh shall see the salvation	Lk 3:6	3956
a men mused in their hearts of	Lk 3:15	3956
John answered, saying unto them *a*	Lk 3:16	537
for *a* the evils which Herod had	Lk 3:19	3956
Added yet this above *a*, that he	Lk 3:20	3956
Now when *a* the people were	Lk 3:21	537
shewed unto him *a* the kingdoms of	Lk 4:5	3956
A this power will I give thee, and	Lk 4:6	537
wilt worship me, *a* shall be thine	Lk 4:7	3956
devil had ended *a* the temptation	Lk 4:13	3956
through *a* the region round about	Lk 4:14	3650
synagogues, being glorified of *a*	Lk 4:15	3956
the eyes of *a* them that were in	Lk 4:20	3956
a bare him witness, and wondered	Lk 4:22	3956
famine was throughout *a* the land	Lk 4:25	3956
a they in the synagogue, when	Lk 4:28	3956
And they were *a* amazed, and spake	Lk 4:36	3956
a they that had any sick with	Lk 4:40	3956
we have toiled *a* the night	Lk 5:5	3650
a that were with him, at the	Lk 5:9	3956
ships to land, they forsook *a*	Lk 5:11	537
And they were *a* amazed, and they	Lk 5:26	537
And he left *a*, rose up, and	Lk 5:28	537
looking round about upon them *a*	Lk 6:10	3956
continued *a* night in prayer to	Lk 6:12	1273
of people out of *a* Judaea	Lk 6:17	3956
out of him, and healed them *a*	Lk 6:19	3956
when *a* men shall speak well of	Lk 6:26	3956
Now when he had ended *a* his	Lk 7:1	3956
And there came a fear on *a*	Lk 7:16	537
went forth throughout *a* Judaea	Lk 7:17	3650
throughout *a* the region round	Lk 7:17	3956
John shewed him of *a* these things	Lk 7:18	3956
a the people that heard him, and	Lk 7:29	3956
is justified of *a* her children	Lk 7:35	3956
for they were *a* waiting for him	Lk 8:40	3956
which had spent *a* her living upon	Lk 8:43	3956
When *a* denied, Peter and they that	Lk 8:45	3956
she declared unto him before *a*	Lk 8:47	3956
And *a* wept, and bewailed her	Lk 8:52	3956
And he put them *a* out, and took her	Lk 8:54	3956
power and authority over *a* devils	Lk 9:1	3956
heard of *a* that was done by him	Lk 9:7	3956
told him *a* that they had done	Lk 9:10	3745
go and buy meat for *a* this people	Lk 9:13	3956
did so, and made them *a* sit down	Lk 9:15	537
And they did eat, and were *a* filled	Lk 9:17	3956
And he said to them *a*, If any man	Lk 9:23	3956
they were *a* amazed at the mighty	Lk 9:43	3956
one at *a* things which Jesus did	Lk 9:43	3956
for he that is least among you *a*	Lk 9:48	
over *a* the power of the enemy	Lk 10:19	3956
A things are delivered to me of	Lk 10:22	3956
the Lord thy God with *a* thy heart	Lk 10:27	3650
with *a* thy soul, and with *a* thy	Lk 10:27	3650
thy strength, and with *a* thy mind	Lk 10:27	3650
he taketh from him *a* his armour	Lk 11:22	3833
a things are clean unto you	Lk 11:41	3956
a manner of herbs, and pass over	Lk 11:42	3956
That the blood of *a* the prophets	Lk 11:50	3956
say unto his disciples first of *a*	Lk 12:1	
hairs of your head are *a* numbered	Lk 12:7	3956
there will I bestow *a* my fruits	Lk 12:18	3956
that Solomon in *a* his glory was	Lk 12:27	3956
For *a* these things do the nations	Lk 12:30	3956
a these things shall be added	Lk 12:31	3956
parable unto us, or even to *a*	Lk 12:41	3956
him ruler over *a* that he hath	Lk 12:44	3956
sinners above *a* the Galilaeans	Lk 13:2	3956
ye shall *a* likewise perish	Lk 13:3	3956
a men that dwelt in Jerusalem	Lk 13:4	3956
ye shall *a* likewise perish	Lk 13:5	3956
a his adversaries were ashamed	Lk 13:17	3956
a the people rejoiced for *a* the	Lk 13:17	3956
from me, *a* ye workers of iniquity	Lk 13:27	3956
a the prophets, in the kingdom of	Lk 13:28	3956
for *a* things are now ready	Lk 14:17	3956
they *a* with one consent began to	Lk 14:18	3956
a that behold it begin to mock	Lk 14:29	3956
that forsaketh not *a* that he hath	Lk 14:33	3956
near unto him *a* the publicans	Lk 15:1	3956
younger son gathered *a* together	Lk 15:13	537
And when he had spent *a*, there	Lk 15:14	3956
me, and *a* that I have is thine	Lk 15:31	3956
covetous, heard *a* these things	Lk 16:14	3956
And beside *a* this, between us and	Lk 16:26	3956
done *a* those things which are	Lk 17:10	3956
flood came, and destroyed them *a*	Lk 17:27	537
from heaven, and destroyed them *a*	Lk 17:29	537
I give tithes of *a* that I possess	Lk 18:12	3956
A these have I kept from my youth	Lk 18:21	3956
sell *a* that thou hast, and	Lk 18:22	3956
Peter said, Lo, we have left *a*	Lk 18:28	3956
a things that are written by the	Lk 18:31	3956
a the people, when they saw it,	Lk 18:43	3956
they *a* murmured, saying, That he	Lk 19:7	537
God with a loud voice for *a* the	Lk 19:37	3956
for *a* the people were very	Lk 19:48	537
a the people will stone us	Lk 20:6	3956
Last of *a* the woman died also	Lk 20:32	3956
for *a* live unto him	Lk 20:38	3956
not ask him any question at *a*	Lk 20:40	

Then in the audience of *a* the Lk 20:45 3956
hath cast in more than they *a* Lk 21:3 3956
For *a* these have of their Lk 21:4 537
cast in *a* the living that she had Lk 21:4 537
But before *a* these, they shall Lk 21:12 537
which *a* your adversaries shall Lk 21:15 3956
ye shall be hated of *a* men for my Lk 21:17 3956
that *a* things which are written Lk 21:22 3956
led away captive into *a* nations Lk 21:24 3956
the fig tree, and *a* the trees Lk 21:29 3956
pass away, till *a* be fulfilled Lk 21:32 3956
a them that dwell on the face of Lk 21:35 3956
be accounted worthy to escape *a* Lk 21:36 3956
a the people came early in the Lk 21:38 3956
Then said they *a*, Art thou then Lk 22:70 3956
teaching throughout *a* Jewry Lk 23:5 3650
And they cried out *a* at once Lk 23:18 3829
there was a darkness over *a* the Lk 23:44 3650
a the people that came together Lk 23:48 3956
a his acquaintance, and the women Lk 23:49 3956
told *a* these things unto the Lk 24:9 3956
unto the eleven, and to *a* the rest Lk 24:9 3956
they talked together of *a* these Lk 24:14 3956
word before God and *a* the people Lk 24:19 3956
and beside *a* this, to day is the Lk 24:21 3956
slow of heart to believe *a* that Lk 24:25 3956
a the prophets, he expounded unto Lk 24:27 3956
in *a* the scriptures the things Lk 24:27 3956
that *a* things must be fulfilled, Lk 24:44 3956
in his name among *a* nations Lk 24:47 3956
A things were made by him Jn 1:3 3956
that *a* men through him might Jn 1:7 3956
of his fulness have *a* we received Jn 1:16 3956
he drove them *a* out of the temple Jn 2:15 3956
unto them, because he knew *a* men Jn 2:24 3956
baptizeth, and *a* men come to him Jn 3:26 3956
that cometh from above is above *a* Jn 3:31 3956
cometh from heaven is above *a* Jn 3:31 3956
hath given *a* things into his hand Jn 3:35 3956
is come, he will tell us *a* things Jn 4:25 3956
which told me *a* things that ever Jn 4:29 3956
He told me *a* that ever I did Jn 4:39 3956
having seen *a* the things that he Jn 4:45 3956
sheweth him *a* things that himself Jn 5:20 3956
but hath committed *a* judgment Jn 5:22 3956
That *a* men should honour the Son, Jn 5:23 3956
in the which *a* that are in the Jn 5:28 3956
A that the Father giveth me shall Jn 6:37 3956
that of *a* which he hath given me Jn 6:39 3956
And they shall be *a* taught of God Jn 6:45 3956
done one work, and ye *a* marvel Jn 7:21 3956
a the people came unto him Jn 8:2 3956
A that ever came before me are Jn 10:8 3956
gave them me, is greater than *a* Jn 10:29 3956
but *a* things that John spake of Jn 10:41 3956
a men will believe on him Jn 11:48 3956
unto them, Ye know nothing at *a* Jn 11:49 3762
earth, will draw *a* men unto me Jn 12:32 3956
had given *a* things into his hands Jn 13:3 3956
and ye are clean, but not *a* Jn 13:10 3956
said he, Ye are not *a* clean Jn 13:11 3956
I speak not of you *a* Jn 13:18 3956
By this shall *a* men know that ye Jn 13:35 3956
name, he shall teach you *a* things Jn 14:26 3956
and bring *a* things to your Jn 14:26 3956
for *a* things that I have heard of Jn 15:15 3956
But *a* these things will they do Jn 15:21 3956
he will guide you into *a* truth Jn 16:13 3956
A things that the Father hath are Jn 16:15 3956
sure that thou knowest *a* things Jn 16:30 3956
hast given him power over *a* flesh Jn 17:2 3956
Now they have known that *a* things Jn 17:7 3956
a mine are thine, and thine are Jn 17:10 3956
That they *a* may be one Jn 17:21 3956
knowing *a* things that should come Jn 18:4 3956
them, I find in him no fault at *a* Jn 18:38
Then cried they *a* again, saying, Jn 18:40 3956
have no power at *a* against me Jn 19:11 3762
Jesus knowing that *a* things were Jn 19:28 3956
for *a* there were so many, yet was Jn 21:11
him, Lord, thou knowest *a* things Jn 21:17 3956
of *a* that Jesus began both to do Acts 1:1 3956
in *a* Judaea, and in Samaria, and Acts 1:8 3956
These *a* continued with one accord Acts 1:14 3956
midst, and *a* his bowels gushed out Acts 1:18 3956
it was known unto *a* the dwellers Acts 1:19 3956
us *a* the time that the Lord Jesus Acts 1:21 3956
which knowest the hearts of *a* men Acts 1:24 3956
they were *a* with one accord in Acts 2:1 537
it filled *a* the house where they Acts 2:2 3650
they were *a* filled with the Holy Acts 2:4 537
And they were *a* amazed and Acts 2:7 3956
are not *a* these which speak Acts 2:7 3956
And they were *a* amazed, and were in. Acts 2:12 3956
a ye that dwell at Jerusalem, be Acts 2:14 537
out of my Spirit upon *a* flesh Acts 2:17 3956
whereof we *a* are witnesses Acts 2:32 3956
Therefore let *a* the house of Acts 2:36 3956
to *a* that are afar off, even as Acts 2:39 3956
a that believed were together Acts 2:44 3956
and had *a* things common Acts 2:44 537
and goods, and parted them to *a* men.. Acts 2:45 3956
having favour with *a* the people Acts 2:47 3650
a the people saw him walking and Acts 3:9 3956
a the people ran together unto Acts 3:11 3956
in the presence of you *a* Acts 3:16 3956
by the mouth of *a* his prophets Acts 3:18 3956
times of restitution of *a* things Acts 3:21 3956
of *a* his holy prophets since the Acts 3:21 3956
him shall ye hear in *a* things Acts 3:22 3956
a the prophets from Samuel and Acts 3:24 3956
in thy seed shall *a* the kindreds Acts 3:25 3956
Be it known unto you *a*, and to *a* Acts 4:10 3956
done by them is manifest to *a* Acts 4:16 3956
a nor teach in the name of Jesus Acts 4:18 2527
for *a* men glorified God for that Acts 4:21 3956
reported *a* that the chief priests Acts 4:23 3745
and the sea, and *a* that in them is Acts 4:24 3956
that with *a* boldness they may Acts 4:29 3956
they were *a* filled with the Holy Acts 4:31 537
but they had *a* things common Acts 4:32 537
and great grace was upon them *a* Acts 4:33 3956
great fear came on *a* them that Acts 5:5 3956
great fear came upon *a* the church Acts 5:11 3650
they were *a* with one accord in Acts 5:12 537
a they that were with him, (which Acts 5:17 3956
people *a* the words of this life Acts 5:20 3956
a the senate of the children of Acts 5:21 3956
truly found we shut with *a* safety Acts 5:23 3956
in reputation among *a* the people Acts 5:34 3956
and *a*, as many as obeyed him, were Acts 5:36 3956
and *a*, even as many as obeyed him, Acts 5:37 3956
a that sat in the council, Acts 6:15 537
him out of *a* his afflictions Acts 7:10 3956
over Egypt and *a* his house Acts 7:10 3650
a dearth over *a* the land of Egypt Acts 7:11 3650
a his kindred, threescore and Acts 7:14 3956
Moses was learned in *a* the wisdom Acts 7:22 3956
not my hand made *a* these things Acts 7:50 3956
they were *a* scattered abroad Acts 8:1 3956
To whom they *a* gave heed, from Acts 8:10 3956
had the charge of *a* her treasure Acts 8:27 3956
thou believest with *a* thine heart Acts 8:37 3650
he preached in *a* the cities Acts 8:40 3956
to bind *a* that call on thy name Acts 9:14 3956
But *a* that heard him were amazed, Acts 9:21 3956
but they were *a* afraid of him Acts 9:26 3956
churches rest throughout *a* Judaea Acts 9:31 3650
passed throughout *a* quarters Acts 9:32 3956
a that dwelt at Lydda and Saron Acts 9:35 3956
a the widows stood by him weeping Acts 9:39 3956
But Peter put them *a* forth Acts 9:40 3956
it was known throughout *a* Joppa Acts 9:42 3650
that feared God with *a* his house Acts 10:2 3956
when he had declared *a* these Acts 10:8 537
Wherein were *a* manner of Acts 10:12 3956
of good report among *a* the nation Acts 10:22 3650
Now therefore are we *a* here Acts 10:33 3956
to hear *a* things that are Acts 10:33 3956
(he is Lord of *a* Acts 10:36 3956
was published throughout *a* Judaea Acts 10:37 3650
healing *a* that were oppressed of Acts 10:38 3956
we are witnesses of *a* things Acts 10:39 3956
Not to *a* the people, but unto Acts 10:41 3956
To him give *a* the prophets Acts 10:43 3956
the Holy Ghost fell on *a* them Acts 10:44 3956
a were drawn up again into heaven Acts 11:10 537
a thy house shall be saved Acts 11:14 3956
God, was glad, and exhorted them *a* Acts 11:23 3956
dearth throughout *a* the world Acts 11:28 3650
from *a* the expectation of the Acts 12:11 3956
And said, O full of *a* subtilty Acts 13:10 3956
a mischief, thou child of the Acts 13:10 3956
thou enemy of *a* righteousness Acts 13:10 3956
which shall fulfil *a* my will Acts 13:22 3956
to *a* the people of Israel Acts 13:24 3956
a that was written of him Acts 13:29 537
by him *a* that believe are Acts 13:39 3956
are justified from *a* things Acts 13:39 3956
published throughout *a* the region Acts 13:49 3650
a things that are therein Acts 14:15 3956
Who in times past suffered *a* Acts 14:16 3956
they rehearsed *a* that God had Acts 14:27 3745
great joy unto *a* the brethren Acts 15:3 3956
they declared *a* things that God Acts 15:4 3745
Then *a* the multitude kept silence Acts 15:12 3956
a the Gentiles, upon whom my name Acts 15:17 3956
Lord, who doeth *a* these things Acts 15:17 3956
Known unto God are *a* his works Acts 15:18 3956
for they knew *a* that his father Acts 16:3 537
immediately *a* the doors were Acts 16:26 3956
for we are *a* here Acts 16:28 537
to *a* that were in his house Acts 16:32 3956
he and *a* his, straightway Acts 16:33 3956
believing in God with *a* his house Acts 16:34 3832
set *a* the city on an uproar, and Acts 17:5
these *a* do contrary to the Acts 17:7 3956
the word with *a* readiness of mind Acts 17:11 3956
for to come to him with *a* speed Acts 17:15
(For *a* the Athenians and strangers Acts 17:21 3956
I perceive that in *a* things ye Acts 17:22 3956
a things therein, seeing that he Acts 17:24 3956
a life, and breath, and *a* things Acts 17:25 3956
hath made of one blood *a* nations Acts 17:26 3956
dwell on *a* the face of the earth Acts 17:26 3956
but now commandeth *a* men every Acts 17:30 3956
hath given assurance unto *a* men Acts 17:31 3956
a Jews to depart from Rome Acts 18:2 3956
on the Lord with *a* his house Acts 18:8 3650
Then *a* the Greeks took Sosthenes, Acts 18:17 3956
I must by *a* means keep this feast Acts 18:21 3843
went over *a* the country of Acts 18:23
strengthening *a* the disciples Acts 18:23 3956
a the men were about twelve Acts 19:7 3956
so that *a* they which dwelt in Acts 19:10 3956
And this was known to *a* the Jews Acts 19:17 3956
and fear fell on them *a*, and the Acts 19:17 3956
and burned them before *a* men Acts 19:19 3956
but almost throughout *a* Asia Acts 19:26 3956
should be destroyed, whom *a* Asia Acts 19:27 3650
a with one voice about the space Acts 19:34 3956
I have been with you at *a* seasons Acts 20:18 3956
the Lord with *a* humility of mind Acts 20:19 3956
And now, behold, I know that ye *a* Acts 20:25 3956
I am pure from the blood of *a* men Acts 20:26 3956
unto you *a* the counsel of God Acts 20:27 3956
to *a* the flock, over the which Acts 20:28 3956
among *a* them which are sanctified Acts 20:32 3956
I have shewed you *a* things Acts 20:35 3956
down, and prayed with them *a* Acts 20:36 3956
they *a* wept sore, and fell on Acts 20:37 3956
Sorrowing most of *a* for the words Acts 20:38 3122
they *a* brought us on our way, Acts 21:5 3956
a the elders were present Acts 21:18 3956
they are *a* zealous of the law Acts 21:20 3956
that thou teachest *a* the Jews Acts 21:21 3956
a may know that those things, Acts 21:24 3956
temple, stirred up *a* the people Acts 21:27 3956
that teacheth *a* men every where Acts 21:28 3956
a the city was moved, and the Acts 21:30 3650
that *a* Jerusalem was in an uproar Acts 21:31 3650
toward God, as ye *a* are this day Acts 22:3 3956
a the estate of the elders Acts 22:5 3956
a things which are appointed for Acts 22:10 3956
having a good report of *a* the Acts 22:12 3956
unto *a* men of what thou hast seen Acts 22:15 3956
a their council to appear, and Acts 22:30 3650
I have lived in *a* good conscience Acts 23:1 3956
accept it always, and in *a* places Acts 24:3 3837
noble Felix, with *a* thankfulness Acts 24:3 3956
a mover of sedition among *a* the Acts 24:5 3956
take knowledge of *a* these things Acts 24:8 3956
believing *a* things which are Acts 24:14 3956
have I offended any thing at *a* Acts 25:8
a men which are here present with Acts 25:24 3956
about whom *a* the multitude of the Acts 25:24 3956
this day before thee touching *a* Acts 26:2 3956
thee to be expert in *a* customs Acts 26:3 3956
at Jerusalem, know *a* the Jews Acts 26:4 3956
when we were *a* fallen to the Acts 26:14 3956
throughout *a* the coasts of Judaea Acts 26:20 3956
but also *a* that hear me this day, Acts 26:29 3956
a hope that we should be saved Acts 27:20 3956
God hath given thee *a* them that Acts 27:24 3956
Paul besought them *a* to take meat Acts 27:33 537
to God in presence of them *a* Acts 27:35 3956
Then were they *a* of good cheer Acts 27:36 3956
we were in *a* in the ship two Acts 27:37 3956
that they escaped *a* safe to land Acts 27:44 3956
received *a* that came in unto him, Acts 28:30 3956
with *a* confidence, no man Acts 28:31 3956
to the faith among *a* nations Rom 1:5 3956
To *a* that be in Rome, beloved of Rom 1:7 3956
through Jesus Christ for you *a* Rom 1:8 3956
from heaven against *a* ungodliness Rom 1:18 3956
filled with *a* unrighteousness Rom 1:29 3956
that they are *a* under sin Rom 3:9 3956
They are *a* gone out of the way, Rom 3:12 3956
a the world may become guilty Rom 3:19 3956
a and upon *a* them that believe Rom 3:22 3956
For *a* have sinned, and come short Rom 3:23 3956
the father of *a* them that believe Rom 4:11 3956
might be sure to *a* the seed Rom 4:16 3956
who is the father of us *a* Rom 4:16 3956
a men, for that *a* have sinned Rom 5:12 3956
came upon *a* men to condemnation Rom 5:18 3956
a men unto justification of life Rom 5:18 3956
wrought in me *a* manner of Rom 7:8 3956
we know that *a* things work Rom 8:28 3956
but delivered him up for us *a* Rom 8:32 3956
him also freely give us *a* things Rom 8:32 3956
sake we are killed *a* the day long Rom 8:36 3650
in *a* these things we are more Rom 8:37 3956
flesh Christ came, who is over *a* Rom 9:5 3956
For they are not *a* Israel Rom 9:6 3956
of Abraham, are they *a* children Rom 9:7 3956
declared throughout *a* the earth Rom 9:17 3956
for the same Lord over *a* is rich Rom 10:12 3956
unto *a* that call upon him Rom 10:12 3956
they have not *a* obeyed the gospel Rom 10:16 3956
their sound went into *a* the earth Rom 10:18 3956
A day long I have stretched forth Rom 10:21 3650
so *a* Israel shall be saved Rom 11:26 3956
hath concluded them *a* in unbelief Rom 11:32 3956
that he might have mercy upon *a* Rom 11:32 3956
him, and to him, are *a* things Rom 11:36 3956
a members have not the same Rom 12:4 3956
honest in the sight of *a* men Rom 12:17 3956
in you, live peaceably with *a* men Rom 12:18 3956
Render therefore to *a* their dues Rom 13:7 3956
that he may eat *a* things Rom 14:2 3956
for we shall *a* stand before the Rom 14:10 3956
A things indeed are pure Rom 14:20 3956
Praise the Lord, *a* ye Gentiles Rom 15:11 3956
and laud him, *a* ye people Rom 15:11 3956
God of hope fill you with *a* joy Rom 15:13 3956
goodness, filled with *a* knowledge Rom 15:14 3956
the God of peace be with you *a* Rom 15:33 3956
but also *a* the churches of the Rom 16:4 3956
a the saints which are with them Rom 16:15 3956
is come abroad unto *a* men Rom 16:19 3956
Lord Jesus Christ be with you *a* Rom 16:24 3956
made known to *a* nations for the Rom 16:26 3956
with *a* that in every place call 1Cor 1:2 3956
a utterance, and in *a* knowledge 1Cor 1:5 3956
that ye *a* speak the same thing, 1Cor 1:10 3956
for the Spirit searcheth *a* things 1Cor 2:10 3956
is spiritual judgeth *a* things 1Cor 2:15 3956
For *a* things are yours 1Cor 3:21 3956
a are yours 1Cor 3:22 3956
of *a* things unto this day 1Cor 4:13 3956
A things are lawful unto me 1Cor 6:12 3956
but *a* things are not expedient 1Cor 6:12 3956
a things are lawful for me, but I 1Cor 6:12 3956
For I would that *a* men were even 1Cor 7:7 3956
And so ordain I in *a* churches 1Cor 7:17 3956
we know that we *a* have knowledge 1Cor 8:1 3956
the Father, of whom are *a* things 1Cor 8:6 3956
Christ, by whom are *a* things 1Cor 8:6 3956
but suffer *a* things, lest we 1Cor 9:12 3956
For though I be free from *a* men 1Cor 9:19 3956
have I made myself servant unto *a* 1Cor 9:19 3956

I am made a things to a men, 1Cor 9:22 3956
that I might by a means save some 1Cor 9:22 3956
they which run in a race run a 1Cor 9:24 3956
mastery is temperate in a things 1Cor 9:25 3956
how that a our fathers were under 1Cor 10:1 3956
and a passed through the sea 1Cor 10:1 3956
were a baptized unto Moses in the 1Cor 10:2 3956
did a eat the same spiritual meat 1Cor 10:3 3956
did a drink the same spiritual 1Cor 10:4 3956
Now a these things happened unto 1Cor 10:11 3956
for we are a partakers of that 1Cor 10:17 3956
A things are lawful for me 1Cor 10:23 3956
but a things are not expedient 1Cor 10:23 3956
a things are lawful for me 1Cor 10:23 3956
but a things edify not 1Cor 10:23 3956
ye do, do a to the glory of God 1Cor 10:31 3956
as I please a men in a things 1Cor 10:33 3956
that ye remember me in a things 1Cor 11:2 3956
for that is even a one as if she 1Cor 11:5
but a things of God 1Cor 11:12 3956
For first of a, when ye come 1Cor 11:18
same God which worketh a in a 1Cor 12:6 3956
But a these worketh that one and 1Cor 12:11 3956
a the members of that one body, 1Cor 12:12 3956
are we a baptized into one body 1Cor 12:13 3956
have been a made to drink into 1Cor 12:13 3956
And if they were a one member 1Cor 12:19 3956
a the members suffer with it 1Cor 12:26 3956
a the members rejoice with it 1Cor 12:26 3956
Are a apostles 1Cor 12:29 3956
are a prophets 1Cor 12:29 3956
are a teachers 1Cor 12:29 3956
are a workers of miracles 1Cor 12:29 3956
Have a the gifts of healing 1Cor 12:30 3956
do a speak with 1Cor 12:30 3956
do a interpret? 1Cor 12:30 3956
a mysteries, and a knowledge 1Cor 13:2 3956
and though I have a faith, so that 1Cor 13:2 3956
though I bestow a my goods to 1Cor 13:3 3956
a things, believeth a things 1Cor 13:7 3956
a things, endureth a things 1Cor 13:7 3956
I would that ye a spake with 1Cor 14:5 3956
speak with tongues more than ye a 1Cor 14:18 3956
yet for a that will they not hear 1Cor 14:21 3779
a speak with tongues, and there 1Cor 14:23 3956
But if a prophesy, and there come 1Cor 14:24 3956
of a, he is judged of a 1Cor 14:24 3956
Let a things be done unto 1Cor 14:26 3956
For ye may a prophesy one by one, 1Cor 14:31 3956
that a may learn, and a may be 1Cor 14:31 3956
as in a churches of the saints 1Cor 14:33 3956
Let a things be done decently and 1Cor 14:40 3956
of a that which I also received 1Cor 15:3
then of a the apostles 1Cor 15:7 3956
last of a he was seen of me also, 1Cor 15:8 3956
more abundantly than they a 1Cor 15:10 3956
we are of a men most miserable 1Cor 15:19 3956
For as in Adam a die, even so in 1Cor 15:22 3956
in Christ shall a be made alive 1Cor 15:22 3956
a rule and a authority and power 1Cor 15:24 3956
till he hath put a enemies under 1Cor 15:25 3956
For he hath put a things under 1Cor 15:27 3956
But when he saith a things are 1Cor 15:27 3956
which did put a things under him 1Cor 15:27 3956
when a things shall be subdued 1Cor 15:28 3956
him that put a things under him 1Cor 15:28 3956
that God may be a in a 1Cor 15:28 3956
dead, if the dead rise not at a 1Cor 15:29 3654
A flesh is not the same flesh 1Cor 15:39 4561
We shall not a sleep 1Cor 15:51 3956
but we shall a be changed 1Cor 15:51 3956
was not at a to come at this time 1Cor 16:12 3843
Let a your things be done with 1Cor 16:14 3956
A the brethren greet you 1Cor 16:20 3956
be with you a in Christ Jesus 1Cor 16:24 3956
is at Corinth, with a 2Cor 1:1 3956
the saints which are in a Achaia 2Cor 1:1 3650
mercies, and the God of a comfort 2Cor 1:3 3956
us in a our tribulation, that we 2Cor 1:4 3650
For a the promises of God in him 2Cor 1:20 3745
having confidence in you a 2Cor 2:3 3956
that my joy is the joy of you a 2Cor 2:3 3956
that I may not overcharge you a 2Cor 2:5 3956
ye be obedient in a things 2Cor 2:9 3956
hearts, known and read of a men 2Cor 3:2 3956
But we a, with open face 2Cor 3:18 3956
For a things are for your sakes, 2Cor 4:15 3956
For we must a appear before the 2Cor 5:10 3956
died for a, then were a dead 2Cor 5:14 3956
And that he died for a, that they 2Cor 5:15 3956
behold, a things are become new 2Cor 5:17 3956
a things are of God, who hath 2Cor 5:18 3956
But in a things approving 2Cor 6:4 3956
and yet possessing a things 2Cor 6:10 3956
from a filthiness of the flesh 2Cor 7:1 3956
joyful in a our tribulation 2Cor 7:4 3956
In a things ye have approved 2Cor 7:11 3956
his spirit was refreshed by you a 2Cor 7:13 3956
but as we spake a things to you 2Cor 7:14 3956
the obedience of you a, how with 2Cor 7:15 3956
confidence in you in a things 2Cor 7:16 3956
in a diligence, and in your love 2Cor 8:7 3956
gospel throughout a the churches 2Cor 8:18 3956
God is able to make a grace 2Cor 9:8 3956
a sufficiency in a things 2Cor 9:8 3956
in every thing to a bountifulness 2Cor 9:11 3956
unto them, and unto a men 2Cor 9:13 3956
to revenge a disobedience 2Cor 10:6 3956
manifest among you in a things 2Cor 11:6 3956
in a things I have kept myself 2Cor 11:9 3956
the care of a the churches 2Cor 11:28 3956
wrought among you in a patience 2Cor 12:12 3956
but we do a things, dearly 2Cor 12:19 3956
to a other, that, if I come again 2Cor 13:2 3956
A the saints salute you 2Cor 13:13 3956
of the Holy Ghost, be with you a 2Cor 13:14 3956
a the brethren which are with me, Gal 1:2 3956
I said unto Peter before them a Gal 2:14 3956
In thee shall a nations be Gal 3:8 3956
one that continueth not in a Gal 3:10 3956
hath concluded a under sin Gal 3:22 3956
For ye are a the children of God Gal 3:26 3956
for ye are a one in Christ Jesus Gal 3:28 3956
a servant, though he be lord of a Gal 4:1 3956
ye have not injured me at a Gal 4:12 3762
free, which is the mother of us a Gal 4:26 3956
For a the law is fulfilled in one Gal 5:14 3956
that teacheth in a good things Gal 6:6 3956
let us do good unto a men Gal 6:10 3956
who hath blessed us with a Eph 1:3 3956
abounded toward us in a wisdom Eph 1:8 3956
in one a things in Christ Eph 1:10 3956
the purpose of him who worketh a Eph 1:11 3956
Jesus, and love unto a the saints, Eph 1:15 3956
Far above a principality, and Eph 1:21 3956
hath put a things under his feet, Eph 1:22 3956
head over a things to the church Eph 1:22 3956
of him that filleth a in a Eph 1:23 3956
Among whom also we a had our Eph 2:3 3956
In whom a the building fitly Eph 2:21 3956
less than the least of a saints Eph 3:8 3956
to make a men see what is the Eph 3:9 3956
who created a things by Jesus Eph 3:9 3956
with a saints what is the breadth Eph 3:18 3956
filled with a the fulness of God Eph 3:19 3956
above a that we ask or think Eph 3:20 3956
by Christ Jesus throughout a ages Eph 3:21 3956
With a lowliness and meekness, Eph 4:2 3956
and Father of a, who is above a Eph 4:6 3956
and through a, and in you a Eph 4:6 3956
ascended up far above a heavens Eph 4:10 3956
that he might fill a things Eph 4:10 3956
Till we a come in the unity of Eph 4:13 3956
may grow up into him in a things Eph 4:15 3956
to work a uncleanness with Eph 4:19 3956
Let a bitterness, and wrath, and Eph 4:31 3956
put away from you, with a malice Eph 4:31 3956
a uncleanness, or covetousness, Eph 5:3 3956
of the Spirit is in a goodness Eph 5:9 3956
But a things that are reproved Eph 5:13 3956
always for a things unto God Eph 5:20 3956
in the evil day, and having done a Eph 6:13 537
Above a, taking the shield of Eph 6:16 3956
ye shall be able to quench a the Eph 6:16 3956
Praying always with a prayer Eph 6:18 3956
thereunto with a perseverance Eph 6:18 3956
and supplication for a saints Eph 6:18 3956
shall make known to you a things Eph 6:21 3956
Grace be with a them that love Eph 6:24 3956
to a the saints in Christ Jesus Phil 1:1 3956
for you a making request with joy Phil 1:4 3956
for me to think this of you a Phil 1:7 3956
ye a are partakers of my grace Phil 1:7 3956
how greatly I long after you a in Phil 1:8 3956
in knowledge and in a judgment Phil 1:9 3956
are manifest in a the palace Phil 1:13 3650
and in a other places Phil 1:13 3956
ashamed, but that with a boldness Phil 1:20 3956
continue with you a for your Phil 1:25 3956
Do a things without murmurings and Phil 2:14 3956
I joy, and rejoice with you a Phil 2:17 3956
For a seek their own, not the Phil 2:21 3956
For he longed after you a Phil 2:26 3956
in the Lord with a gladness Phil 2:29 3956
I count a things but loss for the Phil 3:8 3956
suffered the loss of a things Phil 3:8 3956
to subdue a things unto himself Phil 3:21 3956
moderation be known unto a men Phil 4:5 3956
which passeth a understanding Phil 4:7 3956
in a things I am instructed both Phil 4:12 3956
I can do a things through Christ Phil 4:13 3956
But I have a, and abound Phil 4:18 3956
But my God shall supply a your Phil 4:19 3956
A the saints salute you, chiefly Phil 4:22 3956
Lord Jesus Christ be with you a Phil 4:23 3956
which ye have to a the saints Col 1:4 3956
unto you, as it is in a the world Col 1:6 3956
knowledge of his will in a wisdom Col 1:9 3956
of the Lord unto a pleasing Col 1:10 3956
Strengthened with a might Col 1:11 3956
unto a patience and longsuffering Col 1:11 3956
For by him were a things created Col 1:16 3956
a things were created by him, and Col 1:16 3956
And he is before a things Col 1:17 3956
and by him a things consist Col 1:17 3956
that in a things he might have Col 1:18 3956
in him should a fulness dwell Col 1:19 3956
reconcile a things unto himself Col 1:20 3956
and teaching every man in a wisdom Col 1:28 3956
unto a riches of the full Col 2:2 3956
In whom are hid a the treasures Col 2:3 3956
For in him dwelleth a the fulness Col 2:9 3956
is the head of a principality Col 2:10 3956
having forgiven you a trespasses Col 2:13 3956
from which a the body by joints Col 2:19 3956
Which a are to perish with the Col 2:22 3956
But now ye also put off a these Col 3:8 3956
but Christ is a, and in a Col 3:11 3956
above a these things put on Col 3:14 3956
dwell in you richly in a wisdom Col 3:16 3956
do a in the name of the Lord Col 3:17 3956
obey your parents in a things Col 3:20 3956
obey in a things your masters Col 3:22 3956
A my state shall Tychicus declare Col 4:7 3956
you a things which are done here Col 4:9 3956
complete in a the will of God Col 4:12 3956
thanks to God always for you a 1Th 1:2 3956
to a that believe in Macedonia 1Th 1:7 3956
not God, and are contrary to a men 1Th 2:15 3956
over you in a our affliction 1Th 3:7 3956
for a the joy wherewith we joy 1Th 3:9 3956
toward another, and toward a men 1Th 3:12 3956
Jesus Christ with a his saints 1Th 3:13 3956
the Lord is the avenger of a such 1Th 4:6 3956
indeed ye do it toward a the 1Th 4:10 3956
brethren which are in a Macedonia 1Th 4:10 3650
Ye are a the children of light, 1Th 5:5 3956
the weak, be patient toward a men 1Th 5:14 3956
among yourselves, and to a men 1Th 5:15 3956
Prove a things 1Th 5:21 3956
Abstain from a appearance of evil 1Th 5:22 3956
Greet a the brethren with an holy 1Th 5:26 3956
be read unto a the holy brethren 1Th 5:27 3956
you a toward each other aboundeth 2Th 1:3 3956
faith in a your persecutions and 2Th 1:4 3956
to be admired in a them that 2Th 1:10 3956
fulfil a the good pleasure of his 2Th 1:11 3956
above a that is called God 2Th 2:4 3956
the working of Satan with a power 2Th 2:9 3956
And with a deceivableness of 2Th 2:10 3956
That they a might be damned who 2Th 2:12 3956
for a men have not faith 2Th 3:2 3956
you disorderly, working not at a 2Th 3:11 3367
give you peace always by a means 2Th 3:16 3956
The Lord be with you a 2Th 3:16 3956
Lord Jesus Christ be with you a 2Th 3:18 3956
worthy of a acceptation, that 1Ti 1:15 3956
might shew forth a longsuffering 1Ti 1:16 3956
therefore, that, first of a 1Ti 2:1 3956
of thanks, be made for a men 1Ti 2:1 3956
for a that are in authority 1Ti 2:2 3956
and peaceable life in a godliness 1Ti 2:2 3956
Who will have a men to be saved, 1Ti 2:4
Who gave himself a ransom for a 1Ti 2:6 3956
in silence with a subjection 1Ti 2:11 3956
in subjection with a gravity 1Ti 3:4 3956
sober, faithful in a things 1Ti 3:11 3956
is profitable unto a things 1Ti 4:8 3956
saying and worthy of a acceptation 1Ti 4:9 3956
God, who is the Saviour of a men 1Ti 4:10 3956
thy profiting may appear to a 1Ti 4:15 3956
younger as sisters, with a purity 1Ti 5:2 3956
Them that sin rebuke before a 1Ti 5:20 3956
own masters worthy of a honour 1Ti 6:1 3956
of money is the root of a evil 1Ti 6:10 3956
of God, who quickeneth a things 1Ti 6:13 3956
us richly a things to enjoy 1Ti 6:17 3956
that a they which are in Asia be 2Ti 1:15 3956
thee understanding in a things 2Ti 2:7 3956
Therefore I endure a things for 2Ti 2:10 3956
but be gentle unto a men, apt to 2Ti 2:24 3956
shall be manifest unto a men 2Ti 3:9 3956
but out of them a the Lord 2Ti 3:11 3956
a that will live godly in Christ 2Ti 3:12 3956
A scripture is given by 2Ti 3:16 3956
furnished unto a good works 2Ti 3:17 3956
exhort with a longsuffering and 2Ti 4:2 3956
But watch thou in a things 2Ti 4:5 3956
but unto a them also that love 2Ti 4:8 3956
with me, but a men forsook me 2Ti 4:16 3956
that a the Gentiles might hear 2Ti 4:17 3956
and Claudia, and a the brethren 2Ti 4:21 3956
Unto the pure a things are pure Titus 1:15 3956
In a things shewing thyself a Titus 2:7 3956
to please them well in a things Titus 2:9 3956
but shewing a good fidelity Titus 2:10 3956
of God our Saviour in a things Titus 2:10 3956
salvation hath appeared to a men Titus 2:11 3956
might redeem us from a iniquity Titus 2:14 3956
and rebuke with a authority Titus 2:15 3956
shewing a meekness unto a men Titus 3:2 3956
A that are with me salute thee Titus 3:15 3956
Grace be with you a Titus 3:15 3956
Lord Jesus, and toward a saints Philem 5 3956
hath appointed heir of a things Heb 1:2 3956
upholding a things by the word of Heb 1:3 3956
let a the angels of God worship Heb 1:6 3956
they a shall wax old as doth a Heb 1:11 3956
Are they not a ministering Heb 1:14 3956
Thou hast put a things in Heb 2:8 3956
For in that he put a in Heb 2:8 3956
not yet a things put under him Heb 2:8 3956
became him, for whom are a things Heb 2:10 3956
and by whom are a things Heb 2:10 3956
who are sanctified are a of one Heb 2:11 3956
were a their lifetime subject to Heb 2:15 3956
Wherefore in a things it behoved Heb 2:17 3956
Moses was faithful in a his house Heb 3:2 3650
but he that built a things is God Heb 3:4 3956
was faithful in a his house Heb 3:5 3650
howbeit not a that came out of Heb 3:16 3956
the seventh day from a his works Heb 4:4 3956
but a things are naked and opened Heb 4:13 3956
but was in a points tempted like Heb 4:15 3956
unto a them that obey him Heb 5:9 3956
is to them an end of a strife Heb 6:16 3956
Abraham gave a tenth part of a Heb 7:2 3956
without a contradiction the less Heb 7:7 3956
that thou make a things according Heb 8:5 3956
for a shall know me, from the Heb 8:11 3956
which is called the Holiest of a Heb 9:3
of a was not yet made manifest Heb 9:8
it is of no strength at a while Heb 9:17 4219
had spoken every precept to a the Heb 9:19 3956
both the book, and a the people, Heb 9:19 3956
a the vessels of the ministry Heb 9:21 3956
almost a things are by the law Heb 9:22 3956
body of Jesus Christ once for a Heb 10:10 2178
These a died in faith, not having Heb 11:13 3956
And these a, having obtained a Heb 11:39 3956
whereof a are partakers, then are Heb 12:8 3956
Follow peace with a men, and Heb 12:14 3956

heaven, and to God the Judge of a ... Heb 12:23 3956
Marriage is honourable in a ... Heb 13:4 3956
in a things willing to live ... Heb 13:18 3956
Salute a them that have the rule ... Heb 13:24 3956
rule over you, and a the saints ... Heb 13:24 3956
Grace be with you a ... Heb 13:25 3956
count it a joy when ye fall into ... Jas 1:2 3956
that giveth to a men liberally ... Jas 1:5 3956
man is unstable in a his ways ... Jas 1:8 3956
Wherefore lay apart a filthiness ... Jas 1:21 3956
in one point, he is guilty of a ... Jas 2:10 3956
For in many things we offend a ... Jas 3:2 537
a such rejoicing is evil ... Jas 4:16 3956
But above a things, my brethren, ... Jas 5:12 3956
so be ye holy in a manner of ... 1Pet 1:15 3956
For a flesh is as grass ... 1Pet 1:24 3956
a the glory of man as the flower ... 1Pet 1:24 3956
Wherefore laying aside a malice ... 1Pet 2:1 3956
a guile, and hypocrisies ... 1Pet 2:1 3956
and envies, and a evil speakings, ... 1Pet 2:1 3956
Honour a men ... 1Pet 2:17 3956
to your masters with a fear ... 1Pet 2:18 3956
be ye a of one mind, having ... 1Pet 3:8 3956
But the end of a things is at ... 1Pet 4:7 3956
above a things have fervent ... 1Pet 4:8 3956
that God in a things may be ... 1Pet 4:11 3956
a of you be subject one to ... 1Pet 5:5 3956
Casting a your care upon him ... 1Pet 5:7 3956
But the God of a grace, who hath ... 1Pet 5:10 3956
Peace be with you a that are in ... 1Pet 5:14 3956
a things that pertain unto life ... 2Pet 1:3 3956
giving a diligence, add to your ... 2Pet 1:5
a things continue as they were ... 2Pet 3:4 3956
but that a should come to ... 2Pet 3:9
Seeing then that a these things ... 2Pet 3:11 3956
ye to be in a holy conversation ... 2Pet 3:11
As also in a his epistles, ... 2Pet 3:16 3956
and in him is no darkness at a ... 1Jn 1:5 3762
his Son cleanseth us from a sin ... 1Jn 1:7 3956
cleanse us from a unrighteousness ... 1Jn 1:9 3956
For a that is in the world, the ... 1Jn 2:16 3956
that they were not a of us ... 1Jn 2:19 3956
the Holy One, and ye know a things ... 1Jn 2:20 3956
teacheth you of a things, and is ... 1Jn 2:27 3956
our heart, and knoweth a things ... 1Jn 3:20 3956
A unrighteousness is sin ... 1Jn 5:17 3956
but also a they that have known ... 2Jn 1 3956
I wish above a things that thou ... 3Jn 2 3956
hath good report of a men ... 3Jn 12 3956
when I gave a diligence to write ... Jude 3 3956
To execute judgment upon a ... Jude 15 3956
to convince a that are ungodly ... Jude 15 3956
a their ungodly deeds which they ... Jude 15 3956
of a their hard speeches which ... Jude 15 3956
and of a things that he saw ... Rev 1:2 3745
a kindreds of the earth shall ... Rev 1:7 3956
a the churches shall know that I ... Rev 2:23 3956
which shall come upon a the world ... Rev 3:10 3650
for thou hast created a things ... Rev 4:11 3956
God sent forth into a the earth ... Rev 5:6 3956
a that are in them, heard I ... Rev 5:13 3956
four thousand of a the tribes of ... Rev 7:4 3956
of a nations, and kindreds, and ... Rev 7:9 3956
a the angels stood round about ... Rev 7:11 3956
God shall wipe away a tears from ... Rev 7:17 3956
of a saints upon the golden altar ... Rev 8:3 3956
a green grass was burnt up ... Rev 8:7 3956
to smite the earth with a plagues ... Rev 11:6 3956
who was to rule a nations with a ... Rev 12:5 3956
a the world wondered after the ... Rev 13:3 3650
was given him over a kindreds ... Rev 13:7 3956
a that dwell upon the earth shall ... Rev 13:8 3956
he exerciseth a the power of the ... Rev 13:12 3956
And he causeth a, both small and ... Rev 13:16 3956
because she made a nations drink ... Rev 14:8 3956
for a nations shall come and ... Rev 15:4 3956
For a nations have drunk of the ... Rev 18:3 3956
a thyine wood, and a manner ... Rev 18:12 3956
a manner vessels of most precious ... Rev 18:12 3956
a things which were dainty and ... Rev 18:14 3956
thou shalt find them no more at a ... Rev 18:14 3364
a the company in ships, and ... Rev 18:17 3956
wherein were made rich a that had ... Rev 18:19 3956
and shall be found no more at a ... Rev 18:21 3364
be heard no more at a in thee ... Rev 18:22 3364
be heard no more at a in thee ... Rev 18:22 3364
shall shine no more at a in thee ... Rev 18:23 3364
be heard no more at a in thee ... Rev 18:23 3364
sorceries were a nations deceived ... Rev 18:23 3956
of a that were slain upon the ... Rev 18:24 3956
a ye his servants, and ye that ... Rev 19:5 3956
saying to a the fowls that fly in ... Rev 19:17 3956
on them, and the flesh of a men ... Rev 19:18 3956
a the fowls were filled with ... Rev 19:21 3956
God shall wipe away a tears from ... Rev 21:4 3956
said, Behold, I make a things new ... Rev 21:5 3956
overcometh shall inherit a things ... Rev 21:7 3956
a liars, shall have their part in ... Rev 21:8 3956
with a manner of precious stones ... Rev 21:19 3956
it shall not be shut at a by day ... Rev 21:25 3364
Lord Jesus Christ be with you a ... Rev 22:21 3956

ALLAMMELECH See ALAMMELECH.

ALLEGING
Opening and a, that Christ must ... Acts 17:3 3908

ALLEGORY
Which things are an a ... Gal 4:24 238

ALLELUIA (al-le-loo'-yah) *Greek form of Hallelujah.*
much people in heaven, saying, A ... Rev 19:1 239
And again they said, A ... Rev 19:3 239
saying, Amen; A. ... Rev 19:4 239
of mighty thunderings, saying, A ... Rev 19:6 239

ALLIED
of our God, was a unto Tobiah ... Neh 13:4 7138

ALLON (al'-lon) See ALLON-BACHUTH, ELON.
1. A city in Naphtali.
from A to Zaanannim, and Adami, ... Josh 19:33 438
2. A chief of a Simeonite family.
the son of Shiphi, the son of A ... 1Chr 4:37 438

ALLON-BACHUTH (al'-lon-bak'-ooth) *A place near Bethel.*
and the name of it was called A ... Gen 35:8 439

ALLOW
ye a the deeds of your fathers ... Lk 11:48 4909
God, which they themselves also a ... Acts 24:15 4327
For that which I do I a not ... Rom 7:15 1097

ALLOWANCE
his a was a continual a ... 2Kin 25:30 737

ALLOWED
But as we were a of God to be put ... 1Th 2:4 1381

ALLOWETH
himself in that thing which he a ... Rom 14:22 1381

ALLURE
Therefore, behold, I will a her ... Hos 2:14 6601
they a through the lusts of the ... 2Pet 2:18 1185

ALMIGHTY *A term for God meaning sufficient or all-powerful.*
and said unto him, I am the A God ... Gen 17:1 7706
God A bless thee, and make thee ... Gen 28:3 7706
And God said unto him, I am God A ... Gen 35:11 7706
God A give you mercy before the ... Gen 43:14 7706
God A appeared unto me at Luz in ... Gen 48:3 7706
and by the A, who shall bless thee ... Gen 49:25 7706
unto Jacob, by the name of God A ... Ex 6:3 7706
which saw the vision of the A ... Num 24:4 7706
which saw the vision of the A ... Num 24:16 7706
for the A hath dealt very ... Ruth 1:20 7706
me, and the A hath afflicted me ... Ruth 1:21 7706
not thou the chastening of the A ... Job 5:17 7706
the arrows of the A are within me ... Job 6:4 7706
he forsaketh the fear of the A ... Job 6:14 7706
or doth the A pervert justice ... Job 8:3 7706
and make thy supplication to the A ... Job 8:5 7706
find out the A unto perfection ... Job 11:7 7706
Surely I would speak to the A ... Job 13:3 7706
himself against the A ... Job 15:25 7706
What is the A, that we should ... Job 21:15 7706
shall drink of the wrath of the A ... Job 21:20 7706
Is it any pleasure to the A ... Job 22:3 7706
and what can the A do for them ... Job 22:17 7706
If thou return to the A, thou ... Job 22:23 7706
the A shall be thy defence, and ... Job 22:25 7706
thou have thy delight in the A ... Job 22:26 7706
heart soft, and the A troubleth me ... Job 23:16 7706
times are not hidden from the A ... Job 24:1 7706
and the A, who hath vexed my soul ... Job 27:2 7706
Will he delight himself in the A ... Job 27:10 7706
is with the A will I not conceal ... Job 27:11 7706
which they shall receive of the A ... Job 27:13 7706
When the A was yet with me, when ... Job 29:5 7706
inheritance of the A from on high ... Job 31:2 7706
that the A would answer me, and ... Job 31:35 7706
the inspiration of the A giveth ... Job 32:8 7706
the breath of the A hath given me ... Job 33:4 7706
and from the A, that he should ... Job 34:10 7706
will the A pervert judgment ... Job 34:12 7706
neither will the A regard it ... Job 35:13 7706
Touching the A, we cannot find ... Job 37:23 7706
with the A instruct him ... Job 40:2 7706
When the A scattered kings in it, ... Ps 68:14 7706
abide under the shadow of the A ... Ps 91:1 7706
come as a destruction from the A ... Is 13:6 7706
waters, as the voice of the A ... Eze 1:24 7706
as the voice of the A God when he ... Eze 10:5 7706
from the A shall it come ... Joel 1:15 7706
and daughters, saith the Lord A ... 2Cor 6:18 3841
was, and which is to come, the A ... Rev 1:8 3841
Holy, holy, holy, Lord God A ... Rev 4:8 3841
We give thee thanks, O Lord God A ... Rev 11:17 3841
are thy works, Lord God A ... Rev 15:3 3841
altar say, Even so, Lord God A ... Rev 16:7 3841
battle of that great day of God A ... Rev 16:14 3841
the fierceness and wrath of A God ... Rev 19:15 3841
for the Lord God A and the Lamb ... Rev 21:22 3841

ALMODAD (al-mo'-dad) *A descendant of Shem.*
And Joktan begat A, and Sheleph, and Gen 10:26 486
And Joktan begat A, and Sheleph, and 1Chr 1:20 486

ALMON (al'-mon) *A Levitical town in Benjamin.*
suburbs, and A with her suburbs ... Josh 21:18 5960

ALMOND
the a tree shall flourish, and the ... Eccl 12:5 8247
I said, I see a rod of an a tree ... Jer 1:11 8247

ALMON-DIBLATHAIM (al'-mon-dib-lath-a'-im) *An encampment of Israel in the Wilderness.*
from Dibon-gad, and encamped in A ... Num 33:46 5963
And they removed from A, and ... Num 33:47 5963

ALMONDS
spices, and myrrh, nuts, and a ... Gen 43:11 8247
Three bowls made like unto a ... Ex 25:33 8246
made like a in the other branch ... Ex 25:33 8246
be four bowls made like unto a ... Ex 25:34 8246
the fashion of a in one branch ... Ex 37:19 8246
made like a in another branch ... Ex 37:19 8246
were four bowls made like a ... Ex 37:20 8246
and bloomed blossoms, and yielded a ... Num 17:8 8247

ALMOST
they be a ready to stone me ... Ex 17:4 4592
as for me, my feet were a gone ... Ps 73:2 4592
my soul had a dwelt in silence ... Ps 94:17 4592
They had a consumed me upon earth ... Ps 119:87 4592
I was a in all evil in the midst ... Prov 5:14 4592
the next sabbath day came a the ... Acts 13:44 4975
but a throughout all Asia, this ... Acts 19:26 4975
when the seven days were a ended ... Acts 21:27 3195
A thou persuadest me to be a ... Acts 26:28
hear me this day, were both a ... Acts 26:29
a all things are by the law ... Heb 9:22 4975

ALMS
that ye do not your a before men ... Mt 6:1 1654
Therefore when thou doest thine a ... Mt 6:2 1654
But when thou doest a, let not ... Mt 6:3 1654
That thine a may be in secret ... Mt 6:4 1654
But rather give a of such things ... Lk 11:41 1654
Sell that ye have, and give a ... Lk 12:33 1654
to ask a of them that entered ... Acts 3:2 1654
to go into the temple asked an a ... Acts 3:3 1654
a at the Beautiful gate of the ... Acts 3:10 1654
which gave much a to the people ... Acts 10:2 1654
thine a are come up for a ... Acts 10:4 1654
thine a are had in remembrance in ... Acts 10:31 1654
I came to bring a to my nation ... Acts 24:17 1654

ALMSDEEDS
of good works and a which she did ... Acts 9:36 1654

ALMUG
Ophir great plenty of a trees ... 1Kin 10:11 484
the king made of the a trees ... 1Kin 10:12 484
there came no such a trees ... 1Kin 10:12 484

ALOES
as the trees of lign a which the ... Num 24:6 174
thy garments smell of myrrh, and a ... Ps 45:8 174
perfumed my bed with myrrh, a ... Prov 7:17 174
myrrh and a, with all the chief ... Song 4:14 174
brought a mixture of myrrh and a ... Jn 19:39 250

ALONE
not good that the man should be a ... Gen 2:18 905
And Jacob was left a ... Gen 32:24 905
brother is dead, and he is left a ... Gen 42:38 905
he a is left of his mother, and ... Gen 44:20 905
thee in Egypt, saying, Let us a ... Ex 14:12 2308
why sittest thou thyself a ... Ex 18:14 905
not able to perform it thyself a ... Ex 18:18 905
Moses a shall come near the LORD ... Ex 24:2 905
Now therefore let me a, that my ... Ex 32:10
he shall dwell a ... Lev 13:46 909
able to bear all this people a ... Num 11:14 905
that thou bear it not thyself a ... Num 11:17 905
lo, the people shall dwell a ... Num 23:9 909
am not able to bear you myself a ... Deut 1:9 905
How can I myself a bear your ... Deut 1:12 905
Let me a, that I may destroy them ... Deut 9:14 7503
So the LORD a did lead him, and ... Deut 32:12 909
then shall dwell in safety a ... Deut 33:28 909
perished not a in his iniquity ... Josh 22:20 259
which he had for himself a ... Judg 3:20 905
let me a two months, that I may ... Judg 11:37 7503
and said unto him, Why art thou a ... 1Sa 21:1 905
let him a, and let him curse ... 2Sa 16:11
looked, and behold a man running a ... 2Sa 18:24 905
And the king said, If he be a ... 2Sa 18:25 905
Behold another man running a ... 2Sa 18:26 905
and they two were a in the field ... 1Kin 11:29 905
And the man of God said, Let her a ... 2Kin 4:27 7503
thou art the God, even thou a ... 2Kin 19:15 905
And he said, Let him a ... 2Kin 23:18
So they let his bones a, with the ... 2Kin 23:18 4422
whom a God hath chosen, is yet ... 1Chr 29:1 259
the work of this house of God a ... Ezr 6:7 7662
Thou, even thou, art LORD a ... Neh 9:6 905
scorn to lay hands on Mordecai a ... Est 3:6 905
I only am escaped a to tell thee ... Job 1:15 905
I only am escaped a to tell thee ... Job 1:16 905
I only am escaped a to tell thee ... Job 1:17 905
I only am escaped a to tell thee ... Job 1:19 905
let me a ... Job 7:16 2308
nor let me a till I swallow down ... Job 7:19 7503
Which a spreadeth out the heavens ... Job 9:8 905
cease then, and let me a, that I ... Job 10:20 7896
Hold your peace, let me a ... Job 13:13
Unto whom a the earth was given, ... Job 15:19 905
Or have eaten my morsel myself a ... Job 31:17 905
thou, whose name a is JEHOVAH ... Ps 83:18 905
thou art God a ... Ps 86:10 905
am as a sparrow a upon the house ... Ps 102:7 909
To him who a doeth great wonders ... Ps 136:4 905
for his name a is excellent ... Ps 148:13 905
scornest, thou a shalt bear it ... Prov 9:12 905
There is one a, and there is not a ... Eccl 4:8
to him that is a when he falleth ... Eccl 4:10 259
but how can one be warm a ... Eccl 4:11
the LORD a shall be exalted in ... Is 2:11 905
the LORD a shall be exalted in ... Is 2:17 905
that they may be placed a in the ... Is 5:8 905
none shall be a in his appointed ... Is 14:31 909
thou art the God, even thou a ... Is 37:16 905
stretcheth forth the heavens a ... Is 44:24 905
Behold, I was left a ... Is 49:21 905
for I called him a, and blessed ... Is 51:2 259
I have trodden the winepress a ... Is 63:3 905
I sat a because of thy hand ... Jer 15:17 909
gates nor bars, which dwell a ... Jer 49:31 909
He sitteth a and keepeth silence, ... Lam 3:28 905
I Daniel a saw the vision ... Dan 10:7 905
Therefore I was left a, and saw ... Dan 10:8 905
let him a ... Hos 4:17
Assyria, a wild ass a by himself ... Hos 8:9 909
Man shall not live by bread a ... Mt 4:4 3441

evening was come, he was there *a* ... Mt 14:23 3441
Let them *a* ... Mt 15:14 863
his fault between thee and him *a* ... Mt 18:15 3441
Saying, Let us *a* ... Mk 1:24 1439
And when he was *a*, they that were ... Mk 4:10 2651
and when they were *a*, he expounded.. Mk 4:34
of the sea, and he *a* on the land ... Mk 6:47 3441
And Jesus said, Let her *a* ... Mk 14:6 863
gave him to drink, saying, Let *a* ... Mk 15:36 863
man shall not live by bread *a* ... Lk 4:4 3441
Saying, Let us *a* ... Lk 4:34 1439
Who can forgive sins, but God *a* ... Lk 5:21 3441
to eat but for the priests *a* ... Lk 6:4 3441
came to pass, as he was *a* praying ... Lk 9:18 2651
voice was past, Jesus was found *a* ... Lk 9:36 3441
my sister hath left me to serve *a* ... Lk 10:40 3441
let it *a* this year also, till I ... Lk 13:8 863
again into a mountain himself *a* ... Jn 6:15 3441
his disciples were gone away *a* ... Jn 6:22 3441
and Jesus was left *a*, and the woman... Jn 8:9 3441
for I am not *a*, but I and the ... Jn 8:16 3441
the Father hath not left me *a* ... Jn 8:29 3441
If we let him thus *a*, all men ... Jn 11:48 863
Then said Jesus, Let her *a* ... Jn 12:7 863
the ground and die, it abideth *a* ... Jn 12:24 3441
to his own, and shall leave me *a* ... Jn 16:32 3441
and yet I am not *a*, because the ... Jn 16:32 3441
Neither pray I for these *a* ... Jn 17:20 3440
from these men, and let them *a* ... Acts 5:38 1439
that not *a* at Ephesus, but almost ... Acts 19:26 3440
it was not written for his sake *a* ... Rom 4:23 3440
and I am left *a*, and they seek my ... Rom 11:3 3441
he have rejoicing in himself *a* ... Gal 6:4 3441
it good to be left at Athens *a* ... 1Th 3:1 3441
the high priest *a* once every year ... Heb 9:7 3441
hath not works, is dead, being *a* ... Jas 2:17

ALONG

her maidens walked *a* by the ... Ex 2:5
the fire ran *a* upon the ground ... Ex 9:23
but we will go *a* by the king's ... Num 21:22
of Zin *a* by the coast of Edom ... Num 34:3
I will go *a* by the high way, I ... Deut 2:27
chased them *a* the way that goeth ... Josh 10:10
and passed *a* to Zin, and ascended ... Josh 15:3
passed *a* to Hezron, and went up to ... Josh 15:3
and passed *a* by the north of ... Josh 15:6
passed *a* unto the side of mount ... Josh 15:10
passed *a* to mount Baalah, and went ... Josh 15:11
passeth *a* unto the borders of ... Josh 16:2
the border went *a* on the right ... Josh 17:7
passed *a* toward the side over ... Josh 18:18
the border passed *a* to the side ... Josh 18:19
from thence passeth on *a* on the ... Josh 19:13
the children of the east lay *a* in ... Judg 7:12
it, that the tent lay *a* ... Judg 7:13
all that came *a* that way by them ... Judg 9:25
another company come *a* by the ... Judg 9:37
Then they went *a* through the ... Judg 11:18
that be *a* by the coasts of Arnon ... Judg 11:26
liers in wait drew themselves *a* ... Judg 20:37
went *a* the highway, lowing as ... 1Sa 6:12 1980
straightway all *a* on the earth ... 1Sa 28:20
her husband went with her *a* ... 2Sa 3:16 1980
Shimei went *a* on the hill's side ... 2Sa 16:13
a by the altar and the temple ... 2Kin 11:11
a by the altar and the temple, by ... 2Chr 23:10
them, weeping all *a* as he went ... Jer 41:6 1980

ALOOF

my friends stand *a* from my sore ... Ps 38:11 5048

ALOTH (*a'-loth*) See BEALOTH. *A region near Asher.*

of Hushai was in Asher and in *A* ... 1Kin 4:16 1175

ALOUD

And he wept *a* ... Gen 45:2
mocked them, and said, Cry *a* ... 1Kin 18:27
And they cried *a*, and cut ... 1Kin 18:28
and many shouted *a* for joy ... Ezr 3:12
I cry *a*, but there is no judgment ... Job 19:7 7768
shall sing *a* of thy righteousness ... Ps 51:14 7442
and at noon, will I pray, and cry *a* ... Ps 55:17 1993
I will sing *a* of thy mercy in the ... Ps 59:16 7442
Sing *a* unto God our strength ... Ps 81:1 7442
her saints shall shout *a* for joy ... Ps 132:16 7442
let them sing *a* upon their beds ... Ps 149:5 7442
they shall cry *a* from the sea ... Is 24:14 6670
forth into singing, and cry *a* ... Is 54:1 6670
Cry *a*, spare not, lift up thy ... Is 58:1 1627
Then an herald cried *a*, To you it ... Dan 3:4 2429
He cried *a*, and said thus, Hew ... Dan 4:14 2429
The king cried *a* to bring in the ... Dan 5:7 2429
cry *a* at Beth-aven, after thee, O ... Hos 5:8 7321
Now why dost thou cry out *a* ... Mic 4:9 7452
the multitude crying *a* began to ... Mk 15:8 310

ALPHA (*al'-fah*) *First letter of Greek alphabet.*

I am *A* and Omega, the beginning and Rev 1:8 1
Saying, I am *A* and Omega, the ... Rev 1:11 1
I am *A* and Omega, the beginning and Rev 21:6 1
I am *A* and Omega, the beginning and Rev 22:13 1

ALPHAEUS (*al-fe'-us*) See CLEOPAS.

1. Father of the apostle James.

James the son of *A*, and Lebbaeus ... Mt 10:3 256
and Thomas, and James the son of *A* .. Mk 3:18 256
and Thomas, James the son of *A* ... Lk 6:15 256
and Matthew, James the son of *A* ... Acts 1:13 256

2. Father of the apostle Levi.

he saw Levi the son of *A* sitting ... Mk 2:14 256

ALREADY

have offended against the LORD *a* ... 2Chr 28:13
are brought unto bondage *a* ... Neh 5:5
it hath been *a* of old time ... Eccl 1:10 3528
even that which hath been *a* done ... Eccl 2:12 3528
that which is to be hath *a* been ... Eccl 3:15 3528
I praised the dead which are *a* ... Eccl 4:2 3528
That which hath been is named *a* ... Eccl 6:10 3528
yea, I have cursed them *a* ... Mal 2:2
adultery with her *a* in his heart ... Mt 5:28 2235
unto you, That Elias is come *a* ... Mt 17:12 2235
marvelled if he were *a* dead ... Mk 15:44 2235
what will I, if it be *a* kindled ... Lk 12:49 2235
that believeth not is condemned *a* ... Jn 3:18 2235
for they are white *a* to harvest ... Jn 4:35 2235
for the Jews had agreed *a* ... Jn 9:22 2235
answered them, I have told you *a* ... Jn 9:27 2235
had lain in the grave four days *a* ... Jn 11:17 2235
Jesus, and saw that he was dead *a* ... Jn 19:33 2235
there were three men *a* come unto ... Acts 11:11
because the fast was now *a* past ... Acts 27:9 2235
present in spirit, have judged *a* ... 1Cor 5:3 2235
bewail many which have sinned *a* ... 2Cor 12:21 4258
Not as though I had *a* attained ... Phil 3:12 2235
attained, either were *a* perfect ... Phil 3:12 2235
whereto we have *a* attained ... Phil 3:16 5348
mystery of iniquity doth *a* work ... 2Th 2:7 2235
For some are *a* turned aside after ... 1Ti 5:15 2235
that the resurrection is past *a* ... 2Ti 2:18 2235
even now *a* is it in the world ... 1Jn 4:3 2235
ye have *a* hold fast till I come ... Rev 2:25

ALSO

he made the stars *a* ... Gen 1:16
the tree of life *a* in the midst ... Gen 2:9
gave *a* unto her husband with her ... Gen 3:6 1571
Thorns *a* and thistles shall it ... Gen 3:18
Unto Adam *a* and to his wife did ... Gen 3:21
take *a* of the tree of life, and ... Gen 3:22 1571
he *a* brought of the firstlings of ... Gen 4:4 1571
she *a* bare Tubal-cain, an ... Gen 4:22 1571
to him *a* there was born a son ... Gen 4:26 1571
with man, for that he *a* is flesh ... Gen 6:3 7683
a after that, when the sons of ... Gen 6:4 1571
The earth *a* was corrupt before ... Gen 6:11
Of fowls *a* of the air by sevens ... Gen 7:3 1571
The fountains *a* of the deep ... Gen 8:2
A he sent forth a dove from him ... Gen 8:8
Unto Shem *a*, the father of all ... Gen 10:21 1571
The princes *a* of Pharaoh saw her ... Gen 12:15
And Lot *a*, which went with Abram ... Gen 13:5 1571
then shall thy seed *a* be numbered ... Gen 13:16 1571
a the Amorites, that dwelt in ... Gen 14:7 1571
a brought again his brother Lot ... Gen 14:16 1571
and his goods, and the women *a* ... Gen 14:16 1571
a that nation, whom they shall ... Gen 15:14 1571
Have I *a* here looked after him ... Gen 16:13 1571
her, and give thee a son *a* of her ... Gen 17:16 1571
pleasure, my lord being old *a* ... Gen 18:12
Wilt thou *a* destroy the righteous ... Gen 18:23 637
wilt thou *a* destroy and not spare ... Gen 18:24 637
thee concerning this thing *a* ... Gen 19:21 1571
make him drink wine this night *a* ... Gen 19:34 1571
father drink wine that night *a* ... Gen 19:35 1571
she *a* bare a son, and called his ... Gen 19:38 1571
wilt thou slay *a* a righteous ... Gen 20:4 1571
for I *a* withheld thee from ... Gen 20:6
a of the son of the bondwoman ... Gen 21:13
she hath *a* born children unto thy ... Gen 22:20
name was Reumah, she bare *a* Tebah .. Gen 22:24
and I will give thy camels drink *a* ... Gen 24:14
will draw water for thy camels *a* ... Gen 24:19
I will *a* draw for thy camels ... Gen 24:44 1571
and I will give thy camels drink *a* ... Gen 24:46 1571
and she made the camels drink *a* ... Gen 24:46 1571
he gave *a* to her brother and to ... Gen 24:53
well, and strove for that *a* ... Gen 26:21 1571
he *a* had made savoury meat, and ... Gen 27:31 1571
his father, Bless me, even me *a* ... Gen 27:34 1571
bless me, even me *a*, O my father ... Gen 27:38 1571
deprived *a* of you both in one day ... Gen 27:45 1571
we will give thee this *a* for the ... Gen 29:27 1571
him Rachel his daughter to wife *a* ... Gen 29:28
he went in *a* unto Rachel ... Gen 29:30 1571
he loved *a* Rachel more than Leah ... Gen 29:30 1571
therefore given me this son *a* ... Gen 29:33 1571
that I may *a* have children by her ... Gen 30:3 1571
hath *a* heard my voice, and hath ... Gen 30:6 1571
take away my son's mandrakes *a* ... Gen 30:15 1571
I provide for mine own house *a* ... Gen 30:30 1571
hath quite devoured *a* our money ... Gen 31:15 1571
a he cometh to meet thee, and four ... Gen 32:6 1571
and, behold, *a* he is behind us ... Gen 32:18 1571
Leah *a* with her children came ... Gen 33:7 1571
thou shalt have this son *a* ... Gen 35:17 1571
sheaf arose, and *a* stood upright ... Gen 37:7 1571
wherefore he slew him *a* ... Gen 38:10 1571
said, Lest peradventure he die *a* ... Gen 38:11 1571
a the men of the place said, that ... Gen 38:22 1571
and *a*, behold, she is with child ... Gen 38:24 1571
here *a* have I done nothing that ... Gen 40:15 1571
I *a* was in my dream, and, behold ... Gen 40:16 637
behold, *a* his blood is required ... Gen 42:22 1571
we, and thou, and *a* our little ones ... Gen 43:8 1571
Take *a* your brother, and arise, go ... Gen 43:13
we *a* will be my lord's bondmen ... Gen 44:9 1571
Now *a* let it be according unto ... Gen 44:10 1571
he *a* with whom the cup is found ... Gen 44:16 1571
And if ye take this *a* from me ... Gen 44:29 1571
A regard not your stuff ... Gen 45:20
I will *a* surely bring thee up ... Gen 46:4 1571
now, both we, and *a* our fathers ... Gen 46:34 1571
both we, and *a* our fathers ... Gen 47:3 1571
my lord *a* hath our herds of ... Gen 47:18
lo, God hath shewed me *a* thy seed ... Gen 48:11 1571
he *a* shall become a people ... Gen 48:19 1571
and he *a* shall be great ... Gen 48:19 1571
And his brethren *a* went and fell ... Gen 50:18 1571
the children *a* of Machir the son ... Gen 50:23 1571
they join *a* unto our enemies, and ... Ex 1:10 1571
a drew water enough for us, and ... Ex 2:19 1571
I have *a* seen the oppression ... Ex 3:9 1571
not believe *a* these two signs ... Ex 4:9 1571
And *a*, behold, he cometh forth to ... Ex 4:14 1571
I have *a* established my covenant ... Ex 6:4 1571
I have *a* heard the groaning of ... Ex 6:5 1571
Then Pharaoh *a* called the wise ... Ex 7:11 1571
they *a* did in like manner with ... Ex 7:11 1571
did he set his heart to this *a* ... Ex 7:23 1571
a the ground whereon they are ... Ex 8:21 1571
hardened his heart at this time *a* ... Ex 8:32 1571
your little ones *a* go with you ... Ex 10:24 1571
Thou must give us *a* sacrifices ... Ex 10:25 1571
Our cattle *a* shall go with us ... Ex 10:26 1571
A take your flocks and your herds ... Ex 12:32 1571
and bless me *a* ... Ex 12:32 1571
multitude went up *a* with them ... Ex 12:38 1571
his chosen captains *a* are drowned ... Ex 15:4
all this people shall *a* go to ... Ex 18:23 1571
And let the priests *a*, which come ... Ex 19:22 1571
he shall *a* bring him to the door ... Ex 21:6
his owner *a* shall be put to death ... Ex 21:29 1571
the dead ox *a* they shall divide ... Ex 21:35 1571
A thou shalt not oppress a ... Ex 23:9
a they saw God, and did eat and ... Ex 24:11
Thou shalt *a* make a table of ... Ex 25:23
Thou shalt *a* take one ram ... Ex 29:15
A thou shalt take of the ram the ... Ex 29:22
I will sanctify *a* both Aaron ... Ex 29:44
Thou shalt *a* make a laver of ... Ex 30:18
and his foot *a* of brass ... Ex 30:18
Take thou *a* unto thee principal ... Ex 30:23
Speak thou *a* unto the children of ... Ex 31:13
thou hast *a* found grace in my ... Ex 33:12 1571
I will do this thing *a* that thou ... Ex 33:17 1571
The candlestick *a* for the light ... Ex 35:14
A he made thereunto a border of ... Ex 37:12
a he made unto it a crown of gold ... Ex 37:26
he *a* shall be unclean, and guilty ... Lev 5:2
on the morrow *a* the remainder of ... Lev 7:16
a he put in the breastplate the ... Lev 8:8
a upon the mitre, even upon his ... Lev 8:9
A a bullock and a ram for peace ... Lev 9:4
He slew *a* the bullock and the ram ... Lev 9:18
These *a* shall be unclean unto you ... Lev 11:29
he *a* that beareth the carcase of ... Lev 11:40
The flesh *a*, in which, even in ... Lev 13:18
If a man *a* or a woman have in the ... Lev 13:38
The garment *a* that the plague of ... Lev 13:47
a he shall wash his flesh in ... Lev 14:9
The woman *a* with whom man shall ... Lev 15:18
every thing *a* that she sitteth ... Lev 15:20
A thou shalt not approach unto a ... Lev 18:19
That the land spue not you out *a* ... Lev 18:28
If a man *a* lie with mankind, as ... Lev 20:13
A man *a* or woman that hath a ... Lev 20:27
If the priest's daughter *a* be ... Lev 22:12
A on the tenth day of this ... Lev 23:27 389
A in the fifteenth day of the ... Lev 23:39 389
I *a* will do this unto you ... Lev 26:16 637
I will *a* send wild beasts among ... Lev 26:22
Then will I *a* walk contrary unto ... Lev 26:24 637
walk contrary unto you *a* in fury ... Lev 26:28
a in the iniquities of their ... Lev 26:39 637
that *a* they have walked contrary ... Lev 26:40 637
that I *a* have walked contrary ... Lev 26:41 637
a my covenant with Isaac, and *a* ... Lev 26:42 637
The land *a* shall be left of them ... Lev 26:43
These *a* are the generations of ... Num 3:1
Take *a* the sum of the sons of ... Num 4:22 1571
shall offer *a* his meat offering ... Num 6:17
Israel *a* keep the passover at his ... Num 9:2
A in the day of your gladness, and ... Num 10:10
children of Israel *a* wept again ... Num 11:4 1571
Moses *a* was displeased ... Num 11:10
hath he not spoken *a* by us ... Num 12:2 1571
and *a* for the stranger that ... Num 15:15
and seek ye the priesthood *a* ... Num 16:10 1571
thou *a*, and Aaron, each of you his ... Num 16:17
Lest the earth swallow us up *a* ... Num 16:34
thy brethren *a* of the tribe of ... Num 18:2 1571
that neither they, nor ye *a* ... Num 18:3 1571
I *a* have given thee the charge of ... Num 18:8
Thus ye *a* shall offer an heave ... Num 18:28 1571
drank, and their beasts *a* ... Num 20:11
tarry ye *a* here this night, that ... Num 22:19 1571
surely now *a* I had slain thee, and ... Num 22:33 1571
Spake I not *a* to thy messengers ... Num 24:12 1571
Seir *a* shall be a possession for ... Num 24:18
he *a* shall perish for ever ... Num 24:24 1571
and Balak *a* went his way ... Num 24:25 1571
thou *a* shalt be gathered unto thy ... Num 27:13 1571
A in the day of the firstfruits ... Num 28:26
If a woman *a* vow a vow unto the ... Num 30:3
Balaam *a* the son of Beor they ... Num 31:8
upon their gods *a* the LORD ... Num 33:4
ye shall give *a* unto the Levites ... Num 35:2
A the LORD was angry with me for ... Deut 1:37 1571
Thou *a* shalt not go in thither ... Deut 1:37 1571
ye shall *a* buy water of them for ... Deut 2:6 1571
Which *a* were accounted giants, as ... Deut 2:11 637
The Horims *a* dwelt in Seir ... Deut 2:12
(That *a* was accounted a land of ... Deut 2:20 637
God delivered into our hands Og *a* ... Deut 3:3 1571
The plain *a*, and Jordan, and the ... Deut 3:17
until they *a* possess the land ... Deut 3:20 1571
he will *a* bless the fruit of thy ... Deut 7:13
Thou shalt *a* consider in thine ... Deut 8:5
A in Horeb ye provoked the LORD ... Deut 9:8
hearkened unto me at that time *a* ... Deut 9:19 1571
prayed for Aaron *a* the same time ... Deut 9:20 1571
hearkened unto me at that time *a* ... Deut 10:10 1571

Context	Reference	Number
the LORD's thy God, the earth *a*	Deut 10:14	
a unto thy maidservant thou shalt	Deut 15:17	637
The firstfruit *a* of thy corn	Deut 18:4	
let him *a* go and return unto his	Deut 20:6	
have a place *a* without the camp	Deut 23:12	
a have given them unto the Levite	Deut 26:13	1571
which *a* shall not leave thee	Deut 28:51	
A every sickness, and every plague	Deut 28:61	1571
a with him that is not here with	Deut 29:15	
a the LORD hath said unto me,	Deut 31:2	
I will *a* send the teeth of beasts	Deut 32:24	
the suckling *a* with the man of	Deut 32:25	
a his heavens shall drop down dew	Deut 33:28	637
they *a* have possessed the land	Josh 1:15	1571
that ye will *a* shew kindness unto	Josh 2:12	1571
they have *a* transgressed my	Josh 7:11	1571
have *a* stolen, and dissembled *a*	Josh 7:11	1571
And the LORD delivered it *a*	Josh 10:30	1571
as he had done *a* to Libnah	Josh 10:39	
a the Avites	Josh 13:3	
Balaam *a* the son of Beor, the	Josh 13:22	
give me *a* springs of water	Josh 15:19	
There was *a* a lot for the tribe	Josh 17:1	
There was *a* a lot for the rest of	Josh 17:2	
the coast of Manasseh *a* was on	Josh 17:9	
Ummah *a*, and Aphek, and Rehob	Josh 19:30	
The LORD *a* spake unto Joshua,	Josh 20:1	
sent them away *a* unto their tents	Josh 22:7	1571
I sent Moses *a* and Aaron, and I	Josh 24:5	
will we *a* serve the LORD	Josh 24:18	1571
give me *a* springs of water	Judg 1:15	
A Judah took Gaza with the coast	Judg 1:18	
they *a* went up against Beth-el	Judg 1:22	1571
Wherefore I *a* said, I will not	Judg 2:3	1571
a all that generation were	Judg 2:10	1571
I *a* will not henceforth drive out	Judg 2:21	1571
the haft *a* went in after the	Judg 3:22	1571
and he *a* delivered Israel	Judg 3:31	1571
the clouds *a* dropped water	Judg 5:4	1571
even Issachar, and *a* Barak	Judg 5:15	3651
who *a* was gathered after him	Judg 6:35	1571
then blow ye the trumpets *a* on	Judg 7:18	1571
he spake *a* unto the men of Penuel	Judg 8:9	1571
and thy son, and thy son's son *a*	Judg 8:22	1571
she *a* bare him a son, whose name	Judg 8:31	1571
remember *a* that I am your bone and	Judg 9:2	
and let him *a* rejoice in you	Judg 9:19	1571
of the tower of Shechem died *a*	Judg 9:49	1571
Jordan to fight *a* against Judah	Judg 10:9	1571
our God, and *a* served Baalim	Judg 10:10	
The Zidonians *a*, and the	Judg 10:12	1571
a the standing corn, with the	Judg 15:5	5704
spakest of *a* in mine ears, behold	Judg 17:2	1571
his concubine *a* was with him	Judg 19:10	
which was *a* of mount Ephraim	Judg 19:16	
wine *a* for me, and for thy	Judg 19:19	1571
a they set on fire all the cities	Judg 20:48	
and Chilion died *a* both of them	Ruth 1:5	1571
should have an husband *a* to night	Ruth 1:12	
and should *a* bear sons	Ruth 1:12	1571
the LORD do so to me, and more *a*	Ruth 1:17	3541
let fall *a* some of the handfuls	Ruth 2:16	1571
Moabitess said, He said unto me *a*	Ruth 2:21	
A he said, Bring the vail that	Ruth 3:15	
thou must buy it *a* of Ruth the	Ruth 4:5	
her adversary *a* provoked her sore	1Sa 1:6	1571
Therefore *a* I have lent him to	1Sa 1:28	1571
A before they burnt the fat, the	1Sa 2:15	1571
both with the LORD, and *a* with men	1Sa 2:26	1571
I begin, I will *a* make an end	1Sa 3:12	
God do so to thee, and more *a*	1Sa 3:17	3541
there hath been *a* a great	1Sa 4:17	1571
the people, and thy two sons *a*	1Sa 4:17	1571
gods, so do they *a* unto thee	1Sa 8:8	1571
That we *a* may be like all the	1Sa 8:20	1571
Is Saul *a* among the prophets	1Sa 10:11	1571
Is Saul *a* among the prophets	1Sa 10:12	1571
Saul *a* went home to Gibeah	1Sa 10:26	1571
a the king that reigneth over you	1Sa 12:14	1571
and that Israel *a* was had in	1Sa 13:4	1571
they *a* trembled, and the earth	1Sa 14:15	1571
even they *a* turned to be with the	1Sa 14:21	1571
even they *a* followed hard after	1Sa 14:22	1571
answered, God do so and more *a*	1Sa 14:44	3541
Samuel *a* said unto Saul, The LORD	1Sa 15:1	
he hath *a* rejected thee from	1Sa 15:23	
a the Strength of Israel will not	1Sa 15:29	1571
a he armed him with a coat of	1Sa 17:38	
a in the sight of Saul's servants	1Sa 18:5	1571
Saul *a* sent messengers unto	1Sa 19:11	
of Saul, and they *a* prophesied	1Sa 19:20	1571
third time, and they prophesied *a*	1Sa 19:21	1571
Then went he *a* to Ramah, and came	1Sa 19:22	1571
the Spirit of God was upon him *a*	1Sa 19:23	1571
And he stript off his clothes *a*	1Sa 19:24	1571
Is Saul *a* among the prophets	1Sa 19:24	1571
But *a* thou shalt not cut off thy	1Sa 20:15	
their hand *a* is with David	1Sa 22:17	1571
that *a* Saul my father knoweth	1Sa 23:17	1571
Saul *a* and his men went to seek	1Sa 23:25	
David *a* arose afterward, and went	1Sa 24:8	
David *a* girded on his sword	1Sa 25:13	1571
more *a* do God unto the enemies of	1Sa 25:22	3541
David *a* took Ahinoam of Jezreel	1Sa 25:43	
they were *a* both of them his	1Sa 25:43	
things, and *a* shalt still prevail	1Sa 26:25	1571
Moreover the LORD will *a* deliver	1Sa 28:19	1571
the LORD *a* shall deliver the host	1Sa 28:19	1571
hearken thou *a* unto the voice of	1Sa 28:22	1571
whom they had made *a* to abide at	1Sa 30:21	
many of the people *a* are fallen	2Sa 1:4	1571
and Jonathan his son are dead *a*	2Sa 1:4	1571
(*A* he bade them teach the	2Sa 1:18	
up thither, and his two wives *a*	2Sa 2:2	1571
I *a* will requite you this	2Sa 2:6	1571
a the house of Judah have	2Sa 2:7	1571
Joab *a* and Abishai pursued after	2Sa 2:24	
So do God to Abner, and more *a*	2Sa 3:9	3541
saying *a*, Make thy league with me	2Sa 3:12	
Abner *a* spake in the ears of	2Sa 3:19	1571
Abner went *a* to speak in the ears	2Sa 3:19	1571
So do God to me, and more *a*	2Sa 3:35	3541
(for Beeroth *a* was reckoned to	2Sa 4:2	1571
A in time past, when Saul was	2Sa 5:2	1571
Ibhar *a*, and Elishua, and Nepheg,	2Sa 5:15	
The Philistines *a* came and spread	2Sa 5:18	
A the LORD telleth thee that he	2Sa 7:11	
but thou hast spoken *a* of thy	2Sa 7:19	1571
David smote *a* Hadadezer, the son	2Sa 8:3	
Which *a* king David did dedicate	2Sa 8:11	
then fled they *a* before Abishai	2Sa 10:14	
to Uriah, Tarry here to day *a*	2Sa 11:12	1571
and Uriah the Hittite died *a*	2Sa 11:17	1571
Uriah the Hittite is dead *a*	2Sa 11:21	1571
Uriah the Hittite is dead *a*	2Sa 11:24	1571
The LORD *a* hath put away thy sin	2Sa 12:13	1571
the child *a* that is born unto	2Sa 12:14	1571
and the king *a* and all his servants	2Sa 13:36	1571
and we will destroy the heir *a*	2Sa 14:7	1571
Wherefore goest thou *a* with us	2Sa 15:19	1571
art a stranger, and *a* an exile	2Sa 15:19	1571
even there *a* will thy servant be	2Sa 15:21	
the king *a* himself passed over	2Sa 15:23	
And lo Zadok *a*, and all the Levites	2Sa 15:24	1571
The king said *a* unto Zadok the	2Sa 15:27	
so will I now *a* be thy servant	2Sa 15:34	
Call now Hushai the Archite *a*	2Sa 17:5	1571
he *a* that is valiant, whose heart	2Sa 17:10	1571
surely go forth with you myself *a*	2Sa 18:2	1571
I pray thee, *a* run after Cushi	2Sa 18:22	1571
king said, He *a* bringeth tidings	2Sa 18:26	1571
God do so to me, and more *a*	2Sa 19:13	3541
a half the people of Israel	2Sa 19:40	1571
we have *a* more right in David	2Sa 19:43	1571
together, and went *a* after him	2Sa 20:14	637
Ira *a* the Jairite was a chief	2Sa 20:26	1571
he *a* was born to the giant	2Sa 21:20	1571
He bowed the heavens *a*, and came	2Sa 22:10	
me forth *a* into a large place	2Sa 22:20	
I was *a* upright before him, and	2Sa 22:24	
Thou hast *a* given me the shield	2Sa 22:36	
Thou *a* hast delivered me from the	2Sa 22:44	
thou *a* hast lifted me up on high	2Sa 22:49	
he went down *a* and slew a lion in	2Sa 23:20	
he *a* was a very goodly man	1Kin 1:6	1571
I *a* will come in after thee, and	1Kin 1:14	
Nathan the prophet *a* came in	1Kin 1:22	
The king *a* said unto them, Take	1Kin 1:33	
a Solomon sitteth on the throne	1Kin 1:46	1571
a thus said the king, Blessed be	1Kin 1:48	1571
Moreover thou knowest *a* what Joab	1Kin 2:5	1571
ask for him the kingdom *a*	1Kin 2:22	
God do so to me, and more *a*	1Kin 2:23	3541
I have *a* given thee that which	1Kin 3:13	1571
that this woman was delivered *a*	1Kin 3:18	1571
to him *a* pertained the region of	1Kin 4:13	
he *a* took Basmath the daughter of	1Kin 4:15	1571
Barley *a* and straw for the horses	1Kin 4:28	
he spake *a* of beasts, and of fowl,	1Kin 4:33	
a the whole altar that was by the	1Kin 6:22	
The two doors *a* were of olive	1Kin 6:32	
So *a* made he for the door of the	1Kin 6:33	
He built *a* the house of the	1Kin 7:2	
Solomon made *a* an house for	1Kin 7:8	
pillars had pomegranates *a* above	1Kin 7:20	1571
a upon the mouth of it were	1Kin 7:31	1571
thou spakest *a* with thy mouth, and	1Kin 8:24	
Israel *a* were not able utterly to	1Kin 9:21	
And the navy *a* of Hiram, that	1Kin 10:11	1571
and for the king's house, harps *a*	1Kin 10:12	
my father *a* chastised you with	1Kin 12:14	
The altar *a* was rent, and the	1Kin 13:5	
them they told *a* to their father	1Kin 13:11	
him, I am a prophet *a* as thou art	1Kin 13:18	1571
the lion *a* stood by the carcase	1Kin 13:24	
For they *a* built them high places	1Kin 14:23	1571
there were *a* sodomites in the	1Kin 14:24	1571
a Maachah his mother, even her he	1Kin 15:13	1571
a by the hand of the prophet Jehu	1Kin 16:7	1571
and hath *a* slain the king	1Kin 16:16	1571
hast thou *a* brought evil upon the	1Kin 17:20	
he filled the trench *a* with water	1Kin 18:35	1571
let the gods do to me, and more *a*	1Kin 19:2	3541
thy wives *a* and thy children, even	1Kin 20:3	
The gods do so unto me, and more *a*	1Kin 20:10	3541
killed, and *a* taken possession	1Kin 21:19	1571
of Jezebel *a* spake the LORD,	1Kin 21:23	1571
shalt persuade him, and prevail *a*	1Kin 22:22	1571
Again *a* he sent unto him another	2Kin 1:11	
He took up *a* the mantle of Elijah	2Kin 2:13	
when he *a* had smitten the waters,	2Kin 2:14	
the Moabites *a* into your hand	2Kin 3:18	
he was *a* a mighty man in valour,	2Kin 5:1	
more *a* to me, if the head of	2Kin 6:31	3541
and if we sit still here, we die *a*	2Kin 7:4	
another tent, and carried thence *a*	2Kin 7:8	
it shall *a* come upon the land	2Kin 8:1	1571
Smite him *a* in the chariot	2Kin 9:27	1571
and horses, a fenced city *a*	2Kin 10:2	
was over the city, the elders *a*	2Kin 10:5	
between the king *a* and the people	2Kin 11:17	
remained the grove *a* in Samaria	2Kin 13:6	1571
he brought *a* the brasen altar,	2Kin 16:14	
A Judah kept not the commandments	2Kin 17:19	1571
His mother's name *a* was Abi	2Kin 18:2	
hath made Judah *a* to sin with his	2Kin 21:11	1571
I *a* have heard thee, saith the	2Kin 22:19	1571
them *a* that burned incense unto	2Kin 23:5	
all the houses *a* of the high	2Kin 23:19	1571
remove Judah *a* out of my sight	2Kin 23:27	1571
a for the innocent blood that he	2Kin 24:4	1571
The Jebusite *a*, and the Amorite,	1Chr 1:14	
Hadoram *a*, and Uzal, and Diklah,	1Chr 1:21	
Hadad died *a*	1Chr 1:51	
The sons *a* of Hezron, that were	1Chr 2:9	
Jerahmeel had *a* another wife	1Chr 2:26	
She bare *a* Shaaph the father of	1Chr 2:49	1571
Ibhar *a*, and Elishama, and	1Chr 3:6	
Malchiram *a*, and Pedaiah, and	1Chr 3:18	
The sons *a* of Aaron	1Chr 6:3	
Their brethren *a* the Levites were	1Chr 6:48	
they gave *a* Gezer with her	1Chr 6:67	
Kedemoth *a* with her suburbs, and	1Chr 6:79	
The sons *a* of Jediael	1Chr 7:10	
Shuppim *a*, and Huppim, the	1Chr 7:12	
a Resheph, and Telah his son, and	1Chr 7:25	
Shechem *a* and the towns thereof,	1Chr 7:28	
Beriah *a*, and Shema, who were	1Chr 8:13	
Ishmerai *a*, and Jezliah, and Jobab,	1Chr 8:18	
these *a* dwelt with their brethren	1Chr 8:32	637
Some of them *a* were appointed to	1Chr 9:29	
they *a* dwelt with their brethren	1Chr 9:38	637
a for asking counsel of one that	1Chr 10:13	1571
These *a* are the chief of the	1Chr 11:10	
a he went down and slew a lion in	1Chr 11:22	
A the valiant men of the armies	1Chr 11:26	
all the rest *a* of Israel were of	1Chr 12:38	1571
with them *a* to the priests and	1Chr 13:2	
David *a* had upon him an ephod of	1Chr 15:27	
Benaiah *a* and Jahaziel the priests	1Chr 16:6	
he *a* is to be feared above all	1Chr 16:25	
the world *a* shall be stable, that	1Chr 16:30	637
Obed-edom *a* the son of Jeduthun	1Chr 16:38	
A I will ordain a place for my	1Chr 17:9	
for thou hast *a* spoken of thy	1Chr 17:17	
David *a* houghed all the chariot	1Chr 18:4	
Them *a* king David dedicated unto	1Chr 18:11	1571
he brought *a* exceeding much spoil	1Chr 20:2	
he *a* was the son of the giant	1Chr 20:6	1571
the oxen *a* for burnt offerings	1Chr 21:23	
A cedar trees in abundance	1Chr 22:4	
timber *a* and stone have I prepared	1Chr 22:14	
David *a* commanded all the princes	1Chr 22:17	
And *a* unto the Levites	1Chr 23:26	1571
The sons *a* of Mushi	1Chr 24:30	
A unto Shemaiah his son were sons	1Chr 26:6	
A Hosah, of the children of	1Chr 26:10	
course was Mikloth *a* the ruler	1Chr 27:4	
Over the camels *a* was Obil the	1Chr 27:30	
A Jonathan David's uncle was a	1Chr 27:32	
A for the courses of the priests	1Chr 28:13	
silver *a* for all instruments of	1Chr 28:14	
and *a* for the lamps thereof,	1Chr 28:15	
A pure gold for the fleshhooks,	1Chr 28:17	
a the princes and all the people	1Chr 28:21	
David the king *a* rejoiced with	1Chr 29:9	1571
I know *a*, my God, that thou	1Chr 29:17	
Send me *a* cedar trees, fir trees,	2Chr 2:8	
a to grave any manner of graving,	2Chr 2:14	
He overlaid *a* the house, the	2Chr 3:7	
the other wing was five cubits *a*	2Chr 3:12	
A he made before the house two	2Chr 3:15	
A he made a molten sea of ten	2Chr 4:2	
He made *a* ten lavers, and put five	2Chr 4:6	
He made *a* ten tables, and placed	2Chr 4:8	
He made *a* bases, and lavers made	2Chr 4:14	
The pots *a*, and the shovels, and	2Chr 4:16	
house of God, the golden altar *a*	2Chr 4:19	
A king Solomon, and all the	2Chr 5:6	
A the Levites which were the	2Chr 5:12	
the Levites *a* with instruments of	2Chr 7:6	
A at the same time Solomon kept	2Chr 7:8	
A he built Beth-horon the upper,	2Chr 8:5	
the porters *a* by their courses at	2Chr 8:14	
his cupbearers *a*, and their	2Chr 9:4	
And the servants *a* of Huram	2Chr 9:10	1571
therefore have I *a* left you in	2Chr 12:5	
he carried away *a* the shields of	2Chr 12:9	
a in Judah things went well	2Chr 12:12	1571
His mother's name *a* was Michaiah	2Chr 13:2	
Jeroboam *a* set the battle in	2Chr 13:3	
the shewbread *a* set they in order	2Chr 13:11	
A he took away out of all the	2Chr 14:5	
They smote *a* the tents of cattle,	2Chr 14:15	1571
a concerning Maachah the mother	2Chr 15:16	1571
A in the third year of his reign	2Chr 17:7	
A some of the Philistines brought	2Chr 17:11	
him, and thou shalt *a* prevail	2Chr 18:21	1571
a the Levites shall be officers	2Chr 19:11	
It came to pass after this *a*	2Chr 20:1	
divers *a* of the princes of Israel	2Chr 21:4	1571
The same time *a* did Libnah revolt	2Chr 21:10	
a hast slain thy brethren of thy	2Chr 21:13	1571
the king's house, and his sons *a*	2Chr 21:17	1571
His mother's name *a* was Athaliah	2Chr 22:2	
He *a* walked in the ways of the	2Chr 22:3	1571
He walked *a* after their counsel,	2Chr 22:5	1571
a the singers with instruments of	2Chr 23:13	1571
A Jehoiada appointed the offices	2Chr 23:18	
His mother's name *a* was Zibiah of	2Chr 24:1	
a all the dedicated things of the	2Chr 24:7	1571
a such as wrought iron and brass	2Chr 24:12	1571
the LORD, he hath *a* forsaken you	2Chr 24:20	
He hired *a* an hundred thousand	2Chr 25:6	
the king's house, the hostages *a*	2Chr 25:24	
His mother's name *a* was Jecoliah	2Chr 26:3	
A he built towers in the desert,	2Chr 26:10	
husbandmen *a*, and vine dressers in	2Chr 26:10	
yea, himself hasted *a* to go out	2Chr 26:20	1571
His mother's name *a* was Jerushah	2Chr 27:1	
He fought *a* with the king of the	2Chr 27:5	
made *a* molten images for Baalim	2Chr 28:2	1571

Context	Reference	Number
He sacrificed *a* and burnt incense	2Chr 28:4	
he was *a* delivered into the hand	2Chr 28:5	
took *a* away much spoil from them,	2Chr 28:8	1571
The Philistines *a* had invaded the	2Chr 28:18	
the villages thereof, Gimzo *a*	2Chr 28:18	
A they have shut up the doors of	2Chr 29:7	1571
they killed *a* the lambs, and they	2Chr 29:22	
LORD began *a* with the trumpets	2Chr 29:27	
a the burnt offerings were in	2Chr 29:35	1571
and wrote letters *a* to Ephraim	2Chr 30:1	1571
A in Judah the hand of God was to	2Chr 30:12	1571
Judah and Benjamin, in Ephraim *a*	2Chr 31:1	
He appointed *a* the king's portion	2Chr 31:3	
they *a* brought in the tithe of	2Chr 31:6	1571
A of the sons of Aaron the	2Chr 31:19	
A he strengthened himself, and	2Chr 32:5	
He wrote *a* letters to rail on the	2Chr 32:17	
Storehouses *a* for the increase of	2Chr 32:28	
This same Hezekiah *a* stopped the	2Chr 32:30	
A he built altars in the house of	2Chr 33:4	
a he observed times, and used	2Chr 33:6	
His prayer *a*, and how God was	2Chr 33:19	
A they were over the bearers of	2Chr 34:13	
I have even heard thee *a*, saith	2Chr 34:27	1571
Conaniah *a*, and Shemaiah and	2Chr 35:9	
Nebuchadnezzar *a* carried of the	2Chr 36:7	
he *a* rebelled against king	2Chr 36:13	1571
put it *a* in writing, saying,	2Chr 36:22	1571
put it *a* in writing, saying,	Ezr 1:1	1571
A Cyrus the king brought forth	Ezr 1:7	
They kept *a* the feast of	Ezr 3:4	
They gave money *a* unto the masons	Ezr 3:7	
mighty kings *a* over Jerusalem	Ezr 4:20	
We asked their names *a*, to	Ezr 5:10	638
And the vessels *a* of gold and	Ezr 5:14	638
a let the golden and silver	Ezr 6:5	638
A I have made a decree, that	Ezr 6:11	
The vessels *a* that are given thee	Ezr 7:19	
A we certify you, that touching	Ezr 7:24	
Of the sons *a* of Adin	Ezr 8:6	
Of the sons *a* of Bigvai	Ezr 8:14	
a for Joiarib, and for Elnathan,	Ezr 8:16	
A of the Nethinims, whom David and	Ezr 8:20	
A twenty basons of gold, of a	Ezr 8:27	
the vessels are holy *a*	Ezr 8:28	
A the children of those that had	Ezr 8:35	
we *a* will be with thee	Ezr 10:4	
A of the Levites	Ezr 10:23	
Of the singers *a*	Ezr 10:24	
Of the sons *a* of Bebai	Ezr 10:28	
of Jerusalem *a* is broken down	Neh 1:3	
(the queen *a* sitting by him,) For	Neh 2:6	
as *a* the king's words that he had	Neh 2:18	637
who *a* laid the beams thereof, and	Neh 3:3	
Next unto him *a* repaired Hananiah	Neh 3:8	
After him repaired *a* Shemaiah the	Neh 3:29	
Some *a* there were that said, We	Neh 5:3	
There were *a* that said, We have	Neh 5:4	
A I said, It is not good that ye	Neh 5:9	
a the hundredth part of the money	Neh 5:11	
A I shook my lap, and said, So God	Neh 5:13	1571
a I continued in the work of this	Neh 5:16	1571
a fowls were prepared for me, and	Neh 5:18	
thou hast *a* appointed prophets to	Neh 6:7	1571
A they reported his good deeds	Neh 6:19	1571
which went up *a* from Tel-melah	Neh 7:61	
A Jeshua, and Bani, and Sherebiah,	Neh 8:7	
A day by day, from the first day	Neh 8:18	
camest down *a* upon mount Sinai	Neh 9:13	
Thou gavest *a* thy good spirit to	Neh 9:20	
Their children *a* multipliedst	Neh 9:23	
a they have dominion over our	Neh 9:37	
A we made ordinances for us, to	Neh 10:32	
A the firstborn of our sons, and	Neh 10:36	
rest of the people *a* cast lots	Neh 11:1	
A of the Levites	Neh 11:15	
The overseer *a* of the Levites at	Neh 11:22	
The children *a* of Benjamin from	Neh 11:31	
A Bakbukiah and Unni, their	Neh 12:9	
Joiakim *a* begat Eliashib, and	Neh 12:10	
a the priests, to the reign of	Neh 12:22	
A from the house of Gilgal, and	Neh 12:29	
A that day they offered great	Neh 12:43	
the wives *a* and the children	Neh 12:43	
as *a* wine, grapes, and figs, and	Neh 13:15	637
There dwelt men of Tyre *a* therein	Neh 13:16	
me, O my God, concerning this *a*	Neh 13:22	1571
In those days *a* saw I Jews that	Neh 13:23	1571
A Vashti the queen made a feast	Est 1:9	1571
but *a* to all the princes, and to	Est 1:16	
brought *a* unto the king's house	Est 2:8	
is given to thee, the people *a*	Est 3:11	
A he gave him the copy of the	Est 4:8	
I *a* and my maidens will fast	Est 4:16	1571
invited unto her *a* with the king	Est 5:12	1571
queen *a* before me in the house	Est 7:8	1571
said before the king, Behold *a*	Est 7:9	1571
Write ye *a* for the Jews, as it	Est 8:8	
a according unto this day's	Est 9:13	1571
day *a* of the month Adar, and slew	Est 9:15	1571
His substance *a* was seven	Job 1:3	
LORD, and Satan came *a* among them	Job 1:6	1571
speaking, there came *a* another	Job 1:16	
speaking, there came *a* another	Job 1:17	
speaking, there came *a* another	Job 1:18	
Satan came *a* among them to	Job 2:1	1571
Thou shalt know *a* that thy seed	Job 5:25	
are not his days *a* like the days	Job 7:1	
he passeth on *a*, but I perceive	Job 9:11	
it shall *a* prove me perverse	Job 9:20	
he seeth wickedness *a*	Job 11:11	
A thou shalt lie down, and none	Job 11:19	
a he sendeth them out, and they	Job 12:15	
ye know, the same do I know *a*	Job 13:2	1571
He *a* shall be my salvation	Job 13:16	1571
puttest my feet *a* in the stocks	Job 13:27	
he fleeth *a* as a shadow, and	Job 14:2	
I *a* could speak as ye do	Job 16:4	1571
he hath *a* taken me by my neck, and	Job 16:12	
a my prayer is pure	Job 16:17	
A now, behold, my witness is in	Job 16:19	1571
He hath made me *a* a byword of the	Job 17:6	
Mine eye *a* is dim by reason of	Job 17:7	
The righteous *a* shall hold on his	Job 17:9	
He hath *a* kindled his wrath	Job 19:11	
The eye *a* which saw him shall see	Job 20:9	
Thou shalt *a* decree a thing, and	Job 22:28	
The eye *a* of the adulterer	Job 24:15	
He draweth *a* the mighty with his	Job 24:22	
they have *a* let loose the bridle	Job 30:11	
My harp *a* is turned to mourning,	Job 30:31	
This *a* were an iniquity to be	Job 31:28	1571
A against his three friends was	Job 32:3	
I *a* will shew mine opinion	Job 32:10	637
I said, I will answer *a* my part	Job 32:17	637
I *a* will shew mine opinion	Job 32:17	637
I *a* am formed out of the clay	Job 33:6	1571
He is chastened *a* with pain upon	Job 33:19	
Elihu *a* proceeded, and said,	Job 36:1	
He openeth *a* their ear to	Job 36:10	
A can any understand the	Job 36:29	637
the cattle *a* concerning the	Job 36:33	637
At this *a* my heart trembleth, and	Job 37:1	637
A by watering he wearieth the	Job 37:11	637
Her young ones *a* suck up blood	Job 39:30	
Wilt thou *a* disannul my judgment	Job 40:8	637
Then will I *a* confess unto thee	Job 40:14	1571
the LORD *a* accepted Job	Job 42:9	
a the LORD gave Job twice as much	Job 42:10	
every man *a* gave him a piece of	Job 42:11	
He had *a* seven sons and three	Job 42:13	
his leaf *a* shall not wither	Ps 1:3	
let them *a* that love thy name be	Ps 5:11	
My soul is *a* sore vexed	Ps 6:3	
He hath *a* prepared for him the	Ps 7:13	
The LORD *a* will be a refuge for	Ps 9:9	
my reins *a* instruct me in the	Ps 16:7	637
my flesh *a* shall rest in hope	Ps 16:9	637
the foundations *a* of the hills	Ps 18:7	
He bowed the heavens *a*, and came	Ps 18:9	
The LORD *a* thundered in the	Ps 18:13	
me forth *a* into a large place	Ps 18:19	
I was *a* upright before him, and I	Ps 18:23	
Thou hast *a* given me the shield	Ps 18:35	
Thou hast *a* given me the necks of	Ps 18:40	
sweeter *a* than honey and the	Ps 19:10	
Keep back thy servant *a* from	Ps 19:13	1571
I have trusted *a* in the LORD	Ps 26:1	
have mercy *a* upon me, and answer	Ps 27:7	
feed them *a*, and lift them up for	Ps 28:9	
He maketh them *a* to skip like a	Ps 29:6	
Draw out *a* the spear, and stop the	Ps 35:3	
Delight thyself *a* in the LORD	Ps 37:4	
trust *a* in him	Ps 37:5	
mine eyes, it *a* is gone from me	Ps 38:10	1571
They *a* that seek after my life	Ps 38:12	
They *a* that render evil for good	Ps 38:20	
He brought me up *a* out of an	Ps 40:2	
forget *a* thine own people, and thy	Ps 45:10	
The righteous *a* shall see	Ps 52:6	
mischief *a* and sorrow are in the	Ps 55:10	
Ephraim *a* is the strength of mine	Ps 60:7	
A unto thee, O Lord, belongeth	Ps 62:12	
They *a* that dwell in the	Ps 65:8	
the valleys *a* are covered over	Ps 65:13	
they shout for joy, they *a* sing	Ps 65:13	637
let them *a* that hate him flee	Ps 68:1	
the heavens *a* dropped at the	Ps 68:8	637
yea, for the rebellious *a*	Ps 68:18	637
I made sackcloth *a* my garment	Ps 69:11	
They gave me *a* gall for my meat	Ps 69:21	
This *a* shall please the LORD	Ps 69:31	
The seed *a* of his servants shall	Ps 69:36	
Now *a* when I am old and greyheaded	Ps 71:18	1571
Thy righteousness *a*, O God, is	Ps 71:19	
I will *a* praise thee with the	Ps 71:22	1571
My tongue *a* shall talk of thy	Ps 71:24	1571
have dominion *a* from sea to sea	Ps 72:8	
the poor *a*, and him that hath no	Ps 72:12	
prayer *a* shall be made for him	Ps 72:15	
is thine, the night *a* is thine	Ps 74:16	637
of the wicked *a* will I cut off	Ps 75:10	
In Salem *a* is his tabernacle, and	Ps 76:2	
I will meditate *a* of all thy work	Ps 77:12	
the depths *a* were troubled	Ps 77:16	637
thine arrows *a* went abroad	Ps 77:17	637
In the daytime *a* he led them with	Ps 78:14	
brought streams *a* out of the rock	Ps 78:16	
can he give bread *a*	Ps 78:20	1571
anger *a* came up against Israel	Ps 78:21	1571
He rained flesh *a* upon them as	Ps 78:27	
He gave *a* their increase unto the	Ps 78:46	
up their cattle *a* to the hail	Ps 78:48	
out the heathen *a* before them	Ps 78:55	
his people over *a* unto the sword	Ps 78:62	
He chose David *a* his servant	Ps 78:70	
He should have fed them *a* with	Ps 81:16	
Assur *a* is joined with them	Ps 83:8	1571
the rain *a* filleth the pools	Ps 84:6	1571
thy faithfulness *a* in the	Ps 89:5	637
are thine, the earth *a* is thine	Ps 89:11	637
mine arm *a* shall strengthen him	Ps 89:21	637
I will set his hand *a* in the sea	Ps 89:25	
A I will make him my firstborn,	Ps 89:27	637
His seed *a* will I make to endure	Ps 89:29	
Thou hast *a* turned the edge of	Ps 89:43	637
Mine eye *a* shall see my desire on	Ps 92:11	
the world *a* is stablished, that	Ps 93:1	389
strength of the hills is his *a*	Ps 95:4	
the world *a* shall be established	Ps 96:10	637
king's strength *a* loveth judgment	Ps 99:4	
Israel *a* came into Egypt	Ps 105:23	
He smote their vines *a* and their	Ps 105:33	
He smote *a* all the firstborn in	Ps 105:36	
brought them forth *a* with silver	Ps 105:37	
He rebuked the Red sea *a*, and it	Ps 106:9	
They envied Moses *a* in the camp	Ps 106:16	
their seed *a* among the nations	Ps 106:27	
themselves *a* unto Baal-peor	Ps 106:28	
They angered him *a* at the waters	Ps 106:32	
Their enemies *a* oppressed them,	Ps 106:42	
He made them *a* to be pitied of	Ps 106:46	
Let them exalt him *a* in the	Ps 107:32	
He blesseth them *a*, so that they	Ps 107:38	
Ephraim *a* is the strength of mine	Ps 108:8	
me about *a* with words of hatred	Ps 109:3	
let them seek their bread *a* out	Ps 109:10	
I became *a* a reproach unto them	Ps 109:25	
They *a* do no iniquity	Ps 119:3	637
Princes *a* did sit and speak	Ps 119:23	1571
Thy testimonies *a* are my delight	Ps 119:24	
Let thy mercies come *a* unto me	Ps 119:41	
of thy testimonies *a* before kings	Ps 119:46	
My hands *a* will I lift up unto	Ps 119:48	
their children shall *a* sit upon	Ps 132:12	1571
I will *a* clothe her priests with	Ps 132:16	
How precious *a* are thy thoughts	Ps 139:17	
for yet my prayer *a* shall be in	Ps 141:5	
he *a* will hear their cry, and will	Ps 145:19	
He hath *a* stablished them for	Ps 148:6	
He *a* exalteth the horn of his	Ps 148:14	
I *a* will laugh at your calamity	Prov 1:26	1571
He taught me *a*, and said unto me,	Prov 4:4	
she hath *a* furnished her table	Prov 9:2	637
shall be watered *a* himself	Prov 11:25	1571
A to punish the just is not good,	Prov 17:26	1571
cometh, then cometh *a* contempt	Prov 18:3	1571
He *a* that is slothful in his work	Prov 18:9	1571
A, that the soul be without	Prov 19:2	1571
he *a* shall cry himself, but shall	Prov 21:13	1571
a wisdom, and instruction, and	Prov 23:23	
She *a* lieth in wait as for a prey	Prov 23:28	637
These things *a* belong to the wise	Prov 24:23	1571
These are *a* proverbs of Solomon,	Prov 25:1	1571
lest thou *a* be like unto him	Prov 26:4	1571
is *a* a great oppressor	Prov 28:16	
an he goat *a*	Prov 30:31	176
She riseth *a* while it is yet	Prov 31:15	
her husband *a*, and he praiseth her	Prov 31:28	
The sun *a* ariseth, and the sun	Eccl 1:5	
that this *a* is vexation of spirit	Eccl 1:17	1571
and, behold, this *a* is vanity	Eccl 2:1	1571
a I had great possessions of	Eccl 2:7	1571
I gathered me *a* silver and gold,	Eccl 2:8	1571
a my wisdom remained with me	Eccl 2:9	637
I myself perceived *a* that one	Eccl 2:14	1571
my heart, that this *a* is vanity	Eccl 2:15	1571
This is *a* vanity	Eccl 2:19	1571
This *a* is vanity and a great evil	Eccl 2:21	1571
This is *a* vanity	Eccl 2:23	1571
This *a* I saw, that it was from	Eccl 2:24	1571
This *a* is vanity and vexation of	Eccl 2:26	1571
a he hath set the world in their	Eccl 3:11	1571
a that every man should eat and	Eccl 3:13	1571
This is *a* vanity and vexation of	Eccl 4:4	1571
This is *a* vanity, yea, it is a	Eccl 4:8	1571
whereas *a* he that is born in his	Eccl 4:14	1571
they *a* that come after shall not	Eccl 4:16	1571
Surely this *a* is vanity and	Eccl 4:16	1571
words there are *a* divers vanities	Eccl 5:7	
this is *a* vanity	Eccl 5:10	1571
this *a* is a sore evil, that in	Eccl 5:16	1571
All his days *a* he eateth in	Eccl 5:17	1571
Every man *a* to whom God hath	Eccl 5:19	1571
good, and *a* that he have no burial	Eccl 6:3	1571
this is *a* vanity and vexation of	Eccl 6:9	1571
this *a* is vanity	Eccl 7:6	1571
God *a* hath set the one over	Eccl 7:14	1571
a from this withdraw not thine	Eccl 7:18	1571
A take no heed unto all words	Eccl 7:21	1571
For oftentimes *a* thine own heart	Eccl 7:22	1571
this is *a* vanity	Eccl 8:10	1571
I said that this *a* is vanity	Eccl 8:14	1571
(for *a* there is that neither day	Eccl 8:16	1571
a the heart of the sons of men is	Eccl 9:3	1571
A their love, and their hatred, and	Eccl 9:6	1571
For man *a* knoweth not his time	Eccl 9:12	1571
have I seen *a* under the sun	Eccl 9:13	1571
Yea *a*, when he that is a fool	Eccl 10:3	1571
A fool *a* is full of words	Eccl 10:14	
a portion to seven, and *a* to eight	Eccl 11:2	1571
A when they shall be afraid of	Eccl 12:5	1571
a our bed is green	Song 1:16	637
now *a* thy breasts shall be as	Song 7:8	
Their land *a* is full of silver and	Is 2:7	
their land is *a* full of horses,	Is 2:7	
Their land *a* is full of idols	Is 2:8	
a made a winepress therein	Is 5:2	1571
I will *a* command the clouds that	Is 5:6	
that king Uzziah died I saw *a* the	Is 6:1	
A I heard the voice of the Lord,	Is 6:8	
men, but will ye weary my God *a*	Is 7:13	1571
it shall *a* consume the beard	Is 7:20	1571
The LORD spake *a* unto me again	Is 8:5	
The wolf *a* shall dwell with the	Is 11:6	
The envy *a* of Ephraim shall	Is 11:13	
he *a* is become my salvation	Is 12:2	
I have *a* called my mighty ones	Is 13:3	1571
Their children *a* shall be dashed	Is 13:16	
Their bows *a* shall dash the young	Is 13:18	
Art thou *a* become weak as we	Is 14:10	1571
I will sit *a* upon the mount of	Is 14:13	

I will *a* make it a possession for Is 14:23
The fortress *a* shall cease from Is 17:3
The fishers *a* shall mourn Is 19:8
they have *a* seduced Egypt, even Is 19:13
morning cometh, and *a* the night Is 21:12 1571
Ye have seen *a* the breaches of Is 22:9
Ye made *a* a ditch between the two Is 22:11
there *a* shalt thou have no rest Is 23:12 1571
The earth *a* is defiled under the Is 24:5
for thou *a* hast wrought all our Is 26:12
the earth *a* shall disclose her Is 26:21
But they *a* have erred through Is 28:7 1571
Judgment *a* will I lay to the line Is 28:17
This *a* cometh forth from the LORD Is 28:29 1571
The meek *a* shall increase their Is 29:19
They *a* that erred in spirit shall Is 29:24
but a shame, and *a* a reproach Is 30:5 1571
Ye shall defile *a* the covering of Is 30:22
Yet he *a* is wise, and will bring Is 31:2 1571
defending *a* he will deliver it Is 31:5
The heart *a* of the rash shall Is 32:4
The instruments *a* of the churl Is 32:7
our salvation *a* in the time of Is 33:2 637
Their slain *a* shall be cast out Is 34:3
the owl *a* and the raven shall Is 34:11
a meet with the wild beasts of Is 34:14
the screech owl *a* shall rest Is 34:14 389
shall the vultures *a* be gathered Is 34:15 389
Hezekiah *a* had said, What is the Is 38:22
he shall *a* blow upon them, and Is 40:24 1571
a I have baked bread upon the Is 44:19 637
a confounded, all of them Is 45:16 1571
I will *a* bring it to pass Is 46:11 637
have purposed it, I will *a* do it Is 46:11 637
I am the first, I *a* am the last Is 48:12 637
Mine hand *a* hath laid the Is 48:13 637
Thy seed *a* had been as the sand Is 48:19
he clave the rock *a*, and the Is 48:21
I will *a* give thee for a light to Is 49:6
princes *a* shall worship, because Is 49:7
A the sons of the stranger, that Is 56:6
Behind the doors *a* and the posts Is 57:8
with him *a* that is of a contrite Is 57:15
I will lead him *a*, and restore Is 57:18
The sons *a* of them that afflicted Is 60:14
Thou shalt *a* suck the milk of the Is 60:16
I will *a* make thy officers peace Is 60:17
Thy people *a* shall be all Is 60:21
Thou shalt *a* be a crown of glory Is 62:3
I *a* will choose their delusions Is 66:4 1571
I will *a* take of them for priests Is 66:21 1571
It came *a* in the days of Jer 1:3
the pastors *a* transgressed Jer 2:8
A the children of Noph and Jer 2:16 1571
therefore hast thou *a* taught the Jer 2:33 1571
A in thy skirts is found the Jer 2:34 1571
thou *a* shalt be ashamed of Egypt Jer 2:36 1571
The LORD said *a* unto me in the Jer 3:6
but went and played the harlot *a* Jer 3:8 1571
now *a* will I give sentence Jer 4:12 1571
They have healed *a* the hurt of Jer 6:14
A I set watchmen over you, saying Jer 6:17
thou shalt *a* call unto them Jer 7:27
scatter them *a* among the heathen Jer 9:16
neither *a* is it in them to do Jer 10:5 1571
then may ye *a* do good, that are Jer 13:23 1571
the hind *a* calved in the field Jer 14:5 1571
word of the LORD came *a* unto me Jer 16:1
Thou shalt not *a* go into the Jer 16:8
They have built *a* the high places Jer 19:5
who was *a* chief governor in the Jer 20:1
I have seen *a* in the prophets of Jer 23:14
they strengthen *a* the hands of Jer 23:14
shall serve themselves of them *a* Jer 25:14 1571
there was *a* a man that prophesied Jer 26:20 1571
field have I given *a* to serve him Jer 27:6 1571
I spake *a* to Zedekiah king of Jer 27:12
A I spake to the priests and to Jer 27:16
him the beasts of the field *a* Jer 28:14 1571
Thus shalt thou *a* speak to Jer 29:24
I will *a* glorify them, and they Jer 30:19
Their children *a* shall be as Jer 30:20
then the seed of Israel *a* shall Jer 31:36 1571
I will *a* cast off all the seed of Jer 31:37 1571
Then may *a* my covenant be broken Jer 33:21 1571
I have sent *a* unto you all my Jer 35:15
a thou shalt read them in the Jer 36:6 1571
a what the king said unto thee Jer 38:25
a the king of Babylon slew all Jer 39:6
Go back *a* to Gedaliah the son of Jer 40:5
Ishmael *a* slew all the Jews that Jer 41:3
He shall break *a* the images of Jer 43:13
A her hired men are in the midst Jer 46:21 1571
for they *a* are turned back, and Jer 46:21 1571
A thou shalt be cut down, O Jer 48:2 1571
treasures, thou shalt *a* be taken Jer 48:7 1571
the valley *a* shall perish, and the Jer 48:8
Moab *a* shall wallow in his vomit Jer 48:26
he *a* shall be in derision Jer 48:26 1571
for the waters *a* of Nimrim shall Jer 48:34 1571
A Edom shall be a desolation Jer 49:17
for thee, and thou art *a* taken Jer 50:24 1571
a caught, because thou hast Jer 50:24 1571
With thee *a* will I break in Jer 51:22
I will *a* break in pieces with Jer 51:23
he slew *a* all the princes of Jer 52:10 1571
A the pillars of brass that were Jer 52:17
The caldrons *a*, and the shovels Jer 52:18
The second pillar *a* and the Jer 52:22
He took *a* out of the city an Jer 52:25
her prophets *a* find no vision Lam 2:9 1571
A when I cry and shout, he Lam 3:8 1571
He hath *a* broken my teeth with Lam 3:16
the cup *a* shall pass through unto Lam 4:21 1571

A out of the midst thereof came Eze 1:5
they four *a* had the face of an Eze 1:10
I heard *a* the noise of the wings Eze 3:13
a thou hast delivered thy soul Eze 3:21
Thou *a*, son of man, take thee a Eze 4:1
set the camp *a* against it Eze 4:2
Lie thou *a* upon thy left side, and Eze 4:4
Take thou *a* unto thee wheat, and Eze 4:9
shalt drink *a* water by measure Eze 4:11
Thou shalt *a* take thereof a few Eze 5:3
therefore will I *a* diminish thee Eze 5:11 1571
A, thou son of man, thus saith Eze 7:2
They shall *a* gird themselves with Eze 7:18
My face will I turn *a* from them Eze 7:22
I will *a* make the pomp of the Eze 7:24
He said *a* unto me, Turn thee yet Eze 8:13
Therefore will I *a* deal in fury Eze 8:18 1571
He cried *a* in mine ears with a Eze 9:1
And as for me *a*, mine eye shall Eze 9:10 1571
the same wheels *a* turned not from Eze 10:16 1571
up, these lifted up themselves *a* Eze 10:17
the wheels *a* were beside them, and Eze 10:19
word of the LORD *a* came unto me Eze 12:1
My net *a* will I spread upon him Eze 12:13
Your kerchiefs *a* will I tear Eze 13:21
I clothed thee *a* with broidered Eze 16:10
I decked thee *a* with ornaments Eze 16:11
Thou hast *a* taken thy fair jewels Eze 16:17
My meat *a* which I gave thee, fine Eze 16:19
That thou hast *a* built unto thee Eze 16:24
Thou hast *a* committed fornication Eze 16:26
the whore *a* with the Assyrians Eze 16:28
I will *a* give thee into their Eze 16:39
shall strip thee *a* of thy clothes Eze 16:39
They shall *a* bring up a company Eze 16:40
thou *a* shalt give no hire any Eze 16:41 1571
therefore I *a* will recompense thy Eze 16:43 1571
Thou *a*, which hast judged thy Eze 16:52 1571
yea, be thou confounded *a* Eze 16:52 1571
He took *a* of the seed of the land Eze 17:5
There was *a* another great eagle Eze 17:7
he hath *a* taken the mighty of the Eze 17:13
I will *a* take of the highest Eze 17:22
so *a* the soul of the son is mine Eze 18:4
The nations *a* heard of him Eze 19:4
Moreover *a* I gave them my Eze 20:12 1571
Yet *a* I lifted up my hand unto Eze 20:15 1571
unto them *a* in the wilderness Eze 20:23 1571
Wherefore I gave them *a* statutes Eze 20:25 1571
there *a* they made their sweet Eze 20:28
one his idols, and hereafter *a* Eze 20:39
is sharpened, and *a* furbished Eze 21:9 1571
I will *a* smite mine hands Eze 21:17 1571
A, thou son of man, appoint thee Eze 21:19
They shall *a* strip thee out of Eze 23:26
bear thou *a* thy lewdness and thy Eze 23:35 1571
have *a* caused their sons, whom Eze 23:37 1571
it on, and *a* pour water into it Eze 24:3 1571
burn *a* the bones under it, and Eze 24:5 1571
A the word of the LORD came unto Eze 24:15
A, thou son of man, shall it not Eze 24:25
I will *a* stretch out mine hand Eze 25:13
I will *a* scrape her dust from her Eze 26:4
Dan *a* and Javan going to and fro Eze 27:19
They *a* that uphold Egypt shall Eze 30:6
I will *a* make the multitude of Eze 30:10
I will *a* destroy the idols, and I Eze 30:13
At Tehaphnehes *a* the day shall be Eze 30:18
They *a* went down into hell with Eze 31:17 1571
I will *a* water with thy blood the Eze 32:6
I will *a* vex the hearts of many Eze 32:9
I will destroy *a* all the beasts Eze 32:13
It came to pass *a* in the twelfth Eze 32:17
A, thou son of man, the children Eze 33:30
A, thou son of man, prophesy unto Eze 36:1
A new heart *a* will I give you, and Eze 36:26
I will *a* save you from all your Eze 36:29
will *a* cause you to dwell in the Eze 36:33
they shall *a* walk in my judgments Eze 37:24
My tabernacle *a* shall be with Eze 37:27
It shall *a* come to pass, that at Eze 38:10
a the name of the city shall be Eze 39:16 1571
He measured *a* the porch of the Eze 40:8
The space *a* before the little Eze 40:12
He made *a* posts of threescore Eze 40:14
whereupon *a* they laid the Eze 40:42
I saw *a* the height of the house Eze 41:8
A the breadth of the face of the Eze 41:14
the bullock *a* of the sin offering Eze 43:21
they shall *a* prepare a young Eze 43:25
ye shall *a* give unto the priest Eze 44:30
breadth, shall *a* the Levites, the Eze 45:5
The west side *a* shall be the Eze 47:20
a before thee, O king, have I Dan 6:22 638
the beast had *a* four heads Dan 7:6
through his policy *a* he shall Dan 8:25
he shall *a* stand up against the Dan 8:25
His body *a* was like the beryl, and Dan 10:6
A I in the first year of Darius Dan 11:1
shall *a* carry captives into Egypt Dan 11:8 1571
a the robbers of thy people shall Dan 11:14
He shall *a* set his face to enter Dan 11:17
a the prince of the covenant Dan 11:22 1571
He shall enter *a* into the Dan 11:41
his hand *a* upon the countries Dan 11:42
I will *a* cause all her mirth to Hos 2:11
so will I *a* be for thee Hos 3:3 1571
of the sea *a* shall be taken away Hos 4:3 1571
the prophet *a* shall fall with Hos 4:5 1571
I will *a* reject thee, that thou Hos 4:6
I will *a* forget thy children Hos 4:6 1571
Judah *a* shall fall with them Hos 5:5 1571
A, O Judah, he hath set an Hos 6:11 1571
Ephraim *a* is like a silly dove Hos 7:11

For from Israel was it *a* Hos 8:6
woe *a* to them when I depart from Hos 9:12 1571
It shall be *a* carried unto Hos 10:6 1571
The high places *a* of Aven Hos 10:8
I taught Ephraim *a* to go, taking Hos 11:3
The LORD hath *a* a controversy Hos 12:2
I have *a* spoken by the prophets Hos 12:10
pomegranate tree, the palm tree *a* Joel 1:12 1571
of the field cry *a* unto thee Joel 1:20 1571
Therefore *a* now, saith the LORD Joel 2:12 1571
a upon the servants and upon the Joel 2:29 1571
I will *a* gather all nations, and Joel 3:2
The children *a* of Judah and the Joel 3:6
The LORD *a* shall roar out of Zion Joel 3:16
I will break *a* the bar of Amos 1:5
A I brought you up from the land Amos 2:10
of Israel upon him I will *a* visit Amos 3:14
I *a* have given you cleanness of Amos 4:6 1571
a I have withholden the rain from Amos 4:7 1571
This *a* shall not be, saith the Amos 7:6
A Amaziah said unto Amos, O thou Amos 7:12
they shall *a* make gardens, and eat Amos 9:14
and *a* much cattle Jonah 4:11
Who *a* eat the flesh of my people Mic 3:3
Now *a* many nations are gathered Mic 4:11
graven images *a* will I cut off Mic 5:13
Therefore *a* will I make thee sick Mic 6:13 1571
In that day *a* he shall come even Mic 7:12
her young children *a* were dashed Nah 3:10 1571
Thou *a* shalt be drunken Nah 3:11 1571
thou *a* shalt seek strength Nah 3:11 1571
Their horses *a* are swifter than Hab 1:8
Yea *a*, because he transgresseth Hab 2:5 637
to him, and makest him drunken *a* Hab 2:15 637
drink thou *a*, and let thy foreskin Hab 2:16 1571
I will *a* stretch out mine hand Zeph 1:4
In the same day *a* will I punish Zeph 1:9
they shall *a* build houses, but Zeph 1:13
Ye Ethiopians *a*, ye shall be Zeph 2:12 1571
I will *a* leave in the midst of Zeph 3:12
then thou shalt *a* judge my house Zec 3:7 1571
shalt *a* keep my courts, and I will Zec 3:7 1571
his hands shall *a* finish it Zec 4:9
should it *a* be marvellous in mine Zec 8:6 1571
I will go *a* Zec 8:21 1571
Hamath *a* shall border thereby Zec 9:2 1571
Gaza *a* shall see it, and be very Zec 9:5
As for thee *a*, by the blood of Zec 9:11 1571
I will bring them again *a* out of Zec 10:10
Three shepherds *a* I cut off in Zec 11:8
them, and their soul *a* abhorred me Zec 11:8 1571
The LORD *a* shall save the tents Zec 12:7
a I will cause the prophets and Zec 13:2 1571
Judah *a* shall fight at Jerusalem Zec 14:14 1571
Ye said *a*, Behold, what a Mal 1:13
Therefore have I *a* made you Mal 2:9 1571
that I may come and worship him *a* Mt 2:8 *2504*
now *a* the ax is laid unto the Mt 3:10 *2532*
cheek, turn to him the other *a* Mt 5:39 *2532*
coat, let him have thy cloke *a* Mt 5:40 *2532*
Father will *a* forgive you Mt 6:14 *2532*
is, there will your heart be *a* Mt 6:21 *2532*
Iscariot, who *a* betrayed him Mt 10:4 *2532*
him will I confess *a* before my Mt 10:32 *2504*
him will I *a* deny before my Mt 10:33 *2504*
Even so shall it be *a* unto this Mt 12:45 *2532*
He *a* that received seed among the Mt 13:22 *1161*
which *a* beareth fruit, and Mt 13:23 *1211*
fruit, then appeared the tares *a* Mt 13:26 *2532*
ye root up *a* the wheat with them Mt 13:29 *260*
Why do ye *a* transgress the Mt 15:3 *2532*
Jesus said, Are ye *a* yet without Mt 15:16 *2532*
The Pharisees *a* with the Mt 16:1 *2532*
I say *a* unto thee, That thou art Mt 16:18 *1161*
Likewise shall *a* the Son of man Mt 17:12 *2532*
Shouldest not thou *a* have had Mt 18:33 *2532*
my heavenly Father do *a* unto you Mt 18:35 *2532*
The Pharisees *a* came unto him Mt 19:3 *2532*
ye *a* shall sit upon twelve Mt 19:28 *2532*
Go ye *a* into the vineyard, and Mt 20:4 *2532*
Go ye *a* into the vineyard Mt 20:7 *2532*
but *a* if ye shall say unto this Mt 21:21 *2579*
I *a* will ask you one thing, which Mt 21:24 *2504*
Likewise the second *a*, and the Mt 22:26 *2532*
And last of all the woman died *a* Mt 22:27 *2532*
outside of them may be clean *a* Mt 23:26 *2532*
Even so ye *a* outwardly appear Mt 23:28 *2532*
so shall *a* the coming of the Son Mt 24:27 *2532*
so shall *a* the coming of the Son Mt 24:37 *2532*
so shall *a* the coming of the Son Mt 24:39 *2532*
Therefore be ye *a* ready Mt 24:44 *2532*
Afterward came *a* the other Mt 25:11 *2532*
two, he *a* gained other two Mt 25:17 *2532*
He *a* that had received two Mt 25:22 *2532*
Then shall he say *a* unto them on Mt 25:41 *2532*
Then shall they *a* answer him Mt 25:44 *2532*
whole world, there shall *a* this Mt 26:13 *2532*
Likewise *a* said all the disciples Mt 26:35 *2532*
Thou *a* wast with Jesus of Galilee Mt 26:69 *2532*
This fellow was *a* with Jesus of Mt 26:71 *2532*
Surely thou *a* art one of them Mt 26:73 *2532*
Likewise *a* the chief priests Mt 27:41 *1161*
The thieves *a*, which were Mt 27:44 *2532*
who *a* himself was Jesus' disciple Mt 27:57 *2532*
who *a* were in the ship mending Mk 1:19 *2532*
towns, that I may preach there *a* Mk 1:38 *2546*
sinners sat *a* together with Jesus Mk 2:15 *2532*
No man *a* seweth a piece of new Mk 2:21 *2532*
gave *a* to them which were with Mk 2:26 *2532*
of man is Lord *a* of the sabbath Mk 2:28 *2532*
Iscariot, which *a* betrayed him Mk 3:19 *2532*
there were *a* with him other Mk 4:36 *2532*
devil, and *a* concerning the swine Mk 5:16 *2532*
Are ye so without understanding *a* Mk 7:18 *2532*

to set them *a* before them	Mk 8:7	*2532*
unto him with his disciples *a*	Mk 8:34	
of him *a* shall the Son of man be	Mk 8:38	*2532*
that your Father *a* which is in	Mk 11:25	*2532*
I will *a* ask of you one question,	Mk 11:29	*2504*
he sent him *a* last unto them,	Mk 12:6	*2532*
last of all the woman died *a*	Mk 12:22	*2532*
this *a* that she hath done shall	Mk 14:9	*2532*
Likewise *a* said they all	Mk 14:31	*2532*
thou *a* wast with Jesus of	Mk 14:67	*2532*
Likewise *a* the chief priests	Mk 15:31	*2532*
There were *a* women looking on	Mk 15:40	*2532*
(Who *a*, when he was in Galilee,	Mk 15:41	*2532*
which *a* waited for the kingdom of	Mk 15:43	*2532*
It seemed good to me *a*, having	Lk 1:3	*2504*
therefore *a* that holy thing which	Lk 1:35	*2532*
she hath *a* conceived a son in her	Lk 1:36	*2532*
Joseph *a* went up from Galilee,	Lk 2:4	*2532*
pierce through thy own soul *a*	Lk 2:35	*2532*
now *a* the axe is laid unto the	Lk 3:9	*2532*
Then came *a* publicans to be	Lk 3:12	*2532*
that Jesus *a* being baptized, and	Lk 3:21	*2532*
do *a* here in thy country	Lk 4:23	*2532*
devils *a* came out of many, crying	Lk 4:41	*2532*
kingdom of God to other cities *a*	Lk 4:43	*2532*
And so was *a* James, and John, the	Lk 5:10	*2532*
he spake *a* a parable unto them	Lk 5:36	*2532*
No man *a* having drunk old wine	Lk 5:39	*2532*
gave *a* to them that were with him	Lk 6:4	*2532*
of man is Lord *a* of the sabbath	Lk 6:5	*2532*
it came to pass *a* on another	Lk 6:6	*2532*
twelve, whom *a* he named apostles	Lk 6:13	*2532*
(whom he *a* named Peter,) and	Lk 6:14	*2532*
Iscariot, which *a* was the traitor	Lk 6:16	*2532*
the one cheek offer *a* the other	Lk 6:29	*2532*
forbid not to take thy coat *a*	Lk 6:29	*2532*
to you, do ye *a* to them likewise	Lk 6:31	*2532*
for sinners *a* love those that	Lk 6:32	*2532*
for sinners *a* do even the same	Lk 6:33	*2532*
for sinners *a* lend to sinners, to	Lk 6:34	*2532*
as your Father *a* is merciful	Lk 6:36	*2532*
For I *a* am a man set under	Lk 7:8	*2532*
Who is this that forgiveth sins *a*	Lk 7:49	*2532*
They *a* which saw it told them by	Lk 8:36	*2532*
And another *a* said, Lord, I will	Lk 9:61	*2532*
Lord appointed other seventy *a*	Lk 10:1	*2532*
which *a* sat at Jesus' feet, and	Lk 10:39	*2532*
as John *a* taught his disciples	Lk 11:1	*2532*
for we *a* forgive every one that	Lk 11:4	*2532*
If Satan *a* be divided against	Lk 11:18	*2532*
so shall *a* the Son of man be to	Lk 11:30	*2532*
thy whole body *a* is full of light	Lk 11:34	*2532*
thy body *a* is full of darkness	Lk 11:34	*2532*
make that which is within *a*	Lk 11:40	*2532*
thus saying thou reproachest us *a*	Lk 11:45	*2532*
And he said, Woe unto you *a*	Lk 11:46	*2532*
Therefore *a* said the wisdom of	Lk 11:49	*2532*
A I say unto you, Whosoever shall	Lk 12:8	*1161*
him shall the Son of man *a*	Lk 12:8	*2532*
is, there will your heart be *a*	Lk 12:34	*2532*
Be ye therefore ready *a*	Lk 12:40	*2532*
he said *a* to the people, When ye	Lk 12:54	*2532*
He spake *a* this parable	Lk 13:6	*1161*
Lord, let it alone this year *a*	Lk 13:8	*2532*
Then said he *a* to him that bade	Lk 14:12	*2532*
lest they *a* bid thee again, and a	Lk 14:12	*2532*
sisters, yea, and his own life *a*	Lk 14:26	*2532*
he said *a* unto his disciples,	Lk 16:1	*2532*
is least is faithful *a* in much	Lk 16:10	*2532*
in the least is unjust *a* in much	Lk 16:10	*2532*
And the Pharisees *a*, who were	Lk 16:14	*2532*
the rich man *a* died, and was	Lk 16:22	*2532*
lest they *a* come into this place	Lk 16:28	*2532*
so shall *a* the Son of man be in	Lk 17:24	*2532*
so shall it be *a* in the days of	Lk 17:26	*2532*
Likewise *a* as it was in the days	Lk 17:28	*2532*
they brought unto him *a* infants	Lk 18:15	*2532*
forsomuch as he *a* is a son of	Lk 19:9	*2532*
Be thou *a* over five cities	Lk 19:19	*2532*
I will *a* ask you one thing	Lk 20:3	*2504*
and they beat him *a*, and entreated	Lk 20:11	*2528*
and they wounded him *a*, and cast	Lk 20:12	*2532*
and in like manner the seven *a*	Lk 20:31	*2532*
Last of all the woman died *a*	Lk 20:32	*2532*
he saw *a* a certain poor widow	Lk 21:2	*2532*
Likewise *a* the cup after supper,	Lk 22:20	*2532*
there was *a* a strife among them,	Lk 22:24	*2532*
and his disciples *a* followed him	Lk 22:39	*2532*
and said, This man was *a* with him	Lk 22:56	*2532*
him, and said, Thou art *a* of them	Lk 22:58	*2532*
truth this fellow *a* was with him	Lk 22:59	*2532*
if I *a* ask you, ye will not	Lk 22:68	*2532*
who himself *a* was at Jerusalem at	Lk 23:7	*2532*
which *a* bewailed and lamented him	Lk 23:27	*2532*
And there were *a* two others	Lk 23:32	*2532*
the rulers *a* with them derided	Lk 23:35	*2532*
And the soldiers *a* mocked him	Lk 23:36	*2532*
a superscription *a* was written	Lk 23:38	*2532*
who *a* himself waited for the	Lk 23:51	*2532*
And the women *a*, which came with	Lk 23:55	*2532*
certain women *a* of our company	Lk 24:22	*2532*
that they had *a* seen a vision of	Lk 24:23	*2532*
John *a* was baptizing in Aenon	Jn 3:23	*2532*
for they *a* went unto the feast	Jn 4:45	*2532*
but said *a* that God was his	Jn 5:18	*2532*
these *a* doeth the Son likewise	Jn 5:19	*2532*
authority to execute judgment *a*	Jn 5:27	*2532*
they *a* took shipping, and came to	Jn 6:24	*2532*
That ye *a* have seen me, and	Jn 6:36	*2532*
the twelve, Will ye *a* go away	Jn 6:67	*2532*
that thy disciples *a* may see the	Jn 7:3	*2532*
then went he *a* up unto the feast,	Jn 7:10	*2532*
the Pharisees, Are ye *a* deceived	Jn 7:47	*2532*
unto him, Art thou *a* of Galilee	Jn 7:52	*2532*
It is *a* written in your law, that	Jn 8:17	*2532*
ye should have known my Father *a*	Jn 8:19	*2532*
Then again the Pharisees *a* asked	Jn 9:15	*2532*
will ye *a* be his disciples	Jn 9:27	*2532*
and said unto him, Are we blind *a*	Jn 9:40	*2532*
them *a* I must bring, and they	Jn 10:16	*2548*
his fellowdisciples, Let us *a* go	Jn 11:16	*2532*
the Jews *a* weeping which came	Jn 11:33	*2532*
but that *a* he should gather	Jn 11:52	*2532*
but that they might see Lazarus *a*	Jn 12:9	*2532*
they might put Lazarus *a* to death	Jn 12:10	*2532*
this cause the people *a* met him	Jn 12:18	*2532*
there shall *a* my servant be	Jn 12:26	*2532*
rulers *a* many believed on him	Jn 12:42	*2532*
but *a* my hands and my head	Jn 13:9	*2532*
ye *a* ought to wash one another's	Jn 13:14	*2532*
God shall *a* glorify him in	Jn 13:32	*2532*
that ye *a* love one another	Jn 13:34	*2532*
believe in God, believe *a* in me	Jn 14:1	*2532*
where I am, there ye may be *a*	Jn 14:3	*2532*
ye should have known my Father *a*	Jn 14:7	*2532*
the works that I do shall he do *a*	Jn 14:12	*2548*
because I live, ye shall live *a*	Jn 14:19	*2532*
they will *a* persecute you	Jn 15:20	*2532*
my saying, they will keep yours *a*	Jn 15:20	*2532*
that hateth me hateth my Father *a*	Jn 15:23	*2532*
ye *a* shall bear witness, because	Jn 15:27	*2532*
that thy Son *a* may glorify thee	Jn 17:1	*2532*
even so have I *a* sent them into	Jn 17:18	*2504*
that they *a* might be sanctified	Jn 17:19	*2532*
but for them *a* which shall	Jn 17:20	*2532*
that they *a* may be one in us	Jn 17:21	*2532*
Father, I will that they *a*	Jn 17:24	*2548*
And Judas *a*, which betrayed him,	Jn 18:2	*2532*
And Judas *a*, which betrayed him,	Jn 18:5	*2532*
Art not thou *a* one of this man's	Jn 18:17	*2532*
Art not thou *a* one of his	Jn 18:25	*2532*
and *a* his coat	Jn 19:23	*2532*
And there came *a* Nicodemus	Jn 19:39	*2532*
Then went in *a* that other	Jn 20:8	*2532*
say unto him, We *a* go with thee	Jn 21:3	*2532*
which *a* leaned on his breast at	Jn 21:20	*2532*
there are *a* many other things	Jn 21:25	*2532*
To whom *a* he shewed himself alive	Acts 1:3	*2532*
Which *a* said, Ye men of Galilee,	Acts 1:11	*2532*
of you, as ye yourselves *a* know	Acts 2:22	*2532*
moreover *a* my flesh shall rest in	Acts 2:26	*2532*
ye did it, as did *a* your rulers	Acts 3:17	*2532*
his wife *a* being privy to it, and	Acts 5:2	*2532*
There came *a* a multitude out of	Acts 5:16	*2532*
so is *a* the Holy Ghost, whom God	Acts 5:32	*2532*
he *a* perished	Acts 5:37	*2548*
Which *a* our fathers that came	Acts 7:45	*2532*
Then Simon himself believed *a*	Acts 8:13	*2532*
Give me *a* this power, that on	Acts 8:19	*2504*
he came down *a* to the saints	Acts 9:32	*2532*
I myself *a* am a man	Acts 10:26	*2504*
because that on the Gentiles *a*	Acts 10:45	*2532*
had *a* received the word of God	Acts 11:1	*2532*
Then hath God *a* to the Gentiles	Acts 11:18	*2532*
Which *a* they did, and sent it to	Acts 11:30	*2532*
proceeded further to take Peter *a*	Acts 12:3	*2532*
they had *a* John to their minister	Acts 13:5	*2532*
(who *a* is called Paul,) filled	Acts 13:9	*2532*
to whom *a* he gave testimony, and	Acts 13:22	*2532*
as it is *a* written in the second	Acts 13:33	*2532*
he saith *a* in another psalm	Acts 13:35	*2532*
Jews and *a* of the Greeks believed	Acts 14:1	*2532*
a of the Jews with their rulers,	Acts 14:5	
We *a* are men of like passions	Acts 14:15	*2532*
who shall *a* tell you the same	Acts 15:27	*2532*
being prophets *a* themselves	Acts 15:32	*2532*
Paul *a* and Barnabas continued in	Acts 15:35	*1161*
of the Lord, with many others *a*	Acts 15:35	*2532*
upside down are come hither *a*	Acts 17:6	*2532*
a of honourable women which were	Acts 17:12	*2532*
at Berea, they came thither *a*	Acts 17:13	*2546*
as certain *a* of your own poets	Acts 17:28	*2532*
For we are *a* his offspring	Acts 17:28	*2532*
Greeks *a* dwelling at Ephesus	Acts 19:17	*2532*
Many of them *a* which used curious	Acts 19:19	*1161*
been there, I must *a* see Rome	Acts 19:21	*2532*
but *a* that the temple of the	Acts 19:27	*2532*
a to the Greeks, repentance	Acts 20:21	*2532*
A of your own selves shall men	Acts 20:30	*2532*
but *a* to die at Jerusalem for the	Acts 21:13	*2532*
There went with us *a* certain of	Acts 21:16	*2532*
thou thyself *a* walkest orderly	Acts 21:24	*2532*
brought Greeks *a* into the temple	Acts 21:28	*2532*
As *a* the high priest doth bear me	Acts 22:5	*2532*
from whom *a* I received letters	Acts 22:5	*2532*
was shed, I *a* was standing by, and	Acts 22:20	*2532*
and the chief captain *a* was afraid	Acts 22:29	*2532*
must thou bear witness *a* at Rome	Acts 23:11	*2532*
commandment to his accusers *a* to	Acts 23:30	*2532*
presented Paul *a* before him	Acts 23:33	*2532*
when thine accusers are *a* come	Acts 23:35	*2532*
Who *a* hath gone about to profane	Acts 24:6	*2532*
And the Jews *a* assented, saying	Acts 24:9	*2532*
which they themselves *a* allow	Acts 24:15	*2532*
He hoped *a* that money should have	Acts 24:26	
I would *a* hear the man myself	Acts 25:22	*2532*
a here, crying that he ought not	Acts 25:24	
Which thing I *a* did in Jerusalem	Acts 26:10	*2532*
before whom *a* I speak freely	Acts 26:26	*2532*
but *a* all that hear me this day,	Acts 26:29	*2532*
and ship, but *a* of our lives	Acts 27:10	*2532*
part advised to depart thence *a*	Acts 27:12	*2547*
cheer, and they *a* took some meat	Acts 27:36	*2532*
So when this was done, others *a*	Acts 28:9	*2532*
Who *a* honoured us with many	Acts 28:10	*2532*
Among whom are ye *a* the called of	Rom 1:6	*2532*
might have some fruit among you *a*	Rom 1:13	*2532*
gospel to you that are at Rome *a*	Rom 1:15	*2532*
the Jew first, and *a* to the Greek	Rom 1:16	*2532*
Wherefore God *a* gave them up to	Rom 1:24	*2532*
And likewise *a* the men, leaving	Rom 1:27	*2532*
Jew first, and *a* of the Gentile	Rom 2:9	*2532*
Jew first, and *a* to the Gentile	Rom 2:10	*2532*
law shall *a* perish without law	Rom 2:12	*2532*
conscience *a* bearing witness	Rom 2:15	*4828*
why yet am I *a* judged as a sinner	Rom 3:7	*2504*
is he not *a* of the Gentiles	Rom 3:29	*2532*
Yes, of the Gentiles *a*	Rom 3:29	*2532*
Even as David *a* describeth the	Rom 4:6	*2532*
or upon the uncircumcision *a*	Rom 4:9	*2532*
might be imputed unto them *a*	Rom 4:11	*2532*
but who *a* walk in the steps of	Rom 4:12	*2532*
but to that *a* which is of the	Rom 4:16	*2532*
he was able *a* to perform	Rom 4:21	*2532*
But for us *a*, to whom it shall be	Rom 4:24	*2532*
By whom *a* we have access by faith	Rom 5:2	*2532*
but we glory in tribulations *a*	Rom 5:3	*2532*
but we *a* joy in God through our	Rom 5:11	*2532*
offence, so *a* is the free gift	Rom 5:15	*2532*
even so we *a* should walk in	Rom 6:4	*2532*
we shall be *a* in the likeness of	Rom 6:5	*2532*
that we shall *a* live with him	Rom 6:8	*2532*
Likewise reckon ye *a* yourselves	Rom 6:11	*2532*
ye *a* are become dead to the law	Rom 7:4	*2532*
a quicken your mortal bodies by	Rom 8:11	*2532*
that we may be *a* glorified	Rom 8:17	*2532*
a shall be delivered from the	Rom 8:21	*2532*
And not only they, but ourselves *a*	Rom 8:23	*2532*
Likewise the Spirit *a* helpeth our	Rom 8:26	*2532*
he *a* did predestinate to be	Rom 8:29	*2532*
predestinate, them he *a* called	Rom 8:30	*2532*
he called, them he *a* justified	Rom 8:30	*2532*
he justified, them he *a* glorified	Rom 8:30	*2532*
him *a* freely give us all things	Rom 8:32	*2532*
who *a* maketh intercession for us	Rom 8:34	*2532*
my conscience *a* bearing me	Rom 9:1	*4828*
but when Rebecca *a* had conceived	Rom 9:10	*2532*
Jews only, but *a* of the Gentiles	Rom 9:24	*2532*
As he saith *a* in Osee, I will	Rom 9:25	*2532*
Esaias *a* crieth concerning Israel	Rom 9:27	*1161*
For I *a* am an Israelite, of the	Rom 11:1	*2532*
so then at this present time *a*	Rom 11:5	*2532*
be holy, the lump is *a* holy	Rom 11:16	*2532*
heed lest he *a* spare not thee	Rom 11:21	*3761*
otherwise thou *a* shalt be cut off	Rom 11:22	*2532*
And they *a*, if they abide not	Rom 11:23	*1161*
so have these *a* now not believed	Rom 11:31	*2532*
mercy they *a* may obtain mercy	Rom 11:31	*2532*
but *a* for conscience sake	Rom 13:5	*2532*
for this cause pay ye tribute *a*	Rom 13:6	*2532*
as Christ *a* received us to the	Rom 15:7	*2532*
I myself *a* am persuaded of you,	Rom 15:14	*2532*
that ye *a* are full of goodness,	Rom 15:14	*2532*
able *a* to admonish one another	Rom 15:14	*2532*
For which cause *a* I have been	Rom 15:22	*2532*
their duty is *a* to minister unto	Rom 15:27	*2532*
succourer of many, and of myself *a*	Rom 16:2	*2532*
but *a* all the churches of the	Rom 16:4	*2532*
who *a* were in Christ before me	Rom 16:7	*2532*
Who shall *a* confirm you unto the	1Cor 1:8	*2532*
I baptized *a* the household of	1Cor 1:16	*2532*
Which things *a* we speak, not in	1Cor 2:13	*2532*
that we *a* might reign with you	1Cor 4:8	*2532*
to judge them *a* that are without	1Cor 5:12	*2532*
will *a* raise up us by his own	1Cor 6:14	*2532*
likewise *a* the wife unto the	1Cor 7:3	*2532*
likewise *a* the husband hath not	1Cor 7:4	*2532*
likewise *a* he that is called,	1Cor 7:22	*2532*
is difference *a* between a wife	1Cor 7:34	
I think *a* that I have the Spirit	1Cor 7:40	*2504*
or saith not the law the same *a*	1Cor 9:8	*2532*
evil things, as they *a* lusted	1Cor 10:6	*2548*
Christ, as some of them *a* tempted	1Cor 10:9	*2532*
ye, as some of them *a* murmured	1Cor 10:10	*2532*
temptation *a* make a way to escape	1Cor 10:13	*2532*
of me, even as I *a* am of Christ	1Cor 11:1	*2504*
not covered, let her *a* be shorn	1Cor 11:6	*2532*
even so is the man *a* by the woman	1Cor 11:12	*2532*
For there must be *a* heresies	1Cor 11:19	*2532*
that which *a* I delivered unto you	1Cor 11:23	*2532*
the same manner *a* he took the cup	1Cor 11:25	*2532*
so *a* is Christ	1Cor 12:12	*2532*
shall I know even as *a* I am known	1Cor 13:12	*2532*
pray with the understanding *a*	1Cor 14:15	*2532*
sing with the understanding *a*	1Cor 14:15	*2532*
my voice I might teach others *a*	1Cor 14:19	*2532*
obedience, as *a* saith the law	1Cor 14:34	*2532*
which *a* ye have received, and	1Cor 15:1	*2532*
By which *a* ye are saved, if ye	1Cor 15:2	*2532*
of all that which I *a* received	1Cor 15:3	*2532*
last of all he was seen of me *a*	1Cor 15:8	*2504*
vain, and your faith is *a* vain	1Cor 15:14	*2532*
Then they *a* which are fallen	1Cor 15:18	*2532*
by man came *a* the resurrection of	1Cor 15:21	*2532*
then shall the Son *a* himself be	1Cor 15:28	*2532*
There are *a* celestial bodies, and	1Cor 15:40	*2532*
So *a* is the resurrection of the	1Cor 15:42	*2532*
such are they *a* that are earthy	1Cor 15:48	*2532*
such are they *a* that are heavenly	1Cor 15:48	*2532*
we shall *a* bear the image of the	1Cor 15:49	*2532*
And if it be meet that I go *a*	1Cor 16:4	*2504*
the work of the Lord, as I *a* do	1Cor 16:10	*2532*
so our consolation *a* aboundeth by	2Cor 1:5	*2532*
same sufferings which we *a* suffer	2Cor 1:6	*2532*
so shall ye be *a* of the	2Cor 1:7	*2532*
Ye *a* helping together by prayer	2Cor 1:11	*2532*
As *a* ye have acknowledged us in	2Cor 1:14	*2532*
even as ye *a* are ours in the day	2Cor 1:14	*2532*
Who hath *a* sealed us, and given	2Cor 1:22	*2532*
For to this end *a* did I write	2Cor 2:9	*2532*
ye forgive any thing, I forgive *a*	2Cor 2:10	*2532*
Who *a* hath made us able ministers	2Cor 3:6	*2532*

that the life *a* of Jesus might be 2Cor 4:10 2532
that the life *a* of Jesus might be 2Cor 4:11 2532
we *a* believe, and therefore speak 2Cor 4:13 2532
shall raise up us *a* by Jesus 2Cor 4:14 2532
who *a* hath given unto us the 2Cor 5:5 2532
I trust *a* are made manifest in 2Cor 5:11 2532
beseech you *a* that ye receive not 2Cor 6:1 2532
my children,) be ye *a* enlarged 2Cor 6:13 2532
a finish in you the same grace *a* 2Cor 8:6 2532
that ye abound in this grace *a* 2Cor 8:7 2532
but *a* to be forward a year ago 2Cor 8:10 2532
a out of that which ye have 2Cor 8:11 2532
that their abundance *a* may be a 2Cor 8:14 2532
but who was *a* chosen of the 2Cor 8:19 2532
but *a* in the sight of men 2Cor 8:21 2532
sparingly shall reap *a* sparingly 2Cor 9:6 2532
shall reap *a* bountifully 2Cor 9:6 2532
but is abundant *a* by many 2Cor 9:12 2532
such will we be *a* in deed when we 2Cor 10:11 2532
you *a* in preaching the gospel of 2Cor 10:14 2532
a be transformed as the ministers 2Cor 11:15 2532
after the flesh, I will glory *a* 2Cor 11:18 2504
(I speak foolishly,) I am bold *a* 2Cor 11:21 2504
For we *a* are weak in him, but we 2Cor 13:4 2532
this *a* we wish, even your 2Cor 13:9 2532
Barnabas, and took Titus with me *a* Gal 2:1 2532
the same which I *a* was forward to Gal 2:10 2532
insomuch that Barnabas *a* was Gal 2:13 2532
we ourselves *a* are found sinners, Gal 2:17 2532
as I have *a* told you in time past Gal 5:21 2532
let us *a* walk in the Spirit Gal 5:25 2532
thyself, lest thou *a* be tempted Gal 6:1 2532
man soweth, that shall he *a* reap Gal 6:7 2532
In whom *a* we have obtained an Eph 1:11 2532
In whom ye *a* trusted, after that Eph 1:13 2532
in whom *a* after that ye believed, Eph 1:13 2532
Wherefore I *a*, after I heard of Eph 1:15 2504
but *a* in that which is to come Eph 1:21 2532
Among whom *a* we all had our Eph 2:3 2532
In whom ye *a* are builded together Eph 2:22 2532
what is it but that he *a* Eph 4:9 2532
He that descended is the same *a* Eph 4:10 2532
as Christ *a* hath loved us, and Eph 5:2 2532
even as Christ *a* loved the church Eph 5:25 2532
that your Master *a* is in heaven Eph 6:9 2532
But that ye *a* may know my affairs Eph 6:21 2532
and some *a* of good will Phil 1:15 2532
always, so now *a* Christ shall be Phil 1:20 2532
but *a* to suffer for his sake Phil 1:29 2532
but every man *a* on the things of Phil 2:4 2532
which was *a* in Christ Jesus Phil 2:5 2532
Wherefore God *a* hath highly Phil 2:9 2532
For the same cause *a* do ye joy Phil 2:18 2532
that I *a* may be of good comfort, Phil 2:19 2504
I *a* myself shall come shortly Phil 2:24 2532
and not on him only, but on me *a* Phil 2:27 2532
Though I might *a* have confidence Phil 3:4 2532
a I am apprehended of Christ Phil 3:12 2532
from whence *a* we look for the Phil 3:20 2532
And I intreat thee *a*, true Phil 4:3 2532
me in the gospel, with Clement *a* Phil 4:3 2532
wherein ye were *a* careful Phil 4:10 2532
Now ye Philippians know *a* Phil 4:15 2532
forth fruit, as it doth *a* in you Col 1:6 2532
As ye *a* learned of Epaphras our Col 1:7 2532
Who *a* declared unto us your love Col 1:8 2532
For this cause we *a*, since the Col 1:9 2532
Whereunto I *a* labour, striving Col 1:29 2532
In whom *a* ye are circumcised with Col 2:11 2532
wherein *a* ye are risen with him Col 2:12 2532
then shall ye *a* appear with him Col 3:4 2532
In the which ye *a* walked some Col 3:7 2532
But now ye *a* put off all these Col 3:8 2532
as Christ forgave you, so *a* do ye Col 3:13 2532
to the which *a* ye are called in Col 3:15 2532
knowing that ye *a* have a Master Col 4:1 2532
Withal praying *a* for us, that God Col 4:3 2532
Christ, for which I am *a* in bonds Col 4:3 2532
cause that it be read *a* in the Col 4:16 2532
but *a* in power, and in the Holy 1Th 1:5 2532
but *a* in every place your faith 1Th 1:8 2532
but *a* our own souls, because ye 1Th 2:8 2532
Ye are witnesses, and God *a* 1Th 2:10 2532
For this cause *a* thank we God 1Th 2:13 2532
worketh *a* in you that believe 1Th 2:13 2532
for ye *a* have suffered like 1Th 2:14 2532
to see us, as we *a* to see you 1Th 3:6 2532
as we *a* have forewarned you and 1Th 4:6 2532
who hath *a* given unto us his holy 1Th 4:8 2532
even so them *a* which sleep in 1Th 4:14 2532
one another, even as *a* ye do 1Th 5:11 2532
calleth you, who *a* will do it 1Th 5:24 2532
of God, for which ye *a* suffer 2Th 1:5 2532
Wherefore *a* we pray always for 2Th 1:11 2532
In like manner *a*, that women 1Ti 2:9 2532
let these *a* first be proved 1Ti 3:10 2532
and not only idle, but tattlers *a* 1Ti 5:13 2532
all, that others *a* may fear 1Ti 5:20 2532
Likewise *a* the good works of some 1Ti 5:25 2532
life, whereunto thou art *a* called 1Ti 6:12 2532
and I am persuaded that in thee *a* 2Ti 1:5 2532
cause I *a* suffer these things 2Ti 1:12 2532
shall be able to teach others *a* 2Ti 2:2 2532
if a man *a* strive for masteries, 2Ti 2:5 2532
that they may *a* obtain the 2Ti 2:10 2532
him, we shall *a* live with him 2Ti 2:11 2532
we shall *a* reign with him 2Ti 2:12 2532
if we deny him, he *a* will deny us 2Ti 2:12 2548
but *a* of wood and of earth 2Ti 2:20 2532
Flee *a* youthful lusts 2Ti 2:22 1161
This know *a*, that in the last 2Ti 3:1 1161
so do these *a* resist the truth 2Ti 3:8 2532
unto all men, as theirs *a* was 2Ti 3:9 2532
but unto all them *a* that love his 2Ti 4:8 2532

Of whom be thou ware *a* 2Ti 4:15 2532
For we ourselves *a* were sometimes Titus 3:3 2532
let ours *a* learn to maintain good Titus 3:14 2532
now *a* a prisoner of Jesus Christ Philem 9 2532
thou wilt *a* do more than I say Philem 21 2532
But withal prepare me *a* a lodging Philem 22 2532
by whom *a* he made the worlds Heb 1:2 2532
God *a* bearing them witness, both Heb 2:4 4901
he *a* himself likewise took part Heb 2:14 2532
as *a* Moses was faithful in all Heb 3:2 2532
he *a* hath ceased from his own Heb 4:10 2532
for that he himself *a* is Heb 5:2 2532
so *a* for himself, to offer for Heb 5:3 2532
So *a* Christ glorified not himself Heb 5:5 2532
As he saith *a* in another place, Heb 5:6 2532
To whom *a* Abraham gave a tenth Heb 7:2 2532
after that *a* King of Salem, which Heb 7:2 2532
And as I may so say, Levi *a* Heb 7:9 2532
necessity a change *a* of the law Heb 7:12 2532
Wherefore he is able *a* to save Heb 7:25 2532
this man have somewhat *a* to offer Heb 8:3 2532
by how much *a* he is the mediator Heb 8:6 2532
a ordinances of divine service Heb 9:1 2532
there must *a* of necessity be the Heb 9:16
Holy Ghost *a* is a witness to us Heb 10:15 2532
Through faith *a* Sara herself Heb 11:11 2532
from whence *a* he received him in Heb 11:19 2532
of David *a*, and Samuel, and of the Heb 11:32 5037
Wherefore seeing we *a* are Heb 12:1 2532
not the earth only, but *a* heaven Heb 12:26 2532
as being yourselves *a* in the body Heb 13:3 2532
Wherefore Jesus *a*, that he might Heb 13:12 2532
so *a* shall the rich man fade away Jas 1:11 2532
there come in *a* a poor man in Jas 2:2 2532
Do not commit adultery, said *a* Jas 2:11 2532
the devils *a* believe, and tremble Jas 2:19 2532
Likewise *a* was not Rahab the Jas 2:25 2532
so faith without works is dead *a* Jas 2:26 2532
able *a* to bridle the whole body Jas 3:2 2532
Behold *a* the ships, which though Jas 3:4 2532
Be ye *a* patient Jas 5:8 2532
Ye *a*, as lively stones, are built 1Pet 2:5 2532
Wherefore *a* it is contained in 1Pet 2:6 2532
whereunto *a* they were appointed 1Pet 2:8 2532
and gentle, but *a* to the froward 1Pet 2:18 2532
because Christ *a* suffered for us, 1Pet 2:21 2532
they *a* may without the word be 1Pet 3:1 2532
in the old time the holy women *a* 1Pet 3:5 2532
For Christ *a* hath once suffered 1Pet 3:18 2532
By which *a* he went and preached 1Pet 3:19 2532
whereunto even baptism doth *a* now 1Pet 3:21 2532
preached *a* to them that are dead 1Pet 4:6 2532
ye may be glad *a* with exceeding 1Pet 4:13 2532
who am *a* an elder, and a witness 1Pet 5:1 2532
a a partaker of the glory that 1Pet 5:1 2532
We have *a* a more sure word of 2Pet 1:19 2532
false prophets *a* among the people 2Pet 2:1 2532
with fervent heat, the earth *a* 2Pet 3:10 2532
as our beloved brother Paul *a* 2Pet 3:15 2532
As *a* in all his epistles, 2Pet 3:16 2532
as they do *a* the other scriptures 2Pet 3:16 2532
things before, beware lest ye *a* 2Pet 3:17 4879
that ye *a* may have fellowship 1Jn 1:3 2532
but *a* for the sins of the whole 1Jn 2:2 2532
in him ought himself *a* so to walk 1Jn 2:6 2532
the Son hath the Father *a* 1Jn 2:23 2532
ye *a* shall continue in the Son, 1Jn 2:24 2532
sin transgresseth *a* the law 1Jn 3:4 2532
we ought *a* to love one another 1Jn 4:11 2532
who loveth God love his brother *a* 1Jn 4:21 2532
him *a* that is begotten of him 1Jn 5:1 2532
but *a* all they that have known 2Jn 1 2532
yea, and we *a* bear record 3Jn 12 2532
Likewise *a* these filthy dreamers Jude 8 2532
And Enoch *a*, the seventh from Adam Jude 14 2532
him, and they *a* which pierced him Rev 1:7
who *a* am your brother, and Rev 1:9 2532
the Nicolaitanes, which I *a* hate Rev 2:6 2504
So hast thou *a* them that hold the Rev 2:15 2532
I *a* will keep thee from the hour Rev 3:10 2504
my throne, even as I *a* overcame Rev 3:21 2504
until their fellowservants *a* Rev 6:11 2532
where *a* our Lord was crucified Rev 11:8 2532
he *a* having a sharp sickle Rev 14:17 2532

ALTAR

Noah builded an *a* unto the LORD Gen 8:20 4196
offered burnt offerings on the *a* Gen 8:20 4196
builded he an *a* unto the LORD Gen 12:7 4196
he builded an *a* unto the LORD Gen 12:8 4196
Unto the place of the *a*, which he Gen 13:4 4196
and built there an *a* unto the LORD Gen 13:18 4196
and Abraham built an *a* there Gen 22:9 4196
laid him on the *a* upon the wood Gen 22:9 4196
And he builded an *a* there, and Gen 26:25 4196
And he erected there an *a*, and Gen 33:20 4196
and make there an *a* unto God Gen 35:1 4196
I will make there an *a* unto God Gen 35:3 4196
And he built there an *a*, and called Gen 35:7 4196
And Moses built an *a*, and called Ex 17:15 4196
An *a* of earth thou shalt make Ex 20:24 4196
thou wilt make me an *a* of stone Ex 20:25 4196
thou go up by steps unto mine *a* Ex 20:26 4196
thou shalt take him from mine *a* Ex 21:14 4196
builded an *a* under the hill, and Ex 24:4 4196
the blood he sprinkled on the *a* Ex 24:6 4196
shalt make an *a* of shittim wood Ex 27:1 4196
the *a* shall be foursquare Ex 27:1 4196
the compass of the *a* beneath Ex 27:5 4196
may be even to the midst of the *a* Ex 27:5 4196
thou shalt make staves for the *a* Ex 27:6 4196
be upon the two sides of the *a* Ex 27:7 4196
a to minister in the holy place Ex 28:43 4196
horns of the *a* with thy finger Ex 29:12 4196

blood beside the bottom of the *a* Ex 29:12 4196
them, and burn them upon the *a* Ex 29:13 4196
it round about upon the *a* Ex 29:16 4196
burn the whole ram upon the *a* Ex 29:18 4196
the blood upon the *a* round about Ex 29:20 4196
of the blood that is upon the *a* Ex 29:21 4196
burn them upon the *a* for a burnt Ex 29:25 4196
and thou shalt cleanse the *a* Ex 29:36 4196
shalt make an atonement for the *a* Ex 29:37 4196
and it shall be an *a* most holy Ex 29:37 4196
toucheth the *a* shall be holy Ex 29:37 4196
which thou shalt offer upon the *a* Ex 29:38 4196
of the congregation, and the *a* Ex 29:44 4196
thou shalt make an *a* to burn Ex 30:1 4196
of the congregation and the *a* Ex 30:18 4196
come near to the *a* to minister Ex 30:20 4196
his vessels, and the *a* of incense, Ex 30:27 4196
the *a* of burnt offering with all Ex 30:28 4196
furniture, and the *a* of incense, Ex 31:8 4196
the *a* of burnt offering with all Ex 31:9 4196
saw it, he built an *a* before it Ex 32:5 4196
And the incense *a*, and his staves, Ex 35:15 4196
The *a* of burnt offering, with his Ex 35:16 4196
the incense *a* of shittim wood Ex 37:25 4196
he made the *a* of burnt offering Ex 38:1 4196
he made all the vessels of the *a* Ex 38:3 4196
he made for the *a* a brasen grate Ex 38:4 4196
the rings on the sides of the *a* Ex 38:7 4196
he made the *a* hollow with boards Ex 38:7
the congregation, and the brasen *a* Ex 38:30 4196
it, and all the vessels of the *a* Ex 38:30 4196
And the golden *a*, and the anointing Ex 39:38 4196
The brasen *a*, and his grate of Ex 39:39 4196
thou shalt set the *a* of gold for Ex 40:5 4196
thou shalt set the *a* of the burnt Ex 40:6 4196
tent of the congregation and the *a* Ex 40:7 4196
the *a* of the burnt offering Ex 40:10 4196
his vessels, and sanctify the *a* Ex 40:10 4196
and it shall be an *a* most holy Ex 40:10 4196
he put the golden *a* in the tent Ex 40:26 4196
he put the *a* of burnt offering by Ex 40:29 4196
tent of the congregation and the *a* Ex 40:30 4196
and when they came near unto the *a* Ex 40:32 4196
about the tabernacle and the *a* Ex 40:33 4196
the *a* that is by the door of the Lev 1:5 4196
priest shall put fire upon the *a* Lev 1:7 4196
on the fire which is upon the *a* Lev 1:8 4196
priest shall burn all on the *a* Lev 1:9 4196
the *a* northward before the LORD Lev 1:11 4196
his blood round about upon the *a* Lev 1:11 4196
on the fire which is upon the *a* Lev 1:12 4196
it all, and burn it upon the *a* Lev 1:13 4196
priest shall bring it unto the *a* Lev 1:15 4196
off his head, and burn it on the *a* Lev 1:15 4196
be wrung out at the side of the *a* Lev 1:15 4196
it beside the *a* on the east part Lev 1:16 4196
priest shall burn it upon the *a* Lev 1:17 4196
the memorial of it upon the *a* Lev 2:2 4196
he shall bring it unto the *a* Lev 2:8 4196
and shall burn it upon the *a* Lev 2:9 4196
burnt on the *a* for a sweet savour Lev 2:12 4196
the blood upon the *a* round about Lev 3:2 4196
on the *a* upon the burnt sacrifice Lev 3:5 4196
thereof round about upon the *a* Lev 3:8 4196
priest shall burn it upon the *a* Lev 3:11 4196
thereof upon the *a* round about Lev 3:13 4196
priest shall burn them upon the *a* Lev 3:16 4196
the *a* of sweet incense before the Lev 4:7 4196
of the *a* of the burnt offering Lev 4:7 4196
upon the *a* of the burnt offering Lev 4:10 4196
of the *a* which is before the LORD Lev 4:18 4196
of the *a* of the burnt offering Lev 4:18 4196
from him, and burn it upon the *a* Lev 4:19 4196
horns of the *a* of burnt offering Lev 4:25 4196
bottom of the *a* of burnt offering Lev 4:25 4196
shall burn all his fat upon the *a* Lev 4:26 4196
horns of the *a* of burnt offering Lev 4:30 4196
thereof at the bottom of the *a* Lev 4:30 4196
the *a* for a sweet savour unto the Lev 4:31 4196
horns of the *a* of burnt offering Lev 4:34 4196
thereof at the bottom of the *a* Lev 4:34 4196
priest shall burn them upon the *a* Lev 4:35 4196
offering upon the side of the *a* Lev 5:9 4196
wrung out at the bottom of the *a* Lev 5:9 4196
thereof, and burn it on the *a* Lev 5:12 4196
the *a* all night unto the morning Lev 6:9 4196
the fire of the *a* shall be Lev 6:9 4196
with the burnt offering on the *a* Lev 6:10 4196
and he shall put them beside the *a* Lev 6:10 4196
the fire upon the *a* shall be Lev 6:12 4196
shall ever be burning upon the *a* Lev 6:13 4196
it before the LORD, before the *a* Lev 6:14 4196
it upon the *a* for a sweet savour Lev 6:15 4196
sprinkle round about upon the *a* Lev 7:2 4196
a for an offering made by fire Lev 7:5 4196
shall burn the fat upon the *a* Lev 7:31 4196
thereof upon the *a* seven times Lev 8:11 4196
seven times, and anointed the *a* Lev 8:11 4196
the *a* round about with his finger Lev 8:15 4196
his finger, and purified the *a* Lev 8:15 4196
the blood at the bottom of the *a* Lev 8:15 4196
and Moses burned it upon the *a* Lev 8:16 4196
the blood upon the *a* round about Lev 8:19 4196
burnt the whole ram upon the *a* Lev 8:21 4196
the blood upon the *a* round about Lev 8:24 4196
burnt them on the *a* upon the Lev 8:28 4196
of the blood which was upon the *a* Lev 8:30 4196
said unto Aaron, Go unto the *a* Lev 9:7 4196
Aaron therefore went unto the *a* Lev 9:8 4196
and put it upon the horns of the *a* Lev 9:9 4196
the blood at the bottom of the *a* Lev 9:9 4196
sin offering, he burnt upon the *a* Lev 9:10 4196
sprinkled round about upon the *a* Lev 9:12 4196
and he burnt them upon the *a* Lev 9:13 4196

upon the burnt offering on the *a* Lev 9:14 4196
thereof, and burnt it upon the *a* Lev 9:17 4196
sprinkled upon the *a* round about Lev 9:18 4196
and he burnt the fat upon the *a* Lev 9:20 4196
consumed upon the *a* the burnt Lev 9:24 4196
it without leaven beside the *a* Lev 10:12 4196
and the meat offering upon the *a* Lev 14:20 4196
from off the *a* before the LORD Lev 16:12 4196
the *a* that is before the LORD Lev 16:18 4196
the horns of the *a* round about Lev 16:18 4196
of the congregation, and the *a* Lev 16:20 4196
offering shall he burn upon the *a* Lev 16:25 4196
of the congregation, and for the *a* Lev 16:33 4196
sprinkle the blood upon the *a* of Lev 17:6 4196
a to make an atonement for your Lev 17:11 4196
vail, nor come nigh unto the *a* Lev 21:23 4196
of them upon the *a* unto the LORD Lev 22:22 4196
by the *a* round about, and the Num 3:26 4196
upon the golden *a* they shall Num 4:11 4196
take away the ashes from the *a* Num 4:13 4196
basons, all the vessels of the *a* Num 4:14 4196
by the *a* round about, and their Num 4:26 4196
the LORD, and offer it upon the *a* Num 5:25 4196
thereof, and burn it upon the *a* Num 5:26 4196
instruments thereof, both the *a* Num 7:1 4196
offered for dedicating of the *a* Num 7:10 4196
their offering before the *a* Num 7:10 4196
day, for the dedicating of the *a* Num 7:11 4196
This was the dedication of the *a* Num 7:84 4196
This was the dedication of the *a* Num 7:88 4196
plates for a covering of the *a* Num 16:38 4196
plates for a covering of the *a* Num 16:39 4196
put fire therein from off the *a* Num 16:46 4196
vessels of the sanctuary and the *a* Num 18:3 4196
sanctuary, and the charge of the *a* Num 18:5 4196
office for every thing of the *a* Num 18:7 4196
sprinkle their blood upon the *a* Num 18:17 4196
offered on every *a* a bullock Num 23:2 4196
offered upon every *a* a bullock Num 23:4 4196
a bullock and a ram on every *a* Num 23:14 4196
a bullock and a ram on every *a* Num 23:30 4196
upon the *a* of the LORD thy God Deut 12:27 4196
upon the *a* of the LORD thy God Deut 12:27 4196
unto the *a* of the LORD thy God Deut 16:21 4196
before the *a* of the LORD thy God Deut 26:4 4196
there shalt thou build an *a* Deut 27:5 4196
the LORD thy God, an *a* of stones Deut 27:5 4196
Thou shalt build the *a* of the Deut 27:6 4196
burnt sacrifice upon thine *a* Deut 33:10 4196
Then Joshua built an *a* unto the Josh 8:30 4196
an *a* of whole stones, over which Josh 8:31 4196
for the *a* of the LORD, even unto Josh 9:27 4196
a by Jordan, a great *a* Josh 22:10 4196
a over against the land of Canaan Josh 22:11 4196
in that ye have builded you an *a* Josh 22:16 4196
an *a* beside the *a* of the LORD Josh 22:19 4196
That we have built us an *a* to Josh 22:23 4196
us now prepare to build us an *a* Josh 22:26 4196
the pattern of the *a* of the LORD Josh 22:28 4196
to build an *a* for burnt offerings Josh 22:29 4196
beside the *a* of the LORD our God Josh 22:29 4196
children of Gad called the *a* Ed Josh 22:34 4196
built an *a* there unto the LORD Judg 6:24 4196
throw down the *a* of Baal that thy Judg 6:25 4196
build an *a* unto the LORD thy God Judg 6:26 4196
the *a* of Baal was cast down, and Judg 6:28 4196
offered upon the *a* that was built Judg 6:28 4196
he hath cast down the *a* of Baal Judg 6:30 4196
because one hath cast down his *a* Judg 6:31 4196
because he hath thrown down his *a* Judg 6:32 4196
up toward heaven from off the *a* Judg 13:20 4196
ascended in the flame of the *a* Judg 13:20 4196
rose early, and built there an *a* Judg 21:4 4196
my priest, to offer upon mine *a* 1Sa 2:28 4196
I shall not cut off from mine *a* 1Sa 2:33 4196
there he built an *a* unto the LORD 1Sa 7:17 4196
And Saul built an *a* unto the LORD 1Sa 14:35 4196
the same was the first *a* that he 1Sa 14:35 4196
rear an *a* unto the LORD in the 2Sa 24:18 4196
to build an *a* unto the LORD, that 2Sa 24:21 4196
built there an *a* unto the LORD 2Sa 24:25 4196
caught hold on the horns of the *a* 1Kin 1:50 4196
caught hold on the horns of the *a* 1Kin 1:51 4196
they brought him down from the *a* 1Kin 1:53 4196
caught hold on the horns of the *a* 1Kin 2:28 4196
and, behold, he is by the *a* 1Kin 2:29 4196
did Solomon offer upon that *a* 1Kin 3:4 4196
so covered the *a* which was of 1Kin 6:20 4196
also the whole *a* that was by the 1Kin 6:22 4196
the *a* of gold, and the table of 1Kin 7:48 4196
Solomon stood before the *a* of the 1Kin 8:22 4196
come before thine *a* in this house 1Kin 8:31 4196
from before the *a* of the LORD 1Kin 8:54 4196
because the brasen *a* that was 1Kin 8:64 4196
peace offerings upon the *a* which 1Kin 9:25 4196
the *a* that was before the LORD 1Kin 9:25 4196
Judah, and he offered upon the *a* 1Kin 12:32 4196
So he offered upon the *a* which he 1Kin 12:33 4196
and he offered upon the *a*, and 1Kin 12:33 4196
stood by the *a* to burn incense 1Kin 13:1 4196
he cried against the *a* in the 1Kin 13:2 4196
of the LORD, and said, O *a*, *a* 1Kin 13:2 4196
the *a* shall be rent, and the ashes 1Kin 13:3 4196
cried against the *a* in Beth-el 1Kin 13:4 4196
he put forth his hand from the *a* 1Kin 13:4 4196
The *a* also was rent 1Kin 13:5 4196
the ashes poured out from the *a* 1Kin 13:5 4196
the LORD against the *a* in Beth-el 1Kin 13:32 4196
he reared up an *a* for Baal in the 1Kin 16:32 4196
leaped upon the *a* which was made 1Kin 18:26 4196
he repaired the *a* of the LORD 1Kin 18:30 4196
an *a* in the name of the LORD 1Kin 18:32 4196
and he made a trench about the *a* 1Kin 18:32 4196
the water ran round about the *a* 1Kin 18:35 4196

of the temple, along by the *a* 2Kin 11:11 4196
lid of it, and set it beside the *a* 2Kin 12:9 4196
saw an *a* that was at Damascus 2Kin 16:10 4196
the priest the fashion of the *a* 2Kin 16:10 4196
Urijah the priest built an *a* 2Kin 16:11 4196
from Damascus, the king saw the *a* 2Kin 16:12 4196
and the king approached to the *a* 2Kin 16:12 4196
his peace offerings, upon the *a* 2Kin 16:13 4196
And he brought also the brasen *a* 2Kin 16:14 4196
of the house, from between the *a* 2Kin 16:14 4196
put it on the north side of the *a* 2Kin 16:14 4196
Upon the great *a* burn the morning 2Kin 16:15 4196
the brasen *a* shall be for me to 2Kin 16:15 4196
before this *a* in Jerusalem 2Kin 18:22 4196
to the *a* of the LORD in Jerusalem 2Kin 23:9 4196
Moreover the *a* that was at 2Kin 23:15 4196
to sin, had made, both that *a* 2Kin 23:15 4196
and burned them upon the *a* 2Kin 23:16 4196
done against the *a* of Beth-el 2Kin 23:17 4196
upon the *a* of the burnt offering 1Chr 6:49 4196
on the *a* of incense, and were 1Chr 6:49 4196
upon the *a* of the burnt offering 1Chr 16:40 4196
set up an *a* unto the LORD in the 1Chr 21:18 4196
that I may build an *a* therein 1Chr 21:22 4196
built there an *a* unto the LORD 1Chr 21:26 4196
fire upon the *a* of burnt offering 1Chr 21:26 4196
the *a* of the burnt offering, were 1Chr 21:29 4196
this is the *a* of the burnt 1Chr 22:1 4196
for the *a* of incense refined gold 1Chr 28:18 4196
Moreover the brasen *a*, that 2Chr 1:5 4196
to the brasen *a* before the LORD 2Chr 1:6 4196
Moreover he made an *a* of brass 2Chr 4:1 4196
house of God, the golden *a* also 2Chr 4:19 4196
stood at the east end of the *a* 2Chr 5:12 4196
he stood before the *a* of the LORD 2Chr 6:12 4196
come before thine *a* in this house 2Chr 6:22 4196
because the brasen *a* which 2Chr 7:7 4196
dedication of the *a* seven days 2Chr 7:9 4196
the LORD on the *a* of the LORD 2Chr 8:12 4196
and renewed the *a* of the LORD 2Chr 15:8 4196
of the temple, along by the *a* 2Chr 23:10 4196
incense upon the *a* of incense 2Chr 26:16 4196
LORD, from beside the incense *a* 2Chr 26:19 4196
the *a* of burnt offering, with all 2Chr 29:18 4196
they are before the *a* of the LORD 2Chr 29:19 4196
offer them on the *a* of the LORD 2Chr 29:21 4196
blood, and sprinkled it on the *a* 2Chr 29:22 4196
sprinkled the blood upon the *a* 2Chr 29:22 4196
sprinkled the blood upon the *a* 2Chr 29:22 4196
with their blood upon the *a* 2Chr 29:24 4196
the burnt offering upon the *a* 2Chr 29:27 4196
Ye shall worship before one *a* 2Chr 32:12 4196
And he repaired the *a* of the LORD 2Chr 33:16 4196
offerings upon the *a* of the LORD 2Chr 35:16 4196
builded the *a* of the God of Ezr 3:2 4196
they set the *a* upon his bases Ezr 3:3 4196
offer them upon the *a* of the Ezr 7:17 4056
to burn upon the *a* of the LORD Neh 10:34 4196
so will I compass thine *a* Ps 26:6 4196
Then will I go unto the *a* of God Ps 43:4 4196
they offer bullocks upon thine *a* Ps 51:19 4196
even unto the horns of the *a* Ps 118:27 4196
with the tongs from off the *a* Is 6:6 4196
In that day shall there be an *a* Is 19:19 4196
a as chalkstones that are beaten Is 27:9 4196
Ye shall worship before this *a* Is 36:7 4196
shall be accepted upon mine *a* Is 56:7 4196
come up with acceptance on mine *a* Is 60:7 4196
The Lord hath cast off his *a* Lam 2:7 4196
northward at the gate of the *a* Eze 8:5 4196
LORD, between the porch and the *a* Eze 8:16 4196
in, and stood beside the brasen *a* Eze 9:2 4196
keepers of the charge of the *a* Eze 40:46 4196
the *a* that was before the house Eze 40:47 4196
The *a* of wood was three cubits Eze 41:22 4196
of the *a* after the cubits Eze 43:13 4196
be the higher place of the *a* Eze 43:13 4196
So the *a* shall be four cubits Eze 43:15 741
and from the *a* and upward shall be Eze 43:15 741
the *a* shall be twelve cubits long Eze 43:16 741
a in the day when they shall make Eze 43:18 4196
and they shall cleanse the *a* Eze 43:22 4196
Seven days shall they purge the *a* Eze 43:26 4196
your burnt offerings upon the *a* Eze 43:27 4196
corners of the settle of the *a* Eze 45:19 4196
house, at the south side of the *a* Eze 47:1 4196
howl, ye ministers of the *a* Joel 1:13 4196
weep between the porch and the *a* Joel 2:17 4196
clothes laid to pledge by every *a* Amos 2:8 4196
horns of the *a* shall be cut off Amos 3:14 4196
saw the Lord standing upon the *a* Amos 9:1 4196
bowls, and as the corners of the *a* Zec 9:15 4196
be like the bowls before the *a* Zec 14:20 4196
offer polluted bread upon mine *a* Mal 1:7 4196
kindle fire on mine *a* for nought Mal 1:10 4196
covering the *a* of the LORD with Mal 2:13 4196
if thou bring thy gift to the *a* Mt 5:23 *2379*
Leave there thy gift before the *a* Mt 5:24 *2379*
Whosoever shall swear by the *a* Mt 23:18 *2379*
or the *a* that sanctifieth the Mt 23:19 *2379*
therefore shall swear by the *a* Mt 23:20 *2379*
slew between the temple and the *a* Mt 23:35 *2379*
right side of the *a* of incense Lk 1:11 *2379*
which perished between the *a* Lk 11:51 *2379*
devotions, I found an *a* with this Acts 17:23 *1041*
a are partakers with the *a* 1Cor 9:13 *2379*
the sacrifices partakers of the *a* 1Cor 10:18 *2379*
no man gave attendance at the *a* Heb 7:13 *2379*
We have an *a*, whereof they have Heb 13:10 *2379*
offered Isaac his son upon the *a* Jas 2:21 *2379*
I saw under the *a* the souls of Rev 6:9 *2379*
angel came and stood at the *a* Rev 8:3 *2379*
a which was before the throne Rev 8:3 *2379*
and filled it with fire of the *a* Rev 8:5 *2379*

the golden *a* which is before God Rev 9:13 *2379*
the temple of God, and the *a* Rev 11:1 *2379*
another angel came out from the *a* Rev 14:18 *2379*
I heard another out of the *a* say Rev 16:7 *2379*

ALTARS

But ye shall destroy their *a* Ex 34:13 4196
and the candlestick, and the *a* Num 3:31 4196
unto Balak, Build me here seven *a* Num 23:1 4196
unto him, I have prepared seven *a* Num 23:4 4196
top of Pisgah, and built seven *a* Num 23:14 4196
unto Balak, Build me here seven *a* Num 23:29 4196
ye shall destroy their *a*, and Deut 7:5 4196
And ye shall overthrow their *a* Deut 12:3 4196
ye shall throw down their *a* Judg 2:2 4196
thy covenant, thrown down thine *a* 1Kin 19:10 4196
thy covenant, thrown down thine *a* 1Kin 19:14 4196
his *a* and his images brake they in 2Kin 11:18 4196
the priest of Baal before the *a* 2Kin 11:18 4196
whose *a* Hezekiah hath taken away, 2Kin 18:22 4196
and he reared up *a* for Baal 2Kin 21:3 4196
he built *a* in the house of the 2Kin 21:4 4196
he built *a* for all the host of 2Kin 21:5 4196
the *a* that were on the top of the 2Kin 23:12 4196
the *a* which Manasseh had made in 2Kin 23:12 4196
places that were there upon the *a* 2Kin 23:20 4196
away the *a* of the strange gods 2Chr 14:3 4196
and brake it down, and brake his *a* 2Chr 23:17 4196
the priest of Baal before the *a* 2Chr 23:17 4196
he made him *a* in every corner of 2Chr 28:24 4196
took away the *a* that were in 2Chr 30:14 4196
all the *a* for incense took they 2Chr 30:14
the *a* out of all Judah and 2Chr 31:1 4196
away his high places and his *a* 2Chr 32:12 4196
and he reared up *a* for Baalim 2Chr 33:3 4196
Also he built *a* in the house of 2Chr 33:4 4196
he built *a* for all the host of 2Chr 33:5 4196
all the *a* that he had built in 2Chr 33:15 4196
they brake down the *a* of Baalim 2Chr 34:4 4196
bones of the priests upon their *a* 2Chr 34:5 4196
And when he had broken down the *a* 2Chr 34:7 4196
may lay her young, even thine *a* Ps 84:3 4196
And he shall not look to the *a* Is 17:8 4196
whose *a* Hezekiah hath taken away, Is 36:7 4196
burneth incense upon *a* of brick Is 65:3
set up *a* to that shameful thing Jer 11:13 4196
even *a* to burn incense unto Baal Jer 11:13 4196
and upon the horns of your *a* Jer 17:1 4196
their children remember their *a* Jer 17:2 4196
your *a* shall be desolate, and your Eze 6:4 4196
your bones round about your *a* Eze 6:5 4196
that your *a* may be laid waste and Eze 6:6 4196
their idols round about their *a* Eze 6:13 4196
Ephraim hath made many *a* to sin Hos 8:11 4196
a shall be unto him to sin Hos 8:11 4196
his fruit he hath increased the *a* Hos 10:1 4196
he shall break down their *a* Hos 10:2 4196
thistle shall come up on their *a* Hos 10:8 4196
their *a* are as heaps in the Hos 12:11 4196
will also visit the *a* of Beth-el Amos 3:14 4196
prophets, and digged down thine *a* Rom 11:3 *2379*

ALTASCHITH

To the chief Musician, *A*, Michtam Ps 57:*t* 516
To the chief Musician, *A*, Michtam Ps 58:*t* 516
To the chief Musician, *A*, Michtam Ps 59:*t* 516
To the chief Musician, *A*, A Psalm Ps 75:*t* 516

AL-TASHHETH See ALTASCHITH.

ALTER

He shall not *a* it, nor change it, Lev 27:10 2498
that whosoever shall *a* this word Ezr 6:11 8133
that shall put to their hand to *a* Ezr 6:12 8133
nor *a* the thing that is gone out Ps 89:34 8138

ALTERED

and the Medes, that it be not *a* Est 1:19 5674
fashion of his countenance was *a* Lk 9:29

ALTERETH

Medes and Persians, which *a* not Dan 6:8 5709
Medes and Persians, which *a* not Dan 6:12 5709

ALTHOUGH

the Philistines, *a* that was near Ex 13:17 3588
a there was a plague in the Josh 22:17
A my house be not so with God 2Sa 23:5 3588
desire, *a* he make it not to grow 2Sa 23:5 3588
A I have sent unto thee, saying, 1Kin 20:5 3588
a the enemy could not countervail Est 7:4 3588
a thou movedst me against him, to Job 2:3
A affliction cometh not forth of Job 5:6 3588
A thou sayest thou shalt not see Job 35:14
a I was an husband unto them, Jer 31:32
is sold, *a* they were yet alive Eze 7:13
A I have cast them far off among Eze 11:16 3588
a I have scattered them among the Eze 11:16 272
A the fig tree shall not blossom, Hab 3:17 272
A all shall be offended, yet will Mk 14:29
a the works were finished from Heb 4:3 *2543*

ALTOGETHER

done *a* according to the cry of it Gen 18:21 3617
surely thrust you out hence *a* Ex 11:1 3617
And mount Sinai was *a* on a smoke Ex 19:18 3605
make thyself *a* a prince over us Num 16:13 1571
behold, thou hast blessed them *a* Num 23:11
thou hast *a* blessed them these Num 24:10
But if her husband *a* hold his Num 30:14
That which is *a* just shalt thou Deut 16:20
that he would not destroy him *a* 2Chr 12:12 3617
For if thou *a* holdest thy peace Est 4:14
that ye would *a* hold your peace Job 13:5
why then are ye thus *a* vain Job 27:12
the LORD are true and righteous *a* Ps 19:9 3162
man at his best state is *a* vanity Ps 39:5 3605
I was *a* such an one as thyself Ps 50:21

they are *a* become filthy ... Ps 53:3 3162
they are *a* lighter than vanity ... Ps 62:9 3162
lo, O LORD, thou knowest it *a* ... Ps 139:4 3605
yea, he is *a* lovely ... Song 5:16 3605
saith, Are not my princes *a* kings ... Is 10:8 3162
but these have *a* broken the yoke, ... Jer 5:5 3162
But they are *a* brutish and foolish ... Jer 10:8 259
wilt thou be *a* unto me as a liar, ... Jer 15:18
will not leave thee *a* unpunished ... Jer 30:11
he that shall *a* go unpunished ... Jer 49:12
Thou wast *a* born in sins, and dost ... Jn 9:34 *3650*
a such as I am, except these ... Acts 26:29
Yet not *a* with the fornicators of ... 1Cor 5:10 *3843*
Or saith he it *a* for our sakes ... 1Cor 9:10 *3843*

ALUSH (*a'-lush*) *An Israelite encampment during the Exodus.*
from Dophkah, and encamped in *A* ... Num 33:13 442
And they removed from *A*, and ... Num 33:14 442

ALVAH (*al'-vah*) See ALIAH. *An Edomite chief.*
duke Timnah, duke *A*, duke Jetheth ... Gen 36:40 5933

ALVAN (*al'-van*) See ALIAN. *A son of Shobal the Horite.*
A, and Manahath, and Ebal, Shepho, ... Gen 36:23 5935

ALWAY
the table shewbread before me *a* ... Ex 25:30 8548
So it was *a* ... Num 9:16 8548
judgments, and his commandments, *a*. Deut 11:1
be only oppressed and crushed *a* ... Deut 28:33
son shall eat bread *a* at my table ... 2Sa 9:10 8548
a light *a* before me in Jerusalem ... 1Kin 11:36
him to give him *a* a light ... 2Kin 8:19
I would not live *a* ... Job 7:16 5769
needy shall not *a* be forgotten ... Ps 9:18 5331
heart to perform thy statutes *a* ... Ps 119:112 5769
Happy is the man that feareth *a* ... Prov 28:14 8548
and, lo, I am with you *a*, even ... Mt 28:20
but your time is *a* ready ... Jn 7:6 *3842*
to the people, and prayed to God *a* ... Acts 10:2 *1275*
not see, and bow down their back *a* ... Rom 11:10 *1275*
For we which live are *a* delivered ... 2Cor 4:11 *104*
As sorrowful, yet *a* rejoicing ... 2Cor 6:10 *104*
Rejoice in the Lord *a* ... Phil 4:4 *104*
Let your speech be *a* with grace ... Col 4:6 *104*
be saved, to fill up their sins *a* ... 1Th 2:16 *104*
to give thanks *a* to God for you ... 2Th 2:13 *104*
said, The Cretians are *a* liars ... Titus 1:12 *104*
They do *a* err in their heart ... Heb 3:10 *104*

ALWAYS
shall not *a* strive with man ... Gen 6:3 5769
to cause the lamp to burn *a* ... Ex 27:20 8548
it shall be *a* upon his forehead, ... Ex 28:38 8548
me, and keep all my commandments *a* Deut 5:29
the LORD our God, for our good *a* ... Deut 6:24
of the LORD thy God are *a* upon it ... Deut 11:12 8548
learn to fear the LORD thy God *a* ... Deut 14:23
Be ye mindful *a* of his covenant ... 1Chr 16:15 5769
good unto me, but *a* evil ... 2Chr 18:7
will he *a* call upon God ... Job 27:10
Great men are not *a* wise ... Job 32:9
His ways are *a* grievous ... Ps 10:5
I have set the LORD *a* before me ... Ps 16:8 8548
He will not *a* chide ... Ps 103:9 5331
be thou ravished *a* with her love ... Prov 5:19 8548
delight, rejoicing *a* before him ... Prov 8:30
Let thy garments be *a* white ... Eccl 9:8
ever, neither will I be *a* wroth ... Is 57:16 5331
and her womb to be *a* great with me ... Jer 20:17 5769
Israel, which have been *a* waste ... Eze 38:8 8548
do *a* behold the face of my Father ... Mt 18:10
For ye have the poor *a* with you ... Mt 26:11 *3842*
but me ye have not *a* ... Mt 26:11 *3842*
And *a*, night and day, he was in the ... Mk 5:5 *1275*
For ye have the poor with you *a* ... Mk 14:7 *3842*
but me ye have not *a* ... Mk 14:7 *3842*
end, that men ought *a* to pray ... Lk 18:1 *3842*
Watch ye therefore, and pray *a* ... Lk 21:36
for I do *a* those things that ... Jn 8:29 *3842*
And I knew that thou hearest me *a* ... Jn 11:42 *3842*
For the poor *a* ye have with you ... Jn 12:8 *3842*
but me ye have not *a* ... Jn 12:8 *3842*
temple, whither the Jews *a* resort ... Jn 18:20 *3842*
foresaw the Lord *a* before my face ... Acts 2:25
ye do *a* resist the Holy Ghost ... Acts 7:51 *104*
We accept it *a*, and in all places, ... Acts 24:3 *3839*
to have *a* a conscience void of ... Acts 24:16 *1275*
mention of you *a* in my prayers ... Rom 1:9 *3842*
I thank my God *a* on your behalf ... 1Cor 1:4 *3842*
a abounding in the work of the ... 1Cor 15:58 *3842*
which *a* causeth us to triumph in ... 2Cor 2:14 *3842*
A bearing about in the body the ... 2Cor 4:10 *3842*
Therefore we are *a* confident ... 2Cor 5:6 *3842*
a having all sufficiency in all ... 2Cor 9:8 *3842*
affected *a* in a good thing ... Gal 4:18 *3842*
Giving thanks *a* for all things ... Eph 5:20 *3842*
Praying *a* with all prayer and ... Eph 6:18
A in every prayer of mine for you ... Phil 1:4 *3842*
but that with all boldness, as *a* ... Phil 1:20 *3842*
my beloved, as ye have *a* obeyed ... Phil 2:12 *3842*
Jesus Christ, praying *a* for you ... Col 1:3 *3842*
a labouring fervently for you in ... Col 4:12 *3842*
give thanks to God *a* for you all ... 1Th 1:2 *3842*
ye have good remembrance of us *a* ... 1Th 3:6 *3842*
are bound to thank God *a* for you ... 2Th 1:3 *3842*
Wherefore also we pray *a* for you ... 2Th 1:11 *3842*
give you peace *a* by all means ... 2Th 3:16
mention of thee *a* in my prayers ... Philem 4 *3842*
the priests went *a* into the first ... Heb 9:6 *1275*
be ready *a* to give an answer to ... 1Pet 3:15 *104*
not be negligent to put you *a* in ... 2Pet 1:12 *104*
these things *a* in remembrance ... 2Pet 1:15 *1539*

AM
A I my brother's keeper ... Gen 4:9
I *a* thy shield, and thy exceeding ... Gen 15:1
I *a* the LORD that brought thee ... Gen 15:7
unto him, I *a* the Almighty God ... Gen 17:1
After I *a* waxed old shall I have ... Gen 18:12
surety bear a child, which *a* old ... Gen 18:13
which *a* but dust and ashes ... Gen 18:27
and he said, Behold, here I *a* ... Gen 22:1
and he said, Here *a* I, my son ... Gen 22:7
and he said, Here *a* I ... Gen 22:11
I *a* a stranger and a sojourner ... Gen 23:4
I *a* the daughter of Bethuel the ... Gen 24:24
And he said, I *a* Abraham's servant ... Gen 24:34
said, If it be so, why *a* I thus ... Gen 25:22
for I *a* faint ... Gen 25:30
Behold, I *a* at the point to die ... Gen 25:32
I *a* the God of Abraham thy father ... Gen 26:24
for I *a* with thee, and will bless ... Gen 26:24
said unto him, Behold, here *a* I ... Gen 27:1
I *a* old, I know not the day of my ... Gen 27:2
a hairy man, and I *a* a smooth man ... Gen 27:11
and he said, Here *a* I ... Gen 27:18
father, I *a* Esau thy firstborn ... Gen 27:19
And he said, I *a* ... Gen 27:24
I *a* thy son, thy firstborn Esau ... Gen 27:32
I *a* weary of my life because of ... Gen 27:46
I *a* the LORD God of Abraham thy ... Gen 28:13
I *a* with thee, and will keep thee ... Gen 28:15
A I in God's stead, who hath ... Gen 30:2
And Leah said, Happy *a* I, for the ... Gen 30:13
And I said, Here *a* I ... Gen 31:11
I *a* the God of Beth-el, where ... Gen 31:13
I *a* not worthy of the least of ... Gen 32:10
and now I *a* become two bands ... Gen 32:10
said unto him, I *a* God Almighty ... Gen 35:11
And he said to him, Here *a* I ... Gen 37:13
whose these are, *a* I with child ... Gen 38:25
I *a* Pharaoh, and without thee ... Gen 41:44
of my children, I *a* bereaved ... Gen 43:14
unto his brethren, I *a* Joseph ... Gen 45:3
I *a* Joseph your brother, whom ye ... Gen 45:4
And he said, Here *a* I ... Gen 46:2
I *a* God, the God of thy father ... Gen 46:3
I *a* to be gathered unto my people ... Gen 49:29
for *a* I in the place of God ... Gen 50:19
And he said, Here *a* I ... Ex 3:4
I *a* the God of thy father, the ... Ex 3:6
I *a* come down to deliver them out ... Ex 3:8
And Moses said unto God, Who *a* I ... Ex 3:11
said unto Moses, I *A* THAT I *A* ... Ex 3:14 1961
I *A* hath sent me unto you ... Ex 3:14 1961
I *a* sure that the king of Egypt ... Ex 3:19
I *a* not eloquent, neither ... Ex 4:10
but I *a* slow of speech, and of a ... Ex 4:10
and said unto him, I *a* the LORD ... Ex 6:2
I *a* the LORD, and I will bring you ... Ex 6:6
know that I *a* the LORD your God ... Ex 6:7
I *a* the LORD ... Ex 6:8
who *a* of uncircumcised lips ... Ex 6:12
unto Moses, saying, I *a* the LORD ... Ex 6:29
I *a* of uncircumcised lips, and how ... Ex 6:30
shall know that I *a* the LORD ... Ex 7:5
thou shalt know that I *a* the LORD ... Ex 7:17
I *a* the LORD in the midst of the ... Ex 8:22
As soon as I *a* gone out of the ... Ex 9:29
ye may know how that I *a* the LORD ... Ex 10:2
I *a* the LORD ... Ex 12:12
may know that I *a* the LORD ... Ex 14:4
shall know that I *a* the LORD ... Ex 14:18
for I *a* the LORD that healeth ... Ex 15:26
know that I *a* the LORD your God ... Ex 16:12
in law Jethro *a* come unto thee ... Ex 18:6
I *a* the LORD thy God, which have ... Ex 20:2
the LORD thy God *a* a jealous God ... Ex 20:5
for I *a* gracious ... Ex 22:27
know that I *a* the LORD their God ... Ex 29:46
I *a* the LORD their God ... Ex 29:46
that ye may know that I *a* the ... Ex 31:13
for so I *a* commanded ... Lev 8:35
for so I *a* commanded ... Lev 10:13
For I *a* the LORD your God ... Lev 11:44
for I *a* holy ... Lev 11:44
For I *a* the LORD that bringeth ... Lev 11:45
therefore be holy, for I *a* holy ... Lev 11:45
unto them, I *a* the LORD your God ... Lev 18:2
I *a* the LORD your God ... Lev 18:4
I *a* the LORD ... Lev 18:5
I *a* the LORD ... Lev 18:6
I *a* the LORD ... Lev 18:21
I *a* the LORD your God ... Lev 18:30
for I the LORD your God *a* holy ... Lev 19:2
I *a* the LORD your God ... Lev 19:3
I *a* the LORD your God ... Lev 19:4
I *a* the LORD your God ... Lev 19:10
I *a* the LORD ... Lev 19:12
I *a* the LORD ... Lev 19:14
I *a* the LORD ... Lev 19:16
I *a* the LORD ... Lev 19:18
I *a* the LORD your God ... Lev 19:25
I *a* the LORD ... Lev 19:28
I *a* the LORD ... Lev 19:30
I *a* the LORD your God ... Lev 19:31
I *a* the LORD ... Lev 19:32
I *a* the LORD your God ... Lev 19:34
I *a* the LORD your God, which ... Lev 19:36
I *a* the LORD ... Lev 19:37
for I *a* the LORD your God ... Lev 20:7
I *a* the LORD which sanctify you ... Lev 20:8
I *a* the LORD your God, which have ... Lev 20:24
for I the LORD *a* holy, and have ... Lev 20:26
LORD, which sanctify you, *a* holy ... Lev 21:8
I *a* the LORD ... Lev 21:12
I *a* the LORD ... Lev 22:2
I *a* the LORD ... Lev 22:3
I *a* the LORD ... Lev 22:8
I *a* the LORD ... Lev 22:30
I *a* the LORD ... Lev 22:31
I *a* the LORD which hallow you, ... Lev 22:32
I *a* the LORD ... Lev 22:33
I *a* the LORD your God ... Lev 23:22
I *a* the LORD your God ... Lev 23:43
for I *a* the LORD your God ... Lev 24:22
for I *a* the LORD your God ... Lev 25:17
I *a* the LORD your God, which ... Lev 25:38
I *a* the LORD your God ... Lev 25:55
for I *a* the LORD your God ... Lev 26:1
I *a* the LORD ... Lev 26:2
I *a* the LORD your God, which ... Lev 26:13
for I *a* the LORD their God ... Lev 26:44
I *a* the LORD ... Lev 26:45
I *a* the LORD ... Num 3:13
take the Levites for me (I *a* the ... Num 3:41
I *a* the LORD ... Num 3:45
I *a* the LORD your God ... Num 10:10
I *a* not able to bear all this ... Num 11:14
said, The people, among whom I *a* ... Num 11:21
I *a* the LORD your God, which ... Num 15:41
I *a* the LORD your God ... Num 15:41
I *a* thy part and thine inheritance ... Num 18:20
A not I thine ass, upon which ... Num 22:30
a I not able indeed to promote ... Num 22:37
Balak, Lo, I *a* come unto thee ... Num 22:38
I *a* not able to bear you myself ... Deut 1:9
for I *a* not among you ... Deut 1:42
I *a* the LORD thy God, which ... Deut 5:6
the LORD thy God *a* a jealous God ... Deut 5:9
that I *a* come unto the country ... Deut 26:3
know that I *a* the LORD your God ... Deut 29:6
I *a* an hundred and twenty years ... Deut 31:2
while I *a* yet alive with you this ... Deut 31:27
a he, and there is no god with me ... Deut 32:39
the host of the LORD *a* I now come ... Josh 5:14
I *a* this day fourscore and five ... Josh 14:10
As yet I *a* as strong this day as ... Josh 14:11
seeing I *a* a great people, ... Josh 17:14
I *a* old and stricken in age ... Josh 23:2
this day I *a* going the way of all ... Josh 23:14
for I *a* thirsty ... Judg 4:19
unto you, I *a* the LORD your God ... Judg 6:10
I *a* the least in my father's ... Judg 6:15
I *a* pursuing after Zebah and ... Judg 8:5
remember also that I *a* your bone ... Judg 9:2
And he said, I *a* ... Judg 13:11
I *a* a Levite of Beth-lehem-judah, ... Judg 17:9
hath hired me, and I *a* his priest ... Judg 18:4
from thence *a* I ... Judg 19:18
but I *a* now going to the house of ... Judg 19:18
for I *a* too old to have an ... Ruth 1:12
of me, seeing I *a* a stranger ... Ruth 2:10
answered, I *a* Ruth thine handmaid ... Ruth 3:9
is true that I *a* thy near kinsman ... Ruth 3:12
and I *a* after thee ... Ruth 4:4
a not I better to thee than ten ... 1Sa 1:8
I *a* a woman of a sorrowful spirit ... 1Sa 1:15
I *a* the woman that stood by thee ... 1Sa 1:26
and he answered, Here *a* I ... 1Sa 3:4
ran unto Eli, and said, Here *a* I ... 1Sa 3:5
and went to Eli, and said, Here *a* I ... 1Sa 3:6
and went to Eli, and said, Here *a* I ... 1Sa 3:8
And he answered, Here *a* I ... 1Sa 3:16
I *a* he that came out of the army, ... 1Sa 4:16
Saul, and said, I *a* the seer ... 1Sa 9:19
A not I a Benjamite, of the ... 1Sa 9:21
and I *a* old and grayheaded ... 1Sa 12:2
Behold, here I *a* ... 1Sa 12:3
I *a* with thee according to thy ... 1Sa 14:7
I *a* come to sacrifice to the LORD ... 1Sa 16:2
I *a* come to sacrifice unto the ... 1Sa 16:5
a not I a Philistine, and ye ... 1Sa 17:8
A I a dog, that thou comest to me ... 1Sa 17:43
I *a* the son of thy servant Jesse ... 1Sa 17:58
And David said unto Saul, Who *a* I ... 1Sa 18:18
law, seeing that I *a* a poor man ... 1Sa 18:23
And he answered, Here I *a*, my lord ... 1Sa 22:12
answered, I *a* sore distressed ... 1Sa 28:15
I *a* a young man of Egypt, servant ... 1Sa 30:13
of the camp of Israel *a* I escaped ... 2Sa 1:3
And I answered, Here *a* I ... 2Sa 1:7
I answered him, I *a* an Amalekite ... 2Sa 1:8
I *a* the son of a stranger, an ... 2Sa 1:13
I *a* distressed for thee, my ... 2Sa 1:26
And he answered, I *a* ... 2Sa 2:20
A I a dog's head, which against ... 2Sa 3:8
I *a* this day weak, though ... 2Sa 3:39
the LORD, and he said, Who *a* I ... 2Sa 7:18
look upon such a dead dog as I *a* ... 2Sa 9:8
David, and said, I *a* with child ... 2Sa 11:5
I *a* indeed a widow woman, and mine ... 2Sa 14:5
Now therefore that I *a* come to ... 2Sa 14:15
Wherefore *a* I come from Geshur ... 2Sa 14:32
behold, here *a* I, let him do to ... 2Sa 15:26
I *a* come the first this day of ... 2Sa 19:20
for do not I know that I *a* this ... 2Sa 19:22
I *a* this day fourscore years old ... 2Sa 19:35
And he answered, I *a* he ... 2Sa 20:17
I *a* one of them that are ... 2Sa 20:19
unto Gad, I *a* in a great strait ... 2Sa 24:14
and I *a* but a little child ... 1Kin 3:7
I *a* risen up in the room of David ... 1Kin 8:20
And he said, I *a* ... 1Kin 13:14
I *a* a prophet also as thou art ... 1Kin 13:18
his sons, saying, When I *a* dead ... 1Kin 13:31
for I *a* sent to thee with heavy ... 1Kin 14:6
I *a* gathering two sticks, that I ... 1Kin 17:12
And he answered him, I *a* ... 1Kin 18:8
as soon as I *a* gone from thee, ... 1Kin 18:12
that I *a* thy servant, and that I ... 1Kin 18:36

for I *a* not better than my	1Kin 19:4	
and I, even I only, *a* left	1Kin 19:10	
and I, even I only, *a* left	1Kin 19:14	
I *a* thine, and all that I have	1Kin 20:4	
thou shalt know that I *a* the LORD	1Kin 20:13	
ye shall know that I *a* the LORD	1Kin 20:28	
I *a* as thou art, my people as thy	1Kin 22:4	
for I *a* wounded	1Kin 22:34	
see me when I *a* taken from thee	2Kin 2:10	
I *a* as thou art, my people as thy	2Kin 3:7	
A I God, to kill and to make alive	2Kin 5:7	
I *a* thy servant and thy son	2Kin 16:7	
A I now come up without the LORD	2Kin 18:25	
I *a* come up to the height of the	2Kin 19:23	
I *a* bringing such evil upon	2Kin 21:12	
before the LORD, and said, Who *a* I	1Chr 17:16	
unto Gad, I *a* in a great strait	1Chr 21:13	
But who *a* I, and what is my people	1Chr 29:14	
who *a* I then, that I should build	2Chr 2:6	
for the house which I *a* about to	2Chr 2:9	
for I *a* risen up in the room of	2Chr 6:10	
a set on the throne of Israel, as	2Chr 6:10	
I *a* as thou art, and my people as	2Chr 18:3	
for I *a* wounded	2Chr 18:33	
for I *a* sore wounded	2Chr 35:23	
I *a* ashamed and blush to lift up	Ezr 9:6	
I *a* doing a great work, so that I	Neh 6:3	
who is there, that, being as I *a*	Neh 6:11	
to morrow *a* I invited unto her	Est 5:12	
I only *a* escaped alone to tell	Job 1:15	
I only *a* escaped alone to tell	Job 1:16	
I only *a* escaped alone to tell	Job 1:17	
I only *a* escaped alone to tell	Job 1:19	
So *a* I made to possess months of	Job 7:3	
I *a* full of tossings to and fro	Job 7:4	
eyes are upon me, and I *a* not	Job 7:8	
A I a sea, or a whale, that thou	Job 7:12	
so that I *a* a burden to myself	Job 7:20	
I *a* perfect, it shall also prove	Job 9:20	
I *a* afraid of all my sorrows, I	Job 9:28	
For he is not a man, as I *a*	Job 9:32	
Thou knowest that I *a* not wicked	Job 10:7	
I *a* full of confusion	Job 10:15	
pure, and I *a* clean in thine eyes	Job 11:4	
I *a* not inferior to you	Job 12:3	1961
I *a* as one mocked of his	Job 12:4	
I *a* not inferior unto you	Job 13:2	
though I forbear, what *a* I eased	Job 16:6	
out of wrong, but I *a* not heard	Job 19:7	
me on every side, and I *a* gone	Job 19:10	
I *a* an alien in their sight	Job 19:15	
I *a* escaped with the skin of my	Job 19:20	
Even when I remember I *a* afraid	Job 21:6	
Therefore *a* I troubled at his	Job 23:15	
I consider, I *a* afraid of him	Job 23:15	
now *a* I their song, yea, I *a*	Job 30:9	
I *a* become like dust and ashes	Job 30:19	
I *a* a brother to dragons, and a	Job 30:29	
I *a* young, and ye are very old	Job 32:6	
For I *a* full of matter	Job 32:18	
I *a* according to thy wish in	Job 33:6	
I also *a* formed out of the clay	Job 33:6	
I *a* clean without transgression,	Job 33:9	
I *a* innocent	Job 33:9	
For Job hath said, I *a* righteous	Job 34:5	
Behold, I *a* vile	Job 40:4	
for I *a* weak	Ps 6:2	
I *a* weary with my groaning	Ps 6:6	
trouble me rejoice when I *a* moved	Ps 13:4	
I *a* purposed that my mouth shall	Ps 17:3	
the night season, and *a* not silent	Ps 22:2	
But I *a* a worm, and no man	Ps 22:6	
I *a* poured out like water, and all	Ps 22:14	
for I *a* desolate and afflicted	Ps 25:16	
trusted in him, and I *a* helped	Ps 28:7	
me, O LORD, for I *a* in trouble	Ps 31:9	
I *a* forgotten as a dead man out	Ps 31:12	
I *a* like a broken vessel	Ps 31:12	
I *a* cut off from before thine	Ps 31:22	
unto my soul, I *a* thy salvation	Ps 35:3	
I have been young, and now *a* old	Ps 37:25	
I *a* troubled	Ps 38:6	
I *a* bowed down greatly	Ps 38:6	1961
I *a* feeble and sore broken	Ps 38:8	
For I *a* ready to halt, and my	Ps 38:17	
that I may know how frail I *a*	Ps 39:4	
I *a* consumed by the blow of thine	Ps 39:10	
for I *a* a stranger with thee, and	Ps 39:12	
so that I *a* not able to look up	Ps 40:12	
But I *a* poor and needy	Ps 40:17	
Be still, and know that I *a* God	Ps 46:10	
I *a* God, even thy God	Ps 50:7	
But I *a* like a green olive tree	Ps 52:8	
What time I *a* afraid, I will	Ps 56:3	
I *a* come into deep waters, where	Ps 69:2	
I *a* weary of my crying	Ps 69:3	
I *a* become a stranger unto my	Ps 69:8	
for I *a* in trouble	Ps 69:17	
and I *a* full of heaviness	Ps 69:20	
But I *a* poor and sorrowful	Ps 69:29	
But I *a* poor and needy	Ps 70:5	
I *a* as a wonder unto many	Ps 71:7	
Now also when I *a* old and	Ps 71:18	
Nevertheless I *a* continually with	Ps 73:23	
I *a* so troubled that I cannot	Ps 77:4	
I *a* the LORD thy God, which	Ps 81:10	
for I *a* poor and needy	Ps 86:1	
for I *a* holy	Ps 86:2	
I *a* counted with them that go	Ps 88:4	
I *a* as a man that hath no	Ps 88:4	1961
I *a* shut up, and I cannot come	Ps 88:8	
I *a* afflicted and ready to die	Ps 88:15	
suffer thy terrors I *a* distracted	Ps 88:15	
me in the day when I *a* in trouble	Ps 102:2	
I *a* like a pelican of the	Ps 102:6	1961
I *a* like an owl of the desert	Ps 102:6	1961
a as a sparrow alone upon the	Ps 102:7	
and I *a* withered like grass	Ps 102:11	
For I *a* poor and needy, and my	Ps 109:22	
I *a* gone like the shadow when it	Ps 109:23	
I *a* tossed up and down as the	Ps 109:23	
O LORD, truly I *a* thy servant	Ps 116:16	
I *a* thy servant, and the son of	Ps 116:16	
I *a* a stranger in the earth	Ps 119:19	
I *a* a companion of all them that	Ps 119:63	
For I *a* become like a bottle in	Ps 119:83	
I *a* thine, save me	Ps 119:94	
I *a* afflicted very much	Ps 119:107	
I *a* afraid of thy judgments	Ps 119:120	
I *a* thy servant	Ps 119:125	
I *a* small and despised	Ps 119:141	
I *a* for peace	Ps 120:7	
for I *a* fearfully and wonderfully	Ps 139:14	
when I awake, I *a* still with thee	Ps 139:18	
a not I grieved with those that	Ps 139:21	
for I *a* brought very low	Ps 142:6	
for I *a* thy servant	Ps 143:12	
I *a* understanding	Prov 8:14	
heart clean, I *a* pure from my sin	Prov 20:9	
and saith, *A* not I in sport	Prov 26:19	
Surely I *a* more brutish than any	Prov 30:2	
I *a* come to great estate, and have	Eccl 1:16	
I *a* black, but comely, O ye	Song 1:5	
not upon me, because I *a* black	Song 1:6	
I *a* the rose of Sharon, and the	Song 2:1	
for I *a* sick of love	Song 2:5	
My beloved is mine, and I *a* his	Song 2:16	
I *a* come into my garden, my	Song 5:1	
tell him, that I *a* sick of love	Song 5:8	
I *a* my beloved's, and my beloved	Song 6:3	
I *a* my beloved's, and his desire	Song 7:10	
I *a* a wall, and my breasts like	Song 8:10	
I *a* full of the burnt offerings	Is 1:11	
I *a* weary to bear them	Is 1:14	
for I *a* undone	Is 6:5	
because I *a* a man of unclean lips	Is 6:5	
Then said I, Here *a* I	Is 6:8	
for I *a* prudent	Is 10:13	
I *a* the son of the wise, the son	Is 19:11	
I *a* set in my ward whole nights	Is 21:8	
and he saith, I *a* not learned	Is 29:12	
shall not say, I *a* sick	Is 33:24	
a I now come up without the LORD	Is 36:10	
a I come up to the height of the	Is 37:24	
I *a* deprived of the residue of my	Is 38:10	
O LORD, I *a* oppressed	Is 38:14	
I *a* he	Is 41:4	
for I *a* with thee	Is 41:10	
for I *a* thy God	Is 41:10	
I *a* the LORD	Is 42:8	
For I *a* the LORD thy God, the	Is 43:3	
for I *a* with thee	Is 43:5	
me, and understand that I *a* he	Is 43:10	
I, even I, *a* the LORD	Is 43:11	
saith the LORD, that I *a* God	Is 43:12	
Yea, before the day was I *a* he	Is 43:13	
I *a* the LORD, your Holy One, the	Is 43:15	
a he that blotteth out thy	Is 43:25	
One shall say, I *a* the LORD'S	Is 44:5	
I *a* the first, and I *a* the last	Is 44:6	
I *a* warm, I have seen the fire	Is 44:16	
I *a* the LORD that maketh all	Is 44:24	
by thy name, *a* the God of Israel	Is 45:3	
I *a* the LORD, and there is none	Is 45:5	
I *a* the LORD, and there is none	Is 45:6	
I *a* the LORD	Is 45:18	
for I *a* God, and there is none	Is 45:22	
And even to your old age I *a* he	Is 46:4	
for I *a* God, and there is none	Is 46:9	
I *a* God, and there is none like me	Is 46:9	
that sayest in thine heart, I *a*	Is 47:8	
hast said in thine heart, I *a*	Is 47:10	
I *a* he	Is 48:12	
I *a* the first, I also *a* the last	Is 48:12	
the time that it was, there *a* I	Is 48:16	
I *a* the LORD thy God which	Is 48:17	
a desolate, a captive, and	Is 49:21	
thou shalt know that I *a* the LORD	Is 49:23	
that I the LORD *a* thy Saviour	Is 49:26	
even I, *a* he that comforteth you	Is 51:12	
But I *a* the LORD thy God, that	Is 51:15	
day that I *a* he that doth speak	Is 52:6	
say, Behold, I *a* a dry tree	Is 56:3	
cry, and he shall say, Here I *a*	Is 58:9	
that I the LORD *a* thy Saviour	Is 60:16	
I *a* sought of them that asked not	Is 65:1	
I *a* found of them that sought me	Is 65:1	
for I *a* holier than thou	Is 65:5	
for I *a* a child	Jer 1:6	
unto me, Say not, I *a* a child	Jer 1:7	
for I *a* with thee to deliver thee	Jer 1:8	
for I *a* with thee, saith the LORD	Jer 1:19	
I *a* not polluted, I have not gone	Jer 2:23	
thou sayest, Because I *a* innocent	Jer 2:35	
for I *a* merciful, saith the LORD,	Jer 3:12	
for I *a* married unto you	Jer 3:14	
I *a* pained at my very heart	Jer 4:19	
Therefore I *a* full of the fury of	Jer 6:11	
I *a* weary with holding in	Jer 6:11	
daughter of my people *a* I hurt	Jer 8:21	
I *a* black	Jer 8:21	
that I *a* the LORD which exercise	Jer 9:24	
I *a* weary with repenting	Jer 15:6	
for I *a* called by thy name, O	Jer 15:16	
for I *a* with thee to save thee and	Jer 15:20	
I *a* in derision daily, every one	Jer 20:7	
I *a* against thee, O inhabitant of	Jer 21:13	
I *a* like a drunken man, and like a	Jer 23:9	
A I a God at hand, saith the LORD	Jer 23:23	
I *a* against the prophets, saith	Jer 23:30	
I *a* against the prophets, saith	Jer 23:31	
I *a* against them that prophesy	Jer 23:32	
to know me, that I *a* the LORD	Jer 24:7	
for me, behold, I *a* in your hand	Jer 26:14	
a a witness, saith the LORD	Jer 29:23	
For I *a* with thee, saith the LORD	Jer 30:11	
for I *a* a father to Israel, and	Jer 31:9	
I *a* the LORD, the God of all	Jer 32:27	
Baruch, saying, I *a* shut up	Jer 36:5	
I *a* afraid of the Jews that are	Jer 38:19	
for I *a* with you to save you, and	Jer 42:11	
for I *a* with thee	Jer 46:28	
I *a* against thee, O thou most	Jer 50:31	1961
I *a* against thee, O destroying	Jer 51:25	
for I *a* become vile	Lam 1:11	
from whom I *a* not able to rise up	Lam 1:14	
for I *a* in distress	Lam 1:20	
I *a* the man that hath seen	Lam 3:1	
then I said, I *a* cut off	Lam 3:54	
I *a* their musick	Lam 3:63	
a against thee, and will execute	Eze 5:8	
ye shall know that I *a* the LORD	Eze 6:7	
because I *a* broken with their	Eze 6:9	
they shall know that I *a* the LORD	Eze 6:10	
shall ye know that I *a* the LORD	Eze 6:13	
they shall know that I *a* the LORD	Eze 6:14	
ye shall know that I *a* the LORD	Eze 7:4	
ye shall know that I *a* the LORD	Eze 7:9	
they shall know that I *a* the LORD	Eze 7:27	
ye shall know that I *a* the LORD	Eze 11:10	
ye shall know that I *a* the LORD	Eze 11:12	
Say, I *a* your sign	Eze 12:11	
they shall know that I *a* the LORD	Eze 12:15	
they shall know that I *a* the LORD	Eze 12:16	
ye shall know that I *a* the LORD	Eze 12:20	
For I *a* the LORD	Eze 12:25	
I *a* against you, saith the Lord	Eze 13:8	
shall know that I *a* the Lord GOD	Eze 13:9	
ye shall know that I *a* the LORD	Eze 13:14	
I *a* against your pillows,	Eze 13:20	
ye shall know that I *a* the LORD	Eze 13:21	
ye shall know that I *a* the LORD	Eze 13:23	
ye shall know that I *a* the LORD	Eze 14:8	
ye shall know that I *a* the LORD	Eze 15:7	
thou shalt know that I *a* the LORD	Eze 16:62	
when I *a* pacified toward thee for	Eze 16:63	
saying, I *a* the LORD your God	Eze 20:5	
I *a* the LORD your God	Eze 20:7	
I *a* the LORD that sanctify them	Eze 20:12	
I *a* the LORD your God	Eze 20:19	
know that I *a* the LORD your God	Eze 20:20	
they might know that I *a* the LORD	Eze 20:26	
ye shall know that I *a* the LORD	Eze 20:38	
ye shall know that I *a* the LORD	Eze 20:42	
ye shall know that I *a* the LORD	Eze 20:44	
I *a* against thee, and will draw	Eze 21:3	
thou shalt know that I *a* the LORD	Eze 22:16	
and I *a* profaned among them	Eze 22:26	
shall know that I *a* the Lord GOD	Eze 23:49	
shall know that I *a* the Lord GOD	Eze 24:24	
they shall know that I *a* the LORD	Eze 24:27	
ye shall know that I *a* the LORD	Eze 25:5	
thou shalt know that I *a* the LORD	Eze 25:7	
they shall know that I *a* the LORD	Eze 25:11	
they shall know that I *a* the LORD	Eze 25:17	
I *a* against thee, O Tyrus, and	Eze 26:3	
they shall know that I *a* the LORD	Eze 26:6	
hast said, I *a* of perfect beauty	Eze 27:3	
I *a* a God, I sit in the seat of	Eze 28:2	
him that slayeth thee, I *a* God	Eze 00:0	
I *a* against thee, O Zidon	Eze 28:22	
they shall know that I *a* the LORD	Eze 28:22	
they shall know that I *a* the LORD	Eze 28:23	
shall know that I *a* the Lord GOD	Eze 28:24	
know that I *a* the LORD their God	Eze 28:26	
I *a* against thee, Pharaoh king of	Eze 29:3	
shall know that I *a* the LORD	Eze 29:6	
they shall know that I *a* the LORD	Eze 29:9	
therefore I *a* against thee, and	Eze 29:10	
shall know that I *a* the Lord GOD	Eze 29:16	
they shall know that I *a* the LORD	Eze 29:21	
they shall know that I *a* the LORD	Eze 30:8	
they shall know that I *a* the LORD	Eze 30:19	
I *a* against Pharaoh king of Egypt	Eze 30:22	
they shall know that I *a* the LORD	Eze 30:25	
they shall know that I *a* the LORD	Eze 30:26	
shall they know that I *a* the LORD	Eze 32:15	
shall they know that I *a* the LORD	Eze 33:29	
I *a* against the shepherds	Eze 34:10	
and shall know that I *a* the LORD	Eze 34:27	
I the LORD their God *a* with them	Eze 34:30	
I *a* your God, saith the Lord GOD	Eze 34:31	
I *a* against thee, and I will	Eze 35:3	
thou shalt know that I *a* the LORD	Eze 35:4	
ye shall know that I *a* the LORD	Eze 35:9	
thou shalt know that I *a* the LORD	Eze 35:12	
they shall know that I *a* the LORD	Eze 35:15	
I *a* for you, and I will turn unto	Eze 36:9	
ye shall know that I *a* the Lord	Eze 36:11	
shall know that I *a* the LORD	Eze 36:23	
they shall know that I *a* the LORD	Eze 36:38	
ye shall know that I *a* the LORD	Eze 37:6	
ye shall know that I *a* the LORD	Eze 37:13	
I *a* against thee, O Gog, the	Eze 38:3	
they shall know that I *a* the LORD	Eze 38:23	
I *a* against thee, O Gog, the	Eze 39:1	
they shall know that I *a* the LORD	Eze 39:6	
shall know that I *a* the LORD	Eze 39:7	
of Israel shall know that I *a* the	Eze 39:22	
a sanctified in them in the sight	Eze 39:27	
know that I *a* the LORD their God	Eze 39:28	
I *a* their inheritance	Eze 44:28	

I *a* their possession Eze 44:28
I *a* now come forth to give thee Dan 9:22
forth, and I *a* come to shew thee Dan 9:23
for unto thee *a* I now sent Dan 10:11
heard, and I *a* come for thy words Dan 10:12
Now I *a* come to make thee Dan 10:14
when I *a* gone forth, lo, the Dan 10:20
my wife, neither *a* I her husband Hos 2:2
for I *a* God, and not man Hos 11:9
Yet I *a* become rich, I have found Hos 12:8
I that *a* the LORD thy God from Hos 12:9
Yet I *a* the LORD thy God from the Hos 13:4
I *a* like a green fir tree Hos 14:8
ye shall know that I *a* in the Joel 2:27
that I *a* the LORD your God, and Joel 2:27
let the weak say, I *a* strong Joel 3:10
So shall ye know that I *a* the Joel 3:17
I *a* pressed under you, as a cart Amos 2:13
he said unto them, I *a* an Hebrew Jonah 1:9
I *a* cast out of thy sight Jonah 2:4
But truly I *a* full of power by Mic 3:8
for I *a* as when they have Mic 7:1
I *a* against thee, saith the LORD Nah 2:13
I *a* against thee, saith the LORD Nah 3:5
I shall answer when I *a* reproved Hab 2:1
that said in her heart, I *a* Zeph 2:15
I *a* with you, saith the LORD Hag 1:13
for I *a* with you, saith the LORD Hag 2:4
I *a* jealous for Jerusalem and for Zec 1:14
I *a* very sore displeased with the Zec 1:15
I *a* returned to Jerusalem with Zec 1:16
I *a* returned unto Zion, and will Zec 8:3
for I *a* the LORD their God, and Zec 10:6
for I *a* rich Zec 11:5
a no prophet, I *a* an husbandman Zec 13:5
for I *a* a great King, saith the Mal 1:14
For I *a* the LORD, I change not Mal 3:6
whose shoes I *a* not worthy to Mt 3:11 1510
Son, in whom I *a* well pleased Mt 3:17
Think not that I *a* come to Mt 5:17
I *a* not come to destroy, but to Mt 5:17
Lord, I *a* not worthy that thou Mt 8:8 1510
For I *a* a man under authority, Mt 8:9 1510
for I *a* not come to call the Mt 9:13
ye that I *a* able to do this Mt 9:28
Think not that I *a* come to send Mt 10:34
For I *a* come to set a man at Mt 10:35
for I *a* meek and lowly in heart Mt 11:29 1510
I *a* not sent but unto the lost Mt 15:24
men say that I the Son of man *a* Mt 16:13 1511
them, But whom say ye that I *a* Mt 16:15 1511
Son, in whom I *a* well pleased Mt 17:5
there *a* I in the midst of them Mt 18:20 1510
thine eye evil, because I *a* good Mt 20:15 1510
baptism that I *a* baptized with Mt 20:22
baptism that I *a* baptized with Mt 20:23
I *a* the God of Abraham, and the Mt 22:32 1510
in my name, saying, I *a* Christ Mt 24:5 1510
But after I *a* risen again Mt 26:32
I *a* able to destroy the temple of Mt 26:61
I *a* innocent of the blood of this Mt 27:24 1510
for he said, I *a* the Son of God Mt 27:43 1510
I *a* with you alway, even unto the Mt 28:20 1510
I *a* not worthy to stoop down Mk 1:7 1510
Son, in whom I *a* well pleased Mk 1:11
them, Whom do men say that I *a* Mk 8:27 1511
them, But whom say ye that I *a* Mk 8:29 1511
baptism that I *a* baptized with Mk 10:38
with the baptism that I *a* Mk 10:39
I *a* the God of Abraham, and the Mk 12:26
in my name, saying, I *a* Christ Mk 13:6 1510
But after that I *a* risen, I will Mk 14:28
And Jesus said, I *a* Mk 14:62 1510
for I *a* an old man, and my wife Lk 1:18
I *a* Gabriel, that stand in the Lk 1:19 1510
a sent to speak unto thee, and to Lk 1:19
shoes I *a* not worthy to unloose Lk 3:16 1510
in thee I *a* well pleased Lk 3:22
for therefore *a* I sent Lk 4:43
for I *a* a sinful man, O Lord Lk 5:8 1510
for I *a* not worthy that thou Lk 7:6 1510
For I also *a* a man set under Lk 7:8 1510
Whom say the people that I *a* Lk 9:18 1511
them, But whom say ye that I *a* Lk 9:20 1511
I *a* come to send fire on the Lk 12:49
how *a* I straitened till it be Lk 12:50
Suppose ye that I *a* come to give Lk 12:51
a no more worthy to be called thy Lk 15:19 1510
a no more worthy to be called thy Lk 15:21 1510
to beg I *a* ashamed Lk 16:3
I *a* resolved what to do Lk 16:4
when I *a* put out of the Lk 16:4
for I *a* tormented in this flame Lk 16:24
that I *a* not as other men are, Lk 18:11 1510
in my name, saying, I *a* Christ Lk 21:8 1510
but I *a* among you as he that Lk 22:27 1510
I *a* ready to go with thee, both Lk 22:33 1510
And Peter said, Man, I *a* not Lk 22:58 1510
said unto them, Ye say that I *a* Lk 22:70 1510
but confessed, I *a* not the Christ Jn 1:20 1510
And he saith, I *a* not Jn 1:21 1510
I *a* the voice of one crying in Jn 1:23
latchet I *a* not worthy to unloose Jn 1:27 1510
therefore *a* I come baptizing with Jn 1:31
I *a* not the Christ, but that I *a* Jn 3:28 1510
which *a* a woman of Samaria Jn 4:9 5607
her, I that speak unto thee *a* he Jn 4:26 1510
but while I *a* coming, another Jn 5:7
I *a* come in my Father's name, and Jn 5:43
unto them, I *a* the bread of life Jn 6:35 1510
I *a* the bread which came down Jn 6:41 1510
I *a* that bread of life Jn 6:48 1510
I *a* the living bread which came Jn 6:51 1510
know me, and ye know whence I *a* Jn 7:28 1510
I *a* not come of myself, but he Jn 7:28
for I *a* from him, and he hath sent Jn 7:29 1510
Yet a little while *a* I with you Jn 7:33 1510
and where I *a*, thither ye cannot Jn 7:34 1510
and where I *a*, thither ye cannot Jn 7:36 1510
I *a* the light of the world Jn 8:12 1510
for I *a* not alone, but I and the Jn 8:16 1510
I *a* one that bear witness of Jn 8:18 1510
I *a* from above Jn 8:23 1510
I *a* not of this world Jn 8:23 1510
for if ye believe not that I *a* he Jn 8:24 1510
then shall ye know that I *a* he Jn 8:28 1510
unto you, Before Abraham was, I *a* Jn 8:58 1510
As long as I *a* in the world Jn 9:5 1510
I *a* the light of the world Jn 9:5 1510
but he said, I *a* he Jn 9:9 1510
For judgment I *a* come into this Jn 9:39
I *a* the door of the sheep Jn 10:7 1510
I *a* the door Jn 10:9 1510
I *a* come that they might have Jn 10:10
I *a* the good shepherd Jn 10:11 1510
I *a* the good shepherd Jn 10:14 1510
know my sheep, and *a* known of mine Jn 10:14
I said, I *a* the Son of God Jn 10:36
I *a* glad for your sakes that I Jn 11:15
I *a* the resurrection, and the life Jn 11:25 1510
and where I *a*, there shall also my Jn 12:26 1510
I *a* come a light into the world, Jn 12:46
for so I *a* Jn 13:13 1510
pass, ye may believe that I *a* he Jn 13:19 1510
yet a little while I *a* with you Jn 13:33 1510
that where I *a*, there ye may be Jn 14:3 1510
I *a* the way, the truth, and the Jn 14:6 1510
thou not that I *a* in the Father Jn 14:10
Believe me that I *a* in the Father Jn 14:11
shall know that I *a* in my Father Jn 14:20
I *a* the true vine, and my Father Jn 15:1 1510
I *a* the vine, ye are the branches Jn 15:5 1510
Father, and *a* come into the world Jn 16:28
yet I *a* not alone, because the Jn 16:32 1510
and I *a* glorified in them Jn 17:10
now I *a* no more in the world, but Jn 17:11 1510
even as I *a* not of the world Jn 17:14 1510
even as I *a* not of the world Jn 17:16 1510
given me, be with me where I *a* Jn 17:24 1510
Jesus saith unto them, I *a* he Jn 18:5 1510
I *a* he, they went backward, and Jn 18:6 1510
I have told you that I *a* he Jn 18:8 1510
He saith, I *a* not Jn 18:17 1510
He denied it, and said, I *a* not Jn 18:25 1510
Pilate answered, *A* I a Jew Jn 18:35 1510
Thou sayest that I *a* a king Jn 18:37 1510
he said, I *a* King of the Jews Jn 19:21 1510
for I *a* not yet ascended to my Jn 20:17
I *a* the God of thy fathers, the Acts 7:32
a come down to deliver them Acts 7:34
I *a* Jesus whom thou persecutest Acts 9:5 1510
he said, Behold, I *a* here, Lord Acts 9:10
said, Behold, I *a* he whom ye seek Acts 10:21 1510
I myself also *a* a man Acts 10:26 1510
he said, Whom think ye that I *a* Acts 13:25 1511
I *a* not he Acts 13:25 1510
his feet I *a* not worthy to loose Acts 13:25 1510
I *a* clean Acts 18:6
For I *a* with thee, and no man Acts 18:10 1510
that I *a* pure from the blood of Acts 20:26
for I *a* ready not to be bound Acts 21:13
I *a* a man which *a* a Jew of Acts 21:39 1510
I *a* verily a man which *a* a Jew, Acts 22:3 1510
I *a* Jesus of Nazareth, whom thou Acts 22:8 1510
I *a* a Pharisee, the son of a Acts 23:6 1510
the dead I *a* called in question Acts 23:6
a called in question by you this Acts 24:21
whereof I *a* accused of the Jews Acts 26:2
a judged for the hope of the Acts 26:6
Agrippa, I *a* accused of the Jews Acts 26:7
I *a* Jesus whom thou persecutest Acts 26:15 1510
I *a* not mad, most noble Festus Acts 26:25
for I *a* persuaded that none of Acts 26:26
almost, and altogether such as I *a* Acts 26:29 1510
night the angel of God, whose I *a* Acts 27:23 1510
Israel I *a* bound with this chain Acts 28:20
I *a* debtor both to the Greeks, and Rom 1:14 1510
I *a* ready to preach the gospel to Rom 1:15
For I *a* not ashamed of the gospel Rom 1:16
why yet *a* I also judged as a Rom 3:7
but I *a* carnal, sold under sin Rom 7:14 1510
O wretched man that I *a* Rom 7:24
For I *a* persuaded, that neither Rom 8:38
For I also *a* an Israelite, of the Rom 11:1 1510
I *a* left alone, and they seek my Rom 11:3
inasmuch as I *a* the apostle of Rom 11:13 1510
a persuaded by the Lord Jesus, Rom 14:14
I myself also *a* persuaded of you, Rom 15:14
I *a* sure that, when I come unto Rom 15:29
I *a* glad therefore on your behalf Rom 16:19
one of you saith, I *a* of Paul 1Cor 1:12 1510
For while one saith, I *a* of Paul 1Cor 3:4 1510
and another, I *a* of Apollos 1Cor 3:4
yet *a* I not hereby justified 1Cor 4:4
A I not an apostle 1Cor 9:1 1510
a I not free? 1Cor 9:1 1510
others, yet doubtless I *a* to you 1Cor 9:2 1510
I *a* made all things to all men, 1Cor 9:22
why *a* I evil spoken of for that 1Cor 10:30
of me, even as I also *a* of Christ 1Cor 11:1
Because I *a* not the hand, I *a* 1Cor 12:15 1510
Because I *a* not the eye, I *a* not 1Cor 12:16 1510
I *a* become as sounding brass, or 1Cor 13:1
and have not charity, I *a* nothing 1Cor 13:2 1510
I know even as also I *a* known 1Cor 13:12
For I *a* the least of the apostles 1Cor 15:9 1510
that *a* not meet to be called an 1Cor 15:9 1510
by the grace of God I *a* what I *a* 1Cor 15:10 1510
I *a* glad of the coming of 1Cor 16:17
I *a* filled with comfort 2Cor 7:4
I *a* exceeding joyful in all our 2Cor 7:4
to him of you, I *a* not ashamed 2Cor 7:14
who in presence *a* base among you 2Cor 10:1
being absent *a* bold toward you 2Cor 10:1
I *a* present with that confidence 2Cor 10:2
For I *a* jealous over you with 2Cor 11:2
I speak foolishly,) I *a* bold also 2Cor 11:21
so *a* I 2Cor 11:22
so *a* I 2Cor 11:22
so *a* I 2Cor 11:22
(I speak as a fool) I *a* more 2Cor 11:23
Who is weak, and I *a* not weak 2Cor 11:29
when I *a* weak, then *a* I strong 2Cor 12:10 1510
I *a* become a fool in glorying 2Cor 12:11
for in nothing *a* I behind the 2Cor 12:11
the third time I *a* ready to come 2Cor 12:14
the third time I *a* coming to you 2Cor 13:1
through the law *a* dead to the law Gal 2:19
I *a* crucified with Christ Gal 2:20
I *a* afraid of you, lest I have Gal 4:11
I beseech you, be as I *a* Gal 4:12
for I *a* as ye are Gal 4:12
A I therefore become your enemy, Gal 4:16
not only when I *a* present with Gal 4:18
who *a* less than the least of all Eph 3:8
For which I *a* an ambassador in Eph 6:20
knowing that I *a* set for the Phil 1:17
For I *a* in a strait betwixt two, Phil 1:23
I *a* apprehended of Christ Jesus Phil 3:12
learned, in whatsoever state I *a* Phil 4:11 1510
in all things I *a* instructed both Phil 4:12
I *a* full, having received of Phil 4:18
whereof I Paul *a* made a minister Col 1:23
Whereof I *a* made a minister, Col 1:25
yet *a* I with you in the spirit, Col 2:5 1510
for which I *a* also in bonds Col 4:3
of whom I *a* chief 1Ti 1:15 1510
Whereunto I *a* ordained a preacher 1Ti 2:7
I *a* persuaded that in thee also 2Ti 1:5
Whereunto I *a* appointed a 2Ti 1:11
nevertheless I *a* not ashamed 2Ti 1:12
a persuaded that he is able to 2Ti 1:12
For I *a* now ready to be offered, 2Ti 4:6
he is tempted, I *a* tempted of God Jas 1:13
for I *a* holy 1Pet 1:16 1510
who *a* also an elder, and a witness 1Pet 5:1
as long as I *a* in this tabernacle 2Pet 1:13 1510
Son, in whom I *a* well pleased 2Pet 1:17
I *a* Alpha and Omega, the beginning Rev 1:8 1510
who also *a* your brother, and Rev 1:9
I *a* Alpha and Omega, the first and Rev 1:11 1510
I *a* the first and the last Rev 1:17 1510
I *a* he that liveth, and was dead Rev 1:18 1510
I *a* alive for evermore, Amen Rev 1:18 1510
I *a* he which searcheth the reins Rev 2:23 1510
I *a* rich, and increased with goods Rev 3:17 1510
a set down with my Father in his Rev 3:21
a no widow, and shall see no Rev 18:7 1510
I *a* thy fellowservant, and of thy Rev 19:10 1510
I *a* Alpha and Omega, the beginning Rev 21:6 1510
for I *a* thy fellowservant, and of Rev 22:9 1510
I *a* Alpha and Omega, the beginning Rev 22:13 1510
I *a* the root and the offspring of Rev 22:16 1510

AMAD (*a'-mad*) *A town on the border of Asher.*
And Alammelech, and *A*, and Misheal Josh 19:26 6008

AMAL (*a'-mal*) *A descendant of Asher.*
and Imna, and Shelesh, and *A* 1Chr 7:35 6000

AMALEK (*am'-al-ek*) See AMALEKITE.
1. The son of Eliphaz.
and she bare to Eliphaz *A* Gen 36:12 6002
duke Gatam, and duke *A* Gen 36:16 6002
and Gatam, Kenaz, and Timna, and *A* 1Chr 1:36 6002
2. Descendants of Amalek.
Then came *A*, and fought with Ex 17:8 6002
out men, and go out, fight with *A* Ex 17:9 6002
had said to him, and fought with *A* Ex 17:10 6002
he let down his hand, *A* prevailed Ex 17:11 6002
And Joshua discomfited *A* and his Ex 17:13 6002
of *A* from under heaven Ex 17:14 6002
the LORD will have war with *A* Ex 17:16 6002
And when he looked on *A*, he took Num 24:20 6002
A was the first of the nations Num 24:20 6002
Remember what *A* did unto thee by Deut 25:17 6002
of *A* from under heaven Deut 25:19 6002
him the children of Ammon and *A* Judg 3:13 6002
there a root of them against *A* Judg 5:14 6002
that which *A* did to Israel 1Sa 15:2 6002
Now go and smite *A*, and utterly 1Sa 15:3 6002
And Saul came to a city of *A* 1Sa 15:5 6002
have brought Agag the king of *A* 1Sa 15:20 6002
his fierce wrath upon *A*, 1Sa 28:18 6002
and of the Philistines, and of *A* 2Sa 8:12 6002
from the Philistines and, from *A* 1Chr 18:11 6002
Gebal, and Ammon, and *A* Ps 83:7 6002

AMALEKITE (*am'-al-ek-ite*) See AMALEKITES.
A descendant of Amalek.
man of Egypt, servant to an *A* 1Sa 30:13 6003
And I answered him, I am an *A* 2Sa 1:8 6003
I am the son of a stranger, an *A* 2Sa 1:13 6003

AMALEKITES (*am'-al-ek-ites*)
and smote all the country of the *A* Gen 14:7 6003
The *A* dwell in the land of the Num 13:29 6003
(Now the *A* and the Canaanites Num 14:25 6003
For the *A* and the Canaanites are Num 14:43 6003
Then the *A* came down, and the Num 14:45 6003
the Midianites came up, and the *A* Judg 6:3 6003
Then all the Midianites and the *A* Judg 6:33 6003
And the Midianites and the *A* Judg 7:12 6003
The Zidonians also, and the *A* Judg 10:12 6003

of Ephraim, in the mount of the A .... Judg 12:15 6003
gathered an host, and smote the A 1Sa 14:48 6003
get you down from among the A 1Sa 15:6 6003
Kenites departed from among the A 1Sa 15:6 6003
Saul smote the A from Havilah 1Sa 15:7 6003
took Agag the king of the A alive......... 1Sa 15:8 6003
They have brought them from the A ... 1Sa 15:15 6003
utterly destroy the sinners the A.......... 1Sa 15:18 6003
and have utterly destroyed the A.......... 1Sa 15:20 6003
to me Agag the king of the A 1Sa 15:32 6003
and the Gezrites, and the A.................. 1Sa 27:8 6003
that the A had invaded the south, ... 1Sa 30:1 6003
all that the A had carried away 1Sa 30:18 6003
from the slaughter of the A.................. 2Sa 1:1 6003
rest of the A that were escaped............ 1Chr 4:43 6003

AMAM (*a'-mam*) *A city near Shema and Moladah.*
A, and Shema, and Moladah,.................. Josh 15:26 538

AMANA (*am-a'-nah*) *A city in southern Judah.*
look from the top of A, from the.......... Song 4:8 549

AMARIAH (*am-a-ri'-ah*)
1. A descendant of Aaron.
begat A, and A begat Ahitub,................ 1Chr 6:7 568
A his son, Ahitub his son,.................... 1Chr 6:52 568
The son of A, the son of Azariah, ... Ezr 7:3 568
2. A High Priest during Solomon's reign.
begat Amariah, and A begat Ahitub,.... 1Chr 6:11 568
3. A descendant of Kohath.
A the second, Jahaziel the third, ... 1Chr 23:19 568
A the second, Jahaziel the third, ... 1Chr 24:23 568
4. Chief priest during Jehoshaphat's reign.
A the chief priest is over you in 2Chr 19:11 568
5. A Levite in Hezekiah's time.
and Jeshua, and Shemaiah, A.............. 2Chr 31:15 568
6. Married a foreign wife in exile.
Shallum, A, and Joseph.......................... Ezr 10:42 568
7. A priest who sealed the covenant with Nehemiah.
Pashur, A, Malchijah,.............................. Neh 10:3 568
A, Malluch, Hattush,.............................. Neh 12:2 568
of A, Jehohanan...................................... Neh 12:13 568
8. A descendant of Judah.
son of Zechariah, the son of A.............. Neh 11:4 568
9. An ancestor of Zephaniah the prophet.
the son of Gedaliah, the son of A.......... Zeph 1:1 568

AMASA (*am'-a-sah*)
1. David's nephew.
Absalom made A captain of the............. 2Sa 17:25 6021
which A was a man's son, whose.......... 2Sa 17:25 6021
And say ye to A, Art thou not of 2Sa 19:13 6021
Then said the king to A, Assemble 2Sa 20:4 6021
So A went to assemble the men of 2Sa 20:5 6021
is in Gibeon, A went before them......... 2Sa 20:8 6021
And Joab said to A, Art thou in 2Sa 20:9 6021
And Joab took A, by the beard with 2Sa 20:9 6021
But A took no heed to the sword......... 2Sa 20:10 6021
A wallowed in blood in the midst......... 2Sa 20:12 6021
he removed A out of the highway 2Sa 20:12 6021
unto A the son of Jether, whom he...... 1Kin 2:5 6021
A the son of Jether, captain of............ 1Kin 2:32 6021
And Abigail bare A 1Chr 2:17 6021
the father of A was Jether the.............. 1Chr 2:17 6021
2. An Ephraimite who opposed the slavery of the Jews.
A the son of Hadlai, stood up................ 2Chr 28:12 6021

AMASAI (*am'-as-ahee*)
1. A descendant of Kohath.
A, and Ahimoth 1Chr 6:25 6022
the son of Mahath, the son of A........... 1Chr 6:35 6022
arose, Mahath the son of A 2Chr 29:12 6022
2. A captain in David's army.
Then the spirit came upon A................. 1Chr 12:18 6022
3. A Levite who helped relocate the Ark.
Jehoshaphat, and Nethaneel, and A....... 1Chr 15:24 6022

AMASHAI (*am'-ash-ahee*) *A priest of the Emmer family.*
A the son of Azareel, the son of........... Neh 11:13 6023

AMASHSAI See AMASHI.

AMASIAH (*am-a-si'-ah*) *Chief captain of Jehoshaphat's army.*
next him was A the son of Zichri,......... 2Chr 17:16 6007

AMAZED
Then the dukes of Edom shall be a ...... Ex 15:15 926
again, the men of Benjamin were a....... Judg 20:41 926
They were a, they answered no............ Job 32:15 2865
they shall be a one at another .... Is 13:8 8539
I will make many people a at thee......... Eze 32:10 8074
And all the people were a, and said...... Mt 12:23 1839
heard it, they were exceedingly a.......... Mt 19:25 1605
And they were all a, insomuch that...... Mk 1:27 2284
insomuch that they were all a .... Mk 2:12 1839
they were sore a in themselves............ Mk 6:51 1839
they beheld him, were greatly a .... Mk 9:15 1568
and they were a.................................... Mk 10:32 2284
and John, and began to be sore a.......... Mk 14:33 1568
for they trembled and were a............... Mk 16:8 1611
And when they saw him, they were a.. Lk 2:48 1605
And they were all a, and spake............ Lk 4:36
And they were all a, and they............... Lk 5:26
they were all a at the mighty............... Lk 9:43 1605
And they were all a and marvelled,...... Acts 2:7 1839
And they were all a, and were in .... Acts 2:12 1839
But all that heard him were a .... Acts 9:21 1839

AMAZEMENT
a at that which had happened unto...... Acts 3:10 1611
and are not afraid with any a................ 1Pet 3:6 4423

AMAZIAH (*am-a-zi'-ah*)
1. Son and successor of King Joash of Judah.
A his son reigned in his stead 2Kin 12:21 558
he fought against A king of Judah 2Kin 13:12 558
A the son of Joash king of Judah......... 2Kin 14:1 558
Then A sent messengers to Jehoash....... 2Kin 14:8 558
of Israel sent to A king of Judah.......... 2Kin 14:9 558
But A would not hear............................ 2Kin 14:11 558
A king of Judah looked one................... 2Kin 14:11 558
of Israel took A king of Judah.............. 2Kin 14:13 558
he fought with A king of Judah 2Kin 14:15 558
A the son of Joash king of Judah......... 2Kin 14:17 558
And the rest of the acts of A................. 2Kin 14:18 558
him king instead of his father A.......... 2Kin 14:21 558
In the fifteenth year of A the............... 2Kin 14:23 558
son of A king of Judah to reign............ 2Kin 15:1 558
to all that his father A had done 2Kin 15:3 558
A his son, Azariah his son,................... 1Chr 3:12 558
A his son reigned in his stead 2Chr 24:27 558
A was twenty and five years old 2Chr 25:1 558
Moreover A gathered Judah 2Chr 25:5 558
A said to the man of God, But............... 2Chr 25:9 558
Then A separated them, to wit,............. 2Chr 25:10 558
A strengthened himself, and led 2Chr 25:11 558
of the army which A sent back 2Chr 25:13 558
after that A was come from the 2Chr 25:14 558
of the LORD was kindled against A 2Chr 25:15 558
Then A king of Judah took advice,........ 2Chr 25:17 558
of Israel sent to A king of Judah.......... 2Chr 25:18 558
But A would not hear............................ 2Chr 25:20 558
A king of Judah, at Beth-shemesh,....... 2Chr 25:21 558
of Israel took A king of Judah.............. 2Chr 25:23 558
A the son of Joash king of Judah......... 2Chr 25:25 558
Now the rest of the acts of A................ 2Chr 25:26 558
Now after the time that A did............... 2Chr 25:27 558
king in the room of his father A.......... 2Chr 26:1 558
to all that his father A did.................. 2Chr 26:4 558
2. A Simeonite.
Jamlech, and Joshah the son of A........ 1Chr 4:34 558
3. A Levite from the Merari family.
son of Hashabiah, the son of A............ 1Chr 6:45 558
4. Priest of the idols at Bethel.
Then A the priest of Beth-el sent .... Amos 7:10 558
Also A said unto Amos, O thou .... Amos 7:12 558
Then answered Amos, and said to A ..... Amos 7:14 558

AMBASSADOR
but a faithful a is health......................... Prov 13:17 6735
an a is sent unto the heathen,............... Jer 49:14 6735
an a is sent among the heathen,............ Obad 1 6735
For which I am an a in bonds............... Eph 6:20 4243

AMBASSADORS
and made as if they had been a .... Josh 9:4 6735
the a of the princes of Babylon............ 2Chr 32:31 3887
But he sent a to him, saying,................ 2Chr 35:21 4397
That sendeth a by the sea..................... Is 18:2 6735
at Zoan, and his a came to Hanes......... Is 30:4 4397
the a of peace shall weep .... Is 33:7 4397
him in sending his a into Egypt............ Eze 17:15 4397
Now then we are a for Christ 2Cor 5:20 4243

AMBASSAGE
a great way off, he sendeth an a .... Lk 14:32 4242

AMBER
midst thereof as the colour of a............ Eze 1:4 2830
And I saw as the colour of a................. Eze 1:27 2830
of brightness, as the colour of a .... Eze 8:2 2830

AMBUSH
lay thee an a for the city behind .... Josh 8:2 693
Then ye shall rise up from the a........... Josh 8:7 693
and they went to lie in a, and .... Josh 8:9 693
them to lie in a between Beth-el .... Josh 8:12 693
in a against him behind the city .... Josh 8:14 693
the a arose quickly out of their .... Josh 8:19 693
saw that the a had taken the city .... Josh 8:21 693

AMBUSHES
up the watchmen, prepare the a.......... Jer 51:12 693

AMBUSHMENT
But Jeroboam caused an a to come...... 2Chr 13:13 3993
Judah, and the a was behind them....... 2Chr 13:13 3993

AMBUSHMENTS
the LORD set a against the 2Chr 20:22 693

AMEN
1. A term meaning "so be it."
And the woman shall say, A, a .... Num 5:22 543
the people shall answer and say, A....... Deut 27:15 543
and all the people shall say, A............ Deut 27:16 543
And all the people shall say, A............ Deut 27:17 543
And all the people shall say, A............ Deut 27:18 543
And all the people shall say, A............ Deut 27:19 543
And all the people shall say, A............ Deut 27:20 543
And all the people shall say, A............ Deut 27:21 543
And all the people shall say, A............ Deut 27:22 543
And all the people shall say, A............ Deut 27:23 543
And all the people shall say, A............ Deut 27:24 543
And all the people shall say, A............ Deut 27:25 543
And all the people shall say, A............ Deut 27:26 543
answered the king, and said, A............ 1Kin 1:36 543
And all the people said, A.................... 1Chr 16:36 543
And all the congregation said, A .... Neh 5:13 543
all the people answered, A, A.............. Neh 8:6 543
A, and A .... Ps 41:13 543
A, and A .... Ps 72:19 543
A, and A .... Ps 89:52 543
and let all the people say, A .... Ps 106:48 543
Even the prophet Jeremiah said, A .... Jer 28:6 543
and the glory, for ever. A...................... Mt 6:13 281
the end of the world. A......................... Mt 28:20 281
with signs following. A......................... Mk 16:20 281
praising and blessing God. A................. Lk 24:53 281
that should be written. A....................... Jn 21:25 281
who is blessed for ever. A..................... Rom 1:25 281
God blessed for ever. A......................... Rom 9:5 281
to whom be glory for ever. A................ Rom 11:36 281
peace be with you all. A....................... Rom 15:33 281
Jesus Christ be with you. A.................. Rom 16:20 281
Jesus Christ be with you all. A............. Rom 16:24 281
through Jesus Christ for ever. A. .... Rom 16:27 281
say A at thy giving of thanks................ 1Cor 14:16 281
with you all in Christ Jesus. A.............. 1Cor 16:24 281
God in him are yea, and in him A......... 2Cor 1:20 281
Holy Ghost, be with you all. A............. 2Cor 13:14 281
be glory for ever and ever. A............... Gal 1:5 281
Christ be with your spirit. A................. Gal 6:18 281
all ages, world without end. A............. Eph 3:21 281
Lord Jesus Christ in sincerity. A.......... Eph 6:24 281
be glory for ever and ever. A............... Phil 4:20 281
Jesus Christ be with you all. A............. Phil 4:23 281
Grace be with you. A............................ Col 4:18 281
Jesus Christ be with you. A.................. 1Th 5:28 281
Jesus Christ be with you all. A............. 2Th 3:18 281
glory for ever and ever. A.................... 1Ti 1:17 281
honour and power everlasting. A. 1Ti 6:16 281
Grace be with thee. A........................... 1Ti 6:21 281
be glory for ever and ever. A............... 2Ti 4:18 281
Grace be with you. A............................ 2Ti 4:22 281
Grace be with you all. A....................... Titus 3:15 281
Christ be with your spirit. A................. Philem 25 281
be glory for ever and ever. A............... Heb 13:21 281
Grace be with you all. A....................... Heb 13:25 281
dominion for ever and ever. A.............. 1Pet 4:11 281
dominion for ever and ever. A.............. 1Pet 5:11 281
all that are in Christ Jesus. A............... 1Pet 5:14 281
glory both now and for ever. A............. 2Pet 3:18 281
keep yourselves from idols. A............... 1Jn 5:21 281
thy elect sister greet thee. A................ 2Jn 13 281
power, both now and ever. A................. Jude 25 281
dominion for ever and ever. A.............. Rev 1:6 281
Even so, A .... Rev 1:7 281
I am alive for evermore, A.................... Rev 1:18 281
And the four beasts said, A.................. Rev 5:14 281
Saying, A: Blessing, and glory.............. Rev 7:12 281
our God for ever and ever. A................ Rev 7:12 281
sat on the throne, saying, A;................ Rev 19:4 281
Surely I come quickly. A....................... Rev 22:20 281
Jesus Christ be with you all. A............. Rev 22:21 281
2. A title of Christ.
These things saith the A, the................ Rev 3:14 281

AMEND
LORD, to repair and a the house 2Chr 34:10 2388
A your ways and your doings, and I .... Jer 7:3 3190
For if ye throughly a your ways........... Jer 7:5 3190
Therefore now a your ways.................... Jer 26:13 3190
a your doings, and go not after .... Jer 35:15 3190
them the hour when he began to a ...... Jn 4:52 2192

AMENDS
he shall make a for the harm that .... Lev 5:16 7999

AMERCE
they shall a him in an hundred............. Deut 22:19 6064

AMETHYST
row a ligure, an agate, and an a........... Ex 28:19 306
row, a ligure, an agate, and an a.......... Ex 39:12 306
the twelfth, an a .... Rev 21:20 271

AMI (*a'-mi*) *A family of returned exiles.*
of Zebaim, the children of A.................. Ezr 2:57 532

AMIABLE
How a are thy tabernacles, O LORD...... Ps 84:1 3039

AMINADAB (*a-min'-a-dab*) See AMMINADAB.
Son of Aram; ancestor of Jesus.
And Aram begat A .... Mt 1:4 284
and A begat Naasson.............................. Mt 1:4 284
Which was the son of A, which was .... Lk 3:33 284

AMISS
We have sinned, we have done a 2Chr 6:37 5753
which speak any thing a against.......... Dan 3:29 7955
but this man hath done nothing a .... Lk 23:41 824
and receive not, because ye ask a......... Jas 4:3 2560

AMITTAI (*a-mit'-tahee*) *Father of Jonah.*
his servant Jonah, the son of A 2Kin 14:25 573
LORD came unto Jonah the son of A.... Jonah 1:1 573

AMMAH (*am'-mah*) See METHEG-AMMAH. *A hill near Gibeon.*
they were come to the hill of A............ 2Sa 2:24 522

AMMI (*am'-mi*) See AMMI-NADIB, BEN-AMMI, LO-AMMI. *A name given to Israel by Hosea meaning "my people."*
Say ye unto your brethren, A................ Hos 2:1 5971

AMMIEL (*am'-me-el*) See ELIAM.
1. A spy for Moses.
of Dan, A the son of Gemalli................ Num 13:12 5988
2. A Manassehite of Lodebar.
the house of Machir, the son of A......... 2Sa 9:4 5988
the house of Machir, the son of A......... 2Sa 9:5 5988
Machir the son of A of Lo-debar 2Sa 17:27 5988
3. Father of a wife of David.
of Bath-shua the daughter of A 1Chr 3:5 5988
4. A Levite Tabernacle servant.
A the sixth, Issachar the seventh.......... 1Chr 26:5 5988

AMMIHUD (*am-mi'-hud*)
1. Father of Elishama.
Elishama the son of A........................... Num 1:10 5989
shall be Elishama the son of A.............. Num 2:18 5989
seventh day Elishama the son of A....... Num 7:48 5989
offering of Elishama the son of A......... Num 7:53 5989
host was Elishama the son of A .... Num 10:22 5989
A his son, Elishama his son, ... 1Chr 7:26 5989
2. A Simeonite.
of Simeon, Shemuel the son of A .... Num 34:20 5989

3. *A Naphtalite.*
of Naphtali, Pedahel the son of A .... Num 34:28 5989
4. *Father of the king of Geshur.*
and went to Talmai, the son of A........... 2Sa 13:37 5989
5. *A son of Omri.*
Uthai the son of A, the son of............... 1Chr 9:4 5989

AMMINADAB (*am-min'-a-dab*) See AMINADAB, AMMI-NADIB.
1. *Aaron's father-in-law.*
took him Elisheba, daughter of A.......... Ex 6:23 5992
2. *A prince of Judah.*
Nahshon the son of A .... Num 1:7 5992
Nahshon the son of A shall be............... Num 2:3 5992
day was Nahshon the son of A............... Num 7:12 5992
offering of Nahshon the son of A............ Num 7:17 5992
his host was Nahshon the son of A...... Num 10:14 5992
Hezron begat Ram, and Ram begat A.. Ruth 4:19 5992
A begat Nahshon, and Nahshon begat. Ruth 4:20 5992
And Ram begat A................................ 1Chr 2:10 5992
A begat Nahshon, prince of the............ 1Chr 2:10 5992
3. *A son of Kohath.*
A his son, Korah his son, Assir............. 1Chr 6:22 5992
4. *A Levite who relocated the Ark.*
A the chief, and his brethren an........... 1Chr 15:10 5992
and Joel, Shemaiah, and Eliel, and A.... 1Chr 15:11 5992

AMMI-NADIB
made me like the chariots of A............ Song 6:12 5993

AMMISHADDAI (*am-mi-shad'-dahee*) *Father of the chief of the tribe of Dan.*
Ahiezer the son of A.............................. Num 1:12 5996
Dan shall be Ahiezer the son of A .... Num 2:25 5996
tenth day Ahiezer the son of A............ Num 7:66 5996
offering of Ahiezer the son of A .... Num 7:71 5996
his host was Ahiezer the son of A .... Num 10:25 5996

AMMIZABAD (*am-miz'-a-bad*) *Son of a captain of David.*
and in his course was A his son............ 1Chr 27:6 5990

AMMON (*am'-mon*) *Territory in Jordan.*
the children of A unto this day............ Gen 19:38 5983
even unto the children of A.................. Num 21:24 5983
of the children of A was strong .... Num 21:24 5983
over against the children of A.............. Deut 2:19 5983
the children of A any possession .... Deut 2:19 5983
the children of A thou camest not......... Deut 2:37 5983
in Rabbath of the children of A............. Deut 3:11 5983
the border of the children of A .... Deut 3:16 5983
the border of the children of A .... Josh 12:2 5983
the border of the children of A .... Josh 13:10 5983
the land of the children of A .... Josh 13:25 5983
unto him the children of A .... Judg 3:13 5983
and the gods of the children of A.......... Judg 10:6 5983
the hands of the children of A .... Judg 10:7 5983
Moreover the children of A passed........ Judg 10:9 5983
Amorites, from the children of A .... Judg 10:11 5983
Then the children of A were................. Judg 10:17 5983
fight against the children of A .... Judg 10:18 5983
that the children of A made war .... Judg 11:4 5983
of A made war against Israel .... Judg 11:5 5983
may fight with the children of A........... Judg 11:6 5983
fight against the children of A .... Judg 11:8 5983
fight against the children of A .... Judg 11:9 5983
the king of the children of A................ Judg 11:12 5983
the king of the children of A................ Judg 11:13 5983
the king of the children of A................ Judg 11:14 5983
nor the land of the children of A .... Judg 11:15 5983
of Israel and the children of A .... Judg 11:27 5983
the king of the children of A .... Judg 11:28 5983
over unto the children of A .... Judg 11:29 5983
the children of A into mine hands .... Judg 11:30 5983
in peace from the children of A .... Judg 11:31 5983
of A to fight against them.................... Judg 11:32 5983
Thus the children of A were.................. Judg 11:33 5983
even of the children of A...................... Judg 11:36 5983
fight against the children of A .... Judg 12:1 5983
strife with the children of A .... Judg 12:2 5983
over against the children of A............... Judg 12:3 5983
children of A came against you 1Sa 12:12 5983
and against the children of A................ 1Sa 14:47 5983
of Moab, and of the children of A 2Sa 8:12 5983
king of the children of A died 2Sa 10:1 5983
the land of the children of A 2Sa 10:2 5983
of A said unto Hanun their lord 2Sa 10:3 5983
when the children of A saw that............ 2Sa 10:6 5983
David, the children of A sent 2Sa 10:6 5983
And the children of A came out 2Sa 10:8 5983
array against the children of A 2Sa 10:10 5983
of A be too strong for thee 2Sa 10:11 5983
when the children of A saw that............ 2Sa 10:14 5983
returned from the children of A 2Sa 10:14 5983
help the children of A any more............ 2Sa 10:19 5983
they destroyed the children of A 2Sa 11:1 5983
the sword of the children of A 2Sa 12:9 5983
Rabbah of the children of A 2Sa 12:26 5983
the cities of the children of A............... 2Sa 12:31 5983
of Rabbah of the children of A 2Sa 17:27 5983
abomination of the children of A 1Kin 11:7 5983
the god of the children of A 1Kin 11:33 5983
abomination of the children of A 2Kin 23:13 5983
and bands of the children of A.............. 2Kin 24:2 5983
Moab, and from the children of A.......... 1Chr 18:11 5983
king of the children of A died 1Chr 19:1 5983
of the children of A to Hanun................ 1Chr 19:2 5983
the children of A said to Hanun 1Chr 19:3 5983
when the children of A saw that............ 1Chr 19:6 5983
the children of A sent a thousand......... 1Chr 19:6 5983
the children of A gathered................... 1Chr 19:7 5983
And the children of A came out 1Chr 19:9 5983
array against the children of A 1Chr 19:11 5983
of A be too strong for thee 1Chr 19:12 5983
when the children of A saw that........... 1Chr 19:15 5983
help the children of A any more........... 1Chr 19:19 5983
the country of the children of A........... 1Chr 20:1 5983
the cities of the children of A.............. 1Chr 20:3 5983
of Moab, and the children of A 2Chr 20:1 5983
And now, behold, the children of A 2Chr 20:10 5983
against the children of A 2Chr 20:22 5983
For the children of A and Moab 2Chr 20:23 5983
the children of A gave him the.............. 2Chr 27:5 5983
the children of A pay unto him 2Chr 27:5 5983
had married wives of Ashdod, of A....... Neh 13:23 5983
Gebal, and A, and Amalek .... Ps 83:7 5983
the children of A shall obey them .... Is 11:14 5983
and Edom, and the children of A........... Jer 9:26 5983
and Moab, and the children of A .... Jer 25:21 5983
captivity of the children of A .... Jer 49:6 5983
and the chief of the children of A .... Dan 11:41 5983
of the children of A, and for four......... Amos 1:13 5983
revilings of the children of A............... Zeph 2:8 5983
and the children of A as Gomorrah ...... Zeph 2:9 5983

AMMONITE (*am'-mon-ite*) See AMMONITES, AMMONITESS. *A descendant of Ammon.*
An A or Moabite shall not enter........... Deut 23:3 5984
Then Nahash the A came up................. 1Sa 11:1 5984
Nahash the A answered them, On 1Sa 11:2 5984
Zelek the A, Nahari the........................ 2Sa 23:37 5984
Zelek the A, Naharai the..................... 1Chr 11:39 5984
and Tobiah the servant, the A .... Neh 2:10 5984
and Tobiah the servant, the A .... Neh 2:19 5984
Now Tobiah the A was by him .... Neh 4:3 5984
was found written, that the A............... Neh 13:1 5984

AMMONITES (*am'-mon-ites*)
the A call them Zamzummims............... Deut 2:20 5984
slew the A until the heat of the............ 1Sa 11:11 5984
Pharaoh, women of the Moabites, A 1Kin 11:1 5984
Milcom the abomination of the A 1Kin 11:5 5984
and with them other beside the A......... 2Chr 20:1 5984
the A gave gifts to Uzziah 2Chr 26:8 5984
also with the king of the A.................. 2Chr 27:5 5984
Perizzites, the Jebusites, the A............ Ezr 9:1 5984
Tobiah, and the Arabians, and the A.... Neh 4:7 5984
of Moab, and to the king of the A .... Jer 27:3 5984
that were in Moab, and among the A .. Jer 40:11 5984
that Baalis the king of the A .... Jer 40:14 5984
and departed to go over to the A .... Jer 41:10 5984
with eight men, and went to the A....... Jer 41:15 5984
Concerning The A, thus saith the .... Jer 49:1 5984
to be heard in Rabbah of the A .... Jer 49:2 5984
may come to Rabbath of the A............. Eze 21:20 5984
the Lord GOD concerning the A............ Eze 21:28 5984
man, set thy face against the A........... Eze 25:2 5984
And say unto the A, Hear the word ..... Eze 25:3 5984
the A a couchingplace for flocks .... Eze 25:5 5984
the men of the east with the A............. Eze 25:10 5984
that the A may not be remembered...... Eze 25:10 5984

AMMONITESS (*am'-mon-i-tess*)
his mother's name was Naamah an A.. 1Kin 14:21 5984
his mother's name was Naamah an A.. 1Kin 14:31 5984
his mother's name was Naamah an A.. 2Chr 12:13 5984
Zabad the son of Shimeath an A.......... 2Chr 24:26 5984

AMNON (*am'-non*) See AMNON'S.
1. *A son of David.*
and his firstborn was A, of..................... 2Sa 3:2 550
A the son of David loved her 2Sa 13:1 550
A was so vexed, that he fell sick 2Sa 13:2 550
A thought it hard for him to do............ 2Sa 13:2 550
But A had a friend, whose name 2Sa 13:3 550
A said unto him, I love Tamar, my........ 2Sa 13:4 550
So A lay down, and made himself.......... 2Sa 13:6 550
A said unto the king, I pray thee.......... 2Sa 13:6 550
A said, Have out all men from me 2Sa 13:9 550
A said unto Tamar, Bring the meat...... 2Sa 13:10 550
into the chamber to A her brother....... 2Sa 13:10 550
Then A hated her exceedingly 2Sa 13:15 550
A said unto her, Arise, be gone............ 2Sa 13:15 550
Hath A thy brother been with thee 2Sa 13:20 550
brother A neither good nor bad............ 2Sa 13:22 550
for Absalom hated A, because he.......... 2Sa 13:22 550
thee, let my brother A go with us......... 2Sa 13:26 550
pressed him, that he let A 2Sa 13:27 550
and when I say unto you, Smite A 2Sa 13:28 550
unto A as Absalom had commanded.... 2Sa 13:29 550
for A only is dead................................ 2Sa 13:32 550
for A only is dead................................ 2Sa 13:33 550
for he was comforted concerning A...... 2Sa 13:39 550
the firstborn A, of Ahinoam the 1Chr 3:1 550
2. *A son of Shimon.*
And the sons of Shimon were, A............ 1Chr 4:20 550

AMNON'S (*am'-nons*) *Refers to Amnon 1.*
Go now to thy brother A house............ 2Sa 13:7 550
Tamar went to her brother A house..... 2Sa 13:8 550
Mark ye now when A heart is merry ... 2Sa 13:28 550

AMOK (*a'-mok*) *A priest who returned from exile under Zerubbabel.*
Sallu, A, Hilkiah, Jedaiah...................... Neh 12:7 5987
of A, Eber .... Neh 12:20 5987

AMON (*a'-mon*)
1. *A governor of Samaria.*
carry him back unto A the.................... 1Kin 22:26 526
carry him back to A the governor 2Chr 18:25 526
2. *Son and successor of King Manasseh of Judah.*
A his son reigned in his stead 2Kin 21:18 526
A was twenty and two years old........... 2Kin 21:19 526
the servants of A conspired 2Kin 21:23 526
that had conspired against king A 2Kin 21:24 526
of the acts of A which he did............... 2Kin 21:25 526
A his son, Josiah his son..................... 1Chr 3:14 526
A his son reigned in his stead 2Chr 33:20 526
A was two and twenty years old........... 2Chr 33:21 526
for A sacrificed unto all the................. 2Chr 33:22 526
but A trespassed more and more.......... 2Chr 33:23 526
that had conspired against king A 2Chr 33:25 526
Josiah the son of A king of Judah.......... Jer 1:2 526
Josiah the son of A king of Judah.......... Jer 25:3 526
the days of Josiah the son of A .... Zeph 1:1 526
and Manasses begat A........................... Mt 1:10 *300*
and A begat Josias .... Mt 1:10 *300*
3. *A descendant of Solomon who returned from the Exile under Zerubbabel.*
of Zebaim, the children of A.................. Neh 7:59 526

AMONG
Every man child a you shall be............. Gen 17:10
old shall be circumcised a you .... Gen 17:12
every male a the men of Abraham's..... Gen 17:23
thou art a mighty prince a us .... Gen 23:6 8432
Ephron dwelt a the children of............. Gen 23:10 8432
of the Canaanites, a whom I dwell .... Gen 24:3 7130
all the brown cattle a the sheep .... Gen 30:32
spotted and speckled a the goats.......... Gen 30:32
spotted a the goats............................... Gen 30:33
brown a the sheep, that shall be.......... Gen 30:33
it, and all the brown a the sheep.......... Gen 30:35
they might conceive a the rods............. Gen 30:41
if every male a us be circumcised .... Gen 34:22
a the inhabitants of the land................ Gen 34:30
a the Canaanites and the Perizzites...... Gen 34:30
the strange gods that are a you............ Gen 35:2 8432
a their dukes in the land of Seir........... Gen 36:30
of the chief baker a his servants .... Gen 40:20 8432
to buy corn a those that came............. Gen 42:5 8432
any men of activity a them.................. Gen 47:6
when she saw the ark a the flags......... Ex 2:5 8432
children of Israel from a them .... Ex 7:5 8432
feared the word of the LORD a the........ Ex 9:20
my signs which I have done a them..... Ex 10:2
and get you forth from a my people..... Ex 12:31 8432
stranger that sojourneth a you............ Ex 12:49 8432
the womb a the children of Israel......... Ex 13:2
all the firstborn of man a thy.............. Ex 13:13
unto thee, O LORD, a the gods .... Ex 15:11
LORD, saying, Is the LORD a us .... Ex 17:7 7130
that I may dwell a them...................... Ex 25:8 8432
from a the children of Israel,................ Ex 28:1 8432
I will dwell a the children of .... Ex 29:45 8432
of Egypt, that I may dwell a them....... Ex 29:46 8432
that there be no plague a them .... Ex 30:12
passeth a them that are numbered ...... Ex 30:13 5921
passeth a them that are numbered ...... Ex 30:14 5921
be cut off from a his people................. Ex 31:14 7130
unto their shame a their enemies......... Ex 32:25
let my Lord, I pray thee, go a us........... Ex 34:9 7130
all the people a which thou art............ Ex 34:10 7310
and every firstling a thy cattle............ Ex 34:19
Take ye from a you an offering............ Ex 35:5
wise hearted a you shall come............. Ex 35:10
every wise hearted man a them........... Ex 36:8
All the males a the children of............. Lev 6:18
All the males a the priests shall.......... Lev 6:29
Every male a the priests shall .... Lev 7:6
He a the sons of Aaron, that................ Lev 7:33
from a the children of Israel................ Lev 7:34
the beasts which ye shall eat a............ Lev 11:2
a the beasts, that shall ye eat.............. Lev 11:3
have in abomination a the fowls .... Lev 11:13 4480
a all manner of beasts that go on.......... Lev 11:27
a the creeping things that creep.......... Lev 11:29
unclean to you a all that creep .... Lev 11:31
or whatsoever hath more feet a........... Lev 11:42
my tabernacle that is a them .... Lev 15:31 8432
that remaineth a them in the............... Lev 16:16 854
a stranger that sojourneth a you.......... Lev 16:29 8432
be cut off from a his people................. Lev 17:4 7130
the strangers which sojourn a you ...... Lev 17:8 8432
be cut off from a his people................. Lev 17:9
the strangers that sojourn a you.......... Lev 17:10 8432
cut him off from a his people .... Lev 17:10 7130
that sojourneth a you eat blood .... Lev 17:12 8432
the strangers that sojourn a you.......... Lev 17:13 8432
stranger that sojourneth a you............. Lev 18:26 8432
be cut off from a their people................ Lev 18:29 7130
be cut off from a his people.................. Lev 19:8
down as a talebearer a thy people .... Lev 19:16
be unto you as one born a you.............. Lev 19:34 854
cut him off from a his people .... Lev 20:3 7130
with Molech, from a their people .... Lev 20:5 7130
cut him off from a his people .... Lev 20:6 7130
that there be no wickedness a you .... Lev 20:14 8432
be cut off from a their people............... Lev 20:18 7130
defiled for the dead a his people.......... Lev 21:1
being a chief man a his people............. Lev 21:4
is the high priest a his brethren........... Lev 21:10
he profane his seed a his people .... Lev 21:15
all your seed a your generations.......... Lev 22:3
hallowed a the children of Israel........... Lev 22:32 8432
be cut off from a his people................. Lev 23:29
will I destroy from a his people .... Lev 23:30 7130
went out a the children of Israel........... Lev 24:10 8432
a the children of Israel......................... Lev 25:33 8432
strangers that do sojourn a you .... Lev 25:45
And I will set my tabernacle a you....... Lev 26:11 8432
And I will walk a you, and will be........ Lev 26:12 8432
will also send wild beasts a you........... Lev 26:22
I will send the pestilence a you .... Lev 26:25 8432
I will scatter you a the heathen .... Lev 26:33
And ye shall perish a the heathen......... Lev 26:38
fathers were not numbered a them...... Num 1:47 8432
of them a the children of Israel........... Num 1:49 8432
numbered a the children of Israel......... Num 2:33 8432
I have taken the Levites from a .... Num 3:12 8432
matrix a the children of Israel .... Num 3:12
a the children of Israel......................... Num 3:41
a the cattle of the children of.............. Num 3:41
all the firstborn a the children .... Num 3:42

a the children of Israel, and the ... Num 3:45
of Kohath from *a* the sons of Levi ... Num 4:2 8432
the Kohathites from *a* the Levites ... Num 4:18 8432
an oath *a* thy people, when the ... Num 5:21 8432
shall be a curse *a* her people ... Num 5:27 7130
Take the Levites from *a* the ... Num 8:6 8432
from *a* the children of Israel ... Num 8:14 8432
me from *a* the children of Israel ... Num 8:16 8432
to his sons from *a* the children ... Num 8:19 8432
plague *a* the children of Israel ... Num 8:19
season *a* the children of Israel ... Num 9:7 8432
be cut off from *a* his people ... Num 9:13
if a stranger shall sojourn *a* you ... Num 9:14 854
the fire of the LORD burnt *a* them ... Num 11:1
the fire of the LORD burnt *a* them ... Num 11:3
that was *a* them fell a lusting ... Num 11:4 7130
despised the LORD which is *a* you ... Num 11:20 7130
a whom I am, are six hundred ... Num 11:21 7130
If there be a prophet *a* you ... Num 12:6
a man, every one a ruler *a* them ... Num 13:2
signs which I have shewed *a* them ... Num 14:11 7130
people in thy might from *a* them ... Num 14:13 7130
that thou LORD art *a* this people ... Num 14:14 7130
not up, for the LORD is not *a* you ... Num 14:42 7130
or whosoever be *a* you in your ... Num 15:14 8432
henceforward *a* your generations ... Num 15:23
stranger that sojourneth *a* them ... Num 15:26 8432
is born *a* the children of Israel ... Num 15:29
stranger that sojourneth *a* them ... Num 15:29 8432
be cut off from *a* his people ... Num 15:30 7130
of them, and the LORD is *a* them ... Num 16:3 8432
from *a* this congregation, that I ... Num 16:21 8432
perished from *a* the congregation ... Num 16:33 8432
Get you up from *a* this ... Num 16:45 8432
the plague was begun *a* the people ... Num 16:47
the rod of Aaron was *a* their rods ... Num 17:6 8432
from *a* the children of Israel ... Num 18:6 8432
shalt thou have any part *a* them ... Num 18:20 8432
thine inheritance *a* the children ... Num 18:20 8432
that *a* the children of Israel ... Num 18:23 8432
A the children of Israel they ... Num 18:24 8432
stranger that sojourneth *a* them ... Num 19:10 8432
cut off from *a* the congregation ... Num 19:20 8432
sent fiery serpents *a* the people ... Num 21:6
not be reckoned *a* the nations ... Num 23:9
and the shout of a king is *a* them ... Num 23:21
saw it, he rose up from *a* the ... Num 25:7 8432
he was zealous for my sake *a* them ... Num 25:11 8432
of a chief house *a* the Simeonites ... Num 25:14
numbered *a* the children of Israel ... Num 26:62 8432
them *a* the children of Israel ... Num 26:62 8432
But *a* these there was not a man ... Num 26:64
be done away from *a* his family ... Num 27:4 8432
a the brethren of our father ... Num 27:4 8432
a their father's brethren ... Num 27:7 8432
Peor, and there was a plague *a* the ... Num 31:16
kill every male *a* the little ones ... Num 31:17
a you in the land of Canaan ... Num 32:30 8432
which the LORD had smitten *a* them ... Num 33:4
an inheritance *a* your families ... Num 33:54
a the cities which ye shall give ... Num 35:6 854
and for the sojourner *a* them ... Num 35:15 8432
for I the LORD dwell *a* the ... Num 35:34 8432
known *a* your tribes, and I will ... Deut 1:13
tens, and officers *a* your tribes ... Deut 1:15
for I am not *a* you ... Deut 1:42 7130
were wasted out from *a* the host ... Deut 2:14 7130
to destroy them from *a* the host ... Deut 2:15 7130
and dead from *a* the people, ... Deut 2:16 7130
hath destroyed them from *a* you ... Deut 4:3 7130
shall scatter you *a* the nations ... Deut 4:27
left few in number *a* the heathen ... Deut 4:27
LORD thy God is a jealous God *a* ... Deut 6:15 7130
a you, or *a* your cattle ... Deut 7:14
God will send the hornet *a* them ... Deut 7:20
for the LORD thy God is *a* you ... Deut 7:21 7130
If there arise *a* you a prophet ... Deut 13:1 7130
such wickedness as this is *a* you ... Deut 13:11 7130
Belial, are gone out from *a* you ... Deut 13:13 7130
such abomination is wrought *a* you ... Deut 13:14 7130
and cheweth the cud *a* the beasts ... Deut 14:6
when there shall be no poor *a* you ... Deut 15:4
If there be *a* you a poor man of ... Deut 15:7
and the widow, that are *a* you ... Deut 16:11 7130
If there be found *a* you, within ... Deut 17:2 7130
put the evil away from *a* you ... Deut 17:7 7130
one from *a* thy brethren shalt ... Deut 17:15 7130
no inheritance *a* their brethren ... Deut 18:2 7130
There shall not be found *a* you ... Deut 18:10
a Prophet from *a* their brethren ... Deut 18:18 7130
thou put the evil away from *a* you ... Deut 19:19 7130
no more any such evil *a* you ... Deut 19:20 7130
of innocent blood from *a* you ... Deut 21:9 7130
seest *a* the captives a beautiful ... Deut 21:11
thou put evil away from *a* you ... Deut 21:21 7130
thou put evil away from *a* you ... Deut 22:21 7130
shalt put away evil from *a* you ... Deut 22:24 7130
If there be *a* you any man ... Deut 23:10
shall dwell with thee, even *a* you ... Deut 23:16 7130
shalt put evil away from *a* you ... Deut 24:7 7130
and the stranger that is *a* you ... Deut 26:11 7130
a all nations whither the LORD ... Deut 28:37
that the man that is tender *a* you ... Deut 28:54
tender and delicate woman *a* you ... Deut 28:56
shall scatter thee *a* all people ... Deut 28:64
a these nations shalt thou find ... Deut 28:65
silver and gold, which were *a* them ... Deut 29:17
Lest there should be *a* you man ... Deut 29:18
lest there should be *a* you a root ... Deut 29:18
them to mind *a* all the nations ... Deut 30:1
whither they go to be *a* them ... Deut 31:16 7130
us, because our God is not *a* us ... Deut 31:17 7130
of them to cease from *a* men ... Deut 32:26
me, and sealed up *a* my treasures ... Deut 32:34

which I testify *a* you this day ... Deut 32:46
ye trespassed against me *a* the ... Deut 32:51 8432
the LORD will do wonders *a* you ... Josh 3:5 7130
know that the living God is *a* you ... Josh 3:10 7130
That this may be a sign *a* you ... Josh 4:6 7130
put it even *a* their own stuff ... Josh 7:11
destroy the accursed from *a* you ... Josh 7:12 7130
the accursed thing from *a* you ... Josh 7:13 7130
When I saw *a* the spoils a goodly ... Josh 7:21
lodged that night *a* the people ... Josh 8:9 8432
as he that was born *a* them ... Josh 8:33
that were conversant *a* them ... Josh 8:35 7130
Peradventure ye dwell *a* us ... Josh 9:7 7130
and that they dwelt *a* them ... Josh 9:16 7130
when ye dwell *a* us ... Josh 9:22 7130
peace with Israel, and were *a* them ... Josh 10:1 7130
the Maachathites dwell *a* the ... Josh 13:13 7130
a them that were slain by them ... Josh 13:22 413
he gave none inheritance *a* them ... Josh 14:3 8432
was a great man *a* the Anakims ... Josh 14:15
a part *a* the children of Judah ... Josh 15:13 8432
the children of Ephraim were *a* ... Josh 16:9 8432
but the Canaanites dwell *a* the ... Josh 16:10 7130
us an inheritance *a* our brethren ... Josh 17:4 8432
he gave them an inheritance *a* the ... Josh 17:4 8432
had an inheritance *a* his sons ... Josh 17:6 8432
are *a* the cities of Manasseh ... Josh 17:9 8432
there remained *a* the children of ... Josh 18:2
Give out from *a* you three men for ... Josh 18:4
the Levites have no part *a* you ... Josh 18:7 7130
to Joshua the son of Nun *a* them ... Josh 19:49 8432
a place, that he may dwell *a* them ... Josh 20:4 5973
stranger that sojourneth *a* them ... Josh 20:9 8432
a their brethren on this side ... Josh 22:7 5973
fathers *a* the thousands of Israel ... Josh 22:14
dwelleth, and take possession *a* us ... Josh 22:19 8432
we perceive that the LORD is *a* us ... Josh 22:31 8432
That ye come not *a* these nations ... Josh 23:7
these that remain *a* you ... Josh 23:7
even these that remain *a* you ... Josh 23:12 854
to that which I did *a* them ... Josh 24:5 7130
a all the people through whom we ... Josh 24:17
the strange gods which are *a* you ... Josh 24:23 7130
they went and dwelt *a* the people ... Judg 1:16 854
Canaanites dwelt in Gezer *a* them ... Judg 1:29 7130
but the Canaanites dwelt *a* them ... Judg 1:30 7130
Asherites dwelt *a* the Canaanites ... Judg 1:32 7130
but he dwelt *a* the Canaanites, ... Judg 1:33 7130
of Israel dwelt *a* the Canaanites ... Judg 3:5 7130
seen *a* forty thousand in Israel ... Judg 5:8
themselves willingly *a* the people ... Judg 5:9
over the nobles *a* the people ... Judg 5:13
thee, Benjamin, *a* thy people ... Judg 5:14
Why abodest thou *a* the sheepfolds ... Judg 5:16 996
away the strange gods from *a* them ... Judg 10:16 7130
of Ephraim *a* the Ephraimites ... Judg 12:4 8432
and *a* the Manassites ... Judg 12:4 8432
Is there never a woman *a* the ... Judg 14:3
or *a* all my people, that thou ... Judg 14:3
unto them *a* the tribes of Israel ... Judg 18:1 8432
Let not thy voice be heard *a* us ... Judg 18:25
is this that is done *a* you ... Judg 20:12
A all this people there were ... Judg 20:16
Who is there *a* all the tribes of ... Judg 21:5
they found *a* the inhabitants of ... Judg 21:12
after the reapers *a* the sheaves ... Ruth 2:7 996
Let her glean even *a* the sheaves ... Ruth 2:15
not cut off from *a* his brethren ... Ruth 4:10 5973
dunghill, to set them *a* princes ... 1Sa 2:8 5973
us, that, when it cometh *a* us ... 1Sa 4:3 7130
a great slaughter *a* the people ... 1Sa 4:17
he had wrought wonderfully *a* them ... 1Sa 6:6
gods and Ashtaroth from *a* you ... 1Sa 7:3 8432
there was not *a* the children of ... 1Sa 9:2
place *a* them that were bidden ... 1Sa 9:22
upon him, and he prophesied *a* them ... 1Sa 10:10 8432
he prophesied *a* the prophets ... 1Sa 10:11 5973
Is Saul also *a* the prophets ... 1Sa 10:11
Is Saul also *a* the prophets ... 1Sa 10:12
he hath hid himself *a* the stuff ... 1Sa 10:22 413
and when he stood *a* the people ... 1Sa 10:23 8432
is none like him *a* all the people ... 1Sa 10:24
in the field, and *a* all the people ... 1Sa 14:15
slaughter *a* the Philistines ... 1Sa 14:30
Disperse yourselves *a* the people ... 1Sa 14:34
But there was not a man *a* all the ... 1Sa 14:39
you down from *a* the Amalekites ... 1Sa 15:6 8432
departed from *a* the Amalekites ... 1Sa 15:6 8432
thy mother be childless *a* women ... 1Sa 15:33
provided me a king *a* his sons ... 1Sa 16:1
the man went *a* men for an old man ... 1Sa 17:12
say, Is Saul also *a* the prophets ... 1Sa 19:24
who is so faithful *a* all thy ... 1Sa 22:14
of their idols, and *a* the people ... 1Sa 31:9 854
he dealt *a* all the people ... 2Sa 6:19
even *a* the whole multitude of ... 2Sa 6:19
Ahithophel is *a* the conspirators ... 2Sa 15:31
Give counsel *a* you what we shall ... 2Sa 16:20
There is a slaughter *a* the people ... 2Sa 17:9
a them that did eat at thine own ... 2Sa 19:28
thee, O LORD, *a* the heathen, and I ... 2Sa 22:50
in the seat, chief *a* the captains ... 2Sa 23:8
son of Zeruiah, was chief *a* three ... 2Sa 23:18
them, and had the name *a* three ... 2Sa 23:18
had the name *a* three mighty men ... 2Sa 23:22
a the kings like unto thee all ... 1Kin 3:13
a us any that can skill to hew ... 1Kin 5:6
I will dwell *a* the children of ... 1Kin 6:13 8432
did he put *a* the treasures of the ... 1Kin 7:51
a all the people of the earth ... 1Kin 8:53
proverb and a byword *a* all people ... 1Kin 9:7
household *a* the sons of Pharaoh ... 1Kin 11:20 8432
I exalted thee from *a* the people ... 1Kin 14:7 8432
set Naboth on high *a* the people ... 1Kin 21:9

set Naboth on high *a* the people ... 1Kin 21:12
I dwell *a* mine own people ... 2Kin 4:13 8432
him arise up from *a* his brethren ... 2Kin 9:2 8432
stole him from *a* the king's sons ... 2Kin 11:2 8432
the LORD sent lions *a* them ... 2Kin 17:25
he hath sent lions *a* them ... 2Kin 17:26
like him *a* all the kings of Judah ... 2Kin 18:5
Who are they *a* all the gods of ... 2Kin 18:35
there is nothing *a* my treasures ... 2Kin 20:15
unleavened bread *a* their brethren ... 2Kin 23:9 8432
and those that dwelt *a* plants ... 1Chr 4:23
their brethren *a* all the families ... 1Chr 7:5
them, and had a name *a* the three ... 1Chr 11:20
had the name *a* the three mighties ... 1Chr 11:24
he was honourable *a* the thirty ... 1Chr 11:25 4480
they were *a* the mighty men, ... 1Chr 12:1
a mighty man *a* the thirty ... 1Chr 12:4
make known his deeds *a* the people ... 1Chr 16:8
Declare his glory *a* the heathen ... 1Chr 16:24
marvellous works *a* all nations ... 1Chr 16:24
and let men say *a* the nations ... 1Chr 16:31
and justice *a* all his people ... 1Chr 18:14
and Benjamin counted he not *a* them ... 1Chr 21:6 8432
into courses *a* the sons of Levi ... 1Chr 23:6
A the sons of Eleazar there were ... 1Chr 24:4
eight *a* the sons of Ithamar ... 1Chr 24:4
A these were the divisions of the ... 1Chr 26:12
even *a* the chief men, having ... 1Chr 26:12
of the porters *a* the sons of Kore ... 1Chr 26:19
and *a* the sons of Merari ... 1Chr 26:19
were officers *a* them of Israel on ... 1Chr 26:30 5921
A the Hebronites was Jerijah the ... 1Chr 26:31
even *a* the Hebronites, according ... 1Chr 26:31
there were found *a* them mighty ... 1Chr 26:31
who was mighty *a* the thirty ... 1Chr 27:6
a the sons of my father he liked ... 1Chr 28:4
put he *a* the treasures of the ... 2Chr 5:1
a all the tribes of Israel to ... 2Chr 6:5
if I send pestilence *a* my people ... 2Chr 7:13
proverb and a byword *a* all nations ... 2Chr 7:20
to be ruler *a* his brethren ... 2Chr 11:22
they found *a* them in abundance ... 2Chr 20:25
stole him from *a* the king's sons ... 2Chr 22:11 8432
in the city of David *a* the kings ... 2Chr 24:16 5973
of the people from *a* the people ... 2Chr 24:23
Ashdod, and *a* the Philistines ... 2Chr 26:6
all that were naked *a* them ... 2Chr 28:15
to all the males *a* the priests ... 2Chr 31:19
by genealogies *a* the Levites ... 2Chr 31:19
Who was there *a* all the gods of ... 2Chr 32:14
which took Manasseh *a* the thorns ... 2Chr 33:11
they are written *a* the sayings of ... 2Chr 33:19 5921
them speedily *a* all the people ... 2Chr 35:13
Who is there *a* you of all his ... 2Chr 36:23
Who is there *a* you of all his ... Ezr 1:3
a those that were reckoned by ... Ezr 2:62
there were *a* them two hundred ... Ezr 2:65
a the sons of the priests there ... Ezr 10:18
scatter you abroad *a* the nations ... Neh 1:8
till we come in the midst *a* them ... Neh 4:11 8432
those that came unto us from *a* ... Neh 5:17 4480
It is reported *a* the heathen ... Neh 6:6
a those that were reckoned by ... Neh 7:64
wonders that thou didst *a* them ... Neh 9:17 5973
And we cast the lots *a* the priests ... Neh 10:34
the second *a* his brethren ... Neh 11:17
yet *a* many nations was there no ... Neh 13:26
let it be written *a* the laws of ... Est 1:19
dispersed *a* the people in all the ... Est 3:8 996
was great mourning *a* the Jews ... Est 4:3
To stablish this *a* them, that ... Est 9:21 5921
should not fail from *a* the Jews ... Est 9:28 8432
great *a* the Jews, and accepted of ... Est 10:3
LORD, and Satan came also *a* them ... Job 1:6 8432
Satan came also *a* them to present ... Job 2:1 8432
and he sat down *a* the ashes ... Job 2:8 8432
and no stranger passed *a* them ... Job 15:19 8432
I cannot find one wise man *a* you ... Job 17:10
have son nor nephew *a* his people ... Job 18:19
He cutteth out rivers *a* the rocks ... Job 28:10
They were driven forth from *a* men ... Job 30:5 1460
A the bushes they brayed ... Job 30:7 996
one *a* a thousand, to shew unto ... Job 33:23 4480
let us know *a* ourselves what is ... Job 34:4 996
sin, he clappeth his hands *a* us ... Job 34:37 996
and their life is *a* the unclean ... Job 36:14
He saith *a* the trumpets, Ha, ha ... Job 39:25 1767
they part him *a* the merchants ... Job 41:6 996
them inheritance *a* their brethren ... Job 42:15 8432
declare *a* the people his doings ... Ps 9:11
fail from *a* the children of men ... Ps 12:1
a the heathen, and sing praises ... Ps 18:49
their seed from *a* the children of ... Ps 21:10
They part my garments *a* them ... Ps 22:18
he is the governor *a* the nations ... Ps 22:28
was a reproach *a* all mine enemies ... Ps 31:11
but especially *a* my neighbours ... Ps 31:11
I will praise thee *a* much people ... Ps 35:18
hast scattered us *a* the heathen ... Ps 44:11
makest us a byword *a* the heathen ... Ps 44:14
shaking of the head *a* the people ... Ps 44:14
were *a* thy honourable women ... Ps 45:9
even the rich *a* the people shall ... Ps 45:12
I will be exalted *a* the heathen ... Ps 46:10
is in their dwellings, and *a* them ... Ps 55:15 7130
My soul is *a* lions ... Ps 57:4 8432
I lie even *a* them that are set on ... Ps 57:4
praise thee, O Lord, *a* the people ... Ps 57:9
will sing unto thee *a* the nations ... Ps 57:9
thy saving health *a* all nations ... Ps 67:2
Though ye have lien *a* the pots ... Ps 68:13 996
the Lord is *a* them, as in Sinai, ... Ps 68:17
the LORD God might dwell *a* them ... Ps 68:18
a them were the damsels playing ... Ps 68:25 8432

neither is there *a* us any that Ps 74:9 854
thy strength *a* the people Ps 77:14
sent divers sorts of flies *a* them Ps 78:45
by sending evil angels *a* them Ps 78:49
the tent which he placed *a* men Ps 78:60
let him be known *a* the heathen in Ps 79:10
and our enemies laugh *a* themselves Ps 80:6
he judgeth *a* the gods Ps 82:1 8432
A the gods there is none like Ps 86:8
Free *a* the dead, like the slain Ps 88:5
who *a* the sons of the mighty can Ps 89:6
ye brutish *a* the people Ps 94:8
Declare his glory *a* the heathen Ps 96:3
his wonders *a* all people Ps 96:3
Say *a* the heathen that the LORD Ps 96:10
Aaron *a* his priests Ps 99:6
Samuel *a* them that call upon his Ps 99:6
valleys, which run *a* the hills Ps 104:10 996
which sing *a* the branches Ps 104:12 996
make known his deeds *a* the people Ps 105:1
They shewed his signs *a* them Ps 105:27
one feeble person *a* their tribes Ps 105:37
their seed also *a* the nations Ps 106:27
But were mingled *a* the heathen Ps 106:35
and gather us from *a* the heathen Ps 106:47
praise thee, O LORD, *a* the people Ps 108:3
praises unto thee *a* the nations Ps 108:3
I will praise him *a* the multitude Ps 109:30 8432
He shall judge *a* the heathen Ps 110:6
then said they *a* the heathen Ps 126:2
And brought out Israel from *a* them Ps 136:11 8432
Cast in thy lot *a* us Prov 1:14 8432
he that soweth discord *a* brethren Prov 6:19 996
And beheld *a* the simple ones Prov 7:7
I discerned *a* the youths Prov 7:7
but *a* the righteous there is Prov 14:9 996
of life abideth *a* the wise Prov 15:31 7130
of the inheritance *a* the brethren Prov 17:2 8432
Be not *a* winebibbers Prov 23:20
a riotous eaters of flesh Prov 23:20
the transgressors *a* men Prov 23:28
in a mortar *a* wheat with a pestle Prov 27:22 8432
earth, and the needy from *a* men Prov 30:14
lion which is strongest *a* beasts Prov 30:30
when he sitteth *a* the elders of Prov 31:23 5973
the sun, and it is common *a* men Eccl 6:1 5921
one man *a* a thousand have I found Eccl 7:28
but a woman *a* all those have I Eccl 7:28
This is an evil *a* all things that Eccl 9:3
cry of him that ruleth *a* fools Eccl 9:17
know not, O thou fairest *a* women Song 1:8
As the lily *a* thorns Song 2:2 996
so is my love *a* the daughters Song 2:2 996
As the apple tree *a* the trees of Song 2:3
wood, so is my beloved *a* the sons Song 2:3 996
he feedeth *a* the lilies Song 2:16
twins, and none is barren *a* them Song 4:2
twins, which feed *a* the lilies Song 4:5
beloved, O thou fairest *a* women Song 5:9
the chiefest *a* ten thousand Song 5:10
gone, O thou fairest *a* women Song 6:1
he feedeth *a* the lilies Song 6:3
and there is not one barren *a* them Song 6:6
And he shall judge *a* the nations Is 2:4 996
written *a* the living in Jerusalem Is 4:3
shall be weary nor stumble *a* them Is 5:27
many *a* them shall stumble, and Is 8:15
seal the law *a* my disciples Is 8:16
send *a* his fat ones leanness Is 10:16
declare his doings *a* the people Is 12:4
midst of the land *a* the people Is 24:13 8432
a marvellous work *a* this people Is 29:14
the poor *a* men shall rejoice in Is 29:19
Who *a* us shall dwell with the Is 33:14
who *a* us shall dwell with Is 33:14
Who are they *a* all the gods of Is 36:20
there is nothing *a* my treasures Is 39:4
even *a* them, and there was no Is 41:28
Who *a* you will give ear to this Is 42:23
who *a* them can declare this, and Is 43:9
there was no strange god *a* you Is 43:12
shall spring up as *a* the grass Is 44:4 996
himself *a* the trees of the forest Is 44:14
which *a* them hath declared these Is 48:14
Who is *a* you that feareth the Is 50:10
her *a* all the sons whom she hath Is 51:18
A the smooth stones of the stream Is 57:6
shall be known *a* the Gentiles Is 61:9
and their offspring *a* the people Is 61:9 8432
Which remain *a* the graves Is 65:4
And I will set a sign *a* them Is 66:19
declare my glory *a* the Gentiles Is 66:19
shall I put thee *a* the children Jer 3:19
ground, and sow not *a* thorns Jer 4:3 413
For *a* my people are found wicked Jer 5:26
they shall fall *a* them that fall Jer 6:15
O congregation, what is *a* them Jer 6:18
a tower and a fortress *a* my people Jer 6:27
shall they fall *a* them that fall Jer 8:12
a you, which will not be charmed, Jer 8:17
scatter them also *a* the heathen Jer 9:16
forasmuch as *a* all the wise men Jer 10:7
is found *a* the men of Judah Jer 11:9
a the inhabitants of Jerusalem Jer 11:9
the house of Judah from *a* them Jer 12:14 8432
Are there any *a* the vanities of Jer 14:22
Ask ye now *a* the heathen, who Jer 18:13
a them, till they be consumed Jer 24:10
the sword that I will send *a* them Jer 25:16 996
the sword which I will send *a* you Jer 25:27 996
a all the nations whither I have Jer 29:18
have a man to dwell *a* this people Jer 29:32 8432
shout *a* the chief of the nations Jer 31:7
day, and in Israel, and *a* other men Jer 32:20

came in and went out *a* the people Jer 37:4 8432
remained but wounded men *a* them Jer 37:10
so he dwelt *a* the people Jer 39:14 8432
a all that were carried away Jer 40:1 8432
and dwell with him *a* the people Jer 40:5 8432
dwelt with him *a* the people that Jer 40:6 8432
a the Ammonites, and in Edom, and Jer 40:11
But ten men were found *a* them Jer 41:8
slew them not *a* their brethren Jer 41:8 8432
a reproach *a* all the nations of Jer 44:8
as Tabor is *a* the mountains Jer 46:18
was he found *a* thieves Jer 48:27
make thee small *a* the heathen Jer 49:15
and despised *a* men Jer 49:15
Declare ye *a* the nations, and Jer 50:2
become a desolation *a* the nations Jer 50:23
and the cry is heard *a* the nations Jer 50:46
blow the trumpet *a* the nations Jer 51:27
an astonishment *a* the nations Jer 51:41
she that was great *a* the nations Lam 1:1
princess *a* the provinces, how is Lam 1:1
a all her lovers she hath none to Lam 1:2
she dwelleth *a* the heathen Lam 1:3
is as a menstruous woman *a* them Lam 1:17 996
and her princes are *a* the Gentiles Lam 2:9
they said *a* the heathen, They Lam 4:15
we shall live *a* the heathen Lam 4:20
as I was *a* the captives by the Eze 1:1 8432
down *a* the living creatures Eze 1:13 996
there hath been a prophet *a* them Eze 2:5 8432
and thou dost dwell *a* scorpions Eze 2:6 413
astonished *a* them seven days Eze 3:15 8432
and thou shalt not go out *a* them Eze 3:25 8432
defiled bread *a* the Gentiles Eze 4:13
a reproach *a* the nations that are Eze 5:14
escape the sword *a* the nations Eze 6:8
a the nations whither they shall Eze 6:9
a their idols round about their Eze 6:13 8432
one man *a* them was clothed with Eze 9:2 8432
a whom I saw Jaazaniah the son of Eze 11:1 8432
and will execute judgments *a* you Eze 11:9
cast them far off *a* the heathen Eze 11:16
scattered them *a* the countries Eze 11:16
house of Israel that are *a* them Eze 12:10 8432
the prince that is *a* them shall Eze 12:12 8432
shall scatter them *a* the nations Eze 12:15
a the heathen whither they come Eze 12:16
will ye pollute me *a* my people Eze 13:19 413
is *a* the trees of the forest Eze 15:2
As the vine tree *a* the trees of Eze 15:6
thy renown went forth *a* the Eze 16:14
which is not good *a* his people Eze 18:18 8432
she lay down *a* lions, she Eze 19:2 996
her whelps *a* young lions Eze 19:2 8432
down *a* the lions, he became a Eze 19:6 8432
was exalted *a* the thick branches Eze 19:11 996
a whom they were, in whose sight Eze 20:9 8432
would scatter them *a* the heathen Eze 20:23
purge out from *a* you the rebels Eze 20:38
I will scatter thee *a* the heathen Eze 22:15
sabbaths, and I am profaned *a* them Eze 22:26 8432
And I sought for a man *a* them Eze 22:30
and she became famous *a* women Eze 23:10
not be remembered *a* the nations Eze 25:10
made of cedar, *a* thy merchandise Eze 27:24
The merchants *a* the people shall Eze 27:36
All they that know thee *a* the Eze 28:19
people *a* whom they are scattered Eze 28:25
her cities *a* the cities that are Eze 29:12 8432
the Egyptians *a* the nations Eze 29:12
the Egyptians *a* the nations Eze 30:23
the Egyptians *a* the nations Eze 30:26
and disperse them *a* the countries Eze 30:26
his top was *a* the thick boughs Eze 31:3 996
up his top *a* the thick boughs Eze 31:10 996
up their top *a* the thick boughs Eze 31:14 413
in greatness *a* the trees of Eden Eze 31:18
thy destruction *a* the nations Eze 32:9
The strong *a* the mighty shall Eze 32:21
and take any person from *a* them Eze 33:6
that a prophet hath been *a* them Eze 33:33 8432
is *a* his sheep that are scattered Eze 34:12 8432
my servant David a prince *a* them Eze 34:24 8432
I will make myself known *a* them Eze 35:11
And I scattered them *a* the heathen Eze 36:19
Israel had profaned *a* the heathen Eze 36:21
ye have profaned *a* the heathen Eze 36:22
which was profaned *a* the heathen Eze 36:23
will take you from *a* the heathen Eze 36:24
reproach of famine *a* the heathen Eze 36:30
of Israel from *a* the heathen Eze 37:21 996
a them that dwell carelessly in Eze 39:6
I will set my glory *a* the heathen Eze 39:21
led into captivity *a* the heathen Eze 39:28 413
sons of Zadok *a* the sons of Levi Eze 40:46
that is *a* the children of Israel Eze 44:9 8432
the strangers that sojourn *a* you Eze 47:22 8432
which shall beget children *a* you Eze 47:22 8432
country *a* the children of Israel Eze 47:22
with you *a* the tribes of Israel Eze 47:22 8432
Now *a* these were of the children Dan 1:6
a them all was found none like Dan 1:19
a the inhabitants of the earth Dan 4:35
there came up *a* them another Dan 7:8 997
he shall scatter *a* them the prey Dan 11:24
they that understand *a* the people Dan 11:33
a the tribes of Israel have I Hos 5:9
there is none *a* them that calleth Hos 7:7
hath mixed himself *a* the people Hos 7:8
now shall they be *a* the Gentiles Hos 8:8
they have hired *a* the nations Hos 8:10
shall be wanderers *a* the nations Hos 9:17
shall a tumult arise *a* thy people Hos 10:14
he be fruitful *a* his brethren Hos 13:15 996

should they say *a* the people Joel 2:17
make you a reproach *a* the heathen Joel 2:19
my great army which I sent *a* you Joel 2:25
they have scattered *a* the nations Joel 3:2
Proclaim ye this *a* the Gentiles Joel 3:9
who was *a* the herdmen of Tekoa, Amos 1:1
he that is courageous *a* the Amos 2:16
I have sent *a* you the pestilence Amos 4:10
the house of Israel *a* all nations Amos 9:9
ambassador is sent *a* the heathen Obad 1
made thee small *a* the heathen Obad 2
thou set thy nest *a* the stars Obad 4 996
and say, Is not the LORD *a* us Mic 3:11 7130
And he shall judge *a* many people Mic 4:3 996
though thou be little *a* the Mic 5:2
be *a* the Gentiles in the midst of Mic 5:8
a lion *a* the beasts of the forest Mic 5:8
as a young lion *a* the flocks of Mic 5:8
and there is none upright *a* men Mic 7:2
No, that was situate *a* the rivers Nah 3:8
Behold ye *a* the heathen, and Hab 1:5
a praise *a* all people of the Zeph 3:20
Who is left *a* you that saw this Hag 2:3
so my spirit remaineth *a* you Hag 2:5 8432
he stood *a* the myrtle trees that Zec 1:8 996
the man that stood *a* the myrtle Zec 1:10 996
that stood *a* the myrtle trees Zec 1:11 996
to walk *a* these that stand by Zec 3:7 996
a all the nations whom they knew Zec 7:14 5921
as ye were a curse *a* the heathen Zec 8:13
And I will sow them *a* the people Zec 10:9
like an hearth of fire *a* the wood Zec 12:6
he that is feeble *a* them at that Zec 12:8
from the LORD shall be *a* them Zec 14:13
Who is there even *a* you that Mal 1:10
shall be great *a* the Gentiles Mal 1:11
name shall be great *a* the heathen Mal 1:11
my name is dreadful *a* the heathen Mal 1:14
art not the least *a* the princes Mt 2:6 *1722*
manner of disease *a* the people Mt 4:23 *1722*
and every disease *a* the people Mt 9:35 *1722*
A them that are born of women Mt 11:11 *1722*
What man shall there be *a* you Mt 12:11 *1537*
And some fell *a* thorns Mt 13:7 *1909*
He also that received seed *a* the Mt 13:22 *1519*
grown, it is the greatest *a* herbs Mt 13:32
sever the wicked from *a* the just Mt 13:49 *3319*
And they reasoned *a* themselves Mt 16:7 *1722*
faith, why reason ye *a* yourselves Mt 16:8 *1722*
But it shall not be so *a* you Mt 20:26 *1722*
but whosoever will be great *a* you Mt 20:26 *1722*
And whosoever will be chief *a* you Mt 20:27 *1722*
they said *a* themselves, This is Mt 21:38 *1722*
But he that is greatest *a* you Mt 23:11
there be an uproar *a* the people Mt 26:5 *1722*
They parted my garments *a* them Mt 27:35
A which was Mary Magdalene, and Mt 27:56 *1722*
a the Jews until this day Mt 28:15 *1722*
that they questioned *a* themselves Mk 1:27 *4314*
And some fell *a* thorns, and the Mk 4:7 *1519*
are they which are sown *a* thorns Mk 4:18 *1519*
Who had his dwelling *a* the tombs Mk 5:3 *1722*
a his own kin, and in his own Mk 6:4 *1722*
two fishes divided he *a* them all Mk 6:41
And they reasoned *a* themselves Mk 8:16 *4314*
the five loaves *a* five thousand Mk 8:19 *1519*
And when the seven *a* four thousand Mk 8:20 *1519*
disputed *a* yourselves by the way Mk 9:33 *4314*
they had disputed *a* themselves Mk 9:34 *4314*
saying *a* themselves, Who then can Mk 10:26 *4314*
But so shall it not be *a* you Mk 10:43 *1722*
but whosoever will be great *a* you Mk 10:43 *1722*
husbandmen said *a* themselves Mk 12:7 *4314*
first be published *a* all nations Mk 13:10 *1519*
a themselves with the scribes Mk 15:31 *4314*
a whom was Mary Magdalene, and Mk 15:40 *1722*
they said *a* themselves, Who shall Mk 16:3 *4314*
are most surely believed *a* us Lk 1:1 *1722*
to take away my reproach *a* men Lk 1:25 *1722*
blessed art thou *a* women Lk 1:28 *1722*
and said, Blessed art thou *a* women Lk 1:42 *1722*
they sought him *a* their kinsfolk Lk 2:44 *1722*
spake *a* themselves, saying, What Lk 4:36 *4314*
a great prophet is risen up *a* us Lk 7:16 *1722*
A those that are born of women Lk 7:28 *1722*
that which fell *a* thorns are they Lk 8:14 *1519*
there arose a reasoning *a* them Lk 9:46 *1722*
for he that is least *a* you all Lk 9:48 *1722*
fell *a* thieves, which stripped Lk 10:30 *4045*
unto him that fell *a* the thieves Lk 10:36 *1519*
that which is highly esteemed *a* Lk 16:15 *1722*
was the chief *a* the publicans Lk 19:2
some of the Pharisees from *a* the Lk 19:39
him, they reasoned *a* themselves Lk 20:14 *4314*
this, and divide it *a* yourselves Lk 22:17
began to enquire *a* themselves Lk 22:23 *4314*
And there was also a strife *a* them Lk 22:24 *1722*
but he that is greatest *a* you Lk 22:26 *1722*
in me, And he was reckoned *a* the Lk 22:37 *3326*
together, Peter sat down *a* them Lk 22:55 *3319*
Why seek ye the living *a* the dead Lk 24:5 *3326*
in his name *a* all nations Lk 24:47 *1519*
was made flesh, and dwelt *a* us Jn 1:14 *1722*
but what are they *a* so many Jn 6:9 *1519*
them, Murmur not *a* yourselves Jn 6:43 *3326*
therefore strove *a* themselves Jn 6:52 *4314*
there was much murmuring *a* the Jn 7:12 *1722*
Then said the Jews *a* themselves Jn 7:35 *4314*
unto the dispersed *a* the Gentiles Jn 7:35
So there was a division *a* the Jn 7:43 *1722*
He that is without sin *a* you Jn 8:7
And there was a division *a* them Jn 9:16 *1722*
a the Jews for these sayings Jn 10:19 *1722*
walked no more openly *a* the Jews Jn 11:54 *1722*

spake *a* themselves, as they stood ... Jn 11:56 3326
therefore said *a* themselves ... Jn 12:19 4314
there were certain Greeks *a* them ... Jn 12:20 1537
Nevertheless *a* the chief rulers ... Jn 12:42 1537
If I had not done *a* them the ... Jn 15:24 1722
of his disciples *a* themselves ... Jn 16:17 4314
Do ye enquire *a* yourselves of ... Jn 16:19 3326
They said therefore *a* themselves ... Jn 19:24 4314
They parted my raiment *a* them ... Jn 19:24
this saying abroad *a* the brethren ... Jn 21:23 1519
Lord Jesus went in and out *a* us ... Acts 1:21 1909
approved of God *a* you by miracles ... Acts 2:22 1519
be destroyed from *a* the people ... Acts 3:23
name under heaven given *a* men ... Acts 4:12 1722
they conferred *a* themselves ... Acts 4:15 4315
it spread no further *a* the people ... Acts 4:17 1519
was there any *a* them that lacked ... Acts 4:34 1722
and wonders wrought *a* the people ... Acts 5:12 1722
in reputation *a* all the people ... Acts 5:34
look ye out *a* you seven men of ... Acts 6:3 1537
wonders and miracles *a* the people ... Acts 6:8 1722
of good report *a* all the nation ... Acts 10:22 5259
was no small stir *a* the soldiers ... Acts 12:18 1722
whosoever *a* you feareth God, to ... Acts 13:26 1722
ran in *a* the people, crying out, ... Acts 14:14 1519
while ago God made choice *a* us ... Acts 15:7 1722
wrought *a* the Gentiles by them ... Acts 15:12 1722
which from *a* the Gentiles are ... Acts 15:19 575
Silas, chief men *a* the brethren ... Acts 15:22 1722
So Paul departed from *a* them ... Acts 17:33 3319
a the which was Dionysius the ... Acts 17:34 1722
teaching the word of God *a* them ... Acts 18:11 1722
a whom I have gone preaching the ... Acts 20:25 1722
grievous wolves enter in *a* you ... Acts 20:29 1519
to give you an inheritance *a* all ... Acts 20:32 1722
what things God had wrought *a* the ... Acts 21:19 1722
a the Gentiles to forsake Moses ... Acts 21:21 2596
some another, *a* the multitude ... Acts 21:34 1722
to take him by force from *a* them ... Acts 23:10 3319
a mover of sedition *a* all the ... Acts 24:5
that I cried standing *a* them ... Acts 24:21 1722
which *a* you are able, go down ... Acts 25:5 1722
when he had tarried *a* them more ... Acts 25:6 1722
and questions which are *a* the Jews ... Acts 26:3 2596
which was at the first *a* mine own ... Acts 26:4 1722
inheritance *a* them which are ... Acts 26:18 1722
no loss of any man's life *a* you ... Acts 27:22 1537
they said *a* themselves, No doubt ... Acts 28:4 4314
when they agreed not *a* themselves ... Acts 28:25 4314
had great reasoning *a* themselves ... Acts 28:29 1722
to the faith *a* all nations ... Rom 1:5 1722
A whom are ye also the called of ... Rom 1:6 1722
might have some fruit *a* you also ... Rom 1:13 1722
even as *a* other Gentiles ... Rom 1:13 1722
a the Gentiles through you ... Rom 2:24 1722
be the firstborn *a* many brethren ... Rom 8:29 1722
tree, wert graffed in *a* them ... Rom 11:17 1722
me, to every man that is *a* you ... Rom 12:3 1722
confess to thee *a* the Gentiles ... Rom 15:9 1722
who are of note *a* the apostles ... Rom 16:7 1722
that there be no divisions *a* you ... 1Cor 1:10 1722
that there are contentions *a* you ... 1Cor 1:11 1722
not to know any thing *a* you ... 1Cor 2:2 1722
wisdom *a* them that are perfect ... 1Cor 2:6 1722
whereas there is *a* you envying ... 1Cor 3:3 1722
If any man *a* you seemeth to be ... 1Cor 3:18 1722
that there is fornication *a* you ... 1Cor 5:1 1722
so much as named *a* the Gentiles ... 1Cor 5:1 1722
might be taken away from *a* you ... 1Cor 5:2 3319
Therefore put away from *a* ... 1Cor 5:13
there is not a wise man *a* you ... 1Cor 6:5 1722
there is utterly a fault *a* you ... 1Cor 6:7 1722
that there be divisions *a* you ... 1Cor 11:18 1722
there must be also heresies *a* you ... 1Cor 11:19 1722
may be made manifest *a* you ... 1Cor 11:19 1722
many are weak and sickly *a* you ... 1Cor 11:30 1722
how say some *a* you that there is ... 1Cor 15:12 1722
who was preached *a* you by us ... 2Cor 1:19 1722
Wherefore come out from *a* them ... 2Cor 6:17 3319
who in presence am base *a* you ... 2Cor 10:1 1722
comparing themselves *a* themselves ... 2Cor 10:12
made manifest *a* you in all things ... 2Cor 11:6 1519
in perils *a* false brethren ... 2Cor 11:26 1722
wrought *a* you in all patience ... 2Cor 12:12 1722
my God will humble me *a* you ... 2Cor 12:21 4314
I might preach him *a* the heathen ... Gal 1:16 1722
which I preach *a* the Gentiles ... Gal 2:2 1722
set forth, crucified *a* you ... Gal 3:1 1722
Spirit, and worketh miracles *a* you ... Gal 3:5 1722
A whom also we all had our ... Eph 2:3 1722
that I should preach *a* the ... Eph 3:8 1722
let it not be once named *a* you ... Eph 5:3 1722
a whom ye shine as lights in the ... Phil 2:15 1722
of this mystery *a* the Gentiles ... Col 1:27 1722
when this epistle is read *a* you ... Col 4:16 3844
men we were *a* you for your sake ... 1Th 1:5 1722
But we were gentle *a* you, even as ... 1Th 2:7 1722
ourselves *a* you that believe ... 1Th 2:10
to know them which labour *a* you ... 1Th 5:12 1722
And be at peace *a* yourselves ... 1Th 5:13 1722
both *a* yourselves, and to all men ... 1Th 5:15 1519
a you was believed) in that day ... 2Th 1:10 1909
not ourselves disorderly *a* you ... 2Th 3:7 1722
some which walk *a* you disorderly ... 2Th 3:11 1722
hast heard of me *a* many witnesses ... 2Ti 2:2 1223
from *a* men is ordained for men in ... Heb 5:1 3319
If any man *a* you seem to be ... Jas 1:26 1722
so is the tongue *a* our members ... Jas 3:6 1722
and endued with knowledge *a* you ... Jas 3:13 1722
come wars and fightings *a* you ... Jas 4:1 1722
Is any *a* you afflicted ... Jas 5:13 1722
Is any sick *a* you ... Jas 5:14 1722
honest *a* the Gentiles ... 1Pet 2:12 1722
have fervent charity *a* yourselves ... 1Pet 4:8 1519
elders which are *a* you I exhort ... 1Pet 5:1 1722
the flock of God which is *a* you ... 1Pet 5:2 1722
false prophets also *a* the people ... 2Pet 2:1 1722
shall be false teachers *a* you ... 2Pet 2:1 1722
righteous man dwelling *a* them ... 2Pet 2:8 1722
to have the preeminence *a* them ... 3Jn 9 1722
convince all that are ungodly *a* ... Jude 15
martyr, who was slain *a* you ... Rev 2:13 3844
on the throne shall dwell *a* them ... Rev 7:15 1909
These were redeemed from *a* men ... Rev 14:4

AMONGST
God *a* the trees of the garden ... Gen 3:8 8432
of a buryingplace *a* you ... Gen 23:9 8432

AMORITE (*am'-o-rite*) *A descendant of Canaan, Ham's son.*
And the Jebusite, and the *A* ... Gen 10:16 567
dwelt in the plain of Mamre the *A* ... Gen 14:13 567
the hand of the *A* with my sword ... Gen 48:22 567
drive out the Canaanite, the *A* ... Ex 33:2 567
I drive out before thee the *A* ... Ex 34:11 567
the *A* which was in it ... Num 32:39 567
given into thine hand Sihon the *A* ... Deut 2:24 567
Lebanon, the Hittite, and the *A* ... Josh 9:1 567
east and on the west, and to the *A* ... Josh 11:3 567
The Jebusite also, and the *A* ... 1Chr 1:14 567
thy father was an *A*, and thy ... Eze 16:3 567
an Hittite, and your father an *A* ... Eze 16:45 567
Yet destroyed I the *A* before them ... Amos 2:9 567
to possess the land of the *A* ... Amos 2:10 567

AMORITES (*am'-o-rites*)
of the Amalekites, and also the *A* ... Gen 14:7 567
iniquity of the *A* is not yet full ... Gen 15:16 567
And the *A*, and the Canaanites, and ... Gen 15:21 567
and the Hittites, and the *A* ... Ex 3:8 567
and the Hittites, and the *A* ... Ex 3:17 567
and the Hittites, and the *A* ... Ex 13:5 567
thee, and bring thee in unto the *A* ... Ex 23:23 567
and the Jebusites, and the *A* ... Num 13:29 567
cometh out of the coasts of the *A* ... Num 21:13 567
of Moab, between Moab and the *A* ... Num 21:13 567
unto Sihon king of the *A*, saying, ... Num 21:21 567
dwelt in all the cities of the *A* ... Num 21:25 567
city of Sihon the king of the *A* ... Num 21:26 567
unto Sihon king of the *A* ... Num 21:29 567
Israel dwelt in the land of the *A* ... Num 21:31 567
drove out the *A* that were there ... Num 21:32 567
didst unto Sihon king of the *A* ... Num 21:34 567
all that Israel had done to the *A* ... Num 22:2 567
kingdom of Sihon king of the *A* ... Num 32:33 567
had slain Sihon the king of the *A* ... Deut 1:4 567
and go to the mount of the *A* ... Deut 1:7 567
the way of the mountain of the *A* ... Deut 1:19 567
come unto the mountain of the *A* ... Deut 1:20 567
deliver us into the hand of the *A* ... Deut 1:27 567
And the *A*, which dwelt in that ... Deut 1:44 567
didst unto Sihon king of the *A* ... Deut 3:2 567
hand of the two kings of the *A* ... Deut 3:8 567
and the *A* call it Shenir ... Deut 3:9 567
the land of Sihon king of the *A* ... Deut 4:46 567
of Bashan, two kings of the *A* ... Deut 4:47 567
and the Girgashites, and the *A* ... Deut 7:1 567
namely, the Hittites, and the *A* ... Deut 20:17 567
to Sihon and to Og, kings of the *A* ... Deut 31:4 567
did unto the two kings of the *A* ... Josh 2:10 567
and the Girgashites, and the *A* ... Josh 3:10 567
pass, when all the kings of the *A* ... Josh 5:1 567
deliver us into the hand of the *A* ... Josh 7:7 567
he did to the two kings of the *A* ... Josh 9:10 567
Therefore the five kings of the *A* ... Josh 10:5 567
for all the kings of the *A* that ... Josh 10:6 567
A before the children of Israel ... Josh 10:12 567
Sihon king of the *A*, who dwelt in ... Josh 12:2 567
the Hittites, the *A*, and the ... Josh 12:8 567
Aphek, to the borders of the *A* ... Josh 13:4 567
the cities of Sihon king of the *A* ... Josh 13:10 567
kingdom of Sihon king of the *A* ... Josh 13:21 567
you into the land of the *A* ... Josh 24:8 567
Jericho fought against you, the *A* ... Josh 24:11 567
you, even the two kings of the *A* ... Josh 24:12 567
the flood, or the gods of the *A* ... Josh 24:15 567
even the *A* which dwelt in the ... Josh 24:18 567
the *A* forced the children of Dan ... Judg 1:34 567
But the *A* would dwell in mount ... Judg 1:35 567
the coast of the *A* was from the ... Judg 1:36 567
the Canaanites, Hittites, and *A* ... Judg 3:5 567
fear not the gods of the *A* ... Judg 6:10 567
side Jordan in the land of the *A* ... Judg 10:8 567
from the Egyptians, and from the *A* ... Judg 10:11 567
unto Sihon king of the *A*, the ... Judg 11:19 567
possessed all the land of the *A* ... Judg 11:21 567
possessed all the coasts of the *A* ... Judg 11:22 567
A from before his people Israel ... Judg 11:23 567
was peace between Israel and the *A* ... 1Sa 7:14 567
but of the remnant of the *A* ... 2Sa 21:2 567
country of Sihon king of the *A* ... 1Kin 4:19 567
people that were left of the *A* ... 1Kin 9:20 567
to all things as did the *A* ... 1Kin 21:26 567
wickedly above all that the *A* did ... 2Kin 21:11 567
left of the Hittites, and the *A* ... 2Chr 8:7 567
Moabites, the Egyptians, and the *A* ... Ezr 9:1 567
Canaanites, the Hittites, the *A* ... Neh 9:8 567
Sihon king of the *A*, and Og king ... Ps 135:11 567
Sihon king of the *A* ... Ps 136:19 567

AMOS (*a'-mos*)
1. A prophet during the reign of Uzziah.
The words of *A*, who was among the ... Amos 1:1 5986
And the LORD said unto me, *A* ... Amos 7:8 5986
A hath conspired against thee in ... Amos 7:10 5986
For thus *A* saith, Jeroboam shall ... Amos 7:11 5986
Also Amaziah said unto *A*, O thou ... Amos 7:12 5986
Then answered *A*, and said to ... Amos 7:14 5986
And he said, *A*, what seest thou ... Amos 8:2 5986
2. Son of Naum; an ancestor of Jesus.
which was the son of *A*, which ... Lk 3:25 301

AMOUNTING
gold, *a* to six hundred talents ... 2Chr 3:8

AMOZ (*a'-moz*) *Father of Isaiah.*
Isaiah the prophet the son of *A* ... 2Kin 19:2 531
the son of *A* sent to Hezekiah ... 2Kin 19:20 531
Isaiah the son of *A* came to him ... 2Kin 20:1 531
Isaiah the prophet, the son of *A* ... 2Chr 26:22 531
the prophet Isaiah the son of *A* ... 2Chr 32:20 531
Isaiah the prophet, the son or *A* ... 2Chr 32:32 531
The vision of Isaiah the son of *A* ... Is 1:1 531
the son of *A* saw concerning Judah ... Is 2:1 531
which Isaiah the son of *A* did see ... Is 13:1 531
the LORD by Isaiah the son of *A* ... Is 20:2 531
Isaiah the prophet the son of *A* ... Is 37:2 531
the son of *A* sent unto Hezekiah ... Is 37:21 531
the son of *A* came unto him ... Is 38:1 531

AMPHIPOLIS (*am-fip'-o-lis*) *A city in Macedonia.*
when they had passed through *A* ... Acts 17:1 295

AMPLIAS (*am'-ple-as*) *A Christian acquaintance of Paul's.*
Greet *A* my beloved in the Lord ... Rom 16:8 291

AMRAM (*am'-ram*) See AMRAMITES, AMRAM'S, HEMDAN.
1. Father of Moses and Aaron.
A, and Izhar, and Hebron, and Uzziel ... Ex 6:18 6019
A took him Jochebed his father's ... Ex 6:20 6019
of the life of *A* were an hundred ... Ex 6:20 6019
A, and Izehar, Hebron, and Uzziel ... Num 3:19 6019
And Kohath begat *A* ... Num 26:58 6019
and she bare unto *A* Aaron and Moses Num 26:59 6019
A, Izhar, and Hebron, and Uzziel ... 1Chr 6:2 6019
And the children of *A* ... 1Chr 6:3 6019
And the sons of Kohath were, *A* ... 1Chr 6:18 6019
A, Izhar, Hebron, and Uzziel, four ... 1Chr 23:12 6019
The sons of *A* ... 1Chr 23:13 6019
Of the sons of *A* ... 1Chr 24:20 6019
2. Married a foreign wife in exile.
Maadai, *A*, and Uel, ... Ezr 10:34 6019
3. A son of Dishon.
A, and Eshban, and Ithran, and ... 1Chr 1:41 2566

AMRAMITES (*am'-ram-ites*) *Descendants of Amram 1.*
of Kohath was the family of the *A* ... Num 3:27 6020
Of the *A*, and the Izharites, the ... 1Chr 26:23 6020

AMRAM'S (*am'-rams*)
the name of *A* wife was Jochebed, ... Num 26:59 6019

AMRAPHEL (*am'-raf-el*) *King of Shinar in Abraham's time.*
in the days of *A* king of Shinar ... Gen 14:1 569
A king of Shinar, and Arioch king ... Gen 14:9 569

AMZI (*am'-zi*)
1. A son of Merari.
The son of *A*, the son of Bani, ... 1Chr 6:46 557
2. Ancestor of Adaiah.
the son of Pelaliah, the son of *A* ... Neh 11:12 557

AN See PREFACE.

ANAB (*a'-nab*) *A Canaanite city.*
from Hebron, from Debir, from *A* ... Josh 11:21 6024
And *A*, and Eshtemoh, and Anim, ... Josh 15:50 6024

ANAH (*a'-nah*)
1. A daughter of Zibeon.
of *A* the daughter of Zibeon the ... Gen 36:2 6034
the daughter of *A* the daughter of ... Gen 36:14 6034
of Aholibamah the daughter of *A* ... Gen 36:18 6034
And the children of *A* were these ... Gen 36:25 6034
and Aholibamah the daughter of *A* ... Gen 36:25 6034
2. A son of Seir.
Lotan, and Shobal, and Zibeon, and *A*. Gen 36:20 6034
duke Shobal, duke Zibeon, duke *A* ... Gen 36:29 6034
Lotan, and Shobal, and Zibeon, and *A*. 1Chr 1:38 6034
3. A son of Zibeon.
both Ajah, and *A* ... Gen 36:24 6034
this was that *A* that found the ... Gen 36:24 6034
Aiah, and *A* ... 1Chr 1:40 6034
The sons of *A* ... 1Chr 1:41 6034

ANAHARATH (*an-a-ha'-rath*) *A town in Issachar.*
And Haphraim, and Shihon, and *A* ... Josh 19:19 588

ANAIAH (*an-a-i'-ah*)
1. A priest who assisted Ezra.
stood Mattithiah, and Shema, and *A* ... Neh 8:4 6043
2. A Jew who sealed the covenant.
Pelatiah, Hanan, *A*, ... Neh 10:22 6043

ANAK (*a'-nak*) See ANAKIMS. *The son of Arba.*
and Talmai, the children of *A* ... Num 13:22 6061
we saw the children of *A* there ... Num 13:28 6061
we saw the giants, the sons of *A* ... Num 13:33 6061
stand before the children of *A* ... Deut 9:2 6061
the city of Arba the father of *A* ... Josh 15:13 6061
drove thence the three sons of *A* ... Josh 15:14 6061
and Talmai, the children of *A* ... Josh 15:14 6061
the city of Arba the father of *A* ... Josh 21:11 6061
thence the three sons of *A* ... Judg 1:20 6061

ANAKIM See ANAKIMS.

ANAKIMS (*an'-ak-ims*) *Descendants of Anak.*
have seen the sons of the *A* there ... Deut 1:28 6062
great, and many, and tall, as the *A* ... Deut 2:10 6062
were accounted giants, as the *A* ... Deut 2:11 6062
great, and many, and tall, as the *A* ... Deut 2:21 6062
and tall, the children of the *A* ... Deut 9:2 6062
cut off the *A* from the mountains, ... Josh 11:21 6062
There was none of the *A* left in ... Josh 11:22 6062

in that day how the *A* were there Josh 14:12 6062
Arba was a great man among the *A* Josh 14:15 6062

ANAKITES See ANAKIMS.

ANAMIM *(an'-am-im) A people of northern Egypt.*
And Mizraim begat Ludim, and *A* Gen 10:13 6047
And Mizraim begat Ludim, and *A* 1Chr 1:11 6047

ANAMITES See ANAMIM.

ANAMMELECH *(a-nam'-mel-ek) A god of the Babylonians.*
in fire to Adrammelech and *A* 2Kin 17:31 6048

ANAN *(a'-nan) An Israelite who sealed the covenant under Nehemiah.*
And Ahijah, Hanan, *A*, Neh 10:26 6052

ANANI *(an-a'-ni) A son of Elioneai.*
and Johanan, and Dalaiah, and *A* 1Chr 3:24 6054

ANANIAH *(an-an-i'-ah)* See ANANIAS.
1. Grandfather of Azariah.
the son of *A* by his house Neh 3:23 6055
2. A town in Benjamin.
And at Anathoth, Nob, *A*, Neh 11:32 6055

ANANIAS *(an-an-i'-as)* See ANANIAH.
1. A Christian who tried to deceive the apostles.
But a certain man named *A* Acts 5:1 367
But Peter said, *A*, why hath Satan Acts 5:3 367
A hearing these words fell down, Acts 5:5 367
2. A Christian who aided Paul.
disciple at Damascus, named *A* Acts 9:10 367
him said the Lord in a vision, *A* Acts 9:10 367
a vision a man named *A* coming in Acts 9:12 367
Then *A* answered, Lord, I have Acts 9:13 367
A went his way, and entered into Acts 9:17 367
And one *A*, a devout man according Acts 22:12 367
3. The High Priest who interrogated Paul.
the high priest *A* commanded them Acts 23:2 367
after five days *A* the high priest Acts 24:1 367

ANATH *(a'-nath)* See BETH-ANATH. *Father of Shamgar the judge.*
him was Shamgar the son of *A* Judg 3:31 6067
the days of Shamgar the son of *A* Judg 5:6 6067

ANATHEMA *(a-nath'-em-ah) Greek word for "accursed."*
Christ, let him be *A* Maranatha 1Cor 16:22 331

ANATHOTH *(an'-a-thoth)* See ANETOTITHE.
1. A Levitical city in Benjamin.
A with her suburbs, and Almon with Josh 21:18 6068
said the king, Get thee to *A* 1Kin 2:26 6068
suburbs, and *A* with her suburbs 1Chr 6:60 6068
The men of *A*, an hundred twenty Ezr 2:23 6068
The men of *A*, an hundred twenty Neh 7:27 6068
And at *A*, Nob, Ananiah, Neh 11:32 6068
to be heard unto Laish, O poor *A* Is 10:30 6068
were in *A* in the land of Benjamin Jer 1:1 6068
saith the LORD of the men of *A* Jer 11:21 6068
will bring evil upon the men of *A* Jer 11:23 6068
thou not reproved Jeremiah of *A* Jer 29:27 6068
Buy thee my field that is in *A* Jer 32:7 6068
field, I pray thee, that is in *A* Jer 32:8 6068
my uncle's son, that was in *A* Jer 32:9 6068
2. A son of Becher.
Omri, and Jerimoth, and Abiah, and *A* 1Chr 7:8 6068
3. An Israelite who sealed the covenant under Nehemiah.
Hariph, *A*, Nebai, Neh 10:19 6068

ANATHOTHITE See ANTOTHITE.

ANCESTORS
remember the covenant of their *a* Lev 26:45 7223

ANCHOR
hope we have as an *a* of the soul Heb 6:19 45

ANCHORS
they cast four *a* out of the stern Acts 27:29 45
have cast *a* out of the foreship Acts 27:30
And when they had taken up the *a* Acts 27:40 45

ANCIENT
chief things of the *a* mountains Deut 33:15 6924
that *a* river, the river Kishon Judg 5:21 6917
of *a* times that I have formed it 2Kin 19:25 6924
And these are *a* things 1Chr 4:22 6267
of the fathers, who were *a* men Ezr 3:12 2204
With the *a* is wisdom Job 12:12 3453
days of old, the years of *a* times Ps 77:5 5769
Remove not the *a* landmark Prov 22:28 5769
prophet, and the prudent, and the *a* Is 3:2 2204
himself proudly against the *a* Is 3:5 2204
The *a* and honourable, he is the Is 9:15 2204
of the wise, the son of *a* kings Is 19:11 6924
whose antiquity is of *a* days Is 23:7 6924
of *a* times, that I have formed it Is 37:26 6924
since I appointed the *a* people Is 44:7 5769
hath declared this from *a* time Is 45:21 6924
from *a* times the things that are Is 46:10 6924
upon the *a* hast thou very heavily Is 47:6 2204
awake, as in the *a* days, in the Is 51:9 6924
mighty nation, it is an *a* nation Jer 5:15 5769
in their ways from the *a* paths Jer 18:15 5769
Then they began at the *a* men Eze 9:6 2204
even the *a* high places are ours Eze 36:2 5769
the *A* of days did sit, whose Dan 7:9 6268
heaven, and came to the *A* of days Dan 7:13 6268
Until the *A* of days came, and Dan 7:22 6268

ANCIENTS
As saith the proverb of the *a* 1Sa 24:13 6931
I understand more than the *a* Ps 119:100 2204
judgment with the *a* of his people Is 3:14 2204
and before his *a* gloriously Is 24:23 2204
take of the *a* of the people Jer 19:1 2204
and of the *a* of the priests Jer 19:1 2204
the priest, and counsel from the *a* Eze 7:26 2204
of the *a* of the house of Israel Eze 8:11 2204
hast thou seen what the *a* of the Eze 8:12 2204
The *a* of Gebal and the wise men Eze 27:9 2204

ANCLE
a bones received strength Acts 3:7 4974

ANCLES
the waters were to the *a* Eze 47:3 657

AND See PREFACE.

ANDREW *(an'-drew) One of the twelve disciples.*
A his brother, casting a net into Mt 4:18 406
is called Peter, and *A* his brother Mt 10:2 406
A his brother casting a net into Mk 1:16 406
into the house of Simon and *A* Mk 1:29 406
And *A*, and Philip, and Bartholomew, Mk 3:18 406
and John and *A* asked him privately, Mk 13:3 406
A his brother, James and John, Lk 6:14 406
speak, and followed him, was *A* Jn 1:40 406
was of Bethsaida, the city of *A* Jn 1:44 406
One of his disciples, *A*, Simon Jn 6:8 406
Philip cometh and telleth *A* Jn 12:22 406
and again *A* and Philip tell Jesus Jn 12:22 406
Peter, and James, and John, and *A* Acts 1:13 406

ANDRONICUS *(an-dro-ni'-cus) A relative of Paul.*
Salute *A* and Junia, my kinsmen, and Rom 16:7 408

ANEM *(a'-nem)* See EN-GANNIM. *A Levitical city in Issachar.*
suburbs, and *A* with her suburbs 1Chr 6:73 6046

ANER *(a'-nur)*
1. An ally of Abraham.
of Eshcol, and brother of *A* Gen 14:13 6063
of the men which went with me, *A* Gen 14:24 6063
2. A Levitical city in Manasseh.
A with her suburbs, and Bileam 1Chr 6:70 6063

ANETHOTHITE *(an'-e-thoth-ite)* See ANETOTHITE. *A native of Anathoth.*
Abiezer the *A*, Mebunnai the 2Sa 23:27 6069

ANETOTHITE *(an'-e-toth-ite)* See ANETHOTHITE, ANTOTHITE. *Same as Anethothite.*
the ninth month was Abiezer the *A* 1Chr 27:12 6069

ANGEL
the *a* of the LORD found her by a Gen 16:7 4397
the *a* of the LORD said unto her, Gen 16:9 4397
the *a* of the LORD said unto her, Gen 16:10 4397
the *a* of the LORD said unto her, Gen 16:11 4397
the *a* of God called to Hagar out Gen 21:17 4397
the *a* of the LORD called unto him Gen 22:11 4397
the *a* of the LORD called unto Gen 22:15 4397
he shall send his *a* before thee Gen 24:7 4397
I walk, will send his *a* with thee Gen 24:40 4397
the *a* of God spake unto me in a Gen 31:11 4397
The *a* which redeemed me from all Gen 48:16 4397
the *a* of the LORD appeared unto Ex 3:2 4397
the *a* of God, which went before Ex 14:19 4397
I send an *A* before thee, to keep Ex 23:20 4397
For mine *A* shall go before thee, Ex 23:23 4397
mine *A* shall go before thee Ex 32:34 4397
And I will send an *a* before thee Ex 33:2 4397
he heard our voice, and sent an *a* Num 20:16 4397
the *a* of the LORD stood in the Num 22:22 4397
the ass saw the *a* of the LORD Num 22:23 4397
But the *a* of the LORD stood in a Num 22:24 4397
the ass saw the *a* of the LORD Num 22:25 4397
the *a* of the LORD went further, Num 22:26 4397
the ass saw the *a* of the LORD Num 22:27 4397
he saw the *a* of the LORD standing Num 22:31 4397
the *a* of the LORD said unto him, Num 22:32 4397
said unto the *a* of the LORD Num 22:34 4397
the *a* of the LORD said unto Num 22:35 4397
an *a* of the LORD came up from Judg 2:1 4397
when the *a* of the LORD spake Judg 2:4 4397
said the *a* of the LORD, curse ye Judg 5:23 4397
And there came an *a* of the LORD Judg 6:11 4397
the *a* of the LORD appeared unto Judg 6:12 4397
the *a* of God said unto him, Take Judg 6:20 4397
Then the *a* of the LORD put forth Judg 6:21 4397
Then the *a* of the LORD departed Judg 6:21 4397
that he was an *a* of the LORD Judg 6:22 4397
an *a* of the LORD face to face Judg 6:22 4397
the *a* of the LORD appeared unto Judg 13:3 4397
the countenance of an *a* of God Judg 13:6 4397
the *a* of God came again unto the Judg 13:9 4397
the *a* of the LORD said unto Judg 13:13 4397
said unto the *a* of the LORD Judg 13:15 4397
the *a* of the LORD said unto Judg 13:16 4397
not that he was an *a* of the LORD Judg 13:16 4397
said unto the *a* of the LORD Judg 13:17 4397
the *a* of the LORD said unto him, Judg 13:18 4397
and the *a* did wonderously Judg 13:19
that the *a* of the LORD ascended Judg 13:20 4397
But the *a* of the LORD did no more Judg 13:21 4397
knew that he was an *a* of the LORD Judg 13:21 4397
good in my sight, as an *a* of God 1Sa 29:9 4397
for as an *a* of God, so is my lord 2Sa 14:17 4397
to the wisdom of an *a* of God 2Sa 14:20 4397
lord the king is as an *a* of God 2Sa 19:27 4397
when the *a* stretched out his hand 2Sa 24:16 4397
said to the *a* that destroyed the 2Sa 24:16 4397
the *a* of the LORD was by the 2Sa 24:16 4397
saw the *a* that smote the people 2Sa 24:17 4397
an *a* spake unto me by the word of 1Kin 13:18 4397
then an *a* touched him, and said 1Kin 19:5 4397
the *a* of the LORD came again the 1Kin 19:7 4397
But the *a* of the LORD said to 2Kin 1:3 4397
the *a* of the LORD said unto 2Kin 1:15 4397
that the *a* of the LORD went out, 2Kin 19:35 4397
the *a* of the LORD destroying 1Chr 21:12 4397
God sent an *a* unto Jerusalem to 1Chr 21:15 4397
said to the *a* that destroyed, It 1Chr 21:15 4397
the *a* of the LORD stood by the 1Chr 21:15 4397
saw the *a* of the LORD stand 1Chr 21:16 4397
Then the *a* of the LORD commanded 1Chr 21:18 4397
Ornan turned back, and saw the *a* 1Chr 21:20 4397
And the LORD commanded the *a* 1Chr 21:27 4397
of the sword of the *a* of the LORD 1Chr 21:30 4397
And the LORD sent an *a*, which cut 2Chr 32:21 4397
The *a* of the LORD encampeth round Ps 34:7 4397
let the *a* of the LORD chase them Ps 35:5 4397
let the *a* of the LORD persecute Ps 35:6 4397
neither say thou before the *a* Eccl 5:6 4397
Then the *a* of the LORD went forth Is 37:36 4397
the *a* of his presence saved them Is 63:9 4397
and Abed-nego, who hath sent his *a* Dan 3:28 4398
My God hath sent his *a*, and hath Dan 6:22 4398
Yea, he had power over the *a* Hos 12:4 4397
the *a* that talked with me said Zec 1:9 4397
they answered the *a* of the LORD Zec 1:11 4397
Then the *a* of the LORD answered Zec 1:12 4397
the LORD answered the *a* that Zec 1:13 4397
So the *a* that communed with me Zec 1:14 4397
I said unto the *a* that talked Zec 1:19 4397
the *a* that talked with me went Zec 2:3 4397
another *a* went out to meet him, Zec 2:3 4397
standing before the *a* of the LORD Zec 3:1 4397
garments, and stood before the *a* Zec 3:3 4397
the *a* of the LORD stood by Zec 3:5 4397
the *a* of the LORD protested unto Zec 3:6 4397
the *a* that talked with me came Zec 4:1 4397
spake to the *a* that talked with Zec 4:4 4397
Then the *a* that talked with me Zec 4:5 4397
Then the *a* that talked with me Zec 5:5 4397
Then said I to the *a* that talked Zec 5:10 4397
said unto the *a* that talked with Zec 6:4 4397
the *a* answered and said unto me, Zec 6:5 4397
as the *a* of the LORD before them Zec 12:8 4397
the *a* of the Lord appeared unto Mt 1:20 32
the *a* of the Lord had bidden him Mt 1:24 32
the *a* of the Lord appeareth to Mt 2:13 32
an *a* of the Lord appeareth in a Mt 2:19 32
for the *a* of the Lord descended Mt 28:2 32
the *a* answered and said unto the Mt 28:5 32
there appeared unto him an *a* of Lk 1:11 32
But the *a* said unto him, Fear not Lk 1:13 32
And Zacharias said unto the *a* Lk 1:18 32
the *a* answering said unto him, I Lk 1:19 32
in the sixth month the *a* Gabriel Lk 1:26 32
the *a* came in unto her, and said, Lk 1:28 32
the *a* said unto her, Fear not, Lk 1:30 32
Then said Mary unto the *a* Lk 1:34 32
the *a* answered and said unto her, Lk 1:35 32
And the *a* departed from her Lk 1:38 32
the *a* of the Lord came upon them, Lk 2:9 32
the *a* said unto them, Fear not Lk 2:10 32
the *a* a multitude of the heavenly Lk 2:13 32
which was so named of the *a* Lk 2:21 32
there appeared an *a* unto him from Lk 22:43 32
For an *a* went down at a certain Jn 5:4 32
others said, An *a* spake to him Jn 12:29 32
But the *a* of the Lord by night Acts 5:19 32
as it had been the face of an *a* Acts 6:15 32
a of the Lord in a flame of fire Acts 7:30 32
a which appeared to him in the Acts 7:35 32
in the wilderness with the *a* Acts 7:38 32
the *a* of the Lord spake unto Acts 8:26 32
day an *a* of God coming in to him Acts 10:3 32
when the *a* which spake unto Acts 10:7 32
was warned from God by an holy *a* Acts 10:22 32
how he had seen an *a* in his house Acts 11:13 32
the *a* of the Lord came upon him, Acts 12:7 32
the *a* said unto him, Gird thyself Acts 12:8 32
was true which was done by the *a* Acts 12:9 32
forthwith the *a* departed from him Acts 12:10 32
that the Lord hath sent his *a* Acts 12:11 32
Then said they, It is his *a* Acts 12:15
immediately the *a* of the Lord Acts 12:23 32
is no resurrection, neither *a* Acts 23:8 32
spirit or an *a* hath spoken to him Acts 23:9 32
by me this night the *a* of God Acts 27:23 32
is transformed into an *a* of light 2Cor 11:14 32
or an *a* from heaven, preach any Gal 1:8 32
but received me as an *a* of God Gal 4:14 32
signified it by his *a* unto his Rev 1:1 32
Unto the *a* of the church of Rev 2:1 32
unto the *a* of the church in Rev 2:8 32
to the *a* of the church in Rev 2:12 32
unto the *a* of the church in Rev 2:18 32
unto the *a* of the church in Rev 3:1 32
to the *a* of the church in Rev 3:7 32
unto the *a* of the church of the Rev 3:14 32
I saw a strong *a* proclaiming with Rev 5:2 32
I saw another *a* ascending from Rev 7:2 32
And another *a* came and stood at the Rev 8:3 32
the *a* took the censer, and filled Rev 8:5 32
The first *a* sounded, and there Rev 8:7 32
And the second *a* sounded, and as it Rev 8:8 32
And the third *a* sounded, and there Rev 8:10 32
And the fourth *a* sounded, and the Rev 8:12 32
heard an *a* flying through the Rev 8:13 32
And the fifth *a* sounded, and I saw Rev 9:1 32
which is the *a* of the bottomless Rev 9:11 32
And the sixth *a* sounded, and I Rev 9:13
Saying to the sixth *a* which had Rev 9:14 32
I saw another mighty *a* come down Rev 10:1 32
the *a* which I saw stand upon the Rev 10:5 32
of the voice of the seventh *a* Rev 10:7 32
is open in the hand of the *a* Rev 10:8 32
And I went unto the *a*, and said Rev 10:9 32
the *a* stood, saying, Rise, and Rev 11:1 32

And the seventh *a* sounded Rev 11:15 32
I saw another *a* fly in the midst Rev 14:6 32
And there followed another *a* Rev 14:8 32
the third *a* followed them, saying Rev 14:9 32
another *a* came out of the temple, Rev 14:15 32
another *a* came out of the temple Rev 14:17 32
another *a* came out from the altar Rev 14:18 32
the *a* thrust in his sickle into Rev 14:19 32
the second *a* poured out his vial Rev 16:3 32
the third *a* poured out his vial Rev 16:4 32
I heard the *a* of the waters say, Rev 16:5 32
the fourth *a* poured out his vial, Rev 16:8 32
the fifth *a* poured out his vial Rev 16:10 32
the sixth *a* poured out his vial Rev 16:12 32
the seventh *a* poured out his vial Rev 16:17 32
the *a* said unto me, Wherefore Rev 17:7 32
another *a* come down from heaven Rev 18:1 32
a mighty *a* took up a stone like a Rev 18:21 32
I saw an *a* standing in the sun Rev 19:17 32
I saw an *a* come down from heaven, Rev 20:1 32
of a man, that is, of the *a* Rev 21:17 32
a to shew unto his servants the Rev 22:6 32
a which shewed me these things Rev 22:8 32
I Jesus have sent mine *a* to Rev 22:16 32

ANGEL'S

up before God out of the *a* hand Rev 8:4 32
the little book out of the *a* hand Rev 10:10 32

ANGELS

there came two *a* to Sodom at even Gen 19:1 4397
then the *a* hastened Lot, saying, Gen 19:15 4397
behold the *a* of God ascending and Gen 28:12 4397
his way, and the *a* of God met him Gen 32:1 4397
his *a* he charged with folly Job 4:18 4397
him a little lower than the *a* Ps 8:5 430
thousand, even thousands of *a* Ps 68:17 8136
by sending evil *a* among them Ps 78:49 4397
shall give his *a* charge over thee Ps 91:11 4397
Bless the LORD, ye his *a*, that Ps 103:20 4397
Who maketh his *a* spirits Ps 104:4 4397
Praise ye him, all his *a* Ps 148:2 4397
He shall give his *a* charge Mt 4:6 32
a came and ministered unto him Mt 4:11 32
and the reapers are the *a* Mt 13:39 32
Son of man shall send forth his *a* Mt 13:41 32
the *a* shall come forth, and sever Mt 13:49 32
glory of his Father with his *a* Mt 16:27 32
That in heaven their *a* do always Mt 18:10 32
but are as the *a* of God in heaven Mt 22:30 32
he shall send his *a* with a great Mt 24:31 32
not the *a* of heaven, but my Mt 24:36 32
glory, and all the holy *a* with him Mt 25:31 32
prepared for the devil and his *a* Mt 25:41 32
me more than twelve legions of *a* Mt 26:53 32
the *a* ministered unto him Mk 1:13 32
of his Father with the holy *a* Mk 8:38 32
but are as the *a* which are in Mk 12:25 32
And then shall he send his *a* Mk 13:27 32
not the *a* which are in heaven, Mk 13:32 32
as the *a* were gone away from them Lk 2:15 32
shall give his *a* charge over thee Lk 4:10 32
in his Father's, and of the holy *a* Lk 9:26 32
also confess before the *a* of God Lk 12:8 32
be denied before the *a* of God Lk 12:9 32
the *a* of God over one sinner that Lk 15:10 32
was carried by the *a* into Lk 16:22 32
for they are equal unto the *a* Lk 20:36 2465
they had also seen a vision of *a* Lk 24:23 32
the *a* of God ascending and Jn 1:51 32
seeth two *a* in white sitting, the Jn 20:12 32
the law by the disposition of *a* Acts 7:53 32
neither death, nor life, nor *a* Rom 8:38 32
spectacle unto the world, and to *a* 1Cor 4:9 32
Know ye not that we shall judge *a* 1Cor 6:3 32
on her head because of the *a* 1Cor 11:10 32
with the tongues of men and of *a* 1Cor 13:1 32
it was ordained by *a* in the hand Gal 3:19 32
humility and worshipping of *a* Col 2:18 32
from heaven with his mighty *a* 2Th 1:7 32
in the Spirit, seen of *a*, 1Ti 3:16 32
Lord Jesus Christ, and the elect *a* 1Ti 5:21 32
made so much better than the *a* Heb 1:4 32
of the *a* said he at any time Heb 1:5 32
let all the *a* of God worship him Heb 1:6 32
of the *a* he saith Heb 1:7 32
Who maketh his *a* spirits Heb 1:7 32
But to which of the *a* said he at Heb 1:13 32
the word spoken by *a* was stedfast Heb 2:2 32
For unto the *a* hath he not put in Heb 2:5 32
him a little lower than the *a* Heb 2:7 32
the *a* for the suffering of death Heb 2:9 32
took not on him the nature of *a* Heb 2:16 32
and to an innumerable company of *a* Heb 12:22 32
some have entertained *a* unawares Heb 13:2 32
which things the *a* desire to look 1Pet 1:12 32
a and authorities and powers being 1Pet 3:22 32
God spared not the *a* that sinned 2Pet 2:4 32
Whereas *a*, which are greater in 2Pet 2:11 32
the *a* which kept not their first Jude 6 32
are the *a* of the seven churches Rev 1:20 32
before my Father, and before his *a* Rev 3:5 32
of many *a* round about the throne Rev 5:11 32
after these things I saw four *a* Rev 7:1 32
with a loud voice to the four *a* Rev 7:2 32
all the *a* stood round about the Rev 7:11 32
I saw the seven *a* which stood Rev 8:2 32
the seven *a* which had the seven Rev 8:6 32
of the trumpet of the three *a* Rev 8:13 32
Loose the four *a* which are bound Rev 9:14 32
the four *a* were loosed, which Rev 9:15 32
his *a* fought against the dragon Rev 12:7 32
and the dragon fought and his *a* Rev 12:7 32
his *a* were cast out with him Rev 12:9 32
in the presence of the holy *a* Rev 14:10 32
seven *a* having the seven last Rev 15:1 32
the seven *a* came out of the Rev 15:6 32
a seven golden vials full of the Rev 15:7 32
of the seven *a* were fulfilled Rev 15:8 32
the temple saying to the seven *a* Rev 16:1 32
seven *a* which had the seven vials Rev 17:1 32
came unto me one of the seven *a* Rev 21:9 32
gates, and at the gates twelve *a* Rev 21:12 32

ANGELS'

Man did eat *a* food Ps 78:25 47

ANGER

brother's *a* turn away from thee Gen 27:45 639
Jacob's *a* was kindled against Gen 30:2 639
let not thine *a* burn against thy Gen 44:18 639
for in their *a* they slew a man, Gen 49:6 639
Cursed be their *a*, for it was Gen 49:7 639
the *a* of the LORD was kindled Ex 4:14 639
out from Pharaoh in a great *a* Ex 11:8 639
Moses' *a* waxed hot, and he cast Ex 32:19 639
Let not the *a* of my lord wax hot Ex 32:22 639
and his *a* was kindled Num 11:1 639
the *a* of the LORD was kindled Num 11:10 639
the *a* of the LORD was kindled Num 12:9 639
God's *a* was kindled because he Num 22:22 639
Balaam's *a* was kindled, and he Num 22:27 639
Balak's *a* was kindled against Num 24:10 639
the *a* of the LORD was kindled Num 25:3 639
that the fierce *a* of the LORD may Num 25:4 639
the LORD's *a* was kindled the same Num 32:10 639
the LORD's *a* was kindled against Num 32:13 639
a of the LORD toward Israel Num 32:14 639
LORD thy God, to provoke him to *a* Deut 4:25 3707
a of the LORD thy God be kindled Deut 6:15 639
so will the *a* of the LORD be Deut 7:4 639
of the LORD, to provoke him to *a* Deut 9:18 3707
For I was afraid of the *a* Deut 9:19 639
turn from the fierceness of his *a* Deut 13:17 639
him, but then the *a* of the LORD Deut 29:20 639
which the LORD overthrew in his *a* Deut 29:23 639
meaneth the heat of this great *a* Deut 29:24 639
the *a* of the LORD was kindled Deut 29:27 639
them out of their land in *a* Deut 29:28 639
Then my *a* shall be kindled Deut 31:17 639
to provoke him to *a* through the Deut 31:29 3707
provoked they him to *a* Deut 32:16 3707
me to *a* with their vanities Deut 32:21 3707
them to *a* with a foolish nation Deut 32:21
For a fire is kindled in mine *a* Deut 32:22 639
the *a* of the LORD was kindled Josh 7:1 639
from the fierceness of his *a* Josh 7:26 639
then shall the *a* of the LORD be Josh 23:16 639
them, and provoked the LORD to *a* Judg 2:12 3707
the *a* of the LORD was hot against Judg 2:14 639
the *a* of the LORD was hot against Judg 2:20 639
Therefore the *a* of the LORD was Judg 3:8 639
Let not thine *a* be hot against me Judg 6:39 639
Then their *a* was abated toward Judg 8:3 7307
son of Ebed, his *a* was kindled Judg 9:30 639
the *a* of the LORD was hot against Judg 10:7 639
his *a* was kindled, and he went up Judg 14:19 639
his *a* was kindled greatly 1Sa 11:6 639
Eliab's *a* was kindled against 1Sa 17:28 639
Then Saul's *a* was kindled against 1Sa 20:30 639
arose from the table in fierce *a* 1Sa 20:34 639
the *a* of the LORD was kindled 2Sa 6:7 639
David's *a* was greatly kindled 2Sa 12:5 639
again the *a* of the LORD was 2Sa 24:1 639
molten images, to provoke me to *a* 1Kin 14:9 3707
groves, provoking the LORD to *a* 1Kin 14:15 3707
the LORD God of Israel to *a* 1Kin 15:30 3707
to provoke me to *a* with their sins 1Kin 16:2 3707
in provoking him to *a* with the 1Kin 16:7 3707
Israel to *a* with their vanities 1Kin 16:13 3707
Israel to *a* with their vanities 1Kin 16:26 3707
the LORD God of Israel to *a* than 1Kin 16:33 3707
thou hast provoked me to *a* 1Kin 21:22 3707
provoked to *a* the LORD God of 1Kin 22:53 3707
the *a* of the LORD was kindled 2Kin 13:3 639
things to provoke the LORD to *a* 2Kin 17:11 3707
of the LORD, to provoke him to *a* 2Kin 17:17 3707
of the LORD, to provoke him to *a* 2Kin 21:6 3707
sight, and have provoked me to *a* 2Kin 21:15 3707
to *a* with all the works of their 2Kin 22:17 3707
had made to provoke the LORD to *a* 2Kin 23:19 3707
wherewith his *a* was kindled 2Kin 23:26 639
For through the *a* of the LORD it 2Kin 24:20 639
the *a* of the LORD was kindled 1Chr 13:10 639
wherefore their *a* was greatly 2Chr 25:10 639
and they returned home in great *a* 2Chr 25:10 639
Wherefore the *a* of the LORD was 2Chr 25:15 639
provoked to *a* the LORD God of his 2Chr 28:25 3707
of the LORD, to provoke him to *a* 2Chr 33:6 3707
to *a* with all the works of their 2Chr 34:25 3707
thee to *a* before the builders Neh 4:5 3707
gracious and merciful, slow to *a* Neh 9:17 639
wroth, and his *a* burned in him Est 1:12 2534
which overturneth them in his *a* Job 9:5 639
If God will not withdraw his *a* Job 9:13 639
He teareth himself in his *a* Job 18:4 639
God distributeth sorrows in his *a* Job 21:17 639
not so, he hath visited in his *a* Job 35:15 639
O lord, rebuke me not in thine *a* Ps 6:1 639
Arise, O LORD, in thine *a* Ps 7:6 639
fiery oven in the time of thine *a* Ps 21:9 6440
put not thy servant away in *a* Ps 27:9 639
For his *a* endureth but a moment Ps 30:5 639
Cease from *a*, and forsake wrath Ps 37:8 639
in my flesh because of thine *a* Ps 38:3 2195
in thine *a* cast down the people, Ps 56:7 639
let thy wrathful *a* take hold of Ps 69:24 639
why doth thine *a* smoke against Ps 74:1 639
hath he in *a* shut up his tender Ps 77:9 639
a also came up against Israel Ps 78:21 639
many a time turned he his *a* away Ps 78:38 639
upon them the fierceness of his *a* Ps 78:49 639
He made a way to his *a* Ps 78:50 639
him to *a* with their high places Ps 78:58 3707
from the fierceness of thine *a* Ps 85:3 639
cause thine *a* toward us to cease Ps 85:4 3708
out thine *a* to all generations Ps 85:5 639
For we are consumed by thine *a* Ps 90:7 639
Who knoweth the power of thine *a* Ps 90:11 639
merciful and gracious, slow to *a* Ps 103:8 639
will he keep his *a* for ever Ps 103:9 639
him to *a* with their inventions Ps 106:29 3707
slow to *a*, and of great mercy Ps 145:8 639
but grievous words stir up *a* Prov 15:1 639
is slow to *a* appeaseth strife Prov 15:18 639
He that is slow to *a* is better Prov 16:32 639
of a man deferreth his *a* Prov 19:11 639
whoso provoketh him to *a* sinneth Prov 20:2 5674
A gift in secret pacifieth *a* Prov 21:14 639
and the rod of his *a* shall fail Prov 22:8 5678
is cruel, and *a* is outrageous Prov 27:4 639
for *a* resteth in the bosom of Eccl 7:9 3708
the Holy One of Israel unto *a* Is 1:4 5006
Therefore is the *a* of the LORD Is 5:25 639
For all this his *a* is not turned Is 5:25 639
for the fierce *a* of Rezin with Is 7:4 639
For all this his *a* is not turned Is 9:12 639
For all this his *a* is not turned Is 9:17 639
For all this his *a* is not turned Is 9:21 639
For all this his *a* is not turned Is 10:4 639
O Assyrian, the rod of mine *a* Is 10:5 639
mine *a* in their destruction Is 10:25 639
thine *a* is turned away, and thou Is 12:1 639
called my mighty ones for mine *a* Is 13:3 639
cruel both with wrath and fierce *a* Is 13:9 639
and in the day of his fierce *a* Is 13:13 639
he that ruled the nations in *a* Is 14:6 639
from far, burning with his *a* Is 30:27 639
with the indignation of his *a* Is 30:30 639
poured upon him the fury of his *a* Is 42:25 639
name's sake will I defer mine *a* Is 48:9 639
for I will tread them in mine *a* Is 63:3 639
tread down the people in mine *a* Is 63:6 639
me to *a* continually to my face Is 65:3 3707
to render his *a* with fury Is 66:15 639
surely his *a* shall turn from me Jer 2:35 639
Will he reserve his *a* for ever Jer 3:5
not cause mine *a* to fall upon you Jer 3:12 6440
and I will not keep *a* for ever Jer 3:12
for the fierce *a* of the LORD is Jer 4:8 639
of the LORD, and by his fierce *a* Jer 4:26 639
that they may provoke me to *a* Jer 7:18 3707
Do they provoke me to *a* Jer 7:19 3707
Behold, mine *a* and my fury shall Jer 7:20 639
me to *a* with their graven images Jer 8:19 3707
not in thine *a*, lest thou bring Jer 10:24 639
themselves to provoke me to *a* in Jer 11:17 3707
of the fierce *a* of the LORD Jer 12:13 639
for a fire is kindled in mine *a* Jer 15:14 639
ye have kindled a fire in mine *a* Jer 17:4 639
with them in the time of thine *a* Jer 18:23 639
and with a strong arm, even in *a* Jer 21:5 639
The *a* of the LORD shall not Jer 23:20 639
provoke me not to *a* with the Jer 25:6 3707
that ye might provoke me to *a* Jer 25:7 3707
of the fierce *a* of the LORD Jer 25:37 639
and because of his fierce *a* Jer 25:38 639
The fierce *a* of the LORD shall Jer 30:24 639
other gods, to provoke me to *a* Jer 32:29 3707
to *a* with the work of their hands Jer 32:30 3707
to me as a provocation of mine *a* Jer 32:31 639
they have done to provoke me to *a* Jer 32:32 3707
I have driven them in mine *a* Jer 32:37 639
men, whom I have slain in mine *a* Jer 33:5 639
for great is the *a* and the fury Jer 36:7 639
As mine *a* and my fury hath been Jer 42:18 639
have committed to provoke me to *a* Jer 44:3 3707
mine *a* was poured forth, and was Jer 44:6 639
evil upon them, even my fierce *a* Jer 49:37 639
from the fierce *a* of the LORD Jer 51:45 639
For through the *a* of the LORD it Jer 52:3 639
me in the day of his fierce *a* Lam 1:12 639
of Zion with a cloud in his *a* Lam 2:1 639
his footstool in the day of his *a* Lam 2:1 639
fierce *a* all the horn of Israel Lam 2:3 639
the indignation of his *a* the king Lam 2:6 639
slain them in the day of thine *a* Lam 2:21 639
a none escaped nor remained Lam 2:22 639
Thou hast covered with *a*, and Lam 3:43 639
destroy them in *a* from under the Lam 3:66 639
he hath poured out his fierce *a* Lam 4:11 639
The *a* of the LORD hath divided Lam 4:16 6440
Thus shall mine *a* be accomplished Eze 5:13 639
execute judgments in thee in *a* Eze 5:15 639
and I will send mine *a* upon thee Eze 7:3 639
and accomplish mine *a* upon thee Eze 7:8 639
have returned to provoke me to *a* Eze 8:17 3707
an overflowing shower in mine *a* Eze 13:13 639
thy whoredoms, to provoke me to *a* Eze 16:26 3707
to accomplish my *a* against them Eze 20:8 639
to accomplish my *a* against them Eze 20:21 639
so will I gather you in mine *a* Eze 22:20 639
do in Edom according to mine *a* Eze 25:14 639
will even do according to thine *a* Eze 35:11 639
I have consumed them in mine *a* Eze 43:8 639
I beseech thee, let thine *a* Dan 9:16 639
shall be destroyed, neither in *a* Dan 11:20 639
mine *a* is kindled against them Hos 8:5 639
execute the fierceness of mine *a* Hos 11:9 639
provoked him to *a* most bitterly Hos 12:14 3707
I gave thee a king in mine *a* Hos 13:11 639
for mine *a* is turned away from Hos 14:4 639
gracious and merciful, slow to *a* Joel 2:13 639
his *a* did tear perpetually, and he Amos 1:11 639

and turn away from his fierce *a* Jonah 3:9 639
God, and merciful, slow to *a* Jonah 4:2 639
And I will execute vengeance in *a* Mic 5:15 639
he retaineth not his *a* for ever Mic 7:18 639
The LORD is slow to *a*, and great Nah 1:3 639
abide in the fierceness of his *a* Nah 1:6 639
was thine *a* against the rivers Hab 3:8 639
didst thresh the heathen in *a* Hab 3:12 639
before the fierce *a* of the LORD Zeph 2:2 639
day of the LORD's *a* come upon you Zeph 2:2 639
be hid in the day of the LORD's *a* Zeph 2:3 639
indignation, even all my fierce *a* Zeph 3:8 639
Mine *a* was kindled against the Zec 10:3 639
looked round about on them with *a* Mk 3:5 *3709*
by a foolish nation I will *a* you Rom 10:19 *3949*
all bitterness, and wrath, and *a* Eph 4:31 *3709*
a, wrath, malice, blasphemy, Col 3:8 *3709*
provoke not your children to *a* Col 3:21

ANGERED
They *a* him also at the waters of Ps 106:32 7107

ANGLE
all they that cast *a* into the Is 19:8 2443
take up all of them with the *a* Hab 1:15 2443

ANGRY
him, Oh let not the LORD be *a* Gen 18:30 2734
he said, Oh let not the Lord be *a* Gen 18:32 2734
nor *a* with yourselves, that ye Gen 45:5 2734
he was *a* with Eleazar and Ithamar, Lev 10:16 7107
Also the LORD was *a* with me for Deut 1:37 599
LORD was *a* with me for your sakes Deut 4:21 599
so that the LORD was *a* with you Deut 9:8 599
the LORD was very *a* with Aaron to Deut 9:20 599
lest *a* fellows run upon thee, and Judg 18:25 5315
then be ye *a* for this matter 2Sa 19:42 2734
thou be *a* with them, and deliver 1Kin 8:46 599
And the LORD was *a* with Solomon 1Kin 11:9 599
the LORD was very *a* with Israel 2Kin 17:18 599
thou be *a* with them, and deliver 2Chr 6:36 599
wouldest not thou be *a* with us Ezr 9:14 599
I was very *a* when I heard their Neh 5:6 2734
Kiss the Son, lest he be *a* Ps 2:12 599
God is *a* with the wicked every Ps 7:11 2194
in thy sight when once thou art *a* Ps 76:7 639
wilt thou be *a* for ever Ps 79:5 599
how long wilt thou be *a* against Ps 80:4 6225
Wilt thou be *a* with us for ever Ps 85:5 599
He that is soon *a* dealeth Prov 14:17 639
with a contentious and an *a* woman Prov 21:19 3708
Make no friendship with an *a* man Prov 22:24 639
so doth an *a* countenance a Prov 25:23 2194
An *a* man stirreth up strife, and a Prov 29:22 639
should God be *a* at thy voice Eccl 5:6 7107
not hasty in thy spirit to be *a* Eccl 7:9 3707
mother's children were *a* with me Song 1:6 2734
though thou wast *a* with me Is 12:1 599
be quiet, and will be no more *a* Eze 16:42 3707
For this cause the king was *a* Dan 2:12 1149
exceedingly, and he was very *a* Jonah 4:1 2734
the LORD, Doest thou well to be *a* Jonah 4:4 2734
thou well to be *a* for the gourd Jonah 4:9 2734
And he said, I do well to be *a* Jonah 4:9 2734
That whosoever is *a* with his Mt 5:22 *3710*
house being *a* said to his servant Lk 14:21 *3710*
And he was *a*, and would not go in Lk 15:28 *3710*
are ye *a* at me, because I have Jn 7:23 *5520*
Be ye *a*, and sin not Eph 4:26 *3710*
not selfwilled, not soon *a* Titus 1:7 *3711*
And the nations were *a*, and thy Rev 11:18 *3710*

ANGUISH
in that we saw the *a* of his soul Gen 42:21 6869
not unto Moses for *a* of spirit Ex 6:9 7115
and be in *a* because of thee Deut 2:25 2342
for *a* is come upon me, because my 2Sa 1:9 7661
will speak in the *a* of my spirit Job 7:11 6862
and *a* shall make him afraid Job 15:24 4691
and *a* have taken hold on me Ps 119:143 4689
distress and *a* cometh upon you Prov 1:27 6695
trouble and darkness, dimness of *a* Is 8:22 6695
into the land of trouble and *a* Is 30:6 6695
the *a* as of her that bringeth Jer 4:31 6869
a hath taken hold of us, and pain, Jer 6:24 6869
a and sorrows have taken her, as a Jer 49:24 6869
a took hold of him, and pangs as Jer 50:43 6869
she remembereth no more the *a* Jn 16:21 *2347*
Tribulation and *a*, upon every soul Rom 2:9 *4730*
a of heart I wrote unto you with 2Cor 2:4 *4928*

ANIAM (*a'-ne-am*) *A son of Shemida.*
Ahian, and Shechem, and Likhi, and *A* 1Chr 7:19 593

ANIM (*a'-nim*) *A city in Judah.*
And Anab, and Eshtemoh, and *A* Josh 15:50 6044

ANISE
for ye pay tithe of mint and *a* Mt 23:23 *432*

ANNA (*an'-nah*) *A prophetess.*
And there was one *A*, a prophetess, Lk 2:36 *451*

ANNAS (*an'-nas*) *A High Priest during Jesus' ministry.*
A and Caiaphas being the high Lk 3:2 *452*
And led him away to *A* first Jn 18:13 *452*
Now *A* had sent him bound unto Jn 18:24 *452*
A the high priest, and Caiaphas, Acts 4:6 *452*

ANOINT
and shalt *a* them, and consecrate Ex 28:41 4886
pour it upon his head, and *a* him Ex 29:7 4886
for it, and thou shalt *a* it Ex 29:36 4886
thou shalt *a* the tabernacle of Ex 30:26 4886
And thou shalt *a* Aaron and his sons Ex 30:30 4886
a the tabernacle, and all that is Ex 40:9 4886
thou shalt *a* the altar of the Ex 40:10 4886
And thou shalt *a* the laver Ex 40:11 4886
and *a* him, and sanctify him Ex 40:13 4886
And thou shalt *a* them Ex 40:15 4886
as thou didst *a* their father Ex 40:15 4886
And the priest, whom he shall *a* Lev 16:32 4886
but thou shalt not *a* thyself with Deut 28:40 5480
on a time to *a* a king over them Judg 9:8 4886
If in truth ye *a* me king over you Judg 9:15 4886
a thee, and put thy raiment upon Ruth 3:3 5480
thou shalt *a* him to be captain 1Sa 9:16 4886
The LORD sent me to *a* thee to be 1Sa 15:1 4886
thou shalt *a* unto me him whom I 1Sa 16:3 4886
And the LORD said, Arise, *a* him 1Sa 16:12 4886
a not thyself with oil, but be as 2Sa 14:2 5480
Nathan the prophet *a* him there 1Kin 1:34 4886
a Hazael to be king over Syria 1Kin 19:15 4886
thou *a* to be king over Israel 1Kin 19:16 4886
thou *a* to be prophet in thy room 1Kin 19:16 4886
ye princes, and *a* the shield Is 21:5 4886
prophecy, and to *a* the most Holy Dan 9:24 4886
neither did I *a* myself at all Dan 10:3 5480
a themselves with the chief Amos 6:6 4886
thou shalt not *a* thee with oil Mic 6:15 5480
a thine head, and wash thy face Mt 6:17 *218*
to *a* my body to the burying Mk 14:8 *3462*
that they might come and *a* him Mk 16:1 *218*
My head with oil thou didst not *a* Lk 7:46 *218*
a thine eyes with eyesalve, that Rev 3:18 *1472*

ANOINTED
and wafers unleavened *a* with oil Ex 29:2 4886
to be *a* therein, and to be Ex 29:29 4888
or unleavened wafers *a* with oil Lev 2:4 4886
If the priest that is *a* do sin Lev 4:3 4899
the priest that is *a* shall take Lev 4:5 4899
the priest that is *a* shall bring Lev 4:16 4899
the LORD in the day when he is *a* Lev 6:20 4886
is *a* in his stead shall offer it Lev 6:22 4899
and unleavened wafers *a* with oil Lev 7:12 4886
Israel, in the day that he *a* them Lev 7:36 4886
a the tabernacle and all that was Lev 8:10 4886
a the altar and all his vessels, Lev 8:11 4886
head, and *a* him, to sanctify him Lev 8:12 4886
Aaron, the priests which were *a* Num 3:3 4886
of unleavened bread *a* with oil Num 6:15 4886
up the tabernacle, and had *a* it Num 7:1 4886
had *a* them, and sanctified them Num 7:1 4886
altar in the day that it was *a* Num 7:10 4886
altar, in the day when it was *a* Num 7:84 4886
of the altar, after that it was *a* Num 7:88 4886
which was *a* with the holy oil Num 35:25 4886
king, and exalt the horn of his *a* 1Sa 2:10 4899
shall walk before mine *a* for ever 1Sa 2:35 4899
a thee to be captain over his 1Sa 10:1 4886
before the LORD, and before his *a* 1Sa 12:3 4899
his *a* is witness this day, that 1Sa 12:5 4899
the LORD *a* thee king over Israel 1Sa 15:17 4886
Surely the LORD's *a* is before him 1Sa 16:6 4899
a him in the midst of his 1Sa 16:13 4886
unto my master, the LORD's *a* 1Sa 24:6 4899
seeing he is the *a* of the LORD 1Sa 24:6 4899
for he is the LORD's *a* 1Sa 24:10 4899
his hand against the LORD's *a* 1Sa 26:9 4899
mine hand against the LORD's *a* 1Sa 26:11 4899
kept your master, the LORD's *a* 1Sa 26:16 4899
mine hand against the LORD's *a* 1Sa 26:23 4899
hand to destroy the LORD's *a* 2Sa 1:14 4899
saying, I have slain the LORD's *a* 2Sa 1:16 4899
though he had not been *a* with oil 2Sa 1:21 4899
there they *a* David king over the 2Sa 2:4 4886
of Judah have *a* me king over them 2Sa 2:7 4886
I am this day weak, though *a* king 2Sa 3:39 4886
they *a* David king over Israel 2Sa 5:3 4886
they had *a* David king over Israel 2Sa 5:17 4886
I *a* thee king over Israel, and I 2Sa 12:7 4886
a himself, and changed his apparel 2Sa 12:20 5480
And Absalom, whom we *a* over us 2Sa 19:10 4886
because he cursed the LORD's *a* 2Sa 19:21 4899
and sheweth mercy to his *a* 2Sa 22:51 4899
the *a* of the God of Jacob, and the 2Sa 23:1 4899
of the tabernacle, and *a* Solomon 1Kin 1:39 4886
prophet have *a* him king in Gihon 1Kin 1:45 4886
had *a* him king in the room of his 1Kin 5:1 4886
I have *a* thee king over Israel 2Kin 9:3 4886
I have *a* thee king over the 2Kin 9:6 4886
I have *a* thee king over Israel 2Kin 9:12 4886
and they made him king, and *a* him 2Kin 11:12 4886
a him, and made him king in his 2Kin 23:30 4886
they *a* David king over Israel, 1Chr 11:3 4886
David was *a* king over all Israel 1Chr 14:8 4886
Saying, Touch not mine *a*, and do 1Chr 16:22 4899
a him unto the LORD to be the 1Chr 29:22 4886
turn not away the face of thine *a* 2Chr 6:42 4899
whom the LORD had *a* to cut off 2Chr 22:7 4886
And Jehoiada and his sons *a* him 2Chr 23:11 4886
a them, and carried all the feeble 2Chr 28:15 4886
the LORD, and against his *a* Ps 2:2 4899
and sheweth mercy to his *a* Ps 18:50 4899
know I that the LORD saveth his *a* Ps 20:6 4899
is the saving strength of his *a* Ps 28:8 4899
hath *a* thee with the oil of Ps 45:7 4886
and look upon the face of thine *a* Ps 84:9 4899
with my holy oil have I *a* him Ps 89:20 4886
thou hast been wroth with thine *a* Ps 89:38 4899
the footsteps of thine *a* Ps 89:51 4899
I shall be *a* with fresh oil Ps 92:10 1101
Saying, Touch not mine *a*, and do Ps 105:15 4899
turn not away the face of thine *a* Ps 132:10 4899
I have ordained a lamp for mine *a* Ps 132:17 4899
Thus saith the LORD to his *a* Is 45:1 4899
because the LORD hath *a* me to Is 61:1 4886
the *a* of the LORD, was taken in Lam 4:20 4899
from thee, and I *a* thee with oil Eze 16:9 5480
Thou art the *a* cherub that Eze 28:14 4473
even for salvation with thine *a* Hab 3:13 4899
said he, These are the two *a* ones Zec 4:14 3323
a with oil many that were sick, Mk 6:13 *218*
because he hath *a* me to preach Lk 4:18 *5548*
feet, and *a* them with the ointment Lk 7:38 *218*
but this woman hath *a* my feet Lk 7:46 *218*
he *a* the eyes of the blind man Jn 9:6 *1909*
a mine eyes, and said unto me, Go Jn 9:11 *2025*
which *a* the Lord with ointment Jn 11:2 *218*
a the feet of Jesus, and wiped his Jn 12:3 *218*
child Jesus, whom thou hast *a* Acts 4:27 *5548*
How God *a* Jesus of Nazareth with Acts 10:38 *5548*
with you in Christ, and hath *a* us 2Cor 1:21 *5548*
hath *a* thee with the oil of Heb 1:9 *5548*

ANOINTEDST
Beth-el, where thou *a* the pillar Gen 31:13 4886

ANOINTEST
thou *a* my head with oil Ps 23:5 1878

ANOINTING
for the light, spices for *a* oil Ex 25:6 4888
Then shalt thou take the *a* oil Ex 29:7 4888
upon the altar, and of the *a* oil Ex 29:21 4888
it shall be an holy *a* oil Ex 30:25 4888
This shall be an holy *a* oil unto Ex 30:31 4888
And the *a* oil, and sweet incense Ex 31:11 4888
the light, and spices for *a* oil Ex 35:8 4888
and his staves, and the *a* oil Ex 35:15 4888
for the light, and for the *a* oil Ex 35:28 4888
And he made the holy *a* oil Ex 37:29 4888
And the golden altar, and the *a* oil Ex 39:38 4888
And thou shalt take the *a* oil Ex 40:9 4888
for their *a* shall surely be an Ex 40:15 4888
is the portion of the *a* of Aaron Lev 7:35 4888
of the *a* of his sons, out of the Lev 7:35 4888
and the garments, and the *a* oil Lev 8:2 4888
And Moses took the *a* oil, and Lev 8:10 4888
he poured of the *a* oil upon Lev 8:12 4888
And Moses took of the *a* oil Lev 8:30 4888
for the *a* oil of the LORD is upon Lev 10:7 4888
whose head the *a* oil was poured Lev 21:10 4888
for the crown of the *a* oil of his Lev 21:12 4888
daily meat offering, and the *a* oil Num 4:16 4888
I given them by reason of the *a* Num 18:8 4888
be destroyed because of the *a* Is 10:27 8081
a him with oil in the name of the Jas 5:14 *218*
But the *a* which ye have received 1Jn 2:27 *5545*
but as the same *a* teacheth you of 1Jn 2:27 *5545*

ANON
word, and *a* with joy receiveth it Mt 13:20 *2117*
fever, and *a* they tell him of her Mk 1:30 *2112*

ANOTHER
hath appointed me *a* seed instead Gen 4:25 312
And they said one to *a*, Go to, let Gen 11:3 7453
and laid each piece one against *a* Gen 15:10 7453
And they digged *a* well, and strove Gen 26:21 312
from thence, and digged *a* well Gen 26:22 312
in the morning, and sware one to *a* Gen 26:31 312
that I should give her to *a* man Gen 29:19 312
The LORD shall add to me *a* son Gen 30:24 312
when we are absent one from *a* Gen 31:49 7453
And he dreamed yet *a* dream Gen 37:9 312
And they said one to *a*, Behold, Gen 37:19 250
sons, Why do ye look one upon *a* Gen 42:1
And they said one to *a*, We are Gen 42:21 250
they were afraid, saying one to *a* Gen 42:28 250
have ye *a* brother Gen 43:7
and the men marvelled one at *a* Gen 43:33 7453
They saw not one *a*, neither rose Ex 10:23 250
Israel saw it, they said one to *a* Ex 16:15 250
and I judge between one and *a* Ex 18:16 7453
If he take him *a* wife Ex 21:10 312
one smite *a* with a stone, or with Ex 21:18 7453
and shall feed in *a* man's field Ex 22:5 312
which *a* challengeth to be his, Ex 22:9
their faces shall look one to *a* Ex 25:20 250
be coupled together one to *a* Ex 26:3 269
shall be coupled one to *a* Ex 26:3 269
the uttermost edge of *a* curtain Ex 26:4
the loops may take hold one of *a* Ex 26:5 269
board, set in order one against *a* Ex 26:17 269
two sockets under *a* board for his Ex 26:19 259
and two sockets under *a* board Ex 26:21 259
and two sockets under *a* board Ex 26:25 259
the five curtains one unto *a* Ex 36:10 259
curtains he coupled one unto *a* Ex 36:10 259
the uttermost side of *a* curtain Ex 36:11
the loops held one curtain to *a* Ex 36:12 259
one unto *a* with the taches Ex 36:13 259
equally distant one from *a* Ex 36:22 259
two sockets under *a* board for his Ex 36:24 259
and two sockets under *a* board Ex 36:26 259
a cherub on the other end on that Ex 37:8 259
seat, with their faces one to *a* Ex 37:9 250
made like almonds in *a* branch Ex 37:19 259
of Aaron have, one as much as *a* Lev 7:10 250
falsely, neither lie one to *a* Lev 19:11 5997
adultery with *a* man's wife Lev 20:10
hand, ye shall not oppress one *a* Lev 25:14 250
shall not therefore oppress one *a* Lev 25:17 5997
not rule one over *a* with rigour Lev 25:46 250
And they shall fall one upon *a* Lev 26:37 250
he have sold the field to *a* man Lev 27:20 312
with *a* instead of thy husband Num 5:19
aside to *a* instead of thy husband Num 5:20
aside to *a* instead of her husband Num 5:29
a young bullock shalt thou take Num 8:8 8145
And they said one to *a*, Let us Num 14:4 250
because he had *a* spirit with him, Num 14:24 312
I pray thee, with me unto *a* place Num 23:13 312
I will bring thee unto *a* place Num 23:27 312
remove from one tribe to *a* tribe Num 36:9 312
nation from the midst of *a* nation Deut 4:34

the battle, and a man dedicate it	Deut 20:5	312
in the battle, and a man eat of it	Deut 20:6	312
in the battle, and a man take her	Deut 20:7	312
a hated, and they have born him	Deut 21:15	259
she may go and be a man's wife	Deut 24:2	312
men strive together one with a	Deut 25:11	250
wife, and a man shall lie with her	Deut 28:30	312
shall be given unto a people	Deut 28:32	312
and cast them into a land	Deut 29:28	312
there arose a generation after	Judg 2:10	312
And they said one to a, Who hath	Judg 6:29	7453
a company come along by the plain	Judg 9:37	259
princes of Gilead said one to a	Judg 10:18	7453
shall I be weak, and be as a man	Judg 16:7	259
shall I be weak, and be as a man	Judg 16:11	259
Go not to glean in a field	Ruth 2:8	312
rose up before one could know a	Ruth 3:14	7453
If one man sin against a, the	1Sa 2:25	376
a carrying three loaves of bread,	1Sa 10:3	259
a carrying a bottle of wine	1Sa 10:3	259
and shalt be turned into a man	1Sa 10:6	312
from Samuel, God gave him a heart	1Sa 10:9	312
then the people said one to a	1Sa 10:11	7453
a company turned the way to	1Sa 13:18	259
a company turned to the way of	1Sa 13:18	259
they went on beating down one a	1Sa 14:16	
And he turned from him toward a	1Sa 17:30	312
answered one a as they played	1Sa 18:7	
one a, and wept one with a	1Sa 20:41	7453
sing one to a of him in dances	1Sa 21:11	
whom they sang one to a in dances	1Sa 29:5	
sword devoureth one as well as a	2Sa 11:25	2090
but thou shalt bear tidings a day	2Sa 18:20	312
watchman saw a man running	2Sa 18:26	312
Behold a man running alone	2Sa 18:26	
their wings touched one a in the	1Kin 6:27	3671
had a court within the porch	1Kin 7:8	312
And God stirred him up a adversary	1Kin 11:23	
So he went a way, and returned not	1Kin 13:10	312
shall feign herself to be a woman	1Kin 14:5	5234
why feignest thou thyself to be a	1Kin 14:6	5234
Obadiah went a way by himself	1Kin 18:6	259
Then he found a man, and said,	1Kin 20:37	312
will give thee a vineyard for it	1Kin 21:6	312
manner, and a said on that manner	1Kin 22:20	2088
Again also he sent unto him a	2Kin 1:11	312
slain, and they have smitten one a	2Kin 3:23	7453
and they said one to a, Why sit we	2Kin 7:3	7453
and they said one to a, Lo, the	2Kin 7:6	250
again, and entered into a tent	2Kin 7:8	312
Then they said one to a, We do	2Kin 7:9	7453
Baal was full from one end to a	2Kin 10:21	
let us look one a in the face	2Kin 14:8	
king of Judah looked one a in the	2Kin 14:11	
Jerusalem from one end to a	2Kin 21:16	
Jerahmeel had also a wife	1Chr 2:26	312
and from one kingdom to a people	1Chr 16:20	312
tent, and from one tabernacle to a	1Chr 17:5	
divided by lot, one sort with a	1Chr 24:5	
men, having wards one against a	1Chr 26:12	251
a saying after that manner	2Chr 18:19	2088
every one helped to destroy a	2Chr 20:23	7453
let us see one a in the face	2Chr 25:17	
and they saw one a in the face	2Chr 25:21	
a wall without, and repaired Millo	2Chr 32:5	312
until a commandment shall be	Ezr 4:21	
end to a with their uncleanness	Ezr 9:11	
a piece over against the going up	Neh 3:19	8145
of Urijah the son of Koz a piece	Neh 3:21	8145
Binnui the son of Henadad a piece	Neh 3:24	8145
the Tekoites repaired a piece	Neh 3:27	8145
the sixth son of Zalaph, a piece	Neh 3:30	8145
upon the wall, one far from a	Neh 4:19	250
a fourth part they confessed, and	Neh 9:3	
vessels being diverse one from a	Est 1:7	
unto a that is better than she	Est 1:19	7468
arise to the Jews from a place	Est 4:14	312
and of sending portions one to a	Est 9:19	7453
and of sending portions one to a	Est 9:22	7453
yet speaking, there came also a	Job 1:16	2088
yet speaking, there came also a	Job 1:17	2088
yet speaking, there came also a	Job 1:18	2088
or as one man mocketh a, do ye so	Job 13:9	
mine eyes shall behold, and not a	Job 19:27	2114
a dieth in the bitterness of his	Job 21:25	2088
Then let me sow, and let a eat	Job 31:8	312
Then let my wife grind unto a	Job 31:10	312
One is so near to a, that no air	Job 41:16	259
They are joined one to a, they	Job 41:17	250
that hasten after a god	Ps 16:4	312
putteth down one, and setteth up a	Ps 75:7	2088
they went from one nation to a	Ps 105:13	
from one kingdom to a people	Ps 105:13	312
and let a take his office	Ps 109:8	312
shall praise thy works to a	Ps 145:4	
and discover not a secret to a	Prov 25:9	312
Let a man praise thee, and not	Prov 27:2	2114
away, and a generation cometh	Eccl 1:4	
for he hath not a to help him up	Eccl 4:10	8145
man ruleth over a to his own hurt	Eccl 8:9	
thy beloved more than a beloved	Song 5:9	
thy beloved more than a beloved	Song 5:9	
be oppressed, every one by a	Is 3:5	
And one cried unto a, and said,	Is 6:3	2088
they shall be amazed one at a	Is 13:8	7453
a tongue will he speak to this	Is 28:11	312
and my glory will I not give to a	Is 42:8	312
a shall call himself by the name	Is 44:5	2088
a shall subscribe with his hand	Is 44:5	2088
I will not give my glory unto a	Is 48:11	312
discovered thyself to a than me	Is 57:8	
and call his servants by a name	Is 65:15	312
shall not build, and a inhabit	Is 65:22	312
they shall not plant, and a eat	Is 65:22	312
pass, that from one new moon to a	Is 66:23	
a, and from one sabbath to a	Is 66:23	
go from him, and become a man's	Jer 3:1	312
And I will dash them one against a	Jer 13:14	250
so he made it again a vessel	Jer 18:4	312
come from a place be forsaken	Jer 18:14	2114
into a country, where ye were not	Jer 22:26	312
north, far and near, one with a	Jer 25:26	250
Take thee again a roll, and write	Jer 36:28	312
Then took Jeremiah a roll	Jer 36:32	312
to fall, yea, one fell upon a	Jer 46:16	7453
One post shall run to meet a	Jer 51:31	
and one messenger to meet a	Jer 51:31	
after that in a year shall come a	Jer 51:46	
Their wings were joined one to a	Eze 1:9	269
of every one were joined one to a	Eze 1:11	376
creatures that touched one a	Eze 3:13	269
not turn thee from one side to a	Eze 4:8	
water, and be astonied one with a	Eze 4:17	250
a wheel by a cherub	Eze 10:9	259
and a wheel by a cherub	Eze 10:9	259
place to a place in their sight	Eze 12:3	312
fire, and a fire shall devour them	Eze 15:7	
There was also a great eagle with	Eze 17:7	259
then she took a of her whelps	Eze 19:5	259
a hath lewdly defiled his	Eze 22:11	376
a in thee hath humbled his sister	Eze 22:11	376
iniquities, and mourn one toward a	Eze 24:23	250
of the houses, and speak one to a	Eze 33:30	259
then take a stick, and write upon	Eze 37:16	259
join them one to a into one stick	Eze 37:17	259
little chamber to the roof of a	Eze 40:13	
a on that side, upon the posts	Eze 40:26	259
on this side, and a on that side	Eze 40:49	259
chambers were three, one over a	Eze 41:6	
north, and a door toward the south	Eze 41:11	259
inherit it, one as well as a	Eze 47:14	250
after thee shall arise a kingdom	Dan 2:39	317
a third kingdom of brass, which	Dan 2:39	317
they shall not cleave one to a	Dan 2:43	1836
and his knees smote one against a	Dan 5:6	1668
thyself, and give thy rewards to a	Dan 5:17	321
from the sea, diverse one from a	Dan 7:3	1668
And behold a beast, a second, like	Dan 7:5	317
After this I beheld, and lo a	Dan 7:6	317
came up among them a little horn	Dan 7:8	317
and a shall rise after them	Dan 7:24	312
a saint said unto that certain	Dan 8:13	259
and thou shalt not be for a man	Hos 3:3	
let no man strive, nor reprove a	Hos 4:4	376
and their children a generation	Joel 1:3	312
Neither shall one thrust a	Joel 2:8	250
caused it not to rain upon a city	Amos 4:7	259
one against a in the broad ways	Nah 2:4	8264
a angel went out to meet him,	Zec 2:3	312
of one city shall go to a	Zec 8:21	259
rest eat every one the flesh of a	Zec 11:9	7468
the LORD spake often one to a	Mal 3:16	7453
into their own country a way	Mt 2:12	243
and to a, Come, and he cometh	Mt 8:9	243
a of his disciples said unto him,	Mt 8:21	2087
you in this city, flee ye into a	Mt 10:23	243
should come, or do we look for a	Mt 11:3	2087
A parable put he forth unto them,	Mt 13:24	243
A parable put he forth unto them,	Mt 13:31	243
A parable spake he unto them	Mt 13:33	243
for fornication, and shall marry a	Mt 19:9	243
Hear a parable	Mt 21:33	243
and killed a, and stoned a	Mt 21:35	3739
to his farm, a to his merchandise	Mt 22:5	
not be left here one stone upon a	Mt 24:2	
one a, and shall hate one a	Mt 24:10	240
to a two, and to a one	Mt 25:15	3739
he shall separate them one from a	Mt 25:32	240
a maid saw him, and said unto them	Mt 26:71	243
the right hand, and a on the left	Mt 27:38	1520
exceedingly, and said one to a	Mk 4:41	240
questioning one with a what the	Mk 9:10	1438
and have peace one with a	Mk 9:50	240
put away his wife, and marry a	Mk 10:11	243
her husband, and be married to a	Mk 10:12	243
again he sent unto them a servant	Mk 12:4	243
And again he sent a	Mk 12:5	243
not be left one stone upon a	Mk 13:2	
and a said, Is it I	Mk 14:19	243
I will build a made without hands	Mk 14:58	243
in a form unto two of them	Mk 16:12	2087
the shepherds said one to a	Lk 2:15	240
it came to pass also on a sabbath	Lk 6:6	2087
communed one with a what they	Lk 6:11	240
and to a, Come, and he cometh	Lk 7:8	243
or look we for a	Lk 7:19	243
or look we for a	Lk 7:20	243
marketplace, and calling one to a	Lk 7:32	240
afraid wondered, saying one to a	Lk 8:25	240
And they went to a village	Lk 9:56	2087
And he said unto a, Follow me	Lk 9:59	2087
a also said, Lord, I will follow	Lk 9:61	2087
that they trode one upon a	Lk 12:1	240
a said, I have bought five yoke	Lk 14:19	2087
a said, I have married a wife, and	Lk 14:20	2087
going to make war against a king	Lk 14:31	2087
Then said he to a, And how much	Lk 16:7	2087
faithful in that which is a man's	Lk 16:12	245
away his wife, and marrieth a	Lk 16:18	2087
a came, saying, Lord, behold,	Lk 19:20	2087
leave in thee one stone upon a	Lk 19:44	
And again he sent a servant	Lk 20:11	2087
not be left one stone upon a	Lk 21:6	
And after a little while a saw him	Lk 22:58	2087
hour after a confidently affirmed	Lk 22:59	243
are these that ye have one to a	Lk 24:17	240
And they said one to a, Did not	Lk 24:32	240
said the disciples one to a	Jn 4:33	240
true, One soweth, and a reapeth	Jn 4:37	243
a steppeth down before me	Jn 5:7	243
There is a that beareth witness	Jn 5:32	243
if a shall come in his own name,	Jn 5:43	243
which receive honour one of a	Jn 5:44	240
the disciples looked one on a	Jn 13:22	240
give unto you, That ye love one a	Jn 13:34	240
you, that ye also love one a	Jn 13:34	240
if ye have love one to a	Jn 13:35	240
and he shall give you a Comforter	Jn 14:16	243
commandment, That ye love one a	Jn 15:12	240
I command you, that ye love one a	Jn 15:17	240
Jesus, and so did a disciple	Jn 18:15	243
again a scripture saith, They	Jn 19:37	2087
a shall gird thee, and carry thee	Jn 21:18	243
and his bishoprick let a take	Acts 1:20	2087
and marvelled, saying one to a	Acts 2:7	240
and were in doubt, saying one to a	Acts 2:12	243
Till a king arose, which knew not	Acts 7:18	2087
why do ye wrong one to a	Acts 7:26	240
or come unto one of a nation	Acts 10:28	246
he departed, and went into a place	Acts 12:17	2087
he saith also in a psalm, Thou	Acts 13:35	2087
saying that there is a king	Acts 17:7	2087
cried one thing, and some a	Acts 19:32	243
let them implead one a	Acts 19:38	240
we had taken our leave one of a	Acts 21:6	240
And some cried one thing, some a	Acts 21:34	243
burned in their lust one toward a	Rom 1:27	240
for wherein thou judgest a	Rom 2:1	2087
accusing or else excusing one a	Rom 2:15	240
Thou therefore which teachest a	Rom 2:21	2087
liveth, she be married to a man	Rom 7:3	2087
though she be married to a man	Rom 7:3	2087
that ye should be married to a	Rom 7:4	2087
But I see a law in my members,	Rom 7:23	2087
unto honour, and a unto dishonour	Rom 9:21	3739
and every one members one of a	Rom 12:5	240
one to a with brotherly love	Rom 12:10	240
in honour preferring one a	Rom 12:10	240
Be of the same mind one toward a	Rom 12:16	240
man any thing, but to love one a	Rom 13:8	240
for he that loveth a hath	Rom 13:8	2087
a, who is weak, eateth herbs	Rom 14:2	3739
thou that judgest a man's servant	Rom 14:4	245
One man esteemeth one day above a	Rom 14:5	
a esteemeth every day alike	Rom 14:5	3739
therefore judge one a any more	Rom 14:13	240
things wherewith one may edify a	Rom 14:19	240
a according to Christ Jesus	Rom 15:5	240
Wherefore receive ye one a	Rom 15:7	240
able also to admonish one a	Rom 15:14	240
build upon a man's foundation	Rom 15:20	245
Salute one a with an holy kiss	Rom 16:16	240
and a, I am of Apollos	1Cor 3:4	2087
foundation, and a buildeth thereon	1Cor 3:10	243
be puffed up for one against a	1Cor 4:6	2087
who maketh thee to differ from a	1Cor 4:7	
of you, having a matter against a	1Cor 6:1	2087
because ye go to law one with a	1Cor 6:7	1438
this manner, and a after that	1Cor 7:7	3588
judged of a man's conscience	1Cor 10:29	243
and one is hungry, and a is drunken	1Cor 11:21	3739
together to eat, tarry one for a	1Cor 11:33	240
to a the word of knowledge by the	1Cor 12:8	243
To a faith by the same Spirit	1Cor 12:9	2087
to a the gifts of healing by the	1Cor 12:9	243
To a the working of miracles	1Cor 12:10	243
to a prophecy	1Cor 12:10	243
to a discerning of spirits	1Cor 12:10	243
to a divers kinds of tongues	1Cor 12:10	2087
to a the interpretation of	1Cor 12:10	243
have the same care one for a	1Cor 12:25	240
be revealed to a that sitteth by	1Cor 14:30	243
a flesh of beasts, a of	1Cor 15:39	243
a of fishes, and a of birds	1Cor 15:39	243
the glory of the terrestrial is a	1Cor 15:40	2087
a glory of the moon, and a	1Cor 15:41	243
differeth from a star in glory	1Cor 15:41	
Greet ye one a with an holy kiss	1Cor 16:20	240
not to boast in a man's line of	2Cor 10:16	245
he that cometh preacheth a Jesus	2Cor 11:4	243
or if ye receive a spirit	2Cor 11:4	2087
or a gospel, which ye have not	2Cor 11:4	2087
Greet one a with an holy kiss	2Cor 13:12	240
the grace of Christ unto a gospel	Gal 1:6	2087
Which is not a	Gal 1:7	243
flesh, but by love serve one a	Gal 5:13	240
But if ye bite and devour one a	Gal 5:15	240
that ye be not consumed one of a	Gal 5:15	240
one a, envying one a	Gal 5:26	240
in himself alone, and not in a	Gal 6:4	2087
forbearing one a in love	Eph 4:2	240
for we are members one of a	Eph 4:25	240
And be ye kind one to a,	Eph 4:32	240
tenderhearted, forgiving one a	Eph 4:32	1438
one to a in the fear of God	Eph 5:21	240
Lie not one to a, seeing that ye	Col 3:9	240
one a, and forgiving one a	Col 3:13	1438
and admonishing one a in psalms	Col 3:16	1438
and abound in love one toward a	1Th 3:12	240
are taught of God to love one a	1Th 4:9	240
comfort one a with these words	1Th 4:18	240
together, and edify one a, even as	1Th 5:11	1520
without preferring one before a	1Ti 5:21	4299
and envy, hateful, and hating one a	Titus 3:3	240
But exhort one a daily, while it	Heb 3:13	1438
afterward have spoken of a day	Heb 4:8	243
As he saith also in a place	Heb 5:6	2087
further need was there that a	Heb 7:11	2087
are spoken pertaineth to a tribe	Heb 7:13	2087
there ariseth a priest,	Heb 7:15	2087
let us consider one a to provoke	Heb 10:24	240
but exhorting one a	Heb 10:25	

and had sent them out *a* way	Jas 2:25	2087
Speak not evil one of *a*, brethren	Jas 4:11	240
who art thou that judgest *a*	Jas 4:12	2087
Grudge not one against *a*,	Jas 5:9	240
one to *a*, and pray one for *a*	Jas 5:16	240
see that ye love one *a* with a	1Pet 1:22	240
mind, having compassion one of *a*	1Pet 3:8	4835
one to *a* without grudging	1Pet 4:9	240
so minister the same one to *a*	1Pet 4:10	1438
all of you be subject one to *a*	1Pet 5:5	240
Greet ye one *a* with a kiss of	1Pet 5:14	240
we have fellowship one with *a*	1Jn 1:7	240
that we should love one *a*	1Jn 3:11	240
Son Jesus Christ, and love one *a*	1Jn 3:23	240
Beloved, let us love one *a*	1Jn 4:7	240
us, we ought also to love one *a*	1Jn 4:11	240
If we love one *a*, God dwelleth in	1Jn 4:12	240
the beginning, that we love one *a*	2Jn 5	240
there went out *a* horse that was	Rev 6:4	243
and that they should kill one *a*	Rev 6:4	240
I saw *a* angel ascending from the	Rev 7:2	243
a angel came and stood at the	Rev 8:3	243
I saw *a* mighty angel come down	Rev 10:1	243
and shall send gifts one to *a*	Rev 11:10	240
there appeared *a* wonder in heaven	Rev 12:3	243
I beheld *a* beast coming up out of	Rev 13:11	243
I saw *a* angel fly in the midst of	Rev 14:6	243
And there followed *a* angel	Rev 14:8	243
a angel came out of the temple,	Rev 14:15	243
a angel came out of the temple	Rev 14:17	243
a angel came out from the altar,	Rev 14:18	243
I saw *a* sign in heaven, great and	Rev 15:1	243
I heard *a* out of the altar say,	Rev 16:7	243
after these things I saw *a* angel	Rev 18:1	243
I heard *a* voice from heaven,	Rev 18:4	243
a book was opened, which is the	Rev 20:12	243

ANOTHER'S

may not understand one *a* speech	Gen 11:7	7453
And if one man's ox hurt *a*	Ex 21:35	7453
ye also ought to wash one *a* feet	Jn 13:14	240
his own, but every man *a* wealth	1Cor 10:24	2087
Bear ye one *a* burdens, and so	Gal 6:2	240

ANSWER

a for me in time to come, when it	Gen 30:33	6030
shall give Pharaoh an *a* of peace	Gen 41:16	6030
And his brethren could not *a* him	Gen 45:3	6030
be, if it make thee *a* of peace	Deut 20:11	6030
And they shall *a* and say, Our hands	Deut 21:7	6030
and spit in his face, and shall *a*	Deut 25:9	6030
And all the people shall *a*	Deut 27:15	6030
Then ye shall *a* them, That the	Josh 4:7	559
yea, she returned *a* to herself	Judg 5:29	559
then he would *a* him, Nay	1Sa 2:16	559
what if thy father *a* thee roughly	1Sa 20:10	6030
he could not *a* Abner a word again	2Sa 3:11	7725
see what *a* I shall return to him	2Sa 24:13	1697
And they shall *a*, Because they	1Kin 9:9	559
advise that I may *a* this people	1Kin 12:6	1697
a them, and speak good words to	1Kin 12:7	6030
give ye that we may *a* this people	1Kin 12:9	1697
was neither voice, nor any to *a*	1Kin 18:29	6030
any salute thee, *a* him not again	2Kin 4:29	6030
was, saying, *A* him not	2Kin 18:36	6030
ye me to return *a* to this people	2Chr 10:6	1697
we may return *a* to this people	2Chr 10:9	1697
Thus shalt thou *a* the people that	2Chr 10:10	559
Then sent the king an *a* unto	Ezr 4:17	6600
then they returned *a* by letter	Ezr 5:5	8421
And thus they returned us *a*	Ezr 5:11	6600
peace, and found nothing to *a*	Neh 5:8	1696
Mordecai commanded to *a* Esther	Est 4:13	7725
bade them return Mordecai this *a*	Est 4:15	
if there be any that will *a* thee	Job 5:1	6030
he cannot *a* him one of a thousand	Job 9:3	6030
How much less shall I *a* him	Job 9:14	6030
were righteous, yet would I not *a*	Job 9:15	6030
man, as I am, that I should *a* him	Job 9:32	6030
Then call thou, and I will *a*	Job 13:22	6030
or let me speak, and *a* thou me	Job 13:22	7725
Thou shalt call, and I will *a* thee	Job 14:15	6030
my servant, and he gave me no *a*	Job 19:16	6030
do my thoughts cause me to *a*	Job 20:2	7725
my understanding causeth me to *a*	Job 20:3	6030
the words which he would *a* me	Job 23:5	6030
he visiteth, what shall I *a* him	Job 31:14	7725
is, that the Almighty would *a* me	Job 31:35	6030
these three men ceased to *a* Job	Job 32:1	6030
because they had found no *a*	Job 32:3	4617
Elihu saw that there was no *a* in	Job 32:5	4617
neither will I *a* him with your	Job 32:14	7725
I will *a* also my part, I also	Job 32:17	6030
I will open my lips and *a*	Job 32:20	6030
If thou canst *a* me, set thy words	Job 33:5	7725
I will *a* thee, that God is	Job 33:12	6030
thou hast any thing to say, *a* me	Job 33:32	7725
I will *a* thee, and thy companions	Job 35:4	4405
There they cry, but none giveth *a*	Job 35:12	6030
will demand of thee, and *a* thou me	Job 38:3	3045
that reproveth God, let him *a* it	Job 40:2	6030
what shall I *a* thee	Job 40:4	7725
but I will not *a*	Job 40:5	6030
have mercy also upon me, and *a* me	Ps 27:7	6030
in righteousness wilt thou *a* us	Ps 65:5	6030
for thou wilt *a* me	Ps 86:7	6030
call upon me, and I will *a* him	Ps 91:15	6030
the day when I call *a* me speedily	Ps 102:2	6030
save with thy right hand, and *a* me	Ps 108:6	6030
to *a* him that reproacheth me	Ps 119:42	6030
in thy faithfulness *a* me, and in	Ps 143:1	6030
call upon me, but I will not *a*	Prov 1:28	6030
A soft *a* turneth away wrath	Prov 15:1	4617
hath joy by the *a* of his mouth	Prov 15:23	4617
of the righteous studieth to *a*	Prov 15:28	6030
the *a* of the tongue, is from the	Prov 16:1	4617
that thou mightest *a* the words of	Prov 22:21	7725
his lips that giveth a right *a*	Prov 24:26	1697
A not a fool according to his	Prov 26:4	6030
A a fool according to his folly,	Prov 26:5	6030
that I may *a* him that reproacheth	Prov 27:11	1697
he understand he will not *a*	Prov 29:19	4617
I called him, but he gave me no *a*	Song 5:6	6030
What shall one then *a* the	Is 14:32	6030
he shall hear it, he will *a* thee	Is 30:19	6030
was, saying, *A* him not	Is 36:21	6030
I asked of them, could *a* a word	Is 41:28	7725
cry unto him, yet can he not *a*	Is 46:7	6030
I called, was there none to *a*	Is 50:2	6030
thou call, and the LORD shall *a*	Is 58:9	6030
when I called, ye did not *a*	Is 65:12	6030
that before they call, I will *a*	Is 65:24	6030
because when I called, none did *a*	Is 66:4	6030
then shalt thou *a* them, Like as	Jer 5:19	559
but they will not *a* thee	Jer 7:27	6030
Then they shall *a*, Because they	Jer 22:9	559
Call unto me, and I will *a* thee	Jer 33:3	6030
thing the LORD shall *a* you	Jer 42:4	6030
people which had given him that *a*	Jer 44:20	6030
I the LORD will *a* him that cometh	Eze 14:4	6030
I the LORD will *a* him by myself	Eze 14:7	6030
that thou shalt *a*, For the	Eze 21:7	559
careful to *a* thee in this matter	Dan 3:16	8421
Yea, the LORD will *a* and say unto	Joel 2:19	6030
for there is no *a* of God	Mic 3:7	4617
what I shall *a* when I am reproved	Hab 2:1	7725
beam out of the timber shall *a* it	Hab 2:11	6030
Then he shall *a*, Those with which	Zec 13:6	559
no man was able to *a* him a word	Mt 22:46	611
Then shall the righteous *a* him	Mt 25:37	611
And the King shall *a* and say unto	Mt 25:40	611
Then shall they also *a* him	Mt 25:44	611
Then shall he *a* them, saying,	Mt 25:45	611
a me, and I will tell you by what	Mk 11:29	611
a me	Mk 11:30	611
neither wist they what to *a* him	Mk 14:40	611
And he from within shall *a*	Lk 11:7	611
how or what thing ye shall *a*	Lk 12:11	626
and he shall *a* and say unto you, I	Lk 13:25	611
they could not *a* him again to	Lk 14:6	470
and *a* me	Lk 20:3	2036
and they marvelled at his *a*	Lk 20:26	612
meditate before what ye shall *a*	Lk 21:14	626
I also ask you, ye will not *a* me	Lk 22:68	611
that we may give an *a* to them	Jn 1:22	612
But Jesus gave him no *a*	Jn 19:9	612
the more cheerfully *a* for myself	Acts 24:10	626
have licence to *a* for himself	Acts 25:16	627
because I shall *a* for myself this	Acts 26:2	626
what saith the *a* of God unto him	Rom 11:4	5538
Mine *a* to them that do examine me	1Cor 9:3	627
that ye may have somewhat to *a*	2Cor 5:12	
know how ye ought to *a* every man	Col 4:6	611
At my first *a* no man stood with	2Ti 4:16	627
be ready always to give an *a* to	1Pet 3:15	627
but the *a* of a good conscience	1Pet 3:21	1906

ANSWERABLE

a to the hangings of the court	Ex 38:18	5980

ANSWERED

And Abraham *a* and said, Behold now,	Gen 18:27	6030
And the children of Heth *a* Abraham	Gen 23:5	6030
Ephron the Hittite *a* Abraham in	Gen 23:10	6030
Ephron *a* Abraham, saying unto him	Gen 23:14	6030
Then Laban and Bethuel *a* and said,	Gen 24:50	6030
And Isaac *a* and said unto Esau,	Gen 27:37	6030
And Isaac his father *a* and said	Gen 27:39	6030
And Rachel and Leah *a* and said unto	Gen 31:14	6030
And Jacob *a* and said to Laban,	Gen 31:31	6030
and Jacob *a* and said to Laban, What	Gen 31:36	6030
And Laban *a* and said unto Jacob,	Gen 31:43	6030
And the sons of Jacob *a* Shechem	Gen 34:13	6030
who *a* me in the day of my	Gen 35:3	6030
And Joseph *a* and said, This is the	Gen 40:18	6030
Joseph *a* Pharaoh, saying, It is	Gen 41:16	6030
And Reuben *a* them, saying, Spake I	Gen 42:22	6030
And they *a*, Thy servant our father	Gen 43:28	559
And Moses *a* and said, But, behold,	Ex 4:1	6030
And Miriam *a* them, Sing ye to the	Ex 15:21	6030
And all the people *a* together	Ex 19:8	6030
spake, and God *a* him by a voice	Ex 19:19	6030
all the people *a* with one voice	Ex 24:3	6030
of Moses, one of his young men, *a*	Num 11:28	6030
And Balaam *a* and said unto the	Num 22:18	6030
And he *a* and said, Must I not take	Num 23:12	6030
But Balaam *a* and said unto Balak,	Num 23:26	6030
Gad and the children of Reuben *a*	Num 32:31	6030
And ye *a* me, and said, The thing	Deut 1:14	6030
Then ye *a* and said unto me, We	Deut 1:41	6030
they *a* Joshua, saying, All that	Josh 1:16	6030
And the men *a* her, Our life for	Josh 2:14	559
Achan *a* Joshua, and said, Indeed I	Josh 7:20	6030
they *a* Joshua, and said, Because	Josh 9:24	6030
Who *a*, Give me a blessing	Josh 15:19	559
And Joshua *a* them, If thou be a	Josh 17:15	559
and the half tribe of Manasseh *a*	Josh 22:21	6030
And the people *a* and said, God	Josh 24:16	6030
Her wise ladies *a* her, yea, she	Judg 5:29	6030
And his fellow *a* and said, This is	Judg 7:14	6030
the men of Penuel *a* him as the	Judg 8:8	6030
as the men of Succoth had *a* him	Judg 8:8	6030
And they *a*, As thou art, so were	Judg 8:18	559
And they *a*, We will willingly give	Judg 8:25	559
king of the children of Ammon *a*	Judg 11:13	559
And they *a*, Samson, the son in law	Judg 15:6	559
And they *a*, To bind Samson are we	Judg 15:10	559
Then *a* the five men that went to	Judg 18:14	6030
But none *a*	Judg 19:28	6030
of the woman that was slain, *a*	Judg 20:4	6030
And they *a* him, The LORD bless	Ruth 2:4	559
that was set over the reapers *a*	Ruth 2:6	6030
And Boaz *a* and said unto her, It	Ruth 2:11	6030
And she *a*, I am Ruth thine	Ruth 3:9	559
And Hannah *a* and said, No, my lord,	1Sa 1:15	6030
Then Eli *a* and said, Go in peace	1Sa 1:17	6030
and he *a*, Here am I	1Sa 3:4	559
And he *a*, I called not, my son	1Sa 3:6	559
Then Samuel *a*, Speak	1Sa 3:10	559
And he *a*, Here am I	1Sa 3:16	559
And the messenger *a* and said,	1Sa 4:17	6030
But she *a* not, neither did she	1Sa 4:20	6030
And they *a*, Let the ark of the God	1Sa 5:8	559
They *a*, Five golden emerods, and	1Sa 6:4	559
And the servant *a* Saul again	1Sa 9:8	6030
And they *a* them, and said, He is	1Sa 9:12	6030
And Samuel *a* Saul, and said, I am	1Sa 9:19	6030
And Saul *a* and said, Am not I a	1Sa 9:21	6030
And one of the same place *a*	1Sa 10:12	6030
And the LORD *a*, Behold, he hath	1Sa 10:22	559
And Nahash the Ammonite *a* them	1Sa 11:2	559
And they *a*, He is witness	1Sa 12:5	559
men of the garrison *a* Jonathan	1Sa 14:12	6030
Then *a* one of the people, and said	1Sa 14:28	6030
But he *a* him not that day	1Sa 14:37	6030
among all the people that *a* him	1Sa 14:39	6030
And Saul *a*, God do so and more also	1Sa 14:44	559
Then *a* one of the servants, and	1Sa 16:18	6030
the people *a* him after this	1Sa 17:27	559
the people *a* him again after the	1Sa 17:30	1697
And David *a*, I am the son of thy	1Sa 17:58	559
the women *a* one another as they	1Sa 18:7	6030
And Michal *a* Saul, He said unto me	1Sa 19:17	559
And Jonathan *a* Saul, David	1Sa 20:28	6030
Jonathan *a* Saul his father, and	1Sa 20:32	6030
And the priest *a* David, and said,	1Sa 21:4	6030
David *a* the priest, and said unto	1Sa 21:5	6030
Then *a* Doeg the Edomite, which	1Sa 22:9	6030
And he *a*, Here I am, my lord	1Sa 22:12	559
Then Ahimelech *a* the king	1Sa 22:14	6030
And the LORD *a* him and said, Arise,	1Sa 23:4	6030
Nabal *a* David's servants, and said	1Sa 25:10	6030
Then *a* David and said to Ahimelech	1Sa 26:6	6030
Then Abner *a* and said, Who art	1Sa 26:14	6030
And David *a* and said, Behold the	1Sa 26:22	6030
of the LORD, the LORD *a* him not	1Sa 28:6	6030
And Saul *a*, I am sore distressed	1Sa 28:15	6030
And Achish *a* and said to David, I	1Sa 29:9	6030
And he *a* him, Pursue	1Sa 30:8	559
Then *a* all the wicked men and men	1Sa 30:22	6030
And he *a*, That the people are fled	2Sa 1:4	559
And I *a*, Here am I	2Sa 1:7	559
I *a* him, I am an Amalekite	2Sa 1:8	559
And he *a*, I am the son of a	2Sa 1:13	559
And he *a*, I am	2Sa 2:20	559
David *a* Rechab and Baanah his	2Sa 4:9	6030
And he *a*, Behold thy servant	2Sa 9:6	559
And she *a* him, Nay, my brother, do	2Sa 13:12	559
son of Shimeah David's brother, *a*	2Sa 13:32	6030
And she *a*, I am indeed a widow	2Sa 14:5	559
Then the king *a* and said unto the	2Sa 14:18	6030
And the woman *a* and said, As thy	2Sa 14:19	6030
And Absalom *a* Joab, Behold, I sent	2Sa 14:32	559
Ittai *a* the king, and said, As the	2Sa 15:21	6030
But the people *a*, Thou shalt not	2Sa 18:3	559
And Ahimaaz *a*, When Joab sent the	2Sa 18:29	559
And Cushi *a*, The enemies of my	2Sa 18:32	559
But Abishai the son of Zeruiah *a*	2Sa 19:21	6030
And he *a*, My lord, O king, my	2Sa 19:26	559
And the king *a*, Chimham shall go	2Sa 19:38	559
men of Judah *a* the men of Israel	2Sa 19:42	6030
men of Israel *a* the men of Judah	2Sa 19:43	6030
And he *a*, I am he	2Sa 20:17	559
And he *a*, I do hear	2Sa 20:17	559
And Joab *a* and said, Far be it, far	2Sa 20:20	6030
And the LORD *a*, It is for Saul, and	2Sa 21:1	559
they *a* the king, The man that	2Sa 21:5	559
unto the LORD, but he *a* them not	2Sa 22:42	6030
Then king David *a* and said, Call	1Kin 1:28	6030
the son of Jehoiada *a* the king	1Kin 1:36	6030
And Jonathan *a* and said to Adonijah	1Kin 1:43	6030
And king Solomon *a* and said unto	1Kin 2:22	6030
Thus said Joab, and thus he *a* me	1Kin 2:30	6030
Then the king *a* and said, Give her	1Kin 3:27	6030
And he *a*, Nothing	1Kin 11:22	559
the king *a* the people roughly, and	1Kin 12:13	6030
unto them, the people *a* the king	1Kin 12:16	1697
And the king *a* and said unto the	1Kin 13:6	6030
And he *a* him, I am	1Kin 18:8	559
And he *a*, I have not troubled	1Kin 18:18	559
the people *a* him not a word	1Kin 18:21	6030
And all the people *a* and said, It	1Kin 18:24	6030
was no voice, nor any that *a*	1Kin 18:26	6030
And the king of Israel *a* and said,	1Kin 20:4	6030
And the king of Israel *a* and said,	1Kin 20:11	6030
And he *a*, Thou	1Kin 20:14	559
and he *a*, I will not give thee my	1Kin 21:6	559
And he *a*, I have found thee	1Kin 21:20	559
And he *a* him, Go, and prosper	1Kin 22:15	559
And they *a* him, He was an hairy	2Kin 1:8	559
And Elijah *a* and said to the	2Kin 1:10	6030
And he *a* and said unto him, O man	2Kin 1:11	6030
And Elijah *a* and said unto them, If	2Kin 1:12	6030
And he *a*, Yea, I know it	2Kin 2:5	559
And he *a*, The way through the	2Kin 3:8	559
the king of Israel's servants *a*	2Kin 3:11	6030
And she *a*, I dwell among mine own	2Kin 4:13	559
And Gehazi *a*, Verily she hath no	2Kin 4:14	559
And she *a*, It is well	2Kin 4:26	559
And he *a*, Go ye	2Kin 6:2	559
And he *a*, I will go	2Kin 6:3	559
And he *a*, Fear not	2Kin 6:16	559
And he *a*, Thou shalt not smite	2Kin 6:22	559
And she *a*, This woman said unto me	2Kin 6:28	559

the king leaned *a* the man of God 2Kin 7:2 6030
And one of his servants *a* and said, 2Kin 7:13 6030
that lord *a* the man of God, and 2Kin 7:19 6030
And he *a*, Because I know the evil 2Kin 8:12 559
And Elisha *a*, The LORD hath shewed 2Kin 8:13 559
And he *a*, He told me that thou 2Kin 8:14 559
And Jehu *a*, What hast thou to do 2Kin 9:19 559
And he *a*, What peace, so long as 2Kin 9:22 559
And they *a*, We are the brethren of 2Kin 10:13 559
And Jehonadab *a*, It is 2Kin 10:15 559
their peace, and *a* him not a word 2Kin 18:36 6030
And Hezekiah *a*, It is a light 2Kin 20:10 559
And Hezekiah *a*, All the things 2Kin 20:15 559
David went out to meet them, and *a* 1Chr 12:17 6030
And Joab *a*, The LORD make his 1Chr 21:3 559
he *a* him from heaven by fire upon 1Chr 21:26 6030
David saw that the LORD had *a* him 1Chr 21:28 6030
the king of Tyre *a* in writing 2Chr 2:11 559
And it shall be *a*, Because they 2Chr 7:22 559
And the king *a* them roughly 2Chr 10:13 6030
a them after the advice of the 2Chr 10:14 1697
unto them, the people *a* the king 2Chr 10:16 7725
he *a* him, I am as thou art, and my 2Chr 18:3 559
And the man of God *a*, The LORD is 2Chr 25:9 559
Then Hezekiah *a* and said, Now ye 2Chr 29:31 6030
of the house of Zadok *a* him 2Chr 31:10 559
And Hilkiah *a* and said to Shaphan 2Chr 34:15 6030
she *a* them, Thus saith the LORD 2Chr 34:23 559
one of the sons of Elam, *a* Ezr 10:2 6030
Then all the congregation *a* Ezr 10:12 6030
Then *a* I them, and said unto them, Neh 2:20 1697
I *a* them after the same manner Neh 6:4 7725
And all the people *a*, Amen, Amen, Neh 8:6 6030
Memucan *a* before the king and the Est 1:16 559
And Esther *a*, If it seem good unto Est 5:4 559
Then *a* Esther, and said, My Est 5:7 6039
Haman *a* the king, For the man Est 6:7 559
Then Esther the queen *a* and said, Est 7:3 6030
Then the king Ahasuerus *a* Est 7:5 559
Then Satan *a* the LORD, and said, Job 1:7 6030
Then Satan *a* the LORD, and said, Job 1:9 6030
Satan *a* the LORD, and said, From Job 2:2 6030
Satan *a* the LORD, and said, Skin Job 2:4 6030
Then Eliphaz the Temanite *a* Job 4:1 6030
But Job *a* and said, Job 6:1 6030
Then *a* Bildad the Shuhite, and Job 8:1 6030
Then Job *a* and said, Job 9:1 6030
If I had called, and he had *a* me Job 9:16 6030
Then *a* Zophar the Naamathite, and Job 11:1 6030
not the multitude of words be *a* Job 11:2 6030
And Job *a* and said, Job 12:1 6030
Then *a* Eliphaz the Temanite, and Job 15:1 6030
Then Job *a* and said, Job 16:1 6030
Then *a* Bildad the Shuhite, and Job 18:1 6030
Then Job *a* and said, Job 19:1 6030
Then *a* Zophar the Naamathite, and Job 20:1 6030
But Job *a* and said, Job 21:1 6030
Then Eliphaz the Temanite *a* Job 22:1 6030
Then Job *a* and said, Job 23:1 6030
Then *a* Bildad the Shuhite, and Job 25:1 6030
But Job *a* and said, Job 26:1 6030
the son of Barachel the Buzite *a* Job 32:6 6030
Job, or that *a* his words Job 32:12 6030
They were amazed, they *a* no more Job 32:15 6030
but stood still, and *a* no more Job 32:16 6030
Furthermore Elihu *a* and said, Job 34:1 6030
Then the LORD *a* Job out of the Job 38:1 6030
Moreover the LORD *a* Job, and said, Job 40:1 6030
Then Job *a* the LORD, and said, Job 40:3 6030
Then *a* the LORD unto Job out of Job 40:6 6030
Then Job *a* the LORD, and said, Job 42:1 6030
unto the LORD, but he *a* them not Ps 18:41 6030
I *a* thee in the secret place of Ps 81:7 6030
upon the LORD, and he *a* them Ps 99:6 6030
the LORD *a* me, and set me in a Ps 118:5 6030
And he *a*, Until the cities be Is 6:11 559
And he *a* and said, Babylon is Is 21:9 6030
their peace, and *a* him not a word Is 36:21 6030
And Hezekiah *a*, All that is in Is 39:4 559
and I called you, but ye *a* not Jer 7:13 6030
Then *a* I, and said, So be it, O Jer 11:5 6030
his brother, What hath the LORD *a* Jer 23:35 6030
What hath the LORD *a* thee Jer 23:37 6030
unto them, but they have not *a* Jer 35:17 6030
Then Baruch *a* them, He pronounced Jer 36:18 559
in Pathros, *a* Jeremiah, saying, Jer 44:15 6030
Then I *a* them, The word of the Eze 24:20 559
And I *a*, O Lord GOD, thou knowest Eze 37:3 559
The king *a* and said to the Dan 2:5 6032
They *a* again and said, Let the Dan 2:7 6032
The king *a* and said, I know of Dan 2:8 6032
The Chaldeans *a* before the king, Dan 2:10 6032
Then Daniel *a* with counsel and Dan 2:14 8421
He *a* and said to Arioch the king's Dan 2:15 6032
Daniel *a* and said, Blessed be the Dan 2:20 6032
The king *a* and said to Daniel, Dan 2:26 6032
Daniel *a* in the presence of the Dan 2:27 6032
The king *a* unto Daniel, and said, Dan 2:47 6032
Meshach, and Abed-nego, *a* Dan 3:16 6032
They *a* and said unto the king, Dan 3:24 6032
He *a* and said, Lo, I see four men Dan 3:25 6032
Belteshazzar *a* and said, My lord, Dan 4:19 6032
Then Daniel *a* and said before the Dan 5:17 6032
The king *a* and said, The thing is Dan 6:12 6032
Then *a* they and said before the Dan 6:13 6032
Then *a* Amos, and said to Amaziah, Amos 7:14 6030
what Balaam the son of Beor *a* him Mic 6:5 6030
And the LORD *a* me, and said, Write Hab 2:2 6030
And the priests *a* and said, No Hag 2:12 6030
And the priests *a* and said, It Hag 2:13 6030
Then *a* Haggai, and said, So is Hag 2:14 6030
stood among the myrtle trees *a* Zec 1:10 6030
they *a* the angel of the LORD that Zec 1:11 6030
Then the angel of the LORD *a* Zec 1:12 6030
the LORD *a* the angel that talked Zec 1:13 6030
And he *a* me, These are the horns Zec 1:19 559
And he *a* and spake unto those that Zec 3:4 6030
So I *a* and spake to the angel that Zec 4:4 6030
the angel that talked with me *a* Zec 4:5 6030
Then he *a* and spake unto me, Zec 4:6 6030
Then *a* I, and said unto him, What Zec 4:11 6030
I *a* again, and said unto him, What Zec 4:12 6030
And he *a* me and said, Knowest thou Zec 4:13 559
And I *a*, I see a flying roll Zec 5:2 559
Then I *a* and said unto the angel Zec 6:4 6030
And the angel *a* and said unto me, Zec 6:5 6030
But he *a* and said, It is written, Mt 4:4 611
The centurion *a* and said, Lord, I Mt 8:8 611
Jesus *a* and said unto them, Go and Mt 11:4 611
At that time Jesus *a* and said, I Mt 11:25 611
the scribes and of the Pharisees *a* Mt 12:38 611
But he *a* and said unto them, An Mt 12:39 611
But he *a* and said unto him that Mt 12:48 611
He *a* and said unto them, Because Mt 13:11 611
He *a* and said unto them, He that Mt 13:37 611
And Peter *a* him and said, Lord, if Mt 14:28 611
But he *a* and said unto them, Why Mt 15:3 611
But he *a* and said, Every plant, Mt 15:13 611
Then *a* Peter and said unto him, Mt 15:15 611
But he *a* her not a word Mt 15:23 611
But he *a* and said, I am not sent Mt 15:24 611
But he *a* and said, It is not meet Mt 15:26 611
Then Jesus *a* and said unto her, O Mt 15:28 611
He *a* and said unto them, When it Mt 16:2 611
And Simon Peter *a* and said, Thou Mt 16:16 611
And Jesus *a* and said unto him, Mt 16:17 611
Then *a* Peter, and said unto Jesus, Mt 17:4 611
And Jesus *a* and said unto them, Mt 17:11 611
Then Jesus *a* and said, O faithless Mt 17:17 611
And he *a* and said unto them, Have Mt 19:4 611
Then *a* Peter and said unto him, Mt 19:27 611
But he *a* one of them, and said, Mt 20:13 611
But Jesus *a* and said, Ye know not Mt 20:22 611
Jesus *a* and said unto them, Verily Mt 21:21 611
And Jesus *a* and said unto them, I Mt 21:24 611
they *a* Jesus, and said, We cannot Mt 21:27 611
He *a* and said, I will not Mt 21:29 611
And he *a* and said, I go sir Mt 21:30 611
And Jesus *a* and spake unto them Mt 22:1 611
Jesus *a* and said unto them, Ye do Mt 22:29 611
And Jesus *a* and said unto them, Mt 24:4 611
But the wise *a*, saying, Not so Mt 25:9 611
But he *a* and said, Verily I say Mt 25:12 611
His lord *a* and said unto him, Thou Mt 25:26 611
And he *a* and said, He that dippeth Mt 26:23 611
Then Judas, which betrayed him, *a* Mt 26:25 611
Peter *a* and said unto him, Though Mt 26:33 611
And the high priest *a* and said unto Mt 26:63 611
They *a* and said, He is guilty of Mt 26:66 611
priests and elders, he *a* nothing Mt 27:12 611
And he *a* him to never a word Mt 27:14 611
The governor *a* and said unto them, Mt 27:21 611
Then *a* all the people, and said, Mt 27:25 611
And the angel *a* and said unto the Mt 28:5 611
he *a* them, saying, Who is my Mk 3:33 611
And he *a*, saying, My name is Mk 5:9 611
He *a* and said unto them, Give ye Mk 6:37 611
He *a* and said unto them, Well hath Mk 7:6 611
And she *a* and said unto him, Yes, Mk 7:28 611
And his disciples *a* him, From Mk 8:4 611
And they *a*, John the Baptist Mk 8:28 611
And Peter *a* and said to Jesus, Mk 9:5 611
And he *a* and told them, Elias Mk 9:12 611
And one of the multitude *a* Mk 9:17 611
And John *a* him, saying, Master, we Mk 9:38 611
And he *a* and said unto them, What Mk 10:3 611
And Jesus *a* and said unto them, For Mk 10:5 611
And he *a* and said unto him, Master, Mk 10:20 611
And Jesus *a* and said, Verily I say Mk 10:29 611
And Jesus *a* and said unto him, What Mk 10:51 611
And Jesus *a* and said unto it, No Mk 11:14 611
And Jesus *a* and said unto them, I Mk 11:29 611
And they *a* and said unto Jesus, We Mk 11:33 611
that he had *a* them well, asked Mk 12:28 611
And Jesus *a* him, The first of all Mk 12:29 611
Jesus saw that he *a* discreetly Mk 12:34 611
And Jesus *a* and said, while he Mk 12:35 611
And he *a* and said unto them, It is Mk 14:20 611
And Jesus *a* and said unto them, Are Mk 14:48 611
he held his peace, and *a* nothing Mk 14:61 611
but he *a* nothing Mk 15:3 611
But Jesus yet *a* nothing Mk 15:5 611
But Pilate *a* them, saying, Will Mk 15:9 611
And Pilate *a* and said again unto Mk 15:12 611
And the angel *a* and said unto her, Lk 1:35 611
And his mother *a* and said, Not so Lk 1:60 611
John *a*, saying unto them all, I Lk 3:16 611
And Jesus *a* him, saying, It is Lk 4:4 611
And Jesus *a* and said unto him, Get Lk 4:8 611
Simon *a* and said, I suppose that Lk 7:43 611
And he *a* and said unto them, My Lk 8:21 611
he *a* him, saying, Fear not Lk 8:50 611
And John *a* and said, Master, we saw Lk 9:49 611
said unto him, Thou hast *a* right Lk 10:28 611
And Jesus *a* and said unto her, Lk 10:41 611
Then *a* one of the lawyers, and Lk 11:45 611
the synagogue *a* with indignation Lk 13:14 611
The Lord then *a* him, and said, Lk 13:15 611
a them, saying, Which of you Lk 14:5 611
he *a* them and said, The kingdom of Lk 17:20 611
And they *a* and said unto him, Where Lk 17:37 611
And he *a* and said unto them, I tell Lk 19:40 611
And he *a* and said unto them, I will Lk 20:3 611
And they *a*, that they could not Lk 20:7 611
They *a* and said, Caesar's Lk 20:24 611
And Jesus *a* and said, Suffer ye Lk 22:51 611
he *a* him and said, Thou sayest it Lk 23:3 611
but he *a* him nothing Lk 23:9 611
And he *a*, No Jn 1:21 611
John *a* them, saying, I baptize Jn 1:26 611
Jesus *a* and said unto him, Before Jn 1:48 611
Nathanael *a* and saith unto him, Jn 1:49 611
Jesus *a* and said unto him, Because Jn 1:50 611
Then *a* the Jews and said unto him, Jn 2:18 611
Jesus *a* and said unto them, Jn 2:19 611
Jesus *a* and said unto him, Verily, Jn 3:3 611
Jesus *a*, Verily, verily, I say Jn 3:5 611
Nicodemus *a* and said unto him, How Jn 3:9 611
Jesus *a* and said unto him, Art Jn 3:10 611
John *a* and said, A man can receive Jn 3:27 611
Jesus *a* and said unto her, If thou Jn 4:10 611
Jesus *a* and said unto her, Jn 4:13 611
The woman *a* and said, I have no Jn 4:17 611
The impotent man *a* him, Sir, I Jn 5:7 611
He *a* them, He that made me whole, Jn 5:11 611
But Jesus *a* them, My Father Jn 5:17 611
Then *a* Jesus and said unto them, Jn 5:19 611
Philip *a* him, Two hundred Jn 6:7 611
Jesus *a* them and said, Verily, Jn 6:26 611
Jesus *a* and said unto them, This Jn 6:29 611
Jesus therefore *a* and said unto Jn 6:43 611
Then Simon Peter *a* him, Lord, to Jn 6:68 611
Jesus *a* them, Have not I chosen Jn 6:70 611
Jesus *a* them, and said, My Jn 7:16 611
The people *a* and said, Thou hast a Jn 7:20 611
Jesus *a* and said unto them, I have Jn 7:21 611
The officers *a*, Never man spake Jn 7:46 611
Then *a* them the Pharisees, Are ye Jn 7:47 611
They *a* and said unto him, Art thou Jn 7:52 611
Jesus *a* and said unto them, Though Jn 8:14 611
Jesus *a*, Ye neither know me, nor Jn 8:19 611
They *a* him, We be Abraham's seed, Jn 8:33 611
Jesus *a* them, Verily, verily, I Jn 8:34 611
They *a* and said unto him, Abraham Jn 8:39 611
Then *a* the Jews, and said unto him Jn 8:48 611
Jesus *a*, I have not a devil Jn 8:49 611
Jesus *a*, If I honour myself, my Jn 8:54 611
Jesus *a*, Neither hath this man Jn 9:3 611
He *a* and said, A man that is Jn 9:11 611
His parents *a* them and said, We Jn 9:20 611
He *a* and said, Whether he be a Jn 9:25 611
He *a* them, I have told you Jn 9:27 611
The man *a* and said unto them, Why Jn 9:30 611
They *a* and said unto him, Thou Jn 9:34 611
He *a* and said, Who is he, Lord, Jn 9:36 611
Jesus *a* them, I told you, and ye Jn 10:25 611
Jesus *a* them, Many good works Jn 10:32 611
The Jews *a* him, saying, For a Jn 10:33 611
Jesus *a* them, Is it not written Jn 10:34 611
Jesus *a*, Are there not twelve Jn 11:9 611
And Jesus *a* them, saying, The hour Jn 12:23 611
Jesus *a* and said, This voice came Jn 12:30 611
The people *a* him, We have heard Jn 12:34 611
Jesus *a* and said unto him, What I Jn 13:7 611
Jesus *a* him, If I wash thee not, Jn 13:8 611
Jesus *a*, He it is, to whom I Jn 13:26 611
Jesus *a* him, Whither I go, thou Jn 13:36 611
Jesus *a* him, Wilt thou lay down Jn 13:38 611
Jesus *a* and said unto him, If a Jn 14:23 611
Jesus *a* them, Do ye now believe Jn 16:31 611
They *a* him, Jesus of Nazareth Jn 18:5 611
Jesus *a*, I have told you that I Jn 18:8 611
Jesus *a* him, I spake openly to Jn 18:20 611
Jesus *a* him, If I have spoken Jn 18:23 611
They *a* and said unto him, If he Jn 18:30 611
Jesus *a* him, Sayest thou this Jn 18:34 611
Pilate *a*, Am I a Jew Jn 18:35 611
Jesus *a*, My kingdom is not of Jn 18:36 611
Jesus *a*, Thou sayest that I am a Jn 18:37 611
The Jews *a* him, We have a law, and Jn 19:7 611
Jesus *a*, Thou couldest have no Jn 19:11 611
The chief priests *a*, We have no Jn 19:15 611
Pilate *a*, What I have written I Jn 19:22 611
And Thomas *a* and said unto him, My Jn 20:28 611
They *a* him, No Jn 21:5 611
he *a* unto the people, Ye men of Acts 3:12 611
But Peter and John *a* and said unto Acts 4:19 611
Peter *a* unto her, Tell me whether Acts 5:8 611
Peter and the other apostles *a* Acts 5:29 611
Then *a* Simon, and said, Pray ye to Acts 8:24 611
And the eunuch *a* Philip, and said, Acts 8:34 611
And he *a* and said, I believe that Acts 8:37 611
Then Ananias *a*, Lord, I have Acts 9:13 611
Then *a* Peter, Acts 10:46 611
But the voice *a* me again from Acts 11:9 611
had held their peace, James *a* Acts 15:13 611
And the evil spirit *a* and said, Acts 19:15 611
Then Paul *a*, What mean ye to weep Acts 21:13 611
And I *a*, Who art thou, Lord Acts 22:8 611
And the chief captain *a*, With a Acts 22:28 611
had beckoned unto him to speak, *a* Acts 24:10 611
to come, Felix trembled, and *a* Acts 24:25 611
But Festus *a*, that Paul should be Acts 25:4 611
While he *a* for himself, Neither Acts 25:8 626
a Paul, and said, Wilt thou go up Acts 25:9 611
had conferred with the council, *a* Acts 25:12 611
To whom I *a*, It is not the manner Acts 25:16 611
forth the hand, and *a* for himself Acts 26:1 626
And one of the elders *a*, saying Rev 7:13 611

ANSWEREDST

Thou *a* them, O LORD our God Ps 99:8 6030
In the day when I cried thou *a* me Ps 138:3 6030

ANSWEREST

of Ner, saying, *A* thou not, Abner 1Sa 26:14 6030
what emboldeneth thee that thou *a* Job 16:3 6030
and said unto him, *A* thou nothing Mt 26:62 611
Jesus, saying, *A* thou nothing Mk 14:60 611
him again, saying, *A* thou nothing Mk 15:4 611
A thou the high priest so Jn 18:22 611

ANSWERETH
a me no more, neither by prophets 1Sa 28:15 6030
and the God that *a* by fire 1Kin 18:24 6030
who calleth upon God, and he *a* him ... Job 12:4 6030
He that *a* a matter before he Prov 18:13 7725
but the rich *a* roughly Prov 18:23 6030
As in water face *a* to face Prov 27:19
because God *a* him in the joy of Eccl 5:20 6030
but money *a* all things Eccl 10:19 6030
And Peter *a* and saith unto him, Mk 8:29 *611*
He *a* him, and saith, O faithless Mk 9:19 *611*
But Jesus *a* again, and saith unto Mk 10:24 *611*
He *a* and saith unto them, He that Lk 3:11 *611*
a to Jerusalem which now is, and Gal 4:25 *4960*

ANSWERING
Jesus *a* said unto him, Suffer it Mt 3:15 *611*
Jesus *a* saith unto them, Have Mk 11:22 *611*
Jesus *a* saith unto them, Neither Mk 11:33 *611*
Jesus *a* said unto them, Render to Mk 12:17 *611*
Jesus *a* said unto them, Do ye not Mk 12:24 *611*
Jesus *a* said unto him, Seest thou Mk 13:2 *611*
Jesus *a* them began to say, Take Mk 13:5 *611*
he *a* said unto him, Thou sayest Mk 15:2 *611*
the angel *a* said unto him, I am Lk 1:19 *611*
Jesus *a* said unto him, It is said Lk 4:12 *611*
Simon *a* said unto him, Master, we Lk 5:5 *611*
he *a* said unto them, What reason Lk 5:22 *611*
Jesus *a* said unto them, They that Lk 5:31 *611*
Jesus *a* them said, Have ye not Lk 6:3 *611*
Then Jesus *a* said unto them, Go Lk 7:22 *611*
Jesus *a* said unto him, Simon, I Lk 7:40 *611*
They *a* said, John the Baptist Lk 9:19 *611*
Peter *a* said, The Christ of God Lk 9:20 *611*
And Jesus *a* said, O faithless and Lk 9:41 *611*
he *a* said, Thou shalt love the Lk 10:27 *611*
And Jesus *a* said, A certain man Lk 10:30 *5274*
Jesus *a* said unto them, Suppose Lk 13:2 *611*
he *a* said unto him, Lord, let it Lk 13:8 *611*
Jesus *a* spake unto the lawyers and Lk 14:3 *611*
he *a* said to his father, Lo, Lk 15:29 *611*
And Jesus *a* said, Were there not Lk 17:17 *611*
Jesus *a* said unto them, The Lk 20:34 *611*
certain of the scribes *a* said Lk 20:39 *611*
But the other *a* rebuked him Lk 23:40 *611*
a said unto him, Art thou only a Lk 24:18 *611*
not *a* again Titus 2:9 *488*

ANSWERS
seeing in your *a* there remaineth Job 21:34 8666
because of his *a* for wicked men Job 34:36 8666
at his understanding and *a* Lk 2:47 *612*

ANT
Go to the *a*, thou sluggard Prov 6:6 5244

ANTHOTHIJAH See ANTOTHIJAH.

ANTICHRIST
ye have heard that *a* shall come 1Jn 2:18 *500*
He is *a*, that denieth the Father 1Jn 2:22 *500*
and this is that spirit of *a* 1Jn 4:3 *500*
This is a deceiver and an *a* 2Jn 7 *500*

ANTICHRISTS
come, even now are there many *a* 1Jn 2:18 *500*

ANTIOCH (*an'-te-ok*)
1. A city in Syria.
and Nicolas a proselyte of *A* Acts 6:5 *491*
far as Phenice, and Cyprus, and *A* Acts 11:19 *490*
which, when they were come to *A* Acts 11:20 *490*
that he should go as far as *A* Acts 11:22 *490*
found him, he brought him unto *A* Acts 11:26 *490*
were called Christians first in *A* Acts 11:26 *490*
prophets from Jerusalem unto *A* Acts 11:27 *490*
that was at *A* certain prophets Acts 13:1 *490*
And thence sailed to *A*, from Acts 14:26 *490*
their own company to *A* with Paul Acts 15:22 *490*
which are of the Gentiles in *A* Acts 15:23 *490*
were dismissed, they came to *A* Acts 15:30 *490*
also and Barnabas continued in *A* Acts 15:35 *490*
the church, he went down to *A* Acts 18:22 *490*
But when Peter was come to *A* Gal 2:11 *490*
2. A city in Pisidia.
Perga, they came to *A* in Pisidia Acts 13:14 *490*
came thither certain Jews from *A* Acts 14:19 *490*
to Lystra, and to Iconium, and *A* Acts 14:21 *490*
which came unto me at *A*, at 2Ti 3:11 *490*

ANTIPAS (*an'-tip-as*) *A Christian martyr.*
wherein *A* was my faithful martyr Rev 2:13 *493*

ANTIPATRIS (*an-tip'-at-ris*) *A city in northern Palestine.*
and brought him by night to *A* Acts 23:31 *494*

ANTIQUITY
whose *a* is of ancient days Is 23:7 6927

ANTOTHIJAH (*an-to-thi'-jah*) *Son of Shashak.*
And Hananiah, and Elam, and *A* 1Chr 8:24 6070

ANTOTHITE (*an'-to-thite*) See ANETOTHITE. *A native of Anathoth.*
Ikkesh the Tekoite, Abiezer the *A* 1Chr 11:28 6069
and Berachah, and Jehu the *A* 1Chr 12:3 6069

ANTS
The *a* are a people not strong, Prov 30:25 5244

ANUB (*a'-nub*) *A descendant of Judah.*
And Coz begat *A*, and Zobebah, and 1Chr 4:8 6036

ANVIL
the hammer him that smote the *a* Is 41:7 6471

ANY
a beast of the field which the Gen 3:1 3605
lest *a* finding him should kill Gen 4:15 3605
not again unto him *a* more Gen 8:12 5750
the ground *a* more for man's sake Gen 8:21 5750
smite *a* more every thing living Gen 8:21 5750
shall all flesh be cut off *a* more Gen 9:11 5750
neither shall there *a* more be a Gen 9:11 5750
not take *a* thing that is thine Gen 14:23 3605
thy name *a* more be called Abram Gen 17:5 5750
bought with money of *a* stranger Gen 17:12 3605
Is *a* thing too hard for the LORD Gen 18:14
Lot, Hast thou here *a* besides Gen 19:12 4310
for I cannot do *a* thing till thou Gen 19:22
neither do thou *a* thing unto him Gen 22:12 3972
neither had *a* man known her Gen 24:16
Thou shalt not give me *a* thing Gen 30:31 3972
Is there yet *a* portion or Gen 31:14
shall not be called *a* more Jacob Gen 35:10 5750
before there reigned *a* king over Gen 36:31
back *a* thing from me but thee Gen 39:9 3972
of the prison looked not to *a* Gen 39:23 3972
whether there be *a* truth in you Gen 42:16
five times so much as *a* of theirs Gen 43:34
if thou knowest *a* men of activity Gen 47:6
when there falleth out *a* war Ex 1:10
not Pharaoh deal deceitfully *a* Ex 8:29 3254
shall there be *a* more hail Ex 9:29 5750
there remained not *a* green thing Ex 10:15
neither rose *a* from his place for Ex 10:23 376
it, nor shall be like it *a* more Ex 11:6 3254
But against *a* of the children of Ex 11:7 3605
prepared for themselves *a* victual Ex 12:39
neither was there *a* worm therein Ex 16:24
not make unto thee *a* graven image Ex 20:4
or *a* likeness of *a* thing that Ex 20:4 3605
in it thou shalt not do *a* work Ex 20:10 3605
his ass, nor *a* thing that is thy Ex 20:17 3605
if *a* mischief follow, then thou Ex 21:23
or for *a* manner of lost thing, Ex 22:9 3605
or a sheep, or *a* beast, to keep Ex 22:10 3605
He that sacrificeth unto *a* god Ex 22:20
Ye shall not afflict *a* widow Ex 22:22 3605
If thou afflict them in *a* wise Ex 22:23
If thou lend money to *a* of my Ex 22:25
neither shall ye eat *a* flesh that Ex 22:31
if *a* man have *a* matters to do, Ex 24:14
shall ye make *a* other like it Ex 30:32
Whosoever compoundeth *a* like it Ex 30:33
or whosoever putteth *a* of it upon Ex 30:33
whosoever doeth *a* work therein Ex 31:14 3605
whosoever doeth *a* work in the Ex 31:15 3605
unto them, Whosoever hath *a* gold Ex 32:24
neither let *a* man be seen Ex 34:3
in all the earth, nor in *a* nation Ex 34:10 3605
neither shall *a* man desire thy Ex 34:24
wood for *a* work of the service Ex 35:24 3605
to make *a* manner of cunning work Ex 35:33 3605
even of them that do *a* work Ex 35:35 3605
a more work for the offering of Ex 36:6 5750
If *a* man of you bring an offering Lev 1:2
when *a* will offer a meat offering Lev 2:1 5315
nor *a* honey, in *a* offering of Lev 2:11 3605
sin through ignorance against *a* Lev 4:2 3605
and shall do against *a* of them Lev 4:2 259
a of the commandments of the LORD Lev 4:13 259
through ignorance against *a* of Lev 4:22 259
if *a* one of the common people sin Lev 4:27 5315
a of the commandments of the LORD Lev 4:27 259
if a soul touch *a* unclean thing Lev 5:2 3605
he put *a* frankincense thereon Lev 5:11
commit *a* of these things which Lev 5:17 259
in *a* of all these that a man Lev 6:3 259
it shall be forgiven him for *a* Lev 6:7 259
the blood thereof upon *a* garment Lev 6:27
whereof *a* of the blood is brought Lev 6:30
offereth *a* man's burnt offering Lev 7:8
he shall not leave *a* of it until Lev 7:15
And if *a* of the flesh of the Lev 7:18
the flesh that toucheth *a* unclean Lev 7:19 3605
that shall touch *a* unclean thing Lev 7:21 3605
or *a* unclean beast Lev 7:21
or *a* abominable unclean thing, and Lev 7:21 3605
may be used in *a* other use Lev 7:24
of beast, in *a* of your dwellings Lev 7:26 3605
be that eateth *a* manner of blood Lev 7:27 3605
of *a* living thing which is in the Lev 11:10 3605
And upon whatsoever *a* of them Lev 11:32
whether it be *a* vessel of wood, Lev 11:32 3605
wherein *a* work is done, it must Lev 11:32
whereinto *a* of them falleth, Lev 11:33
every thing whereupon *a* part of Lev 11:35
if *a* part of their carcase fall Lev 11:37
a sowing seed which is to be sown Lev 11:37 3605
But if *a* water be put upon the Lev 11:38
a part of their carcase fall Lev 11:38
if *a* beast, of which ye may eat, Lev 11:39
a creeping thing that creepeth Lev 11:43 3605
a manner of creeping thing that Lev 11:44 3605
Or if there be *a* flesh, in the Lev 13:24
or in *a* thing made of skin Lev 13:48 3605
the woof, or in *a* thing of skin Lev 13:49 3605
or in *a* work that is made of skin Lev 13:51 3605
or *a* thing of skin, wherein the Lev 13:52 3605
the woof, or in *a* thing of skin Lev 13:53 3605
the woof, or in *a* thing of skin Lev 13:57 3605
or *a* thing of skins, to pronounce Lev 13:59 3605
When *a* man hath a running issue Lev 15:2 376
he that sitteth on *a* thing Lev 15:6
whosoever toucheth *a* thing that Lev 15:10 3605
he that beareth *a* of those things Lev 15:10
if *a* man's seed of copulation go Lev 15:16
whosoever toucheth *a* thing that Lev 15:22 3605
or on *a* thing whereon she sitteth Lev 15:23
if *a* man lie with her at all, and Lev 15:24
that eateth *a* manner of blood Lev 17:10 3605
neither shall *a* stranger that Lev 17:12
catcheth *a* beast or fowl that may Lev 17:13
to *a* that is near of kin to him Lev 18:6 376
thou shalt not let *a* of thy seed Lev 18:21
with *a* beast to defile thyself Lev 18:23 3605
neither shall *a* woman stand Lev 18:23
yourselves in *a* of these things Lev 18:24 3605
shall not commit *a* of these Lev 18:26 3605
neither *a* of your own nation Lev 18:26
nor *a* stranger that sojourneth Lev 18:26
commit *a* of these abominations Lev 18:29 3605
that ye commit not *a* one of these Lev 18:30
thou shalt in *a* wise rebuke thy Lev 19:17
nor bear *a* grudge against the Lev 19:18
Ye shall not eat *a* thing with the Lev 19:26
Ye shall not make *a* cuttings in Lev 19:28
nor print *a* marks upon you Lev 19:28
that giveth *a* of his seed unto Lev 20:2
if the people of the land do *a* Lev 20:4
if a woman approach unto *a* beast Lev 20:16 3605
or by *a* manner of living thing Lev 20:25 3605
nor make *a* cuttings in their Lev 21:5
And the daughter of *a* priest Lev 21:9 376
shall he go in to *a* dead body Lev 21:11 3605
generations that hath *a* blemish Lev 21:17
nose, or *a* thing superfluous, Lev 21:18
whoso toucheth *a* thing that is Lev 22:4 3605
toucheth *a* creeping thing Lev 22:5 3605
a such shall be unclean until Lev 22:6
priest buy *a* soul with his money Lev 22:11
a bullock or a lamb that hath *a* Lev 22:23
neither shall ye make *a* offering Lev 22:24
bread of your God of *a* of these Lev 22:25 3605
gather *a* gleaning of thy harvest Lev 23:22
doeth *a* work in that same day Lev 23:30 3605
he that killeth *a* man shall Lev 24:17 3605
if *a* of his kin come to redeem it Lev 25:25
may the Levites redeem at *a* time Lev 25:32 5769
or *a* that is nigh of kin unto him Lev 25:49
neither shall ye set up *a* image Lev 26:1
all that *a* man giveth of such Lev 27:9
if it be *a* unclean beast, of Lev 27:11 3605
field will in *a* wise redeem it Lev 27:19
it shall not be redeemed *a* more Lev 27:20
they shall not touch *a* holy thing Num 4:15
commit *a* sin that men commit Num 5:6 3605
whatsoever *a* man giveth the Num 5:10
If *a* man's wife go aside, and Num 5:12 376
shall he drink *a* liquor of grapes Num 6:3 3605
if *a* man die very suddenly by him Num 6:9
If *a* man of you or of your Num 9:10 376
morning, nor break *a* bone of it Num 9:12
neither shall *a* of them that Num 14:23 3605
if *a* soul sin through ignorance, Num 15:27 259
Whosoever cometh *a* thing near Num 17:13
that there be no wrath *a* more Num 18:5
shalt thou have *a* part among them Num 18:20
that toucheth the dead body of *a* Num 19:11 3605
dead body of *a* man that is dead Num 19:13 3605
neither is there *a* water to drink Num 20:5
only, without doing *a* thing else Num 20:19
bread, neither is there *a* water Num 21:5
if a serpent had bitten *a* man Num 21:9
a power at all to say *a* thing Num 22:38
neither is there *a* divination Num 23:23
ye shall not do *a* work therein Num 29:7 3605
not *a* of her vows, or of her Num 30:5 3605
But if he shall *a* ways make them Num 30:15
whosoever hath killed *a* person Num 31:19
and whosoever hath touched *a* slain Num 31:19
which killeth *a* person at Num 35:11
a person unawares may flee Num 35:15
or have cast upon him *a* thing Num 35:22 3605
Or with *a* stone, wherewith a man Num 35:23 3605
But if the slayer shall at *a* time Num 35:26
Whoso killeth *a* person, the Num 35:30
shall not testify against *a* Num 35:30
if they be married to *a* of the Num 36:3 259
possesseth an inheritance in *a* Num 36:8
children of Ammon *a* possession Deut 2:19
nor unto *a* place of the river Deut 2:37 3605
image, the similitude of *a* figure Deut 4:16 3605
The likeness of *a* beast that is Deut 4:17 3605
the likeness of *a* winged fowl Deut 4:17 3605
The likeness of *a* thing that Deut 4:18 3605
the likeness of *a* fish that is in Deut 4:18 3605
image, or the likeness of *a* thing Deut 4:23 3605
image, or the likeness of *a* thing Deut 4:25 3605
whether there hath been *a* such Deut 4:32
not make thee *a* graven image Deut 5:8 3605
or *a* likeness of *a* thing that Deut 5:8 3605
in it thou shalt not do *a* work Deut 5:14 3605
nor *a* of thy cattle, nor thy Deut 5:14 3605
his ass, or *a* thing that is thy Deut 5:21 3605
voice of the LORD our God *a* more Deut 5:25
were more in number than *a* people Deut 7:7 3605
thou shalt not lack *a* thing in it Deut 8:9 3605
nor *a* of thy vows which thou Deut 12:17 3605
fear, and shall do no more *a* such Deut 13:11 1697
nor make *a* baldness between your Deut 14:1
shalt not eat *a* abominable thing Deut 14:3 3605
Ye shall not eat of *a* thing that Deut 14:21 3605
of one of thy brethren within *a* Deut 15:7 259
if there be *a* blemish therein, as Deut 15:21
or have *a* ill blemish, thou shalt Deut 15:21 3605
shall there *a* thing of the flesh Deut 16:4
passover within *a* of thy gates Deut 16:5 259
of *a* trees near unto the altar of Deut 16:21 3605
shalt thou set thee up *a* image Deut 16:22
unto the LORD thy God *a* bullock Deut 17:1
is blemish, or *a* evilfavouredness Deut 17:1 3605
within *a* of thy gates which the Deut 17:2 259
or *a* of the host of heaven, which Deut 17:3 3605
Thou shalt in *a* wise set him king Deut 17:15
if a Levite come from *a* of thy Deut 18:6 259
shall not be found among you *a* Deut 18:10
let me see this great fire *a* more Deut 18:16

But if a man hate his neighbour, Deut 19:11
up against a man for a iniquity Deut 19:15 3605
a sin, in a sin that he sinneth Deut 19:15 3605
a man to testify against him that Deut 19:16
no more a such evil among you Deut 19:20 1697
but thou shalt in a wise bury him Deut 21:23
thou shalt in a case bring them Deut 22:1
before thee in the way in a tree Deut 22:6 3605
But thou shalt in a wise let the Deut 22:7
if a man fall from thence Deut 22:8
If a man take a wife, and go in Deut 22:13
If there be among you a man Deut 23:10
of the LORD thy God for a vow Deut 23:18 3605
usury of a thing that is lent Deut 23:19 3605
shalt not put a in thy vessel Deut 23:24
he be charged with a business Deut 24:5 3605
If a man be found stealing a of Deut 24:7 5315
dost lend thy brother a thing Deut 24:10 3972
In a case thou shalt deliver him Deut 24:13
ought thereof for a unclean use Deut 26:14
not lift up a iron tool upon them Deut 27:5
maketh a graven or molten image Deut 27:15
that lieth with a manner of beast Deut 27:21 3605
a of the words which I command Deut 28:14 3605
to a of them of the flesh of his Deut 28:55 259
nor a grass groweth therein, like Deut 29:23 3605
If a of thine be driven out unto Deut 30:4
which have not known a thing Deut 31:13
neither is there a understanding Deut 32:28
neither is there a that can Deut 32:39
There shall not a man be able to Josh 1:5
remain a more courage in a man Josh 2:11
our head, if a hand be upon him Josh 2:19
was there spirit in them a more Josh 5:1
children of Israel manna a more Josh 5:12
nor make a noise with your voice, Josh 6:10
neither shall a word proceed out Josh 6:10
in a wise keep yourselves from Josh 6:18
neither will I be with you a more Josh 7:12
which no man hath lift up a iron Josh 8:31
a of the children of Israel Josh 10:21
there was not a left to breathe Josh 11:11 3605
neither left they a to breathe Josh 11:14 3605
Levi Moses gave not a inheritance Josh 13:33 3605
that killeth a person unawares Josh 20:3
that whosoever killeth a person Josh 20:9
There failed not ought of a good Josh 21:45 3605
Else if ye do in a wise go back Josh 23:12
a of these nations from before Josh 23:13
so that they could not a longer Judg 2:14
will not henceforth drive out a Judg 2:21
when a man doth come and enquire Judg 4:20
thee, and say, Is there a man here Judg 4:20
now art thou a thing better than Judg 11:25
drink, and eat not a unclean thing Judg 13:4 3605
neither eat a unclean thing Judg 13:7 3605
She may not eat of a thing that Judg 13:14 3605
drink, nor eat a unclean thing Judg 13:14 3605
weak, and be like a other man Judg 16:17 3605
put them to shame in a thing Judg 18:7
and had no business with a man Judg 18:7
of a thing that is in the earth Judg 18:10 3605
they had no business with a man Judg 18:28
there is no want of a thing Judg 19:19 3605
We will not a of us go to his Judg 20:8 376
neither will we a of us turn into Judg 20:8 376
There shall not a of us give his Judg 21:1 376
known no man by lying with a male Judg 21:12
are there yet a more sons in my Ruth 1:11
meet thee not in a other field Ruth 2:22
neither is there a rock like our 1Sa 2:2
when a man offered sacrifice, the 1Sa 2:13 3605
if a man said unto him, Let them 1Sa 2:16
if thou hide a thing from me of 1Sa 3:17
nor a that come into Dagon's 1Sa 5:5 3605
but in a wise return him a 1Sa 6:3
was higher than a of the people 1Sa 9:2 3605
he was higher than a of the 1Sa 10:23 3605
a bribe to blind mine eyes 1Sa 12:3
thou taken ought of a man's hand 1Sa 12:4
of a of the people that were with 1Sa 13:22 3605
that eateth a food until evening 1Sa 14:24
none of the people tasted a food 1Sa 14:24 3605
man that eateth a food this day 1Sa 14:28
and when Saul saw a strong man 1Sa 14:52 3605
or a valiant man, he took him 1Sa 14:52 3605
The king desireth not a dowry 1Sa 18:25
my father about to morrow a time 1Sa 20:12
Saul spake not a thing that day 1Sa 20:26 3972
But the lad knew not a thing 1Sa 20:39 3972
Let no man know a thing of the 1Sa 21:2 3972
impute a thing unto his servant 1Sa 22:15 3605
hurt, neither missed we a thing 1Sa 25:15 3972
to him by the morning light a 1Sa 25:22
a that pisseth against the wall 1Sa 25:34
me a more in a coast of Israel 1Sa 27:1 3605
they slew not a, either great or 1Sa 30:2 376
eaten no bread, nor drunk a water 1Sa 30:12
nor a thing that they had taken 1Sa 30:19 3605
Shall I go up into a of the 2Sa 2:1 259
more, neither fought they a more 2Sa 2:28
in a house since the time that I 2Sa 7:6
with a of the tribes of Israel 2Sa 7:7 259
of wickedness afflict them a more 2Sa 7:10
is there a God beside thee 2Sa 7:22
Is there yet a that is left of 2Sa 9:1
is there not yet a of the house 2Sa 9:3 376
help the children of Ammon a more 2Sa 10:19
hard for him to do a thing to her 2Sa 13:2 3972
and he shall not touch thee a more 2Sa 14:10
of blood to destroy a more 2Sa 14:11
neither doth God respect a person 2Sa 14:14
if there be a iniquity in me, let 2Sa 14:32
that when a man that had a 2Sa 15:2 3605
that every man which hath a suit 2Sa 15:4
that when a man came nigh to him 2Sa 15:5
and they knew not a thing 2Sa 15:11 3605
shall there a man be put to death 2Sa 19:22
I yet to cry a more unto the king 2Sa 19:28
Why speakest thou a more of thy 2Sa 19:29
can I hear a more the voice of 2Sa 19:35
or hath he given us a gift 2Sa 19:42
shalt thou kill a man in Israel 2Sa 21:4
in a of the coasts of Israel 2Sa 21:5 3605
him at a time in saying, Why hast 1Kin 1:6
and go not forth thence a whither 1Kin 2:36
out, and walkest abroad a whither 1Kin 2:42
thee shall a arise like unto thee 1Kin 3:12
so that there shall not be a 1Kin 3:13 376
that there is not among us a that 1Kin 5:6 376
was neither hammer nor axe nor a 1Kin 6:7 3605
If a man trespass against his 1Kin 8:31
soever be made by a man, or by 1Kin 8:38 3605
there was not a thing hid from 1Kin 10:3
not the like made in a kingdom 1Kin 10:20 3605
howbeit let me go in a wise 1Kin 11:22
turned not aside from a thing 1Kin 15:5 3605
that he might not suffer a to go 1Kin 15:17
not to Jeroboam a that breathed 1Kin 15:29 3605
was no voice, nor a that answered 1Kin 18:26
nor a to answer, nor a that 1Kin 18:29
a thing would come from him 1Kin 20:33
if by a means he be missing, then 1Kin 20:39
a more death or barren land 2Kin 2:21
hath not a thing in the house 2Kin 4:2 3605
if thou meet a man, salute him 2Kin 4:29
if a salute thee, answer him not 2Kin 4:29 376
I wait for the LORD a longer 2Kin 6:33
we will not make a king 2Kin 10:5 376
neither left he a of them 2Kin 10:14 376
If a of the men whom I have 2Kin 10:24
a man's heart to bring into the 2Kin 12:4
wheresoever a breach shall be 2Kin 12:5 376
a vessels of gold, or vessels of 2Kin 12:13
for there was not a shut up 2Kin 14:26
a left, nor a helper for Israel 2Kin 14:26
nor a that were before him 2Kin 18:5
Hath a of the gods of the nations 2Kin 18:33 376
a more out of the land which I 2Kin 21:8
after him arose there a like him 2Kin 23:25
not again a more out of his land 2Kin 24:7
in the land of Edom before a king 1Chr 1:43
spake I a word to a of the judges 1Chr 17:6 259
of wickedness waste them a more 1Chr 17:9
is there a God beside thee 1Chr 17:20
help the children of Ammon a more 1Chr 19:19
nor a vessels of it for the 1Chr 23:26 3605
whosoever had dedicated a thing 1Chr 26:28
king in a matter of the courses 1Chr 27:1 3605
man, for a manner of service 1Chr 28:21 3605
on a king before him in Israel 1Chr 29:25 3605
neither shall there a after thee 2Chr 1:12
also to grave a manner of graving 2Chr 2:14 3605
neither chose I a man to be a 2Chr 6:5
soever shall be made of a man 2Chr 6:29 3605
and Levites concerning a matter 2Chr 8:15 3605
neither was there a such spice as 2Chr 9:9
not the like made in a kingdom 2Chr 9:19 3605
it was not a thing accounted of 2Chr 9:20 3972
in a thing should enter in 2Chr 23:19 3605
a ways able to deliver their 2Chr 32:13
for no god of a nation or kingdom 2Chr 32:15 3605
Neither will I a more remove the 2Chr 33:8
the work in a manner of service 2Chr 34:13 3605
whosoever remaineth in a place Ezr 1:4 3605
that touching a of the priests and Ezr 7:24 3606
neither told I a man what my God Neh 2:12
neither was there a beast with me Neh 2:12
wall, neither bought we a land Neh 5:16
of the land bring ware or a Neh 10:31
for ever without a regarding it Job 4:20
if there be a that will answer Job 5:1
is there a to deliver them Job 5:4
or is there a taste in the white Job 6:6
shall his place know him a more Job 7:10
it withereth before a other herb Job 8:12 3605
Neither is there a daysman Job 9:33
shadow of death, without a order Job 10:22
is there a secret thing with thee Job 15:11
Not for a injustice in mine hands Job 16:17
nor a remaining in his dwellings Job 18:19
shall his place a more behold him Job 20:9
Shall a teach God knowledge Job 21:22
Is it a pleasure to the Almighty, Job 22:3
Is there a number of his armies Job 25:3
if a blot hath cleaved to mine Job 31:7
If I have seen a perish for want Job 31:19
or a poor without covering Job 31:19
accept a man's person, neither Job 32:21
not account of a of his matters Job 33:13 3605
if a say, I have sinned, and Job 33:27
If thou hast a thing to say Job 33:32
would not consider a of his ways Job 34:27 3605
I will not offend a more Job 34:31
God is mighty, and despiseth not a Job 36:5
Also can a understand the Job 36:29
he respecteth not a that are wise Job 37:24 3605
that say, Who will shew us a good Ps 4:6
there were a that did understand Ps 14:2
deliver a by his great strength Ps 33:17
LORD shall not want a good thing Ps 34:10 3605
not thyself in a wise to do evil Ps 37:8
neither is there a rest in my Ps 38:3
None of them can by a means Ps 49:7
there were a that did understand Ps 53:2
be not merciful to a wicked Ps 59:5 3605
there is no more a prophet Ps 74:9
among us a that knoweth how long Ps 74:9
shalt thou worship a strange god Ps 81:9
neither are there a works like Ps 86:8
neither shall a plague come nigh Ps 91:10
neither let there be a to favour Ps 109:12
neither a that go down into Ps 115:17 3605
let not a iniquity have dominion Ps 119:133 3605
neither is there a breath in Ps 135:17
see if there be a wicked way in Ps 139:24
not my heart to a evil thing Ps 141:4
unto my God while I have a being Ps 146:2
hath not dealt so with a nation Ps 147:20 3605
is spread in the sight of a bird Prov 1:17 3605
He will not regard a ransom Prov 6:35 3605
but sin is a reproach to a people Prov 14:34
of a person shall flee to the pit Prov 28:17
I am more brutish than a man Prov 30:2
beasts, and turneth not away for a Prov 30:30 3605
judgment of a of the afflicted Prov 31:5 3605
Is there a thing whereof it may Eccl 1:10
neither shall there be a Eccl 1:11
withheld not my heart from a joy Eccl 2:10 3605
nor a thing taken from it Eccl 3:14
hasty to utter a thing before God Eccl 5:2
seen the sun, nor known a thing Eccl 6:5
but the dead know not a thing Eccl 9:5 3972
neither have they a more a reward Eccl 9:5
neither have they a more a Eccl 9:6
in a thing that is done under the Eccl 9:6 3605
Why should ye be stricken a more Is 1:5
shall they learn war a more Is 2:4
neither is there a end of their Is 2:7
neither is there a end of their Is 2:7
shall there be a work for Egypt Is 19:15
we have not wrought a deliverance Is 26:18
lest a hurt it, I will keep it Is 27:3
be removed into a corner a more Is 30:20
neither shall a of the cords Is 33:20 3605
nor a ravenous beast shall go up Is 35:9
Hath a of the gods of the nations Is 36:18 376
I know not a Is 44:8
neither is there a that taketh Is 51:18
was so marred more than a man Is 52:14
neither was a deceit in his mouth Is 53:9
reproach of thy widowhood a more Is 54:4
his hand from doing a evil Is 56:2 3605
justice, nor a pleadeth for truth Is 59:4
neither shall thy land a more be Is 62:4
neither shall that be done a more Jer 3:16
neither shall they walk a more Jer 3:17
if there be a that executeth Jer 5:1
and trust ye not in a brother Jer 9:4 3605
to stretch forth my tent a more Jer 10:20
Are there a among the vanities of Jer 14:22
sabbath day, neither do ye a work Jer 17:22 3605
not give heed to a of his words Jer 18:18 3605
nor speak a more in his name Jer 20:9
shall not return thither a more Jer 22:11
David, and ruling a more in Judah Jer 22:30
Can a hide himself in secret Jer 23:24 376
shall not sorrow a more at all Jer 31:12
nor thrown down a more for ever Jer 31:40
is there a thing too hard for me Jer 32:27 3605
so that I will not take a of his Jer 33:26
serve themselves of them a more Jer 34:10
nor plant vineyard, nor have a Jer 35:7
nor a of his servants that heard Jer 36:24 3605
Is there a word from the LORD Jer 37:17
that can do a thing against you Jer 38:5
nor a thing for the which he hath Jer 42:21 3605
more be named in the mouth of a Jer 44:26 3605
without a to dwell therein Jer 48:9
nor a son of man dwell in it Jer 49:33
neither shall a son of man dwell Jer 50:40
neither doth a son of man pass Jer 51:43
not flow together a more unto him Jer 51:44
see if there be a sorrow like Lam 1:12
not, without a intermission, Lam 3:49
I will not do a more the like Eze 5:9
spare, neither will I have a pity Eze 5:11
multitude, nor of a of theirs Eze 7:11 1991
neither shall a strengthen Eze 7:13 376
but come not near a man upon whom. Eze 9:6 3605
more a vain vision nor flattering Eze 12:24
of my words be prolonged a more Eze 12:28 3605
be polluted a more with all their Eze 14:11 3605
is the vine tree more than a tree Eze 15:2
be taken thereof to do a work Eze 15:3
of it to hang a vessel thereon Eze 15:3 3605
Is it meet for a work Eze 15:4
shall it be meet yet for a work Eze 15:5
to do a of these unto thee, to Eze 16:5 259
also shalt give no hire a more Eze 16:41
never open thy mouth a more Eze 16:63
ye shall not have occasion a more Eze 18:3
And hath not oppressed a, but hath Eze 18:7 376
neither hath taken a increase Eze 18:8
the like to a one of these things Eze 18:10
that doeth not a of those duties, Eze 18:11 3605
Neither hath oppressed a, hath Eze 18:16 376
Have I a pleasure at all that the Eze 18:23
it shall not return a more Eze 21:5
them, nor remember Egypt a more Eze 23:27
purged from thy filthiness a more Eze 24:13
terror, and never shalt be a more Eze 27:36
and never shalt thou be a more Eze 28:19
nor a grieving thorn of all that Eze 28:24
itself a more above the nations Eze 29:15
nor a tree in the garden of God Eze 31:8 3605
foot of man trouble them a more Eze 32:13
take a person from among them, he Eze 33:6
shepherds feed themselves a more Eze 34:10
the shame of the heathen a more Eze 34:29
bereave thy nations a more Eze 36:14
the shame of the heathen a more Eze 36:15

the reproach of the people *a* more........ Eze 36:15
cause thy nations to fall *a* more........ Eze 36:15
into two kingdoms *a* more at all........ Eze 37:22
a more with their idols, nor with........ Eze 37:23
things, nor with *a* of their........ Eze 37:23 3605
them pollute my holy name *a* more........ Eze 39:7
neither cut down *a* out of the........ Eze 39:10
when *a* seeth a man's bone, then........ Eze 39:15
left none of them *a* more there........ Eze 39:28
I hide my face *a* more from them........ Eze 39:29
of *a* stranger that is among the........ Eze 44:9 3605
come near to *a* of my holy things........ Eze 44:13 3605
with *a* thing that causeth sweat........ Eze 44:18
Neither shall *a* priest drink wine........ Eze 44:21 3605
of *a* thing that is dead of itself........ Eze 44:31 3605
give a gift unto *a* of his sons........ Eze 46:16 376
asked such things at *a* magician........ Dan 2:10 3606
is not revealed to me for *a*........ Dan 2:30
that I have more than *a* living........ Dan 2:30 3606
might not serve nor worship *a* god........ Dan 3:28 3606
which speak *a* thing amiss against........ Dan 3:29
neither was there *a* error or........ Dan 6:4 3606
We shall not find *a* occasion........ Dan 6:5 3606
shall ask a petition of *a* God or........ Dan 6:7 3606
that shall ask a petition of *a*........ Dan 6:12 3606
neither was there *a* that could........ Dan 8:4
there be *a* strength to withstand........ Dan 11:15
desire of women, nor regard *a* god........ Dan 11:37 3605
where is *a* other that may save........ Hos 13:10
neither will we say *a* more to the........ Hos 14:3
have I to do *a* more with idols........ Hos 14:8
neither shall be *a* more after it........ Joel 2:2
strangers pass through her *a* more........ Joel 3:17
house, Is there yet *a* with thee........ Amos 6:10
not again pass by them *a* more........ Amos 7:8
not again *a* more at Beth-el........ Amos 7:13
not again pass by them *a* more........ Amos 8:2
never forget *a* of their works........ Amos 8:7 3605
there shall not be *a* remaining of........ Obad 18
herd nor flock, taste *a* thing........ Jonah 3:7 3792
shall they learn war *a* more........ Mic 4:3
thou shalt not see evil *a* more........ Zeph 3:15
or *a* meat, shall it be holy........ Hag 2:12 3605
by a dead body touch *a* of these........ Hag 2:13 3605
for man, nor *a* hire for beast........ Zec 8:10
neither was there *a* peace to him........ Zec 8:10
shall pass through them *a* more........ Zec 9:8
that when *a* shall yet prophesy,........ Zec 13:3 376
regardeth not the offering *a* more........ Mal 2:13
lest at *a* time thou dash thy foot........ Mt 4:6 *3379*
lest at *a* time the adversary........ Mt 5:25 *3379*
if *a* man will sue thee at the law........ Mt 5:40
into *a* city of the Samaritans........ Mt 10:5
neither knoweth *a* man the Father........ Mt 11:27 *5100*
neither shall *a* man hear his........ Mt 12:19 *5100*
lest at *a* time they should see........ Mt 13:15 *3379*
When *a* one heareth the word of........ Mt 13:19 *3956*
If *a* man will come after me, let........ Mt 16:24 *1536*
a thing that they shall ask........ Mt 18:19 *3956*
if *a* man say ought unto you, ye........ Mt 21:3 *5100*
neither carest thou for *a* man........ Mt 22:16 *3762*
neither durst *a* man from that day........ Mt 22:46 *5100*
forth ask him *a* more questions........ Mt 22:46 *3765*
to take *a* thing out of his house........ Mt 24:17 *5100*
Then if *a* man shall say unto you,........ Mt 24:23 *5100*
See thou say nothing to *a* man........ Mk 1:44 *3367*
lest at *a* time they should be........ Mk 4:12 *3379*
neither was *a* thing kept secret,........ Mk 4:22 *5100*
If *a* man have ears to hear, let........ Mk 4:23 *1536*
neither could *a* man tame him........ Mk 5:4 *3762*
thou the Master *a* further........ Mk 5:35 *2089*
If *a* man have ears to hear, let........ Mk 7:16 *1536*
nor tell it to *a* in the town........ Mk 8:26 *5100*
about, they saw no man *a* more........ Mk 9:8 *3765*
but if thou canst do *a* thing........ Mk 9:22 *1535*
he would not that *a* man should........ Mk 9:30 *5100*
If *a* man desire to be first, the........ Mk 9:35 *1536*
if *a* man say unto you, Why do ye........ Mk 11:3 *1536*
he might find *a* thing thereon........ Mk 11:13 *1536*
would not suffer that *a* man........ Mk 11:16 *1536*
carry *a* vessel through the temple........ Mk 11:16
if ye have ought against *a*........ Mk 11:25 *1536*
and died, neither left he *a* seed........ Mk 12:21
that durst ask him *a* question........ Mk 12:34
Take heed lest *a* man deceive you........ Mk 13:5 *5100*
to take *a* thing out of his house........ Mk 13:15 *5100*
then if *a* man shall say to you,........ Mk 13:21 *5100*
I will not deny thee in *a* wise........ Mk 14:31 *3364*
What need we *a* further witnesses........ Mk 14:63 *2089*
whether he had been *a* while dead........ Mk 15:44
neither said they *a* thing to *a*........ Mk 16:8 *3762*
and if they drink *a* deadly thing........ Mk 16:18 *5100*
no man, neither accuse *a* falsely........ Lk 3:14
lest at *a* time thou dash thy foot........ Lk 4:11 *3379*
all they that had *a* sick with........ Lk 4:40
neither *a* thing hid, that shall........ Lk 8:17
clothes, neither abode in *a* house........ Lk 8:27
neither could be healed of *a*........ Lk 8:43 *3762*
If *a* man will come after me, let........ Lk 9:23 *5100*
told no man in those days *a* of........ Lk 9:36 *3762*
nothing shall by *a* means hurt you........ Lk 10:19 *3364*
of *a* of you that is a father........ Lk 11:11 *5100*
art bidden of *a* man to a wedding........ Lk 14:8 *5100*
If *a* man come to me, and hate not........ Lk 14:26 *1536*
I at *a* time thy commandment........ Lk 15:29 *3763*
if I have taken *a* thing........ Lk 19:8 *5100*
from *a* man by false accusation........ Lk 19:8 *1536*
if *a* man ask you, Why do ye loose........ Lk 19:31 *5100*
acceptest thou the person of *a*........ Lk 20:21
deny that there is *a* resurrection........ Lk 20:27 *3361*
If *a* man's brother die, having a........ Lk 20:28 *5100*
Neither can they die *a* more........ Lk 20:36 *2089*
not ask him *a* question at all........ Lk 20:40 *3762*
lest at *a* time your hearts be........ Lk 21:34 *3379*
I will not *a* more eat thereof,........ Lk 22:16 *3765*
and shoes, lacked ye *a* thing........ Lk 22:35 *5100*
What need we *a* further witness........ Lk 22:71 *2089*
unto them, Have ye here *a* meat........ Lk 24:41 *5100*
without him was not *a* thing made........ Jn 1:3 *1520*
No man hath seen God at *a* time........ Jn 1:18 *4455*
Can there *a* good thing come out........ Jn 1:46 *5100*
needed not that *a* should testify........ Jn 2:25 *5100*
Hath *a* man brought him ought to........ Jn 4:33 *3387*
neither heard his voice at *a* time........ Jn 5:37 *4455*
Not that *a* man hath seen the........ Jn 6:46 *5100*
if *a* man eat of this bread, he........ Jn 6:51 *5100*
man that doeth *a* thing in secret........ Jn 7:4 *5100*
If *a* man will do his will, he........ Jn 7:17 *5100*
If *a* man thirst, let him come........ Jn 7:37 *5100*
Have *a* of the rulers or of the........ Jn 7:48 *3387*
Doth our law judge *a* man, before........ Jn 7:51 *3588*
and were never in bondage to *a* man........ Jn 8:33 *3762*
that if *a* man did confess that he........ Jn 9:22 *5100*
but if *a* man be a worshipper of........ Jn 9:31 *5100*
began was it not heard that *a* man........ Jn 9:32 *5100*
by me if *a* man enter in, he shall........ Jn 10:9 *5100*
neither shall *a* man pluck them........ Jn 10:28 *5100*
If *a* man walk in the day, he........ Jn 11:9 *5100*
if *a* man knew where he were, he........ Jn 11:57 *5100*
If *a* man serve me, let him follow........ Jn 12:26 *5100*
if *a* man serve me, him will my........ Jn 12:26 *5100*
if *a* man hear my words, and........ Jn 12:47 *5100*
If ye shall ask *a* thing in my........ Jn 14:14 *5100*
needest not that *a* man should ask........ Jn 16:30 *5100*
for us to put *a* man to death........ Jn 18:31 *3762*
them, Children, have ye *a* meat........ Jn 21:5 *3387*
is there salvation in *a* other........ Acts 4:12 *3762*
neither said *a* of them that ought........ Acts 4:32 *1520*
Neither was there *a* among them........ Acts 4:34 *5100*
that if he found *a* of this way........ Acts 9:2 *5100*
for I have never eaten *a* thing........ Acts 10:14 *3956*
not call *a* man common or unclean........ Acts 10:28 *3367*
Can *a* man forbid water, that........ Acts 10:47 *5100*
common or unclean hath at *a* time........ Acts 11:8 *3763*
if ye have *a* word of exhortation........ Acts 13:15 *5150*
as though he needed *a* thing........ Acts 17:25 *5100*
whether there be *a* Holy Ghost........ Acts 19:2
him, have a matter against *a* man........ Acts 19:38 *5100*
But if ye enquire *a* thing........ Acts 19:39 *5100*
the temple disputing with *a* man........ Acts 24:12 *5100*
have found *a* evil doing in me........ Acts 24:20 *1536*
if there be *a* wickedness in him........ Acts 25:5 *1536*
have I offended *a* thing at all........ Acts 25:8 *5100*
or have committed *a* thing worthy........ Acts 25:11 *5100*
Romans to deliver *a* man to die........ Acts 25:16 *5100*
without *a* delay on the morrow I........ Acts 25:17 *3362*
he ought not to live *a* longer........ Acts 25:24 *3370*
if by *a* means they might attain........ Acts 27:12 *4458*
no loss of *a* man's life among you........ Acts 27:22 *3762*
fall from the head of *a* of you........ Acts 27:34 *3762*
lest *a* of them should swim out,........ Acts 27:42 *5100*
neither *a* of the brethren that........ Acts 28:21 *5100*
shewed or spake *a* harm of thee........ Acts 28:21 *5100*
if by *a* means now at length I........ Rom 1:10 *4458*
to sin, live *a* longer therein........ Rom 6:2 *2089*
Now if *a* man have not the Spirit........ Rom 8:9 *5100*
Who shall lay *a* thing to the........ Rom 8:33
nor *a* other creature, shall be........ Rom 8:39 *5100*
having done *a* good or evil........ Rom 9:11 *5100*
If by *a* means I may provoke to........ Rom 11:14 *4458*
Owe no man *a* thing, but to love........ Rom 13:8 *3367*
if there be *a* other commandment,........ Rom 13:9 *1536*
judge one another *a* more........ Rom 14:13 *3370*
esteemeth *a* thing to be unclean........ Rom 14:14 *5100*
nor *a* thing whereby thy brother........ Rom 14:21 *3362*
of *a* of those things which Christ........ Rom 15:18 *5100*
Lest *a* should say that I had........ 1Cor 1:15 *3387*
not whether I baptized *a* other........ 1Cor 1:16 *1536*
not to know *a* thing among you........ 1Cor 2:2 *5100*
is he that planteth *a* thing........ 1Cor 3:7 *5100*
Now if *a* man build upon this........ 1Cor 3:12 *5100*
If *a* man's work abide which he........ 1Cor 3:14 *1536*
If *a* man's work shall be burned,........ 1Cor 3:15 *1536*
If *a* man defile the temple of God........ 1Cor 3:17 *1536*
If *a* man among you seemeth to be........ 1Cor 3:18 *1536*
if *a* man that is called a brother........ 1Cor 5:11 *5100*
Dare *a* of you, having a matter........ 1Cor 6:1 *5100*
be brought under the power of *a*........ 1Cor 6:12 *5100*
If *a* brother hath a wife that........ 1Cor 7:12 *1536*
Is *a* man called being circumcised........ 1Cor 7:18 *5100*
Is *a* called in uncircumcision........ 1Cor 7:18 *5100*
But if *a* man think that he........ 1Cor 7:36 *5100*
if *a* man think that he knoweth........ 1Cor 8:2 *5100*
man think that he knoweth *a* thing........ 1Cor 8:2 *5100*
But if *a* man love God, the same........ 1Cor 8:3 *5100*
But take heed lest by *a* means........ 1Cor 8:9 *3381*
For if *a* man see thee which hast........ 1Cor 8:10 *5100*
Who goeth a warfare *a* time at his........ 1Cor 9:7 *4218*
than that *a* man should make my........ 1Cor 9:15 *5100*
lest that by *a* means, when I have........ 1Cor 9:27 *3381*
that the idol is *a* thing, or that........ 1Cor 10:19 *5100*
in sacrifice to idols is *a* thing........ 1Cor 10:19 *5100*
If *a* of them that believe not bid........ 1Cor 10:27 *5100*
But if *a* man say unto you, This........ 1Cor 10:28 *5100*
But if *a* man seem to be........ 1Cor 11:16 *5100*
if *a* man hunger, let him eat at........ 1Cor 11:34 *5100*
If *a* man speak in an unknown........ 1Cor 14:27 *5100*
If *a* thing be revealed to another........ 1Cor 14:30
And if they will learn *a* thing........ 1Cor 14:35 *5100*
If *a* man think himself to be a........ 1Cor 14:37 *1536*
But if *a* man be ignorant, let him........ 1Cor 14:38 *1536*
If *a* man love not the Lord Jesus........ 1Cor 16:22 *1536*
them which are in *a* trouble........ 2Cor 1:4 *3956*
But if *a* have caused grief, he........ 2Cor 2:5 *5100*
To whom ye forgive *a* thing........ 2Cor 2:10 *5100*
for if I forgave *a* thing, to whom........ 2Cor 2:10 *1536*
to think *a* thing as of ourselves........ 2Cor 3:5 *5100*
Therefore if *a* man be in Christ,........ 2Cor 5:17 *1536*
Giving no offence in *a* thing........ 2Cor 6:3 *3367*
boasted *a* thing to him of you........ 2Cor 7:14 *1536*
Whether *a* do enquire of Titus, he........ 2Cor 8:23
If *a* man trust to himself that he........ 2Cor 10:7 *5100*
But I fear, lest by *a* means........ 2Cor 11:3 *3381*
Howbeit whereinsoever *a* is bold........ 2Cor 11:21 *5100*
lest *a* man should think of me........ 2Cor 12:6 *5100*
Did I make a gain of you by *a* of........ 2Cor 12:17 *5100*
preach *a* other gospel unto you........ Gal 1:8
If *a* man preach *a* other gospel........ Gal 1:9 *1536*
lest by *a* means I should run, or........ Gal 2:2 *3381*
circumcision availeth *a* thing........ Gal 5:6 *5100*
circumcision availeth *a* thing........ Gal 6:15 *5100*
of works, lest *a* man should boast........ Eph 2:9 *5100*
hath *a* inheritance in the kingdom........ Eph 5:5
spot, or wrinkle, or *a* such thing........ Eph 5:27 *5100*
whatsoever good thing *a* man doeth........ Eph 6:8 *1538*
therefore *a* consolation in Christ........ Phil 2:1 *1536*
if *a* comfort of love........ Phil 2:1 *1536*
if *a* fellowship of the Spirit........ Phil 2:1 *1536*
if *a* bowels and mercies........ Phil 2:1 *1536*
If *a* other man thinketh that he........ Phil 3:4 *1536*
If by *a* means I might attain unto........ Phil 3:11 *4458*
if in *a* thing ye be otherwise........ Phil 3:15 *1536*
if there be *a* virtue, and if there........ Phil 4:8 *1536*
lest *a* man should beguile you........ Col 2:4 *3387*
Beware lest *a* man spoil you........ Col 2:8 *3387*
not in *a* honour to the satisfying........ Col 2:23 *5100*
a man have a quarrel against *a*........ Col 3:13 *5100*
that we need not to speak *a* thing........ 1Th 1:8 *5100*
For neither at *a* time used we........ 1Th 2:5 *4218*
not be chargeable unto *a* of you........ 1Th 2:9 *5100*
defraud his brother in *a* matter........ 1Th 4:6
render evil for evil unto *a* man........ 1Th 5:15 *5100*
Let no man deceive you by *a* means........ 2Th 2:3 *3367*
Neither did we eat *a* man's bread........ 2Th 3:8 *5100*
not be chargeable to *a* of you........ 2Th 3:8 *5100*
that if *a* would not work, neither........ 2Th 3:10 *1536*
if *a* man obey not our word by........ 2Th 3:14 *5100*
if there be *a* other thing that is........ 1Ti 1:10 *1536*
But if *a* widow have children or........ 1Ti 5:4 *5100*
But if *a* provide not for his own,........ 1Ti 5:8 *5100*
If *a* man or woman that believeth........ 1Ti 5:16 *1536*
If *a* man teach otherwise, and........ 1Ti 6:3 *1536*
If *a* be blameless, the husband of........ Titus 1:6 *1536*
of the angels said he at *a* time........ Heb 1:5 *4218*
of the angels said he at *a* times........ Heb 1:13 *4218*
lest at *a* time we should let them........ Heb 2:1 *3379*
lest there be in *a* of you an evil........ Heb 3:12 *5100*
lest *a* of you be hardened through........ Heb 3:13 *5100*
a of you should seem to come........ Heb 4:1 *5100*
lest *a* man fall after the same........ Heb 4:11 *5100*
sharper than *a* twoedged sword,........ Heb 4:12 *3956*
Neither is there *a* creature that........ Heb 4:13
but if *a* man draw back, my soul........ Heb 10:38
Looking diligently lest *a* man........ Heb 12:15 *5100*
lest *a* root of bitterness........ Heb 12:15 *5100*
Lest there be *a* fornicator........ Heb 12:16 *5100*
not be spoken to them *a* more........ Heb 12:19 *2089*
If *a* of you lack wisdom, let him........ Jas 1:5 *5100*
shall receive *a* thing of the Lord........ Jas 1:7 *5100*
evil, neither tempteth he *a* man........ Jas 1:13 *3762*
For if *a* be a hearer of the word,........ Jas 1:23 *1536*
If *a* man among you seem to be........ Jas 1:26 *1536*
If *a* man offend not in word, the........ Jas 3:2 *1536*
earth, neither by *a* other oath........ Jas 5:12 *5100*
Is *a* among you afflicted........ Jas 5:13 *5100*
Is *a* merry?........ Jas 5:13 *5100*
Is *a* sick among you........ Jas 5:14 *5100*
if *a* of you do err from the truth........ Jas 5:19 *1536*
if *a* obey not the word, they also........ 1Pet 3:1 *5100*
are not afraid with *a* amazement........ 1Pet 3:6 *1536*
If *a* man speak, let him speak as........ 1Pet 4:11 *1536*
if *a* man minister, let him do it........ 1Pet 4:11 *1536*
Yet if *a* man suffer as a........ 1Pet 4:16
is of *a* private interpretation........ 2Pet 1:20
not willing that *a* should perish........ 2Pet 3:9 *5100*
if *a* man sin, we have an advocate........ 1Jn 2:1 *5100*
If *a* man love the world, the love........ 1Jn 2:15 *5100*
ye need not that *a* man teach you........ 1Jn 2:27 *5100*
No man hath seen God at *a* time........ 1Jn 4:12 *4455*
if we ask *a* thing according to........ 1Jn 5:14 *5100*
If *a* man see his brother sin a........ 1Jn 5:16 *1536*
If there come *a* unto you, and........ 2Jn 10 *1536*
if *a* man hear my voice, and open........ Rev 3:20 *1536*
nor on the sea, nor on *a* tree........ Rev 7:1 *3956*
no more, neither thirst *a* more........ Rev 7:16 *2089*
the sun light on them, nor *a* heat........ Rev 7:16 *3956*
a green thing, neither *a* tree........ Rev 9:4 *3956*
if *a* man will hurt them, fire........ Rev 11:5 *1536*
if *a* man will hurt them, he must........ Rev 11:5 *1536*
place found *a* more in heaven........ Rev 12:8 *2089*
If *a* man have an ear, let him........ Rev 13:9 *1536*
If *a* man worship the beast and his........ Rev 14:9 *1536*
buyeth their merchandise *a* more........ Rev 18:11 *3765*
be, shall be found *a* more in thee........ Rev 18:22 *2089*
shall there be *a* more pain........ Rev 21:4 *2089*
into it *a* thing that defileth........ Rev 21:27 *3956*
If *a* man shall add unto these........ Rev 22:18 *5100*
if *a* man shall take away from the........ Rev 22:19 *5100*

APACE
And he came *a*, and drew near........ 2Sa 18:25
Kings of armies did flee *a*........ Ps 68:12
are beaten down, and are fled *a*........ Jer 46:5

APART
That thou shalt set *a* unto the........ Ex 13:12 5674
she shall be put *a* seven days........ Lev 15:19 5079
she is put *a* for her uncleanness........ Lev 18:19 5079
a him that is godly for himself........ Ps 4:3 6395
her that was set *a* for pollution........ Eze 22:10 5079
family of the house of David *a*........ Zec 12:12 905
of David *a*, and their wives *a*........ Zec 12:12 905
of Nathan *a*, and their wives *a*........ Zec 12:12 905

of Levi a, and their wives a Zec 12:13 905
of Shimei a, and their wives a Zec 12:13 905
family a, and their wives a Zec 12:14 905
by ship into a desert place a Mt 14:13 2596
went up into a mountain a to pray Mt 14:23 2596
them up into an high mountain a Mt 17:1 2596
came the disciples to Jesus a Mt 17:19 2596
the twelve disciples a in the way Mt 20:17 2596
Come ye yourselves a into a Mk 6:31 2596
an high mountain a by themselves Mk 9:2 2596
Wherefore lay a all filthiness and Jas 1:21 659

APELLES (*a-pel'-leze*) *A Christian acquaintance of Paul.*
Salute A approved in Christ Rom 16:10 559

APES
gold, and silver, ivory, and a 1Kin 10:22 6971
gold, and silver, ivory, and a 2Chr 9:21 6971

APHARSACHITES (*a-far'-sak-ites*) See APHARSATHCHITES. *An Assyrian tribe.*
and his companions the A, which Ezr 5:6 671
and your companions the A Ezr 6:6 671

APHARSATHCHITES (*a-far'-sath-kites*) See APHARSACHITES, APHARSITES. *Same as Apharsachites.*
the Dinaites, the A, the Ezr 4:9 671

APHARSITES (*a-far'-sites*) See APHARSATHCHITES. *Same as Apharsachites*
the Tarpelites, the A, the Ezr 4:9 670

APHEK (*a'-fek*) See APHIK.
1. A Canaanite city.
The king of A, one Josh 12:18 663
and the Philistines pitched in A 1Sa 4:1 663
together all their armies to A 1Sa 29:1 663
2. A city in Asher.
is beside the Sidonians, unto A Josh 13:4 663
Ummah also, and A, and Rehob Josh 19:30 663
3. Place where Ahab defeated Benhadad.
the Syrians, and went up to A 1Kin 20:26 663
But the rest fled to A, into the 1Kin 20:30 663
thou shalt smite the Syrians in A 2Kin 13:17 663

APHEKAH (*af-e'-kah*) *A city in Judah.*
And Janum, and Beth-tappuah, and A Josh 15:53 664

APHIAH (*af-i'-ah*) *An ancestor of Saul.*
son of Bechorath, the son of A 1Sa 9:1 647

APHIK (*a'-fik*) See APHEK. *Same as Aphek 2.*
Achzib, nor of Helbah, nor of A Judg 1:31 663

APHRAH (*af'-rah*) See BETH-LEAPHRAH, OPHRAH. *A city in Benjamin.*
in the house of A roll thyself in Mic 1:10 1036

APHSES (*af'-seze*) *A Levite chief.*
to Hezir, the eighteenth to A 1Chr 24:15 6483

APIECE
take five shekels a by the poll Num 3:47
incense, weighing ten shekels a Num 7:86
of their princes gave him a rod a Num 17:6
brass, of eighteen cubits high a 1Kin 7:15 259
Every one had four faces a Eze 10:21 259
And the doors had two leaves a Eze 41:24
neither have two coats a Lk 9:3 303
containing two or three firkins a Jn 2:6 303

APOLLONIA (*ap-ol-lo'-ne-ah*) *A city in Macedonia.*
passed through Amphipolis and A Acts 17:1 624

APOLLOS (*ap-ol'-los*) *A Christian Jew from Alexandria.*
And a certain Jew named A, born at Acts 18:24 625
while A was at Corinth, Paul Acts 19:1 625
and I of A 1Cor 1:12 625
and another, I am of A 1Cor 3:4 625
Who then is Paul, and who is A 1Cor 3:5 625
I have planted, A watered 1Cor 3:6 625
Whether Paul, or A, or Cephas, or 1Cor 3:22 625
to myself and to A for your sakes 1Cor 4:6 625
As touching our brother A 1Cor 16:12 625
A on their journey diligently, Titus 3:13 625

APOLLYON (*ap-ol'-le-on*) *The angel of the Abyss.*
the Greek tongue hath his name A Rev 9:11 623

APOSTLE
Jesus Christ, called to be an a Rom 1:1 652
as I am the a of the Gentiles Rom 11:13 652
called to be an a of Jesus Christ 1Cor 1:1 652
Am I not an a 1Cor 9:1 652
If I be not an a unto others 1Cor 9:2 652
am not meet to be called an a 1Cor 15:9 652
an a of Jesus Christ by the will 2Cor 1:1 652
Truly the signs of an a were 2Cor 12:12 652
Paul, an a, (not of men, neither Gal 1:1 652
an a of Jesus Christ by the will Eph 1:1 652
an a of Jesus Christ by the will Col 1:1 652
an a of Jesus Christ by the 1Ti 1:1 652
I am ordained a preacher, and an a 1Ti 2:7 652
an a of Jesus Christ by the will 2Ti 1:1 652
am appointed a preacher, and an a 2Ti 1:11 652
an a of Jesus Christ, according Titus 1:1 652
heavenly calling, consider the A Heb 3:1 652
an a of Jesus Christ, to the 1Pet 1:1 652
an a of Jesus Christ, to them 2Pet 1:1 652

APOSTLES
names of the twelve a are these Mt 10:2 652
the a gathered themselves Mk 6:30 652
twelve, whom also he named a Lk 6:13 652
And the a, when they were returned Lk 9:10 652
I will send them prophets and a Lk 11:49 652
the a said unto the Lord, Lk 17:5 652
down, and the twelve a with him Lk 22:14 652
told these things unto the a Lk 24:10 652
unto the a whom he had chosen Acts 1:2 652
he was numbered with the eleven a Acts 1:26 652
Peter and to the rest of the a Acts 2:37 652
and signs were done by the a Acts 2:43 652
with great power gave the a Acts 4:33 652
who by the a was surnamed Acts 4:36 652
hands of the a were many signs Acts 5:12 652
And laid their hands on the a Acts 5:18 652
Peter and the other a answered Acts 5:29 652
to put the a forth a little space Acts 5:34 652
and when they had called the a Acts 5:40 652
Whom they set before the a Acts 6:6 652
Judaea and Samaria, except the a Acts 8:1 652
Now when the a which were at Acts 8:14 652
took him, and brought him to the a Acts 9:27 652
And the a and brethren that were in Acts 11:1 652
with the Jews, and part with the a Acts 14:4 652
Which when the a, Barnabas and Acts 14:14 652
go up to Jerusalem unto the a Acts 15:2 652
of the church, and of the a Acts 15:4 652
And the a and elders came together Acts 15:6 652
Then pleased it the a and elders, Acts 15:22 652
The a and elders and brethren send Acts 15:23 652
from the brethren unto the a Acts 15:33
keep, that were ordained of the a Acts 16:4 652
who are of note among the a Rom 16:7 652
God hath set forth us the a last 1Cor 4:9 652
a wife, as well as other a 1Cor 9:5 652
set some in the church, first a 1Cor 12:28 652
Are all a? 1Cor 12:29 652
then of all the a 1Cor 15:7 652
For I am the least of the a 1Cor 15:9 652
a whit behind the very chiefest a 2Cor 11:5 652
For such are false a, deceitful 2Cor 11:13 652
themselves into the a of Christ 2Cor 11:13 5570
am I behind the very chiefest a 2Cor 12:11 652
to them which were a before me Gal 1:17 652
But other of the a saw I none Gal 1:19 652
upon the foundation of the a Eph 2:20 652
is now revealed unto his holy a Eph 3:5 652
And he gave some, a Eph 4:11 652
burdensome, as the a of Christ 1Th 2:6 652
of us the a of the Lord and 2Pet 3:2 652
of the a of our Lord Jesus Christ Jude 17 652
tried them which say they are a Rev 2:2 652
her, thou heaven, and ye holy a Rev 18:20 652
names of the twelve a of the Lamb Rev 21:14 652

APOSTLES'
stedfastly in the a doctrine Acts 2:42 652
And laid them down at the a feet Acts 4:35 652
money, and laid it at the a feet Acts 4:37 652
part, and laid it at the a feet Acts 5:2 652
that through laying on of the a Acts 8:18 652

APOSTLESHIP
take part of this ministry and a Acts 1:25 651
whom we have received grace and a Rom 1:5 651
seal of mine a are ye in the Lord 1Cor 9:2 651
to the a of the circumcision Gal 2:8 651

APOTHECARIES
Hananiah the son of one of the a Neh 3:8 7543

APOTHECARIES'
of spices prepared by the a art 2Chr 16:14 4842

APOTHECARY
compound after the art of the a Ex 30:25 7543
confection after the art of the a Ex 30:35 7543
according to the work of the a Ex 37:29 7543
a to send forth a stinking savour Eccl 10:1 7543

APPAIM (*ap'-pa-im*) *A son of Nadab.*
Seled, and A 1Chr 2:30 649
And the sons of A 1Chr 2:31 649

APPAREL
by the year, and a suit of a Judg 17:10 899
asses, and the camels, and the a 1Sa 27:9 899
on ornaments of gold upon your a 2Sa 1:24 3830
himself, and changed his a 2Sa 12:20 8071
mourner, and put on now mourning a 2Sa 14:2 899
of his ministers, and their a 1Kin 10:5 4403
of his ministers, and their a 2Chr 9:4 4403
his cupbearers also, and their a 2Chr 9:4 4403
priests in their a with trumpets Ezr 3:10 3847
that Esther put on her royal a Est 5:1
Let the royal a be brought which Est 6:8 3830
And let this a and horse be Est 6:9 3830
Haman, Make haste, and take the a Est 6:10 3830
Then took Haman the a and the Est 6:11 3830
of the king in royal a of blue Est 8:15 3830
The changeable suits of a Is 3:22 4254
our own bread, and wear our own a Is 4:1 8071
this that is glorious in his a Is 63:1 3830
Wherefore art thou red in thine a Is 63:2 3830
work, and in chests of rich a Eze 27:24 1264
as are clothed with strange a Zeph 1:8 4403
together, gold, and silver, and a Zec 14:14 899
two men stood by them in white a Acts 1:10 2066
set day Herod, arrayed in royal a Acts 12:21 2066
no man's silver, or gold, or a Acts 20:33 2441
adorn themselves in modest a 1Ti 2:9 2689
man with a gold ring, in goodly a Jas 2:2 2066
of gold, or of putting on of a 1Pet 3:3 2440

APPARELLED
daughters that were virgins a 2Sa 13:18 3847
they which are gorgeously a Lk 7:25 2441

APPARENTLY
I speak mouth to mouth, even a Num 12:8 4758

APPEAL
I a unto Caesar Acts 25:11 1941
was constrained to a unto Caesar Acts 28:19 1941

APPEALED
answered, Hast thou a unto Caesar Acts 25:12 1941
But when Paul had a to be Acts 25:21 1941
he himself hath a to Augustus Acts 25:25 1941
if he had not a unto Caesar Acts 26:32 1941

APPEAR
one place, and let the dry land a Gen 1:9 7200
made the white a which was in the Gen 30:37 4286
none shall a before me empty Ex 23:15 7200
males shall a before the Lord GOD Ex 23:17 7200
none shall a before me empty Ex 34:20 7200
children a before the Lord GOD Ex 34:23 7200
when thou shalt go up to a before Ex 34:24 7200
to day the LORD will a unto you Lev 9:4 7200
of the LORD shall a unto you Lev 9:6 7200
if it a still in the garment, Lev 13:57 7200
for I will a in the cloud upon Lev 16:2 7200
in a year shall all thy males a Deut 16:16 7200
they shall not a before the LORD Deut 16:16 7200
When all Israel is come to a Deut 31:11 7200
the LORD did no more a to Manoah Judg 13:21 7200
that he may a before the LORD, and 1Sa 1:22 7200
Did I plainly a unto the house of 1Sa 2:27 1540
that night did God a unto Solomon 2Chr 1:7 7200
when shall I come and a before God Ps 42:2 7200
Let thy work a unto thy servants, Ps 90:16 7200
up Zion, he shall a in his glory Ps 102:16 7200
The flowers a on the earth Song 2:12 7200
goats, that a from mount Gilead Song 4:1 1570
flock of goats that a from Gilead Song 6:5 1570
whether the tender grape a Song 7:12 6524
When ye come to a before me Is 1:12 7200
but he shall a to your joy Is 66:5 7200
thy face, that thy shame may a Jer 13:26 7200
in all your doings your sins do a Eze 21:24 7200
that they may a unto men to fast Mt 6:16 5316
That thou a not unto men to fast, Mt 6:18 5316
which indeed a beautiful outward, Mt 23:27 5316
outwardly a righteous unto men Mt 23:28 5316
then shall a the sign of the Son Mt 24:30 5316
for ye are as graves which a not Lk 11:44 82
of God should immediately a Lk 19:11 398
priests and all their council to a Acts 22:30 2064
in the which I will a unto thee Acts 26:16 3700
But sin, that it might a sin Rom 7:13 5316
For we must all a before the 2Cor 5:10 5319
the sight of God might a unto you 2Cor 7:12 5319
not that we should a approved 2Cor 13:7 5316
Christ, who is our life, shall a Col 3:4 5319
shall ye also a with him in glory Col 3:4 5319
that thy profiting may a to all 1Ti 4:15 5318
now to a in the presence of God Heb 9:24 1718
he a the second time without sin Heb 9:28 3700
not made of things which do a Heb 11:3 5316
shall the ungodly and the sinner a 1Pet 4:18 5316
when the chief Shepherd shall a 1Pet 5:4 5319
that, when he shall a, we may 1Jn 2:28 5319
it doth not yet a what we shall 1Jn 3:2 5319
but we know that, when he shall a 1Jn 3:2 5319
shame of thy nakedness do not a Rev 3:18 5319

APPEARANCE
as it were the a of fire, until Num 9:15 4758
by day, and the a of fire by night Num 9:16 4758
for man looketh on the outward a 1Sa 16:7 5869
And this was their a Eze 1:5 4758
their a was like burning coals of Eze 1:13 4758
and like the a of lamps Eze 1:13 4758
returned as the a of a flash of Eze 1:14 4758
The a of the wheels and their work Eze 1:16 4758
and their a and their work was as Eze 1:16 4758
as the a of a sapphire stone Eze 1:26 4758
as the a of a man above upon it Eze 1:26 4758
as the a of fire round about Eze 1:27 4758
from the a of his loins even Eze 1:27 4758
from the a of his loins even Eze 1:27 4758
I saw as it were the a of fire Eze 1:27 4758
As the a of the bow that is in Eze 1:28 4758
so was the a of the brightness Eze 1:28 4758
This was the a of the likeness of Eze 1:28 4758
and lo a likeness as the a of fire Eze 8:2 4758
from the a of his loins even Eze 8:2 4758
as the a of brightness, as the Eze 8:2 4758
as the a of the likeness of a Eze 10:1 4758
the a of the wheels was as the Eze 10:9 4758
whose a was like the a Eze 40:3 4758
the a of the one as the a Eze 41:21 4758
the a of the chambers which were Eze 42:11 4758
it was according to the a of the Eze 43:3 4758
stood before me as the a of a man Dan 8:15 4758
and his face as the a of lightning Dan 10:6 4758
me one like the a of a man Dan 10:18 4758
a of them is as the a of horses Joel 2:4 4758
Judge not according to the a Jn 7:24 3799
to answer them which glory in a 2Cor 5:12 4383
on things after the outward a 2Cor 10:7 4383
Abstain from all a of evil 1Th 5:22 1491

APPEARANCES
And as for their a, they four had Eze 10:10 4758
by the river of Chebar, their a Eze 10:22 4758

APPEARED
the LORD a unto Abram, and said, Gen 12:7 7200
unto the LORD, who a unto him Gen 12:7 7200
old and nine, the LORD a to Abram Gen 17:1 7200
the LORD a unto him in the plains Gen 18:1 7200
And the LORD a unto him, and said, Gen 26:2 7200
the LORD a unto him the same Gen 26:24 7200
that a unto thee when thou Gen 35:1 7200
because there God a unto him Gen 35:7 1540
God a unto Jacob again, when he Gen 35:9 7200
God Almighty a unto me at Luz in Gen 48:3 7200
the angel of the LORD a unto him Ex 3:2 7200
a unto me, saying, I have surely Ex 3:16 7200

The LORD hath not a unto thee ... Ex 4:1 7200
God of Jacob, hath a unto thee ... Ex 4:5 7200
I a unto Abraham, unto Isaac, and ... Ex 6:3 7200
his strength when the morning a ... Ex 14:27 6437
glory of the LORD a in the cloud ... Ex 16:10 7200
of the LORD a unto all the people ... Lev 9:23 7200
the glory of the LORD a in the ... Num 14:10 7200
the glory of the LORD a unto all ... Num 16:19 7200
it, and the glory of the LORD a ... Num 16:42 7200
the glory of the LORD a unto them ... Num 20:6 7200
the LORD a in the tabernacle in a ... Deut 31:15 7200
the angel of the LORD a unto him ... Judg 6:12 7200
of the LORD a unto the woman ... Judg 13:3 7200
Behold, the man hath a unto me ... Judg 13:10 7200
the LORD a again in Shiloh ... 1Sa 3:21 7200
And the channels of the sea a ... 2Sa 22:16 7200
In Gibeon the LORD a to Solomon ... 1Kin 3:5 7200
That the LORD a to Solomon the ... 1Kin 9:2 7200
as he had a unto him at Gibeon ... 1Kin 9:2 7200
which had a unto him twice ... 1Kin 11:9 7200
there a a chariot of fire, and ... 2Kin 2:11
where the LORD a unto David his ... 2Chr 3:1 7200
the LORD a to Solomon by night, ... 2Chr 7:12 7200
of the morning till the stars a ... Neh 4:21 3318
The LORD hath a of old unto me, ... Jer 31:3 7200
a over them as it were a sapphire ... Eze 10:1 7200
there a in the cherubims the form ... Eze 10:8 7200
she a in her height with the ... Eze 19:11 7200
days their countenances a fairer ... Dan 1:15 7200
Belshazzar a vision a unto me ... Dan 8:1 7200
after that which a unto me at the ... Dan 8:1 7200
of the Lord a unto him in a dream ... Mt 1:20 5316
diligently what time the star a ... Mt 2:7 5316
fruit, then a the tares also ... Mt 13:26 5316
there a unto them Moses and Elias ... Mt 17:3 3700
the holy city, and a unto many ... Mt 27:53 1718
there a unto them Elias with ... Mk 9:4 3700
he a first to Mary Magdalene, out ... Mk 16:9 5316
After that he a in another form ... Mk 16:12 5319
Afterward he a unto the eleven as ... Mk 16:14 5319
there a unto him an angel of the ... Lk 1:11 3700
And of some, that Elias had a ... Lk 9:8 5316
Who a in glory, and spake of his ... Lk 9:31 3700
there a an angel unto him from ... Lk 22:43 3700
risen indeed, and hath a to Simon ... Lk 24:34 3700
there a unto them cloven tongues ... Acts 2:3 3700
The God of glory a unto our ... Acts 7:2 3700
there a to him in the wilderness ... Acts 7:30 3700
angel which a to him in the bush ... Acts 7:35 3700
that a unto thee in the way as ... Acts 9:17 3700
a vision a to Paul in the night ... Acts 16:9 3700
for I have a unto thee for this ... Acts 26:16 3700
sun nor stars in many days a ... Acts 27:20 2014
salvation hath a to all men ... Titus 2:11 2014
of God our Saviour toward man a ... Titus 3:4 2014
hath he a to put away sin by the ... Heb 9:26 5319
there a a great wonder in heaven ... Rev 12:1 3700
there a another wonder in heaven ... Rev 12:3 3700

APPEARETH

But when raw flesh a in him ... Lev 13:14 7200
as the leprosy a in the skin of ... Lev 13:43 4758
him into thy hand, as a this day ... Deut 2:30
one of them in Zion a before God ... Ps 84:7 7200
The hay a, and the tender grass ... Prov 27:25 1540
for evil a out of the north, and ... Jer 6:1 8259
and who shall stand when he a ... Mal 3:2 7200
the Lord a to Joseph in a dream ... Mt 2:13 5316
an angel of the Lord a in a dream ... Mt 2:19 5316
that a for a little time, and then ... Jas 4:14 5316

APPEARING

until the a of our Lord Jesus ... 1Ti 6:14 2015
the a of our Saviour Jesus Christ ... 2Ti 1:10 2015
the quick and the dead at his a ... 2Ti 4:1 2015
all them also that love his a ... 2Ti 4:8 2015
the glorious a of the great God ... Titus 2:13 2015
glory at the a of Jesus Christ ... 1Pet 1:7 602

APPEASE

I will a him with the present ... Gen 32:20 6440

APPEASED

the wrath of king Ahasuerus was a ... Est 2:1 7918
the townclerk had a the people ... Acts 19:35 2687

APPEASETH

he that is slow to anger a strife ... Prov 15:18 8252

APPERTAIN

up, with all that a unto them ... Num 16:30
for to thee doth it a ... Jer 10:7 2969

APPERTAINED

and all the men that a unto Korah ... Num 16:32
They, and all that a to them ... Num 16:33
the palace which a to the house ... Neh 2:8

APPERTAINETH

and give it unto him to whom it a ... Lev 6:5
It a not unto thee, Uzziah, to ... 2Chr 26:18

APPETITE

or fill the a of the young lions, ... Job 38:39 2416
if thou be a man given to a ... Prov 23:2 5315
mouth, and yet the a is not filled ... Eccl 6:7 5315
he is faint, and his soul hath a ... Is 29:8 8264

APPHIA *(af'-fee-ah) A Christian acquaintance of Paul.*

And to our beloved A, and Archippus .. Philem 2 682

APPII *(ap'-pe-i) A place south of Rome.*

came to meet us as far as A forum ... Acts 28:15 675

APPIUS See APPII.

APPLE

he kept him as the a of his eye ... Deut 32:10 380
Keep me as the a of the eye ... Ps 17:8 1323
and my law as the a of thine eye ... Prov 7:2 380
As the a tree among the trees of ... Song 2:3 8598
I raised thee up under the a tree ... Song 8:5 8598
let not the a of thine eye cease ... Lam 2:18 1323
the a tree, even all the trees of ... Joel 1:12 8598
you toucheth the a of his eye ... Zec 2:8 892

APPLES

A word fitly spoken is like a of ... Prov 25:11 8598
with flagons, comfort me with a ... Song 2:5 8598
and the smell of thy nose like a ... Song 7:8 8598

APPLIED

I a mine heart to know, and to ... Eccl 7:25 5437
a my heart unto every work that ... Eccl 8:9 5414
When I a mine heart to know ... Eccl 8:16 5414

APPLY

that we may a our hearts unto ... Ps 90:12 935
a thine heart to understanding ... Prov 2:2 5186
a thine heart unto my knowledge ... Prov 22:17 7896
A thine heart unto instruction, ... Prov 23:12 935

APPOINT

A me thy wages, and I will give it ... Gen 30:28 5344
let him a officers over the land, ... Gen 41:34 6485
then I will a thee a place ... Ex 21:13 7760
shalt a it for the service of the ... Ex 30:16 5414
I will even a over you terror, ... Lev 26:16 6485
But thou shalt a the Levites over ... Num 1:50 6485
And thou shalt a Aaron and his sons ... Num 3:10 6485
a them every one to his service ... Num 4:19 7760
ye shall a unto them in charge ... Num 4:27 6485
refuge, which ye shall a for the ... Num 35:6 5414
Then ye shall a you cities to be ... Num 35:11 7136
A out for you cities of refuge, ... Josh 20:2 5414
a them for himself, for his ... 1Sa 8:11 7760
he will a him captains over ... 1Sa 8:12 7760
to a me ruler over the people of ... 2Sa 6:21 6680
Moreover I will a a place for my ... 2Sa 7:10 7760
my lord the king shall a ... 2Sa 15:15 977
to all that thou shalt a ... 1Kin 5:6 559
the place that thou shalt a me ... 1Kin 5:9 7971
to a their brethren to be the ... 1Chr 15:16 5975
a watches of the inhabitants of ... Neh 7:3 5975
let the king a officers in all ... Est 2:3 6485
thou wouldest a me a set time ... Job 14:13 7896
salvation will God a for walls ... Is 26:1 7896
To a unto them that mourn in Zion ... Is 61:3 7760
I will a over them four kinds, ... Jer 15:3 6485
chosen man, that I may a over her ... Jer 49:19 6485
and who will a me the time ... Jer 49:19 3259
chosen man, that I may a over her ... Jer 50:44 6485
and who will a me the time ... Jer 50:44 3259
a a captain against her ... Jer 51:27 6485
a thee two ways, that the sword ... Eze 21:19 7760
A a way, that the sword may come ... Eze 21:20 7760
to a captains, to open the mouth ... Eze 21:22 7760
to a battering rams against the ... Eze 21:22 7760
ye shall a the possession of the ... Eze 45:6 5414
a themselves one head, and they ... Hos 1:11 7760
a him his portion with the ... Mt 24:51 5087
will a him his portion with the ... Lk 12:46 5087
I a unto you a kingdom, as my ... Lk 22:29 1303
whom we may a over this business ... Acts 6:3 2525

APPOINTED

hath a me another seed instead of ... Gen 4:25 7896
At the time a I will return unto ... Gen 18:14 4150
thou hast a for thy servant Isaac ... Gen 24:14 3198
hath a out for my master's son ... Gen 24:44 3198
the LORD a a set time, saying, To ... Ex 9:5 7760
in the time a of the month Abib ... Ex 23:15 4150
keep the passover at his a season ... Num 9:2 4150
ye shall keep it in his a season ... Num 9:3 4150
a season among the children of ... Num 9:7 4150
of the LORD in his a season ... Num 9:13 4150
he and all his people, at a time a ... Josh 8:14 4150
they a Kedesh in Galilee in mount ... Josh 20:7 6942
These were the cities a for all ... Josh 20:9 4152
six hundred men a with weapons of ... Judg 18:11 2296
the six hundred men a with their ... Judg 18:16 2296
that were a with weapons of war ... Judg 18:17 2296
Now there was an a sign between ... Judg 20:38 4150
to the set time that Samuel had a ... 1Sa 13:8
thou camest not within the days a ... 1Sa 13:11 4150
and Samuel standing as a over them ... 1Sa 19:20 5324
field at the time a with David ... 1Sa 20:35 4150
I have a my servants to such and ... 1Sa 21:2 3045
shall have a thee ruler over ... 1Sa 25:30 6680
his place which thou hast a him ... 1Sa 29:4 6485
For the LORD had a to defeat the ... 2Sa 17:14 6680
the set time which he had a him ... 2Sa 20:5 3259
the morning even to the time a ... 2Sa 24:15 4150
I have a him to be ruler over ... 1Kin 1:35 6680
a him victuals, and gave him land ... 1Kin 11:18 559
the third day, as the king had a ... 1Kin 12:12 1696
man whom I a to utter destruction ... 1Kin 20:42 2764
the king a the lord on whose hand ... 2Kin 7:17 6485
So the king a unto her a certain ... 2Kin 8:6 5414
Jehu a fourscore men without, and ... 2Kin 10:24 7760
the priest a officers over the ... 2Kin 11:18 7760
the king of Assyria a unto ... 2Kin 18:14 7760
a unto all manner of service of ... 1Chr 6:48 5414
were a for all the work of the ... 1Chr 6:49
were a to oversee the vessels ... 1Chr 9:29 4487
So the Levites a Heman the son of ... 1Chr 15:17 5975
were a to sound with cymbals of ... 1Chr 15:19
he a certain of the Levites to ... 1Chr 16:4 5414
And he a, according to the order ... 2Chr 8:14 5975
he a singers unto the LORD, and ... 2Chr 20:21 5975
Also Jehoiada a the offices of ... 2Chr 23:18 7760
Hezekiah a the courses of the ... 2Chr 31:2 5975
He a also the king's portion of ... 2Chr 31:3
which I have a for your fathers ... 2Chr 33:8 5975
and they that the king had a ... 2Chr 34:22
a the Levites, from twenty years ... Ezr 3:8 5975
the princes had a for the service ... Ezr 8:20 5414
in our cities come at a times ... Ezr 10:14 2163
from the time that I was a to be ... Neh 5:14 6680
thou hast also a prophets to ... Neh 6:7 5975
the singers and the Levites were a ... Neh 7:1 6485
in their rebellion a a captain to ... Neh 9:17 5414
at times a year by year, to burn ... Neh 10:34 2163
a two great companies of them ... Neh 12:31 5975
at that time were some a over the ... Neh 12:44 6485
a the wards of the priests and the ... Neh 13:30 5975
for the wood offering, at times a ... Neh 13:31 2163
for so the king had a to all the ... Est 1:8 3245
the keeper of the women, a ... Est 2:15 559
whom he had a to attend upon her, ... Est 4:5 5975
to their a time every year ... Est 9:27
days of Purim in their times a ... Est 9:31
Is there not an a time to man ... Job 7:1 6635
and wearisome nights are a to me ... Job 7:3 4487
thou hast a his bounds that he ... Job 14:5 6213
the days of my a time will I wait ... Job 14:14 6635
the heritage a unto him by God ... Job 20:29 561
the thing that is a for me ... Job 23:14 2706
to the house a for all living ... Job 30:23 4150
given us like sheep a for meat ... Ps 44:11
a a law in Israel, which he ... Ps 78:5 7760
thou those that are a to die ... Ps 79:11 1121
in the new moon, in the time a ... Ps 81:3 3677
loose those that are a to death ... Ps 102:20 1121
He a the moon for seasons ... Ps 104:19 6213
and will come home at the day a ... Prov 7:20 3677
when he a the foundations of the ... Prov 8:29 2710
all such as are a to destruction ... Prov 31:8 1121
your a feasts my soul hateth ... Is 1:14 4150
shall be alone in his a times ... Is 14:31 4151
the a barley and the rie in their ... Is 28:25 5567
since I a the ancient people ... Is 44:7 7760
us the a weeks of the harvest ... Jer 5:24 2708
in the heaven knoweth her a times ... Jer 8:7 4150
if I have not a the ordinances of ... Jer 33:25 7760
he hath passed the time a ... Jer 46:17 4150
there hath he a it ... Jer 47:7 3259
I have a thee each day for a year ... Eze 4:6 5414
which have a my land into their ... Eze 36:5 5414
it in the a place of the house ... Eze 43:21 4662
the king a them a daily provision ... Dan 1:5 4487
who hath a your meat and your ... Dan 1:10 4487
for at the time a the end shall ... Dan 8:19 4150
was true, but the time a was long ... Dan 10:1 6635
the end shall be at the time a ... Dan 11:27 4150
At the time a he shall return, and ... Dan 11:29 4150
because it is yet for a time a ... Dan 11:35 4150
hear ye the rod, and who hath a it ... Mic 6:9 3259
the vision is yet for an a time ... Hab 2:3 4150
disciples did as Jesus had a them ... Mt 26:19 4929
potter's field, as the Lord a me ... Mt 27:10 4929
a mountain where Jesus had a them ... Mt 28:16 5021
no more than that which is a you ... Lk 3:13 1299
the Lord a other seventy also ... Lk 10:1 322
as my Father hath a unto me ... Lk 22:29 1303
And they a two, Joseph called ... Acts 1:23 1476
in the wilderness, as he had a ... Acts 7:44 1299
determined the times before a ... Acts 17:26 4384
Because he hath a a day, in the ... Acts 17:31 2476
for so had he a, minding himself ... Acts 20:13 1299
things which are a for thee to do ... Acts 22:10 5021
And when they had a him a day ... Acts 28:23 5021
last, as it were a to death ... 1Cor 4:9 1935
until the time a of the father ... Gal 4:2 4287
know that we are a thereunto ... 1Th 3:3 2749
For God hath not a us to wrath ... 1Th 5:9 5087
Whereunto I am a a preacher ... 2Ti 1:11 5087
in every city, as I had a thee ... Titus 1:5 1299
whom he hath a heir of all things ... Heb 1:2 5087
was faithful to him that a him ... Heb 3:2 4160
as it is a unto men once to die, ... Heb 9:27 606
whereunto also they were a ... 1Pet 2:8 5087

APPOINTETH

that he a over it whomsoever he ... Dan 5:21 6966

APPOINTMENT

At the a of Aaron and his sons ... Num 4:27 6310
for by the a of Absalom this hath ... 2Sa 13:32 6310
according to the a of the priests ... Ezr 6:9 3883
for they had made an a together ... Job 2:11 3259

APPREHEND

with a garrison, desirous to a me ... 2Cor 11:32 4084
if that I may a that for which ... Phil 3:12 2638

APPREHENDED

And when he had a him, he put him ... Acts 12:4 4084
which also I am a of Christ Jesus ... Phil 3:12 2638
I count not myself to have a ... Phil 3:13 2638

APPROACH

None of you shall a to any that ... Lev 18:6 7126
thou shalt not a to his wife ... Lev 18:14 7126
Also thou shalt not a unto a ... Lev 18:19 7126
if a woman a unto any beast, and ... Lev 20:16 7126
let him not a to offer the bread ... Lev 21:17 7126
hath a blemish, he shall not a ... Lev 21:18 7126
when they a unto the most holy ... Num 4:19 5066
battle, that the priest shall a ... Deut 20:2 5066
ye a this day unto battle against ... Deut 20:3 7126
thy days a that thou must die ... Deut 31:14 7126
are with me, will a unto the city ... Josh 8:5 7126
can make his sword to a unto him ... Job 40:19 5066
and causest to a unto thee ... Ps 65:4 7126
draw near, and he shall a unto me ... Jer 30:21 5066
engaged his heart to a unto me ... Jer 30:21 5066
where the priests that a unto the ... Eze 42:13 7138
shall a to those things which are ... Eze 42:14 7126
which a unto me, to minister unto ... Eze 43:19 7126
the light which no man can a unto ... 1Ti 6:16 676

APPROACHED
Wherefore *a* ye so nigh unto the... 2Sa 11:20 5066
the king *a* to the altar, and... 2Kin 16:12 7126

APPROACHETH
faileth not, where no thief *a*... Lk 12:33 *1448*

APPROACHING
they take delight in *a* to God... Is 58:2 7132
the more, as ye see the day *a*... Heb 10:25 *1448*

APPROVE
their posterity *a* their sayings... Ps 49:13 7520
ye shall *a* by your letters... 1Cor 16:3 *1381*
That ye may *a* things that are... Phil 1:10 *1381*

APPROVED
a man *a* of God among you by... Acts 2:22 *584*
is acceptable to God, and *a* of men... Rom 14:18 *1384*
Salute Apelles *a* in Christ... Rom 16:10 *1384*
that they which are *a* may be made... 1Cor 11:19 *1384*
In all things ye have *a*... 2Cor 7:11 *4921*
he that commendeth himself is *a*... 2Cor 10:18 *1384*
not that we should appear *a*... 2Cor 13:7 *1384*
Study to shew thyself *a* unto God... 2Ti 2:15 *1384*

APPROVEST
a the things that are more... Rom 2:18 *1381*

APPROVETH
man in his cause, the Lord *a* not... Lam 3:36 7200

APPROVING
But in all things *a* ourselves as... 2Cor 6:4 *4921*

APRONS
together, and made themselves *a*... Gen 3:7 2290
unto the sick handkerchiefs or *a*... Acts 19:12 *4612*

APT
a for war, even them the king of... 2Kin 24:16 6213
of them that were *a* to the war... 1Chr 7:40
given to hospitality, *a* to teach... 1Ti 3:2 *1317*
all men, *a* to teach, patient,... 2Ti 2:24 *1317*

AQUILA (*ac'-quil-ah*) *A Christian acquaintance of Paul.*
And found a certain Jew named *A*... Acts 18:2 *207*
Syria, and with him Priscilla and *A*... Acts 18:18 *207*
whom when *A* and Priscilla had... Acts 18:26 *207*
A my helpers in Christ Jesus... Rom 16:3 *207*
A and Priscilla salute you much in... 1Cor 16:19 *207*
Salute Prisca and *A*, and the... 2Ti 4:19 *207*

AR (*ar*) *The capital of Moab.*
goeth down to the dwelling of *A*... Num 21:15 6144
it hath consumed *A* of Moab... Num 21:28 6144
because I have given *A* unto the... Deut 2:9 6144
Thou art to pass over through *A*... Deut 2:18 6144
and the Moabites which dwell in *A*... Deut 2:29 6144
Because in the night *A* of Moab is... Is 15:1 6144

ARA (*a'-rah*) *A son of Jether.*
Jephunneh, and Pispah, and *A*... 1Chr 7:38 690

ARAB (*a'-rab*) See ARBITE. *A city in Judah.*
A, and Dumah, and Eshean,... Josh 15:52 694

ARABAH (*ar'-ab-ah*) See BETH-ARABAH. *The Jordan Valley.*
the side over against *A* northward... Josh 18:18 6160
and went down unto *A*... Josh 18:18 6160

ARABIA (*a-ra'-be-ah*) *The northern part of the Arabian peninsula.*
and of all the kings of *A*... 1Kin 10:15 6152
And all the kings of *A* and... 2Chr 9:14 6152
The burden upon *A*... Is 21:13 6152
In the forest in *A* shall ye lodge... Is 21:13 6152
And all the kings of *A*, and all the... Jer 25:24 6152
A, and all the princes of Kedar,... Eze 27:21 6152
but I went into *A*, and returned... Gal 1:17 *688*
For this Agar is mount Sinai in *A*... Gal 4:25 *688*

ARABIAN (*a-ra'-be-un*) See ARABIANS. *An inhabitant of Arabia.*
the Ammonite, and Geshem the *A*... Neh 2:19 6163
and Tobiah, and Geshem the *A*... Neh 6:1 6163
shall the *A* pitch tent there... Is 13:20 6153
as the *A* in the wilderness... Jer 3:2 6163

ARABIANS (*a-ra'-be-uns*)
the *A* brought him flocks, seven... 2Chr 17:11 6163
of the Philistines, and of the *A*... 2Chr 21:16 6163
A to the camp had slain all the... 2Chr 22:1 6163
against the *A* that dwelt in... 2Chr 26:7 6163
Sanballat, and Tobiah, and the *A*... Neh 4:7 6163
Cretes and *A*, we do hear them... Acts 2:11 *690*

ARABS See ARABIANS.

ARAD (*a'-rad*)
1. A Canaanite king.
when king *A* the Canaanite, which... Num 21:1 6166
king *A* the Canaanite, which dwelt... Num 33:40 6166
2. A district in Judah.
the king of *A*, one... Josh 12:14 6166
which lieth in the south of *A*... Judg 1:16 6166
3. A son of Beriah.
And Zebadiah, and *A*, and Ader,... 1Chr 8:15 6166

ARAH (*a'-rah*)
1. A son of Ulla.
A, and Haniel, and Rezia... 1Chr 7:39 733
2. A family of exiles who returned under Zerubbabel.
The children of *A*, seven hundred... Ezr 2:5 733
The children of *A*, six hundred... Neh 7:10 733
3. Grandfather of Tobiah's wife.
in law of Shechaniah the son of *A*... Neh 6:18 733

ARAM (*a'-ram*) See ARAMITESS, ARAM-NAHARAIM, ARAM-ZOBAH, BETH-ARAM, PADAN-ARAM, SYRIA.
1. The son of Shem.
and Arphaxad, and Lud, and *A*... Gen 10:22 758
And the children of *A*... Gen 10:23 758
and Arphaxad, and Lud, and *A*... 1Chr 1:17 758
2. The son of Kemuel.
and Kemuel the father of *A*... Gen 22:21 758
3. Another name for Syria.
of Moab hath brought me from *A*... Num 23:7 758
4. A district of Canaan.
And he took Geshur, and *A*, with the.. 1Chr 2:23 758
5. The son of Shamer.
Ahi, and Rohgah, Jehubbah, and *A*... 1Chr 7:34 758
and Esrom begat *A*... Mt 1:3 *689*
And *A* begat Aminadab... Mt 1:4 *689*
Aminadab, which was the son of *A*... Lk 3:33 *689*

ARAMEAN See ARAMITESS.

ARAMITESS (*a'-ram-i-tes*) See SYRIAN. *Manasseh's concubine.*
(but his concubine the *A* bare... 1Chr 7:14 761

ARAM-NAHARAIM (*a'-ram-na-ha-ra'-im*) See MESOPOTAMIA. *The area between the Tigris and Euphrates rivers.*
when he strove with *A* and with... Ps 60:*t* 763

ARAM-ZOBAH (*a'-ram-zo'-bah*) *The area between the Orontes and Euphrates rivers.*
with Aram-naharaim and with *A*... Ps 60:*t* 760

ARAN (*a'-ran*) See BETH-ARAN. *The son of Seir the Horite.*
of Dishan are these; Uz, and *A*... Gen 36:28 765
sons of Dishan; Uz, and *A*... 1Chr 1:42 765

ARARAT (*ar'-ar-at*) See ARMENIA. *A district in Armenia.*
month, upon the mountains of *A*... Gen 8:4 780
against her the kingdoms of *A*... Jer 51:27 780

ARAUNAH (*a-raw'-nah*) See ORNAN. *A Jebusite.*
threshingplace of *A* the Jebusite... 2Sa 24:16 728
threshingfloor of *A* the Jebusite... 2Sa 24:18 728
A looked, and saw the king and his... 2Sa 24:20 728
A went out, and bowed himself... 2Sa 24:20 728
A said, Wherefore is my lord the... 2Sa 24:21 728
A said unto David, Let my lord... 2Sa 24:22 728
All these things did *A*, as a king... 2Sa 24:23 728
A said unto the king, The LORD... 2Sa 24:23 728
And the king said unto *A*, Nay... 2Sa 24:24 728

ARBA (*ar'-bah*) See ARBAH, ARBATHITE, ARBITE, KIRJATH-ABBA. *Father of Anakim.*
even the city of *A* the father of... Josh 15:13 704
the city of *A* the father of Anak... Josh 21:11 704

ARBAH (*ar'-bah*) See ARBA. *Another name for Hebron.*
unto Mamre, unto the city of *A*... Gen 35:27 704

ARBATHITE (*ar'-bath-ite*) *A native of Arbah.*
Abi-albon the *A*, Azmaveth the... 2Sa 23:31 6164
the brooks of Gaash, Abiel the *A*... 1Chr 11:32 6164

ARBITE (*ar'-bite*) *A native of Arab.*
the Carmelite, Paarai the *A*... 2Sa 23:35 701

ARCHANGEL
a shout, with the voice of the *a*... 1Th 4:16 *743*
Yet Michael the *a*, when... Jude 9 *743*

ARCHELAUS (*ar-ke-la'-us*) *A son of Herod the Great.*
But when he heard that *A* did... Mt 2:22 *745*

ARCHER
in the wilderness, and became an *a*... Gen 21:20 7198
bendeth let the *a* bend his bow... Jer 51:3 1869

ARCHERS
The *a* have sorely grieved him, and... Gen 49:23 1167
a in the places of drawing water... Judg 5:11 2686
against Saul, and the *a* hit him... 1Sa 31:3 3384
and he was sore wounded of the *a*... 1Sa 31:3 3384
Ulam were mighty men of valour, *a*... 1Chr 8:40 7198
the *a* hit him... 1Chr 10:3 7198
and he was wounded of the *a*... 1Chr 10:3 3384
the *a* shot at king Josiah... 2Chr 35:23 3384
His *a* compass me round about, he... Job 16:13 7228
And the residue of the number of *a*... Is 21:17 7198
together, they are bound by the *a*... Is 22:3 7198
together the *a* against Babylon... Jer 50:29 7228

ARCHES
round about, and likewise to the *a*... Eze 40:16 361
the *a* thereof were after the... Eze 40:21 361
And their windows, and their *a*... Eze 40:22 361
the *a* thereof were before them... Eze 40:22 361
the *a* thereof according to these... Eze 40:24 361
in the *a* thereof round about,... Eze 40:25 361
the *a* thereof were before them... Eze 40:26 361
the *a* thereof, according to these... Eze 40:29 361
in the *a* thereof round about... Eze 40:29 361
the *a* round about were five and... Eze 40:30 361
the *a* thereof were toward the... Eze 40:31 361
the *a* thereof, were according to... Eze 40:33 361
in the *a* thereof round about... Eze 40:33 361
the *a* thereof were toward the... Eze 40:34 361
the *a* thereof, and the windows to... Eze 40:36 361

ARCHEVITES (*ar'-ke-vites*) *Chaldean settlers in Samaria.*
Tarpelites, the Apharsites, the *A*... Ezr 4:9 756

ARCHI (*ar'-kee*) See ARCHITE. *A border city of Ephraim.*
unto the borders of *A* to Ataroth... Josh 16:2 757

ARCHIPPUS (*ar-kip'-pus*) *A Christian acquaintance of Paul.*
And say to *A*, Take heed to the... Col 4:17 *751*
A our fellowsoldier, and to the... Philem 2 *751*

ARCHITE (*ar'-kite*) See ARCHI. *A friend of David.*
Hushai the *A* came to meet him... 2Sa 15:32 757
came to pass, when Hushai the *A*... 2Sa 16:16 757
Call now Hushai the *A* also... 2Sa 17:5 757
The counsel of Hushai the *A* is... 2Sa 17:14 757
Hushai the *A* was the king's... 1Chr 27:33 757

ARCHITES See ARCHI.

ARCTURUS (*ark-tu'-rus*) *Another name for "the Great Bear."*
Which maketh *A*, Orion, and... Job 9:9 5906
canst thou guide *A* with his sons... Job 38:32 5906

ARD (*ard*) See ARDITES.
1. A son of Benjamin.
Muppim, and Huppim, and *A*... Gen 46:21 714
2. A son of Bela.
And the sons of Bela were *A*... Num 26:40 714
of *A*, the family of the Ardites... Num 26:40 714

ARDITES (*ar'-dites*) *Descendants of Bela.*
of Ard, the family of the *A*... Num 26:40 716

ARDON (*ar'-don*) *A son of Caleb.*
Jesher, and Shobab, and *A*... 1Chr 2:18 715

ARE See PREFACE.

ARELI (*a-re'-li*) See ARELITES. *A son of Gad.*
and Ezbon, Eri, and Arodi, and *A*... Gen 46:16 692
of *A*, the family of the Arelites... Num 26:17 692

ARELITES (*a-re'-lites*) See ARELI. *Descendants of Areli.*
of Areli, the family of the *A*... Num 26:17 692

AREOPAGITE (*a-re-op'-a-jite*) *A title of Dionysius.*
the which was Dionysius the *A*... Acts 17:34 *698*

AREOPAGUS (*a-re-op'-a-gus*) See AREOPAGITE, MARS'-HILL. *A plaza in Athens.*
took him, and brought him unto *A*... Acts 17:19 *697*

ARETAS (*ar'-e-tas*) *A north Arabian ruler.*
A the king kept the city of the... 2Cor 11:32 *702*

ARGOB (*ar'-gob*)
1. A district of Og in Bashan.
cities, all the region of *A*... Deut 3:4 709
all the region of *A*, with all... Deut 3:13 709
took all the country of *A* unto... Deut 3:14 709
also pertained the region of *A*... 1Kin 4:13 709
2. An official of King Pekah of Israel.
of the king's house, with *A*... 2Kin 15:25 709

ARGUING
but what doth your *a* reprove... Job 6:25 3198

ARGUMENTS
him, and fill my mouth with *a*... Job 23:4 8433

ARIDAI (*a-rid'-a-i*) *A son of Haman.*
And Parmashta, and Arisai, and *A*... Est 9:9 742

ARIDATHA (*a-rid'-a-thah*) *A son of Haman.*
And Poratha, and Adalia, and *A*... Est 9:8 743

ARIEH (*a-ri'-eh*) *A companion of Argob.*
the king's house, with Argob and *A*... 2Kin 15:25 745

ARIEL (*a'-re-el*) See JERUSALEM.
1. An emissary of Ezra.
Then sent I for Eliezer, for *A*... Ezr 8:16 740
2. A name for Jerusalem.
Woe to Ariel, to *A*, the city... Is 29:1 740
Yet I will distress *A*, and there... Is 29:2 740
and it shall be unto me as *A*... Is 29:2 740
the nations that fight against *A*... Is 29:7 740

ARIGHT
a will I shew the salvation of... Ps 50:23
that set not their heart *a*... Ps 78:8 3559
of the wise useth knowledge *a*... Prov 15:2 3190
the cup, when it moveth itself *a*... Prov 23:31 4339
and heard, but they spake not *a*... Jer 8:6 3651

ARIMATHAEA (*ar-im-ath-e'-ah*) *Another name for Ramah.*
come, there came a rich man of *A*... Mt 27:57 *707*
Joseph of *A*, an honourable... Mk 15:43 *707*
he was of *A*, a city of the Jews... Lk 23:51 *707*
And after this Joseph of *A*... Jn 19:38 *707*

ARIMATHEA See ARIMATHAEA.

ARIOCH (*a'-re-ok*)
1. King of Ellasar in Assyria.
A king of Ellasar, Chedorlaomer... Gen 14:1 746
of Shinar, and *A* king of Ellasar... Gen 14:9 746
2. Captain of Nebuchadnezzar's guard.
wisdom to *A* the captain of the... Dan 2:14 746
said to *A* the king's captain, Why... Dan 2:15 746
Then *A* made the thing known to... Dan 2:15 746
Therefore Daniel went in unto *A*... Dan 2:24 746
Then *A* brought in Daniel before... Dan 2:25 746

ARISAI (*a-ris'-a-i*) *A son of Haman.*
And Parmashta, and *A*, and... Est 9:9 747

ARISE
A, walk through the land in the... Gen 13:17 6965
angels hastened Lot, saying, *A*... Gen 19:15 6965
A, lift up the lad, and hold him... Gen 21:18 6965
a, I pray thee, sit and eat of my... Gen 27:19 6965
unto his father, Let my father *a*... Gen 27:31 6965
and *a*, flee thou to Laban my... Gen 27:43 6965
A, go to Padan-aram, to the house... Gen 28:2 6965
now *a*, get thee out from this... Gen 31:13 6965
And God said unto Jacob, *A*... Gen 35:1 6965
And let us *a*, and go up to Beth-el... Gen 35:3 6965
there shall *a* after them seven... Gen 41:30 6965

the lad with me, and we will a Gen 43:8 6965
Take also your brother, and a Gen 43:13 6965
And the LORD said unto me, A Deut 9:12 6965
And the LORD said unto me, A Deut 10:11 6965
If there a among you a prophet, Deut 13:1 6965
If there a a matter too hard for Deut 17:8 6965
then shalt thou a, and get thee up Deut 17:8
now therefore a, go over this Josh 1:2 6965
the people of war with thee, and a Josh 8:1 6965
a, Barak, and lead thy captivity Judg 5:12 6965
that the LORD said unto him, A Judg 7:9 6965
the host of Israel, and said, A Judg 7:15 6965
And they said, A, that we may go Judg 18:9 6965
to a up out of the city with a Judg 20:40 5927
of the servants with thee, and a 1Sa 9:3 6965
And the LORD said, A, anoint him 1Sa 16:12 6965
the LORD answered him and said, A 1Sa 23:4 6965
to Joab, Let the young men now a 2Sa 2:14 6965
And Joab said, Let them a 2Sa 2:14 6965
Abner said unto David, I will a 2Sa 3:21 6965
if so be that the king's wrath a 2Sa 11:20 5927
And Amnon said unto her, A 2Sa 13:15 6965
were with him at Jerusalem, A 2Sa 15:14 6965
twelve thousand men, and I will a 2Sa 17:1 6965
king David, and said unto David, A 2Sa 17:21 6965
Now therefore a, go forth, and 2Sa 19:7 6965
them, that they could not a 2Sa 22:39 6965
thee shall any a like unto thee 1Kin 3:12 6965
And Jeroboam said to his wife, A 1Kin 14:2 6965
A thou therefore, get thee to 1Kin 14:12 6965
A, get thee to Zarephath, which 1Kin 17:9 6965
touched him, and said unto him, A 1Kin 19:5 6965
time, and touched him, and said, A 1Kin 19:7 6965
a, and eat bread, and let thine 1Kin 21:7 6965
that Jezebel said to Ahab, A 1Kin 21:15 6965
A, go down to meet Ahab king of 1Kin 21:18 6965
said to Elijah the Tishbite, A 2Kin 1:3 6965
had restored to life, saying, A 2Kin 8:1 6965
make him a up from among his 2Kin 9:2 6965
A therefore, and be doing, and the 1Chr 22:16 6965
a therefore, and build ye the 1Chr 22:19 6965
Now therefore a, O LORD God, into 2Chr 6:41 6965
A; for this matter belongeth Ezr 10:4 6965
therefore we his servants will a Neh 2:20 6965
Thus shall there a too much Est 1:18
deliverance a to the Jews from Est 4:14 5975
I lie down, I say, When shall I a Job 7:4 6965
and upon whom doth not his light a Job 25:3 6965
A, O LORD Ps 3:7 6965
A, O LORD, in thine anger, lift Ps 7:6 6965
A, O LORD Ps 9:19 6965
A, O LORD Ps 10:12 6965
of the needy, now will I a Ps 12:5 6965
A, O LORD, disappoint him, cast Ps 17:13 6965
a, cast us not off for ever Ps 44:23 6974
A for our help, and redeem us for Ps 44:26 6965
Let God a, let his enemies be Ps 68:1 6965
A, O God, plead thine own cause Ps 74:22 6965
who should a and declare them to Ps 78:6 6965
A, O God, judge the earth Ps 82:8 6965
shall the dead a and praise thee Ps 88:10 6965
when the waves thereof a, thou Ps 89:9 7721
Thou shalt a, and have mercy upon Ps 102:13 6965
when they a, let them be ashamed Ps 109:28 6965
A, O LORD, into thy rest Ps 132:8 6965
when wilt thou a out of thy sleep Prov 6:9 6965
Her children a up, and call her Prov 31:28 6965
A, my love, my fair one, and come Song 2:13 6965
a, ye princes, and anoint the Is 21:5 6965
a, pass over to Chittim Is 23:12 6965
with my dead body shall they a Is 26:19 6965
but will a against the house of Is 31:2 6965
of rulers, Kings shall see and a Is 49:7 6965
a, and sit down, O Jerusalem Is 52:2 6965
A, shine; Is 60:1 6965
but the LORD shall a upon thee Is 60:2 2224
therefore gird up thy loins, and a Jer 1:17 6965
of their trouble they will say, A Jer 2:27 6965
let them a, if they can save thee Jer 2:28 6965
a, and let us go up at noon Jer 6:4 6965
A, and let us go by night, and let Jer 6:5 6965
Shall they fall, and not a Jer 8:4 6965
which is upon thy loins, and a Jer 13:4 6965
that the LORD said unto me, A Jer 13:6 6965
A, and go down to the potter's Jer 18:2 6965
A ye, and let us go up to Zion Jer 31:6 6965
and they said, A, and let us go Jer 46:16 6965
A ye, go up to Kedar, and spoil Jer 49:28 6965
A, get you up unto the wealthy Jer 49:31 6965
A, cry out in the night Lam 2:19 6965
and he said unto me, A, go forth Eze 3:22 6965
after thee shall a another Dan 2:39 6966
and they said thus unto it, A Dan 7:5 6966
which shall a out of the earth Dan 7:17 6966
are ten kings that shall a Dan 7:24 6966
shall a tumult a among thy people Hos 10:14 6965
by whom shall Jacob a Amos 7:2 6965
by whom shall Jacob a Amos 7:5 6965
A ye, and let us rise up against Obad 1 6965
A, go to Nineveh, that great city Jonah 1:2 6965
a, call upon thy God, if so be Jonah 1:6 6965
A, go unto Nineveh, that great Jonah 3:2 6965
came to pass, when the sun did a Jonah 4:8 2224
A ye, and depart Mic 2:10 6965
A and thresh, O daughter of Zion Mic 4:13 6965
A, contend thou before the Mic 6:1 6965
when I fall, I shall a Mic 7:8 6965
to the dumb stone, A, it shall Hab 2:19 5782
a with healing in his wings Mal 4:2 2224
to Joseph in a dream, saying, A Mt 2:13 1453
Saying, A, and take the young Mt 2:20 1453
or to say, A, and walk Mt 9:5 1453
he to the sick of the palsy,) A Mt 9:6 1453
came and touched them, and said, A Mt 17:7 1453
For there shall a false Christs Mt 24:24 1453
or to say, A, and take up thy bed, Mk 2:9 1453
I say unto thee, A, and take up Mk 2:11 1453
Damsel, I say unto thee, a Mk 5:41 1453
of the palsy,) I say unto thee, A Lk 5:24 1453
Young man, I say unto thee, A Lk 7:14 1453
hand, and called, saying, Maid, a Lk 8:54 1453
I will a and go to my father, and Lk 15:18 450
And he said unto him, A, go thy Lk 17:19 450
why do thoughts a in your hearts Lk 24:38 305
A, let us go hence Jn 14:31 1453
Lord spake unto Philip, saying, A Acts 8:26 450
And the Lord said unto him, A Acts 9:6 450
And the Lord said unto him, A Acts 9:11 450
a, and make thy bed Acts 9:34 450
him to the body said, Tabitha, a Acts 9:40 450
A therefore, and get thee down, and Acts 10:20 450
I heard a voice saying unto me, A Acts 11:7 450
him up, saying, A up quickly Acts 12:7 450
of your own selves shall men a Acts 20:30 450
And the Lord said unto me, A Acts 22:10 450
a, and be baptized, and wash away Acts 22:16 450
a from the dead, and Christ shall Eph 5:14 450
the day star a in your hearts 2Pet 1:19 393

ARISETH
there a a little cloud out of the 1Kin 18:44 5927
The sun a, they gather themselves Ps 104:22 2224
there a a light in the darkness Ps 112:4 2224
The sun also a, and the sun goeth Eccl 1:5 2224
when he a to shake terribly the Is 2:19 6965
when he a to shake terribly the Is 2:21 6965
but when the sun a they flee away Nah 3:17 2224
persecution a because of the word Mt 13:21 1096
persecution a for the word's sake Mk 4:17 1096
for out of Galilee a no prophet Jn 7:52 1453
there a another priest, Heb 7:15 450

ARISING
the king a from the banquet of Est 7:7 6965

ARISTARCHUS (*ar-is-tar'-cus*) *A companion of Paul.*
and having caught Gaius and A Acts 19:29 708
and of the Thessalonians, A Acts 20:4 708
one A, a Macedonian of Acts 27:2 708
A my fellowprisoner saluteth you, Col 4:10 708
Marcus, A, Demas, Lucas, my Philem 24 708

ARISTOBULUS See ARISTOBULUS'.

ARISTOBULUS' (*a-rus-to-bu'-luz*) *A Christian acquaintance of Paul.*
them which are of A household Rom 16:10 711

ARK
Make thee an a of gopher wood Gen 6:14 8392
rooms shalt thou make in the a Gen 6:14 8392
The length of the a shall be Gen 6:15 8392
A window shalt thou make to the a Gen 6:16 8392
the door of the a shalt thou set Gen 6:16 8392
and thou shalt come into the a Gen 6:18 8392
sort shalt thou bring into the a Gen 6:19 8392
thou and all thy house into the a Gen 7:1 8392
sons' wives with him, into the a Gen 7:7 8392
two and two unto Noah into the a Gen 7:9 8392
of his sons with them, into the a Gen 7:13 8392
they went in unto Noah into the a Gen 7:15 8392
increased, and bare up the a Gen 7:17 8392
the a went upon the face of the Gen 7:18 8392
they that were with him in the a Gen 7:23 8392
cattle that was with him in the a Gen 8:1 8392
the a rested in the seventh month Gen 8:4 8392
window of the a which he had made Gen 8:6 8392
she returned unto him into the a Gen 8:9 8392
pulled her in unto him into the a Gen 8:9 8392
sent forth the dove out of the a Gen 8:10 8392
removed the covering of the a Gen 8:13 8392
Go forth of the a, thou, and thy Gen 8:16 8392
kinds, went forth out of the a Gen 8:19 8392
from all that go out of the a Gen 9:10 8392
of Noah, that went forth of the a Gen 9:18 8392
took for him an a of bulrushes Ex 2:3 8392
she saw the a among the flags Ex 2:5 8392
shall make an a of shittim wood Ex 25:10 727
the rings by the sides of the a Ex 25:14 727
that the a may be borne with them Ex 25:14 727
shall be in the rings of the a Ex 25:15 727
thou shalt put into the a the Ex 25:16 727
the mercy seat above upon the a Ex 25:21 727
in the a thou shalt put the Ex 25:21 727
are upon the a of the testimony Ex 25:22 727
the vail the a of the testimony Ex 26:33 727
put the mercy seat upon the a of Ex 26:34 727
that is by the a of the testimony Ex 30:6 727
and the a of the testimony, Ex 30:26 727
the a of the testimony, and the Ex 31:7 727
The a, and the staves thereof, Ex 35:12 727
made the a of shittim wood Ex 37:1 727
sides of the a, to bear the a Ex 37:5 727
The a of the testimony, and the Ex 39:35 727
therein the a of the testimony Ex 40:3 727
cover the a with the vail Ex 40:3 727
before the a of the testimony Ex 40:5 727
and put the testimony into the a Ex 40:20 727
and set the staves on the a Ex 40:20 727
the mercy seat above upon the a Ex 40:20 727
he brought the a into the Ex 40:21 727
covered the a of the testimony Ex 40:21 727
mercy seat, which is upon the a Lev 16:2 727
And their charge shall be the a Num 3:31 727
cover the a of testimony with it Num 4:5 727
that was upon the a of testimony Num 7:89 727
the a of the covenant of the LORD Num 10:33 727
when the a set forward, that Num 10:35 727
nevertheless the a of the Num 14:44 727
mount, and make thee an a of wood Deut 10:1 727
and thou shalt put them in the a Deut 10:2 727
I made an a of shittim wood, and Deut 10:3 727
tables in the a which I had made Deut 10:5 727
to bear the a of the covenant of Deut 10:8 727
which bare the a of the covenant Deut 31:9 727
which bare the a of the covenant Deut 31:25 727
put it in the side of the a of Deut 31:26 727
When ye see the a of the covenant Josh 3:3 727
Take up the a of the covenant, and Josh 3:6 727
took up the a of the covenant Josh 3:6 727
that bear the a of the covenant Josh 3:8 727
the a of the covenant of the Lord Josh 3:11 727
that bear the a of the LORD Josh 3:13 727
the priests bearing the a of the Josh 3:14 727
bare the a were come unto Jordan Josh 3:15 727
of the priests that bare the a Josh 3:15 727
the priests that bare the a of Josh 3:17 727
Pass over before the a of the Josh 4:5 727
the a of the covenant of the LORD Josh 4:7 727
bare the a of the covenant stood Josh 4:9 727
a stood in the midst of Jordan Josh 4:10 727
that the a of the LORD passed Josh 4:11 727
that bear the a of the testimony Josh 4:16 727
the a of the covenant of the LORD Josh 4:18 727
a seven trumpets of rams' horns Josh 6:4 727
Take up the a of the covenant, and Josh 6:6 727
horns before the a of the LORD Josh 6:6 727
pass on before the a of the LORD Josh 6:7 727
the a of the covenant of the LORD Josh 6:8 727
and the rereward came after the a Josh 6:9 727
So the a of the LORD compassed Josh 6:11 727
priests took up the a of the LORD Josh 6:12 727
of rams' horns before the a of Josh 6:13 727
came after the a of the LORD Josh 6:13 727
a of the LORD until the eventide Josh 7:6 727
judges, stood on this side the a Josh 8:33 727
which bare the a of the covenant Josh 8:33 727
(for the a of the covenant of God Judg 20:27 727
where the a of God was, and Samuel 1Sa 3:3 727
Let us fetch the a of the 1Sa 4:3 727
might bring from thence the a of 1Sa 4:4 727
were there with the a of the 1Sa 4:4 727
when the a of the covenant of the 1Sa 4:5 727
they understood that the a of the 1Sa 4:6 727
And the a of God was taken 1Sa 4:11 727
heart trembled for the a of God 1Sa 4:13 727
dead, and the a of God is taken 1Sa 4:17 727
he made mention of the a of God 1Sa 4:18 727
that the a of God was taken 1Sa 4:19 727
because the a of God was taken, 1Sa 4:21 727
for the a of God is taken 1Sa 4:22 727
the Philistines took the a of God 1Sa 5:1 727
the Philistines took the a of God 1Sa 5:2 727
earth before the a of the LORD 1Sa 5:3 727
ground before the a of the LORD 1Sa 5:4 727
The a of the God of Israel shall 1Sa 5:7 727
with the a of the God of Israel 1Sa 5:8 727
Let the a of the God of Israel be 1Sa 5:8 727
they carried the a of the God of 1Sa 5:8 727
they sent the a of God to Ekron 1Sa 5:10 727
as the a of God came to Ekron, 1Sa 5:10 727
the a of the God of Israel to us 1Sa 5:10 727
Send away the a of the God of 1Sa 5:11 727
the a of the LORD was in the 1Sa 6:1 727
shall we do to the a of the LORD 1Sa 6:2 727
If ye send away the a of the God 1Sa 6:3 727
take the a of the LORD, and lay it 1Sa 6:8 727
they laid the a of the LORD upon 1Sa 6:11 727
up their eyes, and saw the a 1Sa 6:13 727
took down the a of the LORD 1Sa 6:15 727
they set down the a of the LORD 1Sa 6:18 727
had looked into the a of the LORD 1Sa 6:19 727
brought again the a of the LORD 1Sa 6:21 727
and brought up the a of the LORD 1Sa 7:1 727
his son to keep the a of the LORD 1Sa 7:1 727
to pass, while the a abode in 1Sa 7:2 727
Ahiah, Bring hither the a of God 1Sa 14:18 727
For the a of God was at that time 1Sa 14:18 727
bring up from thence the a of God 2Sa 6:2 727
they set the a of God upon a new 2Sa 6:3 727
Gibeah, accompanying the a of God 2Sa 6:4 727
and Ahio went before the a 2Sa 6:4 727
forth his hand to the a of God 2Sa 6:6 727
and there he died by the a of God 2Sa 6:7 727
How shall the a of the LORD come 2Sa 6:9 727
a of the LORD unto him into the 2Sa 6:10 727
the a of the LORD continued in 2Sa 6:11 727
unto him, because of the a of God 2Sa 6:12 727
brought up the a of God from the 2Sa 6:12 727
that when they that bare the a of 2Sa 6:13 727
the a of the LORD with shouting 2Sa 6:15 727
as the a of the LORD came into 2Sa 6:16 727
they brought in the a of the LORD 2Sa 6:17 727
but the a of God dwelleth within 2Sa 7:2 727
And Uriah said unto David, The a 2Sa 11:11 727
bearing the a of the covenant of 2Sa 15:24 727
and they set down the a of God 2Sa 15:24 727
Carry back the a of God into the 2Sa 15:25 727
Abiathar carried the a of God 2Sa 15:29 727
because thou barest the a of the 1Kin 2:26 727
stood before the a of the 1Kin 3:15 727
to set there the a of the 1Kin 6:19 727
that they might bring up the a of 1Kin 8:1 727
and the priests took up the a 1Kin 8:3 727
they brought up the a of the LORD 1Kin 8:4 727
him, were with him before the a 1Kin 8:5 727
the priests brought in the a of 1Kin 8:6 727
two wings over the place of the a 1Kin 8:7 727
and the cherubims covered the a 1Kin 8:7 727
There was nothing in the a save 1Kin 8:9 727
have set there a place for the a 1Kin 8:21 727
LORD, after that the a had rest 1Chr 6:31 727
again the a of our God to us 1Chr 13:3 727
to bring the a of God from 1Chr 13:5 727

up thence the *a* of God the LORD 1Chr 13:6 727
they carried the *a* of God in a 1Chr 13:7 727
put forth his hand to hold the *a* 1Chr 13:9 727
because he put his hand to the *a* 1Chr 13:10 727
I bring the *a* of God home to me 1Chr 13:12 727
So David brought not the *a* home 1Chr 13:13 727
the *a* of God remained with the 1Chr 13:14 727
prepared a place for the *a* of God 1Chr 15:1 727
the *a* of God but the Levites 1Chr 15:2 727
LORD chosen to carry the *a* of God 1Chr 15:2 727
to bring up the *a* of the LORD 1Chr 15:3 727
that ye may bring up the *a* of the 1Chr 15:12 727
the *a* of the LORD God of Israel 1Chr 15:14 727
of the Levites bare the *a* of God 1Chr 15:15 727
were doorkeepers for the *a* 1Chr 15:23 727
the trumpets before the *a* of God 1Chr 15:24 727
Jehiah were doorkeepers for the *a* 1Chr 15:24 727
went to bring up the *a* of the 1Chr 15:25 727
the Levites that bare the *a* of 1Chr 15:26 727
all the Levites that bare the *a* 1Chr 15:27 727
the *a* of the covenant of the LORD 1Chr 15:28 727
as the *a* of the covenant of the 1Chr 15:29 727
So they brought the *a* of God 1Chr 16:1 727
minister before the *a* of the LORD 1Chr 16:4 727
the *a* of the covenant of God 1Chr 16:6 727
the *a* of the covenant of the LORD 1Chr 16:37 727
minister before the *a* continually 1Chr 16:37 727
but the *a* of the covenant of the 1Chr 17:1 727
to bring the *a* of the covenant of 1Chr 22:19 727
the *a* of the covenant of the LORD 1Chr 28:2 727
covered the *a* of the covenant of 1Chr 28:18 727
But the *a* of God had David 2Chr 1:4 727
to bring up the *a* of the covenant 2Chr 5:2 727
and the Levites took up the *a* 2Chr 5:4 727
And they brought up the *a*, and the 2Chr 5:5 727
assembled unto him before the *a* 2Chr 5:6 727
the priests brought in the *a* of 2Chr 5:7 727
wings over the place of the *a* 2Chr 5:8 727
and the cherubims covered the *a* 2Chr 5:8 727
they drew out the staves of the *a* 2Chr 5:9 727
seen from the *a* before the oracle 2Chr 5:9
There was nothing in the *a* save 2Chr 5:10 727
And in it have I put the *a* 2Chr 6:11 727
thou, and the *a* of thy strength 2Chr 6:41 727
whereunto the *a* of the LORD hath 2Chr 8:11 727
Put the holy *a* in the house which 2Chr 35:3 727
thou, and the *a* of thy strength Ps 132:8 727
The *a* of the covenant of the LORD Jer 3:16 727
day that Noe entered into the *a* Mt 24:38 *2787*
day that Noe entered into the *a* Lk 17:27 *2787*
the *a* of the covenant overlaid Heb 9:4 *2787*
prepared an *a* to the saving of Heb 11:7 *2787*
while the *a* was a preparing, 1Pet 3:20 *2787*
his temple the *a* of his testament Rev 11:19 *2787*

ARKITE *(ar'-kite) A tribe descended from Canaan.*
And the Hivite, and the *A*, and the Gen 10:17 6208
And the Hivite, and the *A*, and the 1Chr 1:15 6208

ARKITES See ARCHI.

ARM
redeem you with a stretched out *a* Ex 6:6 2220
by the greatness of thine *a* they Ex 15:16 2220
A some of yourselves unto the war Num 31:3 2502
hand, and by a stretched out *a* Deut 4:34 2220
hand and by a stretched out *a* Deut 5:15 2220
hand, and the stretched out *a* Deut 7:19 2220
power and by thy stretched out *a* Deut 9:29 2220
hand, and his stretched out *a* Deut 11:2 2220
hand, and with an outstretched *a* Deut 26:8 2220
teareth the *a* with the crown of Deut 33:20 2220
come, that I will cut off thine *a* 1Sa 2:31 2220
the *a* of thy father's house, that 1Sa 2:31 2220
and the bracelet that was on his *a* 2Sa 1:10 2220
hand, and of thy stretched out *a* 1Kin 8:42 2220
great power and a stretched out *a* 2Kin 17:36 2220
hand, and thy stretched out *a* 2Chr 6:32 2220
With his is an *a* of flesh 2Chr 32:8 2220
how savest thou the *a* that hath Job 26:2 2220
Then let mine *a* fall from my Job 31:22 3802
mine *a* be broken from the bone Job 31:22 248
by reason of the *a* of the mighty Job 35:9 2220
the high *a* shall be broken Job 38:15 2220
Hast thou an *a* like God Job 40:9 2220
Break thou the *a* of the wicked Ps 10:15 2220
neither did their own *a* save them Ps 44:3 2220
but thy right hand, and thine *a* Ps 44:3 2220
with thine *a* redeemed thy people Ps 77:15 2220
thine enemies with thy strong *a* Ps 89:10 2220
Thou hast a mighty *a* Ps 89:13 2220
mine *a* also shall strengthen him Ps 89:21 2220
his right hand, and his holy *a* Ps 98:1 2220
hand, and with a stretched out *a* Ps 136:12 2220
heart, as a seal upon thine *a* Song 8:6 2220
every man the flesh of his own *a* Is 9:20 2220
and reapeth the ears with his *a* Is 17:5 2220
shew the lighting down of his *a* Is 30:30 2220
be thou their *a* every morning Is 33:2 2220
hand, and his *a* shall rule for him Is 40:10 2220
shall gather the lambs with his *a* Is 40:11 2220
his *a* shall be on the Chaldeans Is 48:14 2220
on mine *a* shall they trust Is 51:5 2220
put on strength, O *a* of the LORD Is 51:9 2220
LORD hath made bare his holy *a* in Is 52:10 2220
to whom is the *a* of the LORD Is 53:1 2220
therefore his *a* brought salvation Is 59:16 2220
by the *a* of his strength, Surely Is 62:8 2220
therefore mine own *a* brought Is 63:5 2220
hand of Moses with his glorious *a* Is 63:12 2220
in man, and maketh flesh his *a* Jer 17:5 2220
hand and with a strong *a*, even in Jer 21:5 2220
power and by my outstretched *a* Jer 27:5 2220
great power and stretched out *a* Jer 32:17 2220
hand, and with a stretched out *a* Jer 32:21 248
his *a* is broken, saith the LORD Jer 48:25 2220
thine *a* shall be uncovered, and Eze 4:7 2220
hand, and with a stretched out *a* Eze 20:33 2220
hand, and with a stretched out *a* Eze 20:34 2220
I have broken the *a* of Pharaoh Eze 30:21 2220
and they that were his *a*, that Eze 31:17 2220
not retain the power of the *a* Dan 11:6 2220
neither shall he stand, nor his *a* Dan 11:6 2220
the sword shall be upon his *a* Zec 11:17 2220
his *a* shall be clean dried up, and Zec 11:17 2220
hath shewed strength with his *a* Lk 1:51 *1023*
to whom hath the *a* of the Lord Jn 12:38 *1023*
with an high *a* brought he them Acts 13:17 *1023*
a yourselves likewise with the 1Pet 4:1 *3695*

ARMAGEDDON *(ar-mag-ed'-don) Scene of the last great battle of time.*
called in the Hebrew tongue *A* Rev 16:16 717

ARMED
he *a* his trained servants, born Gen 14:14 7324
tribe, twelve thousand *a* for war Num 31:5 2502
a before the children of Israel Num 32:17 2502
if ye will go *a* before the LORD Num 32:20 2502
will go all of you *a* over Jordan Num 32:21 2502
pass over, every man *a* for war Num 32:27 2502
Jordan, every man *a* to battle Num 32:29 2502
will not pass over with you *a* Num 32:30 2502
We will pass over *a* before the Num 32:32 2502
ye shall pass over *a* before your Deut 3:18 2502
shall pass before your brethren *a* Josh 1:14 2571
passed over *a* before the children Josh 4:12 2571
let him that is *a* pass on before Josh 6:7 2502
the *a* men went before the priests Josh 6:9 2502
the *a* men went before them Josh 6:13 2502
the *a* men that were in the host Judg 7:11 2571
he was *a* with a coat of mail 1Sa 17:5 3847
Saul *a* David with his armour, and 1Sa 17:38 3847
also he *a* him with a coat of mail 1Sa 17:38 3847
They were *a* with bows, and could 1Chr 12:2 5401
that were ready *a* to the war 1Chr 12:23 2502
eight hundred, ready *a* to the war 1Chr 12:24 2502
with him *a* men with bow and shield 2Chr 17:17 5401
So the *a* men left the captives and 2Chr 28:14 2502
he goeth on to meet the *a* men Job 39:21 5402
The children of Ephraim, being *a* Ps 78:9 5401
and thy want as an *a* man Prov 6:11 4043
and thy want as an *a* man Prov 24:34 4043
therefore the *a* soldiers of Moab Is 15:4 2502
When a strong man *a* keepeth his Lk 11:21 *2528*

ARMENIA *(ar-me'-ne-ah) A region between the lower ends of the Black and Caspian seas.*
they escaped into the land of *A* 2Kin 19:37 780
they escaped into the land of *A* Is 37:38 780

ARMHOLES
under thine *a* under the cords Jer 38:12
women that sew pillows to all *a* Eze 13:18

ARMIES
of Egypt according to their *a* Ex 6:26 6635
upon Egypt, and bring forth mine *a* Ex 7:4 6635
day have I brought your *a* out of Ex 12:17 6635
of the land of Egypt by their *a* Ex 12:51 6635
shall number them by their *a* Num 1:3 6635
of Judah pitch throughout their *a* Num 2:3 6635
four hundred, throughout their *a* Num 2:9 6635
of Reuben according to their *a* Num 2:10 6635
and fifty, throughout their *a* Num 2:16 6635
of Ephraim according to their *a* Num 2:18 6635
and an hundred, throughout their *a* Num 2:24 6635
be on the north side by their *a* Num 2:25 6635
of Judah according to their *a* Num 10:14 6635
set forward according to their *a* Num 10:18 6635
set forward according to their *a* Num 10:22 6635
of Israel according to their *a* Num 10:28 6635
their *a* under the hand of Moses Num 33:1 6635
of the *a* to lead the people Deut 20:9 6635
together their *a* to battle 1Sa 17:1 4264
and cried unto the *a* of Israel 1Sa 17:8 4634
I defy the *a* of Israel this day 1Sa 17:10 4634
out of the *a* of the Philistines, 1Sa 17:23 4630
defy the *a* of the living God 1Sa 17:26 4634
defied the *a* of the living God 1Sa 17:36 4634
hosts, the God of the *a* of Israel 1Sa 17:45 4634
against the *a* of the Philistines 1Sa 23:3 4634
their *a* together for warfare 1Sa 28:1 4264
together all their *a* to Aphek 1Sa 29:1 4264
And when all the captains of the *a* 2Kin 25:23 2428
great, and the captains of the *a* 2Kin 25:26 2428
the valiant men of the *a* were 1Chr 11:26 2428
sent the captains of his *a* 2Chr 16:4 2428
Is there any number of his *a* Job 25:3 1416
and goest not forth with our *a* Ps 44:9 6635
which didst not go out with our *a* Ps 60:10 6635
Kings of *a* did flee apace Ps 68:12 6635
As it were the company of two *a* Song 6:13 4264
and his fury upon all their *a* Is 34:2 6635
and he sent forth his *a*, and Mt 22:7 *4753*
see Jerusalem compassed with *a* Lk 21:20 *4760*
to flight the *a* of the aliens Heb 11:34 *3925*
the *a* which were in heaven Rev 19:14 *4753*
kings of the earth, and their *a* Rev 19:19 *4753*

ARMONI *(ar-mo'-ni) A son of King Saul.*
Aiah, whom she bare unto Saul, *A* 2Sa 21:8 764

ARMOUR
the young man that bare his *a* 1Sa 14:1 3627
to the young man that bare his *a* 1Sa 14:6 3627
And Saul armed David with his *a* 1Sa 17:38 4055
David girded his sword upon his *a* 1Sa 17:39 4055
but he put his *a* in his tent 1Sa 17:54 3627
his head, and stripped off his *a* 1Sa 31:9 3627
they put his *a* in the house of 1Sa 31:10 3627
the young men, and take thee his *a* 2Sa 2:21 2488
bare Joab's *a* compassed about 2Sa 18:15 3627
of gold, and garments, and *a* 1Kin 10:25 5402
and they washed his *a* 1Kin 22:38 2185
all that were able to put on *a* 2Kin 3:21 2290
horses, a fenced city also, and *a* 2Kin 10:2 5402
and all the house of his *a* 2Kin 20:13 3627
him, they took his head, and his *a* 1Chr 10:9 3627
they put his *a* in the house of 1Chr 10:10 3627
the *a* of the house of the forest Is 22:8 5402
and all the house of his *a* Is 39:2 3627
them clothed with all sorts of *a* Eze 38:4 3627
him all his *a* wherein he trusted Lk 11:22 *3833*
and let us put on the *a* of light Rom 13:12 *3696*
by the *a* of righteousness on the 2Cor 6:7 *3696*
Put on the whole *a* of God Eph 6:11 *3833*
take unto you the whole *a* of God Eph 6:13 *3833*

ARMOURBEARER
hastily unto the young man his *a* Judg 9:54 3627
his *a* said unto him, Do all that 1Sa 14:7 3627
answered Jonathan and his *a* 1Sa 14:12 3627
And Jonathan said unto his *a* 1Sa 14:12 3627
upon his feet, and his *a* after him 1Sa 14:13 3627
and his *a* slew after him 1Sa 14:13 3627
his *a* made, was about twenty men, 1Sa 14:14 3627
Jonathan and his *a* were not there 1Sa 14:17 3627
and he became his *a* 1Sa 16:21 3627
Then said Saul unto his *a* 1Sa 31:4 3627
But his *a* would not 1Sa 31:4 3627
when his *a* saw that Saul was dead 1Sa 31:5 3627
died, and his three sons, and his *a* 1Sa 31:6 3627
a to Joab the son of Zeruiah, 2Sa 23:37 3627
Then said Saul to his *a*, Draw thy 1Chr 10:4 3627
But his *a* would not 1Chr 10:4 3627
when his *a* saw that Saul was dead 1Chr 10:5 3627
the *a* of Joab the son of Zeruiah, 1Chr 11:39 3627

ARMOURY
the *a* at the turning of the wall Neh 3:19 5402
tower of David builded for an *a* Song 4:4 8530
The LORD hath opened his *a* Jer 50:25 214

ARMS
the *a* of his hands were made Gen 49:24 2220
underneath are the everlasting *a* Deut 33:27 2220
the cords that were upon his *a* Judg 15:14 2220
them from off his *a* like a thread Judg 16:12 2220
bow of steel is broken by mine *a* 2Sa 22:35 2220
and smote Jehoram between his *a* 2Kin 9:24 2220
the *a* of the fatherless have been Job 22:9 2220
bow of steel is broken by mine *a* Ps 18:34 2220
For the *a* of the wicked shall be Ps 37:17 2220
strength, and strengtheneth her *a* Prov 31:17 2220
it with the strength of his *a* Is 44:12 2220
shall bring thy sons in their *a* Is 49:22 2684
mine *a* shall judge the people Is 51:5 2220
and I will tear them from your *a* Eze 13:20 2220
of Egypt, and will break his *a* Eze 30:22 2220
I will strengthen the *a* of the Eze 30:24 2220
but I will break Pharaoh's *a* Eze 30:24 2220
the *a* of the king of Babylon Eze 30:25 2220
the *a* of Pharaoh shall fall down Eze 30:25 2220
his *a* of silver, his belly and his Dan 2:32 1672
eyes as lamps of fire, and his *a* Dan 10:6 2220
the *a* of the south shall not Dan 11:15 2220
with the *a* of a flood shall they Dan 11:22 2220
a shall stand on his part, and Dan 11:31 2220
bound and strengthened their *a* Hos 7:15 2220
to go, taking them by their *a* Hos 11:3 2220
and when he had taken him in his *a* Mk 9:36 *1723*
And he took them up in his *a* Mk 10:16 *1723*
Then took he him up in his *a* Lk 2:28 *43*

ARMY
the chief captain of his *a* Gen 26:26 6635
and his horsemen, and his *a* Ex 14:9 2428
what he did unto the *a* of Egypt Deut 11:4 2428
Sisera, the captain of Jabin's *a* Judg 4:7 6635
we should give bread unto thine *a* Judg 8:6 6635
to Abimelech, Increase thine *a* Judg 9:29 6635
they slew of the *a* in the field 1Sa 4:2 4634
a man of Benjamin out of the *a* 1Sa 4:12 4634
I am he that came out of the *a* 1Sa 4:16 4634
and I fled to day out of the *a* 1Sa 4:16 4634
battle in array, *a* against *a* 1Sa 17:21 4634
battle in array, *a* against *a* 1Sa 17:21 2428
the carriage, and ran into the *a* 1Sa 17:22 4634
ran toward the *a* to meet the 1Sa 17:48 4634
the *a* which followed them 1Kin 20:19 2428
And number thee an *a* 1Kin 20:25 2428
like the *a* that thou hast lost, 1Kin 20:25 2428
the *a* of the Chaldees pursued 2Kin 25:5 2428
all his *a* were scattered from him 2Kin 25:5 2428
all the *a* of the Chaldees, that 2Kin 25:10 2428
Joab led forth the power of the *a* 1Chr 20:1 6635
general of the king's *a* was Joab 1Chr 27:34 6635
with an *a* of valiant men of war 2Chr 13:3 2428
Asa had an *a* of men that bare 2Chr 14:8 2428
as they went out before the *a* 2Chr 20:21 2502
For the *a* of the Syrians came 2Chr 24:24 2428
let not the *a* of Israel go with 2Chr 25:7 6635
I have given to the *a* of Israel 2Chr 25:9 1416
the *a* that was come to him out of 2Chr 25:10 1416
of the *a* which Amaziah sent back 2Chr 25:13 1416
And under their hand was an *a* 2Chr 26:13 6635
king had sent captains of the *a* Neh 2:9 2428
the *a* of Samaria, and said, What Neh 4:2 2428
and dwelt as a king in the *a* Job 29:25 1416
terrible as an *a* with banners Song 6:4
and terrible as an *a* with banners Song 6:10
unto king Hezekiah with a great *a* Is 36:2 2426
forth the chariot and horse, the *a* Is 43:17 2428
of Babylon's *a* besieged Jerusalem Jer 32:2 2428
king of Babylon, and all his *a* Jer 34:1 2428
a fought against Jerusalem Jer 34:7 2428

hand of the king of Babylon's *a* Jer 34:21 2428
fear of the *a* of the Chaldeans Jer 35:11 2428
for fear of the *a* of the Syrians Jer 35:11 2428
Then Pharaoh's *a* was come forth Jer 37:5 2428
Behold, Pharaoh's *a*, which is Jer 37:7 2428
a of the Chaldeans that fight Jer 37:10 2428
that when the *a* of the Chaldeans Jer 37:11 2428
Jerusalem for fear of Pharaoh's *a* Jer 37:11 2428
hand of the king of Babylon's *a* Jer 38:3 2428
all his *a* against Jerusalem, and Jer 39:1 2428
Chaldeans' *a* pursued after them Jer 39:5 2428
against the *a* of Pharaoh-necho Jer 46:2 2428
for they shall march with an *a* Jer 46:22 2428
of Babylon came, he and all his *a* Jer 52:4 2428
But the *a* of the Chaldeans Jer 52:8 2428
all his *a* was scattered from him Jer 52:8 2428
all the *a* of the Chaldeans, that Jer 52:14 2428
shall Pharaoh with his mighty *a* Eze 17:17 2428
of Lud and of Phut were in thine *a* Eze 27:10 2428
The men of Arvad with thine *a* Eze 27:11 2428
his *a* to serve a great service Eze 29:18 2428
yet had he no wages, nor his *a* Eze 29:18 2428
it shall be the wages for his *a* Eze 29:19 2428
all his *a* slain by the sword, Eze 32:31 2428
their feet, an exceeding great *a* Eze 37:10 2428
bring thee forth, and all thine *a* Eze 38:4 2428
a great company, and a mighty *a* Eze 38:15 2428
were in his *a* to bind Shadrach Dan 3:20 2429
to his will in the *a* of heaven Dan 4:35 2429
which shall come with an *a* Dan 11:7 2428
certain years with a great *a* Dan 11:13 2428
king of the south with a great *a* Dan 11:25 2428
with a very great and mighty *a* Dan 11:25 2428
him, and his *a* shall overflow Dan 11:26 2428
utter his voice before his *a* Joel 2:11 2428
far off from you the northern *a* Joel 2:20
my great *a* which I sent among you Joel 2:25 2428
about mine house because of the *a* Zec 9:8 4675
then came I with an *a*, and rescued Acts 23:27 4753
the number of the *a* of the Rev 9:16 4753
on the horse, and against his *a* Rev 19:19 4753

ARNAN (*ar'-nan*) *Descendants of David.*
sons of Rephaiah, the sons of *A* 1Chr 3:21 770

ARNON (*ar'-non*) *A river in southern Canaan.*
and pitched on the other side of *A* Num 21:13 769
for *A* is the border of Moab, Num 21:13 769
Red sea, and in the brooks of *A* Num 21:14 769
his land from *A* unto Jabbok Num 21:24 769
land out of his hand, even unto *A* Num 21:26 769
the lords of the high places of *A* Num 21:28 769
Moab, which is in the border of *A* Num 22:36 769
journey, and pass over the river *A* Deut 2:24 769
is by the brink of the river of *A* Deut 2:36 769
the river of *A* unto mount Hermon Deut 3:8 769
Aroer, which is by the river *A* Deut 3:12 769
unto the river *A* half the valley Deut 3:16 769
is by the bank of the river *A* Deut 4:48 769
from the river *A* unto mount Josh 12:1 769
is upon the bank of the river *A* Josh 12:2 769
is upon the bank of the river *A* Josh 13:9 769
is on the bank of the river *A* Josh 13:16 769
from *A* even unto Jabbok, and unto Judg 11:13 769
and pitched on the other side of *A* Judg 11:18 769
for *A* was the border of Moab Judg 11:18 769
from *A* even unto Jabbok, and from Judg 11:22 769
that be along by the coasts of *A* Judg 11:26 769
Aroer, which is by the river *A* 2Kin 10:33 769
Moab shall be at the fords of *A* Is 16:2 769
tell ye it in *A*, that Moab is Jer 48:20 769

AROD (*a'-rod*) See ARODITES. *A son of Gad.*
Of *A*, the family of the Arodites Num 26:17 720

ARODI (*ar'-o-di*) See ARODITES. *Descendants of Arod.*
Haggi, Shuni, and Ezbon, Eri, and *A* Gen 46:16 722

ARODITES (*a'-ro-dites*) *Same as Arodi.*
Of Arod, the family of the *A* Num 26:17 722

AROER (*ar'-o-ur*)
1. A city in the valley of Jabbok.
Gad built Dibon, and Ataroth, and *A* Num 32:34 6177
unto *A* that is before Rabbah Josh 13:25 6177
over Jordan, and pitched in *A* 2Sa 24:5 6177
The cities of *A* are forsaken Is 17:2 6177
2. An Amorite city.
From *A*, which is by the brink of Deut 2:36 6177
we possessed at that time, from *A* Deut 3:12 6177
From *A*, which is by the bank of Deut 4:48 6177
dwelt in Heshbon, and ruled from *A* Josh 12:2 6177
From *A*, that is upon the bank of Josh 13:9 6177
And their coast was from *A* Josh 13:16 6177
in Heshbon and her towns, and in *A* Judg 11:26 6177
And he smote them from *A*, even Judg 11:33 6177
and the Manassites, from *A* 2Kin 10:33 6177
the son of Joel, who dwelt in *A* 1Chr 5:8 6177
O inhabitant of *A*, stand by the Jer 48:19 6177
3. A city in southern Judah.
And to them which were in *A* 1Sa 30:28 6177

AROERITE (*ar'-o-ur-ite*) *A native of Aroer.*
Jehiel the sons of Hothan the *A* 1Chr 11:44 6200

AROSE
And when the morning *a*, then the Gen 19:15 5927
when she lay down, nor when she *a* Gen 19:33 6965
and the younger *a*, and lay with him Gen 19:35 6965
when she lay down, nor when she *a* Gen 19:35 6965
and he *a*, and went to Mesopotamia, Gen 24:10 6965
And Rebekah *a*, and her damsels, and Gen 24:61 6965
in the field, and, lo, my sheaf *a* Gen 37:7 6965
And she *a*, and went away, and laid Gen 38:19 6965
Now there *a* up a new king over Ex 1:8 6965
there *a* not a prophet since in Deut 34:10 6965
So Joshua *a*, and all the people of Josh 8:3 6965
the ambush *a* quickly out of their Josh 8:19 6965
And the men *a*, and went away Josh 18:8 6965
son of Zippor, king of Moab, *a* Josh 24:9 6965
there *a* another generation after Judg 2:10 6965
And he *a* out of his seat Judg 3:20 6965
And Deborah *a*, and went with Barak Judg 4:9 6965
in Israel, until that I Deborah *a* Judg 5:7 6965
that I *a* a mother in Israel Judg 5:7 6965
the city *a* early in the morning Judg 6:28 7925
And Gideon *a*, and slew Zebah and Judg 8:21 6965
after Abimelech there *a* to defend Judg 10:1 6965
And after him *a* Jair, a Gileadite, Judg 10:3 6965
And Manoah *a*, and went after his Judg 13:11 6965
a at midnight, and took the doors Judg 16:3 6965
And her husband *a*, and went after Judg 19:3 6965
when they *a* early in the morning, Judg 19:5 7925
he *a* early in the morning on the Judg 19:8 7925
And all the people *a* as one man Judg 20:8 6965
And the children of Israel *a* Judg 20:18 6965
Then she *a* with her daughters in Ruth 1:6 6965
And Samuel *a* and went to Eli, and 1Sa 3:6 6965
And he *a* and went to Eli, and said, 1Sa 3:8 6965
of Ashdod *a* early on the morrow 1Sa 5:3 7925
when they *a* early on the morrow 1Sa 5:4 7925
And they *a* early 1Sa 9:26 7925
And Saul *a*, and they went out both 1Sa 9:26 6965
And Samuel *a*, and gat him up from 1Sa 13:15 6965
when he *a* against me, I caught 1Sa 17:35 6965
to pass, when the Philistine *a* 1Sa 17:48 6965
the men of Israel and of Judah *a* 1Sa 17:52 6965
Wherefore David *a* and went, he and 1Sa 18:27 6965
and Jonathan *a*, and Abner sat by 1Sa 20:25 6965
So Jonathan *a* from the table in 1Sa 20:34 6965
David *a* out of a place toward the 1Sa 20:41 6965
And he *a* and departed 1Sa 20:42 6965
And David *a*, and fled that day for 1Sa 21:10 6965
which were about six hundred, *a* 1Sa 23:13 6965
And Jonathan Saul's son *a*, and went 1Sa 23:16 6965
And they *a*, and went to Ziph before 1Sa 23:24 6965
Then David *a*, and cut off the 1Sa 24:4 6965
David also *a* afterward, and went 1Sa 24:8 6965
And David *a*, and went down to the 1Sa 25:1 6965
And she *a*, and bowed herself on her 1Sa 25:41 6965
And Abigail hasted, and *a*, and rode 1Sa 25:42 6965
Then Saul *a*, and went down to the 1Sa 26:2 6965
And David *a*, and came to the place 1Sa 26:5 6965
And David *a*, and he passed over 1Sa 27:2 6965
So he *a* from the earth, and sat 1Sa 28:23 6965
All the valiant men *a*, and went 1Sa 31:12 6965
Then there *a* and went over by 2Sa 2:15 6965
And David *a*, and went with all the 2Sa 6:2 6965
that David *a* from off his bed, and 2Sa 11:2 6965
And the elders of his house *a* 2Sa 12:17 6965
Then David *a* from the earth, and 2Sa 12:20 6965
Then all the king's sons *a* 2Sa 13:29 6965
Then the king *a*, and tare his 2Sa 13:31 6965
So Joab *a* and went to Geshur, and 2Sa 14:23 6965
Then Joab *a*, and came to Absalom 2Sa 14:31 6965
So he *a*, and went to Hebron 2Sa 15:9 6965
Then David *a*, and all the people 2Sa 17:22 6965
he saddled his ass, and *a* 2Sa 17:23 6965
Then the king *a*, and sat in the 2Sa 19:8 6965
He *a*, and smote the Philistines 2Sa 23:10 6965
feared because of Solomon, and *a* 1Kin 1:50 6965
And Shimei *a*, and saddled his ass, 1Kin 2:40 6965
she *a* at midnight, and took my son 1Kin 3:20 6965
he *a* from before the altar of the 1Kin 8:54 6965
they *a* out of Midian, and came to 1Kin 11:18 6965
And Jeroboam *a*, and fled into Egypt 1Kin 11:40 6965
And Jeroboam's wife did so, and *a* 1Kin 14:4 6965
And Jeroboam's wife *a*, and departed 1Kin 14:17 6965
So he *a* and went to Zarephath 1Kin 17:10 6965
And when he saw that, he *a* 1Kin 19:3 6965
And he *a*, and did eat and drink, and 1Kin 19:8 6965
Then he *a*, and went after Elijah, 1Kin 19:21 6965
And he *a*, and went down with him 2Kin 1:15 6965
And he *a*, and followed her 2Kin 4:30 6965
Wherefore they *a* and fled in the 2Kin 7:7 6965
the king *a* in the night, and said 2Kin 7:12 6965
And the woman *a*, and did after the 2Kin 8:2 6965
And he *a*, and went into the house 2Kin 9:6 6965
And he *a* and departed, and came to 2Kin 10:12 6965
saw that her son was dead, she *a* 2Kin 11:1 6965
And his servants *a*, and made a 2Kin 12:20 6965
when they *a* early in the morning, 2Kin 19:35 7925
neither after him *a* there any 2Kin 23:25 6965
and the captains of the armies, *a* 2Kin 25:26 6965
They *a*, all the valiant men, and 1Chr 10:12 6965
that there *a* war at Gezer with 1Chr 20:4 5975
saw that her son was dead, she *a* 2Chr 22:10 6965
Then the Levites *a*, Mahath the 2Chr 29:12 6965
And they *a* and took away the altars 2Chr 30:14 6965
Then the priests the Levites *a* 2Chr 30:27 6965
of the LORD *a* against his people 2Chr 36:16 5927
I *a* up from my heaviness Ezr 9:5 6965
Then *a* Ezra, and made the chief Ezr 10:5 6965
I *a* in the night, I and some few Neh 2:12 6965
So Esther *a*, and stood before the Est 8:4 6965
Then Job *a*, and rent his mantle, Job 1:20 6965
I *a*, and they spake against me Job 19:18 6965
and the aged *a*, and stood up Job 29:8 6965
When God *a* to judgment, to save Ps 76:9 6965
hasteth to his place where he *a* Eccl 1:5 2224
when they *a* early in the morning, Is 37:36 2224
Then *a* Ishmael the son of Jer 41:2 6965
Then I *a*, and went forth into the Eze 3:23 6965
Then the king *a* very early in the Dan 6:19 6966
So Jonah *a*, and went unto Nineveh, Jonah 3:3 6965
he *a* from his throne, and he laid Jonah 3:6 6965
When he *a*, he took the young Mt 2:14 1453
And he *a*, and took the young child Mt 2:21 1453
and she *a*, and ministered unto them Mt 8:15 1453
there *a* a great tempest in the Mt 8:24 1096
Then he *a*, and rebuked the winds Mt 8:26 1453
And he *a*, and departed to his house Mt 9:7 1453
And he *a*, and followed him Mt 9:9 450
And Jesus *a*, and followed him, and Mt 9:19 1453
her by the hand, and the maid *a* Mt 9:25 1453
Then all those virgins *a*, and Mt 25:7 1453
And the high priest *a*, and said Mt 26:62 450
of the saints which slept *a* Mt 27:52 1453
And immediately he *a*, took up the Mk 2:12 1453
And he *a* and followed him Mk 2:14 450
there *a* a great storm of wind, and Mk 4:37 1096
And he *a*, and rebuked the wind, and Mk 4:39 1326
And straightway the damsel *a* Mk 5:42 450
And from thence he *a*, and went into Mk 7:24 450
and he *a* Mk 9:27 450
he *a* from thence, and cometh into Mk 10:1 450
there *a* certain, and bare false Mk 14:57 450
Mary *a* in those days, and went Lk 1:39 450
he *a* out of the synagogue, and Lk 4:38 450
and immediately she *a* and Lk 4:39 450
And he *a* and stood forth Lk 6:8 450
and when the flood *a*, the stream Lk 6:48 1096
Then he *a*, and rebuked the wind and Lk 8:24 1453
came again, and she *a* straightway Lk 8:55 450
Then there *a* a reasoning among Lk 9:46 1525
there *a* a mighty famine in that Lk 15:14 1096
And he *a*, and came to his father Lk 15:20 450
And the whole multitude of them *a* Lk 23:1 450
Then *a* Peter, and ran unto the Lk 24:12 450
Then there *a* a question between Jn 3:25 1096
the sea *a* by reason of a great Jn 6:18 1326
she *a* quickly, and came unto him Jn 11:29 1453
And the young men *a*, wound him up, Acts 5:6 450
there *a* a murmuring of the Acts 6:1 1096
Then there *a* certain of the Acts 6:9 450
Till another king *a*, which knew Acts 7:18 450
And he *a* and went Acts 8:27 450
And Saul *a* from the earth Acts 9:8 1453
he received sight forthwith, and *a* Acts 9:18 450
And he *a* immediately Acts 9:34 450
Then Peter *a* and went with them Acts 9:39 450
upon the persecution that *a* about Acts 11:19 1096
the same time there *a* no small Acts 19:23 1096
there *a* a dissension between the Acts 23:7 1096
And there *a* a great cry Acts 23:9 1096
were of the Pharisees' part *a* Acts 23:9 450
when there *a* a great dissension, Acts 23:10 1096
But not long after there *a* Acts 27:14 906
there *a* a smoke out of the pit, Rev 9:2 305

ARPAD (*ar'pad*) *A city near Hamath.*
are the gods of Hamath, and of *A* 2Kin 18:34 774
king of Hamath, and the king of *A* 2Kin 19:13 774
is not Hamath as *A* Is 10:9 774
Hamath is confounded, and *A* Jer 49:23 774

ARPHAD (*ar'-fad*) See ARPAD. *Same as Arpad.*
Where are the gods of Hamath and *A* Is 36:19 774
king of Hamath, and the king of *A* Is 37:13 774

ARPHAXAD
Elam, and Asshur, and *A* Gen 10:22 775
And *A* begat Salah Gen 10:24 775
begat *A* two years after the flood Gen 11:10 775
he begat *A* five hundred years Gen 11:11 775
A lived five and thirty years, and Gen 11:12 775
A lived after he begat Salah four Gen 11:13 775
Elam, and Asshur, and *A* 1Chr 1:17 775
A begat Shelah, and Shelah begat 1Chr 1:18 775
Shem, *A*, Shelah, 1Chr 1:24 775
of Cainan, which was the son of *A* Lk 3:36 742

ARRAY
a to fight against them at Gibeah Judg 20:20 6186
set their battle again in *a* in Judg 20:22 6186
put themselves in *a* the first day Judg 20:22 6186
themselves in *a* against Gibeah Judg 20:30 6186
put themselves in *a* at Baal-tamar Judg 20:33 6186
themselves in *a* against Israel 1Sa 4:2 6186
set the battle in *a* against the 1Sa 17:2 6186
come out to set your battle in *a* 1Sa 17:8 6186
had put the battle in *a*, army 1Sa 17:21 6186
put the battle in *a* at the 2Sa 10:8 6186
put them in *a* against the Syrians 2Sa 10:9 6186
that he might put them in *a* 2Sa 10:10 6186
set themselves in *a* against David 2Sa 10:17 6186
his servants, Set yourselves in *a* 1Kin 20:12
themselves in *a* against the city 1Kin 20:12
put the battle in *a* before the 1Chr 19:9 6186
put them in *a* against the Syrians 1Chr 19:10 6186
they set themselves in *a* against 1Chr 19:11 6186
set the battle in *a* against them 1Chr 19:17 6186
battle in *a* against the Syrians 1Chr 19:17 6186
Abijah set the battle in *a* with 2Chr 13:3 631
a against him with eight hundred 2Chr 13:3 6186
they set the battle in *a* in the 2Chr 14:10 6186
that they may *a* the man withal Est 6:9 3847
do set themselves in *a* against me Job 6:4 6186
a thyself with glory and beauty Job 40:10 3847
set themselves in *a* at the gate Is 22:7 7896
set in *a* as men for war against Jer 6:23 6186
he shall *a* himself with the land Jer 43:12 5844
set themselves in *a* against her Jer 50:9 6186
Put yourselves in *a* against Jer 50:14 6186
upon horses, every one put in *a* Jer 50:42 6186
a strong people set in battle *a* Joel 2:5 6186
or gold, or pearls, or costly *a* 1Ti 2:9 2441

ARRAYED
a him in vestures of fine linen, Gen 41:42 3847
being *a* in white linen, having 2Chr 5:12 3847
a them, and shod them, and gave 2Chr 28:15 3847
a Mordecai, and brought him on Est 6:11 3847
glory was not *a* like one of these Mt 6:29 4016
glory was not *a* like one of these Lk 12:27 4016
a him in a gorgeous robe, and sent Lk 23:11 4016
a in royal apparel, sat upon his Acts 12:21 1746

these which are *a* in white robes ... Rev 7:13 *4016*
And the woman was *a* in purple ... Rev 17:4 *4016*
she should be *a* in fine linen ... Rev 19:8 *4016*

ARRIVED
they *a* at the country of the ... Lk 8:26 *2668*
and the next day we *a* at Samos ... Acts 20:15 *3846*

ARROGANCY
let not *a* come out of your mouth ... 1Sa 2:3 6277
pride, and *a*, and the evil way, and ... Prov 8:13 1347
I will cause the *a* of the proud ... Is 13:11 1347
proud) his loftiness, and his *a* ... Jer 48:29 1347

ARROW
lad ran, he shot an *a* beyond him ... 1Sa 20:36 2678
of the *a* which Jonathan had shot ... 1Sa 20:37 2678
and said, Is not the *a* beyond thee ... 1Sa 20:37 2678
the *a* went out at his heart, and ... 2Kin 9:24 2678
The *a* of the LORD's deliverance, ... 2Kin 13:17 2671
the *a* of deliverance from Syria ... 2Kin 13:17 2671
this city, nor shoot an *a* there ... 2Kin 19:32 2671
The *a* cannot make him flee ... Job 41:28
ready their *a* upon the string ... Ps 11:2 2671
God shall shoot at them with an *a* ... Ps 64:7 2671
nor for the *a* that flieth by day ... Ps 91:5 2671
a maul, and a sword, and a sharp *a* ... Prov 25:18 2671
this city, nor shoot an *a* there ... Is 37:33 2671
Their tongue is as an *a* shot out ... Jer 9:8 2671
and set me as a mark for the *a* ... Lam 3:12 2671
his *a* shall go forth as the ... Zec 9:14 2671

ARROWS
and pierce them through with his *a* ... Num 24:8 2671
I will spend mine *a* upon them ... Deut 32:23 2671
will make mine *a* drunk with blood ... Deut 32:42 2671
I will shoot three *a* on the side ... 1Sa 20:20 2671
a lad, saying, Go, find out the *a* ... 1Sa 20:21 2671
the *a* are on this side of thee, ... 1Sa 20:21 2671
Behold, the *a* are beyond thee ... 1Sa 20:22 2671
find out now the *a* which I shoot ... 1Sa 20:36 2671
Jonathan's lad gathered up the *a* ... 1Sa 20:38 2678
And he sent out *a*, and scattered ... 2Sa 22:15 2671
said unto him, Take bow and *a* ... 2Kin 13:15 2671
And he took unto him bow and *a* ... 2Kin 13:15 2671
And he said, Take the *a* ... 2Kin 13:18 2671
shooting *a* out of a bow, even of ... 1Chr 12:2 2671
and upon the bulwarks, to shoot *a* ... 2Chr 26:15 2671
For the *a* of the Almighty are ... Job 6:4 2671
he ordaineth his *a* against the ... Ps 7:13 2671
Yea, he sent out his *a*, and ... Ps 18:14 2671
thou shalt make ready thine *a* ... Ps 21:12
For thine *a* stick fast in me, and ... Ps 38:2 2671
Thine *a* are sharp in the heart of ... Ps 45:5 2671
men, whose teeth are spears and *a* ... Ps 57:4 2671
he bendeth his bow to shoot his *a* ... Ps 58:7 2671
bend their bows to shoot their *a* ... Ps 64:3 2671
There brake he the *a* of the bow ... Ps 76:3 7565
thine *a* also went abroad ... Ps 77:17 2687
Sharp *a* of the mighty, with coals ... Ps 120:4 2671
As *a* are in the hand of a mighty ... Ps 127:4 2671
shoot out thine *a*, and destroy ... Ps 144:6 2671
mad man who casteth firebrands, *a* ... Prov 26:18 2671
Whose *a* are sharp, and all their ... Is 5:28 2671
With *a* and with bows shall men ... Is 7:24 2671
their *a* shall be as of a mighty ... Jer 50:9 2671
the bow, shoot at her, spare no *a* ... Jer 50:14 2671
Make bright the *a* ... Jer 51:11 1121
He hath caused the *a* of his ... Lam 3:13 2671
upon them the evil *a* of famine ... Eze 5:16 2671
he made his *a* bright, he ... Eze 21:21 2671
will cause thine *a* to fall out of ... Eze 39:3 2671
the bucklers, the bows and the *a* ... Eze 39:9 2671
at the light of thine *a* they went ... Hab 3:11 2671

ART
and said unto him, Where *a* thou ... Gen 3:9
thou *a* cursed above all cattle, ... Gen 3:14
for dust thou *a*, and unto dust ... Gen 3:19
said unto Cain, Why *a* thou wroth ... Gen 4:6
now *a* thou cursed from the earth, ... Gen 4:11
I know that thou *a* a fair woman ... Gen 12:11
I pray thee, thou *a* my sister ... Gen 12:13
the place where thou *a* northward ... Gen 13:14
thou *a* with child, and shalt bear ... Gen 16:11
land wherein thou *a* a stranger ... Gen 17:8
thou *a* but a dead man, for the ... Gen 20:3
thou *a* a mighty prince among us ... Gen 23:6
And said, Whose daughter *a* thou ... Gen 24:23
and said, Whose daughter *a* thou ... Gen 24:47
Thou *a* our sister, be thou the ... Gen 24:60
for thou *a* much mightier than we ... Gen 26:16
thou *a* now the blessed of the ... Gen 26:29
who *a* thou, my son ... Gen 27:18
he said, *A* thou my very son Esau ... Gen 27:24
father said unto him, Who *a* thou ... Gen 27:32
land wherein thou *a* a stranger ... Gen 28:4
to him, Surely thou *a* my bone ... Gen 29:14
Jacob, Because thou *a* my brother ... Gen 29:15
asketh thee, saying, Whose *a* thou ... Gen 32:17
but thee, because thou *a* his wife ... Gen 39:9
so discreet and wise as thou *a* ... Gen 41:39
for thou *a* even as Pharaoh ... Gen 44:18
Now thou *a* commanded, this do ye ... Gen 45:19
face, because thou *a* yet alive ... Gen 46:30
said unto Jacob, How old *a* thou ... Gen 47:8
thou *a* my firstborn, my might, and ... Gen 49:3
thou *a* he whom thy brethren shall ... Gen 49:8
the prey, my son, thou *a* gone up ... Gen 49:9
a bloody husband *a* thou to me ... Ex 4:25
she said, A bloody husband thou *a* ... Ex 4:26
thou *a* not able to perform it ... Ex 18:18
after the *a* of the apothecary ... Ex 30:25 4640
after the *a* of the apothecary ... Ex 30:35 4640
for thou *a* a stiffnecked people ... Ex 33:3
a shall see the work of the LORD ... Ex 34:10

who *a* the priest, so shall it be ... Lev 27:12
thou LORD *a* among this people ... Num 14:14
that thou LORD *a* seen face to ... Num 14:14
thou *a* undone, O people of ... Num 21:29
Thou *a* to pass over through Ar, ... Deut 2:18
When thou *a* in tribulation, and ... Deut 4:30
greater and mightier than thou *a* ... Deut 4:38
For thou *a* an holy people unto ... Deut 7:6
the people of whom thou *a* afraid ... Deut 7:19
a full, then thou shalt bless the ... Deut 8:10
a full, and hast built goodly ... Deut 8:12
Thou *a* to pass over Jordan this ... Deut 9:1
for thou *a* a stiffnecked people ... Deut 9:6
For thou *a* an holy people unto ... Deut 14:2
for thou *a* an holy people unto ... Deut 14:21
so that thou *a* not able to carry ... Deut 14:24
When thou *a* come unto the land ... Deut 17:14
When thou *a* come into the land ... Deut 18:9
when thou *a* come in unto the land ... Deut 26:1
when thou *a* passed over, that ... Deut 27:3
this day thou *a* become the people ... Deut 27:9
the earth shall see that thou *a* ... Deut 28:10
thou *a* waxen fat, thou *a* grown ... Deut 32:15
thou *a* covered with fatness ... Deut 32:15
that begat thee thou *a* unmindful ... Deut 32:18
Happy *a* thou, O Israel ... Deut 33:29
A thou for us, or for our ... Josh 5:13
LORD said unto him, Thou *a* old ... Josh 13:1
Thou *a* a great people, and hast ... Josh 17:17
And they answered, As thou *a* ... Judg 8:18
for thou *a* the son of a strange ... Judg 11:2
that thou *a* come against me to ... Judg 11:12
now *a* thou any thing better than ... Judg 11:25
thou *a* one of them that trouble ... Judg 11:35
unto him, *A* thou an Ephraimite ... Judg 12:5
thou *a* barren, and bearest not ... Judg 13:3
A thou the man that spakest unto ... Judg 13:11
and when thou *a* athirst, go unto ... Ruth 2:9
a come unto a people which thou ... Ruth 2:11
whose wings thou *a* come to trust ... Ruth 2:12
And he said, Who *a* thou ... Ruth 3:9
for thou *a* a near kinsman ... Ruth 3:9
know that thou *a* a virtuous woman ... Ruth 3:11
she said, Who *a* thou, my daughter ... Ruth 3:16
said unto him, Behold, thou *a* old ... 1Sa 8:5
When thou *a* departed from me to ... 1Sa 10:2
when thou *a* come thither to the ... 1Sa 10:5
for thou *a* come down that thou ... 1Sa 17:28
Thou *a* not able to go against ... 1Sa 17:33
for thou *a* but a youth, and he a ... 1Sa 17:33
said to him, Whose son *a* thou ... 1Sa 17:58
father in the field where thou *a* ... 1Sa 19:3
Why *a* thou alone, and no man with ... 1Sa 21:1
Thou *a* more righteous than I ... 1Sa 24:17
Who *a* thou that criest to the ... 1Sa 26:14
Abner, *A* not thou a valiant man ... 1Sa 26:15
for thou *a* Saul ... 1Sa 28:12
know that thou *a* good in my sight ... 1Sa 29:9
and whence *a* thou ... 1Sa 30:13
And he said unto me, Who *a* thou ... 2Sa 1:8
man that told him, Whence *a* thou ... 2Sa 1:13
him, and said, *A* thou Asahel ... 2Sa 2:20
Wherefore thou *a* great, O LORD ... 2Sa 7:22
and thou, LORD, *a* become their God ... 2Sa 7:24
thou *a* that God, and thy words be ... 2Sa 7:28
king said unto him, *A* thou Ziba ... 2Sa 9:2
said to David, Thou *a* the man ... 2Sa 12:7
Why *a* thou, being the king's son, ... 2Sa 13:4
him, and said, Of what city *a* thou ... 2Sa 15:2
for thou *a* a stranger, and also an ... 2Sa 15:19
the priest, *A* not thou a seer ... 2Sa 15:27
thou *a* taken in thy mischief, ... 2Sa 16:8
because thou *a* a bloody man ... 2Sa 16:8
thou *a* abhorred of thy father ... 2Sa 16:21
but now thou *a* worth ten thousand ... 2Sa 18:3
A thou not of my bone, and of my ... 2Sa 19:13
A thou in health, my brother ... 2Sa 20:9
her, the woman said, *A* thou Joab ... 2Sa 20:17
For thou *a* my lamp, O LORD ... 2Sa 22:29
for thou *a* a valiant man, and ... 1Kin 1:42
for thou *a* a wise man, and knowest ... 1Kin 2:9
for thou *a* worthy of death ... 1Kin 2:26
house which thou *a* in building ... 1Kin 6:12
A thou the man of God that camest ... 1Kin 13:14
I am a prophet also as thou *a* ... 1Kin 13:18
a thou come unto me to call my ... 1Kin 17:18
I know that thou *a* a man of God ... 1Kin 17:24
A thou that my lord Elijah ... 1Kin 18:7
A thou he that troubleth Israel ... 1Kin 18:17
day that thou *a* God in Israel ... 1Kin 18:36
may know that thou *a* the LORD God ... 1Kin 18:37
as soon as thou *a* departed from ... 1Kin 20:36
king of Israel, I am as thou *a* ... 1Kin 22:4
that bed on which thou *a* gone up ... 2Kin 1:4
that bed on which thou *a* gone up ... 2Kin 1:6
that bed on which thou *a* gone up ... 2Kin 1:16
I am as thou *a*, my people as thy ... 2Kin 3:7
And when thou *a* come in, thou ... 2Kin 4:4
thou *a* the God, even thou alone, ... 2Kin 19:15
may know that thou *a* the LORD God ... 2Kin 19:19
And now, LORD, thou *a* God, and hast ... 1Chr 17:26
thou *a* exalted as head above all ... 1Chr 29:11
O LORD, thou *a* our God ... 2Chr 14:11
prepared by the apothecaries' *a* ... 2Chr 16:14 4640
he answered him, I am as thou *a* ... 2Chr 18:3
fathers, *a* not thou God in heaven ... 2Chr 20:6
A not thou our God, who didst ... 2Chr 20:7
A thou made of the king's counsel ... 2Chr 25:16
as thou *a* sent of the king ... Ezr 7:14
God of Israel, thou *a* righteous ... Ezr 9:15
sad, seeing thou *a* not sick ... Neh 2:2
Thou, even thou, *a* LORD alone ... Neh 9:6
Thou *a* the LORD the God, who ... Neh 9:7
for thou *a* righteous ... Neh 9:8

but thou *a* a God ready to pardon, ... Neh 9:17
for thou *a* a gracious and merciful ... Neh 9:31
Howbeit thou *a* just in all that ... Neh 9:33
who knoweth whether thou *a* come ... Est 4:14
toucheth thee, and thou *a* troubled ... Job 4:5
A thou the first man that was ... Job 15:7
to corruption, Thou *a* my father ... Job 17:14
Thou *a* my mother, and my sister ... Job 17:14
Almighty, that thou *a* righteous ... Job 22:3
Thou *a* become cruel to me ... Job 30:21
fine gold, Thou *a* my confidence ... Job 31:24
Behold, in this thou *a* not just ... Job 33:12
to say to a king, Thou *a* wicked ... Job 34:18
may hurt a man as thou *a* ... Job 35:8
hath said unto me, Thou *a* my Son ... Ps 2:7
thou, O LORD, *a* a shield for me ... Ps 3:3
For thou *a* not a God that hath ... Ps 5:4
that thou *a* mindful of him ... Ps 8:4
thou *a* the helper of the ... Ps 10:14
unto the LORD, Thou *a* my LORD ... Ps 16:2
why *a* thou so far from helping me ... Ps 22:1
But thou *a* holy, O thou that ... Ps 22:3
But thou *a* he that took me out of ... Ps 22:9
thou *a* my God from my mother's ... Ps 22:10
for thou *a* with me ... Ps 23:4
for thou *a* the God of my ... Ps 25:5
For thou *a* my rock and my fortress ... Ps 31:3
for thou *a* my strength ... Ps 31:4
I said, Thou *a* my God ... Ps 31:14
Thou *a* my hiding place ... Ps 32:7
thou *a* my help and my deliverer ... Ps 40:17
Why *a* thou cast down, O my soul ... Ps 42:5
why *a* thou disquieted in me ... Ps 42:5
Why *a* thou cast down, O my soul ... Ps 42:11
why *a* thou disquieted within me ... Ps 42:11
For thou *a* the God of my strength ... Ps 43:2
Why *a* thou cast down, O my soul ... Ps 43:5
why *a* thou disquieted within me ... Ps 43:5
Thou *a* my King, O God ... Ps 44:4
Thou *a* fairer than the children ... Ps 45:2
O god, thou *a* my God ... Ps 63:1
who *a* the confidence of all the ... Ps 65:5
How terrible *a* thou in thy works ... Ps 66:3
thou *a* terrible out of thy holy ... Ps 68:35
thou *a* my help and my deliverer ... Ps 70:5
to save me, for thou *a* my rock ... Ps 71:3
For thou *a* my hope, O Lord GOD ... Ps 71:5
thou *a* my trust from my youth ... Ps 71:5
thou *a* he that took me out of my ... Ps 71:6
but thou *a* my strong refuge ... Ps 71:7
Thou *a* more glorious and excellent ... Ps 76:4
Thou, even thou, *a* to be feared ... Ps 76:7
thy sight when once thou *a* angry ... Ps 76:7
Thou *a* the God that doest wonders ... Ps 77:14
a the most high over all the ... Ps 83:18
a good, and ready to forgive ... Ps 86:5
For thou *a* great, and doest ... Ps 86:10
thou *a* God alone ... Ps 86:10
a a God full of compassion, and ... Ps 86:15
For thou *a* the glory of their ... Ps 89:17
Thou *a* my father, my God, and the ... Ps 89:26
to everlasting, thou *a* God ... Ps 90:2
LORD, *a* most high for evermore ... Ps 92:8
thou *a* from everlasting ... Ps 93:2
a high above all the earth ... Ps 97:9
thou *a* exalted far above all gods ... Ps 97:9
But thou *a* the same, and thy years ... Ps 102:27
O LORD my God, thou *a* very great ... Ps 104:1
thou *a* clothed with honour and ... Ps 104:1
Thou *a* a priest for ever after ... Ps 110:4
me, and *a* become my salvation ... Ps 118:21
Thou *a* my God, and I will praise ... Ps 118:28
thou *a* my God, I will exalt thee ... Ps 118:28
Blessed *a* thou, O LORD ... Ps 119:12
Thou *a* my portion, O LORD ... Ps 119:57
Thou *a* good, and doest good ... Ps 119:68
Thou *a* my hiding place and my ... Ps 119:114
Righteous *a* thou, O LORD, and ... Ps 119:137
Thou *a* near, O LORD ... Ps 119:151
of Babylon, who *a* to be destroyed ... Ps 137:8
a acquainted with all my ways ... Ps 139:3
up into heaven, thou *a* there ... Ps 139:8
bed in hell, behold, thou *a* there ... Ps 139:8
said unto the LORD, Thou *a* my God ... Ps 140:6
Thou *a* my refuge and my portion in ... Ps 142:5
for thou *a* my God ... Ps 143:10
Thou *a* snared with the words of ... Prov 6:2
thou *a* taken with the words of ... Prov 6:2
when thou *a* come into the hand of ... Prov 6:3
Say unto wisdom, Thou *a* my sister ... Prov 7:4
unto the wicked, Thou *a* righteous ... Prov 24:24
Blessed *a* thou, O land, when thy ... Eccl 10:17
Behold, thou *a* fair, my love ... Song 1:15
behold, thou *a* fair ... Song 1:15
Behold, thou *a* fair, my beloved, ... Song 1:16
that *a* in the clefts of the rock, ... Song 2:14
Behold, thou *a* fair, my love ... Song 4:1
behold, thou *a* fair ... Song 4:1
Thou *a* all fair, my love ... Song 4:7
Thou *a* beautiful, O my love, as ... Song 6:4
How fair and how pleasant *a* thou ... Song 7:6
saying, Since thou *a* laid down ... Is 14:8
A thou also become weak as we ... Is 14:10
a thou become like unto us ... Is 14:10
How *a* thou fallen from heaven, O ... Is 14:12
how *a* thou cut down to the ground ... Is 14:12
But thou *a* cast out of thy grave ... Is 14:19
whole Palestina, *a* dissolved ... Is 14:31
that thou *a* wholly gone up to the ... Is 22:1
Thou that *a* full of stirs, a ... Is 22:2
O lord, thou *a* my God ... Is 25:1
thou *a* glorified ... Is 26:15
thou *a* the God, even thou alone, ... Is 37:16
may know that thou *a* the LORD ... Is 37:20

a my servant, Jacob whom I have ... Is 41:8
said unto thee, Thou *a* my servant ... Is 41:9
thou *a* mine ... Is 43:1
for thou *a* my god ... Is 44:17
for thou *a* my servant ... Is 44:21
thou *a* my servant ... Is 44:21
Verily thou *a* a God that hidest ... Is 45:15
thou that *a* given to pleasures, ... Is 47:8
Thou *a* wearied in the multitude ... Is 47:13
I knew that thou *a* obstinate ... Is 48:4
Thou *a* my servant, O Israel, in ... Is 49:3
A thou not it that hath cut Rahab ... Is 51:9
A thou not it which hath dried ... Is 51:10
who *a* thou, that thou shouldest ... Is 51:12
say unto Zion, Thou *a* my people ... Is 51:16
to another than me, and *a* gone up ... Is 57:8
Thou *a* wearied in the greatness ... Is 57:10
Wherefore *a* thou red in thine ... Is 63:2
Doubtless thou *a* our father ... Is 63:16
a our father, our redeemer ... Is 63:16
behold, thou *a* wroth ... Is 64:5
now, O LORD, thou *a* our father ... Is 64:8
how then *a* thou turned into the ... Jer 2:21
thou *a* a swift dromedary ... Jer 2:23
to a stock, Thou *a* my father ... Jer 2:27
thou *a* the guide of my youth ... Jer 3:4
for thou *a* the LORD our God ... Jer 3:22
And when thou *a* spoiled, what wilt ... Jer 4:30
thou *a* great, and thy name is ... Jer 10:6
Righteous *a* thou, O LORD, when I ... Jer 12:1
thou *a* near in their mouth, and ... Jer 12:2
a in the midst of us, and we are ... Jer 14:9
a not thou he, O LORD our God ... Jer 14:22
the LORD, thou *a* gone backward ... Jer 15:6
for thou *a* my praise ... Jer 17:14
thou *a* my hope in the day of evil ... Jer 17:17
thou *a* stronger than I, and hast ... Jer 20:7
Thou *a* Gilead unto me, and the ... Jer 22:6
for thou *a* the LORD my God ... Jer 31:18
of the men of whom thou *a* afraid ... Jer 39:17
a thou he that shall altogether ... Jer 49:12
thou *a* also taken, O Babylon, and ... Jer 50:24
thou *a* found, and also caught, ... Jer 50:24
Thou *a* my battle ax and weapons of ... Jer 51:20
thou *a* very wroth against us ... Lam 5:22
For thou *a* not sent to a people ... Eze 3:5
and thou *a* come to excellent ... Eze 16:7
thee, therefore thou *a* contrary ... Eze 16:34
Thou *a* thy mother's daughter, ... Eze 16:45
thou *a* the sister of thy sisters, ... Eze 16:45
in that thou *a* a comfort unto ... Eze 16:54
Thou *a* become guilty in thy blood ... Eze 22:4
a come even unto thy years ... Eze 22:4
which *a* infamous and much vexed ... Eze 22:5
Thou *a* the land that is not ... Eze 22:24
because thou *a* polluted with ... Eze 23:30
How *a* thou destroyed, that wast ... Eze 26:17
O thou that *a* situate at the ... Eze 27:3
which *a* a merchant of the people ... Eze 27:3
yet thou *a* a man, and not God, ... Eze 28:2
Behold, thou *a* wiser than Daniel ... Eze 28:3
Thou *a* the anointed cherub that ... Eze 28:14
Whom *a* thou like in thy greatness ... Eze 31:2
To whom *a* thou thus like in glory ... Eze 31:18
Thou *a* like a young lion of the ... Eze 32:2
thou *a* as a whale in the seas ... Eze 32:2
thou *a* unto them as a very lovely ... Eze 33:32
A thou come to take a spoil ... Eze 38:13
A thou he of whom I have spoken ... Eze 38:17
unto thee *a* thou brought hither ... Eze 40:4
A thou able to make known unto me ... Dan 2:26 383
Thou, O king, *a* a king of kings ... Dan 2:37
Thou *a* this head of gold ... Dan 2:38
but thou *a* able ... Dan 4:18
that *a* grown and become strong ... Dan 4:22
A thou that Daniel, which *a* of ... Dan 5:13
Thou *a* weighed in the balances, ... Dan 5:27
the balances, and *a* found wanting ... Dan 5:27
for thou *a* greatly beloved ... Dan 9:23
not my people, Thou *a* my people ... Hos 2:23
and they shall say, Thou *a* my God ... Hos 2:23
thou *a* greatly despised ... Obad 2
by night, (how *a* thou cut off ... Obad 5
and of what people *a* thou ... Jonah 1:8
I knew that thou *a* a gracious God ... Jonah 4:2
O thou that *a* named the house of ... Mic 2:7
for thou *a* vile ... Nah 1:14
A thou better than populous No, ... Nah 3:8
A thou not from everlasting, O ... Hab 1:12
Thou *a* of purer eyes than to ... Hab 1:13
Thou *a* filled with shame for ... Hab 2:16
Who *a* thou, O great mountain ... Zec 4:7
a not the least among the princes ... Mt 2:6 *1488*
whiles thou *a* in the way with him ... Mt 5:25 *1488*
Our Father which *a* in heaven ... Mt 6:9
a thou come hither to torment us ... Mt 8:29
A thou he that should come, or do ... Mt 11:3 *1488*
which *a* exalted unto heaven, ... Mt 11:23
Of a truth thou *a* the Son of God ... Mt 14:33 *1488*
say that thou *a* John the Baptist ... Mt 16:14
Thou *a* the Christ, the Son of the ... Mt 16:16 *1488*
and said unto him, Blessed *a* thou ... Mt 16:17 *1488*
also unto thee, That thou *a* Peter ... Mt 16:18 *1488*
thou *a* an offence unto me ... Mt 16:23 *1488*
Master, we know that thou *a* true ... Mt 22:16 *1488*
knew thee that thou *a* an hard man ... Mt 25:24 *1488*
Friend, wherefore *a* thou come ... Mt 26:50
Surely thou also *a* one of them ... Mt 26:73 *1488*
A thou the King of the Jews ... Mt 27:11 *1488*
Thou *a* my beloved Son, in whom I ... Mk 1:11 *1488*
a thou come to destroy us ... Mk 1:24
I know thee who thou *a*, the Holy ... Mk 1:24 *1488*
saying, Thou *a* the Son of God ... Mk 3:11 *1488*
saith unto him, Thou *a* the Christ ... Mk 8:29 *1488*
Master, we know that thou *a* true ... Mk 12:14 *1488*
Thou *a* not far from the kingdom ... Mk 12:34 *1488*
A thou the Christ, the Son of the ... Mk 14:61 *1488*
Peter, Surely thou *a* one of them ... Mk 14:70 *1488*
for thou *a* a Galilaean, and thy ... Mk 14:70 *1488*
A thou the King of the Jews ... Mk 15:2 *1488*
thou that *a* highly favoured, the ... Lk 1:28
blessed *a* thou among women ... Lk 1:28
Blessed *a* thou among women, and ... Lk 1:42
which said, Thou *a* my beloved Son ... Lk 3:22 *1488*
a thou come to destroy us ... Lk 4:34
I know thee who thou *a* ... Lk 4:34 *1488*
Thou *a* Christ the Son of God ... Lk 4:41 *1488*
A thou he that should come ... Lk 7:19 *1488*
A thou he that should come ... Lk 7:20 *1488*
which *a* exalted to heaven, shalt ... Lk 10:15
thou *a* careful and troubled about ... Lk 10:41
say, Our Father which *a* in heaven ... Lk 11:2
as thou *a* in the way, give ... Lk 12:58
Woman, thou *a* loosed from thine ... Lk 13:12
When thou *a* bidden of any man to ... Lk 14:8
But when thou *a* bidden, go and sit ... Lk 14:10
thou *a* ever with me, and all that ... Lk 15:31 *1488*
is comforted, and thou *a* tormented ... Lk 16:25
because thou *a* an austere man ... Lk 19:21
and when thou *a* converted, ... Lk 22:32
him, and said, Thou *a* also of them ... Lk 22:58 *1488*
A thou the Christ ... Lk 22:67 *1488*
A thou then the Son of God ... Lk 22:70 *1488*
A thou the King of the Jews ... Lk 23:3 *1488*
seeing thou *a* in the same ... Lk 23:40 *1488*
A thou only a stranger in ... Lk 24:18
Jerusalem to ask him, Who *a* thou ... Jn 1:19 *1488*
A thou Elias? ... Jn 1:21 *1488*
A thou that prophet ... Jn 1:21 *1488*
said they unto him, Who *a* thou ... Jn 1:22 *1488*
Thou *a* Simon the son of Jona ... Jn 1:42 *1488*
him, Rabbi, thou *a* the Son of God ... Jn 1:49 *1488*
thou *a* the King of Israel ... Jn 1:49 *1488*
we know that thou *a* a teacher ... Jn 3:2
A thou a master of Israel, and ... Jn 3:10 *1488*
A thou greater than our father ... Jn 4:12 *1488*
I perceive that thou *a* a prophet ... Jn 4:19 *1488*
him, Behold, thou *a* made whole ... Jn 5:14
are sure that thou *a* that Christ ... Jn 6:69 *1488*
unto him, *A* thou also of Galilee ... Jn 7:52 *1488*
said they unto him, Who *a* thou ... Jn 8:25 *1488*
not well that thou *a* a Samaritan ... Jn 8:48 *1488*
A thou greater than our father ... Jn 8:53 *1488*
Thou *a* not yet fifty years old, ... Jn 8:57 *2192*
him, and said, Thou *a* his disciple ... Jn 9:28 *1488*
I believe that thou *a* the Christ ... Jn 11:27 *1488*
a in me, and I in thee, that they ... Jn 17:21
A not thou also one of this man's ... Jn 18:17 *1488*
A not thou also one of his ... Jn 18:25 *1488*
A thou the King of the Jews ... Jn 18:33 *1488*
said unto him, *A* thou a king then ... Jn 18:37 *1488*
saith unto Jesus, Whence *a* thou ... Jn 19:9 *1488*
thou *a* not Caesar's friend ... Jn 19:12 *1488*
durst ask him, Who *a* thou ... Jn 21:12 *1488*
accord, and said, Lord, thou *a* God ... Acts 4:24
For I perceive that thou *a* in the ... Acts 8:23
And he said, Who *a* thou, Lord ... Acts 9:5 *1488*
hast well done that thou *a* come ... Acts 10:33
And they said unto her, Thou *a* mad ... Acts 12:15
Thou *a* my Son, this day have I ... Acts 13:33 *1488*
or silver, or stone, graven by *a* ... Acts 17:29 *5073*
they will hear that thou *a* come ... Acts 21:22
A not thou that Egyptian, which ... Acts 21:38 *1488*
And I answered, Who *a* thou, Lord ... Acts 22:8 *1488*
unto him, Tell me, *a* thou a Roman ... Acts 22:27 *1488*
Thou *a* permitted to speak for ... Acts 26:1
And I said, Who *a* thou, Lord ... Acts 26:15 *1488*
Paul, thou *a* beside thyself ... Acts 26:24
Therefore thou *a* inexcusable ... Rom 2:1 *1488*
whosoever thou *a* that judgest ... Rom 2:1 *1488*
thou *a* called a Jew, and restest ... Rom 2:17
a confident that thou thyself *a* ... Rom 2:19
overcome when thou *a* judged ... Rom 3:4
who *a* thou that repliest against ... Rom 9:20 *1488*
Who *a* thou that judgest another ... Rom 14:4 *1488*
A thou called being a servant ... 1Cor 7:21
A thou bound unto a wife ... 1Cor 7:27
A thou loosed from a wife ... 1Cor 7:27
Wherefore thou *a* no more a ... Gal 4:7 *1488*
whereunto thou *a* also called ... 1Ti 6:12
Thou *a* my Son, this day have I ... Heb 1:5 *1488*
but thou *a* the same, and thy years ... Heb 1:12 *1488*
that thou *a* mindful of him ... Heb 2:6
Thou *a* my Son, to day have I ... Heb 5:5 *1488*
Thou *a* a priest for ever after ... Heb 5:6
Thou *a* a priest for ever after ... Heb 7:17
Thou *a* a priest for ever after ... Heb 7:21
faint when thou *a* rebuked of him ... Heb 12:5
thou *a* become a transgressor of ... Jas 2:11
thou *a* not a doer of the law, but ... Jas 4:11 *1488*
who *a* thou that judgest another ... Jas 4:12 *1488*
from whence thou *a* fallen ... Rev 2:5
and poverty, (but thou *a* rich) ... Rev 2:9 *1488*
name that thou livest, and *a* dead ... Rev 3:1 *1488*
that thou *a* neither cold nor hot ... Rev 3:15 *1488*
So then because thou *a* lukewarm ... Rev 3:16 *1488*
knowest not that thou *a* wretched ... Rev 3:17 *1488*
Thou *a* worthy, O Lord, to receive ... Rev 4:11 *1488*
Thou *a* worthy to take the book, ... Rev 5:9 *1488*
which *a*, and wast, and *a* to come ... Rev 11:17
for thou only *a* holy ... Rev 15:4
a righteous, O Lord, which *a* ... Rev 16:5 *5607*

ARTAXERXES (*ar-tax-erx'-ees*) See ARTAXERXES'.
1. A Persian king known as Longimanus.
And in the days of *A* wrote Bishlam ... Ezr 4:7 783
companions, unto *A* king of Persia ... Ezr 4:7 783
to *A* the king in this sort ... Ezr 4:8 783
unto him, even unto *A* the king ... Ezr 4:11 783
2. A Persian king known as Cambyses.
and Darius, and *A* king of Persia ... Ezr 6:14 783
3. A Persian king known as Darius.
in the reign of *A* king of Persia ... Ezr 7:1 783
in the seventh year of *A* the king ... Ezr 7:7 783
king *A* gave unto Ezra the priest ... Ezr 7:11 783
A, king of kings, unto Ezra the ... Ezr 7:12 783
even I *A* the king, do make a ... Ezr 7:21 783
in the reign of *A* the king ... Ezr 8:1 783
the twentieth year of *A* the king ... Neh 2:1 783
and thirtieth year of *A* the king ... Neh 5:14 783
thirtieth year of *A* king of ... Neh 13:6 783

ARTAXERXES' (*ar-tax-erx'-eez*) *Refers to Artaxerxes 1.*
Now when the copy of king *A* ... Ezr 4:23 783

ARTEMAS (*ar'-te-mas*) *A companion of Paul.*
When I shall send *A* unto thee ... Titus 3:12 734

ARTEMIS See DIANA.

ARTIFICER
an instructer of every *a* in brass ... Gen 4:22 2794
the counsellor, and the cunning *a* ... Is 3:3 2796

ARTIFICERS
work to be made by the hands of *a* ... 1Chr 29:5 2796
Even to the *a* and builders gave ... 2Chr 34:11 2796

ARTILLERY
Jonathan gave his *a* unto his lad ... 1Sa 20:40 3627

ARTS
a brought their books together ... Acts 19:19 *4021*

ARUBBOTH See ARUBOTH.

ARUBOTH (*ar'-u-both*) *A district of Solomon's rule.*
The son of Hesed, in *A* ... 1Kin 4:10 700

ARUMAH (*a-ru'-mah*) *A place in Ephraim.*
And Abimelech dwelt at *A* ... Judg 9:41 725

ARVAD (*ar'-vad*) See ARVADITE. *An island near Zidon.*
of Zidon and *A* were thy mariners ... Eze 27:8 719
The men of *A* with thine army were ... Eze 27:11 719

ARVADITE (*ar'-vad-ite*) *Descendants of Canaan.*
And the *A*, and the Zemarite, and the . Gen 10:18 721
And the *A*, and the Zemarite, and the . 1Chr 1:16 721

ARVADITES See ARVADITE.

ARZA (*ar'-zah*) *A steward of King Elah of Israel.*
himself drunk in the house of *A* ... 1Kin 16:9 777

AS See PREFACE.

ASA (*a'-sah*) See ASA'S.
1. A king of Judah.
A his son reigned in his stead ... 1Kin 15:8 609
of Israel reigned *A* over Judah ... 1Kin 15:9 609
A did that which was right in the ... 1Kin 15:11 609
A destroyed her idol, and burnt it ... 1Kin 15:13 609
And there was war between *A* ... 1Kin 15:16 609
out or come in to *A* king of Judah ... 1Kin 15:17 609
Then *A* took all the silver and the ... 1Kin 15:18 609
king *A* sent them to Ben-hadad, ... 1Kin 15:18 609
Ben-hadad hearkened unto king *A* ... 1Kin 15:20 609
Then king *A* made a proclamation ... 1Kin 15:22 609
king *A* built with them Geba of ... 1Kin 15:22 609
The rest of all the acts of *A* ... 1Kin 15:23 609
A slept with his fathers, and was ... 1Kin 15:24 609
second year of *A* king of Judah ... 1Kin 15:25 609
Even in the third year of *A* king ... 1Kin 15:28 609
And there was war between *A* ... 1Kin 15:32 609
In the third year of *A* king of ... 1Kin 15:33 609
sixth year of *A* king of Judah ... 1Kin 16:8 609
seventh year of *A* king of Judah ... 1Kin 16:10 609
seventh year of *A* king of Judah ... 1Kin 16:15 609
first year of *A* king of Judah ... 1Kin 16:23 609
eighth year of *A* king of Judah ... 1Kin 16:29 609
Jehoshaphat the son of *A* began to ... 1Kin 22:41 609
in all the ways of *A* his father ... 1Kin 22:43 609
in the days of his father *A* ... 1Kin 22:46 609
A his son, Jehoshaphat his son, ... 1Chr 3:10 609
A his son reigned in his stead ... 2Chr 14:1 609
A did that which was good and ... 2Chr 14:2 609
A had an army of men that bare ... 2Chr 14:8 609
Then *A* went out against him, and ... 2Chr 14:10 609
A cried unto the LORD his God, and ... 2Chr 14:11 609
smote the Ethiopians before *A* ... 2Chr 14:12 609
And *A* and the people that were with .. 2Chr 14:13 609
And he went out to meet *A*, and said .. 2Chr 15:2 609
and said unto him, Hear ye me, *A* ... 2Chr 15:2 609
when *A* heard these words, and the ... 2Chr 15:8 609
fifteenth year of the reign of *A* ... 2Chr 15:10 609
Maachah the mother of *A* the king ... 2Chr 15:16 609
A cut down her idol, and stamped ... 2Chr 15:16 609
of *A* was perfect all his days ... 2Chr 15:17 609
thirtieth year of the reign of *A* ... 2Chr 15:19 609
A Baasha king of Israel came up ... 2Chr 16:1 609
out or come in to *A* king of Judah ... 2Chr 16:1 609
Then *A* brought out silver and gold ... 2Chr 16:2 609
Ben-hadad hearkened unto king *A* ... 2Chr 16:4 609
Then *A* the king took all Judah ... 2Chr 16:6 609
the seer came to *A* king of Judah ... 2Chr 16:7 609
Then *A* was wroth with the seer, ... 2Chr 16:10 609
A oppressed some of the people ... 2Chr 16:10 609
And, behold, the acts of *A* ... 2Chr 16:11 609
A in the thirty and ninth year of ... 2Chr 16:12 609
A slept with his fathers, and died ... 2Chr 16:13 609
which *A* his father had taken ... 2Chr 17:2 609

walked in the way of A his father 2Chr 20:32 609
in the ways of A king of Judah 2Chr 21:12 609
was it which A the king had made Jer 41:9 609
and Abia begat A Mt 1:7 760
And A begat Josaphat Mt 1:8 760
2. Chief of a Levite family.
and Berechiah the son of A 1Chr 9:16 609

ASAHEL (*as'-a-hel*)
1. The son of Zeruiah, David's sister.
there, Joab, and Abishai, and A 2Sa 2:18 760
A was as light of foot as a wild 2Sa 2:18 6214
And A pursued after Abner 2Sa 2:19 6214
behind him, and said, Art thou A 2Sa 2:20 6214
But A would not turn aside from 2Sa 2:21 6214
And Abner said again to A, Turn 2Sa 2:22 6214
to the place where A fell down 2Sa 2:23 6214
servants nineteen men and A 2Sa 2:30 6214
And they took up A, and buried him 2Sa 2:32 6214
for the blood of A his brother 2Sa 3:27 6214
brother A at Gibeon in the battle 2Sa 3:30 6214
A the brother of Joab was one of 2Sa 23:24 6214
Abishai, and Joab, and A, three 1Chr 2:16 6214
A the brother of Joab, Elhanan 1Chr 11:26 6214
month was A the brother of Joab 1Chr 27:7 6214
2. A Levite teacher.
and Nethaniah, and Zebadiah, and A 2Chr 17:8 6214
3. A Levite officer.
and Azaziah, and Nahath, and A 2Chr 31:13 6214
4. Father of Jonathan.
Only Jonathan the son of A Ezr 10:15 6214

ASAHIAH (*as-a-hi'-ah*) See ASAIAH. *An officer of King Josiah.*
A a servant of the king's, saying 2Kin 22:12 6222
and Achbor, and Shaphan, and A 2Kin 22:14 6222

ASAIAH (*as-a'-yah*)
1. A descendant of Simeon.
and Jaakobah, and Jeshohaiah, and A 1Chr 4:36 6222
2. A descendant of Libni.
son, Haggiah his son, A his son 1Chr 6:30 6222
3. A Shilonite of Jerusalem.
A the firstborn, and his sons 1Chr 9:5 6222
4. A descendant of Merari.
A the chief, and his brethren two 1Chr 15:6 6222
and for the Levites, for Uriel, A 1Chr 15:11 6222
5. Same as Asahiah.
A a servant of the king's, saying 2Chr 34:20 6222

ASAPH (*a'-saf*) See ASAPH'S.
1. Father of Joah.
and Joah the son of A the recorder 2Kin 18:18 623
and Joah the son of A the recorder 2Kin 18:37 623
the scribe, and Joah, the son of A Is 36:22 623
2. A musician of David and Solomon.
And his brother A, who stood on 1Chr 6:39 623
even A the son of Berachiah, the 1Chr 6:39 623
brethren, A the son of Berechiah 1Chr 15:17 623
So the singers, Heman, A, and 1Chr 15:19 623
A the chief, and next to him 1Chr 16:5 623
but A made a sound with cymbals 1Chr 16:5 623
thank the LORD into the hand of A 1Chr 16:7 623
ark of the covenant of the LORD A 1Chr 16:37 623
to the service of the sons of A 1Chr 25:1 623
Of the sons of A 1Chr 25:2 623
of Asaph under the hands of A 1Chr 25:2 623
to the king's order to A 1Chr 25:6 623
lot came forth for A to Joseph 1Chr 25:9 623
the singers, all of them of A 2Chr 5:12 623
a Levite of the sons of A 2Chr 20:14 623
and of the sons of A 2Chr 29:13 623
words of David, and of A the seer 2Chr 29:30 623
the sons of A were in their place 2Chr 35:15 623
to the commandment of David, and A 2Chr 35:15 623
the children of A, an hundred Ezr 2:41 623
the sons of A with cymbals Ezr 3:10 623
the children of A, an hundred Neh 7:44 623
the son of Zabdi, the son of A Neh 11:17 623
Of the sons of A, the singers Neh 11:22 623
the son of Zaccur, the son of A Neh 12:35 623
A of old there were chief of the Neh 12:46 623
A Psalm of A Ps 50:t 623
A Psalm of A Ps 73:t 623
Maschil of A Ps 74:t 623
Altaschith, A Psalm or Song of A Ps 75:t 623
on Neginoth, A Psalm or Song of A Ps 76:t 623
to Jeduthun, A Psalm of A Ps 77:t 623
Maschil of A Ps 78:t 623
A Psalm of A Ps 79:t 623
Shoshannim-Eduth, A Psalm of A Ps 80:t 623
upon Gittith, A Psalm of A Ps 81:t 623
A Psalm of A Ps 82:t 623
A Song or Psalm of A Ps 83:t 623
3. A Levite family in post-exilic Jerusalem.
the son of Zichri, the son of A 1Chr 9:15 623
4. Descendants of Merari.
the son of Kore, of the sons of A 1Chr 26:1 623
5. A Persian official.
a letter unto A the keeper of the Neh 2:8 623

ASAPH'S (*a'-safs*) *Refers to Asaph 1.*
and Joah, A son, the recorder Is 36:3 623

ASAREEL (*a-sar'-e-el*) *A son of Jehaleleel.*
Ziph, and Ziphah, Tiria, and A 1Chr 4:16 840

ASARELAH (*as-a-re'-lah*) See JESHARELAH. *A son of a musician of David.*
and Joseph, and Nethaniah, and A 1Chr 25:2 841

ASA'S (*a'-sahz*) *Refers to Asa 1.*
nevertheless A heart was perfect 1Kin 15:14 609

ASCEND
the people shall a up every man Josh 6:5 5927
Who shall a into the hill of the Ps 24:3 5927
He causeth the vapours to a from Ps 135:7 5927
If I a up into heaven, thou art Ps 139:8 5927
I will a into heaven, I will Is 14:13 5927
I will a above the heights of the Is 14:14 5927
he causeth the vapors to a from Jer 10:13 5927
he causeth the vapors to a from Jer 51:16 5927
Thou shalt a and come like a storm Eze 38:9 5927
of man a up where he was before Jn 6:62 305
I a unto my Father, and your Jn 20:17 305
heart, Who shall a into heaven Rom 10:6 305
shall a out of the bottomless pit Rev 17:8 305

ASCENDED
the smoke thereof a as the smoke Ex 19:18 5927
they a by the south, and came unto Num 13:22 5927
smoke of the city a up to heaven Josh 8:20 5927
and that the smoke of the city a Josh 8:21 5927
So Joshua a from Gilgal, he, and Josh 10:7 5927
a up on the south side unto Josh 15:3 5927
LORD a in the flame of the altar Judg 13:20 5927
flame of the city a up to heaven Judg 20:40 5927
Thou hast a on high, thou hast Ps 68:18 5927
Who hath a up into heaven, or Prov 30:4 5927
no man hath a up to heaven, but Jn 3:13 305
for I am not yet a to my Father Jn 20:17 305
David is not a into the heavens Acts 2:34 305
after three days he a from Acts 25:1 305
When he a up on high, he led Eph 4:8 305
(Now that he a, what is it but Eph 4:9 305
that a up far above all heavens Eph 4:10 305
a up before God out of the Rev 8:4 305
they a up to heaven in a cloud Rev 11:12 305

ASCENDETH
the beast that a out of the Rev 11:7 305
of their torment a up for ever Rev 14:11 305

ASCENDING
and behold the angels of God a Gen 28:12 5927
I saw gods a out of the earth 1Sa 28:13 5927
he went before, a up to Jerusalem Lk 19:28 305
open, and the angels of God a Jn 1:51 305
saw another angel a from the east Rev 7:2 305

ASCENT
the south to the a of Akrabbim Num 34:4 4608
went up by the a of mount Olivet 2Sa 15:30 4608
his a by which he went up unto 1Kin 10:5 5930
his a by which he went up into 2Chr 9:4 5944

ASCRIBE
a ye greatness unto our God Deut 32:3 3051
will a righteousness to my Maker Job 36:3 5414
A ye strength unto God Ps 68:34 5414

ASCRIBED
They have a unto David ten 1Sa 18:8 5414
to me they have a but thousands 1Sa 18:8 5414

ASENATH (*as'-e-nath*) *A great-grandson of Solomon.*
he gave him to wife A the Gen 41:45 621
came, which A the daughter of Gen 41:50 621
Ephraim, which A the daughter of Gen 46:20 621

ASER (*a'-sur*) See ASHER. *Greek form of Asher.*
of Phanuel, of the tribe of A Lk 2:36 768
Of the tribe of A were sealed Rev 7:6 768

ASH
he planteth an a, and the rain Is 44:14 766

ASHAMED
man and his wife, and were not a Gen 2:25 954
should she not be a seven days Num 12:14 3637
And they tarried till they were a Judg 3:25 954
because the men were greatly a 2Sa 10:5 3637
as people being a steal away when 2Sa 19:3 3637
when they urged him till he was a 2Kin 2:17 954
stedfastly, until he was a 2Kin 8:11 954
for the men were greatly a 1Chr 19:5 3637
the priests and the Levites were a 2Chr 30:15 3637
For I was a to require of the Ezr 8:22 954
And said, O my God, I am a Ezr 9:6 954
they came thither, and were a Job 6:20 2659
mockest, shall no man make thee a Job 11:3 3637
ye are not a that ye make Job 19:3 954
Let all mine enemies be a Ps 6:10 954
let them return and be a suddenly Ps 6:10 954
let me not be a, let not mine Ps 25:2 954
let none that wait on thee be a Ps 25:3 954
let them be a which transgress Ps 25:3 954
let me not be a Ps 25:20 954
let me never be a Ps 31:1 954
Let me not be a, O LORD Ps 31:17 954
let the wicked be a, and let them Ps 31:17 954
and their faces were not a Ps 34:5 2659
Let them be a and brought to Ps 35:26 954
shall not be a in the evil time Ps 37:19 954
Let them be a and confounded Ps 40:14 954
GOD of hosts, be a for my sake Ps 69:6 954
Let them be a and confounded that Ps 70:2 954
O let not the oppressed return a Ps 74:21 3637
which hate me may see it, and be a Ps 86:17 954
when they arise, let them be a Ps 109:28 954
Then shall I not be a, when I Ps 119:6 954
before kings, and will not be a Ps 119:46 954
Let the proud be a Ps 119:78 954
that I be not a Ps 119:80 954
and let me not be a of my hope Ps 119:116 954
they shall not be a, but they Ps 127:5 954
but she that maketh a is as Prov 12:4 954
For they shall be a of the oaks Is 1:29 954
a of Ethiopia their expectation Is 20:5 954
Be thou a, O Zidon Is 23:4 954
shall be confounded, and the sun a Is 24:23 954
be a for their envy at the people Is 26:11 954
Jacob, Jacob shall not now be a Is 29:22 954
They were all a of a people that Is 30:5 954
Lebanon is a and hewn down Is 33:9 2659
incensed against thee shall be a Is 41:11 954
back, they shall be greatly a Is 42:17 954
that they may be a Is 44:9 954
all his fellows shall be a Is 44:11 954
fear, and they shall be a together Is 44:11 954
They shall be a, and also Is 45:16 954
ye shall not be a nor confounded Is 45:17 954
incensed against him shall be a Is 45:24 954
shall not be a that wait for me Is 49:23 954
and I know that I shall not be a Is 50:7 954
for thou shalt not be a Is 54:4 954
shall rejoice, but ye shall be a Is 65:13 954
to your joy, and they shall be a Is 66:5 954
As the thief is a when he is Jer 2:26 1322
so is the house of Israel a Jer 2:26 954
thou also shalt be a of Egypt Jer 2:36 954
as thou wast a of Assyria Jer 2:36 954
forehead, thou refusedst to be a Jer 3:3 3637
Were they a when they had Jer 6:15 954
nay, they were not at all a Jer 6:15 954
The wise men are a, they are Jer 8:9 954
Were they a when they had Jer 8:12 954
nay, they were not at all a Jer 8:12 954
they shall be a of your revenues Jer 12:13 954
they were a and confounded, and Jer 14:3 954
in the earth, the plowmen were a Jer 14:4 954
she hath been a and confounded Jer 15:9 954
all that forsake thee shall be a Jer 17:13 954
they shall be greatly a Jer 20:11 954
surely then shalt thou be a Jer 22:22 954
I was a, yea, even confounded Jer 31:19 954
And Moab shall be a of Chemosh Jer 48:13 954
as the house of Israel was a of Jer 48:13 954
she that bare you shall be a Jer 50:12 2659
which are a of thy lewd way Eze 16:27 3637
shalt remember thy ways, and be a Eze 16:61 3637
terror they are a of their might Eze 32:30 954
be a and confounded for your own Eze 36:32 954
that they may be a of their Eze 43:10 3637
if they be a of all that they Eze 43:11 3637
they shall be a because of their Hos 4:19 954
Israel shall be a of his own Hos 10:6 954
Be ye a, O ye husbandmen Joel 1:11 954
and my people shall never be a Joel 2:26 954
and my people shall never be a Joel 2:27 954
Then shall the seers be a Mic 3:7 954
thou not be a for all thy doings Zeph 3:11 954
for her expectation shall be a Zec 9:5 954
be a every one of his vision Zec 13:4 954
therefore shall be a of me Mk 8:38 1870
also shall the Son of man be a Mk 8:38 1870
For whosoever shall be a of me Lk 9:26 1870
of him shall the Son of man be a Lk 9:26 1870
all his adversaries were a Lk 13:17 2617
to beg I am a Lk 16:3 153
For I am not a of the gospel of Rom 1:16 1870
And hope maketh not a Rom 5:5 2617
those things whereof ye are now a Rom 6:21 1870
believeth on him shall not be a Rom 9:33 2617
believeth on him shall not be a Rom 10:11 2617
thing to him of you, I am not a 2Cor 7:14 2617
ye) should be a in this same 2Cor 9:4 2617
destruction, I should not be a 2Cor 10:8 153
that in nothing I shall be a Phil 1:20 153
with him, that he may be a 2Th 3:14 1788
Be not thou therefore a of the 2Ti 1:8 1870
nevertheless I am not a 2Ti 1:12 1870
me, and was not a of my chain 2Ti 1:16 1870
workman that needeth not to be a 2Ti 2:15 422
is of the contrary part may be a Titus 2:8 1788
he is not a to call them brethren Heb 2:11 1870
wherefore God is not a to be Heb 11:16 1870
they may be a that falsely accuse 1Pet 3:16 2617
as a Christian, let him not be a 1Pet 4:16 153
not be a before him at his coming 1Jn 2:28 153

ASHAN (*a'-shan*) See COR-ASHAN. *A Levitical city in Judah.*
Libnah, and Ether, and A Josh 15:42 6228
Ain, Remmon, and Ether, and A Josh 19:7 6228
and Ain, Rimmon, and Tochen, and A 1Chr 4:32 6228
And A with her suburbs, and 1Chr 6:59 6228

ASHARELAH See ASARELAH.

ASHBEA (*ash'-be-ah*) *Descendants of Shelah.*
fine linen, of the house of A 1Chr 4:21 791

ASHBEL (*ash'-bel*) See ASHBELITES. *A son of Benjamin.*
were Belah, and Becher, and A Gen 46:21 788
of A, the family of the Num 26:38 788
A the second, and Aharah the third 1Chr 8:1 788

ASHBELITES (*ash'-bel-ites*) *Descendants of Ashbel.*
of Ashbel, the family of the A Num 26:38 789

ASHCHENAZ (*ash'-ke-naz*) See ASHKENAZ.
1. A son of Gomer.
A, and Riphath, and Togarmah 1Chr 1:6 813
2. A tribe near Armenia.
kingdoms of Ararat, Minni, and A Jer 51:27 813

ASHDOD (*ash'-dod*) See ASHDODITES, AZOTUS.
A Philistine city.
only in Gaza, in Gath, and in A Josh 11:22 795
unto the sea, all that lay near A Josh 15:46 795
A with her towns and her villages Josh 15:47 795
brought it from Eben-ezer unto A 1Sa 5:1 795
when they of A arose early on the 1Sa 5:3 795
of Dagon in A unto this day 1Sa 5:5 795
the LORD was heavy upon them of A 1Sa 5:6 795
smote them with emerods, even A 1Sa 5:6 795
when the men of A saw that it was 1Sa 5:7 795
for A one, for Gaza one, for 1Sa 6:17 795
wall of Jabneh, and the wall of A 2Chr 26:6 795

and built cities about A 2Chr 26:6 795
Jews that had married wives of A Neh 13:23 795
spake half in the speech of A Neh 13:24 795
the year that Tartan came unto A Is 20:1 795
sent him,) and fought against A Is 20:1 795
and Ekron, and the remnant of A Jer 25:20 795
cut off the inhabitant from A Amos 1:8 795
Publish in the palaces at A Amos 3:9 795
shall drive out A at the noonday Zeph 2:4 795
And a bastard shall dwell in A Zec 9:6 795

ASHDODITES (*ash'-dod-ites*) See ASHDOTHITES. *Inhabitants of Ashdod.*
and the Ammonites, and the A Neh 4:7 796

ASHDOTHITES (*ash'-doth-ites*) See ASHDODITES. *Same as Ashdodites.*
the Gazathites, and the A, the Josh 13:3 796

ASHDOTH-PISGAH (*ash''-doth-piz'gah*) *The eastern slope of Mt. Pisgah.*
the salt sea, under A eastward Deut 3:17
and from the south, under A Josh 12:3
And Beth-peor, and A, and Josh 13:20

ASHER (*ash'-ur*) See ASER, ASHERITES.
1. A son of Jacob by Zilpah.
and she called his name A Gen 30:13 836
Gad, and A: these are the sons Gen 35:26 836
And the sons of A Gen 46:17 836
Out of A his bread shall be fat, Gen 49:20 836
Dan, and Naphtali, Gad, and A Ex 1:4 836
of the daughter of A was Sarah Num 26:46 836
and Benjamin, Naphtali, Gad, and A 1Chr 2:2 836
The sons of A; Imnah, and Isuah 1Chr 7:30 836
All these were the children of A 1Chr 7:40 836
2. A tribe descended from Asher 1.
Of A Num 1:13 836
Of the children of A, by their Num 1:40 836
of them, even of the tribe of A Num 1:41 836
by him shall be the tribe of A Num 2:27 836
of A shall be Pagiel the son of Num 2:27 836
prince of the children of A Num 7:72 836
of A was Pagiel the son of Ocran Num 10:26 836
Of the tribe of A, Sethur the son Num 13:13 836
Of the children of A after their Num 26:44 836
of A according to those that were Num 26:47 836
of the tribe of the children of A Num 34:27 836
Reuben, Gad, and A, and Zebulun, Deut 27:13 836
of A he said, Let Asher be Deut 33:24 836
of A according to their families Josh 19:24 836
of A according to their families Josh 19:31 836
reacheth to A on the west side, Josh 19:34 836
and out of the tribe of A Josh 21:6 836
And out of the tribe of A, Mishal Josh 21:30 836
Neither did A drive out the Judg 1:31 836
A continued on the sea shore, and Judg 5:17 836
and he sent messengers unto A Judg 6:35 836
out of Naphtali, and out of A Judg 7:23 836
and out of the tribe of A 1Chr 6:62 836
And out of the tribe of A 1Chr 6:74 836
And of A, such as went forth to 1Chr 12:36 836
Nevertheless divers of A and 2Chr 30:11 836
the west side, a portion for A Eze 48:2 836
And by the border of A, from the Eze 48:3 836
one gate of Gad, one gate of A Eze 48:34 836
3. A town in Manasseh.
Manasseh was from A to Michmethah Josh 17:7 836
met together in A on the north Josh 17:10 836
in A Beth-shean and her towns Josh 17:11 836
Baanah the son of Hushai was in A 1Kin 4:16 836

ASHERITES (*ash'-ur-ites*) *Same as Asher 2.*
But the A dwelt among the Judg 1:32 843

ASHES
the Lord, which am but dust and a Gen 18:27 665
you handfuls of a of the furnace Ex 9:8 6368
they took a of the furnace, and Ex 9:10 6368
make his pans to receive his a Ex 27:3 1878
east part, by the place of the a Lev 1:16 1880
where the a are poured out, and Lev 4:12 1880
where the a are poured out shall Lev 4:12 1880
take up the a which the fire hath Lev 6:10 1880
carry forth the a without the Lev 6:11 1880
take away the a from the altar Num 4:13 1878
gather up the a of the heifer Num 19:9 665
he that gathereth the a of the Num 19:10 665
of the a of the burnt heifer of Num 19:17 6083
Tamar put a on her head, and rent 2Sa 13:19 665
the a that are upon it shall be 1Kin 13:3 1880
the a poured out from the altar, 1Kin 13:5 1880
himself with a upon his face 1Kin 20:38 665
took the a away from his face 1Kin 20:41 665
carried the a of them unto 2Kin 23:4 6083
and put on sackcloth with a Est 4:1 665
and many lay in sackcloth and a Est 4:3 665
and he sat down among the a Job 2:8 665
Your remembrances are like unto a Job 13:12 665
and I am become like dust and a Job 30:19 665
myself, and repent in dust and a Job 42:6 665
For I have eaten a like bread Ps 102:9 665
scattereth the hoar frost like a Ps 147:16 665
He feedeth on a Is 44:20 665
spread sackcloth and a under him Is 58:5 665
to give unto them beauty for a Is 61:3 665
sackcloth, and wallow thyself in a Jer 6:26 665
and wallow yourselves in the a Jer 25:34
of the dead bodies, and of the a Jer 31:40 1880
stones, he hath covered me with a Lam 3:16 665
shall wallow themselves in the a Eze 27:30 665
I will bring thee to a upon the Eze 28:18 665
with fasting, and sackcloth, and a Dan 9:3 665
him with sackcloth, and sat in a Jonah 3:6 665
for they shall be a under the Mal 4:3 665
long ago in sackcloth and a Mt 11:21 *4700*
sitting in sackcloth and a Lk 10:13 *4700*
the a of an heifer sprinkling the Heb 9:13 *4700*
Gomorrah into a condemned them 2Pet 2:6 *5077*

ASHHUR See ASHUR.

ASHIMA (*ash'-im-ah*) *An idol of Hamath.*
and the men of Hamath made A 2Kin 17:30 807

ASHKELON (*ash'-ke-lon*) See ASKELON, ESHKALONITES. *A Philistine city.*
upon him, and he went down to A Judg 14:19 831
the land of the Philistines, and A Jer 25:20 831
A is cut off with the remnant of Jer 47:5 831
hath given it a charge against A Jer 47:7 831
that holdeth the sceptre from A Amos 1:8 831
be forsaken, and A a desolation Zeph 2:4 831
in the houses of A shall they lie Zeph 2:7 831
A shall see it, and fear Zec 9:5 831
Gaza, and A shall not be inhabited Zec 9:5 831

ASHKENAZ (*ash'-ke-naz*) See ASHCHENAZ. *A son oftine city.*
A, and Riphath, and Togarmah Gen 10:3 813

ASHNAH (*ash'-nah*)
1. A town in Judah near Dan.
valley, Eshtaol, and Zoreah, and A Josh 15:33 823
2. A town in Judah on the plains.
And Jiphtah, and A, and Nezib, Josh 15:43 823

ASHPENAZ (*ash'-pe-naz*) *A prince of the eunuchs under Nebuchadnezzar.*
the king spake unto A the master Dan 1:3 828

ASHRIEL (*ash'-re-el*) See ASRIEL. *A grandson of Manasseh.*
A, whom she bare 1Chr 7:14 845

ASHTAROTH (*ash'-ta-roth*) See ASHTERATHITE, ASHTEROTH, ASTORETH, ASTAROTH, BEESHTERAH.
1. A god of the Philistines, Phoenicians, and Zidonians.
the LORD, and served Baal and A Judg 2:13 6252
the LORD, and served Baalim, and A Judg 10:6 6252
A from among you, and prepare your 1Sa 7:3 6252
Israel did put away Baalim and A 1Sa 7:4 6252
LORD, and have served Baalim and A 1Sa 12:10 6252
put his armour in the house of A 1Sa 31:10 6252
2. A city in Bashan.
Og king of Bashan, which was at A Josh 9:10 6252
of the giants, that dwelt at A Josh 12:4 6252
Og in Bashan, which reigned in A Josh 13:12 6252
And half Gilead, and A, and Edrei, Josh 13:31 6252
3. A Levitical city in Manasseh.
suburbs, and A with her suburbs 1Chr 6:71 6252

ASHTERATHITE (*ash'-ter-a-thite*) *Family name of Uzziah.*
Uzzia the A, Shama and Jehiel the 1Chr 11:44 6254

ASHTEROTH (*ash'-te-roth*) *A city in Og.*
smote the Rephaims in A Karnaim Gen 14:5 6255

ASHTEROTH-KARNAIM See ASHTEROTH.

ASHTORETH (*ash'-to-reth*) See ASHTAROTH. *Same as Ashtaroth 1.*
For Solomon went after A the 1Kin 11:5 6252
have worshipped A the goddess of 1Kin 11:33 6252
for A the abomination of the 2Kin 23:13 6252

ASHUR (*ash'-ur*) See ASHURITES, ASSHUR, ASSUR, ASSYRIA. *A son of Hezvon.*
bare him A the father of Tekoa 1Chr 2:24 804
A the father of Tekoa had two 1Chr 4:5 804

ASHURBANIPAL See ASNAPPER.

ASHURITES (*ash'-ur-ites*) See ASSHURIM. *A tribe in the plain of Esdraelon.*
king over Gilead, and over the A 2Sa 2:9 843
the company of the A have made Eze 27:6 843

ASHVATH (*ash'-vath*) *A descendant of Asher.*
Pasach, and Bimhal, and A 1Chr 7:33 6220

ASIA (*a'-she-ah*)
1. A Roman province.
and Cappadocia, in Pontus, and A Acts 2:9 773
and of them of Cilicia and of A Acts 6:9 773
Ghost to preach the word in A Acts 16:6 773
in A heard the word of the Lord Acts 19:10 773
himself stayed in A for a season Acts 19:22 773
And certain of the chief of A Acts 19:31 775
him into A Sopater of Berea Acts 20:4 773
and of A, Tychicus and Trophimus Acts 20:4 773
he would not spend the time in A Acts 20:16 773
the first day that I came into A Acts 20:18 773
The churches of A salute you 1Cor 16:19 773
our trouble which came to us in A 2Cor 1:8 773
are in A be turned away from me 2Ti 1:15 773
Pontus, Galatia, Cappadocia, A 1Pet 1:1 773
the seven churches which are in A Rev 1:4 773
the seven churches which are in A Rev 1:11 773
2. Another name for Asia Minor.
but almost throughout all A Acts 19:26 773
should be destroyed, whom all A Acts 19:27 773
ended, the Jews which were of A Acts 21:27 773
Whereupon certain Jews from A Acts 24:18 773
to sail by the coasts of A Acts 27:2 773

ASIDE
And Moses said, I will now turn a Ex 3:3
LORD saw that he turned a to see Ex 3:4
They have turned a quickly out of Ex 32:8
unto them, If any man's wife go a Num 5:12 7847
if thou hast not gone a to Num 5:19 7847
But if thou hast gone a to Num 5:20 7847
when a wife goeth a to another Num 5:29 7847
the ass turned a out of the way Num 22:23 5186
ye shall not turn a to the right Deut 5:32
turned a out of the way which I Deut 9:12
ye had turned a quickly out of Deut 9:16
be not deceived, and ye turn a Deut 11:16
but turn a out of the way which I Deut 11:28
that he turn not a from the Deut 17:20
thou shalt not go a from any of Deut 28:14 5493
turn a from the way which I have Deut 31:29
that ye turn not a therefrom to Josh 23:6
he turned a to see the carcase of Judg 14:8
We will not turn a hither into Judg 19:12
And they turned a thither, to go Judg 19:15
turn a, sit down here Ruth 4:1
And he turned a, and sat down Ruth 4:1
turned not a to the right hand or 1Sa 6:12
but turned a after lucre, and took 1Sa 8:3 5186
yet turn not a from following the 1Sa 12:20
And turn ye not a 1Sa 12:21
Turn thee a to thy right hand or 2Sa 2:21 5186
not turn a from following of him 2Sa 2:21
Turn thee a from following me 2Sa 2:22
Howbeit he refused to turn a 2Sa 2:23
Joab took him a in the gate to 2Sa 3:27 5186
but David carried it a into the 2Sa 6:10 5186
And the king said unto him, Turn a 2Sa 18:30 5437
And he turned a, and stood still 2Sa 18:30 5437
turned not a from any thing that 1Kin 15:5
and, behold, a man turned a 1Kin 20:39
they turned a to fight against 1Kin 22:32
he turned not a from it, doing 1Kin 22:43
thou shalt set a that which is 2Kin 4:4 5265
turned not a to the right hand or 2Kin 22:2 5493
but carried it a into the house 1Chr 13:13 5186
paths of their way are turned a Job 6:18 3943
They are all gone a, they are all Ps 14:3 5493
proud, nor such as turn a to lies Ps 40:4 7847
they were turned a like a Ps 78:57 2015
hate the work of them that turn a Ps 101:3 7750
As for such as turn a unto their Ps 125:5 5186
a by the flocks of thy companions Song 1:7 5844
whither is thy beloved turned a Song 6:1 6437
To turn a the needy from judgment Is 10:2 5186
turn a the just for a thing of Is 29:21 5186
turn a out of the path, cause the Is 30:11 5186
deceived heart hath turned him a Is 44:20 5186
turneth a to tarry for a night Jer 14:8 5186
or who shall go a to ask how thou Jer 15:5 5493
He hath turned a my ways, and Lam 3:11
To turn a the right of a man Lam 3:35 5186
turn a the way of the meek Amos 2:7 5186
they turn a the poor in the gate Amos 5:12 5186
that turn a the stranger from his Mal 3:5 5186
he turned a into the parts of Mt 2:22 *402*
For laying a the commandment of Mk 7:8 *863*
he took him a from the multitude Mk 7:33 *2596*
went a privately into a desert Lk 9:10 *5298*
supper, and laid a his garments Jn 13:4 *5087*
them to go a out of the council Acts 4:15 *565*
and went with him a privately Acts 23:19 *402*
And when they were gone a, they Acts 26:31 *402*
have turned a unto vain jangling 1Ti 1:6 *1824*
are already turned a after Satan 1Ti 5:15 *1824*
let us lay a every weight, and the Heb 12:1 *659*
Wherefore laying a all malice 1Pet 2:1 *659*

ASIEL (*a''-se'-el*) *Grandfather of Jehu.*
the son of Seraiah, the son of A 1Chr 4:35 6221

ASK
it that thou dost a after my name Gen 32:29 7592
A me never so much dowry and gift, Gen 34:12
who shall a counsel for him after Num 27:21 7592
For a now of the days that are Deut 4:32 7592
a from the one side of heaven Deut 4:32
and make search, and a diligently Deut 13:14 7592
a thy father, and he will shew Deut 32:7 7592
that when your children a their Josh 4:6 7592
When your children shall a their Josh 4:21 7592
him to a of her father a field Josh 15:18 7592
him to a of her father a field Judg 1:14 7592
A counsel, we pray thee, of God, Judg 18:5 7592
sins this evil, to a us a king 1Sa 12:19 7592
A thy young men, and they will 1Sa 25:8 7592
Wherefore then dost thou a of me 1Sa 28:16 7592
the thing that I shall a thee 2Sa 14:18 7592
shall surely a counsel at Abel 2Sa 20:18 7592
now I a one petition of thee, 1Kin 2:16 7592
said unto her, A on, my mother 1Kin 2:20 7592
why dost thou a Abishag the 1Kin 2:22 7592
a for him the kingdom also 1Kin 2:22 7592
said, A what I shall give thee 1Kin 3:5 7592
to a a thing of thee for her son 1Kin 14:5 1875
A what I shall do for thee, 2Kin 2:9 7592
him, A what I shall give thee 2Chr 1:7 7592
together, to a help of the LORD 2Chr 20:4 1245
But a now the beasts, and they Job 12:7 7592
A of me, and I shall give thee the Ps 2:8 7592
A thee a sign of the LORD thy God Is 7:11 7592
a it either in the depth, or in Is 7:11 7592
But Ahaz said, I will not a Is 7:12 7592
A me of things to come concerning Is 45:11 7592
they a of me the ordinances of Is 58:2 7592
a for the old paths, where is the Jer 6:16 7592
go aside to a how thou doest Jer 15:5 7592
A ye now among the heathen, who Jer 18:13 7592
or a priest, shall a thee Jer 23:33 7592
A ye now, and see whether a man Jer 30:6 7592
Jeremiah, I will a thee a thing Jer 38:14 7592
a him that fleeth, and her that Jer 48:19 7592
They shall a the way to Zion with Jer 50:5 7592
the young children a bread Lam 4:4 7592
that whosoever shall a a petition Dan 6:7 1156
that every man that shall a a Dan 6:12 1156
My people a counsel at their Hos 4:12 7592
A now the priests concerning the Hag 2:11 7592
A ye of the LORD rain in the time Zec 10:1 7592
ye have need of, before ye a him Mt 6:8 *154*

A, and it shall be given you	Mt 7:7	*154*
of you, whom if his son *a* bread	Mt 7:9	*154*
Or if he *a* a fish, will he give	Mt 7:10	*154*
good things to them that *a* him	Mt 7:11	*154*
give her whatsoever she would *a*	Mt 14:7	*154*
any thing that they shall *a*	Mt 18:19	*154*
and said, Ye know not what ye *a*	Mt 20:22	*154*
whatsoever ye shall *a* in prayer	Mt 21:22	*154*
I also will *a* you one thing,	Mt 21:24	*2065*
forth *a* him any more questions	Mt 22:46	*1905*
that they should *a* Barabbas	Mt 27:20	*154*
A of me whatsoever thou wilt, and	Mk 6:22	*154*
Whatsoever thou shalt *a* of me	Mk 6:23	*154*
unto her mother, What shall I *a*	Mk 6:24	*154*
saying, and were afraid to *a* him	Mk 9:32	*1905*
unto them, Ye know not what ye *a*	Mk 10:38	*154*
I will also *a* of you one question	Mk 11:29	*1905*
that durst *a* him any question	Mk 12:34	*1905*
unto them, I will *a* you one thing	Lk 6:9	*1905*
away thy goods *a* them not again	Lk 6:30	*523*
they feared to *a* him of that	Lk 9:45	*2065*
And I say unto you, *A*, and it shall	Lk 11:9	*154*
If a son shall *a* bread of any of	Lk 11:11	*154*
or if he *a* a fish, will he for a	Lk 11:11	
Or if he shall *a* an egg, will he	Lk 11:12	*154*
Holy Spirit to them that *a* him	Lk 11:13	*154*
much, of him they will *a* the more	Lk 12:48	*154*
And if any man *a* you, Why do ye	Lk 19:31	*2065*
I will also *a* you one thing	Lk 20:3	*2065*
not *a* him any question at all	Lk 20:40	*1905*
And if I also *a* you, ye will not	Lk 22:68	*2065*
Levites from Jerusalem to *a* him	Jn 1:19	*2065*
a him: he shall speak	Jn 9:21	*2065*
He is of age; *a* him	Jn 9:23	*2065*
whatsoever thou wilt *a* of God	Jn 11:22	*154*
that he should *a* who it should be	Jn 13:24	*4441*
whatsoever ye shall *a* in my name	Jn 14:13	*154*
If ye shall *a* any thing in my	Jn 14:14	*154*
ye shall *a* what ye will, and it	Jn 15:7	*154*
shall *a* of the Father in my name	Jn 15:16	*154*
that they were desirous to *a* him	Jn 16:19	*2065*
in that day ye shall *a* me nothing	Jn 16:23	*2065*
Whatsoever ye shall *a* the Father	Jn 16:23	*154*
a, and ye shall receive, that your	Jn 16:24	*154*
At that day ye shall *a* in my name	Jn 16:26	*154*
not that any man should *a* thee	Jn 16:30	*2065*
a them which heard me, what I	Jn 18:21	*1905*
none of the disciples durst *a* him	Jn 21:12	*1833*
to *a* alms of them that entered	Acts 3:2	*154*
I *a* therefore for what intent ye	Acts 10:29	*4441*
let them *a* their husbands at home	1Cor 14:35	*1905*
above all that we *a* or think	Eph 3:20	*154*
you lack wisdom, let him *a* of God	Jas 1:5	*154*
But let him *a* in faith, nothing	Jas 1:6	*154*
yet ye have not, because ye *a* not	Jas 4:2	*154*
Ye *a*, and receive not	Jas 4:3	*154*
because ye *a* amiss	Jas 4:3	*154*
And whatsoever we *a*, we receive of	1Jn 3:22	*154*
if we *a* any thing according to	1Jn 5:14	*154*
that he hear us, whatsoever we *a*	1Jn 5:15	*154*
is not unto death, he shall *a*	1Jn 5:16	*154*

ASKED

I *a* her, and said, Whose daughter	Gen 24:47	7592
of the place *a* him of his wife	Gen 26:7	7592
And Jacob *a* him, and said, Tell me,	Gen 32:29	7592
and the man *a* him, saying, What	Gen 37:15	7592
Then he *a* the men of that place,	Gen 38:21	7592
he *a* Pharaoh's officers that were	Gen 40:7	7592
The man *a* us straitly of our	Gen 43:7	7592
he *a* them of their welfare, and	Gen 43:27	7592
My lord *a* his servants, saying,	Gen 44:19	7592
they *a* each other of their	Ex 18:7	7592
a not counsel at the mouth of the	Josh 9:14	7592
they gave him the city which he *a*	Josh 19:50	7592
the children of Israel *a* the LORD	Judg 1:1	7592
He *a* water, and she gave him milk	Judg 5:25	7592
And when they enquired and *a*	Judg 6:29	1245
but I *a* him not whence he was,	Judg 13:6	7592
a counsel of God, and said, Which	Judg 20:18	7592
a counsel of the LORD, saying,	Judg 20:23	7592
petition that thou hast *a* of him	1Sa 1:17	7592
Because I have *a* him of the LORD	1Sa 1:20	7592
me my petition which I *a* of him	1Sa 1:27	7592
the people that *a* of him a king	1Sa 8:10	7592
Saul *a* counsel of God, Shall I go	1Sa 14:37	7592
and he *a* and said, Where are Samuel	1Sa 19:22	7592
David earnestly *a* leave of me	1Sa 20:6	7592
David earnestly *a* leave of me to	1Sa 20:28	7592
that Solomon had *a* this thing	1Kin 3:10	7592
Because thou hast *a* this thing	1Kin 3:11	7592
hast not *a* for thyself long life	1Kin 3:11	7592
neither hast *a* riches for thyself	1Kin 3:11	7592
nor hast *a* the life of thine	1Kin 3:11	7592
but hast *a* for thyself	1Kin 3:11	7592
thee that which thou hast not *a*	1Kin 3:13	7592
all her desire, whatsoever she *a*	1Kin 10:13	7592
he said, Thou hast *a* a hard thing	2Kin 2:10	7592
And when the king *a* the woman	2Kin 8:6	7592
heart, and thou hast not *a* riches	2Chr 1:11	7592
neither yet hast *a* long life	2Chr 1:11	7592
but hast *a* wisdom and knowledge	2Chr 1:11	7592
all her desire, whatsoever she *a*	2Chr 9:12	7592
Then *a* we those elders, and said	Ezr 5:9	7593
We *a* their names also, to certify	Ezr 5:10	7593
I *a* them concerning the Jews that	Neh 1:2	7592
Have ye not *a* them that go by the	Job 21:29	7592
He *a* life of thee, and thou gavest	Ps 21:4	7592
The people *a*, and he brought	Ps 105:40	7592
Egypt, and have not *a* at my mouth	Is 30:2	7592
when I *a* of them, could answer a	Is 41:28	7592
sought of them that *a* not for me	Is 65:1	7592
they *a* Baruch, saying, Tell us	Jer 36:17	7592
the king *a* him secretly in his	Jer 37:17	7592
princes unto Jeremiah, and *a* him	Jer 38:27	7592
that *a* such things at any	Dan 2:10	7593
a him the truth of all this	Dan 7:16	1156
And they *a* him, saying, Is it	Mt 12:10	*1905*
he *a* his disciples, saying, Whom	Mt 16:13	*2065*
And his disciples *a* him, saying,	Mt 17:10	*1905*
is no resurrection, and *a* him,	Mt 22:23	*1905*
a him a question, tempting him,	Mt 22:35	*1905*
gathered together, Jesus *a* them	Mt 22:41	*1905*
and the governor *a* him, saying,	Mt 27:11	*1905*
the twelve *a* of him the parable	Mk 4:10	*2065*
he *a* him, What is thy name	Mk 5:9	*1905*
with haste unto the king, and *a*	Mk 6:25	*154*
the Pharisees and scribes *a* him	Mk 7:5	*1905*
his disciples *a* him concerning	Mk 7:17	*1905*
he *a* them, How many loaves have	Mk 8:5	*1905*
him, he *a* him if he saw ought	Mk 8:23	*1905*
and by the way he *a* his disciples	Mk 8:27	*1905*
And they *a* him, saying, Why say	Mk 9:11	*1905*
he *a* the scribes, What question	Mk 9:16	*1905*
he *a* his father, How long is it	Mk 9:21	*1905*
his disciples *a* him privately	Mk 9:28	*1905*
and being in the house he *a* them	Mk 9:33	*1905*
a him, Is it lawful for a man to	Mk 10:2	*1905*
in the house his disciples *a* him	Mk 10:10	*1905*
a him, Good Master, what shall I	Mk 10:17	*1905*
and they *a* him, saying,	Mk 12:18	*1905*
a him, Which is the first	Mk 12:28	*1905*
John and Andrew *a* him privately,	Mk 13:3	*1905*
a Jesus, saying, Answerest thou	Mk 14:60	*1905*
Again the high priest *a* him	Mk 14:61	*1905*
And Pilate *a* him, Art thou the	Mk 15:2	*1905*
Pilate *a* him again, saying,	Mk 15:4	*1905*
he *a* him whether he had been any	Mk 15:44	*1905*
he *a* for a writing table, and	Lk 1:63	*154*
And the people *a* him, saying, What	Lk 3:10	*1905*
And his disciples *a* him, saying,	Lk 8:9	*1905*
And Jesus *a* him, saying, What is	Lk 8:30	*1905*
he *a* them, saying, Whom say the	Lk 9:18	*1905*
a what these things meant	Lk 15:26	*4441*
And a certain ruler *a* him, saying,	Lk 18:18	*1905*
pass by, he *a* what it meant	Lk 18:36	*4441*
when he was come near, he *a* him,	Lk 18:40	*1905*
And they *a* him, saying, Master, we	Lk 20:21	*1905*
and they *a* him,	Lk 20:27	*1905*
And they *a* him, saying, Master,	Lk 21:7	*1905*
a him, saying, Prophesy, who is	Lk 22:64	*1905*
And Pilate *a* him, saying, Art thou	Lk 23:3	*1905*
he *a* whether the man were a	Lk 23:6	*1905*
And they *a* him, What then	Jn 1:21	*2065*
And they *a* him, and said unto him,	Jn 1:25	*2065*
thou wouldest have *a* of him	Jn 4:10	*154*
Then *a* they him, What man is that	Jn 5:12	*2065*
And his disciples *a* him, saying,	Jn 9:2	*2065*
a him how he had received his	Jn 9:15	*2065*
And they *a* them, saying, Is this	Jn 9:19	*2065*
Hitherto have ye *a* nothing in my	Jn 16:24	*154*
Then *a* he them again, Whom seek	Jn 18:7	*1905*
The high priest then *a* Jesus of	Jn 18:19	*2065*
they *a* of him, saying, Lord, wilt	Acts 1:6	*1905*
to go into the temple *a* an alms	Acts 3:3	*2065*
had set them in the midst, they *a*	Acts 4:7	*4441*
and the high priest *a* them	Acts 5:27	*1905*
a whether Simon, which was	Acts 10:18	*4441*
a him, What is that thou hast to	Acts 23:19	*2065*
he *a* of what province he was	Acts 23:34	*1905*
I *a* him whether he would go to	Acts 25:20	*3004*
unto them that *a* not after me	Rom 10:20	*1905*

ASKELON (*as'-ke-lon*) See ASHKELON. *A Philistine city.*

A with the coast thereof, and	Judg 1:18	831
one for Gaza one, for *A* one	1Sa 6:17	831
it not in the streets of *A*	2Sa 1:20	831

ASKEST

Why *a* thou thus after my name,	Judg 13:18	7592
a drink of me, which am a woman	Jn 4:9	*154*
Why *a* thou me?	Jn 18:21	*1905*

ASKETH

a thee, saying, Whose art thou	Gen 32:17	7592
thy son *a* thee in time to come	Ex 13:14	7592
when thy son *a* thee in time to	Deut 6:20	7592
hands earnestly, the prince *a*	Mic 7:3	7592
and the judge *a* for a reward	Mic 7:3	7592
Give to him that *a* thee, and from	Mt 5:42	*154*
For every one that *a* receiveth	Mt 7:8	*154*
Give to every man that *a* of thee	Lk 6:30	*154*
For every one that *a* receiveth	Lk 11:10	*154*
and none of you *a* me, Whither	Jn 16:5	*2065*
an answer to every man that *a* you	1Pet 3:15	*154*

ASKING

of the LORD, in *a* you a king	1Sa 12:17	7592
also for *a* counsel of one that	1Chr 10:13	7592
heart by *a* meat for their lust	Ps 78:18	7592
hearing them, and *a* them questions	Lk 2:46	*1905*
So when they continued *a* him	Jn 8:7	*2065*
a no question for conscience sake	1Cor 10:25	*350*
a no question for conscience sake	1Cor 10:27	*350*

ASLEEP

for he was fast *a* and weary	Judg 4:21	7290
for they were all *a*	1Sa 26:12	3463
lips of those that are *a* to speak	Song 7:9	3463
and he lay, and was fast *a*	Jonah 1:5	7290
but he was *a*	Mt 8:24	*2518*
the disciples, and findeth them *a*	Mt 26:40	*2518*
And he came and found them *a* again	Mt 26:43	*2518*
part of the ship, *a* on a pillow	Mk 4:38	*2518*
returned, he found them *a* again	Mk 14:40	*2518*
But as they sailed he fell *a*	Lk 8:23	*879*
when he had said this, he fell *a*	Acts 7:60	*2837*
present, but some are fallen *a*	1Cor 15:6	*2837*
fallen *a* in Christ are perished	1Cor 15:18	*2837*
concerning them which are *a*	1Th 4:13	*2837*
not prevent them which are *a*	1Th 4:15	*2837*
for since the fathers fell *a*	2Pet 3:4	*2837*

ASNAH (*as'-nah*) *A family of exiles.*

The children of *A*, the children	Ezr 2:50	619

ASNAPPER (*as-nap'-pur*) *An Assyrian king.*

noble *A* brought over, and set in	Ezr 4:10	620

ASP

shall play on the hole of the *a*	Is 11:8	6620

ASPATHA (*as'-pa-thah*) *A son of Haman.*

and Dalphon, and *A*	Est 9:7	630

ASPS

dragons, and the cruel venom of *a*	Deut 32:33	6620
it is the gall of *a* within him	Job 20:14	6620
He shall suck the poison of *a*	Job 20:16	6620
the poison of *a* is under their	Rom 3:13	*785*

ASRIEL (*as'-re-el*) See ASHRIEL, ASRIELITES. *A grandson of Manasseh.*

And of *A*, the family of the	Num 26:31	844
Helek, and for the children of *A*	Josh 17:2	844

ASRIELITES (*as'-re-el-ites*) *Descendants of Asriel.*

And of Asriel, the family of the *A*	Num 26:31	845

ASS

in the morning, and saddled his *a*	Gen 22:3	2543
men, Abide ye here with the *a*	Gen 22:5	2543
give his *a* provender in the inn	Gen 42:27	2543
clothes, and laded every man his *a*	Gen 44:13	2543
Issachar is a strong *a* couching	Gen 49:14	2543
his sons, and set them upon an *a*	Ex 4:20	2543
every firstling of an *a* thou	Ex 13:13	2543
nor his ox, nor his *a*, nor any	Ex 20:17	2543
an ox or an *a* fall therein	Ex 21:33	2543
alive, whether it be ox, or *a*	Ex 22:4	2543
whether it be for ox, for *a*	Ex 22:9	2543
deliver unto his neighbour an *a*	Ex 22:10	2543
enemy's ox or his *a* going astray	Ex 23:4	2543
If thou see the *a* of him that	Ex 23:5	2543
thine *a* may rest, and the son of	Ex 23:12	2543
But the firstling of an *a* thou	Ex 34:20	2543
I have not taken one *a* from them	Num 16:15	2543
in the morning, and saddled his *a*	Num 22:21	860
Now he was riding upon his *a*	Num 22:22	860
the *a* saw the angel of the LORD	Num 22:23	860
the *a* turned aside out of the way	Num 22:23	860
and Balaam smote the *a*, to turn	Num 22:23	860
when the *a* saw the angel of the	Num 22:25	860
when the *a* saw the angel of the	Num 22:27	860
and he smote the *a* with a staff	Num 22:27	860
LORD opened the mouth of the *a*	Num 22:28	860
And Balaam said unto the *a*	Num 22:29	860
the *a* said unto Balaam	Num 22:30	860
Am not I thine *a*,	Num 22:30	860
smitten thine *a* these three times	Num 22:32	860
the *a* saw me, and turned from me	Num 22:33	860
nor thine ox, nor thine *a*	Deut 5:14	2543
his maidservant, his ox, or his *a*	Deut 5:21	2543
manner shalt thou do with his *a*	Deut 22:3	2543
shalt not see thy brother's *a* or	Deut 22:4	2543
plow with an ox and an *a* together	Deut 22:10	2543
thine *a* shall be violently taken	Deut 28:31	2543
and old, and ox, and sheep, and *a*	Josh 6:21	2543
and she lighted off her *a*	Josh 15:18	2543
and she lighted from off her *a*	Judg 1:14	2543
neither sheep, nor ox, nor *a*	Judg 6:4	2543
sons that rode on thirty *a* colts	Judg 10:4	5895
rode on threescore and ten *a* colts	Judg 12:14	5895
And he found a new jawbone of an *a*	Judg 15:15	2543
said, With the jawbone of an *a*	Judg 15:16	2543
with the jaw of an *a* have I slain	Judg 15:16	2543
the man took her up upon an *a*	Judg 19:28	2543
or whose *a* have I taken	1Sa 12:3	2543
suckling, ox and sheep, camel and *a*	1Sa 15:3	2543
Jesse took an *a* laden with bread,	1Sa 16:20	2543
it was so, as she rode on the *a*	1Sa 25:20	2543
she hasted, and lighted off the *a*	1Sa 25:23	2543
and arose, and rode upon an *a*	1Sa 25:42	2543
not followed, he saddled his *a*	2Sa 17:23	2543
said, I will saddle me an *a*	2Sa 19:26	2543
And Shimei arose, and saddled his *a*	1Kin 2:40	2543
unto his sons, Saddle me the *a*	1Kin 13:13	2543
So they saddled him the *a*	1Kin 13:13	2543
that he saddled for him the *a*	1Kin 13:23	2543
the *a* stood by it, the lion also	1Kin 13:24	2543
his sons, saying, Saddle me the *a*	1Kin 13:27	2543
carcase cast in the way, and the *a*	1Kin 13:28	2543
eaten the carcase, nor torn the *a*	1Kin 13:28	2543
man of God, and laid it upon the *a*	1Kin 13:29	2543
Then she saddled an *a*, and said to	2Kin 4:24	860
Doth the wild *a* bray when he hath	Job 6:5	6501
away the *a* of the fatherless	Job 24:3	2543
Who hath sent out the wild *a* free	Job 39:5	5601
loosed the bands of the wild *a*	Job 39:5	6171
for the horse, a bridle for the *a*	Prov 26:3	2543
owner, and the *a* his master's crib	Is 1:3	2543
the feet of the ox and the *a*	Is 32:20	2543
A wild *a* used to the wilderness,	Jer 2:24	6501
be buried with the burial of an *a*	Jer 22:19	2543
a wild *a* alone by himself	Hos 8:9	6501
lowly, and riding upon an *a*	Zec 9:9	2543
and upon a colt the foal of an *a*	Zec 9:9	860
mule, of the camel, and of the *a*	Zec 14:15	2543
ye shall find an *a* tied, and a	Mt 21:2	3688
thee, meek, and sitting upon an *a*	Mt 21:5	3688
and a colt the foal of an *a*	Mt 21:5	5268
And brought the *a*, and the colt, and	Mt 21:7	3688
his ox or his *a* from the stall	Lk 13:15	3688
an *a* or an ox fallen into a pit	Lk 14:5	3688
when he had found a young *a*	Jn 12:14	3678
the dumb *a* speaking with man's	2Pet 2:16	*5268*

ASSAULT
and province that would *a* them — Est 8:11 — 6696
when there was an *a* made both of — Acts 14:5 — *3730*

ASSAULTED
a the house of Jason, and sought — Acts 17:5 — *2186*

ASSAY
If we *a* to commune with thee, — Job 4:2 — 5254

ASSAYED
Or hath God *a* to go and take him a — Deut 4:34 — 5254
upon his armour, and he *a* to go — 1Sa 17:39 — 2974
he *a* to join himself to the — Acts 9:26 — *3987*
they *a* to go into Bithynia — Acts 16:7 — *3985*

ASSAYING
Egyptians *a* to do were drowned — Heb 11:29 — *3984*

ASSEMBLE
them, all the assembly shall *a* — Num 10:3 — 3259
A me the men of Judah within — 2Sa 20:4 — 2199
Amasa went to *a* the men of Judah — 2Sa 20:5 — 2199
shall *a* the outcasts of Israel, — Is 11:12 — 622
A yourselves and come — Is 45:20 — 6908
All ye, *a* yourselves, and hear — Is 48:14 — 6908
A yourselves, and let us go into — Jer 4:5 — 622
a yourselves, and let us enter — Jer 8:14 — 622
a all the beasts of the field, — Jer 12:9 — 622
I will *a* them into the midst of — Jer 21:4 — 622
a you out of the countries where — Eze 11:17 — 622
the field, *A* yourselves, and come — Eze 39:17 — 6908
shall *a* a multitude of great — Dan 11:10 — 622
they *a* themselves for corn and — Hos 7:14 — 1481
a the elders, gather the children — Joel 2:16 — 6908
A yourselves, and come, all ye — Joel 3:11 — 5789
A yourselves upon the mountains — Amos 3:9 — 622
I will surely *a*, O Jacob, all of — Mic 2:12 — 622
will I *a* her that halteth, and I — Mic 4:6 — 622
that I may *a* the kingdoms, to — Zeph 3:8 — 6908

ASSEMBLED
which *a* at the door of the — Ex 38:8 — 6638
they *a* all the congregation — Num 1:18 — 6950
of Israel *a* together at Shiloh — Josh 18:1 — 6950
of Israel *a* themselves together — Judg 10:17 — 622
they lay with the women that *a* at — 1Sa 2:22 — 6633
that were with him *a* themselves — 1Sa 14:20 — 2199
Then Solomon *a* the elders of — 1Kin 8:1 — 6950
And all the men of Israel *a* — 1Kin 8:2 — 6950
of Israel, that were *a* unto him — 1Kin 8:5 — 3259
he *a* all the house of Judah, with — 1Kin 12:21 — 6950
David *a* the children of Aaron, and — 1Chr 15:4 — 662
David *a* all the princes of Israel — 1Chr 28:1 — 6950
Then Solomon *a* the elders of — 2Chr 5:2 — 6950
a themselves unto the king in the — 2Chr 5:3 — 6950
of Israel that were *a* unto him — 2Chr 5:6 — 3259
And on the fourth day they *a* — 2Chr 20:26 — 6950
there *a* at Jerusalem much people — 2Chr 30:13 — 622
Then were *a* unto me every one — Ezr 9:4 — 622
there *a* unto him out of Israel a — Ezr 10:1 — 6908
of Israel were *a* with fasting — Neh 9:1 — 622
the Jews that were at Shushan *a* — Est 9:18 — 6950
For, lo, the kings were *a* — Ps 48:4 — 3259
together, and let the people be *a* — Is 43:9
a themselves by troops in the — Jer 5:7 — 1413
thy company that are *a* unto thee — Eze 38:7 — 6950
princes *a* together to the king, — Dan 6:6 — 7284
Then these men *a*, and found Daniel — Dan 6:11 — 7284
Then these men *a* unto the king — Dan 6:15 — 7284
Then *a* together the chief priests — Mt 26:3 — *4863*
the scribes and the elders were *a* — Mt 26:57 — *4863*
when they were *a* with the elders, — Mt 28:12 — *4863*
with him were *a* all the chief — Mk 14:53 — *4905*
were *a* for fear of the Jews — Jn 20:19 — *4863*
being *a* together with them, — Acts 1:4 — *4871*
shaken where they were *a* together — Acts 4:31 — *4863*
to pass, that a whole year they *a* — Acts 11:26 — *4863*
being *a* with one accord, to send — Acts 15:25 — *1096*

ASSEMBLIES
the *a* of violent men have sought — Ps 86:14 — 5712
fastened by the masters of *a* — Eccl 12:11 — 627
and sabbaths, the calling of *a* — Is 1:13 — 4744
of mount Zion, and upon her *a* — Is 4:5 — 4744
laws and my statutes in all mine *a* — Eze 44:24 — 4150
I will not smell in your solemn *a* — Amos 5:21 — 6116

ASSEMBLING
the lookingglasses of the women *a* — Ex 38:8 — 6633
Not forsaking the *a* of ourselves — Heb 10:25 — *1997*

ASSEMBLY
unto their *a*, mine honour, be not — Gen 49:6 — 6951
the whole *a* of the congregation — Ex 12:6 — 6951
to kill this whole *a* with hunger — Ex 16:3 — 6951
be hid from the eyes of the *a* — Lev 4:13 — 6951
the *a* was gathered together unto — Lev 8:4 — 5712
it is a solemn *a* — Lev 23:36 — 6116
whole *a* of the children of Israel — Num 8:9 — 5712
use them for the calling of the *a* — Num 10:2 — 5712
them, all the *a* shall assemble — Num 10:3 — 5712
the *a* of the congregation of the — Num 14:5 — 6951
hundred and fifty princes of the *a* — Num 16:2 — 5712
went from the presence of the *a* — Num 20:6 — 6951
and gather thou the *a* together — Num 20:8 — 5712
day ye shall have a solemn *a* — Num 29:35 — 6116
the LORD spake unto all your *a* in — Deut 5:22 — 6951
of the fire in the day of the *a* — Deut 9:10 — 6951
of the fire in the day of the *a* — Deut 10:4 — 6951
be a solemn *a* to the LORD thy God — Deut 16:8 — 6116
God in Horeb in the day of the *a* — Deut 18:16 — 6951
in the *a* of the people of God — Judg 20:2 — 6951
camp from Jabesh-gilead to the *a* — Judg 21:8 — 6951
all this *a* shall know that the — 1Sa 17:47 — 6951
Proclaim a solemn *a* for Baal — 2Kin 10:20 — 6116
eighth day they made a solemn *a* — 2Chr 7:9 — 6116
the whole *a* took counsel to keep — 2Chr 30:23 — 6951
And I set a great *a* against them — Neh 5:7 — 6952
on the eighth day was a solemn *a* — Neh 8:18 — 6116
the *a* of the wicked have inclosed — Ps 22:16 — 5712
be feared in the *a* of the saints — Ps 89:7 — 5475
praise him in the *a* of the elders — Ps 107:32 — 4186
in the *a* of the upright, and in — Ps 111:1 — 5475
midst of the congregation and *a* — Prov 5:14 — 5712
upon the *a* of young men together — Jer 6:11 — 5475
an *a* of treacherous men — Jer 9:2 — 6116
I sat not in the *a* of the mockers — Jer 15:17 — 5475
spake to all the *a* of the people — Jer 26:17 — 6951
to come up against Babylon an *a* — Jer 50:9 — 6951
he hath called an *a* against me to — Lam 1:15 — 4150
destroyed his places of the *a* — Lam 2:6 — 4150
not be in the *a* of my people — Eze 13:9 — 5475
with an *a* of people, which shall — Eze 23:24 — 6951
ye a fast, call a solemn *a* — Joel 1:14 — 6116
sanctify a fast, call a solemn *a* — Joel 2:15 — 6116
are sorrowful for the solemn *a* — Zeph 3:18 — 4150
for the *a* was confused — Acts 19:32 — *1577*
shall be determined in a lawful *a* — Acts 19:39 — *1577*
thus spoken, he dismissed the *a* — Acts 19:41 — *1577*
To the general *a* and church of the — Heb 12:23 — *3831*
your *a* a man with a gold ring — Jas 2:2 — *4864*

ASSENT
good to the king with one *a* — 2Chr 18:12 — 6310

ASSENTED
And the Jews also *a*, saying that — Acts 24:9 — *4934*

ASSES
and he had sheep, and oxen, and he *a*. — Gen 12:16 — 2543
and maidservants, and she *a* — Gen 12:16 — 860
and maidservants, and camels, and *a* — Gen 24:35 — 2543
and menservants, and camels, and *a* — Gen 30:43 — 2543
And I have oxen, and *a*, flocks, and — Gen 32:5 — 2543
kine, and ten bulls, twenty she *a* — Gen 32:15 — 860
sheep, and their oxen, and their *a* — Gen 34:28 — 2543
as he fed the *a* of Zibeon his — Gen 36:24 — 2543
they laded their *a* with the corn — Gen 42:26 — 2543
and take us for bondmen, and our *a* — Gen 43:18 — 2543
and he gave their *a* provender — Gen 43:24 — 2543
were sent away, they and their *a* — Gen 44:3 — 2543
ten *a* laden with the good things — Gen 45:23 — 860
ten she *a* laden with corn and — Gen 45:23 — 2543
cattle of the herds, and for the *a* — Gen 47:17 — 2543
upon the horses, upon the *a* — Ex 9:3 — 2543
and of the beeves, and of the *a* — Num 31:28 — 2543
persons, of the beeves, of the *a* — Num 31:30 — 2543
And threescore and one thousand *a* — Num 31:34 — 2543
the *a* were thirty thousand and — Num 31:39 — 2543
And thirty thousand *a* and five — Num 31:45 — 2543
daughters, and his oxen, and his *a* — Josh 7:24 — 2543
and took old sacks upon their *a* — Josh 9:4 — 2543
Speak, ye that ride on white *a* — Judg 5:10 — 860
with him, and a couple of *a* — Judg 19:3 — 2543
there were with him two *a* saddled — Judg 19:10 — 2543
both straw and provender for our *a* — Judg 19:19 — 2543
and gave provender unto the *a* — Judg 19:21 — 2543
goodliest young men, and your *a* — 1Sa 8:16 — 2543
the *a* of Kish Saul's father were — 1Sa 9:3 — 860
thee, and arise, go seek the *a* — 1Sa 9:3 — 860
my father leave caring for the *a* — 1Sa 9:5 — 860
as for thine *a* that were lost — 1Sa 9:20 — 860
The *a* which thou wentest to seek — 1Sa 10:2 — 860
hath left the care of the *a* — 1Sa 10:2 — 860
And he said, To seek the *a* — 1Sa 10:14 — 860
us plainly that the *a* were found — 1Sa 10:16 — 860
and sucklings, and oxen, and *a* — 1Sa 22:19 — 2543
cakes of figs, and laid them on *a* — 1Sa 25:18 — 2543
the sheep, and the oxen, and the *a* — 1Sa 27:9 — 2543
him, with a couple of *a* saddled — 2Sa 16:1 — 2543
The *a* be for the king's household — 2Sa 16:2 — 2543
of the young men, and one of the *a* — 2Kin 4:22 — 860
and their horses, and their *a* — 2Kin 7:7 — 2543
a tied, and the tents as they were — 2Kin 7:10 — 2543
of *a* two thousand, and of men an — 1Chr 5:21 — 2543
and Naphtali, brought bread on *a* — 1Chr 12:40 — 2543
over the *a* was Jehdeiah the — 1Chr 27:30 — 860
all the feeble of them upon *a* — 2Chr 28:15 — 2543
their *a*, six thousand seven — Ezr 2:67 — 2543
seven hundred and twenty *a* — Neh 7:69 — 2543
bringing in sheaves, and lading *a* — Neh 13:15 — 2543
of oxen, and five hundred she *a* — Job 1:3 — 860
the *a* feeding beside them — Job 1:14 — 860
as wild *a* in the desert, go they — Job 24:5 — 6501
yoke of oxen, and a thousand she *a* — Job 42:12 — 860
the wild *a* quench their thirst — Ps 104:11 — 6501
of horsemen, a chariot of *a* — Is 21:7 — 2543
upon the shoulders of young *a* — Is 30:6 — 5895
the young *a* that ear the ground — Is 30:24 — 5895
dens for ever, a joy of wild *a* — Is 32:14 — 6501
the wild *a* did stand in the high — Jer 14:6 — 6501
whose flesh is as the flesh of *a* — Eze 23:20 — 2543
his dwelling was with the wild *a* — Dan 5:21 — 6167

ASSHUR (*ash'-ur*) See ASHUR, ASSUR, ASSYRIA.
1. The builder of Nineveh.
Out of that land went forth *A* — Gen 10:11 — 804
2. A son of Shem.
Elam, and *A*, and Arphaxad, and Lud, — Gen 10:22 — 804
Elam, and *A*, and Arphaxad, and Lud, — 1Chr 1:17 — 804
3. Another name for Assyria.
until *A* shall carry thee away — Num 24:22 — 804
of Chittim, and shall afflict *A* — Num 24:24 — 804
Eden, the merchants of Sheba, *A* — Eze 27:23 — 804
A is there and all her company — Eze 32:22 — 804
A shall not save us — Hos 14:3 — 804

ASSHURIM (*ash'-u-rim*) See ASHURITES. *Descendants of Dedan.*
And the sons of Dedan were *A* — Gen 25:3 — 805

ASSHURITES See ASSHURIM.

ASSIGNED
had a portion *a* them of Pharaoh — Gen 47:22
they *a* Bezer in the wilderness — Josh 20:8 — 5414
that he *a* Uriah unto a place — 2Sa 11:16 — 5414

ASSIR (*as'-sur*)
1. A son of Korah.
A, and Elkanah, and Abiasaph — Ex 6:24 — 617
son, Korah his son, *A* his son, — 1Chr 6:22 — 617
2. A son of Ebiasaph.
Ebiasaph his son, and *A* his son, — 1Chr 6:23 — 617
The son of Tahath, the son of *A* — 1Chr 6:37 — 617
3. A son of Jeconiah.
A, Salathiel his son, — 1Chr 3:17 — 617

ASSIST
that ye *a* her in whatsoever — Rom 16:2 — *3936*

ASSOCIATE
A yourselves, O ye people, and ye — Is 8:9 — 7489

ASSOS (*as'-sos*) *A seaport of Mysia in Asia Minor.*
before to ship, and sailed unto *A* — Acts 20:13 — *789*
And when he met with us at *A* — Acts 20:14 — *789*

ASS'S
his *a* colt unto the choice vine — Gen 49:11 — 860
until an *a* head was sold for — 2Kin 6:25 — 2543
man be born like a wild *a* colt — Job 11:12 — 6501
King cometh, sitting on an *a* colt — Jn 12:15 — *3688*

ASSUR (*As'-sur*) See ASSHUR. *Same as Asshur 3.*
the days of Esar-haddon king of *A* — Ezr 4:2 — 804
A also is joined with them — Ps 83:8 — 804

ASSURANCE
and shalt have none *a* of thy life — Deut 28:66 — 539
quietness and *a* for ever — Is 32:17 — 983
he hath given *a* unto all men — Acts 17:31 — *4102*
of the full *a* of understanding — Col 2:2 — *4136*
in the Holy Ghost, and in much *a* — 1Th 1:5 — *4136*
the full *a* of hope unto the end — Heb 6:11 — *4136*
a true heart in full *a* of faith — Heb 10:22 — *4136*

ASSURE
shall *a* our hearts before him — 1Jn 3:19 — *3983*

ASSURED
unto it, and it shall be *a* to him — Lev 27:19 — 6966
give you *a* peace in this place — Jer 14:13 — 571
hast learned and hast been *a* of — 2Ti 3:14 — *4104*

ASSUREDLY
said unto David, Know thou *a* — 1Sa 28:1 — 3045
A Solomon thy son shall reign — 1Kin 1:13 — 3588
A Solomon thy son shall reign — 1Kin 1:17 — 3588
A Solomon thy son shall reign — 1Kin 1:30 — 3588
this land *a* with my whole heart — Jer 32:41 — 571
If thou wilt *a* go forth unto the — Jer 38:17 — 3318
drink of the cup have *a* drunken — Jer 49:12 — 8354
all the house of Israel know *a* — Acts 2:36 — *806*
a gathering that the Lord had — Acts 16:10 — *4822*

ASSWAGE
of my lips should *a* your grief — Job 16:5 — 2820

ASSWAGED
over the earth, and the waters *a* — Gen 8:1 — 7918
Though I speak, my grief is not *a* — Job 16:6 — 2820

ASSYRIA (*as-sir'-e-ah*) See ASSHUR, ASSYRIAN.
A Mesopotamian empire.
which goeth toward the east of *A* — Gen 2:14 — 804
Egypt, as thou goest toward *A* — Gen 25:18 — 804
Pul the king of *A* came against — 2Kin 15:19 — 804
silver, to give to the king of *A* — 2Kin 15:20 — 804
So the king of *A* turned back — 2Kin 15:20 — 804
came Tiglath-pileser king of *A* — 2Kin 15:29 — 804
and carried them captive to *A* — 2Kin 15:29 — 804
to Tiglath-pileser king of *A* — 2Kin 16:7 — 804
it for a present to the king of *A* — 2Kin 16:8 — 804
the king of *A* hearkened unto him — 2Kin 16:9 — 804
for the king of *A* went up against — 2Kin 16:9 — 804
to meet Tiglath-pileser king of *A* — 2Kin 16:10 — 804
of the LORD for the king of *A* — 2Kin 16:18 — 804
him came up Shalmaneser king of *A* — 2Kin 17:3 — 804
the king of *A* found conspiracy in — 2Kin 17:4 — 804
no present to the king of *A* — 2Kin 17:4 — 804
the king of *A* shut him up — 2Kin 17:4 — 804
Then the king of *A* came up — 2Kin 17:5 — 804
Hoshea the king of *A* took Samaria — 2Kin 17:6 — 804
and carried Israel away into *A* — 2Kin 17:6 — 804
their own land to *A* unto this day — 2Kin 17:23 — 804
the king of *A* brought men from — 2Kin 17:24 — 804
they spake to the king of *A* — 2Kin 17:26 — 804
Then the king of *A* commanded — 2Kin 17:27 — 804
he rebelled against the king of *A* — 2Kin 18:7 — 804
king of *A* came up against Samaria — 2Kin 18:9 — 804
the king of *A* did carry away — 2Kin 18:11 — 804
did carry away Israel unto *A* — 2Kin 18:11 — 804
did Sennacherib king of *A* come up — 2Kin 18:13 — 804
sent to the king of *A* to Lachish — 2Kin 18:14 — 804
the king of *A* appointed unto — 2Kin 18:14 — 804
and gave it to the king of *A* — 2Kin 18:16 — 804
And the king of *A* sent Tartan — 2Kin 18:17 — 804
the great king, the king of *A* — 2Kin 18:19 — 804
pledges to my lord the king of *A* — 2Kin 18:23 — 804
of the great king, the king of *A* — 2Kin 18:28 — 804
into the hand of the king of *A* — 2Kin 18:30 — 804
for thus saith the king of *A* — 2Kin 18:31 — 804
out of the hand of the king of *A* — 2Kin 18:33 — 804
whom the king of *A* his master — 2Kin 19:4 — 804
the king of *A* have blasphemed me — 2Kin 19:6 — 804
found the king of *A* warring — 2Kin 19:8 — 804
into the hand of the king of *A* — 2Kin 19:10 — 804
kings of *A* have done to all lands — 2Kin 19:11 — 804
the kings of *A* have destroyed the — 2Kin 19:17 — 804

king of *A* I have heard... 2Kin 19:20 804
the LORD concerning the king of *A*... 2Kin 19:32 804
So Sennacherib king of *A* departed... 2Kin 19:36 804
out of the hand of the king of *A*... 2Kin 20:6 804
king of *A* to the river Euphrates... 2Kin 23:29 804
king of *A* carried away captive... 1Chr 5:6 804
up the spirit of Pul king of *A*... 1Chr 5:26 804
of Tilgath-pilneser king of *A*... 1Chr 5:26 804
unto the kings of *A* to help him... 2Chr 28:16 804
king of *A* came unto him, and... 2Chr 28:20 804
and gave it unto the king of *A*... 2Chr 28:21 804
out of the hand of the kings of *A*... 2Chr 30:6 804
Sennacherib king of *A* came... 2Chr 32:1 804
Why should the kings of *A* come... 2Chr 32:4 804
nor dismayed for the king of *A*... 2Chr 32:7 804
this did Sennacherib king of *A*... 2Chr 32:9 804
Thus saith Sennacherib king of *A*... 2Chr 32:10 804
out of the hand of the king of *A*... 2Chr 32:11 804
in the camp of the king of *A*... 2Chr 32:21 804
hand of Sennacherib the king of *A*... 2Chr 32:22 804
of the host of the king of *A*... 2Chr 33:11 804
heart of the king of *A* unto them... Ezr 6:22 804
of the kings of *A* unto this day... Neh 9:32 804
even the king of *A*... Is 7:17 804
the bee that is in the land of *A*... Is 7:18 804
the river, by the king of *A*... Is 7:20 804
taken away before the king of *A*... Is 8:4 804
and many, even the king of *A*... Is 8:7 804
the stout heart of the king of *A*... Is 10:12 804
which shall be left, from *A*... Is 11:11 804
which shall be left, from *A*... Is 11:16 804
be a highway out of Egypt to *A*... Is 19:23 804
Egypt, and the Egyptian into *A*... Is 19:23 804
be the third with Egypt and with *A*... Is 19:24 804
A the work of my hands, and Israel... Is 19:25 804
Sargon the king of *A* sent him... Is 20:1 804
So shall the king of *A* lead away... Is 20:4 804
be delivered from the king of *A*... Is 20:6 804
ready to perish in the land of *A*... Is 27:13 804
king of *A* came up against all the... Is 36:1 804
the king of *A* sent Rabshakeh from... Is 36:2 804
the great king, the king of *A*... Is 36:4 804
thee, to my master the king of *A*... Is 36:8 804
of the great king, the king of *A*... Is 36:13 804
into the hand of the king of *A*... Is 36:15 804
for thus saith the king of *A*... Is 36:16 804
out of the hand of the king of *A*... Is 36:18 804
whom the king of *A* his master... Is 37:4 804
the king of *A* have blasphemed me... Is 37:6 804
found the king of *A* warring... Is 37:8 804
into the hand of the king of *A*... Is 37:10 804
of *A* have done to all lands by... Is 37:11 804
the kings of *A* have laid waste... Is 37:18 804
me against Sennacherib king of *A*... Is 37:21 804
the LORD concerning the king of *A*... Is 37:33 804
So Sennacherib king of *A* departed... Is 37:37 804
out of the hand of the king of *A*... Is 38:6 804
hast thou to do in the way of *A*... Jer 2:18 804
Egypt, as thou wast ashamed of *A*... Jer 2:36 804
the king of *A* hath devoured him... Jer 50:17 804
as I have punished the king of *A*... Jer 50:18 804
that were the chosen men of *A*... Eze 23:7 804
they call to Egypt, they go to *A*... Hos 7:11 804
For they are gone up to *A*... Hos 8:9 804
shall eat unclean things in *A*... Hos 9:3 804
A for a present to king Jareb... Hos 10:6 804
and as a dove out of the land of *A*... Hos 11:11 804
the land of *A* with the sword... Mic 5:6 804
he shall come even to thee from *A*... Mic 7:12 804
shepherds slumber, O king of *A*... Nah 3:18 804
against the north, and destroy *A*... Zeph 2:13 804
of Egypt, and gather them out of *A*... Zec 10:10 804
the pride of *A* shall be brought... Zec 10:11 804

ASSYRIAN (*as-sir'-e'-un*) See ASSYRIANS. *An inhabitant of Assyria.*
O *A*, the rod of mine anger, and... Is 10:5 804
in Zion, be not afraid of the *A*... Is 10:24 804
I will break the *A* in my land... Is 14:25 804
the *A* shall come into Egypt, and... Is 19:23 804
til the *A* founded it for them... Is 23:13 804
LORD shall the *A* be beaten down... Is 30:31 804
Then shall the *A* fall with the... Is 31:8 804
the *A* oppressed them without... Is 52:4 804
the *A* was a cedar in Lebanon with... Eze 31:3 804
wound, then went Ephraim to the *A*... Hos 5:13 804
but the *A* shall be his king... Hos 11:5 804
when the *A* shall come into our... Mic 5:5 804
shall he deliver us from the *A*... Mic 5:6 804

ASSYRIANS (*as-sir'-e-uns*)
of the *A* an hundred fourscore... 2Kin 19:35 804
Egyptians shall serve with the *A*... Is 19:23 804
in the camp of the *A* an hundred... Is 37:36 804
to the Egyptians, and to the *A*... Lam 5:6 804
played the whore also with the *A*... Eze 16:28 804
lovers, on the *A* her neighbours,... Eze 23:5 804
lovers, into the hand of the *A*... Eze 23:9 804
doted upon the *A* her neighbours... Eze 23:12 804
and Koa, and all the *A* with them... Eze 23:23 804
do make a covenant with the *A*... Hos 12:1 804

ASTAROTH (*as'-ta-roth*) See ASHTAROTH. *A city in Bashan.*
Bashan, which dwelt at *A* in Edrei... Deut 1:4 6252

ASTONIED
and of my beard, and sat down *a*... Ezr 9:3 8074
I sat *a* until the evening... Ezr 9:4 8074
Upright men shall be *a* at this... Job 17:8 8074
after him shall be *a* at his day... Job 18:20 8074
As many were *a* at thee... Is 52:14 8074
Why shouldest thou be as a man *a*... Jer 14:9 1724
be *a* one with another, and consume... Eze 4:17 8074
Nebuchadnezzar the king was *a*... Dan 3:24 8429
was *a* for one hour, and his... Dan 4:19 8075
in him, and his lords were *a*... Dan 5:9 7672

ASTONISHED
dwell therein shall be *a* at it... Lev 26:32 8074
one that passeth by it shall be *a*... 1Kin 9:8 8074
Mark me, and be *a*, and lay your... Job 21:5 8074
tremble, and are *a* at his reproof... Job 26:11 8539
Be *a*, O ye heavens, at this, and... Jer 2:12 8074
and the priests shall be *a*... Jer 4:9 8074
that passeth thereby shall be *a*... Jer 18:16 8074
that passeth thereby shall be *a*... Jer 19:8 8074
one that goeth by it shall be *a*... Jer 49:17 8074
that goeth by Babylon shall be *a*... Jer 50:13 8074
remained there *a* among them seven... Eze 3:15 8074
at every moment, and be *a* at thee... Eze 26:16 8074
of the isles shall be *a* at thee... Eze 27:35 8074
the people shall be *a* at thee... Eze 28:19 8074
I was *a* at the vision, but none... Dan 8:27 8074
the people were *a* at his doctrine... Mt 7:28 *1605*
insomuch that they were *a*... Mt 13:54 *1605*
they were *a* at his doctrine... Mt 22:33 *1605*
they were *a* at his doctrine... Mk 1:22 *1605*
And they were *a* with a great... Mk 5:42 *1839*
and many hearing him were *a*... Mk 6:2 *1605*
And were beyond measure *a*, saying,... Mk 7:37 *1605*
the disciples were *a* at his words... Mk 10:24 *2284*
they were *a* out of measure,... Mk 10:26 *1605*
the people was *a* at his doctrine... Mk 11:18 *1605*
him were *a* at his understanding... Lk 2:47 *1839*
they were *a* at his doctrine... Lk 4:32 *1605*
For he was *a*, and all that were... Lk 5:9 *4023*
And her parents were *a*... Lk 8:56 *1839*
also of our company made us *a*... Lk 24:22 *1839*
a said, Lord, what wilt thou have... Acts 9:6 *2284*
which believed were *a*, as many as... Acts 10:45 *1839*
the door, and saw him, they were *a*... Acts 12:16 *1839*
being *a* at the doctrine of the... Acts 13:12 *1605*

ASTONISHMENT
and blindness, and *a* of heart... Deut 28:28 8541
And thou shalt become an *a*... Deut 28:37 8047
shall be an *a* to every one that... 2Chr 7:21 8074
delivered them to trouble, to *a*... 2Chr 29:8 8047
made us to drink the wine of *a*... Ps 60:3 8653
a hath taken hold on me... Jer 8:21 8047
destroy them, and make them an *a*... Jer 25:9 8047
shall be a desolation, and an *a*... Jer 25:11 8047
to make them a desolation, and an *a*... Jer 25:18 8047
the earth, to be a curse, and an *a*... Jer 29:18 8047
shall be an execration, and an *a*... Jer 42:18 8047
shall be an execration, and an *a*... Jer 44:12 8047
your land a desolation, and an *a*... Jer 44:22 8047
dwelling place for dragons, an *a*... Jer 51:37 8047
become an *a* among the nations... Jer 51:41 8047
drink water by measure, and with *a*... Eze 4:16 8078
an *a* unto the nations that are... Eze 5:15 8047
and drink their water with *a*... Eze 12:19 8078
and sorrow, with the cup of *a*... Eze 23:33 8047
I will smite every horse with *a*... Zec 12:4 8541
were astonished with a great *a*... Mk 5:42 *1611*

ASTRAY
enemy's ox or his ass going *a*... Ex 23:4 8582
brother's ox or his sheep go *a*... Deut 22:1 5080
they go *a* as soon as they be born... Ps 58:3 8582
Before I was afflicted I went *a*... Ps 119:67 7683
I have gone *a* like a lost sheep... Ps 119:176 8582
of his folly he shall go *a*... Prov 5:23 7686
her ways, go not *a* in her paths... Prov 7:25 8582
righteous to go *a* in an evil way... Prov 28:10 7686
All we like sheep have gone *a*... Is 53:6 8582
have caused them to go *a*, they... Jer 50:6 8582
Israel may go no more *a* from me... Eze 14:11 8582
far from me, when Israel went *a*... Eze 44:10 8582
which went *a* away from me after... Eze 44:10 8582
children of Israel went *a* from me... Eze 44:15 8582
which went not *a* when the... Eze 48:11 8582
the children of Israel went *a*... Eze 48:11 8582
as the Levites went *a*... Eze 48:11 8582
sheep, and one of them be gone *a*... Mt 18:12 *4105*
and seeketh that which is gone *a*... Mt 18:12 *4105*
ninety and nine which went not *a*... Mt 18:13 *4105*
For ye were as sheep going *a*... 1Pet 2:25 *4105*
the right way, and are gone *a*... 2Pet 2:15 *4105*

ASTROLOGER
such things at any magician, or *a*... Dan 2:10 826

ASTROLOGERS
Let now the *a*, the stargazers,... Is 47:13 1895
a that were in all his realm... Dan 1:20 825
to call the magicians, and the *a*... Dan 2:2 825
cannot the wise men, the *a*... Dan 2:27 826
Then came in the magicians, the *a*... Dan 4:7 826
cried aloud to bring in the *a*... Dan 5:7 826
made master of the magicians, *a*... Dan 5:11 826
And now the wise men, the *a*... Dan 5:15 826

ASUNDER
but shall not divide it *a*... Lev 1:17
neck, but shall not divide it *a*... Lev 5:8
clave *a* that was under them... Num 16:31
of fire, and parted them both *a*... 2Kin 2:11 996
at ease, but he hath broken me *a*... Job 16:12
about, he cleaveth my reins *a*... Job 16:13
Let us break their bands *a*... Ps 2:3
he hath cut *a* the cords of the... Ps 129:4
of the whole earth cut in *a*... Jer 50:23
great pain, and No shall be rent *a*... Eze 30:16
he beheld, and drove *a* the nations... Hab 3:6
staff, even Beauty, and cut it *a*... Zec 11:10
Then I cut *a* mine other staff,... Zec 11:14
together, let not man put *a*... Mt 19:6 *5563*
And shall cut him *a*, and appoint... Mt 24:51 *1371*
chains had been plucked *a* by him... Mk 5:4 *1288*
together, let not man put *a*... Mk 10:9 *5563*
he burst *a* in the midst, and all... Acts 1:18 *2997*
departed in *a* one from the other... Acts 15:39 *673*
even to the dividing *a* of soul... Heb 4:12
were stoned, they were sawn *a*... Heb 11:37 *4249*

ASUPPIM *Storage for temple gods.*
and to his sons the house of *A*... 1Chr 26:15 624
four a day, and toward *A* two... 1Chr 26:17 624

ASYNCRITUS (*a-sin'-cri-tus*) *A Christian acquaintance of Paul.*
Salute *A*, Phlegon, Hermas,... Rom 16:14 *799*

AT
he placed *a* the east of the... Gen 3:24
not well, sin lieth *a* the door... Gen 4:7
and it grieved him *a* his heart... Gen 6:6 413
it came to pass *a* the end of... Gen 8:6
a the hand of every beast will I... Gen 9:5
require it, and *a* the hand of man... Gen 9:5
a the hand of every man's brother... Gen 9:5
his tent had been *a* the beginning... Gen 13:3
he had made there *a* the first... Gen 13:4
a the valley of Shaveh, which is... Gen 14:17 413
Sarah shall bear unto thee *a* this... Gen 17:21
A the time appointed I will... Gen 18:14
came two angels to Sodom *a* even... Gen 19:1
Lot went out *a* the door unto them... Gen 19:6
were *a* the door of the house with... Gen 19:11
a every place whither we shall... Gen 20:13 413
a the set time of which God had... Gen 21:2
And it came to pass *a* that time... Gen 21:22
they made a covenant *a* Beer-sheba... Gen 21:32
and Abraham dwelt *a* Beer-sheba... Gen 22:19
went in *a* the gate of his city... Gen 23:10
went in *a* the gate of his city... Gen 23:18
water *a* the time of the evening... Gen 24:11
the man wondering *a* her held his... Gen 24:21
he stood by the camels *a* the well... Gen 24:30 5921
us a few days, *a* the least ten... Gen 24:55 176
damsel, and enquire *a* her mouth... Gen 24:57
in the field *a* the eventide... Gen 24:63
Behold, I am *a* the point to die... Gen 25:32
Philistines looked out *a* a window... Gen 26:8 1157
mourning for my father are *a* hand... Gen 27:41 7126
city was called Luz *a* the first... Gen 28:19
it came to pass *a* the time that... Gen 31:10
then receive my present *a* my hand... Gen 33:10
a the hand of the children of... Gen 33:19
And it came to pass *a* that time... Gen 38:1
and he was *a* Chezib, when she bare... Gen 38:5
Remain a widow *a* thy father's... Gen 38:11
it came to pass *a* the end of two... Gen 41:1
ill favoured, as *a* the beginning... Gen 41:21
men shall dine with me *a* noon... Gen 43:16
a the first time are we brought... Gen 43:18
with him *a* the door of the house... Gen 43:19
we came indeed down *a* the first... Gen 43:20
against Joseph came *a* noon... Gen 43:25
the men marvelled one *a* another... Gen 43:33 413
began *a* the eldest, and left *a*... Gen 44:12
eldest, and left *a* the youngest... Gen 44:12
they were troubled *a* his presence... Gen 45:3
me *a* Luz in the land of Canaan... Gen 48:3
Zebulun shall dwell *a* the haven... Gen 49:13
but he shall overcome *a* the last... Gen 49:19
sorely grieved him, and shot *a* him... Gen 49:23
a night he shall divide the spoil... Gen 49:27
down to wash herself *a* the river... Ex 2:5 5921
cast it *a* his feet, and said,... Ex 4:25
thou delivered thy people *a* all... Ex 5:23
his heart *a* this time also... Ex 8:32
For I will *a* this time send all... Ex 9:14
nor sodden *a* all with water, but... Ex 12:9
day of the month *a* even, ye shall... Ex 12:18
twentieth day of the month *a* even... Ex 12:18
none of you shall go out *a* the... Ex 12:22
that *a* midnight the LORD smote... Ex 12:29
it came to pass *a* the end of the... Ex 12:41
A even, then ye shall know that... Ex 16:6
A even ye shall eat flesh, and in... Ex 16:12 996
that *a* even the quails came up,... Ex 16:13
he encamped *a* the mount of God... Ex 18:5
judge the people *a* all seasons... Ex 18:22
judged the people *a* all seasons... Ex 18:26
come not *a* your wives... Ex 19:15 413
they stood *a* the nether part of... Ex 19:17
they cry *a* all unto me, I will... Ex 22:23
If thou *a* all take thy... Ex 22:26
joined *a* the two edges thereof... Ex 28:7 413
chains of pure gold *a* the ends... Ex 28:14
upon the breastplate chains *a* the... Ex 28:22
lamb thou shalt offer *a* even... Ex 29:39 996
lamb thou shalt offer *a* even... Ex 29:41 996
throughout your generations *a* the... Ex 29:42
Aaron lighteth the lamps *a* even... Ex 30:8 996
And he received them *a* their hand... Ex 32:4
stood every man *a* his tent door... Ex 33:8
and stood *a* the door of the... Ex 33:9
stand *a* the tabernacle door... Ex 33:10
of ingathering *a* the year's end... Ex 34:22
the door *a* the entering in of the... Ex 35:15
together *a* the head thereof... Ex 36:29 413
which assembled *a* the door of the... Ex 38:8
the breastplate chains *a* the ends... Ex 39:15
up the hanging *a* the court gate... Ex 40:8
he set up the hanging *a* the door... Ex 40:28
it of his own voluntary will *a*... Lev 1:3 413
wrung out *a* the side of the altar... Lev 1:15 5921
kill it *a* the door of the... Lev 3:2
all the blood of the bullock *a*... Lev 4:7 413
which is *a* the door of the... Lev 4:7
shall pour out all the blood *a*... Lev 4:18 413
which is *a* the door of the... Lev 4:18
shall pour out his blood *a* the... Lev 4:25 413
thereof *a* the bottom of the altar... Lev 4:30 413

thereof *a* the bottom of the altar	Lev 4:34	413
out *a* the bottom of the altar	Lev 5:9	413
morning, and half thereof *a* night	Lev 6:20	
be eaten *a* all on the third day	Lev 7:18	
poured the blood *a* the bottom of	Lev 8:15	413
Boil the flesh *a* the door of the	Lev 8:31	
of your consecration be *a* an end	Lev 8:33	3117
Therefore shall ye abide *a* the	Lev 8:35	5921
poured out the blood *a* the bottom	Lev 9:9	413
plague in his sight be *a* a stay	Lev 13:5	
scall be in his sight *a* a stay	Lev 13:37	
a the door of the tabernacle of	Lev 14:11	
And if any man lie with her *a* all	Lev 15:24	
that he come not *a* all times into	Lev 16:2	
present them before the LORD *a*	Lev 16:7	
your souls, and do no work *a* all	Lev 16:29	
upon the altar of the LORD *a* the	Lev 17:6	
whether she be born *a* home	Lev 18:9	
ye shall offer it *a* your own will	Lev 19:5	
if it be eaten *a* all on the third	Lev 19:7	
not *a* all redeemed, nor freedom	Lev 19:20	
Ye shall offer *a* your own will a	Lev 22:19	
LORD, offer it *a* your own will	Lev 22:29	
day of the first month *a* even is	Lev 23:5	996
the ninth day of the month *a* even	Lev 23:32	
may the Levites redeem *a* any time	Lev 25:32	
therein shall be astonished *a* it	Lev 26:32	5921
if he shall *a* all change beast	Lev 27:10	
But if he will *a* all redeem it	Lev 27:13	
valued *a* fifty shekels of silver	Lev 27:16	
if a man will *a* all redeem ought	Lev 27:31	
and if he change it *a* all, then	Lev 27:33	
Aaron numbered *a* the commandment	Num 3:39	5921
A the appointment of Aaron and his	Num 4:27	5921
LORD he shall come *a* no dead body	Num 6:6	5921
the head of his separation *a* the	Num 6:18	
passover *a* his appointed season	Num 9:2	
a even, ye shall keep it in his	Num 9:3	996
day of the first month *a* even in	Num 9:5	996
month *a* even they shall keep it	Num 9:11	996
a even there was upon the	Num 9:15	
A the commandment of the LORD the	Num 9:18	5921
a the commandment of the LORD	Num 9:18	5921
A the commandment of the LORD	Num 9:23	5921
a the commandment of the LORD	Num 9:23	5921
a the commandment of the LORD by	Num 9:23	5921
assemble themselves to thee *a* the	Num 10:3	413
there is nothing *a* all, beside	Num 11:6	
until it come out *a* your nostrils	Num 11:20	
and abode *a* Hazeroth	Num 11:35	
and said, Let us go up *a* once	Num 13:30	
about them fled *a* the cry of them	Num 16:34	
water, and shall be clean *a* even	Num 19:19	
my word *a* the water of Meribah	Num 20:24	
pitched *a* Ije-abarim, in the	Num 21:11	
a the stream of the brooks that	Num 21:15	
We have shot *a* them	Num 21:30	
his people, to the battle *a* Edrei	Num 21:33	
Amorites, which dwelt *a* Heshbon	Num 21:34	
king of the Moabites *a* that time	Num 22:4	
And God came unto Balaam *a* night	Num 22:20	
any power *a* all to say any thing	Num 22:38	
them *a* all, nor bless them *a* all	Num 23:25	
as *a* other times, to seek for	Num 24:1	
to sanctify me *a* the water before	Num 27:14	
a his word shall they go out, and	Num 27:21	5921
a his word they shall come in,	Num 27:21	5921
lamb shalt thou offer *a* even	Num 28:4	996
lamb shalt thou offer *a* even	Num 28:8	996
father shall hold his peace *a* her	Num 30:4	
if she had *a* all an husband, when	Num 30:6	
held his peace *a* her in the day	Num 30:7	
heard it, and held his peace *a* her	Num 30:11	
his peace *a* her from day to day	Num 30:14	
because he held his peace *a* her	Num 30:14	
unto the camp *a* the plains of	Num 31:12	413
Alush, and encamped *a* Rephidim	Num 33:14	
pitched *a* Kibroth-hattaavah	Num 33:16	
and encamped *a* Hazeroth	Num 33:17	
and pitched *a* Rimmon-parez	Num 33:19	
from Libnah, and pitched *a* Rissah	Num 33:21	
Makheloth, and encamped *a* Tahath	Num 33:26	
from Tahath, and pitched *a* Tarah	Num 33:27	
and encamped *a* Moseroth	Num 33:30	
and encamped *a* Hor-hagidgad	Num 33:32	
Jotbathah, and encamped *a* Ebronah	Num 33:34	
and encamped *a* Ezion-gaber	Num 33:35	
Hor *a* the commandment of the LORD	Num 33:38	
out of it shall be *a* the sea	Num 34:5	5921
out of it shall be *a* Hazar-enan	Num 34:9	
out of it shall be *a* the salt sea	Num 34:12	
killeth any person *a* unawares	Num 35:11	
or hurl *a* him by laying of wait,	Num 35:20	
But if the slayer shall *a* any	Num 35:26	
which dwelt *a* Astaroth in Edrei	Deut 1:4	
And I spake unto you *a* that time	Deut 1:9	
I charged your judges *a* that time	Deut 1:16	
I commanded you *a* that time all	Deut 1:18	
all his people, to fight *a* Jahaz	Deut 2:32	
took all his cities *a* that time	Deut 2:34	
all his people, to battle *a* Edrei	Deut 3:1	
Amorites, which dwelt *a* Heshbon	Deut 3:2	
took all his cities *a* that time	Deut 3:4	
we took *a* that time out of the	Deut 3:8	
which we possessed *a* that time	Deut 3:12	
And I commanded you *a* that time	Deut 3:18	
And I commanded Joshua *a* that time.	Deut 3:21	
I besought the LORD *a* that time	Deut 3:23	
the LORD commanded me *a* that time	Deut 4:14	
the Amorites, who dwelt *a* Heshbon	Deut 4:46	
you *a* that time, to shew you the	Deut 5:5	
us alive, as it is *a* this day	Deut 6:24	
shalt not be affrighted *a* them	Deut 7:21	6440
mayest not consume them *a* once	Deut 7:22	4118
to do thee good *a* thy latter end	Deut 8:16	
if thou do *a* all forget the LORD	Deut 8:19	
it came to pass *a* the end of	Deut 9:11	
as *a* the first, forty days and	Deut 9:18	
unto me *a* that time also	Deut 9:19	
a Taberah, and *a* Massah, and *a*	Deut 9:22	
a Kibroth-hattaavah, ye provoked	Deut 9:22	
as I fell down *a* the first	Deut 9:25	
A that time the LORD said unto me	Deut 10:1	
A that time the LORD separated	Deut 10:8	
unto me *a* that time also, and the	Deut 10:10	
A the end of three years thou	Deut 14:28	
A the end of every seven years	Deut 15:1	
the year of release, is *a* hand	Deut 15:9	7126
sacrificedst the first day *a* even	Deut 16:4	
But *a* the place which the LORD	Deut 16:6	413
sacrifice the passover *a* even	Deut 16:6	
a the going down of the sun, *a*	Deut 16:6	
A the mouth of two witnesses, or	Deut 17:6	5921
but *a* the mouth of one witness he	Deut 17:6	5921
a the mouth of two witnesses, or	Deut 19:15	5921
or *a* the mouth of three witnesses	Deut 19:15	5921
not sell her *a* all for money	Deut 21:14	
thy fill *a* thine own pleasure	Deut 23:24	
he shall be free *a* home one year	Deut 24:5	
A his day thou shalt give him his	Deut 24:15	
And thou shalt grope *a* noonday	Deut 28:29	
a even thou shalt say, Would God	Deut 28:67	
A the end of every seven years,	Deut 31:10	
day of their calamity is *a* hand	Deut 32:35	7138
a the waters of Meribah-kadesh	Deut 32:51	
and they sat down *a* thy feet	Deut 33:3	
whom thou didst prove *a* Massah	Deut 33:8	5921
strive *a* the waters of Meribah	Deut 33:8	
A that time the LORD said unto	Josh 5:2	
the children of Israel *a* the hill	Josh 5:3	413
a even in the plains of Jericho	Josh 5:10	
it came to pass *a* the seventh	Josh 6:16	
Joshua adjured them *a* that time	Josh 6:26	
wherefore hast thou *a* all brought	Josh 7:7	
as *a* the first, that we will flee	Josh 8:5	
flee before us, as *a* the first	Josh 8:6	
a a time appointed, before the	Josh 8:14	
cast it *a* the entering of the	Josh 8:29	413
to Joshua unto the camp *a* Gilgal	Josh 9:6	
of Bashan, which was *a* Ashtaroth	Josh 9:10	
asked not counsel *a* the mouth of	Josh 9:14	
it came to pass *a* the end of	Josh 9:16	
with a great slaughter *a* Gibeon	Josh 10:10	
themselves in a cave *a* Makkedah	Josh 10:16	
found hid in a cave *a* Makkedah	Josh 10:17	
to Joshua *a* Makkedah in peace	Josh 10:21	
it came to pass *a* the time of the	Josh 10:27	
land did Joshua take *a* one time	Josh 10:42	
pitched together *a* the waters of	Josh 11:5	413
Joshua *a* that time turned back,	Josh 11:10	
a that time came Joshua, and cut	Josh 11:21	
dwelt *a* Ashtaroth and *a* Edrei,	Josh 12:4	
out of that coast were *a* the sea	Josh 15:4	
was from the bay of the sea *a* the	Josh 15:5	5704
out thereof were *a* En-rogel	Josh 15:7	413
which is *a* the end of the valley	Josh 15:8	
out of the border were *a* the sea	Josh 15:11	
Judah *a* Jerusalem unto this day	Josh 15:63	
goings out thereof are *a* the sea	Josh 16:3	
to Jericho, and went out *a* Jordan	Josh 16:7	
goings out thereof were *a* the sea	Josh 16:8	
outgoings of it were *a* the sea	Josh 17:9	
assembled together *a* Shiloh	Josh 18:1	
to Joshua to the host *a* Shiloh	Josh 18:9	
a the wilderness of Beth-aven	Josh 18:12	
out thereof were *a* Kirjath-baal	Josh 18:14	413
outgoings of the border were *a*	Josh 18:19	
sea *a* the south end of Jordan	Josh 18:19	
of their border were *a* Jordan	Josh 19:22	
are *a* the sea from the coast to	Josh 19:29	
outgoings thereof were *a* Jordan	Josh 19:33	
a the door of the tabernacle of	Josh 19:51	
a the entering of the gate of the	Josh 20:4	
a unawares might flee thither	Josh 20:9	
they spake unto them *a* Shiloh in	Josh 21:2	
a the commandment of the LORD,	Josh 21:3	413
a the passage of the children of	Josh 22:11	413
themselves together *a* Shiloh	Josh 22:12	
a the least such as before knew	Judg 3:2	7535
they slew of Moab *a* that time	Judg 3:29	
she judged Israel *a* that time	Judg 4:4	
with ten thousand men *a* his feet	Judg 4:10	
A her feet he bowed, he fell, he	Judg 5:27	996
a her feet he bowed, he fell	Judg 5:27	996
of Sisera looked out *a* a window	Judg 5:28	1157
Zeeb they slew *a* the winepress of	Judg 7:25	
were they whom ye slew *a* Tabor	Judg 8:18	
unto his father's house *a* Ophrah	Judg 9:5	
And Abimelech dwelt *a* Arumah	Judg 9:41	
it came to pass *a* the end of two	Judg 11:39	
my people were *a* great strife	Judg 12:2	
slew him *a* the passages of Jordan	Judg 12:6	413
there fell *a* that time of the	Judg 12:6	
Ibzan, and was buried *a* Beth-lehem	Judg 12:10	
and a meat offering *a* our hands	Judg 13:23	
nor would as *a* this time have	Judg 13:23	
him *a* times in the camp of Dan	Judg 13:25	
for *a* that time the Philistines	Judg 14:4	
arose *a* midnight, and took the	Judg 16:3	
I will go out as *a* other times	Judg 16:20	
that I may be *a* once avenged of	Judg 16:28	
So the dead which he slew *a* his	Judg 16:30	
unto a people that were *a* quiet	Judg 18:27	
of the city was Laish *a* the first	Judg 18:29	
his work out of the field *a* even	Judg 19:16	
beat *a* the door, and spake to the	Judg 19:22	5921
fell down *a* the door of the man's	Judg 19:26	
down *a* the door of the house	Judg 19:27	
of Benjamin were numbered *a* that	Judg 20:15	
sling stones *a* an hair breadth	Judg 20:16	413
to fight against them *a* Gibeah	Judg 20:20	
against Gibeah, as *a* other times	Judg 20:30	
as *a* other times, in the highways	Judg 20:31	
down before us, as *a* the first	Judg 20:32	
themselves in array *a* Baal-tamar	Judg 20:33	
Benjamin came again *a* that time	Judg 21:14	
not give unto them *a* this time	Judg 21:22	
departed thence *a* that time	Judg 21:24	
A mealtime come thou hither, and	Ruth 2:14	
he went to lie down *a* the end of	Ruth 3:7	
And it came to pass *a* midnight	Ruth 3:8	
behold, a woman lay *a* his feet	Ruth 3:8	
latter end than *a* the beginning	Ruth 3:10	
she lay *a* his feet until the	Ruth 3:14	
a the door of the tabernacle of	1Sa 2:22	
Wherefore kick ye *a* my sacrifice	1Sa 2:29	
a mine offering, which I have	1Sa 2:29	
And it came to pass *a* that time	1Sa 3:2	
called as *a* other times, Samuel,	1Sa 3:10	
a which both the ears of every	1Sa 3:11	
and shut up their calves *a* home	1Sa 6:10	
I have here *a* hand the fourth	1Sa 9:8	
the border of Benjamin *a* Zelzah	1Sa 10:2	
themselves together *a* Michmash	1Sa 13:11	
For the ark of God was *a* that	1Sa 14:18	
of the town trembled *a* his coming	1Sa 16:4	
were gathered together *a* Shochoh	1Sa 17:1	
his father's sheep *a* Beth-lehem	1Sa 17:15	
with his hand, as *a* other times	1Sa 18:10	
But it came to pass *a* the time	1Sa 18:19	
David is *a* Naioth in Ramah	1Sa 19:19	
they be *a* Naioth in Ramah	1Sa 19:22	
fail to sit with the king *a* meat	1Sa 20:5	
field unto the third day *a* even	1Sa 20:5	
If thy father *a* all miss me	1Sa 20:6	
it *a* the hand of David's enemies	1Sa 20:16	
as though I shot *a* a mark	1Sa 20:20	
as *a* other times, even upon a	1Sa 20:25	
cast a javelin *a* him to smite him	1Sa 20:33	5921
went out into the field *a* the	1Sa 20:35	
was afraid *a* the meeting of David	1Sa 21:1	
themselves *a* least from women	1Sa 21:4	389
me, to lie in wait, as *a* this day	1Sa 22:8	
me, to lie in wait, as *a* this day	1Sa 22:13	
goeth *a* thy bidding, and is	1Sa 22:14	413
dwelt in strong holds *a* En-gedi	1Sa 23:29	
buried him in his house *a* Ramah	1Sa 25:1	
fell *a* his feet, and said, Upon me	1Sa 25:24	5921
stuck in the ground *a* his bolster	1Sa 26:7	
spear even to the earth *a* once	1Sa 26:8	
the spear that is *a* his bolster	1Sa 26:11	
of water that was *a* his bolster	1Sa 26:16	
And David dwelt with Achish *a* Gath	1Sa 27:3	
hath a familiar spirit *a* En-dor	1Sa 28:7	
And David enquired *a* the LORD	1Sa 30:8	
also to abide *a* the brook Besor	1Sa 30:21	
buried them under a tree *a* Jabesh	1Sa 31:13	
came to Hebron *a* break of day	2Sa 2:32	
Asahel *a* Gibeon in the battle	2Sa 3:30	
wept *a* the grave of Abner	2Sa 3:32	
who lay on a bed *a* noon	2Sa 4:5	
of Abinadab which was *a* Gibeah	2Sa 6:4	
his border *a* the river Euphrates	2Sa 8:3	
eat bread *a* my table continually	2Sa 9:7	5921
shall eat bread alway *a* my table	2Sa 9:10	5921
the king, he shall eat *a* my table	2Sa 9:11	5921
continually *a* the king's table	2Sa 9:13	5921
Tarry *a* Jericho until your beards	2Sa 10:5	
put the battle in array *a* the	2Sa 10:8	
a the time when kings go forth to	2Sa 11:1	
David tarried still *a* Jerusalem	2Sa 11:1	
But Uriah slept *a* the door of the	2Sa 11:9	
a even he went out to lie on his	2Sa 11:13	
may see it, and eat it *a* her hand	2Sa 13:5	
sight, that I may eat *a* her hand	2Sa 13:6	
(for it was *a* every year's end	2Sa 14:26	
a two hundred shekels after the	2Sa 14:26	
while I abode *a* Geshur in Syria	2Sa 15:8	
that were with him *a* Jerusalem	2Sa 15:14	
Behold, he abideth *a* Jerusalem	2Sa 16:3	
And he cast stones *a* David	2Sa 16:6	
a all the servants of king David	2Sa 16:6	
as he went, and threw stones *a* him	2Sa 16:13	5980
had enquired *a* the oracle of God	2Sa 16:23	
given is not good *a* this time	2Sa 17:7	
of them be overthrown *a* the first	2Sa 17:9	
all the people were *a* strife	2Sa 19:9	
that did eat *a* thine own table	2Sa 19:28	
while he lay *a* Mahanaim	2Sa 19:32	
have we eaten *a* all of the king's	2Sa 19:42	
came to his house *a* Jerusalem	2Sa 20:3	
When they were *a* the great stone	2Sa 20:8	5973
shall surely ask counsel *a* Abel	2Sa 20:18	
battle with the Philistines *a* Gob	2Sa 21:18	
a the rebuking of the LORD, *a*	2Sa 22:16	
hundred, whom he slew *a* one time	2Sa 23:8	
a the end of nine months and	2Sa 24:8	
surely buy it of thee *a* a price	2Sa 24:24	
him *a* any time in saying, Why	1Kin 1:6	
be of those that eat *a* thy table	1Kin 2:7	
he came down to meet me *a* Jordan	1Kin 2:8	
but I will not *a* this time put	1Kin 2:26	
it came to pass *a* the end of	1Kin 2:39	
And she arose *a* midnight, and took	1Kin 3:20	
in Lebanon, and two months *a* home	1Kin 5:14	
a the side of every addition	1Kin 7:30	
themselves unto king Solomon *a*	1Kin 8:2	
which Moses put there *a* Horeb	1Kin 8:9	
of his people Israel *a* all times	1Kin 8:59	
his commandments, as *a* this day	1Kin 8:61	
a that time Solomon held a feast,	1Kin 8:65	
he had appeared unto him *a* Gibeon	1Kin 9:2	

But if ye shall *a* all turn from 1Kin 9:6
a this house, which is high, 1Kin 9:8
it came to pass *a* the end of 1Kin 9:10
For the king had *a* sea a navy of 1Kin 10:22
and with the king *a* Jerusalem 1Kin 10:26
received the linen yarn *a* a price 1Kin 10:28
it came to pass *a* that time when 1Kin 11:29
the house of the LORD *a* Jerusalem 1Kin 12:27
to pass, as they sat *a* the table 1Kin 13:20 413
A that time Abijah the son of 1Kin 14:1
feet, as she came in *a* the door 1Kin 14:6
of Syria, that dwelt *a* Damascus 1Kin 15:18
and Baasha smote him *a* Gibbethon 1Kin 15:27
which eat *a* Jezebel's table 1Kin 18:19
And it came to pass *a* noon 1Kin 18:27
it came to pass *a* the time of the 1Kin 18:36
done all these things *a* thy word 1Kin 18:36
it came to pass *a* the seventh 1Kin 18:44
and a cruse of water *a* his head 1Kin 19:6
thy servant *a* the first I will do 1Kin 20:9
And they went out *a* noon 1Kin 20:16
for *a* the return of the year the 1Kin 20:22
it came to pass *a* the return of 1Kin 20:26
a the word of the LORD to day 1Kin 22:5
may go up and fall *a* Ramoth-gilead 1Kin 22:20
If thou return *a* all in peace 1Kin 22:28
man drew a bow *a* a venture 1Kin 22:34
the Syrians, and died *a* even 1Kin 22:35
ships were broken *a* Ezion-geber 1Kin 22:48
a Beth-el came forth to Elisha 2Kin 2:3
were *a* Jericho came to Elisha 2Kin 2:5
were to view *a* Jericho saw him 2Kin 2:15
to him, (for he tarried *a* Jericho 2Kin 2:18
bare a son *a* that season that 2Kin 4:17
fell *a* his feet, and bowed herself 2Kin 4:37 5921
stood *a* the door of the house of 2Kin 5:9
in not receiving *a* his hands that 2Kin 5:20
door, and hold him fast *a* the door 2Kin 6:32
men *a* the entering in of the gate 2Kin 7:3
it came to pass *a* the seven 2Kin 8:3
Libnah revolted *a* the same time 2Kin 8:22
the Syrians had given him *a* Ramah 2Kin 8:29
the LORD, *a* the hand of Jezebel 2Kin 9:7
and the arrow went out *a* his heart 2Kin 9:24
they did so *a* the going up to Gur 2Kin 9:27
head, and looked out *a* a window 2Kin 9:30 1157
And as Jehu entered in *a* the gate 2Kin 9:31
Lay ye them in two heaps *a* the 2Kin 10:8
as he was *a* the shearing house in 2Kin 10:12
slew them *a* the pit of the 2Kin 10:14
part shall be *a* the gate of Sur 2Kin 11:6
a third part *a* the gate behind 2Kin 11:6
the money that every man is set *a* 2Kin 12:4
land *a* the coming in of the year 2Kin 13:20
glory of this, and tarry *a* home 2Kin 14:10
in the face *a* Beth-shemesh 2Kin 14:11
a Beth-shemesh, and came to 2Kin 14:13
he was buried *a* Jerusalem with 2Kin 14:20
A that time Rezin king of Syria 2Kin 16:6
saw an altar that was *a* Damascus 2Kin 16:10
so it was *a* the beginning of 2Kin 17:25
a the end of three years they 2Kin 18:10
A that time did Hezekiah cut off 2Kin 18:16
gods of the nations delivered *a* 2Kin 18:33
hath shaken her head *a* thee 2Kin 19:21
and returned, and dwelt *a* Nineveh 2Kin 19:36
A that time Berodach-baladan, the 2Kin 20:12
burned it *a* the brook Kidron, and 2Kin 23:6
left hand *a* the gate of the city 2Kin 23:8
a the entering in of the house of 2Kin 23:11
the altar that was *a* Beth-el 2Kin 23:15
and he slew him *a* Megiddo, when he 2Kin 23:29
a Riblah in the land of Hamath 2Kin 23:33
Surely *a* the commandment of the 2Kin 24:3 5921
A that time the servants of 2Kin 24:10
slew them *a* Riblah in the land of 2Kin 25:21
that were with him *a* Mizpah 2Kin 25:25
the scribes which dwelt *a* Jabez 1Chr 2:55
And they dwelt *a* Beer-sheba 1Chr 4:28
a Bilhah, and *a* Ezem, and *a* Tolad 1Chr 4:29
a Bethuel, and *a* Hormah, and *a* 1Chr 4:30
a Beth-marcaboth, and Hazar-susim, 1Chr 4:31
a Beth-birei, and *a* Shaaraim 1Chr 4:31
a Gibeon dwelt the father of 1Chr 8:29
these dwelt *a* Jerusalem 1Chr 9:34
with their brethren *a* Jerusalem 1Chr 9:38
hundred slain by him *a* one time 1Chr 11:11
He was with David *a* Pas-dammim 1Chr 11:13
garrison was then *a* Beth-lehem 1Chr 11:16
of Beth-lehem, that is *a* the gate 1Chr 11:17
For *a* that time day by day there 1Chr 12:22
brethren were *a* their commandment 1Chr 12:32 5921
for we enquired not *a* it in the 1Chr 13:3
David took more wives *a* Jerusalem 1Chr 14:3
because ye did it not *a* the first 1Chr 15:13
daughter of Saul looking out *a* a 1Chr 15:29 1157
out *a* the presence of the LORD 1Chr 16:33
the high place that was *a* Gibeon 1Chr 16:39
any more, as *a* the beginning, 1Chr 17:9
Tarry *a* Jericho until your beards 1Chr 19:5
a the time that kings go out to 1Chr 20:1
But David tarried *a* Jerusalem 1Chr 20:1
that there arose war *a* Gezer with 1Chr 20:4
a which time Sibbechai the 1Chr 20:4
And yet again there was war *a* Gath 1Chr 20:6
David went up *a* the saying of Gad 1Chr 21:19
A that time when David saw that 1Chr 21:28
were *a* that season in the high 1Chr 21:29
season in the high place *a* Gibeon 1Chr 21:29
the LORD, and likewise *a* even 1Chr 23:30
A Parbar westward, four *a* the 1Chr 26:18
a the causeway, and two *a* Parbar 1Chr 26:18
men of valour *a* Jazer of Gilead 1Chr 26:31
and my judgments, as *a* this day 1Chr 28:7
will be wholly *a* thy commandment 1Chr 28:21
the high place that was *a* Gibeon 2Chr 1:3
pitched a tent for it *a* Jerusalem 2Chr 1:4
which was *a* the tabernacle of the 2Chr 1:6
that was *a* Gibeon to Jerusalem 2Chr 1:13
and with the king *a* Jerusalem 2Chr 1:14
gold *a* Jerusalem as plenteous as 2Chr 1:15
received the linen yarn *a* a price 2Chr 1:16
LORD *a* Jerusalem in mount Moriah 2Chr 3:1
which Moses put therein *a* Horeb 2Chr 5:10
stood *a* the east end of the altar 2Chr 5:12
Also *a* the same time Solomon kept 2Chr 7:8
it came to pass *a* the end of 2Chr 8:1
by their courses *a* every gate 2Chr 8:14
a the sea side in the land of 2Chr 8:17 5921
with hard questions *a* Jerusalem 2Chr 9:1
and with the king *a* Jerusalem 2Chr 9:25
were brought under *a* that time 2Chr 13:18
valley of Zephathah *a* Mareshah 2Chr 14:10
a Jerusalem in the third month 2Chr 15:10
And all Judah rejoiced *a* the oath 2Chr 15:15 5921
burnt it *a* the brook Kidron 2Chr 15:16
of Syria, that dwelt *a* Damascus 2Chr 16:2
a that time Hanani the seer came 2Chr 16:7
a the word of the LORD to day 2Chr 18:4
they sat in a void place *a* the 2Chr 18:9
may go up and fall *a* Ramoth-gilead 2Chr 18:19
man drew a bow *a* a venture 2Chr 18:33
And Jehoshaphat dwelt *a* Jerusalem 2Chr 19:4
ye shall find them *a* the end of 2Chr 20:16
king of Syria *a* Ramoth-gilead 2Chr 22:5
which were given him *a* Ramah 2Chr 22:6
Jehoram the son of Ahab *a* Jezreel 2Chr 22:6
part shall be *a* the king's house 2Chr 23:5
a third part *a* the gate of the 2Chr 23:5
a his pillar *a* the entering in 2Chr 23:13 5921
he set the porters *a* the gates of 2Chr 23:19 5921
a the king's commandment they 2Chr 24:8
set it without *a* the gate of the 2Chr 24:8
that *a* what time the chest was 2Chr 24:11
stoned him with stones *a* the 2Chr 24:21
it came to pass *a* the end of the 2Chr 24:23
abide now *a* home 2Chr 25:19
a Beth-shemesh, which belongeth 2Chr 25:21
a Beth-shemesh, and brought him to 2Chr 25:23
in Jerusalem *a* the corner gate 2Chr 26:9 5921
a the valley gate, and *a* the 2Chr 26:9 5921
A that time did king Ahaz send 2Chr 28:16
the house of the LORD *a* Jerusalem 2Chr 30:1
could not keep it *a* that time 2Chr 30:3
LORD God of Israel *a* Jerusalem 2Chr 30:5
there assembled *a* Jerusalem much 2Chr 30:13
a Jerusalem kept the feast of 2Chr 30:21
a the commandment of Hezekiah the 2Chr 31:13
all Judah that were *a* Jerusalem 2Chr 32:9
did him honour *a* his death 2Chr 32:33
the entering in *a* the fish gate 2Chr 33:14
the porters waited *a* every gate 2Chr 35:15
kept the passover *a* that time 2Chr 35:17
And the archers shot *a* king Josiah 2Chr 35:23
of Egypt put him down *a* Jerusalem 2Chr 36:3
put them in his temple *a* Babylon 2Chr 36:7
to build him an house *a* Jerusalem Ezr 1:2
of the LORD which is *a* Jerusalem Ezr 2:68
unto the house of God *a* Jerusalem Ezr 3:8
side the river, and *a* such a time Ezr 4:10
side the river, and *a* such a time Ezr 4:11
river, Peace, and *a* such a time Ezr 4:17
house of God which is *a* Jerusalem Ezr 4:24
house of God which is *a* Jerusalem Ezr 5:2
A the same time came to them Ezr 5:3
house, which is there *a* Babylon Ezr 5:17
this house of God *a* Jerusalem Ezr 5:17
And there was found *a* Achmetha Ezr 6:2
the house of God *a* Jerusalem Ezr 6:3
the temple which is *a* Jerusalem Ezr 6:5
the temple which is *a* Jerusalem Ezr 6:5
the priests which are *a* Jerusalem Ezr 6:9
house of God which is *a* Jerusalem Ezr 6:12
offered *a* the dedication of this Ezr 6:17
of God, which is *a* Jerusalem Ezr 6:18
perfect peace, and *a* such a time Ezr 7:12
the chief *a* the place Casiphia Ezr 8:17
a the place Casiphia, that they Ezr 8:17
a the river of Ahava, that we Ezr 8:21 5921
a Jerusalem, in the chambers of Ezr 8:29
weight was written *a* that time Ezr 8:34
a the words of the God of Israel Ezr 9:4
a the evening sacrifice I arose Ezr 9:5
of those that tremble *a* the Ezr 10:3
our cities come *a* appointed times Ezr 10:14
put in my heart to do *a* Jerusalem Neh 2:12
armoury *a* the turning of the wall Neh 3:19
Likewise *a* the same time said I Neh 4:22
there were *a* my table an hundred Neh 5:17 5921
(though *a* that time I had not set Neh 6:1 5704
to preach of thee *a* Jerusalem Neh 6:7
of them which came up *a* the first Neh 7:5
a their pleasure, and we are in Neh 9:37
a times appointed year by year, Neh 10:34
of the people dwelt *a* Jerusalem Neh 11:1
themselves to dwell *a* Jerusalem Neh 11:2
a Jerusalem dwelt certain of the Neh 11:4
a Jerusalem were four hundred Neh 11:6
overseer also of the Levites *a* Neh 11:22
was *a* the king's hand in all Neh 11:24
of Judah dwelt *a* Kirjath-arba Neh 11:25
a Dibon, and in the villages Neh 11:25
a Jekabzeel, and in the villages Neh 11:25
a Jeshua, and *a* Moladah, and *a* Neh 11:26
a Hazar-shual, and *a* Beer-sheba, Neh 11:27
a Ziklag, and *a* Mekonah, and in Neh 11:28
a En-rimmon, and *a* Zareah, and *a* Neh 11:29
a Lachish, and the fields thereof, Neh 11:30
a Azekah, and in the villages Neh 11:30
from Geba dwelt *a* Michmash Neh 11:31
a Anathoth, Nob, Ananiah, Neh 11:32
a the thresholds of the gates Neh 12:25
a the dedication of the wall of Neh 12:27 5921
a the fountain gate, which was Neh 12:37
a the going up of the wall, above Neh 12:37
a that time were some appointed Neh 12:44
this time was not I *a* Jerusalem Neh 13:6
of my servants set I *a* the gates Neh 13:19 5921
a times appointed, and for the Neh 13:31
queen Vashti refused to come *a* Est 1:12
given *a* Shushan to destroy them Est 4:8
holdest thy peace *a* this time Est 4:14
unto Esther *a* the banquet of wine Est 5:6
the Jew sitting *a* the king's gate Est 5:13
that sitteth *a* the king's gate Est 6:10
second day *a* the banquet of wine Est 7:2
my life be given me *a* my petition Est 7:3
and my people *a* my request Est 7:3
the king, and fell down *a* his feet Est 8:3 6440
a that time in the third month Est 8:9
was given *a* Shushan the palace Est 8:14
and the decree was given *a* Shushan Est 9:14
slew three hundred men *a* Shushan Est 9:15
But the Jews that were *a* Shushan Est 9:18
we receive good *a* the hand of God Job 2:10
then had I been *a* rest, Job 3:13
and there the weary be *a* rest Job 3:17
A destruction and famine thou Job 5:22
field shall be *a* peace with thee Job 5:23
he will laugh *a* the trial of the Job 9:23
the thought of him that is *a* ease Job 12:5
and what do thy eyes wink *a* Job 15:12
of darkness is ready *a* his hand Job 15:23
you, and shake mine head *a* you Job 16:4
I was *a* ease, but he hath broken Job 16:12
men shall be astonied *a* this Job 17:8 5921
shall be ready *a* his side Job 18:12
him shall be astonied *a* his day Job 18:20 5921
that he shall stand *a* the latter Job 19:25
rejoice *a* the sound of the organ Job 21:12
strength, being wholly *a* ease Job 21:23
thyself with him, and be *a* peace Job 22:21
am I troubled *a* his presence Job 23:15
and are astonished *a* his reproof Job 26:11
Men shall clap their hands *a* him Job 27:23 5921
and kept silence *a* my counsel Job 29:21 3926
laid wait *a* my neighbour's door Job 31:9 5921
If I rejoiced *a* the destruction Job 31:29
shall be troubled *a* midnight Job 34:20
A this also my heart trembleth, Job 37:1
He mocketh *a* fear, and is not Job 39:22
the eagle mount up *a* thy command Job 39:27 5291
cast down even *a* the sight of him Job 41:9
him that layeth *a* him cannot hold Job 41:26
he laugheth *a* the shaking of a Job 41:29
unto him that was *a* peace with me Ps 7:4
fall and perish *a* thy presence Ps 9:3
his enemies, he puffeth *a* them Ps 10:5
shoot *a* the upright in heart Ps 11:2
from him that puffeth *a* him Ps 12:5
because he is *a* my right hand Ps 16:8
a thy right hand there are Ps 16:11
A the brightness that was before Ps 18:12
were discovered *a* thy rebuke Ps 18:15
a the blast of the breath of thy Ps 18:15
His soul shall dwell *a* ease Ps 25:13
Song *a* the dedication of the Ps 30:*t*
give thanks *a* the remembrance of Ps 30:4
I will bless the LORD *a* all times Ps 34:1
come upon him *a* unawares Ps 35:8
together that rejoice *a* mine hurt Ps 35:26
The LORD shall laugh *a* him Ps 37:13
verily every man *a* his best state Ps 39:5
hold not thy peace *a* my tears Ps 39:12 413
Deep calleth unto deep *a* the Ps 42:7
and fear, and shall laugh *a* him Ps 52:6 5921
would I fly away, and be *a* rest Ps 55:6
a noon, will I pray, and cry aloud Ps 55:17
such as be *a* peace with him Ps 55:20
They return *a* evening Ps 59:6
thou, O LORD, shalt laugh *a* them Ps 59:8
a evening let them return Ps 59:14
Trust in him *a* all times Ps 62:8
may shoot in secret *a* the perfect Ps 64:4
suddenly do they shoot *a* him Ps 64:4
shall shoot *a* them with an arrow Ps 64:7
parts are afraid *a* thy tokens Ps 65:8
perish *a* the presence of God Ps 68:2
dropped *a* the presence of God Ps 68:8
was moved *a* the presence of God Ps 68:8
she that tarried *a* home divided Ps 68:12
Because of thy temple *a* Jerusalem Ps 68:29 5921
For I was envious *a* the foolish Ps 73:3
work thereof *a* once with axes Ps 74:6 3162
A thy rebuke, O God of Jacob, Ps 76:6
they perish *a* the rebuke of thy Ps 80:16
I proved thee *a* the waters of Ps 81:7 5291
as to Jabin, *a* the brook of Kison Ps 83:9
Which perished *a* En-dor Ps 83:10
that wasteth *a* noonday Ps 91:6
A thousand shall fall *a* thy side Ps 91:7
ten thousand *a* thy right hand Ps 91:7
wax *a* the presence of the LORD Ps 97:5
a the presence of the LORD of the Ps 97:5
give thanks *a* the remembrance of Ps 97:12
God, and worship *a* his footstool Ps 99:5
God, and worship *a* his holy hill Ps 99:9
A thy rebuke they fled Ps 104:7 4480
a the voice of thy thunder they Ps 104:7 4480
bind his princes *a* his pleasure Ps 105:22
doeth righteousness *a* all times Ps 106:3
a the sea, even *a* the Red sea Ps 106:7 5921

him also *a* the waters of strife Ps 106:32 5921
man, and are *a* their wit's end Ps 107:27
let Satan stand *a* his right hand Ps 109:6 5921
For he shall stand *a* the right Ps 109:31
Sit thou *a* my right hand, until I Ps 110:1
The LORD *a* thy right hand shall Ps 110:5 5921
a the presence of the Lord, *a* Ps 114:7
sore *a* me that I might fall Ps 118:13
unto thy judgments *a* all times Ps 119:20
And I will walk *a* liberty Ps 119:45
A midnight I will rise to give Ps 119:62
I rejoice *a* thy word, as one that Ps 119:162 5921
scorning of those that are *a* ease Ps 123:4
Lo, we heard of it *a* Ephratah Ps 132:6
we will worship *a* his footstool Ps 132:7
Zion, which dwelleth *a* Jerusalem Ps 135:21
are scattered *a* the grave's mouth Ps 141:7
Turn you *a* my reproof Prov 1:23
But ye have set *a* nought all my Prov 1:25 6544
I also will laugh *a* your calamity Prov 1:26
they know not *a* what they stumble Prov 4:19
And thou mourn *a* the last, when Prov 5:11
breasts satisfy thee *a* all times Prov 5:19
For *a* the window of my house I Prov 7:6
and lieth in wait *a* every corner Prov 7:12 681
For the goodman is not *a* home Prov 7:19
him, and will come home *a* the day Prov 7:20
She crieth *a* the gates, *a* the Prov 8:3 3027
a the coming in *a* the doors Prov 8:3
me, watching daily *a* my gates Prov 8:34 5921
waiting *a* the posts of my doors Prov 8:34
For she sitteth *a* the door of her Prov 9:14
Fools make a mock *a* sin Prov 14:9
the wicked *a* the gates of the Prov 14:19
enemies to be *a* peace with him Prov 16:7 5921
he that is glad *a* calamities Prov 17:5
A friend loveth *a* all times Prov 17:17
be gotten hastily *a* the beginning Prov 20:21
his ears *a* the cry of the poor Prov 21:13
They that tarry long *a* the wine Prov 23:30 5921
A the last it biteth like a Prov 23:32
be thou envious *a* the wicked Prov 24:19
in his ways shall fall *a* once Prov 28:18
him become his son *a* the length Prov 29:21
The eye that mocketh *a* his father Prov 30:17
should God be angry *a* thy voice Eccl 5:6 5921
province, marvel not *a* the matter Eccl 5:8 5921
man's heart is *a* his right hand Eccl 10:2
but a fool's heart *a* his left Eccl 10:2
he shall rise up *a* the voice of Eccl 12:4
pitcher be broken *a* the fountain Eccl 12:6 5921
or the wheel broken *a* the cistern Eccl 12:6 413
makest thy flock to rest *a* noon Song 1:7
the king sitteth *a* his table Song 1:12
he looketh forth *a* the windows Song 2:9 4480
a our gates are all manner of Song 7:13 5921
had a vineyard *a* Baal-hamon Song 8:11
hath required this *a* your hand Is 1:12
restore thy judges as *a* the first Is 1:26
counsellors as *a* the beginning Is 1:26
a the voice of him that cried Is 6:4
a the end of the conduit of the Is 7:3 413
vines *a* a thousand silverlings Is 7:23
when *a* the first he lightly Is 9:1
of Midian *a* the rock of Oreb Is 10:26
a Michmash he hath laid up his Is 10:28
taken up their lodging *a* Geba Is 10:29
shall he remain *a* Nob that day Is 10:32
for the day of the LORD is *a* hand Is 13:6 7138
shall be amazed one *a* another Is 13:8 413
The whole earth is *a* rest Is 14:7
Yea, the fir trees rejoice *a* thee Is 14:8
thee to meet thee *a* thy coming Is 14:9
shall be *a* the fords of Arnon Is 16:2
for the extortioner is *a* an end Is 16:4
A that day shall a man look to Is 17:7
behold *a* eveningtide trouble Is 17:14
shall be moved *a* his presence Is 19:1
a pillar *a* the border thereof to Is 19:19 681
A the same time spake the LORD by Is 20:2
I was bowed down *a* the hearing of Is 21:3
I was dismayed *a* the seeing of it Is 21:3
themselves in array *a* the gate Is 22:7
As *a* the report concerning Egypt, Is 23:5
pained *a* the report of Tyre Is 23:5
for their envy *a* the people Is 26:11
in the holy mount *a* Jerusalem Is 27:13
and with hell are we *a* agreement Is 28:15
it shall be *a* an instant suddenly Is 29:5
and have not asked *a* my mouth Is 30:2
For his princes were *a* Zoan Is 30:4
cometh suddenly *a* an instant Is 30:13
shall flee *a* the rebuke of one Is 30:17 6440
a the rebuke of five shall ye Is 30:17 6440
shall dwell in Zion *a* Jerusalem Is 30:19
unto thee *a* the voice of thy cry Is 30:19
Rise up, ye women that are *a* ease Is 32:9
Tremble, ye women that are *a* ease Is 32:11
A the noise of the tumult the Is 33:3
a the lifting up of thyself the Is 33:3
hath shaken her head *a* thee Is 37:22
and returned, and dwelt *a* Nineveh Is 37:37
A that time Merodach-baladan, the Is 39:1
I will destroy and devour *a* once Is 42:14 3162
shall not be a coal to warm *a* Is 47:14
Is my hand shortened *a* all Is 50:2
a my rebuke I dry up the sea, I Is 50:2
which hast drunk *a* the hand of Is 51:17
they lie *a* the head of all the Is 51:20
As many were astonied *a* thee Is 52:14
shall shut their mouths *a* him Is 52:15
we stumble *a* noonday as in the Is 59:10
shall be nursed *a* thy side Is 60:4 5921
down *a* the soles of thy feet Is 60:14 5921
might flow down *a* thy presence Is 64:1
may tremble *a* thy presence Is 64:2
flowed down *a* thy presence Is 64:3
spirit, and trembleth *a* my word Is 66:2 5921
LORD, ye that tremble *a* his word Is 66:5 413
or shall a nation be born *a* once Is 66:8
a the entering of the gates of Jer 1:15
be not dismayed *a* their faces Jer 1:17
a this, and be horribly afraid, be Jer 2:12 5921
up the wind *a* her pleasure Jer 2:24
A that time they shall call Jer 3:17
it shall come to pass *a* that day Jer 4:9
A that time shall it be said to Jer 4:11
I am pained *a* my very heart Jer 4:19
down *a* the presence of the LORD Jer 4:26
will ye not tremble *a* my presence Jer 5:22
arise, and let us go up *a* noon Jer 6:4
nay, they were not *a* all ashamed Jer 6:15
a the time that I visit them they Jer 6:15
that enter in *a* these gates to Jer 7:2
where I set my name *a* the first Jer 7:12
A that time, saith the LORD, they Jer 8:1
nay, they were not *a* all ashamed Jer 8:12
the whole land trembled *a* the Jer 8:16
be not dismayed *a* the signs of Jer 10:2
the heathen are dismayed *a* them Jer 10:2
a his wrath the earth shall Jer 10:10
of the land *a* this once, and will Jer 10:18
them *a* all in the time of their Jer 11:12
the young men a spoiler *a* noonday Jer 15:8
a his end shall be a fool Jer 17:11
even entering in *a* the gates of Jer 17:27
A what instant I shall speak Jer 18:7
a what instant I shall speak Jer 18:9
and the shouting *a* noontide Jer 20:16
Am I a God *a* hand, saith the LORD Jer 23:23
not profit this people *a* all Jer 23:32
wine cup of this fury *a* my hand Jer 25:15
took I the cup *a* the LORD's hand Jer 25:17
the cup *a* thine hand to drink Jer 25:28
be *a* that day from one end of the Jer 25:33
all Judah put him *a* all to death Jer 26:19
a Jerusalem, go not to Babylon Jer 27:18
a Babylon I will visit you Jer 29:10
the people that are *a* Jerusalem Jer 29:25
A the same time, saith the LORD, Jer 31:1
shall not sorrow any more *a* all Jer 31:12
made thee a name, as *a* this day Jer 32:20 5704
will build them, as *a* the first Jer 33:7
as *a* the first, saith the LORD Jer 33:11
a that time, will I cause the Jer 33:15
the people which were *a* Jerusalem Jer 34:8
A the end of seven years let ye Jer 34:14
set *a* liberty *a* their pleasure Jer 34:16
so we dwell *a* Jerusalem Jer 35:11
a the entry of the new gate of Jer 36:10
write all these words *a* his mouth Jer 36:17
wrote *a* the mouth of Jeremiah Jer 36:27
and fields *a* the same time Jer 39:10
I will dwell *a* Mizpah to serve Jer 40:10
a Mizpah, and the Chaldeans that Jer 41:3
which is *a* the entry of Pharaoh's Jer 43:9
of Egypt, which dwell *a* Migdol Jer 44:1
a Tahpanhes, and *a* Noph, and in Jer 44:1
wasted and desolate, as *a* this day Jer 44:6
an inhabitant, as *a* this day Jer 44:22
happened unto you, as *a* this day Jer 44:23
in a book *a* the mouth of Jeremiah Jer 45:1
a ease, and none shall make him Jer 46:27
A the noise of the stamping of Jer 47:3
a the rushing of his chariots, and Jer 47:3
a the rumbling of his wheels, the Jer 47:3
Moab hath been *a* ease from his Jer 48:11
a that day shall be as the heart Jer 48:41
shall hiss *a* all the plagues Jer 49:17 5921
The earth is moved *a* the noise of Jer 49:21
a the cry the noise thereof was Jer 49:21
a that day shall the heart of the Jer 49:22
grown fat as the heifer *a* grass Jer 50:11
and hiss *a* all her plagues Jer 50:13 5921
ye that bend the bow, shoot *a* her Jer 50:14 413
A the noise of the taking of Jer 50:46
that his city is taken *a* one end Jer 51:31
so *a* Babylon shall fall the slain Jer 51:49
her, and did mock *a* her sabbaths Lam 1:7 5921
a home there is as death Lam 1:20
pass by clap their hands *a* thee Lam 2:15 5921
wag their head *a* the daughter of Lam 2:15 5921
ear *a* my breathing, *a* my cry Lam 3:56
nor be dismayed *a* their looks Eze 2:6
neither be dismayed *a* their looks Eze 3:9
them of the captivity *a* Tel-abib Eze 3:15
it came to pass *a* the end of Eze 3:16
hear the word *a* my mouth, and give Eze 3:17
blood will I require *a* thine hand Eze 3:18
blood will I require *a* thine hand Eze 3:20
behold northward *a* the gate of Eze 8:5
a the door of the temple of the Eze 8:16
and begin *a* my sanctuary Eze 9:6
Then they began *a* the ancient men Eze 9:6
every one stood *a* the door of the Eze 10:19
behold *a* the door of the gate Eze 11:1
go forth *a* even in their sight Eze 12:4
unto them, The days are *a* hand Eze 12:23 7196
I be enquired of *a* all by them Eze 14:3
salted *a* all, nor swaddled *a* all Eze 16:4
place *a* every head of the way Eze 16:25 413
that dwell *a* thy left hand Eze 16:46 5921
that dwelleth *a* thy right hand, Eze 16:46
as *a* the time of thy reproach of Eze 16:57
Have I any pleasure *a* all that Eze 18:23
into your mind shall not be *a* all Eze 20:32
choose it *a* the head of the way Eze 21:19
stood *a* the parting of the way Eze 21:21 413
a the head of the two ways, to Eze 21:21
A his right hand was the Eze 21:22
I have smitten mine hand *a* thy Eze 22:13 413
a thy blood which hath been in Eze 22:13 5921
being *a* ease was with her Eze 23:42
and *a* even my wife died Eze 24:18
thy walls shall shake *a* the noise Eze 26:10
shake *a* the sound of thy fall Eze 26:15
and shall tremble *a* every moment Eze 26:16
moment, and be astonished *a* thee Eze 26:16
shall be troubled *a* thy departure Eze 26:18
situate *a* the entry of the sea Eze 27:3 5921
The suburbs shall shake *a* the Eze 27:28
isles shall be astonished *a* thee Eze 27:35 5921
the people shall hiss *a* thee Eze 27:36 5921
people shall be astonished *a* thee Eze 28:19 5921
all their loins to be *a* a stand Eze 29:7
A the end of forty years will I Eze 29:13
A Tehaphnehes also the day shall Eze 30:18
to shake *a* the sound of his fall Eze 31:16
make many people amazed *a* thee Eze 32:10
they shall tremble *a* every moment Eze 32:10
I require *a* the watchman's hand Eze 33:6
shalt hear the word *a* my mouth Eze 33:7
blood will I require *a* thine hand Eze 33:8
require my flock *a* their hand Eze 34:10
As thou didst rejoice *a* the Eze 35:15
for they are *a* hand to come Eze 36:8 7126
unto you than *a* your beginnings Eze 36:11
into two kingdoms any more *a* all Eze 37:22
that *a* the same time shall things Eze 38:10
I will go to them that are *a* rest Eze 38:11
it shall come to pass *a* the same Eze 38:18
earth, shall shake *a* my presence Eze 38:20
be filled *a* my table with horses Eze 39:20 5921
a the side without, as one goeth Eze 40:40 413
which was *a* the porch of the gate Eze 40:40
which was *a* the side of the north Eze 40:44 413
one *a* the side of the east gate Eze 40:44 413
a the end toward the west was Eze 41:12
having charge *a* the gates of the Eze 44:11 413
that when they enter in *a* the Eze 44:17 413
they shall come *a* no dead person Eze 44:25 413
he shall worship *a* the threshold Eze 46:2 5921
of the land shall worship *a* the Eze 46:3
which was *a* the side of the gate, Eze 46:19 5921
a the south side of the altar Eze 47:1
a the bank of the river were very Eze 47:7 413
a the south side southward, the Eze 48:28 413
a the east side four thousand and Eze 48:32 413
a the south side four thousand and Eze 48:33
A the west side four thousand and Eze 48:34
that *a* the end thereof they might Dan 1:5
a the end of ten days their Dan 1:15
Now *a* the end of the days that Dan 1:18
asked such things *a* any magician Dan 2:10
That *a* what time ye hear the Dan 3:5
Therefore *a* that time, when all Dan 3:7
Wherefore *a* that time certain Dan 3:8
Now if ye be ready that *a* what Dan 3:15
was *a* rest in mine house, and Dan 4:4
But *a* the last Daniel came in Dan 4:8 5706
A the end of twelve months he Dan 4:29
And *a* the end of the days I Dan 4:34
A the same time my reason Dan 4:36
of God which was *a* Jerusalem Dan 5:3
they came *a* the bottom of the den Dan 6:24
appeared unto me *a* the first Dan 8:1
that I was *a* Shushan in the Dan 8:2
for *a* the time of the end shall Dan 8:17
for *a* the time appointed the end Dan 8:19
and I was astonished *a* the vision Dan 8:27 5921
confusion of faces, as *a* this day Dan 9:7
gotten thee renown, as *a* this day Dan 9:15
in the vision *a* the beginning Dan 9:21
A the beginning of thy Dan 9:23
neither did I anoint myself *a* all Dan 10:3
they shall speak lies *a* one table Dan 11:27 5921
end shall be *a* the time appointed Dan 11:27
A the time appointed he shall Dan 11:29
a the time of the end shall the Dan 11:40
the king of the south push *a* him Dan 11:40
Ethiopians shall be *a* his steps Dan 11:43
a that time shall Michael stand Dan 12:1
a that time thy people shall be Dan 12:1
stand in thy lot *a* the end of the Dan 12:13
it shall come to pass *a* that day Hos 1:5
And it shall be *a* that day Hos 2:16
people ask counsel *a* their stocks Hos 4:12
cry aloud *a* Beth-aven, after thee Hos 5:8
in the fig tree *a* her first time Hos 9:10
none *a* all would exalt him Hos 11:7 3162
for the day of the LORD is *a* hand Joel 1:15 7138
cometh, for it is nigh *a* hand Joel 2:1
they shall enter in *a* the windows Joel 2:9 1157
and have taken nothing *a* all Amos 3:5
Publish in the palaces *a* Ashdod Amos 3:9
And ye shall go out *a* the breaches Amos 4:3
every cow *a* that which is before Amos 4:3
a Gilgal multiply transgression Amos 4:4
to them that are *a* ease in Zion Amos 6:1
not again any more *a* Beth-el Amos 7:13
cause the sun to go down *a* noon Amos 8:9
the men that were *a* peace with Obad 7
it not *a* Gath, weep ye not *a* all Mic 1:10
his face from them *a* that time Mic 3:4
be confounded *a* all their might Mic 7:16
will not *a* all acquit the wicked Nah 1:3
The mountains quake *a* him Nah 1:5
earth is burned *a* his presence Nah 1:5
a the top of all the streets Nah 3:10
And they shall scoff *a* the kings Hab 1:10
but *a* the end it shall speak, and Hab 2:3
proud man, neither keepeth *a* home Hab 2:5

there is no breath *a* all in the Hab 2:19
coals went forth *a* his feet Hab 3:5
a the light of thine arrows they Hab 3:11
a the shining of thy glittering Hab 3:11
my lips quivered *a* the voice Hab 3:16
Hold thy peace *a* the presence of Zeph 1:7
for the day of the LORD is *a* hand Zeph 1:7
it shall come to pass *a* that time Zeph 1:12
drive out Ashdod *a* the noonday Zeph 2:4
a that time I will undo all that Zeph 3:19
A that time will I bring you Zeph 3:20
earth sitteth still, and is *a* rest Zec 1:11
with the heathen that are *a* ease Zec 1:15
Satan standing *a* his right hand Zec 3:1 5921
for they are men wondered *a* Zec 3:8
did ye *a* all fast unto me, even Zec 7:5
price that I was prised *a* of them Zec 11:13
them *a* that day shall be as David Zec 12:8
that *a* evening time it shall be Zec 14:7
also shall fight *a* Jerusalem Zec 14:14
I accept an offering *a* your hand Mal 1:10
and ye have snuffed *a* it, saith Mal 1:13
should seek the law *a* his mouth Mal 2:7
caused many to stumble *a* the law Mal 2:8
it with good will *a* your hand Mal 2:13
the kingdom of heaven is *a* hand Mt 3:2 *1448*
lest *a* any time thou dash thy Mt 4:6 *3379*
the kingdom of heaven is *a* hand Mt 4:17 *1448*
lest *a* any time the adversary Mt 5:25 *3379*
I say unto you, Swear not *a* all Mt 5:34 *2527*
any man will sue thee *a* the law Mt 5:40 *2919*
Enter ye in *a* the strait gate Mt 7:13 *1223*
were astonished *a* his doctrine Mt 7:28 *1909*
my servant lieth *a* home sick of Mt 8:6 *1722*
sitting *a* the receipt of custom Mt 9:9 *1909*
as Jesus sat *a* meat in the house, Mt 9:10 *345*
The kingdom of heaven is *a* hand Mt 10:7 *1448*
For I am come to set a man *a* Mt 10:35 *1369*
Sidon *a* the day of judgment, than Mt 11:22 *1722*
A that time Jesus answered and Mt 11:25 *1722*
A that time Jesus went on the Mt 12:1 *1722*
because they repented *a* the Mt 12:41 *1519*
lest *a* any time they should see Mt 13:15 *3379*
So shall it be *a* the end of the Mt 13:49 *1722*
A that time Herod the tetrarch Mt 14:1 *1722*
and them which sat with him *a* meat Mt 14:9 *4873*
that whatsoever entereth in *a* the Mt 15:17 *1519*
and cast them down *a* Jesus' feet Mt 15:30 *3844*
A the same time came the Mt 18:1 *1722*
fell down *a* his feet, and besought Mt 18:29 *1519*
that he which made them *a* the Mt 19:4 *575*
were astonished *a* his doctrine Mt 22:33 *1909*
love the uppermost rooms *a* feasts Mt 23:6 *1722*
guides, which strain *a* a gnat Mt 23:24 *1368*
that it is near, even *a* the doors Mt 24:33 *1909*
shall be grinding *a* the mill Mt 24:41 *1722*
a midnight there was a cry made, Mt 25:6
then *a* my coming I should have Mt 25:27
it on his head, as he sat *a* meat Mt 26:7 *345*
Master saith, My time is *a* hand Mt 26:18 *1451*
I will keep the passover *a* thy Mt 26:18 *4314*
behold, the hour is *a* hand Mt 26:45 *1448*
he is *a* hand that doth betray me Mt 26:46 *1448*
A the last came two false Mt 26:60
Now *a* that feast the governor was Mt 27:15 *2596*
and the kingdom of God is *a* hand Mk 1:15 *1448*
were astonished *a* his doctrine Mk 1:22 *1909*
a even, when the sun did set, Mk 1:32
was gathered together *a* the door Mk 1:33 *4314*
sitting *a* the receipt of custom Mk 2:14 *1909*
as Jesus sat *a* meat in his house, Mk 2:15 *2621*
lest *a* any time they should be Mk 4:12 *3379*
he saw him, he fell *a* his feet, Mk 5:22 *4314*
lieth *a* the point of death Mk 5:23
And they were offended *a* him Mk 6:3 *1722*
him, and came and fell *a* his feet Mk 7:25 *4314*
many things, and be set *a* nought Mk 9:12 *1847*
he was sad *a* that saying, and went Mk 10:22 *1909*
were astonished *a* his words Mk 10:24 *1909*
a the mount of Olives, he sendeth Mk 11:1 *4314*
was astonished *a* his doctrine Mk 11:18 *1909*
a the season he sent to the Mk 12:2
a him they cast stones, and Mk 12:4
And they marvelled *a* him Mk 12:17 *1909*
and the uppermost rooms *a* feasts Mk 12:39 *1722*
that it is nigh, even *a* the doors Mk 13:29 *1909*
a even, or *a* midnight, or *a* the Mk 13:35
Simon the leper, as he sat *a* meat Mk 14:3 *2621*
he that betrayeth me is *a* hand Mk 14:42 *1448*
and warmed himself *a* the fire Mk 14:54 *4314*
Now *a* that feast he released unto Mk 15:6 *2596*
a the ninth hour Jesus cried with Mk 15:34
sepulchre *a* the rising of the sun Mk 16:2
the eleven as they sat *a* meat Mk 16:14 *345*
without *a* the time of incense Lk 1:10
and many shall rejoice *a* his birth Lk 1:14 *1909*
she was troubled *a* his saying Lk 1:29 *1909*
a those things which were told Lk 2:18 *4012*
his mother marvelled *a* those Lk 2:33 *1909*
year *a* the feast of the passover Lk 2:41
astonished *a* his understanding Lk 2:47 *1909*
lest *a* any time thou dash thy Lk 4:11 *3379*
to set *a* liberty them that are Lk 4:18 *1722*
wondered *a* the gracious words Lk 4:22 *1909*
were astonished *a* his doctrine Lk 4:32 *1909*
nevertheless *a* thy word I will Lk 5:5 *1909*
it, he fell down *a* Jesus' knees Lk 5:8 *4363*
a the draught of the fishes which Lk 5:9 *1909*
sitting *a* the receipt of custom Lk 5:27 *1909*
these things, he marvelled *a* him Lk 7:9
a meat in the Pharisee's house Lk 7:37 *345*
stood *a* his feet behind him Lk 7:38 *3844*
they that sat *a* meat with him Lk 7:49 *345*
could not come *a* him for the Lk 8:19 *1519*
they arrived *a* the country of the Lk 8:26 *1519*
sitting *a* the feet of Jesus, Lk 8:35 *3844*
and he fell down *a* Jesus' feet Lk 8:41 *3844*
he should accomplish *a* Jerusalem Lk 9:31 *1722*
they were all amazed *a* the mighty Lk 9:43 *1909*
one *a* all things which Jesus did Lk 9:43 *1909*
which are *a* home *a* my house Lk 9:61 *1519*
which are *a* home *a* my house Lk 9:61 *1519*
Sidon *a* the judgment, than for Lk 10:14 *1722*
a Levite, when he was *a* the place Lk 10:32 *2596*
which also sat *a* Jesus' feet Lk 10:39 *3844*
and shall go unto him *a* midnight Lk 11:5 *3317*
for they repented *a* the preaching Lk 11:32 *1519*
a an hour when ye think not Lk 12:40
a an hour when he is not aware, Lk 12:46 *1722*
There were present *a* that season Lk 13:1 *1722*
to enter in *a* the strait gate Lk 13:24 *1223*
without, and to knock *a* the door Lk 13:25
of them that sit *a* meat with thee Lk 14:10 *4873*
a the resurrection of the just Lk 14:14 *1722*
sat *a* meat with him heard these Lk 14:15 *4873*
sent his servant *a* supper time to Lk 14:17
neither transgressed I *a* any time Lk 15:29 *3763*
which was laid *a* his gate Lk 16:20 *4314*
fell down on his face *a* his feet Lk 17:16 *3844*
to day I must abide *a* thy house Lk 19:5 *1722*
that *a* my coming I might have Lk 19:23
a the mount called the mount of Lk 19:29 *4314*
in the which *a* your entering ye Lk 19:30 *1531*
even now *a* the descent of the Lk 19:37 *4314*
a least in this thy day, the Lk 19:42 *1065*
a the season he sent a servant to Lk 20:10 *1722*
and they marvelled *a* his answer Lk 20:26 *1909*
even Moses shewed *a* the bush Lk 20:37 *1909*
not ask him any question *a* all Lk 20:40
and the chief rooms *a* feasts Lk 20:46 *1722*
that summer is now nigh *a* hand Lk 21:30 *1451*
the kingdom of God is nigh *a* hand Lk 21:31 *1451*
lest *a* any time your hearts be Lk 21:34 *3379*
a night he went out, and abode in Lk 21:37 *3571*
greater, he that sitteth *a* meat Lk 22:27 *345*
is not he that sitteth *a* meat Lk 22:27 *345*
drink *a* my table in my kingdom, Lk 22:30 *1909*
And when he was *a* the place Lk 22:40 *1909*
also was *a* Jerusalem *a* that time Lk 23:7 *1722*
his men of war set him *a* nought Lk 23:11 *1848*
for before they were *a* enmity Lk 23:12 *1722*
release one unto them *a* the feast Lk 23:17 *2596*
And they cried out all *a* once Lk 23:18 *3826*
wondering in himself *a* that which Lk 24:12
which were early *a* the sepulchre Lk 24:22 *1909*
And beginning *a* Moses and all the Lk 24:27 *575*
as he sat *a* meat with them, he Lk 24:30 *2625*
nations, beginning *a* Jerusalem Lk 24:47 *575*
No man hath seen God *a* any time Jn 1:18 *4455*
Every man *a* the beginning doth Jn 2:10 *4412*
And the Jews' passover was *a* hand Jn 2:13 *1451*
was in Jerusalem *a* the passover Jn 2:23 *1722*
nor yet *a* Jerusalem, worship the Jn 4:21 *1722*
he did *a* Jerusalem *a* the feast Jn 4:45 *1722*
whose son was sick *a* Capernaum Jn 4:46 *1722*
for he was *a* the point of death Jn 4:47 *3195*
Yesterday *a* the seventh hour the Jn 4:52
knew that it was *a* the same hour Jn 4:53 *1722*
Now there is *a* Jerusalem by the Jn 5:2 *1722*
For an angel went down *a* a Jn 5:4 *2596*
Marvel not *a* this Jn 5:28
heard his voice *a* any time Jn 5:37 *4455*
immediately the ship was *a* the Jn 6:21 *1909*
raise it up again *a* the last day Jn 6:39 *1722*
will raise him up *a* the last day Jn 6:40
The Jews then murmured *a* him Jn 6:41 *4012*
will raise him up *a* the last day Jn 6:44
will raise him up *a* the last day Jn 6:54
that his disciples murmured *a* it Jn 6:61 *4012*
feast of tabernacles was *a* hand Jn 7:2 *1451*
the Jews sought him *a* the feast Jn 7:11 *1722*
are ye angry *a* me, because I have Jn 7:23
let him first cast a stone *a* her Jn 8:7 *1909*
beginning *a* the eldest, even unto Jn 8:9 *575*
took they up stones to cast *a* him Jn 8:59 *1909*
it was *a* Jerusalem the feast of Jn 10:22 *1722*
place where John *a* first baptized Jn 10:40
the resurrection *a* the last day Jn 11:24 *1722*
saw him, she fell down *a* his feet Jn 11:32 *1519*
unto them, Ye know nothing *a* all Jn 11:49 *3762*
Jews' passover was nigh *a* hand Jn 11:55 *1451*
that sat *a* the table with him Jn 12:2 *4873*
not his disciples *a* the first Jn 12:16 *4412*
came up to worship *a* the feast Jn 12:20 *1722*
Now no man *a* the table knew for Jn 13:28 *345*
A that day ye shall know that I Jn 14:20 *1722*
said not unto you *a* the beginning Jn 16:4 *1537*
A that day ye shall ask in my Jn 16:26 *1722*
But Peter stood *a* the door Jn 18:16 *4314*
I find in him no fault *a* all Jn 18:38
unto you one *a* the passover Jn 18:39 *1722*
have no power *a* all against me Jn 19:11
which *a* the first came to Jesus Jn 19:39
for the sepulchre was nigh *a* hand Jn 19:42 *1451*
without *a* the sepulchre weeping Jn 20:11 *4314*
the one *a* the head Jn 20:12 *4314*
and the other *a* the feet Jn 20:12 *1722*
Then the same day *a* evening Jn 20:19
disciples *a* the sea of Tiberias Jn 21:1 *1909*
leaned on his breast *a* supper Jn 21:20 *1722*
wilt thou *a* this time restore Acts 1:6 *1722*
unto all the dwellers *a* Jerusalem Acts 1:19
were dwelling *a* Jerusalem Jews Acts 2:5 *1722*
and all ye that dwell *a* Jerusalem Acts 2:14
the temple *a* the hour of prayer Acts 3:1 *1909*
whom they laid daily *a* the gate Acts 3:2 *4314*
alms *a* the Beautiful gate of the Acts 3:10 *1909*
amazement *a* that which had Acts 3:10 *1909*
of Israel, why marvel ye *a* this Acts 3:12 *1909*
gathered together *a* Jerusalem Acts 4:6 *1519*
was set *a* nought of you builders Acts 4:11 *1848*
commanded them not to speak *a* all Acts 4:18 *2527*
laid them down *a* the apostles' Acts 4:35 *3844*
laid it *a* the apostles' feet Acts 4:37 *3844*
laid it *a* the apostles' feet Acts 5:2 *3844*
buried thy husband are *a* the door Acts 5:9 *1909*
she down straightway *a* his feet Acts 5:10 *3844*
that *a* the least the shadow of Acts 5:15 *2579*
a the second time Joseph was made Acts 7:13 *1722*
would have set them *a* one again Acts 7:26 *1519*
Then fled Moses *a* this saying Acts 7:29 *1722*
saw it, he wondered *a* the sight Acts 7:31
clothes *a* a young man's feet Acts 7:58 *3844*
a that time there was a great Acts 8:1 *1722*
the church which was *a* Jerusalem Acts 8:1 *1722*
a Jerusalem heard that Samaria Acts 8:14 *1722*
began *a* the same scripture, and Acts 8:35 *575*
But Philip was found *a* Azotus Acts 8:40 *1519*
was a certain disciple *a* Damascus Acts 9:10 *1722*
done to thy saints *a* Jerusalem Acts 9:13 *1722*
disciples which were *a* Damascus Acts 9:19 *1722*
the Jews which dwelt *a* Damascus Acts 9:22 *1722*
how he had preached boldly *a* Acts 9:27 *1722*
in and going out *a* Jerusalem Acts 9:28 *1722*
to the saints which dwelt *a* Lydda Acts 9:32
And all that dwelt *a* Lydda Acts 9:35
Now there was *a* Joppa a certain Acts 9:36 *1722*
sheet knit *a* the four corners Acts 10:11
met him, and fell down *a* his feet Acts 10:25 *1909*
a the ninth hour I prayed in my Acts 10:30
a any time entered into my mouth Acts 11:8 3763
on them, as on us *a* the beginning Acts 11:15 *1722*
as Peter knocked *a* the door of Acts 12:13
was *a* Antioch certain prophets Acts 13:1 *1722*
And when they were *a* Salamis Acts 13:5 *1722*
being astonished *a* the doctrine Acts 13:12 *1909*
For they that dwell *a* Jerusalem Acts 13:27 *1722*
there sat a certain man *a* Lystra Acts 14:8 *1722*
how God *a* the first did visit the Acts 15:14
the brethren that were *a* Lystra Acts 16:2 *1722*
and elders which were *a* Jerusalem Acts 16:4 *1722*
a midnight Paul and Silas prayed, Acts 16:25 *2596*
God was preached of Paul *a* Berea Acts 17:13 *1722*
Paul waited for them *a* Athens Acts 17:16 *1722*
of this ignorance God winked *a* Acts 17:30
And when he had landed *a* Caesarea Acts 18:22 *1519*
born *a* Alexandria, an eloquent Acts 18:24
that, while Apollos was *a* Corinth Acts 19:1 *1722*
and Greeks also dwelling *a* Ephesus Acts 19:17
and hear, that not alone *a* Ephesus Acts 19:26
is in danger to be set *a* nought Acts 19:27 *1519*
before tarried for us *a* Troas Acts 20:5 *1722*
And when he met with us *a* Assos Acts 20:14 *1519*
the next day we arrived *a* Samos Acts 20:15 *1519*
a Samos, and tarried *a* Trogyllium Acts 20:15 *1722*
to be *a* Jerusalem the day of Acts 20:16 *1519*
have been with you *a* all seasons Acts 20:18
into Syria, and landed *a* Tyre Acts 21:3 *1519*
So shall the Jews *a* Jerusalem Acts 21:11 *1722*
but also to die *a* Jerusalem for Acts 21:13 *1519*
be *a* charges with them, that they Acts 21:24 *1159*
this city *a* the feet of Gamaliel Acts 22:3 *3844*
thou bear witness also *a* Rome Acts 23:11 *1519*
a the third hour of the night Acts 23:23 *575*
Paul should be kept *a* Caesarea Acts 25:4 *1722*
have I offended any thing *a* all Acts 25:8
I stand *a* Caesar's judgment seat, Acts 25:10 *1909*
whom, when I was *a* Jerusalem Acts 25:15 *1519*
a Festus' commandment Paul was Acts 25:23
both *a* Jerusalem, and also here, Acts 25:24 *1722*
which was *a* the first among mine Acts 26:4 *575*
among mine own nation *a* Jerusalem Acts 26:4 *1722*
A midday, O king, I saw in the Acts 26:13
a Jerusalem, and throughout all Acts 26:20
man might have been set *a* liberty Acts 26:32 *630*
the next day we touched *a* Sidon Acts 27:3 *1519*
landing *a* Syracuse, we tarried Acts 28:12 *1519*
if by any means now *a* length I Rom 1:10 *4218*
to you that are *a* Rome also Rom 1:15 *1722*
a this time his righteousness Rom 3:26 *1722*
He staggered not *a* the promise of Rom 4:20 *1519*
who is even *a* the right hand of Rom 8:34 *1722*
A this time will I come, and Sarah Rom 9:9 *2596*
For they stumbled *a* that Rom 9:32
Even so then *a* this present time Rom 11:5 *1722*
is far spent, the day is *a* hand Rom 13:12 *1448*
thou set *a* nought thy brother Rom 14:10 *1848*
poor saints which are *a* Jerusalem Rom 15:26 *1722*
of the church which is *a* Cenchrea Rom 16:1 *1722*
servant of the church *a* Cenchrea Rom *s* *1722*
church of God which is *a* Corinth 1Cor 1:2 *1722*
she is *a* liberty to be married to 1Cor 7:39 *1657*
sit *a* meat in the idol's temple 1Cor 8:10 *2621*
any time *a* his own charges 1Cor 9:7 *4218*
they which wait *a* the altar are 1Cor 9:13
man hunger, let him eat *a* home 1Cor 11:34 *1722*
say Amen *a* thy giving of thanks 1Cor 14:16 *1909*
or *a* the most by three, and that 1Cor 14:27
them ask their husbands *a* home 1Cor 14:35 *1722*
five hundred brethren *a* once 1Cor 15:6 *2178*
that are Christ's *a* his coming 1Cor 15:23 *1722*
dead, if the dead rise not *a* all 1Cor 15:29 *3654*
have fought with beasts *a* Ephesus 1Cor 15:32 *1722*
of an eye, *a* the last trump 1Cor 15:52 *1722*
But I will tarry *a* Ephesus until 1Cor 16:8 *1722*
but his will was not *a* all to 1Cor 16:12 *3843*
not *a* all to come *a* this time 1Cor 16:12 *3568*
church of God which is *a* Corinth 2Cor 1:1 *1722*
While we look not *a* the things 2Cor 4:18 *4648*
but *a* the things which are not 2Cor 4:18 *4648*
whilst we are *a* home in the body, 2Cor 5:6 *1722*
that now *a* this time your 2Cor 8:14 *1722*

ye have not injured me *a* all Gal 4:12 *3762*
the gospel unto you *a* the first Gal 4:13
to the saints which are *a* Ephesus Eph 1:1 *1722*
set him *a* his own right hand in Eph 1:20 *1722*
That *a* that time ye were without Eph 2:12 *1722*
not *a* my tribulations for you Eph 3:13 *1722*
Christ Jesus which are *a* Philippi Phil 1:1 *1722*
That *a* the name of Jesus every Phil 2:10 *1722*
The Lord is *a* hand Phil 4:5 *1451*
that now *a* the last your care of Phil 4:10 *4218*
in Christ which are *a* Colosse Col 1:2 *1722*
for you, and for them *a* Laodicea Col 2:1 *1722*
a Philippi, we were bold in our 1Th 2:2 *1722*
For neither *a* any time used we 1Th 2:5 *4218*
Lord Jesus Christ *a* his coming 1Th 2:19 *1722*
it good to be left *a* Athens alone 1Th 3:1 *1722*
a the coming of our Lord Jesus 1Th 3:13 *1722*
be *a* peace among yourselves 1Th 5:13 *1722*
that the day of Christ is *a* hand 2Th 2:2 *1764*
you disorderly, working not *a* all 2Th 3:11 *3367*
thee to abide still *a* Ephesus 1Ti 1:3 *1722*
learn first to shew piety *a* home 1Ti 5:4
he ministered unto me *a* Ephesus 2Ti 1:18 *1722*
taken captive by him *a* his will 2Ti 2:26 *1519*
a Antioch, *a* Iconium, *a* Lystra 2Ti 3:11 *1722*
the dead *a* his appearing and his 2Ti 4:1 *2596*
time of my departure is *a* hand 2Ti 4:6 *2186*
judge, shall give me *a* that day 2Ti 4:8 *1722*
that I left *a* Troas with Carpus 2Ti 4:13 *1722*
A my first answer no man stood 2Ti 4:16 *1722*
Erastus abode *a* Corinth 2Ti 4:20 *1722*
have I left *a* Miletum sick 2Ti 4:20 *1722*
discreet, chaste, keepers *a* home Titus 2:5 *3626*
who *a* sundry times and in divers Heb 1:1
of the angels said he *a* any time Heb 1:5 *4218*
of the angels said he *a* any times Heb 1:13 *4218*
lest *a* any time we should let Heb 2:1 *3379*
which *a* the first began to be Heb 2:3
man gave attendance *a* the altar Heb 7:13
a all while the testator liveth Heb 9:17 *3379*
is set down *a* the right hand of Heb 12:2 *1722*
brother Timothy is set *a* liberty Heb 13:23 *630*
a the same place sweet water Jas 3:11 *1537*
glory *a* the appearing of Jesus 1Pet 1:7 *1722*
a the revelation of Jesus Christ 1Pet 1:13 *1722*
to them which stumble *a* the word 1Pet 2:8
the end of all things is *a* hand 1Pet 4:7 *1448*
must begin *a* the house of God 1Pet 4:17 *575*
and if it first begin *a* us 1Pet 4:17 *575*
The church that is *a* Babylon 1Pet 5:13 *1722*
and in him is no darkness *a* all 1Jn 1:5 *3762*
ashamed before him *a* his coming 1Jn 2:28 *1722*
No man hath seen God *a* any time 1Jn 4:12 *4455*
for the time is *a* hand Rev 1:3 *1451*
I fell *a* his feet as dead Rev 1:17 *4314*
I stand *a* the door, and knock Rev 3:20 *1909*
stood *a* the altar, having a Rev 8:3 *1909*
shalt find them no more *a* all Rev 18:14
and shall be found no more *a* all Rev 18:21
be heard no more *a* all in thee Rev 18:22
be heard no more *a* all in thee Rev 18:22
shall shine no more *a* all in thee Rev 18:23
be heard no more *a* all in thee Rev 18:23
blood of his servants *a* her hand Rev 19:2 *1537*
I fell *a* his feet to worship him Rev 19:10 *1710*
a the gates twelve angels, and Rev 21:12 *1909*
it shall not be shut *a* all by day Rev 21:25
for the time is *a* hand Rev 22:10 *1451*

ATAD (*a'-tad*) See ABEL-MIZRAIM. *A place east of the Jordan.*
came to the threshingfloor of *A* Gen 50:10 329
the mourning in the floor of *A* Gen 50:11 329

ATARAH (*at'-a-rah*) *A wife of Jerahmeel.*
another wife, whose name was *A* 1Chr 2:26 5851

ATAROTH (*at'-a-roth*) See ATAROTH-ADAR, ATROTH.
1. A city east of the Jordan.
A, and Dibon, and Jazer, and Nimrah, Num 32:3 5852
children of Gad built Dibon, and *A* Num 32:34 5852
2. A city in Ephraim.
unto the borders of Archi to *A* Josh 16:2 5852
And it went down from Janohah to *A*. Josh 16:7 5852
3. A city in Judah.
and the Netophathites, *A*, the 1Chr 2:54 5852

ATAROTH-ADAR (*at''-a-roth-a'-dar*) See ATAROTH-ADDAR. *A city on the border of Benjamin.*
and the border descended to *A* Josh 18:13 5853

ATAROTH-ADDAR (*at''-a-roth-ad'-dar*) See ATAROTH-ADAR. *Same as Ataroth-adar.*
on the east side was *A*, unto Josh 16:5 5853

ATE
a the sacrifices of the dead Ps 106:28 398
I *a* no pleasant bread, neither Dan 10:3 398
of the angel's hand, and *a* it up Rev 10:10 *2719*

ATER (*a'-tur*)
1. An ancestor of an exiled family.
The children of *A* of Hezekiah Ezr 2:16 333
The children of *A* of Hezekiah Neh 7:21 333
2. An exiled family who returned under Zerubbabel.
of Shallum, the children of *A* Ezr 2:42 333
of Shallum, the children of *A* Neh 7:45 333
3. An Israelite who sealed the covenant with Nehemiah.
A, Hizkijah, Azzur, Neh 10:17 333

ATHACH (*a'-thak*) *A city in Judah.*
and to them which were in *A* 1Sa 30:30 6269

ATHAIAH (*ath-a-i'-ah*) *A son of Uzziah*
A the son of Uzziah, the son of Neh 11:4 6265

ATHALIAH (*ath-a-li'-ah*)
1. Daughter of Jezebel.
And his mother's name was *A* 2Kin 8:26 6271
when *A* the mother of Ahaziah saw 2Kin 11:1 6271
nurse, in the bedchamber from *A* 2Kin 11:2 6271
A did reign over the land 2Kin 11:3 6271
when *A* heard the noise of the 2Kin 11:13 6271
A rent her clothes, and cried, 2Kin 11:14 6271
they slew *A* with the sword beside 2Kin 11:20 6271
also was *A* the daughter of Omri 2Chr 22:2 6271
But when *A* the mother of Ahaziah 2Chr 22:10 6271
of Ahaziah,) hid him from *A* 2Chr 22:11 6271
and *A* reigned over the land 2Chr 22:12 6271
Now when *A* heard the noise of the 2Chr 23:12 6271
Then *A* rent her clothes, and said, 2Chr 23:13 6271
they had slain *A* with the sword 2Chr 23:21 6271
For the sons of *A*, that wicked 2Chr 24:7 6271
2. A son of Jeroham.
and Shehariah, and *A* 1Chr 8:26 6271
3. Father of Jeshiah.
Jeshaiah the son of *A*, and with Ezr 8:7 6271

ATHENIANS (*a-the'-ne-uns*) *Citizens of Athens.*
(For all the *A* and strangers which Acts 17:21 *117*

ATHENS (*ath'-ens*) See ATHENIANS. *A city in Greece.*
conducted Paul brought him unto *A* Acts 17:15 *116*
while Paul waited for them at *A* Acts 17:16 *116*
Mars' hill, and said, Ye men of *A* Acts 17:22 *117*
these things Paul departed from *A* Acts 18:1 *116*
it good to be left at *A* alone 1Th 3:1 *116*
Thessalonians was written from *A* 1Th s *116*
Thessalonians was written from *A* 2Th s *116*

ATHIRST
And he was sore *a*, and called on Judg 15:18 6770
and when thou art *a*, go unto the Ruth 2:9 6770
when saw we thee an hungred, or *a* Mt 25:44 *1372*
I will give unto him that is *a* of Rev 21:6 *1372*
And let him that is *a* come Rev 22:17 *1372*

ATHLAI (*ath'-lahee*) *Married a foreign wife in exile.*
Jehohanan, Hananiah, Zabbai, and *A* Ezr 10:28 6270

ATONEMENT
things wherewith the *a* was made Ex 29:33 3722
bullock for a sin offering for *a* Ex 29:36 3725
when thou hast made an *a* for it Ex 29:36 3722
shalt make an *a* for the altar Ex 29:37 3722
Aaron shall make an *a* upon the Ex 30:10 3722
he make *a* upon it throughout your Ex 30:10 3722
to make an *a* for your souls Ex 30:15 3722
thou shalt take the *a* money of Ex 30:16 3725
to make an *a* for your souls Ex 30:16 3722
I shall make an *a* for your sin Ex 32:30 3722
for him to make *a* for him Lev 1:4 3722
priest shall make an *a* for them Lev 4:20 3722
the priest shall make an *a* for Lev 4:26 3722
priest shall make an *a* for him Lev 4:31 3722
an *a* for his sin that he hath Lev 4:35 3722
the priest shall make an *a* for Lev 5:6 3722
the priest shall make an *a* for Lev 5:10 3722
the priest shall make an *a* for Lev 5:13 3722
the priest shall make an *a* for Lev 5:16 3722
make an *a* for him concerning his Lev 5:18 3722
make an *a* for him before the LORD Lev 6:7 3722
the priest that maketh *a* Lev 7:7 3722
to do, to make an *a* for you Lev 8:34 3722
make an *a* for thyself, and for the Lev 9:7 3722
the people, and make an *a* for them Lev 9:7 3722
to make *a* for them before the Lev 10:17 3722
the LORD, and make an *a* for her Lev 12:7 3722
priest shall make an *a* for her Lev 12:8 3722
make an *a* for him before the LORD Lev 14:18 3722
make an *a* for him that is to be Lev 14:19 3722
priest shall make an *a* for him Lev 14:20 3722
to be waved, to make an *a* for him Lev 14:21 3722
to make an *a* for him before the Lev 14:29 3722
the priest shall make an *a* for Lev 14:31 3722
and make an *a* for the house Lev 14:53 3722
the priest shall make an *a* for Lev 15:15 3722
the priest shall make an *a* for Lev 15:30 3722
make an *a* for himself, and for his Lev 16:6 3722
the LORD, to make an *a* with him Lev 16:10 3722
and shall make an *a* for himself Lev 16:11 3722
he shall make an *a* for the holy Lev 16:16 3722
in to make an *a* in the holy place Lev 16:17 3722
and have made an *a* for himself Lev 16:17 3722
the LORD, and make an *a* for it Lev 16:18 3722
make an *a* for himself, and for the Lev 16:24 3722
in to make *a* in the holy place Lev 16:27 3722
the priest make an *a* for you Lev 16:30 3722
father's stead, shall make the *a* Lev 16:32 3722
he shall make an *a* for the holy Lev 16:33 3722
he shall make an *a* for the Lev 16:33 3722
shall make an *a* for the priests Lev 16:33 3722
to make an *a* for the children of Lev 16:34 3722
altar to make an *a* for your souls Lev 17:11 3722
that maketh an *a* for the soul Lev 17:11 3722
the priest shall make an *a* for Lev 19:22 3722
month there shall be a day of *a* Lev 23:27 3725
for it is a day of *a* Lev 23:28 3725
to make an *a* for you before the Lev 23:28 3722
in the day of *a* shall ye make the Lev 25:9 3725
beside the ram of the *a* Num 5:8 3725
whereby an *a* shall be made for Num 5:8 3722
offering, and make an *a* for him Num 6:11 3722
to make an *a* for the Levites Num 8:12 3722
to make an *a* for the children of Num 8:19 3722
Aaron made an *a* for them to Num 8:21 3722
the priest shall make an *a* for Num 15:25 3722
the priest shall make an *a* for Num 15:28 3722
the LORD, to make an *a* for him Num 15:28 3722
and make an *a* for them Num 16:46 3722
and made an *a* for the people Num 16:47 3722
made an *a* for the children of Num 25:13 3722
offering, to make an *a* for you Num 28:22 3722
the goats, to make an *a* for you Num 28:30 3722
offering, to make an *a* for you Num 29:5 3722
beside the sin offering of *a* Num 29:11 3725
to make an *a* for our souls before Num 31:50 3722
and wherewith shall I make the *a* 2Sa 21:3 3722
holy, and to make an *a* for Israel 1Chr 6:49 3722
to make an *a* for all Israel 2Chr 29:24 3722
offerings to make an *a* for Israel Neh 10:33 3722
whom we have now received the *a* Rom 5:11 *2643*

ATONEMENTS
blood of the sin offering of *a* Ex 30:10 3725

ATROTH (*a'-troth*) See ATAROTH. *A city in Gad.*
And *A*, Shophan, and Jaazer, and Num 32:35 5855

ATROTH BETH JOAB See ATROTH.

ATTAI (*at'-tahee*)
1. A grandson of Sheshan.
and she bare him *A* 1Chr 2:35 6262
A begat Nathan, and Nathan begat 1Chr 2:36 6262
2. A Gadite in David's army.
A the sixth, Eliel the seventh, 1Chr 12:11 6262
3. A son of Rehoboam.
which bare him Abijah, and *A* 2Chr 11:20 6262

ATTAIN
it is high, I cannot *a* unto it Ps 139:6
shall *a* unto wise counsels Prov 1:5 7069
as his hand shall *a* unto, and an Eze 46:7 5381
it be ere they *a* to innocency Hos 8:5 3201
any means they might *a* to Phenice Acts 27:12 *2658*
If by any means I might *a* unto Phil 3:11 *2658*

ATTAINED
have not *a* unto the days of the Gen 47:9 5381
howbeit he *a* not unto the first 2Sa 23:19 935
but he *a* not to the first three 2Sa 23:23 935
howbeit he *a* not to the first 1Chr 11:21 935
but *a* not to the first three 1Chr 11:25 935
have *a* to righteousness, even the Rom 9:30 *2638*
hath not *a* to the law of Rom 9:31 *5348*
Not as though I had already *a* Phil 3:12 *2983*
whereto we have already *a* Phil 3:16 *5348*
doctrine, whereunto thou hast *a* 1Ti 4:6 *3877*

ATTALIA (*at-ta-li'-ah*) *A seaport near Perga.*
in Perga, they went down into *A* Acts 14:25 *825*

ATTEND
he had appointed to *a* upon her Est 4:5 6440
a unto my cry, give ear unto my Ps 17:1 7181
A unto me, and hear me Ps 55:2 7181
a unto my prayer Ps 61:1 7181
and *a* to the voice of my Ps 86:6 7181
A unto my cry Ps 142:6 7181
and *a* to know understanding Prov 4:1 7181
My son, *a* to my words Prov 4:20 7181
a unto my wisdom, and bow thine Prov 5:1 7181
a to the words of my mouth Prov 7:24 7181
that ye may *a* upon the Lord 1Cor 7:35 *2145*

ATTENDANCE
the *a* of his ministers, and their 1Kin 10:5 4612
the *a* of his ministers, and their 2Chr 9:4 4612
give *a* to reading, to exhortation 1Ti 4:13 *4337*
which no man gave *a* at the altar Heb 7:13 *4337*

ATTENDED
I *a* unto you, and, behold, there Job 32:12 995
he hath *a* to the voice of my Ps 66:19 7181
that she *a* unto the things which Acts 16:14 *4337*

ATTENDING
a continually upon this very Rom 13:6 *4343*

ATTENT
let thine ears be *a* unto the 2Chr 6:40 7183
mine ears *a* unto the prayer that 2Chr 7:15 7183

ATTENTIVE
Let thine ear now be *a*, and thine Neh 1:6 7183
let now thine ear be *a* to the Neh 1:11 7183
were *a* unto the book of the law Neh 8:3
let thine ears be *a* to the voice Ps 130:2 7183
people were very *a* to hear him Lk 19:48 *1582*

ATTENTIVELY
Hear *a* the noise of his voice, and Job 37:2 8085

ATTIRE
a woman with the *a* of an harlot Prov 7:10 7897
her ornaments, or a bride her *a* Jer 2:32 7196
in dyed *a* upon their heads Eze 23:15 2871

ATTIRED
the linen mitre shall he be *a* Lev 16:4 6801

AUDIENCE
in the *a* of the children of Heth Gen 23:10 241
the *a* of the people of the land Gen 23:13 241
in the *a* of the sons of Heth Gen 23:16 241
read in the *a* of the people Ex 24:7 241
I pray thee, speak in thine *a* 1Sa 25:24 241
in the *a* of our God, keep and seek 1Chr 28:8 241
of Moses in the *a* of the people Neh 13:1 241
sayings in the *a* of the people Lk 7:1 *189*
Then in the *a* of all the people Lk 20:45 *191*
and ye that fear God, give *a* Acts 13:16 *191*
gave *a* to Barnabas and Paul, Acts 15:12 *191*
they gave him *a* unto this word, Acts 22:22 *191*

AUGMENT
to *a* yet the fierce anger of the ... Num 32:14 5595

AUGUSTAN See AUGUSTUS.

AUGUSTUS (*aw-gus'-tus*) See AUGUSTUS', CAESAR. *An emperor of Rome.*
went out a decree from Caesar *A* ... Lk 2:1 *828*
be reserved unto the hearing of *A* ... Acts 25:21 *828*
he himself hath appealed to *A* ... Acts 25:25 *828*

AUGUSTUS' (*aw-gus'-tus*)
Julius, a centurion of *A* band ... Acts 27:1 *828*

AUL
bore his ear through with an *a* ... Ex 21:6 4836
Then thou shalt take an *a* ... Deut 15:17 4836

AUNT
she is thine *a* ... Lev 18:14 1733

AUSTERE
thee, because thou art an *a* man ... Lk 19:21 *840*
Thou knewest that I was an *a* man ... Lk 19:22 *840*

AUTHOR
For God is not the *a* of confusion ... 1Cor 14:33
he became the *a* of eternal ... Heb 5:9 *159*
Looking unto Jesus the *a* and ... Heb 12:2 *747*

AUTHORITIES
angels and *a* and powers being made ... 1Pet 3:22 *1849*

AUTHORITY
the Jew, wrote with all *a* ... Est 9:29 8633
When the righteous are in *a* ... Prov 29:2 7235
he taught them as one having *a* ... Mt 7:29 *1849*
For I am a man under *a*, having ... Mt 8:9 *1849*
are great exercise *a* upon them ... Mt 20:25 *2715*
By what *a* doest thou these things ... Mt 21:23 *1849*
and who gave thee this *a* ... Mt 21:23 *1849*
you by what *a* I do these things ... Mt 21:24 *1849*
I you by what *a* I do these things ... Mt 21:27 *1849*
he taught them as one that had *a* ... Mk 1:22 *1849*
for with *a* commandeth he even the ... Mk 1:27 *1849*
great ones exercise *a* upon them ... Mk 10:42 *2715*
By what *a* doest thou these things ... Mk 11:28 *1849*
thee this *a* to do these things ... Mk 11:28 *1849*
you by what *a* I do these things ... Mk 11:29 *1849*
you by what *a* I do these things ... Mk 11:33 *1849*
gave *a* to his servants, and to ... Mk 13:34 *1849*
for with *a* and power he commandeth ... Lk 4:36 *1849*
For I also am a man set under *a* ... Lk 7:8 *1849*
a over all devils, and to cure ... Lk 9:1 *1849*
have thou *a* over ten cities ... Lk 19:17 *1849*
by what *a* doest thou these things ... Lk 20:2 *1849*
who is he that gave thee this *a* ... Lk 20:2 *1849*
I you by what *a* I do these things ... Lk 20:8 *1849*
the power and *a* of the governor ... Lk 20:20 *1849*
they that exercise *a* upon them ... Lk 22:25 *1850*
hath given him *a* to execute ... Jn 5:27 *1849*
an eunuch of great *a* under ... Acts 8:27 *1413*
here he hath *a* from the chief ... Acts 9:14 *1849*
having received *a* from the chief ... Acts 26:10 *1849*
as I went to Damascus with *a* ... Acts 26:12 *1849*
have put down all rule and all *a* ... 1Cor 15:24 *1849*
boast somewhat more of our *a* ... 2Cor 10:8 *1849*
kings, and for all that are in *a* ... 1Ti 2:2 *5247*
nor to usurp *a* over the man ... 1Ti 2:12 *831*
and exhort, and rebuke with all *a* ... Titus 2:15 *2003*
power, and his seat, and great *a* ... Rev 13:2 *1849*

AVA (*a'-vah*) See IVAH. *An area near Babylon.*
and from Cuthah, and from *A* ... 2Kin 17:24 5755

AVAILETH
Yet all this *a* me nothing ... Est 5:13 7737
neither circumcision *a* any thing ... Gal 5:6 *2480*
neither circumcision *a* any thing ... Gal 6:15 *2480*
prayer of a righteous man *a* much ... Jas 5:16 *2480*

AVEN See BETH-AVEN. *Another name for Heliopolis, in Egypt.*
The young men of *A* and of ... Eze 30:17 206
The high places also of *A* ... Hos 10:8 206
inhabitant from the plain of *A* ... Amos 1:5 206

AVENGE
Thou shalt not *a*, nor bear any ... Lev 19:18 5358
that shall *a* the quarrel of my ... Lev 26:25 5358
A the children of Israel of the ... Num 31:2
and *a* the LORD of Midian ... Num 31:3
for he will *a* the blood of his ... Deut 32:43 5358
and thee, and the LORD *a* me of thee ... 1Sa 24:12 5358
that I may *a* the blood of my ... 2Kin 9:7 5358
to *a* themselves on their enemies ... Est 8:13 5358
and *a* me of mine enemies ... Is 1:24 5358
that he may *a* him of his ... Jer 46:10 5358
I will *a* the blood of Jezreel ... Hos 1:4 6485
saying, *A* me of mine adversary ... Lk 18:3 *1556*
widow troubleth me, I will *a* her ... Lk 18:5 *1556*
And shall not God *a* his own elect ... Lk 18:7
you that he will *a* them speedily ... Lk 18:8
a not yourselves, but rather give ... Rom 12:19 *1556*
a our blood on them that dwell on ... Rev 6:10 *1556*

AVENGED
If Cain shall be *a* sevenfold ... Gen 4:24 5358
until the people had *a* themselves ... Josh 10:13 5358
done this, yet will I be *a* of you ... Judg 15:7 5358
that I may be at once *a* of the ... Judg 16:28 5358
that I may be *a* on mine enemies ... 1Sa 14:24 5358
to be *a* of the king's enemies ... 1Sa 18:25 5358
or that my lord hath *a* himself ... 1Sa 25:31 3467
the LORD hath *a* my lord the king ... 2Sa 4:8
LORD hath *a* him of his enemies ... 2Sa 18:19 8199
for the LORD hath *a* thee this day ... 2Sa 18:31 8199
shall not my soul be *a* on such a ... Jer 5:9 5358
shall not my soul be *a* on such a ... Jer 5:29 5358
shall not my soul be *a* on such a ... Jer 9:9 5358
a him that was oppressed, and ... Acts 7:24
for God hath *a* you on her ... Rev 18:20
hath *a* the blood of his servants ... Rev 19:2 *1556*

AVENGER
you cities for refuge from the *a* ... Num 35:12 1350
Lest the *a* of the blood pursue ... Deut 19:6 1350
into the hand of the *a* of blood ... Deut 19:12 1350
your refuge from the *a* of blood ... Josh 20:3 1350
if the *a* of blood pursue after ... Josh 20:5 1350
die by the hand of the *a* of blood ... Josh 20:9 1350
mightest still the enemy and the *a* ... Ps 8:2 5358
by reason of the enemy and *a* ... Ps 44:16 5358
the Lord is the *a* of all such ... 1Th 4:6 *1558*

AVENGETH
It is God that *a* me, and that ... 2Sa 22:48
It is God that *a* me, and subdueth ... Ps 18:47

AVENGING
ye the LORD for the *a* of Israel ... Judg 5:2
from *a* thyself with thine own ... 1Sa 25:26 3467
from *a* myself with mine own hand ... 1Sa 25:33 3467

AVERSE
by securely as men *a* from war ... Mic 2:8 7725

AVIM (*a'-vim*) See AVIMS, AVITES. *A city near Bethel.*
And *A*, and Parah, and Ophrah, ... Josh 18:23 5761

AVIMS (*a'-vims*) See AVIM. *A Canaanite tribe.*
the *A* which dwelt in Hazerim, ... Deut 2:23 5757

AVITES (*a'-vites*) See AVIM.
1. Same as Avims.
and the Ekronites; also the *A* ... Josh 13:3 5757
2. A tribe moved to Samaria.
the *A* made Nibhaz and Tartak, and ... 2Kin 17:31 5757

AVITH (*a'-vith*) *Capital of Edom.*
and the name of his city was *A* ... Gen 36:35 5762
and the name of his city was *A* ... 1Chr 1:46 5762

AVOID
A it, pass not by it, turn from ... Prov 4:15 6544
and *a* them ... Rom 16:17 *1578*
to *a* fornication, let every man ... 1Cor 7:2 *1223*
foolish and unlearned questions *a* ... 2Ti 2:23 *3868*
But *a* foolish questions, and ... Titus 3:9 *4026*

AVOIDED
David *a* out of his presence twice ... 1Sa 18:11 5437

AVOIDING
A this, that no man should blame ... 2Cor 8:20 *4724*
a profane and vain babblings, and ... 1Ti 6:20 *1624*

AVOUCHED
Thou hast *a* the LORD this day to ... Deut 26:17 559
the LORD hath *a* thee this day to ... Deut 26:18 559

AVVA See AVA.

AVVIM See AVITES.

AWAIT
But their laying *a* was known of ... Acts 9:24 *1917*

AWAKE
A, *a*, Deborah ... Judg 5:12 5782
a, *a*, utter a song ... Judg 5:12 5782
surely now he would *a* for thee ... Job 8:6 5782
be no more, they shall not *a* ... Job 14:12 6974
a for me to the judgment that ... Ps 7:6 5782
I shall be satisfied, when I *a* ... Ps 17:15 6974
a to my judgment, even unto my ... Ps 35:23 6974
A, why sleepest thou, O Lord ... Ps 44:23 5782
A up, my glory ... Ps 57:8 5782
a, psaltery and harp ... Ps 57:8 5782
I myself will *a* early ... Ps 57:8 5782
a to help me, and behold ... Ps 59:4 5782
a to visit all the heathen ... Ps 59:5 6974
A, psaltery and harp ... Ps 108:2 5782
I myself will *a* early ... Ps 108:2 5782
when I *a*, I am still with thee ... Ps 139:18 6974
when shall I *a* ... Prov 23:35 6974
nor *a* my love, till he please ... Song 2:7 5782
nor *a* my love, till he please ... Song 3:5 5782
A, O north wind ... Song 4:16 5782
nor *a* my love, until he please ... Song 8:4 5782
A and sing, ye that dwell in dust ... Is 26:19 6974
A, *a*, put on strength, O arm ... Is 51:9 5782
a, as in the ancient days, in the ... Is 51:9 5782
A, *a*, stand up, O Jerusalem, ... Is 51:17 5782
A, *a*; put on thy strength ... Is 52:1 5782
in the dust of the earth shall *a* ... Dan 12:2 6974
A, ye drunkards, and weep ... Joel 1:5 6974
a that shall vex thee, and thou ... Hab 2:7 6974
him that saith to the wood, *A* ... Hab 2:19 6974
A, O sword, against my shepherd, ... Zec 13:7 5782
and they *a* him, and say unto him, ... Mk 4:38 *1326*
and when they were *a*, they saw his ... Lk 9:32 *1235*
that I may *a* him out of sleep ... Jn 11:11 *1852*
it is high time to *a* out of sleep ... Rom 13:11 *1453*
A to righteousness, and sin not ... 1Cor 15:34 *1594*
A thou that sleepest, and arise ... Eph 5:14 *1453*

AWAKED
Jacob *a* out of his sleep, and he ... Gen 28:16 3364
he *a* out of his sleep, and went ... Judg 16:14 3364
saw it, nor knew it, neither *a* ... 1Sa 26:12 6974
he sleepeth, and must be *a* ... 1Kin 18:27 3364
him, saying, The child is not *a* ... 2Kin 4:31 6974
I *a*; for the LORD sustained me ... Ps 3:5 6974
Then the Lord *a* as one out of ... Ps 78:65 3364
Upon this I *a*, and beheld ... Jer 31:26 6974

AWAKEST
so, O Lord, when thou *a*, thou ... Ps 73:20 5782
and when thou *a*, it shall talk ... Prov 6:22 6974

AWAKETH
As a dream when one *a* ... Ps 73:20 6974
but he *a*, and his soul is empty ... Is 29:8 6974
but he *a*, and, behold, he is faint ... Is 29:8 6974

AWAKING
of the prison *a* out of his sleep ... Acts 16:27

AWARE
Or ever I was *a*, my soul made me ... Song 6:12 3045
O Babylon, and thou wast not *a* ... Jer 50:24 3045
and in an hour that he is not *a* of ... Mt 24:50 *1097*
walk over them are not *a* of them ... Lk 11:44 *1492*
and at an hour when he is not *a* ... Lk 12:46 *1097*

AWAY
and they sent him *a*, and his wife, ... Gen 12:20
the carcases, Abram drove them *a* ... Gen 15:11
favour in thy sight, pass not *a* ... Gen 18:3
and the child, and sent her *a* ... Gen 21:14
servants had violently taken *a* ... Gen 21:25
he said, Send me *a* unto my master ... Gen 24:54
send me *a* that I may go to my ... Gen 24:56
they sent *a* Rebekah their sister, ... Gen 24:59
sent them *a* from Isaac his son, ... Gen 25:6
me, and have sent me *a* from you ... Gen 26:27
and have sent thee *a* in peace ... Gen 26:29
and Isaac sent them *a*, and they ... Gen 26:31
hath taken *a* thy blessing ... Gen 27:35
he took *a* my birthright ... Gen 27:36
now he hath taken *a* my blessing ... Gen 27:36
until thy brother's fury turn *a* ... Gen 27:44
brother's anger turn *a* from thee ... Gen 27:45
And Isaac sent *a* Jacob ... Gen 28:5
sent him *a* to Padan-aram, to take ... Gen 28:6
wouldest thou take *a* my son's ... Gen 30:15
God hath taken *a* my reproach ... Gen 30:23
Jacob said unto Laban, Send me *a* ... Gen 30:25
Jacob hath taken *a* all that was ... Gen 31:1
Thus God hath taken *a* the cattle ... Gen 31:9
he carried *a* all his cattle, and ... Gen 31:18
Jacob stole *a* unawares to Laban ... Gen 31:20
thou hast stolen *a* unawares to me ... Gen 31:26
carried *a* my daughters, as ... Gen 31:26
a secretly, and steal *a* from me ... Gen 31:27
might have sent thee *a* with mirth ... Gen 31:27
thou hadst sent me *a* now empty ... Gen 31:42
Put *a* the strange gods that are ... Gen 35:2
And she arose, and went *a*, and laid ... Gen 38:19
For indeed I was stolen *a* out of ... Gen 40:15
not, and ye will take Benjamin *a* ... Gen 42:36
that he may send *a* your other ... Gen 43:14
was light, the men were sent *a* ... Gen 44:3
So he sent his brethren *a* ... Gen 45:24
said unto her, Take this child *a* ... Ex 2:9
shepherds came and drove them *a* ... Ex 2:17
that he may take *a* the frogs from ... Ex 8:8
only ye shall not go very far *a* ... Ex 8:28
that he may take *a* from me this ... Ex 10:17
which took *a* the locusts, and cast ... Ex 10:19
put *a* leaven out of your houses ... Ex 12:15
And the children of Israel went *a* ... Ex 12:28
up my bones *a* hence with you ... Ex 13:19
He took not *a* the pillar of the ... Ex 13:22
hast thou taken us *a* to die in ... Ex 14:11
of Canaan shall melt *a* ... Ex 15:15
Thou wilt surely wear *a*, both ... Ex 18:18
And the LORD said unto him, *A* ... Ex 19:24 3212
it die, or be hurt, or driven *a* ... Ex 22:10
I will take sickness *a* from the ... Ex 23:25
And I will take *a* mine hand ... Ex 33:23
he shall pluck *a* his crop with ... Lev 1:16
the kidneys, it shall he take *a* ... Lev 3:4
the kidneys, it shall he take *a* ... Lev 3:10
the kidneys, it shall he take *a* ... Lev 3:15
the kidneys, it shall he take *a* ... Lev 4:9
he shall take *a* all the fat ... Lev 4:31
as the fat is taken *a* from off ... Lev 4:31
he shall take *a* all the fat ... Lev 4:35
a from the sacrifice of the peace ... Lev 4:35
or in a thing taken *a* by violence ... Lev 6:2
that which he took violently *a* ... Lev 6:4
the kidneys, it shall he take *a* ... Lev 7:4
shall command that they take *a* ... Lev 14:40
that he hath taken *a* the stones ... Lev 14:43
shall send him *a* by the hand of a ... Lev 16:21
a woman put *a* from her husband ... Lev 21:7
poor, and hath sold *a* some of his ... Lev 25:25
pine *a* in their iniquity in your ... Lev 26:39
shall they pine *a* with them ... Lev 26:39
enemies, I will not cast them *a* ... Lev 26:44
they shall take *a* the ashes from ... Num 4:13
But now our soul is dried *a* ... Num 11:6
ye are turned *a* from the LORD ... Num 14:43 310
thou shalt quite take *a* their ... Num 17:10
Israel turned *a* from him ... Num 20:21
that he take *a* the serpents from ... Num 21:7
Asshur shall carry thee *a* captive ... Num 24:22
LORD may be turned *a* from Israel ... Num 25:4
hath turned my wrath *a* from the ... Num 25:11
be done *a* from among his family ... Num 27:4 1639
For if ye turn *a* from after him ... Num 32:15
their inheritance be taken *a* from ... Num 36:4
For they will turn *a* thy son from ... Deut 7:4
the LORD will take *a* from thee ... Deut 7:15
turn you *a* from the LORD your God ... Deut 13:5
the evil *a* from the midst of thee ... Deut 13:5 1197
thee *a* from the LORD thy God ... Deut 13:10
thou shalt not let him go *a* empty ... Deut 15:13
thee, I will not go *a* from thee ... Deut 15:16 3318
thou sendest him *a* free from thee ... Deut 15:18
put the evil *a* from among you ... Deut 17:7 1197
thou shalt put *a* the evil from ... Deut 17:12 1197
that his heart turn not *a* ... Deut 17:17
but thou shalt put *a* the guilt of ... Deut 19:13 1197

put the evil *a* from among you	Deut 19:19	1197
So shalt thou put *a* the guilt of	Deut 21:9	1197
thou put evil *a* from among you	Deut 21:21	1197
he may not put her *a* all his days	Deut 22:19	
thou put evil *a* from among you	Deut 22:21	1197
shalt thou put *a* evil from Israel	Deut 22:22	1197
so thou shalt put *a* evil from	Deut 22:24	1197
he may not put her *a* all his days	Deut 22:29	
in thee, and turn *a* from thee	Deut 23:14	
former husband, which sent her *a*	Deut 24:4	
shalt put evil *a* from among you	Deut 24:7	1197
I have brought *a* the hallowed	Deut 26:13	1197
neither have I taken *a* ought	Deut 26:14	1197
and no man shall fray them *a*	Deut 28:26	
taken *a* from before thy face	Deut 28:31	
whose heart turneth *a* this day	Deut 29:18	5493
But if thine heart turn *a*	Deut 30:17	
not hear, but shalt be drawn *a*	Deut 30:17	
And she sent them *a*, and they	Josh 2:21	
This day have I rolled *a* the	Josh 5:9	
until ye take *a* the accursed	Josh 7:13	
valour, and sent them *a* by night	Josh 8:3	
were drawn *a* from the city	Josh 8:16	
And the men arose, and went *a*	Josh 18:8	
blessed them, and sent them *a*	Josh 22:6	
sent them *a* also unto their tents	Josh 22:7	
to turn *a* this day from following	Josh 22:16	
But that ye must turn *a* this day	Josh 22:18	
put *a* the gods which your fathers	Josh 24:14	5493
Now therefore put *a*, said he, the	Josh 24:23	5493
he sent *a* the people that bare	Judg 3:18	
chariot, and fled *a* on his feet	Judg 4:15	
Howbeit Sisera fled *a* on his feet	Judg 4:17	
The river of Kishon swept them *a*	Judg 5:21	
took *a* the ornaments that were on	Judg 8:21	
And Jotham ran *a*, and fled, and went	Judg 9:21	
they put *a* the strange gods from	Judg 10:16	5493
Because Israel took *a* my land	Judg 11:13	
Israel took not *a* the land of	Judg 11:15	
he sent her *a* for two months	Judg 11:38	
that he cast *a* the jawbone out of	Judg 15:17	
went *a* with them, bar and all, and	Judg 16:3	5265
went *a* with the pin of the beam,	Judg 16:14	5265
Ye have taken *a* my gods which I	Judg 18:24	
and the priest, and ye are gone *a*	Judg 18:24	
went *a* from him unto her father's	Judg 19:2	
death, and put *a* evil from Israel	Judg 20:13	1197
were drawn *a* from the city	Judg 20:31	
put *a* thy wine from thee	1Sa 1:14	5493
Send *a* the ark of the God of	1Sa 5:11	
If ye send *a* the ark of the God	1Sa 6:3	
and send it *a*, that it may go	1Sa 6:8	
then put *a* the strange gods and	1Sa 7:3	5493
of Israel did put *a* Baalim	1Sa 7:4	5493
Up, that I may send thee *a*	1Sa 9:26	
And Samuel sent all the people *a*	1Sa 10:25	
behold, the multitude melted *a*	1Sa 14:16	
And as Samuel turned about to go *a*	1Sa 15:27	
taketh *a* the reproach from Israel	1Sa 17:26	
but he slipped *a* out of Saul's	1Sa 19:10	
sent *a* mine enemy, that he is	1Sa 19:17	
will shew it thee, and send thee *a*	1Sa 20:13	
for the LORD hath sent thee *a*	1Sa 20:22	
in thine eyes, let me get *a*	1Sa 20:29	4422
in the day when it was taken *a*	1Sa 21:6	
brought *a* their cattle, and smote	1Sa 23:5	
haste to get *a* for fear of Saul	1Sa 23:26	3212
enemy, will he let him go well *a*	1Sa 24:19	1870
break *a* every man from his master	1Sa 25:10	
and they gat them *a*, and no man saw.	1Sa 26:12	3212
took *a* the sheep, and the oxen, and	1Sa 27:9	
Saul had put *a* those that had	1Sa 28:3	5493
rose up, and went *a* that night	1Sa 28:25	
or small, but carried them *a*	1Sa 30:2	
that the Amalekites had carried *a*	1Sa 30:18	
that they may lead them *a*	1Sa 30:22	
of the mighty is vilely cast *a*	2Sa 1:21	
And David sent Abner *a*	2Sa 3:21	
for he had sent him *a*, and he was	2Sa 3:22	
the king, and he hath sent him *a*	2Sa 3:23	
is it that thou hast sent him *a*	2Sa 3:24	
gat them *a* through the plain all	2Sa 4:7	3212
take you *a* from the earth	2Sa 4:11	
Except thou take *a* the blind	2Sa 5:6	5493
mercy shall not depart *a* from him	2Sa 7:15	
Saul, whom I put *a* before thee	2Sa 7:15	5493
to their buttocks, and sent them *a*	2Sa 10:4	
The LORD also hath put *a* thy sin	2Sa 12:13	5674
this evil in sending me *a* is	2Sa 13:16	
they went both of them *a* quickly	2Sa 17:18	
for if we flee *a*, they will not	2Sa 18:3	
mule that was under him went *a*	2Sa 18:9	
steal *a* when they flee in battle	2Sa 19:3	
the men of Judah stolen thee *a*	2Sa 19:41	
Strangers shall fade *a*, and they	2Sa 22:46	
be all of them as thorns thrust *a*	2Sa 23:6	5074
and the men of Israel were gone *a*	2Sa 23:9	
take *a* the iniquity of thy	2Sa 24:10	5674
mayest take *a* the innocent blood	1Kin 2:31	5493
of the servants of Shimei ran *a*	1Kin 2:39	
so that they carry them *a*	1Kin 8:46	7617
enemies, which led them *a* captive	1Kin 8:48	7617
eighth day he sent the people *a*	1Kin 8:66	
for surely they will turn *a* your	1Kin 11:2	
and his wives turned *a* his heart	1Kin 11:3	
that his wives turned *a* his heart	1Kin 11:4	
I will not rend *a* all the kingdom	1Kin 11:13	
rent the kingdom *a* from the house	1Kin 14:8	
will take *a* the remnant of the	1Kin 14:10	
Jeroboam, as a man taketh *a* dung	1Kin 14:10	
he took *a* the treasures of the	1Kin 14:26	
he even took *a* all	1Kin 14:26	
he took *a* all the shields of gold	1Kin 14:26	
he took *a* the sodomites out of	1Kin 15:12	
they took *a* the stones of Ramah,	1Kin 15:22	
I will take *a* the posterity of	1Kin 16:3	
now, O LORD, take *a* my life	1Kin 19:4	
they seek my life, to take it *a*	1Kin 19:10	
they seek my life, to take it *a*	1Kin 19:14	
it in their hand, and take it *a*	1Kin 20:6	
do this thing, Take the kings *a*	1Kin 20:24	
I will send thee *a* with this	1Kin 20:34	
covenant with him, and sent him *a*	1Kin 20:34	
and took the ashes *a* from his face	1Kin 20:41	5493
turned *a* his face, and would eat	1Kin 21:4	
will take *a* thy posterity, and	1Kin 21:21	
the high places were not taken *a*	1Kin 22:43	5493
thou that the LORD will take *a*	2Kin 2:3	
thou that the LORD will take *a*	2Kin 2:5	
before I be taken *a* from thee	2Kin 2:9	
for he put *a* the image of Baal	2Kin 3:2	5493
Gehazi came near to thrust her *a*	2Kin 4:27	
had brought *a* captive out of the	2Kin 5:2	
But Naaman was wroth, and went *a*	2Kin 5:11	
So he turned and went *a* in a rage	2Kin 5:12	
eaten and drunk, he sent them *a*	2Kin 6:23	
hath sent to take *a* mine head	2Kin 6:32	
Syrians had cast *a* in their haste	2Kin 7:15	
the high places were not taken *a*	2Kin 12:3	5493
and he went *a* from Jerusalem	2Kin 12:18	
the high places were not taken *a*	2Kin 14:4	5493
and carried Israel *a* into Assyria	2Kin 17:6	1540
the LORD carried *a* before them	2Kin 17:11	1540
So was Israel carried *a* out of	2Kin 17:23	1540
had carried *a* from Samaria came	2Kin 17:28	1540
whom they carried *a* from thence	2Kin 17:33	1540
did carry *a* Israel unto Assyria	2Kin 18:11	1540
altars Hezekiah hath taken *a*	2Kin 18:22	5493
How then wilt thou turn *a* the	2Kin 18:24	
take you *a* to a land like your	2Kin 18:32	
shalt beget, shall they take *a*	2Kin 20:18	
he took *a* the horses that the	2Kin 23:11	7673
the LORD to anger, Josiah took *a*	2Kin 23:19	5493
and in Jerusalem, did Josiah put *a*	2Kin 23:24	1197
to Jehoiakim, and took Jehoahaz *a*	2Kin 23:34	
he carried *a* all Jerusalem, and	2Kin 24:14	1540
he carried *a* Jehoiachin to	2Kin 24:15	1540
fell *a* to the king of Babylon	2Kin 25:11	
the captain of the guard carry *a*	2Kin 25:11	1540
they ministered, took they *a*	2Kin 25:14	
the captain of the guard took *a*	2Kin 25:15	
was carried *a* out of their land	2Kin 25:21	1540
king of Assyria carried *a* captive	1Chr 5:6	1540
And they took *a* their cattle	1Chr 5:21	7617
of Assyria, and he carried them *a*	1Chr 5:26	1540
when the LORD carried *a* Judah	1Chr 6:15	1540
came down to take *a* their cattle	1Chr 7:21	
of Moab, after he had sent them *a*	1Chr 8:8	
who drove *a* the inhabitants of	1Chr 8:13	1272
who were carried *a* to Babylon for	1Chr 9:1	1540
took *a* the body of Saul, and the	1Chr 10:12	
upon advisement sent him *a*	1Chr 12:19	
turn *a* from them, and come upon	1Chr 14:14	
will not take my mercy *a* from him	1Chr 17:13	5493
by their buttocks, and sent them *a*	1Chr 19:4	
do *a* the iniquity of thy servant	1Chr 21:8	5674
they carry them *a* captives unto a	2Chr 6:36	7617
turn not *a* the face of thine	2Chr 6:42	
the people *a* into their tents	2Chr 7:10	
But if ye turn *a*, and forsake my	2Chr 7:19	
went *a* to her own land, she and	2Chr 9:12	
took *a* the treasures of the house	2Chr 12:9	
he carried *a* also the shields of	2Chr 12:9	
For he took *a* the altars of the	2Chr 14:3	5493
Also he took *a* out of all the	2Chr 14:5	5493
they carried *a* very much spoil	2Chr 14:13	
of cattle, and carried *a* sheep	2Chr 14:15	7617
put *a* the abominable idols out of	2Chr 15:8	5674
were not taken *a* out of Israel	2Chr 15:17	5493
they carried *a* the stones of	2Chr 16:6	
he took *a* the high places	2Chr 17:6	5493
in that thou hast taken *a* the	2Chr 19:3	1197
came to take *a* the spoil of them	2Chr 20:25	
more than they could carry *a*	2Chr 20:25	
the high places were not taken *a*	2Chr 20:33	5493
carried *a* all the substance that	2Chr 21:17	7617
children of Judah carry *a* captive	2Chr 25:12	
a from following the LORD they	2Chr 25:27	
carried *a* a great multitude of	2Chr 28:5	7617
a captive of their brethren two	2Chr 28:8	
took also *a* much spoil from them,	2Chr 28:8	
Judah, and carried *a* captives	2Chr 28:17	
For Ahaz took *a* a portion out of	2Chr 28:21	
have turned *a* their faces from	2Chr 29:6	
fierce wrath may turn *a* from us	2Chr 29:10	
did cast *a* in his transgression	2Chr 29:19	
of his wrath may turn *a* from you	2Chr 30:8	
will not turn *a* his face from you	2Chr 30:9	
took *a* the altars that were in	2Chr 30:14	5493
altars for incense took they *a*	2Chr 30:14	5493
Hezekiah taken *a* his high places	2Chr 32:12	5493
he took *a* the strange gods, and	2Chr 33:15	5493
And Josiah took *a* all the	2Chr 34:33	5493
said to his servants, Have me *a*	2Chr 35:23	5674
the sword carried he *a* to Babylon	2Chr 36:20	1540
of those which had been carried *a*	Ezr 2:1	1473
had carried *a* unto Babylon	Ezr 2:1	1540
carried the people *a* into Babylon	Ezr 5:12	1541
of those that had been carried *a*	Ezr 8:35	1473
of those that had been carried *a*	Ezr 9:4	1473
our God to put *a* all the wives	Ezr 10:3	3318
of them that had been carried *a*	Ezr 10:6	1473
of those that had been carried *a*	Ezr 10:8	1473
that they would put *a* their wives	Ezr 10:19	3318
of those that had been carried *a*	Neh 7:6	1473
the king of Babylon had carried *a*	Neh 7:6	1546
Who had been carried *a* from	Est 2:6	1546
which had been carried *a* with	Est 2:6	1546
the king of Babylon had carried *a*	Est 2:6	1546
to take *a* his sackcloth from him	Est 4:4	5493
put *a* the mischief of Haman the	Est 8:3	5674
fell upon them, and took them *a*	Job 1:15	
camels, and have carried them *a*	Job 1:17	
gave, and the LORD hath taken *a*	Job 1:21	
excellency which is in them go *a*	Job 4:21	5265
the stream of brooks they pass *a*	Job 6:15	
cloud is consumed and vanisheth *a*	Job 7:9	
and take *a* mine iniquity	Job 7:21	5674
he have cast them *a* for their	Job 8:4	
God will not cast *a* a perfect man	Job 8:20	
Behold, he taketh *a*, who can	Job 9:12	2862
they flee *a*, they see no good	Job 9:25	
They are passed *a* as the swift	Job 9:26	
Let him take his rod *a* from me	Job 9:34	5493
be in thine hand, put it far *a*	Job 11:14	
remember it as waters that pass *a*	Job 11:16	
He leadeth counsellors *a* spoiled	Job 12:17	
He leadeth princes *a* spoiled	Job 12:19	
He removeth *a* the speech of the	Job 12:20	
taketh *a* the understanding of the	Job 12:20	
He taketh *a* the heart of the	Job 12:24	5493
But man dieth, and wasteth *a*	Job 14:10	
thou washest *a* the things which	Job 14:19	
his countenance, and sendest him *a*	Job 14:20	
Why doth thine heart carry thee *a*	Job 15:12	
breath of his mouth shall he go *a*	Job 15:30	
He shall fly *a* as a dream	Job 20:8	
he shall be chased *a* as a vision	Job 20:8	
a an house which he builded not	Job 20:19	1497
his goods shall flow *a* in the day	Job 20:28	
chaff that the storm carrieth *a*	Job 21:18	1589
Thou hast sent widows *a* empty	Job 22:9	
thou shalt put *a* iniquity far	Job 22:23	7368
they violently take *a* flocks	Job 24:2	
They drive *a* the ass of the	Job 24:3	
they take *a* the sheaf from the	Job 24:10	
who hath taken *a* my judgment	Job 27:2	5493
when God taketh *a* his soul	Job 27:8	7953
stealeth him *a* in the night	Job 27:20	
The east wind carrieth him *a*	Job 27:21	
up, they are gone *a* from men	Job 28:4	
they push *a* my feet, and they	Job 30:12	
my welfare passeth *a* as a cloud	Job 30:15	
my maker would soon take me *a*	Job 32:22	
His flesh is consumed *a*, that it	Job 33:21	
and God hath taken *a* my judgment	Job 34:5	5493
troubled at midnight, and pass *a*	Job 34:20	
shall be taken *a* without hand	Job 34:20	5493
he take thee *a* with his stroke	Job 36:18	5496
chaff which the wind driveth *a*	Ps 1:4	
cast *a* their cords from us	Ps 2:3	
I did not put *a* his statutes from	Ps 18:22	5493
The strangers shall fade *a*	Ps 18:45	
put not thy servant *a* in anger	Ps 27:9	5186
Draw me not *a* with the wicked, and	Ps 28:3	
they devised to take *a* my life	Ps 31:13	
who drove him *a*, and he departed	Ps 34:*t*	
into smoke shall they consume *a*	Ps 37:20	
Yet he passed *a*, and, lo, he was	Ps 37:36	
Remove thy stroke *a* from me	Ps 39:10	
beauty to consume *a* like a moth	Ps 39:11	
they were troubled, and hasted *a*	Ps 48:5	
he dieth he shall carry nothing *a*	Ps 49:17	
Cast me not *a* from thy presence	Ps 51:11	
for ever, he shall take thee *a*	Ps 52:5	2846
for then would I fly *a*, and be at	Ps 55:6	
Let them melt *a* as waters which	Ps 58:7	
let every one of them pass *a*	Ps 58:8	
he shall take them *a* as with a	Ps 58:9	
all that see them shall flee *a*	Ps 64:8	
thou shalt purge them *a*	Ps 65:3	
which hath not turned *a* my prayer	Ps 66:20	
is driven *a*, so drive them *a*	Ps 68:2	
restored that which I took not *a*	Ps 69:4	1497
many a time turned he his anger *a*	Ps 78:38	
a wind that passeth *a*, and cometh	Ps 78:39	
purge *a* our sins, for thy name's	Ps 79:9	
Thou hast taken *a* all thy wrath	Ps 85:3	
Thou hast put *a* mine acquaintance	Ps 88:8	7368
carriest them *a* as with a flood	Ps 90:5	
days are passed *a* in thy wrath	Ps 90:9	
it is soon cut off, and we fly *a*	Ps 90:10	
take me not *a* in the midst of my	Ps 102:24	
of thy thunder they hasted *a*	Ps 104:7	
thou takest *a* their breath, they	Ps 104:29	
to turn *a* his wrath, lest he	Ps 106:23	
gnash with his teeth, and melt *a*	Ps 112:10	
Turn *a* mine eyes from beholding	Ps 119:37	
Turn *a* my reproach which I fear	Ps 119:39	
Thou puttest *a* all the wicked of	Ps 119:119	
not *a* the face of thine anointed	Ps 132:10	
a captive required of us a song	Ps 137:3	
are as a shadow that passeth *a*	Ps 144:4	
which taketh *a* the life of the	Prov 1:19	
For the turning *a* of the simple	Prov 1:32	
by it, turn from it, and pass *a*	Prov 4:15	
and their sleep is taken *a*	Prov 4:16	1497
Put *a* from thee a froward mouth,	Prov 4:24	5493
his reproach shall not be wiped *a*	Prov 6:33	
but he casteth *a* the substance of	Prov 10:3	1920
is driven *a* in his wickedness	Prov 14:32	
A soft answer turneth *a* wrath	Prov 15:1	
chaseth *a* his mother, is a son	Prov 19:26	
a all evil with his eyes	Prov 20:8	
of a wound cleanseth *a* evil	Prov 20:30	
why should he take *a* thy bed from	Prov 22:27	
they fly *a* as an eagle toward	Prov 23:5	
he turn *a* his wrath from him	Prov 24:18	
Take *a* the dross from the silver,	Prov 25:4	1898
Take *a* the wicked from before the	Prov 25:5	1898
shame, and thine infamy turn not *a*	Prov 25:10	
As he that taketh *a* a garment in	Prov 25:20	5710

The north wind driveth *a* rain ... Prov 25:23
He that turneth *a* his ear from ... Prov 28:9
but wise men turn *a* wrath ... Prov 29:8
beasts, and turneth not *a* for any ... Prov 30:30
One generation passeth *a*, and ... Eccl 1:4
A time to cast *a* stones, and a ... Eccl 3:5
time to keep, and a time to cast *a* ... Eccl 3:6
which he may carry *a* in his hand ... Eccl 5:15
put *a* evil from thy flesh ... Eccl 11:10 5493
my love, my fair one, and come *a* ... Song 2:10
my love, my fair one, and come *a* ... Song 2:13
day break, and the shadows flee *a* ... Song 2:17
day break, and the shadows flee *a* ... Song 4:6
the walls took *a* my veil from me ... Song 5:7
Turn *a* thine eyes from me, for ... Song 6:5
anger, they are gone *a* backward ... Is 1:4
of assemblies, I cannot *a* with ... Is 1:13
put *a* the evil of your doings ... Is 1:16 5493
thee, and purely purge *a* thy dross ... Is 1:25
and take *a* all thy tin ... Is 1:25 5493
doth take *a* from Jerusalem and ... Is 3:1 5493
a the bravery of their tinkling ... Is 3:18 5493
thy name, to take *a* our reproach ... Is 4:1
a the filth of the daughters of ... Is 4:4
I will take *a* the hedge thereof ... Is 5:5 5493
take *a* the righteousness of the ... Is 5:23 5493
because they have cast *a* the law ... Is 5:24
this his anger is not turned *a* ... Is 5:25
prey, and shall carry it *a* safe ... Is 5:29
and thine iniquity is taken *a* ... Is 6:7 5493
the LORD have removed men far *a* ... Is 6:12
a before the king of Assyria ... Is 8:4
this his anger is not turned *a* ... Is 9:12
this his anger is not turned *a* ... Is 9:17
this his anger is not turned *a* ... Is 9:21
to take *a* the right from the poor ... Is 10:2 1497
this his anger is not turned *a* ... Is 10:4
be taken *a* from off thy shoulder ... Is 10:27 5493
with me, thine anger is turned *a* ... Is 12:1
for the hay is withered *a* ... Is 15:6
shall they carry *a* to the brook ... Is 15:7
And gladness is taken *a*, and joy ... Is 16:10
is taken *a* from being a city ... Is 17:1 5493
with pruninghooks, and take *a* ... Is 18:5 5493
they shall turn the rivers far *a* ... Is 19:6
brooks, shall wither, be driven *a* ... Is 19:7
lead *a* the Egyptians prisoners ... Is 20:4
Therefore said I, Look *a* from me ... Is 22:4
thee *a* with a mighty captivity ... Is 22:17
The earth mourneth and fadeth *a* ... Is 24:4
the world languisheth and fadeth *a* ... Is 24:4
the Lord GOD will wipe *a* tears ... Is 25:8
he take *a* from off all the earth ... Is 25:8 5493
all the fruit to take *a* his sin ... Is 27:9 5493
shall sweep *a* the refuge of lies ... Is 28:17
shall be as chaff that passeth *a* ... Is 29:5
thou shalt cast them *a* as a ... Is 30:22 2219
shall cast *a* his idols of silver ... Is 31:7 3988
and sorrow and sighing shall flee *a* ... Is 35:10
altars Hezekiah hath taken *a* ... Is 36:7 5493
How then wilt thou turn *a* the ... Is 36:9
take you *a* to a land like your ... Is 36:17
shall beget, shall they take *a* ... Is 39:7
shall take them *a* as stubble ... Is 40:24
chosen thee, and not cast thee *a* ... Is 41:9
and the wind shall carry them *a* ... Is 41:16
swallowed thee up shall be far *a* ... Is 49:19
of the mighty shall be taken *a* ... Is 49:25
divorcement, whom I have put *a* ... Is 50:1
is your mother put *a* ... Is 50:1
rebellious, neither turned *a* back ... Is 50:5
heavens shall vanish *a* like smoke ... Is 51:6
sorrow and mourning shall flee *a* ... Is 51:11
my people is taken *a* for nought ... Is 52:5
and merciful men are taken *a* ... Is 57:1
is taken *a* from the evil to come ... Is 57:1
the wind shall carry them all *a* ... Is 57:13
If thou take *a* from the midst of ... Is 58:9 5493
If thou turn *a* thy foot from the ... Is 58:13
departing *a* from our God ... Is 59:13
And judgment is turned *a* backward ... Is 59:14
like the wind, have taken us *a* ... Is 64:6
unto the carrying *a* of Jerusalem ... Jer 1:3
her occasion who can turn her *a* ... Jer 2:24
They say, If a man put *a* his wife ... Jer 3:1
adultery I had put her *a*, and ... Jer 3:8
and shalt not turn *a* from me ... Jer 3:19
and if thou wilt put *a* thine ... Jer 4:1 5493
take *a* the foreskins of your ... Jer 4:4 5493
take *a* her battlements ... Jer 5:10 5493
have turned *a* these things ... Jer 5:25
for the day goeth *a*, for the ... Jer 6:4
for the wicked are not plucked *a* ... Jer 6:29
hair, O Jerusalem, and cast it *a* ... Jer 7:29
and none shall fray them *a* ... Jer 7:33
shall he turn *a*, and not return ... Jer 8:4
given them shall pass *a* from them ... Jer 8:13
LORD's flock is carried *a* captive ... Jer 13:17
be carried *a* captive all of it ... Jer 13:19
shall be wholly carried *a* captive ... Jer 13:19
as the stubble that passeth *a* by ... Jer 13:24
take me not *a* in thy ... Jer 15:15
for I have taken *a* my peace from ... Jer 16:5
to turn *a* thy wrath from them ... Jer 18:20
weep sore for him that goeth *a* ... Jer 22:10
my flock, and driven them *a* ... Jer 23:2
a captive Jeconiah the son of ... Jer 24:1
are carried *a* captive of Judah ... Jer 24:5
when he carried *a* captive ... Jer 27:20
of Babylon took *a* from this place ... Jer 28:3
and all that is carried *a* captive ... Jer 28:6
which were carried *a* captives ... Jer 29:1
a captive from Jerusalem to ... Jer 29:1
all that are carried *a* captives ... Jer 29:4
a from Jerusalem unto Babylon ... Jer 29:4
you to be carried *a* captives ... Jer 29:7
I will turn *a* your captivity, and ... Jer 29:14
you to be carried *a* captive ... Jer 29:14
that I will not turn *a* from them ... Jer 32:40
Then will I cast *a* the seed of ... Jer 33:26
Thou fallest *a* to the Chaldeans ... Jer 37:13
I fall not *a* to the Chaldeans ... Jer 37:14
mire, and they are turned *a* back ... Jer 38:22
a captive into Babylon the ... Jer 39:9
in the city, and those that fell *a* ... Jer 39:9
carried *a* captive of Jerusalem ... Jer 40:1
which were carried *a* captive unto ... Jer 40:1
not carried *a* captive to Babylon ... Jer 40:7
Then Ishmael carried *a* captive ... Jer 41:10
Nethaniah carried them *a* captive ... Jer 41:10
a captive from Mizpah cast about ... Jer 41:14
carry us *a* captives into Babylon ... Jer 43:3
them, and carry them *a* captives ... Jer 43:12
them dismayed and turned *a* back ... Jer 46:5
Let not the swift flee *a*, nor the ... Jer 46:6
Why are thy valiant men swept *a* ... Jer 46:15
back, and are fled *a* together ... Jer 46:21
Moab, that it may flee and get *a* ... Jer 48:9 3318
suddenly make him run *a* from her ... Jer 49:19
and their flocks shall they take *a* ... Jer 49:29
turned them *a* on the mountains ... Jer 50:6
the lions have driven him *a* ... Jer 50:17
make them suddenly run *a* from her ... Jer 50:44
that have escaped the sword, go *a* ... Jer 51:50
captain of the guard carried *a* ... Jer 52:15
in the city, and those that fell *a* ... Jer 52:15
they ministered, took they *a* ... Jer 52:18
took the captain of the guard *a* ... Jer 52:19
Thus Judah was carried *a* captive ... Jer 52:27
Nebuchadrezzar carried *a* captive ... Jer 52:28
a captive from Jerusalem eight ... Jer 52:29
a captive of the Jews seven ... Jer 52:30
violently taken *a* his tabernacle ... Lam 2:6
iniquity, to turn *a* thy captivity ... Lam 2:14
for these pine *a*, stricken ... Lam 4:9
when they fled *a* and wandered ... Lam 4:15
more carry thee *a* into captivity ... Lam 4:22
spirit lifted me up, and took me *a* ... Eze 3:14
consume *a* for their iniquity ... Eze 4:17
they shall take *a* all the ... Eze 11:18 5493
turn *a* your faces from all your ... Eze 14:6
I throughly washed *a* thy blood ... Eze 16:9
I took them *a* as I saw good ... Eze 16:50 5493
turneth *a* from his righteousness ... Eze 18:24
turneth *a* from his righteousness ... Eze 18:26
a from his wickedness that he ... Eze 18:27
and turneth *a* from all his ... Eze 18:28
Cast *a* from you all your ... Eze 18:31
them, Cast ye *a* every man the ... Eze 20:7
they did not every man cast *a* the ... Eze 20:8
they shall take *a* thy nose ... Eze 23:25 5493
and take *a* thy fair jewels ... Eze 23:26
shall take *a* all thy labour, and ... Eze 23:29
I take *a* from thee the desire of ... Eze 24:16
but ye shall pine *a* for your ... Eze 24:23
lay *a* their robes, and put off ... Eze 26:16 5493
they shall take *a* her multitude ... Eze 30:4
if the sword come, and take him *a* ... Eze 33:4
he is taken *a* in his iniquity ... Eze 33:6
be upon us, and we pine *a* in them ... Eze 33:10
again that which was driven *a* ... Eze 34:4
again that which was driven *a* ... Eze 34:16
I will take *a* the stony heart out ... Eze 36:26 5493
to carry *a* silver and gold, to ... Eze 38:13
silver and gold, to take *a* cattle ... Eze 38:13
Now let them put *a* their whoredom ... Eze 43:9 7368
that are gone *a* far from me ... Eze 44:10
which went astray *a* from me after ... Eze 44:10
a widow, nor her that is put *a* ... Eze 44:22
take *a* your exactions from my ... Eze 45:9 7311
Thus Melzar took *a* the portion of ... Dan 1:16
and the wind carried them *a* ... Dan 2:35
the beasts get *a* from under it ... Dan 4:14 5111
they had their dominion taken *a* ... Dan 7:12 5709
dominion, which shall not pass *a* ... Dan 7:14 5709
and they shall take *a* his dominion ... Dan 7:26 5709
and the daily sacrifice was taken *a* ... Dan 8:11 7311
thy fury be turned *a* from thy ... Dan 9:16
he hath taken *a* the multitude ... Dan 11:12
shall take *a* the daily sacrifice ... Dan 11:31 5493
and utterly to make *a* many ... Dan 11:44 2763
daily sacrifice shall be taken *a* ... Dan 12:11 5493
but I will utterly take them *a* ... Hos 1:6
let her therefore put *a* her ... Hos 2:2 5493
take *a* my corn in the time ... Hos 2:9
For I will take *a* the names of ... Hos 2:17 5493
of the sea also shall be taken *a* ... Hos 4:3
wine and new wine take *a* the heart ... Hos 4:11
I, even I, will tear and go *a* ... Hos 5:14
I will take *a*, and none shall ... Hos 5:14
and as the early dew it goeth *a* ... Hos 6:4
glory shall fly *a* like a bird ... Hos 9:11
My God will cast them *a*, because ... Hos 9:17
as the early dew that passeth *a* ... Hos 13:3
anger, and took him *a* in my wrath ... Hos 13:11
Take *a* all iniquity, and receive ... Hos 14:2
mine anger is turned *a* from him ... Hos 14:4
made it clean bare, and cast it *a* ... Joel 1:7
withered *a* from the sons of men ... Joel 1:12
I will not turn *a* the punishment ... Amos 1:3
I will not turn *a* the punishment ... Amos 1:6
because they carried *a* captive ... Amos 1:6
I will not turn *a* the punishment ... Amos 1:9
I will not turn *a* the punishment ... Amos 1:11
I will not turn *a* the punishment ... Amos 1:13
I will not turn *a* the punishment ... Amos 2:1
I will not turn *a* the punishment ... Amos 2:4
I will not turn *a* the punishment ... Amos 2:6
shall flee *a* naked in that day ... Amos 2:16
he will take you *a* with hooks ... Amos 4:2
and have taken *a* your horses ... Amos 4:10 7628
Take thou *a* from me the noise of ... Amos 5:23 5493
Ye that put far *a* the evil day ... Amos 6:3 5077
Israel shall surely be led *a* ... Amos 7:11
flee thee *a* into the land of ... Amos 7:12
fleeth of them shall not flee *a* ... Amos 9:1
carried *a* captive his forces ... Obad 11
turn *a* from his fierce anger ... Jonah 3:9
Pass ye *a*, thou inhabitant of ... Mic 1:11
and houses, and take them *a* ... Mic 2:2 7726
turning *a* he hath divided our ... Mic 2:4
have ye taken *a* my glory for ever ... Mic 2:9
turned *a* the excellency of Jacob ... Nah 2:2
And Huzzab shall be led *a* captive ... Nah 2:7 1540
yet they shall flee *a* ... Nah 2:8
Yet was she carried *a*, she went ... Nah 3:10 1473
cankerworm spoileth, and fleeth *a* ... Nah 3:16
when the sun ariseth they flee *a* ... Nah 3:17
them, and turn *a* their captivity ... Zeph 2:7
for then I will take *a* out of the ... Zeph 3:11 5493
LORD hath taken *a* thy judgments ... Zeph 3:15 5493
Take *a* the filthy garments from ... Zec 3:4 5493
pulled *a* the shoulder, and stopped ... Zec 7:11
I will take *a* his blood out of ... Zec 9:7 5493
sceptre of Egypt shall depart *a* ... Zec 10:11
Their flesh shall consume *a* while ... Zec 14:12
shall consume *a* in their holes ... Zec 14:12
shall consume *a* in their mouth ... Zec 14:12
and one shall take you *a* with it ... Mal 2:3
and did turn many *a* from iniquity ... Mal 2:6
saith that he hateth putting *a* ... Mal 2:16
are gone *a* from mine ordinances ... Mal 3:7 5493
they were carried *a* to Babylon ... Mt 1:11 *3350*
a into Babylon are fourteen ... Mt 1:17 *3350*
from the carrying *a* into Babylon ... Mt 1:17 *3350*
was minded to put her *a* privily ... Mt 1:19 *630*
Whosoever shall put *a* his wife ... Mt 5:31 *630*
whosoever shall put *a* his wife ... Mt 5:32 *630*
take *a* thy coat, let him have thy ... Mt 5:40
borrow of thee turn not thou *a* ... Mt 5:42 *654*
suffer us to go *a* into the herd ... Mt 8:31 *565*
they had no root, they withered *a* ... Mt 13:6
be taken *a* even that he hath ... Mt 13:12 *142*
catcheth *a* that which was sown in ... Mt 13:19 *726*
Then Jesus sent the multitude *a* ... Mt 13:36 *863*
into vessels, but cast the bad *a* ... Mt 13:48 *1854*
send the multitude *a*, that they ... Mt 14:15 *630*
while he sent the multitudes *a* ... Mt 14:22 *630*
when he had sent the multitudes *a* ... Mt 14:23 *630*
besought him, saying, Send her *a* ... Mt 15:23 *630*
and I will not send them *a* fasting ... Mt 15:32 *630*
he sent *a* the multitude, and took ... Mt 15:39 *630*
to put *a* his wife for every cause ... Mt 19:3 *630*
of divorcement, and to put her *a* ... Mt 19:7 *630*
suffered you to put *a* your wives ... Mt 19:8 *630*
Whosoever shall put *a* his wife ... Mt 19:9 *630*
is put *a* doth commit adultery ... Mt 19:9 *630*
that saying, he went *a* sorrowful ... Mt 19:22 *565*
presently the fig tree withered *a* ... Mt 21:19
soon is the fig tree withered *a* ... Mt 21:20
him hand and foot, and take him *a* ... Mt 22:13 *142*
Heaven and earth shall pass *a* ... Mt 24:35 *3928*
but my words shall not pass *a* ... Mt 24:35 *3928*
flood came, and took them all *a* ... Mt 24:39 *142*
taken *a* even that which he hath ... Mt 25:29 *142*
these shall go *a* into everlasting ... Mt 25:46 *565*
He went *a* again the second time ... Mt 26:42 *565*
this cup may not pass *a* from me ... Mt 26:42 *3928*
went *a* again, and prayed the third ... Mt 26:44 *565*
him *a* to Caiaphas the high priest ... Mt 26:57 *520*
had bound him, they led him *a* ... Mt 27:2 *520*
him, and led him *a* to crucify him ... Mt 27:31 *520*
come by night, and steal him *a* ... Mt 27:64
stole him *a* while we slept ... Mt 28:13
disciples went *a* into Galilee ... Mt 28:16
him, and forthwith sent him *a* ... Mk 1:43 *1544*
shall be taken *a* from them ... Mk 2:20 *522*
it up taketh *a* from the old ... Mk 2:21 *142*
it had no root, it withered *a* ... Mk 4:6
taketh *a* the word that was sown ... Mk 4:15 *142*
they had sent *a* the multitude ... Mk 4:36 *863*
send them *a* out of the country ... Mk 5:10 *649*
Send them *a*, that they may go ... Mk 6:36 *630*
while he sent *a* the people ... Mk 6:45 *630*
And when he had sent them *a* ... Mk 6:46 *657*
if I send them *a* fasting to their ... Mk 8:3 *630*
and he sent them *a* ... Mk 8:9 *630*
he sent him *a* to his house ... Mk 8:26 *649*
with his teeth, and pineth *a* ... Mk 9:18
for a man to put *a* his wife ... Mk 10:2 *630*
of divorcement, and to put her *a* ... Mk 10:4 *630*
Whosoever shall put *a* his wife ... Mk 10:11 *630*
a woman shall put *a* her husband ... Mk 10:12 *630*
at that saying, and went *a* grieved ... Mk 10:22 *565*
casting *a* his garment, rose, and ... Mk 10:50 *577*
which thou cursedst is withered *a* ... Mk 11:21
and beat him, and sent him *a* empty ... Mk 12:3 *649*
sent him *a* shamefully handled ... Mk 12:4 *649*
Heaven and earth shall pass *a* ... Mk 13:31 *3928*
but my words shall not pass *a* ... Mk 13:31 *3928*
take *a* this cup from me ... Mk 14:36 *3911*
And again he went *a*, and prayed, and ... Mk 14:39 *565*
take him, and lead him *a* safely ... Mk 14:44 *520*
they led Jesus *a* to the high ... Mk 14:53 *520*
and bound Jesus, and carried him *a* ... Mk 15:1 *667*
soldiers led him *a* into the hall ... Mk 15:16 *520*
Who shall roll us *a* the stone ... Mk 16:3 *617*
saw that the stone was rolled *a* ... Mk 16:4 *617*
to take *a* my reproach among men ... Lk 1:25 *851*
and the rich he hath sent empty *a* ... Lk 1:53 *1821*
were gone *a* from them into heaven ... Lk 2:15 *565*
shall be taken *a* from them ... Lk 5:35 *851*

him that taketh *a* thy cloke ..... Lk 6:29 *142*
of him that taketh *a* thy goods ..... Lk 6:30 *142*
it was sprung up, it withered *a* ..... Lk 8:6
taketh *a* the word out of their ..... Lk 8:12 *142*
and in time of temptation fall *a* ..... Lk 8:13 *868*
but Jesus sent him *a*, saying, ... Lk 8:38 *630*
And when the day began to wear *a* ..... Lk 9:12
unto him, Send the multitude *a* ..... Lk 9:12 *630*
and lose himself, or be cast *a* ..... Lk 9:25 *2210*
shall not be taken *a* from her ..... Lk 10:42 *851*
for ye have taken *a* the key of ..... Lk 11:52
stall, and lead him *a* to watering ..... Lk 13:15 *520*
for my lord taketh *a* from me the ..... Lk 16:3 *851*
Whosoever putteth *a* his wife ..... Lk 16:18 *630*
marrieth her that is put *a* from ..... Lk 16:18 *630*
him not come down to take it *a* ..... Lk 17:31
he hath shall be taken *a* from him ..... Lk 19:26
beat him, and sent him *a* empty ..... Lk 20:10 *1821*
shamefully, and sent him *a* empty ..... Lk 20:11 *1821*
shall be led *a* captive into all ..... Lk 21:24
This generation shall not pass *a* ..... Lk 21:32
Heaven and earth shall pass *a* ..... Lk 21:33
but my words shall not pass *a* ..... Lk 21:33
A with this man, and release unto ..... Lk 23:18
And as they led him *a*, they laid ..... Lk 23:26 *520*
stone rolled *a* from the sepulchre ..... Lk 24:2 *617*
which taketh *a* the sin of the ..... Jn 1:29
gone *a* unto the city to buy meat ..... Jn 4:8 *565*
for Jesus had conveyed himself *a* ..... Jn 5:13 *1593*
his disciples were gone *a* alone ..... Jn 6:22 *565*
the twelve, Will ye also go *a* ..... Jn 6:67 *5217*
went *a* again beyond Jordan into ..... Jn 10:40 *565*
Jesus said, Take ye *a* the stone ..... Jn 11:39
Then they took *a* the stone from ..... Jn 11:41
take *a* both our place and nation ..... Jn 11:48
of him many of the Jews went *a* ..... Jn 12:11 *5217*
heard how I said unto you, I go *a* ..... Jn 14:28 *5217*
beareth not fruit he taketh *a* ..... Jn 15:2
is expedient for you that I go *a* ..... Jn 16:7 *565*
for if I go not *a*, the Comforter ..... Jn 16:7 *565*
And led him *a* to Annas first ..... Jn 18:13 *520*
A with him, *a* with him, ... Jn 19:15 *142*
And they took Jesus, and led him *a* ..... Jn 19:16 *520*
and that they might be taken *a* ..... Jn 19:31
he might take *a* the body of Jesus ..... Jn 19:38
stone taken *a* from the sepulchre ..... Jn 20:1
They have taken *a* the Lord out of ..... Jn 20:2
Then the disciples went *a* again ..... Jn 20:10 *565*
Because they have taken *a* my Lord ..... Jn 20:13
laid him, and I will take him *a* ..... Jn 20:15
in turning *a* every one of you ..... Acts 3:26 *654*
drew *a* much people after him ..... Acts 5:37 *868*
his neighbour wrong thrust him *a* ..... Acts 7:27 *683*
I will carry you *a* beyond Babylon ..... Acts 7:43 *3351*
his judgment was taken *a* ..... Acts 8:33
of the Lord caught *a* Philip ..... Acts 8:39 *726*
the morrow Peter went *a* with them ..... Acts 10:23 *1831*
hands on them, they sent them *a* ..... Acts 13:3 *630*
seeking to turn *a* the deputy from ..... Acts 13:8 *1294*
brethren immediately sent *a* Paul ..... Acts 17:10 *1599*
a Paul to go as it were to the ..... Acts 17:14 *1821*
turned *a* much people, saying that ..... Acts 19:26 *3179*
we sailed *a* from Philippi after ..... Acts 20:6 *1602*
to draw *a* disciples after them ..... Acts 20:30 *645*
after, crying, *A* with him ..... Acts 21:36 *142*
wash *a* thy sins, calling on the ..... Acts 22:16 *628*
A with such a fellow from the ..... Acts 22:22 *142*
took him *a* out of our hands ..... Acts 24:7 *520*
should be saved was then taken *a* ..... Acts 27:20 *4014*
then, Hath God cast *a* his people ..... Rom 11:1 *683*
God hath not cast *a* his people ..... Rom 11:2 *683*
For if the casting *a* of them be ..... Rom 11:15 *580*
shall turn *a* ungodliness from ..... Rom 11:26 *654*
when I shall take *a* their sins ..... Rom 11:27 *851*
might be taken *a* from among you 1Cor 5:2
Therefore put *a* from among 1Cor 5:13 *1808*
not the husband put *a* his wife 1Cor 7:11 *863*
with him, let him not put her *a* 1Cor 7:12 *863*
fashion of this world passeth *a* 1Cor 7:31
carried *a* unto these dumb idols, ... 1Cor 12:2 *520*
be knowledge, it shall vanish *a* 1Cor 13:8 *2673*
which is in part shall be done *a* 1Cor 13:10 *2673*
a man, I put *a* childish things 1Cor 13:11 *2673*
which glory was to be done *a* 2Cor 3:7 *2673*
that which is done *a* was glorious 2Cor 3:11 *2673*
a in the reading of the old 2Cor 3:14 *343*
which vail is done *a* in Christ 2Cor 3:14 *2673*
Lord, the vail shall be taken *a* 2Cor 3:16 *4014*
old things are passed *a* 2Cor 5:17
a with their dissimulation ..... Gal 2:13 *4879*
Wherefore putting *a* lying ..... Eph 4:25 *659*
be put *a* from you, with all ..... Eph 4:31
be not moved *a* from the hope of ..... Col 1:23 *3334*
there come a falling *a* first 2Th 2:3 *646*
which some having put *a* 1Ti 1:19 *683*
are in Asia be turned *a* from me 2Ti 1:15 *654*
from such turn *a* 2Ti 3:5 *665*
sins, led *a* with divers lusts, ... 2Ti 3:6
they shall turn *a* their ears from 2Ti 4:4 *654*
If they shall fall *a*, to renew ..... Heb 6:6 *3895*
waxeth old is ready to vanish *a* ..... Heb 8:13
world hath he appeared to put *a* ..... Heb 9:26 *115*
and of goats should take *a* sins ..... Heb 10:4 *851*
He taketh *a* the first, that he ..... Heb 10:9 *337*
which can never take *a* sins ..... Heb 10:11 *4014*
Cast not *a* therefore your ..... Heb 10:35 *577*
if we turn *a* from him that ..... Heb 12:25 *654*
of the grass he shall pass *a* ..... Jas 1:10
the rich man fade *a* in his ways ..... Jas 1:11
he is drawn *a* of his own lust ..... Jas 1:14
little time, and then vanisheth *a* ..... Jas 4:14
undefiled, and that fadeth not *a* 1Pet 1:4
and the flower thereof falleth *a* 1Pet 1:24 *1601*
a of the filth of the flesh 1Pet 3:21 *595*
crown of glory that fadeth not *a* 1Pet 5:4
shall pass *a* with a great noise 2Pet 3:10
being led *a* with the error of the 2Pet 3:17 *4879*
And the world passeth *a*, and the 1Jn 2:17
was manifested to take *a* our sins 1Jn 3:5
God shall wipe *a* all tears from ..... Rev 7:17 *1813*
her to be carried *a* of the flood ..... Rev 12:15
And every island fled *a*, and the ..... Rev 16:20
So he carried me *a* in the spirit ..... Rev 17:3 *667*
the earth and the heaven fled *a* ..... Rev 20:11
and the first earth were passed *a* ..... Rev 21:1
God shall wipe *a* all tears from ..... Rev 21:4 *1813*
the former things are passed *a* ..... Rev 21:4 *565*
he carried me *a* in the spirit to ..... Rev 21:10 *667*
if any man shall take *a* from the ..... Rev 22:19 *851*
God shall take *a* his part out of ..... Rev 22:19 *851*

AWE
Stand in *a*, and sin not ..... Ps 4:4 7264
of the world stand in *a* of him ..... Ps 33:8 1481
heart standeth in *a* of thy word ..... Ps 119:161 6342

AWOKE
Noah *a* from his wine, and knew ..... Gen 9:24 3364
So Pharaoh *a* ..... Gen 41:4 3364
And Pharaoh *a*, and, behold, it was ..... Gen 41:7 3364
So I *a* ..... Gen 41:21 3364
he *a* out of his sleep, and said, I ..... Judg 16:20 3364
And Solomon *a* 1Kin 3:15 3364
a him, saying, Lord, save us ..... Mt 8:25 *1453*
a him, saying, Master, master, we ..... Lk 8:24 *1326*

AX
by forcing an *a* against them ..... Deut 20:19 1631
share, and his coulter, and his *a* 1Sa 13:20 7134
the *a* head fell into the water 2Kin 6:5 1270
Shall the *a* boast itself against ..... Is 10:15 1631
hands of the workman, with the *a* ..... Jer 10:3 4621
Thou art my battle *a* and weapons ..... Jer 51:20 4601
now also the *a* is laid unto the ..... Mt 3:10 *513*

AXE
with the *a* to cut down the tree ..... Deut 19:5 1631
Abimelech took an *a* in his hand ..... Judg 9:48 7134
there was neither hammer nor *a* 1Kin 6:7 1631
now also the *a* is laid unto the ..... Lk 3:9 *513*

AXES
and for the forks, and for the *a* 1Sa 13:21 7134
under *a* of iron, and made them 2Sa 12:31 4037
with harrows of iron, and with *a* 1Chr 20:3 4050
lifted up *a* upon the thick trees ..... Ps 74:5 7134
work thereof at once with *a* ..... Ps 74:6 3781
army, and come against her with *a* ..... Jer 46:22 7134
with his *a* he shall break down ..... Eze 26:9 2719

AXLETREES
the *a* of the wheels were joined 1Kin 7:32 3027
their *a*, and their naves, and their 1Kin 7:33 3027

AZAL (*a'-zal*) *A place near Jerusalem.*
the mountains shall reach unto *A* ..... Zec 14:5 682

AZALIAH (*az-a-li'-ah*) *Father of Shaphan.*
king sent Shaphan the son of *A* 2Kin 22:3 683
he sent Shaphan the son of *A* 2Chr 34:8 683

AZANIAH (*az-a-ni'-ah*) *Father of Jeshua.*
both Jeshua the son of *A*, Binnui ..... Neh 10:9 245

AZARAEL (*a-zar'-a-el*) See AZAREEL. *A priest from the Immer family.*
And his brethren, Shemaiah, and *A* ..... Neh 12:36 5832

AZAREEL (*a-zar'-e-el*) See AZARAEL.
1. A Korahite in David's army.
Elkanah, and Jesiah, and *A*, and 1Chr 12:6 5832
2. A priest during David's time.
The eleventh to *A*, he, his sons, ... 1Chr 25:18 5832
3. A Danite prince during David's time.
Of Dan, *A* the son of Jeroham 1Chr 27:22 5832
4. Married a foreign wife in exile.
A, and Shelemiah, Shemariah, ... Ezr 10:41 5832
5. Same as Azarael.
and Amashai the son of *A*, the son ..... Neh 11:13 5832

AZAREL See AZAREEL.

AZARIAH (*az-a-ri'-ah*) See AHAZIAH.
1. A descendant of Zadok.
A the son of Zadok the priest, ... 1Kin 4:2 5838
2. Captain of Solomon's guard.
A the son of Nathan was over the 1Kin 4:5 5838
3. A king of Judah.
And all the people of Judah took *A* 2Kin 14:21 5838
Jeroboam king of Israel began *A* 2Kin 15:1 5838
And the rest of the acts of *A* 2Kin 15:6 5838
So *A* slept with his fathers 2Kin 15:7 5838
eighth year of *A* king of Judah 2Kin 15:8 5838
thirtieth year of *A* king of Judah 2Kin 15:17 5838
In the fiftieth year of *A* king of 2Kin 15:23 5838
fiftieth year of *A* king of Judah 2Kin 15:27 5838
A his son, Jotham his son, ... 1Chr 3:12 5838
4. A descendant of Judah.
the sons of Ethan; *A* 1Chr 2:8 5838
5. A descendant of Jerahmeel.
Obed begat Jehu, and Jehu begat *A* 1Chr 2:38 5838
A begat Helez, and Helez begat 1Chr 2:39 5838
6. A son of Ahimaaz.
And Ahimaaz begat *A*, and Azariah 1Chr 6:9 5838
7. Grandson of Ahimaah.
And Johanan begat *A*, (he it is 1Chr 6:10 5838
A begat Amariah, and Amariah begat 1Chr 6:11 5838
8. A son of Hilkiah.
begat Hilkiah, and Hilkiah begat *A* 1Chr 6:13 5838
A begat Seraiah, and Seraiah begat 1Chr 6:14 5838
A the son of Hilkiah, the son of 1Chr 9:11 5838
the son of Seraiah, the son of *A* ..... Ezr 7:1 5838
9. A descendant of Kohath.
the son of Joel, the son of *A* 1Chr 6:36 5838
10. A prophet sent to King Asa.
God came upon *A* the son of Oded 2Chr 15:1 5838
11. A son of King Jehoshaphat.
the sons of Jehoshaphat, *A* 2Chr 21:2 5838
12. A brother of King Jehoram.
and Jehiel, and Zechariah, and *A* 2Chr 21:2 5838
13. A son of King Jehoram.
A the son of Jehoram king of 2Chr 22:6 5838
14. A conspirator with Joash.
A the son of Jeroham, and Ishmael 2Chr 23:1 5838
15. Another conspirator with Joash.
A the son of Obed, and Maaseiah 2Chr 23:1 5838
16. A High Priest.
A the priest went in after him, ... 2Chr 26:17 5838
A the chief priest, and all the 2Chr 26:20 5838
17. A chief of Ephraim.
A the son of Johanan, Berechiah 2Chr 28:12 5838
18. Father of Joel.
of Amasai, and Joel the son of *A* 2Chr 29:12 5838
19. Helped cleanse the Temple.
Abdi, and *A* the son of Jehalelel 2Chr 29:12 5838
20. A chief priest.
A the chief priest of the house 2Chr 31:10 5838
A the ruler of the house of God 2Chr 31:13 5838
21. Great-grandfather of Zadok.
The son of Amariah, the son of *A* ..... Ezr 7:3 5838
22. A repairer of the Jerusalem walls.
After him repaired *A* the son of ..... Neh 3:23 5838
from the house of *A* unto the ..... Neh 3:24 5838
23. An exile with Zerubbabel.
Zerubbabel, Jeshua, Nehemiah, *A* ..... Neh 7:7 5838
24. A priest with Ezra.
Hodijah, Maaseiah, Kelita, *A* ..... Neh 8:7 5838
25. A priest who renewed the covenant.
Seraiah, *A*, Jeremiah, ... Neh 10:2 5838
26. A prince of Judah.
And *A*, Ezra, and Meshullam, ... Neh 12:33 5838
27. The son of Hoshaiah.
Then spake *A* the son of Hoshaiah, ... Jer 43:2 5838
28. A companion of Daniel.
Daniel, Hananiah, Mishael, and *A* ..... Dan 1:6 5838
and to *A*, of Abed-nego ..... Dan 1:7 5838
Daniel, Hananiah, Mishael, and *A* ..... Dan 1:11 5838
Daniel, Hananiah, Mishael, and *A* ..... Dan 1:19 5838
known to Hananiah, Mishael, and *A* ..... Dan 2:17 5839

AZARYAHU See AZARIAH.

AZAZ (*a'-zaz*) *Father of Bela.*
And Bela the son of *A*, the son of 1Chr 5:8 5811

AZAZIAH (*az-a-zi'-ah*)
1. A Levite who relocated the Ark.
and Obed-edom, and Jeiel, and *A* 1Chr 15:21 5812
2. Father of Hoshea.
of Ephraim, Hoshea the son of *A* 1Chr 27:20 5812
3. A Levite during Hezekiah's reign.
And Jehiel, and *A*, and Nahath, and 2Chr 31:13 5812

AZBUK (*az'-buk*) *Father of Nehemiah.*
repaired Nehemiah the son of *A* ..... Neh 3:16 5802

AZEKAH (*a-ze'-kah*) *A town in Judah.*
to Beth-horon, and smote them to *A* ..... Josh 10:10 5825
from heaven upon them unto *A* ..... Josh 10:11 5825
Jarmuth, and Adullam, Socoh, and *A* ..... Josh 15:35 5825
and pitched between Shochoh and *A* 1Sa 17:1 5825
And Adoraim, and Lachish, and *A* 2Chr 11:9 5825
and the fields thereof, at *A* ..... Neh 11:30 5825
against Lachish, and against *A* ..... Jer 34:7 5825

AZEL (*a'-zel*) See JAAZIEL. *A descendant of King Saul.*
son, Eleasah his son, *A* his son 1Chr 8:37 682
A had six sons, whose names are 1Chr 8:38 682
All these were the sons of *A* 1Chr 8:38 682
son, Eleasah his son, *A* his son 1Chr 9:43 682
A had six sons, whose names are 1Chr 9:44 682
these were the sons of *A* 1Chr 9:44 682

AZEM (*a'-zem*) See EZEM. *A city in Judah.*
Baalah, and Iim, and *A*, ... Josh 15:29 6107
And Hazar-shual, and Balah, and *A* ..... Josh 19:3 6107

AZGAD (*az'-gad*)
1. A family of exiles.
The children of *A*, a thousand two ..... Ezr 2:12 5803
The children of *A*, two thousand ..... Neh 7:17 5803
2. An exile with Ezra.
And of the sons of *A* ..... Ezr 8:12 5803
3. A family who sealed the covenant.
Bunni, *A*, Bebai, ... Neh 10:15 5803

AZIEL (*a'-ze-el*) *A Levite who relocated the Ark.*
And Zechariah, and *A*, and 1Chr 15:20 5815

AZIZA (*a-zi'-zah*) *Married a foreigner in exile.*
and Jeremoth, and Zabad, and *A* ..... Ezr 10:27 5819

AZMAVETH (*az-ma'-veth*) See BETH-AZMAVETH.
1. A "mighty man" of David.
the Arbathite, *A* the Barhumite, ... 2Sa 23:31 5820
A the Baharumite, Eliahba the 1Chr 11:33 5820
2. A descendant of Jonathan.
and Jehoadah begat Alemeth, and *A* 1Chr 8:36 5820
and Jarah begat Alemeth, and *A* 1Chr 9:42 5820
3. Father of Jeziel and Pelet.
Jeziel, and Pelet, the sons of *A* 1Chr 12:3 5820
4. A village on the border of Judah.
The children of *A*, forty and two ..... Ezr 2:24 5820
and out of the fields of Geba and *A* ..... Neh 12:29 5820
5. A treasurer of David.
treasures was *A* the son of Adiel 1Chr 27:25 5820

AZMON (*az'-mon*) See HESHMON. *A place in southern Canaan.*
to Hazar-addar, and pass on to *A* ..... Num 34:4 6111

from A unto the river of Egypt ... Num 34:5 6111
From thence it passed toward A ... Josh 15:4 6111

AZNOTH-TABOR (*az''-noth-ta'-bor*) *Hills on the border of Naphtali.*
the coast turneth westward to A ... Josh 19:34 243

AZOR (*a'-zor*) *Great-grandson of Zorobabel.*
and Eliakim begat A ... Mt 1:13 *107*
And A begat Sadoc ... Mt 1:14 *107*

AZOTUS (*a-zo'-tus*) See ASHDOD. *Greek form of Ashdod.*
But Philip was found at A ... Acts 8:40 *108*

AZRIEL (*az'-re-el*)
1. Chief of a family of Manasseh.
Epher, and Ishi, and Eliel, and A ... 1Chr 5:24 5837
2. Father of Jerimoth
Naphtali, Jerimoth the son of A ... 1Chr 27:19 5837
3. Father of Seraiah.
and Seraiah the son of A, and ... Jer 36:26 5837

AZRIKAM (*az'-ri-kam*)
1. A son of Neariah.
Elioenai, and Hezekiah, and A ... 1Chr 3:23 5840
2. A son of Azel.
sons, whose names are these, A ... 1Chr 8:38 5840
sons, whose names are these, A ... 1Chr 9:44 5840
3. A descendant of Merari.
the son of Hasshub, the son of A ... 1Chr 9:14 5840
the son of Hashub, the son of A ... Neh 11:15 5840
4. Governor of the house of King Ahaz.
A the governor of the house, and ... 2Chr 28:7 5840

AZUBAH (*a-zu'-bah*)
1. Mother of King Jehoshaphat.
his mother's name was A the ... 1Kin 22:42 5806
his mother's name was A the ... 2Chr 20:31 5806
2. Wife of Caleb.
begat children of A his wife ... 1Chr 2:18 5806
when A was dead, Caleb took unto ... 1Chr 2:19 5806

AZUR (*a'-zur*) See AZZUR.
1. Father of Hananiah.
Hananiah the son of A the prophet ... Jer 28:1 5809
2. Father of Jaazaniah.
whom I saw Jaazaniah the son of A ... Eze 11:1 5809

AZZAH (*az'-zah*) See GAZA. *A Philistine city.*
dwelt in Hazerim, even unto A ... Deut 2:23 5804
the river, from Tiphsah even to A ... 1Kin 4:24 5804
Philistines, and Ashkelon, and A ... Jer 25:20 5804

AZZAN (*az'-zan*) *A prince of Issachar.*
of Issachar, Paltiel the son of A ... Num 34:26 5821

AZZUR (*az'-zur*) *An Israelite who sealed the covenant under Nehemiah.*
Ater, Hizkijah, A, ... Neh 10:17 5809

B

BAAL (*ba'-al*) See BAAL-BERITH, BAALE, BAAL-GAD, BAAL-HAMON, BAAL-HANAN, BAAL-HAZOR, BAAL-HERMON, BAALIM, BAAL-MEON, BAAL-PEOR, BAAL-PERAZIM, BAAL-SHALISHA, BAAL-TAMAR.
1. Chief god of the Canaanites.
him up into the high places of B ... Num 22:41 1168
forsook the LORD, and served B ... Judg 2:13 1168
altar of B that thy father hath ... Judg 6:25 1168
the altar of B was cast down, and ... Judg 6:28 1168
he hath cast down the altar of B ... Judg 6:30 1168
against him, Will ye plead for B ... Judg 6:31 1168
Let B plead against him, because ... Judg 6:32 1168
Zidonians, and went and served B ... 1Kin 16:31 1168
altar for B in the house of B ... 1Kin 16:32 1168
and the prophets of B four hundred ... 1Kin 18:19 1168
but if B, then follow him ... 1Kin 18:21 1168
said unto the prophets of B ... 1Kin 18:25 1168
called on the name of B from ... 1Kin 18:26 1168
even until noon, saying, O B ... 1Kin 18:26 1168
unto them, Take the prophets of B ... 1Kin 18:40 1168
knees which have not bowed unto B ... 1Kin 19:18 1168
For he served B, and worshipped ... 1Kin 22:53 1168
of B that his father had made ... 2Kin 3:2 1168
unto them, Ahab served B a little ... 2Kin 10:18 1168
unto me all the prophets of B ... 2Kin 10:19 1168
have a great sacrifice to do to B ... 2Kin 10:19 1168
destroy the worshippers of B ... 2Kin 10:19 1168
Proclaim a solemn assembly for B ... 2Kin 10:20 1168
and all the worshippers of B came ... 2Kin 10:21 1168
And they came into the house of B ... 2Kin 10:21 1168
the house of B was full from one ... 2Kin 10:21 1168
for all the worshippers of B ... 2Kin 10:22 1168
of Rechab, into the house of B ... 2Kin 10:23 1168
and said unto the worshippers of B ... 2Kin 10:23 1168
but the worshippers of B only ... 2Kin 10:23 1168
to the city of the house of B ... 2Kin 10:25 1168
the images out of the house of B ... 2Kin 10:26 1168
And they brake down the image of B ... 2Kin 10:27 1168
and brake down the house of B ... 2Kin 10:27 1168
Jehu destroyed B out of Israel ... 2Kin 10:28 1168
the land went into the house of B ... 2Kin 11:18 1168
the priest of B before the altars ... 2Kin 11:18 1168
the host of heaven, and served B ... 2Kin 17:16 1168
and he reared up altars for B ... 2Kin 21:3 1168
the vessels that were made for B ... 2Kin 23:4 1168
also that burned incense unto B ... 2Kin 23:5 1168
the people went to the house of B ... 2Chr 23:17 1168
the priest of B before the altars ... 2Chr 23:17 1168
and the prophets prophesied by B ... Jer 2:8 1168
falsely, and burn incense unto B ... Jer 7:9 1168
altars to burn incense unto B ... Jer 11:13 1168
anger in offering incense unto B ... Jer 11:17 1168
taught my people to swear by B ... Jer 12:16 1168
built also the high places of B ... Jer 19:5 1168
fire for burnt offerings unto B ... Jer 19:5 1168
they prophesied in B, and caused ... Jer 23:13 1168
have forgotten my name for B ... Jer 23:27 1168
they have offered incense unto B ... Jer 32:29 1168
they built the high places of B ... Jer 32:35 1168
gold, which they prepared for B ... Hos 2:8 1168
but when he offended in B ... Hos 13:1 1168
the remnant of B from this place ... Zeph 1:4 1168
bowed the knee to the image of B ... Rom 11:4 *896*
2. A city in Simeon.
about the same cities, unto B ... 1Chr 4:33 1168
3. A descendant of Reuben.
son, Reaia his son, B his son, ... 1Chr 5:5 1168
4. A descendant of Benjamin.
son Abdon, and Zur, and Kish, and B ... 1Chr 8:30 1168
Abdon, then Zur, and Kish, and B ... 1Chr 9:36 1168

BAALAH (*ba'-al-ah*) See BAALE, BALEH, BILHAH, KIRJATH-BAAL.
1. A city in Judah.
and the border was drawn to B ... Josh 15:9 1173
from B westward unto mount Seir ... Josh 15:10 1173
B, and Iim, and Azem ... Josh 15:29 1173
went up, and all Israel, to B ... 1Chr 13:6 1173
2. A hill in Judah.
and passed along to mount B ... Josh 15:11 1173

BAALATH (*ba'-al-ath*) See BAALATH-BEER. *A town in Dan.*
And Eltekeh, and Gibbethon, and B ... Josh 19:44 1191
And B, and Tadmor in the wilderness ... 1Kin 9:18 1191
And B, and all the store cities ... 2Chr 8:6 1191

BAALATH-BEER (*ba''-al-ath-be'-ur*) *A city in Simeon.*
round about these cities to B ... Josh 19:8 1192

BAAL-BERITH (*ba''-al-be'-rith*) *An idol.*
after Baalim, and made B their god ... Judg 8:33 1170
of silver out of the house of B ... Judg 9:4 1170

BAALE (*ba'-al-eh*) *A form of Baalah.*
were with him from B of Judah ... 2Sa 6:2 1184

BAALE-JUDAH See BAALE.

BAAL-GAD (*ba''-al-gad'*) *A Canaanite city.*
even unto B in the valley of ... Josh 11:17 1171
from B in the valley of Lebanon ... Josh 12:7 1171
from B under mount Hermon unto ... Josh 13:5 1171

BAAL-HAMON (*ba''-al-ha'-mon*) *A place near Samaria.*
Solomon had a vineyard at B ... Song 8:11 1174

BAAL-HANAN (*ba''-al-ha'-nan*)
1. A king of Edom.
B the son of Achbor reigned in ... Gen 36:38 1177
B the son of Achbor died, and ... Gen 36:39 1177
B the son of Achbor reigned in ... 1Chr 1:49 1177
when B was dead, Hadad reigned in ... 1Chr 1:50 1177
2. A superintendent for David.
the low plains was B the Gederite ... 1Chr 27:28 1177

BAAL-HAZOR (*ba''-al-ha'-zor*) See HAZOR. *A place near Ephraim.*
Absalom had sheepshearers in B ... 2Sa 13:23 1178

BAAL-HERMON (*ba''-al-her'-mon*) *A city near Mt. Hermon.*
from mount B unto the entering in ... Judg 3:3 1179
they increased from Bashan unto B ... 1Chr 5:23 1179

BAALI (*ba'-al-i*) *A rejected title of God.*
and shalt call me no more B ... Hos 2:16 1180

BAALIM (*ba'-al-im*) See BAAL. *Plural of Baal.*
sight of the LORD, and served B ... Judg 2:11 1168
the LORD their God, and served B ... Judg 3:7 1168
again, and went a whoring after B ... Judg 8:33 1168
sight of the LORD, and served B ... Judg 10:6 1168
our God, and also served B ... Judg 10:10 1168
children of Israel did put away B ... 1Sa 7:4 1168
the LORD, and have served B ... 1Sa 12:10 1168
the LORD, and thou hast followed B ... 1Kin 18:18 1168
David, and sought not unto B ... 2Chr 17:3 1168
the LORD did they bestow upon B ... 2Chr 24:7 1168
and made also molten images for B ... 2Chr 28:2 1168
and he reared up altars for B ... 2Chr 33:3 1168
the altars of B in his presence ... 2Chr 34:4 1168
polluted, I have not gone after B ... Jer 2:23 1168
of their own heart, and after B ... Jer 9:14 1168
will visit upon her the days of B ... Hos 2:13 1168
the names of B out of her mouth ... Hos 2:17 1168
they sacrificed unto B, and burned ... Hos 11:2 1168

BAALIS (*ba'-al-is*) *A king of the Ammonites.*
Dost thou certainly know that B ... Jer 40:14 1185

BAAL-MEON (*ba''-al-me'-on*) See BETH-BAAL-MEON. *A Reubenite town.*
And Nebo, and B, (their names being ... Num 32:38 1186
in Aroer, even unto Nebo and B ... 1Chr 5:8 1186
of the country, Beth-jeshimoth, B ... Eze 25:9 1186

BAAL-PEOR (*ba''-al-pe'-or*) See PEOR. *A Moabite idol.*
And Israel joined himself unto B ... Num 25:3 1187
his men that were joined unto B ... Num 25:5 1187
what the LORD did because of B ... Deut 4:3 1187
for all the men that followed B ... Deut 4:3 1187
joined themselves also unto B ... Ps 106:28 1187
but they went to B, and separated ... Hos 9:10 1187

BAAL-PERAZIM (*ba''-al-per'-a-zim*) *A place near the valley of Rephaim.*
And David came to B, and David ... 2Sa 5:20 1188
called the name of that place B ... 2Sa 5:20 1188
So they came up to B ... 1Chr 14:11 1188
called the name of that place B ... 1Chr 14:11 1188

BAAL'S (*ba'-als*)
but B prophets are four hundred ... 1Kin 18:22 1168

BAAL-SHALISHA (*ba''-al-shal'-i-shah*) *A place in Ephraim*
And there came a man from B ... 2Kin 4:42 1190

BAAL-TAMAR (*ba''-al-ta'-mar*) *A place in Benjamin.*
and put themselves in array at B ... Judg 20:33 1193

BAAL-ZEBUB (*ba''-al-ze'-bub*) See BEELZEBUB. *A Philistine idol.*
enquire of B the god of Ekron ... 2Kin 1:2 1176
to enquire of B the god of Ekron ... 2Kin 1:3 1176
to enquire of B the god of Ekron ... 2Kin 1:6 1176
to enquire of B the god of Ekron ... 2Kin 1:16 1176

BAAL-ZEPHON (*ba''-al-ze'-fon*) *A place near the Rea Sea crossing.*
Migdol and the sea, over against B ... Ex 14:2 1189
sea, beside Pi-hahiroth, before B ... Ex 14:9 1189
Pi-hahiroth, which is before B ... Num 33:7 1189

BAANA (*ba'-an-ah*) See BAANAH.
1. An officer in Solomon's army.
B the son of Ahilud ... 1Kin 4:12 1195
2. Father of Zadok.
them repaired Zadok the son of B ... Neh 3:4 1195

BAANAH (*ba'-an-ah*) See BAANA.
1. A captain in Ishbosheth's army.
the name of the one was B ... 2Sa 4:2 1195
the Beerothite, Rechab and B ... 2Sa 4:5 1195
Rechab and B his brother escaped ... 2Sa 4:6 1195
B his brother, the sons of Rimmon ... 2Sa 4:9 1195
2. Father of Heleb.
Heleb the son of B, a ... 2Sa 23:29 1195
the son of B the Netophathite ... 1Chr 11:30 1195
3. An officer in Solomon's army.
B the son of Hushai was in Asher ... 1Kin 4:16 1195
4. An exile who returned with Zerubbabel.
Bilshan, Mizpar, Bigvai, Rehum, B ... Ezr 2:2 1195
Mispereth, Bigvai, Nehum, B ... Neh 7:7 1195
Malluch, Harim, B ... Neh 10:27 1195

BAARA (*ba'-ar-ah*) *A wife of Shaharaim.*
Hushim and B were his wives ... 1Chr 8:8 1199

BAASEIAH (*ba-as-i'-ah*) *A Gersonite Levite.*
The son of Michael, the son of B ... 1Chr 6:40 1202

BAASHA (*ba'-ash-ah*) *A king of Israel.*
B king of Israel all their days ... 1Kin 15:16 1201
B king of Israel went up against ... 1Kin 15:17 1201
thy league with B king of Israel ... 1Kin 15:19 1201
when B heard thereof, that he ... 1Kin 15:21 1201
thereof, wherewith B had builded ... 1Kin 15:22 1201
B the son of Ahijah, of the house ... 1Kin 15:27 1201
B smote him at Gibbethon, which ... 1Kin 15:27 1201
Asa king of Judah did B slay him ... 1Kin 15:28 1201
B king of Israel all their days ... 1Kin 15:32 1201
B the son of Ahijah to reign over ... 1Kin 15:33 1201
Jehu the son of Hanani against B ... 1Kin 16:1 1201
will take away the posterity of B ... 1Kin 16:3 1201
Him that dieth of B in the city ... 1Kin 16:4 1201
Now the rest of the acts of B ... 1Kin 16:5 1201
So B slept with his fathers, and ... 1Kin 16:6 1201
the word of the LORD against B ... 1Kin 16:7 1201
B to reign over Israel in Tirzah ... 1Kin 16:8 1201
that he slew all the house of B ... 1Kin 16:11 1201
Zimri destroy all the house of B ... 1Kin 16:12 1201
against B by Jehu the prophet ... 1Kin 16:12 1201
For all the sins of B, and the ... 1Kin 16:13 1201
the house of B the son of Ahijah ... 1Kin 21:22 1201
the house of B the son of Ahijah ... 2Kin 9:9 1201
year of the reign of Asa B king ... 2Chr 16:1 1201
thy league with B king of Israel ... 2Chr 16:3 1201
when B heard it, that he left off ... 2Chr 16:5 1201
thereof, wherewith B was building ... 2Chr 16:6 1201
made for fear of B king of Israel ... Jer 41:9 1201

BABBLER
and a b is no better ... Eccl 10:11
some said, What will this b say ... Acts 17:18 *4691*

BABBLING
who hath b ... Prov 23:29 7879

BABBLINGS
trust, avoiding profane and vain b ... 1Ti 6:20 *2757*
But shun profane and vain b ... 2Ti 2:16 *2757*

BABE
and, behold, the *b* wept — Ex 2:6 — 5288
of Mary, the *b* leaped in her womb — Lk 1:41 — *1025*
the *b* leaped in my womb for joy — Lk 1:44 — *1025*
Ye shall find the *b* wrapped in — Lk 2:12 — *1025*
and the *b* lying in a manger — Lk 2:16 — *1025*
for he is a *b* — Heb 5:13 — *3516*

BABEL (*ba'-bel*) See BABYLON. *A city in the plain of Shinar.*
beginning of his kingdom was *B* — Gen 10:10 — 894
is the name of it called *B* — Gen 11:9 — 894

BABES
Out of the mouth of *b* and — Ps 8:2 — 5768
of their substance to their *b* — Ps 17:14 — 5768
and *b* shall rule over them — Is 3:4 — 8586
and hast revealed them unto *b* — Mt 11:25 — *3516*
never read, Out of the mouth of *b* — Mt 21:16 — *3516*
and hast revealed them unto *b* — Lk 10:21 — *3516*
of the foolish, a teacher of *b* — Rom 2:20 — *3516*
carnal, even as unto *b* in Christ — 1Cor 3:1 — *3516*
As newborn *b*, desire the sincere — 1Pet 2:2 — *1025*

BABYLON (*bab'-il-un*) See BABEL, BABYLONIANS, BABYLONISH, BABYLON'S, CHALDEA, SHESHACH. *Capital of the Babylonian Empire; located on the Euphrates River.*
of Assyria brought men from *B* — 2Kin 17:24 — 894
the men of *B* made Succoth-benoth, — 2Kin 17:30 — 894
the son of Baladan, king of *B* — 2Kin 20:12 — 894
from a far country, even from *B* — 2Kin 20:14 — 894
this day, shall be carried into *B* — 2Kin 20:17 — 894
in the palace of the king of *B* — 2Kin 20:18 — 894
Nebuchadnezzar king of *B* came up — 2Kin 24:1 — 894
for the king of *B* had taken from — 2Kin 24:7 — 894
of *B* came up against Jerusalem — 2Kin 24:10 — 894
king of *B* came against the city — 2Kin 24:11 — 894
Judah went out to the king of *B* — 2Kin 24:12 — 894
the king of *B* took him in the — 2Kin 24:12 — 894
he carried away Jehoiachin to *B* — 2Kin 24:15 — 894
captivity from Jerusalem to *B* — 2Kin 24:15 — 894
of *B* brought captive to *B* — 2Kin 24:16 — 894
the king of *B* made Mattaniah his — 2Kin 24:17 — 894
rebelled against the king of *B* — 2Kin 24:20 — 894
Nebuchadnezzar king of *B* came — 2Kin 25:1 — 894
him up to the king of *B* to Riblah — 2Kin 25:6 — 894
of brass, and carried him to *B* — 2Kin 25:7 — 894
of king Nebuchadnezzar king of *B* — 2Kin 25:8 — 894
guard, a servant of the king of *B* — 2Kin 25:8 — 894
that fell away to the king of *B* — 2Kin 25:11 — 894
and carried the brass of them to *B* — 2Kin 25:13 — 894
them to the king of *B* to Riblah — 2Kin 25:20 — 894
And the king of *B* smote them — 2Kin 25:21 — 894
Nebuchadnezzar king of *B* had left — 2Kin 25:22 — 894
heard that the king of *B* had made — 2Kin 25:23 — 894
the land, and serve the king of *B* — 2Kin 25:24 — 894
that Evil-merodach king of *B* in — 2Kin 25:27 — 894
the kings that were with him in *B* — 2Kin 25:28 — 894
away to *B* for their transgression — 1Chr 9:1 — 894
ambassadors of the princes of *B* — 2Chr 32:31 — 894
with fetters, and carried him to *B* — 2Chr 33:11 — 894
came up Nebuchadnezzar king of *B* — 2Chr 36:6 — 894
him in fetters, to carry him to *B* — 2Chr 36:6 — 894
of the house of the LORD to *B* — 2Chr 36:7 — 894
and put them in his temple at *B* — 2Chr 36:7 — 894
sent, and brought him to *B* — 2Chr 36:10 — 894
all these he brought to *B* — 2Chr 36:18 — 894
the sword carried he away to *B* — 2Chr 36:20 — 894
brought up from *B* unto Jerusalem — Ezr 1:11 — 894
B had carried away unto *B* — Ezr 2:1 — 894
of Nebuchadnezzar the king of *B* — Ezr 5:12 — 895
and carried the people away into *B* — Ezr 5:12 — 895
of *B* the same king Cyrus made a — Ezr 5:13 — 895
brought them into the temple of *B* — Ezr 5:14 — 895
king take out of the temple of *B* — Ezr 5:14 — 895
house, which is there at *B* — Ezr 5:17 — 895
the treasures were laid up in *B* — Ezr 6:1 — 895
at Jerusalem, and brought unto *B* — Ezr 6:5 — 895
This Ezra went up from *B* — Ezr 7:6 — 894
month began he to go up from *B* — Ezr 7:9 — 894
find in all the province of *B* — Ezr 7:16 — 895
them that went up with me from *B* — Ezr 8:1 — 894
the king of *B* had carried away — Neh 7:6 — 894
king of *B* came I unto the king — Neh 13:6 — 894
the king of *B* had carried away — Est 2:6 — 894
Rahab and *B* to them that know me — Ps 87:4 — 894
By the rivers of *B*, there we sat — Ps 137:1 — 894
O daughter of *B*, who art to be — Ps 137:8 — 894
The burden of *B*, which Isaiah the — Is 13:1 — 894
And *B*, the glory of kingdoms, the — Is 13:19 — 894
proverb against the king of *B* — Is 14:4 — 894
hosts, and cut off from *B* the name — Is 14:22 — 894
and said, *B* is fallen, is fallen — Is 21:9 — 894
the son of Baladan, king of *B* — Is 39:1 — 894
far country unto me, even from *B* — Is 39:3 — 894
this day, shall be carried to *B* — Is 39:6 — 894
in the palace of the king of *B* — Is 39:7 — 894
For your sake I have sent to *B* — Is 43:14 — 894
the dust, O virgin daughter of *B* — Is 47:1 — 894
he will do his pleasure on *B* — Is 48:14 — 894
Go ye forth of *B*, flee ye from — Is 48:20 — 894
into the hand of the king of *B* — Jer 20:4 — 894
shall carry them captive into *B* — Jer 20:4 — 894
and take them, and carry them to *B* — Jer 20:5 — 894
and thou shalt come to *B*, and there — Jer 20:6 — 894
king of *B* maketh war against us — Jer 21:2 — 894
ye fight against the king of *B* — Jer 21:4 — 894
hand of Nebuchadrezzar king of *B* — Jer 21:7 — 894
into the hand of the king of *B* — Jer 21:10 — 894
hand of Nebuchadrezzar king of *B* — Jer 22:25 — 894
of *B* had carried away captive — Jer 24:1 — 894
and had brought them to *B* — Jer 24:1 — 894
year of Nebuchadrezzar king of *B* — Jer 25:1 — 894
and Nebuchadrezzar the king of *B* — Jer 25:9 — 894
serve the king of *B* seventy years — Jer 25:11 — 894
that I will punish the king of *B* — Jer 25:12 — 894
of Nebuchadnezzar the king of *B* — Jer 27:6 — 894
same Nebuchadnezzar the king of *B* — Jer 27:8 — 894
under the yoke of the king of *B* — Jer 27:8 — 894
Ye shall not serve the king of *B* — Jer 27:9 — 894
under the yoke of the king of *B* — Jer 27:11 — 894
under the yoke of the king of *B* — Jer 27:12 — 894
that will not serve the king of *B* — Jer 27:13 — 894
Ye shall not serve the king of *B* — Jer 27:14 — 894
shortly be brought again from *B* — Jer 27:16 — 894
serve the king of *B*, and live — Jer 27:17 — 894
and at Jerusalem, go not to *B* — Jer 27:18 — 894
Nebuchadnezzar king of *B* took not — Jer 27:20 — 894
king of Judah from Jerusalem to *B* — Jer 27:20 — 894
They shall be carried to *B* — Jer 27:22 — 894
broken the yoke of the king of *B* — Jer 28:2 — 894
of *B* took away from this place — Jer 28:3 — 894
this place, and carried them to *B* — Jer 28:3 — 894
of Judah, that went into *B* — Jer 28:4 — 894
break the yoke of the king of *B* — Jer 28:4 — 894
captive, from *B* into this place — Jer 28:6 — 894
of *B* from the neck of all nations — Jer 28:11 — 894
serve Nebuchadnezzar king of *B* — Jer 28:14 — 894
away captive from Jerusalem to *B* — Jer 29:1 — 894
king of Judah sent unto *B* to — Jer 29:3 — 894
Nebuchadnezzar king of *B*) saying — Jer 29:3 — 894
away from Jerusalem unto *B* — Jer 29:4 — 894
at *B* I will visit you, and perform — Jer 29:10 — 894
hath raised us up prophets in *B* — Jer 29:15 — 894
I have sent from Jerusalem to *B* — Jer 29:20 — 894
hand of Nebuchadrezzar king of *B* — Jer 29:21 — 894
captivity of Judah which are in *B* — Jer 29:22 — 894
whom the king of *B* roasted in the — Jer 29:22 — 894
therefore he sent unto us in *B* — Jer 29:28 — 894
into the hand of the king of *B* — Jer 32:3 — 894
into the hand of the king of *B* — Jer 32:4 — 894
And he shall lead Zedekiah to *B* — Jer 32:5 — 894
hand of Nebuchadrezzar king of *B* — Jer 32:28 — 894
of the king of *B* by the sword — Jer 32:36 — 894
when Nebuchadnezzar king of *B* — Jer 34:1 — 894
into the hand of the king of *B* — Jer 34:2 — 894
behold the eyes of the king of *B* — Jer 34:3 — 894
to mouth, and thou shalt go to *B* — Jer 34:3 — 894
king of *B* came up into the land — Jer 35:11 — 894
The king of *B* shall certainly — Jer 36:29 — 894
whom Nebuchadrezzar king of *B* — Jer 37:1 — 894
into the hand of the king of *B* — Jer 37:17 — 894
The king of *B* shall not come — Jer 37:19 — 894
by the hand of the king of *B* — Jer 38:23 — 894
came Nebuchadrezzar king of *B* — Jer 39:1 — 894
princes of the king of *B* came in — Jer 39:3 — 894
of the princes o the king of *B* — Jer 39:3 — 894
up to Nebuchadnezzar king of *B* to — Jer 39:5 — 894
Then the king of *B* slew the sons — Jer 39:6 — 894
also the king of *B* slew all the — Jer 39:6 — 894
with chains, to carry him to *B* — Jer 39:7 — 894
B the remnant of the people that — Jer 39:9 — 894
Now Nebuchadrezzar king of *B* gave — Jer 39:11 — 894
were carried away captive unto *B* — Jer 40:1 — 894
unto thee to come with me into *B* — Jer 40:4 — 894
unto thee to come with me into *B* — Jer 40:4 — 894
whom the king of *B* hath made — Jer 40:5 — 894
heard that the king of *B* had made — Jer 40:7 — 894
not carried away captive to *B* — Jer 40:7 — 894
the land, and serve the king of *B* — Jer 40:9 — 894
heard that the king of *B* had left — Jer 40:11 — 894
whom the king of *B* had made — Jer 41:2 — 894
whom the king of *B* made governor — Jer 41:18 — 894
Be not afraid of the king of *B* — Jer 42:11 — 894
and carry us away captives into *B* — Jer 43:3 — 894
take Nebuchadrezzar the king of *B* — Jer 43:10 — 894
hand of Nebuchadrezzar king of *B* — Jer 44:30 — 894
of *B* smote in the fourth year of — Jer 46:2 — 894
king of *B* should come and smite — Jer 46:13 — 894
hand of Nebuchadrezzar king of *B* — Jer 46:26 — 894
king of *B* shall smite, thus saith — Jer 49:28 — 894
for Nebuchadrezzar king of *B* hath — Jer 49:30 — 894
that the LORD spake against *B* — Jer 50:1 — 894
B is taken, Bel is confounded, — Jer 50:2 — 894
Remove out of the midst of *B* — Jer 50:8 — 894
cause to come up against *B* an — Jer 50:9 — 894
goeth by *B* shall be astonished — Jer 50:13 — 894
in array against *B* round about — Jer 50:14 — 894
Cut off the sower from *B*, and him — Jer 50:16 — 894
king of *B* hath broken his bones — Jer 50:17 — 894
I will punish the king of *B* — Jer 50:18 — 894
how is *B* become a desolation — Jer 50:23 — 894
thee, and thou art also taken, O *B* — Jer 50:24 — 894
and escape out of the land of *B* — Jer 50:28 — 894
together the archers against *B* — Jer 50:29 — 894
and disquiet the inhabitants of *B* — Jer 50:34 — 894
and upon the inhabitants of *B* — Jer 50:35 — 894
against thee, O daughter of *B* — Jer 50:42 — 894
The king of *B* hath heard the — Jer 50:43 — 894
that he hath taken against *B* — Jer 50:45 — 894
taking of *B* the earth is moved — Jer 50:46 — 894
Behold, I will raise up against *B* — Jer 51:1 — 894
And will send unto *B* fanners — Jer 51:2 — 894
Flee out of the midst of *B* — Jer 51:6 — 894
B hath been a golden cup in the — Jer 51:7 — 894
B is suddenly fallen and destroyed — Jer 51:8 — 894
We would have healed *B*, but she — Jer 51:9 — 894
for his device is against *B* — Jer 51:11 — 894
the standard upon the walls of *B* — Jer 51:12 — 894
against the inhabitants of *B* — Jer 51:12 — 894
And I will render unto *B* and to all — Jer 51:24 — 894
LORD shall be performed against *B* — Jer 51:29 — 894
to make the land of *B* a — Jer 51:29 — 894
The mighty men of *B* have forborn — Jer 51:30 — 894
to shew the king of *B* that his — Jer 51:31 — 894
The daughter of *B* is like a — Jer 51:33 — 894
the king of *B* hath devoured me — Jer 51:34 — 894
to me and to my flesh be upon *B* — Jer 51:35 — 894
B shall become heaps, a dwelling — Jer 51:37 — 894
how is *B* become an astonishment — Jer 51:41 — 894
The sea is come up upon *B* — Jer 51:42 — 894
And I will punish Bel in *B* — Jer 51:44 — 894
yea, the wall of *B* shall fall — Jer 51:44 — 894
upon the graven images of *B* — Jer 51:47 — 894
that is therein, shall sing for *B* — Jer 51:48 — 894
As *B* hath caused the slain of — Jer 51:49 — 894
so at *B* shall fall the slain of — Jer 51:49 — 894
Though *B* should mount up to — Jer 51:53 — 894
A sound of a cry cometh from *B* — Jer 51:54 — 894
Because the LORD hath spoiled *B* — Jer 51:55 — 894
is come upon her, even upon *B* — Jer 51:56 — 894
The broad walls of *B* shall be — Jer 51:58 — 894
B in the fourth year of his reign — Jer 51:59 — 894
the evil that should come upon *B* — Jer 51:60 — 894
words that are written against *B* — Jer 51:60 — 894
to Seraiah, When thou comest to *B* — Jer 51:61 — 894
thou shalt say, Thus shall *B* sink — Jer 51:64 — 894
rebelled against the king of *B* — Jer 52:3 — 894
Nebuchadrezzar king of *B* came — Jer 52:4 — 894
B to Riblah in the land of Hamath — Jer 52:9 — 894
the king of *B* slew the sons of — Jer 52:10 — 894
the king of *B* bound him in chains — Jer 52:11 — 894
and carried him to *B* — Jer 52:11 — 894
year of Nebuchadrezzar king of *B* — Jer 52:12 — 894
guard, which served the king of *B* — Jer 52:12 — 894
away, that fell to the king of *B* — Jer 52:15 — 894
all the brass of them to *B* — Jer 52:17 — 894
them to the king of *B* to Riblah — Jer 52:26 — 894
And the king of *B* smote them — Jer 52:27 — 894
that Evil-merodach king of *B* in — Jer 52:31 — 894
the kings that were with him in *B* — Jer 52:32 — 894
diet given him of the king of *B* — Jer 52:34 — 894
I will bring him to *B* to the land — Eze 12:13 — 894
Behold, the king of *B* is come to — Eze 17:12 — 894
and led them with him to *B* — Eze 17:12 — 894
in the midst of *B* he shall die — Eze 17:16 — 894
snare, and I will bring him to *B* — Eze 17:20 — 894
and brought him to the king of *B* — Eze 19:9 — 894
sword of the king of *B* may come — Eze 21:19 — 894
For the king of *B* stood at the — Eze 21:21 — 894
the king of *B* set himself against — Eze 24:2 — 894
Tyrus Nebuchadrezzar king of *B* — Eze 26:7 — 894
Nebuchadrezzar king of *B* caused — Eze 29:18 — 894
unto Nebuchadrezzar king of *B* — Eze 29:19 — 894
hand of Nebuchadrezzar king of *B* — Eze 30:10 — 894
the arms of the king of *B* — Eze 30:24 — 894
the arms of the king of *B* — Eze 30:25 — 894
into the hand of the king of *B* — Eze 30:25 — 894
king of *B* shall come upon thee — Eze 32:11 — 894
king of *B* unto Jerusalem, and — Dan 1:1 — 894
to destroy all the wise men of *B* — Dan 2:12 — 895
forth to slay the wise men of *B* — Dan 2:14 — 895
the rest of the wise men of *B* — Dan 2:18 — 895
to destroy the wise men of *B* — Dan 2:24 — 895
Destroy not the wise men of *B* — Dan 2:24 — 895
over the whole province of *B* — Dan 2:48 — 895
over all the wise men of *B* — Dan 2:48 — 895
the affairs of the province of *B* — Dan 2:49 — 895
of Dura, in the province of *B* — Dan 3:1 — 895
the affairs of the province of *B* — Dan 3:12 — 895
Abed-nego, in the province of *B* — Dan 3:30 — 895
all the wise men of *B* before me — Dan 4:6 — 895
in the palace of the kingdom of *B* — Dan 4:29 — 895
and said, Is not this great *B* — Dan 4:30 — 895
and said to the wise men of *B* — Dan 5:7 — 895
king of *B* Daniel had a dream — Dan 7:1 — 895
field, and thou shalt go even to *B* — Mic 4:10 — 894
dwellest with the daughter of *B* — Zec 2:7 — 894
of Jedaiah, which are come from *B* — Zec 6:10 — 894
time they were carried away to *B* — Mt 1:11 — 897
And after they were brought to *B* — Mt 1:12 — 897
into *B* are fourteen generations — Mt 1:17 — 897
into *B* unto Christ are fourteen — Mt 1:17 — 897
and I will carry you away beyond *B* — Acts 7:43 — 897
The church that is at *B*, elected — 1Pet 5:13 — 897
B is fallen, is fallen, that — Rev 14:8 — 897
great *B* came in remembrance — Rev 16:19 — 897
B THE GREAT, THE MOTHER OF — Rev 17:5 — 897
B the great is fallen, is fallen, — Rev 18:2 — 897
Alas, alas that great city *B* — Rev 18:10 — 897
that great city *B* be thrown down — Rev 18:21 — 897

BABYLONIA See BABYLONISH.

BABYLONIAN See CHALDEANS'.

BABYLONIANS (*bab-il-o'-ne-ans*) See CHALDEANS. *Inhabitants of Babylonia.*
Apharsites, the Archevites, the *B* — Ezr 4:9 — 896
the manner of the *B* of Chaldea — Eze 23:15
the *B* came to her into the bed of — Eze 23:17
The *B*, and all the Chaldeans, — Eze 23:23

BABYLONISH (*bab-il-o'-nish*) See BABYLONIANS.
the spoils a goodly *B* garment — Josh 7:21 — 8152

BABYLON'S (*bab'-il-ons*)
For then the king of *B* army — Jer 32:2 — 894
When the king of *B* army fought — Jer 34:7 — 894
the hand of the king of *B* army — Jer 34:21 — 894
the hand of the king of *B* army — Jer 38:3 — 894
forth unto the king of *B* princes — Jer 38:17 — 894
go forth to the king of *B* princes — Jer 38:18 — 894
forth to the king of *B* princes — Jer 38:22 — 894
and all the king of *B* princes — Jer 39:13 — 894

BACA (*ba'-cah*) *A valley near Jerusalem.*
the valley of *B* make it a well — Ps 84:6 — 1056

BACHRITES (*bak'-rites*) *Descendants of Becher.*
of Becher, the family of the *B* — Num 26:35 — 1076

BACK
he brought *b* all the goods, and Gen 14:16 7725
And they said, Stand *b* Gen 19:9 1973
his wife looked *b* from behind him Gen 19:26
to pass, as he drew *b* his hand Gen 38:29 7725
neither hath he kept *b* any thing Gen 39:9 2820
the LORD caused the sea to go *b* Ex 14:21
wife, after he had sent her *b* Ex 18:2
surely bring it *b* to him again Ex 23:4 7725
and thou shalt see my *b* parts Ex 33:23 268
wherefore are we kept *b*, that we Num 9:7 1639
brought *b* word unto them, and unto Num 13:26 7725
thee, I will get me *b* again Num 22:34 7725
LORD hath kept thee *b* from honour Num 24:11 4513
dig therewith, and shalt turn *b* Deut 23:13 7725
turned *b* upon the pursuers Josh 8:20 2015
For Joshua drew not his hand *b* Josh 8:26 7725
And Joshua at that time turned *b* Josh 11:10 7725
Else if ye do in any wise go *b* Josh 23:12 7725
unto the LORD, and I cannot go *b* Judg 11:35 7725
turned and went *b* unto his house Judg 18:26 7725
in law is gone *b* unto her people Ruth 1:15 7725
b with Naomi out of the country Ruth 2:6 7725
turned his *b* to go from Samuel 1Sa 10:9 7926
for he is turned *b* from following 1Sa 15:11 7725
hath kept me *b* from hurting thee 1Sa 25:34 4513
the bow of Jonathan turned not *b* 2Sa 1:22 268
can I bring him *b* again 2Sa 12:23 7725
thou, and take *b* thy brethren 2Sa 15:20 7725
Carry *b* the ark of God into the 2Sa 15:25 7725
I will bring *b* all the people 2Sa 17:3 7725
for Joab held *b* the people 2Sa 18:16 2820
not a word of bringing the king *b* 2Sa 19:10 7725
to bring the king *b* to his house 2Sa 19:11 7725
ye the last to bring *b* the king 2Sa 19:12 7725
turn *b* again, that I may die in 2Sa 19:37 7725
first had in bringing *b* our king 2Sa 19:43 7725
Bring him *b* with thee into thine 1Kin 13:18 7725
So he went *b* with him, and did eat 1Kin 13:19 7725
the prophet that brought him *b* 1Kin 13:20 7725
But camest *b*, and hast eaten bread 1Kin 13:22 7725
the prophet whom he had brought *b* 1Kin 13:23 7725
him *b* from the way heard thereof 1Kin 13:26 7725
it upon the ass, and brought it *b* 1Kin 13:29 7725
and hast cast me behind thy *b* 1Kin 14:9 1458
brought them *b* into the guard 1Kin 14:28 7725
hast turned their heart *b* again 1Kin 18:37 322
And he said unto him, Go *b* again 1Kin 19:20 7725
And he returned *b* from him 1Kin 19:21 7725
carry him *b* unto Amon the 1Kin 22:26 7725
that they turned *b* from pursuing 1Kin 22:33 7725
the messengers turned *b* unto him 2Kin 1:5 7725
them, Why are ye now turned *b* 2Kin 1:5 7725
that fell from him, and went *b* 2Kin 2:13 7725
And he turned *b*, and looked on them 2Kin 2:24 310
king Joram went *b* to be healed in 2Kin 8:29 7725
So the king of Assyria turned *b* 2Kin 15:20 7725
I will turn thee *b* by the way by 2Kin 19:28 7725
ten degrees, or go *b* ten degrees 2Kin 20:9 7725
And Ornan turned *b*, and saw the 1Chr 21:20 7725
And when Judah looked *b*, behold, 2Chr 13:14 6437
carry him *b* to Amon the governor 2Chr 18:25 7725
they turned *b* again from pursuing 2Chr 18:32 7725
brought them *b* unto the LORD God 2Chr 19:4 7725
of the army which Amaziah sent *b* 2Chr 25:13 7725
and brought the king word *b* again 2Chr 34:16 7725
and viewed the wall, and turned *b* Neh 2:15 7725
Neither have I gone *b* from the Job 23:12 4185
He holdeth *b* the face of his Job 26:9
He keepeth *b* his soul from the Job 33:18 2820
To bring *b* his soul from the pit, Job 33:30 7725
Because they turned *b* from him Job 34:27 5493
turneth he *b* from the sword Job 39:22 7725
When mine enemies are turned *b* Ps 9:3 268
when the LORD bringeth *b* the Ps 14:7 7725
Keep *b* thy servant also from Ps 19:13 2820
shalt thou make them turn their *b* Ps 21:12 7926
let them be turned *b* and brought Ps 35:4 268
us to turn *b* from the enemy Ps 44:10 268
Our heart is not turned *b* Ps 44:18 268
Every one of them is gone *b* Ps 53:3 5472
When God bringeth *b* the captivity Ps 53:6 7725
then shall mine enemies turn *b* Ps 56:9 268
Let them be turned *b* for a reward Ps 70:3 7725
turned *b* in the day of battle Ps 78:9 2015
Yea, they turned *b* and tempted God Ps 78:41 7725
But turned *b*, and dealt Ps 78:57 5472
So will not we go *b* from thee Ps 80:18 5472
thou hast brought *b* the captivity Ps 85:1 7725
Jordan was driven *b* Ps 114:3 268
Jordan, that thou wast driven *b* Ps 114:5 268
The plowers plowed upon my *b* Ps 129:3 1354
and turned *b* that hate Zion Ps 129:5 268
but a rod is for the *b* of him Prov 10:13 1458
and stripes for the *b* of fools Prov 19:29 1458
ass, and a rod for the fool's *b* Prov 26:3 1458
out, and who shall turn it *b* Is 14:27 7725
and will not call *b* his words Is 31:2 5493
I will turn thee *b* by the way by Is 37:29 7725
cast all my sins behind thy *b* Is 38:17 1458
They shall be turned *b*, they Is 42:17 268
and to the south, Keep not *b* Is 43:6 3607
rebellious, neither turned away *b* Is 50:5 268
I gave my *b* to the smiters, and my Is 50:6 1458
they have turned their *b* unto me Jer 2:27 6203
the LORD is not turned *b* from us Jer 4:8 7725
neither will I turn *b* from it Jer 4:28 7725
turn *b* thine hand as a Jer 6:9 7725
b by a perpetual backsliding Jer 8:5 7725
They are turned *b* to the Jer 11:10 7725
I will shew them the *b*, and not Jer 18:17 6203
I will turn *b* the weapons of war Jer 21:4 5437
And they have turned unto me the *b* Jer 32:33 6203
mire, and they are turned away *b* Jer 38:22 268
Now while he was not yet gone *b* Jer 40:5 7725
Go *b* also to Gedaliah the son of Jer 40:5 7725
I will keep nothing *b* from you Jer 42:4 4513
them dismayed and turned away *b* Jer 46:5 268
and are fled apace, and look not *b* Jer 46:5 6437
for they also are turned *b* Jer 46:21 6437
not look *b* to their children for Jer 47:3 6437
keepeth *b* his sword from blood Jer 48:10 4513
hath Moab turned the *b* with shame Jer 48:39 6203
Flee ye, turn *b*, dwell deep, O Jer 49:8 6437
for my feet, he hath turned me *b* Lam 1:13 268
he hath drawn *b* his right hand Lam 2:3 268
me, and cast me behind thy *b* Eze 23:35 1458
I will not go *b*, neither will I Eze 24:14 6544
And I will turn thee *b*, and put Eze 38:4 7725
that is brought *b* from the sword Eze 38:8 7725
And I will turn thee *b*, and leave Eze 39:2 7725
Then he brought me *b* the way of Eze 44:1 7725
which had upon the *b* of it four Dan 7:6 1355
For Israel slideth *b* as a Hos 4:16 5637
but none shall look *b* Nah 2:8 6437
that are turned *b* from the LORD Zeph 1:6 5253
when I turn *b* your captivity Zeph 3:20 7725
return *b* to take his clothes Mt 24:18 *3694*
rolled *b* the stone from the door, Mt 28:2 *617*
turn *b* again for to take up his Mk 13:16 *617*
they turned *b* again to Jerusalem, Lk 2:45 *5290*
the ship, and returned *b* again Lk 8:37 *5290*
hand to the plough, and looking *b* Lk 9:62 *3694*
saw that he was healed, turned *b* Lk 17:15 *5290*
let him likewise not return *b* Lk 17:31 *3694*
time many of his disciples went *b* Jn 6:66 *3694*
thus said, she turned herself *b* Jn 20:14 *3694*
kept *b* part of the price, his Acts 5:2 *3557*
to keep *b* part of the price of Acts 5:3 *3557*
hearts turned *b* again into Egypt Acts 7:39 *4762*
how I kept *b* nothing that was Acts 20:20 *5288*
see, and bow down their *b* alway Rom 11:10 *3577*
but if any man draw *b*, my soul Heb 10:38 *5288*
of them who draw *b* unto perdition Heb 10:39 *5289*
which is of you kept *b* by fraud Jas 5:4 *650*

BACKBITERS
B, haters of God, despiteful, Rom 1:30 *2637*

BACKBITETH
He that *b* not with his tongue, Ps 15:3 7270

BACKBITING
an angry countenance a *b* tongue Prov 25:23 5643

BACKBITINGS
envyings, wraths, strifes, *b* 2Cor 12:20 *2636*

BACKBONE
shall he take off hard by the *b* Lev 3:9 6096

BACKS
enemies turn their *b* unto thee Ex 23:27 6203
their *b* before their enemies Josh 7:8 6203
but turned their *b* before their Josh 7:12 6203
Therefore they turned their *b* Judg 20:42
of the LORD, and turned their *b* 2Chr 29:6 6203
and cast thy law behind their *b* Neh 9:26 1458
with their *b* toward the temple of Eze 8:16 268
And their whole body, and their *b* Eze 10:12 1354

BACKSIDE
the flock to the *b* of the desert Ex 3:1 310
hang over the *b* of the tabernacle Ex 26:12 268
a book written within and on the *b* Rev 5:1 *3693*

BACKSLIDER
The *b* in heart shall be filled Prov 14:14 5472

BACKSLIDING
that which *b* Israel hath done Jer 3:6 4878
b Israel committed adultery I had Jer 3:8 4878
The *b* Israel hath justified Jer 3:11 4878
thou *b* Israel, saith the LORD Jer 3:12 4878
O *b* children, saith the LORD Jer 3:14 7726
ye *b* children, and I will heal Jer 3:22 7726
slidden back by a perpetual *b* Jer 8:5 4878
thou go about, O thou *b* daughter Jer 31:22 7728
thy flowing valley, O *b* daughter Jer 49:4 7728
Israel slideth back as a *b* heifer Hos 4:16 5637
my people are bent to *b* from me Hos 11:7 4878
I will heal their *b*, I will love Hos 14:4 4878

BACKSLIDINGS
thee, and thy *b* shall reprove thee Jer 2:19 4878
children, and I will heal your *b* Jer 3:22 4878
many, and their *b* are increased Jer 5:6 4878
for our *b* are many Jer 14:7 4878

BACKWARD
both their shoulders, and went *b* Gen 9:23 322
and their faces were *b*, and they Gen 9:23 322
so that his rider shall fall *b* Gen 49:17 268
seat *b* by the side of the gate 1Sa 4:18 322
the shadow return *b* ten degrees 2Kin 20:10 322
brought the shadow ten degrees *b* 2Kin 20:11 322
and *b*, but I cannot perceive him Job 23:8 268
let them be driven *b* and put to Ps 40:14 268
let them be turned *b*, and put to Ps 70:2 268
unto anger, they are gone away *b* Is 1:4 268
that they might go, and fall *b* Is 28:13 268
sun dial of Ahaz, ten degrees *b* Is 38:8 322
that turneth wise men *b*, and Is 44:25 268
And judgment is turned away *b* Is 59:14 268
of their evil heart, and went *b* Jer 7:24 268
saith the LORD, thou art gone *b* Jer 15:6 268
yea, she sigheth, and turneth *b* Lam 1:8 268
unto them, I am he, they went *b* Jn 18:6

BAD
cannot speak unto thee *b* or good Gen 24:50 7451
not to Jacob either good or *b* Gen 31:24 7451
not to Jacob either good or *b* Gen 31:29 7451
good for a *b*, or a *b* for a good Lev 27:10 7451
value it, whether it be good or *b* Lev 27:12 7451
it, whether it be good or *b* Lev 27:14 7451
search whether it be good or *b* Lev 27:33 7451
dwell in, whether it be good or *b* Num 13:19 7451
either good or *b* of mine own mind Num 24:13 7451
brother Amnon neither good nor *b* 2Sa 13:22 7451
the king to discern good and *b* 2Sa 14:17 7451
I may discern between good and *b* 1Kin 3:9 7451
the *b* city, and have set up the Ezr 4:12 873
not be eaten, they were so *b* Jer 24:2 7451
into vessels, but cast the *b* away Mt 13:48 *4550*
all as many as they found, both *b* Mt 22:10 *4190*
done, whether it be good or *b* 2Cor 5:10 *2556*

BADE
And the man did as Joseph *b* Gen 43:17 559
up till the morning, as Moses *b* Ex 16:24 6680
b stone them with stones Num 14:10 559
did unto them as the LORD *b* him Josh 11:9 559
all that her mother in law *b* her Ruth 3:6 6680
and some *b* me kill thee 1Sa 24:10 559
(Also he *b* them teach the 2Sa 1:18 559
for thy servant Joab, he *b* me 2Sa 14:19 6680
on the third day, as the king *b* 2Chr 10:12 1696
Then Esther *b* them return Est 4:15 559
understood they how that he *b* Mt 16:12 *2036*
And he that *b* thee and him come and Lk 14:9 *2564*
that when he that *b* thee cometh Lk 14:10 *2564*
said he also to him that *b* him Lk 14:12 *2564*
made a great supper, and *b* many Lk 14:16 *2564*
the Spirit *b* me go with them, Acts 11:12 *2036*
But *b* them farewell, saying, I Acts 18:21 *657*
b that he should be examined by Acts 22:24 *2036*

BADEST
have done according as thou *b* me Gen 27:19 1696

BADGERS'
b skins, and shittim wood, Ex 25:5 8476
and a covering above of *b* skins Ex 26:14 8476
b skins, and shittim wood, Ex 35:7 8476
of rams, and *b* skins, brought them Ex 35:23 8476
a covering of *b* skins above that Ex 36:19 8476
red, and the covering of *b* skins Ex 39:34 8476
thereon the covering of *b* skins Num 4:6 8476
same with a covering of *b* skins Num 4:8 8476
within a covering of *b* skins Num 4:10 8476
it with a covering of *b* skins Num 4:11 8476
them with a covering of *b* skins Num 4:12 8476
upon it a covering of *b* skins Num 4:14 8476
the covering of the *b* skins that Num 4:25 8476
work, and shod thee with *b* skin Eze 16:10 8476

BADNESS
in all the land of Egypt for *b* Gen 41:19 7455

BAG
not have in thy *b* divers weights Deut 25:13 3599
in a shepherd's *b* which he had 1Sa 17:40 3627
And David put his hand in his *b* 1Sa 17:49 3627
transgression is sealed up in a *b* Job 14:17 6872
He hath taken a *b* of money with Prov 7:20 6872
the weights of the *b* are his work Prov 16:11 3599
They lavish gold out of the *b* Is 46:6 3599
with the *b* of deceitful weights Mic 6:11 3599
to put it into a *b* with holes Hag 1:6 6872
he was a thief, and had the *b* Jn 12:6 *1101*
thought, because Judas had the *b* Jn 13:29 *1101*

BAGS
two talents of silver in two *b* 2Kin 5:23 2754
came up, and they put up in *b* 2Kin 12:10 6696
yourselves *b* which wax not old Lk 12:33 *905*

BAHARUMITE (*ba-ha'-rum-ite*) See BARHUMITE. *Inhabitants of Bahurim.*
Azmaveth the *B*, Eliahba the 1Chr 11:33 978

BAHURIM (*ba-hu'-rim*) See BAHARUMITE. *A village near Jerusalem.*
her along weeping behind her to *B* 2Sa 3:16 980
And when king David came to *B* 2Sa 16:5 980
and came to a man's house in *B* 2Sa 17:18 980
Gera, a Benjamite, which was of *B* 2Sa 19:16 980
the son of Gera, a Benjamite of *B* 1Kin 2:8 980

BAJITH (*ba'-jith*) *A temple in Moab.*
He is gone up to *B*, and to Dibon, Is 15:2 1006

BAKBAKKAR (*bak-bak'-kar*) *A Levite who returned from exile.*
And *B*, Heresh, and Galal, and 1Chr 9:15 1230

BAKBUK (*bak'-buk*) *A family who returned from exile.*
The children of *B*, the children Ezr 2:51 1227
The children of *B*, the children Neh 7:53 1227

BAKBUKIAH (*bak-buk-i'-ah*) *A Levite exile who resettled in Jerusalem.*
B the second among his brethren, Neh 11:17 1229
Also *B* and Unni, their brethren, Neh 12:9 1229
Mattaniah, and *B*, Obadiah, Neh 12:25 1229

BAKE
did *b* unleavened bread, and they Gen 19:3 644
b that which ye will *b* to day, Ex 16:23 644
flour, and *b* twelve cakes thereof Lev 24:5 644
ten women shall *b* your bread in Lev 26:26 644
did *b* unleavened bread thereof 1Sa 28:24 644
in his sight, and did *b* the cakes 2Sa 13:8 1310
thou shalt *b* it with dung that Eze 4:12 5746
where they shall *b* the meat Eze 46:20 644

BAKED
they *b* unleavened cakes of the Ex 12:39 644
b it in pans, and made cakes of it Num 11:8 1310
and for that which is *b* in the pan 1Chr 23:29
also I have *b* bread upon the Is 44:19 644

BAKEMEATS
of all manner of *b* for Pharaoh ... Gen 40:17

BAKEN
of a meat offering *b* in the oven ... Lev 2:4 644
be a meat offering *b* in a pan ... Lev 2:5
meat offering *b* in the frying pan ... Lev 2:7
It shall not be *b* with leaven ... Lev 6:17 644
and when it is *b*, thou shalt bring ... Lev 6:21 7246
the *b* pieces of the meat offering ... Lev 6:21 8601
offering that is *b* in the oven ... Lev 7:9 644
they shall be *b* with leaven ... Lev 23:17 644
there was a cake *b* on the coals ... 1Kin 19:6

BAKER
his *b* had offended their lord the ... Gen 40:1 644
the *b* of the king of Egypt, which ... Gen 40:5 644
When the chief *b* saw that the ... Gen 40:16 644
of the chief *b* among his servants ... Gen 40:20 644
But he hanged the chief *b* ... Gen 40:22 644
house, both me and the chief *b* ... Gen 41:10 644
as an oven heated by the *b* ... Hos 7:4 644
their *b* sleepeth all the night ... Hos 7:6 644

BAKERS
and against the chief of the *b* ... Gen 40:2 644
and to be cooks, and to be *b* ... 1Sa 8:13 644

BAKERS'
of bread out of the *b* street ... Jer 37:21 644

BAKETH
yea, he kindleth it, and *b* bread ... Is 44:15 644

BALAAM (*ba'-la-am*) See BALAAM'S. *Son of Beor.*
unto *B* the son of Beor to Pethor ... Num 22:5 1109
and they came unto *B*, and spake ... Num 22:7 1109
the princes of Moab abode with *B* ... Num 22:8 1109
And God came unto *B*, and said, What Num 22:9 1109
B said unto God, Balak the son of ... Num 22:10 1109
And God said unto *B*, Thou shalt ... Num 22:12 1109
B rose up in the morning, and said ... Num 22:13 1109
B refuseth to come with us ... Num 22:14 1109
And they came to *B*, and said to him ... Num 22:16 1109
B answered and said unto the ... Num 22:18 1109
And God came unto *B* at night ... Num 22:20 1109
B rose up in the morning, and ... Num 22:21 1109
B smote the ass, to turn her into ... Num 22:23 1109
the LORD, she fell down under *B* ... Num 22:27 1109
of the ass, and she said unto *B* ... Num 22:28 1109
B said unto the ass, Because thou ... Num 22:29 1109
And the ass said unto *B*, Am not I ... Num 22:30 1109
the LORD opened the eyes of *B* ... Num 22:31 1109
B said unto the angel of the LORD ... Num 22:34 1109
the angel of the LORD said unto *B* ... Num 22:35 1109
So *B* went with the princes of ... Num 22:35 1109
when Balak heard that *B* was come ... Num 22:36 1109
And Balak said unto *B*, Did I not ... Num 22:37 1109
B said unto Balak, Lo, I am come ... Num 22:38 1109
B went with Balak, and they came ... Num 22:39 1109
oxen and sheep, and sent to *B* ... Num 22:40 1109
on the morrow, that Balak took *B* ... Num 22:41 1109
B said unto Balak, Build me here ... Num 23:1 1109
And Balak did as *B* had spoken ... Num 23:2 1109
B offered on every altar a ... Num 23:2 1109
B said unto Balak, Stand by thy ... Num 23:3 1109
And God met *B* ... Num 23:4 1109
And Balak said unto *B*, What hast ... Num 23:11 1109
And the LORD met *B*, and put a word .. Num 23:16 1109
And Balak said unto *B*, Neither ... Num 23:25 1109
But *B* answered and said unto Balak ... Num 23:26 1109
And Balak said unto *B*, Come, I ... Num 23:27 1109
Balak brought *B* unto the top of ... Num 23:28 1109
B said unto Balak, Build me here ... Num 23:29 1109
And Balak did as *B* had said ... Num 23:30 1109
when *B* saw that it pleased the ... Num 24:1 1109
B lifted up his eyes, and he saw ... Num 24:2 1109
B the son of Beor hath said, and ... Num 24:3 1109
anger was kindled against *B* ... Num 24:10 1109
and Balak said unto *B*, I called ... Num 24:10 1109
B said unto Balak, Spake I not ... Num 24:12 1109
B the son of Beor hath said, and ... Num 24:15 1109
B rose up, and went and returned to ... Num 24:25 1109
B also the son of Beor they slew ... Num 31:8 1109
Israel, through the counsel of *B* ... Num 31:16 1109
B the son of Beor of Pethor of ... Deut 23:4 1109
thy God would not hearken unto *B* ... Deut 23:5 1109
B also the son of Beor, the ... Josh 13:22 1109
called *B* the son of Beor to curse ... Josh 24:9 1109
But I would not hearken unto *B* ... Josh 24:10 1109
but hired *B* against them, that he ... Neh 13:2 1109
what *B* the son of Beor answered ... Mic 6:5 1109
the way of *B* the son of Bosor ... 2Pet 2:15 *903*
after the error of *B* for reward ... Jude 11 *903*
them that hold the doctrine of *B* ... Rev 2:14 *903*

BALAAM'S
crushed *B* foot against the wall ... Num 22:25 1109
B anger was kindled, and he smote ... Num 22:27 1109
And the LORD put a word in *B* mouth .. Num 23:5 1109

BALAC (*ba'-lak*) See BALAK. *Greek form of Balak.*
of Balaam, who taught *B* to cast a ... Rev 2:14 *904*

BALADAN (*bal'-adan*) See BERODACH-BALADAN, MERODACH-BALADAN. *Father of a Babylonian king.*
Berodach-baladan, the son of *B* ... 2Kin 20:12 1081
Merodach-baladan, the son of *B* ... Is 39:1 1081

BALAH (*ba'-lah*) See BAALAH. *A city in Simeon.*
And Hazar-shual, and *B*, and Azem, ... Josh 19:3 1088

BALAK (*ba'-lak*) See BALAC, BALAK'S. *A king of Moab.*
B the son of Zippor saw all that ... Num 22:2 1111
B the son of Zippor was king of ... Num 22:4 1111
and spake unto him the words of *B* ... Num 22:7 1111
B the son of Zippor, king of Moab ... Num 22:10 1111
and said unto the princes of *B* ... Num 22:13 1111
Moab rose up, and they went unto *B* ... Num 22:14 1111
B sent yet again princes, more ... Num 22:15 1111
Thus saith *B* the son of Zippor ... Num 22:16 1111
and said unto the servants of *B* ... Num 22:18 1111
If *B* would give me his house full ... Num 22:18 1111
Balaam went with the princes of *B* ... Num 22:35 1111
when *B* heard that Balaam was come .. Num 22:36 1111
B said unto Balaam, Did I not ... Num 22:37 1111
And Balaam said unto *B*, Lo, I am ... Num 22:38 1111
And Balaam went with *B*, and they ... Num 22:39 1111
B offered oxen and sheep, and sent ... Num 22:40 1111
that *B* took Balaam, and brought ... Num 22:41 1111
And Balaam said unto *B*, Build me ... Num 23:1 1111
B did as Balaam had spoken ... Num 23:2 1111
and *B* and Balaam offered on every ... Num 23:2 1111
And Balaam said unto *B*, Stand by ... Num 23:3 1111
mouth, and said, Return unto *B* ... Num 23:5 1111
B the king of Moab hath brought ... Num 23:7 1111
B said unto Balaam, What hast ... Num 23:11 1111
B said unto him, Come, I pray ... Num 23:13 1111
And he said unto *B*, Stand here by ... Num 23:15 1111
mouth, and said, Go again unto *B* ... Num 23:16 1111
B said unto him, What hath the ... Num 23:17 1111
his parable, and said, Rise up, *B* ... Num 23:18 1111
B said unto Balaam, Neither curse ... Num 23:25 1111
Balaam answered and said unto *B* ... Num 23:26 1111
B said unto Balaam, Come, I pray ... Num 23:27 1111
B brought Balaam unto the top of ... Num 23:28 1111
And Balaam said unto *B*, Build me ... Num 23:29 1111
B did as Balaam had said, and ... Num 23:30 1111
B said unto Balaam, I called thee ... Num 24:10 1111
And Balaam said unto *B*, Spake I ... Num 24:12 1111
If *B* would give me his house full ... Num 24:13 1111
and *B* also went his way ... Num 24:25 1111
Then *B* the son of Zippor, king of ... Josh 24:9 1111
better than *B* the son of Zippor ... Judg 11:25 1111
remember now what *B* king of Moab ... Mic 6:5 1111

BALAK'S (*ba'-laks*)
B anger was kindled against ... Num 24:10 1111

BALANCE
Let me be weighed in an even *b* ... Job 31:6 3976
to be laid in the *b*, they are ... Ps 62:9 3976
A false *b* is abomination to the ... Prov 11:1 3976
A just weight and *b* are the LORD's ... Prov 16:11 3976
and a false *b* is not good ... Prov 20:23 3976
in scales, and the hills in a *b* ... Is 40:12 3976
as the small dust of the *b* ... Is 40:15 3976
the bag, and weigh silver in the *b* ... Is 46:6 7070

BALANCES
Just *b*, just weights, a just ... Lev 19:36 3976
calamity laid in the *b* together ... Job 6:2 3976
and weighed him the money in the *b* ... Jer 32:10 3976
then take thee *b* to weigh ... Eze 5:1 3976
Ye shall have just *b*, and a just ... Eze 45:10 3976
Thou art weighed in the *b* ... Dan 5:27 3977
the *b* of deceit are in his hand ... Hos 12:7 3976
and falsifying the *b* by deceit ... Amos 8:5 3976
count them pure with the wicked *b* ... Mic 6:11 3976
him had a pair of *b* in his hand ... Rev 6:5

BALANCINGS
thou know the *b* of the clouds ... Job 37:16 4657

BALD
the *b* locust after his kind, and ... Lev 11:22 5556
is fallen off his head, he is *b* ... Lev 13:40 7142
toward his face, he is forehead *b* ... Lev 13:41 1371
And if there be in the *b* head ... Lev 13:42 7146
or *b* forehead, a white reddish ... Lev 13:42 1372
his *b* head, or his *b* forehead ... Lev 13:42 1372
b head, or in his *b* forehead ... Lev 13:43 1372
said unto him, Go up, thou *b* head ... 2Kin 2:23 7142
go up, thou *b* head ... 2Kin 2:23 7142
nor make themselves *b* for them ... Jer 16:6 7139
For every head shall be *b* ... Jer 48:37 7144
themselves utterly *b* for thee ... Eze 27:31 7139
every head was made *b*, and every ... Eze 29:18 7139
Make thee *b*, and poll thee for thy ... Mic 1:16 7139

BALDNESS
shall not make *b* upon their head ... Lev 21:5 7144
nor make any *b* between your eyes ... Deut 14:1 7144
and instead of well set hair *b* ... Is 3:24 7144
on all their heads shall be *b* ... Is 15:2 7144
weeping, and to mourning, and to *b* ... Is 22:12 7144
B is come upon Gaza ... Jer 47:5 7144
faces, and *b* upon all their heads ... Eze 7:18 7144
all loins, and *b* upon every head ... Amos 8:10 7144
enlarge thy *b* as the eagle ... Mic 1:16 7144

BALL
toss thee like a *b* into a large ... Is 22:18 1754

BALM
their camels bearing spicery and *b* ... Gen 37:25 6875
the man a present, a little *b* ... Gen 43:11 6875
Is there no *b* in Gilead ... Jer 8:22 6875
Go up into Gilead, and take *b* ... Jer 46:11 6875
take *b* for her pain, if so be she ... Jer 51:8 6875
and Pannag, and honey, and oil, and *b* Eze 27:17 6875

BAMAH (*ba'-mah*) See BAMOTH. *Places where Israel sacrificed to idols.*
thereof is called *B* unto this day ... Eze 20:29 1117

BAMOTH (*ba'-moth*) See BAMOTH-BAAL. *A city on the Arnon River.*
and from Nahaliel to *B* ... Num 21:19 1120
from *B* in the valley, that is in ... Num 21:20 1120

BAMOTH-BAAL (*ba''-moth-ba'-al*) *A Moabite town.*
Dibon, and *B*, and Beth-baal-meon, ... Josh 13:17 1120

BAND
with a *b* round about the hole, ... Ex 39:23 8193
and there went with him a *b* of men ... 1Sa 10:26 2428
him, and became captain over a *b* ... 1Kin 11:24 1416
behold, they spied a *b* of men ... 2Kin 13:21 1416
and made them captains of the *b* ... 1Chr 12:18 1416
David against the *b* of the rovers ... 1Chr 12:21 1416
for the *b* of men that came with ... 2Chr 22:1 1416
of the king a *b* of soldiers ... Ezr 8:22 2428
unicorn with his *b* in the furrow ... Job 39:10 5688
the earth, even with a *b* of iron ... Dan 4:15 613
the earth, even with a *b* of iron ... Dan 4:23 613
unto him the whole *b* of soldiers ... Mt 27:27 *4686*
and they call together the whole *b* ... Mk 15:16 *4686*
then, having received a *b* of men ... Jn 18:3 *4686*
Then the *b* and the captain and ... Jn 18:12 *4686*
of the *b* called the Italian *b* ... Acts 10:1 *4686*
unto the chief captain of the *b* ... Acts 21:31 *4686*
a centurion of Augustus' *b* ... Acts 27:1 *4686*

BANDED
certain of the Jews *b* together ... Acts 23:12

BANDS
herds, and the camels, into two *b* ... Gen 32:7 4264
and now I am become two *b* ... Gen 32:10 4264
I have broken the *b* of your yoke ... Lev 26:13 4133
his *b* loosed from off his hands ... Judg 15:14 612
two men that were captains of *b* ... 2Sa 4:2 1416
So the *b* of Syria came no more ... 2Kin 6:23 1416
the *b* of the Moabites invaded the ... 2Kin 13:20 1416
Pharaoh-nechoh put him in *b* at ... 2Kin 23:33 631
against him *b* of the Chaldees ... 2Kin 24:2 1416
b of the Syrians, and *b* of the ... 2Kin 24:2 1416
b of the children of Ammon, and ... 2Kin 24:2 1416
were *b* of soldiers for war, six ... 1Chr 7:4 1416
b that were ready armed to the ... 1Chr 12:23 7218
men, that went out to war by *b* ... 2Chr 26:11 1416
The Chaldeans made out three *b* ... Job 1:17 7218
Pleiades, or loose the *b* of Orion ... Job 38:31 4189
hath loosed the *b* of the wild ass ... Job 39:5 4147
Let us break their *b* asunder ... Ps 2:3 4147
For there are no *b* in their death ... Ps 73:4 2784
death, and brake their *b* in sunder ... Ps 107:14 4147
The *b* of the wicked have robbed ... Ps 119:61 2256
go they forth all of them by *b* ... Prov 30:27 2683
snares and nets, and her hands as *b* ... Eccl 7:26 612
lest your *b* be made strong ... Is 28:22 4147
thyself from the *b* of thy neck ... Is 52:2 4147
to loose the *b* of wickedness, to ... Is 58:6 2784
broken thy yoke, and burst thy *b* ... Jer 2:20 4147
they shall put *b* upon thee ... Eze 3:25 5688
behold, I will lay *b* upon thee ... Eze 4:8 5688
him to help him, and all his *b* ... Eze 12:14 102
all his *b* shall fall by the sword ... Eze 17:21 102
I have broken the *b* of their yoke ... Eze 34:27 4133
Gomer, and all his *b* ... Eze 38:6 102
the north quarters, and all his *b* ... Eze 38:6 102
the land, thou, and all thy *b* ... Eze 38:9 102
will rain upon him, and upon his *b* ... Eze 38:22 102
of Israel, thou, and all thy *b* ... Eze 39:4 102
cords of a man, with *b* of love ... Hos 11:4 5688
Beauty, and the other I called *B* ... Zec 11:7 2256
asunder mine other staff, even *B* ... Zec 11:14 2256
and he brake the *b*, and was driven ... Lk 8:29 *1199*
and every one's *b* were loosed ... Acts 16:26 *1199*
Jews, he loosed him from his *b* ... Acts 22:30 *1199*
the sea, and loosed the rudder *b* ... Acts 27:40 *2202*
b having nourishment ministered, ... Col 2:19 *4886*

BANI (*ba'-ni*)
1. A "mighty man" of David.
of Nathan of Zobah, *B* the Gadite, ... 2Sa 23:36 1137
2. A Levite descendant of Merari.
The son of Amzi, the son of *B* ... 1Chr 6:46 1137
3. A descendant of Pharez.
the son of Imri, the son of *B* ... 1Chr 9:4 1137
4. A family of exiles.
The children of *B*, six hundred ... Ezr 2:10 1137
And of the sons of *B* ... Ezr 10:29 1137
5. Father whose sons married foreign wives.
Of the sons of *B* ... Ezr 10:34 1137
6. A Jewish descendant of a foreign woman.
And *B*, and Binnui, Shimei, ... Ezr 10:38 1137
7. Father of Rehum.
the Levites, Rehum the son of *B* ... Neh 3:17 1137
Also Jeshua, and *B*, and Sherebiah, ... Neh 8:7 1137
of the Levites, Jeshua, and *B* ... Neh 9:4 1137
Levites, Jeshua, and Kadmiel, *B* ... Neh 9:5 1137
8. A priest who assisted Ezra.
Shebaniah, Bunni, Sherebiah, *B* ... Neh 9:4 1137
Hodijah, *B*, Beninu ... Neh 10:13 1137
9. An Israelite who renewed the covenant under Nehemiah.
Pahath-moab, Elam, Zatthu, *B* ... Neh 10:14 1137
10. A family of exiles.
Jerusalem was Uzzi the son of *B* ... Neh 11:22 1137

BANISHED
doth not fetch home again his *b* ... 2Sa 14:13 5080
that his *b* be not expelled from ... 2Sa 14:14 5080

BANISHMENT
whether it be unto death, or to *b* ... Ezr 7:26 8331
thee false burdens and causes of *b* ... Lam 2:14 4065

BANK
I stood upon the *b* of the river ... Gen 41:17 8193
which is by the *b* of the river ... Deut 4:48 8193
which is upon the *b* of the river ... Josh 12:2 8193
that is upon the *b* of the river ... Josh 13:9 8193
that is on the *b* of the river ... Josh 13:16 8193
they cast up a *b* against the city ... 2Sa 20:15 5550
back, and stood by the *b* of Jordan ... 2Kin 2:13 8193
shield, nor cast a *b* against it ... 2Kin 19:32 5550
shields, nor cast a *b* against it ... Is 37:33 5550
at the *b* of the river were very ... Eze 47:7 8193

by the river upon the *b* thereof ... Eze 47:12 8193
this side of the *b* of the river ... Dan 12:5 8193
that side of the *b* of the river ... Dan 12:5 8193
not thou my money into the *b* ... Lk 19:23 *5132*

BANKS
all his *b* all the time of harvest ... Josh 3:15 1415
place, and flowed over all his *b* ... Josh 4:18 1415
when it had overflown all his *b* ... 1Chr 12:15 1428
channels, and go over all his *b* ... Is 8:7 1415
man's voice between the *b* of Ulai ... Dan 8:16

BANNER
Thou hast given a *b* to them that ... Ps 60:4 5251
house, and his *b* over me was love ... Song 2:4 1714
Lift ye up a *b* upon the high ... Is 13:2 5251

BANNERS
of our God we will set up our *b* ... Ps 20:5 1713
terrible as an army with *b* ... Song 6:4 1713
and terrible as an army with *b* ... Song 6:10 1713

BANQUET
b that I have prepared for him ... Est 5:4 4960
Haman came to the *b* that Esther ... Est 5:5 4960
said unto Esther at the *b* of wine ... Est 5:6 4960
Haman come to the *b* that I shall ... Est 5:8 4960
the *b* that she had prepared but ... Est 5:12 4960
merrily with the king unto the *b* ... Est 5:14 4960
the *b* that Esther had prepared ... Est 6:14 4960
Haman came to *b* with Esther the ... Est 7:1 8354
the second day at the *b* of wine ... Est 7:2 4960
the king arising from the *b* of ... Est 7:7 4960
into the place of the *b* of wine ... Est 7:8 4960
the companions make a *b* of him ... Job 41:6 3738
his lords, came into the *b* house ... Dan 5:10 4961
the *b* of them that stretched ... Amos 6:7 4797

BANQUETING
He brought me to the *b* house ... Song 2:4 3196

BANQUETINGS
excess of wine, revellings, *b* ... 1Pet 4:3 *4224*

BAPTISM
and Sadducees come to his *b* ... Mt 3:7 *908*
the *b* that I am baptized with ... Mt 20:22 *908*
be baptized with the *b* that I am ... Mt 20:23 *908*
The *b* of John, whence was it ... Mt 21:25 *908*
preach the *b* of repentance for ... Mk 1:4 *908*
be baptized with the *b* that I am ... Mk 10:38 *908*
with the *b* that I am baptized ... Mk 10:39 *908*
The *b* of John, was it from heaven ... Mk 11:30 *908*
preaching the *b* of repentance for ... Lk 3:3 *908*
being baptized with the *b* of John ... Lk 7:29 *908*
But I have a *b* to be baptized ... Lk 12:50 *908*
The *b* of John, was it from heaven ... Lk 20:4 *908*
Beginning from the *b* of John ... Acts 1:22 *908*
after the *b* which John preached ... Acts 10:37 *908*
preached before his coming the *b* ... Acts 13:24 *908*
Lord, knowing only the *b* of John ... Acts 18:25 *908*
And they said, Unto John's *b* ... Acts 19:3 *908*
baptized with the *b* of repentance ... Acts 19:4 *908*
buried with him by *b* into death ... Rom 6:4 *908*
One Lord, one faith, one *b* ... Eph 4:5 *908*
Buried with him in *b*, wherein ... Col 2:12 *908*
b doth also now save us (not the ... 1Pet 3:21 *908*

BAPTISMS
Of the doctrine of *b*, and of ... Heb 6:2 *909*

BAPTIST (*bap'-tist*) See BAPTIST'S. *John, the forerunner of Jesus.*
In those days came John the *B* ... Mt 3:1 *910*
risen a greater than John the *B* ... Mt 11:11 *910*
from the days of John the *B* until ... Mt 11:12 *910*
his servants, This is John the *B* ... Mt 14:2 *910*
Some say that thou art John the *B* ... Mt 16:14 *910*
he spake unto them of John the *B* ... Mt 17:13 *910*
That John the *B* was risen from ... Mk 6:14 *907*
she said, The head of John the *B* ... Mk 6:24 *910*
a charger the head of John the *B* ... Mk 6:25 *910*
And they answered, John the *B* ... Mk 8:28 *910*
John *B* hath sent us unto thee, ... Lk 7:20 *910*
a greater prophet than John the *B* ... Lk 7:28 *910*
For John the *B* came neither ... Lk 7:33 *910*
They answering said, John the *B* ... Lk 9:19 *910*

BAPTIST'S (*bap'-tists*)
me here John *B* head in a charger ... Mt 14:8 *910*

BAPTIZE
I indeed *b* you with water unto ... Mt 3:11 *907*
he shall *b* you with the Holy ... Mt 3:11 *907*
John did *b* in the wilderness, and ... Mk 1:4 *907*
but he shall *b* you with the Holy ... Mk 1:8 *907*
I indeed *b* you with water ... Lk 3:16 *907*
he shall *b* you with the Holy ... Lk 3:16 *907*
them, saying, I *b* with water ... Jn 1:26 *907*
he that sent me to *b* with water ... Jn 1:33 *907*
For Christ sent me not to *b* ... 1Cor 1:17 *907*

BAPTIZED
And were *b* of him in Jordan, ... Mt 3:6 *907*
Jordan unto John, to be *b* of him ... Mt 3:13 *907*
I have need to be *b* of thee ... Mt 3:14 *907*
And Jesus, when he was *b*, went up ... Mt 3:16 *907*
b with the baptism that I am *b* ... Mt 20:22 *907*
b with the baptism that I am *b* ... Mt 20:23 *907*
were all *b* of him in the river of ... Mk 1:5 *907*
I indeed have *b* you with water ... Mk 1:8 *907*
and was *b* of John in Jordan ... Mk 1:9 *907*
b with the baptism that I am *b* ... Mk 10:38 *907*
am *b* withal shall ye be *b* ... Mk 10:39 *907*
believeth and is *b* shall be saved ... Mk 16:16 *907*
that came forth to be *b* of him ... Lk 3:7 *907*
Then came also publicans to be *b* ... Lk 3:12 *907*
Now when all the people were *b* ... Lk 3:21 *907*
to pass, that Jesus also being *b* ... Lk 3:21 *907*
being *b* with the baptism of John ... Lk 7:29 *907*
themselves, being not *b* of him ... Lk 7:30 *907*
But I have a baptism to be *b* with ... Lk 12:50 *907*
there he tarried with them, and *b* ... Jn 3:22 *907*
and they came, and were *b* ... Jn 3:23 *907*
b more disciples than John, ... Jn 4:1 *907*
(Though Jesus himself *b* not ... Jn 4:2 *907*
the place where John at first *b* ... Jn 10:40 *907*
For John truly *b* with water ... Acts 1:5 *907*
but ye shall be *b* with the Holy ... Acts 1:5 *907*
be *b* every one of you in the name ... Acts 2:38 *907*
gladly received his word were *b* ... Acts 2:41 *907*
name of Jesus Christ, they were *b* ... Acts 8:12 *907*
and when he was *b*, he continued ... Acts 8:13 *907*
only they were *b* in the name of ... Acts 8:16 *907*
what doth hinder me to be *b* ... Acts 8:36 *907*
and he *b* him ... Acts 8:38 *907*
forthwith, and arose, and was *b* ... Acts 9:18 *907*
water, that these should not be *b* ... Acts 10:47 *907*
to be *b* in the name of the Lord ... Acts 10:48 *907*
he said, John indeed *b* with water ... Acts 11:16 *907*
but ye shall be *b* with the Holy ... Acts 11:16 *907*
And when she was *b*, and her ... Acts 16:15 *907*
and was *b*, he and all his, ... Acts 16:33 *907*
hearing believed, and were *b* ... Acts 18:8 *907*
them, Unto what then were ye *b* ... Acts 19:3 *907*
John verily *b* with the baptism of ... Acts 19:4 *907*
they were *b* in the name of the ... Acts 19:5 *907*
arise, and be *b*, and wash away thy ... Acts 22:16 *907*
that so many of us as were *b* into ... Rom 6:3 *907*
Christ were *b* into his death ... Rom 6:3 *907*
or were ye *b* in the name of Paul ... 1Cor 1:13 *907*
I thank God that I *b* none of you ... 1Cor 1:14 *907*
say that I had *b* in mine own name ... 1Cor 1:15 *907*
I *b* also the household of ... 1Cor 1:16 *907*
I know not whether I *b* any other ... 1Cor 1:16 *907*
were all *b* unto Moses in the ... 1Cor 10:2 *907*
Spirit are we all *b* into one body ... 1Cor 12:13 *907*
they do which are *b* for the dead ... 1Cor 15:29 *907*
why are they then *b* for the dead ... 1Cor 15:29 *907*
b into Christ have put on Christ ... Gal 3:27 *907*

BAPTIZEST
Why *b* thou then, if thou be not ... Jn 1:25 *907*

BAPTIZETH
is he which *b* with the Holy Ghost ... Jn 1:33 *907*
witness, behold, the same *b* ... Jn 3:26 *907*

BAPTIZING
b them in the name of the Father, ... Mt 28:19 *907*
beyond Jordan, where John was *b* ... Jn 1:28 *907*
therefore am I come *b* with water ... Jn 1:31 *907*
John also was *b* in Aenon near to ... Jn 3:23 *907*

BAR
the middle *b* in the midst of the ... Ex 26:28 1280
he made the middle *b* to shoot ... Ex 36:33 1280
skins, and shall put it upon a *b* ... Num 4:10 4132
skins, and shall put them on a *b* ... Num 4:12 4132
posts, and went away with them, *b* ... Judg 16:3 1280
them shut the doors, and *b* them ... Neh 7:3 270
will break also the *b* of Damascus ... Amos 1:5 1280

BARABBAS (*ba-rab'-bas*) *A criminal released instead of Jesus.*
then a notable prisoner, called *B* ... Mt 27:16 *912*
B, or Jesus which is called ... Mt 27:17 *912*
multitude that they should ask *B* ... Mt 27:20 *912*
They said, *B* ... Mt 27:21 *912*
Then released he *B* unto them ... Mt 27:26 *912*
And there was one named *B*, which ... Mk 15:7 *912*
should rather release *B* unto them ... Mk 15:11 *912*
people, released *B* unto them, and ... Mk 15:15 *912*
this man, and release unto us *B* ... Lk 23:18 *912*
saying, Not this man, but *B* ... Jn 18:40 *912*
Now *B* was a robber ... Jn 18:40 *912*

BARACHEL (*bar'-ak-el*) *Father of Elihu.*
of Elihu the son of *B* the Buzite ... Job 32:2 1292
Elihu the son of *B* the Buzite ... Job 32:6 1292

BARACHIAH See BARACHIAS.

BARACHIAS (*bar'-ak-i'-as*) *Father of Zachariah.*
the blood of Zacharias son of *B* ... Mt 23:35 *914*

BARAK (*ba'rak*) *A captain in Deborah's army.*
called *B* the son of Abinoam out ... Judg 4:6 1301
B said unto her, If thou wilt go ... Judg 4:8 1301
arose, and went with *B* to Kedesh ... Judg 4:9 1301
B called Zebulun and Naphtali to ... Judg 4:10 1301
they shewed Sisera that *B* the son ... Judg 4:12 1301
And Deborah said unto *B*, Up ... Judg 4:14 1301
So *B* went down from mount Tabor, ... Judg 4:14 1301
the edge of the sword before *B* ... Judg 4:15 1301
But *B* pursued after the chariots, ... Judg 4:16 1301
as *B* pursued Sisera, Jael came ... Judg 4:22 1301
B the son of Abinoam on that day, ... Judg 5:1 1301
arise, *B*, and lead thy captivity ... Judg 5:12 1301
even Issachar, and also *B* ... Judg 5:15 1301
me to tell of Gedeon, and of *B* ... Heb 11:32 *913*

BARAKEL See BARACHEL.

BARBARIAN
be unto him that speaketh a *b* ... 1Cor 14:11 *915*
speaketh shall be a *b* unto me ... 1Cor 14:11 *915*
nor uncircumcision, *B*, Scythian, ... Col 3:11 *915*

BARBARIANS
when the *b* saw the venomous beast ... Acts 28:4 *915*
both to the Greeks, and to the *B* ... Rom 1:14 *915*

BARBAROUS
the *b* people shewed us no little ... Acts 28:2 *915*

BARBED
thou fill his skin with *b* irons ... Job 41:7 7905

BARBER'S
sharp knife, take thee a *b* razor ... Eze 5:1 1532

BARE
b Cain, and said, I have gotten a ... Gen 4:1 3205
she again *b* his brother Abel ... Gen 4:2 3205
and she conceived, and *b* Enoch ... Gen 4:17 3205
And Adah *b* Jabal ... Gen 4:20 3205
she also *b* Tubal-cain, an ... Gen 4:22 3205
she *b* a son, and called his name ... Gen 4:25 3205
they *b* children to them, the same ... Gen 6:4 3205
b up the ark, and it was lift up ... Gen 7:17 5375
Abram's wife *b* him no children ... Gen 16:1 3205
And Hagar *b* Abram a son ... Gen 16:15 3205
his son's name, which Hagar *b* ... Gen 16:15 3205
when Hagar *b* Ishmael to Abram ... Gen 16:16 3205
And the firstborn *b* a son, and ... Gen 19:37 3205
And the younger, she also *b* a son ... Gen 19:38 3205
and they *b* children ... Gen 20:17 3205
b Abraham a son in his old age, ... Gen 21:2 3205
unto him, whom Sarah *b* to him ... Gen 21:3 3205
she *b* also Tebah, and Gaham, and ... Gen 22:24 3205
of Milcah, which she *b* unto Nahor ... Gen 24:24 3205
Sarah my master's wife *b* a son to ... Gen 24:36 3205
son, whom Milcah *b* unto him ... Gen 24:47 3205
she *b* him Zimran, and Jokshan, and ... Gen 25:2 3205
Sarah's handmaid, *b* unto Abraham ... Gen 25:12 3205
years old when she *b* them ... Gen 25:26 3205
b a son, and she called his name ... Gen 29:32 3205
she conceived again, and *b* a son ... Gen 29:33 3205
she conceived again, and *b* a son ... Gen 29:34 3205
she conceived again, and *b* a son ... Gen 29:35 3205
saw that she *b* Jacob no children ... Gen 30:1 3205
conceived, and *b* Jacob a son ... Gen 30:5 3205
again, and *b* Jacob a second son ... Gen 30:7 3205
Zilpah Leah's maid *b* Jacob a son ... Gen 30:10 3205
Leah's maid *b* Jacob a second son ... Gen 30:12 3205
and *b* Jacob the fifth son ... Gen 30:17 3205
again, and *b* Jacob the sixth son ... Gen 30:19 3205
And afterwards she *b* a daughter ... Gen 30:21 3205
And she conceived, and *b* a son ... Gen 30:23 3205
then all the cattle *b* speckled ... Gen 31:8 3205
then *b* all the cattle ringstraked ... Gen 31:8 3205
I *b* the loss of it ... Gen 31:39 2308
which she *b* unto Jacob, went out ... Gen 34:1 3205
And Adah *b* to Esau Eliphaz ... Gen 36:4 3205
and Bashemath *b* Reuel ... Gen 36:4 3205
And Aholibamah *b* Jeush, and Jaalam, ... Gen 36:5 3205
and she *b* to Eliphaz Amalek ... Gen 36:12 3205
she *b* to Esau Jeush, and Jaalam, ... Gen 36:14 3205
And she conceived, and *b* a son ... Gen 38:3 3205
she conceived again, and *b* a son ... Gen 38:4 3205
yet again conceived, and *b* a son ... Gen 38:5 3205
he was at Chezib, when she *b* him ... Gen 38:5 3205
priest of On *b* unto him ... Gen 41:50 3205
know that my wife *b* me two sons ... Gen 44:27 3205
which she *b* unto Jacob in ... Gen 46:15 3205
these she *b* unto Jacob, even ... Gen 46:18 3205
priest of On *b* unto him ... Gen 46:20 3205
and she *b* these unto Jacob ... Gen 46:25 3205
the woman conceived, and *b* a son ... Ex 2:2 3205
she *b* him a son, and he called his ... Ex 2:22 3205
and she *b* him Aaron and Moses ... Ex 6:20 3205
she *b* him Nadab, and Abihu, ... Ex 6:23 3205
and she *b* him Phinehas ... Ex 6:25 3205
how I *b* you on eagles' wings, and ... Ex 19:4 5375
shall be rent, and his head *b* ... Lev 13:45 6544
whether it be *b* within or without ... Lev 13:55 7146
they *b* it between two upon a ... Num 13:23 5375
whom her mother *b* to Levi in ... Num 26:59 3205
she *b* unto Amram Aaron and Moses, ... Num 26:59 3205
how that the LORD thy God *b* thee ... Deut 1:31 5375
which *b* the ark of the covenant ... Deut 31:9 5375
which *b* the ark of the covenant ... Deut 31:25 5375
as they that *b* the ark were come ... Josh 3:15 5375
the feet of the priests that *b* ... Josh 3:15 5375
the priests that *b* the ark of the ... Josh 3:17 5375
b the ark of the covenant stood ... Josh 4:9 5375
For the priests which *b* the ark ... Josh 4:10 5375
when the priests that *b* the ark ... Josh 4:18 5375
which *b* the ark of the covenant ... Josh 8:33 5375
the people that *b* the present ... Judg 3:18 5375
she also *b* him a son, whose name ... Judg 8:31 3205
And Gilead's wife *b* him sons ... Judg 11:2 3205
and his wife was barren, and *b* not ... Judg 13:2 3205
And the woman *b* a son, and called ... Judg 13:24 3205
Pharez, whom Tamar *b* unto Judah ... Ruth 4:12 3205
her conception, and she *b* a son ... Ruth 4:13 3205
had conceived, that she *b* a son ... 1Sa 1:20 3205
b three sons and two daughters ... 1Sa 2:21 3205
the young man that *b* his armour ... 1Sa 14:1 5375
the young man that *b* his armour ... 1Sa 14:6 5375
the man that *b* the shield went ... 1Sa 17:41 5375
that when they that *b* the ark of ... 2Sa 6:13 5375
became his wife, and *b* him a son ... 2Sa 11:27 3205
that Uriah's wife *b* unto David ... 2Sa 12:15 3205
she *b* a son, and he called his ... 2Sa 12:24 3205
ten young men that *b* Joab's ... 2Sa 18:15 5375
whom she *b* unto Saul, Armoni and ... 2Sa 21:8 3205
his mother *b* him after Absalom ... 1Kin 1:6 3205
and ten thousand that *b* burdens ... 1Kin 5:15 5375
which *b* rule over the people that ... 1Kin 9:23 7287
train, with camels that *b* spices ... 1Kin 10:2 5375
Tahpenes *b* him Genubath his son ... 1Kin 11:20 3205
the LORD, that the guard *b* them ... 1Kin 14:28 5375
b a son at that season that ... 2Kin 4:17 3205
and they *b* them before him ... 2Kin 5:23 5375
she *b* Zimran, and Jokshan, and ... 1Chr 1:32 3205
his daughter in law *b* him Pharez ... 1Chr 2:4 3205

And Abigail *b* Amasa 1Chr 2:17 3205
unto him Ephrath, which *b* him Hur 1Chr 2:19 3205
and she *b* him Segub 1Chr 2:21 3205
then Abiah Hezron's wife *b* him 1Chr 2:24 3205
she *b* him Ahban, and Molid 1Chr 2:29 3205
and she *b* him Attai 1Chr 2:35 3205
b Haran, and Moza, and Gazez 1Chr 2:46 3205
concubine, *b* Sheber, and Tirhanah 1Chr 2:48 3205
She *b* also Shaaph the father of 1Chr 2:49 3205
Naarah *b* him Ahuzam, and Hepher, 1Chr 4:6 3205
Because I *b* him with sorrow 1Chr 4:9 3205
she *b* Miriam, and Shammai, and 1Chr 4:17 2029
his wife Jehudijah *b* Jered the 1Chr 4:18 3205
Ashriel, whom she *b* 1Chr 7:14 3205
b Machir the father of Gilead 1Chr 7:14 3205
the wife of Machir *b* a son 1Chr 7:16 3205
And his sister Hammoleketh *b* Ishod 1Chr 7:18 3205
b a son, and he called his name 1Chr 7:23 3205
children of Judah that *b* shield 1Chr 12:24 5375
b the ark of God upon their 1Chr 15:15 5375
God helped the Levites that *b* the 1Chr 15:26 5375
and all the Levites that *b* the ark 1Chr 15:27 5375
that *b* rule over the people 2Chr 8:10 7287
company, and camels that *b* spices 2Chr 9:1 5375
Which *b* him children 2Chr 11:19 3205
which *b* him Abijah, and Attai, and 2Chr 11:20 3205
had an army of men that *b* targets 2Chr 14:8 5375
that *b* shields and drew bows, two 2Chr 14:8 5375
the wall, and they that *b* burdens Neh 4:17 5375
even their servants *b* rule over Neh 5:15 7980
and bitterness to her that *b* him Prov 17:25 3205
she that *b* thee shall rejoice Prov 23:25 3205
the choice one of her that *b* her Song 6:9 3205
brought thee forth that *b* thee Song 8:5 3205
and she conceived, and *b* a son Is 8:3 3205
Elam *b* the quiver with chariots Is 22:6 5375
strip you, and make you *b*, and gird Is 32:11 6209
make *b* the leg, uncover the thigh Is 47:2 2834
father, and unto Sarah that *b* you Is 51:2 2342
The LORD hath made *b* his holy arm Is 52:10 2834
he *b* the sin of many, and made Is 53:12 5375
he *b* them, and carried them all Is 63:9 5190
discovered, and thy heels made *b* Jer 13:22 2554
their mothers that *b* them Jer 16:3 3205
wherein my mother *b* me be blessed Jer 20:14 3205
out, and thy mother that *b* thee Jer 22:26 3205
But I have made Esau *b*, I have Jer 49:10 2834
she that *b* you shall be ashamed Jer 50:12 3205
I *b* it upon my shoulder in their Eze 12:7 5375
whereas thou wast naked and *b* Eze 16:7 6181
youth, when thou wast naked and *b* Eze 16:22 6181
jewels, and leave thee naked and *b* Eze 16:39 6181
the sceptres of them that *b* rule Eze 19:11 4910
and they were mine, and they *b* sons Eze 23:4 3205
and shall leave thee naked and *b* Eze 23:29 6181
their sons, whom they *b* unto me Eze 23:37 3205
which conceived, and *b* him a son Hos 1:3 3205
conceived again, and *b* a daughter Hos 1:6 3205
she conceived, and *b* a son Hos 1:8 3205
he hath made it clean *b*, and cast Joel 1:7 2834
infirmities, and *b* our sicknesses Mt 8:17 *941*
For many *b* false witness against Mk 14:56 *5576*
b false witness against him, Mk 14:57 *5576*
all *b* him witness, and wondered at Lk 4:22 *3140*
they that *b* him stood still Lk 7:14 *941*
up, and *b* fruit an hundredfold Lk 8:8 *4160*
Blessed is the womb that *b* thee Lk 11:27 *941*
barren, and the wombs that never *b* Lk 23:29 *1080*
John *b* witness of him, and cried, Jn 1:15 *3140*
John *b* record, saying, I saw the Jn 1:32 *3140*
b record that this is the Son of Jn 1:34 *3140*
And they *b* it Jn 2:8 *5342*
he *b* witness unto the truth Jn 5:33 *3140*
bag, and *b* what was put therein Jn 12:6 *941*
him from the dead, *b* record Jn 12:17 *3140*
And he that saw it *b* record Jn 19:35 *3140*
b them witness, giving them the Acts 15:8 *3140*
but *b* grain, it may chance of 1Cor 15:37 *1131*
Who his own self *b* our sins in 1Pet 2:24 *399*
Who *b* record of the word of God, Rev 1:2 *3140*
which *b* twelve manner of fruits, Rev 22:2 *4160*

BAREFOOT
his head covered, and he went *b* 2Sa 15:30 3182
And he did so, walking naked and *b* Is 20:2 3182
b three years for a sign and Is 20:3 3182
young and old, naked and *b* Is 20:4 3182

BAREST
because thou *b* the ark of the 1Kin 2:26 5375
thou never *b* rule over them Is 63:19 4910
Jordan, to whom thou *b* witness Jn 3:26 *3140*

BARHUMITE (*bar'hu-mite*) See BAHARUMITE. *A form of Baharumite.*
the Arbathite, Azmaveth the *B* 2Sa 23:31 1273

BARIAH (*ba-ri'-ah*) *Grandson of Shechaniah.*
Hattush, and Igeal, and *B*, and 1Chr 3:22 1282

BAR-JESUS (*bar-je'-sus*) See ELYMAS. *Another name of Elymas.*
prophet, a Jew, whose name was *B* Acts 13:6 *919*

BAR-JONA (*bar-jo'-nah*) See SIMON. *Another name of Simon Peter.*
him, Blessed art thou, Simon *B* Mt 16:17 *920*

BAR-JONAH See BAR-JONA.

BARK
are all dumb dogs, they cannot *b* Is 56:10 5024

BARKED
my vine waste, and *b* my fig tree Joel 1:7 7111

BARKOS (*bar'-cos*) *A family who returned from the Exile.*
The children of *B*, the children Ezr 2:53 1302
The children of *B*, the children Neh 7:55 1302

BARLEY
And the flax and the *b* was smitten Ex 9:31 8184
for the *b* was in the ear, and the Ex 9:31 8184
a homer of *b* seed shall be valued Lev 27:16 8184
tenth part of an ephah of *b* meal Num 5:15 8184
A land of wheat, and *b*, and vines, Deut 8:8 8184
a cake of *b* bread tumbled into Judg 7:13 8184
in the beginning of *b* harvest Ruth 1:22 8184
and it was about an ephah of *b* Ruth 2:17 8184
glean unto the end of *b* harvest Ruth 2:23 8184
he winnoweth *b* to night in the Ruth 3:2 8184
it, he measured six measures of *b* Ruth 3:15 8184
six measures of *b* gave he me Ruth 3:17 8184
is near mine, and he hath *b* there 2Sa 14:30 8184
earthen vessels, and wheat, and *b* 2Sa 17:28 8184
in the beginning of *b* harvest 2Sa 21:9 8184
B also and straw for the horses and 1Kin 4:28 8184
firstfruits, twenty loaves of *b* 2Kin 4:42 8184
and two measures of *b* for a shekel 2Kin 7:1 8184
and two measures of *b* for a shekel 2Kin 7:16 8184
Two measures of *b* for a shekel 2Kin 7:18 8184
was a parcel of ground full of *b* 1Chr 11:13 8184
and twenty thousand measures of *b* 2Chr 2:10 8184
Now therefore the wheat, and the *b* 2Chr 2:15 8184
of wheat, and ten thousand of *b* 2Chr 27:5 8184
of wheat, and cockle instead of *b* Job 31:40 8184
wheat and the appointed *b* and the Is 28:25 8184
in the field, of wheat, and of *b* Jer 41:8 8184
thou also unto thee wheat, and *b* Eze 4:9 8184
And thou shalt eat it as *b* cakes Eze 4:12 8184
among my people for handfuls of *b* Eze 13:19 8184
part of an ephah of an homer of *b* Eze 45:13 8184
of *b*, and an half homer of *b* Hos 3:2 8184
for the wheat and for the *b* Joel 1:11 8184
here, which hath five *b* loaves Jn 6:9 *2916*
fragments of the five *b* loaves Jn 6:13 *2916*
three measures of *b* for a penny Rev 6:6 *2915*

BARN
thy seed, and gather it into thy *b* Job 39:12 1637
Is the seed yet in the *b* Hag 2:19 4035
but gather the wheat into my *b* Mt 13:30 *596*
neither have storehouse nor *b* Lk 12:24 *596*

BARNABAS (*bar'-na-bas*) See JOSES. *A companion of Paul.*
by the apostles was surnamed *B* Acts 4:36 *921*
But *B* took him, and brought him to Acts 9:27 *921*
and they sent forth *B*, that he Acts 11:22 *921*
Then departed *B* to Tarsus Acts 11:25 *921*
to the elders by the hands of *B* Acts 11:30 *921*
And *B* and Saul returned from Acts 12:25 *921*
as *B*, and Simeon that was called Acts 13:1 *921*
Holy Ghost said, Separate me *B* Acts 13:2 *921*
who called for *B* and Saul, and Acts 13:7 *921*
proselytes followed Paul and *B* Acts 13:43 *921*
B waxed bold, and said, It was Acts 13:46 *921*
persecution against Paul and *B* Acts 13:50 *921*
And they called *B*, Jupiter Acts 14:12 *921*
Which when the apostles, *B* Acts 14:14 *921*
day he departed with *B* to Derbe Acts 14:20 *921*
B had no small dissension and Acts 15:2 *921*
they determined that Paul and *B* Acts 15:2 *921*
silence, and gave audience to *B* Acts 15:12 *921*
company to Antioch with Paul and *B* Acts 15:22 *921*
men unto you with our beloved *B* Acts 15:25 *921*
B continued in Antioch, teaching Acts 15:35 *921*
some days after Paul said unto *B* Acts 15:36 *921*
B determined to take with them Acts 15:37 *921*
so *B* took Mark, and sailed unto Acts 15:39 *921*
Or I only and *B*, have not we power 1Cor 9:6 *921*
went up again to Jerusalem with *B* Gal 2:1 *921*
B the right hands of fellowship Gal 2:9 *921*
insomuch that *B* also was carried Gal 2:13 *921*
you, and Marcus, sister's son to *B* Col 4:10 *921*

BARNFLOOR
out of the *b*, or out of the 2Kin 6:27 1637

BARNS
So shall thy *b* be filled with Prov 3:10 618
desolate, the *b* are broken down Joel 1:17 4460
do they reap, nor gather into *b* Mt 6:26 *596*
I will pull down my *b*, and build Lk 12:18 *596*

BARREL
but an handful of meal in a *b* 1Kin 17:12 3537
The *b* of meal shall not waste, 1Kin 17:14 3537
the *b* of meal wasted not, neither 1Kin 17:16 3537

BARRELS
Fill four *b* with water, and pour 1Kin 18:33 3537

BARREN
But Sarai was *b* Gen 11:30 6135
for his wife, because she was *b* Gen 25:21 6135
but Rachel was *b* Gen 29:31 6135
cast their young, nor be *b* Ex 23:26 6135
not be male or female *b* among you Deut 7:14 6135
and his wife was *b*, and bare not Judg 13:2 6135
unto her, Behold now, thou art *b* Judg 13:3 6135
so that the *b* hath born seven 1Sa 2:5 6135
water is naught, and the ground *b* 2Kin 2:19 7921
thence any more death or *b* land 2Kin 2:21 7921
entreateth the *b* that beareth not Job 24:21 6135
and the *b* land his dwellings Job 39:6 4420
He maketh the *b* woman to keep Ps 113:9 6135
and the *b* womb Prov 30:16 6115
twins, and none is *b* among them Song 4:2 7909
and there is not one *b* among them Song 6:6 7909
Sing, O *b*, thou that didst not Is 54:1 6135
and will drive him into a land *b* Joel 2:20 6723
because that Elisabeth was *b* Lk 1:7 *4722*
month with her, who was called *b* Lk 1:36 *4722*
they shall say, Blessed are the *b* Lk 23:29 *4722*
Rejoice, thou *b* that bearest not Gal 4:27 *4722*
you that ye shall neither be *b* 2Pet 1:8 *692*

BARRENNESS
A fruitful land into *b*, for the Ps 107:34 4420

BARS
thou shalt make *b* of shittim wood Ex 26:26 1280
five *b* for the boards of the Ex 26:27 1280
five *b* for the boards of the side Ex 26:27 1280
of gold for places for the *b* Ex 26:29 1280
shalt overlay the *b* with gold Ex 26:29 1280
his taches, and his boards, his *b* Ex 35:11 1280
he made *b* of shittim wood Ex 36:31 1280
five *b* for the boards of the Ex 36:32 1280
five *b* for the boards of the Ex 36:32 1280
b, and overlaid the *b* with gold Ex 36:34 1280
his taches, his boards, his *b* Ex 39:33 1280
thereof, and put in the *b* thereof Ex 40:18 1280
the *b* thereof, and the pillars Num 3:36 1280
the *b* thereof, and the pillars Num 4:31 1280
with high walls, gates, and *b* Deut 3:5 1280
into a town that hath gates and *b* 1Sa 23:7 1280
cities with walls and brasen *b* 1Kin 4:13 1280
cities, with walls, gates, and *b* 2Chr 8:5 1280
walls, and towers, gates, and *b* 2Chr 14:7 1280
locks thereof, and the *b* thereof Neh 3:3 1280
locks thereof, and the *b* thereof Neh 3:6 1280
the *b* thereof, and a thousand Neh 3:13 1280
locks thereof, and the *b* thereof Neh 3:14 1280
the *b* thereof, and the wall of the Neh 3:15 1280
shall go down to the *b* of the pit Job 17:16 905
for it my decreed place, and set *b* Job 38:10 1280
his bones are like *b* of iron Job 40:18 4800
cut the *b* of iron in sunder Ps 107:16 1280
strengthened the *b* of thy gates Ps 147:13 1280
are like the *b* of a castle Prov 18:19 1280
and cut in sunder the *b* of iron Is 45:2 1280
which have neither gates nor *b* Jer 49:31 1280
her *b* are broken Jer 51:30 1280
he hath destroyed and broken her *b* Lam 2:9 1280
and having neither *b* nor gates Eze 38:11 1280
the earth with her *b* was about me Jonah 2:6 1280
the fire shall devour thy *b* Nah 3:13 1280

BARSABAS (*bar'-sab-as*) See JOSEPH, JUDAS, JUSTUS.
1. The successor of Judas as apostle.
appointed two, Joseph called *B* Acts 1:23 *923*
2. A disciple sent to Antioch with Silas.
namely, Judas surnamed *B*, and Acts 15:22 *923*

BARSABBAS See BARSABAS.

BARTHOLOMEW (*bar-thol'-o-mew*) See NATHANAEL. *One of Jesus' twelve disciples.*
Philip, and *B*; Thomas, and Mt 10:3 *918*
And Andrew, and Philip, and *B* Mk 3:18 *918*
James and John, Philip and *B* Lk 6:14 *918*
and Andrew, Philip, and Thomas, *B* Acts 1:13 *918*

BARTIMAEUS (*bar-ti-me'-us*) *A blind beggar.*
a great number of people, blind *B* Mk 10:46 *924*

BARUCH (*ba'-rook*)
1. A son of Zabbai.
After him *B* the son of Zabbai Neh 3:20 1263
Daniel, Ginnethon, *B*, Neh 10:6 1263
2. A descendant of Perez.
And Maaseiah the son of *B*, the son Neh 11:5 1263
3. The scribe of Jeremiah.
purchase unto *B* the son of Neriah Jer 32:12 1263
I charged *B* before them, saying, Jer 32:13 1263
purchase unto *B* the son of Neriah Jer 32:16 1263
called *B* the son of Neriah Jer 36:4 1263
B wrote from the mouth of Jer 36:4 1263
And Jeremiah commanded *B*, saying, Jer 36:5 1263
B the son of Neriah did according Jer 36:8 1263
Then read *B* in the book the words Jer 36:10 1263
when *B* read the book in the ears Jer 36:13 1263
the son of Cushi, unto *B* Jer 36:14 1263
So *B* the son of Neriah took the Jer 36:14 1263
So *B* read it in their ears Jer 36:15 1263
both one and other, and said unto *B* Jer 36:16 1263
And they asked *B*, saying, Tell us Jer 36:17 1263
Then *B* answered them, He Jer 36:18 1263
Then said the princes unto *B* Jer 36:19 1263
to take *B* the scribe and Jeremiah Jer 36:26 1263
the words which *B* wrote at the Jer 36:27 1263
roll, and gave it to *B* the scribe Jer 36:32 1263
But *B* the son of Neriah setteth Jer 43:3 1263
prophet, and *B* the son of Neriah Jer 43:6 1263
spake unto *B* the son of Neriah Jer 45:1 1263
the God of Israel, unto thee, O *B* Jer 45:2 1263

BARZILLAI (*bar-zil'-la-i*)
1. A friend of David.
B the Gileadite of Rogelim, 2Sa 17:27 1271
B the Gileadite came down from 2Sa 19:31 1271
Now *B* was a very aged man, even 2Sa 19:32 1271
And the king said unto *B*, Come 2Sa 19:33 1271
B said unto the king, How long 2Sa 19:34 1271
was come over, the king kissed *B* 2Sa 19:39 1271
unto the sons of *B* the Gileadite 1Kin 2:7 1271
of Koz, the children of *B* Ezr 2:61 1271
the daughters of *B* the Gileadite Ezr 2:61 1271
of Koz, the children of *B* Neh 7:63 1271
of *B* the Gileadite to wife Neh 7:63 1271
2. Husband of Merab.
the son of *B* the Meholathite 2Sa 21:8 1271

BASE
will be *b* in mine own sight 2Sa 6:22 8217
cubits was the length of one *b* 1Kin 7:27 4350
the ledges there was a *b* above 1Kin 7:29 3653
every *b* had four brasen wheels, 1Kin 7:30 4350
was round after the work of the *b* 1Kin 7:31 3653
the wheels were joined to the *b* 1Kin 7:32 4350
to the four corners of one *b* 1Kin 7:34 4350

were of the very *b* itself — 1Kin 7:34 4350
in the top of the *b* was there a — 1Kin 7:35 4350
on the top of the *b* the ledges — 1Kin 7:35 4350
of fools, yea, children of *b* men — Job 30:8
the *b* against the honourable — Is 3:5 7034
That the kingdom might be *b* — Eze 17:14 8217
they shall be there a *b* kingdom — Eze 29:14 8217
and set there upon her own *b* — Zec 5:11 4369
and *b* before all the people, — Mal 2:9 8217
b things of the world, and things — 1Cor 1:28 *36*
who in presence am *b* among you — 2Cor 10:1 *5011*

BASEMATH See Basmath.

BASER
lewd fellows of the *b* sort — Acts 17:5 *60*

BASES
And he made ten *b* of brass — 1Kin 7:27 4350
the work of the *b* was on this — 1Kin 7:28 4350
this manner he made the ten *b* — 1Kin 7:37 4350
every one of the ten *b* one laver — 1Kin 7:38 4350
he put five *b* on the right side — 1Kin 7:39 4350
ten *b*, and ten lavers on the *b* — 1Kin 7:43 4350
Ahaz cut off the borders of the *b* — 2Kin 16:17 4350
the house of the Lord, and the *b* — 2Kin 25:13 4350
the *b* which Solomon had made for — 2Kin 25:16 4350
b, and lavers made he upon the *b* — 2Chr 4:14 4350
And they set the altar upon his *b* — Ezr 3:3 4350
the sea, and concerning the *b* — Jer 27:19 4369
the house of the Lord, and the *b* — Jer 52:17 4350
bulls that were under the *b* — Jer 52:20 4350

BASEST
It shall be the *b* of the kingdoms — Eze 29:15 8217
setteth up over it the *b* of men — Dan 4:17 8215

BASHAN (*ba'-shan*) See Bashan-havoth-jair.
Kingdom of King Og.
turned and went up by the way of *B* — Num 21:33 1316
Og the king of *B* went out against — Num 21:33 1316
and the kingdom of Og king of *B* — Num 32:33 1316
in Heshbon, and Og the king of *B* — Deut 1:4 1316
turned, and went up the way to *B* — Deut 3:1 1316
Og the king of *B* came out against — Deut 3:1 1316
our hands Og also, the king of *B* — Deut 3:3 1316
of Argob, the kingdom of Og in *B* — Deut 3:4 1316
plain, and all Gilead, and all *B* — Deut 3:10 1316
cities of the kingdom of Og in *B* — Deut 3:10 1316
For only Og king of *B* remained of — Deut 3:11 1316
And the rest of Gilead, and all *B* — Deut 3:13 1316
the region of Argob, with all *B* — Deut 3:13 1316
and Golan in *B*, of the Manassites — Deut 4:43 1316
land, and the land of Og king of *B* — Deut 4:47 1316
of Heshbon, and Og the king of *B* — Deut 29:7 1316
lambs, and rams of the breed of *B* — Deut 32:14 1316
he shall leap from *B* — Deut 33:22 1316
of Heshbon, and to Og king of *B* — Josh 9:10 1316
And the coast of Og king of *B* — Josh 12:4 1316
Hermon, and in Salcah, and in all *B* — Josh 12:5 1316
Hermon, and all *B* unto Salcah — Josh 13:11 1316
All the kingdom of Og in *B* — Josh 13:12 1316
coast was from Mahanaim, all *B* — Josh 13:30 1316
all the kingdom of Og king of *B* — Josh 13:30 1316
the towns of Jair, which are in *B* — Josh 13:30 1316
cities of the kingdom of Og in *B* — Josh 13:31 1316
war, therefore he had Gilead and *B* — Josh 17:1 1316
beside the land of Gilead and *B* — Josh 17:5 1316
Golan in *B* out of the tribe of — Josh 20:8 1316
the half tribe of Manasseh in *B* — Josh 21:6 1316
gave Golan in *B* with her suburbs — Josh 21:27 1316
Moses had given possession in *B* — Josh 22:7 1316
region of Argob, which is in *B* — 1Kin 4:13 1316
the Amorites, and of Og king of *B* — 1Kin 4:19 1316
the river Arnon, even Gilead and *B* — 2Kin 10:33 1316
in the land of *B* unto Salchah — 1Chr 5:11 1316
next, and Jaanai, and Shaphat in *B* — 1Chr 5:12 1316
And they dwelt in Gilead in *B* — 1Chr 5:16 1316
increased from *B* unto Baal-hermon — 1Chr 5:23 1316
out of the tribe of Manasseh in *B* — 1Chr 6:62 1316
Golan in *B* with her suburbs, and — 1Chr 6:71 1316
and the land of Og king of *B* — Neh 9:22 1316
strong bulls of *B* have beset me — Ps 22:12 1316
hill of God is as the hill of *B* — Ps 68:15 1316
an high hill as the hill of *B* — Ps 68:15 1316
said, I will bring again from *B* — Ps 68:22 1316
of the Amorites, and Og king of *B* — Ps 135:11 1316
And Og the king of *B* — Ps 136:20 1316
up, and upon all the oaks of *B* — Is 2:13 1316
and *B* and Carmel shake off their — Is 33:9 1316
and lift up thy voice in *B* — Jer 22:20 1316
and he shall feed on Carmel and *B* — Jer 50:19 1316
Of the oaks of *B* have they made — Eze 27:6 1316
all of them fatlings of *B* — Eze 39:18 1316
Hear this word, ye kine of *B* — Amos 4:1 1316
let them feed in *B* and Gilead, as — Mic 7:14 1316
B languisheth, and Carmel, and the — Nah 1:4 1316
howl, O ye oaks of *B* — Zec 11:2 1316

BASHAN-HAVOTH-JAIR (*ba'''-shan-ha''-voth-ja'-ur) Same as Argob.*
called them after his own name, *B* — Deut 3:14

BASHEMATH (*bash'-e-math*) See Basmath.
1. Daughter of Elon the Hittite.
B the daughter of Elon the — Gen 26:34 1315
2. Daughter of Ishmael.
B Ishmael's daughter, sister of — Gen 36:3 1315
and *B* bare Reuel — Gen 36:4 1315
the son of *B* the wife of Esau — Gen 36:10 1315
were the sons of *B* Esau's wife — Gen 36:13 1315
are the sons of *B* Esau's wife — Gen 36:17 1315

BASKET
in the uppermost *b* there was of — Gen 40:17 5536
them out of the *b* upon my head — Gen 40:17 5536
b, and bring them in the *b* — Ex 29:3 5536
one wafer out of the *b* of the — Ex 29:23 5536
and the bread that is in the *b* — Ex 29:32 5536
rams, and a *b* of unleavened bread — Lev 8:2 5536
out of the *b* of unleavened bread, — Lev 8:26 5536
that is in the *b* of consecrations — Lev 8:31 5536
a *b* of unleavened bread, cakes of — Num 6:15 5536
with the *b* of unleavened bread — Num 6:17 5536
one unleavened cake out of the *b* — Num 6:19 5536
thee, and shalt put it in a *b* — Deut 26:2 2935
take the *b* out of thine hand — Deut 26:4 2935
Blessed shall be thy *b* and thy — Deut 28:5 2935
Cursed shall be thy *b* and thy — Deut 28:17 2935
the flesh he put in a *b*, and he — Judg 6:19 5536
One *b* had very good figs, even — Jer 24:2 1731
the other *b* had very naughty figs — Jer 24:2 1731
behold a *b* of summer fruit — Amos 8:1 3619
And I said, A *b* of summer fruit — Amos 8:2 3619
let him down by the wall in a *b* — Acts 9:25 *4711*
through a window in a *b* was I let — 2Cor 11:33 *4553*

BASKETS
I had three white *b* on my head — Gen 40:16 5536
The three *b* are three days — Gen 40:18 5536
persons, and put their heads in *b* — 2Kin 10:7 1731
as a grapegatherer into the *b* — Jer 6:9 5552
two *b* of figs were set before the — Jer 24:1 1736
that remained twelve *b* full — Mt 14:20 *2894*
meat that was left seven *b* full — Mt 15:37 *4711*
and how many *b* ye took up — Mt 16:9 *2894*
and how many *b* ye took up — Mt 16:10 *4711*
they took up twelve *b* full of the — Mk 6:43 *2894*
broken meat that was left seven *b* — Mk 8:8 *4711*
how many *b* full of fragments took — Mk 8:19 *2894*
how many *b* full of fragments took — Mk 8:20 *4711*
that remained to them twelve *b* — Lk 9:17 *2894*
and filled twelve *b* with the — Jn 6:13 *2894*

BASMATH (*bas'-math*) See Bashemath. *A daughter of Solomon.*
he also took *B* the daughter of — 1Kin 4:15 1315

BASON
it in the blood that is in the *b* — Ex 12:22 5592
with the blood that is in the *b* — Ex 12:22 5592
gave gold by weight for every *b* — 1Chr 28:17 3713
by weight for every *b* of silver — 1Chr 28:17 3713
that he poureth water into a *b* — Jn 13:5 *3537*

BASONS
half of the blood, and put it in *b* — Ex 24:6 101
ashes, and his shovels, and his *b* — Ex 27:3 4219
pots, and the shovels, and the *b* — Ex 38:3 4219
and the shovels, and the *b* — Num 4:14 4219
Brought beds, and *b*, and earthen — 2Sa 17:28 5592
lavers, and the shovels, and the *b* — 1Kin 7:40 4219
pots, and the shovels, and the *b* — 1Kin 7:45 4219
bowls, and the snuffers, and the *b* — 1Kin 7:50 4219
Lord bowls of silver, snuffers, *b* — 2Kin 12:13 4219
for the golden *b* he gave gold by — 1Chr 28:17 3713
And he made an hundred *b* of gold — 2Chr 4:8 4219
pots, and the shovels, and the *b* — 2Chr 4:11 4219
And the snuffers, and the *b* — 2Chr 4:22 4219
Thirty *b* of gold, silver *b* — Ezr 1:10 3713
Also twenty *b* of gold, of a — Ezr 8:27 3713
a thousand drams of gold, fifty *b* — Neh 7:70 4219
And the *b*, and the firepans, and the — Jer 52:19 5592

BASTARD
A *b* shall not enter into the — Deut 23:2 4464
a *b* shall dwell in Ashdod, and I — Zec 9:6 4464

BASTARDS
all are partakers, then are ye *b* — Heb 12:8 *3541*

BAT
kind, and the lapwing, and the *b* — Lev 11:19 5847
kind, and the lapwing, and the *b* — Deut 14:18 5847

BATH
of vineyard shall yield one *b* — Is 5:10 1324
and a just ephah, and a just *b* — Eze 45:10 1324
the *b* shall be of one measure, — Eze 45:11 1324
that the *b* may contain the tenth — Eze 45:11 1324
the *b* of oil, ye shall offer the — Eze 45:14 1324
tenth part of a *b* out of the cor — Eze 45:14 1324

BATHE
b himself in water, and be unclean — Lev 15:5 7364
b himself in water, and be unclean — Lev 15:6 7364
b himself in water, and be unclean — Lev 15:7 7364
b himself in water, and be unclean — Lev 15:8 7364
b himself in water, and be unclean — Lev 15:10 7364
b himself in water, and be unclean — Lev 15:11 7364
b his flesh in running water, and — Lev 15:13 7364
they shall both *b* themselves in — Lev 15:18 7364
b himself in water, and be unclean — Lev 15:21 7364
b himself in water, and be unclean — Lev 15:22 7364
b himself in water, and be unclean — Lev 15:27 7364
and *b* his flesh in water, and — Lev 16:26 7364
and *b* his flesh in water, and — Lev 16:28 7364
b himself in water, and be unclean — Lev 17:15 7364
he wash them not, nor *b* his flesh — Lev 17:16 7364
he shall *b* his flesh in water, and — Num 19:7 7364
b his flesh in water, and shall be — Num 19:8 7364
b himself in water, and shall be — Num 19:19 7364

BATHED
For my sword shall be *b* in heaven — Is 34:5 7301

BATH-RABBIM (*bath-rab'-bim*) *A gate at Heshbon.*
in Heshbon, by the gate of *B* — Song 7:4 1337

BATHS
it contained two thousand *b* — 1Kin 7:26 1324
one laver contained forty *b* — 1Kin 7:38 1324
and twenty thousand *b* of wine — 2Chr 2:10 1324
and twenty thousand *b* of oil — 2Chr 2:10 1324
received and held three thousand *b* — 2Chr 4:5 1324
wheat, and to an hundred *b* of wine — Ezr 7:22 1325
and to an hundred *b* of oil — Ezr 7:22 1324
cor, which is an homer of ten *b* — Eze 45:14 1324
for ten *b* are an homer — Eze 45:14 1324

BATH-SHEBA (*bath'-she-bah*) See Bath-shua.
A wife of David.
And one said, Is not this *B* — 2Sa 11:3 1339
And David comforted *B* his wife — 2Sa 12:24 1339
unto *B* the mother of Solomon — 1Kin 1:11 1339
B went in unto the king into the — 1Kin 1:15 1339
B bowed, and did obeisance unto — 1Kin 1:16 1339
David answered and said, Call me *B* — 1Kin 1:28 1339
Then *B* bowed with her face to the — 1Kin 1:31 1339
came to *B* the mother of Solomon — 1Kin 2:13 1339
And *B* said, Well — 1Kin 2:18 1339
B therefore went unto king — 1Kin 2:19 1339
him, after he had gone in to *B* — Ps 51:*t* 1339

BATH-SHUA (*bath'-shu-ah*) See Bath-sheba.
A form of Bath-sheba.
of *B* the daughter of Ammiel — 1Chr 3:5 1340

BATS
worship, to the moles and to the *b* — Is 2:20 5847

BATTERED
that were with Joab *b* the wall — 2Sa 20:15 7843

BATTERING
set *b* rams against it round about — Eze 4:2
to appoint *b* rams against the — Eze 21:22

BATTLE
they joined *b* with them in the — Gen 14:8 4421
all his people, to the *b* at Edrei — Num 21:33 4421
hundreds, which came from the *b* — Num 31:14
men of war which went to the *b* — Num 31:21 4421
war upon them, who went out to *b* — Num 31:27 6635
men of war which went out to *b* — Num 31:28 6635
for war, before the Lord to *b* — Num 32:27 4421
over Jordan, every man armed to *b* — Num 32:29 4421
neither contend with them in *b* — Deut 2:9 4421
it, and contend with him in *b* — Deut 2:24 4421
and all his people, to *b* at Edrei — Deut 3:1 4421
out to *b* against thine enemies — Deut 20:1 4421
when ye are come nigh unto the *b* — Deut 20:2 4421
day unto *b* against your enemies — Deut 20:3 4421
his house, lest he die in the *b* — Deut 20:5 4421
his house, lest he die in the *b* — Deut 20:6 4421
his house, lest he die in the *b* — Deut 20:7 4421
came out against us unto *b* — Deut 29:7 4421
over before the Lord unto *b* — Josh 4:13 4421
city went out against Israel to *b* — Josh 8:14 4421
all other they took in *b* — Josh 11:19 4421
should come against Israel in *b* — Josh 11:20 4421
intend to go up against them in *b* — Josh 22:33 6635
from *b* before the sun was up — Judg 8:13 4421
to go out to *b* against the — Judg 20:14 4421
to the *b* against the children of — Judg 20:18 4421
went out to *b* against Benjamin — Judg 20:20 4421
set their *b* again in array in the — Judg 20:22 4421
Shall I go up again to *b* against — Judg 20:23 4421
out to *b* against the children of — Judg 20:28 4421
of all Israel, and the *b* was sore — Judg 20:34 4421
men of Israel retired in the *b* — Judg 20:39 4421
down before us, as in the first *b* — Judg 20:39 4421
but the *b* overtook them — Judg 20:42 4421
out against the Philistines to *b* — 1Sa 4:1 4421
and when they joined *b*, Israel was — 1Sa 4:2 4421
drew near to *b* against Israel — 1Sa 7:10 4421
it came to pass in the day of *b* — 1Sa 13:22 4421
themselves, and they came to the *b* — 1Sa 14:20 4421
followed hard after them in the *b* — 1Sa 14:22 4421
the *b* passed over unto Beth-aven — 1Sa 14:23 4421
together their armies to *b* — 1Sa 17:1 4421
set the *b* in array against the — 1Sa 17:2 4421
come out to set your *b* in array — 1Sa 17:8 4421
went and followed Saul to the *b* — 1Sa 17:13 4421
the *b* were Eliab the first born — 1Sa 17:13 4421
the fight, and shouted for the *b* — 1Sa 17:20 4421
had put the *b* in array, army — 1Sa 17:21
down that thou mightest see the *b* — 1Sa 17:28 4421
for the *b* is the Lord's, and he — 1Sa 17:47 4421
or he shall descend into *b* — 1Sa 26:10 4421
thou shalt go out with me to *b* — 1Sa 28:1 4264
let him not go down with us to *b* — 1Sa 29:4 4421
lest in the *b* he be an adversary — 1Sa 29:4 4421
shall not go up with us to the *b* — 1Sa 29:9 4421
part is that goeth down to the *b* — 1Sa 30:24 4421
the *b* went sore against Saul, and — 1Sa 31:3 4421
the people are fled from the *b* — 2Sa 1:4 4421
fallen in the midst of the *b* — 2Sa 1:25 4421
there was a very sore *b* that day — 2Sa 2:17 4421
brother Asahel at Gibeon in the *b* — 2Sa 3:30 4421
put the *b* in array at the — 2Sa 10:8 4221
of the *b* was against him before — 2Sa 10:9 4421
unto the *b* against the Syrians — 2Sa 10:13 4421
the time when kings go forth to *b* — 2Sa 11:1
in the forefront of the hottest *b* — 2Sa 11:15 4421
make thy *b* more strong against — 2Sa 11:25 4421
that thou go to *b* in thine own — 2Sa 17:11 7128
the *b* was in the wood of Ephraim — 2Sa 18:6 4421
For the *b* was there scattered — 2Sa 18:8 4421
steal away when they flee in *b* — 2Sa 19:3 4421
we anointed over us, is dead in *b* — 2Sa 19:10 4421
shalt go no more out with us to *b* — 2Sa 21:17 4421
that there was again a *b* with the — 2Sa 21:18 4421
there was again a *b* in Gob with — 2Sa 21:19 4421
And there was yet a *b* in Gath — 2Sa 21:20 4421
hast girded me with strength to *b* — 2Sa 22:40 4421
were there gathered together to *b* — 2Sa 23:9 4421
go out to *b* against their enemy — 1Kin 8:44 4421
he said, Who shall order the *b* — 1Kin 20:14 4421
the seventh day the *b* was joined — 1Kin 20:29 4421
went out into the midst of the *b* — 1Kin 20:39 4421
go with me to *b* to Ramoth-gilead — 1Kin 22:4 4421
I go against Ramoth-gilead to *b* — 1Kin 22:6 4421
we go against Ramoth-gilead to *b* — 1Kin 22:15 4421

myself, and enter into the *b* 1Kin 22:30 4421
himself, and went into the *b* 1Kin 22:30 4421
And the *b* increased that day 1Kin 22:35 4421
thou go with me against Moab to *b* 2Kin 3:7 4421
that the *b* was too sore for him 2Kin 3:26 4421
for they cried to God in the *b* 1Chr 5:20 4421
fit to go out for war and *b* 1Chr 7:11 4421
to *b* was twenty and six thousand 1Chr 7:40 4421
the *b* went sore against Saul, and 1Chr 10:3 4421
were gathered together to *b* 1Chr 11:13 4421
and men of war fit for the *b* 1Chr 12:8 4421
the Philistines against Saul to *b* 1Chr 12:19 4421
Zebulun, such as went forth to *b* 1Chr 12:33 6635
of Asher, such as went forth to *b* 1Chr 12:36 6635
of instruments of war for the *b* 1Chr 12:37 4421
that then thou shalt go out to *b* 1Chr 14:15 4421
from their cities, and came to *b* 1Chr 19:7 4421
put the *b* in array before the 1Chr 19:9 4421
the *b* was set against him before 1Chr 19:10 4421
before the Syrians unto the *b* 1Chr 19:14 4421
set the *b* in array against them 1Chr 19:17
So when David had put the *b* in 1Chr 19:17 4421
the time that kings go out to *b* 1Chr 20:1
Abijah set the *b* in array with an 2Chr 13:3 4421
Jeroboam also set the *b* in array 2Chr 13:3
the *b* was before and behind 2Chr 13:14 4421
they set the *b* in array in the 2Chr 14:10 4421
Shall we go to Ramoth-gilead to *b* 2Chr 18:5 4421
shall we go to Ramoth-gilead to *b* 2Chr 18:14 4421
myself, and will go to the *b* 2Chr 18:29 4421
and they went to the *b* 2Chr 18:29 4421
And the *b* increased that day 2Chr 18:34 4421
came against Jehoshaphat to *b* 2Chr 20:1 4421
for the *b* is not yours, but God's 2Chr 20:15 4421
shall not need to fight in this *b* 2Chr 20:17
go, do it, be strong for the *b* 2Chr 25:8 4421
they should not go with him to *b* 2Chr 25:13 4421
him, as a king ready to the *b* Job 15:24 3593
of trouble, against the day of *b* Job 38:23 7128
and he smelleth the *b* afar off Job 39:25 4421
hand upon him, remember the *b* Job 41:8 4421
me with strength unto the *b* Ps 18:39 4421
and mighty, the LORD mighty in *b* Ps 24:8 4421
from the *b* that was against me Ps 55:18 7128
shield, and the sword, and the *b* Ps 76:3 4421
bows, turned back in the day of *b* Ps 78:9 7128
not made him to stand in the *b* Ps 89:43 4421
covered my head in the day of *b* Ps 140:7 5402
is prepared against the day of *b* Prov 21:31 4421
nor the *b* to the strong, neither Eccl 9:11 4421
For every *b* of the warrior is Is 9:5 5430
hosts mustereth the host of the *b* Is 13:4 4421
with the sword, nor dead in *b* Is 22:2 4421
briers and thorns against me in *b* Is 27:4 4421
them that turn the *b* to the gate Is 28:6 4421
his anger, and the strength of *b* Is 42:25 4421
as the horse rusheth into the *b* Jer 8:6 4421
men be slain by the sword in *b* Jer 18:21 4421
and shield, and draw near to *b* Jer 46:3 4421
against her, and rise up to the *b* Jer 49:14 4421
A sound of *b* is in the land, and Jer 50:22 4421
put in array, like a man to the *b* Jer 50:42 4421
Thou art my *b* ax and weapons of Jer 51:20 4661
but none goeth to the *b* Eze 7:14 4421
in the *b* in the day of the LORD Eze 13:5 4421
neither in anger, nor in *b* Dan 11:20 4421
stirred up to *b* with a very great Dan 11:25 4421
by bow, nor by sword, nor by *b* Hos 1:7 4421
the *b* out of the earth, and will Hos 2:18 4421
the *b* in Gibeah against the Hos 10:9 4421
Beth-arbel in the day of *b* Hos 10:14 4421
as a strong people set in *b* array Joel 2:5 4421
with shouting in the day of *b* Amos 1:14 4421
let us rise up against her in *b* Obad 1 4421
the *b* bow shall be cut off Zec 9:10 4421
them as his goodly horse in the *b* Zec 10:3 4421
the nail, out of him the *b* bow Zec 10:4 4421
the mire of the streets in the *b* Zec 10:5 4421
nations against Jerusalem to *b* Zec 14:2 4421
as when he fought in the day of *b* Zec 14:3 7128
shall prepare himself to the *b* 1Cor 14:8 *4171*
like unto horses prepared unto *b* Rev 9:7 *4171*
of many horses running to *b* Rev 9:9 *4171*
to gather them to the *b* of that Rev 16:14 *4171*
to gather them together to *b* Rev 20:8 *4171*

BATTLEMENT
thou shalt make a *b* for thy roof Deut 22:8 4624

BATTLEMENTS
take away her *b* Jer 5:10 5189

BATTLES
go out before us, and fight our *b* 1Sa 8:20 4421
for me, and fight the LORD's *b* 1Sa 18:17 4421
lord fighteth the *b* of the LORD 1Sa 25:28 4421
Out of the spoils won in *b* did 1Chr 26:27 4421
God to help us, and to fight our *b* 2Chr 32:8 4421
in *b* of shaking will he fight Is 30:32 4421

BAVAI (*bav'-a-i*) *A descendant of Henadad.*
B the son of Henadad, the ruler Neh 3:18 942

BAVVAI See BAVAI.

BAY
from the *b* that looketh southward Josh 15:2 3956
the *b* of the sea at the uttermost Josh 15:5 3956
b of the salt sea at the south Josh 18:19 3956
himself like a green *b* tree Ps 37:35 249
chariot grisled and *b* horses Zec 6:3 554
the *b* went forth, and sought to go Zec 6:7 554

BAZLITH (*baz'-lith*) See BAZLUTH. *A family who returned from exile.*
The children of *B*, the children Neh 7:54 1213

BAZLUTH (*baz'-luth*) See BAZLITH. *A form of Bazlith.*
The children of *B*, the children Ezr 2:52 1213

BDELLIUM
there is *b* and the onyx stone Gen 2:12 916
colour thereof as the colour of *b* Num 11:7 916

BE See PREFACE.

BEACON
till ye be left as a *b* upon the Is 30:17 8650

BEALIAH (*be-a-li'-ah*) *A warrior in David's army.*
Eluzai, and Jerimoth, and *B* 1Chr 12:5 1183

BEALOTH (*be'-a-loth*) See ALOTH. *A city in Judah.*
Ziph, and Telem, and *B*, Josh 15:24 1175

BEAM
went away with the pin of the *b* Judg 16:14 708
his spear was like a weaver's *b* 1Sa 17:7 4500
whose spear was like a weaver's *b* 2Sa 21:19 4500
the thick *b* were before them 1Kin 7:6 5646
and take thence every man a *b* 2Kin 6:2 6982
But as one was felling a *b* 2Kin 6:5 6982
was a spear like a weaver's *b* 1Chr 11:23 4500
spear staff was like a weaver's *b* 1Chr 20:5 4500
the *b* out of the timber shall Hab 2:11 3714
but considerest not the *b* that is Mt 7:3 *1385*
behold, a *b* is in thine own eye Mt 7:4 *1385*
first cast out the *b* out of thine Mt 7:5 *1385*
but perceivest not the *b* that is Lk 6:41 *1385*
the *b* that is in thine own eye Lk 6:42 *1385*
cast out first the *b* out of thine Lk 6:42 *1385*

BEAMS
that the *b* should not be fastened 1Kin 6:6
and covered the house with *b* 1Kin 6:9 1356
hewed stone, and a row of cedar *b* 1Kin 6:36 3773
with cedar *b* upon the pillars 1Kin 7:2 3773
with cedar above upon the *b* 1Kin 7:3 6763
hewed stones, and a row of cedar *b* 1Kin 7:12 3773
He overlaid also the house, the *b* 2Chr 3:7 6982
b for the gates of the palace Neh 2:8 7136
who also laid the *b* thereof Neh 3:3 7136
they laid the *b* thereof, and set Neh 3:6 7136
Who layeth the *b* of his chambers Ps 104:3 7136
The *b* of our house are cedar, and Song 1:17 6982

BEANS
and flour, and parched corn, and *b* 2Sa 17:28 6321
unto thee wheat, and barley, and *b* Eze 4:9 6321

BEAR
is greater than I can *b* Gen 4:13 5375
the land was not able to *b* them Gen 13:6 5375
art with child, and shalt *b* a son Gen 16:11 3205
that is ninety years old, *b* Gen 17:17 3205
wife shall *b* thee a son indeed Gen 17:19 3205
which Sarah shall *b* unto thee at Gen 17:21 3205
Shall I of a surety *b* a child Gen 18:13 3205
these eight Milcah did *b* to Nahor Gen 22:23 3205
she shall *b* upon my knees, that I Gen 30:3 3205
b them because of their cattle Gen 36:7 5375
then let me *b* the blame for ever Gen 43:9 2398
then I shall *b* the blame to my Gen 44:32 2398
and bowed his shoulder to *b* Gen 49:15 5445
they shall *b* the burden with thee Ex 18:22 5375
Thou shalt not *b* false witness Ex 20:16 6030
of the staves to *b* the table Ex 25:27 5375
two sides of the altar, to *b* it Ex 27:7 5375
Aaron shall *b* their names before Ex 28:12 5375
Aaron shall *b* the names of the Ex 28:29 5375
Aaron shall *b* the judgment of the Ex 28:30 5375
that Aaron may *b* the iniquity of Ex 28:38 5375
that they *b* not iniquity, and die Ex 28:43 5375
for the staves to *b* it withal Ex 30:4 5375
sides of the ark, to *b* the ark Ex 37:5 5375
for the staves to *b* the table Ex 37:14 5375
them with gold, to *b* the table Ex 37:15 5375
for the staves to *b* it withal Ex 37:27 5375
of the altar, to *b* it withal Ex 38:7 5375
it, then he shall *b* his iniquity Lev 5:1 5375
guilty, and shall *b* his iniquity Lev 5:17 5375
eateth of it shall *b* his iniquity Lev 7:18 5375
it you to *b* the iniquity of the Lev 10:17 5375
But if she *b* a maid child, then Lev 12:5 3205
the goat shall *b* upon him all Lev 16:22 5375
then he shall *b* his iniquity Lev 17:16 5375
eateth it shall *b* his iniquity Lev 19:8 5375
nor *b* any grudge against the Lev 19:18 5201
he shall *b* his iniquity Lev 20:17 5375
they shall *b* their iniquity Lev 20:19 5375
they shall *b* their sin Lev 20:20 5375
lest they *b* sin for it, and die Lev 22:9 5375
Or suffer them to *b* the iniquity Lev 22:16 5375
curseth his God shall *b* his sin Lev 24:15 5375
they shall *b* the tabernacle, and Num 1:50 5375
sons of Kohath shall come to *b* it Num 4:15 5375
they shall *b* the curtains of the Num 4:25 5375
this woman shall *b* her iniquity Num 5:31 5375
should *b* upon their shoulders Num 7:9 5375
season, that man shall *b* his sin Num 9:13 5375
I am not able to *b* all this Num 11:14 5375
they shall *b* the burden of the Num 11:17 5375
that thou *b* it not thyself alone Num 11:17 5375
How long shall I *b* with this evil Num 14:27
b your whoredoms, until your Num 14:33 5375
shall ye *b* your iniquities, even Num 14:34 5375
b the iniquity of the sanctuary Num 18:1 5375
thy sons with thee shall *b* the Num 18:1 5375
the congregation, lest they *b* sin Num 18:22 5375
they shall *b* their iniquity Num 18:23 5375
ye shall *b* no sin by reason of it Num 18:32 5375
then he shall *b* her iniquity Num 30:15 5375
am not able to *b* you myself alone Deut 1:9 5375
I myself alone *b* your cumbrance Deut 1:12 5375
thee, as a man doth *b* his son Deut 1:31 5375
Neither shalt thou *b* false Deut 5:20 6030
to *b* the ark of the covenant of Deut 10:8 5375
her children which she shall *b* Deut 28:57 3205
that *b* the ark of the covenant Josh 3:8 5375
that *b* the ark of the LORD Josh 3:13 5375
that *b* the ark of the testimony Josh 4:16 5375
seven priests shall *b* before the Josh 6:4 5375
let seven priests *b* seven Josh 6:6 5375
thou shalt conceive, and *b* a son Judg 13:3 3205
thou shalt conceive, and *b* a son Judg 13:5 3205
thou shalt conceive, and *b* a son Judg 13:7 3205
to night, and should also *b* sons Ruth 1:12 3205
and there came a lion, and a *b* 1Sa 17:34 1677
slew both the lion and the *b* 1Sa 17:36 1677
lion, and out of the paw of the *b* 1Sa 17:37 1677
as a *b* robbed of her whelps in 2Sa 17:8 1677
b the king tidings, how that the 2Sa 18:19 1319
Thou shalt not *b* tidings this day 2Sa 18:20 1319
but thou shalt *b* tidings another 2Sa 18:20 1319
this day thou shalt *b* no tidings 2Sa 18:20 1319
it was not my son, which I did *b* 1Kin 3:21 3205
to *b* witness against him, saying 1Kin 21:10 5749
which thou puttest on me will I *b* 2Kin 18:14 5375
root downward, and *b* fruit upward 2Kin 19:30 6213
men, men able to *b* buckler 1Chr 5:18 5375
and ten thousand men to *b* burdens 2Chr 2:2 5445
should *b* rule in his own house Est 1:22 8323
I *b* up the pillars of it Ps 75:3 8505
how I do *b* in my bosom the Ps 89:50 5375
They shall *b* thee up in their Ps 91:12 5375
scornest, thou alone shalt *b* it Prov 9:12 5375
hand of the diligent shall *b* rule Prov 12:24 4910
Let a *b* robbed of her whelps meet Prov 17:12 1677
but a wounded spirit who can *b* Prov 18:14 5375
As a roaring lion, and a ranging *b* Prov 28:15 1677
and for four which it cannot *b* Prov 30:21 5375
whereof every one *b* twins Song 4:2 8382
I am weary to *b* them Is 1:14 5375
b a son, and shall call his name Is 7:14 3205
And the cow and the *b* shall feed Is 11:7 1677
root downward, and *b* fruit upward Is 37:31 6213
I have made, and I will *b* Is 46:4 5375
They *b* him upon the shoulder Is 46:7 5375
that *b* the vessels of the LORD Is 52:11 5375
for he shall *b* their iniquities Is 53:11 5445
O barren, thou that didst not *b* Is 54:1 5375
the priests *b* rule by their means Jer 5:31 7287
this is a grief, and I must *b* it Jer 10:19 5375
b no burden on the sabbath day Jer 17:21 5375
not to *b* a burden, even entering Jer 17:27 5375
to husbands, that they may *b* sons Jer 29:6 3205
because I did *b* the reproach of Jer 31:19 5375
that the LORD could no longer *b* Jer 44:22 5375
was unto me as a *b* lying in wait Lam 3:10 1677
that he *b* the yoke in his youth Lam 3:27 5375
it thou shalt *b* their iniquity Eze 4:4 5375
so shalt thou *b* the iniquity of Eze 4:5 5375
thou shalt *b* the iniquity of the Eze 4:6 5375
thou *b* it upon thy shoulders Eze 12:6 5375
shall *b* upon his shoulder in the Eze 12:12 5375
they shall *b* the punishment of Eze 14:10 5375
b thine own shame for thy sins Eze 16:52 5375
b thy shame, in that thou hast Eze 16:52 5375
thou mayest *b* thine own shame Eze 16:54 5375
and that it might *b* fruit Eze 17:8 5375
b fruit, and be a goodly cedar Eze 17:23 6213
doth not the son *b* the iniquity Eze 18:19 5375
The son shall not *b* the iniquity Eze 18:20 5375
father *b* the iniquity of the son Eze 18:20 5375
therefore *b* thou also thy Eze 23:35 5375
ye shall *b* the sins of your idols Eze 23:49 5375
b their shame with them that go Eze 32:30 5375
neither *b* the shame of the Eze 34:29 5375
you, they shall *b* their shame Eze 36:7 5375
neither shalt thou *b* the reproach Eze 36:15 5375
they shall even *b* their iniquity Eze 44:10 5375
they shall *b* their iniquity Eze 44:12 5375
but they shall *b* their shame Eze 44:13 5375
that they *b* them not out into the Eze 46:20 3318
which shall *b* rule over all the Dan 2:39 7981
beast, a second, like to a *b* Dan 7:5 1678
dried up, they shall *b* no fruit Hos 9:16 6213
I will meet them as a *b* that is Hos 13:8 1677
flee from a lion, and a *b* met him Amos 5:19 1677
is not able to *b* all his words Amos 7:10 3557
therefore ye shall *b* the reproach Mic 6:16 5375
I will *b* the indignation of the Mic 7:9 5375
all they that *b* silver are cut Zeph 1:11 5187
If one *b* holy flesh in the skirt Hag 2:12 5375
me, Whither do these *b* the ephah Zec 5:10 3212
he shall *b* the glory, and shall Zec 6:13 5375
whose shoes I am not worthy to *b* Mt 3:11 *941*
their hands they shall *b* thee up Mt 4:6 *142*
Thou shalt not *b* false witness Mt 19:18 *5576*
him they compelled to *b* his cross Mt 27:32 *142*
Do not *b* false witness, Defraud Mk 10:19 *5576*
and Rufus, to *b* his cross Mk 15:21 *142*
wife Elisabeth shall *b* thee a son Lk 1:13 *1080*
their hands they shall *b* thee up Lk 4:11 *142*
Truly ye *b* witness that ye allow Lk 11:48 *3140*
And if it *b* fruit, well Lk 13:9 *4160*
And whosoever doth not *b* his cross Lk 14:27 *941*
though he *b* long with them Lk 18:7 *3114*
Do not *b* false witness, Honour Lk 18:20 *5576*
that he might *b* it after Jesus Lk 23:26 *5342*
to *b* witness of the Light, that Jn 1:7 *3140*
but was sent to *b* witness of that Jn 1:8 *3140*
b unto the governor of the feast Jn 2:8 *5342*
Ye yourselves *b* me witness Jn 3:28 *3140*
If I *b* witness of myself, my Jn 5:31 *3140*
b witness of me, that the Father Jn 5:36 *3140*

Though I *b* record of myself, yet Jn 8:14 *3140*
I am one that *b* witness of myself Jn 8:18 *3140*
name, they *b* witness of me Jn 10:25 *3140*
branch cannot *b* fruit of itself Jn 15:4 *5342*
glorified, that ye *b* much fruit Jn 15:8 *5342*
And ye also shall *b* witness Jn 15:27 *3140*
you, but ye cannot *b* them now Jn 16:12 *941*
evil, *b* witness of the evil Jn 18:23 *3140*
that I should *b* witness unto the Jn 18:37 *3140*
to *b* my name before the Gentiles, Acts 9:15 *941*
our fathers nor we were able to *b* Acts 15:10 *941*
would that I should *b* with you Acts 18:14 *430*
the high priest doth *b* me witness Acts 22:5 *3140*
so must thou *b* witness also at Acts 23:11 *3140*
could not *b* up into the wind, we Acts 27:15 *503*
For I *b* them record that they Rom 10:2 *3140*
Thou shalt not *b* false witness Rom 13:9 *5576*
to *b* the infirmities of the weak Rom 15:1 *941*
hitherto ye were not able to *b* it 1Cor 3:2
that ye may be able to *b* it 1Cor 10:13 *5297*
we shall also *b* the image of the 1Cor 15:49 *5409*
I *b* record, yea, and beyond their 2Cor 8:3 *3140*
Would to God ye could *b* with me a 2Cor 11:1 *430*
and indeed *b* with me 2Cor 11:1 *430*
ye might well *b* with him 2Cor 11:4 *430*
for I *b* you record, that, if it Gal 4:15 *3140*
you shall *b* his judgment, Gal 5:10 *941*
B ye one another's burdens, and so Gal 6:2 *941*
every man shall *b* his own burden Gal 6:5 *941*
for I *b* in my body the marks of Gal 6:17 *941*
For I *b* him record, that he hath Col 4:13 *3140*
b children, guide the house, give 1Ti 5:14 *5041*
offered to *b* the sins of many Heb 9:28 *399*
my brethren, *b* olive berries Jas 3:12 *4160*
b witness, and shew unto you that 1Jn 1:2 *3140*
are three that *b* record in heaven 1Jn 5:7 *3140*
are three that *b* witness in earth 1Jn 5:8 *3140*
yea, and we also *b* record 3Jn 12
how thou canst not *b* them which Rev 2:2 *941*
his feet were as the feet of a *b* Rev 13:2 *715*

BEARD
a plague upon the head or the *b* Lev 13:29 2206
even a leprosy upon the head or *b* Lev 13:30 2206
his hair off his head and his *b* Lev 14:9 2206
thou mar the corners of thy *b* Lev 19:27 2206
shave off the corner of their *b* Lev 21:5 2206
against me, I caught him by his *b* 1Sa 17:35 2206
his spittle fall down upon his *b* 1Sa 21:13 2206
his feet, nor trimmed his *b* 2Sa 19:24 8222
by the *b* with the right hand to 2Sa 20:9 2206
the hair of my head and of my *b* Ezr 9:3 2206
upon the *b*, even Aaron's *b* Ps 133:2 2206
and it shall also consume the *b* Is 7:20 2206
be baldness, and every *b* cut off Is 15:2 2206
shall be bald, and every *b* clipped Jer 48:37 2206
upon thine head and upon thy *b* Eze 5:1 2206

BEARDS
off the one half of their *b* 2Sa 10:4 2206
at Jericho until your *b* be grown 2Sa 10:5 2206
at Jericho until your *b* be grown 1Chr 19:5 2206
men, having their *b* shaven Jer 41:5 2206

BEARERS
of them to be *b* of burdens 2Chr 2:18 5449
they were over the *b* of burdens 2Chr 34:13 5449
The strength of the *b* of burdens Neh 4:10 5449

BEAREST
now, thou art barren, and *b* not Judg 13:3 3205
that thou *b* unto thy people Ps 106:4
him, Thou *b* record of thyself Jn 8:13 *3140*
thou *b* not the root, but the root Rom 11:18 *941*
Rejoice, thou barren that *b* not Gal 4:27 5088

BEARETH
whosoever *b* ought of the carcase Lev 11:25 5375
he that *b* the carcase of them Lev 11:28 5375
he also that *b* the carcase of it Lev 11:40 5375
he that *b* any of those things Lev 15:10 5375
father *b* the sucking child Num 11:12 5375
b shall succeed in the name of Deut 25:6 3205
be among you a root that *b* gall Deut 29:18 6509
that it is not sown, nor *b* Deut 29:23 6779
taketh them, *b* them on her wings Deut 32:11 5375
up in me *b* witness to my face Job 16:8 6030
entreateth the barren that *b* not Job 24:21 3205
A man that *b* false witness Prov 25:18 6030
but when the wicked *b* rule Prov 29:2 4910
whereof every one *b* twins Song 6:6 8382
spring, for the tree *b* her fruit Joel 2:22 5375
which also *b* fruit, and bringeth Mt 13:23 *2592*
is another that *b* witness of me Jn 5:32 *3140*
that sent me *b* witness of me Jn 8:18 *3140*
Every branch in me that *b* not Jn 15:2 *5342*
and every branch that *b* fruit Jn 15:2 *5342*
The Spirit itself *b* witness with Rom 8:16 *4828*
for he *b* not the sword in vain Rom 13:4 *5409*
B all things, believeth all 1Cor 13:7 *4722*
But that which *b* thorns and briers Heb 6:8 *1627*
it is the Spirit that *b* witness 1Jn 5:6 *3140*

BEARING
have given you every herb *b* seed Gen 1:29 2232
LORD hath restrained me from *b* Gen 16:2 3205
his name Judah; and left *b* Gen 29:35 3205
When Leah saw that she had left *b* Gen 30:9 3205
with their camels *b* spicery Gen 37:25 5375
set forward, *b* the tabernacle Num 10:17 5375
set forward, *b* the sanctuary Num 10:21 5375
and the priests the Levites *b* it Josh 3:3 5375
the priests *b* the ark of the Josh 3:14 5375
that the seven priests *b* the Josh 6:8 5375
seven priests *b* seven trumpets of Josh 6:13 5375
one *b* a shield went before him 1Sa 17:7 5375
b the ark of the covenant of God 2Sa 15:24 5375

b precious seed, shall doubtless Ps 126:6 5375
you a man *b* a pitcher of water Mk 14:13 *941*
meet you, *b* a pitcher of water Lk 22:10 *941*
he *b* his cross went forth into a Jn 19:17 *941*
their conscience also *b* witness Rom 2:15 *4828*
my conscience also *b* me witness Rom 9:1 *4828*
Always *b* about in the body the 2Cor 4:10 *4064*
God also *b* them witness, both Heb 2:4 *4901*
without the camp, *b* his reproach Heb 13:13 *5342*

BEARS
forth two she *b* out of the wood 2Kin 2:24 1677
We roar all like *b*, and mourn sore Is 59:11 1677

BEAST
b of the earth after his kind Gen 1:24 2416
God made the *b* of the earth after Gen 1:25 2416
to every *b* of the earth, and to Gen 1:30 2416
God formed every *b* of the field Gen 2:19 2416
air, and to every *b* of the field Gen 2:20 2416
was more subtil than any *b* of the Gen 3:1 2416
above every *b* of the field Gen 3:14 2416
both man, and *b*, and the creeping Gen 6:7 929
Of every clean *b* thou shalt take Gen 7:2 929
every *b* after his kind, and all Gen 7:14 2416
of fowl, and of cattle, and of *b* Gen 7:21 2416
Every *b*, every creeping thing, and Gen 8:19 2416
and took of every clean *b*, and of Gen 8:20 929
be upon every *b* of the earth Gen 9:2 2416
hand of every *b* will I require it Gen 9:5 2416
of every *b* of the earth with you Gen 9:10 2416
the ark, to every *b* of the earth Gen 9:10 2416
every *b* of theirs be ours Gen 34:23 929
Some evil *b* hath devoured him Gen 37:20 2416
an evil *b* hath devoured him Gen 37:33 2416
and it became lice in man, and in *b* Ex 8:17 929
were lice upon man, and upon *b* Ex 8:18 929
with blains upon man, and upon *b* Ex 9:9 929
with blains upon man, and upon *b* Ex 9:10 929
b which shall be found in the Ex 9:19 929
of Egypt, upon man, and upon *b* Ex 9:22 929
was in the field, both man and *b* Ex 9:25 929
move his tongue, against man or *b* Ex 11:7 929
the land of Egypt, both man and *b* Ex 12:12 929
of Israel, both of man and of *b* Ex 13:2 929
cometh of a *b* which thou hast Ex 13:12 929
of man, and the firstborn of *b* Ex 13:15 929
whether it be *b* or man, it shall Ex 19:13 929
and the dead *b* shall be his Ex 21:34
be eaten, and shall put in his *b* Ex 22:5 1165
or an ox, or a sheep, or any *b* Ex 22:10 929
Whosoever lieth with a *b* shall Ex 22:19 929
the *b* of the field multiply Ex 23:29 2416
it be a carcase of an unclean *b* Lev 5:2 2416
of man, or any unclean *b*, or any Lev 7:21 929
the fat of the *b* that dieth of Lev 7:24 5038
whosoever eateth the fat of the *b* Lev 7:25 929
whether it be of fowl or of *b* Lev 7:26 929
The carcases of every *b* which Lev 11:26 929
And if any *b*, of which ye may eat, Lev 11:39 929
between the *b* that may be eaten Lev 11:47 2416
the *b* that may not be eaten Lev 11:47 2416
catcheth any *b* or fowl that may Lev 17:13 2416
any *b* to defile thyself therewith Lev 18:23 929
before a *b* to lie down thereto Lev 18:23 929
And if a man lie with a *b*, he Lev 20:15 929
and ye shall slay the *b* Lev 20:15 929
And if a woman approach unto any *b* Lev 20:16 929
shalt kill the woman, and the *b* Lev 20:16 929
make your souls abominable by *b* Lev 20:25 929
he that killeth a *b* shall make it Lev 24:18
shall make it good; *b* for *b* Lev 24:18 5315
shall make it good; *b* for *b* Lev 24:18 929
And he that killeth a *b*, he shall Lev 24:21 929
for the *b* that are in thy land, Lev 25:7 2416
And if it be a *b*, whereof men Lev 27:9 929
shall at all change *b* for *b* Lev 27:10 929
And if it be any unclean *b* Lev 27:11 929
present the *b* before the priest Lev 27:11 929
And if it be of an unclean *b* Lev 27:27 929
that he hath, both of man and *b* Lev 27:28 929
in Israel, both man and *b* Num 3:13 929
of Israel are mine, both man and *b* Num 8:17 929
was taken, both of man and of *b* Num 31:26 929
of fifty, both of man and of *b* Num 31:47 929
The likeness of any *b* that is on Deut 4:17 929
every *b* that parteth the hoof, and Deut 14:6 929
that lieth with any manner of *b* Deut 27:21 929
the men of every city, as the *b* Judg 20:48 929
by a wild *b* that was in Lebanon 2Kin 14:9 2416
by a wild *b* that was in Lebanon 2Chr 25:18 2416
neither was there any *b* with me Neh 2:12 929
save the *b* that I rode upon Neh 2:12 929
the *b* that was under me to pass Neh 2:14 929
or that the wild *b* may break them Job 39:15 2416
O LORD, thou preservest man and *b* Ps 36:6 929
For every *b* of the forest is mine Ps 50:10 2416
I was as a *b* before thee Ps 73:22 929
the wild *b* of the field doth Ps 80:13 2123
drink to every *b* of the field Ps 104:11 2416
of Egypt, both of man and *b* Ps 135:8 929
He giveth to the *b* his food Ps 147:9 929
man regardeth the life of his *b* Prov 12:10 929
man hath no preeminence above a *b* Eccl 3:19 929
the spirit of the *b* that goeth Eccl 3:21 929
nor any ravenous *b* shall go up Is 35:9 2416
The *b* of the field shall honour Is 43:20 2416
they are a burden to the weary *b* Is 46:1
As a *b* goeth down into the valley Is 63:14 929
this place, upon man, and upon *b* Jer 7:20 929
of the heavens and the *b* are fled Jer 9:10 929
of this city, both man and *b* Jer 21:6 929
the *b* that are upon the ground, Jer 27:5 929
of man, and with the seed of *b* Jer 31:27 929
It is desolate without man or *b* Jer 32:43 929

desolate without man and without *b* Jer 33:10 929
without inhabitant, and without *b* Jer 33:10 929
desolate without man and without *b* Jer 33:12 929
to cease from thence man and *b* Jer 36:29 929
they shall depart, both man and *b* Jer 50:3 929
remain in it, neither man nor *b* Jer 51:62 929
and will cut off man and *b* from it Eze 14:13 929
that I cut off man and *b* from it Eze 14:17 929
to cut off from it man and *b* Eze 14:19 929
and the famine, and the noisome *b* Eze 14:21 2416
to cut off from it man and *b* Eze 14:21 929
and will cut off man and *b* from it Eze 25:13 929
and cut off man and *b* out of thee Eze 29:8 929
nor foot of *b* shall pass through Eze 29:11 929
meat to every *b* of the field Eze 34:8 2416
neither shall the *b* of the land Eze 34:28 2416
I will multiply upon you man and *b* Eze 36:11 929
to every *b* of the field, Assemble Eze 39:17 2416
or torn, whether it be fowl or *b* Eze 44:31 929
And behold another *b*, a second, Dan 7:5 2423
the *b* had also four heads Dan 7:6 2423
visions, and behold a fourth *b* Dan 7:7 2423
beheld even till the *b* was slain Dan 7:11 2423
know the truth of the fourth *b* Dan 7:19 2423
The fourth *b* shall be the fourth Dan 7:23 2423
the wild *b* shall tear them Hos 13:8 2416
saying, Let neither man nor *b* Jonah 3:7 929
b be covered with sackcloth, and Jonah 3:8 929
bind the chariot to the swift *b* Mic 1:13 7409
I will consume man and *b* Zeph 1:3 929
hire for man, nor any hire for *b* Zec 8:10 929
and wine, and set him on his own *b* Lk 10:34 *2934*
the venomous *b* hang on his hand Acts 28:4 *2342*
he shook off the *b* into the fire Acts 28:5 *2342*
if so much as a *b* touch the Heb 12:20 *2342*
the first *b* was like a lion, and Rev 4:7 *2226*
the second *b* like a calf Rev 4:7 *2226*
the third *b* had a face as a man, Rev 4:7 *2226*
the fourth *b* was like a flying Rev 4:7 *2226*
seal, I heard the second *b* say Rev 6:3 *2226*
seal, I heard the third *b* say Rev 6:5 *2226*
the voice of the fourth *b* say Rev 6:7 *2226*
the *b* that ascendeth out of the Rev 11:7 *2342*
saw a *b* rise up out of the sea, Rev 13:1 *2342*
the *b* which I saw was like unto a Rev 13:2 *2342*
the world wondered after the *b* Rev 13:3 *2342*
which gave power unto the *b* Rev 13:4 *2342*
and they worshipped the *b* Rev 13:4 *2342*
saying, Who is like unto the *b* Rev 13:4 *2342*
I beheld another *b* coming up out Rev 13:11 *2342*
power of the first *b* before him Rev 13:12 *2342*
therein to worship the first *b* Rev 13:12 *2342*
power to do in the sight of the *b* Rev 13:14 *2342*
should make an image to the *b* Rev 13:14 *2342*
give life unto the image of the *b* Rev 13:15 *2342*
image of the *b* should both speak Rev 13:15 *2342*
image of the *b* should be killed Rev 13:15 *2342*
the mark, or the name of the *b* Rev 13:17 *2342*
count the number of the *b* Rev 13:18 *2342*
voice, If any man worship the *b* Rev 14:9 *2342*
day nor night, who worship the *b* Rev 14:11 *2342*
had gotten the victory over the *b* Rev 15:2 *2342*
men which had the mark of the *b* Rev 16:2 *2342*
his vial upon the seat of the *b* Rev 16:10 *2342*
and out of the mouth of the *b* Rev 16:13 *2342*
sit upon a scarlet coloured *b* Rev 17:3 *2342*
of the *b* that carrieth her, which Rev 17:7 *2342*
The *b* that thou sawest was, and is Rev 17:8 *2342*
when they behold the *b* that was Rev 17:8 *2342*
the *b* that was, and is not, even Rev 17:11 *2342*
as kings one hour with the *b* Rev 17:12 *2342*
power and strength unto the *b* Rev 17:13 *2342*
which thou sawest upon the *b* Rev 17:16 *2342*
and give their kingdom unto the *b* Rev 17:17 *2342*
And I saw the *b*, and the kings of Rev 19:19 *2342*
the *b* was taken, and with him the Rev 19:20 *2342*
had received the mark of the *b* Rev 19:20 *2342*
and which had not worshipped the *b* Rev 20:4 *2342*
of fire and brimstone, where the *b* Rev 20:10 *2342*

BEAST'S
let a *b* heart be given unto him Dan 4:16 2423

BEASTS
of *b* that are not clean by two, Gen 7:2 929
Of clean *b*, and of *b* that are Gen 7:8 929
That which was torn of *b* I Gen 31:39 2966
and his cattle, and all his *b* Gen 36:6 929
lade your *b*, and go, get you unto Gen 45:17 1165
and all the firstborn of *b* Ex 11:5 929
that is torn of *b* in the field Ex 22:31 2966
what they leave the *b* of the Ex 23:11 2416
fat of that which is torn with *b* Lev 7:24 2966
These are the *b* which ye shall Lev 11:2 2416
all the *b* that are on the earth Lev 11:2 929
and cheweth the cud, among the *b* Lev 11:3 929
manner of *b* that go on all four Lev 11:27 2416
This is the law of the *b*, and of Lev 11:46 929
or that which was torn with *b* Lev 17:15 2966
put difference between clean *b* Lev 20:25 929
of itself, or is torn with *b* Lev 22:8 2966
I will rid evil *b* out of the land Lev 26:6 2416
I will also send wild *b* among you Lev 26:22 2416
Only the firstling of the *b* Lev 27:26 929
LORD, whether it be of men or *b* Num 18:15 929
of unclean *b* shalt thou redeem Num 18:15 929
the congregation and their *b* drink Num 20:8 1165
drank, and their *b* also Num 20:11 1165
all the prey, both of men and of *b* Num 31:11 929
of the flocks, of all manner of *b* Num 31:30 929
their goods, and for all their *b* Num 35:3 2416
lest the *b* of the field increase Deut 7:22 2416
These are the *b* which ye shall Deut 14:4 929
and cheweth the cud among the *b* Deut 14:6 929
unto the *b* of the earth, and no Deut 28:26 929

send the teeth of *b* upon them Deut 32:24 929
the air, and to the *b* of the field 1Sa 17:44 929
to the wild *b* of the earth 1Sa 17:46 2416
nor the *b* of the field by night 2Sa 21:10 2416
he spake also of *b*, and of fowl, 1Kin 4:33 929
alive, that we lose not all the *b* 1Kin 18:5 929
ye, and your cattle, and your *b* 2Kin 3:17 929
and stalls for all manner of *b* 2Chr 32:28 929
gold, and with goods, and with *b* Ezr 1:4 929
with gold, with goods, and with *b* Ezr 1:6 929
be afraid of the *b* of the earth Job 5:22 2416
the *b* of the field shall be at Job 5:23 2416
But ask now the *b*, and they shall Job 12:7 929
Wherefore are we counted as *b* Job 18:3 929
us more than the *b* of the earth Job 35:11 929
Then the *b* go into dens, and Job 37:8 2416
where all the *b* of the field play Job 40:20 2416
oxen, yea, and the *b* of the field Ps 8:7 929
he is like the *b* that perish Ps 49:12 929
not, is like the *b* that perish Ps 49:20 929
the wild *b* of the field are mine Ps 50:11 2123
saints unto the *b* of the earth Ps 79:2 2416
wherein all the *b* of the forest Ps 104:20 2416
both small and great *b* Ps 104:25 2416
B, and all cattle Ps 148:10 2416
She hath killed her *b* Prov 9:2 2874
A lion which is strongest among *b* Prov 30:30 929
see that they themselves are *b* Eccl 3:18 929
the sons of men befalleth *b* Eccl 3:19 929
of rams, and the fat of fed *b* Is 1:11 4806
But wild *b* of the desert shall Is 13:21 6728
the wild *b* of the islands shall Is 13:22 338
and to the *b* of the earth Is 18:6 929
all the *b* of the earth shall Is 18:6 929
The burden of the *b* of the south Is 30:6 929
The wild *b* of the desert shall Is 34:14 6728
with the wild *b* of the island Is 34:14 338
nor the *b* thereof sufficient for Is 40:16 2416
their idols were upon the *b* Is 46:1 2416
All ye *b* of the field, come to Is 56:9 2416
yea, all ye *b* in the forest Is 56:9 2416
and upon mules, and upon swift *b* Is 66:20 3753
heaven, and for the *b* of the earth Jer 7:33 929
the *b* are consumed, and the birds Jer 12:4 929
assemble all the *b* of the field Jer 12:9 2416
the *b* of the earth, to devour and Jer 15:3 929
heaven, and for the *b* of the earth Jer 16:4 929
heaven, and for the *b* of the earth Jer 19:7 929
the *b* of the field have I given Jer 27:6 2416
given him the *b* of the field also Jer 28:14 2416
heaven, and to the *b* of the earth Jer 34:20 929
Therefore the wild *b* of the Jer 50:39 6728
wild *b* of the islands shall dwell Jer 50:39 338
I send upon you famine and evil *b* Eze 5:17 2416
creeping things, and abominable *b* Eze 8:10 929
If I cause noisome *b* to pass Eze 14:15 2416
may pass through because of the *b* Eze 14:15 2416
for meat to the *b* of the field Eze 29:5 2416
b of the field bring forth their Eze 31:6 2416
all the *b* of the field shall be Eze 31:13 2416
I will fill the *b* of the whole Eze 32:4 2416
I will destroy also all the *b* Eze 32:13 929
nor the hoofs of *b* trouble them Eze 32:13 929
I give to the *b* to be devoured Eze 33:27 2416
meat to all the *b* of the field Eze 34:5 2416
will cause the evil *b* to cease Eze 34:25 2416
the *b* of the field, and all Eze 38:20 2416
to the *b* of the field to be Eze 39:4 2416
the *b* of the field and the fowls Dan 2:38 2423
the *b* of the field had shadow Dan 4:12 2423
let the *b* get away from under it, Dan 4:14 2423
the *b* in the grass of the earth Dan 4:15 2423
under which the *b* of the field Dan 4:21 2423
be with the *b* of the field Dan 4:23 2423
shall be with the *b* of the field Dan 4:25 2423
shall be with the *b* of the field Dan 4:32 2423
and his heart was made like the *b* Dan 5:21 2423
four great *b* came up from the sea Dan 7:3 2423
all the *b* that were before it Dan 7:7 2423
As concerning the rest of the *b* Dan 7:12 2423
These great *b*, which are four, Dan 7:17 2423
so that no *b* might stand before Dan 8:4 2416
the *b* of the field shall eat them Hos 2:12 2416
for them with the *b* of the field Hos 2:18 2416
with the *b* of the field, and with Hos 4:3 2416
How do the *b* groan Joel 1:18 929
The *b* of the field cry also unto Joel 1:20 929
Be not afraid, ye *b* of the field Joel 2:22 929
the peace offerings of your fat *b* Amos 5:22 4806
a lion among the *b* of the forest Mic 5:8 929
cover thee, and the spoil of *b* Hab 2:17 929
of her, all the *b* of the nations Zeph 2:14 2416
a place for *b* to lie down in Zeph 2:15 2416
of all the *b* that shall be in Zec 14:15 929
and was with the wild *b* Mk 1:13 *2342*
have ye offered to me slain *b* Acts 7:42 *4968*
of fourfooted *b* of the earth Acts 10:12 *5074*
b of the earth, and wild *b* Acts 10:12 *2342*
b of the earth, and wild *b* Acts 11:6 *2342*
And provide them *b*, that they may Acts 23:24 *2934*
man, and to birds, and fourfooted *b* Rom 1:23 *5074*
I have fought with *b* at Ephesus 1Cor 15:32 *2341*
flesh of men, another flesh of *b* 1Cor 15:39 *2934*
Cretians are alway liars, evil *b* Titus 1:12 *2342*
For the bodies of those *b* Heb 13:11 *2226*
For every kind of *b*, and of birds, Jas 3:7 *2342*
But these, as natural brute *b* 2Pet 2:12 *2226*
they know naturally, as brute *b* Jude 10 *2226*
were four *b* full of eyes before Rev 4:6 *2226*
the four *b* had each of them six Rev 4:8 *2226*
And when those *b* give glory Rev 4:9 *2226*
of the throne and of the four *b* Rev 5:6 *2226*
he had taken the book, the four *b* Rev 5:8 *2226*
round about the throne and the *b* Rev 5:11 *2226*
And the four *b* said, Amen Rev 5:14 *2226*
thunder, one of the four *b* saying Rev 6:1 *2226*
in the midst of the four *b* say Rev 6:6 *2226*
death, and with the *b* of the earth Rev 6:8 *2342*
and about the elders and the four *b* Rev 7:11 *2226*
the throne, and before the four *b* Rev 14:3 *2226*
one of the four *b* gave unto the Rev 15:7 *2226*
and fine flour, and wheat, and *b* Rev 18:13 *2934*
elders and the four *b* fell down and Rev 19:4 *2226*

BEAT
thou shalt *b* some of it very Ex 30:36 7833
they did *b* the gold into thin Ex 39:3 7554
or *b* it in a mortar, and baked it Num 11:8 1743
b him above these with many Deut 25:3 5221
he *b* down the tower of Penuel, and Judg 8:17 5422
b down the city, and sowed it with Judg 9:45 5422
b at the door, and spake to the Judg 19:22 1849
b out that she had gleaned Ruth 2:17 2251
Then did I *b* them as small as the 2Sa 22:43 7833
they *b* down the cities, and on 2Kin 3:25 2040
Three times did Joash *b* him 2Kin 13:25 5221
of the LORD, did the king *b* down 2Kin 23:12 5422
Then did I *b* them small as the Ps 18:42 7833
I will *b* down his foes before his Ps 89:23 3807
Thou shalt *b* him with the rod, and Prov 23:14 5221
they shall *b* their swords into Is 2:4 3807
ye that ye *b* my people to pieces Is 3:15 1792
that the LORD shall *b* off from Is 27:12 2251
b them small, and shalt make the Is 41:15 1854
B your plowshares into swords, and Joel 3:10 3807
the sun *b* upon the head of Jonah, Jonah 4:8 5221
they shall *b* their swords into Mic 4:3 3807
thou shalt *b* in pieces many Mic 4:13 1854
winds blew, and *b* upon that house Mt 7:25 *4363*
winds blew, and *b* upon that house Mt 7:27 *4350*
b one, and killed another, and Mt 21:35 *1194*
the waves *b* into the ship, so Mk 4:37 *1911*
b him, and sent him away empty Mk 12:3 *1194*
the stream *b* vehemently upon that Lk 6:48 *4366*
which the stream did *b* vehemently Lk 6:49 *4366*
shall begin to *b* the menservants Lk 12:45 *5180*
but the husbandmen *b* him, and sent Lk 20:10 *1194*
they *b* him also, and entreated him Lk 20:11 *1194*
clothes, and commanded to *b* them Acts 16:22 *4463*
b him before the judgment seat Acts 18:17 *5180*
b in every synagogue them that Acts 22:19 *1194*

BEATEN
had set over them, were *b* Ex 5:14 5221
and, behold, thy servants are *b* Ex 5:16 5221
of *b* work shalt thou make them, Ex 25:18 4749
of *b* work shall the candlestick Ex 25:31 4749
shall be one *b* work of pure gold Ex 25:36 4749
pure oil olive *b* for the light Ex 27:20 3795
fourth part of an hin of *b* oil Ex 29:40 3795
b out of one piece made he them, Ex 37:7 4749
of *b* work made he the candlestick Ex 37:17 4749
of it was one *b* work of pure gold Ex 37:22 4749
even corn *b* out of full ears Lev 2:14 1643
part of the *b* corn thereof, and Lev 2:16 1643
full of sweet incense *b* small Lev 16:12 1851
pure oil olive *b* for the light Lev 24:2 3795
of the candlestick was of *b* gold Num 8:4 4749
the flowers thereof, was *b* work Num 8:4 4749
fourth part of an hin of *b* oil Num 28:5 3795
the wicked man be worthy to be *b* Deut 25:2 5221
down, and to be *b* before his face, Deut 25:2 5221
as if they were *b* before them Josh 8:15 5060
and Abner was *b*, and the men of 2Sa 2:17 5062
two hundred targets of *b* gold 1Kin 10:16 7820
three hundred shields of *b* gold 1Kin 10:17 7820
thousand measures of *b* wheat 2Chr 2:10 4347
two hundred targets of *b* gold 2Chr 9:15 7820
six hundred shekels of *b* gold 2Chr 9:15 7820
hundred shields made he of *b* gold 2Chr 9:16 7820
had *b* the graven images into 2Chr 34:7 3807
they have *b* me, and I felt it not Prov 23:35 1986
chalkstones that are *b* in sunder Is 27:9 5310
fitches are *b* out with a staff Is 28:27 2251
LORD shall the Assyrian be *b* down Is 30:31 2865
and their mighty ones are *b* down Jer 46:5 3807
thereof shall be *b* to pieces Mic 1:7 3807
in the synagogues ye shall be *b* Mk 13:9 *1194*
shall be *b* with many stripes Lk 12:47 *1194*
shall be *b* with few stripes Lk 12:48 *1194*
b them, they commanded that they Acts 5:40 *1194*
They have *b* us openly uncondemned Acts 16:37 *1194*
Thrice was I *b* with rods, once 2Cor 11:25 *4463*

BEATEST
When thou *b* thine olive tree, Deut 24:20 2251
for if thou *b* him with the rod, Prov 23:13 5221

BEATETH
I, not as one that *b* the air 1Cor 9:26 *1194*

BEATING
they went on *b* down one another 1Sa 14:16 1986
b some, and killing some Mk 12:5 *1194*
the soldiers, they left *b* of Paul Acts 21:32 *5180*

BEAUTIES
in the *b* of holiness from the Ps 110:3 1926

BEAUTIFUL
but Rachel was *b* and well favoured Gen 29:17
among the captives a *b* woman Deut 21:11
and withal of a *b* countenance 1Sa 16:12 3303
and of a *b* countenance 1Sa 25:3 3303
the woman was very *b* to look upon 2Sa 11:2 2896
mother, and the maid was fair and *b* Est 2:7
B for situation, the joy of the Ps 48:2 3303
made every thing *b* in his time Eccl 3:11 3303
Thou art *b*, O my love, as Tirzah, Song 6:4 3303
How *b* are thy feet with shoes, O Song 7:1 3303
shall the branch of the LORD be *b* Is 4:2 6643
put on thy *b* garments, O Is 52:1 8597
How *b* upon the mountains are the Is 52:7 4998
our *b* house, where our fathers Is 64:11 8597
that was given thee, thy *b* flock Jer 13:20 8597
strong staff broken, and the *b* rod Jer 48:17 8597
a *b* crown upon thine head Eze 16:12 8597
and thou wast exceeding *b*, and thou Eze 16:13 3303
b crowns upon their heads Eze 23:42 8597
which indeed appear *b* outward Mt 23:27 *5611*
of the temple which is called *B* Acts 3:2 *5611*
alms at the *B* gate of the temple Acts 3:10 *5611*
How *b* are the feet of them that Rom 10:15 *5611*

BEAUTIFY
to *b* the house of the LORD which Ezr 7:27 6286
he will *b* the meek with salvation Ps 149:4 6286
to *b* the place of my sanctuary Is 60:13 6286

BEAUTY
thy brother for glory and for *b* Ex 28:2 8597
make for them, for glory and for *b* Ex 28:40 8597
The *b* of Israel is slain upon thy 2Sa 1:19 6643
much praised as Absalom for his *b* 2Sa 14:25 3308
the LORD in the *b* of holiness 1Chr 16:29 1927
house with precious stones for *b* 2Chr 3:6 8597
should praise the *b* of holiness 2Chr 20:21 1927
the people and the princes her *b* Est 1:11 3308
and array thyself with glory and *b* Job 40:10 1926
life, to behold the *b* of the LORD Ps 27:4 5278
the LORD in the *b* of holiness Ps 29:2 1927
thou makest his *b* to consume away Ps 39:11 2530
the king greatly desire thy *b* Ps 45:11 3308
their *b* shall consume in the Ps 49:14 6736
Out of Zion, the perfection of *b* Ps 50:2 3308
let the *b* of the LORD our God be Ps 90:17 5278
and *b* are in his sanctuary Ps 96:6 8597
the LORD in the *b* of holiness Ps 96:9 1927
not after her *b* in thine heart Prov 6:25 3308
the *b* of old men is the grey head Prov 20:29 1926
Favour is deceitful, and *b* is vain Prov 31:30 3308
and burning instead of *b* Is 3:24 3308
the *b* of the Chaldees' excellency Is 13:19 8597
whose glorious *b* is a fading Is 28:1 8597
And the glorious *b*, which is on Is 28:4 8597
of glory, and for a diadem of *b* Is 28:5 8597
eyes shall see the king in his *b* Is 33:17 3308
man, according to the *b* of a man Is 44:13 8597
there is no *b* that we should Is 53:2 4758
to give unto them *b* for ashes Is 61:3 6287
of Zion all her *b* is departed Lam 1:6 1926
unto the earth the *b* of Israel Lam 2:1 8597
that men call The perfection of *b* Lam 2:15 3308
As for the *b* of his ornament, he Eze 7:20 6643
forth among the heathen for thy *b* Eze 16:14 3308
thou didst trust in thine own *b* Eze 16:15 3308
hast made thy *b* to be abhorred Eze 16:25 3308
thou hast said, I am of perfect *b* Eze 27:3 3308
thy builders have perfected thy *b* Eze 27:4 3308
they have made thy *b* perfect Eze 27:11 3308
against the *b* of thy wisdom Eze 28:7 3308
full of wisdom, and perfect in *b* Eze 28:12 3308
was lifted up because of thy *b* Eze 28:17 3308
of God was like unto him in his *b* Eze 31:8 3308
Whom dost thou pass in *b* Eze 32:19 5276
his *b* shall be as the olive tree, Hos 14:6 1935
goodness, and how great is his *b* Zec 9:17 3308
the one I called *B*, and the other Zec 11:7 5278
And I took my staff, even *B* Zec 11:10 5278

BEBAI (beb'-a-i)
1. Father of returned exiles.
The children of B, six hundred Ezr 2:11 893
The children of B, six hundred Neh 7:16 893
2. Father of returned exiles with Ezra.
And of the sons of B Ezr 8:11 893
Zechariah the son of B, and with Ezr 8:11 893
Of the sons also of B Ezr 10:28 893
3. One who sealed the covenant.
Bunni, Azgad, B, Neh 10:15 893

BECAME
and man *b* a living soul Gen 2:7 1961
was parted, and *b* into four heads Gen 2:10 1961
the same *b* mighty men which were Gen 6:4
him, and she *b* a pillar of salt Gen 19:26 1961
and she *b* my wife Gen 20:12 1961
in the wilderness, and *b* an archer Gen 21:20 1961
took Rebekah, and she *b* his wife Gen 24:67 1961
and grew until he *b* very great Gen 26:13 1431
For thy servant *b* surety for the Gen 44:32 6148
so the land *b* Pharaoh's Gen 47:20 1961
only, which *b* not Pharaoh's Gen 47:26 1961
bear, and *b* a servant unto tribute Gen 49:15 1961
daughter, and he *b* her son Ex 2:10 1961
on the ground, and it *b* a serpent Ex 4:3 1961
it, and it *b* a rod in his hand Ex 4:4 1961
his servants, and it *b* a serpent Ex 7:10 1961
man his rod, and they *b* serpents Ex 7:12 1961
it *b* lice in man, and in beast Ex 8:17 1961
all the dust of the land *b* lice Ex 8:17 1961
it *b* a boil breaking forth with Ex 9:10 1961
land of Egypt since it *b* a nation Ex 9:24 1961
so it *b* one tabernacle Ex 36:13 1961
Miriam *b* leprous, white as snow Num 12:10
and they *b* a sign Num 26:10 1961
b there a nation, great, mighty, Deut 26:5 1961
the people melted, and *b* as water Josh 7:5 1961
Hebron therefore *b* the Josh 14:14 1961
it *b* the inheritance of the Josh 24:32 1961
among them, and *b* tributaries Judg 1:30 1961
of Beth-anath *b* tributaries unto Judg 1:33 1961
so that they *b* tributaries Judg 1:35 1961
which thing *b* a snare unto Gideon Judg 8:27 1961
b as flax that was burnt with Judg 15:14 1961
one of his sons, who *b* his priest Judg 17:5 1961
and the young man *b* his priest Judg 17:12 1961

in her bosom, and *b* nurse unto it Ruth 4:16 1961
Therefore it *b* a proverb, Is Saul 1Sa 10:12 1961
and he *b* his armourbearer 1Sa 16:21 1961
Saul *b* David's enemy continually 1Sa 18:29 1961
and he *b* a captain over them 1Sa 22:2 1961
within him, and he *b* as a stone 1Sa 25:37 1961
of David, and *b* his wife 1Sa 25:42 1961
b one troop, and stood on the top 2Sa 2:25 1961
to flee, that he fell, and *b* lame 2Sa 4:4 6452
so the Moabites *b* David's 2Sa 8:2 1961
the Syrians *b* servants to David, 2Sa 8:6 1961
they of Edom *b* David's servants 2Sa 8:14 1961
she *b* his wife, and bare him a son 2Sa 11:27 1961
b captain over a band, when David 1Kin 11:24 1961
And this thing *b* a sin 1Kin 12:30 1961
him again, and *b* as it was before 1Kin 13:6 1961
he *b* one of the priests of the 1Kin 13:33 1961
this thing *b* sin unto the house 1Kin 13:34 1961
Hoshea *b* his servant, and gave him 2Kin 17:3 1961
b vain, and went after the heathen 2Kin 17:15 1891
Jehoiakim *b* his servant three 2Kin 24:1 1961
the Moabites *b* David's servants, 1Chr 18:2 1961
the Syrians *b* David's servants, 1Chr 18:6 1961
the Edomites *b* David's servants 1Chr 18:13 1961
with David, and *b* his servants 1Chr 19:19 5647
So Jotham *b* mighty, because he 2Chr 27:6 2388
b fat, and delighted themselves in Neh 9:25 8080
of the people of the land *b* Jews Est 8:17 3054
and I *b* a proverb to them Ps 69:11 1961
they *b* as dung for the earth Ps 83:10 1961
I *b* also a reproach unto them Ps 109:25 1961
they *b* as women Jer 51:30 1961
b a spreading vine of low stature Eze 17:6 1961
so it *b* a vine, and brought forth Eze 17:6 1961
it *b* a young lion, and it learned Eze 19:3 1961
he *b* a young lion, and learned to Eze 19:6 1961
and she *b* famous among women Eze 23:10 1961
his branches *b* long because of Eze 31:5 748
they *b* meat to all the beasts of Eze 34:5 1961
surely because my flock *b* a prey Eze 34:8 1961
my flock *b* meat to every beast of Eze 34:8 1961
which *b* a prey and derision to the Eze 36:4 1961
b like the chaff of the summer Dan 2:35 1934
the image *b* a great mountain Dan 2:35 1934
according to his will, and *b* great Dan 8:4 1431
toward the ground, and I *b* dumb Dan 10:15 481
in the day that he *b* a stranger Obad 12 5235
did shake, and *b* as dead men Mt 28:4 *1096*
And his raiment *b* shining, Mk 9:3 *1096*
he *b* very hungry, and would have Acts 10:10 *1096*
but *b* vain in their imaginations, Rom 1:21 *3154*
to be wise, they *b* fools, Rom 1:22 *3471*
from sin, ye *b* the servants of Rom 6:18 *1402*
And unto the Jews I *b* as a Jew 1Cor 9:20 *1096*
To the weak *b* I as weak, that I 1Cor 9:22 *1096*
but when I *b* a man, I put away 1Cor 13:11 *1096*
yet for your sakes he *b* poor 2Cor 8:9 *4433*
b obedient unto death, even the Phil 2:8 *1096*
ye *b* followers of us, and of the 1Th 1:6 *1096*
b followers of the churches of 1Th 2:14 *1096*
For it *b* him, for whom are all Heb 2:10 *4241*
he *b* the author of eternal Heb 5:9 *1096*
For such an high priest *b* us Heb 7:26 *4241*
whilst ye *b* companions of them Heb 10:33 *1096*
b heir of the righteousness which Heb 11:7 *1096*
the sun *b* black as sackcloth of Rev 6:12 *1096*
of hair, and the moon *b* as blood Rev 6:12 *1096*
the third part of the sea *b* blood Rev 8:8 *1096*
part of the waters *b* wormwood Rev 8:11
it *b* as the blood of a dead man Rev 16:3 *1096*
and they *b* blood Rev 16:4 *1096*

BECAMEST

and thou, LORD, *b* their God 1Chr 17:22 1961
the Lord GOD, and thou *b* mine Eze 16:8 1961

BECAUSE

b that in it he had rested from Gen 2:3 3588
b she was taken out of Man Gen 2:23 3588
and I was afraid, *b* I was naked Gen 3:10 3588
B thou hast done this, thou art Gen 3:14 3588
B thou hast hearkened unto the Gen 3:17 3588
b she was the mother of all Gen 3:20 3588
b of the ground which the LORD Gen 5:29 4480
b of the waters of the flood Gen 7:7 6440
b the LORD did there confound the Gen 11:9 3588
and my soul shall live *b* of thee Gen 12:13 1558
plagues *b* of Sarai Abram's wife Gen 12:17 1697
b the LORD hath heard thy Gen 16:11 3588
B the cry of Sodom and Gomorrah is Gen 18:20 3588
b their sin is very grievous Gen 18:20 3588
b the cry of them is waxen great Gen 19:13 3588
B I thought, Surely the fear of Gen 20:11 3588
b of Sarah Abraham's wife Gen 20:18
in Abraham's sight *b* of his son Gen 21:11
in thy sight *b* of the lad Gen 21:12 5921
of the lad, and *b* of thy bondwoman Gen 21:12 5921
I make a nation, *b* he is thy seed Gen 21:13 3588
Abimelech *b* of a well of water Gen 21:25
b there they sware both of them Gen 21:31 3588
for *b* thou hast done this thing, Gen 22:16
b thou hast obeyed my voice Gen 22:18
for his wife, *b* she was barren Gen 25:21 3588
b he did eat of his venison Gen 25:28 3588
B that Abraham obeyed my voice, Gen 26:5 6119
b she was fair to look upon Gen 26:7 3588
B I said, Lest I die for her Gen 26:9 3588
b they strove with him Gen 26:20 3588
B the LORD thy God brought it to Gen 27:20 3588
b his hands were hairy, as his Gen 27:23 3588
Esau hated Jacob *b* of the Gen 27:41 5921
I am weary of my life *b* of the Gen 27:46 6440
all night, *b* the sun was set Gen 28:11 3588
B thou art my brother, shouldest Gen 29:15 3588
B the LORD hath heard that I was Gen 29:33 3588
b I have born him three sons Gen 29:34 3588
b I have given my maiden to my Gen 30:18 834
b I have born him six sons Gen 30:20 3588
b thou sore longedst after thy Gen 31:30 3588
and said to Laban, *B* I was afraid Gen 31:31 3588
b he touched the hollow of Gen 32:32 3588
b God hath dealt graciously with Gen 33:11 3588
with me, and *b* I have enough Gen 33:11 3588
b he had wrought folly in Israel Gen 34:7 3588
b he had defiled Dinah their Gen 34:13 834
b he had delight in Jacob's Gen 34:19 3588
b they had defiled their sister Gen 34:27 834
b there God appeared unto him, Gen 35:7 3588
not bear them *b* of their cattle Gen 36:7 6440
b he was the son of his old age Gen 37:3 3588
b she had covered her face Gen 38:15 3588
b that I gave her not to Shelah Gen 38:26 3588
me but thee, *b* thou art his wife Gen 39:9 834
b the LORD was with him, and that Gen 39:23 834
it is *b* the thing is established Gen 41:32 3588
b that the famine was so sore in Gen 41:57 3588
b they were brought into Joseph's Gen 43:18 3588
B of the money that was returned Gen 43:18
b the Egyptians might not eat Gen 43:32 3588
thy face, *b* thou art yet alive Gen 46:30 3588
b the famine prevailed over them Gen 47:20 3588
b thou wentest up to thy father's Gen 49:4 3588
they were grieved *b* of the Ex 1:12 6440
B the Hebrew women are not as the Ex 1:19 3588
b the midwives feared God, that Ex 1:21 3588
B I drew him out of the water Ex 2:10 3588
thou art, *b* of the circumcision Ex 4:26
b ye have made our savour to be Ex 5:21 834
LORD *b* of the frogs which he had Ex 8:12
stand before Moses *b* of the boils Ex 9:11 6440
b they were thrust out of Egypt, Ex 12:39 3588
This is done *b* of that which the Ex 13:8 5668
B there were no graves in Egypt, Ex 14:11 1115
b of the chiding of the children Ex 17:7 5921
b they tempted the LORD, saying, Ex 17:7 5921
B the LORD hath sworn that the Ex 17:16 3588
B the people come unto me to Ex 18:15 3588
b the LORD descended upon it in Ex 19:18
not eat thereof, *b* they are holy Ex 29:33 3588
shall not be eaten, *b* it is holy Ex 29:34 3588
b they made the calf, which Aaron Ex 32:35
b the cloud abode thereon, and the Ex 40:35 3588
b he hath sinned, and is guilty, Lev 6:4 3588
b of the burning upon the altar Lev 6:9 5921
b it is thy due, and thy sons' due Lev 10:13 3588
b he cheweth the cud, but Lev 11:4 3588
b he cheweth the cud, but Lev 11:5 3588
b he cheweth the cud, but Lev 11:6 3588
clean, *b* the plague is healed Lev 14:48 3588
b of his issue he is unclean Lev 15:2
b of the uncleanness of the Lev 16:16
b of their transgressions in all Lev 16:16
b he hath profaned the hallowed Lev 19:8 3588
put to death, *b* she was not free Lev 19:20 3588
b he hath given of his seed unto Lev 20:3 3588
the altar, *b* he hath a blemish Lev 21:23 3588
b it is his food Lev 22:7 3588
b their corruption is in them, and Lev 22:25 3588
bring forth the old *b* of the new Lev 26:10 6440
b it did not rest in your Lev 26:35
b, even *b* they despised my Lev 26:43 3282
b their soul abhorred my statutes Lev 26:43
B all the firstborn are mine Num 3:13 3588
b the consecration of his God is Num 6:7 3588
b his separation was defiled Num 6:12 3588
b the service of the sanctuary Num 7:9 3588
b he brought not the offering of Num 9:13 3588
b the fire of the LORD burnt Num 11:3 3588
alone, *b* it is too heavy for me Num 11:14 3588
b that ye have despised the LORD Num 11:20 3282
b there they buried the people Num 11:34 3588
Aaron spake against Moses *b* of Num 12:1
b of the cluster of grapes which Num 13:24
B the LORD was not able to bring Num 14:16 1115
B all those men which have seen Num 14:22 3588
b he had another spirit with him, Num 14:24 6118
b ye are turned away from the Num 14:43
B he hath despised the word of Num 15:31 3588
b it was not declared what should Num 15:34 3588
b the water of separation was not Num 19:13 3588
b he hath defiled the sanctuary Num 19:20 3588
B ye believed me not, to sanctify Num 20:12 3282
b the children of Israel strove Num 20:13 834
b ye rebelled against my word at Num 20:24
was much discouraged *b* of the way Num 21:4
of the people, *b* they were many Num 22:3 3588
Moab was distressed *b* of the Num 22:3 6440
God's anger was kindled *b* he went Num 22:22 3588
the ass, *B* thou hast mocked me Num 22:29 3588
b thy way is perverse before me Num 22:32 3588
b he was zealous for his God, and Num 25:13
b there was no inheritance given Num 26:62 3588
his family, *b* he hath no son Num 27:4 3588
b her father disallowed her Num 30:5 3588
b he held his peace at her in the Num 30:14 3588
b they have not wholly followed Num 32:11 3588
dwell in the fenced cities *b* of Num 32:17 6440
b our inheritance is fallen to us Num 32:19 3588
B he should have remained in the Num 35:28 3588
B the LORD hated us, he hath Deut 1:27
b he hath wholly followed the Deut 1:36
b I have given mount Seir unto Deut 2:5 3588
b I have given Ar unto the Deut 2:9 3588
b I have given it unto the Deut 2:19 3588
and be in anguish *b* of thee Deut 2:25 6440
what the LORD did *b* of Baal-peor Deut 4:3
b he loved thy fathers, therefore Deut 4:37
b ye were more in number than any Deut 7:7
But *b* the LORD loved you, and Deut 7:8 3588
b he would keep the oath which he Deut 7:8
b ye would not be obedient unto Deut 8:20 6118
b of all your sins which ye Deut 9:18 3588
b the LORD had said he would Deut 9:25 3588
B the LORD was not able to bring Deut 9:28 3588
b he hated them, he hath brought Deut 9:28 3588
b thy soul longeth to eat flesh Deut 12:20 3588
b he hath spoken to turn you away Deut 13:5 3588
b he hath sought to thrust thee Deut 13:10 3588
b it divideth the hoof, yet Deut 14:8 3588
Levite, (*b* he hath no part nor Deut 14:29 3588
b it is called the LORD's release Deut 15:2 3588
b that for this thing the LORD Deut 15:10 3588
b he loveth thee and thine house, Deut 15:16 3588
house, *b* he is well with thee Deut 15:16 3588
b the LORD thy God shall bless Deut 16:15 3588
b of these abominations the LORD Deut 18:12 1558
b the way is long, and slay him Deut 19:6 3588
neither be ye terrified *b* of them Deut 20:3 6440
of her, *b* thou hast humbled her Deut 21:14
b he hath brought up an evil name Deut 22:19 3588
b she hath wrought folly in Deut 22:21 3588
b she cried not, being in the Deut 22:24
b he hath humbled his neighbour's Deut 22:24
b he hath humbled her, he may not Deut 22:29
B they met you not with bread and Deut 23:4
b they hired against thee Balaam Deut 23:4 3588
b the LORD thy God loved thee Deut 23:5 3588
b thou wast a stranger in his Deut 23:7 3588
b he hath found some uncleanness Deut 24:1 3588
b he uncovereth his father's Deut 27:20 3588
b of the wickedness of thy doings Deut 28:20 6440
b thou hearkenedst not unto the Deut 28:45 3588
B thou servedst not the LORD thy Deut 28:47
b he hath nothing left him in the Deut 28:55
b thou wouldest not obey the Deut 28:62 3588
B they have forsaken the covenant Deut 29:25
b our God is not among us Deut 31:17 3588
b ye will do evil in the sight of Deut 31:29 3588
B I will publish the name of the Deut 32:3 3588
b of the provoking of his sons, Deut 32:19
b it is your life Deut 32:47 3588
B ye trespassed against me among Deut 32:51
b ye sanctified me not in the Deut 32:51 3588
b there, in a portion of the Deut 33:21 3588
of the land faint *b* of you Josh 2:9 6440
more courage in any man, *b* of you Josh 2:11 6440
of the country do faint *b* of us Josh 2:24 6440
b of the children of Israel Josh 5:1 6440
b they obeyed not the voice of Josh 5:6 834
b they had not circumcised them Josh 5:7 3588
up *b* of the children of Israel Josh 6:1 6440
b she hid the messengers that we Josh 6:17 3588
b she hid the messengers, which Josh 6:25 3588
enemies, *b* they were accursed Josh 7:12 3588
b he hath transgressed the Josh 7:15 3588
b he hath wrought folly in Israel Josh 7:15 3588
country thy servants are come *b* Josh 9:9
b the princes of the congregation Josh 9:18 3588
b of the oath which we sware unto Josh 9:20 5921
B it was certainly told thy Josh 9:24 3588
sore afraid of our lives *b* of you Josh 9:24 6440
b Gibeon was a great city, as one Josh 10:2 3588
b it was greater than Ai, and all Josh 10:2 3588
b the LORD God of Israel fought Josh 10:42 3588
Joshua, Be not afraid *b* of them Josh 11:6 6440
b thou hast wholly followed the Josh 14:9 3588
b that he wholly followed the Josh 14:14 3282
b he was a man of war, therefore Josh 17:1 3588
B the daughters of Manasseh had Josh 17:6 3588
b he smote his neighbour Josh 20:5 3588
b ye have not committed this Josh 22:31 834
unto all these nations *b* of you Josh 23:3 6440
b they had chariots of iron Judg 1:19 3588
for it repented the LORD *b* of Judg 2:18 6440
he said, *B* that this people hath Judg 2:20 3282
b they had done evil in the sight Judg 3:12
b they came not to the help of Judg 5:23 3588
b of the Midianites the children Judg 6:2 6440
impoverished *b* of the Midianites Judg 6:6 6440
unto the LORD *b* of the Midianites Judg 6:7
for *b* I have seen an angel of the Judg 6:22
it was, *b* he feared his father's Judg 6:27 834
b he hath cast down the altar of Judg 6:30 3588
b he hath cut down the grove that Judg 6:30 3588
b one hath cast down his altar Judg 6:31 3588
b he hath thrown down his altar Judg 6:32 3588
he feared, *b* he was yet a youth Judg 8:20 3588
earrings, *b* they were Ishmaelites Judg 8:24 3588
of Shechem, *b* he is your brother Judg 9:18 3588
both *b* we have forsaken our God, Judg 10:10 3588
B Israel took away my land, when Judg 11:13 3588
b they said, Ye Gileadites are Judg 12:4 3588
surely die, *b* we have seen God Judg 13:22 3588
told her, *b* she lay sore upon him Judg 14:17 3588
b he had taken his wife, and given Judg 15:6 3588
b it was far from Zidon, and they Judg 18:28 3588
b they trusted unto the liers in Judg 20:36 3588
b that the LORD had made a breach Judg 21:15 3588
b we reserved not to each man his Judg 21:22 3588
b the LORD had shut up her womb 1Sa 1:6 3588
B I have asked him of the LORD 1Sa 1:20 3588
b I rejoice in thy salvation 1Sa 2:1 3588
b the LORD would slay them 1Sa 2:25 3588
b his sons made themselves vile, 1Sa 3:13 3588
b the ark of God was taken, and 1Sa 4:21 413
b of her father in law and her 1Sa 4:21 413
b they had looked into the ark of 1Sa 6:19 3588
b the LORD had smitten many of 1Sa 6:19 3588
day *b* of your king which ye shall 1Sa 8:18 6440
b he doth bless the sacrifice 1Sa 9:13 3588
b their cry is come unto me 1Sa 9:16 3588
Is it not *b* the LORD hath 1Sa 10:1 3588
b we have forsaken the LORD, and 1Sa 12:10 3588

b it hath pleased the LORD to ... 1Sa 12:22 3588
B I saw that the people were ... 1Sa 13:11 3588
b thou hast not kept that which ... 1Sa 13:14 3588
b I tasted a little of this honey ... 1Sa 14:29 3588
B thou hast rejected the word of ... 1Sa 15:23 3282
b I feared the people, and obeyed ... 1Sa 15:24 3588
b I have refused him ... 1Sa 16:7 3588
Let no man's heart fail *b* of him ... 1Sa 17:32 5921
b he loved him as his own soul ... 1Sa 18:3
b the LORD was with him, and was ... 1Sa 18:12 3588
b he went out and came in before ... 1Sa 18:16 3588
b he hath not sinned against thee ... 1Sa 19:4 3588
thee, and *b* his works have been to ... 1Sa 19:4 3588
to swear again, *b* he loved him ... 1Sa 20:17
missed, *b* thy seat will be empty ... 1Sa 20:18 3588
b his father had done him shame ... 1Sa 20:34 3588
b the king's business required ... 1Sa 21:8 3588
b their hand also is with David, ... 1Sa 22:17 3588
b they knew when he fled, and did ... 1Sa 22:17 3588
b he had cut off Saul's skirt ... 1Sa 24:5
b my lord fighteth the battles of ... 1Sa 25:28 3588
b a deep sleep from the LORD was ... 1Sa 26:12 3588
b ye have not kept your master, ... 1Sa 26:16 834
b my soul was precious in thine ... 1Sa 26:21
B thou obeyedst not the voice of ... 1Sa 28:18 834
afraid, *b* of the words of Samuel ... 1Sa 28:20
b the soul of all the people was ... 1Sa 30:6 3588
b three days agone I fell sick ... 1Sa 30:13 3588
b of all the great spoil that ... 1Sa 30:16
B they went not with us, we will ... 1Sa 30:22 3282
b my life is yet whole in me ... 2Sa 1:9 3588
b I was sure that he could not ... 2Sa 1:10 3588
b they were fallen by the sword ... 2Sa 1:12 3588
b ye have done this thing ... 2Sa 2:6 834
a word again, *b* he feared him ... 2Sa 3:11
b he had slain their brother ... 2Sa 3:30
b the LORD had made a breach upon ... 2Sa 6:8
unto him, *b* of the ark of God ... 2Sa 6:12 5668
b he had fought against Hadadezer ... 2Sa 8:10
b the men were greatly ashamed ... 2Sa 10:5 3588
b he did this thing, and *b* ... 2Sa 12:6
b thou hast despised me, and hast ... 2Sa 12:10
b by this deed thou hast given ... 2Sa 12:14 3588
his name Jedidiah, *b* of the LORD ... 2Sa 12:25 5668
b he had forced his sister Tamar ... 2Sa 13:22
it is *b* the people have made me ... 2Sa 14:15 3588
b the hair was heavy on him, ... 2Sa 14:26 3588
mischief, *b* thou art a bloody man ... 2Sa 16:8 3588
b the LORD hath said unto him, ... 2Sa 16:10 3588
tidings, *b* the king's son is dead ... 2Sa 18:20
b he cursed the LORD's anointed ... 2Sa 19:21 3588
b thy servant is lame ... 2Sa 19:26 3588
B the king is near of kin to us ... 2Sa 19:42 3588
house, *b* he slew the Gibeonites ... 2Sa 21:1
b of the LORD's oath that was ... 2Sa 21:7 5921
moved and shook, *b* he was wroth ... 2Sa 22:8 3588
me, *b* he delighted in me ... 2Sa 22:20 3588
b they cannot be taken with hands ... 2Sa 23:6 3588
And Adonijah feared *b* of Solomon ... 1Kin 1:50 6440
I fled *b* of Absalom thy brother ... 1Kin 2:7 6440
b thou barest the ark of the Lord ... 1Kin 2:26 3588
b thou hast been afflicted in all ... 1Kin 2:26 3588
b there was no house built unto ... 1Kin 3:2 3588
B thou hast asked this thing, and ... 1Kin 3:11 3282
b she overlaid it ... 1Kin 3:19 834
b they were exceeding many ... 1Kin 7:47
stand to minister *b* of the cloud ... 1Kin 8:11 6440
b they have sinned against thee, ... 1Kin 8:33 834
b they have sinned against thee ... 1Kin 8:35 3588
b the brasen altar that was ... 1Kin 8:64 3588
B they forsook the LORD their God ... 1Kin 9:9
b the LORD loved Israel for ever, ... 1Kin 10:9
b his heart was turned from the ... 1Kin 11:9 3588
B that they have forsaken me, and ... 1Kin 11:33
b he kept my commandments and my ... 1Kin 11:34 834
b in him there is found some good ... 1Kin 14:13 3282
b they have made their groves, ... 1Kin 14:15 834
up *b* of the sins of Jeroboam ... 1Kin 14:16 1558
B David did that which was right ... 1Kin 15:5 834
b she had made an idol in a grove ... 1Kin 15:13 834
B of the sins of Jeroboam which ... 1Kin 15:30 5921
and *b* he killed him ... 1Kin 16:7 834
b there had been no rain in the ... 1Kin 17:7 3588
b the journey is too great for ... 1Kin 19:7 3588
b the children of Israel have ... 1Kin 19:14 3588
B the Syrians have said, The LORD ... 1Kin 20:28
B thou hast not obeyed the voice ... 1Kin 20:36
B thou hast let go out of thy ... 1Kin 20:42 3282
b it is near unto my house ... 1Kin 21:2 3588
displeased *b* of the word which ... 1Kin 21:4 5921
B I spake unto Naboth the ... 1Kin 21:6 3588
b thou hast sold thyself to work ... 1Kin 21:20 3588
b he humbleth himself before me, ... 1Kin 21:29 3588
Is it not *b* there is not a God in ... 2Kin 1:3
Is it not *b* there is not a God in ... 2Kin 1:6
is it not *b* there is no God in ... 2Kin 1:16
b he had no son ... 2Kin 1:17 3588
b by him the LORD had given ... 2Kin 5:1 3588
B I know the evil that thou wilt ... 2Kin 8:12 3588
of Ahab in Jezreel, *b* he was sick ... 2Kin 8:29 3588
b of Hazael king of Syria ... 2Kin 9:14 6440
Jehu, *B* thou hast done well in ... 2Kin 10:30
b the king of Syria oppressed ... 2Kin 13:4 3588
b of his covenant with Abraham, ... 2Kin 13:23 4616
b they opened not to him, ... 2Kin 15:16 3588
b they know not the manner of the ... 2Kin 17:26 834
B they obeyed not the voice of ... 2Kin 18:12
B thy rage against me and thy ... 2Kin 19:28 3282
B Manasseh king of Judah hath ... 2Kin 21:11
B they have done that which was ... 2Kin 21:15
hand, *b* they dealt faithfully ... 2Kin 22:7 3588
b our fathers have not hearkened ... 2Kin 22:13
B they have forsaken me, and have ... 2Kin 22:17
B thine heart was tender, and thou ... 2Kin 22:19 3282
b of all the provocations that ... 2Kin 23:26 5921
b in his days the earth was ... 1Chr 1:19 3588
saying, *B* I bare him with sorrow ... 1Chr 4:9 3588
b there was pasture there for ... 1Chr 4:41 3588
b their cattle were multiplied in ... 1Chr 5:9 3588
b they put their trust in him ... 1Chr 5:20 3588
many slain, *b* the war was of God ... 1Chr 5:22 3588
b they came down to take away ... 1Chr 7:21 3588
b it went evil with his house ... 1Chr 7:23 3588
b the charge was upon them, and ... 1Chr 9:27 3588
close *b* of Saul the son of Kish ... 1Chr 12:1 6440
b he put his hand to the ark ... 1Chr 13:10
b the LORD had made a breach upon ... 1Chr 13:11 3588
on high, *b* of his people Israel ... 1Chr 14:2 5668
For *b* ye did it not at the first, ... 1Chr 15:13 3588
about the song, *b* he was skilful ... 1Chr 15:22 3588
b he cometh to judge the earth ... 1Chr 16:33 3588
b his mercy endureth for ever ... 1Chr 16:41 3588
b he had fought against Hadarezer ... 1Chr 18:10
b his father shewed kindness to ... 1Chr 19:2 3588
greatly, *b* I have done this thing ... 1Chr 21:8 834
for he was afraid *b* of the sword ... 1Chr 21:30 6440
b thou hast shed much blood upon ... 1Chr 22:8 3588
B their office was to wait on the ... 1Chr 23:28 3588
b the LORD had said he would ... 1Chr 27:23 3588
b there fell wrath for it against ... 1Chr 27:24
b thou hast been a man of war, and ... 1Chr 28:3 3588
b I have set my affection to the ... 1Chr 29:3
b with perfect heart they offered ... 1Chr 29:9 3588
B this was in thine heart, and ... 2Chr 1:11
B the LORD hath loved his people, ... 2Chr 2:11
b they have sinned against thee ... 2Chr 6:24 3588
b they have sinned against thee ... 2Chr 6:26 3588
b the glory of the LORD had ... 2Chr 7:2 3588
b his mercy endureth for ever, ... 2Chr 7:6 3588
b the brasen altar which Solomon ... 2Chr 7:7 3588
B they forsook the LORD God of ... 2Chr 7:22
b the places are holy, whereunto ... 2Chr 8:11 3588
b thy God loved Israel, to ... 2Chr 9:8
b they had transgressed against ... 2Chr 12:2 3588
to Jerusalem *b* of Shishak ... 2Chr 12:5 6448
b he prepared not his heart to ... 2Chr 12:14 3588
b they relied upon the LORD God ... 2Chr 13:18 3588
b the LORD had given him rest ... 2Chr 14:6 3588
b we have sought the LORD our God ... 2Chr 14:7 3588
b she had made an idol in a grove ... 2Chr 15:16 834
B thou hast relied on the king of ... 2Chr 16:7
b thou didst rely on the LORD, he ... 2Chr 16:8
a rage with him *b* of this thing ... 2Chr 16:10 5921
b he walked in the first ways of ... 2Chr 17:3 3588
B thou hast joined thyself with ... 2Chr 20:37
b he was the firstborn ... 2Chr 21:3 3588
b of the covenant that he had ... 2Chr 21:7 3282
b he had forsaken the LORD God of ... 2Chr 21:10 3588
B thou hast not walked in the ... 2Chr 21:12
to be healed in Jezreel *b* of the ... 2Chr 22:6 3588
of Ahab at Jezreel, *b* he was sick ... 2Chr 22:6 3588
B, said they, he is the son of ... 2Chr 22:9 3588
b he had done good in Israel, ... 2Chr 24:16 3588
b ye have forsaken the LORD, he ... 2Chr 24:20 3588
b they had forsaken the LORD God ... 2Chr 24:24 3588
b thou hast done this, and hast ... 2Chr 25:16 3588
b they sought after the gods of ... 2Chr 25:20 3588
b the LORD had smitten him ... 2Chr 26:20 3588
b he prepared his ways before the ... 2Chr 27:6 3588
b they had forsaken the LORD God ... 2Chr 28:6
b the LORD God of your fathers ... 2Chr 28:9
low *b* of Ahaz king of Israel ... 2Chr 28:19 5668
B the gods of the kings of Syria ... 2Chr 28:23 3588
b the priests had not sanctified ... 2Chr 30:3 3588
b our fathers have not kept the ... 2Chr 34:21
B they have forsaken me, and have ... 2Chr 34:25
B thine heart was tender, and thou ... 2Chr 34:27 3282
b the priests the sons of Aaron ... 2Chr 35:14 3588
b he had compassion on his people ... 2Chr 36:15 3588
them *b* of the people of those ... Ezr 3:3
b he is good, for his mercy ... Ezr 3:11 3588
b the foundation of the house of ... Ezr 3:11 5921
Now *b* we have maintenance from ... Ezr 4:14
b we had spoken unto the king, ... Ezr 8:22 3588
b of the transgression of those ... Ezr 9:4 5921
stand before thee *b* of this ... Ezr 9:15 5921
for he mourned *b* of the ... Ezr 10:6 3588
trembling *b* of this matter, and ... Ezr 10:9 3588
them day and night, *b* of them ... Neh 4:9 6440
might buy corn, *b* of the dearth ... Neh 5:3
b of the reproach of the heathen ... Neh 5:9
did not I, *b* of the fear of God ... Neh 5:15 6440
b the bondage was heavy upon this ... Neh 5:18 3588
b he was the son in law of ... Neh 6:18 3588
b they had understood the words ... Neh 8:12 3588
hast set over us *b* of our sins ... Neh 9:37
b of all this we make a sure ... Neh 9:38
B they met not the children of ... Neh 13:2 3588
O my God, *b* they have defiled the ... Neh 13:29 5921
b she hath not performed the ... Est 1:15
b he laid his hand upon the Jews ... Est 8:7
b the fear of Mordecai fell upon ... Est 9:3 3588
B Haman the son of Hammedatha, ... Est 9:24 3588
B it shut not up the doors of my ... Job 3:10 3588
were confounded *b* they had hoped ... Job 6:20 3588
b our days upon earth are a ... Job 8:9 3588
b thou shalt forget thy misery, ... Job 11:16 3588
shalt be secure, *b* there is hope ... Job 11:18 3588
B he covereth his face with his ... Job 15:27 3588
the light is short *b* of darkness ... Job 17:12 6440
tabernacle, *b* it is none of his ... Job 18:15
B he hath oppressed and hath ... Job 20:19 3588
b he hath violently taken away an ... Job 20:19
B I was not cut off before the ... Job 23:17 3588
B I delivered the poor that cried ... Job 29:12 3588
B he hath loosed my cord, and ... Job 30:11 3588
If I rejoiced *b* my wealth was ... Job 31:25 3588
b mine hand had gotten much ... Job 31:25 3588
b he was righteous in his own ... Job 32:1 3588
b he justified himself rather ... Job 32:2 5921
b they had found no answer, and ... Job 32:3
b they were elder than he ... Job 32:4 3588
B they turned back from him, and ... Job 34:27
b of his answers for wicked men ... Job 34:36 5921
b of the pride of evil men ... Job 35:12 6440
b it is not so, he hath visited ... Job 35:15 3588
B there is wrath, beware lest he ... Job 36:18 3588
thou it, *b* thou wast then born ... Job 38:21 3588
or *b* the number of thy days is ... Job 38:21
him, *b* his strength is great ... Job 39:11 3588
B God hath deprived her of wisdom ... Job 39:17 3588
righteousness *b* of mine enemies ... Ps 5:8 4616
for joy, *b* thou defendest them ... Ps 5:11
Mine eye is consumed *b* of grief ... Ps 6:7
it waxeth old *b* of all mine ... Ps 6:7
lift up thyself *b* of the rage of ... Ps 7:6
strength *b* of thine enemies ... Ps 8:2 4616
b he hath dealt bountifully with ... Ps 13:6 3588
poor, *b* the LORD is his refuge ... Ps 14:6 3588
b he is at my right hand, I shall ... Ps 16:8 3588
and were shaken, *b* he was wroth ... Ps 18:7 3588
me, *b* he delighted in me ... Ps 18:19 3588
a plain path, *b* of mine enemies ... Ps 27:11 4616
B they regard not the works of ... Ps 28:5 3588
b he hath heard the voice of my ... Ps 28:6 3588
faileth *b* of mine iniquity ... Ps 31:10
b we have trusted in his holy ... Ps 33:21 3588
Fret not thyself *b* of evildoers ... Ps 37:1
fret not thyself *b* of him who ... Ps 37:7
b of the man who bringeth wicked ... Ps 37:7
and save them, *b* they trust in him ... Ps 37:40 3588
in my flesh *b* of thine anger ... Ps 38:3 6440
any rest in my bones *b* of my sin ... Ps 38:3 6440
are corrupt *b* of my foolishness ... Ps 38:5 6440
b I follow the thing that good is ... Ps 38:20 8478
b thou didst it ... Ps 39:9 3588
b mine enemy doth not triumph ... Ps 41:11 3588
why go I mourning *b* of the ... Ps 42:9
Why go I mourning *b* of the ... Ps 43:2
b thou hadst a favour unto them ... Ps 44:3 3588
ride prosperously *b* of truth ... Ps 45:4
Judah be glad, *b* of thy judgments ... Ps 48:11 4616
for ever, *b* thou hast done it ... Ps 52:9 3588
shame, *b* God hath despised them ... Ps 53:5 3588
B of the voice of the enemy, ... Ps 55:3
b of the oppression of the wicked ... Ps 55:3 6440
B they have no changes, therefore ... Ps 55:19 834
B of his strength will I wait ... Ps 59:9
may be displayed *b* of the truth ... Ps 60:4 6440
Philistia, triumph thou *b* of me ... Ps 60:8 5921
B thy lovingkindness is better ... Ps 63:3 3588
B thou hast been my help, ... Ps 63:7 3588
B of thy temple at Jerusalem ... Ps 68:29
B for thy sake I have borne ... Ps 69:7 3588
deliver me *b* of mine enemies ... Ps 69:18 4616
B they believed not in God, and ... Ps 78:22 3588
b thou, LORD, hast holpen me, and ... Ps 86:17 3588
B thou hast made the LORD, which ... Ps 91:9 3588
B he hath set his love upon me, ... Ps 91:14 3588
on high, *b* he hath known my name ... Ps 91:14 3588
Judah rejoiced *b* of thy judgments ... Ps 97:8 4616
B of thine indignation and thy ... Ps 102:10 6440
B they provoked his spirit, so ... Ps 106:33 3588
B they rebelled against the words ... Ps 107:11 3588
b of their transgression, and ... Ps 107:17 1870
b of their iniquities, are ... Ps 107:17
their soul is melted *b* of trouble ... Ps 107:26
are they glad *b* they be quiet ... Ps 107:30 3588
B that he remembered not to shew ... Ps 109:16 3282
b thy mercy is good, deliver thou ... Ps 109:21 3588
b he hath heard my voice and my ... Ps 116:1 3588
B he hath inclined his ear unto ... Ps 116:2 3588
b his mercy endureth for ever ... Ps 118:1 3588
b of the wicked that forsake thy ... Ps 119:53 3588
This I had, *b* I kept thy precepts ... Ps 119:56 3588
thee *b* of thy righteous judgments ... Ps 119:62 5921
b I have hoped in thy word ... Ps 119:74 3588
ancients, *b* I keep thy precepts ... Ps 119:100 3588
eyes, *b* they keep not thy law ... Ps 119:136 5921
b mine enemies have forgotten thy ... Ps 119:139 3588
b they kept not thy word ... Ps 119:158 834
thee *b* of thy righteous judgments ... Ps 119:164 5921
B of the house of the LORD our ... Ps 122:9 4616
B I have called, and ye refused ... Prov 1:24 3282
b they refuse to do judgment ... Prov 21:7 3588
Rob not the poor, *b* he is poor ... Prov 22:22 3588
son, eat thou honey, *b* it is good ... Prov 24:13 3588
Fret not thyself *b* of evil men ... Prov 24:19
b the work that is wrought under ... Eccl 2:17 3588
b I should leave it unto the man ... Eccl 2:18
b they have a good reward for ... Eccl 4:9 834
b God answereth him in the joy of ... Eccl 5:20 3588
B to every purpose there is time ... Eccl 8:6 3588
B sentence against an evil work ... Eccl 8:11 834
b he feareth not before God ... Eccl 8:13 834
b a man hath no better thing ... Eccl 8:15 834
b though a man labour to seek it ... Eccl 8:17 834
b he knoweth not how to go to the ... Eccl 10:15 834
the grinders cease *b* they are few ... Eccl 12:3 3588
b man goeth to his long home, and ... Eccl 12:5 3588
b the preacher was wise, he still ... Eccl 12:9
B of the savour of thy good ... Song 1:3
b I am black, *b* the sun ... Song 1:6
his thigh *b* of fear in the night ... Song 3:8
b they be replenished from the ... Is 2:6 3588
b their tongue and their doings ... Is 3:8 3588
B the daughters of Zion are ... Is 3:16
b they have no knowledge ... Is 5:13
b they have cast away the law of ... Is 5:24 3588
b I am a man of unclean lips, and ... Is 6:5 3588
B Syria, Ephraim, and the son of ... Is 7:5
b all the land shall become ... Is 7:24 3588

it is *b* there is no light in them	Is 8:20	834
be destroyed *b* of the anointing	Is 10:27	6440
b thou hast destroyed thy land,	Is 14:20	3588
b the rod of him that smote thee	Is 14:29	3588
B in the night Ar of Moab is laid	Is 15:1	3588
b in the night Kir of Moab is	Is 15:1	3588
which they left *b* of the children	Is 17:9	6440
B thou hast forgotten the God of	Is 17:10	3588
fear *b* of the shaking of the hand	Is 19:16	6440
b of the counsel of the LORD of	Is 19:17	6440
unto the LORD *b* of the oppressors	Is 19:20	6440
b of the spoiling of the daughter	Is 22:4	5921
b they have transgressed the laws	Is 24:5	3588
b he trusteth in thee	Is 26:3	3588
B ye have said, We have made a	Is 28:15	3588
b he will not ever be threshing	Is 28:28	3588
B ye despise this word, and trust	Is 30:12	3282
in chariots, *b* they are many	Is 31:1	3588
horsemen, *b* they are very strong	Is 31:1	3588
B the palaces shall be forsaken	Is 32:14	3588
B thy rage against me, and thy	Is 37:29	3282
b the spirit of the LORD bloweth	Is 40:7	3588
b I give waters in the wilderness	Is 43:20	3588
B I knew that thou art obstinate,	Is 48:4	
b of the LORD that is faithful,	Is 49:7	4616
b there is no water, and dieth for	Is 50:2	
b of the fury of the oppressor	Is 51:13	6440
b he had done no violence,	Is 53:9	5921
b he hath poured out his soul	Is 53:12	
unto thee *b* of the LORD thy God	Is 55:5	4616
b the abundance of the sea shall	Is 60:5	3588
Israel, *b* he hath glorified thee	Is 60:9	3588
b the LORD hath anointed me to	Is 61:1	3282
consumed us, *b* of our iniquities	Is 64:7	3027
b when I called, ye did not	Is 65:12	3282
b the former troubles are	Is 65:16	3588
b they are hid from mine eyes	Is 65:16	3588
b when I called, none did answer	Is 66:4	3282
B I am innocent, surely his anger	Jer 2:35	3588
b thou sayest, I have not sinned	Jer 2:35	5921
it *b* of the evil of your doings	Jer 4:4	6440
b she hath been rebellious	Jer 4:17	3588
b it is bitter, *b* it	Jer 4:18	3588
b thou hast heard, O my soul, the	Jer 4:19	3588
b I have spoken it, I have	Jer 4:28	
my soul is wearied *b* of murderers	Jer 4:31	
b their transgressions are many,	Jer 5:6	3588
B ye speak this word, behold, I	Jer 5:14	3282
b they have not hearkened unto my	Jer 6:19	
b the LORD hath rejected them	Jer 6:30	3588
b ye have done all these works,	Jer 7:13	3282
b we have sinned against the LORD	Jer 8:14	3588
b of them that dwell in a far	Jer 8:19	
b they are burned up, so that	Jer 9:10	3588
B they have forsaken my law which	Jer 9:13	5921
b we have forsaken the land,	Jer 9:19	3588
b our dwellings have cast us out	Jer 9:19	3588
needs be borne, *b* they cannot go	Jer 10:5	3588
b they said, He shall not see our	Jer 12:4	3588
b no man layeth it to heart	Jer 12:11	3588
be ashamed of your revenues *b* of	Jer 12:13	
b the LORD's flock is carried	Jer 13:17	3588
b thou hast forgotten me, and	Jer 13:25	834
B the ground is chapt, for there	Jer 14:4	5668
forsook it, *b* there was no grass	Jer 14:5	3588
did fail, *b* there was no grass	Jer 14:6	3588
of Jerusalem *b* of the famine	Jer 14:16	6440
b of Manasseh the son of Hezekiah	Jer 15:4	1558
I sat alone *b* of thy hand	Jer 15:17	6440
B your fathers have forsaken me,	Jer 16:11	
b they have defiled my land, they	Jer 16:18	5921
b they have forsaken the LORD,	Jer 17:13	3588
B my people hath forgotten me,	Jer 18:15	3588
B they have forsaken me, and have	Jer 19:4	
hiss *b* of all the plagues thereof	Jer 19:8	5921
b of all the houses upon whose	Jer 19:13	3605
b they have hardened their necks,	Jer 19:15	3588
b the word of the LORD was made a	Jer 20:8	3588
B he slew me not from the womb	Jer 20:17	834
b of the evil of your doings	Jer 21:12	6440
B they have forsaken the covenant	Jer 22:9	
b thou closest thyself in cedar	Jer 22:15	3588
me is broken *b* of the prophets	Jer 23:9	
b of the LORD	Jer 23:9	6440
b of the words of his holiness	Jer 23:9	3588
for *b* of swearing the land	Jer 23:10	6440
B ye say this word, The burden of	Jer 23:38	3282
B ye have not heard my words,	Jer 25:8	
b of the sword that I will send	Jer 25:16	6440
b of the sword which I will send	Jer 25:27	6440
habitations are cut down *b* of the	Jer 25:37	6440
b of the fierceness of the	Jer 25:38	6440
and *b* of his fierce anger	Jer 25:38	6440
b of the evil of their doings	Jer 26:3	6440
b thou hast taught rebellion	Jer 28:16	3588
B ye have said, The LORD hath	Jer 29:15	3588
B they have not hearkened to my	Jer 29:19	
B they have committed villany in	Jer 29:23	
B thou hast sent letters in thy	Jer 29:25	
B that Shemaiah hath prophesied	Jer 29:31	
b he hath taught rebellion	Jer 29:32	3588
b thy sins were increased	Jer 30:14	
b thy sins were increased, I have	Jer 30:15	
b they called thee an Outcast,	Jer 30:17	3588
for her children, *b* they were not	Jer 31:15	3588
b I did bear the reproach of my	Jer 31:19	3588
b of the sword, and of the famine,	Jer 32:24	6440
B of all the evil of the children	Jer 32:32	5921
B the sons of Jonadab the son of	Jer 35:16	3588
b I have spoken unto them, but	Jer 35:17	3282
B ye have obeyed the commandment	Jer 35:18	
b thou hast put thy trust in me,	Jer 39:18	3588
b ye have sinned against the LORD	Jer 40:3	3588
whom he had slain *b* of Gedaliah	Jer 41:9	3027
B of the Chaldeans	Jer 41:18	6440
b Ishmael the son of Nethaniah	Jer 41:18	3588
B of their wickedness which they	Jer 44:3	6440
b of the evil of your doings, and	Jer 44:22	6440
b of the abominations which ye	Jer 44:22	6440
B ye have burned incense, and	Jer 44:23	
b ye have sinned against the LORD	Jer 44:23	834
b the LORD did drive them	Jer 46:15	3588
b the day of their calamity was	Jer 46:21	3588
b they are more than the	Jer 46:23	3588
B of the day that cometh to spoil	Jer 47:4	5921
For *b* thou hast trusted in thy	Jer 48:7	
b the riches that he hath gotten	Jer 48:36	
b he hath magnified himself	Jer 48:42	
shadow of Heshbon *b* of the force	Jer 48:45	
b they have sinned against the	Jer 50:7	
B ye were glad, *b* ye rejoiced	Jer 50:11	3588
b ye are grown fat as the heifer	Jer 50:11	3588
B of the wrath of the LORD it	Jer 50:13	
b thou hast striven against the	Jer 50:24	3588
b it is the vengeance of the LORD	Jer 51:11	3588
b we have heard reproach	Jer 51:51	3588
B the LORD hath spoiled Babylon,	Jer 51:55	3588
B the spoiler is come upon her,	Jer 51:56	3588
into captivity *b* of affliction	Lam 1:3	
and *b* of great servitude	Lam 1:3	
b none come to the solemn feasts	Lam 1:4	
b they have seen her nakedness	Lam 1:8	3588
b the comforter that should	Lam 1:16	3588
desolate, *b* the enemy prevailed	Lam 1:16	3588
b the children and the sucklings	Lam 2:11	
b his compassions fail not	Lam 3:22	3588
b he hath borne it upon him	Lam 3:28	3588
Mine eye affecteth mine heart *b*	Lam 3:51	
with the peril of our lives *b* of	Lam 5:9	6440
an oven *b* of the terrible famine	Lam 5:10	6440
B of the mountain of Zion, which	Lam 5:18	5921
b thou hast not given him warning	Eze 3:20	3588
shall surely live, *b* he is warned	Eze 3:21	3588
B ye multiplied more than the	Eze 5:7	3282
b of all thine abominations	Eze 5:9	3282
b thou hast defiled my sanctuary	Eze 5:11	3282
b I am broken with their whorish	Eze 6:9	834
b it is the stumblingblock of	Eze 7:19	3588
b of the violence of all them	Eze 12:19	
B ye have spoken vanity, and seen	Eze 13:8	3282
B, even *b* they have seduced	Eze 13:10	3282
B with lies ye have made the	Eze 13:22	3282
b they are all estranged from me	Eze 14:5	834
may pass through *b* of the beasts	Eze 14:15	6440
b they have committed a trespass,	Eze 15:8	3282
the harlot *b* of thy renown	Eze 16:15	5921
Assyrians, *b* thou wast unsatiable	Eze 16:28	1115
B thy filthiness was poured out,	Eze 16:36	3282
B thou hast not remembered the	Eze 16:43	
thy mouth any more *b* of thy shame	Eze 16:63	6440
b he cruelly oppressed, spoiled	Eze 18:18	3588
B he considereth, and turneth away	Eze 18:28	
B they despised my judgments, and	Eze 20:16	3282
B they had not executed my	Eze 20:24	3282
b it cometh	Eze 21:7	3588
B it is a trial, and what if the	Eze 21:13	3588
B ye have made your iniquity to	Eze 21:24	3282
b, I say, that ye are come to	Eze 21:24	3282
to consume *b* of the glittering	Eze 21:28	4616
B ye are all become dross, behold	Eze 22:19	3282
b thou hast gone a whoring after	Eze 23:30	
b thou art polluted with their	Eze 23:30	
B thou hast forgotten me, and cast	Eze 23:35	3282
b they are adulteresses, and blood	Eze 23:45	3588
b I have purged thee, and thou	Eze 24:13	3282
B thou saidst, Aha, against my	Eze 25:3	3282
B thou hast clapped thine hands,	Eze 25:6	3282
B that Moab and Seir do say,	Eze 25:8	3282
B that Edom hath dealt against	Eze 25:12	3282
B the Philistines have dealt by	Eze 25:15	3282
b that Tyrus hath said against	Eze 26:2	3282
B thine heart is lifted up, and	Eze 28:2	3282
is lifted up *b* of thy riches	Eze 28:5	
B thou hast set thine heart as	Eze 28:6	3282
was lifted up *b* of thy beauty	Eze 28:17	
b they have been a staff of reed	Eze 29:6	3282
b he hath said, The river is mine	Eze 29:9	3282
b they wrought for me, saith the	Eze 29:20	834
his branches became long *b* of the	Eze 31:5	
B thou hast lifted up thyself in	Eze 31:10	
laid the land most desolate *b* of	Eze 33:29	5921
scattered, *b* there is no shepherd	Eze 34:5	
surely *b* my flock became a prey,	Eze 34:8	3282
b there was no shepherd, neither	Eze 34:8	
B ye have thrust with side and	Eze 34:21	3282
B thou hast had a perpetual	Eze 35:5	3588
B thou hast said, These two	Eze 35:10	3282
b it was desolate, so will I do	Eze 35:15	
B the enemy hath said against you	Eze 36:2	3282
B they have made you desolate, and	Eze 36:3	3282
b ye have borne the shame of the	Eze 36:6	3282
B they say unto you, Thou land	Eze 36:13	3282
b they trespassed against me,	Eze 39:23	
b the LORD, the God of Israel,	Eze 44:2	3588
b of all your abominations	Eze 44:7	413
B they ministered unto them	Eze 44:12	
b these waters shall come thither	Eze 47:9	3588
b their waters they they issued	Eze 47:12	3588
b ye see the thing is gone from	Dan 2:8	
Therefore *b* the king's	Dan 3:22	
b there is no other God that can	Dan 3:29	
b I know that the spirit of the	Dan 4:9	1768
b an excellent spirit was in him	Dan 6:3	
him, *b* he believed in his God	Dan 6:23	1768
I beheld then *b* of the voice of	Dan 7:11	4481
b of their trespass that they	Dan 9:7	
b we have sinned against thee	Dan 9:8	834
b we have sinned against him	Dan 9:11	3588
b for our sins, and for the	Dan 9:16	3588
b it is yet for a time appointed	Dan 11:35	
b there is no truth, nor mercy,	Hos 4:1	3588
b thou hast rejected knowledge, I	Hos 4:6	3588
b they have left off to take heed	Hos 4:10	3588
b the shadow thereof is good	Hos 4:13	3588
be ashamed *b* of their sacrifices	Hos 4:19	
b ye have been a snare on Mizpah,	Hos 5:1	3588
b he willingly walked after the	Hos 5:11	3588
b they have transgressed against	Hos 7:13	3588
b they have transgressed my	Hos 8:1	3588
B Ephraim hath made many altars	Hos 8:11	3282
they are gone *b* of destruction	Hos 9:6	
b they did not hearken unto him	Hos 9:17	3588
no king, *b* we feared not the LORD	Hos 10:3	3588
of Samaria shall fear *b* of the	Hos 10:5	
thereof, *b* it is departed from it	Hos 10:5	3588
b thou didst trust in thy way, in	Hos 10:13	3588
you *b* of your great wickedness	Hos 10:15	6440
king, *b* they refused to return	Hos 11:5	3588
them, *b* of their own counsels	Hos 11:6	
of wine, *b* of the new wine	Joel 1:5	5921
b the harvest of the field is	Joel 1:11	3588
b joy is withered away from the	Joel 1:12	3588
perplexed, *b* they have no pasture	Joel 1:18	3588
b he hath done great things	Joel 2:20	3588
B ye have taken my silver and my	Joel 3:5	834
b they have shed innocent blood	Joel 3:19	834
b they have threshed Gilead with	Amos 1:3	5921
b they carried away captive the	Amos 1:6	5921
b they delivered up the whole	Amos 1:9	5921
b he did pursue his brother with	Amos 1:11	5921
b they have ripped up the women	Amos 1:13	5921
b he burned the bones of the king	Amos 2:1	5921
b they have despised the law of	Amos 2:4	5921
b they sold the righteous for	Amos 2:6	5921
b I will do this unto thee,	Amos 4:12	
of the LORD, *b* he had told them	Jonah 1:10	3588
b it is in the power of their	Mic 2:1	3588
b it is polluted, it shall	Mic 2:10	5668
thee desolate *b* of thy sins	Mic 6:13	5921
b I have sinned against him,	Mic 7:9	3588
b of them that dwell therein	Mic 7:13	5921
our God, and shall fear *b* of thee	Mic 7:17	
ever, *b* he delighteth in mercy	Mic 7:18	3588
B of the multitude of the	Nah 3:4	
seek strength *b* of the enemy	Nah 3:11	
b by them their portion is fat,	Hab 1:16	3588
b it will surely come, it will	Hab 2:3	3588
b he transgresseth by wine, he is	Hab 2:5	3588
B thou hast spoiled many nations,	Hab 2:8	3588
b of men's blood, and for the	Hab 2:8	3588
b of men's blood, and for the	Hab 2:17	
b they have sinned against the	Zeph 1:17	3588
b they have reproached and	Zeph 2:10	3588
be haughty *b* of my holy mountain	Zeph 3:11	
B of mine house that is waste, and	Hag 1:9	3282
or came in *b* of the affliction	Zec 8:10	4480
about mine house *b* of the army	Zec 9:8	
b of him that passeth by	Zec 9:8	
and *b* of him that returneth	Zec 9:8	
troubled, *b* there was no shepherd	Zec 10:2	3588
b the LORD is with them, and the	Zec 10:5	3588
b the mighty are spoiled	Zec 11:2	834
b ye do not lay it to heart	Mal 2:2	3588
B the LORD hath been witness	Mal 2:14	
not be comforted, *b* they are not	Mt 2:18	*3754*
b thou canst not make one hair	Mt 5:36	*3754*
B strait is the gate, and narrow	Mt 7:14	*3754*
b they fainted, and were scattered	Mt 9:36	*3754*
were done, *b* they repented not	Mt 11:20	*3754*
b thou hast hid these things from	Mt 11:25	*3754*
b they repented at the preaching	Mt 12:41	*3754*
b they had no deepness of earth	Mt 13:5	*1223*
b they had no root, they withered	Mt 13:6	*1223*
B it is given unto you to know	Mt 13:11	*3754*
b they seeing see not	Mt 13:13	*3754*
persecution ariseth *b* of the word	Mt 13:21	*1223*
works there *b* of their unbelief	Mt 13:58	*1223*
b they counted him as a prophet	Mt 14:5	*3754*
b they continue with me now three	Mt 15:32	*3754*
It is *b* we have taken no bread	Mt 16:7	*3754*
b ye have brought no bread	Mt 16:8	*3754*
unto them, *B* of your unbelief	Mt 17:20	*1223*
Woe unto the world *b* of offences	Mt 18:7	*575*
that debt, *b* thou desiredst me	Mt 18:32	*1893*
Moses *b* of the hardness of your	Mt 19:8	*4314*
unto him, *B* no man hath hired us	Mt 20:7	*3754*
Is thine eye evil, *b* I am good	Mt 20:15	*3754*
b they should hold their peace	Mt 20:31	*2443*
b they took him for a prophet	Mt 21:46	*1894*
b ye build the tombs of the	Mt 23:29	*3754*
b iniquity shall abound, the love	Mt 24:12	*1223*
be offended *b* of me this night	Mt 26:31	*1722*
men shall be offended *b* of thee	Mt 26:33	*1722*
b it is the price of blood	Mt 27:6	*1893*
this day in a dream *b* of him	Mt 27:19	*1223*
devils to speak, *b* they knew him	Mk 1:34	*3754*
wait on him *b* of the multitude	Mk 3:9	*1223*
B they said, He hath an unclean	Mk 3:30	*3754*
b it had no depth of earth	Mk 4:5	*1223*
b it had no root, it withered	Mk 4:6	*1223*
the sickle, *b* the harvest is come	Mk 4:29	*3754*
B that he had been often bound	Mk 5:4	*1223*
he marvelled *b* of their unbelief	Mk 6:6	*1223*
b they were as sheep not having a	Mk 6:34	*3754*
B it entereth not into his heart,	Mk 7:19	*3754*
b they have now been with me	Mk 8:2	*3754*
saying, It is *b* we have no bread	Mk 8:16	*3754*
Why reason ye, *b* ye have no bread	Mk 8:17	*3754*
forbad him, *b* he followeth not us	Mk 9:38	*3754*
b ye belong to Christ, verily I	Mk 9:41	*3754*
b all the people was astonished	Mk 11:18	*3754*
b ye know not the scriptures,	Mk 12:24	*3754*

be offended *b* of me this night Mk 14:27 *1722*
b it was the preparation, that is Mk 15:42 *1893*
b they believed not them which Mk 16:14 *3754*
b that Elisabeth was barren, and Lk 1:7 *2530*
b thou believest not my words, Lk 1:20
(*b* he was of the house and lineage Lk 2:4 *1223*
b there was no room for them in Lk 2:7 *1360*
b he hath anointed me to preach Lk 4:18
bring him in *b* of the multitude Lk 5:19 *1223*
away, *b* it lacked moisture Lk 8:6 *1223*
b many devils were entered into Lk 8:30 *3754*
b that it was said of some, that Lk 9:7 *1223*
b he followeth not with us Lk 9:49 *3754*
b his face was as though he would Lk 9:53 *3754*
b your names are written in Lk 10:20 *3754*
b he is his friend, yet *b* Lk 11:8 *1223*
b ye say that I cast out devils Lk 11:18 *3754*
b I have no room where to bestow Lk 12:17 *3754*
b they suffered such things Lk 13:2 *3754*
b that Jesus had healed on the Lk 13:14 *3754*
b he hath received him safe and Lk 15:27 *3754*
steward, *b* he had done wisely Lk 16:8 *3754*
Doth he thank that servant *b* he Lk 17:9 *3754*
Yet *b* this widow troubleth me, I Lk 18:5 *1223*
b he was little of stature Lk 19:3 *3754*
b he was nigh to Jerusalem, and Lk 19:11 *1223*
b they thought that the kingdom Lk 19:11
b thou hast been faithful in a Lk 19:17 *3754*
b thou art an austere man Lk 19:21 *3754*
B the Lord hath need of him Lk 19:31 *3754*
b thou knewest not the time of Lk 19:44
b he had heard many things of him Lk 23:8 *1223*
B I said unto thee, I saw thee Jn 1:50 *3754*
unto them, *b* he knew all men, Jn 2:24 *1223*
b he hath not believed in the Jn 3:18 *3754*
light, *b* their deeds were evil Jn 3:19 *1063*
b there was much water there Jn 3:23 *3754*
rejoiceth greatly *b* of the Jn 3:29 *1223*
more believed *b* of his own word Jn 4:41 *1223*
we believe, not *b* of thy saying Jn 4:42 *1223*
b he had done these things on the Jn 5:16 *3754*
b he not only had broken the Jn 5:18 *3754*
also, *b* he is the Son of man Jn 5:27 *3754*
b I seek not mine own will, but Jn 5:30 *3754*
b they saw his miracles which he Jn 6:2 *3754*
not *b* ye saw the miracles, but Jn 6:26 *3754*
but *b* ye did eat of the loaves, Jn 6:26 *3754*
b he said, I am the bread which Jn 6:41 *3754*
b the Jews sought to kill him Jn 7:1 *3754*
b I testify of it, that the works Jn 7:7 *3754*
(not *b* it is of Moses, but of the Jn 7:22 *3754*
b I have made a man every whit Jn 7:23 *3754*
b his hour was not yet come Jn 7:30 *3754*
b that Jesus was not yet Jn 7:39 *3754*
among the people *b* of him Jn 7:43 *1223*
b he saith, Whither I go, ye Jn 8:22 *3754*
b my word hath no place in you Jn 8:37 *3754*
even *b* ye cannot hear my word Jn 8:43 *3754*
b there is no truth in him Jn 8:44 *3754*
b I tell you the truth, ye Jn 8:45 *3754*
them not, *b* ye are not of God Jn 8:47 *3754*
b he keepeth not the sabbath day Jn 9:16 *3754*
parents, *b* they feared the Jews Jn 9:22 *3754*
b he is an hireling, and careth Jn 10:13 *3754*
b I lay down my life, that I Jn 10:17 *3754*
b ye are not of my sheep, as I Jn 10:26 *1063*
b that thou, being a man, makest Jn 10:33 *3754*
b I said, I am the Son of God Jn 10:36 *3754*
b he seeth the light of this Jn 11:9 *3754*
b there is no light in him Jn 11:10 *3754*
but *b* of the people which stand Jn 11:42 *1223*
but *b* he was a thief, and had the Jn 12:6 *3754*
B that by reason of him many of Jn 12:11 *3754*
said, This voice came not *b* of me Jn 12:30 *1223*
b that Esaias said again, Jn 12:39 *3754*
but *b* of the Pharisees they did Jn 12:42 *1223*
b Judas had the bag, that Jesus Jn 13:29 *1893*
b I go unto my Father Jn 14:12 *3754*
b it seeth him not, neither Jn 14:17 *3754*
b I live, ye shall live also Jn 14:19 *3754*
b I said, I go unto the Father Jn 14:28 *3754*
but *b* ye are not of the world, Jn 15:19 *3754*
b they know not him that sent me Jn 15:21 *3754*
b ye have been with me from the Jn 15:27 *3754*
b they have not known the Father, Jn 16:3 *3754*
the beginning, *b* I was with you Jn 16:4 *3754*
But *b* I have said these things Jn 16:6 *3754*
Of sin, *b* they believe not on me Jn 16:9 *3754*
b I go to my Father, and ye see me Jn 16:10 *3754*
b the prince of this world is Jn 16:11 *3754*
see me, *b* I go to the Father Jn 16:16 *3754*
and, *B* I go to the Father Jn 16:17 *3754*
hath sorrow, *b* her hour is come Jn 16:21 *3754*
b ye have loved me, and have Jn 16:27 *3754*
alone, *b* the Father is with me Jn 16:32 *3754*
b they are not of the world, even Jn 17:14 *3754*
b he made himself the Son of God Jn 19:7 *3754*
b it was the preparation, that Jn 19:31 *1893*
b of the Jews' preparation day Jn 19:42 *1223*
B they have taken away my Lord, Jn 20:13 *3754*
b thou hast seen me, thou hast Jn 20:29 *3754*
Peter was grieved *b* he said unto Jn 21:17 *3754*
b that every man heard them speak Acts 2:6 *3754*
b it was not possible that he Acts 2:24 *2530*
B thou wilt not leave my soul in Acts 2:27 *3754*
punish them, *b* of the people Acts 4:21 *1223*
b their widows were neglected in Acts 6:1 *3754*
b that of long time he had Acts 8:11 *1223*
b thou hast thought that the gift Acts 8:20 *3754*
b that on the Gentiles also was Acts 10:45 *3754*
b he saw it pleased the Jews, he Acts 12:3
b their country was nourished by Acts 12:20 *1223*
b he gave not God the glory Acts 12:23
b they knew him not, nor yet the Acts 13:27

b he was the chief speaker Acts 14:12 *1894*
circumcised him *b* of the Jews Acts 16:3 *1223*
b he preached unto them Jesus, and Acts 17:18 *3754*
B he hath appointed a day, in the Acts 17:31 *1360*
(*b* that Claudius had commanded Acts 18:2 *1223*
b he was of the same craft, he Acts 18:3 *1223*
b he would not spend the time in Acts 20:16 *3704*
a Roman, and *b* he had bound him Acts 22:29 *3754*
b he would have known the Acts 22:30
B that thou mayest understand, Acts 24:11
b I doubted of such manner of Acts 25:20
b I shall answer for myself this Acts 26:2
Especially *b* I know thee to be Acts 26:3
b the winds were contrary Acts 27:4 *1223*
b the fast was now already past, Acts 27:9 *1223*
b the haven was not commodious to Acts 27:12
b of the present rain, and *b* Acts 28:2 *1223*
b there was no cause of death in Acts 28:18 *1223*
b that for the hope of Israel I Acts 28:20 *1063*
B that which may be known of God Rom 1:19 *1360*
B that, when they knew God, they Rom 1:21 *1360*
b that unto them were committed Rom 3:2 *3754*
B the law worketh wrath Rom 4:15 *1063*
b the love of God is shed abroad Rom 5:5 *3754*
b we are not under the law, but Rom 6:15 *3754*
b of the infirmity of your flesh Rom 6:19 *1223*
B the carnal mind is enmity Rom 8:7 *1360*
in you, the body is dead *b* of sin Rom 8:10 *1223*
Spirit is life *b* of righteousness Rom 8:10 *1223*
B the creature itself also shall Rom 8:21 *3754*
b he maketh intercession for the Rom 8:27 *3754*
b they are the seed of Abraham, Rom 9:7 *3754*
b a short work will the Lord make Rom 9:28 *3754*
B they sought it not by faith, Rom 9:32 *3754*
b of unbelief they were broken Rom 11:20
he eat, *b* he eateth not of faith Rom 14:23 *3754*
b of the grace that is given to Rom 15:15 *1223*
B the foolishness of God is wiser 1Cor 1:25 *3754*
b they are spiritually discerned 1Cor 2:14 *3754*
b it shall be revealed by fire 1Cor 3:13 *3754*
b ye go to law one with another 1Cor 6:7 *3754*
power on her head *b* of the angels 1Cor 11:10 *1223*
B I am not the hand, I am not of 1Cor 12:15 *3754*
B I am not the eye, I am not of 1Cor 12:16 *3754*
b I persecuted the church of God 1Cor 15:9 *1360*
b we have testified of God that 1Cor 15:15 *3754*
b I found not Titus my brother 2Cor 2:13
b we thus judge, that if one died 2Cor 5:14
b his spirit was refreshed by you 2Cor 7:13 *3754*
b I have preached to you the 2Cor 11:7 *3754*
b I love you not 2Cor 11:11 *3754*
that *b* of false brethren unawares Gal 2:4 *1223*
the face, *b* he was to be blamed Gal 2:11 *3754*
It was added *b* of transgressions, Gal 3:19 *5484*
b ye are sons, God hath sent Gal 4:6 *3754*
enemy, *b* I tell you the truth Gal 4:16
b of the blindness of their heart Eph 4:18 *1223*
for *b* of these things cometh the Eph 5:6 *1223*
the time, *b* the days are evil Eph 5:16 *3754*
you all, *b* I have you in my heart Phil 1:7 *1223*
b that ye had heard that he had Phil 2:26 *1360*
B for the work of Christ he was Phil 2:30 *3754*
Not *b* I desire a gift Phil 4:17 *3754*
own souls, *b* ye were dear unto us 1Th 2:8 *1360*
b we would not be chargeable unto 1Th 2:9 *4314*
thank we God without ceasing, *b* 1Th 2:13 *3754*
b that the Lord is the avenger of 1Th 4:6 *1360*
b that your faith groweth 2Th 1:3 *3754*
in all them that believe (*b* our 2Th 1:10 *3754*
b they received not the love of 2Th 2:10
b God hath from the beginning 2Th 2:13 *3754*
Not *b* we have not power, but to 2Th 3:9 *3754*
b I did it ignorantly in unbelief 1Ti 1:13 *3754*
b we trust in the living God, who 1Ti 4:10 *3754*
b they have cast off their first 1Ti 5:12 *3754*
despise them, *b* they are brethren 1Ti 6:2 *3754*
b they are faithful and beloved, 1Ti 6:2 *3754*
b the bowels of the saints are Philem 7 *3754*
could not enter in *b* of unbelief Heb 3:19 *1223*
entered not in *b* of unbelief Heb 4:6 *1223*
b he could swear by no greater, Heb 6:13 *1893*
b they were not suffered to Heb 7:23 *1223*
b he continueth ever, hath an Heb 7:24 *1223*
b they continued not in my Heb 8:9 *3754*
b that the worshippers once Heb 10:2 *1223*
found, *b* God had translated him Heb 11:5 *1360*
b she judged him faithful who had Heb 11:11 *1893*
b they saw he was a proper child Heb 11:23 *1360*
b as the flower of the grass he Jas 1:10 *3754*
yet ye have not, *b* ye ask not Jas 4:2 *1223*
b ye ask amiss, that ye may Jas 4:3 *1360*
B it is written, Be ye holy 1Pet 1:16 *1360*
b Christ also suffered for us, 1Pet 2:21 *3754*
b your adversary the devil, as a 1Pet 5:8 *3754*
b the darkness is past, and the 1Jn 2:8 *3754*
b that darkness hath blinded his 1Jn 2:11 *3754*
b your sins are forgiven you for 1Jn 2:12 *3754*
b ye have known him that is from 1Jn 2:13 *3754*
b ye have overcome the wicked one 1Jn 2:13 *3754*
b ye have known the Father 1Jn 2:13 *3754*
b ye have known him that is from 1Jn 2:14 *3754*
b ye are strong, and the word of 1Jn 2:14 *3754*
unto you *b* ye know not the truth 1Jn 2:21 *3754*
but *b* ye know it, and that no lie 1Jn 2:21 *3754*
knoweth us not, *b* it knew him not 1Jn 3:1 *3754*
cannot sin, *b* he is born of God 1Jn 3:9 *3754*
B his own works were evil, and his 1Jn 3:12 *3754*
unto life, *b* we love the brethren 1Jn 3:14 *3754*
b he laid down his life for us 1Jn 3:16 *3754*
b we keep his commandments, and do 1Jn 3:22 *3754*
b many false prophets are gone 1Jn 4:1 *3754*
b greater is he that is in you, 1Jn 4:4 *3754*
b that God sent his only begotten 1Jn 4:9 *3754*
b he hath given us of his Spirit 1Jn 4:13 *3754*

b as he is, so are we in this 1Jn 4:17 *3754*
b fear hath torment 1Jn 4:18 *3754*
We love him, *b* he first loved us 1Jn 4:19 *3754*
witness, *b* the Spirit is truth 1Jn 5:6 *3754*
b he believeth not the record 1Jn 5:10 *3754*
B that for his name's sake they 3Jn 7 *1063*
in admiration *b* of advantage Jude 16 *5484*
of the earth shall wail *b* of him Rev 1:7 *1909*
b thou hast left thy first love Rev 2:4 *3754*
b thou hast there them that hold Rev 2:14 *3754*
b thou sufferest that woman Rev 2:20 *3754*
B thou hast kept the word of my Rev 3:10 *3754*
So then *b* thou art lukewarm, and Rev 3:16 *3754*
B thou sayest, I am rich, and Rev 3:17 *3754*
b no man was found worthy to open Rev 5:4 *3754*
waters, *b* they were made bitter Rev 8:11 *3754*
b these two prophets tormented Rev 11:10 *3754*
b thou hast taken to thee thy Rev 11:17 *3754*
b he knoweth that he hath but a Rev 12:12
b she made all nations drink of Rev 14:8 *3754*
shalt be, *b* thou hast judged thus Rev 16:5 *3754*
God of heaven *b* of their pains Rev 16:11 *1537*
men blasphemed God *b* of the Rev 16:21 *1537*

BECHER (*be'-ker*) See BACHRITES.
1. A son of Benjamin.
sons of Benjamin were Belah, and *B* Gen 46:21 1071
Bela, and *B*, and Jediael, three 1Chr 7:6 1071
And the sons of *B* 1Chr 7:8 1071
All these are the sons of *B* 1Chr 7:8 1071
2. A son of Ephraim.
of *B*, the family of the Bachrites Num 26:35 1071

BECHERITES See BACHRITES.

BECHORATH (*be-ko'-rath*) *An ancestor of King Saul.*
the son of Zeror, the son of *B* 1Sa 9:1 1064

BECKONED
for he *b* unto them, and remained Lk 1:22 *1269*
they *b* unto their partners, which Lk 5:7 *2656*
Simon Peter therefore *b* to him Jn 13:24 *3506*
Alexander *b* with the hand, and Acts 19:33 *2678*
b with the hand unto the people Acts 21:40 *2678*
governor had *b* unto him to speak Acts 24:10 *3506*

BECKONING
b unto them with the hand to hold Acts 12:17 *2678*
b with his hand said, Men of Acts 13:16 *2678*

BECOME
the man is *b* as one of us, to Gen 3:22 1961
the waters shall no more *b* a Gen 9:15 1961
Abraham shall surely *b* a great Gen 18:18 1961
and he is *b* great Gen 24:35 1431
and now I am *b* two bands Gen 32:10 1961
with you, and we will *b* one people Gen 34:16 1961
see what will *b* of his dreams Gen 37:20 1961
he also shall *b* a people, and he Gen 48:19 1961
his seed shall *b* a multitude of Gen 48:19 1961
shall *b* blood upon the dry land Ex 4:9 1961
Pharaoh, and it shall *b* a serpent Ex 7:9 1961
of water, that they may *b* blood Ex 7:19 1961
that it may *b* lice throughout all Ex 8:16 1961
it shall *b* small dust in all the Ex 9:9 1961
and song, and he is *b* my salvation Ex 15:2 1961
O LORD, is *b* glorious in power Ex 15:6 142
lest the land *b* desolate, and the Ex 23:29 1961
we wot not what is *b* of him Ex 32:1 1961
we wot not what is *b* of him Ex 32:23 1961
the land *b* full of wickedness Lev 19:29 4390
shall enter into her, and *b* bitter Num 5:24
b bitter, and her belly shall Num 5:27
this day thou art *b* the people of Deut 27:9 1961
thou shalt *b* an astonishment, a Deut 28:37 1961
our shoes are *b* old by reason of Josh 9:13 1086
go from me, and I shall *b* weak Judg 16:17 2470
from thee, and is *b* thine enemy 1Sa 28:16 1961
and thou, LORD, art *b* their God 2Sa 7:24 1961
about, and is *b* my brother's 1Kin 2:15 1961
thee what shall *b* of the child 1Kin 14:3 1961
and they shall *b* a prey and a spoil 2Kin 21:14 1961
that they should *b* a desolation 2Kin 22:19 1961
did, and what should *b* of her Est 2:11 6213
my skin is broken, and *b* loathsome Job 7:5 3988
which are ready to *b* heaps Job 15:28
b old, yea, are mighty in power Job 21:7 6275
I am *b* like dust and ashes Job 30:19 4911
Thou art *b* cruel to me Job 30:21 2015
they are all together *b* filthy Ps 14:3 444
I *b* like them that go down into Ps 28:1 4911
they are altogether *b* filthy Ps 53:3 444
and *b* not vain in robbery Ps 62:10 1891
I am *b* a stranger unto my Ps 69:8 1961
Let their table *b* a snare before Ps 69:22 1961
their welfare, let it *b* a trap Ps 69:22
We are *b* a reproach to our Ps 79:4 1961
and let his prayer *b* sin Ps 109:7 1961
and song, and is *b* my salvation Ps 118:14 1961
heard me, and art *b* my salvation Ps 118:21 1961
is *b* the head stone of the corner Ps 118:22 1961
For I am *b* like a bottle in the Ps 119:83 1961
have him *b* his son at the length Prov 29:21 1961
is the faithful city *b* an harlot Is 1:21 1961
Thy silver is *b* dross, thy wine Is 1:22 1961
all the land shall *b* briers Is 7:24 1961
he also is *b* my salvation Is 12:2 1961
thee, Art thou also *b* weak as we Is 14:10 2470
art thou *b* like unto us Is 14:10 4911
of Pharaoh is *b* brutish Is 19:11 1197
The princes of Zoan are *b* fools Is 19:13 2973
the vision of all is *b* unto you Is 29:11 1961
thereof shall *b* burning pitch Is 34:9 1961
the parched ground shall *b* a pool Is 35:7 1961
Their webs shall not *b* garments Is 59:6 1961
A little one shall *b* a thousand Is 60:22 1961

after vanity, and are *b* vain Jer 2:5 1891
b another man's, shall he return Jer 3:1 1961
And the prophets shall *b* wind Jer 5:13 1961
therefore they are *b* great Jer 5:27 6238
b a den of robbers in your eyes Jer 7:11 1961
For the pastors are *b* brutish Jer 10:21 1197
this house shall *b* a desolation Jer 22:5 1961
field, and Jerusalem shall *b* heaps Jer 26:18 1961
that Bozrah shall *b* a desolation Jer 49:13 1961
how is Babylon *b* a desolation Jer 50:23 1961
and they shall *b* as women Jer 50:37 1961
And Babylon shall *b* heaps, a Jer 51:37 1961
how is Babylon *b* an astonishment Jer 51:41 1961
how is she *b* as a widow Lam 1:1 1961
provinces, how is she *b* tributary Lam 1:1 1961
with her, they are *b* her enemies Lam 1:2 1961
her princes are *b* like harts that Lam 1:6 1961
for I am *b* vile Lam 1:11 1961
How is the gold *b* dim Lam 4:1 6004
daughter of my people is *b* cruel Lam 4:3
is withered, it is *b* like a stick Lam 4:8 1961
Thou art *b* guilty in thy blood Eze 22:4 816
house of Israel is to me *b* dross Eze 22:18 1961
Because ye are all *b* dross Eze 22:19 1961
it shall *b* a spoil to the nations Eze 26:5 1961
is *b* like the garden of Eden Eze 36:35 1961
and ruined cities are *b* fenced Eze 36:35
they shall *b* one in thine hand Eze 37:17 1961
king, that art grown and *b* strong Dan 4:22 8631
thy people are *b* a reproach to Dan 9:16
shall *b* strong with a small Dan 11:23 6105
And Ephraim said, Yet I am *b* rich Hos 12:8 6238
and his spring shall *b* dry Hos 13:15
Samaria shall *b* desolate Hos 13:16 816
see what would *b* of the city Jonah 4:5 1961
field, and Jerusalem shall *b* heaps Mic 3:12 1961
their goods shall *b* a booty Zeph 1:13 1961
how is she *b* a desolation, a Zeph 2:15 1961
Zerubbabel thou shalt *b* a plain Zec 4:7
b as little children, ye shall Mt 18:3 *1096*
the same is *b* the head of the Mt 21:42
will make you to *b* fishers of men Mk 1:17 *1096*
is *b* the head of the corner Mk 12:10
the same is *b* the head of the Lk 20:17
he power to *b* the sons of God Jn 1:12 *1096*
which is *b* the head of the corner Acts 4:11
we wot not what is *b* of him Acts 7:40 *1096*
the soldiers, what was *b* of Peter Acts 12:18 *1096*
they are together *b* unprofitable Rom 3:12 *889*
the world may *b* guilty before God Rom 3:19 *1096*
that he might *b* the father of Rom 4:18 *1096*
b servants to God, ye have your Rom 6:22 *1402*
ye also are *b* dead to the law by Rom 7:4 *2289*
might *b* exceeding sinful Rom 7:13 *1096*
in this world, let him *b* a fool 1Cor 3:18 *1096*
let him not *b* uncircumcised 1Cor 7:18 *1986*
b a stumblingblock to them that 1Cor 8:9 *1096*
I am *b* as sounding brass, or a 1Cor 13:1 *1096*
b the firstfruits of them that 1Cor 15:20 *1096*
behold, all things are *b* new 2Cor 5:17 *1096*
I am *b* a fool in glorying 2Cor 12:11 *1096*
Am I therefore *b* your enemy Gal 4:16 *1096*
Christ is *b* of no effect unto you Gal 5:4 *2673*
the things which *b* sound doctrine Titus 2:1 *4241*
b effectual by the acknowledging Philem 6 *1096*
are *b* such as have need of milk, Heb 5:12 *1096*
are *b* judges of evil thoughts Jas 2:4 *1096*
thou art *b* a transgressor of the Jas 2:11 *1096*
are *b* the kingdoms of our Lord Rev 11:15 *1096*
is *b* the habitation of devils, and Rev 18:2 *1096*

BECOMETH
holiness *b* thine house, O LORD Ps 93:5 4998
He *b* poor that dealeth with a Prov 10:4
Excellent speech *b* not a fool Prov 17:7 5000
b surety in the presence of his Prov 17:18 6148
is born in his kingdom *b* poor Eccl 4:14
for thus it *b* us to fulfil all Mt 3:15 *4241*
the word, and he *b* unfruitful Mt 13:22 *1096*
b a tree, so that the birds of Mt 13:32 *1096*
the word, and it *b* unfruitful Mk 4:19 *1096*
b greater than all herbs, and Mk 4:32 *1096*
as *b* saints, and that ye assist Rom 16:2 *516*
once named among you, as *b* saints Eph 5:3 *4241*
be as it *b* the gospel of Christ Phil 1:27 *516*
But (which *b* women professing 1Ti 2:10 *516*
be in behaviour as *b* holiness Titus 2:3 *2412*

BECORATH See BECHORATH.

BED
himself, and sat upon the *b* Gen 48:2 4296
thou wentest up to thy father's *b* Gen 49:4 4904
gathered up his feet into the *b* Gen 49:33 4296
thy bedchamber, and upon thy *b* Ex 8:3 4296
and he die not, but keepeth his *b* Ex 21:18 4904
Every *b*, whereon he lieth that Lev 15:4 4904
his *b* shall wash his clothes Lev 15:5 4904
her *b* shall wash his clothes Lev 15:21 4904
And if it be on her *b*, or on any Lev 15:23 4904
all the *b* whereon he lieth shall Lev 15:24 4904
Every *b* whereon she lieth all the Lev 15:26 4904
her as the *b* of her separation Lev 15:26 4904
an image, and laid it in the *b* 1Sa 19:13 4296
Bring him up to me in the *b* 1Sa 19:15 4296
there was an image in the *b* 1Sa 19:16 4296
from the earth, and sat upon the *b* 1Sa 28:23 4296
who lay on a *b* at noon 2Sa 4:5 4904
he lay on his *b* in his bedchamber 2Sa 4:7 4296
in his own house upon his *b* 2Sa 4:11 4904
that David arose from off his *b* 2Sa 11:2 4904
b with the servants of his lord 2Sa 11:13 4904
unto him, Lay thee down on thy *b* 2Sa 13:5 4904
the king bowed himself upon the *b* 1Kin 1:47 4904
abode, and laid him upon his own *b* 1Kin 17:19 4296
And he laid him down upon his *b* 1Kin 21:4 4296
that *b* on which thou art gone up 2Kin 1:4 4296
that *b* on which thou art gone up 2Kin 1:6 4296
that *b* on which thou art gone up 2Kin 1:16 4296
and let us set for him there a *b* 2Kin 4:10 4296
laid him on the *b* of the man of 2Kin 4:21 4296
was dead, and laid upon his *b* 2Kin 4:32 4296
as he defiled his father's *b* 1Chr 5:1 3326
laid him in the *b* which was 2Chr 16:14 4904
the priest, and slew him on his *b* 2Chr 24:25 4296
upon the *b* whereon Esther was Est 7:8 4296
My *b* shall comfort me, my couch Job 7:13 6210
I have made my *b* in the darkness Job 17:13 3326
men, in slumberings upon the *b* Job 33:15 4904
also with pain upon his *b* Job 33:19 4904
with your own heart upon your *b* Ps 4:4 4904
all the night make I my *b* to swim Ps 6:6 4296
He deviseth mischief upon his *b* Ps 36:4 4904
him upon the *b* of languishing Ps 41:3 6210
make all his *b* in his sickness Ps 41:3 4904
When I remember thee upon my *b* Ps 63:6 3326
of my house, nor go up into my *b* Ps 132:3
if I make my *b* in hell, behold, Ps 139:8 3331
I have decked my *b* with coverings Prov 7:16 6210
I have perfumed my *b* with myrrh Prov 7:17 4904
take away thy *b* from under thee Prov 22:27 4904
so doth the slothful upon his *b* Prov 26:14 4296
also our *b* is green Song 1:16 6210
By night on my *b* I sought him Song 3:1 4904
Behold his *b*, which is Solomon's Song 3:7 4296
His cheeks are as a *b* of spices Song 5:13 6170
For the *b* is shorter than that a Is 28:20 4702
high mountain hast thou set thy *b* Is 57:7 4904
thou hast enlarged thy *b*, and made Is 57:8 4904
thou lovedst their *b* where thou Is 57:8 4904
came to her into the *b* of love Eze 23:17 4904
And satest upon a stately *b* Eze 23:41 4296
They have set her a *b* in the Eze 32:25 4904
visions of thy head upon thy *b* Dan 2:28 4903
came into thy mind upon thy *b* Dan 2:29 4903
afraid, and the thoughts upon my *b* Dan 4:5 4903
the visions of mine head in my *b* Dan 4:10 4903
the visions of my head upon my *b* Dan 4:13 4903
and visions of his head upon his *b* Dan 7:1 4903
in Samaria in the corner of a *b* Amos 3:12 4296
sick of the palsy, lying on a *b* Mt 9:2 *2825*
the palsy,) Arise, take up thy *b* Mt 9:6 *2825*
they let down the *b* wherein the Mk 2:4 *2895*
to say, Arise, and take up thy *b* Mk 2:9 *2895*
thee, Arise, and take up thy *b* Mk 2:11 *2895*
he arose, took up the *b*, and went Mk 2:12 *2895*
put under a bushel, or under a *b* Mk 4:21 *2825*
and her daughter laid upon the *b* Mk 7:30 *2825*
men brought in a *b* a man which Lk 5:18 *2825*
a vessel, or putteth it under a *b* Lk 8:16 *2825*
and my children are with me in *b* Lk 11:7 *2845*
there shall be two men in one *b* Lk 17:34 *2825*
unto him, Rise, take up thy *b* Jn 5:8 *2895*
was made whole, and took up his *b* Jn 5:9 *2895*
lawful for thee to carry thy *b* Jn 5:10 *2895*
same said unto me, Take up thy *b* Jn 5:11 *2895*
said unto thee, Take up thy *b* Jn 5:12 *2895*
which had kept his *b* eight years Acts 9:33 *2895*
arise, and make thy *b* Acts 9:34 *4766*
in all, and the *b* undefiled Heb 13:4 *2845*
Behold, I will cast her into a *b* Rev 2:22 *2825*

BEDAD (*be'-dad*) *Father of Hadad.*
died, and Hadad the son of *B* Gen 36:35 911
was dead, Hadad the son of *B* 1Chr 1:46 911

BEDAN (*be'-dan*)
1. A judge of Israel.
And the LORD sent Jerubbaal, and *B* 1Sa 12:11 917
2. A descendant of Manasseh.
And the sons of Ulam; *B* 1Chr 7:17 917

BEDCHAMBER
into thine house, and into thy *b* Ex 8:3
house, he lay on his bed in his *b* 2Sa 4:7
words that thou speakest in thy *b* 2Kin 6:12
in the *b* from Athaliah, so that 2Kin 11:2
and put him and his nurse in a *b* 2Chr 22:11
and curse not the rich in thy *b* Eccl 10:20

BEDEIAH (*be-de'-yah*) *Married a foreign wife in exile.*
Benaiah, *B*, Chelluh, Ezr 10:35 912

BED'S
bowed himself upon the *b* head Gen 47:31 4296

BEDS
Brought *b*, and basons, and earthen 2Sa 17:28 4904
the *b* were of gold and silver, Est 1:6 4296
let them sing aloud upon their *b* Ps 149:5 4904
to the *b* of spices, to feed in Song 6:2 6170
they shall rest in their *b* Is 57:2 4904
when they howled upon their *b* Hos 7:14 4904
That lie upon *b* of ivory, and Amos 6:4 4296
and work evil upon their *b* Mic 2:1 4904
about in *b* those that were sick Mk 6:55 *2895*
the streets, and laid them on *b* Acts 5:15 *2825*

BEDSTEAD
his *b* was a *b* of iron Deut 3:11 6210

BEE
for the *b* that is in the land of Is 7:18 1682

BEELIADA (*be-e-li'-ad-ah*) *A son of David.*
And Elishama, and *B*, and Eliphalet 1Chr 14:7 1182

BEELZEBUB (*be-el'-ze-bub*) See BAAL-ZEBUB.
Chief of evil spirits.
called the master of the house *B* Mt 10:25 *954*
but by *B* the prince of the devils Mt 12:24 *954*
if I by *B* cast out devils, by Mt 12:27 *954*
from Jerusalem said, He hath *B* Mk 3:22 *954*
through *B* the chief of the devils Lk 11:15 *954*
that I cast out devils through *B* Lk 11:18 *954*
if I by *B* cast out devils, by Lk 11:19 *954*

BEELZEBULL See BEELZEBUB.

BEEN
his tent had *b* at the beginning Gen 13:3 1961
when he had *b* there a long time Gen 26:8
God of my father hath *b* with me Gen 31:5 1961
twenty years have I *b* with thee Gen 31:38
Thus have I *b* twenty years in thy Gen 31:41
had *b* with me, surely thou hadst Gen 31:42 1961
She hath *b* more righteous than I Gen 38:26
hath the famine *b* in the land Gen 45:6
their trade hath *b* to feed cattle Gen 46:32 1961
Thy servants' trade hath *b* about Gen 46:34 1961
days of the years of my life *b* Gen 47:9 1961
I have *b* a stranger in a strange Ex 2:22 1961
such as hath not *b* in Egypt since Ex 9:18 1961
For it had *b* better for us to Ex 14:12
I have *b* an alien in a strange Ex 18:3 1961
it hath *b* testified to his owner, Ex 21:29
such as have not *b* done in all Ex 34:10
should it have *b* accepted in the Lev 10:19
after that he hath *b* seen of the Lev 13:7
hath not *b* sprinkled upon him Num 19:20 1961
the LORD thy God hath *b* with thee Deut 2:7
whether there hath *b* any such Deut 4:32 1961
thing is, or hath *b* heard like it Deut 4:32
ye have *b* rebellious against the Deut 9:7 1961
Ye have *b* rebellious against the Deut 9:24 1961
for he hath *b* worth a double Deut 15:18
which hath not *b* wrought with Deut 21:3
ye have *b* rebellious against the Deut 31:27 1961
would to God we had *b* content Josh 7:7
made as if they had *b* ambassadors Josh 9:4
the cave wherein they had *b* hid Josh 10:27
no man hath *b* able to stand Josh 23:9
green withs which had not *b* dried Judg 16:8
for I have *b* a Nazarite unto God Judg 16:17
her, It hath fully *b* shewed me Ruth 2:11
Eli thought she had *b* drunken 1Sa 1:13
for there hath not *b* such a thing 1Sa 4:7 1961
Hebrews, as they have *b* to you 1Sa 4:9
there hath *b* also a great 1Sa 4:17 1961
it *b* kept for thee since I said 1Sa 9:24
how mine eyes have *b* enlightened 1Sa 14:29
for had there not *b* now a much 1Sa 14:30
wherein this sin hath *b* this day 1Sa 14:38 1961
should have *b* utterly destroyed 1Sa 15:21
should have *b* given to David 1Sa 18:19
have *b* to thee-ward very good 1Sa 19:4
as he hath *b* with my father 1Sa 20:13 1961
Of a truth women have *b* kept from 1Sa 21:5
evil hath not *b* found in thee all 1Sa 25:28
surely there had not *b* left unto 1Sa 25:34
which hath *b* with me these days, 1Sa 29:3 1961
LORD liveth, thou hast *b* upright 1Sa 29:6
I have *b* with thee unto this day 1Sa 29:8 1961
he had not *b* anointed with oil 2Sa 1:21
very pleasant hast thou *b* unto me 2Sa 1:26
and if that had *b* too little 2Sa 12:8
Amnon thy brother *b* with thee 2Sa 13:20 1961
of Absalom this hath *b* determined 2Sa 13:32 1961
it had *b* good for me to have *b* 2Sa 14:32
as I have *b* thy father's servant 2Sa 15:34 1961
As the LORD hath *b* with my lord 1Kin 1:37 1961
because thou hast *b* afflicted in 1Kin 2:26
yet thou hast not *b* as my servant 1Kin 14:8 1961
as if it had *b* a light thing for 1Kin 16:31
because there had *b* no rain in 1Kin 17:7 1961
I have *b* very jealous for the 1Kin 19:10
I have *b* very jealous for the 1Kin 19:14
thou hast *b* careful for us with 2Kin 4:13
heard that Hezekiah had *b* sick 2Kin 20:12 1961
I have *b* with thee whithersoever 1Chr 17:8 1961
because thou hast *b* a man of war 1Chr 28:3
not *b* on any king before him in 1Chr 29:25 1961
have had that have *b* before thee 2Chr 1:12
hath *b* without the true God 2Chr 15:3
that had *b* king David's, which 2Chr 23:9
of those which had *b* carried away Ezr 2:1
us hath *b* plainly read before me Ezr 4:18
commanded, and search hath *b* made Ezr 4:19
and sedition have *b* made therein Ezr 4:19
There have *b* mighty kings also Ezr 4:20 1934
until now hath it *b* in building Ezr 5:16
of those that had *b* carried away Ezr 8:35
rulers hath *b* chief in this Ezr 9:2 1961
of those that had *b* carried away Ezr 9:4
b in a great trespass unto this Ezr 9:7
b delivered into the hand of the Ezr 9:7
b shewed from the LORD our God Ezr 9:8
of them that had *b* carried away Ezr 10:6
of those that had *b* carried away Ezr 10:8
Now I had not *b* beforetime sad in Neh 2:1 1961
the former governors that had *b* Neh 5:15
of those that had *b* carried away Neh 7:6
the Levites had not *b* given them Neh 13:10
Who had *b* carried away from Est 2:6
with the captivity which had *b* Est 2:6
that she had *b* twelve months Est 2:12 1961
but I have not *b* called to come Est 4:11
dignity hath *b* done to Mordecai Est 6:3
But if we had *b* sold for bondmen Est 7:4
b quiet, I should have slept Job 3:13
then had I *b* at rest, Job 3:13
hidden untimely birth I had not *b* Job 3:16 1961
have *b* as though I had not *b* Job 10:19 1961
I should have *b* carried from the Job 10:19
of the fatherless have *b* broken Job 22:9
If mine heart have *b* deceived by Job 31:9
my heart hath *b* secretly enticed, Job 31:27
gates of death *b* opened unto thee Job 38:17

all they that had *b* of his ... Job 42:11
for they have *b* ever of old ... Ps 25:6
thou hast *b* my help ... Ps 27:9 1961
he had *b* my friend or brother ... Ps 35:14
I have *b* young, and now am old ... Ps 37:25 1961
My tears have *b* my meat day ... Ps 42:3 1961
to have *b* continually before me ... Ps 50:8
hast *b* partaker with adulterers ... Ps 50:18
for thou hast *b* my defence ... Ps 59:16 1961
us, thou hast *b* displeased ... Ps 60:1
For thou hast *b* a shelter for me, ... Ps 61:3 1961
Because thou hast *b* my help ... Ps 63:7 1961
should have *b* for their welfare ... Ps 69:22
By thee have I *b* holden up from ... Ps 71:6 1961
all the day long have I *b* plagued ... Ps 73:14 1961
thou hast *b* favourable unto thy ... Ps 85:1
thou hast *b* wroth with thine ... Ps 89:38
thou hast *b* our dwelling place in ... Ps 90:1 1961
Unless the LORD had *b* my help ... Ps 94:17
The LORD hath *b* mindful of us ... Ps 115:12
Thy statutes have *b* my songs in ... Ps 119:54 1961
for me that I have *b* afflicted ... Ps 119:71
Unless thy law had *b* my delights ... Ps 119:92
If it had not *b* the LORD who was ... Ps 124:1 1961
If it had not *b* the LORD who was ... Ps 124:2 1961
as those that have *b* long dead ... Ps 143:3
strong men have *b* slain by her ... Prov 7:26
The thing that hath *b*, it is that ... Eccl 1:9 1961
it hath *b* already of old time, ... Eccl 1:10 1961
have *b* before me in Jerusalem ... Eccl 1:16 1961
that which hath *b* already done ... Eccl 2:12
That which hath *b* is now ... Eccl 3:15 1961
which is to be hath already *b* ... Eccl 3:15 1961
both they, which hath not yet *b* ... Eccl 4:3 1961
of all that have *b* before them ... Eccl 4:16 1961
That which hath *b* is named ... Eccl 6:10 1961
they have not *b* closed, neither ... Is 1:6
we should have *b* as Sodom ... Is 1:9 1961
we should have *b* like unto ... Is 1:9
What could have *b* done more to my ... Is 5:4
hast not *b* mindful of the rock of ... Is 17:10
thou harlot that hast *b* forgotten ... Is 23:16
For thou hast *b* a strength to the ... Is 25:4 1961
so have we *b* in thy sight, O LORD ... Is 26:17 1961
b with child, we have *b* ... Is 26:18
which hath *b* winnowed with the ... Is 30:24
king of Judah, when he had *b* sick ... Is 38:9
he had heard that he had *b* sick ... Is 39:1
hath it not *b* told you from the ... Is 40:21
I have *b* still, and refrained ... Is 42:14 1961
thou hast *b* honourable, and I have ... Is 43:4
but thou hast *b* weary of me ... Is 43:22
then had thy peace *b* as a river ... Is 48:18 1961
Thy seed also had *b* as the sand ... Is 48:19 1961
his name should not have *b* cut ... Is 48:19
these, where had they *b* ... Is 49:21
for that which had not *b* told ... Is 52:15
whom hast thou *b* afraid or feared ... Is 57:11
Whereas thou hast *b* forsaken ... Is 60:15 1961
made, and all those things have *b* ... Is 66:2 1961
Have I *b* a wilderness unto Israel ... Jer 2:31 1961
where thou hast not *b* lien with ... Jer 3:2
the showers have *b* withholden ... Jer 3:3
there hath *b* no latter rain ... Jer 3:3 1961
because she hath *b* rebellious ... Jer 4:17
she hath *b* ashamed and confounded ... Jer 15:9 1961
my mother might have *b* my grave ... Jer 20:17 1961
This hath *b* thy manner from thy ... Jer 22:21
prophets that have *b* before me ... Jer 28:8 1961
For this city hath *b* to me as a ... Jer 32:31 1961
which hath *b* sold unto thee ... Jer 34:14 1961
my fury hath *b* poured forth upon ... Jer 42:18
whither they had *b* driven ... Jer 43:5
have *b* consumed by the sword and ... Jer 44:18
Moab hath *b* at ease from his ... Jer 48:11
hath not *b* emptied from vessel to ... Jer 48:11 1961
My people hath *b* lost sheep ... Jer 50:6 1961
for she hath *b* proud against the ... Jer 50:29
For Israel hath not *b* forsaken ... Jer 51:5
Babylon hath *b* a golden cup in ... Jer 51:7
there hath *b* a prophet among them ... Eze 2:5 1961
my soul hath not *b* polluted ... Eze 4:14
as if a wheel had *b* in the midst ... Eze 10:10 1961
where ye have *b* scattered ... Eze 11:17
hast not *b* as an harlot, in that ... Eze 16:31 1961
wherein ye have *b* scattered ... Eze 20:41
doings, wherein ye have *b* defiled ... Eze 20:43
which hath *b* in the midst of thee ... Eze 22:13 1961
Thou hast *b* in Eden the garden of ... Eze 28:13 1961
because they have *b* a staff of ... Eze 29:6 1961
that a prophet hath *b* among them ... Eze 33:33 1961
have *b* scattered in the cloudy ... Eze 34:12
which have *b* always waste ... Eze 38:8 1961
have *b* brought in before me, that ... Dan 5:15
not *b* done as hath *b* done upon ... Dan 9:12
because ye have *b* a snare on ... Hos 5:1 1961
though I have *b* a rebuker of them ... Hos 5:2
Hath this *b* in your days, or even ... Joel 1:2 1961
there hath not *b* ever the like ... Joel 2:2 1961
shall be as though they had not *b* ... Obad 16 1961
goings forth have *b* from of old ... Mic 5:2
where they have *b* put to shame ... Zeph 3:19
The LORD hath *b* sore displeased ... Zec 1:2
this hath *b* by your means ... Mal 1:9 1961
but have *b* partial in the law ... Mal 2:9
LORD hath *b* witness between thee ... Mal 2:14
Your words have *b* stout against ... Mal 3:13
her that had *b* the wife of Urias ... Mt 1:6
It hath *b* said, Whosoever shall ... Mt 5:31
hath *b* said by them of old time ... Mt 5:33
Ye have heard that it hath *b* said ... Mt 5:38
Ye have heard that it hath *b* said ... Mt 5:43
had *b* done in Tyre and Sidon, they ... Mt 11:21
which have *b* done in thee ... Mt 11:23
had *b* done in Sodom, it would ... Mt 11:23
I will utter things which have *b* ... Mt 13:35
If we had *b* in the days of our ... Mt 23:30 2258
we would not have *b* partakers ... Mt 23:30 2258
thou hast *b* faithful over a few ... Mt 25:21 2258
thou hast *b* faithful over a few ... Mt 25:23 2258
might have *b* sold for much ... Mt 26:9
it had *b* good for that man if he ... Mt 26:24 2258
for that man if he had not *b* born ... Mt 26:24
Because that he had *b* often bound ... Mk 5:4
the chains had *b* plucked asunder ... Mk 5:4
he that had *b* possessed with the ... Mk 5:18
they supposed it had *b* a spirit ... Mk 6:49 *1511*
have now *b* with me three days ... Mk 8:2 *4357*
For it might have *b* sold for more ... Mk 14:5
and have *b* given to the poor ... Mk 14:5
that man if he had never *b* born ... Mk 14:21
whether he had *b* any while dead ... Mk 15:44
and told them that had *b* with him ... Mk 16:10 *1096*
had *b* seen of her, believed not ... Mk 16:11
wherein thou hast *b* instructed ... Lk 1:4
which have *b* since the world ... Lk 1:70
him to have *b* in the company ... Lk 2:44 *1511*
where he had *b* brought up ... Lk 4:16
the servant whole that had *b* sick ... Lk 7:10
which had *b* healed of evil ... Lk 8:2
mighty works had *b* done in Tyre ... Lk 10:13
which have *b* done in you, they ... Lk 10:13
If therefore ye have not *b* ... Lk 16:11 *1096*
if ye have not *b* faithful in that ... Lk 16:12 *1096*
because thou hast *b* faithful in a ... Lk 19:17 *1096*
But we trusted that it had *b* he ... Lk 24:21 *2076*
knew that he had *b* now a long ... Jn 5:6 *2192*
him, that he had *b* blind, and ... Jn 9:18 *2258*
Jesus, Lord, if thou hadst *b* here ... Jn 11:21 *2258*
him, Lord, if thou hadst *b* here ... Jn 11:32 *2258*
for he hath *b* dead four days ... Jn 11:39 *2076*
Lazarus was which had *b* dead ... Jn 12:1
the arm of the Lord *b* revealed ... Jn 12:38
Have I *b* so long time with you, ... Jn 14:9 *1510*
because ye have *b* with me from ... Jn 15:27 *2075*
must needs have *b* fulfilled ... Acts 1:16
them, that they had *b* with Jesus ... Acts 4:13 2258
indeed a notable miracle hath *b* ... Acts 4:16
lest they should have *b* stoned ... Acts 5:26
as it had *b* the face of an angel ... Acts 6:15
of whom ye have *b* now the ... Acts 7:52 *1096*
from his eyes as it had *b* scales ... Acts 9:18
as it had *b* a great sheet knit at ... Acts 10:11
as it had *b* a great sheet, let ... Acts 11:5
which had *b* brought up with Herod ... Acts 13:1
should first have *b* spoken to you ... Acts 13:46
the city, supposing he had *b* dead ... Acts 14:19
Antioch, from whence they had *b* ... Acts 14:26
when there had *b* much disputing ... Acts 15:7 *1096*
that the prisoners had *b* fled ... Acts 16:27
saying, After I have *b* there ... Acts 19:21 *1096*
I have *b* with you at all seasons ... Acts 20:18 *1096*
have *b* pulled in pieces of them ... Acts 23:10
should have *b* killed of them ... Acts 23:27
as I know that thou hast *b* of ... Acts 24:10 *5607*
ought to have *b* here before thee ... Acts 24:19 *3918*
should have *b* given him of Paul ... Acts 24:26
when they had *b* there many days, ... Acts 25:14 *1304*
man might have *b* set at liberty ... Acts 26:32 *1096*
For if we have *b* planted together ... Rom 6:5
we had *b* as Sodoma, and *b* made ... Rom 9:29 *1096*
or who hath *b* his counsellor ... Rom 11:34 *1096*
For which cause also I have *b* ... Rom 15:22
have *b* made partakers of their ... Rom 15:27
for she hath *b* a succourer of ... Rom 16:2 *1096*
For it hath *b* declared unto me of ... 1Cor 1:11
have *b* all made to drink into one ... 1Cor 12:13
but we have *b* throughly made ... 2Cor 11:6
reproach, as though we had *b* weak ... 2Cor 11:21
and a day I have *b* in the deep ... 2Cor 11:25 *4160*
ought to have *b* commended of you ... 2Cor 12:11
Christ hath *b* evidently set forth ... Gal 3:1
for if there had *b* a law given ... Gal 3:21
should have *b* by the law ... Gal 3:21 2258
For as many of you as have *b* ... Gal 3:27
that, if it had *b* possible ... Gal 4:15
ye have *b* called unto liberty ... Gal 5:13
of the world hath *b* hid in God ... Eph 3:9
have *b* taught by him, as the ... Eph 4:21
ye had heard that he had *b* sick ... Phil 2:26 *1096*
which hath *b* hid from ages ... Col 1:26
in the faith, as ye have *b* taught ... Col 2:7
which have *b* a comfort unto me ... Col 4:11 *1096*
when we might have *b* burdensome ... 1Th 2:6
traditions which ye have *b* taught ... 2Th 2:15
having *b* the wife of one man, ... 1Ti 5:9 *1096*
hast *b* assured of, knowing of ... 2Ti 3:14
faithful word as he hath *b* taught ... Titus 1:9
first covenant had *b* faultless ... Heb 8:7 2258
have *b* sought for the second ... Heb 8:7
if they had *b* mindful of that ... Heb 11:15
them that have *b* occupied therein ... Heb 13:9
tamed, and hath *b* tamed of mankind ... Jas 3:7
on the earth, and *b* wanton ... Jas 5:5
For it had *b* better for them not ... 2Pet 2:21 2258
for if they had *b* of us, they ... 1Jn 2:19 2258
stood a Lamb as it had *b* slain ... Rev 5:6
inhabitants of the earth have *b* ... Rev 17:2

BEER (*be'-ur*) See BAALITH-BEER, BEER-ELIM, BEER-LAHAI-ROI, BEER-SHEBA.
1. An Israelite post beyond the Arnon River.
And from thence they went to *B* ... Num 21:16 876
2. A town in Judah.
ran away, and fled, and went to *B* ... Judg 9:21 876

BEERA (*be-e'-rah*) *Son of Zophah.*
and Shilshah, and Ithran, and *B* ... 1Chr 7:37 878

BEERAH (*be-e'-rah*) *A Reubenite prince.*
B his son, whom Tilgath-pilneser ... 1Chr 5:6 880

BEER-ELIM (*be''-ur-e'-lim*) *A well in Moab.*
and the howling thereof unto *B* ... Is 15:8 879

BEERI (*be-e'-ri*)
1. Father of Judith.
the daughter of *B* the Hittite ... Gen 26:34 882
2. Father of Hosea.
came unto Hosea, the son of *B* ... Hos 1:1 882

BEER-LAHAI-ROI (*be'''-ur-la''-hahe-ro'-e*) *A well.*
Wherefore the well was called *B* ... Gen 16:14 883

BEEROTH (*be-e'-roth*) See BEROTHITE.
1. An Israelite encampment during the Exodus.
B of the children of Jaakan to ... Deut 10:6 881
2. A Hivvite city in Canaan.
were Gibeon, and Chephirah, and *B* ... Josh 9:17 881
Gibeon, and Ramah, and *B*, ... Josh 18:25 881
(for *B* also was reckoned to ... 2Sa 4:2 881
of Kirjath-arim, Chephirah, and *B* ... Ezr 2:25 881
Kirjath-jearim, Chephirah, and *B* ... Neh 7:29 881

BEEROTHITE (*be-er'-o-thite*) See BEEROTHITES, BEROTHITE. *An inhabitant of Beeroth.*
Rechab, the sons of Rimmon a *B* ... 2Sa 4:2 886
And the sons of Rimmon the *B* ... 2Sa 4:5 886
brother, the sons of Rimmon the *B* ... 2Sa 4:9 886
Zelek the Ammonite, Nahari the *B* ... 2Sa 23:37 886

BEEROTHITES (*be-er'-o-thites*)
the *B* fled to Gittaim, and were ... 2Sa 4:3 886

BEER-SHEBA (*be-ur'-she-bah*) *A Canaanite city.*
wandered in the wilderness of *B* ... Gen 21:14 884
Wherefore he called that place *B* ... Gen 21:31 884
Thus they made a covenant at *B* ... Gen 21:32 884
And Abraham planted a grove in *B* ... Gen 21:33 884
rose up and went together to *B* ... Gen 22:19 884
and Abraham dwelt at *B* ... Gen 22:19 884
And he went up from thence to *B* ... Gen 26:23 884
of the city is *B* unto this day ... Gen 26:33 884
And Jacob went out from *B*, and went ... Gen 28:10 884
all that he had, and came to *B* ... Gen 46:1 884
And Jacob rose up from *B* ... Gen 46:5 884
And Hazar-shual, and *B*, and ... Josh 15:28 884
they had in their inheritance *B* ... Josh 19:2 884
as one man, from Dan even to *B* ... Judg 20:1 884
even to *B* knew that Samuel was ... 1Sa 3:20 884
they were judges in *B* ... 1Sa 8:2 884
and over Judah, from Dan even to *B* ... 2Sa 3:10 884
unto thee, from Dan even to *B* ... 2Sa 17:11 884
of Israel, from Dan even to *B* ... 2Sa 24:2 884
to the south of Judah, even to *B* ... 2Sa 24:7 884
even to *B* seventy thousand men ... 2Sa 24:15 884
his fig tree, from Dan even to *B* ... 1Kin 4:25 884
went for his life, and came to *B* ... 1Kin 19:3 884
his mother's name was Zibiah of *B* ... 2Kin 12:1 884
burned incense, from Geba to *B* ... 2Kin 23:8 884
And they dwelt at *B*, and Moladah, ... 1Chr 4:28 884
number Israel from *B* even to Dan ... 1Chr 21:2 884
people from *B* to mount Ephraim ... 2Chr 19:4 884
name also was Zibiah of *B* ... 2Chr 24:1 884
from *B* even to Dan, that they ... 2Chr 30:5 884
And at Hazar-shual, and at *B* ... Neh 11:27 884
they dwelt from *B* unto the valley ... Neh 11:30 884
into Gilgal, and pass not to *B* ... Amos 5:5 884
and, The manner of *B* liveth ... Amos 8:14 884

BEES
you, and chased you, as *b* do ... Deut 1:44 1682
behold, there was a swarm of *b* ... Judg 14:8 1682
They compassed me about like *b* ... Ps 118:12 1682

BE-ESHTARAH See BEESH-TERAH.

BEESH-TERAH (*be-esh'te-rah*) See ASHTAROTH. *A Levitical city in Manasseh.*
and *B* with her suburbs ... Josh 21:27 1203

BEETLE
the *b* after his kind, and the ... Lev 11:22 2728

BEEVES
a male without blemish, of the *b* ... Lev 22:19 1241
a freewill offering in *b* or sheep ... Lev 22:21 1241
both of the persons, and of the *b* ... Num 31:28 1241
fifty, of the persons, of the *b* ... Num 31:30 1241
threescore and twelve thousand *b* ... Num 31:33 1241
the *b* were thirty and six thousand ... Num 31:38 1241
And thirty and six thousand *b* ... Num 31:44 1241

BEFALL
Lest peradventure mischief *b* him ... Gen 42:4 7122
if mischief *b* him by the way in ... Gen 42:38 7122
also from me, and mischief *b* him ... Gen 44:29 7136
shall *b* you in the last days ... Gen 49:1 7122
evils and troubles shall *b* them ... Deut 31:17 4672
evil will *b* you in the latter ... Deut 31:29 7122
There shall no evil *b* thee ... Ps 91:10 579
b thy people in the latter days ... Dan 10:14 7136
the things that shall *b* me there ... Acts 20:22 4876

BEFALLEN
and such things have *b* me ... Lev 10:19 7122
all the travel that hath *b* us ... Num 20:14 4672
many evils and troubles are *b* them ... Deut 31:21 4672
us, why then is all this *b* us ... Judg 6:13 4672
he thought, Something hath *b* him ... 1Sa 20:26 4745
every thing that had *b* him ... Est 6:13 7136
what was *b* to the possessed of ... Mt 8:33 4876

BEFALLETH
b the sons of men *b* beasts... Eccl 3:19 4745
even one thing *b* them... Eccl 3:19 4745

BEFELL
and told him all that *b* unto them... Gen 42:29 7136
told him all things that *b* them... Josh 2:23 4672
thee than all the evil that *b*... 2Sa 19:7 935
that saw it told them how it *b* to... Mk 5:16 *1096*
which *b* me by the lying in wait... Acts 20:19 *4819*

BEFORE
the field *b* it was in the earth... Gen 2:5 2962
every herb of the field *b* it grew... Gen 2:5 2962
The earth also was corrupt *b* God... Gen 6:11 6440
The end of all flesh is come *b* me... Gen 6:13 6440
righteous *b* me in this generation... Gen 7:1 6440
He was a mighty hunter *b* the LORD... Gen 10:9 6440
the mighty hunter *b* the LORD... Gen 10:9 6440
Haran died *b* his father Terah in... Gen 11:28
her, and commended her *b* Pharaoh... Gen 12:15 413
Is not the whole land *b* thee... Gen 13:9 6440
b the LORD destroyed Sodom and... Gen 13:10 6440
sinners *b* the LORD exceedingly... Gen 13:13
walk *b* me, and be thou perfect... Gen 17:1 6440
O that Ishmael might live *b* thee... Gen 17:18 6440
he had dressed, and set it *b* them... Gen 18:8 6440
but Abraham stood yet *b* the LORD... Gen 18:22 6440
But *b* they lay down, the men of... Gen 19:4 2962
great *b* the face of the LORD... Gen 19:13 854
place where he stood *b* the LORD... Gen 19:27
said, Behold, my land is *b* thee... Gen 20:15 6440
Abraham stood up from *b* his dead... Gen 23:3
himself *b* the people of the land... Gen 23:12 6440
in Machpelah, which was *b* Mamre... Gen 23:17 6440
b all that went in at the gate of... Gen 23:18 6440
of the field of Machpelah *b* Mamre... Gen 23:19
he shall send his angel *b* thee... Gen 24:7 6440
b he had done speaking, that,... Gen 24:15 6440
there was set meat *b* him to eat... Gen 24:33 6440
b whom I walk, will send his... Gen 24:40 6440
b I had done speaking in mine... Gen 24:45 2962
Behold, Rebekah is *b* thee... Gen 24:51 6440
the Hittite, which is *b* Mamre... Gen 25:9
unto Shur, that is *b* Egypt... Gen 25:18
my soul may bless thee *b* I die... Gen 27:4 2962
thee *b* the LORD *b* my death... Gen 27:7 6440
he may bless thee *b* his death... Gen 27:10 6440
I have eaten of all *b* thou camest... Gen 27:33 2962
give the younger *b* the firstborn... Gen 29:26 6440
little which thou hadst *b* I came... Gen 30:30 6440
shall come for my hire *b* thy face... Gen 30:33
b the flocks in the gutters in... Gen 30:38 5227
the flocks conceived *b* the rods... Gen 30:39 413
that Jacob laid the rods *b* the... Gen 30:41
it was not toward him as *b*... Gen 31:2
that it is not toward me as *b*... Gen 31:5
b our brethren discern thou what... Gen 31:32 5048
lord that I cannot rise up *b* thee... Gen 31:35 6440
set it here *b* my brethren... Gen 31:37 5048
Jacob sent messengers *b* him to... Gen 32:3 6440
unto his servants, Pass over *b* me... Gen 32:16 6440
and whose are these *b* thee... Gen 32:17 6440
with the present that goeth *b* me... Gen 32:20 6440
So went the present over *b* him... Gen 32:21
And he passed over *b* them, and... Gen 33:3 6440
and let us go, and I will go *b* thee... Gen 33:12 5048
thee, pass over *b* his servant... Gen 33:14 6440
as the cattle that goeth *b* me... Gen 33:14 6440
and pitched his tent *b* the city... Gen 33:18
and the land shall be *b* you... Gen 34:10 6440
b there reigned any king over the... Gen 36:31 6440
even *b* he came near unto them,... Gen 37:18 2962
my dream, behold, a vine was *b* me... Gen 40:9 6440
and they cried *b* him, Bow the knee... Gen 41:43 6440
he stood *b* Pharaoh king of Egypt... Gen 41:46 6440
sons *b* the years of famine came... Gen 41:50 2962
bowed down themselves *b* him with... Gen 42:6
Simeon, and bound him *b* their eyes... Gen 42:24
not unto thee, and set him *b* thee... Gen 43:9 6440
Almighty give you mercy *b* the man... Gen 43:14 6440
down to Egypt, and stood *b* Joseph... Gen 43:15 6440
And they sat *b* him, the firstborn... Gen 43:33 6440
sent messes unto them from *b* him... Gen 43:34 6440
they fell *b* him on the ground... Gen 44:14 6440
could not refrain himself *b* all... Gen 45:1
for God did send me *b* you to... Gen 45:5 6440
God sent me *b* you to preserve you... Gen 45:7 6440
I will go and see him *b* I die... Gen 45:28 2962
he sent Judah *b* him unto Joseph,... Gen 46:28 6440
The land of Egypt is *b* thee... Gen 47:6 6440
his father, and set him *b* Pharaoh... Gen 47:7 6440
and went out from *b* Pharaoh... Gen 47:10 6440
shall we die *b* thine eyes... Gen 47:19
b I came unto thee into Egypt... Gen 48:5 5704
b whom my fathers Abraham and... Gen 48:15 6440
and he set Ephraim *b* Manasseh... Gen 48:20 6440
children shall bow down *b* thee... Gen 49:8
of Machpelah, which is *b* Mamre... Gen 49:30
of Ephron the Hittite, *b* Mamre... Gen 50:13
Thy father did command *b* he died... Gen 50:16 6440
also went and fell down *b* his face... Gen 50:18
and Moses fled from *b* it... Ex 4:3 6440
do all those wonders *b* Pharaoh... Ex 4:21 6440
And Moses spake *b* the LORD... Ex 6:12 6440
And Moses said *b* the LORD, Behold,... Ex 6:30 6440
thy rod, and cast it *b* Pharaoh... Ex 7:9 6440
Aaron cast down his rod *b* Pharaoh... Ex 7:10 6440
b his servants, and it became a... Ex 7:10 6440
the morning, and stand *b* Pharaoh... Ex 8:20 6440
of the Egyptians *b* their eyes... Ex 8:26
the furnace, and stood *b* Pharaoh... Ex 9:10 6440
b Moses because of the boils... Ex 9:11 6440
stand *b* Pharaoh, and say unto him,... Ex 9:13 6440
I might shew these my signs *b* him... Ex 10:1 7130
refuse to humble thyself *b* me... Ex 10:3 6440
for evil is *b* you... Ex 10:10 6440
b them there were no such locusts... Ex 10:14 6440
did all these wonders *b* Pharaoh... Ex 11:10 6440
their dough *b* it was leavened... Ex 12:34 2962
the LORD went *b* them by day in a... Ex 13:21 6440
fire by night, from *b* the people... Ex 13:22 6440
encamp *b* Pi-hahiroth, between... Ex 14:2 6440
b it shall ye encamp by the sea... Ex 14:2 5226
beside Pi-hahiroth, *b* Baal-zephon... Ex 14:9 6440
which went *b* the camp of Israel,... Ex 14:19 6440
the cloud went from *b* their face... Ex 14:19 6440
of Israel, Come near *b* the LORD... Ex 16:9 6440
therein, and lay it up *b* the LORD... Ex 16:33 6440
Aaron laid it up *b* the Testimony... Ex 16:34 6440
Go on *b* the people, and take with... Ex 17:5 6440
I will stand *b* thee there upon... Ex 17:6 6440
with Moses' father in law *b* God... Ex 18:12 6440
there Israel camped *b* the mount... Ex 19:2 5048
laid *b* their faces all these... Ex 19:7
shalt have no other gods *b* me... Ex 20:3
that his fear may be *b* your faces... Ex 20:20 5021
which thou shalt set *b* them... Ex 21:1 6440
parties shall come *b* the judges... Ex 22:9 5703
and none shall appear *b* me empty... Ex 23:15 6440
males shall appear *b* the Lord GOD... Ex 23:17
Behold, I send an Angel *b* thee... Ex 23:20 6440
For mine Angel shall go *b* thee... Ex 23:23 6440
I will send my fear *b* thee... Ex 23:27 6440
And I will send hornets *b* thee... Ex 23:28 6440
and the Hittite, from *b* thee... Ex 23:28 6440
them out from *b* thee in one year... Ex 23:29 6440
I will drive them out from *b* thee... Ex 23:30 6440
thou shalt drive them out *b* thee... Ex 23:31 6440
the table shewbread *b* me alway... Ex 25:30 6440
which is *b* the testimony, Aaron... Ex 27:21 5921
evening to morning *b* the LORD... Ex 27:21 6440
Aaron shall bear their names *b*... Ex 28:12 6440
shoulderpieces of the ephod *b* it... Ex 28:25
for a memorial *b* the LORD... Ex 28:29 6440
when he goeth in *b* the LORD... Ex 28:30 6440
his heart *b* the LORD continually... Ex 28:30 6440
in unto the holy place *b* the LORD... Ex 28:35 6440
they may be accepted *b* the LORD... Ex 28:38 6440
brought *b* the tabernacle of the... Ex 29:10 6440
shalt kill the bullock *b* the LORD... Ex 29:11 6440
bread that is *b* the LORD... Ex 29:23 6440
for a wave offering *b* the LORD... Ex 29:24 6440
for a sweet savour *b* the LORD... Ex 29:25 6440
it for a wave offering *b* the LORD... Ex 29:26 6440
of the congregation *b* the LORD... Ex 29:42 6440
thou shalt put it *b* the vail that... Ex 30:6 6440
b the mercy seat that is over the... Ex 30:6 6440
a perpetual incense *b* the LORD... Ex 30:8 6440
the children of Israel *b* the LORD... Ex 30:16 6440
put of it *b* the testimony in the... Ex 30:36 6440
make us gods, which shall go *b* us... Ex 32:1 6440
saw it, he built an altar *b* it... Ex 32:5 6440
Make us gods, which shall go *b* us... Ex 32:23 6440
mine Angel shall go *b* thee... Ex 32:34 6440
And I will send an angel *b* thee... Ex 33:2 6440
make all my goodness pass *b* thee... Ex 33:19
the name of the LORD *b* thee... Ex 33:19 6440
nor herds feed *b* that mount... Ex 34:3
And the LORD passed by *b* him... Ex 34:6
b all thy people I will do... Ex 34:10 5048
I drive out *b* thee the Amorite,... Ex 34:11 6440
And none shall appear *b* me empty... Ex 34:20 6440
children appear *b* the Lord GOD... Ex 34:23 6440
will cast out the nations *b* thee... Ex 34:24 6440
b the LORD thy God thrice in the... Ex 34:24
But when Moses went in *b* the LORD... Ex 34:34 6440
shoulderpieces of the ephod, *b* it... Ex 39:18
b the ark of the testimony... Ex 40:5 6440
b the door of the tabernacle of... Ex 40:6 6440
bread in order upon it *b* the LORD... Ex 40:23 6440
he lighted the lamps *b* the LORD... Ex 40:25 6440
of the congregation *b* the vail... Ex 40:26 6440
of the congregation *b* the LORD... Lev 1:3 6440
shall kill the bullock *b* the LORD... Lev 1:5 6440
of the altar northward *b* the LORD... Lev 1:11 6440
it without blemish *b* the LORD... Lev 3:1 6440
then shall he offer it *b* the LORD... Lev 3:7 6440
kill it *b* the tabernacle of the... Lev 3:8 6440
then he shall offer it *b* the LORD... Lev 3:12 6440
kill it *b* the tabernacle of the... Lev 3:13 6440
of the congregation *b* the LORD... Lev 4:4 6440
and kill the bullock *b* the LORD... Lev 4:4 6440
the blood seven times *b* the LORD... Lev 4:6 6440
b the vail of the sanctuary... Lev 4:6 6440
altar of sweet incense *b* the LORD... Lev 4:7 6440
bring him *b* the tabernacle of the... Lev 4:14 6440
head of the bullock *b* the LORD... Lev 4:15 6440
shall be killed *b* the LORD... Lev 4:15 6440
b the LORD, even *b* the vail... Lev 4:17 6440
of the altar which is *b* the LORD... Lev 4:18 6440
the burnt offering *b* the LORD... Lev 4:24 6440
an atonement for him *b* the LORD... Lev 6:7 6440
it *b* the LORD, *b* the altar... Lev 6:14 6440
sin offering be killed *b* the LORD... Lev 6:25 6440
for a wave offering *b* the LORD... Lev 7:30 6440
bread, that was *b* the LORD... Lev 8:26 6440
for a wave offering *b* the LORD... Lev 8:27 6440
it for a wave offering *b* the LORD... Lev 8:29 6440
blemish, and offer them *b* the LORD... Lev 9:2 6440
to sacrifice *b* the LORD... Lev 9:4 6440
commanded *b* the tabernacle of the... Lev 9:5
drew near and stood *b* the LORD... Lev 9:5 6440
for a wave offering *b* the LORD... Lev 9:21 6440
came a fire out from *b* the LORD... Lev 9:24 6440
offered strange fire *b* the LORD... Lev 10:1 6440
them, and they died *b* the LORD... Lev 10:2 6440
b all the people I will be... Lev 10:3
carry your brethren from *b* the... Lev 10:4 6440
it for a wave offering *b* the LORD... Lev 10:15 6440
atonement for them *b* the LORD... Lev 10:17 6440
their burnt offering *b* the LORD... Lev 10:19 6440
Who shall offer it *b* the LORD... Lev 12:7 6440
b the LORD, at the door of the... Lev 14:11 6440
for a wave offering *b* the LORD... Lev 14:12 6440
his finger seven times *b* the LORD... Lev 14:16 6440
an atonement for him *b* the LORD... Lev 14:18 6440
of the congregation, *b* the LORD... Lev 14:23 6440
for a wave offering *b* the LORD... Lev 14:24 6440
left hand seven times *b* the LORD... Lev 14:27 6440
an atonement for him *b* the LORD... Lev 14:29 6440
that is to be cleansed *b* the LORD... Lev 14:31 6440
b the priest go into it to see... Lev 14:36 2962
come *b* the LORD unto the door of... Lev 15:14 6440
for him *b* the LORD for his issue... Lev 15:15 6440
b the LORD for the issue of her... Lev 15:30 6440
when they offered *b* the LORD... Lev 16:1 6440
within the vail *b* the mercy seat... Lev 16:2
present them *b* the LORD at the... Lev 16:7 6440
be presented alive *b* the LORD... Lev 16:10 6440
from off the altar *b* the LORD... Lev 16:12 6440
incense upon the fire *b* the LORD... Lev 16:13 6440
b the mercy seat shall he... Lev 16:14 6440
mercy seat, and *b* the mercy seat... Lev 16:15 6440
unto the altar that is *b* the LORD... Lev 16:18 6440
from all your sins *b* the LORD... Lev 16:30 6440
LORD *b* the tabernacle of the LORD... Lev 17:4 6440
b a beast to lie down thereto... Lev 18:23 6440
defiled which I cast out *b* you... Lev 18:24 6440
the land done, which were *b* you... Lev 18:27 6440
out the nations that were *b* you... Lev 18:28 6440
which were committed *b* you... Lev 18:30 6440
put a stumblingblock *b* the blind... Lev 19:14 6440
ram of the trespass offering *b*... Lev 19:22 6440
shalt rise up *b* the hoary head... Lev 19:32 6440
nation, which I cast out *b* you... Lev 20:23 6440
shall wave the sheaf *b* the LORD... Lev 23:11 6440
for a wave offering *b* the LORD... Lev 23:20 6440
for you *b* the LORD your God... Lev 23:28 6440
ye shall rejoice *b* the LORD your... Lev 23:40 6440
morning *b* the LORD continually... Lev 24:3 6440
b the LORD continually... Lev 24:4 6440
upon the pure table *b* the LORD... Lev 24:6 6440
in order *b* the LORD continually... Lev 24:8 6440
they shall fall *b* you by the... Lev 26:7 6440
shall fall *b* you by the sword... Lev 26:8 6440
ye shall be slain *b* your enemies... Lev 26:17 6440
another, as it were *b* a sword... Lev 26:37 6440
no power to stand *b* your enemies... Lev 26:37 6440
present himself *b* the priest... Lev 27:8 6440
present the beast *b* the priest... Lev 27:11 6440
and Abihu died *b* the LORD... Num 3:4 6440
offered strange fire *b* the LORD... Num 3:4 6440
present them *b* Aaron the priest,... Num 3:6 6440
b the tabernacle of the... Num 3:7 6440
But those that encamp *b* the... Num 3:38 6440
even *b* the tabernacle of the... Num 3:38 6440
her near, and set her *b* the LORD... Num 5:16 6440
shall set the woman *b* the LORD... Num 5:18 6440
wave the offering *b* the LORD... Num 5:25 6440
and shall set the woman *b* the LORD... Num 5:30 6440
days that were *b* shall be lost... Num 6:12 7223
shall bring them *b* the LORD... Num 6:16 6440
for a wave offering *b* the LORD... Num 6:20 6440
brought their offering *b* the LORD... Num 7:3 6440
brought them *b* the tabernacle... Num 7:3 6440
their offering *b* the altar... Num 7:10 6440
Levites *b* the tabernacle of the... Num 8:9 6440
bring the Levites *b* the LORD... Num 8:10 6440
Aaron shall offer the Levites *b*... Num 8:11 6440
shalt set the Levites *b* Aaron... Num 8:13 6440
b his sons, and offer them for an... Num 8:13 6440
them as an offering *b* the LORD... Num 8:21 6440
b Aaron, and *b* his sons... Num 8:22 6440
b Moses and *b* Aaron on that day... Num 9:6 6440
be remembered *b* the LORD your God... Num 10:9 6440
to you for a memorial *b* your God... Num 10:10 6440
the covenant of the LORD went *b*... Num 10:33 6440
them that hate thee flee *b* thee... Num 10:35 6440
beside this manna, *b* our eyes... Num 11:6
is among you, and have wept *b* him... Num 11:20 6440
built seven years *b* Zoan in Egypt... Num 13:22 6440
Caleb stilled the people *b* Moses... Num 13:30 413
faces *b* all the assembly of the... Num 14:5 6440
b all the children of Israel... Num 14:10 413
them, and that thou goest *b* them... Num 14:14 6440
died by the plague *b* the LORD... Num 14:37 6440
ye be not smitten *b* your enemies... Num 14:42 6440
and the Canaanites are there *b* you... Num 14:43 6440
shall the stranger be *b* the LORD... Num 15:15 6440
and their sin offering *b* the LORD... Num 15:25 6440
sinneth by ignorance *b* the LORD... Num 15:28 6440
And they rose up *b* Moses, with... Num 16:2 6440
in them *b* the LORD to morrow... Num 16:7 6440
to stand *b* the congregation to... Num 16:9 6440
and all thy company *b* the LORD... Num 16:16 6440
bring ye *b* the LORD every man his... Num 16:17 6440
for they offered them *b* the LORD... Num 16:38 6440
near to offer incense *b* the LORD... Num 16:40 6440
Aaron came *b* the tabernacle of... Num 16:43
the congregation *b* the testimony... Num 17:4 6440
Moses laid up the rods *b* the LORD... Num 17:7 6440
brought out all the rods from *b*... Num 17:9 6440
Aaron's rod again *b* the testimony... Num 17:10 6440
b the tabernacle of witness... Num 18:2 6440
for ever *b* the LORD unto thee... Num 18:19 6440
and one shall slay her *b* his face... Num 19:3 6440
directly *b* the tabernacle of the... Num 19:4 6440
when our brethren died *b* the LORD... Num 20:3 6440
ye unto the rock *b* their eyes... Num 20:8
took the rod from *b* the LORD... Num 20:9 6440
congregation together *b* the rock... Num 20:10
in the wilderness which is *b* Moab... Num 21:11

because thy way is perverse *b* me Num 22:32 5048
hang them up *b* the LORD against Num 25:4
who were weeping *b* the door of Num 25:6
offered strange fire *b* the LORD Num 26:61 6440
And they stood *b* Moses Num 27:2 6440
b Eleazar the priest Num 27:2 6440
and *b* the princes and all the Num 27:2 6440
brought their cause *b* the LORD Num 27:5 6440
me at the water *b* their eyes Num 27:14
Which may go out *b* them Num 27:17 6440
and which may go in *b* them Num 27:17 6440
set him *b* Eleazar the priest Num 27:19 6440
and *b* all the congregation Num 27:19 6440
he shall stand *b* Eleazar the Num 27:21 6440
the judgment of Urim *b* the LORD Num 27:21 6440
set him *b* Eleazar the priest, and Num 27:22 6440
priest, and *b* all the congregation Num 27:22 6440
for our souls *b* the LORD Num 31:50 6440
the children of Israel *b* the LORD Num 31:54 6440
b the congregation of Israel Num 32:4 6440
armed *b* the children of Israel Num 32:17 6440
will go armed *b* the LORD to war Num 32:20 6440
you armed over Jordan *b* the LORD Num 32:21 6440
driven out his enemies from *b* him Num 32:21 6440
And the land be subdued *b* the LORD Num 32:22 6440
b the LORD, and *b* Israel Num 32:22
be your possession *b* the LORD Num 32:22 6440
b the LORD to battle, as my lord Num 32:27 6440
b the LORD, and the land shall be Num 32:29 6440
the land shall be subdued *b* you Num 32:29 6440
We will pass over armed *b* the Num 32:32 6440
which is *b* Baal-zephon Num 33:7
and they pitched *b* Migdol Num 33:7 6440
they departed from *b* Pi-hahiroth Num 33:8 6440
the mountains of Abarim, *b* Nebo Num 33:47 6440
of the land from *b* you, and Num 33:52 6440
of the land from *b* you Num 33:55 6440
until he stand *b* the congregation Num 35:12 6440
came near, and spake *b* Moses Num 36:1 6440
b the princes, the chief fathers Num 36:1 6440
Behold, I have set the land *b* you Deut 1:8 6440
thy God hath set the land *b* thee Deut 1:21 6440
and said, We will send men *b* us Deut 1:22 6440
LORD your God which goeth *b* you Deut 1:30 6440
did for you in Egypt *b* your eyes Deut 1:30
Who went in the way *b* you Deut 1:33 6440
son of Nun, which standeth *b* thee Deut 1:38 6440
lest ye be smitten *b* your enemies Deut 1:42 6440
And ye returned and wept *b* the LORD. Deut 1:45 6440
had destroyed them from *b* them Deut 2:12 6440
the LORD destroyed them *b* them Deut 2:21 6440
destroyed the Horims from *b* them Deut 2:22 6440
to give Sihon and his land *b* thee Deut 2:31 6440
LORD our God delivered him *b* us Deut 2:33 6440
ye shall pass over armed *b* your Deut 3:18 6440
he shall go over *b* this people Deut 3:28 6440
which I set *b* you this day Deut 4:8 6440
b the LORD thy God in Horeb Deut 4:10 6440
that are past, which were *b* thee Deut 4:32 6440
did for you in Egypt *b* your eyes Deut 4:34
out nations from *b* thee greater Deut 4:38 6440
set *b* the children of Israel Deut 4:44 6440
shalt have none other gods *b* me Deut 5:7
out all thine enemies from *b* thee Deut 6:19 6440
all his household, *b* our eyes Deut 6:22
commandments *b* the LORD our God Deut 6:25 6440
hath cast out many nations *b* thee Deut 7:1 6440
thy God shall deliver them *b* thee Deut 7:2 6440
those nations *b* thee by little Deut 7:22 6440
no man be able to stand *b* thee Deut 7:24 6440
the LORD destroyeth *b* your face Deut 8:20
Who can stand *b* the children of Deut 9:2 6440
God is he which goeth over *b* thee Deut 9:3 6440
shall bring them down *b* thy face Deut 9:3
hath cast them out from *b* thee Deut 9:4 6440
doth drive them out from *b* thee Deut 9:4 6440
doth drive them out from *b* thee Deut 9:5 6440
hands, and brake them *b* your eyes Deut 9:17
And I fell down *b* the LORD Deut 9:18 6440
Thus I fell down *b* the LORD forty Deut 9:25 6440
to stand *b* the LORD to minister Deut 10:8 6440
take thy journey *b* the people Deut 10:11 6440
out all these nations from *b* you Deut 11:23 6440
no man be able to stand *b* you Deut 11:25 6440
I set *b* you this day a blessing Deut 11:26 6440
which I set *b* you this day Deut 11:32 6440
ye shall eat *b* the LORD your God Deut 12:7 6440
ye shall rejoice *b* the LORD your Deut 12:12 6440
But thou must eat them *b* the LORD Deut 12:18 6440
thou shalt rejoice *b* the LORD thy Deut 12:18 6440
cut off the nations from *b* thee Deut 12:29 6440
they be destroyed from *b* thee Deut 12:30 6440
thou shalt eat *b* the LORD thy God Deut 14:23 6440
eat there *b* the LORD thy God Deut 14:26 6440
Thou shalt eat it *b* the LORD thy Deut 15:20 6440
shalt rejoice *b* the LORD thy God Deut 16:11 6440
b the LORD thy God in the place Deut 16:16
shall not appear *b* the LORD empty Deut 16:16
minister there *b* the LORD thy God Deut 17:12 854
is *b* the priests the Levites Deut 17:18 6440
do, which stand there *b* the LORD Deut 18:7 6440
doth drive them out from *b* thee Deut 18:12 6440
is, shall stand *b* the LORD Deut 19:17 6440
b the priests and the judges, Deut 19:17 6440
firstborn *b* the son of the hated Deut 21:16 6440
be *b* thee in the way in any tree Deut 22:6 6440
cloth *b* the elders of the city Deut 22:17 6440
to give up thine enemies *b* thee Deut 23:14 6440
that is abomination *b* the LORD Deut 24:4 6440
unto thee *b* the LORD thy God Deut 24:13 6440
down, and to be beaten *b* his face Deut 25:2
set it down *b* the altar of the Deut 26:4 6440
say *b* the LORD thy God, A Syrian Deut 26:5 6440
shalt set it *b* the LORD thy God Deut 26:10 6440
worship *b* the LORD thy God Deut 26:10 6440
thou shalt say *b* the LORD thy God Deut 26:13 6440
rejoice *b* the LORD thy God Deut 27:7 6440
thee to be smitten *b* thy face Deut 28:7
way, and flee *b* thee seven ways Deut 28:7 6440
to be smitten *b* thine enemies Deut 28:25 6440
them, and flee seven ways *b* them Deut 28:25 6440
ox shall be slain *b* thine eyes Deut 28:31
taken away from *b* thy face Deut 28:31
life shall hang in doubt *b* thee Deut 28:66 5048
b your eyes in the land of Egypt Deut 29:2
all of you *b* the LORD your God Deut 29:10 6440
us this day *b* the LORD our God Deut 29:15 6440
curse, which I have set *b* thee Deut 30:1 6440
I have set *b* thee this day life Deut 30:15 6440
you, that I have set *b* you life Deut 30:19 6440
thy God, he will go over *b* thee Deut 31:3 6440
destroy these nations from *b* thee Deut 31:3 6440
Joshua, he shall go over *b* thee Deut 31:3 6440
shall give them up *b* your face Deut 31:5
he it is that doth go *b* thee Deut 31:8 6440
all Israel is come to appear *b* Deut 31:11
thou shalt read this law *b* all Deut 31:11 5048
b I have brought them into the Deut 31:21 2962
thou shalt see the land *b* thee Deut 32:52 5048
children of Israel *b* his death Deut 33:1 6440
they shall put incense *b* thee Deut 33:10 639
thrust out the enemy from *b* thee Deut 33:27 6440
not any man be able to stand *b* Josh 1:5 6440
but ye shall pass *b* your brethren Josh 1:14 6440
b they were laid down, she came Josh 2:8 2962
lodged there *b* they passed over Josh 3:1 2962
and pass over *b* the people Josh 3:6 6440
covenant, and went *b* the people Josh 3:6 6440
out from *b* you the Canaanites Josh 3:10 6440
passeth over *b* you into Jordan Josh 3:11 6440
ark of the covenant *b* the people Josh 3:14 6440
Pass over *b* the ark of the LORD Josh 4:5 6440
waters of Jordan were cut off *b* Josh 4:7 6440
passed over armed *b* the children Josh 4:12 6440
over *b* the LORD unto battle Josh 4:13 6440
over all his banks, as they did *b* Josh 4:18
the waters of Jordan from *b* you Josh 4:23 6440
sea, which he dried up from *b* us Josh 4:23 6440
from *b* the children of Israel Josh 5:1 6440
seven priests shall bear *b* the Josh 6:4 6440
up every man straight *b* him Josh 6:5 5048
rams' horns *b* the ark of the LORD Josh 6:6 6440
pass on *b* the ark of the LORD Josh 6:7 6440
rams' horns passed on *b* the LORD Josh 6:8 6440
the armed men went *b* the priests Josh 6:9 6440
b the ark of the LORD went on Josh 6:13 6440
and the armed men went *b* them Josh 6:13 6440
city, every man straight *b* him Josh 6:20 5048
Cursed be the man *b* the LORD Josh 6:26 6440
they fled *b* the men of Ai Josh 7:4 6440
for they chased them from *b* the Josh 7:5 6440
b the ark of the LORD until the Josh 7:6 6440
their backs *b* their enemies Josh 7:8 6440
could not stand *b* their enemies Josh 7:12 6440
their backs *b* their enemies Josh 7:12 6440
canst not stand *b* thine enemies Josh 7:13 6440
and laid them out *b* the LORD Josh 7:23 6440
first, that we will flee *b* them Josh 8:5 6440
for they will say, They flee *b* us Josh 8:6 6440
therefore we will flee *b* them Josh 8:6 6440
of Israel, *b* the people to Ai Josh 8:10 6440
came *b* the city, and pitched on Josh 8:11 5048
at a time appointed, *b* the plain Josh 8:14 6440
as if they were beaten *b* them Josh 8:15 6440
on that side *b* the priests the Josh 8:33 5048
of the LORD had commanded *b* Josh 8:33 7223
which Joshua read not *b* all the Josh 8:35 5048
of the land from *b* you, therefore Josh 9:24 6440
their hosts, and encamped *b* Gibeon Josh 10:5 5921
not a man of them stand *b* thee Josh 10:8 6440
LORD discomfited them *b* Israel Josh 10:10 6440
pass, as they fled from *b* Israel Josh 10:11 6440
Amorites *b* the children of Israel Josh 10:12 6440
no day like that *b* it or after it Josh 10:14 6440
them up all slain *b* Israel Josh 11:6 6440
From Sihor, which is *b* Egypt Josh 13:3
out from *b* the children of Israel Josh 13:6 6440
unto Aroer that is *b* Rabbah Josh 13:25
name of Hebron *b* was Kirjath-arba Josh 14:15 6440
that is *b* the going up to Adummim Josh 15:7 5227
b the valley of Hinnom westward Josh 15:8
and the name of Debir *b* was Josh 15:15 6440
they came near *b* Eleazar the Josh 17:4 6440
b Joshua the son of Nun, and Josh 17:4 6440
b the princes, saying, The LORD Josh 17:4 6440
Michmethah, that lieth *b* Shechem Josh 17:7
And the land was subdued *b* them Josh 18:1 6440
for you here *b* the LORD our God Josh 18:6 6440
lots for you *b* the LORD in Shiloh Josh 18:8 6440
for them in Shiloh *b* the LORD Josh 18:10 6440
that lieth *b* Beth-horon southward Josh 18:14
end of the mountain that lieth *b* Josh 18:16
to the river that is *b* Jokneam Josh 19:11
Rakkon, with the border *b* Japho Josh 19:46 4136
by lot in Shiloh *b* the LORD Josh 19:51 6440
until he stand *b* the congregation Josh 20:6 6440
until he stood *b* the congregation Josh 20:9 6440
a man of all their enemies *b* them Josh 21:44 6440
do the service of the LORD *b* him Josh 22:27 6440
our God that is *b* his tabernacle Josh 22:29 6440
he shall expel them from *b* you Josh 23:5 6440
out from *b* you great nations Josh 23:9 6440
able to stand *b* you unto this day Josh 23:9 6440
any of these nations from *b* you Josh 23:13 6440
they presented themselves *b* God Josh 24:1 6440
and I destroyed them from *b* you Josh 24:8 6440
And I sent the hornet *b* you Josh 24:12 6440
which drave them out from *b* you Josh 24:12 6440
out from *b* us all the people Josh 24:18 6440
name of Hebron *b* was Kirjath-arba Judg 1:10 6440
and the name of Debir *b* was Judg 1:11 6440
the name of the city *b* was Luz Judg 1:23 6440
not drive them out from *b* you Judg 2:3 6440
any longer stand *b* their enemies Judg 2:14 6440
from *b* them of the nations which Judg 2:21 6440
such as *b* knew nothing thereof Judg 3:2 6440
him from the mount, and he *b* them Judg 3:27 6440
is not the LORD gone out *b* thee Judg 4:14 6440
the edge of the sword *b* Barak Judg 4:15 6440
Canaan *b* the children of Israel Judg 4:23 6440
mountains melted from *b* the LORD Judg 5:5 6440
even that Sinai from *b* the LORD Judg 5:5 6440
you, and drave them out from *b* you Judg 6:9 6440
my present, and set it *b* thee Judg 6:18 6440
take *b* them the waters unto Judg 7:24
from battle *b* the sun was up Judg 8:13 4608
subdued *b* the children of Israel Judg 8:28 6440
Gaal went out *b* the men of Judg 9:39 6440
chased him, and he fled *b* him Judg 9:40 6440
and the LORD deliver them *b* me Judg 11:9 6440
his words *b* the LORD in Mizpeh Judg 11:11 6440
Amorites from *b* his people Israel Judg 11:23 6440
our God shall drive out from *b* us Judg 11:24 6440
subdued *b* the children of Israel Judg 11:33 6440
of Jordan *b* the Ephraimites Judg 12:5
And Samson's wife wept *b* him Judg 14:16 5921
she wept *b* him the seven days, Judg 14:17 5921
seventh day *b* the sun went down Judg 14:18 2962
top of an hill that is *b* Hebron Judg 16:3
I will go out as at other times *b* Judg 16:20 6471
b the LORD is your way wherein ye Judg 18:6 5227
the cattle and the carriage *b* them Judg 18:21 6440
wept *b* the LORD until even, and Judg 20:23 6440
and wept, and sat there *b* the LORD Judg 20:26 6440
and peace offerings *b* the LORD Judg 20:26 6440
stood *b* it in those days,) saying Judg 20:28 6440
said, They are smitten down *b* us Judg 20:32 6440
the LORD smote Benjamin *b* Israel Judg 20:35 6440
Surely they are smitten down *b* us Judg 20:39 6440
they turned their backs *b* the men Judg 20:42 6440
and abode there till even *b* God Judg 21:2 6440
she rose up *b* one could know Ruth 3:14 2958
Buy it *b* the inhabitants, and Ruth 4:4 5048
b the elders of my people Ruth 4:4 5048
she continued praying *b* the LORD 1Sa 1:12 6440
poured out my soul *b* the LORD 1Sa 1:15 6440
early, and worshipped *b* the LORD 1Sa 1:19 6440
that he may appear *b* the LORD 1Sa 1:22
unto the LORD *b* Eli the priest 1Sa 2:11
Also *b* they burnt the fat, the 1Sa 2:15 2962
men was very great *b* the LORD 1Sa 2:17
But Samuel ministered *b* the LORD 1Sa 2:18
the child Samuel grew *b* the LORD 1Sa 2:21 5973
incense, to wear an ephod *b* me 1Sa 2:28 6440
father, should walk *b* me for ever 1Sa 2:30 6440
he shall walk *b* mine anointed for 1Sa 2:35 6440
ministered unto the LORD *b* Eli 1Sa 3:1 6440
was smitten *b* the Philistines 1Sa 4:2 6440
us to day *b* the Philistines 1Sa 4:3 6440
Israel is fled *b* the Philistines, 1Sa 4:17 6440
the earth *b* the ark of the LORD 1Sa 5:3 6440
the ground *b* the ark of the LORD 1Sa 5:4 6440
to stand *b* this holy LORD God 1Sa 6:20 6440
and poured it out *b* the LORD 1Sa 7:6 6440
and they were smitten *b* Israel 1Sa 7:10 6440
and some shall run *b* his chariots 1Sa 8:11 6440
king may judge us, and go out *b* us 1Sa 8:20 6440
behold, he is *b* you 1Sa 9:12 6440
b he go up to the high place to 1Sa 9:13 2962
in his ear a day *b* Saul came 1Sa 9:15 6440
go up *b* me unto the high place 1Sa 9:19 6440
was upon it, and set it *b* Saul 1Sa 9:24 6440
set it *b* thee, and eat 1Sa 9:24 6440
Bid the servant pass on *b* us 1Sa 9:27 6440
and a pipe, and a harp, *b* them 1Sa 10:5 6440
thou shalt go down *b* me to Gilgal 1Sa 10:8 6440
b the LORD by your tribes 1Sa 10:19 6440
a book, and laid it up *b* the LORD 1Sa 10:25 6440
Saul king *b* the LORD in Gilgal 1Sa 11:15 6440
of peace offerings *b* the LORD 1Sa 11:15 6440
behold, the king walketh *b* you 1Sa 12:2 6440
I have walked *b* you from my 1Sa 12:2 6440
b the LORD, and *b* his anointed 1Sa 12:3 5048
that I may reason with you *b* the 1Sa 12:7 6440
the LORD will do *b* your eyes 1Sa 12:16
and they fell *b* Jonathan 1Sa 14:13 6440
with the Philistines *b* that time 1Sa 14:21 865
b the elders of my people, and 1Sa 15:30 5048
b Israel, and turn again with me, 1Sa 15:30 5048
in pieces *b* the LORD in Gilgal 1Sa 15:33 6440
the LORD's anointed is *b* him 1Sa 16:6 5048
and made him pass *b* Samuel 1Sa 16:8 6440
of his sons to pass *b* Samuel 1Sa 16:10 6440
thy servants, which are *b* thee 1Sa 16:16 6440
came to Saul, and stood *b* him 1Sa 16:21 6440
David, I pray thee, stand *b* me 1Sa 16:22 6440
one bearing a shield went *b* him 1Sa 17:7 6440
spake, they rehearsed them *b* Saul 1Sa 17:31 6440
that bare the shield went *b* him 1Sa 17:41 6440
brought him *b* Saul with the head 1Sa 17:57 6440
went out and came in *b* the people 1Sa 18:13 6440
he went out and came in *b* them 1Sa 18:16 6440
prophesied *b* Samuel in like 1Sa 19:24 6440
said *b* Jonathan, What have I done 1Sa 20:1 6440
and what is my sin *b* thy father 1Sa 20:1 6440
that was taken from *b* the LORD 1Sa 21:6 6440
that day, detained *b* the LORD 1Sa 21:7 6440
he changed his behaviour *b* them 1Sa 21:13 5869
he brought them *b* the king of 1Sa 22:4
two made a covenant *b* the LORD 1Sa 23:18 6440
arose, and went to Ziph *b* Saul 1Sa 23:24 6440
unto her servants, Go on *b* me 1Sa 25:19 6440

fell *b* David on her face, and	1Sa 25:23	639
of Hachilah, which is *b* Jeshimon	1Sa 26:1	
of Hachilah, which is *b* Jeshimon	1Sa 26:3	
of men, cursed be they *b* the LORD	1Sa 26:19	6440
the earth *b* the face of the LORD	1Sa 26:20	5048
me set a morsel of bread *b* thee	1Sa 28:22	6440
it *b* Saul, and *b* his servants	1Sa 28:25	6440
which they drave *b* those other	1Sa 30:20	6440
fled from *b* the Philistines	1Sa 31:1	6440
young men now arise, and play *b* us	2Sa 2:14	6440
Israel, *b* the servants of David	2Sa 2:17	6440
that lieth *b* Giah by the way of	2Sa 2:24	
my kingdom are guiltless *b* the	2Sa 3:28	5973
with sackcloth, and mourn *b* Abner	2Sa 3:31	6440
as a man falleth *b* wicked men	2Sa 3:34	6440
with them in Hebron *b* the LORD	2Sa 5:3	6440
forth upon mine enemies *b* me	2Sa 5:20	6440
then shall the LORD go out *b* thee	2Sa 5:24	6440
and Ahio went *b* the ark	2Sa 6:4	6440
b the LORD on all manner of	2Sa 6:5	6440
David danced *b* the LORD with all	2Sa 6:14	6440
leaping and dancing *b* the LORD	2Sa 6:16	6440
and peace offerings *b* the LORD	2Sa 6:17	6440
It was *b* the LORD, which chose me	2Sa 6:21	6440
which chose me *b* thy father	2Sa 6:21	
b all his house, to appoint me	2Sa 6:21	
therefore will I play *b* the LORD	2Sa 6:21	6440
from Saul, whom I put away *b* thee	2Sa 7:15	6440
be established for ever *b* thee	2Sa 7:16	6440
sat *b* the LORD, and he said, Who	2Sa 7:18	6440
land, *b* thy people, which thou	2Sa 7:23	6440
David be established *b* thee	2Sa 7:26	6440
it may continue for ever *b* thee	2Sa 7:29	6440
Ammon saw that they stank *b* David	2Sa 10:6	
of the battle was against him *b*	2Sa 10:9	6440
and they fled *b* him	2Sa 10:13	6440
then fled they also *b* Abishai	2Sa 10:14	6440
that they were smitten *b* Israel	2Sa 10:15	6440
the host of Hadarezer went *b* them	2Sa 10:16	6440
And the Syrians fled *b* Israel	2Sa 10:18	6440
that they were smitten *b* Israel	2Sa 10:19	6440
him, he did eat and drink *b* him	2Sa 11:13	6440
will take thy wives *b* thine eyes	2Sa 12:11	
b all Israel, and *b* the sun	2Sa 12:12	5048
he required, they set bread *b* him	2Sa 12:20	
a pan, and poured them out *b* him	2Sa 13:9	6440
his face to the ground *b* the king	2Sa 14:33	6440
horses, and fifty men to run *b* him	2Sa 15:1	6440
from Gath, passed on *b* the king	2Sa 15:18	
slain *b* the servants of David	2Sa 18:7	6440
earth upon his face *b* the king	2Sa 18:28	
And all the people came *b* the king	2Sa 19:8	6440
b me continually in the room of	2Sa 19:13	6440
they went over Jordan *b* the king	2Sa 19:17	6440
son of Gera fell down *b* the king	2Sa 19:18	6440
but dead men *b* my lord the king	2Sa 19:28	6440
is in Gibeon, Amasa went *b* them	2Sa 20:8	6440
them in the hill *b* the LORD	2Sa 21:9	6440
Through the brightness *b* him were	2Sa 22:13	5048
For all his judgments were *b* me	2Sa 22:23	5048
I was also upright *b* him, and have	2Sa 22:24	
flee three months *b* thine enemies	2Sa 24:13	6440
bowed himself *b* the king on his	2Sa 24:20	
and let her stand *b* the king	1Kin 1:2	6440
and fifty men to run *b* him	1Kin 1:5	6440
And when he was come in *b* the king	1Kin 1:23	6440
he bowed himself *b* the king with	1Kin 1:23	6440
behold, they eat and drink *b* him	1Kin 1:25	6440
presence, and stood *b* the king	1Kin 1:28	6440
And they came *b* the king	1Kin 1:32	6440
to walk *b* me in truth with all	1Kin 2:4	6440
of the Lord GOD *b* David my father	1Kin 2:26	6440
established *b* the LORD for ever	1Kin 2:45	6440
as he walked *b* thee in truth	1Kin 3:6	6440
there was none like thee *b* thee	1Kin 3:12	6440
stood *b* the ark of the covenant	1Kin 3:15	6440
unto the king, and stood *b* him	1Kin 3:16	6440
Thus they spake *b* the king	1Kin 3:22	6440
they brought a sword *b* the king	1Kin 3:24	6440
the porch *b* the temple of the	1Kin 6:3	
the breadth thereof *b* the house	1Kin 6:3	
ready *b* it was brought thither	1Kin 6:7	4551
house, that is, the temple *b* it	1Kin 6:17	3942
the chains of gold *b* the oracle	1Kin 6:21	6440
and the porch was *b* them	1Kin 7:6	
and the thick beam were *b* them	1Kin 7:6	
b the oracle, with the flowers,	1Kin 7:49	6440
unto him, were with him *b* the ark	1Kin 8:5	6440
in the holy place *b* the oracle	1Kin 8:8	
Solomon stood *b* the altar of the	1Kin 8:22	6440
walk *b* thee with all their heart	1Kin 8:23	6440
b me as thou hast walked *b* me	1Kin 8:25	6440
thy servant prayeth *b* thee to day	1Kin 8:28	6440
the oath come *b* thine altar in	1Kin 8:31	6440
be smitten down *b* the enemy	1Kin 8:33	6440
give them compassion *b* them who	1Kin 8:50	6440
he arose from *b* the altar of the	1Kin 8:54	6440
have made supplication *b* the LORD	1Kin 8:59	6440
him, offered sacrifice *b* the LORD	1Kin 8:62	6440
that was *b* the house of the LORD	1Kin 8:64	6440
the brasen altar that was *b* the	1Kin 8:64	6440
b the LORD our God, seven days and	1Kin 8:65	6440
that thou hast made *b* me	1Kin 9:3	6440
And if thou wilt walk *b* me	1Kin 9:4	6440
statutes which I have set *b* you	1Kin 9:6	6440
the altar that was *b* the LORD	1Kin 9:25	6440
which stand continually *b* thee	1Kin 10:8	6440
in the hill that is *b* Jerusalem	1Kin 11:7	
a light alway *b* me in Jerusalem	1Kin 11:36	6440
that stood *b* Solomon his father	1Kin 12:6	
up with him, and which stood *b* him	1Kin 12:8	6440
people went to worship *b* the one	1Kin 12:30	6440
him again, and became as it was *b*	1Kin 13:6	7223
evil above all that were *b* thee	1Kin 14:9	6440
cast out *b* the children of Israel	1Kin 14:24	6440
father, which he had done *b* him	1Kin 15:3	6440
worse than all that were *b* him	1Kin 16:25	6440
LORD above all that were *b* him	1Kin 16:30	6440
kings of Israel that were *b* him	1Kin 16:33	6440
b whom I stand, there shall not	1Kin 17:1	6440
brook Cherith, that is *b* Jordan	1Kin 17:3	
brook Cherith, that is *b* Jordan	1Kin 17:5	
b whom I stand, I will surely	1Kin 18:15	6440
ran *b* Ahab to the entrance of	1Kin 18:46	6440
stand upon the mount *b* the LORD	1Kin 19:11	6440
in pieces the rocks *b* the LORD	1Kin 19:11	6440
with twelve yoke of oxen *b* him	1Kin 19:19	6440
b them like two little flocks of	1Kin 20:27	5048
b him, to bear witness against	1Kin 21:10	5048
children of Belial, and sat *b* him	1Kin 21:13	5048
cast out *b* the children of Israel	1Kin 21:26	6440
how Ahab humbleth himself *b* me	1Kin 21:29	6440
because he humbleth himself *b* me	1Kin 21:29	6440
the prophets prophesied *b* them	1Kin 22:10	6440
stood *b* the LORD, and said, I will	1Kin 22:21	6440
and fell on his knees *b* Elijah	2Kin 1:13	5048
b I be taken away from thee	2Kin 2:9	2962
themselves to the ground *b* him	2Kin 2:15	
b whom I stand, surely, were it	2Kin 3:14	6440
so that they fled *b* them	2Kin 3:24	6440
had called her, she stood *b* him	2Kin 4:12	6440
And Gehazi passed on *b* them	2Kin 4:31	6440
the prophets were sitting *b* him	2Kin 4:38	6440
I set this *b* an hundred men	2Kin 4:43	6440
So he set it *b* them, and they did	2Kin 4:44	6440
company, and came, and stood *b* him	2Kin 5:15	6440
b whom I stand, I will receive	2Kin 5:16	6440
and they bare them *b* him	2Kin 5:23	6440
he went in, and stood *b* his master	2Kin 5:25	413
set bread and water *b* them	2Kin 6:22	6440
and the king sent a man from *b* him	2Kin 6:32	6440
burden, and came and stood *b* him	2Kin 8:9	6440
Behold, two kings stood not *b* him	2Kin 10:4	6440
the priest of Baal *b* the altars	2Kin 11:18	6440
was put to the worse *b* Israel	2Kin 14:12	6440
smote him *b* the people, and slew	2Kin 15:10	6905
out from *b* the children of Israel	2Kin 16:3	6440
altar, which was *b* the LORD	2Kin 16:14	6440
kings of Israel that were *b* him	2Kin 17:2	6440
out from *b* the children of Israel	2Kin 17:8	6440
whom the LORD carried away *b* them	2Kin 17:11	6440
of Judah, nor any that were *b* him	2Kin 18:5	6440
Ye shall worship *b* this altar in	2Kin 18:22	6440
the LORD, and spread it *b* the LORD	2Kin 19:14	6440
And Hezekiah prayed *b* the LORD	2Kin 19:15	6440
as corn blasted *b* it be grown up	2Kin 19:26	6440
nor come *b* it with shield, nor	2Kin 19:32	6924
how I have walked *b* thee in truth	2Kin 20:3	6440
cast out *b* the children of Israel	2Kin 21:2	6440
b the children of Israel	2Kin 21:9	6440
Amorites did, which were *b* him	2Kin 21:11	6440
And Shaphan read it *b* the king	2Kin 22:10	6440
hast humbled thyself *b* the LORD	2Kin 22:19	6440
rent thy clothes, and wept *b* me	2Kin 22:19	6440
and made a covenant *b* the LORD	2Kin 23:3	6440
high places that were *b* Jerusalem	2Kin 23:13	
unto him was there no king *b* him	2Kin 23:25	6440
the sons of Zedekiah *b* his eyes	2Kin 25:7	6440
b him all the days of his life	2Kin 25:29	6440
Edom *b* any king reigned over the	1Chr 1:43	6440
land, whom God destroyed *b* them	1Chr 5:25	6440
they ministered *b* the dwelling	1Chr 6:32	6440
fled from *b* the Philistines	1Chr 10:1	6440
with them in Hebron *b* the LORD	1Chr 11:3	6440
fled from *b* the Philistines	1Chr 11:13	6440
all Israel played *b* God with all	1Chr 13:8	6440
and there he died *b* God	1Chr 13:10	6440
for God is gone forth *b* thee to	1Chr 14:15	6440
the trumpets *b* the ark of God	1Chr 15:24	6440
and peace offerings *b* God	1Chr 16:1	6440
to minister *b* the ark of the LORD	1Chr 16:4	6440
with trumpets continually *b* the	1Chr 16:6	6440
bring an offering, and come *b* him	1Chr 16:29	6440
Fear *b* him, all the earth	1Chr 16:30	6440
So he left there *b* the ark of the	1Chr 16:37	6440
to minister *b* the ark continually	1Chr 16:37	6440
b the tabernacle of the LORD in	1Chr 16:39	6440
off all thine enemies from *b* thee	1Chr 17:8	6440
took it from him that was *b* thee	1Chr 17:13	6440
sat *b* the LORD, and said, Who am I	1Chr 17:16	6440
out nations from *b* thy people	1Chr 17:21	6440
thy servant be established *b* thee	1Chr 17:24	6440
found in his heart to pray *b* thee	1Chr 17:25	6440
that it may be *b* thee for ever	1Chr 17:27	6440
who came and pitched *b* Medeba	1Chr 19:7	6440
in array *b* the gate of the city	1Chr 19:9	
the battle was set against him *b*	1Chr 19:10	6440
b the Syrians unto the battle	1Chr 19:14	6440
and they fled *b* him	1Chr 19:14	6440
they likewise fled *b* Abishai his	1Chr 19:15	6440
were put to the worse *b* Israel	1Chr 19:16	6440
the host of Hadarezer went *b* them	1Chr 19:16	6440
But the Syrians fled *b* Israel	1Chr 19:18	6440
were put to the worse *b* Israel	1Chr 19:19	6440
months to be destroyed *b* thy foes	1Chr 21:12	6440
not go *b* it to enquire of God	1Chr 21:30	6440
prepared abundantly *b* his death	1Chr 22:5	6440
b the LORD, and *b* his people	1Chr 22:18	6440
ever, to burn incense *b* the LORD	1Chr 23:13	6440
unto them, continually *b* the LORD	1Chr 23:31	6440
Abihu died *b* their father, and had	1Chr 24:2	6440
Levites, wrote them *b* the king	1Chr 24:6	6440
b the chief of the fathers of the	1Chr 24:6	
b all the house of my father to	1Chr 28:4	
the LORD *b* all the congregation	1Chr 29:10	5869
For we are strangers *b* thee	1Chr 29:15	6440
drink *b* the LORD on that day with	1Chr 29:22	6440
been on any king *b* him in Israel	1Chr 29:25	6440
he put *b* the tabernacle of the	2Chr 1:5	6440
to the brasen altar *b* the LORD	2Chr 1:6	6440
go out and come in *b* this people	2Chr 1:10	6440
have had that have been *b* thee	2Chr 1:12	6440
from *b* the tabernacle of the	2Chr 1:13	6440
to burn *b* him sweet incense, and	2Chr 2:4	6440
save only to burn sacrifice *b* him	2Chr 2:6	6440
Also he made *b* the house two	2Chr 3:15	6440
up the pillars *b* the temple	2Chr 3:17	5921
after the manner *b* the oracle	2Chr 4:20	6440
were assembled unto him *b* the ark	2Chr 5:6	6440
seen from the ark *b* the oracle	2Chr 5:9	
he stood *b* the altar of the LORD	2Chr 6:12	6440
kneeled down upon his knees *b* all	2Chr 6:13	5048
that walk *b* thee with all their	2Chr 6:14	6440
my law, as thou hast walked *b* me	2Chr 6:16	6440
which thy servant prayeth *b* thee	2Chr 6:19	6440
the oath come *b* thine altar in	2Chr 6:22	6440
be put to the worse *b* the enemy	2Chr 6:24	6440
make supplication *b* thee in this	2Chr 6:24	6440
deliver them over *b* their enemies	2Chr 6:36	6440
offered sacrifices *b* the LORD	2Chr 7:4	6440
priests sounded trumpets *b* them	2Chr 7:6	5048
that was *b* the house of the LORD	2Chr 7:7	6440
for thee, if thou wilt walk *b* me	2Chr 7:17	6440
which I have set *b* you, and shall	2Chr 7:19	6440
which he had built *b* the porch	2Chr 8:12	6440
minister *b* the priests, as the	2Chr 8:14	5048
which stand continually *b* thee	2Chr 9:7	6440
such seen *b* in the land of Judah	2Chr 9:11	6440
b Solomon his father while he yet	2Chr 10:6	6440
up with him, that stood *b* him	2Chr 10:8	6440
so they were *b* Judah, and the	2Chr 13:13	6440
back, behold, the battle was *b*	2Chr 13:14	6440
Jeroboam and all Israel *b* Abijah	2Chr 13:15	6440
children of Israel fled *b* Judah	2Chr 13:16	6440
and the kingdom was quiet *b* him	2Chr 14:5	6440
bars, while the land is yet *b* us	2Chr 14:7	6440
LORD smote the Ethiopians *b* Asa	2Chr 14:12	6440
Ethiopians *b* Asa, and *b* Judah	2Chr 14:12	6440
b the LORD, and *b* his host	2Chr 14:13	6440
that was *b* the porch of the LORD	2Chr 15:8	6440
the prophets prophesied *b* them	2Chr 18:9	6440
stood *b* the LORD, and said, I will	2Chr 18:20	6440
wrath upon thee from *b* the LORD	2Chr 19:2	6440
Levites shall be officers *b* you	2Chr 19:11	6440
of the LORD, *b* the new court,	2Chr 20:5	6440
of this land *b* thy people Israel	2Chr 20:7	6440
we stand *b* this house, and in thy	2Chr 20:9	6440
And all Judah stood *b* the LORD	2Chr 20:13	6440
b the wilderness of Jeruel	2Chr 20:16	6440
of Jerusalem fell *b* the LORD	2Chr 20:18	6440
as they went out *b* the army	2Chr 20:21	6440
the priest of Baal *b* the altars	2Chr 23:17	6440
the rest of the money *b* the king	2Chr 24:14	6440
shall make thee fall *b* the enemy	2Chr 25:8	6440
and bowed down himself *b* them	2Chr 25:14	6440
was put to the worse *b* Israel	2Chr 25:22	6440
even rose up in his forehead *b*	2Chr 26:19	6440
his ways *b* the LORD his God	2Chr 27:6	6440
cast out *b* the children of Israel	2Chr 28:3	6440
he went out *b* the host that came	2Chr 28:9	6440
the spoil *b* the princes and all	2Chr 28:14	6440
hath chosen you to stand *b* him	2Chr 29:11	6440
they are *b* the altar of the LORD	2Chr 29:19	6440
for the sin offering *b* the king	2Chr 29:23	6440
b them that lead them captive	2Chr 30:9	6440
right and truth *b* the LORD his God	2Chr 31:20	6440
Ye shall worship *b* one altar	2Chr 32:12	6440
cast out *b* the children of Israel	2Chr 33:2	6440
which I have chosen *b* all the	2Chr 33:7	
b the children of Israel	2Chr 33:9	6440
greatly *b* the God of his fathers	2Chr 33:12	
graven images, *b* he was humbled	2Chr 33:19	6440
And humbled not himself *b* the LORD	2Chr 33:23	6440
And Shaphan read it *b* the king	2Chr 34:18	6440
have read *b* the king of Judah	2Chr 34:24	6440
thou didst humble thyself *b* God	2Chr 34:27	6440
and humbledst thyself *b* me	2Chr 34:27	6440
rend thy clothes, and weep *b* me	2Chr 34:27	6440
and made a covenant *b* the LORD	2Chr 34:31	6440
humbled not himself *b* Jeremiah	2Chr 36:12	6440
this house was laid *b* their eyes	Ezr 3:12	6440
us hath been plainly read *b* me	Ezr 4:18	6925
letter was read *b* Rehum, and	Ezr 4:23	6925
those deliver thou *b* the God of	Ezr 7:19	6925
extended mercy unto me *b* the king	Ezr 7:28	6440
b all the king's mighty princes	Ezr 7:28	6440
might afflict ourselves *b* our God	Ezr 8:21	6440
until ye weigh them *b* the chief	Ezr 8:29	6440
we are *b* thee in our trespasses	Ezr 9:15	6440
for we cannot stand *b* thee	Ezr 9:15	6440
himself down *b* the house of God	Ezr 10:1	6440
rose up from *b* the house of God	Ezr 10:6	6440
prayed *b* the God of heaven,	Neh 1:4	6440
servant, which I pray *b* thee now	Neh 1:6	6440
the king, that wine was *b* him	Neh 2:1	6440
even *b* the dragon well, and to the	Neh 2:13	
he spake *b* his brethren and the	Neh 4:2	6440
sin be blotted out from *b* thee	Neh 4:5	6440
thee to anger *b* the builders	Neh 4:5	5048
b me were chargeable unto the	Neh 5:15	6440
they reported his good deeds *b* me	Neh 6:19	6440
street that was *b* the water gate	Neh 8:1	6440
b the congregation both of men	Neh 8:2	6440
b the street that was *b* the	Neh 8:3	6440
b the men and the women, and those	Neh 8:3	5048
his heart faithful *b* thee	Neh 9:8	6440
thou didst divide the sea *b* them	Neh 9:11	6440
thou subduedst *b* them the	Neh 9:24	6440
rest, they did evil again *b* thee	Neh 9:28	6440
the trouble seem little *b* thee	Neh 9:32	6440
fat land which thou gavest *b* them	Neh 9:35	6440
of God, and Ezra the scribe *b* them	Neh 12:36	6440

b this, Eliashib the priest, Neh 13:4 6440
began to be dark *b* the sabbath Neh 13:19 6440
of the provinces, being *b* him Est 1:3 6440
To bring Vashti the queen *b* the Est 1:11 6440
And Memucan answered *b* the king Est 1:16 6440
the queen to be brought in *b* him Est 1:17 6440
come no more *b* king Ahasuerus Est 1:19 6440
Mordecai walked every day *b* the Est 2:11 6440
book of the chronicles *b* the king Est 2:23 6440
b Haman from day to day, and from Est 3:7 6440
came even *b* the king's gate Est 4:2 6440
which was *b* the king's gate Est 4:6 6440
to make request *b* him for her Est 4:8 6440
and they were read *b* the king Est 6:1 6440
of the city, and proclaim *b* him Est 6:9 6440
of the city, and proclaimed *b* him Est 6:11 6440
b whom thou hast begun to fall, Est 6:13 6440
him, but shalt surely fall *b* him Est 6:13 6440
Then Haman was afraid *b* the king Est 7:6 6440
the queen also *b* me in the house Est 7:8 5973
said *b* the king, Behold also, the Est 7:9 6440
And Mordecai came *b* the king Est 8:1 6440
Esther spake yet again *b* the king Est 8:3 6440
arose, and stood *b* the king, Est 8:4 6440
the thing seem right *b* the king Est 8:5 6440
the palace was brought *b* the king Est 9:11 6440
But when Esther came *b* the king Est 9:25 6440
to present themselves *b* the LORD Job 1:6 5921
to present themselves *b* the LORD Job 2:1 5921
to present himself *b* the LORD Job 2:1 6440
For my sighing cometh *b* I eat Job 3:24 6440
Then a spirit passed *b* my face Job 4:15 5921
an image was *b* mine eyes, there Job 4:16 5048
which are crushed *b* the moth Job 4:19 6440
it withereth *b* any other herb Job 8:12 6440
He is green *b* the sun, and his Job 8:16 6440
B I go whence I shall not return, Job 10:21 2962
will maintain mine own ways *b* him Job 13:15
an hypocrite shall not come *b* him Job 13:16 6440
fear, and restrainest prayer *b* God Job 15:4 6440
or wast thou made *b* the hills Job 15:7 6440
shall be accomplished *b* his time Job 15:32 3808
they that went *b* were affrighted Job 18:20 6931
and their offspring *b* their eyes Job 21:8
They are as stubble *b* the wind Job 21:18 6440
as there are innumerable *b* him Job 21:33 6440
I would order my cause *b* him Job 23:4 6440
I was not cut off *b* the darkness Job 23:17 6440
Hell is naked *b* him, and Job 26:6 5048
also let loose the bridle *b* me Job 30:11 6440
me, set thy words in order *b* me Job 33:5 6440
see him, yet judgment is *b* him Job 35:14 6440
who then is able to stand *b* me Job 41:10 6440
sorrow is turned into joy *b* him Job 41:22 6440
Job twice as much as he had *b* Job 42:10
had been of his acquaintance *b* Job 42:11 6440
make thy way straight *b* my face Ps 5:8
I have set the LORD always *b* me Ps 16:8 5048
his temple, and my cry came *b* him Ps 18:6 6440
At the brightness that was *b* him Ps 18:12 5048
For all his judgments were *b* me Ps 18:22 5048
I was also upright *b* him, and I Ps 18:23 5973
them small as the dust *b* the wind Ps 18:42
pay my vows *b* them that fear him Ps 22:25 6440
the nations shall worship *b* thee Ps 22:27 6440
down to the dust shall bow *b* him Ps 22:29 6440
Thou preparest a table *b* me in Ps 23:5 6440
thy lovingkindness is *b* mine eyes Ps 26:3 5048
trust in thee *b* the sons of men Ps 31:19 5048
I am cut off from *b* thine eyes Ps 31:22 5048
changed his behaviour *b* Abimelech Ps 34:t 6440
Let them be as chaff *b* the wind Ps 35:5 6440
is no fear of God *b* his eyes Ps 36:1 5048
Lord, all my desire is *b* thee Ps 38:9 5048
and my sorrow is continually *b* me Ps 38:17 5048
bridle, while the wicked is *b* me Ps 39:1 5048
and mine age is as nothing *b* thee Ps 39:5 5048
b I go hence, and be no more Ps 39:13 2962
settest me *b* thy face for ever Ps 41:12
when shall I come and appear *b* God Ps 42:2 6440
My confusion is continually *b* me Ps 44:15 5048
a fire shall devour *b* him Ps 50:3 6440
to have been continually *b* me Ps 50:8 5048
and set them in order *b* thine eyes Ps 50:21
and my sin is ever *b* me Ps 51:3 5048
for it is good *b* thy saints Ps 52:9 5048
they have not set God *b* them Ps 54:3 5048
that I may walk *b* God in the Ps 56:13 6440
they have digged a pit *b* me Ps 57:6 6440
B your pots can feel the thorns, Ps 58:9 2962
He shall abide *b* God for ever Ps 61:7 6440
people, pour out your heart *b* him Ps 62:8 6440
also that hate him flee *b* him Ps 68:1 6440
as wax melteth *b* the fire Ps 68:2 6440
let them rejoice *b* God Ps 68:3 6440
by his name JAH, and rejoice *b* him Ps 68:4 6440
thou wentest forth *b* thy people Ps 68:7 6440
The singers went *b*, the players Ps 68:25 6924
mine adversaries are all *b* thee Ps 69:19 5048
their table become a snare *b* them Ps 69:22 6440
in the wilderness shall bow *b* him Ps 72:9 6440
all kings shall fall down *b* him Ps 72:11
I was as a beast *b* thee Ps 73:22 5973
cast out the heathen also *b* them Ps 78:55 6440
of the prisoner come *b* thee Ps 79:11 6440
B Ephraim and Benjamin Ps 80:2 6440
Thou preparedst room *b* it Ps 80:9 6440
as the stubble *b* the wind Ps 83:13 6440
of them in Zion appeareth *b* God Ps 84:7 413
Righteousness shall go *b* him Ps 85:13 6440
made shall come and worship *b* thee Ps 86:9 6440
and have not set thee *b* them Ps 86:14 5048
I have cried day and night *b* thee Ps 88:1 5048
Let my prayer come *b* thee Ps 88:2 6440

and truth shall go *b* thy face Ps 89:14
beat down his foes *b* his face Ps 89:23
and his throne as the sun *b* me Ps 89:36 6440
B the mountains were brought Ps 90:2 2962
hast set our iniquities *b* thee Ps 90:8 5048
Let us come *b* his presence with Ps 95:2 6924
let us kneel *b* the LORD our maker Ps 95:6 6440
Honour and majesty are *b* him Ps 96:6 6440
fear *b* him, all the earth Ps 96:9 6440
B the LORD Ps 96:13 6440
A fire goeth *b* him, and burneth up Ps 97:3 6440
make a joyful noise *b* the LORD Ps 98:6 6440
B the LORD Ps 98:9 6440
come *b* his presence with singing Ps 100:2
set no wicked thing *b* mine eyes Ps 101:3 6440
out his complaint *b* the LORD Ps 102:t 6440
seed shall be established *b* thee Ps 102:28 6440
He sent a man *b* them, even Joseph Ps 105:17 6440
chosen stood *b* him in the breach Ps 106:23 6440
Let them be *b* the LORD Ps 109:15 5048
I will walk *b* the LORD in the Ps 116:9 6440
thy judgments have I laid *b* me Ps 119:30
of thy testimonies also *b* kings Ps 119:46 5048
B I was afflicted I went astray Ps 119:67 2962
for all my ways are *b* thee Ps 119:168 5048
Let my cry come near *b* thee Ps 119:169 6440
Let my supplication come *b* thee Ps 119:170 6440
b the gods will I sing praise Ps 138:1 5048
Thou hast beset me behind and *b* Ps 139:5 6924
be set forth *b* thee as incense Ps 141:2 6440
Set a watch, O LORD, *b* my mouth Ps 141:3
I poured out my complaint *b* him Ps 142:2 6440
I shewed *b* him my trouble Ps 142:2 6440
who can stand *b* his cold Ps 147:17 6440
eyelids look straight *b* thee Prov 4:25 5048
of man are *b* the eyes of the LORD Prov 5:21 5227
of his way, *b* his works of old Prov 8:22 6924
B the mountains were settled, Prov 8:25 2962
b the hills was I brought forth Prov 8:25 6440
delight, rejoicing always *b* him Prov 8:30 6440
The evil bow *b* the good Prov 14:19 6440
and destruction are *b* the LORD Prov 15:11 6440
and *b* honour is humility Prov 15:33 6440
Pride goeth *b* destruction Prov 16:18 6440
and an haughty spirit *b* a fall Prov 16:18 6440
contention, *b* it be meddled with Prov 17:14 6440
Wisdom is *b* him that hath Prov 17:24
B destruction the heart of man is Prov 18:12 6440
and *b* honour is humility Prov 18:12 6440
a matter *b* he heareth it, it is Prov 18:13 2962
him, and bringeth him *b* great men Prov 18:16 6440
he shall stand *b* kings Prov 22:29 6440
he shall not stand *b* mean men Prov 22:29 6440
diligently what is *b* thee Prov 23:1 6440
away the wicked from *b* the king Prov 25:5 6440
b the wicked is as a troubled Prov 25:26 6440
shewed *b* the whole congregation Prov 26:26
but who is able to stand *b* envy Prov 27:4 6440
deny me them not *b* I die Prov 30:7 2962
of old time, which was *b* us Eccl 1:10 6440
that have been *b* me in Jerusalem Eccl 1:16 6440
all that were in Jerusalem *b* me Eccl 2:7 6440
all that were *b* me in Jerusalem Eccl 2:9 6440
give to him that is good *b* God Eccl 2:26 6440
it, that men should fear *b* him Eccl 3:14 6440
even of all that have been *b* them Eccl 4:16 6440
be hasty to utter any thing *b* God Eccl 5:2 6440
neither say thou *b* the angel Eccl 5:6 6440
that knoweth to walk *b* the living Eccl 6:8 5048
why shouldest thou die *b* thy time Eccl 7:17 3808
that fear God, which fear *b* him Eccl 8:12 6440
because he feareth not *b* God Eccl 8:13 6440
or hatred by all that is *b* them Eccl 9:1 6440
vineyard, which is mine, is *b* me Song 8:12 6440
When ye come to appear *b* me Is 1:12 6440
of your doings from *b* mine eyes Is 1:16 5048
For *b* the child shall know to Is 7:16 2962
For *b* the child shall have Is 8:4 2962
taken away *b* the king of Assyria Is 8:4 6440
they joy *b* thee according to the Is 9:3 6440
The Syrians *b*, and the Philistines Is 9:12 6924
be dashed to pieces *b* their eyes Is 13:16
chaff of the mountains *b* the wind Is 17:13 6440
a rolling thing *b* the whirlwind Is 17:13 6440
and *b* the morning he is not Is 17:14 2962
be for them that dwell *b* the LORD Is 23:18 6440
b his ancients gloriously Is 24:23 5048
as the hasty fruit *b* the summer Is 28:4 2962
write it *b* them in a table, and Is 30:8 854
One of Israel to cease from *b* us Is 30:11 6440
Ye shall worship *b* this altar Is 36:7 6440
the LORD, and spread it *b* the LORD Is 37:14 6440
as corn blasted *b* it be grown up Is 37:27 6440
nor come *b* it with shields, nor Is 37:33 6924
how I have walked *b* thee in truth Is 38:3 6440
is with him, and his work *b* him Is 40:10 6440
All nations *b* him are as nothing Is 40:17 5048
Keep silence *b* me, O islands Is 41:1 413
his foot, gave the nations *b* him Is 41:2 6440
b they spring forth I tell you of Is 42:9 2962
I will make darkness light *b* them Is 42:16 6440
b me there was no God formed, Is 43:10 6440
Yea, *b* the day was I am he Is 43:13
holden, to subdue nations *b* him Is 45:1 6440
to open *b* him the two leaved Is 45:1 6440
I will go *b* thee, and make the Is 45:2 6440
to warm at, nor fire to sit *b* it Is 47:14 5048
b it came to pass I shewed it Is 48:5 2962
even *b* the day when thou heardest Is 48:7 6440
cut off nor destroyed from *b* me Is 48:19 6440
thy walls are continually *b* me Is 49:16 5048
for the LORD will go *b* you Is 52:12 6440
For he shall grow up *b* him as a Is 53:2 6440
as a sheep *b* her shearers is dumb Is 53:7 6440

break forth *b* you into singing Is 55:12 6440
for the spirit should fail *b* me Is 57:16 6440
thy righteousness shall go *b* thee Is 58:8 6440
are multiplied *b* thee, and our Is 59:12 5048
to spring forth *b* all the nations Is 61:11 5048
is with him, and his work *b* him Is 62:11 6440
arm, dividing the water *b* them Is 63:12 6440
Behold, it is written *b* me Is 65:6 6440
but did evil *b* mine eyes, and did Is 65:12
that *b* they call, I will answer Is 65:24 2962
but they did evil *b* mine eyes Is 66:4
B she travailed, she brought Is 66:7 2962
b her pain came, she was Is 66:7 2962
I will make, shall remain *b* me Is 66:22 6440
all flesh come to worship *b* me Is 66:23 6440
B I formed thee in the belly I Jer 1:5 2962
b thou camest forth out of the Jer 1:5 2962
lest I confound thee *b* them Jer 1:17 6440
yet thine iniquity is marked *b* me Jer 2:22 6440
b me continually is grief and Jer 6:7
lay stumblingblocks *b* this people Jer 6:21 413
stand *b* me in this house, which Jer 7:10 6440
they shall spread them *b* the sun Jer 8:2
my law which I set *b* them Jer 9:13 6440
b he cause darkness, and *b* Jer 13:16 2962
Moses and Samuel stood *b* me Jer 15:1 6440
to the sword *b* their enemies Jer 15:9 6440
again, and thou shalt stand *b* me Jer 15:19 6440
out of my lips was right *b* thee Jer 17:16 5227
as with an east wind *b* the enemy Jer 18:17 6440
Remember that I stood *b* thee to Jer 18:20 6440
but let them be overthrown *b* thee Jer 18:23 6440
fall by the sword *b* their enemies Jer 19:7 6440
I set *b* you the way of life, and Jer 21:8 6440
were set *b* the temple of the LORD Jer 24:1 6440
in my law, which I have set *b* you Jer 26:4 6440
The prophets that have been *b* me Jer 28:8 6440
b thee of old prophesied both Jer 28:8 6440
and he shall slay them *b* your eyes Jer 29:21
shall be established *b* me Jer 30:20 6440
those ordinances depart from *b* me Jer 31:36 6440
from being a nation *b* me for ever Jer 31:36 6440
b all the Jews that sat in the Jer 32:12 5869
And I charged Baruch *b* them Jer 32:13 5869
done evil *b* me from their youth Jer 32:30 5869
I should remove it from *b* my face Jer 32:31 5921
an honour *b* all the nations of Jer 33:9
man *b* me to offer burnt offerings Jer 33:18 6440
should be no more a nation *b* them Jer 33:24 6440
former kings which were *b* thee Jer 34:5 6440
ye had made a covenant *b* me in Jer 34:15 6440
covenant which they had made *b* me Jer 34:18 6440
I set *b* the sons of the house of Jer 35:5 6440
want a man to stand *b* me for ever Jer 35:19 6440
their supplication *b* the LORD Jer 36:7 6440
that they proclaimed a fast *b* the Jer 36:9 6440
fire on the hearth burning *b* him Jer 36:22 6440
I pray thee, be accepted *b* thee Jer 37:20 6440
out of the dungeon, *b* he die Jer 38:10 2962
my supplication *b* the king Jer 38:26 6440
of Zedekiah in Riblah *b* his eyes Jer 39:6
accomplished in that day *b* thee Jer 39:16 6440
behold, all the land is *b* thee Jer 40:4 6440
supplication be accepted *b* thee Jer 42:2 6440
present your supplication *b* him Jer 42:9 6440
set *b* you and *b* your fathers Jer 44:10 6440
b that Pharaoh smote Gaza Jer 47:1 6440
shepherd that will stand *b* me Jer 49:19 6440
to be dismayed *b* their enemies Jer 49:37 6440
b them that seek their life Jer 49:37 6440
be as the he goats *b* the flocks Jer 50:8 6440
shepherd that will stand *b* me Jer 50:44 6440
the sons of Zedekiah *b* his eyes Jer 52:10
b him all the days of his life Jer 52:33 6440
gone into captivity *b* the enemy Lam 1:5 6440
without strength *b* the pursuer Lam 1:6 6440
all their wickedness come *b* thee Lam 1:22 6440
his right hand from *b* the enemy Lam 2:3 6440
like water *b* the face of the Lord Lam 2:19 5227
a man *b* the face of the most High Lam 3:35 5048
And he spread it *b* me Eze 2:10 6440
and I lay a stumblingblock *b* him Eze 3:20 6440
thee a tile, and lay it *b* thee Eze 4:1 6440
down your slain men *b* your idols Eze 6:4 6440
children of Israel *b* their idols Eze 6:5 6440
and the elders of Judah sat *b* me Eze 8:1 6440
there stood *b* them seventy men of Eze 8:11 6440
men which were *b* the house Eze 9:6 6440
of Israel unto me, and sat *b* me Eze 14:1 6440
of their iniquity *b* their face Eze 14:3 5227
of his iniquity *b* his face Eze 14:4 5227
of his iniquity *b* his face Eze 14:7 5227
mine oil and mine incense *b* them Eze 16:18 6440
thou hast even set it *b* them for Eze 16:19 6440
and committed abomination *b* me Eze 16:50 6440
B thy wickedness was discovered, Eze 16:57 2962
enquire of the LORD, and sat *b* me Eze 20:1 6440
not be polluted *b* the heathen Eze 20:9 5869
not be polluted *b* the heathen Eze 20:14 5869
sanctified in you *b* the heathen Eze 20:41 5869
with bitterness sigh *b* their eyes Eze 21:6
in the gap *b* me for the land Eze 22:30 6440
and I will set judgment *b* them Eze 23:24 6440
bed, and a table prepared *b* it Eze 23:41 6440
Wilt thou yet say *b* him that Eze 28:9 6440
ground, I will lay thee *b* kings Eze 28:17 6440
he shall groan *b* him with the Eze 30:24 6440
I shall brandish my sword *b* them Eze 32:10 5921
they sit *b* thee as my people, and Eze 33:31 6440
their way was *b* me as the Eze 36:17 6440
be sanctified in you *b* their eyes Eze 36:23
be in thine hand *b* their eyes Eze 37:20
in thee, O Gog, *b* their eyes Eze 38:16
The space also *b* the little Eze 40:12 6440

and the arches thereof were *b* them	Eze 40:22	6440
and the arches thereof were *b* them	Eze 40:26	6440
and the altar that was *b* the house	Eze 40:47	6440
twenty cubits, *b* the temple	Eze 41:4	
Now the building that was *b* the	Eze 41:12	
is the table that is *b* the LORD	Eze 41:22	6440
which was *b* the building toward	Eze 42:1	6440
B the length of an hundred cubits	Eze 42:2	
b the chambers was a walk of ten	Eze 42:4	6440
b the temple were an hundred	Eze 42:8	
the way *b* them was like the	Eze 42:11	6440
even the way directly *b* the wall	Eze 42:12	6440
which are *b* the separate place,	Eze 42:13	
thou shalt offer them *b* the LORD	Eze 43:24	6440
sit in it to eat bread *b* the LORD	Eze 44:3	6440
way of the north gate *b* the house	Eze 44:4	
they shall stand *b* them to	Eze 44:11	6440
unto them *b* their idols, and	Eze 44:12	6440
they shall stand *b* me to offer	Eze 44:15	6440
or a widow that had a priest *b*	Eze 44:22	
b the oblation of the holy	Eze 45:7	
b the possession of the city,	Eze 45:7	
gate *b* the LORD in the sabbaths	Eze 46:3	6440
b the LORD in the solemn feasts	Eze 46:9	6440
they might stand *b* the king	Dan 1:5	6440
be looked upon *b* thee, and the	Dan 1:13	6440
brought them in *b* Nebuchadnezzar	Dan 1:18	6440
therefore stood they *b* the king	Dan 1:19	6440
So they came and stood *b* the king	Dan 2:2	6440
and corrupt words to speak *b* me	Dan 2:9	6925
The Chaldeans answered *b* the king	Dan 2:10	6925
other that can shew it *b* the king	Dan 2:11	6925
bring me in *b* the king, and I will	Dan 2:24	6925
in Daniel *b* the king in haste	Dan 2:25	6925
was excellent, stood *b* thee	Dan 2:31	6903
interpretation thereof *b* the king	Dan 2:36	6925
they stood *b* the image that	Dan 3:3	6903
they brought these men *b* the king	Dan 3:13	6925
all the wise men of Babylon *b* me	Dan 4:6	6925
and I told the dream *b* them	Dan 4:7	6925
at the last Daniel came in *b* me	Dan 4:8	
b him I told the dream, saying,	Dan 4:8	6925
drank wine *b* the thousand	Dan 5:1	6903
was Daniel brought in *b* the king	Dan 5:13	6925
have been brought in *b* me	Dan 5:15	6925
said *b* the king, Let thy gifts be	Dan 5:17	6925
trembled and feared *b* him	Dan 5:19	
the vessels of his house *b* thee	Dan 5:23	6925
prayed, and gave thanks *b* his God	Dan 6:10	6925
and making supplication *b* his God	Dan 6:11	6925
spake *b* the king concerning the	Dan 6:12	6925
said *b* the king, That Daniel,	Dan 6:13	6925
of musick brought *b* him	Dan 6:18	6925
forasmuch as *b* him innocency was	Dan 6:22	6925
and also *b* thee, O king, have I	Dan 6:22	6925
and fear *b* the God of Daniel	Dan 6:26	
all the beasts that were *b* it	Dan 7:7	6925
b whom there were three of the	Dan 7:8	6925
issued and came forth from *b* him	Dan 7:10	6925
times ten thousand stood *b* him	Dan 7:10	6925
and they brought him near *b* him	Dan 7:13	6925
came up, and *b* whom three fell	Dan 7:20	
there stood *b* the river a ram	Dan 8:3	6440
that no beasts might stand *b* him	Dan 8:4	6440
I had seen standing *b* the river	Dan 8:6	6440
power in the ram to stand *b* him	Dan 8:7	6440
behold, there stood *b* me as the	Dan 8:15	5048
which he set *b* us by his servants	Dan 9:10	6440
not our prayer *b* the LORD our God	Dan 9:13	
b thee for our righteousnesses	Dan 9:18	6440
presenting my supplication *b* the	Dan 9:20	6440
and to chasten thyself *b* thy God	Dan 10:12	6440
and said unto him that stood *b* me	Dan 10:16	6440
will, and none shall stand *b* him	Dan 11:16	6440
they be overflown from *b* him	Dan 11:22	6440
they are *b* my face	Hos 7:2	5048
not the meat cut off *b* our eyes	Joel 1:16	5048
A fire devoureth *b* them	Joel 2:3	6440
is as the garden of Eden *b* them	Joel 2:3	6440
B their face the people shall be	Joel 2:6	
The earth shall quake *b* them	Joel 2:10	6440
shall utter his voice *b* his army	Joel 2:11	6440
b the great and the terrible day	Joel 2:31	6440
two years *b* the earthquake	Amos 1:1	6440
destroyed I the Amorite *b* them	Amos 2:9	6440
every cow at that which is *b* her	Amos 4:3	5084
go into captivity *b* their enemies	Amos 9:4	6440
their wickedness is come up *b* me	Jonah 1:2	6440
Therefore I fled *b* unto Tarshish	Jonah 4:2	6924
as wax *b* the fire, and as the	Mic 1:4	6440
The breaker is come up *b* them	Mic 2:13	6440
and their king shall pass *b* them	Mic 2:13	6440
contend thou *b* the mountains, and	Mic 6:1	854
I sent *b* thee Moses, Aaron, and	Mic 6:4	6440
Wherewith shall I come *b* the LORD	Mic 6:6	6924
bow myself *b* the high God	Mic 6:6	
shall I come *b* him with burnt	Mic 6:6	6924
Who can stand *b* his indignation	Nah 1:6	6440
in pieces is come up *b* thy face	Nah 2:1	5921
for spoiling and violence are *b* me	Hab 1:3	5048
all the earth keep silence *b* him	Hab 2:20	6440
B him went the pestilence, and	Hab 3:5	6440
B the decree bring forth, *b*	Zeph 2:2	6440
b the day pass as the chaff,	Zeph 2:2	6440
b the fierce anger of the LORD	Zeph 2:2	6440
b the day of the LORD's anger	Zeph 2:2	6440
back your captivity *b* your eyes	Zeph 3:20	
and the people did fear *b* the LORD	Hag 1:12	6440
people, and so is this nation *b* me	Hag 2:14	6440
from *b* a stone was laid upon a	Hag 2:15	2962
silent, O all flesh, *b* the LORD	Zec 2:13	6440
standing *b* the angel of the LORD	Zec 3:1	6440
garments, and stood *b* the angel	Zec 3:3	6440
spake unto those that stood *b* him	Zec 3:4	6440

and thy fellows that sit *b* thee	Zec 3:8	6440
stone that I have laid *b* Joshua	Zec 3:9	6440
b Zerubbabel thou shalt become a	Zec 4:7	6440
b the Lord of all the earth	Zec 6:5	5921
and their men, to pray *b* the LORD,	Zec 7:2	
For *b* these days there was no	Zec 8:10	6440
us go speedily to pray *b* the LORD	Zec 8:21	
Jerusalem, and to pray *b* the LORD	Zec 8:22	
as the angel of the LORD *b* them	Zec 12:8	6440
which is *b* Jerusalem on the east,	Zec 14:4	
like as ye fled from *b* the	Zec 14:5	6440
be like the bowls *b* the altar	Zec 14:20	6440
me, and was afraid *b* my name	Mal 2:5	6440
base *b* all the people, according	Mal 2:9	
and he shall prepare the way *b* me	Mal 3:1	6440
her fruit *b* the time in the field	Mal 3:11	
mournfully *b* the LORD of hosts	Mal 3:14	6440
b him for them that feared the	Mal 3:16	6440
prophet *b* the coming of the great	Mal 4:5	6440
b they came together, she was	Mt 1:18	
they saw in the east, went *b* them	Mt 2:9	4254
the prophets which were *b* you	Mt 5:12	4253
Let your light so shine *b* men	Mt 5:16	1715
Leave there thy gift *b* the altar	Mt 5:24	1715
that ye do not your alms *b* men	Mt 6:1	1715
do not sound a trumpet *b* thee	Mt 6:2	1715
ye have need of, *b* ye ask him	Mt 6:8	4253
cast ye your pearls *b* swine	Mt 7:6	1715
hither to torment us *b* the time	Mt 8:29	4253
ye shall be brought *b* governors	Mt 10:18	1909
therefore shall confess me *b* men	Mt 10:32	1715
him will I confess also *b* my	Mt 10:32	1715
But whosoever shall deny me *b* men	Mt 10:33	1715
him will I also deny *b* my Father	Mt 10:33	1715
I send my messenger *b* thy face	Mt 11:10	4253
shall prepare thy way *b* thee	Mt 11:10	1715
of Herodias danced *b* them	Mt 14:6	3319
being *b* instructed of her mother,	Mt 14:8	4264
to go *b* him unto the other side,	Mt 14:22	4254
And was transfigured *b* them	Mt 17:2	1715
And the multitudes that went *b*	Mt 21:9	4254
go into the kingdom of God *b* you	Mt 21:31	4254
Behold, I have told you *b*	Mt 24:25	4280
were *b* the flood they were eating	Mt 24:38	4253
b him shall be gathered all	Mt 25:32	1715
I will go *b* you into Galilee	Mt 26:32	4254
b the cock crow, thou shalt deny	Mt 26:34	4250
But he denied *b* them all, saying,	Mt 26:70	1715
B the cock crow, thou shalt deny	Mt 26:75	4250
Jesus stood *b* the governor	Mt 27:11	1715
washed his hands *b* the multitude	Mt 27:24	561
and they bowed the knee *b* him	Mt 27:29	1715
he goeth *b* you into Galilee	Mt 28:7	4254
I send my messenger *b* thy face	Mk 1:2	4253
shall prepare thy way *b* thee	Mk 1:2	1715
rising up a great while *b* day	Mk 1:35	1773
the bed, and went forth *b* them all	Mk 2:12	1726
they saw him, fell down *b* him	Mk 3:11	4363
in her, came and fell down *b* him	Mk 5:33	4363
to his disciples to set *b* them	Mk 6:41	3908
the other side *b* unto Bethsaida	Mk 6:45	4254
to his disciples to set *b* them	Mk 8:6	3908
and they did set them *b* the people	Mk 8:6	3908
commanded to set them also *b* them	Mk 8:7	3908
and he was transfigured *b* them	Mk 9:2	1715
and Jesus went *b* them	Mk 10:32	4254
And they that went *b*, and they that	Mk 11:9	4254
and ye shall be brought *b* rulers	Mk 13:9	1909
I will go *b* you into Galilee	Mk 14:28	4254
b the cock crow twice, thou shalt	Mk 14:30	
B the cock crow twice, thou shalt	Mk 14:72	4250
that is, the day *b* the sabbath,	Mk 15:42	4315
that he goeth *b* you into Galilee	Mk 16:7	4254
And they were both righteous *b* God	Lk 1:6	1799
b God in the order of his course	Lk 1:8	1725
he shall go *b* him in the spirit	Lk 1:17	1799
holiness and righteousness *b* him	Lk 1:75	1799
for thou shalt go *b* the face of	Lk 1:76	4253
b he was conceived in the womb	Lk 2:21	4253
b he had seen the Lord's Christ	Lk 2:26	
prepared *b* the face of all people	Lk 2:31	2596
bring him in, and to lay him *b* him	Lk 5:18	1799
his couch into the midst *b* Jesus	Lk 5:19	1715
And immediately he rose up *b* them	Lk 5:25	1799
I send my messenger *b* thy face	Lk 7:27	4253
shall prepare thy way *b* thee	Lk 7:27	1715
he cried out, and fell down *b* him	Lk 8:28	4363
trembling, and falling down *b* him	Lk 8:47	4363
she declared unto him *b* all the	Lk 8:47	1799
disciples to set *b* the multitude	Lk 9:16	3908
And sent messengers *b* his face	Lk 9:52	4253
two *b* his face into every city and	Lk 10:1	4253
eat such things as are set *b* you	Lk 10:8	3908
and I have nothing to set *b* him	Lk 11:6	3908
he had not first washed *b* dinner	Lk 11:38	4253
one of them is forgotten *b* God	Lk 12:6	1799
Whosoever shall confess me *b* men	Lk 12:8	1715
also confess *b* the angels of God	Lk 12:8	1715
But he that denieth me *b* men	Lk 12:9	1799
be denied *b* the angels of God	Lk 12:9	1799
there was a certain man *b* him	Lk 14:2	1715
sinned against heaven, and *b* thee,	Lk 15:18	1799
which justify yourselves *b* men	Lk 16:15	1799
And they which went *b* rebuked him	Lk 18:39	4254
And he ran *b*, and climbed up into a	Lk 19:4	1715
bring hither, and slay them *b* me	Lk 19:27	1715
he had thus spoken, he went *b*	Lk 19:28	1715
hold of his words *b* the people	Lk 20:26	1726
But *b* all these, they shall lay	Lk 21:12	4253
prisons, being brought *b* kings	Lk 21:12	1909
not to meditate *b* what ye shall	Lk 21:14	4304
to stand *b* the Son of man	Lk 21:36	1715
this passover with you *b* I suffer	Lk 22:15	4253
b that thou shalt thrice deny	Lk 22:34	

one of the twelve, went *b* them	Lk 22:47	4281
B the cock crow, thou shalt deny	Lk 22:61	4250
for *b* they were at enmity between	Lk 23:12	4391
I, having examined him *b* you	Lk 23:14	1799
wherein never man *b* was laid	Lk 23:53	3764
mighty in deed and word *b* God	Lk 24:19	1726
And he took it, and did eat *b* them	Lk 24:43	1799
cometh after me is preferred *b* me	Jn 1:15	1715
for he was *b* me	Jn 1:15	4413
coming after me is preferred *b* me	Jn 1:27	1715
a man which is preferred *b* me	Jn 1:30	1715
for he was *b* me	Jn 1:30	4413
B that Philip called thee, when	Jn 1:48	4253
Christ, but that I am sent *b* him	Jn 3:28	1715
another steppeth down *b* me	Jn 5:7	4253
of man ascend up where he was *b*	Jn 6:62	4386
b it hear him, and know what he	Jn 7:51	
say unto you, *B* Abraham was, I am	Jn 8:58	4250
they which *b* had seen him that he	Jn 9:8	4386
his own sheep, he goeth *b* them	Jn 10:4	1715
that ever came *b* me are thieves	Jn 10:8	4253
up to Jerusalem *b* the passover	Jn 11:55	4253
Then Jesus six days *b* the	Jn 12:1	4253
had done so many miracles *b* them	Jn 12:37	1715
Now *b* the feast of the passover,	Jn 13:1	4253
Now I tell you *b* it come, that,	Jn 13:19	4253
I have told you *b* it come to pass	Jn 14:29	4250
that it hated me *b* it hated you	Jn 15:18	4412
I had with thee *b* the world was	Jn 17:5	4253
for thou lovedst me *b* the	Jn 17:24	4253
of David spake *b* concerning Judas	Acts 1:16	4277
b that great and notable day of	Acts 2:20	
foresaw the Lord always *b* my face	Acts 2:25	1799
He seeing this *b* spake of the	Acts 2:31	4275
which God *b* had shewed by the	Acts 3:18	4293
which *b* was preached unto you	Acts 3:20	4296
this man stand here *b* you whole	Acts 4:10	1799
counsel determined *b* to be done	Acts 4:28	4309
standing without *b* the doors	Acts 5:23	4253
them, they set them *b* the council	Acts 5:27	1722
For *b* these days rose up Theudas,	Acts 5:36	4253
Whom they set *b* the apostles	Acts 6:6	1799
b he dwelt in Charran,	Acts 7:2	
Aaron, Make us gods to go *b* us	Acts 7:40	4313
whom God drave out *b* the face of	Acts 7:45	575
Who found favour *b* God, and	Acts 7:46	1799
have slain them which shewed *b* of	Acts 7:52	4293
and like a lamb dumb *b* his shearer	Acts 8:32	1726
to bear my name *b* the Gentiles	Acts 9:15	1799
are come up for a memorial *b* God	Acts 10:4	1799
house, and stood *b* the gate,	Acts 10:17	1909
a man stood *b* me in bright	Acts 10:30	1799
are we all here present *b* God	Acts 10:33	1799
unto witnesses chosen *b* of God	Acts 10:41	4401
the keepers *b* the door kept the	Acts 12:6	4253
told how Peter stood *b* the gate	Acts 12:14	4253
b his coming the baptism of	Acts 13:24	
which was *b* their city, brought	Acts 14:13	4253
trembling, and fell down *b* Paul	Acts 16:29	4363
his house, he set meat *b* them	Acts 16:34	3908
determined the times *b* appointed	Acts 17:26	4384
beat him *b* the judgment seat	Acts 18:17	1715
evil of that way *b* the multitude	Acts 19:9	1799
and burned them *b* all men	Acts 19:19	1799
These going *b* tarried for us at	Acts 20:5	4281
And we went *b* to ship, and sailed	Acts 20:13	4281
(For they had seen *b* with him in	Acts 21:29	4308
which *b* these days madest an	Acts 21:38	4253
Paul down, and set him *b* them	Acts 22:30	1519
conscience *b* God until this day	Acts 23:1	
to his accusers also to say *b*	Acts 23:30	1909
presented Paul also *b* him	Acts 23:33	
ought to have been here *b* thee	Acts 24:19	1909
me, while I stood *b* the council	Acts 24:20	1909
be judged of these things *b* me	Acts 25:9	1909
b that he which is accused have	Acts 25:16	4250
b you, and specially *b* thee	Acts 25:26	1909
answer for myself this day *b* thee	Acts 26:2	1909
b whom also I speak freely	Acts 26:26	4314
thou must be brought *b* Caesar	Acts 27:24	3936
hearers of the law are just *b* God	Rom 2:13	3844
for we have *b* proved both Jews and	Rom 3:9	4256
is no fear of God *b* their eyes	Rom 3:18	561
the world may become guilty *b* God	Rom 3:19	
but not *b* God	Rom 4:2	4314
b him whom he believed, even God	Rom 4:17	2713
And as Esaias said *b*, Except the	Rom 9:29	4280
for we shall all stand *b* the	Rom 14:10	3936
have it to thyself *b* God	Rom 14:22	1799
who also were in Christ *b* me	Rom 16:7	4253
which God ordained *b* the world	1Cor 2:7	4253
judge nothing *b* the time, until	1Cor 4:5	4253
go to law *b* the unjust, and not	1Cor 6:1	1909
the unjust, and not *b* the saints	1Cor 6:1	1909
and that *b* the unbelievers	1Cor 6:6	1909
whatsoever is set *b* you, eat,	1Cor 10:27	3908
one taketh *b* other his own supper	1Cor 11:21	4301
I was minded to come unto you *b*	2Cor 1:15	4386
For we must all appear *b* the	2Cor 5:10	1715
for I have said *b*, that ye are in	2Cor 7:3	4280
boasting, which I made *b* Titus	2Cor 7:14	1909
for you, who have begun *b*	2Cor 8:10	4278
b the churches, the proof of your	2Cor 8:24	
that they would go *b* unto you	2Cor 9:5	4281
bounty, whereof ye had notice *b*	2Cor 9:5	4293
we speak *b* God in Christ	2Cor 12:19	2714
I told you *b*, and foretell you, as	2Cor 13:2	4280
As we said *b*, so say I now again,	Gal 1:9	4280
to them which were apostles *b* me	Gal 1:17	4253
you, behold, *b* God, I lie not	Gal 1:20	1799
For *b* that certain came from	Gal 2:12	4253
I said unto Peter *b* them all	Gal 2:14	1715
b whose eyes Jesus Christ hath	Gal 3:1	2596
preached *b* the gospel unto	Gal 3:8	4283

was confirmed *b* of God in Christ Gal 3:17 4300
But *b* faith came, we were kept Gal 3:23 4253
of the which I tell you *b* Gal 5:21 4302
him *b* the foundation of the world Eph 1:4 4253
and without blame *b* him in love Eph 1:4 2714
which God hath *b* ordained that we Eph 2:10 4282
unto those things which are *b* Phil 3:13 1715
whereof ye heard *b* in the word of Col 1:5 4257
he is *b* all things, and by him all Col 1:17 4253
even after that we had suffered *b* 1Th 2:2 4310
we told you *b* that we should 1Th 3:4 4302
we joy for your sakes *b* our God 1Th 3:9 1715
unblameable in holiness *b* God 1Th 3:13 1715
Who was *b* a blasphemer, and a 1Ti 1:13 4386
prophecies which went *b* on thee 1Ti 1:18 4254
that is good and acceptable *b* God 1Ti 5:4 1799
but *b* two or three witnesses 1Ti 5:19 1909
Them that sin rebuke *b* all 1Ti 5:20 1799
I charge thee *b* God, and the Lord 1Ti 5:21 1799
without preferring one *b* another 1Ti 5:21 4299
beforehand, going *b* to judgment 1Ti 5:24 4254
good profession *b* many witnesses 1Ti 6:12 1799
all things, and *b* Christ Jesus 1Ti 6:13
who *b* Pontius Pilate witnessed a 1Ti 6:13 1909
in Christ Jesus *b* the world began 2Ti 1:9 4253
charging them *b* the Lord that 2Ti 2:14 1799
I charge thee therefore *b* God 2Ti 4:1 1799
Do thy diligence to come *b* winter 2Ti 4:21 4253
brought *b* Nero the second time 2Ti s 1799
promised *b* the world began Titus 1:2 4253
lay hold upon the hope set *b* us Heb 6:18 4295
going *b* for the weakness and Heb 7:18 4254
for after that he had said *b* Heb 10:15 4280
for *b* his translation he had this Heb 11:5 4253
the race that is set *b* us Heb 12:1 4295
was set *b* him endured the cross Heb 12:2 4295
Pure religion and undefiled *b* God Jas 1:27 3844
draw you *b* the judgment seats Jas 2:6 1519
the judge standeth *b* the door Jas 5:9 4253
b the foundation of the world 1Pet 1:20 4253
against them *b* the Lord 2Pet 2:11 3844
spoken *b* by the holy prophets 2Pet 3:2 4280
seeing ye know these things *b* 2Pet 3:17 4267
not be ashamed *b* him at his 1Jn 2:28 575
and shall assure our hearts *b* him 1Jn 3:19 1715
of thy charity *b* the church 3Jn 6 1799
who were *b* of old ordained to Jude 4 4270
b of the apostles of our Lord Jude 17 4280
to present you faultless *b* the Jude 24 2714
Spirits which are *b* his throne Rev 1:4 1799
b the children of Israel, to eat Rev 2:14 1799
not found thy works perfect *b* God Rev 3:2 1799
b my Father, and *b* his angels Rev 3:5 1799
I have set *b* thee an open door, Rev 3:8 1799
worship *b* thy feet, and to know Rev 3:9 1799
of fire burning *b* the throne Rev 4:5 1799
b the throne there was a sea of Rev 4:6 1799
were four beasts full of eyes *b* Rev 4:6 1715
twenty elders fall down *b* him Rev 4:10 1799
and cast their crowns *b* the throne Rev 4:10 1799
elders fell down *b* the Lamb Rev 5:8 1799
stood *b* the throne, and *b* the Rev 7:9 1799
fell *b* the throne on their faces, Rev 7:11 1799
are they *b* the throne of God Rev 7:15 1799
seven angels which stood *b* God Rev 8:2 1799
altar which was *b* the throne Rev 8:3 1799
ascended up *b* God out of the Rev 8:4 1799
the golden altar which is *b* God Rev 9:13 1799
prophesy again *b* many peoples Rev 10:11 1909
standing *b* the God of the earth Rev 11:4 1799
which sat *b* God on their seats, Rev 11:16 1799
the dragon stood *b* the woman Rev 12:4 1799
which accused them *b* our God day Rev 12:10 1799
power of the first beast *b* him Rev 13:12 1799
it were a new song *b* the throne Rev 14:3 1799
b the four beasts, and the elders Rev 14:3 1799
without fault *b* the throne of God Rev 14:5 1799
shall come and worship *b* thee Rev 15:4 1799
Babylon came in remembrance *b* God Rev 16:19 1799
that wrought miracles *b* him Rev 19:20 1799
dead, small and great, stand *b* God Rev 20:12 1799
I fell down to worship *b* the feet Rev 22:8 1715

BEFOREHAND

take no thought *b* what ye shall Mk 13:11 4305
make up *b* your bounty, whereof ye 2Cor 9:5 4294
Some men's sins are open *b* 1Ti 5:24 4271
good works of some are manifest *b* 1Ti 5:25 4271
signify, when it testified *b* the 1Pet 1:11 4303

BEFORETIME

The Horims also dwelt in Seir *b* Deut 2:12 6440
for Hazor *b* was the head of all Josh 11:10 6440
unwittingly, and hated him not *b* Josh 20:5
(*B* in Israel, when a man went to 1Sa 9:9 6440
a Prophet was *b* called a Seer 1Sa 9:9 6440
when all that knew him *b* saw that 1Sa 10:11
afflict them any more, as *b* 2Sa 7:10 7223
Israel dwelt in their tents, as *b* 2Kin 13:5 6440
Now I had not been *b* sad in his Neh 2:1
and *b*, that we may say, He is Is 41:26 6440
which *b* in the same city used Acts 8:9 4391

BEG

be continually vagabonds, and *b* Ps 109:10 7592
therefore shall he *b* in harvest Prov 20:4 7592
to *b* I am ashamed Lk 16:3 1871

BEGAN

then *b* men to call upon the name Gen 4:26 2490
when men *b* to multiply on the Gen 6:1 2490
Noah *b* to be an husbandman, and he Gen 9:20 2490
he *b* to be a mighty one in the Gen 10:8 2490
seven years of dearth *b* to come Gen 41:54 2490
b at the eldest, and left at the Gen 44:12 2490
the people *b* to commit whoredom Num 25:1 2490
b Moses to declare this law, Deut 1:5 2974
the Spirit of the LORD *b* to move Judg 13:25 2490
she *b* to afflict him, and his Judg 16:19 2490
head *b* to grow again after he was Judg 16:22 2490
and when the day *b* to spring Judg 19:25 5927
they *b* to smite of the people, and Judg 20:31 2490
the battle, Benjamin *b* to smite Judg 20:39 2490
But when the flame *b* to arise up Judg 20:40 2490
his eyes *b* to wax dim, that he 1Sa 3:2 2490
when he *b* to reign over Israel 2Sa 2:10
years old when he *b* to reign 2Sa 5:4
that he *b* to build the house of 1Kin 6:1
one years old when he *b* to reign 1Kin 14:21
Nadab the son of Jeroboam *b* to 1Kin 15:25
b Baasha the son of Ahijah to 1Kin 15:33
b Elah the son of Baasha to reign 1Kin 16:8
when he *b* to reign, as soon as he 1Kin 16:11
Judah *b* Omri to reign over Israel 1Kin 16:23
year of Asa king of Judah *b* Ahab 1Kin 16:29
Asa *b* to reign over Judah in the 1Kin 22:41
five years old when he *b* to reign 1Kin 22:42
Ahaziah the son of Ahab *b* to 1Kin 22:51
Now Jehoram the son of Ahab *b* to 2Kin 3:1
king of Judah *b* to reign 2Kin 8:16
old was he when he *b* to reign 2Kin 8:17
was Ahaziah when he *b* to reign 2Kin 8:26
b Ahaziah to reign over Judah 2Kin 9:29
the LORD *b* to cut Israel short 2Kin 10:32 2490
was Jehoash when he *b* to reign 2Kin 11:21
year of Jehu Jehoash *b* to reign 2Kin 12:1
Judah Jehoahaz the son of Jehu *b* 2Kin 13:1
year of Joash king of Judah *b* 2Kin 13:10
five years old when he *b* to reign 2Kin 14:2
of Israel *b* to reign in Samaria 2Kin 14:23
b Azariah son of Amaziah king of 2Kin 15:1
old was he when he *b* to reign 2Kin 15:2
of Jabesh *b* to reign in the nine 2Kin 15:13
b Menahem the son of Gadi to 2Kin 15:17
Pekahiah the son of Menahem *b* to 2Kin 15:23
b to reign over Israel in Samaria 2Kin 15:27
b Jotham the son of Uzziah king 2Kin 15:32
old was he when he *b* to reign 2Kin 15:33
In those days the LORD *b* to send 2Kin 15:37 2490
Jotham king of Judah *b* to reign 2Kin 16:1
old was Ahaz when he *b* to reign 2Kin 16:2
year of Ahaz king of Judah *b* 2Kin 17:1
of Ahaz king of Judah *b* to reign 2Kin 18:1
old was he when he *b* to reign 2Kin 18:2
years old when he *b* to reign 2Kin 21:1
two years old when he *b* to reign 2Kin 21:19
years old when he *b* to reign 2Kin 22:1
years old when he *b* to reign 2Kin 23:31
five years old when he *b* to reign 2Kin 23:36
years old when he *b* to reign 2Kin 24:8
one years old when he *b* to reign 2Kin 24:18
b to reign did lift up the head 2Kin 25:27
he *b* to be mighty upon the earth 1Chr 1:10 2490
the son of Zeruiah *b* to number 1Chr 27:24 2490
Then Solomon *b* to build the house 2Chr 3:1 2490
he *b* to build in the second day 2Chr 3:2 2490
years old when he *b* to reign 2Chr 12:13
year of king Jeroboam *b* Abijah to 2Chr 13:1
And when they *b* to sing and to 2Chr 20:22 2490
five years old when he *b* to reign 2Chr 20:31
two years old when he *b* to reign 2Chr 21:5
old was he when he *b* to reign 2Chr 21:20
was Ahaziah when he *b* to reign 2Chr 22:2
years old when he *b* to reign 2Chr 24:1
five years old when he *b* to reign 2Chr 25:1
old was Uzziah when he *b* to reign 2Chr 26:3
five years old when he *b* to reign 2Chr 27:1
years old when he *b* to reign 2Chr 27:8
years old when he *b* to reign 2Chr 28:1
Hezekiah *b* to reign when he was 2Chr 29:1
Now they *b* on the first day of 2Chr 29:17 2490
And when the burnt offering *b* 2Chr 29:27 2490
the song of the LORD *b* also with 2Chr 29:27 2490
In the third month they *b* to lay 2Chr 31:7 2490
Since the people *b* to bring the 2Chr 31:10 2490
in every work that he *b* in the 2Chr 31:21 2490
years old when he *b* to reign 2Chr 33:1
years old when he *b* to reign 2Chr 33:21
years old when he *b* to reign 2Chr 34:1
he *b* to seek after the God of 2Chr 34:3 2490
twelfth year he *b* to purge Judah 2Chr 34:3 2490
years old when he *b* to reign 2Chr 36:2
five years old when he *b* to reign 2Chr 36:5
years old when he *b* to reign 2Chr 36:9
years old when he *b* to reign 2Chr 36:11
b they to offer burnt offerings Ezr 3:6 2490
b Zerubbabel the son of Shealtiel Ezr 3:8 2490
b to build the house of God which Ezr 5:2 8271
month *b* he to go up from Babylon Ezr 7:9 3246
that the breaches *b* to be stopped Neh 4:7 2490
when the gates of Jerusalem *b* to Neh 13:19 6751
years old when he *b* to reign Jer 52:1
Then they *b* at the ancient men Eze 9:6 2490
Jonah *b* to enter into the city a Jonah 3:4 2490
From that time Jesus *b* to preach Mt 4:17 756
departed, Jesus *b* to say unto the Mt 11:7 756
Then *b* he to upbraid the cities Mt 11:20 756
b to pluck the ears of corn, and Mt 12:1 756
From that time forth *b* Jesus to Mt 16:21 756
b to rebuke him, saying, Be it Mt 16:22 756
b every one of them to say unto Mt 26:22 756
b to be sorrowful and very heavy Mt 26:37 756
Then *b* he to curse and to swear, Mt 26:74 756
as it *b* to dawn toward the first Mt 28:1 2020
b to publish it much, and to blaze Mk 1:45 756
and his disciples *b*, as they went, Mk 2:23 756
he *b* again to teach by the sea Mk 4:1 756
they *b* to pray him to depart out Mk 5:17 756
b to publish in Decapolis how Mk 5:20 756
he *b* to teach in the synagogue Mk 6:2 756
b to send them forth by two and Mk 6:7 756
he *b* to teach them many things Mk 6:34 756
b to carry about in beds those Mk 6:55 756
b to question with him, seeking Mk 8:11 756
he *b* to teach them, that the Son Mk 8:31 756
took him, and *b* to rebuke him Mk 8:32 756
Then Peter *b* to say unto him, Lo, Mk 10:28 756
b to tell them what things should Mk 10:32 756
they *b* to be much displeased with Mk 10:41 756
he *b* to cry out, and say, Jesus, Mk 10:47 756
b to cast out them that sold and Mk 11:15 756
he *b* to speak unto them by Mk 12:1 756
And Jesus answering them *b* to say Mk 13:5 756
they *b* to be sorrowful, and to say Mk 14:19 756
b to be sore amazed, and to be Mk 14:33 756
some *b* to spit on him, and to Mk 14:65 756
b to say to them that stood by, Mk 14:69 756
But he *b* to curse and to swear, Mk 14:71 756
the multitude crying aloud *b* to Mk 15:8 756
b to salute him, Hail, King of Mk 15:18 756
which have been since the world *b* Lk 1:70
Jesus himself *b* to be about Lk 3:23 756
he *b* to say unto them, This day Lk 4:21 756
the ships, so that they *b* to sink Lk 5:7
and the Pharisees *b* to reason Lk 5:21 756
was dead sat up, and *b* to speak Lk 7:15 756
he *b* to speak unto the people Lk 7:24 756
b to wash his feet with tears, and Lk 7:38 756
him *b* to say within themselves Lk 7:49 756
And when the day *b* to wear away Lk 9:12 756
he *b* to say, This is an evil Lk 11:29 756
the Pharisees *b* to urge him Lk 11:53 756
he *b* to say unto his disciples Lk 12:1 756
with one consent *b* to make excuse Lk 14:18 756
Saying, This man *b* to build Lk 14:30 756
and he *b* to be in want Lk 15:14 756
And they *b* to be merry Lk 15:24 756
of the disciples *b* to rejoice Lk 19:37 756
b to cast out them that sold Lk 19:45 756
Then *b* he to speak to the people Lk 20:9 756
And they *b* to enquire among Lk 22:23 756
they *b* to accuse him, saying, We Lk 23:2 756
them the hour when he *b* to amend Jn 4:52 2192
Since the world *b* was it not Jn 9:32
b to wash the disciples' feet, and Jn 13:5 756
of all that Jesus *b* both to do Acts 1:1 756
b to speak with other tongues, as Acts 2:4 756
holy prophets since the world *b* Acts 3:21
b at the same scripture, and Acts 8:35 756
b from Galilee, after the baptism Acts 10:37 756
as I *b* to speak, the Holy Ghost Acts 11:15 756
he *b* to speak boldly in the Acts 18:26 756
Tertullus *b* to accuse him, saying Acts 24:2 756
he had broken it, he *b* to eat Acts 27:35 756
was kept secret since the world *b* Rom 16:25
Christ Jesus before the world *b* 2Ti 1:9
lie, promised before the world *b* Titus 1:2
which at the first *b* to be spoken Heb 2:3

BEGAT

and Irad *b* Mehujael Gen 4:18 3205
and Mehujael *b* Methusael Gen 4:18 3205
and Methusael *b* Lamech Gen 4:18 3205
b a son in his own likeness, Gen 5:3 3205
and he *b* sons and daughters Gen 5:4 3205
hundred and five years, and *b* Enos Gen 5:6 3205
after he *b* Enos eight hundred Gen 5:7 3205
years, and *b* sons and daughters Gen 5:7 3205
lived ninety years, and *b* Cainan Gen 5:9 3205
Enos lived after he *b* Cainan Gen 5:10 3205
years, and *b* sons and daughters Gen 5:10 3205
seventy years, and *b* Mahalaleel Gen 5:12 3205
And Cainan lived after he *b* Gen 5:13 3205
years, and *b* sons and daughters Gen 5:13 3205
sixty and five years, and *b* Jared Gen 5:15 3205
after he *b* Jared eight hundred Gen 5:16 3205
years, and *b* sons and daughters Gen 5:16 3205
sixty and two years, and he *b* Enoch Gen 5:18 3205
Jared lived after he *b* Enoch Gen 5:19 3205
years, and *b* sons and daughters Gen 5:19 3205
and five years, and *b* Methuselah Gen 5:21 3205
b Methuselah three hundred years Gen 5:22 3205
and *b* sons and daughters Gen 5:22 3205
and seven years, and *b* Lamech Gen 5:25 3205
Methuselah lived after he *b* Gen 5:26 3205
two years, and *b* sons and daughters Gen 5:26 3205
eighty and two years, and *b* a son Gen 5:28 3205
Lamech lived after he *b* Noah five Gen 5:30 3205
years, and *b* sons and daughters Gen 5:30 3205
and Noah *b* Shem, Ham, and Japheth Gen 5:32 3205
Noah *b* three sons, Shem, Ham, and Gen 6:10 3205
And Cush *b* Nimrod Gen 10:8 3205
And Mizraim *b* Ludim, and Gen 10:13 3205
Canaan *b* Sidon his firstborn, and Gen 10:15 3205
And Arphaxad *b* Salah Gen 10:24 3205
and Salah *b* Eber Gen 10:24 3205
Joktan *b* Almodad, and Sheleph, and Gen 10:26 3205
b Arphaxad two years after the Gen 11:10 3205
Shem lived after he *b* Arphaxad Gen 11:11 3205
years, and *b* sons and daughters Gen 11:11 3205
five and thirty years, and *b* Salah Gen 11:12 3205
after he *b* Salah four hundred Gen 11:13 3205
years, and *b* sons and daughters Gen 11:13 3205
lived thirty years, and *b* Eber Gen 11:14 3205
after he *b* Eber four hundred Gen 11:15 3205
years, and *b* sons and daughters Gen 11:15 3205
four and thirty years, and *b* Peleg Gen 11:16 3205
after he *b* Peleg four hundred Gen 11:17 3205
years, and *b* sons and daughters Gen 11:17 3205
lived thirty years, and *b* Reu Gen 11:18 3205
lived after he *b* Reu two hundred Gen 11:19 3205
years, and *b* sons and daughters Gen 11:19 3205
two and thirty years, and *b* Serug Gen 11:20 3205
after he *b* Serug two hundred Gen 11:21 3205

years, and *b* sons and daughters	Gen 11:21	3205
lived thirty years, and *b* Nahor	Gen 11:22	3205
Serug lived after he *b* Nahor two	Gen 11:23	3205
years, and *b* sons and daughters	Gen 11:23	3205
nine and twenty years, and *b* Terah	Gen 11:24	3205
lived after he *b* Terah an hundred	Gen 11:25	3205
years, and *b* sons and daughters	Gen 11:25	3205
and *b* Abram, Nahor, and Haran	Gen 11:26	3205
Terah *b* Abram, Nahor, and Haran	Gen 11:27	3205
and Haran *b* Lot	Gen 11:27	3205
And Bethuel *b* Rebekah	Gen 22:23	3205
And Jokshan *b* Sheba, and Dedan	Gen 25:3	3205
Abraham *b* Isaac	Gen 25:19	3205
which they *b* in your land	Lev 25:45	3205
and Machir *b* Gilead	Num 26:29	3205
And Kohath *b* Amram	Num 26:58	3205
Of the Rock that *b* thee thou art	Deut 32:18	3205
and Gilead *b* Jephthah	Judg 11:1	3205
Pharez *b* Hezron,	Ruth 4:18	3205
And Hezron *b* Ram	Ruth 4:19	3205
and Ram *b* Amminadab	Ruth 4:19	3205
And Amminadab *b* Nahshon, and	Ruth 4:20	3205
Nahshon, and Nahshon *b* Salmon	Ruth 4:20	3205
Salmon *b* Boaz, and Boaz *b* Obed	Ruth 4:21	3205
Obed *b* Jesse	Ruth 4:22	3205
and Jesse *b* David	Ruth 4:22	3205
And Cush *b* Nimrod	1Chr 1:10	3205
And Mizraim *b* Ludim, and	1Chr 1:11	3205
Canaan *b* Zidon his firstborn, and	1Chr 1:13	3205
And Arphaxad *b* Shelah	1Chr 1:18	3205
and Shelah *b* Eber	1Chr 1:18	3205
Joktan *b* Almodad, and Sheleph, and	1Chr 1:20	3205
And Abraham *b* Isaac	1Chr 1:34	3205
And Ram *b* Amminadab	1Chr 2:10	3205
and Amminadab *b* Nahshon, prince of	1Chr 2:10	3205
And Nahshon *b* Salma	1Chr 2:11	3205
and Salma *b* Boaz	1Chr 2:11	3205
Boaz *b* Obed, and Obed *b* Jesse,	1Chr 2:12	3205
Jesse *b* his firstborn Eliab, and	1Chr 2:13	3205
Caleb the son of Hezron *b*	1Chr 2:18	3205
Hur *b* Uri, and Uri *b* Bezaleel	1Chr 2:20	3205
And Segub *b* Jair, who had three and	1Chr 2:22	3205
Attai *b* Nathan	1Chr 2:36	3205
and Nathan *b* Zabad	1Chr 2:36	3205
Zabad *b* Ephlal	1Chr 2:37	3205
Ephlal *b* Obed	1Chr 2:37	3205
And Obed *b* Jehu	1Chr 2:38	3205
and Jehu *b* Azariah	1Chr 2:38	3205
And Azariah *b* Helez	1Chr 2:39	3205
and Helez *b* Eleasah	1Chr 2:39	3205
And Eleasah *b* Sisamai	1Chr 2:40	3205
and Sisamai *b* Shallum	1Chr 2:40	3205
Shallum *b* Jekamiah	1Chr 2:41	3205
and Jekamiah *b* Elishama	1Chr 2:41	3205
And Shema *b* Raham, the father of	1Chr 2:44	3205
and Rekem *b* Shammai	1Chr 2:44	3205
and Haran *b* Gazez	1Chr 2:46	3205
Reaiah the son of Shobal *b* Jahath	1Chr 4:2	3205
and Jahath *b* Ahumai, and Lahad	1Chr 4:2	3205
Coz *b* Anub, and Zobebah, and the	1Chr 4:8	3205
the brother of Shuah *b* Mehir	1Chr 4:11	3205
Eshton *b* Beth-rapha, and Paseah,	1Chr 4:12	3205
And Meonothai *b* Ophrah	1Chr 4:14	3205
and Seraiah *b* Joab, the father of	1Chr 4:14	3205
Eleazar *b* Phinehas	1Chr 6:4	3205
Phinehas *b* Abishua	1Chr 6:4	3205
And Abishua *b* Bukki	1Chr 6:5	3205
and Bukki *b* Uzzi	1Chr 6:5	3205
And Uzzi *b* Zerahiah	1Chr 6:6	3205
and Zerahiah *b* Meraioth	1Chr 6:6	3205
Meraioth *b* Amariah	1Chr 6:7	3205
and Amariah *b* Ahitub	1Chr 6:7	3205
And Ahitub *b* Zadok	1Chr 6:8	3205
and Zadok *b* Ahimaaz	1Chr 6:8	3205
And Ahimaaz *b* Azariah	1Chr 6:9	3205
and Azariah *b* Johanan	1Chr 6:9	3205
And Johanan *b* Azariah, (he it is	1Chr 6:10	3205
And Azariah *b* Amariah	1Chr 6:11	3205
and Amariah *b* Ahitub	1Chr 6:11	3205
And Ahitub *b* Zadok	1Chr 6:12	3205
and Zadok *b* Shallum	1Chr 6:12	3205
And Shallum *b* Hilkiah	1Chr 6:13	3205
and Hilkiah *b* Azariah	1Chr 6:13	3205
And Azariah *b* Seraiah	1Chr 6:14	3205
and Seraiah *b* Jehozadak	1Chr 6:14	3205
Heber *b* Japhlet, and Shomer, and	1Chr 7:32	3205
Now Benjamin *b* Bela his firstborn	1Chr 8:1	3205
them, and *b* Uzza, and Ahihud	1Chr 8:7	3205
Shaharaim *b* children in the	1Chr 8:8	3205
he *b* of Hodesh his wife, Jobab,	1Chr 8:9	3205
And of Hushim he *b* Abitub, and	1Chr 8:11	3205
And Mikloth *b* Shimeah	1Chr 8:32	3205
And Ner *b* Kish, and Kish *b* Saul	1Chr 8:33	3205
Saul *b* Jonathan, and Malchi-shua,	1Chr 8:33	3205
and Merib-baal *b* Micah	1Chr 8:34	3205
And Ahaz *b* Jehoadah	1Chr 8:36	3205
and Jehoadah *b* Alemeth, and	1Chr 8:36	3205
and Zimri *b* Moza,	1Chr 8:36	3205
And Moza *b* Binea	1Chr 8:37	3205
And Mikloth *b* Shimeam	1Chr 9:38	3205
And Ner *b* Kish	1Chr 9:39	3205
and Kish *b* Saul	1Chr 9:39	3205
Saul *b* Jonathan, and Malchi-shua,	1Chr 9:39	3205
and Merib-baal *b* Micah	1Chr 9:40	3205
And Ahaz *b* Jarah	1Chr 9:42	3205
Jarah *b* Alemeth, and Azmaveth, and	1Chr 9:42	3205
and Zimri *b* Moza	1Chr 9:42	3205
And Moza *b* Binea	1Chr 9:43	3205
David *b* more sons and daughters	1Chr 14:3	3205
b twenty and eight sons, and	2Chr 11:21	3205
b twenty and two sons, and sixteen	2Chr 13:21	3205
and he *b* sons and daughters	2Chr 24:3	3205
Jeshua *b* Joiakim	Neh 12:10	3205
Joiakim also *b* Eliashib	Neh 12:10	3205
and Eliashib *b* Joiada	Neh 12:10	3205
Joiada *b* Jonathan	Neh 12:11	3205
and Jonathan *b* Jaddua	Neh 12:11	3205
unto thy father that *b* thee	Prov 23:22	3205
fathers that *b* them in this land	Jer 16:3	3205
brought her, and he that *b* her	Dan 11:6	3205
his mother that *b* him shall say	Zec 13:3	3205
his mother that *b* him shall	Zec 13:3	3205
Abraham *b* Isaac	Mt 1:2	*1080*
and Isaac *b* Jacob	Mt 1:2	*1080*
and Jacob *b* Judas and his brethren	Mt 1:2	*1080*
Judas *b* Phares and Zara of Thamar	Mt 1:3	*1080*
and Phares *b* Esrom	Mt 1:3	*1080*
and Esrom *b* Aram	Mt 1:3	*1080*
And Aram *b* Aminadab	Mt 1:4	*1080*
and Aminadab *b* Naasson	Mt 1:4	*1080*
and Naasson *b* Salmon	Mt 1:4	*1080*
And Salmon *b* Booz of Rachab	Mt 1:5	*1080*
and Booz *b* Obed of Ruth	Mt 1:5	*1080*
and Obed *b* Jesse	Mt 1:5	*1080*
And Jesse *b* David the king	Mt 1:6	*1080*
David the king *b* Solomon of her	Mt 1:6	*1080*
And Solomon *b* Roboam	Mt 1:7	*1080*
and Roboam *b* Abia	Mt 1:7	*1080*
and Abia *b* Asa	Mt 1:7	*1080*
And Asa *b* Josaphat	Mt 1:8	*1080*
and Josaphat *b* Joram	Mt 1:8	*1080*
and Joram *b* Ozias	Mt 1:8	*1080*
And Ozias *b* Joatham	Mt 1:9	*1080*
and Joatham *b* Achaz	Mt 1:9	*1080*
and Achaz *b* Ezekias	Mt 1:9	*1080*
And Ezekias *b* Manasses	Mt 1:10	*1080*
and Manasses *b* Amon	Mt 1:10	*1080*
and Amon *b* Josias	Mt 1:10	*1080*
Josias *b* Jechonias and his	Mt 1:11	*1080*
to Babylon, Jechonias *b* Salathiel	Mt 1:12	*1080*
and Salathiel *b* Zorobabel	Mt 1:12	*1080*
And Zorobabel *b* Abiud	Mt 1:13	*1080*
and Abiud *b* Eliakim	Mt 1:13	*1080*
and Eliakim *b* Azor	Mt 1:13	*1080*
And Azor *b* Sadoc	Mt 1:14	*1080*
and Sadoc *b* Achim	Mt 1:14	*1080*
and Achim *b* Eliud	Mt 1:14	*1080*
And Eliud *b* Eleazar	Mt 1:15	*1080*
and Eleazar *b* Matthan	Mt 1:15	*1080*
and Matthan *b* Jacob	Mt 1:15	*1080*
Jacob *b* Joseph the husband of	Mt 1:16	*1080*
and so Abraham *b* Isaac, and	Acts 7:8	*1080*
and Isaac *b* Jacob	Acts 7:8	
Jacob *b* the twelve patriarchs	Acts 7:8	*1080*
of Madian, where he *b* two sons	Acts 7:29	*1080*
Of his own will *b* he us with the	Jas 1:18	*616*
that *b* loveth him also that is	1Jn 5:1	*1080*

BEGET

twelve princes shall he *b*	Gen 17:20	3205
When thou shalt *b* children	Deut 4:25	3205
Thou shalt *b* sons and daughters,	Deut 28:41	3205
from thee, which thou shalt *b*	2Kin 20:18	3205
If a man *b* an hundred children,	Eccl 6:3	3205
from thee, which thou shall *b*	Is 39:7	3205
ye wives, and *b* sons and daughters	Jer 29:6	3205
If he *b* a son that is a robber, a	Eze 18:10	3205
Now, lo, if he *b* a son, that	Eze 18:14	3205
which shall *b* children among you	Eze 47:22	3205

BEGETTEST

issue, which thou *b* after them	Gen 48:6	3205
unto his father, What *b* thou	Is 45:10	3205

BEGETTETH

He that *b* a fool doeth it to his	Prov 17:21	3205
he that *b* a wise child shall have	Prov 23:24	3205
he *b* a son, and there is nothing	Eccl 5:14	3205

BEGGAR

lifteth up the *b* from the	1Sa 2:8	34
was a certain *b* named Lazarus	Lk 16:20	*4434*
it came to pass, that the *b* died	Lk 16:22	*4434*

BEGGARLY

b elements, whereunto ye desire	Gal 4:9	*4434*

BEGGED

to Pilate, and *b* the body of Jesus	Mt 27:58	*154*
Pilate, and *b* the body of Jesus	Lk 23:52	*154*
Is not this he that sat and *b*	Jn 9:8	*4319*

BEGGING

forsaken, nor his seed *b* bread	Ps 37:25	1245
sat by the highway side *b*	Mk 10:46	*4319*
blind man sat by the way side *b*	Lk 18:35	*4319*

BEGIN

and this they *b* to do	Gen 11:6	2490
b to possess it, and contend with	Deut 2:24	2490
This day will I *b* to put the	Deut 2:25	2490
b to possess, that thou mayest	Deut 2:31	2490
b to number the seven weeks from	Deut 16:9	2490
This day will I *b* to magnify thee	Josh 3:7	2490
What man is he that will *b* to	Judg 10:18	2490
he shall *b* to deliver Israel out	Judg 13:5	2490
when I *b*, I will also make an end	1Sa 3:12	2490
Did I then *b* to enquire of God	1Sa 22:15	2490
Jehoram king of Judah *b* to reign	2Kin 8:25	
was the principal to *b* the	Neh 11:17	8462
I *b* to bring evil on the city	Jer 25:29	2490
and *b* at my sanctuary	Eze 9:6	2490
And shall *b* to smite his	Mt 24:49	*756*
b not to say within yourselves,	Lk 3:8	*756*
shall *b* to beat the menservants	Lk 12:45	*756*
ye *b* to stand without, and to	Lk 13:25	*756*
Then shall ye *b* to say, We have	Lk 13:26	*756*
thou *b* with shame to take the	Lk 14:9	*756*
all that behold it *b* to mock him	Lk 14:29	*756*
these things *b* to come to pass	Lk 21:28	*756*
Then shall they *b* to say to the	Lk 23:30	*756*
Do we *b* again to commend	2Cor 3:1	*756*
must *b* at the house of God	1Pet 4:17	*756*
and if it first *b* at us, what	1Pet 4:17	
angel, when he shall *b* to sound	Rev 10:7	*3195*

BEGINNEST

weeks from such time as thou *b* to	Deut 16:9	2490

BEGINNING

In the *b* God created the heaven	Gen 1:1	7225
the *b* of his kingdom was Babel	Gen 10:10	7225
where his tent had been at the *b*	Gen 13:3	8462
still ill favoured, as at the *b*	Gen 41:21	8462
the *b* of my strength, the	Gen 49:3	7225
shall be unto you the *b* of months	Ex 12:2	7218
from the *b* of the year even unto	Deut 11:12	7225
for he is the *b* of his strength	Deut 21:17	7225
from the *b* of revenges upon the	Deut 32:42	7218
camp in the *b* of the middle watch	Judg 7:19	7218
in the *b* of barley harvest	Ruth 1:22	8462
in the latter end than at the *b*	Ruth 3:10	7223
in the *b* of barley harvest	2Sa 21:9	8462
from the *b* of harvest until water	2Sa 21:10	8462
so it was at the *b* of their	2Kin 17:25	8462
waste them any more, as at the *b*	1Chr 17:9	7223
in the *b* of his reign, wrote they	Ezr 4:6	8462
Though thy *b* was small, yet thy	Job 8:7	7225
latter end of Job more than his *b*	Job 42:12	7225
of the LORD is the *b* of wisdom	Ps 111:10	7225
Thy word is true from the *b*	Ps 119:160	7218
of the LORD is the *b* of knowledge	Prov 1:7	7225
possessed me in the *b* of his way	Prov 8:22	7225
up from everlasting, from the *b*	Prov 8:23	7218
of the LORD is the *b* of wisdom	Prov 9:10	8462
The *b* of strife is as when one	Prov 17:14	7225
may be gotten hastily at the *b*	Prov 20:21	7223
God maketh from the *b* to the end	Eccl 3:11	7218
end of a thing than the *b* thereof	Eccl 7:8	7225
The *b* of the words of his mouth	Eccl 10:13	8462
and thy counsellors as at the *b*	Is 1:26	8462
terrible from their *b* hitherto	Is 18:2	1931
terrible from their *b* hitherto	Is 18:7	1931
it not been told you from the *b*	Is 40:21	7218
the generations from the *b*	Is 41:4	7218
Who hath declared from the *b*	Is 41:26	7218
Declaring the end from the *b*	Is 46:10	7225
the former things from the *b*	Is 48:3	227
from the *b* declared it to thee	Is 48:5	227
created now, and not from the *b*	Is 48:7	227
not spoken in secret from the *b*	Is 48:16	7218
For since the *b* of the world men	Is 64:4	5769
b is the place of our sanctuary	Jer 17:12	7223
In the *b* of the reign of	Jer 26:1	7225
In the *b* of the reign of	Jer 27:1	7225
in the *b* of the reign of Zedekiah	Jer 28:1	7225
b of the reign of Zedekiah king	Jer 49:34	7225
in the *b* of the watches pour out	Lam 2:19	7218
in the *b* of the year, in the	Eze 40:1	7218
I had seen in the vision at the *b*	Dan 9:21	8462
At the *b* of thy supplications the	Dan 9:23	8462
The *b* of the word of the LORD by	Hos 1:2	8462
the *b* of the shooting up of the	Amos 7:1	8462
she is the *b* of the sin to the	Mic 1:13	7225
b to sink, he cried, saying, Lord	Mt 14:30	*756*
made them at the *b* made them male	Mt 19:4	*746*
but from the *b* it was not so	Mt 19:8	*746*
b from the last unto the first	Mt 20:8	*756*
All these are the *b* of sorrows	Mt 24:8	*746*
the *b* of the world to this time	Mt 24:21	*746*
The *b* of the gospel of Jesus	Mk 1:1	*746*
But from the *b* of the creation	Mk 10:6	*746*
such as was not from the *b* of the	Mk 13:19	*746*
unto us, which from the *b* were	Lk 1:2	*746*
b from Galilee to this place	Lk 23:5	*756*
b at Moses and all the prophets,	Lk 24:27	*756*
among all nations, *b* at Jerusalem	Lk 24:47	*756*
In the *b* was the Word, and the	Jn 1:1	*746*
The same was in the *b* with God	Jn 1:2	*746*
Every man at the *b* doth set forth	Jn 2:10	*4412*
This *b* of miracles did Jesus in	Jn 2:11	*746*
For Jesus knew from the *b* who	Jn 6:64	*746*
b at the eldest, even unto the	Jn 8:9	*756*
that I said unto you from the *b*	Jn 8:25	*746*
He was a murderer from the *b*	Jn 8:44	*746*
ye have been with me from the *b*	Jn 15:27	*746*
I said not unto you at the *b*	Jn 16:4	*746*
B from the baptism of John, unto	Acts 1:22	*756*
rehearsed the matter from the *b*	Acts 11:4	*756*
fell on them, as on us at the *b*	Acts 11:15	*746*
his works from the *b* of the world	Acts 15:18	
Which knew me from the *b*, if they	Acts 26:5	509
which from the *b* of the world	Eph 3:9	
that in the *b* of the gospel, when	Phil 4:15	*746*
who is the *b*, the firstborn from	Col 1:18	*746*
because God hath from the *b*	2Th 2:13	*746*
in the *b* hast laid the foundation	Heb 1:10	*746*
Christ, if we hold the *b* of our	Heb 3:14	*746*
descent, having neither *b* of days	Heb 7:3	*746*
end is worse with them than the *b*	2Pet 2:20	*4413*
were from the *b* of the creation	2Pet 3:4	*746*
That which was from the *b*	1Jn 1:1	*746*
which ye had from the *b*	1Jn 2:7	*746*
which ye have heard from the *b*	1Jn 2:7	*746*
have known him that is from the *b*	1Jn 2:13	*746*
have known him that is from the *b*	1Jn 2:14	*746*
which ye have heard from the *b*	1Jn 2:24	*746*
from the *b* shall remain in you	1Jn 2:24	*746*
for the devil sinneth from the *b*	1Jn 3:8	*746*
message that ye heard from the *b*	1Jn 3:11	*746*
but that which we had from the *b*	2Jn 5	*746*
That, as ye have heard from the *b*	2Jn 6	*746*
I am Alpha and Omega, the *b*	Rev 1:8	*746*
the *b* of the creation of God	Rev 3:14	*746*
I am Alpha and Omega, the *b*	Rev 21:6	*746*
I am Alpha and Omega, the *b*	Rev 22:13	*746*

BEGINNINGS
in the *b* of your months, ye shall	Num 10:10	7218
in the *b* of your months ye shall	Num 28:11	7218
do better unto you than at your *b*	Eze 36:11	7221
these are the *b* of sorrows	Mk 13:8	746

BEGOTTEN
b Seth were eight hundred years	Gen 5:4	3205
b of thy father, she is thy	Lev 18:11	4138
have I *b* them, that thou	Num 11:12	3205
The children that are *b* of them	Deut 23:8	3205
and ten sons of his body *b*	Judg 8:30	3318
or who hath *b* the drops of dew	Job 38:28	3205
this day have I *b* thee	Ps 2:7	3205
thine heart, Who hath *b* me these	Is 49:21	3205
for they have *b* strange children	Hos 5:7	3205
as of the only *b* of the Father	Jn 1:14	3439
the only *b* Son, which is in the	Jn 1:18	3439
that he gave his only *b* Son	Jn 3:16	3439
the name of the only *b* Son of God	Jn 3:18	3439
my Son, this day have I *b* thee	Acts 13:33	1080
I have *b* you through the gospel	1Cor 4:15	1080
whom I have *b* in my bonds	Philem 10	1080
my Son, this day have I *b* thee	Heb 1:5	1080
art my Son, to day have I *b* thee	Heb 5:5	1080
offered up his only *b* son	Heb 11:17	3439
to his abundant mercy hath *b* us	1Pet 1:3	313
his only *b* Son into the world	1Jn 4:9	3439
loveth him also that is *b* of him	1Jn 5:1	1080
but he that is *b* of God keepeth	1Jn 5:18	1080
the first *b* of the dead, and the	Rev 1:5	4416

BEGUILE
lest any man should *b* you with	Col 2:4	3884
Let no man *b* you of your reward	Col 2:18	2603

BEGUILED
the woman said, The serpent *b* me	Gen 3:13	5377
wherefore then hast thou *b* me	Gen 29:25	7411
wherewith they have *b* you in the	Num 25:18	5230
saying, Wherefore have ye *b* us	Josh 9:22	7411
as the serpent *b* Eve through his	2Cor 11:3	1818

BEGUILING
b unstable souls	2Pet 2:14	1185

BEGUN
the plague is *b*	Num 16:46	2490
the plague was *b* among the people	Num 16:47	2490
I have *b* to give Sihon and his	Deut 2:31	2490
thou hast *b* to shew thy servant	Deut 3:24	2490
before whom thou hast *b* to fall	Est 6:13	2490
undertook to do as they had *b*	Est 9:23	2490
And when he had *b* to reckon	Mt 18:24	756
desired Titus, that as he had *b*	2Cor 8:6	4278
for you, who have *b* before	2Cor 8:10	4278
having *b* in the Spirit, are ye	Gal 3:3	1728
that he which hath *b* a good work	Phil 1:6	1728
for when they have *b* to wax	1Ti 5:11	2691

BEHALF
the *b* of the children of Israel	Ex 27:21	854
sent messengers to David on his *b*	2Sa 3:12	8478
to shew himself strong in the *b*	2Chr 16:9	5973
I have yet to speak on God's *b*	Job 36:2	
own *b* shall cause the reproach	Dan 11:18	
I am glad therefore on your *b*	Rom 16:19	1909
I thank my God always on your *b*	1Cor 1:4	4012
may be given by many on our *b*	2Cor 1:11	5228
you occasion to glory on our *b*	2Cor 5:12	5228
and of our boasting on your *b*	2Cor 8:24	5228
you should be in vain in this *b*	2Cor 9:3	3313
it is given in the *b* of Christ	Phil 1:29	5228
but let him glorify God on this *b*	1Pet 4:16	3313

BEHAVE
should *b* themselves strangely	Deut 32:27	5234
let us *b* ourselves valiantly for	1Chr 19:13	2388
I will *b* myself wisely in a	Ps 101:2	7919
the child shall *b* himself proudly	Is 3:5	7292
Doth not *b* itself unseemly,	1Cor 13:5	807
know how thou oughtest to *b*	1Ti 3:15	390

BEHAVED
sent him, and *b* himself wisely	1Sa 18:5	7919
David *b* himself wisely in all his	1Sa 18:14	7919
saw that he *b* himself very wisely	1Sa 18:15	7919
that David *b* himself more wisely	1Sa 18:30	7919
I *b* myself as though he had been	Ps 35:14	1980
Surely I have *b* and quieted myself	Ps 131:2	7737
as they have *b* themselves ill in	Mic 3:4	7489
unblameably we *b* ourselves among	1Th 2:10	1096
for we *b* not ourselves disorderly	2Th 3:7	812

BEHAVETH
he *b* himself uncomely toward his	1Cor 7:36	807

BEHAVIOUR
And he changed his *b* before them	1Sa 21:13	2940
he changed his *b* before Abimelech	Ps 34:*t*	2940
wife, vigilant, sober, of good *b*	1Ti 3:2	2887
that they be in *b* as becometh	Titus 2:3	2688

BEHEADED
heifer that is *b* in the valley	Deut 21:6	6202
b him, and took his head, and gat	2Sa 4:7	
he sent, and *b* John in the prison	Mt 14:10	607
he said, It is John, whom I *b*	Mk 6:16	607
he went and *b* him in the prison,	Mk 6:27	607
And Herod said, John have I *b*	Lk 9:9	607
were *b* for the witness of Jesus	Rev 20:4	3990

BEHELD
the Egyptians *b* the woman that	Gen 12:14	7200
b all the plain of Jordan, that	Gen 13:10	7200
all the land of the plain, and *b*	Gen 19:28	7200
Jacob *b* the countenance of Laban,	Gen 31:2	7200
Israel *b* Joseph's sons, and said,	Gen 48:8	7200
when he *b* the serpent of brass,	Num 21:9	5027
He hath not *b* iniquity in Jacob,	Num 23:21	5027
that *b* while Samson made sport	Judg 16:27	7200
David *b* the place where Saul lay,	1Sa 26:5	7200
as he was destroying, the LORD *b*	1Chr 21:15	7200
If I *b* the sun when it shined, or	Job 31:26	7200
I *b* the transgressors, and was	Ps 119:158	7200
I looked on my right hand, and *b*	Ps 142:4	7200
b among the simple ones, I	Prov 7:7	7200
Then I *b* all the work of God,	Eccl 8:17	7200
For I *b*, and there was no man	Is 41:28	7200
I *b* the earth, and, lo, it was	Jer 4:23	7200
I *b* the mountains, and, lo, they	Jer 4:24	7200
I *b*, and, lo, there was no man, and	Jer 4:25	7200
I *b*, and, lo, the fruitful place	Jer 4:26	7200
Upon this I awaked, and *b*	Jer 31:26	7200
Now as I *b* the living creatures,	Eze 1:15	7200
Then I *b*, and lo a likeness as the	Eze 8:2	7200
And when I *b*, lo, the sinews and	Eze 37:8	7200
I *b* till the wings thereof were	Dan 7:4	
After this I *b*, and lo another,	Dan 7:6	
I *b* till the thrones were cast	Dan 7:9	
I *b* then because of the voice of	Dan 7:11	
I *b* even till the beast was slain	Dan 7:11	
I *b*, and the same horn made war	Dan 7:21	
he *b*, and drove asunder the	Hab 3:6	7200
But Jesus *b* them, and said unto	Mt 19:26	1689
all the people, when they *b* him	Mk 9:15	1492
b how the people cast money into	Mk 12:41	2334
of Joses *b* where he was laid	Mk 15:47	2334
I *b* Satan as lightning fall from	Lk 10:18	2334
he *b* the city, and wept over it,	Lk 19:41	1492
he *b* them, and said, What is this	Lk 20:17	1689
But a certain maid *b* him as he	Lk 22:56	1492
b the sepulchre, and how his body	Lk 23:55	2300
he *b* the linen clothes laid by	Lk 24:12	991
we *b* his glory, the glory as of	Jn 1:14	2300
And when Jesus *b* him, he said,	Jn 1:42	1689
spoken these things, while they *b*	Acts 1:9	991
b your devotions, I found an	Acts 17:23	333
And I *b*, and, lo, in the midst of	Rev 5:6	1492
And I *b*, and I heard the voice of	Rev 5:11	1492
And I *b*, and lo a black horse	Rev 6:5	1492
I *b* when he had opened the sixth	Rev 6:12	1492
After this I *b*, and, lo, a great	Rev 7:9	1492
And I *b*, and heard an angel flying	Rev 8:13	1492
and their enemies *b* them	Rev 11:12	2334
I *b* another beast coming up out	Rev 13:11	1492

BEHEMOTH
Behold now *b*, which I made with	Job 40:15	930

BEHIND
in the tent door, which was *b* him	Gen 18:10	310
look not *b* thee, neither stay	Gen 19:17	310
his wife looked back from *b* him	Gen 19:26	310
behold *b* him a ram caught in a	Gen 22:13	310
and, behold, also he is *b* us	Gen 32:18	310
Behold, thy servant Jacob is *b* us	Gen 32:20	310
there shall not an hoof be left *b*	Ex 10:26	
maidservant that is *b* the mill	Ex 11:5	310
of Israel, removed and went *b* them	Ex 14:19	310
their face, and stood *b* them	Ex 14:19	310
If there be yet many years *b*	Lev 25:51	
pitch *b* the tabernacle westward	Num 3:23	310
even all that were feeble *b* thee	Deut 25:18	310
thee an ambush for the city *b* it	Josh 8:2	310
against the city, even *b* the city	Josh 8:4	310
in ambush against him *b* the city	Josh 8:14	310
when the men of Ai looked *b* them	Josh 8:20	310
behold, it is *b* Kirjath-jearim	Judg 18:12	310
the Benjamites looked *b* them	Judg 20:40	310
wrapped in a cloth *b* the ephod	1Sa 21:9	310
And when Saul looked *b* him	1Sa 24:8	310
those that were left *b* stayed	1Sa 30:9	3498
for two hundred abode *b*, which	1Sa 30:10	5975
And when he looked *b* him, he saw	2Sa 1:7	310
Then Abner looked *b* him, and said,	2Sa 2:20	310
that the spear came out *b* him	2Sa 2:23	310
along weeping *b* her to Bahurim	2Sa 3:16	310
but fetch a compass *b* them	2Sa 5:23	310
was against him before and *b*	2Sa 10:9	268
by the way of the hill side *b* him	2Sa 13:34	310
the top of the throne was round *b*	1Kin 10:19	310
anger, and hast cast me *b* thy back	1Kin 14:9	310
sound of his master's feet *b* him	2Kin 6:32	310
turn thee *b* me	2Kin 9:18	310
turn thee *b* me	2Kin 9:19	310
part at the gate *b* the guard	2Kin 11:6	310
was set against him before and *b*	1Chr 19:10	268
ambushment to come about *b* them	2Chr 13:13	310
and the ambushment was *b* them	2Chr 13:13	310
the battle was before and *b*	2Chr 13:14	268
I in the lower places *b* the wall	Neh 4:13	310
the rulers were *b* all the house	Neh 4:16	310
and cast thy law *b* their backs	Neh 9:26	310
and castest my words *b* thee	Ps 50:17	310
Thou hast beset me *b* and before,	Ps 139:5	268
behold, he standeth *b* our wall	Song 2:9	310
before, and the Philistines *b*	Is 9:12	268
ears shall hear a word *b* thee	Is 30:21	310
hast cast all my sins *b* thy back	Is 38:17	310
B the doors also and the posts	Is 57:8	310
gardens *b* one tree in the midst	Is 66:17	310
I heard *b* me a voice of a great	Eze 3:12	310
cast me *b* thy back, therefore	Eze 23:35	310
the separate place which was *b* it	Eze 41:15	310
and *b* them a flame burneth	Joel 2:3	310
b them a desolate wilderness	Joel 2:3	310
repent, and leave a blessing *b* him	Joel 2:14	310
b him were there red horses,	Zec 1:8	310
of blood twelve years, came *b* him	Mt 9:20	3693
and said unto Peter, Get thee *b* me	Mt 16:23	3694
of Jesus, came in the press *b*	Mk 5:27	3693
Peter, saying, Get thee *b* me	Mk 8:33	3694
die, and leave his wife *b* him	Mk 12:19	2641
Jesus tarried *b* in Jerusalem	Lk 2:43	5278
and said unto him, Get thee *b* me	Lk 4:8	3694
stood at his feet *b* him weeping	Lk 7:38	3694
Came *b* him, and touched the border	Lk 8:44	3693
So that ye come *b* in no gift	1Cor 1:7	5302
whit *b* the very chiefest apostles	2Cor 11:5	5302
for in nothing am I *b* the very	2Cor 12:11	5302
those things which are *b*, and	Phil 3:13	3694
fill up that which is *b* of the	Col 1:24	5302
heard *b* me a great voice, as of a	Rev 1:10	3694
beasts full of eyes before and *b*	Rev 4:6	3693

BEHOLD
And God said, *B*, I have given you	Gen 1:29	2009
thing that he had made, and, *b*	Gen 1:31	2009
And the LORD God said, *B*, the man	Gen 3:22	2005
B, thou hast driven me out this	Gen 4:14	2005
God looked upon the earth, and, *b*	Gen 6:12	2009
and, *b*, I will destroy them with	Gen 6:13	2005
And, *b*, I, even I, do bring a	Gen 6:17	2005
of the ark, and looked, and, *b*	Gen 8:13	2009
And I, *b*, I establish my covenant	Gen 9:9	2005
And the LORD said, *B*, the people	Gen 11:6	2005
B now, I know that thou art a	Gen 12:11	2009
now therefore *b* thy wife, take	Gen 12:19	2009
And Abram said, *B*, to me thou hast	Gen 15:3	2005
And, *b*, the word of the LORD came	Gen 15:4	2009
b a smoking furnace, and a burning	Gen 15:17	2009
B now, the LORD hath restrained	Gen 16:2	2009
But Abram said unto Sarai, *B*	Gen 16:6	2009
of the LORD said unto her, *B*	Gen 16:11	2009
b, it is between Kadesh and Bered	Gen 16:14	2009
As for me, *b*, my covenant is with	Gen 17:4	2009
B, I have blessed him, and will	Gen 17:20	2009
And he said, *B*, in the tent	Gen 18:9	2009
B now, I have taken upon me to	Gen 18:27	2009
B now, I have taken upon me to	Gen 18:31	2009
B now, my lords, turn in, I pray	Gen 19:2	2009
B now, I have two daughters which	Gen 19:8	2009
B now, thy servant hath found	Gen 19:19	2009
B now, this city is near to flee	Gen 19:20	2009
said unto the younger, *B*, I lay	Gen 19:34	2005
dream by night, and said to him, *B*	Gen 20:3	2009
And Abimelech said, *B*, my land is	Gen 20:15	2009
And unto Sarah he said, *B*, I have	Gen 20:16	2009
b, he is to thee a covering of	Gen 20:16	2009
and he said, *B*, here I am	Gen 22:1	2009
he said, *B* the fire and the wood	Gen 22:7	2009
b behind him a ram caught in a	Gen 22:13	2009
it was told Abraham, saying, *B*	Gen 22:20	2009
B, I stand here by the well of	Gen 24:13	2009
he had done speaking, that, *b*	Gen 24:15	2009
and, *b*, he stood by the camels at	Gen 24:30	2009
B, I stand by the well of water	Gen 24:43	2009
done speaking in mine heart, *b*	Gen 24:45	2009
B, Rebekah is before thee, take	Gen 24:51	2009
lifted up his eyes, and saw, and, *b*	Gen 24:63	2009
to be delivered were fulfilled, *b*	Gen 25:24	2009
And Esau said, *B*, I am at the	Gen 25:32	2009
out at a window, and saw, and, *b*	Gen 26:8	2009
called Isaac, and said, *B*, of a	Gen 26:9	2009
and he said unto him, *B*, here am I	Gen 27:1	2009
B now, I am old, I know not the	Gen 27:2	2009
unto Jacob her son, saying, *B*	Gen 27:6	2009
said to Rebekah his mother, *B*	Gen 27:11	2005
and, *b*, now he hath taken away my	Gen 27:36	2009
answered and said unto Esau, *B*	Gen 27:37	2005
answered and said unto him, *B*	Gen 27:39	2009
younger son, and said unto him, *B*	Gen 27:42	2009
b a ladder set up on the earth,	Gen 28:12	2009
b the angels of God ascending and	Gen 28:12	2009
And, *b*, the LORD stood above it,	Gen 28:13	2009
And, *b*, I am with thee, and will	Gen 28:15	2009
b a well in the field, and, lo,	Gen 29:2	2009
and, *b*, Rachel his daughter cometh	Gen 29:6	2009
to pass, that in the morning, *b*	Gen 29:25	2009
B my maid Bilhah, go in unto her	Gen 30:3	2009
And Laban said, *B*, I would it	Gen 30:34	2005
the countenance of Laban, and, *b*	Gen 31:2	2009
eyes, and saw in a dream, and, *b*	Gen 31:10	2009
B this heap, and *b* this	Gen 31:51	2009
and, *b*, also he is behind us	Gen 32:18	2009
And say ye moreover, *B*, thy	Gen 32:20	2009
up his eyes, and looked, and, *b*	Gen 33:1	2009
for the land, *b*, it is large	Gen 34:21	2009
For, *b*, we were binding sheaves	Gen 37:7	2009
and, *b*, your sheaves stood round	Gen 37:7	2009
told it his brethren, and said, *B*	Gen 37:9	2009
and, *b*, the sun and the moon and the	Gen 37:9	2009
And a certain man found him, and, *b*	Gen 37:15	2009
And they said one to another, *B*	Gen 37:19	2009
up their eyes and looked, and, *b*	Gen 37:25	2009
and, *b*, Joseph was not in the pit	Gen 37:29	2009
B thy father in law goeth up to	Gen 38:13	2009
b, I sent this kid, and thou hast	Gen 38:23	2009
and also, *b*, she is with child by	Gen 38:24	2009
the time of her travail, that, *b*	Gen 38:27	2009
as he drew back his hand, that, *b*	Gen 38:29	2009
and said unto his master's wife, *B*	Gen 39:8	2005
and looked upon them, and, *b*	Gen 40:6	2009
and said to him, In my dream, *b*	Gen 40:9	2009
I also was in my dream, and, *b*	Gen 40:16	2009
and, *b*, he stood by the river	Gen 41:1	2009
And, *b*, there came up out of the	Gen 41:2	2009
And, *b*, seven other kine came up	Gen 41:3	2009
and, *b*, seven ears of corn came up	Gen 41:5	2009
And, *b*, seven thin ears and blasted	Gen 41:6	2009
And Pharaoh awoke, and, *b*, it was a	Gen 41:7	2009
said unto Joseph, In my dream, *b*	Gen 41:17	2005
And, *b*, there came up out of the	Gen 41:18	2009
And, *b*, seven other kine came up	Gen 41:19	2009
And I saw in my dream, and, *b*	Gen 41:22	2009
And, *b*, seven ears, withered, thin	Gen 41:23	2009
B, there come seven years of	Gen 41:29	2009
And he said, *B*, I have heard that	Gen 42:2	2009

and, *b*, the youngest is this day Gen 42:13 2009
therefore, *b*, also his blood is Gen 42:22 2009
for, *b*, it was in his sack's Gen 42:27 2009
they emptied their sacks, that, *b* Gen 42:35 2009
that we opened our sacks, and, *b* Gen 43:21 2009
B, the money, which we found in Gen 44:8 2005
b, we are my lord's servants, Gen 44:16 2009
And, *b*, your eyes see, and the eyes Gen 45:12 2009
and, *b*, they are in the land of Gen 47:1 2009
Joseph said unto the people, *B* Gen 47:23 2009
things, that one told Joseph, *B* Gen 48:1 2009
And one told Jacob, and said, *B* Gen 48:2 2009
And said unto me, *B*, I will make Gen 48:4 2005
And Israel said unto Joseph, *B* Gen 48:21 2009
and they said, *B*, we be thy Gen 50:18 2009
And he said unto his people, *B* Ex 1:9 2009
and, *b*, the babe wept Ex 2:6 2009
he went out the second day, *b* Ex 2:13 2009
and he looked, and, *b*, the bush Ex 3:2 2009
Now therefore, *b*, the cry of the Ex 3:9 2009
And Moses said unto God, *B* Ex 3:13 2009
And Moses answered and said, But, *b* Ex 4:1 2005
and when he took it out, *b* Ex 4:6 2009
it out of his bosom, and, *b* Ex 4:7 2009
And also, *b*, he cometh forth to Ex 4:14 2009
if thou refuse to let him go, *b* Ex 4:23 2009
And Pharaoh said, *B*, the people of Ex 5:5 2005
and, *b*, thy servants are beaten Ex 5:16 2009
spake before the LORD, saying, *B* Ex 6:12 2005
And Moses said before the LORD, *B* Ex 6:30 2005
and, *b*, hitherto thou wouldest not Ex 7:16 2009
b, I will smite with the rod that Ex 7:17 2009
if thou refuse to let them go, *b* Ex 8:2 2009
thou wilt not let my people go, *b* Ex 8:21 2005
And Moses said, *B*, I go out from Ex 8:29 2009
B, the hand of the LORD is upon Ex 9:3 2009
And Pharaoh sent, and, *b*, there was Ex 9:7 2009
B, to morrow about this time I Ex 9:18 2005
refuse to let my people go, *b* Ex 10:4 2005
lifted up their eyes, and, *b* Ex 14:10 2009
And I, *b*, I will harden the hearts Ex 14:17 2005
Then said the LORD unto Moses, *B* Ex 16:4 2005
toward the wilderness, and, *b* Ex 16:10 2009
the dew that lay was gone up, *b* Ex 16:14 2009
B, I will stand before thee there Ex 17:6 2005
B, I send an Angel before thee, Ex 23:20 2009
B the blood of the covenant, Ex 24:8 2009
and, *b*, Aaron and Hur are with you Ex 24:14 2009
And I, *b*, I have given with him Ex 31:6 2009
I have seen this people, and, *b* Ex 32:9 2009
b, mine Angel shall go before Ex 32:34 2009
And the LORD said, *B*, there is a Ex 33:21 2009
And he said, *B*, I make a covenant Ex 34:10 2009
b, I drive out before thee the Ex 34:11 2005
children of Israel saw Moses, *b* Ex 34:30 2009
did look upon all the work, and, *b* Ex 39:43 2009
goat of the sin offering, and, *b* Lev 10:16 2009
B, the blood of it was not Lev 10:18 2005
And Aaron said unto Moses, *B* Lev 10:19 2005
and, *b*, if the plague in his sight Lev 13:5 2009
and, *b*, if the plague be somewhat Lev 13:6 2009
And if the priest see that, *b* Lev 13:8 2009
and, *b*, if the rising be white in Lev 13:10 2009
and, *b*, if the leprosy have Lev 13:13 2009
and, *b*, if the plague be turned Lev 13:17 2009
if, when the priest seeth it, *b* Lev 13:20 2009
if the priest look on it, and, *b* Lev 13:21 2009
and, *b*, if the hair in the bright Lev 13:25 2009
if the priest look on it, and, *b* Lev 13:26 2009
and, *b*, if it be in sight deeper Lev 13:30 2009
on the plague of the scall, and, *b* Lev 13:31 2009
and, *b*, if the scall spread not, Lev 13:32 2009
and, *b*, if the scall be not spread Lev 13:34 2009
and, *b*, if the scall be spread in Lev 13:36 2009
and, *b*, if the bright spots in the Lev 13:39 2009
and, *b*, if the rising of the sore Lev 13:43 2009
if the priest shall look, and, *b* Lev 13:53 2009
and, *b*, if the plague have not Lev 13:55 2009
And if the priest look, and, *b* Lev 13:56 2009
and the priest shall look, and, *b* Lev 14:3 2009
shall look on the plague, and, *b* Lev 14:37 2009
and, *b*, if the plague be spread in Lev 14:39 2009
priest shall come and look, and, *b* Lev 14:44 2009
come in, and look upon it, and, *b* Lev 14:48 2009
b, we shall not sow, nor gather Lev 25:20 2005
And I, *b*, I have taken the Levites Num 3:12 2009
similitude of the LORD shall he *b* Num 12:8 5027
and, *b*, Miriam became leprous, Num 12:10 2009
Aaron looked upon Miriam, and, *b* Num 12:10 2009
and, *b*, the cloud covered it, and Num 16:42 2009
and, *b*, the plague was begun among Num 16:47 2009
and, *b*, the rod of Aaron for the Num 17:8 2009
spake unto Moses, saying, *B* Num 17:12 2005
And I, *b*, I have taken your Num 18:6 2009
And the LORD spake unto Aaron, *B* Num 18:8 2009
And, *b*, I have given the children Num 18:21 2009
and, *b*, we are in Kadesh, a city Num 20:16 2009
people, to call him, saying, *B* Num 22:5 2009
b, they cover the face of the Num 22:5 2009
B, there is a people come out of Num 22:11 2009
b, I went out to withstand thee, Num 22:32 2009
him, and from the hills I *b* him Num 23:9 7789
thee to curse mine enemies, and, *b* Num 23:11 2009
And when he came to him, *b* Num 23:17 2009
B, I have received commandment to Num 23:20 2009
B, the people shall rise up as a Num 23:24 2005
thee to curse mine enemies, and, *b* Num 24:10 2009
And now, *b*, I go unto my people Num 24:14 2005
I shall *b* him, but not nigh Num 24:17 7789
And, *b*, one of the children of Num 25:6 2009
Wherefore say, *B*, I give unto him Num 25:12 2005
B, these caused the children of Num 31:16 2005
and the land of Gilead, that, *b* Num 32:1 2009
And, *b*, ye are risen up in your Num 32:14 2009

But if ye will not do so, *b* Num 32:23 2009
B, I have set the land before you Deut 1:8 7200
God hath multiplied you, and, *b* Deut 1:10 2009
B, the LORD thy God hath set the Deut 1:21 7200
b, I have given into thine hand Deut 2:24 7200
And the LORD said unto me, *B* Deut 2:31 7200
b, his bedstead was a bedstead of Deut 3:11 2009
eastward, and *b* it with thine eyes Deut 3:27 7200
B, I have taught you statutes and Deut 4:5 7200
And ye said, *B*, the LORD our God Deut 5:24 2005
I have seen this people, and, *b* Deut 9:13 2009
And I looked, and, *b*, ye had sinned Deut 9:16 2009
B, the heaven and the heaven of Deut 10:14 2005
B, I set before you this day a Deut 11:26 7200
and, *b*, if it be truth, and the Deut 13:14 2009
it, and enquired diligently, and, *b* Deut 17:4 2009
and, *b*, if the witness be a false Deut 19:18 2009
And now, *b*, I have brought the Deut 26:10 2009
And the LORD said unto Moses, *B* Deut 31:14 2005
And the LORD said unto Moses, *B* Deut 31:16 2009
b, while I am yet alive with you Deut 31:27 2005
b the land of Canaan, which I Deut 32:49 7200
the king of Jericho, saying, *B* Josh 2:2 2009
B, when we come into the land, Josh 2:18 2009
B, the ark of the covenant of the Josh 3:11 2009
up his eyes and looked, and, *b* Josh 5:13 2009
and, *b*, they are hid in the earth Josh 7:21 2009
and, *b*, it was hid in his tent, and Josh 7:22 2009
And he commanded them, saying, *B* Josh 8:4 7200
behind them, they saw, and, *b* Josh 8:20 2009
but now, *b*, it is dry, and it is Josh 9:12 2009
and, *b*, they be rent Josh 9:13 2009
And now, *b*, we are in thine hand Josh 9:25 2005
And now, *b*, the LORD hath kept me Josh 14:10 2009
children of Israel heard say, *B* Josh 22:11 2009
B the pattern of the altar of the Josh 22:28 7200
B, I have divided unto you by lot Josh 23:4 7200
And, *b*, this day I am going the Josh 23:14 2009
said unto all the people, *B* Josh 24:27 2009
b, I have delivered the land into Judg 1:2 2009
and when they saw that, *b*, the Judg 3:24 2009
and, *b*, he opened not the doors of Judg 3:25 2009
and, *b*, their lord was fallen down Judg 3:25 2009
And, *b*, as Barak pursued Sisera, Judg 4:22 2009
And when he came into her tent, *b* Judg 4:22 2009
b, my family is poor in Manasseh, Judg 6:15 2009
arose early in the morning, *b* Judg 6:28 2009
B, I will put a fleece of wool in Judg 6:37 2009
And when Gideon was come, *b* Judg 7:13 2009
dream unto his fellow, and said, *B* Judg 7:13 2009
and, *b*, when I come to the outside Judg 7:17 2009
B Zebah and Zalmunna Judg 8:15 2009
unto Abimelech privily, saying, *B* Judg 9:31 2009
and, *b*, they fortify the city Judg 9:31 2009
and, *b*, when he and the people that Judg 9:33 2009
the people, he said to Zebul, *B* Judg 9:36 2009
in the field, and looked, and, *b* Judg 9:43 2009
to Mizpeh unto his house, and, *b* Judg 11:34 2009
B now, thou art barren, and Judg 13:3 2009
But he said unto me, *B*, thou Judg 13:7 2009
her husband, and said unto him, *B* Judg 13:10 2009
and, *b*, a young lion roared Judg 14:5 2009
and, *b*, there was a swarm of bees Judg 14:8 2009
And he said unto her, *B*, I have Judg 14:16 2009
And Delilah said unto Samson, *B* Judg 16:10 2009
spakest of also in mine ears, *b* Judg 17:2 2009
for we have seen the land, and, *b* Judg 18:9 2009
b, it is behind Kirjath-jearim Judg 18:12 2009
damsel's father, said unto him, *B* Judg 19:9 2009
b, the day groweth to an end, Judg 19:9 2009
And, *b*, there came an old man from Judg 19:16 2009
were making their hearts merry, *b* Judg 19:22 2009
B, here is my daughter a maiden, Judg 19:24 2009
and, *b*, the woman his concubine Judg 19:27 2009
B, ye are all children of Israel Judg 20:7 2009
looked behind them, and, *b* Judg 20:40 2009
And, *b*, there came none to the Judg 21:8 2009
the people were numbered, and, *b* Judg 21:9 2009
Then they said, *B*, there is a Judg 21:19 2009
And see, and, *b*, if the daughters Judg 21:21 2009
And she said, *B*, thy sister in law Ruth 1:15 2009
And, *b*, Boaz came from Beth-lehem, Ruth 2:4 2009
B, he winnoweth barley to night Ruth 3:2 2009
and, *b*, a woman lay at his feet Ruth 3:8 2009
and, *b*, the kinsman of whom Boaz Ruth 4:1 2009
B, the days come, that I will cut 1Sa 2:31 2009
And the LORD said to Samuel, *B* 1Sa 3:11 2009
arose early on the morrow, *b* 1Sa 5:3 2009
early on the morrow morning, *b* 1Sa 5:4 2009
And said unto him, *B*, thou art old 1Sa 8:5 2009
B now, there is in this city a 1Sa 9:6 2009
said Saul to his servant, But, *b* 1Sa 9:7 2009
answered Saul again, and said, *B* 1Sa 9:8 2009
b, he is before you 1Sa 9:12 2009
they were come into the city, *b* 1Sa 9:14 2009
B the man whom I spake to thee of 1Sa 9:17 2009
Samuel said, *B* that which is left 1Sa 9:24 2009
and, *b*, I will come down unto thee 1Sa 10:8 2009
they came thither to the hill, *b* 1Sa 10:10 2009
knew him beforetime saw that, *b* 1Sa 10:11 2009
And the LORD answered, *B*, he hath 1Sa 10:22 2009
And, *b*, Saul came after the herd 1Sa 11:5 2009
And Samuel said unto all Israel, *B* 1Sa 12:1 2009
And now, *b*, the king walketh 1Sa 12:2 2009
and, *b*, my sons are with you 1Sa 12:2 2009
B, here I am 1Sa 12:3 2009
Now therefore *b* the king whom ye 1Sa 12:13 2009
and, *b*, the LORD hath set a king 1Sa 12:13 2009
of offering the burnt offering, *b* 1Sa 13:10 2009
b, I am with thee according to 1Sa 14:7 2005
Then said Jonathan, *B*, we will 1Sa 14:8 2009
and the Philistines said, *B* 1Sa 14:11 2009
and, *b*, the multitude melted away, 1Sa 14:16 2009
And when they had numbered, *b* 1Sa 14:17 2009

and, *b*, every man's sword was 1Sa 14:20 2009
people were come into the wood, *b* 1Sa 14:26 2009
Then they told Saul, saying, *B* 1Sa 14:33 2009
Saul came to Carmel, and, *b* 1Sa 15:12 2009
B, to obey is better than 1Sa 15:22 2009
remaineth yet the youngest, and, *b* 1Sa 16:11 2009
B now, an evil spirit from God 1Sa 16:15 2009
one of the servants, and said, *B* 1Sa 16:18 2009
And as he talked with them, *b* 1Sa 17:23 2009
B my elder daughter Merab, her 1Sa 18:17 2009
with David secretly, and say, *B* 1Sa 18:22 2009
the messengers were come in, *b* 1Sa 19:16 2009
And it was told Saul, saying, *B* 1Sa 19:19 2009
And one said, *B*, they be at Naioth 1Sa 19:22 2009
b, my father will do nothing 1Sa 20:2 2009
And David said unto Jonathan, *B* 1Sa 20:5 2009
any time, or the third day, and, *b* 1Sa 20:12 2009
And, *b*, I will send a lad, saying, 1Sa 20:21 2009
I expressly say unto the lad, *B* 1Sa 20:21 2009
I say thus unto the young man, *B* 1Sa 20:22 2009
which thou and I have spoken of, *b* 1Sa 20:23 2009
slewest in the valley of Elah, *b* 1Sa 21:9 2009
Then they told David, saying, *B* 1Sa 23:1 2009
And David's men said unto him, *B* 1Sa 23:3 2009
that it was told him, saying, *B* 1Sa 24:1 2009
B the day of which the LORD said 1Sa 24:4 2009
which the LORD said unto thee, *B* 1Sa 24:4 2009
thou men's words, saying, *B* 1Sa 24:9 2009
B, this day thine eyes have seen 1Sa 24:10 2009
And now, *b*, I know well that thou 1Sa 24:20 2009
Abigail, Nabal's wife, saying, *B* 1Sa 25:14 2009
b, I come after you 1Sa 25:19 2005
by the covert of the hill, and, *b* 1Sa 25:20 2009
and, *b*, he held a feast in his 1Sa 25:36 2009
her face to the earth, and said, *B* 1Sa 25:41 2009
and, *b*, Saul lay sleeping within 1Sa 26:7 2009
b, I have played the fool, and 1Sa 26:21 2009
and said, *B* the king's spear 1Sa 26:22 2009
And, *b*, as thy life was much set 1Sa 26:24 2009
And his servants said to him, *B* 1Sa 28:7 2009
And the woman said unto him, *B* 1Sa 28:9 2009
troubled, and said unto him, *B* 1Sa 28:21 2009
his men came to the city, and, *b* 1Sa 30:3 2009
when he had brought him down, *b* 1Sa 30:16 2009
B a present for you of the spoil 1Sa 30:26 2009
to pass on the third day, that, *b* 2Sa 1:2 2009
by chance upon mount Gilboa, *b* 2Sa 1:6 2009
b, it is written in the book of 2Sa 1:18 2009
Make thy league with me, and, *b* 2Sa 3:12 2009
And, *b*, the servants of David and 2Sa 3:22 2009
b, Abner came unto thee 2Sa 3:24 2009
B the head of Ish-bosheth the son 2Sa 4:8 2009
When one told me, saying, *B* 2Sa 4:10 2009
unto Hebron, and spake, saying, *B* 2Sa 5:1 2005
And Ziba said unto the king, *B* 2Sa 9:4 2009
And he answered, *B* thy servant 2Sa 9:6 2009
Thus saith the LORD, *B*, I will 2Sa 12:11 2005
for they said, *B*, while the child 2Sa 12:18 2009
and said, *B* now, thy servant hath 2Sa 13:24 2009
up his eyes, and looked, and, *b* 2Sa 13:34 2009
And Jonadab said unto the king, *B* 2Sa 13:35 2009
made an end of speaking, that, *b* 2Sa 13:36 2009
And, *b*, the whole family is risen 2Sa 14:7 2009
B now, I have done this thing 2Sa 14:21 2009
And Absalom answered Joab, *B* 2Sa 14:32 2009
servants said unto the king, *B* 2Sa 15:15 2009
b, here am I, let him do to me as 2Sa 15:26 2005
mount, where he worshipped God, *b* 2Sa 15:32 2009
B, they have there with them 2Sa 15:36 2009
past the top of the hill, *b* 2Sa 16:1 2009
And Ziba said unto the king, *B* 2Sa 16:3 2009
Then said the king to Ziba, *B* 2Sa 16:4 2009
king David came to Bahurim, *b* 2Sa 16:5 2009
and, *b*, thou art taken in thy 2Sa 16:8 2009
and to all his servants, *B* 2Sa 16:11 2009
B, he is hid now in some pit, or 2Sa 17:9 2009
saw it, and told Joab, and said, *B* 2Sa 18:10 2009
unto the man that told him, And, *b* 2Sa 18:11 2009
looked, and *b* a man running alone 2Sa 18:24 2009
B another man running alone 2Sa 18:26 2009
And, *b*, Cushi came 2Sa 18:31 2009
And it was told Joab, *B*, the king 2Sa 19:1 2009
unto all the people, saying, *B* 2Sa 19:8 2009
therefore, *b*, I am come the first 2Sa 19:20 2009
But *b* thy servant Chimham 2Sa 19:37 2009
And, *b*, all the men of Israel came 2Sa 19:41 2009
And the woman said unto Joab, *B* 2Sa 20:21 2009
b, here be oxen for burnt 2Sa 24:22 7200
B, while thou yet talkest there 1Kin 1:14 2009
And now, *b*, Adonijah reigneth 1Kin 1:18 2009
saying, *B* Nathan the prophet 1Kin 1:23 2009
and, *b*, they eat and drink before 1Kin 1:25 2009
And while he yet spake, *b*, 1Kin 1:42 2009
And it was told Solomon, saying, *B* 1Kin 1:51 2009
And, *b*, thou hast with thee Shimei 1Kin 2:8 2009
and, *b*, he is by the altar 1Kin 2:29 2009
And they told Shimei, saying, *B* 1Kin 2:39 2009
B, I have done according to thy 1Kin 3:12 2009
and, *b*, it was a dream 1Kin 3:15 2009
morning to give my child suck, *b* 1Kin 3:21 2009
considered it in the morning, *b* 1Kin 3:21 2009
And, *b*, I purpose to build an 1Kin 5:5 2005
b, the heaven and heaven of 1Kin 8:27 2009
and, *b*, the half was not told me 1Kin 10:7 2009
hast thou lacked with me, that, *b* 1Kin 11:22 2009
the LORD, the God of Israel, *B* 1Kin 11:31 2005
b thy gods, O Israel, which 1Kin 12:28 2009
And, *b*, there came a man of God 1Kin 13:1 2009
B, a child shall be born unto the 1Kin 13:2 2009
B, the altar shall be rent, and 1Kin 13:3 2009
And, *b*, men passed by, and saw the 1Kin 13:25 2009
b, there is Ahijah the prophet, 1Kin 14:2 2009
And the LORD said unto Ahijah, *B* 1Kin 14:5 2009
Therefore, *b*, I will bring evil 1Kin 14:10 2005

he warred, and how he reigned, *b*	1Kin 14:19	2009
b, I have sent unto thee a	1Kin 15:19	2009
B, I will take away the posterity	1Kin 16:3	2005
b, I have commanded a widow	1Kin 17:9	2009
came to the gate of the city, *b*	1Kin 17:10	2009
and, *b*, I am gathering two sticks,	1Kin 17:12	2005
And as Obadiah was in the way, *b*	1Kin 18:7	2009
go, tell thy lord, *B*, Elijah is	1Kin 18:8	2009
thou sayest, Go, tell thy lord, *B*	1Kin 18:11	2009
thou sayest, Go, tell thy lord, *B*	1Kin 18:14	2009
the seventh time, that he said, *B*	1Kin 18:44	2009
and slept under a juniper tree, *b*	1Kin 19:5	2009
And he looked, and, *b*, there was a	1Kin 19:6	2009
and, *b*, the word of the LORD came	1Kin 19:9	2009
And, *b*, the LORD passed by, and a	1Kin 19:11	2009
And, *b*, there came a voice unto	1Kin 19:13	2009
And, *b*, there came a prophet unto	1Kin 20:13	2009
b, I will deliver it into thine	1Kin 20:13	2005
B now, we have heard that the	1Kin 20:31	2009
obeyed the voice of the LORD, *b*	1Kin 20:36	2009
and, *b*, a man turned aside, and	1Kin 20:39	2009
b, he is in the vineyard of	1Kin 21:18	2009
B, I will bring evil upon thee,	1Kin 21:21	2005
B now, the words of the prophets	1Kin 22:13	2009
Now therefore, *b*, the LORD hath	1Kin 22:23	2009
And Micaiah said, *B*, thou shalt	1Kin 22:25	2009
and, *b*, he sat on the top of an	2Kin 1:9	2009
B, there came fire down from	2Kin 1:14	2009
still went on, and talked, that, *b*	2Kin 2:11	2009
B now, there be with thy servants	2Kin 2:16	2009
of the city said unto Elisha, *B*	2Kin 2:19	2009
offering was offered, that, *b*	2Kin 3:20	2009
B now, I perceive that this is an	2Kin 4:9	2009
unto him, Say now unto her, *B*	2Kin 4:13	2009
he said to Gehazi his servant, *B*	2Kin 4:25	2009
Elisha was come into the house, *b*	2Kin 4:32	2009
this letter is come unto thee, *b*	2Kin 5:6	2009
wroth, and went away, and said, *B*	2Kin 5:11	2009
and he said, *B*, now I know that	2Kin 5:15	2009
of Elisha the man of God, said, *B*	2Kin 5:20	2009
My master hath sent me, saying, *B*	2Kin 5:22	2009
B now, the place where we dwell	2Kin 6:1	2009
And it was told him, saying, *B*	2Kin 6:13	2009
was risen early, and gone forth, *b*	2Kin 6:15	2009
and, *b*, the mountain was full of	2Kin 6:17	2009
and, *b*, they were in the midst of	2Kin 6:20	2009
and, *b*, they besieged it, until an	2Kin 6:25	2009
wall, and the people looked, and, *b*	2Kin 6:30	2009
while he yet talked with them, *b*	2Kin 6:33	2009
and he said, *B*, this evil is of	2Kin 6:33	2009
the man of God, and said, *B*	2Kin 7:2	2009
And he said, *B*, thou shalt see it	2Kin 7:2	2009
part of the camp of Syria, *b*	2Kin 7:5	2009
to the camp of the Syrians, and, *b*	2Kin 7:10	2009
which are left in the city, (*b*	2Kin 7:13	2009
b, I say, they are even as all	2Kin 7:13	2009
the man of God, and said, Now, *b*	2Kin 7:19	2009
And he said, *B*, thou shalt see it	2Kin 7:19	2009
a dead body to life, that, *b*	2Kin 8:5	2009
And when he came, *b*, the captains	2Kin 9:5	2009
exceedingly afraid, and said, *B*	2Kin 10:4	2009
b, I conspired against my master,	2Kin 10:9	2009
And when she looked, *b*, the king	2Kin 11:14	2009
they were burying a man, that, *b*	2Kin 13:21	2009
rest of the acts of Zachariah, *b*	2Kin 15:11	2009
his conspiracy which he made, *b*	2Kin 15:15	2009
Pekahiah, and all that he did, *b*	2Kin 15:26	2009
of Pekah, and all that he did, *b*	2Kin 15:31	2009
hath sent lions among them, and, *b*	2Kin 17:26	2009
Now, *b*, thou trustest upon the	2Kin 18:21	2009
B, I will send a blast upon him,	2Kin 19:7	2005
of Tirhakah king of Ethiopia, *B*	2Kin 19:9	2009
B, thou hast heard what the kings	2Kin 19:11	2009
arose early in the morning, *b*	2Kin 19:35	2009
b, I will heal thee	2Kin 20:5	2005
B, the days come, that all that	2Kin 20:17	2009
saith the LORD God of Israel, *B*	2Kin 21:12	2009
Thus saith the LORD, *B*, I will	2Kin 22:16	2005
B therefore, I will gather thee	2Kin 22:20	2005
and, *b*, they were written in the	1Chr 9:1	2009
to David unto Hebron, saying, *B*	1Chr 11:1	2009
B, he was honourable among the	1Chr 11:25	2009
B, a son shall be born to thee,	1Chr 22:9	2009
Now, *b*, in my trouble I have	1Chr 22:14	2009
And, *b*, the courses of the priests	1Chr 28:21	2009
David the king, first and last, *b*	1Chr 29:29	2009
B, I build an house to the name	2Chr 2:4	2009
and, *b*, my servants shall be with	2Chr 2:8	2009
And, *b*, I will give to thy	2Chr 2:10	2009
b, heaven and the heaven of	2Chr 6:18	2009
and, *b*, the one half of the	2Chr 9:6	2009
And, *b*, God himself is with us for	2Chr 13:12	2009
And when Judah looked back, *b*	2Chr 13:14	2009
b, I have sent thee silver and	2Chr 16:3	2009
And, *b*, the acts of Asa, first and	2Chr 16:11	2009
Micaiah spake to him, saying, *B*	2Chr 18:12	2009
Now therefore, *b*, the LORD hath	2Chr 18:22	2009
And Micaiah said, *B*, thou shalt	2Chr 18:24	2009
And, *b*, Amariah the chief priest	2Chr 19:11	2009
and, *b*, they be in Hazazon-tamar,	2Chr 20:2	2009
And now, *b*, the children of Ammon	2Chr 20:10	2009
B, I say, how they reward us, to	2Chr 20:11	2009
b, they come up by the cliff of	2Chr 20:16	2009
looked unto the multitude, and, *b*	2Chr 20:24	2009
of Jehoshaphat, first and last, *b*	2Chr 20:34	2009
B, with a great plague will the	2Chr 21:14	2009
And he said unto them, *B*, the	2Chr 23:3	2009
And she looked, and, *b*, the king	2Chr 23:13	2009
repairing of the house of God, *b*	2Chr 24:27	2009
acts of Amaziah, first and last, *b*	2Chr 25:26	2009
priests, looked upon him, and, *b*	2Chr 26:20	2009
to Samaria, and said unto them, *B*	2Chr 28:9	2009
of all his ways, first and last, *b*	2Chr 28:26	2009
we prepared and sanctified, and, *b*	2Chr 29:19	2009
of Hezekiah, and his goodness, *b*	2Chr 32:32	2009
name of the LORD God of Israel, *b*	2Chr 33:18	2009
b, they are written among the	2Chr 33:19	2009
Thus saith the LORD, *B*, I will	2Chr 34:24	2005
B, I will gather thee to thy	2Chr 34:28	2005
and, *b*, they are written in the	2Chr 35:25	2009
And his deeds, first and last, *b*	2Chr 35:27	2009
and that which was found in him, *b*	2Chr 36:8	2009
b, we are before thee in our	Ezr 9:15	2005
B, we are servants this day, and	Neh 9:36	2009
thereof and the good thereof, *b*	Neh 9:36	2009
king's servants said unto him, *B*	Est 6:5	2009
B also, the gallows fifty cubits	Est 7:9	2009
queen and to Mordecai the Jew, *B*	Est 8:7	2009
And the LORD said unto Satan, *B*	Job 1:12	2009
And, *b*, there came a great wind	Job 1:19	2009
And the LORD said unto Satan, *B*	Job 2:6	2009
B, thou hast instructed many, and	Job 4:3	2009
B, he put no trust in his	Job 4:18	2005
B, happy is the man whom God	Job 5:17	2009
B, this is the joy of his way, and	Job 8:19	2005
B, God will not cast away a	Job 8:20	2005
B, he taketh away, who can hinder	Job 9:12	2005
B, he breaketh down, and it cannot	Job 12:14	2005
B, he withholdeth the waters, and	Job 12:15	2005
B now, I have ordered my cause	Job 13:18	2009
B, he putteth no trust in his	Job 15:15	2005
Also now, *b*, my witness is in	Job 16:19	2009
B, I cry out of wrong, but I am	Job 19:7	2005
for myself, and mine eyes shall *b*	Job 19:27	7200
shall his place any more *b* him	Job 20:9	7789
B, I know your thoughts, and the	Job 21:27	2005
b the height of the stars, how	Job 22:12	7200
B, I go forward, but he is not	Job 23:8	2005
he doth work, but I cannot *b* him	Job 23:9	2372
B, as wild asses in the desert,	Job 24:5	2005
B even to the moon, and it shineth	Job 25:5	2005
B, all ye yourselves have seen it	Job 27:12	2005
And unto man he said, *B*, the fear	Job 28:28	2005
b, my desire is, that the	Job 31:35	2005
B, I waited for your words	Job 32:11	2005
Yea, I attended unto you, and, *b*	Job 32:12	2009
B, my belly is as wine which hath	Job 32:19	2009
B, now I have opened my mouth, my	Job 33:2	2009
B, I am according to thy wish in	Job 33:6	2005
B, my terror shall not make thee	Job 33:7	2009
B, he findeth occasions against	Job 33:10	2005
B, in this thou art not just	Job 33:12	2005
his face, who then can *b* him	Job 34:29	7789
b the clouds which are higher	Job 35:5	7789
B, God is mighty, and despiseth	Job 36:5	2005
B, God exalteth by his power	Job 36:22	2005
magnify his work, which men *b*	Job 36:24	7891
man may *b* it afar off	Job 36:25	5027
B, God is great, and we know him	Job 36:26	2005
B, he spreadeth his light upon it	Job 36:30	2005
the prey, and her eyes *b* afar off	Job 39:29	5027
B, I am vile	Job 40:4	2005
b every one that is proud, and	Job 40:11	7200
B now behemoth, which I made with	Job 40:15	2009
B, he drinketh up a river, and	Job 40:23	2005
B, the hope of him is in vain	Job 41:9	2005
B, he travaileth with iniquity,	Ps 7:14	2009
his eyes *b*, his eyelids try, the	Ps 11:4	2372
countenance doth *b* the upright	Ps 11:7	2372
let thine eyes *b* the things that	Ps 17:2	2372
As for me, I will *b* thy face in	Ps 17:15	2372
to *b* the beauty of the LORD, and	Ps 27:4	2372
B, the eye of the LORD is upon	Ps 33:18	2009
the perfect man, and *b* the upright	Ps 37:37	7200
B, thou hast made my days as an	Ps 39:5	2009
b the works of the LORD, what	Ps 46:8	2372
B, I was shapen in iniquity	Ps 51:5	2005
B, thou desirest truth in the	Ps 51:6	2005
B, God is mine helper	Ps 54:4	2009
awake to help me, and *b*	Ps 59:4	7200
B, they belch out with their	Ps 59:7	2009
his eyes *b* the nations	Ps 66:7	6822
B, these are the ungodly, who	Ps 73:12	2009
b, I should offend against the	Ps 73:15	2009
B, he smote the rock, that the	Ps 78:20	2005
look down from heaven, and *b*	Ps 80:14	7200
B, O God our shield, and look upon	Ps 84:9	7200
b Philistia, and Tyre, with	Ps 87:4	2009
Only with thine eyes shalt thou *b*	Ps 91:8	5027
heaven did the LORD *b* the earth	Ps 102:19	5027
Who humbleth himself to *b* the	Ps 113:6	7200
that I may *b* wondrous things out	Ps 119:18	5027
B, I have longed after thy	Ps 119:40	2009
B, he that keepeth Israel shall	Ps 121:4	2009
B, as the eyes of servants look	Ps 123:2	2009
B, that thus shall the man be	Ps 128:4	2009
B, how good and how pleasant it is	Ps 133:1	2009
B, bless ye the LORD, all ye	Ps 134:1	2009
if I make my bed in hell, *b*	Ps 139:8	2009
b, I will pour out my spirit unto	Prov 1:23	2009
And, *b*, there met him a woman with	Prov 7:10	2009
B, the righteous shall be	Prov 11:31	2005
Thine eyes shall *b* strange women	Prov 23:33	7200
If thou sayest, *B*, we knew it not	Prov 24:12	2005
and, *b*, all is vanity and vexation	Eccl 1:14	2009
and, *b*, this also is vanity	Eccl 2:1	2009
and, *b*, all was vanity and vexation	Eccl 2:11	2009
And I turned myself to *b* wisdom	Eccl 2:12	7200
b the tears of such as were	Eccl 4:1	2009
B that which I have seen	Eccl 5:18	2009
B, this have I found, saith the	Eccl 7:27	7200
it is for the eyes to *b* the sun	Eccl 11:7	7200
B, thou art fair, my love	Song 1:15	2009
b, thou art fair	Song 1:15	2009
B, thou art fair, my beloved, yea	Song 1:16	2009
b, he cometh leaping upon the	Song 2:8	2009
b, he standeth behind our wall,	Song 2:9	2009
B his bed, which is Solomon's	Song 3:7	2009
b king Solomon with the crown	Song 3:11	7200
B, thou art fair, my love	Song 4:1	2009
b, thou art fair	Song 4:1	2009
For, *b*, the Lord, the LORD of	Is 3:1	2009
for judgment, but *b* oppression	Is 5:7	2009
for righteousness, but *b* a cry	Is 5:7	2009
and, *b*, they shall come with speed	Is 5:26	2009
b darkness and sorrow, and the	Is 5:30	2009
B, a virgin shall conceive, and	Is 7:14	2009
Now therefore, *b*, the Lord	Is 8:7	2009
B, I and the children whom the	Is 8:18	2009
b trouble and darkness, dimness of	Is 8:22	2009
B, the Lord, the LORD of hosts,	Is 10:33	2009
B, God is my salvation	Is 12:2	2009
B, the day of the LORD cometh,	Is 13:9	2009
B, I will stir up the Medes	Is 13:17	2005
B, Damascus is taken away from	Is 17:1	2009
And *b* at eveningtide trouble	Is 17:14	2009
B, the LORD rideth upon a swift	Is 19:1	2009
isle shall say in that day, *B*	Is 20:6	2009
And, *b*, here cometh a chariot of	Is 21:9	2009
b joy and gladness, slaying oxen,	Is 22:13	2009
B, the LORD will carry thee away	Is 22:17	2009
B the land of the Chaldeans	Is 23:13	2005
B, the LORD maketh the earth	Is 24:1	2009
will not *b* the majesty of the	Is 26:10	7200
For, *b*, the LORD cometh out of	Is 26:21	2009
B, the Lord hath a mighty and	Is 28:2	2009
thus saith the Lord GOD, *B*	Is 28:16	2005
an hungry man dreameth, and, *b*	Is 29:8	2009
a thirsty man dreameth, and, *b*	Is 29:8	2009
but he awaketh, and, *b*, he is	Is 29:8	2009
Therefore, *b*, I will proceed to	Is 29:14	2005
B, the name of the LORD cometh	Is 30:27	2009
B, a king shall reign in	Is 32:1	2005
B, their valiant ones shall cry	Is 33:7	2005
they shall *b* the land that is	Is 33:17	7200
b, it shall come down upon Idumea	Is 34:5	2009
b, your God will come with	Is 35:4	2009
B, I will send a blast upon him,	Is 37:7	2005
B, thou hast heard what the kings	Is 37:11	2009
arose early in the morning, *b*	Is 37:36	2009
b, I will add unto thy days	Is 38:5	2005
B, I will bring again the shadow	Is 38:8	2005
I shall *b* man no more with the	Is 38:11	7200
B, for peace I had great	Is 38:17	2009
B, the days come, that all that	Is 39:6	2009
the cities of Judah, *B* your God	Is 40:9	2009
B, the Lord GOD will come with	Is 40:10	2009
b, his reward is with him, and his	Is 40:10	2009
B, the nations are as a drop of a	Is 40:15	2005
b, he taketh up the isles as a	Is 40:15	2005
b who hath created these things,	Is 40:26	7200
B, all they that were incensed	Is 41:11	2005
B, I will make thee a new sharp	Is 41:15	2009
may be dismayed, and *b* it together	Is 41:23	7200
B, ye are of nothing, and your	Is 41:24	2005
shall say to Zion, *B*, *b* them	Is 41:27	2009
B, they are all vanity	Is 41:29	2005
B my servant, whom I uphold	Is 42:1	2005
B, the former things are come to	Is 42:9	2009
B, I will do a new thing	Is 43:19	2005
B, all his fellows shall be	Is 44:11	2005
B, they shall be as stubble	Is 47:14	2009
lest thou shouldest say, *B*	Is 48:7	2009
B, I have refined thee, but not	Is 48:10	2009
B, these shall come from far	Is 49:12	2009
B, I have graven thee upon the	Is 49:16	2005
up thine eyes round about, and *b*	Is 49:18	7200
B, I was left alone	Is 49:21	2005
Thus saith the Lord GOD, *B*	Is 49:22	2009
B, for your iniquities have ye	Is 50:1	2005
b, at my rebuke I dry up the sea,	Is 50:2	2005
B, the Lord GOD will help me	Is 50:9	2005
B, all ye that kindle a fire,	Is 50:11	2005
the cause of his people, *B*	Is 51:22	2009
b, it is I	Is 52:6	2009
B, my servant shall deal	Is 52:13	2009
with tempest, and not comforted, *b*	Is 54:11	2009
B, they shall surely gather	Is 54:15	2005
B, I have created the smith that	Is 54:16	2005
B, I have given him for a witness	Is 55:4	2005
B, thou shalt call a nation that	Is 55:5	2005
neither let the eunuch say, *B*	Is 56:3	2005
B, in the day of your fast ye	Is 58:3	2005
B, ye fast for strife and debate,	Is 58:4	2005
B, the LORD's hand is not	Is 59:1	2005
wait for light, but *b* obscurity	Is 59:9	2009
For, *b*, the darkness shall cover	Is 60:2	2009
B, the LORD hath proclaimed unto	Is 62:11	2009
Say ye to the daughter of Zion, *B*	Is 62:11	2009
b, his reward is with him, and his	Is 62:11	2009
b from the habitation of thy	Is 63:15	7200
b, thou art wroth	Is 64:5	2005
b, see, we beseech thee, we are	Is 64:9	2005
B me, *b* me, unto a nation	Is 65:1	2009
b me, unto a nation that was not	Is 65:1	2009
B, it is written before me	Is 65:6	2009
thus saith the Lord GOD, *B*	Is 65:13	2009
b, my servants shall drink, but	Is 65:13	2009
b, my servants shall rejoice, but	Is 65:13	2009
B, my servants shall sing for joy	Is 65:14	2009
For, *b*, I create new heavens and a	Is 65:17	2005
for, *b*, I create Jerusalem a	Is 65:18	2005
For thus saith the LORD, *B*	Is 66:12	2005
For, *b*, the LORD will come with	Is 66:15	2009
b, I cannot speak	Jer 1:6	2009
And the LORD said unto me, *B*	Jer 1:9	2009
For, *b*, I have made thee this day	Jer 1:18	2009
B, I will plead with thee,	Jer 2:35	2005
B, thou hast spoken and done evil	Jer 3:5	2009
B, we come unto thee	Jer 3:22	2005
B, he shall come up as clouds, and	Jer 4:13	2009
b, publish against Jerusalem,	Jer 4:16	2009

Context	Reference	Strong's
Because ye speak this word, *b*	Jer 5:14	2005
b, their ear is uncircumcised, and	Jer 6:10	2009
b, the word of the LORD is unto	Jer 6:10	2009
b, I will bring evil upon this	Jer 6:19	2009
Therefore thus saith the LORD, *B*	Jer 6:21	2005
Thus saith the LORD, *B*, a people	Jer 6:22	2009
B, ye trust in lying words, that	Jer 7:8	2009
B, even I have seen it, saith the	Jer 7:11	2009
B, mine anger and my fury shall be	Jer 7:20	2009
Therefore, *b*, the days come,	Jer 7:32	2009
a time of health, and *b* trouble	Jer 8:15	2009
For, *b*, I will send serpents,	Jer 8:17	2005
B the voice of the cry of the	Jer 8:19	2009
thus saith the LORD of hosts, *B*	Jer 9:7	2005
B, I will feed them, even this	Jer 9:15	2005
B, the days come, saith the LORD,	Jer 9:25	2009
For thus saith the LORD, *B*	Jer 10:18	2005
B, the noise of the bruit is come	Jer 10:22	2009
Therefore thus saith the LORD, *B*	Jer 11:11	2005
thus saith the LORD of hosts, *B*	Jer 11:22	2005
B, I will pluck them out of their	Jer 12:14	2005
and, *b*, the girdle was marred, it	Jer 13:7	2009
unto them, Thus saith the LORD, *B*	Jer 13:13	2005
b them that come from the north	Jer 13:20	7200
b, the prophets say unto them, Ye	Jer 14:13	2009
then *b* the slain with the sword	Jer 14:18	2009
then *b* them that are sick with	Jer 14:18	2009
the time of healing, and *b* trouble	Jer 14:19	2009
B, I will cause to cease out of	Jer 16:9	2005
for, *b*, ye walk every one after	Jer 16:12	2009
Therefore, *b*, the days come,	Jer 16:14	2009
B, I will send for many fishers,	Jer 16:16	2005
Therefore, *b*, I will this once	Jer 16:21	2005
B, they say unto me, Where is the	Jer 17:15	2009
down to the potter's house, and, *b*	Jer 18:3	2009
B, as the clay is in the potter's	Jer 18:6	2009
B, I frame evil against you, and	Jer 18:11	2009
B, I will bring evil upon this	Jer 19:3	2005
Therefore, *b*, the days come,	Jer 19:6	2009
B, I will bring upon this city and	Jer 19:15	2005
For thus saith the LORD, *B*	Jer 20:4	2005
enemies, and thine eyes shall *b* it	Jer 20:4	7200
B, I will turn back the weapons	Jer 21:4	2005
B, I set before you the way of	Jer 21:8	2005
B, I am against thee, O	Jer 21:13	2005
b, I will visit upon you the evil	Jer 23:2	2005
B, the days come, saith the LORD,	Jer 23:5	2009
Therefore, *b*, the days come,	Jer 23:7	2009
B, I will feed them with wormwood	Jer 23:15	2005
B, a whirlwind of the LORD is	Jer 23:19	2009
Therefore, *b*, I am against the	Jer 23:30	2005
B, I am against the prophets,	Jer 23:31	2005
B, I am against them that	Jer 23:32	2005
Therefore, *b*, I, even I, will	Jer 23:39	2005
The LORD shewed me, and, *b*	Jer 24:1	2009
B, I will send and take all the	Jer 25:9	2005
Thus saith the LORD of hosts, *B*	Jer 25:32	2009
As for me, *b*, I am in your hand	Jer 26:14	2005
that prophesy unto you, saying, *B*	Jer 27:16	2009
B, I will cast thee from off the	Jer 28:16	2005
B, I will send upon them the	Jer 29:17	2005
B, I will deliver them into the	Jer 29:21	2009
B, I will punish Shemaiah the	Jer 29:32	2005
neither shall he *b* the good that	Jer 29:32	7200
B, I will bring again the	Jer 30:18	2005
B, the whirlwind of the LORD	Jer 30:23	2009
B, I will bring them from the	Jer 31:8	2005
B, the days come, saith the LORD,	Jer 31:27	2009
B, the days come, saith the LORD,	Jer 31:31	2009
B, the days come, saith the LORD,	Jer 31:38	2009
and say, Thus saith the LORD, *B*	Jer 32:3	2005
and his eyes shall *b* his eyes	Jer 32:4	7200
B, Hanameel the son of Shallum	Jer 32:7	2009
b, thou hast made the heaven and	Jer 32:17	2009
B the mounts, they are come unto	Jer 32:24	2009
and, *b*, thou seest it	Jer 32:24	2009
B, I am the LORD, the God of all	Jer 32:27	2009
B, I will give this city into the	Jer 32:28	2005
B, I will gather them out of all	Jer 32:37	2005
B, I will bring it health and cure	Jer 33:6	2005
B, the days come, saith the LORD,	Jer 33:14	2009
B, I will give this city into the	Jer 34:2	2005
thine eyes shall *b* the eyes of	Jer 34:3	7200
b, I proclaim a liberty for you,	Jer 34:17	2005
B, I will command, saith the LORD	Jer 34:22	2005
B, I will bring upon Judah and	Jer 35:17	2005
B, Pharaoh's army, which is come	Jer 37:7	2005
Then Zedekiah the king said, *B*	Jer 38:5	2009
And, *b*, all the women that are	Jer 38:22	2009
B, I will bring my words upon	Jer 39:16	2005
And now, *b*, I loose thee this day	Jer 40:4	2009
b, all the land is before thee	Jer 40:4	7200
As for me, *b*, I will dwell at	Jer 40:10	2005
of many, as thine eyes do *b* us	Jer 42:2	7200
b, I will pray unto the LORD your	Jer 42:4	2005
B, I will send and take	Jer 43:10	2005
and, *b*, this day they are a	Jer 44:2	2009
B, I will set my face against you	Jer 44:11	2005
B, I have sworn by my great name,	Jer 44:26	2005
B, I will watch over them for	Jer 44:27	2005
B, I will give Pharaoh-hophra	Jer 44:30	2005
B, that which I have built will I	Jer 45:4	2009
for, *b*, I will bring evil upon	Jer 45:5	2005
B, I will punish the multitude of	Jer 46:25	2005
for, *b*, I will save thee from	Jer 46:27	2005
B, waters rise up out of the	Jer 47:2	2009
Therefore, *b*, the days come,	Jer 48:12	2009
B, he shall fly as an eagle, and	Jer 48:40	2009
Therefore, *b*, the days come,	Jer 49:2	2009
B, I will bring a fear upon thee,	Jer 49:5	2005
B, they whose judgment was not to	Jer 49:12	2009
B, he shall come up like a lion	Jer 49:19	2009
B, he shall come up and fly as the	Jer 49:22	2009
B, I will break the bow of Elam,	Jer 49:35	2005
b, the hindermost of the nations	Jer 50:12	2009
B, I will punish the king of	Jer 50:18	2005
B, I am against thee, O thou most	Jer 50:31	2005
B, a people shall come from the	Jer 50:41	2009
B, he shall come up like a lion	Jer 50:44	2009
B, I will raise up against	Jer 51:1	2005
B, I am against thee, O	Jer 51:25	2005
B, I will plead thy cause, and	Jer 51:36	2005
Therefore, *b*, the days come, that	Jer 51:47	2009
Wherefore, *b*, the days come,	Jer 51:52	2009
O LORD, *b* my affliction	Lam 1:9	7200
b, and see if there be any sorrow	Lam 1:12	5027
you, all people, and *b* my sorrow	Lam 1:18	7200
B, O LORD	Lam 1:20	7200
B, O LORD, and consider to whom	Lam 2:20	7200
LORD look down, and *b* from heaven	Lam 3:50	7200
B their sitting down, and their	Lam 3:63	5027
consider, and *b* our reproach	Lam 5:1	7200
And I looked, and, *b*, a whirlwind	Eze 1:4	2009
b one wheel upon the earth by the	Eze 1:15	2009
And when I looked, *b*, an hand was	Eze 2:9	2009
B, I have made thy face strong	Eze 3:8	2009
and, *b*, the glory of the LORD	Eze 3:23	2009
But thou, O son of man, *b*	Eze 3:25	2009
And, *b*, I will lay bands upon thee	Eze 4:8	2009
b, my soul hath not been polluted	Eze 4:14	2009
he said unto me, Son of man, *b*	Eze 4:16	2005
B, I, even I, am against thee, and	Eze 5:8	2005
B, I, even I, will bring a sword	Eze 6:3	2005
An evil, an only evil, *b*, is come	Eze 7:5	2009
b, it is come	Eze 7:6	2009
B the day, *b*, it is come	Eze 7:10	2009
And, *b*, the glory of the God of	Eze 8:4	2009
b northward at the gate of the	Eze 8:5	2009
I looked, *b* a hole in the wall	Eze 8:7	2009
had digged in the wall, *b* a door	Eze 8:8	2009
b the wicked abominations that	Eze 8:9	7200
b every form of creeping things,	Eze 8:10	2009
and, *b*, there sat women weeping	Eze 8:14	2009
court of the LORD's house, and, *b*	Eze 8:16	2009
And, *b*, six men came from the way	Eze 9:2	2009
And, *b*, the man clothed with linen	Eze 9:11	2009
Then I looked, and, *b*, in the	Eze 10:1	2009
looked, *b* the four wheels by the	Eze 10:9	2009
b at the door of the gate five and	Eze 11:1	2009
Son of man, *b*, they of the house	Eze 12:27	2009
and seen lies, therefore, *b*	Eze 13:8	2005
B, I am against your pillows,	Eze 13:20	2005
Yet, *b*, therein shall be left a	Eze 14:22	2009
b, they shall come forth unto you	Eze 14:22	2009
B, it is cast into the fire for	Eze 15:4	2009
B, when it was whole, it was meet	Eze 15:5	2009
by thee, and looked upon thee, *b*	Eze 16:8	2009
B, therefore I have stretched out	Eze 16:27	2009
B, therefore I will gather all	Eze 16:37	2005
b, therefore I also will	Eze 16:43	1887
B, every one that useth proverbs	Eze 16:44	2009
B, this was the iniquity of thy	Eze 16:49	2009
and, *b*, this vine did bend her	Eze 17:7	2009
Yea, *b*, being planted, shall it	Eze 17:10	2009
tell them, *B*, the king of Babylon	Eze 17:12	2009
B, all souls are mine	Eze 18:4	2005
B, I will kindle a fire in thee,	Eze 20:47	2005
B, I am against thee, and will	Eze 21:3	2005
b, it cometh, and shall be brought	Eze 21:7	2009
B, the princes of Israel, every	Eze 22:6	2009
B, therefore I have smitten mine	Eze 22:13	2009
ye are all become dross, *b*	Eze 22:19	2005
B, I will raise up thy lovers	Eze 23:22	2005
B, I will deliver thee into the	Eze 23:28	2005
Son of man, *b*, I take away from	Eze 24:16	2005
B, I will profane my sanctuary	Eze 24:21	2005
B, therefore I will deliver thee	Eze 25:4	2005
B, therefore I will stretch out	Eze 25:7	2005
that Moab and Seir do say, *B*	Eze 25:8	2009
Therefore, *b*, I will open the	Eze 25:9	2005
B, I will stretch out mine hand	Eze 25:16	2005
B, I am against thee, O Tyrus, and	Eze 26:3	2005
B, I will bring upon Tyrus	Eze 26:7	2005
B, thou art wiser than Daniel	Eze 28:3	2009
B, therefore I will bring	Eze 28:7	2005
kings, that they may *b* thee	Eze 28:17	7200
the sight of all them that *b* thee	Eze 28:18	7200
B, I am against thee, O Zidon	Eze 28:22	2005
B, I am against thee, Pharaoh	Eze 29:3	2005
B, I will bring a sword upon thee	Eze 29:8	2005
B, therefore I am against thee,	Eze 29:10	2005
B, I will give the land of Egypt	Eze 29:19	2005
B, I am against Pharaoh king of	Eze 30:22	2005
B, the Assyrian was a cedar in	Eze 31:3	2009
B, I am against the shepherds	Eze 34:10	2005
B, I, even I, will both search my	Eze 34:11	2005
B, I judge between cattle and	Eze 34:17	2005
B, I, even I, will judge between	Eze 34:20	2005
B, O mount Seir, I am against	Eze 35:3	2005
B, I have spoken in my jealousy	Eze 36:6	2005
For, *b*, I am for you, and I will	Eze 36:9	2005
and, *b*, there were very many in	Eze 37:2	2009
B, I will cause breath to enter	Eze 37:5	2005
b a shaking, and the bones came	Eze 37:7	2009
b, they say, Our bones are dried,	Eze 37:11	2009
B, O my people, I will open your	Eze 37:12	2009
B, I will take the stick of	Eze 37:19	2009
B, I will take the children of	Eze 37:21	2009
B, I am against thee, O Gog, the	Eze 38:3	2005
B, I am against thee, O Gog, the	Eze 39:1	2005
B, it is come, and it is done,	Eze 39:8	2009
And he brought me thither, and, *b*	Eze 40:3	2009
b with thine eyes, and hear with	Eze 40:4	7200
b a wall on the outside of the	Eze 40:5	2009
b a gate toward the south	Eze 40:24	2009
And, *b*, the glory of the God of	Eze 43:2	2009
and, *b*, the glory of the LORD	Eze 43:5	2009
B, this is the law of the house	Eze 43:12	2009
and I looked, and, *b*, the glory of	Eze 44:4	2009
b with thine eyes, and hear with	Eze 44:5	7200
and, *b*, there was a place on the	Eze 46:19	2009
and, *b*, in every corner of the	Eze 46:21	2009
and, *b*, waters issued out from	Eze 47:1	2009
and, *b*, there ran out waters on	Eze 47:2	2009
Now when I had returned, *b*	Eze 47:7	2009
king, sawest, and *b* a great image	Dan 2:31	431
b a tree in the midst of the	Dan 4:10	431
of my head upon my bed, and, *b*	Dan 4:13	431
saw in my vision by night, and, *b*	Dan 7:2	718
b another beast, a second, like	Dan 7:5	718
b a fourth beast, dreadful and	Dan 7:7	718
I considered the horns, and, *b*	Dan 7:8	431
and, *b*, in this horn were eyes	Dan 7:8	431
I saw in the night visions, and, *b*	Dan 7:13	718
up mine eyes, and saw, and, *b*	Dan 8:3	2009
And as I was considering, *b*	Dan 8:5	2009
sought for the meaning, then, *b*	Dan 8:15	2009
And he said, *B*, I will make thee	Dan 8:19	2005
b our desolations, and the city	Dan 9:18	7200
b a certain man clothed in linen,	Dan 10:5	2009
And, *b*, an hand touched me, which	Dan 10:10	2009
And, *b*, one like the similitude of	Dan 10:16	2009
B, there shall stand up yet three	Dan 11:2	2009
Then I Daniel looked, and, *b*	Dan 12:5	2009
Therefore, *b*, I will hedge up thy	Hos 2:6	2005
Therefore, *b*, I will allure her,	Hos 2:14	2009
answer and say unto his people, *B*	Joel 2:19	2005
For, *b*, in those days, and in that	Joel 3:1	2009
B, I will raise them out of the	Joel 3:7	2005
B, I am pressed under you, as a	Amos 2:13	2009
b the great tumults in the midst	Amos 3:9	7200
For, *b*, the LORD commandeth, and	Amos 6:11	2009
But, *b*, I will raise up against	Amos 6:14	2005
and, *b*, he formed grasshoppers in	Amos 7:1	2009
and, *b*, the Lord GOD called to	Amos 7:4	2009
and, *b*, the Lord stood upon a wall	Amos 7:7	2009
Then said the Lord, *B*, I will set	Amos 7:8	2005
b a basket of summer fruit	Amos 8:1	2009
B, the days come, saith the Lord	Amos 8:11	2009
B, the eyes of the Lord GOD are	Amos 9:8	2009
B, the days come, saith the LORD,	Amos 9:13	2009
B, I have made thee small among	Obad 2	2009
For, *b*, the LORD cometh forth out	Mic 1:3	2009
B, against this family do I	Mic 2:3	2005
I shall *b* his righteousness	Mic 7:9	7200
mine eyes shall *b* her	Mic 7:10	7200
B upon the mountains the feet of	Nah 1:15	2209
B, I am against thee, saith the	Nah 2:13	2205
B, I am against thee, saith the	Nah 3:5	2205
B, thy people in the midst of	Nah 3:13	2009
and cause me to *b* grievance	Hab 1:3	5027
B ye among the heathen, and regard	Hab 1:5	7200
art of purer eyes than to *b* evil	Hab 1:13	7200
B, his soul which is lifted up is	Hab 2:4	2009
B, is it not of the LORD of hosts	Hab 2:13	2009
B, it is laid over with gold and	Hab 2:19	2009
B, at that time I will undo all	Zeph 3:19	2005
b a man riding upon a red horse,	Zec 1:8	2009
and fro through the earth, and, *b*	Zec 1:11	2009
eyes, and saw, and *b* four horns	Zec 1:18	2009
b a man with a measuring line in	Zec 2:1	2009
And, *b*, the angel that talked with	Zec 2:3	2009
For, *b*, I will shake mine hand	Zec 2:9	2005
And unto him he said, *B*, I have	Zec 3:4	7200
for, *b*, I will bring forth my	Zec 3:8	2005
For *b* the stone that I have laid	Zec 3:9	2009
b, I will engrave the graving	Zec 3:9	2005
b a candlestick all of gold, with	Zec 4:2	2005
and looked, and *b* a flying roll	Zec 5:1	2009
And, *b*, there was lifted up a	Zec 5:7	2009
I up mine eyes, and looked, and, *b*	Zec 5:9	2009
up mine eyes, and looked, and, *b*	Zec 6:1	2009
me, and spake unto me, saying, *B*	Zec 6:8	7200
B the man whose name is The	Zec 6:12	2009
B, I will save my people from the	Zec 8:7	2005
B, the Lord will cast her out, and	Zec 9:4	2009
b, thy King cometh unto thee	Zec 9:9	2009
B, I will make Jerusalem a cup of	Zec 12:2	2009
B, the day of the LORD cometh, and	Zec 14:1	2009
Ye said also, *B*, what a weariness	Mal 1:13	2009
B, I will corrupt your seed, and	Mal 2:3	2005
B, I will send my messenger, and	Mal 3:1	2005
b, he shall come, saith the LORD	Mal 3:1	2009
For, *b*, the day cometh, that	Mal 4:1	2009
B, I will send you Elijah the	Mal 4:5	2009
he thought on these things, *b*	Mt 1:20	*2400*
B, a virgin shall be with child,	Mt 1:23	*2400*
in the days of Herod the king, *b*	Mt 2:1	*2400*
And when they were departed, *b*	Mt 2:13	*2400*
But when Herod was dead, *b*	Mt 2:19	*2400*
Then the devil leaveth him, and, *b*	Mt 4:11	*2400*
B the fowls of the air	Mt 6:26	*1689*
and, *b*, a beam is in thine own eye	Mt 7:4	*2400*
And, *b*, there came a leper and	Mt 8:2	*2400*
And, *b*, there arose a great	Mt 8:24	*2400*
And, *b*, they cried out, saying,	Mt 8:29	*2400*
and, *b*, the whole herd of swine	Mt 8:32	*2400*
And, *b*, the whole city came out to	Mt 8:34	*2400*
And, *b*, they brought to him a man	Mt 9:2	*2400*
And, *b*, certain of the scribes	Mt 9:3	*2400*
Jesus sat at meat in the house, *b*	Mt 9:10	*2400*
spake these things unto them, *b*	Mt 9:18	*2400*
And, *b*, a woman, which was	Mt 9:20	*2400*
As they went out, *b*, they brought	Mt 9:32	*2400*
B, I send you forth as sheep in	Mt 10:16	*2400*
b, they that wear soft clothing	Mt 11:8	*2400*
is he, of whom it is written, *B*	Mt 11:10	*2400*
say, *B* a man gluttonous, and a	Mt 11:19	*2400*
saw it, they said unto him, *B*	Mt 12:2	*2400*
And, *b*, there was a man which had	Mt 12:10	*2400*
B my servant, whom I have chosen	Mt 12:18	*2400*
and, *b*, a greater than Jonas is	Mt 12:41	*2400*

and, *b*, a greater than Solomon is	Mt 12:42	2400
he yet talked to the people, *b*	Mt 12:46	2400
Then one said unto him, *B*	Mt 12:47	2400
B my mother and my brethren	Mt 12:49	2400
unto them in parables, saying, *B*	Mt 13:3	2400
And, *b*, a woman of Canaan came out.	Mt 15:22	2400
And, *b*, there appeared unto them	Mt 17:3	2400
While he yet spake, *b*, a bright	Mt 17:5	2400
b a voice out of the cloud, which	Mt 17:5	2400
heaven their angels do always *b*	Mt 18:10	991
And, *b*, one came and said unto him,	Mt 19:16	2400
Peter and said unto him, *B*	Mt 19:27	2400
B, we go up to Jerusalem	Mt 20:18	2400
And, *b*, two blind men sitting by	Mt 20:30	2400
Tell ye the daughter of Sion, *B*	Mt 21:5	2400
Tell them which are bidden, *B*	Mt 22:4	2400
Wherefore, *b*, I send unto you	Mt 23:34	2400
B, your house is left unto you	Mt 23:38	2400
B, I have told you before	Mt 24:25	2400
if they shall say unto you, *B*	Mt 24:26	2400
b, he is in the secret chambers	Mt 24:26	2400
midnight there was a cry made, *B*	Mt 25:6	2400
b, I have gained beside them five	Mt 25:20	2396
b, I have gained two other	Mt 25:22	2396
b, the hour is at hand, and the	Mt 26:45	2400
b, he is at hand that doth betray	Mt 26:46	2400
And, *b*, one of them which were	Mt 26:51	2400
b, now ye have heard his	Mt 26:65	2396
And, *b*, the veil of the temple was	Mt 27:51	2400
And, *b*, there was a great	Mt 28:2	2400
and, *b*, he goeth before you into	Mt 28:7	2400
went to tell his disciples, *b*	Mt 28:9	2400
Now when they were going, *b*	Mt 28:11	2400
it is written in the prophets, *B*	Mk 1:2	2400
And the Pharisees said unto him, *B*	Mk 2:24	2396
him, and they said unto him, *B*	Mk 3:32	2396
B my mother and my brethren	Mk 3:34	2396
B, there went out a sower to sow	Mk 4:3	2400
And, *b*, there cometh one of the	Mk 5:22	2400
Saying, *B*, we go up to Jerusalem	Mk 10:33	2400
saith unto him, Master, *b*	Mk 11:21	2396
b, I have foretold you all things	Mk 13:23	2400
b, the Son of man is betrayed	Mk 14:41	2400
b how many things they witness	Mk 15:4	2396
by, when they heard it said, *B*	Mk 15:35	2400
b the place where they laid him	Mk 16:6	2396
And, *b*, thou shalt be dumb, and not	Lk 1:20	2400
And, *b*, thou shalt conceive in thy	Lk 1:31	2400
And, *b*, thy cousin Elisabeth, she	Lk 1:36	2400
B the handmaid of the Lord	Lk 1:38	2400
for, *b*, from henceforth all	Lk 1:48	2400
for, *b*, I bring you good tidings	Lk 2:10	2400
And, *b*, there was a man in	Lk 2:25	2400
and said unto Mary his mother, *B*	Lk 2:34	2400
b, thy father and I have sought	Lk 2:48	2400
city, *b* a man full of leprosy	Lk 5:12	2400
And, *b*, men brought in a bed a man	Lk 5:18	2400
for, *b*, your reward is great in	Lk 6:23	2400
nigh to the gate of the city, *b*	Lk 7:12	2400
B, they which are gorgeously	Lk 7:25	2400
is he, of whom it is written, *B*	Lk 7:27	2400
ye say, *B* a gluttonous man, and a	Lk 7:34	2400
And, *b*, a woman in the city, which	Lk 7:37	2400
And, *b*, there came a man named	Lk 8:41	2400
And, *b*, there talked with him two	Lk 9:30	2400
And, *b*, a man of the company cried	Lk 9:38	2400
b, I send you forth as lambs	Lk 10:3	2400
B, I give unto you power to tread	Lk 10:19	2400
And, *b*, a certain lawyer stood up,	Lk 10:25	2400
and, *b*, a greater than Solomon is	Lk 11:31	2400
and, *b*, a greater than Jonas is	Lk 11:32	2400
and, *b*, all things are clean unto	Lk 11:41	2400
the dresser of his vineyard, *B*	Lk 13:7	2400
And, *b*, there was a woman which	Lk 13:11	2400
And, *b*, there are last which shall	Lk 13:30	2400
them, Go ye, and tell that fox, *B*	Lk 13:32	2400
B, your house is left unto you	Lk 13:35	2400
And, *b*, there was a certain man	Lk 14:2	2400
all that *b* it begin to mock him,	Lk 14:29	2334
for, *b*, the kingdom of God is	Lk 17:21	2400
the twelve, and said unto them, *B*	Lk 18:31	2400
And, *b*, there was a man named	Lk 19:2	2400
B, Lord, the half of my goods I	Lk 19:8	2400
And another came, saying, Lord, *b*	Lk 19:20	2400
As for these things which ye *b*	Lk 21:6	2334
B the fig tree, and all the trees	Lk 21:29	1492
And he said unto them, *B*, when ye	Lk 22:10	2400
But, *b*, the hand of him that	Lk 22:21	2400
And the Lord said, Simon, Simon, *b*	Lk 22:31	2400
And they said, Lord, *b*, here are	Lk 22:38	2400
b a multitude, and he that was	Lk 22:47	2400
and, *b*, I, having examined him	Lk 23:14	2400
For, *b*, the days are coming, in	Lk 23:29	2400
And, *b*, there was a man named	Lk 23:50	2400
were much perplexed thereabout, *b*	Lk 24:4	2400
And, *b*, two of them went that same	Lk 24:13	2400
B my hands and my feet, that it is	Lk 24:39	1492
And, *b*, I send the promise of my	Lk 24:49	2400
B the Lamb of God, which taketh	Jn 1:29	2396
he saith, *B* the Lamb of God	Jn 1:36	2396
B an Israelite indeed, in whom is	Jn 1:47	2396
to whom thou barest witness, *b*	Jn 3:26	2396
b, I say unto you, Lift up your	Jn 4:35	2400
the temple, and said unto him, *B*	Jn 5:14	2396
sent unto him, saying, Lord, *b*	Jn 11:3	2396
said the Jews, *B* how he loved him	Jn 11:36	2396
b, thy King cometh, sitting on an	Jn 12:15	2400
b, the world is gone after him	Jn 12:19	2396
B, the hour cometh, yea, is now	Jn 16:32	2400
that they may *b* my glory, which	Jn 17:24	2334
b, they know what I said	Jn 18:21	2396
again, and saith unto them, *B*	Jn 19:4	2396
Pilate saith unto them, *B* the man	Jn 19:5	2396
saith unto the Jews, *B* your King	Jn 19:14	2396
unto his mother, Woman, *b* thy son	Jn 19:26	2400
he to the disciple, *B* thy mother	Jn 19:27	2400
hither thy finger, and *b* my hands	Jn 20:27	2396
toward heaven as he went up, *b*	Acts 1:10	2400
saying one to another, *B*	Acts 2:7	2400
now, Lord, *b* their threatenings	Acts 4:29	1896
b, the feet of them which have	Acts 5:9	2400
came one and told them, saying, *B*	Acts 5:25	2400
and, *b*, ye have filled Jerusalem	Acts 5:28	2400
and as he drew near to *b* it	Acts 7:31	2657
Moses trembled, and durst not *b*	Acts 7:32	2657
And said, *B*, I see the heavens	Acts 7:56	2400
and, *b*, a man of Ethiopia, an	Acts 8:27	2400
And he said, *B*, I am here, Lord	Acts 9:10	2400
for, *b*, he prayeth,	Acts 9:11	2400
which he had seen should mean, *b*	Acts 10:17	2400
the Spirit said unto him, *B*	Acts 10:19	2400
and said, *B*, I am he whom ye seek	Acts 10:21	2400
hour I prayed in my house, and, *b*	Acts 10:30	2400
And, *b*, immediately there were	Acts 11:11	2400
And, *b*, the angel of the Lord came	Acts 12:7	2400
And now, *b*, the hand of the Lord	Acts 13:11	2400
But, *b*, there cometh one after me	Acts 13:25	2400
B, ye despisers, and wonder, and	Acts 13:41	1492
and, *b*, a certain disciple was	Acts 16:1	2400
And now, *b*, I go bound in the	Acts 20:22	2400
And now, *b*, I know that ye all,	Acts 20:25	2400
B, thou art called a Jew, and	Rom 2:17	2396
As it is written, *B*, I lay in	Rom 9:33	2400
B therefore the goodness and	Rom 11:22	1492
B Israel after the flesh	1Cor 10:18	991
B, I shew you a mystery	1Cor 15:51	2400
of Israel could not stedfastly *b*	2Cor 3:7	816
b, all things are become new	2Cor 5:17	2400
b, now is the accepted time	2Cor 6:2	2400
b, now is the day of salvation	2Cor 6:2	2400
as dying, and, *b*, we live	2Cor 6:9	2400
For *b* this selfsame thing, that	2Cor 7:11	2400
B, the third time I am ready to	2Cor 12:14	2400
things which I write unto you, *b*	Gal 1:20	2400
B, I Paul say unto you, that if	Gal 5:2	2396
B I and the children which God	Heb 2:13	2400
fault with them, he saith, *B*	Heb 8:8	2400
B, we put bits in the horses'	Jas 3:3	2400
B also the ships, which though	Jas 3:4	2400
B, how great a matter a little	Jas 3:5	2400
B, the hire of the labourers who	Jas 5:4	2400
B, the husbandman waiteth for the	Jas 5:7	2400
b, the judge standeth before the	Jas 5:9	2400
B, we count them happy which	Jas 5:11	2400
is contained in the scripture, *B*	1Pet 2:6	2400
good works, which they shall *b*	1Pet 2:12	2029
While they *b* your chaste	1Pet 3:2	2029
B, what manner of love the Father	1Jn 3:1	1492
prophesied of these, saying, *B*	Jude 14	2400
B, he cometh with clouds	Rev 1:7	2400
and, *b*, I am alive for evermore,	Rev 1:18	2400
b, the devil shall cast some of	Rev 2:10	2400
B, I will cast her into a bed, and	Rev 2:22	2400
b, I have set before thee an open	Rev 3:8	2400
B, I will make them of the	Rev 3:9	2400
b, I will make them to come and	Rev 3:9	2400
B, I come quickly	Rev 3:11	2400
B, I stand at the door, and knock	Rev 3:20	2400
After this I looked, and, *b*	Rev 4:1	2400
and, *b*, a throne was set in heaven	Rev 4:2	2400
b, the Lion of the tribe of Juda,	Rev 5:5	2400
And I saw, and *b* a white horse	Rev 6:2	2400
And I looked, and *b* a pale horse	Rev 6:8	2400
and, *b*, there come two woes more	Rev 9:12	2400
and, *b*, the third woe cometh	Rev 11:14	2400
b a great red dragon, having	Rev 12:3	2400
b a white cloud, and upon the	Rev 14:14	2400
And after that I looked, and, *b*	Rev 15:5	2400
B, I come as a thief	Rev 16:15	2400
when they *b* the beast that was,	Rev 17:8	991
heaven opened, and *b* a white horse	Rev 19:11	2400
voice out of heaven saying, *B*	Rev 21:3	2400
that sat upon the throne said, *B*	Rev 21:5	2400
B, I come quickly	Rev 22:7	2400
And, *b*, I come quickly	Rev 22:12	2400

BEHOLDEST

for thou *b* mischief and spite, to	Ps 10:14	5027
why *b* thou the mote that is in	Mt 7:3	991
why *b* thou the mote that is in	Lk 6:41	991
when thou thyself *b* not the beam	Lk 6:42	991

BEHOLDETH

he *b* not the way of the vineyards	Job 24:18	6437
He *b* all high things	Job 41:34	7200
he *b* all the sons of men	Ps 33:13	7200
For he *b* himself, and goeth his	Jas 1:24	2657

BEHOLDING

Turn away mine eyes from *b* vanity	Ps 119:37	7200
place, *b* the evil and the good	Prov 15:3	6822
saving the *b* of them with their	Eccl 5:11	7200
many women were there *b* afar off	Mt 27:55	2334
Then Jesus *b* him loved him, and	Mk 10:21	1689
And the people stood *b*	Lk 23:35	2334
b the things which were done,	Lk 23:48	2334
stood afar off, *b* these things	Lk 23:49	3708
b the man which was healed	Acts 4:14	991
b the miracles and signs which	Acts 8:13	2334
who stedfastly *b* him, and	Acts 14:9	816
earnestly *b* the council, said,	Acts 23:1	816
with open face *b* as in a glass	2Cor 3:18	2734
b your order, and the stedfastness	Col 2:5	991
he is like unto a man *b* his	Jas 1:23	2657

BEHOVED

thus it *b* Christ to suffer, and to	Lk 24:46	1163
Wherefore in all things it *b* him	Heb 2:17	3784

BEING

have pleasure, my lord *b* old also	Gen 18:12	
the LORD *b* merciful unto him	Gen 19:16	
his son Isaac *b* eight days old	Gen 21:4	
I *b* in the way, the LORD led me	Gen 24:27	
I *b* few in number, they shall	Gen 34:30	
his people, *b* old and full of days	Gen 35:29	
b seventeen years old, was	Gen 37:2	
b an hundred and ten years old	Gen 50:26	
their kneadingtroughs *b* bound up	Ex 12:34	
that openeth the matrix, *b* males	Ex 13:15	
the owner thereof *b* not with it	Ex 22:14	
Foursquare it shall be *b* doubled	Ex 28:16	
of them that cry for *b* overcome	Ex 32:18	
the breadth thereof, *b* doubled	Ex 39:9	
b a chief man among his people,	Lev 21:4	
b taken from the children of	Lev 24:8	
princes of Israel, *b* twelve men	Num 1:44	
a wall *b* on this side, and a wall	Num 22:24	
b in her father's house in her	Num 30:3	
b yet in her youth in her	Num 30:16	
b the rest of the prey which the	Num 31:32	
Baal-meon, (their names *b* changed	Num 32:38	
b the kingdom of Og, gave I unto	Deut 3:13	
b matters of controversy within	Deut 17:8	
she cried not, *b* in the city	Deut 22:24	
our enemies themselves *b* judges	Deut 32:31	
of you be freed from *b* bondmen	Josh 9:23	
Aaron, *b* of the families of the	Josh 21:10	
b an hundred and ten years old	Josh 24:29	
b an hundred and ten years old	Judg 2:8	
b threescore and ten persons, upon	Judg 9:5	
b a child, girded with a linen	1Sa 2:18	
also rejected thee from *b* king	1Sa 15:23	
thee from *b* king over Israel	1Sa 15:26	
a great space *b* between them	1Sa 26:13	
of salt, *b* eighteen thousand men	2Sa 8:13	
b the king's son, lean from day	2Sa 13:4	
b stronger than she, forced her,	2Sa 13:14	
as people *b* ashamed steal away	2Sa 19:3	
he *b* girded with a new sword,	2Sa 21:16	
noise of the city *b* in an uproar	1Kin 1:41	
from *b* priest unto the LORD	1Kin 2:27	1961
Hadad *b* yet a little child	1Kin 11:17	
even her he removed from *b* queen	1Kin 15:13	
in *b* like the house of Jeroboam	1Kin 16:7	1961
of Israel, *b* seven thousand	1Kin 20:15	
Jehoshaphat *b* then king of Judah,	2Kin 8:16	
b seventy persons, were with the	2Kin 10:6	
b told, into the hands of them	2Kin 12:11	
b over the host of the LORD, were	1Chr 9:19	
household *b* taken for Eleazar	1Chr 24:6	
b arrayed in white linen, having	2Chr 5:12	
men, *b* mighty men of valour	2Chr 13:3	
king, he removed her from *b* queen	2Chr 15:16	
and departed without *b* desired	2Chr 21:20	
in a several house, *b* a leper	2Chr 26:21	
b set up, let him be hanged	Ezr 6:11	
b guilty, they offered a ram of	Ezr 10:19	
b as I am, would go into the	Neh 6:11	
of the provinces, *b* before him	Est 1:3	
(the vessels *b* diverse one from	Est 1:7	
out, *b* hastened by the king's	Est 3:15	
b hastened and pressed on by the	Est 8:14	
who ever perished, *b* innocent	Job 4:7	
b wholly at ease and quiet	Job 21:23	
Job died, *b* old and full of days	Job 42:17	
Nevertheless man *b* in honour	Ps 49:12	
b girded with power	Ps 65:6	
b mine enemies wrongfully, are	Ps 69:4	
b armed, and carrying bows, turned	Ps 78:9	
b full of compassion, forgave	Ps 78:38	
us cut them off from *b* a nation	Ps 83:4	
to my God while I have my *b*	Ps 104:33	5750
b bound in affliction and iron	Ps 107:10	
see my substance, yet *b* unperfect	Ps 139:16	
unto my God while I have any *b*	Ps 146:2	5750
shall keep thy foot from *b* taken	Prov 3:26	
that *b* often reproved hardeneth	Prov 29:1	
all hold swords, *b* expert in war	Song 3:8	
midst thereof *b* paved with love	Song 3:10	
she *b* desolate shall sit upon the	Is 3:26	
is taken away from *b* a city	Is 17:1	
or *b* his counsellor hath taught	Is 40:13	
but the sinner *b* an hundred years	Is 65:20	
Withhold thy foot from *b* unshod	Jer 2:25	
b desolate it mourneth unto me	Jer 12:11	
from *b* a pastor to follow thee	Jer 17:16	
b a nation before me for ever	Jer 31:36	1961
b an Hebrew or an Hebrewess, go	Jer 34:9	
when he had taken him *b* bound in	Jer 40:1	
let us cut it off from *b* a nation	Jer 48:2	
be destroyed from *b* a people	Jer 48:42	
b planted, shall it prosper	Eze 17:10	
multitude *b* at ease was with her	Eze 23:42	
which *b* brought forth into the	Eze 47:8	1961
b in the midst of that which is	Eze 48:22	
b gathered together, saw these	Dan 3:27	
b about threescore and two years	Dan 5:31	
his windows *b* open in his chamber	Dan 6:10	
Now that *b* broken, whereas four	Dan 8:22	
b caused to fly swiftly, touched	Dan 9:21	
b a just man, and not willing to	Mt 1:19	5607
which *b* interpreted is, God with	Mt 1:23	
Then Joseph *b* raised from sleep	Mt 1:24	
b warned of God in a dream that	Mt 2:12	
b warned of God in a dream, he	Mt 2:22	
b evil, know how to give good	Mt 7:11	5607
b evil, speak good things	Mt 12:34	5607
b before instructed of her mother	Mt 14:8	
b grieved for the hardness of	Mk 3:5	
b interpreted, Damsel, I say unto	Mk 5:41	
days the multitude *b* very great	Mk 8:1	5607
b in the house he asked them,	Mk 9:33	1096

b in Bethany in the house of	Mk 14:3	5607
b interpreted, The place of a	Mk 15:22	
b interpreted, My God, my God,	Mk 15:34	
b delivered out of the hand of	Lk 1:74	
espoused wife, b great with child	Lk 2:5	5607
Pontius Pilate b governor of	Lk 3:1	
Herod b tetrarch of Galilee, and	Lk 3:1	
Caiaphas b the high priests, the	Lk 3:2	1909
b reproved by him for Herodias	Lk 3:19	
pass, that Jesus also b baptized	Lk 3:21	
b (as was supposed) the son of	Lk 3:23	5607
Jesus b full of the Holy Ghost	Lk 4:1	
B forty days tempted of the devil	Lk 4:2	
synagogues, b glorified of all	Lk 4:15	
b baptized with the baptism of	Lk 7:29	
themselves, b not baptized of him	Lk 7:30	
they b afraid wondered, saying	Lk 8:25	
b evil, know how to give good	Lk 11:13	5225
b a daughter of Abraham, whom	Lk 13:16	5607
house b angry said to his servant	Lk 14:21	
b in torments, and seeth Abraham	Lk 16:23	5225
of God, b the children of the	Lk 20:36	5607
b brought before kings and rulers	Lk 21:12	
b of the number of the twelve	Lk 22:3	5607
b in an agony he prayed more	Lk 22:44	1096
b interpreted, Master,) where	Jn 1:38	
b interpreted, the Christ	Jn 1:41	
b wearied with his journey, sat	Jn 4:6	
b a Jew, askest drink of me,	Jn 4:9	5607
a multitude b in that place	Jn 5:13	5607
betray him, b one of the twelve	Jn 6:71	5607
Jesus by night, b one of them,)	Jn 7:50	5607
it, b convicted by their own	Jn 8:9	
b a man, makest thyself God	Jn 10:33	5607
b the high priest that same year,	Jn 11:49	5607
but b high priest that year, he	Jn 11:51	5607
And supper b ended, the devil	Jn 13:2	
unto you, b yet present with you	Jn 14:25	
b his kinsman whose ear Peter cut	Jn 18:26	5607
b a disciple of Jesus, but	Jn 19:38	5607
b the first day of the week, when	Jn 20:19	
then came Jesus, the doors b shut	Jn 20:26	
b seen of them forty days, and	Acts 1:3	
b assembled together with them,	Acts 1:4	
b delivered by the determinate	Acts 2:23	
Therefore b a prophet, and knowing	Acts 2:30	5225
Therefore b by the right hand of	Acts 2:33	
hour of prayer, b the ninth hour	Acts 3:1	
B grieved that they taught the	Acts 4:2	
B let go, they went to their own	Acts 4:23	
b interpreted, The son of	Acts 4:36	
his wife also b privy to it	Acts 5:2	
b full of the Holy Ghost, looked	Acts 7:55	5225
b sent forth by the Holy Ghost,	Acts 13:4	
b astonished at the doctrine of	Acts 13:12	
b a cripple from his mother's	Acts 14:8	5225
b brought on their way by the	Acts 15:3	
b read in the synagogues every	Acts 15:21	
b assembled with one accord, to	Acts 15:25	
b prophets also themselves,	Acts 15:32	5607
b recommended by the brethren	Acts 15:40	
b grieved, turned and said to the	Acts 16:18	5607
b Jews, do exceedingly trouble	Acts 16:20	5225
neither to observe, b Romans	Acts 16:21	5605
b Romans, and have cast us into	Acts 16:37	5225
we live, and move, and have our b	Acts 17:28	2070
b fervent in the spirit, he spake	Acts 18:25	
there b no cause whereby we may	Acts 19:40	5225
b fallen into a deep sleep	Acts 20:9	
b led by the hand of them that	Acts 22:11	
b exceedingly mad against them, I	Acts 26:11	
of Thessalonica, b with us	Acts 27:2	5607
we b exceedingly tossed with a	Acts 27:18	
b understood by the things that	Rom 1:20	
B filled with all unrighteousness	Rom 1:29	
b instructed out of the law	Rom 2:18	
b witnessed by the law and the	Rom 3:21	
B justified freely by his grace	Rom 3:24	
which he had yet b uncircumcised	Rom 4:11	
which he had b yet uncircumcised	Rom 4:12	
And b not weak in faith, he	Rom 4:19	
b fully persuaded that, what he	Rom 4:21	
Therefore b justified by faith,	Rom 5:1	
b now justified by his blood, we	Rom 5:9	
b reconciled, we shall be saved	Rom 5:10	
Knowing that Christ b raised from	Rom 6:9	
B then made free from sin, ye	Rom 6:18	
But now b made free from sin, and	Rom 6:22	
that b dead wherein we were held	Rom 7:6	
(For the children b not yet born	Rom 9:11	
For they b ignorant of God's	Rom 10:3	
b a wild olive tree, wert graffed	Rom 11:17	5607
b many, are one body in Christ,	Rom 12:5	
b sanctified by the Holy Ghost	Rom 15:16	
b reviled, we bless	1Cor 4:12	
b persecuted, we suffer it	1Cor 4:12	
B defamed, we intreat	1Cor 4:13	
Is any man called b circumcised	1Cor 7:18	
Art thou called b a servant	1Cor 7:21	
b a servant, is the Lord's	1Cor 7:22	
b free, is Christ's servant	1Cor 7:22	
conscience b weak is defiled	1Cor 8:7	5607
(b not without law to God, but	1Cor 9:21	5607
For we b many are one bread, and	1Cor 10:17	
one body, b many, are one body	1Cor 12:12	5607
If so be that b clothed we shall	2Cor 5:3	
tabernacle do groan, b burdened	2Cor 5:4	
but b more forward, of his own	2Cor 8:17	5225
B enriched in every thing to all	2Cor 9:11	
but b absent am bold toward you	2Cor 10:1	
myself from b burdensome unto you	2Cor 11:9	
b crafty, I caught you with guile	2Cor 12:16	5225
b absent now I write to them	2Cor 13:2	
I write these things b absent	2Cor 13:10	
lest b present I should use	2Cor 13:10	
b more exceedingly zealous of the	Gal 1:14	5225
b a Greek, was compelled to be	Gal 2:3	5607
b a Jew, livest after the manner	Gal 2:14	5225
of the law, b made a curse for us	Gal 3:13	
b predestinated according to the	Eph 1:11	
your understanding b enlightened	Eph 1:18	
that ye b in time past Gentiles	Eph 2:11	
b aliens from the commonwealth of	Eph 2:12	
Jesus Christ himself b the chief	Eph 2:20	5607
b rooted and grounded in love,	Eph 3:17	
b alienated from the life of God	Eph 4:18	5607
Who b past feeling have given	Eph 4:19	
B confident of this very thing,	Phil 1:6	
B filled with the fruits of	Phil 1:11	
b of one accord, of one mind	Phil 2:2	
b in the form of God, thought it	Phil 2:6	5225
b found in fashion as a man, he	Phil 2:8	
b made conformable unto his death	Phil 3:10	
b fruitful in every good work, and	Col 1:10	
b knit together in love, and unto	Col 2:2	
b dead in your sins and the	Col 2:13	5607
So b affectionately desirous of	1Th 2:8	
b taken from you for a short time	1Th 2:17	
but the woman b deceived was in	1Ti 2:14	
lest b lifted up with pride he	1Ti 3:6	
of a deacon, b found blameless	1Ti 3:10	5607
b mindful of thy tears, that I	2Ti 1:4	
worse, deceiving, and b deceived	2Ti 3:13	
b abominable, and disobedient, and	Titus 1:16	5607
That b justified by his grace, we	Titus 3:7	
sinneth, b condemned of himself	Titus 3:11	5607
b such an one as Paul the aged,	Philem 9	5607
Who b the brightness of his glory	Heb 1:3	
B made so much better than the	Heb 1:4	
himself hath suffered b tempted	Heb 2:18	
a promise b left us of entering	Heb 4:1	
not b mixed with faith in them	Heb 4:2	
b made perfect, he became the	Heb 5:9	
first b by interpretation King of	Heb 7:2	
For the priesthood b changed	Heb 7:12	
But Christ b come an high priest	Heb 9:11	
by it he b dead yet speaketh	Heb 11:4	
b warned of God of things not	Heb 11:7	
b destitute, afflicted, tormented	Heb 11:37	
as b yourselves also in the body	Heb 13:3	5607
he b not a forgetful hearer, but	Jas 1:25	1096
hath not works, is dead, b alone	Jas 2:17	
b much more precious than of gold	1Pet 1:7	1096
B born again, not of corruptible	1Pet 1:23	
at the word, b disobedient	1Pet 2:8	
b dead to sins, should live unto	1Pet 2:24	
b in subjection unto their own	1Pet 3:5	
as b heirs together of the grace	1Pet 3:7	
b put to death in the flesh, but	1Pet 3:18	
powers b made subject unto him	1Pet 3:22	
Neither as b lords over God's	1Pet 5:3	
but b ensamples to the flock	1Pet 5:3	1096
b overflowed with water, perished	2Pet 3:6	
wherein the heavens b on fire	2Pet 3:12	
b led away with the error of the	2Pet 3:17	
b turned, I saw seven golden	Rev 1:12	
And she b with child cried,	Rev 12:2	2192
b the firstfruits unto God and to	Rev 14:4	

BEKAH

A b for every man, that is, half	Ex 38:26	1235

BEKERITE See BACHRITES.

BEL (bel) See BAAL. *A Babylonian god.*

B boweth down, Nebo stoopeth,	Is 46:1	1078
B is confounded, Merodach is	Jer 50:2	1078
And I will punish B in Babylon	Jer 51:44	1078

BELA (be'-lah) See BELAH, BELAITES.

1. Another name for Zoar.

king of Zeboiim, and the king of B	Gen 14:2	1106
the king of B (the same is Zoar	Gen 14:8	1106

2. An Edomite king.

B the son of Beor reigned in Edom	Gen 36:32	1106
B died, and Jobab the son of Zerah	Gen 36:33	1106
B the son of Beor	1Chr 1:43	1106
when B was dead, Jobab the son of	1Chr 1:44	1106

3. A son of Benjamin.

of B, the family of the Belaites	Num 26:38	1106
And the sons of B were Ard	Num 26:40	1106
B, and Becher, and Jediael, three	1Chr 7:6	1106
And the sons of B	1Chr 7:7	1106
Benjamin begat B his firstborn	1Chr 8:1	1106
And the sons of B were, Addar, and	1Chr 8:3	1106

4. A son of Azaz the Reubenite.

B the son of Azaz, the son of	1Chr 5:8	1106

BELAH (be'-lah) See BELA. *A form of Bela.*

And the sons of Benjamin were B	Gen 46:21	1106

BELAITES (be'-lah-ites) *Descendants of Bela.*

of Bela, the family of the B	Num 26:38	1108

BELCH

they b out with their mouth	Ps 59:7	5042

BELIAL (be'-le-al) *A title for a "worthless person."*

Certain men, the children of B	Deut 13:13	1100
of the city, certain sons of B	Judg 19:22	1100
us the men, the children of B	Judg 20:13	1100
handmaid for a daughter of B	1Sa 1:16	1100
the sons of Eli were sons of B	1Sa 2:12	1100
But the children of B said	1Sa 10:27	1100
for he is such a son of B	1Sa 25:17	1100
I pray thee, regard this man of B	1Sa 25:25	1100
all the wicked men and men of B	1Sa 30:22	1100
thou bloody man, and thou man of B	2Sa 16:7	1100
happened to be there a man of B	2Sa 20:1	1100
But the sons of B shall be all of	2Sa 23:6	1100
And set two men, sons of B	1Kin 21:10	1100
came in two men, children of B	1Kin 21:13	1100
the men of B witnessed against	1Kin 21:13	1100
him vain men, the children of B	2Chr 13:7	1100
what concord hath Christ with B	2Cor 6:15	955

BELIED

They have b the LORD, and said, It	Jer 5:12	3584

BELIEF

of the Spirit and b of the truth	2Th 2:13	4102

BELIEVE

But, behold, they will not b me	Ex 4:1	539
That they may b that the LORD God	Ex 4:5	539
to pass, if they will not b thee	Ex 4:8	539
that they will b the voice of the	Ex 4:8	539
if they will not b also these two	Ex 4:9	539
with thee, and b thee for ever	Ex 19:9	539
how long will it be ere they b me	Num 14:11	539
ye did not b the LORD your God	Deut 1:32	539
that did not b in the LORD their	2Kin 17:14	539
B in the LORD your God, so shall	2Chr 20:20	539
b his prophets, so shall ye	2Chr 20:20	539
on this manner, neither yet b him	2Chr 32:15	539
yet would I not b that he had	Job 9:16	539
Wilt thou b him, that he will	Job 39:12	539
When he speaketh fair, b him not	Prov 26:25	539
If ye will not b, surely ye shall	Is 7:9	539
b me, and understand that I am he	Is 43:10	539
b them not, though they speak	Jer 12:6	539
in your days, which ye will not b	Hab 1:5	539
B ye that I am able to do this	Mt 9:28	4100
these little ones which b in me	Mt 18:6	4100
us, Why did ye not then b him	Mt 21:25	4100
afterward, that ye might b him	Mt 21:32	4100
b it not	Mt 24:23	4100
b it not	Mt 24:26	4100
from the cross, and we will b him	Mt 27:42	4100
repent ye, and b the gospel	Mk 1:15	
synagogue, Be not afraid, only b	Mk 5:36	4100
said unto him, If thou canst b	Mk 9:23	4100
and said with tears, Lord, I b	Mk 9:24	4100
of these little ones that b in me	Mk 9:42	4100
but shall b that those things	Mk 11:23	4100
b that ye receive them, and ye	Mk 11:24	4100
say, Why then did ye not b him	Mk 11:31	4100
b him not	Mk 13:21	4100
the cross, that we may see and b	Mk 15:32	4100
signs shall follow them that b	Mk 16:17	4100
their hearts, lest they should b	Lk 8:12	4100
have no root, which for a while b	Lk 8:13	4100
b only, and she shall be made	Lk 8:50	4100
If I tell you, ye will not b	Lk 22:67	4100
slow of heart to b all that the	Lk 24:25	
that all men through him might b	Jn 1:7	4100
even to them that b on his name	Jn 1:12	4100
and ye b not, how shall ye b	Jn 3:12	4100
b me, the hour cometh, when ye	Jn 4:21	4100
And said unto the woman, Now we b	Jn 4:42	4100
signs and wonders, ye will not b	Jn 4:48	4100
whom he hath sent, him ye b not	Jn 5:38	4100
How can ye b, which receive	Jn 5:44	4100
But if ye b not his writings	Jn 5:47	4100
how shall ye b my words	Jn 5:47	4100
that ye b on him whom he hath	Jn 6:29	4100
then, that we may see, and b thee	Jn 6:30	4100
ye also have seen me, and b not	Jn 6:36	4100
there are some of you that b not	Jn 6:64	4100
And we b and are sure that thou art	Jn 6:69	4100
neither did his brethren b in him	Jn 7:5	4100
which they that b on him should	Jn 7:39	4100
for if ye b not that I am he, ye	Jn 8:24	4100
I tell you the truth, ye b me not	Jn 8:45	4100
say the truth, why do ye not b me	Jn 8:46	4100
the Jews did not b concerning him	Jn 9:18	4100
Dost thou b on the Son of God	Jn 9:35	4100
he, Lord, that I might b on him	Jn 9:36	4100
And he said, Lord, I b	Jn 9:38	4100
But ye b not, because ye are not	Jn 10:26	4100
the works of my Father, b me not	Jn 10:37	4100
ye b not me, b the works	Jn 10:38	4100
that ye may know, and b, that the	Jn 10:38	4100
not there, to the intent ye may b	Jn 11:15	4100
I b that thou art the Christ, the	Jn 11:27	4100
thee, that, if thou wouldest b	Jn 11:40	4100
that they may b that thou hast	Jn 11:42	4100
thus alone, all men will b on him	Jn 11:48	4100
b in the light, that ye may be	Jn 12:36	4100
Therefore they could not b	Jn 12:39	4100
words, and b not, I judge him not	Jn 12:47	4100
to pass, ye may b that I am he	Jn 13:19	4100
ye b in God, b also in me	Jn 14:1	4100
B me that I am in the Father, and	Jn 14:11	4100
or else b me for the very works'	Jn 14:11	4100
it is come to pass, ye might b	Jn 14:29	4100
Of sin, because they b not on me	Jn 16:9	4100
by this we b that thou camest	Jn 16:30	4100
Jesus answered them, Do ye now b	Jn 16:31	4100
shall b on me through their word	Jn 17:20	4100
that the world may b that thou	Jn 17:21	4100
he saith true, that ye might b	Jn 19:35	4100
hand into his side, I will not b	Jn 20:25	4100
that ye might b that Jesus is the	Jn 20:31	4100
I b that Jesus Christ is the Son	Acts 8:37	4100
by him all that b are justified	Acts 13:39	4100
work which ye shall in no wise b	Acts 13:41	4100
hear the word of the gospel, and b	Acts 15:7	4100
But we b that through the grace	Acts 15:11	4100
B on the Lord Jesus Christ, and	Acts 16:31	4100
that they should b on him which	Acts 19:4	4100
of Jews there are which b	Acts 21:20	4100
As touching the Gentiles which b	Acts 21:25	4100
for I b God, that it shall be	Acts 27:25	4100
For what if some did not b	Rom 3:3	569
unto all and upon all them that b	Rom 3:22	4100

B

be the father of all them that *b* Rom 4:11 4100
if we *b* on him that raised up Rom 4:24 4100
we *b* that we shall also live with Rom 6:8 4100
shalt *b* in thine heart that God Rom 10:9 4100
how shall they *b* in him of whom Rom 10:14 4100
from them that do not *b* in Judaea Rom 15:31 544
of preaching to save them that *b* 1Cor 1:21 4100
If any of them that *b* not bid you 1Cor 10:27 571
and I partly *b* it 1Cor 11:18 4100
for a sign, not to them that *b* 1Cor 14:22 4100
but to them that *b* not 1Cor 14:22 571
serveth not for them that *b* 1Cor 14:22 571
but for them which *b* 1Cor 14:22 4100
the minds of them which *b* not 2Cor 4:4 571
we also *b*, and therefore speak 2Cor 4:13 4100
might be given to them that *b* Gal 3:22 4100
of his power to us-ward who *b* Eph 1:19 4100
of Christ, not only to *b* on him Phil 1:29 4100
to all that *b* in Macedonia 1Th 1:7 4100
ourselves among you that *b* 1Th 2:10 4100
worketh also in you that *b* 1Th 2:13 4100
For if we *b* that Jesus died and 1Th 4:14 4100
b (because our testimony among 2Th 1:10 4100
that they should *b* a lie 2Th 2:11 4100
b on him to life everlasting 1Ti 1:16 4100
with thanksgiving of them which *b* 1Ti 4:3 4103
men, specially of those that *b* 1Ti 4:10 4103
If we *b* not, yet he abideth 2Ti 2:13 569
but of them that *b* to the saving Heb 10:39 4102
cometh to God must *b* that he is Heb 11:6 4100
the devils also *b*, and tremble Jas 2:19 4100
Who by him do *b* in God, that 1Pet 1:21 4100
therefore which *b* he is precious 1Pet 2:7 4100
That we should *b* on the name of 1Jn 3:23 4100
b not every spirit, but try the 1Jn 4:1 4100
have I written unto you that *b* on 1Jn 5:13 4100
that ye may *b* on the name of the 1Jn 5:13 4100

BELIEVED

And he *b* in the LORD Gen 15:6 539
heart fainted, for he *b* them not Gen 45:26 539
And the people *b* Ex 4:31 539
b the LORD, and his servant Moses Ex 14:31 539
and Aaron, Because ye *b* me not Num 20:12 539
ye *b* him not, nor hearkened to Deut 9:23 539
And Achish *b* David, saying, He 1Sa 27:12 539
Howbeit I *b* not the words, until 1Kin 10:7 539
Howbeit I *b* not their words 2Chr 9:6 539
I laughed on them, they *b* it not Job 29:24 539
unless I had *b* to see the Ps 27:13 539
Because they *b* not in God Ps 78:22 539
b not for his wondrous works Ps 78:32 539
Then *b* they his words Ps 106:12 539
land, they *b* not his word Ps 106:24 539
I *b*, therefore have I spoken Ps 116:10 539
for I have *b* thy commandments Ps 119:66 539
Who hath *b* our report Is 53:1 539
the son of Ahikam *b* them not Jer 40:14 539
would not have *b* that the Lam 4:12 539
upon him, because he *b* in his God Dan 6:23 540
So the people of Nineveh *b* God Jonah 3:5 539
and as thou hast *b*, so be it done Mt 8:13 4100
of righteousness, and ye *b* him not Mt 21:32 4100
publicans and the harlots *b* him Mt 21:32 4100
and had been seen of her, *b* not Mk 16:11 569
neither *b* they them Mk 16:13 4100
because they *b* not them which had Mk 16:14 4100
which are most surely *b* among us Lk 1:1 4135
And blessed is she that *b* Lk 1:45 4100
will say, Why then *b* ye him not Lk 20:5 4100
as idle tales, and they *b* them not Lk 24:11 569
And while they yet *b* not for joy Lk 24:41 569
and his disciples *b* on him Jn 2:11 4100
they *b* the scripture, and the word Jn 2:22 4100
many *b* in his name, when they saw Jn 2:23 4100
because he hath not *b* in the name Jn 3:18 4100
b on him for the saying of the Jn 4:39 4100
many more *b* because of his own Jn 4:41 4100
the man *b* the word that Jesus had Jn 4:50 4100
and himself *b*, and his whole house Jn 4:53 4100
b Moses, ye would have *b* me Jn 5:46 4100
who they were that *b* not, and who Jn 6:64 4100
And many of the people *b* on him Jn 7:31 4100
or of the Pharisees *b* on him Jn 7:48 4100
spake these words, many *b* on him Jn 8:30 4100
to those Jews which *b* on him Jn 8:31 4100
them, I told you, and ye *b* not Jn 10:25 4100
And many *b* on him there Jn 10:42 4100
things which Jesus did, *b* on him Jn 11:45 4100
the Jews went away, and *b* on Jesus Jn 12:11 4100
them, yet they *b* not on him Jn 12:37 4100
Lord, who hath *b* our report Jn 12:38 4100
chief rulers also many *b* on him Jn 12:42 4100
have *b* that I came out from God Jn 16:27 4100
they have *b* that thou didst send Jn 17:8 4100
to the sepulchre, and he saw, and *b* Jn 20:8 4100
thou hast seen me, thou hast *b* Jn 20:29 4100
that have not seen, and yet have *b* Jn 20:29 4100
all that *b* were together, and had Acts 2:44 4100
of them which heard the word *b* Acts 4:4 4100
of them that *b* were of one heart Acts 4:32 4100
But when they *b* Philip preaching Acts 8:12 4100
Then Simon himself *b* also Acts 8:13 4100
b not that he was a disciple Acts 9:26 4100
and many *b* in the Lord Acts 9:42 4100
which *b* were astonished, as many Acts 10:45 4103
who *b* on the Lord Jesus Christ Acts 11:17 4100
and a great number *b*, and turned Acts 11:21 4100
when he saw what was done, *b* Acts 13:12 4100
were ordained to eternal life *b* Acts 13:48 4100
the Jews and also of the Greeks *b* Acts 14:1 4100
them to the Lord, on whom they *b* Acts 14:23 4100
the sect of the Pharisees which *b* Acts 15:5 4100
woman, which was a Jewess, and *b* Acts 16:1 4103
And some of them *b*, and consorted Acts 17:4 3982
But the Jews which *b* not, moved Acts 17:5 544
Therefore many of them *b* Acts 17:12 4100
certain men clave unto him, and *b* Acts 17:34 4100
b on the Lord with all his house Acts 18:8 4100
many of the Corinthians hearing *b* Acts 18:8 4100
much which had *b* through grace Acts 18:27 4100
the Holy Ghost since ye *b* Acts 19:2 4100
b not, but spake evil of that way Acts 19:9 544
And many that *b* came, and confessed Acts 19:18 4100
synagogue them that *b* on thee Acts 22:19 4100
the centurion *b* the master Acts 27:11 3982
some *b* the things which were Acts 28:24 3982
which were spoken, and some *b* not Acts 28:24
Abraham *b* God, and it was counted Rom 4:3
nations,) before him whom he *b* Rom 4:17 4100
Who against hope *b* in hope Rom 4:18 4100
on him in whom they have not *b* Rom 10:14 4100
Lord, who hath *b* our report Rom 10:16 4100
ye in times past have not *b* God Rom 11:30 544
Even so have these also now not *b* Rom 11:31 544
salvation nearer than when we *b* Rom 13:11 4100
but ministers by whom ye *b* 1Cor 3:5 4100
you, unless ye have *b* in vain 1Cor 15:2 4100
or they, so we preach, and so ye *b* 1Cor 15:11 4100
according as it is written, I *b* 2Cor 4:13 4100
even we have *b* in Jesus Christ Gal 2:16 4100
Even as Abraham *b* God, and it was Gal 3:6 4100
in whom also after that ye *b* Eph 1:13 4100
among you was *b*) in that day 2Th 1:10 4100
be damned who *b* not the truth 2Th 2:12 4100
b on in the world, received up 1Ti 3:16 4100
for I know whom I have *b*, and am 2Ti 1:12 4100
that they which have *b* in God Titus 3:8 4100
his rest, but to them that *b* not Heb 3:18 544
For we which have *b* do enter into Heb 4:3 4100
perished not with them that *b* not Heb 11:31 544
which saith, Abraham *b* God Jas 2:23 4100
b the love that God hath to us 1Jn 4:16 4100
destroyed them that *b* not Jude 5 4100

BELIEVERS

b were the more added to the Lord Acts 5:14 4100
but be thou an example of the *b* 1Ti 4:12 4103

BELIEVEST

because thou *b* not my words Lk 1:20 4100
thee under the fig tree, *b* thou Jn 1:50 4100
B thou this Jn 11:26 4100
B thou not that I am in the Jn 14:10 4100
If thou *b* with all thine heart Acts 8:37 4100
King Agrippa, *b* thou the prophets Acts 26:27 4100
I know that thou *b* Acts 26:27 4100
Thou *b* that there is one God Jas 2:19 4100

BELIEVETH

He *b* not that he shall return out Job 15:22 539
neither *b* he that it is the sound Job 39:24 539
The simple *b* every word Prov 14:15 539
he that *b* shall not make haste Is 28:16 539
things are possible to him that *b* Mk 9:23 4100
He that *b* and is baptized shall be Mk 16:16 4100
but he that *b* not shall be damned Mk 16:16 569
That whosoever *b* in him should Jn 3:15 4100
that whosoever *b* in him should Jn 3:16 4100
He that *b* on him is not condemned Jn 3:18 4100
but he that *b* not is condemned Jn 3:18 4100
He that *b* on the Son hath Jn 3:36 4100
he that *b* not the Son shall not Jn 3:36 544
b on him that sent me, hath Jn 5:24 4100
he that *b* on me shall never Jn 6:35 4100
b on him, may have everlasting Jn 6:40 4100
He that *b* on me hath everlasting Jn 6:47 4100
He that *b* on me, as the scripture Jn 7:38 4100
he that *b* in me, though he were Jn 11:25 4100
liveth and *b* in me shall never die Jn 11:26 4100
cried and said, He that *b* on me Jn 12:44 4100
b not on me, but on him that sent Jn 12:44 4100
that whosoever *b* on me should not Jn 12:46 4100
I say unto you, He that *b* on me Jn 14:12 4100
b in him shall receive remission Acts 10:43 4100
salvation to every one that *b* Rom 1:16 4100
justifier of him which *b* in Jesus Rom 3:26
but *b* on him that justifieth the Rom 4:5 4100
whosoever *b* on him shall not be Rom 9:33 4100
righteousness to every one that *b* Rom 10:4 4100
heart man *b* unto righteousness Rom 10:10 4100
Whosoever *b* on him shall not be Rom 10:11 4100
For one *b* that he may eat all Rom 14:2 4100
brother hath a wife that *b* not 1Cor 7:12 571
which hath an husband that *b* not 1Cor 7:13 571
b all things, hopeth all things 1Cor 13:7 4100
and there come in one that *b* not 1Cor 14:24 571
hath he that *b* with an infidel 2Cor 6:15 4103
man or woman that *b* have widows 1Ti 5:16 4103
he that *b* on him shall not be 1Pet 2:6 4100
Whosoever *b* that Jesus is the 1Jn 5:1 4100
but he that *b* that Jesus is the 1Jn 5:5 4100
He that *b* on the Son of God hath 1Jn 5:10 4100
he that *b* not God hath made him a 1Jn 5:10 4100
because he *b* not the record that 1Jn 5:10 4100

BELIEVING

ye shall ask in prayer, *b* Mt 21:22 4100
and be not faithless, but *b* Jn 20:27 4103
that *b* ye might have life through Jn 20:31 4100
b in God with all his house Acts 16:34 4100
b all things which are written in Acts 24:14 4100
you with all joy and peace in *b* Rom 15:13 4100
And they that have *b* masters 1Ti 6:2 4103
though now ye see him not, yet *b* 1Pet 1:8 4100

BELL

A golden *b* and a pomegranate Ex 28:34 6472
and a pomegranate, a golden *b* Ex 28:34 6472
A *b* and a pomegranate, a *b* and a Ex 39:26 6472

BELLIES

alway liars, evil beasts, slow *b* Titus 1:12 1064

BELLOW

heifer at grass, and *b* as bulls Jer 50:11 6670

BELLOWS

The *b* are burned, the lead is Jer 6:29 4647

BELLS

b of gold between them round Ex 28:33 6472
they made *b* of pure gold Ex 39:25 6472
and put the *b* between the Ex 39:25 6472
there be upon the *b* of the horses Zec 14:20 4698

BELLY

upon thy *b* shalt thou go, and dust Gen 3:14 1512
Whatsoever goeth upon the *b* Lev 11:42 1512
thigh to rot, and thy *b* to swell Num 5:21 990
bowels, to make thy *b* to swell Num 5:22 990
her *b* shall swell, and her thigh Num 5:27 990
and the woman through her *b* Num 25:8 6897
thigh, and thrust it into his *b* Judg 3:21 990
not draw the dagger out of his *b* Judg 3:22 990
over against the *b* which was by 1Kin 7:20 990
ghost when I came out of the *b* Job 3:11 990
fill his *b* with the east wind Job 15:2 990
and their *b* prepareth deceit Job 15:35 990
God shall cast them out of his *b* Job 20:15 990
shall not feel quietness in his *b* Job 20:20 990
When he is about to fill his *b* Job 20:23 990
my *b* is as wine which hath no Job 32:19 990
force is in the navel of his *b* Job 40:16 990
whose *b* thou fillest with thy hid Ps 17:14 990
art my God from my mother's *b* Ps 22:10 990
with grief, yea, my soul and my *b* Ps 31:9 990
our *b* cleaveth unto the earth Ps 44:25 990
but the *b* of the wicked shall Prov 13:25 990
into the innermost parts of the *b* Prov 18:8 990
A man's *b* shall be satisfied with Prov 18:20 990
all the inward parts of the *b* Prov 20:27 990
stripes the inward parts of the *b* Prov 20:30 990
into the innermost parts of the *b* Prov 26:22 990
his *b* is as bright ivory overlaid Song 5:14 4578
thy *b* is like an heap of wheat Song 7:2 990
which are borne by me from the *b* Is 46:3 990
formed thee in the *b* I knew thee Jer 1:5 990
filled his *b* with my delicates Jer 51:34 3770
Son of man, cause thy *b* to eat Eze 3:3 990
and his arms of silver, his *b* Dan 2:32 4577
Jonah was in the *b* of the fish Jonah 1:17 4578
LORD his God out of the fish's *b* Jonah 2:1 4578
out of the *b* of hell cried I, and Jonah 2:2 990
When I heard, my *b* trembled Hab 3:16 990
and three nights in the whale's *b* Mt 12:40 2836
in at the mouth goeth into the *b* Mt 15:17 2836
into his heart, but into the *b* Mk 7:19 2836
b with the husks that the swine Lk 15:16 2836
out of his *b* shall flow rivers of Jn 7:38 2836
Jesus Christ, but their own *b* Rom 16:18 2836
Meats for the *b*, and the *b* for 1Cor 6:13 2836
destruction, whose God is their *b* Phil 3:19 2836
and it shall make thy *b* bitter Rev 10:9 2836
I had eaten it, my *b* was bitter Rev 10:10 2836

BELONG

Do not interpretations *b* to God Gen 40:8
the possession of the land did *b* Lev 27:24
and over all things that *b* to it Num 1:50
The secret things *b* unto the LORD Deut 29:29
which are revealed *b* unto us Deut 29:29
shields of the earth *b* unto God Ps 47:9
unto GOD the Lord *b* the issues Ps 68:20
These things also *b* to the wise Prov 24:23
To the Lord our God *b* mercies Dan 9:9
my name, because ye *b* to Christ Mk 9:41 1510
the things which *b* unto thy peace Lk 19:42
for the things that *b* to the Lord 1Cor 7:32

BELONGED

on the border of Manasseh *b* to Josh 17:8
of the herdmen that *b* to Saul 1Sa 21:7
the mighty men which *b* to David 1Kin 1:8
which *b* to the Philistines 1Kin 15:27
which *b* to the Philistines 1Kin 16:15
which *b* to Judah, for Israel, are 2Kin 14:28
All these *b* to the sons of Machir 1Chr 2:23
which *b* to Judah, to bring up 1Chr 13:6
the burial which *b* to the kings 2Chr 26:23
house which *b* to king Ahasuerus Est 1:9
with such things as *b* to her Est 2:9 4490
he *b* unto Herod's jurisdiction Lk 23:7 1510

BELONGEST

said unto him, To whom *b* thou 1Sa 30:13

BELONGETH

This is it that *b* unto the Num 8:24
To me *b* vengeance, and recompence Deut 32:35
by Gibeah, which *b* to Benjamin Judg 19:14
into Gibeah that *b* to Benjamin Judg 20:4
which *b* to Judah, and pitched 1Sa 17:1
upon the coast which *b* to Judah 1Sa 30:14
which *b* to Zidon, and dwell there 1Kin 17:9
which *b* to Judah, and left his 1Kin 19:3
at Beth-shemesh, which *b* to Judah 2Kin 14:11
at Beth-shemesh, which *b* to Judah 2Chr 25:21
for this matter *b* unto thee Ezr 10:4
Salvation *b* unto the LORD Ps 3:8
that power *b* unto God Ps 62:11
Also unto thee, O Lord, *b* mercy Ps 62:12
O LORD God, to whom vengeance *b* Ps 94:1
O God, to whom vengeance *b* Ps 94:1
O Lord, righteousness *b* unto thee Dan 9:7
to us *b* confusion of face, to our Dan 9:8
But strong meat *b* to them that Heb 5:14 1510
hath said, Vengeance *b* unto me Heb 10:30

BELONGING
the service of the sanctuary b Num 7:9
a part of the field b unto Boaz Ruth 2:3
Philistines b to the five lords 1Sa 6:18
meddleth with strife b not to him Prov 26:17
b to the city called Bethsaida Lk 9:10

BELOVED
If a man have two wives, one b Deut 21:15 157
born him children, both the b Deut 21:15 157
he may not make the son of the b Deut 21:16 157
The b of the LORD shall dwell in Deut 33:12 3039
who was b of his God, and God made Neh 13:26 157
That thy b may be delivered Ps 60:5 3039
That thy b may be delivered Ps 108:6 3039
for so he giveth his b sleep Ps 127:2 3039
only b in the sight of my mother Prov 4:3
My b is unto me as a cluster of Song 1:14 1730
Behold, thou art fair, my b Song 1:16 157
so is my b among the sons Song 2:3 1730
The voice of my b Song 2:8 1730
My b is like a roe or a young Song 2:9 1730
My b spake, and said unto me, Rise Song 2:10 1730
My b is mine, and I am his Song 2:16 1730
the shadows flee away, turn, my b Song 2:17 1730
Let my b come into his garden, and Song 4:16 1730
drink, yea, drink abundantly, O b Song 5:1 1730
the voice of my b that knocketh Song 5:2 1730
My b put in his hand by the hole Song 5:4 1730
I rose up to open to my b Song 5:5 1730
I opened to my b Song 5:6 1730
but my b had withdrawn himself Song 5:6 1730
of Jerusalem, if ye find my b Song 5:8 1730
thy b more than another b Song 5:9 1730
thy b more than another b Song 5:9 1730
My b is white and ruddy, the Song 5:10 1730
This is my b, and this is my Song 5:16 1730
Whither is thy b gone, O thou Song 6:1 1730
whither is thy b turned aside Song 6:1 1730
My b is gone down into his garden Song 6:2 1730
am my beloved's, and my b is mine Song 6:3 1730
mouth like the best wine for my b Song 7:9 1730
Come, my b, let us go forth into Song 7:11 1730
I have laid up for thee, O my b Song 7:13 1730
wilderness, leaning upon her b Song 8:5 1730
Make haste, my b, and be thou like Song 8:14 1730
of my b touching his vineyard Is 5:1 1730
What hath my b to do in mine Jer 11:15 3039
I have given the dearly b of my Jer 12:7 3033
for thou art greatly b Dan 9:23 2530
me, O Daniel, a man greatly b Dan 10:11 2530
And said, O man greatly b, fear Dan 10:19 2530
love a woman b of her friend, yet Hos 3:1 157
even the b fruit of their womb Hos 9:16 4261
heaven, saying, This is my b Son Mt 3:17 27
my b, in whom my soul is well Mt 12:18 27
which said, This is my b Son Mt 17:5 27
heaven, saying, Thou art my b Son Mk 1:11 27
cloud, saying, This is my b Son Mk 9:7 27
which said, Thou art my b Son Lk 3:22 27
cloud, saying, This is my b Son Lk 9:35 27
I will send my b son Lk 20:13 27
men unto you with our b Barnabas Acts 15:25 27
b of God, called to be saints Rom 1:7 27
and her b, which was not b Rom 9:25 27
they are b for the fathers' sakes Rom 11:28 27
Dearly b, avenge not yourselves Rom 12:19 27
Greet Amplias my b in the Lord Rom 16:8 27
helper in Christ, and Stachys my b Rom 16:9 27
Salute the b Persis, which Rom 16:12 27
but as my b sons I warn you 1Cor 4:14 27
you Timotheus, who is my b son 1Cor 4:17 27
Wherefore, my dearly b, flee from 1Cor 10:14 27
my b brethren, be ye stedfast, 1Cor 15:58 27
therefore these promises dearly b 2Cor 7:1 27
but we do all things, dearly b 2Cor 12:19 27
he hath made us accepted in the b Eph 1:6 25
a b brother and faithful minister Eph 6:21 27
Wherefore, my b, as ye have Phil 2:12 27
Therefore, my brethren dearly b Phil 4:1 27
fast in the Lord, my dearly b Phil 4:1 27
as the elect of God, holy and b Col 3:12 25
unto you, who is a b brother Col 4:7 27
b brother, who is one of you Col 4:9 27
the b physician, and Demas, greet Col 4:14 27
Knowing, brethren b, your 1Th 1:4 25
brethren b of the Lord, because 2Th 2:13 25
because they are faithful and b 1Ti 6:2 27
To Timothy, my dearly b son 2Ti 1:2 27
unto Philemon our dearly b Philem 1 27
And to our b Apphia, and Archippus Philem 2 27
but above a servant, a brother b Philem 16 27
But, b, we are persuaded better Heb 6:9 27
Do not err, my b brethren Jas 1:16 27
my b brethren, let every man be Jas 1:19 27
my b brethren, Hath not God Jas 2:5 27
Dearly b, I beseech you as 1Pet 2:11 27
B, think it not strange 1Pet 4:12 27
excellent glory, This is my b Son 2Pet 1:17 27
This second epistle, b, I now 2Pet 3:1 27
But, b, be not ignorant of this 2Pet 3:8 27
Wherefore, b, seeing that ye look 2Pet 3:14 27
even as our b brother Paul also 2Pet 3:15 27
Ye therefore, b, seeing ye know 2Pet 3:17 27
B, now are we the sons of God, and 1Jn 3:2 27
B, if our heart condemn us not, 1Jn 3:21 27
B, believe not every spirit, but 1Jn 4:1 27
B, let us love one another 1Jn 4:7 27
B, if God so loved us, we ought 1Jn 4:11 27
B, I wish above all things that 3Jn 2 27
B, thou doest faithfully 3Jn 5 27
B, follow not that which is evil, 3Jn 11 27
B, when I gave all diligence to Jude 3 27
But, b, remember ye the words Jude 17 27
But ye, b, building up yourselves Jude 20 27
the saints about, and the b city Rev 20:9 25

BELOVED'S
I am my b, and my beloved is mine Song 6:3 1730
I am my b, and his desire is Song 7:10 1730

BELSHAZZAR (*bel-shaz'-ar*) *A Babylonian king.*
B the king made a great feast to Dan 5:1 1113
B, whiles he tasted the wine, Dan 5:2 1113
Then was king B greatly troubled, Dan 5:9 1113
And thou his son, O B, hast not Dan 5:22 1113
Then commanded B, and they clothed. Dan 5:29 1113
In that night was B the king of Dan 5:30 1113
In the first year of B king of Dan 7:1 1113
king B a vision appeared unto me Dan 8:1 1113

BELTESHAZZAR (*bel-te-shaz'-ar*) See DANIEL. *The Babylonian name given to Daniel.*
he gave unto Daniel the name of B Dan 1:7 1095
said to Daniel, whose name was B Dan 2:26 1096
in before me, whose name was B Dan 4:8 1096
O B, master of the magicians, Dan 4:9 1096
Now thou, O B, declare the Dan 4:18 1096
Then Daniel, whose name was B Dan 4:19 1096
The king spake, and said, B Dan 4:19 1096
B answered and said, My lord, the Dan 4:19 1096
Daniel, whom the king named B Dan 5:12 1096
Daniel, whose name was called B Dan 10:1 1095

BEMOAN
or who shall b thee Jer 15:5 5110
neither go to lament nor b them Jer 16:5 5110
not for the dead, neither b him Jer 22:10 5110
All ye that are about him, b him Jer 48:17 5110
who will b her Nah 3:7 5110

BEMOANED
and they b him, and comforted him Job 42:11 5110

BEMOANING
heard Ephraim b himself thus Jer 31:18 5110

BEN (*ben*) *A Levite.*
the second degree, Zechariah, B 1Chr 15:18 1122

BENAIAH (*ben-ay'-ah*)
1. An officer of David.
B the son of Jehoiada was over 2Sa 8:18 1141
B the son of Jehoiada was over 2Sa 20:23 1141
B the son of Jehoiada, the son of 2Sa 23:20 1141
These things did B the son of 2Sa 23:22 1141
B the son of Jehoiada, and Nathan 1Kin 1:8 1141
But Nathan the prophet, and B 1Kin 1:10 1141
B the son of Jehoiada, and thy 1Kin 1:26 1141
prophet, and B the son of Jehoiada 1Kin 1:32 1141
B the son of Jehoiada answered 1Kin 1:36 1141
B the son of Jehoiada, and the 1Kin 1:38 1141
B the son of Jehoiada, and the 1Kin 1:44 1141
the hand of B the son of Jehoiada 1Kin 2:25 1141
Then Solomon sent B the son of 1Kin 2:29 1141
B came to the tabernacle of the 1Kin 2:30 1141
B brought the king word again, 1Kin 2:30 1141
So B the son of Jehoiada went up, 1Kin 2:34 1141
the king put B the son of 1Kin 2:35 1141
commanded B the son of Jehoiada 1Kin 2:46 1141
B the son of Jehoiada was over 1Kin 4:4 1141
B the son of Jehoiada, the son of 1Chr 11:22 1141
These things did B the son of 1Chr 11:24 1141
B the son of Jehoiada was over 1Chr 18:17 1141
month was B the son of Jehoiada 1Chr 27:5 1141
This is that B, who was mighty 1Chr 27:6 1141
2. A "mighty man" of David.
B the Pirathonite, Hiddai of the 2Sa 23:30 1141
of Benjamin, B the Pirathonite, 1Chr 11:31 1141
month was B the Pirathonite 1Chr 27:14 1141
3. A Simeonite family chief.
and Adiel, and Jesimiel, and B 1Chr 4:36 1141
4. A priest of David.
and Jehiel, and Unni, Eliab, and B 1Chr 15:18 1141
Unni, and Eliab, and Maaseiah, and B 1Chr 15:20 1141
and Amasai, and Zechariah, and B 1Chr 15:24 1141
and Mattithiah, and Eliab, and B 1Chr 16:5 1141
B also and Jahaziel the priests 1Chr 16:6 1141
5. Father of Jehoiada.
was Jehoiada the son of B 1Chr 27:34 1141
6. Grandfather of Jehaziel.
son of Zechariah, the son of B 2Chr 20:14 1141
7. A Levite during Hezekiah's reign.
and Ismachiah, and Mahath, and B 2Chr 31:13 1141
8. A descendant of Parosh.
and Eleazar, and Malchijah, and B Ezr 10:25 1141
9. A son of Pahath-moab.
Adna, and Chelal, B, Maaseiah, Ezr 10:30 1141
10. A son of Bani.
B, Bedeiah, Chelluh, Ezr 10:35 1141
11. A son of Nebo.
Zabad, Zebina, Jadau, and Joel, B Ezr 10:43 1141
12. Father of Pelatiah.
of Azur, and Pelatiah the son of B Eze 11:1 1141
that Pelatiah the son of B died Eze 11:13 1141

BEN-AMMI (*ben-am'-mi*) *A son of Lot.*
bare a son, and called his name B Gen 19:38 1151

BENCHES
have made thy b of ivory, brought Eze 27:6 7175

BEND
For, lo, the wicked b their bow Ps 11:2 1869
b their bows to shoot their Ps 64:3 1869
they b their tongues like their Jer 9:3 1869
Lydians, that handle and b the bow Jer 46:9 1869
all ye that b the bow, shoot at Jer 50:14 1869
all ye that b the bow, camp Jer 50:29 1869
bendeth let the archer b his bow Jer 51:3 1869
this vine did b her roots toward Eze 17:7 3719

BEN DEKER See DEKAR.

BENDETH
when he b his bow to shoot his Ps 58:7 1869
Against him that b let the archer Jer 51:3 1869

BENDING
thee shall come b unto thee Is 60:14 7817

BENEATH
she was buried b Beth-el under an Gen 35:8 8478
above, or that is in the earth b Ex 20:4 8478
they shall be coupled together b Ex 26:24 4295
under the compass of the altar b Ex 27:5 4295
b upon the hem of it thou shalt Ex 28:33
hands, and brake them b the mount Ex 32:19 8478
And they were coupled b, and Ex 36:29 4295
thereof b unto the midst of it Ex 38:4 4295
that is in the waters b the earth Deut 4:18 8478
heaven above, and upon the earth b Deut 4:39 8478
above, or that is in the earth b Deut 5:8 8478
that is in the waters b the earth Deut 5:8 8478
only, and thou shalt not be b Deut 28:13 4295
and for the deep that coucheth b Deut 33:13 8478
in heaven above, and in earth b Josh 2:11 8478
of Midian was b him in the valley Judg 7:8 8478
which is by Zartanah b Jezreel 1Kin 4:12 8478
b the lions and oxen were certain 1Kin 7:29 8478
in heaven above, or on earth b 1Kin 8:23 8478
His roots shall be dried up b Job 18:16 8478
that he may depart from hell b Prov 15:24 4295
Hell from b is moved for thee to Is 14:9 8478
heavens, and look upon the earth b Is 51:6 8478
of the earth searched out b Jer 31:37 4295
from above, and his roots from b Amos 2:9 8478
as Peter was b in the palace, Mk 14:66 2736
he said unto them, Ye are from b Jn 8:23 2736
above, and signs in the earth b Acts 2:19 2736

BENE BARAK See BENE-BERAK.

BENE-BERAK (*be'-ne-be'-rak*) *A city in Dan.*
And Jehud, and B, and Gath-rimmon, Josh 19:45 1138

BENEFACTORS
authority upon them are called b Lk 22:25 2110

BENEFIT
according to the b done unto him 2Chr 32:25 1576
wherewith I said I would b them Jer 18:10 3190
that ye might have a second b 2Cor 1:15 5485
and beloved, partakers of the b 1Ti 6:2 2108
that thy b should not be as it Philem 14 18

BENEFITS
Lord, who daily loadeth us with b Ps 68:19
my soul, and forget not all his b Ps 103:2 1576
the LORD for all his b toward me Ps 116:12 8408

BENE JAAKAN See BENE.

BENE-JAAKAN (*be'-ne-ja'-a-kan*) *Namesake of several wells.*
from Moseroth, and pitched in B Num 33:31 1142
And they removed from B, and Num 33:32 1142

BENEVOLENCE
render unto the wife due b 1Cor 7:3 2133

BEN-HADAD (*ben'ha-dad*)
1. A Syrian king, son of Tabrimon.
and king Asa sent them to B 1Kin 15:18 1131
So B hearkened unto king Asa, and 1Kin 15:20 1131
sent to B king of Syria, that 2Chr 16:2 1130
B hearkened unto king Asa, and 2Chr 16:4 1130
2. A Syrian king during Ahab's reign.
B the king of Syria gathered all 1Kin 20:1 1131
and said unto him, Thus saith B 1Kin 20:2 1131
again, and said, Thus speaketh B 1Kin 20:5 1131
he said unto the messengers of B 1Kin 20:9 1131
B sent unto him, and said, The 1Kin 20:10 1131
when B heard this message, as he 1Kin 20:12
But B was drinking himself drunk 1Kin 20:16 1130
B sent out, and they told him, 1Kin 20:17 1130
B the king of Syria escaped on an 1Kin 20:20 1130
that B numbered the Syrians, and 1Kin 20:26 1130
B fled, and came into the city, 1Kin 20:30 1130
and said, Thy servant B saith 1Kin 20:32 1130
and they said, Thy brother B 1Kin 20:33 1130
Then B came forth to him 1Kin 20:33 1130
B said unto him, The cities, 1Kin 20:34
that B king of Syria gathered all 2Kin 6:24 1130
B the king of Syria was sick 2Kin 8:7 1130
Thy son B king of Syria hath sent 2Kin 8:9 1130
3. A Syrian king, son of Hazael.
into the hand of B the son of 2Kin 13:3 1130
B his son reigned in his stead 2Kin 13:24 1130
of B the son of Hazael the cities 2Kin 13:25 1130
shall devour the palaces of B Amos 1:4 1130
4. A title for all the Syrian kings.
it shall consume the palaces of B Jer 49:27 1130

BEN-HAIL (*ben-ha'-il*) *A prince of Judah.*
he sent to his princes, even to B 2Chr 17:7 1134

BEN-HANAN (*ben-ha'-nan*) *A son of Shimon.*
Shimon were, Amnon, and Rinnah, B 1Chr 4:20 1135

BENINU (*ben'-i-nu*) *A Levite who renewed the covenant.*
Hodijah, Bani, B Neh 10:13 1148

BENJAMIN (*ben'-ja-min*) See BENJAMIN'S, BENJAMITE.
1. Youngest son of Jacob.
but his father called him B Gen 35:18 1144
Joseph, and B Gen 35:24 1144
But B, Joseph's brother, Jacob Gen 42:4 1144
is not, and ye will take B away Gen 42:36 1144
away your other brother, and B Gen 43:14 1144
double money in their hand, and B Gen 43:15 1144
And when Joseph saw B with them Gen 43:16 1144

up his eyes, and saw his brother *B*........ Gen 43:29 1144
see, and the eyes of my brother *B*......... Gen 45:12 1144
and *B* wept upon his neck..................... Gen 45:14 1144
but to *B* he gave three hundred.............. Gen 45:22 1144
Joseph, and *B* .... Gen 46:19 1144
And the sons of *B* were Belah .... Gen 46:21 1144
Issachar, Zebulun, and *B*,..................... Ex 1:3 1144
Dan, Joseph, and *B*, Naphtali, Gad,....... 1Chr 2:2 1144
The sons of *B*... 1Chr 7:6 1144
Now *B* begat Bela his firstborn,............ 1Chr 8:1 1144
2. One of the twelve tribes comprising Israel.
B shall ravin as a wolf:........................... Gen 49:27 1144
Of *B*.. Num 1:11 1144
Of the children of *B*, by their .... Num 1:36 1144
of them, even of the tribe of *B*.............. Num 1:37 1144
Then the tribe of *B*................................. Num 2:22 1144
of *B* shall be Abidan the son of............. Num 2:22 1144
prince of the children of *B* .... Num 7:60 1144
B was Abidan the son of Gideoni .... Num 10:24 1144
Of the tribe of *B*, Palti the son .... Num 13:9 1144
The sons of *B* after their....................... Num 26:38 1144
sons of *B* after their families................ Num 26:41 1144
Of the tribe of *B*, Elidad the son .... Num 34:21 1144
and Issachar, and Joseph, and *B*............ Deut 27:12 1144
of *B* he said, The beloved of the .... Deut 33:12 1144
of *B* came up according to their .... Josh 18:11 1144
inheritance of the children of *B*............ Josh 18:20 1144
of *B* according to their families............ Josh 18:21 1144
of *B* according to their families............ Josh 18:28 1144
Simeon, and out of the tribe of *B*.......... Josh 21:4 1144
And out of the tribe of *B*, Gibeon.......... Josh 21:17 1144
the children of *B* did not drive .... Judg 1:21 1144
of *B* in Jerusalem unto this day .... Judg 1:21 1144
after thee, *B*, among thy people............ Judg 5:14 1144
also against Judah, and against *B* .... Judg 10:9 1144
by Gibeah, which belongeth to *B*........... Judg 19:14 1144
(Now the children of *B* heard that......... Judg 20:3 1144
into Gibeah that belongeth to *B*........... Judg 20:4 1144
do, when they come to Gibeah of *B*........ Judg 20:10 1144
men through all the tribe of *B* .... Judg 20:12 1144
But the children of *B* would not............ Judg 20:13 1144
But the children of *B* gathered.............. Judg 20:14 1144
the children of *B* were numbered........... Judg 20:15 1144
And the men of Israel, beside *B*............. Judg 20:17 1144
battle against the children of *B*............ Judg 20:18 1144
went out to battle against *B* .... Judg 20:20 1144
the children of *B* came forth out .... Judg 20:21 1144
the children of *B* my brother................. Judg 20:23 1144
the children of *B* the second day........... Judg 20:24 1144
B went forth against them out of........... Judg 20:25 1144
the children of *B* my brother................. Judg 20:28 1144
children of *B* on the third day............... Judg 20:30 1144
the children of *B* went out..................... Judg 20:31 1144
And the children of *B* said .... Judg 20:32 1144
And the LORD smote *B* before Israel..... Judg 20:35 1144
So the children of *B* saw that............... Judg 20:36 1144
B began to smite and kill of the .... Judg 20:39 1144
again, the men of *B* were amazed.......... Judg 20:41 1144
there fell of *B* eighteen thousand .... Judg 20:44 1144
fell that day of *B* were twenty .... Judg 20:46 1144
again upon the children of *B*................. Judg 20:48 1144
give his daughter unto *B* to wife........... Judg 21:1 1144
repented them for *B* their brother......... Judg 21:6 1144
to speak to the children of *B*................ Judg 21:13 1144
B came again at that time..................... Judg 21:14 1144
And the people repented them for *B* ..... Judg 21:15 1144
the women are destroyed out of *B*........ Judg 21:16 1144
for them that be escaped of *B*............... Judg 21:17 1144
be he that giveth a wife to *B*................ Judg 21:18 1144
they commanded the children of *B*........ Judg 21:20 1144
of Shiloh, and go to the land of *B* .... Judg 21:21 1144
And the children of *B* did so................. Judg 21:23 1144
ran a man of *B* out of the army.............. 1Sa 4:12 1144
Now there was a man of *B*, whose.......... 1Sa 9:1 1144
thee a man out of the land of *B*............ 1Sa 9:16 1144
the families of the tribe of *B*............... 1Sa 9:21 1144
in the border of *B* at Zelzah 1Sa 10:2 1144
near, the tribe of *B* was taken............... 1Sa 10:20 1144
B to come near by their families............ 1Sa 10:21 1144
were with Jonathan in Gibeah of *B* 1Sa 13:2 1144
up from Gilgal unto Gibeah of *B* 1Sa 13:15 1144
with them, abode in Gibeah of *B*........... 1Sa 13:16 1144
of Saul in Gibeah of *B* looked 1Sa 14:16 1144
and over Ephraim, and over *B* 2Sa 2:9 1144
went over by number twelve of *B*........... 2Sa 2:15 1144
the children of *B* gathered.................... 2Sa 2:25 1144
of David had smitten of *B* 2Sa 2:31 1144
Abner also spake in the ears of *B*.......... 2Sa 3:19 1144
good to the whole house of *B* 2Sa 3:19 1144
Beerothite, of the children of *B*............ 2Sa 4:2 1144
Beeroth also was reckoned to *B* 2Sa 4:2 1144
were a thousand men of *B* with him 2Sa 19:17 1144
they in the country of *B* in Zelah.......... 2Sa 21:14 1144
of Gibeah of the children of *B*.............. 2Sa 23:29 1144
Shimei the son of Elah, in *B* 1Kin 4:18 1144
of Judah, with the tribe of *B* 1Kin 12:21 1144
unto all the house of Judah and *B* 1Kin 12:23 1144
Asa built with them Geba of *B* 1Kin 15:22 1144
And out of the tribe of *B*...................... 1Chr 6:60 1144
of the tribe of the children of *B*........... 1Chr 6:65 1144
All these are of the sons of *B* 1Chr 8:40 1144
of Judah, and of the children of *B*........ 1Chr 9:3 1144
And of the sons of *B*............................. 1Chr 9:7 1144
pertained to the children of *B* 1Chr 11:31 1144
bow, even of Saul's brethren of *B* 1Chr 12:2 1144
there came of the children of *B* 1Chr 12:16 1144
And of the children of *B*, the................ 1Chr 12:29 1144
B counted he not among them.............. 1Chr 21:6 1144
of *B*, Jaasiel the son of Abner................ 1Chr 27:21 1144
B an hundred and fourscore 2Chr 11:1 1144
and to all Israel in Judah and *B*............ 2Chr 11:3 1144
in Judah and in *B* fenced cities............. 2Chr 11:10 1144
having Judah and *B* on his side 2Chr 11:12 1144
all the countries of Judah and *B*........... 2Chr 11:23 1144
and out of *B*, that bare shields and....... 2Chr 14:8 1144
ye me, Asa, and all Judah and *B*........... 2Chr 15:2 1144
out of all the land of Judah and *B* 2Chr 15:8 1144
And he gathered all Judah and *B*.......... 2Chr 15:9 1144
And of *B* 2Chr 17:17 1144
throughout all Judah and *B*.................. 2Chr 25:5 1144
the altars out of all Judah and *B*.......... 2Chr 31:1 1144
of Israel, and of all Judah and *B*.......... 2Chr 34:9 1144
in Jerusalem and *B* to stand to it 2Chr 34:32 1144
of the fathers of Judah and *B*............... Ezr 1:5 1144
B heard that the children of the........... Ezr 4:1 1144
B gathered themselves together............ Ezr 10:9 1144
of Judah, and of the children of *B*......... Neh 11:4 1144
And these are the sons of *B*................. Neh 11:7 1144
The children also of *B* from Geba .... Neh 11:31 1144
were divisions in Judah, and in *B*.......... Neh 11:36 1144
There is little *B* with their.................... Ps 68:27 1144
Before Ephraim and *B* and Manasseh... Ps 80:2 1144
were in Anathoth in the land of *B* .... Jer 1:1 1144
O ye children of *B*, gather..................... Jer 6:1 1144
Jerusalem, and from the land of *B*........ Jer 17:26 1144
which is in the country of *B*................. Jer 32:8 1144
take witnesses in the land of *B*............. Jer 32:44 1144
of the south, and in the land of *B* .... Jer 33:13 1144
to go into the land of *B*, to .... Jer 37:12 1144
of Judah and the border of *B*............... Eze 48:22 1144
west side, *B* shall have a portion .... Eze 48:23 1144
And by the border of *B*, from the.......... Eze 48:24 1144
one gate of Joseph, one gate of *B* .... Eze 48:32 1144
at Beth-aven, after thee, O *B*............... Hos 5:8 1144
and *B* shall possess Gilead..................... Obad 19 1144
of Cis, a man of the tribe of *B*.............. Acts 13:21 *953*
of Abraham, of the tribe of *B* .... Rom 11:1 *953*
of Israel, of the tribe of *B*..................... Phil 3:5 *953*
Of the tribe of *B* were sealed................. Rev 7:8 *953*
3. Great-grandson of Benjamin 1.
Jeush, and *B*, and Ehud, and 1Chr 7:10 1144
4. A descendant of Harim.
B, Malluch, and Shemariah..................... Ezr 10:32 1144
5. A repairer of the Jerusalem wall.
After him repaired *B* and Hashub.......... Neh 3:23 1144
6. Purified the Jerusalem wall.
Judah, and *B*, and Shemaiah, and .... Neh 12:34 1144
7. A gate of Jerusalem.
that were in the high gate of *B*............. Jer 20:2 1144
And when he was in the gate of *B*........ Jer 37:13 1144
then sitting in the gate of *B*................. Jer 38:7 1144

BENJAMIN'S (*ben'-ja-mins*)
1. Refers to Benjamin 1.
but *B* mess was five times so much ...... Gen 43:34 1144
and the cup was found in *B* sack .... Gen 44:12 1144
he fell upon his brother *B* neck .... Gen 45:14 1144
2. Refers to Benjamin 7.
from *B* gate unto the place of the......... Zec 14:10 1144

BENJAMITE (*ben'-ja-mite*) See BENJAMITES. *A descendant of Benjamin.*
Ehud the son of Gera, a *B*..................... Judg 3:15 1145
Bechorath, the son of Aphiah, a *B* 1Sa 9:1 1145
answered and said, Am not I a *B* 1Sa 9:21 1145
much more now may this *B* do it............ 2Sa 16:11 1145
And Shimei the son of Gera, a *B*........... 2Sa 19:16 1145
was Sheba, the son of Bichri, a *B*......... 2Sa 20:1 1145
a *B* of Bahurim, which cursed me.......... 1Kin 2:8 1145
of Shimei, the son of Kish, a *B*............ Est 2:5 1145
the words of Cush the *B*........................ Ps 7:*t* 1145

BENJAMITES (*ben'-ja-mites*)
but the men of the place were *B* .... Judg 19:16 1145
of the *B* that day twenty and five .... Judg 20:35 1145
men of Israel gave place to the *B*......... Judg 20:36 1145
the *B* looked behind them, and,............ Judg 20:40 1145
they inclosed the *B* round about........... Judg 20:43 1145
passed through the land of the *B* 1Sa 9:4 1145
stood about him, Hear now, ye *B*.......... 1Sa 22:7 1145
Abiezer the Anetothite, of the *B*........... 1Chr 27:12 1145

BENO (*be'-no*) *A descendant of Merari.*
sons of Jaaziah; *B*.................................. 1Chr 24:26 1121
B, and Shoham, and Zaccur, and Ibri... 1Chr 24:27 1121

BEN-ONI (*ben-o'-ni*) *Rachel's second son.*
died) that she called his name *B*.......... Gen 35:18 1126

BENT
he hath *b* his bow, and made it .... Ps 7:12 1869
have *b* their bow, to cast down .... Ps 37:14 1869
are sharp, and all their bows *b*.............. Is 5:28 1869
drawn sword, and from the *b* bow......... Is 21:15 1869
He hath *b* his bow like an enemy.......... Lam 2:4 1869
He hath *b* his bow, and set me as a...... Lam 3:12 1869
my people are *b* to backsliding .... Hos 11:7 8511
When I have *b* Judah for me,................ Zec 9:13 1869

BEN-ZOHETH (*ben-zo'-heth*) *A descendant of Caleb.*
sons of Ishi were, Zoheth, and *B*.......... 1Chr 4:20 1132

BEON (*be'-on*) *A place east of the Jordan River.*
Elealeh, and Shebam, and Nebo, and *B* Num 32:3 1194

BEOR (*be'-or*)
1. Father of Bela.
Bela the son of *B* reigned in Edom........ Gen 36:32 1160
Bela the son of *B* 1Chr 1:43 1160
2. Father of Balaam.
Balaam the son of *B* to Pethor............... Num 22:5 1160
Balaam the son of *B* hath said .... Num 24:3 1160
Balaam the son of *B* hath said .... Num 24:15 1160
Balaam also the son of *B* they............... Num 31:8 1160
son of *B* of Pethor of Mesopotamia .... Deut 23:4 1160
Balaam also the son of *B*, the................ Josh 13:22 1160
Balaam the son of *B* to curse you .... Josh 24:9 1160
what Balaam the son of *B* answered .... Mic 6:5 1160

BERA (*be'-rah*) *King of Sodom.*
made war with *B* king of Sodom............ Gen 14:2 1298

BERACAH See BERACHAH.

BERACHAH (*ber'-a-kah*)
1. A Benjamite warrior in David's army.
and *B*, and Jehu the Antothite,.............. 1Chr 12:3 1294
2. A valley in Judah.
themselves in the valley of *B*................. 2Chr 20:26 1294
place was called, The valley of *B*.......... 2Chr 20:26 1294

BERACHIAH (*ber-a-ki'-ah*) See BERECHIAH. *Father of Asaph.*
hand, even Asaph the son of *B* 1Chr 6:39 1296

BERAIAH (*ber-a-i'-ah*) *A son of Shimhi.*
And Adaiah, and *B*, and Shimrath, the 1Chr 8:21 1256

BERAKIAH See BERACHIAH.

BEREA (*be-re'-a*) *A city in Macedonia.*
Paul and Silas by night unto *B* .... Acts 17:10 *960*
of God was preached of Paul at *B*......... Acts 17:13 *960*
him into Asia Sopater of *B*.................... Acts 20:4 *960*

BEREAVE
do I labour, and *b* my soul of good........ Eccl 4:8 2637
I will *b* them of children, I will............. Jer 15:7 7921
evil beasts, and they shall *b* thee.......... Eze 5:17 7921
no more henceforth *b* them of men....... Eze 36:12 7921
neither *b* thy nations any more,............ Eze 36:14
their children, yet will I *b* them............ Hos 9:12 7921

BEREAVED
Me have ye *b* of my children.................. Gen 42:36 7921
b of my children, I am *b*........................ Gen 43:14 7921
wives be *b* of their children .... Jer 18:21 7909
up men, and hast *b* thy nations............ Eze 36:13 7921
as a bear that is *b* of her whelps .... Hos 13:8 7909

BEREAVETH
abroad the sword *b*, at home there....... Lam 1:20 7921

BERECHIAH (*ber-e-ki'-ah*) See BERACHIAH.
1. A descendant of King Jehoiakim.
And Hashubah, and Ohel, and *B*........... 1Chr 3:20 1296
2. Same as Berachiah.
his brethren, Asaph the son of *B*.......... 1Chr 15:17 1296
3. A Levite near Jerusalem.
B the son of Asa, the son of 1Chr 9:16 1296
4. A Levite doorkeeper.
And *B* and Elkanah were doorkeepers. 1Chr 15:23 1296
5. An Ephraimite.
B the son of Meshillemoth, and 2Chr 28:12 1296
6. Father of Meshullam.
repaired Meshullam the son of *B*.......... Neh 3:4 1296
son of *B* over against his chamber........ Neh 3:30 1296
of Meshullam the son of *B*.................... Neh 6:18 1296
7. Father of Zechariah.
LORD unto Zechariah, the son of *B*........ Zec 1:1 1296
LORD unto Zechariah, the son of *B*........ Zec 1:7 1296

BERED (*be'-red*)
1. A place in southern Canaan.
behold, it is between Kadesh and *B*...... Gen 16:14 1260
2. An Ephraimite.
B his son, and Tahath his son, and 1Chr 7:20 1260

BEREKIAH See BERECHIAH.

BERI (*be'-ri*) See BERITES. *Son of Zophah.*
and Harnepher, and Shual, and *B*......... 1Chr 7:36 1275

BERIAH (*be-ri'-ah*) See BERIITES.
1. A son of Asher.
Jimnah, and Ishuah, and Isui, and *B* .... Gen 46:17 1283
and the sons of *B*.................................... Gen 46:17 1283
of *B*, the family of the Beriites .... Num 26:44 1283
Of the sons of *B* .... Num 26:45 1283
Imnah, and Isuah, and Ishuai, and *B* ... 1Chr 7:30 1283
And the sons of *B*.................................... 1Chr 7:31 1283
2. A son of Ephraim.
a son, and he called his name *B*............ 1Chr 7:23 1283
3. A son of Elpaal.
B also, and Shema, who were heads..... 1Chr 8:13 1283
and Ispah, and Joha, the sons of *B* 1Chr 8:16 1283
4. A Levite.
Jahath, Zina, and Jeush, and *B* 1Chr 23:10 1283
but Jeush and *B* had not many sons..... 1Chr 23:11 1283

BERIITES (*be-ri'-ites*) *Descendants of Beriah 1.*
of Beriah, the family of the *B*............... Num 26:44 1284

BERITES (*be'-rites*) *Descendants of Beri.*
and to Beth-maachah, and all the *B* 2Sa 20:14 1276

BERITH (*be'-rith*) See BAAL-BERITH. *Idol at Shechem.*
an hold of the house of the god *B*......... Judg 9:46 1286

BERNICE (*bur-ni'-see*) *Daughter of Herod Agrippa.*
B came unto Caesarea to salute .... Acts 25:13 *959*
when Agrippa was come, and *B*............ Acts 25:23 *959*
rose up, and the governor, and *B*.......... Acts 26:30 *959*

BERODACH-BALADAN (*ber-o'-dak-bal'-a-dan*) See MERODACH-BALADAN. *A king of Babylon.*
At that time *B*, the son of 2Kin 20:12 1255

BEROEA See BEREA.

BEROTHAH (*ber-o'-thah*) See BEROTHAI, BEROTHITE. *A city near Hamath.*
Hamath, *B*, Sibraim, which is................. Eze 47:16 1268

BEROTHAI (*ber'-o-thahee*) See BEROTHAH. *A city of Hadadezer.*
And from Betah, and from *B*, cities 2Sa 8:8 1268

BEROTHITE (*be'-ro-thite*) See BEEROTHITE. *A native of Beeroth.*
Zelek the Ammonite, Naharai the *B*..... 1Chr 11:39 1307

BERRIES
two or three *b* in the top of the... Is 17:6 1620
tree, my brethren, bear olive *b*... Jas 3:12 *1636*

BERYL
And the fourth row a *b*, and an onyx .. Ex 28:20 8658
And the fourth row, a *b*, an onyx,... Ex 39:13 8658
are as gold rings set with the *b*... Song 5:14 8658
was like unto the colour of a *b*... Eze 1:16 8658
was as the colour of a *b* stone... Eze 10:9 8658
topaz, and the diamond, the *b*... Eze 28:13 8658
His body also was like the *b*... Dan 10:6 8658
the eighth, *b*... Rev 21:20 *969*

BESAI (*be'-sahee*) *A family of exiles.*
of Paseah, the children of *B*... Ezr 2:49 1153
The children of *B*, the children... Neh 7:52 1153

BESEECH
we *b* thee, three days' journey... Ex 3:18 4994
I *b* thee, shew me thy glory... Ex 33:18 4994
I *b* thee, lay not the sin upon us... Num 12:11 4994
Heal her now, O God, I *b* thee... Num 12:13 4994
I *b* thee, let the power of my... Num 14:17 4994
I *b* thee, the iniquity of this... Num 14:19 4994
I *b* thee, tell thy servant... 1Sa 23:11 4994
I *b* thee, and his servants go with... 2Sa 13:24 4994
I humbly *b* thee that I may find... 2Sa 16:4
I *b* thee, O LORD, take away the... 2Sa 24:10 4994
I *b* thee, save thou us out of his... 2Kin 19:19 4994
I *b* thee, O LORD, remember now... 2Kin 20:3 577
I *b* thee, do away the iniquity of... 1Chr 21:8 4994
I *b* thee, thine eyes be open, and... 2Chr 6:40 4994
I *b* thee, O LORD God of heaven,... Neh 1:5 577
I *b* thee, the word that thou... Neh 1:8 4994
I *b* thee, let now thine ear be... Neh 1:11 577
I *b* thee, that thou hast made me... Job 10:9 4994
I *b* thee, and I will speak... Job 42:4 4994
we *b* thee, O God of hosts... Ps 80:14 4994
I *b* thee, deliver my soul... Ps 116:4 577
Save now, I *b* thee, O LORD... Ps 118:25 577
I *b* thee, send now prosperity... Ps 118:25 577
I *b* thee, the freewill offerings... Ps 119:108 4994
I *b* thee, how I have walked... Is 38:3 577
we *b* thee, we are all thy people... Is 64:9 4994
We *b* thee, let this man be put to... Jer 38:4 4994
I *b* thee, the voice of the LORD,... Jer 38:20 4994
we *b* thee, our supplication be... Jer 42:2 4994
thy servants, I *b* thee, ten days... Dan 1:12 4994
I *b* thee, let thine anger and thy... Dan 9:16 4994
O Lord GOD, forgive, I *b* thee... Amos 7:2 4994
I, O Lord GOD, cease, I *b* thee... Amos 7:5 4994
We *b* thee, O LORD, we *b*... Jonah 1:14 577
I *b* thee, my life from me... Jonah 4:3 4994
b God that he will be gracious... Mal 1:9
they *b* him to put his hand upon... Mk 7:32 *3870*
I *b* thee, torment me not... Lk 8:28 *1189*
I *b* thee, look upon my son... Lk 9:38 *1189*
I *b* thee, suffer me to speak unto... Acts 21:39 *1189*
wherefore I *b* thee to hear me... Acts 26:3 *1189*
I *b* you therefore, brethren, by... Rom 12:1 *3870*
Now I *b* you, brethren, for the... Rom 15:30 *3870*
Now I *b* you, brethren, mark them... Rom 16:17 *3870*
Now I *b* you, brethren, by the... 1Cor 1:10 *3870*
Wherefore I *b* you, be ye... 1Cor 4:16 *3870*
I *b* you, brethren, (ye know the... 1Cor 16:15 *3870*
Wherefore I *b* you that ye would... 2Cor 2:8 *3870*
as though God did *b* you by us... 2Cor 5:20 *3870*
b you also that ye receive not... 2Cor 6:1 *3870*
Now I Paul myself *b* you by the... 2Cor 10:1 *3870*
But I *b* you, that I may not be... 2Cor 10:2 *1189*
Brethren, I *b* you, be as I am... Gal 4:12 *1189*
b you that ye walk worthy of the... Eph 4:1 *3870*
I *b* Euodias, and *b* Syntyche,... Phil 4:2 *3870*
b Syntyche, that they be of the... Phil 4:2 *3870*
Furthermore then we *b* you... 1Th 4:1 *2065*
but we *b* you, brethren, that ye... 1Th 4:10 *3870*
we *b* you, brethren, to know them... 1Th 5:12 *2065*
Now we *b* you, brethren, by the... 2Th 2:1 *2065*
for love's sake I rather *b* thee... Philem 9 *3870*
I *b* thee for my son Onesimus,... Philem 10 *3870*
But I *b* you the rather to do this... Heb 13:19 *3870*
I *b* you, brethren, suffer the... Heb 13:22 *3870*
I *b* you as strangers and pilgrims,... 1Pet 2:11 *3870*
And now I *b* thee, lady, not as... 2Jn 5 *2065*

BESEECHING
came unto him a centurion, *b* him,... Mt 8:5 *3870*
b him, and kneeling down to him,... Mk 1:40 *3870*
b him that he would come and heal... Lk 7:3 *2065*

BESET
b the house round about, and beat... Judg 19:22 5437
b the house round about upon me... Judg 20:5 5437
bulls of Bashan have *b* me round... Ps 22:12 3803
Thou hast *b* me behind and before,... Ps 139:5 6696
own doings have *b* them about... Hos 7:2 5437
the sin which doth so easily *b* us... Heb 12:1 *2139*

BESIDE
b the first famine that was in... Gen 26:1 905
take other wives *b* my daughters... Gen 31:50 5921
on foot that were men, *b* children... Ex 12:37 905
b Pi-hahiroth, before Baal-zephon... Ex 14:9 5921
pour all the blood *b* the bottom... Ex 29:12 413
cast it *b* the altar on the east... Lev 1:16 681
and he shall put them *b* the altar... Lev 6:10 681
b the burnt sacrifice of the... Lev 9:17 905
eat it without leaven *b* the altar... Lev 10:12 681
b the other in her life time... Lev 18:18 5921
B the sabbaths of the LORD, and... Lev 23:38 905
b your gifts, and *b* all your... Lev 23:38 905
b all your freewill offerings,... Lev 23:38 905
b the ram of the atonement,... Num 5:8 905
lain with thee *b* thine husband... Num 5:20 1107
b that that his hand shall get... Num 6:21 905
b this manna, before our eyes... Num 11:6 1115
b them that died about the matter... Num 16:49 905
and as cedar trees *b* the waters... Num 24:6 5921
b the continual burnt offering,... Num 28:10 5921
b the continual burnt offering,... Num 28:15 5921
Ye shall offer these *b* the burnt... Num 28:23 905
it shall be offered *b* the... Num 28:24 5921
Ye shall offer them *b* the... Num 28:31 905
B the burnt offering of the month... Num 29:6 905
b the sin offering of atonement,... Num 29:11 905
b the continual burnt offering,... Num 29:16 905
b the continual burnt offering,... Num 29:19 905
b the continual burnt offering,... Num 29:22 905
b the continual burnt offering,... Num 29:25 905
b the continual burnt offering,... Num 29:28 905
b the continual burnt offering,... Num 29:31 905
b the continual burnt offering,... Num 29:34 905
b the continual burnt offering,... Num 29:38 905
b your vows, and your freewill... Num 29:39 905
b the rest of them that were... Num 31:8 5921
b unwalled towns a great many... Deut 3:5 905
there is none else *b* him... Deut 4:35 905
Gilgal, *b* the plains of Moreh... Deut 11:30 681
b that which cometh of the sale... Deut 18:8 905
more for thee, *b* these three... Deut 19:9 5921
b the covenant which he made with... Deut 29:1 905
the city Adam, that is *b* Zaretan... Josh 3:16 6654
which is *b* Beth-aven, on the east... Josh 7:2 5973
king of Ai, which is *b* Beth-el... Josh 12:9 6654
and Mearah that is *b* the Sidonians... Josh 13:4
b the land of Gilead and Bashan,... Josh 17:5 905
in building you an altar *b* the... Josh 22:19 1107
b the altar of the LORD our God... Josh 22:29 905
and it be dry upon all the earth *b*... Judg 6:37
pitched *b* the well of Harod... Judg 7:1 5921
b ornaments, and collars, and... Judg 8:26 905
b the chains that were about... Judg 8:26 905
b her he had neither son nor... Judg 11:34
b the inhabitants of Gibeah,... Judg 20:15 905
b Benjamin, were numbered four... Judg 20:17 905
wait which they had set *b* Gibeah... Judg 20:36 413
And she sat *b* the reapers... Ruth 2:14 6654
there is none to redeem it *b* thee... Ruth 4:4 2108
for there is none *b* thee... 1Sa 2:2 1115
to battle, and pitched *b* Eben-ezer... 1Sa 4:1 5921
stand *b* my father in the field... 1Sa 19:3 3027
neither is there any God *b* thee... 2Sa 7:22 2108
in Baal-hazor, which is *b* Ephraim... 2Sa 13:23 5973
stood *b* the way of the gate... 2Sa 15:2
all his servants passed on *b* him... 2Sa 15:18
and took my son from *b* me... 1Kin 3:20 681
sheep, *b* harts, and roebucks, and... 1Kin 4:23 905
B the chief of Solomon's officers... 1Kin 5:16 905
in Ezion-geber, which is *b* Eloth... 1Kin 9:26 854
b that which Solomon gave her of... 1Kin 10:13 905
B that he had of the merchantmen,... 1Kin 10:15 905
and two lions stood *b* the stays... 1Kin 10:19 681
b the mischief that Hadad did... 1Kin 11:25 854
lay my bones *b* his bones... 1Kin 13:31 681
with the sword *b* the king's house... 2Kin 11:20
set it *b* the altar, on the right... 2Kin 12:9 681
b his sin wherewith he made Judah... 2Kin 21:16 905
b the sons of the concubines, and... 1Chr 3:9 905
neither is there any God *b* thee... 1Chr 17:20 2108
b that which she had brought unto... 2Chr 9:12 905
B that which chapmen and merchants... 2Chr 9:14 905
b those whom the king put in the... 2Chr 17:19 905
with them other *b* the Ammonites... 2Chr 20:1
LORD, from *b* the incense altar... 2Chr 26:19 5921
B their genealogy of males, from... 2Chr 31:16 905
b the freewill offering for the... Ezr 1:4 5973
b all that was willingly offered... Ezr 1:6
B their servants and their maids,... Ezr 2:65 905
b forty shekels of silver... Neh 5:15 310
b those that came unto us from... Neh 5:17
B their manservants and their... Neh 7:67 905
b him stood Mattithiah, and Shema,... Neh 8:4 681
and the asses feeding *b* them... Job 1:14
he leadeth me *b* the still waters... Ps 23:2 5921
upon earth that I desire *b* thee... Ps 73:25 5973
feed thy kids *b* the shepherds'... Song 1:8 5921
are ye that sow *b* all waters... Is 32:20 5921
and *b* me there is no saviour... Is 43:11 1107
and *b* me there is no God... Is 44:6 1107
Is there a God *b* me... Is 44:8 1107
none else, there is no God *b* me... Is 45:5 2108
the west, that there is none *b* me... Is 45:6 1107
and there is no God else *b* me... Is 45:21 1107
there is none *b* me... Is 45:21 2108
heart, I am, and none else *b* me... Is 47:8 657
heart, I am, and none else *b* me... Is 47:10 657
b those that are gathered unto... Is 56:8
b thee, what he hath prepared for... Is 64:4 2108
princes which stood *b* the king... Jer 36:21 5921
in, and stood *b* the brasen altar... Eze 9:2 681
he went in, and stood *b* the wheels... Eze 10:6 681
also turned not from *b* them... Eze 10:16 681
out, the wheels also were *b* them... Eze 10:19 5980
their wings, and the wheels *b* them... Eze 11:22 5980
thereof from *b* the great waters... Eze 32:13 5921
up, even for others *b* those... Dan 11:4 905
for there is no saviour *b* me... Hos 13:4 1115
I am, and there is none *b* me... Zeph 2:15 657
thousand men, *b* women and children... Mt 14:21 *5565*
thousand men, *b* women and children... Mt 15:38 *5565*
I have gained *b* them five talents... Mt 25:20 *1909*
gained two other talents *b* them... Mt 25:22 *1909*
for they said, He is *b* himself... Mk 3:21 *1839*
b all this, between us and you... Lk 16:26 *1909*
b all this, to day is the third... Lk 24:21 *4862*
voice, Paul, thou art *b* thyself... Acts 26:24 *3105*
For whether we be *b* ourselves... 2Cor 5:13 *1839*
B those things that are without,... 2Cor 11:28 *5565*
b this, giving all diligence, add... 2Pet 1:5 *846*

BESIDES
unto Lot, Hast thou here any *b*... Gen 19:12 5750
b Jacob's sons' wives, all the... Gen 46:26 905
B the cakes, he shall offer for... Lev 7:13 5921
not here a prophet of the LORD *b*... 1Kin 22:7 5750
not here a prophet of the LORD *b*... 2Chr 18:6 5750
other lords *b* thee have had... Is 26:13 2108
there were added *b* unto them many... Jer 36:32 5750
b, I know not whether I baptized... 1Cor 1:16 *3063*
unto me even thine own self *b*... Philem 19 *4359*

BESIEGE
thee, then thou shalt *b* it... Deut 20:12 6696
When thou shalt *b* a city a long... Deut 20:19 6696
he shall *b* thee in all thy gates,... Deut 28:52 6887
he shall *b* thee in all thy gates... Deut 28:52 6887
to Keilah, to *b* David and his men... 1Sa 23:8 6696
if their enemy *b* them in the land... 1Kin 8:37 6887
city, and his servants did *b* it... 2Kin 24:11 6696
if their enemies *b* them in the... 2Chr 6:28 6696
b, O Media... Is 21:2 6696
which *b* you without the walls, and... Jer 21:4 6696
to the Chaldeans that *b* you... Jer 21:9 6696

BESIEGED
children of Ammon, and *b* Rabbah... 2Sa 11:1 6696
b him in Abel of Beth-maachah, and... 2Sa 20:15 6696
Israel with him, and they *b* Tirzah... 1Kin 16:17 6696
b Samaria, and warred against it... 1Kin 20:1 6696
host, and went up, and *b* Samaria... 2Kin 6:24 6696
and, behold, they *b* it, until an... 2Kin 6:25 6696
and they *b* Ahaz, but could not... 2Kin 16:5 6696
to Samaria, and *b* it three years... 2Kin 17:5 6696
came up against Samaria, and *b* it... 2Kin 18:9 6696
up all the rivers of *b* places... 2Kin 19:24 4693
Jerusalem, and the city was *b*... 2Kin 24:10
the city was *b* unto the eleventh... 2Kin 25:2
of Ammon, and came and *b* Rabbah... 1Chr 20:1 6696
b it, and built great bulwarks... Eccl 9:14 5437
garden of cucumbers, as a *b* city... Is 1:8 5341
up all the rivers of the *b* places... Is 37:25 4693
of Babylon's army *b* Jerusalem... Jer 32:2 6696
when the Chaldeans that *b*... Jer 37:5 6696
against Jerusalem, and they *b* it... Jer 39:1 6696
So the city was *b* unto the... Jer 52:5
face against it, and it shall be *b*... Eze 4:3 4692
is *b* shall die by the famine... Eze 6:12 5341
Babylon unto Jerusalem, and *b* it... Dan 1:1 6696

BESODEIAH (*bes-o-di'-ah*) *A repairer of Jerusalem's walls.*
Paseah, and Meshullam the son of *B*... Neh 3:6 1152

BESOM
it with the *b* of destruction... Is 14:23 4292

BESOR (*be'-sor*) *A brook in southern Judah.*
with him, and came to the brook *B*... 1Sa 30:9 1308
could not go over the brook *B*... 1Sa 30:10 1308
made also to abide at the brook *B*... 1Sa 30:21 1308

BESOUGHT
anguish of his soul, when he *b* us... Gen 42:21 2603
Moses *b* the LORD his God, and said... Ex 32:11 2470
I *b* the LORD at that time, saying... Deut 3:23 2603
David therefore *b* God for the... 2Sa 12:16 1245
And the man of God *b* the LORD... 1Kin 13:6 2470
b him, and said unto him, O man of... 2Kin 1:13 2603
And Jehoahaz *b* the LORD, and the... 2Kin 13:4 2470
he *b* the LORD his God, and humbled... 2Chr 33:12 2470
we fasted and *b* our God for this... Ezr 8:23 1245
b him with tears to put away the... Est 8:3 2603
b the LORD, and the LORD repented... Jer 26:19 2470
So the devils *b* him, saying, If... Mt 8:31 *3870*
they *b* him that he would depart... Mt 8:34 *3870*
b him that they might only touch... Mt 14:36 *3870*
b him, saying, Send her away... Mt 15:23 *2065*
b him, saying, Have patience with... Mt 18:29 *3870*
he *b* him much that he would not... Mk 5:10 *3870*
And all the devils *b* him, saying,... Mk 5:12 *3870*
b him greatly, saying, My little... Mk 5:23 *3870*
b him that they might touch if it... Mk 6:56 *3870*
she *b* him that he would cast... Mk 7:26 *2065*
unto him, and *b* him to touch him... Mk 8:22 *3870*
and they *b* him for her... Lk 4:38 *2065*
b him, saying, Lord, if thou wilt... Lk 5:12 *1189*
they *b* him instantly, saying,... Lk 7:4 *3870*
they *b* him that he would not... Lk 8:31 *3870*
they *b* him that he would suffer... Lk 8:32 *3870*
about *b* him to depart from them... Lk 8:37 *2065*
b him that he might be with him... Lk 8:38 *1189*
b him that he would come into his... Lk 8:41 *3870*
I *b* thy disciples to cast him out... Lk 9:40 *1189*
a certain Pharisee *b* him to dine... Lk 11:37 *2065*
they *b* him that he would tarry... Jn 4:40 *2065*
b him that he would come down, and.. Jn 4:47 *2065*
) *b* Pilate that their legs might... Jn 19:31 *2065*
b Pilate that he might take away... Jn 19:38 *2065*
the Gentiles *b* that these words... Acts 13:42 *3870*
and her household, she *b* us... Acts 16:15 *3870*
b them, and brought them out, and... Acts 16:39 *3870*
b him not to go up to Jerusalem... Acts 21:12 *3870*
him against Paul, and *b* him,... Acts 25:2 *3870*
Paul *b* them all to take meat,... Acts 27:33 *3870*
this thing I *b* the Lord thrice... 2Cor 12:8 *3870*
As I *b* thee to abide still at... 1Ti 1:3 *3870*

BEST
take of the *b* fruits in the land... Gen 43:11 2173
in the *b* of the land make thy... Gen 47:6 4315
in the *b* of the land, in the land... Gen 47:11 4315
of the *b* of his own field... Ex 22:5 4315
of the *b* of his own vineyard,... Ex 22:5 4315
All the *b* of the oil... Num 18:12 2459
all the *b* of the wine, and of the... Num 18:12 2459
of the LORD, of all the *b* thereof... Num 18:29 2459
have heaved the *b* thereof from it... Num 18:30 2459

B

have heaved from it the *b* of it — Num 18:32 2459
them marry to whom they think *b* — Num 36:6 2896
thy gates, where it liketh him *b* — Deut 23:16 2896
oliveyards, even the *b* of them — 1Sa 8:14 2896
the *b* of the sheep, and of the — 1Sa 15:9 4315
people spared the *b* of the sheep — 1Sa 15:15 4315
What seemeth you *b* I will do — 2Sa 18:4 3190
and overlaid it with the *b* gold — 1Kin 10:18 6338
Look even out the *b* and meetest of — 2Kin 10:3 2896
her maids unto the *b* place of the — Est 2:9 2896
verily every man at his *b* state — Ps 39:5 5324
like the *b* wine for my beloved — Song 7:9 2896
b of Lebanon, all that drink — Eze 31:16 2896
The *b* of them is as a brier — Mic 7:4 2896
servants, Bring forth the *b* robe — Lk 15:22 *4413*
But covet earnestly the *b* gifts — 1Cor 12:31 *2909*

BESTEAD
shall pass through it, hardly *b* — Is 8:21

BESTIR
that then thou shalt *b* thyself — 2Sa 5:24 2782

BESTOW
that he may *b* upon you a blessing — Ex 32:29 5414
thou shalt *b* that money for — Deut 14:26 5414
the LORD did they *b* upon Baalim — 2Chr 24:7 6213
thou shalt have occasion to *b* — Ezr 7:20 5415
b it out of the king's treasure — Ezr 7:20 5415
have no room where to *b* my fruits — Lk 12:17 *4863*
there will I *b* all my fruits and — Lk 12:18 *4863*
upon these we *b* more abundant — 1Cor 12:23 *4060*
though I *b* all my goods to feed — 1Cor 13:3 *5595*

BESTOWED
whom he *b* in the cities for — 1Kin 10:26 3240
hand, and *b* them in the house — 2Kin 5:24 6485
the money to be *b* on workmen — 2Kin 12:15 5414
b upon him such royal majesty as — 1Chr 29:25 5414
whom he *b* in the chariot cities — 2Chr 9:25 3240
to all that the LORD hath *b* on us — Is 63:7 1580
which he hath *b* on them according — Is 63:7 1580
reap that whereon ye *b* no labour — Jn 4:38 *2872*
Mary, who *b* much labour on us — Rom 16:6 *2872*
his grace which was *b* upon me was — 1Cor 15:10
that for the gift *b* upon us by — 2Cor 1:11
b on the churches of Macedonia — 2Cor 8:1 *1325*
lest I have *b* upon you labour in — Gal 4:11 *2872*
of love the Father hath *b* upon us — 1Jn 3:1 *1325*

BETAH (*be'-tah*) *A city of Hadadezer.*
And from B, and from Berothai, — 2Sa 8:8 984

BETEN (*be'-ten*) *A city in Asher.*
border was Helkath, and Hali, and B — Josh 19:25 991

BETHABARA (*beth-ab'-ar-ah*) See BETHBARAH. *A place east of the Jordan River.*
were done in B beyond Jordan — Jn 1:28 *962*

BETH ACACIA See BETH-SHITTAH.

BETH-ANATH (*beth'-a-nath*) *A city in Naphtali.*
Iron, and Migdal-el, Horem, and B — Josh 19:38 1043
nor the inhabitants of B — Judg 1:33 1043
of B became tributaries unto them — Judg 1:33 1043

BETH-ANOTH (*beth'-a-noth*) *A city in Judah.*
And Maarath, and B, and Eltekon — Josh 15:59 1042

BETHANY (*beth'-a-ny*) *A village near Jerusalem.*
and went out of the city into B — Mt 21:17 *963*
Now when Jesus was in B, in the — Mt 26:6 *963*
to Jerusalem, unto Bethphage and B — Mk 11:1 *963*
went out unto B with the twelve — Mk 11:11 *963*
when they were come from B — Mk 11:12 *963*
being in B in the house of Simon — Mk 14:3 *963*
was come nigh to Bethphage and B — Lk 19:29 *963*
And he led them out as far as to B — Lk 24:50 *963*
man was sick, named Lazarus, of B — Jn 11:1 *963*
Now B was nigh unto Jerusalem, — Jn 11:18 *963*
before the passover came to B — Jn 12:1 *963*

BETH APHRAH See APHRAH.

BETH-ARABAH (*beth-ar'-ab-ah*) *A city of the Arabah.*
and passed along by the north of B — Josh 15:6 1026
In the wilderness, B, Middin, and — Josh 15:61 1026
And B, and Zemaraim, and Beth-el, — Josh 18:22 1026

BETH-ARAM (*beth'-a-ram*) *A city in Gad.*
And in the valley, B, and — Josh 13:27 1027

BETH-ARBEL (*beth-ar'-bel*) *A city destroyed by the Assyrians.*
as Shalman spoiled B in the day — Hos 10:14 1009

BETH ASHBEA See ASHBEA.

BETH-AVEN (*beth-a'-ven*) *A town in Benjamin.*
Jericho to Ai, which is beside B — Josh 7:2 1007
were at the wilderness of B — Josh 18:12 1007
in Michmash, eastward from B — 1Sa 13:5 1007
and the battle passed over unto B — 1Sa 14:23 1007
Gilgal, neither go ye up to B — Hos 4:15 1007
cry aloud at B, after thee, O — Hos 5:8 1007
fear because of the calves of B — Hos 10:5 1007

BETH-AZMAVETH (*beth-az'-maveth*) See AZMAVETH. *A village in Judah.*
The men of B, forty and two — Neh 7:28 1041

BETH-BAAL-MEON (*beth-ba'-al-me'-on*) *A Moabite town.*
Dibon, and Bamoth-baal, and B — Josh 13:17 1010

BETH-BARAH (*beth-ba'-rah*) See BETHABARA. *A place in Gad.*
before them the waters unto B — Judg 7:24 1012
and took the waters unto B — Judg 7:24 1012

BETH-BIREI (*beth-bir-e-i*) See BETH-LEBAOTH. *A town in Simeon.*
and Hazar-susim, and at B, and at — 1Chr 4:31 1011

BETH BIRI See BETH-BIREI.

BETH-CAR (*beth'-car*) *A Philistine stronghold in Judah.*
them, until they came under B — 1Sa 7:11 1033

BETH-DAGON (*beth-da'-gon*)
1. A town in Judah.
And Gederoth, B, and Naamah, and — Josh 15:41 1016
2. A town in Asher.
turneth toward the sunrising to B — Josh 19:27 1016

BETH-DIBLATHAIM (*beth-dib-lath-a'-im*) *A Moabite town.*
Dibon, and upon Nebo, and upon B — Jer 48:22 1015

BETH-EL
unto a mountain on the east of B — Gen 12:8 1008
having B on the west, and Hai on — Gen 12:8 1008
journeys from the south even to B — Gen 13:3 1008
been at the beginning, between B — Gen 13:3 1008
called the name of that place B — Gen 28:19 1008
I am the God of B, where thou — Gen 31:13 1008
unto Jacob, Arise, go up to B — Gen 35:1 1008
And let us arise, and go up to B — Gen 35:3 1008
in the land of Canaan, that is, B — Gen 35:6 1008
was buried beneath B under an oak — Gen 35:8 1008
place where God spake with him, B — Gen 35:15 1008
And they journeyed from B — Gen 35:16 1008
Beth-aven, on the east side of B — Josh 7:2 1008
lie in ambush, and abode between B — Josh 8:9 1008
them to lie in ambush between B — Josh 8:12 1008
was not a man left in Ai or B — Josh 8:17 1008
the king of Ai, which is beside B — Josh 12:9 1008
the king of B, one — Josh 12:16 1008
from Jericho throughout mount B — Josh 16:1 1008
And goeth out from B to Luz — Josh 16:2 1008
to the side of Luz, which is B — Josh 18:13 1008
and Zemaraim, and B — Josh 18:22 1008
they also went up against B — Judg 1:22 1008
house of Joseph sent to descry B — Judg 1:23 1008
Ramah and B in mount Ephraim — Judg 4:5 1008
which is on the north side of B — Judg 21:19 1008
that goeth up from B to Shechem — Judg 21:19 1008
from year to year in circuit to B — 1Sa 7:16 1008
three men going up to God to B — 1Sa 10:3 1008
Saul in Michmash and in mount B — 1Sa 13:2 1008
To them which were in B, and to — 1Sa 30:27 1008
And he set the one in B, and the — 1Kin 12:29 1008
So did he in B, sacrificing unto — 1Kin 12:32 1008
he placed in B the priests of the — 1Kin 12:32 1008
the altar which he had made in B — 1Kin 12:33 1008
by the word of the LORD unto B — 1Kin 13:1 1008
had cried against the altar in B — 1Kin 13:4 1008
not by the way that he came to B — 1Kin 13:10 1008
there dwelt an old prophet in B — 1Kin 13:11 1008
man of God had done that day in B — 1Kin 13:11 1008
the LORD against the altar in B — 1Kin 13:32 1008
for the LORD hath sent me to B — 2Kin 2:2 1008
So they went down to B — 2Kin 2:2 1008
were at B came forth to Elisha — 2Kin 2:3 1008
And he went up from thence unto B — 2Kin 2:23 1008
the golden calves that were in B — 2Kin 10:29 1008
from Samaria came and dwelt in B — 2Kin 17:28 1008
carried the ashes of them unto B — 2Kin 23:4 1008
Moreover the altar that was at B — 2Kin 23:15 1008
hast done against the altar of B — 2Kin 23:17 1008
the acts that he had done in B — 2Kin 23:19 1008
and habitations were, B and the — 1Chr 7:28 1008
B with the towns thereof, and — 2Chr 13:19 1008
The men of B and Ai, two hundred — Ezr 2:28 1008
The men of B and Ai, an hundred — Neh 7:32 1008
dwelt at Michmash, and Aija, and B — Neh 11:31 1008
was ashamed of B their confidence — Jer 48:13 1008
So shall B do unto you because of — Hos 10:15 1008
he found him in B, and there he — Hos 12:4 1008
I will also visit the altars of B — Amos 3:14 1008
Come to B, and transgress — Amos 4:4 1008
But seek not B, nor enter into — Amos 5:5 1008
and B shall come to nought — Amos 5:5 1008
there be none to quench it in B — Amos 5:6 1008
Then Amaziah the priest of B sent — Amos 7:10 1008
prophesy not again any more at B — Amos 7:13 1008

BETH-ELITE (*beth'-el-ite*) *A native of Bethel.*
days did Hiel the B build Jericho — 1Kin 16:34 1017

BETH-EMEK (*beth-e'-mek*) *A town in Asher.*
toward the north side of B — Josh 19:27 1025

BETHER (*be'-thur*) *A district in the Jordan valley.*
hart upon the mountains of B — Song 2:17 1336

BETHESDA (*beth-ez'-dah*) *A pool in Jerusalem.*
is called in the Hebrew tongue B — Jn 5:2 *964*

BETH-EZEL (*beth-e'-zel*) *A city in Judah.*
not forth in the mourning of B — Mic 1:11 1018

BETH-GADER (*beth-ga'-der*) See GEDER. *A descendant of Caleb.*
Hareph the father of B — 1Chr 2:51 1013

BETH-GAMUL (*beth-ga'-mul*) *A Moabite town.*
And upon Kiriathaim, and upon B — Jer 48:23 1014

BETH-HACCEREM (*beth-hak'-se-rem*) *A town in Judah.*
of Rechab, the ruler of part of B — Neh 3:14 1021
and set up a sign of fire in B — Jer 6:1 1021

BETH HAKKEREM See BETH-HACCEREM.

BETH-HARAN (*beth-ha'-ran*) See ELON-BETH-HARAN. *A city in Gad.*
And Beth-nimrah, and B, fenced — Num 32:36 1028

BETH-HOGLA (*beth-hog'-lah*) See BETH-HOGLAH. *A city in Benjamin.*
And the border went up to B — Josh 15:6 1031

BETH HOGLAH See BETH-HOGLA.

BETH-HOGLAH (*beth-hog'-lah*) See BETH-HOGLA. *Same as Beth-hogla.*
along to the side of B northward — Josh 18:19 1031
their families were Jericho, and B — Josh 18:21 1031

BETH-HORON (*beth-ho'-ron*) *Two cities in Ephraim, near Benjamin.*
along the way that goeth up to B — Josh 10:10 1032
and were in the going down to B — Josh 10:11 1032
unto the coast of B the nether — Josh 16:3 1032
Ataroth-addar, unto B the upper — Josh 16:5 1032
on the south side of the nether B — Josh 18:13 1032
that lieth before B southward — Josh 18:14 1032
suburbs, and B with her suburbs — Josh 21:22 1032
company turned the way to B — 1Sa 13:18 1032
built Gezer, and B the nether, — 1Kin 9:17 1032
suburbs, and B with her suburbs, — 1Chr 6:68 1032
who built B the nether, and the — 1Chr 7:24 1032
Also he built B the upper — 2Chr 8:5 1032
B the nether, fenced cities, with — 2Chr 8:5 1032
Judah, from Samaria even unto B — 2Chr 25:13 1032

BETHINK
Yet if they shall *b* themselves in — 1Kin 8:47
Yet if they *b* themselves in the — 2Chr 6:37

BETH JESHIMOTH See JESIMOTH.

BETH-JESHIMOTH (*beth-jesh'-im-oth*) See BETH-JESIMOTH. *Same as Beth-jesimoth.*
sea on the east, the way to B — Josh 12:3 1020
and Ashdoth-pisgah, and B, — Josh 13:20 1020
the glory of the country, B — Eze 25:9 1020

BETH-JESIMOTH (*beth-jes'-im-oth*) See BETH-JESHIMOTH. *A Moabite city.*
from B even unto Abel-shittim in — Num 33:49 1020

BETH-LE-APHRAH See APHRAH.

BETH-LEBAOTH (*beth-leb'-a-oth*) See BETH-BISEI. *A town in Simeon.*
And B, and Sharuhen — Josh 19:6 1034

BETH-LEHEM (*beth'-le-hem*) See BETH-LEHEMITE, BETH-LEHEM-JUDAH.
1. A city in Judah.
in the way to Ephrath, which is B — Gen 35:19 1035
the same is B — Gen 48:7 1035
two went until they came to B — Ruth 1:19 1035
to pass, when they were come to B — Ruth 1:19 1035
they came to B in the beginning — Ruth 1:22 1035
And, behold, Boaz came from B — Ruth 2:4 1035
in Ephratah, and be famous in B — Ruth 4:11 1035
the LORD spake, and came to B — 1Sa 16:4 1035
to feed his father's sheep at B — 1Sa 17:15 1035
that he might run to B his city — 1Sa 20:6 1035
asked leave of me to go to B — 1Sa 20:28 1035
of his father, which was in B — 2Sa 2:32 1035
of the Philistines was then in B — 2Sa 23:14 1035
of the water of the well of B — 2Sa 23:15 1035
drew water out of the well of B — 2Sa 23:16 1035
Elhanan the son of Dodo of B — 2Sa 23:24 1035
garrison was then at B — 1Chr 11:16 1035
of the water of the well of B — 1Chr 11:17 1035
drew water out of the well of B — 1Chr 11:18 1035
Elhanan the son of Dodo of B — 1Chr 11:26 1035
He built even B, and Etam, and — 2Chr 11:6 1035
The children of B, an hundred — Ezr 2:21 1035
The men of B and Netophah, an — Neh 7:26 1035
B Ephratah, though thou be little — Mic 5:2 1035
2. A town in Zebulun.
and Shimron, and Idalah, and B — Josh 19:15 1035
3. A town in Ephraim.
him Ibzan of B judged Israel — Judg 12:8 1035
died Ibzan, and was buried at B — Judg 12:10 1035
4. A descendant of Caleb.
Salma the father of B, Hareph the — 1Chr 2:51 1035
B, and the Netophathites, Ataroth, — 1Chr 2:54 1035
of Ephratah, the father of B — 1Chr 4:4 1035

BETHLEHEM *A town in Judea.*
of Chimham, which is by B — Jer 41:17 1035
Now when Jesus was born in B of — Mt 2:1 *965*
said unto him, In B of Judaea — Mt 2:5 *965*
And thou B, in the land of Juda, — Mt 2:6 *965*
And he sent them to B, and said, Go — Mt 2:8 *965*
all the children that were in B — Mt 2:16 *965*
city of David, which is called B — Lk 2:4 *965*
Let us now go even unto B — Lk 2:15 *965*
of David, and out of the town of B — Jn 7:42 *965*

BETH-LEHEMITE (*beth'-le-hem-ite*) *A native of Bethlehem.*
I will send thee to Jesse the B — 1Sa 16:1 1022
I have seen a son of Jesse the B — 1Sa 16:18 1022
son of thy servant Jesse the B — 1Sa 17:58 1022
the son of Jaare-oregim, a B — 2Sa 21:19 1022

BETH-LEHEM-JUDAH (*beth'-le-hem-ju'-dah*) *Same as Beth-lehem 1.*
out of B of the family of Judah — Judg 17:7 1035
departed out of the city from B — Judg 17:8 1035
said unto him, I am a Levite of B — Judg 17:9 1035
took to him a concubine out of B — Judg 19:1 1035
him unto her father's house to B — Judg 19:2 1035
We are passing from B toward the — Judg 19:18 1035
and I went to B, but I am now — Judg 19:18 1035

a certain man of B went to Ruth 1:1 1035
and Chilion, Ephrathites of B Ruth 1:2 1035
the son of that Ephrathite of B 1Sa 17:12 1035

BETH MAACAH

BETH-MAACHAH (*beth-ma'-a-kah*) See ABEL-BETH-MAACHAH. *A city in Manasseh.*
of Israel unto Abel, and to B 2Sa 20:14 1038
came and besieged him in Abel of B 2Sa 20:15 1038

BETH-MARCABOTH (*beth-mar'-cab-oth*) *A city in Judah.*
And Ziklag, and B, and Hazar-susah, Josh 19:5 1024
And at B, and Hazar-susim, and at 1Chr 4:31 1024

BETH-MEON (*beth-me'-on*) See BETH-BAAL-MEON. *A Moabite city.*
and upon Beth-gamul, and upon B Jer 48:23 1010

BETH-NIMRAH (*beth-nim'-rah*) See NIMRAH. *A city in Gad.*
And B, and Beth-haran, fenced Num 32:36 1039
And in the valley, Beth-aram, and B Josh 13:27 1039

BETH OPHRAH See APHRAH.

BETH-PALET (*beth-pa'-let*) See BETH-PELET. *A town in Judah.*
and Heshmon, and B Josh 15:27 1046

BETH-PAZZEZ (*beth-paz'-zez*) *A town in Issachar.*
and En-haddah, and B Josh 19:21 1048

BETH PELET See BETH-PALET.

BETH-PEOR (*beth-pe'-or*) *A Moabite city.*
in the valley over against B Deut 3:29 1047
in the valley over against B Deut 4:46 1047
the land of Moab, over against B Deut 34:6 1047
And B, and Ashdoth-pisgah, and Josh 13:20 1047

BETHPHAGE (*beth'-fa-je*) *A village near Jerusalem.*
unto Jerusalem, and were come to B Mt 21:1 967
came nigh to Jerusalem, unto B Mk 11:1 967
pass, when he was come nigh to B Lk 19:29 967

BETH-PHELET (*beth'-fe-let*) See BETH-PALET. *A town in Judah.*
at Jeshua, and at Moladah, and at B Neh 11:26 1046

BETH-RAPHA (*beth'-ra-fah*) *Son of Eshton.*
And Eshton begat B, and Paseah, and 1Chr 4:12 1051

BETH-REHOB (*beth'-re-hob*) *A place in northern Canaan.*
was in the valley that lieth by B Judg 18:28 1050
sent and hired the Syrians of B 2Sa 10:6 1050

BETHSAIDA (*beth-sa'-dah*)
1. A city in Galilee.
woe unto thee, B Mt 11:21 966
to the other side before unto B Mk 6:45 966
woe unto thee, B Lk 10:13 966
Now Philip was of B, the city of Jn 1:44 966
Philip, which was of B of Galilee Jn 12:21 966
2. A place east of Lake Gennesareth.
And he cometh to B Mk 8:22 966
belonging to the city called B Lk 9:10 966

BETH SHAN See BETH-SHEAN.

BETH-SHAN (*beth'-shan*) See BETH-SHEAN. *A city in Manasseh.*
his body to the wall of B 1Sa 31:10 1052
of his sons from the wall of B 1Sa 31:12 1052
stolen them from the street of B 2Sa 21:12 1052

BETH-SHEAN (*beth-she'-an*) See BETH-SHAN. *Same as Beth-shan.*
had in Issachar and in Asher B Josh 17:11 1052
of iron, both they who are of B Josh 17:16 1052
drive out the inhabitants of B Judg 1:27 1052
Taanach and Megiddo, and all B 1Kin 4:12 1052
from B to Abel-meholah, even unto 1Kin 4:12 1052
of the children of Manasseh, B 1Chr 7:29 1052

BETH SHEMESH See SHEMESH.

BETH-SHEMESH (*beth'-she-mesh*) See BETH-SHEMITE.
1. A town in Judah.
the north side, and went down to B Josh 15:10 1053
suburbs, and B with her suburbs Josh 21:16 1053
by the way of his own coast to B 1Sa 6:9 1053
the straight way to the way of B 1Sa 6:12 1053
after them unto the border of B 1Sa 6:12 1053
they of B were reaping their 1Sa 6:13 1053
the men of B offered burnt 1Sa 6:15 1053
And he smote the men of B, because 1Sa 6:19 1053
And the men of B said, Who is able 1Sa 6:20 1053
in Makaz, and in Shaalbim, and B 1Kin 4:9 1053
one another in the face at B 2Kin 14:11 1053
Jehoash the son of Ahaziah, at B 2Kin 14:13 1053
suburbs, and B with her suburbs 1Chr 6:59 1053
he and Amaziah king of Judah, at B 2Chr 25:21 1053
Joash, the son of Jehoahaz, at B 2Chr 25:23 1053
south of Judah, and had taken B 2Chr 28:18 1053
2. A city in Issachar.
to Tabor, and Shahazimah, and B Josh 19:22 1053
3. A city in Naphtali.
Horem, and Beth-anath, and B Josh 19:38 1053
drive out the inhabitants of B Judg 1:33 1053
nevertheless the inhabitants of B Judg 1:33 1053
4. A temple in Egypt.
shall break also the images of B Jer 43:13 1053

BETH-SHEMITE (*beth'-shem-ite*) *An inhabitant of Beth-shemesh.*
into the field of Joshua, a B 1Sa 6:14 1030
day in the field of Joshua, the B 1Sa 6:18 1030

BETH-SHITTAH (*beth-shit'-tah*) *A place in the Jordan valley.*
and the host fled to B in Zererath Judg 7:22 1029

BETH-TAPPUAH (*beth-tap'-pu-ah*) *A city in Judah.*
And Janum, and B, and Aphekah, Josh 15:53 1054

BETHUEL (*beth-u'-el*) See BETHUL.
1. Son of Nahor.
and Pildash, and Jidlaph, and B Gen 22:22 1328
And B begat Rebekah Gen 22:23 1328
came out, who was born to B Gen 24:15 1328
daughter of B the son of Milcah Gen 24:24 1328
And she said, The daughter of B Gen 24:47 1328
B answered and said, The thing Gen 24:50 1328
the daughter of B the Syrian of Gen 25:20 1328
to the house of B thy mother's Gen 28:2 1328
son of B the Syrian, the brother Gen 28:5 1328
2. A town in Simeon.
And at B, and at Hormah, and at 1Chr 4:30 1328

BETHUL (*beth'-ul*) See BETHUEL. *A city in Simeon.*
And Eltolad, and B, and Hormah, Josh 19:4 1329

BETHZATHA See BETHESDA.

BETHZOR See BETH-ZUR.

BETH-ZUR (*beth'-zur*)
1. A town in Judah.
Halhul, B, and Gedor, Josh 15:58 1049
And B, and Shoco, and Adullam, 2Chr 11:7 1049
the ruler of the half part of B Neh 3:16 1049
2. A descendant of Caleb.
and Maon was the father of B 1Chr 2:45 1049

BETIMES
they rose up b in the morning, and Gen 26:31 7925
by his messengers, rising up b 2Chr 36:15 7925
If thou wouldest seek unto God b Job 8:5 7836
rising b for a prey Job 24:5 7836
that loveth him chasteneth him b Prov 13:24 7836

BETONIM (*bet'-o-nim*) *A town in Gad.*
Heshbon unto Ramath-mizpeh, and B Josh 13:26 993

BETRAY
be come to b me to mine enemies 1Chr 12:17 7411
shall b one another, and shall Mt 24:10 3860
he sought opportunity to b him Mt 26:16 3860
you, that one of you shall b me Mt 26:21 3860
in the dish, the same shall b me Mt 26:23 3860
he is at hand that doth b me Mt 26:46 3860
shall b the brother to death Mk 13:12 3860
chief priests, to b him unto them Mk 14:10 3860
how he might conveniently b him Mk 14:11 3860
which eateth with me shall b me Mk 14:18 3860
how he might b him unto them Lk 22:4 3860
sought opportunity to b him unto Lk 22:6 3860
believed not, and who should b him Jn 6:64 3860
for he it was that should b him Jn 6:71 3860
Simon's son, which should b him Jn 12:4 3860
Iscariot, Simon's son, to b him Jn 13:2 3860
For he knew who should b him Jn 13:11 3860
you, that one of you shall b me Jn 13:21 3860

BETRAYED
and Judas Iscariot, who also b him Mt 10:4 3860
shall be b into the hands of men Mt 17:22 3860
shall be b unto the chief priests Mt 20:18 3860
Son of man is b to be crucified Mt 26:2 3860
man by whom the Son of man is b Mt 26:24 3860
Then Judas, which b him, answered Mt 26:25 3860
the Son of man is b into the Mt 26:45 3860
Now he that b him gave them a Mt 26:48 3860
that I have b the innocent blood Mt 27:4 3860
Judas Iscariot, which also b him Mk 3:19 3860
man by whom the Son of man is b Mk 14:21 3860
the Son of man is b into the Mk 14:41 3860
he that b him had given them a Mk 14:44 3860
ye shall be b both by parents, and Lk 21:16 3860
woe unto that man by whom he is b Lk 22:22 3860
And Judas also, which b him Jn 18:2 3860
And Judas also, which b him Jn 18:5 3860
in which he was b took bread 1Cor 11:23 3860

BETRAYERS
of whom ye have been now the b Acts 7:52 4273

BETRAYEST
b thou the Son of man with a kiss Lk 22:48 3860

BETRAYETH
Then Judas, which had b him Mt 27:3
lo, he that b me is at hand Mk 14:42 3860
the hand of him that b me is with Lk 22:21 3860
Lord, which is he that b thee Jn 21:20 3860

BETROTH
Thou shalt b a wife, and another Deut 28:30 781
I will b thee unto me for ever Hos 2:19 781
yea, I will b thee unto me in Hos 2:19 781
I will even b thee unto me in Hos 2:20 781

BETROTHED
who hath b her to himself, then Ex 21:8 3259
if he have b her unto his son, he Ex 21:9 3259
a man entice a maid that is not b Ex 22:16 781
b to an husband, and not at all Lev 19:20 2778
man is there that hath b a wife Deut 20:7 781
is a virgin be b unto an husband Deut 22:23 781
man find a b damsel in the field Deut 22:25 781
the b damsel cried, and there was Deut 22:27 781
that is a virgin, which is not b Deut 22:28 781

BETTER
It is b that I give her to thee, Gen 29:19 2896
For it had been b for us to serve Ex 14:12 2896
were it not b for us to return Num 14:3 2896
of the grapes of Ephraim b than Judg 8:2 2896
of Shechem, Whether is b for you Judg 9:2 2896
now art thou any thing b than Judg 11:25 2896
is it b for thee to be a priest Judg 18:19 2896
which is b to thee than seven Ruth 4:15 2896
am not I b to thee than ten sons 1Sa 1:8 2896
to obey is b than sacrifice, and 1Sa 15:22 2896
of thine, that is b than thou 1Sa 15:28 2896
there is nothing b for me than 1Sa 27:1 2896
of Hushai the Archite is b than 2Sa 17:14 2896
therefore now it is b that thou 2Sa 18:3 2896
name of Solomon b than thy name 1Kin 1:47 3190
b than he, and slew them with the 1Kin 2:32 2896
for I am not b than my fathers 1Kin 19:4 2896
thee for it a b vineyard than it 1Kin 21:2 2896
b than all the waters of Israel 2Kin 5:12 2896
which were b than thyself 2Chr 21:13 2896
unto another that is b than she Est 1:19 2896
that a righteous man hath is b Ps 37:16 2896
thy lovingkindness is b than life Ps 63:3 2896
b than an ox or bullock that hath Ps 69:31 3190
thy courts is b than a thousand Ps 84:10 2896
It is b to trust in the LORD than Ps 118:8 2896
It is b to trust in the LORD than Ps 118:9 2896
The law of thy mouth is b unto me Ps 119:72 2896
For the merchandise of it is b Prov 3:14 2896
For wisdom is b than rubies Prov 8:11 2896
My fruit is b than gold, yea, Prov 8:19 2896
is b than he that honoureth Prov 12:9 2896
B is little with the fear of the Prov 15:16 2896
B is a dinner of herbs where love Prov 15:17 2896
B is a little with righteousness Prov 16:8 2896
How much b is it to get wisdom Prov 16:16 2896
B it is to be of an humble spirit Prov 16:19 2896
to anger is b than the mighty Prov 16:32 2896
B is a dry morsel, and quietness Prov 17:1 2896
B is the poor that walketh in his Prov 19:1 2896
and a poor man is b than a liar Prov 19:22 2896
It is b to dwell in a corner of Prov 21:9 2896
It is b to dwell in the Prov 21:19 2896
For b it is that it be said unto Prov 25:7 2896
It is b to dwell in the corner of Prov 25:24 2896
Open rebuke is b than secret love Prov 27:5 2896
for b is a neighbour that is near Prov 27:10 2896
B is the poor that walketh in his Prov 28:6 2896
There is nothing b for a man Eccl 2:24 2896
perceive that there is nothing b Eccl 3:22 2896
b is he than both they, which Eccl 4:3 2896
B is an handful with quietness, Eccl 4:6 2896
Two are b than one Eccl 4:9 2896
B is a poor and a wise child than Eccl 4:13 2896
B is it that thou shouldest not Eccl 5:5 2896
an untimely birth is b than he Eccl 6:3 2896
B is the sight of the eyes than Eccl 6:9 2896
vanity, what is man the b Eccl 6:11 3148
A good name is b than precious Eccl 7:1 2896
It is b to go to the house of Eccl 7:2 2896
Sorrow is b than laughter Eccl 7:3 2896
countenance the heart is made b Eccl 7:3 3190
It is b to hear the rebuke of the Eccl 7:5 2896
B is the end of a thing than the Eccl 7:8 2896
is b than the proud in spirit Eccl 7:8 2896
the former days were b than these Eccl 7:10 2896
man hath no b thing under the sun Eccl 8:15 2896
living dog is b than a dead lion Eccl 9:4 2896
Wisdom is b than strength Eccl 9:16 2896
Wisdom is b than weapons of war Eccl 9:18 2896
and a babbler is no b Eccl 10:11 3504
for thy love is b than wine Song 1:2 2896
how much b is thy love than wine Song 4:10 2896
a name b than of sons and of Is 56:5 2896
be slain with the sword are b Lam 4:9 2896
will do b unto you than at your Eze 36:11 2896
times b than all the magicians Dan 1:20 3027
for then was it b with me than Hos 2:7 2896
be they b than these kingdoms Amos 6:2 2896
for it is b for me to die than to Jonah 4:3 2896
It is b for me to die than to Jonah 4:8 2896
Art thou b than populous No, that Nah 3:8 3190
Are ye not much b than they Mt 6:26 1308
much then is a man b than a sheep Mt 12:12 1308
in me, it were b for him that a Mt 18:6 4851
it is b for thee to enter into Mt 18:8 2570
it is b for thee to enter into Mt 18:9 2570
it is b for him that a millstone Mk 9:42
it is b for thee to enter into Mk 9:43 2570
it is b for thee to enter halt Mk 9:45 2570
it is b for thee to enter into Mk 9:47 2570
for he saith, The old is b Lk 5:39 5543
much more are ye b than the fowls Lk 12:24 1308
It were b for him that a Lk 17:2 3081
are we b than they Rom 3:9 4284
for it is b to marry than to burn 1Cor 7:9 2909
her not in marriage doeth b 1Cor 7:38 2573
neither, if we eat, are we the b 1Cor 8:8 4052
for it were b for me to die, than 1Cor 9:15
ye come together not for the b 1Cor 11:17 2909
which is far b Phil 1:23 2909
esteem other b than themselves Phil 2:3 5242
made so much b than the angels Heb 1:4 2909
we are persuaded b things of you Heb 6:9 2909
the less is blessed of the b Heb 7:7 2909
the bringing in of a b hope did Heb 7:19 2909
made a surety of a b testament Heb 7:22 2909
is the mediator of a b covenant Heb 8:6 2909
was established upon b promises Heb 8:6 2909
with b sacrifices than these Heb 9:23 2909
that ye have in heaven a b Heb 10:34 2909
But now they desire a b country Heb 11:16 2909
might obtain a b resurrection Heb 11:35 2909
provided some b thing for us Heb 11:40 2909
that speaketh b things than that Heb 12:24 2909
For it is b, if the will of God 1Pet 3:17 2909
For it had been b for them not to 2Pet 2:21 2909

B

BETTERED
that she had, and was nothing *b* … Mk 5:26 *5623*

BETWEEN
And I will put enmity *b* thee … Gen 3:15 996
woman, and *b* thy seed and her seed … Gen 3:15 996
of the covenant which I make *b* me … Gen 9:12 996
be for a token of a covenant *b* me … Gen 9:13 996
my covenant, which is *b* me … Gen 9:15 996
the everlasting covenant *b* God … Gen 9:16 996
which I have established *b* me … Gen 9:17 996
And Resen *b* Nineveh and Calah … Gen 10:12 996
the beginning, *b* Beth-el and Hai … Gen 13:3 996
there was a strife *b* the herdmen … Gen 13:7 996
b my herdmen and thy herdmen … Gen 13:8 996
lamp that passed *b* those pieces … Gen 15:17 996
the LORD judge *b* me and thee … Gen 16:5 996
behold, it is *b* Kadesh and Bered … Gen 16:14 996
And I will make my covenant *b* me … Gen 17:2 996
I will establish my covenant *b* me … Gen 17:7 996
b me and you and thy seed after … Gen 17:10 996
country, and dwelled *b* Kadesh … Gen 20:1 996
and let it be for a witness *b* me … Gen 31:44 996
said, This heap is a witness *b* me … Gen 31:48 996
for he said, The LORD watch *b* me … Gen 31:49 996
brought them out from *b* his knees … Gen 48:12 5973
nor a lawgiver from *b* his feet … Gen 49:10 996
ass couching down *b* two burdens … Gen 49:14 996
I will put a division *b* my people … Ex 8:23 996
sever *b* the cattle of Israel … Ex 9:4 996
put a difference *b* the Egyptians … Ex 11:7 996
and for a memorial *b* thine eyes … Ex 13:9 996
and for frontlets *b* thine eyes … Ex 13:16 996
b Migdol and the sea, over against … Ex 14:2 996
it came *b* the camp of the … Ex 14:20 996
of Sin, which is *b* Elim and Sinai, … Ex 16:1 996
and I judge *b* one and another, and I … Ex 18:16 996
oath of the LORD be *b* them both … Ex 22:11 996
from *b* the two cherubims which … Ex 25:22 996
divide unto you *b* the holy place … Ex 26:33 996
bells of gold *b* them round about … Ex 28:33 8432
and thou shalt put it *b* the … Ex 30:18 996
for it is a sign *b* me and you … Ex 31:13 996
It is a sign *b* me and the children … Ex 31:17 996
put the bells *b* the pomegranates … Ex 39:25 8432
round about *b* the pomegranates … Ex 39:25 8432
thou shalt set the laver *b* the … Ex 40:7 996
he set the laver *b* the tent of … Ex 40:30 996
that ye may put difference *b* holy … Lev 10:10 996
and unholy, and *b* unclean and clean … Lev 10:10 996
make a difference *b* the unclean … Lev 11:47 996
b the beast that may be eaten and … Lev 11:47 996
put difference *b* clean beasts … Lev 20:25 996
and *b* unclean fowls and clean … Lev 20:25 996
laws, which the LORD made *b* him … Lev 26:46 996
from *b* the two cherubims … Num 7:89 996
the flesh was yet *b* their teeth … Num 11:33 996
they bare it *b* two upon a staff … Num 13:23 996
And he stood *b* the dead and the … Num 16:48 996
of Moab, *b* Moab and the Amorites … Num 21:13 996
thereof be divided *b* many … Num 26:56 996
b a man and his wife, *b* the … Num 30:16 996
b them that took the war upon … Num 31:27 996
battle, and *b* all the congregation … Num 31:27 996
shall judge *b* the slayer and the … Num 35:24 996
b Paran, and Tophel, and Laban, and … Deut 1:1 996
Hear the causes *b* your brethren … Deut 1:16 996
and judge righteously *b* every man … Deut 1:16 996
that day had no knowledge *b* good … Deut 1:39
(I stood *b* the LORD and you at … Deut 5:5 996
be as frontlets *b* thine eyes … Deut 6:8 996
may be as frontlets *b* your eyes … Deut 11:18 996
nor make any baldness *b* your eyes … Deut 14:1 996
b blood and blood, *b* plea and … Deut 17:8 996
b stroke and stroke, being matters … Deut 17:8 996
b whom the controversy is, shall … Deut 19:17
If there be a controversy *b* men … Deut 25:1 996
that cometh out from *b* her feet … Deut 28:57 996
and he shall dwell *b* his shoulders … Deut 33:12 996
Yet there shall be a space *b* you … Josh 3:4 996
abode *b* Beth-el and Ai, on the … Josh 8:9 996
now there was a valley *b* them … Josh 8:11 996
them to lie in ambush *b* Beth-el … Josh 8:12 996
forth *b* the children of Judah … Josh 18:11 996
hath made Jordan a border *b* us … Josh 22:25 996
But that it may be a witness *b* us … Josh 22:27 996
but it is a witness *b* us and you … Josh 22:28 996
witness *b* us that the LORD is God … Josh 22:34 996
the LORD, he put darkness *b* you … Josh 24:7 996
the palm tree of Deborah *b* Ramah … Judg 4:5 996
for there was peace *b* Jabin the … Judg 4:17 996
sent an evil spirit *b* Abimelech … Judg 9:23 996
The LORD be witness *b* us … Judg 11:10 996
this day *b* the children of Israel … Judg 11:27 996
times in the camp of Dan *b* Zorah … Judg 13:25 996
in the midst *b* two tails … Judg 15:4 996
and they set him *b* the pillars … Judg 16:25 996
him up, and buried him *b* Zorah … Judg 16:31 996
sign *b* the men of Israel and the … Judg 20:38 5973
which dwelleth *b* the cherubims … 1Sa 4:4
took a stone, and set it *b* Mizpeh … 1Sa 7:12 996
And there was peace *b* Israel … 1Sa 7:14 996
b the passages, by which Jonathan … 1Sa 14:4 996
And Saul said, Cast lots *b* me … 1Sa 14:42 996
to Judah, and pitched *b* Shochoh … 1Sa 17:1 996
and there was a valley *b* them … 1Sa 17:3 996
a target of brass *b* his shoulders … 1Sa 17:6 996
liveth, there is but a step *b* me … 1Sa 20:3 996
of, behold, the LORD be *b* thee … 1Sa 20:23 996
LORD, saying, The LORD be *b* me … 1Sa 20:42 996
b my seed and thy seed for ever … 1Sa 20:42 996
The LORD judge *b* me and thee, and … 1Sa 24:12 996
therefore be judge, and judge *b* me … 1Sa 24:15 996
a great space being *b* them … 1Sa 26:13 996
was long war *b* the house of Saul … 2Sa 3:1 996
there was war *b* the house of Saul … 2Sa 3:6 996
that dwelleth *b* the cherubims … 2Sa 6:2
and he was taken up *b* the heaven … 2Sa 18:9 996
David sat *b* the two gates … 2Sa 18:24 996
and can I discern *b* good and evil … 2Sa 19:35 996
the LORD's oath that was *b* them … 2Sa 21:7 996
b David and Jonathan the son of … 2Sa 21:7 996
people, that I may discern *b* good … 1Kin 3:9 996
and there was peace *b* Hiram … 1Kin 5:12 996
and the borders were *b* the ledges … 1Kin 7:28 996
that were *b* the ledges were lions … 1Kin 7:29 996
in the clay ground *b* Succoth … 1Kin 7:46 996
And there was war *b* Rehoboam … 1Kin 14:30 996
And there was war *b* Rehoboam … 1Kin 15:6 996
And there was war *b* Abijam … 1Kin 15:7 996
And there was war *b* Asa and Baasha … 1Kin 15:16 996
There is a league *b* me and thee, … 1Kin 15:19 996
b my father and thy father … 1Kin 15:19 996
And there was war *b* Asa and Baasha … 1Kin 15:32 996
So they divided the land *b* them … 1Kin 18:6
How long halt ye *b* two opinions … 1Kin 18:21 5921
and put his face *b* his knees … 1Kin 18:42 996
three years without war *b* Syria … 1Kin 22:1 996
smote the king of Israel *b* the … 1Kin 22:34 996
and smote Jehoram *b* his arms … 2Kin 9:24 996
made a covenant *b* the LORD … 2Kin 11:17 996
b the king also and the people … 2Kin 11:17 996
from *b* the altar and the house of … 2Kin 16:14 996
which dwellest *b* the cherubims … 2Kin 19:15
the way of the gate *b* two walls … 2Kin 25:4 996
that dwelleth *b* the cherubims … 1Chr 13:6
of the LORD stand *b* the earth … 1Chr 21:16 996
in the clay ground *b* Succoth … 2Chr 4:17 996
And there were wars *b* Rehoboam … 2Chr 12:15
And there was war *b* Abijah … 2Chr 13:2 996
There is a league *b* me and thee, … 2Chr 16:3 996
as there was *b* my father … 2Chr 16:3 996
smote the king of Israel *b* the … 2Chr 18:33 996
b blood and blood, *b* law and … 2Chr 19:10 996
And Jehoiada made a covenant *b* him … 2Chr 23:16 996
b all the people, and *b* the … 2Chr 23:16 996
b the going up of the corner unto … Neh 3:32 996
that no air can come *b* them … Job 41:16 996
that dwellest *b* the cherubims … Ps 80:1
he sitteth *b* the cherubims … Ps 99:1
to cease, and parteth *b* the mighty … Prov 18:18 996
Ye made also a ditch *b* the two … Is 22:11 996
that dwellest *b* the cherubims … Is 37:16
iniquities have separated *b* you … Is 59:2 996
execute judgment *b* a man and his … Jer 7:5 996
passed *b* the parts thereof, … Jer 34:18 996
which passed *b* the parts of the … Jer 34:19 996
a true and faithful witness *b* us … Jer 42:5 996
way of the gate *b* the two walls … Jer 52:7 996
overtook her *b* the straits … Lam 1:3 996
set it for a wall of iron *b* thee … Eze 4:3 996
spirit lifted me up *b* the earth … Eze 8:3 996
b the porch and the altar, were … Eze 8:16 996
Go in *b* the wheels, even under … Eze 10:2 996
of fire from *b* the cherubims … Eze 10:2 996
the wheels, from *b* the cherubims … Eze 10:6 996
b the cherubims unto the fire … Eze 10:7 996
the fire that was *b* the cherubims … Eze 10:7 996
hath executed true judgment *b* man … Eze 18:8 996
my sabbaths, to be a sign *b* me … Eze 20:12 996
and they shall be a sign *b* me … Eze 20:20 996
have put no difference *b* the holy … Eze 22:26 996
shewed difference *b* the unclean … Eze 22:26 996
Behold, I judge *b* cattle and … Eze 34:17 996
b the rams and the he goats … Eze 34:17
will judge *b* the fat cattle and … Eze 34:20 996
fat cattle and *b* the lean cattle … Eze 34:20 996
and I will judge *b* cattle and … Eze 34:22 996
b the little chambers were five … Eze 40:7 996
b the chambers was the wideness … Eze 41:10 996
that a palm tree was *b* a cherub … Eze 41:18 996
make a separation *b* the sanctuary … Eze 42:20 996
by my posts, and the wall *b* me … Eze 43:8 996
people the difference *b* the holy … Eze 44:23 996
them to discern *b* the unclean … Eze 44:23 996
which is *b* the border of Damascus … Eze 47:16 996
b the border of Judah and the … Eze 48:22 996
the mouth of it *b* the teeth of it … Dan 7:5 997
had a notable horn *b* his eyes … Dan 8:5 996
a man's voice *b* the banks of Ulai … Dan 8:16 996
the great horn that is *b* his eyes … Dan 8:21 996
b the seas in the glorious holy … Dan 11:45 996
her adulteries from *b* her breasts … Hos 2:2 996
weep *b* the porch and the altar, and … Joel 2:17 996
cannot discern *b* their right hand … Jonah 4:11 996
lifted up the ephah *b* the earth … Zec 5:9 996
chariots out from *b* two mountains … Zec 6:1 996
of peace shall be *b* them both … Zec 6:13 996
his abominations from *b* his teeth … Zec 9:7 996
break the brotherhood *b* Judah … Zec 11:14 996
the LORD hath been witness *b* thee … Mal 2:14 996
discern *b* the righteous and the … Mal 3:18 996
b him that serveth God and him … Mal 3:18 996
go and tell him his fault *b* thee … Mt 18:15 *3342*
whom ye slew *b* the temple … Mt 23:35 *3342*
which perished *b* the altar … Lk 11:51 *3342*
b us and you there is a great gulf … Lk 16:26 *3342*
they were at enmity *b* themselves … Lk 23:12 *4314*
b some of John's disciples … Jn 3:25
Peter was sleeping *b* two soldiers … Acts 12:6 *3342*
And put no difference *b* us … Acts 15:9 *3342*
contention was so sharp *b* them … Acts 15:39
a dissension *b* the Pharisees … Acts 23:7
aside, they talked *b* themselves … Acts 26:31 *4314*
their own bodies *b* themselves … Rom 1:24 *1722*
there is no difference *b* the Jew … Rom 10:12
be able to judge *b* his brethren … 1Cor 6:5
There is difference also *b* a wife … 1Cor 7:34 3307
the middle wall of partition *b* us … Eph 2:14
is one God, and one mediator *b* God … 1Ti 2:5

BETWIXT
be a token of the covenant *b* me … Gen 17:11 996
what is that *b* me and thee … Gen 23:15 996
now an oath *b* us, even *b* us … Gen 26:28 996
set three days' journey *b* himself … Gen 30:36 996
that they may judge *b* us both … Gen 31:37 996
see, God is witness *b* me and thee … Gen 31:50 996
pillar, which I have cast *b* me … Gen 31:51 996
God of their father, judge *b* us … Gen 31:53 996
before me, and put a space *b* drove … Gen 32:16 996
Neither is there any daysman *b* us … Job 9:33 996
shine by the cloud that cometh *b* … Job 36:32 6293
shall lie all night *b* my breasts … Song 1:13 996
I pray you, *b* me and my vineyard … Is 5:3 996
by the gate *b* the two walls … Jer 39:4 996
For I am in a strait *b* two … Phil 1:23 *1537*

BEULAH (*be-u'-lah*) *A name of restored Israel.*
called Hephzi-bah, and thy land *B* … Is 62:4 1166

BEWAIL
b the burning which the LORD hath … Lev 10:6 1058
b her father and her mother a full … Deut 21:13 1058
b my virginity, I and my fellows … Judg 11:37 1058
Therefore I will *b* with the … Is 16:9 1058
that I shall *b* many which have … 2Cor 12:21 *3996*
deliciously with her, shall *b* her … Rev 18:9 *2799*

BEWAILED
and *b* her virginity upon the … Judg 11:38 1058
And all wept, and *b* her … Lk 8:52 *2875*
people, and of women, which also *b* … Lk 23:27 *2875*

BEWAILETH
that *b* herself, that spreadeth … Jer 4:31 3306

BEWARE
B thou that thou bring not my son … Gen 24:6 8104
B of him, and obey his voice, … Ex 23:21 8104
Then *b* lest thou forget the LORD, … Deut 6:12 8104
B that thou forget not the LORD … Deut 8:11 8104
B that there be not a thought in … Deut 15:9 8104
Now therefore *b*, I pray thee, and … Judg 13:4 8104
I said unto the woman let her *b* … Judg 13:13 8104
B that none touch the young man … 2Sa 18:12 8104
B that thou pass not such a place … 2Kin 6:9 8104
b lest he take thee away with his … Job 36:18
a scorner, and the simple will *b* … Prov 19:25 6191
B lest Hezekiah persuade you, … Is 36:18
B of false prophets, which come … Mt 7:15 *4337*
But *b* of men … Mt 10:17 *4337*
b of the leaven of the Pharisees … Mt 16:6 *4337*
that ye should *b* of the leaven of … Mt 16:11 *4337*
them not *b* of the leaven of bread … Mt 16:12 *4337*
b of the leaven of the Pharisees, … Mk 8:15 *991*
B of the scribes, which love to … Mk 12:38 *991*
B ye of the leaven of the … Lk 12:1 *4337*
Take heed, and *b* of covetousness … Lk 12:15 *5442*
B of the scribes, which desire to … Lk 20:46 *4337*
B therefore, lest that come upon … Acts 13:40 *991*
B of dogs, *b* of evil workers … Phil 3:2 *991*
b of the concision … Phil 3:2 *991*
B lest any man spoil you through … Col 2:8 *991*
b lest ye also, being led away … 2Pet 3:17 *5442*

BEWITCHED
b the people of Samaria, giving … Acts 8:9 *1839*
time he had *b* them with sorceries … Acts 8:11 *1839*
foolish Galatians, who hath *b* you … Gal 3:1 *940*

BEWRAY
b not him that wandereth … Is 16:3 1540

BEWRAYETH
of his right hand, which *b* itself … Prov 27:16 7121
he heareth cursing, and *b* it not … Prov 29:24 5046
for thy speech *b* thee … Mt 26:73

BEYOND
spread his tent *b* the tower of … Gen 35:21 1973
of Atad, which is *b* Jordan … Gen 50:10 5676
Abel-mizraim, which is *b* Jordan … Gen 50:11 5676
or if it run *b* the time of her … Lev 15:25 5921
I cannot go *b* the word of the … Num 22:18 5674
I cannot go *b* the commandment of … Num 24:13 5674
your God hath given them *b* Jordan … Deut 3:20 5676
the good land that is *b* Jordan … Deut 3:25 5676
Neither is it *b* the sea, that … Deut 30:13 5676
the Amorites, that were *b* Jordan … Josh 9:10 5676
b Jordan eastward, even as Moses … Josh 13:8 5676
inheritance *b* Jordan on the east … Josh 18:7 5676
passed *b* the quarries, and escaped … Judg 3:26 5674
Gilead abode *b* Jordan … Judg 5:17 5676
Behold, the arrows are *b* thee … 1Sa 20:22 1973
lad ran, he shot an arrow *b* him … 1Sa 20:36 5674
and said, Is not the arrow *b* thee … 1Sa 20:37 1973
the Syrians that were *b* the river … 2Sa 10:16 5676
unto the place that is *b* Jokneam … 1Kin 4:12 5676
and shall scatter them *b* the river … 1Kin 14:15 5676
the Syrians that were *b* the river … 1Chr 19:16 5676
from *b* the sea on this side Syria … 2Chr 20:2 5676
and unto the rest *b* the river … Ezr 4:17 5675
over all countries *b* the river … Ezr 4:20 5675
Tatnai, governor *b* the river, … Ezr 6:6 5675
which are *b* the river, be ye far … Ezr 6:6 5675
even of the tribute *b* the river … Ezr 6:8 5675
treasurers which are *b* the river … Ezr 7:21 5675
the people that are *b* the river … Ezr 7:25 5675
me to the governors *b* the river … Neh 2:7 5676
came to the governors *b* the river … Neh 2:9 5676
from *b* the tower of the furnaces … Neh 12:38 5921
by them *b* the river, by the king … Is 7:20 5676
b Jordan, in Galilee of the … Is 9:1 5676
which is *b* the rivers of Ethiopia … Is 18:1 5676
cast forth *b* the gates of … Jer 22:19 1973
of the isles which are *b* the sea … Jer 25:22 5676

to go into captivity *b* Damascus.......... Amos 5:27 1973
From *b* the rivers of Ethiopia my.......... Zeph 3:10 5676
b Jordan, Galilee of the Gentiles.......... Mt 4:15 *4008*
and from Judaea, and from *b* Jordan.... Mt 4:25 *4008*
the coasts of Judaea *b* Jordan.......... Mt 19:1 *4008*
and from Idumaea, and from *b* Jordan Mk 3:8 *4008*
amazed in themselves *b* measure.......... Mk 6:51
were *b* measure astonished, saying....... Mk 7:37 *5249*
were done in Bethabara *b* Jordan........ Jn 1:28 *4008*
he that was with thee *b* Jordan........ Jn 3:26 *4008*
went away again *b* Jordan into the....... Jn 10:40 *4008*
I will carry you away *b* Babylon........ Acts 7:43 *1900*
b their power they were willing.......... 2Cor 8:3 *5228*
not ourselves *b* our measure.............. 2Cor 10:14 *5239*
the gospel in the regions *b* you.......... 2Cor 10:16 *5238*
how that *b* measure I persecuted.......... Gal 1:13
That no man go *b* and defraud his........ 1Th 4:6 *5233*

BEZAI (*be'-zahee*)
1. A family of exiles.
The children of *B*, three hundred.......... Ezr 2:17 1209
The children of *B*, three hundred.......... Neh 7:23 1209
2. A family who renewed the covenant.
Hodijah, Hashum, *B*,.............................. Neh 10:18 1209

BEZALEEL (*be-zal'-e-el*)
1. A craftsman.
called by name *B* the son of Uri.......... Ex 31:2 1212
called by name *B* the son of Uri.......... Ex 35:30 1212
Then wrought *B* and Aholiab, and........ Ex 36:1 1212
And Moses called *B* and Aholiab, and.. Ex 36:2 1212
B made the ark of shittim wood.......... Ex 37:1 1212
B the son of Uri, the son of Hur,.......... Ex 38:22 1212
And Hur begat Uri, and Uri begat *B*...... 1Chr 2:20 1212
that *B* the son of Uri, the son of.......... 2Chr 1:5 1212
2. Married a foreign wife in exile.
Benaiah, Maaseiah, Mattaniah, *B*.......... Ezr 10:30 1212

BEZALEL See BEZALEEL.

BEZEK (*be'-zek*) See ADONI-BEZEK. *A place in the Jordan valley.*
of them in *B* ten thousand men.......... Judg 1:4 966
And they found Adoni-bezek in *B*.......... Judg 1:5 966
And when he numbered them in *B*.......... 1Sa 11:8 966

BEZER (*be'-zer*)
1. A city of refuge.
B in the wilderness, in the plain.......... Deut 4:43 1221
they assigned *B* in the wilderness.......... Josh 20:8 1221
B with her suburbs, and Jahazah.......... Josh 21:36 1221
B in the wilderness with her.............. 1Chr 6:78 1221
2. A son of Liph.
B, and Hod, and Shamma.................. 1Chr 7:37 1221

BICHRI (*bik'-ri*) *Father of Sheba.*
name was Sheba, the son of *B*.......... 2Sa 20:1 1075
and followed Sheba the son of *B*.......... 2Sa 20:2 1075
son of *B* do us more harm than did...... 2Sa 20:6 1075
pursue after Sheba the son of *B*.......... 2Sa 20:7 1075
pursued after Sheba the son of *B*.......... 2Sa 20:10 1075
pursue after Sheba the son of *B*.......... 2Sa 20:13 1075
Sheba the son of *B* by name.............. 2Sa 20:21 1075
the head of Sheba the son of *B*.......... 2Sa 20:22 1075

BICHRITES See BERITES.

BICRI See BICHRI.

BID
b them that they make them.............. Num 15:38 559
until the day I *b* you shout.............. Josh 6:10 559
B the servant pass on before us,.......... 1Sa 9:27 559
ere thou *b* the people return from.......... 2Sa 2:26 559
riding for me, except I *b* thee.............. 2Kin 4:24 559
if the prophet had *b* thee do some........ 2Kin 5:13 1696
will do all that thou shalt *b* us.......... 2Kin 10:5 559
it the preaching that I *b* thee.............. Jonah 3:2 1696
a sacrifice, he hath *b* his guests.......... Zeph 1:7 6942
b me come unto thee on the water...... Mt 14:28 *2753*
ye shall find, *b* to the marriage.......... Mt 22:9 *2564*
whatsoever they *b* you observe.......... Mt 23:3 *2036*
let me first go *b* them farewell.......... Lk 9:61 *657*
b her therefore that she help me.......... Lk 10:40 *2036*
lest they also *b* thee again.............. Lk 14:12 *479*
that believe not *b* you to a feast.......... 1Cor 10:27 *2564*
house, neither *b* him God speed.......... 2Jn 10 *3004*

BIDDEN
and afterwards they eat that be *b*.......... 1Sa 9:13 7121
place among them that were *b*.......... 1Sa 9:22 7121
for the LORD hath *b* him.............. 2Sa 16:11 559
the angel of the Lord had *b* him.......... Mt 1:24 *4367*
them that were *b* to the wedding.......... Mt 22:3 *2564*
saying, Tell them which are *b*.......... Mt 22:4 *2564*
they which were *b* were not worthy........ Mt 22:8 *2564*
Pharisee which had *b* him saw it.......... Lk 7:39 *2564*
a parable to those which were *b*.......... Lk 14:7 *2564*
When thou art *b* of any man to a.......... Lk 14:8 *2564*
man than thou be *b* of him.............. Lk 14:8 *2564*
But when thou art *b*, go and sit.......... Lk 14:10 *2564*
time to say to them that were *b*.......... Lk 14:17 *2564*
were *b* shall taste of my supper.......... Lk 14:24 *2564*

BIDDETH
For he that *b* him God speed is.......... 2Jn 11 *3004*

BIDDING
son in law, and goeth at thy *b*.......... 1Sa 22:14 4928

BIDKAR (*bid'-kar*) *A captain of Jehu.*
Then said Jehu to *B* his captain.......... 2Kin 9:25 920

BIER
king David himself followed the *b*.......... 2Sa 3:31 4296
And he came and touched the *b*.......... Lk 7:14 *4673*

BIGTHA (*big'-thah*) *A servant of Ahasuerus.*
Mehuman, Biztha, Harbona, *B*.......... Est 1:10 903

BIGTHAN (*big'-than*) See BIGTHANA. *A conspirator against Ahasuerus.*
two of the king's chamberlains, *B*.......... Est 2:21 904

BIGTHANA (*big'-than-ah*) See BIGTHAN. *Same as Bigthan.*
that Mordecai had told of *B*.............. Est 6:2 904

BIGVAI (*big'-vahee*)
1. A family chief with Zerubbabel.
Mordecai, Bilshan, Mizpar, *B*.............. Ezr 2:2 902
Mordecai, Bilshan, Mispereth, *B*.......... Neh 7:7 902
2. A family of exiles with Zerubbabel.
The children of *B*, two thousand.......... Ezr 2:14 902
The children of *B*, two thousand.......... Neh 7:19 902
3. A family of exiles with Ezra.
Of the sons also of *B*.............................. Ezr 8:14 902
4. A family who renewed the covenant.
Adonijah, *B*, Adin,.............................. Neh 10:16 902

BILDAD (*bil'-dad*) *A friend of Job.*
B the Shuhite, and Zophar the.......... Job 2:11 1085
Then answered *B* the Shuhite.............. Job 8:1 1085
Then answered *B* the Shuhite.............. Job 18:1 1085
Then answered *B* the Shuhite.............. Job 25:1 1085
B the Shuhite and Zophar the.............. Job 42:9 1085

BILEAM (*bil'-e-am*) See IBLEAM. *A Levitical city in Manasseh.*
B with her suburbs, for the.............. 1Chr 6:70 1109

BILGAH (*bil'-gah*)
1. A priest during David's time.
The fifteenth to *B*, the sixteenth.......... 1Chr 24:14 1083
2. A priest with Zerubbabel.
Miamin, Maadiah, *B*,.............................. Neh 12:5 1083
Of *B*, Shammua.............................. Neh 12:18 1083

BILGAI (*bil'-gahee*) *A priest with Zerubbabel.*
Maaziah, *B*, Shemaiah.............................. Neh 10:8 1084

BILHAH (*bil'-hah*) See BALAH.
1. Mother of Dan and Naphtali.
B his handmaid to be her maid.......... Gen 29:29 1090
And she said, Behold my maid *B*.......... Gen 30:3 1090
she gave him *B* her handmaid to.......... Gen 30:4 1090
B conceived, and bare Jacob a son........ Gen 30:5 1090
B Rachel's maid conceived again,.......... Gen 30:7 1090
lay with *B* his father's concubine.......... Gen 35:22 1090
And the sons of *B*, Rachel's.............. Gen 35:25 1090
and the lad was with the sons of *B*...... Gen 37:2 1090
These are the sons of *B*, which.......... Gen 46:25 1090
Jezer, and Shallum, the sons of *B*.......... 1Chr 7:13 1090
2. A town in Simeon.
And at *B*, and at Ezem, and at Tolad,.. 1Chr 4:29 1090

BILHAN (*bil'-han*)
1. Son of Ezer.
B, and Zaavan, and Akan.............. Gen 36:27 1092
B, and Zavan, and Jakan.............. 1Chr 1:42 1092
2. Son of Jediael.
also of Jediael; *B*.............................. 1Chr 7:10 1092
and the sons of *B*.............................. 1Chr 7:10 1092

BILL
him write her a *b* of divorcement.......... Deut 24:1 5612
write her a *b* of divorcement, and.......... Deut 24:3 5612
Where is the *b* of your mother's.......... Is 50:1 5612
away, and given her a *b* of divorce........ Jer 3:8 5612
to write a *b* of divorcement.............. Mk 10:4 *975*
And he said unto him, Take thy *b*.......... Lk 16:6 *1121*
And he said unto him, Take thy *b*.......... Lk 16:7 *1121*

BILLOWS
waves and thy *b* are gone over me........ Ps 42:7 1530
all thy *b* and thy waves passed.......... Jonah 2:3 4867

BILSHAN (*bil'-shan*) *A Jewish prince with Zerubbabel.*
Seraiah, Reelaiah, Mordecai, *B*.......... Ezr 2:2 1114
Raamiah, Nahamani, Mordecai, *B*.......... Neh 7:7 1114

BIMHAL (*bim'-hal*) *A son of Japlet.*
Pasach, and *B*, and Ashvath.............. 1Chr 7:33 1118

BIND
they shall *b* the breastplate by.......... Ex 28:28 7405
they did *b* the breastplate by his.......... Ex 39:21 7405
or swear an oath to *b* his soul.......... Num 30:2 631
b herself by a bond, being in her.......... Num 30:3 631
thou shalt *b* them for a sign upon.......... Deut 6:8 7194
b them for a sign upon your hand,.......... Deut 11:18 7194
b up the money in thine hand, and........ Deut 14:25 6887
thou shalt *b* this line of scarlet.......... Josh 2:18 7194
To *b* Samson are we come up, to do.... Judg 15:10 631
him, We are come down to *b* thee.......... Judg 15:12 631
but we will *b* thee fast, and.............. Judg 15:13 631
that we may *b* him to afflict him.......... Judg 16:5 631
If they *b* me with seven green.......... Judg 16:7 631
If they *b* me fast with new ropes.......... Judg 16:11 631
and *b* it as a crown to me.............. Job 31:36 6029
Canst thou *b* the sweet influences.......... Job 38:31 7194
Canst thou *b* the unicorn with his.......... Job 39:10 7194
and *b* their faces in secret.............. Job 40:13 2280
or wilt thou *b* him for thy.............. Job 41:5 7194
To *b* his princes at his pleasure.......... Ps 105:22 631
b the sacrifice with cords, even.......... Ps 118:27 631
To *b* their kings with chains, and.......... Ps 149:8 631
b them about thy neck.............. Prov 3:3 7194
B them continually upon thine.......... Prov 6:21 7194
B them upon thy fingers, write.......... Prov 7:3 7194
B up the testimony, seal the law.......... Is 8:16 6887
b them on thee, as a bride doeth.......... Is 49:18 7194
he hath sent me to *b* up the.............. Is 61:1 2280
that thou shalt *b* a stone to it.......... Jer 51:63 7164
shall *b* thee with them, and thou.......... Eze 3:25 631
number, and *b* them in thy skirts.......... Eze 5:3 6887
b the tire of thine head upon.......... Eze 24:17 2280

healed, to put a roller to *b* it.......... Eze 30:21 2280
will *b* up that which was broken,.......... Eze 34:16 2280
were in his army to *b* Shadrach.......... Dan 3:20 3729
hath smitten, and he will *b* us up.......... Hos 6:1 2280
when they shall *b* themselves in.......... Hos 10:10 631
b the chariot to the swift beast.......... Mic 1:13 7573
except he first *b* the strong man.......... Mt 12:29 *1210*
b them in bundles to burn them.......... Mt 13:30 *1210*
whatsoever thou shalt *b* on earth.......... Mt 16:19 *1210*
Whatsoever ye shall *b* on earth.......... Mt 18:18 *1210*
B him hand and foot, and take him...... Mt 22:13 *1210*
For they *b* heavy burdens and.......... Mt 23:4 *1195*
he will first *b* the strong man.......... Mk 3:27 *1210*
and no man could *b* him, no, not.......... Mk 5:3 *1210*
to *b* all that call on thy name.......... Acts 9:14 *1210*
Gird thyself, and *b* on thy sandals........ Acts 12:8 *5265*
So shall the Jews at Jerusalem *b*.......... Acts 21:11 *1210*

BINDETH
For he maketh sore, and *b* up.......... Job 5:18 2280
He *b* up the waters in his thick.......... Job 26:8 6887
He *b* the floods from overflowing.......... Job 28:11 2280
it *b* me about as the collar of my.......... Job 30:18 247
they cry not when he *b* them.............. Job 36:13 631
nor he that *b* sheaves his bosom.......... Ps 129:7 6014
in heart, and *b* up their wounds.......... Ps 147:3 2280
As he that *b* a stone in a sling,.......... Prov 26:8 6887
in the day that the LORD *b* up the.......... Is 30:26 2280

BINDING
we were *b* sheaves in the field,.......... Gen 37:7 481
B his foal unto the vine, and his.......... Gen 49:11 681
it shall have a *b* of woven work.......... Ex 28:32 8193
every *b* oath to afflict the soul,.......... Num 30:13 632
this way unto the death, *b*.............. Acts 22:4 *1195*

BINEA (*bin'-e-ah*) *A son of Moza.*
And Moza begat *B*.............................. 1Chr 8:37 1150
And Moza begat *B*.............................. 1Chr 9:43 1150

BINNUI (*bin'-nu-ee*)
1. A Levite who returned from exile.
Jeshua, and Noadiah the son of *B*.......... Ezr 8:33 1131
2. A descendant of Pahath-moab.
Mattaniah, Bezaleel, and *B*.............. Ezr 10:30 1131
3. A descendant of Bani.
And Bani, and *B*, Shimei,.............. Ezr 10:38 1131
4. A descendant of Henadad.
After him repaired *B* the son of.......... Neh 3:24 1131
B of the sons of Henadad, Kadmiel........ Neh 10:9 1131
5. A family who returned from exile.
The children of *B*, six hundred.......... Neh 7:15 1131
6. A Levite with Zerubbabel.
Jeshua, *B*, Kadmiel, Sherebiah,.......... Neh 12:8 1131

BIRD
his kind, every *b* of every sort.......... Gen 7:14 6833
As for the living *b*, he shall.............. Lev 14:6 6833
the living *b* in the blood of the.......... Lev 14:6 6833
of the *b* that was killed over the.......... Lev 14:6 6833
shall let the living *b* loose into.......... Lev 14:7 6833
and the scarlet, and the living *b*.......... Lev 14:51 6833
them in the blood of the slain *b*.......... Lev 14:51 6833
the house with the blood of the *b*.......... Lev 14:52 6833
water, and with the living *b*.............. Lev 14:52 6833
b out of the city into the open.......... Lev 14:53 6833
thou play with him as with a *b*.......... Job 41:5 6833
Flee as a *b* to your mountain.......... Ps 11:1 6833
Our soul is escaped as a *b* out of.......... Ps 124:7 6833
is spread in the sight of any *b*.......... Prov 1:17
as a *b* from the hand of the.............. Prov 6:5 6833
as a *b* hasteth to the snare, and.......... Prov 7:23 6833
As the *b* by wandering, as the.......... Prov 26:2 6833
As a *b* that wandereth from her.......... Prov 27:8 6833
for a *b* of the air shall carry.......... Eccl 10:20 5775
rise up at the voice of the *b*.......... Eccl 12:4 6833
as a wandering *b* cast out of the.......... Is 16:2 5775
a ravenous *b* from the east.............. Is 46:11 5861
is unto me as a speckled *b*.............. Jer 12:9 5861
enemies chased me sore, like a *b*.......... Lam 3:52 6833
glory shall fly away like a *b*.......... Hos 9:11 5775
shall tremble as a *b* out of Egypt.......... Hos 11:11 6833
Can a *b* fall in a snare upon the.......... Amos 3:5 6833
of every unclean and hateful *b*.......... Rev 18:2 *3732*

BIRD'S
If a *b* nest chance to be before.......... Deut 22:6 6833

BIRDS
but the *b* divided he not.............. Gen 15:10 6833
the *b* did eat them out of the.......... Gen 40:17 5775
the *b* shall eat thy flesh from.......... Gen 40:19 5775
is to be cleansed two *b* alive.......... Lev 14:4 6833
shall command that one of the *b*.......... Lev 14:5 6833
take to cleanse the house two *b*.......... Lev 14:49 6833
the *b* in an earthen vessel over.......... Lev 14:50 6833
Of all clean *b* ye shall eat.............. Deut 14:11 6833
suffered neither the *b* of the air.......... 2Sa 21:10 5775
Where the *b* make their nests.......... Ps 104:17 6833
as the *b* that are caught in the.......... Eccl 9:12 6833
time of the singing of *b* is come.......... Song 2:12
As *b* flying, so will the LORD of.......... Is 31:5 6833
all the *b* of the heavens were.......... Jer 4:25 5775
As a cage is full of *b*, so are.......... Jer 5:27 5775
the beasts are consumed, and the *b*...... Jer 12:4 5775
the *b* round about are against her........ Jer 12:9 5861
unto the ravenous *b* of every sort.......... Eze 39:4 6833
the *b* of the air have nests.............. Mt 8:20 *4071*
so that the *b* of the air come and.......... Mt 13:32 *4071*
holes, and *b* of the air have nests.......... Lk 9:58 *4071*
like to corruptible man, and to *b*.......... Rom 1:23 *4071*
of fishes, and another of *b*.............. 1Cor 15:39 *4421*
For every kind of beasts, and of *b*........ Jas 3:7 *4071*

BIRDS'
and his nails like b claws Dan 4:33 6853

BIRSHA (*bur'-shah*) *A king of Gomorrah.*
with B king of Gomorrah, Shinab Gen 14:2 1306

BIRTH
other stone, according to their b Ex 28:10 8435
the children are come to the b 2Kin 19:3 4866
hidden untimely b I had not been Job 3:16 5309
like the untimely b of a woman Ps 58:8 5309
that an untimely b is better than Eccl 6:3 5309
of death than the day of one's b Eccl 7:1 3205
the children are come to the b Is 37:3 4866
Shall I bring to the b, and not Is 66:9 7665
Thy b and thy nativity is of the Eze 16:3 4351
fly away like a bird, from the b Hos 9:11 3205
Now the b of Jesus Christ was on Mt 1:18 *1083*
and many shall rejoice at his b Lk 1:14 *1083*
a man which was blind from his b Jn 9:1 *1079*
of whom I travail in b again Gal 4:19 *5605*
with child cried, travailing in b Rev 12:2 *5605*

BIRTHDAY
third day, which was Pharaoh's b Gen 40:20
But when Herod's b was kept Mt 14:6 *1077*
that Herod on his b made a supper Mk 6:21 *1077*

BIRTHRIGHT
said, Sell me this day thy b Gen 25:31 1062
what profit shall this b do to me Gen 25:32 1062
and he sold his b unto Jacob Gen 25:33 1062
thus Esau despised his b Gen 25:34 1062
he took away my b Gen 27:36 1062
the firstborn according to his b Gen 43:33 1062
his b was given unto the sons of 1Chr 5:1 1062
is not to be reckoned after the b 1Chr 5:1 1062
but the b was Joseph's 1Chr 5:2 1062
for one morsel of meat sold his b Heb 12:16 *4415*

BIRZAITH See BIRZAVITH.

BIRZAVITH (*bur'za-vith*) *A descendant of Asher.*
Malchiel, who is the father of B 1Chr 7:31 1269

BISHLAM (*bish'-lam*) *A commissioner of Artaxerxes.*
in the days of Artaxerxes wrote B Ezr 4:7 1312

BISHOP
If a man desire the office of a b 1Ti 3:1 *1984*
A b then must be blameless, the 1Ti 3:2 *1985*
ordained the first b of the 2Ti s *1985*
For a b must be blameless, as the Titus 1:7 *1985*
ordained the first b of the Titus s *1985*
the Shepherd and B of your souls 1Pet 2:25 *1985*

BISHOPRICK
and his b let another take Acts 1:20 *1984*

BISHOPS
which are at Philippi, with the b Phil 1:1 *1985*

BIT
the people, and they b the people Num 21:6 5391
mouth must be held in with b Ps 32:9 4964
on the wall, and a serpent b him Amos 5:19 5391

BITE
an hedge, a serpent shall b him Eccl 10:8 5391
will b without enchantment Eccl 10:11 5391
be charmed, and they shall b you Jer 8:17 5391
the serpent, and he shall b them Amos 9:3 5391
that b with their teeth, and cry, Mic 3:5 5391
up suddenly that shall b thee Hab 2:7 5391
But if ye b and devour one another Gal 5:15 *1143*

BITETH
that b the horse heels, so that Gen 49:17 5391
At the last it b like a serpent Prov 23:32 5391

BITHIA See BITHIAH.

BITHIAH (*bith-i'-ah*) *Daughter of Pharaoh.*
these are the sons of B the 1Chr 4:18 1332

BITHRON (*bith'-ron*) *A district in Arabah.*
Jordan, and went through all B 2Sa 2:29 1338

BITHYNIA (*bith-in'-e-ah*) *A Roman province in Asia Minor.*
Mysia, they assayed to go into B Acts 16:7 *978*
Galatia, Cappadocia, Asia, and B 1Pet 1:1 *978*

BITS
we put b in the horses' mouths, Jas 3:3 *5469*

BITTEN
to pass, that every one that is b Num 21:8 5391
that if a serpent had b any man Num 21:9 5391

BITTER
with a great and exceeding b cry Gen 27:34 4751
their lives b with hard bondage Ex 1:14 4843
with b herbs they shall eat it Ex 12:8 4844
waters of Marah, for they were b Ex 15:23 4751
shall have in his hand the b Num 5:18 4751
be thou free from this b water Num 5:19 4751
blot them out with the b water Num 5:23 4751
b water that causeth the curse Num 5:24 4751
shall enter into her, and become b Num 5:24 4751
shall enter into her, and become b Num 5:27 4751
with unleavened bread and b herbs Num 9:11 4844
heat, and with b destruction Deut 32:24 4815
of gall, their clusters are b Deut 32:32 4846
of Israel, that it was very b 2Kin 14:26 4784
and cried with a loud and a b cry Est 4:1 4751
and life unto the b in soul Job 3:20 4751
For thou writest b things against Job 13:26 4846
Even to day is my complaint b Job 23:2 4805
shoot their arrows, even b words Ps 64:3 4751
But her end is b as wormwood Prov 5:4 4751
soul every b thing is sweet Prov 27:7 4751
I find more b than death the Eccl 7:26 4751
b for sweet, and sweet for b Is 5:20 4751
shall be b to them that drink it Is 24:9 4843
see that it is an evil thing and b Jer 2:19 4751
thy wickedness, because it is b Jer 4:18 4751
an only son, most b lamentation Jer 6:26 8563
Ramah, lamentation, and b weeping Jer 31:15 8563
bitterness of heart and b wailing Eze 27:31 4751
and the end thereof as a b day Amos 8:10 4751
I raise up the Chaldeans, that b Hab 1:6 4751
wives, and be not b against them Col 3:19 *4087*
the same place sweet water and b Jas 3:11 *4089*
But if ye have b envying and Jas 3:14 *4089*
waters, because they were made b Rev 8:11 *4087*
and it shall make thy belly b Rev 10:9 *4087*
as I had eaten it, my belly was b Rev 10:10 *4087*

BITTERLY
curse ye b the inhabitants Judg 5:23 779
hath dealt very b with me Ruth 1:20 4843
I will weep b, labour not to Is 22:4 4843
ambassadors of peace shall weep b Is 33:7 4751
against thee, and shall cry b Eze 27:30 4751
provoked him to anger most b Hos 12:14 8563
the mighty man shall cry there b Zeph 1:14 4751
And he went out, and wept b Mt 26:75 *4090*
And Peter went out, and wept b Lk 22:62 *4090*

BITTERN
make it a possession for the b Is 14:23 7090
and the b shall possess it Is 34:11 7090
the b shall lodge in the upper Zeph 2:14 7090

BITTERNESS
And she was in b of soul, and 1Sa 1:10 4751
Surely the b of death is past 1Sa 15:32 4751
it will be b in the latter end 2Sa 2:26 4751
will complain in the b of my soul Job 7:11 4751
my breath, but filleth me with b Job 9:18 4472
I will speak in the b of my soul Job 10:1 4751
dieth in the b of his soul Job 21:25 4751
The heart knoweth his own b Prov 14:10 4751
father, and b to her that bare him Prov 17:25 4470
all my years in the b of my soul Is 38:15 4751
Behold, for peace I had great b Is 38:17 4843
are afflicted, and she is in b Lam 1:4 4843
He hath filled me with b, he hath Lam 3:15 4844
and took me away, and I went in b Eze 3:14 4751
with b sigh before their eyes Eze 21:6 4814
weep for thee with b of heart Eze 27:31 4751
son, and shall be in b for him Zec 12:10 4843
that is in b for his firstborn Zec 12:10 4843
that thou art in the gall of b Acts 8:23 *4088*
mouth is full of cursing and b Rom 3:14 *4088*
Let all b, and wrath, and anger, and Eph 4:31 *4088*
lest any root of b springing up Heb 12:15 *4088*

BIZIOTHIAH See BIZJOTHJAH.

BIZJOTHJAH (*biz-joth'-jah*) *A town in Judah.*
Hazar-shual, and Beer-sheba, and B Josh 15:28 964

BIZTHA (*biz'-thah*) *An eunuch of Ahasuerus.*
wine, he commanded Mehuman, B Est 1:10 968

BLACK
and that there is no b hair in it Lev 13:31 7838
that there is b hair grown up Lev 13:37 7838
that the heaven was b with clouds 1Kin 18:45 6937
of red, and blue, and white, and b Est 1:6 5508
My skin is b upon me, and my bones Job 30:30 7835
in the evening, in the b Prov 7:9 380
I am b, but comely, O ye Song 1:5 7838
Look not upon me, because I am b Song 1:6 7840
locks are bushy, and b as a raven Song 5:11 7838
mourn, and the heavens above be b Jer 4:28 6937
I am b Jer 8:21 6937
they are b unto the ground Jer 14:2 6937
Our skin was b like an oven Lam 5:10 3648
and in the second chariot b horses Zec 6:2 7838
The b horses which are therein go Zec 6:6 7838
not make one hair white or b Mt 5:36 *3189*
And I beheld, and lo a b horse Rev 6:5 *3189*
the sun became b as sackcloth of Rev 6:12 *3189*

BLACKER
Their visage is b than a coal Lam 4:8 2821

BLACKISH
Which are b by reason of the ice, Job 6:16 6937

BLACKNESS
let the b of the day terrify it Job 3:5 3650
I clothe the heavens with b Is 50:3 6940
all faces shall gather b Joel 2:6 6289
and the faces of them all gather b Nah 2:10 6289
that burned with fire, nor unto b Heb 12:18 *1105*
the b of darkness for ever Jude 13 *2217*

BLADE
the haft also went in after the b Judg 3:22 3851
and the fat closed upon the b Judg 3:22 3851
mine arm fall from my shoulder b Job 31:22 7929
But when the b was sprung up, and Mt 13:26 *5528*
first the b, then the ear, after Mk 4:28 *5528*

BLAINS
breaking forth with b upon man Ex 9:9 76
breaking forth with b upon man Ex 9:10 76

BLAME
then let me bear the b for ever Gen 43:9 2398
bear the b to my father for ever Gen 44:32 2398
that no man should b us in this 2Cor 8:20 *3469*
without b before him in love Eph 1:4 *299*

BLAMED
thing, that the ministry be not b 2Cor 6:3 *3469*
the face, because he was to be b Gal 2:11 *2607*

BLAMELESS
and ye shall be b Gen 44:10 5355
We will be b of this thine oath Josh 2:17 5355
Now shall I be more b than the Judg 15:3 5352
profane the sabbath, and are b Mt 12:5 *338*
and ordinances of the Lord b Lk 1:6 *273*
that ye may be b in the day of 1Cor 1:8 *410*
That ye may be b and harmless, the Phil 2:15 *273*
which is in the law, b Phil 3:6 *273*
body be preserved b unto the 1Th 5:23 *274*
A bishop then must be b, the 1Ti 3:2 *483*
office of a deacon, being found b 1Ti 3:10 *410*
in charge, that they may be b 1Ti 5:7 *483*
If any be b, the husband of one Titus 1:6 *410*
For a bishop must be b, as the Titus 1:7 *410*
him in peace, without spot, and b 2Pet 3:14 *298*

BLASPHEME
to the enemies of the LORD to b 2Sa 12:14 5006
him, saying, Thou didst b God 1Kin 21:10 1288
people, saying, Naboth did b God 1Kin 21:13 1288
shall the enemy b thy name for Ps 74:10 5006
wherewith soever they shall b Mk 3:28 *987*
But he that shall b against the Mk 3:29 *987*
synagogue, and compelled them to b Acts 26:11 *987*
that they may learn not to b 1Ti 1:20 *987*
Do not they b that worthy name by Jas 2:7 *987*
to b his name, and his tabernacle, Rev 13:6 *987*

BLASPHEMED
son b the name of the LORD Lev 24:11 5344
of the king of Assyria have b me 2Kin 19:6 1442
Whom hast thou reproached and b 2Kin 19:22 1442
foolish people have b thy name Ps 74:18 5006
of the king of Assyria have b me Is 37:6 1442
Whom hast thou reproached and b Is 37:23 1442
name continually every day is b Is 52:5 5006
mountains, and b me upon the hills Is 65:7 2778
in this your fathers have b me Eze 20:27 1442
they opposed themselves, and b Acts 18:6 *987*
For the name of God is b among Rom 2:24 *987*
of God and his doctrine be not b 1Ti 6:1 *987*
that the word of God be not b Titus 2:5 *987*
b the name of God, which hath Rev 16:9 *987*
b the God of heaven because of Rev 16:11 *987*
men b God because of the plague Rev 16:21 *987*

BLASPHEMER
Who was before a b, and a 1Ti 1:13 *989*

BLASPHEMERS
nor yet b of your goddess Acts 19:37 *987*
covetous, boasters, proud, b 2Ti 3:2 *989*

BLASPHEMEST
and sent into the world, Thou b Jn 10:36 *987*

BLASPHEMETH
he that b the name of the LORD, Lev 24:16 5344
when he b the name of the LORD, Lev 24:16 5344
of him that reproacheth and b Ps 44:16 1442
within themselves, This man b Mt 9:3 *987*
but unto him that b against the Lk 12:10 *987*

BLASPHEMIES
that I have heard all thy b which Eze 35:12 5007
thefts, false witness, b Mt 15:19 *988*
Why doth this man thus speak b Mk 2:7 *988*
b wherewith soever they shall Mk 3:28 *988*
Who is this which speaketh b Lk 5:21 *988*
mouth speaking great things and b Rev 13:5 *988*

BLASPHEMING
by Paul, contradicting and b Acts 13:45 *987*

BLASPHEMOUS
him speak b words against Moses Acts 6:11 *989*
b words against this holy place Acts 6:13 *989*

BLASPHEMOUSLY
many other things b spake they Lk 22:65 *987*

BLASPHEMY
of trouble, and of rebuke, and b 2Kin 19:3 5007
of trouble, and of rebuke, and of b Is 37:3 5007
b shall be forgiven unto men Mt 12:31 *988*
but the b against the Holy Ghost Mt 12:31 *988*
clothes, saying, He hath spoken b Mt 26:65 *987*
behold, now ye have heard his b Mt 26:65 *988*
lasciviousness, an evil eye, b Mk 7:22 *988*
Ye have heard the b Mk 14:64 *988*
stone thee not; but for b Jn 10:33 *988*
anger, wrath, malice, b, filthy Col 3:8 *988*
I know the b of them which say Rev 2:9 *988*
and upon his heads the name of b Rev 13:1 *988*
opened his mouth in b against God Rev 13:6 *988*
beast, full of names of b Rev 17:3 *988*

BLAST
with the b of thy nostrils the Ex 15:8 7307
make a long b with the ram's horn Josh 6:5
at the b of the breath of his 2Sa 22:16 5397
Behold, I will send a b upon him 2Kin 19:7 7307
By the b of God they perish, and Job 4:9 5397
at the b of the breath of thy Ps 18:15 5397
when the b of the terrible ones Is 25:4 7307
Behold, I will send a b upon him Is 37:7 7307

BLASTED
b with the east wind sprung up Gen 41:6 7710
b with the east wind, sprung up Gen 41:23 7710
the seven empty ears b with the Gen 41:27 7710
as corn b before it be grown up 2Kin 19:26 7711
as corn b before it be grown up Is 37:27 7709

BLASTING
and with the sword, and with b Deut 28:22 7711
famine, if there be pestilence, b 1Kin 8:37 7711
be pestilence, if there be b 2Chr 6:28 7711
I have smitten you with b Amos 4:9 7711
I smote you with b and with mildew Hag 2:17 7711

BLASTUS (*blas'-tus*) *A servant of Herod Agrippa I.*
him, and, having made *B* the king's...... Acts 12:20 *986*

BLAZE
to *b* abroad the matter, insomuch......... Mk 1:45 *1310*

BLEATING
What meaneth then this *b* of the.......... 1Sa 15:14 6963

BLEATINGS
to hear the *b* of the flocks..................... Judg 5:16 8292

BLEMISH
Your lamb shall be without *b*................ Ex 12:5 8549
bullock, and two rams without *b*........... Ex 29:1 8549
let him offer a male without *b*............... Lev 1:3 8549
shall bring it a male without *b*............... Lev 1:10 8549
it without *b* before the LORD.................. Lev 3:1 8549
he shall offer it without *b*...................... Lev 3:6 8549
without *b* unto the LORD for a sin .... Lev 4:3 8549
of the goats, a male without *b*.............. Lev 4:23 8549
of the goats, a female without *b*........... Lev 4:28 8549
shall bring it a female without *b*.......... Lev 4:32 8549
a ram without *b* out of the flocks......... Lev 5:15 8549
a ram without *b* out of the flock........... Lev 5:18 8549
a ram without *b* out of the flock,.......... Lev 6:6 8549
for a burnt offering, without *b*.............. Lev 9:2 8549
both of the first year, without *b*........... Lev 9:3 8549
shall take two he lambs without *b*........ Lev 14:10 8549
lamb of the first year without *b*............ Lev 14:10 8549
their generations that hath any *b*.......... Lev 21:17 3971
man he be that hath a *b*, he shall .... Lev 21:18 3971
or that hath a *b* in his eye .... Lev 21:20 8400
No man that hath a *b* of the seed.......... Lev 21:21 3971
he hath a *b*.. Lev 21:21 3971
the altar, because he hath a *b*............... Lev 21:23 3971
at your own will a male without *b*........ Lev 22:19 8549
But whatsoever hath a *b*, that .... Lev 22:20 3971
there shall be no *b* therein .... Lev 22:21 3971
the sheaf an he lamb without *b* of........ Lev 23:12 8549
lambs without *b* of the first year.......... Lev 23:18 8549
a man cause a *b* in his neighbour.......... Lev 24:19 3971
as he hath caused a *b* in a man............ Lev 24:20 3971
without *b* for a burnt offering.............. Num 6:14 8549
year without *b* for a sin offering........... Num 6:14 8549
one ram without *b* for peace.................. Num 6:14 8549
without spot, wherein is no *b*................. Num 19:2 3971
they shall be unto you without *b*.......... Num 28:19 8549
they shall be unto you without *b*)......... Num 28:31 8549
lambs of the first year without *b*.......... Num 29:2 8549
they shall be unto you without *b*.......... Num 29:8 8549
they shall be without *b*........................... Num 29:13 8549
lambs of the first year without *b*.......... Num 29:20 8549
lambs of the first year without *b*.......... Num 29:23 8549
lambs of the first year without *b*.......... Num 29:29 8549
lambs of the first year without *b*.......... Num 29:32 8549
lambs of the first year without *b*.......... Num 29:36 8549
And if there be any *b* therein.............. Deut 15:21 3971
lame, or blind, or have any ill *b*.......... Deut 15:21 3971
bullock, or sheep, wherein is *b*............. Deut 17:1 3971
of his head there was no *b* in him......... 2Sa 14:25 3971
without *b* for a sin offering................... Eze 43:22 8549
offer a young bullock without *b*............ Eze 43:23 8549
a ram out of the flock without *b*........... Eze 43:23 8549
a ram out of the flock, without *b*.......... Eze 43:25 8549
take a young bullock without *b*.............. Eze 45:18 8549
seven rams without *b* daily the.............. Eze 45:23 8549
day shall be six lambs without *b*........... Eze 46:4 8549
b, and a ram without *b*........................ Eze 46:4 8549
be a young bullock without *b*................ Eze 46:6 8549
they shall be without *b*........................... Eze 46:6 8549
lamb of the first year without *b*............ Eze 46:13 8549
Children in whom was no *b*..................... Dan 1:4 3971
it should be holy and without *b*............... Eph 5:27 *299*
of Christ, as of a lamb without *b*.......... 1Pet 1:19 *299*

BLEMISHES
is in them, and *b* be in them................... Lev 22:25 3971
Spots they are and *b*, sporting 2Pet 2:13 *3470*

BLESS
a great nation, and I will *b* thee.............. Gen 12:2 1288
And I will *b* them that *b* thee................. Gen 12:3 1288
And I will *b* her, and give thee a........... Gen 17:16 1288
yea, I will *b* her, and she shall .... Gen 17:16 1288
That in blessing I will *b* thee.................. Gen 22:17 1288
will be with thee, and will *b* thee.......... Gen 26:3 1288
I am with thee, and will *b* thee.............. Gen 26:24 1288
that my soul may *b* thee before I........... Gen 27:4 1288
b thee before the LORD before my........... Gen 27:7 1288
that he may *b* thee before his................. Gen 27:10 1288
venison, that thy soul may *b* me............ Gen 27:19 1288
venison, that my soul may *b* thee........... Gen 27:25 1288
venison, that thy soul may *b* me............ Gen 27:31 1288
B me, even me also, O my father............ Gen 27:34 1288
b me, even me also, O my father............ Gen 27:38 1288
And God Almighty *b* thee, and make........ Gen 28:3 1288
not let thee go, except thou *b* me........... Gen 32:26 1288
thee, unto me, and I will *b* them........... Gen 48:9 1288
me from all evil, *b* the lads.................... Gen 48:16 1288
saying, In thee shall Israel *b*................. Gen 48:20 1288
who shall *b* thee with blessings............ Gen 49:25 1288
and *b* me also.. Ex 12:32 1288
come unto thee, and I will *b* thee.......... Ex 20:24 1288
he shall *b* thy bread, and thy................. Ex 23:25 1288
On this wise ye shall *b* the.................... Num 6:23 1288
The LORD *b* thee, and keep thee............. Num 6:24 1288
and I will *b* them................................... Num 6:27 1288
I have received commandment to *b*......... Num 23:20 1288
them at all, nor *b* them at all................ Num 23:25 1288
it pleased the LORD to *b* Israel............... Num 24:1 1288
b you, as he hath promised you............. Deut 1:11 1288
thee, and *b* thee, and multiply thee........ Deut 7:13 1288
he will also *b* the fruit of thy................ Deut 7:13 1288
then thou shalt *b* the LORD thy.............. Deut 8:10 1288
to *b* in his name, unto this day.............. Deut 10:8 1288
that the LORD thy God may *b* thee.......... Deut 14:29 1288
for the LORD shall greatly *b* thee............ Deut 15:4 1288
God shall *b* thee in all thy works........... Deut 15:10 1288
the LORD thy God shall *b* thee in........... Deut 15:18 1288
b thee in all thine increase..................... Deut 16:15 1288
to *b* in the name of the LORD................. Deut 21:5 1288
that the LORD thy God may *b* thee.......... Deut 23:20 1288
in his own raiment, and *b* thee.............. Deut 24:13 1288
that the LORD thy God may *b* thee.......... Deut 24:19 1288
b thy people Israel, and the land............ Deut 26:15 1288
mount Gerizim to *b* the people................ Deut 27:12 1288
he shall *b* thee in the land which........... Deut 28:8 1288
to *b* all the work of thine hand.............. Deut 28:12 1288
that he *b* himself in his heart,................ Deut 29:19 1288
the LORD thy God shall *b* thee in .... Deut 30:16 1288
B, LORD, his substance, and accept .... Deut 33:11 1288
that they should *b* the people of............ Josh 8:33 1288
B ye the LORD... Judg 5:9 1288
answered him, The LORD *b* thee.............. Ruth 2:4 1288
because he doth *b* the sacrifice.............. 1Sa 9:13 1288
David returned to *b* his household.......... 2Sa 6:20 1288
to *b* the house of thy servant................. 2Sa 7:29 1288
to *b* him, because he had fought............. 2Sa 8:10 1288
that ye may *b* the inheritance of............ 2Sa 21:3 1288
came to *b* our lord king David............... 1Kin 1:47 1288
Oh that thou wouldest *b* me indeed........ 1Chr 4:10 1288
and David returned to *b* his house.......... 1Chr 16:43 1288
to *b* the house of thy servant................. 1Chr 17:27 1288
to *b* in his name for ever...................... 1Chr 23:13 1288
Now *b* the LORD your God...................... 1Chr 29:20 1288
b the LORD your God for ever and........... Neh 9:5 1288
thou, LORD, wilt *b* the righteous............. Ps 5:12 1288
I will *b* the LORD, who hath given .... Ps 16:7 1288
congregations will I *b* the LORD............. Ps 26:12 1288
people, and *b* thine inheritance.............. Ps 28:9 1288
the LORD will *b* his people with .... Ps 29:11 1288
I will *b* the LORD at all times................. Ps 34:1 1288
they *b* with their mouth, but they .... Ps 62:4 1288
Thus will I *b* thee while I live................ Ps 63:4 1288
O *b* our God, ye people, and make.......... Ps 66:8 1288
God be merciful unto us, and *b* us......... Ps 67:1 1288
God, even our own God, shall *b* us........ Ps 67:6 1288
God shall *b* us .... Ps 67:7 1288
B ye God in the congregations,............... Ps 68:26 1288
Sing unto the LORD, *b* his name............. Ps 96:2 1288
thankful unto him, and *b* his name .... Ps 100:4 1288
B the LORD, O my soul.......................... Ps 103:1 1288
is within me, *b* his holy name .... Ps 103:1
B the LORD, O my soul, and forget......... Ps 103:2 1288
B the LORD, ye his angels, that............. Ps 103:20 1288
B ye the LORD, all ye his hosts............... Ps 103:21 1288
B the LORD, all his works in all............ Ps 103:22 1288
b the LORD, O my soul........................... Ps 103:22 1288
B the LORD, O my soul........................... Ps 104:1 1288
B thou the LORD, O my soul................... Ps 104:35 1288
Let them curse, but *b* thou.................... Ps 109:28 1288
he will *b* us.. Ps 115:12 1288
he will *b* the house of Israel .... Ps 115:12 1288
he will *b* the house of Aaron................. Ps 115:12 1288
He will *b* them that fear the LORD......... Ps 115:13 1288
But we will *b* the LORD from this........... Ps 115:18 1288
The LORD shall *b* thee out of Zion......... Ps 128:5 1288
we *b* you in the name of the LORD .... Ps 129:8 1288
I will abundantly *b* her provision.......... Ps 132:15 1288
b ye the LORD, all ye servants of............ Ps 134:1 1288
in the sanctuary, and *b* the LORD........... Ps 134:2 1288
and earth *b* thee out of Zion................. Ps 134:3 1288
B the LORD, O house of Israel .... Ps 135:19 1288
b the LORD, O house of Aaron............... Ps 135:19 1288
B the LORD, O house of Levi.................. Ps 135:20 1288
ye that fear the LORD, *b* the LORD.......... Ps 135:20 1288
I will *b* thy name for ever and.............. Ps 145:1 1288
Every day will I *b* thee........................... Ps 145:2 1288
and thy saints shall *b* thee..................... Ps 145:10 1288
let all flesh *b* his holy name for .... Ps 145:21 1288
and doth not *b* their mother................... Prov 30:11 1288
Whom the LORD of hosts shall *b*............. Is 19:25 1288
himself in the earth shall *b*.................... Is 65:16 1288
nations shall *b* themselves in him .... Jer 4:2 1288
The LORD *b* thee, O habitation of.......... Jer 31:23 1288
from this day will I *b* you..................... Hag 2:19 1288
b them that curse you, do good to......... Mt 5:44 *2127*
B them that curse you, and pray .... Lk 6:28 *2127*
his Son Jesus, sent him to *b* you............ Acts 3:26 *2127*
B them which persecute you.................. Rom 12:14 *2127*
b, and curse not...................................... Rom 12:14 *2127*
being reviled, we *b*................................ 1Cor 4:12 *2127*
The cup of blessing which we *b*.............. 1Cor 10:16 *2127*
when thou shalt *b* with the spirit............ 1Cor 14:16 *2127*
Surely blessing I will *b* thee................... Heb 6:14 *2127*
Therewith *b* we God, even the................ Jas 3:9 *2127*

BLESSED
God *b* them, saying, Be fruitful,.............. Gen 1:22 1288
God *b* them, and God said unto them...... Gen 1:28 1288
God *b* the seventh day, and.................... Gen 2:3 1288
b them, and called their name Adam....... Gen 5:2 1288
God *b* Noah and his sons, and said......... Gen 9:1 1288
B be the LORD God of Shem .... Gen 9:26 1288
all families of the earth be *b*.................. Gen 12:3 1288
he *b* him, and said................................. Gen 14:19 1288
B be Abram of the most high God,......... Gen 14:19 1288
b be the most high God, which.............. Gen 14:20 1288
Behold, I have *b* him, and will.............. Gen 17:20 1288
of the earth shall be *b* in him................ Gen 18:18 1288
all the nations of the earth be *b*............. Gen 22:18 1288
the LORD had *b* Abraham in all.............. Gen 24:1 1288
B be the LORD God of my master............ Gen 24:27 1288
said, Come in, thou *b* of the LORD......... Gen 24:31 1288
the LORD hath *b* my master greatly......... Gen 24:35 1288
b the LORD God of my master................. Gen 24:48 1288
they *b* Rebekah, and said unto her,......... Gen 24:60 1288
Abraham, that God *b* his son Isaac......... Gen 25:11 1288
all the nations of the earth be *b*............. Gen 26:4 1288
and the LORD *b* him................................ Gen 26:12 1288
thou art now the *b* of the LORD.............. Gen 26:29 1288
so he *b* him... Gen 27:23 1288
b him, and said, See, the smell of........... Gen 27:27 1288
of a field which the LORD hath *b*............. Gen 27:27 1288
b be he that blesseth thee....................... Gen 27:29 1288
before thou camest, and have *b* him........ Gen 27:33 1288
yea, and he shall be *b*.............................. Gen 27:33 1288
wherewith his father *b* him..................... Gen 27:41 1288
b him, and charged him, and said .... Gen 28:1 1288
Esau saw that Isaac had *b* Jacob .... Gen 28:6 1288
that as he *b* him he gave him a.............. Gen 28:6 1288
the families of the earth be *b* .... Gen 28:14 1288
for the daughters will call me *b*............... Gen 30:13 833
the LORD hath *b* me for thy sake............ Gen 30:27 1288
the LORD hath *b* thee since my............... Gen 30:30 1288
sons and his daughters, and *b* them........ Gen 31:55 1288
And he *b* him there................................. Gen 32:29 1288
came out of Padan-aram, and *b* him........ Gen 35:9 1288
that the LORD *b* the Egyptian's............... Gen 39:5 1288
and Jacob *b* Pharaoh.............................. Gen 47:7 1288
Jacob *b* Pharaoh, and went out from....... Gen 47:10 1288
in the land of Canaan, and *b* me,............ Gen 48:3 1288
he *b* Joseph, and said, God, before......... Gen 48:15 1288
he *b* them that day, saying, In................ Gen 48:20 1288
father spake unto them, and *b* them........ Gen 49:28 1288
to his blessing he *b* them........................ Gen 49:28 1288
B be the LORD, who hath delivered......... Ex 18:10 1288
the LORD *b* the sabbath day.................... Ex 20:11 1288
and Moses *b* them.................................. Ex 39:43 1288
b them, and came down from .... Lev 9:22 1288
and came out, and *b* the people.............. Lev 9:23 1288
that he whom thou blessest is *b*............... Num 22:6 1288
for they are *b*... Num 22:12 1288
thou hast *b* them altogether.................... Num 23:11 1288
and he hath *b*.. Num 23:20 1288
B is he that blesseth thee, and.............. Num 24:9 1288
thou hast altogether *b* them these........... Num 24:10 1288
For the LORD thy God hath *b* thee.......... Deut 2:7 1288
Thou shalt be *b* above all people............ Deut 7:14 1288
the LORD thy God hath *b* thee................ Deut 12:7 1288
when the LORD thy God hath *b* thee........ Deut 14:24 1288
b thee thou shalt give unto him.............. Deut 15:14 1288
as the LORD thy God hath *b* thee............ Deut 16:10 1288
B shalt thou be in the city, and .... Deut 28:3 1288
b shalt thou be in the field..................... Deut 28:3 1288
B shall be the fruit of thy body,............ Deut 28:4 1288
B shall be thy basket and thy................. Deut 28:5 1288
B shalt thou be when thou comest .... Deut 28:6 1288
b shalt thou be when thou goest............. Deut 28:6 1288
b the children of Israel before................ Deut 33:1 1288
B of the LORD be his land, for .... Deut 33:13 1288
B be he that enlargeth Gad.................... Deut 33:20 1288
Let Asher be *b* with children.................. Deut 33:24 1288
And Joshua *b* him, and gave unto .... Josh 14:13 1288
as the LORD hath *b* me hitherto............... Josh 17:14 1288
So Joshua *b* them, and sent them............ Josh 22:6 1288
unto their tents, then he *b* them .... Josh 22:7 1288
and the children of Israel *b* God............. Josh 22:33 1288
therefore he *b* you still........................... Josh 24:10 1288
B above women shall Jael the wife......... Judg 5:24 1288
b shall she be above women in the......... Judg 5:24 1288
the child grew, and the LORD *b* him........ Judg 13:24 1288
B be thou of the LORD, my son.............. Judg 17:2 1288
b be he that did take knowledge............. Ruth 2:19 1288
B be he of the LORD, who hath not......... Ruth 2:20 1288
B be thou of the LORD, my.................... Ruth 3:10 1288
B be the LORD, which hath not.............. Ruth 4:14 1288
Eli *b* Elkanah and his wife, and............. 1Sa 2:20 1288
unto him, *B* be thou of the LORD............ 1Sa 15:13 1288
And Saul said, *B* be ye of the LORD....... 1Sa 23:21 1288
B be the LORD God of Israel,................. 1Sa 25:32 1288
b be thy advice, and *b* be 1Sa 25:33 1288
B be the LORD, that hath pleaded........... 1Sa 25:39 1288
to David, *B* be thou, my son David......... 1Sa 26:25 1288
B be ye of the LORD, that ye have.......... 2Sa 2:5 1288
the LORD *b* Obed-edom, and all his......... 2Sa 6:11 1288
The LORD hath *b* the house of................ 2Sa 6:12 1288
he *b* the people in the name of................ 2Sa 6:18 1288
of thy servant be *b* for ever..................... 2Sa 7:29 1288
he would not go, but *b* him.................... 2Sa 13:25 1288
B be the LORD thy God, which hath........ 2Sa 18:28 1288
king kissed Barzillai, and *b* him............. 2Sa 19:39 1288
and *b* be my rock................................... 2Sa 22:47 1288
B be the LORD God of Israel,................. 1Kin 1:48 1288
And king Solomon shall be *b*................... 1Kin 2:45 1288
B be the LORD this day, which 1Kin 5:7 1288
b all the congregation of Israel.............. 1Kin 8:14 1288
B be the LORD God of Israel,................. 1Kin 8:15 1288
b all the congregation of Israel.............. 1Kin 8:55 1288
B be the LORD, that hath given.............. 1Kin 8:56 1288
they *b* the king, and went unto.............. 1Kin 8:66 1288
B be the LORD thy God, which............... 1Kin 10:9 1288
the LORD *b* the house of Obed-edom....... 1Chr 13:14 1288
he *b* the people in the name of............... 1Chr 16:2 1288
B be the LORD God of Israel for............. 1Chr 16:36 1288
O LORD, and it shall be *b* for ever.......... 1Chr 17:27 1288
for God *b* him... 1Chr 26:5 1288
Wherefore David *b* the LORD before........ 1Chr 29:10 1288
B be thou, LORD God of Israel our......... 1Chr 29:10 1288
all the congregation *b* the LORD............ 1Chr 29:20 1288
B be the LORD God of Israel, that.......... 2Chr 2:12 1288
b the whole congregation of.................... 2Chr 6:3 1288
B be the LORD God of Israel, who.......... 2Chr 6:4 1288
B be the LORD thy God, which............... 2Chr 9:8 1288
for there they *b* the LORD...................... 2Chr 20:26 1288
the Levites arose and *b* the people.......... 2Chr 30:27 1288
they *b* the LORD, and his people............ 2Chr 31:8 1288
for the LORD hath *b* his people............... 2Chr 31:10 1288
B be the LORD God of our fathers,......... Ezr 7:27 1288
Ezra *b* the LORD, the great God.............. Neh 8:6 1288
b be thy glorious name, which is............ Neh 9:5 1288
the people *b* all the men, that................ Neh 11:2 1288
thou hast *b* the work of his hands.......... Job 1:10 1288

b be the name of the LORD	Job 1:21	1288
the ear heard me, then it *b* me	Job 29:11	833
If his loins have not *b* me	Job 31:20	1288
So the LORD *b* the latter end of	Job 42:12	1288
B is the man that walketh not in	Ps 1:1	835
B are all they that put their	Ps 2:12	835
and *b* be my rock	Ps 18:46	1288
hast made him most *b* for ever	Ps 21:6	1293
B be the LORD, because he hath	Ps 28:6	1288
B be the LORD	Ps 31:21	1288
B is he whose transgression is	Ps 32:1	835
B is the man unto whom the LORD	Ps 32:2	835
B is the nation whose God is the	Ps 33:12	835
b is the man that trusteth in him	Ps 34:8	835
For such as be *b* of him shall	Ps 37:22	1288
and his seed is *b*	Ps 37:26	1293
B is that man that maketh the	Ps 40:4	835
B is he that considereth the poor	Ps 41:1	835
he shall be *b* upon the earth	Ps 41:2	833
B be the LORD God of Israel from	Ps 41:13	1288
God hath *b* thee for ever	Ps 45:2	1288
while he lived he *b* his soul	Ps 49:18	1288
B is the man whom thou choosest,	Ps 65:4	835
B be God, which hath not turned	Ps 66:20	1288
B be the Lord, who daily loadeth	Ps 68:19	1288
B be God	Ps 68:35	1288
and men shall be *b* in him	Ps 72:17	1288
all nations shall call him *b*	Ps 72:17	833
B be the LORD God, the God of	Ps 72:18	1288
b be his glorious name for ever	Ps 72:19	1288
B are they that dwell in thy	Ps 84:4	835
B is the man whose strength is in	Ps 84:5	835
b is the man that trusteth in	Ps 84:12	835
B is the people that know the	Ps 89:15	835
B be the LORD for evermore	Ps 89:52	1288
B is the man whom thou chastenest	Ps 94:12	835
B are they that keep judgment, and	Ps 106:3	835
B be the LORD God of Israel from	Ps 106:48	1288
B is the man that feareth the	Ps 112:1	835
of the upright shall be *b*	Ps 112:2	1288
B be the name of the LORD from	Ps 113:2	1288
Ye are *b* of the LORD which made	Ps 115:15	1288
B be he that cometh in the name	Ps 118:26	1288
we have *b* you out of the house of	Ps 118:26	1288
B are the undefiled in the way,	Ps 119:1	835
B are they that keep his	Ps 119:2	835
B art thou, O LORD	Ps 119:12	1288
B be the LORD, who hath not given	Ps 124:6	1288
B is every one that feareth the	Ps 128:1	835
man be *b* that feareth the LORD	Ps 128:4	1288
B be the LORD out of Zion, which	Ps 135:21	1288
B be the LORD my strength, which	Ps 144:1	1288
he hath *b* thy children within	Ps 147:13	1288
Let thy fountain be *b*	Prov 5:18	1288
for *b* are they that keep my ways	Prov 8:32	835
B is the man that heareth me,	Prov 8:34	835
The memory of the just is *b*	Prov 10:7	1293
his children are *b* after him	Prov 20:7	835
the end thereof shall not be *b*	Prov 20:21	1288
hath a bountiful eye shall be *b*	Prov 22:9	1288
children arise up, and call her *b*	Prov 31:28	833
B art thou, O land, when thy king	Eccl 10:17	835
The daughters saw her, and *b* her	Song 6:9	833
B be Egypt my people, and Assyria	Is 19:25	1288
b are all they that wait for him	Is 30:18	835
B are ye that sow beside all	Is 32:20	835
alone, and *b* him, and increased him	Is 51:2	1288
B is the man that doeth this, and	Is 56:2	835
the seed which the LORD hath *b*	Is 61:9	1288
are the seed of the *b* of the LORD	Is 65:23	1288
incense, as if he *b* an idol	Is 66:3	1288
B is the man that trusteth in the	Jer 17:7	1288
wherein my mother bare me be *b*	Jer 20:14	1288
B be the glory of the LORD from	Eze 3:12	1288
Then Daniel *b* the God of heaven	Dan 2:19	1289
B be the name of God for ever and	Dan 2:20	1289
B be the God of Shadrach, Meshach	Dan 3:28	1289
I *b* the most High, and I praised	Dan 4:34	1289
B is he that waiteth, and cometh	Dan 12:12	835
that sell them say, *B* be the LORD	Zec 11:5	1288
And all nations shall call you *b*	Mal 3:12	833
B are the poor in spirit	Mt 5:3	*3107*
B are they that mourn	Mt 5:4	*3107*
B are the meek	Mt 5:5	*3107*
B are they which do hunger and	Mt 5:6	*3107*
B are the merciful	Mt 5:7	*3107*
B are the pure in heart	Mt 5:8	*3107*
B are the peacemakers	Mt 5:9	*3107*
B are they which are persecuted	Mt 5:10	*3107*
B are ye, when men shall revile	Mt 5:11	*3107*
b is he, whosoever shall not be	Mt 11:6	*3107*
But *b* are your eyes, for they see	Mt 13:16	*3107*
and looking up to heaven, he *b*	Mt 14:19	*2127*
B art thou, Simon Bar-jona	Mt 16:17	*3107*
B is he that cometh in the name	Mt 21:9	*2127*
B is he that cometh in the name	Mt 23:39	*2127*
B is that servant, whom his lord	Mt 24:46	*3107*
ye *b* of my Father, inherit the	Mt 25:34	*2127*
b it, and brake it, and gave it to	Mt 26:26	*2127*
he looked up to heaven, and *b*	Mk 6:41	*2127*
and he *b*, and commanded to set them	Mk 8:7	*2127*
his hands upon them, and *b* them	Mk 10:16	*2127*
B is he that cometh in the name	Mk 11:9	*2127*
B be the kingdom of our father	Mk 11:10	*2127*
did eat, Jesus took bread, and *b*	Mk 14:22	*2127*
thou the Christ, the Son of the *B*	Mk 14:61	*2128*
b art thou among women	Lk 1:28	*2127*
B art thou among women, and	Lk 1:42	*2127*
b is the fruit of thy womb	Lk 1:42	*2127*
And *b* is she that believed	Lk 1:45	*3107*
all generations shall call me *b*	Lk 1:48	*3106*
B be the Lord God of Israel	Lk 1:68	*2128*
in his arms, and *b* God, and said,	Lk 2:28	*2127*
And Simeon *b* them, and said unto	Lk 2:34	*2127*
disciples, and said, *B* be ye poor	Lk 6:20	*3107*
B are ye that hunger now	Lk 6:21	*3107*
B are ye that weep now	Lk 6:21	*3107*
B are ye, when men shall hate you	Lk 6:22	*3107*
b is he, whosoever shall not be	Lk 7:23	
he *b* them, and brake, and gave to	Lk 9:16	*2127*
B are the eyes which see the	Lk 10:23	*3107*
B is the womb that bare thee, and	Lk 11:27	*3107*
b are they that hear the word of	Lk 11:28	*3107*
B are those servants, whom the	Lk 12:37	*3107*
them so, *b* are those servants	Lk 12:38	*3107*
B is that servant, whom his lord	Lk 12:43	*3107*
B is he that cometh in the name	Lk 13:35	*2127*
And thou shalt be *b*	Lk 14:14	*3107*
B is he that shall eat bread in	Lk 14:15	*3107*
B be the King that cometh in the	Lk 19:38	*2127*
B are the barren, and the wombs	Lk 23:29	*3107*
b it, and brake, and gave to them	Lk 24:30	*2127*
he lifted up his hands, and *b* them	Lk 24:50	*2127*
it came to pass, while he *b* them	Lk 24:51	*2127*
B is the King of Israel that	Jn 12:13	*2127*
b are they that have not seen, and	Jn 20:29	*3107*
the kindreds of the earth be *b*	Acts 3:25	*1757*
It is more *b* to give than to	Acts 20:35	*3107*
the Creator, who is *b* for ever	Rom 1:25	*2128*
B are they whose iniquities are	Rom 4:7	*3107*
B is the man to whom the Lord	Rom 4:8	*3107*
who is over all, God *b* for ever	Rom 9:5	*2128*
B be God, even the Father of our	2Cor 1:3	*2128*
which is *b* for evermore, knoweth	2Cor 11:31	*2128*
In thee shall all nations be *b*	Gal 3:8	*1757*
faith are *b* with faithful Abraham	Gal 3:9	*2127*
B be the God and Father of our	Eph 1:3	*2128*
who hath *b* us with all spiritual	Eph 1:3	*2127*
the glorious gospel of the *b* God	1Ti 1:11	*3107*
times he shall shew, who is the *b*	1Ti 6:15	*3107*
Looking for that *b* hope, and the	Titus 2:13	*3107*
slaughter of the kings, and *b* him	Heb 7:1	*2127*
b him that had the promises	Heb 7:6	*2127*
the less is *b* of the better	Heb 7:7	*2127*
By faith Isaac *b* Jacob and Esau	Heb 11:20	*2127*
b both the sons of Joseph	Heb 11:21	*2127*
B is the man that endureth	Jas 1:12	*3107*
this man shall be *b* in his deed	Jas 1:25	*3107*
B be the God and Father of our	1Pet 1:3	*2128*
B is he that readeth, and they	Rev 1:3	*3107*
B are the dead which die in the	Rev 14:13	*3107*
B is he that watcheth, and keepeth	Rev 16:15	*3107*
B are they which are called unto	Rev 19:9	*3107*
B and holy is he that hath part in	Rev 20:6	*3107*
b is he that keepeth the sayings	Rev 22:7	*3107*
B are they that do his	Rev 22:14	*3107*

BLESSEDNESS

also describeth the *b* of the man	Rom 4:6	*3108*
Cometh this *b* then upon the	Rom 4:9	*3108*
Where is then the *b* ye spake of	Gal 4:15	*3108*

BLESSEST

that he whom thou *b* is blessed	Num 22:6	1288
for thou *b*, O LORD, and it shall	1Chr 17:27	1288
thou *b* the springing thereof	Ps 65:10	1288

BLESSETH

and blessed be he that *b* thee	Gen 27:29	1288
Blessed is he that *b* thee	Num 24:9	1288
For the LORD thy God *b* thee	Deut 15:6	1288
b the covetous, whom the LORD	Ps 10:3	1288
He *b* them also, so that they are	Ps 107:38	1288
but he *b* the habitation of the	Prov 3:33	1288
He that *b* his friend with a loud	Prov 27:14	1288
That he who *b* himself in the	Is 65:16	1288

BLESSING

and thou shalt be a *b*	Gen 12:2	1293
That in *b* I will bless thee, and	Gen 22:17	1288
bring a curse upon me, and not a *b*	Gen 27:12	1293
Isaac had made an end of *b* Jacob	Gen 27:30	1293
and hath taken away thy *b*	Gen 27:35	1293
now he hath taken away my *b*	Gen 27:36	1293
Hast thou not reserved a *b* for me	Gen 27:36	1293
his father, Hast thou but one *b*	Gen 27:38	1293
b wherewith his father blessed	Gen 27:41	1293
And give thee the *b* of Abraham	Gen 28:4	1293
my *b* that is brought to thee	Gen 33:11	1293
the *b* of the LORD was upon all	Gen 39:5	1293
to his *b* he blessed them	Gen 49:28	1293
may bestow upon you a *b* this day	Ex 32:29	1293
Then I will command my *b* upon you	Lev 25:21	1293
I set before you this day a *b*	Deut 11:26	1293
A *b*, if ye obey the commandments	Deut 11:27	1293
put the *b* upon mount Gerizim	Deut 11:29	1293
according to the *b* of the LORD	Deut 12:15	1293
according to the *b* of the LORD	Deut 16:17	1293
the curse into a *b* unto thee	Deut 23:5	1293
The LORD shall command the *b* upon	Deut 28:8	1293
things are come upon thee, the *b*	Deut 30:1	1293
set before you life and death, *b*	Deut 30:19	1293
And this is the *b*, wherewith Moses	Deut 33:1	1293
And this is the *b* of Judah	Deut 33:7	
let the *b* come upon the head of	Deut 33:16	
and full with the *b* of the LORD	Deut 33:23	1293
Who answered, Give me a *b*	Josh 15:19	1293
And she said unto him, Give me a *b*	Judg 1:15	1293
now this *b* which thine handmaid	1Sa 25:27	1293
with thy *b* let the house of thy	2Sa 7:29	1293
thee, take a *b* of thy servant	2Kin 5:15	1293
which is exalted above all *b*	Neh 9:5	1293
our God turned the curse into a *b*	Neh 13:2	1293
The *b* of him that was ready to	Job 29:13	1293
thy *b* is upon thy people	Ps 3:8	1293
shall receive the *b* from the LORD	Ps 24:5	1293
as he delighted not in *b*, so let	Ps 109:17	1293
The *b* of the LORD be upon you	Ps 129:8	1293
there the LORD commanded the *b*	Ps 133:3	1293
The *b* of the LORD, it maketh rich	Prov 10:22	1293
By the *b* of the upright the city	Prov 11:11	1293
but *b* shall be upon the head of	Prov 11:26	1293
a good *b* shall come upon them	Prov 24:25	1293
even a *b* in the midst of the land	Is 19:24	1293
my *b* upon thine offspring	Is 44:3	1293
for a *b* is in it	Is 65:8	1293
places round about my hill a *b*	Eze 34:26	1293
there shall be showers of *b*	Eze 34:26	1293
that he may cause the *b* to rest	Eze 44:30	1293
repent, and leave a *b* behind him	Joel 2:14	1293
I save you, and ye shall be a *b*	Zec 8:13	1293
of heaven, and pour you out a *b*	Mal 3:10	1293
in the temple, praising and *b* God	Lk 24:53	*2127*
of the *b* of the gospel of Christ	Rom 15:29	*2129*
The cup of *b* which we bless, is	1Cor 10:16	*2129*
That the *b* of Abraham might come	Gal 3:14	*2129*
is dressed, receiveth *b* from God	Heb 6:7	*2129*
Surely *b* I will bless thee, and	Heb 6:14	*2129*
he would have inherited the *b*	Heb 12:17	*2129*
of the same mouth proceedeth *b*	Jas 3:10	*2129*
but contrariwise *b*	1Pet 3:9	*2129*
that ye should inherit a *b*	1Pet 3:9	*2129*
and honour, and glory, and *b*	Rev 5:12	*2129*
are in them, heard I saying, *B*	Rev 5:13	*2129*
B, and glory, and wisdom, and	Rev 7:12	*2129*

BLESSINGS

bless thee with *b* of heaven above	Gen 49:25	1293
b of the deep that lieth under,	Gen 49:25	1293
b of the breasts, and of the womb	Gen 49:25	1293
The *b* of thy father have	Gen 49:26	1293
the *b* of my progenitors unto the	Gen 49:26	1293
all these *b* shall come on thee,	Deut 28:2	1293
all the words of the law, the *b*	Josh 8:34	1293
him with the *b* of goodness	Ps 21:3	1293
B are upon the head of the just	Prov 10:6	1293
faithful man shall abound with *b*	Prov 28:20	1293
upon you, and I will curse your *b*	Mal 2:2	1293
b in heavenly places in Christ	Eph 1:3	*2129*

BLEW

the LORD, and *b* with the trumpets	Josh 6:8	8628
priests that *b* with the trumpets	Josh 6:9	8628
and *b* with the trumpets	Josh 6:13	8628
when the priests *b* with the	Josh 6:16	8628
the priests *b* with the trumpets	Josh 6:20	8628
that he *b* a trumpet in the	Judg 3:27	8628
upon Gideon, and he *b* a trumpet	Judg 6:34	8628
they *b* the trumpets, and brake the	Judg 7:19	8628
three companies *b* the trumpets	Judg 7:20	8628
the three hundred *b* the trumpets	Judg 7:22	8628
Saul *b* the trumpet throughout all	1Sa 13:3	8628
So Joab *b* a trumpet, and all the	2Sa 2:28	8628
Joab *b* the trumpet, and the people	2Sa 18:16	8628
he *b* a trumpet, and said, We have	2Sa 20:1	8628
he *b* a trumpet, and they retired	2Sa 20:22	8628
And they *b* the trumpet	1Kin 1:39	8628
b with trumpets, saying, Jehu is	2Kin 9:13	8628
land rejoiced, and *b* with trumpets	2Kin 11:14	8628
the floods came, and the winds *b*	Mt 7:25	*4154*
the floods came, and the winds *b*	Mt 7:27	*4154*
by reason of a great wind that *b*	Jn 6:18	*4154*
And when the south wind *b* softly	Acts 27:13	*5285*
and after one day the south wind *b*	Acts 28:13	*1920*

BLIND

or deaf, or the seeing, or the *b*	Ex 4:11	5787
put a stumblingblock before the *b*	Lev 19:14	5787
a *b* man, or a lame, or he that	Lev 21:18	5787
B, or broken, or maimed, or	Lev 22:22	5788
therein, as if it be lame, or *b*	Deut 15:21	5787
for a gift doth *b* the eyes of the	Deut 16:19	5786
the *b* to wander out of the way	Deut 27:18	5787
as the *b* gropeth in darkness, and	Deut 28:29	5787
bribe to *b* mine eyes therewith	1Sa 12:3	5956
Except thou take away the *b*	2Sa 5:6	5787
Jebusites, and the lame and the *b*	2Sa 5:8	5787
Wherefore they said, The *b*	2Sa 5:8	5787
I was eyes to the *b*, and feet was	Job 29:15	5787
LORD openeth the eyes of the *b*	Ps 146:8	5787
the eyes of the *b* shall see out	Is 29:18	5787
the eyes of the *b* shall be opened	Is 35:5	5787
To open the *b* eyes, to bring out	Is 42:7	5787
I will bring the *b* by a way that	Is 42:16	5787
and look, ye *b*, that ye may see	Is 42:18	5787
Who is *b*, but my servant	Is 42:19	5787
who is *b* as he that is perfect,	Is 42:19	5787
and *b* as the LORD's servant	Is 42:19	5787
Bring forth the *b* people that	Is 43:8	5787
His watchmen are *b*	Is 56:10	5787
We grope for the wall like the *b*	Is 59:10	5787
of the earth, and with them the *b*	Jer 31:8	5787
wandered as *b* men in the streets	Lam 4:14	5787
that they shall walk like *b* men	Zeph 1:17	5787
if ye offer the *b* for sacrifice	Mal 1:8	5787
two *b* men followed him, crying,	Mt 9:27	*5185*
the house, the *b* men came to him	Mt 9:28	*5185*
The *b* receive their sight, and the	Mt 11:5	*5185*
him one possessed with a devil, *b*	Mt 12:22	*5185*
healed him, insomuch that the *b*	Mt 12:22	*5185*
they be *b* leaders of the *b*	Mt 15:14	*5185*
they be *b* leaders of the *b*	Mt 15:14	*5185*
if the *b* lead the *b*, both	Mt 15:14	*5185*
And if the *b* lead the *b*	Mt 15:14	*5185*
with them those that were lame, *b*	Mt 15:30	*5185*
the lame to walk, and the *b* to see	Mt 15:31	*5185*
two *b* men sitting by the way side	Mt 20:30	*5185*
And the *b* and the lame came to him	Mt 21:14	*5185*
ye *b* guides, which say, Whosoever	Mt 23:16	*5185*
Ye fools and *b*:	Mt 23:17	*5185*
Ye fools and *b*:	Mt 23:19	*5185*
Ye *b* guides, which strain at a	Mt 23:24	*5185*
Thou *b* Pharisee, cleanse first	Mt 23:26	*5185*
and they bring a *b* man unto him	Mk 8:22	*5185*
he took the *b* man by the hand, and	Mk 8:23	*5185*

b Bartimaeus, the son of Timaeus, Mk 10:46 5185
And they call the *b* man, saying Mk 10:49 5185
The *b* man said unto him, Lord, Mk 10:51 5185
and recovering of sight to the *b* Lk 4:18 5185
them, Can the *b* lead the *b* Lk 6:39 5185
many that were *b* he gave sight Lk 7:21 5185
how that the *b* see, the lame walk Lk 7:22 5185
poor, the maimed, the lame, the *b* Lk 14:13 5185
the maimed, and the halt, and the *b* Lk 14:21 5185
a certain *b* man sat by the way Lk 18:35 5185
multitude of impotent folk, of *b* Jn 5:3 5185
a man which was *b* from his birth Jn 9:1 5185
his parents, that he was born *b* Jn 9:2 5185
eyes of the *b* man with the clay Jn 9:6 5185
before had seen him that he was *b* Jn 9:8 5185
him that aforetime was *b* Jn 9:13 5185
They say unto the *b* man again Jn 9:17 5185
him, that he had been *b*, and Jn 9:18 5185
your son, who ye say was born *b* Jn 9:19 5185
is our son, and that he was born *b* Jn 9:20 5185
called they the man that was *b* Jn 9:24 5185
I know, that, whereas I was *b* Jn 9:25 5185
the eyes of one that was born *b* Jn 9:32 5185
they which see might be made *b* Jn 9:39 5185
and said unto him, Are we *b* also Jn 9:40 5185
said unto them, If ye were *b* Jn 9:41 5185
a devil open the eyes of the *b* Jn 10:21 5185
which opened the eyes of the *b* Jn 11:37 5185
is upon thee, and thou shalt be *b* Acts 13:11 5185
thou thyself art a guide of the *b* Rom 2:19 5185
he that lacketh these things is *b* 2Pet 1:9 5185
and miserable, and poor, and *b* Rev 3:17 5185

BLINDED

He hath *b* their eyes, and hardened Jn 12:40 5186
obtained it, and the rest were *b* Rom 11:7 4456
But their minds were *b* 2Cor 3:14 4456
b the minds of them which believe 2Cor 4:4 5186
that darkness hath *b* his eyes 1Jn 2:11 5186

BLINDETH

for the gift *b* the wise, and Ex 23:8 5786

BLINDFOLDED

And when they had *b* him, they Lk 22:64 4028

BLINDNESS

at the door of the house with *b* Gen 19:11 5575
smite thee with madness, and *b* Deut 28:28 5788
this people, I pray thee, with *b* 2Kin 6:18 5575
he smote them with *b* according to 2Kin 6:18 5575
every horse of the people with *b* Zec 12:4 5788
that *b* in part is happened to Rom 11:25 4457
because of the *b* of their heart Eph 4:18 4457

BLOOD

the voice of thy brother's *b* Gen 4:10 1818
thy brother's *b* from thy hand Gen 4:11 1818
thereof, which is the *b* thereof Gen 9:4 1818
surely your *b* of your lives will Gen 9:5 1818
Whoso sheddeth man's *b*, Gen 9:6 1818
by man shall his *b* be shed Gen 9:6 1818
Reuben said unto them, Shed no *b* Gen 37:22 1818
our brother, and conceal his *b* Gen 37:26 1818
and dipped the coat in the *b* Gen 37:31 1818
behold, also his *b* is required Gen 42:22 1818
and his clothes in the *b* of grapes Gen 49:11 1818
shall become *b* upon the dry land Ex 4:9 1818
and they shall be turned to *b* Ex 7:17 1818
of water, that they may become *b* Ex 7:19 1818
that there may be *b* throughout Ex 7:19 1818
in the river were turned to *b* Ex 7:20 1818
there was *b* throughout all the Ex 7:21 1818
And they shall take of the *b* Ex 12:7 1818
the *b* shall be to you for a token Ex 12:13 1818
and when I see the *b*, I will pass Ex 12:13 1818
dip it in the *b* that is in the Ex 12:22 1818
with the *b* that is in the bason Ex 12:22 1818
he seeth the *b* upon the lintel Ex 12:23 1818
there shall no *b* be shed for him Ex 22:2 1818
there shall be *b* shed for him Ex 22:3 1818
Thou shalt not offer the *b* of my Ex 23:18 1818
And Moses took half of the *b* Ex 24:6 1818
half of the *b* he sprinkled on the Ex 24:6 1818
And Moses took the *b*, and sprinkled Ex 24:8 1818
Behold the *b* of the covenant, Ex 24:8 1818
take of the *b* of the bullock Ex 29:12 1818
pour all the *b* beside the bottom Ex 29:12 1818
the ram, and thou shalt take his *b* Ex 29:16 1818
kill the ram, and take of his *b* Ex 29:20 1818
sprinkle the *b* upon the altar Ex 29:20 1818
of the *b* that is upon the altar Ex 29:21 1818
with the *b* of the sin offering of Ex 30:10 1818
Thou shalt not offer the *b* of my Ex 34:25 1818
Aaron's sons, shall bring the *b* Lev 1:5 1818
sprinkle the *b* round about upon Lev 1:5 1818
shall sprinkle his *b* round about Lev 1:11 1818
the *b* thereof shall be wrung out Lev 1:15 1818
the *b* upon the altar round about Lev 3:2 1818
b thereof round about upon the Lev 3:8 1818
of Aaron shall sprinkle the *b* Lev 3:13 1818
that ye eat neither fat nor *b* Lev 3:17 1818
shall take of the bullock's *b* Lev 4:5 1818
shall dip his finger in the *b* Lev 4:6 1818
sprinkle of the *b* seven times Lev 4:6 1818
priest shall put some of the *b* Lev 4:7 1818
shall pour all the *b* of the Lev 4:7 1818
b to the tabernacle of the Lev 4:16 1818
dip his finger in some of the *b* Lev 4:17 1818
he shall put some of the *b* upon Lev 4:18 1818
shall pour out all the *b* at the Lev 4:18 1818
b of the sin offering with his Lev 4:25 1818
shall pour out his *b* at the Lev 4:25 1818
of the *b* thereof with his finger Lev 4:30 1818
shall pour out all the *b* thereof Lev 4:30 1818
b of the sin offering with his Lev 4:34 1818
shall pour out all the *b* thereof Lev 4:34 1818
he shall sprinkle of the *b* of the Lev 5:9 1818
the rest of the *b* shall be wrung Lev 5:9 1818
of the *b* thereof upon any garment Lev 6:27 1818
whereof any of the *b* is brought Lev 6:30 1818
the *b* thereof shall he sprinkle Lev 7:2 1818
the *b* of the peace offerings Lev 7:14 1818
ye shall eat no manner of *b* Lev 7:26 1818
it be that eateth any manner of *b* Lev 7:27 1818
that offereth the *b* of the peace Lev 7:33 1818
and Moses took the *b*, and put it Lev 8:15 1818
poured the *b* at the bottom of the Lev 8:15 1818
Moses sprinkled the *b* upon the Lev 8:19 1818
and Moses took of the *b* of it Lev 8:23 1818
Moses put of the *b* upon the tip Lev 8:24 1818
Moses sprinkled the *b* upon the Lev 8:24 1818
of the *b* which was upon the altar Lev 8:30 1818
of Aaron brought the *b* unto him Lev 9:9 1818
and he dipped his finger in the *b* Lev 9:9 1818
poured out the *b* at the bottom of Lev 9:9 1818
sons presented unto him the *b* Lev 9:12 1818
sons presented unto him the *b* Lev 9:18 1818
the *b* of it was not brought in Lev 10:18 1818
in the *b* of her purifying three Lev 12:4 1818
she shall continue in the *b* of Lev 12:5 1818
cleansed from the issue of her *b* Lev 12:7 1818
the living bird in the *b* of the Lev 14:6 1818
of the *b* of the trespass offering Lev 14:14 1818
upon the *b* of the trespass Lev 14:17 1818
of the *b* of the trespass offering Lev 14:25 1818
upon the place of the *b* of the Lev 14:28 1818
dip them in the *b* of the slain Lev 14:51 1818
the house with the *b* of the bird Lev 14:52 1818
and her issue in her flesh be *b* Lev 15:19 1818
b many days out of the time of Lev 15:25 1818
take of the *b* of the bullock Lev 16:14 1818
the *b* with his finger seven times Lev 16:14 1818
bring his *b* within the vail, and Lev 16:15 1818
do with that *b* as he did with the Lev 16:15 1818
he did with the *b* of the bullock Lev 16:15 1818
take of the *b* of the bullock Lev 16:18 1818
of the *b* of the goat, and put it Lev 16:18 1818
he shall sprinkle of the *b* upon Lev 16:19 1818
whose *b* was brought in to make Lev 16:27 1818
b shall be imputed unto that man Lev 17:4 1818
he hath shed *b* Lev 17:4 1818
b upon the altar of the LORD at Lev 17:6 1818
you, that eateth any manner of *b* Lev 17:10 1818
against that soul that eateth *b* Lev 17:10 1818
the life of the flesh is in the *b* Lev 17:11 1818
for it is the *b* that maketh an Lev 17:11 1818
No soul of you shall eat *b* Lev 17:12 1818
that sojourneth among you eat *b* Lev 17:12 1818
shall even pour out the *b* thereof Lev 17:13 1818
the *b* of it is for the life Lev 17:14 1818
Ye shall eat the *b* of no manner Lev 17:14 1818
of all flesh is the *b* thereof Lev 17:14 1818
against the *b* of thy neighbour Lev 19:16 1818
not eat any thing with the *b* Lev 19:26 1818
his *b* shall be upon him Lev 20:9 1818
their *b* shall be upon them Lev 20:11 1818
their *b* shall be upon them Lev 20:12 1818
their *b* shall be upon them Lev 20:13 1818
their *b* shall be upon them Lev 20:16 1818
uncovered the fountain of her *b* Lev 20:18 1818
their *b* shall be upon them Lev 20:27 1818
sprinkle their *b* upon the altar Num 18:17 1818
take of her *b* with his finger Num 19:4 1818
sprinkle of her *b* directly before Num 19:4 1818
her skin, and her flesh, and her *b* Num 19:5 1818
prey, and drink the *b* of the slain Num 23:24 1818
The revenger of *b* himself shall Num 35:19 1818
the revenger of *b* shall slay the Num 35:21 1818
the revenger of *b* according to Num 35:24 1818
of the hand of the revenger of *b* Num 35:25 1818
the revenger of *b* find him Num 35:27 1818
the revenger of *b* kill the slayer Num 35:27 1818
he shall not be guilty of *b* Num 35:27 1818
for *b* it defileth the land Num 35:33 1818
of the *b* that is shed therein Num 35:33 1818
but by the *b* of him that shed it Num 35:33 1818
Only ye shall not eat the *b* Deut 12:16 1818
be sure that thou eat not the *b* Deut 12:23 1818
for the *b* is the life Deut 12:23 1818
offerings, the flesh and the *b* Deut 12:27 1818
the *b* of thy sacrifices shall be Deut 12:27 1818
thou shalt not eat the *b* thereof Deut 15:23 1818
in judgment, between *b* and *b* Deut 17:8 1818
of the *b* pursue the slayer Deut 19:6 1818
That innocent *b* be not shed in Deut 19:10 1818
inheritance, and so *b* be upon thee Deut 19:10 1818
into the hand of the avenger of *b* Deut 19:12 1818
guilt of innocent *b* from Israel Deut 19:13 1818
Our hands have not shed this *b* Deut 21:7 1818
lay not innocent *b* unto thy Deut 21:8 1818
the *b* shall be forgiven them Deut 21:8 1818
of innocent *b* from among you Deut 21:9 1818
thou bring not *b* upon thine house Deut 22:8 1818
drink the pure *b* of the grape Deut 32:14 1818
make mine arrows drunk with *b* Deut 32:42 1818
and that with the *b* of the slain Deut 32:42 1818
will avenge the *b* of his servants Deut 32:43 1818
his *b* shall be upon his head, and Josh 2:19 1818
his *b* shall be on our head, if Josh 2:19 1818
your refuge from the avenger of *b* Josh 20:3 1818
the avenger of *b* pursue after him Josh 20:5 1818
by the hand of the avenger of *b* Josh 20:9 1818
their *b* be laid upon Abimelech Judg 9:24 1818
people did eat them with the *b* 1Sa 14:32 1818
LORD, in that they eat with the *b* 1Sa 14:33 1818
the LORD in eating with the *b* 1Sa 14:34 1818
wilt thou sin against innocent *b* 1Sa 19:5 1818
thee from coming to shed *b* 1Sa 25:26 1818
that thou hast shed *b* causeless 1Sa 25:31 1818
me this day from coming to shed *b* 1Sa 25:33 1818
let not my *b* fall to the earth 1Sa 26:20 1818
unto him, Thy *b* be upon thy head 2Sa 1:16 1818
From the *b* of the slain, from the 2Sa 1:22 1818
for the *b* of Asahel his brother 2Sa 3:27 1818
the *b* of Abner the son of Ner 2Sa 3:28 1818
now require his *b* of your hand 2Sa 4:11 1818
of *b* to destroy any more, lest 2Sa 14:11 1818
all the *b* of the house of Saul 2Sa 16:8 1818
Amasa wallowed in *b* in the midst 2Sa 20:12 1818
is not this the *b* of the men that 2Sa 23:17 1818
shed the *b* of war in peace, and 1Kin 2:5 1818
put the *b* of war upon his girdle 1Kin 2:5 1818
thou down to the grave with *b* 1Kin 2:9 1818
mayest take away the innocent *b* 1Kin 2:31 1818
return his *b* upon his own head 1Kin 2:32 1818
Their *b* shall therefore return 1Kin 2:33 1818
thy *b* shall be upon thine own 1Kin 2:37 1818
till the *b* gushed out upon them 1Kin 18:28 1818
b of Naboth shall dogs lick thy 1Kin 21:19 1818
of Naboth shall dogs lick thy *b* 1Kin 21:19 1818
the *b* ran out of the wound into 1Kin 22:35 1818
and the dogs licked up his *b* 1Kin 22:38 1818
on the other side as red as *b* 2Kin 3:22 1818
And they said, This is *b* 2Kin 3:23 1818
that I may avenge the *b* of my 2Kin 9:7 1818
the *b* of all the servants of the 2Kin 9:7 1818
seen yesterday the *b* of Naboth 2Kin 9:26 1818
the *b* of his sons, saith the LORD 2Kin 9:26 1818
some of her *b* was sprinkled on 2Kin 9:33 1818
sprinkled the *b* of his peace 2Kin 16:13 1818
all the *b* of the burnt offering 2Kin 16:15 1818
all the *b* of the sacrifice 2Kin 16:15 1818
shed innocent *b* very much 2Kin 21:16 1818
for the innocent *b* that he shed 2Kin 24:4 1818
filled Jerusalem with innocent *b* 2Kin 24:4 1818
shall I drink the *b* of these men 1Chr 11:19 1818
Thou hast shed *b* abundantly 1Chr 22:8 1818
much *b* upon the earth in my sight 1Chr 22:8 1818
been a man of war, and hast shed *b* 1Chr 28:3 1818
their cities, between *b* and *b* 2Chr 19:10 1818
the *b* of the sons of Jehoiada the 2Chr 24:25 1818
and the priests received the *b* 2Chr 29:22 1818
sprinkled the *b* upon the altar 2Chr 29:22 1818
sprinkled the *b* upon the altar 2Chr 29:22 1818
with their *b* upon the altar 2Chr 29:24 1818
the priests sprinkled the *b* 2Chr 30:16 1818
sprinkled the *b* from their hands 2Chr 35:11 1818
O earth, cover not thou my *b* Job 16:18 1818
Her young ones also suck up *b* Job 39:30 1818
When he maketh inquisition for *b* Ps 9:12 1818
offerings of *b* will I not offer Ps 16:4 1818
What profit is there in my *b* Ps 30:9 1818
of bulls, or drink the *b* of goats Ps 50:13 1818
his feet in the *b* of the wicked Ps 58:10 1818
dipped in the *b* of thine enemies Ps 68:23 1818
shall their *b* be in his sight Ps 72:14 1818
And had turned their rivers into *b* Ps 78:44 1818
Their *b* have they shed like water Ps 79:3 1818
b of thy servants which is shed Ps 79:10 1818
and condemn the innocent *b* Ps 94:21 1818
He turned their waters into *b* Ps 105:29 1818
And shed innocent *b* Ps 106:38 1818
even the *b* of their sons and of Ps 106:38 1818
and the land was polluted with *b* Ps 106:38 1818
with us, let us lay wait for *b* Prov 1:11 1818
to evil, and make haste to shed *b* Prov 1:16 1818
And they lay wait for their own *b* Prov 1:18 1818
and hands that shed innocent *b* Prov 6:17 1818
wicked are to lie in wait for *b* Prov 12:6 1818
man that doeth violence to the *b* Prov 28:17 1818
of the nose bringeth forth *b* Prov 30:33 1818
delight not in the *b* of bullocks Is 1:11 1818
your hands are full of *b* Is 1:15 1818
shall have purged the *b* of Is 4:4 1818
noise, and garments rolled in *b* Is 9:5 1818
of Dimon shall be full of *b* Is 15:9 1818
earth also shall disclose her *b* Is 26:21 1818
his ears from hearing of *b* Is 33:15 1818
shall be melted with their *b* Is 34:3 1818
of the LORD is filled with *b* Is 34:6 1818
fatness, and with the *b* of lambs Is 34:6 1818
their land shall be soaked with *b* Is 34:7 1818
shall be drunken with their own *b* Is 49:26 1818
For your hands are defiled with *b* Is 59:3 1818
make haste to shed innocent *b* Is 59:7 1818
their *b* shall be sprinkled upon Is 63:3 5332
as if he offered swine's *b* Is 66:3 1818
the *b* of the souls of the poor Jer 2:34 1818
shed not innocent *b* in this place Jer 7:6 1818
pour out their *b* by the force of Jer 18:21
place with the *b* of innocents Jer 19:4 1818
shed innocent *b* in this place Jer 22:3 1818
and for to shed innocent *b* Jer 22:17 1818
bring innocent *b* upon yourselves Jer 26:15 1818
and made drunk with their *b* Jer 46:10 1818
keepeth back his sword from *b* Jer 48:10 1818
my *b* upon the inhabitants of Jer 51:35 1818
that have shed the *b* of the just Lam 4:13 1818
have polluted themselves with *b* Lam 4:14 1818
but his *b* will I require at thine Eze 3:18 1818
but his *b* will I require at thine Eze 3:20 1818
b shall pass through thee Eze 5:17 1818
great, and the land is full of *b* Eze 9:9 1818
and pour out my fury upon it in *b* Eze 14:19 1818
saw thee polluted in thine own *b* Eze 16:6 1818
unto thee when thou wast in thy *b* Eze 16:6 1818
unto thee when thou wast in thy *b* Eze 16:6 1818
washed away thy *b* from thee Eze 16:9 1818
bare, and wast polluted in thy *b* Eze 16:22 1818
by the *b* of thy children, which Eze 16:36 1818
wedlock and shed *b* are judged Eze 16:38 1818
and I will give thee *b* in fury Eze 16:38 1818
that is a robber, a shedder of *b* Eze 18:10 1818

B

Context	Reference	No.
his *b* shall be upon him	Eze 18:13	1818
mother is like a vine in thy *b*	Eze 19:10	1818
thy *b* shall be in the midst of	Eze 21:32	1818
The city sheddeth *b* in the midst	Eze 22:3	1818
in thy *b* that thou hast shed	Eze 22:4	1818
in thee to their power to shed *b*	Eze 22:6	1818
men that carry tales to shed *b*	Eze 22:9	1818
have they taken gifts to shed *b*	Eze 22:12	1818
at thy *b* which hath been in the	Eze 22:13	1818
ravening the prey, to shed *b*	Eze 22:27	1818
b is in their hands, and with	Eze 23:37	1818
the manner of women that shed *b*	Eze 23:45	1818
and *b* is in their hands	Eze 23:45	1818
For her *b* is in the midst of her	Eze 24:7	1818
I have set her *b* upon the top of	Eze 24:8	1818
pestilence, and *b* into her street	Eze 28:23	1818
I will also water with thy *b* the	Eze 32:6	1818
his *b* shall be upon his own head	Eze 33:4	1818
his *b* shall be upon him	Eze 33:5	1818
but his *b* will I require at the	Eze 33:6	1818
but his *b* will I require at thine	Eze 33:8	1818
Ye eat with the *b*, and lift up	Eze 33:25	1818
eyes toward your idols, and shed *b*	Eze 33:25	1818
hast shed the *b* of the children	Eze 35:5	
b, and *b* shall pursue thee	Eze 35:6	1818
b, even *b* shall pursue thee	Eze 35:6	1818
my fury upon them for the *b* that	Eze 36:18	1818
him with pestilence and with *b*	Eze 38:22	1818
that ye may eat flesh, and drink *b*	Eze 39:17	1818
drink the *b* of the princes of the	Eze 39:18	1818
drink *b* till ye be drunken, of my	Eze 39:19	1818
thereon, and to sprinkle *b* thereon	Eze 43:18	1818
thou shalt take of the *b* thereof	Eze 43:20	1818
offer my bread, the fat and the *b*	Eze 44:7	1818
to offer unto me the fat and the *b*	Eze 44:15	1818
take of the *b* of the sin offering	Eze 45:19	1818
I will avenge the *b* of Jezreel	Hos 1:4	1818
break out, and *b* toucheth *b*	Hos 4:2	1818
iniquity, and is polluted with *b*	Hos 6:8	1818
shall he leave his *b* upon him	Hos 12:14	1818
in the heavens and in the earth, *b*	Joel 2:30	1818
into darkness, and the moon into *b*	Joel 2:31	1818
shed innocent *b* in their land	Joel 3:19	1818
their *b* that I have not cleansed	Joel 3:21	1818
and lay not upon us innocent *b*	Jonah 1:14	1818
They build up Zion with *b*	Mic 3:10	1818
they all lie in wait for *b*	Mic 7:2	1818
because of men's *b*, and for the	Hab 2:8	1818
him that buildeth a town with *b*	Hab 2:12	1818
them afraid, because of men's *b*	Hab 2:17	1818
their *b* shall be poured out as	Zeph 1:17	1818
take away his *b* out of his mouth	Zec 9:7	1818
by the *b* of thy covenant I have	Zec 9:11	1818
with an issue of *b* twelve years	Mt 9:20	*131*
b hath not revealed it unto thee,	Mt 16:17	*129*
them in the *b* of the prophets	Mt 23:30	*129*
righteous *b* shed upon the earth	Mt 23:35	*129*
b of righteous Abel unto the *b*	Mt 23:35	*129*
For this is my *b* of the new	Mt 26:28	*129*
I have betrayed the innocent *b*	Mt 27:4	*129*
because it is the price of *b*	Mt 27:6	*129*
field was called, The field of *b*	Mt 27:8	*129*
of the *b* of this just person	Mt 27:24	*129*
His *b* be on us, and on our	Mt 27:25	*129*
had an issue of *b* twelve years	Mk 5:25	*129*
fountain of her *b* was dried up	Mk 5:29	*129*
This is my *b* of the new testament	Mk 14:24	*129*
having an issue of *b* twelve years	Lk 8:43	*129*
her issue of *b* stanched	Lk 8:44	*129*
That the *b* of all the prophets,	Lk 11:50	*129*
From the *b* of Abel unto the *b*	Lk 11:51	*129*
whose *b* Pilate had mingled with	Lk 13:1	*129*
cup is the new testament in my *b*	Lk 22:20	*129*
of *b* falling down to the ground	Lk 22:44	*129*
Which were born, not of *b*	Jn 1:13	*129*
of the Son of man, and drink his *b*	Jn 6:53	*129*
eateth my flesh, and drinketh my *b*	Jn 6:54	*129*
indeed, and my *b* is drink indeed	Jn 6:55	*129*
eateth my flesh, and drinketh my *b*	Jn 6:56	*129*
and forthwith came there out *b*	Jn 19:34	*129*
that is to say, The field of *b*	Acts 1:19	*129*
b, and fire, and vapour of smoke	Acts 2:19	*129*
into darkness, and the moon into *b*	Acts 2:20	*129*
to bring this man's *b* upon us	Acts 5:28	*129*
from things strangled, and from *b*	Acts 15:20	*129*
meats offered to idols, and from *b*	Acts 15:29	*129*
hath made of one *b* all nations of	Acts 17:26	*129*
Your *b* be upon your own heads	Acts 18:6	*129*
I am pure from the *b* of all men	Acts 20:26	*129*
he hath purchased with his own *b*	Acts 20:28	*129*
offered to idols, and from *b*	Acts 21:25	*129*
when the *b* of thy martyr Stephen	Acts 22:20	*129*
Their feet are swift to shed *b*	Rom 3:15	*129*
through faith in his *b*, to	Rom 3:25	*129*
being now justified by his *b*	Rom 5:9	*129*
the communion of the *b* of Christ	1Cor 10:16	*129*
cup is the new testament in my *b*	1Cor 11:25	*129*
of the body and *b* of the Lord	1Cor 11:27	*129*
b cannot inherit the kingdom of	1Cor 15:50	*129*
I conferred not with flesh and *b*	Gal 1:16	*129*
we have redemption through his *b*	Eph 1:7	*129*
are made nigh by the *b* of Christ	Eph 2:13	*129*
we wrestle not against flesh and *b*	Eph 6:12	*129*
we have redemption through his *b*	Col 1:14	*129*
peace through the *b* of his cross	Col 1:20	*129*
are partakers of flesh and *b*	Heb 2:14	*129*
once every year, not without *b*	Heb 9:7	*129*
Neither by the *b* of goats	Heb 9:12	*129*
but by his own *b* he entered in	Heb 9:12	*129*
For if the *b* of bulls and of goats	Heb 9:13	*129*
much more shall the *b* of Christ	Heb 9:14	*129*
testament was dedicated without *b*	Heb 9:18	*129*
the law, he took the *b* of calves	Heb 9:19	*129*
This is the *b* of the testament	Heb 9:20	*129*
with *b* both the tabernacle	Heb 9:21	*129*
are by the law purged with *b*	Heb 9:22	*129*
shedding of *b* is no remission	Heb 9:22	*130*
place every year with *b* of others	Heb 9:25	*129*
not possible that the *b* of bulls	Heb 10:4	*129*
the holiest by the *b* of Jesus	Heb 10:19	*129*
counted the *b* of the covenant	Heb 10:29	*129*
passover, and the sprinkling of *b*	Heb 11:28	*129*
Ye have not yet resisted unto *b*	Heb 12:4	*129*
to the *b* of sprinkling, that	Heb 12:24	*129*
whose *b* is brought into the	Heb 13:11	*129*
the people with his own *b*	Heb 13:12	*129*
through the *b* of the everlasting	Heb 13:20	*129*
of the *b* of Jesus Christ	1Pet 1:2	*129*
But with the precious *b* of Christ	1Pet 1:19	*129*
the *b* of Jesus Christ his Son	1Jn 1:7	*129*
is he that came by water and *b*	1Jn 5:6	*129*
by water only, but by water and *b*	1Jn 5:6	*129*
spirit, and the water, and the *b*	1Jn 5:8	*129*
us from our sins in his own *b*	Rev 1:5	*129*
God by thy *b* out of every kindred	Rev 5:9	*129*
avenge our *b* on them that dwell	Rev 6:10	*129*
of hair, and the moon became as *b*	Rev 6:12	*129*
them white in the *b* of the Lamb	Rev 7:14	*129*
hail and fire mingled with *b*	Rev 8:7	*129*
third part of the sea became *b*	Rev 8:8	*129*
over waters to turn them to *b*	Rev 11:6	*129*
overcame him by the *b* of the Lamb	Rev 12:11	*129*
b came out of the winepress, even	Rev 14:20	*129*
it became as the *b* of a dead man	Rev 16:3	*129*
and they became *b*	Rev 16:4	*129*
they have shed the *b* of saints	Rev 16:6	*129*
thou hast given them *b* to drink	Rev 16:6	*129*
drunken with the *b* of the saints	Rev 17:6	*129*
with the *b* of the martyrs of	Rev 17:6	*129*
her was found the *b* of prophets	Rev 18:24	*129*
hath avenged the *b* of his	Rev 19:2	*129*
with a vesture dipped in *b*	Rev 19:13	*129*

BLOODGUILTINESS

Context	Reference	No.
Deliver me from *b*, O God, thou	Ps 51:14	1818

BLOODTHIRSTY

Context	Reference	No.
The *b* hate the upright	Prov 29:10	

BLOODY

Context	Reference	No.
Surely a *b* husband art thou to me	Ex 4:25	1818
A *b* husband thou art, because of	Ex 4:26	1818
Come out, come out, thou *b* man	2Sa 16:7	1818
because thou art a *b* man	2Sa 16:8	1818
is for Saul, and for his *b* house	2Sa 21:1	1818
the LORD will abhor the *b*	Ps 5:6	1818
sinners, nor my life with *b* men	Ps 26:9	1818
b and deceitful men shall not live	Ps 55:23	1818
iniquity, and save me from *b* men	Ps 59:2	1818
from me therefore, ye *b* men	Ps 139:19	1818
for the land is full of *b* crimes	Eze 7:23	1818
judge, wilt thou judge the *b* city	Eze 22:2	1818
Woe to the *b* city, to the pot	Eze 24:6	1818
Woe to the *b* city	Eze 24:9	1818
Woe to the *b* city	Nah 3:1	1818
sick of a fever and of a *b* flux	Acts 28:8	*1420*

BLOOMED

Context	Reference	No.
b blossoms, and yielded almonds	Num 17:8	6692

BLOSSOM

Context	Reference	No.
rod, whom I shall choose, shall *b*	Num 17:5	6524
their *b* shall go up as dust	Is 5:24	6525
Israel shall *b* and bud, and fill	Is 27:6	6692
shall rejoice, and *b* as the rose	Is 35:1	6524
It shall *b* abundantly, and rejoice	Is 35:2	6524
Although the fig tree shall not *b*	Hab 3:17	6524

BLOSSOMED

Context	Reference	No.
the rod hath *b*, pride hath budded	Eze 7:10	6692

BLOSSOMS

Context	Reference	No.
it budded, and her *b* shot forth	Gen 40:10	5322
brought forth buds, and bloomed *b*	Num 17:8	6731

BLOT

Context	Reference	No.
b me, I pray thee, out of thy	Ex 32:32	4229
him will I *b* out of my book	Ex 32:33	4229
he shall *b* them out with the	Num 5:23	4229
b out their name from under	Deut 9:14	4229
that thou shalt *b* out the	Deut 25:19	4229
the LORD shall *b* out his name	Deut 29:20	4229
b out the name of Israel from	2Kin 14:27	4229
if any *b* hath cleaved to mine	Job 31:7	3971
mercies *b* out my transgressions	Ps 51:1	4229
b out all mine iniquities	Ps 51:9	4229
a wicked man getteth himself a *b*	Prov 9:7	3971
neither *b* out their sin from thy	Jer 18:23	4229
I will not *b* out his name out of	Rev 3:5	*1813*

BLOTTED

Context	Reference	No.
sin be *b* out from before thee	Neh 4:5	4229
Let them be *b* out of the book of	Ps 69:28	4229
following let their name be *b* out	Ps 109:13	4229
the sin of his mother be *b* out	Ps 109:14	4229
I have *b* out, as a thick cloud,	Is 44:22	4229
that your sins may be *b* out	Acts 3:19	*1813*

BLOTTETH

Context	Reference	No.
I, even I, am he that *b* out thy	Is 43:25	4229

BLOTTING

Context	Reference	No.
B out the handwriting of	Col 2:14	*1813*

BLOW

Context	Reference	No.
Thou didst *b* with thy wind, the	Ex 15:10	5398
And when they shall *b* with them	Num 10:3	8628
if they *b* but with one trumpet,	Num 10:4	8628
When ye *b* an alarm, then the	Num 10:5	8628
When ye *b* an alarm the second	Num 10:6	8628
they shall *b* an alarm for their	Num 10:6	8628
be gathered together, ye shall *b*	Num 10:7	8628
shall *b* with the trumpets	Num 10:8	8628
then ye shall *b* an alarm with the	Num 10:9	7321
ye shall *b* with the trumpets over	Num 10:10	8628
and the trumpets to *b* in his hand	Num 31:6	8643
priests shall *b* with the trumpets	Josh 6:4	8628
When I *b* with a trumpet, I and all	Judg 7:18	8628
then *b* ye the trumpets also on	Judg 7:18	8628
in their right hands to *b* withal	Judg 7:20	8628
b ye with the trumpet, and say,	1Kin 1:34	8628
did *b* with the trumpets before	1Chr 15:24	2690
consumed by the *b* of thine hand	Ps 39:10	8409
an east wind to *b* in the heaven	Ps 78:26	5265
B up the trumpet in the new moon,	Ps 81:3	8628
he causeth his wind to *b*, and the	Ps 147:18	5380
b upon my garden, that the spices	Song 4:16	6315
and he shall also *b* upon them	Is 40:24	5398
B ye the trumpet in the land	Jer 4:5	8628
b the trumpet in Tekoa, and set up	Jer 6:1	8628
breach, with a very grievous *b*	Jer 14:17	4347
b the trumpet among the nations,	Jer 51:27	8628
I will *b* against thee in the fire	Eze 21:31	6315
to *b* the fire upon it, to melt it	Eze 22:20	5301
b upon you in the fire of my	Eze 22:21	5301
he *b* the trumpet, and warn the	Eze 33:3	8628
b not the trumpet, and the people	Eze 33:6	8628
B ye the cornet in Gibeah, and the	Hos 5:8	8628
B ye the trumpet in Zion, and	Joel 2:1	8628
B the trumpet in Zion, sanctify a	Joel 2:15	8628
brought it home, I did *b* upon it	Hag 1:9	5301
the Lord GOD shall *b* the trumpet	Zec 9:14	8628
And when ye see the south wind *b*	Lk 12:55	*4154*
wind should not *b* on the earth	Rev 7:1	*4154*

BLOWETH

Context	Reference	No.
when he *b* a trumpet, hear ye	Is 18:3	8628
the spirit of the LORD *b* upon it	Is 40:7	5380
that *b* the coals in the fire	Is 54:16	5301
The wind *b* where it listeth, and	Jn 3:8	*4154*

BLOWING

Context	Reference	No.
a memorial of *b* of trumpets	Lev 23:24	8643
it is a day of *b* the trumpets	Num 29:1	8643
going on, and *b* with the trumpets	Josh 6:9	8628
going on, and *b* with the trumpets	Josh 6:13	8628

BLOWN

Context	Reference	No.
a fire not *b* shall consume him	Job 20:26	5301
that the great trumpet shall be *b*	Is 27:13	8628
They have *b* the trumpet, even to	Eze 7:14	8628
Shall a trumpet be *b* in the city	Amos 3:6	8628

BLUE

Context	Reference	No.
And *b*, and purple, and scarlet, and	Ex 25:4	8504
of fine twined linen, and *b*	Ex 26:1	8504
of *b* upon the edge of the one	Ex 26:4	8504
And thou shalt make a vail of *b*	Ex 26:31	8504
for the door of the tent, of *b*	Ex 26:36	8504
an hanging of twenty cubits, of *b*	Ex 27:16	8504
And they shall take gold, and *b*	Ex 28:5	8504
make the ephod of gold, of *b*	Ex 28:6	8504
even of gold, of *b*, and purple, and	Ex 28:8	8504
of gold, of *b*, and of purple, and	Ex 28:15	8504
of the ephod with a lace of *b*	Ex 28:28	8504
the robe of the ephod all of *b*	Ex 28:31	8504
thou shalt make pomegranates of *b*	Ex 28:33	8504
And thou shalt put it on a *b* lace	Ex 28:37	8504
And *b*, and purple, and scarlet, and	Ex 35:6	8504
every man, with whom was found *b*	Ex 35:23	8504
which they had spun, both of *b*	Ex 35:25	8504
and of the embroiderer, in *b*	Ex 35:35	8504
of fine twined linen, and *b*	Ex 36:8	8504
he made loops of *b* on the edge of	Ex 36:11	8504
And he made a vail of *b*, and purple	Ex 36:35	8504
for the tabernacle door of *b*	Ex 36:37	8504
of the court was needlework, of *b*	Ex 38:18	8504
workman, and an embroiderer in *b*	Ex 38:23	8504
And of the *b*, and purple, and	Ex 39:1	8504
And he made the ephod of gold, *b*	Ex 39:2	8504
into wires, to work it in the *b*	Ex 39:3	8504
of gold, *b*, and purple, and scarlet	Ex 39:5	8504
of gold, *b*, and purple, and scarlet	Ex 39:8	8504
of the ephod with a lace of *b*	Ex 39:21	8504
the ephod of woven work, all of *b*	Ex 39:22	8504
of the robe pomegranates of *b*	Ex 39:24	8504
girdle of fine twined linen, and *b*	Ex 39:29	8504
And they tied unto it a lace of *b*	Ex 39:31	8504
over it a cloth wholly of *b*	Num 4:6	8504
they shall spread a cloth of *b*	Num 4:7	8504
And they shall take a cloth of *b*	Num 4:9	8504
they shall spread a cloth of *b*	Num 4:11	8504
and put them in a cloth of *b*	Num 4:12	8504
of the borders a ribband of *b*	Num 15:38	8504
and in purple, and crimson, and *b*	2Chr 2:7	8504
and in timber, in purple, in *b*	2Chr 2:14	8504
And he made the vail of *b*, and	2Chr 3:14	8504
Where were white, green, and *b*	Est 1:6	8504
upon a pavement of red, and *b*	Est 1:6	8504
of the king in royal apparel of *b*	Est 8:15	8504
b and purple is their clothing	Jer 10:9	8504
Which were clothed with *b*	Eze 23:6	8504
b and purple from the isles of	Eze 27:7	8504
in *b* clothes, and broidered work,	Eze 27:24	8504

BLUENESS

Context	Reference	No.
The *b* of a wound cleanseth away	Prov 20:30	2250

BLUNT

Context	Reference	No.
If the iron be *b*, and he do not	Eccl 10:10	6949

BLUSH

Context	Reference	No.
b to lift up my face to thee, my	Ezr 9:6	3637
all ashamed, neither could they *b*	Jer 6:15	3637
all ashamed, neither could they *b*	Jer 8:12	3637

BOANERGES (*bo-an-er'-jees*) *Surname of James and John, the sons of Zebedee.*

Context	Reference	No.
and he surnamed them *B*, which is,	Mk 3:17	*993*

BOAR
The *b* out of the wood doth waste ... Ps 80:13 2386

BOARD
cubits shall be the length of a *b* ... Ex 26:16 7175
shall be the breadth of one *b* ... Ex 26:16 7175
tenons shall there be in one *b* ... Ex 26:17 7175
under one *b* for his two tenons ... Ex 26:19 7175
another *b* for his two tenons ... Ex 26:19 7175
two sockets under one *b* ... Ex 26:21 7175
and two sockets under another *b* ... Ex 26:21 7175
two sockets under one *b* ... Ex 26:25 7175
and two sockets under another *b* ... Ex 26:25 7175
The length of a *b* was ten cubits ... Ex 36:21 7175
and the breadth of a *b* one cubit ... Ex 36:21 7175
One *b* had two tenons, equally ... Ex 36:22 7175
under one *b* for his two tenons ... Ex 36:24 7175
another *b* for his two tenons ... Ex 36:24 7175
two sockets under one *b* ... Ex 36:26 7175
and two sockets under another *b* ... Ex 36:26 7175
silver, under every *b* two sockets ... Ex 36:30 7175

BOARDS
thou shalt make *b* for the ... Ex 26:15 7175
for all the *b* of the tabernacle ... Ex 26:17 7175
make the *b* for the tabernacle ... Ex 26:18 7175
twenty *b* on the south side ... Ex 26:18 7175
of silver under the twenty *b* ... Ex 26:19 7175
side there shall be twenty *b* ... Ex 26:20 7175
westward thou shalt make six *b* ... Ex 26:22 7175
two *b* shalt thou make for the ... Ex 26:23 7175
And they shall be eight *b*, and ... Ex 26:25 7175
five for the *b* of the one side of ... Ex 26:26 7175
five bars for the *b* of the other ... Ex 26:27 7175
five bars for the *b* of the side ... Ex 26:27 7175
the *b* shall reach from end to end ... Ex 26:28 7175
shalt overlay the *b* with gold ... Ex 26:29 7175
Hollow with *b* shalt thou make it ... Ex 27:8 3871
covering, his taches, and his *b* ... Ex 35:11 7175
he made *b* for the tabernacle of ... Ex 36:20 7175
for all the *b* of the tabernacle ... Ex 36:22 7175
he made the *b* for the tabernacle ... Ex 36:23 7175
twenty *b* for the south side ... Ex 36:23 7175
silver he made under the twenty *b* ... Ex 36:24 7175
north corner, he made twenty *b* ... Ex 36:25 7175
tabernacle westward he made six *b* ... Ex 36:27 7175
two *b* made he for the corners of ... Ex 36:28 7175
And there were eight *b* ... Ex 36:30 7175
five for the *b* of the one side of ... Ex 36:31 7175
five bars for the *b* of the other ... Ex 36:32 7175
five bars for the *b* of the ... Ex 36:32 7175
b from the one end to the other ... Ex 36:33 7175
And he overlaid the *b* with gold ... Ex 36:34 7175
he made the altar hollow with *b* ... Ex 38:7 3871
his furniture, his taches, his *b* ... Ex 39:33 7175
sockets, and set up the *b* thereof ... Ex 40:18 7175
shall be the *b* of the tabernacle ... Num 3:36 7175
the *b* of the tabernacle, and the ... Num 4:31 7175
house with beams and *b* of cedar ... 1Kin 6:9 7713
the house within with *b* of cedar ... 1Kin 6:15 6763
and the walls with *b* of cedar ... 1Kin 6:16 6763
will inclose her with *b* of cedar ... Song 8:9 3871
thy ship *b* of fir trees of Senir ... Eze 27:5 3871
And the rest, some on *b*, and some ... Acts 27:44 *4548*

BOAST
b himself as he that putteth it ... 1Kin 20:11 1984
thine heart lifteth thee up to *b* ... 2Chr 25:19 3513
soul shall make her *b* in the LORD ... Ps 34:2 1984
In God we *b* all the day long, and ... Ps 44:8 1984
b themselves in the multitude of ... Ps 49:6 1984
workers of iniquity *b* themselves ... Ps 94:4 559
that *b* themselves of idols ... Ps 97:7 1984
B not thyself of to morrow ... Prov 27:1 1984
Shall the ax *b* itself against him ... Is 10:15 6286
their glory shall ye *b* yourselves ... Is 61:6 3235
the law, and makest thy *b* of God ... Rom 2:17 *2744*
Thou that makest thy *b* of the law ... Rom 2:23 *2744*
B not against the branches ... Rom 11:18 *2620*
But if thou *b*, thou bearest not ... Rom 11:18
for which I *b* of you to them of ... 2Cor 9:2 *2744*
For though I should *b* somewhat ... 2Cor 10:8 *2744*
But we will not *b* of things ... 2Cor 10:13 *2744*
not to *b* in another man's line of ... 2Cor 10:16 *2744*
that I may *b* myself a little ... 2Cor 11:16 *2744*
of works, lest any man should *b* ... Eph 2:9 *2744*

BOASTED
your mouth ye have *b* against me ... Eze 35:13 1431
For if I have *b* any thing to him ... 2Cor 7:14 *2744*

BOASTERS
of God, despiteful, proud, *b* ... Rom 1:30 *213*
of their own selves, covetous, *b* ... 2Ti 3:2 *213*

BOASTEST
Why *b* thou thyself in mischief, O ... Ps 52:1 1984

BOASTETH
For the wicked *b* of his heart's ... Ps 10:3 1984
he is gone his way, then he *b* ... Prov 20:14 1984
Whoso *b* himself of a false gift ... Prov 25:14 1984
little member, and *b* great things ... Jas 3:5 *3166*

BOASTING
Theudas, *b* himself to be somebody ... Acts 5:36 *3004*
Where is *b* then ... Rom 3:27 *2746*
to you in truth, even so our *b* ... 2Cor 7:14 *2746*
love, and of our *b* on your behalf ... 2Cor 8:24 *2746*
lest our *b* of you should be in ... 2Cor 9:3 *2745*
ashamed in this same confident *b* ... 2Cor 9:4 *2746*
Not *b* of things without our ... 2Cor 10:15 *2744*
this *b* in the regions of Achaia ... 2Cor 11:10 *2746*
in this confidence of *b* ... 2Cor 11:17 *2746*

BOASTINGS
But now ye rejoice in your *b* ... Jas 4:16 *212*

BOAT
there went over a ferry *b* to ... 2Sa 19:18 5679
that there was none other *b* there ... Jn 6:22 *4142*
not with his disciples into the *b* ... Jn 6:22 *4142*
we had much work to come by the *b* ... Acts 27:16 *4627*
had let down the *b* into the sea ... Acts 27:30 *4627*
cut off the ropes of the *b* ... Acts 27:32 *4627*

BOATS
(Howbeit there came other *b* from ... Jn 6:23 *4142*

BOAZ (*bo'-az*) See Booz.
1. Husband of Ruth.
and his name was *B* ... Ruth 2:1 1162
of the field belonging unto *B* ... Ruth 2:3 1162
B came from Beth-lehem, and said ... Ruth 2:4 1162
Then said *B* unto his servant that ... Ruth 2:5 1162
Then said *B* unto Ruth, Hearest ... Ruth 2:8 1162
B answered and said unto her, It ... Ruth 2:11 1162
B said unto her, At mealtime come ... Ruth 2:14 1162
B commanded his young men, saying ... Ruth 2:15 1162
with whom I wrought to day is *B* ... Ruth 2:19 1162
B to glean unto the end of barley ... Ruth 2:23 1162
now is not *B* of our kindred, with ... Ruth 3:2 1162
when *B* had eaten and drunk, and his ... Ruth 3:7 1162
Then went *B* up to the gate, and ... Ruth 4:1 1162
kinsman of whom *B* spake came by ... Ruth 4:1 1162
Then said *B*, What day thou buyest ... Ruth 4:5 1162
Therefore the kinsman said unto *B* ... Ruth 4:8 1162
B said unto the elders, and unto ... Ruth 4:9 1162
So *B* took Ruth, and she was his ... Ruth 4:13 1162
And Salmon begat *B* ... Ruth 4:21 1162
and *B* begat Obed ... Ruth 4:21 1162
begat Salma, and Salma begat *B* ... 1Chr 2:11 1162
B begat Obed, and Obed begat Jesse ... 1Chr 2:12 1162
2. A pillar in Solomon's Temple.
and called the name thereof *B* ... 1Kin 7:21 1162
and the name of that on the left *B* ... 2Chr 3:17 1162

BOCHERU (*bok'-er-u*) *A relative of Saul.*
whose names are these, Azrikam, *B* ... 1Chr 8:38 1074
whose names are these, Azrikam, *B* ... 1Chr 9:44 1074

BOCHIM (*bo'-kim*) *A place near Gilgal.*
the LORD came up from Gilgal to *B* ... Judg 2:1 1066
called the name of that place *B* ... Judg 2:5 1066

BODIES
the sight of my lord, but our *b* ... Gen 47:18 1472
the *b* of his sons from the wall ... 1Sa 31:12 1472
the *b* of his sons, and brought ... 1Chr 10:12 1480
they were dead *b* fallen to the ... 2Chr 20:24 6297
both riches with the dead *b* ... 2Chr 20:25 6297
they have dominion over our *b* ... Neh 9:37 1472
ashes, your *b* to *b* of clay ... Job 13:12 1354
ashes, your *b* to *b* of clay ... Job 13:12 1472
The dead *b* of thy servants have ... Ps 79:2 5038
fill the places with the dead *b* ... Ps 110:6 1472
And the whole valley of the dead *b* ... Jer 31:40 6297
fill them with the dead *b* of men ... Jer 33:5 6297
their dead *b* shall be for meat ... Jer 34:20 5038
cast all the dead *b* of the men ... Jer 41:9 6297
another, and two covered their *b* ... Eze 1:11 1472
covered on that side, their *b* ... Eze 1:23 1472
upon whose *b* the fire had no ... Dan 3:27 1655
king's word, and yielded their *b* ... Dan 3:28 1655
be many dead *b* in every place ... Amos 8:3 6297
many *b* of the saints which slept ... Mt 27:52 *4983*
that the *b* should not remain upon ... Jn 19:31 *4983*
their own *b* between themselves ... Rom 1:24 *4983*
b by his Spirit that dwelleth in ... Rom 8:11 *4983*
present your *b* a living sacrifice ... Rom 12:1 *4983*
Know ye not that your *b* are the ... 1Cor 6:15 *4983*
There are also celestial *b* ... 1Cor 15:40 *4983*
and *b* terrestrial ... 1Cor 15:40 *4983*
love their wives as their own *b* ... Eph 5:28 *4983*
our *b* washed with pure water ... Heb 10:22 *4983*
For the *b* of those beasts, whose ... Heb 13:11 *4983*
their dead *b* shall lie in the ... Rev 11:8 *4430*
shall see their dead *b* three days ... Rev 11:9 *4430*
their dead *b* to be put in graves ... Rev 11:9 *4430*

BODILY
in a *b* shape like a dove upon him ... Lk 3:22 *4984*
but his *b* presence is weak, and ... 2Cor 10:10 *4983*
all the fulness of the Godhead *b* ... Col 2:9 *4985*
For *b* exercise profiteth little ... 1Ti 4:8 *4984*

BODY
as it were the *b* of heaven in his ... Ex 24:10 6106
shall he go in to any dead *b* ... Lev 21:11 5315
LORD he shall come at no dead *b* ... Num 6:6 5315
defiled by the dead *b* of a man ... Num 9:6 5315
defiled by the dead *b* of a man ... Num 9:7 5315
be unclean by reason of a dead *b* ... Num 9:10 5315
He that toucheth the dead *b* of ... Num 19:11 5315
dead *b* of any man that is dead ... Num 19:13 5315
in the open fields, or a dead *b* ... Num 19:16 5315
His *b* shall not remain all night ... Deut 21:23 5038
shall be the fruit of thy *b* ... Deut 28:4 990
in goods, in the fruit of thy *b* ... Deut 28:11 990
shall be the fruit of thy *b* ... Deut 28:18 990
eat the fruit of thine own *b* ... Deut 28:53 990
thine hand, in the fruit of thy *b* ... Deut 30:9 990
and ten sons of his *b* begotten ... Judg 8:30 3409
they fastened his *b* to the wall ... 1Sa 31:10 1472
all night, and took the *b* of Saul ... 1Sa 31:12 1472
he had restored a dead *b* to life ... 2Kin 8:5
men, and took away the *b* of Saul ... 1Chr 10:12 1480
the children's sake of mine own *b* ... Job 19:17 990
my skin worms destroy this *b* ... Job 19:26
is drawn, and cometh out of the *b* ... Job 20:25 1465
Of the fruit of thy *b* will I set ... Ps 132:11 990
thy flesh and thy *b* are consumed, ... Prov 5:11 7607
fruitful field, both soul and *b* ... Is 10:18 1320
with my dead *b* shall they arise ... Is 26:19 5038
hast laid thy *b* as the ground ... Is 51:23 1460
cast his dead *b* into the graves ... Jer 26:23 5038
his dead *b* shall be cast out in ... Jer 36:30 5038
were more ruddy in *b* than rubies ... Lam 4:7 6106
And their whole *b*, and their backs, ... Eze 10:12 1320
his *b* was wet with the dew of ... Dan 4:33 1655
his *b* was wet with the dew of ... Dan 5:21 1655
his *b* destroyed, and given to the ... Dan 7:11 1655
in my spirit in the midst of my *b* ... Dan 7:15 5085
His *b* also was like the beryl, and ... Dan 10:6 1472
the fruit of my *b* for the sin of ... Mic 6:7 990
by a dead *b* touch any of these ... Hag 2:13 5315
not that thy whole *b* should be ... Mt 5:29 *4983*
not that thy whole *b* should be ... Mt 5:30 *4983*
The light of the *b* is the eye ... Mt 6:22 *4983*
thy whole *b* shall be full of ... Mt 6:22 *4983*
thy whole *b* shall be full of ... Mt 6:23 *4983*
nor yet for your *b*, what ye shall ... Mt 6:25 *4983*
than meat, and the *b* than raiment ... Mt 6:25 *4983*
And fear not them which kill the *b* ... Mt 10:28 *4983*
to destroy both soul and *b* in hell ... Mt 10:28 *4983*
disciples came, and took up the *b* ... Mt 14:12 *4983*
hath poured this ointment on my *b* ... Mt 26:12 *4983*
this is my *b* ... Mt 26:26 *4983*
Pilate, and begged the *b* of Jesus ... Mt 27:58 *4983*
commanded the *b* to be delivered ... Mt 27:58 *4983*
And when Joseph had taken the *b* ... Mt 27:59 *4983*
she felt in her *b* that she was ... Mk 5:29 *4983*
to anoint my *b* to the burying ... Mk 14:8 *4983*
this is my *b* ... Mk 14:22 *4983*
cloth cast about his naked *b* ... Mk 14:51 *4983*
Pilate, and craved the *b* of Jesus ... Mk 15:43 *4983*
he gave the *b* to Joseph ... Mk 15:45 *4983*
The light of the *b* is the eye ... Lk 11:34 *4983*
thy whole *b* also is full of light ... Lk 11:34 *4983*
thy *b* also is full of darkness ... Lk 11:34 *4983*
If thy whole *b* therefore be full ... Lk 11:36 *4983*
afraid of them that kill the *b* ... Lk 12:4 *4983*
neither for the *b*, what ye shall ... Lk 12:22 *4983*
the *b* is more than raiment ... Lk 12:23 *4983*
unto them, Wheresoever the *b* is ... Lk 17:37 *4983*
This is my *b* which is given for ... Lk 22:19 *4983*
Pilate, and begged the *b* of Jesus ... Lk 23:52 *4983*
sepulchre, and how his *b* was laid ... Lk 23:55 *4983*
found not the *b* of the Lord Jesus ... Lk 24:3 *4983*
And when they found not his *b* ... Lk 24:23 *4983*
he spake of the temple of his *b* ... Jn 2:21 *4983*
he might take away the *b* of Jesus ... Jn 19:38 *4983*
therefore, and took the *b* of Jesus ... Jn 19:38 *4983*
Then took they the *b* of Jesus ... Jn 19:40 *4983*
where the *b* of Jesus had lain ... Jn 20:12 *4983*
and turning him to the *b* said ... Acts 9:40 *4983*
So that from his *b* were brought ... Acts 19:12 *5559*
considered not his own *b* now dead ... Rom 4:19 *4983*
that the *b* of sin might be ... Rom 6:6 *4983*
therefore reign in your mortal *b* ... Rom 6:12 *4983*
to the law by the *b* of Christ ... Rom 7:4 *4983*
me from the *b* of this death ... Rom 7:24 *4983*
the *b* is dead because of sin ... Rom 8:10 *4983*
do mortify the deeds of the *b* ... Rom 8:13 *4983*
to wit, the redemption of our *b* ... Rom 8:23 *4983*
as we have many members in one *b* ... Rom 12:4 *4983*
are one *b* in Christ, and every one ... Rom 12:5 *4983*
For I verily, as absent in *b* ... 1Cor 5:3 *4983*
Now the *b* is not for fornication, ... 1Cor 6:13 *4983*
and the Lord for the *b* ... 1Cor 6:13 *4983*
is joined to an harlot is one *b* ... 1Cor 6:16 *4983*
that a man doeth is without the *b* ... 1Cor 6:18 *4983*
sinneth against his own *b* ... 1Cor 6:18 *4983*
know ye not that your *b* is the ... 1Cor 6:19 *4983*
therefore glorify God in your *b* ... 1Cor 6:20 *4983*
wife hath not power of her own *b* ... 1Cor 7:4 *4983*
hath not power of his own *b* ... 1Cor 7:4 *4983*
that she may be holy both in *b* ... 1Cor 7:34 *4983*
But I keep under my *b*, and bring ... 1Cor 9:27 *4983*
the communion of the *b* of Christ ... 1Cor 10:16 *4983*
many are one bread, and one *b* ... 1Cor 10:17 *4983*
this is my *b*, which is broken for ... 1Cor 11:24 *4983*
shall be guilty of the *b* ... 1Cor 11:27 *4983*
not discerning the Lord's *b* ... 1Cor 11:29 *4983*
For as the *b* is one, and hath many ... 1Cor 12:12 *4983*
one *b*, being many, are one *b* ... 1Cor 12:12 *4983*
are we all baptized into one *b* ... 1Cor 12:13 *4983*
For the *b* is not one member, but ... 1Cor 12:14 *4983*
not the hand, I am not of the *b* ... 1Cor 12:15 *4983*
is it therefore not of the *b* ... 1Cor 12:15 *4983*
am not the eye, I am not of the *b* ... 1Cor 12:16 *4983*
is it therefore not of the *b* ... 1Cor 12:16 *4983*
If the whole *b* were an eye ... 1Cor 12:17 *4983*
every one of them in the *b* ... 1Cor 12:18 *4983*
all one member, where were the *b* ... 1Cor 12:19 *4983*
they many members, yet but one *b* ... 1Cor 12:20 *4983*
much more those members of the *b* ... 1Cor 12:22 *4983*
And those members of the *b* ... 1Cor 12:23 *4983*
God hath tempered the *b* together ... 1Cor 12:24 *4983*
should be no schism in the *b* ... 1Cor 12:25 *4983*
Now ye are the *b* of Christ ... 1Cor 12:27 *4983*
though I give my *b* to be burned ... 1Cor 13:3 *4983*
and with what *b* do they come ... 1Cor 15:35 *4983*
sowest not that *b* that shall be ... 1Cor 15:37 *4983*
But God giveth it a *b* as it hath ... 1Cor 15:38 *4983*
him, and to every seed his own *b* ... 1Cor 15:38 *4983*
It is sown a natural *b* ... 1Cor 15:44 *4983*
it is raised a spiritual *b* ... 1Cor 15:44 *4983*
There is a natural *b* ... 1Cor 15:44 *4983*
and there is a spiritual *b* ... 1Cor 15:44 *4983*
the *b* the dying of the Lord Jesus ... 2Cor 4:10 *4983*
might be made manifest in our *b* ... 2Cor 4:10 *4983*
whilst we are at home in the *b* ... 2Cor 5:6 *4983*
rather to be absent from the *b* ... 2Cor 5:8 *4983*
receive the things done in his *b* ... 2Cor 5:10 *4983*
years ago, (whether in the *b* ... 2Cor 12:2 *4983*
or whether out of the *b*, I cannot ... 2Cor 12:2 *4983*

in the b, or out of the b 2Cor 12:3 4983
for I bear in my b the marks of Gal 6:17 4983
Which is his b, the fulness of Eph 1:23 4983
unto God in one b by the cross Eph 2:16 4983
be fellowheirs, and of the same b Eph 3:6 4954
There is one b, and one Spirit, Eph 4:4 4983
the edifying of the b of Christ Eph 4:12 4983
From whom the whole b fitly Eph 4:16 4983
maketh increase of the b unto the Eph 4:16 4983
and he is the saviour of the b Eph 5:23 4983
For we are members of his b Eph 5:30 4983
Christ shall be magnified in my b Phil 1:20 4983
Who shall change our vile b Phil 3:21 4983
like unto his glorious b, Phil 3:21 4983
And he is the head of the b Col 1:18 4983
In the b of his flesh through Col 1:22 4983
in putting off the b of the sins Col 2:11 4983
but the b is of Christ Col 2:17 4983
from which all the b by joints Col 2:19 4983
humility, and neglecting of the b Col 2:23 4983
which also ye are called in one b Col 3:15 4983
b be preserved blameless unto the 1Th 5:23 4983
but a b hast thou prepared me Heb 10:5 4983
through the offering of the b of Heb 10:10 4983
as being yourselves also in the b Heb 13:3 4983
things which are needful to the b Jas 2:16 4983
For as the b without the spirit Jas 2:26 4983
able also to bridle the whole b Jas 3:2 4983
and we turn about their whole b Jas 3:3 4983
that it defileth the whole b Jas 3:6 4983
our sins in his own b on the tree 1Pet 2:24 4983
he disputed about the b of Moses Jude 9 4983

BODY'S
Christ in my flesh for his b sake Col 1:24 4983

BOHAN (bo'-han) *A namesake of a border stone.*
the stone of B the son of Reuben Josh 15:6 932
the stone of B the son of Reuben Josh 18:17 932

BOIL
shall be a b breaking forth with Ex 9:9 7822
it became a b breaking forth with Ex 9:10 7822
for the b was upon the magicians, Ex 9:11 7822
B the flesh at the door of the Lev 8:31 1310
even in the skin thereof, was a b Lev 13:18 7822
in the place of the b there be a Lev 13:19 7822
of leprosy broken out of the b Lev 13:20 7822
and spread not, it is a burning b Lev 13:23 7822
And they took and laid it on the b 2Kin 20:7 7822
maketh the deep to b like a pot Job 41:31 7570
lay it for a plaister upon the b Is 38:21 7822
the fire causeth the waters to b Is 64:2 1158
bones under it, and make it b well Eze 24:5 7570
shall b the trespass offering Eze 46:20 1310
are the places of them that b Eze 46:24 1310
b the sacrifice of the people Eze 46:24 1310

BOILED
them, and b their flesh with the 1Kin 19:21 1310
So we b my son, and did eat him 2Kin 6:29 1310
My bowels b, and rested not Job 30:27 7570

BOILING
it was made with b places under Eze 46:23 4018

BOILS
before Moses because of the b Ex 9:11 7822
smote Job with sore b from the Job 2:7 7822

BOISTEROUS
But when he saw the wind b Mt 14:30 2478

BOKERU See BOCHERU.

BOKIM See BOCHIM.

BOLD
but the righteous are b as a lion Prov 28:1 982
Then Paul and Barnabas waxed b Acts 13:46 3955
But Esaias is very b, and saith, I Rom 10:20 662
but being absent am b toward you 2Cor 10:1 2292
that I may not be b when I am 2Cor 10:2 2292
I think to be b against some 2Cor 10:2 5111
Howbeit whereinsoever any is b 2Cor 11:21 5111
(I speak foolishly,) I am b also 2Cor 11:21 5111
are much more b to speak the word Phil 1:14 5111
we were b in our God to speak 1Th 2:2 3955
though I might be much b in Philem 8 3954

BOLDLY
sword, and came upon the city b Gen 34:25 983
went in b unto Pilate, and craved Mk 15:43 5111
But, lo, he speaketh b, and they Jn 7:26 3954
how he had preached b at Damascus Acts 9:27 3955
he spake b in the name of the Acts 9:29 3955
abode they speaking b in the Lord Acts 14:3 3955
began to speak b in the synagogue Acts 18:26 3955
spake b for the space of three Acts 19:8 3955
the more b unto you in some sort Rom 15:15 5112
me, that I may open my mouth b Eph 6:19 3954
that therein I may speak b Eph 6:20 3955
Let us therefore come b unto the Heb 4:16 3954
So that we may b say, The Lord is Heb 13:6 2292

BOLDNESS
the b of his face shall be Eccl 8:1 5797
Now when they saw the b of Peter Acts 4:13 3954
that with all b they may speak Acts 4:29 3954
they spake the word of God with b Acts 4:31 3954
Great is my b of speech toward 2Cor 7:4 3954
In whom we have b and access with Eph 3:12 3954
be ashamed, but that with all b Phil 1:20 3954
great b in the faith which is in 1Ti 3:13 3954
b to enter into the holiest by Heb 10:19 3954
that we may have b in the day of 1Jn 4:17 3954

BOLLED
was in the ear, and the flax was b Ex 9:31 1392

BOLSTER
a pillow of goats' hair for his b 1Sa 19:13 4763
a pillow of goats' hair for his b 1Sa 19:16 4763
stuck in the ground at his b 1Sa 26:7 4763
now the spear that is at his b 1Sa 26:11 4763
the cruse of water from Saul's b 1Sa 26:12 4763
cruse of water that was at his b 1Sa 26:16 4763

BOLT
from me, and b the door after her 2Sa 13:17 5274

BOLTED
her out, and b the door after her 2Sa 13:18 5274

BOND
an oath to bind his soul with a b Num 30:2 632
the LORD, and bind herself by a b Num 30:3 632
her b wherewith she hath bound Num 30:4 632
every b wherewith she hath bound Num 30:4 632
her soul by a b with an oath Num 30:10 632
every b wherewith she bound her Num 30:11 632
or concerning the b of her soul Num 30:12 632
He looseth the b of kings Job 12:18 4148
you into the b of the covenant Eze 20:37 4562
from this b on the sabbath day Lk 13:16 1199
and in the b of iniquity Acts 8:23 4886
Gentiles, whether we be b or free 1Cor 12:13 1401
there is neither b nor free Gal 3:28 1401
of the Spirit in the b of peace Eph 4:3 4886
the Lord, whether he be b or free Eph 6:8 1401
Barbarian, Scythian, b nor free Col 3:11 1401
which is the b of perfectness Col 3:14 4886
and great, rich and poor, free and b Rev 13:16 1401
flesh of all men, both free and b Rev 19:18 1401

BONDAGE
their lives bitter with hard b Ex 1:14 5656
Israel sighed by reason of the b Ex 2:23 5656
up unto God by reason of the b Ex 2:23 5656
whom the Egyptians keep in b Ex 6:5 5647
and I will rid you out of their b Ex 6:6 5656
anguish of spirit, and for cruel b Ex 6:9 5656
from Egypt, out of the house of b Ex 13:3 5650
from Egypt, from the house of b Ex 13:14 5650
of Egypt, out of the house of b Ex 20:2 5650
of Egypt, from the house of b Deut 5:6 5650
of Egypt, from the house of b Deut 6:12 5650
of Egypt, from the house of b Deut 8:14 5650
you out of the house of b Deut 13:5 5650
of Egypt, from the house of b Deut 13:10 5650
us, and laid upon us hard b Deut 26:6 5656
of Egypt, from the house of b Josh 24:17 5650
you forth out of the house of b Judg 6:8 5650
us a little reviving in our b Ezr 9:8 5659
God hath not forsaken us in our b Ezr 9:9 5659
and, lo, we bring into b our sons Neh 5:5 3533
are brought unto b already Neh 5:5 3533
because the b was heavy upon this Neh 5:18 5656
a captain to return to their b Neh 9:17 5659
from the hard b wherein thou wast Is 14:3 5656
and were never in b to any man Jn 8:33 1398
they should bring them into b Acts 7:6 1402
they shall be in b will I judge Acts 7:7 1398
the spirit of b again to fear Rom 8:15 1397
shall be delivered from the b of Rom 8:21 1397
is not under b in such cases 1Cor 7:15 1402
suffer, if a man bring you into b 2Cor 11:20 2615
that they might bring us into b Gal 2:4 2615
were in b under the elements of Gal 4:3 1402
ye desire again to be in b Gal 4:9 1398
mount Sinai, which gendereth to b Gal 4:24 1397
is in b with her children Gal 4:25 1398
again with the yoke of b Gal 5:1 1397
all their lifetime subject to b Heb 2:15 1397
of the same is he brought in b 2Pet 2:19 1402

BONDMAID
with a woman, that is a b Lev 19:20 8198
had two sons, the one by a b Gal 4:22 3814

BONDMAIDS
Both thy bondmen, and thy b Lev 25:44 519
of them shall ye buy bondmen and b Lev 25:44 519

BONDMAN
instead of the lad a b to my lord Gen 44:33 5650
wast a b in the land of Egypt Deut 15:15 5650
that thou wast a b in Egypt Deut 16:12 5650
that thou wast a b in Egypt Deut 24:18 5650
wast a b in the land of Egypt Deut 24:22 5650
and the mighty men, and every b Rev 6:15 1401

BONDMEN
and fall upon us, and take us for b Gen 43:18 5650
and we also will be my lord's b Gen 44:9 5650
they shall not be sold as b Lev 25:42 5650
Both thy b, and thy bondmaids, Lev 25:44 5650
of them shall ye buy b and Lev 25:44 5650
they shall be your b for ever Lev 25:46 5647
that ye should not be their b Lev 26:13 5650
son, We were Pharaoh's b in Egypt Deut 6:21 5650
you out of the house of b Deut 7:8 5650
be sold unto your enemies for b Deut 28:68 5650
none of you be freed from being b Josh 9:23 5650
of Israel did Solomon make no b 1Kin 9:22 5650
take unto him my two sons to be b 2Kin 4:1 5650
of Judah and Jerusalem for b 2Chr 28:10 5650
For we were b Ezr 9:9 5650
But if we had been sold for b Est 7:4 5650
of Egypt, out of the house of b Jer 34:13 5650

BONDS
or of her b wherewith she hath Num 30:5 632
her b wherewith she bound her Num 30:7 632
all her vows, or all her b Num 30:14 632
thou hast loosed my b Ps 116:16 4147
broken the yoke, and burst the b Jer 5:5 4147
Make thee b and yokes, and put them Jer 27:2 4147
off thy neck, and will burst thy b Jer 30:8 4147
and will burst thy b in sunder Nah 1:13 4147
in every city, saying that b Acts 20:23 1199
charge worthy of death or of b Acts 23:29 1199
a certain man left in b by Felix Acts 25:14 1198
such as I am, except these b Acts 26:29 1199
nothing worthy of death or of b Acts 26:31 1199
For which I am an ambassador in b Eph 6:20 254
inasmuch as both in my b, and in Phil 1:7 1199
So that my b in Christ are Phil 1:13 1199
Lord, waxing confident by my b Phil 1:14 1199
to add affliction to my b Phil 1:16 1199
Christ, for which I am also in b Col 4:3 1210
Remember my b Col 4:18 1199
as an evil doer, even unto b 2Ti 2:9 1199
whom I have begotten in my b Philem 10 1199
unto me in the b of the gospel Philem 13 1199
ye had compassion of me in my b Heb 10:34 1199
and scourgings, yea, moreover of b Heb 11:36 1199
Remember them that are in b Heb 13:3 1198

BONDSERVANT
not compel him to serve as a b Lev 25:39

BONDSERVICE
levy a tribute of b unto this day 1Kin 9:21 5647

BONDWOMAN
unto Abraham, Cast out this b Gen 21:10 519
for the son of this b shall not Gen 21:10 519
of the lad, and because of thy b Gen 21:12 519
son of the b will I make a nation Gen 21:13 519
But he who was of the b was born Gal 4:23 3814
Cast out the b and her son Gal 4:30 3814
for the son of the b shall not be Gal 4:30 3814
we are not children of the b Gal 4:31 3814

BONDWOMEN
your enemies for bondmen and b Deut 28:68 8198
for bondmen and b unto you 2Chr 28:10 8198
we had been sold for bondmen and b Est 7:4 8198

BONE
said, This is now b of my bones Gen 2:23 6106
said to him, Surely thou art my b Gen 29:14 6106
shall ye break a b thereof Ex 12:46 6106
morning, nor break any b of it Num 9:12 6106
or a b of a man, or a grave, Num 19:16 6106
and upon him that touched a b Num 19:18 6106
remember also that I am your b Judg 9:2 6106
saying, Behold, we are thy b 2Sa 5:1 6106
ye to Amasa, Art thou not of my b 2Sa 19:13 6106
saying, Behold, we are thy b 1Chr 11:1 6106
thine hand now, and touch his b Job 2:5 6106
My b cleaveth to my skin and to my Job 19:20 6106
and mine arm be broken from the b Job 31:22 7070
all mine enemies upon the cheek b Ps 3:7
and a soft tongue breaketh the b Prov 25:15 1634
came together, b to his b Eze 37:7 6106
land, when any seeth a man's b Eze 39:15 6106
A b of him shall not be broken Jn 19:36 3747

BONES
said, This is now bone of my b Gen 2:23 6106
ye shall carry up my b from hence Gen 50:25 6106
Moses took the b of Joseph with Ex 13:19 6106
carry up my b away hence with you Ex 13:19 6106
enemies, and shall break their b Num 24:8 6106
the b of Joseph, which the Josh 24:32 6106
divided her, together with her b Judg 19:29 6106
And they took their b, and buried 1Sa 31:13 6106
Ye are my brethren, ye are my b 2Sa 19:12 6106
David went and took the b of Saul 2Sa 21:12 6106
the b of Jonathan his son from 2Sa 21:12 6106
up from thence the b of Saul 2Sa 21:13 6106
the b of Jonathan his son 2Sa 21:13 6106
they gathered the b of them that 2Sa 21:13 6106
the b of Saul and Jonathan his son 2Sa 21:14 6106
men's b shall be burnt upon thee 1Kin 13:2 6106
lay my b beside his b 1Kin 13:31 6106
down, and touched the b of Elisha 2Kin 13:21 6106
their places with the b of men 2Kin 23:14 6106
took the b out of the sepulchres, 2Kin 23:16 6106
let no man move his b 2Kin 23:18 6106
So they let his b alone 2Kin 23:18 6106
with the b of the prophet that 2Kin 23:18 6106
and burned men's b upon them 2Kin 23:20 6106
buried their b under the oak in 1Chr 10:12 6106
he burnt the b of the priests 2Chr 34:5 6106
which made all my b to shake Job 4:14 6106
flesh, and hast fenced me with b Job 10:11 6106
His b are full of the sin of his Job 20:11 6106
his b are moistened with marrow Job 21:24 6106
My b are pierced in me in the Job 30:17 6106
my b are burned with heat Job 30:30 6106
of his b with strong pain Job 33:19 6106
his b that were not seen stick Job 33:21 6106
His b are as strong pieces of Job 40:18 6106
his b are like bars of iron Job 40:18 1634
for my b are vexed Ps 6:2 6106
all my b are out of joint Ps 22:14 6106
I may tell all my b Ps 22:17 6106
iniquity, and my b are consumed Ps 31:10 6106
my b waxed old through my roaring Ps 32:3 6106
He keepeth all his b Ps 34:20 6106
All my b shall say, LORD, who is Ps 35:10 6106
rest in my b because of my sin Ps 38:3 6106
As with a sword in my b, mine Ps 42:10 6106
that the b which thou hast broken Ps 51:8 6106
for God hath scattered the b of Ps 53:5 6106
my b are burned as an hearth Ps 102:3 6106
groaning my b cleave to my skin Ps 102:5 6106
water, and like oil into his b Ps 109:18 6106
Our b are scattered at the Ps 141:7 6106
to thy navel, and marrow to thy b Prov 3:8 6106

ashamed is as rottenness in his *b* Prov 12:4 6106
but envy the rottenness of the *b* Prov 14:30 6106
and a good report maketh the *b* fat Prov 15:30 6106
to the soul, and health to the *b* Prov 16:24 6106
but a broken spirit drieth the *b* Prov 17:22 1634
nor how the *b* do grow in the womb Eccl 11:5 6106
a lion, so will he break all my *b* Is 38:13 6106
in drought, and make fat thy *b* Is 58:11 6106
your *b* shall flourish like an Is 66:14 6106
out the *b* of the kings of Judah Jer 8:1 6106
the *b* of his princes, and the Jer 8:1 6106
the *b* of the priests, and the Jer 8:1 6106
the *b* of the prophets, and the Jer 8:1 6106
the *b* of the inhabitants of Jer 8:1 6106
as a burning fire shut up in my *b* Jer 20:9 6106
all my *b* shake Jer 23:9 6106
king of Babylon hath broken his *b* Jer 50:17 6106
above hath he sent fire into my *b* Lam 1:13 6106
he hath broken my *b* Lam 3:4 6106
their skin cleaveth to their *b* Lam 4:8 6106
I will scatter your *b* round about Eze 6:5 6106
fill it with the choice *b* Eze 24:4 6106
and burn also the *b* under it Eze 24:5 6106
them seethe the *b* of it therein Eze 24:5 6106
it well, and let the *b* be burned Eze 24:10 6106
iniquities shall be upon their *b* Eze 32:27 6106
of the valley which was full of *b* Eze 37:1 6106
me, Son of man, can these *b* live Eze 37:3 6106
unto me, Prophesy upon these *b* Eze 37:4 6106
and say unto them, O ye dry *b* Eze 37:4 6106
saith the Lord GOD unto these *b* Eze 37:5 6106
the *b* came together, bone to his Eze 37:7 6106
these *b* are the whole house of Eze 37:11 6106
Our *b* are dried, and our hope is Eze 37:11 6106
brake all their *b* in pieces or Dan 6:24 1635
because he burned the *b* of the Amos 2:1 6106
bring out the *b* out of the house Amos 6:10 6106
and their flesh from off their *b* Mic 3:2 6106
and they break their *b*, and chop Mic 3:3 6106
rottenness entered into my *b* Hab 3:16 6106
gnaw not the *b* till the morrow Zeph 3:3 1633
are within full of dead men's *b* Mt 23:27 *3747*
for a spirit hath not flesh and *b* Lk 24:39 *3747*
ancle *b* received strength Acts 3:7 *4974*
body, of his flesh, and of his *b* Eph 5:30 *3747*
gave commandment concerning his *b* Heb 11:22 *3747*

BONNETS
b shalt thou make for them, for Ex 28:40 4021
and his sons, and put the *b* on them Ex 29:9 4021
goodly *b* of fine linen, and linen Ex 39:28 4021
with girdles, and put *b* upon them Lev 8:13 4021
The *b*, and the ornaments of the Is 3:20 6287
have linen *b* upon their heads Eze 44:18 6287

BOOK
This is the *b* of the generations Gen 5:1 5612
Write this for a memorial in a *b* Ex 17:14 5612
he took the *b* of the covenant, and Ex 24:7 5612
out of thy *b* which thou hast Ex 32:32 5612
me, him will I blot out of my *b* Ex 32:33 5612
shall write these curses in a *b* Num 5:23 5612
in the *b* of the wars of the LORD Num 21:14 5612
him a copy of this law in a *b* out Deut 17:18 5612
law that are written in this *b* Deut 28:58 5612
not written in the *b* of this law Deut 28:61 5612
in this *b* shall lie upon him Deut 29:20 5612
are written in this *b* of the law Deut 29:21 5612
curses that are written in this *b* Deut 29:27 5612
are written in this *b* of the law Deut 30:10 5612
the words of this law in a *b* Deut 31:24 5612
Take this *b* of the law, and put it Deut 31:26 5612
This *b* of the law shall not Josh 1:8 5612
in the *b* of the law of Moses Josh 8:31 5612
is written in the *b* of the law Josh 8:34 5612
this written in the *b* of Jasher Josh 10:13 5612
by cities into seven parts in a *b* Josh 18:9 5612
in the *b* of the law of Moses Josh 23:6 5612
words in the *b* of the law of God Josh 24:26 5612
the kingdom, and wrote it in a *b* 1Sa 10:25 5612
it is written in the *b* of Jasher 2Sa 1:18 5612
in the *b* of the acts of Solomon 1Kin 11:41 5612
they are written in the *b* of the 1Kin 14:19 5612
are they not written in the *b* of 1Kin 14:29 5612
are they not written in the *b* of 1Kin 15:7 5612
are they not written in the *b* of 1Kin 15:23 5612
are they not written in the *b* of 1Kin 15:31 5612
are they not written in the *b* of 1Kin 16:5 5612
are they not written in the *b* of 1Kin 16:14 5612
are they not written in the *b* of 1Kin 16:20 5612
are they not written in the *b* of 1Kin 16:27 5612
are they not written in the *b* of 1Kin 22:39 5612
are they not written in the *b* of 1Kin 22:45 5612
are they not written in the *b* of 2Kin 1:18 5612
are they not written in the *b* of 2Kin 8:23 5612
are they not written in the *b* of 2Kin 10:34 5612
are they not written in the *b* of 2Kin 12:19 5612
are they not written in the *b* of 2Kin 13:8 5612
are they not written in the *b* of 2Kin 13:12 5612
in the *b* of the law of Moses 2Kin 14:6 5612
are they not written in the *b* of 2Kin 14:15 5612
are they not written in the *b* of 2Kin 14:18 5612
are they not written in the *b* of 2Kin 14:28 5612
are they not written in the *b* of 2Kin 15:6 5612
they are written in the *b* of the 2Kin 15:11 5612
they are written in the *b* of the 2Kin 15:15 5612
are they not written in the *b* of 2Kin 15:21 5612
they are written in the *b* of the 2Kin 15:26 5612
they are written in the *b* of the 2Kin 15:31 5612
are they not written in the *b* of 2Kin 15:36 5612
are they not written in the *b* of 2Kin 16:19 5612
are they not written in the *b* of 2Kin 20:20 5612
are they not written in the *b* of 2Kin 21:17 5612
b of the chronicles of the kings 2Kin 21:25 5612
I have found the *b* of the law in 2Kin 22:8 5612
And Hilkiah gave the *b* to Shaphan 2Kin 22:8 5612
the priest hath delivered me a *b* 2Kin 22:10 5612
the words of the *b* of the law 2Kin 22:11 5612
the words of this *b* that is found 2Kin 22:13 5612
unto the words of this *b*, to do 2Kin 22:13 5612
even all the words of the *b* which 2Kin 22:16 5612
b of the covenant which was found 2Kin 23:2 5612
that were written in this *b* 2Kin 23:3 5612
written in the *b* of this covenant 2Kin 23:21 5612
b that Hilkiah the priest found 2Kin 23:24 5612
are they not written in the *b* of 2Kin 23:28 5612
are they not written in the *b* of 2Kin 24:5 5612
in the *b* of the kings of Israel 1Chr 9:1 5612
in the *b* of Samuel the seer 1Chr 29:29 1697
in the *b* of Nathan the prophet, 1Chr 29:29 1697
in the *b* of Gad the seer, 1Chr 29:29 1697
in the *b* of Nathan the prophet 2Chr 9:29 1697
in the *b* of Shemaiah the prophet 2Chr 12:15 1697
in the *b* of the kings of Judah 2Chr 16:11 5612
had the *b* of the law of the LORD 2Chr 17:9 5612
they are written in the *b* of Jehu 2Chr 20:34 1697
in the *b* of the kings of Israel 2Chr 20:34 5612
the story of the *b* of the kings 2Chr 24:27 5612
in the law in the *b* of Moses 2Chr 25:4 5612
in the *b* of the kings of Judah 2Chr 25:26 5612
in the *b* of the kings of Israel 2Chr 27:7 5612
in the *b* of the kings of Judah 2Chr 28:26 5612
in the *b* of the kings of Judah and 2Chr 32:32 5612
in the *b* of the kings of Israel 2Chr 33:18 1697
Hilkiah the priest found a *b* of 2Chr 34:14 5612
I have found the *b* of the law in 2Chr 34:15 5612
delivered the *b* to Shaphan 2Chr 34:15 5612
Shaphan carried the *b* to the king 2Chr 34:16 5612
the priest hath given me a *b* 2Chr 34:18 5612
the words of the *b* that is found 2Chr 34:21 5612
all that is written in this *b* 2Chr 34:21 5612
curses that are written in the *b* 2Chr 34:24 5612
b of the covenant that was found 2Chr 34:30 5612
which are written in this *b* 2Chr 34:31 5612
it is written in the *b* of Moses 2Chr 35:12 5612
in the *b* of the kings of Israel 2Chr 35:27 5612
in the *b* of the kings of Israel 2Chr 36:8 5612
b of the records of thy fathers Ezr 4:15 5609
thou find in the *b* of the records Ezr 4:15 5609
it is written in the *b* of Moses Ezr 6:18 5609
bring the *b* of the law of Moses Neh 8:1 5612
attentive unto the *b* of the law Neh 8:3 5612
Ezra opened the *b* in the sight of Neh 8:5 5612
So they read in the *b* in the law Neh 8:8 5612
he read in the *b* of the law of Neh 8:18 5612
read in the *b* of the law of the Neh 9:3 5612
in the *b* of the chronicles Neh 12:23 5612
On that day they read in the *b* of Neh 13:1 5612
it was written in the *b* of the Est 2:23 5612
he commanded to bring the *b* of Est 6:1 5612
and it was written in the *b* Est 9:32 5612
are they not written in the *b* of Est 10:2 5612
oh that they were printed in a *b* Job 19:23 5612
mine adversary had written a *b* Job 31:35 5612
of the *b* it is written of me Ps 40:7 5612
are they not in thy *b* Ps 56:8 5612
out of the *b* of the living Ps 69:28 5612
in thy *b* all my members were Ps 139:16 5612
the words of a *b* that is sealed Is 29:11 5612
the *b* is delivered to him that is Is 29:12 5612
the deaf hear the words of the *b* Is 29:18 5612
in a table, and note it in a *b* Is 30:8 5612
Seek ye out of the *b* of the LORD Is 34:16 5612
all that is written in this *b* Jer 25:13 5612
I have spoken unto thee in a *b* Jer 30:2 5612
subscribed the *b* of the purchase Jer 32:12 5612
Take thee a roll of a *b*, and write Jer 36:2 5612
unto him, upon a roll of a *b* Jer 36:4 5612
reading in the *b* the words of the Jer 36:8 5612
Then read Baruch in the *b* the Jer 36:10 5612
had heard out of the *b* all the Jer 36:11 5612
when Baruch read the *b* in the Jer 36:13 5612
and I wrote them with ink in the *b* Jer 36:18 5612
b which Jehoiakim king of Judah Jer 36:32 5612
in a *b* at the mouth of Jeremiah Jer 45:1 5612
So Jeremiah wrote in a *b* all the Jer 51:60 5612
made an end of reading this *b* Jer 51:63 5612
and, lo, a roll of a *b* was therein Eze 2:9 5612
shall be found written in the *b* Dan 12:1 5612
shut up the words, and seal the *b* Dan 12:4 5612
The *b* of the vision of Nahum the Nah 1:1 5612
a *b* of remembrance was written Mal 3:16 5612
The *b* of the generation of Jesus Mt 1:1 *976*
ye not read in the *b* of Moses Mk 12:26 *976*
As it is written in the *b* of the Lk 3:4 *976*
him the *b* of the prophet Esaias Lk 4:17 *975*
And when he had opened the *b* Lk 4:17 *975*
And he closed the *b*, and he gave it Lk 4:20 *975*
himself saith in the *b* of Psalms Lk 20:42 *976*
which are not written in this *b* Jn 20:30 *975*
it is written in the *b* of Psalms Acts 1:20 *976*
written in the *b* of the prophets Acts 7:42 *976*
in the *b* of the law to do them Gal 3:10 *975*
whose names are in the *b* of life Phil 4:3 *976*
hyssop, and sprinkled both the *b* Heb 9:19 *975*
of the *b* it is written of me Heb 10:7 *975*
and, What thou seest, write in a *b* Rev 1:11 *975*
out his name out of the *b* of life Rev 3:5 *976*
on the throne a *b* written within Rev 5:1 *975*
Who is worthy to open the *b* Rev 5:2 *975*
the earth, was able to open the *b* Rev 5:3 *975*
worthy to open and to read the *b* Rev 5:4 *975*
hath prevailed to open the *b* Rev 5:5 *975*
took the *b* out of the right hand Rev 5:7 *975*
And when he had taken the *b* Rev 5:8 *975*
Thou art worthy to take the *b* Rev 5:9 *975*
had in his hand a little *b* open Rev 10:2 *974*
take the little *b* which is open Rev 10:8 *974*
unto him, Give me the little *b* Rev 10:9 *974*
I took the little *b* out of the Rev 10:10 *974*
names are not written in the *b* of Rev 13:8 *976*
names were not written in the *b* Rev 17:8 *976*
another *b* was opened Rev 20:12 *976*
which is the *b* of life Rev 20:12 *976*
was not found written in the *b* of Rev 20:15 *976*
written in the Lamb's *b* of life Rev 21:27 *975*
sayings of the prophecy of this *b* Rev 22:7 *975*
which keep the sayings of this *b* Rev 22:9 *975*
sayings of the prophecy of this *b* Rev 22:10 *975*
words of the prophecy of this *b* Rev 22:18 *975*
that are written in this *b* Rev 22:18 *975*
words of the *b* of this prophecy Rev 22:19 *976*
his part out of the *b* of life Rev 22:19 *976*
which are written in this *b* Rev 22:19 *975*

BOOKS
of making many *b* there is no end Eccl 12:12 5612
was set, and the *b* were opened Dan 7:10 5609
by *b* the number of the years Dan 9:2 5612
the *b* that should be written Jn 21:25 *975*
arts brought their *b* together Acts 19:19 *976*
comest, bring with thee, and the *b* 2Ti 4:13 *975*
and the *b* were opened Rev 20:12 *975*
which were written in the *b* Rev 20:12 *975*

BOOTH
as a *b* that the keeper maketh Job 27:18 5521
the city, and there made him a *b* Jonah 4:5 5521

BOOTHS
house, and made *b* for his cattle Gen 33:17 5521
Ye shall dwell in *b* seven days Lev 23:42 5521
Israelites born shall dwell in *b* Lev 23:42 5521
children of Israel to dwell in *b* Lev 23:43 5521
of Israel should dwell in *b* in Neh 8:14 5521
of thick trees, to make *b* Neh 8:15 5521
them, and made themselves *b* Neh 8:16 5521
made *b*, and sat under the *b* Neh 8:17 5521

BOOTIES
and thou shalt be for *b* unto them Hab 2:7 4933

BOOTY
And the *b*, being the rest of the Num 31:32 4455
And their camels shall be a *b* Jer 49:32 957
their goods shall become a *b* Zeph 1:13 4953

BOOZ (*bo'-oz*) See BOAZ. *Greek form of Boaz.*
And Salmon begat *B* of Rachab Mt 1:5 *1003*
and *B* begat Obed of Ruth Mt 1:5 *1003*
of Obed, which was the son of *B* Lk 3:32 *1003*

BOR ASHAN See CHOR-ASHAN.

BORDER
the *b* of the Canaanites was from Gen 10:19 1366
his *b* shall be unto Zidon Gen 49:13 3411
the mount, or touch the *b* of it Ex 19:12 7097
thou shalt make unto it a *b* of an Ex 25:25 4526
to the *b* thereof round about Ex 25:25 4526
Over against the *b* shall the Ex 25:27 4526
the breastplate in the *b* thereof Ex 28:26 8193
Also he made thereunto a *b* of an Ex 37:12 4526
for the *b* thereof round about Ex 37:12 4526
Over against the *b* were the rings Ex 37:14 4526
the breastplate, upon the *b* of it Ex 39:19 8193
a city in the uttermost of thy *b* Num 20:16 1366
give Israel passage through his *b* Num 20:21 1366
for Arnon is the *b* of Moab Num 21:13 1366
Ar, and lieth upon the *b* of Moab Num 21:15 1366
Israel to pass through his *b* Num 21:23 1366
for the *b* of the children of Num 21:24 1366
Moab, which is in the *b* of Arnon Num 22:36 1366
in Ije-abarim, in the *b* of Moab Num 33:44 1366
your south *b* shall be the outmost Num 34:3 1366
your *b* shall turn from the south Num 34:4 1366
the *b* shall fetch a compass from Num 34:5 1366
And as for the western *b*, ye shall Num 34:6 1366
even have the great sea for a *b* Num 34:6 1366
this shall be your west *b* Num 34:6 1366
And this shall be your north *b* Num 34:7 1366
b unto the entrance of Hamath Num 34:8
forth of the *b* shall be to Zedad Num 34:8 1366
the *b* shall go on to Ziphron, and Num 34:9 1366
this shall be your north *b* Num 34:9 1366
east *b* from Hazar-enan to Shepham Num 34:10 1366
the *b* shall descend, and shall Num 34:11 1366
the *b* shall go down to Jordan, and Num 34:12 1366
the *b* of the city of his refuge Num 35:26 1366
the *b* even unto the river Jabbok, Deut 3:16 1366
which is the *b* of the children of Deut 3:16 1366
LORD thy God shall enlarge thy *b* Deut 12:20 1366
Gilgal, in the east *b* of Jericho Josh 4:19 7097
which is the *b* of the children of Josh 12:2 1366
unto the *b* of the Geshurites and Josh 12:5 1366
the *b* of Sihon king of Heshbon Josh 12:5 1366
unto the *b* of the children of Josh 13:10 1366
the *b* of the Geshurites and Josh 13:11 1366
the *b* of the children of Reuben Josh 13:23 1366
was Jordan, and the *b* thereof Josh 13:23 1366
from Mahanaim unto the *b* of Debir Josh 13:26 1366
king of Heshbon, Jordan and his *b* Josh 13:27 1366
even to the *b* of Edom the Josh 15:1 1366
their south *b* was from the shore Josh 15:2 1366
the east *b* was the salt sea, even Josh 15:5 1366
their *b* in the north quarter was Josh 15:5 1366
the *b* went up to Beth-hogla, and Josh 15:6 1366
the *b* went up to the stone of Josh 15:6 1366
the *b* went up toward Debir from Josh 15:7 1366
the *b* passed toward the waters of Josh 15:7 1366
the *b* went up by the valley of Josh 15:8 1366
the *b* went up to the top of the Josh 15:8 1366
the *b* was drawn from the top of Josh 15:9 1366
the *b* was drawn to Baalah, which Josh 15:9 1366
the *b* compassed from Baalah Josh 15:10 1366
the *b* went out unto the side of Josh 15:11 1366
the *b* was drawn to Shicron, and Josh 15:11 1366

out of the *b* were at the sea Josh 15:11 1366
the west *b* was to the great sea, Josh 15:12 1366
the great sea, and the *b* thereof Josh 15:47 1366
the *b* of the children of Ephraim Josh 16:5 1366
even the *b* of their inheritance Josh 16:5 1366
the *b* went out toward the sea to Josh 16:6 1366
the *b* went about eastward unto Josh 16:6 1366
The *b* went out from Tappuah Josh 16:8 1366
the *b* went along on the right Josh 17:7 1366
but Tappuah on the *b* of Manasseh Josh 17:8 1366
Manasseh's, and the sea is his *b* Josh 17:10 1366
their *b* on the north side was Josh 18:12 1366
the *b* went up to the side of Josh 18:12 1366
the *b* went over from thence Josh 18:13 1366
the *b* descended to Ataroth-adar, Josh 18:13 1366
the *b* was drawn thence, and Josh 18:14 1366
the *b* went out on the west, and Josh 18:15 1366
the *b* came down to the end of the Josh 18:16 1366
the *b* passed along to the side of Josh 18:19 1366
the outgoings of the *b* were at Josh 18:19 1366
Jordan was the *b* of it on the Josh 18:20 1379
the *b* of their inheritance was Josh 19:10 1366
their *b* went up toward the sea, Josh 19:11 1366
unto the *b* of Chisloth-tabor Josh 19:12 1366
the *b* compasseth it on the north Josh 19:14 1366
their *b* was toward Jezreel, and Josh 19:18 1366
of their *b* were at Jordan Josh 19:22 1366
their *b* was Helkath, and Hali, and Josh 19:25 1366
Rakkon, with the *b* before Japho Josh 19:46 1366
hath made Jordan a *b* between us Josh 22:25 1366
in the *b* of his inheritance in Josh 24:30 1366
in the *b* of his inheritance in Judg 2:9 1366
to the *b* of Abel-meholah, unto Judg 7:22 8193
but came not within the *b* of Moab Judg 11:18 1366
for Arnon was the *b* of Moab Judg 11:18 1366
them unto the *b* of Beth-shemesh 1Sa 6:12 1366
in the *b* of Benjamin at Zelzah 1Sa 10:2 1366
turned to the way of the *b* that 1Sa 13:18 1366
his *b* at the river Euphrates 2Sa 8:3 3027
and unto the *b* of Egypt 1Kin 4:21 1366
and upward, and stood in the *b* 2Kin 3:21 1366
Philistines, and to the *b* of Egypt 2Chr 9:26 1366
them to the *b* of his sanctuary Ps 78:54 1366
will establish the *b* of the widow Prov 15:25 1366
a pillar at the *b* thereof to the Is 19:19 1366
enter into the height of his *b* Is 37:24 7093
shall come again to their own *b* Jer 31:17 1366
against her from the utmost *b* Jer 50:26 7093
will judge you in the *b* of Israel Eze 11:10 1366
will judge you in the *b* of Israel Eze 11:11 1366
Syene even unto the *b* of Ethiopia Eze 29:10 1366
the *b* thereof by the edge thereof Eze 43:13 1366
the *b* about it shall be half a Eze 43:17 1366
settle, and upon the *b* round about Eze 43:20 1366
the west *b* unto the east *b* Eze 45:7 1366
This shall be the *b*, whereby ye Eze 47:13 1366
this shall be the *b* of the land Eze 47:15 1366
is between the *b* of Damascus Eze 47:16 1366
of Damascus and the *b* of Hamath Eze 47:16 1366
the *b* from the sea shall be Eze 47:17 1366
the *b* of Damascus, and the north Eze 47:17 1366
northward, and the *b* of Hamath Eze 47:17 1366
from the *b* unto the east sea Eze 47:18 1366
shall be the great sea from the *b* Eze 47:20 1366
the *b* of Damascus northward, to Eze 48:1 1366
And by the *b* of Dan, from the east Eze 48:2 1366
by the *b* of Asher, from the east Eze 48:3 1366
by the *b* of Naphtali, from the Eze 48:4 1366
by the *b* of Manasseh, from the Eze 48:5 1366
by the *b* of Ephraim, from the Eze 48:6 1366
by the *b* of Reuben, from the east Eze 48:7 1366
by the *b* of Judah, from the east Eze 48:8 1366
most holy by the *b* of the Levites Eze 48:12 1366
over against the *b* of the priests Eze 48:13 1366
of the oblation toward the east *b* Eze 48:21 1366
twenty thousand toward the west *b* Eze 48:21 1366
prince's, between the *b* of Judah Eze 48:22 1366
the *b* of Benjamin, shall be for Eze 48:22 1366
by the *b* of Benjamin, from the Eze 48:24 1366
by the *b* of Simeon, from the east Eze 48:25 1366
by the *b* of Issachar, from the Eze 48:26 1366
by the *b* of Zebulun, from the Eze 48:27 1366
And by the *b* of Gad, at the south Eze 48:28 1366
the *b* shall be even from Tamar Eze 48:28 1366
remove them far from their *b* Joel 3:6 1366
that they might enlarge their *b* Amos 1:13 1366
their *b* greater than your *b* Amos 6:2 1366
have brought thee even to the *b* Obad 7 1366
themselves against their *b* Zeph 2:8 1366
And Hamath also shall *b* thereby Zec 9:2 1379
The *b* of wickedness, and, The Mal 1:4 1366
be magnified from the *b* of Israel Mal 1:5 1366
it were but the *b* of his garment Mk 6:56 *2899*
touched the *b* of his garment Lk 8:44 *2899*

BORDERS

were in all the *b* round about Gen 23:17 1366
to cities from one end of the *b* Gen 47:21 1366
I will smite all thy *b* with frogs Ex 8:2 1366
unto the *b* of the land of Canaan Ex 16:35 7097
before thee, and enlarge thy *b* Ex 34:24 1366
b of their garments throughout Num 15:38 3671
fringe of the *b* a ribband of blue Num 15:38 3671
left, until we have passed thy *b* Num 20:17 1366
high way, until we be past thy *b* Num 21:22 1366
the *b* of the city of his refuge Num 35:27 1366
in the *b* of Dor on the west, Josh 11:2 5299
all the *b* of the Philistines, and Josh 13:2 1552
Egypt, even unto the *b* of Ekron Josh 13:3 1366
Aphek, to the *b* of the Amorites Josh 13:4 1366
unto the *b* of Archi to Ataroth Josh 16:2 1366
they came unto the *b* of Jordan Josh 22:10 1552
in the *b* of Jordan, at the Josh 22:11 1552
they had *b*, and the *b* were 1Kin 7:28 4526
on the *b* that were between the 1Kin 7:29 4526
of it were gravings with their *b* 1Kin 7:31 4526
under the *b* were four wheels 1Kin 7:32 4526
the *b* thereof were of the same 1Kin 7:35 4526
on the *b* thereof, he graved 1Kin 7:36 4526
Ahaz cut off the *b* of the bases 2Kin 16:17 4526
the *b* thereof, from the tower of 2Kin 18:8 1366
enter into the lodgings of his *b* 2Kin 19:23 7093
suburbs of Sharon, upon their *b* 1Chr 5:16 8444
by the *b* of the children of 1Chr 7:29 3027
hast set all the *b* of the earth Ps 74:17 1367
He maketh peace in thy *b*, and Ps 147:14 1366
We will make thee *b* of gold with Song 1:11 8447
is gone round about the *b* of Moab Is 15:8 1366
all thy *b* of pleasant stones Is 54:12 1366
nor destruction within thy *b* Is 60:18 1366
all thy sins, even in all thy *b* Jer 15:13 1366
for sin, throughout all thy *b* Jer 17:3 1366
Thy *b* are in the midst of the Eze 27:4 1366
in all the *b* thereof round about Eze 45:1 1366
and when he treadeth within our *b* Mic 5:6 1366
in the *b* of Zabulon and Nephthalim Mt 4:13 *3725*
enlarge the *b* of their garments, Mt 23:5 *2899*
arose, and went into the *b* of Tyre Mk 7:24 *3181*

BORE

his master shall *b* his ear Ex 21:6 7527
or *b* his jaw through with a thorn Job 41:2 5344

BORED

b a hole in the lid of it, and set 2Kin 12:9 5344

BORN

And unto Enoch was *b* Irad Gen 4:18 3205
to him also there was *b* a son Gen 4:26 3205
and daughters were *b* unto them Gen 6:1 3205
them were sons *b* after the flood Gen 10:1 3205
even to him were children *b* Gen 10:21 3205
And unto Eber were *b* two sons Gen 10:25 3205
b in his own house, three hundred Gen 14:14 3211
one *b* in my house is mine heir Gen 15:3 1121
he that is *b* in the house, or Gen 17:12 3211
He that is *b* in thy house, and he Gen 17:13 3211
Shall a child be *b* unto him that Gen 17:17 3205
and all that were *b* in his house Gen 17:23 3211
b in the house, and bought with Gen 17:27 3211
of his son that was *b* unto him Gen 21:3 3205
when his son Isaac was *b* unto him Gen 21:5 3205
for I have *b* him a son in his old Gen 21:7 3205
which she had *b* unto Abraham Gen 21:9 3205
she hath also *b* children unto thy Gen 22:20 3205
who was *b* to Bethuel, son of Gen 24:15 3205
because I have *b* him three sons Gen 29:34 3205
me, because I have *b* him six sons Gen 30:20 3205
to pass, when Rachel had *b* Joseph Gen 30:25 3205
their children which they have *b* Gen 31:43 3205
which were *b* to him in Padan-aram Gen 35:26 3205
which were *b* unto him in the land Gen 36:5 3205
unto Joseph were *b* two sons Gen 41:50 3205
the land of Egypt were *b* Manasseh Gen 46:20 3205
of Rachel, which were *b* to Jacob Gen 46:22 3205
which were *b* him in Egypt, were Gen 46:27 3205
which were *b* unto thee in the Gen 48:5 3205
Every son that is *b* ye shall cast Ex 1:22 3209
be a stranger, or *b* in the land Ex 12:19 249
be as one that is *b* in the land Ex 12:48 249
she have *b* him sons or daughters Ex 21:4 3205
conceived seed, and *b* a man child Lev 12:2 3205
that hath *b* a male or a female Lev 12:7 3205
mother, whether she be *b* at home Lev 18:9 4138
or *b* abroad, even their nakedness Lev 18:9 4138
be unto you as one *b* among you Lev 19:34 249
he that is *b* in his house Lev 22:11 3211
b shall dwell in booths Lev 23:42 249
as he that is *b* in the land Lev 24:16 249
and for him that was *b* in the land Num 9:14 249
All that are *b* of the country Num 15:13 249
both for him that is *b* among the Num 15:29 249
whether he be *b* in the land Num 15:30 249
And unto Aaron was *b* Nadab Num 26:60 3205
they have *b* him children, both Deut 21:15 3205
but all the people that were *b* in Josh 5:5 3209
as he that was *b* among them Josh 8:33 249
do unto the child that shall be *b* Judg 13:8 3205
father, who was *b* unto Israel Judg 18:29 3205
thee than seven sons, hath *b* him Ruth 4:15 3205
saying, There is a son *b* to Naomi Ruth 4:17 3205
so that the barren hath *b* seven 1Sa 2:5 3205
for thou hast *b* a son 1Sa 4:20 3205
the battle were Eliab the first *b* 1Sa 17:13 3205
unto David were sons *b* in Hebron 2Sa 3:2 3205
These were *b* to David in Hebron 2Sa 3:5 3205
yet sons and daughters *b* to David 2Sa 5:13 3205
that were *b* unto him in Jerusalem 2Sa 5:14 3209
the child also that is *b* unto 2Sa 12:14 3209
Absalom there were *b* three sons 2Sa 14:27 3205
he also was *b* to the giant 2Sa 21:20 3205
These four were *b* to the giant in 2Sa 21:22 3205
a child shall be *b* unto the house 1Kin 13:2 3205
And unto Eber were *b* two sons 1Chr 1:19 3205
which three were *b* unto him of 1Chr 2:3 3205
of Hezron, that were *b* unto him 1Chr 2:9 3205
which were *b* unto him in Hebron 1Chr 3:1 3205
These six were *b* unto him in 1Chr 3:4 3205
And these were *b* unto him in 1Chr 3:5 3205
that were *b* in that land slew 1Chr 7:21 3205
These were *b* unto the giant in 1Chr 20:8 3205
Behold, a son shall be *b* to thee 1Chr 22:9 3205
unto Shemaiah his son were sons *b* 1Chr 26:6 3205
wives, and such as are *b* of them Ezr 10:3 3205
there were *b* unto him seven sons Job 1:2 3205
the day perish wherein I was *b* Job 3:3 3205
Yet man is *b* unto trouble, as the Job 5:7 3205
though man be *b* like a wild ass's Job 11:12 3205
Man that is *b* of a woman is of Job 14:1 3205
Art thou the first man that was *b* Job 15:7 3205
and he which is *b* of a woman Job 15:14 3205
he be clean that is *b* of a woman Job 25:4 3205
thou it, because thou wast then *b* Job 38:21 3205
unto a people that shall be *b* Ps 22:31 3205
go astray as soon as they be *b* Ps 58:3 990
the children which should be *b* Ps 78:6 3205
this man was *b* there Ps 87:4 3205
This and that man was *b* in her Ps 87:5 3205
people, that this man was *b* there Ps 87:6 3205
a brother is *b* for adversity Prov 17:17 3205
and had servants *b* in my house Eccl 2:7 1121
A time to be *b*, and a time to die Eccl 3:2 3205
whereas also he that is *b* in his Eccl 4:14 3205
For unto us a child is *b*, unto us Is 9:6 3205
or shall a nation be *b* at once Is 66:8 3205
that are *b* in this place, and Jer 16:3 3205
Cursed be the day wherein I was *b* Jer 20:14 3205
A man child is *b* unto thee Jer 20:15 3205
country, where ye were not *b* Jer 22:26 3205
in the day thou wast *b* thy navel Eze 16:4 3205
in the day that thou wast *b* Eze 16:5 3205
you as *b* in the country among the Eze 47:22 249
her as in the day that she was *b* Hos 2:3 3205
of Mary, of whom was *b* Jesus Mt 1:16 *1080*
Now when Jesus was *b* in Bethlehem Mt 2:1 *1080*
is he that is *b* King of the Jews Mt 2:2 *5088*
of them where Christ should be *b* Mt 2:4 *1080*
Among them that are *b* of women Mt 11:11 *1084*
which were so *b* from their Mt 19:12 *1080*
for that man if he had not been *b* Mt 26:24 *1080*
that man if he had never been *b* Mk 14:21 *1080*
that holy thing which shall be *b* Lk 1:35 *1080*
For unto you is *b* this day in the Lk 2:11 *5088*
Among those that are *b* of women Lk 7:28 *1084*
Which were *b*, not of blood, nor Jn 1:13 *1080*
thee, Except a man be *b* again Jn 3:3 *1080*
How can a man be *b* when he is old Jn 3:4 *1080*
into his mother's womb, and be *b* Jn 3:4 *1080*
thee, Except a man be *b* of water Jn 3:5 *1080*
That which is *b* of the flesh is Jn 3:6 *1080*
that which is *b* of the Spirit is Jn 3:6 *1080*
unto thee, Ye must be *b* again Jn 3:7 *1080*
every one that is *b* of the Spirit Jn 3:8 *1080*
We be not *b* of fornication Jn 8:41 *1080*
his parents, that he was *b* blind Jn 9:2 *1080*
your son, who ye say was *b* blind Jn 9:19 *1080*
our son, and that he was *b* blind Jn 9:20 *1080*
the eyes of one that was *b* blind Jn 9:32 *1080*
Thou wast altogether *b* in sins Jn 9:34 *1080*
that a man is *b* into the world Jn 16:21 *1080*
To this end was I *b*, and for this Jn 18:37 *1080*
our own tongue, wherein we were *b* Acts 2:8 *1080*
In which time Moses was *b* Acts 7:20 *1080*
b in Pontus, lately come from Acts 18:2 *1085*
b at Alexandria, an eloquent man, Acts 18:24 *1085*
b in Tarsus, a city in Cilicia, Acts 22:3 *1080*
And Paul said, But I was free *b* Acts 22:28 *1080*
(For the children being not yet *b* Rom 9:11 *1080*
as of one *b* out of due time 1Cor 15:8 *1626*
bondwoman was *b* after the flesh Gal 4:23 *1080*
But as then he that was *b* after Gal 4:29 *1080*
him that was *b* after the Spirit Gal 4:29
By faith Moses, when he was *b* Heb 11:23 *1080*
Being *b* again, not of corruptible 1Pet 1:23 *313*
doeth righteousness is *b* of him 1Jn 2:29 *1080*
Whosoever is *b* of God doth not 1Jn 3:9 *1080*
sin, because he is *b* of God 1Jn 3:9 *1080*
every one that loveth is *b* of God 1Jn 4:7 *1080*
Jesus is the Christ is *b* of God 1Jn 5:1 *1080*
For whatsoever is *b* of God 1Jn 5:4 *1080*
whosoever is *b* of God sinneth not 1Jn 5:18 *1080*
her child as soon as it was *b* Rev 12:4 *5088*

BORNE

that the ark may be *b* with them Ex 25:14 5375
that the table may be *b* with them Ex 25:28 5375
stood, and on which it was *b* up Judg 16:29 5564
I have *b* chastisement, I will not Job 34:31 5375
then I could have *b* it Ps 55:12 5375
for thy sake I have *b* reproach Ps 69:7 5375
which are *b* by me from the belly, Is 46:3 6006
Surely he hath *b* our griefs Is 53:4 5375
ye shall be *b* upon her sides, and Is 66:12 5375
they must needs be *b*, because Jer 10:5 5375
She that hath *b* seven languisheth Jer 15:9 3205
that thou hast *b* me a man of Jer 15:10 3205
because he hath *b* it upon him Lam 3:28 5190
we have *b* their iniquities Lam 5:7 5445
whom thou hast *b* unto me Eze 16:20 3205
Thou hast *b* thy lewdness and thine Eze 16:58 5375
yet have they *b* their shame with Eze 32:24 5375
yet have they *b* their shame with Eze 32:25 5375
because ye have *b* the shame of Eze 36:6 5375
that they have *b* their shame Eze 39:26 5375
But ye have *b* the tabernacle of Amos 5:26 5375
unto us, which have *b* the burden Mt 20:12 *941*
heavy burdens and grievous to be *b* Mt 23:4 *1418*
of the palsy, which was *b* of four Mk 2:3 *142*
men with burdens grievous to be *b* Lk 11:46 *1418*
sent me, hath *b* witness of me Jn 5:37
Sir, if thou have *b* him hence Jn 20:15 *941*
that he was *b* of the soldiers for Acts 21:35 *941*
as we have *b* the image of the 1Cor 15:49 *5409*
Which have *b* witness of thy 3Jn 6
And hast *b*, and hast patience, and Rev 2:3 *941*

BORROW

woman shall *b* of her neighbour Ex 3:22 7592
let every man *b* of his neighbour, Ex 11:2 7592
if a man *b* ought of his neighbour Ex 22:14 7592
nations, but thou shalt not *b* Deut 15:6 5670
many nations, and thou shalt not *b* Deut 28:12 3867
b thee vessels abroad of all thy 2Kin 4:3 7592
b not a few 2Kin 4:3

from him that would *b* of thee Mt 5:42 *1155*

BORROWED
they *b* of the Egyptians jewels of Ex 12:35 7592
for it was *b* 2Kin 6:5 7592
We have *b* money for the king's Neh 5:4 3867

BORROWER
the *b* is servant to the lender Prov 22:7 3867
as with the lender, so with the *b* Is 24:2 3867

BORROWETH
The wicked *b*, and payeth not again Ps 37:21 3867

BORSHAN See CHOR-ASHAN.

BOSCATH (*bos'-cath*) See BOSKETH. *A city in Judah.*
the daughter of Adaiah of *B* 2Kin 22:1 1218

BOSOM
I have given my maid into thy *b* Gen 16:5 2436
Put now thine hand into thy *b* Ex 4:6 2436
And he put his hand into his *b* Ex 4:6 2436
Put thine hand into thy *b* again Ex 4:7 2436
he put his hand into his *b* again Ex 4:7 2436
and plucked it out of his *b* Ex 4:7 2436
say unto me, Carry them in thy *b* Num 11:12 2436
daughter, or the wife of thy *b* Deut 13:6 2436
and toward the wife of his *b* Deut 28:54 2436
evil toward the husband of her *b* Deut 28:56 2436
the child, and laid it in her *b* Ruth 4:16 2436
of his own cup, and lay in his *b* 2Sa 12:3 2436
and thy master's wives into thy *b* 2Sa 12:8 2436
him, and let her lie in thy *b* 1Kin 1:2 2436
slept, and laid it in her *b* 1Kin 3:20 2436
and laid her dead child in my *b* 1Kin 3:20 2436
And he took him out of her *b* 1Kin 17:19 2436
by hiding mine iniquity in my *b* Job 31:33 2243
prayer returned into mine own *b* Ps 35:13 2436
pluck it out of thy *b* Ps 74:11 2436
into their *b* their reproach Ps 79:12 2436
how I do bear in my *b* the Ps 89:50 2436
nor he that bindeth sheaves his *b* Ps 129:7 2683
embrace the *b* of a stranger Prov 5:20 2436
Can a man take fire in his *b* Prov 6:27 2436
man taketh a gift out of the *b* to Prov 17:23 2436
man hideth his hand in his *b* Prov 19:24 6747
and a reward in the *b* strong wrath Prov 21:14 2436
slothful hideth his hand in his *b* Prov 26:15 6747
anger resteth in the *b* of fools Eccl 7:9 2436
his arm, and carry them in his *b* Is 40:11 2436
even recompense into their *b* Is 65:6 2436
their former work into their *b* Is 65:7 2436
of the fathers into the *b* of Jer 32:18 2436
poured out into their mothers' *b* Lam 2:12 2436
from her that lieth in thy *b* Mic 7:5 2436
over, shall men give into your *b* Lk 6:38 *2859*
by the angels into Abraham's *b* Lk 16:22 *2859*
afar off, and Lazarus in his *b* Lk 16:23 *2859*
which is in the *b* of the Father Jn 1:18 *2859*
on Jesus' *b* one of his disciples Jn 13:23 *2859*

BOSOR (*bo'-sor*) *Greek form of Besor.*
the way of Balaam the son of *B* 2Pet 2:15 *1007*

BOSSES
upon the thick *b* of his bucklers Job 15:26 1354

BOTCH
smite thee with the *b* of Egypt Deut 28:27 7822
with a sore *b* that cannot be Deut 28:35 7822

BOTH
And they were *b* naked, the man and Gen 2:25 8147
And the eyes of them *b* were opened Gen 3:7 8147
b man, and beast, and the creeping Gen 6:7
b of fowl, and of cattle, and of Gen 7:21
b man, and cattle, and the creeping Gen 7:23
b of fowl, and of cattle, and of Gen 8:17
laid it upon *b* their shoulders Gen 9:23 8147
b old and young, all the people Gen 19:4
with blindness, *b* small and great Gen 19:11
Thus were *b* the daughters of Lot Gen 19:36 8147
b of them made a covenant Gen 21:27 8147
there they sware *b* of them Gen 21:31 8147
they went *b* of them together Gen 22:6 8147
so they went *b* of them together Gen 22:8 8147
unto him, We have *b* straw Gen 24:25 1571
B drink thou, and I will also draw Gen 24:44 8147
deprived also of you *b* in one day Gen 27:45 8147
that they may judge betwixt us *b* Gen 31:37 8147
b Ajah, and Anah Gen 36:24
And they dreamed a dream *b* of them Gen 40:5 8147
house, *b* me and the chief baker Gen 41:10
and when *b* they and their father Gen 42:35
b we, and thou, and also our little Gen 43:8 1571
b let him die, and we also will be Gen 44:9
b we, and he also with whom the Gen 44:16 1571
b we, and also our fathers Gen 46:34 1571
b we, and also our fathers Gen 47:3 1571
thine eyes, *b* we and our land Gen 47:19 1571
And Joseph took them *b*, Ephraim in Gen 48:13 8147
there went up with him *b* chariots Gen 50:9 1571
task in making brick *b* yesterday Ex 5:14 1571
b in vessels of wood, and in Ex 7:19 8147
the frogs shall come up *b* on thee Ex 8:4
was in the field, *b* man and beast Ex 9:25 8147
the land of Egypt, *b* man and beast Ex 12:12 8147
b ye and the children of Israel Ex 12:31 1571
of Israel, *b* of man and of beast Ex 13:2
b the firstborn of man, and the Ex 13:15
b thou, and this people that is Ex 18:18 1571
the cause of *b* parties shall come Ex 22:9 8147
of the LORD be between them *b* Ex 22:11 8147
thus shall it be for them *b* Ex 26:24 8147
I will sanctify also *b* Aaron Ex 29:44
were written on *b* their sides Ex 32:15 8147
b men and women, as many as were Ex 35:22

b of blue, and of purple, and of Ex 35:25
b he, and Aholiab, the son of Ex 35:34
to *b* of them in *b* the corners Ex 36:29 8147
b the top of it, and the sides Ex 37:26
brasen pot, it shall be *b* scoured Lev 6:28
b the laver and his foot, to Lev 8:11
b of the first year, without Lev 9:3
they shall *b* bathe themselves in Lev 15:18
Aaron shall lay *b* his hands upon Lev 16:21 8147
he shall *b* wash his clothes, and Lev 17:15
b of them shall surely be put to Lev 20:11 8147
b of them shall surely be put to Lev 20:12 8147
b of them have committed an Lev 20:13 8147
be burnt with fire, *b* he and they Lev 20:14
b of them shall be cut off from Lev 20:18 8147
b of the most holy, and of the Lev 21:22
kill it and her young *b* in one day Lev 22:28
b he and his children with him, and Lev 25:41
B thy bondmen, and thy bondmaids Lev 25:44
b he, and his children with him Lev 25:54
b of man and beast, and of the Lev 27:28
if he change it at all, then *b* it Lev 27:33
in Israel, *b* man and beast Num 3:13
B male and female shall ye put out Num 5:3
b the altar and all the vessels Num 7:1
b of them were full of fine flour Num 7:13 8147
b of them full of fine flour Num 7:19 8147
b of them full of fine flour Num 7:25 8147
b of them full of fine flour Num 7:31 8147
b of them full of fine flour Num 7:37 8147
b of them full of fine flour Num 7:43 8147
b of them full of fine flour Num 7:49 8147
b of them full of fine flour Num 7:55 8147
b of them full of fine flour Num 7:61 8147
b of them full of fine flour Num 7:67 8147
b of them full of fine flour Num 7:73 8147
b of them full of fine flour Num 7:79 8147
Israel are mine, *b* man and beast Num 8:17
b for the stranger, and for him Num 9:14
and they *b* came forth Num 12:5 8147
One ordinance shall be *b* for you Num 15:15
b for him that is born among the Num 15:29
For which cause *b* thou and all thy Num 16:11
thrust *b* of them through, the man Num 25:8 8147
b he, and all the children of Num 27:21
the prey, *b* of men and of beasts Num 31:11
purify *b* yourselves and your Num 31:19
b of man and of beast, thou, and Num 31:26
b of the persons, and of the Num 31:28
b of man and of beast, and gave Num 31:47
b for the children of Israel, and Num 35:15
Then *b* the men, between whom the Deut 19:17 8147
b the beloved and the hated Deut 21:15
then they shall *b* of them die Deut 22:22
b the man that lay with the woman Deut 22:22
Then ye shall bring them *b* out Deut 22:24 8147
for even *b* these are abomination Deut 23:18 8147
choose life, that *b* thou and thy Deut 30:19
shall destroy *b* the young man Deut 32:25 1571
b man and woman, young and Josh 6:21
b of men and women, were twelve Josh 8:25
b to go out, and to come in Josh 14:11
b they who are of Beth-shean and Josh 17:16
colours of needlework on *b* sides Judg 5:30
for *b* they and their camels were Judg 6:5
b thou, and thy son, and thy son's Judg 8:22 1571
b because we have forsaken our Judg 10:10
burnt up *b* the shocks, and also Judg 15:5
eat and drink *b* of them together Judg 19:6 8147
and they did eat *b* of them Judg 19:8 8147
Yet there is *b* straw and provender Judg 19:19 1571
and Chilion died also *b* of them Ruth 1:5 8147
and was in favour *b* with the LORD 1Sa 2:26 1571
one day they shall die *b* of them 1Sa 2:34 8147
at which *b* the ears of every one 1Sa 3:11 8147
b the palms of his hands were cut 1Sa 5:4 8147
b small and great, and they had 1Sa 5:9
b of fenced cities, and of country 1Sa 6:18 8147
arose, and they went out *b* of them 1Sa 9:26 8147
of the LORD then shall *b* ye 1Sa 12:14 1571
be consumed, *b* ye and your king 1Sa 12:25 1571
b of them discovered themselves 1Sa 14:11 8147
but slay *b* man and woman, infant 1Sa 15:3
Thy servant slew *b* the lion 1Sa 17:36 1571
they went out *b* of them into the 1Sa 20:11 8174
forasmuch as we have sworn *b* of 1Sa 20:42 8174
b men and women, children and 1Sa 22:19
in prosperity, Peace be *b* to thee 1Sa 25:6
were a wall unto us *b* by night 1Sa 25:16 1571
they were also *b* of them his 1Sa 25:43 8147
thou shalt *b* do great things, and 1Sa 26:25 1571
was over *b* the Cherethites 2Sa 8:18
and was lame on *b* his feet 2Sa 9:13 8147
bring me again, and shew me *b* it 2Sa 15:25
of Ahithophel *b* with David 2Sa 16:23 1571
but they went *b* of them away 2Sa 17:18 8147
not asked, *b* riches, and honour 1Kin 3:13 1571
b of the temple and of the oracle 1Kin 6:5
b the floor of the house, and the 1Kin 6:15
b the floor and the walls with 1Kin 6:16
b the cherubims were of one 1Kin 6:25 8147
b for the inner court of the 1Kin 7:12
b for the doors of the inner 1Kin 7:50
of fire, and parted them *b* asunder 2Kin 2:11 8147
b ye, and your cattle, and your 2Kin 3:17
compassed the city *b* with horses 2Kin 6:15
b their children, and their 2Kin 17:41 1571
of it, *b* his ears shall tingle 2Kin 21:12 8147
all the people, *b* small and great 2Kin 23:2
b that altar and the high place he 2Kin 23:15 1571
b small and great, and the captains 2Kin 25:26
could use *b* the right hand and the 1Chr 12:2
b toward the east, and toward the 1Chr 12:15
b ye and your brethren, that ye 1Chr 15:12

b man and woman, to every one a 1Chr 16:3
B for the shewbread, and for the 1Chr 23:29
b Zadok of the sons of Eleazar 1Chr 24:3 8147
b for the candlestick, and also 1Chr 28:15
B riches and honour come of thee 1Chr 29:12
b riches with the dead bodies 2Chr 20:25
b toward God, and toward his house 2Chr 24:16
b he and Amaziah king of Judah, at 2Chr 25:21
b in the low country, and in the 2Chr 26:10
b the second year, and the third 2Chr 27:5
B to the genealogy of the priests 2Chr 31:17
b he and the inhabitants of 2Chr 32:26
b of the new moons, and of all the Ezr 3:5
b young bullocks, and rams, and Ezr 6:9
b I and my father's house have Neh 1:6
half of them held *b* the spears Neh 4:16
before the congregation *b* of men Neh 8:2
b Jeshua the son of Azaniah Neh 10:9
b with thanksgivings, and with Neh 12:27
b out of the plain country round Neh 12:28
b the singers and the porters kept Neh 12:45
b unto great and small, seven days Est 1:5
honour, *b* to great and small Est 1:20
they were *b* hanged on a tree Est 2:23 8147
b young and old, little children Est 3:13
b little ones and women, and to Est 8:11
king Ahasuerus, *b* nigh and far Est 9:20
that might lay his hand upon us *b* Job 9:33 8147
With us are *b* the grayheaded and Job 15:10 1571
I will *b* lay me down in peace, and Ps 4:8 3162
B low and high, rich and poor Ps 49:2 1571
b living, and in his wrath Ps 58:9
b the inward thought of every one Ps 64:6
b the chariot and horse are cast Ps 76:6
b small and great beasts Ps 104:25
fear the LORD, *b* small and great Ps 115:13
of Egypt, *b* of man and beast Ps 135:8
and the light are *b* alike to thee Ps 139:12
B young men, and maidens Ps 148:12
even they *b* are abomination to Prov 17:15 8147
b of them are alike abomination Prov 20:10 8147
the LORD hath made even *b* of them Prov 20:12 8147
and who knoweth the ruin of them *b* Prov 24:22 8147
all things *b* rewardeth the fool Prov 26:10
wrath is heavier than them *b* Prov 27:3 8147
the LORD lighteneth *b* their eyes Prov 29:13 8147
Yea, better is he than *b* they Eccl 4:3 8147
than *b* the hands full with Eccl 4:6
man's heart discerneth *b* time Eccl 8:5
or whether they *b* shall be alike Eccl 11:6 8147
they shall *b* burn together, and Is 1:31 8147
shall be forsaken of *b* her kings Is 7:16 8147
offence to *b* the houses of Israel Is 8:14 8147
fruitful field, *b* soul and body Is 10:18
cruel *b* with wrath and fierce Is 13:9
he shall *b* cut off the sprigs Is 18:5
b he that helpeth shall fall, and Is 31:3 8147
He hath *b* spoken unto me, and Is 38:15
the tongs *b* worketh in the coals Is 44:12
b the former and the latter, in Jer 5:24
b the fowl of the heavens and the Jer 9:10
b the prophet and the priest go Jer 14:18 1571
B the great and the small shall Jer 16:6
of this city, *b* man and beast Jer 21:6
For *b* prophet and priest are Jer 23:11 1571
b rising up early, and sending Jer 26:5
b against many countries, and Jer 28:8
b young men and old together Jer 31:13
b that which was sealed according Jer 32:11
b which is sealed, and this Jer 32:14
the words, they were afraid *b* one Jer 36:16 413
your wives have *b* spoken with Jer 44:25
and they are fallen *b* together Jer 46:12 8147
they shall depart, *b* man and beast Jer 50:3
for the LORD hath *b* devised Jer 51:12 1571
a rumour shall *b* come one year Jer 51:46
is good that a man should *b* hope Lam 3:26
b maids, and little children, and Eze 9:6
forth, *b* sons and daughters Eze 14:22
fire devoureth *b* the ends of it Eze 15:4 8147
b twain shall come forth out of Eze 21:19
defiled, that they took *b* one way Eze 23:13 8147
b thy lewdness and thy whoredoms Eze 23:29
will *b* search my sheep, and seek Eze 34:11
b the shields and the bucklers Eze 39:9
all their goings out were *b* Eze 42:11
to give *b* the sanctuary and the Dan 8:13
b these kings' hearts shall be to Dan 11:27 8147
b treadeth down, and teareth in Mic 5:8
do evil with *b* hands earnestly Mic 7:3
lifteth up *b* the bright sword Nah 3:3
b the cormorant and the bittern Zeph 2:14 1571
of peace shall be between them *b* Zec 6:13 8147
be in the siege *b* against Judah Zec 12:2 1571
new bottles, and *b* are preserved Mt 9:17 *297*
which is able to destroy *b* soul Mt 10:28 *2532*
the blind and dumb *b* spake and saw Mt 12:22 *2532*
Let *b* grow together until the Mt 13:30 *297*
b shall fall into the ditch Mt 15:14 *297*
many as they found, *b* bad and good Mt 22:10 *5037*
b what they had done, and what Mk 6:30 *5037*
he maketh *b* the deaf to hear, and Mk 7:37 *5037*
they were *b* righteous before God Lk 1:6 *297*
they *b* were now well stricken in Lk 1:7 *297*
b hearing them, and asking them Lk 2:46 *2532*
filled *b* the ships, so that they Lk 5:7 *297*
then *b* the new maketh a rent, and Lk 5:36 *2532*
and *b* are preserved Lk 5:38 *297*
shall they not *b* fall into the Lk 6:39 *297*
to pay, he frankly forgave them *b* Lk 7:42 *297*
ye shall be betrayed *b* by parents Lk 21:16 *2532*
b into prison, and to death Lk 22:33 *2532*
b Jesus was called, and his Jn 2:2 *2532*
that *b* he that soweth and he that Jn 4:36 *2532*

Ye *b* know me, and ye know Jn 7:28 2532
unto him, Thou hast *b* seen him Jn 9:37 2532
come and take away *b* our place Jn 11:48 2532
Now *b* the chief priests and the Jn 11:57 2532
I have *b* glorified it, and will Jn 12:28 2532
have they *b* seen and hated *b* me Jn 15:24 2532
So they ran *b* together Jn 20:4 1417
of all that Jesus began *b* to do Acts 1:1 5037
witnesses unto me *b* in Jerusalem Acts 1:8 5037
upper room, where abode *b* Peter Acts 1:13 5037
David, that he is *b* dead and Acts 2:29 2532
have crucified, *b* Lord and Christ Acts 2:36 2532
b Herod, and Pontius Pilate, with Acts 4:27 5037
to the Lord, multitudes *b* of men Acts 5:14 5037
were baptized, *b* men and women Acts 8:12 5037
they went down *b* into the water Acts 8:38 297
b Philip and the eunuch Acts 8:38 5037
he did *b* in the land of the Jews Acts 10:39 5037
that they went *b* together into Acts 14:1
a great multitude *b* of the Jews Acts 14:1 5037
an assault made *b* of the Gentiles Acts 14:5 5037
the Lord Jesus, *b* Jews and Greeks Acts 19:10 5037
Testifying *b* to the Jews, and also Acts 20:21 5037
b we, and they of that place, Acts 21:12 5037
and delivering into prisons *b* men Acts 22:4 5037
but the Pharisees confess *b* Acts 23:8 297
the dead, *b* of the just and unjust Acts 24:15 5037
b at Jerusalem, and also here, Acts 25:24 5037
a witness *b* of these things which Acts 26:16 5037
this day, witnessing *b* to small Acts 26:22 5037
were *b* almost, and altogether such Acts 26:29 2532
b out of the law of Moses, and out Acts 28:23 5037
you by the mutual faith *b* of you Rom 1:12 5037
I am debtor *b* to the Greeks, and Rom 1:14 5037
b to the wise, and to the unwise Rom 1:14 5037
for we have before proved *b* Jews Rom 3:9 5037
of the riches *b* of the wisdom Rom 11:33 2532
For to this end Christ *b* died Rom 14:9 2532
he might be Lord *b* of the dead Rom 14:9 2532
Christ our Lord, *b* theirs and ours 1Cor 1:2 5037
b Jews and Greeks, Christ the 1Cor 1:24 5037
who *b* will bring to light the 1Cor 4:5 2532
this present hour we *b* hunger 1Cor 4:11 2532
but God shall destroy *b* it 1Cor 6:13 2532
God hath *b* raised up the Lord, and 1Cor 6:14 2532
that *b* they that have wives be as 1Cor 7:29 2532
that she may be holy *b* in body 1Cor 7:34 2532
b minister bread for your food 2Cor 9:10 2532
b which are in heaven, and which Eph 1:10 5037
is our peace, who hath made *b* one Eph 2:14 297
that he might reconcile *b* unto Eph 2:16 297
For through him we *b* have access Eph 2:18 297
inasmuch as *b* in my bonds Phil 1:7 5037
which worketh in you *b* to will Phil 2:13 2532
things, which ye have *b* learned Phil 4:9 2532
I know *b* how to be abased, and I Phil 4:12 2532
I am instructed *b* to be full Phil 4:12 2532
b to abound and to suffer need Phil 4:12 2532
Who *b* killed the Lord Jesus, and 1Th 2:15 2532
b among yourselves, and to all men 1Th 5:15 2532
Lord touching you, that ye *b* do 2Th 3:4 2532
For therefore we *b* labour 1Ti 4:10 2532
this thou shalt *b* save thyself 1Ti 4:16 2532
by sound doctrine *b* to exhort Titus 1:9 2532
b in the flesh, and in the Lord Philem 16 2532
b with signs and wonders, and with Heb 2:4 5037
For *b* he that sanctifieth and they Heb 2:11 5037
to God, that he may offer *b* gifts Heb 5:1 5037
exercised to discern *b* good Heb 5:14 5037
b sure and stedfast, and which Heb 6:19 5037
in which were offered *b* gifts Heb 9:9 5037
hyssop, and sprinkled *b* the book Heb 9:19 5037
with blood *b* the tabernacle Heb 9:21 2532
a gazingstock *b* by reproaches Heb 10:33 5037
blessed *b* the sons of Joseph Heb 11:21 1538
no fountain *b* yield salt water Jas 3:12
in *b* which I stir up your pure 2Pet 3:1
To him be glory *b* now and for ever 2Pet 3:18 2532
he hath *b* the Father and the Son 2Jn 9 2532
dominion and power, *b* now and ever Jude 25 2532
image of the beast should *b* speak Rev 13:15 2532
b small and great, rich and poor, Rev 13:16
that fear him, *b* small and great Rev 19:5
b free and bond Rev 19:18 5037
b small and great Rev 19:18 2532
These *b* were cast alive into a Rev 19:20 1417

BOTTLE

a *b* of water, and gave it unto Gen 21:14 2573
And the water was spent in the *b* Gen 21:15 2573
went, and filled the *b* with water Gen 21:19 2573
And she opened a *b* of milk Judg 4:19 4997
a *b* of wine, and brought him unto 1Sa 1:24 5035
and another carrying a *b* of wine 1Sa 10:3 5035
a *b* of wine, and a kid, and sent 1Sa 16:20 4997
of summer fruits, and a *b* of wine 2Sa 16:1 5035
put thou my tears into thy *b* Ps 56:8 4997
I am become like a *b* in the smoke Ps 119:83 4997
Every *b* shall be filled with wine Jer 13:12 5035
every *b* shall be filled with wine Jer 13:12 5035
Go and get a potter's earthen *b* Jer 19:1 1228
Then shalt thou break the *b* in Jer 19:10 1228
drink, that puttest thy *b* to him Hab 2:15 2573

BOTTLES

sacks upon their asses, and wine *b* Josh 9:4 4997
these *b* of wine, which we filled, Josh 9:13 4997
two *b* of wine, and five sheep 1Sa 25:18 5035
it is ready to burst like new *b* Job 32:19 178
or who can stay the *b* of heaven Job 38:37 5035
his vessels, and break their *b* Jer 48:12 5035
have made him sick with *b* of wine Hos 7:5 2573
do men put new wine into old *b* Mt 9:17 779
else the *b* break, and the wine Mt 9:17 779
wine runneth out, and the *b* perish Mt 9:17 779
but they put new wine into new *b* Mt 9:17 779
man putteth new wine into old *b* Mk 2:22 779
the new wine doth burst the *b* Mk 2:22 779
spilled, and the *b* will be marred Mk 2:22 779
new wine must be put into new *b* Mk 2:22 779
man putteth new wine into old *b* Lk 5:37 779
the new wine will burst the *b* Lk 5:37 779
be spilled, and the *b* shall perish Lk 5:37 779
new wine must be put into new *b* Lk 5:38 779

BOTTOM

they sank into the *b* as a stone Ex 15:5 4688
blood beside the *b* of the altar Ex 29:12 3247
the *b* of the altar of the burnt Lev 4:7 3247
the *b* of the altar of the burnt Lev 4:18 3247
b of the altar of burnt offering Lev 4:25 3247
thereof at the *b* of the altar Lev 4:30 3247
thereof at the *b* of the altar Lev 4:34 3247
wrung out at the *b* of the altar Lev 5:9 3247
the blood at the *b* of the altar Lev 8:15 3247
the blood at the *b* of the altar Lev 9:9 3247
it, and covereth the *b* of the sea Job 36:30 8328
the *b* thereof of gold, the Song 3:10 7507
even the *b* shall be a cubit, and Eze 43:13 2436
from the *b* upon the ground even Eze 43:14 2436
the *b* thereof shall be a cubit Eze 43:17 3247
they came at the *b* of the den Dan 6:24 773
from my sight in the *b* of the sea Amos 9:3 7172
myrtle trees that were in the *b* Zec 1:8 4699
in twain from the top to the *b* Mt 27:51 2736
in twain from the top to the *b* Mk 15:38 2736

BOTTOMLESS

was given the key of the *b* pit Rev 9:1 12
And he opened the *b* pit Rev 9:2 12
which is the angel of the *b* pit Rev 9:11 12
b pit shall make war against them Rev 11:7 12
and shall ascend out of the *b* pit Rev 17:8 12
having the key of the *b* pit Rev 20:1 12
And cast him into the *b* pit Rev 20:3 12

BOTTOMS

down to the *b* of the mountains Jonah 2:6 7095

BOUGH

Joseph is a fruitful *b* Gen 49:22 1121
even a fruitful *b* by a well Gen 49:22 1121
cut down a *b* from the trees, and Judg 9:48 7754
likewise cut down every man his *b* Judg 9:49 7754
shall lop the *b* with terror Is 10:33 6288
in the top of the uppermost *b* Is 17:6 534
strong cities be as a forsaken *b* Is 17:9 2793

BOUGHS

first day the *b* of goodly trees Lev 23:40 6529
the *b* of thick trees, and willows Lev 23:40 6057
shalt not go over the *b* again Deut 24:20 6288
under the thick *b* of a great oak 2Sa 18:9 7730
bring forth *b* like a plant Job 14:9 7105
the *b* thereof were like the Ps 80:10 6057
She sent out her *b* unto the sea Ps 80:11 7105
I will take hold of the *b* thereof Song 7:8 5577
When the *b* thereof are withered, Is 27:11 7105
and it shall bring forth *b* Eze 17:23 6057
and his top was among the thick *b* Eze 31:3 5688
his *b* were multiplied, and his Eze 31:5 5634
heaven made their nests in his *b* Eze 31:6 5589
the fir trees were not like his *b* Eze 31:8 5589
shot up his top among the thick *b* Eze 31:10 5688
his *b* are broken by all the Eze 31:12 6288
up their top among the thick *b* Eze 31:14 5688
the heaven dwelt in the *b* thereof Dan 4:12 6056

BOUGHT

or *b* with money of any stranger, Gen 17:12 4736
he that is *b* with thy money, must Gen 17:13 4736
all that were *b* with his money, Gen 17:23 4736
b with money of the stranger, Gen 17:27 4736
he *b* a parcel of a field, where Gen 33:19 7069
b him of the hands of the Gen 39:1 7069
Canaan, for the corn which they *b* Gen 47:14 7666
Joseph *b* all the land of Egypt Gen 47:20 7069
the land of the priests *b* he not Gen 47:22 7069
I have *b* you this day and your Gen 47:23 7069
which Abraham *b* with the field of Gen 49:30 7069
which Abraham *b* with the field Gen 50:13 7069
man's servant that is *b* for money Ex 12:44 4736
b it until the year of jubile Lev 25:28 7069
for ever to him that *b* it Lev 25:30 7069
b him from the year that he was Lev 25:50 7069
of the money that he was *b* for Lev 25:51 4736
the LORD a field which he hath *b* Lev 27:22 4736
return unto him of whom it was *b* Lev 27:24 7069
he thy father that hath *b* thee Deut 32:6 7069
a parcel of ground which Jacob *b* Josh 24:32 7069
that I have *b* all that was Ruth 4:9 7069
little ewe lamb, which he had *b* 2Sa 12:3 7069
So David *b* the threshingfloor and 2Sa 24:24 7069
he *b* the hill Samaria of Shemer 1Kin 16:24 7069
this wall, neither *b* we any land Neh 5:16 7069
Thou hast *b* me no sweet cane with Is 43:24 7069
I *b* the field of Hanameel my Jer 32:9 7069
And fields shall be *b* in this land Jer 32:43 7069
So I *b* her to me for fifteen Hos 3:2 3739
and sold all that he had, and *b* it Mt 13:46 59
b in the temple, and overthrew the Mt 21:12 59
b with them the potter's field, Mt 27:7 59
b in the temple, and overthrew the Mk 11:15 59
he *b* fine linen, and took him down Mk 15:46 59
had *b* sweet spices, that they Mk 16:1 59
I have *b* a piece of ground, and I Lk 14:18 59
I have *b* five yoke of oxen, and I Lk 14:19 59
they did eat, they drank, they *b* Lk 17:28 59
that sold therein, and them that *b* Lk 19:45 59
in the sepulchre that Abraham *b* Acts 7:16 5608
For ye are *b* with a price 1Cor 6:20 59
Ye are *b* with a price 1Cor 7:23 59
even denying the Lord that *b* them 2Pet 2:1 59

BOUND

b Isaac his son, and laid him on Gen 22:9 6123
b upon his hand a scarlet thread, Gen 38:28 7194
where the king's prisoners were *b* Gen 39:20 631
the place where Joseph was *b* Gen 40:3 631
which were *b* in the prison Gen 40:5 631
be *b* in the house of your prison Gen 42:19 631
and *b* him before their eyes Gen 42:24 631
life is *b* up in the lad's life Gen 44:30 7194
utmost *b* of the everlasting hills Gen 49:26 8379
their kneadingtroughs being *b* up Ex 12:34 6887
ephod, and *b* it unto him therewith Lev 8:7 640
which hath no covering *b* upon it Num 19:15 6616
wherewith she hath *b* her soul Num 30:4 631
she hath *b* her soul shall stand Num 30:4 631
wherewith she hath *b* her soul Num 30:5 631
lips, wherewith she *b* her soul Num 30:6 631
she *b* her soul shall stand Num 30:7 631
lips, wherewith she *b* her soul Num 30:8 631
wherewith they have *b* their souls Num 30:9 631
or *b* her soul by a bond with an Num 30:10 631
she *b* her soul shall stand Num 30:11 631
she *b* the scarlet line in the Josh 2:21 7194
bottles, old, and rent, and *b* up Josh 9:4 6887
they *b* him with two new cords, and Judg 15:13 631
mightest be *b* to afflict thee Judg 16:6 631
dried, and she *b* him with them Judg 16:8 631
wherewith thou mightest be *b* Judg 16:10 631
b him therewith, and said unto him Judg 16:12 631
me wherewith thou mightest be *b* Judg 16:13 631
b him with fetters of brass Judg 16:21 631
the soul of my lord shall be *b* in 1Sa 25:29 6887
Thy hands were not *b*, nor thy 2Sa 3:34 631
b two talents of silver in two 2Kin 5:23 6887
shut him up, and *b* him in prison 2Kin 17:4 631
b him with fetters of brass, and 2Kin 25:7 631
b him with fetters, and carried 2Chr 33:11 631
b him in fetters, to carry him to 2Chr 36:6 631
And if they be *b* in fetters Job 36:8 631
take it to the *b* thereof, and that Job 38:20 1366
out those which are *b* with chains Ps 68:6 615
Thou hast set a *b* that they may Ps 104:9 1366
being *b* in affliction and iron Ps 107:10 615
Foolishness is *b* in the heart of Prov 22:15 7194
who hath *b* the waters in a Prov 30:4 6887
not been closed, neither *b* up Is 1:6 2280
they are *b* by the archers Is 22:3 631
are found in thee are *b* together Is 22:3 631
of the prison to them that are *b* Is 61:1 631
the *b* of the sea by a perpetual Jer 5:22 1366
cause, that thou mayest be *b* up Jer 30:13 4205
b him with chains, to carry him Jer 39:7 631
when he had taken him being *b* in Jer 40:1 631
king of Babylon *b* him in chains Jer 52:11 631
transgressions is *b* by his hand Lam 1:14 8244
b with cords, and made of cedar, Eze 27:24 2280
it shall not be *b* up to be healed Eze 30:21 2280
neither have ye *b* up that which Eze 34:4 2280
these men were *b* in their coats Dan 3:21 3729
fell down *b* into the midst of the Dan 3:23 3729
Did not we cast three men *b* into Dan 3:24 3729
The wind hath *b* her up in her Hos 4:19 6887
were like them that remove the *b* Hos 5:10 1366
Though I have *b* and strengthened Hos 7:15 3256
The iniquity of Ephraim is *b* up Hos 13:12 6887
her great men were *b* in chains Nah 3:10 7576
b him, and put him in prison for Mt 14:3 1210
on earth shall be *b* in heaven Mt 16:19 1210
on earth shall be *b* in heaven Mt 18:18 1210
And when they had *b* him, they led Mt 27:2 1210
he had been often *b* with fetters Mk 5:4 1210
b him in prison for Herodias' Mk 6:17 1210
b Jesus, and carried him away, and Mk 15:1 1210
which lay *b* with them that had Mk 15:7 1210
and he was kept *b* with chains Lk 8:29 1196
b up his wounds, pouring in oil Lk 10:34 2611
of Abraham, whom Satan hath *b* Lk 13:16 1210
b hand and foot with graveclothes Jn 11:44 1210
his face was *b* about with a Jn 11:44 4019
of the Jews took Jesus, and *b* him, Jn 18:12 1210
Now Annas had sent him *b* unto Jn 18:24 1210
might bring them *b* unto Jerusalem Acts 9:2 1210
them *b* unto the chief priests Acts 9:21 1210
two soldiers, *b* with two chains Acts 12:6 1210
I go *b* in the spirit unto Acts 20:22 1210
b his own hands and feet, and said, Acts 21:11 1210
for I am ready not to be *b* only Acts 21:13 1210
him to be *b* with two chains Acts 21:33 1210
which were there *b* unto Jerusalem Acts 22:5 1210
as they *b* him with thongs, Paul Acts 22:25 4385
a Roman, and because he had *b* him Acts 22:29 1210
b themselves under a curse, Acts 23:12 332
We have *b* ourselves under a great Acts 23:14 332
which have *b* themselves with an Acts 23:21 332
the Jews a pleasure, left Paul *b* Acts 24:27 1210
of Israel I am *b* with this chain Acts 28:20 4029
is *b* by the law to her husband so Rom 7:2 1210
Art thou *b* unto a wife 1Cor 7:27 1210
The wife is *b* by the law as long 1Cor 7:39 1210
We are *b* to thank God always for 2Th 1:3 3784
But we are *b* to give thanks alway 2Th 2:13 3784
but the word of God is not *b* 2Ti 2:9 1210
that are in bonds, as *b* with them Heb 13:3 4887
b in the great river Euphrates Rev 9:14 1210
Satan, and *b* him a thousand years, Rev 20:2 1210

BOUNDS

thou shalt set *b* unto the people Ex 19:12 1379
Set *b* about the mount, and Ex 19:23 1379
I will set thy *b* from the Red sea Ex 23:31 1366
he set the *b* of the people Deut 32:8 1367
his *b* that he cannot pass Job 14:5 2706
hath compassed the waters with *b* Job 26:10 2706

have removed the *b* of the people .... Is 10:13 1367
the *b* of their habitation .... Acts 17:26 *3734*

BOUNTIFUL
He that hath a *b* eye shall be .... Prov 22:9 2896
nor the churl said to be *b* .... Is 32:5 7771

BOUNTIFULLY
because he hath dealt *b* with me .... Ps 13:6 1580
the LORD hath dealt *b* with thee .... Ps 116:7 1580
Deal *b* with thy servant, that I .... Ps 119:17 1580
for thou shalt deal *b* with me .... Ps 142:7 1580
soweth *b* shall reap also *b* 2Cor 9:6 *2129*

BOUNTIFULNESS
enriched in every thing to all *b* 2Cor 9:11 *572*

BOUNTY
Solomon gave her of his royal *b* 1Kin 10:13 3027
you, and make up beforehand your *b* .. 2Cor 9:5 *2129*
might be ready, as a matter of *b* 2Cor 9:5 *2129*

BOW
I do set my *b* in the cloud, and it .... Gen 9:13 7198
that the *b* shall be seen in the .... Gen 9:14 7198
the *b* shall be in the cloud .... Gen 9:16 7198
thy weapons, thy quiver and thy *b* .... Gen 27:3 7198
thee, and nations *b* down to thee .... Gen 27:29 7812
thy mother's sons *b* down to thee .... Gen 27:29 7812
thy brethren indeed come to *b* .... Gen 37:10 7812
they cried before him, *B* the knee .... Gen 41:43 86
with my sword and with my *b* .... Gen 48:22 7198
children shall *b* down before thee .... Gen 49:8 7812
But his *b* abode in strength, and .... Gen 49:24 7198
b down themselves unto me, saying .... Ex 11:8 7812
Thou shalt not *b* down thyself to .... Ex 20:5 7812
Thou shalt not *b* down to their .... Ex 23:24 7812
in your land, to *b* down unto it .... Lev 26:1 7812
Thou shalt not *b* down thyself .... Deut 5:9 7812
nor *b* yourselves unto them .... Josh 23:7 7812
with thy sword, nor with thy *b* .... Josh 24:12 7198
them, and to *b* down unto them .... Judg 2:19 7812
even to his sword, and to his *b* 1Sa 18:4 7198
of Judah the use of the *b* 2Sa 1:18 7198
the *b* of Jonathan turned not back 2Sa 1:22 7198
so that a *b* of steel is broken by 2Sa 22:35 7198
certain man drew a *b* at a venture 1Kin 22:34 7198
I *b* myself in the house of Rimmon 2Kin 5:18 7812
when I *b* down myself in the house 2Kin 5:18 7812
with thy sword and with thy *b* 2Kin 6:22 7198
Jehu drew a *b* with his full 2Kin 9:24 7198
And Elisha said unto him, Take *b* 2Kin 13:15 7198
And he took unto him *b* and arrows 2Kin 13:15 7198
Israel, Put thine hand upon the *b* 2Kin 13:16 7198
nor *b* yourselves to them, nor 2Kin 17:35 7812
b down thine ear, and hear 2Kin 19:16 5186
and sword, and to shoot with *b* 1Chr 5:18 7198
and shooting arrows out of a *b* 1Chr 12:2 7198
and with him armed men with *b* 2Chr 17:17 7198
certain man drew a *b* at a venture 2Chr 18:33 7198
the *b* of steel shall strike him .... Job 20:24 7198
my *b* was renewed in my hand .... Job 29:20 7198
let others *b* down upon her .... Job 31:10 3766
They *b* themselves, they bring .... Job 39:3 3766
he hath bent his *b*, and made it .... Ps 7:12 7198
For, lo, the wicked bend their *b* .... Ps 11:2 7198
so that a *b* of steel is broken by .... Ps 18:34 7198
to the dust shall *b* before him .... Ps 22:29 3766
B down thine ear to me .... Ps 31:2 5186
the sword, and have bent their *b* .... Ps 37:14 7198
For I will not trust in my *b* .... Ps 44:6 7198
he breaketh the *b*, and cutteth the .... Ps 46:9 7198
bendeth his *b* to shoot his arrows .... Ps 58:7
the wilderness shall *b* before him .... Ps 72:9 3766
brake he the arrows of the *b* .... Ps 76:3 7198
turned aside like a deceitful *b* .... Ps 78:57 7198
B down thine ear, O LORD, hear me .... Ps 86:1 5186
O come, let us worship and *b* down .... Ps 95:6 3766
B thy heavens, O LORD, and come .... Ps 144:5 5186
b thine ear to my understanding .... Prov 5:1 5186
The evil *b* before the good .... Prov 14:19 7817
B down thine ear, and hear the .... Prov 22:17 5186
the strong men shall *b* themselves .... Eccl 12:3 5791
Without me they shall *b* down .... Is 10:4 3766
drawn sword, and from the bent *b* .... Is 21:15 7198
and as driven stubble to his *b* .... Is 41:2 7198
That unto me every knee shall *b* .... Is 45:23 3766
They stoop, they *b* down together .... Is 46:2 3766
they shall *b* down to thee with .... Is 49:23 7812
B down, that we may go over .... Is 51:23 7812
is it to *b* down his head as a .... Is 58:5 3721
they that despised thee shall *b* .... Is 60:14 7812
ye shall all *b* down to the .... Is 65:12 3766
Pul, and Lud, that draw the *b* .... Is 66:19 7198
They shall lay hold on *b* and spear .... Jer 6:23 7198
tongues like their *b* for lies .... Jer 9:3 7198
that handle and bend the *b* .... Jer 46:9 7198
I will break the *b* of Elam .... Jer 49:35 7198
all ye that bend the *b*, shoot at .... Jer 50:14 7198
all ye that bend the *b*, camp .... Jer 50:29 7198
They shall hold the *b* and the .... Jer 50:42 7198
bendeth let the archer bend his *b* .... Jer 51:3 7198
He hath bent his *b* like an enemy .... Lam 2:4 7198
He hath bent his *b*, and set me as .... Lam 3:12 7198
As the appearance of the *b* that .... Eze 1:28 7198
I will smite thy *b* out of thy .... Eze 39:3 7198
that I will break the *b* of Israel .... Hos 1:5 7198
God, and will not save them by *b* .... Hos 1:7 7198
and I will break the *b* and the .... Hos 2:18 7198
they are like a deceitful *b* .... Hos 7:16 7198
he stand that handleth the *b* .... Amos 2:15 7198
b myself before the high God .... Mic 6:6 3721
the perpetual hills did *b* .... Hab 3:6 7817
Thy *b* was made quite naked .... Hab 3:9 7198
the battle *b* shall be cut off .... Zec 9:10 7198
filled the *b* with Ephraim, and .... Zec 9:13 7198
the nail, out of him the battle *b* .... Zec 10:4 7198
see, and *b* down their back alway .... Rom 11:10 *4781*
Lord, every knee shall *b* to me .... Rom 14:11 *2578*
For this cause I *b* my knees unto .... Eph 3:14 *2578*
name of Jesus every knee should *b* .... Phil 2:10 *2578*
and he that sat on him had a *b* .... Rev 6:2 *5115*

BOWED
b himself toward the ground .... Gen 18:2 7812
he *b* himself with his face toward .... Gen 19:1 7812
b himself to the people of the .... Gen 23:7 7812
Abraham *b* down himself before the .... Gen 23:12 7812
the man *b* down his head, and .... Gen 24:26 6915
I *b* down my head, and worshipped .... Gen 24:48 6915
b himself to the ground seven .... Gen 33:3 7812
children, and they *b* themselves .... Gen 33:6 7812
came near, and *b* themselves .... Gen 33:7 7812
and Rachel, and they *b* themselves .... Gen 33:7 7812
b down themselves before him with .... Gen 42:6 7812
b themselves to him to the earth .... Gen 43:26 7812
they *b* down their heads, and made .... Gen 43:28 6915
Israel *b* himself upon the bed's .... Gen 47:31 7812
he *b* himself with his face to the .... Gen 48:12 7812
b his shoulder to bear, and became .... Gen 49:15 5186
then they *b* their heads and .... Ex 4:31 6915
And the people *b* the head and .... Ex 12:27 6915
b his head toward the earth, and .... Ex 34:8 6915
he *b* down his head, and fell flat .... Num 22:31 6915
did eat, and *b* down to their gods .... Num 25:2 7812
gods, and *b* yourselves to them .... Josh 23:16 7812
b themselves unto them, and .... Judg 2:12 7812
gods, and *b* themselves unto them .... Judg 2:17 7812
At her feet he *b*, he fell, he lay .... Judg 5:27 3766
at her feet he *b*, he fell .... Judg 5:27 3766
where he *b*, there he fell down .... Judg 5:27 3766
b down upon their knees to drink .... Judg 7:6 3766
he *b* himself with all his might .... Judg 16:30 5186
b herself to the ground, and said .... Ruth 2:10 7812
she *b* herself and travailed 1Sa 4:19 3766
ground, and *b* himself three times 1Sa 20:41 7812
face to the earth, and *b* himself 1Sa 24:8 7812
face, and *b* herself to the ground 1Sa 25:23 7812
b herself on her face to the 1Sa 25:41 7812
face to the ground, and *b* himself 1Sa 28:14 7812
he *b* himself, and said, What is 2Sa 9:8 7812
b himself, and thanked the king 2Sa 14:22 7812
b himself on his face to the 2Sa 14:33 7812
Cushi *b* himself unto Joab, and ran 2Sa 18:21 7812
he *b* the heart of all the men of 2Sa 19:14 5186
He *b* the heavens also, and came 2Sa 22:10 5186
b himself before the king on his 2Sa 24:20 7812
And Bath-sheba *b*, and did obeisance 1Kin 1:16 6915
he *b* himself before the king with 1Kin 1:23 7812
Then Bath-sheba *b* with her face 1Kin 1:31 6915
the king *b* himself upon the bed 1Kin 1:47 7812
b himself to king Solomon 1Kin 1:53 7812
b himself unto her, and sat down 1Kin 2:19 7812
knees which have not *b* unto Baal 1Kin 19:18 3766
b themselves to the ground before 2Kin 2:15 7812
b herself to the ground, and took 2Kin 4:37 7812
b himself to David with his face 1Chr 21:21 7812
b down their heads, and worshipped 1Chr 29:20 6915
they *b* themselves with their 2Chr 7:3 3766
Jehoshaphat *b* his head with his 2Chr 20:18 6915
b down himself before them, and 2Chr 25:14 7812
present with him *b* themselves 2Chr 29:29 3766
they *b* their heads and worshipped 2Chr 29:30 6915
they *b* their heads, and worshipped .... Neh 8:6 6915
that were in the king's gate, *b* .... Est 3:2 3766
But Mordecai *b* not, nor did him .... Est 3:2 3766
Haman saw that Mordecai *b* not .... Est 3:5 3766
He *b* the heavens also, and came .... Ps 18:9 5186
I *b* down heavily, as one that .... Ps 35:14 7817
I am *b* down greatly .... Ps 38:6 7817
For our soul is *b* down to the .... Ps 44:25 7743
my soul is *b* down .... Ps 57:6 3721
up all those that be *b* down .... Ps 145:14 3721
LORD raiseth them that are *b* down .... Ps 146:8 3721
of men shall be *b* down, and the .... Is 2:11 7817
loftiness of man shall be *b* down .... Is 2:17 7817
I was *b* down at the hearing of it .... Is 21:3 5791
they *b* the knee before him, and .... Mt 27:29 *1120*
was *b* together, and could in no .... Lk 13:11 *4794*
b down their faces to the earth .... Lk 24:5 *2827*
he *b* his head, and gave up the .... Jn 19:30 *2827*
who have not *b* the knee to the .... Rom 11:4 *2578*

BOWELS
thine own *b* shall be thine heir .... Gen 15:4 4578
shall be separated from thy *b* .... Gen 25:23 4578
for his *b* did yearn upon his .... Gen 43:30 7358
the curse shall go into thy *b* .... Num 5:22 4578
which shall proceed out of thy *b* 2Sa 7:12 4578
my son, which came forth of my *b* 2Sa 16:11 4578
shed out his *b* to the ground, and 2Sa 20:10 4578
for her *b* yearned upon her son 1Kin 3:26 7358
sickness by disease of thy *b* 2Chr 21:15 4578
until thy *b* fall out by reason of 2Chr 21:15 4578
his *b* with an incurable disease 2Chr 21:18 4578
his *b* fell out by reason of his 2Chr 21:19 4578
b slew him there with the sword 2Chr 32:21 4578
Yet his meat in his *b* is turned .... Job 20:14 4578
My *b* boiled, and rested not .... Job 30:27 4578
it is melted in the midst of my *b* .... Ps 22:14 4578
that took me out of my mother's *b* .... Ps 71:6 4578
let it come into his *b* like water .... Ps 109:18 7130
door, and my *b* were moved for him .... Song 5:4 4578
Wherefore my *b* shall sound like .... Is 16:11 4578
the offspring of thy *b* like the .... Is 48:19 4578
from the *b* of my mother hath he .... Is 49:1 4578
strength, the sounding of thy *b* .... Is 63:15 4578
My *b*, my *b* .... Jer 4:19 4578
therefore my *b* are troubled for .... Jer 31:20 4578
my *b* are troubled .... Lam 1:20 4578
my *b* are troubled, my liver is .... Lam 2:11 4578
fill thy *b* with this roll that I .... Eze 3:3 4578
their souls, neither fill their *b* .... Eze 7:19 4578
midst, and all his *b* gushed out .... Acts 1:18 *4698*
ye are straitened in your own *b* 2Cor 6:12 *4698*
you all in the *b* of Jesus Christ .... Phil 1:8 *4698*
of the Spirit, if any *b* and .... Phil 2:1 *4698*
beloved, *b* of mercies, kindness .... Col 3:12 *4698*
because the *b* of the saints are .... Philem 7 *4698*
receive him, that is, mine own *b* .... Philem 12 *4698*
refresh my *b* in the Lord .... Philem 20 *4698*
shutteth up his *b* of compassion 1Jn 3:17 *4698*

BOWETH
likewise every one that *b* down .... Judg 7:5 3766
And the mean man *b* down, and the .... Is 2:9 7817
Bel *b* down, Nebo stoopeth, their .... Is 46:1 3766

BOWING
the LORD, *b* himself to the earth .... Gen 24:52
their eyes *b* down to the earth .... Ps 17:11 5186
as a *b* wall shall ye be, and as a .... Ps 62:3 5186
b their knees worshipped him .... Mk 15:19 5087

BOWL
one silver *b* of seventy shekels .... Num 7:13 4219
one silver *b* of seventy shekels .... Num 7:19 4219
one silver *b* of seventy shekels .... Num 7:25 4219
one silver *b* of seventy shekels .... Num 7:31 4219
one silver *b* of seventy shekels .... Num 7:37 4219
a silver *b* of seventy shekels .... Num 7:43 4219
one silver *b* of seventy shekels .... Num 7:49 4219
one silver *b* of seventy shekels .... Num 7:55 4219
one silver *b* of seventy shekels .... Num 7:61 4219
one silver *b* of seventy shekels .... Num 7:67 4219
one silver *b* of seventy shekels .... Num 7:73 4219
one silver *b* of seventy shekels .... Num 7:79 4219
and thirty shekels, each *b* seventy .... Num 7:85 4219
of the fleece, a *b* full of water .... Judg 6:38 5602
loosed, or the golden *b* be broken .... Eccl 12:6 1543
with a *b* upon the top of it, and .... Zec 4:2 1543
one upon the right side of the *b* .... Zec 4:3 1543

BOWLS
b thereof, to cover withal .... Ex 25:29 4518
his shaft, and his branches, his *b* .... Ex 25:31 1375
Three *b* made like unto almonds .... Ex 25:33 1375
three *b* made like almonds in the .... Ex 25:33 1375
be four *b* made like unto almonds .... Ex 25:34 1375
dishes, and his spoons, and his *b* .... Ex 37:16 4518
his shaft, and his branch, his *b* .... Ex 37:17 1375
Three *b* made after the fashion of .... Ex 37:19 1375
three *b* made like almonds in .... Ex 37:19 1375
were four *b* made like almonds .... Ex 37:20 1375
dishes, and the spoons, and the *b* .... Num 4:7 4518
of silver, twelve silver *b* .... Num 7:84 4219
the two *b* of the chapiters that 1Kin 7:41 1543
to cover the two *b* of the 1Kin 7:41 1543
to cover the two *b* of the 1Kin 7:42 1543
And the *b*, and the snuffers, and the 1Kin 7:50 5592
the house of the LORD *b* of silver 2Kin 12:13 5592
And the firepans, and the *b* 2Kin 25:15 4219
gold for the fleshhooks, and the *b* 1Chr 28:17 4219
and the snuffers, and the *b* .... Jer 52:18 4219
basons, and the firepans, and the *b* .... Jer 52:19 4219
That drink wine in *b*, and anoint .... Amos 6:6 4219
and they shall be filled like *b* .... Zec 9:15 4219
be like the *b* before the altar .... Zec 14:20 4219

BOWMEN
the noise of the horsemen and *b* .... Jer 4:29

BOWS
The *b* of the mighty men are 1Sa 2:4 7198
They were armed with *b*, and could 1Chr 12:2 7198
that bare shields and drew *b* 2Chr 14:8 7198
and helmets, and habergeons, and *b* 2Chr 26:14 7198
swords, their spears, and their *b* .... Neh 4:13 7198
the spears, the shields, and the *b* .... Neh 4:16 7198
heart, and their *b* shall be broken .... Ps 37:15 7198
bend their *b* to shoot their .... Ps 64:3
being armed, and carrying *b* .... Ps 78:9 7198
are sharp, and all their *b* bent .... Is 5:28 7198
with *b* shall men come thither .... Is 7:24 7198
Their *b* also shall dash the young .... Is 13:18 7198
every one of their *b* is broken .... Jer 51:56 7198
shields and the bucklers, the *b* .... Eze 39:9 7198

BOWSHOT
a good way off, as it were a *b* .... Gen 21:16

BOX
take this *b* of oil in thine hand 2Kin 9:1 6378
Then take the *b* of oil, and pour 2Kin 9:3 6378
the pine, and the *b* tree together .... Is 41:19 8391
the *b* together, to beautify the .... Is 60:13 8391
b of very precious ointment .... Mt 26:7 *211*
a woman having an alabaster *b* of .... Mk 14:3 *211*
and she brake the *b*, and poured it .... Mk 14:3 *211*
an alabaster *b* of ointment .... Lk 7:37 *211*

BOY
have given a *b* for an harlot, and .... Joel 3:3 3206

BOYS
And the *b* grew .... Gen 25:27 5288
of the city shall be full of *b* .... Zec 8:5 3206

BOZEZ (*bo'-zez*) *A rock near Michmash.*
and the name of the one was *B* 1Sa 14:4 949

BOZKATH (*boz'-kath*) *A city in Judah.*
Lachish, and *B*, and Eglon .... Josh 15:39 1218

BOZRAH (*boz'-rah*)
1. The capital city of Edom.
Zerah of *B* reigned in his stead .... Gen 36:33 1224
Zerah of *B* reigned in his stead 1Chr 1:44 1224
the LORD hath a sacrifice in *B* .... Is 34:6 1224
Edom, with dyed garments from *B* .... Is 63:1 1224
that *B* shall become a desolation .... Jer 49:13 1224

eagle, and spread his wings over B ... Jer 49:22 1224
shall devour the palaces of B ... Amos 1:12 1224
them together as the sheep of B ... Mic 2:12 1224
2. A place in Moab.
And upon Kerioth, and upon B ... Jer 48:24 1224

BRACELET
the b that was on his arm, and ... 2Sa 1:10 685

BRACELETS
two b for her hands of ten ... Gen 24:22 6781
b upon his sister's hands, and ... Gen 24:30 6781
her face, and the b upon her hands ... Gen 24:47 6781
And she said, Thy signet, and thy b ... Gen 38:18 6616
whose are these, the signet, and b ... Gen 38:25 6616
willing hearted, and brought b ... Ex 35:22 2397
of jewels of gold, chains, and b ... Num 31:50 6781
The chains, and the b, and the ... Is 3:19 8285
I put b upon thy hands, and a ... Eze 16:11 6781
which put b upon their hands, and ... Eze 23:42 6781

BRAKE
b every tree of the field ... Ex 9:25 7665
all the people b off the golden ... Ex 32:3 6561
and b them beneath the mount ... Ex 32:19 7665
hands, and b them before your eyes ... Deut 9:17 7665
b the pitchers that were in their ... Judg 7:19 5310
b the pitchers, and held the lamps ... Judg 7:20 7665
head, and all to b his skull ... Judg 9:53 7533
he b the withs, as a thread of ... Judg 16:9 5423
he b them from off his arms like ... Judg 16:12 5423
side of the gate, and his neck b ... 1Sa 4:18 7665
the three mighty men b through ... 2Sa 23:16 1234
b in pieces the rocks before the ... 1Kin 19:11 7665
they b down the image of Baal, and ... 2Kin 10:27 5422
b down the house of Baal, and made ... 2Kin 10:27 5422
the house of Baal, and b it down ... 2Kin 11:18 5422
his images b they in pieces ... 2Kin 11:18 7665
b down the wall of Jerusalem from ... 2Kin 14:13 6555
b the images, and cut down the ... 2Kin 18:4 7665
b in pieces the brasen serpent ... 2Kin 18:4 3807
he b down the houses of the ... 2Kin 23:7 5422
b down the high places of the ... 2Kin 23:8 5422
b them down from thence, and cast ... 2Kin 23:12 7323
he b in pieces the images, and cut ... 2Kin 23:14 7665
altar and the high place he b down ... 2Kin 23:15 5422
b down the walls of Jerusalem ... 2Kin 25:10 5422
the three b through the host of ... 1Chr 11:18 1234
b down the images, and cut down ... 2Chr 14:3 7665
b into it, and carried away all ... 2Chr 21:17 1234
b it down, and b his altars and ... 2Chr 23:17 5422
b down the wall of Jerusalem from ... 2Chr 25:23 6555
b down the wall of Gath, and the ... 2Chr 26:6 6555
b the images in pieces, and cut ... 2Chr 31:1 7665
they b down the altars of Baalim ... 2Chr 34:4 5422
he b in pieces, and made dust of ... 2Chr 34:4 7665
b down the wall of Jerusalem, and ... 2Chr 36:19 5422
I b the jaws of the wicked, and ... Job 29:17 7665
sea with doors, when it b forth ... Job 38:8 1518
b up for it my decreed place, and ... Job 38:10 7665
There b he the arrows of the bow, ... Ps 76:3 7665
he b the whole staff of bread ... Ps 105:16 7665
b the trees of their coasts ... Ps 105:33 7665
the plague b in upon them ... Ps 106:29 6555
death, and their bands in sunder ... Ps 107:14 5423
prophet Jeremiah's neck, and b it ... Jer 28:10 7665
which my covenant they b, ... Jer 31:32 6565
b down the walls of Jerusalem ... Jer 39:8 5422
b down all the walls of Jerusalem ... Jer 52:14 5422
of the LORD, the Chaldeans b ... Jer 52:17 7665
despised, and whose covenant he b ... Eze 17:16 6565
troubled, and his sleep b from him ... Dan 2:1 1961
iron and clay, and b them to pieces ... Dan 2:34 1855
that it b in pieces the iron, the ... Dan 2:45 1855
b all their bones in pieces or ... Dan 6:24 1855
b in pieces, and stamped the ... Dan 7:7 1855
b in pieces, and stamped the ... Dan 7:19 1855
smote the ram, and b his two horns ... Dan 8:7 7665
up to heaven, he blessed, and b ... Mt 14:19 *2806*
b them, and gave to his disciples, ... Mt 15:36 *2806*
b it, and gave it to the disciples ... Mt 26:26 *2806*
b the loaves, and gave them to his ... Mk 6:41 *2622*
loaves, and gave thanks, and b ... Mk 8:6 *2806*
When I b the five loaves among ... Mk 8:19 *2806*
she b the box, and poured it on ... Mk 14:3 *4937*
b it and gave to them, and said, ... Mk 14:22 *2806*
and their net b ... Lk 5:6 *1284*
he b the bands, and was driven of ... Lk 8:29 *1284*
to heaven, he blessed them, and b ... Lk 9:16 *2622*
b it, and gave unto them, saying, ... Lk 22:19 *2806*
took bread, and blessed it, and b ... Lk 24:30 *2806*
b the legs of the first, and of ... Jn 19:32 *2608*
dead already, they b not his legs ... Jn 19:33 *2608*
when he had given thanks, he b it ... 1Cor 11:24 *2806*

BRAKEST
in the first tables, which thou b ... Ex 34:1 7665
in the first tables which thou b ... Deut 10:2 7665
thou b the heads of the dragons ... Ps 74:13 7665
Thou b the heads of leviathan in ... Ps 74:14 7533
they leaned upon thee, thou b ... Eze 29:7 7665

BRAMBLE
said all the trees unto the b ... Judg 9:14 329
the b said unto the trees, If in ... Judg 9:15 329
not, let fire come out of the b ... Judg 9:15 329
nor of a b bush gather they ... Lk 6:44 *942*

BRAMBLES
b in the fortresses thereof ... Is 34:13 2336

BRANCH
with a knop and a flower in one b ... Ex 25:33 7070
made like almonds in the other b ... Ex 25:33 7070
his shaft, and his b, his bowls, ... Ex 37:17 7070
the fashion of almonds in one b ... Ex 37:19 7070
made like almonds in another b ... Ex 37:19 7070
cut down from thence a b with one ... Num 13:23 2156
his b shooteth forth in his ... Job 8:16 3127
that the tender b thereof will ... Job 14:7
time, and his b shall not be green ... Job 15:32 3712
and above shall his b be cut off ... Job 18:16 7105
the dew lay all night upon my b ... Job 29:19 7105
the b that thou madest strong for ... Ps 80:15 1121
righteous shall flourish as a b ... Prov 11:28 5929
In that day shall the b of the ... Is 4:2 6780
off from Israel head and tail, b ... Is 9:14 3712
a B shall grow out of his roots ... Is 11:1 5342
of thy grave like an abominable b ... Is 14:19 5342
forsaken bough, and an uppermost b ... Is 17:9 534
head or tail, b or rush, may do ... Is 19:15 3712
the b of the terrible ones shall ... Is 25:5 2158
the b of my planting, the work of ... Is 60:21 5342
raise unto David a righteous B ... Jer 23:5 6780
that time, will I cause the B of ... Jer 33:15 6780
they put the b to their nose ... Eze 8:17 2156
or than a b which is among the ... Eze 15:2 2156
took the highest b of the cedar ... Eze 17:3 6788
the highest b of the high cedar ... Eze 17:22 6788
But out of a b of her roots shall ... Dan 11:7 5342
will bring forth my servant the B ... Zec 3:8 6780
the man whose name is The B ... Zec 6:12 6780
leave them neither root nor b ... Mal 4:1 6057
When his b is yet tender, and ... Mt 24:32 *2798*
When her b is yet tender, and ... Mk 13:28 *2798*
Every b in me that beareth not ... Jn 15:2 *2814*
every b that beareth fruit, he ... Jn 15:2
As the b cannot bear fruit of ... Jn 15:4 *2814*
in me, he is cast forth as a b ... Jn 15:6 *2814*

BRANCHES
And in the vine were three b ... Gen 40:10 8299
The three b are three days ... Gen 40:12 8299
whose b run over the wall ... Gen 49:22 1121
his shaft, and his b, his bowls, ... Ex 25:31 7070
six b shall come out of the sides ... Ex 25:32 7070
three b of the candlestick out of ... Ex 25:32 7070
three b of the candlestick out of ... Ex 25:32 7070
so in the six b that come out of ... Ex 25:33 7070
be a knop under two b of the same ... Ex 25:35 7070
and a knop under two b of the same ... Ex 25:35 7070
and a knop under two b of the same ... Ex 25:35 7070
according to the six b that ... Ex 25:35 7070
their b shall be of the same ... Ex 25:36 7070
six b going out of the sides ... Ex 37:18 7070
three b of the candlestick out of ... Ex 37:18 7070
three b of the candlestick out of ... Ex 37:18 7070
so throughout the six b going out ... Ex 37:19 7070
And a knop under two b of the same ... Ex 37:21 7070
and a knop under two b of the same ... Ex 37:21 7070
and a knop under two b of the same ... Ex 37:21 7070
to the six b going out of it ... Ex 37:21 7070
knops and their b were of the same ... Ex 37:22 7070
b of palm trees, and the boughs of ... Lev 23:40 3709
fetch olive b, and pine b ... Neh 8:15 5929
and myrtle b, and palm b ... Neh 8:15 5929
b of thick trees, to make booths, ... Neh 8:15 5929
the flame shall dry up his b ... Job 15:30 3127
the sea, and her b unto the river ... Ps 80:11 3127
which sing among the b ... Ps 104:12 6073
her b are stretched out, they are ... Is 16:8 7976
in the outmost fruitful b thereof ... Is 17:6 5585
and take away and cut down the b ... Is 18:5 5189
down, and consume the b thereof ... Is 27:10 5585
it, and the b of it are broken ... Jer 11:16 1808
whose b turned toward him, and the ... Eze 17:6 1808
became a vine, and brought forth b ... Eze 17:6 905
and shot forth her b toward him ... Eze 17:7 1808
that it might bring forth b ... Eze 17:8 6057
in the shadow of the b thereof ... Eze 17:23 1808
full of b by reason of many ... Eze 19:10 6058
was exalted among the thick b ... Eze 19:11 5688
with the multitude of her b ... Eze 19:11 1808
is gone out of a rod of her b ... Eze 19:14 905
a cedar in Lebanon with fair b ... Eze 31:3 6057
his b became long because of the ... Eze 31:5 6288
under his b did all the beasts of ... Eze 31:6 6288
greatness, in the length of his b ... Eze 31:7 1808
chesnut trees were not like his b ... Eze 31:8 6288
fair by the multitude of his b ... Eze 31:9 1808
all the valleys his b are fallen ... Eze 31:12 1808
of the field shall be upon his b ... Eze 31:13 6288
ye shall shoot forth your b ... Eze 36:8 6057
down the tree, and cut off his b ... Dan 4:14 6056
under it, and the fowls from his b ... Dan 4:14 6056
upon whose b the fowls of the ... Dan 4:21 6056
cities, and shall consume his b ... Hos 11:6 905
His b shall spread, and his beauty ... Hos 14:6 3127
the b thereof are made white ... Joel 1:7 8299
them out, and marred their vine b ... Nah 2:2 2156
What be these two olive b which ... Zec 4:12 7641
come and lodge in the b thereof ... Mt 13:32 *2798*
others cut down b from the trees ... Mt 21:8 *2798*
herbs, and shooteth out great b ... Mk 4:32 *2798*
others cut down b off the trees ... Mk 11:8 *4746*
of the air lodged in the b of it ... Lk 13:19 *2798*
Took b of palm trees, and went ... Jn 12:13 *902*
I am the vine, ye are the b ... Jn 15:5 *2814*
if the root be holy, so are the b ... Rom 11:16 *2798*
And if some of the b be broken off ... Rom 11:17 *2798*
Boast not against the b ... Rom 11:18 *2798*
The b were broken off, that I ... Rom 11:19 *2798*
if God spared not the natural b ... Rom 11:21 *2798*
these, which be the natural b ... Rom 11:24

BRAND
is not this a b plucked out of ... Zec 3:2 181

BRANDISH
when I shall b my sword before ... Eze 32:10 5774

BRANDS
And when he had set the b on fire ... Judg 15:5 3940

BRASEN
four b rings in the four corners ... Ex 27:4 5178
burnt offering, with his b grate ... Ex 35:16 5178
he made for the altar a b grate ... Ex 38:4 5178
twenty, and their b sockets twenty ... Ex 38:10 5178
the b altar, and the b grate ... Ex 38:30 5178
The b altar, and his grate of ... Ex 39:39 5178
and if it be sodden in a b pot ... Lev 6:28 5178
the priest took the b censers ... Num 16:39 5178
great cities with walls and b bars ... 1Kin 4:13 5178
And every base had four b wheels ... 1Kin 7:30 5178
because the b altar that was ... 1Kin 8:64 5178
made in their stead b shields ... 1Kin 14:27 5178
And he brought also the b altar ... 2Kin 16:14 5178
the b altar shall be for me to ... 2Kin 16:15 5178
off the b oxen that were under it ... 2Kin 16:17 5178
brake in pieces the b serpent ... 2Kin 18:4 5178
the b sea that was in the house ... 2Kin 25:13 5178
wherewith Solomon made the b sea ... 1Chr 18:8 5178
Moreover the b altar, that ... 2Chr 1:5 5178
to the b altar before the LORD ... 2Chr 1:6 5178
For Solomon had made a b scaffold ... 2Chr 6:13 5178
because the b altar which Solomon ... 2Chr 7:7 5178
b walls against the whole land, ... Jer 1:18 5178
unto this people a fenced b wall ... Jer 15:20 5178
the b sea that was in the house ... Jer 52:17 5178
twelve b bulls that were under ... Jer 52:20 5178
in, and stood beside the b altar ... Eze 9:2 5178
and pots, b vessels, and of tables ... Mk 7:4 *5473*

BRASS
of every artificer in b and iron ... Gen 4:22 5178
gold, and silver, and b, ... Ex 25:3 5178
thou shalt make fifty taches of b ... Ex 26:11 5178
cast five sockets of b for them ... Ex 26:37 5178
and thou shalt overlay it with b ... Ex 27:2 5178
thereof thou shalt make of b ... Ex 27:3 5178
for it a grate of network of b ... Ex 27:4 5178
wood, and overlay them with b ... Ex 27:6 5178
twenty sockets shall be of b ... Ex 27:10 5178
and their twenty sockets of b ... Ex 27:11 5178
of silver, and their sockets of b ... Ex 27:17 5178
linen, and their sockets of b ... Ex 27:18 5178
pins of the court, shall be of b ... Ex 27:19 5178
Thou shalt also make a laver of b ... Ex 30:18 5178
and his foot also of b ... Ex 30:18 5178
in gold, and in silver, and in b ... Ex 31:4 5178
gold, and silver, and b, ... Ex 35:5 5178
b brought the LORD's offering ... Ex 35:24 5178
in gold, and in silver, and in b ... Ex 35:32 5178
he made fifty taches of b to ... Ex 36:18 5178
but their five sockets were of b ... Ex 36:38 5178
and he overlaid it with b ... Ex 38:2 5178
the vessels thereof made he of b ... Ex 38:3 5178
the four ends of the grate of b ... Ex 38:5 5178
wood, and overlaid them with b ... Ex 38:6 5178
And he made the laver of b ... Ex 38:8 5178
and the foot of it of b ... Ex 38:8 5178
and their sockets of b twenty ... Ex 38:11 5178
sockets for the pillars were of b ... Ex 38:17 5178
four, and their sockets of b four ... Ex 38:19 5178
the court round about, were of b ... Ex 38:20 5178
the b of the offering was seventy ... Ex 38:29 5178
brasen altar, and his grate of b ... Ex 39:39 5178
as iron, and your earth as b ... Lev 26:19 5154
And Moses made a serpent of b ... Num 21:9 5178
when he beheld the serpent of b ... Num 21:9 5178
the gold, and the silver, the b ... Num 31:22 5178
of whose hills thou mayest dig b ... Deut 8:9 5178
that is over thy head shall be b ... Deut 28:23 5178
Thy shoes shall be iron and b ... Deut 33:25 5178
silver, and gold, and vessels of b ... Josh 6:19 5178
and the gold, and the vessels of b ... Josh 6:24 5178
silver, and with gold, and with b ... Josh 22:8 5178
and bound him with fetters of b ... Judg 16:21 5178
had an helmet of b upon his head ... 1Sa 17:5 5178
was five thousand shekels of b ... 1Sa 17:5 5178
he had greaves of b upon his legs ... 1Sa 17:6 5178
a target of b between his ... 1Sa 17:6 5178
put an helmet of b upon his head ... 1Sa 17:38 5178
king David took exceeding much b ... 2Sa 8:8 5178
vessels of gold, and vessels of b ... 2Sa 8:10 5178
hundred shekels of b in weight ... 2Sa 21:16 5178
was a man of Tyre, a worker in b ... 1Kin 7:14 5178
and cunning to work all works in b ... 1Kin 7:14 5178
For he cast two pillars of b ... 1Kin 7:15 5178
he made two chapiters of molten b ... 1Kin 7:16 5178
And he made ten bases of b ... 1Kin 7:27 5178
brasen wheels, and plates of b ... 1Kin 7:30 5178
Then made he ten lavers of b ... 1Kin 7:38 5178
of the LORD, were of bright b ... 1Kin 7:45 5178
was the weight of the b found out ... 1Kin 7:47 5178
and bound him with fetters of b ... 2Kin 25:7 5178
the pillars of b that were in the ... 2Kin 25:13 5178
carried the b of them to Babylon ... 2Kin 25:13 5178
all the vessels of b wherewith ... 2Kin 25:14 5178
the b of all these vessels was ... 2Kin 25:16 5178
and the chapiter upon it was b ... 2Kin 25:17 5178
chapiter round about, all of b ... 2Kin 25:17 5178
to sound with cymbals of b ... 1Chr 15:19 5178
brought David very much b ... 1Chr 18:8 5178
the pillars, and the vessels of b ... 1Chr 18:8 5178
of vessels of gold and silver and b ... 1Chr 18:10 5178
b in abundance without weight ... 1Chr 22:3 5178
and of b and iron without weight ... 1Chr 22:14 5178
Of the gold, the silver, and the b ... 1Chr 22:16 5178
and the b for things of b ... 1Chr 29:2 5178

of *b* eighteen thousand talents, 1Chr 29:7 5178
in gold, and in silver, and in *b* 2Chr 2:7 5178
work in gold, and in silver, in *b* 2Chr 2:14 5178
Moreover he made an altar of *b* 2Chr 4:1 5178
overlaid the doors of them with *b* 2Chr 4:9 5178
the house of the LORD of bright *b* 2Chr 4:16 5178
for the weight of the *b* could not 2Chr 4:18 5178
king Rehoboam made shields of *b* 2Chr 12:10 5178
b to mend the house of the LORD 2Chr 24:12 5178
or is my flesh of *b* Job 6:12 5153
b is molten out of the stone Job 28:2 5154
bones are as strong pieces of *b* Job 40:18 5154
as straw, and *b* as rotten wood Job 41:27 5154
For he hath broken the gates of *b* Ps 107:16 5178
break in pieces the gates of *b* Is 45:2 5154
is an iron sinew, and thy brow *b* Is 48:4 5154
For *b* I will bring gold, and for Is 60:17 5178
will bring silver, and for wood *b* Is 60:17 5178
they are *b* and iron Jer 6:28 5178
Also the pillars of *b* that were Jer 52:17 5178
carried all the *b* of them to Jer 52:17 5178
all the vessels of *b* wherewith Jer 52:18 5178
the *b* of all these vessels was Jer 52:20 5178
And a chapiter of *b* was upon it Jer 52:22 5178
chapiters round about, all of *b* Jer 52:22 5178
like the colour of burnished *b* Eze 1:7 5178
all they are *b*, and tin, and iron, Eze 22:18 5178
As they gather silver, and *b* Eze 22:20 5178
that the *b* of it may be hot, and Eze 24:11 5178
vessels of *b* in thy market Eze 27:13 5178
was like the appearance of *b* Eze 40:3 5178
his belly and his thighs of *b* Dan 2:32 5174
was the iron, the clay, the *b* Dan 2:35 5174
and another third kingdom of *b* Dan 2:39 5174
brake in pieces the iron, the *b* Dan 2:45 5174
even with a band of iron and *b* Dan 4:15 5174
even with a band of iron and *b* Dan 4:23 5174
gods of gold, and of silver, of *b* Dan 5:4 5174
the gods of silver, and gold, of *b* Dan 5:23 5174
were of iron, and his nails of *b* Dan 7:19 5174
feet like in colour to polished *b* Dan 10:6 5178
iron, and I will make thy hoofs *b* Mic 4:13 5154
the mountains were mountains of *b* Zec 6:1 5178
nor silver, nor *b* in your purses, Mt 10:9 5475
I am become as sounding *b* 1Cor 13:1 5475
And his feet like unto fine *b* Rev 1:15 5474
fire, and his feet are like fine *b* Rev 2:18 5474
and idols of gold, and silver, and *b* Rev 9:20 5470
of most precious wood, and of *b* Rev 18:12 5475

BRAVERY
the *b* of their tinkling ornaments Is 3:18 8597

BRAWLER
but patient, not a *b*, not 1Ti 3:3 269

BRAWLERS
speak evil of no man, to be no *b* Titus 3:2 269

BRAWLING
the housetop, than with a *b* woman Prov 21:9 4090
the housetop, than with a *b* woman Prov 25:24 4090

BRAY
Doth the wild ass *b* when he hath Job 6:5 5101
Though thou shouldest *b* a fool in Prov 27:22 3806

BRAYED
Among the bushes they *b* Job 30:7 5101

BREACH
this *b* be upon thee Gen 38:29 6556
B for *b*, eye for eye, tooth Lev 24:20 7667
and ye shall know my *b* of promise Num 14:34 8569
made a *b* in the tribes of Israel Judg 21:15 6556
before me, as the *b* of waters 2Sa 5:20 6556
the LORD had made a *b* upon Uzzah 2Sa 6:8 6556
wheresoever any *b* shall be found 2Kin 12:5 919
the LORD had made a *b* upon Uzza 1Chr 13:11 6556
the LORD our God made a *b* upon us 1Chr 15:13 6555
that there was no *b* left therein Neh 6:1 6556
He breaketh me with *b* upon *b* Job 16:14 6556
chosen stood before him in the *b* Ps 106:23 6556
therein is a *b* in the spirit Prov 15:4 7667
let us make a *b* therein for us, Is 7:6 1234
be to you as a *b* ready to fall Is 30:13 6556
bindeth up the *b* of his people Is 30:26 7667
be called, The repairer of the *b* Is 58:12 6556
people is broken with a great *b* Jer 14:17 7667
for thy *b* is great like the sea Lam 2:13 7667
into a city wherein is made a *b* Eze 26:10 1234

BREACHES
the sea shore, and abode in his *b* Judg 5:17 4664
repaired the *b* of the city of 1Kin 11:27 6556
them repair the *b* of the house 2Kin 12:5 919
not repaired the *b* of the house 2Kin 12:6 919
repair ye not the *b* of the house 2Kin 12:7 919
deliver it for the *b* of the house 2Kin 12:7 919
to repair the *b* of the house 2Kin 12:8 919
the *b* of the house of the LORD 2Kin 12:12 919
to repair the *b* of the house 2Kin 22:5 919
that the *b* began to be stopped, Neh 4:7 6555
heal the *b* thereof Ps 60:2 7667
also the *b* of the city of David Is 22:9 1233
And ye shall go out at the *b* Amos 4:3 6556
will smite the great house with *b* Amos 6:11 7447
fallen, and close up the *b* thereof Amos 9:11 6556

BREAD
of thy face shalt thou eat *b* Gen 3:19 3899
king of Salem brought forth *b* Gen 14:18 3899
And I will fetch a morsel of *b* Gen 18:5 3899
a feast, and did bake unleavened *b* Gen 19:3
early in the morning, and took *b* Gen 21:14 3899
Then Jacob gave Esau *b* and pottage Gen 25:34 3899
gave the savoury meat and the *b* Gen 27:17 3899
I go, and will give me *b* to eat Gen 28:20 3899
and called his brethren to eat *b* Gen 31:54 3899
and they did eat *b*, and tarried all Gen 31:54 3899
And they sat down to eat *b* Gen 37:25 3899
save the *b* which he did eat Gen 39:6 3899
all the land of Egypt there was *b* Gen 41:54 3899
the people cried to Pharaoh for *b* Gen 41:55 3899
that they should eat *b* there Gen 43:25 3899
himself, and said, Set on *b* Gen 43:31 3899
might not eat *b* with the Hebrews Gen 43:32 3899
she asses laden with corn and *b* Gen 45:23 3899
his father's household, with *b* Gen 47:12 3899
there was no *b* in all the land Gen 47:13 3899
unto Joseph, and said, Give us *b* Gen 47:15 3899
Joseph gave them *b* in exchange Gen 47:17 3899
he fed them with *b* for all their Gen 47:17 3899
buy us and our land for *b*, and we Gen 47:19 3899
Out of Asher his *b* shall be fat Gen 49:20 3899
call him, that he may eat *b* Ex 2:20 3899
roast with fire, and unleavened *b* Ex 12:8
days shall ye eat unleavened *b* Ex 12:15
b from the first day until the Ex 12:15
observe the feast of unleavened *b* Ex 12:17
even, ye shall eat unleavened *b* Ex 12:18
shall ye eat unleavened *b* Ex 12:20
shall no leavened *b* be eaten Ex 13:3
days thou shalt eat unleavened *b* Ex 13:6
Unleavened *b* shall be eaten seven Ex 13:7
no leavened *b* be seen with thee Ex 13:7
and when we did eat *b* to the full Ex 16:3 3899
I will rain *b* from heaven for you Ex 16:4 3899
and in the morning *b* to the full Ex 16:8 3899
morning ye shall be filled with *b* Ex 16:12 3899
This is the *b* which the LORD hath Ex 16:15 3899
day they gathered twice as much *b* Ex 16:22 3899
the sixth day the *b* of two days Ex 16:29 3899
that they may see the *b* wherewith Ex 16:32 3899
to eat *b* with Moses' father in Ex 18:12 3899
keep the feast of unleavened *b* Ex 23:15
shalt eat unleavened *b* seven days Ex 23:15
of my sacrifice with leavened *b* Ex 23:18
your God, and he shall bless thy *b* Ex 23:25 3899
And unleavened *b*, and cakes Ex 29:2 3899
one loaf of *b*, and one cake of oiled Ex 29:23 3899
b that is before the LORD Ex 29:23
the *b* that is in the basket, by Ex 29:32 3899
of the consecrations, or of the *b* Ex 29:34 3899
of unleavened *b* shalt thou keep Ex 34:18
days thou shalt eat unleavened *b* Ex 34:18
he did neither eat *b*, nor drink Ex 34:28 3899
he set the *b* in order upon it Ex 40:23 3899
with unleavened *b* shall it be Lev 6:16
leavened *b* with the sacrifice of Lev 7:13 3899
rams, and a basket of unleavened *b* Lev 8:2
out of the basket of unleavened *b* Lev 8:26
cake, and a cake of oiled *b* Lev 8:26
there eat it with the *b* that is Lev 8:31 3899
of the *b* shall ye burn with fire Lev 8:32 3899
the *b* of their God, they do offer Lev 21:6 3899
for he offereth the *b* of thy God Lev 21:8 3899
to offer the *b* of his God Lev 21:17 3899
nigh to offer the *b* of his God Lev 21:21 3899
He shall eat the *b* of his God Lev 21:22 3899
hand shall ye offer the *b* of your Lev 22:25 3899
of unleavened *b* unto the LORD Lev 23:6
days ye must eat unleavened *b* Lev 23:6
And ye shall eat neither *b* Lev 23:14 3899
ye shall offer with the *b* seven Lev 23:18 3899
b of the first fruits for a wave Lev 23:20 3899
it may be on the *b* for a memorial Lev 24:7 3899
ye shall eat your *b* to the full Lev 26:5 3899
I have broken the staff of your *b* Lev 26:26 3899
shall bake your *b* in one oven Lev 26:26 3899
you your *b* again by weight Lev 26:26 3899
the continual *b* shall be thereon Num 4:7 3899
And a basket of unleavened *b* Num 6:15
of unleavened *b* anointed with oil Num 6:15
with the basket of unleavened *b* Num 6:17
it, and eat it with unleavened *b* Num 9:11
for they are *b* for us Num 14:9 3899
when ye eat of the *b* of the land Num 15:19 3899
for there is no *b*, neither is Num 21:5 3899
and our soul loatheth this light *b* Num 21:5 3899
my *b* for my sacrifices made by Num 28:2 3899
days shall unleavened *b* be eaten Num 28:17
that man doth not live by *b* only Deut 8:3 3899
shalt eat *b* without scarceness Deut 8:9 3899
neither did eat *b* nor drink water Deut 9:9 3899
I did neither eat *b*, nor drink Deut 9:18 3899
shalt eat no leavened *b* with it Deut 16:3
thou eat unleavened *b* therewith Deut 16:3
even the *b* of affliction Deut 16:3 3899
there shall be no leavened *b* seen Deut 16:4
days thou shalt eat unleavened *b* Deut 16:8
in the feast of unleavened *b* Deut 16:16
Because they met you not with *b* Deut 23:4 3899
Ye have not eaten *b*, neither have Deut 29:6 3899
all the *b* of their provision was Josh 9:5 3899
This our *b* we took hot for our Josh 9:12 3899
a cake of barley *b* tumbled into Judg 7:13 3899
loaves of *b* unto the people that Judg 8:5 3899
we should give *b* unto thine army Judg 8:6 3899
that we should give *b* unto thy Judg 8:15 3899
me, I will not eat of thy *b* Judg 13:16 3899
thine heart with a morsel of *b* Judg 19:5 3899
and there is *b* and wine also for me Judg 19:19 3899
his people in giving them *b* Ruth 1:6 3899
come thou hither, and eat of the *b* Ruth 2:14 3899
have hired out themselves for *b* 1Sa 2:5 3899
piece of silver and a morsel of *b* 1Sa 2:36 3899
that I may eat a piece of *b* 1Sa 2:36 3899
for the *b* is spent in our vessels 1Sa 9:7 3899
carrying three loaves of *b* 1Sa 10:3 3899
and give thee two loaves of *b* 1Sa 10:4 3899
And Jesse took an ass laden with *b* 1Sa 16:20 3899
me five loaves of *b* in mine hand 1Sa 21:3 3899
is no common *b* under mine hand 1Sa 21:4 3899
but there is hallowed *b* 1Sa 21:4 3899
the *b* is in a manner common, yea, 1Sa 21:5
So the priest gave him hallowed *b* 1Sa 21:6
for there was no *b* there but the 1Sa 21:6 3899
to put hot *b* in the day when it 1Sa 21:6 3899
in that thou hast given him *b* 1Sa 22:13 3899
Shall I then take my *b*, and my 1Sa 25:11 3899
for he had eaten no *b* all the day 1Sa 28:20 3899
me set a morsel of *b* before thee 1Sa 28:22 3899
and did bake unleavened *b* thereof 1Sa 28:24
him to David, and gave him *b* 1Sa 30:11 3899
for he had eaten no *b*, nor drunk 1Sa 30:12 3899
on the sword, or that lacketh *b* 2Sa 3:29 3899
to me, and more also, if I taste *b* 2Sa 3:35 3899
as men, to every one a cake of *b* 2Sa 6:19 3899
thou shalt eat *b* at my table 2Sa 9:7 3899
son shall eat *b* alway at my table 2Sa 9:10 3899
neither did he eat *b* with them 2Sa 12:17 3899
they set *b* before him, and he did 2Sa 12:20 3899
dead, thou didst rise and eat *b* 2Sa 12:21 3899
upon them two hundred loaves of *b* 2Sa 16:1 3899
and the *b* and summer fruit for the 2Sa 16:2 3899
neither will I eat *b* nor drink 1Kin 13:8 3899
of the LORD, saying, Eat no *b* 1Kin 13:9 3899
him, Come home with me, and eat *b* 1Kin 13:15 3899
neither will I eat *b* nor drink 1Kin 13:16 3899
Thou shalt eat no *b* nor drink 1Kin 13:17 3899
thine house, that he may eat *b* 1Kin 13:18 3899
did eat *b* in his house, and drank 1Kin 13:19 3899
But camest back, and hast eaten *b* 1Kin 13:22 3899
LORD did say to thee, Eat no *b* 1Kin 13:22 3899
to pass, after he had eaten *b* 1Kin 13:23 3899
And the ravens brought him *b* 1Kin 17:6 3899
and flesh in the morning, and *b* 1Kin 17:6 3899
a morsel of *b* in thine hand 1Kin 17:11 3899
in a cave, and fed them with *b* 1Kin 18:4 3899
in a cave, and fed them with *b* 1Kin 18:13 3899
away his face, and would eat no *b* 1Kin 21:4 3899
so sad, that thou eatest no *b* 1Kin 21:5 3899
arise, and eat *b*, and let thine 1Kin 21:7 3899
and feed him with *b* of affliction 1Kin 22:27 3899
and she constrained him to eat *b* 2Kin 4:8 3899
by, he turned in thither to eat *b* 2Kin 4:8 3899
man of God *b* of the firstfruits 2Kin 4:42 3899
set *b* and water before them, that 2Kin 6:22 3899
land of corn and wine, a land of *b* 2Kin 18:32 3899
unleavened *b* among their brethren 2Kin 23:9
there was no *b* for the people of 2Kin 25:3 3899
he did eat *b* continually before 2Kin 25:29 3899
brought *b* on asses, and on camels, 1Chr 12:40 3899
woman, to every one a loaf of *b* 1Chr 16:3 3899
even in the feast of unleavened *b* 2Chr 8:13
and feed him with *b* of affliction 2Chr 18:26 3899
unleavened *b* in the second month 2Chr 30:13
kept the feast of unleavened *b* 2Chr 30:21
feast of unleavened *b* seven days 2Chr 35:17
unleavened *b* seven days with joy Ezr 6:22
he came thither, he did eat no *b* Ezr 10:6 3899
not eaten the *b* of the governor Neh 5:14 3899
people, and had taken of them *b* Neh 5:15 3899
not I the *b* of the governor Neh 5:18 3899
gavest them *b* from heaven for Neh 9:15 3899
not the children of Israel with *b* Neh 13:2 3899
He wandereth abroad for *b* Job 15:23 3899
hast withholden *b* from the hungry Job 22:7 3899
shall not be satisfied with *b* Job 27:14 3899
for the earth, out of it cometh *b* Job 28:5 3899
So that his life abhorreth *b* Job 33:20 3899
did eat *b* with him in his house Job 42:11 3899
eat up my people as they eat *b* Ps 14:4 3899
forsaken, nor his seed begging *b* Ps 37:25 3899
I trusted, which did eat of my *b* Ps 41:9 3899
eat up my people as they eat *b* Ps 53:4 3899
can he give *b* also Ps 78:20 3899
feedest them with the *b* of tears Ps 80:5 3899
so that I forget to eat my *b* Ps 102:4 3899
For I have eaten ashes like *b* Ps 102:9 3899
b which strengtheneth man's heart Ps 104:15 3899
he brake the whole staff of *b* Ps 105:16 3899
them with the *b* of heaven Ps 105:40 3899
let them seek their *b* also out of Ps 109:10
up late, to eat the *b* of sorrows Ps 127:2 3899
I will satisfy her poor with *b* Ps 132:15 3899
For they eat the *b* of wickedness Prov 4:17 3899
a man is brought to a piece of *b* Prov 6:26 3899
Come, eat of my *b*, and drink of Prov 9:5 3899
b eaten in secret is pleasant Prov 9:17 3899
honoureth himself, and lacketh *b* Prov 12:9 3899
land shall be satisfied with *b* Prov 12:11 3899
and thou shalt be satisfied with *b* Prov 20:13 3899
B of deceit is sweet to a man Prov 20:17 3899
he giveth of his *b* to the poor Prov 22:9 3899
Eat thou not the *b* of him that Prov 23:6 3899
be hungry, give him *b* to eat Prov 25:21 3899
his land shall have plenty of *b* Prov 28:19 3899
for for a piece of *b* that man Prov 28:21 3899
and eateth not the *b* of idleness Prov 31:27 3899
eat thy *b* with joy, and drink thy Eccl 9:7 3899
strong, neither yet *b* to the wise Eccl 9:11 3899
Cast thy *b* upon the waters Eccl 11:1 3899
and the staff, the whole stay of *b* Is 3:1 3899
house is neither *b* nor clothing Is 3:7 3899
saying, We will eat our own *b* Is 4:1 3899
with their *b* him that fled Is 21:14 3899
B corn is bruised Is 28:28 3899
Lord give you the *b* of adversity Is 30:20 3899
b of the increase of the earth, Is 30:23 3899
b shall be given him Is 33:16 3899
land of corn and wine, a land of *b* Is 36:17 3899
yea, he kindleth it, and baketh *b* Is 44:15 3899
also I have baked *b* upon the Is 44:19 3899
pit, nor that his *b* should fail Is 51:14 3899

money for that which is not *b*	Is 55:2	3899
to the sower, and *b* to the eater	Is 55:10	3899
not to deal thy *b* to the hungry	Is 58:7	3899
eat up thine harvest, and thy *b*	Jer 5:17	3899
of *b* out of the bakers' street	Jer 37:21	3899
until all the *b* in the city were	Jer 37:21	3899
there is no more *b* in the city	Jer 38:9	3899
they did eat *b* together in Mizpah	Jer 41:1	3899
the trumpet, nor have hunger of *b*	Jer 42:14	3899
so that there was no *b* for the	Jer 52:6	3899
he did continually eat *b* before	Jer 52:33	3899
All her people sigh, they seek *b*	Lam 1:11	3899
the young children ask *b*, and no	Lam 4:4	3899
Assyrians, to be satisfied with *b*	Lam 5:6	3899
We gat our *b* with the peril of	Lam 5:9	3899
vessel, and make thee *b* thereof	Eze 4:9	3899
defiled *b* among the Gentiles	Eze 4:13	3899
shalt prepare thy *b* therewith	Eze 4:15	3899
break the staff of *b* in Jerusalem	Eze 4:16	3899
and they shall eat *b* by weight	Eze 4:16	3899
That they may want *b* and water, and.	Eze 4:17	3899
and will break your staff of *b*	Eze 5:16	3899
eat thy *b* with quaking, and drink	Eze 12:18	3899
eat their *b* with carefulness	Eze 12:19	3899
of barley and for pieces of *b*	Eze 13:19	3899
break the staff of the *b* thereof	Eze 14:13	3899
sister Sodom, pride, fulness of *b*	Eze 16:49	3899
hath given his *b* to the hungry	Eze 18:7	3899
hath given his *b* to the hungry	Eze 18:16	3899
thy lips, and eat not the *b* of men	Eze 24:17	3899
your lips, nor eat the *b* of men	Eze 24:22	3899
in it to eat *b* before the LORD	Eze 44:3	3899
even my house, when ye offer my *b*	Eze 44:7	3899
unleavened *b* shall be eaten	Eze 45:21	
I ate no pleasant *b*, neither came	Dan 10:3	3899
my lovers, that give me my *b*	Hos 2:5	3899
be unto them as the *b* of mourners	Hos 9:4	3899
for their *b* for their soul shall	Hos 9:4	3899
want of *b* in all your places	Amos 4:6	3899
the land of Judah, and there eat *b*	Amos 7:12	3899
in the land, not a famine of *b*	Amos 8:11	3899
they that eat thy *b* have laid a	Obad 7	3899
and with his skirt do touch *b*	Hag 2:12	3899
offer polluted *b* upon mine altar	Mal 1:7	3899
that these stones be made *b*	Mt 4:3	740
Man shall not live by *b* alone	Mt 4:4	740
Give us this day our daily *b*	Mt 6:11	740
of you, whom if his son ask *b*	Mt 7:9	740
not their hands when they eat *b*	Mt 15:2	740
not meet to take the children's *b*	Mt 15:26	740
have so much *b* in the wilderness	Mt 15:33	740
they had forgotten to take *b*	Mt 16:5	740
It is because we have taken no *b*	Mt 16:7	740
because ye have brought no *b*	Mt 16:8	740
spake it not to you concerning *b*	Mt 16:11	740
not beware of the leaven of *b*	Mt 16:12	740
b the disciples came to Jesus	Mt 26:17	
as they were eating, Jesus took *b*	Mt 26:26	740
they could not so much as eat *b*	Mk 3:20	740
no scrip, no *b*, no money in their	Mk 6:8	740
the villages, and buy themselves *b*	Mk 6:36	740
buy two hundred pennyworth of *b*	Mk 6:37	740
his disciples eat *b* with defiled	Mk 7:2	740
but eat *b* with unwashen hands	Mk 7:5	740
not meet to take the children's *b*	Mk 7:27	740
men with *b* here in the wilderness	Mk 8:4	740
disciples had forgotten to take *b*	Mk 8:14	740
It is because we have no *b*	Mk 8:16	740
reason ye, because ye have no *b*	Mk 8:17	740
the passover, and of unleavened *b*	Mk 14:1	
And the first day of unleavened *b*	Mk 14:12	
And as they did eat, Jesus took *b*	Mk 14:22	740
this stone that it be made *b*	Lk 4:3	740
man shall not live by *b* alone	Lk 4:4	740
eating *b* nor drinking wine	Lk 7:33	740
staves, nor scrip, neither *b*	Lk 9:3	740
Give us day by day our daily *b*	Lk 11:3	740
If a son shall ask *b* of any of	Lk 11:11	740
to eat *b* on the sabbath day	Lk 14:1	740
shall eat *b* in the kingdom of God	Lk 14:15	740
of my father's have *b* enough	Lk 15:17	740
feast of unleavened *b* drew nigh	Lk 22:1	
Then came the day of unleavened *b*	Lk 22:7	
And he took *b*, and gave thanks, and	Lk 22:19	740
sat at meat with them, he took *b*	Lk 24:30	740
known of them in breaking of *b*	Lk 24:35	740
Philip, Whence shall we buy *b*	Jn 6:5	740
Two hundred pennyworth of *b* is	Jn 6:7	740
the place where they did eat *b*	Jn 6:23	740
He gave them *b* from heaven to eat	Jn 6:31	740
gave you not that *b* from heaven	Jn 6:32	740
giveth you the true *b* from heaven	Jn 6:32	740
For the *b* of God is he which	Jn 6:33	740
Lord, evermore give us this *b*	Jn 6:34	740
unto them, I am the *b* of life	Jn 6:35	740
I am the *b* which came down from	Jn 6:41	740
I am that *b* of life	Jn 6:48	740
This is the *b* which cometh down	Jn 6:50	740
I am the living *b* which came down	Jn 6:51	740
if any man eat of this *b*, he	Jn 6:51	740
the *b* that I will give is my	Jn 6:51	740
This is that *b* which came down	Jn 6:58	740
of this *b* shall live for ever	Jn 6:58	740
He that eateth *b* with me hath	Jn 13:18	740
there, and fish laid thereon, and *b*	Jn 21:9	740
Jesus then cometh, and taketh *b*	Jn 21:13	740
fellowship, and in breaking of *b*	Acts 2:42	740
breaking *b* from house to house,	Acts 2:46	740
were the days of unleavened *b*	Acts 12:3	
after the days of unleavened *b*	Acts 20:6	
came together to break *b*, Paul	Acts 20:7	740
come up again, and had broken *b*	Acts 20:11	740
he had thus spoken, he took *b*	Acts 27:35	740
the unleavened *b* of sincerity	1Cor 5:8	
The *b* which we break, is it not	1Cor 10:16	740
For we being many are one *b*	1Cor 10:17	740
are all partakers of that one *b*	1Cor 10:17	740
in which he was betrayed took *b*	1Cor 11:23	740
For as often as ye eat this *b*	1Cor 11:26	740
whosoever shall eat this *b*	1Cor 11:27	740
and so let him eat of that *b*	1Cor 11:28	740
both minister *b* for your food	2Cor 9:10	740
did we eat any man's *b* for nought	2Th 3:8	740
they work, and eat their own *b*	2Th 3:12	740

BREADTH

the *b* of it fifty cubits, and the	Gen 6:15	7341
length of it and in the *b* of it	Gen 13:17	7341
a cubit and a half the *b* thereof	Ex 25:10	7341
a cubit and a half the *b* thereof	Ex 25:17	7341
thereof, and a cubit the *b* thereof	Ex 25:23	7341
a border of an hand *b* round about	Ex 25:25	2948
the *b* of one curtain four cubits	Ex 26:2	7341
the *b* of one curtain four cubits	Ex 26:8	7341
half shall be the *b* of one board	Ex 26:16	7341
for the *b* of the court on the	Ex 27:12	7341
the *b* of the court on the east	Ex 27:13	7341
the *b* fifty every where, and the	Ex 27:18	7341
and a span shall be the *b* thereof	Ex 28:16	7341
thereof, and a cubit the *b* thereof	Ex 30:2	7341
the *b* of one curtain four cubits	Ex 36:9	7341
cubits was the *b* of one curtain	Ex 36:15	7341
the *b* of a board one cubit and a	Ex 36:21	7341
and a cubit and a half the *b* of it	Ex 37:1	7341
one cubit and a half the *b* thereof	Ex 37:6	7341
thereof, and a cubit the *b* thereof	Ex 37:10	7341
a cubit, and the *b* of it a cubit	Ex 37:25	7341
and five cubits the *b* thereof	Ex 38:1	7341
height in the *b* was five cubits	Ex 38:18	7341
thereof, and a span the *b* thereof	Ex 39:9	7341
and four cubits the *b* of it	Deut 3:11	7341
could sling stones at an hair *b*	Judg 20:16	
the *b* thereof twenty cubits, and	1Kin 6:2	7341
according to the *b* of the house	1Kin 6:3	7341
ten cubits was the *b* thereof	1Kin 6:3	7341
in length, and twenty cubits in *b*	1Kin 6:20	7341
the *b* thereof fifty cubits, and	1Kin 7:2	7341
the *b* thereof thirty cubits	1Kin 7:6	7341
And it was an hand *b* thick	1Kin 7:26	2947
and four cubits the *b* thereof	1Kin 7:27	7341
cubits, and the *b* twenty cubits	2Chr 3:3	7341
according to the *b* of the house	2Chr 3:4	7341
according to the *b* of the house	2Chr 3:8	7341
the *b* thereof twenty cubits	2Chr 3:8	7341
and twenty cubits the *b* thereof	2Chr 4:1	7341
the *b* thereof threescore cubits	Ezr 6:3	6613
the *b* of the waters is straitened	Job 37:10	7341
thou perceived the *b* of the earth	Job 38:18	7338
shall fill the *b* of thy land	Is 8:8	7341
long by the cubit and an hand *b*	Eze 40:5	2948
he measured the *b* of the building	Eze 40:5	7341
he measured the *b* of the entry of	Eze 40:11	7341
the *b* was five and twenty cubits	Eze 40:13	7341
Then he measured the *b* from the	Eze 40:19	7341
length thereof, and the *b* thereof	Eze 40:20	7341
the *b* five and twenty cubits	Eze 40:21	7341
the *b* five and twenty cubits	Eze 40:25	7341
the *b* five and twenty cubits	Eze 40:36	7341
the *b* of the gate was three	Eze 40:48	7341
cubits, and the *b* eleven cubits	Eze 40:49	7341
which was the *b* of the tabernacle	Eze 41:1	7341
the *b* of the door was ten cubits	Eze 41:2	7341
and the *b*, twenty cubits	Eze 41:2	7341
the *b* of the door, seven cubits	Eze 41:3	7341
and the *b*, twenty cubits, before	Eze 41:4	7341
the *b* of every side chamber, four	Eze 41:5	7341
therefore the *b* of the house was	Eze 41:7	7341
the *b* of the place that was left	Eze 41:11	7341
Also the *b* of the face of the	Eze 41:14	7341
door, and the *b* was fifty cubits	Eze 42:2	7341
was a walk of ten cubits *b* inward	Eze 42:4	7341
The cubit is a cubit and an hand *b*	Eze 43:13	2948
the *b* a cubit, and the border	Eze 43:13	7341
be two cubits, and the *b* one cubit	Eze 43:14	7341
four cubits, and the *b* one cubit	Eze 43:14	7341
the *b* shall be ten thousand	Eze 45:1	7341
in length, with five hundred in *b*	Eze 45:2	7341
and the *b* of ten thousand	Eze 45:3	7341
length, and the ten thousand of *b*	Eze 45:5	7341
and twenty thousand reeds in *b*	Eze 48:8	7341
length, and of ten thousand in *b*	Eze 48:9	7341
toward the west ten thousand in *b*	Eze 48:10	7341
toward the east ten thousand in *b*	Eze 48:10	7341
in length, and ten thousand in *b*	Eze 48:13	7341
thousand, and the *b* ten thousand	Eze 48:13	7341
that are left in the *b* over	Eze 48:15	7341
and the *b* thereof six cubits	Dan 3:1	6613
march through the *b* of the land	Hab 1:6	4800
to see what is the *b* thereof	Zec 2:2	7341
and the *b* thereof ten cubits	Zec 5:2	7341
with all saints what is the *b*	Eph 3:18	4114
went up on the *b* of the earth	Rev 20:9	4114
the length is as large as the *b*	Rev 21:16	4114
The length and the *b* and the height	Rev 21:16	4114

BREAK

Lot, and came near to *b* the door	Gen 19:9	7665
that thou shalt *b* his yoke from	Gen 27:40	6561
neither shall ye *b* a bone thereof	Ex 12:46	7665
it, then thou shalt *b* his neck	Ex 13:13	6202
lest they *b* through unto the LORD	Ex 19:21	2040
lest the LORD *b* forth upon them	Ex 19:22	6555
the people *b* through to come up	Ex 19:24	2040
lest he *b* forth upon them	Ex 19:24	6555
If fire *b* out, and catch in thorns	Ex 22:6	3318
quite *b* down their images	Ex 23:24	7665
B off the golden earrings, which	Ex 32:2	6561
hath any gold, let them *b* it off	Ex 32:24	6561
b their images, and cut down their	Ex 34:13	7665
not, then shalt thou *b* his neck	Ex 34:20	6202
and ye shall *b* it	Lev 11:33	7665
if a leprosy *b* out abroad in the	Lev 13:12	6524
b out in the house, after that he	Lev 14:43	6524
he shall *b* down the house, the	Lev 14:45	5422
but that ye *b* my covenant	Lev 26:15	6565
I will *b* the pride of your power	Lev 26:19	7665
to *b* my covenant with them	Lev 26:44	6565
the morning, nor *b* any bone of it	Num 9:12	7665
shall *b* their bones, and pierce	Num 24:8	1633
he shall not *b* his word, he shall	Num 30:2	2490
b down their images, and cut down	Deut 7:5	7665
b their pillars, and burn their	Deut 12:3	7665
b my covenant which I have made	Deut 31:16	6565
and provoke me, and *b* my covenant	Deut 31:20	6565
I will never *b* my covenant with	Judg 2:1	6565
peace, I will *b* down this tower	Judg 8:9	5422
many servants now a days that *b*	1Sa 25:10	6555
they came to Hebron at *b* of day	2Sa 2:32	215
b thy league with Baasha king of	1Kin 15:19	6565
to *b* through even unto the king	2Kin 3:26	1234
did the Chaldees *b* in pieces	2Kin 25:13	7665
b thy league with Baasha king of	2Chr 16:3	6565
Should we again *b* thy	Ezr 9:14	6565
he shall even *b* down their stone	Neh 4:3	6565
Wilt thou *b* a leaf driven to and	Job 13:25	6206
b me in pieces with words	Job 19:2	1792
He shall *b* in pieces mighty men	Job 34:24	7489
or that the wild beast may *b* them	Job 39:15	1758
Let us *b* their bands asunder, and	Ps 2:3	5423
Thou shalt *b* them with a rod of	Ps 2:9	7489
B thou the arm of the wicked and	Ps 10:15	7665
B their teeth, O God, in their	Ps 58:6	2040
b out the great teeth of the	Ps 58:6	5422
shall *b* in pieces the oppressor	Ps 72:4	1792
But now they *b* down the carved	Ps 74:6	1986
If they *b* my statutes, and keep	Ps 89:31	2490
My covenant will I not *b*, nor	Ps 89:34	2490
They *b* in pieces thy people, O	Ps 94:5	1792
oil, which shall not *b* my head	Ps 141:5	5106
a time to *b* down, and a time to	Eccl 3:3	6555
Until the day *b*, and the shadows	Song 2:17	6315
Until the day *b*, and the shadows	Song 4:6	6315
b down the wall thereof, and it	Is 5:5	6555
they *b* forth into singing	Is 14:7	6476
That I will *b* the Assyrian in my	Is 14:25	7665
b the clods of his ground	Is 28:24	7702
nor *b* it with the wheel of his	Is 28:28	2000
he shall *b* it as the breaking of	Is 30:14	7665
the wilderness shall waters *b* out	Is 35:6	1234
so will he *b* all my bones	Is 38:13	7665
A bruised reed shall he not *b*	Is 42:3	7665
b forth into singing, ye	Is 44:23	6476
I will *b* in pieces the gates of	Is 45:2	7665
b forth into singing, O mountains	Is 49:13	6476
B forth into joy, sing together,	Is 52:9	6476
b forth into singing, and cry	Is 54:1	6476
For thou shalt *b* forth on the	Is 54:3	6555
the hills shall *b* forth before	Is 55:12	6476
go free, and that ye *b* every yoke	Is 58:6	5423
thy light *b* forth as the morning	Is 58:8	1234
b forth upon all the inhabitants	Jer 1:14	6605
B up your fallow ground, and sow	Jer 4:3	5214
b not thy covenant with us	Jer 14:21	6565
Shall iron *b* the northern iron and	Jer 15:12	7489
Then shalt thou *b* the bottle in	Jer 19:10	7665
Even so will I *b* this people	Jer 19:11	7665
for I will *b* the yoke of the king	Jer 28:4	7665
Even so will I *b* the yoke of	Jer 28:11	7665
that I will *b* his yoke from off	Jer 30:8	7665
to *b* down, and to throw down, and	Jer 31:28	5422
If ye can *b* my covenant of the	Jer 33:20	6565
He shall *b* also the images of	Jer 43:13	7665
which I have built will I *b* down	Jer 45:4	2040
his vessels, and *b* their bottles	Jer 48:12	5310
I will *b* the bow of Elam, the	Jer 49:35	7665
for with thee will I *b* in pieces	Jer 51:20	5310
with thee will I *b* in pieces the	Jer 51:21	5310
with thee will I *b* in pieces the	Jer 51:21	5310
thee also will I *b* in pieces man	Jer 51:22	5310
with thee will I *b* in pieces old	Jer 51:22	5310
with thee will I *b* in pieces the	Jer 51:22	5310
I will also *b* in pieces with thee	Jer 51:23	5310
with thee will I *b* in pieces the	Jer 51:23	5310
with thee will I *b* in pieces	Jer 51:23	5310
I will *b* the staff of bread in	Eze 4:16	7665
will *b* your staff of bread	Eze 5:16	7665
So will I *b* down the wall that ye	Eze 13:14	2040
will *b* the staff of the bread	Eze 14:13	7665
thee, as women that *b* wedlock	Eze 16:38	5003
shall *b* down thy high places	Eze 16:39	5422
or shall he *b* the covenant, and be	Eze 17:15	6565
thou shalt *b* the sherds thereof,	Eze 23:34	1633
of Tyrus, and *b* down her towers	Eze 26:4	2040
axes he shall *b* down thy towers	Eze 26:9	5422
they shall *b* down thy walls, and	Eze 26:12	2040
of thee by thy hand, thou didst *b*	Eze 29:7	7533
when I shall *b* there the yokes of	Eze 30:18	7665
will *b* his arms, the strong, and	Eze 30:22	7665
but I will *b* Pharaoh's arms, and	Eze 30:24	7665
shall it *b* in pieces and bruise	Dan 2:40	1854
people, but it shall *b* in pieces	Dan 2:44	1854
b off thy sins by righteousness,	Dan 4:27	6562
tread it down, and *b* it in pieces	Dan 7:23	1854
that I will *b* the bow of Israel	Hos 1:5	7665
I will *b* the bow and the sword and	Hos 2:18	7665
committing adultery, they *b* out	Hos 4:2	6555
he shall *b* down their altars, he	Hos 10:2	6202
plow, and Jacob shall *b* his clods	Hos 10:11	7702
b up your fallow ground	Hos 10:12	5214
and they shall not *b* their ranks	Joel 2:7	5670
I will *b* also the bar of Damascus	Amos 1:5	7665
lest he *b* out like fire in the	Amos 5:6	6743
they *b* their bones, and chop them	Mic 3:3	6746

For now will I *b* his yoke from ... Nah 1:13 7665
that I might *b* my covenant which ... Zec 11:10 6565
that I might *b* the brotherhood ... Zec 11:14 6565
Whosoever therefore shall *b* one ... Mt 5:19 *3089*
and where thieves *b* through ... Mt 6:19 *1358*
do not *b* through nor steal ... Mt 6:20 *1358*
else the bottles *b*, and the wine ... Mt 9:17 *4486*
A bruised reed shall he not *b* ... Mt 12:20 *2608*
came together to *b* bread, Paul ... Acts 20:7 *2806*
a long while, even till *b* of day ... Acts 20:11 *827*
ye to weep and to *b* mine heart ... Acts 21:13 *4919*
The bread which we *b*, is it not ... 1Cor 10:16 *2806*
b forth and cry, thou that ... Gal 4:27 *4486*

BREAKER
The *b* is come up before them ... Mic 2:13 6555
but if thou be a *b* of the law ... Rom 2:25 *3848*

BREAKEST
Thou *b* the ships of Tarshish with ... Ps 48:7 7665

BREAKETH
he said, Let me go, for the day *b* ... Gen 32:26 5927
For he *b* me with a tempest, and ... Job 9:17 7779
he *b* down, and it cannot be built ... Job 12:14 2040
He *b* me with breach upon breach, ... Job 16:14 6555
The flood *b* out from the ... Job 28:4 6555
voice of the LORD *b* the cedars ... Ps 29:5 7665
the LORD *b* the cedars of Lebanon ... Ps 29:5 7665
he *b* the bow, and cutteth the ... Ps 46:9 7665
My soul *b* for the longing that it ... Ps 119:20 1638
and a soft tongue *b* the bone ... Prov 25:15 7665
whoso *b* an hedge, a serpent shall ... Eccl 10:8 6555
is crushed *b* out into a viper ... Is 59:5 1234
as one *b* a potter's vessel, that ... Jer 19:11 7665
hammer that *b* the rock in pieces ... Jer 23:29 6327
bread, and no man *b* it unto them ... Lam 4:4 6566
forasmuch as iron *b* in pieces ... Dan 2:40 1855
and as iron that *b* all these ... Dan 2:40 7940

BREAKING
with him until the *b* of the day ... Gen 32:24 5927
shall be a boil *b* forth with ... Ex 9:9 6524
it became a boil *b* forth with ... Ex 9:10 6524
If a thief be found *b* up, and be ... Ex 22:2 4290
hand like the *b* forth of waters ... 1Chr 14:11 6556
upon me as a wide *b* in of waters ... Job 30:14 6556
that there be no *b* in, nor going ... Ps 144:14 6556
b down the walls, and of crying to ... Is 22:5 6979
whose *b* cometh suddenly at an ... Is 30:13 7667
he shall break it as the *b* of the ... Is 30:14 7667
the oath in *b* the covenant ... Eze 16:59 6565
the oath by *b* the covenant ... Eze 17:18 6565
of man, with the *b* of thy loins ... Eze 21:6 7670
place of the *b* forth of children ... Hos 13:13 4866
was known of them in *b* of bread ... Lk 24:35 *2800*
in *b* of bread, and in prayers ... Acts 2:42 *2800*
b bread from house to house, did ... Acts 2:46 *2806*
through *b* the law dishonourest ... Rom 2:23 *3847*

BREAKINGS
by reason of *b* they purify ... Job 41:25 7667

BREAST
thou shalt take the *b* of the ram ... Ex 29:26 2373
the *b* of the wave offering ... Ex 29:27 2373
made by fire, the fat with the *b* ... Lev 7:30 2373
that the *b* may be waved for a ... Lev 7:30 2373
but the *b* shall be Aaron's and his ... Lev 7:31 2373
For the wave *b* and the heave ... Lev 7:34 2373
And Moses took the *b*, and waved it ... Lev 8:29 2373
And the wave *b* and heave shoulder ... Lev 10:14 2373
the wave *b* shall they bring with ... Lev 10:15 2373
for the priest, with the wave *b* ... Num 6:20 2373
shall be thine, as the wave *b* ... Num 18:18 2373
pluck the fatherless from the *b* ... Job 24:9 7699
and shalt suck the *b* of kings ... Is 60:16 7699
the sea monsters draw out the *b* ... Lam 4:3 7699
head was of fine gold, his *b* ... Dan 2:32 2306
unto heaven, but smote upon his *b* ... Lk 18:13 *4738*
lying on Jesus' *b* saith unto him ... Jn 13:25 *4738*
also leaned on his *b* at supper ... Jn 21:20 *4738*

BREASTPLATE
be set in the ephod, and in the *b* ... Ex 25:7 2833
a *b*, and an ephod, and a robe, and a ... Ex 28:4 2833
thou shalt make the *b* of judgment ... Ex 28:15 2833
thou shalt make upon the *b* chains ... Ex 28:22 2833
make upon the *b* two rings of gold ... Ex 28:23 2833
rings on the two ends of the *b* ... Ex 28:23 2833
which are on the ends of the *b* ... Ex 28:24 2833
of the *b* in the border thereof ... Ex 28:26 2833
they shall bind the *b* by the ... Ex 28:28 2833
that the *b* be not loosed from the ... Ex 28:28 2833
the *b* of judgment upon his heart ... Ex 28:29 2833
put in the *b* of judgment the Urim ... Ex 28:30 2833
the ephod, and the ephod, and the *b* ... Ex 29:5 2833
set for the ephod, and for the *b* ... Ex 35:9 2833
set, for the ephod, and for the *b* ... Ex 35:27 2833
he made the *b* of cunning work, ... Ex 39:8 2833
they made the *b* double ... Ex 39:9 2833
upon the *b* chains at the ends ... Ex 39:15 2833
rings in the two ends of the *b* ... Ex 39:16 2833
two rings on the ends of the *b* ... Ex 39:17 2833
put them on the two ends of the *b* ... Ex 39:19 2833
they did bind the *b* by his rings ... Ex 39:21 2833
that the *b* might not be loosed ... Ex 39:21 2833
And he put the *b* upon him ... Lev 8:8 2833
also he put in the *b* the Urim ... Lev 8:8 2833
he put on righteousness as a *b* ... Is 59:17 8302
having on the *b* of righteousness ... Eph 6:14 *2382*
sober, putting on the *b* of faith ... 1Th 5:8 *2382*

BREASTPLATES
And they had *b* ... Rev 9:9 *2382*
as it were *b* of iron ... Rev 9:9 *2382*
having *b* of fire, and of jacinth, ... Rev 9:17 *2382*

BREASTS
lieth under, blessings of the *b* ... Gen 49:25 7699
And they put the fat upon the *b* ... Lev 9:20 2373
And the *b* and the right shoulder ... Lev 9:21 2373
or why the *b* that I should suck ... Job 3:12 7699
His *b* are full of milk, and his ... Job 21:24 5845
when I was upon my mother's *b* ... Ps 22:9 7699
let her *b* satisfy thee at all ... Prov 5:19 1717
shall lie all night betwixt my *b* ... Song 1:13 7699
Thy two *b* are like two young roes ... Song 4:5 7699
Thy two *b* are like two young roes ... Song 7:3 7699
thy *b* to clusters of grapes ... Song 7:7 7699
now also thy *b* shall be as ... Song 7:8 7699
that sucked the *b* of my mother ... Song 8:1 7699
a little sister, and she hath no *b* ... Song 8:8 7699
I am a wall, and my *b* like towers ... Song 8:10 7699
the milk, and drawn from the *b* ... Is 28:9 7699
with the *b* of her consolations ... Is 66:11 7699
thy *b* are fashioned, and thine ... Eze 16:7 7699
there were their *b* pressed ... Eze 23:3 7699
bruised the *b* of her virginity ... Eze 23:8 1717
thereof, and pluck off thine own *b* ... Eze 23:34 7699
her adulteries from between her *b* ... Hos 2:2 7699
them a miscarrying womb and dry *b* ... Hos 9:14 7699
and those that suck the *b* ... Joel 2:16 7699
of doves, tabering upon their *b* ... Nah 2:7 3824
which were done, smote their *b* ... Lk 23:48 *4738*
having their *b* girded with golden ... Rev 15:6 *4738*

BREATH
into his nostrils the *b* of life ... Gen 2:7 5397
flesh, wherein is the *b* of life ... Gen 6:17 7307
flesh, wherein is the *b* of life ... Gen 7:15 7307
whose nostrils was the *b* of life ... Gen 7:22 5397
blast of the *b* of his nostrils ... 2Sa 22:16 7307
that there was no *b* left in him ... 1Kin 17:17 5397
by the *b* of his nostrils are they ... Job 4:9 7307
will not suffer me to take my *b* ... Job 9:18 7307
thing, and the *b* of all mankind ... Job 12:10 7307
by the *b* of his mouth shall he go ... Job 15:30 7307
My *b* is corrupt, my days are ... Job 17:1 7307
My *b* is strange to my wife, ... Job 19:17 7307
All the while my *b* is in me ... Job 27:3 5397
the *b* of the Almighty hath given ... Job 33:4 5397
unto himself his spirit and his *b* ... Job 34:14 5397
By the *b* of God frost is given ... Job 37:10 5397
His *b* kindleth coals, and a flame ... Job 41:21 5315
blast of the *b* of thy nostrils ... Ps 18:15 7307
of them by the *b* of his mouth ... Ps 33:6 7307
thou takest away their *b*, they ... Ps 104:29 7307
is there any *b* in their mouths ... Ps 135:17 7307
His *b* goeth forth, he returneth ... Ps 146:4 7307
thing that hath *b* praise the LORD ... Ps 150:6 5397
yea, they have all one *b* ... Eccl 3:19 7307
whose *b* is in his nostrils ... Is 2:22 5397
with the *b* of his lips shall he ... Is 11:4 7307
And his *b*, as an overflowing ... Is 30:28 7307
the *b* of the LORD, like a stream ... Is 30:33 5397
your *b*, as fire, shall devour you ... Is 33:11 7307
he that giveth *b* unto the people ... Is 42:5 5397
and there is no *b* in them ... Jer 10:14 7307
and there is no *b* in them ... Jer 51:17 7307
The *b* of our nostrils, the ... Lam 4:20 7307
I will cause *b* to enter into you, ... Eze 37:5 7307
put *b* in you, and ye shall live ... Eze 37:6 7307
but there was no *b* in them ... Eze 37:8 7307
Come from the four winds, O *b* ... Eze 37:9 7307
the *b* came into them, and they ... Eze 37:10 7307
and the God in whose hand thy *b* is ... Dan 5:23 5396
me, neither is there *b* left in me ... Dan 10:17 5397
there is no *b* at all in the midst ... Hab 2:19 7307
he giveth to all life, and *b* ... Acts 17:25 *4157*

BREATHE
there was not any left to *b* ... Josh 11:11 5397
them, neither left they any to *b* ... Josh 11:14 5397
me, and such as *b* out cruelty ... Ps 27:12 3307
b upon these slain, that they may ... Eze 37:9 5301

BREATHED
b into his nostrils the breath of ... Gen 2:7 5301
but utterly destroyed all that *b* ... Josh 10:40 5397
left not to Jeroboam any that *b* ... 1Kin 15:29 5397
he *b* on them, and saith unto them, ... Jn 20:22 *1720*

BREATHETH
shalt save alive nothing that *b* ... Deut 20:16 5397

BREATHING
hide not thine ear at my *b* ... Lam 3:56 7309
yet *b* out threatenings and ... Acts 9:1 *1709*

BRED
morning, and it *b* worms, and stank ... Ex 16:20 7311

BREECHES
linen *b* to cover their nakedness ... Ex 28:42 4370
linen *b* of fine twined linen, ... Ex 39:28 4370
his linen *b* shall he put upon his ... Lev 6:10 4370
have the linen *b* upon his flesh ... Lev 16:4 4370
have linen *b* upon their loins ... Eze 44:18 4370

BREED
that they may *b* abundantly in the ... Gen 8:17 8317
lambs, and rams of the *b* of Bashan ... Deut 32:14 1121

BREEDING
even the *b* of nettles, and ... Zeph 2:9 4476

BRETHREN
father, and told his two *b* without ... Gen 9:22 251
servants shall he be unto his *b* ... Gen 9:25 251
for we be *b* ... Gen 13:8 251
in the presence of all his *b* ... Gen 16:12 251
And said, I pray you, *b*, do not so ... Gen 19:7 251
me to the house of my master's *b* ... Gen 24:27 251
died in the presence of all his *b* ... Gen 25:18 251
be lord over thy *b*, and let thy ... Gen 27:29 251
all his *b* have I given to him for ... Gen 27:37 251
And Jacob said unto them, My *b* ... Gen 29:4 251
And he took his *b* with him ... Gen 31:23 251
Laban with his *b* pitched in the ... Gen 31:25 251
before our *b* discern thou what is ... Gen 31:32 251
here before my *b* and thy *b* ... Gen 31:37 251
And Jacob said unto his *b*, Gather ... Gen 31:46 251
called his *b* to eat bread ... Gen 31:54 251
unto her father and unto her *b* ... Gen 34:11 251
Jacob, Simeon and Levi, Dinah's *b* ... Gen 34:25 251
was feeding the flock with his *b* ... Gen 37:2 251
when his *b* saw that their father ... Gen 37:4 251
loved him more than all his *b* ... Gen 37:4 251
a dream, and he told it his *b* ... Gen 37:5 251
his *b* said to him, Shalt thou ... Gen 37:8 251
another dream, and told it his *b* ... Gen 37:9 251
it to his father, and to his *b* ... Gen 37:10 251
thy *b* indeed come to bow down ... Gen 37:10 251
And his *b* envied him ... Gen 37:11 251
his *b* went to feed their father's ... Gen 37:12 251
Do not thy *b* feed the flock in ... Gen 37:13 251
see whether it be well with thy *b* ... Gen 37:14 251
And he said, I seek my *b* ... Gen 37:16 251
And Joseph went after his *b* ... Gen 37:17 251
when Joseph was come unto his *b* ... Gen 37:23 251
And Judah said unto his *b*, What ... Gen 37:26 251
And his *b* were content ... Gen 37:27 251
And he returned unto his *b* ... Gen 37:30 251
that Judah went down from his *b* ... Gen 38:1 251
he die also, as his *b* did ... Gen 38:11 251
Joseph's ten *b* went down to buy ... Gen 42:3 251
Jacob sent not with his *b* ... Gen 42:4 251
and Joseph's *b* came, and bowed ... Gen 42:6 251
And Joseph saw his *b*, and he knew ... Gen 42:7 251
And Joseph knew his *b*, but they ... Gen 42:8 251
said, Thy servants are twelve *b* ... Gen 42:13 251
let one of your *b* be bound in the ... Gen 42:19 251
And he said unto his *b*, My money ... Gen 42:28 251
We be twelve *b*, sons of our ... Gen 42:32 251
leave one of your *b* here with me ... Gen 42:33 251
his *b* came to Joseph's house ... Gen 44:14 251
and let the lad go up with his *b* ... Gen 44:33 251
made himself known unto his *b* ... Gen 45:1 251
And Joseph said unto his *b* ... Gen 45:3 251
his *b* could not answer him ... Gen 45:3 251
And Joseph said unto his *b* ... Gen 45:4 251
Moreover he kissed all his *b* ... Gen 45:15 251
after that his *b* talked with him ... Gen 45:15 251
saying, Joseph's *b* are come ... Gen 45:16 251
said unto Joseph, Say unto thy *b* ... Gen 45:17 251
So he sent his *b* away, and they ... Gen 45:24 251
And Joseph said unto his *b* ... Gen 46:31 251
Pharaoh, and say unto him, My *b* ... Gen 46:31 251
and said, My father and my *b* ... Gen 47:1 251
And he took some of his *b*, even ... Gen 47:2 251
And Pharaoh said unto his *b* ... Gen 47:3 251
and thy *b* are come unto thee ... Gen 47:5 251
make thy father and *b* to dwell ... Gen 47:6 251
Joseph placed his father and his *b* ... Gen 47:11 251
nourished his father, and his *b* ... Gen 47:12 251
of their *b* in their inheritance ... Gen 48:6 251
to thee one portion above thy *b* ... Gen 48:22 251
Simeon and Levi are *b* ... Gen 49:5 251
art he whom thy *b* shall praise ... Gen 49:8 251
him that was separate from his *b* ... Gen 49:26 251
all the house of Joseph, and his *b* ... Gen 50:8 251
returned into Egypt, he, and his *b* ... Gen 50:14 251
when Joseph's *b* saw that their ... Gen 50:15 251
thee now, the trespass of thy *b* ... Gen 50:17 251
his *b* also went and fell down ... Gen 50:18 251
And Joseph said unto his *b* ... Gen 50:24 251
And Joseph died, and all his *b* ... Ex 1:6 251
that he went out unto his *b* ... Ex 2:11 251
smiting an Hebrew, one of his *b* ... Ex 2:11 251
return unto my *b* which are in ... Ex 4:18 251
carry your *b* from before the ... Lev 10:4 251
but let your *b*, the whole house ... Lev 10:6 251
is the high priest among his *b* ... Lev 21:10 251
but over your *b* the children of ... Lev 25:46 251
one of his *b* may redeem him ... Lev 25:48 251
their *b* in the tabernacle of the ... Num 8:26 251
all thy *b* the sons of Levi with ... Num 16:10 251
thy *b* also of the tribe of Levi, ... Num 18:2 251
I have taken your *b* the Levites ... Num 18:6 251
when our *b* died before the LORD ... Num 20:3 251
brought unto his *b* a Midianitish ... Num 25:6 251
among the *b* of our father ... Num 27:4 251
among their father's *b* ... Num 27:7 251
give his inheritance unto his *b* ... Num 27:9 251
And if he have no *b*, then ye shall ... Num 27:10 251
inheritance unto his father's *b* ... Num 27:10 251
And if his father have no *b* ... Num 27:11 251
of Reuben, Shall your *b* go to war ... Num 32:6 251
Hear the causes between your *b* ... Deut 1:16 251
our *b* have discouraged our heart, ... Deut 1:28 251
of your *b* the children of Esau ... Deut 2:4 251
from our *b* the children of Esau ... Deut 2:8 251
your *b* the children of Israel ... Deut 3:18 251
LORD have given rest unto your *b* ... Deut 3:20 251
part nor inheritance with his *b* ... Deut 10:9 251
you a poor man of one of thy *b* ... Deut 15:7 251
one from among thy *b* shalt thou ... Deut 17:15 251
be not lifted up above his *b* ... Deut 17:20 251
have no inheritance among their *b* ... Deut 18:2 251
as all his *b* the Levites do, ... Deut 18:7 251
from the midst of thee, of thy *b* ... Deut 18:15 251
up a Prophet from among their *b* ... Deut 18:18 251
his *b* of the children of Israel ... Deut 24:7 251
and needy, whether he be of thy *b* ... Deut 24:14 251
If *b* dwell together, and one of ... Deut 25:5 251
neither did he acknowledge his *b* ... Deut 33:9 251
him that was separated from his *b* ... Deut 33:16 251
let him be acceptable to his *b* ... Deut 33:24 251

ye shall pass before your *b* armed	Josh 1:14	251
the LORD have given your *b* rest	Josh 1:15	251
my father, and my mother, and my *b*	Josh 2:13	251
father, and thy mother, and thy *b*	Josh 2:18	251
father, and her mother, and her *b*	Josh 6:23	251
Nevertheless my *b* that went up	Josh 14:8	251
us an inheritance among our *b*	Josh 17:4	251
among the *b* of their father	Josh 17:4	251
Ye have not left your *b* these	Josh 22:3	251
God hath given rest unto your *b*	Josh 22:4	251
b on this side Jordan westward	Josh 22:7	251
spoil of your enemies with your *b*	Josh 22:8	251
And he said, They were my *b*	Judg 8:19	251
to Shechem unto his mother's *b*	Judg 9:1	251
his mother's *b* spake of him in	Judg 9:3	251
slew his *b* the sons of Jerubbaal,	Judg 9:5	251
aided him in the killing of his *b*	Judg 9:24	251
the son of Ebed came with his *b*	Judg 9:26	251
Ebed and his *b* be come to Shechem	Judg 9:31	251
and Zebul thrust out Gaal and his *b*	Judg 9:41	251
father, in slaying his seventy *b*	Judg 9:56	251
Then Jephthah fled from his *b*	Judg 11:3	251
among the daughters of thy *b*	Judg 14:3	251
Then his *b* and all the house of	Judg 16:31	251
they came unto their *b* to Zorah	Judg 18:8	251
their *b* said unto them, What say	Judg 18:8	251
of Laish, and said unto their *b*	Judg 18:14	251
and said unto them, Nay, my *b*	Judg 19:23	251
of their *b* the children of Israel	Judg 20:13	251
their *b* come unto us to complain	Judg 21:22	251
be not cut off from among his *b*	Ruth 4:10	251
him in the midst of his *b*	1Sa 16:13	251
Take now for thy *b* an ephah of	1Sa 17:17	251
and run to the camp to thy *b*	1Sa 17:17	251
thousand, and look how thy *b* fare	1Sa 17:18	251
army, and came and saluted his *b*	1Sa 17:22	251
away, I pray thee, and see my *b*	1Sa 20:29	251
and when his *b* and all his father's	1Sa 22:1	251
David, Ye shall not do so, my *b*	1Sa 30:23	251
return from following their *b*	2Sa 2:26	251
of Saul thy father, to his *b*	2Sa 3:8	251
return thou, and take back thy *b*	2Sa 15:20	251
Ye are my *b*, ye are my bones and	2Sa 19:12	251
Why have our *b* the men of Judah	2Sa 19:41	251
called all his *b* the king's sons,	1Kin 1:9	251
your *b* the children of Israel	1Kin 12:24	251
him arise up from among his *b*	2Kin 9:2	251
Jehu met with the *b* of Ahaziah	2Kin 10:13	251
answered, We are the *b* of Ahaziah	2Kin 10:13	251
unleavened bread among their *b*	2Kin 23:9	251
was more honourable than his *b*	1Chr 4:9	251
but his *b* had not many children,	1Chr 4:27	251
For Judah prevailed above his *b*	1Chr 5:2	251
his *b* by their families, when the	1Chr 5:7	251
their *b* of the house of their	1Chr 5:13	251
their *b* the sons of Merari stood	1Chr 6:44	251
Their *b* also the Levites were	1Chr 6:48	251
their *b* among all the families of	1Chr 7:5	251
his *b* came to comfort him	1Chr 7:22	251
dwelt with their *b* in Jerusalem	1Chr 8:32	251
Jeuel, and their *b*, six hundred and	1Chr 9:6	251
And their *b*, according to their	1Chr 9:9	251
And their *b*, heads of the house of	1Chr 9:13	251
and Talmon, and Ahiman, and their *b*	1Chr 9:17	251
the son of Korah, and his *b*	1Chr 9:19	251
And their *b*, which were in their	1Chr 9:25	251
And other of their *b*, of the sons	1Chr 9:32	251
dwelt with their *b* at Jerusalem	1Chr 9:38	251
over against their *b*	1Chr 9:38	251
bow, even of Saul's *b* of Benjamin	1Chr 12:2	251
all their *b* were at their	1Chr 12:32	251
for their *b* had prepared for them	1Chr 12:39	251
abroad unto our *b* every where	1Chr 13:2	251
his *b* an hundred and twenty	1Chr 15:5	251
his *b* two hundred and twenty	1Chr 15:6	251
his *b* an hundred and thirty	1Chr 15:7	251
the chief, and his *b* two hundred	1Chr 15:8	251
the chief, and his *b* fourscore	1Chr 15:9	251
his *b* an hundred and twelve	1Chr 15:10	251
yourselves, both ye and your *b*	1Chr 15:12	251
their *b* to be the singers with	1Chr 15:16	251
and of his *b*, Asaph the son of	1Chr 15:17	251
and of the sons of Merari their *b*	1Chr 15:17	251
with them their *b* of the second	1Chr 15:18	251
into the hand of Asaph and his *b*	1Chr 16:7	251
of the LORD Asaph and his *b*	1Chr 16:37	251
And Obed-edom with their *b*	1Chr 16:38	251
his *b* the priests, before the	1Chr 16:39	251
their *b* the sons of Kish took	1Chr 23:22	251
of the sons of Aaron their *b*	1Chr 23:32	251
their *b* the sons of Aaron in the	1Chr 24:31	251
over against their younger *b*	1Chr 24:31	251
with their *b* that were instructed	1Chr 25:7	251
to Gedaliah, who with his *b*	1Chr 25:9	251
to Zaccur, he, his sons, and his *b*	1Chr 25:10	251
to Izri, he, his sons, and his *b*	1Chr 25:11	251
Nethaniah, he, his sons, and his *b*	1Chr 25:12	251
Bukkiah, he, his sons, and his *b*	1Chr 25:13	251
he, his sons, and his *b*, were	1Chr 25:14	251
Jeshaiah, he, his sons, and his *b*	1Chr 25:15	251
Mattaniah, he, his sons, and his *b*	1Chr 25:16	251
to Shimei, he, his sons, and his *b*	1Chr 25:17	251
Azareel, he, his sons, and his *b*	1Chr 25:18	251
Hashabiah, he, his sons, and his *b*	1Chr 25:19	251
Shubael, he, his sons, and his *b*	1Chr 25:20	251
he, his sons, and his *b*, were	1Chr 25:21	251
Jeremoth, he, his sons, and his *b*	1Chr 25:22	251
Hananiah, he, his sons, and his *b*	1Chr 25:23	251
he, his sons, and his *b*, were	1Chr 25:24	251
to Hanani, he, his sons, and his *b*	1Chr 25:25	251
Mallothi, he, his sons, and his *b*	1Chr 25:26	251
Eliathah, he, his sons, and his *b*	1Chr 25:27	251
to Hothir, he, his sons, and his *b*	1Chr 25:28	251
Giddalti, he, his sons, and his *b*	1Chr 25:29	251
Mahazioth, he, his sons, and his *b*	1Chr 25:30	251
he, his sons, and his *b*, were	1Chr 25:31	251
whose *b* were strong men, Elihu,	1Chr 26:7	251
they and their sons and their *b*	1Chr 26:8	251
And Meshelemiah had sons and *b*	1Chr 26:9	251
sons and *b* of Hosah were thirteen	1Chr 26:11	251
And his *b* by Eliezer	1Chr 26:25	251
his *b* were over all the treasures	1Chr 26:26	251
hand of Shelomith, and of his *b*	1Chr 26:28	251
Hebronites, Hashabiah and his *b*	1Chr 26:30	251
And his *b*, men of valour, were two	1Chr 26:32	251
Elihu, one of the *b* of David	1Chr 27:18	251
his feet, and said, Hear me, my *b*	1Chr 28:2	251
with their sons and their *b*	2Chr 5:12	251
go up, nor fight against your *b*	2Chr 11:4	251
chief, to be ruler among his *b*	2Chr 11:22	251
shall come to you of your *b* that	2Chr 19:10	251
come upon you, and upon your *b*	2Chr 19:10	251
he had his *b* the sons of Jehoshaphat,	2Chr 21:2	251
slew all his *b* with the sword, and	2Chr 21:4	251
also hast slain thy *b* of thy	2Chr 21:13	251
and the sons of the *b* of Ahaziah	2Chr 22:8	251
of their *b* two hundred thousand	2Chr 28:8	251
ye have taken captive of your *b*	2Chr 28:11	251
city of palm trees, to their *b*	2Chr 28:15	251
And they gathered their *b*, and	2Chr 29:15	251
wherefore their *b* the Levites did	2Chr 29:34	251
like your fathers, and like your *b*	2Chr 30:7	251
turn again unto the LORD, your *b*	2Chr 30:9	251
to give to their *b* by courses	2Chr 31:15	251
the fathers of your *b* the people	2Chr 35:5	251
yourselves, and prepare your *b*	2Chr 35:6	251
and Shemaiah and Nethaneel, his *b*	2Chr 35:9	251
for their *b* the Levites prepared	2Chr 35:15	251
his *b* the priests, and Zerubbabel	Ezr 3:2	251
the son of Shealtiel, and his *b*	Ezr 3:2	251
remnant of their *b* the priests	Ezr 3:8	251
Jeshua with his sons and his *b*	Ezr 3:9	251
their sons and their *b* the Levites	Ezr 3:9	251
for their *b* the priests, and for	Ezr 6:20	251
seem good to thee, and to thy *b*	Ezr 7:18	252
to his *b* the Nethinims, at the	Ezr 8:17	251
Sherebiah, with his sons and his *b*	Ezr 8:18	251
of the sons of Merari, his *b*	Ezr 8:19	251
and ten of their *b* with them	Ezr 8:24	251
the son of Jozadak, and his *b*	Ezr 10:18	251
That Hanani, one of my *b*, came,	Neh 1:2	251
rose up with his *b* the priests	Neh 3:1	251
After him repaired their *b*	Neh 3:18	251
And he spake before his *b* and the	Neh 4:2	251
and terrible, and fight for your *b*	Neh 4:14	251
So neither I, nor my *b*, nor my	Neh 4:23	251
wives against their *b* the Jews	Neh 5:1	251
flesh is as the flesh of our *b*	Neh 5:5	251
have redeemed our *b* the Jews	Neh 5:8	251
and will ye even sell your *b*	Neh 5:8	251
I likewise, and my *b*, and my	Neh 5:10	251
my *b* have not eaten the bread of	Neh 5:14	251
And their *b*, Shebaniah, Hodijah,	Neh 10:10	251
They clave to their *b*, their	Neh 10:29	251
their *b* that did the work of the	Neh 11:12	251
And his *b*, chief of the fathers,	Neh 11:13	251
And their *b*, mighty men of valour,	Neh 11:14	251
Bakbukiah the second among his *b*	Neh 11:17	251
their *b* that kept the gates, were	Neh 11:19	251
of their *b* in the days of Jeshua	Neh 12:7	251
the thanksgiving, he and his *b*	Neh 12:8	251
Also Bakbukiah and Unni, their *b*	Neh 12:9	251
with their *b* over against them,	Neh 12:24	251
And his *b*, Shemaiah, and Azarael,	Neh 12:36	251
was to distribute unto their *b*	Neh 13:13	251
of the multitude of his *b*	Est 10:3	251
My *b* have dealt deceitfully as a	Job 6:15	251
He hath put my *b* far from me	Job 19:13	251
came there unto him all his *b*	Job 42:11	251
them inheritance among their *b*	Job 42:15	251
I will declare thy name unto my *b*	Ps 22:22	251
I am become a stranger unto my *b*	Ps 69:8	251
For my *b* and companions' sakes, I	Ps 122:8	251
how pleasant it is for *b* to dwell	Ps 133:1	251
and he that soweth discord among *b*	Prov 6:19	251
of the inheritance among the *b*	Prov 17:2	251
All the *b* of the poor do hate him	Prov 19:7	251
Your *b* that hated you, that cast	Is 66:5	251
they shall bring all your *b* for	Is 66:20	251
as I have cast out all your *b*	Jer 7:15	251
For even thy *b*, and the house of	Jer 12:6	251
of your *b* that are not gone forth	Jer 29:16	251
the son of Habaziniah, and his *b*	Jer 35:3	251
and slew them not among their *b*	Jer 41:8	251
his seed is spoiled, and his *b*	Jer 49:10	251
of man, thy *b*, even thy *b*	Eze 11:15	251
Say ye unto your *b*, Ammi	Hos 2:1	251
Though he be fruitful among his *b*	Hos 13:15	251
then the remnant of his *b* shall	Mic 5:3	251
and Jacob begat Judas and his *b*	Mt 1:2	80
Josias begat Jechonias and his *b*	Mt 1:11	80
by the sea of Galilee, saw two *b*	Mt 4:18	80
from thence, he saw other two *b*	Mt 4:21	80
And if ye salute your *b* only	Mt 5:47	80
his *b* stood without, desiring to	Mt 12:46	80
thy *b* stand without, desiring to	Mt 12:47	80
and who are my *b*	Mt 12:48	80
and said, Behold my mother and my *b*	Mt 12:49	80
and his *b*, James, and Joses, and	Mt 13:55	80
that hath forsaken houses, or *b*	Mt 19:29	80
indignation against the two *b*	Mt 20:24	80
Now there were with us seven *b*	Mt 22:25	80
and all ye are *b*	Mt 23:8	80
one of the least of these my *b*	Mt 25:40	80
go tell my *b* that they go into	Mt 28:10	80
There came then his *b* and his	Mk 3:31	80
thy *b* without seek for thee	Mk 3:32	80
saying, Who is my mother, or my *b*	Mk 3:33	80
and said, Behold my mother and my *b*	Mk 3:34	80
no man that hath left house, or *b*	Mk 10:29	80
now in this time, houses, and *b*	Mk 10:30	80
Now there were seven *b*	Mk 12:20	80
came to him his mother and his *b*	Lk 8:19	80
thy *b* stand without, desiring to	Lk 8:20	80
my *b* are these which hear the	Lk 8:21	80
call not thy friends, nor thy *b*	Lk 14:12	80
and wife, and children, and *b*	Lk 14:26	80
For I have five *b*	Lk 16:28	80
hath left house, or parents, or *b*	Lk 18:29	80
There were therefore seven *b*	Lk 20:29	80
be betrayed both by parents, and *b*	Lk 21:16	80
art converted, strengthen thy *b*	Lk 22:32	80
he, and his mother, and his *b*	Jn 2:12	80
His *b* therefore said unto him,	Jn 7:3	80
neither did his *b* believe in him	Jn 7:5	80
But when his *b* were gone up	Jn 7:10	80
but go to my *b*, and say unto them,	Jn 20:17	80
this saying abroad among the *b*	Jn 21:23	80
mother of Jesus, and with his *b*	Acts 1:14	80
Men and *b*, this scripture must	Acts 1:16	80
Men and *b*, let me freely speak	Acts 2:29	80
rest of the apostles, Men and *b*	Acts 2:37	80
And now, *b*, I wot that through	Acts 3:17	80
God raise up unto you of your *b*	Acts 3:22	80
Wherefore, *b*, look ye out among	Acts 6:3	80
And he said, Men, *b*, and fathers,	Acts 7:2	80
Joseph was made known to his *b*	Acts 7:13	80
his *b* the children of Israel	Acts 7:23	80
For he supposed his *b* would have	Acts 7:25	80
one again, saying, Sirs, ye are *b*	Acts 7:26	80
God raise up unto you of your *b*	Acts 7:37	80
Which when the *b* knew, they	Acts 9:30	80
certain *b* from Joppa accompanied	Acts 10:23	80
b that were in Judaea heard that	Acts 11:1	80
these six *b* accompanied me	Acts 11:12	80
unto the *b* which dwelt in Judaea	Acts 11:29	80
things unto James, and to the *b*	Acts 12:17	80
unto them, saying, Ye men and *b*	Acts 13:15	80
Men and *b*, children of the stock	Acts 13:26	80
unto you therefore, men and *b*	Acts 13:38	80
minds evil affected against the *b*	Acts 14:2	80
down from Judaea taught the *b*	Acts 15:1	80
caused great joy unto all the *b*	Acts 15:3	80
up, and said unto them, Men and *b*	Acts 15:7	80
James answered, saying, Men and *b*	Acts 15:13	80
and Silas, chief men among the *b*	Acts 15:22	80
b send greeting unto the *b*	Acts 15:23	80
exhorted the *b* with many words,	Acts 15:32	80
from the *b* unto the apostles	Acts 15:33	80
visit our *b* in every city where	Acts 15:36	80
by the *b* unto the grace of God	Acts 15:40	80
of by the *b* that were at Lystra	Acts 16:2	80
and when they had seen the *b*	Acts 16:40	80
certain *b* unto the rulers of the	Acts 17:6	80
the *b* immediately sent away Paul	Acts 17:10	80
then immediately the *b* sent away	Acts 17:14	80
and then took his leave of the *b*	Acts 18:18	80
the *b* wrote, exhorting the	Acts 18:27	80
And now, *b*, I commend you to God,	Acts 20:32	80
to Ptolemais, and saluted the *b*	Acts 21:7	80
the *b* received us gladly	Acts 21:17	80
Men, *b*, and fathers, hear ye my	Acts 22:1	80
I received letters unto the *b*	Acts 22:5	80
the council, said, Men and *b*	Acts 23:1	80
Then said Paul, I wist not, *b*	Acts 23:5	80
out in the council, Men and *b*	Acts 23:6	80
Where we found *b*, and were desired	Acts 28:14	80
when the *b* heard of us, they came	Acts 28:15	80
he said unto them, Men and *b*	Acts 28:17	80
neither any of the *b* that came	Acts 28:21	80
I would not have you ignorant, *b*	Rom 1:13	80
Know ye not, *b*, (for I speak to	Rom 7:1	80
Wherefore, my *b*, ye also are	Rom 7:4	80
Therefore, *b*, we are debtors, not	Rom 8:12	80
be the firstborn among many *b*	Rom 8:29	80
accursed from Christ for my *b*	Rom 9:3	80
B, my heart's desire and prayer to	Rom 10:1	80
For I would not, *b*, that ye	Rom 11:25	80
I beseech you therefore, *b*	Rom 12:1	80
also am persuaded of you, my *b*	Rom 15:14	80
Nevertheless, *b*, I have written	Rom 15:15	80
Now I beseech you, *b*, for the	Rom 15:30	80
the *b* which are with them	Rom 16:14	80
Now I beseech you, *b*, mark them	Rom 16:17	80
Now I beseech you, *b*, by the name	1Cor 1:10	80
declared unto me of you, my *b*	1Cor 1:11	80
For ye see your calling, *b*	1Cor 1:26	80
And I, *b*, when I came to you, came	1Cor 2:1	80
And I, *b*, could not speak unto you	1Cor 3:1	80
And these things, *b*, I have in a	1Cor 4:6	80
be able to judge between his *b*	1Cor 6:5	80
wrong, and defraud, and that your *b*	1Cor 6:8	80
B, let every man, wherein he is	1Cor 7:24	80
But this I say, *b*, the time is	1Cor 7:29	80
But when ye sin so against the *b*	1Cor 8:12	80
as the *b* of the Lord, and Cephas	1Cor 9:5	80
Moreover, *b*, I would not that ye	1Cor 10:1	80
Now I praise you, *b*, that ye	1Cor 11:2	80
Wherefore, my *b*, when ye come	1Cor 11:33	80
Now concerning spiritual gifts, *b*	1Cor 12:1	80
Now, *b*, if I come unto you	1Cor 14:6	80
B, be not children in	1Cor 14:20	80
How is it then, *b*	1Cor 14:26	80
Wherefore, *b*, covet to prophesy,	1Cor 14:39	80
Moreover, *b*, I declare unto you	1Cor 15:1	80
of above five hundred *b* at once	1Cor 15:6	80
Now this I say, *b*, that flesh and	1Cor 15:50	80
Therefore, my beloved *b*, be ye	1Cor 15:58	80
for I look for him with the *b*	1Cor 16:11	80
him to come unto you with the *b*	1Cor 16:12	80
I beseech you, *b*, (ye know the	1Cor 16:15	80
All the *b* greet you	1Cor 16:20	80

For we would not, *b*, have you	2Cor 1:8	80
Moreover, *b*, we do you to wit of	2Cor 8:1	80
or our *b* be enquired of, they are	2Cor 8:23	80
Yet have I sent the *b*, lest our	2Cor 9:3	80
it necessary to exhort the *b*	2Cor 9:5	80
the *b* which came from Macedonia	2Cor 11:9	80
the sea, in perils among false *b*	2Cor 11:26	5569
Finally, *b*, farewell	2Cor 13:11	80
all the *b* which are with me, unto	Gal 1:2	80
But I certify you, *b*, that the	Gal 1:11	80
of false *b* unawares brought in	Gal 2:4	5569
B, I speak after the manner of	Gal 3:15	80
B, I beseech you, be as I am	Gal 4:12	80
Now we, *b*, as Isaac was, are the	Gal 4:28	80
So then, *b*, we are not children	Gal 4:31	80
And I, *b*, if I yet preach	Gal 5:11	80
For, *b*, ye have been called unto	Gal 5:13	80
B, if a man be overtaken in a	Gal 6:1	80
B, the grace of our Lord Jesus	Gal 6:18	80
Finally, my *b*, be strong in the	Eph 6:10	80
Peace be to the *b*, and love with	Eph 6:23	80
I would ye should understand, *b*	Phil 1:12	80
And many of the *b* in the Lord	Phil 1:14	80
Finally, my *b*, rejoice in the	Phil 3:1	80
B, I count not myself to have	Phil 3:13	80
B, be followers together of me,	Phil 3:17	80
my *b* dearly beloved and longed for	Phil 4:1	80
Finally, *b*, whatsoever things are	Phil 4:8	80
The *b* which are with me greet you	Phil 4:21	80
faithful *b* in Christ which are at	Col 1:2	80
Salute the *b* which are in	Col 4:15	80
b beloved, your election of God	1Th 1:4	80
For yourselves, *b*, know our	1Th 2:1	80
For ye remember, *b*, our labour and	1Th 2:9	80
For ye, *b*, became followers of	1Th 2:14	80
But we, *b*, being taken from you	1Th 2:17	80
Therefore, *b*, we were comforted	1Th 3:7	80
then we beseech you, *b*, and exhort	1Th 4:1	80
the *b* which are in all Macedonia	1Th 4:10	80
but we beseech you, *b*, that ye	1Th 4:10	80
not have you to be ignorant, *b*	1Th 4:13	80
of the times and the seasons, *b*	1Th 5:1	80
But ye, *b*, are not in darkness,	1Th 5:4	80
And we beseech you, *b*, to know	1Th 5:12	80
Now we exhort you, *b*, warn them	1Th 5:14	80
B, pray for us	1Th 5:25	80
Greet all the *b* with an holy kiss	1Th 5:26	80
be read unto all the holy *b*	1Th 5:27	80
to thank God always for you, *b*	2Th 1:3	80
Now we beseech you, *b*, by the	2Th 2:1	80
b beloved of the Lord, because	2Th 2:13	80
Therefore, *b*, stand fast, and hold	2Th 2:15	80
Finally, *b*, pray for us, that the	2Th 3:1	80
Now we command you, *b*, in the	2Th 3:6	80
But ye, *b*, be not weary in well	2Th 3:13	80
If thou put the *b* in remembrance	1Ti 4:6	80
and the younger men as *b*	1Ti 5:1	80
despise them, because they are *b*	1Ti 6:2	80
Linus, and Claudia, and all the *b*	2Ti 4:21	80
he is not ashamed to call them *b*	Heb 2:11	80
I will declare thy name unto my *b*	Heb 2:12	80
him to be made like unto his *b*	Heb 2:17	80
Wherefore, holy *b*, partakers of	Heb 3:1	80
Take heed, *b*, lest there be in	Heb 3:12	80
to the law, that is, of their *b*	Heb 7:5	80
Having therefore, *b*, boldness to	Heb 10:19	80
And I beseech you, *b*, suffer the	Heb 13:22	80
My *b*, count it all joy when ye	Jas 1:2	80
Do not err, my beloved *b*	Jas 1:16	80
Wherefore, my beloved *b*, let	Jas 1:19	80
My *b*, have not the faith of our	Jas 2:1	80
Hearken, my beloved *b*, Hath not	Jas 2:5	80
What doth it profit, my *b*	Jas 2:14	80
My *b*, be not many masters,	Jas 3:1	80
My *b*, these things ought not so	Jas 3:10	80
Can the fig tree, my *b*, bear	Jas 3:12	80
Speak not evil one of another, *b*	Jas 4:11	80
Be patient therefore, *b*, unto the	Jas 5:7	80
Grudge not one against another, *b*	Jas 5:9	80
Take, my *b*, the prophets, who	Jas 5:10	80
But above all things, my *b*	Jas 5:12	80
B, if any of you do err from the	Jas 5:19	80
unto unfeigned love of the *b*	1Pet 1:22	5360
one of another, love as *b*	1Pet 3:8	5361
in your *b* that are in the world	1Pet 5:9	81
Wherefore the rather, *b*, give	2Pet 1:10	80
B, I write no new commandment	1Jn 2:7	80
Marvel not, my *b*, if the world	1Jn 3:13	80
unto life, because we love the *b*	1Jn 3:14	80
to lay down our lives for the *b*	1Jn 3:16	80
rejoiced greatly, when the *b* came	3Jn 3	80
whatsoever thou doest to the *b*	3Jn 5	80
doth he himself receive the *b*	3Jn 10	80
fellowservants also and their *b*	Rev 6:11	80
the accuser of our *b* is cast down	Rev 12:10	80
of thy *b* that have the testimony	Rev 19:10	80
of thy *b* the prophets, and of them	Rev 22:9	80

BRETHREN'S

lest his *b* heart faint as well as	Deut 20:8	251

BRIBE

b to blind mine eyes therewith	1Sa 12:3	3724
afflict the just, they take a *b*	Amos 5:12	3724

BRIBERY

consume the tabernacles of *b*	Job 15:34	7810

BRIBES

aside after lucre, and took *b*	1Sa 8:3	7810
and their right hand is full of *b*	Ps 26:10	7810
his hands from holding of *b*	Is 33:15	7810

BRICK

to another, Go to, let us make *b*	Gen 11:3	3835
they had *b* for stone, and slime	Gen 11:3	3843
hard bondage, in morter, and in *b*	Ex 1:14	3843
give the people straw to make *b*	Ex 5:7	3835
task in making *b* both yesterday	Ex 5:14	3835
and they say to us, Make *b*	Ex 5:16	3843
burneth incense upon altars of *b*	Is 65:3	3843

BRICKKILN

and made them pass through the *b*	2Sa 12:31	4404
and hide them in the clay in the *b*	Jer 43:9	4404
the morter, make strong the *b*	Nah 3:14	4404

BRICKS

And the tale of the *b*, which they	Ex 5:8	3843
shall ye deliver the tale of *b*	Ex 5:18	3843
from your *b* of your daily task	Ex 5:19	3843
The *b* are fallen down, but we	Is 9:10	3843

BRIDE

bind them on thee, as a *b* doeth	Is 49:18	3618
as a *b* adorneth herself with her	Is 61:10	3618
bridegroom rejoiceth over the *b*	Is 62:5	3618
her ornaments, or a *b* her attire	Jer 2:32	3618
bridegroom, and the voice of the *b*	Jer 7:34	3618
bridegroom, and the voice of the *b*	Jer 16:9	3618
bridegroom, and the voice of the *b*	Jer 25:10	3618
bridegroom, and the voice of the *b*	Jer 33:11	3618
and the *b* out of her closet	Joel 2:16	3618
He that hath the *b* is the	Jn 3:29	3565
of the *b* shall be heard no more	Rev 18:23	3565
prepared as a *b* adorned for her	Rev 21:2	3565
hither, I will shew thee the *b*	Rev 21:9	3565
And the Spirit and the *b* say	Rev 22:17	3565

BRIDECHAMBER

Can the children of the *b* mourn	Mt 9:15	3567
Can the children of the *b* fast	Mk 2:19	3567
make the children of the *b* fast	Lk 5:34	3567

BRIDEGROOM

Which is as a *b* coming out of his	Ps 19:5	2860
as a *b* decketh himself with	Is 61:10	2860
as the *b* rejoiceth over the bride	Is 62:5	2860
of gladness, the voice of the *b*	Jer 7:34	2860
of gladness, the voice of the *b*	Jer 16:9	2860
of gladness, the voice of the *b*	Jer 25:10	2860
of gladness, the voice of the *b*	Jer 33:11	2860
let the *b* go forth of his chamber	Joel 2:16	2860
as long as the *b* is with them	Mt 9:15	3566
when the *b* shall be taken from	Mt 9:15	3566
and went forth to meet the *b*	Mt 25:1	3566
While the *b* tarried, they all	Mt 25:5	3566
a cry made, Behold, the *b* cometh	Mt 25:6	3566
they went to buy, the *b* came	Mt 25:10	3566
fast, while the *b* is with them	Mk 2:19	3566
long as they have the *b* with them	Mk 2:19	3566
when the *b* shall be taken away	Mk 2:20	3566
fast, while the *b* is with them	Lk 5:34	3566
when the *b* shall be taken away	Lk 5:35	3566
of the feast called the *b*	Jn 2:9	3566
He that hath the bride is the *b*	Jn 3:29	3566
but the friend of the *b*, which	Jn 3:29	3566
and the voice of the *b* and of the	Rev 18:23	3566

BRIDEGROOM'S

greatly because of the *b* voice	Jn 3:29	3566

BRIDLE

my *b* in thy lips, and I will turn	2Kin 19:28	4964
also let loose the *b* before me	Job 30:11	7448
can come to him with his double *b*	Job 41:13	7448
must be held in with bit and *b*	Ps 32:9	7448
I will keep my mouth with a *b*	Ps 39:1	4269
a *b* for the ass, and a rod for the	Prov 26:3	4964
there shall be a *b* in the jaws of	Is 30:28	7448
my *b* in thy lips, and I will turn	Is 37:29	4964
able also to *b* the whole body	Jas 3:2	5469

BRIDLES

winepress, even unto the horse *b*	Rev 14:20	5469

BRIDLETH

b not his tongue, but deceiveth	Jas 1:26	5468

BRIEFLY

it is *b* comprehended in this	Rom 13:9	346
as I suppose, I have written *b*	1Pet 5:12	

BRIER

instead of the *b* shall come up	Is 55:13	5636
b unto the house of Israel	Eze 28:24	5544
The best of them is as a *b*	Mic 7:4	2312

BRIERS

of the wilderness and with *b*	Judg 8:7	1303
and thorns of the wilderness and *b*	Judg 8:16	1303
but there shall come up *b*	Is 5:6	8068
it shall even be for *b* and thorns	Is 7:23	8068
all the land shall become *b*	Is 7:24	8068
not come thither the fear of *b*	Is 7:25	8068
it shall devour the *b* and thorns,	Is 9:18	8068
his thorns and his *b* in one day	Is 10:17	8068
who would set the *b* and thorns	Is 27:4	8068
people shall come up thorns and *b*	Is 32:13	8068
afraid of their words, though *b*	Eze 2:6	5621
b is rejected, and is nigh unto	Heb 6:8	5146

BRIGANDINE

that lifteth himself up in his *b*	Jer 51:3	5630

BRIGANDINES

the spears, and put on the *b*	Jer 46:4	5630

BRIGHT

or *b* spot, and it be in the skin	Lev 13:2	934
If the *b* spot be white in the	Lev 13:4	934
be a white rising, or a *b* spot	Lev 13:19	934
But if the *b* spot stay in his	Lev 13:23	934
that burneth have a white *b* spot	Lev 13:24	934
if the hair in the *b* spot be	Lev 13:25	934
be no white hair in the *b* spot	Lev 13:26	934
if the *b* spot stay in his place,	Lev 13:28	934
b spots, even white *b* spots	Lev 13:38	934
if the *b* spots in the skin of	Lev 13:39	934
and for a scab, and for a *b* spot	Lev 14:56	934
of the LORD, were of *b* brass	1Kin 7:45	4803
the house of the LORD of *b* brass	2Chr 4:16	4838
he scattereth his *b* cloud	Job 37:11	216
now men see not the *b* light which	Job 37:21	925
his belly is as *b* ivory overlaid	Song 5:14	6247
Make *b* the arrows	Jer 51:11	1305
and the fire was *b*, and out of the	Eze 1:13	5051
it is made *b*, it is wrapped up	Eze 21:15	1300
he made his arrows *b*, he	Eze 21:21	7043
b iron, cassia, and calamus, were	Eze 27:19	6219
All the *b* lights of heaven will I	Eze 32:8	3974
lifteth up both the *b* sword	Nah 3:3	3851
so the LORD shall make *b* clouds	Zec 10:1	2385
a *b* cloud overshadowed them	Mt 17:5	5460
as when the *b* shining of a candle	Lk 11:36	796
man stood before me in *b* clothing	Acts 10:30	2986
the offspring of David, and the *b*	Rev 22:16	2986

BRIGHTNESS

Through the *b* before him were	2Sa 22:13	5051
shined, or the moon walking in *b*	Job 31:26	3368
At the *b* that was before him his	Ps 18:12	5051
for *b*, but we walk in darkness	Is 59:9	5054
kings to the *b* of thy rising	Is 60:3	5051
neither for *b* shall the moon give	Is 60:19	5051
thereof go forth as *b*, and the	Is 62:1	5051
a *b* was about it, and out of the	Eze 1:4	5051
of fire, and it had *b* round about	Eze 1:27	5051
appearance of the *b* round about	Eze 1:28	5051
upward, as the appearance of *b*	Eze 8:2	2096
full of the *b* of the LORD's glory	Eze 10:4	5051
and they shall defile thy *b*	Eze 28:7	3314
thy wisdom by reason of thy *b*	Eze 28:17	3314
whose *b* was excellent, stood	Dan 2:31	2122
mine honour and *b* returned unto me	Dan 4:36	2122
shine as the *b* of the firmament	Dan 12:3	2096
even very dark, and no *b* in it	Amos 5:20	5051
And his *b* was as the light	Hab 3:4	5051
above the *b* of the sun, shining	Acts 26:13	2987
destroy with the *b* of his coming	2Th 2:8	2015
Who being the *b* of his glory	Heb 1:3	541

BRIM

were dipped in the *b* of the water	Josh 3:15	7097
from the one *b* to the other	1Kin 7:23	8193
under the *b* of it round about	1Kin 7:24	8193
the *b* thereof was wrought like	1Kin 7:26	8193
was wrought like the *b* of a cup	1Kin 7:26	8193
sea of ten cubits from *b* to *b*	2Chr 4:2	8193
the *b* of it like the work of the	2Chr 4:5	8193
like the work of the *b* of a cup	2Chr 4:5	8193
And they filled them up to the *b*	Jn 2:7	507

BRIMSTONE

upon Sodom and upon Gomorrah *b*	Gen 19:24	1614
that the whole land thereof is *b*	Deut 29:23	1614
b shall be scattered upon his	Job 18:15	1614
he shall rain snares, fire and *b*	Ps 11:6	1614
of the LORD, like a stream of *b*	Is 30:33	1614
pitch, and the dust thereof into *b*	Is 34:9	1614
and great hailstones, fire, and *b*	Eze 38:22	1614
b from heaven, and destroyed them	Lk 17:29	2303
of fire, and of jacinth, and *b*	Rev 9:17	2306
mouths issued fire and smoke and *b*	Rev 9:17	2303
and by the smoke, and by the *b*	Rev 9:18	2303
b in the presence of the holy	Rev 14:10	2303
a lake of fire burning with *b*	Rev 19:20	2303
cast into the lake of fire and *b*	Rev 20:10	2303
lake which burneth with fire and *b*	Rev 21:8	2303

BRING

said, Let the earth *b* forth grass	Gen 1:11	1876
Let the waters *b* forth abundantly	Gen 1:20	8317
Let the earth *b* forth the living	Gen 1:24	3318
thou shalt *b* forth children	Gen 3:16	3205
thistles shall it *b* forth to thee	Gen 3:18	6779
do *b* a flood of waters upon the	Gen 6:17	935
sort shalt thou *b* into the ark	Gen 6:19	935
B forth with thee every living	Gen 8:17	3318
b forth abundantly in the earth	Gen 9:7	8317
when I *b* a cloud over the earth,	Gen 9:14	6049
with them to *b* them on the way	Gen 18:16	7971
that the LORD may *b* upon Abraham	Gen 18:19	935
b them out unto us, that we may	Gen 19:5	3318
b them out unto you, and do ye to	Gen 19:8	3318
city, *b* them out of this place	Gen 19:12	3318
must I needs *b* thy son again unto	Gen 24:5	7725
Beware thou that thou *b* not my	Gen 24:6	7725
only *b* not my son thither again	Gen 24:8	7725
b it to me, that I may eat	Gen 27:4	935
to hunt for venison, and to *b* it	Gen 27:5	935
B me venison, and make me savoury	Gen 27:7	935
thou shalt *b* it to thy father,	Gen 27:10	935
I shall *b* a curse upon me, and not	Gen 27:12	935
B it near to me, and I will eat of	Gen 27:25	5066
will *b* thee again into this land	Gen 28:15	7725
and *b* me word again	Gen 37:14	7725
B her forth, and let her be burnt	Gen 38:24	3318
and *b* me out of this house	Gen 40:14	3318
and God will shortly *b* it to pass	Gen 41:32	6213
But *b* your youngest brother unto	Gen 42:20	935
b your youngest brother unto me	Gen 42:34	935
two sons, if I *b* him not to thee	Gen 42:37	935
I will *b* him to thee again	Gen 42:37	7725
then shall ye *b* down my gray	Gen 42:38	3381
he would say, *B* your brother down	Gen 43:7	3381
if I *b* him not unto thee, and set	Gen 43:9	935
B these men home, and slay, and	Gen 43:16	935
B him down unto me, that I may	Gen 44:21	3381
ye shall *b* down my gray hairs	Gen 44:29	3381
thy servants shall *b* down the	Gen 44:31	3381
If I *b* him not unto thee, then I	Gen 44:32	935
haste and *b* down my father hither	Gen 45:13	3381

wives, and *b* your father, and come...... Gen 45:19 5375
will also surely *b* thee up again .... Gen 46:4 5927
B them, I pray thee, unto me, and........ Gen 48:9 3947
b you again unto the land of your........ Gen 48:21 7725
to *b* to pass, as it is this day,................ Gen 50:20 6213
b you out of this land unto the........... Gen 50:24 5927
to *b* them up out of that land .... Ex 3:8 5927
that thou mayest *b* forth my................. Ex 3:10 3318
that I should *b* forth the....................... Ex 3:11 3318
I will *b* you up out of the...................... Ex 3:17 5927
I will *b* you out from under the........... Ex 6:6 3318
I will *b* you in unto the land, ... Ex 6:8 935
to *b* the children of Israel out.............. Ex 6:13 935
B out the children of Israel from.......... Ex 6:26 3318
to *b* out the children of Israel............... Ex 6:27 3318
b forth mine armies, and my people..... Ex 7:4 3318
b out the children of Israel from........... Ex 7:5 3318
the river shall *b* forth frogs.................. Ex 8:3 8317
enchantments to *b* forth lice .... Ex 8:18 3318
to morrow will I *b* the locusts................ Ex 10:4 935
Yet will I *b* one plague more upon .... Ex 11:1 935
that the LORD did *b* the children .... Ex 12:51 3318
shall *b* thee into the land of the............ Ex 13:5 935
shall *b* thee into the land of the .... Ex 13:11 935
Thou shalt *b* them in, and plant .... Ex 15:17 935
prepare that which they *b* in.................. Ex 16:5 935
that thou mayest *b* the causes .... Ex 18:19 935
matter they shall *b* unto thee................ Ex 18:22 935
shall *b* him unto the judges .... Ex 21:6 5066
he shall also *b* him to the door, ... Ex 21:6 5066
then let him *b* it for witness, and......... Ex 22:13 935
thou shalt surely *b* it back to................ Ex 23:4 7725
of thy land thou shalt *b* into the .... Ex 23:19 935
to *b* thee into the place which I .... Ex 23:20 935
b thee in unto the Amorites, and .... Ex 23:23 935
that they *b* me an offering .... Ex 25:2 3947
that thou mayest *b* in thither................. Ex 26:33 935
that they *b* thee pure oil olive............... Ex 27:20 3947
b them in the basket, with the............... Ex 29:3 7126
his sons thou shalt *b* unto the............... Ex 29:4 7126
And thou shalt *b* his sons, and put .... Ex 29:8 7126
your daughters, and *b* them unto me... Ex 32:2 935
For mischief did he *b* them out.............. Ex 32:12 3318
sayest unto me, *B* up this people........... Ex 33:12 5927
of thy land thou shalt *b* unto the........... Ex 34:26 935
of a willing heart, let him *b* it .... Ex 35:5 935
to *b* for all manner of work .... Ex 35:29
The people *b* much more than .... Ex 36:5 935
thou shalt *b* in the table, and set.......... Ex 40:4 935
thou shalt *b* in the candlestick,.............. Ex 40:4 935
And thou shalt *b* Aaron and his sons... Ex 40:12 7126
And thou shalt *b* his sons, and.............. Ex 40:14 7126
If any man of you *b* an offering .... Lev 1:2 7126
ye shall *b* your offering of the.............. Lev 1:2 7126
shall *b* the blood, and sprinkle .... Lev 1:5 7126
he shall *b* it a male without.................. Lev 1:10 7126
and the priest shall *b* it all .... Lev 1:13 7126
then he shall *b* his offering of .... Lev 1:14 7126
the priest shall *b* it unto the................. Lev 1:15 7126
he shall *b* it to Aaron's sons the........... Lev 2:2 935
if thou *b* an oblation of a meat............... Lev 2:4 7126
thou shalt *b* the meat offering .... Lev 2:8 935
he shall *b* it unto the altar .... Lev 2:8 5066
which ye shall *b* unto the LORD.............. Lev 2:11 7126
then let him *b* for his sin .... Lev 4:3 7126
he shall *b* the bullock unto the............... Lev 4:4 935
b it to the tabernacle of the.................... Lev 4:5 935
b him before the tabernacle of............... Lev 4:14 935
b of the bullock's blood to the................ Lev 4:16 935
he shall *b* his offering, a kid of.............. Lev 4:23 935
then he shall *b* his offering .... Lev 4:28 935
if he *b* a lamb for a sin offering .... Lev 4:32 935
he shall *b* it a female without................ Lev 4:32 935
he shall *b* his trespass offering .... Lev 5:6 935
And if he be not able to *b* a lamb.......... Lev 5:7 5060
then he shall *b* for his trespass, ... Lev 5:7 935
he shall *b* them unto the priest,............. Lev 5:8 935
be not able to *b* two turtledoves.......... Lev 5:11 5381
then he that sinned shall *b* for.............. Lev 5:11 935
Then shall he *b* it to the priest,............. Lev 5:12 935
Then he shall *b* for his trespass .... Lev 5:15 935
he shall *b* a ram without blemish .... Lev 5:18 935
he shall *b* his trespass offering .... Lev 6:6 935
it is baken, thou shalt *b* it in .... Lev 6:21 935
b his oblation unto the LORD of .... Lev 7:29 935
His own hands shall *b* the..................... Lev 7:30 935
with the breast, it shall he *b*................. Lev 7:30 935
the wave breast shall they *b* with .... Lev 10:15 935
she shall *b* a lamb of the first................ Lev 12:6 935
And if she be not able to *b* a lamb....... Lev 12:8 4672
then she shall *b* two turtles .... Lev 12:8 3947
he shall *b* them on the eighth day .... Lev 14:23 935
b them unto the priest, to the............... Lev 15:29 935
Aaron shall *b* the goat upon which........ Lev 16:9 7126
Aaron shall *b* the bullock of the............ Lev 16:11 7126
small, and *b* it within the vail............... Lev 16:12 935
b his blood within the vail, and .... Lev 16:15 935
altar, he shall *b* the live goat................ Lev 16:20 7126
of Israel may *b* their sacrifices............. Lev 17:5 935
they may *b* them unto the LORD .... Lev 17:5 935
land of Canaan, whither I *b* you .... Lev 18:3 935
he shall *b* his trespass offering.............. Lev 19:21 935
whither I *b* you to dwell therein, ... Lev 20:22 935
then ye shall *b* a sheaf of the................. Lev 23:10 935
Ye shall *b* out of your .... Lev 23:17 935
that they *b* unto thee pure oil................ Lev 24:2 3947
B forth him that hath cursed.................. Lev 24:14 3318
that they should *b* forth him that .... Lev 24:23 3318
it shall *b* forth fruit for three................ Lev 25:21 6213
b forth the old because of the............... Lev 26:10 3318
I will *b* seven times more plagues......... Lev 26:21 3254
I will *b* a sword upon you, that .... Lev 26:25 935
waste, and *b* your sanctuaries unto .... Lev 26:31 8074
I will *b* the land into desolation............. Lev 26:32 8074

whereof men *b* an offering unto............ Lev 27:9 7126
B the tribe of Levi near, and................. Num 3:6 7126
which they *b* unto the priest,................ Num 5:9 7126
Then shall the man *b* his wife............... Num 5:15 935
he shall *b* her offering for her,.............. Num 5:15 935
And the priest shall *b* her near .... Num 5:16 7126
eighth day he shall *b* two turtles.......... Num 6:10 935
shall *b* a lamb of the first year .... Num 6:12 935
the priest shall *b* them before.............. Num 6:16 7126
thou shalt *b* the Levites before .... Num 8:9 7126
thou shalt *b* the Levites before .... Num 8:10 7126
b them unto the tabernacle of the .... Num 11:16 3947
b of the fruit of the land......................... Num 13:20 3947
then he will *b* us into this land,............. Num 14:8 935
the LORD was not able to *b* this............ Num 14:16 935
him will I *b* into the land .... Num 14:24 935
be a prey, them will I *b* in..................... Num 14:31 935
Even those men that did *b* up the.......... Num 14:37 3318
his offering unto the LORD *b* a .... Num 15:4 7126
Then shall he *b* with a bullock a .... Num 15:9 7126
thou shalt *b* for a drink offering........... Num 15:10 7126
into the land whither I *b* you............... Num 15:18 935
they shall *b* their offering, a .... Num 15:25 935
then he shall *b* a she goat of the.......... Num 15:27 7126
to *b* you near to himself to do .... Num 16:9 7126
b ye before the LORD every man .... Num 16:17 7126
B Aaron's rod again before the .... Num 17:10 7725
b thou with thee, that they may............ Num 18:2 7126
which they shall *b* unto the LORD.......... Num 18:13 935
which they *b* unto the LORD,................. Num 18:15 7126
that they *b* thee a red heifer................ Num 19:2 3947
that he may *b* her forth without .... Num 19:3 3318
to *b* us in unto this evil place................ Num 20:5 935
thou shalt *b* forth to them water........... Num 20:8 3318
therefore ye shall not *b* this................. Num 20:12 935
son, and *b* them up unto mount Hor.... Num 20:25 5927
I will *b* you word again, as the .... Num 22:8 7725
I will *b* thee unto another place .... Num 23:27 3947
them out, and which may *b* them in .... Num 27:17 935
when ye *b* a new meat offering .... Num 28:26 7126
and *b* us not over Jordan .... Num 32:5 5674
b it unto me, and I will hear it............... Deut 1:17 7126
b us word again by what way we .... Deut 1:22 7725
to *b* thee in, to give thee their .... Deut 4:38 935
thence, that he might *b* us in .... Deut 6:23 935
When the LORD thy God shall *b*............. Deut 7:1 935
Neither shalt thou *b* an......................... Deut 7:26 935
he shall *b* them down before thy.......... Deut 9:3 3665
the LORD was not able to *b* them .... Deut 9:28 935
thither ye shall *b* your burnt .... Deut 12:6 935
thither shall ye *b* all that I.................. Deut 12:11 935
b forth all the tithe of thine................. Deut 14:28 3318
Then shalt thou *b* forth that man .... Deut 17:5 3318
b down the heifer unto a rough .... Deut 21:4 2381
Then thou shalt *b* her home to .... Deut 21:12 935
b him out unto the elders of his .... Deut 21:19 3318
thou shalt in any case *b* them .... Deut 22:1 7725
then thou shalt *b* it unto thine .... Deut 22:2 622
that thou *b* not blood upon thine.......... Deut 22:8 7760
b up an evil name upon her, and........... Deut 22:14 3318
b forth the tokens of the .... Deut 22:15 3318
Then they shall *b* out the damsel .... Deut 22:21 3318
Then ye shall *b* them both out............... Deut 22:24 3318
Thou shalt not *b* the hire of a .... Deut 23:18 935
to whom thou dost lend shall *b* .... Deut 24:11 3318
which thou shalt *b* of thy land............... Deut 26:2 935
The LORD shall *b* thee, and thy............. Deut 28:36 3212
The LORD shall *b* a nation against.......... Deut 28:49 5375
Moreover he will *b* upon thee all........... Deut 28:60 7725
them will the LORD *b* upon thee .... Deut 28:61 5927
you, and to *b* you to nought.................. Deut 28:63 8045
the LORD shall *b* thee into Egypt .... Deut 28:68 7725
to *b* upon it all the curses that............. Deut 29:27 935
the LORD thy God will *b* thee into.......... Deut 30:5 935
b it unto us, that we may hear it .... Deut 30:12 3947
b it unto us, that we may hear it .... Deut 30:13 3947
for thou shalt *b* the children of............. Deut 31:23 935
Judah, and *b* him unto his people .... Deut 33:7 935
B forth the men that are come to .... Josh 2:3 3318
and thou shalt *b* thy father.................... Josh 2:18 622
b out thence the woman, and all........... Josh 6:22 3318
b out those five kings unto me .... Josh 10:22 3318
b the description hither to me,............. Josh 18:6 935
so shall the LORD *b* upon you all .... Josh 23:15 935
not the LORD *b* us up from Egypt........... Judg 6:13 5927
b forth my present, and set it................ Judg 6:18 3318
B out thy son, that he may die .... Judg 6:30 3318
b them down unto the water, and I...... Judg 7:4 338
If ye *b* me home again to fight .... Judg 11:9 7725
to *b* her again, having his..................... Judg 19:3 7725
B forth the man that came into .... Judg 19:22 3318
them I will *b* out now, and humble .... Judg 19:24 3318
B the vail that thou hast upon.............. Ruth 3:15 3051
be weaned, and then I will *b* him........... 1Sa 1:22 935
that they might *b* from thence the 1Sa 4:4 5375
b their calves home from them 1Sa 6:7 7725
if we go, what shall we *b* the man......... 1Sa 9:7 935
a present to *b* to the man of God.......... 1Sa 9:7 935
B the portion which I gave thee,............ 1Sa 9:23 5414
b the men, that we may put them 1Sa 11:12 5414
B hither a burnt offering to me,............. 1Sa 13:9 5066
Ahiah, *B* hither the ark of God.............. 1Sa 14:18 5066
B me hither every man his ox, and 1Sa 14:34 5066
B ye hither to me Agag the king 1Sa 15:32 5066
can play well, and *b* him to me.............. 1Sa 16:17 935
B him up to me in the bed, that I 1Sa 19:15 5927
shouldest thou *b* me to thy father 1Sa 20:8 935
the priest, *B* hither the ephod............... 1Sa 23:9 5066
to *b* tidings to Gath, saying,.................. 1Sa 27:11 935
b me him up, whom I shall name............ 1Sa 28:8 5927
Whom shall I *b* up unto thee 1Sa 28:11 5927
And he said, *B* me up Samuel 1Sa 28:11 5927
thou disquieted me, to *b* me up 1Sa 28:15 5927
pray thee, *b* me hither the ephod.......... 1Sa 30:7 5066

Canst thou *b* me down to this 1Sa 30:15 3381
I will *b* thee down to this...................... 1Sa 30:15 3381
that were with him did David *b* up........ 2Sa 2:3 5927
to *b* about all Israel unto thee 2Sa 3:12 5437
except thou first *b* Michal Saul's 2Sa 3:13 935
to *b* up from thence the ark of 2Sa 6:2 5927
thou shalt *b* in the fruits, that.............. 2Sa 9:10 935
can I *b* him back again 2Sa 12:23 7725
B the meat into the chamber, that........ 2Sa 13:10 935
b him to me, and he shall not 2Sa 14:10 935
b the young man Absalom again............ 2Sa 14:21 7725
If the LORD shall *b* me again 2Sa 15:8 7725
b evil upon us, and smite the city 2Sa 15:14 5080
he will *b* me again, and shew me 2Sa 15:25 7725
I will *b* back all the people unto........... 2Sa 17:3 7725
all Israel *b* ropes to that city 2Sa 17:13 5375
LORD might *b* evil upon Absalom 2Sa 17:14 935
Why are ye the last to *b* the king 2Sa 19:11 7725
ye the last to *b* back the king 2Sa 19:12 7725
that thou mayest *b* them down 2Sa 22:28 8213
own mule, and *b* him down to Gihon... 1Kin 1:33 3381
but his hoar head *b* thou down to.......... 1Kin 2:9 3381
And the king said, *B* me a sword........... 1Kin 3:24 3947
My servants shall *b* them down............ 1Kin 5:9 3381
that they might *b* up the ark of............. 1Kin 8:1 5927
the priests and the Levites *b* up........... 1Kin 8:4 5927
to *b* his way upon his head.................... 1Kin 8:32 5414
b them again unto the land which........ 1Kin 8:34 7725
did they *b* them out by their 1Kin 10:29 3318
to *b* the kingdom again to..................... 1Kin 12:21 7725
B him back with thee into thine........... 1Kin 13:18 7725
I will *b* evil upon the house of.............. 1Kin 14:10 935
B me, I pray thee, a morsel of............... 1Kin 17:11 3947
b it unto me, and after make for.......... 1Kin 17:13 3318
Then he said, Go ye, *b* him 1Kin 20:33 3947
I will *b* evil upon thee, and will 1Kin 21:21 935
I will not *b* the evil in his days 1Kin 21:29 935
will I *b* the evil upon his house............. 1Kin 21:29 935
B me a new cruse, and put salt............. 2Kin 2:20 3947
And they *b* it to him.............................. 2Kin 2:20 935
But now *b* me a minstrel........................ 2Kin 3:15 3947
unto her son, *B* me yet a vessel 2Kin 4:6 5066
But he said, Then *b* meal...................... 2Kin 4:41 3947
I will *b* you to the man whom ye........... 2Kin 6:19 3212
B forth vestments for all the 2Kin 10:22 3318
to *b* into the house of the LORD............. 2Kin 12:4 935
there is not strength to *b* forth 2Kin 19:3 3205
I will *b* evil upon this place, and 2Kin 22:16 935
which I will *b* upon this place............... 2Kin 22:20 935
to *b* forth out of the temple of.............. 2Kin 23:4 3318
that they should *b* them in 1Chr 9:28
let us *b* again the ark of our God........... 1Chr 13:3 5437
Hemath, to *b* the ark of God from......... 1Chr 13:5 935
to *b* up thence the ark of God the.......... 1Chr 13:6 5927
How shall I *b* the ark of God home........ 1Chr 13:12 935
to *b* up the ark of the LORD unto 1Chr 15:3 5927
that ye may *b* up the ark of the 1Chr 15:12 5927
sanctified themselves to *b* up the 1Chr 15:14 5927
went to *b* up the ark of the 1Chr 15:25 5927
b an offering, and come before him....... 1Chr 16:29 5375
b the number of them to me, that......... 1Chr 21:2 935
shall *b* again to him that sent me......... 1Chr 21:12 7725
to *b* the ark of the covenant of.............. 1Chr 22:19 935
we will *b* it to thee in flotes by 2Chr 2:16 935
to *b* up the ark of the covenant............ 2Chr 5:2 5927
the priests and the Levites *b* up.......... 2Chr 5:5 5927
b them again unto the land which......... 2Chr 6:25 7725
that he might *b* the kingdom again........ 2Chr 11:1 7725
the Levites to *b* in out of Judah 2Chr 24:6 935
to *b* in to the LORD the 2Chr 24:9 935
to *b* them again unto the LORD............ 2Chr 24:19 7725
Ye shall not *b* in the captives................. 2Chr 28:13 935
b sacrifices and thank offerings 2Chr 29:31 935
Since the people began to *b* the 2Chr 31:10 935
I will *b* evil upon this place, and 2Chr 34:24 935
that I will *b* upon this place 2Chr 34:28 935
those did Cyrus king of Persia *b*............ Ezr 1:8 3318
All these did Sheshbazzar *b* up.............. Ezr 1:11 5927
to *b* cedar trees from Lebanon to........... Ezr 3:7 935
that they should *b* unto us.................... Ezr 8:17 935
to *b* them to Jerusalem unto the........... Ezr 8:30 935
will *b* them unto the place that I .... Neh 1:9 935
we *b* into bondage our sons and our .... Neh 5:5 3533
to *b* the book of the law of Moses .... Neh 8:1 935
that thou mightest *b* them again........... Neh 9:29 7725
if the people of the land *b* ware .... Neh 10:31 935
to *b* it into the house of our God .... Neh 10:34 935
to *b* the firstfruits of our...................... Neh 10:35 935
to *b* to the house of our God,................ Neh 10:36 935
that we should *b* the firstfruits .... Neh 10:37 935
the Levites shall *b* up the tithe .... Neh 10:38 5927
shall *b* the offering of the corn .... Neh 10:39 935
to *b* one of ten to dwell in..................... Neh 11:1 935
to *b* them to Jerusalem, to keep............ Neh 12:27 935
did not our God *b* all this evil .... Neh 13:18 935
yet ye *b* more wrath upon Israel............ Neh 13:18 935
To *b* Vashti the queen before the.......... Est 1:11 935
business, to *b* it into the king's............ Est 3:9 935
he commanded to *b* the book of............ Est 6:1 935
b him on horseback through the............ Est 6:9 7392
hasted to *b* Haman unto the.................. Est 6:14 935
Did I say, *B* unto me .... Job 6:22 3051
wilt thou *b* me into dust again.............. Job 10:9 7725
Who can *b* a clean thing out of an .... Job 14:4 5414
b forth boughs like a plant.................... Job 14:9 6213
b forth vanity, and their belly .... Job 15:35 3205
it shall *b* him to the king of.................. Job 18:14 6805
know that thou wilt *b* me to death........ Job 30:23 7725
To *b* back his soul from the pit,............. Job 33:30 7725
Canst thou *b* forth Mazzaroth in............ Job 38:32 3318
wild goats of the rock *b* forth .... Job 39:1 3205
thou the time when they *b* forth............ Job 39:2 3205
they *b* forth their young ones,............... Job 39:3 6398
that he will *b* home thy seed, and......... Job 39:12 7725

one that is proud, and *b* him low .... Job 40:12 3665
the mountains *b* him forth food............ Job 40:20 5375
but wilt *b* down high looks.................... Ps 18:27 8213
O *b* thou me out of my distresses .... Ps 25:17 3318
and he shall *b* it to pass.......................... Ps 37:5 6213
And he shall *b* forth thy......................... Ps 37:6 3318
of David, to *b* to remembrance .... Ps 38:t 2142
let them *b* me unto thy holy hill, ... Ps 43:3 935
shalt *b* them down into the pit of .... Ps 55:23 3381
b them down, O Lord our shield............ Ps 59:11 3381
Who will *b* me into the strong .... Ps 60:9 2986
I will *b* again from Bashan..................... Ps 68:22 7725
I will *b* my people again from the......... Ps 68:22 7725
shall kings *b* presents unto thee .... Ps 68:29 2986
of David, to *b* to remembrance .... Ps 70:t 2142
shalt *b* me up again from the................. Ps 71:20 5927
shall *b* peace to the people..................... Ps 72:3 5375
and of the isles shall *b* presents .... Ps 72:10 7725
b presents unto him that ought to......... Ps 76:11 2986
b hither the timbrel, the .... Ps 81:2 5414
They shall still *b* forth fruit in............... Ps 92:14 5107
he shall *b* upon them their own............. Ps 94:23 7725
b an offering, and come into his .... Ps 96:8 5375
that he may *b* forth food out of............. Ps 104:14 3318
Who will *b* me into the strong .... Ps 108:10 2986
B my soul out of prison, that I............... Ps 142:7 3318
sake *b* my soul out of trouble .... Ps 143:11 3318
our sheep may *b* forth thousands........... Ps 144:13 503
she shall *b* thee to honour, when .... Prov 4:8 3513
will not so much as *b* it to his................ Prov 19:24 7725
it grieveth him to *b* it again to.............. Prov 26:15 7725
not what a day may *b* forth.................... Prov 27:1 3205
Scornful men *b* a city into a................... Prov 29:8 6315
A man's pride shall *b* him low............... Prov 29:23 8213
for who shall *b* him to see what .... Eccl 3:22 935
God will *b* thee into judgment .... Eccl 11:9 935
For God shall *b* every work into............. Eccl 12:14 935
b thee into my mother's house, ... Song 8:2 935
to *b* a thousand pieces of silver .... Song 8:11 935
B no more vain oblations........................ Is 1:13 935
that it should *b* forth grapes.................. Is 5:2 6213
that it should *b* forth grapes.................. Is 5:4 6213
The LORD shall *b* upon thee.................... Is 7:17 935
them, and *b* them to their place .... Is 14:2 935
for I will *b* more upon Dimon,............... Is 15:9 7896
nor *b* forth children, neither do .... Is 23:4 3205
up young men, nor *b* up virgins .... Is 23:4 7311
to *b* into contempt all the .... Is 23:9 7034
Thou shalt *b* down the noise of.............. Is 25:5 3665
he shall *b* down their pride .... Is 25:11 8213
fort of thy walls shall he *b* down........... Is 25:12 7817
b to the ground, even to the dust.......... Is 25:12 5060
b to pass his act, his strange .... Is 28:21 5647
he also is wise, and will *b* evil .... Is 31:2 935
chaff, ye shall *b* forth stubble............... Is 33:11 3205
there is not strength to *b* forth............. Is 37:3 3205
I will *b* again the shadow of the............ Is 38:8 7725
b forth your strong reasons, ... Is 41:21 5066
Let them *b* them forth, and shew us ...... Is 41:22 5066
he shall *b* forth judgment to the .... Is 42:1 3318
he shall *b* forth judgment unto.............. Is 42:3 3318
to *b* out the prisoners from the.............. Is 42:7 3318
I will *b* the blind by a way that .... Is 42:16 3212
I will *b* thy seed from the east,............. Is 43:5 935
b my sons from far, and my.................... Is 43:6 935
B forth the blind people that .... Is 43:8 3318
let them *b* forth their witnesses,........... Is 43:9 5414
let them *b* forth salvation, and.............. Is 45:8 6509
Tell ye, and *b* them near........................ Is 45:21 5066
b it again to mind, O ye......................... Is 46:8 7725
it, I will also *b* it to pass .... Is 46:11 935
I *b* near my righteousness .... Is 46:13 7126
to *b* Jacob again to him, Though........... Is 49:5 7725
they shall *b* thy sons in their................. Is 49:22 935
when the LORD shall *b* again Zion .... Is 52:8 7725
the earth, and maketh it *b* forth............ Is 55:10 3205
Even them will I *b* to my holy .... Is 56:7 935
that thou *b* the poor that are .... Is 58:7 935
mischief, and *b* forth iniquity .... Is 59:4 3205
they shall *b* gold and incense .... Is 60:6 5375
to *b* thy sons from far, their .... Is 60:9 935
that men may *b* unto thee the................ Is 60:11 935
For brass I will *b* gold .... Is 60:17 935
and for iron I will *b* silver .... Is 60:17 935
I will *b* down their strength to.............. Is 63:6 3381
I will *b* forth a seed out of..................... Is 65:9 3318
in vain, nor *b* forth for trouble.............. Is 65:23 3205
will *b* their fears upon them .... Is 66:4 935
be made to *b* forth in one day............... Is 66:8 2342
Shall I *b* to the birth............................... Is 66:9 7665
and not cause to *b* forth .... Is 66:9 3205
shall I cause to *b* forth, and shut .... Is 66:9 3205
they shall *b* all your brethren .... Is 66:20 935
as the children of Israel *b* an................. Is 66:20 935
a family, and I will *b* you to Zion .... Jer 3:14 935
for I will *b* evil from the north,............. Jer 4:6 935
I will *b* a nation upon you from .... Jer 5:15 935
I will *b* evil upon this people,................ Jer 6:19 935
they shall *b* out the bones of the........... Jer 8:1 3318
lest thou *b* me to nothing....................... Jer 10:24
therefore I will *b* upon them all............. Jer 11:8 935
I will *b* evil upon them, which .... Jer 11:11 935
for I will *b* evil upon the men of .... Jer 11:23 935
grow, yea, they *b* forth fruit.................. Jer 12:2 6213
will *b* them again, every man to............ Jer 12:15 7725
return, then will I *b* thee again............. Jer 15:19 7725
I will *b* them again into their .... Jer 16:15 7725
b upon them the day of evil, and .... Jer 17:18 935
nor *b* it in by the gates of .... Jer 17:21 935
to *b* in no burden through the .... Jer 17:24 935
when thou shalt *b* a troop...................... Jer 18:22 935
I will *b* evil upon this place,.................. Jer 19:3 935
I will *b* upon this city and upon .... Jer 19:15 935
will *b* them again to their folds............. Jer 23:3 7725
for I will *b* evil upon them, even .... Jer 23:12 935
I will *b* an everlasting reproach .... Jer 23:40 5414
I will *b* them again to this land .... Jer 24:6 7725
will *b* them against this land, and .... Jer 25:9 935
I will *b* upon that land all my .... Jer 25:13 935
I begin to *b* evil on the city .... Jer 25:29
ye shall surely *b* innocent blood .... Jer 26:15 5414
But the nations that *b* their neck.......... Jer 27:11 935
B your necks under the yoke of .... Jer 27:12 935
then will I *b* them up, and restore .... Jer 27:22 5927
Within two full years will I *b* .... Jer 28:3 7725
I will *b* again to this place...................... Jer 28:4 7725
to *b* again the vessels of the.................. Jer 28:6 7725
I will *b* you again into the place............ Jer 29:14 7725
that I will *b* again the captivity .... Jer 30:3 7725
I will *b* again the captivity of................. Jer 30:18 7725
I will *b* them from the north .... Jer 31:8 935
when I shall *b* again their .... Jer 31:23 7725
b them out of the land of Egypt .... Jer 31:32 3318
I will *b* them again unto this................. Jer 32:37 7725
so will I *b* upon them all the .... Jer 32:42 935
I will *b* it health and cure, and I .... Jer 33:6 4608
and of them that shall *b* the.................. Jer 33:11 935
b them into the house of the LORD .... Jer 35:2 935
I will *b* upon Judah and upon all........... Jer 35:17 935
I will *b* upon them, and upon the........... Jer 36:31 935
So they shall *b* out all thy wives .... Jer 38:23 4672
I will *b* my words upon this city............. Jer 39:16 935
to *b* them to the house of the .... Jer 41:5 935
the evil that I will *b* upon them............ Jer 42:17 935
I will *b* evil upon all flesh,.................... Jer 45:5 935
for I will *b* upon it, even upon .... Jer 48:44 935
Yet will I *b* again the captivity.............. Jer 48:47 7725
I will *b* a fear upon thee, saith .... Jer 49:5 935
afterward I will *b* again the.................. Jer 49:6 7725
for I will *b* the calamity of Esau .... Jer 49:8 935
I will *b* thee down from thence, ... Jer 49:16 3381
I will *b* their calamity from all............... Jer 49:32 935
upon Elam will I *b* the four winds .... Jer 49:36 935
I will *b* evil upon them, even my........... Jer 49:37 935
that I will *b* again the captivity .... Jer 49:39 7725
I will *b* Israel again to his .... Jer 50:19 7725
I will *b* them down like lambs to........... Jer 51:40 3381
I will *b* forth out of his mouth .... Jer 51:44 3318
the evil that I will *b* upon her............... Jer 51:64 935
thou wilt *b* the day that thou................. Lam 1:21 935
I will *b* the sword upon thee .... Eze 5:17 935
will *b* a sword upon you, and I .... Eze 6:3 935
Wherefore I will *b* the worst of .... Eze 7:24 935
but I will *b* you forth out of the............ Eze 11:7 3318
I will *b* a sword upon you, saith .... Eze 11:8 935
I will *b* you out of the midst................. Eze 11:9 3318
Then shalt thou *b* forth thy stuff .... Eze 12:4 3318
I will *b* him to Babylon to the............... Eze 12:13 935
b it down to the ground, so that .... Eze 13:14 5060
Or if I *b* a sword upon that land, ... Eze 14:17 935
They shall also *b* up a company .... Eze 16:40 5927
When I shall *b* again their .... Eze 16:53 7725
then will I *b* again the captivity .... Eze 16:53
that it might *b* forth branches,............. Eze 17:8 6213
I will *b* him to Babylon, and will .... Eze 17:20 935
it shall *b* forth boughs, and bear.......... Eze 17:23 5375
to *b* them forth of the land of .... Eze 20:6 3318
that I would not *b* them into the .... Eze 20:15 935
I will *b* you out from the people,.......... Eze 20:34 3318
I will *b* you into the wilderness .... Eze 20:35 935
I will *b* you into the bond of the .... Eze 20:37 935
I will *b* them forth out of the................ Eze 20:38 3318
when I *b* you out from the people, ... Eze 20:41 3318
when I shall *b* you into the land .... Eze 20:42 935
to *b* thee upon the necks of them .... Eze 21:29 5414
I will *b* them against thee on.............. Eze 23:22 935
I will *b* up a company upon them, ... Eze 23:46 5927
b it out piece by piece .... Eze 24:6 3318
Behold, I will *b* upon Tyrus .... Eze 26:7 935
when I shall *b* up the deep upon .... Eze 26:19 5927
When I shall *b* thee down with .... Eze 26:20 3381
therefore I will *b* strangers upon........... Eze 28:7 935
They shall *b* thee down to the pit .... Eze 28:8 3381
therefore will I *b* forth a fire .... Eze 28:18 3318
I will *b* thee to ashes upon the .... Eze 28:18 5414
I will *b* thee up out of the midst............ Eze 29:4 5927
I will *b* a sword upon thee, and .... Eze 29:8 935
I will *b* again the captivity of................ Eze 29:14 7725
of the field *b* forth their young .... Eze 31:6 3205
they shall *b* thee up in my net .... Eze 32:3 5927
when I shall *b* thy destruction .... Eze 32:9 935
When I *b* the sword upon a land,............ Eze 33:2 935
I will *b* them out from the people.......... Eze 34:13 3318
will *b* them to their own land, and........ Eze 34:13 935
b again that which was driven................ Eze 34:16 7725
and they shall increase and *b* fruit......... Eze 36:11 6509
will *b* you into your own land............... Eze 36:24 935
will *b* up flesh upon you, and .... Eze 37:6 5927
b you into the land of Israel.................. Eze 37:12 935
b them into their own land.................... Eze 37:21 935
I will *b* thee forth, and all thine............ Eze 38:4 3318
I will *b* thee against my land,................ Eze 38:16 935
that I would *b* thee against them.......... Eze 38:17 935
will *b* thee upon the mountains of .... Eze 39:2 935
Now will I *b* again the captivity .... Eze 39:25 7725
it shall *b* forth new fruit .... Eze 47:12 1069
that he should *b* certain of the .... Dan 1:3 935
king had said he should *b* them in......... Dan 1:18 935
b me in before the king, and I .... Dan 2:24 5924
and fury commanded to *b* Shadrach .... Dan 3:13 858
Therefore made I a decree to *b* in.......... Dan 4:6 5924
wine, commanded to *b* the golden .... Dan 5:2 858
aloud to *b* in the astrologers................. Dan 5:7 5924
to *b* in everlasting righteousness .... Dan 9:24 935
b her into the wilderness, and............... Hos 2:14 1980
I will *b* them down as the fowls .... Hos 7:12 3381
Though they *b* up their children,............ Hos 9:12 1431
but Ephraim shall *b* forth his .... Hos 9:13 3318
yea, though they *b* forth, yet.................. Hos 9:16 3205
time, when I shall *b* again the................ Joel 3:1 7725
will *b* them down into the valley............. Joel 3:2 3381
he shall *b* down thy strength from........ Amos 3:11 3381
which say to their masters, *B*................. Amos 4:1 935
b your sacrifices every morning,............ Amos 4:4 935
to *b* out the bones out of the .... Amos 6:10 3318
I will *b* up sackcloth upon all................ Amos 8:10 5927
heaven, thence will I *b* them down........ Amos 9:2 3381
I will *b* again the captivity of................ Amos 9:14 7725
Who shall *b* me down to the ground.... Obad 3 3381
stars, thence will I *b* thee down .... Obad 4 3381
rowed hard to *b* it to the land............... Jonah 1:13 7725
Yet will I *b* an heir unto thee, O .... Mic 1:15 935
Be in pain, and labour to *b* forth .... Mic 4:10 1518
he will *b* me forth to the light,.............. Mic 7:9 3318
I will *b* distress upon men, that .... Zeph 1:17
Before the decree *b* forth....................... Zeph 2:2 3205
doth he *b* his judgment to light .... Zeph 3:5 5414
dispersed, shall *b* mine offering............. Zeph 3:10 2986
At that time will I *b* you again.............. Zeph 3:20 935
Ye have sown much, and *b* in little ...... Hag 1:6 935
b wood, and build the house.................. Hag 1:8 935
I will *b* forth my servant the................. Zec 3:8 935
he shall *b* forth the headstone.............. Zec 4:7 3318
I will *b* it forth, saith the LORD .... Zec 5:4 3318
And I will *b* them, and they shall.......... Zec 8:8 935
I will *b* them again to place them .... Zec 10:6 7725
I will *b* them again also out of.............. Zec 10:10 7725
I will *b* them into the land of................ Zec 10:10 935
I will *b* the third part through .... Zec 13:9 935
B ye all the tithes into the .... Mal 3:10 935
she shall *b* forth a son, and thou .... Mt 1:21 5088
shall *b* forth a son, and they.................. Mt 1:23 5088
b me word again, that I may come......... Mt 2:8 518
be thou there until I *b* thee word......... Mt 2:13 2036
B forth therefore fruits meet for.......... Mt 3:8 4160
Therefore if thou *b* thy gift to.............. Mt 5:23 4374
tree cannot *b* forth evil fruit................ Mt 7:18 4160
a corrupt tree *b* forth good fruit........... Mt 7:18 4160
He said, *B* them hither to me .... Mt 14:18 5342
b him hither to me................................. Mt 17:17 5342
loose them, and *b* them unto me............ Mt 21:2 71
did run to *b* his disciples word............. Mt 28:8 518
b forth fruit, some thirtyfold,............... Mk 4:20 2592
they *b* unto him one that was deaf........ Mk 7:32 5342
they *b* a blind man unto him, and.......... Mk 8:22 5342
b him unto me....................................... Mk 9:19 5342
loose him, and *b* him .... Mk 11:2 71
b me a penny, that I may see it.............. Mk 12:15 5342
they *b* him unto the place..................... Mk 15:22 5342
b forth a son, and shalt call his.............. Lk 1:31 5088
I *b* you good tidings of great joy........... Lk 2:10 2097
B forth therefore fruits worthy .... Lk 3:8 4160
and they sought means to *b* him in........ Lk 5:18 1533
b him in because of the multitude .... Lk 5:19 1533
a corrupt tree *b* forth good fruit........... Lk 6:43 4160
life, and *b* no fruit to perfection .... Lk 8:14 5052
b forth fruit with patience..................... Lk 8:15 2592
B thy son hither.................................... Lk 9:41 4317
And when they *b* you unto the............... Lk 12:11 4374
b in hither the poor, and the .... Lk 14:21 1521
B forth the best robe, and put it............ Lk 15:22 1627
b hither the fatted calf, and kill............ Lk 15:23 5342
b hither, and slay them before me .... Lk 19:27 71
loose him, and *b* him hither.................. Lk 19:30 71
them also I must *b*, and they shall........ Jn 10:16 71
b all things to your remembrance, ... Jn 14:26 5179
that it may *b* forth more fruit .... Jn 15:2 5342
b forth fruit, and that your fruit............ Jn 15:16 5342
What accusation *b* ye against this .... Jn 18:29 5342
I *b* him forth to you, that ye may .... Jn 19:4 71
B of the fish which ye have now........... Jn 21:10 5342
intend to *b* this man's blood upon......... Acts 5:28 1863
that they should *b* them into................. Acts 7:6 1402
he might *b* them bound unto .... Acts 9:2 71
that he might *b* them bound unto.......... Acts 9:21 71
to *b* him forth to the people .... Acts 12:4 321
sought to *b* them out to the .... Acts 17:5 71
to *b* them which were there bound......... Acts 22:5 71
them, and to *b* him into the castle......... Acts 23:10 71
he *b* him down unto you to morrow ...... Acts 23:15 2609
B this young man unto the chief........... Acts 23:17 520
prayed me to *b* this young man .... Acts 23:18 71
b down Paul to morrow into the .... Acts 23:20 2609
b him safe unto Felix the .... Acts 23:24 1295
I came to *b* alms to my nation.............. Acts 24:17 4160
that we should *b* forth fruit unto .... Rom 7:4 2592
to *b* forth fruit unto death .... Rom 7:5 2592
to *b* Christ down from above .... Rom 10:6 2609
to *b* up Christ again from the .... Rom 10:7 321
b glad tidings of good things .... Rom 10:15 2097
wise, and will *b* to nothing the 1Cor 1:19 114
to *b* to nought things that are 1Cor 1:28 2673
who both will *b* to light the.................. 1Cor 4:5 5461
who shall *b* you into remembrance........ 1Cor 4:17 363
my body, and *b* it into subjection 1Cor 9:27 1396
them will I send to *b* your 1Cor 16:3 667
that ye may *b* me on my journey........... 1Cor 16:6 4311
if a man *b* you into bondage, if a 2Cor 11:20 2615
that they might *b* us into bondage......... Gal 2:4 2615
schoolmaster to *b* us unto Christ .... Gal 3:24
but *b* them up in the nurture and.......... Eph 6:4 1625
in Jesus will God *b* with him................. 1Th 4:14 71
Take Mark, and *b* him with thee............. 2Ti 4:11 71
b with thee, and the books, but............. 2Ti 4:13 5342
B Zenas the lawyer and Apollos on .... Titus 3:13 4311
unjust, that he might *b* us to God 1Pet 3:18 4317
who privily shall *b* in damnable............ 2Pet 2:1 3919
them, and *b* upon themselves swift 2Pet 2:1 1863
b not railing accusation against............. 2Pet 2:11 5342
b not this doctrine, receive him............ 2Jn 10 5342
whom if thou *b* forward on their........... 3Jn 6 4311
durst not *b* against him a railing .... Jude 9 2018

of the earth do *b* their glory Rev 21:24 *5342*
And they shall *b* the glory Rev 21:26 *5342*

BRINGERS
the *b* up of the children, sent to 2Kin 10:5 539

BRINGEST
a valiant man, and *b* good tidings 1Kin 1:42 1319
b me into judgment with thee Job 14:3 935
that *b* good tidings, get thee up Is 40:9 1319
that *b* good tidings, lift up thy Is 40:9 1319
For thou *b* certain strange things Acts 17:20 *1533*

BRINGETH
which *b* you out from under the Ex 6:7 3318
For I am the LORD that *b* you up Lev 11:45 5927
b it not unto the door of the Lev 17:4 935
b it not unto the door of the Lev 17:9 935
For the LORD thy God *b* thee into Deut 8:7 935
that the field *b* forth year by Deut 14:22 3318
he *b* down to the grave, and 1Sa 2:6 3381
down to the grave, and *b* up 1Sa 2:6 5927
he *b* low, and lifteth up 1Sa 2:7 8213
the king said, He also *b* tidings 2Sa 18:26 1319
that *b* down the people under me, 2Sa 22:48 3381
that *b* me forth from mine enemies 2Sa 22:49 3318
into whose hand God *b* abundantly Job 12:6 935
b out to light the shadow of Job 12:22 3318
for wrath *b* the punishments of Job 19:29
that is hid *b* he forth to light Job 28:11 3318
that *b* forth his fruit in his Ps 1:3 5414
when the LORD *b* back the Ps 14:7 7725
The LORD *b* the counsel of the Ps 33:10 6331
man who *b* wicked devices to pass Ps 37:7 6213
When God *b* back the captivity of Ps 53:6 7725
he *b* out those which are bound Ps 68:6 3318
he *b* them out of their distresses Ps 107:28 3318
so he *b* them unto their desired Ps 107:30 5148
he *b* the wind out of his Ps 135:7 3318
mouth of the just *b* forth wisdom Prov 10:31 5107
moving his lips he *b* evil to pass Prov 16:30 3615
him, and *b* him before great men Prov 18:16 5148
that causeth shame, and *b* reproach Prov 19:26 2659
wicked, and *b* the wheel over them Prov 20:26 7725
when he *b* it with a wicked mind Prov 21:27 935
to himself *b* his mother to shame Prov 29:15
He that delicately *b* up his Prov 29:21 6445
The fear of man *b* a snare Prov 29:25 5414
churning of milk *b* forth butter Prov 30:33 3318
of the nose *b* forth blood Prov 30:33 3318
forcing of wrath *b* forth strife Prov 30:33 3318
she *b* her food from afar Prov 31:14 935
the wood that *b* forth trees Eccl 2:6 6779
the Lord *b* up upon them the Is 8:7 5927
For he *b* down them that dwell on Is 26:5 7817
he *b* it even to the dust Is 26:5 5060
That *b* the princes to nothing Is 40:23 5414
that *b* out their host by number Is 40:26 3318
Jerusalem one that *b* good tidings Is 41:27 1319
Which *b* forth the chariot and Is 43:17 3318
feet of him that *b* good tidings Is 52:7 1319
that *b* good tidings of good, that Is 52:7 1319
that *b* forth an instrument for Is 54:16 3318
For as the earth *b* forth her bud Is 61:11 3318
her that *b* forth her first child Jer 4:31 1069
b forth the wind out of his Jer 10:13 3318
b forth the wind out of his Jer 51:16 3318
which *b* their iniquity to Eze 29:16 2142
he *b* forth fruit unto himself Hos 10:1 7737
feet of him that *b* good tidings Nah 1:15 1319
that which the ground *b* forth Hag 1:11 3318
therefore every tree which *b* not Mt 3:10 *4160*
good tree *b* forth good fruit Mt 7:17 *4160*
a corrupt tree *b* forth evil fruit Mt 7:17 *4160*
Every tree that *b* not forth good Mt 7:19 *4160*
of the heart *b* forth good things Mt 12:35 *1544*
evil treasure *b* forth evil things Mt 12:35 *1544*
b forth, some an hundredfold, Mt 13:23 *4160*
which *b* forth out of his treasure Mt 13:52 *1544*
b them up into an high mountain Mt 17:1 *399*
For the earth *b* forth fruit of Mk 4:28 *2592*
every tree therefore which *b* not Lk 3:9 *4160*
For a good tree *b* not forth Lk 6:43 *4160*
heart *b* forth that which is good Lk 6:45 *4393*
heart *b* forth that which is evil Lk 6:45 *4393*
if it die, it *b* forth much fruit Jn 12:24 *5342*
the same *b* forth much fruit Jn 15:5 *5342*
b forth fruit, as it doth also in Col 1:6 *2592*
For the grace of God that *b* Titus 2:11 *4992*
when he *b* in the firstbegotten Heb 1:6 *1521*
b forth herbs meet for them by Heb 6:7 *5088*
hath conceived, it *b* forth sin Jas 1:15 *616*
it is finished, *b* forth death Jas 1:15 *5088*

BRINGING
b them out from the land of Egypt Ex 12:42 3318
the people were restrained from *b* Ex 36:6 935
b iniquity to remembrance Num 5:15 2142
by *b* up a slander upon the land Num 14:36 3318
ye not a word of *b* the king back 2Sa 19:10 7725
be first had in *b* back our king 2Sa 19:43 7725
b gold, and silver, ivory, and apes 1Kin 10:22 5375
I am *b* such evil upon Jerusalem 2Kin 21:12 935
came the ships of Tarshish *b* gold 2Chr 9:21 5375
b in sheaves, and lading asses Neh 13:15 935
rejoicing, *b* his sheaves with him Ps 126:6 5375
b burnt offerings, and sacrifices, Jer 17:26 935
b sacrifices of praise, unto the Jer 17:26 935
in *b* them forth out of the land Eze 20:9 3318
by *b* upon us a great evil Dan 9:12 935
given to a nation *b* forth the Mt 21:43 *4160*
b one sick of the palsy, which Mk 2:3 *5342*
b the spices which they had Lk 24:1 *5342*
b sick folks, and them which were Acts 5:16 *5342*
b me into captivity to the law of Rom 7:23 *163*
b into captivity every thought to 2Cor 10:5 *163*

in *b* many sons unto glory, to Heb 2:10 *71*
but the *b* in of a better hope did Heb 7:19 *1898*
b in the flood upon the world of 2Pet 2:5 *1863*

BRINK
kine upon the *b* of the river Gen 41:3 8193
it in the flags by the river's *b* Ex 2:3 8193
by the river's *b* against he come Ex 7:15 8193
which is by the *b* of the river of Deut 2:36 8193
to the *b* of the water of Jordan Josh 3:8 7097
to return to the *b* of the river Eze 47:6 8193

BROAD
cubits long, and five cubits *b* Ex 27:1 7341
let them make them *b* plates for a Num 16:38 7555
they were made *b* plates for a Num 16:39 7554
chamber was five cubits *b* 1Kin 6:6 7341
and the middle was six cubits *b* 1Kin 6:6 7341
and the third was seven cubits *b* 1Kin 6:6 7341
cubits long, and five cubits *b* 2Chr 6:13 7341
Jerusalem unto the *b* wall Neh 3:8 7342
the furnaces even unto the *b* wall Neh 12:38 7342
out of the strait into a *b* place Job 36:16 7338
thy commandment is exceeding *b* Ps 119:96 7342
in the *b* ways I will seek him Song 3:2 7339
be unto us a place of *b* rivers Is 33:21
seek in the *b* places thereof, if Jer 5:1 7339
The *b* walls of Babylon shall be Jer 51:58 7342
of the gate, which was one reed *b* Eze 40:6 7341
of the gate, which was one reed *b* Eze 40:6 7341
was one reed long, and one reed *b* Eze 40:7 7341
long, and five and twenty cubits *b* Eze 40:29 7341
cubits long, and five cubits *b* Eze 40:30 7341
long, and five and twenty cubits *b* Eze 40:33 7341
long, and a cubit and an half *b* Eze 40:42 7341
And within were hooks, an hand *b* Eze 40:43
long, and an hundred cubits *b* Eze 40:47 7341
six cubits *b* on the one side, and Eze 41:1 7341
six cubits *b* on the other side, Eze 41:1 7341
the west was seventy cubits *b* Eze 41:12 7341
as long as they, and as *b* as they Eze 42:11 7342
reeds long, and five hundred *b* Eze 42:20 7341
be twelve cubits long, twelve *b* Eze 43:16 7341
fourteen *b* in the four squares Eze 43:17 7341
of the city five thousand *b* Eze 45:6 7341
of forty cubits long and thirty *b* Eze 46:22 7341
one against another in the *b* ways Nah 2:4 7339
b is the way, that leadeth to Mt 7:13 *2149*
they make *b* their phylacteries, Mt 23:5 *4115*

BROADER
than the earth, and *b* than the sea Job 11:9 7342

BROIDED
not with *b* hair, or gold, or 1Ti 2:9 *4117*

BROIDERED
a *b* coat, a mitre, and a girdle Ex 28:4 8665
I clothed thee also with *b* work Eze 16:10 7553
of fine linen, and silk, and *b* work Eze 16:13 7553
And tookest thy *b* garments Eze 16:18 7553
and put off their *b* garments Eze 26:16 7553
Fine linen with *b* work from Egypt Eze 27:7 7553
b work, and fine linen, and coral, Eze 27:16 7553
b work, and in chests of rich Eze 27:24 7553

BROILED
they gave him a piece of a *b* fish Lk 24:42 *3702*

BROKEN
fountains of the great deep *b* up Gen 7:11 1234
he hath *b* my covenant Gen 17:14 6565
she said, How hast thou *b* forth Gen 38:29 6555
wherein it is sodden shall be *b* Lev 6:28 7665
for pots, they shall be *b* down Lev 11:35 5422
of leprosy *b* out of the boil Lev 13:20 6524
it is a leprosy *b* out of the Lev 13:25 6524
which hath the issue, shall be *b* Lev 15:12 7665
or scabbed, or hath his stones *b* Lev 21:20 4790
Blind, or *b*, or maimed, or having Lev 22:22 7665
is bruised, or crushed, or *b* Lev 22:24 5423
I have *b* the bands of your yoke, Lev 26:13 7665
when I have *b* the staff of your Lev 26:26 7665
hath *b* his commandment, that soul Num 15:31 6565
Then were the horsehoofs *b* by the Judg 5:22 1986
as a thread of tow is *b* when it Judg 16:9 5423
The bows of the mighty men are *b* 1Sa 2:4 2844
of the LORD shall be *b* to pieces 1Sa 2:10 2865
The LORD hath *b* forth upon mine 2Sa 5:20 6555
a bow of steel is *b* by mine arms 2Sa 22:35 5181
altar of the LORD that was *b* down 1Kin 18:30 2040
the ships were *b* at Ezion-geber 1Kin 22:48 7665
the house, that it be not *b* down 2Kin 11:6 4535
And the city was *b* up, and all the 2Kin 25:4 1234
God hath *b* in upon mine enemies 1Chr 14:11 6555
the LORD hath *b* thy works 2Chr 20:37 6555
And the ships were *b*, that they 2Chr 20:37 7665
had *b* up the house of God 2Chr 24:7 6555
that they all were *b* in pieces 2Chr 25:12 1234
built up all the wall that was *b* 2Chr 32:5 6555
Hezekiah his father had *b* down 2Chr 33:3 5422
when he had *b* down the altars and 2Chr 34:7 5422
wall of Jerusalem also is *b* down Neh 1:3 6555
of Jerusalem, which were *b* down Neh 2:13 6555
teeth of the young lions, are *b* Job 4:10 5421
my skin is *b*, and become loathsome Job 7:5 7280
at ease, but he hath *b* me asunder Job 16:12 6565
are past, my purposes are *b* off Job 17:11 5423
of the fatherless have been *b* Job 22:9 1792
wickedness shall be *b* as a tree Job 24:20 7665
mine arm be *b* from the bone Job 31:22 7665
and the high arm shall be *b* Job 38:15 7665
thou hast *b* the teeth of the Ps 3:7 7665
a bow of steel is *b* by mine arms Ps 18:34 5181
I am like a *b* vessel Ps 31:12 6
unto them that are of a *b* heart Ps 34:18 7665
not one of them is *b* Ps 34:20 7665

heart, and their bows shall be *b* Ps 37:15 7665
the arms of the wicked shall be *b* Ps 37:17 7665
I am feeble and sore *b* Ps 38:8 1794
Though thou hast sore *b* us in the Ps 44:19 1794
which thou hast *b* may rejoice Ps 51:8 1794
sacrifices of God are a *b* spirit Ps 51:17 7665
a *b* and a contrite heart, O God, Ps 51:17 7665
he hath *b* his covenant Ps 55:20 2490
thou hast *b* it Ps 60:2 6480
Reproach hath *b* my heart Ps 69:20 7665
hast thou then *b* down her hedges Ps 80:12 6555
Thou hast *b* Rahab in pieces, as Ps 89:10 1792
Thou hast *b* down all his hedges Ps 89:40 6555
For he hath *b* the gates of brass, Ps 107:16 7665
he might even slay the *b* in heart Ps 109:16 5218
the snare is *b*, and we are escaped Ps 124:7 7665
He healeth the *b* in heart Ps 147:3 7665
his knowledge the depths are *b* up Prov 3:20 1234
shall he be *b* without remedy Prov 6:15 7665
of the heart the spirit is *b* Prov 15:13 5218
but a *b* spirit drieth the bones Prov 17:22 5218
the stone wall thereof was *b* down Prov 24:31 2040
time of trouble is like a *b* tooth Prov 25:19 7465
is like a city that is *b* down Prov 25:28 6555
a threefold cord is not quickly *b* Eccl 4:12 5423
loosed, or the golden bowl be *b* Eccl 12:6 7533
the pitcher be *b* at the fountain Eccl 12:6 7665
or the wheel *b* at the cistern Eccl 12:6 7533
the latchet of their shoes be *b* Is 5:27 5423
and five years shall Ephraim be *b* Is 7:8 2844
and ye shall be *b* in pieces Is 8:9 2844
and ye shall be *b* in pieces Is 8:9 2844
and ye shall be *b* in pieces Is 8:9 2844
shall stumble, and fall, and be *b* Is 8:15 7665
For thou hast *b* the yoke of his Is 9:4 2865
The LORD hath *b* the staff of the Is 14:5 7665
rod of him that smote thee is *b* Is 14:29 7665
have *b* down the principal plants Is 16:8 1986
they shall be *b* in the purposes Is 19:10 1792
gods he hath *b* unto the ground Is 21:9 7665
the houses have ye *b* down to Is 22:10 5422
b the everlasting covenant Is 24:5 6565
The city of confusion is *b* down Is 24:10 7665
The earth is utterly *b* down Is 24:19 7489
are withered, they shall be *b* off Is 27:11 7665
go, and fall backward, and be *b* Is 28:13 7665
vessel that is *b* in pieces Is 30:14 3807
he hath *b* the covenant, he hath Is 33:8 6565
any of the cords thereof be *b* Is 33:20 5423
in the staff of this *b* reed Is 36:6 7533
b cisterns, that can hold no Jer 2:13 7665
Tahapanes have *b* the crown of thy Jer 2:16 7462
For of old time I have *b* thy yoke Jer 2:20 7665
b down at the presence of the Jer 4:26 5422
these have altogether *b* the yoke Jer 5:5 7665
is spoiled, and all my cords are *b* Jer 10:20 5423
the house of Judah have *b* my Jer 11:10 6565
it, and the branches of it are *b* Jer 11:16 7489
people is *b* with a great breach Jer 14:17 7665
this man Coniah a despised *b* idol Jer 22:28 5310
me is *b* because of the prophets Jer 23:9 7665
I have *b* the yoke of the king of Jer 28:2 7665
b the yoke from off the neck of Jer 28:12 7665
Thou hast *b* the yokes of wood Jer 28:13 7665
be *b* with David my servant Jer 33:21 6565
b up from Jerusalem for fear of Jer 37:11 5927
of the month, the city was *b* up Jer 39:2 1234
say, How is the strong staff *b* Jer 48:17 7665
for it is *b* down Jer 48:20 2865
Moab is cut off, and his arm is *b* Jer 48:25 7665
for I have *b* Moab like a vessel Jer 48:38 7665
howl, saying, How is it *b* down Jer 48:39 2865
Merodach is *b* in pieces Jer 50:2 2844
her images are *b* in pieces Jer 50:2 2865
king of Babylon hath *b* his bones Jer 50:17 6105
whole earth cut in asunder and *b* Jer 50:23 7665
her bars are *b* Jer 51:30 7665
every one of their bows is *b* Jer 51:56 2865
of Babylon shall be utterly *b* Jer 51:58 6209
Then the city was *b* up, and all Jer 52:7 1234
he hath destroyed and *b* her bars Lam 2:9 7665
he hath *b* my bones Lam 3:4 7665
He hath also *b* my teeth with Lam 3:16 1638
and your images shall be *b* Eze 6:4 7665
desolate, and your idols may be *b* Eze 6:6 7665
because I am *b* with their whorish Eze 6:9 7665
and my covenant that he hath *b* Eze 17:19 6331
her strong rods were *b* and Eze 19:12 6531
she is *b* that was the gates of Eze 26:2 7665
the east wind hath *b* thee in the Eze 27:26 7665
be *b* by the seas in the depths of Eze 27:34 7665
her foundations shall be *b* down Eze 30:4 2040
I have *b* the arm of Pharaoh king Eze 30:21 7665
the strong, and that which was *b* Eze 30:22 7665
his boughs are *b* by all the Eze 31:12 7665
thou shalt be *b* in the midst of Eze 32:28 7665
have ye bound up that which was *b* Eze 34:4 7665
and will bind up that which was *b* Eze 34:16 7665
when I have *b* the bands of their Eze 34:27 7665
they have *b* my covenant because Eze 44:7 6565
b to pieces together, and became Dan 2:35 1854
be partly strong, and partly *b* Dan 2:42 8406
was strong, the great horn was *b* Dan 8:8 7665
Now that being *b*, whereas four Dan 8:22 7665
but he shall be *b* without hand Dan 8:25 7665
stand up, his kingdom shall be *b* Dan 11:4 7665
from before him, and shall be *b* Dan 11:22 7665
b in judgment, because he Hos 5:11 7533
of Samaria shall be *b* in pieces Hos 8:6 7616
desolate, the barns are *b* down Joel 1:17 2040
so that the ship was like to be *b* Jonah 1:4 7665
they have *b* up, and have passed Mic 2:13 6555
And it was *b* in that day Zec 11:11 6565
one, nor heal that that is *b* Zec 11:16 7665

they took up of the *b* meat that Mt 15:37 *2801*
fall on this stone shall be *b* Mt 21:44 *4917*
suffered his house to be *b* up Mt 24:43 *1358*
and when they had *b* it up, they Mk 2:4 *1846*
him, and the fetters *b* in pieces Mk 5:4 *4937*
they took up of the *b* meat that Mk 8:8 *2801*
his house to be *b* through Lk 12:39 *1358*
fall upon that stone shall be *b* Lk 20:18 *4917*
he not only had *b* the sabbath Jn 5:18 *3089*
the law of Moses should not be *b* Jn 7:23 *3089*
and the scripture cannot be *b* Jn 10:35 *3089*
Pilate that their legs might be *b* Jn 19:31 *2608*
A bone of him shall not be *b* Jn 19:36 *4937*
so many, yet was not the net *b* Jn 21:11 *4977*
when the congregation was *b* up Acts 13:43 *3089*
had *b* bread, and eaten, and talked Acts 20:11 *2806*
and when he had *b* it, he began to Acts 27:35 *2806*
but the hinder part was *b* with Acts 27:41 *3089*
some on *b* pieces of the ship Acts 27:44
if some of the branches be *b* off Rom 11:17 *1575*
say then, The branches were *b* off Rom 11:19 *1575*
of unbelief they were *b* off Rom 11:20 *1575*
is my body, which is *b* for you 1Cor 11:24 *2806*
hath *b* down the middle wall of Eph 2:14 *3089*
potter shall they be *b* to shivers Rev 2:27 *4937*

BROKENFOOTED
Or a man that is *b*, or Lev 21:19

BROKENHANDED
a man that is brokenfooted, or *b* Lev 21:19

BROKENHEARTED
he hath sent me to bind up the *b* Is 61:1
he hath sent me to heal the *b* Lk 4:18

BROOD
doth gather her *b* under her wings Lk 13:34 *3555*

BROOK
them, and sent them over the *b* Gen 32:23 5158
thick trees, and willows of the *b* Lev 23:40 5158
And they came unto the *b* of Eshcol Num 13:23 5158
The place was called the *b* Eshcol Num 13:24 5158
I, and get you over the *b* Zered Deut 2:13 5158
And we went over the *b* Zered Deut 2:13 5158
we were come over the *b* Zered Deut 2:14 5158
cast the dust thereof into the *b* Deut 9:21 5158
five smooth stones out of the *b* 1Sa 17:40 5158
with him, and came to the *b* Besor 1Sa 30:9 5158
could not go over the *b* Besor 1Sa 30:10 5158
made also to abide at the *b* Besor 1Sa 30:21 5158
himself passed over the *b* Kidron 2Sa 15:23 5158
They be gone over the *b* of water 2Sa 17:20 4323
out, and passest over the *b* Kidron 1Kin 2:37 5158
idol, and burnt it by the *b* Kidron 1Kin 15:13 5158
and hide thyself by the *b* Cherith 1Kin 17:3 5158
that thou shalt drink of the *b* 1Kin 17:4 5158
he went and dwelt by the *b* Cherith 1Kin 17:5 5158
and he drank of the *b* 1Kin 17:6 5158
a while, that the *b* dried up 1Kin 17:7 5158
brought them down to the *b* Kishon 1Kin 18:40 5158
Jerusalem, unto the *b* Kidron 2Kin 23:6 5158
and burned it at the *b* Kidron 2Kin 23:6 5158
dust of them into the *b* Kidron 2Kin 23:12 5158
it, and burnt it at the *b* Kidron 2Chr 15:16 5158
find them at the end of the *b* 2Chr 20:16 5158
it out abroad into the *b* Kidron 2Chr 29:16 5158
and cast them into the *b* Kidron 2Chr 30:14 5158
the *b* that ran through the midst 2Chr 32:4 5158
went I up in the night by the *b* Neh 2:15 5158
have dealt deceitfully as a *b* Job 6:15 5158
of the *b* compass him about Job 40:22 5158
as to Jabin, at the *b* of Kison Ps 83:9 5158
shall drink of the *b* in the way Ps 110:7 5158
of wisdom as a flowing *b* Prov 18:4 5158
away to the *b* of the willows Is 15:7 5158
the fields unto the *b* of Kidron Jer 31:40 5158
his disciples over the *b* Cedron Jn 18:1 *5493*

BROOKS
Red sea, and in the *b* of Arnon, Num 21:14 5158
at the stream of the *b* that goeth Num 21:15 5158
a good land, a land of *b* of water Deut 8:7 5158
Hiddai of the *b* of Gaash 2Sa 23:30 5158
fountains of water, and unto all *b* 1Kin 18:5 5158
Hurai of the *b* of Gaash, Abiel 1Chr 11:32 5158
as the stream of *b* they pass away Job 6:15 5158
floods, the *b* of honey and butter Job 20:17 5158
of Ophir as the stones of the *b* Job 22:24 5158
hart panteth after the water *b* Ps 42:1 650
the *b* of defence shall be emptied Is 19:6 2975
the *b*, by the mouth of the *b* Is 19:7 2975
and every thing sown by the *b* Is 19:7 2975
angle into the *b* shall lament Is 19:8 2975

BROTH
basket, and he put the *b* in a pot Judg 6:19 4839
upon this rock, and pour out the *b* Judg 6:20 4839
b of abominable things is in Is 65:4 6564

BROTHER
And she again bare his *b* Abel Gen 4:2 251
And Cain talked with Abel his *b* Gen 4:8 251
Cain rose up against Abel his *b* Gen 4:8 251
unto Cain, Where is Abel thy *b* Gen 4:9 251
at the hand of every man's *b* will Gen 9:5 251
the *b* of Japheth the elder, even Gen 10:21 251
b of Eshcol, and *b* of Aner Gen 14:13 251
b of Eshcol, and *b* of Aner Gen 14:13 251
that his *b* was taken captive Gen 14:14 251
and also brought again his *b* Lot Gen 14:16 251
even she herself said, He is my *b* Gen 20:5 251
shall come, say of me, He is my *b* Gen 20:13 251
I have given thy *b* a thousand Gen 20:16 251
born children unto thy *b* Nahor Gen 22:20 251
Huz his firstborn, and Buz his *b* Gen 22:21 251
did bear to Nahor, Abraham's *b* Gen 22:23 251
the wife of Nahor, Abraham's *b* Gen 24:15 251
And Rebekah had a *b*, and his name Gen 24:29 251
he gave also to her *b* and to her Gen 24:53 251
And her *b* and her mother said, Let Gen 24:55 251
And after that came his *b* out Gen 25:26 251
thy father speak unto Esau thy *b* Gen 27:6 251
Esau my *b* is a hairy man, and I am Gen 27:11 251
were hairy, as his *b* Esau's hands Gen 27:23 251
that Esau his *b* came in from his Gen 27:30 251
Thy *b* came with subtilty, and hath Gen 27:35 251
thou live, and shalt serve thy *b* Gen 27:40 251
then will I slay my *b* Jacob Gen 27:41 251
thy *b* Esau, as touching thee, Gen 27:42 251
flee thou to Laban my *b* to Haran Gen 27:43 251
daughters of Laban thy mother's *b* Gen 28:2 251
the *b* of Rebekah, Jacob's and Gen 28:5 251
daughter of Laban his mother's *b* Gen 29:10 251
the sheep of Laban his mother's *b* Gen 29:10 251
the flock of Laban his mother's *b* Gen 29:10 251
Rachel that he was her father's *b* Gen 29:12 251
unto Jacob, Because thou art my *b* Gen 29:15 251
Esau his *b* unto the land of Seir Gen 32:3 251
saying, We came to thy *b* Esau Gen 32:6 251
pray thee, from the hand of my *b* Gen 32:11 251
his hand a present for Esau his *b* Gen 32:13 251
When Esau my *b* meeteth thee Gen 32:17 251
until he came near to his *b* Gen 33:3 251
And Esau said, I have enough, my *b* Gen 33:9 251
from the face of Esau thy *b* Gen 35:1 251
he fled from the face of his *b* Gen 35:7 251
from the face of his *b* Jacob Gen 36:6 251
profit is it if we slay our *b* Gen 37:26 251
for he is our *b* and our flesh Gen 37:27 251
her, and raise up seed to thy *b* Gen 38:8 251
that he should give seed to his *b* Gen 38:9 251
that, behold, his *b* came out Gen 38:29 251
And afterward came out his *b* Gen 38:30 251
But Benjamin, Joseph's *b*, Jacob Gen 42:4 251
your youngest *b* come hither Gen 42:15 251
of you, and let him fetch your *b* Gen 42:16 251
But bring your youngest *b* unto me Gen 42:20 251
verily guilty concerning our *b* Gen 42:21 251
And bring your youngest *b* unto me Gen 42:34 251
so will I deliver you your *b* Gen 42:34 251
for his *b* is dead, and he is left Gen 42:38 251
face, except your *b* be with you Gen 43:3 251
If thou wilt send our *b* with us Gen 43:4 251
face, except your *b* be with you Gen 43:5 251
the man whether ye had yet a *b* Gen 43:6 251
have ye another *b* Gen 43:7 251
he would say, Bring your *b* down Gen 43:7 251
Take also your *b*, and arise, go Gen 43:13 251
he may send away your other *b* Gen 43:14 251
saw his *b* Benjamin, his mother's Gen 43:29 251
and said, Is this your younger *b* Gen 43:29 251
his bowels did yearn upon his *b* Gen 43:30 251
saying, Have ye a father, or a *b* Gen 44:19 251
his *b* is dead, and he alone is Gen 44:20 251
youngest *b* come down with you Gen 44:23 251
if our youngest *b* be with us Gen 44:26 251
except our youngest *b* be with us Gen 44:26 251
And he said, I am Joseph your *b* Gen 45:4 251
see, and the eyes of my *b* Benjamin Gen 45:12 251
fell upon his *b* Benjamin's neck Gen 45:14 251
but truly his younger *b* shall be Gen 48:19 251
Is not Aaron the Levite thy *b* Ex 4:14 251
Aaron thy *b* shall be thy prophet Ex 7:1 251
Aaron thy *b* shall speak unto Ex 7:2 251
take thou unto thee Aaron thy *b* Ex 28:1 251
for Aaron thy *b* for glory Ex 28:2 251
holy garments for Aaron thy *b* Ex 28:4 251
shalt put them upon Aaron thy *b* Ex 28:41 251
the camp, and slay every man his *b* Ex 32:27 251
man upon his son, and upon his *b* Ex 32:29 251
Moses, Speak unto Aaron thy *b* Lev 16:2 251
the nakedness of thy father's *b* Lev 18:14 251
not hate thy *b* in thine heart Lev 19:17 251
and for his daughter, and for his *b* Lev 21:2 251
If thy *b* be waxen poor, and hath Lev 25:25 251
he redeem that which his *b* sold Lev 25:25 251
if thy *b* be waxen poor, and fallen Lev 25:35 251
that thy *b* may live with thee Lev 25:36 251
if thy *b* that dwelleth by thee be Lev 25:39 251
thy *b* that dwelleth by him wax Lev 25:47 251
or for his mother, for his *b* Num 6:7 251
together, thou, and Aaron thy *b* Num 20:8 251
of Edom, Thus saith thy *b* Israel Num 20:14 251
as Aaron thy *b* was gathered Num 27:13 251
our *b* unto his daughters Num 36:2 251
between every man and his *b* Deut 1:16 251
If thy *b*, the son of thy mother, Deut 13:6 251
it of his neighbour, or of his *b* Deut 15:2 251
thy *b* thine hand shall release Deut 15:3 251
shut thine hand from thy poor *b* Deut 15:7 251
eye be evil against thy poor *b* Deut 15:9 251
open thine hand wide unto thy *b* Deut 15:11 251
And if thy *b*, an Hebrew man, or an Deut 15:12 251
over thee, which is not thy *b* Deut 17:15 251
testified falsely against his *b* Deut 19:18 251
thought to have done unto his *b* Deut 19:19 251
case bring them again unto thy *b* Deut 22:1 251
if thy *b* be not nigh unto thee, Deut 22:2 251
thee until thy *b* seek after it Deut 22:2 251
for he is thy *b* Deut 23:7 251
not lend upon usury to thy *b* Deut 23:19 251
but unto thy *b* thou shalt not Deut 23:20 251
thou dost lend thy *b* any thing Deut 24:10 7453
then thy *b* should seem vile unto Deut 25:3 251
her husband's *b* shall go in unto Deut 25:5 2993
duty of an husband's *b* unto her Deut 25:5 2992
the name of his *b* which is dead Deut 25:6 251
My husband's *b* refuseth to raise Deut 25:7 2993
up unto his *b* a name in Israel Deut 25:7 251
the duty of my husband's *b* Deut 25:7 2992
eye shall be evil toward his *b* Deut 28:54 251
as Aaron thy *b* died in mount Hor, Deut 32:50 251
of Kenaz, the *b* of Caleb, took it Josh 15:17 251
And Judah said unto Simeon his *b* Judg 1:3 251
son of Kenaz, Caleb's younger *b* Judg 1:13 251
And Judah went with Simeon his *b* Judg 1:17 251
son of Kenaz, Caleb's younger *b* Judg 3:9 251
for they said, He is our *b* Judg 9:3 251
of Shechem, because he is your *b* Judg 9:18 251
for fear of Abimelech his *b* Judg 9:21 251
be laid upon Abimelech their *b* Judg 9:24 251
the children of Benjamin my *b* Judg 20:23 251
the children of Benjamin my *b* Judg 20:28 251
them for Benjamin their *b* Judg 21:6 251
land, which was our *b* Elimelech's Ruth 4:3 251
the son of Ahitub, I-chabod's *b* 1Sa 14:3 251
Eliab his eldest *b* heard when he 1Sa 17:28 251
and my *b*, he hath commanded me to 1Sa 20:29 251
b to Joab, saying, Who will go 1Sa 26:6 251
for thee, my *b* Jonathan 2Sa 1:26 251
I hold up my face to Joab thy *b* 2Sa 2:22 251
up every one from following his *b* 2Sa 2:27 251
for the blood of Asahel his *b* 2Sa 3:27 251
Joab and Abishai his *b* slew Abner 2Sa 3:30 251
because he had slain their *b* 2Sa 3:30 251
and Rechab and Baanah his *b* escaped 2Sa 4:6 251
answered Rechab and Baanah his *b* 2Sa 4:9 251
into the hand of Abishai his *b* 2Sa 10:10 251
the son of Shimeah David's *b* 2Sa 13:3 251
love Tamar, my *b* Absalom's sister 2Sa 13:4 251
Go now to thy *b* Amnon's house 2Sa 13:7 251
Tamar went to her *b* Amnon's house 2Sa 13:8 251
into the chamber to Amnon her *b* 2Sa 13:10 251
And she answered him, Nay, my *b* 2Sa 13:12 251
Absalom her *b* said unto her 2Sa 13:20 251
Hath Amnon thy *b* been with thee 2Sa 13:20 251
he is thy *b* 2Sa 13:20 251
desolate in her *b* Absalom's house 2Sa 13:20 251
Absalom spake unto his *b* Amnon 2Sa 13:22
let my *b* Amnon go with us 2Sa 13:26 251
the son of Shimeah David's *b* 2Sa 13:32 251
Deliver him that smote his *b* 2Sa 14:7 251
the life of his *b* whom he slew 2Sa 14:7 251
the son of Zeruiah, Joab's *b* 2Sa 18:2 251
Amasa, Art thou in health, my *b* 2Sa 20:9 251
Abishai his *b* pursued after Sheba 2Sa 20:10 251
slew the *b* of Goliath the Gittite 2Sa 21:19
Shimeah the *b* of David slew him 2Sa 21:21 251
the *b* of Joab, the son of Zeruiah 2Sa 23:18 251
Asahel the *b* of Joab was one of 2Sa 23:24 251
the mighty men, and Solomon his *b* 1Kin 1:10 251
I fled because of Absalom thy *b* 1Kin 2:7 251
given to Adonijah thy *b* to wife 1Kin 2:21 251
for he is mine elder *b* 1Kin 2:22 251
which thou hast given me, my *b* 1Kin 9:13 251
over him, saying, Alas, my *b* 1Kin 13:30 251
he is my *b* 1Kin 20:32 251
and they said, Thy *b* Ben-hadad 1Kin 20:33 251
his father's *b* king in his stead 2Kin 24:17 251
the sons of Jada the *b* of Shammai 1Chr 2:32 251
of Caleb the *b* of Jerahmeel were 1Chr 2:42 251
Chelub the *b* of Shuah begat Mehir 1Chr 4:11 251
his *b* Asaph, who stood on his 1Chr 6:39 251
and the name of his *b* was Sheresh 1Chr 7:16 251
And the sons of his *b* Helem 1Chr 7:35 251
And the sons of Eshek his *b* were 1Chr 8:39 251
And Abishai the *b* of Joab, he was 1Chr 11:20 251
armies were, Asahel the *b* of Joab 1Chr 11:26 251
Joel the *b* of Nathan, Mibhar the 1Chr 11:38 251
the son of Shimri, and Joha his *b* 1Chr 11:45 251
unto the hand of Abishai his *b* 1Chr 19:11 251
fled before Abishai his *b* 1Chr 19:15 251
the *b* of Goliath the Gittite 1Chr 20:5 251
son of Shimea David's *b* slew him 1Chr 20:7 251
The *b* of Michah was Isshiah 1Chr 24:25 1730
Zetham, and Joel his *b*, which were 1Chr 26:22 251
month was Asahel the *b* of Joab 1Chr 27:7 251
Shimei his *b* was the next 2Chr 31:12 251
hand of Cononiah and Shimei his *b* 2Chr 31:13 251
Eliakim his *b* king over Judah 2Chr 36:4 251
And Necho took Jehoahaz his *b* 2Chr 36:4 251
Zedekiah his *b* king over Judah 2Chr 36:10 251
exact usury, every one of his *b* Neh 5:7 251
That I gave my *b* Hanani, and Neh 7:2 251
a pledge from thy *b* for nought Job 22:6 251
I am a *b* to dragons, and a Job 30:29 251
though he had been my friend or *b* Ps 35:14 251
can by any means redeem his *b* Ps 49:7 251
sittest and speakest against thy *b* Ps 50:20 251
a *b* is born for adversity Prov 17:17 251
b to him that is a great waster Prov 18:9 251
A *b* offended is harder to be won Prov 18:19 251
that sticketh closer than a *b* Prov 18:24 251
that is near than a *b* far off Prov 27:10 251
yea, he hath neither child nor *b* Eccl 4:8 251
O that thou wert as my *b*, that Song 8:1 251
his *b* of the house of his father Is 3:6 251
no man shall spare his *b* Is 9:19 251
fight every one against his *b* Is 19:2 251
and every one said to his *b* Is 41:6 251
and trust ye not in any *b* Jer 9:4 251
for every *b* will utterly supplant Jer 9:4 251
lament for him, saying, Ah my *b* Jer 22:18 251
neighbour, and every one to his *b* Jer 23:35 251
his neighbour, and every man his *b* Jer 31:34 251
of them, to wit, of a Jew his *b* Jer 34:9 251
ye go every man his *b* an Hebrew Jer 34:14 251
liberty, every one to his *b* Jer 34:17 251
spoiled his *b* by violence Eze 18:18 251
to another, every one to his *b* Eze 33:30 251
sword shall be against his *b* Eze 38:21 251
for son, or for daughter, for *b* Eze 44:25 251
He took his *b* by the heel in the Hos 12:3 251
did pursue his *b* with the sword Amos 1:11 251

b Jacob shame shall cover thee — Obad 10 — 251
thy *b* in the day that he became a — Obad 12 — 251
hunt every man his *b* with a net — Mic 7:2 — 251
every one by the sword of his *b* — Hag 2:22 — 251
and compassions every man to his *b* — Zec 7:9 — 251
evil against his *b* in your heart — Zec 7:10 — 251
Was not Esau Jacob's *b* — Mal 1:2 — 251
every man against his *b*, by — Mal 2:10 — 251
called Peter, and Andrew his *b* — Mt 4:18 — 80
the son of Zebedee, and John his *b* — Mt 4:21 — 80
his *b* without a cause shall be in — Mt 5:22 — 80
and whosoever shall say to his *b* — Mt 5:22 — 80
thy *b* hath ought against thee — Mt 5:23 — 80
first be reconciled to thy *b* — Mt 5:24 — 80
Or how wilt thou say to thy *b* — Mt 7:4 — 80
is called Peter, and Andrew his *b* — Mt 10:2 — 80
the son of Zebedee, and John his *b* — Mt 10:2 — 80
b shall deliver up the *b* to death — Mt 10:21 — 80
is in heaven, the same is my *b* — Mt 12:50 — 80
sake, his *b* Philip's wife — Mt 14:3 — 80
Peter, James, and John his *b* — Mt 17:1 — 80
Moreover if thy *b* shall trespass — Mt 18:15 — 80
hear thee, thou hast gained thy *b* — Mt 18:15 — 80
how oft shall my *b* sin against me — Mt 18:21 — 80
every one his *b* their trespasses — Mt 18:35 — 80
his *b* shall marry his wife — Mt 22:24 — 80
and raise up seed unto his *b* — Mt 22:24 — 80
issue, left his wife unto his *b* — Mt 22:25 — 80
Andrew his *b* casting a net into — Mk 1:16 — 80
the son of Zebedee, and John his *b* — Mk 1:19 — 80
Zebedee, and John the *b* of James — Mk 3:17 — 80
the will of God, the same is my *b* — Mk 3:35 — 80
and James, and John the *b* of James — Mk 5:37 — 80
the *b* of James, and Joses, and of — Mk 6:3 — 80
sake, his *b* Philip's wife — Mk 6:17 — 80
wrote unto us, If a man's *b* die — Mk 12:19 — 80
that his *b* should take his wife, — Mk 12:19 — 80
and raise up seed unto his *b* — Mk 12:19 — 80
b shall betray the *b* to death — Mk 13:12 — 80
his *b* Philip tetrarch of Ituraea — Lk 3:1 — 80
for Herodias his *b* Philip's wife — Lk 3:19 — 80
named Peter,) and Andrew his *b* — Lk 6:14 — 80
And Judas the *b* of James, and Judas — Lk 6:16
canst thou say to thy *b*, B — Lk 6:42 — 80
unto him, Master, speak to my *b* — Lk 12:13 — 80
he said unto him, Thy *b* is come — Lk 15:27 — 80
for this thy *b* was dead, and is — Lk 15:32 — 80
If thy *b* trespass against thee, — Lk 17:3 — 80
wrote unto us, If any man's *b* die — Lk 20:28 — 80
that his *b* should take his wife, — Lk 20:28 — 80
wife, and raise up seed unto his *b* — Lk 20:28 — 80
him, was Andrew, Simon Peter's *b* — Jn 1:40 — 80
He first findeth his own *b* Simon — Jn 1:41 — 80
Andrew, Simon Peter's *b*, saith — Jn 6:8 — 80
hair, whose *b* Lazarus was sick — Jn 11:2 — 80
comfort them concerning their *b* — Jn 11:19 — 80
been here, my *b* had not died — Jn 11:21 — 80
unto her, Thy *b* shall rise again — Jn 11:23 — 80
been here, my *b* had not died — Jn 11:32 — 80
Zelotes, and Judas the *b* of James — Acts 1:13
B Saul, the Lord, even Jesus, — Acts 9:17 — 80
he killed James the *b* of John — Acts 12:2 — 80
and said unto him, Thou seest, *b* — Acts 21:20 — 80
B Saul, receive thy sight — Acts 22:13 — 80
But why dost thou judge thy *b* — Rom 14:10 — 80
why dost thou set at nought thy *b* — Rom 14:10 — 80
But if thy *b* be grieved with thy — Rom 14:15 — 80
any thing whereby thy *b* stumbleth — Rom 14:21 — 80
city saluteth you, and Quartus a *b* — Rom 16:23 — 80
will of God, and Sosthenes our *b* — 1Cor 1:1 — 80
is called a *b* be a fornicator — 1Cor 5:11 — 80
But *b* goeth to law with *b*, — 1Cor 6:6 — 80
If any *b* hath a wife that — 1Cor 7:12 — 80
A *b* or a sister is not under — 1Cor 7:15 — 80
knowledge shall the weak *b* perish — 1Cor 8:11 — 80
if meat make my *b* to offend — 1Cor 8:13 — 80
lest I make my *b* to offend — 1Cor 8:13 — 80
As touching our *b* Apollos — 1Cor 16:12 — 80
the will of God, and Timothy our *b* — 2Cor 1:1 — 80
because I found not Titus my *b* — 2Cor 2:13 — 80
And we have sent with him the *b* — 2Cor 8:18 — 80
And we have sent with them our *b* — 2Cor 8:22 — 80
Titus, and with him I sent a *b* — 2Cor 12:18 — 80
I none, save James the Lord's *b* — Gal 1:19 — 80
how I do, Tychicus, a beloved *b* — Eph 6:21 — 80
to send to you Epaphroditus, my *b* — Phil 2:25 — 80
will of God, and Timotheus our *b* — Col 1:1 — 80
unto you, who is a beloved *b* — Col 4:7 — 80
Onesimus, a faithful and beloved *b* — Col 4:9 — 80
And sent Timotheus, our *b*, and — 1Th 3:2 — 80
defraud his *b* in any matter — 1Th 4:6 — 80
every *b* that walketh disorderly — 2Th 3:6 — 80
an enemy, but admonish him as a *b* — 2Th 3:15 — 80
of Jesus Christ, and Timothy our *b* — Philem 1 — 80
saints are refreshed by thee, *b* — Philem 7 — 80
a *b* beloved, specially to me, but — Philem 16 — 80
Yea, *b*, let me have joy of thee — Philem 20 — 80
his neighbour, and every man his *b* — Heb 8:11 — 80
Know ye that our *b* Timothy is set — Heb 13:23 — 80
Let the *b* of low degree rejoice — Jas 1:9 — 80
If a *b* or sister be naked, and — Jas 2:15 — 80
He that speaketh evil of his *b* — Jas 4:11 — 80
of his *b*, and judgeth his *b* — Jas 4:11 — 80
Silvanus, a faithful *b* unto you — 1Pet 5:12 — 80
even as our beloved *b* Paul also — 2Pet 3:15 — 80
is in the light, and hateth his *b* — 1Jn 2:9 — 80
He that loveth his *b* abideth in — 1Jn 2:10 — 80
that hateth his *b* is in darkness — 1Jn 2:11 — 80
neither he that loveth not his *b* — 1Jn 3:10 — 80
of that wicked one, and slew his *b* — 1Jn 3:12 — 80
loveth not his *b* abideth in death — 1Jn 3:14 — 80
hateth his *b* is a murderer — 1Jn 3:15 — 80
good, and seeth his *b* have need — 1Jn 3:17 — 80
say, I love God, and hateth his *b* — 1Jn 4:20 — 80
not his *b* whom he hath seen — 1Jn 4:20 — 80
he who loveth God love his *b* also — 1Jn 4:21 — 80
If any man see his *b* sin a sin — 1Jn 5:16 — 80
b of James, to them that are — Jude 1 — 80
I John, who also am your *b* — Rev 1:9 — 80

BROTHERHOOD

I might break the *b* between Judah — Zec 11:14 — 264
Love the *b* — 1Pet 2:17 — 81

BROTHERLY

and remembered not the *b* covenant — Amos 1:9 — 251
one to another with *b* love — Rom 12:10 — 5360
But as touching *b* love ye need — 1Th 4:9 — 5360
Let *b* love continue — Heb 13:1 — 5360
And to godliness *b* kindness — 2Pet 1:7 — 5360
and to *b* kindness charity — 2Pet 1:7 — 5360

BROTHER'S

Am I my *b* keeper — Gen 4:9 — 251
the voice of thy *b* blood crieth — Gen 4:10 — 251
receive thy *b* blood from thy hand — Gen 4:11 — 251
And his *b* name was Jubal — Gen 4:21 — 251
and his *b* name was Joktan — Gen 10:25 — 251
Sarai his wife, and Lot his *b* son — Gen 12:5 — 251
And they took Lot, Abram's *b* son — Gen 14:12 — 251
master's *b* daughter unto his son — Gen 24:48 — 251
until thy *b* fury turn away — Gen 27:44 — 251
Until thy *b* anger turn away from — Gen 27:45 — 251
unto Onan, Go in unto thy *b* wife — Gen 38:8 — 251
when he went in unto his *b* wife — Gen 38:9 — 251
the nakedness of thy *b* wife — Lev 18:16 — 251
it is thy *b* nakedness — Lev 18:16 — 251
And if a man shall take his *b* wife — Lev 20:21 — 251
he hath uncovered his *b* nakedness — Lev 20:21 — 251
Thou shalt not see thy *b* ox or — Deut 22:1 — 251
and with all lost things of thy *b* — Deut 22:3 — 251
Thou shalt not see thy *b* ass or — Deut 22:4 — 251
man like not to take his *b* wife — Deut 25:7 — 2994
then let his *b* wife go up to the — Deut 25:7 — 2994
Then shall his *b* wife come unto — Deut 25:9 — 2994
will not build up his *b* house — Deut 25:9 — 251
turned about, and is become my *b* — 1Kin 2:15 — 251
and his *b* name was Joktan — 1Chr 1:19 — 251
wine in their eldest *b* house — Job 1:13 — 251
wine in their eldest *b* house — Job 1:18 — 251
neither go into thy *b* house in — Prov 27:10 — 251
the mote that is in thy *b* eye — Mt 7:3 — 80
out the mote out of thy *b* eye — Mt 7:5 — 80
for thee to have thy *b* wife — Mk 6:18 — 80
the mote that is in thy *b* eye — Lk 6:41 — 80
out the mote that is in thy *b* eye — Lk 6:42 — 80
an occasion to fall in his *b* way — Rom 14:13 — 80
were evil, and his *b* righteous — 1Jn 3:12 — 80

BROTHERS'

unto their father's *b* sons — Num 36:11 — 1730

BROUGHT

the earth *b* forth grass, and herb — Gen 1:12 — 3318
the waters *b* forth abundantly — Gen 1:21 — 8317
b them unto Adam to see what he — Gen 2:19 — 935
he a woman, and *b* her unto the man — Gen 2:22 — 935
that Cain *b* of the fruit of the — Gen 4:3 — 935
he also *b* of the firstlings of — Gen 4:4 — 935
he *b* back all the goods — Gen 14:16 — 7725
also *b* again his brother Lot, and — Gen 14:16 — 7725
king of Salem *b* forth bread — Gen 14:18 — 3318
he *b* him forth abroad, and said, — Gen 15:5 — 3318
I am the LORD that *b* thee out of — Gen 15:7 — 3318
they *b* him forth, and set him — Gen 19:16 — 3318
when they had *b* them forth abroad — Gen 19:17 — 3318
thee, that thou hast *b* on me — Gen 20:9 — 935
the servant *b* forth jewels of — Gen 24:53 — 3318
Isaac *b* her into his mother — Gen 24:67 — 935
have *b* guiltiness upon us — Gen 26:10 — 935
fetched, and *b* them to his mother — Gen 27:14 — 935
the LORD thy God *b* it to me — Gen 27:20 — 7136
he *b* it near to him, and he did — Gen 27:25 — 5066
he *b* him wine, and he drank — Gen 27:25 — 935
b it unto his father, and said — Gen 27:31 — 935
b it me, and I have eaten of all — Gen 27:33 — 935
kissed him, and *b* him to his house — Gen 29:13 — 935
his daughter, and *b* her to him — Gen 29:23 — 935
b them unto his mother Leah — Gen 30:14 — 935
b forth cattle ringstraked, — Gen 30:39 — 3205
torn of beasts I *b* not unto thee — Gen 31:39 — 935
my blessing that is *b* to thee — Gen 33:11 — 935
Joseph *b* unto his father their — Gen 37:2 — 935
and they *b* Joseph into Egypt — Gen 37:28 — 935
they *b* it to their father — Gen 37:32 — 935
When she was *b* forth, she sent to — Gen 38:25 — 3318
Joseph was *b* down to Egypt — Gen 39:1 — 3381
which had *b* him down thither — Gen 39:1 — 3381
he hath *b* in an Hebrew unto us to — Gen 39:14 — 935
which thou hast *b* unto us — Gen 39:17 — 935
thereof *b* forth ripe grapes — Gen 40:10 — 1310
they *b* him hastily out of the — Gen 41:14 — 7323
the earth *b* forth by handfuls — Gen 41:47 — 6213
which they had *b* out of Egypt — Gen 43:2 — 935
the money that was *b* again in the — Gen 43:12 — 7725
the man *b* the men into Joseph's — Gen 43:17 — 935
because they were *b* into Joseph's — Gen 43:18 — 935
at the first time are we *b* in — Gen 43:18 — 935
we have *b* it again in our hand — Gen 43:21 — 7725
other money have we *b* down in our — Gen 43:22 — 3381
he *b* Simeon out unto them — Gen 43:23 — 3318
the man *b* the men into Joseph's — Gen 43:24 — 935
they *b* him the present which was — Gen 43:26 — 935
we *b* again unto thee out of the — Gen 44:8 — 7725
all his seed *b* he with him into — Gen 46:7 — 935
they have *b* their flocks, and — Gen 46:32 — 935
Joseph *b* in Jacob his father, and — Gen 47:7 — 935
Joseph *b* the money into Pharaoh's — Gen 47:14 — 935
they *b* their cattle unto Joseph — Gen 47:17 — 935
And he *b* them near unto him — Gen 48:10 — 5066
Joseph *b* them out from between — Gen 48:12 — 3318
hand, and *b* them near unto him — Gen 48:13 — 5066
were *b* up upon Joseph's knees — Gen 50:23 — 3205
she *b* him unto Pharaoh's daughter — Ex 2:10 — 935
When thou hast *b* forth the people — Ex 3:12 — 3318
b up frogs upon the land of Egypt — Ex 8:7 — 5927
which he had *b* against Pharaoh — Ex 8:12 — 7760
the field, and shall not be *b* home — Ex 9:19 — 622
Aaron were *b* again unto Pharaoh — Ex 10:8 — 7725
the LORD *b* an east wind upon the — Ex 10:13 — 5090
the east wind *b* the locusts — Ex 10:13 — 5375
b your armies out of the land of — Ex 12:17 — 3318
which they *b* forth out of Egypt — Ex 12:39 — 3318
LORD *b* you out from this place — Ex 13:3 — 3318
hath the LORD *b* thee out of Egypt — Ex 13:9 — 3318
hand the LORD *b* us out from Egypt — Ex 13:14 — 3318
the LORD *b* us forth out of Egypt — Ex 13:16 — 3318
the LORD *b* again the waters of — Ex 15:19 — 7725
So Moses *b* Israel from the Red — Ex 15:22 — 5265
which I have *b* upon the Egyptians — Ex 15:26 — 7760
for ye have *b* us forth into this — Ex 16:3 — 3318
shall know that the LORD hath *b* — Ex 16:6 — 3318
when I *b* you forth from the land — Ex 16:32 — 3318
thou hast *b* us up out of Egypt — Ex 17:3 — 5927
that the LORD had *b* Israel out of — Ex 18:1 — 3318
the hard causes they *b* unto Moses — Ex 18:26 — 935
wings, and *b* you unto myself — Ex 19:4 — 935
Moses *b* forth the people out of — Ex 19:17 — 3318
which have *b* thee out of the land — Ex 20:2 — 3318
house shall be *b* unto the judges — Ex 22:8 — 7126
shalt cause a bullock to be *b* — Ex 29:10 — 7126
that *b* them forth out of the land — Ex 29:46 — 3318
the man that *b* us up out of the — Ex 32:1 — 5927
their ears, and *b* them unto Aaron — Ex 32:3 — 935
which *b* thee up out of the land — Ex 32:4 — 5927
offerings, and *b* peace offerings — Ex 32:6 — 5066
which have *b* thee up out of the — Ex 32:8 — 5927
which thou hast *b* forth out of — Ex 32:11 — 3318
that thou hast *b* so great a sin — Ex 32:21 — 935
the man that *b* us up out of the — Ex 32:23 — 5927
the people which thou hast *b* up — Ex 33:1 — 5927
they *b* the LORD's offering to the — Ex 35:21 — 935
b bracelets, and earrings, and — Ex 35:22 — 935
rams, and badgers' skins, *b* them — Ex 35:23 — 935
brass *b* the LORD's offering — Ex 35:24 — 935
for any work of the service, *b* it — Ex 35:24 — 935
b that which they had spun, both — Ex 35:25 — 935
the rulers *b* onyx stones, and — Ex 35:27 — 935
The children of Israel *b* a — Ex 35:29 — 935
the children of Israel had *b* for — Ex 36:3 — 935
And they *b* yet unto him free — Ex 36:3 — 935
they *b* the tabernacle unto Moses, — Ex 39:33 — 935
he *b* the ark into the tabernacle, — Ex 40:21 — 935
is *b* into the tabernacle of the — Lev 6:30 — 935
And Moses *b* Aaron and his sons, and — Lev 8:6 — 7126
Moses *b* Aaron's sons, and put — Lev 8:13 — 7126
he *b* the bullock for the sin — Lev 8:14 — 5066
he *b* the ram for the burnt — Lev 8:18 — 7126
he *b* the other ram, the ram of — Lev 8:22 — 7126
he *b* Aaron's sons, and Moses put — Lev 8:24 — 7126
they *b* that which Moses commanded — Lev 9:5 — 3947
the sons of Aaron *b* the blood — Lev 9:9 — 7126
he *b* the people's offering, and — Lev 9:15 — 7126
he *b* the burnt offering, and — Lev 9:16 — 7126
he *b* the meat offering, and took — Lev 9:17 — 7126
the blood of it was not *b* in — Lev 10:18 — 935
then he shall be *b* unto Aaron the — Lev 13:2 — 935
he shall be *b* unto the priest — Lev 13:9 — 935
He shall be *b* unto the priest — Lev 14:2 — 935
whose blood was *b* in to make — Lev 16:27 — 935
which *b* you out of the land of — Lev 19:36 — 3318
is *b* forth, then it shall be — Lev 22:27 — 3205
That *b* you out of the land of — Lev 22:33 — 3318
have *b* an offering unto your God — Lev 23:14 — 935
from the day that ye *b* the sheaf — Lev 23:15 — 935
when I *b* them out of the land of — Lev 23:43 — 3318
And they *b* him unto Moses — Lev 24:11 — 935
which *b* you forth out of the land — Lev 25:38 — 3318
which I *b* forth out of the land — Lev 25:42 — 3318
they are my servants whom I *b* — Lev 25:55 — 3318
which *b* you forth out of the land — Lev 26:13 — 3318
have *b* them into the land of — Lev 26:41 — 935
whom I *b* forth out of the land of — Lev 26:45 — 3318
he shall be *b* unto the door of — Num 6:13 — 935
they *b* their offering before the — Num 7:3 — 935
they *b* them before the tabernacle — Num 7:3 — 7126
because he *b* not the offering of — Num 9:13 — 7126
b quails from the sea, and let — Num 11:31 — 1468
not till Miriam was *b* in again — Num 12:15 — 622
they *b* of the pomegranates, and of — Num 13:23
b back word unto them, and unto — Num 13:26 — 7725
they *b* up an evil report of the — Num 13:32 — 3318
hath the LORD *b* us unto this land — Num 14:3 — 935
gathering sticks *b* him unto Moses — Num 15:33 — 7126
b him without the camp, and stoned — Num 15:36 — 3318
which *b* you out of the land of — Num 15:41 — 3318
he hath *b* thee near to him, and — Num 16:10 — 7126
hast *b* us up out of a land that — Num 16:13 — 5927
Moreover thou hast not *b* us into — Num 16:14 — 935
b forth buds, and bloomed blossoms — Num 17:8 — 3318
Moses *b* out all the rods from — Num 17:9 — 3318
why have ye *b* up the congregation — Num 20:4 — 935
hath *b* us forth out of Egypt — Num 20:16 — 3318
Wherefore have ye *b* us up out of — Num 21:5 — 5927
b him up into the high places of — Num 22:41 — 5927
king of Moab hath *b* me from Aram — Num 23:7 — 5148
he *b* him into the field of Zophim — Num 23:14 — 3947
God *b* them out of Egypt — Num 23:22 — 3318
Balak *b* Balaam unto the top of — Num 23:28 — 3947
God *b* him forth out of Egypt — Num 24:8 — 3318
b unto his brethren a Midianitish — Num 25:6 — 7126
Moses *b* their cause before the — Num 27:5 — 7126
they *b* the captives, and the prey, — Num 31:12 — 935
We have therefore *b* an oblation — Num 31:50 — 7126

Context	Reference	Strong's
b it into the tabernacle of the	Num 31:54	935
until we have *b* them unto their	Num 32:17	935
b it down unto us	Deut 1:25	3381
b us word again, and said, It is a	Deut 1:25	7725
he hath *b* us forth out of the	Deut 1:27	3318
b you forth out of the iron	Deut 4:20	3318
b thee out in his sight with his	Deut 4:37	3318
which *b* thee out of the land of	Deut 5:6	3318
that the LORD thy God *b* thee out	Deut 5:15	3318
b thee into the land which he	Deut 6:10	935
which *b* thee forth out of the	Deut 6:12	3318
the LORD *b* us out of Egypt with a	Deut 6:21	3318
he *b* us out from thence, that he	Deut 6:23	3318
hath the LORD *b* you out with a	Deut 7:8	3318
the LORD thy God *b* thee out	Deut 7:19	3318
which *b* thee forth out of the	Deut 8:14	3318
who *b* thee forth water out of the	Deut 8:15	3318
hath *b* me in to possess this land	Deut 9:4	935
hast *b* forth out of Egypt have	Deut 9:12	3318
which thou hast *b* forth out of	Deut 9:26	3318
he hath *b* them out to slay them	Deut 9:28	3318
when the LORD thy God hath *b* thee	Deut 11:29	935
which *b* you out of the land of	Deut 13:5	3318
which *b* thee out of the land of	Deut 13:10	3318
God *b* thee forth out of Egypt by	Deut 16:1	3318
which *b* thee up out of the land	Deut 20:1	5927
because he hath *b* up an evil name	Deut 22:19	3318
the LORD *b* us forth out of Egypt	Deut 26:8	3318
he hath *b* us into this place, and	Deut 26:9	935
I have *b* the firstfruits of the	Deut 26:10	935
I have *b* away the hallowed things	Deut 26:13	1197
b them forth out of the land of	Deut 29:25	3318
For when I shall have *b* them into	Deut 31:20	935
before I have *b* them into the	Deut 31:21	935
fruits *b* forth by the sun	Deut 33:14	
But she had *b* them up to the roof	Josh 2:6	5927
b out Rahab, and her father, and	Josh 6:23	3318
they *b* out all her kindred, and	Josh 6:23	3318
at all *b* this people over Jordan	Josh 7:7	5674
be *b* according to your tribes	Josh 7:14	7126
and *b* Israel by their tribes	Josh 7:16	7126
And he *b* the family of Judah	Josh 7:17	7126
he *b* the family of the Zarhites	Josh 7:17	7126
he *b* his household man by man	Josh 7:18	7126
b them unto Joshua, and unto all	Josh 7:23	935
they *b* them unto the valley of	Josh 7:24	5927
took alive, and *b* him to Joshua	Josh 8:23	7126
b forth those five kings unto him	Josh 10:23	3318
when they *b* out those kings unto	Josh 10:24	3318
I *b* him word again as it was in	Josh 14:7	7725
of Israel, and *b* them word again	Josh 22:32	7725
and afterward I *b* you out	Josh 24:5	3318
I *b* your fathers out of Egypt	Josh 24:6	3318
b the sea upon them, and covered	Josh 24:7	935
I *b* you into the land of the	Josh 24:8	935
our God, he it is that *b* us up	Josh 24:17	5927
of Israel *b* up out of Egypt	Josh 24:32	5927
they *b* him to Jerusalem, and there	Judg 1:7	935
have *b* you unto the land which I	Judg 2:1	935
which *b* them out of the land of	Judg 2:12	3318
he *b* the present unto Eglon king	Judg 3:17	7126
she *b* forth butter in a lordly	Judg 5:25	7126
I *b* you up from Egypt	Judg 6:8	5927
b you forth out of the house of	Judg 6:8	3318
b it out unto him under the oak,	Judg 6:19	3318
So he *b* down the people unto the	Judg 7:5	3381
b the heads of Oreb and Zeeb to	Judg 7:25	935
thou hast *b* me very low, and thou	Judg 11:35	3766
that they *b* thirty companions to	Judg 14:11	3947
cords, and *b* him up from the rock	Judg 15:13	5927
b up to her seven green withs	Judg 16:8	5927
her, and *b* money in their hand	Judg 16:18	5927
b him down to Gaza, and bound him	Judg 16:21	3381
b him up, and buried him between	Judg 16:31	5927
said unto him, Who *b* thee hither	Judg 18:3	935
she *b* him into her father's house	Judg 19:3	935
So he *b* him into his house, and	Judg 19:21	935
and *b* her forth unto them	Judg 19:25	3318
they *b* them unto the camp to	Judg 21:12	935
the LORD hath *b* me home again	Ruth 1:21	7725
she *b* forth, and gave to her that	Ruth 2:18	3318
b him unto the house of the LORD	1Sa 1:24	935
a bullock, and *b* the child to Eli	1Sa 1:25	935
all that the fleshhook *b* up the	1Sa 2:14	5927
b it to him from year to year,	1Sa 2:19	5927
b it from Eben-ezer unto Ashdod	1Sa 5:1	935
they *b* it into the house of Dagon	1Sa 5:2	935
They have *b* about the ark of the	1Sa 5:10	5437
The Philistines have *b* again the	1Sa 6:21	7725
b up the ark of the LORD, and	1Sa 7:1	935
b it into the house of Abinadab	1Sa 7:1	935
b them up out of Egypt even unto	1Sa 8:8	5927
b them into the parlour, and made	1Sa 9:22	935
I *b* up Israel out of Egypt, and	1Sa 10:18	5927
him, and *b* him no presents	1Sa 10:27	935
that *b* your fathers up out of the	1Sa 12:6	5927
which *b* forth your fathers out of	1Sa 12:8	3318
all the people *b* every man his ox	1Sa 14:34	5066
They have *b* them from the	1Sa 15:15	935
have *b* Agag the king of Amalek,	1Sa 15:20	935
And he sent, and *b* him in	1Sa 16:12	935
Philistine, and *b* it to Jerusalem	1Sa 17:54	935
b him before Saul with the head	1Sa 17:57	935
David *b* their foreskins, and they	1Sa 18:27	935
Jonathan *b* David to Saul, and he	1Sa 19:7	935
for thou hast *b* thy servant into	1Sa 20:8	935
for I have neither *b* my sword nor	1Sa 21:8	3947
then have ye *b* him to me	1Sa 21:14	935
that ye have *b* this fellow to	1Sa 21:15	935
he *b* them before the king of Moab	1Sa 22:4	5148
b away their cattle, and smote	1Sa 23:5	5090
handmaid hath *b* unto my lord	1Sa 25:27	935
her hand that which she had *b* him	1Sa 25:35	935
she *b* it before Saul, and before	1Sa 28:25	5066
Abiathar *b* thither the ephod to	1Sa 30:7	5066
b him to David, and gave him bread	1Sa 30:11	3947
And when he had *b* him down	1Sa 30:16	3381
have *b* them hither unto my lord	2Sa 1:10	935
Saul, and *b* him over to Mahanaim	2Sa 2:8	5674
b in a great spoil with them	2Sa 3:22	935
which *b* him again from the well	2Sa 3:26	7725
they *b* the head of Ish-bosheth	2Sa 4:8	935
thinking to have *b* good tidings	2Sa 4:10	1319
b it out of the house of Abinadab	2Sa 6:3	5375
they *b* it out of the house of	2Sa 6:4	5375
b up the ark of God from the	2Sa 6:12	5927
all the house of Israel *b* up the	2Sa 6:15	5927
they *b* in the ark of the LORD, and	2Sa 6:17	935
I *b* up the children of Israel out	2Sa 7:6	5927
that thou hast *b* me hitherto	2Sa 7:18	935
David's servants, and *b* gifts	2Sa 8:2	5375
servants to David, and *b* gifts	2Sa 8:6	5375
Hadadezer, and *b* them to Jerusalem	2Sa 8:7	935
Joram *b* with him vessels of	2Sa 8:10	1961
b out the Syrians that were	2Sa 10:16	3318
he *b* forth the spoil of the city	2Sa 12:30	3318
he *b* forth the people that were	2Sa 12:31	3318
b them into the chamber to Amnon	2Sa 13:10	935
when she had *b* them unto him to	2Sa 13:11	5066
Then his servant *b* her out	2Sa 13:18	3318
Geshur, and *b* Absalom to Jerusalem	2Sa 14:23	935
B beds, and basons, and earthen	2Sa 17:28	5066
have *b* the king, and his household	2Sa 19:41	5674
whom she *b* up for Adriel the son	2Sa 21:8	3205
he *b* up from thence the bones of	2Sa 21:13	5927
He *b* me forth also into a large	2Sa 22:20	3318
and took it, and *b* it to David	2Sa 23:16	935
Shunammite, and *b* her to the king	1Kin 1:3	935
David's mule, and *b* him to Gihon	1Kin 1:38	3212
they *b* him down from the altar	1Kin 1:53	3381
Benaiah *b* the king word again,	1Kin 2:30	7725
went, and *b* his servants from Gath	1Kin 2:40	935
b her into the city of David,	1Kin 3:1	935
they *b* a sword before the king	1Kin 3:24	935
they *b* presents, and served	1Kin 4:21	5066
dromedaries *b* they unto the place	1Kin 4:28	935
they *b* great stones, costly	1Kin 5:17	5265
ready before it was *b* thither	1Kin 6:7	4551
Solomon *b* in the things which	1Kin 7:51	935
they *b* up the ark of the LORD, and	1Kin 8:4	5927
the priests *b* in the ark of the	1Kin 8:6	935
Since the day that I *b* forth my	1Kin 8:16	3318
when he *b* them out of the land of	1Kin 8:21	3318
who *b* forth their fathers out of	1Kin 9:9	3318
LORD *b* upon them all this evil	1Kin 9:9	935
talents, and *b* it to king Solomon	1Kin 9:28	935
that *b* gold from Ophir	1Kin 10:11	5375
b in from Ophir great plenty of	1Kin 10:11	935
they *b* every man his present,	1Kin 10:25	935
Solomon had horses *b* out of Egypt	1Kin 10:28	4161
which *b* thee up out of the land	1Kin 12:28	5927
unto the prophet that *b* him back	1Kin 13:20	7725
the prophet whom he had *b* back	1Kin 13:23	7725
when the prophet that *b* him back	1Kin 13:26	7725
it upon the ass, and *b* it back	1Kin 13:29	7725
b them back into the guard	1Kin 14:28	7725
he *b* in the things which his	1Kin 15:15	935
And the ravens *b* him bread	1Kin 17:6	935
hast thou also *b* evil upon the	1Kin 17:20	
b him down out of the chamber	1Kin 17:23	3381
Elijah *b* them down to the brook	1Kin 18:40	3381
departed, and *b* him word again	1Kin 20:9	7725
b a man unto me, and said, Keep	1Kin 20:39	935
king died, and was *b* to Samaria	1Kin 22:37	935
sons, who *b* the vessels to her	2Kin 4:5	5066
b him to his mother, he sat on	2Kin 4:20	935
b the man of God bread of the	2Kin 4:42	935
had *b* away captive out of the	2Kin 5:2	7617
he *b* the letter to the king of	2Kin 5:6	935
at his hands that which he *b*	2Kin 5:20	935
to them that *b* up Ahab's children	2Kin 10:1	539
men of the city, which *b* them up	2Kin 10:6	1431
They have *b* the heads of the	2Kin 10:8	935
he *b* them forth vestments	2Kin 10:22	3318
I have *b* into your hands escape	2Kin 10:24	935
they *b* forth the images out of	2Kin 10:26	3318
b them to him into the house of	2Kin 11:4	935
he *b* forth the king's son, and put	2Kin 11:12	3318
they *b* down the king from the	2Kin 11:19	3381
is *b* into the house of the LORD	2Kin 12:4	935
was *b* into the house of the LORD	2Kin 12:9	935
of the money that was *b* into the	2Kin 12:13	935
sin money was not *b* into the	2Kin 12:16	935
And they *b* him on horses	2Kin 14:20	5375
he *b* also the brasen altar, which	2Kin 16:14	7126
b no present to the king of	2Kin 17:4	5927
which had *b* them up out of the	2Kin 17:7	5927
of Assyria *b* men from Babylon	2Kin 17:24	935
the priests whom ye *b* from thence	2Kin 17:27	1540
who *b* you up out of the land of	2Kin 17:36	5927
now have I *b* it to pass, that	2Kin 19:25	935
he *b* the shadow ten degrees	2Kin 20:11	7725
b water into the city, are they	2Kin 20:20	935
is *b* into the house of the LORD	2Kin 22:4	935
b the king word again, and said,	2Kin 22:9	7725
they *b* the king word again	2Kin 22:20	7725
he *b* out the grove from the house	2Kin 23:6	3318
he *b* all the priests out of the	2Kin 23:8	935
b him to Jerusalem, and buried him	2Kin 23:30	935
of Babylon *b* captive to Babylon	2Kin 24:16	935
b him up to the king of Babylon	2Kin 25:6	5927
b them to the king of Babylon to	2Kin 25:20	3212
b them unto Halah, and Habor, and	1Chr 5:26	935
b them to Jabesh, and buried their	1Chr 10:12	935
and took it, and *b* it to David	1Chr 11:18	935
jeopardy of their lives they *b* it	1Chr 11:19	935
b bread on asses, and on camels,	1Chr 12:40	935
So David *b* not the ark home to	1Chr 13:13	5493
the LORD *b* the fear of him upon	1Chr 14:17	5414
Thus all Israel *b* up the ark of	1Chr 15:28	5927
So they *b* the ark of God, and set	1Chr 16:1	935
that I *b* up Israel unto this day	1Chr 17:5	5927
that thou hast *b* me hitherto	1Chr 17:16	935
David's servants, and *b* gifts	1Chr 18:2	5375
David's servants, and *b* gifts	1Chr 18:6	5375
Hadarezer, and *b* them to Jerusalem	1Chr 18:7	935
b David very much brass,	1Chr 18:8	3947
the gold that he *b* from all these	1Chr 18:11	5375
he *b* also exceeding much spoil	1Chr 20:2	3318
he *b* out the people that were in	1Chr 20:3	3318
they of Tyre *b* much cedar wood to	1Chr 22:4	935
But the ark of God had David *b* up	2Chr 1:4	5927
Solomon had horses *b* out of Egypt	2Chr 1:16	4161
b forth out of Egypt a chariot	2Chr 1:17	3318
so *b* they out horses for all the	2Chr 1:17	3318
Solomon *b* in all the things that	2Chr 5:1	935
they *b* up the ark, and the	2Chr 5:5	5927
the priests *b* in the ark of the	2Chr 5:7	935
Since the day that I *b* forth my	2Chr 6:5	3318
which *b* them forth out of the	2Chr 7:22	3318
therefore hath he *b* all this evil	2Chr 7:22	935
Solomon *b* up the daughter of	2Chr 8:11	5927
gold, and *b* them to king Solomon	2Chr 8:18	935
which *b* gold from Ophir, *b*	2Chr 9:10	935
which she had *b* unto the king	2Chr 9:12	935
that which chapmen and merchants *b*.	2Chr 9:14	935
governors of the country *b* gold	2Chr 9:14	935
they *b* every man his present,	2Chr 9:24	935
they *b* unto Solomon horses out of	2Chr 9:28	3318
young men that were *b* up with him	2Chr 10:8	1431
the young men that were *b* up with	2Chr 10:10	1431
b them again into the guard	2Chr 12:11	7725
Israel were *b* under at that time	2Chr 13:18	3665
of the spoil which they had *b*	2Chr 15:11	935
he *b* into the house of God the	2Chr 15:18	935
Then Asa *b* out silver and gold out	2Chr 16:2	3318
all Judah *b* to Jehoshaphat	2Chr 17:5	5414
b Jehoshaphat presents, and	2Chr 17:11	935
and the Arabians *b* him flocks	2Chr 17:11	935
b them back unto the LORD God of	2Chr 19:4	7725
hid in Samaria,) and *b* him to Jehu	2Chr 22:9	935
Then they *b* out the king's son,	2Chr 23:11	3318
Then Jehoiada the priest *b* out	2Chr 23:14	3318
b down the king from the house of	2Chr 23:20	3381
b in, and cast into the chest,	2Chr 24:10	935
b unto the king's office by the	2Chr 24:11	935
they *b* the rest of the money	2Chr 24:14	935
b them unto the top of the rock,	2Chr 25:12	935
that he *b* the gods of the	2Chr 25:14	935
b him to Jerusalem, and brake down	2Chr 25:23	935
they *b* him upon horses, and buried	2Chr 25:28	5375
captives, and *b* them to Damascus	2Chr 28:5	935
them, and *b* the spoil to Samaria	2Chr 28:8	935
b them to Jericho, the city of	2Chr 28:15	935
For the LORD *b* Judah low because	2Chr 28:19	3665
but they *b* him not into the	2Chr 28:27	935
he *b* in the priests and the	2Chr 29:4	935
b out all the uncleanness that	2Chr 29:16	3318
they *b* seven bullocks, and seven	2Chr 29:21	935
they *b* forth the he goats for the	2Chr 29:23	5066
the congregation *b* in sacrifices	2Chr 29:31	935
which the congregation *b*	2Chr 29:32	935
b in the burnt offerings into the	2Chr 30:15	935
the children of Israel *b* in	2Chr 31:5	935
all things *b* they in abundantly	2Chr 31:5	935
they also *b* in the tithe of oxen	2Chr 31:6	935
b in the offerings and the tithes	2Chr 31:12	935
many *b* gifts unto the LORD to	2Chr 32:23	935
b it straight down to the west	2Chr 32:30	3474
Wherefore the LORD *b* upon them	2Chr 33:11	935
b him again to Jerusalem into his	2Chr 33:13	7725
that was *b* into the house of God	2Chr 34:9	935
when they *b* out the money that	2Chr 34:14	3318
was *b* into the house of the LORD	2Chr 34:14	935
b the king word back again,	2Chr 34:16	7725
So they *b* the king word again	2Chr 34:28	7725
they *b* him to Jerusalem, and he	2Chr 35:24	3212
b him to Babylon, with the goodly	2Chr 36:10	935
Therefore he *b* upon them the king	2Chr 36:17	5927
all these he *b* to Babylon	2Chr 36:18	935
Also Cyrus the king *b* forth the	Ezr 1:7	3318
had *b* forth out of Jerusalem	Ezr 1:7	3318
b up from Babylon unto Jerusalem	Ezr 1:11	5927
of Assur, which *b* us up hither	Ezr 4:2	5927
great and noble Asnapper *b* over	Ezr 4:10	1541
b them into the temple of Babylon	Ezr 5:14	2987
b unto Babylon, be restored, and	Ezr 6:5	2987
b again unto the temple which is	Ezr 6:5	1946
they *b* us a man of understanding	Ezr 8:18	935
God had *b* their counsel to nought	Neh 4:15	6565
are *b* unto bondage already	Neh 5:5	3533
Ezra the priest *b* the law before	Neh 8:2	935
b them, and made themselves booths	Neh 8:16	935
God that *b* thee up out of Egypt	Neh 9:18	5927
art just in all that is *b* upon us	Neh 9:33	935
Then I *b* up the princes of Judah	Neh 12:31	5927
thither *b* I again the vessels of	Neh 13:9	7725
Then *b* all Judah the tithe of the	Neh 13:12	935
which they *b* into Jerusalem on	Neh 13:15	935
Tyre also therein, which *b* fish	Neh 13:16	935
burden be *b* in on the sabbath day	Neh 13:19	935
the queen to be *b* in before him	Est 1:17	935
he *b* up Hadassah, that is, Esther	Est 2:7	539
that Esther was *b* also unto the	Est 2:8	3947
as when she was *b* up with him	Est 2:20	539
Let the royal apparel be *b* which	Est 6:8	935
b him on horseback through the	Est 6:11	7392
the palace was *b* before the king	Est 9:11	935
Now a thing was secretly *b* to me	Job 4:12	1589
thou *b* me forth out of the womb	Job 10:18	3318
and they are *b* low, but he	Job 14:21	6819
they shall be *b* forth to the day	Job 21:30	2986

Context	Reference	No.
Yet shall he be *b* to the grave	Job 21:32	2986
while, but are gone and *b* low	Job 24:24	4355
from my youth he was *b* up with me	Job 31:18	1431
evil that the LORD had *b* upon him	Job 42:11	935
mischief, and *b* forth falsehood	Ps 7:14	3205
He *b* me forth also into a large	Ps 18:19	3318
They are *b* down and fallen	Ps 20:8	3766
thou hast *b* me into the dust of	Ps 22:15	8239
thou hast *b* up my soul from the	Ps 30:3	5927
b to confusion that devise my	Ps 35:4	2659
b to confusion together that	Ps 35:26	2659
He *b* me up also out of an	Ps 40:2	5927
She shall be *b* unto the king in	Ps 45:14	2986
follow her shall be *b* unto thee	Ps 45:14	935
and rejoicing shall they be *b*	Ps 45:15	2986
for they are *b* unto shame	Ps 71:24	2659
How are they *b* into desolation,	Ps 73:19	
He *b* streams also out of the rock	Ps 78:16	3318
by his power he *b* in the south	Ps 78:26	5090
he *b* them to the border of his	Ps 78:54	935
he *b* him to feed Jacob his people	Ps 78:71	935
for we are *b* very low	Ps 79:8	1809
Thou hast *b* a vine out of Egypt	Ps 80:8	5265
which *b* thee out of the land of	Ps 81:10	5927
thou hast *b* back the captivity of	Ps 85:1	7725
thou hast *b* his strong holds to	Ps 89:40	7760
Before the mountains were *b* forth	Ps 90:2	3205
Their land *b* forth frogs in	Ps 105:30	8317
He *b* them forth also with silver	Ps 105:37	3318
he *b* quails, and satisifed them	Ps 105:40	935
he *b* forth his people with joy,	Ps 105:43	3318
they were *b* into subjection under	Ps 106:42	3665
were *b* low for their iniquity	Ps 106:43	4355
Therefore he *b* down their heart	Ps 107:12	3665
He *b* them out of darkness and the	Ps 107:14	3318
b low through oppression,	Ps 107:39	7817
I was *b* low, and he helped me	Ps 116:6	1809
b out Israel from among them	Ps 136:11	3318
for I am *b* very low	Ps 142:6	1809
a man is *b* to a piece of bread	Prov 6:26	
were no depths, I was *b* forth	Prov 8:24	2342
before the hills was I *b* forth	Prov 8:25	2342
was by him, as one *b* up with him	Prov 8:30	539
of musick shall be *b* low	Eccl 12:4	7817
the king hath *b* me into his	Song 1:4	935
He *b* me to the banqueting house,	Song 2:4	935
until I had *b* him into my	Song 3:4	935
there thy mother *b* thee forth	Song 8:5	2254
there she *b* thee forth that bare	Song 8:5	2254
b up children, and they have	Is 1:2	7311
and he shall be *b* low	Is 2:12	8213
grapes, and it *b* forth wild grapes	Is 5:2	6213
grapes, *b* it forth wild grapes	Is 5:4	6213
And the mean man shall be *b* down	Is 5:15	7817
Thy pomp is *b* down to the grave,	Is 14:11	3381
Yet thou shalt be *b* down to hell	Is 14:15	3381
is laid waste, and *b* to silence	Is 15:1	1820
is laid waste, and *b* to silence	Is 15:1	1820
be *b* unto the LORD of hosts of a	Is 18:7	2986
b water to him that was thirsty	Is 21:14	857
and he *b* it to ruin	Is 23:13	7760
the terrible ones shall be *b* low	Is 25:5	6030
we have as it were *b* forth wind	Is 26:18	3205
And thou shalt be *b* down, and shalt	Is 29:4	8213
the terrible one is *b* to nought	Is 29:20	656
now have I *b* it to pass, that	Is 37:26	935
have *b* down all their nobles, and	Is 43:14	3381
Thou hast not *b* me the small	Is 43:23	935
the woman, What hast thou *b* forth	Is 45:10	2342
I have *b* him, and he shall make	Is 48:15	935
and who hath *b* up these	Is 49:21	1431
the sons whom she hath *b* forth	Is 51:18	3205
all the sons that she hath *b* up	Is 51:18	1431
he is *b* as a lamb to the	Is 53:7	2986
therefore his arm *b* salvation	Is 59:16	3467
and that their kings may be *b*	Is 60:11	5090
they that have *b* it together	Is 62:9	6908
mine own arm *b* salvation unto me	Is 63:5	3467
Where is he that *b* them up out of	Is 63:11	5927
Before she travailed, she *b* forth	Is 66:7	3205
she *b* forth her children	Is 66:8	3205
Where is the LORD that *b* us up	Jer 2:6	5927
I *b* you into a plentiful country,	Jer 2:7	935
to a stone, Thou hast *b* me forth	Jer 2:27	3205
them in the day that I *b* them out	Jer 7:22	3318
into plates is *b* from Tarshish	Jer 10:9	935
I *b* them forth out of the land of	Jer 11:4	3318
I *b* them up out of the land of	Jer 11:7	5927
an ox that is *b* to the slaughter	Jer 11:19	2986
I have *b* upon them against the	Jer 15:8	935
that *b* up the children of Israel	Jer 16:14	5927
that *b* up the children of Israel	Jer 16:15	5927
that Pashur *b* forth Jeremiah out	Jer 20:3	3318
man who *b* tidings to my father	Jer 20:15	1319
which *b* up the children of Israel	Jer 23:7	5927
But, The LORD liveth, which *b* up	Jer 23:8	5927
and had *b* them to Babylon	Jer 24:1	935
b him unto Jehoiakim the king	Jer 26:23	935
shortly be *b* again from Babylon	Jer 27:16	7725
hast *b* forth thy people Israel	Jer 32:21	3318
Like as I have *b* all this great	Jer 32:42	935
b them into subjection for	Jer 34:11	3533
I *b* them forth out of the land of	Jer 34:13	3318
b them into subjection, to be	Jer 34:16	3533
I *b* them into the house of the	Jer 35:4	935
Jeremiah, and *b* him to the princes	Jer 37:14	935
b forth to the king of Babylon's	Jer 38:22	3318
they *b* him up to Nebuchadnezzar	Jer 39:5	5927
Now the LORD hath *b* it, and done	Jer 40:3	935
whom he had *b* again from Gibeon	Jer 41:16	7725
evil that I have *b* upon Jerusalem	Jer 44:2	935
hath *b* forth the weapons of his	Jer 50:25	3318
The LORD hath *b* forth our	Jer 51:10	3318
b them to the king of Babylon to	Jer 52:26	3212

Context	Reference	No.
b him forth out of prison,	Jer 52:31	3218
he hath *b* them down to the ground	Lam 2:2	5060
b up hath mine enemy consumed	Lam 2:22	7235
b me into darkness, but not into	Lam 3:2	3212
they that were *b* up in scarlet	Lam 4:5	539
b me in the visions of God to	Eze 8:3	935
he *b* me to the door of the court	Eze 8:7	935
Then he *b* me to the door of the	Eze 8:14	935
he *b* me into the inner court of	Eze 8:16	935
b me unto the east gate of the	Eze 11:1	935
b me in a vision by the Spirit of	Eze 11:24	935
I *b* forth my stuff by day, as	Eze 12:7	3318
I *b* it forth in the twilight, and	Eze 12:7	3318
a remnant that shall be *b* forth	Eze 14:22	3318
evil that I have *b* upon Jerusalem	Eze 14:22	935
all that I have *b* upon it	Eze 14:22	935
b forth branches, and shot forth	Eze 17:6	5375
LORD have *b* down the high tree	Eze 17:24	8213
she *b* up one of her whelps	Eze 19:3	5927
they *b* him with chains unto the	Eze 19:4	935
b him to the king of Babylon	Eze 19:9	935
they *b* him into holds, that his	Eze 19:9	935
b them into the wilderness	Eze 20:10	935
in whose sight I *b* them out	Eze 20:14	3318
in whose sight I *b* them forth	Eze 20:22	3318
For when I had *b* them into the	Eze 20:28	935
it cometh, and shall be *b* to pass	Eze 21:7	1961
she her whoredoms *b* from Egypt	Eze 23:8	
thy whoredom *b* from the land of	Eze 23:27	
b Sabeans from the wilderness	Eze 23:42	935
b out of the isles of Chittim	Eze 27:6	
they *b* thee for a present horns	Eze 27:15	7725
Thy rowers have *b* thee into great	Eze 27:26	935
thou shalt not be *b* together	Eze 29:5	622
shall be *b* to destroy the land	Eze 30:11	935
yet shalt thou be *b* down with the	Eze 31:18	3381
neither have ye *b* again that	Eze 34:4	7725
b you up out of your graves,	Eze 37:13	5927
that is *b* back from the sword	Eze 38:8	7725
but it is *b* forth out of the	Eze 38:8	3318
When I have *b* them again from the	Eze 39:27	7725
was upon me, and *b* me thither	Eze 40:1	935
In the visions of God *b* he me	Eze 40:2	935
he *b* me thither, and, behold,	Eze 40:3	935
them unto thee art thou *b* hither	Eze 40:4	935
Then *b* he me into the outward	Eze 40:17	935
After that he *b* me toward the	Eze 40:24	3212
he *b* me to the inner court by the	Eze 40:28	935
he *b* me into the inner court	Eze 40:32	935
he *b* me to the north gate, and	Eze 40:35	935
he *b* me to the porch of the house	Eze 40:48	935
he *b* me by the steps whereby they	Eze 40:49	
Afterward he *b* me to the temple,	Eze 41:1	935
Then he *b* me forth into the utter	Eze 42:1	3318
he *b* me into the chamber that was	Eze 42:1	935
he *b* me forth toward the gate	Eze 42:15	3318
Afterward he *b* me to the gate,	Eze 43:1	3212
b me into the inner court	Eze 43:5	935
Then he *b* me back the way of the	Eze 44:1	7725
Then *b* he me the way of the north	Eze 44:4	935
In that ye have *b* into my	Eze 44:7	935
After he *b* me through the entry,	Eze 46:19	935
Then he *b* me forth into the utter	Eze 46:21	3318
Afterward he *b* me again unto the	Eze 47:1	7725
Then *b* he me out of the way of	Eze 47:2	3318
he *b* me through the waters	Eze 47:3	5674
and *b* me through the waters	Eze 47:4	5674
a thousand, and *b* me through	Eze 47:4	5674
Then he *b* me, and caused me to	Eze 47:6	3212
which being *b* forth into the sea,	Eze 47:8	3318
he *b* the vessels into the	Dan 1:2	935
Now God had *b* Daniel into favour	Dan 1:9	5414
b them in before Nebuchadnezzar	Dan 1:18	935
Then Arioch *b* in Daniel before	Dan 2:25	5954
Then they *b* these men before the	Dan 3:13	858
Then they *b* the golden vessels	Dan 5:3	858
Then was Daniel *b* in before the	Dan 5:13	5954
the king my father *b* out of Jewry	Dan 5:13	858
have been *b* in before me, that	Dan 5:15	5954
they have *b* the vessels of his	Dan 5:23	858
they *b* Daniel, and cast him into	Dan 6:16	858
And a stone was *b*, and laid upon	Dan 6:17	858
of musick *b* before him	Dan 6:18	5954
they *b* those men which had	Dan 6:24	858
they *b* him near before him	Dan 7:13	7127
upon the evil, and *b* it upon us	Dan 9:14	935
that hast *b* thy people forth out	Dan 9:15	3318
be given up, and they that *b* her	Dan 11:6	935
the LORD *b* Israel out of Egypt	Hos 12:13	5927
Also I *b* you up from the land of	Amos 2:10	5927
the whole family which I *b* up	Amos 3:1	5927
Have not I *b* up Israel out of the	Amos 9:7	5927
have *b* thee even to the border	Obad 7	7971
yet hast thou *b* up my life from	Jonah 2:6	5927
she which travaileth hath *b* forth	Mic 5:3	3205
For I *b* thee up out of the land	Mic 6:4	5927
away captive, she shall be *b* up	Nah 2:7	5927
and when ye *b* it home, I did blow	Hag 1:9	935
the olive tree, hath not *b* forth	Hag 2:19	5375
pride of Assyria shall be *b* down	Zec 10:11	3381
ye *b* that which was torn, and the	Mal 1:13	935
thus ye *b* an offering	Mal 1:13	935
And after they were *b* to Babylon	Mt 1:12	*3350*
she had *b* forth her firstborn son	Mt 1:25	*5088*
they *b* unto him all sick people	Mt 4:24	*4374*
they *b* unto him many that were	Mt 8:16	*4374*
they *b* to him a man sick of the	Mt 9:2	*4374*
behold, they *b* to him a dumb man	Mt 9:32	*4374*
ye shall be *b* before governors and	Mt 10:18	*71*
heaven, shalt be *b* down to hell	Mt 11:23	*2601*
Then was *b* unto him one possessed	Mt 12:22	*4374*
against itself is *b* to desolation	Mt 12:25	*2049*
ground, and *b* forth fruit, some an	Mt 13:8	*1325*
b forth fruit, then appeared the	Mt 13:26	*4160*

Context	Reference	No.
And his head was *b* in a charger	Mt 14:11	*5342*
and she *b* it to her mother	Mt 14:11	*5342*
b unto him all that were diseased	Mt 14:35	*4374*
because ye have *b* no bread	Mt 16:8	*2989*
I *b* him to thy disciples, and they	Mt 17:16	*4374*
one was *b* unto him, which owed	Mt 18:24	*4374*
Then were there *b* unto him little	Mt 19:13	*4374*
b the ass, and the colt, and put on	Mt 21:7	*71*
And they *b* unto him a penny	Mt 22:19	*4374*
b other five talents, saying,	Mt 25:20	*4374*
b again the thirty pieces of	Mt 27:3	*654*
they *b* unto him all that were	Mk 1:32	*5342*
b forth, some thirty, and some	Mk 4:8	*5342*
Is a candle *b* to be put under a	Mk 4:21	*2064*
But when the fruit is *b* forth	Mk 4:29	*3860*
and commanded his head to be *b*	Mk 6:27	*5342*
b his head in a charger, and gave	Mk 6:28	*5342*
I have *b* unto thee my son, which	Mk 9:17	*5342*
And they *b* him unto him	Mk 9:20	*5342*
they *b* young children to him,	Mk 10:13	*4374*
rebuked those that *b* them	Mk 10:13	*4374*
they *b* the colt to Jesus, and cast	Mk 11:7	*71*
And they *b* it	Mk 12:16	*5342*
ye shall be *b* before rulers and	Mk 13:9	*2476*
and she *b* forth a son	Lk 1:57	*1080*
she *b* forth her firstborn son, and	Lk 2:7	*5088*
they *b* him to Jerusalem, to	Lk 2:22	*321*
when the parents *b* in the child	Lk 2:27	*1521*
mountain and hill shall be *b* low	Lk 3:5	*5013*
he *b* him to Jerusalem, and set him	Lk 4:9	*71*
Nazareth, where he had been *b* up	Lk 4:16	*5142*
divers diseases *b* them unto him	Lk 4:40	*71*
when they had *b* their ships to	Lk 5:11	*2609*
men *b* in a bed a man which was	Lk 5:18	*5342*
b an alabaster box of ointment,	Lk 7:37	*2865*
b him to an inn, and took care of	Lk 10:34	*71*
against itself is *b* to desolation	Lk 11:17	*2049*
rich man *b* forth plentifully	Lk 12:16	*2164*
they *b* unto him also infants,	Lk 18:15	*4374*
and commanded him to be *b* unto him	Lk 18:40	*71*
And they *b* him to Jesus	Lk 19:35	*71*
being *b* before kings and rulers	Lk 21:12	*71*
b him into the high priest's	Lk 22:54	*1521*
Ye have *b* this man unto me, as	Lk 23:14	*4374*
And he *b* him to Jesus	Jn 1:42	*71*
Hath any man *b* him ought to eat	Jn 4:33	*5342*
unto them, Why have ye not *b* him	Jn 7:45	*71*
Pharisees *b* unto him a woman	Jn 8:3	*71*
They *b* to the Pharisees him that	Jn 9:13	*71*
that kept the door, and *b* in Peter	Jn 18:16	*1521*
he *b* Jesus forth, and sat down in	Jn 19:13	*71*
b a mixture of myrrh and aloes,	Jn 19:39	*5342*
b the prices of the things that	Acts 4:34	*5342*
b the money, and laid it at the	Acts 4:37	*5342*
b a certain part, and laid it at	Acts 5:2	*5342*
Insomuch that they *b* forth the	Acts 5:15	*1627*
doors, and *b* them forth, and said,	Acts 5:19	*1806*
sent to the prison to have them *b*	Acts 5:21	*71*
and *b* them without violence	Acts 5:26	*71*
And when they had *b* them, they set	Acts 5:27	*71*
were scattered, and *b* to nought	Acts 5:36	*1096*
him, and *b* him to the council,	Acts 6:12	*71*
He *b* them out, after that he had	Acts 7:36	*1806*
which *b* us out of the land of	Acts 7:40	*1806*
after *b* in with Jesus into the	Acts 7:45	*1521*
the hand, and *b* him into Damascus	Acts 9:8	*1521*
b him to the apostles, and	Acts 9:27	*71*
they *b* him down to Caesarea, and	Acts 9:30	*2609*
they *b* him into the upper chamber	Acts 9:39	*321*
found him, he *b* him unto Antioch	Acts 11:26	*71*
when Herod would have *b* him forth	Acts 12:6	*4254*
Lord had *b* him out of the prison	Acts 12:17	*1806*
which had been *b* up with Herod	Acts 13:1	*4939*
with an high arm *b* he them out of	Acts 13:17	*1806*
b oxen and garlands unto the gates	Acts 14:13	*5342*
being *b* on their way by the	Acts 15:3	*4311*
which *b* her masters much gain by	Acts 16:16	*3930*
b them to the magistrates, saying	Acts 16:20	*4317*
b them out, and said, Sirs, what	Acts 16:30	*4254*
when he had *b* them into his house	Acts 16:34	*321*
b them out, and desired them to	Acts 16:39	*1806*
conducted Paul *b* him unto Athens	Acts 17:15	*71*
b him unto Areopagus, saying, May	Acts 17:19	*71*
b him to the judgment seat,	Acts 18:12	*71*
So that from his body were *b* unto	Acts 19:12	*2018*
arts *b* their books together	Acts 19:19	*4851*
Diana, *b* no small gain unto the	Acts 19:24	*3930*
For ye have *b* hither these men,	Acts 19:37	*71*
they *b* the young man alive, and	Acts 20:12	*71*
they all *b* us on our way, with	Acts 21:5	*4311*
b with them one Mnason of Cyprus,	Acts 21:16	*71*
further *b* Greeks also into the	Acts 21:28	*1521*
that Paul had *b* into the temple	Acts 21:29	*1521*
yet *b* up in this city at the feet	Acts 22:3	*397*
him to be *b* into the castle	Acts 22:24	*71*
b Paul down, and set him before	Acts 22:30	*2609*
b him to the chief captain, and	Acts 23:18	*71*
I *b* him forth into their council	Acts 23:28	*2609*
b him by night to Antipatris	Acts 23:31	*71*
seat commanded Paul to be *b*	Acts 25:6	*71*
commanded the man to be *b* forth	Acts 25:17	*71*
they *b* none accusation of such	Acts 25:18	*2018*
commandment Paul was *b* forth	Acts 25:23	*71*
Wherefore I have *b* him forth	Acts 25:26	*4254*
thou must be *b* before Caesar	Acts 27:24	*3936*
to be *b* on my way thitherward by	Rom 15:24	*4311*
but I will not be *b* under the	1Cor 6:12	*1850*
then shall be *b* to pass the	1Cor 15:54	*1096*
of you to be *b* on my way toward	2Cor 1:16	*4311*
of false brethren unawares *b* in	Gal 2:4	*3920*
b us good tidings of your faith	1Th 3:6	*2097*
if she have *b* up children	1Ti 5:10	*5044*
For we *b* nothing into this world,	1Ti 6:7	*1533*
abolished death, and hath *b* life	2Ti 1:10	*5461*

when Paul was *b* before Nero the 2Ti s *3936*
whose blood is *b* into the Heb 13:11 *1533*
that *b* again from the dead our Heb 13:20 *321*
the earth *b* forth her fruit Jas 5:18 *985*
b unto you at the revelation of 1Pet 1:13 *5342*
of the same is he *b* in bondage 2Pet 2:19 *1402*
she *b* forth a man child, who was Rev 12:5 *5088*
woman which *b* forth the man child Rev 12:13 *5088*

BROUGHTEST
which thou *b* out of the land of Ex 32:7 5927
(for thou *b* up this people in thy Num 14:13 5927
the land whence thou *b* us out say Deut 9:28 3318
which thou *b* out by thy mighty Deut 9:29 3318
that leddest out and *b* in Israel 2Sa 5:2 935
which thou *b* forth out of Egypt, 1Kin 8:51 3318
when thou *b* our fathers out of 1Kin 8:53 3318
that leddest out and *b* in Israel 1Chr 11:2 935
b him forth out of Ur of the Neh 9:7 3318
b forth water for them out of the Neh 9:15 3318
b them into the land, concerning Neh 9:23 935
Thou *b* us into the net Ps 66:11 935
but thou *b* us out into a wealthy Ps 66:12 3318

BROW
is an iron sinew, and thy *b* brass Is 48:4 4696
led him unto the *b* of the hill Lk 4:29 *3790*

BROWN
all the *b* cattle among the sheep, Gen 30:32 2345
b among the sheep, that shall be Gen 30:33 2345
all the *b* among the sheep, and Gen 30:35 2345
all the *b* in the flock of Laban Gen 30:40 2345

BRUISE
it shall *b* thy head, and thou Gen 3:15 7779
head, and thou shalt *b* his heel Gen 3:15 7779
nor *b* it with his horsemen Is 28:28 1854
Yet it pleased the LORD to *b* him Is 53:10 1792
Thy *b* is incurable, and thy wound Jer 30:12 7667
shall it break in pieces and *b* Dan 2:40 7490
There is no healing of thy *b* Nah 3:19 7667
the God of peace shall *b* Satan Rom 16:20 *4937*

BRUISED
unto the LORD that which is *b* Lev 22:24 4600
upon the staff of this *b* reed 2Kin 18:21 7533
Bread corn is *b* Is 28:28 1854
A *b* reed shall he not break, and Is 42:3 7533
he was *b* for our iniquities Is 53:5 1792
there they *b* the teats of their Eze 23:3 6213
they *b* the breasts of her Eze 23:8 6213
A *b* reed shall he not break, and Mt 12:20 *4937*
to set at liberty them that are *b* Lk 4:18 *2352*

BRUISES
but wounds, and *b*, and putrifying Is 1:6 2250

BRUISING
in *b* thy teats by the Egyptians Eze 23:21 6213
b him hardly departeth from him Lk 9:39 *4937*

BRUIT
the noise of the *b* is come Jer 10:22 8052
all that hear the *b* of thee shall Nah 3:19 8088

BRUTE
But these, as natural *b* beasts 2Pet 2:12 *249*
as *b* beasts, in those things they Jude 10 *249*

BRUTISH
the *b* person perish, and leave Ps 49:10 1197
A *b* man knoweth not Ps 92:6 1197
Understand, ye *b* among the people Ps 94:8 1197
but he that hateth reproof is *b* Prov 12:1 1197
Surely I am more *b* than any man Prov 30:2 1197
of Pharaoh is become *b* Is 19:11 1197
But they are altogether *b* Jer 10:8 1197
Every man is *b* in his knowledge Jer 10:14 1197
For the pastors are become *b* Jer 10:21 1197
Every man is *b* by his knowledge Jer 51:17 1197
thee into the hand of *b* men Eze 21:31 1197

BUCKET
the nations are as a drop of a *b* Is 40:15 1805

BUCKETS
shall pour the water out of his *b* Num 24:7 1805

BUCKLER
he is a *b* to all them that trust 2Sa 22:31 4043
valiant men, men able to bear *b* 1Chr 5:18 4043
that could handle shield and *b* 1Chr 12:8 7420
my *b*, and the horn of my salvation Ps 18:2 4043
he is a *b* to all those that trust Ps 18:30 4043
Take hold of shield and *b*, and Ps 35:2 6793
truth shall be thy shield and *b* Ps 91:4 5507
he is a *b* to them that walk Prov 2:7 4043
Order ye the *b* and shield, and draw Jer 46:3 4043
which shall set against thee *b* Eze 23:24 6793
lift up the *b* against thee Eze 26:8 6793

BUCKLERS
captains of hundreds spears, and *b* 2Chr 23:9 4043
upon the thick bosses of his *b* Job 15:26 4043
whereon there hang a thousand *b* Song 4:4 4043
even a great company with *b* Eze 38:4 6793
both the shields and the *b* Eze 39:9 6793

BUD
the scent of water it will *b* Job 14:9 6524
to cause the *b* of the tender herb Job 38:27 4161
I make the horn of David to *b* Ps 132:17 6779
and the pomegranates *b* forth Song 7:12 5132
when the *b* is perfect, and the Is 18:5 6525
Israel shall blossom and *b* Is 27:6 6524
and maketh it bring forth and *b* Is 55:10 6779
as the earth bringeth forth her *b* Is 61:11 6779
to multiply as the *b* of the field Eze 16:7 6779
of the house of Israel to *b* forth Eze 29:21 6779
the *b* shall yield no meal Hos 8:7 6779

BUDDED
and it was as though it *b*, and her Gen 40:10 6524
Aaron for the house of Levi was *b* Num 17:8 6524
flourished, and the pomegranates *b* Song 6:11 5132
rod hath blossomed, pride hath *b* Eze 7:10 6524
had manna, and Aaron's rod that *b* Heb 9:4 *985*

BUDS
was budded, and brought forth *b* Num 17:8 6525

BUFFET
to *b* him, and to say unto him, Mk 14:65 *2852*
the messenger of Satan to *b* me 2Cor 12:7 *2852*

BUFFETED
they spit in his face, and *b* him Mt 26:67 *2852*
and thirst, and are naked, and are *b* 1Cor 4:11 *2852*
when ye be *b* for your faults, ye 1Pet 2:20 *2852*

BUILD
let us *b* us a city and a tower, Gen 11:4 1129
and they left off to *b* the city Gen 11:8 1129
thou shalt not *b* it of hewn stone Ex 20:25 1129
B me here seven altars, and Num 23:1 1129
B me here seven altars, and Num 23:29 1129
We will *b* sheepfolds here for our Num 32:16 1129
B you cities for your little ones Num 32:24 1129
thou shalt *b* bulwarks against the Deut 20:20 1129
will not *b* up his brother's house Deut 25:9 1129
there shalt thou *b* an altar unto Deut 27:5 1129
Thou shalt *b* the altar of the Deut 27:6 1129
thou shalt *b* an house, and thou Deut 28:30 1129
us now prepare to *b* us an altar Josh 22:26 1129
to *b* an altar for burnt offerings Josh 22:29 1129
b an altar unto the LORD thy God Judg 6:26 1129
which two did *b* the house of Ruth 4:11 1129
I will *b* him a sure house 1Sa 2:35 1129
Shalt thou *b* me an house for me 2Sa 7:5 1129
Why *b* ye not me an house of cedar 2Sa 7:7 1129
He shall *b* an house for my name, 2Sa 7:13 1129
saying, I will *b* thee an house 2Sa 7:27 1129
to *b* an altar unto the LORD, that 2Sa 24:21 1129
B thee an house in Jerusalem, and 1Kin 2:36 1129
b an house unto the name of the 1Kin 5:3 1129
I purpose to *b* an house unto the 1Kin 5:5 1129
he shall *b* an house unto my name 1Kin 5:5 1129
timber and stones to *b* the house 1Kin 5:18 1129
that he began to *b* the house of 1Kin 6:1 1129
tribes of Israel to *b* an house 1Kin 8:16 1129
to *b* an house for the name of the 1Kin 8:17 1129
heart to *b* an house unto my name 1Kin 8:18 1129
thou shalt not *b* the house 1Kin 8:19 1129
he shall *b* the house unto my name 1Kin 8:19 1129
for to *b* the house of the LORD, 1Kin 9:15 1129
Solomon desired to *b* in Jerusalem 1Kin 9:19 1129
then did he *b* Millo 1Kin 9:24 1129
Then did Solomon *b* an high place 1Kin 11:7 1129
b thee a sure house, as I built 1Kin 11:38 1129
did Hiel the Beth-elite *b* Jericho 1Kin 16:34 1129
and carpenters, to *b* him an house 1Chr 14:1 1129
Thou shalt not *b* me an house to 1Chr 17:4 1129
the LORD will *b* thee an house 1Chr 17:10 1129
He shall *b* me an house, and I will 1Chr 17:12 1129
that thou wilt *b* him an house 1Chr 17:25 1129
that I may *b* an altar therein 1Chr 21:22 1129
stones to *b* the house of God 1Chr 22:2 1129
charged him to *b* an house for the 1Chr 22:6 1129
it was in my mind to *b* an house 1Chr 22:7 1129
thou shalt not *b* an house unto my 1Chr 22:8 1129
He shall *b* an house for my name 1Chr 22:10 1129
b the house of the LORD thy God, 1Chr 22:11 1129
b ye the sanctuary of the LORD 1Chr 22:19 1129
I had in mine heart to *b* an house 1Chr 28:2 1129
Thou shalt not *b* an house for my 1Chr 28:3 1129
thy son, he shall *b* my house 1Chr 28:6 1129
to *b* an house for the sanctuary 1Chr 28:10 1129
to *b* thee an house for thine holy 1Chr 29:16 1129
to *b* the palace, for the which I 1Chr 29:19 1129
Solomon determined to *b* an house 2Chr 2:1 1129
didst send him cedars to *b* him an 2Chr 2:3 1129
I *b* an house to the name of the 2Chr 2:4 1129
And the house which I *b* is great 2Chr 2:5 1129
But who is able to *b* him an house 2Chr 2:6 1129
that I should *b* him an house 2Chr 2:6 1129
to *b* shall be wonderful great 2Chr 2:9 1129
that might *b* an house for the 2Chr 2:12 1129
Then Solomon began to *b* the house 2Chr 3:1 1129
he began to *b* in the second day 2Chr 3:2 1129
tribes of Israel to *b* an house in 2Chr 6:5 1129
to *b* an house for the name of the 2Chr 6:7 1129
heart to *b* an house for my name 2Chr 6:8 1129
thou shalt not *b* the house 2Chr 6:9 1129
he shall *b* the house for my name 2Chr 6:9 1129
Solomon desired to *b* in Jerusalem 2Chr 8:6 1129
Let us *b* these cities, and make 2Chr 14:7 1129
son of David king of Israel did *b* 2Chr 35:3 1129
he hath charged me to *b* him an 2Chr 36:23 1129
he hath charged me to *b* him an Ezr 1:2 1129
b the house of the LORD God of Ezr 1:3 1129
to go up to *b* the house of the Ezr 1:5 1129
said unto them, Let us *b* with you Ezr 4:2 1129
us to *b* an house unto our God Ezr 4:3 1129
b unto the LORD God of Israel Ezr 4:3 1129
began to *b* the house of God which Ezr 5:2 1124
commanded you to *b* this house Ezr 5:3 1124
Who commanded you to *b* this house Ezr 5:9 1124
b the house that was builded Ezr 5:11 1124
a decree to *b* this house of God Ezr 5:13 1124
was made of Cyrus the king to *b* Ezr 5:17 1124
the elders of the Jews *b* this Ezr 6:7 1124
sepulchres, that I may *b* it Neh 2:5 1129
let us *b* up the wall of Jerusalem Neh 2:17 1129
And they said, Let us rise up and *b* Neh 2:18 1129
we his servants will arise and *b* Neh 2:20 1129
gate did the sons of Hassenaah *b* Neh 3:3 1129
he *b* it, and set up the doors Neh 3:14 1129
he said, Even that which they *b* Neh 4:3 1129
we are not able to *b* the wall Neh 4:10 1129
destroy them, and not *b* them up Ps 28:5 1129
b thou the walls of Jerusalem Ps 51:18 1129
will *b* the cities of Judah Ps 69:35 1129
ever, and *b* up thy throne to all Ps 89:4 1129
When the LORD shall *b* up Zion Ps 102:16 1129
Except the LORD *b* the house Ps 127:1 1129
they labour in vain that *b* it Ps 127:1 1129
The LORD doth *b* up Jerusalem Ps 147:2 1129
and afterwards *b* thine house Prov 24:27 1129
to break down, and a time to *b* up Eccl 3:3 1129
we will *b* upon her a palace of Song 8:9 1129
but we will *b* with hewn stones Is 9:10 1129
he shall *b* my city, and he shall Is 45:13 1129
thee shall *b* the old waste places Is 58:12 1129
of strangers shall *b* up thy walls Is 60:10 1129
they shall *b* the old wastes, they Is 61:4 1129
And they shall *b* houses, and Is 65:21 1129
They shall not *b*, and another Is 65:22 1129
is the house that ye *b* unto me Is 66:1 1129
destroy, and to throw down, to *b* Jer 1:10 1129
and concerning a kingdom, to *b* Jer 18:9 1129
I will *b* me a wide house and large Jer 22:14 1129
and I will *b* them, and not pull Jer 24:6 1129
B ye houses, and dwell in them Jer 29:5 1129
b ye houses, and dwell in them Jer 29:28 1129
Again I will *b* thee, and thou Jer 31:4 1129
so will I watch over them, to *b* Jer 31:28 1129
Israel to return, and will *b* them Jer 33:7 1129
Neither shall ye *b* house, nor sow Jer 35:7 1129
Nor to *b* houses for us to dwell Jer 35:9 1129
in this land, then will I *b* you Jer 42:10 1129
b a fort against it, and cast a Eze 4:2 1129
let us *b* houses Eze 11:3 1129
to cast a mount, and to *b* a fort Eze 21:22 1129
and shall *b* houses, and plant Eze 28:26 1129
I the LORD *b* the ruined places Eze 36:36 1129
to *b* Jerusalem unto the Messiah Dan 9:25 1129
I will *b* it as in the days of old Amos 9:11 1129
they shall *b* the waste cities, and Amos 9:14 1129
They *b* up Zion with blood, and Mic 3:10 1129
they shall also *b* houses, but not Zeph 1:13 1129
and bring wood, and *b* the house Hag 1:8 1129
To *b* it an house in the land of Zec 5:11 1129
he shall *b* the temple of the LORD Zec 6:12 1129
Even he shall *b* the temple of the Zec 6:13 1129
b in the temple of the LORD, and Zec 6:15 1129
Tyrus did *b* herself a strong hold Zec 9:3 1129
return and *b* the desolate places Mal 1:4 1129
the LORD of hosts, They shall *b* Mal 1:4 1129
upon this rock I will *b* my church Mt 16:18 *3618*
because ye *b* the tombs of the Mt 23:29 *3618*
of God, and to *b* it in three days Mt 26:61 *3618*
within three days I will *b* Mk 14:58 *3618*
Woe unto you for ye *b* the Lk 11:47 *3618*
them, and ye *b* their sepulchres Lk 11:48 *3618*
pull down my barns, and *b* greater Lk 12:18 *3618*
of you, intending to *b* a tower Lk 14:28 *3618*
Saying, This man began to *b* Lk 14:30 *3618*
what house will ye *b* me Acts 7:49 *3618*
will *b* again the tabernacle of Acts 15:16 *456*
I will *b* again the ruins thereof, Acts 15:16 *456*
grace, which is able to *b* you up Acts 20:32 *2026*
lest I should *b* upon another Rom 15:20 *3618*
Now if any man *b* upon this 1Cor 3:12 *2026*
For if I *b* again the things which Gal 2:18 *3618*

BUILDED
he *b* a city, and called the name Gen 4:17 1129
Noah *b* an altar unto the LORD Gen 8:20 1129
b Nineveh, and the city Rehoboth, Gen 10:11 1129
which the children of men *b* Gen 11:5 1129
there *b* he an altar unto the LORD Gen 12:7 1129
there he *b* an altar unto the LORD Gen 12:8 1129
he *b* an altar there, and called Gen 26:25 1129
b an altar under the hill, and Ex 24:4 1129
unto the cities which they *b* Num 32:38 1129
in that ye have *b* you an altar Josh 22:16 1129
less this house that I have *b* 1Kin 8:27 1129
that this house, which I have *b* 1Kin 8:43 1129
thereof, wherewith Baasha had *b* 1Kin 15:22 1129
b for Ashtoreth the abomination 2Kin 23:13 1129
the house that is to be *b* for the 1Chr 22:5 1129
b the altar of the God of Israel, Ezr 3:2 1129
the children of the captivity *b* Ezr 4:1 1129
the king, that, if this city be *b* Ezr 4:13 1124
that, if this city be *b* again Ezr 4:16 1124
cease, and that this city be not *b* Ezr 4:21 1124
which is *b* with great stones, and Ezr 5:8 1124
that was *b* these many years ago Ezr 5:11 1124
which a great king of Israel *b* Ezr 5:11 1124
house of God be *b* in his place Ezr 5:15 1124
at Jerusalem, Let the house be *b* Ezr 6:3 1124
And the elders of the Jews *b* Ezr 6:14 1124
And they *b*, and finished it, Ezr 6:14 1124
priests, and they *b* the sheep gate Neh 3:1 1129
next unto him *b* the men of Neh 3:2 1129
next to them *b* Zaccur the son of Neh 3:2 1129
heard that we *b* the wall, he was Neh 4:1 1129
They which *b* on the wall, and they Neh 4:17 1129
sword girded by his side, and so *b* Neh 4:18 1129
heard that I had *b* the wall Neh 6:1 1129
therein, and the houses were not *b* Neh 7:4 1129
for the singers had *b* them Neh 12:29 1129
away an house which he *b* not Job 20:19 1129
Jerusalem is *b* as a city that is Ps 122:3 1129
Wisdom hath *b* her house, she hath Prov 9:1 1129
Through wisdom is an house *b* Prov 24:3 1129
I *b* me houses Eccl 2:4 1129
tower of David *b* for an armoury Song 4:4 1129
city shall be *b* upon her own heap Jer 30:18 1129
He hath *b* against me, and Lam 3:5 1129
and the wastes shall be *b* Eze 36:10 1129

cities, and the wastes shall be *b* Eze 36:33 1129
they sold, they planted, they *b* Lk 17:28 *3618*
In whom ye also are *b* together Eph 2:22 *4925*
inasmuch as he who hath *b* the Heb 3:3 *2680*
For every house is *b* by some man Heb 3:4 *2680*

BUILDEDST
goodly cities, which thou *b* not Deut 6:10 1129

BUILDER
which hath foundations, whose *b* Heb 11:10 *5079*

BUILDERS
Solomon's *b* and Hiram's *b* 1Kin 5:18 1129
it out to the carpenters and *b* 2Kin 12:11 1129
Unto carpenters, and *b*, and masons, 2Kin 22:6 1129
b gave they it, to buy hewn stone 2Chr 34:11 1129
when the *b* laid the foundation of Ezr 3:10 1129
thee to anger before the *b* Neh 4:5 1129
For the *b*, every one had his Neh 4:18 1129
The stone which the *b* refused is Ps 118:22 1129
thy *b* have perfected thy beauty Eze 27:4 1129
The stone which the *b* rejected Mt 21:42 *3618*
The stone which the *b* rejected is Mk 12:10 *3618*
The stone which the *b* rejected Lk 20:17 *3618*
which was set at nought of you *b* Acts 4:11 *3618*
the stone which the *b* disallowed 1Pet 2:7 *3618*

BUILDEST
When thou *b* a new house, then Deut 22:8 1129
for which cause thou *b* the wall Neh 6:6 1129
In that thou *b* thine eminent Eze 16:31 1129
b it in three days, save thyself Mt 27:40 *3618*
temple, and *b* it in three days, Mk 15:29 *3618*

BUILDETH
riseth up and *b* this city Jericho Josh 6:26 1129
He *b* his house as a moth, and as a Job 27:18 1129
Every wise woman *b* her house Prov 14:1 1129
Woe unto him that *b* his house by Jer 22:13 1129
forgotten his Maker, and *b* temples Hos 8:14 1129
It is he that *b* his stories in Amos 9:6 1129
Woe to him that *b* a town with Hab 2:12 1129
foundation, and another *b* thereon 1Cor 3:10 *2026*
man take heed how he *b* thereupon 1Cor 3:10 *2026*

BUILDING
in *b* you an altar beside the Josh 22:19 1129
made an end of *b* his own house 1Kin 3:1 1129
And the house, when it was in *b* 1Kin 6:7 1129
in the house, while it was in *b* 1Kin 6:7 1129
this house which thou art in *b* 1Kin 6:12 1129
So was he seven years in *b* it 1Kin 6:38 1129
But Solomon was *b* his own house 1Kin 7:1 1129
the *b* of the house of the LORD 1Kin 9:1 1129
that he left off *b* of Ramah 1Kin 15:21 1129
God, and had made ready for the *b* 1Chr 28:2 1129
for the *b* of the house of God 2Chr 3:3 1129
it, that he left off *b* of Ramah 2Chr 16:5 1129
thereof, wherewith Baasha was *b* 2Chr 16:6 1129
of Judah, and troubled them in *b* Ezr 4:4 1129
b the rebellious and the bad city, Ezr 4:12 1124
names of the men that make this *b* Ezr 5:4 1147
even until now hath it been in *b* Ezr 5:16 1124
for the *b* of this house of God Ezr 6:8 1124
much slothfulness the *b* decayeth Eccl 10:18 4746
b forts, to cut off many persons Eze 17:17 1129
he measured the breadth of the *b* Eze 40:5 1146
Now the *b* that was before the Eze 41:12 1146
the wall of the *b* was five cubits Eze 41:12 1146
and the separate place, and the *b* Eze 41:13 1140
he measured the length of the *b* Eze 41:15 1146
was before the *b* toward the north Eze 42:1 1146
and than the middlemost of the *b* Eze 42:5 1146
therefore the *b* was straitened Eze 42:6
place, and over against the *b* Eze 42:10 1146
there was a row of *b* round about Eze 46:23
and six years was this temple in *b* Jn 2:20 *3618*
God's husbandry, ye are God's *b* 1Cor 3:9 *3619*
dissolved, we have a *b* of God 2Cor 5:1 *3619*
In whom all the *b* fitly framed Eph 2:21 *3619*
that is to say, not of this *b* Heb 9:11 *2937*
b up yourselves on your most holy Jude 20 *2026*
the *b* of the wall of it was of Rev 21:18 *1739*

BUILDINGS
to shew him the *b* of the temple Mt 24:1 *3619*
of stones and what *b* are here Mk 13:1 *3619*
him, Seest thou these great *b* Mk 13:2 *3619*

BUILT
b there an altar unto the LORD Gen 13:18 1129
Abraham *b* an altar there, and laid Gen 22:9 1129
b him an house, and made booths Gen 33:17 1129
he *b* there an altar, and called Gen 35:7 1129
they *b* for Pharaoh treasure Ex 1:11 1129
Moses *b* an altar, and called the Ex 17:15 1129
saw it, he *b* an altar before it Ex 32:5 1129
(Now Hebron was *b* seven years Num 13:22 1129
let the city of Sihon be *b* Num 21:27 1129
b seven altars, and offered a Num 23:14 1129
And the children of Gad *b* Dibon Num 32:34 1129
the children of Reuben *b* Heshbon Num 32:37 1129
hast *b* goodly houses, and dwelt Deut 8:12 1129
it shall not be *b* again Deut 13:16 1129
is there that hath *b* a new house Deut 20:5 1129
Then Joshua *b* an altar unto the Josh 8:30 1129
he *b* the city, and dwelt therein Josh 19:50 1129
b there an altar by Jordan Josh 22:10 1129
b an altar over against the land Josh 22:11 1129
That we have *b* us an altar to Josh 22:23 1129
labour, and cities which ye *b* not Josh 24:13 1129
b a city, and called the name Judg 1:26 1129
Then Gideon *b* an altar there unto Judg 6:24 1129
offered upon the altar that was *b* Judg 6:28 1129
they *b* a city, and dwelt therein Judg 18:28 1129
b there an altar, and offered Judg 21:4 1129
there he *b* an altar unto the LORD 1Sa 7:17 1129
Saul *b* an altar unto the LORD 1Sa 14:35 1129
altar that he *b* unto the LORD 1Sa 14:35 1129
David *b* round about from Millo and 2Sa 5:9 1129
and they *b* David an house 2Sa 5:11 1129
David *b* there an altar unto the 2Sa 24:25 1129
house *b* unto the name of the LORD 1Kin 3:2 1129
which king Solomon *b* for the LORD 1Kin 6:2 1129
house he *b* chambers round about 1Kin 6:5 1129
was *b* of stone made ready before 1Kin 6:7 1129
So he *b* the house, and finished it 1Kin 6:9 1129
then he *b* chambers against all 1Kin 6:10 1129
So Solomon *b* the house, and 1Kin 6:14 1129
he *b* the walls of the house 1Kin 6:15 1129
he *b* twenty cubits on the sides 1Kin 6:16 1129
he even *b* them for it within, 1Kin 6:16 1129
he *b* the inner court with three 1Kin 6:36 1129
He *b* also the house of the forest 1Kin 7:2 1129
I have surely *b* thee an house to 1Kin 8:13 1129
have *b* an house for the name of 1Kin 8:20 1129
house that I have *b* for thy name 1Kin 8:44 1129
house which I have *b* for thy name 1Kin 8:48 1129
this house, which thou hast *b* 1Kin 9:3 1129
when Solomon had *b* the two houses 1Kin 9:10 1129
And Solomon *b* Gezer 1Kin 9:17 1129
house which Solomon had *b* for her 1Kin 9:24 1129
altar which he *b* unto the LORD 1Kin 9:25 1129
and the house that he had *b* 1Kin 10:4 1129
Solomon *b* Millo, and repaired the 1Kin 11:27 1129
as I *b* for David, and will give 1Kin 11:38 1129
Then Jeroboam *b* Shechem in mount 1Kin 12:25 1129
went out from thence, and *b* Penuel 1Kin 12:25 1129
For they also *b* them high places, 1Kin 14:23 1129
b Ramah, that he might not suffer 1Kin 15:17 1129
king Asa *b* with them Geba of 1Kin 15:22 1129
he did, and the cities which he *b* 1Kin 15:23 1129
b on the hill, and called the name 1Kin 16:24 1129
the name of the city which he *b* 1Kin 16:24 1129
Baal, which he had *b* in Samaria 1Kin 16:32 1129
with the stones he *b* an altar in 1Kin 18:32 1129
made, and all the cities that he *b* 1Kin 22:39 1129
He *b* Elath, and restored it to 2Kin 14:22 1129
He *b* the higher gate of the house 2Kin 15:35 1129
Urijah the priest *b* an altar 2Kin 16:11 1129
that they had *b* in the house 2Kin 16:18 1129
they *b* them high places in all 2Kin 17:9 1129
For he *b* up again the high places 2Kin 21:3 1129
he *b* altars in the house of the 2Kin 21:4 1129
he *b* altars for all the host of 2Kin 21:5 1129
they *b* forts against it round 2Kin 25:1 1129
that Solomon *b* in Jerusalem 1Chr 6:10 1129
until Solomon had *b* the house of 1Chr 6:32 1129
who *b* Beth-horon the nether, and 1Chr 7:24 1129
and Misham, and Shamed, who *b* Ono 1Chr 8:12 1129
he *b* the city round about, even 1Chr 11:8 1129
Why have ye not *b* me an house of 1Chr 17:6 1129
David *b* there an altar unto the 1Chr 21:26 1129
to be *b* to the name of the LORD 1Chr 22:19 1129
But I have surely *b* an house of 2Chr 6:2 1129
have *b* the house for the name of 2Chr 6:10 1129
less this house which I have *b* 2Chr 6:18 1129
I have *b* is called by thy name 2Chr 6:33 1129
house which I have *b* for thy name 2Chr 6:34 1129
house which I have *b* for thy name 2Chr 6:38 1129
wherein Solomon had *b* the house 2Chr 8:1 1129
to Solomon, Solomon *b* them 2Chr 8:2 1129
he *b* Tadmor in the wilderness, and 2Chr 8:4 1129
cities, which he *b* in Hamath 2Chr 8:4 1129
Also he *b* Beth-horon the upper, 2Chr 8:5 1129
the house that he had *b* for her 2Chr 8:11 1129
which he had *b* before the porch, 2Chr 8:12 1129
and the house that he had *b* 2Chr 9:3 1129
b cities for defence in Judah 2Chr 11:5 1129
He *b* even Beth-lehem, and Etam, and 2Chr 11:6 1129
he *b* fenced cities in Judah 2Chr 14:6 1129
So they *b* and prospered 2Chr 14:7 1129
b Ramah, to the intent that he 2Chr 16:1 1129
he *b* therewith Geba and Mizpah 2Chr 16:6 1129
he *b* in Judah castles, and cities 2Chr 17:12 1129
have *b* thee a sanctuary therein 2Chr 20:8 1129
He *b* Eloth, and restored it to 2Chr 26:2 1129
b cities about Ashdod, and among 2Chr 26:6 1129
Moreover Uzziah *b* towers in 2Chr 26:9 1129
Also he *b* towers in the desert, 2Chr 26:10 1129
He *b* the high gate of the house 2Chr 27:3 1129
and on the wall of Ophel he *b* much 2Chr 27:3 1129
Moreover he *b* cities in the 2Chr 27:4 1129
and in the forests he *b* castles 2Chr 27:4 1129
b up all the wall that was broken 2Chr 32:5 1129
For he *b* again the high places 2Chr 33:3 1129
Also he *b* altars in the house of 2Chr 33:4 1129
he *b* altars for all the host of 2Chr 33:5 1129
Now after this he *b* a wall 2Chr 33:14 1129
all the altars that he had *b* in 2Chr 33:15 1129
places wherein he *b* high places 2Chr 33:19 1129
they *b* it, and set up the doors Neh 3:13 1129
he *b* it, and covered it, and set up Neh 3:15 1129
So *b* we the wall Neh 4:6 1129
came to pass, when the wall was *b* Neh 7:1 1129
which *b* desolate places for Job 3:14 1129
down, and it cannot be *b* again Job 12:14 1129
the Almighty, thou shalt be *b* up Job 22:23 1129
he *b* his sanctuary like high Ps 78:69 1129
Mercy shall be *b* up for ever Ps 89:2 1129
b great bulwarks against it Eccl 9:14 1129
b a tower in the midst of it, and Is 5:2 1129
it shall never be *b* Is 25:2 1129
cities of Judah, Ye shall be *b* Is 44:26 1129
to Jerusalem, Thou shalt be *b* Is 44:28 1129
they have *b* the high places of Jer 7:31 1129
then shall they be *b* in the midst Jer 12:16 1129
They have *b* also the high places Jer 19:5 1129
build thee, and thou shalt be *b* Jer 31:4 1129
that the city shall be *b* to the Jer 31:38 1129
that they *b* it even unto this day Jer 32:31 1129
they *b* the high places of Baal, Jer 32:35 1129
which I have *b* will I break down Jer 45:4 1129
b forts against it round about Jer 52:4 1129
one *b* up a wall, and, lo, others Eze 13:10 1129
That thou hast also *b* unto thee Eze 16:24 1129
Thou hast *b* thy high place at Eze 16:25 1129
thou shalt be *b* no more Eze 26:14 1129
that I have *b* for the house of Dan 4:30 1124
the street shall be *b* again Dan 9:25 1129
ye have *b* houses of hewn stone, Amos 5:11 1129
day that thy walls are to be *b* Mic 7:11 1129
that the LORD's house should be *b* Hag 1:2 1129
my house shall be *b* in it Zec 1:16 1129
laid, that the temple might be *b* Zec 8:9 1129
which *b* his house upon a rock Mt 7:24 *3618*
which *b* his house upon the sand Mt 7:26 *3618*
b a tower, and let it out to Mt 21:33 *3618*
b a tower, and let it out to Mk 12:1 *3618*
the hill whereon their city was *b* Lk 4:29 *3618*
He is like a man which *b* an house Lk 6:48 *3618*
b an house upon the earth Lk 6:49 *3618*
and he hath *b* us a synagogue Lk 7:5 *3618*
But Solomon *b* him an house Acts 7:47 *3618*
abide which he hath *b* thereupon 1Cor 3:14 *2026*
are *b* upon the foundation of the Eph 2:20 *2026*
b up in him, and stablished in the Col 2:7 *2026*
but he that *b* all things is God Heb 3:4 *2680*
are *b* up a spiritual house, an 1Pet 2:5 *3618*

BUKKI (*buk'-ki*)
1. A high priest.
And Abishua begat *B* 1Chr 6:5 1231
and *B* begat Uzzi 1Chr 6:5 1231
B his son, Uzzi his son, Zerahiah 1Chr 6:51 1231
the son of Uzzi, the son of *B* Ezr 7:4 1231
2. A Danite prince.
of Dan, *B* the son of Jogli Num 34:22 1231

BUKKIAH (*buk-ki'-ah*) *A Levite musician.*
B, Mattaniah, Uzziel, Shebuel, and 1Chr 25:4 1232
The sixth to *B*, he, his sons, and 1Chr 25:13 1232

BUL (*bul*) *Eighth month of the Hebrew year.*
the eleventh year, in the month *B* 1Kin 6:38 945

BULL
Their *b* gendereth, and faileth not Job 21:10 7794
the streets, as a wild *b* in a net Is 51:20 8377

BULLOCK
Take one young *b*, and two rams Ex 29:1 6499
them in the basket, with the *b* Ex 29:3 6499
thou shalt cause a *b* to be Ex 29:10 6499
hands upon the head of the *b* Ex 29:10 6499
shalt kill the *b* before the LORD Ex 29:11 6499
shalt take of the blood of the *b* Ex 29:12 6499
But the flesh of the *b*, and his Ex 29:14 6499
day a *b* for a sin offering for Ex 29:36 6499
shall kill the *b* before the LORD Lev 1:5
a young *b* without blemish unto Lev 4:3 6499
he shall bring the *b* unto the Lev 4:4 6499
kill the *b* before the LORD Lev 4:4 6499
b at the bottom of the altar of Lev 4:7 6499
fat of the *b* for the sin offering Lev 4:8 6499
the *b* of the sacrifice of peace Lev 4:10 7794
And the skin of the *b*, and all his Lev 4:11 6499
Even the whole *b* shall he carry Lev 4:12 6499
shall offer a young *b* for the sin Lev 4:14 6499
the head of the *b* before the LORD Lev 4:15 6499
the *b* shall be killed before the Lev 4:15 6499
he shall do with the *b* as he did Lev 4:20 6499
did with the *b* for a sin offering Lev 4:20 6499
forth the *b* without the camp Lev 4:21 6499
burn him as he burned the first *b* Lev 4:21 6499
a *b* for the sin offering, and two Lev 8:2 6499
he brought the *b* for the sin Lev 8:14 6499
of the *b* for the sin offering Lev 8:14 6499
But the *b*, and his hide, his flesh Lev 8:17 6499
Also a *b* and a ram for peace Lev 9:4 7794
He slew also the *b* and the ram for Lev 9:18 7794
And the fat of the *b* and of the ram Lev 9:19 7794
with a young *b* for a sin offering Lev 16:3 6499
offer his *b* of the sin offering Lev 16:6 6499
bring the *b* of the sin offering Lev 16:11 6499
shall kill the *b* of the sin Lev 16:11 6499
shall take of the blood of the *b* Lev 16:14 6499
as he did with the blood of the *b* Lev 16:15 6499
shall take of the blood of the *b* Lev 16:18 6499
the *b* for the sin offering, and Lev 16:27 6499
Either a *b* or a lamb that hath Lev 22:23 7794
When a *b*, or a sheep, or a goat, Lev 22:27 7794
of the first year, and one young *b* Lev 23:18 6499
One young *b*, one ram, one lamb of Num 7:15 6499
One young *b*, one ram, one lamb of Num 7:21 6499
One young *b*, one ram, one lamb of Num 7:27 6499
One young *b*, one ram, one lamb of Num 7:33 6499
One young *b*, one ram, one lamb of Num 7:39 6499
One young *b*, one ram, one lamb of Num 7:45 6499
One young *b*, one ram, one lamb of Num 7:51 6499
One young *b*, one ram, one lamb of Num 7:57 6499
One young *b*, one ram, one lamb of Num 7:63 6499
One young *b*, one ram, one lamb of Num 7:69 6499
One young *b*, one ram, one lamb of Num 7:75 6499
One young *b*, one ram, one lamb of Num 7:81 6499
a young *b* with his meat offering Num 8:8 6499
another young *b* shalt thou take Num 8:8 6499
a *b* for a burnt offering, or for Num 15:8
Then shall he bring with a *b* a Num 15:9
Thus shall it be done for one *b* Num 15:11 7794
one young *b* for a burnt offering Num 15:24 6499
Balaam offered on every altar a *b* Num 23:2 6499
have offered upon every altar a *b* Num 23:4 6499
seven altars, and offered a *b* Num 23:14 6499
Balaam had said, and offered a *b* Num 23:30 6499
mingled with oil, for one *b* Num 28:12 6499
be half an hin of wine unto a *b* Num 28:14 6499

deals shall ye offer for a *b* Num 28:20 6499
oil, three tenth deals unto one *b* Num 28:28 6499
one young *b*, one ram, and seven Num 29:2 6499
oil, three tenth deals for a *b* Num 29:3 6499
one young *b*, one ram, and seven Num 29:8 6499
oil, three tenth deals to a *b* Num 29:9 6499
every *b* of the thirteen bullocks Num 29:14 6499
one *b*, one ram, seven lambs of Num 29:36 6499
their drink offerings for the *b* Num 29:37 6499
work with the firstling of thy *b* Deut 15:19 7794
unto the LORD thy God any *b* Deut 17:1 7794
is like the firstling of his *b* Deut 33:17 7794
him, Take thy father's young *b* Judg 6:25 6499
even the second *b* of seven years Judg 6:25 6499
place, and take the second *b* Judg 6:26 6499
the second *b* was offered upon the Judg 6:28 6499
And they slew a *b*, and brought the 1Sa 1:25 6499
them choose one *b* for themselves 1Kin 18:23 6499
and I will dress the other *b* 1Kin 18:23 6499
Choose you one *b* for yourselves 1Kin 18:25 6499
they took the *b* which was given 1Kin 18:26 6499
cut the *b* in pieces, and laid him 1Kin 18:33 6499
consecrate himself with a young *b* 2Chr 13:9 6499
I will take no *b* out of thy house Ps 50:9 6499
than an ox or *b* that hath horns Ps 69:31 6499
lion shall eat straw like the *b* Is 65:25 1241
as a *b* unaccustomed to the yoke Jer 31:18 5695
a young *b* for a sin offering Eze 43:19 6499
Thou shalt take the *b* also of the Eze 43:21 6499
as they did cleanse it with the *b* Eze 43:22 6499
offer a young *b* without blemish Eze 43:23 6499
they shall also prepare a young *b* Eze 43:25 6499
take a young *b* without blemish Eze 45:18 6499
the land a *b* for a sin offering Eze 45:22 6499
meat offering of an ephah for a *b* Eze 45:24 6499
be a young *b* without blemish Eze 46:6 6499
a meat offering, an ephah for a *b* Eze 46:7 6499
offering shall be an ephah to a *b* Eze 46:11 6499

BULLOCK'S
lay his hand upon the *b* head Lev 4:4 6499
shall take of the *b* blood Lev 4:5 6499
b blood to the tabernacle of the Lev 4:16 6499

BULLOCKS
the burnt offering were twelve *b* Num 7:87 6499
offerings were twenty and four *b* Num 7:88 6499
hands upon the heads of the *b* Num 8:12 6499
and prepare me here seven *b* Num 23:29 6499
two young *b*, and one ram, seven Num 28:11 6499
two young *b*, and one ram, and seven Num 28:19 6499
two young *b*, one ram, seven lambs Num 28:27 6499
thirteen young *b*, two rams, and Num 29:13 6499
every bullock of the thirteen *b* Num 29:14 6499
day ye shall offer twelve young *b* Num 29:17 6499
their drink offerings for the *b* Num 29:18 6499
And on the third day eleven *b* Num 29:20 6499
their drink offerings for the *b* Num 29:21 6499
And on the fourth day ten *b* Num 29:23 6499
their drink offerings for the *b* Num 29:24 6499
And on the fifth day nine *b* Num 29:26 6499
their drink offerings for the *b* Num 29:27 6499
And on the sixth day eight *b* Num 29:29 6499
their drink offerings for the *b* Num 29:30 6499
And on the seventh day seven *b* Num 29:32 6499
their drink offerings for the *b* Num 29:33 6499
him up with her, with three *b* 1Sa 1:24 6499
Let them therefore give us two *b* 1Kin 18:23 6499
LORD, that they offered seven *b* 1Chr 15:26 6499
after that day, even a thousand *b* 1Chr 29:21 6499
And they brought seven *b*, and seven 2Chr 29:21 6499
So they killed the *b*, and the 2Chr 29:22 1241
brought, was threescore and ten *b* 2Chr 29:32 1241
to the congregation a thousand *b* 2Chr 30:24 6499
to the congregation a thousand *b* 2Chr 30:24 6499
thousand, and three thousand *b* 2Chr 35:7 1241
they have need of, both young *b* Ezr 6:9 8450
of this house of God an hundred *b* Ezr 6:17 8450
buy speedily with this money *b* Ezr 7:17 8450
twelve *b* for all Israel, ninety Ezr 8:35 6499
take unto you now seven *b* Job 42:8 6499
they offer *b* upon thine altar Ps 51:19 6499
I will offer *b* with goats Ps 66:15 1241
I delight not in the blood of *b* Is 1:11 6499
them, and the *b* with the bulls Is 34:7 6499
in the midst of her like fatted *b* Jer 46:21 5695
Slay all her *b* Jer 50:27 6499
rams, of lambs, and of goats, of *b* Eze 39:18 6499
offering to the LORD, seven *b* Eze 45:23 6499
they sacrifice *b* in Gilgal Hos 12:11 7794

BULLS
their colts, forty kine, and ten *b* Gen 32:15 6499
Many *b* have compassed me Ps 22:12 6499
strong *b* of Bashan have beset me Ps 22:12
Will I eat the flesh of *b* Ps 50:13 47
spearmen, the multitude of the *b* Ps 68:30 47
them, and the bullocks with the *b* Is 34:7 47
heifer at grass, and bellow as *b* Jer 50:11 47
twelve brasen *b* that were under Jer 52:20 1241
For if the blood of *b* and of goats Heb 9:13 *5022*
not possible that the blood of *b* Heb 10:4 *5022*

BULRUSH
is it to bow down his head as a *b* Is 58:5 100

BULRUSHES
him, she took for him an ark of *b* Ex 2:3 1573
in vessels of *b* upon the waters Is 18:2 1573

BULWARKS
thou shalt build *b* against the Deut 20:20 4692
to be on the towers and upon the *b* 2Chr 26:15 6438
Mark ye well her *b*, consider her Ps 48:13 2430
it, and built great *b* against it Eccl 9:14 4685
will God appoint for walls and *b* Is 26:1 2426

BUNAH (*boo'-nah*) *Son of Jerahmeel.*
were, Ram the firstborn, and *B* 1Chr 2:25 946

BUNCH
And ye shall take a *b* of hyssop Ex 12:22 92

BUNCHES
bread, and an hundred *b* of raisins 2Sa 16:1 6778
b of raisins, and wine, and oil, and 1Chr 12:40 6778
treasures upon the *b* of camels Is 30:6 1707

BUNDLE
every man's *b* of money was in his Gen 42:35 6872
b of life with the LORD thy God 1Sa 25:29 6872
A *b* of myrrh is my wellbeloved Song 1:13 6872
Paul had gathered a *b* of sticks Acts 28:3 *4128*

BUNDLES
their father saw the *b* of money Gen 42:35 6872
and bind them in *b* to burn them Mt 13:30 *1197*

BUNNI (*bun'-ni*)
1. A Levite with Ezra.
and Bani, Kadmiel, Shebaniah, *B* Neh 9:4 1137
2. Father of Hashabiah.
son of Hashabiah, the son of *B* Neh 11:15 1137
3. A family who renewed the covenant.
B, Azgad, Bebai, Neh 10:15 1137

BURDEN
they shall bear the *b* with thee Ex 18:22
hateth thee lying under his *b* Ex 23:5 4853
These things are the *b* of the Num 4:15 4853
one to his service and to his *b* Num 4:19 4853
And this is the charge of their *b* Num 4:31 4853
of the charge of their *b* Num 4:32 4853
the service of the *b* in the Num 4:47 4853
service, and according to his *b* Num 4:49 4853
that thou layest the *b* of all Num 11:11 4853
they shall bear the *b* of the Num 11:17 4853
bear your cumbrance, and your *b* Deut 1:12 4853
then thou shalt be a *b* unto me 2Sa 15:33 4853
be yet a *b* unto my lord the king 2Sa 19:35 4853
thy servant two mules' *b* of earth 2Kin 5:17 4853
of Damascus, forty camels' *b* 2Kin 8:9 4853
the LORD laid this *b* upon him 2Kin 9:25 4853
it shall not be a *b* upon your 2Chr 35:3 4853
that there should no *b* be brought Neh 13:19 4853
thee, so that I am a *b* to myself Job 7:20 4853
as an heavy *b* they are too heavy Ps 38:4 4853
Cast thy *b* upon the LORD, and he Ps 55:22 3053
I removed his shoulder from the *b* Ps 81:6 5449
and the grasshopper shall be a *b* Eccl 12:5 5445
hast broken the yoke of his *b* Is 9:4 5448
that his *b* shall be taken away Is 10:27 5448
The *b* of Babylon, which Isaiah Is 13:1 4853
his *b* depart from off their Is 14:25 5448
that king Ahaz died was this *b* Is 14:28 4853
The *b* of Moab Is 15:1 4853
The *b* of Damascus Is 17:1 4853
The *b* of Egypt Is 19:1 4853
The *b* of the desert of the sea Is 21:1 4853
The *b* of Dumah Is 21:11 4853
The *b* upon Arabia Is 21:13 4853
The *b* of the valley of vision Is 22:1 4853
the *b* that was upon it shall be Is 22:25 4853
The *b* of Tyre Is 23:1 4853
The *b* of the beasts of the south Is 30:6 4853
anger, and the *b* thereof is heavy Is 30:27 4858
they are a *b* to the weary beast Is 46:1 4853
they could not deliver the *b* Is 46:2 4853
bear no *b* on the sabbath day, nor Jer 17:21 4853
Neither carry forth a *b* out of Jer 17:22 4853
to bring in no *b* through the Jer 17:24 4853
sabbath day, and not to bear a *b* Jer 17:27 4853
saying, What is the *b* of the LORD Jer 23:33 4853
shalt then say unto them, What *b* Jer 23:33 4853
The *b* of the LORD, I will even Jer 23:34 4853
the *b* of the LORD shall ye Jer 23:36 4853
every man's word shall be his *b* Jer 23:36 4853
since ye say, The *b* of the LORD Jer 23:38 4853
The *b* of the LORD, and I have sent Jer 23:38 4853
shall not say, The *b* of the LORD Jer 23:38 4853
This *b* concerneth the prince in Eze 12:10 4853
for the *b* of the king of princes Hos 8:10 4853
The *b* of Nineveh Nah 1:1 4853
The *b* which Habakkuk the prophet Hab 1:1 4853
whom the reproach of it was a *b* Zeph 3:18 4864
The *b* of the word of the LORD in Zec 9:1 4853
The *b* of the word of the LORD for Zec 12:1 4853
all that *b* themselves with it Zec 12:3 6006
The *b* of the word of the LORD to Mal 1:1 4853
my yoke is easy, and my *b* is light Mt 11:30 *5413*
unto us, which have borne the *b* Mt 20:12 *922*
to lay upon you no greater *b* than Acts 15:28 *922*
the ship was to unlade her *b* Acts 21:3 *1117*
But be it so, I did not *b* you 2Cor 12:16 *2599*
every man shall bear his own *b* Gal 6:5 *5413*
I will put upon you none other *b* Rev 2:24 *922*

BURDENED
this tabernacle do groan, being *b* 2Cor 5:4 *916*
that other men be eased, and ye *b* 2Cor 8:13 *2347*

BURDENS
ass couching down between two *b* Gen 49:14 4942
to afflict them with their *b* Ex 1:11 5450
brethren, and looked on their *b* Ex 2:11 5450
get you unto your *b* Ex 5:4 5450
and ye make them rest from their *b* Ex 5:5 5450
from under the *b* of the Egyptians Ex 6:6 5450
from under the *b* of the Egyptians Ex 6:7 5450
Gershonites, to serve, and for *b* Num 4:24 4853
the Gershonites, in all their *b* Num 4:27 4853
unto them in charge all their *b* Num 4:27 4853
and ten thousand that bare *b* 1Kin 5:15 5449
and ten thousand men to bear *b* 2Chr 2:2 5449
of them to be bearers of *b* 2Chr 2:18 5449
greatness of the *b* laid upon him 2Chr 24:27 4853
they were over the bearers of *b* 2Chr 34:13 5449
of the bearers of *b* is decayed Neh 4:10 5449
on the wall, and they that bare *b* Neh 4:17 5447
and figs, and all manner of *b* Neh 13:15 4853
wickedness, to undo the heavy *b* Is 58:6 92
but have seen for thee false *b* Lam 2:14 4864
and ye take from him *b* of wheat Amos 5:11 4864
For they bind heavy *b* and grievous Mt 23:4 *5413*
men with *b* grievous to be borne Lk 11:46 *5413*
the *b* with one of your fingers Lk 11:46 *5413*
Bear ye one another's *b*, and so Gal 6:2 *922*

BURDENSOME
a *b* stone for all people Zec 12:3 4614
kept myself from being *b* unto you 2Cor 11:9 *4*
be that I myself was not *b* to you 2Cor 12:13 *2655*
and I will not be *b* to you 2Cor 12:14 *2655*
others, when we might have been *b* 1Th 2:6

BURIAL
the *b* which belonged to the kings 2Chr 26:23 6900
good, and also that he have no *b* Eccl 6:3 6900
not be joined with them in *b* Is 14:20 6900
be buried with the *b* of an ass Jer 22:19 6900
on my body, she did it for my *b* Mt 26:12 *1779*
men carried Stephen to his *b* Acts 8:2

BURIED
thou shalt be *b* in a good old age Gen 15:15 6912
Abraham *b* Sarah his wife in the Gen 23:19 6912
Ishmael *b* him in the cave of Gen 25:9 6912
there was Abraham *b*, and Sarah his Gen 25:10 6912
she was *b* beneath Beth-el under Gen 35:8 6912
was *b* in the way to Ephrath, Gen 35:19 6912
and his sons Esau and Jacob *b* him Gen 35:29 6912
I *b* her there in the way of Gen 48:7 6912
There they *b* Abraham and Sarah his Gen 49:31 6912
there they *b* Isaac and Rebekah his Gen 49:31 6912
and there I *b* Leah Gen 49:31 6912
b him in the cave of the field of Gen 50:13 6912
father, after he had *b* his father Gen 50:14 6912
because there they *b* the people Num 11:34 6912
Miriam died there, and was *b* there Num 20:1 6912
For the Egyptians *b* all their Num 33:4 6912
Aaron died, and there he was *b* Deut 10:6 6912
he *b* him in a valley in the land Deut 34:6 6912
they *b* him in the border of his Josh 24:30 6912
b they in Shechem, in a parcel of Josh 24:32 6912
they *b* him in a hill that Josh 24:33 6912
they *b* him in the border of his Judg 2:9 6912
was *b* in the sepulchre of Joash Judg 8:32 6912
and died, and was *b* in Shamir Judg 10:2 6912
And Jair died, and was *b* in Camon Judg 10:5 6912
was *b* in one of the cities of Judg 12:7 6912
Ibzan, and was *b* at Beth-lehem Judg 12:10 6912
was *b* in Aijalon in the country Judg 12:12 6912
was *b* in Pirathon in the land of Judg 12:15 6912
b him between Zorah and Eshtaol in Judg 16:31 6912
will I die, and there will I be *b* Ruth 1:17 6912
b him in his house at Ramah 1Sa 25:1 6912
b him in Ramah, even in his own 1Sa 28:3 6912
b them under a tree at Jabesh, and 1Sa 31:13 6912
were they that *b* Saul 2Sa 2:4 6912
even unto Saul, and have *b* him 2Sa 2:5 6912
b him in the sepulchre of his 2Sa 2:32 6912
And they *b* Abner in Hebron 2Sa 3:32 6912
b it in the sepulchre of Abner in 2Sa 4:12 6912
was *b* in the sepulchre of his 2Sa 17:23 6912
be *b* by the grave of my father and 2Sa 19:37 6912
Jonathan his son *b* they in the 2Sa 21:14 6912
was *b* in the city of David 1Kin 2:10 6912
he was *b* in his own house in the 1Kin 2:34 6912
was *b* in the city of David his 1Kin 11:43 6912
came to pass, after he had *b* him 1Kin 13:31 6912
wherein the man of God is *b* 1Kin 13:31 6912
And they *b* him 1Kin 14:18 6912
was *b* with his fathers in the 1Kin 14:31 6912
they *b* him in the city of David 1Kin 15:8 6912
was *b* with his fathers in the 1Kin 15:24 6912
his fathers, and was *b* in Tirzah 1Kin 16:6 6912
his fathers, and was *b* in Samaria 1Kin 16:28 6912
they *b* the king in Samaria 1Kin 22:37 6912
was *b* with his fathers in the 1Kin 22:50 6912
was *b* with his fathers in the 2Kin 8:24 6912
b him in his sepulchre with his 2Kin 9:28 6912
and they *b* him in Samaria 2Kin 10:35 6912
they *b* him with his fathers in 2Kin 12:21 6912
and they *b* him in Samaria 2Kin 13:9 6912
Joash was *b* in Samaria with the 2Kin 13:13 6912
And Elisha died, and they *b* him 2Kin 13:20 6912
was *b* in Samaria with the kings 2Kin 14:16 6912
he was *b* at Jerusalem with his 2Kin 14:20 6912
they *b* him with his fathers in 2Kin 15:7 6912
was *b* with his fathers in the 2Kin 15:38 6912
was *b* with his fathers in the 2Kin 16:20 6912
was *b* in the garden of his own 2Kin 21:18 6912
he was *b* in his sepulchre in the 2Kin 21:26 6912
b him in his own sepulchre 2Kin 23:30 6912
b their bones under the oak in 1Chr 10:12 6912
he was *b* in the city of David his 2Chr 9:31 6912
was *b* in the city of David 2Chr 12:16 6912
they *b* him in the city of David 2Chr 14:1 6912
they *b* him in his own sepulchres, 2Chr 16:14 6912
was *b* with his fathers in the 2Chr 21:1 6912
Howbeit they *b* him in the city of 2Chr 21:20 6912
they had slain him, they *b* him 2Chr 22:9 6912
they *b* him in the city of David 2Chr 24:16 6912
they *b* him in the city of David, 2Chr 24:25 6912
but they *b* him not in the 2Chr 24:25 6912
b him with his fathers in the 2Chr 25:28 6912
they *b* him with his fathers in 2Chr 26:23 6912
they *b* him in the city of David 2Chr 27:9 6912
they *b* him in the city, even in 2Chr 28:27 6912
they *b* him in the chiefest of the 2Chr 32:33 6912

they *b* him in his own house 2Chr 33:20 6912
was *b* in one of the sepulchres of 2Chr 35:24 6912
remain of him shall be *b* in death Job 27:15 6912
And so I saw the wicked *b*, who had Eccl 8:10 6912
shall not be gathered, nor be *b* Jer 8:2 6912
neither shall they be *b* Jer 16:4 6912
they shall not be *b*, neither Jer 16:6 6912
shalt die, and shalt be *b* there Jer 20:6 6912
He shall be *b* with the burial of Jer 22:19 6912
lamented, neither gathered, nor *b* Jer 25:33 6912
till the buriers have *b* it in the Eze 39:15 6912
b it, and went and told Jesus Mt 14:12 *2290*
the rich man also died, and was *b* Lk 16:22 *2290*
David, that he is both dead and *b* Acts 2:29 *2290*
up, and carried him out, and *b* him Acts 5:6 *2290*
b thy husband are at the door Acts 5:9 *2290*
her forth, *b* her by her husband Acts 5:10 *2290*
Therefore we are *b* with him by Rom 6:4 *4916*
And that he was *b*, and that he rose 1Cor 15:4 *2290*
B with him in baptism, wherein Col 2:12 *4916*

BURIERS

till the *b* have buried it in the Eze 39:15 6912

BURN

make brick, and *b* them throughly Gen 11:3 8313
thine anger *b* against thy servant Gen 44:18 2734
the morning ye shall *b* with fire Ex 12:10 8313
to cause the lamp to *b* always Ex 27:20 5927
them, and *b* them upon the altar Ex 29:13 6999
shalt thou *b* with fire without Ex 29:14 8313
thou shalt *b* the whole ram upon Ex 29:18 6999
b them upon the altar for a burnt Ex 29:25 6999
then thou shalt *b* the remainder Ex 29:34 8313
make an altar to *b* incense upon Ex 30:1 4729
Aaron shall *b* thereon sweet Ex 30:7 6999
he shall *b* incense upon it Ex 30:7 6999
he shall *b* incense upon it, a Ex 30:8 6999
to *b* offering made by fire unto Ex 30:20 6999
priest shall *b* all on the altar Lev 1:9 6999
it all, and *b* it upon the altar Lev 1:13 6999
his head, and *b* it on the altar Lev 1:15 6999
the priest shall *b* it upon the Lev 1:17 6999
the priest shall *b* the memorial Lev 2:2 6999
shall *b* it upon the altar Lev 2:9 6999
for ye shall *b* no leaven, nor any Lev 2:11 6999
the priest shall *b* the memorial Lev 2:16 6999
Aaron's sons shall *b* it on the Lev 3:5 6999
the priest shall *b* it upon the Lev 3:11 6999
the priest shall *b* them upon the Lev 3:16 6999
the priest shall *b* them upon the Lev 4:10 6999
b him on the wood with fire Lev 4:12 8313
from him, and *b* it upon the altar Lev 4:19 6999
b him as he burned the first Lev 4:21 8313
he shall *b* all his fat upon the Lev 4:26 6999
the priest shall *b* it upon the Lev 4:31 6999
the priest shall *b* them upon the Lev 4:35 6999
b it on the altar, according to Lev 5:12 6999
the priest shall *b* wood on it Lev 6:12 1197
he shall *b* thereon the fat of the Lev 6:12 6999
shall *b* it upon the altar for a Lev 6:15 6999
the priest shall *b* them upon the Lev 7:5 6999
the priest shall *b* the fat upon Lev 7:31 6999
of the bread shall ye *b* with fire Lev 8:32 8313
He shall therefore *b* that garment Lev 13:52 8313
thou shalt *b* it in the fire Lev 13:55 8313
thou shalt *b* that wherein the Lev 13:57 8313
shall he *b* upon the altar Lev 16:25 6999
they shall *b* in the fire their Lev 16:27 8313
b the fat for a sweet savour unto Lev 17:6 6999
cause the lamps to *b* continually Lev 24:2 5927
b it upon the altar, and afterward Num 5:26 6999
shalt *b* their fat for an offering Num 18:17 6999
one shall *b* the heifer in his Num 19:5 8313
blood, with her dung, shall he *b* Num 19:5 8313
(for the mountain did *b* with fire Deut 5:23 1197
b their graven images with fire Deut 7:5 8313
their gods shall ye *b* with fire Deut 7:25 8313
and *b* their groves with fire Deut 12:3 8313
shalt *b* with fire the city, and Deut 13:16 8313
shall *b* unto the lowest hell, and Deut 32:22 3344
b their chariots with fire Josh 11:6 8313
that did Joshua *b* Josh 11:13 8313
of the tower to *b* it with fire Judg 9:52 8313
we will *b* thine house upon thee Judg 12:1 8313
us the riddle, lest we *b* thee Judg 14:15 8313
not fail to *b* the fat presently 1Sa 2:16 6999
to *b* incense, to wear an ephod 1Sa 2:28 6999
stood by the altar to *b* incense 1Kin 13:1 6999
places that *b* incense upon thee 1Kin 13:2 6999
Upon the great altar *b* the 2Kin 16:15 6999
of Israel did *b* incense to it 2Kin 18:4 6999
b incense in the high places in 2Kin 23:5 6999
to *b* incense before the LORD, to 1Chr 23:13 6999
to *b* before him sweet incense, and 2Chr 2:4 6999
save only to *b* sacrifice before 2Chr 2:6 6999
that they should *b* after the 2Chr 4:20 1197
they *b* unto the LORD every 2Chr 13:11 6999
lamps thereof, to *b* every evening 2Chr 13:11 1197
to *b* incense upon the altar of 2Chr 26:16 6999
to *b* incense unto the LORD, but 2Chr 26:18 6999
that are consecrated to *b* incense 2Chr 26:18 6999
a censer in his hand to *b* incense 2Chr 26:19 6999
to *b* incense unto other gods 2Chr 28:25 6999
minister unto him, and *b* incense 2Chr 29:11 6999
one altar, and *b* incense upon it 2Chr 32:12 6999
to *b* upon the altar of the LORD Neh 10:34 1197
shall thy jealousy *b* like fire Ps 79:5 1197
shall thy wrath *b* like fire Ps 89:46 1197
and they shall both *b* together Is 1:31 1197
and it shall *b* and devour his Is 10:17 1197
them, I would *b* them together Is 27:4 6702
And Lebanon is not sufficient to *b* Is 40:16 1197
Then shall it be for a man to *b* Is 44:15 1197
the fire shall *b* them Is 47:14 8313
b that none can quench it because Jer 4:4 1197
b incense unto Baal, and walk Jer 7:9 6999
and it shall *b*, and shall not be Jer 7:20 1197
Hinnom, to *b* their sons and their Jer 7:31 8313
even altars to *b* incense unto Jer 11:13 6999
anger, which shall *b* upon you Jer 15:14 3344
anger, which shall *b* for ever Jer 17:4 3344
to *b* their sons with fire for Jer 19:5 8313
and he shall *b* it with fire Jer 21:10 8313
b that none can quench it, Jer 21:12 1197
b it with the houses, upon whose Jer 32:29 8313
and he shall *b* it with fire Jer 34:2 8313
so shall they *b* odours for thee Jer 34:5 8313
and and take it, and *b* it with fire Jer 34:22 8313
king that he would not *b* the roll Jer 36:25 8313
and take it, and *b* it with fire Jer 37:8 8313
tent, and *b* this city with fire Jer 37:10 8313
they shall *b* it with fire, and Jer 38:18 8313
and he shall *b* them, and carry them Jer 43:12 8313
Egyptians shall he *b* with fire Jer 43:13 8313
in that they went to *b* incense Jer 44:3 6999
to *b* no incense unto other gods Jer 44:5 6999
to *b* incense unto the queen of Jer 44:17 6999
But since we left off to *b* Jer 44:18 6999
to *b* incense to the queen of Jer 44:25 6999
Thou shalt *b* with fire a third Eze 5:2 1197
the fire, and *b* them in the fire Eze 5:4 8313
they shall *b* thine houses with Eze 16:41 8313
b up their houses with fire Eze 23:47 8313
b also the bones under it, and Eze 24:5 1754
brass of it may be hot, and may *b* Eze 24:11 2787
b the weapons, both the shields Eze 39:9 5400
they shall *b* them with fire seven Eze 39:9 1197
for they shall *b* the weapons with Eze 39:10 1197
he shall *b* it in the appointed Eze 43:21 8313
b incense upon the hills, under Hos 4:13 6999
I will *b* her chariots in the Nah 2:13 1197
b incense unto their drag Hab 1:16 6999
cometh, that shall *b* as an oven Mal 4:1 1197
day that cometh shall *b* them up Mal 4:1 3857
but he will *b* up the chaff with Mt 3:12 *2618*
and bind them in bundles to *b* them Mt 13:30 *2618*
his lot was to *b* incense when he Lk 1:9 *2370*
but the chaff he will *b* with fire Lk 3:17 *2618*
Did not our heart *b* within us Lk 24:32 *2545*
it is better to marry than to *b* 1Cor 7:9 *4448*
who is offended, and I *b* not 2Cor 11:29 *4448*
eat her flesh, and *b* her with fire Rev 17:16 *2618*

BURNED

the bush *b* with fire, and the bush Ex 3:2 1197
burn him as he *b* the first Lev 4:21 8313
Moses *b* it upon the altar Lev 8:16 6999
the mountain *b* with fire unto the Deut 4:11 1197
mount, and the mount *b* with fire Deut 9:15 1197
b them with fire, after they had Josh 7:25 8313
Israel *b* none of them, save Hazor Josh 11:13 8313
smitten Ziklag, and *b* it with fire 1Sa 30:1 8313
and, behold, it was *b* with fire 1Sa 30:3 8313
and we *b* Ziklag with fire 1Sa 30:14 8313
and David and his men *b* them 2Sa 5:21 5375
they shall be utterly *b* with fire 2Sa 23:7 8313
of the house of Baal, and *b* them 2Kin 10:26 8313
b incense still in the high 2Kin 15:35 6999
have *b* incense unto other gods, 2Kin 22:17 6999
he *b* them without Jerusalem in 2Kin 23:4 8313
them also that *b* incense unto 2Kin 23:5 6999
b it at the brook Kidron, and 2Kin 23:6 8313
where the priests had *b* incense 2Kin 23:8 6999
b the chariots of the sun with 2Kin 23:11 8313
b the high place, and stamped it 2Kin 23:15 8313
small to powder, and *b* the grove 2Kin 23:15 8313
b them upon the altar, and 2Kin 23:16 8313
b men's bones upon them, and 2Kin 23:20 8313
and they were *b* with fire 1Chr 14:12 8313
them, and *b* incense unto them 2Chr 25:14 6999
have not *b* incense nor offered 2Chr 29:7 6999
have *b* incense unto other gods, 2Chr 34:25 6999
the gates thereof are *b* with fire Neh 1:3 3341
the gates thereof are *b* with fire Neh 2:17 3341
heaps of the rubbish which are *b* Neh 4:2 8313
very wroth, and his anger *b* in him Est 1:12 1197
hath *b* up the sheep, and the Job 1:16 1197
me, and my bones are *b* with heat Job 30:30 2787
while I was musing the fire *b* Ps 39:3 1197
they have *b* up all the synagogues Ps 74:8 8313
It is *b* with fire, it is cut down Ps 80:16 8313
and my bones are *b* as an hearth Ps 102:3 2787
the flame *b* up the wicked Ps 106:18 3857
bosom, and his clothes not be *b* Prov 6:27 8313
hot coals, and his feet not be *b* Prov 6:28 3554
your cities are *b* with fire Is 1:7 8313
inhabitants of the earth are *b* Is 24:6 2787
up shall they be *b* in the fire Is 33:12 3341
it *b* him, yet he laid it not to Is 42:25 1197
the fire, thou shalt not be *b* Is 43:2 3554
I have *b* part of it in the fire Is 44:19 8314
praised thee, is *b* up with fire Is 64:11 8316
which have *b* incense upon the Is 65:7 6999
have *b* incense unto other gods, Jer 1:16 6999
his cities are *b* without Jer 2:15 3341
The bellows are *b*, the lead is Jer 6:29 2787
because they are *b* up, so that Jer 9:10 3341
is *b* up like a wilderness, that Jer 9:12 3341
they have *b* incense to vanity, and Jer 18:15 6999
have *b* incense in it unto other Jer 19:4 6999
upon whose roofs they have *b* Jer 19:13 6999
that the king had *b* the roll Jer 36:27 8313
the king of Judah hath *b* Jer 36:28 8313
Thou hast *b* this roll, saying, Jer 36:29 8313
king of Judah had *b* in the fire Jer 36:32 8313
city shall not be *b* with fire Jer 38:17 8313
cause this city to be *b* with fire Jer 38:23 8313
the Chaldeans *b* the king's house, Jer 39:8 8313
had *b* incense unto other gods Jer 44:15 6999
when we *b* incense to the queen of Jer 44:19 6999
The incense that ye *b* in the Jer 44:21 6999
Because ye have *b* incense Jer 44:23 6999
daughters shall be *b* with fire Jer 49:2 3341
they have *b* her dwellingplaces Jer 51:30 3341
the reeds they have *b* with fire Jer 51:32 8313
high gates shall be *b* with fire Jer 51:58 3341
b the house of the LORD, and the Jer 52:13 8313
of the great men, *b* he with fire Jer 52:13 8313
he *b* against Jacob like a flaming Lam 2:3 1197
of it, and the midst of it is *b* Eze 15:4 2787
fire hath devoured it, and it is *b* Eze 15:5 2787
to the north shall be *b* therein Eze 20:47 6866
it well, and let the bones be *b* Eze 24:10 2787
wherein she *b* incense to them, and Hos 2:13 6999
b incense to graven images Hos 11:2 6999
the flame hath *b* all the trees of Joel 1:19 3857
because he *b* the bones of the Amos 2:1 8313
thereof shall be *b* with the fire Mic 1:7 8313
the earth is *b* at his presence, Nah 1:5 5375
are gathered and *b* in the fire Mt 13:40 *2618*
murderers, and *b* up their city Mt 22:7 *1714*
them into the fire, and they are *b* Jn 15:6 *2545*
and *b* them before all men Acts 19:19 *2618*
b in their lust one toward Rom 1:27 *1572*
If any man's work shall be *b* 1Cor 3:15 *2618*
and though I give my body to be *b* 1Cor 13:3 *2545*
whose end is to be *b* Heb 6:8 *2740*
that *b* with fire, nor unto Heb 12:18 *2545*
for sin, are *b* without the camp Heb 13:11 *2618*
that are therein shall be *b* up 2Pet 3:10 *2618*
as if they *b* in a furnace Rev 1:15 *4448*
she shall be utterly *b* with fire Rev 18:8 *2618*

BURNETH

the quick flesh that *b* have a Lev 13:24 4348
he that *b* them shall wash his Lev 16:28 8313
he that *b* her shall wash his Num 19:8 8313
he *b* the chariot in the fire Ps 46:9 8313
As the fire *b* a wood, and as the Ps 83:14 1197
b up his enemies round about Ps 97:3 3857
For wickedness *b* as the fire Is 9:18 1197
He *b* part thereof in the fire Is 44:16 8313
thereof as a lamp that *b* Is 62:1 1197
As when the melting fire *b* Is 64:2 6919
b incense upon altars of brick Is 65:3 6999
nose, a fire that *b* all the day Is 65:5 3344
he that *b* incense, as if he Is 66:3 2142
him that *b* incense to his gods Jer 48:35 6999
morning it *b* as a flaming fire Hos 7:6 1197
and behind them a flame *b* Joel 2:3 3857
take him up, and he that *b* him Amos 6:10 5635
in the lake which *b* with fire Rev 21:8 *2545*

BURNING

a *b* lamp that passed between Gen 15:17 784
B for *b*, wound for wound, Ex 21:25 3555
B for *b*, wound for wound, Ex 21:25 3345
because of the *b* upon the altar Lev 6:9 4169
of the altar shall be *b* in it Lev 6:9 3344
upon the altar shall be *b* in it Lev 6:12 3344
shall ever be *b* upon the altar Lev 6:13 3344
bewail the *b* which the LORD hath Lev 10:6 8316
and spread not, it is a *b* boil Lev 13:23 6867
the skin whereof there is a hot *b* Lev 13:24 4348
is a leprosy broken out of the *b* Lev 13:25 4348
it is a rising of the *b*, and the Lev 13:28 4348
it is an inflammation of the *b* Lev 13:28 4348
of *b* coals of fire from off the Lev 16:12 784
the *b* ague, that shall consume Lev 26:16 6920
take up the censers out of the *b* Num 16:37 8316
the midst of the *b* of the heifer Num 19:6 8316
and with an extreme *b*, and with Deut 28:22 2746
is brimstone, and salt, and *b* Deut 29:23 8316
hunger, and devoured with *b* heat Deut 32:24
they made a very great *b* for him 2Chr 16:14 8316
And his people made no *b* for him 2Chr 21:19 8316
like the *b* of his fathers 2Chr 21:19 8316
Out of his mouth go *b* lamps Job 41:19 3940
Let *b* coals fall upon them Ps 140:10 784
in his lips there is as a *b* fire Prov 16:27 6867
As coals are to *b* coals, and wood Prov 26:21 1513
B lips and a wicked heart are like Prov 26:23 1814
and *b* instead of beauty Is 3:24 3587
judgment, and by the spirit of *b* Is 4:4 1197
but this shall be with *b* and fuel Is 9:5 8316
a *b* like the *b* of a fire Is 10:16 3350
a *b* like the *b* of a fire Is 10:16 3345
b with his anger, and the burden Is 30:27 1197
land thereof shall become *b* pitch Is 34:9 1197
as a *b* fire shut up in my bones Jer 20:9 1197
a fire on the hearth *b* before him Jer 36:22 1197
b incense unto other gods in the Jer 44:8 6999
was like *b* coals of fire, and like Eze 1:13 1197
the midst of a *b* fiery furnace Dan 3:6 3345
the midst of a *b* fiery furnace Dan 3:11 3345
the midst of a *b* fiery furnace Dan 3:15 3345
us from the *b* fiery furnace Dan 3:17 3345
them into the *b* fiery furnace Dan 3:20 3345
the midst of the *b* fiery furnace Dan 3:21 3345
the midst of the *b* fiery furnace Dan 3:23 3345
the mouth of the *b* fiery furnace Dan 3:26 3345
flame, and his wheels as *b* fire Dan 7:9 1815
and given to the *b* flame Dan 7:11 3346
a firebrand plucked out of the *b* Amos 4:11 8316
b coals went forth at his feet Hab 3:5 7565
be girded about, and your lights *b* Lk 12:35 *2545*
He was a *b* and a shining light Jn 5:35 *2545*
is no sooner risen with a *b* heat Jas 1:11 *2742*
lamps of fire *b* before the throne Rev 4:5 *2545*
as it were a great mountain *b* Rev 8:8 *2545*
b as it were a lamp, and it fell Rev 8:10 *2545*
they shall see the smoke of her *b* Rev 18:9 *4451*
when they saw the smoke of her *b* Rev 18:18 *4451*

a lake of fire *b* with brimstone	Rev 19:20	*2545*

BURNINGS

people shall be as the *b* of lime	Is 33:12	4955
us shall dwell with everlasting *b*	Is 33:14	4168
with the *b* of thy fathers, the	Jer 34:5	4955

BURNISHED

like the colour of *b* brass	Eze 1:7	7044

BURNT

offered *b* offerings on the altar	Gen 8:20	5930
offer him there for a *b* offering	Gen 22:2	5930
clave the wood for the *b* offering	Gen 22:3	5930
took the wood of the *b* offering	Gen 22:6	5930
is the lamb for a *b* offering	Gen 22:7	5930
himself a lamb for a *b* offering	Gen 22:8	5930
offered him up for a *b* offering	Gen 22:13	5930
Bring her forth, and let her be *b*	Gen 38:24	8313
sight, why the bush is not *b*	Ex 3:3	1197
and *b* offerings, that we may	Ex 10:25	5930
took a *b* offering and sacrifices	Ex 18:12	5930
sacrifice thereon thy *b* offerings	Ex 20:24	5930
Israel, which offered *b* offerings	Ex 24:5	5930
it is a *b* offering unto the LORD	Ex 29:18	5930
upon the altar for a *b* offering	Ex 29:25	5930
b offering throughout your	Ex 29:42	5930
nor *b* sacrifice, nor meat	Ex 30:9	5930
the altar of *b* offering with all	Ex 30:28	5930
the altar of *b* offering with all	Ex 31:9	5930
offered *b* offerings, and brought	Ex 32:6	5930
b it in the fire, and ground it to	Ex 32:20	8313
The altar of *b* offering, with his	Ex 35:16	5930
he made the altar of *b* offering	Ex 38:1	5930
b offering before the door of the	Ex 40:6	5930
the altar of the *b* offering	Ex 40:10	5930
he *b* sweet incense thereon	Ex 40:27	6999
he put the altar of *b* offering by	Ex 40:29	5930
and offered upon it the *b* offering	Ex 40:29	5930
If his offering be a *b* sacrifice	Lev 1:3	5930
upon the head of the *b* offering	Lev 1:4	5930
And he shall flay the *b* offering	Lev 1:6	5930
to be a *b* sacrifice, an offering	Lev 1:9	5930
of the goats, for a *b* sacrifice	Lev 1:10	5930
it is a *b* sacrifice, an offering	Lev 1:13	5930
if the *b* sacrifice for his	Lev 1:14	5930
it is a *b* sacrifice, an offering	Lev 1:17	5930
but they shall not be *b* on the	Lev 2:12	5927
on the altar upon the *b* sacrifice	Lev 3:5	5930
of the altar of the *b* offering	Lev 4:7	5930
upon the altar of the *b* offering	Lev 4:10	5930
are poured out shall he be *b*	Lev 4:12	8313
of the altar of the *b* offering	Lev 4:18	5930
the *b* offering before the LORD	Lev 4:24	5930
horns of the altar of *b* offering	Lev 4:25	5930
bottom of the altar of *b* offering	Lev 4:25	5930
in the place of the *b* offering	Lev 4:29	5930
horns of the altar of *b* offering	Lev 4:30	5930
where they kill the *b* offering	Lev 4:33	5930
horns of the altar of *b* offering	Lev 4:34	5930
and the other for a *b* offering	Lev 5:7	5930
offer the second for a *b* offering	Lev 5:10	5930
This is the law of the *b* offering	Lev 6:9	5930
It is the *b* offering, because of	Lev 6:9	5930
with the *b* offering on the altar	Lev 6:10	5930
lay the *b* offering in order upon	Lev 6:12	6999
it shall be wholly *b*	Lev 6:22	6999
for the priest shall be wholly *b*	Lev 6:23	
In the place where the *b* offering	Lev 6:25	5930
it shall be *b* in the fire	Lev 6:30	8313
b offering shall they kill the	Lev 7:2	5930
offereth any man's *b* offering	Lev 7:8	5930
b offering which he hath offered	Lev 7:8	5930
third day shall be *b* with fire	Lev 7:17	8313
it shall be *b* with fire	Lev 7:19	8313
This is the law of the *b* offering	Lev 7:37	5930
he *b* with fire without the camp	Lev 8:17	8313
the ram for the *b* offering	Lev 8:18	5930
Moses *b* the head, and the pieces,	Lev 8:20	6999
Moses *b* the whole ram upon the	Lev 8:21	6999
it was a *b* sacrifice for a sweet	Lev 8:21	5930
b them on the altar upon the	Lev 8:28	6999
on the altar upon the *b* offering	Lev 8:28	5930
and a ram for a *b* offering	Lev 9:2	5930
without blemish, for a *b* offering	Lev 9:3	5930
thy *b* offering, and make an	Lev 9:7	5930
sin offering, he *b* upon the altar	Lev 9:10	6999
the hide he *b* with fire without	Lev 9:11	8313
And he slew the *b* offering	Lev 9:12	5930
presented the *b* offering unto him	Lev 9:13	5930
and he *b* them upon the altar	Lev 9:13	6999
b them upon the *b* offering on	Lev 9:14	6999
b them upon the *b* offering on	Lev 9:14	5930
And he brought the *b* offering	Lev 9:16	5930
b it upon the altar	Lev 9:17	6999
beside the *b* sacrifice of the	Lev 9:17	5930
he *b* the fat upon the altar	Lev 9:20	6999
and the *b* offering, and peace	Lev 9:22	5930
upon the altar the *b* offering	Lev 9:24	5930
offering, and, behold, it was *b*	Lev 10:16	8313
their *b* offering before the LORD	Lev 10:19	5930
the first year for a *b* offering	Lev 12:6	5930
the one for the *b* offering	Lev 12:8	5930
it shall be *b* in the fire	Lev 13:52	8313
the *b* offering, in the holy place	Lev 14:13	5930
he shall kill the *b* offering	Lev 14:19	5930
priest shall offer the *b* offering	Lev 14:20	5930
and the other a *b* offering	Lev 14:22	5930
and the other for a *b* offering	Lev 14:31	5930
and the other for a *b* offering	Lev 15:15	5930
and the other for a *b* offering	Lev 15:30	5930
and a ram for a *b* offering	Lev 16:3	5930
and one ram for a *b* offering	Lev 16:5	5930
forth, and offer his *b* offering	Lev 16:24	5930
the *b* offering of the people, and	Lev 16:24	5930
that offereth a *b* offering or	Lev 17:8	5930
day, it shall be *b* in the fire	Lev 19:6	8313
they shall be *b* with fire	Lev 20:14	8313
she shall be *b* with fire	Lev 21:9	8313
unto the LORD for a *b* offering	Lev 22:18	5930
for a *b* offering unto the LORD	Lev 23:12	5930
they shall be for a *b* offering	Lev 23:18	5930
a *b* offering, and a meat offering,	Lev 23:37	5930
and the other for a *b* offering	Num 6:11	5930
without blemish for a *b* offering	Num 6:14	5930
sin offering, and his *b* offering	Num 6:16	5930
the first year, for a *b* offering	Num 7:15	5930
the first year, for a *b* offering	Num 7:21	5930
the first year, for a *b* offering	Num 7:27	5930
the first year, for a *b* offering	Num 7:33	5930
the first year, for a *b* offering	Num 7:39	5930
the first year, for a *b* offering	Num 7:45	5930
the first year, for a *b* offering	Num 7:51	5930
the first year, for a *b* offering	Num 7:57	5930
the first year, for a *b* offering	Num 7:63	5930
the first year, for a *b* offering	Num 7:69	5930
the first year, for a *b* offering	Num 7:75	5930
the first year, for a *b* offering	Num 7:81	5930
All the oxen for the *b* offering	Num 7:87	5930
and the other for a *b* offering	Num 8:12	5930
trumpets over your *b* offerings	Num 10:10	5930
the fire of the LORD *b* among them	Num 11:1	1197
the fire of the LORD *b* among them	Num 11:3	1197
a *b* offering, or a sacrifice in	Num 15:3	5930
with the *b* offering or sacrifice	Num 15:5	5930
a bullock for a *b* offering	Num 15:8	5930
young bullock for a *b* offering	Num 15:24	5930
they that were *b* had offered	Num 16:39	8313
b heifer of purification for sin	Num 19:17	8316
Balak, Stand by thy *b* offering	Num 23:3	5930
lo, he stood by his *b* sacrifice	Num 23:6	5930
Stand here by thy *b* offering	Num 23:15	5930
he stood by his *b* offering	Num 23:17	5930
day, for a continual *b* offering	Num 28:3	5930
It is a continual *b* offering	Num 28:6	5930
This is the *b* offering of every	Num 28:10	5930
beside the continual *b* offering	Num 28:10	5930
offer a *b* offering unto the LORD	Num 28:11	5930
for a *b* offering of a sweet	Num 28:13	5930
this is the *b* offering of every	Num 28:14	5930
beside the continual *b* offering	Num 28:15	5930
for a *b* offering unto the LORD	Num 28:19	5930
the *b* offering in the morning	Num 28:23	5930
is for a continual *b* offering	Num 28:23	5930
beside the continual *b* offering	Num 28:24	5930
But ye shall offer the *b* offering	Num 28:27	5930
beside the continual *b* offering	Num 28:31	5930
ye shall offer a *b* offering for a	Num 29:2	5930
Beside the *b* offering of the	Num 29:6	5930
offering, and the daily *b* offering	Num 29:6	5930
But ye shall offer a *b* offering	Num 29:8	5930
and the continual *b* offering	Num 29:11	5930
And ye shall offer a *b* offering	Num 29:13	5930
beside the continual *b* offering	Num 29:16	5930
beside the continual *b* offering	Num 29:19	5930
beside the continual *b* offering	Num 29:22	5930
beside the continual *b* offering	Num 29:25	5930
beside the continual *b* offering	Num 29:28	5930
beside the continual *b* offering	Num 29:31	5930
beside the continual *b* offering	Num 29:34	5930
But ye shall offer a *b* offering	Num 29:36	5930
beside the continual *b* offering	Num 29:38	5930
for your *b* offerings, and for your	Num 29:39	5930
they *b* all their cities wherein	Num 31:10	8313
b it with fire, and stamped it, and	Deut 9:21	8313
ye shall bring your *b* offerings	Deut 12:6	5930
your *b* offerings, and your	Deut 12:11	5930
b offerings in every place that	Deut 12:13	5930
thou shalt offer thy *b* offerings	Deut 12:14	5930
thou shalt offer thy *b* offerings	Deut 12:27	5930
have *b* in the fire to their gods	Deut 12:31	8313
thou shalt offer *b* offerings	Deut 27:6	5930
They shall be *b* with hunger	Deut 32:24	4198
whole *b* sacrifice upon thine	Deut 33:10	3632
they *b* the city with fire, and all	Josh 6:24	8313
thing shall be *b* with fire	Josh 7:15	8313
And Joshua *b* Ai, and made it an	Josh 8:28	8313
they offered thereon *b* offerings	Josh 8:31	5930
b their chariots with fire	Josh 11:9	8313
and he *b* Hazor with fire	Josh 11:11	8313
or if to offer thereon *b* offering	Josh 22:23	5930
not for *b* offering, nor for	Josh 22:26	5930
before him with our *b* offerings	Josh 22:27	5930
not for *b* offerings, nor for	Josh 22:28	5930
to build an altar for *b* offerings	Josh 22:29	5930
offer a *b* sacrifice with the wood	Judg 6:26	5930
will offer it up for a *b* offering	Judg 11:31	5930
if thou wilt offer a *b* offering	Judg 13:16	5930
not have received a *b* offering	Judg 13:23	5930
b up both the shocks, and also the	Judg 15:5	1197
b her and her father with fire	Judg 15:6	8313
as flax that was *b* with fire	Judg 15:14	1197
sword, and *b* the city with fire	Judg 18:27	8313
offered *b* offerings and peace	Judg 20:26	5930
offered *b* offerings and peace	Judg 21:4	5930
Also before they *b* the fat	1Sa 2:15	6999
offered the kine a *b* offering	1Sa 6:14	5930
Beth-shemesh offered *b* offerings	1Sa 6:15	5930
offered it for a *b* offering	1Sa 7:9	5930
was offering up the *b* offering	1Sa 7:10	5930
to offer *b* offerings, and to	1Sa 10:8	5930
Bring hither a *b* offering to me	1Sa 13:9	5930
And he offered the *b* offering	1Sa 13:9	5930
an end of offering the *b* offering	1Sa 13:10	5930
and offered a *b* offering	1Sa 13:12	5930
as great delight in *b* offerings	1Sa 15:22	5930
came to Jabesh, and *b* them there	1Sa 31:12	8313
and David offered *b* offerings	2Sa 6:17	5930
an end of offering *b* offerings	2Sa 6:18	5930
here be oxen for *b* sacrifice	2Sa 24:22	5930
neither will I offer *b* offerings	2Sa 24:24	5930
offered *b* offerings and peace	2Sa 24:25	5930
and *b* incense in high places	1Kin 3:3	6999
a thousand *b* offerings did	1Kin 3:4	5930
LORD, and offered up *b* offerings	1Kin 3:15	5930
for there he offered *b* offerings	1Kin 8:64	5930
little to receive the *b* offerings	1Kin 8:64	5930
b it with fire, and slain the	1Kin 9:16	8313
did Solomon offer *b* offerings	1Kin 9:25	5930
he *b* incense upon the altar that	1Kin 9:25	6999
which *b* incense and sacrificed	1Kin 11:8	6999
upon the altar, and *b* incense	1Kin 12:33	6999
men's bones shall be *b* upon thee	1Kin 13:2	8313
idol, and *b* it by the brook Kidron	1Kin 15:13	8313
b the king's house over him with	1Kin 16:18	8313
and pour it on the *b* sacrifice	1Kin 18:33	5930
fell, and consumed the *b* sacrifice	1Kin 18:38	5930
b incense yet in the high places	1Kin 22:43	6999
b up the two captains of the	2Kin 1:14	398
offered him for a *b* offering upon	2Kin 3:27	5930
b offering nor sacrifice unto	2Kin 5:17	5930
b offerings, Jehu appointed	2Kin 10:24	5930
an end of offering the *b* offering	2Kin 10:25	5930
b incense in the high places	2Kin 12:3	6999
b incense on the high places	2Kin 14:4	6999
b incense still on the high	2Kin 15:4	6999
b incense in the high places, and	2Kin 16:4	6999
And he *b* his *b* offering	2Kin 16:13	6999
altar burn the morning *b* offering	2Kin 16:15	5930
and the king's *b* sacrifice	2Kin 16:15	5930
with the *b* offering of all the	2Kin 16:15	5930
all the blood of the *b* offering	2Kin 16:15	5930
there they *b* incense in all the	2Kin 17:11	6999
the Sepharvites *b* their children	2Kin 17:31	8313
he *b* the house of the LORD, and	2Kin 25:9	8313
great man's house *b* he with fire	2Kin 25:9	8313
upon the altar of the *b* offering	1Chr 6:49	5930
and they offered *b* sacrifices	1Chr 16:1	5930
end of offering the *b* offerings	1Chr 16:2	5930
To offer *b* offerings unto the	1Chr 16:40	5930
b offering continually morning	1Chr 16:40	5930
the oxen also for *b* offerings	1Chr 21:23	5930
nor offer *b* offerings without	1Chr 21:24	5930
offered *b* offerings and peace	1Chr 21:26	5930
fire upon the altar of *b* offering	1Chr 21:26	5930
and the altar of the *b* offering	1Chr 21:29	5930
of the *b* offering for Israel	1Chr 22:1	5930
to offer all *b* sacrifices unto	1Chr 23:31	5930
offered *b* offerings unto the LORD	1Chr 29:21	5930
a thousand *b* offerings upon it	2Chr 1:6	5930
for the *b* offerings morning and	2Chr 2:4	5930
b offering they washed in them	2Chr 4:6	5930
and consumed the *b* offering	2Chr 7:1	5930
for there he offered *b* offerings	2Chr 7:7	5930
able to receive the *b* offerings	2Chr 7:7	5930
Then Solomon offered *b* offerings	2Chr 8:12	5930
and every evening *b* sacrifices	2Chr 13:11	5930
it, and *b* it at the brook Kidron	2Chr 15:16	8313
to offer the *b* offerings of the	2Chr 23:18	5930
they offered *b* offerings in the	2Chr 24:14	5930
Moreover he *b* incense in the	2Chr 28:3	6999
b his children in the fire, after	2Chr 28:3	1197
b incense in the high places, and	2Chr 28:4	6999
b offerings in the holy place	2Chr 29:7	5930
LORD, and the altar of *b* offering	2Chr 29:18	5930
commanded that the *b* offering	2Chr 29:24	5930
the *b* offering upon the altar	2Chr 29:27	5930
when the *b* offering began, the	2Chr 29:27	5930
until the *b* offering was finished	2Chr 29:28	5930
were of a free heart *b* offerings	2Chr 29:31	5930
And the number of the *b* offerings	2Chr 29:32	5930
were for a *b* offering to the LORD	2Chr 29:32	5930
not flay all the *b* offerings	2Chr 29:34	5930
also the *b* offerings were in	2Chr 29:35	5930
offerings for every *b* offering	2Chr 29:35	5930
brought in the *b* offerings into	2Chr 30:15	5930
and Levites for *b* offerings	2Chr 31:2	5930
his substance for the *b* offerings	2Chr 31:3	5930
evening *b* offerings, and the *b*	2Chr 31:3	5930
he *b* the bones of the priests	2Chr 34:5	8313
And they removed the *b* offerings	2Chr 35:12	5930
busied in offering of *b* offerings	2Chr 35:14	5930
to offer *b* offerings upon the	2Chr 35:16	5930
they *b* the house of God, and brake	2Chr 36:19	8313
b all the palaces thereof with	2Chr 36:19	8313
to offer *b* offerings thereon, as	Ezr 3:2	5930
they offered *b* offerings thereon	Ezr 3:3	5930
even *b* offerings morning and	Ezr 3:3	5930
offered the daily *b* offerings by	Ezr 3:4	5930
offered the continual *b* offering	Ezr 3:5	5930
offer *b* offerings unto the LORD	Ezr 3:6	5930
for the *b* offerings of the God of	Ezr 6:9	5928
offered *b* offerings unto the God	Ezr 8:35	5930
all this was a *b* offering unto	Ezr 8:35	5930
and for the continual *b* offering	Neh 10:33	5930
offered *b* offerings according to	Job 1:5	5930
up for yourselves a *b* offering	Job 42:8	5930
and accept thy *b* sacrifice	Ps 20:3	5930
b offering and sin offering hast	Ps 40:6	5930
thy sacrifices or thy *b* offerings	Ps 50:8	5930
thou delightest not in *b* offering	Ps 51:16	5930
b offering and whole *b* offering	Ps 51:19	5930
into thy house with *b* offerings	Ps 66:13	5930
thee *b* sacrifices of fatlings	Ps 66:15	5930
I am full of the *b* offerings of	Is 1:11	5930
sufficient for a *b* offering	Is 40:16	5930
small cattle of thy *b* offerings	Is 43:23	5930
their *b* offerings and their	Is 56:7	5930
I hate robbery for *b* offering	Is 61:8	5930
your *b* offerings are not	Jer 6:20	5930
Put your *b* offerings unto your	Jer 7:21	5930
concerning *b* offerings or	Jer 7:22	5930
and when they offer *b* offering	Jer 14:12	5930

south, bringing *b* offerings, and ... Jer 17:26 5930
fire for *b* offerings unto Baal ... Jer 19:5 5930
before me to offer *b* offerings ... Jer 33:18 5930
and will make thee a *b* mountain ... Jer 51:25 8316
where they washed the *b* offering ... Eze 40:38 5930
to slay thereon the *b* offering ... Eze 40:39 5930
of hewn stone for the *b* offering ... Eze 40:42 5930
they slew the *b* offering and the ... Eze 40:42 5930
to offer *b* offerings thereon, and ... Eze 43:18 5930
up for a *b* offering unto the LORD ... Eze 43:24 5930
your *b* offerings upon the altar ... Eze 43:27 5930
they shall slay the *b* offering ... Eze 44:11 5930
for a *b* offering, and for peace ... Eze 45:15 5930
prince's part to give *b* offerings ... Eze 45:17 5930
the *b* offering, and the peace ... Eze 45:17 5930
prepare a *b* offering to the LORD ... Eze 45:23 5930
according to the *b* offering ... Eze 45:25 5930
shall prepare his *b* offering ... Eze 46:2 5930
the *b* offering that the prince ... Eze 46:4 5930
shall prepare a voluntary *b* ... Eze 46:12 5930
he shall prepare his *b* offering ... Eze 46:12 5930
Thou shalt daily prepare a *b* ... Eze 46:13 5930
for a continual *b* offering ... Eze 46:15 5930
of God more than *b* offerings ... Hos 6:6 5930
Though ye offer me *b* offerings ... Amos 5:22 5930
come before him with *b* offerings ... Mic 6:6 5930
more than all whole *b* offerings ... Mk 12:33 *3646*
In *b* offerings and sacrifices for ... Heb 10:6 *3646*
b offerings and offering for sin ... Heb 10:8 *3646*
the third part of trees was *b* up ... Rev 8:7 *2618*
and all green grass was *b* up ... Rev 8:7 *2618*

BURST
it is ready to *b* like new bottles ... Job 32:19 1234
presses shall *b* out with new wine ... Prov 3:10 6555
broken thy yoke, and *b* thy bands ... Jer 2:20 5423
broken the yoke, and *b* the bonds ... Jer 5:5 5423
will *b* thy bonds, and strangers ... Jer 30:8 5423
will *b* thy bonds in sunder ... Nah 1:13 5423
the new wine doth *b* the bottles ... Mk 2:22 *4486*
the new wine will *b* the bottles ... Lk 5:37 *4486*
he *b* asunder in the midst, and all ... Acts 1:18 *2997*

BURSTING
b of it a sherd to take fire from ... Is 30:14 4386

BURY
that I may *b* my dead out of my ... Gen 23:4 6912
of our sepulchres *b* thy dead ... Gen 23:6 6912
but that thou mayest *b* thy dead ... Gen 23:6 6912
should *b* my dead out of my sight ... Gen 23:8 6912
b thy dead ... Gen 23:11 6912
of me, and I will *b* my dead there ... Gen 23:13 6912
b therefore thy dead ... Gen 23:15 6912
b me not, I pray thee, in Egypt ... Gen 47:29 6912
b me in their buryingplace ... Gen 47:30 6912
b me with my fathers in the cave ... Gen 49:29 6912
of Canaan, there shalt thou *b* me ... Gen 50:5 6912
b my father, and I will come again ... Gen 50:5 6912
b thy father, according as he ... Gen 50:6 6912
And Joseph went up to *b* his father ... Gen 50:7 6912
went up with him to *b* his father ... Gen 50:14 6912
shalt in any wise *b* him that day ... Deut 21:23 6912
said, and fall upon him, and *b* him ... 1Kin 2:31 6912
host was gone up to *b* the slain ... 1Kin 11:15 6912
to the city, to mourn and to *b* him ... 1Kin 13:29 6912
then *b* me in the sepulchre ... 1Kin 13:31 6912
shall mourn for him, and *b* him ... 1Kin 14:13 6912
and there shall be none to *b* her ... 2Kin 9:10 6912
now this cursed woman, and *b* her ... 2Kin 9:34 6912
And they went to *b* her ... 2Kin 9:35 6912
and there was none to *b* them ... Ps 79:3 6912
for they shall *b* in Tophet ... Jer 7:32 6912
and they shall have none to *b* them ... Jer 14:16 6912
they shall *b* them in Tophet ... Jer 19:11 6912
till there be no place to *b* ... Jer 19:11 6912
and there shall they *b* Gog ... Eze 39:11 6912
people of the land shall *b* them ... Eze 39:13 6912
passing through the land to *b* ... Eze 39:14 6912
them up, Memphis shall *b* them ... Hos 9:6 6912
me first to go and *b* my father ... Mt 8:21 *2290*
and let the dead *b* their dead ... Mt 8:22 *2290*
potter's field, to *b* strangers in ... Mt 27:7 *5027*
me first to go and *b* my father ... Lk 9:59 *2290*
him, Let the dead *b* their dead ... Lk 9:60 *2290*
as the manner of the Jews is to *b* ... Jn 19:40 *1779*

BURYING
to pass, as they were *b* a man ... 2Kin 13:21 6912
the house of Israel be *b* of them ... Eze 39:12 6912
to anoint my body to the *b* ... Mk 14:8 *1780*
day of my *b* hath she kept this ... Jn 12:7 *1780*

BURYINGPLACE
me a possession of a *b* with you ... Gen 23:4 6913
a possession of a *b* amongst you ... Gen 23:9 6913
of a *b* by the sons of Heth ... Gen 23:20 6913
of Egypt, and bury me in their *b* ... Gen 47:30 6913
Hittite for a possession of a *b* ... Gen 49:30 6913
of a *b* of Ephron the Hittite ... Gen 50:13 6913
Eshtaol in the *b* of Manoah his ... Judg 16:31 6913

BUSH
of fire out of the midst of a *b* ... Ex 3:2 5572
the *b* burned with fire ... Ex 3:2 5572
and the *b* was not consumed ... Ex 3:2 5572
sight, why the *b* is not burnt ... Ex 3:3 5572
him out of the midst of the *b* ... Ex 3:4 5572
will of him that dwelt in the *b* ... Deut 33:16 5572
how in the *b* God spake unto him, ... Mk 12:26 *942*
nor of a bramble *b* gather they ... Lk 6:44 *942*
even Moses shewed at the *b* ... Lk 20:37 *942*
Lord in a flame of fire in a *b* ... Acts 7:30 *942*
which appeared to him in the *b* ... Acts 7:35 *942*

BUSHEL
a candle, and put it under a *b* ... Mt 5:15 *3426*
brought to be put under a *b* ... Mk 4:21 *3426*
a secret place, neither under a *b* ... Lk 11:33 *3426*

BUSHES
Who cut up mallows by the *b* ... Job 30:4 7880
Among the *b* they brayed ... Job 30:7 7880
and upon all thorns, and upon all *b* ... Is 7:19 5097

BUSHY
most fine gold, his locks are *b* ... Song 5:11 8534

BUSIED
b in offering of burnt offerings ... 2Chr 35:14

BUSINESS
went into the house to do his *b* ... Gen 39:11 4399
shall he be charged with any *b* ... Deut 24:5 1697
yours, if ye utter not this our *b* ... Josh 2:14 1697
And if thou utter this our *b* ... Josh 2:20 1697
and had no *b* with any man ... Judg 18:7 1697
they had no *b* with any man ... Judg 18:28 1697
thyself when the *b* was in hand ... 1Sa 20:19 4639
The king hath commanded me a *b* ... 1Sa 21:2 1697
of the *b* whereabout I send thee ... 1Sa 21:2 1697
the king's *b* required haste ... 1Sa 21:8 1697
for the outward *b* over Israel ... 1Chr 26:29 4399
westward in all the *b* of the LORD ... 1Chr 26:30 4399
and the Levites wait upon their *b* ... 2Chr 13:10 4399
he had much *b* in the cities of ... 2Chr 17:13 4399
Howbeit in the *b* of the ... 2Chr 32:31
the outward *b* of the house of God ... Neh 11:16 4399
over the *b* of the house of God ... Neh 11:22 4399
the Levites, every one in his *b* ... Neh 13:30 4399
that have the charge of the *b* ... Est 3:9 4399
that do *b* in great waters ... Ps 107:23 4399
thou a man diligent in his *b* ... Prov 22:29 4399
cometh through the multitude of *b* ... Eccl 5:3 6045
to see the *b* that is done upon ... Eccl 8:16 6045
I rose up, and did the king's *b* ... Dan 8:27 4399
I must be about my Father's *b* ... Lk 2:49
whom we may appoint over this *b* ... Acts 6:3 *5532*
Not slothful in *b* ... Rom 12:11 *4710*
whatsoever *b* she hath need of you ... Rom 16:2 *4229*
to be quiet, and to do your own *b* ... 1Th 4:11 *2398*

BUSY
And as thy servant was *b* here ... 1Kin 20:40 6213

BUSYBODIES
working not at all, but are *b* ... 2Th 3:11 *4020*
only idle, but tattlers also and *b* ... 1Ti 5:13 *4021*

BUSYBODY
or as a *b* in other men's matters ... 1Pet 4:15 *244*

BUT See PREFACE.

BUTLER
that the *b* of the king of Egypt ... Gen 40:1 4945
of his dream, the *b* and the baker ... Gen 40:5 4945
the chief *b* told his dream to ... Gen 40:9 4945
manner when thou wast his *b* ... Gen 40:13 4945
lifted up the head of the chief *b* ... Gen 40:20 4945
he restored the chief *b* unto his ... Gen 40:21 4945
not the chief *b* remember Joseph ... Gen 40:23 4945
spake the chief *b* unto Pharaoh ... Gen 41:9 4945

BUTLERS
against the chief of the *b* ... Gen 40:2 4945

BUTLERSHIP
the chief butler unto his *b* again ... Gen 40:21 4945

BUTTER
And he took *b*, and milk, and the ... Gen 18:8 2529
B of kine, and milk of sheep, with ... Deut 32:14 2529
brought forth *b* in a lordly dish ... Judg 5:25 2529
And honey, and *b*, and sheep, and ... 2Sa 17:29 2529
floods, the brooks of honey and *b* ... Job 20:17 2529
When I washed my steps with *b* ... Job 29:6 2529
of his mouth were smoother than *b* ... Ps 55:21 4260
churning of milk bringeth forth *b* ... Prov 30:33 2529
B and honey shall he eat, that he ... Is 7:15 2529
they shall give, he shall eat *b* ... Is 7:22 2529
for *b* and honey shall every one ... Is 7:22 2529

BUTTOCKS
in the middle, even to their *b* ... 2Sa 10:4 8357
in the midst hard by their *b* ... 1Chr 19:4 4667
even with their *b* uncovered ... Is 20:4 8357

BUY
Egypt to Joseph for to *b* corn ... Gen 41:57 7666
thither, and *b* for us from thence ... Gen 42:2 7666
went down to *b* corn in Egypt ... Gen 42:3 7666
to *b* corn among those that came ... Gen 42:5 7666
From the land of Canaan to *b* food ... Gen 42:7 7666
but to *b* food are thy servants ... Gen 42:10 7666
Go again, *b* us a little food ... Gen 43:2 7666
we will go down and *b* thee food ... Gen 43:4 7666
down at the first time to *b* food ... Gen 43:20 7666
down in our hands to *b* food ... Gen 43:22 7666
Go again, and *b* us a little food ... Gen 44:25 7666
b us and our land for bread, and we ... Gen 47:19 7069
If thou *b* an Hebrew servant, six ... Ex 21:2 7069
But if the priest *b* any soul with ... Lev 22:11 7069
thou shalt *b* of thy neighbour ... Lev 25:15 7069
of them shall ye *b* bondmen ... Lev 25:44 7069
among you, of them shall ye *b* ... Lev 25:45 7069
Ye shall *b* meat of them for money ... Deut 2:6 7666
ye shall also *b* water of them for ... Deut 2:6 3739
bondwomen, and no man shall *b* you ... Deut 28:68 7069
B it before the inhabitants, and ... Ruth 4:4 7069
thou must *b* it also of Ruth the ... Ruth 4:5 7069
said unto Boaz, *B* it for thee ... Ruth 4:8 7069
To *b* the threshingfloor of thee, ... 2Sa 24:21 7069
but I will surely *b* it of thee at ... 2Sa 24:24 7069
to *b* timber and hewed stone to ... 2Kin 12:12 7069
to *b* timber and hewn stone to ... 2Kin 22:6 7069
but I will verily *b* it for the ... 1Chr 21:24 7069
to *b* hewn stone, and timber for ... 2Chr 34:11 7069
That thou mayest *b* speedily with ... Ezr 7:17 7066
and houses, that we might *b* corn ... Neh 5:3 3947
that we would not *b* it of them on ... Neh 10:31 3947
B the truth, and sell it not ... Prov 23:23 7069
come ye, *b*, and eat ... Is 55:1 7666
b wine and milk without money and ... Is 55:1 7666
B thee my field that is in ... Jer 32:7 7069
of redemption is thine to *b* it ... Jer 32:7 7069
B my field, I pray thee, that is ... Jer 32:8 7069
b it for thyself ... Jer 32:8 7069
B thee the field for money, and ... Jer 32:25 7069
Men shall *b* fields for money, and ... Jer 32:44 7069
That we may *b* the poor for silver ... Amos 8:6 7069
and *b* themselves victuals ... Mt 14:15 *59*
that sell, and *b* for yourselves ... Mt 25:9 *59*
And while they went to *b*, the ... Mt 25:10 *59*
villages, and *b* themselves bread ... Mk 6:36 *59*
b two hundred pennyworth of bread ... Mk 6:37 *59*
b meat for all this people ... Lk 9:13 *59*
him sell his garment, and *b* one ... Lk 22:36 *59*
gone away unto the city to *b* meat ... Jn 4:8 *59*
Philip, Whence shall we *b* bread ... Jn 6:5 *59*
B those things that we have need ... Jn 13:29 *59*
and they that *b*, as though they ... 1Cor 7:30 *59*
and continue there a year, and *b* ... Jas 4:13 *1710*
I counsel thee to *b* of me gold ... Rev 3:18 *59*
And that no man might *b* or sell ... Rev 13:17 *59*

BUYER
naught, it is naught, saith the *b* ... Prov 20:14 7069
as with the *b*, so with the seller ... Is 24:2 7069
let not the *b* rejoice, nor the ... Eze 7:12 7069

BUYEST
or *b* ought of thy neighbour's ... Lev 25:14 7069
What day thou *b* the field of the ... Ruth 4:5 7069

BUYETH
She considereth a field, and *b* it ... Prov 31:16 3947
all that he hath, and *b* that field ... Mt 13:44 *59*
for no man *b* their merchandise ... Rev 18:11 *59*

BUZ (*buz*)
1. Son of Nahor.
B his brother, and Kemuel the ... Gen 22:21 938
2. A Gadite.
the son of Jahdo, the son of *B* ... 1Chr 5:14 938
3. A tribe in northern Arabia.
Dedan, and Tema, and *B*, and all that ... Jer 25:23 938

BUZI (*boo'-zi*) See BUZITE. *Father of Ezekiel.*
Ezekiel the priest, the son of *B* ... Eze 1:3 941

BUZITE (*boo'-zite*) *A member of Buz 3.*
Elihu the son of Barachel the *B* ... Job 32:2 940
son of Barachel the *B* answered ... Job 32:6 940

BY See PREFACE.

BYWAYS
the travellers walked through *b* ... Judg 5:6

BYWORD
astonishment, a proverb, and a *b* ... Deut 28:37 8148
a proverb and a *b* among all people ... 1Kin 9:7 8148
proverb and a *b* among all nations ... 2Chr 7:20 8148
made me also a *b* of the people ... Job 17:6 4914
I their song, yea, I am their *b* ... Job 30:9 4405
Thou makest us a *b* among the ... Ps 44:14 4912

C

CAB
the fourth part of a c of dove's 2Kin 6:25 6894

CABBON (*cab'-bon*) *A town in Judah.*
And C, and Lahmam, and Kithlish, Josh 15:40 3522

CABINS
into the dungeon, and into the c Jer 37:16 2588

CABUL (*ca'-bul*) *A town in Asher.*
goeth out to C on the left hand, Josh 19:27 3521
them the land of C unto this day 1Kin 9:13 3521

CAESAR (*se'-zur*) See CAESAR'S. *Title for the Roman emperor.*
it lawful to give tribute unto C Mt 22:17 2541
Render therefore unto C the Mt 22:21 2541
Is it lawful to give tribute to C Mk 12:14 2541
Render to C the things that are Mk 12:17 2541
went out a decree from C Augustus Lk 2:1 2541
year of the reign of Tiberius C Lk 3:1 2541
for us to give tribute unto C Lk 20:22 2541
Render therefore unto C the Lk 20:25 2541
forbidding to give tribute to C Lk 23:2 2541
himself a king speaketh against C Jn 19:12 2541
answered, We have no king but C Jn 19:15 2541
to pass in the days of Claudius C Acts 11:28 2541
do contrary to the decrees of C Acts 17:7 2541
the temple, nor yet against C Acts 25:8 2541
I appeal unto C Acts 25:11 2541
Hast thou appealed unto C Acts 25:12 2541
unto C shalt thou go Acts 25:12 2541
kept till I might send him to C Acts 25:21 2541
if he had not appealed unto C Acts 26:32 2541
thou must be brought before C Acts 27:24 2541
was constrained to appeal unto C Acts 28:19 2541

CAESAREA (*ses-a-re'-ah*)
1. A town north of Galilee.
into the coasts of C Philippi Mt 16:13 2542
into the towns of C Philippi Mk 8:27 2542
2. A Judean Mediterranean port.
all the cities, till he came to C Acts 8:40 2542
knew, they brought him down to C Acts 9:30 2542
certain man in C called Cornelius Acts 10:1 2542
morrow after they entered into C Acts 10:24 2542
where I was, sent from C unto me Acts 11:11 2542
And he went down from Judaea to C Acts 12:19 2542
And when he had landed at C Acts 18:22 2542
company departed, and came unto C Acts 21:8 2542
certain of the disciples of C Acts 21:16 2542
two hundred soldiers to go to C Acts 23:23 2542
Who, when they came to C, and Acts 23:33 2542
he ascended from C to Jerusalem Acts 25:1 2542
that Paul should be kept at C Acts 25:4 2542
ten days, he went down unto C Acts 25:6 2542
came unto C to salute Festus Acts 25:13 2542

CAESAR'S (*se'-zurs*)
They say unto him, C Mt 22:21 2541
Caesar the things which are C Mt 22:21 2541
And they said unto him, C Mk 12:16 2541
to Caesar the things that are C Mk 12:17 2541
They answered and said, C Lk 20:24 2541
unto Caesar the things which be C Lk 20:25 2541
man go, thou art not C friend Jn 19:12 2541
I stand at C judgment seat, where Acts 25:10 2541
they that are of C household Phil 4:22 2541

CAGE
As a c is full of birds, so are Jer 5:27 3619
a c of every unclean and hateful Rev 18:2 5438

CAIAPHAS (*cah'-ya-fus*) *A High Priest during Jesus' time.*
the high priest, who was called C Mt 26:3 2533
led him away to C the high priest Mt 26:57 2533
C being the high priests, the Lk 3:2 2533
And one of them, named C, being Jn 11:49 2533
for he was father in law to C Jn 18:13 2533
Now C was he, which gave counsel Jn 18:14 2533
him bound unto C the high priest Jn 18:24 2533
Then led they Jesus from C unto Jn 18:28 2533
And Annas the high priest, and C Acts 4:6 2533

CAIN See TUBAL-CAIN.
1. Eldest son of Adam and Eve.
and she conceived, and bare C Gen 4:1 7014
but C was a tiller of the ground Gen 4:2 7014
that C brought of the fruit of Gen 4:3 7014
But unto C and to his offering he Gen 4:5 7014
And C was very wroth, and his Gen 4:5 7014
And the LORD said unto C, Why art Gen 4:6 7014
C talked with Abel his brother Gen 4:8 7014
that C rose up against Abel his Gen 4:8 7014
And the LORD said unto C, Where is Gen 4:9 7014
And C said unto the LORD, My Gen 4:13 7014
Therefore whosoever slayeth C Gen 4:15 7014
And the LORD set a mark upon C Gen 4:15 7014
C went out from the presence of Gen 4:16 7014
And C knew his wife Gen 4:17 7014
If C shall be avenged sevenfold, Gen 4:24 7014
seed instead of Abel, whom C slew Gen 4:25 7014
a more excellent sacrifice than C Heb 11:4 2535
Not as C, who was of that wicked 1Jn 3:12 2535
they have gone in the way of C Jude 11 2535
2. A town in Judah.
C, Gibeah, and Timnah Josh 15:57 7014

CAINAN (*ca'-nun*) See KENAN. *Son of Enos.*
lived ninety years, and begat C Gen 5:9 7018
after he begat C eight hundred Gen 5:10 7018
C lived seventy years, and begat Gen 5:12 7018
C lived after he begat Mahalaleel Gen 5:13 7018
all the days of C were nine Gen 5:14 7018
Which was the son of C, which was Lk 3:36 2536
Maleleel, which was the son of C Lk 3:37 2536

CAKE
one c of oiled bread, and one Ex 29:23 2471
LORD, he took one unleavened c Lev 8:26 2471
a c of oiled bread, and one wafer, Lev 8:26 2471
two tenth deals shall be in one c Lev 24:5 2471
one unleavened c out of the Num 6:19 2471
Ye shall offer up a c of the Num 15:20 2471
a c of barley bread tumbled into Judg 7:13 6742
gave him a piece of a c of figs 1Sa 30:12 1690
as men, to every one a c of bread 2Sa 6:19 2471
thy God liveth, I have not a c 1Kin 17:12 4580
make me thereof a little c first 1Kin 17:13 5692
there was a c baken on the coals, 1Kin 19:6 5692
Ephraim is a c not turned Hos 7:8 5692

CAKES
it, and make c upon the hearth Gen 18:6 5692
they baked unleavened c of the Ex 12:39 5692
c unleavened tempered with oil, Ex 29:2 2471
it shall be unleavened c of fine Lev 2:4 2471
unleavened c mingled with oil Lev 7:12 2471
c mingled with oil, of fine flour Lev 7:12 2471
Besides the c, he shall offer for Lev 7:13 2471
flour, and bake twelve c thereof Lev 24:5 2471
c of fine flour mingled with oil, Num 6:15 2471
baked it in pans, and made c of it Num 11:8 5692
after the passover, unleavened c Josh 5:11 4682
unleavened c of an ephah of flour Judg 6:19 4682
the flesh and the unleavened c Judg 6:20 4682
the flesh and the unleavened c Judg 6:21 4682
the flesh and the unleavened c Judg 6:21 2471
raisins, and two hundred c of figs 1Sa 25:18 1690
make me a couple of c in my sight 2Sa 13:6 3834
made c in his sight, and did bake 2Sa 13:8 3823
in his sight, and did bake the c 2Sa 13:8 3834
Tamar took the c which she had 2Sa 13:10 3834
c of figs, and bunches of raisins, 1Chr 12:40 1690
offering, and for the unleavened c 1Chr 23:29 7550
to make c to the queen of heaven, Jer 7:18 3561
did we make her c to worship her, Jer 44:19 3561
And thou shalt eat it as barley c Eze 4:12 5692

CALAH (*ca'-lah*) *An Assyrian city.*
and the city Rehoboth, and C Gen 10:11 3625
And Resen between Nineveh and C Gen 10:12 3625

CALAMITIES
refuge, until these c be overpast Ps 57:1 1942
prayer also shall be in their c Ps 141:5 7451
he that is glad at c shall not be Prov 17:5 343

CALAMITY
for the day of their c is at hand Deut 32:35 343
prevented me in the day of my c 2Sa 22:19 343
my c laid in the balances Job 6:2 1942
my path, they set forward my c Job 30:13 1942
prevented me in the day of my c Ps 18:18 343
I also will laugh at your c Prov 1:26 343
shall his c come suddenly Prov 6:15 343
son is the c of his father Prov 19:13 1942
For their c shall rise suddenly Prov 24:22 343
house in the day of thy c Prov 27:10 343
the face, in the day of their c Jer 18:17 343
day of their c was come upon them Jer 46:21 343
The c of Moab is near to come, and Jer 48:16 343
will bring the c of Esau upon him Jer 49:8 343
I will bring their c from all Jer 49:32 343
the sword in the time of their c Eze 35:5 343
my people in the day of their c Obad 13 343
affliction in the day of their c Obad 13 343
substance in the day of their c Obad 13 343

CALAMUS
of sweet c two hundred and fifty Ex 30:23 7070
c and cinnamon, with all trees of Song 4:14 7070
bright iron, cassia, and c Eze 27:19 7070

CALCOL (*cal'-col*) See CHALCOL. *A son of Zerah.*
Zimri, and Ethan, and Heman, and C 1Chr 2:6 3633

CALDRON
it into the pan, or kettle, or c 1Sa 2:14 7037
as out of a seething pot or c Job 41:20 100
this city is the c, and we be the Eze 11:3 5518
the flesh, and this city is the c Eze 11:7 5518
This city shall not be your c Eze 11:11 5518
the pot, and as flesh within the c Mic 3:3 7037

CALDRONS
sod they in pots, and in c 2Chr 35:13 1731
The c also, and the shovels, and Jer 52:18 5518
firepans, and the bowls, and the c Jer 52:19 5518

CALEB (*ca'-leb*) See CALEB'S, CALEB-EPHRATAH, CHELLUBAI.
1. A son of Jephunneh.
of Judah, C the son of Jephunneh Num 13:6 3612
C stilled the people before Moses Num 13:30 3612
C the son of Jephunneh, which Num 14:6 3612
But my servant C, because he had Num 14:24 3612
save C the son of Jephunneh, and Num 14:30 3612
C the son of Jephunneh, which Num 14:38 3612
save C the son of Jephunneh, and Num 26:65 3612
Save C the son of Jephunneh the Num 32:12 3612
of Judah, C the son of Jephunneh Num 34:19 3612
Save C the son of Jephunneh Deut 1:36 3612
C the son of Jephunneh the Josh 14:6 3612
gave unto C the son of Jephunneh Josh 14:13 3612
of C the son of Jephunneh the Josh 14:14 3612
unto C the son of Jephunneh he Josh 15:13 3612
C drove thence the three sons of Josh 15:14 3612
And C said, He that smiteth Josh 15:16 3612
son of Kenaz, the brother of C Josh 15:17 3612
C said unto her, What wouldest Josh 15:18 3612
gave they to C the son of Josh 21:12 3612
And C said, He that smiteth Judg 1:12 3612
C said unto her, What wilt thou Judg 1:14 3612
C gave her the upper springs and Judg 1:15 3612
And they gave Hebron unto C Judg 1:20 3612
and he was of the house of C 1Sa 25:3 3612
to Judah, and upon the south of C 1Sa 30:14 3612
and the daughter of C was Achsa 1Chr 2:49 3612
And the sons of C the son of 1Chr 4:15 3612
they gave to C the son of 1Chr 6:56 3612
2. A son of Hezron.
C the son of Hezron begat 1Chr 2:18 3612
C took unto him Ephrath, which 1Chr 2:19 3612
Now the sons of C the brother of 1Chr 2:42 3612
3. A son of Hur.
were the sons of C the son of Hur 1Chr 2:50 3612

CALEB-EPHRATAH (*ca''-leb-ef'-ra-tah*) *The place where Hezron died.*
after that Hezron was dead in C 1Chr 2:24 3613

CALEB-EPHRATHAH See CALEB-EPHRATAH.

CALEB'S (*ca'-lebs*) *Refers to Caleb 1.*
C younger brother, took it Judg 1:13 3612
son of Kenaz, C younger brother Judg 3:9 3612
C concubine, bare Haran, and Moza, 1Chr 2:46 3612
C concubine, bare Sheber, and 1Chr 2:48 3612

CALF
the herd, and fetcht a c tender Gen 18:7
the c which he had dressed, and Gen 18:8
after he had made it a molten c Ex 32:4 5695
they have made them a molten c Ex 32:8 5695
unto the camp, that he saw the c Ex 32:19 5695
he took the c which they had made Ex 32:20 5695
fire, and there came out this c Ex 32:24 5695
people, because they made the c Ex 32:35 5695
Take thee a young c for a sin Lev 9:2 5695
and a c and a lamb, both of the Lev 9:3 5695
slew the c of the sin offering, Lev 9:8 5695
God, and had made you a molten c Deut 9:16 5695
the c which ye had made, and burnt Deut 9:21 5695
woman had a fat c in the house 1Sa 28:24 5695
they had made them a molten c Neh 9:18 5695
cow calveth, and casteth not her c Job 21:10
maketh them also to skip like a c Ps 29:6 5695
They made a c in Horeb, and Ps 106:19 5695
and the c and the young lion and the Is 11:6 5695
there shall the c feed, and there Is 27:10 5695
me, when they cut the c in twain Jer 34:18 5695
passed between the parts of the c Jer 34:19 5695
Thy c, O Samaria, hath cast thee Hos 8:5 5695
but the c of Samaria shall be Hos 8:6 5695
And bring hither the fatted c Lk 15:23 3448
father hath killed the fatted c Lk 15:27 3448
hast killed for him the fatted c Lk 15:30 3448
they made a c in those days, and Acts 7:41 3447
and the second beast like a c Rev 4:7 3448

CALF'S
was like the sole of a c foot Eze 1:7 5695

CALKERS
men thereof were in thee thy c Eze 27:9
mariners, and thy pilots, thy c Eze 27:27

CALL
Adam to see what he would c them Gen 2:19 7121
then began men to c upon the name Gen 4:26 7121
son, and shalt c his name Ishmael Gen 16:11 7121
thou shalt not c her name Sarai Gen 17:15 7121
thou shalt c his name Isaac Gen 17:19 7121
We will c the damsel, and enquire Gen 24:57 7121
the daughters will c me blessed Gen 30:13 833
to pass, when Pharaoh shall c you Gen 46:33 7121
c to thee a nurse of the Hebrew Ex 2:7 7121
c him, that he may eat bread Ex 2:20 7121
one c thee, and thou eat of his Ex 34:15 7121
And Moses sent to c Dathan Num 16:12 7121
to c him, saying, Behold, there Num 22:5 7121
him, If the men come to c thee Num 22:20 7121
send unto thee to c thee Num 22:37 7121
but the Moabites c them Emims Deut 2:11 7121
the Ammonites c them Zamzummims Deut 2:20 7121
Hermon the Sidonians c Sirion Deut 3:9 7121
and the Amorites c it Shenir Deut 3:9 7121
all things that we c upon him for Deut 4:7 7121
I c heaven and earth to witness Deut 4:26 5749
elders of his city shall c him Deut 25:8 7121
thou shalt c them to mind among Deut 30:1 7725
I c heaven and earth to record Deut 30:19 5749
c Joshua, and present yourselves Deut 31:14 7121
c heaven and earth to record Deut 31:28 5749
They shall c the people unto the Deut 33:19 7121
didst not c us to go with thee Judg 12:1 7121
C for Samson, that he may make us Judg 16:25 7121
and to c peaceably unto them Judg 21:13 7121
C me not Naomi, c me Mara Ruth 1:20 7121
why then c ye me Naomi, seeing Ruth 1:21 7121
for thou didst c me 1Sa 3:6 7121
for thou didst c me 1Sa 3:8 7121
and it shall be, if he c thee 1Sa 3:9 7121
I will c unto the LORD, and he 1Sa 12:17 7121
c Jesse to the sacrifice, and I 1Sa 16:3 7121

sent to c Ahimelech the priest 1Sa 22:11 7121
C now Hushai the Archite also, and 2Sa 17:5 7121
I will c on the LORD, who is 2Sa 22:4 7121
answered and said, C me Bath-sheba 1Kin 1:28 7121
C me Zadok the priest, and Nathan 1Kin 1:32 7121
in all that they c for unto thee 1Kin 8:52 7121
me to c my sin to remembrance 1Kin 17:18 2142
c ye on the name of your gods, and 1Kin 18:24 7121
I will c on the name of the LORD 1Kin 18:24 7121
c on the name of your gods, but 1Kin 18:25 7121
gone to c Micaiah spake unto him 1Kin 22:13 7121
his servant, C this Shunammite 2Kin 4:12 7121
And he said, C her 2Kin 4:15 7121
and said, C this Shunammite 2Kin 4:36 7121
c on the name of the LORD his God 2Kin 5:11 7121
Now therefore c unto me all the 2Kin 10:19 7121
c upon his name, make known his 1Chr 16:8 7121
went to c Micaiah spake to him 2Chr 18:12 7121
C now, if there be any that will Job 5:1 7121
Then c thou, and I will answer Job 13:22 7121
Thou shalt c, and I will answer Job 14:15 7121
will he always c upon God Job 27:10 7121
Hear me when I c, O God of my Ps 4:1 7121
LORD will hear when I c unto him Ps 4:3 7121
eat bread, and c not upon the LORD Ps 14:4 7121
I will c upon the LORD, who is Ps 18:3 7121
let the king hear us when we c Ps 20:9 7121
they c their lands after their Ps 49:11 7121
He shall c to the heavens from Ps 50:4 7121
c upon me in the day of trouble Ps 50:15 7121
As for me, I will c upon God Ps 55:16 7121
all nations shall c him blessed Ps 72:17 833
I c to remembrance my song in the Ps 77:6 2142
us, and we will c upon thy name Ps 80:18 7121
unto all them that c upon thee Ps 86:5 7121
of my trouble I will c upon thee Ps 86:7 7121
He shall c upon me, and I will Ps 91:15 7121
among them that c upon his name Ps 99:6 7121
in the day when I c answer me Ps 102:2 7121
c upon his name Ps 105:1 7121
therefore will I c upon him as Ps 116:2 7121
c upon the name of the LORD Ps 116:13 7121
will c upon the name of the LORD Ps 116:17 7121
unto all them that c upon him Ps 145:18 7121
to all that c upon him in truth Ps 145:18 7121
Then shall they c upon me Prov 1:28 7121
c understanding thy kinswoman Prov 7:4 7121
Unto you, O men, I c Prov 8:4 7121
To c passengers who go right on Prov 9:15 7121
arise up, and c her blessed Prov 31:28 833
Woe unto them that c evil good Is 5:20 559
shall c his name Immanuel Is 7:14 7121
C his name Maher-shalal-hash-baz Is 8:3 7121
c upon his name, declare his Is 12:4 7121
Lord GOD of hosts c to weeping Is 22:12 7121
that I will c my servant Eliakim Is 22:20 7121
will not c back his words Is 31:2 5493
They shall c the nobles thereof Is 34:12 7121
the sun shall he c upon my name Is 41:25 7121
another shall c himself by the Is 44:5 7121
And who, as I, shall c, and shall Is 44:7 7121
which c thee by thy name, am the Is 45:3 7121
For they c themselves of the holy Is 48:2 7121
when I c unto them, they stand up Is 48:13 7121
thou shalt c a nation that thou Is 55:5 7121
c ye upon him while he is near Is 55:6 7121
wilt thou c this a fast, and an Is 58:5 7121
Then shalt thou c, and the LORD Is 58:9 7121
c the sabbath a delight, the holy Is 58:13 7121
and they shall c thee, The city of Is 60:14 7121
but thou shalt c thy walls Is 60:18 7121
shall c you the Ministers of our Is 61:6 7121
And they shall c them, The holy Is 62:12 7121
c his servants by another name Is 65:15 7121
come to pass, that before they c Is 65:24 7121
I will c all the families of the Jer 1:15 7121
At that time they shall c Jer 3:17 7121
and I said, Thou shalt c me Jer 3:19 7121
Reprobate silver shall men c them Jer 6:30 7121
thou shalt also c unto them Jer 7:27 7121
c for the mourning women, that Jer 9:17 7121
families that c not on thy name Jer 10:25 7121
for I will c for a sword upon all Jer 25:29 7121
Then shall ye c upon me, and ye Jer 29:12 7121
C unto me, and I will answer thee, Jer 33:3 7121
C together the archers against Jer 50:29 8085
c together against her the Jer 51:27 8085
men c The perfection of beauty Lam 2:15 559
but he will c to remembrance the Eze 21:23 2142
I will c for the corn, and will Eze 36:29 7121
I will c for a sword against him Eze 38:21 7121
they shall c it The valley of Eze 39:11 7121
king commanded to c the magicians Dan 2:2 7121
said unto him, C his name Jezreel Hos 1:4 7121
unto him, C her name Lo-ruhamah Hos 1:6 7121
Then said God, C his name Lo-ammi Hos 1:9 7121
LORD, that thou shalt c me Ishi Hos 2:16 7121
and shalt c me no more Baali Hos 2:16 7121
they c to Egypt, they go to Hos 7:11 7121
c a solemn assembly, gather the Joel 1:14 7121
a fast, c a solemn assembly Joel 2:15 7121
that whosoever shall c on the Joel 2:32 7121
the remnant whom the LORD shall c Joel 2:32 7121
they shall c the husbandman to Amos 5:16 7121
c upon thy God, if so be that God Jonah 1:6 7121
that they may all c upon the name Zeph 3:9 7121
hosts, shall ye c every man his Zec 3:10 7121
they shall c on my name, and I Zec 13:9 7121
and they shall c them, The border Mal 1:4 7121
all nations shall c you blessed Mal 3:12 833
And now we c the proud happy Mal 3:15 833
thou shalt c his name JESUS Mt 1:21 *2564*
they shall c his name Emmanuel, Mt 1:23 *2564*
I am not come to c the righteous Mt 9:13 *2564*
they c them of his household Mt 10:25 *2564*
C the labourers, and give them Mt 20:8 *2564*
sent forth his servants to c them Mt 22:3 *2564*
doth David in spirit c him Lord Mt 22:43 *2564*
If David then c him Lord Mt 22:45 *2564*
c no man your father upon the Mt 23:9 *2564*
I came not to c the righteous Mk 2:17 *2564*
they c the blind man, saying unto Mk 10:49 *5455*
whom ye c the King of the Jews Mk 15:12 *3004*
they c together the whole band Mk 15:16 *4779*
thou shalt c his name John Lk 1:13 *2564*
a son, and shalt c his name JESUS Lk 1:31 *2564*
generations shall c me blessed Lk 1:48 *3106*
I came not to c the righteous Lk 5:32 *2564*
why c ye me, Lord, Lord, and do Lk 6:46 *2564*
c not thy friends, nor thy Lk 14:12 *5455*
c the poor, the maimed, the lame, Lk 14:13 *2564*
c thy husband, and come hither Jn 4:16 *5455*
Ye c me Master and Lord Jn 13:13 *5455*
Henceforth I c you not servants Jn 15:15 *3004*
that whosoever shall c on the Acts 2:21 *1941*
many as the Lord our God shall c Acts 2:39 *4341*
to bind all that c on thy name Acts 9:14 *1941*
c for one Simon, whose surname is Acts 10:5 *3343*
cleansed, that c not thou common Acts 10:15 *2840*
not c any man common or unclean Acts 10:28 *3004*
c hither Simon, whose surname is Acts 10:32 *3333*
cleansed, that c not thou common Acts 11:9 *2840*
c for Simon, whose surname is Acts 11:13 *3343*
took upon them to c over them Acts 19:13 *3687*
after the way which they c heresy Acts 24:14 *3004*
season, I will c for thee Acts 24:25 *3333*
I will c them my people, which Rom 9:25 *2564*
is rich unto all that c upon him Rom 10:12 *1941*
For whosoever shall c upon the Rom 10:13 *1941*
How then shall they c on him in Rom 10:14 *1941*
with all that in every place c 1Cor 1:2 *1941*
Moreover I c God for a record 2Cor 1:23 *1941*
When I c to remembrance the 2Ti 1:5 *2983*
with them that c on the Lord out 2Ti 2:22 *1941*
is not ashamed to c them brethren Heb 2:11 *2564*
But c to remembrance the former Heb 10:32 *363*
let him c for the elders of the Jas 5:14 *4341*
if ye c on the Father, who 1Pet 1:17 *1941*

CALLED

God c the light Day, and the Gen 1:5 7121
Day, and the darkness he c Night Gen 1:5 7121
God c the firmament Heaven Gen 1:8 7121
And God c the dry land Earth Gen 1:10 7121
together of the waters c he Seas Gen 1:10 7121
whatsoever Adam c every living Gen 2:19 7121
she shall be c Woman, because she Gen 2:23 7121
And the LORD God c unto Adam Gen 3:9 7121
Adam c his wife's name Eve Gen 3:20 7121
c the name of the city, after the Gen 4:17 7121
bare a son, and c his name Seth Gen 4:25 7121
and he c his name Enos Gen 4:26 7121
c their name Adam, in the day Gen 5:2 7121
and c his name Seth Gen 5:3 7121
he c his name Noah, saying, This Gen 5:29 7121
is the name of it c Babel Gen 11:9 7121
c upon the name of the LORD Gen 12:8 7121
And Pharaoh c Abram, and said Gen 12:18 7121
there Abram c on the name of the Gen 13:4 7121
she c the name of the LORD that Gen 16:13 7121
the well was c Beer-lahai-roi Gen 16:14 7121
Abram c his son's name, which Gen 16:15 7121
thy name any more be c Abram Gen 17:5 7121
they c unto Lot, and said unto him Gen 19:5 7121
the name of the city was c Zoar Gen 19:22 7121
bare a son, and c his name Moab Gen 19:37 7121
a son, and c his name Ben-ammi Gen 19:38 7121
c all his servants, and told all Gen 20:8 7121
Then Abimelech c Abraham, and said Gen 20:9 7121
Abraham c the name of his son Gen 21:3 7121
for in Isaac shall thy seed be c Gen 21:12 7121
the angel of God c to Hagar out Gen 21:17 7121
Wherefore he c that place Gen 21:31 7121
c there on the name of the LORD, Gen 21:33 7121
the angel of the LORD c unto him Gen 22:11 7121
Abraham c the name of that place Gen 22:14 7121
the angel of the LORD c unto Gen 22:15 7121
they c Rebekah, and said unto her, Gen 24:58 7121
and they c his name Esau Gen 25:25 7121
and his name was c Jacob Gen 25:26 7121
therefore was his name c Edom Gen 25:30 7121
And Abimelech c Isaac, and said, Gen 26:9 7121
he c their names after the names Gen 26:18 7121
by which his father had c them Gen 26:18 7121
he c the name of the well Esek Gen 26:20 7121
he c the name of it Sitnah Gen 26:21 7121
he c the name of it Rehoboth Gen 26:22 7121
c upon the name of the LORD, and Gen 26:25 7121
And he c it Shebah Gen 26:33 7121
he c Esau his eldest son, and said Gen 27:1 7121
c Jacob her younger son, and said Gen 27:42 7121
And Isaac c Jacob, and blessed him, Gen 28:1 7121
he c the name of that place Gen 28:19 7121
that city was c Luz at the first Gen 28:19
a son, and she c his name Reuben Gen 29:32 7121
and she c his name Simeon Gen 29:33 7121
therefore was his name c Levi Gen 29:34 7121
therefore she c his name Judah Gen 29:35 7121
therefore c she his name Dan Gen 30:6 7121
and she c his name Naphtali Gen 30:8 7121
and she c his name Gad Gen 30:11 7121
and she c his name Asher Gen 30:13 7121
and she c his name Issachar Gen 30:18 7121
and she c his name Zebulun Gen 30:20 7121
a daughter, and c her name Dinah Gen 30:21 7121
And she c his name Joseph Gen 30:24 7121
c Rachel and Leah to the field Gen 31:4 7121
Laban c it Jegar-sahadutha Gen 31:47 7121
but Jacob c it Galeed Gen 31:47 7121
was the name of it c Galeed Gen 31:48 7121
c his brethren to eat bread Gen 31:54 7121
he c the name of that place Gen 32:2 7121
Thy name shall be c no more Jacob Gen 32:28 559
Jacob c the name of the place Gen 32:30 7121
name of the place is c Succoth Gen 33:17 7121
an altar, and c it El-elohe-Israel Gen 33:20 7121
altar, and c the place El-beth-el Gen 35:7 7121
name of it was c Allon-bachuth Gen 35:8 7121
shall not be c any more Jacob Gen 35:10 7121
and he c his name Israel Gen 35:10 7121
Jacob c the name of the place Gen 35:15 7121
died) that she c his name Ben-oni Gen 35:18 7121
but his father c him Benjamin Gen 35:18 7121
and he c his name Er Gen 38:3 7121
and she c his name Onan Gen 38:4 7121
and c his name Shelah Gen 38:5 7121
therefore his name was c Pharez Gen 38:29 7121
and his name was c Zarah Gen 38:30 7121
That she c unto the men of her Gen 39:14 7121
c for all the magicians of Egypt, Gen 41:8 7121
c Joseph, and they brought him Gen 41:14 7121
And Pharaoh c Joseph's name Gen 41:45 7121
And Joseph c the name of the Gen 41:51 7121
name of the second c he Ephraim Gen 41:52 7121
he c his son Joseph, and said unto Gen 47:29 7121
shall be c after the name of Gen 48:6 7121
Jacob c unto his sons, and said, Gen 49:1 7121
the name of it was c Abel-mizraim Gen 50:11 7121
king of Egypt c for the midwives Ex 1:18 7121
maid went and c the child's mother Ex 2:8 7121
And she c his name Moses Ex 2:10 7121
a son, and he c his name Gershom Ex 2:22 7121
God c unto him out of the midst Ex 3:4 7121
Then Pharaoh also c the wise men Ex 7:11 7121
Then Pharaoh c for Moses and Aaron Ex 8:8 7121
Pharaoh c for Moses and for Aaron, Ex 8:25 7121
c for Moses and Aaron, and said Ex 9:27 7121
Then Pharaoh c for Moses and Aaron Ex 10:16 7121
Pharaoh c unto Moses, and said, Go Ex 10:24 7121
Then Moses c for all the elders Ex 12:21 7121
he c for Moses and Aaron by night, Ex 12:31 7121
the name of it was c Marah Ex 15:23 7121
the house of Israel c the name Ex 16:31 7121
he c the name of the place Massah Ex 17:7 7121
c the name of it Jehovah-nissi Ex 17:15 7121
the LORD c unto him out of the Ex 19:3 7121
c for the elders of the people, Ex 19:7 7121
the LORD c Moses up to the top of Ex 19:20 7121
the seventh day he c unto Moses Ex 24:16 7121
I have c by name Bezaleel the son Ex 31:2 7121
c it the Tabernacle of the Ex 33:7 7121
And Moses c unto them Ex 34:31 7121
the LORD hath c by name Bezaleel Ex 35:30 7121
Moses c Bezaleel and Aholiab, and Ex 36:2 7121
the LORD c unto Moses, and spake Lev 1:1 7121
eighth day, that Moses c Aaron Lev 9:1 7121
Moses c Mishael and Elzaphan, and Lev 10:4 7121
he c the name of the place Num 11:3 7121
he c the name of that place Num 11:34 7121
tabernacle, and c Aaron and Miriam Num 12:5 7121
Moses c Oshea the son of Nun Num 13:16 7121
The place was c the brook Eshcol, Num 13:24 7121
he c the name of the place Hormah Num 21:3 7121
I c thee to curse mine enemies, Num 24:10 7121
they c the people unto the Num 25:2 7121
thereof, and c them Havoth-jair Num 32:41 7121
c it Nobah, after his own name Num 32:42 7121
which was c the land of giants Deut 3:13 7121
c them after his own name, Deut 3:14 7121
Moses c all Israel, and said unto Deut 5:1 7121
because it is c the LORD's Deut 15:2 7121
And his name shall be c in Israel Deut 25:10 7121
art c by the name of the LORD Deut 28:10 7121
Moses c unto all Israel, and said Deut 29:2 7121
Moses c unto Joshua, and said unto Deut 31:7 7121
Then Joshua c the twelve men, Josh 4:4 7121
place is c Gilgal unto this day Josh 5:9 7121
the son of Nun c the priests Josh 6:6 7121
the name of that place was c Josh 7:26 7121
c together to pursue after them Josh 8:16 2199
Joshua c for them, and he spake Josh 9:22 7121
that Joshua c for all the men of Josh 10:24 7121
c Leshem, Dan, after the name of Josh 19:47 7121
Then Joshua c the Reubenites, and Josh 22:1 7121
children of Gad c the altar Ed Josh 22:34 7121
Joshua c for all Israel, and for Josh 23:2 7121
c for the elders of Israel, and Josh 24:1 7121
c Balaam the son of Beor to curse Josh 24:9 7121
the name of the city was c Hormah Judg 1:17 7121
a city, and c the name thereof Luz Judg 1:26 7121
they c the name of that place Judg 2:5 7121
c Barak the son of Abinoam out of Judg 4:6 7121
Barak c Zebulun and Naphtali to Judg 4:10 2199
the LORD, and c it Jehovah-shalom Judg 6:24 7121
on that day he c him Jerubbaal Judg 6:32 7121
a son, whose name he c Abimelech Judg 8:31 7760
Then he c hastily unto the young Judg 9:54 7121
which are c Havoth-jair unto this Judg 10:4 7121
and when I c you, ye delivered me Judg 12:2 2199
bare a son, and c his name Samson Judg 13:24 7121
have ye c us to take that we have Judg 14:15 7121
hand, and c that place Ramath-lehi Judg 15:17 7121
c on the LORD, and said, Thou hast Judg 15:18 7121
wherefore he c the name thereof Judg 15:19 7121
sent and c for the lords of the Judg 16:18 7121
she c for a man, and she caused Judg 16:19 7121
they c for Samson out of the Judg 16:25 7121
Samson c unto the LORD, and said, Judg 16:28 7121
wherefore they c that place Judg 18:12 7121
they c the name of the city Dan, Judg 18:29 7121
and they c his name Obed Ruth 4:17 7121
c his name Samuel, saying, 1Sa 1:20 7121

Context	Reference	Number
That the LORD c Samuel	1Sa 3:4	7121
And he said, I c not	1Sa 3:5	7121
the LORD c yet again, Samuel	1Sa 3:6	7121
And he answered, I c not, my son	1Sa 3:6	7121
the LORD c Samuel again the third	1Sa 3:8	7121
that the LORD had c the child	1Sa 3:8	7121
c as at other times, Samuel,	1Sa 3:10	7121
Then Eli c Samuel, and said,	1Sa 3:16	7121
the Philistines c for the priests	1Sa 6:2	7121
c the name of it Eben-ezer,	1Sa 7:12	7121
for he that is now c a Prophet	1Sa 9:9	
a Prophet was beforetime c a Seer	1Sa 9:9	7121
that Samuel c Saul to the top of	1Sa 9:26	7121
Samuel c the people together unto	1Sa 10:17	6817
So Samuel c unto the LORD	1Sa 12:18	7121
the people were c together after	1Sa 13:4	6817
sons, and c them to the sacrifice	1Sa 16:5	7121
Then Jesse c Abinadab, and made	1Sa 16:8	7121
And Jonathan c David, and Jonathan	1Sa 19:7	7121
Saul c all the people together to	1Sa 23:8	8085
therefore they c that place	1Sa 23:28	7121
therefore I have c thee, that	1Sa 28:15	7121
Then Achish c David, and said unto	1Sa 29:6	7121
him, he saw me, and c unto me	2Sa 1:7	7121
David c one of the young men, and	2Sa 1:15	7121
that place was c Helkath-hazzurim	2Sa 2:16	7121
Then Abner c to Joab, and said,	2Sa 2:26	7121
fort, and c it the city of David	2Sa 5:9	7121
Therefore he c the name of that	2Sa 5:20	7121
whose name is c by the name of	2Sa 6:2	7121
he c the name of the place	2Sa 6:8	7121
when they had c him unto David,	2Sa 9:2	7121
Then the king c to Ziba, Saul's	2Sa 9:9	7121
And when David had c him, he did	2Sa 11:13	7121
a son, and he c his name Solomon	2Sa 12:24	7121
he c his name Jedidiah, because	2Sa 12:25	7121
city, and it be c after my name	2Sa 12:28	7121
Then he c his servant that	2Sa 13:17	7121
and when he had c for Absalom	2Sa 14:33	7121
judgment, then Absalom c unto him	2Sa 15:2	7121
men out of Jerusalem, that were c	2Sa 15:11	7121
he c the pillar after his own	2Sa 18:18	7121
it is c unto this day, Absalom's	2Sa 18:18	7121
the watchman c unto the porter,	2Sa 18:26	7121
And Ahimaaz c, and said unto the	2Sa 18:28	7121
the king c the Gibeonites, and	2Sa 21:2	7121
In my distress I c upon the LORD	2Sa 22:7	7121
c all his brethren the king's	1Kin 1:9	7121
and Solomon his brother, he c not	1Kin 1:10	7121
hath c all the sons of the king,	1Kin 1:19	7121
Solomon thy servant hath he not c	1Kin 1:19	7121
hath c all the king's sons, and	1Kin 1:25	7121
servant Solomon, hath he not c	1Kin 1:26	7121
c for Shimei, and said unto him,	1Kin 2:36	7121
c for Shimei, and said unto him,	1Kin 2:42	7121
c the name thereof Jachin	1Kin 7:21	7121
and c the name thereof Boaz	1Kin 7:21	7121
I have builded, is c by thy name	1Kin 8:43	7121
he c them the land of Cabul unto	1Kin 9:13	7121
That they sent and c him	1Kin 12:3	7121
c him unto the congregation, and	1Kin 12:20	7121
c the name of the city which he	1Kin 16:24	7121
he c to her, and said, Fetch me, I	1Kin 17:10	7121
he c to her, and said, Bring me, I	1Kin 17:11	7121
Ahab c Obadiah, which was the	1Kin 18:3	7121
c on the name of Baal from	1Kin 18:26	7121
Then the king of Israel c all the	1Kin 20:7	7121
the king of Israel c an officer	1Kin 22:9	7121
that the LORD hath c these three	2Kin 3:10	7121
for the LORD hath c these three	2Kin 3:13	7121
And when he had c her, she stood	2Kin 4:12	7121
And when he had c her, she stood	2Kin 4:15	7121
she c unto her husband, and said,	2Kin 4:22	7121
he c Gehazi, and said, Call this	2Kin 4:36	7121
So he c her	2Kin 4:36	7121
he c his servants, and said unto	2Kin 6:11	7121
c unto the porter of the city	2Kin 7:10	7121
And he c the porters	2Kin 7:11	7121
for the LORD hath c for a famine	2Kin 8:1	7121
Elisha the prophet c one of the	2Kin 9:1	7121
Then king Jehoash c for Jehoiada	2Kin 12:7	7121
c the name of it Joktheel unto	2Kin 14:7	7121
and he c it Nehushtan	2Kin 18:4	7121
And when they had c to the king	2Kin 18:18	7121
his mother c his name Jabez,	1Chr 4:9	7121
Jabez c on the God of Israel,	1Chr 4:10	7121
which are c by their names	1Chr 6:65	7121
a son, and she c his name Peresh	1Chr 7:16	7121
he c his name Beriah, because it	1Chr 7:23	7121
therefore they c it the city of	1Chr 11:7	7121
cherubims, whose name is c on it	1Chr 13:6	7121
place is c Perez-uzza to this day	1Chr 13:11	7121
therefore they c the name of that	1Chr 14:11	7121
David c for Zadok and Abiathar the	1Chr 15:11	7121
offerings, and c upon the LORD	1Chr 21:26	7121
Then he c for Solomon his son, and	1Chr 22:6	7121
c the name of that on the right	2Chr 3:17	7121
I have built is c by thy name	2Chr 6:33	7121
which are c by my name, shall	2Chr 7:14	7121
And they sent and c him	2Chr 10:3	7121
the king of Israel c for one of	2Chr 18:8	7121
the name of the same place was c	2Chr 20:26	7121
the king c for Jehoiada the chief	2Chr 24:6	7121
and was c after their name	Ezr 2:61	7121
Then I c the priests, and took an	Neh 5:12	7121
wife, and was c after their name	Neh 7:63	7121
her, and that she were c by name	Est 2:14	7121
c on the thirteenth day of the	Est 3:12	7121
Then c Esther for Hatach, one of	Est 4:5	7121
the inner court, who is not c	Est 4:11	7121
but I have not been c to come in	Est 4:11	7121
c for his friends, and Zeresh his	Est 5:10	935
Then were the king's scribes c at	Est 8:9	7121
Wherefore they c these days Purim	Est 9:26	7121
c for their three sisters to eat	Job 1:4	7121
If I had c, and he had answered me	Job 9:16	7121
I c my servant, and he gave me no	Job 19:16	7121
he c the name of the first,	Job 42:14	7121
I have c upon thee, for thou wilt	Ps 17:6	7121
In my distress I c upon the LORD	Ps 18:6	7121
for I have c upon thee	Ps 31:17	7121
c the earth from the rising of	Ps 50:1	7121
they have not c upon God	Ps 53:4	7121
that have not c upon thy name	Ps 79:6	7121
I have c daily upon thee, I have	Ps 88:9	7121
they c upon the LORD, and he	Ps 99:6	7121
Moreover he c for a famine upon	Ps 105:16	7121
Then c I upon the name of the	Ps 116:4	7121
I c upon the LORD in distress	Ps 118:5	7121
Because I have c, and ye refused	Prov 1:24	7121
wise in heart shall be c prudent	Prov 16:21	7121
shall be c a mischievous person	Prov 24:8	7121
I c him, but he gave me no answer	Song 5:6	7121
afterward thou shalt be c	Is 1:26	7121
only let us be c by thy name	Is 4:1	7121
in Jerusalem, shall be c holy	Is 4:3	559
and his name shall be c Wonderful	Is 9:6	7121
I have also c my mighty ones for	Is 13:3	7121
one shall be c, The city of	Is 19:18	559
shepherds is c forth against him	Is 31:4	7121
person shall be no more c liberal	Is 32:5	7121
it shall be c The way of holiness	Is 35:8	7121
c him to his foot, gave the	Is 41:2	7121
c thee from the chief men thereof	Is 41:9	7121
I the LORD have c thee in	Is 42:6	7121
I have c thee by thy name	Is 43:1	7121
every one that is c by my name	Is 43:7	7121
But thou hast not c upon me	Is 43:22	7121
I have even c thee by thy name	Is 45:4	7121
thou shalt no more be c tender	Is 47:1	7121
for thou shalt no more be c	Is 47:5	7121
which are c by the name of Israel	Is 48:1	7121
wast c a transgressor from the	Is 48:8	7121
unto me, O Jacob and Israel, my c	Is 48:12	7121
yea, I have c him	Is 48:15	7121
The LORD hath c me from the womb	Is 49:1	7121
when I c, was there none to	Is 50:2	7121
for I c him alone, and blessed him	Is 51:2	7121
of the whole earth shall he be c	Is 54:5	7121
For the LORD hath c thee as a	Is 54:6	7121
for mine house shall be c an	Is 56:7	7121
and thou shalt be c, The repairer	Is 58:12	7121
that they might be c trees of	Is 61:3	7121
and thou shalt be c by a new name	Is 62:2	7121
but thou shalt be c Hephzi-bah	Is 62:4	7121
and thou shalt be c, Sought out, A	Is 62:12	7121
they were not c by thy name	Is 63:19	7121
nation that was not c by my name	Is 65:1	7121
because when I c, ye did not	Is 65:12	7121
because when I c, none did answer	Is 66:4	7121
which is c by my name, and say, We	Jer 7:10	7121
which is c by my name, become a	Jer 7:11	7121
I c you, but ye answered not	Jer 7:13	7121
which is c by my name, wherein ye	Jer 7:14	7121
the house which is c by my name	Jer 7:30	7121
that it shall no more be c Tophet	Jer 7:32	559
The LORD c thy name, A green	Jer 11:16	7121
they have c a multitude after	Jer 12:6	7121
of us, and we are c by thy name	Jer 14:9	7121
for I am c by thy name, O LORD	Jer 15:16	7121
place shall no more be c Tophet	Jer 19:6	7121
LORD hath not c thy name Pashur	Jer 20:3	7121
is his name whereby he shall be c	Jer 23:6	7121
on the city which is c by my name	Jer 25:29	7121
because they c thee an Outcast,	Jer 30:17	7121
which is c by my name, to defile	Jer 32:34	7121
the name wherewith she shall be c	Jer 33:16	7121
the house which is c by my name	Jer 34:15	7121
I have c unto them, but they have	Jer 35:17	7121
Then Jeremiah c Baruch the son of	Jer 36:4	7121
Then c he Johanan the son of	Jer 42:8	7121
he hath c an assembly against me	Lam 1:15	7121
I c for my lovers, but they	Lam 1:19	7121
bring the day that thou hast c	Lam 1:21	7121
Thou hast c as in a solemn day my	Lam 2:22	7121
I c upon thy name, O LORD, out of	Lam 3:55	7121
in the day that I c upon thee	Lam 3:57	7121
he c to the man clothed with	Eze 9:3	7121
thereof is c Bamah unto this day	Eze 20:29	7121
now let Daniel be c, and he will	Dan 5:12	7123
the banks of Ulai, which c	Dan 8:16	7121
the city which is c by thy name	Dan 9:18	7121
and thy people are c by thy name	Dan 9:19	7121
whose name was c Belteshazzar	Dan 10:1	7121
him, and c my son out of Egypt	Hos 11:1	7121
As they c them, so they went from	Hos 11:2	7121
though they c them to the most	Hos 11:7	7121
the Lord GOD c to contend by fire	Amos 7:4	7121
which are c by my name, saith the	Amos 9:12	7121
I c for a drought upon the land,	Hag 1:11	7121
shall be c a city of truth	Zec 8:3	7121
two staves; the one I c Beauty	Zec 11:7	7121
Beauty, and the other I c Bands	Zec 11:7	7121
was born Jesus, who is c Christ	Mt 1:16	*3004*
and he c his name JESUS	Mt 1:25	*2564*
he had privily c the wise men	Mt 2:7	*2564*
Out of Egypt have I c my son	Mt 2:15	*2564*
and dwelt in a city c Nazareth	Mt 2:23	*3004*
He shall be c a Nazarene	Mt 2:23	*2564*
saw two brethren, Simon c Peter	Mt 4:18	*3004*
and he c them	Mt 4:21	*2564*
for they shall be c the children	Mt 5:9	*2564*
he shall be c the least in the	Mt 5:19	*2564*
the same shall be c great in the	Mt 5:19	*2564*
when he had c unto him his twelve	Mt 10:1	*4341*
The first, Simon, who is c Peter	Mt 10:2	*3004*
If they have c the master of the	Mt 10:25	*2564*
is not his mother c Mary	Mt 13:55	*3004*
he c the multitude, and said unto	Mt 15:10	*4341*
Then Jesus c his disciples unto	Mt 15:32	*4341*
Jesus c a little child unto him,	Mt 18:2	*4341*
his lord, after that he had c him	Mt 18:32	*4341*
for many be c, but few chosen	Mt 20:16	*2822*
But Jesus c them unto him, and	Mt 20:25	*4341*
c them, and said, What will ye	Mt 20:32	*5455*
My house shall be c the house of	Mt 21:13	*2564*
For many are c, but few are	Mt 22:14	*2822*
to be c of men, Rabbi, Rabbi	Mt 23:7	*2564*
But be not ye c Rabbi	Mt 23:8	*2564*
Neither be ye c masters	Mt 23:10	*2564*
who c his own servants, and	Mt 25:14	*2564*
high priest, who was c Caiaphas,	Mt 26:3	*3004*
c Judas Iscariot, went unto the	Mt 26:14	*3004*
them unto a place c Gethsemane	Mt 26:36	*3004*
Wherefore that field was c	Mt 27:8	*2564*
a notable prisoner, c Barabbas	Mt 27:16	*3004*
or Jesus which is c Christ	Mt 27:17	*3004*
then with Jesus which is c Christ	Mt 27:22	*3004*
were come unto a place c Golgotha	Mt 27:33	*3004*
And straightway he c them	Mk 1:20	*2564*
he c them unto him, and said unto	Mk 3:23	*4341*
he c unto him the twelve, and	Mk 6:7	*4341*
when he had c all the people unto	Mk 7:14	*4341*
Jesus c his disciples unto him,	Mk 8:1	*4341*
when he had c the people unto him	Mk 8:34	*4341*
c the twelve, and saith unto them,	Mk 9:35	*5455*
But Jesus c them to him, and saith	Mk 10:42	*4341*
still, and commanded him to be c	Mk 10:49	*5455*
My house shall be c of all	Mk 11:17	*2564*
he c unto him his disciples, and	Mk 12:43	*4341*
Peter c to mind the word that	Mk 14:72	*363*
away into the hall, c Praetorium	Mk 15:16	
shall be c the Son of the Highest	Lk 1:32	*2564*
of thee shall be c the Son of God	Lk 1:35	*2564*
month with her, who was c barren	Lk 1:36	*2564*
they c him Zacharias, after the	Lk 1:59	*2564*
but he shall be c John	Lk 1:60	*2564*
kindred that is c by this name	Lk 1:61	*2564*
father, how he would have him c	Lk 1:62	*2564*
shalt be c the prophet of the	Lk 1:76	*2564*
of David, which is c Bethlehem	Lk 2:4	*2564*
the child, his name was c JESUS	Lk 2:21	*2564*
womb shall be c holy to the Lord	Lk 2:23	*2564*
he c unto him his disciples	Lk 6:13	*4377*
of Alphaeus, and Simon c Zelotes,	Lk 6:15	*2564*
that he went into a city c Nain	Lk 7:11	*2564*
Mary c Magdalene, out of whom	Lk 8:2	*2564*
and took her by the hand, and c	Lk 8:54	*5455*
Then he c his twelve disciples	Lk 9:1	*4779*
belonging to the city c Bethsaida	Lk 9:10	*2564*
And she had a sister c Mary	Lk 10:39	*2564*
he c her to him, and said unto her	Lk 13:12	*4377*
am no more worthy to be c thy son	Lk 15:19	*2564*
am no more worthy to be c thy son	Lk 15:21	*2564*
he c one of the servants, and	Lk 15:26	*4341*
he c him, and said unto him, How	Lk 16:2	*5455*
So he c every one of his lord's	Lk 16:5	*4341*
But Jesus c them unto him, and	Lk 18:16	*4341*
he c his ten servants, and	Lk 19:13	*2564*
these servants to be c unto him	Lk 19:15	*5455*
at the mount c the mount of	Lk 19:29	*2564*
that is c the mount of Olives	Lk 21:37	*2564*
nigh, which is c the Passover	Lk 22:1	*3004*
upon them are c benefactors	Lk 22:25	*2564*
multitude, and he that was c Judas	Lk 22:47	*3004*
when he had c together the chief	Lk 23:13	*4779*
to the place, which is c Calvary	Lk 23:33	*2564*
same day to a village c Emmaus	Lk 24:13	*3686*
thou shalt be c Cephas, which is	Jn 1:42	*2564*
him, Before that Philip c thee	Jn 1:48	*5455*
And both Jesus was c, and his	Jn 2:2	*2564*
of the feast c the bridegroom	Jn 2:9	*5455*
of Samaria, which is c Sychar	Jn 4:5	*3004*
Messias cometh, which is c Christ	Jn 4:25	*3044*
which is c in the Hebrew tongue	Jn 5:2	*1951*
A man that is c Jesus made clay,	Jn 9:11	*3004*
until they c the parents of him	Jn 9:18	*5455*
Then again c they the man that	Jn 9:24	*5455*
If he c them gods, unto whom the	Jn 10:35	*2036*
said Thomas, which is c Didymus	Jn 11:16	*3004*
c Mary her sister secretly,	Jn 11:28	*5455*
wilderness, into a city c Ephraim	Jn 11:54	*3004*
he c Lazarus out of his grave	Jn 12:17	*5455*
but I have c you friends	Jn 15:15	*2046*
c Jesus, and said unto him, Art	Jn 18:33	*5455*
in a place that is c the Pavement	Jn 19:13	*3004*
a place c the place of a skull	Jn 19:17	*3004*
which is c in the Hebrew Golgotha	Jn 19:17	*3004*
c Didymus, was not with them when	Jn 20:24	*3004*
Thomas c Didymus, and Nathanael of	Jn 21:2	*3004*
Jerusalem from the mount c Olivet	Acts 1:12	*2564*
field is c in their proper tongue	Acts 1:19	*2564*
Joseph c Barsabas, who was	Acts 1:23	*2564*
the temple which is c Beautiful	Acts 3:2	*3004*
in the porch that is c Solomon's	Acts 3:11	*2564*
And they c them, and commanded	Acts 4:18	*2564*
c the council together, and all	Acts 5:21	*4779*
and when they had c the apostles	Acts 5:40	*4341*
Then the twelve c the multitude	Acts 6:2	*4341*
which is c the synagogue of the	Acts 6:9	*3004*
c his father Jacob to him, and all	Acts 7:14	*3333*
c Simon, which beforetime in the	Acts 8:9	*3686*
the street which is c Straight	Acts 9:11	*2564*
the house of Judas for one c Saul	Acts 9:11	*3686*
which c on this name in Jerusalem	Acts 9:21	*1941*
by interpretation is c Dorcas	Acts 9:36	*3004*
up, and when he had c the saints	Acts 9:41	*5455*
man in Caesarea c Cornelius	Acts 10:1	*3686*
of the band c the Italian band	Acts 10:1	*2564*
he c two of his household	Acts 10:7	*5455*
And c, and asked whether Simon,	Acts 10:18	*5455*
Then c he them in, and lodged them	Acts 10:23	*1528*

had c together his kinsmen and Acts 10:24 4779
the disciples were c Christians Acts 11:26 5537
and Simeon that was c Niger Acts 13:1 2564
the work whereunto I have c them Acts 13:2 4341
who c for Barnabas and Saul, and Acts 13:7 4341
Then Saul, (who also is c Paul Acts 13:9
And they c Barnabas, Jupiter Acts 14:12 2564
Gentiles, upon whom my name is c Acts 15:17 1941
had c us for to preach the gospel Acts 16:10 4341
Then he c for a light, and sprang Acts 16:29 154
Whom he c together with the Acts 19:25 4867
be c in question for this day's Acts 19:40 1458
Paul c unto him the disciples, and Acts 20:1 4341
c the elders of the church Acts 20:17 3333
of the dead I am c in question Acts 23:6 2919
Then Paul c one of the centurions Acts 23:17 4341
Paul the prisoner c me unto him Acts 23:18 4341
he c unto him two centurions, Acts 23:23 4341
And when he was c forth, Tertullus Acts 24:2 2564
am c in question by you this day Acts 24:21 2919
place which is c The fair havens Acts 27:8 2564
a tempestuous wind, c Euroclydon Acts 27:14 2564
certain island which is c Clauda Acts 27:16 2564
knew that the island was c Melita Acts 28:1 2564
that after three days Paul c the Acts 28:17 4779
cause therefore have I c for you Acts 28:20 3870
c to be an apostle, separated Rom 1:1 2822
are ye also the c of Jesus Christ Rom 1:6 2822
beloved of God, c to be saints Rom 1:7 2822
Behold, thou art c a Jew, and Rom 2:17 2028
she shall be c an adulteress Rom 7:3 5537
to them who are the c according Rom 8:28 2822
did predestinate, them he also c Rom 8:30 2564
and whom he c, them he also Rom 8:30 2564
but, In Isaac shall thy seed be c Rom 9:7 2564
Even us, whom he hath c, not of Rom 9:24 2564
there shall they be c the Rom 9:26 2564
c to be an apostle of Jesus 1Cor 1:1 2822
c to be saints, with all that in 1Cor 1:2 2822
by whom ye were c unto the 1Cor 1:9 2564
But unto them which are c 1Cor 1:24 2822
mighty, not many noble, are c 1Cor 1:26
if any man that is c a brother be 1Cor 5:11 3687
but God hath c us to peace 1Cor 7:15 2564
man, as the Lord hath c every one 1Cor 7:17 2564
Is any man c being circumcised 1Cor 7:18 2564
Is any c in uncircumcision 1Cor 7:18 2564
the same calling wherein he was c 1Cor 7:20 2564
Art thou c being a servant 1Cor 7:21 2564
For he that is c in the Lord 1Cor 7:22 2564
likewise also he that is c 1Cor 7:22 2564
let every man, wherein he is c 1Cor 7:24 2564
though there be that are c gods 1Cor 8:5 3004
am not meet to be c an apostle 1Cor 15:9 2564
c you into the grace of Christ Gal 1:6 2564
womb, and c me by his grace, Gal 1:15 2564
ye have been c unto liberty Gal 5:13 2564
who are c Uncircumcision by that Eph 2:11 3004
c the Circumcision in the flesh Eph 2:11 3004
the vocation wherewith ye are c Eph 4:1 2564
even as ye are c in one hope of Eph 4:4 2564
which also ye are c in one body Col 3:15 2564
And Jesus, which is c Justus Col 4:11 3004
who hath c you unto his kingdom 1Th 2:12 2564
For God hath not c us unto 1Th 4:7 2564
himself above all that is c God 2Th 2:4 3004
Whereunto he c you by our gospel, 2Th 2:14 2564
life, whereunto thou art also c 1Ti 6:12 2564
of science falsely so c 1Ti 6:20 5581
c us with an holy calling, not 2Ti 1:9 2564
daily, while it is c To day Heb 3:13 2564
himself, but he that is c of God Heb 5:4 2564
C of God an high priest after the Heb 5:10 4316
not be c after the order of Aaron Heb 7:11 3004
which is c the sanctuary Heb 9:2 3004
which is c the Holiest of all Heb 9:3 3004
they which are c might receive Heb 9:15 2564
when he was c to go out into a Heb 11:8 2564
is not ashamed to be c their God Heb 11:16 1941
That in Isaac shall thy seed be c Heb 11:18 2564
refused to be c the son of Heb 11:24 3004
worthy name by the which ye are c Jas 2:7 1941
he was c the Friend of God Jas 2:23 2564
as he which hath c you is holy 1Pet 1:15 2564
the praises of him who hath c you 1Pet 2:9 2564
For even hereunto were ye c 1Pet 2:21 2564
knowing that ye are thereunto c 1Pet 3:9 2564
who hath c us unto his eternal 1Pet 5:10 2564
of him that hath c us to glory 2Pet 1:3 2564
we should be c the sons of God 1Jn 3:1 2564
preserved in Jesus Christ, and c Jude 1 2822
was in the isle that is c Patmos Rev 1:9 2564
name of the star is c Wormwood Rev 8:11 3004
which spiritually is c Sodom Rev 11:8 2564
c the Devil, and Satan, which Rev 12:9 2564
them together into a place c in Rev 16:16 2564
and they that are with him are c Rev 17:14 2822
Blessed are they which are c unto Rev 19:9 2564
that sat upon him was c Faithful Rev 19:11 2564
his name is c The Word of God Rev 19:13 2564

CALLEDST
us thus, that thou c us not Judg 8:1 7121
for thou c me 1Sa 3:5 7121
Thou c in trouble, and I delivered Ps 81:7 7121
Thus thou c to remembrance the Eze 23:21 6485

CALLEST
said unto him, Why c thou me good Mt 19:17 3004
said unto him, Why c thou me good Mk 10:18 3004
said unto him, Why c thou me good Lk 18:19 3004

CALLETH
that the stranger c to thee for 1Kin 8:43 7121
that the stranger c to thee for 2Chr 6:33 7121
who c upon God, and he answereth Job 12:4 7121
Deep c unto deep at the noise of Ps 42:7 7121
he c them all by their names Ps 147:4 7121
and his mouth c for strokes Prov 18:6 7121
He c to me out of Seir, Watchman, Is 21:11 7121
he c them all by names by the Is 40:26 7121
None c for justice, nor any Is 59:4 7121
is none that c upon thy name Is 64:7 7121
is none among them that c unto me Hos 7:7 7121
that c for the waters of the sea, Amos 5:8 7121
he that c for the waters of the Amos 9:6 7121
that, said, This man c for Elias Mt 27:47 5455
and c unto him whom he would Mk 3:13 4341
he c thee Mk 10:49 5455
therefore himself c him Lord Mk 12:37 3004
heard it said, Behold, he c Elias Mk 15:35 5455
he c together his friends and Lk 15:6 4779
it, she c her friends and her Lk 15:9 4779
when he c the Lord the God of Lk 20:37 3004
David therefore c him Lord Lk 20:44 2564
he c his own sheep by name, and Jn 10:3 2564
The Master is come, and c for thee Jn 11:28 5455
c those things which be not as Rom 4:17 2564
not of works, but of him that c Rom 9:11 2564
Spirit of God c Jesus accursed 1Cor 12:3 3004
cometh not of him that c you Gal 5:8 2564
Faithful is he that c you 1Th 5:24 2564
which c herself a prophetess, to Rev 2:20 3004

CALLING
them for the c of the assembly Num 10:2 4744
the c of assemblies, I cannot Is 1:13 7121
c the generations from the Is 41:4 7121
C a ravenous bird from the east, Is 46:11 7121
in c to remembrance the days of Eze 23:19 2142
markets, and c unto their fellows, Mt 11:16 4377
without, sent unto him, c him Mk 3:31 5455
Peter c to remembrance saith unto Mk 11:21 363
c unto him the centurion, he Mk 15:44 4341
John c unto him two of his Lk 7:19 4341
c one to another, and saying, We Lk 7:32 4377
c upon God, and saying, Lord Jesus Acts 7:59 1941
c on the name of the Lord Acts 22:16 1941
c of God are without repentance Rom 11:29 2821
For ye see your c, brethren, how 1Cor 1:26 2821
the same c wherein he was called 1Cor 7:20 2821
know what is the hope of his c Eph 1:18 2821
are called in one hope of your c Eph 4:4 2821
the high c of God in Christ Jesus Phil 3:14 2821
would count you worthy of this c 2Th 1:11 2821
us, and called us with an holy c 2Ti 1:9 2821
partakers of the heavenly c Heb 3:1 2821
Sarah obeyed Abraham, c him lord 1Pet 3:6 2564
give diligence to make your c 2Pet 1:10 2821

CALM
He maketh the storm a c, so that Ps 107:29 1827
that the sea may be c unto us Jonah 1:11 8367
so shall the sea be c unto you Jonah 1:12 8367
and there was a great c Mt 8:26 1055
ceased, and there was a great c Mk 4:39 1055
and they ceased, and there was a c Lk 8:24 1055

CALNEH (*cal'-neh*) See CALNO, CANNEH. *A center of Babylonian worship.*
Babel, and Erech, and Accad, and C Gen 10:10 3641
Pass ye unto C, and see Amos 6:2 3641

CALNO (*cal'-no*) See CALNEH. *Same as Calneh.*
Is not C as Carchemish Is 10:9 3641

CALVARY
to the place, which is called C Lk 23:33 2898

CALVE
thou mark when the hinds do c Job 39:1 2342
of the LORD maketh the hinds to c Ps 29:9 2342

CALVED
Yea, the hind also c in the field Jer 14:5 3205

CALVES
bring their c home from them 1Sa 6:7 1121
cart, and shut up their c at home 1Sa 6:10 1121
and took sheep, and oxen, and c 1Sa 14:32
counsel, and made two c of gold 1Kin 12:28 5695
unto the c that he had made 1Kin 12:32 5695
the golden c that were in Beth-el 2Kin 10:29 5695
them molten images, even two c 2Kin 17:16 5695
for the c which he had made 2Chr 11:15 5695
and there are with you golden c 2Chr 13:8 5695
with the c of the people, till Ps 68:30 5695
because of the c of Beth-aven Hos 10:5 5697
the men that sacrifice kiss the c Hos 13:2 5697
will we render the c of our lips Hos 14:2 6499
the c out of the midst of the Amos 6:4 5695
offerings, with c of a year old Mic 6:6 5695
grow up as c of the stall Mal 4:2 5695
by the blood of goats and c Heb 9:12 3448
the law, he took the blood of c Heb 9:19 3448

CALVETH
their cow c, and casteth not her Job 21:10 6403

CAME
in process of time it c to pass Gen 4:3 1961
it c to pass, when they were in Gen 4:8 1961
it c to pass, when men began to Gen 6:1 1961
when the sons of God c in unto Gen 6:4 935
it c to pass after seven days, Gen 7:10 1961
it c to pass at the end of forty Gen 8:6 1961
the dove c in to him in the Gen 8:11 935
it c to pass in the six hundredth Gen 8:13 1961
(out of whom c Philistim Gen 10:14 3318
it c to pass, as they journeyed Gen 11:2 1961
the LORD c down to see the city Gen 11:5 3381
they c unto Haran, and dwelt there Gen 11:31 935
and into the land of Canaan they c Gen 12:5 935
it c to pass, when he was come Gen 12:11 1961
it c to pass, that, when Abram Gen 12:14 1961
Then Abram removed his tent, and c Gen 13:18 935
it c to pass in the days of Gen 14:1 1961
fourteenth year c Chedorlaomer Gen 14:5 935
c to En-mishpat, which is Kadesh, Gen 14:7 935
there c one that had escaped, and Gen 14:13 935
the LORD c unto Abram in a vision Gen 15:1 1961
the word of the LORD c unto him Gen 15:4
when the fowls c down upon the Gen 15:11 3381
it c to pass, that, when the sun Gen 15:17 1961
there c two angels to Sodom at Gen 19:1 935
men which c in to thee this night Gen 19:5 935
for therefore c they under the Gen 19:8 935
This one fellow c in to sojourn Gen 19:9 935
Lot, and c near to break the door Gen 19:9 5066
it c to pass, when they had Gen 19:17 1961
it c to pass, when God destroyed Gen 19:29 1961
it c to pass on the morrow, that Gen 19:34 1961
But God c to Abimelech in a dream Gen 20:3 935
it c to pass, when God caused me Gen 20:13 1961
it c to pass at that time, that Gen 21:22 1961
it c to pass after these things, Gen 22:1 1961
they c to the place which God had Gen 22:9 935
it c to pass after these things, Gen 22:20 1961
Abraham c to mourn for Sarah, and Gen 23:2 935
it c to pass, before he had done Gen 24:15 1961
that, behold, Rebekah c out Gen 24:15 3318
and filled her pitcher, and c up Gen 24:16 5927
it c to pass, as the camels had Gen 24:22 1961
it c to pass, when he saw the Gen 24:30 1961
that he c unto the man Gen 24:30 935
And the man c into the house Gen 24:32 935
I c this day unto the well, and Gen 24:42 935
Rebekah c forth with her pitcher Gen 24:45 3318
And it c to pass, that, when Gen 24:52 1961
Isaac c from the way of the well Gen 24:62 935
it c to pass after the death of Gen 25:11 1061
And the first c out red, all over Gen 25:25 3318
after that c his brother out, and Gen 25:26 3318
Esau c from the field, and he was Gen 25:29 935
it c to pass, when he had been Gen 26:8 1961
it c to pass the same day Gen 26:32 1961
that Isaac's servants c, and told him Gen 26:32 935
it c to pass, that when Isaac was Gen 27:1 1961
he c unto his father, and said, My Gen 27:18 935
And he c near, and kissed him Gen 27:27 5066
it c to pass, as soon as Isaac Gen 27:30 1961
his brother c in from his hunting Gen 27:30 935
Thy brother c with subtilty, and Gen 27:35 935
c into the land of the people of Gen 29:1 3212
Rachel c with her father's sheep Gen 29:9 935
it c to pass, when Jacob saw Gen 29:10 1961
it c to pass, when Laban heard Gen 29:13 1961
it c to pass in the evening, that Gen 29:23 1961
it c to pass, that in the morning Gen 29:25 1961
Jacob c out of the field in the Gen 30:16 935
it c to pass, when Rachel had Gen 30:25 1961
which thou hadst before I c Gen 30:30
when the flocks c to drink Gen 30:38 935
conceive when they c to drink Gen 30:38 935
it c to pass, whensoever the Gen 30:41 1961
it c to pass at the time that the Gen 31:10 1961
God c to Laban the Syrian in a Gen 31:24 935
We c to thy brother Esau, and also Gen 32:6 935
took of that which c to his hand Gen 32:13 935
and looked, and, behold, Esau c Gen 33:1 935
until he c near to his brother Gen 33:3 5066
Then the handmaidens c near Gen 33:6 5066
also with her children c near Gen 33:7 5066
after c Joseph near and Rachel, and Gen 33:7 5066
Jacob c to Shalem, a city of Gen 33:18 935
when he c from Padan-aram Gen 33:18 935
the sons of Jacob c out of the Gen 34:7 935
Shechem his son c unto the gate Gen 34:20 935
it c to pass on the third day, Gen 34:25 1961
c upon the city boldly, and slew Gen 34:25 935
sons of Jacob c upon the slain Gen 34:27 935
So Jacob c to Luz, which is in Gen 35:6 935
when he c out of Padan-aram, and Gen 35:9 935
it c to pass, when she was in Gen 35:17 935
it c to pass, as her soul was in Gen 35:18 935
it c to pass, when Israel dwelt Gen 35:22 1961
Jacob c unto Isaac his father Gen 35:27 935
these are the dukes that c of Gen 36:16
these are the dukes that c of Gen 36:17
these were the dukes that c of Gen 36:18
the dukes that c of the Horites Gen 36:29
are the dukes that c of Hori Gen 36:30 935
names of the dukes that c of Esau Gen 36:40
of Hebron, and he c to Shechem Gen 37:14 935
even before he c near unto them Gen 37:18 7126
it c to pass, when Joseph was Gen 37:23 1961
a company of Ishmeelites c from Gen 37:25 935
it c to pass at that time, that Gen 38:1 1961
it c to pass, when he went in Gen 38:9 1961
c in unto her, and she conceived Gen 38:18 935
it c to pass about three months Gen 38:24 1961
it c to pass in the time of her Gen 38:27 1961
it c to pass, when she travailed, Gen 38:28 1961
thread, saying, This c out first Gen 38:28 3318
it c to pass, as he drew back his Gen 38:29 1961
that, behold, his brother c out Gen 38:29 3318
afterward c out his brother, that Gen 38:30 3318
it c to pass from the time that Gen 39:5 1961
it c to pass after these things, Gen 39:7 1961
it c to pass, as she spake to Gen 39:10 1961
it c to pass about this time, Gen 39:11 1961
it c to pass, when she saw that Gen 39:13 1961
he c in unto me to lie with me, Gen 39:14 935
it c to pass, when he heard that Gen 39:15 1961
by her, until his lord c home Gen 39:16 935
unto us, c in unto me to mock me Gen 39:17 935
it c to pass, as I lifted up my Gen 39:18 1961
it c to pass, when his master Gen 39:19 1961

it c to pass after these things,	Gen 40:1	1961
Joseph c in unto them in the	Gen 40:6	935
it c to pass the third day, which	Gen 40:20	1961
it c to pass at the end of two	Gen 41:1	1961
there c up out of the river seven	Gen 41:2	5927
seven other kine c up after them	Gen 41:3	5927
ears of corn c up upon one stalk	Gen 41:5	5927
it c to pass in the morning that	Gen 41:8	1961
it c to pass, as he interpreted	Gen 41:13	1961
his raiment, and c in unto Pharaoh	Gen 41:14	935
there c up out of the river seven	Gen 41:18	5927
seven other kine c up after them	Gen 41:19	5927
seven ears c up in one stalk,	Gen 41:22	5927
ill favoured kine that c up after	Gen 41:27	5927
sons before the years of famine c	Gen 41:50	935
all countries c into Egypt to	Gen 41:57	935
the sons of Israel c to buy corn	Gen 42:5	935
to buy corn among those that c	Gen 42:5	935
and Joseph's brethren c, and bowed	Gen 42:6	935
they c unto Jacob their father	Gen 42:29	935
it c to pass as they emptied	Gen 42:35	1961
it c to pass, when they had eaten	Gen 43:2	1961
they c near to the steward of	Gen 43:19	5066
we c indeed down at the first	Gen 43:20	3381
And it c to pass	Gen 43:21	1961
when we c to the inn, that we	Gen 43:21	935
present against Joseph c at noon	Gen 43:25	935
And when Joseph c home, they	Gen 43:26	935
his brethren c to Joseph's house	Gen 44:14	935
Then Judah c near unto him, and	Gen 44:18	5066
it c to pass when we c up unto	Gen 44:24	1961
it c to pass when we c up unto	Gen 44:24	5927
And they c near	Gen 45:4	5066
c into the land of Canaan unto	Gen 45:25	935
c to Beer-sheba, and offered	Gen 46:1	935
c into Egypt, Jacob, and all his	Gen 46:6	935
which c into Egypt, Jacob and his	Gen 46:8	935
All the souls that c with Jacob	Gen 46:26	935
which c out of his loins, besides	Gen 46:26	3318
Jacob, which c into Egypt, were	Gen 46:27	935
they c into the land of Goshen	Gen 46:28	935
Then Joseph c and told Pharaoh, and	Gen 47:1	935
all the Egyptians c unto Joseph	Gen 47:15	935
they c unto him the second year,	Gen 47:18	935
it c to pass after these things,	Gen 48:1	1961
before I c unto thee into Egypt	Gen 48:5	935
when I c from Padan, Rachel died	Gen 48:7	935
they c to the threshingfloor of	Gen 50:10	935
of Israel, which c into Egypt	Ex 1:1	935
man and his household c with Jacob	Ex 1:1	935
all the souls that c out of the	Ex 1:5	3318
it c to pass, because the	Ex 1:21	1961
the daughter of Pharaoh c down to	Ex 2:5	3381
it c to pass in those days, when	Ex 2:11	1961
and they c and drew water, and	Ex 2:16	935
And the shepherds c and drove them	Ex 2:17	935
when they c to Reuel their father	Ex 2:18	935
it c to pass in process of time,	Ex 2:23	1961
their cry c up unto God by reason	Ex 2:23	5927
c to the mountain of God, even to	Ex 3:1	935
it c to pass by the way in the	Ex 4:24	1961
of the children of Israel c	Ex 5:15	935
as they c forth from Pharaoh	Ex 5:20	3318
For since I c to Pharaoh to speak	Ex 5:23	935
it c to pass on the day when the	Ex 6:28	1961
and the frogs c up, and covered the	Ex 8:6	5927
there c a grievous swarm of flies	Ex 8:24	935
Aaron c in unto Pharaoh, and said	Ex 10:3	935
it c to pass, that at midnight	Ex 12:29	1961
it c to pass at the end of the	Ex 12:41	1961
the selfsame day it c to pass	Ex 12:41	1961
it c to pass the selfsame day,	Ex 12:51	1961
in which ye c out from Egypt, out	Ex 13:3	3318
This day c ye out in the month	Ex 13:4	3318
me when I c forth out of Egypt	Ex 13:8	3318
it c to pass, when Pharaoh would	Ex 13:15	1961
it c to pass, when Pharaoh had	Ex 13:17	1961
it c between the camp of the	Ex 14:20	935
so that the one c not near the	Ex 14:20	7126
it c to pass, that in the morning	Ex 14:24	1961
that c into the sea after them	Ex 14:28	935
And when they c to Marah, they	Ex 15:23	935
they c to Elim, where were twelve	Ex 15:27	935
of the children of Israel c unto	Ex 16:1	935
it c to pass, as Aaron spake unto	Ex 16:10	1961
it c to pass, that at even the	Ex 16:13	1961
that at even the quails c up	Ex 16:13	5927
it c to pass, that on the sixth	Ex 16:22	1961
the rulers of the congregation c	Ex 16:22	935
it c to pass, that there went out	Ex 16:27	1961
until they c to a land inhabited	Ex 16:35	935
until they c unto the borders of	Ex 16:35	935
Then c Amalek, and fought with	Ex 17:8	935
it c to pass, when Moses held up	Ex 17:11	1961
c with his sons and his wife unto	Ex 18:5	935
and they c into the tent	Ex 18:7	935
and Aaron c, and all the elders of	Ex 18:12	935
it c to pass on the morrow, that	Ex 18:13	1961
the same day c they into the	Ex 19:1	935
And Moses c and called for the	Ex 19:7	935
it c to pass on the third day in	Ex 19:16	1961
the LORD c down upon mount Sinai,	Ex 19:20	3381
If he c in by himself, he shall	Ex 21:3	935
an hired thing, it c for his hire	Ex 22:15	935
And Moses c and told the people all	Ex 24:3	935
And it c to pass	Ex 32:19	7126
as soon as he c nigh unto the	Ex 32:19	935
fire, and there c out this calf	Ex 32:24	3318
it c to pass on the morrow, that	Ex 32:30	1961
it c to pass, that every one	Ex 33:7	1961
it c to pass, when Moses went out	Ex 33:8	1961
it c to pass, as Moses entered	Ex 33:9	1961
And it c to pass	Ex 34:29	1961
when Moses c down from mount	Ex 34:29	3381
when he c down from the mount,	Ex 34:29	3381
all the children of Israel c nigh	Ex 34:32	5066
took the vail off, until he c out	Ex 34:34	3318
he c out, and spake unto the	Ex 34:34	3318
And they c, every one whose heart	Ex 35:21	935
And they c, both men and women, as	Ex 35:22	935
c every man from his work which	Ex 36:4	935
it c to pass in the first month	Ex 40:17	1961
when they c near unto the altar,	Ex 40:32	7126
it c to pass on the eighth day,	Lev 9:1	935
c down from offering of the sin	Lev 9:22	3381
c out, and blessed the people	Lev 9:23	3318
there c a fire out from before	Lev 9:24	3318
every one that c to do the	Num 4:47	935
it c to pass on the day that	Num 7:1	1961
they c before Moses and before	Num 9:6	7126
it c to pass on the twentieth day	Num 10:11	1961
up the tabernacle against they c	Num 10:21	935
it c to pass, when the ark set	Num 10:35	1961
Why c we forth out of Egypt	Num 11:20	3318
the LORD c down in a cloud, and	Num 11:25	3381
it c to pass, that, when the	Num 11:25	1961
And they three c out	Num 12:4	3318
the LORD c down in the pillar of	Num 12:5	3381
and they both c forth	Num 12:5	3318
by the south, and c unto Hebron	Num 13:22	935
they c unto the brook of Eshcol,	Num 13:23	935
c to Moses, and to Aaron, and to	Num 13:26	935
We c unto the land whither thou	Num 13:27	935
Then the Amalekites c down	Num 14:45	3381
and Dathan and Abiram c out	Num 16:27	3318
it c to pass, as he had made an	Num 16:31	1961
there c out a fire from the LORD,	Num 16:35	3318
And it c to pass, when the	Num 16:42	1961
Aaron c before the tabernacle of	Num 16:43	935
it c to pass, that on the morrow	Num 17:8	1961
and upon which never c yoke	Num 19:2	5927
Then c the children of Israel,	Num 20:1	935
the water c out abundantly, and	Num 20:11	3318
Edom c out against him with much	Num 20:20	3318
from Kadesh, and c unto mount Hor	Num 20:22	935
Eleazar c down from the mount	Num 20:28	3381
heard tell that Israel c by the	Num 21:1	935
Therefore the people c to Moses	Num 21:7	935
it c to pass, that if a serpent	Num 21:9	1961
he c to Jahaz, and fought against	Num 21:23	935
they c unto Balaam, and spake unto	Num 22:7	935
God c unto Balaam, and said, What	Num 22:9	935
they c to Balaam, and said to him,	Num 22:16	935
God c unto Balaam at night, and	Num 22:20	935
they c unto Kirjath-huzoth	Num 22:39	935
it c to pass on the morrow, that	Num 22:41	1961
And when he c to him, behold, he	Num 23:17	935
and the spirit of God c upon him	Num 24:2	1961
one of the children of Israel c	Num 25:6	935
it c to pass after the plague,	Num 26:1	1961
Then c the daughters of	Num 27:1	7126
hundreds, which c from the battle	Num 31:14	935
of hundreds, c near unto Moses	Num 31:48	7126
Gad and the children of Reuben c	Num 32:2	935
of the men that c up out of Egypt	Num 32:11	5927
they c near unto him, and said, We	Num 32:16	5066
from Marah, and c unto Elim	Num 33:9	935
c near, and spake before Moses, and	Num 36:1	7126
it c to pass in the fortieth year	Deut 1:3	1961
and we c to Kadesh-barnea	Deut 1:19	935
ye c near unto me every one of	Deut 1:22	7126
c unto the valley of Eshcol, and	Deut 1:24	935
until ye c into this place	Deut 1:31	935
c out against you, and chased you,	Deut 1:44	3318
in which we c from Kadesh-barnea	Deut 2:14	1980
So it c to pass, when all the men	Deut 2:16	1961
which c forth out of Caphtor,	Deut 2:23	3318
Then Sihon c out against us, he	Deut 2:32	3318
king of Bashan c out against us	Deut 3:1	3318
ye c near and stood under the	Deut 4:11	7126
after they c forth out of Egypt,	Deut 4:45	3318
it c to pass, when ye heard the	Deut 5:23	1961
that ye c near unto me, even all	Deut 5:23	7126
until ye c unto this place, ye	Deut 9:7	935
it c to pass at the end of forty	Deut 9:11	1961
c down from the mount, and the	Deut 9:15	3381
c down from the mount, and put the	Deut 10:5	3381
until ye c into this place	Deut 11:5	935
of Egypt, from whence ye c out	Deut 11:10	3318
this woman, and when I c to her	Deut 22:14	7126
when ye c forth out of Egypt	Deut 23:4	3318
when ye c unto this place, Sihon	Deut 29:7	935
c out against us unto battle, and	Deut 29:7	3318
how we c through the nations	Deut 29:16	5674
it c to pass, when Moses had made	Deut 31:24	1961
not, to new gods that c newly up	Deut 32:17	935
And Moses c and spake all the words	Deut 32:44	935
The LORD c from Sinai, and rose up	Deut 33:2	935
he c with ten thousands of saints	Deut 33:2	857
he c with the heads of the people	Deut 33:21	857
servant of the LORD it c to pass	Josh 1:1	1961
c into an harlot's house, named	Josh 2:1	935
there c men in hither to night of	Josh 2:2	935
There c men unto me, but I wist	Josh 2:4	935
it c to pass about the time of	Josh 2:5	1961
she c up unto them upon the roof	Josh 2:8	5927
for you, when ye c out of Egypt	Josh 2:10	3318
c unto the mountain, and abode	Josh 2:22	935
c to Joshua the son of Nun, and	Josh 2:23	935
c to Jordan, he and all the	Josh 3:1	935
it c to pass after three days,	Josh 3:2	1961
it c to pass, when the people	Josh 3:14	1961
which c down from above stood	Josh 3:16	3381
those that c down toward the sea	Josh 3:16	3381
it c to pass, when all the people	Josh 4:1	1961
it c to pass, when all the people	Josh 4:11	1961
it c to pass, when the priests	Josh 4:18	1961
the people c up out of Jordan on	Josh 4:19	5927
Israel c over this Jordan on dry	Josh 4:22	5674
it c to pass, when all the kings	Josh 5:1	1961
the people that c out of Egypt	Josh 5:4	3318
after they c out of Egypt	Josh 5:4	3318
that c out were circumcised	Josh 5:5	3318
way as they c forth out of Egypt	Josh 5:5	3318
which c out of Egypt, were	Josh 5:6	3318
it c to pass, when they had done	Josh 5:8	1961
it c to pass, when Joshua was by	Josh 5:13	1961
none went out, and none c in	Josh 6:1	935
it c to pass, when Joshua had	Josh 6:8	1961
the rereward c after the ark, the	Josh 6:9	1980
they c into the camp, and lodged	Josh 6:11	935
but the rereward c after the ark	Josh 6:13	1980
it c to pass on the seventh day,	Josh 6:15	1961
it c to pass at the seventh time,	Josh 6:16	1961
it c to pass, when the people	Josh 6:20	1961
c before the city, and pitched on	Josh 8:11	935
it c to pass, when the king of Ai	Josh 8:14	1961
it c to pass, when Israel had	Josh 8:24	1961
it c to pass, when all the kings	Josh 9:1	1961
the day we c forth to go unto you	Josh 9:12	3318
it c to pass at the end of three	Josh 9:16	1961
c unto their cities on the third	Josh 9:17	935
Now it c to pass, when	Josh 10:1	1961
Joshua therefore c unto them	Josh 10:9	935
it c to pass, as they fled from	Josh 10:11	1961
it c to pass, when Joshua and the	Josh 10:20	1961
it c to pass, when they brought	Josh 10:24	1961
And they c near, and put their feet	Josh 10:24	7126
it c to pass at the time of the	Josh 10:27	1961
of Gezer c up to help Lachish	Josh 10:33	5927
it c to pass, when Jabin king of	Josh 11:1	1961
kings were met together, they c	Josh 11:5	935
So Joshua c, and all the people of	Josh 11:7	935
And at that time c Joshua, and cut	Josh 11:21	935
of Judah c unto Joshua in Gilgal	Josh 14:6	5066
And it c to pass	Josh 15:18	1961
as she c unto him, that she moved	Josh 15:18	935
c to Jericho, and went out at	Josh 16:7	6293
they c near before Eleazar the	Josh 17:4	7126
Yet it c to pass, when the	Josh 17:13	1961
c again to Joshua to the host at	Josh 18:9	935
of the children of Benjamin c up	Josh 18:11	5927
the coast of their lot c forth	Josh 18:11	3318
the border c down to the end of	Josh 18:16	3381
the second lot c forth to Simeon,	Josh 19:1	3318
the third lot c up for the	Josh 19:10	5927
the fourth lot c out to Issachar,	Josh 19:17	3318
the fifth lot c out for the tribe	Josh 19:24	3318
The sixth lot c out to the	Josh 19:32	3318
the seventh lot c out for the	Josh 19:40	3318
Then c near the heads of the	Josh 21:1	5066
the lot c out for the families of	Josh 21:4	3318
all c to pass	Josh 21:45	935
when they c unto the borders of	Josh 22:10	935
they c unto the children of	Josh 22:15	935
it c to pass a long time after	Josh 23:1	1961
and ye c unto the sea	Josh 24:6	935
over Jordan, and c unto Jericho	Josh 24:11	935
it c to pass after these things,	Josh 24:29	1961
the death of Joshua it c to pass	Judg 1:1	1961
And it c to pass	Judg 1:14	1961
when she c to him	Judg 1:14	935
it c to pass, when Israel was	Judg 1:28	1961
an angel of the LORD c up from	Judg 2:1	5927
it c to pass, when the angel of	Judg 2:4	1961
it c to pass, when the judge was	Judg 2:19	1961
the spirit of the LORD c upon him	Judg 3:10	1961
And Ehud c unto him	Judg 3:20	935
and the dirt c out	Judg 3:22	3318
he was gone out, his servants c	Judg 3:24	935
it c to pass, when he was come,	Judg 3:27	1961
Israel c up to her for judgment	Judg 4:5	5927
Jael c out to meet him, and said	Judg 4:22	3318
when he c into her tent, behold,	Judg 4:22	935
out of Machir c down governors,	Judg 5:14	3381
The kings c and fought	Judg 5:19	935
because they c not to the help of	Judg 5:23	935
sown, that the Midianites c up	Judg 6:3	5927
even they c up against them	Judg 6:3	5927
For they c up with their cattle	Judg 6:5	5927
they c as grasshoppers for	Judg 6:5	935
it c to pass, when the children	Judg 6:7	1961
there c an angel of the LORD, and	Judg 6:11	935
it c to pass the same night, that	Judg 6:25	1961
Spirit of the LORD c upon Gideon	Judg 6:34	3847
and they c up to meet them	Judg 6:35	5927
it c to pass the same night, that	Judg 7:9	1961
c unto a tent, and smote it that	Judg 7:13	935
c unto the outside of the camp in	Judg 7:19	935
Gideon c to Jordan, and passed	Judg 8:4	935
he c unto the men of Succoth, and	Judg 8:15	935
it c to pass, as soon as Gideon	Judg 8:33	1961
they robbed all that c along that	Judg 9:25	5674
son of Ebed c with his brethren	Judg 9:26	935
it c to pass on the morrow, that	Judg 9:42	1961
Abimelech c unto the tower, and	Judg 9:52	935
upon them c the curse of Jotham	Judg 9:57	935
it c to pass in process of time,	Judg 11:4	1961
when they c up out of Egypt, from	Judg 11:13	5927
But when Israel c up from Egypt	Judg 11:16	5927
unto the Red sea, and c to Kadesh	Judg 11:16	935
c by the east side of the land of	Judg 11:18	935
but c not within the border of	Judg 11:18	935
of the LORD c upon Jephthah	Judg 11:29	1961
Jephthah c to Mizpeh unto his	Judg 11:34	935
his daughter c out to meet him	Judg 11:34	3318
it c to pass, when he saw her,	Judg 11:35	1961
it c to pass at the end of two	Judg 11:39	1961
Then the woman c and told her	Judg 13:6	935
saying, A man of God c unto me	Judg 13:6	935
the angel of God c again unto the	Judg 13:9	935
that c unto me the other day	Judg 13:10	935

Context	Reference	No.
c to the man, and said unto him,	Judg 13:11	935
For it c to pass, when the flame	Judg 13:20	1961
And he c up, and told his father and	Judg 14:2	5927
c to the vineyards of Timnath	Judg 14:5	935
of the LORD c mightily upon him	Judg 14:6	6743
c to his father and mother, and	Judg 14:9	1980
it c to pass, when they saw him,	Judg 14:11	1961
Out of the eater c forth meat	Judg 14:14	3318
of the strong c forth sweetness	Judg 14:14	3318
it c to pass on the seventh day,	Judg 14:15	1961
it c to pass on the seventh day,	Judg 14:17	1961
the Spirit of the LORD c upon him	Judg 14:19	6743
But it c to pass within a while	Judg 15:1	1961
And the Philistines c up, and burnt	Judg 15:6	5927
And when he c unto Lehi, the	Judg 15:14	935
of the LORD c mightily upon him	Judg 15:14	
it c to pass, when he had made an	Judg 15:17	1961
jaw, and there c water thereout	Judg 15:19	3318
he had drunk, his spirit c again	Judg 15:19	7725
it c to pass afterward, that he	Judg 16:4	1961
of the Philistines c up unto her	Judg 16:5	5927
it c to pass, when she pressed	Judg 16:16	1961
of the Philistines c up unto her	Judg 16:18	5927
it c to pass, when their hearts	Judg 16:25	1961
the house of his father c down	Judg 16:31	3381
he c to mount Ephraim to the	Judg 17:8	935
who when they c to mount Ephraim,	Judg 18:2	935
c to Laish, and saw the people	Judg 18:7	935
they c unto their brethren to	Judg 18:8	935
c unto the house of Micah	Judg 18:13	935
c to the house of the young man	Judg 18:15	935
c in thither, and took the graven	Judg 18:17	935
c unto Laish, unto a people that	Judg 18:27	935
it c to pass in those days, when	Judg 19:1	1961
it c to pass on the fourth day,	Judg 19:5	1961
c over against Jebus, which is	Judg 19:10	935
there c an old man from his work	Judg 19:16	935
the man that c into thine house	Judg 19:22	935
Then c the woman in the dawning	Judg 19:26	935
c up out of the land of Egypt	Judg 19:30	5927
I c into Gibeah that belongeth to	Judg 20:4	935
of Benjamin c forth out of Gibeah	Judg 20:21	3318
the children of Israel c near	Judg 20:24	7126
c unto the house of God, and wept,	Judg 20:26	935
c forth out of their places	Judg 20:33	1518
there c against Gibeah ten	Judg 20:34	935
them which c out of the cities	Judg 20:42	
the beast, and all that c to hand	Judg 20:48	4672
all the cities that they c to	Judg 20:48	4672
the people c to the house of God,	Judg 21:2	935
it c to pass on the morrow, that	Judg 21:4	1961
c not up with the congregation	Judg 21:5	5927
c not up to the LORD to Mizpeh	Judg 21:5	5927
c not up to Mizpeh to the LORD	Judg 21:8	5927
there c none to the camp from	Judg 21:8	935
Benjamin c again at that time	Judg 21:14	7725
Now it c to pass in the days when	Ruth 1:1	1961
they c into the country of Moab,	Ruth 1:2	935
went until they c to Beth-lehem	Ruth 1:19	935
it c to pass, when they were come	Ruth 1:19	1961
they c to Beth-lehem in the	Ruth 1:22	935
And she went, and c, and gleaned in	Ruth 2:3	935
Boaz c from Beth-lehem, and said	Ruth 2:4	935
that c back with Naomi out of the	Ruth 2:6	7725
so she c, and hath continued even	Ruth 2:7	935
she c softly, and uncovered his	Ruth 3:7	935
it c to pass at midnight, that	Ruth 3:8	1961
that a woman c into the floor	Ruth 3:14	935
when she c to her mother in law,	Ruth 3:16	935
kinsman of whom Boaz spake c by	Ruth 4:1	5674
it c to pass, as she continued	1Sa 1:12	1961
c to their house to Ramah	1Sa 1:19	935
Wherefore it c to pass, when the	1Sa 1:20	1961
sacrifice, the priest's servant c	1Sa 2:13	935
all the Israelites that c thither	1Sa 2:14	935
the fat, the priest's servant c	1Sa 2:15	935
when she c up with her husband to	1Sa 2:19	5927
there c a man of God unto Eli, and	1Sa 2:27	935
it c to pass at that time, when	1Sa 3:2	1961
And the LORD c, and stood, and	1Sa 3:10	935
word of Samuel c to all Israel	1Sa 4:1	1961
of the LORD c into the camp	1Sa 4:5	935
c to Shiloh the same day with his	1Sa 4:12	935
And when he c, lo, Eli sat upon a	1Sa 4:13	935
when the man c into the city, and	1Sa 4:13	935
the man c in hastily, and told Eli	1Sa 4:14	935
I am he that c out of the army,	1Sa 4:16	935
it c to pass, when he made	1Sa 4:18	1961
for her pains c upon her	1Sa 4:19	2015
And it c to pass	1Sa 5:10	1961
as the ark of God c to Ekron	1Sa 5:10	935
the cart c into the field of	1Sa 6:14	935
And the men of Kirjath-jearim c	1Sa 7:1	935
it c to pass, while the ark abode	1Sa 7:2	1961
until they c under Beth-car	1Sa 7:11	
they c no more into the coast of	1Sa 7:13	935
it c to pass, when Samuel was old	1Sa 8:1	1961
and c to Samuel unto Ramah,	1Sa 8:4	935
for he c to day to the city	1Sa 9:12	935
Samuel c out against them, for to	1Sa 9:14	3318
in his ear a day before Saul c	1Sa 9:15	935
it c to pass about the spring of	1Sa 9:26	1961
all those signs c to pass that	1Sa 10:9	935
when they c thither to the hill,	1Sa 10:10	935
and the Spirit of God c upon him	1Sa 10:10	6743
it c to pass, when all that knew	1Sa 10:11	1961
he c to the high place	1Sa 10:13	935
were no where, we c to Samuel	1Sa 10:14	935
Then Nahash the Ammonite c up	1Sa 11:1	5927
Then c the messengers to Gibeah	1Sa 11:4	935
Saul c after the herd out of the	1Sa 11:5	935
the Spirit of God c upon Saul	1Sa 11:6	6743
they c out with one consent	1Sa 11:7	3318
said unto the messengers that c	1Sa 11:9	935
And the messengers c and shewed it	1Sa 11:9	935
they c into the midst of the host	1Sa 11:11	935
it c to pass, that they which	1Sa 11:11	1961
children of Ammon c against you	1Sa 12:12	935
and they c up, and pitched in	1Sa 13:5	5927
but Samuel c not to Gilgal	1Sa 13:8	935
it c to pass, that as soon as he	1Sa 13:10	1961
burnt offering, behold, Samuel c	1Sa 13:10	935
the spoilers c out of the camp of	1Sa 13:17	3318
So it c to pass in the day of	1Sa 13:22	1961
Now it c to pass upon a day, that	1Sa 14:1	1961
it c to pass, while Saul talked	1Sa 14:19	1961
and they c to the battle	1Sa 14:20	935
all they of the land c to a wood	1Sa 14:25	935
the way, when he c up from Egypt	1Sa 15:2	5927
Saul c to a city of Amalek, and	1Sa 15:5	935
when they c up out of Egypt	1Sa 15:6	5927
Then c the word of the LORD unto	1Sa 15:10	1961
Saul c to Carmel, and, behold, he	1Sa 15:12	935
And Samuel c to Saul	1Sa 15:13	935
Agag c unto him delicately	1Sa 15:32	1980
Samuel c no more to see Saul	1Sa 15:35	
LORD spake, and c to Beth-lehem	1Sa 16:4	935
it c to pass, when they were come	1Sa 16:6	1961
the Spirit of the LORD c upon	1Sa 16:13	6743
David c to Saul, and stood before	1Sa 16:21	935
it c to pass, when the evil	1Sa 16:23	1961
he c to the trench, as the host	1Sa 17:20	935
and ran into the army, and c	1Sa 17:22	935
there c up the champion, the	1Sa 17:23	5927
there c a lion, and a bear, and	1Sa 17:34	935
And the Philistine c on and drew	1Sa 17:41	3212
it c to pass, when the Philistine	1Sa 17:48	1961
when the Philistine arose, and c	1Sa 17:48	3212
it c to pass, when he had made an	1Sa 18:1	1961
And it c to pass	1Sa 18:6	1961
as they c, when David was returned	1Sa 18:6	935
that the women c out of all	1Sa 18:6	3318
it c to pass on the morrow, that	1Sa 18:10	1961
evil spirit from God c upon Saul	1Sa 18:10	6473
out and c in before the people	1Sa 18:13	935
he went out and c in before them	1Sa 18:16	935
But it c to pass at the time when	1Sa 18:19	1961
it c to pass, after they went	1Sa 18:30	1961
c to Samuel to Ramah, and told him	1Sa 19:18	935
c to a great well that is in	1Sa 19:22	935
until he c to Naioth in Ramah	1Sa 19:23	935
fled from Naioth in Ramah, and c	1Sa 20:1	935
it c to pass on the morrow, which	1Sa 20:27	1961
it c to pass in the morning, that	1Sa 20:35	1961
up the arrows, and c to his master	1Sa 20:38	935
Then c David to Nob to Ahimelech	1Sa 21:1	935
these three days, since I c out	1Sa 21:5	3318
c into the forest of Hareth	1Sa 22:5	935
they c all of them to the king	1Sa 22:11	935
it c to pass, when Abiathar the	1Sa 23:6	1961
that he c down with an ephod in	1Sa 23:6	3381
Then c up the Ziphites to Saul to	1Sa 23:19	5927
wherefore he c down into a rock,	1Sa 23:25	3381
But there c a messenger unto Saul	1Sa 23:27	935
it c to pass, when Saul was	1Sa 24:1	1961
he c to the sheepcotes by the way	1Sa 24:3	935
it c to pass afterward, that	1Sa 24:5	1961
it c to pass, when David had made	1Sa 24:16	1961
And when David's young men c	1Sa 25:9	935
their way, and went again, and c	1Sa 25:12	935
that she c down by the covert of	1Sa 25:20	3381
his men c down against her	1Sa 25:20	3381
And Abigail c to Nabal	1Sa 25:36	935
But it c to pass in the morning,	1Sa 25:37	1916
it c to pass about ten days after	1Sa 25:38	1916
the Ziphites c unto Saul to	1Sa 26:1	935
he saw that Saul c after him into	1Sa 26:3	935
c to the place where Saul had	1Sa 26:5	935
Abishai c to the people by night	1Sa 26:7	935
for there c one of the people in	1Sa 26:15	935
and returned, and c to Achish	1Sa 27:9	935
it c to pass in those days, that	1Sa 28:1	1961
themselves together, and c	1Sa 28:4	935
they c to the woman by night	1Sa 28:8	935
And the woman c unto Saul, and saw	1Sa 28:21	935
it c to pass, when David and his	1Sa 30:1	1961
his men c to the city, and, behold	1Sa 30:3	935
c to the brook Besor, where those	1Sa 30:9	935
his spirit c again to him	1Sa 30:12	7725
David c to the two hundred men,	1Sa 30:21	935
when David c near to the people,	1Sa 30:21	5066
that c against us into our hand	1Sa 30:23	935
And when David c to Ziklag	1Sa 30:26	935
and the Philistines c and dwelt in	1Sa 31:7	935
it c to pass on the morrow, when	1Sa 31:8	1691
Philistines c to strip the slain	1Sa 31:8	935
c to Jabesh, and burnt them there	1Sa 31:12	935
Now it c to pass after the death	2Sa 1:1	1961
It c even to pass on the third	2Sa 1:2	1961
a man c out of the camp from Saul	2Sa 1:2	935
when he c to David, that he fell	2Sa 1:2	935
it c to pass after this, that	2Sa 2:1	1961
And the men of Judah c, and there	2Sa 2:4	935
that the spear c out behind him	2Sa 2:23	3318
it c to pass, that as many as	2Sa 2:23	935
that as many as c to the place	2Sa 2:23	935
Bithron, and they c to Mahanaim	2Sa 2:29	935
they c to Hebron at break of day	2Sa 2:32	935
it c to pass, while there was war	2Sa 3:6	1961
So Abner c to David to Hebron, and	2Sa 3:20	935
Joab c from pursuing a troop, and	2Sa 3:22	935
the son of Ner c to the king	2Sa 3:23	935
Then Joab c to the king, and said,	2Sa 3:24	935
behold, Abner c unto thee	2Sa 3:24	935
that he c to deceive thee, and to	2Sa 3:25	935
when all the people c to cause	2Sa 3:35	935
old when the tidings c of Saul	2Sa 4:4	935
it c to pass, as she made haste	2Sa 4:4	1961
c about the heat of the day to	2Sa 4:5	935
they c thither into the midst of	2Sa 4:6	935
For when they c into the house,	2Sa 4:7	935
Then c all the tribes of Israel	2Sa 5:1	935
of Israel c to the king to Hebron	2Sa 5:3	935
Philistines c up to seek David	2Sa 5:17	5927
The Philistines also c and spread	2Sa 5:18	935
David c to Baal-perazim, and David	2Sa 5:20	935
And the Philistines c up yet again	2Sa 5:22	5927
And when they c to Nachon's	2Sa 6:6	935
the LORD c into the city of David	2Sa 6:16	935
of Saul c out to meet David	2Sa 6:20	3318
it c to pass, when the king sat	2Sa 7:1	1961
it c to pass that night, that the	2Sa 7:4	1961
word of the LORD c unto Nathan	2Sa 7:4	1961
And after this it c to pass	2Sa 8:1	1961
c to succour Hadadezer king of	2Sa 8:5	935
it c to pass after this, that the	2Sa 10:1	1961
David's servants c into the land	2Sa 10:2	935
And the children of Ammon c out	2Sa 10:8	3318
of Ammon, and c to Jerusalem	2Sa 10:14	935
and they c to Helam	2Sa 10:16	935
passed over Jordan, and c to Helam	2Sa 10:17	935
it c to pass, after the year was	2Sa 11:1	1961
it c to pass in an eveningtide,	2Sa 11:2	1961
she c in unto him, and he lay with	2Sa 11:4	935
it c to pass in the morning, that	2Sa 11:14	1961
it c to pass, when Joab observed	2Sa 11:16	1961
So the messenger went, and c	2Sa 11:22	935
c out unto us into the field, and	2Sa 11:23	3318
he c unto him, and said unto him,	2Sa 12:1	935
there c a traveller unto the rich	2Sa 12:4	935
it c to pass on the seventh day,	2Sa 12:18	1961
c into the house of the LORD, and	2Sa 12:20	935
then he c to his own house	2Sa 12:20	935
it c to pass after this, that	2Sa 13:1	1961
it c to pass after two full years	2Sa 13:23	1961
Absalom c to the king, and said,	2Sa 13:24	935
it c to pass, while they were in	2Sa 13:30	1961
the way, that tidings c to David	2Sa 13:30	935
there c much people by the way of	2Sa 13:34	1980
it c to pass, as soon as he had	2Sa 13:36	1961
that, behold, the king's sons c	2Sa 13:36	935
c to Absalom unto his house, and	2Sa 14:31	935
So Joab c to the king, and told	2Sa 14:33	935
he c to the king, and bowed	2Sa 14:33	935
it c to pass after this, that	2Sa 15:1	1961
c to the king for judgment	2Sa 15:2	935
that when any man c nigh to him	2Sa 15:5	7126
that c to the king for judgment	2Sa 15:6	935
it c to pass after forty years,	2Sa 15:7	1961
there c a messenger to David,	2Sa 15:13	935
men which c after him from Gath	2Sa 15:18	935
it c to pass, that when David was	2Sa 15:32	1961
Hushai the Archite c to meet him	2Sa 15:32	
David's friend c into the city	2Sa 15:37	935
and Absalom c into Jerusalem	2Sa 15:37	935
And when king David c to Bahurim	2Sa 16:5	935
thence c out a man of the family	2Sa 16:5	3318
c forth, and cursed still as he c	2Sa 16:5	3318
which c forth of my bowels,	2Sa 16:11	3318
c weary, and refreshed themselves	2Sa 16:14	935
c to Jerusalem, and Ahithophel	2Sa 16:15	935
it c to pass, when Hushai the	2Sa 16:16	1961
c to a man's house in Bahurim,	2Sa 17:18	935
when Absalom's servants c to the	2Sa 17:20	935
it c to pass, after they were	2Sa 17:21	1961
that they c up out of the well,	2Sa 17:21	5927
Then David c to Mahanaim	2Sa 17:24	935
it c to pass, when David was come	2Sa 17:27	1961
all the people c out by hundreds	2Sa 18:4	3318
And he c apace, and drew near	2Sa 18:25	3212
And, behold, Cushi c	2Sa 18:31	935
Joab c into the house to the king	2Sa 19:5	935
all the people c before the king	2Sa 19:8	935
the king returned, and c to Jordan	2Sa 19:15	935
Judah c to Gilgal, to go to meet	2Sa 19:15	935
c down with the men of Judah to	2Sa 19:16	3381
of Saul c down to meet the king	2Sa 19:24	3381
until the day he c again in peace	2Sa 19:24	935
it c to pass, when he was come to	2Sa 19:25	1961
the Gileadite c down from Rogelim	2Sa 19:31	3381
the men of Israel c to the king	2Sa 19:41	935
David c to his house at Jerusalem	2Sa 20:3	935
one that c by him stood still	2Sa 20:12	935
And they c and besieged him in Abel	2Sa 20:15	935
it c to pass after this, that	2Sa 21:18	1961
bowed the heavens also, and c down	2Sa 22:10	3381
c to David in the harvest time	2Sa 23:13	935
Then they c to Gilead, and to the	2Sa 24:6	935
they c to Dan-jaan, and about to	2Sa 24:6	935
c to the strong hold of Tyre, and	2Sa 24:7	935
they c to Jerusalem at the end of	2Sa 24:8	935
the LORD c unto the prophet Gad	2Sa 24:11	1961
So Gad c to David, and told him,	2Sa 24:13	935
Gad c that day to David, and said	2Sa 24:18	935
Nathan the prophet also c in	1Kin 1:22	935
she c into the king's presence,	1Kin 1:28	935
And they c before the king	1Kin 1:32	935
And all the people c up after him	1Kin 1:40	5927
the son of Abiathar the priest c	1Kin 1:42	935
c to bless our lord king David	1Kin 1:47	935
And he c and bowed himself to king	1Kin 1:53	7126
for so they c to me when I fled	1Kin 2:7	7126
but he c down to meet me at	1Kin 2:8	3381
c to Bath-sheba the mother of	1Kin 2:13	935
Then tidings c to Joab	1Kin 2:28	935
Benaiah c to the tabernacle of	1Kin 2:30	935
it c to pass at the end of three	1Kin 2:39	1961
he c to Jerusalem, and stood	1Kin 3:15	935
Then c there two women, that were	1Kin 3:16	935
it c to pass the third day after	1Kin 3:18	1961
and for all that c unto king	1Kin 4:27	7131
there c of all people to hear the	1Kin 4:34	935

it c to pass, when Hiram heard	1Kin 5:7	1961
it c to pass in the four hundred	1Kin 6:1	1961
the word of the LORD c to Solomon	1Kin 6:11	1961
he c to king Solomon, and wrought	1Kin 7:14	935
And all the elders of Israel c	1Kin 8:3	935
when they c out of the land of	1Kin 8:9	3318
it c to pass, when the priests	1Kin 8:10	1961
it c to pass, when Solomon had	1Kin 9:1	1961
it c to pass at the end of twenty	1Kin 9:10	1961
Hiram c out from Tyre to see the	1Kin 9:12	3318
But Pharaoh's daughter c up out	1Kin 9:24	5927
they c to Ophir, and fetched from	1Kin 9:28	935
she c to prove him with hard	1Kin 10:1	935
she c to Jerusalem with a very	1Kin 10:2	935
believed not the words, until I c	1Kin 10:7	935
there c no more such abundance of	1Kin 10:10	935
there c no such almug trees, nor	1Kin 10:12	935
Now the weight of gold that c to	1Kin 10:14	935
once in three years c the navy of	1Kin 10:22	935
And a chariot c up and went out of	1Kin 10:29	5927
For it c to pass, when Solomon	1Kin 11:4	1961
For it c to pass, when David was	1Kin 11:15	1961
out of Midian, and c to Paran	1Kin 11:18	935
they c to Egypt, unto Pharaoh	1Kin 11:18	935
it c to pass at that time when	1Kin 11:29	1961
it c to pass, when Jeroboam the	1Kin 12:2	1961
all the congregation of Israel c	1Kin 12:3	935
all the people c to Rehoboam the	1Kin 12:12	935
it c to pass, when all Israel	1Kin 12:20	1961
But the word of God c unto	1Kin 12:22	1961
there c a man of God out of Judah	1Kin 13:1	935
it c to pass, when king Jeroboam	1Kin 13:4	1961
by the way that he c to Beth-el	1Kin 13:10	935
and his sons c and told him all the	1Kin 13:11	935
of God went, which c from Judah	1Kin 13:12	935
it c to pass, as they sat at the	1Kin 13:20	1961
that the word of the LORD c unto	1Kin 13:20	1961
the man of God that c from Judah	1Kin 13:21	935
it c to pass, after he had eaten	1Kin 13:23	1961
and they c and told it in the city	1Kin 13:25	935
and the old prophet c to the city	1Kin 13:29	935
it c to pass, after he had buried	1Kin 13:31	1961
and c to the house of Ahijah	1Kin 14:4	935
as she c in at the door, that he	1Kin 14:6	935
and departed, and c to Tirzah	1Kin 14:17	935
when she c to the threshold of	1Kin 14:17	935
it c to pass in the fifth year of	1Kin 14:25	1961
of Egypt c up against Jerusalem	1Kin 14:25	5927
it c to pass, when Baasha heard	1Kin 15:21	1961
it c to pass, when he reigned,	1Kin 15:29	1961
LORD c to Jehu the son of Hanani	1Kin 16:1	1961
c the word of the LORD against	1Kin 16:7	1961
it c to pass, when he began to	1Kin 16:11	1961
it c to pass, when Zimri saw that	1Kin 16:18	1961
it c to pass, as if it had been a	1Kin 16:31	1961
the word of the LORD c unto him	1Kin 17:2	1961
it c to pass after a while, that	1Kin 17:7	1961
the word of the LORD c unto him	1Kin 17:8	1961
when he c to the gate of the city	1Kin 17:10	935
it c to pass after these things,	1Kin 17:17	1961
of the child c into him again	1Kin 17:22	7725
it c to pass after many days,	1Kin 18:1	1961
that the word of the LORD c to	1Kin 18:1	1961
it c to pass, when Ahab saw	1Kin 18:17	1961
Elijah c unto all the people, and	1Kin 18:21	5066
it c to pass at noon, that Elijah	1Kin 18:27	1961
it c to pass, when midday was	1Kin 18:29	1961
And all the people c near unto him	1Kin 18:30	5066
unto whom the word of the LORD c	1Kin 18:31	1961
it c to pass at the time of the	1Kin 18:36	1961
that Elijah the prophet c near	1Kin 18:36	5066
it c to pass at the seventh time,	1Kin 18:44	1961
it c to pass in the mean while,	1Kin 18:45	1961
c to Beer-sheba, which belongeth	1Kin 19:3	935
journey into the wilderness, and c	1Kin 19:4	935
the LORD c again the second time	1Kin 19:7	7725
he c thither unto a cave, and	1Kin 19:9	935
the word of the LORD c to him	1Kin 19:9	
there c a voice unto him, and said	1Kin 19:13	935
And the messengers c again	1Kin 20:5	7725
it c to pass, when Ben-hadad	1Kin 20:12	1961
there c a prophet unto Ahab king	1Kin 20:13	5066
the provinces c out of the city	1Kin 20:19	3318
the prophet c to the king of	1Kin 20:22	5066
it c to pass at the return of the	1Kin 20:26	1961
there c a man of God, and spake	1Kin 20:28	5066
c into the city, into an inner	1Kin 20:30	935
c to the king of Israel, and said,	1Kin 20:32	935
Then Ben-hadad c forth to him	1Kin 20:33	3318
and displeased, and c to Samaria	1Kin 20:43	935
it c to pass after these things,	1Kin 21:1	1961
Ahab c into his house heavy and	1Kin 21:4	935
But Jezebel his wife c to him	1Kin 21:5	935
there c in two men, children of	1Kin 21:13	935
it c to pass, when Jezebel heard	1Kin 21:15	1961
it c to pass, when Ahab heard	1Kin 21:16	1961
the word of the LORD c to Elijah	1Kin 21:17	1961
it c to pass, when Ahab heard	1Kin 21:27	1961
the word of the LORD c to Elijah	1Kin 21:28	1961
it c to pass in the third year,	1Kin 22:2	1961
c down to the king of Israel	1Kin 22:2	3381
So he c to the king	1Kin 22:15	935
there c forth a spirit, and stood	1Kin 22:21	3318
it c to pass, when the captains	1Kin 22:32	1961
it c to pass, when the captains	1Kin 22:33	1961
There c a man up to meet us, and	2Kin 1:6	5927
man was he which c up to meet you	2Kin 1:7	5927
there c down fire from heaven, and	2Kin 1:10	3381
the fire of God c down from	2Kin 1:12	3381
captain of fifty went up, and c	2Kin 1:13	935
there c fire down from heaven, and	2Kin 1:14	3381
it c to pass, when the LORD would	2Kin 2:1	1961
were at Beth-el c forth to Elisha	2Kin 2:3	3318
So they c to Jericho	2Kin 2:4	935
that were at Jericho c to Elisha	2Kin 2:5	5066
it c to pass, when they were gone	2Kin 2:9	1961
it c to pass, as they still went	2Kin 2:11	1961
they c to meet him, and bowed	2Kin 2:15	935
when they c again to him, (for he	2Kin 2:18	7725
there c forth little children out	2Kin 2:23	3318
there c forth two she bears out	2Kin 2:24	3318
But it c to pass, when Ahab was	2Kin 3:5	1961
it c to pass, when the minstrel	2Kin 3:15	1961
the hand of the LORD c upon him	2Kin 3:15	1961
it c to pass in the morning, when	2Kin 3:20	1961
there c water by the way of Edom,	2Kin 3:20	935
when they c to the camp of Israel	2Kin 3:24	935
it c to pass, when the vessels	2Kin 4:6	1961
Then she c and told the man of God	2Kin 4:7	935
fell on a day, that he c thither	2Kin 4:11	935
c unto the man of God to mount	2Kin 4:25	935
it c to pass, when the man of God	2Kin 4:25	1961
when she c to the man of God to	2Kin 4:27	935
but Gehazi c near to thrust her	2Kin 4:27	5066
And Elisha c again to Gilgal	2Kin 4:38	7725
wild gourds his lap full, and c	2Kin 4:39	935
it c to pass, as they were eating	2Kin 4:40	1961
there c a man from Baal-shalisha,	2Kin 4:42	935
it c to pass, when the king of	2Kin 5:7	1961
So Naaman c with his horses and	2Kin 5:9	935
And his servants c near, and spake	2Kin 5:13	5066
his flesh c again like unto the	2Kin 5:14	7725
God, he and all his company, and c	2Kin 5:15	935
when he c to the tower, he took	2Kin 5:24	935
And when they c to Jordan, they	2Kin 6:4	935
they c by night, and compassed the	2Kin 6:14	935
when they c down to him, Elisha	2Kin 6:18	3381
it c to pass, when they were come	2Kin 6:20	1961
So the bands of Syria c no more	2Kin 6:23	935
it c to pass after this, that	2Kin 6:24	1961
it c to pass, when the king heard	2Kin 6:30	1961
but ere the messenger c to him	2Kin 6:32	935
the messenger c down unto him	2Kin 6:33	3381
when these lepers c to the	2Kin 7:8	935
c again, and entered into another	2Kin 7:8	7725
So they c and called unto the	2Kin 7:10	935
We c to the camp of the Syrians,	2Kin 7:10	935
spake when the king c down to him	2Kin 7:17	3381
it c to pass as the man of God	2Kin 7:18	1961
it c to pass at the seven years'	2Kin 8:3	1961
it c to pass, as he was telling	2Kin 8:5	1961
And Elisha c to Damascus	2Kin 8:7	935
forty camels' burden, and c	2Kin 8:9	935
from Elisha, and c to his master	2Kin 8:14	935
it c to pass on the morrow, that	2Kin 8:15	1961
And when he c, behold, the	2Kin 9:5	935
Then Jehu c forth to the servants	2Kin 9:11	3318
wherefore c this mad fellow to	2Kin 9:11	935
spied the company of Jehu as he c	2Kin 9:17	935
saying, The messenger c to them	2Kin 9:18	935
which c to them, and said, Thus	2Kin 9:19	935
He c even unto them, and cometh	2Kin 9:20	935
it c to pass, when Joram saw Jehu	2Kin 9:22	1961
Wherefore they c again, and told	2Kin 9:36	7725
And it c to pass	2Kin 10:7	1961
when the letter c to them	2Kin 10:7	935
there c a messenger, and told him,	2Kin 10:8	935
it c to pass in the morning, that	2Kin 10:9	1961
and departed, and c to Samaria	2Kin 10:12	1980
when he c to Samaria, he slew all	2Kin 10:17	935
and all the worshippers of Baal c	2Kin 10:21	935
was not a man left that c not	2Kin 10:21	935
they c into the house of Baal	2Kin 10:21	935
it c to pass, as soon as he had	2Kin 10:25	1961
and c to Jehoiada the priest	2Kin 11:9	935
she c to the people into the	2Kin 11:13	935
horses c into the king's house	2Kin 11:16	3996
c by the way of the gate of the	2Kin 11:19	935
scribe and the high priest c up	2Kin 12:10	5927
king of Israel c down unto him	2Kin 13:14	3381
it c to pass, as they were	2Kin 13:21	1961
it c to pass, as soon as the	2Kin 14:5	1961
c to Jerusalem, and brake down the	2Kin 14:13	935
And so it c to pass	2Kin 15:12	1961
c to Samaria, and smote Shallum	2Kin 15:14	935
of Assyria c against the land	2Kin 15:19	935
days of Pekah king of Israel c	2Kin 15:29	935
Israel c up to Jerusalem to war	2Kin 16:5	5927
and the Syrians c to Elath	2Kin 16:6	935
against king Ahaz c from Damascus	2Kin 16:11	935
Against him c up Shalmaneser king	2Kin 17:3	5927
Then the king of Assyria c up	2Kin 17:5	5927
had carried away from Samaria c	2Kin 17:28	935
Now it c to pass in the third	2Kin 18:1	1961
it c to pass in the fourth year	2Kin 18:9	1961
of Assyria c up against Samaria	2Kin 18:9	5957
And they went up and c to Jerusalem	2Kin 18:17	935
And when they were come up, they c	2Kin 18:17	935
there c out to them Eliakim the	2Kin 18:18	3318
Then c Eliakim the son of Hilkiah	2Kin 18:37	935
it c to pass, when king Hezekiah	2Kin 19:1	1961
of king Hezekiah c to Isaiah	2Kin 19:5	935
By the way that he c, by the same	2Kin 19:33	935
it c to pass that night, that the	2Kin 19:35	1961
And it c to pass, as he was	2Kin 19:37	1961
Isaiah the son of Amoz c to him	2Kin 20:1	935
it c to pass, afore Isaiah was	2Kin 20:4	1961
the word of the LORD c to him	2Kin 20:4	1961
Then c Isaiah the prophet unto	2Kin 20:14	935
from whence c they unto thee	2Kin 20:14	935
fathers c forth out of Egypt	2Kin 21:15	3318
it c to pass in the eighteenth	2Kin 22:3	1961
Shaphan the scribe c to the king	2Kin 22:9	935
it c to pass, when the king had	2Kin 22:11	1961
the priests of the high places c	2Kin 23:9	5927
which c from Judah, and proclaimed	2Kin 23:17	935
the prophet that c out of Samaria	2Kin 23:18	935
he c to Egypt, and died there	2Kin 23:34	935
king of Babylon c up, and	2Kin 24:1	5927
of the LORD c this upon Judah	2Kin 24:3	1961
the king of Egypt c not again any	2Kin 24:7	3318
of Babylon c up against Jerusalem	2Kin 24:10	5927
of Babylon c against the city	2Kin 24:11	935
LORD it c to pass in Jerusalem	2Kin 24:20	1961
it c to pass in the ninth year of	2Kin 25:1	1961
Nebuchadnezzar king of Babylon c	2Kin 25:1	935
c Nebuzar-adan, captain of the	2Kin 25:8	935
there c to Gedaliah to Mizpah,	2Kin 25:23	935
But it c to pass in the seventh	2Kin 25:25	1961
of Elishama, of the seed royal, c	2Kin 25:25	935
the armies, arose, and c to Egypt	2Kin 25:26	935
it c to pass in the seven and	2Kin 25:27	1961
(of whom c the Philistines,) and	1Chr 1:12	3318
of them c the Zareathites, and the	1Chr 2:53	3318
are the Kenites that c of Hemath	1Chr 2:55	935
these written by name c in the	1Chr 4:41	935
and of him c the chief ruler	1Chr 5:2	
because they c down to take away	1Chr 7:21	3381
his brethren c to comfort him	1Chr 7:22	935
and the Philistines c and dwelt in	1Chr 10:7	935
it c to pass on the morrow, when	1Chr 10:8	1961
Philistines c to strip the slain	1Chr 10:8	935
Therefore c all the elders of	1Chr 11:3	935
they that c to David to Ziklag	1Chr 12:1	935
there c of the children of	1Chr 12:16	935
Then the spirit c upon Amasai	1Chr 12:18	3847
when he c with the Philistines	1Chr 12:19	935
day there c to David to help him	1Chr 12:22	935
c to David to Hebron, to turn the	1Chr 12:23	935
c with a perfect heart to Hebron,	1Chr 12:38	935
And when they c unto the	1Chr 13:9	935
And the Philistines c and spread	1Chr 14:9	935
So they c up to Baal-perazim	1Chr 14:11	5927
it c to pass, when God helped the	1Chr 15:26	1961
it c to pass, as the ark of the	1Chr 15:29	1961
the LORD c to the city of David	1Chr 15:29	935
Now it c to pass, as David sat in	1Chr 17:1	1961
it c to pass the same night, that	1Chr 17:3	1961
that the word of God c to Nathan	1Chr 17:3	935
And David the king c and sat before	1Chr 17:16	935
Now after this it c to pass	1Chr 18:1	1961
when the Syrians of Damascus c to	1Chr 18:5	935
Now it c to pass after this, that	1Chr 19:1	1961
So the servants of David c into	1Chr 19:2	935
who c and pitched before Medeba	1Chr 19:7	935
from their cities, and c to battle	1Chr 19:7	935
And the children of Ammon c out	1Chr 19:9	3318
Then Joab c to Jerusalem	1Chr 19:15	935
c upon them, and set the battle in	1Chr 19:17	935
it c to pass, that after the year	1Chr 20:1	1961
of the children of Ammon, and c	1Chr 20:1	935
it c to pass after this, that	1Chr 20:4	1961
all Israel, and c to Jerusalem	1Chr 21:4	935
So Gad c to David, and said unto	1Chr 21:11	935
And as David c to Ornan, Ornan	1Chr 21:21	935
But the word of the LORD c to me	1Chr 22:8	1961
Now the first lot c forth to	1Chr 24:7	3318
Of Mahli c Eleazar, who had no	1Chr 24:28	
Now the first lot c forth for	1Chr 25:9	3318
and his lot c out northward	1Chr 26:14	3318
Hosah the lot c forth westward,	1Chr 26:16	
matter of the courses, which c in	1Chr 27:1	935
Then Solomon c from his journey	2Chr 1:13	935
And all the elders of Israel c	2Chr 5:4	935
Israel, when they c out of Egypt	2Chr 5:10	3318
it c to pass, when the priests	2Chr 5:11	1961
It c even to pass, as the	2Chr 5:13	1961
the fire c down from heaven, and	2Chr 7:1	3381
of Israel saw how the fire c down	2Chr 7:3	3381
all that c into Solomon's heart	2Chr 7:11	935
it c to pass at the end of twenty	2Chr 8:1	1961
she c to prove Solomon with hard	2Chr 9:1	935
not their words, until I c	2Chr 9:6	935
Now the weight of gold that c to	2Chr 9:13	935
every three years once c the	2Chr 9:21	935
it c to pass, when Jeroboam the	2Chr 10:2	1961
So Jeroboam and all Israel c	2Chr 10:3	935
all the people c to Rehoboam on	2Chr 10:12	935
But the word of the LORD c to	2Chr 11:2	1961
and c to Judah and Jerusalem	2Chr 11:14	3212
LORD God of Israel c to Jerusalem	2Chr 11:16	935
it c to pass, when Rehoboam had	2Chr 12:1	1961
it c to pass, that in the fifth	2Chr 12:2	1961
of Egypt c up against Jerusalem	2Chr 12:2	5927
that c with him out of Egypt	2Chr 12:3	935
to Judah, and c to Jerusalem	2Chr 12:4	935
Then c Shemaiah the prophet to	2Chr 12:5	935
word of the LORD c to Shemaiah	2Chr 12:7	1961
of Egypt c up against Jerusalem	2Chr 12:9	5927
house of the LORD, the guard c	2Chr 12:11	935
it c to pass, that God smote	2Chr 13:15	1961
there c out against them Zerah	2Chr 14:9	3318
and c unto Mareshah	2Chr 14:9	935
the fear of the LORD c upon them	2Chr 14:14	1961
the Spirit of God c upon Azariah	2Chr 15:1	1961
went out, nor to him that c in	2Chr 15:5	935
king of Israel c up against Judah	2Chr 16:1	5927
it c to pass, when Baasha heard	2Chr 16:5	1961
the seer c to Asa king of Judah	2Chr 16:7	935
Then there c out a spirit, and	2Chr 18:20	3318
the son of Chenaanah c near	2Chr 18:23	5066
it c to pass, when the captains	2Chr 18:31	1961
For it c to pass, that, when the	2Chr 18:32	1961
It c to pass after this also,	2Chr 20:1	1961
c against Jehoshaphat to battle	2Chr 20:1	935
Then there c some that told	2Chr 20:2	935
of Judah they c to seek the LORD	2Chr 20:4	935
when they c out of the land of	2Chr 20:10	935
c the Spirit of the LORD in the	2Chr 20:14	1961
when Judah c toward the watch	2Chr 20:24	935
his people c to take away the	2Chr 20:25	935
And they c to Jerusalem with	2Chr 20:28	935

Context	Reference	Number
there c a writing to him from	2Chr 21:12	935
they c up into Judah, and brake	2Chr 21:17	5927
it c to pass, that in process of	2Chr 21:19	1961
for the band of men that c with	2Chr 22:1	935
it c to pass, that, when Jehu was	2Chr 22:8	1961
of Israel, and they c to Jerusalem	2Chr 23:2	935
she c to the people into the	2Chr 23:12	935
they c through the high gate into	2Chr 23:20	935
it c to pass after this, that	2Chr 24:4	1961
Now it c to pass, that at what	2Chr 24:11	1961
and the high priest's officer c	2Chr 24:11	935
Jehoiada c the princes of Judah	2Chr 24:17	935
wrath c upon Judah and Jerusalem	2Chr 24:18	1961
And the Spirit of God c upon	2Chr 24:20	3847
it c to pass at the end of the	2Chr 24:23	1961
host of Syria c up against him	2Chr 24:23	5927
they c to Judah and Jerusalem, and	2Chr 24:23	935
c with a small company of men	2Chr 24:24	935
Now it c to pass, when the	2Chr 25:3	1961
But there c a man of God to him,	2Chr 25:7	935
Now it c to pass, after that	2Chr 25:14	1961
it c to pass, as he talked with	2Chr 25:16	1961
for it c of God, that he might	2Chr 25:20	
before the host that c to Samaria	2Chr 28:9	935
against them that c from the war	2Chr 28:12	935
king of Assyria c unto him	2Chr 28:20	935
and sanctified themselves, and c	2Chr 29:15	935
c they to the porch of the LORD	2Chr 29:17	935
themselves, and c to Jerusalem	2Chr 30:11	935
congregation that c out of Israel	2Chr 30:25	935
the strangers that c out of the	2Chr 30:25	935
their prayer c up to his holy	2Chr 30:27	935
soon as the commandment c abroad	2Chr 31:5	6555
And when Hezekiah and the princes c	2Chr 31:8	935
Sennacherib king of Assyria c	2Chr 32:1	935
they that c forth of his own	2Chr 32:21	3329
c not upon them in the days of	2Chr 32:26	935
when they c to Hilkiah the high	2Chr 34:9	935
it c to pass, when the king had	2Chr 34:19	1961
Necho king of Egypt c up to fight	2Chr 35:20	5927
c to fight in the valley of	2Chr 35:22	935
Against him c up Nebuchadnezzar	2Chr 36:6	5927
c again unto Jerusalem and Judah,	Ezr 2:1	7725
Which c with Zerubbabel	Ezr 2:2	935
when they c to the house of the	Ezr 2:68	935
Then they c to Zerubbabel, and to	Ezr 4:2	5066
that the Jews which c up from	Ezr 4:12	5559
At the same time c to them Tatnai	Ezr 5:3	858
till the matter c to Darius	Ezr 5:5	1946
Then c the same Sheshbazzar, and	Ezr 5:16	858
he c to Jerusalem in the fifth	Ezr 7:8	935
the fifth month c he to Jerusalem	Ezr 7:9	935
we c to Jerusalem, and abode there	Ezr 8:32	935
were done, the princes c to me	Ezr 9:1	5066
and when he c thither, he did eat	Ezr 10:6	3212
it c to pass in the month Chisleu	Neh 1:1	1961
Hanani, one of my brethren, c	Neh 1:2	935
it c to pass, when I heard these	Neh 1:4	1961
it c to pass in the month Nisan,	Neh 2:1	1961
Then I c to the governors beyond	Neh 2:9	935
So I c to Jerusalem, and was there	Neh 2:11	935
But it c to pass, that when	Neh 4:1	1961
But it c to pass, that when	Neh 4:7	1961
it c to pass, that when the Jews	Neh 4:12	1961
the Jews which dwelt by them c	Neh 4:12	935
it c to pass, when our enemies	Neh 4:15	1961
it c to pass from that time forth	Neh 4:16	1961
beside those that c unto us from	Neh 5:17	935
Now it c to pass, when Sanballat,	Neh 6:1	1961
Afterward I c unto the house of	Neh 6:10	935
it c to pass, that when all our	Neh 6:16	1961
the letters of Tobiah c unto them	Neh 6:17	935
Now it c to pass, when the wall	Neh 7:1	1961
of them which c up at the first	Neh 7:5	5927
c again to Jerusalem and to Judah,	Neh 7:6	7725
Who c with Zerubbabel, Jeshua,	Neh 7:7	935
and when the seventh month c	Neh 7:73	5060
Now it c to pass, when they had	Neh 13:3	1961
king of Babylon c I unto the king	Neh 13:6	935
I c to Jerusalem, and understood	Neh 13:7	935
it c to pass, that when the gates	Neh 13:19	1961
From that time forth c they no	Neh 13:21	935
Now it c to pass in the days of	Est 1:1	1961
in before him, but she c not	Est 1:17	935
So it c to pass, when the king's	Est 2:8	1961
Then thus c every maiden unto the	Est 2:13	935
she c in unto the king no more,	Est 2:14	935
Now it c to pass, when they spake	Est 3:4	1961
c even before the king's gate	Est 4:2	935
commandment and his decree c	Est 4:3	5060
maids and her chamberlains c	Est 4:4	935
And Hatach c and told Esther the	Est 4:9	935
Now it c to pass on the third day	Est 5:1	1961
Haman c to the banquet that	Est 5:5	935
and when he c home, he sent and	Est 5:10	935
So Haman c in	Est 6:6	935
Mordecai c again to the king's	Est 6:12	7725
c the king's chamberlains, and	Est 6:14	935
Haman c to banquet with Esther	Est 7:1	935
Mordecai c before the king	Est 8:1	935
commandment and his decree c	Est 8:17	5060
But when Esther c before the king	Est 9:25	935
c to present themselves before	Job 1:6	935
LORD, and Satan c also among them	Job 1:6	935
there c a messenger unto Job, and	Job 1:14	935
there c also another, and said,	Job 1:16	935
there c also another, and said,	Job 1:17	935
there c also another, and said,	Job 1:18	935
there c a great wind from the	Job 1:19	935
Naked c I out of my mother's womb	Job 1:21	3318
c to present themselves before	Job 2:1	935
Satan c also among them to	Job 2:1	935
they c every one from his own	Job 2:11	935
ghost when I c out of the belly	Job 3:11	3318
yet trouble c	Job 3:26	935
Fear c upon me, and trembling,	Job 4:14	7122
they c thither, and were ashamed	Job 6:20	935
and whose spirit c from thee	Job 26:4	3318
was ready to perish c upon me	Job 29:13	935
They c upon me as a wide breaking	Job 30:14	857
for good, then evil c unto me	Job 30:26	935
for light, there c darkness	Job 30:26	935
Out of whose womb c the ice	Job 38:29	3318
Then c there unto him all his	Job 42:11	935
my cry c before him, even into	Ps 18:6	935
bowed the heavens also, and c down	Ps 18:9	3381
c upon me to eat up my flesh,	Ps 27:2	7126
Nathan the prophet c unto him	Ps 51:t	935
of David, when Doeg the Edomite c	Ps 52:t	935
of David, when the Ziphims c	Ps 54:t	935
anger also c up against Israel	Ps 78:21	5927
The wrath of God c upon them	Ps 78:31	5927
They c round about me daily like	Ps 88:17	5437
Until the time that his word c	Ps 105:19	935
Israel also c into Egypt	Ps 105:23	935
there c divers sorts of flies, and	Ps 105:31	935
He spake, and the locusts c	Ps 105:34	935
Therefore c I forth to meet thee,	Prov 7:15	3318
As he c forth of his mother's	Eccl 5:15	3318
shall he return to go as he c	Eccl 5:15	935
evil, that in all points as he c	Eccl 5:16	935
there c a great king against it,	Eccl 9:14	935
which c up from the washing	Song 4:2	5927
it c to pass in the days of Ahaz	Is 7:1	1961
he c up out of the land of Egypt	Is 11:16	5927
year that Tartan c unto Ashdod	Is 20:1	935
and his ambassadors c to Hanes	Is 30:4	5060
Now it c to pass in the	Is 36:1	1961
c up against all the defenced	Is 36:1	5927
Then c forth unto him Eliakim,	Is 36:3	3318
Then c Eliakim, the son of	Is 36:22	935
it c to pass, when king Hezekiah	Is 37:1	1961
of king Hezekiah c to Isaiah	Is 37:5	935
By the way that he c, by the same	Is 37:34	935
And it c to pass, as he was	Is 37:38	1961
the son of Amoz c unto him	Is 38:1	935
Then c the word of the LORD to	Is 38:4	1961
Then c Isaiah the prophet unto	Is 39:3	935
from whence c they unto thee	Is 39:3	935
were afraid, drew near, and c	Is 41:5	857
them suddenly, and they c to pass	Is 48:3	935
before it c to pass I shewed it	Is 48:5	935
Wherefore, when I c, was there no	Is 50:2	935
before her pain c, she was	Is 66:7	935
To whom the word of the LORD c in	Jer 1:2	1961
It c also in the days of	Jer 1:3	1961
the word of the LORD c unto me	Jer 1:4	1961
the word of the LORD c unto me	Jer 1:11	1961
the word of the LORD c unto me	Jer 1:13	1961
the word of the LORD c to me	Jer 2:1	1961
And it c to pass through the	Jer 3:9	1961
The word that c to Jeremiah from	Jer 7:1	1961
c forth out of the land of Egypt	Jer 7:25	3318
neither c it into my heart	Jer 7:31	5927
looked for peace, but no good c	Jer 8:15	
The word that c to Jeremiah from	Jer 11:1	1961
the word of the LORD c unto me	Jer 13:3	1961
it c to pass after many days,	Jer 13:6	1961
the word of the LORD c unto me	Jer 13:8	1961
The word of the LORD that c to	Jer 14:1	1961
they c to the pits, and found no	Jer 14:3	935
word of the LORD c also unto me	Jer 16:1	1961
that which c out of my lips was	Jer 17:16	4161
The word which c to Jeremiah from	Jer 18:1	1961
Then the word of the LORD c to me	Jer 18:5	1961
neither c it into my mind	Jer 19:5	5927
Then c Jeremiah from Tophet,	Jer 19:14	935
it c to pass on the morrow, that	Jer 20:3	1961
Wherefore c I forth out of the	Jer 20:18	3318
The word which c unto Jeremiah	Jer 21:1	1961
the word of the LORD c unto me	Jer 24:4	1961
The word that c to Jeremiah	Jer 25:1	1961
Judah c this word from the LORD	Jer 26:1	1961
Now it c to pass, when Jeremiah	Jer 26:8	1961
then they c up from the king's	Jer 26:10	5927
c this word unto Jeremiah from	Jer 27:1	1961
it c to pass the same year, in	Jer 28:1	1961
LORD c unto Jeremiah the prophet	Jer 28:12	1961
Then c the word of the LORD unto	Jer 29:30	1961
The word that c to Jeremiah from	Jer 30:1	1961
The word that c to Jeremiah from	Jer 32:1	1961
The word of the LORD c unto me	Jer 32:6	1961
son c to me in the court of the	Jer 32:8	935
And they c in, and possessed it	Jer 32:23	935
Then c the word of the LORD unto	Jer 32:26	1961
neither c it into my mind, that	Jer 32:35	5927
c unto Jeremiah the second time	Jer 33:1	1961
word of the LORD c unto Jeremiah	Jer 33:19	1961
word of the LORD c to Jeremiah	Jer 33:23	1961
The word which c unto Jeremiah	Jer 34:1	1961
This is the word that c unto	Jer 34:8	1961
LORD c to Jeremiah from the LORD	Jer 34:12	1961
The word which c unto Jeremiah	Jer 35:1	1961
But it c to pass, when	Jer 35:11	1961
of Babylon c up into the land	Jer 35:11	5927
Then c the word of the LORD unto	Jer 35:12	1961
it c to pass in the fourth year	Jer 36:1	1961
that this word c unto Jeremiah	Jer 36:1	1961
it c to pass in the fifth year of	Jer 36:9	1961
to all the people that c from the	Jer 36:9	935
roll in his hand, and c unto them	Jer 36:14	935
Now it c to pass, when they had	Jer 36:16	1961
it c to pass, that when Jehudi	Jer 36:23	1961
word of the LORD c to Jeremiah	Jer 36:27	1961
Now Jeremiah c in and went out	Jer 37:4	935
Then c the word of the LORD unto	Jer 37:6	1961
it c to pass, that when the army	Jer 37:11	1961
Then c all the princes unto	Jer 38:27	935
c Nebuchadrezzar king of Babylon	Jer 39:1	935
of the king of Babylon c in	Jer 39:3	935
it c to pass, that when Zedekiah	Jer 39:4	1961
word of the LORD c unto Jeremiah	Jer 39:15	1961
The word that c to Jeremiah from	Jer 40:1	1961
Then they c to Gedaliah to Mizpah	Jer 40:8	935
c to the land of Judah, to	Jer 40:12	935
fields, c to Gedaliah to Mizpah,	Jer 40:13	935
Now it c to pass in the seventh	Jer 41:1	1961
c unto Gedaliah the son of Ahikam	Jer 41:1	935
it c to pass the second day after	Jer 41:4	1961
That there c certain from Shechem	Jer 41:5	935
it c to pass, as he met them, he	Jer 41:6	1961
when they c into the midst of the	Jer 41:7	935
Now it c to pass, that when all	Jer 41:13	1961
even unto the greatest, c near,	Jer 42:1	5066
it c to pass after ten days, that	Jer 42:7	1961
word of the LORD c unto Jeremiah	Jer 42:7	1961
it c to pass, that when Jeremiah	Jer 43:1	1961
So they c into the land of Egypt	Jer 43:7	935
thus c they even to Tahpanhes	Jer 43:7	935
Then c the word of the LORD unto	Jer 43:8	1961
The word that c to Jeremiah	Jer 44:1	1961
them, and c it not into his mind	Jer 44:21	5927
The word of the LORD which c to	Jer 46:1	1961
The word of the LORD that c to	Jer 47:1	1961
The word of the LORD that c to	Jer 49:34	1961
LORD it c to pass in Jerusalem	Jer 52:3	1961
it c to pass in the ninth year of	Jer 52:4	1961
Nebuchadrezzar king of Babylon c	Jer 52:4	935
c Nebuzar-adan, captain of the	Jer 52:12	935
it c to pass in the seven and	Jer 52:31	1961
therefore she c down wonderfully	Lam 1:9	3381
Now it c to pass in the thirtieth	Eze 1:1	1961
The word of the LORD c expressly	Eze 1:3	1961
a whirlwind c out of the north, a	Eze 1:4	935
c the likeness of four living	Eze 1:5	
Then I c to them of the captivity	Eze 3:15	935
it c to pass at the end of seven	Eze 3:16	1961
the word of the LORD c unto me	Eze 3:16	1961
neither c there abominable flesh	Eze 4:14	935
And the word of the LORD c unto me	Eze 6:1	1961
the word of the LORD c unto me	Eze 7:1	1961
it c to pass in the sixth year,	Eze 8:1	1961
six men c from the way of the	Eze 9:2	935
it c to pass, while they were	Eze 9:8	1961
it c to pass, that when he had	Eze 10:6	1961
it c to pass, when I prophesied,	Eze 11:13	1961
the word of the LORD c unto me	Eze 11:14	1961
word of the LORD also c unto me	Eze 12:1	1961
in the morning c the word of the	Eze 12:8	1961
the word of the LORD c to me	Eze 12:17	1961
And the word of the LORD c unto me	Eze 12:21	1961
the word of the LORD c to me	Eze 12:26	1961
And the word of the LORD c unto me	Eze 13:1	1961
Then c certain of the elders of	Eze 14:1	935
And the word of the LORD c unto me	Eze 14:2	1961
word of the LORD c again to me	Eze 14:12	1961
And the word of the LORD c unto me	Eze 15:1	1961
the word of the LORD c unto me	Eze 16:1	1961
it c to pass after all thy	Eze 16:23	1961
And the word of the LORD c unto me	Eze 17:1	1961
c unto Lebanon, and took the	Eze 17:3	935
the word of the LORD c unto me	Eze 17:11	1961
word of the LORD c unto me again	Eze 18:1	1961
it c to pass in the seventh year,	Eze 20:1	1961
Israel c to enquire of the LORD	Eze 20:1	935
Then c the word of the LORD unto	Eze 20:2	1961
the word of the LORD c unto me	Eze 20:45	1961
And the word of the LORD c unto me	Eze 21:1	1961
the word of the LORD c unto me	Eze 21:8	1961
word of the LORD c unto me again	Eze 21:18	1961
the word of the LORD c unto me	Eze 22:1	1961
And the word of the LORD c unto me	Eze 22:17	1961
And the word of the LORD c unto me	Eze 22:23	1961
word of the LORD c again unto me	Eze 23:1	1961
the Babylonians c to her into the	Eze 23:17	935
then they c the same day into my	Eze 23:39	935
and, lo, they c	Eze 23:40	935
the word of the LORD c unto me	Eze 24:1	1961
the word of the LORD c unto me	Eze 24:15	1961
The word of the LORD c unto me	Eze 24:20	1961
word of the LORD c again unto me	Eze 25:1	1961
it c to pass in the eleventh year	Eze 26:1	1961
the word of the LORD c unto me	Eze 26:1	1961
word of the LORD c again unto me	Eze 27:1	1961
word of the LORD c again unto me	Eze 28:1	1961
the word of the LORD c unto me	Eze 28:11	1961
the word of the LORD c unto me	Eze 28:20	1961
the word of the LORD c unto me	Eze 29:1	1961
it c to pass in the seven and	Eze 29:17	1961
the word of the LORD c unto me	Eze 29:17	1961
word of the LORD c again unto me	Eze 30:1	1961
it c to pass in the eleventh year	Eze 30:20	1961
the word of the LORD c unto me	Eze 30:20	1961
it c to pass in the eleventh year	Eze 31:1	1961
the word of the LORD c unto me	Eze 31:1	1961
it c to pass in the twelfth year,	Eze 32:1	1961
the word of the LORD c unto me	Eze 32:1	1961
It c to pass also in the twelfth	Eze 32:17	1961
the word of the LORD c unto me	Eze 32:17	1961
the word of the LORD c unto me	Eze 33:1	1961
it c to pass in the twelfth year	Eze 33:21	1961
out of Jerusalem c unto me	Eze 33:21	935
afore he that was escaped c	Eze 33:22	935
until he c to me in the morning	Eze 33:22	935
the word of the LORD c unto me	Eze 33:23	1961
And the word of the Lord c unto me	Eze 34:1	1961
the word of the LORD c unto me	Eze 35:1	1961
the word of the LORD c unto me	Eze 36:16	1961
shaking, and the bones c together	Eze 37:7	7126
the flesh c up upon them, and the	Eze 37:8	5927
me, and the breath c into them	Eze 37:10	935
word of the LORD c again unto me	Eze 37:15	1961

Context	Reference	Number
And the word of the LORD c unto me	Eze 38:1	1961
Then c he unto the gate which	Eze 40:6	935
Israel c from the way of the east	Eze 43:2	935
saw when I c to destroy the city	Eze 43:3	935
the glory of the LORD c into the	Eze 43:4	935
way of the gate whereby he c in	Eze 46:9	935
the waters c down from under from	Eze 47:1	3381
of Jehoiakim king of Judah c	Dan 1:1	935
So they c and stood before the	Dan 2:2	935
thy thoughts c into thy mind upon	Dan 2:29	5559
time certain Chaldeans c near	Dan 3:8	7127
Then Nebuchadnezzar c near to the	Dan 3:26	7127
c forth of the midst of the fire	Dan 3:26	5312
Then c in the magicians, the	Dan 4:7	5954
at the last Daniel c in before me	Dan 4:8	5954
an holy one c down from heaven	Dan 4:13	5182
All this c upon the king	Dan 4:28	4291
In the same hour c forth fingers	Dan 5:5	5312
Then c in all the king's wise men	Dan 5:8	5954
lords, c into the banquet house	Dan 5:10	5954
Then they c near, and spake before	Dan 6:12	7127
when he c to the den, he cried	Dan 6:20	7127
they c at the bottom of the den	Dan 6:24	4291
great beasts c up from the sea	Dan 7:3	5559
there c up among them another	Dan 7:8	5559
issued and c forth from before him	Dan 7:10	5312
one like the Son of man c with	Dan 7:13	
c to the Ancient of days, and they	Dan 7:13	4291
I c near unto one of them that	Dan 7:16	7127
head, and of the other which c up	Dan 7:20	5559
Until the Ancient of days c	Dan 7:22	858
the time c that the saints	Dan 7:22	4291
it c to pass, when I saw, that I	Dan 8:2	1961
other, and the higher c up last	Dan 8:3	5927
an he goat c from the west on the	Dan 8:5	935
he c to the ram that had two	Dan 8:6	935
for it c up four notable ones	Dan 8:8	5927
out of one of them c forth a	Dan 8:9	3318
it c to pass, when I, even I	Dan 8:15	1961
So he c near where I stood	Dan 8:17	935
and when he c, I was afraid, and	Dan 8:17	935
LORD c to Jeremiah the prophet	Dan 9:2	1961
the commandment c forth, and I am	Dan 9:23	3318
neither c flesh nor wine in my	Dan 10:3	935
the chief princes, c to help me	Dan 10:13	935
Then there c again and touched me	Dan 10:18	
of the LORD that c unto Hosea	Hos 1:1	1961
as in the day when she c up out	Hos 2:15	5927
The word of the LORD that c to	Joel 1:1	1961
to whom the house of Israel c	Amos 6:1	935
it c to pass, that when they had	Amos 7:2	1961
If thieves c to thee, if robbers	Obad 5	935
if the grapegatherers c to thee	Obad 5	935
Now the word of the LORD c unto	Jonah 1:1	1961
So the shipmaster c to him	Jonah 1:6	7126
my prayer c in unto thee, into	Jonah 2:7	935
the word of the LORD c unto Jonah	Jonah 3:1	1961
For word c unto the king of	Jonah 3:6	5060
it c to pass, when the sun did	Jonah 4:8	1961
which c up in a night, and	Jonah 4:10	1961
The word of the LORD that c to	Mic 1:1	1961
the inhabitant of Zaanan c not	Mic 1:11	3318
but evil c down from the LORD	Mic 1:12	3381
God c from Teman, and the Holy One	Hab 3:3	935
they c out as a whirlwind to	Hab 3:14	
The word of the LORD which c unto	Zeph 1:1	1961
c the word of the LORD by Haggai	Hag 1:1	1961
Then c the word of the LORD by	Hag 1:3	1961
for much, and, lo, it c to little	Hag 1:9	
and they c and did work in the	Hag 1:14	935
c the word of the LORD by the	Hag 2:1	1961
with you when ye c out of Egypt	Hag 2:5	3318
c the word of the LORD by Haggai	Hag 2:10	1961
when one c to an heap of twenty	Hag 2:16	935
when one c to the pressfat for to	Hag 2:16	935
LORD c unto Haggai in the four	Hag 2:20	1961
c the word of the LORD unto	Zec 1:1	1961
c the word of the LORD unto	Zec 1:7	1961
angel that talked with me c again	Zec 4:1	7725
the word of the LORD c unto me	Zec 4:8	1961
there c out two women, and the	Zec 5:9	3318
there c four chariots out from	Zec 6:1	3318
And the word of the LORD c unto me	Zec 6:9	1961
it c to pass in the fourth year	Zec 7:1	1961
that the word of the LORD c unto	Zec 7:1	1961
Then c the word of the LORD of	Zec 7:4	1961
word of the LORD c unto Zechariah	Zec 7:8	1961
therefore c a great wrath from	Zec 7:12	1961
word of the LORD of hosts c to me	Zec 8:1	1961
or c in because of the affliction	Zec 8:10	935
of the LORD of hosts c unto me	Zec 8:18	1961
Out of him c forth the corner,	Zec 10:4	3318
left of all the nations which c	Zec 14:16	935
to Joseph, before they c together	Mt 1:18	4905
there c wise men from the east to	Mt 2:1	3854
east, went before them, till it c	Mt 2:9	2064
c into the land of Israel	Mt 2:21	2064
And he c and dwelt in a city called	Mt 2:23	2064
In those days c John the Baptist,	Mt 3:1	3854
And when the tempter c to him	Mt 4:3	4334
leaveth him, and, behold, angels c	Mt 4:11	4334
And leaving Nazareth, he c	Mt 4:13	2064
was set, his disciples c unto him	Mt 5:1	4334
rain descended, and the floods c	Mt 7:25	2064
rain descended, and the floods c	Mt 7:27	2064
it c to pass, when Jesus had	Mt 7:28	1096
there c a leper and worshipped him	Mt 8:2	2064
there c unto him a centurion,	Mt 8:5	4334
And a certain scribe c, and said	Mt 8:19	4334
And his disciples c to him	Mt 8:25	4334
the whole city c out to meet	Mt 8:34	1831
over, and c into his own city	Mt 9:1	2064
it c to pass, as Jesus sat at	Mt 9:10	1096
many publicans and sinners c	Mt 9:10	2064
Then c to him the disciples of	Mt 9:14	4334
there c a certain ruler, and	Mt 9:18	2064
c behind him, and touched the hem	Mt 9:20	4334
when Jesus c into the ruler's	Mt 9:23	2064
the house, the blind men c to him	Mt 9:28	4334
I c not to send peace, but a	Mt 10:34	2064
it c to pass, when Jesus had made	Mt 11:1	1096
For John c neither eating nor	Mt 11:18	2064
The Son of man c eating and	Mt 11:19	2064
for she c from the uttermost	Mt 12:42	2064
into my house from whence I c out	Mt 12:44	1831
by the way side, and the fowls c	Mt 13:4	2064
And the disciples c, and said unto	Mt 13:10	4334
But while men slept, his enemy c	Mt 13:25	2064
the servants of the householder c	Mt 13:27	4334
and his disciples c unto him	Mt 13:36	4334
it c to pass, that when Jesus had	Mt 13:53	1096
And his disciples c, and took up	Mt 14:12	4334
evening, his disciples c to him	Mt 14:15	4334
Then they that were in the ship c	Mt 14:33	2064
over, they c into the land of	Mt 14:34	2064
Then c to Jesus scribes and	Mt 15:1	4334
Then c his disciples, and said	Mt 15:12	4334
a woman of Canaan c out of the	Mt 15:22	1831
And his disciples c and besought	Mt 15:23	4334
Then c she and worshipped him,	Mt 15:25	2064
c nigh unto the sea of Galilee	Mt 15:29	2064
And great multitudes c unto him	Mt 15:30	4334
c into the coasts of Magdala	Mt 15:39	2064
also with the Sadducees c	Mt 16:1	4334
When Jesus c into the coasts of	Mt 16:13	2064
And Jesus c and touched them, and	Mt 17:7	4334
as they c down from the mountain,	Mt 17:9	2597
there c to him a certain man,	Mt 17:14	4334
Then c the disciples to Jesus	Mt 17:19	4334
received tribute money c to Peter	Mt 17:24	4334
At the same time c the disciples	Mt 18:1	4334
Then c Peter to him, and said,	Mt 18:21	4334
done, they were very sorry, and c	Mt 18:31	2064
it c to pass, that when Jesus had	Mt 19:1	1096
c into the coasts of Judaea	Mt 19:1	2064
The Pharisees also c unto him	Mt 19:3	4334
And, behold, one c and said unto	Mt 19:16	4334
when they c that were hired about	Mt 20:9	2064
But when the first c, they	Mt 20:10	2064
Then c to him the mother of	Mt 20:20	4334
Even as the Son of man c not to	Mt 20:28	2064
the lame c to him in the temple	Mt 21:14	4334
he c to it, and found nothing	Mt 21:19	2064
the elders of the people c unto	Mt 21:23	4334
he c to the first, and said, Son,	Mt 21:28	4334
he c to the second, and said	Mt 21:30	4334
For John c unto you in the way of	Mt 21:32	2064
when the king c in to see the	Mt 22:11	1525
The same day c to him the	Mt 22:23	4334
his disciples c to him for to	Mt 24:1	4334
Olives, the disciples c unto him	Mt 24:3	4334
And knew not until the flood c	Mt 24:39	2064
went to buy, the bridegroom c	Mt 25:10	2064
Afterward c also the other	Mt 25:11	2064
that had received five talents c	Mt 25:20	4334
that had received two talents c	Mt 25:22	4334
had received the one talent c	Mt 25:24	4334
I was in prison, and ye c unto me	Mt 25:36	2064
or in prison, and c unto thee	Mt 25:39	2064
it c to pass, when Jesus had	Mt 26:1	1096
There c unto him a woman having	Mt 26:7	4334
bread the disciples c to Jesus	Mt 26:17	4334
And he c and found them asleep	Mt 26:43	2064
lo, Judas, one of the twelve, c	Mt 26:47	2064
And forthwith he c to Jesus	Mt 26:49	4334
Then c they, and laid hands on	Mt 26:50	4334
though many false witnesses c	Mt 26:60	4334
At the last c two false witnesses	Mt 26:60	4334
and a damsel c unto him, saying,	Mt 26:69	4334
after a while c unto him they	Mt 26:73	4334
And as they c out, they found a	Mt 27:32	1831
c out of the graves after his	Mt 27:53	1831
there c a rich man of Arimathaea,	Mt 27:57	2064
Pharisees c together unto Pilate,	Mt 27:62	4863
c Mary Magdalene and the other	Mt 28:1	2064
Lord descended from heaven, and c	Mt 28:2	4334
And they c and held him by the feet	Mt 28:9	4334
some of the watch c into the city	Mt 28:11	2064
Say ye, His disciples c by night	Mt 28:13	2064
And Jesus c and spake unto them,	Mt 28:18	4334
it c to pass in those days, that	Mk 1:9	1096
that Jesus c from Nazareth of	Mk 1:9	2064
there c a voice from heaven,	Mk 1:11	1096
Jesus c into Galilee, preaching	Mk 1:14	2064
a loud voice, he c out of him	Mk 1:26	1831
And he c and took her by the hand,	Mk 1:31	4334
for therefore c I forth	Mk 1:38	1831
And there c a leper to him,	Mk 1:40	2064
they c to him from every quarter	Mk 1:45	2064
it c to pass, that, as Jesus sat	Mk 2:15	1096
I c not to call the righteous,	Mk 2:17	2064
it c to pass, that he went	Mk 2:23	1096
great things he did, c unto him	Mk 3:8	2064
and they c unto him	Mk 3:13	565
the scribes which c down from	Mk 3:22	2597
There c then his brethren and his	Mk 3:31	2064
it c to pass, as he sowed, some	Mk 4:4	1096
side, and the fowls of the air c	Mk 4:4	2064
they c over unto the other side	Mk 5:1	2064
c in the press behind, and touched	Mk 5:27	2064
knowing what was done in her, c	Mk 5:33	2064
there c from the ruler of the	Mk 5:35	2064
thence, and c into his own country	Mk 6:1	2064
of the said Herodias c in	Mk 6:22	1525
she c in straightway with haste	Mk 6:25	1525
his disciples heard of it, they c	Mk 6:29	2064
them, and c together unto him	Mk 6:33	4905
And Jesus, when he c out, saw much	Mk 6:34	1831
spent, his disciples c unto him	Mk 6:35	4334
over, they c into the land of	Mk 6:53	2064
Then c together unto him the	Mk 7:1	4863
scribes, which c from Jerusalem	Mk 7:1	2064
spirit, heard of him, and c	Mk 7:25	2064
he c unto the sea of Galilee,	Mk 7:31	2064
for divers of them c from far	Mk 8:3	2240
c into the parts of Dalmanutha	Mk 8:10	2064
And the Pharisees c forth, and	Mk 8:11	1831
a voice c out of the cloud,	Mk 9:7	2064
as they c down from the mountain,	Mk 9:9	2597
when he c to his disciples, he	Mk 9:14	2064
is it ago since this c unto him	Mk 9:21	1096
the people c running together	Mk 9:25	1998
and rent him sore, and c out of him	Mk 9:26	1831
And he c to Capernaum	Mk 9:33	2064
And the Pharisees c to him	Mk 10:2	4334
there c one running, and kneeled	Mk 10:17	4370
For even the Son of man c not to	Mk 10:45	2064
And they c to Jericho	Mk 10:46	2064
his garment, rose, and c to Jesus	Mk 10:50	2064
when they c nigh to Jerusalem,	Mk 11:1	1448
tree afar off having leaves, he c	Mk 11:13	2064
and when he c to it, he found	Mk 11:13	2064
And one of the scribes c, and	Mk 12:28	4334
there c a certain poor widow, and	Mk 12:42	2064
there c a woman having an	Mk 14:3	2064
c into the city, and found as he	Mk 14:16	2064
they c to a place which was named	Mk 14:32	2064
many other women which c up with	Mk 15:41	4872
waited for the kingdom of God, c	Mk 15:43	2064
they c unto the sepulchre at the	Mk 16:2	2064
it c to pass, that while he	Lk 1:8	1096
And when he c out, he could not	Lk 1:22	1831
it c to pass, that, as soon as	Lk 1:23	1096
the angel c in unto her, and said,	Lk 1:28	1525
And it c to pass, that, when	Lk 1:41	1096
Now Elisabeth's full time c that	Lk 1:57	4130
it c to pass, that on the eighth	Lk 1:59	1096
they c to circumcise the child	Lk 1:59	2064
fear c on all that dwelt round	Lk 1:65	1096
it c to pass in those days, that	Lk 2:1	1096
the angel of the Lord c upon them	Lk 2:9	2186
it c to pass, as the angels were	Lk 2:15	1096
they c with haste, and found Mary,	Lk 2:16	2064
he c by the Spirit into the	Lk 2:27	2064
it c to pass, that after three	Lk 2:46	1096
c to Nazareth, and was subject	Lk 2:51	2064
the word of God c unto John the	Lk 3:2	1096
he c into all the country about	Lk 3:3	2064
c forth to be baptized of him	Lk 3:7	1607
Then c also publicans to be	Lk 3:12	2064
it c to pass, that Jesus also	Lk 3:21	1096
a voice c from heaven, which said	Lk 3:22	1096
he c to Nazareth, where he had	Lk 4:16	2064
c down to Capernaum, a city of	Lk 4:31	2718
he c out of him, and hurt him not	Lk 4:35	1831
And devils also c out of many	Lk 4:41	1831
c unto him, and stayed him, that	Lk 4:42	2064
it c to pass, that, as the people	Lk 5:1	1096
And they c, and filled both the	Lk 5:7	2064
it c to pass, when he was in a	Lk 5:12	1096
multitudes c together to hear	Lk 5:15	4905
it c to pass on a certain day, as	Lk 5:17	1096
I c not to call the righteous,	Lk 5:32	2064
it c to pass on the second	Lk 6:1	1096
it c to pass also on another	Lk 6:6	1096
it c to pass in those days, that	Lk 6:12	1096
he c down with them, and stood in	Lk 6:17	2597
which c to hear him, and to be	Lk 6:17	2064
And when they c to Jesus, they	Lk 7:4	3854
it c to pass the day after, that	Lk 7:11	1096
Now when he c nigh to the gate of	Lk 7:12	1448
And he c and touched the bier	Lk 7:14	4334
And there c a fear on all	Lk 7:16	2983
For John the Baptist c neither	Lk 7:33	2064
I c in hath not ceased to kiss my	Lk 7:45	1525
it c to pass afterward, that he	Lk 8:1	1096
Then c to him his mother and his	Lk 8:19	3854
Now it c to pass on a certain day	Lk 8:22	1096
there c down a storm of wind on	Lk 8:23	2597
they c to him, and awoke him,	Lk 8:24	4334
c to Jesus, and found the man, out	Lk 8:35	2064
it c to pass, that, when Jesus	Lk 8:40	1096
there c a man named Jairus, and he	Lk 8:41	2064
C behind him, and touched the	Lk 8:44	4334
she c trembling, and falling down	Lk 8:47	2064
when he c into the house, he	Lk 8:51	1525
And her spirit c again, and she	Lk 8:55	1994
then c the twelve, and said unto	Lk 9:12	4334
it c to pass, as he was alone	Lk 9:18	1096
it c to pass about an eight days	Lk 9:28	1096
it c to pass, as they departed	Lk 9:33	1096
there c a cloud, and overshadowed	Lk 9:34	1096
there c a voice out of the cloud,	Lk 9:35	1096
it c to pass, that on the next	Lk 9:37	1096
it c to pass, when the time was	Lk 9:51	1096
it c to pass, that, as they went	Lk 9:57	1096
by chance there c down a certain	Lk 10:31	2597
when he was at the place, c	Lk 10:32	2064
as he journeyed, c where he was	Lk 10:33	2064
Now it c to pass, as they went,	Lk 10:38	1096
c to him, and said, Lord, dost	Lk 10:40	2186
it c to pass, that, as he was	Lk 11:1	1096
it c to pass, when the devil was	Lk 11:14	1096
unto my house whence I c out	Lk 11:24	1831
it c to pass, as he spake these	Lk 11:27	1096
for she c from the utmost parts	Lk 11:31	2064
and he c and sought fruit thereon,	Lk 13:6	2064
The same day there c certain of	Lk 13:31	4334
it c to pass, as he went into the	Lk 14:1	1096
So that servant c, and shewed his	Lk 14:21	3854
when he c to himself, he said,	Lk 15:17	2064
And he arose, and c to his father	Lk 15:20	2064

and as he c and drew nigh to the Lk 15:25 *2064*
therefore c his father out, and Lk 15:28 *1831*
moreover the dogs c and licked his Lk 16:21 *2064*
it c to pass, that the beggar Lk 16:22 *1096*
it c to pass, as he went to Lk 17:11 *1096*
it c to pass, that, as they went, Lk 17:14 *1096*
into the ark, and the flood c Lk 17:27 *2064*
she c unto him, saying, Avenge me Lk 18:3 *2064*
it c to pass, that as he was come Lk 18:35 *1096*
when Jesus c to the place, he Lk 19:5 *2064*
c down, and received him joyfully Lk 19:6 *2597*
it c to pass, that when he was Lk 19:15 *1096*
Then c the first, saying, Lord, Lk 19:16 *3854*
And the second c, saying, Lord, Lk 19:18 *2064*
And another c, saying, Lord, Lk 19:20 *2064*
it c to pass, when he was come Lk 19:29 *1096*
it c to pass, that on one of Lk 20:1 *1096*
the scribes c upon him with the Lk 20:1 *2186*
Then c to him certain of the Lk 20:27 *4334*
all the people c early in the Lk 21:38 *3719*
Then c the day of unleavened Lk 22:7 *2064*
he c out, and went, as he was wont Lk 22:39 *1831*
priests and the scribes c together Lk 22:66 *4863*
all the people that c together to Lk 23:48 *4836*
which c with him from Galilee, Lk 23:55 *4905*
they c unto the sepulchre, Lk 24:1 *2064*
it c to pass, as they were much Lk 24:4 *1096*
it c to pass, that, while they Lk 24:15 *1096*
they found not his body, they c Lk 24:23 *2064*
it c to pass, as he sat at meat Lk 24:30 *1096*
it c to pass, while he blessed Lk 24:51 *1096*
The same c for a witness, to bear Jn 1:7 *2064*
He c unto his own, and his own Jn 1:11 *2064*
grace and truth c by Jesus Christ Jn 1:17 *1096*
They c and saw where he dwelt, and Jn 1:39 *2064*
The same c to Jesus by night, and Jn 3:2 *2064*
but he that c down from heaven, Jn 3:13 *2597*
After these things c Jesus Jn 3:22 *2064*
and they c, and were baptized Jn 3:23 *3854*
they c unto John, and said unto Jn 3:26 *2064*
upon this c his disciples, and Jn 4:27 *2064*
out of the city, and c unto him Jn 4:30 *2064*
So Jesus c again into Cana of Jn 4:46 *2064*
(Howbeit there c other boats from Jn 6:23 *2064*
c to Capernaum, seeking for Jesus Jn 6:24 *2064*
For I c down from heaven, not to Jn 6:38 *2597*
bread which c down from heaven Jn 6:41 *2597*
he saith, I c down from heaven Jn 6:42 *2597*
bread which c down from heaven Jn 6:51 *2597*
bread which c down from heaven Jn 6:58 *2597*
Then c the officers to the chief Jn 7:45 *2064*
(he that c to Jesus by night, Jn 7:50 *2064*
And early in the morning he c Jn 8:2 *3854*
he c again into the temple Jn 8:2 *3854*
and all the people c unto him Jn 8:2 *2064*
for I know whence I c, and whither Jn 8:14 *2064*
I proceeded forth and c from God Jn 8:42 *2240*
neither c I of myself, but he Jn 8:42 *2064*
therefore, and washed, and c seeing Jn 9:7 *2064*
All that ever c before me are Jn 10:8 *2064*
Then c the Jews round about him, Jn 10:24 *2944*
gods, unto whom the word of God c Jn 10:35 *1096*
Then when Jesus c, he found that Jn 11:17 *2064*
And many of the Jews c to Martha Jn 11:19 *2064*
she arose quickly, and c unto him Jn 11:29 *2064*
also weeping which c with her Jn 11:33 *4905*
And he that was dead c forth Jn 11:44 *1831*
many of the Jews which c to Mary Jn 11:45 *2064*
before the passover c to Bethany Jn 12:1 *2064*
they c not for Jesus' sake only, Jn 12:9 *2064*
that c up to worship at the feast Jn 12:20 *305*
The same c therefore to Philip, Jn 12:21 *4334*
for this cause c I unto this hour Jn 12:27 *2064*
Then c there a voice from heaven, Jn 12:28 *2064*
This voice c not because of me, Jn 12:30 *1096*
for I c not to judge the world, Jn 12:47 *2064*
believed that I c out from God Jn 16:27 *1831*
I c forth from the Father, and am Jn 16:28 *1831*
surely that I c out from thee Jn 17:8 *1831*
for this cause c I into the world Jn 18:37 *2064*
Then c Jesus forth, wearing the Jn 19:5 *1831*
Then c the soldiers, and brake the Jn 19:32 *2064*
But when they c to Jesus, and saw Jn 19:33 *2064*
forthwith c there out blood and Jn 19:34 *1831*
He c therefore, and took the body Jn 19:38 *2064*
there c also Nicodemus, which at Jn 19:39 *2064*
at the first c to Jesus by night Jn 19:39 *2064*
disciple, and c to the sepulchre Jn 20:3 *2064*
and c first to the sepulchre Jn 20:4 *2064*
which c first to the sepulchre, Jn 20:8 *2064*
Mary Magdalene c and told the Jn 20:18 *2064*
c Jesus and stood in the midst, and Jn 20:19 *2064*
was not with them when Jesus c Jn 20:24 *2064*
then c Jesus, the doors being Jn 20:26 *2064*
disciples c in a little ship Jn 21:8 *2064*
suddenly there c a sound from Acts 2:2 *1096*
abroad, the multitude c together Acts 2:6 *4905*
And fear c upon every soul Acts 2:43 *1096*
and the Sadducees, c upon them, Acts 4:1 *2186*
it c to pass on the morrow, that Acts 4:5 *1096*
great fear c on all them that Acts 5:5 *1096*
not knowing what was done, c in Acts 5:7 *1525*
and the young men c in, and found Acts 5:10 *1525*
great fear c upon all the church, Acts 5:11 *1096*
There c also a multitude out of Acts 5:16 *4905*
But the high priest c, and they Acts 5:21 *3854*
But when the officers c, and found Acts 5:22 *3854*
Then c one and told them, saying, Acts 5:25 *3854*
c upon him, and caught him, and Acts 6:12 *2186*
Then c he out of the land of the Acts 7:4 *1831*
Now there c a dearth over all the Acts 7:11 *2064*
it c into his heart to visit his Acts 7:23 *305*
the voice of the Lord c unto him Acts 7:31 *1096*
c after brought in with Jesus Acts 7:45 *1237*
c out of many that were possessed Acts 8:7 *1831*
they c unto a certain water Acts 8:36 *2064*
the cities, till he c to Caesarea Acts 8:40 *2064*
he journeyed, he c near Damascus Acts 9:3 *1096*
c hither for that intent, that he Acts 9:21 *2064*
it c to pass, as Peter passed Acts 9:32 *1096*
he c down also to the saints Acts 9:32 *2718*
it c to pass in those days, that Acts 9:37 *1096*
it c to pass, that he tarried Acts 9:43 *1096*
there c a voice to him, Rise, Acts 10:13 *1096*
Therefore c I unto you without Acts 10:29 *2064*
as many as c with Peter, because Acts 10:45 *4905*
and it c even to me Acts 11:5 *2064*
c unto the ears of the church Acts 11:22 *191*
Who, when he c, and had seen the Acts 11:23 *3854*
it c to pass, that a whole year Acts 11:26 *1096*
in these days c prophets from Acts 11:27 *2718*
which c to pass in the days of Acts 11:28 *1096*
the angel of the Lord c upon him Acts 12:7 *2186*
they c unto the iron gate that Acts 12:10 *2064*
he c to the house of Mary the Acts 12:12 *2064*
a damsel c to hearken, named Acts 12:13 *4334*
but they c with one accord to him Acts 12:20 *3918*
they c to Perga in Pamphylia Acts 13:13 *2064*
they c to Antioch in Pisidia, and Acts 13:14 *3854*
c up with him from Galilee to Acts 13:31 *4872*
the next sabbath day c almost the Acts 13:44 *4863*
against them, and c unto Iconium Acts 13:51 *2064*
it c to pass in Iconium, that Acts 14:1 *1096*
there c thither certain Jews from Acts 14:19 *1904*
he rose up, and c into the city Acts 14:20 *1525*
Pisidia, they c to Pamphylia Acts 14:24 *2064*
certain men which c down from Acts 15:1 *2718*
elders c together for to consider Acts 15:6 *4863*
were dismissed, they c to Antioch Acts 15:30 *2064*
Then c he to Derbe and Lystra Acts 16:1 *2658*
passing by Mysia c down to Troas Acts 16:8 *2597*
we c with a straight course to Acts 16:11 *2113*
it c to pass, as we went to Acts 16:16 *1096*
And he c out the same hour Acts 16:18 *1831*
c trembling, and fell down before Acts 16:29 *1096*
And they c and besought them, and Acts 16:39 *2064*
they c to Thessalonica, where was Acts 17:1 *2064*
they c thither also, and stirred Acts 17:13 *2064*
from Athens, and c to Corinth Acts 18:1 *2064*
Rome:) and c unto them Acts 18:2 *4334*
he c to Ephesus, and left them Acts 18:19 *2658*
in the scriptures, c to Ephesus Acts 18:24 *2658*
it c to pass, that, while Apollos Acts 19:1 *1096*
the upper coasts c to Ephesus Acts 19:1 *2064*
them, the Holy Ghost c on them Acts 19:6 *2064*
And many that believed c, and Acts 19:18 *2064*
exhortation, he c into Greece, Acts 20:2 *2064*
c unto them to Troas in five days Acts 20:6 *2064*
when the disciples c together to Acts 20:7 *4863*
we took him in, and c to Mitylene Acts 20:14 *2064*
c the next day over against Chios Acts 20:15 *2064*
and the next day we c to Miletus Acts 20:15 *2658*
the first day that I c into Asia Acts 20:18 *1910*
it c to pass, that after we were Acts 21:1 *1096*
we c with a straight course unto Acts 21:1 *2064*
we c to Ptolemais, and saluted the Acts 21:7 *2658*
departed, and c unto Caesarea Acts 21:8 *2064*
there c down from Judaea a Acts 21:10 *2718*
tidings c unto the chief captain Acts 21:31 *305*
Then the chief captain c near Acts 21:33 *1448*
when he c upon the stairs, so it Acts 21:35 *1096*
it c to pass, that, as I made my Acts 22:6 *1096*
were with me, I c into Damascus Acts 22:11 *2064*
C unto me, and stood, and said unto Acts 22:13 *2064*
it c to pass, that, when I was Acts 22:17 *1096*
Then the chief captain c, and said Acts 22:27 *4334*
they c to the chief priests and Acts 23:14 *4334*
then c I with an army, and rescued Acts 23:27 *2186*
when they c to Caesarea, and Acts 23:33 *1525*
chief captain Lysias c upon us Acts 24:7 *3928*
Now after many years I c to bring Acts 24:17 *3854*
when Felix c with his wife Acts 24:24 *3854*
Porcius Festus c into Felix' room Acts 24:27
the Jews which c down from Acts 25:7 *2597*
Bernice c unto Caesarea to salute Acts 25:13 *2658*
we c to Myra, a city of Lycia Acts 27:5 *2718*
c unto a place which is called Acts 27:8 *2064*
so it c to pass, that they Acts 27:44 *1096*
there c a viper out of the heat, Acts 28:3 *1831*
it c to pass, that the father of Acts 28:8 *1096*
had diseases in the island, c Acts 28:9 *4334*
a compass, and c to Rhegium Acts 28:13 *2658*
we c the next day to Puteoli Acts 28:13 *2064*
they c to meet us as far as Appii Acts 28:15 *1831*
And when we c to Rome, the Acts 28:16 *2064*
it c to pass, that after three Acts 28:17 *1096*
any of the brethren that c shewed Acts 28:21 *3854*
there c many to him into his Acts 28:23 *2240*
received all that c in unto him Acts 28:30 *1531*
c upon all men to condemnation Rom 5:18
of one the free gift c upon all Rom 5:18
but when the commandment c Rom 7:9 *2064*
as concerning the flesh Christ c Rom 9:5
And I, brethren, when I c to you 1Cor 2:1 *2064*
c not with excellency of speech 1Cor 2:1 *2064*
c the word of God out from you 1Cor 14:36 *1831*
or c it unto you only 1Cor 14:36 *2658*
For since by man c death 1Cor 15:21
by man c also the resurrection of 1Cor 15:21 *2064*
our trouble which c to us in Asia 2Cor 1:8 *1096*
that to spare you I c not as yet 2Cor 1:23 *2064*
same unto you, lest, when I c 2Cor 2:3 *2064*
when I c to Troas to preach 2Cor 2:12 *2064*
which c from Macedonia supplied 2Cor 11:9 *2064*
Afterwards I c into the regions Gal 1:21 *2064*
who c in privily to spy out our Gal 2:4 *3922*
before that certain c from James Gal 2:12 *2064*
But before faith c, we were kept Gal 3:23 *2064*
And c and preached peace to you Eph 2:17 *2064*
For our gospel c not unto you in 1Th 1:5 *1096*
even as it c to pass, and ye know 1Th 3:4 *1096*
when Timotheus c from you unto us 1Th 3:6 *2064*
that Christ Jesus c into the 1Ti 1:15 *2064*
which c unto me at Antioch, at 2Ti 3:11 *1096*
howbeit not all that c out of Heb 3:16 *1831*
country from whence they c out Heb 11:15 *1831*
when there c such a voice to him 2Pet 1:17 *5342*
this voice which c from heaven we 2Pet 1:18 *5342*
For the prophecy c not in old 2Pet 1:21 *5342*
This is he that c by water 1Jn 5:6 *2064*
greatly, when the brethren c 3Jn 3 *2064*
And he c and took the book out of Rev 5:7 *2064*
and whence c they Rev 7:13 *2064*
These are they which c out of Rev 7:14 *2064*
And another angel c and stood at Rev 8:3 *2064*
which c with the prayers of the Rev 8:4
there c out of the smoke locusts Rev 9:3 *1831*
another angel c out of the temple Rev 14:15 *1831*
another angel c out of the temple Rev 14:17 *1831*
another angel c out from the Rev 14:18 *1831*
blood c out of the winepress, Rev 14:20 *1831*
the seven angels c out of the Rev 15:6 *1831*
there c a great voice out of the Rev 16:17 *1831*
great Babylon c in remembrance Rev 16:19 *3415*
there c one of the seven angels Rev 17:1 *2064*
a voice c out of the throne, Rev 19:5 *1831*
fire c down from God out of Rev 20:9 *2597*
there c unto me one of the seven Rev 21:9 *2064*

C

CAMEL

saw Isaac, she lighted off the c Gen 24:64 1581
as the c, because he cheweth the Lev 11:4 1581
as the c, and the hare, and the Deut 14:7 1581
and suckling, ox and sheep, c 1Sa 15:3 1581
the horse, of the mule, of the c Zec 14:15 1581
It is easier for a c to go Mt 19:24 *2574*
strain at a gnat, and swallow a c Mt 23:24 *2574*
It is easier for a c to go Mk 10:25 *2574*
For it is easier for a c to go Lk 18:25 *2574*

CAMEL'S

and put them in the c furniture Gen 31:34 1581
John had his raiment of c hair Mt 3:4 *2574*
And John was clothed with c hair Mk 1:6 *2574*

CAMELS

maidservants, and she asses, and c Gen 12:16 1581
ten c of the c of his master Gen 24:10 1581
he made his c to kneel down Gen 24:11 1581
and I will give thy c drink also Gen 24:14 1581
I will draw water for thy c also Gen 24:19 1581
draw water, and drew for all his c Gen 24:20 1581
as the c had done drinking, that Gen 24:22 1581
he stood by the c at the well Gen 24:30 1581
the house, and room for the c Gen 24:31 1581
and he ungirded his c Gen 24:32 1581
gave straw and provender for the c Gen 24:32 1581
and maidservants, and c, and asses Gen 24:35 1581
and I will also draw for thy c Gen 24:44 1581
and I will give thy c drink also Gen 24:46 1581
and she made the c drink also Gen 24:46 1581
damsels, and they rode upon the c Gen 24:61 1581
and, behold, the c were coming Gen 24:63 1581
and menservants, and c, and asses Gen 30:43 1581
set his sons and his wives upon c Gen 31:17 1581
and the flocks, and herds, and the c Gen 32:7 1581
Thirty milch c with their colts, Gen 32:15 1581
with their c bearing spicery Gen 37:25 1581
upon the asses, upon the c Ex 9:3 1581
their c were without number Judg 6:5 1581
their c were without number, as Judg 7:12 1581
the oxen, and the asses, and the c 1Sa 27:9 1581
young men, which rode upon c 1Sa 30:17 1581
with c that bare spices, and very 1Kin 10:2 1581
of their c fifty thousand, and of 1Chr 5:21 1581
brought bread on asses, and on c 1Chr 12:40 1581
Over the c also was Obil the 1Chr 27:30 1581
c that bare spices, and gold in 2Chr 9:1 1581
c in abundance, and returned to 2Chr 14:15 1581
Their c, four hundred thirty and Ezr 2:67 1581
Their c, four hundred thirty and Neh 7:69 1581
horseback, and riders on mules, c Est 8:10 327
c went out, being hastened and Est 8:14 327
sheep, and three thousand c Job 1:3 1581
three bands, and fell upon the c Job 1:17 1581
thousand sheep, and six thousand c Job 42:12 1581
of asses, and a chariot of c Is 21:7 1581
treasures upon the bunches of c Is 30:6 1581
multitude of c shall cover thee Is 60:6 1581
and all their vessels, and their c Jer 49:29 1581
their c shall be a booty, and the Jer 49:32 1581
I will make Rabbah a stable for c Eze 25:5 1581

CAMELS'

that were on their c necks Judg 8:21 1581
that were about their c necks Judg 8:26 1581
forty c burden, and came and stood 2Kin 8:9 1581

CAMEST

Sarai's maid, whence c thou Gen 16:8 935
unto the land from whence thou c Gen 24:5 3318
I have eaten of all before thou c Gen 27:33 935
for in it thou c out from Egypt Ex 23:15 3318
month Abib thou c out from Egypt Ex 34:18 3318
wherefore c thou not unto me Num 22:37 1980
the children of Ammon thou c not Deut 2:37 7126
for thou c forth out of the land Deut 16:3 3318
remember the day when thou c Deut 16:3 3318
that thou c forth out of Egypt Deut 16:6 3318
that thou c not within the days 1Sa 13:11 935
he said, Why c thou down hither 1Sa 17:28 3381
C thou not from thy journey 2Sa 11:10 935
Whereas thou c but yesterday, 2Sa 15:20 935
again by the same way that thou c 1Kin 13:9 1980

the man of God that c from Judah	1Kin 13:14	935
to go by the way that thou c	1Kin 13:17	1980
But c back, and hast eaten bread	1Kin 13:22	7725
back by the way by which thou c	2Kin 19:28	935
Thou c down also upon mount Sinai	Neh 9:13	3381
back by the way by which thou c	Is 37:29	935
we looked not for, thou c down	Is 64:3	3381
before thou c forth out of the	Jer 1:5	3318
thou c forth with thy rivers, and	Eze 32:2	1518
how c thou in hither not having a	Mt 22:12	*1525*
him, Rabbi, when c thou hither	Jn 6:25	*1096*
that thou c forth from God	Jn 16:30	*1831*
unto thee in the way as thou c	Acts 9:17	*2064*

CAMON (*ca'-mon*) *A town in Gilead.*

And Jair died, and was buried in C	Judg 10:5	7056

CAMP

which went before the c of Israel	Ex 14:19	4264
between the c of the Egyptians	Ex 14:20	4264
the Egyptians and the c of Israel	Ex 14:20	4264
quails came up, and covered the c	Ex 16:13	4264
people that was in the c trembled	Ex 19:16	4264
out of the c to meet with God	Ex 19:17	4264
thou burn with fire without the c	Ex 29:14	4264
There is a noise of war in the c	Ex 32:17	4264
soon as he came nigh unto the c	Ex 32:19	4264
Moses stood in the gate of the c	Ex 32:26	4264
gate to gate throughout the c	Ex 32:27	4264
the c, afar off from the c	Ex 33:7	4264
which was without the c	Ex 33:7	4264
And he turned again into the c	Ex 33:11	4264
to be proclaimed throughout the c	Ex 36:6	4264
without the c unto a clean place	Lev 4:12	4264
forth the bullock without the c	Lev 4:21	4264
without the c unto a clean place	Lev 6:11	4264
he burnt with fire without the c	Lev 8:17	4264
he burnt with fire without the c	Lev 9:11	4264
before the sanctuary out of the c	Lev 10:4	4264
them in their coats out of the c	Lev 10:5	4264
without the c shall his	Lev 13:46	4264
shall go forth out of the c	Lev 14:3	4264
that he shall come into the c	Lev 14:8	4264
and afterward come into the c	Lev 16:26	4264
one carry forth without the c	Lev 16:27	4264
he shall come into the c	Lev 16:28	4264
an ox, or lamb, or goat, in the c	Lev 17:3	4264
or that killeth it out of the c	Lev 17:3	4264
Israel strove together in the c	Lev 24:10	4264
that hath cursed without the c	Lev 24:14	4264
him that had cursed out of the c	Lev 24:23	4264
tents, every man by his own c	Num 1:52	4264
they of the standard of the c of	Num 2:3	4264
in the c of Judah were an hundred	Num 2:9	4264
c of Reuben according to their	Num 2:10	4264
the c of Reuben were an hundred	Num 2:16	4264
shall set forward with the c of	Num 2:17	4264
the Levites in the midst of the c	Num 2:17	4264
shall be the standard of the c of	Num 2:18	4264
the c of Ephraim were an hundred	Num 2:24	4264
The standard of the c of Dan	Num 2:25	4264
they that were numbered in the c	Num 2:31	4264
when the c setteth forward, Aaron	Num 4:5	4264
as the c is to set forward	Num 4:15	4264
they put out of the c every leper	Num 5:2	4264
without the c shall ye put them	Num 5:3	4264
so, and put them out without the c	Num 5:4	4264
of the c of the children of Judah	Num 10:14	4264
the standard of the c of Reuben	Num 10:18	4264
the standard of the c of the	Num 10:22	4264
the standard of the c of the	Num 10:25	4264
day, when they went out of the c	Num 10:34	4264
in the uttermost parts of the c	Num 11:1	4264
dew fell upon the c in the night	Num 11:9	4264
remained two of the men in the c	Num 11:26	4264
and they prophesied in the c	Num 11:26	4264
and Medad do prophesy in the c	Num 11:27	4264
And Moses gat him into the c	Num 11:30	4264
sea, and let them fall by the c	Num 11:31	4264
the other side, round about the c	Num 11:31	4264
for themselves round about the c	Num 11:32	4264
be shut out from the c seven days	Num 12:14	4264
shut out from the c seven days	Num 12:15	4264
Moses, departed not out of the c	Num 14:44	4264
him with stones without the c	Num 15:35	4264
brought him without the c	Num 15:36	4264
may bring her forth without the c	Num 19:3	4264
he shall come into the c, and the	Num 19:7	4264
up without the c in a clean place	Num 19:9	4264
unto the c at the plains of Moab	Num 31:12	4264
forth to meet them without the c	Num 31:13	4264
ye abide without the c seven days	Num 31:19	4264
ye shall come into the c	Num 31:24	4264
shall he go abroad out of the c	Deut 23:10	4264
he shall not come within the c	Deut 23:10	4264
he shall come into the c again	Deut 23:11	4264
have a place also without the c	Deut 23:12	4264
God walketh in the midst of thy c	Deut 23:14	4264
therefore shall thy c be holy	Deut 23:14	4264
and thy stranger that is in thy c	Deut 29:11	4264
abode in their places in the c	Josh 5:8	4264
into the c, and lodged in the c	Josh 6:11	4264
city once, and returned into the c	Josh 6:14	4264
make the c of Israel a curse, and	Josh 6:18	4264
left them without the c of Israel	Josh 6:23	4264
to Joshua unto the c at Gilgal	Josh 9:6	4264
unto Joshua to the c to Gilgal	Josh 10:6	4264
with him, unto the c to Gilgal	Josh 10:15	4264
c to Joshua at Makkedah in peace	Josh 10:21	4264
with him, unto the c to Gilgal	Josh 10:43	4264
I come to the outside of the c	Judg 7:17	4264
also on every side of all the c	Judg 7:18	4264
came unto the outside of the c in	Judg 7:19	4264
in his place round about the c	Judg 7:21	4264
in the c of Dan between Zorah	Judg 13:25	4264
there came none to the c from	Judg 21:8	4264
brought them unto the c to Shiloh	Judg 21:12	4264
the people were come into the c	1Sa 4:3	4264
of the LORD came into the c	1Sa 4:5	4264
shout in the c of the Hebrews	1Sa 4:6	4264
of the LORD was come into the c	1Sa 4:6	4264
they said, God is come into the c	1Sa 4:7	4264
the c of the Philistines in three	1Sa 13:17	4264
went up with them into the c from	1Sa 14:21	4264
out of the c of the Philistines	1Sa 17:4	4264
run to the c to thy brethren	1Sa 17:17	4264
go down with me to Saul to the c	1Sa 26:6	4264
a man came out of the c from Saul	2Sa 1:2	4264
Out of the c of Israel am I	2Sa 1:3	4264
over Israel that day in the c	1Kin 16:16	4264
when they came to the c of Israel	2Kin 3:24	4264
and such a place shall be my c	2Kin 6:8	8466
to go unto the c of the Syrians	2Kin 7:5	4264
uttermost part of the c of Syria	2Kin 7:5	4264
even the c as it was, and fled for	2Kin 7:7	4264
to the uttermost part of the c	2Kin 7:8	4264
We came to the c of the Syrians	2Kin 7:10	4264
are they gone out of the c to	2Kin 7:12	4264
smote in the c of the Assyrians	2Kin 19:35	4264
to the c had slain all the eldest	2Chr 22:1	4264
captains in the c of the king of	2Chr 32:21	4264
it fall in the midst of their c	Ps 78:28	4264
They envied Moses also in the c	Ps 106:16	4264
I will c against thee round about	Is 29:3	2583
smote in the c of the Assyrians	Is 37:36	4264
the bow, c against it round about	Jer 50:29	2583
set the c also against it, and set	Eze 4:2	4264
for his c is very great	Joel 2:11	4264
which c in the hedges in the cold	Nah 3:17	2583
for sin, are burned without the c	Heb 13:11	*3925*
therefore unto him without the c	Heb 13:13	*3925*
compassed the c of the saints	Rev 20:9	*3925*

CAMPED

there Israel c before the mount	Ex 19:2	2583

CAMPHIRE

is unto me as a cluster of c in	Song 1:14	3724
c, with spikenard,	Song 4:13	3724

CAMPS

c throughout their hosts were six	Num 2:32	4264
that they defile not their c	Num 5:3	4264
and for the journeying of the c	Num 10:2	4264
then the c that lie on the east	Num 10:5	4264
then the c that lie on the south	Num 10:6	4264
all the c throughout their hosts	Num 10:25	4264
c to come up unto your nostrils	Amos 4:10	4264

CAN

is greater than I c bear	Gen 4:13	
so that if a man c number the	Gen 13:16	3201
what c I do this day unto these	Gen 31:43	
how then c I do this great	Gen 39:9	
there is none that c interpret it	Gen 41:15	
C we find such a one as this is,	Gen 41:38	
food, as much as they c carry	Gen 44:1	3201
a man as I c certainly divine	Gen 44:15	
I know that he c speak well	Ex 4:14	
get you straw where ye c find it	Ex 5:11	
young pigeons, such as he c get	Lev 14:30	
Who c count the dust of Jacob, and	Num 23:10	
How c I myself alone bear your	Deut 1:12	
that c do according to thy works,	Deut 3:24	
how c I dispossess them	Deut 7:17	3201
Who c stand before the children	Deut 9:2	
I c no more go out and come in	Deut 31:2	3201
any that c deliver out of my hand	Deut 32:39	
if ye c certainly declare it me	Judg 14:12	
peradventure he c shew us our way	1Sa 9:6	
And Samuel said, How c I go	1Sa 16:2	
me now a man that c play well	1Sa 16:17	
what c he have more but the	1Sa 18:8	
for who c stretch forth his hand	1Sa 26:9	
shalt know what thy servant c do	1Sa 28:2	
what c David say more unto thee	2Sa 7:20	
Who c tell whether GOD will be	2Sa 12:22	
c I bring him back again	2Sa 12:23	3201
none c turn to the right hand or	2Sa 14:19	
me every thing that ye c hear	2Sa 15:36	
c I discern between good and evil	2Sa 19:35	
c thy servant taste what I eat or	2Sa 19:35	
c I hear any more the voice of	2Sa 19:35	
c skill to hew timber like unto	1Kin 5:6	
What c David speak more to thee	1Chr 17:18	
for who c judge this thy people,	2Chr 1:10	
that c skill to grave with the	2Chr 2:7	
for I know that thy servants c	2Chr 2:8	
For how c I endure to see the	Est 8:6	3201
or how c I endure to see the	Est 8:6	3201
when they c find the grave	Job 3:22	
but who c withhold himself from	Job 4:2	3201
C that which is unsavoury be	Job 6:6	
C the rush grow up without mire	Job 8:11	
c the flag grow without water	Job 8:11	
he taketh away, who c hinder him	Job 9:12	
there is none that c deliver out	Job 10:7	
together, then who c hinder him	Job 11:10	
a man, and there c be no opening	Job 12:14	
Who c bring a clean thing out of	Job 14:4	
wherewith he c do no good	Job 15:3	
C a man be profitable unto God,	Job 22:2	
c he judge through the dark cloud	Job 22:13	
what c the Almighty do for them	Job 22:17	
is in one mind, and who c turn him	Job 23:13	
How then c man be justified with	Job 25:4	
or how c he be clean that is born	Job 25:4	
of his power who c understand	Job 26:14	
who then c make trouble	Job 34:29	
his face, who then c behold him	Job 34:29	
or who c say, Thou hast wrought	Job 36:23	
neither c the number of his years	Job 36:26	
Also c any understand the	Job 36:29	
Who c number the clouds in wisdom	Job 38:37	
or who c stay the bottles of	Job 38:37	
thine own right hand c save thee	Job 40:14	
he that made him c make his sword	Job 40:19	
he trusteth that he c draw up	Job 40:23	
Who c discover the face of his	Job 41:13	
or who c come to him with his	Job 41:13	
Who c open the doors of his face	Job 41:14	
that no air c come between them	Job 41:16	
that no thought c be withholden	Job 42:2	
what c the righteous do	Ps 11:3	
Who c understand his errors	Ps 19:12	
none c keep alive his own soul	Ps 22:29	
they are more than c be numbered	Ps 40:5	
None of them c by any means	Ps 49:7	
not fear what flesh c do unto me	Ps 56:4	
be afraid what man c do unto me	Ps 56:11	
your pots c feel the thorns	Ps 58:9	
C God furnish a table in the	Ps 78:19	3201
c he give bread also	Ps 78:20	3201
c he provide flesh for his people	Ps 78:20	3201
For who in the heaven c be	Ps 89:6	
mighty c be likened unto the LORD	Ps 89:6	
Who c utter the mighty acts of	Ps 106:2	
who c shew forth all his praise	Ps 106:2	
what c man do unto me	Ps 118:6	
who c stand before his cold	Ps 147:17	
C a man take fire in his bosom,	Prov 6:27	
C one go upon hot coals, and his	Prov 6:28	
but a wounded spirit who c bear	Prov 18:14	
but a faithful man who c find	Prov 20:6	
Who c say, I have made my heart	Prov 20:9	
how c a man then understand his	Prov 20:24	
seven men that c render a reason	Prov 26:16	
Who c find a virtuous woman	Prov 31:10	
for what c the man do that cometh	Eccl 2:12	
For who c eat, or who else c	Eccl 2:25	
or who else c hasten hereunto,	Eccl 2:25	
so that no man c find out the	Eccl 3:11	
nothing c be put to it, nor any	Eccl 3:14	
but how c one be warm alone	Eccl 4:11	
for who c tell a man what shall	Eccl 6:12	
for who c make that straight,	Eccl 7:13	3201
exceeding deep, who c find it out	Eccl 7:24	
for who c tell him when it shall	Eccl 8:7	
be after him, who c tell him	Eccl 10:14	
neither c the floods drown it	Song 8:7	
a man c stretch himself on it	Is 28:20	
than that he c wrap himself in it	Is 28:20	
death c not celebrate thee	Is 38:18	3201
who among them c declare this	Is 43:9	
there is none that c deliver out	Is 43:13	
yet c he not answer, nor save him	Is 46:7	
C a woman forget her sucking	Is 49:15	
dogs which c never have enough	Is 56:11	3045
cisterns, that c hold no water	Jer 2:13	
her occasion who c turn her away	Jer 2:24	
if they c save thee in the time	Jer 2:28	
C a maid forget her ornaments, or	Jer 2:32	
burn that none c quench it	Jer 4:4	
if ye c find a man, if there be	Jer 5:1	
yet c they not prevail	Jer 5:22	
yet c they not pass over it	Jer 5:22	3201
so that none c pass through them	Jer 9:10	3201
neither c men hear the voice of	Jer 9:10	3201
C the Ethiopian change his skin,	Jer 13:23	
of the Gentiles that c cause rain	Jer 14:22	
or c the heavens give showers	Jer 14:22	
who c know it?	Jer 17:9	
and burn that none c quench it	Jer 21:12	
C any hide himself in secret	Jer 23:24	
If heaven above c be measured	Jer 31:37	
If ye c break my covenant of the	Jer 33:20	
that c do any thing against you	Jer 38:5	3201
How c it be quiet, seeing the	Jer 47:7	
who c heal thee?	Lam 2:13	
C thine heart endure, or c	Eze 22:14	
or c thine hands be strong, in	Eze 22:14	
secret that they c hide from thee	Eze 28:3	
c play well on an instrument	Eze 33:32	
Son of man, c these bones live	Eze 37:3	
I shall know that ye c shew me	Dan 2:9	
that c shew the king's matter	Dan 2:10	3202
that c shew it before the king	Dan 2:11	
that c deliver after this sort	Dan 3:29	3202
none c stay his hand, or say unto	Dan 4:35	
For how c the servant of this my	Dan 10:17	3201
and who c abide it?	Joel 2:11	
C two walk together, except they	Amos 3:3	
C a bird fall in a snare upon the	Amos 3:5	
hath spoken, who c but prophesy	Amos 3:8	
Who c tell if God will turn and	Jonah 3:9	
none evil c come upon us	Mic 3:11	
in pieces, and none c deliver	Mic 5:8	
Who c stand before his	Nah 1:6	
who c abide in the fierceness of	Nah 1:6	
No man c serve two masters	Mt 6:24	*1410*
c add one cubit unto his stature	Mt 6:27	*1410*
neither c a corrupt tree bring	Mt 7:18	
unto them, C the children of the	Mt 9:15	*1410*
Or else how c one enter into a	Mt 12:29	*1410*
O generation of vipers, how c ye	Mt 12:34	*1410*
ye c discern the face of the sky	Mt 16:3	*1097*
but c ye not discern the signs of	Mt 16:3	*1410*
saying, Who then c be saved	Mt 19:25	*1410*
how c ye escape the damnation of	Mt 23:33	
your way, make it as sure as ye c	Mt 27:65	*1492*
who c forgive sins but God only	Mk 2:7	*1410*
unto them, C the children of the	Mk 2:19	*1410*
How c Satan cast out Satan	Mk 3:23	*1410*
No man c enter into a strong	Mk 3:27	*1410*
entering into him c defile him	Mk 7:15	*1410*

From whence c a man satisfy these Mk 8:4 *1410*
no fuller on earth c white them Mk 9:3 *1410*
This kind c come forth by nothing Mk 9:29 *1410*
that c lightly speak evil of me Mk 9:39 *1410*
themselves, Who then c be saved Mk 10:26 *1410*
c ye drink of the cup that I Mk 10:38 *1410*
And they said unto him, We c Mk 10:39 *1410*
Who c forgive sins, but God alone Lk 5:21 *1410*
C ye make the children of the Lk 5:34 *1410*
C the blind lead the blind Lk 6:39 *1410*
that have no more that they c do Lk 12:4
of you with taking thought c add Lk 12:25 *1410*
ye c discern the face of the sky Lk 12:56 *1492*
No servant c serve two masters Lk 16:13 *1410*
neither c they pass to us, that Lk 16:26 *1410*
it said, Who then c be saved Lk 18:26 *1410*
Neither c they die any more Lk 20:36 *1410*
C there any good thing come out Jn 1:46 *1410*
for no man c do these miracles Jn 3:2 *1410*
How c a man be born when he is Jn 3:4 *1410*
c he enter the second time into Jn 3:4 *1410*
unto him, How c these things be Jn 3:9 *1410*
A man c receive nothing, except Jn 3:27 *1410*
The Son c do nothing of himself, Jn 5:19 *1410*
I c of mine own self do nothing Jn 5:30 *1410*
How c ye believe, which receive Jn 5:44 *1410*
No man c come to me, except the Jn 6:44 *1410*
How c this man give us his flesh Jn 6:52 *1410*
who c hear it? Jn 6:60 *1410*
that no man c come unto me, Jn 6:65 *1410*
night cometh, when no man c work Jn 9:4 *1410*
How c a man that is a sinner do Jn 9:16 *1410*
C a devil open the eyes of the Jn 10:21 *1410*
and how c we know the way Jn 14:5 *1410*
no more c ye, except ye abide in Jn 15:4
for without me ye c do nothing Jn 15:5 *1410*
And he said, How c I, except some Acts 8:31 *1410*
C any man forbid water, that Acts 10:47 *1410*
Neither c they prove the things Acts 24:13 *1410*
law of God, neither indeed c be Rom 8:7 *1410*
be for us, who c be against us Rom 8:31
neither c he know them, because 1Cor 2:14 *1410*
For other foundation c no man lay 1Cor 3:11 *1410*
that no man c say that Jesus is 1Cor 12:3 *1410*
For we c do nothing against the 2Cor 13:8 *1410*
I c do all things through Christ Phil 4:13 *2480*
For what thanks c we render to 1Th 3:9 *1410*
it is certain we c carry nothing 1Ti 6:7 *1410*
which no man c approach unto 1Ti 6:16
whom no man hath seen, nor c see 1Ti 6:16 *1410*
Who c have compassion on the Heb 5:2 *1410*
c never with those sacrifices Heb 10:1 *1410*
which c never take away sins Heb 10:11 *1410*
c faith save him? Jas 2:14 *1410*
But the tongue c no man tame Jas 3:8 *1410*
C the fig tree, my brethren, bear Jas 3:12 *1410*
so c no fountain both yield salt Jas 3:12
how c he love God whom he hath 1Jn 4:20 *1410*
an open door, and no man c shut it Rev 3:8 *1410*
which neither c see, nor hear, Rev 9:20 *1410*

CANA (*ca'-nah*) *A village in Galilee.*
was a marriage in C of Galilee Jn 2:1 *2580*
did Jesus in C of Galilee Jn 2:11 *2580*
came again into C of Galilee Jn 4:46 *2580*
and Nathanael of C in Galilee Jn 21:2 *2580*

CANAAN (*ca'-na-an*) See CANAANITE.
1. Son of Ham.
and Ham is the father of C Gen 9:18 3667
And Ham, the father of C, saw the Gen 9:22 3667
And he said, Cursed be C Gen 9:25 3667
and C shall be his servant Gen 9:26 3667
and C shall be his servant Gen 9:27 3667
Cush, and Mizraim, and Phut, and C Gen 10:6 3667
C begat Sidon his firstborn, and Gen 10:15 3667
Cush, and Mizraim, Put, and C 1Chr 1:8 3667
C begat Zidon his firstborn, and 1Chr 1:13 3667
2. Place where Canaanites dwell.
to go into the land of C Gen 11:31 3667
forth to go into the land of C Gen 12:5 3667
and into the land of C they came Gen 12:5 3667
Abram dwelled in the land of C Gen 13:12 3667
dwelt ten years in the land of C Gen 16:3 3667
art a stranger, all the land of C Gen 17:8 3667
same is Hebron in the land of C Gen 23:2 3667
same is Hebron in the land of C Gen 23:19 3667
take a wife of the daughters of C Gen 28:1 3667
take a wife of the daughters of C Gen 28:6 3667
of C pleased not Isaac his father Gen 28:8 3667
Isaac his father in the land of C Gen 31:18 3667
which is in the land of C Gen 33:18 3667
to Luz, which is in the land of C Gen 35:6 3667
his wives of the daughters of C Gen 36:2 3667
born unto him in the land of C Gen 36:5 3667
which he had got in the land of C Gen 36:6 3667
was a stranger, in the land of C Gen 37:1 3667
the famine was in the land of C Gen 42:5 3667
From the land of C to buy food Gen 42:7 3667
sons of one man in the land of C Gen 42:13 3667
their father unto the land of C Gen 42:29 3667
with our father in the land of C Gen 42:32 3667
unto thee out of the land of C Gen 44:8 3667
and go, get you unto the land of C Gen 45:17 3667
came into the land of C unto Gen 45:25 3667
they had gotten in the land of C Gen 46:6 3667
Er and Onan died in the land of C Gen 46:12 3667
which were in the land of C Gen 46:31 3667
are come out of the land of C Gen 47:1 3667
famine is sore in the land of C Gen 47:4 3667
all the land of C fainted by Gen 47:13 3667
of Egypt, and in the land of C Gen 47:14 3667
of Egypt, and in the land of C Gen 47:15 3667
unto me at Luz in the land of C Gen 48:3 3667
by me in the land of C in the way Gen 48:7 3667
is before Mamre, in the land of C Gen 49:30 3667
digged for me in the land of C Gen 50:5 3667
carried him into the land of C Gen 50:13 3667
them, to give them the land of C Ex 6:4 3667
inhabitants of C shall melt away Ex 15:15 3667
unto the borders of the land of C Ex 16:35 3667
ye be come into the land of C Lev 14:34 3667
after the doings of the land of C Lev 18:3 3667
Egypt, to give you the land of C Lev 25:38 3667
they may search the land of C Num 13:2 3667
them to spy out the land of C Num 13:17 3667
Er and Onan died in the land of C Num 26:19 3667
among you in the land of C Num 32:30 3667
the LORD into the land of C Num 32:32 3667
in the south in the land of C Num 33:40 3667
over Jordan into the land of C Num 33:51 3667
When ye come into the land of C Num 34:2 3667
even the land of C with the Num 34:2 3667
of Israel in the land of C Num 34:29 3667
over Jordan into the land of C Num 35:10 3667
shall ye give in the land of C Num 35:14 3667
and behold the land of C, which I Deut 32:49 3667
fruit of the land of C that year Josh 5:12 3667
Israel inherited in the land of C Josh 14:1 3667
them at Shiloh in the land of C Josh 21:2 3667
Shiloh, which is in the land of C Josh 22:9 3667
Jordan, that are in the land of C Josh 22:10 3667
altar over against the land of C Josh 22:11 3667
of Gilead, unto the land of C Josh 22:32 3667
him throughout all the land of C Josh 24:3 3667
had not known all the wars of C Judg 3:1 3667
into the hand of Jabin king of C Judg 4:2 3667
C before the children of Israel Judg 4:23 3667
against Jabin the king of C Judg 4:24 3667
had destroyed Jabin king of C Judg 4:24 3667
then fought the kings of C in Judg 5:19 3667
Shiloh, which is in the land of C Judg 21:12 3667
thee will I give the land of C 1Chr 16:18 3667
thee will I give the land of C Ps 105:11 3667
sacrificed unto the idols of C Ps 106:38 3667
Bashan, and all the kingdoms of C Ps 135:11 3667
of Egypt speak the language of C Is 19:18 3667
thy nativity is of the land of C Eze 16:3 3667
in the land of C unto Chaldea Eze 16:29 3667
O C, the land of the Philistines, Zeph 2:5 3667
a woman of C came out of the same Mt 15:22 *5478*

CANAANITE (*ca'-na-an-ite*) See CANAANITES, CANAANITESS, CANAANITISH, ZELOTES. *Descendants of Canaan.*
the C was then in the land Gen 12:6 3669
and the C and the Perizzite dwelled Gen 13:7 3669
there a daughter of a certain C Gen 38:2 3669
shall drive out the Hivite, the C Ex 23:28 3669
and I will drive out the C Ex 33:2 3669
before thee the Amorite, and the C Ex 34:11 3669
And when king Arad the C, which Num 21:1 3669
And king Arad the C, which dwelt Num 33:40 3669
Hittite, and the Amorite, the C Josh 9:1 3669
to the C on the east and on the Josh 11:3 3669
which is counted to the C Josh 13:3 3669
the C in the house of the LORD of Zec 14:21 3669
Simon the C, and Judas Iscariot, Mt 10:4 *2581*
and Thaddaeus, and Simon the C Mk 3:18 *2581*

CANAANITES (*ca'-na-an-ites*)
families of the C spread abroad Gen 10:18 3669
border of the C was from Sidon Gen 10:19 3669
And the Amorites, and the C Gen 15:21 3669
my son of the daughters of the C Gen 24:3 3669
my son of the daughters of the C Gen 24:37 3669
of the land, among the C and the Gen 34:30 3669
inhabitants of the land, the C Gen 50:11 3669
unto the place of the C, and the Ex 3:8 3669
of Egypt unto the land of the C Ex 3:17 3669
bring thee into the land of the C Ex 13:5 3669
bring thee into the land of the C Ex 13:11 3669
and the Perizzites, and the C Ex 23:23 3669
the C dwell by the sea, and by the Num 13:29 3669
the C dwelt in the valley Num 14:25 3669
the C are there before you, and ye Num 14:43 3669
the C which dwelt in that hill, Num 14:45 3669
of Israel, and delivered up the C Num 21:3 3669
sea side, to the land of the C Deut 1:7 3669
and the Amorites, and the C Deut 7:1 3669
goeth down, in the land of the C Deut 11:30 3669
Hittites, and the Amorites, the C Deut 20:17 3669
drive out from before you the C Josh 3:10 3669
and all the kings of the C Josh 5:1 3669
For the C and all the inhabitants Josh 7:9 3669
Hittites, the Amorites, and the C Josh 12:8 3669
the south, all the land of the C Josh 13:4 3669
not out the C that dwelt in Gezer Josh 16:10 3669
but the C dwell among the Josh 16:10 3669
but the C would dwell in that Josh 17:12 3669
that they put the C to tribute Josh 17:13 3669
all the C that dwell in the land Josh 17:16 3669
for thou shalt drive out the C Josh 17:18 3669
and the Perizzites, and the C Josh 24:11 3669
go up for us against the C first Judg 1:1 3669
that we may fight against the C Judg 1:3 3669
and the LORD delivered the C Judg 1:4 3669
against him, and they slew the C Judg 1:5 3669
went down to fight against the C Judg 1:9 3669
the C that dwelt in Hebron Judg 1:10 3669
they slew the C that inhabited Judg 1:17 3669
but the C would dwell in that Judg 1:27 3669
that they put the C to tribute Judg 1:28 3669
out the C that dwelt in Gezer Judg 1:29 3669
but the C dwelt in Gezer among Judg 1:29 3669
but the C dwelt among them, and Judg 1:30 3669
the Asherites dwelt among the C Judg 1:32 3669
but he dwelt among the C, the Judg 1:33 3669
of the Philistines, and all the C Judg 3:3 3669
of Israel dwelt among the C Judg 3:5 3669
of the Hivites, and of the C 2Sa 24:7 3669
slain the C that dwelt in the 1Kin 9:16 3669
their abominations, even of the C Ezr 9:1 3669
him to give the land of the C Neh 9:8 3669
inhabitants of the land, the C Neh 9:24 3669
shall possess that of the C Obad 20 3669

CANAANITESS (*ca'-na-an-ite-ess*)
him of the daughter of Shua the C 1Chr 2:3 3669

CANAANITISH (*ca'-na-an-i-tish*)
and Shaul the son of a C woman Gen 46:10 3669
and Shaul the son of a C woman Ex 6:15 3669

CANDACE (*can'-da-see*) *Name for a dynasty of Ethiopian queens.*
under C queen of the Ethiopians Acts 8:27 *2582*

CANDLE
his c shall be put out with him Job 18:6 5216
How oft is the c of the wicked Job 21:17 5216
When his c shined upon my head, Job 29:3 5216
For thou wilt light my c Ps 18:28 5216
of man is the c of the LORD Prov 20:27 5216
the c of the wicked shall be put Prov 24:20 5216
her c goeth not out by night Prov 31:18 5216
millstones, and the light of the c Jer 25:10 5216
Neither do men light a c, and put Mt 5:15 *3088*
Is a c brought to be put under a Mk 4:21 *3088*
No man, when he hath lighted a c Lk 8:16 *3088*
No man, when he hath lighted a c Lk 11:33 *3088*
of a c doth give thee light Lk 11:36 *3088*
one piece, doth not light a c Lk 15:8 *3088*
the light of a c shall shine no Rev 18:23 *3088*
and they need no c, neither light Rev 22:5 *3088*

CANDLES
I will search Jerusalem with c Zeph 1:12 5216

CANDLESTICK
thou shalt make a c of pure gold Ex 25:31 4501
beaten work shall the c be made Ex 25:31 4501
of the c out of the one side Ex 25:32 4501
of the c out of the other side Ex 25:32 4501
branches that come out of the c Ex 25:33 4501
in the c shall be four bowls made Ex 25:34 4501
that proceed out of the c Ex 25:35 4501
the c over against the table on Ex 26:35 4501
and all his vessels, and the c Ex 30:27 4501
the pure c with all his furniture Ex 31:8 4501
The c also for the light, and his Ex 35:14 4501
he made the c of pure gold Ex 37:17 4501
of beaten work made he the c Ex 37:17 4501
three branches of the c out of Ex 37:18 4501
three branches of the c out of Ex 37:18 4501
six branches going out of the c Ex 37:19 4501
in the c were four bowls made Ex 37:20 4501
The pure c, with the lamps Ex 39:37 4501
and thou shalt bring in the c Ex 40:4 4501
he put the c in the tent of the Ex 40:24 4501
c before the LORD continually Lev 24:4 4501
the ark, and the table, and the c Num 3:31 4501
cover the c of the light, and his Num 4:9 4501
give light over against the c Num 8:2 4501
lamps thereof over against the c Num 8:3 4501
this work of the c was of beaten Num 8:4 4501
shewed Moses, so he made the c Num 8:4 4501
and a table, and a stool, and a c 2Kin 4:10 4501
of gold, by weight for every c 1Chr 28:15 4501
silver by weight, both for the c 1Chr 28:15 4501
according to the use of every c 1Chr 28:15 4501
the c of gold with the lamps 2Chr 13:11 4501
wrote over against the c upon the Dan 5:5 5043
behold a c all of gold, with a Zec 4:2 4501
upon the right side of the c Zec 4:11 4501
put it under a bushel, but on a c Mt 5:15 *3087*
and not to be set on a c Mk 4:21 *3087*
but setteth it on a c, that they Lk 8:16 *3087*
under a bushel, but on a c Lk 11:33 *3087*
the first, wherein was the c Heb 9:2 *3087*
will remove thy c out of his Rev 2:5 *3087*

CANDLESTICKS
the c of pure gold, five on the 1Kin 7:49 4501
Even the weight for the c of gold 1Chr 28:15 4501
for the c of silver by weight, 1Chr 28:15 4501
he made ten c of gold according 2Chr 4:7 4501
Moreover the c with their lamps, 2Chr 4:20 4501
bowls, and the caldrons, and the c Jer 52:19 4501
turned, I saw seven golden c Rev 1:12 *3087*
in the midst of the seven c one Rev 1:13 *3087*
right hand, and the seven golden c Rev 1:20 *3087*
the seven c which thou sawest are Rev 1:20 *3087*
the midst of the seven golden c Rev 2:1 *3087*
the two c standing before the God Rev 11:4 *3087*

CANE
bought me no sweet c with money Is 43:24 7070
the sweet c from a far country Jer 6:20 7070

CANKER
their word will eat as doth a c 2Ti 2:17 *1044*

CANKERED
Your gold and silver is c Jas 5:3 *2728*

CANKERWORM
locust hath left hath the c eaten Joel 1:4 *3218*
that which the c hath left hath Joel 1:4 *3218*
that the locust hath eaten, the c Joel 2:25 *3218*
it shall eat thee up like the c Nah 3:15 *3218*
make thyself many as the c Nah 3:15 *3218*
the c spoileth, and fleeth away Nah 3:16 *3218*

CANNEH (*can'-neh*) See CALNEH. *A place in southern Arabia.*
Haran, and C, and Eden, the Eze 27:23 3656

CANNOT

I *c* escape to the mountain, lest	Gen 19:19	
for I *c* do any thing till thou be	Gen 19:22	
we *c* speak unto thee bad or good	Gen 24:50	
And they said, We *c*, until all the	Gen 29:8	
lord that I *c* rise up before thee	Gen 31:35	
which *c* be numbered for multitude	Gen 32:12	3808
We *c* do this thing, to give our	Gen 34:14	
to Judah, and said, I *c* find her	Gen 38:22	3808
we *c* tell who put our money in	Gen 43:22	3808
The lad *c* leave his father	Gen 44:22	
And we said, We *c* go down	Gen 44:26	
that one *c* be able to see the	Ex 10:5	3808
The people *c* come up to mount	Ex 19:23	
if he be poor, and *c* get so much	Lev 14:21	3201
I *c* go beyond the word of the	Num 22:18	
and I *c* reverse it	Num 23:20	3808
I *c* go beyond the commandment of	Num 24:13	
the land *c* be cleansed of the	Num 35:33	3308
a sore botch that *c* be healed	Deut 28:35	
the people, Ye *c* serve the LORD	Josh 24:19	
unto the LORD, and I *c* go back	Judg 11:35	
But if ye *c* declare it me, then	Judg 14:13	
I *c* redeem it for myself, lest I	Ruth 4:6	
for I *c* redeem it	Ruth 4:6	
which *c* profit nor deliver	1Sa 12:21	3308
said unto Saul, I *c* go with these	1Sa 17:39	3808
thy soul liveth, O king, I *c* tell	1Sa 17:55	518
that a man *c* speak to him	1Sa 25:17	
thinking, David *c* come in	2Sa 5:6	3808
which *c* be gathered up again	2Sa 14:14	3808
because they *c* be taken with	2Sa 23:6	3808
that *c* be numbered nor counted	1Kin 3:8	3808
heaven of heavens *c* contain thee	1Kin 8:27	3808
he *c* find thee, he shall slay me	1Kin 18:12	3808
heaven of heavens *c* contain him	2Chr 2:6	3808
heaven of heavens *c* contain thee	2Chr 6:18	3808
of the LORD, that ye *c* prosper	2Chr 24:20	3808
for we *c* stand before thee	Ezr 9:15	3808
great work, so that I *c* come down	Neh 6:3	369
so that their hands *c* perform	Job 5:12	
c my taste discern perverse	Job 6:30	3808
he *c* answer him one of a thousand	Job 9:3	3808
down, and it *c* be built again	Job 12:14	3808
his bounds that he *c* pass	Job 14:5	3808
for I *c* find one wise man among	Job 17:10	3808
fenced up my way that I *c* pass	Job 19:8	3808
and backward, but I *c* perceive him	Job 23:8	3808
he doth work, but I *c* behold him	Job 23:9	3808
the right hand, that I *c* see him	Job 23:9	3808
It *c* be gotten for gold, neither	Job 28:15	3808
It *c* be valued with the gold of	Job 28:16	3808
gold and the crystal *c* equal it	Job 28:17	3808
we *c* be satisfied	Job 31:31	3808
consumed away, that it *c* be seen	Job 33:21	3808
a great ransom *c* deliver thee	Job 36:18	3808
doeth he, which we *c* comprehend	Job 37:5	408
for we *c* order our speech by	Job 37:19	3808
the Almighty, we *c* find him out	Job 37:23	3808
together, that they *c* be sundered	Job 41:17	3808
they *c* be moved	Job 41:23	1077
of him that layeth at him *c* hold	Job 41:26	1097
The arrow *c* make him flee	Job 41:28	3808
they *c* be reckoned up in order	Ps 40:5	408
I am so troubled that I *c* speak	Ps 77:4	3808
I am shut up, and I *c* come forth	Ps 88:8	3201
is stablished, that it *c* be moved	Ps 93:1	1077
which *c* be removed, but abideth	Ps 125:1	3808
it is high, I *c* attain unto it	Ps 139:6	
and for four which it *c* bear	Prov 30:21	
man *c* utter it	Eccl 1:8	
is crooked *c* be made straight	Eccl 1:15	
which is wanting *c* be numbered	Eccl 1:15	
that a man *c* find out the work	Eccl 8:17	
a man *c* tell what shall be	Eccl 10:14	
Many waters *c* quench love	Song 8:7	
of assemblies, I *c* away with	Is 1:13	
and he saith, I *c*	Is 29:11	
For the grave *c* praise thee	Is 38:18	3808
into the pit *c* hope for thy truth	Is 38:18	3808
shut their eyes, that they *c* see	Is 44:18	
hearts, that they *c* understand	Is 44:18	
that he *c* deliver his soul, nor	Is 44:20	3808
and pray unto a god that *c* save	Is 45:20	3808
at all, that it *c* redeem	Is 50:2	
are all dumb dogs, they *c* bark	Is 56:10	
are shepherds that *c* understand	Is 56:11	
the troubled sea, when it *c* rest	Is 57:20	
is not shortened, that it *c* save	Is 59:1	3808
his ear heavy, that it *c* hear	Is 59:1	3808
in the street, and equity *c* enter	Is 59:14	
behold, I *c* speak	Jer 1:6	3808
I *c* hold my peace, because thou	Jer 4:19	3808
decree, that it *c* pass it	Jer 5:22	3201
uncircumcised, and they *c* hearken	Jer 6:10	
in lying words, that *c* profit	Jer 7:8	1115
needs be borne, because they *c* go	Jer 10:5	3808
for they *c* do evil, neither also	Jer 10:5	3808
as a mighty man that *c* save	Jer 14:9	
c I do with you as this potter	Jer 18:6	
that *c* be made whole again	Jer 19:11	
that *c* be eaten, they are so evil	Jer 24:3	3808
which *c* be eaten, they are so	Jer 24:8	3808
that *c* be eaten, they are so evil	Jer 29:17	3808
the host of heaven *c* be numbered	Jer 33:22	3808
I *c* go into the house of the LORD	Jer 36:5	
the LORD, though it *c* be searched	Jer 46:23	3808
it *c* be quiet	Jer 49:23	
hedged me about, that I *c* get out	Lam 3:7	3808
that we *c* go in our streets	Lam 4:18	3808
king hath demanded *c* the wise men	Dan 2:27	
which *c* be measured nor numbered	Hos 1:10	3808
c discern between their right	Jonah 4:11	3808
c be satisfied, but gathereth	Hab 2:5	3808
that is set on an hill *c* be hid	Mt 5:14	
Ye *c* serve God and mammon	Mt 6:24	
A good tree *c* bring forth evil	Mt 7:18	
All men *c* receive this saying	Mt 19:11	*3756*
Jesus, and said, We *c* tell	Mt 21:27	*1492*
Thinkest thou that I *c* now pray	Mt 26:53	
himself he *c* save	Mt 27:42	
bridegroom with them, they *c* fast	Mk 2:19	
itself, that kingdom *c* stand	Mk 3:24	
itself, that house *c* stand	Mk 3:25	
he *c* stand, but hath an end	Mk 3:26	
into the man, it *c* defile him	Mk 7:18	
and said unto Jesus, We *c* tell	Mk 11:33	*1492*
himself he *c* save	Mk 15:31	
I *c* rise and give thee	Lk 11:7	
for it *c* be that a prophet perish	Lk 13:33	
for they *c* recompense thee	Lk 14:14	
a wife, and therefore I *c* come	Lk 14:20	
life also, he *c* be my disciple	Lk 14:26	
come after me, *c* be my disciple	Lk 14:27	
that he hath, he *c* be my disciple	Lk 14:33	
I *c* dig	Lk 16:3	
Ye *c* serve God and mammon	Lk 16:13	
would pass from hence to you *c*	Lk 16:26	
he *c* see the kingdom of God	Jn 3:3	
he *c* enter into the kingdom of	Jn 3:5	
The world *c* hate you	Jn 7:7	
and where I am, thither ye *c* come	Jn 7:34	
and where I am, thither ye *c* come	Jn 7:36	
but ye *c* tell whence I come, and	Jn 8:14	
whither I go, ye *c* come	Jn 8:21	
he saith, Whither I go, ye *c* come	Jn 8:22	
even because ye *c* hear my word	Jn 8:43	
and the scripture *c* be broken	Jn 10:35	
the Jews, Whither I go, ye *c* come	Jn 13:33	
Lord, why *c* I follow thee now	Jn 13:37	
whom the world *c* receive, because	Jn 14:17	
As the branch *c* bear fruit of	Jn 15:4	
unto you, but ye *c* bear them now	Jn 16:12	
we *c* tell what he saith	Jn 16:18	
and we *c* deny it	Acts 4:16	
For we *c* but speak the things	Acts 4:20	
it be of God, ye *c* overthrow it	Acts 5:39	
manner of Moses, ye *c* be saved	Acts 15:1	
these things *c* be spoken against	Acts 19:36	*368*
abide in the ship, ye *c* be saved	Acts 27:31	
are in the flesh *c* please God	Rom 8:8	
with groanings which *c* be uttered	Rom 8:26	*215*
But if they *c* contain, let them	1Cor 7:9	*3756*
Ye *c* drink the cup of the Lord	1Cor 10:21	
ye *c* be partakers of the Lord's	1Cor 10:21	
the eye *c* say unto the hand, I	1Cor 12:21	
blood *c* inherit the kingdom of	1Cor 15:50	
(whether in the body, I *c* tell	2Cor 12:2	
whether out of the body, I *c* tell	2Cor 12:2	
or out of the body, I *c* tell	2Cor 12:3	
c disannul, that it should make	Gal 3:17	*3756*
so that ye *c* do the things that	Gal 5:17	*3361*
they that are otherwise *c* be hid	1Ti 5:25	
he *c* deny himself	2Ti 2:13	
life, which God, that *c* lie	Titus 1:2	*893*
Sound speech, that *c* be condemned	Titus 2:8	*176*
have not an high priest which *c*	Heb 4:15	
of which we *c* now speak	Heb 9:5	
which *c* be shaken may remain	Heb 12:27	*3361*
a kingdom which *c* be moved	Heb 12:28	*761*
for God *c* be tempted with evil	Jas 1:13	*551*
and desire to have, and *c* obtain	Jas 4:2	
c see afar off, and hath forgotten	2Pet 1:9	*3467*
and that *c* cease from sin	2Pet 2:14	*180*
he *c* sin, because he is born of	1Jn 3:9	

CANST

that thou *c* understand a dream to	Gen 41:15	
he said, Thou *c* not see my face	Ex 33:20	3201
whereof thou *c* not be healed	Deut 28:27	3201
thou *c* not stand before thine	Josh 7:13	3201
How *c* thou say, I love thee, when	Judg 16:15	
C thou bring me down to this	1Sa 30:15	
wheresoever thou *c* sojourn	2Kin 8:1	
gold that thou *c* find in all the	Ezr 7:16	
C thou by searching find out God	Job 11:7	
c thou find out the Almighty unto	Job 11:7	
what *c* thou do?	Job 11:8	
what *c* thou know?	Job 11:8	
Or darkness, that thou *c* not see	Job 22:11	
If thou *c* answer me, set thy	Job 33:5	3201
C thou bind the sweet influences	Job 38:31	
C thou bring forth Mazzaroth in	Job 38:32	
or *c* thou guide Arcturus with his	Job 38:32	
c thou set the dominion thereof	Job 38:33	
C thou lift up thy voice to the	Job 38:34	
C thou send lightnings, that they	Job 38:35	
or *c* thou mark when the hinds do	Job 39:1	
C thou number the months that	Job 39:2	
C thou bind the unicorn with his	Job 39:10	
C thou make him afraid as a	Job 39:20	
or *c* thou thunder with a voice	Job 40:9	
C thou draw out leviathan with an	Job 41:1	
C thou put an hook into his nose	Job 41:2	
C thou fill his skin with barbed	Job 41:7	
I know that thou *c* do every thing	Job 42:2	3201
all the things thou *c* desire are	Prov 3:15	
that thou *c* not know them	Prov 5:6	
is his son's name, if thou *c* tell	Prov 30:4	
speech than thou *c* perceive	Is 33:19	
that thou *c* not understand	Is 33:19	
How *c* thou say, I am not polluted	Jer 2:23	
then how *c* thou contend with	Jer 12:5	
whose words thou *c* not understand	Eze 3:6	
that thou *c* make interpretations	Dan 5:16	3202
now if thou *c* read the writing	Dan 5:16	3202
evil, and *c* not look on iniquity	Hab 1:13	3201
because thou *c* not make one hair	Mt 5:36	*1410*
thou wilt, thou *c* make me clean	Mt 8:2	*1410*
thou wilt, thou *c* make me clean	Mk 1:40	*1410*
but if thou *c* do any thing, have	Mk 9:22	*1410*
said unto him, If thou *c* believe	Mk 9:23	*1410*
thou wilt, thou *c* make me clean	Lk 5:12	*1410*
Either how *c* thou say to thy	Lk 6:42	*1410*
but *c* not tell whence it cometh	Jn 3:8	*1492*
I go, thou *c* not follow me now	Jn 13:36	*1410*
Who said, *C* thou speak Greek	Acts 21:37	*1097*
how thou *c* not bear them which	Rev 2:2	*1410*

CAPERNAUM (*ca-pur'-na-um*) *A city in Galilee.*

Nazareth, he came and dwelt in *C*	Mt 4:13	*2584*
And when Jesus was entered into *C*	Mt 8:5	*2584*
And thou, *C*, which art exalted	Mt 11:23	*2584*
And when they were come to *C*	Mt 17:24	*2584*
And they went into *C*	Mk 1:21	*2584*
he entered into *C* after some days	Mk 2:1	*2584*
And he came to *C*	Mk 9:33	*2584*
we have heard done in *C*, do also	Lk 4:23	*2584*
And came down to *C*, a city of	Lk 4:31	*2584*
of the people, he entered into *C*	Lk 7:1	*2584*
And thou, *C*, which art exalted to	Lk 10:15	*2584*
After this he went down to *C*	Jn 2:12	*2584*
nobleman, whose son was sick at *C*	Jn 4:46	*2584*
and went over the sea toward *C*	Jn 6:17	*2584*
also took shipping, and came to *C*	Jn 6:24	*2584*
the synagogue, as he taught in *C*	Jn 6:59	*2584*

CAPHTHORIM (*caf'-tho-rim*) See CAPHTORIM. *People of Caphtor.*

whom came the Philistines,) and *C*	1Chr 1:12	3732

CAPHTOR (*caf'-tor*) See CAPHTORIM. *Original land of the Philistines.*

which came forth out of *C*	Deut 2:23	3731
the remnant of the country of *C*	Jer 47:4	3731
and the Philistines from *C*	Amos 9:7	3731

CAPHTORIM (*caf'-to-rim*) See CAPHTHORIM, CAPHTORIMS. *Same as Caphthorim.*

out of whom came Philistim,) and *C*	Gen 10:14	3732

CAPHTORIMS (*caf'-to-rims*) See CAPHTORIM.

Hazerim, even unto Azzah, the *C*	Deut 2:23	3732

CAPHTORITES See CAPHTORIMS.

CAPPADOCIA (*cap-pa-do'-she-ah*) *A Roman province in Asia Minor.*

Mesopotamia, and in Judaea, and *C*	Acts 2:9	*2587*
throughout Pontus, Galatia, *C*	1Pet 1:1	*2587*

CAPTAIN

Phichol the chief *c* of his host	Gen 21:22	8269
Phichol the chief *c* of his host	Gen 21:32	8269
Phichol the chief *c* of his army	Gen 26:26	8269
of Pharaoh's, and *c* of the guard	Gen 37:36	8269
c of the guard, an Egyptian	Gen 39:1	8269
the house of the *c* of the guard	Gen 40:3	8269
the *c* of the guard charged Joseph	Gen 40:4	8269
in the *c* of the guard's house	Gen 41:10	8269
servant to the *c* of the guard	Gen 41:12	8269
be *c* of the children of Judah	Num 2:3	5387
the son of Zuar shall be *c* of the	Num 2:5	5387
be *c* of the children of Zebulun	Num 2:7	5387
the *c* of the children of Reuben	Num 2:10	5387
the *c* of the children of Simeon	Num 2:12	5387
the *c* of the sons of Gad shall be	Num 2:14	5387
the *c* of the sons of Ephraim	Num 2:18	5387
the *c* of the children of Manasseh	Num 2:20	5387
the *c* of the sons of Benjamin	Num 2:22	5387
the *c* of the children of Dan	Num 2:25	5387
the *c* of the children of Asher	Num 2:27	5387
the *c* of the children of Naphtali	Num 2:29	5387
one to another, Let us make a *c*	Num 14:4	7218
but as *c* of the host of the LORD	Josh 5:14	8269
the *c* of the LORD's host said	Josh 5:15	8269
the *c* of whose host was Sisera	Judg 4:2	8269
the *c* of Jabin's army, with his	Judg 4:7	8269
unto Jephthah, Come, and be our *c*	Judg 11:6	7101
made him head and *c* over them	Judg 11:11	7101
him to be *c* over my people Israel	1Sa 9:16	5057
thee to be *c* over his inheritance	1Sa 10:1	5057
c of the host of Hazor, and into	1Sa 12:9	8269
him to be *c* over his people	1Sa 13:14	5057
the name of the *c* of his host was	1Sa 14:50	8269
unto the *c* of their thousand	1Sa 17:18	8269
the *c* of the host, Abner, whose	1Sa 17:55	8269
made him his *c* over a thousand	1Sa 18:13	8269
and he became a *c* over them	1Sa 22:2	8269
the son of Ner, the *c* of his host	1Sa 26:5	8269
of Ner, *c* of Saul's host, took	2Sa 2:8	8269
and thou shalt be a *c* over Israel	2Sa 5:2	5057
soul, he shall be chief and *c*	2Sa 5:8	
Shobach the *c* of the host of	2Sa 10:16	8269
smote Shobach the *c* of their host	2Sa 10:18	8269
Absalom made Amasa *c* of the host	2Sa 17:25	5921
if thou be not *c* of the host	2Sa 19:13	8269
therefore he was their *c*	2Sa 23:19	8269
said to Joab the *c* of the host	2Sa 24:2	8269
priest, and Joab the *c* of the host	1Kin 1:19	8269
c of the host of Israel, and Amasa	1Kin 2:32	8269
of Jether, *c* of the host of Judah	1Kin 2:32	8269
Joab the *c* of the host was gone	1Kin 11:15	8269
that Joab the *c* of the host was	1Kin 11:21	8269
became *c* over a band, when David	1Kin 11:24	8269
c of half his chariots, conspired	1Kin 16:9	8269
the *c* of the host, king over	1Kin 16:16	8269
him a *c* of fifty with his fifty	2Kin 1:9	8269
and said to the *c* of fifty	2Kin 1:10	8269
another *c* of fifty with his fifty	2Kin 1:11	8269
he sent again a *c* of the third	2Kin 1:13	8269
the third *c* of fifty went up, and	2Kin 1:13	8269
the king, or to the *c* of the host	2Kin 4:13	8269
c of the host of the king of	2Kin 5:1	8269
I have an errand to thee, O *c*	2Kin 9:5	8269

And he said, To thee, O c	2Kin 9:5	8269
Then said Jehu to Bidkar his c	2Kin 9:25	7991
a c of his, conspired against him	2Kin 15:25	7991
one c of the least of my master's	2Kin 18:24	6346
tell Hezekiah the c of my people	2Kin 20:5	5057
c of the guard, a servant of the	2Kin 25:8	7227
that were with the c of the guard	2Kin 25:10	7227
did Nebuzar-adan the c of the	2Kin 25:11	7227
But the c of the guard left of	2Kin 25:12	7227
the c of the guard took away	2Kin 25:15	7227
the c of the guard took Seraiah	2Kin 25:18	7227
Nebuzar-adan c of the guard took	2Kin 25:20	7227
first shall be chief and c	1Chr 11:6	8269
for he was their c	1Chr 11:21	8269
a c of the Reubenites, and thirty	1Chr 11:42	7218
Shophach the c of the host of	1Chr 19:16	8269
killed Shophach the c of the host	1Chr 19:18	8269
The third c of the host for the	1Chr 27:5	8269
The fourth c for the fourth month	1Chr 27:7	
The fifth c for the fifth month	1Chr 27:8	8269
The sixth c for the sixth month	1Chr 27:9	
The seventh c for the seventh	1Chr 27:10	
The eighth c for the eighth month	1Chr 27:11	
The ninth c for the ninth month	1Chr 27:12	
The tenth c for the tenth month	1Chr 27:13	
The eleventh c for the eleventh	1Chr 27:14	
The twelfth c for the twelfth	1Chr 27:15	
God himself is with us for our c	2Chr 13:12	7218
next to him was Jehohanan the c	2Chr 17:15	8269
a c to return to their bondage	Neh 9:17	7218
The c of fifty, and the honourable	Is 3:3	8269
one c of the least of my master's	Is 36:9	6346
a c of the ward was there, whose	Jer 37:13	1167
Then Nebuzar-adan the c of the	Jer 39:9	7227
But Nebuzar-adan the c of the	Jer 39:10	
Nebuzar-adan the c of the guard	Jer 39:11	7227
the c of the guard sent, and	Jer 39:13	7227
the c of the guard had let him go	Jer 40:1	7227
the c of the guard took Jeremiah,	Jer 40:2	7227
So the c of the guard gave him	Jer 40:5	7227
whom Nebuzar-adan the c of the	Jer 41:10	7227
the c of the guard had left with	Jer 43:6	7227
appoint a c against her	Jer 51:27	2951
c of the guard, which served the	Jer 52:12	7227
that were with the c of the guard	Jer 52:14	7227
Then Nebuzar-adan the c of the	Jer 52:15	7227
But Nebuzar-adan the c of the	Jer 52:16	7227
took the c of the guard away	Jer 52:19	7227
the c of the guard took Seraiah	Jer 52:24	7227
So Nebuzar-adan the c of the	Jer 52:26	7227
the c of the guard carried away	Jer 52:30	7227
Arioch the c of the king's guard	Dan 2:14	7229
and said to Arioch the king's c	Dan 2:15	7990
Then the band and the c and	Jn 18:12	*5506*
the c of the temple, and the	Acts 4:1	*4755*
the c of the temple and the chief	Acts 5:24	*4755*
Then went the c with the officers	Acts 5:26	*4755*
came unto the chief c of the band	Acts 21:31	*5506*
and when they saw the chief c	Acts 21:32	*5506*
Then the chief c came near	Acts 21:33	*5506*
castle, he said unto the chief c	Acts 21:37	*5506*
The chief c commanded him to be	Acts 22:24	*5506*
that, he went and told the chief c	Acts 22:26	*5506*
Then the chief c came, and said	Acts 22:27	*5506*
And the chief c answered, With a	Acts 22:28	*5506*
the chief c also was afraid,	Acts 22:29	*5506*
a great dissension, the chief c	Acts 23:10	*5506*
council signify to the chief c	Acts 23:15	*5506*
this young man unto the chief c	Acts 23:17	*5506*
and brought him to the chief c	Acts 23:18	*5506*
Then the chief c took him by the	Acts 23:19	*5506*
So the chief c then let the young	Acts 23:22	*5506*
But the chief c Lysias came upon	Acts 24:7	*5506*
the chief c shall come down	Acts 24:22	*5506*
prisoners to the c of the guard	Acts 28:16	*4759*
to make the c of their salvation	Heb 2:10	*747*

CAPTAINS

and c over every one of them	Ex 14:7	7991
his chosen c also are drowned in	Ex 15:4	7991
with the c over thousands, and	Num 31:14	8269
c over hundreds, which came from	Num 31:14	8269
the c of thousands, and c	Num 31:48	8269
c of hundreds, came near unto	Num 31:48	8269
of the c of thousands, and of the	Num 31:52	8269
of the c of hundreds, was sixteen	Num 31:52	8269
the gold of the c of thousands	Num 31:54	8269
c over thousands, and c	Deut 1:15	8269
c over hundreds, and c over	Deut 1:15	8269
c over fifties, and c over	Deut 1:15	8269
c over tens, and officers among	Deut 1:15	8269
that they shall make c of the	Deut 20:9	8269
your c of your tribes, your	Deut 29:10	7218
said unto the c of the men of war	Josh 10:24	7101
will appoint him c over thousands	1Sa 8:12	8269
over thousands, and c over fifties	1Sa 8:12	8269
and make you all c of thousands	1Sa 22:7	8269
of thousands, and c of hundreds	1Sa 22:7	8269
had two men that were c of bands	2Sa 4:2	8269
set c of thousands and c of	2Sa 18:1	8269
and c of hundreds over them	2Sa 18:1	8269
the c charge concerning Absalom	2Sa 18:5	8269
in the seat, chief among the c	2Sa 23:8	7991
and against the c of the host	2Sa 24:4	8269
the c of the host went out from	2Sa 24:4	8269
the c of the host, and Abiathar	1Kin 1:25	8269
the two c of the hosts of Israel	1Kin 2:5	8269
and his princes, and his c	1Kin 9:22	7991
sent the c of the hosts which he	1Kin 15:20	8269
place, and put c in their rooms	1Kin 20:24	6346
two c that had rule over his	1Kin 22:31	8269
when the c of the chariots saw	1Kin 22:32	8269
when the c of the chariots	1Kin 22:33	8269
burnt up the two c of the former	2Kin 1:14	8269
about, and the c of the chariots	2Kin 8:21	8269
the c of the host were sitting	2Kin 9:5	8269
said to the guard and to the c	2Kin 10:25	7991
the c cast them out, and went to	2Kin 10:25	7991
rulers over hundreds, with the c	2Kin 11:4	3746
the c over hundreds did	2Kin 11:9	8269
to the c over hundreds did the	2Kin 11:10	8269
commanded the c of the hundreds	2Kin 11:15	8269
rulers over hundreds, and the c	2Kin 11:19	3746
when all the c of the armies,	2Kin 25:23	8269
the c of the armies, arose, and	2Kin 25:26	8269
Seir, having for their c Pelatiah	1Chr 4:42	7218
a Hachmonite, the chief of the c	1Chr 11:11	7991
Now three of the thirty c went	1Chr 11:15	7218
of the sons of Gad, c of the host	1Chr 12:14	7218
Amasai, who was chief of the c	1Chr 12:18	7991
them, and made them c of the band	1Chr 12:18	7218
c of the thousands that were of	1Chr 12:20	7218
of valour, and were c in the host	1Chr 12:21	8269
father's house twenty and two c	1Chr 12:28	8269
And of Naphtali a thousand c	1Chr 12:34	8269
consulted with the c of thousands	1Chr 13:1	8269
the c over thousands, went to	1Chr 15:25	8269
the c of the host separated to	1Chr 25:1	8269
the c over thousands and hundreds,	1Chr 26:26	8269
the c of the host, had dedicated	1Chr 26:26	8269
c of thousands and hundreds, and	1Chr 27:1	8269
Perez was the chief of all the c	1Chr 27:3	8269
the c of the companies that	1Chr 28:1	8269
the c over the thousands, and	1Chr 28:1	8269
c over the hundreds, and the	1Chr 28:1	8269
the c of thousands and of hundreds	1Chr 29:6	8269
to the c of thousands and of	2Chr 1:2	8269
men of war, and chief of his c	2Chr 8:9	7991
c of his chariots and horsemen	2Chr 8:9	8269
put c in them, and store of	2Chr 11:11	5057
sent the c of his armies against	2Chr 16:4	8269
Of Judah, the c of thousands	2Chr 17:14	8269
c of the chariots that were with	2Chr 18:30	8269
when the c of the chariots saw	2Chr 18:31	8269
when the c of the chariots	2Chr 18:32	8269
him in, and the c of the chariots	2Chr 21:9	8269
took the c of hundreds, Azariah	2Chr 23:1	8269
to the c of hundreds spears	2Chr 23:9	8269
the priest brought out the c of	2Chr 23:14	8269
And he took the c of hundreds	2Chr 23:20	8269
made them c over thousands, and	2Chr 25:5	8269
c over hundreds, according to the	2Chr 25:5	8269
of Hananiah, one of the king's c	2Chr 26:11	8269
he set c of war over the people,	2Chr 32:6	8269
c in the camp of the king of	2Chr 32:21	8269
the c of the host of the king of	2Chr 33:11	8269
put c of war in all the fenced	2Chr 33:14	8269
the king had sent c of the army	Neh 2:9	8269
afar off, the thunder of the c	Job 39:25	8269
for thou hast taught them to be c	Jer 13:21	441
Now when all the c of the forces	Jer 40:7	8269
all the c of the forces that were	Jer 40:13	8269
all the c of the forces that were	Jer 41:11	8269
all the c of the forces that were	Jer 41:13	8269
all the c of the forces that were	Jer 41:16	8269
Then all the c of the forces, and	Jer 42:1	8269
all the c of the forces which	Jer 42:8	8269
all the c of the forces, and all	Jer 43:4	8269
all the c of the forces, took all	Jer 43:5	8269
thee will I break in pieces c	Jer 51:23	6346
the c thereof, and all the rulers	Jer 51:28	6346
princes, and her wise men, her c	Jer 51:57	6346
for Jerusalem, to appoint c	Eze 21:22	3733
Which were clothed with blue, c	Eze 23:6	6346
the Assyrians her neighbours, c	Eze 23:12	6346
of them desirable young men, c	Eze 23:23	6346
princes, the governors, and the c	Dan 3:2	6347
the princes, the governors, and c	Dan 3:3	6347
And the princes, governors, and c	Dan 3:27	6347
the counsellors, and the c	Dan 6:7	6347
thy c as the great grasshoppers,	Nah 3:17	2951
a supper to his lords, high c	Mk 6:21	*5506*
with the chief priests and c	Lk 22:4	*4755*
c of the temple, and the elders,	Lk 22:52	*4755*
of hearing, with the chief c	Acts 25:23	*5506*
and the rich men, and the chief c	Rev 6:15	*5506*
flesh of kings, and the flesh of c	Rev 19:18	*5506*

CAPTIVE

that his brother was taken c	Gen 14:14	7617
ones, and their wives took they c	Gen 34:29	7617
of the c that was in the dungeon	Ex 12:29	7628
Asshur shall carry thee away c	Num 24:22	7617
hands, and thou hast taken them c	Deut 21:10	7617
Barak, and lead thy captivity c	Judg 5:12	7617
enemies, which led them away c	1Kin 8:48	7617
before them who carried them c	1Kin 8:50	7617
had brought away c out of the	2Kin 5:2	7617
thou hast taken c with thy sword	2Kin 6:22	7617
and carried them c to Assyria	2Kin 15:29	1540
carried the people of it c to Kir	2Kin 16:9	1540
of Babylon brought c to Babylon	2Kin 24:16	1473
king of Assyria carried away c	1Chr 5:6	1540
land whither they are carried c	2Chr 6:37	7617
children of Judah carry away c	2Chr 25:12	7617
c of their brethren two hundred	2Chr 28:8	7617
ye have taken c of your brethren	2Chr 28:11	7617
before them that lead them c	2Chr 30:9	7617
high, thou hast led captivity c	Ps 68:18	7617
us away c required of us a song	Ps 137:3	7617
my children, and am desolate, a c	Is 49:21	1473
mighty, or the lawful c delivered	Is 49:24	7628
The c exile hasteneth that he may	Is 51:14	6808
of thy neck, O c daughter of Zion	Is 52:2	7628
of Jerusalem c in the fifth month	Jer 1:3	1540
LORD's flock is carried away c	Jer 13:17	7617
shall be carried away c all of it	Jer 13:19	1540
it shall be wholly carried away c	Jer 13:19	1540
shall carry them c into Babylon	Jer 20:4	1540
place whither they have led him c	Jer 22:12	1540
of Babylon had carried away c	Jer 24:1	1540
that are carried away c of Judah	Jer 24:5	1546
when he carried away c Jeconiah	Jer 27:20	1540
and all that is carried away c	Jer 28:6	1473
away c from Jerusalem to Babylon	Jer 29:1	1473
I caused you to be carried away c	Jer 29:14	1540
of the guard carried away c into	Jer 39:9	1540
were carried away c of Jerusalem	Jer 40:1	1546
were carried away c unto Babylon	Jer 40:1	1540
not carried away c to Babylon	Jer 40:7	1540
Then Ishmael carried away c all	Jer 41:10	7617
of Nethaniah carried them away c	Jer 41:10	7617
away c from Mizpah cast about	Jer 41:14	7617
of the guard carried away c	Jer 52:15	1540
away c out of his own land	Jer 52:27	1540
Nebuchadrezzar carried away c	Jer 52:28	1540
c from Jerusalem eight hundred	Jer 52:29	1540
of the guard carried away c of	Jer 52:30	1540
away c the whole captivity	Amos 1:6	1540
Therefore now shall they go c	Amos 6:7	1540
c with the first that go c	Amos 6:7	1540
led away c out of their own land	Amos 7:11	1540
carried away c his forces	Obad 11	7617
And Huzzab shall be led away c	Nah 2:7	1540
be led away c into all nations	Lk 21:24	*163*
up on high, he led captivity c	Eph 4:8	*162*
who are taken c by him at his	2Ti 2:26	*2221*
lead c silly women laden with	2Ti 3:6	*162*

CAPTIVES

as c taken with the sword	Gen 31:26	7617
took all the women of Midian c	Num 31:9	7617
And they brought the c, and the	Num 31:12	7628
your c on the third day, and on	Num 31:19	7628
seest among the c a beautiful	Deut 21:11	7633
blood of the slain and of the c	Deut 32:42	7633
And had taken the women c, that	1Sa 30:2	7617
and their daughters, were taken c	1Sa 30:3	7617
And David's two wives were taken c	1Sa 30:5	7617
away c unto the land of the enemy	1Kin 8:46	7617
land whither they were carried c	1Kin 8:47	7617
land of them that carried them c	1Kin 8:47	7617
of valour, even ten thousand c	2Kin 24:14	1540
they carry them away c unto a	2Chr 6:36	7617
whither they have carried them c	2Chr 6:38	7617
away a great multitude of them c	2Chr 28:5	7633
therefore, and deliver the c again	2Chr 28:11	7633
shall not bring in the c hither	2Chr 28:13	7633
So the armed men left the c	2Chr 28:14	7633
by name rose up, and took the c	2Chr 28:15	7633
smitten Judah, and carried away c	2Chr 28:17	7628
of all those that carried them c	Ps 106:46	7617
and they shall take them c	Is 14:2	7617
them c, whose c they were	Is 14:2	7617
prisoners, and the Ethiopians c	Is 20:4	1546
my city, and he shall let go my c	Is 45:13	1546
Even the c of the mighty shall be	Is 49:25	7628
to proclaim liberty to the c	Is 61:1	7628
of Judah, with all the c of Judah	Jer 28:4	1546
elders which were carried away c	Jer 29:1	1473
unto all that are carried away c	Jer 29:4	1473
caused you to be carried away c	Jer 29:7	1540
and carry us away c into Babylon	Jer 43:3	1540
burn them, and carry them away c	Jer 43:12	7617
for thy sons are taken c, and thy	Jer 48:46	7628
c, and thy daughters c	Jer 48:46	7633
that took them c held them fast	Jer 50:33	7617
as I was among the c by the river	Eze 1:1	1473
whither they shall be carried c	Eze 6:9	7617
of thy c in the midst of them	Eze 16:53	7628
found a man of the c of Judah	Dan 2:25	
shall also carry c into Egypt	Dan 11:8	7628
to preach deliverance to the c	Lk 4:18	*164*

CAPTIVITY

into c unto Sihon king of the	Num 21:29	7628
the raiment of her c from off her	Deut 21:13	7633
for they shall go into c	Deut 28:41	7628
the LORD thy God will turn thy c	Deut 30:3	7622
Barak, and lead thy c captive	Judg 5:12	7628
the day of the c of the land	Judg 18:30	1546
those carried he into c from	2Kin 24:15	1473
thirtieth year of the c of	2Kin 25:27	1546
dwelt in their steads until the c	1Chr 5:22	1473
And Jehozadak went into c, when	1Chr 6:15	
unto thee in the land of their c	2Chr 6:37	7633
their soul in the land of their c	2Chr 6:38	7633
and our wives are in c for this	2Chr 29:9	7628
the c that were brought up from	Ezr 1:11	1473
that went up out of the c	Ezr 2:1	7628
come out of the c unto Jerusalem	Ezr 3:8	7628
the c builded the temple unto the	Ezr 4:1	1473
the rest of the children of the c	Ezr 6:16	1547
the children of the c kept the	Ezr 6:19	1473
for all the children of the c	Ezr 6:20	1473
which were come again out of c	Ezr 6:21	1473
which were come out of the c	Ezr 8:35	1473
of the lands, to the sword, to c	Ezr 9:7	7628
unto all the children of the c	Ezr 10:7	1473
And the children of the c did so	Ezr 10:16	1473
escaped, which were left of the c	Neh 1:2	7628
c there in the province are in	Neh 1:3	7628
them for a prey in the land of c	Neh 4:4	7633
that went up out of the c	Neh 7:6	7628
again out of the c made booths	Neh 8:17	7628
the c which had been carried away	Est 2:6	1473
And the LORD turned the c of Job	Job 42:10	7622
bringeth back the c of his people	Ps 14:7	7622
bringeth back the c of his people	Ps 53:6	7622
on high, thou hast led c captive	Ps 68:18	7628
And delivered his strength into c	Ps 78:61	7628
hast brought back the c of Jacob	Ps 85:1	7622
LORD turned again the c of Zion	Ps 126:1	7622

Turn again our c, O LORD, as the Ps 126:4 7622
my people are gone into c Is 5:13 1540
carry thee away with a mighty c Is 22:17 2925
but themselves are gone into c Is 46:2 7628
are for the c, to the c Jer 15:2 7628
in thine house shall go into c Jer 20:6 7628
and thy lovers shall go into c Jer 22:22 7628
and I will turn away your c Jer 29:14 7622
not gone forth with you into c Jer 29:16 1473
word of the LORD, all ye of the c Jer 29:20 1473
c of Judah which are in Babylon Jer 29:22 1546
Babylon, saying, This c is long Jer 29:28
Send to all them of the c Jer 29:31 1473
again the c of my people Israel Jer 30:3 7622
thy seed from the land of their c Jer 30:10 7628
one of them, shall go into c Jer 30:16 7633
again the c of Jacob's tents Jer 30:18 7622
when I shall bring again their c Jer 31:23 7622
I will cause their c to return Jer 32:44 7622
And I will cause the c of Judah Jer 33:7 7622
the c of Israel to return, and Jer 33:7 7622
cause to return the c of the land Jer 33:11 7622
I will cause their c to return Jer 33:26 7622
and such as are for c to c Jer 43:11 7628
and such as are for c to c Jer 43:11 7628
furnish thyself to go into c Jer 46:19 1473
thy seed from the land of their c Jer 46:27 7633
go forth into c with his priests Jer 48:7 1473
neither hath he gone into c Jer 48:11 1473
the c of Moab in the latter days Jer 48:47 7622
for their king shall go into c Jer 49:3 1473
I will bring again the c of the Jer 49:6 7622
I will bring again the c of Elam Jer 49:39 7622
thirtieth year of the c of Jer 52:31 1546
Judah is gone into c because of Lam 1:3 1540
are gone into c before the enemy Lam 1:5 7628
and my young men are gone into c Lam 1:18 7628
iniquity, to turn away thy c Lam 2:14 7622
no more carry thee away into c Lam 4:22 1540
fifth year of king Jehoiachin's c Eze 1:2 1546
And go, get thee to them of the c Eze 3:11 1473
came to them of the c at Tel-abib Eze 3:15 1473
into Chaldea, to them of the c Eze 11:24 1473
c all the things that the LORD Eze 11:25 1473
as they that go forth into c Eze 12:4 1473
my stuff by day, as stuff for c Eze 12:7 1473
they shall remove and go into c Eze 12:11 7628
When I shall bring again their c Eze 16:53 7622
the c of Sodom and her daughters Eze 16:53 7622
the c of Samaria and her daughters Eze 16:53 7622
then will I bring again the c of Eze 16:53 7622
of Judah, when they went into c Eze 25:3 1473
I will bring again the c of Egypt Eze 29:14 7622
and these cities shall go into c Eze 30:17 7628
and her daughters shall go into c Eze 30:18 7628
pass in the twelfth year of our c Eze 33:21 1546
went into c for their iniquity Eze 39:23 1540
will I bring again the c of Jacob Eze 39:25 7622
be led into c among the heathen Eze 39:28 1473
five and twentieth year of our c Eze 40:1 1546
of the children of the c of Judah Dan 5:13 1547
of the children of the c of Judah Dan 6:13 1547
by the sword, and by flame, by c Dan 11:33 7628
I returned the c of my people Hos 6:11 7622
shall bring again the c of Judah Joel 3:1 7622
of Syria shall go into c unto Kir Amos 1:5 1540
carried away captive the whole c Amos 1:6 1546
delivered up the whole c to Edom Amos 1:9 1546
And their king shall go into c Amos 1:15 1473
for Gilgal shall surely go into c Amos 5:5 1540
you to go into c beyond Damascus Amos 5:27 1540
go into c forth of his land Amos 7:17 1540
though they go into c before Amos 9:4 7628
the c of my people of Israel Amos 9:14 7622
the c of this host of the Obad 20 1546
the c of Jerusalem, which is in Obad 20 1546
they are gone into c from thee Mic 1:16 1540
she carried away, she went into c Nah 3:10 7628
shall gather the c as the sand Hab 1:9 7628
visit them, and turn away their c Zeph 2:7 7622
turn back your c before your eyes Zeph 3:20 7622
Take of them of the c, even of Zec 6:10 1473
of the city shall go forth into c Zec 14:2 1473
bringing me into c to the law of Rom 7:23 *163*
bringing into c every thought to 2Cor 10:5 *163*
he led c captive, and gave gifts Eph 4:8 *161*
into c shall go into c Rev 13:10 *161*

CARBUNCLE
be a sardius, a topaz, and a c Ex 28:17 1304
was a sardius, a topaz, and a c Ex 39:10 1304
sapphire, the emerald, and the c Eze 28:13 1304

CARBUNCLES
of agates, and thy gates of c Is 54:12 68

CARCAS (*car'-cas*) *A servant of King Ahasuerus.*
Bigtha, and Abagtha, Zethar, and C Est 1:10 3752

CARCASE
whether it be a c of an unclean Lev 5:2 5038
or a c of unclean cattle, or the Lev 5:2 5038
or the c of unclean creeping Lev 5:2 5038
their c shall ye not touch Lev 11:8 5038
whosoever toucheth the c of them Lev 11:24 5038
c of them shall wash his clothes Lev 11:25 5038
whoso toucheth their c shall be Lev 11:27 5038
he that beareth the c of them Lev 11:28 5038
their c falleth shall be unclean Lev 11:35 5038
toucheth their c shall be unclean Lev 11:36 5038
if any part of their c fall upon Lev 11:37 5038
any part of their c fall thereon Lev 11:38 5038
he that toucheth the c thereof Lev 11:39 5038
he that eateth of the c of it Lev 11:40 5038
he also that beareth the c of it Lev 11:40 5038
flesh, nor touch their dead c Deut 14:8 5038
thy c shall be meat unto all Deut 28:26 5038
take his c down from the tree Josh 8:29 5038
aside to see the c of the lion Judg 14:8 4658
and honey in the c of the lion Judg 14:8 1472
honey out of the c of the lion Judg 14:9 1472
thy c shall not come unto the 1Kin 13:22 5038
his c was cast in the way, and the 1Kin 13:24 5038
it, the lion also stood by the c 1Kin 13:24 5038
saw the c cast in the way 1Kin 13:25 5038
and the lion standing by the c 1Kin 13:25 5038
found his c cast in the way, and 1Kin 13:28 5038
ass and the lion standing by the c 1Kin 13:28 5038
the lion had not eaten the c 1Kin 13:28 5038
took up the c of the man of God 1Kin 13:29 5038
he laid his c in his own grave 1Kin 13:30 5038
the c of Jezebel shall be as dung 2Kin 9:37 5038
as a c trodden under feet Is 14:19 6297
For wheresoever the c is, there Mt 24:28 *4430*

CARCASES
the fowls came down upon the c Gen 15:11 6297
shall have their c in abomination Lev 11:11 5038
The c of every beast which Lev 11:26 6297
cast your c upon the c of Lev 26:30 6297
Your c shall fall in this Num 14:29 6297
But as for you, your c, they Num 14:32 6297
until your c be wasted in the Num 14:33 6297
I will give the c of the host of 1Sa 17:46 6297
their c were torn in the midst of Is 5:25 5038
shall come up out of their c Is 34:3 6297
look upon the c of the men that Is 66:24 6297
the c of this people shall be Jer 7:33 5038
Even the c of men shall fall as Jer 9:22 5038
their c shall be meat for the Jer 16:4 5038
with the c of their detestable Jer 16:18 5038
their c will I give to be meat Jer 19:7 5038
I will lay the dead c of the Eze 6:5 6297
nor by the c of their kings in Eze 43:7 6297
the c of their kings, far from me Eze 43:9 6297
of slain, and a great number of c Nah 3:3 6297
whose c fell in the wilderness Heb 3:17 *2966*

CARCHEMISH (*car'-ke-mish*) See CHARCHEMISH. *A city on the Euphrates River.*
Is not Calno as C Is 10:9 3751
was by the river Euphrates in C Jer 46:2 3751

CARE
hath left the c of the asses 1Sa 10:2 1697
flee away, they will not c for us 2Sa 18:3
of us die, will they c for us 2Sa 18:3
careful for us with all this c 2Kin 4:13 2731
nation, that dwelleth without c Jer 49:31 983
eat bread by weight, and with c Eze 4:16 1674
the c of this world, and the Mt 13:22 *3308*
him to an inn, and took c of him Lk 10:34 *1959*
and said unto him, Take c of him Lk 10:35 *1959*
dost thou not c that my sister Lk 10:40 *3199*
c not for it 1Cor 7:21 *3199*
Doth God take c for oxen 1Cor 9:9 *3199*
have the same c one for another 1Cor 12:25 *3309*
but that our c for you in the 2Cor 7:12 *4710*
which put the same earnest c into 2Cor 8:16 *4710*
the c of all the churches 2Cor 11:28 *3308*
will naturally c for your state Phil 2:20 *3309*
that now at the last your c of me Phil 4:10 *5426*
how shall he take c of the church 1Ti 3:5 *1959*
Casting all your c upon him 1Pet 5:7 *3308*

CAREAH (*ca-re'-ah*) See KAREAH. *Father of Johanan.*
and Johanan the son of C, and 2Kin 25:23 7143

CARED
no man c for my soul Ps 142:4 1875
not that he c for the poor Jn 12:6 *3199*
Gallio c for none of those things Acts 18:17 *3199*

CAREFUL
thou hast been c for us with all 2Kin 4:13 2729
shall not be c in the year of Jer 17:8 1672
we are not c to answer thee in Dan 3:16 2818
her, Martha, Martha, thou art c Lk 10:41 *3309*
Be c for nothing Phil 4:6 *3309*
wherein ye were also c, but ye Phil 4:10 *5426*
might be c to maintain good works Titus 3:8 *5431*

CAREFULLY
Only if thou c hearken unto the Deut 15:5 8085
of Maroth waited c for good Mic 1:12 2470
I sent him therefore the more c Phil 2:28 *4708*
though he sought it c with tears Heb 12:17 *1567*

CAREFULNESS
water with trembling and with c Eze 12:18 1674
They shall eat their bread with c Eze 12:19 1674
But I would have you without c 1Cor 7:32 *275*
what c it wrought in you, yea, 2Cor 7:11 *4710*

CARELESS
were therein, how they dwelt c Judg 18:7 983
hear my voice, ye c daughters Is 32:9 982
shall ye be troubled, ye c women Is 32:10 982
be troubled, ye c ones Is 32:11 982
to make the c Ethiopians afraid Eze 30:9 983

CARELESSLY
to pleasures, that dwellest c Is 47:8 983
them that dwell c in the isles Eze 39:6 983
the rejoicing city that dwelt c Zeph 2:15 983

CARES
the c of this world, and the Mk 4:19 *3303*
go forth, and are choked with c Lk 8:14 *3303*
c of this life, and so that day Lk 21:34 *3303*

CAREST
neither c thou for any man Mt 22:16 *3199*
c thou not that we perish Mk 4:38 *3199*
thou art true, and c for no man Mk 12:14 *3199*

CARETH
land which the LORD thy God c for Deut 11:12 1875
hireling, and c not for the sheep Jn 10:13 *3199*
He that is unmarried c for the 1Cor 7:32 *3309*
But he that is married c for the 1Cor 7:33 *3309*
The unmarried woman c for the 1Cor 7:34 *3309*
but she that is married c for the 1Cor 7:34 *3309*
for he c for you 1Pet 5:7 *3199*

CARING
my father leave c for the asses 1Sa 9:5

CARKAS See CARCAS.

CARMEL (*car'-mel*) See CARMELITE.
1. A mountain range in Canaan.
the king of Jokneam of C, one Josh 12:22 3760
and reacheth to C westward Josh 19:26 3760
Samuel, saying, Saul came to C 1Sa 15:12 3760
to me all Israel unto mount C 1Kin 18:19 3760
prophets together unto mount C 1Kin 18:20 3760
And Elijah went up to the top of C 1Kin 18:42 3760
And he went from thence to mount C 2Kin 2:25 3760
unto the man of God to mount C 2Kin 4:25 3760
and into the forest of his C 2Kin 19:23 3760
in the mountains, and in C 2Chr 26:10 3760
Thine head upon thee is like C Song 7:5 3760
and C shake off their fruits Is 33:9 3760
unto it, the excellency of C Is 35:2 3760
border, and the forest of his C Is 37:24 3760
as C by the sea, so shall he come Jer 46:18 3760
habitation, and he shall feed on C Jer 50:19 3760
the top of C shall wither Amos 1:2 3760
hide themselves in the top of C Amos 9:3 3760
in the wood, in the midst of C Mic 7:14 3760
Bashan languisheth, and C, and the Nah 1:4 3760
2. A town in Judah.
Maon, C, and Ziph, and Juttah, Josh 15:55 3760
Maon, whose possessions were in C 1Sa 25:2 3760
and he was shearing his sheep in C 1Sa 25:2 3760
the young men, Get you up to C 1Sa 25:5 3760
all the while they were in C 1Sa 25:7 3760
David were come to Abigail to C 1Sa 25:40 3760

CARMELITE (*car'-mel-ite*) See CARMELITESS.
An inhabitant of Carmel 2.
Abigail the wife of Nabal the C 1Sa 30:5 3761
and Abigail Nabal's wife the C 2Sa 2:2 3761
Abigail the wife of Nabal the C 2Sa 3:3 3761
Hezrai the C, Paarai the Arbite, 2Sa 23:35 3761
Hezro the C, Naarai the son of 1Chr 11:37 3761

CARMELITESS (*car'-mel-i-tess*)
Jezreelitess, and Abigail the C 1Sa 27:3 3762
second Daniel, of Abigail the C 1Chr 3:1 3762

CARMI (*car'-mi*) See CARMITES.
1. Father of Achan.
for Achan, the son of C, the son Josh 7:1 3756
and Achan, the son of C, the son Josh 7:18 3756
And the sons of C 1Chr 2:7 3756
Pharez, Hezron, and C, and Hur, and 1Chr 4:1 3756
2. A son of Reuben.
and Phallu, and Hezron, and C Gen 46:9 3756
Hanoch, and Pallu, Hezron, and C Ex 6:14 3756
of C, the family of the Carmites Num 26:6 3756
Hanoch, and Pallu, Hezron, and C 1Chr 5:3 3756

CARMITES (*car'-mites*) *Descendants of Carmi 2.*
of Carmi, the family of the C Num 26:6 3757

CARNAL
but I am c, sold under sin Rom 7:14 *4559*
Because the c mind is enmity Rom 8:7 *4561*
to minister unto them in c things Rom 15:27 *4559*
as unto spiritual, but as unto c 1Cor 3:1 *4559*
For ye are yet c 1Cor 3:3 *4559*
and divisions, are ye not c 1Cor 3:3 *4559*
are ye not c? 1Cor 3:4 *4559*
if we shall reap your c things 1Cor 9:11 *4559*
weapons of our warfare are not c 2Cor 10:4 *4559*
after the law of a c commandment Heb 7:16 *4559*
c ordinances, imposed on them Heb 9:10 *4561*

CARNALLY
lie c with thy neighbour's wife Lev 18:20 2233
And whosoever lieth c with a woman Lev 19:20 2233
And a man lie with her c, and it be Num 5:13 2233
For to be c minded is death Rom 8:6 *4561*

CARPENTER
So the c encouraged the goldsmith Is 41:7 2796
The c stretcheth out his rule Is 44:13 2796
Is not this the c, the son of Mk 6:3 *5045*

CARPENTER'S
Is not this the c son Mt 13:55 *5045*

CARPENTERS
to David, and cedar trees, and c 2Sa 5:11 2796
and they laid it out to the c 2Kin 12:11 6086
Unto c, and builders, and masons, 2Kin 22:6 2796
of cedars, with masons and c 1Chr 14:1 2796
c to repair the house of the LORD 2Chr 24:12 2796
also unto the masons, and to the c Ezr 3:7 2796
the princes of Judah, with the c Jer 24:1 2796
of Judah and Jerusalem, and the c Jer 29:2 2796
And the LORD shewed me four c Zec 1:20 2796

CARPUS (*car'-pus*) *A friend of Paul.*
cloke that I left at Troas with C 2Ti 4:13 *2591*

CARRIAGE
the cattle and the c before them Judg 18:21 3520
David left his c in the hand of 1Sa 17:22 3627
the hand of the keeper of the c 1Sa 17:22 3627

CARRIAGES
at Michmash he hath laid up his c........ Is 10:28 3627
your c were heavy loaden........ Is 46:1 5385
after those days we took up our c........ Acts 21:15 *643*

CARRIED
he c away all his cattle, and all........ Gen 31:18 5090
c away my daughters, as captives........ Gen 31:26 5090
of Israel c Jacob their father........ Gen 46:5 5375
For his sons c him into the land........ Gen 50:13 5375
c them in their coats out of the........ Lev 10:5 5375
c them over with them unto the........ Josh 4:8 5674
c them up to the top of an hill........ Judg 16:3 5927
of Israel be c about unto Gath........ 1Sa 5:8 5437
they c the ark of the God of........ 1Sa 5:8 5437
that, after they had c it about........ 1Sa 5:9 5437
but c them away, and went on their........ 1Sa 30:2 5090
that the Amalekites had c away........ 1Sa 30:18 3947
but David c it aside into the........ 2Sa 6:10 5186
Abiathar c the ark of God again........ 2Sa 15:29 7725
land whither they were c captives........ 1Kin 8:47 7617
land of them that c them captives........ 1Kin 8:47 7617
before them who c them captive........ 1Kin 8:50 7617
c him up into a loft, where he........ 1Kin 17:19 5927
Then they c him forth out of the........ 1Kin 21:13 3318
c thence silver, and gold, and........ 2Kin 7:8 5375
c thence also, and went and hid it........ 2Kin 7:8 5375
his servants c him in a chariot........ 2Kin 9:28 7392
c them captive to Assyria........ 2Kin 15:29 1540
c the people of it captive to Kir........ 2Kin 16:9 1540
c Israel away into Assyria, and........ 2Kin 17:6 1540
whom the LORD c away before them........ 2Kin 17:11 1540
So was Israel c away out of their........ 2Kin 17:23 1540
they had c away from Samaria came........ 2Kin 17:28 1540
whom they c away from thence........ 2Kin 17:33 1540
this day, shall be c into Babylon........ 2Kin 20:17 5375
c the ashes of them unto Beth-el........ 2Kin 23:4 5375
his servants c him in a chariot........ 2Kin 23:30 7392
he c out thence all the treasures........ 2Kin 24:13 3318
he c away all Jerusalem, and all........ 2Kin 24:14 1540
he c away Jehoiachin to Babylon,........ 2Kin 24:15 1540
those c he into captivity from........ 2Kin 24:15 1980
of brass, and c him to Babylon........ 2Kin 25:7 935
c the brass of them to Babylon........ 2Kin 25:13 5375
So Judah was c away out of their........ 2Kin 25:21 1540
king of Assyria c away captive........ 1Chr 5:6 1540
and he c them away, even the........ 1Chr 5:26 1540
when the LORD c away Judah........ 1Chr 6:15 1540
who were c away to Babylon for........ 1Chr 9:1 1540
they c the ark of God in a new........ 1Chr 13:7 7392
but c it aside into the house of........ 1Chr 13:13 5186
land whither they are c captive........ 2Chr 6:37 7617
whither they have c them captives........ 2Chr 6:38 7617
he c away also the shields of........ 2Chr 12:9 3947
they c away very much spoil........ 2Chr 14:13 5375
c away sheep and camels in........ 2Chr 14:15 7617
they c away the stones of Ramah,........ 2Chr 16:6 5375
c away all the substance that was........ 2Chr 21:17 7617
it, and c it to his place again........ 2Chr 24:11 7725
c away a great multitude of them........ 2Chr 28:5 7617
the children of Israel c away........ 2Chr 28:8 7617
c all the feeble of them upon........ 2Chr 28:15 5095
smitten Judah, and c away captives........ 2Chr 28:17 7617
with fetters, and c him to Babylon........ 2Chr 33:11 3212
Shaphan c the book to the king,........ 2Chr 34:16 935
his brother, and c him to Egypt........ 2Chr 36:4 935
Nebuchadnezzar also c of the........ 2Chr 36:7 935
the sword c he away to Babylon........ 2Chr 36:20 1473
of those which had been c away........ Ezr 2:1 1540
Babylon had c away unto Babylon........ Ezr 2:1 1540
c the people away into Babylon........ Ezr 5:12 1541
of those that had been c away........ Ezr 8:35 1473
of those that had been c away........ Ezr 9:4 1473
of them that had been c away........ Ezr 10:6 1473
of those that had been c away........ Ezr 10:8 1473
of those that had been c away........ Neh 7:6 1473
the king of Babylon had c away........ Neh 7:6 1540
Who had been c away from........ Est 2:6 1540
been c away with Jeconiah king of........ Est 2:6 1540
the king of Babylon had c away........ Est 2:6 1540
have c them away, yea, and slain........ Job 1:17 3947
of the froward is c headlong........ Job 5:13 4116
I should have been c from the........ Job 10:19 2986
though the mountains be c into........ Ps 46:2 4131
of all those that c them captives........ Ps 106:46 7617
For there they that c us away........ Ps 137:3 7617
this day, shall be c to Babylon........ Is 39:6 5375
which are c from the womb........ Is 46:3 5375
shall be c upon their shoulders........ Is 49:22 5375
our griefs, and c our sorrows........ Is 53:4 5445
c them all the days of old........ Is 63:9 5375
LORD's flock is c away captive........ Jer 13:17 7617
Judah shall be c away captive all........ Jer 13:19 1540
it shall be wholly c away captive........ Jer 13:19 1540
king of Babylon had c away........ Jer 24:1 1540
that are c away captive of Judah........ Jer 24:5 1546
when he c away captive Jeconiah........ Jer 27:20 1546
They shall be c to Babylon........ Jer 27:22 935
this place, and c them to Babylon........ Jer 28:3 935
all that is c away captive, from........ Jer 28:6 1473
elders which were c away captives........ Jer 29:1 1473
c away captive from Jerusalem to........ Jer 29:1 1540
unto all that are c away captives........ Jer 29:4 1473
to be c away from Jerusalem unto........ Jer 29:4 1540
caused you to be c away captives........ Jer 29:7 1540
I caused you to be c away captive........ Jer 29:14 1540
the captain of the guard c away........ Jer 39:9 1540
were c away captive of Jerusalem........ Jer 40:1 1546
which were c away captive unto........ Jer 40:1 1540
of them that were not c away........ Jer 40:7 1540
Then Ishmael c away captive all........ Jer 41:10 7617
of Nethaniah c them away captive........ Jer 41:10 7617
c away captive from Mizpah cast........ Jer 41:14 7617
c him up unto the king of Babylon........ Jer 52:9 5927
c him to Babylon, and put him in........ Jer 52:11 935
the captain of the guard c away........ Jer 52:15 1540
c all the brass of them to........ Jer 52:17 5375
Thus Judah was c away captive out........ Jer 52:27 1540
Nebuchadrezzar c away captive........ Jer 52:28 1540
year of Nebuchadrezzar he c away........ Jer 52:29
the captain of the guard c away........ Jer 52:30 1540
whither they shall be c captives........ Eze 6:9 7617
c it into a land of traffick........ Eze 17:4 935
c me out in the spirit of the........ Eze 37:1 3318
which he c into the land of........ Dan 1:2 935
the wind c them away, that no........ Dan 2:35 5376
It shall be also c unto Assyria........ Hos 10:6 2986
Assyrians, and oil is c into Egypt........ Hos 12:1 2986
have c into your temples my........ Joel 3:5 935
because they c away captive the........ Amos 1:6 1540
c away captive his forces........ Obad 11 7617
Yet was she c away, she went into........ Nah 3:10 1473
time they were c away to Babylon........ Mt 1:11 *3350*
c him away, and delivered him to........ Mk 15:1 *667*
there was a dead man c out........ Lk 7:12 *1580*
died, and was c by the angels into........ Lk 16:22 *667*
from them, and c up into heaven........ Lk 24:51 *339*
lame from his mother's womb was c........ Acts 3:2 *941*
up, and c him out, and buried him........ Acts 5:6 *1627*
were c over into Sychem, and laid........ Acts 7:16 *3346*
devout men c Stephen to his........ Acts 8:2 *4792*
him to be c into the castle........ Acts 21:34 *71*
c away unto these dumb idols,........ 1Cor 12:2 *520*
c away with their dissimulation........ Gal 2:13 *4879*
c about with every wind of........ Eph 4:14 *4064*
Be not c about with divers and........ Heb 13:9 *4064*
clouds that are c with a tempest........ 2Pet 2:17 *1643*
without water, c about of winds........ Jude 12 *4064*
her to be c away of the flood........ Rev 12:15 *4216*
So he c me away in the spirit........ Rev 17:3 *667*
he c me away in the spirit to a........ Rev 21:10 *667*

CARRIEST
Thou c them away as with a flood........ Ps 90:5 2229

CARRIETH
and as chaff that the storm c away........ Job 21:18 1589
The east wind c him away, and he........ Job 27:21 5375
woman, and of the beast that c her........ Rev 17:7 *941*

CARRY
going to c it down to Egypt........ Gen 37:25 3381
c corn for the famine of your........ Gen 42:19 935
c down the man a present, a........ Gen 43:11 3381
sacks, c it again in your hand........ Gen 43:12 7725
with food, as much as they can c........ Gen 44:1 5375
which Joseph had sent to c him........ Gen 45:27 5375
which Pharaoh had sent to c him........ Gen 46:5 5375
thou shalt c me out of Egypt, and........ Gen 47:30 5375
ye shall c up my bones from hence........ Gen 50:25 5927
thou shalt not c forth ought of........ Ex 12:46 3318
ye shall c up my bones away hence........ Ex 13:19 5927
to c us forth out of Egypt........ Ex 14:11 3318
go not with me, c us not up hence........ Ex 33:15 5927
c forth without the camp unto a........ Lev 4:12 3318
he shall c forth the bullock........ Lev 4:21 3318
c forth the ashes without the........ Lev 6:11 3318
c your brethren from before the........ Lev 10:4 5375
he shall c them forth out of the........ Lev 14:45 3318
shall one c forth without the........ Lev 16:27 3318
C them in thy bosom, as a nursing........ Num 11:12 5375
Asshur shall c thee away captive........ Num 24:22 7617
so that thou art not able to c it........ Deut 14:24 5375
Thou shalt c much seed out into........ Deut 28:38 3318
ye shall c them over with you, and........ Josh 4:3 5674
c these ten cheeses unto the........ 1Sa 17:18 935
unto him, Go, c them to the city........ 1Sa 20:40 935
C back the ark of God into the........ 2Sa 15:25 7725
to c over the king's household........ 2Sa 19:18 5674
so that they c them away captives........ 1Kin 8:46 7617
shall c thee whither I know not........ 1Kin 18:12 5375
then c him out, and stone him,........ 1Kin 21:10 3318
c him back unto Amon the governor........ 1Kin 22:26 7725
hand, and c me out of the host........ 1Kin 22:34 3318
to a lad, C him to his mother........ 2Kin 4:19 5375
c him to an inner chamber........ 2Kin 9:2 935
C thither one of the priests whom........ 2Kin 17:27 1980
the king of Assyria did c away........ 2Kin 18:11 1540
the captain of the guard c away........ 2Kin 25:11 1540
to c tidings unto their idols, and........ 1Chr 10:9 1319
None ought to c the ark of God........ 1Chr 15:2 5375
LORD chosen to c the ark of God........ 1Chr 15:2 5375
shall no more c the tabernacle........ 1Chr 23:26 5375
thou shalt c it up to Jerusalem........ 2Chr 2:16 5927
they c them away captives unto a........ 2Chr 6:36 7617
c him back to Amon the governor........ 2Chr 18:25 7725
that thou mayest c me out of the........ 2Chr 18:33 3318
more than they could c away........ 2Chr 20:25 4853
children of Judah c away captive........ 2Chr 25:12 7617
c forth the filthiness out of the........ 2Chr 29:5 3318
to c it out abroad into the brook........ 2Chr 29:16 3318
in fetters, to c him to Babylon........ 2Chr 36:6 3212
c them into the temple that is in........ Ezr 5:15 5182
to c the silver and gold, which........ Ezr 7:15 2987
Why doth thine heart c thee away........ Job 15:12 3947
he dieth he shall c nothing away........ Ps 49:17 3947
which he may c away in his hand........ Eccl 5:15 3212
bird of the air shall c the voice........ Eccl 10:20 3212
shall c it away safe, and none........ Is 5:29 6403
shall they c away to the brook of........ Is 15:7 5375
the LORD will c thee away with a........ Is 22:17 2904
her own feet shall c her afar off........ Is 23:7 2986
they will c their riches upon the........ Is 30:6 5375
c them in his bosom, and shall........ Is 40:11 5375
and the wind shall c them away........ Is 41:16 5375
even to hoar hairs will I c you........ Is 46:4 5445
even I will c, and will deliver........ Is 46:4 5445
him upon the shoulder, they c him........ Is 46:7 5445
the wind shall c them all away........ Is 57:13 5375
Neither c forth a burden out of........ Jer 17:22 3318
he shall c them captive into........ Jer 20:4 1540
take them, and c them to Babylon........ Jer 20:5 935
with chains, to c him to Babylon........ Jer 39:7 935
that he should c him home........ Jer 39:14 3318
c us away captives into Babylon........ Jer 43:3 1540
them, and c them away captives........ Jer 43:12 7617
he will no more c thee away into........ Lam 4:22 1540
in their sight, and c out thereby........ Eze 12:5 3318
c it forth in the twilight........ Eze 12:6 3318
through the wall to c out thereby........ Eze 12:12 3318
men that c tales to shed blood........ Eze 22:9 7400
to c away silver and gold, to take........ Eze 38:13 5375
shall also c captives into Egypt........ Dan 11:8 935
began to c about in beds those........ Mk 6:55 *4046*
c any vessel through the temple........ Mk 11:16 *1308*
C neither purse, nor scrip, nor........ Lk 10:4 *941*
not lawful for thee to c thy bed........ Jn 5:10 *142*
c thee whither thou wouldest not........ Jn 21:18 *5342*
at the door, and shall c thee out........ Acts 5:9 *1627*
I will c you away beyond Babylon........ Acts 7:43 *3351*
is certain we can c nothing out........ 1Ti 6:7 *1627*

CARRYING
one c three kids, and another........ 1Sa 10:3 5375
another c three loaves of bread,........ 1Sa 10:3 5375
another c a bottle of wine........ 1Sa 10:3 5375
c bows, turned back in the day of........ Ps 78:9 7411
unto the c away of Jerusalem........ Jer 1:3 1540
from David until the c away into........ Mt 1:17 *3350*
from the c away into Babylon unto........ Mt 1:17 *3350*
c her forth, buried her by her........ Acts 5:10 *1627*

CARSHENA (*car-she'-nah*) *A Persian prince.*
And the next unto him was C........ Est 1:14 3771

CART
Now therefore make a new c........ 1Sa 6:7 5699
no yoke, and tie the kine to the c........ 1Sa 6:7 5699
of the LORD, and lay it upon the c........ 1Sa 6:8 5699
milch kine, and tied them to the c........ 1Sa 6:10 5699
the ark of the LORD upon the c........ 1Sa 6:11 5699
the c came into the field of........ 1Sa 6:14 5699
and they clave the wood of the c........ 1Sa 6:14 5699
set the ark of God upon a new c........ 2Sa 6:3 5699
sons of Abinadab, drave the new c........ 2Sa 6:3 5699
c out of the house of Abinadab........ 1Chr 13:7 5699
and Uzza and Ahio drave the c........ 1Chr 13:7 5699
and sin as it were with a c rope........ Is 5:18 5699
neither is a c wheel turned about........ Is 28:27 5699
break it with the wheel of his c........ Is 28:28 5699
as a c is pressed that is full of........ Amos 2:13 5699

CARVED
house, and fetched the c image........ Judg 18:18 6459
the house within was c with knops........ 1Kin 6:18 4734
he c all the walls of the house........ 1Kin 6:29 7049
about with c figures of cherubims........ 1Kin 6:29 6603
he c upon them carvings of........ 1Kin 6:32 7049
he c thereon cherubims and palm........ 1Kin 6:35 7049
with gold fitted upon the c work........ 1Kin 6:35 2707
And he set a c image, the idol........ 2Chr 33:7 6459
the c images which Manasseh his........ 2Chr 33:22 6456
the c images, and the molten........ 2Chr 34:3 6456
the c images, and the molten........ 2Chr 34:4 6456
But now they break down the c........ Ps 74:6 6603
with c works, with fine linen of........ Prov 7:16 2405

CARVING
in c of timber, to work in all........ Ex 31:5 2799
in c of wood, to make any manner........ Ex 35:33 2799

CARVINGS
carved upon them c of cherubims........ 1Kin 6:32 4734

CASE
did see that they were in evil c........ Ex 5:19
this is the c of the slayer,........ Deut 19:4 1697
thou shalt in any c bring them........ Deut 22:1 7725
In any c thou shalt deliver him........ Deut 24:13 7725
that people, that is in such a c........ Ps 144:15 3602
ye shall in no c enter into the........ Mt 5:20 *3364*
If the c of the man be so with........ Mt 19:10 *156*
been now a long time in that c........ Jn 5:6

CASEMENT
of my house I looked through my c........ Prov 7:6 822

CASES
is not under bondage in such c........ 1Cor 7:15

CASIPHIA (*cas-if'-e-ah*) *A place in Syria.*
Iddo the chief at the place C........ Ezr 8:17 3703
the Nethinims, at the place C........ Ezr 8:17 3703

CASLUHIM (*cas'-loo-him*) *Descendants of Mizraim.*
And Pathrusim, and C, (out of whom........ Gen 10:14 3695
And Pathrusim, and C........ 1Chr 1:12 3695

CASLUHITES See CASLUHIM.

CASSIA
of c five hundred shekels, after........ Ex 30:24 6916
smell of myrrh, and aloes, and c........ Ps 45:8 7102
bright iron, c, and calamus, were........ Eze 27:19 6916

CAST
C out this bondwoman and her son........ Gen 21:10 1644
she c the child under one of the........ Gen 21:15 7993
she goats have not c their young........ Gen 31:38 7921
pillar, which I have c betwixt me........ Gen 31:51 3384
c him into some pit, and we will........ Gen 37:20 7993
but c him into this pit that is........ Gen 37:22 7993
took him, and c him into a pit........ Gen 37:24 7993
wife c her eyes upon Joseph........ Gen 39:7 5375
is born ye shall c into the river........ Ex 1:22 7993
And he said, C it on the ground........ Ex 4:3 7993
he c it on the ground, and it........ Ex 4:3 7993
c it at his feet, and said, Surely........ Ex 4:25 5060
c it before Pharaoh, and it shall........ Ex 7:9 7993

Context	Reference	Number
Aaron c down his rod before	Ex 7:10	7993
For they c down every man his rod	Ex 7:12	7993
and c them into the Red sea	Ex 10:19	8628
his host hath he c into the sea	Ex 15:4	3384
when he had c into the waters	Ex 15:25	7993
ye shall c it to the dogs	Ex 22:31	7993
There shall nothing c their young	Ex 23:26	7921
thou shalt c four rings of gold	Ex 25:12	3332
thou shalt c five sockets of	Ex 26:37	3332
he c the tables out of his hands,	Ex 32:19	7993
then I c it into the fire, and	Ex 32:24	7993
For I will c out the nations	Ex 34:24	3423
he c for them four sockets of	Ex 36:36	3332
he c for it four rings of gold,	Ex 37:3	3332
he c for it four rings of gold,	Ex 37:13	3332
he c four rings for the four ends	Ex 38:5	3332
c the sockets of the sanctuary	Ex 38:27	3332
c it beside the altar on the east	Lev 1:16	7993
they shall c them into an unclean	Lev 14:40	7993
Aaron shall c lots upon the two	Lev 16:8	5414
defiled which I c out before you	Lev 18:24	7971
nation, which I c out before you	Lev 20:23	7971
c your carcases upon the carcases	Lev 26:30	5414
enemies, I will not c them away	Lev 26:44	3988
c it into the midst of the	Num 19:6	7993
or have c upon him any thing	Num 35:22	7993
c it upon him, that he die, and	Num 35:23	5307
To c out all thine enemies from	Deut 6:19	1920
hath c out many nations before	Deut 7:1	5390
hath c them out from before thee	Deut 9:4	1920
c them out of my two hands, and	Deut 9:17	7993
I c the dust thereof into the	Deut 9:21	7993
for thine olive shall c his fruit	Deut 28:40	5394
c them into another land, as it	Deut 29:28	7993
c it at the entering of the gate	Josh 8:29	7993
that the LORD c down great stones	Josh 10:11	7993
c them into the cave wherein they	Josh 10:27	7993
did Moses smite, and c them out	Josh 13:12	3423
that I may c lots for you here	Josh 18:6	3384
that I may here c lots for you	Josh 18:8	7993
Joshua c lots for them in Shiloh	Josh 18:10	7993
the altar of Baal was c down	Judg 6:28	5422
because he hath c down the altar	Judg 6:30	5422
because one hath c down his altar	Judg 6:31	5422
did c therein every man the	Judg 8:25	7993
a certain woman c a piece of a	Judg 9:53	7993
that he c away the jawbone out of	Judg 15:17	7993
C lots between me and Jonathan my	1Sa 14:42	5307
And Saul c the javelin	1Sa 18:11	2904
Saul c a javelin at him to smite	1Sa 20:33	2904
of the mighty is vilely c away	2Sa 1:21	1602
did not a woman c a piece of a	2Sa 11:21	7993
he c stones at David, and at all	2Sa 16:6	5619
and threw stones at him, and c dust	2Sa 16:13	6080
c him into a great pit in the	2Sa 18:17	7993
c a cloth upon him, when he saw	2Sa 20:12	7993
they c up a bank against the city	2Sa 20:15	8210
of Bichri, and c it out to Joab	2Sa 20:22	7993
For he c two pillars of brass, of	1Kin 7:15	6696
c in two rows, when it was c	1Kin 7:24	3333
of Jordan did the king c them	1Kin 7:46	3332
my name, will I c out of my sight	1Kin 9:7	7971
and his carcase was c in the way	1Kin 13:24	7993
and saw the carcase c in the way	1Kin 13:25	7993
and found his carcase c in the way	1Kin 13:28	7993
hast c me behind thy back	1Kin 14:9	7993
LORD c out before the children of	1Kin 14:24	3403
he c himself down upon the earth,	1Kin 18:42	1457
by him, and c his mantle upon him	1Kin 19:19	7993
whom the LORD c out before the	1Kin 21:26	3423
c him upon some mountain, or into	2Kin 2:16	7993
c the salt in there, and said,	2Kin 2:21	7993
of land c every man his stone	2Kin 3:25	7993
And he c it into the pot	2Kin 4:41	7993
down a stick, and c it in thither	2Kin 6:6	7993
Syrians had c away in their haste	2Kin 7:15	7993
c him in the portion of the field	2Kin 9:25	7993
c him into the plat of ground,	2Kin 9:26	7993
guard and the captains c them out	2Kin 10:25	7993
they c the man into the sepulchre	2Kin 13:21	7993
neither c he them from his	2Kin 13:23	7993
whom the LORD c out from before	2Kin 16:3	3423
whom the LORD c out from before	2Kin 17:8	3423
until he had c them out of his	2Kin 17:20	7993
have c their gods into the fire	2Kin 19:18	5414
shield, nor c a bank against it	2Kin 19:32	8210
whom the LORD c out before the	2Kin 21:2	3423
c the powder thereof upon the	2Kin 23:6	7993
c the dust of them into the brook	2Kin 23:12	7993
will c off this city Jerusalem	2Kin 23:27	3988
until he had c them out from his	2Kin 24:20	7993
These likewise c lots over	1Chr 24:31	5307
And they c lots, ward against ward	1Chr 25:8	5307
And they c lots, as well the small	1Chr 26:13	5307
a wise counsellor, they c lots	1Chr 26:14	5307
he will c thee off for ever	1Chr 28:9	2186
Two rows of oxen were c	2Chr 4:3	3332
when it was c	2Chr 4:3	4166
of Jordan did the king c them	2Chr 4:17	3332
will I c out of my sight, and will	2Chr 7:20	7993
his sons had c them off from	2Chr 11:14	2186
Have ye not c out the priests of	2Chr 13:9	5080
to come to c us out of thy	2Chr 20:11	1644
c into the chest, until they had	2Chr 24:10	7993
hath power to help, and to c down	2Chr 25:8	3782
c them down from the top of the	2Chr 25:12	7993
and bows, and slings to c stones	2Chr 26:14	
had c out before the children of	2Chr 28:3	3423
did c away in his transgression	2Chr 29:19	2186
c them into the brook Kidron	2Chr 30:14	7993
whom the LORD had c out before	2Chr 33:2	3423
and c them out of the city	2Chr 33:15	7993
though there were of you c out	Neh 1:9	5080
they were much c down in their	Neh 6:16	5307
c thy law behind their backs, and	Neh 9:26	7993
we c the lots among the priests,	Neh 10:34	5307
rest of the people also c lots	Neh 11:1	5307
therefore I c forth all the	Neh 13:8	7993
of king Ahasuerus, they c Pur	Est 3:7	5307
to destroy them, and had c Pur	Est 9:24	5307
he have c them away for their	Job 8:4	7971
God will not c away a perfect man	Job 8:20	3988
shall c off his flower as the	Job 15:33	7993
his own counsel shall c him down	Job 18:7	7993
For he is c into a net by his own	Job 18:8	7971
God shall c them out of his belly	Job 20:15	3423
God shall c the fury of his wrath	Job 20:23	7971
When men are c down, then thou	Job 22:29	8213
For God shall c upon him, and not	Job 27:22	7993
of my countenance they c not down	Job 29:24	5307
He hath c me into the mire, and I	Job 30:19	3384
ones, they c out their sorrows	Job 39:3	7971
C abroad the rage of thy wrath	Job 40:11	6327
shall not one be c down even at	Job 41:9	2904
c away their cords from us	Ps 2:3	7993
c them out in the multitude of	Ps 5:10	5080
LORD, disappoint him, c him down	Ps 17:13	3766
I did c them out as the dirt in	Ps 18:42	7324
I was c upon thee from the womb	Ps 22:10	7993
them, and c lots upon my vesture	Ps 22:18	5307
they are c down, and shall not be	Ps 36:12	1760
to c down the poor and needy, and	Ps 37:14	5307
he shall not be utterly c down	Ps 37:24	2904
Why art thou c down, O my soul	Ps 42:5	7817
my soul is c down within me	Ps 42:6	7817
Why art thou c down, O my soul	Ps 42:11	7817
why dost thou c me off	Ps 43:2	2186
Why art thou c down, O my soul	Ps 43:5	7817
afflict the people, and c them out	Ps 44:2	7971
But thou hast c off, and put us to	Ps 44:9	2186
arise, c us not off for ever	Ps 44:23	2186
C me not away from thy presence	Ps 51:11	7993
for they c iniquity upon me, and	Ps 55:3	4131
C thy burden upon the LORD, and he	Ps 55:22	7993
in thine anger c down the people,	Ps 56:7	3381
O God, thou hast c us off	Ps 60:1	2186
over Edom will I c out my shoe	Ps 60:8	7993
thou, O God, which hadst c us off	Ps 60:10	2186
They only consult to c him down	Ps 62:4	5080
C me not off in the time of old	Ps 71:9	7993
why hast thou c us off for ever	Ps 74:1	2186
They have c fire into thy	Ps 74:7	7971
horse are c into a dead sleep	Ps 76:6	7290
Will the Lord c off for ever	Ps 77:7	2186
He c upon them the fierceness of	Ps 78:49	7971
He c out the heathen also before	Ps 78:55	1644
thou hast c out the heathen, and	Ps 80:8	1644
But thou hast c off and abhorred,	Ps 89:38	2186
c his throne down to the ground	Ps 89:44	4048
LORD will not c off his people	Ps 94:14	5203
hast lifted me up, and c me down	Ps 102:10	7993
over Edom will I c out my shoe	Ps 108:9	7993
thou, O God, who hast c us off	Ps 108:11	2186
let them be c into the fire	Ps 140:10	5307
C forth lightning, and scatter	Ps 144:6	1299
C in thy lot among us	Prov 1:14	5307
For she hath c down many wounded	Prov 7:26	5307
The lot is c into the lap	Prov 16:33	2904
C out the scorner, and contention	Prov 22:10	1644
A time to c away stones, and a	Eccl 3:5	7993
time to keep, and a time to c away	Eccl 3:6	7993
C thy bread upon the waters	Eccl 11:1	7971
a man shall c his idols of silver	Is 2:20	7993
because they have c away the law	Is 5:24	3988
in them, when they c their leaves	Is 6:13	7995
But thou art c out of thy grave	Is 14:19	7993
wandering bird c out of the nest	Is 16:2	7971
all they that c angle into the	Is 19:8	7993
of the covering c over all people	Is 25:7	3874
and the earth shall c out the dead	Is 26:19	5307
shall c down to the earth with	Is 28:2	3240
doth he not c abroad the fitches,	Is 28:25	6327
c in the principal wheat and the	Is 28:25	7760
thou shalt c them away as a	Is 30:22	2219
shall c away his idols of silver	Is 31:7	3988
Their slain also shall be c out	Is 34:3	7993
he hath c the lot for them, and	Is 34:17	5307
have c their gods into the fire	Is 37:19	5414
shields, nor c a bank against it	Is 37:33	8210
for thou hast c all my sins	Is 38:17	7993
chosen thee, and not c thee away	Is 41:9	3988
C ye up, c ye up, prepare the	Is 57:14	5549
rest, whose waters c up mire	Is 57:20	1644
poor that are c out to thy house	Is 58:7	4788
c up, c up the highways	Is 62:10	5549
that c you out for my name's sake	Is 66:5	5077
c a mount against Jerusalem	Jer 6:6	8210
I visit them they shall be c down	Jer 6:15	3782
I will c you out of my sight, as	Jer 7:15	7993
as I have c out all your brethren	Jer 7:15	7993
and c it away, and take up a	Jer 7:29	7993
visitation they shall be c down	Jer 8:12	3782
our dwellings have c us out	Jer 9:19	7993
to whom they prophesy shall be c	Jer 14:16	7993
c them out of my sight, and let	Jer 15:1	7971
Therefore will I c you out of	Jer 16:13	2904
walk in paths, in a way not c up	Jer 18:15	5549
cedars, and c them into the fire	Jer 22:7	
c forth beyond the gates of	Jer 22:19	7993
I will c thee out, and thy mother	Jer 22:26	2904
wherefore are they c out, he and	Jer 22:28	7993
are c into a land which they know	Jer 22:28	2904
and c you out of my presence	Jer 23:39	
c his dead body into the graves	Jer 26:23	7993
I will c thee from off the face	Jer 28:16	7971
I will also c off all the seed of	Jer 31:37	3988
chosen, he hath even c them off	Jer 33:24	3988
Then will I c away the seed of	Jer 33:26	3988
c it into the fire that was on	Jer 36:23	7933
his dead body shall be c out in	Jer 36:30	7933
c him into the dungeon of	Jer 38:6	7933
whom they have c into the dungeon	Jer 38:9	7933
and took thence old c clouts	Jer 38:11	5499
Put now these old c clouts	Jer 38:12	5499
c them into the midst of the pit,	Jer 41:7	
c all the dead bodies of the men	Jer 41:9	7993
away captive from Mizpah c about	Jer 41:14	5437
c her up as heaps, and destroy her	Jer 50:26	5549
my delicates, he hath c me out	Jer 51:34	1740
c it into the midst of Euphrates	Jer 51:63	7993
till he had c them out from his	Jer 52:3	7993
c down from heaven unto the earth	Lam 2:1	7993
The Lord hath c off his altar	Lam 2:7	2186
they have c up dust upon their	Lam 2:10	5927
the Lord will not c off for ever	Lam 3:31	2186
the dungeon, and c a stone upon me	Lam 3:53	3034
it, and c a mount against it	Eze 4:2	8210
c them into the midst of the fire	Eze 5:4	7993
I will c down your slain men	Eze 6:4	5307
They shall c their silver in the	Eze 7:19	7993
Although I have c them far off	Eze 11:16	7368
it is c into the fire for fuel	Eze 15:4	5414
but thou wast c out in the open	Eze 16:5	7993
C away from you all your	Eze 18:31	7993
she was c down to the ground, and	Eze 19:12	7993
them, C ye away every man the	Eze 20:7	7993
they did not every man c away the	Eze 20:8	7993
to c a mount, and to build a fort	Eze 21:22	8210
c me behind thy back, therefore	Eze 23:35	7998
c a mount against thee, and lift	Eze 26:8	8210
shall c up dust upon their heads,	Eze 27:30	5927
therefore I will c thee as	Eze 28:16	2490
I will c thee to the ground, I	Eze 28:17	7993
when I c him down to hell with	Eze 31:16	3381
I will c thee forth upon the open	Eze 32:4	2904
c them down, even her, and the	Eze 32:18	3381
minds, to c it out for a prey	Eze 36:5	4054
priests shall c salt upon them	Eze 43:24	7993
shall the same hour be c into the	Dan 3:6	7412
that he should be c into the	Dan 3:11	7412
ye shall be c the same hour into	Dan 3:15	7412
to c them into the burning fiery	Dan 3:20	7412
were c into the midst of the	Dan 3:21	7412
Did not we c three men bound into	Dan 3:24	7412
he shall be c into the den of	Dan 6:7	7412
shall be c into the den of lions	Dan 6:12	7412
c him into the den of lions	Dan 6:16	7412
they c them into the den of lions	Dan 6:24	7412
till the thrones were c down	Dan 7:9	7412
but he c him down to the ground,	Dan 8:7	7993
it c down some of the host and of	Dan 8:10	5307
place of his sanctuary was c down	Dan 8:11	7993
it c down the truth to the ground	Dan 8:12	7993
and he shall c down many ten	Dan 11:12	5307
c up a mount, and take the most	Dan 11:15	8210
Israel hath c off the thing that	Hos 8:3	2186
calf, O Samaria, hath c thee off	Hos 8:5	2186
My God will c them away, because	Hos 9:17	3988
c forth his roots as Lebanon	Hos 14:5	5221
made it clean bare, and c it away	Joel 1:7	7993
they have c lots for my people	Joel 3:3	3032
did c off all pity, and his anger	Amos 1:11	7843
ye shall c them into the palace,	Amos 4:3	7993
they shall c them forth with	Amos 8:3	7993
and it shall be c out and drowned,	Amos 8:8	1644
c lots upon Jerusalem, even thou	Obad 11	3032
c forth the wares that were in	Jonah 1:5	2904
fellow, Come, and let us c lots	Jonah 1:7	5307
So they c lots, and the lot fell	Jonah 1:7	5307
me up, and c me forth into the sea	Jonah 1:12	2904
and c him forth into the sea	Jonah 1:15	2904
For thou hadst c me into the deep	Jonah 2:3	7993
I said, I am c out of thy sight	Jonah 2:4	1644
that shall c a cord by lot in the	Mic 2:5	7993
c out from their pleasant houses	Mic 2:9	1644
her that was c far off a strong	Mic 4:7	1972
thou wilt c all their sins into	Mic 7:19	7993
I will c abominable filth upon	Nah 3:6	7993
they c lots for her honourable	Nah 3:10	3032
he hath c out thine enemy	Zeph 3:15	6437
to c out the horns of the	Zec 1:21	3034
he c it into the midst of the	Zec 5:8	7993
he c the weight of lead upon the	Zec 5:8	7993
Behold, the Lord will c her out	Zec 9:4	3423
be as though I had not c them off	Zec 10:6	2186
unto me, C it unto the potter	Zec 11:13	7993
c them to the potter in the house	Zec 11:13	7993
neither shall your vine c her	Mal 3:11	7921
is hewn down, and c into the fire	Mt 3:10	*906*
be the Son of God, c thyself down	Mt 4:6	*906*
heard that John was c into prison	Mt 4:12	*3860*
good for nothing, but to be c out	Mt 5:13	*906*
officer, and thou be c into prison	Mt 5:25	*906*
pluck it out, and c it from thee	Mt 5:29	*906*
whole body should be c into hell	Mt 5:29	*906*
cut it off, and c it from thee	Mt 5:30	*906*
whole body should be c into hell	Mt 5:30	*906*
to morrow is c into the oven,	Mt 6:30	*906*
first c out the beam out of thine	Mt 7:5	*1544*
to c out the mote out of thy	Mt 7:5	*1544*
neither c ye your pearls before	Mt 7:6	*906*
is hewn down, and c into the fire	Mt 7:19	*906*
and in thy name have c out devils	Mt 7:22	*1544*
be c out into outer darkness	Mt 8:12	*1544*
he c out the spirits with his	Mt 8:16	*1544*
him, saying, If thou c us out	Mt 8:31	*1544*
And when the devil was c out	Mt 9:33	*1544*
to c them out, and to heal all	Mt 10:1	*1544*
raise the dead, c out devils	Mt 10:8	*1544*
This fellow doth not c out devils	Mt 12:24	*1544*
if Satan c out Satan, he is	Mt 12:26	*1544*
And if I by Beelzebub c out devils	Mt 12:27	*1544*

whom do your children c them out Mt 12:27 *1544*
But if I c out devils by the Mt 12:28 *1544*
shall c them into a furnace of Mt 13:42 *906*
that was c into the sea, and Mt 13:47 *906*
into vessels, but c the bad away Mt 13:48 *906*
shall c them into the furnace of Mt 13:50 *906*
is c out into the draught Mt 15:17 *1544*
bread, and to c it to dogs Mt 15:26 *906*
c them down at Jesus' feet Mt 15:30 *4496*
said, Why could not we c him out Mt 17:19 *1544*
c an hook, and take up the fish Mt 17:27 *906*
cut them off, and c them from thee Mt 18:8 *906*
to be c into everlasting fire Mt 18:8 *906*
pluck it out, and c it from thee Mt 18:9 *906*
two eyes to be c into hell fire Mt 18:9 *906*
c him into prison, till he should Mt 18:30 *906*
c out all them that sold and Mt 21:12 *1544*
and be thou c into the sea Mt 21:21 *906*
c him out of the vineyard, and Mt 21:39 *1544*
c him into outer darkness Mt 22:13 *1544*
c ye the unprofitable servant Mt 25:30 *1544*
he c down the pieces of silver in Mt 27:5 *4496*
upon my vesture did they c lots Mt 27:35 *906*
with him, c the same in his teeth Mt 27:44 *3679*
diseases, and c out many devils Mk 1:34 *1544*
all Galilee, and c out devils Mk 1:39 *1544*
sicknesses, and to c out devils Mk 3:15 *1544*
How can Satan c out Satan Mk 3:23 *1544*
as if a man should c seed into Mk 4:26 *906*
they c out many devils, and Mk 6:13 *1544*
c forth the devil out of her Mk 7:26 *1544*
bread, and to c it unto the dogs Mk 7:27 *906*
that they should c him out Mk 9:18 *1544*
ofttimes it hath c him into the Mk 9:22 *906*
Why could not we c him out Mk 9:28 *1544*
neck, and he were c into the sea Mk 9:42 *906*
having two feet to be c into hell Mk 9:45 *906*
two eyes to be c into hell fire Mk 9:47 *906*
Jesus, and c their garments on him Mk 11:7 *1911*
began to c out them that sold and Mk 11:15 *1544*
and be thou c into the sea Mk 11:23 *906*
and at him they c stones, and Mk 12:4 *3036*
c him out of the vineyard Mk 12:8 *1544*
beheld how the people c money Mk 12:41 *906*
and many that were rich c in much Mk 12:41 *906*
this poor widow hath c more in Mk 12:43 *906*
which have c into the treasury Mk 12:43 *906*
For all they did c in of their Mk 12:44 *906*
want did c in all that she had Mk 12:44 *906*
cloth c about his naked body Mk 14:51 *4016*
out of whom he had c seven devils Mk 16:9 *1544*
my name shall they c out devils Mk 16:17 *1544*
c in her mind what manner of Lk 1:29 *1260*
is hewn down, and c into the fire Lk 3:9 *906*
c thyself down from hence Lk 4:9 *906*
that they might c him down Lk 4:29 *2630*
c out your name as evil, for the Lk 6:22 *1544*
c out first the beam out of thine Lk 6:42 *1544*
and lose himself, or be c away Lk 9:25 *2210*
thy disciples to c him out Lk 9:40 *1544*
because ye say that I c out Lk 11:18 *1544*
And if I by Beelzebub c out devils Lk 11:19 *1544*
by whom do your sons c them out Lk 11:19 *1544*
the finger of God c out devils Lk 11:20 *1544*
killed hath power to c into hell Lk 12:5 *1685*
to morrow is c into the oven Lk 12:28 *906*
the officer c thee into prison Lk 12:58 *906*
a man took, and c into his garden Lk 13:19 *906*
I c out devils, and I do cures to Lk 13:32 *1544*
but men c it out Lk 14:35 *906*
he c into the sea, than that he Lk 17:2 *4406*
they c their garments upon the Lk 19:35 *1977*
shall c a trench about thee Lk 19:43 *4016*
began to c out them that sold Lk 19:45 *1544*
wounded him also, and c him out Lk 20:12 *1544*
So they c him out of the vineyard Lk 20:15 *1544*
hath c in more than they all Lk 21:3 *906*
c in unto the offerings of God Lk 21:4 *906*
but she of her penury hath c in Lk 21:4 *906*
from them about a stone's c Lk 22:41 *1000*
and for murder, was c into prison Lk 23:19 *906*
murder was c into prison, whom Lk 23:25 *906*
parted his raiment, and c lots Lk 23:34 *906*
John was not yet c into prison Jn 3:24 *906*
to me I will in no wise c out Jn 6:37 *1544*
let him first c a stone at her Jn 8:7 *906*
took they up stones to c at him Jn 8:59 *906*
And they c him out Jn 9:34 *1544*
heard that they had c him out Jn 9:35 *1544*
the prince of this world be c out Jn 12:31 *1544*
he is c forth as a branch, and is Jn 15:6 *906*
c them into the fire, and they are Jn 15:6 *906*
but c lots for it, whose it shall Jn 19:24 *2975*
and for my vesture they did c lots Jn 19:24 *906*
C the net on the right side of Jn 21:6 *906*
They c therefore, and now they Jn 21:6 *906*
did c himself into the sea Jn 21:7 *906*
so that they c out their young Acts 7:19
And when he was c out, Pharaoh's Acts 7:21 *1620*
c him out of the city, and stoned Acts 7:58 *1544*
C thy garment about thee, and Acts 12:8 *4016*
they c them into prison, charging Acts 16:23 *906*
Romans, and have c us into prison Acts 16:37 *906*
c off their clothes, and threw Acts 22:23 *4496*
the third day we c out with our Acts 27:19 *4496*
Howbeit we must be c upon a Acts 27:26 *1601*
they c four anchors out of the Acts 27:29 *4496*
as though they would have c Acts 27:30 *1614*
c out the wheat into the sea Acts 27:38 *1544*
they which could swim should c Acts 27:43 *641*
Hath God c away his people Rom 11:1 *683*
God hath not c away his people Rom 11:2 *683*
let us therefore c off the works Rom 13:12 *656*
not that I may c a snare upon you 1Cor 7:35 *1911*
c down, but not destroyed 2Cor 4:9 *2598*
comforteth those that are c down 2Cor 7:6 *5011*
C out the bondwoman and her son Gal 4:30 *1544*
because they have c off their 1Ti 5:12 *114*
C not away therefore your Heb 10:35 *577*
but c them down to hell, and 2Pet 2:4 *5020*
the devil shall c some of you Rev 2:10 *906*
Balaam, who taught Balac to c a Rev 2:14 *906*
I will c her into a bed, and them Rev 2:22 *906*
c their crowns before the throne, Rev 4:10 *906*
the altar, and c it into the earth Rev 8:5 *906*
they were c upon the earth Rev 8:7 *906*
with fire was c into the sea Rev 8:8 *906*
and did c them to the earth Rev 12:4 *906*
And the great dragon was c out Rev 12:9 *906*
he was c out into the earth, and Rev 12:9 *906*
and his angels were c out with him Rev 12:9 *906*
accuser of our brethren is c down Rev 12:10 *2598*
saw that he was c unto the earth Rev 12:13 *906*
the serpent c out of his mouth Rev 12:15 *906*
the dragon c out of his mouth Rev 12:16 *906*
c it into the great winepress of Rev 14:19 *906*
they c dust on their heads, and Rev 18:19 *906*
c it into the sea, saying, Thus Rev 18:21 *906*
These both were c alive into a Rev 19:20 *1544*
c him into the bottomless pit, and Rev 20:3 *906*
them was c into the lake of fire Rev 20:10 *906*
hell were c into the lake of fire Rev 20:14 *906*
life was c into the lake of fire Rev 20:15 *906*

CASTAWAY
to others, I myself should be a c 1Cor 9:27 *96*

CASTEDST
thou c them down into destruction Ps 73:18 5307

CASTEST
thou c off fear, and restrainest Job 15:4 6565
and c my words behind thee Ps 50:17 7993
LORD, why c thou off my soul Ps 88:14 2186

CASTETH
cow calveth, and c not her calf Job 21:10 7921
he c the wicked down to the Ps 147:6 8213
He c forth his ice like morsels Ps 147:17 7993
but he c away the substance of Prov 10:3 1920
Slothfulness c into a deep sleep Prov 19:15 5307
c down the strength of the Prov 21:22 3381
As a mad man who c firebrands Prov 26:18 3384
with gold, and c silver chains Is 40:19 6884
As a fountain c out her waters, Jer 6:7 6979
so she c out her wickedness Jer 6:7 6979
He c out devils through the Mt 9:34 *1544*
of the devils c he out devils Mk 3:22 *1544*
He c out devils through Beelzebub Lk 11:15 *1544*
but perfect love c out fear 1Jn 4:18 *906*
and c them out of the church 3Jn 10 *1544*
as a fig tree c her untimely figs Rev 6:13 *906*

CASTING
c them down to the ground 2Sa 8:2 7901
all of them had one c, one 1Kin 7:37 4165
c himself down before the house Ezr 10:1 5307
ye see my c down, and are afraid Job 6:21 2866
they have defiled by c down the Ps 74:7
his crown by c it to the ground Ps 89:39
by c up mounts, and building forts Eze 17:17 8210
thy c down shall be in the midst Mic 6:14 3445
his brother, c a net into the sea Mt 4:18 *906*
and parted his garments, c lots Mt 27:35 *906*
his brother c a net into the sea Mk 1:16 *906*
we saw one c out devils in thy Mk 9:38 *1544*
c away his garment, rose, and came Mk 10:50 *577*
c lots upon them, what every man Mk 15:24 *906*
we saw one c out devils in thy Lk 9:49 *1544*
he was c out a devil, and it was Lk 11:14 *1544*
saw the rich men c their gifts Lk 21:1 *906*
poor widow c in thither two mites Lk 21:2 *906*
For if the c away of them be the Rom 11:15 *580*
C down imaginations, and every 2Cor 10:5 *2507*
C all your care upon him 1Pet 5:7 *1977*

CASTLE
David took the c of Zion, which 1Chr 11:5 4686
And David dwelt in the c 1Chr 11:7 4679
are like the bars of a c Prov 18:19 759
him to be carried into the c Acts 21:34 *3925*
as Paul was to be led into the c Acts 21:37 *3925*
him to be brought into the c Acts 22:24 *3925*
them, and to bring him into the c Acts 23:10 *3925*
he went and entered into the c Acts 23:16 *3925*
go with him, and returned to the c Acts 23:32 *3925*

CASTLES
by their towns, and by their c Gen 25:16 2918
they dwelt, and all their goodly c Num 31:10 2918
their c in their coasts, of the 1Chr 6:54 2918
and in the villages, and in the c 1Chr 27:25 4026
and he built in Judah c, and cities 2Chr 17:12 1003
and in the forests he built c 2Chr 27:4 1003

CASTOR (*cas'-tor*) *Patron god of sailors.*
in the isle, whose sign was *C* Acts 28:11 *1359*

CATCH
c in thorns, so that the stacks Ex 22:6 4672
c you every man his wife of the Judg 21:21 2414
from him, and did hastily c it 1Kin 20:33 2480
we shall c them alive, and get 2Kin 7:12 8610
he lieth in wait to c the poor Ps 10:9 2414
he doth c the poor, when he Ps 10:9 2414
net that he hath hid c himself Ps 35:8 3920
extortioner c all that he hath Ps 109:11 5367
they set a trap, they c men Jer 5:26 3920
lion, and it learned to c the prey Eze 19:3 2963
lion, and learned to c the prey Eze 19:6 2963
they c them in their net, and Hab 1:15 1641
Herodians, to c him in his words Mk 12:13 *64*
from henceforth thou shalt c men Lk 5:10 *2221*
seeking to c something out of his Lk 11:54 *2340*

CATCHETH
c any beast or fowl that may be Lev 17:13 6679
c away that which was sown in his Mt 13:19 *726*
and the wolf c them, and scattereth Jn 10:12 *726*

CATERPILLER
mildew, locust, or if there be c 1Kin 8:37 2625
also their increase unto the c Ps 78:46 2625
like the gathering of the c Is 33:4 2625
hath left hath the c eaten Joel 1:4 2625
eaten, the cankerworm, and the c Joel 2:25 2625

CATERPILLERS
or mildew, locusts, or c 2Chr 6:28 2625
spake, and the locusts came, and c Ps 105:34 3218
fill thee with men, as with c Jer 51:14 3218
horses to come up as the rough c Jer 51:27 3218

CATTLE
living creature after his kind, c Gen 1:24 929
c after their kind, and every Gen 1:25 929
fowl of the air, and over the c Gen 1:26 929
And Adam gave names to all c Gen 2:20 929
this, thou art cursed above all c Gen 3:14 929
in tents, and of such as have c Gen 4:20 4735
of c after their kind, of every Gen 6:20 929
all the c after their kind, and Gen 7:14 929
the earth, both of fowl, and of c Gen 7:21 929
of the ground, both man, and c Gen 7:23 929
all the c that was with him in Gen 8:1 929
all flesh, both of fowl, and of c Gen 8:17 929
with you, of the fowl, of the c Gen 9:10 929
And Abram was very rich in c Gen 13:2 4735
c and the herdmen of Lot's c Gen 13:7 4735
the c should be gathered together Gen 29:7 4735
thee, and how thy c was with me Gen 30:29 4735
all the speckled and spotted c Gen 30:32 7716
all the brown c among the sheep, Gen 30:32 7716
and brought forth c ringstraked Gen 30:39 6629
and put them not unto Laban's c Gen 30:40 6629
the stronger c did conceive Gen 30:41 6629
the eyes of the c in the gutters Gen 30:41 6629
But when the c were feeble Gen 30:42 6629
exceedingly, and had much c Gen 30:43 6629
then all the c bare speckled Gen 31:8 6629
then bare all the c ringstraked Gen 31:8 6629
taken away the c of your father Gen 31:9 4735
at the time that the c conceived Gen 31:10 6629
upon the c were ringstraked Gen 31:10 6629
leap upon the c are ringstraked Gen 31:12 6629
And he carried away all his c Gen 31:18 4735
the c of his getting, which he Gen 31:18 4735
daughters, and six years for thy c Gen 31:41 6629
these c are my c, and all Gen 31:43 6629
according as the c that goeth Gen 33:14 4399
house, and made booths for his c Gen 33:17 4735
sons were with his c in the field Gen 34:5 4735
Shall not their c and their Gen 34:23 4735
persons of his house, and his c Gen 36:6 4735
not bear them because of their c Gen 36:7 4735
And they took their c, and their Gen 46:6 4735
their trade hath been to feed c Gen 46:32 4735
c from our youth even until now Gen 46:34 4735
then make them rulers over my c Gen 47:6 4735
And Joseph said, Give your c Gen 47:16 4735
and I will give you for your c Gen 47:16 4735
they brought their c unto Joseph Gen 47:17 4735
for the c of the herds, and for Gen 47:17 4735
for all their c for that year Gen 47:17 4735
my lord also hath our herds of c Gen 47:18 929
upon thy c which is in the field Ex 9:3 4735
sever between the c of Israel Ex 9:4 4735
of Israel and the c of Egypt Ex 9:4 4735
and all the c of Egypt died Ex 9:6 4735
but of the c of the children of Ex 9:6 4735
of the c of the Israelites dead Ex 9:7 4735
therefore now, and gather thy c Ex 9:19 4735
his c flee into the houses Ex 9:20 4735
servants and his c in the field Ex 9:21 4735
Our c also shall go with us Ex 10:26 4735
and all the firstborn of c Ex 12:29 929
and herds, even very much c Ex 12:38 4735
our children and our c with thirst Ex 17:3 4735
nor thy maidservant, nor thy c Ex 20:10 929
and every firstling among thy c Ex 34:19 4735
bring your offering of the c Lev 1:2 929
beast, or a carcase of unclean c Lev 5:2 929
Thou shalt not let thy c gender Lev 19:19 929
And for thy c, and for the beast Lev 25:7 929
your children, and destroy your c Lev 26:22 929
the c of the Levites instead of Num 3:41 929
the c of the children of Israel Num 3:41 929
the c of the Levites instead of Num 3:45 929
of the Levites instead of their c Num 3:45 926
that we and our c should die there Num 20:4 1165
my c drink of thy water, then I Num 20:19 4735
and took the spoil of all their c Num 31:9 929
had a very great multitude of c Num 32:1 4735
the place was a place for c Num 32:1 4735
c, and thy servants have c Num 32:4 4735
build sheepfolds here for our c Num 32:16 4735
wives, our flocks, and all our c Num 32:26 929
of them shall be for their c Num 35:3 929
Only the c we took for a prey Deut 2:35 929
But all the c, and the spoil of Deut 3:7 929
and your little ones, and your c Deut 3:19 4735
(for I know that ye have much c Deut 3:19 4735
nor thine ass, nor any of thy c Deut 5:14 929
barren among you, or among your c Deut 7:14 929
grass in thy fields for thy c Deut 11:15 929
the c thereof, with the edge of Deut 13:15 929
and the little ones, and the c Deut 20:14 929
thy ground, and the fruit of thy c Deut 28:4 929

body, and in the fruit of thy c	Deut 28:11	929
he shall eat the fruit of thy c	Deut 28:51	929
body, and in the fruit of thy c	Deut 30:9	929
your little ones, and your c	Josh 1:14	4735
the c thereof, shall ye take for	Josh 8:2	929
Only the c and the spoil of that	Josh 8:27	929
spoil of these cities, and the c	Josh 11:14	929
with their suburbs for their c	Josh 14:4	4735
the suburbs thereof for our c	Josh 21:2	929
your tents, and with very much c	Josh 22:8	4735
For they came up with their c	Judg 6:5	4735
and put the little ones and the c	Judg 18:21	4735
and brought away their c, and	1Sa 23:5	4735
they drave before those other c	1Sa 30:20	4735
fat c by the stone of Zoheleth,	1Kin 1:9	4806
And he hath slain oxen and fat c	1Kin 1:19	4806
day, and hath slain oxen and fat c	1Kin 1:25	4806
for the c that followed them	2Kin 3:9	929
ye may drink, both ye, and your c	2Kin 3:17	4735
because their c were multiplied	1Chr 5:9	4735
And they took away their c	1Chr 5:21	929
came down to take away their c	1Chr 7:21	929
They smote also the tents of c	2Chr 14:15	929
for he had much c, both in the	2Chr 26:10	929
thousand and six hundred small c	2Chr 35:8	
offerings five thousand small c	2Chr 35:9	
over our bodies, and over our c	Neh 9:37	929
of our sons, and of our c, as it	Neh 10:36	929
the c also concerning the vapour	Job 36:33	4735
the c upon a thousand hills	Ps 50:10	929
gave up their c also to the hail	Ps 78:48	1165
the grass to grow for the c	Ps 104:14	929
suffereth not their c to decrease	Ps 107:38	929
Beasts, and all c	Ps 148:10	929
small c above all that were in	Eccl 2:7	4735
and for the treading of lesser c	Is 7:25	7716
in that day shall thy c feed in	Is 30:23	4735
small c of thy burnt offerings	Is 43:23	7716
upon the beasts, and upon the c	Is 46:1	929
can men hear the voice of the c	Jer 9:10	4735
the multitude of their c a spoil	Jer 49:32	4734
I judge between c and c	Eze 34:17	7716
fat c and between the lean c	Eze 34:20	7716
I will judge between c and c	Eze 34:22	7716
the nations, which have gotten c	Eze 38:12	4735
silver and gold, to take away c	Eze 38:13	4735
the herds of c are perplexed,	Joel 1:18	1241
and also much c	Jonah 4:11	929
forth, and upon men, and upon c	Hag 1:11	929
the multitude of men and c therein	Zec 2:4	929
taught me to keep c from my youth	Zec 13:5	7069
a servant plowing or feeding c	Lk 17:7	*4165*
and his children, and his c	Jn 4:12	*2353*

CAUDA See CLAUDA.

CAUGHT

behold behind him a ram c in a	Gen 22:13	270
she c him by his garment, saying,	Gen 39:12	8610
c it, and it became a rod in his	Ex 4:4	2388
prey which the men of war had c	Num 31:32	962
c him, and cut off his thumbs and	Judg 1:6	270
c a young man of the men of	Judg 8:14	3920
c three hundred foxes, and took	Judg 15:4	3920
of them that danced, whom they c	Judg 21:23	1497
I c him by his beard, and smote	1Sa 17:35	2388
they c every one his fellow by	2Sa 2:16	2388
his head c hold of the oak, and he	2Sa 18:9	2388
c hold on the horns of the altar	1Kin 1:50	2388
he hath c hold on the horns of	1Kin 1:51	270
c hold on the horns of the altar	1Kin 2:28	2388
Ahijah c the new garment that was	1Kin 11:30	8610
the hill, she c him by the feet	2Kin 4:27	2388
and they c him, (for he was hid in	2Chr 22:9	3920
So she c him, and kissed him, and	Prov 7:13	2388
the birds that are c in the snare	Eccl 9:12	270
thou art found, and also c	Jer 50:24	8610
c him, and said unto him, O thou	Mt 14:31	*1949*
And they c him, and cast him out of	Mt 21:39	*2983*
And they c him, and beat him, and	Mk 12:3	*2983*
For oftentimes it had c him	Lk 8:29	*4884*
and that night they c nothing	Jn 21:3	*4084*
of the fish which ye have now c	Jn 21:10	*4084*
c him, and brought him to the	Acts 6:12	*4884*
Spirit of the Lord c away Philip	Acts 8:39	*726*
their gains was gone, they c Paul	Acts 16:19	*1949*
and having c Gaius and Aristarchus,	Acts 19:29	*4884*
the Jews c me in the temple	Acts 26:21	*4815*
And when the ship was c, and could	Acts 27:15	*4884*
such an one c up to the third	2Cor 12:2	*726*
How that he was c up into	2Cor 12:4	*726*
being crafty, I c you with guile	2Cor 12:16	*2983*
remain shall be c up together	1Th 4:17	*726*
and her child was c up unto God	Rev 12:5	*726*

CAUL

the c that is above the liver, and	Ex 29:13	3508
the c above the liver, and the two	Ex 29:22	3508
the c above the liver, with the	Lev 3:4	3508
the c above the liver, with the	Lev 3:10	3508
the c above the liver, with the	Lev 3:15	3508
the c above the liver, with the	Lev 4:9	3508
the c that is above the liver,	Lev 7:4	3508
the c above the liver, and the two	Lev 8:16	3508
the c above the liver, and the two	Lev 8:25	3508
the c above the liver of the sin	Lev 9:10	3508
kidneys, and the c above the liver	Lev 9:19	3508
will rend the c of their heart,	Hos 13:8	5458

CAULS

about their feet, and their c	Is 3:18	7636

CAUSE

I will c it to rain upon the	Gen 7:4	
C every man to go out from me	Gen 45:1	
c frogs to come up upon the land	Ex 8:5	
for this c have I raised thee up	Ex 9:16	5668
morrow about this time I will c	Ex 9:18	
shall c him to be thoroughly	Ex 21:19	
If a man shall c a field or	Ex 22:5	
the c of both parties shall come	Ex 22:9	1697
neither shalt thou speak in a c	Ex 23:2	7379
countenance a poor man in his c	Ex 23:3	7379
the judgment of thy poor in his c	Ex 23:6	7379
to c the lamp to burn always	Ex 27:20	
thou shalt c a bullock to be	Ex 29:10	
he shall c the house to be	Lev 14:41	
daughter, to c her to be a whore	Lev 19:29	
the light, to c the lamps to burn	Lev 24:2	
if a man c a blemish in his	Lev 24:19	5414
Then shalt thou c the trumpet of	Lev 25:9	
the eyes, and c sorrow of heart	Lev 26:16	
he shall c the woman to drink the	Num 5:24	
afterward shall c the woman to	Num 5:26	
will c him to come near unto him	Num 16:5	
will he c to come near unto him	Num 16:5	
For which c both thou and all thy	Num 16:11	3651
brought their c before the LORD	Num 27:5	4941
thou shalt c the inheritance of	Num 27:7	
then ye shall c his inheritance	Num 27:8	
c the strong wine to be poured	Num 28:7	
any person to c him to die	Num 35:30	
the c that is too hard for you,	Deut 1:17	1697
for he shall c Israel to inherit	Deut 1:38	
he shall c them to inherit the	Deut 3:28	
to c his name to dwell there	Deut 12:11	
nor c the people to return to	Deut 17:16	
thou shalt not c the land to sin,	Deut 24:4	
the judge shall c him to lie down	Deut 25:2	
The LORD shall c thine enemies	Deut 28:7	5414
The LORD shall c thee to be	Deut 28:25	5414
thou shalt c them to inherit it	Deut 31:7	
this is the c why Joshua did	Josh 5:4	1697
shall declare his c in the ears	Josh 20:4	1697
nor c to swear by them, neither	Josh 23:7	
Is there not a c?	1Sa 17:29	1697
blood, to slay David without a c	1Sa 19:5	2600
me and thee, and see, and plead my c	1Sa 24:15	7379
that hath pleaded the c of my	1Sa 25:39	7379
snare for my life, to c me to die	1Sa 28:9	
when all the people came to c	2Sa 3:35	
whither shall I c my shame to go	2Sa 13:13	
she said unto him, There is no c	2Sa 13:16	
any suit or c might come unto me	2Sa 15:4	4941
c Solomon my son to ride upon	1Kin 1:33	
will c them to be discharged	1Kin 5:9	
laid upon him to c him to swear	1Kin 8:31	
supplication, and maintain their c	1Kin 8:45	4941
place, and maintain their c	1Kin 8:49	4941
he maintain the c of his servant	1Kin 8:59	4941
the c of his people Israel at all	1Kin 8:59	4941
this was the c that he lifted up	1Kin 11:27	1697
for the c was from the LORD, that	1Kin 12:15	5438
I will c him to fall by the sword	2Kin 19:7	
why will he be a c of trespass to	1Chr 21:3	
supplication, and maintain their c	2Chr 6:35	4941
and maintain their c, and forgive	2Chr 6:39	4941
for the c was of God, that the	2Chr 10:15	5252
what c soever shall come to you	2Chr 19:10	7379
for this c Hezekiah the king, and	2Chr 32:20	
for which c was this city	Ezr 4:15	
to c these men to cease, and that	Ezr 4:21	
they could not c them to cease	Ezr 5:5	
slay them, and c the work to cease	Neh 4:11	
for which c thou buildest the	Neh 6:6	
him did outlandish women c to sin	Neh 13:26	
to c to perish, all Jews, both	Est 3:13	
C Haman to make haste, that he	Est 5:5	
to c to perish, all the power of	Est 8:11	
him, to destroy him without c	Job 2:3	2600
and unto God would I commit my c	Job 5:8	1700
c me to understand wherein I have	Job 6:24	
multiplieth my wounds without c	Job 9:17	2600
Behold now, I have ordered my c	Job 13:18	4941
do my thoughts c me to answer	Job 20:2	
I would order my c before him	Job 23:4	4941
They c the naked to lodge without	Job 24:7	
They c him to go naked without	Job 24:10	
the c which I knew not I searched	Job 29:16	7379
If I did despise the c of my	Job 31:13	4941
c every man to find according to	Job 34:11	
So that they c the cry of the	Job 34:28	
To c it to rain on the earth,	Job 38:26	
to c the bud of the tender herb	Job 38:27	
him that without c is mine enemy	Ps 7:4	7387
hast maintained my right and my c	Ps 9:4	1779
thou wilt c thine ear to hear	Ps 10:17	
which transgress without c	Ps 25:3	7387
Plead my c, O LORD, with them	Ps 35:1	
For without c have they hid for	Ps 35:7	2600
which without c they have digged	Ps 35:7	2600
the eye that hate me without a c	Ps 35:19	2600
to my judgment, even unto my c	Ps 35:23	7379
glad, that favour my righteous c	Ps 35:27	
plead my c against an ungodly	Ps 43:1	7379
c his face to shine upon us	Ps 67:1	
They that hate me without a c are	Ps 69:4	2600
righteousness, and c me to escape	Ps 71:2	
Arise, O God, plead thine own c	Ps 74:22	7379
Thou didst c judgment to be heard	Ps 76:8	
O God, and c thy face to shine	Ps 80:3	
of hosts, and c thy face to shine	Ps 80:7	
didst c it to take deep root, and	Ps 80:9	
God of hosts, c thy face to shine	Ps 80:19	
c thine anger toward us to cease	Ps 85:4	
and fought against me without a c	Ps 109:3	2600
perversely with me without a c	Ps 119:78	8267
Plead my c, and deliver me	Ps 119:154	7379
have persecuted me without a c	Ps 119:161	2600
maintain the c of the afflicted	Ps 140:12	1779
C me to hear thy lovingkindness	Ps 143:8	
c me to know the way wherein I	Ps 143:8	
for the innocent without c	Prov 1:11	2600
Strive not with a man without c	Prov 3:30	2600
unless they c some to fall	Prov 4:16	
That I may c those that love me	Prov 8:21	
first in his own c seemeth just	Prov 18:17	7379
For the LORD will plead their c	Prov 22:23	7379
he shall plead their c with thee	Prov 23:11	7379
who hath wounds without c	Prov 23:29	2600
against thy neighbour without c	Prov 24:28	2600
Debate thy c with thy neighbour	Prov 25:9	7379
considereth the c of the poor	Prov 29:7	1779
thy mouth for the dumb in the c	Prov 31:8	1779
plead the c of the poor and needy	Prov 31:9	
Therefore I went about to c my	Eccl 2:20	
thy mouth to c thy flesh to sin	Eccl 5:6	
What is the c that the former	Eccl 7:10	1961
Dead flies c the ointment of the	Eccl 10:1	
I would c thee to drink of spiced	Song 8:2	
c me to hear it	Song 8:13	
neither doth the c of the widow	Is 1:23	7379
which lead thee c thee to err	Is 3:12	
of this people c them to err	Is 9:16	
c it to be heard unto Laish, O	Is 10:30	
shall not c her light to shine	Is 13:10	
I will c the arrogancy of the	Is 13:11	
He shall c them that come of	Is 27:6	
ye may c the weary to rest	Is 28:12	
c the Holy One of Israel to cease	Is 30:11	
the LORD shall c his glorious	Is 30:30	
he will c the drink of the	Is 32:6	
I will c him to fall by the sword	Is 37:7	
Produce your c, saith the LORD	Is 41:21	7379
nor c his voice to be heard in	Is 42:2	
to c to inherit the desolate	Is 49:8	
that pleadeth the c of his people	Is 51:22	
Assyrian oppressed them without c	Is 52:4	657
I will c thee to ride upon the	Is 58:14	
the Lord GOD will c righteousness	Is 61:11	
birth, and not c to bring forth	Is 66:9	
shall I c to bring forth, and shut	Is 66:9	
I will not c mine anger to fall	Jer 3:12	
they judge not the c	Jer 5:28	1779
the c of the fatherless, yet they	Jer 5:28	
I will c you to dwell in this	Jer 7:3	
Then will I c you to dwell in	Jer 7:7	
Then will I c to cease from the	Jer 7:34	
unto thee have I revealed my c	Jer 11:20	7379
your God, before he c darkness	Jer 13:16	
of the Gentiles that can c rain	Jer 14:22	
I will c them to be removed into	Jer 15:4	5414
verily I will c the enemy to	Jer 15:11	
I will c to cease out of this	Jer 16:9	
I will this once c them to know	Jer 16:21	
I will c them to know mine hand	Jer 16:21	
I will c thee to serve thine	Jer 17:4	
there I will c thee to hear my	Jer 18:2	
I will c them to fall by the	Jer 19:7	
I will c them to eat the flesh of	Jer 19:9	
for unto thee have I opened my c	Jer 20:12	7379
He judged the c of the poor	Jer 22:16	1779
Which think to c my people to	Jer 23:27	
c my people to err by their lies,	Jer 23:32	
c all the nations, to whom I send	Jer 25:15	
dreams which ye c to be dreamed	Jer 29:8	
I will c them to return to the	Jer 30:3	
There is none to plead thy c	Jer 30:13	1779
I will c him to draw near, and he	Jer 30:21	
when I went to c him to rest	Jer 31:2	
I will c them to walk by the	Jer 31:9	
Hinnom, to c their sons and their	Jer 32:35	4616
abomination, to c Judah to sin	Jer 32:35	
I will c them to dwell safely	Jer 32:37	
for I will c their captivity to	Jer 32:44	
I will c the captivity of Judah	Jer 33:7	
For I will c to return the	Jer 33:11	
that time, will I c the Branch of	Jer 33:15	
for I will c their captivity to	Jer 33:26	
c them to return to this city	Jer 34:22	
shall c to cease from thence man	Jer 36:29	
that thou c me not to return to	Jer 37:20	
thou shalt c this city to be	Jer 38:23	
that he would not c me to return	Jer 38:26	
c you to return to your own land	Jer 42:12	
that shall c him to wander, and	Jer 48:12	
Moreover I will c to cease in	Jer 48:35	
that I will c an alarm of war to	Jer 49:2	
For I will c Elam to be dismayed	Jer 49:37	
c to come up against Babylon an	Jer 50:9	
he shall throughly plead their c	Jer 50:34	7379
c the horses to come up as the	Jer 51:27	
Behold, I will plead thy c	Jer 51:36	7379
But though he c grief, yet will	Lam 3:32	
To subvert a man in his c	Lam 3:36	7379
me sore, like a bird, without c	Lam 3:52	2600
judge thou my c	Lam 3:59	4941
c thy belly to eat, and fill thy	Eze 3:3	
c it to pass upon thine head and	Eze 5:1	
I will c my fury to rest upon	Eze 5:13	
C them that have charge over the	Eze 9:1	
If I c noisome beasts to pass	Eze 14:15	
c all that I have done in it	Eze 14:23	2600
of man, c Jerusalem to know her	Eze 16:2	
delivered them to c them to pass	Eze 16:21	
I will c thee to cease from	Eze 16:41	
c them to know the abominations	Eze 20:4	
I will c you to pass under the	Eze 20:37	
and I will c my fury to rest	Eze 21:17	
Shall I c it to return into his	Eze 21:30	
Thus will I c lewdness to cease	Eze 23:48	
That it might c fury to come up	Eze 24:8	
to c thee to hear it with thine	Eze 24:26	
I will c thee to perish out of	Eze 25:7	

will c many nations to come up	Eze 26:3	
I will c the noise of thy songs	Eze 26:13	
which c their terror to be on all	Eze 26:17	5414
shall c their voice to be heard	Eze 27:30	
I will c the fish of thy rivers	Eze 29:4	
will c them to return into the	Eze 29:14	
In that day will I c the horn of	Eze 29:21	
I will c their images to cease	Eze 30:13	
I will c the sword to fall out of	Eze 30:22	
will c all the fowls of the	Eze 32:4	
will I c thy multitude to fall	Eze 32:12	
c their rivers to run like oil,	Eze 32:14	
c them to cease from feeding the	Eze 34:10	
I will c them to lie down, saith	Eze 34:15	
will c the evil beasts to cease	Eze 34:25	
I will c the shower to come down	Eze 34:26	
I will c men to walk upon you,	Eze 36:12	
Neither will I c men to hear in	Eze 36:15	
neither shalt thou c thy nations	Eze 36:15	
c you to walk in my statutes, and	Eze 36:27	
also c you to dwell in the cities	Eze 36:33	
I will c breath to enter into you	Eze 37:5	
c you to come up out of your	Eze 37:12	
will c thee to come up from the	Eze 39:2	
will c thine arrows to fall out	Eze 39:3	
c them to discern between the	Eze 44:23	
that he may c the blessing to	Eze 44:30	
For this c the king was angry and	Dan 2:12	
his policy also he shall c craft	Dan 8:25	
c thy face to shine upon thy	Dan 9:17	
the week he shall c the sacrifice	Dan 9:27	
c the reproach offered by him to	Dan 11:18	
he shall c it to turn upon him	Dan 11:18	
he shall c them to rule over many	Dan 11:39	
will c to cease the kingdom of	Hos 1:4	
I will also c all her mirth to	Hos 2:11	
he will c to come down for you	Joel 2:23	
thither c thy mighty ones to come	Joel 3:11	
Therefore will I c you to go into	Amos 5:27	
c the seat of violence to come	Amos 6:3	
that I will c the sun to go down	Amos 8:9	
for whose c this evil is upon us	Jonah 1:7	7945
for whose c this evil is upon us	Jonah 1:8	834
against him, until he plead my c	Mic 7:9	7379
and c me to behold grievance	Hab 1:3	
I will c the remnant of this	Zec 8:12	
also I will c the prophets and the	Zec 13:2	
a c shall be in danger of the	Mt 5:22	*1500*
saving for the c of fornication	Mt 5:32	*3056*
c them to be put to death	Mt 10:21	*2289*
to put away his wife for every c	Mt 19:3	*156*
For this c shall a man leave	Mt 19:5	*1752*
For this c shall a man leave his	Mk 10:7	*1752*
shall c them to be put to death	Mk 13:12	*2289*
for what c she had touched him	Lk 8:47	*156*
shall they c to be put to death	Lk 21:16	*2289*
I have found no c of death in him	Lk 23:22	*158*
For this c the people also met	Jn 12:18	*1223*
but for this c came I unto this	Jn 12:27	*1223*
law, They hated me without a c	Jn 15:25	*1432*
for this c came I into the world,	Jn 18:37	
what is the c wherefore ye are	Acts 10:21	*156*
they found no c of death in him	Acts 13:28	*156*
there being no c whereby we may	Acts 19:40	*158*
the c wherefore they accused him	Acts 23:28	*156*
declared Paul's c unto the king	Acts 25:14	
there was no c of death in me	Acts 28:18	*156*
For this c therefore have I	Acts 28:20	*156*
For this c God gave them up unto	Rom 1:26	*1223*
For for this c pay ye tribute	Rom 13:6	*1223*
For this c I will confess to thee	Rom 15:9	*1223*
For which c also I have been much	Rom 15:22	*1352*
mark them which c divisions	Rom 16:17	*4160*
For this c have I sent unto you	1Cor 4:17	*1223*
For this c ought the woman to	1Cor 11:10	*1223*
For this c many are weak and	1Cor 11:30	*1223*
For which c we faint not	2Cor 4:16	*1352*
we be sober, it is for your c	2Cor 5:13	
I did it not for his c that had	2Cor 7:12	*1752*
nor for his c that suffered wrong	2Cor 7:12	*1752*
For this c I Paul, the prisoner	Eph 3:1	*5484*
For this c I bow my knees unto	Eph 3:14	*5484*
For this c shall a man leave his	Eph 5:31	*873*
For the same c also do ye joy, and	Phil 2:18	*846*
For this c we also, since the day	Col 1:9	
c that it be read also in the	Col 4:16	*4160*
For this c also thank we God	1Th 2:13	*1223*
For this c, when I could no	1Th 3:5	*1223*
for this c God shall send them	2Th 2:11	*1223*
for this c I obtained mercy	1Ti 1:16	*1223*
For the which c I also suffer	2Ti 1:12	*156*
For this c left I thee in Crete,	Titus 1:5	*5484*
for which c he is not ashamed to	Heb 2:11	*156*
for this c he is the mediator of	Heb 9:15	*1223*
For for this c was the gospel	1Pet 4:6	
that he might c her to be carried	Rev 12:15	*4160*
c that as many as would not	Rev 13:15	

CAUSED

for the LORD God had not c it to	Gen 2:5	
the LORD God c a deep sleep to	Gen 2:21	
when God c me to wander from my	Gen 20:13	
For God hath c me to be fruitful	Gen 41:52	
the LORD c the sea to go back by	Ex 14:21	
they c it to be proclaimed	Ex 36:6	
as he hath c a blemish in a man,	Lev 24:20	5414
these c the children of Israel,	Num 31:16	1961
I have c thee to see it with	Deut 34:4	
she c him to shave off the seven	Judg 16:19	
when Samuel had c all the tribes	1Sa 10:20	
When he had c the tribe of	1Sa 10:21	
Jonathan c David to swear again,	1Sa 20:17	
have c thee to rest from all	2Sa 7:11	
c Solomon to ride upon king	1Kin 1:38	
they have c him to ride upon the	1Kin 1:44	
c a seat to be set for the king's	1Kin 2:19	
he c him to come up into the	1Kin 20:33	
they c their sons and their	2Kin 17:17	
c the children of Israel to dwell	2Chr 8:2	
But Jeroboam c an ambushment to	2Chr 13:13	
c the inhabitants of Jerusalem to	2Chr 21:11	
he c his children to pass through	2Chr 33:6	
he c all that were present in	2Chr 34:32	
the God that hath c his name to	Ezr 6:12	
c the people to understand the	Neh 8:7	
c them to understand the reading	Neh 8:8	
he c the gallows to be made	Est 5:14	
I c the widow's heart to sing for	Job 29:13	
or have c the eyes of the widow	Job 31:16	
or have c the owners thereof to	Job 31:39	
c the light of his cloud to shine	Job 37:15	
c the dayspring to know his place	Job 38:12	
Thou hast c men to ride over our	Ps 66:12	
sea, and c them to pass through	Ps 78:13	
c waters to run down like rivers	Ps 78:16	
He c an east wind to blow in the	Ps 78:26	
upon which thou hast c me to hope	Ps 119:49	
fair speech she c him to yield	Prov 7:21	
they have c Egypt to err in every	Is 19:14	
I have not c thee to serve with	Is 43:23	
he c the waters to flow out of	Is 48:21	
Spirit of the LORD c him to rest	Is 63:14	
c my people Israel to inherit	Jer 12:14	
so have I c to cleave unto me the	Jer 13:11	
I have c him to fall upon it	Jer 15:8	
they have c them to stumble in	Jer 18:15	
c my people Israel to err	Jer 23:13	
had c my people to hear my words,	Jer 23:22	
whom I have c to be carried away	Jer 29:4	
of the city whither I have c you	Jer 29:7	
again into the place whence I c	Jer 29:14	
he c you to trust in a lie	Jer 29:31	
therefore thou hast c all this	Jer 32:23	
c the servants and the handmaids,	Jer 34:11	
c every man his servant, and every	Jer 34:16	
ones have c a cry to be heard	Jer 48:4	
I have c wine to fail from the	Jer 48:33	
have c them to go astray, they	Jer 50:6	
As Babylon hath c the slain of	Jer 51:49	
the LORD hath c the solemn feasts	Lam 2:6	
he hath c thine enemy to rejoice	Lam 2:17	
He hath c the arrows of his	Lam 3:13	
and he c me to eat that roll	Eze 3:2	
I have c thee to multiply as the	Eze 16:7	5414
Wherefore I c them to go forth	Eze 20:10	
in that they c to pass through	Eze 20:26	
thou hast c thy days to draw near	Eze 22:4	
have also c their sons, whom they	Eze 23:37	
till I have c my fury to rest	Eze 24:13	
c his army to serve a great	Eze 29:18	
down to the grave I c a mourning	Eze 31:15	
I c Lebanon to mourn for him, and	Eze 31:15	
which c terror in the land of the	Eze 32:23	5414
which c their terror in the land	Eze 32:24	5414
though their terror was c in the	Eze 32:25	5414
though they c their terror in the	Eze 32:26	5414
For I have c my terror in the	Eze 32:32	5414
c me to pass by them round about	Eze 37:2	
which c them to be led into	Eze 39:28	
c the house of Israel to fall	Eze 44:12	
c me to pass by the four corners	Eze 46:21	
c me to return to the brink of	Eze 47:6	
being c to fly swiftly, touched	Dan 9:21	
of whoredoms hath c them to err	Hos 4:12	
their lies c them to err, after	Amos 2:4	
I c it to rain upon one city, and	Amos 4:7	
c it not to rain upon another	Amos 4:7	
he c it to be proclaimed and	Jonah 3:7	
I have c thine iniquity to pass	Zec 3:4	
ye have c many to stumble at the	Mal 2:8	
have c that even this man should	Jn 11:37	*4160*
they c great joy unto all the	Acts 15:3	*4160*
But if any have c grief, he hath	2Cor 2:5	*3076*

CAUSELESS

that thou hast shed blood c	1Sa 25:31	2600
so the curse c shall not come	Prov 26:2	2600

CAUSES

thou mayest bring the c unto God	Ex 18:19	1697
the hard c they brought unto	Ex 18:26	1697
Hear the c between your brethren,	Deut 1:16	
when for all the c whereby	Jer 3:8	182
false burdens and c of banishment	Lam 2:14	
hast pleaded the c of my soul	Lam 3:58	7379
For these c the Jews caught me in	Acts 26:21	*1752*

CAUSEST

thou c me to ride upon it, and	Job 30:22	
c to approach unto thee, that he	Ps 65:4	

CAUSETH

the bitter water that c the curse	Num 5:18	
bitter water that c the curse	Num 5:19	
this water that c the curse shall	Num 5:22	
the bitter water that c the curse	Num 5:24	
the water that c the curse shall	Num 5:24	
that the water that c the curse	Num 5:27	
c them to wander in a wilderness	Job 12:24	
my understanding c me to answer	Job 20:3	
He c it to come, whether for	Job 37:13	
He c the grass to grow for the	Ps 104:14	
and c them to wander in the	Ps 107:40	
He c the vapours to ascend from	Ps 135:7	
he c his wind to blow, and the	Ps 147:18	
in harvest is a son that c shame	Prov 10:5	
winketh with the eye c sorrow	Prov 10:10	5414
wrath is against him that c shame	Prov 14:35	
have rule over a son that c shame	Prov 17:2	
The lot c contentions to cease,	Prov 18:18	
his mother, is a son that c shame	Prov 19:26	
that c to err from the words of	Prov 19:27	
Whoso c the righteous to go	Prov 28:10	
as the garden c the things that	Is 61:11	
the fire c the waters to boil, to	Is 64:2	
he c the vapors to ascend from	Jer 10:13	
he c the vapors to ascend from	Jer 51:16	
as the sea c his waves to come up	Eze 26:3	
with any thing that c sweat	Eze 44:18	
c her to commit adultery	Mt 5:32	*4160*
which always c us to triumph in	2Cor 2:14	*2358*
which c through us thanksgiving	2Cor 9:11	*2716*
c the earth and them which dwell	Rev 13:12	*4160*
he c all, both small and great,	Rev 13:16	*4160*

CAUSEWAY

by the c of the going up, ward	1Chr 26:16	4546
At Parbar westward, four at the c	1Chr 26:18	4546

CAUSING

c the lips of those that are	Song 7:9	
jaws of the people, c them to err	Is 30:28	
in c you to return to this place	Jer 29:10	
c their flocks to lie down	Jer 33:12	

CAVE

and he dwelt in a c, he and his two	Gen 19:30	4631
he may give me the c of Machpelah	Gen 23:9	4631
the c that is therein, I give it	Gen 23:11	4631
the c which was therein, and all	Gen 23:17	4631
the c of the field of Machpelah	Gen 23:19	4631
the c that is therein, were made	Gen 23:20	4631
buried him in the c of Machpelah	Gen 25:9	4631
c that is in the field of Ephron	Gen 49:29	4631
In the c that is in the field of	Gen 49:30	4631
of the c that is therein was from	Gen 49:32	4631
buried him in the c of the field	Gen 50:13	4631
hid themselves in a c at Makkedah	Josh 10:16	4631
are found hid in a c at Makkedah	Josh 10:17	4631
stones upon the mouth of the c	Josh 10:18	4631
Joshua, Open the mouth of the c	Josh 10:22	4631
five kings unto me out of the c	Josh 10:22	4631
five kings unto him out of the c	Josh 10:23	4631
cast them into the c wherein they	Josh 10:27	4631
and escaped to the c Adullam	1Sa 22:1	4631
by the way, where was a c	1Sa 24:3	4631
remained in the sides of the c	1Sa 24:3	4631
But Saul rose up out of the c	1Sa 24:7	4631
afterward, and went out of the c	1Sa 24:8	4631
to day into mine hand in the c	1Sa 24:10	4631
time unto the c of Adullam	2Sa 23:13	4631
and hid them by fifty in a c	1Kin 18:4	4631
LORD's prophets by fifty in a c	1Kin 18:13	4631
And he came thither unto a c	1Kin 19:9	4631
stood in the entering in of the c	1Kin 19:13	4631
to David, into the c of Adullam	1Chr 11:15	4631
when he fled from Saul in the c	Ps 57:*t*	4631
A Prayer when he was in the c	Ps 142:*t*	4631
It was a c, and a stone lay upon	Jn 11:38	*4693*

CAVE'S

laid great stones in the c mouth	Josh 10:27	4631

CAVES

which are in the mountains, and c	Judg 6:2	4631
people did hide themselves in c	1Sa 13:6	4631
in c of the earth, and in the	Job 30:6	2356
into the c of the earth, for fear	Is 2:19	4247
in the c shall die of the	Eze 33:27	4631
and in dens and c of the earth	Heb 11:38	*3692*

CEASE

and day and night shall not c	Gen 8:22	7673
and the thunder shall c, neither	Ex 9:29	2308
shall c waiting upon the service	Num 8:25	7725
they prophesied, and did not c	Num 11:25	3254
I will make to c from me the	Num 17:5	7918
shall never c out of the land	Deut 15:11	2308
of them to c from among men	Deut 32:26	7673
children c from fearing the LORD	Josh 22:25	7673
of you, and after that I will c	Judg 15:7	2308
Benjamin my brother, or shall I c	Judg 20:28	2308
C not to cry unto the LORD our	1Sa 7:8	2790
of Ramah, and let his work c	2Chr 16:5	7673
to cause these men to c, and that	Ezr 4:21	989
Jews, and made them to c by force	Ezr 4:23	989
they could not cause them to c	Ezr 5:5	989
slay them, and cause the work to c	Neh 4:11	7673
why should the work c, whilst I	Neh 6:3	7673
There the wicked c from troubling	Job 3:17	2308
c then, and let me alone, that I	Job 10:20	2308
tender branch thereof will not c	Job 14:7	2308
C from anger, and forsake wrath	Ps 37:8	7503
He maketh wars to c unto the end	Ps 46:9	7673
cause thine anger toward us to c	Ps 85:4	6565
Thou hast made his glory to c	Ps 89:44	7673
The lot causeth contentions to c	Prov 18:18	7673
C, my son, to hear the	Prov 19:27	2308
honour for a man to c from strife	Prov 20:3	7647
yea, strife and reproach shall c	Prov 22:10	7673
c from thine own wisdom	Prov 23:4	2308
the grinders c because they are	Eccl 12:3	988
c to do evil	Is 1:16	2308
C ye from man, whose breath is in	Is 2:22	2308
while, and the indignation shall c	Is 10:25	3615
the arrogancy of the proud to c	Is 13:11	7673
made their vintage shouting to c	Is 16:10	7673
also shall c from Ephraim	Is 17:3	7673
sighing thereof have I made to c	Is 21:2	7673
One of Israel to c from before us	Is 30:11	7673
when thou shalt c to spoil	Is 33:1	8552
Then will I cause to c from the	Jer 7:34	7673
night and day, and let them not c	Jer 14:17	1820
I will cause to c out of this	Jer 16:9	7673
neither shall c from yielding	Jer 17:8	4185
c from being a nation before me	Jer 31:36	7673
shall cause to c from thence man	Jer 36:29	7673

I will cause to c in Moab ... Jer 48:35 7673
let not the apple of thine eye c ... Lam 2:18 1826
and your idols may be broken and c ... Eze 6:6 7673
make the pomp of the strong to c ... Eze 7:24 7673
I will make this proverb to c ... Eze 12:23 7673
I will cause thee to c from ... Eze 16:41 7673
make thy lewdness to c from thee ... Eze 23:27 7673
lewdness to c out of the land ... Eze 23:48 7673
cause the noise of thy songs to c ... Eze 26:13 7673
c by the hand of Nebuchadrezzar ... Eze 30:10 7673
their images to c out of Noph ... Eze 30:13 7673
of her strength shall c in her ... Eze 30:18 7673
the pomp of her strength shall c ... Eze 33:28 7673
cause them to c from feeding the ... Eze 34:10 7673
evil beasts to c out of the land ... Eze 34:25 7673
sacrifice and the oblation to c ... Dan 9:27 7673
the reproach offered by him to c ... Dan 11:18 7673
will cause to c the kingdom of ... Hos 1:4 7673
also cause all her mirth to c ... Hos 2:11 7673
Then said I, O Lord GOD, c ... Amos 7:5 2308
wilt thou not c to pervert the ... Acts 13:10 *3973*
there be tongues, they shall c ... 1Cor 13:8 *3973*
C not to give thanks for you, ... Eph 1:16 *3973*
do not c to pray for you, and to ... Col 1:9 *3973*
and that cannot c from sin ... 2Pet 2:14 *180*

CEASED
it c to be with Sarah after the ... Gen 18:11 2308
and the thunders and hail c ... Ex 9:33 2308
the hail and the thunders were c ... Ex 9:34 2308
the manna c on the morrow after ... Josh 5:12 7673
they c not from their own doings, ... Judg 2:19 5307
The inhabitants of the villages c ... Judg 5:7 2308
they c in Israel, until that I ... Judg 5:7 2308
and they that were hungry c ... 1Sa 2:5 2308
words in the name of David, and c ... 1Sa 25:9 5117
Then c the work of the house of ... Ezr 4:24 989
So it c unto the second year of ... Ezr 4:24 989
these three men c to answer Job ... Job 32:1 7673
they did tear me, and c not ... Ps 35:15 1826
sore ran in the night, and c not ... Ps 77:2 6313
and say, How hath the oppressor c ... Is 14:4 7673
the golden city c ... Is 14:4 7673
The elders have c from the gate ... Lam 5:14 7673
The joy of our heart is c ... Lam 5:15 7673
the sea c from her raging ... Jonah 1:15 5975
come into the ship, the wind c ... Mt 14:32 *2869*
And the wind c, and there was a ... Mk 4:39 *2869*
and the wind c ... Mk 6:51 *2869*
in hath not c to kiss my feet ... Lk 7:45 *1257*
and they c, and there was a calm ... Lk 8:24 *3973*
in a certain place, when he c ... Lk 11:1 *3973*
they c not to teach and preach ... Acts 5:42 *3973*
And after the uproar was c ... Acts 20:1 *3973*
I c not to warn every one night ... Acts 20:31 *3973*
he would not be persuaded, we c ... Acts 21:14 *2270*
is the offence of the cross c ... Gal 5:11 *2673*
he also hath c from his own works ... Heb 4:10 *2664*
they not have c to be offered ... Heb 10:2 *3973*
in the flesh hath c from sin ... 1Pet 4:1 *3973*

CEASETH
for the godly man c ... Ps 12:1 1584
is precious, and it c for ever ... Ps 49:8 2308
is no talebearer, the strife c ... Prov 26:20 8367
is at an end, the spoiler c ... Is 16:4 3615
The mirth of tabrets c, the noise ... Is 24:8 7673
endeth, the joy of the harp c ... Is 24:8 7673
lie waste, the wayfaring man c ... Is 33:8 7673
c not, without any intermission, ... Lam 3:49 1820
who c from raising after he hath ... Hos 7:4 7673
said, This man c not to speak ... Acts 6:13 *3973*

CEASING
the LORD in c to pray for you ... 1Sa 12:23 2308
but prayer was made without c of ... Acts 12:5 *1618*
that without c I make mention of ... Rom 1:9 *89*
without c your work of faith ... 1Th 1:3 *89*
cause also thank we God without c ... 1Th 2:13 *89*
Pray without c ... 1Th 5:17 *89*
that without c I have remembrance ... 2Ti 1:3 *83*

CEDAR
c wood, and scarlet, and hyssop ... Lev 14:4 730
the c wood, and the scarlet, and ... Lev 14:6 730
c wood, and scarlet, and hyssop ... Lev 14:49 730
And he shall take the c wood ... Lev 14:51 730
living bird, and with the c wood ... Lev 14:52 730
And the priest shall take c wood ... Num 19:6 730
as c trees beside the waters ... Num 24:6 730
c trees, and carpenters, and masons ... 2Sa 5:11 730
See now, I dwell in an house of c ... 2Sa 7:2 730
Why build ye not me an house of c ... 2Sa 7:7 730
from the c tree that is in ... 1Kin 4:33 730
hew me c trees out of Lebanon ... 1Kin 5:6 730
thy desire concerning timber of c ... 1Kin 5:8 730
So Hiram gave Solomon c trees ... 1Kin 5:10 730
house with beams and boards of c ... 1Kin 6:9 730
on the house with timber of c ... 1Kin 6:10 730
the house within with boards of c ... 1Kin 6:15 730
and the walls with boards of c ... 1Kin 6:16 730
the c of the house within was ... 1Kin 6:18 730
all was c ... 1Kin 6:18 730
covered the altar which was of c ... 1Kin 6:20 730
hewed stone, and a row of c beams ... 1Kin 6:36 730
upon four rows of c pillars ... 1Kin 7:2 730
with c beams upon the pillars ... 1Kin 7:2 730
it was covered with c above upon ... 1Kin 7:3 730
it was covered with c from one ... 1Kin 7:7 730
hewed stones, and a row of c beams ... 1Kin 7:12 730
furnished Solomon with c trees ... 1Kin 9:11 730
sent to the c that was in Lebanon ... 2Kin 14:9 730
cut down the tall c trees thereof ... 2Kin 19:23 730
Also c trees in abundance ... 1Chr 22:4 730
Tyre brought much c wood to David ... 1Chr 22:4 730
c trees made he as the sycomore ... 2Chr 1:15 730
Send me also c trees, fir trees, ... 2Chr 2:8 730
c trees made he as the sycomore ... 2Chr 9:27 730
sent to the c that was in Lebanon ... 2Chr 25:18 730
to bring c trees from Lebanon to ... Ezr 3:7 730
He moveth his tail like a c ... Job 40:17 730
he shall grow like a c in Lebanon ... Ps 92:12 730
The beams of our house are c ... Song 1:17 730
will inclose her with boards of c ... Song 8:9 730
plant in the wilderness the c ... Is 41:19 730
and it is cieled with c, and ... Jer 22:14 730
because thou closest thyself in c ... Jer 22:15 730
took the highest branch of the c ... Eze 17:3 730
the highest branch of the high c ... Eze 17:22 730
and bear fruit, and be a goodly c ... Eze 17:23 730
bound with cords, and made of c ... Eze 27:24 729
the Assyrian was a c in Lebanon ... Eze 31:3 730
for he shall uncover the c work ... Zeph 2:14 731
for the c is fallen ... Zec 11:2 730

CEDARS
and devour the c of Lebanon ... Judg 9:15 730
measures of hewed stones, and c ... 1Kin 7:11 730
c made he to be as the sycomore ... 1Kin 10:27 730
to David, and timber of c, with ... 1Chr 14:1 730
Lo, I dwell in an house of c ... 1Chr 17:1 730
ye not built me an house of c ... 1Chr 17:6 730
didst send him c to build him an ... 2Chr 2:3 730
voice of the LORD breaketh the c ... Ps 29:5 730
LORD breaketh the c of Lebanon ... Ps 29:5 730
thereof were like the goodly c ... Ps 80:10 730
the c of Lebanon, which he hath ... Ps 104:16 730
fruitful trees, and all c ... Ps 148:9 730
is as Lebanon, excellent as the c ... Song 5:15 730
And upon all the c of Lebanon ... Is 2:13 730
but we will change them into c ... Is 9:10 730
the c of Lebanon, saying, Since ... Is 14:8 730
will cut down the tall c thereof ... Is 37:24 730
He heweth him down c, and taketh ... Is 44:14 730
they shall cut down thy choice c ... Jer 22:7 730
that makest thy nest in the c ... Jer 22:23 730
they have taken c from Lebanon to ... Eze 27:5 730
The c in the garden of God could ... Eze 31:8 730
was like the height of the c ... Amos 2:9 730
that the fire may devour thy c ... Zec 11:1 730

CEDRON (*se'-drun*) See KIDRON. *Same as Kidron.*
his disciples over the brook C ... Jn 18:1 *2748*

CELEBRATE
even, shall ye c your sabbath ... Lev 23:32 7673
ye shall c it in the seventh ... Lev 23:41 2278
praise thee, death can not c thee ... Is 38:18 1984

CELESTIAL
There are also c bodies, and ... 1Cor 15:40 *2032*
but the glory of the c is one ... 1Cor 15:40 *2032*

CELLARS
wine c was Zabdi the Shiphmite ... 1Chr 27:27 214
over the c of oil was Joash ... 1Chr 27:28 214

CENCHREA (*sen'-kre-ah*) *Harbor city for Corinth.*
having shorn his head in C ... Acts 18:18 *2747*
of the church which is at C ... Rom 16:1 *2747*
Phebe servant of the church at C ... Rom *s*

CENCHREAE See CENCHREA.

CENSER
Aaron, took either of them his c ... Lev 10:1 4289
he shall take a c full of burning ... Lev 16:12 4289
And take every man his c, and put ... Num 16:17 4289
before the LORD every man his c ... Num 16:17 4289
also, and Aaron, each of you his c ... Num 16:17 4289
And they took every man his c ... Num 16:18 4289
Moses said unto Aaron, Take a c ... Num 16:46 4289
had a c in his hand to burn ... 2Chr 26:19 4730
with every man his c in his hand ... Eze 8:11 4730
Which had the golden c, and the ... Heb 9:4 *2369*
at the altar, having a golden c ... Rev 8:3 *3031*
And the angel took the c, and ... Rev 8:5 *3031*

CENSERS
minister about it, even the c ... Num 4:14 4289
Take you c, Korah, and all his ... Num 16:6 4289
censer, two hundred and fifty c ... Num 16:17 4289
take up the c out of the burning ... Num 16:37 4289
The c of these sinners against ... Num 16:38 4289
the priest took the brasen c ... Num 16:39 4289
the spoons, and the c of pure gold ... 1Kin 7:50 4289
basons, and the spoons, and the c ... 2Chr 4:22 4289

CENTURION
there came unto him a c, ... Mt 8:5 *1543*
The c answered and said, Lord, I ... Mt 8:8 *1543*
And Jesus said unto the c, Go thy ... Mt 8:13 *1543*
Now when the c, and they that were ... Mt 27:54 *1543*
And when the c, which stood over ... Mk 15:39 *2760*
and calling unto him the c ... Mk 15:44 *2760*
And when he knew it of the c ... Mk 15:45 *2760*
the c sent friends to him, saying ... Lk 7:6 *1543*
Now when the c saw what was done, ... Lk 23:47 *1543*
a c of the band called the ... Acts 10:1 *1543*
And they said, Cornelius the c ... Acts 10:22 *1543*
said unto the c that stood by ... Acts 22:25 *1543*
When the c heard that, he went and ... Acts 22:26 *1543*
And he commanded a c to keep Paul ... Acts 24:23 *1543*
Julius, a c of Augustus' band ... Acts 27:1 *1543*
there the c found a ship of ... Acts 27:6 *1543*
Nevertheless the c believed the ... Acts 27:11 *1543*
Paul said to the c and to the ... Acts 27:31 *1543*
But the c, willing to save Paul, ... Acts 27:43 *1543*
the c delivered the prisoners to ... Acts 28:16 *1543*

CENTURION'S
And a certain c servant, who was ... Lk 7:2 *1543*

CENTURIONS
immediately took soldiers and c ... Acts 21:32 *1543*
Paul called one of the c unto him ... Acts 23:17 *1543*
And he called unto him two c ... Acts 23:23 *1543*

CEPHAS (*se'-fas*) See PETER. *Name given to Simon Peter.*
thou shalt be called C, which is ... Jn 1:42 *2786*
and I of C ... 1Cor 1:12 *2786*
Whether Paul, or Apollos, or C ... 1Cor 3:22 *2786*
as the brethren of the Lord, and C ... 1Cor 9:5 *2786*
And that he was seen of C, then of ... 1Cor 15:5 *2786*
And when James, C, and John, who ... Gal 2:9 *2786*

CEREMONIES
and according to all the c thereof ... Num 9:3 4941

CERTAIN
And he lighted upon a c place ... Gen 28:11
a c man found him, and, behold, he ... Gen 37:15
and turned in to a c Adullamite ... Gen 38:1 376
there a daughter of a c Canaanite ... Gen 38:2 376
gather a c rate every day, that I ... Ex 16:4 1697
And there were c men, who were ... Num 9:6
with c of the children of Israel, ... Num 16:2 582
C men, the children of Belial, ... Deut 13:13
if it be truth, and the thing c ... Deut 13:14 3559
it be true, and the thing c ... Deut 17:4 3559
to his fault, by a c number ... Deut 25:2
a c woman cast a piece of a ... Judg 9:53 259
there was a c man of Zorah, of ... Judg 13:2 259
that there was a c Levite ... Judg 19:1 376
c sons of Belial, beset the house ... Judg 19:22 582
a c man of Beth-lehem-judah went ... Ruth 1:1
Now there was a c man of ... 1Sa 1:1 259
Now a c man of the servants of ... 1Sa 21:7
a c man saw it, and told Joab, and ... 2Sa 18:10 259
thou shalt know for c that thou ... 1Kin 2:37 3045
unto thee, saying, Know for a c ... 1Kin 2:42 3045
oxen were c additions made of ... 1Kin 7:29
c Edomites of his father's ... 1Kin 11:17 582
a c man of the sons of the ... 1Kin 20:35 259
a c man drew a bow at a venture, ... 1Kin 22:34
Now there cried a c woman of the ... 2Kin 4:1 259
appointed unto her a c officer ... 2Kin 8:6 259
c of them had the charge of the ... 1Chr 9:28
he appointed c of the Levites to ... 1Chr 16:4
Then there went c, and told David ... 1Chr 19:5
Even after a c rate every day, ... 2Chr 8:13 1697
after c years he went down to ... 2Chr 18:2
a c man drew a bow at a venture, ... 2Chr 18:33
Then c of the heads of the ... 2Chr 28:12 592
with c chief of the fathers, ... Ezr 10:16 592
came, he and c men of Judah ... Neh 1:2
down and wept, and mourned c days ... Neh 1:4
at Jerusalem dwelt c of the ... Neh 11:4
that a c portion should be for ... Neh 11:23
c of the priests' sons with ... Neh 12:35
after c days obtained I leave of ... Neh 13:6
smote c of them, and plucked off ... Neh 13:25 582
the palace there was a c Jew ... Est 2:5 376
There is a c people scattered ... Est 3:8 259
But know ye for c, that if ye put ... Jer 26:15 3045
Then rose up c of the elders of ... Jer 26:17 582
c men with him into Egypt ... Jer 26:22
That there came c from Shechem ... Jer 41:5 582
c of the poor of the people ... Jer 52:15
c of the poor of the land for ... Jer 52:16
Then came c of the elders of ... Eze 14:1 582
that c of the elders of Israel ... Eze 20:1 582
that he should bring c of the ... Dan 1:3
and the dream is c, and the ... Dan 2:45 3330
that time c Chaldeans came near ... Dan 3:8 1400
There are c Jews whom thou hast ... Dan 3:12 1400
unto that c saint which spake ... Dan 8:13 6422
fainted, and was sick c days ... Dan 8:27
behold a c man clothed in linen, ... Dan 10:5 259
after c years with a great army ... Dan 11:13 6256
a c scribe came, and said unto him ... Mt 8:19 *1520*
c of the scribes said within ... Mt 9:3 *5100*
behold, there came a c ruler ... Mt 9:18
Then c of the scribes and of the ... Mt 12:38 *5100*
there came to him a c man ... Mt 17:14
of heaven likened unto a c king ... Mt 18:23 *444*
desiring a c thing of him ... Mt 20:20 *5100*
A c man had two sons ... Mt 21:28
There was a c householder ... Mt 21:33 *5100*
of heaven is like unto a c king ... Mt 22:2 *444*
But there were c of the scribes ... Mk 2:6 *5100*
a c woman, which had an issue of ... Mk 5:25 *5100*
synagogue's house c which said ... Mk 5:35
c of the scribes, which came from ... Mk 7:1 *5100*
For a c woman, whose young ... Mk 7:25
c of them that stood there said ... Mk 11:5 *5100*
A c man planted a vineyard, and ... Mk 12:1
send unto him c of the Pharisees ... Mk 12:13 *5100*
And there came a c poor widow ... Mk 12:42 *1520*
there followed him a c young man ... Mk 14:51 *5100*
And there arose c, and bare false ... Mk 14:57 *5100*
a c priest named Zacharias, of ... Lk 1:5 *5100*
to pass, when he was in a c city ... Lk 5:12 *1520*
And it came to pass on a c day ... Lk 5:17 *1520*
c of the Pharisees said unto them ... Lk 6:2 *5100*
a c centurion's servant, who was ... Lk 7:2 *5100*
There was a c creditor which had ... Lk 7:41 *5100*
c women, which had been healed of ... Lk 8:2 *5100*
it was told him by c which said ... Lk 8:20
Now it came to pass on a c day ... Lk 8:22 *1520*
met him out of the city a c man ... Lk 8:27 *5100*
a c man said unto him, Lord, I ... Lk 9:57 *5100*
a c lawyer stood up, and tempted ... Lk 10:25 *5100*
A c man went down from Jerusalem ... Lk 10:30 *5100*
came down a c priest that way ... Lk 10:31 *5100*

But a c Samaritan, as he — Lk 10:33 *5100*
that he entered into a c village — Lk 10:38 *5100*
a c woman named Martha received — Lk 10:38 *5100*
as he was praying in a c place — Lk 11:1 *5100*
a c woman of the company lifted — Lk 11:27 *5100*
a c Pharisee besought him to dine — Lk 11:37 *5100*
The ground of a c rich man — Lk 12:16 *5100*
A c man had a fig tree planted in — Lk 13:6 *5100*
day there came c of the Pharisees — Lk 13:31 *5100*
there was a c man before him — Lk 14:2 *5100*
A c man made a great supper, and — Lk 14:16 *5100*
And he said, A c man had two sons — Lk 15:11 *5100*
disciples, There was a c rich man — Lk 16:1 *5100*
There was a c rich man, which was — Lk 16:19 *5100*
there was a c beggar named — Lk 16:20 *5100*
And as he entered into a c village — Lk 17:12 *5100*
he spake this parable unto c — Lk 18:9 *5100*
a c ruler asked him, saying, Good — Lk 18:18 *5100*
a c blind man sat by the way side — Lk 18:35 *5100*
A c nobleman went into a far — Lk 19:12 *5100*
A c man planted a vineyard, and — Lk 20:9 *5100*
came to him c of the Sadducees — Lk 20:27 *5100*
Then c of the scribes answering — Lk 20:39 *5100*
he saw also a c poor widow — Lk 21:2 *5100*
But a c maid beheld him as he sat — Lk 22:56 *5100*
(Who for a c sedition made in the — Lk 23:19 *5100*
prepared, and c others with them — Lk 24:1
c women also of our company made — Lk 24:22 *5100*
c of them which were with us went — Lk 24:24 *5100*
And there was a c nobleman — Jn 4:46 *5100*
down at a c season into the pool — Jn 5:4
a c man was there, which had an — Jn 5:5 *5100*
Now a c man was sick, named — Jn 11:1 *5100*
there were c Greeks among them — Jn 12:20 *5100*
a c man lame from his mother's — Acts 3:2 *5100*
But a c man named Ananias, with — Acts 5:1 *5100*
privy to it, and brought a c part — Acts 5:2 *5100*
there arose c of the synagogue — Acts 6:9 *5100*
But there was a c man, called — Acts 8:9 *5100*
way, they came unto a c water — Acts 8:36 *5100*
there was a c disciple at — Acts 9:10 *5100*
Then was Saul c days with the — Acts 9:19 *5100*
he found a c man named Aeneas — Acts 9:33 *5100*
Joppa a c disciple named Tabitha — Acts 9:36 *5100*
There was a c man in Caesarea — Acts 10:1 *5100*
a c vessel descending unto him — Acts 10:11 *5100*
c brethren from Joppa accompanied — Acts 10:23 *5100*
prayed they him to tarry c days — Acts 10:48 *5100*
A c vessel descend, as it had — Acts 11:5 *5100*
his hands to vex c of the church — Acts 12:1 *5100*
that was at Antioch c prophets — Acts 13:1 *5100*
Paphos, they found a c sorcerer — Acts 13:6 *5100*
there sat a c man at Lystra — Acts 14:8 *5100*
came thither c Jews from Antioch — Acts 14:19
c men which came down from Judaea. — Acts 15:1 *5100*
c other of them, should go up to — Acts 15:2 *5100*
But there rose up c of the sect — Acts 15:5 *5100*
that c which went out from us — Acts 15:24 *5100*
a c disciple was there, named — Acts 16:1 *5100*
Timotheus, the son of a c woman — Acts 16:1 *5100*
were in that city abiding c days — Acts 16:12 *5100*
a c woman named Lydia, a seller — Acts 16:14 *5100*
a c damsel possessed with a — Acts 16:16 *5100*
took unto them c lewd fellows of — Acts 17:5 *5100*
c brethren unto the rulers of the — Acts 17:6 *5100*
Then c philosophers of the — Acts 17:18 *5100*
For thou bringest c strange — Acts 17:20 *5100*
as c also of your own poets have — Acts 17:28 *5100*
Howbeit c men clave unto him, and — Acts 17:34 *5100*
found a c Jew named Aquila, born — Acts 18:2 *5100*
and entered into a c man's house — Acts 18:7 *5100*
a c Jew named Apollos, born at — Acts 18:24 *5100*
and finding c disciples, — Acts 19:1 *5100*
Then c of the vagabond Jews, — Acts 19:13 *5100*
For a c man named Demetrius, a — Acts 19:24 *5100*
c of the chief of Asia, which — Acts 19:31 *5100*
there sat in a window a c young — Acts 20:9 *5100*
came down from Judaea a c prophet — Acts 21:10 *5100*
There went with us also c of the — Acts 21:16
c of the Jews banded together, and — Acts 23:12 *5100*
for he hath a c thing to tell him — Acts 23:17 *5100*
with a c orator named Tertullus — Acts 24:1 *5100*
Whereupon c Jews from Asia found — Acts 24:18 *5100*
And after c days, when Felix came — Acts 24:24 *5100*
after c days king Agrippa and — Acts 25:13 *5100*
There is a c man left in bonds by — Acts 25:14 *5100*
But had c questions against him — Acts 25:19 *5100*
Of whom I have no c thing to — Acts 25:26 *804*
c other prisoners unto one named — Acts 27:1 *5100*
running under a c island which is — Acts 27:16 *5100*
we must be cast upon a c island — Acts 27:26 *5100*
discovered a c creek with a shore — Acts 27:39 *5100*
Achaia to make a c contribution — Rom 15:26 *5100*
have no c dwellingplace place — 1Cor 4:11 *790*
For before that c came from James — Gal 2:12 *5100*
it is c we can carry nothing out — 1Ti 6:7 *1212*
But one in a c place testified, — Heb 2:6 *4225*
For he spake in a c place of the — Heb 4:4 *4225*
Again, he limiteth a c day — Heb 4:7 *5100*
But a c fearful looking for of — Heb 10:27 *5100*
For there are c men crept in — Jude 4 *5100*

CERTAINLY

I will c return unto thee — Gen 18:10
We saw c that the LORD was with — Gen 26:28
could we c know that he would say — Gen 43:7
that such a man as I can c divine — Gen 44:15
will c requite us all the evil — Gen 50:15
And he said, C I will be with thee — Ex 3:12 3588
If the theft be c found in his — Ex 22:4
he hath c trespassed against the — Lev 5:19
congregation shall c stone him — Lev 24:16
Because it was c told thy — Josh 9:24
if ye can c declare it me within — Judg 14:12
Thy father c knoweth that I have — 1Sa 20:3
for if I knew c that evil were — 1Sa 20:9
thy servant hath c heard that — 1Sa 23:10
for the LORD will c make my lord — 1Sa 25:28
even so will I c do this day — 1Kin 1:30
unto him, Thou mayest c recover — 2Kin 8:10
If thou c return in peace, then — 2Chr 18:27
for riches c make themselves — Prov 23:5
Lo, c in vain made he it — Jer 8:8 403
Do we not c know that every — Jer 13:12
Ye shall c drink — Jer 25:28
The king of Babylon shall c come — Jer 36:29
Dost thou c know that Baalis the — Jer 40:14
know c that I have admonished you — Jer 42:19
Now therefore know c that ye — Jer 42:22
But we will c do whatsoever thing — Jer 44:17
c this is the day that we looked — Lam 2:16 389
and one shall c come, and overflow, — Dan 11:10
shall c come after certain years — Dan 11:13
C this was a righteous man — Lk 23:47 *3689*

CERTAINTY

Know for a c that the LORD your — Josh 23:13
and come ye again to me with the c — 1Sa 23:23 3559
know the c of the words of truth — Prov 22:21 7189
I know of c that ye would gain — Dan 2:8 3330
know the c of those things — Lk 1:4 *803*
not know the c for the tumult — Acts 21:34 *804*
c wherefore he was accused of the — Acts 22:30 *804*

CERTIFIED

have we sent and c the king — Ezr 4:14 3064
Esther c the king thereof in — Est 2:22 559

CERTIFY

there come word from you to c me — 2Sa 15:28 5046
We c the king that, if this city — Ezr 4:16 3046
to c thee, that we might write — Ezr 5:10 3046
Also we c you, that touching any — Ezr 7:24 3046
But I c you, brethren, that the — Gal 1:11 *1107*

CHAFED

they be c in their minds, as a — 2Sa 17:8 4751

CHAFF

as c that the storm carrieth away — Job 21:18 4671
but are like the c which the wind — Ps 1:4 4671
Let them be as c before the wind — Ps 35:5 4671
and the flame consumeth the c — Is 5:24 2842
shall be chased as the c of the — Is 17:13 4671
shall be as c that passeth away — Is 29:5 4671
Ye shall conceive c, ye shall — Is 33:11 2842
and shalt make the hills as c — Is 41:15 4671
What is the c to the wheat — Jer 23:28 8401
became like the c of the summer — Dan 2:35 5784
as the c that is driven with the — Hos 13:3 4671
before the day pass as the c — Zeph 2:2 4671
up the c with unquenchable fire — Mt 3:12 *892*
but the c he will burn with fire — Lk 3:17 *892*

CHAIN

put a gold c about his neck — Gen 41:42 7242
work, and wreaths of c work — 1Kin 7:17 8333
compasseth them about as a c — Ps 73:6 6059
eyes, with one c of thy neck — Song 4:9 6060
he hath made my c heavy — Lam 3:7 5178
Make a c — Eze 7:23 7659
thy hands, and a c on thy neck — Eze 16:11 7242
have a c of gold about his neck, — Dan 5:7 2002
have a c of gold about thy neck, — Dan 5:16 2002
put a c of gold about his neck, — Dan 5:29 2002
of Israel I am bound with this c — Acts 28:20 *254*
me, and was not ashamed of my c — 2Ti 1:16 *254*
pit and a great c in his hand — Rev 20:1 *254*

CHAINS

two c of pure gold at the ends — Ex 28:14 8333
the wreathen c to the ouches — Ex 28:14 8333
c at the ends of wreathen work of — Ex 28:22 8337
c of gold in the two rings which — Ex 28:24 5688
c thou shalt fasten in the two — Ex 28:25
the breastplate c at the ends — Ex 39:15 8333
they put the two wreathen c of — Ex 39:17 5688
two ends of the two wreathen c — Ex 39:18 5688
hath gotten, of jewels of gold, c — Num 31:50 685
beside the c that were about — Judg 8:26 6060
the c of gold before the oracle — 1Kin 6:21 7569
and set thereon palm trees and c — 2Chr 3:5 8333
And he made c, as in the oracle, — 2Chr 3:16 8333
and put them on the c — 2Chr 3:16 8333
out those which are bound with c — Ps 68:6 3574
To bind their kings with c — Ps 149:8 2131
thy head, and c about thy neck — Prov 1:9 6060
jewels, thy neck with c of gold — Song 1:10 2737
The c, and the bracelets, and the — Is 3:19 5188
with gold, and casteth silver c — Is 40:19 7569
in c they shall come over, and — Is 45:14 2131
eyes, and bound him with c — Jer 39:7 5178
in c among all that were carried — Jer 40:1 246
the c which were upon thine hand — Jer 40:4 246
king of Babylon bound him in c — Jer 52:11 5178
they brought him with c unto the — Eze 19:4 2397
And they put him in ward in c — Eze 19:9 2397
all her great men were bound in c — Nah 3:10 2131
could bind him, no, not with c — Mk 5:3 *254*
often bound with fetters and c — Mk 5:4 *254*
the c had been plucked asunder by — Mk 5:4 *254*
and he was kept bound with c — Lk 8:29 *254*
two soldiers, bound with two c — Acts 12:6 *254*
his c fell off from his hands — Acts 12:7 *254*
him to be bound with two c — Acts 21:33 *254*
delivered them into c of darkness — 2Pet 2:4 *4577*
c under darkness unto the — Jude 6 *1199*

CHALCEDONY

the third, a c — Rev 21:19 *5472*

CHALCOL (*kal'-kol*) See CALCOL. *Son of Mahol.*

the Ezrahite, and Heman, and C — 1Kin 4:31 3633

CHALDAEANS (*kal-de'-uns*) See CHALDEANS. *Inhabitants of southern Babylonia.*

came he out of the land of the C — Acts 7:4 *5466*

CHALDEA (*kal-de'-ah*) See BABYLON, CHALDEAN. *Southern portion of Babylonia.*

And C shall be a spoil — Jer 50:10 3778
to all the inhabitants of C all — Jer 51:24 3778
blood upon the inhabitants of C — Jer 51:35 3778
by the Spirit of God into C — Eze 11:24 3778
in the land of Canaan unto C — Eze 16:29 3778
manner of the Babylonians of C — Eze 23:15 3778
sent messengers unto them into C — Eze 23:16 3778

CHALDEAN (*kal-de'-un*) See BABYLONIAN, CHALDEANS, CHALDEANS'

the king of Babylon, the C — Ezr 5:12 3777
any magician, or astrologer, or C — Dan 2:10 3777

CHALDEANS (*kal-de'-uns*) See BABYLONIANS, CHALDAEANS, CHALDEANS', CHALDEES. *Same as Chaldaeans.*

The C made out three bands, and — Job 1:17 3778
Behold the land of the C — Is 23:13 3778
down all their nobles, and the C — Is 43:14 3778
is no throne, O daughter of the C — Is 47:1 3778
darkness, O daughter of the C — Is 47:5 3778
and his arm shall be on the C — Is 48:14 3778
of Babylon, flee ye from the C — Is 48:20 3778
king of Babylon, and against the C — Jer 21:4 3778
falleth to the C that besiege you — Jer 21:9 3778
and into the hand of the C — Jer 22:25 3778
the land of the C for their good — Jer 24:5 3778
iniquity, and the land of the C — Jer 25:12 3778
escape out of the hand of the C — Jer 32:4 3778
though ye fight with the C — Jer 32:5 3778
is given into the hand of the C — Jer 32:24 3778
is given into the hand of the C — Jer 32:25 3778
this city into the hand of the C — Jer 32:28 3778
And the C, that fight against this — Jer 32:29 3778
is given into the hand of the C — Jer 32:43 3778
They come to fight with the C — Jer 33:5 3778
for fear of the army of the C — Jer 35:11 3778
and when the C that besieged — Jer 37:5 3778
the C shall come again, and fight — Jer 37:8 3778
The C shall surely depart from us — Jer 37:9 3778
of the C that fight against you — Jer 37:10 3778
that when the army of the C was — Jer 37:11 3778
Thou fallest away to the C — Jer 37:13 3778
I fall not away to the C — Jer 37:14 3778
goeth forth to the C shall live — Jer 38:2 3778
be given into the hand of the C — Jer 38:18 3778
the Jews that are fallen to the C — Jer 38:19 3778
wives and thy children to the C — Jer 38:23 3778
the C burned the king's house, and — Jer 39:8 3778
saying, Fear not to serve the C — Jer 40:9 3778
dwell at Mizpah to serve the C — Jer 40:10 3778
the C that were found there, and — Jer 41:3 3778
Because of the C — Jer 41:18 3778
deliver us into the hand of the C — Jer 43:3 3778
of the C by Jeremiah the prophet — Jer 50:1 3778
go forth out of the land of the C — Jer 50:8 3778
GOD of hosts in the land of the C — Jer 50:25 3778
A sword is upon the C, saith the — Jer 50:35 3778
against the land of the C — Jer 50:45 3778
shall fall in the land of the C — Jer 51:4 3778
from the land of the C — Jer 51:54 3778
(now the C were by the city round — Jer 52:7 3778
But the army of the C pursued — Jer 52:8 3779
And all the army of the C, that — Jer 52:14 3779
the C brake, and carried all the — Jer 52:17 3779
in the land of the C by the river — Eze 1:3 3779
to Babylon to the land of the C — Eze 12:13 3779
the images of the C pourtrayed — Eze 23:14 3779
The Babylonians, and all the C — Eze 23:23 3779
learning and the tongue of the C — Dan 1:4 3779
and the sorcerers, and the C — Dan 2:2 3779
Then spake the C to the king in — Dan 2:4 3779
king answered and said to the C — Dan 2:5 3779
The C answered before the king, — Dan 2:10 3779
at that time certain C came near — Dan 3:8 3779
magicians, the astrologers, the C — Dan 4:7 3779
bring in the astrologers, the C — Dan 5:7 3779
of the magicians, astrologers, C — Dan 5:11 3779
the king of the C slain — Dan 5:30 3779
made king over the realm of the C — Dan 9:1 3778
For, lo, I raise up the C — Hab 1:6 3778

CHALDEANS' (*kal-de'-uns*)

But the C army pursued after them — Jer 39:5 3778

CHALDEES (*kal'-dees*) See CHALDEES'. *Same as Chaldeans.*

of his nativity, in Ur of the C — Gen 11:28 3778
forth with them from Ur of the C — Gen 11:31 3778
brought thee out of Ur of the C — Gen 15:7 3778
sent against him bands of the C — 2Kin 24:2 3778
(now the C were against the city — 2Kin 25:4 3778
the army of the C pursued after — 2Kin 25:5 3778
And all the army of the C, that — 2Kin 25:10 3778
did the C break in pieces, and — 2Kin 25:13 3778
not to be the servants of the C — 2Kin 25:24 3778
the C that were with him at — 2Kin 25:25 3778
for they were afraid of the C — 2Kin 25:26 3778
upon them the king of the C — 2Chr 36:17 3778
him forth out of Ur of the C — Neh 9:7 3778

CHALDEES' (*kal'-dees*) See CHALDEANS.
the beauty of the C excellency Is 13:19 3778

CHALKSTONES
as c that are beaten in sunder Is 27:9

CHALLENGETH
thing, which another c to be his Ex 22:9 559

CHAMBER
and he entered into his c, and wept Gen 43:30 2315
covereth his feet in his summer c Judg 3:24 2315
will go in to my wife into the c Judg 15:1 2315
wait, abiding with her in the c Judg 16:9 2315
liers in wait abiding in the c Judg 16:12 2315
Tamar, Bring the meat into the c 2Sa 13:10 2315
into the c to Amnon her brother 2Sa 13:10 2315
and went up to the c over the gate 2Sa 18:33 5944
went in unto the king into the c 1Kin 1:15 2315
The nethermost c was five cubits 1Kin 6:6 3326
The door for the middle c was in 1Kin 6:8 6763
winding stairs into the middle c 1Kin 6:8
them back into the guard c 1Kin 14:28 8372
down out of the c into the house 1Kin 17:23 5944
into the city, into an inner c 1Kin 20:30 2315
into an inner c to hide thyself 1Kin 22:25 2315
his upper c that was in Samaria 2Kin 1:2 5944
Let us make a little c, I pray 2Kin 4:10 5944
thither, and he turned into the c 2Kin 4:11 5944
and carry him to an inner c 2Kin 9:2 2315
by the c of Nathan-melech the 2Kin 23:11 3957
on the top of the upper c of Ahaz 2Kin 23:12 5944
them again into the guard c 2Chr 12:11 8372
into an inner c to hide thyself 2Chr 18:24 2315
went into the c of Johanan the Ezr 10:6 3957
of Berechiah over against his c Neh 3:30 5393
of the c of the house of our God Neh 13:4 3957
he had prepared for him a great c Neh 13:5 3957
in preparing him a c in the Neh 13:7 5393
stuff of Tobiah out of the c Neh 13:8 3957
a bridegroom coming out of his c Ps 19:5 2646
into the c of her that conceived Song 3:4 2315
into the c of the sons of Hanan, Jer 35:4 3957
which was by the c of the princes Jer 35:4 2315
which was above the c of Maaseiah Jer 35:4 3957
in the c of Gemariah the son of Jer 36:10 3957
king's house, into the scribe's c Jer 36:12 3957
in the c of Elishama the scribe Jer 36:20 3957
it out of Elishama the scribe's c Jer 36:21 3957
every little c was one reed long, Eze 40:7 8372
little c to the roof of another Eze 40:13 8372
And he said unto me, This c Eze 40:45 3957
the c whose prospect is toward Eze 40:46 3957
and the breadth of every side c Eze 41:5 6763
c to the highest by the midst Eze 41:7
which was for the side c without Eze 41:9 6763
he brought me into the c that was Eze 42:1 3957
open in his c toward Jerusalem Dan 6:10 5952
the bridegroom go forth of his c Joel 2:16 2315
they laid her in an upper c Acts 9:37 *5253*
they brought him into the upper c Acts 9:39 *5253*
were many lights in the upper c Acts 20:8 *5253*

CHAMBERING
rioting and drunkenness, not in c Rom 13:13 *2845*

CHAMBERLAIN
chamber of Nathan-melech the c 2Kin 23:11 5631
the custody of Hege the king's c Est 2:3 5631
of Shaashgaz, the king's c Est 2:14 5631
but what Hegai the king's c Est 2:15 5631
Blastus the king's c their friend Acts 12:20
Erastus the c of the city Rom 16:23 *3623*

CHAMBERLAINS
the seven c that served in the Est 1:10 5001
the king's commandment by his c Est 1:12 5631
of the king Ahasuerus by the c Est 1:15 5631
king's gate, two of the king's c Est 2:21 5631
her c came and told it her Est 4:4 5631
for Hatach, one of the king's c Est 4:5 5631
and Teresh, two of the king's c Est 6:2 5631
with him, came the king's c Est 6:14 5631
And Harbonah, one of the c Est 7:9 5631

CHAMBERS
the house he built c round about 1Kin 6:5 3326
and he made c round about 1Kin 6:5 6763
then he built c against all the 1Kin 6:10 3326
set office, and were over the c 1Chr 9:26 3957
who remaining in the c were free 1Chr 9:33 3957
LORD, in the courts, and in the c 1Chr 23:28 3957
and of the upper c thereof 1Chr 28:11 5944
of all the c round about, of the 1Chr 28:12 3957
he overlaid the upper c with gold 2Chr 3:9 5944
c in the house of the LORD 2Chr 31:11 3957
in the c of the house of the LORD Ezr 8:29 3957
to the c of the house of our God Neh 10:37 3957
the house of our God, to the c Neh 10:38 3957
new wine, and the oil, unto the c Neh 10:39 3957
over the c for the treasures Neh 12:44 5393
commanded, and they cleansed the c Neh 13:9 3957
Pleiades, and the c of the south Job 9:9 2315
the beams of his c in the waters Ps 104:3 5944
He watereth the hills from his c Ps 104:13 5944
in the c of their kings Ps 105:30 2315
going down to the c of death Prov 7:27 2315
by knowledge shall the c be Prov 24:4 2315
king hath brought me into his c Song 1:4 2315
my people, enter thou into thy c Is 26:20 2315
and his c by wrong Jer 22:13 5944
build me a wide house and large c Jer 22:14 5944
of the LORD, into one of the c Jer 35:2 3957
every man in the c of his imagery Eze 8:12 2315
which entereth into their privy c Eze 21:14 2315
the little c were five cubits Eze 40:7 8372
the little c of the gate eastward Eze 40:10 8372
c was one cubit on this side Eze 40:12 8372
the little c were six cubits on Eze 40:12 8372
narrow windows to the little c Eze 40:16 8372
court, and, lo, there were c Eze 40:17 3957
thirty c were upon the pavement Eze 40:17 3957
the little c thereof were three Eze 40:21 8372
And the little c thereof, and the Eze 40:29 8372
And the little c thereof, and the Eze 40:33 8372
The little c thereof, the posts Eze 40:36 8372
And the c and the entries thereof Eze 40:38 3957
the c of the singers in the inner Eze 40:44 3957
the side c were three, one over Eze 41:6 6763
house for the side c round about Eze 41:6 6763
about still upward to the side c Eze 41:7 6763
the foundations of the side c Eze 41:8 6763
of the side c that were within Eze 41:9 6763
between the c was the wideness of Eze 41:10 3957
the doors of the side c were Eze 41:11 6763
and upon the side c of the house Eze 41:26 6763
before the c was a walk of ten Eze 42:4 3957
Now the upper c were shorter Eze 42:5 3957
was without over against the c Eze 42:7 3957
court on the forepart of the c Eze 42:7 3957
For the length of the c that were Eze 42:8 3957
from under these c was the entry Eze 42:9 3957
The c were in the thickness of Eze 42:10 3957
the c which were toward the north Eze 42:11 3957
according to the doors of the c Eze 42:12 3957
Then said he unto me, The north c Eze 42:13 3957
The north c and the south c Eze 42:13 3957
separate place, they be holy c Eze 42:13 3957
and lay them in the holy c Eze 44:19 3957
for a possession for twenty c Eze 45:5 3957
into the holy c of the priests, Eze 46:19 3957
behold, he is in the secret c Mt 24:26 *5009*

CHAMELEON
And the ferret, and the c, and the Lev 11:30 3581

CHAMOIS
pygarg, and the wild ox, and the c Deut 14:5 2169

CHAMPAIGN
which dwell in the c over against Deut 11:30 6160

CHAMPION
there went out a c out of the 1Sa 17:4 1143
them, behold, there came up the c 1Sa 17:23 1143
Philistines saw their c was dead 1Sa 17:51 1368

CHANAAN (*ka'-na-un*) See CANAAN. *Greek form of Canaan.*
over all the land of Egypt and C Acts 7:11 *5477*
seven nations in the land of C Acts 13:19 *5477*

CHANCE
If a bird's nest c to be before Deut 22:6 7122
it was a c that happened to us 1Sa 6:9 4745
As I happened by c upon mount 2Sa 1:6 7122
time and c happeneth to them all Eccl 9:11 6294
by c there came down a certain Lk 10:31 *4795*
it may c of wheat, or of some 1Cor 15:37 *5177*

CHANCELLOR
Rehum the c and Shimshai the Ezr 4:8
Then wrote Rehum the c, and Ezr 4:9
king an answer unto Rehum the c Ezr 4:17

CHANCETH
uncleanness that c him by night Deut 23:10 4745

CHANGE
and be clean, and c your garments Gen 35:2 2498
He shall not alter it, nor c it Lev 27:10 4171
he shall at all c beast for beast Lev 27:10 4171
or bad, neither shall he c it Lev 27:33 4171
if he c it at all, then both it Lev 27:33 4171
the c thereof shall be holy Lev 27:33 8545
sheets and thirty c of garments Judg 14:12 2487
sheets and thirty c of garments Judg 14:13 2487
gave c of garments unto them Judg 14:19 2487
time will I wait, till my c come Job 14:14 2487
They c the night into day Job 17:12 7760
as a vesture shalt thou c them Ps 102:26 2498
not with them that are given to c Prov 24:21 8138
but we will c them into cedars Is 9:10 2498
thou about so much to c thy way Jer 2:36 8138
Can the Ethiopian c his skin Jer 13:23 2015
most High, and think to c times Dan 7:25 8133
therefore will I c their glory Hos 4:7 4171
Then shall his mind c, and he Hab 1:11 2498
clothe thee with c of raiment Zec 3:4 4254
For I am the LORD, I c not Mal 3:6 8138
shall c the customs which Moses Acts 6:14 *236*
for even their women did c the Rom 1:26 *3337*
with you now, and to c my voice Gal 4:20 *236*
Who shall c our vile body, that Phil 3:21 *3345*
of necessity a c also of the law Heb 7:12 *3331*

CHANGEABLE
The c suits of apparel, and the Is 3:22 4254

CHANGED
me, and c my wages ten times Gen 31:7 2498
thou hast c my wages ten times Gen 31:41 2498
c his raiment, and came in unto Gen 41:14 2498
be c unto white, he shall come Lev 13:16 2015
the plague have not c his colour Lev 13:55 2015
Baal-meon, (their names being c Num 32:38 5437
he c his behaviour before them, 1Sa 21:13 8138
c his apparel, and came into the 2Sa 12:20 2498
stead, and c his name to Zedekiah 2Kin 24:17 5437
And c his prison garments 2Kin 25:29 8132
of my disease is my garment c Job 30:18 2664
when he c his behaviour before Ps 34:*t* 8138
change them, and they shall be c Ps 102:26 2498
Thus they c their glory into the Ps 106:20 4171
boldness of his face shall be c Eccl 8:1 8132
c the ordinance, broken the Is 24:5 2498
Hath a nation c their gods Jer 2:11 4171
but my people have c their glory Jer 2:11 4171
in him, and his scent is not c Jer 48:11 4171
And c his prison garments Jer 52:33 8138
how is the most fine gold c Lam 4:1 8132
she hath c my judgments into Eze 5:6 4171
before me, till the time be c Dan 2:9 8133
his visage was c against Shadrach Dan 3:19 8133
neither were their coats c Dan 3:27 8133
have c the king's word, and Dan 3:28 8133
Let his heart be c from man's Dan 4:16 8133
Then the king's countenance was c Dan 5:6 8133
and his countenance was c in him Dan 5:9 8133
nor let thy countenance be c Dan 5:10 8133
the writing, that it be not c Dan 6:8 8133
the king establisheth may be c Dan 6:15 8133
might not be c concerning Daniel Dan 6:17 8133
me, and my countenance c in me Dan 7:28 8133
he hath c the portion of my Mic 2:4 4171
they c their minds, and said that Acts 28:6 *3328*
c the glory of the uncorruptible Rom 1:23 *236*
Who c the truth of God into a lie Rom 1:25 *3337*
all sleep, but we shall all be c 1Cor 15:51 *236*
incorruptible, and we shall be c 1Cor 15:52 *236*
are c into the same image from 2Cor 3:18 *3339*
fold them up, and they shall be c Heb 1:12 *236*
For the priesthood being c Heb 7:12 *3346*

CHANGERS
doves, and the c of money sitting Jn 2:14 *2773*

CHANGERS'
and poured out the c money Jn 2:15 *2855*

CHANGES
he gave each man c of raiment Gen 45:22 2487
of silver, and five c of raiment Gen 45:22 2487
of gold, and ten c of raiment 2Kin 5:5 2487
of silver, and two c of garments 2Kin 5:22 2487
with two c of garments, and laid 2Kin 5:23 2487
c and war are against me Job 10:17 2487
Because they have no c, therefore Ps 55:19 2487

CHANGEST
thou c his countenance, and Job 14:20 8138

CHANGETH
to his own hurt, and c not Ps 15:4 4171
he c the times and the seasons Dan 2:21 8133

CHANGING
redeeming and concerning c Ruth 4:7 8545

CHANNEL
LORD shall beat off from the c of Is 27:12 7641

CHANNELS
the c of the sea appeared, the 2Sa 22:16 650
Then the c of waters were seen, Ps 18:15 650
he shall come up over all his c Is 8:7 650

CHANT
That c to the sound of the viol, Amos 6:5 6527

CHAPEL
for it is the king's c, and it is Amos 7:13 4720

CHAPITER
of the one c was five cubits 1Kin 7:16 3805
of the other c was five cubits 1Kin 7:16 3805
seven for the one c 1Kin 7:17 3805
and seven for the other c 1Kin 7:17 3805
and so did he for the other c 1Kin 7:18 3805
rows round about upon the other c 1Kin 7:20 3805
And the mouth of it within the c 1Kin 7:31 3805
and the c upon it was brass 2Kin 25:17 3805
the height of the c three cubits 2Kin 25:17 3805
upon the c round about, all of 2Kin 25:17 3805
the c that was on the top of each 2Chr 3:15 6858
And a c of brass was upon it Jer 52:22 3805
height of one c was five cubits Jer 52:22 3805

CHAPITERS
and he overlaid their c and their Ex 36:38 7218
overlaying of their c of silver Ex 38:17 7218
and the overlaying of their c Ex 38:19 7218
the pillars, and overlaid their c Ex 38:28 7218
he made two c of molten brass, to 1Kin 7:16 3805
for the c which were upon the top 1Kin 7:17 3805
to cover the c that were upon the 1Kin 7:18 3805
the c that were upon the top of 1Kin 7:19 3805
the c upon the two pillars had 1Kin 7:20 3805
the two bowls of the c that were 1Kin 7:41 3805
to cover the two bowls of the c 1Kin 7:41 3805
the c that were upon the pillars 1Kin 7:42 3805
the c which were on the top of 2Chr 4:12 3805
c which were on the top of the 2Chr 4:12 3805
the c which were upon the pillars 2Chr 4:13 3805
upon the c round about, all of Jer 52:22 3805

CHAPMEN
Beside that which c and merchants 2Chr 9:14

CHAPT
Because the ground is c, for Jer 14:4 2865

CHARASHIM (*car'-a-shim*) *Place founded by Joab.*
the father of the valley of C 1Chr 4:14 2798

CHARCHEMISH (*car'-ke-mish*) See CARCHEMISH. *Same as Carchemish.*
to fight against C by Euphrates 2Chr 35:20 3751

CHARGE
obeyed my voice, and kept my c Gen 26:5 4931
as he blessed him he gave him a c Gen 28:6 6680
gave them a c unto the children Ex 6:13 6680
c the people, lest they break Ex 19:21 5749
keep the c of the LORD, that ye Lev 8:35 4931
the Levites shall keep the c of Num 1:53 4931
And they shall keep his c, and the Num 3:7 4931

the c of the whole congregation Num 3:7 4931
the c of the children of Israel, Num 3:8 4931
the c of the sons of Gershon in Num 3:25 4931
keeping the c of the sanctuary Num 3:28 4931
their c shall be the ark, and the Num 3:31 4931
that keep the c of the sanctuary Num 3:32 4931
c of the sons of Merari shall be Num 3:36 4931
keeping the c of the sanctuary Num 3:38 4931
the c of the children of Israel Num 3:38 4931
unto them in c all their burdens Num 4:27 4931
their c shall be under the hand Num 4:28 4931
this is the c of their burden, Num 4:31 4931
of the c of their burden Num 4:32 4931
the priest shall c her by an oath Num 5:19 7650
Then the priest shall c the woman Num 5:21 7650
the congregation, to keep the c Num 8:26 4931
unto the Levites touching their c Num 8:26 4931
of Israel kept the c of the LORD Num 9:19 4931
they kept the c of the LORD Num 9:23 4931
And they shall keep thy c, and the Num 18:3 4931
the c of all the tabernacle Num 18:3 4931
keep the c of the tabernacle of Num 18:4 4931
shall keep the c of the sanctuary Num 18:5 4931
sanctuary, and the c of the altar Num 18:5 4931
I also have given thee the c of Num 18:8 4931
give him a c in their sight Num 27:19 6680
hands upon him, and gave him a c Num 27:23 6680
Levites, which keep the c of the Num 31:30 4931
Levites, which kept the c of the Num 31:47 4931
men of war which are under our c Num 31:49 3027
But c Joshua, and encourage him, Deut 3:28 6680
the LORD thy God, and keep his c Deut 11:1 4931
unto thy people of Israel's c Deut 21:8 7130
that I may give him a c Deut 31:14 6680
he gave Joshua the son of Nun a c Deut 31:23 6680
but have kept the c of the Josh 22:3 4931
I will give c concerning thee 2Sa 14:8 6680
the captains c concerning Absalom 2Sa 18:5 6680
keep the c of the LORD thy God, 1Kin 2:3 4931
every man according to his c 1Kin 4:28 4941
all the c of the house of Joseph 1Kin 11:28 5447
leaned to have the c of the gate 2Kin 7:17 5921
because the c was upon them, and 1Chr 9:27 4931
certain of them had the c of the 1Chr 9:28 5921
give thee c concerning Israel, 1Chr 22:12 6680
the c of the tabernacle of the 1Chr 23:32 4931
the c of the holy place, and the 1Chr 23:32 4931
the c of the sons of Aaron their 1Chr 23:32 4931
for we keep the c of the LORD our 2Chr 13:11 4931
therefore the Levites had the c 2Chr 30:17 5921
of the palace, c over Jerusalem Neh 7:2 6680
to c ourselves yearly with the Neh 10:32 5414
that have the c of the business Est 3:9 6213
to c her that she should go in Est 4:8 6680
hath given him a c over the earth Job 34:13 6485
they laid to my c things that I Ps 35:11 7592
shall give his angels c over thee Ps 91:11 6680
I c you, O ye daughters of Song 2:7 7650
I c you, O ye daughters of Song 3:5 7650
I c you, O daughters of Jerusalem Song 5:8 7650
beloved, that thou dost so c us Song 5:9 7650
I c you, O daughters of Jerusalem Song 8:4 7650
of my wrath will I give him a c Is 10:6 6680
king of Babylon gave c concerning Jer 39:11 6680
given it a c against Ashkelon Jer 47:7 6680
which had the c of the men of war Jer 52:25 6496
Cause them that have c over the Eze 9:1 6486
the keepers of the c of the house Eze 40:45 4931
the keepers of the c of the altar Eze 40:46 4931
kept the c of mine holy things Eze 44:8 4931
but ye have set keepers of my c Eze 44:8 4931
having c at the gates of the Eze 44:11 6486
keepers of the c of the house Eze 44:14 4931
that kept the c of my sanctuary Eze 44:15 4931
unto me, and they shall keep my c Eze 44:16 4931
which have kept my c, which went Eze 48:11 4931
ways, and if thou wilt keep my c Zec 3:7 4931
give his angels c concerning thee Mt 4:6 *1781*
I c thee, come out of him, and Mk 9:25 *2004*
shall give his angels c over thee Lk 4:10 *1781*
Lord, lay not this sin to their c Acts 7:60 *2476*
who had the c of all her treasure Acts 8:27 *1909*
Who, having received such a c Acts 16:24 *3852*
his c worthy of death or of bonds Acts 23:29 *1462*
any thing to the c of God's elect Rom 8:33 *1458*
the gospel of Christ without c 1Cor 9:18 *77*
I c you by the Lord that this 1Th 5:27 *3726*
that thou mightest c some that 1Ti 1:3 *3853*
This c I commit unto thee, son 1Ti 1:18 *3852*
And these things give in c 1Ti 5:7 *3853*
I c thee before God, and the Lord 1Ti 5:21 *1263*
I give thee c in the sight of God 1Ti 6:13 *3853*
C them that are rich in this 1Ti 6:17 *3853*
I c thee therefore before God, and 2Ti 4:1 *1263*
it may not be laid to their c 2Ti 4:16 *3049*

CHARGEABLE

now go, lest we be c unto thee 2Sa 13:25 3513
before me were c unto the people Neh 5:15 3513
you, and wanted, I was c to no man 2Cor 11:9 *2655*
we would not be c unto any of you 1Th 2:9 *1912*
we might not be c to any of you 2Th 3:8 *1912*

CHARGED

Abimelech c all his people, Gen 26:11 6680
c him, and said unto him, Thou Gen 28:1 6680
of the guard c Joseph with them Gen 40:4 6485
he c them, and said unto them, I Gen 49:29 6680
Pharaoh c all his people, saying, Ex 1:22 6680
I c your judges at that time, Deut 1:16 6680
shall he be c with any business Deut 24:5
Moses c the people the same day, Deut 27:11 6680
Joshua c them that went to Josh 18:8 6680
the servant of the LORD c you Josh 22:5 6680
have I not c the young men that Ruth 2:9 6680
father c the people with the oath 1Sa 14:27 7650
Thy father straitly c the people 1Sa 14:28 7650
c the messenger, saying, When 2Sa 11:19 6680
in our hearing the king c thee 2Sa 18:12 6680
he c Solomon his son, saying, 1Kin 2:1 6680
that I have c thee with 1Kin 2:43 6680
For so was it c me by the word of 1Kin 13:9 6680
whom the LORD had c them, that 2Kin 17:15 6680
c them, saying, Ye shall not fear 2Kin 17:35 6680
c him to build an house for the 1Chr 22:6 6680
judgments which the LORD c Moses 1Chr 22:13 6680
he c them, saying, Thus shall ye 2Chr 19:9 6680
he hath c me to build him an 2Chr 36:23 6485
he hath c me to build him an Ezr 1:2 6485
c that they should not be opened Neh 13:19 559
for Mordecai had c her that she Est 2:10 6680
as Mordecai had c her Est 2:20 6680
sinned not, nor c God foolishly Job 1:22 5414
and his angels he c with folly Job 4:18 7760
I c Baruch before them, saying, Jer 32:13 6680
father in all that he hath c us Jer 35:8 6680
and Jesus straitly c them, saying, Mt 9:30 *1690*
c them that they should not make Mt 12:16 *2008*
Then c he his disciples that they Mt 16:20 *1291*
from the mountain, Jesus c them Mt 17:9 *1781*
And he straitly c him, and Mk 1:43 *1690*
he straitly c them that they Mk 3:12 *2008*
he c them straitly that no man Mk 5:43 *1291*
he c them that they should tell Mk 7:36 *1291*
but the more he c them, so much Mk 7:36 *1291*
he c them, saying, Take heed, Mk 8:15 *1291*
he c them that they should tell Mk 8:30 *2008*
he c them that they should tell Mk 9:9 *1291*
many c him that he should hold Mk 10:48 *2008*
And he c him to tell no man Lk 5:14 *3853*
but he c them that they should Lk 8:56 *3853*
And he straitly c them, and Lk 9:21 *2008*
c him, See thou tell no man that Acts 23:22 *3853*
c every one of you, as a father 1Th 2:11 *3146*
them, and let not the church be c 1Ti 5:16 *916*

CHARGEDST

for thou c us, saying, Set bounds Ex 19:23 5749

CHARGER

And his offering was one silver c Num 7:13 7086
for his offering one silver c Num 7:19 7086
His offering was one silver c Num 7:25 7086
c of the weight of an hundred Num 7:31 7086
His offering was one silver c Num 7:37 7086
c of the weight of an hundred Num 7:43 7086
His offering was one silver c Num 7:49 7086
c of the weight of an hundred Num 7:55 7086
His offering was one silver c Num 7:61 7086
His offering was one silver c Num 7:67 7086
His offering was one silver c Num 7:73 7086
His offering was one silver c Num 7:79 7086
Each c of silver weighing an Num 7:85 7086
here John Baptist's head in a c Mt 14:8 *4094*
And his head was brought in a c Mt 14:11 *4094*
by in a c the head of John the Mk 6:25 *4094*
And brought his head in a c Mk 6:28 *4094*

CHARGERS

twelve c of silver, twelve silver Num 7:84 7086
thirty c of gold, a thousand Ezr 1:9 105
of gold, a thousand c of silver Ezr 1:9 105

CHARGES

and the Levites to their c 2Chr 8:14 4931
c according to their courses 2Chr 31:16 4931
in their c by their courses 2Chr 31:17 4931
And he set the priests in their c 2Chr 35:2 4931
be at c with them, that they may Acts 21:24 *1159*
a warfare any time at his own c 1Cor 9:7 *3800*

CHARGEST

that thou c me to day with a 2Sa 3:8 6485

CHARGING

c the jailer to keep them safely Acts 16:23 *3853*
c them before the Lord that they 2Ti 2:14 *1263*

CHARIOT

ride in the second c which he had Gen 41:43 4818
And Joseph made ready his c, Gen 46:29 4818
And he made ready his c, and took Ex 14:6 7393
And took off their c wheels Ex 14:25 4818
Sisera lighted down off his c Judg 4:15 4818
Why is his c so long in coming Judg 5:28 7393
and David houghed all the c horses 2Sa 8:4 7393
was like the work of a c wheel 1Kin 7:33 4818
a c came up and went out of Egypt 1Kin 10:29 4818
made speed to get him up to his c 1Kin 12:18 4818
up, say unto Ahab, Prepare thy c 1Kin 18:44
horse for horse, and c for c 1Kin 20:25 7393
horse for horse, and c for c 1Kin 20:25 7393
caused him to come up into the c 1Kin 20:33 4818
he said unto the driver of his c 1Kin 22:34 7395
up in his c against the Syrians 1Kin 22:35 4818
the wound into the midst of the c 1Kin 22:35 7393
one washed the c in the pool of 1Kin 22:38 7393
there appeared a c of fire 2Kin 2:11 7393
the c of Israel, and the horsemen 2Kin 2:12 7393
with his horses and with his c 2Kin 5:9 7393
down from the c to meet him 2Kin 5:21 4818
again from his c to meet thee 2Kin 5:26 4818
They took therefore two c horses 2Kin 7:14 7393
So Jehu rode in a c, and went to 2Kin 9:16
And his c was made ready 2Kin 9:21 7393
of Judah went out, each in his c 2Kin 9:21 7393
heart, and he sunk down in his c 2Kin 9:24 7393
and said, Smite him also in the c 2Kin 9:27 4818
carried him in a c to Jerusalem 2Kin 9:28
he took him up to him into the c 2Kin 10:15 4818
So they made him ride in his c 2Kin 10:16 7393
the c of Israel, and the horsemen 2Kin 13:14 7393
him in a c dead from Megiddo 2Kin 23:30
also houghed all the c horses 1Chr 18:4 7393
pattern of the c of the cherubims 1Chr 28:18 4818
which he placed in the c cities 2Chr 1:14 7393
a c for six hundred shekels of 2Chr 1:17 4818
Solomon had, and all the c cities 2Chr 8:6 7393
whom he bestowed in the c cities 2Chr 9:25 7393
made speed to get him up to his c 2Chr 10:18 4818
therefore he said to his c man 2Chr 18:33 7395
c against the Syrians until the 2Chr 18:34 4818
therefore took him out of that c 2Chr 35:24 4818
him in the second c that he had 2Chr 35:24 7393
he burneth the c in the fire Ps 46:9 5699
O God of Jacob, both the c Ps 76:6 7393
who maketh the clouds his c Ps 104:3 7398
a c of the wood of Lebanon Song 3:9 668
he saw a c with a couple of Is 21:7 7393
a c of asses, and a c of Is 21:7 7393
behold, here cometh a c of men Is 21:9 7393
Which bringeth forth the c Is 43:17 7393
thee will I break in pieces the c Jer 51:21 7393
bind the c to the swift beast Mic 1:13 4818
In the first c were red horses Zec 6:2 4818
and in the second c black horses Zec 6:2 4818
And in the third c white horses Zec 6:3 4818
and in the fourth c grisled Zec 6:3 4818
I will cut off the c from Ephraim Zec 9:10 7393
sitting in his c read Esaias the Acts 8:28 *716*
near, and join thyself to this c Acts 8:29 *716*
he commanded the c to stand still Acts 8:38 *716*

CHARIOTS

And there went up with him both c Gen 50:9 7393
And he took six hundred chosen c Ex 14:7 7393
all the c of Egypt, and captains Ex 14:7 7393
c of Pharaoh, and his horsemen, and Ex 14:9 7393
and upon all his host, upon his c Ex 14:17 7393
honour upon Pharaoh, upon his c Ex 14:18 7393
even all Pharaoh's horses, his c Ex 14:23 7393
upon the Egyptians, upon their c Ex 14:26 7393
waters returned, and covered the c Ex 14:28 7393
Pharaoh's c and his host hath he Ex 15:4 4818
of Pharaoh went in with his c Ex 15:19 7393
unto their horses, and to their c Deut 11:4 7393
enemies, and seest horses, and c Deut 20:1 7393
with horses and c very many Josh 11:4 7393
horses, and burn their c with fire Josh 11:6 4818
and burnt their c with fire Josh 11:9 4818
land of the valley have c of iron Josh 17:16 7393
though they have iron c, and Josh 17:18 7393
pursued after your fathers with c Josh 24:6 7393
because they had c of iron Judg 1:19 7393
for he had nine hundred c of iron Judg 4:3 7393
of Jabin's army, with his c Judg 4:7 7393
gathered together all his c Judg 4:13 7393
even nine hundred c of iron Judg 4:13 7393
discomfited Sisera, and all his c Judg 4:15 7393
But Barak pursued after the c Judg 4:16 7393
Why tarry the wheels of his c Judg 5:28 4818
them for himself, for his c 1Sa 8:11 4818
and some shall run before his c 1Sa 8:11 4818
of war, and instruments of his c 1Sa 8:12 7393
with Israel, thirty thousand c 1Sa 13:5 7393
and, lo, the c and horsemen 2Sa 1:6 7393
David took from him a thousand c 2Sa 8:4
reserved of them for an hundred c 2Sa 8:4 7393
of seven hundred c of the Syrians 2Sa 10:18 7393
this, that Absalom prepared him c 2Sa 15:1 4818
and he prepared him c and horsemen, 1Kin 1:5 7393
stalls of horses for his c 1Kin 4:26 4817
Solomon had, and cities for his c 1Kin 9:19 7393
his captains, and rulers of his c 1Kin 9:22 7393
And Solomon gathered together c 1Kin 10:26 7393
had a thousand and four hundred c 1Kin 10:26 7393
he bestowed in the cities for c 1Kin 10:26 7393
Zimri, captain of half his c 1Kin 16:9 7393
kings with him, and horses, and c 1Kin 20:1 7393
out, and smote the horses and c 1Kin 20:21 7393
captains that had rule over his c 1Kin 22:31 7393
captains of the c saw Jehoshaphat 1Kin 22:32 7393
when the captains of the c 1Kin 22:33 7393
sent he thither horses, and c 2Kin 6:14 7393
the city both with horses and c 2Kin 6:15 7393
c of fire round about Elisha 2Kin 6:17 7393
the Syrians to hear a noise of c 2Kin 7:6 7393
to Zair, and all the c with him 2Kin 8:21 7393
about, and the captains of the c 2Kin 8:21 7393
with you, and there are with you c 2Kin 10:2 7393
but fifty horsemen, and ten c 2Kin 13:7 7393
and put thy trust on Egypt for c 2Kin 18:24 7393
With the multitude of my c I am 2Kin 19:23 7393
burned the c of the sun with fire 2Kin 23:11 4818
David took from him a thousand c 1Chr 18:4 7393
but reserved of them an hundred c 1Chr 18:4 7393
talents of silver to hire them c 1Chr 19:6 7393
hired thirty and two thousand c 1Chr 19:7 7393
thousand men which fought in c 1Chr 19:18 7393
And Solomon gathered c 2Chr 1:14 7393
had a thousand and four hundred c 2Chr 1:14 7393
captains, and captains of his c 2Chr 8:9 7393
thousand stalls for horses and c 2Chr 9:25 4818
With twelve hundred c, and 2Chr 12:3 7393
thousand, and three hundred c 2Chr 14:9 4818
a huge host, with very many c 2Chr 16:8 7393
of the c that were with him 2Chr 18:30 7393
captains of the c saw Jehoshaphat 2Chr 18:31 7393
when the captains of the c 2Chr 18:32 7393
princes, and all his c with him 2Chr 21:9 7393
him in, and the captains of the c 2Chr 21:9 7393
Some trust in c, and some in Ps 20:7 7393
The c of God are twenty thousand, Ps 68:17 7393
company of horses in Pharaoh's c Song 1:9 7393
made me like the c of Ammi-nadib Song 6:12 4818
is there any end of their c Is 2:7 4818

bare the quiver with c of men Is 22:6 7393
valleys shall be full of c Is 22:7 7393
there the c of thy glory shall be Is 22:18 4818
and stay on horses, and trust in c Is 31:1 7393
and put thy trust on Egypt for c Is 36:9 7393
By the multitude of my c am I Is 37:24 7393
with his c like a whirlwind, to Is 66:15 4818
all nations upon horses, and in c Is 66:20 7393
his c shall be as a whirlwind Jer 4:13 4818
the throne of David, riding in c Jer 17:25 7393
the throne of David, riding in c Jer 22:4 7393
and rage, ye c Jer 46:9 7393
horses, at the rushing of his c Jer 47:3 7393
their horses, and upon their c Jer 50:37 7393
shall come against thee with c Eze 23:24 2021
the north, with horses, and with c Eze 26:7 7393
and of the wheels, and of the c Eze 26:10 7393
in precious clothes for c Eze 27:20 7396
at my table with horses and c Eze 39:20 7393
him like a whirlwind, with c Dan 11:40 7393
Like the noise of c on the tops Joel 2:5 4818
of thee, and I will destroy thy c Mic 5:10 4818
the c shall be with flaming Nah 2:3 7393
The c shall rage in the streets, Nah 2:4 7393
and I will burn her c in the smoke Nah 2:13 7393
horses, and of the jumping c Nah 3:2 4818
horses and thy c of salvation Hab 3:8 4818
and I will overthrow the c Hag 2:22 4818
there came four c out from Zec 6:1 4818
of c of many horses running to Rev 9:9 *716*
beasts, and sheep, and horses, and c Rev 18:13 *4480*

CHARITABLY
thy meat, now walkest thou not c Rom 14:15

CHARITY
puffeth up, but c edifieth 1Cor 8:1 *26*
men and of angels, and have not c 1Cor 13:1 *26*
remove mountains, and have not c 1Cor 13:2 *26*
body to be burned, and have not c 1Cor 13:3 *26*
C suffereth long, and is kind 1Cor 13:4 *26*
c envieth not 1Cor 13:4 *26*
c vaunteth not itself, is not 1Cor 13:4 *26*
C never faileth 1Cor 13:8 *26*
And now abideth faith, hope, c 1Cor 13:13 *26*
but the greatest of these is c 1Cor 13:13 *26*
Follow after c, and desire 1Cor 14:1 *26*
all your things be done with c 1Cor 16:14 *26*
above all these things put on c Col 3:14 *26*
good tidings of your faith and c 1Th 3:6 *26*
the c of every one of you all 2Th 1:3 *26*
is c out of a pure heart, and of a 1Ti 1:5 *26*
if they continue in faith and c 1Ti 2:15 *26*
in word, in conversation, in c 1Ti 4:12 *26*
follow righteousness, faith, c 2Ti 2:22 *26*
purpose, faith, longsuffering, c 2Ti 3:10 *26*
temperate, sound in faith, in c Titus 2:2 *26*
have fervent c among yourselves 1Pet 4:8 *26*
for c shall cover the multitude 1Pet 4:8 *26*
ye one another with a kiss of c 1Pet 5:14 *26*
and to brotherly kindness c 2Pet 1:7 *26*
of thy c before the church 3Jn 6 *26*
are spots in your feasts of c Jude 12 *26*
I know thy works, and c, and Rev 2:19 *26*

CHARMED
among you, which will not be c Jer 8:17 3908

CHARMER
Or a c, or a consulter with Deut 18:11

CHARMERS
not hearken to the voice of c Ps 58:5 3907
seek to the idols, and to the c Is 19:3 328

CHARMING
of charmers, c never so wisely Ps 58:5

CHARRAN (*car'-ran*) See HARAN. *Greek form of Haran.*
Mesopotamia, before he dwelt in C Acts 7:2 5488
of the Chaldaeans, and dwelt in C Acts 7:4 5488

CHASE
ye shall c your enemies, and they Lev 26:7 7291
And five of you shall c an hundred Lev 26:8 7291
of a shaken leaf shall c them Lev 26:36 7291
How should one c a thousand Deut 32:30 7291
One man of you shall c a thousand Josh 23:10 7291
let the angel of the LORD c them Ps 35:5 1760

CHASED
c you, as bees do, and destroyed Deut 1:44 7291
for they c them from before the Josh 7:5 7291
wilderness wherein they c them Josh 8:24 7291
c them along the way that goeth Josh 10:10 7291
c them unto great Zidon, and unto Josh 11:8 7291
And Abimelech c him, and he fled Judg 9:40 7291
c them, and trode them down with Judg 20:43 7291
therefore I c him from me Neh 13:28 1272
darkness, and c out of the world Job 18:18 5074
he shall be c away as a vision of Job 20:8 5074
And it shall be as the c roe Is 13:14 5080
shall be c as the chaff of the Is 17:13 7291
Mine enemies c me sore, like a Lam 3:52 6679

CHASETH
c away his mother, is a son that Prov 19:26 1272

CHASING
from c after the Philistines 1Sa 17:53 1814

CHASTE
you as a c virgin to Christ 2Cor 11:2 *53*
To be discreet, c, keepers at Titus 2:5 *53*
While they behold your c 1Pet 3:2 *53*

CHASTEN
I will c him with the rod of men, 2Sa 7:14 3198
anger, neither c me in thy hot Ps 6:1 3256
neither c me in thy hot Ps 38:1 3256
C thy son while there is hope, and Prov 19:18 3256
to c thyself before thy God, thy Dan 10:12 6031
As many as I love, I rebuke and c Rev 3:19 *3811*

CHASTENED
and that, when they have c him Deut 21:18 3256
He is c also with pain upon his Job 33:19 3198
c my soul with fasting, that was Ps 69:10
been plagued, and c every morning Ps 73:14 8433
The LORD hath c me sore Ps 118:18 3256
we are c of the Lord, that we 1Cor 11:32 *3811*
as c, and not killed 2Cor 6:9 *3811*
c us after their own pleasure Heb 12:10 *3811*

CHASTENEST
Blessed is the man whom thou c Ps 94:12 3256

CHASTENETH
heart, that, as a man c his son Deut 8:5 3256
son, so the LORD thy God c thee Deut 8:5 3256
he that loveth him c him betimes Prov 13:24 4148
For whom the Lord loveth he c Heb 12:6 *3811*
son is he whom the father c not Heb 12:7 *3811*

CHASTENING
not thou the c of the Almighty Job 5:17 4148
despise not the c of the LORD Prov 3:11 4148
a prayer when thy c was upon them Is 26:16 4148
not thou the c of the Lord Heb 12:5 *3809*
If ye endure c, God dealeth with Heb 12:7 *3809*
Now no c for the present seemeth Heb 12:11 *3809*

CHASTISE
will c you seven times for your Lev 26:28 3256
city shall take that man and c him Deut 22:18 3256
but I will c you with scorpions 1Kin 12:11 3256
but I will c you with scorpions 1Kin 12:14 3256
but I will c you with scorpions 2Chr 10:11
but I will c you with scorpions 2Chr 10:14
I will c them, as their Hos 7:12 3256
in my desire that I should c them Hos 10:10 3256
I will therefore c him, and Lk 23:16 *3811*
I will therefore c him, and let Lk 23:22 *3811*

CHASTISED
my father hath c you with whips 1Kin 12:11 3256
my father also c you with whips 1Kin 12:14 3256
my father c you with whips, but I 2Chr 10:11 3256
my father c you with whips, but I 2Chr 10:14 3256
hast c me, and I was c Jer 31:18 3256

CHASTISEMENT
seen the c of the LORD your God Deut 11:2 4148
be said unto God, I have borne c Job 34:31
the c of our peace was upon him Is 53:5 4148
with the c of a cruel one, for Jer 30:14 4148
But if ye be without c, whereof Heb 12:8 *3809*

CHASTISETH
He that c the heathen, shall not Ps 94:10 3256

CHATTER
a crane or a swallow, so did I c Is 38:14 6850

CHEBAR (*ke'-bar*) *A river in Mesopotamia.*
the captives by the river of C Eze 1:1 3529
of the Chaldeans by the river C Eze 1:3 3529
that dwelt by the river of C Eze 3:15 3529
which I saw by the river of C Eze 3:23 3529
that I saw by the river of C Eze 10:15 3529
God of Israel by the river of C Eze 10:20 3529
which I saw by the river of C Eze 10:22 3529
vision that I saw by the river C Eze 43:3 3529

CHECK
I have heard the c of my reproach Job 20:3 4148

CHECKER
And nets of c work, and wreaths of 1Kin 7:17 7639

CHEDORLAOMER (*ke'-dor-la'-o-mer*) *An Elamite king.*
C king of Elam, and Tidal king of Gen 14:1 3540
Twelve years they served C Gen 14:4 3540
And in the fourteenth year came C Gen 14:5 3540
With C the king of Elam, and with Gen 14:9 3540
return from the slaughter of C Gen 14:17 3540

CHEEK
near, and smote Micaiah on the c 1Kin 22:24 3895
near, and smote Micaiah upon the c 2Chr 18:23 3895
me upon the c reproachfully Job 16:10 3895
all mine enemies upon the c bone Ps 3:7 3895
He giveth his c to him that Lam 3:30 3895
he hath the c teeth of a great Joel 1:6 4973
of Israel with a rod upon the c Mic 5:1 3895
shall smite thee on thy right c Mt 5:39 *4600*
on the one c offer also the other Lk 6:29 *4600*

CHEEKS
priest the shoulder, and the two c Deut 18:3 3895
Thy c are comely with rows of Song 1:10 3895
His c are as a bed of spices, as Song 5:13 3895
my c to them that plucked off the Is 50:6 3895
night, and her tears are on her c Lam 1:2 3895

CHEER
shall c up his wife which he hath Deut 24:5 8055
let thy heart c thee in the days Eccl 11:9 3190
Son, be of good c Mt 9:2 *2293*
unto them, saying, Be of good c Mt 14:27 *2293*
and saith unto them, Be of good c Mk 6:50 *2293*
but be of good c Jn 16:33 *2293*
by him, and said, Be of good c Acts 23:11 *2293*
now I exhort you to be of good c Acts 27:22 *2114*
Wherefore, sirs, be of good c Acts 27:25 *2114*
Then were they all of good c Acts 27:36 *2114*

CHEERETH
I leave my wine, which c God Judg 9:13 8055

CHEERFUL
heart maketh a c countenance Prov 15:13 3190
joy and gladness, and c feasts Zec 8:19 2896
corn shall make the young men c Zec 9:17 5107
for God loveth a c giver 2Cor 9:7 *2431*

CHEERFULLY
I do the more c answer for myself Acts 24:10 *2115*

CHEERFULNESS
he that sheweth mercy, with c Rom 12:8 *2432*

CHEESE
c of kine, for David, and for the 2Sa 17:29 8194
out as milk, and curdled me like c Job 10:10 1385

CHEESES
carry these ten c unto the 1Sa 17:18

CHELAL (*ke'-lal*) *Married a foreign wife in exile.*
Adna, and C, Benaiah, Maaseiah, Ezr 10:30 3636

CHELLUH (*kel'-loo*) *Married a foreign wife in exile.*
Benaiah, Bedeiah, C, Ezr 10:35 3622

CHELUB (*ke'-lub*)
1. A descendant of Caleb.
C the brother of Shuah begat 1Chr 4:11 3620
2. Father of Ezri.
the ground was Ezri the son of C 1Chr 27:26 3620

CHELUBAI (*ke-loo'-bahee*) *Son of Hezron.*
Jerahmeel, and Ram, and C 1Chr 2:9 3621

CHELUH See CHELLUH.

CHELUHI See CHELLUH.

CHEMARIMS (*kem'-a-rims*) *Idolatrous priests of Judah.*
the name of the C with the Zeph 1:4 3649

CHEMOSH (*ke'-mosh*) *A Moabite god.*
thou art undone, O people of C Num 21:29 3645
not thou possess that which C thy Judg 11:24 3645
Solomon build an high place for C 1Kin 11:7 3645
C the god of the Moabites, and 1Kin 11:33 3645
for C the abomination of the 2Kin 23:13 3645
C shall go forth into captivity Jer 48:7 3645
And Moab shall be ashamed of C Jer 48:13 3645
the people of C perisheth Jer 48:46 3645

CHENAANAH (*ke-na'-a-nah*)
1. Father of Zedekiah.
Zedekiah the son of C made him 1Kin 22:11 3668
Zedekiah the son of C went near 1Kin 22:24 3668
Zedekiah the son of C had made 2Chr 18:10 3668
Zedekiah the son of C came near 2Chr 18:23 3668
2. Brother of Ehud.
and Benjamin, and Ehud, and C 1Chr 7:10 3668

CHENANI (*ken'-a-ni*) *A Levite helper of Ezra.*
Bunni, Sherebiah, Bani, and C Neh 9:4 3662

CHENANIAH (*ken-a-ni'-ah*) See CONONIAH.
1. A chief Levite during David's reign.
And C, chief of the Levites, was 1Chr 15:22 3663
C the master of the song with the 1Chr 15:27 3663
2. An officer in David's army.
Of the Izharites, C and his sons 1Chr 26:29 3663

CHEPHAR-AMMONI See CHEPHAR-HAAMMONAI.

CHEPHAR-HAAMMONAI (*ke'-far-ha-am'-mo-nahee*) *A town in Benjamin.*
And C, and Ophni, and Gaba Josh 18:24 3726

CHEPHIRAH (*ke-fi'-rah*) *A Hittite village in Benjamin.*
their cities were Gibeon, and C Josh 9:17 3716
And Mizpeh, and C, and Mozah, Josh 18:26 3716
The children of Kirjath-arim, C Ezr 2:25 3716
The men of Kirjath-jearim, C Neh 7:29 3716

CHERAN (*ke'-ran*) *Son of Dishon.*
and Eshban, and Ithran, and C Gen 36:26 3763
and Eshban, and Ithran, and C 1Chr 1:41 3763

CHERETHIMS (*ker'-e-thims*) See CHERETHITES. *A Philistine tribe.*
and I will cut off the C, and Eze 25:16 3774

CHERETHITES (*ker'-e-thites*) See CHERETHIMS.
1. Same as Cherethims.
invasion upon the south of the C 1Sa 30:14 3774
sea coast, the nation of the C Zeph 2:5 3774
2. Executioners and runners in David's army.
of Jehoiada was over both the C 2Sa 8:18 3774
and all the C, and all the 2Sa 15:18 3774
after him Joab's men, and the C 2Sa 20:7 3774
son of Jehoiada was over the C 2Sa 20:23 3774
the son of Jehoiada, and the C 1Kin 1:38 3746
the son of Jehoiada, and the C 1Kin 1:44 3774
son of Jehoiada was over the C 1Chr 18:17 3774

CHERISH
before the king, and let her c him 1Kin 1:2 5532

CHERISHED
c the king, and ministered to him 1Kin 1:4 5532

CHERISHETH
c it, even as the Lord the church Eph 5:29 *2282*
even as a nurse c her children 1Th 2:7 *2282*

CHERITH (*ke'-rith*) *A brook in Gilead.*
and hide thyself by the brook C 1Kin 17:3 3747
he went and dwelt by the brook C 1Kin 17:5 3747

CHERUB (*ke'-rub*)
1. A winged celestial being.
make one c on the one end, and the .... Ex 25:19 3742
the other c on the other end .... Ex 25:19 3742
One c on the end on this side, and .... Ex 37:8 3742
another c on the other end on .... Ex 37:8 3742
And he rode upon a c, and did fly 2Sa 22:11 3742
cubits was the one wing of the c 1Kin 6:24 3742
cubits the other wing of the c 1Kin 6:24 3742
the other c was ten cubits 1Kin 6:25 3742
of the one c was ten cubits 1Kin 6:26 3742
and so was it of the other c 1Kin 6:26 3742
the wing of the other c touched 1Kin 6:27 3742
wing of the one c was five cubits 2Chr 3:11
to the wing of the other c 2Chr 3:11 3742
of the other c was five cubits 2Chr 3:12 3742
to the wing of the other c 2Chr 3:12 3742
And he rode upon a c, and did fly .... Ps 18:10 3742
of Israel was gone up from the c .... Eze 9:3 3742
the wheels, even under the c .... Eze 10:2 3742
of the LORD went up from the c .... Eze 10:4 3742
one c stretched forth his hand .... Eze 10:7 3742
the cherubims, one wheel by one c .... Eze 10:9 3742
and another wheel by another c .... Eze 10:9 3742
first face was the face of a c .... Eze 10:14 3742
art the anointed c that covereth .... Eze 28:14 3742
I will destroy thee, O covering c .... Eze 28:16 3742
tree was between a c and a c .... Eze 41:18 3742
and every c had two faces .... Eze 41:18 3742
2. An exile who returned with Zerubbabel.
up from Tel-melah, Tel-harsa, C .... Ezr 2:59 3743
from Tel-melah, Tel-haresha, C .... Neh 7:61 3743

CHERUBIM
the east of the garden of Eden C .... Gen 3:24 3742
the c shall stretch forth their .... Ex 25:20 3742

CHERUBIMS
And thou shalt make two c of gold .... Ex 25:18 3742
the c on the two ends thereof .... Ex 25:19 3742
seat shall the faces of the c be .... Ex 25:20 3742
from between the two c which are .... Ex 25:22 3742
with c of cunning work shalt thou .... Ex 26:1 3742
with c shall it be made .... Ex 26:31 3742
with c of cunning work made he .... Ex 36:8 3742
with c made he it of cunning work .... Ex 36:35 3742
And he made two c of gold, beaten .... Ex 37:7 3742
he the c on the two ends thereof .... Ex 37:8 3742
the c spread out their wings on .... Ex 37:9 3742
seatward were the faces of the c .... Ex 37:9 3742
testimony, from between the two c .... Num 7:89 3742
which dwelleth between the c 1Sa 4:4 3742
hosts that dwelleth between the c 2Sa 6:2 3742
he made two c of olive tree 1Kin 6:23 3742
both the c were of one measure and 1Kin 6:25 3742
he set the c within the inner 1Kin 6:27 3742
forth the wings of the c, so that 1Kin 6:27 3742
And he overlaid the c with gold 1Kin 6:28 3742
about with carved figures of c 1Kin 6:29 3742
he carved upon them carvings of c 1Kin 6:32 3742
gold, and spread gold upon the c 1Kin 6:32 3742
And he carved thereon c and palm 1Kin 6:35 3742
the ledges were lions, oxen, and c 1Kin 7:29 3742
the borders thereof, he graved c 1Kin 7:36 3742
even under the wings of the c 1Kin 8:6 3742
For the c spread forth their two 1Kin 8:7 3742
the c covered the ark and the 1Kin 8:7 3742
which dwellest between the c 2Kin 19:15 3742
LORD, that dwelleth between the c 1Chr 13:6 3742
pattern of the chariot of the c 1Chr 28:18 3742
and graved c on the walls 2Chr 3:7 3742
house he made two c of image work 2Chr 3:10 3742
the wings of the c were twenty 2Chr 3:11 3742
The wings of these c spread 2Chr 3:13 3742
fine linen, and wrought c thereon 2Chr 3:14 3742
even under the wings of the c 2Chr 5:7 3742
For the c spread forth their 2Chr 5:8 3742
the c covered the ark and the 2Chr 5:8 3742
thou that dwellest between the c .... Ps 80:1 3742
he sitteth between the c .... Ps 99:1 3742
that dwellest between the c .... Is 37:16 3742
c there appeared over them as it .... Eze 10:1 3742
coals of fire from between the c .... Eze 10:2 3742
Now the c stood on the right side .... Eze 10:3 3742
the wheels, from between the c .... Eze 10:6 3742
c unto the fire that was between .... Eze 10:7 3742
the fire that was between the c .... Eze 10:7 3742
there appeared in the c the form .... Eze 10:8 3742
behold the four wheels by the c .... Eze 10:9 3742
And the c were lifted up .... Eze 10:15 3742
And when the c went, the wheels .... Eze 10:16 3742
when the c lifted up their wings .... Eze 10:16 3742
of the house, and stood over the c .... Eze 10:18 3742
the c lifted up their wings, and .... Eze 10:19 3742
and I knew that they were the c .... Eze 10:20 3742
Then did the c lift up their .... Eze 11:22 3742
And it was made with c and palm .... Eze 41:18 3742
ground unto above the door were c .... Eze 41:20 3742
on the doors of the temple, c .... Eze 41:25 3742
over it the c of glory shadowing .... Heb 9:5 *5502*

CHERUBIMS'
the sound of the c wings was .... Eze 10:5 3742

CHESALON (*kes'-a-lon*) *A landmark in Judah.*
side of mount Jearim, which is C .... Josh 15:10 3693

CHESED (*ke'-sed*) *A son of Nahor.*
And C, and Hazo, and Pildash, and .... Gen 22:22 3777

CHESIL (*ke'-sil*) *A Canaanite town.*
And Eltolad, and C, and Hormah .... Josh 15:30 3686

CHESNUT
poplar, and of the hazel and c tree .... Gen 30:37 6196
the c trees were not like his .... Eze 31:8 6196

CHEST
But Jehoiada the priest took a c 2Kin 12:9 727
there was much money in the c 2Kin 12:10 727
king's commandment they made a c 2Chr 24:8 727
and brought in, and cast into the c 2Chr 24:10 727
that at what time the c was 2Chr 24:11 727
officer came and emptied the c 2Chr 24:11 727

CHESTS
in c of rich apparel, bound with .... Eze 27:24 1595

CHESULLOTH (*ke-sul'-loth*) See CHISLOTH-TABOR. *A town in Issachar.*
border was toward Jezreel, and C .... Josh 19:18 3694

CHEW
ye not eat of them that c the cud .... Lev 11:4 5927
not eat of them that c the cud .... Deut 14:7 5927
for they c the cud, but divide .... Deut 14:7 5927

CHEWED
between their teeth, ere it was c .... Num 11:33 3772

CHEWETH
c the cud, among the beasts, that .... Lev 11:3 5927
the camel, because he c the cud .... Lev 11:4 5927
the coney, because he c the cud .... Lev 11:5 5927
And the hare, because he c the cud .... Lev 11:6 5927
yet he c not the cud .... Lev 11:7 1647
nor c the cud, are unclean unto .... Lev 11:26 5927
c the cud among the beasts, that .... Deut 14:6 5927
yet c not the cud, it is unclean .... Deut 14:8

CHEZIB (*ke'-zib*) See ACHZIB, CHOZEBA. *A Canaanite village.*
and he was at C, when she bare him .... Gen 38:5 3580

CHICKENS
gathereth her c under her wings .... Mt 23:37 *3556*

CHIDE
the people did c with Moses .... Ex 17:2 7378
said unto them, Why c ye with me .... Ex 17:2 7378
they did c with him sharply .... Judg 8:1 7378
He will not always c .... Ps 103:9 7378

CHIDING
because of the c of the children .... Ex 17:7 7379

CHIDON (*ki'-don*) See NACHON. *Place where Uzzah died.*
came unto the threshingfloor of C 1Chr 13:9 3592

CHIEF
Phichol the c captain of his host .... Gen 21:22
Phichol the c captain of his host .... Gen 21:32
Phichol the c captain of his army .... Gen 26:26
against the c of the butlers, and .... Gen 40:2 8269
against the c of the bakers .... Gen 40:2 8269
the c butler told his dream to .... Gen 40:9 8269
When the c baker saw that the .... Gen 40:16 8269
up the head of the c butler .... Gen 40:20 8269
of the c baker among his servants .... Gen 40:20 8269
he restored the c butler unto his .... Gen 40:21 8269
But he hanged the c baker .... Gen 40:22 8269
Yet did not the c butler remember .... Gen 40:23 8269
Then spake the c butler unto .... Gen 41:9 8269
house, both me and the c baker .... Gen 41:10 8269
being a c man among his people .... Lev 21:4 1167
the c of the house of the father .... Num 3:24 5387
the c of the house of the father .... Num 3:30 5387
c over the c of the Levites .... Num 3:32 5387
the c of the house of the father .... Num 3:35 5387
the c of the congregation .... Num 4:34 5387
the c of Israel numbered, after .... Num 4:46 5387
a prince of a c house among the .... Num 25:14 1
people, and of a c house in Midian .... Num 25:15 1
the c fathers of the congregation .... Num 31:26 7218
the c fathers of the tribes of .... Num 32:28 7218
the c fathers of the families of .... Num 36:1 7218
the c fathers of the children of .... Num 36:1 7218
So I took the c of your tribes .... Deut 1:15 7218
for the c things of the ancient .... Deut 33:15 7218
princes, of each c house a prince .... Josh 22:14 1
the c of all the people, even of .... Judg 20:2 6438
hither, all the c of the people 1Sa 14:38 6438
the c of the things which should 1Sa 15:21 7225
of David's soul, he shall be c 2Sa 5:8
and David's sons were c rulers 2Sa 8:18 3548
Jairite was a c ruler about David 2Sa 20:26 3548
in the seat, c among the captains 2Sa 23:8 7218
three of the thirty c went down 2Sa 23:13 7218
son of Zeruiah, was c among three 2Sa 23:18 7218
Beside the c of Solomon's 1Kin 5:16 8269
the c of the fathers of the 1Kin 8:1 5387
These were the c of the officers 1Kin 9:23 8269
the hands of the c of the guard 1Kin 14:27 8269
guard took Seraiah the c priest 2Kin 25:18 7218
and of him came the c ruler 1Chr 5:2 5059
was reckoned, were the c, Jeiel 1Chr 5:7 7218
Joel the c, and Shapham the next 1Chr 5:12 7218
c of the house of their fathers 1Chr 5:15 7218
all of them c men 1Chr 7:3 7218
men of valour, c of the princes 1Chr 7:40 7218
by their generations, c men 1Chr 8:28 7218
All these men were c of the 1Chr 9:9 7218
Shallum was the c 1Chr 9:17 7218
these Levites, the four c porters 1Chr 9:26 1368
c of the fathers of the Levites 1Chr 9:33 7218
These c fathers of the Levites 1Chr 9:34 7218
fathers of the Levites were c 1Chr 9:34 7218
the Jebusites first shall be c 1Chr 11:6 7218
Zeruiah went first up, and was c 1Chr 11:6 7218
These also are the c of the 1Chr 11:10 7218
Hachmonite, the c of the captains 1Chr 11:11 7218
of Joab, he was c of the three 1Chr 11:20 7218
The c was Ahiezer, then Joash 1Chr 12:3 7218
who was c of the captains, and he 1Chr 12:18 7218
Uriel the c, and his brethren an 1Chr 15:5 8269
Asaiah the c, and his brethren two 1Chr 15:6 8269
Joel the c, and his brethren an 1Chr 15:7 8269
Shemaiah the c, and his brethren 1Chr 15:8 8269
Eliel the c, and his brethren 1Chr 15:9 8269
Amminadab the c, and his brethren 1Chr 15:10 8269
Ye are the c of the fathers of 1Chr 15:12 7218
David spake to the c of the 1Chr 15:16 8269
c of the Levites, was for song 1Chr 15:22 8269
Asaph the c, and next to him 1Chr 16:5 7218
of David were c about the king 1Chr 18:17 7223
the c was Jehiel, and Zetham, and 1Chr 23:8 7218
These were the c of the fathers 1Chr 23:9 7218
And Jahath was the c, and Zizah the 1Chr 23:11 7218
of Gershom, Shebuel was the c 1Chr 23:16 7218
of Eliezer were, Rehabiah the c 1Chr 23:17 7218
Shelomith the c 1Chr 23:18 7218
even the c of the fathers, as 1Chr 23:24 7218
there were more c men found of 1Chr 24:4 7218
c men of the house of their 1Chr 24:4 7218
before the c of the fathers of 1Chr 24:6 7218
the c of the fathers of the 1Chr 24:31 7218
Simri the c, (for though he was 1Chr 26:10 7218
yet his father made him the c 1Chr 26:10 7218
the porters, even among the c men 1Chr 26:12 7218
c fathers, even of Laadan the 1Chr 26:21 7218
the c fathers, the captains over 1Chr 26:26 7218
the Hebronites was Jerijah the c 1Chr 26:31 7218
and seven hundred c fathers 1Chr 26:32 7218
the c fathers and captains of 1Chr 27:1 7218
the children of Perez was the c 1Chr 27:3 7218
the son of Jehoiada, a c priest 1Chr 27:5 7218
Then the c of the fathers and 1Chr 29:6 8269
the LORD to be the c governor 1Chr 29:22 5057
all Israel, the c of the fathers 2Chr 1:2 7218
the c of the fathers of the 2Chr 5:2 5387
c of his captains, and captains of 2Chr 8:9 8269
And these were the c of king 2Chr 8:10 8269
Abijah the son of Maachah the c 2Chr 11:22 7218
the hands of the c of the guard 2Chr 12:10 8269
Adnah the c, and with him mighty 2Chr 17:14 8269
of the c of the fathers of Israel 2Chr 19:8 7218
Amariah the c priest is over you 2Chr 19:11 7218
the c of the fathers of Israel 2Chr 23:2 7218
king called for Jehoiada the c 2Chr 24:6 7218
The whole number of the c of the 2Chr 26:12 7218
And Azariah the c priest, and all 2Chr 26:20 7218
Azariah the c priest of the house 2Chr 31:10 7218
c of the Levites, gave unto the 2Chr 35:9 8269
Moreover all the c of the priests 2Chr 36:14 8269
Then rose up the c of the fathers .... Ezr 1:5 7218
some of the c of the fathers .... Ezr 2:68 7218
c of the fathers, who were .... Ezr 3:12 7218
to the c of the fathers, and said .... Ezr 4:2 7218
the rest of the c of the fathers .... Ezr 4:3 7218
the men that were the c of them .... Ezr 5:10 7217
the son of Aaron the c priest .... Ezr 7:5 7218
of Israel c men to go up with me .... Ezr 7:28 7218
are now the c of their fathers .... Ezr 8:1 7218
and for Meshullam, c men .... Ezr 8:16 7218
Iddo the c at the place Casiphia .... Ezr 8:17 7218
twelve of the c of the priests .... Ezr 8:24 8269
them before the c of the priests .... Ezr 8:29 8269
c of the fathers of Israel, at .... Ezr 8:29 8269
hath been c in this trespass .... Ezr 9:2 7223
arose Ezra, and made the c priests .... Ezr 10:5 8269
with certain c of the fathers .... Ezr 10:16 7218
some of the c of the fathers gave .... Neh 7:70 7218
some of the c of the fathers gave .... Neh 7:71 7218
the c of the fathers of all the .... Neh 8:13 7218
The c of the people .... Neh 10:14 7218
Now these are the c of the .... Neh 11:3 7218
c of the fathers, two hundred .... Neh 11:13 7218
of the c of the Levites, had the .... Neh 11:16 7218
These were the c of the priests .... Neh 12:7 7218
priests, the c of the fathers .... Neh 12:12 7218
were recorded c of the fathers .... Neh 12:22 7218
the c of the fathers, were .... Neh 12:23 7218
And the c of the Levites .... Neh 12:24 7218
old there were c of the singers .... Neh 12:46 7218
the c of the people of the earth .... Job 12:24 7218
I chose out their way, and sat c .... Job 29:25 7218
He is the c of the ways of God .... Job 40:19 7725
To the c Musician on Neginoth, A .... Ps 4:*t* 5329
To the c Musician upon Nehiloth .... Ps 5:*t* 5329
To the c Musician on Neginoth .... Ps 6:*t* 5329
To the c Musician upon Gittith, A .... Ps 8:*t* 5329
To the c Musician upon .... Ps 9:*t* 5329
To the c Musician, A Psalm of .... Ps 11:*t* 5329
To the c Musician upon Sheminith .... Ps 12:*t* 5329
To the c Musician, A Psalm of .... Ps 13:*t* 5329
To the c Musician, A Psalm of .... Ps 14:*t* 5329
To the c Musician, A Psalm of .... Ps 18:*t* 5329
To the c Musician, A Psalm of .... Ps 19:*t* 5329
To the c Musician, A Psalm of .... Ps 20:*t* 5329
To the c Musician, A Psalm of .... Ps 21:*t* 5329
To the c Musician upon Aijeleth .... Ps 22:*t* 5329
To the c Musician, A Psalm of .... Ps 31:*t* 5329
To the c Musician, A Psalm of .... Ps 36:*t* 5329
To the c Musician, even to .... Ps 39:*t* 5329
To the c Musician, A Psalm of .... Ps 40:*t* 5329
To the c Musician, A Psalm of .... Ps 41:*t* 5329
To the c Musician, Maschil, for .... Ps 42:*t* 5329
To the c Musician for the sons of .... Ps 44:*t* 5329
To the c Musician upon Shoshannim .... Ps 45:*t* 5329
To the c Musician for the sons of .... Ps 46:*t* 5329
To the c Musician, A Psalm for .... Ps 47:*t* 5329
To the c Musician, A Psalm for .... Ps 49:*t* 5329
To the c Musician, A Psalm of .... Ps 51:*t* 5329
To the c Musician, Maschil, A .... Ps 52:*t* 5329
To the c Musician upon Mahalath .... Ps 53:*t* 5329
To the c Musician on Neginoth .... Ps 54:*t* 5329
To the c Musician on Neginoth .... Ps 55:*t* 5329
To the c Musician upon .... Ps 56:*t* 5329
To the c Musician, Altaschith .... Ps 57:*t* 5329

To the c Musician, Altaschith,	Ps 58:t	5329
To the c Musician, Altaschith,	Ps 59:t	5329
To the c Musician upon	Ps 60:t	5329
To the c Musician upon Neginah, A	Ps 61:t	5329
To the c Musician, to Jeduthun, A	Ps 62:t	5329
To the c Musician, A Psalm of	Ps 64:t	5329
To the c Musician, A Psalm and	Ps 65:t	5329
To the c Musician, A Song or	Ps 66:t	5329
To the c Musician on Neginoth, A	Ps 67:t	5329
To the c Musician, A Psalm or	Ps 68:t	5329
To the c Musician upon Shoshannim	Ps 69:t	5329
To the c Musician, A Psalm of	Ps 70:t	5329
To the c Musician, Altaschith, A	Ps 75:t	5329
To the c Musician on Neginoth, A	Ps 76:t	5329
To the c Musician, to Jeduthun, A	Ps 77:t	5329
the c of their strength in the	Ps 78:51	7725
To the c Musician upon	Ps 80:t	5329
To the c Musician upon Gittith, A	Ps 81:t	5329
To the c Musician upon Gittith, A	Ps 84:t	5329
To the c Musician, A Psalm for	Ps 85:t	5329
for the sons of Korah to the c	Ps 88:t	5329
the c of all their strength	Ps 105:36	7725
To the c Musician, A Psalm of	Ps 109:t	5329
not Jerusalem above my c joy	Ps 137:6	7218
To the c Musician, A Psalm of	Ps 139:t	5329
To the c Musician, A Psalm of	Ps 140:t	5329
She crieth in the c place of	Prov 1:21	7218
a whisperer separateth c friends	Prov 16:28	441
and aloes, with all the c spices	Song 4:14	7218
even all the c ones of the earth	Is 14:9	6260
thee from the c men thereof	Is 41:9	678
to be captains, and as c over thee	Jer 13:21	7218
who was also c governor in the	Jer 20:1	5051
shout among the c of the nations	Jer 31:7	7218
bow of Elam, the c of their might	Jer 49:35	7225
guard took Seraiah the c priest	Jer 52:24	7218
Her adversaries are the c	Lam 1:5	7218
in thy fairs with c of all spices	Eze 27:22	7218
the c prince of Meshech and Tubal,	Eze 38:2	7218
the c prince of Meshech and Tubal	Eze 38:3	7218
the c prince of Meshech and Tubal	Eze 39:1	7218
c of the governors over all the	Dan 2:48	7229
lo, Michael, one of the c princes	Dan 10:13	7223
the c of the children of Ammon	Dan 11:41	7225
which are named c of the nations	Amos 6:1	7225
themselves with the c ointments	Amos 6:6	7225
To the c singer on my stringed	Hab 3:19	5329
he had gathered all the c priests	Mt 2:4	749
c priests and scribes, and be	Mt 16:21	749
be betrayed unto the c priests	Mt 20:18	749
And whosoever will be c among you	Mt 20:27	4413
And when the c priests and scribes	Mt 21:15	749
the c priests and the elders of	Mt 21:23	749
And when the c priests and	Mt 21:45	749
the c seats in the synagogues,	Mt 23:6	4410
assembled together the c priests	Mt 26:3	749
Iscariot, went unto the c priests	Mt 26:14	749
and staves, from the c priests	Mt 26:47	749
Now the c priests, and elders, and	Mt 26:59	749
was come, all the c priests	Mt 27:1	749
pieces of silver to the c priests	Mt 27:3	749
the c priests took the silver	Mt 27:6	749
he was accused of the c priests	Mt 27:12	749
But the c priests and elders	Mt 27:20	749
Likewise also the c priests	Mt 27:41	749
the c priests and Pharisees came	Mt 27:62	749
shewed unto the c priests all the	Mt 28:11	749
captains, and c estates of Galilee	Mk 6:21	4413
of the c priests, and scribes, and	Mk 8:31	749
be delivered unto the c priests	Mk 10:33	749
c priests heard it, and sought how	Mk 11:18	749
there come to him the c priests	Mk 11:27	749
the c seats in the synagogues, and	Mk 12:39	4410
the c priests and the scribes	Mk 14:1	749
twelve, went unto the c priests	Mk 14:10	749
and staves, from the c priest	Mk 14:43	749
were assembled all the c priests	Mk 14:53	749
the c priests and all the council	Mk 14:55	749
the c priests held a consultation	Mk 15:1	749
the c priests accused him of many	Mk 15:3	749
For he knew that the c priests	Mk 15:10	749
But the c priests moved the	Mk 15:11	749
Likewise also the c priests	Mk 15:31	749
c priests and scribes, and be slain	Lk 9:22	749
Beelzebub the c of the devils	Lk 11:15	758
into the house of one of the c	Lk 14:1	758
how they chose out the c rooms	Lk 14:7	4411
which was the c among the	Lk 19:2	754
But the c priests and the scribes	Lk 19:47	749
the c of the people sought to	Lk 19:47	4413
the c priests and the scribes came	Lk 20:1	749
the c priests and the scribes the	Lk 20:19	749
and the c rooms at feasts	Lk 20:46	4411
the c priests and scribes sought	Lk 22:2	749
and communed with the c priests	Lk 22:4	749
and he that is c, as he that doth	Lk 22:26	2233
Jesus said unto the c priests	Lk 22:52	749
the c priests and the scribes came	Lk 22:66	749
Then said Pilate to the c priests	Lk 23:4	749
the c priests and scribes stood and	Lk 23:10	749
had called together the c priests	Lk 23:13	749
of the c priests prevailed	Lk 23:23	749
And how the c priests and our	Lk 24:20	749
the c priests sent officers to	Jn 7:32	749
the officers to the c priests	Jn 7:45	749
Then gathered the c priests	Jn 11:47	749
Now both the c priests and the	Jn 11:57	749
But the c priests consulted that	Jn 12:10	749
Nevertheless among the c rulers	Jn 12:42	758
and officers from the c priests	Jn 18:3	749
the c priests have delivered thee	Jn 18:35	749
When the c priests therefore and	Jn 19:6	749
The c priests answered, We have	Jn 19:15	749
Then said the c priests of the	Jn 19:21	749
reported all that the c priests	Acts 4:23	749
the c priests heard these things,	Acts 5:24	749
c priests to bind all that call	Acts 9:14	749
them bound unto the c priests	Acts 9:21	749
the c men of the city, and raised	Acts 13:50	4413
because he was the c speaker	Acts 14:12	2233
Silas, c men among the brethren	Acts 15:22	2233
which is the c city of that part	Acts 16:12	4413
and of the c women not a few	Acts 17:4	4413
the c ruler of the synagogue,	Acts 18:8	752
the c ruler of the synagogue, and	Acts 18:17	752
c of the priests, which did so	Acts 19:14	749
And certain of the c of Asia	Acts 19:31	775
unto the c captain of the band	Acts 21:31	5506
and when they saw the c captain	Acts 21:32	5506
Then the c captain came near, and	Acts 21:33	5506
he said unto the c captain	Acts 21:37	5506
The c captain commanded him to be	Acts 22:24	5506
he went and told the c captain	Acts 22:26	5506
Then the c captain came, and said	Acts 22:27	5506
the c captain answered, With a	Acts 22:28	5506
the c captain also was afraid,	Acts 22:29	5506
bands, and commanded the c priests	Acts 22:30	749
the c captain, fearing lest Paul	Acts 23:10	5506
And they came to the c priests	Acts 23:14	749
c captain that he bring him down	Acts 23:15	5506
this young man unto the c captain	Acts 23:17	5506
and brought him to the c captain	Acts 23:18	5506
Then the c captain took him by	Acts 23:19	5506
So the c captain then let the	Acts 23:22	5506
But the c captain Lysias came	Acts 24:7	5506
When Lysias the c captain shall	Acts 24:22	5506
the c of the Jews informed him	Acts 25:2	4413
the c priests and the elders of	Acts 25:15	749
of hearing, with the c captains	Acts 25:23	5506
authority from the c priests	Acts 26:10	749
and commission from the c priests	Acts 26:12	749
of the c man of the island	Acts 28:7	4413
called the c of the Jews together	Acts 28:17	4413
himself being the c corner stone	Eph 2:20	204
of whom I am c	1Ti 1:15	4413
I lay in Sion a c corner stone	1Pet 2:6	204
when the c Shepherd shall appear,	1Pet 5:4	750
the c captains, and the mighty men	Rev 6:15	5506

CHIEFEST

c of all the offerings of Israel	1Sa 2:29	7225
made them sit in the c place	1Sa 9:22	7218
the c of the herdmen that	1Sa 21:7	47
they buried him in the c of the	2Chr 32:33	4608
ruddy, the c among ten thousand	Song 5:10	1713
And whosoever of you will be the c	Mk 10:44	4413
a whit behind the very c apostles	2Cor 11:5	
am I behind the very c apostles	2Cor 12:11	
the c city of Phrygia Pacatiana	1Ti s	3390

CHIEFLY

c, because that unto them were	Rom 3:2	4412
c they that are of Caesar's	Phil 4:22	3122
But c them that walk after the	2Pet 2:10	3122

CHILD

she had no c	Gen 11:30	2056
unto her, Behold, thou art with c	Gen 16:11	2030
Every man c among you shall be	Gen 17:10	
every man c in your generations,	Gen 17:12	
the uncircumcised man c whose	Gen 17:14	
Shall a c be born unto him that	Gen 17:17	
Shall I of a surety bear a c	Gen 18:13	
of Lot with c by their father	Gen 19:36	2029
the c grew, and was weaned	Gen 21:8	3206
it on her shoulder, and the c	Gen 21:14	3206
she cast the c under one of the	Gen 21:15	3206
Let me not see the death of the c	Gen 21:16	3206
brethren, and said, The c is not	Gen 37:30	3206
behold, she is with c by whoredom	Gen 38:24	2030
man, whose these are, am I with c	Gen 38:25	2030
saying, Do not sin against the c	Gen 42:22	3206
a c of his old age, a little one	Gen 44:20	3206
saw him that he was a goodly c	Ex 2:2	
with pitch, and put the c therein	Ex 2:3	3206
she had opened it, she saw the c	Ex 2:6	3206
that she may nurse the c for thee	Ex 2:7	3206
said unto her, Take this c away	Ex 2:9	3206
And the woman took the c, and	Ex 2:9	3206
the c grew, and she brought him	Ex 2:10	3206
strive, and hurt a woman with c	Ex 21:22	2030
any widow, or fatherless c	Ex 22:22	
conceived seed, and born a man c	Lev 12:2	
But if she bear a maid c, then	Lev 12:5	
widow, or divorced, and have no c	Lev 22:13	2233
father beareth the sucking c	Num 11:12	
and one of them die, and have no c	Deut 25:5	1121
and she was his only c	Judg 11:34	3173
for the c shall be a Nazarite	Judg 13:5	5288
for the c shall be a Nazarite to	Judg 13:7	5288
do unto the c that shall be born	Judg 13:8	5288
How shall we order the c, and how	Judg 13:12	5288
the c grew, and the LORD blessed	Judg 13:24	5288
And Naomi took the c, and laid it	Ruth 4:16	3206
give unto thine handmaid a man c	1Sa 1:11	2233
not go up until the c be weaned	1Sa 1:22	5288
and the c was young	1Sa 1:24	5288
bullock, and brought the c to Eli	1Sa 1:25	5288
For this c I prayed	1Sa 1:27	5288
the c did minister unto the LORD	1Sa 2:11	5288
before the LORD, being a c	1Sa 2:18	5288
the c Samuel grew before the LORD	1Sa 2:21	5288
the c Samuel grew on, and was in	1Sa 2:26	5288
the c Samuel ministered unto the	1Sa 3:1	5288
that the LORD had called the c	1Sa 3:8	5288
law, Phinehas' wife, was with c	1Sa 4:19	2030
And she named the c I-chabod	1Sa 4:21	5288
no c unto the day of her death	2Sa 6:23	3206
told David, and said, I am with c	2Sa 11:5	2030
the c also that is born unto thee	2Sa 12:14	1121
the LORD struck the c that	2Sa 12:15	3206
therefore besought God for the c	2Sa 12:16	5288
the seventh day, that the c died	2Sa 12:18	3206
to tell him that the c was dead	2Sa 12:18	3206
while the c was yet alive, we	2Sa 12:18	3206
if we tell him that the c is dead	2Sa 12:18	3206
perceived that the c was dead	2Sa 12:19	3206
unto his servants, Is the c dead	2Sa 12:19	3206
thou didst fast and weep for the c	2Sa 12:21	3206
but when the c was dead, thou	2Sa 12:21	3206
While the c was yet alive, I	2Sa 12:22	3206
to me, that the c may live	2Sa 12:22	3206
and I am but a little c	1Kin 3:7	5288
I was delivered of a c with her	1Kin 3:17	3205
this woman's c died in the night	1Kin 3:19	1121
and laid her dead c in my bosom	1Kin 3:20	1121
in the morning to give my c suck	1Kin 3:21	1121
said, Divide the living c in two	1Kin 3:25	3206
the living c was unto the king	1Kin 3:26	1121
O my lord, give her the living c	1Kin 3:26	3205
and said, Give her the living c	1Kin 3:27	3205
Hadad being yet a little c	1Kin 11:17	5288
a c shall be born unto the house	1Kin 13:2	1121
thee what shall become of the c	1Kin 14:3	5288
into the city, the c shall die	1Kin 14:12	3206
threshold of the door, the c died	1Kin 14:17	5288
himself upon the c three times	1Kin 17:21	3206
the soul of the c came into him	1Kin 17:22	3206
And Elijah took the c, and brought	1Kin 17:23	3206
answered, Verily she hath no c	2Kin 4:14	1121
when the c was grown, it fell on	2Kin 4:18	3206
is it well with the c	2Kin 4:26	3206
my staff upon the face of the c	2Kin 4:29	5288
And the mother of the c said	2Kin 4:30	5288
the staff upon the face of the c	2Kin 4:31	5288
him, saying, The c is not awaked	2Kin 4:31	5288
the c was dead, and laid upon his	2Kin 4:32	5288
And he went up, and lay upon the c	2Kin 4:34	3206
he stretched himself upon the c	2Kin 4:34	
and the flesh of the c waxed warm	2Kin 4:34	3206
the c sneezed seven times	2Kin 4:35	5288
and the c opened his eyes	2Kin 4:35	5288
like unto the flesh of a little c	2Kin 5:14	5288
and rip up their women with c	2Kin 8:12	2030
that were with c he ripped up	2Kin 15:16	2030
said, There is a man c conceived	Job 3:3	
as a c that is weaned of his	Ps 131:2	
my soul is even as a weaned c	Ps 131:2	
Even a c is known by his doings,	Prov 20:11	5288
Train up a c in the way he should	Prov 22:6	5288
is bound in the heart of a c	Prov 22:15	5288
not correction from the c	Prov 23:13	5288
a wise c shall have joy of him	Prov 23:24	
but a c left to himself bringeth	Prov 29:15	5288
a c shall have him become his son	Prov 29:21	5290
he hath neither c nor brother	Eccl 4:8	1121
a wise c than an old and foolish	Eccl 4:13	3206
with the second c that shall	Eccl 4:15	3206
O land, when thy king is a c	Eccl 10:16	5288
in the womb of her that is with c	Eccl 11:5	4392
the c shall behave himself	Is 3:5	5288
For before the c shall know to	Is 7:16	5288
For before the c shall have	Is 8:4	5288
For unto us a c is born, unto us	Is 9:6	3206
be few, that a c may write them	Is 10:19	5288
a little c shall lead them	Is 11:6	5288
the sucking c shall play on the	Is 11:8	
the weaned c shall put his hand	Is 11:8	
Like as a woman with c, that	Is 26:17	2030
We have been with c, we have been	Is 26:18	2029
Can a woman forget her sucking c	Is 49:15	
that didst not travail with c	Is 54:1	
for the c shall die an hundred	Is 65:20	5288
she was delivered of a man c	Is 66:7	
for I am a c	Jer 1:6	5288
said unto me, Say not, I am a c	Jer 1:7	5288
that bringeth forth her first c	Jer 4:31	
A man c is born unto thee	Jer 20:15	1121
whether a man doth travail with c	Jer 30:6	3205
and the lame, the woman with c	Jer 31:8	2030
that travaileth with c together	Jer 31:8	3205
is he a pleasant c	Jer 31:20	3206
cut off from you man and woman, c	Jer 44:7	5768
The tongue of the sucking c	Lam 4:4	
When Israel was a c, then I loved	Hos 11:1	5288
their women with c shall be	Hos 13:16	2030
up the women with c of Gilead	Amos 1:13	2030
found with c of the Holy Ghost	Mt 1:18	
Behold, a virgin shall be with c	Mt 1:23	
search diligently for the young c	Mt 2:8	3813
stood over where the young c was	Mt 2:9	3813
they saw the young c with Mary	Mt 2:11	3813
Arise, and take the young c	Mt 2:13	3813
seek the young c to destroy him	Mt 2:13	3813
he arose, he took the young c	Mt 2:14	3813
Arise, and take the young c	Mt 2:20	3813
And he arose, and took the young c	Mt 2:21	3813
to death, and the father the c	Mt 10:21	5043
the c was cured from that very	Mt 17:18	3816
Jesus called a little c unto him	Mt 18:2	3813
humble himself as this little c	Mt 18:4	3813
little c in my name receiveth me	Mt 18:5	3813
the c of hell than yourselves	Mt 23:15	5207
And woe unto them that are with c	Mt 24:19	
And he said, Of a c	Mk 9:21	3812
the father of the c cried out	Mk 9:24	3813
And he took a c, and set him in the	Mk 9:36	3813
the kingdom of God as a little c	Mk 10:15	3813
But woe to them that are with c	Mk 13:17	
And they had no c, because that	Lk 1:7	5043
day they came to circumcise the c	Lk 1:59	3813
What manner of c shall this be	Lk 1:66	3813
And thou, c, shalt be called the	Lk 1:76	3813

the c grew, and waxed strong in Lk 1:80 *3813*
espoused wife, being great with c Lk 2:5 *1471*
was told them concerning this c Lk 2:17 *3813*
for the circumcising of the c Lk 2:21 *3813*
parents brought in the c Jesus Lk 2:27 *3813*
this c is set for the fall and Lk 2:34
the c grew, and waxed strong in Lk 2:40 *3813*
the c Jesus tarried behind in Lk 2:43 *3816*
for he is mine only c Lk 9:38 *3439*
unclean spirit, and healed the c Lk 9:42 *3816*
thought of their heart, took a c Lk 9:47 *3813*
this c in my name receiveth me Lk 9:48 *3813*
c shall in no wise enter therein Lk 18:17 *3813*
But woe unto them that are with c Lk 21:23
him, Sir, come down ere my c die Jn 4:49 *3813*
soon as she is delivered of the c Jn 16:21 *3813*
a truth against thy holy c Jesus Acts 4:27 *3816*
by the name of thy holy c Jesus Acts 4:30 *3816*
him, when as yet he had no c Acts 7:5 *5043*
thou c of the devil, thou enemy Acts 13:10 *5207*
I was a c, I spake as a c 1Cor 13:11 *3516*
I understood as a c 1Cor 13:11 *3516*
I thought as a c 1Cor 13:11 *3516*
the heir, as long as he is a c Gal 4:1 *3516*
as travail upon a woman with c 1Th 5:3
that from a c thou hast known the 2Ti 3:15 *1025*
was delivered of a c when she was Heb 11:11 *5088*
they saw he was a proper c Heb 11:23 *3813*
And she being with c cried Rev 12:2
for to devour her c as soon as it Rev 12:4 *5043*
And she brought forth a man c Rev 12:5 *5207*
her c was caught up unto God, and Rev 12:5 *5043*
which brought forth the man c Rev 12:13

CHILDBEARING

she shall be saved in c, if they 1Ti 2:15 *5042*

CHILDHOOD

you from my c unto this day 1Sa 12:2 5271
for c and youth are vanity Eccl 11:10 3208

CHILDISH

became a man, I put away c things 1Cor 13:11 *3516*

CHILDLESS

wilt thou give me, seeing I go c Gen 15:2 6185
they shall die c Lev 20:20 6185
they shall be c Lev 20:21 6185
As thy sword hath made women c 1Sa 15:33 7921
shall thy mother be c among women 1Sa 15:33 7921
the LORD, Write ye this man c Jer 22:30 6185
took her to wife, and he died c Lk 20:30 *815*

CHILDREN

sorrow thou shalt bring forth c Gen 3:16 1121
of men, and they bare c to them Gen 6:4
the father of all the c of Eber Gen 10:21 1121
elder, even to him were c born Gen 10:21
The c of Shem Gen 10:22 1121
And the c of Aram Gen 10:23 1121
which the c of men builded Gen 11:5 1121
Sarai Abram's wife bare him no c Gen 16:1
may be that I may obtain c by her Gen 16:2 1129
him, that he will command his c Gen 18:19 1121
of the c of Ammon unto this day Gen 19:38 1121
and they bare c Gen 20:17
Sarah should have given c suck Gen 21:7 1121
she hath also born c unto thy Gen 22:20 1121
the c of Heth answered Abraham, Gen 23:5 1121
the land, even to the c of Heth Gen 23:7 1121
Ephron dwelt among the c of Heth Gen 23:10 1121
in the audience of the c of Heth Gen 23:10 1121
in the presence of the c of Heth Gen 23:18 1121
All these were the c of Keturah Gen 25:4 1121
the c struggled together within Gen 25:22 1121
saw that she bare Jacob no c Gen 30:1
and said unto Jacob, Give me c Gen 30:1 1121
that I may also have c by her Gen 30:3 1129
Give me my wives and my c, for Gen 30:26 3206
and these c are my c Gen 31:43 1121
or unto their c which they have Gen 31:43 1121
me, and the mother with the c Gen 32:11 1121
Therefore the c of Israel eat not Gen 32:32 1121
And he divided the c unto Leah Gen 33:1 3206
their c foremost, and Leah and her Gen 33:2 3206
her c after, and Rachel and Joseph Gen 33:2 3206
eyes, and saw the women and the c Gen 33:5 3206
The c which God hath graciously Gen 33:5 3206
came near, they and their c Gen 33:6 3206
And Leah also with her c came near Gen 33:7 3206
knoweth that the c are tender Gen 33:13 3206
the c be able to endure, until I Gen 33:14 3206
at the hand of the c of Hamor Gen 33:19 1121
the c of Seir in the land of Edom Gen 36:21 1121
the c of Lotan were Hori and Hemam Gen 36:22 1121
the c of Shobal were these Gen 36:23 1121
And these are the c of Zibeon Gen 36:24 1121
And the c of Anah were these Gen 36:25 1121
And these are the c of Dishon Gen 36:26 1121
The c of Ezer are these Gen 36:27 1121
The c of Dishan are these Gen 36:28 1121
any king over the c of Israel Gen 36:31 1121
loved Joseph more than all his c Gen 37:3 1121
them, Me have ye bereaved of my c Gen 42:36
If I be bereaved of my c, I am Gen 43:14
thy c, and thy children's c Gen 45:10 1121
And the c of Israel did so Gen 45:21 1121
are the names of the c of Israel Gen 46:8 1121
thy father's c shall bow down Gen 49:8 1121
is therein was from the c of Heth Gen 49:32 1121
Joseph saw Ephraim's c of the Gen 50:23 1121
the c also of Machir the son of Gen 50:23 1121
took an oath of the c of Israel Gen 50:25 1121
are the names of the c of Israel Ex 1:1 1121
the c of Israel were fruitful, and Ex 1:7 1121
the people of the c of Israel are Ex 1:9 1121
because of the c of Israel Ex 1:12 1121
the Egyptians made the c of Ex 1:13 1121
them, but saved the men c alive Ex 1:17 3206
and have saved the men c alive Ex 1:18 3206
This is one of the Hebrews' c Ex 2:6 3206
the c of Israel sighed by reason Ex 2:23 1121
God looked upon the c of Israel Ex 2:25 1121
the cry of the c of Israel is Ex 3:9 1121
the c of Israel out of Egypt Ex 3:10 1121
the c of Israel out of Egypt Ex 3:11 1121
when I come unto the c of Israel Ex 3:13 1121
thou say unto the c of Israel Ex 3:14 1121
thou say unto the c of Israel Ex 3:15 1121
all the elders of the c of Israel Ex 4:29 1121
LORD had visited the c of Israel Ex 4:31 1121
the officers of the c of Israel Ex 5:14 1121
officers of the c of Israel came Ex 5:15 1121
the officers of the c of Israel Ex 5:19 1121
the groaning of the c of Israel Ex 6:5 1121
say unto the c of Israel, I am Ex 6:6 1121
spake so unto the c of Israel Ex 6:9 1121
that he let the c of Israel go Ex 6:11 1121
Behold, the c of Israel have not Ex 6:12 1121
a charge unto the c of Israel Ex 6:13 1121
to bring the c of Israel out of Ex 6:13 1121
Bring out the c of Israel from Ex 6:26 1121
to bring out the c of Israel from Ex 6:27 1121
that he send the c of Israel out Ex 7:2 1121
and my people the c of Israel Ex 7:4 1121
bring out the c of Israel from Ex 7:5 1121
of the c of Israel died not one Ex 9:6 1121
where the c of Israel were, was Ex 9:26 1121
would he let the c of Israel go Ex 9:35 1121
would not let the c of Israel go Ex 10:20 1121
but all the c of Israel had light Ex 10:23 1121
But against any of the c of Ex 11:7 1121
c of Israel go out of his land Ex 11:10 1121
when your c shall say unto you, Ex 12:26 1121
of the c of Israel in Egypt Ex 12:27 1121
the c of Israel went away, and did Ex 12:28 1121
both ye and the c of Israel Ex 12:31 1121
the c of Israel did according to Ex 12:35 1121
the c of Israel journeyed from Ex 12:37 1121
on foot that were men, beside c Ex 12:37 2945
the sojourning of the c of Israel Ex 12:40 1121
c of Israel in their generations Ex 12:42 1121
Thus did all the c of Israel Ex 12:50 1121
that the LORD did bring the c of Ex 12:51 1121
the womb among the c of Israel Ex 13:2 1121
man among thy c shalt thou redeem Ex 13:13 1121
the firstborn of my c I redeem Ex 13:15 1121
the c of Israel went up harnessed Ex 13:18 1121
straitly sworn the c of Israel Ex 13:19 1121
Speak unto the c of Israel Ex 14:2 1121
will say of the c of Israel Ex 14:3 1121
he pursued after the c of Israel Ex 14:8 1121
the c of Israel went out with an Ex 14:8 1121
the c of Israel lifted up their Ex 14:10 1121
the c of Israel cried out unto Ex 14:10 1121
speak unto the c of Israel Ex 14:15 1121
the c of Israel shall go on dry Ex 14:16 1121
the c of Israel went into the Ex 14:22 1121
But the c of Israel walked upon Ex 14:29 1121
the c of Israel this song unto Ex 15:1 1121
but the c of Israel went on dry Ex 15:19 1121
of the c of Israel came unto the Ex 16:1 1121
the c of Israel murmured against Ex 16:2 1121
the c of Israel said unto them, Ex 16:3 1121
said unto all the c of Israel Ex 16:6 1121
congregation of the c of Israel Ex 16:9 1121
congregation of the c of Israel Ex 16:10 1121
the murmurings of the c of Israel Ex 16:12 1121
when the c of Israel saw it, they Ex 16:15 1121
the c of Israel did so, and Ex 16:17 1121
the c of Israel did eat manna Ex 16:35 1121
all the congregation of the c of Ex 17:1 1121
out of Egypt, to kill us and our c Ex 17:3 1121
of the chiding of the c of Israel Ex 17:7 1121
when the c of Israel were gone Ex 19:1 1121
of Jacob, and tell the c of Israel Ex 19:3 1121
shalt speak unto the c of Israel Ex 19:6 1121
fathers upon the c unto the third Ex 20:5 1121
shalt say unto the c of Israel Ex 20:22 1121
her c shall be her master's, and Ex 21:4 3206
love my master, my wife, and my c Ex 21:5 1121
be widows, and your c fatherless Ex 22:24 1121
sent young men of the c of Israel Ex 24:5 1121
upon the nobles of the c of Ex 24:11 1121
in the eyes of the c of Israel Ex 24:17 1121
Speak unto the c of Israel Ex 25:2 1121
commandment unto the c of Israel Ex 25:22 1121
shalt command the c of Israel Ex 27:20 1121
on the behalf of the c of Israel Ex 27:21 1121
him, from among the c of Israel Ex 28:1 1121
them the names of the c of Israel Ex 28:9 1121
with the names of the c of Israel Ex 28:11 1121
of memorial unto the c of Israel Ex 28:12 1121
with the names of the c of Israel Ex 28:21 1121
shall bear the names of the c of Ex 28:29 1121
shall bear the judgment of the c Ex 28:30 1121
which the c of Israel shall Ex 28:38 1121
for ever from the c of Israel Ex 29:28 1121
c of Israel of the sacrifice of Ex 29:28 1121
I will meet with the c of Israel Ex 29:43 1121
will dwell among the c of Israel Ex 29:45 1121
c of Israel after their number Ex 30:12 1121
money of the c of Israel, and Ex 30:16 1121
the c of Israel before the LORD Ex 30:16 1121
shalt speak unto the c of Israel Ex 30:31 1121
thou also unto the c of Israel Ex 31:13 1121
Wherefore the c of Israel shall Ex 31:16 1121
me and the c of Israel for ever Ex 31:17 1121
made the c of Israel drink of it Ex 32:20 1121
the c of Levi did according to Ex 32:28 1121
Moses, Say unto the c of Israel Ex 33:5 1121
And the c of Israel stripped Ex 33:6 1121
of the fathers upon the c Ex 34:7 1121
and upon the children's c Ex 34:7
men c appear before the Lord GOD Ex 34:23
all the c of Israel saw Moses, Ex 34:30 1121
afterward all the c of Israel Ex 34:32 1121
spake unto the c of Israel that Ex 34:34 1121
the c of Israel saw the face of Ex 34:35 1121
of the c of Israel together Ex 35:1 1121
congregation of the c of Israel Ex 35:4 1121
the c of Israel departed from the Ex 35:20 1121
The c of Israel brought a willing Ex 35:29 1121
Moses said unto the c of Israel Ex 35:30 1121
which the c of Israel had brought Ex 36:3 1121
with the names of the c of Israel Ex 39:6 1121
for a memorial to the c of Israel Ex 39:7 1121
to the names of the c of Israel Ex 39:14 1121
the c of Israel did according to Ex 39:32 1121
so the c of Israel made all the Ex 39:42 1121
the c of Israel went onward in Ex 40:36 1121
Speak unto the c of Israel Lev 1:2 1121
Speak unto the c of Israel Lev 4:2 1121
All the males among the c of Lev 6:18 1121
Speak unto the c of Israel Lev 7:23 1121
Speak unto the c of Israel Lev 7:29 1121
of the c of Israel from off the Lev 7:34 1121
ever from among the c of Israel Lev 7:34 1121
be given them of the c of Israel Lev 7:36 1121
the c of Israel to offer their Lev 7:38 1121
unto the c of Israel thou shalt Lev 9:3 1121
that ye may teach the c of Israel Lev 10:11 1121
offerings of the c of Israel Lev 10:14 1121
Speak unto the c of Israel Lev 11:2 1121
Speak unto the c of Israel Lev 12:2 1121
Speak unto the c of Israel Lev 15:2 1121
the c of Israel from their Lev 15:31 1121
c of Israel two kids of the goats Lev 16:5 1121
uncleanness of the c of Israel Lev 16:16 1121
uncleanness of the c of Israel Lev 16:19 1121
the iniquities of the c of Israel Lev 16:21 1121
c of Israel for all their sins Lev 16:34 1121
sons, and unto all the c of Israel Lev 17:2 1121
To the end that the c of Israel Lev 17:5 1121
I said unto the c of Israel Lev 17:12 1121
man there be of the c of Israel Lev 17:13 1121
I said unto the c of Israel Lev 17:14 1121
Speak unto the c of Israel Lev 18:2 1121
congregation of the c of Israel Lev 19:2 1121
against the c of thy people Lev 19:18 1121
thou shalt say to the c of Israel Lev 20:2 1121
he be of the c of Israel, or of Lev 20:2 1121
sons, and unto all the c of Israel Lev 21:24 1121
holy things of the c of Israel Lev 22:2 1121
which the c of Israel hallow unto Lev 22:3 1121
holy things of the c of Israel Lev 22:15 1121
sons, and unto all the c of Israel Lev 22:18 1121
be hallowed among the c of Israel Lev 22:32 1121
Speak unto the c of Israel Lev 23:2 1121
Speak unto the c of Israel Lev 23:10 1121
Speak unto the c of Israel Lev 23:24 1121
Speak unto the c of Israel Lev 23:34 1121
may know that I made the c of Lev 23:43 1121
Moses declared unto the c of Lev 23:44 1121
Command the c of Israel, that Lev 24:2 1121
being taken from the c of Israel Lev 24:8 1121
went out among the c of Israel Lev 24:10 1121
shalt speak unto the c of Israel Lev 24:15 1121
And Moses spake to the c of Israel Lev 24:23 1121
the c of Israel did as the LORD Lev 24:23 1121
Speak unto the c of Israel Lev 25:2 1121
possession among the c of Israel Lev 25:33 1121
his c with him, and shall return Lev 25:41 1121
Moreover of the c of the Lev 25:45 1121
inheritance for your c after you Lev 25:46 1121
your brethren the c of Israel Lev 25:46 1121
both he, and his c with him Lev 25:54 1121
For unto me the c of Israel are Lev 25:55 1121
which shall rob you of your c Lev 26:22
the c of Israel in mount Sinai by Lev 26:46 1121
Speak unto the c of Israel Lev 27:2 1121
the c of Israel in mount Sinai Lev 27:34 1121
congregation of the c of Israel Num 1:2 1121
Of the c of Joseph Num 1:10 1121
the c of Reuben, Israel's eldest Num 1:20 1121
Of the c of Simeon, by their Num 1:22 1121
Of the c of Gad, by their Num 1:24 1121
Of the c of Judah, by their Num 1:26 1121
Of the c of Issachar, by their Num 1:28 1121
Of the c of Zebulun, by their Num 1:30 1121
Of the c of Joseph, namely, of Num 1:32 1121
of the c of Ephraim, by their Num 1:32 1121
Of the c of Manasseh, by their Num 1:34 1121
Of the c of Benjamin, by their Num 1:36 1121
Of the c of Dan, by their Num 1:38 1121
Of the c of Asher, by their Num 1:40 1121
Of the c of Naphtali, throughout Num 1:42 1121
were numbered of the c of Israel Num 1:45 1121
sum of them among the c of Israel Num 1:49 1121
the c of Israel shall pitch their Num 1:52 1121
congregation of the c of Israel Num 1:53 1121
the c of Israel did according to Num 1:54 1121
Every man of the c of Israel Num 2:2 1121
be captain of the c of Judah Num 2:3 1121
be captain of the c of Issachar Num 2:5 1121
be captain of the c of Zebulun Num 2:7 1121
the captain of the c of Reuben Num 2:10 1121
the captain of the c of Simeon Num 2:12 1121
the captain of the c of Manasseh Num 2:20 1121
the captain of the c of Dan shall Num 2:25 1121
the captain of the c of Asher Num 2:27 1121
the captain of the c of Naphtali Num 2:29 1121
which were numbered of the c of Num 2:32 1121
numbered among the c of Israel Num 2:33 1121

the c of Israel did according to Num 2:34 1121
of Sinai, and they had no c Num 3:4 1121
and the charge of the c of Israel Num 3:8 1121
unto him out of the c of Israel Num 3:9 1121
the Levites from among the c of Num 3:12 1121
the matrix among the c of Israel Num 3:12 1121
Number the c of Levi after the Num 3:15 1121
for the charge of the c of Israel Num 3:38 1121
the c of Israel from a month old Num 3:40 1121
firstborn among the c of Israel Num 3:41 1121
the cattle of the c of Israel Num 3:41 1121
firstborn among the c of Israel Num 3:42 1121
firstborn among the c of Israel Num 3:45 1121
the firstborn of the c of Israel Num 3:46 1121
Of the firstborn of the c of Num 3:50 1121
Command the c of Israel, that Num 5:2 1121
the c of Israel did so, and put Num 5:4 1121
Moses, so did the c of Israel Num 5:4 1121
Speak unto the c of Israel Num 5:6 1121
holy things of the c of Israel Num 5:9 1121
Speak unto the c of Israel Num 5:12 1121
Speak unto the c of Israel Num 6:2 1121
ye shall bless the c of Israel Num 6:23 1121
put my name upon the c of Israel Num 6:27 1121
Helon, prince of the c of Zebulun Num 7:24 1121
prince of the c of Reuben Num 7:30 1121
prince of the c of Simeon Num 7:36 1121
of Deuel, prince of the c of Gad Num 7:42 1121
prince of the c of Ephraim Num 7:48 1121
prince of the c of Manasseh Num 7:54 1121
prince of the c of Benjamin Num 7:60 1121
prince of the c of Dan, offered Num 7:66 1121
Ocran, prince of the c of Asher Num 7:72 1121
Enan, prince of the c of Naphtali Num 7:78 1121
from among the c of Israel Num 8:6 1121
of the c of Israel together Num 8:9 1121
the c of Israel shall put their Num 8:10 1121
an offering of the c of Israel Num 8:11 1121
from among the c of Israel Num 8:14 1121
me from among the c of Israel Num 8:16 1121
firstborn of all the c of Israel Num 8:16 1121
of the c of Israel are mine Num 8:17 1121
the firstborn of the c of Israel Num 8:18 1121
sons from among the c of Israel Num 8:19 1121
to do the service of the c of Num 8:19 1121
an atonement for the c of Israel Num 8:19 1121
no plague among the c of Israel Num 8:19 1121
when the c of Israel come nigh Num 8:19 1121
congregation of the c of Israel Num 8:20 1121
so did the c of Israel unto them Num 8:20 1121
Let the c of Israel also keep the Num 9:2 1121
Moses spake unto the c of Israel Num 9:4 1121
Moses, so did the c of Israel Num 9:5 1121
season among the c of Israel Num 9:7 1121
Speak unto the c of Israel Num 9:10 1121
that the c of Israel journeyed Num 9:17 1121
there the c of Israel pitched Num 9:17 1121
LORD the c of Israel journeyed Num 9:18 1121
then the c of Israel kept the Num 9:19 1121
the c of Israel abode in their Num 9:22 1121
the c of Israel took their Num 10:12 1121
the c of Judah according to their Num 10:14 1121
the host of the tribe of the c of Num 10:15 1121
the host of the tribe of the c of Num 10:16 1121
the host of the tribe of the c of Num 10:19 1121
the host of the tribe of the c of Num 10:20 1121
of the c of Ephraim set forward Num 10:22 1121
c of Manasseh was Gamaliel the Num 10:23 1121
the host of the tribe of the c of Num 10:24 1121
camp of the c of Dan set forward Num 10:25 1121
the host of the tribe of the c of Num 10:26 1121
the host of the tribe of the c of Num 10:27 1121
were the journeyings of the c of Num 10:28 1121
the c of Israel also wept again, Num 11:4 1121
which I give unto the c of Israel Num 13:2 1121
men were heads of the c of Israel Num 13:3 1121
and Talmai, the c of Anak, were Num 13:22 3211
c of Israel cut down from thence Num 13:24 1121
congregation of the c of Israel Num 13:26 1121
we saw the c of Anak there Num 13:28 3211
had searched unto the c of Israel Num 13:32 1121
all the c of Israel murmured Num 14:2 1121
wives and our c should be a prey Num 14:3 2945
congregation of the c of Israel Num 14:5 1121
the company of the c of Israel Num 14:7 1121
before all the c of Israel Num 14:10 1121
fathers upon the c unto the third Num 14:18 1121
the murmurings of the c of Israel Num 14:27 1121
your c shall wander in the Num 14:33 1121
sayings unto all the c of Israel Num 14:39 1121
Speak unto the c of Israel Num 15:2 1121
Speak unto the c of Israel Num 15:18 1121
congregation of the c of Israel Num 15:25 1121
congregation of the c of Israel Num 15:26 1121
is born among the c of Israel Num 15:29 1121
while the c of Israel were in the Num 15:32 1121
Speak unto the c of Israel Num 15:38 1121
with certain of the c of Israel Num 16:2 1121
and their sons, and their little c Num 16:27 2945
be a sign unto the c of Israel Num 16:38 1121
a memorial unto the c of Israel Num 16:40 1121
the c of Israel murmured against Num 16:41 1121
Speak unto the c of Israel Num 17:2 1121
the murmurings of the c of Israel Num 17:5 1121
Moses spake unto the c of Israel Num 17:6 1121
the LORD unto all the c of Israel Num 17:9 1121
the c of Israel spake unto Moses, Num 17:12 1121
any more upon the c of Israel Num 18:5 1121
from among the c of Israel Num 18:6 1121
things of the c of Israel Num 18:8 1121
wave offerings of the c of Israel Num 18:11 1121
which the c of Israel offer unto Num 18:19 1121
inheritance among the c of Israel Num 18:20 1121
I have given the c of Levi all Num 18:21 1121
Neither must the c of Israel Num 18:22 1121
that among the c of Israel they Num 18:23 1121
But the tithes of the c of Israel Num 18:24 1121
Among the c of Israel they shall Num 18:24 1121
When ye take of the c of Israel Num 18:26 1121
ye receive of the c of Israel Num 18:28 1121
holy things of the c of Israel Num 18:32 1121
Speak unto the c of Israel Num 19:2 1121
of the c of Israel for a water of Num 19:9 1121
it shall be unto the c of Israel Num 19:10 1121
Then came the c of Israel Num 20:1 1121
me in the eyes of the c of Israel Num 20:12 1121
because the c of Israel strove Num 20:13 1121
the c of Israel said unto him, We Num 20:19 1121
the c of Israel, even the whole Num 20:22 1121
I have given unto the c of Israel Num 20:24 1121
the c of Israel set forward, and Num 21:10 1121
Jabbok, even unto the c of Ammon Num 21:24 1121
of the c of Ammon was strong Num 21:24 1121
the c of Israel set forward, and Num 22:1 1121
because of the c of Israel Num 22:3 1121
the land of the c of his people Num 22:5 1121
and destroy all the c of Sheth Num 24:17 1121
one of the c of Israel came and Num 25:6 1121
congregation of the c of Israel Num 25:6 1121
was stayed from the c of Israel Num 25:8 1121
wrath away from the c of Israel Num 25:11 1121
that I consumed not the c of Num 25:11 1121
an atonement for the c of Israel Num 25:13 1121
congregation of the c of Israel Num 26:2 1121
the c of Israel, which went forth Num 26:4 1121
the c of Reuben Num 26:5 1121
the c of Korah died not Num 26:11 1121
The c of Gad after their families Num 26:15 1121
These are the families of the c Num 26:18 1121
Of the c of Asher after their Num 26:44 1121
the numbered of the c of Israel Num 26:51 1121
numbered among the c of Israel Num 26:62 1121
given them among the c of Israel Num 26:62 1121
who numbered the c of Israel in Num 26:63 1121
when they numbered the c of Num 26:64 1121
shalt speak unto the c of Israel Num 27:8 1121
it shall be unto the c of Israel Num 27:11 1121
I have given unto the c of Israel Num 27:12 1121
the c of Israel may be obedient Num 27:20 1121
all the c of Israel with him, Num 27:21 1121
Command the c of Israel, and say Num 28:2 1121
Moses told the c of Israel Num 29:40 1121
tribes concerning the c of Israel Num 30:1 1121
Avenge the c of Israel of the Num 31:2 1121
the c of Israel took all the Num 31:9 1121
congregation of the c of Israel Num 31:12 1121
these caused the c of Israel Num 31:16 1121
But all the women c, that have Num 31:18 2945
of the c of Israel's half, thou Num 31:30 1121
of the c of Israel's half, which Num 31:42 1121
Even of the c of Israel's half, Num 31:47 1121
for a memorial for the c of Num 31:54 1121
Now the c of Reuben and the Num 32:1 1121
the c of Gad had a very great Num 32:1 1121
The c of Gad and the c of Num 32:2 1121
And Moses said unto the c of Gad Num 32:6 1121
to the c of Reuben, Shall your Num 32:6 1121
c of Israel from going over into Num 32:7 1121
the heart of the c of Israel Num 32:9 1121
armed before the c of Israel Num 32:17 1121
until the c of Israel have Num 32:18 1121
the c of Gad and the c of Num 32:25 1121
of the tribes of the c of Israel Num 32:28 1121
said unto them, If the c of Gad Num 32:29 1121
the c of Reuben will pass with Num 32:29 1121
the c of Gad and the c of Num 32:31 1121
unto them, even to the c of Gad Num 32:33 1121
to the c of Reuben, and unto half Num 32:33 1121
the c of Gad built Dibon, and Num 32:34 1121
the c of Reuben built Heshbon, and Num 32:37 1121
the c of Machir the son of Num 32:39 1121
the journeys of the c of Israel Num 33:1 1121
morrow after the passover the c Num 33:3 1121
the c of Israel removed from Num 33:5 1121
c of Israel were come out of the Num 33:38 1121
of the coming of the c of Israel Num 33:40 1121
Speak unto the c of Israel Num 33:51 1121
Command the c of Israel, and say Num 34:2 1121
Moses commanded the c of Israel Num 34:13 1121
For the tribe of the c of Reuben Num 34:14 1121
the tribe of the c of Gad Num 34:14 1121
of the tribe of the c of Simeon Num 34:20 1121
of the tribe of the c of Dan Num 34:22 1121
The prince of the c of Joseph Num 34:23 1121
the tribe of the c of Manasseh Num 34:23 1121
of the tribe of the c of Ephraim Num 34:24 1121
of the tribe of the c of Zebulun Num 34:25 1121
of the tribe of the c of Issachar Num 34:26 1121
of the tribe of the c of Asher Num 34:27 1121
of the tribe of the c of Naphtali Num 34:28 1121
c of Israel in the land of Canaan Num 34:29 1121
Command the c of Israel, that Num 35:2 1121
the possession of the c of Israel Num 35:8 1121
Speak unto the c of Israel Num 35:10 1121
refuge, both for the c of Israel Num 35:15 1121
LORD dwell among the c of Israel Num 35:34 1121
the families of the c of Gilead Num 36:1 1121
chief fathers of the c of Israel Num 36:1 1121
by lot to the c of Israel Num 36:2 1121
other tribes of the c of Israel Num 36:3 1121
of the c of Israel shall be Num 36:4 1121
Moses commanded the c of Israel Num 36:5 1121
not the inheritance of the c of Num 36:7 1121
for every one of the c of Israel Num 36:7 1121
in any tribe of the c of Israel Num 36:8 1121
that the c of Israel may enjoy Num 36:8 1121
every one of the tribes of the c Num 36:9 1121
by the hand of Moses unto the c Num 36:13 1121
Moses spake unto the c of Israel Deut 1:3 1121
he hath trodden upon, and to his c Deut 1:36 1121
said should be a prey, and your c Deut 1:39 1121
of your brethren the c of Esau Deut 2:4 1121
from our brethren the c of Esau Deut 2:8 1121
the c of Lot for a possession Deut 2:9 1121
but the c of Esau succeeded them, Deut 2:12 1121
nigh over against the c of Ammon Deut 2:19 1121
of the c of Ammon any possession Deut 2:19 1121
the c of Lot for a possession Deut 2:19 1121
As he did to the c of Esau Deut 2:22 1121
(As the c of Esau which dwell in Deut 2:29 1121
of the c of Ammon thou camest not Deut 2:37 1121
destroying the men, women, and c Deut 3:6 2945
not in Rabbath of the c of Ammon Deut 3:11 1121
is the border of the c of Ammon Deut 3:16 1121
your brethren the c of Israel Deut 3:18 1121
and that they may teach their c Deut 4:10 1121
beget c, and children's c Deut 4:25 1121
with thy c after thee, and that Deut 4:40 1121
Moses set before the c of Israel Deut 4:44 1121
Moses spake unto the c of Israel Deut 4:45 1121
the c of Israel smote, after they Deut 4:46 1121
fathers upon the c unto the third Deut 5:9 1121
them, and with their c for ever Deut 5:29 1121
teach them diligently unto thy c Deut 6:7 1121
the c of the Anakims, whom thou Deut 9:2 1121
can stand before the c of Anak Deut 9:2 1121
the c of Israel took their Deut 10:6 1121
of the c of Jaakan to Mosera Deut 10:6 1121
with your c which have not known Deut 11:2 1121
And ye shall teach them your c Deut 11:19 1121
multiplied, and the days of your c Deut 11:21 1121
with thy c after thee, when thou Deut 12:25 1121
with thy c after thee for ever, Deut 12:28 1121
the c of Belial, are gone out Deut 13:13 1121
Ye are the c of the LORD your God Deut 14:1 1121
days in his kingdom, he, and his c Deut 17:20 1121
hated, and they have born him c Deut 21:15 1121
The c that are begotten of them Deut 23:8 1121
his brethren of the c of Israel Deut 24:7 1121
not be put to death for the c Deut 24:16 1121
neither shall the c be put to Deut 24:16 1121
of his c which he shall leave Deut 28:54 1121
flesh of his c whom he shall eat Deut 28:55 1121
toward her c which she shall bear Deut 28:57 1121
Moses to make with the c of Deut 29:1 1121
c that shall rise up after you Deut 29:22 1121
to our c for ever, that we may do Deut 29:29 1121
thee this day, thou and thy c Deut 30:2 1121
together, men, and women, and c Deut 31:12 2945
And that their c, which have not Deut 31:13 1121
you, and teach it the c of Israel Deut 31:19 1121
for me against the c of Israel Deut 31:19 1121
day, and taught it the c of Israel Deut 31:22 1121
for thou shalt bring the c of Deut 31:23 1121
spot is not the spot of his c Deut 32:5 1121
to the number of the c of Israel Deut 32:8 1121
generation, c in whom is no faith Deut 32:20 1121
command your c to observe to do Deut 32:46 1121
which I give unto the c of Israel Deut 32:49 1121
the c of Israel at the waters of Deut 32:51 1121
in the midst of the c of Israel Deut 32:51 1121
land which I give the c of Israel Deut 32:52 1121
the c of Israel before his death Deut 33:1 1121
his brethren, nor knew his own c Deut 33:9 1121
said, Let Asher be blessed with c Deut 33:24 1121
the c of Israel wept for Moses in Deut 34:8 1121
the c of Israel hearkened unto Deut 34:9 1121
to them, even to the c of Israel Josh 1:2 1121
the c of Israel to search out the Josh 2:2 1121
all the c of Israel, and lodged Josh 3:1 1121
Joshua said unto the c of Israel Josh 3:9 1121
had prepared of the c of Israel Josh 4:4 1121
of the tribes of the c of Israel Josh 4:5 1121
that when your c ask their Josh 4:6 1121
unto the c of Israel for ever Josh 4:7 1121
the c of Israel did so as Joshua Josh 4:8 1121
of the tribes of the c of Israel Josh 4:8 1121
the c of Reuben, and the c Josh 4:12 1121
over armed before the c of Israel Josh 4:12 1121
And he spake unto the c of Israel Josh 4:21 1121
When your c shall ask their Josh 4:21 1121
Then ye shall let your c know Josh 4:22 1121
from before the c of Israel Josh 5:1 1121
more, because of the c of Israel Josh 5:1 1121
circumcise again the c of Israel Josh 5:2 1121
circumcised the c of Israel at Josh 5:3 1121
For the c of Israel walked forty Josh 5:6 1121
And their c, whom he raised up in Josh 5:7 1121
the c of Israel encamped in Josh 5:10 1121
neither had the c of Israel manna Josh 5:12 1121
up because of the c of Israel Josh 6:1 1121
But the c of Israel committed a Josh 7:1 1121
kindled against the c of Israel Josh 7:1 1121
Therefore the c of Israel could Josh 7:12 1121
and unto all the c of Israel Josh 7:23 1121
LORD commanded the c of Israel Josh 8:31 1121
the presence of the c of Israel Josh 8:32 1121
the c of Israel journeyed, and Josh 9:17 1121
the c of Israel smote them not, Josh 9:18 1121
of the hand of the c of Israel Josh 9:26 1121
Joshua and with the c of Israel Josh 10:4 1121
c of Israel slew with the sword Josh 10:11 1121
Amorites before the c of Israel Josh 10:12 1121
the c of Israel had made an end Josh 10:20 1121
against any of the c of Israel Josh 10:21 1121
the c of Israel took for a prey Josh 11:14 1121
made peace with the c of Israel Josh 11:19 1121
in the land of the c of Israel Josh 11:22 1121
which the c of Israel smote, and Josh 12:1 1121
is the border of the c of Ammon Josh 12:2 1121
the LORD and the c of Israel smite Josh 12:6 1121
the c of Israel smote on this Josh 12:7 1121

Context	Reference	Number
out from before the c of Israel	Josh 13:6	1121
unto the border of the c of Ammon	Josh 13:10	1121
Nevertheless the c of Israel	Josh 13:13	1121
gave unto the tribe of the c of	Josh 13:15	1121
did the c of Israel slay with the	Josh 13:22	1121
the border of the c of Reuben was	Josh 13:23	1121
c of Reuben after their families	Josh 13:23	1121
even unto the c of Gad according	Josh 13:24	1121
half the land of the c of Ammon	Josh 13:25	1121
the c of Gad after their families	Josh 13:28	1121
of the half tribe of the c of	Josh 13:29	1121
were pertaining unto the c of	Josh 13:31	1121
the c of Machir by their families	Josh 13:31	1121
are the countries which the c of	Josh 14:1	1121
of the tribes of the c of Israel	Josh 14:1	1121
For the c of Joseph were two	Josh 14:4	1121
so the c of Israel did, and they	Josh 14:5	1121
Then the c of Judah came unto	Josh 14:6	1121
while the c of Israel wandered in	Josh 14:10	
the c of Judah by their families	Josh 15:1	1121
This is the coast of the c of	Josh 15:12	1121
gave a part among the c of Judah	Josh 15:13	1121
Ahiman, and Talmai, the c of Anak	Josh 15:14	3211
the c of Judah according to their	Josh 15:20	1121
cities of the tribe of the c of	Josh 15:21	1121
the c of Judah could not drive	Josh 15:63	1121
the Jebusites dwell with the c of	Josh 15:63	1121
the lot of the c of Joseph fell	Josh 16:1	1121
So the c of Joseph, Manasseh and	Josh 16:4	1121
the border of the c of Ephraim	Josh 16:5	1121
c of Ephraim by their families	Josh 16:8	1121
the c of Ephraim were among the	Josh 16:9	1121
inheritance of the c of Manasseh	Josh 16:9	1121
c of Manasseh by their families	Josh 17:2	1121
for the c of Abiezer	Josh 17:2	1121
for the c of Helek	Josh 17:2	1121
for the c of Asriel	Josh 17:2	1121
for the c of Shechem	Josh 17:2	1121
for the c of Hepher	Josh 17:2	1121
and for the c of Shemida	Josh 17:2	1121
these were the male c of Manasseh	Josh 17:2	1121
belonged to the c of Ephraim	Josh 17:8	1121
Yet the c of Manasseh could not	Josh 17:12	1121
when the c of Israel were waxen	Josh 17:13	1121
the c of Joseph spake unto Joshua	Josh 17:14	1121
the c of Joseph said, The hill is	Josh 17:16	1121
the whole congregation of the c	Josh 18:1	1121
the c of Israel seven tribes	Josh 18:2	1121
Joshua said unto the c of Israel	Josh 18:3	1121
divided the land unto the c of	Josh 18:10	1121
the lot of the tribe of the c of	Josh 18:11	1121
came forth between the c of Judah	Josh 18:11	1121
of Judah and the c of Joseph	Josh 18:11	1121
a city of the c of Judah	Josh 18:14	1121
inheritance of the c of Benjamin	Josh 18:20	1121
c of Benjamin according to their	Josh 18:21	1121
c of Benjamin according to their	Josh 18:28	1121
even for the tribe of the c of	Josh 19:1	1121
the inheritance of the c of Judah	Josh 19:1	1121
c of Simeon according to their	Josh 19:8	1121
Out of the portion of the c of	Josh 19:9	1121
inheritance of the c of Simeon	Josh 19:9	1121
for the part of the c of Judah	Josh 19:9	1121
therefore the c of Simeon had	Josh 19:9	1121
c of Zebulun according to their	Josh 19:10	1121
c of Zebulun according to their	Josh 19:16	1121
for the c of Issachar according	Josh 19:17	1121
c of Issachar according to their	Josh 19:23	1121
the c of Asher according to their	Josh 19:24	1121
the c of Asher according to their	Josh 19:31	1121
lot came out to the c of Naphtali	Josh 19:32	1121
even for the c of Naphtali	Josh 19:32	1121
c of Naphtali according to their	Josh 19:39	1121
the c of Dan according to their	Josh 19:40	1121
the coast of the c of Dan went	Josh 19:47	1121
therefore the c of Dan went up to	Josh 19:47	1121
the c of Dan according to their	Josh 19:48	1121
coasts, the c of Israel gave an	Josh 19:49	1121
of the tribes of the c of Israel	Josh 19:51	1121
Speak to the c of Israel, saying,	Josh 20:2	1121
appointed for all the c of Israel	Josh 20:9	1121
of the tribes of the c of Israel	Josh 21:1	1121
the c of Israel gave unto the	Josh 21:3	1121
the c of Aaron the priest, which	Josh 21:4	1121
the rest of the c of Kohath had	Josh 21:5	1121
the c of Gershon had by lot out	Josh 21:6	1121
The c of Merari by their families	Josh 21:7	1121
the c of Israel gave by lot unto	Josh 21:8	1121
of the tribe of the c of Judah	Josh 21:9	1121
of the tribe of the c of Simeon	Josh 21:9	1121
Which the c of Aaron, being of	Josh 21:10	1121
who were of the c of Levi	Josh 21:10	1121
Thus they gave to the c of Aaron	Josh 21:13	1121
All the cities of the c of Aaron	Josh 21:19	1121
the families of the c of Kohath	Josh 21:20	1121
which remained of the c of Kohath	Josh 21:20	1121
of the c of Kohath that remained	Josh 21:26	1121
unto the c of Gershon, of the	Josh 21:27	1121
the families of the c of Merari	Josh 21:34	1121
So all the cities for the c of	Josh 21:40	1121
of the c of Israel were forty	Josh 21:41	1121
the c of Reuben and the c	Josh 22:9	1121
departed from the c of Israel out	Josh 22:9	1121
the c of Reuben and the c	Josh 22:10	1121
the c of Israel heard say, Behold	Josh 22:11	1121
the c of Reuben and the c	Josh 22:11	1121
at the passage of the c of Israel	Josh 22:11	1121
when the c of Israel heard of it,	Josh 22:12	1121
c of Israel gathered themselves	Josh 22:12	1121
the c of Israel sent unto the	Josh 22:13	1121
Israel sent unto the c of Reuben	Josh 22:13	1121
and to the c of Gad	Josh 22:13	1121
And they came unto the c of Reuben	Josh 22:15	1121
and to the c of Gad	Josh 22:15	1121
Then the c of Reuben and the	Josh 22:21	1121
the c of Gad and the half tribe of	Josh 22:21	1121
c might speak unto our c	Josh 22:24	1121
ye c of Reuben and c of Gad	Josh 22:25	1121
so shall your c make our c	Josh 22:25	1121
your c may not say to our c	Josh 22:27	1121
the words that the c of Reuben	Josh 22:30	1121
the c of Gad and the c of	Josh 22:30	1121
c of Reuben, and to the c of Gad	Josh 22:31	1121
to the c of Manasseh, This day we	Josh 22:31	1121
now ye have delivered the c of	Josh 22:31	1121
returned from the c of Reuben	Josh 22:32	1121
and from the c of Gad	Josh 22:32	1121
to the c of Israel, and brought	Josh 22:32	1121
the thing pleased the c of Israel	Josh 22:33	1121
the c of Israel blessed God, and	Josh 22:33	1121
the land wherein the c of Reuben	Josh 22:33	1121
the c of Reuben and the c of	Josh 22:34	1121
his c went down into Egypt	Josh 24:4	1121
which the c of Israel brought up	Josh 24:32	1121
inheritance of the c of Joseph	Josh 24:32	1121
that the c of Israel asked the	Judg 1:1	1121
Now the c of Judah had fought	Judg 1:8	1121
afterward the c of Judah went	Judg 1:9	1121
the c of the Kenite, Moses'	Judg 1:16	1121
c of Judah into the wilderness of	Judg 1:16	1121
the c of Benjamin did not drive	Judg 1:21	1121
the Jebusites dwell with the c of	Judg 1:21	1121
the Amorites forced the c of Dan	Judg 1:34	1121
words unto all the c of Israel	Judg 2:4	1121
the c of Israel went every man	Judg 2:6	1121
the c of Israel did evil in the	Judg 2:11	1121
of the c of Israel might know	Judg 3:2	1121
the c of Israel dwelt among the	Judg 3:5	1121
the c of Israel did evil in the	Judg 3:7	1121
and the c of Israel served	Judg 3:8	1121
when the c of Israel cried unto	Judg 3:9	1121
up a deliverer to the c of Israel	Judg 3:9	1121
the c of Israel did evil again in	Judg 3:12	1121
gathered unto him the c of Ammon	Judg 3:13	1121
So the c of Israel served Eglon	Judg 3:14	1121
But when the c of Israel cried	Judg 3:15	1121
by him the c of Israel sent a	Judg 3:15	1121
the c of Israel went down with	Judg 3:27	1121
the c of Israel again did evil in	Judg 4:1	1121
the c of Israel cried unto the	Judg 4:3	1121
oppressed the c of Israel	Judg 4:3	1121
the c of Israel came up to her	Judg 4:5	1121
thousand men of the c of Naphtali	Judg 4:6	1121
Naphtali and of the c of Zebulun	Judg 4:6	1121
which was of the c of Hobab the	Judg 4:11	1121
of Canaan before the c of Israel	Judg 4:23	1121
the hand of the c of Israel	Judg 4:24	1121
the c of Israel did evil in the	Judg 6:1	1121
c of Israel made them the dens	Judg 6:2	1121
the c of the east, even they came	Judg 6:3	1121
the c of Israel cried unto the	Judg 6:6	1121
when the c of Israel cried unto	Judg 6:7	1121
a prophet unto the c of Israel	Judg 6:8	1121
the c of the east were gathered	Judg 6:33	1121
all the c of the east lay along	Judg 7:12	1121
the hosts of the c of the east	Judg 8:10	1121
one resembled the c of a king	Judg 8:18	1121
subdued before the c of Israel	Judg 8:28	1121
that the c of Israel turned again	Judg 8:33	1121
the c of Israel remembered not	Judg 8:34	1121
the c of Israel did evil again in	Judg 10:6	1121
and the gods of the c of Ammon	Judg 10:6	1121
into the hands of the c of Ammon	Judg 10:7	1121
and oppressed the c of Israel	Judg 10:8	1121
all the c of Israel that were on	Judg 10:8	1121
Moreover the c of Ammon passed	Judg 10:9	1121
the c of Israel cried unto the	Judg 10:10	1121
LORD said unto the c of Israel	Judg 10:11	1121
the Amorites, from the c of Ammon	Judg 10:11	1121
the c of Israel said unto the	Judg 10:15	1121
Then the c of Ammon were gathered	Judg 10:17	1121
the c of Israel assembled	Judg 10:17	1121
to fight against the c of Ammon	Judg 10:18	1121
that the c of Ammon made war	Judg 11:4	1121
that when the c of Ammon made war	Judg 11:5	1121
we may fight with the c of Ammon	Judg 11:6	1121
and fight against the c of Ammon	Judg 11:8	1121
to fight against the c of Ammon	Judg 11:9	1121
unto the king of the c of Ammon	Judg 11:12	1121
the king of the c of Ammon	Judg 11:13	1121
unto the king of the c of Ammon	Judg 11:14	1121
nor the land of the c of Ammon	Judg 11:15	1121
c of Israel and the c of Ammon	Judg 11:27	1121
Howbeit the king of the c of	Judg 11:28	1121
passed over unto the c of Ammon	Judg 11:29	1121
the c of Ammon into mine hands	Judg 11:30	1121
in peace from the c of Ammon	Judg 11:31	1121
Jephthah passed over unto the c	Judg 11:32	1121
Thus the c of Ammon were subdued	Judg 11:33	1121
subdued before the c of Israel	Judg 11:33	1121
enemies, even of the c of Ammon	Judg 11:36	1121
to fight against the c of Ammon	Judg 12:1	1121
great strife with the c of Ammon	Judg 12:2	1121
over against the c of Ammon	Judg 12:3	1121
the c of Israel did evil again in	Judg 13:1	1121
a riddle unto the c of my people	Judg 14:16	1121
the riddle to the c of her people	Judg 14:17	1121
the c of Dan sent of their family	Judg 18:2	1121
war, which were of the c of Dan	Judg 18:16	1121
and overtook the c of Dan	Judg 18:22	1121
And they cried unto the c of Dan	Judg 18:23	1121
the c of Dan said unto him, Let	Judg 18:25	1121
the c of Dan went their way	Judg 18:26	1121
the c of Dan set up the graven	Judg 18:30	1121
that is not of the c of Israel	Judg 19:12	1121
c of Israel came up out of the	Judg 19:30	1121
Then all the c of Israel went out	Judg 20:1	1121
(Now the c of Benjamin heard that	Judg 20:3	1121
the c of Israel were gone up to	Judg 20:3	1121
Then said the c of Israel	Judg 20:3	1121
Behold, ye are all c of Israel	Judg 20:7	1121
the c of Belial, which are in	Judg 20:13	1121
But the c of Benjamin would not	Judg 20:13	1121
of their brethren the c of Israel	Judg 20:13	1121
But the c of Benjamin gathered	Judg 20:14	1121
to battle against the c of Israel	Judg 20:14	1121
the c of Benjamin were numbered	Judg 20:15	1121
the c of Israel arose, and went up	Judg 20:18	1121
battle against the c of Benjamin	Judg 20:18	1121
the c of Israel rose up in the	Judg 20:19	1121
the c of Benjamin came forth out	Judg 20:21	1121
the c of Israel went up and wept	Judg 20:23	1121
the c of Benjamin my brother	Judg 20:23	1121
the c of Israel came near against	Judg 20:24	1121
the c of Benjamin the second day	Judg 20:24	1121
of the c of Israel again eighteen	Judg 20:25	1121
Then all the c of Israel, and all	Judg 20:26	1121
the c of Israel enquired of the	Judg 20:27	1121
the c of Benjamin my brother	Judg 20:28	1121
the c of Israel went up against	Judg 20:30	1121
c of Benjamin on the third day	Judg 20:30	1121
the c of Benjamin went out	Judg 20:31	1121
the c of Benjamin said, They are	Judg 20:32	1121
But the c of Israel said, Let us	Judg 20:32	1121
the c of Israel destroyed of the	Judg 20:35	1121
So the c of Benjamin saw that	Judg 20:36	1121
again upon the c of Benjamin	Judg 20:48	1121
the c of Israel said, Who is	Judg 21:5	1121
the c of Israel repented them for	Judg 21:6	1121
sword, with the women and the c	Judg 21:10	2945
sent some to speak to the c of	Judg 21:13	1121
for the c of Israel have sworn,	Judg 21:18	1121
they commanded the c of Benjamin	Judg 21:20	1121
the c of Benjamin did so, and took	Judg 21:23	1121
the c of Israel departed thence	Judg 21:24	1121
had c, but Hannah had no c	1Sa 1:2	3206
that hath many c is waxed feeble	1Sa 2:5	1121
made by fire of the c of Israel	1Sa 2:28	1121
Then the c of Israel did put away	1Sa 7:4	1121
Samuel judged the c of Israel in	1Sa 7:6	1121
the c of Israel were gathered	1Sa 7:7	1121
when the c of Israel heard it,	1Sa 7:7	1121
the c of Israel said to Samuel,	1Sa 7:8	1121
there was not among the c of	1Sa 9:2	1121
And said unto the c of Israel	1Sa 10:18	1121
But the c of Belial said, How	1Sa 10:27	1121
the c of Israel were three	1Sa 11:8	1121
the c of Ammon came against you	1Sa 12:12	1121
at that time with the c of Israel	1Sa 14:18	1121
Moab, and against the c of Ammon	1Sa 14:47	1121
kindness to all the c of Israel	1Sa 15:6	1121
unto Jesse, Are here all thy c	1Sa 16:11	5288
the c of Israel returned from	1Sa 17:53	1121
the sword, both men and women, c	1Sa 22:19	5768
but if they be the c of men	1Sa 26:19	1121
to every man his wife and his c	1Sa 30:22	1121
the c of Judah the use of the bow	2Sa 1:18	1121
the c of Benjamin gathered	2Sa 2:25	1121
Beerothite, of the c of Benjamin	2Sa 4:2	1121
up the c of Israel out of Egypt	2Sa 7:6	1121
I have walked with all the c of	2Sa 7:7	1121
neither shall the c of wickedness	2Sa 7:10	1121
with the stripes of the c of men	2Sa 7:14	1121
of the c of Ammon, and of the	2Sa 8:12	1121
the king of the c of Ammon died	2Sa 10:1	1121
into the land of the c of Ammon	2Sa 10:2	1121
the princes of the c of Ammon	2Sa 10:3	1121
when the c of Ammon saw that they	2Sa 10:6	1121
the c of Ammon sent and hired the	2Sa 10:6	1121
the c of Ammon came out, and put	2Sa 10:8	1121
in array against the c of Ammon	2Sa 10:10	1121
but if the c of Ammon be too	2Sa 10:11	1121
when the c of Ammon saw that the	2Sa 10:14	1121
Joab returned from the c of Ammon	2Sa 10:14	1121
to help the c of Ammon any more	2Sa 10:19	1121
and they destroyed the c of Ammon	2Sa 11:1	1121
together with him, and with his c	2Sa 12:3	1121
with the sword of the c of Ammon	2Sa 12:9	1121
against Rabbah of the c of Ammon	2Sa 12:26	1121
all the cities of the c of Ammon	2Sa 12:31	1121
of Rabbah of the c of Ammon	2Sa 17:27	1121
were not of the c of Israel	2Sa 21:2	1121
the c of Israel had sworn unto	2Sa 21:2	1121
in his zeal to the c of Israel	2Sa 21:2	1121
of Gibeah of the c of Benjamin	2Sa 23:29	1121
If thy c take heed to their way,	1Kin 2:4	1121
of all the c of the east country	1Kin 4:30	1121
eightieth year after the c of	1Kin 6:1	1121
will dwell among the c of Israel	1Kin 6:13	1121
of the fathers of the c of Israel	1Kin 8:1	1121
a covenant with the c of Israel	1Kin 8:9	1121
so that thy c take heed to their	1Kin 8:25	1121
the hearts of all the c of men	1Kin 8:39	1121
all the c of Israel dedicated the	1Kin 8:63	1121
from following me, ye or your c	1Kin 9:6	1121
which were not of the c of Israel	1Kin 9:20	1121
Their c that were left after them	1Kin 9:21	1121
whom the c of Israel also were	1Kin 9:21	1121
But of the c of Israel did	1Kin 9:22	1121
LORD said unto the c of Israel	1Kin 11:2	1121
the abomination of the c of Ammon	1Kin 11:7	1121
Milcom the god of the c of Ammon	1Kin 11:33	1121
But as for the c of Israel which	1Kin 12:17	1121
your brethren the c of Israel	1Kin 12:24	1121
a feast unto the c of Israel	1Kin 12:33	1121
cast out before the c of Israel	1Kin 14:24	1121
sent unto all the c of Israel	1Kin 18:20	1121
for the c of Israel have forsaken	1Kin 19:10	1121
because the c of Israel have	1Kin 19:14	1121
thy wives also and thy c, even the	1Kin 20:3	1121
thy gold, and thy wives, and thy c	1Kin 20:5	1121
unto me for my wives, and for my c	1Kin 20:7	1121

people, even all the c of Israel 1Kin 20:15 1121
the c of Israel were numbered, and 1Kin 20:27 1121
the c of Israel pitched before 1Kin 20:27 1121
the c of Israel slew of the 1Kin 20:29 1121
c of Belial, and sat before him 1Kin 21:13 1121
cast out before the c of Israel 1Kin 21:26 1121
forth little c out of the city 2Kin 2:23 5288
and tare forty and two c of them 2Kin 2:24 3206
and live thou and thy c of the rest 2Kin 4:7 1121
thou wilt do unto the c of Israel 2Kin 8:12 1121
the sword, and wilt dash their c 2Kin 8:12 6768
him alway a light, and to his c 2Kin 8:19 1121
one of the c of the prophets 2Kin 9:1 1121
to them that brought up Ahab's c 2Kin 10:1
also, and the bringers up of the c 2Kin 10:5
down to salute the c of the king 2Kin 10:13 1121
of the king and the c of the queen 2Kin 10:13 1121
thy c of the fourth generation 2Kin 10:30 1121
the c of Israel dwelt in their 2Kin 13:5 1121
But the c of the murderers he 2Kin 14:6 1121
not be put to death for the c 2Kin 14:6 1121
nor the c be put to death for the 2Kin 14:6 1121
out from before the c of Israel 2Kin 16:3 1121
that the c of Israel had sinned 2Kin 17:7 1121
out from before the c of Israel 2Kin 17:8 1121
the c of Israel did secretly 2Kin 17:9 1121
For the c of Israel walked in all 2Kin 17:22 1121
instead of the c of Israel 2Kin 17:24 1121
their c in fire to Adrammelech 2Kin 17:31 1121
the LORD commanded the c of Jacob 2Kin 17:34 1121
c, and their children's c 2Kin 17:41 1121
for unto those days the c of 2Kin 18:4 1121
for the c are come to the birth, 2Kin 19:3 1121
the c of Eden which were in 2Kin 19:12 1121
cast out before the c of Israel 2Kin 21:2 1121
destroyed before the c of Israel 2Kin 21:9 1121
the graves of the c of the people 2Kin 23:6 1121
in the valley of the c of Hinnom 2Kin 23:10 1121
the abomination of the c of Ammon 2Kin 23:13 1121
and bands of the c of Ammon 2Kin 24:2 1121
king reigned over the c of Israel 1Chr 1:43 1121
Nahshon, prince of the c of Judah 1Chr 2:10 1121
Hezron begat c of Azubah his wife 1Chr 2:18
but Seled died without c 1Chr 2:30 1121
And the c of Sheshan 1Chr 2:31 1121
and Jether died without c 1Chr 2:32 1121
but his brethren had not many c 1Chr 4:27 1121
multiply, like to the c of Judah 1Chr 4:27 1121
the c of Gad dwelt over against 1Chr 5:11 1121
These are the c of Abihail the 1Chr 5:14 1121
the c of the half tribe of 1Chr 5:23 1121
And the c of Amram 1Chr 6:3 1121
are they that waited with their c 1Chr 6:33 1121
the c of Israel gave to the 1Chr 6:64 1121
of the tribe of the c of Judah 1Chr 6:65 1121
of the tribe of the c of Simeon 1Chr 6:65 1121
of the tribe of the c of Benjamin 1Chr 6:65 1121
Unto the rest of the c of Merari 1Chr 6:77 1121
the c of Ir, and Hushim, the sons 1Chr 7:12 1121
the borders of the c of Manasseh 1Chr 7:29 1121
In these dwelt the c of Joseph 1Chr 7:29 1121
These are the c of Japhlet 1Chr 7:33 1121
All these were the c of Asher 1Chr 7:40 1121
Shaharaim begat c in the country 1Chr 8:8
Jerusalem dwelt of the c of Judah 1Chr 9:3 1121
of the c of Benjamin 1Chr 9:3 1121
of the c of Ephraim, and Manasseh 1Chr 9:3 1121
of the c of Pharez the son of 1Chr 9:4 1121
in the companies of the c of Levi 1Chr 9:18 1121
their c had the oversight of the 1Chr 9:23 1121
pertained to the c of Benjamin 1Chr 11:31 1121
there came of the c of Benjamin 1Chr 12:16 1121
The c of Judah that bare shield 1Chr 12:24 1121
Of the c of Simeon, mighty men of 1Chr 12:25 1121
Of the c of Levi four thousand and 1Chr 12:26 1121
of the c of Benjamin, the kindred 1Chr 12:29 1121
of the c of Ephraim twenty 1Chr 12:30 1121
of the c of Issachar, which were 1Chr 12:32 1121
his c which he had in Jerusalem 1Chr 14:4 3205
And David assembled the c of Aaron 1Chr 15:4 1121
the c of the Levites bare the ark 1Chr 15:15 1121
ye c of Jacob, his chosen ones 1Chr 16:13 1121
neither shall the c of wickedness 1Chr 17:9 1121
from Moab, and from the c of Ammon 1Chr 18:11 1121
the king of the c of Ammon died 1Chr 19:1 1121
land of the c of Ammon to Hanun 1Chr 19:2 1121
of the c of Ammon said to Hanun 1Chr 19:3 1121
when the c of Ammon saw that they 1Chr 19:6 1121
the c of Ammon sent a thousand 1Chr 19:6 1121
And the c of Ammon gathered 1Chr 19:7 1121
the c of Ammon came out, and put 1Chr 19:9 1121
in array against the c of Ammon 1Chr 19:11 1121
but if the c of Ammon be too 1Chr 19:12 1121
when the c of Ammon saw that the 1Chr 19:15 1121
help the c of Ammon any more 1Chr 19:19 1121
the country of the c of Ammon 1Chr 20:1 1121
all the cities of the c of Ammon 1Chr 20:3 1121
that was of the c of the giant 1Chr 20:4 3211
before their father, and had no c 1Chr 24:2 1121
of the c of Merari, had sons 1Chr 26:10 1121
Now the c of Israel after their 1Chr 27:1 1121
Of the c of Perez was the chief 1Chr 27:3 1121
the Pelonite, of the c of Ephraim 1Chr 27:10 1121
Pirathonite, of the c of Ephraim 1Chr 27:14 1121
Of the c of Ephraim, Hoshea the 1Chr 27:20 1121
for your c after you for ever 1Chr 28:8 1121
of the fathers of the c of Israel 2Chr 5:2 1121
a covenant with the c of Israel 2Chr 5:10 1121
that he made with the c of Israel 2Chr 6:11 1121
yet so that thy c take heed to 2Chr 6:16 1121
the hearts of the c of men 2Chr 6:30 1121
when all the c of Israel saw how 2Chr 7:3 1121
caused the c of Israel to dwell 2Chr 8:2 1121
But of their c, who were left 2Chr 8:8 1121
whom the c of Israel consumed not 2Chr 8:8 1121
But of the c of Israel did 2Chr 8:9 1121
But as for the c of Israel that 2Chr 10:17 1121
the c of Israel stoned him with 2Chr 10:18 1121
Which bare him c 2Chr 11:19 1121
dispersed of all his c throughout 2Chr 11:23 1121
men, the c of Belial, and have 2Chr 13:7 1121
O c of Israel, fight ye not 2Chr 13:12 1121
the c of Israel fled before Judah 2Chr 13:16 1121
Thus the c of Israel were brought 2Chr 13:18 1121
the c of Judah prevailed, because 2Chr 13:18 1121
this also, that the c of Moab 2Chr 20:1 1121
the c of Ammon, and with them 2Chr 20:1 1121
the c of Ammon and Moab and mount 2Chr 20:10 1121
ones, their wives, and their c 2Chr 20:13 1121
of the c of the Kohathites, and of 2Chr 20:19 1121
of the c of the Korhites, stood 2Chr 20:19 1121
against the c of Ammon, Moab, and 2Chr 20:22 1121
For the c of Ammon and Moab stood 2Chr 20:23 1121
LORD smite thy people, and thy c 2Chr 21:14 1121
But he slew not their c, but did 2Chr 25:4 1121
fathers shall not die for the c 2Chr 25:4 1121
neither shall the c die for the 2Chr 25:4 1121
to wit, with all the c of Ephraim 2Chr 25:7 1121
smote of the c of Seir ten 2Chr 25:11 1121
the c of Judah carry away captive 2Chr 25:12 1121
brought the gods of the c of Seir 2Chr 25:14 1121
the c of Ammon gave him the same 2Chr 27:5 1121
So much did the c of Ammon pay 2Chr 27:5 1121
burnt his c in the fire, after 2Chr 28:3 1121
cast out before the c of Israel 2Chr 28:3 1121
the c of Israel carried away 2Chr 28:8 1121
to keep under the c of Judah 2Chr 28:10 1121
of the heads of the c of Ephraim 2Chr 28:12 1121
Ye c of Israel, turn again unto 2Chr 30:6 1121
your c shall find compassion 2Chr 30:9 1121
the c of Israel that were present 2Chr 30:21 1121
Then all the c of Israel returned 2Chr 31:1 1121
the c of Israel brought in 2Chr 31:5 1121
And concerning the c of Israel 2Chr 31:6 1121
cast out before the c of Israel 2Chr 33:2 1121
he caused his c to pass through 2Chr 33:6 1121
destroyed before the c of Israel 2Chr 33:9 1121
that pertained to the c of Israel 2Chr 34:33 1121
the c of Israel that were present 2Chr 35:17 1121
Now these are the c of the Ezr 2:1 1121
The c of Parosh, two thousand an Ezr 2:3 1121
The c of Shephatiah, three Ezr 2:4 1121
The c of Arah, seven hundred Ezr 2:5 1121
The c of Pahath-moab Ezr 2:6 1121
of the c of Jeshua and Joab, two Ezr 2:6 1121
The c of Elam, a thousand two Ezr 2:7 1121
The c of Zattu, nine hundred Ezr 2:8 1121
The c of Zaccai, seven hundred and Ezr 2:9 1121
The c of Bani, six hundred forty Ezr 2:10 1121
The c of Bebai, six hundred Ezr 2:11 1121
The c of Azgad, a thousand two Ezr 2:12 1121
The c of Adonikam, six hundred Ezr 2:13 1121
The c of Bigvai, two thousand Ezr 2:14 1121
The c of Adin, four hundred fifty Ezr 2:15 1121
The c of Ater of Hezekiah, ninety Ezr 2:16 1121
The c of Bezai, three hundred Ezr 2:17 1121
The c of Jorah, an hundred and Ezr 2:18 1121
The c of Hashum, two hundred Ezr 2:19 1121
The c of Gibbar, ninety and five Ezr 2:20 1121
The c of Beth-lehem, an hundred Ezr 2:21 1121
The c of Azmaveth, forty and two Ezr 2:24 1121
The c of Kirjath-arim, Chephirah, Ezr 2:25 1121
The c of Ramah and Gaba, six Ezr 2:26 1121
The c of Nebo, fifty and two Ezr 2:29 1121
The c of Magbish, an hundred Ezr 2:30 1121
The c of the other Elam, a Ezr 2:31 1121
The c of Harim, three hundred and Ezr 2:32 1121
of the c of Lod, Hadid, and Ono, Ezr 2:33 1121
The c of Jericho, three hundred Ezr 2:34 1121
The c of Senaah, three thousand Ezr 2:35 1121
the c of Jedaiah, of the house of Ezr 2:36 1121
The c of Immer, a thousand fifty Ezr 2:37 1121
The c of Pashur, a thousand two Ezr 2:38 1121
The c of Harim, a thousand and Ezr 2:39 1121
the c of Jeshua and Kadmiel Ezr 2:40 1121
of the c of Hodaviah, seventy and Ezr 2:40 1121
the c of Asaph, an hundred twenty Ezr 2:41 1121
The c of the porters Ezr 2:42 1121
the c of Shallum Ezr 2:42 1121
the c of Ater Ezr 2:42 1121
the c of Talmon Ezr 2:42 1121
the c of Akkub Ezr 2:42 1121
the c of Hatita Ezr 2:42 1121
the c of Shobai, in all an Ezr 2:42 1121
the c of Ziha Ezr 2:43 1121
the c of Hasupha Ezr 2:43 1121
the c of Tabbaoth Ezr 2:43 1121
The c of Keros Ezr 2:44 1121
the c of Siaha Ezr 2:44 1121
the c of Padon Ezr 2:44 1121
The c of Lebanah Ezr 2:45 1121
the c of Hagabah Ezr 2:45 1121
the c of Akkub Ezr 2:45 1121
The c of Hagab Ezr 2:46 1121
the c of Shalmai Ezr 2:46 1121
the c of Hanan Ezr 2:46 1121
The c of Giddel Ezr 2:47 1121
the c of Gahar Ezr 2:47 1121
the c of Reaiah Ezr 2:47 1121
The c of Rezin Ezr 2:48 1121
the c of Nekoda Ezr 2:48 1121
the c of Gazzam Ezr 2:48 1121
The c of Uzza Ezr 2:49 1121
the c of Paseah Ezr 2:49 1121
the c of Besai Ezr 2:49 1121
The c of Asnah Ezr 2:50 1121
the c of Mehunim Ezr 2:50 1121
the c of Nephusim Ezr 2:50 1121
The c of Bakbuk Ezr 2:51 1121
the c of Hakupha Ezr 2:51 1121
the c of Harhur Ezr 2:51 1121
The c of Bazluth Ezr 2:52 1121
the c of Mehida Ezr 2:52 1121
the c of Harsha Ezr 2:52 1121
The c of Barkos Ezr 2:53 1121
the c of Sisera Ezr 2:53 1121
the c of Thamah Ezr 2:53 1121
The c of Neziah Ezr 2:54 1121
the c of Hatipha Ezr 2:54 1121
The c of Solomon's servants Ezr 2:55 1121
the c of Sotai Ezr 2:55 1121
the c of Sophereth Ezr 2:55 1121
the c of Peruda Ezr 2:55 1121
The c of Jaalah Ezr 2:56 1121
the c of Darkon Ezr 2:56 1121
the c of Giddel Ezr 2:56 1121
The c of Shephatiah Ezr 2:57 1121
the c of Hattil Ezr 2:57 1121
the c of Pochereth of Zebaim Ezr 2:57 1121
the c of Ami Ezr 2:57 1121
the c of Solomon's servants, were Ezr 2:58 1121
The c of Delaiah Ezr 2:60 1121
the c of Tobiah Ezr 2:60 1121
the c of Nekoda, six hundred Ezr 2:60 1121
And of the c of the priests Ezr 2:61 1121
the c of Habaiah Ezr 2:61 1121
the c of Koz Ezr 2:61 1121
the c of Barzillai Ezr 2:61 1121
the c of Israel were in the Ezr 3:1 1121
Benjamin heard that the c of the Ezr 4:1 1121
the c of Israel, the priests, and Ezr 6:16 1121
and the rest of the c of the Ezr 6:16 1121
the c of the captivity kept the Ezr 6:19 1121
for all the c of the captivity Ezr 6:20 1121
the c of Israel, which were come Ezr 6:21 1121
went up some of the c of Israel Ezr 7:7 1121
Also the c of those that had been Ezr 8:35 1121
an inheritance to your c for ever Ezr 9:12 1121
of men and women and c Ezr 10:1 3206
unto all the c of the captivity Ezr 10:7 1121
the c of the captivity did so Ezr 10:16 1121
them had wives by whom they had c Ezr 10:44 1121
for the c of Israel thy servants, Neh 1:6 1121
the sins of the c of Israel Neh 1:6 1121
the welfare of the c of Israel Neh 2:10 1121
brethren, our c as their c Neh 5:5 1121
These are the c of the province, Neh 7:6 1121
The c of Parosh, two thousand an Neh 7:8 1121
The c of Shephatiah, three Neh 7:9 1121
The c of Arah, six hundred fifty Neh 7:10 1121
The c of Pahath-moab Neh 7:11 1121
of the c of Jeshua and Joab, two Neh 7:11 1121
The c of Elam, a thousand two Neh 7:12 1121
The c of Zattu, eight hundred Neh 7:13 1121
The c of Zaccai, seven hundred and Neh 7:14 1121
The c of Binnui, six hundred Neh 7:15 1121
The c of Bebai, six hundred Neh 7:16 1121
The c of Azgad, two thousand Neh 7:17 1121
The c of Adonikam, six hundred Neh 7:18 1121
The c of Bigvai, two thousand Neh 7:19 1121
The c of Adin, six hundred fifty Neh 7:20 1121
The c of Ater of Hezekiah, ninety Neh 7:21 1121
The c of Hashum, three hundred Neh 7:22 1121
The c of Bezai, three hundred Neh 7:23 1121
The c of Hariph, an hundred and Neh 7:24 1121
The c of Gibeon, ninety and five Neh 7:25 1121
The c of the other Elam, a Neh 7:34 1121
The c of Harim, three hundred and Neh 7:35 1121
The c of Jericho, three hundred Neh 7:36 1121
The c of Lod, Hadid, and Ono, Neh 7:37 1121
The c of Senaah, three thousand Neh 7:38 1121
the c of Jedaiah, of the house of Neh 7:39 1121
The c of Immer, a thousand fifty Neh 7:40 1121
The c of Pashur, a thousand two Neh 7:41 1121
The c of Harim, a thousand and Neh 7:42 1121
the c of Jeshua, of Kadmiel, and Neh 7:43 1121
of the c of Hodevah, seventy and Neh 7:43 1121
the c of Asaph, an hundred forty Neh 7:44 1121
the c of Shallum Neh 7:45 1121
the c of Ater Neh 7:45 1121
the c of Talmon Neh 7:45 1121
the c of Akkub Neh 7:45 1121
the c of Hatita Neh 7:45 1121
the c of Shobai, an hundred Neh 7:45 1121
the c of Ziha Neh 7:46 1121
the c of Hashupha Neh 7:46 1121
the c of Tabbaoth Neh 7:46 1121
The c of Keros Neh 7:47 1121
c of Sia, the c of Padon, Neh 7:47 1121
The c of Lebana Neh 7:48 1121
the c of Hagaba Neh 7:48 1121
the c of Shalmai Neh 7:48 1121
The c of Hanan Neh 7:49 1121
the c of Giddel Neh 7:49 1121
the c of Gahar Neh 7:49 1121
The c of Reaiah Neh 7:50 1121
the c of Rezin Neh 7:50 1121
the c of Nekoda Neh 7:50 1121
The c of Gazzam Neh 7:51 1121
the c of Uzza Neh 7:51 1121
the c of Phaseah Neh 7:51 1121
The c of Besai Neh 7:52 1121
the c of Meunim Neh 7:52 1121
the c of Nephishesim Neh 7:52 1121
The c of Bakbuk Neh 7:53 1121
the c of Hakupha Neh 7:53 1121
the c of Harhur Neh 7:53 1121
The c of Bazlith Neh 7:54 1121
the c of Mehida Neh 7:54 1121
the c of Harsha Neh 7:54 1121
The c of Barkos Neh 7:55 1121
the c of Sisera Neh 7:55 1121

C

the *c* of Tamah Neh 7:55 1121
The *c* of Neziah Neh 7:56 1121
the *c* of Hatipha Neh 7:56 1121
The *c* of Solomon's servants Neh 7:57 1121
the *c* of Sotai Neh 7:57 1121
the *c* of Sophereth Neh 7:57 1121
the *c* of Perida Neh 7:57 1121
The *c* of Jaala Neh 7:58 1121
the *c* of Darkon Neh 7:58 1121
the *c* of Giddel Neh 7:58 1121
The *c* of Shephatiah Neh 7:59 1121
the *c* of Hattil Neh 7:59 1121
the *c* of Pochereth of Zebaim Neh 7:59 1121
the *c* of Amon Neh 7:59 1121
the *c* of Solomon's servants, were Neh 7:60 1121
The *c* of Delaiah Neh 7:62 1121
the *c* of Tobiah Neh 7:62 1121
the *c* of Nekoda, six hundred Neh 7:62 1121
the *c* of Habaiah Neh 7:63 1121
the *c* of Koz Neh 7:63 1121
the *c* of Barzillai, which took Neh 7:63 1121
the *c* of Israel were in their Neh 7:73 1121
that the *c* of Israel should dwell Neh 8:14 1121
had not the *c* of Israel done so Neh 8:17 1121
fourth day of this month the *c* of Neh 9:1 1121
Their *c* also multipliedst thou as Neh 9:23 1121
So the *c* went in and possessed the Neh 9:24 1121
For the *c* of Israel and the Neh 10:39 1121
the *c* of Levi shall bring the Neh 10:39 1121
the *c* of Solomon's servants Neh 11:3 1121
dwelt certain of the *c* of Judah Neh 11:4 1121
and of the *c* of Benjamin Neh 11:4 1121
Of the *c* of Judah Neh 11:4 1121
of Mahalaleel, of the *c* of Perez Neh 11:4 1121
of the *c* of Zerah the son of Neh 11:24 1121
some of the *c* of Judah dwelt at Neh 11:25 1121
The *c* also of Benjamin from Geba Neh 11:31 1121
the wives also and the *c* rejoiced Neh 12:43 3206
them unto the *c* of Aaron Neh 12:47 1121
not the *c* of Israel with bread Neh 13:2 1121
the sabbath unto the *c* of Judah Neh 13:16 1121
their *c* spake half in the speech Neh 13:24 1121
Jews, both young and old, little *c* Est 3:13 2945
riches, and the multitude of his *c* Est 5:11 1121
His *c* are far from safety, and Job 5:4 1121
If thy *c* have sinned against him, Job 8:4 1121
even the eyes of his *c* shall fail Job 17:5 1121
Yea, young *c* despised me Job 19:18
His *c* shall seek to please the Job 20:10 1121
like a flock, and their *c* dance Job 21:11 3206
layeth up his iniquity for his *c* Job 21:19 1121
food for them and for their *c* Job 24:5 5288
If his *c* be multiplied, it is for Job 27:14 1121
with me, when my *c* were about me Job 29:5 5288
They were *c* of fools Job 30:8 1121
yea, *c* of base men Job 30:8 1121
is a king over all the *c* of pride Job 41:34 1121
his eyelids try, the *c* of men Ps 11:4 1121
fail from among the *c* of men Ps 12:1 1121
from heaven upon the *c* of men Ps 14:2 1121
they are full of *c*, and leave the Ps 17:14 1121
seed from among the *c* of men Ps 21:10 1121
Come, ye *c*, hearken unto me Ps 34:11 1121
therefore the *c* of men put their Ps 36:7 1121
Thou art fairer than the *c* of men Ps 45:2 1121
of thy fathers shall be thy *c* Ps 45:16 1121
from heaven upon the *c* of men Ps 53:2 1121
in his doing toward the *c* of men Ps 66:5 1121
and an alien unto my mother's *c* Ps 69:8 1121
he shall save the *c* of the needy Ps 72:4 1121
against the generation of thy *c* Ps 73:15 1121
will not hide them from their *c* Ps 78:4 1121
should make them known to their *c* Ps 78:5 1121
even the *c* which should be born Ps 78:6 1121
arise and declare them to their *c* Ps 78:6 1121
The *c* of Ephraim, being armed, and Ps 78:9 1121
all of you are *c* of the most High Ps 82:6 1121
they have holpen the *c* of Lot Ps 83:8 1121
If his *c* forsake my law, and walk Ps 89:30 1121
and sayest, Return, ye *c* of men Ps 90:3 1121
and thy glory unto their *c* Ps 90:16 1121
The *c* of thy servants shall Ps 102:28 1121
his acts unto the *c* of Israel Ps 103:7 1121
Like as a father pitieth his *c* Ps 103:13 1121
righteousness unto children's *c* Ps 103:17 1121
servant, ye *c* of Jacob his chosen Ps 105:6 1121
wonderful works to the *c* of men Ps 107:8 1121
wonderful works to the *c* of men Ps 107:15 1121
wonderful works to the *c* of men Ps 107:21 1121
wonderful works to the *c* of men Ps 107:31 1121
Let his *c* be fatherless, and his Ps 109:9 1121
Let his *c* be continually Ps 109:10 1121
be any to favour his fatherless *c* Ps 109:12
and to be a joyful mother of *c* Ps 113:9 1121
you more and more, you and your *c* Ps 115:14 1121
hath he given to the *c* of men Ps 115:16 1121
c are an heritage of the LORD Ps 127:3 1121
so are *c* of the youth Ps 127:4 1121
thy *c* like olive plants round Ps 128:3 1121
thou shalt see thy children's *c* Ps 128:6 1121
If thy *c* will keep my covenant and Ps 132:12 1121
their *c* shall also sit upon thy Ps 132:12 1121
the *c* of Edom in the day of Ps 137:7 1121
from the hand of strange *c* Ps 144:7 1121
me from the hand of strange *c* Ps 144:11 1121
he hath blessed thy *c* within thee Ps 147:13 1121
old men, and *c* Ps 148:12 5288
even of the *c* of Israel, a people Ps 148:14 1121
let the *c* of Zion be joyful in Ps 149:2 1121
Hear, ye *c*, the instruction of a Prov 4:1 1121
Hear me now therefore, O ye *c* Prov 5:7 1121
unto me now therefore, O ye *c* Prov 7:24 1121
therefore hearken unto me, O ye *c* Prov 8:32 1121
inheritance to his children's *c* Prov 13:22 1121

his *c* shall have a place of Prov 14:26 1121
then the hearts of the *c* of men Prov 15:11 1121
Children's *c* are the crown of old Prov 17:6 1121
the glory of *c* are their fathers Prov 17:6 1121
his *c* are blessed after him Prov 20:7 1121
Her *c* arise up, and call her Prov 31:28 1121
If a man beget an hundred *c* Eccl 6:3
my mother's *c* were angry with me Song 1:6 1121
I have nourished and brought up *c* Is 1:2 1121
evildoers, *c* that are corrupters Is 1:4 1121
themselves in the *c* of strangers Is 2:6 3206
I will give *c* to be their princes Is 3:4 5288
c are their oppressors, and women Is 3:12 5768
the *c* whom the LORD hath given me Is 8:18 3206
the *c* of Ammon shall obey them Is 11:14 1121
Their *c* also shall be dashed to Is 13:16 5768
their eye shall not spare *c* Is 13:18 1121
his *c* for the iniquity of their Is 14:21 1121
as the glory of the *c* of Israel Is 17:3 1121
left because of the *c* of Israel Is 17:9 1121
the mighty men of the *c* of Kedar Is 21:17 1121
I travail not, nor bring forth *c* Is 23:4
one by one, O ye *c* of Israel Is 27:12 1121
But when he seeth his *c*, the work Is 29:23 3206
Woe to the rebellious *c*, saith Is 30:1 1121
is a rebellious people, lying *c* Is 30:9 1121
c that will not hear the law of Is 30:9 1121
c of Israel have deeply revolted Is 31:6 1121
for the *c* are come to the birth, Is 37:3 1121
the *c* of Eden which were in Is 37:12 1121
the father to the *c* shall make Is 38:19 1121
shall I know the loss of *c* Is 47:8
moment in one day, the loss of *c* Is 47:9
Thy *c* shall make haste Is 49:17 1121
The *c* which thou shalt have, Is 49:20 1121
me these, seeing I have lost my *c* Is 49:21
with thee, and I will save thy *c* Is 49:25 1121
for more are the *c* of the Is 54:1 1121
than the *c* of the married wife Is 54:1 1121
all thy *c* shall be taught of the Is 54:13 1121
great shall be the peace of thy *c* Is 54:13 1121
are ye not *c* of transgression, a Is 57:4 3206
slaying the *c* in the valleys Is 57:5 3206
my people, *c* that will not lie Is 63:8 1121
she brought forth her *c* Is 66:8 1121
as the *c* of Israel bring an Is 66:20 1121
your children's *c* will I plead Jer 2:9 1121
Also the *c* of Noph and Tahapanes Jer 2:16 1121
In vain have I smitten your *c* Jer 2:30 1121
Turn, O backsliding *c*, saith the Jer 3:14 1121
How shall I put thee among the *c* Jer 3:19 1121
supplications of the *c* of Israel Jer 3:21 1121
Return, ye backsliding *c*, and I Jer 3:22 1121
they are sottish *c*, and they have Jer 4:22 1121
thy *c* have forsaken me, and sworn Jer 5:7 1121
O ye *c* of Benjamin, gather Jer 6:1 1121
pour it out upon the *c* abroad Jer 6:11 5768
The *c* gather wood, and the fathers Jer 7:18 1121
For the *c* of Judah have done evil Jer 7:30 1121
to cut off the *c* from without Jer 9:21 5768
the *c* of Ammon, and Moab, and all Jer 9:26 1121
my *c* are gone forth of me, and Jer 10:20 1121
I will bereave them of *c*, I will Jer 15:7
that brought up the *c* of Israel Jer 16:14 1121
that brought up the *c* of Israel Jer 16:15 1121
Whilst their *c* remember their Jer 17:2 1121
the gate of the *c* of the people Jer 17:19 1121
deliver up their *c* to the famine Jer 18:21 1121
wives be bereaved of their *c* Jer 18:21
which brought up the *c* of Israel Jer 23:7 1121
and Moab, and the *c* of Ammon Jer 25:21 1121
Their *c* also shall be as Jer 30:20 1121
Rahel weeping for her *c* refused Jer 31:15 1121
refused to be comforted for her *c* Jer 31:15 1121
that thy *c* shall come again to Jer 31:17 1121
the bosom of their *c* after them Jer 32:18 1121
For the *c* of Israel and the Jer 32:30 1121
the *c* of Judah have only done Jer 32:30 1121
for the *c* of Israel have only Jer 32:30 1121
all the evil of the *c* of Israel Jer 32:32 1121
of the *c* of Judah, which they Jer 32:32 1121
of them, and of their *c* after them Jer 32:39 1121
wives and thy *c* to the Chaldeans Jer 38:23 1121
unto him men, and women, and *c* Jer 40:7 2945
of war, and the women, and the *c* Jer 41:16 2945
Even men, and women, and *c*, and the Jer 43:6 2945
their *c* for feebleness of hands Jer 47:3 1121
the captivity of the *c* of Ammon Jer 49:6 1121
Leave thy fatherless *c*, I will Jer 49:11 1121
the *c* of Israel shall come, they Jer 50:4 1121
the *c* of Judah together, going and Jer 50:4 1121
c of Israel and the *c* of Judah Jer 50:33 1121
her *c* are gone into captivity Lam 1:5 5768
my *c* are desolate, because the Lam 1:16 1121
because the *c* and the sucklings Lam 2:11 5768
him for the life of thy young *c* Lam 2:19
their fruit, and *c* of a span long Lam 2:20 5768
willingly nor grieve the *c* of men Lam 3:33 1121
the young *c* ask bread, and no man Lam 4:4 5768
women have sodden their own *c* Lam 4:10 3206
the *c* fell under the wood Lam 5:13 5288
I send thee to the *c* of Israel Eze 2:3 1121
For they are impudent *c* and Eze 2:4 1121
unto the *c* of thy people, and Eze 3:11 1121
Even thus shall the *c* of Israel Eze 4:13 1121
c of Israel before their idols Eze 6:5 1121
and young, both maids, and little *c* Eze 9:6 2945
That thou hast slain my *c* Eze 16:21 1121
and by the blood of thy *c* Eze 16:36 1121
that lotheth her husband and her *c* Eze 16:45 1121
lothed their husbands and their *c* Eze 16:45 1121
unto their *c* in the wilderness Eze 20:18 1121
the *c* rebelled against me Eze 20:21 1121
had slain their *c* to their idols Eze 23:39 1121

in the midst of the *c* of men Eze 31:14 1121
speak to the *c* of thy people, and Eze 33:2 1121
say unto the *c* of thy people, The Eze 33:12 1121
Yet the *c* of thy people say, The Eze 33:17 1121
the *c* of thy people still are Eze 33:30 1121
hast shed the blood of the *c* of Eze 35:5 1121
Judah, and for the *c* of Israel his Eze 37:16 1121
when the *c* of thy people shall Eze 37:18 1121
I will take the *c* of Israel from Eze 37:21 1121
therein, even they, and their *c* Eze 37:25 1121
and their children's *c* for ever Eze 37:25 1121
midst of the *c* of Israel for ever Eze 43:7 1121
that is among the *c* of Israel Eze 44:9 1121
c of Israel went astray from me Eze 44:15 1121
which shall beget *c* among you Eze 47:22 1121
the country among the *c* of Israel Eze 47:22 1121
when the *c* of Israel went astray Eze 48:11 1121
bring certain of the *c* of Israel Dan 1:3 1121
C in whom was no blemish, but Dan 1:4 3206
these were of the *c* of Judah Dan 1:6 1121
than the *c* which are of your sort Dan 1:10 3206
the countenance of the *c* that eat Dan 1:13 3206
c which did eat the portion of Dan 1:15 3206
As for these four *c*, God gave Dan 1:17 3206
And wheresoever the *c* of men dwell Dan 2:38 1123
which art of the *c* of the Dan 5:13 1123
Daniel, which is of the *c* of the Dan 6:13 1123
the den of lions, them, their *c* Dan 6:24 1123
and the chief of the *c* of Ammon Dan 11:41 1121
standeth for the *c* of thy people Dan 12:1 1121
of whoredoms and *c* of whoredoms Hos 1:2 3206
Yet the number of the *c* of Israel Hos 1:10 1121
Then shall the *c* of Judah Hos 1:11 1121
the *c* of Israel be gathered Hos 1:11 1121
I will not have mercy upon her *c* Hos 2:4 1121
for they be the *c* of whoredoms Hos 2:4 1121
the LORD toward the *c* of Israel Hos 3:1 1121
For the *c* of Israel shall abide Hos 3:4 1121
shall the *c* of Israel return Hos 3:5 1121
word of the LORD, ye *c* of Israel Hos 4:1 1121
thy God, I will also forget thy *c* Hos 4:6 1121
for they have begotten strange *c* Hos 5:7 1121
Though they bring up their *c* Hos 9:12 1121
bring forth his *c* to the murderer Hos 9:13 1121
c of iniquity did not overtake Hos 10:9 1121
was dashed in pieces upon her *c* Hos 10:14 1121
then the *c* shall tremble from the Hos 11:10 1121
place of the breaking forth of *c* Hos 13:13 1121
Tell ye your *c* of it Joel 1:3 1121
let your *c* tell their *c*, Joel 1:3 1121
and let your *c* tell their *c* Joel 1:3 1121
assemble the elders, gather the *c* Joel 2:16 5768
ye *c* of Zion, and rejoice in the Joel 2:23 1121
The *c* also of Judah and the Joel 3:6 1121
the *c* of Jerusalem have ye sold Joel 3:6 1121
into the hand of the *c* of Judah Joel 3:8 1121
the strength of the *c* of Israel Joel 3:16 1121
violence against the *c* of Judah Joel 3:19 1121
transgressions of the *c* of Ammon Amos 1:13 1121
not even thus, O ye *c* of Israel Amos 2:11 1121
O *c* of Israel, against the whole Amos 3:1 1121
so shall the *c* of Israel be taken Amos 3:12 1121
O ye *c* of Israel, saith the Lord Amos 4:5 1121
Are ye not as *c* of the Ethiopians Amos 9:7 1121
Ethiopians unto me, O *c* of Israel Amos 9:7 1121
thou have rejoiced over the *c* of Obad 12 1121
captivity of this host of the *c* Obad 20 1121
and poll thee for thy delicate *c* Mic 1:16 1121
from their *c* have ye taken away Mic 2:9 5768
shall return unto the *c* of Israel Mic 5:3 1121
her young *c* also were dashed in Nah 3:10 5768
the princes, and the king's *c* Zeph 1:8 1121
the revilings of the *c* of Ammon Zeph 2:8 1121
the *c* of Ammon as Gomorrah, even Zeph 2:9 1121
their *c* shall see it, and be glad Zec 10:7 1121
and they shall live with their *c* Zec 10:9 1121
the heart of the fathers to the *c* Mal 4:6 1121
heart of the *c* to their fathers Mal 4:6 1121
slew all the *c* that were in Mt 2:16 *3816*
Rachel weeping for her *c* Mt 2:18 *5043*
stones to raise up *c* unto Abraham Mt 3:9 *5043*
they shall be called the *c* of God Mt 5:9 *5207*
That ye may be the *c* of your Mt 5:45 *5207*
to give good gifts unto your *c* Mt 7:11 *5043*
But the *c* of the kingdom shall be Mt 8:12 *5207*
Can the *c* of the bridechamber Mt 9:15 *5207*
the *c* shall rise up against their Mt 10:21 *5043*
It is like unto *c* sitting in the Mt 11:16 *3808*
But wisdom is justified of her *c* Mt 11:19 *5043*
by whom do your *c* cast them out Mt 12:27 *5207*
seed are the *c* of the kingdom Mt 13:38 *5207*
tares are the *c* of the wicked one Mt 13:38 *5207*
thousand men, beside women and *c* Mt 14:21 *3813*
thousand men, beside women and *c* Mt 15:38 *3813*
of their own *c*, or of strangers Mt 17:25 *5207*
unto him, Then are the *c* free Mt 17:26 *5207*
converted, and become as little *c* Mt 18:3 *3813*
him to be sold, and his wife, and *c* Mt 18:25 *5043*
there brought unto him little *c* Mt 19:13 *3813*
But Jesus said, Suffer little *c* Mt 19:14 *3813*
father, or mother, or wife, or *c* Mt 19:29 *5043*
of Zebedee's *c* with her sons Mt 20:20 *5207*
the *c* crying in the temple, and Mt 21:15 *3816*
said, If a man die, having no *c* Mt 22:24 *5043*
that ye are the *c* of them which Mt 23:31 *5207*
I have gathered thy *c* together Mt 23:37 *5043*
whom they of the *c* of Israel did Mt 27:9 *5207*
His blood be on us, and on our *c* Mt 27:25 *5043*
and the mother of Zebedee's *c* Mt 27:56 *5207*
Can the *c* of the bridechamber Mk 2:19 *5207*
Let the *c* first be filled Mk 7:27 *5043*
receive one of such *c* in my name Mk 9:37 *3813*
And they brought young *c* to him Mk 10:13 *3813*
the little *c* to come unto me Mk 10:14 *3813*

again, and saith unto them, C ... Mk 10:24 *5043*
father, or mother, or wife, or c ... Mk 10:29 *5043*
and sisters, and mothers, and c ... Mk 10:30 *5043*
wife behind him, and leave no c ... Mk 12:19 *5043*
c shall rise up against their ... Mk 13:12 *5043*
many of the c of Israel shall he ... Lk 1:16 *5207*
hearts of the fathers to the c ... Lk 1:17 *5043*
stones to raise up c unto Abraham ... Lk 3:8 *5043*
them, Can ye make the c of the ... Lk 5:34 *5207*
ye shall be the c of the Highest ... Lk 6:35 *5207*
They are like unto c sitting in ... Lk 7:32 *3813*
wisdom is justified of all her c ... Lk 7:35 *5043*
shut, and my c are with me in bed ... Lk 11:7 *3813*
to give good gifts unto your c ... Lk 11:13 *5043*
I have gathered thy c together ... Lk 13:34 *5043*
father, and mother, and wife, and c ... Lk 14:26 *5043*
for the c of this world are in ... Lk 16:8 *5207*
wiser than the c of light ... Lk 16:8 *5207*
Suffer little c to come unto me, ... Lk 18:16 *3813*
or brethren, or wife, or c ... Lk 18:29 *5043*
the ground, and thy c within thee ... Lk 19:44 *5043*
a wife, and he die without c ... Lk 20:28 *815*
took a wife, and died without c ... Lk 20:29 *815*
and they left no c, and died ... Lk 20:31 *5043*
The c of this world marry, and are ... Lk 20:34 *5207*
and are the c of God, being the ... Lk 20:36 *5207*
being the c of the resurrection ... Lk 20:36 *5207*
for yourselves, and for your c ... Lk 23:28 *5043*
drank thereof himself, and his c ... Jn 4:12 *5207*
unto them, If ye were Abraham's c ... Jn 8:39 *5043*
the c of God that were scattered ... Jn 11:52 *5043*
that ye may be the c of light ... Jn 12:36 *5207*
Little c, yet a little while I am ... Jn 13:33 *5040*
Then Jesus saith unto them, C ... Jn 21:5 *3813*
promise is unto you, and to your c ... Acts 2:39 *5043*
Ye are the c of the prophets, and ... Acts 3:25 *5207*
all the senate of the c of Israel ... Acts 5:21 *5207*
that they cast out their young c ... Acts 7:19 *1025*
his brethren the c of Israel ... Acts 7:23 *5207*
which said unto the c of Israel ... Acts 7:37 *5207*
and kings, and the c of Israel ... Acts 9:15 *5207*
God sent unto the c of Israel ... Acts 10:36 *5207*
c of the stock of Abraham, and ... Acts 13:26 *5207*
the same unto us their c, in that ... Acts 13:33 *5043*
us on our way, with wives and c ... Acts 21:5 *5043*
ought not to circumcise their c ... Acts 21:21 *5043*
spirit, that we are the c of God ... Rom 8:16 *5043*
And if c, then heirs ... Rom 8:17 *5043*
glorious liberty of the c of God ... Rom 8:21 *5043*
seed of Abraham, are they all c ... Rom 9:7 *5043*
They which are the c of the flesh ... Rom 9:8 *5043*
these are not the c of God ... Rom 9:8 *5043*
but the c of the promise are ... Rom 9:8 *5043*
(For the c being not yet born, ... Rom 9:11
be called the c of the living God ... Rom 9:26 *5207*
Though the number of the c of ... Rom 9:27 *5207*
else were your c unclean ... 1Cor 7:14 *5043*
be not c in understanding ... 1Cor 14:20 *3813*
howbeit in malice be ye c ... 1Cor 14:20 *3515*
so that the c of Israel could not ... 2Cor 3:7 *5207*
that the c of Israel could not ... 2Cor 3:13 *5207*
the same, (I speak as unto my c ... 2Cor 6:13 *5043*
for the c ought not to lay up for ... 2Cor 12:14 *5043*
but the parents for the c ... 2Cor 12:14 *5043*
the same are the c of Abraham ... Gal 3:7 *5207*
For ye are all the c of God by ... Gal 3:26 *5207*
Even so we, when we were c ... Gal 4:3 *3516*
My little c, of whom I travail in ... Gal 4:19 *5040*
is, and is in bondage with her c ... Gal 4:25 *5043*
c than she which hath a husband ... Gal 4:27 *5043*
Isaac was, are the c of promise ... Gal 4:28 *5043*
we are not c of the bondwoman, ... Gal 4:31 *5043*
us unto the adoption of c by ... Eph 1:5 *5206*
worketh in the c of disobedience ... Eph 2:2 *5207*
and were by nature the c of wrath ... Eph 2:3 *5043*
That we henceforth be no more c ... Eph 4:14 *3516*
followers of God, as dear c ... Eph 5:1 *5043*
of God upon the c of disobedience ... Eph 5:6 *5207*
walk as c of light ... Eph 5:8 *5043*
C, obey your parents in the Lord ... Eph 6:1 *5043*
provoke not your c to wrath ... Eph 6:4 *5043*
cometh on the c of disobedience ... Col 3:6 *5207*
C, obey your parents in all ... Col 3:20 *5043*
provoke not your c to anger ... Col 3:21 *5043*
even as a nurse cherisheth her c ... 1Th 2:7 *5043*
of you, as a father doth his c ... 1Th 2:11 *5043*
c of light, and the c of the day ... 1Th 5:5 *5207*
having his c in subjection with ... 1Ti 3:4 *5043*
of one wife, ruling their c ... 1Ti 3:12 *5043*
if any widow have c or nephews ... 1Ti 5:4 *5043*
if she have brought up c, if she ... 1Ti 5:10 *5044*
the younger women marry, bear c ... 1Ti 5:14 *5041*
having faithful c not accused of ... Titus 1:6 *5043*
their husbands, to love their c ... Titus 2:4 *5388*
the c which God hath given me ... Heb 2:13 *3813*
Forasmuch then as the c are ... Heb 2:14 *3813*
the departing of the c of Israel ... Heb 11:22 *5027*
which speaketh unto you as unto c ... Heb 12:5 *5027*
As obedient c, not fashioning ... 1Pet 1:14 *5043*
with covetous practices; cursed c ... 2Pet 2:14 *5043*
My little c, these things write I ... 1Jn 2:1 *5040*
I write unto you, little c ... 1Jn 2:12 *5040*
I write unto you, little c ... 1Jn 2:13 *3813*
Little c, it is the last time ... 1Jn 2:18 *3813*
And now, little c, abide in him ... 1Jn 2:28 *5040*
Little c, let no man deceive you ... 1Jn 3:7 *5040*
In this the c of God are manifest ... 1Jn 3:10 *5043*
and the c of the devil ... 1Jn 3:10 *5043*
My little c, let us not love in ... 1Jn 3:18 *5040*
Ye are of God, little c, and have ... 1Jn 4:4 *5040*
we know that we love the c of God ... 1Jn 5:2 *5043*
Little c, keep yourselves from ... 1Jn 5:21 *5040*
unto the elect lady and her c ... 2Jn 1 *5043*
I found of thy c walking in truth ... 2Jn 4 *5043*
The c of thy elect sister greet ... 2Jn 13 *5043*
to hear that my c walk in truth ... 3Jn 4 *5043*
before the c of Israel, to eat ... Rev 2:14 *5207*
And I will kill her c with death ... Rev 2:23 *5043*
all the tribes of the c of Israel ... Rev 7:4 *5207*
twelve tribes of the c of Israel ... Rev 21:12 *5207*

CHILDREN'S
father, that is ours, and our c ... Gen 31:16 1121
thy c children, and thy flocks, and ... Gen 45:10 1121
of all that is the c of Israel ... Ex 9:4 1121
children, and upon the c children ... Ex 34:7 1121
c children, and ye shall have ... Deut 4:25 1121
thy c for ever, because thou hast ... Josh 14:9 1121
children, and their c children ... 2Kin 17:41 1121
for the c sake of mine own body ... Job 19:17 1121
his righteousness unto c children ... Ps 103:17 1121
thou shalt see thy c children ... Ps 128:6 1121
an inheritance to his c children ... Prov 13:22 1121
C children are the crown of old ... Prov 17:6 1121
with your c children will I plead ... Jer 2:9 1121
the c teeth are set on edge ... Jer 31:29 1121
the c teeth are set on edge ... Eze 18:2 1121
their c children for ever ... Eze 37:25 1121
is not meet to take the c bread ... Mt 15:26 *5043*
is not meet to take the c bread ... Mk 7:27 *5043*
the table eat of the c crumbs ... Mk 7:28 *3813*

CHILD'S
maid went and called the c mother ... Ex 2:8 3206
let this c soul come into him ... 1Kin 17:21 3206
flesh shall be fresher than a c ... Job 33:25 5290
which sought the young c life ... Mt 2:20 *3813*

CHILEAB (*kil'-e-ab*) See DANIEL. *A son of David.*
And his second, C, of Abigail the ... 2Sa 3:3 3609

CHILION (*kil'-e-on*) See CHILION'S. *A son of Elimelech.*
name of his two sons Mahlon and C ... Ruth 1:2 3630
and C died also both of them ... Ruth 1:5 3630

CHILION'S (*kil'-e-ons*)
Elimelech's, and all that was C ... Ruth 4:9 3630

CHILMAD (*kil'-mad*) *An area between Assyria and Arabia.*
merchants of Sheba, Asshur, and C ... Eze 27:23 3638

CHIMHAM (*kim'-ham*) *A servant of David.*
But behold thy servant C ... 2Sa 19:37 3643
C shall go over with me, and I ... 2Sa 19:38 3643
to Gilgal, and C went on with him ... 2Sa 19:40 3643
and dwelt in the habitation of C ... Jer 41:17 3643

CHIMNEY
and as the smoke out of the c ... Hos 13:3 699

CHINNERETH (*kin'-ne-reth*) See CHINNEROTH, CINNEROTH, GENNESARET. *A district around the Sea of Galilee.*
the side of the sea of C eastward ... Num 34:11 3672
from C even unto the sea of the ... Deut 3:17 3672
sea of C on the other side Jordan ... Josh 13:27 3672
Zer, and Hammath, Rakkath, and C ... Josh 19:35 3672

CHINNEROTH (*kin'-ne-roth*) See CHINNERETH. *Same as Chinnereth.*
and of the plains south of C ... Josh 11:2 3672
plain to the sea of C on the east ... Josh 12:3 3672

CHIOS (*ki'-os*) *An island near Greece.*
came the next day over against C ... Acts 20:15 5508

CHISLEU (*kis'-lew*) *Ninth month of the Hebrew year.*
And it came to pass in the month C ... Neh 1:1 3691
day of the ninth month, even in C ... Zec 7:1 3691

CHISLEV See CHISLEU.

CHISLON (*kis'-lon*) *Father of Elidad.*
of Benjamin, Elidad the son of C ... Num 34:21 3692

CHISLOTH-TABOR (*kis'-loth-ta'-bor*) See CHESULLOTH. *A city in Zebulon.*
sunrising unto the border of C ... Josh 19:12 3696

CHITTIM (*kit'-tim*) See KITTIM. *Descendants of Javan.*
come come from the coast of C ... Num 24:24 3794
from the land of C it is revealed ... Is 23:1 3794
arise, pass over to C ... Is 23:12 3794
For pass over the isles of C ... Jer 2:10 3794
brought out of the isles of C ... Eze 27:6 3794
For the ships of C shall come ... Dan 11:30 3794

CHIUN (*ki'-un*) See REMPHAN. *Another name for the god Saturn.*
C your images, the star of your ... Amos 5:26 3594

CHLOE (*clo'-e*) *A Christian acquaintance of Paul.*
them which are of the house of C ... 1Cor 1:11 *5514*

CHLOE'S See CHLOE.

CHODE
Jacob was wroth, and c with Laban ... Gen 31:36 7378
And the people c with Moses ... Num 20:3 7378

CHOICE
in the c of our sepulchres bury ... Gen 23:6 4005
and his ass's colt unto the c vine ... Gen 49:11 8321
all your c vows which ye vow unto ... Deut 12:11 4005
a c young man, and a goodly ... 1Sa 9:2 970
chose of all the c men of Israel ... 2Sa 10:9 977
fenced city, and every c city ... 2Kin 3:19 4005
and the c fir trees thereof ... 2Kin 19:23 4005
heads of their father's house, c ... 1Chr 7:40 1305
chose out of all the c of Israel ... 1Chr 19:10 970
them three hundred thousand c men ... 2Chr 25:5 970
daily was one ox and six c sheep ... Neh 5:18 1305
and knowledge rather than c gold ... Prov 8:10 977
and my revenue than c silver ... Prov 8:19 977
tongue of the just is as c silver ... Prov 10:20 977
she is the c one of her that bare ... Song 6:9 1249
and the c fir trees thereof ... Is 37:24 4005
they shall cut down thy c cedars ... Jer 22:7 4005
fill it with the c bones ... Eze 24:4 4005
Take the c of the flock, and burn ... Eze 24:5 4005
and all the trees of Eden, the c ... Eze 31:16 4005
while ago God made c among us ... Acts 15:7 *1586*

CHOICEST
and planted it with the c vine ... Is 5:2 8321
that thy c valleys shall be full ... Is 22:7 4055

CHOKE
c the word, and he becometh ... Mt 13:22 *4846*
c the word, and it becometh ... Mk 4:19 *4846*

CHOKED
the thorns sprung up, and c them ... Mt 13:7 *638*
c it, and it yielded no fruit ... Mk 4:7 *4846*
and were c in the sea ... Mk 5:13 *4155*
thorns sprang up with it, and c it ... Lk 8:7 *638*
are c with cares and riches and ... Lk 8:14 *4846*
place into the lake, and were c ... Lk 8:33 *638*

CHOLER
he was moved with c against him ... Dan 8:7 4843
the south shall be moved with c ... Dan 11:11 4843

CHOOSE
C us out men, and go out, fight ... Ex 17:9 977
that the man whom the LORD doth c ... Num 16:7 977
the man's rod, whom I shall c ... Num 17:5 977
set his love upon you, nor c you ... Deut 7:7 977
c out of all your tribes to put ... Deut 12:5 977
c to cause his name to dwell ... Deut 12:11 977
LORD shall c in one of thy tribes ... Deut 12:14 977
which the LORD thy God shall c ... Deut 12:18 977
the place which the LORD shall c ... Deut 12:26 977
shall c to place his name there ... Deut 14:23 977
God shall c to set his name there ... Deut 14:24 977
which the LORD thy God shall c ... Deut 14:25 977
the place which the LORD shall c ... Deut 15:20 977
shall c to place his name there ... Deut 16:2 977
God shall c to place his name in ... Deut 16:6 977
which the LORD thy God shall c ... Deut 16:7 977
the place which the LORD shall c ... Deut 16:15 977
God in the place which he shall c ... Deut 16:16 977
which the LORD thy God shall c ... Deut 17:8 977
the LORD shall c shall shew thee ... Deut 17:10 977
whom the LORD thy God shall c ... Deut 17:15 977
the place which the LORD shall c ... Deut 18:6 977
he shall c in one of thy gates ... Deut 23:16 977
shall c to place his name there ... Deut 26:2 977
therefore c life, that both thou ... Deut 30:19 977
God in the place which he shall c ... Deut 31:11 977
in the place which he should c ... Josh 9:27 977
c you this day whom ye will serve ... Josh 24:15 977
did I c him out of all the tribes ... 1Sa 2:28 977
c you a man for you, and let him ... 1Sa 17:8 1262
and all the men of Israel, c ... 2Sa 16:18 977
Let me now c out twelve thousand ... 2Sa 17:1 977
of Saul, whom the LORD did c ... 2Sa 21:6 972
c thee one of them, that I may do ... 2Sa 24:12 977
the city which the LORD did c out ... 1Kin 14:21 977
let them c one bullock for ... 1Kin 18:23 977
C you one bullock for yourselves, ... 1Kin 18:25 977
c thee one of them, that I may do ... 1Chr 21:10 977
him, Thus saith the LORD, C thee ... 1Chr 21:11 6901
LORD the God, who didst c Abram ... Neh 9:7 977
c out my words to reason with him ... Job 9:14 977
Let us c to us judgment ... Job 34:4 977
thou refuse, or whether thou c ... Job 34:33 977
teach in the way that he shall c ... Ps 25:12 977
He shall c our inheritance for us ... Ps 47:4 977
did not c the fear of the LORD ... Prov 1:29 977
oppressor, and c none of his ways ... Prov 3:31 977
to refuse the evil, and c the good ... Is 7:15 977
c the good, the land that thou ... Is 7:16 977
on Jacob, and will yet c Israel ... Is 14:1 977
One of Israel, and he shall c thee ... Is 49:7 977
c the things that please me, and ... Is 56:4 977
did c that wherein I delighted ... Is 65:12 977
I also will c their delusions, and ... Is 66:4 977
c thou a place, c it at the ... Eze 21:19 1254
c it at the head of the way to ... Eze 21:19 1254
Zion, and shall yet c Jerusalem ... Zec 1:17 977
land, and shall c Jerusalem again ... Zec 2:12 977
yet what I shall c I wot not ... Phil 1:22 *138*

CHOOSEST
thou c the tongue of the crafty ... Job 15:5 977
Blessed is the man whom thou c ... Ps 65:4 977

CHOOSETH
So that my soul c strangling ... Job 7:15 977
c a tree that will not rot ... Is 40:20 977
an abomination is he that c you ... Is 41:24 977

CHOOSING
C rather to suffer affliction ... Heb 11:25 *138*

CHOP
c them in pieces, as for the pot, ... Mic 3:3 6566

CHOR-ASHAN (*cor-a'-shan*) *A town in Judah.*
and to them which were in C ... 1Sa 30:30 3565

CHORAZIN (*co-ra'-zin*) *A city near Capernaum.*
Woe unto thee, C ... Mt 11:21 *5523*
Woe unto thee, C ... Lk 10:13 *5523*

CHOSE
them wives of all which they c ... Gen 6:2 977
Then Lot c him all the plain of ... Gen 13:11 977
Moses c able men out of all ... Ex 18:25 977
therefore he c their seed after ... Deut 4:37 977

he c their seed after them, even	Deut 10:15	977
Joshua c out thirty thousand	Josh 8:3	977
They c new gods	Judg 5:8	977
Saul c him three thousand men of	1Sa 13:2	977
c him five smooth stones out of	1Sa 17:40	977
which c me before thy father, and	2Sa 6:21	977
he c of all the choice men of	2Sa 10:9	977
I c no city out of all the tribes	1Kin 8:16	977
but I c David to be over my	1Kin 8:16	977
David my servant's sake, whom I c	1Kin 11:34	977
he c out of all the choice of	1Chr 19:10	977
c me before all the house of my	1Chr 28:4	977
out of the land of Egypt I c no	2Chr 6:5	977
neither c I any man to be a ruler	2Chr 6:5	977
I c out their way, and sat chief,	Job 29:25	977
c not the tribe of Ephraim	Ps 78:67	977
But c the tribe of Judah, the	Ps 78:68	977
He c David also his servant, and	Ps 78:70	977
c that in which I delighted not	Is 66:4	977
In the day when I c Israel	Eze 20:5	977
and of them he c twelve, whom also	Lk 6:13	1586
how they c out the chief rooms	Lk 14:7	1586
they c Stephen, a man full of	Acts 6:5	1586
people of Israel c our fathers	Acts 13:17	1586
Paul c Silas, and departed, being	Acts 15:40	1951

CHOSEN

And he took six hundred c chariots	Ex 14:7	970
his c captains also are drowned	Ex 15:4	4005
even him whom he hath c will he	Num 16:5	977
the LORD thy God hath c thee to	Deut 7:6	977
which the LORD thy God hath c to	Deut 12:21	977
the LORD hath c thee to be a	Deut 14:2	977
hath c to place his name there	Deut 16:11	977
hath c him out of all thy tribes	Deut 18:5	977
God hath c to minister unto him	Deut 21:5	977
that ye have c you the LORD	Josh 24:22	977
cry unto the gods which ye have c	Judg 10:14	977
were numbered seven hundred c men..	Judg 20:15	970
seven hundred c men lefthanded	Judg 20:16	970
thousand c men out of all Israel	Judg 20:34	970
king which ye shall have c you	1Sa 8:18	977
See ye him whom the LORD hath c	1Sa 10:24	977
behold the king whom ye have c	1Sa 12:13	977
Neither hath the LORD c this	1Sa 16:8	977
Neither hath the LORD c this	1Sa 16:9	977
Jesse, The LORD hath not c these	1Sa 16:10	977
do not I know that thou hast c	1Sa 20:30	977
thousand c men out of all Israel	1Sa 24:2	970
having three thousand c men of	1Sa 26:2	970
together all the c men of Israel	2Sa 6:1	970
of thy people which thou hast c	1Kin 3:8	977
toward the city which thou hast c	1Kin 8:44	977
the city which thou hast c	1Kin 8:48	977
Jerusalem's sake which I have c	1Kin 11:13	977
the city which I have c out of	1Kin 11:32	977
the city which I have c me to put	1Kin 11:36	977
and fourscore thousand c men	1Kin 12:21	970
which I have c out of all tribes	2Kin 21:7	977
city Jerusalem which I have c	2Kin 23:27	977
All these which were c to be	1Chr 9:22	1305
for them hath the LORD c to carry	1Chr 15:2	977
ye children of Jacob, his c ones	1Chr 16:13	972
Jeduthun, and the rest that were c	1Chr 16:41	1305
for he hath c Judah to be the	1Chr 28:4	977
he hath c Solomon my son to sit	1Chr 28:5	977
for I have c him to be my son, and	1Chr 28:6	977
for the LORD hath c thee to build	1Chr 28:10	977
my son, whom alone God hath c	1Chr 29:1	977
But I have c Jerusalem, that my	2Chr 6:6	977
have c David to be over my people	2Chr 6:6	977
this city which thou hast c	2Chr 6:34	977
toward the city which thou hast c	2Chr 6:38	977
have c this place to myself for	2Chr 7:12	977
For now have I c and sanctified	2Chr 7:16	977
and fourscore thousand c men	2Chr 11:1	970
the city which the LORD had c out	2Chr 12:13	977
even four hundred thousand c men	2Chr 13:3	970
with eight hundred thousand c men	2Chr 13:3	970
five hundred thousand c men	2Chr 13:17	970
for the LORD hath c you to stand	2Chr 29:11	977
which I have c before all the	2Chr 33:7	977
I have c to set my name there	Neh 1:9	977
for this hast thou c rather than	Job 36:21	977
he hath c for his own inheritance	Ps 33:12	977
and smote down the c men of Israel	Ps 78:31	970
I have made a covenant with my c	Ps 89:3	972
exalted one c out of the people	Ps 89:19	970
ye children of Jacob his c	Ps 105:6	972
and Aaron whom he had c	Ps 105:26	977
with joy, and his c with gladness	Ps 105:43	972
That I may see the good of thy c	Ps 106:5	972
had not Moses his c stood before	Ps 106:23	972
I have c the way of truth	Ps 119:30	977
for I have c thy precepts	Ps 119:173	977
For the LORD hath c Zion	Ps 132:13	977
For the LORD hath c Jacob unto	Ps 135:4	977
rather to be c than silver	Prov 16:16	977
rather to be c than great riches	Prov 22:1	977
for the gardens that ye have c	Is 1:29	977
my servant, Jacob whom I have c	Is 41:8	977
I have c thee, and not cast thee	Is 41:9	977
LORD, and my servant whom I have c.	Is 43:10	977
to give drink to my people, my c	Is 43:20	972
and Israel, whom I have c	Is 44:1	977
and thou, Jesurun, whom I have c	Is 44:2	977
I have c thee in the furnace of	Is 48:10	977
Is it such a fast that I have c	Is 58:5	977
not this the fast that I have c	Is 58:6	977
your name for a curse unto my c	Is 65:15	972
they have c their own ways, and	Is 66:3	977
death shall be c rather than life	Jer 8:3	977
families which the LORD hath c	Jer 33:24	977
his c young men are gone down to	Jer 48:15	4005
and who is a c man, that I may	Jer 49:19	970
and who is a c man, that I may	Jer 50:44	970
that were the c men of Assyria	Eze 23:7	4005
withstand, neither his c people	Dan 11:15	4005
for I have c thee, saith the LORD	Hag 2:23	977
that hath c Jerusalem rebuke thee	Zec 3:2	977
Behold my servant, whom I have c	Mt 12:18	140
for many be called, but few c	Mt 20:16	1588
many are called, but few are c	Mt 22:14	1588
the elect's sake, whom he hath c	Mk 13:20	1586
Mary hath c that good part, which	Lk 10:42	1586
if he be Christ, the c of God	Lk 23:35	1588
them, Have not I c you twelve	Jn 6:70	1586
I know whom I have c	Jn 13:18	1586
not c me, but I have c you	Jn 15:16	1586
but I have c you out of the world	Jn 15:19	1586
unto the apostles whom he had c	Acts 1:2	1586
whether of these two thou hast c	Acts 1:24	1586
for he is a c vessel unto me, to	Acts 9:15	1589
unto witnesses c before of God	Acts 10:41	4401
to send c men of their own	Acts 15:22	1586
to send c men unto you with our	Acts 15:25	1586
God of our fathers hath c thee	Acts 22:14	4400
Salute Rufus c in the Lord	Rom 16:13	1588
But God hath c the foolish things	1Cor 1:27	1586
God hath c the weak things of the	1Cor 1:27	1586
which are despised, hath God c	1Cor 1:28	1586
but who was also c of the	2Cor 8:19	5500
According as he hath c us in him	Eph 1:4	1586
c you to salvation through	2Th 2:13	138
who hath c him to be a soldier	2Ti 2:4	4758
Hath not God c the poor of this	Jas 2:5	1586
but c of God, and precious	1Pet 2:4	1588
But ye are a c generation	1Pet 2:9	1588
are with him are called, and c	Rev 17:14	1588

CHOZEBA (*ko-ze'-bah*) See CHEZIB. *A city in Judah.*

And Jokim, and the men of C	1Chr 4:22	3578

CHRIST (*krist*) See ANTICHRIST, CHRISTIAN, CHRIST'S, CHRISTS, JESUS, MESSIAH. *A title of Jesus of Nazareth; Greek for Messiah.*

book of the generation of Jesus C	Mt 1:1	5547
was born Jesus, who is called C	Mt 1:16	5547
unto C are fourteen generations	Mt 1:17	5547
birth of Jesus C was on this wise	Mt 1:18	5547
of them where C should be born	Mt 2:4	5547
in the prison the works of C	Mt 11:2	5547
answered and said, Thou art the C	Mt 16:16	5547
no man that he was Jesus the C	Mt 16:20	5547
Saying, What think ye of C	Mt 22:42	5547
for one is your Master, even C	Mt 23:8	5547
for one is your Master, even C	Mt 23:10	5547
come in my name, saying, I am C	Mt 24:5	5547
shall say unto you, Lo, here is C	Mt 24:23	5547
tell us whether thou be the C	Mt 26:63	5547
Saying, Prophesy unto us, thou C	Mt 26:68	5547
or Jesus which is called C	Mt 27:17	5547
then with Jesus which is called C	Mt 27:22	5547
of the gospel of Jesus C, the Son	Mk 1:1	5547
and saith unto him, Thou art the C	Mk 8:29	5547
my name, because ye belong to C	Mk 9:41	5547
that C is the son of David	Mk 12:35	5547
come in my name, saying, I am C	Mk 13:6	
shall say to you, Lo, here is C	Mk 13:21	5547
and said unto him, Art thou the C	Mk 14:61	5547
Let C the King of Israel descend	Mk 15:32	5547
a Saviour, which is C the Lord	Lk 2:11	5547
before he had seen the Lord's C	Lk 2:26	5547
of John, whether he were the C	Lk 3:15	5547
Thou art C the Son of God	Lk 4:41	5547
for they knew that he was C	Lk 4:41	5547
answering said, The C of God	Lk 9:20	5547
say they that C is David's son	Lk 20:41	5547
come in my name, saying, I am C	Lk 21:8	
Art thou the C	Lk 22:67	5547
that he himself is C a King	Lk 23:2	5547
let him save himself, if he be C	Lk 23:35	5547
on him, saying, If thou be C	Lk 23:39	5547
Ought not C to have suffered	Lk 24:26	5547
and thus it behoved C to suffer	Lk 24:46	5547
grace and truth came by Jesus C	Jn 1:17	5547
but confessed, I am not the C	Jn 1:20	5547
thou then, if thou be not that C	Jn 1:25	5547
is, being interpreted, the C	Jn 1:41	5547
that I said, I am not the C	Jn 3:28	5547
Messias cometh, which is called C	Jn 4:25	5547
is not this the C	Jn 4:29	5547
and know that this is indeed the C	Jn 4:42	5547
and are sure that thou art that C	Jn 6:69	5547
indeed that this is the very C	Jn 7:26	5547
but when C cometh, no man knoweth	Jn 7:27	5547
When C cometh, will he do more	Jn 7:31	5547
Others said, This is the C	Jn 7:41	5547
Shall C come out of Galilee	Jn 7:41	5547
That C cometh of the seed of	Jn 7:42	5547
any man did confess that he was C	Jn 9:22	5547
If thou be the C, tell us plainly	Jn 10:24	5547
I believe that thou art the C	Jn 11:27	5547
the law that C abideth for ever	Jn 12:34	5547
the only true God, and Jesus C	Jn 17:3	5547
might believe that Jesus is the C	Jn 20:31	5547
he would raise up C to sit on his	Acts 2:30	5547
spake of the resurrection of C	Acts 2:31	5547
ye have crucified, both Lord and C	Acts 2:36	5547
Jesus C for the remission of sins	Acts 2:38	5547
of Jesus C of Nazareth rise up	Acts 3:6	5547
that C should suffer, he hath so	Acts 3:18	5547
And he shall send Jesus C, which	Acts 3:20	5547
the name of Jesus C of Nazareth	Acts 4:10	5547
the Lord, and against his C	Acts 4:26	5547
not to teach and preach Jesus C	Acts 5:42	5547
Samaria, and preached C unto them	Acts 8:5	5547
of God, and the name of Jesus C	Acts 8:12	5547
that Jesus C is the Son of God	Acts 8:37	5547
he preached C in the synagogues	Acts 9:20	5547
proving that this is very C	Acts 9:22	5547
Jesus C maketh thee whole	Acts 9:34	5547
preaching peace by Jesus C	Acts 10:36	5547
who believed on the Lord Jesus C	Acts 11:17	5547
Lord Jesus C we shall be saved	Acts 15:11	5547
for the name of our Lord Jesus C	Acts 15:26	5547
of Jesus C to come out of her	Acts 16:18	5547
said, Believe on the Lord Jesus C	Acts 16:31	5547
that C must needs have suffered,	Acts 17:3	5547
whom I preach unto you, is C	Acts 17:3	5547
to the Jews that Jesus was C	Acts 18:5	5547
the scriptures that Jesus was C	Acts 18:28	5547
after him, that is, on C Jesus	Acts 19:4	5547
and faith toward our Lord Jesus C	Acts 20:21	5547
him concerning the faith in C	Acts 24:24	5547
That C should suffer, and that he	Acts 26:23	5547
which concern the Lord Jesus C	Acts 28:31	5547
Paul, a servant of Jesus C	Rom 1:1	5547
his Son Jesus C our Lord, which	Rom 1:3	5547
are ye also the called of Jesus C	Rom 1:6	5547
our Father, and the Lord Jesus C	Rom 1:7	5547
God through Jesus C for you all	Rom 1:8	5547
am not ashamed of the gospel of C	Rom 1:16	5547
by Jesus C according to my gospel	Rom 2:16	5547
is by faith of Jesus C unto all	Rom 3:22	5547
the redemption that is in C Jesus	Rom 3:24	5547
with God through our Lord Jesus C	Rom 5:1	5547
in due time C died for the	Rom 5:6	5547
were yet sinners, C died for us	Rom 5:8	5547
in God through our Lord Jesus C	Rom 5:11	5547
which is by one man, Jesus C	Rom 5:15	5547
reign in life by one, Jesus C	Rom 5:17	5547
eternal life by Jesus C our Lord	Rom 5:21	5547
C were baptized into his death	Rom 6:3	5547
that like as C was raised up from	Rom 6:4	5547
Now if we be dead with C, we	Rom 6:8	5547
Knowing that C being raised from	Rom 6:9	5547
unto God through Jesus C our Lord	Rom 6:11	5547
life through Jesus C our Lord	Rom 6:23	5547
dead to the law by the body of C	Rom 7:4	5547
God through Jesus C our Lord	Rom 7:25	5547
to them which are in C Jesus	Rom 8:1	5547
in C Jesus hath made me free from	Rom 8:2	5547
any man have not the Spirit of C	Rom 8:9	5547
if C be in you, the body is dead	Rom 8:10	5547
he that raised up C from the dead	Rom 8:11	5547
of God, and joint-heirs with C	Rom 8:17	5477
It is C that died, yea rather,	Rom 8:34	5547
separate us from the love of C	Rom 8:35	5547
which is in C Jesus our Lord	Rom 8:39	5547
I say the truth in C, I lie not,	Rom 9:1	5547
accursed from C for my brethren	Rom 9:3	5547
as concerning the flesh C came	Rom 9:5	5547
For C is the end of the law for	Rom 10:4	5547
to bring C down from above	Rom 10:6	5547
to bring up C again from the dead	Rom 10:7	5547
we, being many, are one body in C	Rom 12:5	5547
But put ye on the Lord Jesus C	Rom 13:14	5547
For to this end C both died	Rom 14:9	5547
before the judgment seat of C	Rom 14:10	5547
with thy meat, for whom C died	Rom 14:15	5547
serveth C is acceptable to God	Rom 14:18	5547
For even C pleased not himself	Rom 15:3	5547
another according to C Jesus	Rom 15:5	5547
the Father of our Lord Jesus C	Rom 15:6	5547
as C also received us to the	Rom 15:7	5547
Now I say that Jesus C was a	Rom 15:8	5547
of Jesus C to the Gentiles	Rom 15:16	5547
I may glory through Jesus C in	Rom 15:17	5547
which C hath not wrought by me	Rom 15:18	5547
fully preached the gospel of C	Rom 15:19	5547
the gospel, not where C was named	Rom 15:20	5547
the blessing of the gospel of C	Rom 15:29	5547
and Aquila my helpers in C Jesus	Rom 16:3	5547
the firstfruits of Achaia unto C	Rom 16:5	5547
who also were in C before me	Rom 16:7	5547
Salute Urbane, our helper in C	Rom 16:9	5547
Salute Apelles approved in C	Rom 16:10	5547
The churches of C salute you	Rom 16:16	5547
such serve not our Lord Jesus C	Rom 16:18	5547
of our Lord Jesus C be with you	Rom 16:20	5547
our Lord Jesus C be with you all	Rom 16:24	5547
and the preaching of Jesus C	Rom 16:25	5547
be glory through Jesus C for ever	Rom 16:27	5547
Jesus C through the will of God	1Cor 1:1	5547
that are sanctified in C Jesus	1Cor 1:2	5547
upon the name of Jesus C our Lord	1Cor 1:2	5547
Father, and from the Lord Jesus C	1Cor 1:3	5547
God which is given you by Jesus C	1Cor 1:4	5547
of C was confirmed in you	1Cor 1:6	5547
the coming of our Lord Jesus C	1Cor 1:7	5547
in the day of our Lord Jesus C	1Cor 1:8	5547
of his Son Jesus C our Lord	1Cor 1:9	5547
by the name of our Lord Jesus C	1Cor 1:10	5547
and I of C	1Cor 1:12	5547
Is C divided?	1Cor 1:13	5547
For C sent me not to baptize, but	1Cor 1:17	5547
lest the cross of C should be	1Cor 1:17	5547
But we preach C crucified	1Cor 1:23	5547
C the power of God, and the wisdom	1Cor 1:24	5547
But of him are ye in C Jesus	1Cor 1:30	5547
any thing among you, save Jesus C	1Cor 2:2	5547
But we have the mind of C	1Cor 2:16	5547
carnal, even as unto babes in C	1Cor 3:1	5547
that is laid, which is Jesus C	1Cor 3:11	5547
and C is God's	1Cor 3:23	5547
of us, as of the ministers of C	1Cor 4:1	5547
sake, but ye are wise in C	1Cor 4:10	5547
ten thousand instructers in C	1Cor 4:15	5547
for in C Jesus I have begotten	1Cor 4:15	5547
of my ways which be in C, as I	1Cor 4:17	5547
In the name of our Lord Jesus C	1Cor 5:4	5547

the power of our Lord Jesus C	1Cor 5:4	5547
For even C our passover is	1Cor 5:7	5547
your bodies are the members of C	1Cor 6:15	5547
I then take the members of C	1Cor 6:15	5547
and one Lord Jesus C, by whom are	1Cor 8:6	5547
brother perish, for whom C died	1Cor 8:11	5547
weak conscience, ye sin against C	1Cor 8:12	5547
have I not seen Jesus C our Lord	1Cor 9:1	5547
we should hinder the gospel of C	1Cor 9:12	5547
the gospel of C without charge	1Cor 9:18	5547
to God, but under the law to C	1Cor 9:21	5547
and that Rock was C	1Cor 10:4	5547
Neither let us tempt C, as some	1Cor 10:9	5547
the communion of the blood of C	1Cor 10:16	5547
the communion of the body of C	1Cor 10:16	5547
of me, even as I also am of C	1Cor 11:1	5547
that the head of every man is C	1Cor 11:3	5547
and the head of C is God	1Cor 11:3	5547
so also is C	1Cor 12:12	5547
Now ye are the body of C, and	1Cor 12:27	5547
how that C died for our sins	1Cor 15:3	5547
Now if C be preached that he rose	1Cor 15:12	5547
of the dead, then is C not risen	1Cor 15:13	5547
if C be not risen, then is our	1Cor 15:14	5547
of God that he raised up C	1Cor 15:15	5547
rise not, then is not C raised	1Cor 15:16	5547
if C be not raised, your faith is	1Cor 15:17	5547
fallen asleep in C are perished	1Cor 15:18	5547
this life only we have hope in C	1Cor 15:19	5547
But now is C risen from the dead,	1Cor 15:20	5547
even so in C shall all be made	1Cor 15:22	5547
C the firstfruits	1Cor 15:23	5547
which I have in C Jesus our Lord	1Cor 15:31	5547
victory through our Lord Jesus C	1Cor 15:57	5547
any man love not the Lord Jesus C	1Cor 16:22	5547
of our Lord Jesus C be with you	1Cor 16:23	5547
love be with you all in C Jesus	1Cor 16:24	5547
of Jesus C by the will of God	2Cor 1:1	5547
Father, and from the Lord Jesus C	2Cor 1:2	5547
the Father of our Lord Jesus C	2Cor 1:3	5547
the sufferings of C abound in us	2Cor 1:5	5547
consolation also aboundeth by C	2Cor 1:5	5547
For the Son of God, Jesus C	2Cor 1:19	5547
stablisheth us with you in C	2Cor 1:21	5547
forgave I it in the person of C	2Cor 2:10	5547
always causeth us to triumph in C	2Cor 2:14	5547
are unto God a sweet savour of C	2Cor 2:15	5547
in the sight of God speak we in C	2Cor 2:17	5547
the epistle of C ministered by us	2Cor 3:3	5547
have we through C to God-ward	2Cor 3:4	5547
which vail is done away in C	2Cor 3:14	5547
light of the glorious gospel of C	2Cor 4:4	5547
ourselves, but C Jesus the Lord	2Cor 4:5	5547
of God in the face of Jesus C	2Cor 4:6	5547
before the judgment seat of C	2Cor 5:10	5547
For the love of C constraineth us	2Cor 5:14	5547
we have known C after the flesh	2Cor 5:16	5547
Therefore if any man be in C	2Cor 5:17	5547
us to himself by Jesus C, and hath	2Cor 5:18	5547
To wit, that God was in C	2Cor 5:19	5547
Now then we are ambassadors for C	2Cor 5:20	5547
what concord hath C with Belial	2Cor 6:15	5547
the grace of our Lord Jesus C	2Cor 8:9	5547
the churches, and the glory of C	2Cor 8:23	5547
subjection into the gospel of C	2Cor 9:13	5547
the meekness and gentleness of C	2Cor 10:1	5547
thought to the obedience of C	2Cor 10:5	5547
also in preaching the gospel of C	2Cor 10:14	5547
you as a chaste virgin to C	2Cor 11:2	5547
from the simplicity that is in C	2Cor 11:3	5547
As the truth of C is in me	2Cor 11:10	5547
themselves into the apostles of C	2Cor 11:13	5547
Are they ministers of C	2Cor 11:23	5547
God and Father of our Lord Jesus C	2Cor 11:31	5547
I knew a man in C above fourteen	2Cor 12:2	5547
the power of C may rest upon me	2Cor 12:9	5547
we speak before God in C	2Cor 12:19	5547
seek a proof of C speaking in me	2Cor 13:3	5547
how that Jesus C is in you	2Cor 13:5	5547
The grace of the Lord Jesus C	2Cor 13:14	5547
neither by man, but by Jesus C	Gal 1:1	5547
Father, and from our Lord Jesus C	Gal 1:3	5547
grace of C unto another gospel	Gal 1:6	5547
and would pervert the gospel of C	Gal 1:7	5547
I should not be the servant of C	Gal 1:10	5547
but by the revelation of Jesus C	Gal 1:12	5547
of Judaea which were in C	Gal 1:22	5547
liberty which we have in C Jesus	Gal 2:4	5547
law, but by the faith of Jesus C	Gal 2:16	5547
even we have believed in Jesus C	Gal 2:16	5547
be justified by the faith of C	Gal 2:16	5547
we seek to be justified by C	Gal 2:17	5547
is therefore C the minister of	Gal 2:17	5547
I am crucified with C	Gal 2:20	5547
yet not I, but C liveth in me	Gal 2:20	5547
the law, then C is dead in vain	Gal 2:21	5547
before whose eyes Jesus C hath	Gal 3:1	5547
C hath redeemed us from the curse	Gal 3:13	5547
on the Gentiles through Jesus C	Gal 3:14	5547
one, And to thy seed, which is C	Gal 3:16	5547
was confirmed before of God in C	Gal 3:17	5547
C might be given to them that	Gal 3:22	5547
schoolmaster to bring us unto C	Gal 3:24	5547
of God by faith in C Jesus	Gal 3:26	5547
baptized into C have put on C	Gal 3:27	5547
for ye are all one in C Jesus	Gal 3:28	5547
then an heir of God through C	Gal 4:7	5547
an angel of God, even as C Jesus	Gal 4:14	5547
again until C be formed in you	Gal 4:19	5547
wherewith C hath made us free	Gal 5:1	5547
C shall profit you nothing	Gal 5:2	5547
C is become of no effect unto you	Gal 5:4	5547
For in Jesus C neither	Gal 5:6	5547
and so fulfil the law of C	Gal 6:2	5547
persecution for the cross of C	Gal 6:12	5547
in the cross of our Lord Jesus C	Gal 6:14	5547
For in C Jesus neither	Gal 6:15	5547
Lord Jesus C be with your spirit	Gal 6:18	5547
of Jesus C by the will of God	Eph 1:1	5547
and to the faithful in C Jesus	Eph 1:1	5547
Father, and from the Lord Jesus C	Eph 1:2	5547
God and Father of our Lord Jesus C	Eph 1:3	5547
blessings in heavenly places in C	Eph 1:3	5547
of children by Jesus C to himself	Eph 1:5	5547
together in one all things in C	Eph 1:10	5547
his glory, who first trusted in C	Eph 1:12	5547
That the God of our Lord Jesus C	Eph 1:17	5547
Which he wrought in C, when he	Eph 1:20	5547
hath quickened us together with C	Eph 2:5	5547
in heavenly places in C Jesus	Eph 2:6	5547
toward us through C Jesus	Eph 2:7	5547
created in C Jesus unto good	Eph 2:10	5547
at that time ye were without C	Eph 2:12	5547
But now in C Jesus ye who	Eph 2:13	5547
are made nigh by the blood of C	Eph 2:13	5547
Jesus C himself being the chief	Eph 2:20	5547
of Jesus C for you Gentiles	Eph 3:1	5547
my knowledge in the mystery of C)	Eph 3:4	5547
of his promise in C by the gospel	Eph 3:6	5547
the unsearchable riches of C	Eph 3:8	5547
who created all things by Jesus C	Eph 3:9	5547
he purposed in C Jesus our Lord	Eph 3:11	5547
the Father of our Lord Jesus C	Eph 3:14	5547
That C may dwell in your hearts	Eph 3:17	5547
And to know the love of C, which	Eph 3:19	5547
by C Jesus throughout all ages	Eph 3:21	5547
to the measure of the gift of C	Eph 4:7	5547
for the edifying of the body of C	Eph 4:12	5547
the stature of the fulness of C	Eph 4:13	5547
things, which is the head, even C	Eph 4:15	5547
But ye have not so learned C	Eph 4:20	5547
as C also hath loved us, and hath	Eph 5:2	5547
inheritance in the kingdom of C	Eph 5:5	5547
dead, and C shall give thee light	Eph 5:14	5547
in the name of our Lord Jesus C	Eph 5:20	5547
even as C is the head of the	Eph 5:23	5547
as the church is subject unto C	Eph 5:24	5547
even as C also loved the church,	Eph 5:25	5547
but I speak concerning C and the	Eph 5:32	5547
of your heart, as unto C	Eph 6:5	5547
but as the servants of C, doing	Eph 6:6	5547
the Father and the Lord Jesus C	Eph 6:23	5547
our Lord Jesus C in sincerity	Eph 6:24	5547
the servants of Jesus C, to all	Phil 1:1	5547
to all the saints in C Jesus	Phil 1:1	5547
Father, and from the Lord Jesus C	Phil 1:2	5547
it until the day of Jesus C	Phil 1:6	5547
you all in the bowels of Jesus C	Phil 1:8	5547
without offence till the day of C	Phil 1:10	5547
which are by Jesus C, unto the	Phil 1:11	5547
So that my bonds in C are	Phil 1:13	5547
Some indeed preach C even of envy	Phil 1:15	5547
The one preach C of contention	Phil 1:16	5547
or in truth, C is preached	Phil 1:18	5547
supply of the Spirit of Jesus C	Phil 1:19	5547
so now also C shall be magnified	Phil 1:20	5547
For to me to live is C, and to die	Phil 1:21	5547
desire to depart, and to be with C	Phil 1:23	5547
C for me by my coming to you	Phil 1:26	5547
be as it becometh the gospel of C	Phil 1:27	5547
it is given in the behalf of C	Phil 1:29	5547
be therefore any consolation in C	Phil 2:1	5547
in you, which was also in C Jesus	Phil 2:5	5547
confess that Jesus C is Lord	Phil 2:11	5547
I may rejoice in the day of C	Phil 2:16	5547
work of C he was nigh unto death	Phil 2:30	5547
the spirit, and rejoice in C Jesus	Phil 3:3	5547
to me, those I counted loss for C	Phil 3:7	5547
the knowledge of C Jesus my Lord	Phil 3:8	5547
them but dung, that I may win C	Phil 3:8	5547
which is through the faith of C	Phil 3:9	5547
also I am apprehended of C Jesus	Phil 3:12	5547
high calling of God in C Jesus	Phil 3:14	5547
are the enemies of the cross of C	Phil 3:18	5547
for the Saviour, the Lord Jesus C	Phil 3:20	5547
hearts and minds through C Jesus	Phil 4:7	5547
through C which strengtheneth me	Phil 4:13	5547
to his riches in glory by C Jesus	Phil 4:19	5547
Salute every saint in C Jesus	Phil 4:21	5547
our Lord Jesus C be with you all	Phil 4:23	5547
of Jesus C by the will of God	Col 1:1	5547
in C which are at Colosse	Col 1:2	5547
our Father and the Lord Jesus C	Col 1:2	5547
and the Father of our Lord Jesus C	Col 1:3	5547
we heard of your faith in C Jesus	Col 1:4	5547
for you a faithful minister of C	Col 1:7	5547
C in my flesh for his body's sake	Col 1:24	5547
which is C in you, the hope of	Col 1:27	5547
every man perfect in C Jesus	Col 1:28	5547
of God, and of the Father, and of C	Col 2:2	5547
stedfastness of your faith in C	Col 2:5	5547
received C Jesus the Lord	Col 2:6	5547
of the world, and not after C	Col 2:8	5547
flesh by the circumcision of C	Col 2:11	5547
but the body is of C	Col 2:17	5547
Wherefore if ye be dead with C	Col 2:20	5547
If ye then be risen with C	Col 3:1	5547
where C sitteth on the right hand	Col 3:1	5547
and your life is hid with C in God	Col 3:3	5547
When C, who is our life, shall	Col 3:4	5547
but C is all, and in all	Col 3:11	5547
even as C forgave you, so also do	Col 3:13	5547
Let the word of C dwell in you	Col 3:16	5547
for ye serve the Lord C	Col 3:24	5547
to speak the mystery of C	Col 4:3	5547
who is one of you, a servant of C	Col 4:12	5547
the Father and in the Lord Jesus C	1Th 1:1	5547
our Father, and the Lord Jesus C	1Th 1:1	5547
of hope in our Lord Jesus C	1Th 1:3	5547
burdensome, as the apostles of C	1Th 2:6	5547
which in Judaea are in C Jesus	1Th 2:14	5547
of our Lord Jesus C at his coming	1Th 2:19	5547
fellowlabourer in the gospel of C	1Th 3:2	5547
our Father, and our Lord Jesus C	1Th 3:11	5547
Lord Jesus C with all his saints	1Th 3:13	5547
the dead in C shall rise first	1Th 4:16	5547
salvation by our Lord Jesus C	1Th 5:9	5547
of God in C Jesus concerning you	1Th 5:18	5547
the coming of our Lord Jesus C	1Th 5:23	5547
of our Lord Jesus C be with you	1Th 5:28	5547
our Father and the Lord Jesus C	2Th 1:1	5547
our Father and the Lord Jesus C	2Th 1:2	5547
the gospel of our Lord Jesus C	2Th 1:8	5547
Jesus C may be glorified in you	2Th 1:12	5547
of our God and the Lord Jesus C	2Th 1:12	5547
by the coming of our Lord Jesus C	2Th 2:1	5547
as that the day of C is at hand	2Th 2:2	5547
of the glory of our Lord Jesus C	2Th 2:14	5547
Now our Lord Jesus C himself	2Th 2:16	5547
and into the patient waiting for C	2Th 3:5	5547
in the name of our Lord Jesus C	2Th 3:6	5547
and exhort by our Lord Jesus C	2Th 3:12	5547
our Lord Jesus C be with you all	2Th 3:18	5547
an apostle of Jesus C by the	1Ti 1:1	5547
God our Saviour, and Lord Jesus C	1Ti 1:1	5547
our Father and Jesus C our Lord	1Ti 1:2	5547
I thank C Jesus our Lord, who	1Ti 1:12	5547
faith and love which is in C Jesus	1Ti 1:14	5547
that C Jesus came into the world	1Ti 1:15	5547
Jesus C might shew forth all	1Ti 1:16	5547
God and men, the man C Jesus	1Ti 2:5	5547
apostle, (I speak the truth in C	1Ti 2:7	5547
in the faith which is in C Jesus	1Ti 3:13	5547
be a good minister of Jesus C	1Ti 4:6	5547
begun to wax wanton against C	1Ti 5:11	5547
before God, and the Lord Jesus C	1Ti 5:21	5547
the words of our Lord Jesus C	1Ti 6:3	5547
all things, and before C Jesus	1Ti 6:13	5547
the appearing of our Lord Jesus C	1Ti 6:14	5547
of Jesus C by the will of God	2Ti 1:1	5547
of life which is in C Jesus	2Ti 1:1	5547
the Father and C Jesus our Lord	2Ti 1:2	5547
which was given us in C Jesus	2Ti 1:9	5547
appearing of our Saviour Jesus C	2Ti 1:10	5547
faith and love which is in C Jesus	2Ti 1:13	5547
in the grace that is in C Jesus	2Ti 2:1	5547
as a good soldier of Jesus C	2Ti 2:3	5547
Remember that Jesus C of the seed	2Ti 2:8	5547
is in C Jesus with eternal glory	2Ti 2:10	5547
name of C depart from iniquity	2Ti 2:19	5547
all that will live godly in C	2Ti 3:12	5547
through faith which is in C Jesus	2Ti 3:15	5547
before God, and the Lord Jesus C	2Ti 4:1	5547
The Lord Jesus C be with thy	2Ti 4:22	5547
of God, and an apostle of Jesus C	Titus 1:1	5547
and the Lord Jesus C our Saviour	Titus 1:4	5547
great God and our Saviour Jesus C	Titus 2:13	5547
through Jesus C our Saviour	Titus 3:6	5547
Paul, a prisoner of Jesus C	Philem 1	5547
our Father and the Lord Jesus C	Philem 3	5547
thing which is in you in C Jesus	Philem 6	5547
in C to enjoin thee that which is	Philem 8	5547
and now also a prisoner of Jesus C	Philem 9	5547
my fellowprisoner in C Jesus	Philem 23	5547
Lord Jesus C be with your spirit	Philem 25	5547
Priest of our profession, C Jesus	Heb 3:1	5547
But C as a son over his own house	Heb 3:6	5547
For we are made partakers of C	Heb 3:14	5547
So also C glorified not himself	Heb 5:5	5547
principles of the doctrine of C	Heb 6:1	5547
But C being come an high priest	Heb 9:11	5547
much more shall the blood of C	Heb 9:14	5547
For C is not entered into the	Heb 9:24	5547
So C was once offered to bear the	Heb 9:28	5547
the body of Jesus C once for all	Heb 10:10	5547
of C greater riches than the	Heb 11:26	5547
Jesus C the same yesterday, and to	Heb 13:8	5547
in his sight, through Jesus C	Heb 13:21	5547
of God and of the Lord Jesus C	Jas 1:1	5547
not the faith of our Lord Jesus C	Jas 2:1	5547
Peter, an apostle of Jesus C	1Pet 1:1	5547
of the blood of Jesus C	1Pet 1:2	5547
God and Father of our Lord Jesus C	1Pet 1:3	5547
of Jesus C from the dead,	1Pet 1:3	5547
glory at the appearing of Jesus C	1Pet 1:7	5547
manner of time the Spirit of C	1Pet 1:11	5547
beforehand the sufferings of C	1Pet 1:11	5547
you at the revelation of Jesus C	1Pet 1:13	5547
But with the precious blood of C	1Pet 1:19	5547
acceptable to God by Jesus C	1Pet 2:5	5547
because C also suffered for us,	1Pet 2:21	5547
your good conversation in C	1Pet 3:16	5547
For C also hath once suffered for	1Pet 3:18	5547
by the resurrection of Jesus C	1Pet 3:21	5547
Forasmuch then as C hath suffered	1Pet 4:1	5547
may be glorified through Jesus C	1Pet 4:11	5547
be reproached for the name of C	1Pet 4:14	5547
a witness of the sufferings of C	1Pet 5:1	5547
unto his eternal glory by C Jesus	1Pet 5:10	5547
with you all that are in C Jesus	1Pet 5:14	5547
servant and an apostle of Jesus C	2Pet 1:1	5547
of God and our Saviour Jesus C	2Pet 1:1	5547
the knowledge of our Lord Jesus C	2Pet 1:8	5547
of our Lord and Saviour Jesus C	2Pet 1:11	5547
our Lord Jesus C hath shewed me	2Pet 1:14	5547
and coming of our Lord Jesus C	2Pet 1:16	5547
of the Lord and Saviour Jesus C	2Pet 2:20	5547
of our Lord and Saviour Jesus C	2Pet 3:18	5547
Father, and with his Son Jesus C	1Jn 1:3	5547
the blood of Jesus C his Son	1Jn 1:7	5547
the Father, Jesus C the righteous	1Jn 2:1	5547
that denieth that Jesus is the C	1Jn 2:22	5547

on the name of his Son Jesus C 1Jn 3:23 5547
that confesseth that Jesus C is 1Jn 4:2 5547
C is come in the flesh is not of 1Jn 4:3 5547
Jesus is the C is born of God 1Jn 5:1 5547
by water and blood, even Jesus C 1Jn 5:6 5547
is true, even in his Son Jesus C 1Jn 5:20 5547
Father, and from the Lord Jesus C 2Jn 3 5547
that Jesus C is come in the flesh 2Jn 7 5547
abideth not in the doctrine of C 2Jn 9 5547
that abideth in the doctrine of C 2Jn 9 5547
Jude, the servant of Jesus C Jude 1 5547
Father, and preserved in Jesus C Jude 1 5547
Lord God, and our Lord Jesus C Jude 4 5547
the apostles of our Lord Jesus C Jude 17 5547
Lord Jesus C unto eternal life Jude 21 5547
The Revelation of Jesus C Rev 1:1 5547
and of the testimony of Jesus C Rev 1:2 5547
And from Jesus C, who is the Rev 1:5 5547
kingdom and patience of Jesus C Rev 1:9 5547
and for the testimony of Jesus C Rev 1:9 5547
kingdoms of our Lord, and of his C Rev 11:15 5547
of our God, and the power of his C Rev 12:10 5547
and have the testimony of Jesus C Rev 12:17 5547
reigned with C a thousand years Rev 20:4 5547
shall be priests of God and of C Rev 20:6 5547
our Lord Jesus C be with you all Rev 22:21 5547

CHRISTIAN (*kris'-tyan*) See CHRISTIANS. *A follower of Jesus Christ.*
thou persuadest me to be a C Acts 26:28 5546
Yet if any man suffer as a C 1Pet 4:16 5546

CHRISTIANS (*kris'-tyans*)
were called C first in Antioch Acts 11:26 5546

CHRIST'S (*krists*)
for the Lord Jesus C sake Rom 15:30 5547
And ye are C 1Cor 3:23 5547
We are fools for C sake, but ye 1Cor 4:10 5547
called, being free, is C servant 1Cor 7:22 5547
they that are C at his coming 1Cor 15:23 5547
came to Troas to preach C gospel 2Cor 2:12 5547
we pray you in C stead, be ye 2Cor 5:20 5547
man trust to himself that he is C 2Cor 10:7 5547
he is C, even so are we C 2Cor 10:7 5547
in distresses for C sake 2Cor 12:10 5547
And if ye be C, then are ye Gal 3:29 5547
they that are C have crucified Gal 5:24 5547
even as God for C sake hath Eph 4:32 5547
not the things which are Jesus C Phil 2:21 5547
ye are partakers of C sufferings 1Pet 4:13 5547

CHRISTS (*krists*)
For there shall arise false C Mt 24:24 5580
For false C and false prophets Mk 13:22 5580

CHRONICLES
of the c of the kings of Israel 1Kin 14:19 1697
of the c of the kings of Judah 1Kin 14:29 1697
of the c of the kings of Judah 1Kin 15:7 1697
of the c of the kings of Judah 1Kin 15:23 1697
of the c of the kings of Israel 1Kin 15:31 1697
of the c of the kings of Israel 1Kin 16:5 1697
of the c of the kings of Israel 1Kin 16:14 1697
of the c of the kings of Israel 1Kin 16:20 1697
of the c of the kings of Israel 1Kin 16:27 1697
of the c of the kings of Israel 1Kin 22:39 1697
of the c of the kings of Judah 1Kin 22:45 1697
of the c of the kings of Israel 2Kin 1:18 1697
of the c of the kings of Judah 2Kin 8:23 1697
of the c of the kings of Israel 2Kin 10:34 1697
of the c of the kings of Judah 2Kin 12:19 1697
of the c of the kings of Israel 2Kin 13:8 1697
of the c of the kings of Israel 2Kin 13:12 1697
of the c of the kings of Israel 2Kin 14:15 1697
of the c of the kings of Judah 2Kin 14:18 1697
of the c of the kings of Israel 2Kin 14:28 1697
of the c of the kings of Judah 2Kin 15:6 1697
of the c of the kings of Israel 2Kin 15:11 1697
of the c of the kings of Israel 2Kin 15:15 1697
of the c of the kings of Israel 2Kin 15:21 1697
of the c of the kings of Israel 2Kin 15:26 1697
of the c of the kings of Israel 2Kin 15:31 1697
of the c of the kings of Judah 2Kin 15:36 1697
of the c of the kings of Judah 2Kin 16:19 1697
of the c of the kings of Judah 2Kin 20:20 1697
of the c of the kings of Judah 2Kin 21:17 1697
of the c of the kings of Judah 2Kin 21:25 1697
of the c of the kings of Judah 2Kin 23:28 1697
of the c of the kings of Judah 2Kin 24:5 1697
account of the C of king David 1Chr 27:24 1697
were written in the book of the c Neh 12:23 1697
the book of the c before the king Est 2:23 1697
the book of records of the c Est 6:1 1697
of the c of the kings of Media Est 10:2 1697

CHRYSOLITE
the seventh, c Rev 21:20 5555

CHRYSOPRASUS
the tenth, a c Rev 21:20 5556

CHUB (*cub*) *Allies of Egypt.*
and all the mingled people, and C Eze 30:5 3552

CHUN (*kun*) *A city in Aran-zobah.*
Likewise from Tibhath, and from C 1Chr 18:8 3560

CHURCH
upon this rock I will build my c Mt 16:18 1577
to hear them, tell it unto the c Mt 18:17 1577
but if he neglect to hear the c Mt 18:17 1577
the Lord added to the c daily Acts 2:47 1577
And great fear came upon all the c Acts 5:11 1577
is he, that was in the c in the Acts 7:38 1577
the c which was at Jerusalem Acts 8:1 1577
for Saul, he made havock of the c Acts 8:3 1577
of the c which was in Jerusalem Acts 11:22 1577
assembled themselves with the c Acts 11:26 1577
his hands to vex certain of the c Acts 12:1 1577
ceasing of the c unto God for him Acts 12:5 1577
Now there were in the c that was Acts 13:1 1577
ordained them elders in every c Acts 14:23 1577
and had gathered the c together Acts 14:27 1577
brought on their way by the c Acts 15:3 1577
they were received of the c Acts 15:4 1577
and elders, with the whole c Acts 15:22 1577
and gone up, and saluted the c Acts 18:22 1577
and called the elders of the c Acts 20:17 1577
overseers, to feed the c of God Acts 20:28 1577
of the c which is at Cenchrea Rom 16:1 1577
Likewise greet the c that is in Rom 16:5 1577
mine host, and of the whole c Rom 16:23 1577
servant of the c at Cenchrea Rom *s* 1577
Unto the c of God which is at 1Cor 1:2 1577
as I teach every where in every c 1Cor 4:17 1577
who are least esteemed in the c 1Cor 6:4 1577
the Gentiles, nor to the c of God 1Cor 10:32 1577
when ye come together in the c 1Cor 11:18 1577
or despise ye the c of God 1Cor 11:22 1577
And God hath set some in the c 1Cor 12:28 1577
that prophesieth edifieth the c 1Cor 14:4 1577
that the c may receive edifying 1Cor 14:5 1577
excel to the edifying of the c 1Cor 14:12 1577
Yet in the c I had rather speak 1Cor 14:19 1577
If therefore the whole c be come 1Cor 14:23 1577
let him keep silence in the c 1Cor 14:28 1577
shame for women to speak in the c 1Cor 14:35 1577
because I persecuted the c of God 1Cor 15:9 1577
with the c that is in their house 1Cor 16:19 1577
unto the c of God which is at 2Cor 1:1 1577
measure I persecuted the c of God Gal 1:13 1577
the head over all things to the c Eph 1:22 1577
the c the manifold wisdom of God Eph 3:10 1577
Unto him be glory in the c by Eph 3:21 1577
as Christ is the head of the c Eph 5:23 1577
Therefore as the c is subject Eph 5:24 1577
even as Christ also loved the c Eph 5:25 1577
it to himself a glorious c Eph 5:27 1577
it, even as the Lord the c Eph 5:29 1577
speak concerning Christ and the c Eph 5:32 1577
zeal, persecuting the c Phil 3:6 1577
no c communicated with me as Phil 4:15 1577
he is the head of the body, the c Col 1:18 1577
his body's sake, which is the c Col 1:24 1577
the c which is in his house Col 4:15 1577
also in the c of the Laodiceans Col 4:16 1577
unto the c of the Thessalonians 1Th 1:1 1577
unto the c of the Thessalonians 2Th 1:1 1577
he take care of the c of God 1Ti 3:5 1577
which is the c of the living God 1Ti 3:15 1577
them, and let not the c be charged 1Ti 5:16 1577
bishop of the c of the Ephesians 2Ti *s* 1577
bishop of the c of the Cretians Titus *s* 1577
and to the c in thy house Philem 2 1577
in the midst of the c will I sing Heb 2:12 1577
c of the firstborn, which are Heb 12:23 1577
him call for the elders of the c Jas 5:14 1577
The c that is at Babylon, elected 1Pet 5:13 1577
of thy charity before the c 3Jn 6 1577
I wrote unto the c 3Jn 9 1577
and casteth them out of the c 3Jn 10 1577
angel of the c of Ephesus write Rev 2:1 1577
angel of the c in Smyrna write Rev 2:8 1577
angel of the c in Pergamos write Rev 2:12 1577
angel of the c in Thyatira write Rev 2:18 1577
angel of the c in Sardis write Rev 3:1 1577
And to the angel of the c in Rev 3:7 1577
unto the angel of the c of the Rev 3:14 1577

CHURCHES
Then had the c rest throughout Acts 9:31 1577
and Cilicia, confirming the c Acts 15:41 1577
so were the c established in the Acts 16:5 1577
which are neither robbers of c Acts 19:37 2417
also all the c of the Gentiles Rom 16:4 1577
The c of Christ salute you Rom 16:16 1577
And so ordain I in all c 1Cor 7:17 1577
such custom, neither the c of God 1Cor 11:16 1577
as in all c of the saints 1Cor 14:33 1577
your women keep silence in the c 1Cor 14:34 1577
given order to the c of Galatia 1Cor 16:1 1577
The c of Asia salute you 1Cor 16:19 1577
bestowed on the c of Macedonia 2Cor 8:1 1577
the gospel throughout all the c 2Cor 8:18 1577
the c to travel with us with this 2Cor 8:19 1577
they are the messengers of the c 2Cor 8:23 1577
shew ye to them, and before the c 2Cor 8:24 1577
I robbed other c, taking wages of 2Cor 11:8 1577
me daily, the care of all the c 2Cor 11:28 1577
ye were inferior to other c 2Cor 12:13 1577
with me, unto the c of Galatia Gal 1:2 1577
was unknown by face unto the c of Gal 1:22 1577
became followers of the c of God 1Th 2:14 1577
in the c of God for your patience 2Th 1:4 1577
to the seven c which are in Asia Rev 1:4 1577
the seven c which are in Asia Rev 1:11 1577
are the angels of the seven c Rev 1:20 1577
which thou sawest are the seven c Rev 1:20 1577
what the Spirit saith unto the c Rev 2:7 1577
what the Spirit saith unto the c Rev 2:11 1577
what the Spirit saith unto the c Rev 2:17 1577
all the c shall know that I am he Rev 2:23 1577
what the Spirit saith unto the c Rev 2:29 1577
what the Spirit saith unto the c Rev 3:6 1577
what the Spirit saith unto the c Rev 3:13 1577
what the Spirit saith unto the c Rev 3:22 1577
unto you these things in the c Rev 22:16 1577

CHURL
nor the c said to be bountiful Is 32:5 3596
also of the c are evil Is 32:7 3596

CHURLISH
but the man was c and evil in his 1Sa 25:3 7186

CHURNING
Surely the c of milk bringeth Prov 30:33 4330

CHUSHAN-RISHATHAIM (*cu'-shan-rish-a-tha'-im*) *A king of Mesopotamia.*
the hand of C king of Mesopotamia Judg 3:8 3573
of Israel served C eight years Judg 3:8 3573
the LORD delivered C king of Judg 3:10 3573
and his hand prevailed against C Judg 3:10 3573

CHUZA (*cu'-zah*) *A steward of Herod Antipas.*
the wife of C Herod's steward Lk 8:3 5529

CIELED
greater house he c with fir tree 2Chr 3:5 2645
it is c with cedar, and painted Jer 22:14 5603
c with wood round about, and from Eze 41:16 7824
O ye, to dwell in your c houses Hag 1:4 5603

CIELING
the house, and the walls of the c 1Kin 6:15 5604

CILICIA (*sil-ish'-yah*) *A Roman province in Asia Minor.*
and Alexandrians, and of them of C Acts 6:9 2791
Gentiles in Antioch and Syria and C Acts 15:23 2791
And he went through Syria and C Acts 15:41 2791
am a Jew of Tarsus, a city in C Acts 21:39 2791
Jew, born in Tarsus, a city in C Acts 22:3 2791
he understood that he was of C Acts 23:34 2791
we had sailed over the sea of C Acts 27:5 2791
into the regions of Syria and C Gal 1:21 2791

CINNAMON
of sweet c half so much, even two Ex 30:23 7076
my bed with myrrh, aloes, and c Prov 7:17 7076
calamus and c, with all trees of Song 4:14 7076
c, and odours, and ointments Rev 18:13 2792

CINNEROTH (*sin'-ne-roth*) See CHINNEROTH. *Same as Chinneroth.*
and Abel-beth-maachah, and all C 1Kin 15:20 3672

CIRCLE
sitteth upon the c of the earth Is 40:22 2329

CIRCUIT
from year to year in c to Beth-el 1Sa 7:16 5437
and he walketh in the c of heaven Job 22:14 2329
his c unto the ends of it Ps 19:6 8622

CIRCUITS
again according to his c Eccl 1:6 5439

CIRCUMCISE
ye shall c the flesh of your Gen 17:11 5243
C therefore the foreskin of your Deut 10:16 4135
LORD thy God will c thine heart Deut 30:6 4135
c again the children of Israel Josh 5:2 4135
is the cause why Joshua did c Josh 5:4 4135
C yourselves to the LORD, and take Jer 4:4 4135
day they came to c the child Lk 1:59 4059
and ye on the sabbath day c a man Jn 7:22 4059
That it was needful to c them Acts 15:5 4059
ought not to c their children Acts 21:21 4059

CIRCUMCISED
man child among you shall be c Gen 17:10 4135
days old shall be c among you Gen 17:12 4135
with thy money, must needs be c Gen 17:13 4135
flesh of his foreskin is not c Gen 17:14 4135
c the flesh of their foreskin in Gen 17:23 4135
when he was c in the flesh of his Gen 17:24 4135
when he was c in the flesh of his Gen 17:25 4135
In the selfsame day was Abraham c Gen 17:26 4135
of the stranger, were c with him Gen 17:27 4135
Abraham c his son Isaac being Gen 21:4 4135
be, that every male of you be c Gen 34:15 4135
will not hearken unto us, to be c Gen 34:17 4135
us be c, as they are c Gen 34:22 4135
and every male was c, all that Gen 34:24 4135
for money, when thou hast c him Ex 12:44 4135
the LORD, let all his males be c Ex 12:48 4135
flesh of his foreskin shall be c Lev 12:3 4135
c the children of Israel at the Josh 5:3 4135
the people that came out were c Josh 5:5 4135
out of Egypt, them they had not c Josh 5:5 4135
up in their stead, them Joshua c Josh 5:7 4135
they had not c them by the way Josh 5:7 4135
are c with the uncircumcised Jer 9:25 4135
Isaac, and c him the eighth day Acts 7:8 4059
Except ye be c after the manner Acts 15:1 4059
your souls, saying, Ye must be c Acts 15:24 4059
c him because of the Jews which Acts 16:3 4059
believe, though they be not c Rom 4:11 203
Is any man called being c 1Cor 7:18 4059
let him not be c 1Cor 7:18 4059
a Greek, was compelled to be c Gal 2:3 4059
say unto you, that if ye be c Gal 5:2 4059
again to every man that is c Gal 5:3 4059
flesh, they constrain you to be c Gal 6:12 4059
themselves who are c keep the law Gal 6:13 4059
but desire to have you c, that Gal 6:13 4059
C the eighth day, of the stock of Phil 3:5 4061
In whom also ye are c with the Col 2:11 4059

CIRCUMCISING
they had done c all the people Josh 5:8 4135
for the c of the child, his name Lk 2:21 4059

CIRCUMCISION
thou art, because of the c Ex 4:26 4139
Moses therefore gave unto you c Jn 7:22 4061
man on the sabbath day receive c Jn 7:23 4061
And he gave him the covenant of c Acts 7:8 4061
they of the c which believed were Acts 10:45 4061
were of the c contended with him Acts 11:2 4061
For c verily profiteth, if thou Rom 2:25 4061

C

thy c is made uncircumcision Rom 2:25 *4061*
uncircumcision be counted for c Rom 2:26 *4061*
c dost transgress the law Rom 2:27 *4061*
neither is that c, which is Rom 2:28 *4061*
c is that of the heart, in the Rom 2:29 *4061*
or what profit is there of c Rom 3:1 *4061*
shall justify the c by faith Rom 3:30 *4061*
blessedness then upon the c only Rom 4:9 *4061*
when he was in c, or in Rom 4:10 *4061*
Not in c, but in uncircumcision Rom 4:10 *4061*
And he received the sign of c Rom 4:11 *4061*
the father of c to them who are Rom 4:12 *4061*
to them who are not of the c only Rom 4:12 *4061*
of the c for the truth of God Rom 15:8 *4061*
C is nothing, and uncircumcision 1Cor 7:19 *4061*
gospel of the c was unto Peter Gal 2:7 *4061*
Peter to the apostleship of the c Gal 2:8 *4061*
the heathen, and they unto the c Gal 2:9 *4061*
fearing them which were of the c Gal 2:12 *4061*
neither c availeth any thing Gal 5:6 *4061*
And I, brethren, if I yet preach c Gal 5:11 *4061*
neither c availeth any thing Gal 6:15 *4061*
the C in the flesh made by hands Eph 2:11 *4061*
For we are the c, which worship Phil 3:3 *4061*
with the c made without hands Col 2:11 *4061*
of the flesh by the c of Christ Col 2:11 *4061*
c nor uncircumcision, Barbarian, Col 3:11 *4061*
called Justus, who are of the c Col 4:11 *4061*
specially they of the c Titus 1:10 *4061*

CIRCUMSPECT
that I have said unto you be c Ex 23:13 8104

CIRCUMSPECTLY
See then that ye walk c, not as Eph 5:15 *199*

CIS (*sis*) See KISH. *Father of King Saul.*
gave unto them Saul the son of C Acts 13:21 *2797*

CISTERN
ye every one the waters of his c 2Kin 18:31 953
Drink waters out of thine own c Prov 5:15 953
or the wheel broken at the c Eccl 12:6 953
every one the waters of his own c Is 36:16 953

CISTERNS
hewed them out c, broken c Jer 2:13 877

CITIES
Lot dwelled in the c of the plain Gen 13:12 5892
And he overthrew those c, and all Gen 19:25 5892
and all the inhabitants of the c Gen 19:25 5892
God destroyed the c of the plain Gen 19:29 5892
when he overthrew the c in the Gen 19:29 5892
the c that were round about them Gen 35:5 5892
and let them keep food in the c Gen 41:35 5892
and laid up the food in the c Gen 41:48 5892
he removed them to c from one end Gen 47:21 5892
they built for Pharaoh treasure c Ex 1:11 5892
the c of the Levites, and the Lev 25:32 5892
the houses of the c of their Lev 25:32 5892
for the houses of the c of the Lev 25:33 5892
of their c may not be sold Lev 25:34 5892
gathered together within your c Lev 26:25 5892
And I will make your c waste Lev 26:31 5892
be desolate, and your c waste Lev 26:33 5892
what c they be that they dwell in Num 13:19 5892
the c are walled, and very great Num 13:28 5892
I will utterly destroy their c Num 21:2 5892
utterly destroyed them and their c Num 21:3 5892
And Israel took all these c Num 21:25 5892
in all the c of the Amorites Num 21:25 5892
all their c wherein they dwelt Num 31:10 5892
cattle, and c for our little ones Num 32:16 5892
c because of the inhabitants of Num 32:17 5892
Build you c for your little ones Num 32:24 5892
shall be there in the c of Gilead Num 32:26 5892
with the c thereof in the coasts, Num 32:33 5892
even the c of the country round Num 32:33 5892
and Beth-haran, fenced c Num 32:36 5892
unto the c which they builded Num 32:38 5892
of their possession c to dwell in Num 35:2 5892
for the c round about them Num 35:2 5892
the c shall they have to dwell in Num 35:3 5892
And the suburbs of the c, which ye Num 35:4 5892
be to them the suburbs of the c Num 35:5 5892
among the c which ye shall give Num 35:6 5892
there shall be six c for refuge Num 35:6 5892
them ye shall add forty and two c Num 35:6 5892
So all the c which ye shall give Num 35:7 5892
Levites shall be forty and eight c Num 35:7 5892
the c which ye shall give shall Num 35:8 5892
every one shall give of his c Num 35:8 5892
c to be c of refuge for you Num 35:11 5892
they shall be unto you c for Num 35:12 5892
of these c which ye shall give Num 35:13 5892
six c shall ye have for refuge Num 35:13 5892
give three c on this side Jordan Num 35:14 5892
three c shall ye give in the land Num 35:14 5892
which shall be c of refuge Num 35:14 5892
These six c shall be a refuge, Num 35:15 5892
into what c we shall come Deut 1:22 5892
the c are great and walled up to Deut 1:28 5892
And we took all his c at that time Deut 2:34 5892
the spoil of the c which we took Deut 2:35 5892
nor unto the c in the mountains, Deut 2:37 5892
And we took all his c at that time Deut 3:4 5892
took not from them, threescore c Deut 3:4 5892
All these c were fenced with high Deut 3:5 5892
the cattle, and the spoil of the c Deut 3:7 5892
All the c of the plain, and all Deut 3:10 5892
c of the kingdom of Og in Bashan Deut 3:10 5892
the c thereof, gave I unto the Deut 3:12 5892
shall abide in your c which I Deut 3:19 5892
Then Moses severed three c on Deut 4:41 5892
unto one of these c he might live Deut 4:42 5892
to give thee great and goodly c Deut 6:10 5892
c great and fenced up to heaven, Deut 9:1 5892
shalt hear say in one of thy c Deut 13:12 5892
them, and dwellest in their c Deut 19:1 5892
Thou shalt separate three c for Deut 19:2 5892
he shall flee unto one of those c Deut 19:5 5892
shalt separate three c for thee Deut 19:7 5892
thou add three c more for thee Deut 19:9 5892
and fleeth into one of these c Deut 19:11 5892
the c which are very far off from Deut 20:15 5892
are not of the c of these nations Deut 20:15 5892
But of the c of these people, Deut 20:16 5892
they shall measure unto the c Deut 21:2 5892
came unto their c on the third Josh 9:17 5892
Now their c were Gibeon, and Josh 9:17 5892
great city, as one of the royal c Josh 10:2 5892
them not to enter into their c Josh 10:19 5892
of them entered into fenced c Josh 10:20 5892
thereof, and all the c thereof Josh 10:37 5892
thereof, and all the c thereof Josh 10:39 5892
all the c of those kings, and all Josh 11:12 5892
But as for the c that stood still Josh 11:13 5892
And all the spoil of these c Josh 11:14 5892
them utterly with their c Josh 11:21 5892
all the c of Sihon king of the Josh 13:10 5892
all her c that are in the plain Josh 13:17 5892
all the c of the plain, and all Josh 13:21 5892
after their families, the c Josh 13:23 5892
all the c of Gilead, and half the Josh 13:25 5892
Gad after their families, the c Josh 13:28 5892
which are in Bashan, threescore c Josh 13:30 5892
c of the kingdom of Og in Bashan, Josh 13:31 5892
save c to dwell in, with their Josh 14:4 5892
that the c were great and fenced Josh 14:12 5892
went out to the c of mount Ephron Josh 15:9 5892
the uttermost c of the tribe of Josh 15:21 5892
all the c are twenty and nine, Josh 15:32 5892
fourteen c with their villages Josh 15:36 5892
sixteen c with their villages Josh 15:41 5892
nine c with their villages Josh 15:44 5892
eleven c with their villages Josh 15:51 5892
nine c with their villages Josh 15:54 5892
ten c with their villages Josh 15:57 5892
six c with their villages Josh 15:59 5892
two c with their villages Josh 15:60 5892
six c with their villages Josh 15:62 5892
the separate c for the children Josh 16:9 5892
all the c with their villages Josh 16:9 5892
these c of Ephraim are among the Josh 17:9 5892
are among the c of Manasseh Josh 17:9 5892
out the inhabitants of those c Josh 17:12 5892
described it by c into seven Josh 18:9 5892
Now the c of the tribe of the Josh 18:21 5892
twelve c with their villages Josh 18:24 5892
fourteen c with their villages Josh 18:28 5892
thirteen c and their villages Josh 19:6 5892
four c and their villages Josh 19:7 5892
about these c to Baalath-beer Josh 19:8 5892
twelve c with their villages Josh 19:15 5892
these c with their villages Josh 19:16 5892
sixteen c with their villages Josh 19:22 5892
to their families, the c and their Josh 19:23 5892
two c with their villages Josh 19:30 5892
these c with their villages Josh 19:31 5892
And the fenced c are Ziddim Josh 19:35 5892
nineteen c with their villages Josh 19:38 5892
to their families, the c and their Josh 19:39 5892
these c with their villages Josh 19:48 5892
Appoint out for you c of refuge Josh 20:2 5892
doth flee unto one of those c Josh 20:4 5892
These were the c appointed for Josh 20:9 5892
of Moses to give us c to dwell in Josh 21:2 5892
commandment of the LORD, these c Josh 21:3 5892
the tribe of Benjamin, thirteen c Josh 21:4 5892
the half tribe of Manasseh, ten c Josh 21:5 5892
of Manasseh in Bashan, thirteen c Josh 21:6 5892
of the tribe of Zebulun, twelve c Josh 21:7 5892
these c with their suburbs Josh 21:8 5892
these c which are here mentioned Josh 21:9 5892
nine c out of those two tribes Josh 21:16 5892
four c Josh 21:18 5892
All the c of the children of Josh 21:19 5892
were thirteen c with their Josh 21:19 5892
even they had the c of their lot Josh 21:20 5892
Beth-horon with her suburbs; four c Josh 21:22 5892
Gath-rimmon with her suburbs; four c Josh 21:24 5892
Gath-rimmon with her suburbs; two c. Josh 21:25 5892
All the c were ten with their Josh 21:26 5892
Beesh-terah with her suburbs; two c Josh 21:27 5892
En-gannim with her suburbs; four c Josh 21:29 5892
Rehob with her suburbs; four c Josh 21:31 5892
Kartan with her suburbs; three c Josh 21:32 5892
All the c of the Gershonites Josh 21:33 5892
thirteen c with their suburbs Josh 21:33 5892
Nahalal with her suburbs; four c Josh 21:35 5892
Mephaath with her suburbs; four c Josh 21:37 5892
four c in all Josh 21:39 5892
So all the c for the children of Josh 21:40 5892
were by their lot twelve c Josh 21:40 5892
All the c of the Levites within Josh 21:41 5892
eight c with their suburbs Josh 21:41 5892
These c were every one with their Josh 21:42 5892
thus were all these c Josh 21:42 5892
c which ye built not, and ye dwell Josh 24:13 5892
ass colts, and they had thirty c Judg 10:4 5892
in all the c that be along by the Judg 11:26 5892
come to Minnith, even twenty c Judg 11:33 5892
buried in one of the c of Gilead Judg 12:7 5892
together out of the c unto Gibeah Judg 20:14 5892
at that time out of the c twenty Judg 20:15 5892
them which came out of the c they Judg 20:42 5892
fire all the c that they came to Judg 20:48 5892
inheritance, and repaired the c Judg 21:23 5892
to the number of all the c of the 1Sa 6:18 5892
the five lords, both of fenced c 1Sa 6:18 5892
the c which the Philistines had 1Sa 7:14 5892
women came out of all c of Israel 1Sa 18:6 5892
in the c of the Jerahmeelites 1Sa 30:29 5892
were in the c of the Kenites 1Sa 30:29 5892
were dead, they forsook the c 1Sa 31:7 5892
go up into any of the c of Judah 2Sa 2:1 5892
and they dwelt in the c of Hebron 2Sa 2:3 5892
c of Hadadezer, king David took 2Sa 8:8 5892
people, and for the c of our God 2Sa 10:12 5892
the c of the children of Ammon 2Sa 12:31 5892
him, lest he get him fenced c 2Sa 20:6 5892
to all the c of the Hivites, and 2Sa 24:7 5892
threescore great c with walls 1Kin 4:13 5892
them in the land of their c 1Kin 8:37 8179
twenty c in the land of Galilee 1Kin 9:11 5892
the c which Solomon had given him 1Kin 9:12 5892
What c are these which thou hast 1Kin 9:13 5892
all the c of store that Solomon 1Kin 9:19 5892
c for his chariots 1Kin 9:19 5892
c for his horsemen, and that which 1Kin 9:19 5892
he bestowed in the c for chariots 1Kin 10:26 5892
which dwelt in the c of Judah 1Kin 12:17 5892
which are in the c of Samaria 1Kin 13:32 5892
he had against the c of Israel 1Kin 15:20 5892
the c which he built, are they 1Kin 15:23 5892
And Ben-hadad said unto him, The c 1Kin 20:34 5892
all the c that he built, are they 1Kin 22:39 5892
And they beat down the c, and on 2Kin 3:25 5892
Ben-hadad the son of Hazael the c 2Kin 13:25 5892
him, and recovered the c of Israel 2Kin 13:25 5892
Gozan, and in the c of the Medes 2Kin 17:6 5892
them high places in all their c 2Kin 17:9 5892
placed them in the c of Samaria 2Kin 17:24 5892
and dwelt in the c thereof 2Kin 17:24 5892
and placed in the c of Samaria 2Kin 17:26 5892
in their c wherein they dwelt 2Kin 17:29 5892
Gozan, and in the c of the Medes 2Kin 18:11 5892
against all the fenced c of Judah 2Kin 18:13 5892
waste fenced c into ruinous heaps 2Kin 19:25 5892
the high places in the c of Judah 2Kin 23:5 5892
the priests out of the c of Judah 2Kin 23:8 5892
that were in the c of Samaria 2Kin 23:19 5892
twenty c in the land of Gilead 1Chr 2:22 5892
towns thereof, even threescore c 1Chr 2:23 5892
These were their c unto the reign 1Chr 4:31 5892
and Tochen, and Ashan, five c 1Chr 4:32 5892
that were round about the same c 1Chr 4:33 5892
of Aaron they gave the c of Judah 1Chr 6:57 5892
All their c throughout their 1Chr 6:60 5892
their families were thirteen c 1Chr 6:60 5892
were c given out of the half 1Chr 6:61
tribe of Manasseh, by lot, ten c 1Chr 6:61 5892
of Manasseh in Bashan, thirteen c 1Chr 6:62 5892
of the tribe of Zebulun, twelve c 1Chr 6:63 5892
these c with their suburbs 1Chr 6:64 5892
the children of Benjamin, these c 1Chr 6:65 5892
of the sons of Kohath had c of 1Chr 6:66 5892
of the c of refuge, Shechem in 1Chr 6:67 5892
their possessions in their c were 1Chr 9:2 5892
dead, then they forsook their c 1Chr 10:7 5892
and Levites which are in their c 1Chr 13:2 5892
c of Hadarezer, brought David 1Chr 18:8 5892
themselves together from their c 1Chr 19:7 5892
people, and for the c of our God 1Chr 19:13 5892
the c of the children of Ammon 1Chr 20:3 5892
in the fields, in the c, and in 1Chr 27:25 5892
which he placed in the chariot c 2Chr 1:14 5892
them in the c of their land 2Chr 6:28 8179
That the c which Huram had 2Chr 8:2 5892
wilderness, and all the store c 2Chr 8:4 5892
Beth-horon the nether, fenced c 2Chr 8:5 5892
all the store c that Solomon had, 2Chr 8:6 5892
and all the chariot c 2Chr 8:6 5892
the c of the horsemen, and all 2Chr 8:6 5892
whom he bestowed in the chariot c 2Chr 9:25 5892
that dwelt in the c of Judah 2Chr 10:17 5892
built c for defence in Judah 2Chr 11:5 5892
in Judah and in Benjamin fenced c 2Chr 11:10 5892
he took the fenced c which 2Chr 12:4 5892
took c from him, Beth-el with the 2Chr 13:19 5892
the c of Judah the high places 2Chr 14:5 5892
And he built fenced c in Judah 2Chr 14:6 5892
unto Judah, Let us build these c 2Chr 14:7 5892
smote all the c round about Gerar 2Chr 14:14 5892
and they spoiled all the c 2Chr 14:14 5892
out of the c which he had taken 2Chr 15:8 5892
armies against the c of Israel 2Chr 16:4 5892
and all the store c of Naphtali 2Chr 16:4 5892
in all the fenced c of Judah 2Chr 17:2 5892
in the c of Ephraim, which Asa 2Chr 17:2 5892
to teach in the c of Judah 2Chr 17:7 5892
throughout all the c of Judah 2Chr 17:9 5892
in Judah castles, and c of store 2Chr 17:12 5892
much business in the c of Judah 2Chr 17:13 5892
the fenced c throughout all Judah 2Chr 17:19 5892
all the fenced c of Judah 2Chr 19:5 5892
brethren that dwell in their c 2Chr 19:10 5892
even out of all the c of Judah 2Chr 20:4 5892
things, with fenced c in Judah 2Chr 21:3 5892
Levites out of all the c of Judah 2Chr 23:2 5892
them, Go out unto the c of Judah 2Chr 24:5 5892
battle, fell upon the c of Judah 2Chr 25:13 5892
built c about Ashdod, and among 2Chr 26:6 5892
Moreover he built c in the 2Chr 27:4 5892
invaded the c of the low country 2Chr 28:18 5892
went out to the c of Judah 2Chr 31:1 5892
his possession, into their own c 2Chr 31:1 5892
that dwelt in the c of Judah 2Chr 31:6 5892
in the c of the priests, in their 2Chr 31:15 5892
fields of the suburbs of their c 2Chr 31:19 5892
and encamped against the fenced c 2Chr 32:1 5892
Moreover he provided him c 2Chr 32:29 5892
war in all the fenced c of Judah 2Chr 33:14 5892
And so did he in the c of Manasseh 2Chr 34:6 5892

the Nethinims, dwelt in their c	Ezr 2:70	5892
and all Israel in their c	Ezr 2:70	5892
children of Israel were in the c	Ezr 3:1	5892
over, and set in the c of Samaria	Ezr 4:10	7141
in our c come at appointed times	Ezr 10:14	5892
and all Israel, dwelt in their c	Neh 7:73	5892
of Israel were in their c	Neh 7:73	5892
and proclaim in all their c	Neh 8:15	5892
And they took strong c, and a fat	Neh 9:25	5892
in all the c of our tillage	Neh 10:37	5892
and nine parts to dwell in other c	Neh 11:1	5892
but in the c of Judah dwelt every	Neh 11:3	5892
one in his possession in their c	Neh 11:3	5892
were in all the c of Judah	Neh 11:20	5892
them out of the fields of the c	Neh 12:44	5892
themselves together in their c	Est 9:2	5892
And he dwelleth in desolate c	Job 15:28	5892
and thou hast destroyed c	Ps 9:6	5892
and will build the c of Judah	Ps 69:35	5892
your c are burned with fire	Is 1:7	5892
Until the c be wasted without	Is 6:11	5892
and destroyed the c thereof	Is 14:17	5892
fill the face of the world with c	Is 14:21	5892
The c of Aroer are forsaken	Is 17:2	5892
strong c be as a forsaken bough	Is 17:9	5892
In that day shall five c in the	Is 19:18	5892
covenant, he hath despised the c	Is 33:8	5892
all the defenced c of Judah	Is 36:1	5892
defenced c into ruinous heaps	Is 37:26	5892
say unto the c of Judah, Behold	Is 40:9	5892
the c thereof lift up their voice	Is 42:11	5892
to the c of Judah, Ye shall be	Is 44:26	5892
the desolate c to be inhabited	Is 54:3	5892
and they shall repair the waste c	Is 61:4	5892
Thy holy c are a wilderness, Zion	Is 64:10	5892
and against all the c of Judah	Jer 1:15	5892
his c are burned without	Jer 2:15	5892
the number of thy c are thy gods	Jer 2:28	5892
and let us go into the defenced c	Jer 4:5	5892
thy c shall be laid waste,	Jer 4:7	5892
voice against the c of Judah	Jer 4:16	5892
all the c thereof were broken	Jer 4:26	5892
leopard shall watch over their c	Jer 5:6	5892
shall impoverish thy fenced c	Jer 5:17	5892
what they do in the c of Judah	Jer 7:17	5892
to cease from the c of Judah	Jer 7:34	5892
let us enter into the defenced c	Jer 8:14	5892
I will make the c of Judah	Jer 9:11	5892
to make the c of Judah desolate,	Jer 10:22	5892
all these words in the c of Judah,	Jer 11:6	5892
Then shall the c of Judah	Jer 11:12	5892
the number of thy c were thy gods	Jer 11:13	5892
The c of the south shall be shut	Jer 13:19	5892
shall come from the c of Judah	Jer 17:26	5892
let that man be as the c which	Jer 20:16	5892
c which are not inhabited	Jer 22:6	5892
the c of Judah, and the kings	Jer 25:18	5892
and speak unto all the c of Judah	Jer 26:2	5892
Israel, turn again to these thy c	Jer 31:21	5892
in the c thereof, when I shall	Jer 31:23	5892
in all the c thereof together,	Jer 31:24	5892
in the c of Judah	Jer 32:44	5892
in the c of the mountains	Jer 32:44	5892
in the c of the valley	Jer 32:44	5892
and in the c of the south	Jer 32:44	5892
beast, even in the c of Judah	Jer 33:10	5892
beast, and in all the c thereof	Jer 33:12	5892
In the c of the mountains	Jer 33:13	5892
in the c of the vale	Jer 33:13	5892
in the c of the south	Jer 33:13	5892
in the c of Judah, shall the	Jer 33:13	5892
and against all the c thereof	Jer 34:1	5892
against all the c of Judah that	Jer 34:7	5892
c remained of the c of Judah	Jer 34:7	5892
I will make the c of Judah a	Jer 34:22	5892
Judah that come out of their c	Jer 36:6	5892
the c of Judah unto Jerusalem	Jer 36:9	5892
made governor over the c of Judah	Jer 40:5	5892
dwell in your c that ye have	Jer 40:10	5892
and upon all the c of Judah	Jer 44:2	5892
and was kindled in the c of Judah	Jer 44:6	5892
in the c of Judah, and in the	Jer 44:17	5892
that ye burned in the c of Judah	Jer 44:21	5892
for the c thereof shall be	Jer 48:9	5892
spoiled, and gone up out of her c	Jer 48:15	5892
upon all the c of the land of	Jer 48:24	5892
that dwell in Moab, leave the c	Jer 48:28	5892
Gad, and his people dwell in his c	Jer 49:1	5892
all the c thereof shall be	Jer 49:13	5892
and the neighbour c thereof	Jer 49:18	5892
and I will kindle a fire in his c	Jer 50:32	5892
and the neighbour c thereof	Jer 50:40	5892
Her c are a desolation, a dry	Jer 51:43	5892
and the maids in the c of Judah	Lam 5:11	5892
the c shall be laid waste	Eze 6:6	5892
the c that are inhabited shall be	Eze 12:20	5892
palaces, and he laid waste their c	Eze 19:7	5892
open the side of Moab from the c	Eze 25:9	5892
from his c which are on his	Eze 25:9	5892
like the c that are not inhabited	Eze 26:19	5892
her c among the c that are	Eze 29:12	5892
her c shall be in the midst of	Eze 30:7	5892
midst of the c that are wasted	Eze 30:7	5892
these c shall go into captivity	Eze 30:17	5892
I will lay thy c waste, and thou	Eze 35:4	5892
and thy c shall not return	Eze 35:9	5892
to the c that are forsaken, which	Eze 36:4	5892
the c shall be inhabited, and the	Eze 36:10	5892
also cause you to dwell in the c	Eze 36:33	5892
ruined c are become fenced, and	Eze 36:35	5892
so shall the waste c be filled	Eze 36:38	5892
they that dwell in the c of	Eze 39:9	5892
mount, and take the most fenced c	Dan 11:15	5892
and Judah hath multiplied fenced c	Hos 8:14	5892
but I will send a fire upon his c	Hos 8:14	5892
And the sword shall abide on his c	Hos 11:6	5892
that may save thee in all thy c	Hos 13:10	5892
cleanness of teeth in all your c	Amos 4:6	5892
So two or three c wandered unto	Amos 4:8	5892
and they shall build the waste c	Amos 9:14	5892
shall possess the c of the south	Obad 20	5892
I will cut off the c of thy land	Mic 5:11	5892
so will I destroy thy c	Mic 5:14	5892
Assyria, and from the fortified c	Mic 7:12	5892
and alarm against the fenced c	Zeph 1:16	5892
their c are destroyed, so that	Zeph 3:6	5892
on the c of Judah, against which	Zec 1:12	5892
My c through prosperity shall yet	Zec 1:17	5892
the c thereof round about her,	Zec 7:7	5892
and the inhabitants of many c	Zec 8:20	5892
And Jesus went about all the c	Mt 9:35	*4172*
have gone over the c of Israel	Mt 10:23	*4172*
to teach and to preach in their c	Mt 11:1	*4172*
the c wherein most of his mighty	Mt 11:20	*4172*
followed him on foot out of the c	Mt 14:13	*4172*
and ran afoot thither out of all c	Mk 6:33	*4172*
he entered, into villages, or c	Mk 6:56	*4172*
kingdom of God to other c also	Lk 4:43	*4172*
And he went through the c and	Lk 13:22	*4172*
have thou authority over ten c	Lk 19:17	*4172*
to him, Be thou also over five c	Lk 19:19	*4172*
the c round about unto Jerusalem	Acts 5:16	*4172*
through he preached in all the c	Acts 8:40	*4172*
c of Lycaonia, and unto the region	Acts 14:6	*4172*
And as they went through the c	Acts 16:4	*4172*
them even unto strange c	Acts 26:11	*4172*
And turning the c of Sodom	2Pet 2:6	*4172*
the c about them in like manner,	Jude 7	*4172*
the c of the nations fell	Rev 16:19	*4172*

CITIZEN

himself to a c of that country	Lk 15:15	*4177*
in Cilicia, a c of no mean city	Acts 21:39	*4177*

CITIZENS

But his c hated him, and sent a	Lk 19:14	*4177*

CITY

and he builded a c	Gen 4:17	5892
and called the name of the c	Gen 4:17	5892
the c Rehoboth, and Calah,	Gen 10:11	5892
the same is a great c	Gen 10:12	5892
said, Go to, let us build us a c	Gen 11:4	5892
the LORD came down to see the c	Gen 11:5	5892
and they left off to build the c	Gen 11:8	5892
be fifty righteous within the c	Gen 18:24	5892
fifty righteous within the c	Gen 18:26	5982
all the c for lack of five	Gen 18:28	5892
they lay down, the men of the c	Gen 19:4	5892
and whatsoever thou hast in the c	Gen 19:12	5892
for the LORD will destroy this c	Gen 19:14	5892
consumed in the iniquity of the c	Gen 19:15	5892
forth, and set him without the c	Gen 19:16	5892
this c is near to flee unto, and	Gen 19:20	5892
that I will not overthrow this c	Gen 19:21	5892
the name of the c was called Zoar	Gen 19:22	5892
that went in at the gate of his c	Gen 23:10	5892
that went in at the gate of his c	Gen 23:18	5892
Mesopotamia, unto the c of Nahor	Gen 24:10	5892
to kneel down without the c by a	Gen 24:11	5892
of the c come out to draw water	Gen 24:13	5892
therefore the name of the c is	Gen 26:33	5892
but the name of that c was called	Gen 28:19	5892
a c of Shechem, which is in the	Gen 33:18	5892
and pitched his tent before the c	Gen 33:18	5892
son came unto the gate of their c	Gen 34:20	5892
communed with the men of their c	Gen 34:20	5892
went out of the gate of his c	Gen 34:24	5892
went out of the gate of his c	Gen 34:24	5892
sword, and came upon the c boldly	Gen 34:25	5892
upon the slain, and spoiled the c	Gen 34:27	5892
asses, and that which was in the c	Gen 34:28	5892
unto Mamre, unto the c of Arbah	Gen 35:27	7151
and the name of his c was Dinhabah	Gen 36:32	5892
and the name of his c was Avith	Gen 36:35	5892
and the name of his c was Pau	Gen 36:39	5892
which was round about every c	Gen 41:48	5892
when they were gone out of the c	Gen 44:4	5892
man his ass, and returned to the c	Gen 44:13	5892
As soon as I am gone out of the c	Ex 9:29	5892
went out of the c from Pharaoh	Ex 9:33	5892
an unclean place without the c	Lev 14:40	5892
the c into an unclean place	Lev 14:41	5892
of the c into an unclean place	Lev 14:45	5892
out of the c into the open fields	Lev 14:53	5892
a dwelling house in a walled c	Lev 25:29	5892
c shall be established for ever	Lev 25:30	5892
the c of his possession, shall go	Lev 25:33	5892
a c in the uttermost of thy	Num 20:16	5892
For Heshbon was the c of Sihon	Num 21:26	5892
let the c of Sihon be built and	Num 21:27	5892
a flame from the c of Sihon	Num 21:28	7151
out to meet him unto a c of Moab	Num 22:36	5892
him that remaineth of the c	Num 24:19	5892
reach from the wall of the c	Num 35:4	5892
c on the east side two thousand	Num 35:5	5892
the c shall be in the midst	Num 35:5	5892
him to the c of his refuge	Num 35:25	5892
the border of the c of his refuge	Num 35:26	5892
borders of the c of his refuge	Num 35:27	5892
c of his refuge until the death	Num 35:28	5892
is fled to the c of his refuge	Num 35:32	5892
and the little ones, of every c	Deut 2:34	5892
from the c that is by the river,	Deut 2:36	5892
was not one c too strong for us	Deut 2:36	7151
there was not a c which we took	Deut 3:4	7151
women, and children, of every c	Deut 3:6	5892
the inhabitants of their c	Deut 13:13	5892
that c with the edge of the sword	Deut 13:15	5892
and shalt burn with fire the c	Deut 13:16	5892
the elders of his c shall send	Deut 19:12	5892
nigh unto a c to fight against it	Deut 20:10	5892
cattle, and all that is in the c	Deut 20:14	5892
shalt besiege a c a long time	Deut 20:19	5892
the c that maketh war with thee	Deut 20:20	5892
that the c which is next unto the	Deut 21:3	5892
of that c shall take an heifer	Deut 21:3	5892
the elders of that c shall bring	Deut 21:4	5892
And all the elders of that c	Deut 21:6	5892
him out unto the elders of his c	Deut 21:19	5892
say unto the elders of his c	Deut 21:20	5892
all the men of his c shall stone	Deut 21:21	5892
the elders of the c in the gate	Deut 22:15	5892
cloth before the elders of the c	Deut 22:17	5892
the elders of that c shall take	Deut 22:18	5892
the men of her c shall stone her	Deut 22:21	5892
and a man find her in the c	Deut 22:23	5892
both out unto the gate of that c	Deut 22:24	5892
she cried not, being in the c	Deut 22:24	5892
elders of his c shall call him	Deut 25:8	5892
Blessed shalt thou be in the c	Deut 28:3	5892
Cursed shalt thou be in the c	Deut 28:16	5892
the c of palm trees, unto Zoar	Deut 34:3	5892
an heap very far from the c Adam	Josh 3:16	5892
And ye shall compass the c	Josh 6:3	5892
war, and go round about the c once	Josh 6:3	5892
shall compass the c seven times	Josh 6:4	5892
the wall of the c shall fall down	Josh 6:5	5892
people, Pass on, and compass the c	Josh 6:7	5892
ark of the LORD compassed the c	Josh 6:11	5892
day they compassed the c once	Josh 6:14	5892
compassed the c after the same	Josh 6:15	5892
they compassed the c seven times	Josh 6:15	5892
for the LORD hath given you the c	Josh 6:16	5892
the c shall be accursed, even it,	Josh 6:17	5892
the people went up into the c	Josh 6:20	5892
before him, and they took the c	Josh 6:20	5892
destroyed all that was in the c	Josh 6:21	5892
And they burnt the c with fire	Josh 6:24	5892
up and buildeth this c Jericho	Josh 6:26	5892
of Ai, and his people, and his c	Josh 8:1	5892
an ambush for the c behind it	Josh 8:2	5892
the c, even behind the c	Josh 8:4	5892
go not very far from the c	Josh 8:4	5892
with me, will approach unto the c	Josh 8:5	5892
we have drawn them from the c	Josh 8:6	5892
the ambush, and seize upon the c	Josh 8:7	5892
be, when ye have taken the c	Josh 8:8	5892
that ye shall set the c on fire	Josh 8:8	5892
drew nigh, and came before the c	Josh 8:11	5892
and Ai, on the west side of the c	Josh 8:12	5892
that was on the north of the c	Josh 8:13	5892
in wait on the west of the c	Josh 8:13	5892
the men of the c went out against	Josh 8:14	5892
ambush against him behind the c	Josh 8:14	5892
and were drawn away from the c	Josh 8:16	5892
and they left the c open, and	Josh 8:17	5892
he had in his hand toward the c	Josh 8:18	5892
and they entered into the c	Josh 8:19	5892
and hasted and set the c on fire	Josh 8:19	5892
the smoke of the c ascended up to	Josh 8:20	5892
that the ambush had taken the c	Josh 8:21	5892
that the smoke of the c ascended	Josh 8:21	5892
issued out of the c against them	Josh 8:22	5892
the spoil of that c Israel took	Josh 8:27	5892
the entering of the gate of the c	Josh 8:29	5892
because Gibeon was a great c	Josh 10:2	5892
There was not a c that made peace	Josh 11:19	5892
the c that is in the midst of the	Josh 13:9	5892
the c that is in the midst of the	Josh 13:16	5892
even the c of Arba the father of	Josh 15:13	7151
father of Anak, which c is Hebron	Josh 15:13	
the c of Salt, and En-gedi	Josh 15:62	5892
a c of the children of Judah	Josh 18:14	5892
to Ramah, and to the strong c Tyre	Josh 19:29	5892
gave him the c which he asked	Josh 19:50	5892
and he built the c, and dwelt	Josh 19:50	5892
the entering of the gate of the c	Josh 20:4	5892
the ears of the elders of that c	Josh 20:4	5892
take him into the c unto them	Josh 20:4	5892
And he shall dwell in that c	Josh 20:6	5892
return, and come unto his own c	Josh 20:6	5892
unto the c from whence he fled	Josh 20:6	5892
they gave them the c of Arba the	Josh 21:11	7151
which c is Hebron, in the hill	Josh 21:11	
But the fields of the c, and the	Josh 21:12	5892
to be a c of refuge for the	Josh 21:13	5892
to be a c of refuge for the	Josh 21:21	5892
to be a c of refuge for the	Josh 21:27	5892
to be a c of refuge for the	Josh 21:32	5892
to be a c of refuge for the	Josh 21:38	5892
the sword, and set the c on fire	Judg 1:8	5892
went up out of the c of palm	Judg 1:16	5892
the name of the c was called	Judg 1:17	5892
the name of the c before was Luz	Judg 1:23	5892
saw a man come forth out of the c	Judg 1:24	5892
thee, the entrance into the c	Judg 1:24	5892
them the entrance into the c	Judg 1:25	5892
they smote the c with the edge of	Judg 1:25	5892
of the Hittites, and built a c	Judg 1:26	5892
and possessed the c of palm trees	Judg 3:13	5892
household, and the men of the c	Judg 6:27	5892
when the men of the c arose early	Judg 6:28	5892
the men of the c said unto Joash	Judg 6:30	5892
And he took the elders of the c	Judg 8:16	5892
Penuel, and slew the men of the c	Judg 8:17	5892
ephod thereof, and put it in his c	Judg 8:27	5892
when Zebul the ruler of the c	Judg 9:30	5892
they fortify the c against thee	Judg 9:31	5892
rise early, and set upon the c	Judg 9:33	5892
the entering of the gate of the c	Judg 9:35	5892
were come forth out of the c	Judg 9:43	5892
the entering of the gate of the c	Judg 9:44	5892

fought against the *c* all that day Judg 9:45 5892
and he took the *c*, and slew the Judg 9:45 5892
was therein, and beat down the *c* Judg 9:45 5892
was a strong tower within the *c* Judg 9:51 5892
and women, and all they of the *c* Judg 9:51 5892
the men of the *c* said unto him on Judg 14:18 5892
all night in the gate of the *c* Judg 16:2 5892
the doors of the gate of the *c* Judg 16:3 5892
of the *c* from Beth-lehem-judah to Judg 17:8 5892
sword, and burnt the *c* with fire Judg 18:27 5892
And they built a *c*, and dwelt Judg 18:28 5892
they called the name of the *c* Dan Judg 18:29 5892
of the *c* was Laish at the first Judg 18:29 5892
in into this *c* of the Jebusites Judg 19:11 5892
hither into the *c* of a stranger Judg 19:12 5892
sat him down in a street of the *c* Judg 19:15 5892
man in the street of the *c* Judg 19:17 5892
merry, behold, the men of the *c* Judg 19:22 5892
were gathered against the *c* Judg 20:11 5892
and were drawn away from the *c* Judg 20:31 5892
them from the *c* unto the highways Judg 20:32 5892
smote all the *c* with the edge of Judg 20:37 5892
with smoke rise up out of the *c* Judg 20:38 5892
of the *c* with a pillar of smoke Judg 20:40 5892
the flame of the *c* ascended up to Judg 20:40 5892
sword, as well the men of every *c* Judg 20:48 5892
that all the *c* was moved about Ruth 1:19 5892
took it up, and went into the *c* Ruth 2:18 5892
for all the *c* of my people doth Ruth 3:11 8179
and she went into the *c* Ruth 3:15 5892
ten men of the elders of the *c* Ruth 4:2 5892
up out of his *c* yearly to worship 1Sa 1:3 5892
And when the man came into the *c* 1Sa 4:13 5892
and told it, all the *c* cried out 1Sa 4:13 5892
of the LORD was against the *c* 1Sa 5:9 5892
and he smote the men of the *c* 1Sa 5:9 5892
destruction throughout all the *c* 1Sa 5:11 5892
the cry of the *c* went up to 1Sa 5:12 5892
Go ye every man unto his *c* 1Sa 8:22 5892
there is in this *c* a man of God 1Sa 9:6 5892
So they went unto the *c* where the 1Sa 9:10 5892
as they went up the hill to the *c* 1Sa 9:11 5892
now, for he came to day to the *c* 1Sa 9:12 5892
As soon as ye be come into the *c* 1Sa 9:13 5892
And they went up into the *c* 1Sa 9:14 5892
and when they were come into the *c* 1Sa 9:14 5892
from the high place into the *c* 1Sa 9:25 5892
going down to the end of the *c* 1Sa 9:27 5892
thou art come thither to the *c* 1Sa 10:5 5892
And Saul came to a *c* of Amalek 1Sa 15:5 5892
he might run to Beth-lehem his *c* 1Sa 20:6 5892
family hath a sacrifice in the *c* 1Sa 20:29 5892
unto him, Go, carry them to the *c* 1Sa 20:40 5892
and Jonathan went into the *c* 1Sa 20:42 5892
the *c* of the priests, smote he 1Sa 22:19 5892
to destroy the *c* for my sake 1Sa 23:10 5892
dwell in the royal *c* with thee 1Sa 27:5 5892
him in Ramah, even in his own *c* 1Sa 28:3 5892
So David and his men came to the *c* 1Sa 30:3 5892
the same is the *c* of David 2Sa 5:7 5892
fort, and called it the *c* of David 2Sa 5:9 5892
LORD unto him into the *c* of David 2Sa 6:10 5892
into the *c* of David with gladness 2Sa 6:12 5892
the LORD came into the *c* of David 2Sa 6:16 5892
unto thee, to search the *c* 2Sa 10:3 5892
Abishai, and entered into the *c* 2Sa 10:14 5892
to pass, when Joab observed the *c* 2Sa 11:16 5892
And the men of the *c* went out 2Sa 11:17 5892
nigh unto the *c* when ye did fight 2Sa 11:20 5892
battle more strong against the *c* 2Sa 11:25 5892
him, There were two men in one *c* 2Sa 12:1 5892
of Ammon, and took the royal *c* 2Sa 12:26 5892
and have taken the *c* of waters 2Sa 12:27 5892
together, and encamp against the *c* 2Sa 12:28 5892
lest I take the *c*, and it be 2Sa 12:28 5892
spoil of the *c* in great abundance 2Sa 12:30 5892
him, and said, Of what *c* art thou 2Sa 15:2 5892
David's counsellor, from his *c* 2Sa 15:12 5892
smite the *c* with the edge of the 2Sa 15:14 5892
had done passing out of the *c* 2Sa 15:24 5892
back the ark of God into the *c* 2Sa 15:25 5892
return into the *c* in peace 2Sa 15:27 5892
But if thou return to the *c* 2Sa 15:34 5892
David's friend came into the *c* 2Sa 15:37 5892
if he be gotten into a *c* 2Sa 17:13 5892
all Israel bring ropes to that *c* 2Sa 17:13 5892
not be seen to come into the *c* 2Sa 17:17 5892
him home to his house, to his *c* 2Sa 17:23 5892
that thou succour us out of the *c* 2Sa 18:3 5892
by stealth that day into the *c* 2Sa 19:3 5892
that I may die in mine own *c* 2Sa 19:37 5892
they cast up a bank against the *c* 2Sa 20:15 5892
cried a wise woman out of the *c* 2Sa 20:16 5892
thou seekest to destroy a *c* 2Sa 20:19 5892
only, and I will depart from the *c* 2Sa 20:21 5892
and they retired from the *c* 2Sa 20:22 5892
on the right side of the *c* that 2Sa 24:5 5892
noise of the *c* being in an uproar 1Kin 1:41 7151
so that the *c* rang again 1Kin 1:45 7151
and was buried in the *c* of David 1Kin 2:10 5892
brought her into the *c* of David 1Kin 3:1 5892
of the LORD out of the *c* of David 1Kin 8:1 5892
I chose no *c* out of all the 1Kin 8:16 5892
the *c* which thou hast chosen 1Kin 8:44 5892
the *c* which thou hast chosen, and 1Kin 8:48 5892
Canaanites that dwelt in the *c* 1Kin 9:16 5892
daughter came up out of the *c* of 1Kin 9:24 5892
of the *c* of David his father 1Kin 11:27 5892
the *c* which I have chosen out of 1Kin 11:32 5892
the *c* which I have chosen me to 1Kin 11:36 5892
was buried in the *c* of David his 1Kin 11:43 5892
told it in the *c* where the old 1Kin 13:25 5892
and the old prophet came to the *c* 1Kin 13:29 5892
in the *c* shall the dogs eat 1Kin 14:11 5892
and when thy feet enter into the *c* 1Kin 14:12 5892
the *c* which the LORD did choose 1Kin 14:21 5892
his fathers in the *c* of David 1Kin 14:31 5892
they buried him in the *c* of David 1Kin 15:8 5892
in the *c* of David his father 1Kin 15:24 5892
in the *c* shall the dogs eat 1Kin 16:4 5892
Zimri saw that the *c* was taken 1Kin 16:18 5892
the name of the *c* which he built 1Kin 16:24 5892
when he came to the gate of the *c* 1Kin 17:10 5892
to Ahab king of Israel into the *c* 1Kin 20:2 5892
themselves in array against the *c* 1Kin 20:12 5892
the provinces came out of the *c* 1Kin 20:19 5892
rest fled to Aphek, into the *c* 1Kin 20:30 5892
fled, and came into the *c*, into an 1Kin 20:30 5892
to the nobles that were in his *c* 1Kin 21:8 5892
And the men of his *c*, even the 1Kin 21:11 5892
who were the inhabitants in his *c* 1Kin 21:11 5892
carried him forth out of the *c* 1Kin 21:13 5892
Ahab in the *c* the dogs shall eat 1Kin 21:24 5892
unto Amon the governor of the *c* 1Kin 22:26 5892
sun, saying, Every man to his *c* 1Kin 22:36 5892
in the *c* of David his father 1Kin 22:50 5892
the men of the *c* said unto Elisha 2Kin 2:19 5892
situation of this *c* is pleasant 2Kin 2:19 5892
little children out of the *c* 2Kin 2:23 5892
And ye shall smite every fenced *c* 2Kin 3:19 5892
fenced *c*, and every choice *c* 2Kin 3:19 5892
night, and compassed the *c* about 2Kin 6:14 5892
compassed the *c* both with horses 2Kin 6:15 5892
the way, neither is this the *c* 2Kin 6:19 5892
we say, We will enter into the *c* 2Kin 7:4 5892
c, then the famine is in the *c* 2Kin 7:4 5892
called unto the porter of the *c* 2Kin 7:10 5892
When they come out of the *c* 2Kin 7:12 5892
them alive, and get into the *c* 2Kin 7:12 5892
remain, which are left in the *c* 2Kin 7:13
his fathers in the *c* of David 2Kin 8:24 5892
the *c* to go to tell it in Jezreel 2Kin 9:15 5892
his fathers in the *c* of David 2Kin 9:28 5892
and horses, a fenced *c* also 2Kin 10:2 5892
house, and he that was over the *c* 2Kin 10:5 5892
were with the great men of the *c* 2Kin 10:6 5892
went to the *c* of the house of 2Kin 10:25 5892
rejoiced, and the *c* was in quiet 2Kin 11:20 5892
his fathers in the *c* of David 2Kin 12:21 5892
his fathers in the *c* of David 2Kin 14:20 5892
his fathers in the *c* of David 2Kin 15:7 5892
in the *c* of David his father 2Kin 15:38 5892
his fathers in the *c* of David 2Kin 16:20 5892
of the watchmen to the fenced *c* 2Kin 17:9 5892
of the watchmen to the fenced *c* 2Kin 18:8 5892
this *c* shall not be delivered 2Kin 18:30 5892
the king of the *c* of Sepharvaim 2Kin 19:13 5892
He shall not come into this *c* 2Kin 19:32 5892
and shall not come into this *c* 2Kin 19:33 5892
For I will defend this *c*, to save 2Kin 19:34 5892
this *c* out of the hand of the 2Kin 20:6 5892
defend this *c* for mine own sake 2Kin 20:6 5892
and brought water into the *c* 2Kin 20:20 5892
of Joshua the governor of the *c* 2Kin 23:8 5892
left hand at the gate of the *c* 2Kin 23:8 5892
And the men of the *c* told him 2Kin 23:17 5892
will cast off this *c* Jerusalem 2Kin 23:27 5892
Jerusalem, and the *c* was besieged 2Kin 24:10 5892
of Babylon came against the *c* 2Kin 24:11 5892
the *c* was besieged unto the 2Kin 25:2 5892
the famine prevailed in the *c* 2Kin 25:3 5892
the *c* was broken up, and all the 2Kin 25:4 5892
were against the *c* round about 2Kin 25:4 5892
people that were left in the *c* 2Kin 25:11 5892
out of the *c* he took an officer 2Kin 25:19 5892
which were found in the *c* 2Kin 25:19 5892
the land that were found in the *c* 2Kin 25:19 5892
and the name of his *c* was Dinhabah 1Chr 1:43 5892
and the name of his *c* was Avith 1Chr 1:46 5892
and the name of his *c* was Pai 1Chr 1:50 5892
But the fields of the *c*, and the 1Chr 6:56 5892
the *c* of refuge, and Libnah with 1Chr 6:57
of Zion, which is the *c* of David 1Chr 11:5 5892
they called it the *c* of David 1Chr 11:7 5892
And he built the *c* round about 1Chr 11:8 5892
Joab repaired the rest of the *c* 1Chr 11:8 5892
home to himself to the *c* of David 1Chr 13:13 5892
made him houses in the *c* of David 1Chr 15:1 5892
the LORD came to the *c* of David 1Chr 15:29 5892
in array before the gate of the *c* 1Chr 19:9 5892
brother, and entered into the *c* 1Chr 19:15 5892
exceeding much spoil out of the *c* 1Chr 20:2 5892
of the LORD out of the *c* of David 2Chr 5:2 5892
c among all the tribes of Israel 2Chr 6:5 5892
this *c* which thou hast chosen 2Chr 6:34 5892
toward the *c* which thou hast 2Chr 6:38 5892
daughter of Pharaoh out of the *c* 2Chr 8:11 5892
in the *c* of David his father 2Chr 9:31 5892
in every several *c* he put shields 2Chr 11:12 5892
and Benjamin, unto every fenced *c* 2Chr 11:23 5892
the *c* which the LORD had chosen 2Chr 12:13 5892
and was buried in the *c* of David 2Chr 12:16 5892
they buried him in the *c* of David 2Chr 14:1 5892
destroyed of nation, and *c* of *c* 2Chr 15:6 5892
for himself in the *c* of David 2Chr 16:14 5892
to Amon the governor of the *c* 2Chr 18:25 5892
fenced cities of Judah, *c* by *c* 2Chr 19:5 5892
his fathers in the *c* of David 2Chr 21:1 5892
they buried him in the *c* of David 2Chr 21:20 5892
the *c* was quiet, after that they 2Chr 23:21 5892
they buried him in the *c* of David 2Chr 24:16 5892
they buried him in the *c* of David 2Chr 24:25 5892
his fathers in the *c* of Judah 2Chr 25:28 5892
they buried him in the *c* of David 2Chr 27:9 5892
the *c* of palm trees, to their 2Chr 28:15 5892
in every several *c* of Judah he 2Chr 28:25 5892
and they buried him in the *c* 2Chr 28:27 5892
and gathered the rulers of the *c* 2Chr 29:20 5892
the posts passed from *c* to *c* 2Chr 30:10 5892
their cities, in every several *c* 2Chr 31:19 5892
which were without the *c* 2Chr 32:3 5892
repaired Millo in the *c* of David 2Chr 32:5 5892
the street of the gate of the *c* 2Chr 32:6 5892
that they might take the *c* 2Chr 32:18 5892
the west side of the *c* of David 2Chr 32:30 5892
a wall without the *c* of David 2Chr 33:14 5892
and cast them out of the *c* 2Chr 33:15 5892
and Maaseiah the governor of the *c* 2Chr 34:8 5892
and Judah, every one unto his *c* Ezr 2:1 5892
the rebellious and the bad *c* Ezr 4:12 7149
if this *c* be builded, and the Ezr 4:13 7149
that this *c* is a rebellious *c* Ezr 4:15 7149
which cause was this *c* destroyed Ezr 4:15 7149
if this *c* be builded again, and Ezr 4:16 7149
that this *c* of old time hath made Ezr 4:19 7149
that this *c* be not builded, until Ezr 4:21 7179
with them the elders of every *c* Ezr 10:14 5892
my countenance be sad, when the *c* Neh 2:3 5892
unto the *c* of my fathers' Neh 2:5 5892
house, and for the wall of the *c* Neh 2:8 5892
that go down from the *c* of David Neh 3:15 5892
Now the *c* was large and great Neh 7:4 5892
and to Judah, every one unto his *c* Neh 7:6 5892
to dwell in Jerusalem the holy *c* Neh 11:1 5892
of Senuah was second over the *c* Neh 11:9 5892
holy *c* were two hundred fourscore Neh 11:18 5892
by the stairs of the *c* of David Neh 12:37 5892
this evil upon us, and upon this *c* Neh 13:18 5892
but the *c* Shushan was perplexed Est 3:15 5892
went out into the midst of the *c* Est 4:1 5892
Mordecai unto the street of the *c* Est 4:6 5892
through the street of the *c* Est 6:9 5892
through the street of the *c* Est 6:11 5892
the Jews which were in every *c* to Est 8:11 5892
the *c* of Shushan rejoiced and was Est 8:15 5892
in every province, and in every *c* Est 8:17 5892
every province, and every *c* Est 9:28 5892
Men groan from out of the *c* Job 24:12 5892
out to the gate through the *c* Job 29:7 7176
scorneth the multitude of the *c* Job 39:7 7151
marvellous kindness in a strong *c* Ps 31:21 5892
shall make glad the *c* of God Ps 46:4 5892
to be praised in the *c* of our God Ps 48:1 5892
north, the *c* of the great King Ps 48:2 7151
in the *c* of the LORD of hosts Ps 48:8 5892
in the *c* of our God Ps 48:8 5892
seen violence and strife in the *c* Ps 55:9 5892
a dog, and go round about the *c* Ps 59:6 5892
a dog, and go round about the *c* Ps 59:14 5892
will bring me into the strong *c* Ps 60:9 5892
they of the *c* shall flourish like Ps 72:16 5892
are spoken of thee, O *c* of God Ps 87:3 5892
doers from the *c* of the LORD Ps 101:8 5892
they found no *c* to dwell in Ps 107:4 5892
might go to a *c* of habitation Ps 107:7 5892
may prepare a *c* for habitation Ps 107:36 5892
will bring me into the strong *c* Ps 108:10 5892
as a *c* that is compact together Ps 122:3 5892
except the LORD keep the *c* Ps 127:1 5892
in the *c* she uttereth her words, Prov 1:21 5892
the gates, at the entry of the *c* Prov 8:3 7176
upon the highest places of the *c* Prov 9:3 7176
seat in the high places of the *c* Prov 9:14 7176
rich man's wealth is his strong *c* Prov 10:15 7151
the righteous, the *c* rejoiceth Prov 11:10 7151
of the upright the *c* is exalted Prov 11:11 7176
spirit than he that taketh a *c* Prov 16:32 5892
rich man's wealth is his strong *c* Prov 18:11 7151
harder to be won than a strong *c* Prov 18:19 7151
man scaleth the *c* of the mighty Prov 21:22 5892
is like a *c* that is broken down Prov 25:28 5892
men bring a *c* into a snare Prov 29:8 7151
ten mighty men which are in the *c* Eccl 7:19 5892
in the *c* where they had so done Eccl 8:10 5892
There was a little *c*, and few men Eccl 9:14 5892
he by his wisdom delivered the *c* Eccl 9:15 5892
he knoweth not how to go to the *c* Eccl 10:15 5892
go about the *c* in the streets, and Song 3:2 5892
that go about the *c* found me Song 3:3 5892
that went about the *c* found me Song 5:7 5892
of cucumbers, as a besieged *c* Is 1:8 5892
the faithful *c* become an harlot Is 1:21 7151
The *c* of righteousness, the Is 1:26 5892
of righteousness, the faithful *c* Is 1:26 7151
the golden *c* ceased Is 14:4 4062
cry, O *c* Is 14:31 5892
is taken away from being a *c* Is 17:1 5892
c against *c*, and kingdom Is 19:2 5892
be called, The *c* of destruction Is 19:18 5892
art full of stirs, a tumultuous *c* Is 22:2 5892
a joyous *c*: thy slain men Is 22:2 7151
the breaches of the *c* of David Is 22:9 5892
Is this your joyous *c*, whose Is 23:7
against Tyre, the crowning *c* Is 23:8
against the merchant *c*, to Is 23:11
Take an harp, go about the *c* Is 23:16 5892
The *c* of confusion is broken down Is 24:10 7151
In the *c* is left desolation, and Is 24:12 5892
For thou hast made of a *c* an heap Is 25:2 5892
of a defenced *c* a ruin Is 25:2 7151
a palace of strangers to be no *c* Is 25:2 5892
the *c* of the terrible nations Is 25:3 7151
We have a strong *c* Is 26:1 5892
the lofty *c*, he layeth it low Is 26:5 7151
Yet the defenced *c* shall be Is 27:10 5892
to Ariel, the *c* where David dwelt Is 29:1 7151
the houses of joy in the joyous *c* Is 32:13 7151
multitude of the *c* shall be left Is 32:14 5892
the *c* shall be low in a low place Is 32:19 5892
Zion, the *c* of our solemnities Is 33:20 7151
this *c* shall not be delivered Is 36:15 5892
the king of the *c* of Sepharvaim Is 37:13 5892

He shall not come into this c Is 37:33 5892
and shall not come into this c Is 37:34 5892
For I will defend this c to save Is 37:35 5892
this c out of the hand of the Is 38:6 5892
and I will defend this c Is 38:6 5892
he shall build my c, and he shall Is 45:13 5892
call themselves of the holy c Is 48:2 5892
garments, O Jerusalem, the holy c Is 52:1 5892
The c of the LORD, The Zion of Is 60:14 5892
Sought out, A c not forsaken Is 62:12 5892
A voice of noise from the c Is 66:6 5892
made thee this day a defenced c Jer 1:18 5892
and I will take you one of a c Jer 3:14 5892
The whole c shall flee for the Jer 4:29 5892
every c shall be forsaken, and not Jer 4:29 5892
this is the c to be visited Jer 6:6 5892
the c, and those that dwell Jer 8:16 5892
and if I enter into the c, then Jer 14:18 5892
suddenly, and terrors upon the c Jer 15:8 5892
of this c on the sabbath day Jer 17:24 5892
into the gates of this c kings Jer 17:25 5892
this c shall remain for ever Jer 17:25 5892
And I will make this c desolate Jer 19:8 5892
I break this people and this c Jer 19:11 5892
and even make this c as Tophet Jer 19:12 5892
Behold, I will bring upon this c Jer 19:15 5892
all the strength of this c Jer 20:5 5892
them into the midst of this c Jer 21:4 5892
smite the inhabitants of this c Jer 21:6 5892
in this c from the pestilence Jer 21:7 5892
in this c shall die by the sword Jer 21:9 5892
my face against this c for evil Jer 21:10 5892
many nations shall pass by this c Jer 22:8 5892
LORD done thus unto this great c Jer 22:8 5892
the c that I gave you and your Jer 23:39 5892
the c which is called by my name Jer 25:29 5892
will make this c a curse to all Jer 26:6 5892
this c shall be desolate without Jer 26:9 5892
he hath prophesied against this c Jer 26:11 5892
against this c all the words that Jer 26:12 5892
upon yourselves, and upon this c Jer 26:15 5892
who prophesied against this c Jer 26:20 5892
should this c be laid waste Jer 27:17 5892
the vessels that remain in this c Jer 27:19 5892
seek the peace of the c whither I Jer 29:7 5892
people that dwelleth in this c Jer 29:16 5892
the c shall be builded upon her Jer 30:18 5892
that the c shall be built to the Jer 31:38 5892
I will give this c into the hand Jer 32:3 5892
are come unto the c to take it Jer 32:24 5892
the c is given into the hand of Jer 32:24 5892
for the c is given into the hand Jer 32:25 5892
I will give this c into the hand Jer 32:28 5892
that fight against this c Jer 32:29 5892
shall come and set fire on this c Jer 32:29 5892
For this c hath been to me as a Jer 32:31 5892
God of Israel, concerning this c Jer 32:36 5892
concerning the houses of this c Jer 33:4 5892
I have hid my face from this c Jer 33:5 5892
I will give this c into the hand Jer 34:2 5892
and cause them to return to this c Jer 34:22 5892
again, and fight against this c Jer 37:8 5892
tent, and burn this c with fire Jer 37:10 5892
all the bread in the c were spent Jer 37:21 5892
in this c shall die by the sword Jer 38:2 5892
This c shall surely be given into Jer 38:3 5892
men of war that remain in this c Jer 38:4 5892
there is no more bread in the c Jer 38:9 5892
this c shall not be burned with Jer 38:17 5892
then shall this c be given into Jer 38:18 5892
thou shalt cause this c to be Jer 38:23 5892
of the month, the c was broken up Jer 39:2 5892
went forth out of the c by night Jer 39:4 5892
the people that remained in the c Jer 39:9 5892
my words upon this c for evil Jer 39:16 5892
they came into the midst of the c Jer 41:7 5892
I will destroy the c and the Jer 46:8 5892
the c, and them that dwell therein Jer 47:2 5892
every c, and no c shall escape Jer 48:8 5892
How is the c of praise not left, Jer 49:25 5892
praise not left, the c of my joy Jer 49:25 7151
that his c is taken at one end Jer 51:31 5892
So the c was besieged unto the Jer 52:5 5892
the famine was sore in the c Jer 52:6 5892
Then the c was broken up, and all Jer 52:7 5892
went forth out of the c by night Jer 52:7 5892
were by the c round about Jer 52:7 5892
the people that remained in the c Jer 52:15 5892
took also out of the c an eunuch Jer 52:25 5892
person, which were found in the c Jer 52:25 5892
were found in the midst of the c Jer 52:25 5892
How doth the c sit solitary Lam 1:1 5892
elders gave up the ghost in the c Lam 1:19 5892
swoon in the streets of the c Lam 2:11 7151
wounded in the streets of the c Lam 2:12 5892
Is this the c that men call The Lam 2:15 5892
of all the daughters of my c Lam 3:51 5892
thee, and pourtray upon it the c Eze 4:1 5892
of iron between thee and the c Eze 4:3 5892
third part in the midst of the c Eze 5:2 5892
and he that is in the c, famine and Eze 7:15 5892
the c is full of violence Eze 7:23 5892
charge over the c to draw near Eze 9:1 5892
Go through the midst of the c Eze 9:4 5892
Go ye after him through the c Eze 9:5 5892
they went forth, and slew in the c Eze 9:7 5892
the c full of perverseness Eze 9:9 5892
and scatter them over the c Eze 10:2 5892
and give wicked counsel in this c Eze 11:2 5892
this c is the caldron, and we be Eze 11:3
multiplied your slain in this c Eze 11:6 5892
flesh, and this c is the caldron Eze 11:7
This c shall not be your caldron, Eze 11:11
went up from the midst of the c Eze 11:23 5892
is on the east side of the c Eze 11:23 5892
he set it in a c of merchants Eze 17:4 5892
at the head of the way to the c Eze 21:19 5892
wilt thou judge the bloody c Eze 22:2 5892
The c sheddeth blood in the midst Eze 22:3 5892
Woe to the bloody c, to the pot Eze 24:6 5892
Woe to the bloody c Eze 24:9 5892
as men enter into a c wherein is Eze 26:10 5892
of seafaring men, the renowned c Eze 26:17 5892
I shall make thee a desolate c Eze 26:19 5892
What c is like Tyrus, like the Eze 27:32
unto me, saying, The c is smitten Eze 33:21 5892
name of the c shall be Hamonah Eze 39:16 5892
year after that the c was smitten Eze 40:1 5892
as the frame of a c on the south Eze 40:2 5892
saw when I came to destroy the c Eze 43:3 5892
of the c five thousand broad Eze 45:6 5892
and of the possession of the c Eze 45:7 5892
and before the possession of the c Eze 45:7 5892
be a profane place for the c Eze 48:15 5892
the c shall be in the midst Eze 48:15 5892
the suburbs of the c shall be Eze 48:17 5892
food unto them that serve the c Eze 48:18 5892
they that serve the c shall serve Eze 48:19 5892
with the possession of the c Eze 48:20 5892
and of the possession of the c Eze 48:21 5892
and from the possession of the c Eze 48:22 5892
out of the c on the north side Eze 48:30 5892
the gates of the c shall be after Eze 48:31 5892
the name of the c from that day Eze 48:35 5892
turned away from thy c Jerusalem Dan 9:16 5892
the c which is called by thy name Dan 9:18 5892
for thy c and thy people are Dan 9:19 5892
thy people and upon thy holy c Dan 9:24 5892
shall come shall destroy the c Dan 9:26 5892
Gilead is a c of them that work Hos 6:8 7151
and I will not enter into the c Hos 11:9 5892
They shall run to and fro in the c Joel 2:9 5892
Shall a trumpet be blown in the c Amos 3:6 5892
shall there be evil in a c Amos 3:6 5892
and I caused it to rain upon one c Amos 4:7 5892
it not to rain upon another c Amos 4:7 5892
three cities wandered unto one c Amos 4:8 5892
The c that went out by a thousand Amos 5:3 5892
up the c with all that is therein Amos 6:8 5892
wife shall be an harlot in the c Amos 7:17 5892
go to Nineveh, that great c Jonah 1:2 5892
go unto Nineveh, that great c Jonah 3:2 5892
great c of three days' journey Jonah 3:3 5892
enter into the c a day's journey Jonah 3:4 5892
So Jonah went out of the c Jonah 4:5 5892
and sat on the east side of the c Jonah 4:5 5892
see what would become of the c Jonah 4:5 5892
not I spare Nineveh, that great c Jonah 4:11 5892
shalt thou go forth out of the c Mic 4:10 7151
LORD's voice crieth unto the c Mic 6:9 5892
Woe to the bloody c Nah 3:1 5892
violence of the land, of the c Hab 2:8 7151
and stablisheth a c by iniquity Hab 2:12 7151
violence of the land, of the c Hab 2:17 7151
rejoicing c that dwelt carelessly Zeph 2:15 5892
and polluted, to the oppressing c Zeph 3:1 5892
shall be called a c of truth Zec 8:3 5892
the streets of the c shall be Zec 8:5 5892
of one c shall go to another Zec 8:21
the c shall be taken, and the Zec 14:2 5892
half of the c shall go forth into Zec 14:2 5892
shall not be cut off from the c Zec 14:2 5892
dwelt in a c called Nazareth Mt 2:23 4172
taketh him up into the holy c Mt 4:5 4172
A c that is set on an hill cannot Mt 5:14 4172
for it is the c of the great King Mt 5:35 4172
and went their ways into the c Mt 8:33 4172
the whole c came out to meet Mt 8:34 4172
over, and came into his own c Mt 9:1 4172
into any c of the Samaritans Mt 10:5 4172
into whatsoever c or town ye Mt 10:11 4172
ye depart out of that house or c Mt 10:14 4172
day of judgment, than for that c Mt 10:15 4172
when they persecute you in this c Mt 10:23 4172
every c or house divided against Mt 12:25 4172
all the c was moved, saying, Who Mt 21:10 4172
and went out of the c into Bethany Mt 21:17 4172
morning as he returned into the c Mt 21:18 4172
murderers, and burned up their c Mt 22:7 4172
and persecute them from c to c Mt 23:34 4172
Go into the c to such a man, and Mt 26:18 4172
and went into the holy c, and Mt 27:53 4172
some of the watch came into the c Mt 28:11 4172
all the c was gathered together Mk 1:33 4172
no more openly enter into the c Mk 1:45 4172
swine fled, and told it in the c Mk 5:14 4172
day of judgment, than for that c Mk 6:11 4172
was come, he went out of the c Mk 11:19 4172
saith unto them, Go ye into the c Mk 14:13 4172
went forth, and came into the c Mk 14:16 4172
sent from God unto a c of Galilee Lk 1:26 4172
with haste, into a c of Juda Lk 1:39 4172
taxed, every one into his own c Lk 2:3 4172
out of the c of Nazareth Lk 2:4 4172
into Judaea, unto the c of David Lk 2:4 4172
day in the c of David a Saviour Lk 2:11 4172
Galilee, to their own c Nazareth Lk 2:39 4172
a c of Sidon, unto a woman that Lk 4:26
up, and thrust him out of the c Lk 4:29 4172
hill whereon their c was built Lk 4:29 4172
a c of Galilee, and taught them on Lk 4:31 4172
pass, when he was in a certain c Lk 5:12 4172
that he went into a c called Nain Lk 7:11 4172
he came nigh to the gate of the c Lk 7:12 4172
much people of the c was with her Lk 7:12 4172
And, behold, a woman in the c Lk 7:37 4172
that he went throughout every c Lk 8:1 4172
were come to him out of every c Lk 8:4 4172
him out of the c a certain man Lk 8:27 4172
fled, and went and told it in the c Lk 8:34 4172
published throughout the whole c Lk 8:39 4172
you, when ye go out of that c Lk 9:5 4172
to the c called Bethsaida Lk 9:10 4172
two before his face into every c Lk 10:1 4172
And into whatsoever c ye enter Lk 10:8 4172
But into whatsoever c ye enter Lk 10:10 4172
Even the very dust of your c Lk 10:11 4172
day for Sodom, than for that c Lk 10:12 4172
the streets and lanes of the c Lk 14:21 4172
Saying, There was in a c a judge Lk 18:2 4172
And there was a widow in that c Lk 18:3 4172
he was come near, he beheld the c Lk 19:41 4172
when ye are entered into the c Lk 22:10 4172
a certain sedition made in the c Lk 23:19 4172
of Arimathaea, a c of the Jews Lk 23:51 4172
tarry ye in the c of Jerusalem Lk 24:49 4172
the c of Andrew and Peter Jn 1:44 4172
Then cometh he to a c of Samaria Jn 4:5 4172
gone away unto the c to buy meat Jn 4:8 4172
and went her way into the c Jn 4:28 4172
Then they went out of the c Jn 4:30 4172
c believed on him for the saying Jn 4:39 4172
into a c called Ephraim, and there Jn 11:54 4172
was crucified was nigh to the c Jn 19:20 4172
And cast him out of the c, and Acts 7:58 4172
went down to the c of Samaria Acts 8:5 4172
And there was great joy in that c Acts 8:8 4172
in the same c used sorcery Acts 8:9 4172
unto him, Arise, and go into the c Acts 9:6 4172
journey, and drew nigh unto the c Acts 10:9 4172
I was in the c of Joppa praying Acts 11:5 4172
iron gate that leadeth unto the c Acts 12:10 4172
day came almost the whole c Acts 13:44 4172
women, and the chief men of the c Acts 13:50 4172
multitude of the c was divided Acts 14:4 4172
Jupiter, which was before their c Acts 14:13 4172
Paul, drew him out of the c Acts 14:19 4172
he rose up, and came into the c Acts 14:20 4172
had preached the gospel to that c Acts 14:21 4172
in every c them that preach him Acts 15:21 4172
visit our brethren in every c Acts 15:36 4172
which is the chief c of that part Acts 16:12 4172
we were in that c abiding certain Acts 16:12 4172
went out of the c by a river side Acts 16:13 4172
of the c of Thyatira, which Acts 16:14 4172
do exceedingly trouble our c Acts 16:20 4172
them to depart out of the c Acts 16:39 4172
set all the c on an uproar, and Acts 17:5 4172
brethren unto the rulers of the c Acts 17:6 4173
the people and the rulers of the c Acts 17:8 4173
when he saw the c wholly given to Acts 17:16 4172
for I have much people in this c Acts 18:10 4172
the whole c was filled with Acts 19:29 4172
that the c of the Ephesians is a Acts 19:35 4172
Holy Ghost witnesseth in every c Acts 20:23 4172
till we were out of the c Acts 21:5 4172
in the c Trophimus an Ephesian Acts 21:29 4172
all the c was moved, and the Acts 21:30 4172
a Jew of Tarsus, a c in Cilicia Acts 21:39
a citizen of no mean c Acts 21:39 4172
born in Tarsus, a c Acts 22:3
yet brought up in this c at the Acts 22:3 4172
in the synagogues, nor in the c Acts 24:12 4172
and principal men of the c Acts 25:23 4172
we came to Myra, a c of Lycia Acts 27:5
nigh whereunto was the c of Lasea Acts 27:8 4172
chamberlain of the c saluteth you Rom 16:23 4172
the heathen, in perils in the c 2Cor 11:26 4172
the c of the Damascenes with a 2Cor 11:32 4172
a c of Macedonia, by Titus and 2Cor s
chiefest c of Phrygia Pacatiana 1Ti s 3390
and ordain elders in every c Titus 1:5 4172
For he looked for a c which hath Heb 11:10 4172
for he hath prepared for them a c Heb 11:16 4172
unto the c of the living God, the Heb 12:22 4172
For here have we no continuing c Heb 13:14 4172
morrow we will go into such a c Jas 4:13 4172
and the name of the c of my God Rev 3:12 4172
the holy c shall they tread under Rev 11:2 4172
lie in the street of the great c Rev 11:8 4172
and the tenth part of the c fell Rev 11:13 4172
fallen, is fallen, that great c Rev 14:8 4172
was trodden without the c Rev 14:20 4172
the great c was divided into Rev 16:19 4172
which thou sawest is that great c Rev 17:18 4172
great c Babylon, that mighty c Rev 18:10 4172
saying, Alas, alas that great c Rev 18:16 4172
c is like unto this great c Rev 18:18 4172
saying, Alas, alas that great c Rev 18:19 4172
great c Babylon be thrown down Rev 18:21 4172
saints about, and the beloved c Rev 20:9 4172
And I John saw the holy c, new Rev 21:2 4172
and shewed me that great c Rev 21:10 4172
the wall of the c had twelve Rev 21:14 4172
a golden reed to measure the c Rev 21:15 4172
the c lieth foursquare, and the Rev 21:16 4172
he measured the c with the reed Rev 21:16 4172
the c was pure gold, like unto Rev 21:18 4172
c were garnished with all manner Rev 21:19 4172
the street of the c was pure gold Rev 21:21 4172
the c had no need of the sun, Rev 21:23 4172
in through the gates into the c Rev 22:14 4172
of life, and out of the holy c Rev 22:19 4172

CLAD

he had c himself with a new 1Kin 11:29 3680
was c with zeal as a cloke Is 59:17 5844

CLAMOROUS
A foolish woman is *c* ... Prov 9:13 1993

CLAMOUR
and wrath, and anger, and *c* ... Eph 4:31 *2906*

CLAP
Men shall *c* their hands at him, ... Job 27:23 5606
O *c* your hands, all ye people ... Ps 47:1 8628
Let the floods *c* their hands ... Ps 98:8 4222
of the field shall *c* their hands ... Is 55:12 4222
All that pass by *c* their hands at ... Lam 2:15 5606
thee shall *c* the hands over thee ... Nah 3:19 8628

CLAPPED
they *c* their hands, and said, God ... 2Kin 11:12 5221
Because thou hast *c* thine hands ... Eze 25:6 4222

CLAPPETH
he *c* his hands among us, and ... Job 34:37 5606

CLAUDA (*claw'-dah*) *An island near Crete.*
certain island which is called *C* ... Acts 27:16 *2802*

CLAUDIA (*claw'-de-ah*) *A Roman Christian.*
thee, and Pudens, and Linus, and *C* ... 2Ti 4:21 *2803*

CLAUDIUS (*claw'-de-us*)
1. A Roman emperor.
to pass in the days of *C* Caesar ... Acts 11:28 *2804*
(because that *C* had commanded all ... Acts 18:2 *2804*
2. A Roman officer in Jerusalem.
C Lysias unto the most excellent ... Acts 23:26 *2804*

CLAVE
c the wood for the burnt offering ... Gen 22:3 1234
his soul *c* unto Dinah the ... Gen 34:3 1692
that the ground *c* asunder that ... Num 16:31 1234
But God *c* an hollow place that ... Judg 15:19 1234
but Ruth *c* unto her ... Ruth 1:14 1692
they *c* the wood of the cart, and ... 1Sa 6:14 1234
men of Judah *c* unto their king ... 2Sa 20:2 1692
his hand *c* unto the sword ... 2Sa 23:10 1692
Solomon *c* unto these in love ... 1Kin 11:2 1692
For he *c* to the LORD, and departed ... 2Kin 18:6 1692
They *c* to their brethren, their ... Neh 10:29 2388
He *c* the rocks in the wilderness, ... Ps 78:15 1234
he *c* the rock also, and the waters ... Is 48:21 1234
Howbeit certain men *c* unto him ... Acts 17:34 *2853*

CLAWS
and cleaveth the cleft into two *c* ... Deut 14:6 6541
and his nails like birds' *c* ... Dan 4:33
fat, and tear their *c* in pieces ... Zec 11:16 6541

CLAY
in the *c* ground between Succoth ... 1Kin 7:46 4568
in the *c* ground between Succoth ... 2Chr 4:17 4568
in them that dwell in houses of *c* ... Job 4:19 2563
that thou hast made me as the *c* ... Job 10:9 2563
ashes, your bodies to bodies of *c* ... Job 13:12 2563
dust, and prepare raiment as the *c* ... Job 27:16 2563
I also am formed out of the *c* ... Job 33:6 2563
It is turned as *c* to the seal ... Job 38:14 2563
horrible pit, out of the miry *c* ... Ps 40:2 2916
be esteemed as the potter's *c* ... Is 29:16 2563
and as the potter treadeth *c* ... Is 41:25 2916
Shall the *c* say to him that ... Is 45:9 2563
we are the *c*, and thou our potter ... Is 64:8 2563
the vessel that he made of *c* was ... Jer 18:4 2563
as the *c* is in the potter's hand, ... Jer 18:6 2563
them in the *c* in the brickkiln ... Jer 43:9 4423
feet part of iron and part of *c* ... Dan 2:33 2635
his feet that were of iron and *c* ... Dan 2:34 2635
Then was the iron, the *c*, the ... Dan 2:35 2635
feet and toes, part of potters' *c* ... Dan 2:41 2635
sawest the iron mixed with miry *c* ... Dan 2:41 2635
were part of iron, and part of *c* ... Dan 2:42 2635
sawest iron mixed with miry *c* ... Dan 2:43 2635
even as iron is not mixed with *c* ... Dan 2:43 2635
pieces the iron, the brass, the *c* ... Dan 2:45 2635
go into *c*, and tread the morter, ... Nah 3:14 2916
that ladeth himself with thick *c* ... Hab 2:6 5671
made *c* of the spittle, and he ... Jn 9:6 *4081*
eyes of the blind man with the *c* ... Jn 9:6 *4081*
A man that is called Jesus made *c* ... Jn 9:11 *4081*
sabbath day when Jesus made the *c* ... Jn 9:14 *4081*
He put *c* upon mine eyes, and I ... Jn 9:15 *4081*
not the potter power over the *c* ... Rom 9:21 *4081*

CLEAN
Of every *c* beast thou shalt take ... Gen 7:2 2889
of beasts that are not *c* by two ... Gen 7:2 2889
Of *c* beasts, and of beasts that ... Gen 7:8 2889
and of beasts that are not *c* ... Gen 7:8 2889
c beast, and of every *c* fowl ... Gen 8:20 2889
gods that are among you, and be *c* ... Gen 35:2 2891
without the camp unto a *c* place ... Lev 4:12 2889
without the camp unto a *c* place ... Lev 6:11 2889
all that be *c* shall eat thereof ... Lev 7:19 2889
unholy, and between unclean and *c* ... Lev 10:10 2889
shall ye eat in a *c* place ... Lev 10:14 2889
is plenty of water, shall be *c* ... Lev 11:36 2889
is to be sown, it shall be *c* ... Lev 11:37 2889
between the unclean and the *c* ... Lev 11:47 2889
for her, and she shall be *c* ... Lev 12:8 2891
the priest shall pronounce him *c* ... Lev 13:6 2891
shall wash his clothes, and be *c* ... Lev 13:6 2891
him *c* that hath the plague ... Lev 13:13 2891
he is *c* ... Lev 13:13 2889
him *c* that hath the plague ... Lev 13:17 2891
he is *c* ... Lev 13:17 2889
the priest shall pronounce him *c* ... Lev 13:23 2891
the priest shall pronounce him *c* ... Lev 13:28 2891
the priest shall pronounce him *c* ... Lev 13:34 2891
shall wash his clothes, and be *c* ... Lev 13:34 2891
the scall is healed, he is *c* ... Lev 13:37 2889
the priest shall pronounce him *c* ... Lev 13:37 2891
he is *c* ... Lev 13:39 2889
yet is he *c* ... Lev 13:40 2889
yet is he *c* ... Lev 13:41 2889
the second time, and shall be *c* ... Lev 13:58 2891
thing of skins, to pronounce it *c* ... Lev 13:59 2891
be cleansed two birds alive and *c* ... Lev 14:4 2889
times, and shall pronounce him *c* ... Lev 14:7 2891
in water, that he may be *c* ... Lev 14:8 2891
flesh in water, and he shall be *c* ... Lev 14:9 2891
the priest that maketh him *c* ... Lev 14:11 2891
the man that is to be made *c* ... Lev 14:11 2891
for him, and he shall be *c* ... Lev 14:20 2891
shall pronounce the house *c* ... Lev 14:48 2891
and it shall be *c* ... Lev 14:53 2891
it is unclean, and when it is *c* ... Lev 14:57 2889
the issue spit upon him that is *c* ... Lev 15:8 2889
in running water, and shall be *c* ... Lev 15:13 2891
and after that she shall be *c* ... Lev 15:28 2891
that ye may be *c* from all your ... Lev 16:30 2891
then shall he be *c* ... Lev 17:15 2891
put difference between *c* beasts ... Lev 20:25 2889
and between unclean fowls and *c* ... Lev 20:25 2889
of the holy things, until he be *c* ... Lev 22:4 2891
the sun is down, he shall be *c* ... Lev 22:7 2891
thou shalt not make *c* riddance of ... Lev 23:22
woman be not defiled, but be *c* ... Num 5:28 2889
clothes, and so make themselves *c* ... Num 8:7 2891
But the man that is *c*, and is not ... Num 9:13 2889
every one that is *c* in thy house ... Num 18:11 2889
every one that is *c* in thine ... Num 18:13 2889
a man that is *c* shall gather up ... Num 19:9 2889
up without the camp in a *c* place ... Num 19:9 2889
on the seventh day he shall be *c* ... Num 19:12 2891
the seventh day he shall not be *c* ... Num 19:12 2891
a *c* person shall take hyssop, and ... Num 19:18 2889
the *c* person shall sprinkle upon ... Num 19:19 2889
in water, and shall be *c* at even ... Num 19:19 2891
the fire, and it shall be *c* ... Num 31:23 2891
the seventh day, and ye shall be *c* ... Num 31:24 2891
the *c* may eat thereof, as of the ... Deut 12:15 2889
the *c* shall eat of them alike ... Deut 12:22 2889
Of all *c* birds ye shall eat ... Deut 14:11 2889
But of all *c* fowls ye may eat ... Deut 14:20 2889
the *c* person shall eat it alike, ... Deut 15:22 2889
that is not *c* by reason of ... Deut 23:10 2889
people were passed *c* over Jordan ... Josh 3:17 8552
people were *c* passed over Jordan ... Josh 4:1 8552
all the people were *c* passed over ... Josh 4:11 8552
hath befallen him, he is not *c* ... 1Sa 20:26 2889
surely he is not *c* ... 1Sa 20:26 2889
again to thee, and thou shalt be *c* ... 2Kin 5:10 2891
may I not wash in them, and be *c* ... 2Kin 5:12 2891
he saith to thee, Wash, and be *c* ... 2Kin 5:13 2891
of a little child, and he was *c* ... 2Kin 5:14 2891
for every one that was not *c* ... 2Chr 30:17 2889
and make my hands never so *c* ... Job 9:30 2141
is pure, and I am *c* in thine eyes ... Job 11:4 1249
Who can bring a *c* thing out of an ... Job 14:4 2889
What is man, that he should be *c* ... Job 15:14 2135
heavens are not *c* in his sight ... Job 15:15 2141
he that hath *c* hands shall be ... Job 17:9 2891
or how can he be *c* that is born ... Job 25:4 2135
I am *c* without transgression, I ... Job 33:9 2134
The fear of the LORD is *c* ... Ps 19:9 2889
He that hath *c* hands, and a pure ... Ps 24:4 5355
me with hyssop, and I shall be *c* ... Ps 51:7 2891
Create in me a *c* heart, O God ... Ps 51:10 2889
even to such as are of a *c* heart ... Ps 73:1 1249
Is his mercy *c* gone for ever ... Ps 77:8 656
Where no oxen are, the crib is *c* ... Prov 14:4 1249
of a man are *c* in his own eyes ... Prov 16:2 2134
can say, I have made my heart *c* ... Prov 20:9 2135
to the good and to the *c*, and to ... Eccl 9:2 2889
Wash you, make you *c* ... Is 1:16 2135
down, the earth is *c* dissolved ... Is 24:19 6565
so that there is no place *c* ... Is 28:8
the ground shall eat *c* provender ... Is 30:24 2548
be ye *c*, that bear the vessels of ... Is 52:11 1305
a *c* vessel into the house of the ... Is 66:20 2889
wilt thou not be made *c* ... Jer 13:27 2891
between the unclean and the *c* ... Eze 22:26 2889
will I sprinkle *c* water upon you ... Eze 36:25 2889
and ye shall be *c* ... Eze 36:25 2891
between the unclean and the *c* ... Eze 44:23 2889
he hath made it *c* bare, and cast ... Joel 1:7
his arm shall be *c* dried up ... Zec 11:17
thou wilt, thou canst make me *c* ... Mt 8:2
be thou *c* ... Mt 8:3
for ye make *c* the outside of the ... Mt 23:25
the outside of them may be *c* also ... Mt 23:26 *2513*
he wrapped it in a *c* linen cloth ... Mt 27:59 *2513*
thou wilt, thou canst make me *c* ... Mk 1:40 *2511*
be thou *c* ... Mk 1:41 *2511*
thou wilt, thou canst make me *c* ... Lk 5:12 *2511*
be thou *c* ... Lk 5:13 *2511*
make *c* the outside of the cup ... Lk 11:39 *2511*
behold, all things are *c* unto you ... Lk 11:41 *2513*
his feet, but is *c* every whit ... Jn 13:10 *2513*
and ye are *c*, but not all ... Jn 13:10 *2513*
said he, Ye are not all *c* ... Jn 13:11 *2513*
Now ye are *c* through the word ... Jn 15:3 *2513*
I am *c* ... Acts 18:6 *2513*
those that were *c* escaped from ... 2Pet 2:18 3689
be arrayed in fine linen, *c* ... Rev 19:8 *2513*
clothed in fine linen, white and *c* ... Rev 19:14 *2513*

CLEANNESS
according to the *c* of my hands ... 2Sa 22:21 1252
according to my *c* in his eye ... 2Sa 22:25 1252
according to the *c* of my hands ... Ps 18:20 1252
according to the *c* of my hands in ... Ps 18:24 1252
I also have given you *c* of teeth ... Amos 4:6 5356

CLEANSE
and thou shalt *c* the altar ... Ex 29:36 2398
he shall take to *c* the house two ... Lev 14:49 2398
he shall *c* the house with the ... Lev 14:52 2398
c it, and hallow it from the ... Lev 16:19 2891
to *c* you, that ye may be clean ... Lev 16:30 2891
the children of Israel, and *c* them ... Num 8:6 2891
thou do unto them, to *c* them ... Num 8:7 2891
and thou shalt *c* them, and offer ... Num 8:15 2891
an atonement for them to *c* them ... Num 8:21 2891
to *c* the house of the LORD ... 2Chr 29:15 2891
of the house of the LORD, to *c* it ... 2Chr 29:16 2891
that they should *c* themselves ... Neh 13:22 2891
c thou me from secret faults ... Ps 19:12 5352
iniquity, and *c* me from my sin ... Ps 51:2 5352
shall a young man *c* his way ... Ps 119:9 2135
my people, not to fan, nor to *c* ... Jer 4:11 1305
I will *c* them from all their ... Jer 33:8 2891
from all your idols, will I *c* you ... Eze 36:25 2891
they have sinned, and will *c* them ... Eze 37:23 2891
of them, that they may *c* the land ... Eze 39:12 2891
the face of the earth, to *c* it ... Eze 39:14 2891
Thus shall they *c* the land ... Eze 39:16 2891
thus shalt thou *c* and purge it ... Eze 43:20 2398
and they shall *c* the altar ... Eze 43:22 2398
as they did *c* it with the bullock ... Eze 43:22 2398
blemish, and *c* the sanctuary ... Eze 45:18 2398
For I will *c* their blood that I ... Joel 3:21 5352
c the lepers, raise the dead, ... Mt 10:8 *2511*
c first that which is within the ... Mt 23:26 *2511*
let us *c* ourselves from all ... 2Cor 7:1 *2511*
c it with the washing of water by ... Eph 5:26 *2511*
C your hands, ye sinners ... Jas 4:8 *2511*
to *c* us from all unrighteousness ... 1Jn 1:9 *2511*

CLEANSED
so it shall be *c* ... Lev 11:32 2891
she shall be *c* from the issue of ... Lev 12:7 2891
that is to be *c* two birds alive ... Lev 14:4 2891
be *c* from the leprosy seven times ... Lev 14:7 2891
he that is to be *c* shall wash his ... Lev 14:8 2891
right ear of him that is to be *c* ... Lev 14:14 2891
right ear of him that is to be *c* ... Lev 14:17 2891
the head of him that is to be *c* ... Lev 14:18 2891
is to be *c* from his uncleanness ... Lev 14:19 2891
right ear of him that is to be *c* ... Lev 14:25 2891
right ear of him that is to be *c* ... Lev 14:28 2891
the head of him that is to be *c* ... Lev 14:29 2891
that is to be *c* before the LORD ... Lev 14:31 2891
hath an issue is *c* of his issue ... Lev 15:13 2891
But if she be *c* of her issue ... Lev 15:28 2891
the land cannot be *c* of the blood ... Num 35:33 3722
which we are not *c* until this day ... Josh 22:17 2891
We have *c* all the house of the ... 2Chr 29:18 2891
had not *c* themselves, yet did ... 2Chr 30:18 2891
though he be not *c* according to ... 2Chr 30:19
altars, and *c* Judah and Jerusalem ... 2Chr 34:5 2891
commanded, and they *c* the chambers ... Neh 13:9 2891
Thus *c* I them from all strangers, ... Neh 13:30 2891
I have, if I be *c* from my sin ... Job 35:3
Verily I have *c* my heart in vain, ... Ps 73:13 2135
Thou art the land that is not *c* ... Eze 22:24 2891
In the day that I shall have *c* ... Eze 36:33 2891
And after he is *c*, they shall ... Eze 44:26 2893
then shall the sanctuary be *c* ... Dan 8:14 6663
their blood that I have not *c* ... Joel 3:21 5352
And immediately his leprosy was *c* ... Mt 8:3 *2511*
the lame walk, the lepers are *c* ... Mt 11:5 *2511*
departed from him, and he was *c* ... Mk 1:42 *2511*
and none of them was *c*, saving ... Lk 4:27 *2511*
the lame walk, the lepers are *c* ... Lk 7:22 *2511*
that, as they went, they were *c* ... Lk 17:14 *2511*
said, Were there not ten *c* ... Lk 17:17 *2511*
the second time, What God hath *c* ... Acts 10:15 *2511*
from heaven, What God hath *c* ... Acts 11:9 *2511*

CLEANSETH
but the wind passeth, and *c* them ... Job 37:21 2891
blueness of a wound *c* away evil ... Prov 20:30 8562
Christ his Son *c* us from all sin ... 1Jn 1:7 *2511*

CLEANSING
been seen of the priest for his *c* ... Lev 13:7 2893
much in the skin after his *c* ... Lev 13:35 2893
of the leper in the day of his *c* ... Lev 14:2 2893
day for his *c* unto the priest ... Lev 14:23 2893
that which pertaineth to his *c* ... Lev 14:32 2893
to himself seven days for his *c* ... Lev 15:13 2893
his head in the day of his *c* ... Num 6:9 2893
thou hast made an end of *c* it ... Eze 43:23 2893
offer for thy *c* those things ... Mk 1:44 *2512*
to the priest, and offer for thy *c* ... Lk 5:14 *2512*

CLEAR
thou shalt be *c* from this my oath ... Gen 24:8 5352
shalt thou be *c* from this my oath ... Gen 24:41 5352
one, thou shalt be *c* from my oath ... Gen 24:41 5355
or how shall we *c* ourselves ... Gen 44:16 6663
will by no means *c* the guilty ... Ex 34:7 5352
the earth by *c* shining after rain ... 2Sa 23:4
and be *c* when thou judgest ... Ps 51:4 2135
c as the sun, and terrible as an ... Song 6:10 1249
place like a *c* heat upon herbs ... Is 18:4 6703
darken the earth in the *c* day ... Amos 8:9 216
that the light shall not be *c* ... Zec 14:6 3368
yourselves to be *c* in this matter ... 2Cor 7:11 *53*
like a jasper stone, *c* as crystal ... Rev 21:11 *2929*
was pure gold, like unto *c* glass ... Rev 21:18 *2513*
c as crystal, proceeding out of ... Rev 22:1 *2986*

CLEARER
age shall be *c* than the noonday ... Job 11:17 6965

CLEARING
and by no means *c* the guilty ... Num 14:18 5352
what *c* of yourselves, yea, what ... 2Cor 7:11 *627*

CLEARLY
my lips shall utter knowledge *c* ... Job 33:3 1305
then shalt thou see *c* to cast out ... Mt 7:5 *1227*

was restored, and saw every man c ... Mk 8:25 *5081*
then shalt thou see c to pull out ... Lk 6:42 *1227*
creation of the world are c seen ... Rom 1:20 *2529*

CLEARNESS
were the body of heaven in his *c* ... Ex 24:10 2892

CLEAVE
mother, and shall c unto his wife ... Gen 2:24 1692
he shall c it with the wings ... Lev 1:17 8156
But ye that did c unto the LORD ... Deut 4:4 1695
serve, and to him shalt thou c ... Deut 10:20 1692
in all his ways, and to c unto him ... Deut 11:22 1692
ye shall serve him, and c unto him ... Deut 13:4 1692
there shall c nought of the ... Deut 13:17 1692
make the pestilence c unto thee ... Deut 28:21 1692
and they shall c unto thee ... Deut 28:60 1692
and that thou mayest c unto him ... Deut 30:20 1692
to c unto him, and to serve him ... Josh 22:5 1692
But c unto the LORD your God, as ... Josh 23:8 1692
c unto the remnant of these ... Josh 23:12 1692
of Naaman shall c unto thee ... 2Kin 5:27 1692
the clods c fast together ... Job 38:38 1692
Thou didst c the fountain and the ... Ps 74:15 1234
it shall not c to me ... Ps 101:3 1692
my groaning my bones c to my skin ... Ps 102:5 1692
let my tongue c to the roof of my ... Ps 137:6 1692
they shall c to the house of ... Is 14:1 5596
so have I caused to c unto me the ... Jer 13:11 1692
I will make thy tongue c to the ... Eze 3:26 1692
they shall not c one to another ... Dan 2:43 1692
but many shall c to them with ... Dan 11:34 3867
Thou didst c the earth with ... Hab 3:9 1234
the mount of Olives shall c in ... Zec 14:4 1234
and mother, and shall c to his wife ... Mt 19:5 *4347*
and mother, and c to his wife ... Mk 10:7 *4347*
heart they would c unto the Lord ... Acts 11:23 *4347*
c to that which is good ... Rom 12:9 *2853*

CLEAVED
Nevertheless he c unto the sins ... 2Kin 3:3 1692
their tongue c to the roof of ... Job 29:10 1692
if any blot hath c to mine hands ... Job 31:7 1692

CLEAVETH
c the cleft into two claws, and ... Deut 14:6 8157
he c my reins asunder, and doth ... Job 16:13 6398
My bone c to my skin and to my ... Job 19:20 1692
and my tongue c to my jaws ... Ps 22:15 1692
say they, c fast unto him ... Ps 41:8 3332
our belly c unto the earth ... Ps 44:25 1692
My soul c unto the dust ... Ps 119:25 1692
cutteth and c wood upon the earth ... Ps 141:7 1234
and he that c wood shall be ... Eccl 10:9 1234
For as the girdle c to the loins ... Jer 13:11 1692
c to the roof of his mouth for ... Lam 4:4 1692
their skin c to their bones ... Lam 4:8 6821
dust of your city, which c on us ... Lk 10:11 *2853*

CLEFT
cleaveth the c into two claws, and ... Deut 14:6 8156
him, and the valleys shall be c ... Mic 1:4 1234

CLEFTS
that art in the c of the rock ... Song 2:14 2288
To go into the c of the rocks ... Is 2:21 5366
dwellest in the c of the rock ... Jer 49:16 2288
and the little house with c ... Amos 6:11 1233
dwellest in the c of the rock ... Obad 3 2288

CLEMENCY
hear us of thy c a few words ... Acts 24:4 *1932*

CLEMENT (*clem'-ent*) *A companion of Paul.*
me in the gospel, with C also ... Phil 4:3 *2815*

CLEOPAS (*cle'-o-pas*) See ALPHAEUS, CLEOPHAS. *A disciple on Emmaus Road.*
the one of them, whose name was C ... Lk 24:18 *2810*

CLEOPHAS (*cle'-o-fas*) See CLEOPAS. *Husband of Mary.*
sister, Mary the wife of C ... Jn 19:25 *2832*

CLIFF
they come up by the c of Ziz ... 2Chr 20:16 4608

CLIFFS
To dwell in the c of the valleys ... Job 30:6 6178

CLIFT
will put thee in a c of the rock ... Ex 33:22 5366

CLIFTS
valleys under the c of the rocks ... Is 57:5 5585

CLIMB
thickets, and c up upon the rocks ... Jer 4:29 5927
they shall c the wall like men of ... Joel 2:7 5927
they shall c up upon the houses ... Joel 2:9 5927
though they c up to heaven, ... Amos 9:2 5927

CLIMBED
Jonathan c up upon his hands and ... 1Sa 14:13 5927
c up into a sycomore tree to see ... Lk 19:4 *305*

CLIMBETH
but c up some other way, the same ... Jn 10:1 *305*

CLIPPED
shall be bald, and every beard c ... Jer 48:37 1639

CLODS
clothed with worms and c of dust ... Job 7:5 1487
The c of the valley shall be ... Job 21:33 7263
the c cleave fast together ... Job 38:38 7263
break the c of his ground ... Is 28:24 7702
plow, and Jacob shall break his c ... Hos 10:11 7702
The seed is rotten under their c ... Joel 1:17 4053

CLOKE
and was clad with zeal as a c ... Is 59:17 4598
thy coat, let him have thy c also ... Mt 5:40 *2440*
him that taketh away thy c forbid ... Lk 6:29 *2440*
now they have no c for their sin ... Jn 15:22 *4392*
ye know, nor a c of covetousness ... 1Th 2:5 *4392*
The c that I left at Troas with ... 2Ti 4:13 *5341*
liberty for a c of maliciousness ... 1Pet 2:16 *1942*

CLOPAS See CLEOPHAS.

CLOSE
eyes of her husband, and be kept c ... Num 5:13 5956
be afraid out of their c places ... 2Sa 22:46 4526
while he yet kept himself c ... 1Chr 12:1 6113
kept c from the fowls of the air ... Job 28:21 5641
shut up together as with a c seal ... Job 41:15 6862
be afraid out of their c places ... Ps 18:45 4526
shall follow c after you there in ... Jer 42:16 1692
And I saw him come c unto the ram ... Dan 8:7 681
c up the breaches thereof ... Amos 9:11 1443
And they kept it c, and told no man ... Lk 9:36 *4601*
thence, they sailed c by Crete ... Acts 27:13 *788*

CLOSED
c up the flesh instead thereof ... Gen 2:21 5462
For the LORD had fast c up all ... Gen 20:18 6113
the pit, and the earth c upon them ... Num 16:33 3680
the fat c upon the blade, so that ... Judg 3:22 5462
they have not been c, neither ... Is 1:6 2115
deep sleep, and hath c your eyes ... Is 29:10 6105
for the words are c up and sealed ... Dan 12:9 5640
the depth c me round about, the ... Jonah 2:5 5437
and their eyes they have c ... Mt 13:15 *2576*
he c the book, and he gave it ... Lk 4:20 *4428*
and their eyes have they c ... Acts 28:27 *2576*

CLOSER
that sticketh c than a brother ... Prov 18:24

CLOSEST
because thou c thyself in cedar ... Jer 22:15 8474

CLOSET
and the bride out of her c ... Joel 2:16 2646
thou prayest, enter into thy c ... Mt 6:6 *5009*

CLOSETS
in c shall be proclaimed upon the ... Lk 12:3 *5009*

CLOTH
spread over it a c wholly of blue ... Num 4:6 899
they shall spread a c of blue ... Num 4:7 899
spread upon them a c of scarlet ... Num 4:8 899
And they shall take a c of blue ... Num 4:9 899
they shall spread a c of blue ... Num 4:11 899
and put them in a c of blue ... Num 4:12 899
and spread a purple c thereon ... Num 4:13 899
they shall spread the c before ... Deut 22:17 8071
bolster, and covered it with a c ... 1Sa 19:13 899
wrapped in a c behind the ephod ... 1Sa 21:9 8071
cast a c upon him, when he saw ... 2Sa 20:12 899
morrow, that he took a thick c ... 2Kin 8:15 4346
cast them away as a menstruous c ... Is 30:22
of new c unto an old garment ... Mt 9:16 *4470*
he wrapped it in a clean linen c ... Mt 27:59 *4616*
piece of new c on an old garment ... Mk 2:21 *4470*
having a linen c cast about his ... Mk 14:51 *4616*
And he left the linen c, and fled ... Mk 14:52 *4616*

CLOTHE
his sons, and c them with coats ... Ex 40:14 3847
and she sent raiment to c Mordecai ... Est 4:4 3847
I will also c her priests with ... Ps 132:16 3847
His enemies will I c with shame ... Ps 132:18 3847
shall c a man with rags ... Prov 23:21 3847
I will c him with thy robe, and ... Is 22:21 3847
thou shalt surely c thee with ... Is 49:18 3847
I c the heavens with blackness, ... Is 50:3 3847
they shall c themselves with ... Eze 26:16 3847
ye c you with the wool, ye kill ... Eze 34:3 3847
ye c you, but there is none warm ... Hag 1:6 3847
I will c thee with change of ... Zec 3:4 3847
if God so c the grass of the ... Mt 6:30 *294*
shall he not much more c you ... Mt 6:30
If then God so c the grass ... Lk 12:28 *294*
how much more will he c you ... Lk 12:28

CLOTHED
make coats of skins, and c them ... Gen 3:21 3847
c him with the robe, and put the ... Lev 8:7 3847
who c you in scarlet, with other ... 2Sa 1:24 3847
David was c with a robe of fine ... 1Chr 15:27 3736
who were c in sackcloth, fell ... 1Chr 21:16 3680
be c with salvation, and let thy ... 2Chr 6:41 3847
c in their robes, and they sat in ... 2Chr 18:9 3847
with the spoil c all that were ... 2Chr 28:15 3847
the king's gate c with sackcloth ... Est 4:2 3830
My flesh is c with worms and clods ... Job 7:5 3847
hate thee shall be c with shame ... Job 8:22 3847
Thou hast c me with skin and flesh ... Job 10:11 3847
put on righteousness, and it c me ... Job 29:14 3847
hast thou c his neck with thunder ... Job 39:19 3847
let them be c with shame and ... Ps 35:26 3847
The pastures are c with flocks ... Ps 65:13 3847
reigneth, he is c with majesty ... Ps 93:1 3847
the LORD is c with strength, ... Ps 93:1 3847
thou art c with honour and majesty ... Ps 104:1 3847
As he c himself with cursing like ... Ps 109:18 3847
mine adversaries be c with shame ... Ps 109:29 3847
priests be c with righteousness ... Ps 132:9 3847
her household are c with scarlet ... Prov 31:21 3847
for he hath c me with the ... Is 61:10 3847
prince shall be c with desolation ... Eze 7:27 3847
man among them was c with linen ... Eze 9:2 3847
he called to the man c with linen ... Eze 9:3 3847
the man c with linen, which had ... Eze 9:11 3847
spake unto the man c with linen ... Eze 10:2 3847
commanded the man c with linen ... Eze 10:6 3847
of him that was c with linen ... Eze 10:7 3847
I c thee also with broidered work ... Eze 16:10 3847
Which were c with blue, captains ... Eze 23:6 3847
rulers c most gorgeously, ... Eze 23:12 3847
all of them c with all sorts of ... Eze 38:4 3847
they shall be c with linen ... Eze 44:17 3847
shall be c with scarlet, and have ... Dan 5:7 3848
thou shalt be c with scarlet ... Dan 5:16 3848
they c Daniel with scarlet, and ... Dan 5:29 3848
behold a certain man c in linen ... Dan 10:5 3847
And one said to the man c in linen ... Dan 12:6 3847
And I heard the man c in linen ... Dan 12:7 3847
all such as are c with strange ... Zeph 1:8 3847
Now Joshua was c with filthy ... Zec 3:3 3847
his head, and c him with garments ... Zec 3:5 3847
or, Wherewithal shall we be c ... Mt 6:31 *4016*
A man c in soft raiment ... Mt 11:8 *294*
Naked, and ye c me ... Mt 25:36 *4016*
or naked, and c thee ... Mt 25:38 *4016*
naked, and ye c me not ... Mt 25:43 *4016*
John was c with camel's hair, and ... Mk 1:6 *1746*
and had the legion, sitting, and c ... Mk 5:15 *2439*
they c him with purple, and ... Mk 15:17 *1746*
c in a long white garment ... Mk 16:5 *4016*
A man c in soft raiment ... Lk 7:25 *294*
sitting at the feet of Jesus, c ... Lk 8:35 *2439*
rich man, which was c in purple ... Lk 16:19 *1737*
earnestly desiring to be c upon ... 2Cor 5:2 *1902*
If so be that being c we shall ... 2Cor 5:3 *1746*
but c upon, that mortality might ... 2Cor 5:4 *1902*
to another, and be c with humility ... 1Pet 5:5 *1463*
c with a garment down to the foot ... Rev 1:13 *1746*
same shall be c in white raiment ... Rev 3:5 *4016*
raiment, that thou mayest be c ... Rev 3:18 *4016*
sitting, c in white raiment ... Rev 4:4 *4016*
c with white robes, and palms in ... Rev 7:9 *4016*
down from heaven, c with a cloud ... Rev 10:1 *4016*
threescore days, c in sackcloth ... Rev 11:3 *4016*
a woman c with the sun, and the ... Rev 12:1 *4016*
c in pure and white linen, and ... Rev 15:6 *1746*
that was c in fine linen, and ... Rev 18:16 *4016*
he was c with a vesture dipped in ... Rev 19:13 *4016*
c in fine linen, white and clean ... Rev 19:14 *1746*

CLOTHES
and he rent his c ... Gen 37:29 899
And Jacob rent his c, and put ... Gen 37:34 8071
Then they rent their c, and laded ... Gen 44:13 8071
his c in the blood of grapes ... Gen 49:11 5497
in their c upon their shoulders ... Ex 12:34 8071
morrow, and let them wash their c ... Ex 19:10 8071
and they washed their c ... Ex 19:14 8071
your heads, neither rend your c ... Lev 10:6 899
carcase of them shall wash his c ... Lev 11:25 899
carcase of them shall wash his c ... Lev 11:28 899
carcase of it shall wash his c ... Lev 11:40 899
carcase of it shall wash his c ... Lev 11:40 899
and he shall wash his c, and be ... Lev 13:6 899
and he shall wash his c, and be ... Lev 13:34 899
his c shall be rent, and his head ... Lev 13:45 899
to be cleansed shall wash his c ... Lev 14:8 899
and he shall wash his c, also he ... Lev 14:9 899
in the house shall wash his c ... Lev 14:47 899
in the house shall wash his c ... Lev 14:47 899
toucheth his bed shall wash his c ... Lev 15:5 899
hath the issue shall wash his c ... Lev 15:6 899
hath the issue shall wash his c ... Lev 15:7 899
then he shall wash his c, and ... Lev 15:8 899
of those things shall wash his c ... Lev 15:10 899
in water, he shall wash his c ... Lev 15:11 899
for his cleansing, and wash his c ... Lev 15:13 899
toucheth her bed shall wash his c ... Lev 15:21 899
she sat upon shall wash his c ... Lev 15:22 899
be unclean, and shall wash his c ... Lev 15:27 899
the scapegoat shall wash his c ... Lev 16:26 899
burneth them shall wash his c ... Lev 16:28 899
and shall put on the linen c ... Lev 16:32 899
he shall both wash his c ... Lev 17:15 899
uncover his head, nor rend his c ... Lev 21:10 899
flesh, and let them wash their c ... Num 8:7 899
purified, and they washed their c ... Num 8:21 899
searched the land, rent their c ... Num 14:6 899
Then the priest shall wash his c ... Num 19:7 899
her shall wash his c in water ... Num 19:8 899
of the heifer shall wash his c ... Num 19:10 899
purify himself, and wash his c ... Num 19:19 899
of separation shall wash his c ... Num 19:21 899
wash your c on the seventh day ... Num 31:24 899
your c are not waxen old upon you ... Deut 29:5 8008
And Joshua rent his c, and fell to ... Josh 7:6 8071
he saw her, that he rent his c ... Judg 11:35 899
the same day with his c rent ... 1Sa 4:12 4055
And he stript off his c also ... 1Sa 19:24 899
camp from Saul with his c rent ... 2Sa 1:2 899
Then David took hold on his c ... 2Sa 1:11 899
that were with him, Rend your c ... 2Sa 3:31 899
stood by with their c rent ... 2Sa 13:31 899
his beard, nor washed his c ... 2Sa 19:24 899
and they covered him with c ... 1Kin 1:1 899
those words, that he rent his c ... 1Kin 21:27 899
and he took hold of his own c ... 2Kin 2:12 899
the letter, that he rent his c ... 2Kin 5:7 899
the king of Israel had rent his c ... 2Kin 5:8 899
Wherefore hast thou rent thy c ... 2Kin 5:8 899
of the woman, that he rent his c ... 2Kin 6:30 899
and Athaliah rent her c, and cried, ... 2Kin 11:14 899
to Hezekiah with their c rent ... 2Kin 18:37 899
heard it, that he rent his c ... 2Kin 19:1 899
of the law, that he rent his c ... 2Kin 22:11 899
and a curse, and hast rent thy c ... 2Kin 22:19 899
Then Athaliah rent her c, and said ... 2Chr 23:13 899
of the law, that he rent his c ... 2Chr 34:19 899
before me, and didst rend thy c ... 2Chr 34:27 899
me, none of us put off our c ... Neh 4:23 899
their c waxed not old, and their ... Neh 9:21 8008
was done, Mordecai rent his c ... Est 4:1 899
mine own c shall abhor me ... Job 9:31 8008
his bosom, and his c not be burned ... Prov 6:27 899

to Hezekiah with their c rent Is 36:22 899
heard it, that he rent his c Is 37:1 899
beards shaven, and their c rent Jer 41:5 899
shall strip thee also of thy c Eze 16:39 899
also strip thee out of thy c Eze 23:26 899
in precious c for chariots Eze 27:20 899
in all sorts of things, in blue c Eze 27:24 1545
c laid to pledge by every altar Amos 2:8 899
the colt, and put on them their c Mt 21:7 *2440*
field return back to take his c Mt 24:18 *2440*
Then the high priest rent his c Mt 26:65 *2440*
said, If I may touch but his c Mk 5:28 *2440*
press, and said, Who touched my c Mk 5:30 *2440*
Then the high priest rent his c Mk 14:63 *5509*
from him, and put his own c on him Mk 15:20 *2440*
and wrapped him in swaddling c Lk 2:7 *4683*
the babe wrapped in swaddling c Lk 2:12 *4683*
devils long time, and ware no c Lk 8:27 *2440*
they spread their c in the way Lk 19:36 *2440*
the linen c laid by themselves Lk 24:12 *3608*
it in linen c with the spices Jn 19:40 *3608*
looking in, saw the linen c lying Jn 20:5 *3608*
and seeth the linen c lie Jn 20:6 *3608*
head, not lying with the linen c Jn 20:7 *3608*
their c at a young man's feet Acts 7:58 *2440*
Paul, heard of, they rent their c Acts 14:14 *2440*
the magistrates rent off their c Acts 16:22 *2440*
cried out, and cast off their c Acts 22:23 *2440*

CLOTHEST
Though thou c thyself with Jer 4:30 3847

CLOTHING
and stripped the naked of their c Job 22:6 899
the naked to lodge without c Job 24:7 3830
cause him to go naked without c Job 24:10 3830
seen any perish for want of c Job 31:19 3830
were sick, my c was sackcloth Ps 35:13 3830
her c is of wrought gold Ps 45:13 3830
The lambs are for thy c, and the Prov 27:26 3830
her c is silk and purple Prov 31:22 3830
Strength and honour are her c Prov 31:25 3830
his father, saying, Thou hast c Is 3:6 8071
my house is neither bread nor c Is 3:7 8071
sufficiently, and for durable c Is 23:18 4374
the garments of vengeance for c Is 59:17 8516
blue and purple is their c Jer 10:9 3830
which come to you in sheep's c Mt 7:15 *1742*
they that wear soft c are in Mt 11:8
which love to go in long c Mk 12:38 *4749*
a man stood before me in bright c Acts 10:30 *2066*
to him that weareth the gay c Jas 2:3 *2066*

CLOTHS
the c of service, and the holy Ex 31:10 899
The c of service, to do service Ex 35:19 899
they made c of service, to do Ex 39:1 899
The c of service to do service in Ex 39:41 899

CLOUD
I do set my bow in the c, and it Gen 9:13 6051
when I bring a c over the earth Gen 9:14 6051
the bow shall be seen in the c Gen 9:14 6051
And the bow shall be in the c Gen 9:16 6051
them by day in a pillar of a c Ex 13:21 6051
away the pillar of the c by day Ex 13:22 6051
the pillar of the c went from Ex 14:19 6051
and it was a c and darkness to them Ex 14:20 6051
the pillar of fire and of the c Ex 14:24 6051
of the LORD appeared in the c Ex 16:10 6051
Lo, I come unto thee in a thick c Ex 19:9 6051
a thick c upon the mount, and the Ex 19:16 6051
mount, and a c covered the mount Ex 24:15 6051
the c covered it six days Ex 24:16 6051
Moses out of the midst of the c Ex 24:16 6051
went into the midst of the c Ex 24:18 6051
And the LORD descended in the c Ex 34:5 6051
Then a c covered the tent of the Ex 40:34 6051
because the c abode thereon, and Ex 40:35 6051
when the c was taken up from over Ex 40:36 6051
But if the c were not taken up, Ex 40:37 6051
For the c of the LORD was upon Ex 40:38 6051
in the c upon the mercy seat Lev 16:2 6051
that the c of the incense may Lev 16:13 6051
up the c covered the tabernacle Num 9:15 6051
the c covered it by day, and the Num 9:16 6051
when the c was taken up from the Num 9:17 6051
and in the place where the c abode Num 9:17 6051
as long as the c abode upon the Num 9:18 6051
when the c tarried long upon the Num 9:19 6051
when the c was a few days upon Num 9:20 6051
when the c abode from even unto Num 9:21 6051
that the c was taken up in the Num 9:21 6051
by night that the c was taken up Num 9:21 6051
that the c tarried upon the Num 9:22 6051
that the c was taken up from off Num 10:11 6051
the c rested in the wilderness of Num 10:12 6051
the c of the LORD was upon them Num 10:34 6051
And the LORD came down in a c Num 11:25 6051
came down in the pillar of the c Num 12:5 6051
the c departed from off the Num 12:10 6051
that thy c standeth over them, and Num 14:14 6051
by daytime in a pillar of a c Num 14:14 6051
the c covered it, and the glory of Num 16:42 6051
ye should go, and in a c by day Deut 1:33 6051
the midst of the fire, of the c Deut 5:22 6051
the tabernacle in a pillar of a c Deut 31:15 6051
the pillar of the c stood over Deut 31:15 6051
that the c filled the house of 1Kin 8:10 6051
to minister because of the c 1Kin 8:11 6051
ariseth a little c out of the sea 1Kin 18:44 5645
the house was filled with a c 2Chr 5:13 6051
to minister by reason of the c 2Chr 5:14 6051
the pillar of the c departed not Neh 9:19 6051
let a c dwell upon it Job 3:5 6053
As the c is consumed and vanisheth Job 7:9 6051
can he judge through the dark c Job 22:13 6205
the c is not rent under them Job 26:8 6051
and spreadeth his c upon it Job 26:9 6051
and my welfare passeth away as a c Job 30:15 5645
by the c that cometh betwixt Job 36:32
watering he wearieth the thick c Job 37:11 5645
he scattereth his bright c Job 37:11 6051
the light of his c to shine Job 37:15 6051
When I made the c the garment Job 38:9 6051
daytime also he led them with a c Ps 78:14 6051
He spread a c for a covering Ps 105:39 6051
is as a c of the latter rain Prov 16:15 5645
Zion, and upon her assemblies, a c Is 4:5 6051
like a c of dew in the heat of Is 18:4 5645
the LORD rideth upon a swift c Is 19:1 5645
the heat with the shadow of a c Is 25:5 5645
I have blotted out, as a thick c Is 44:22 5645
thy transgressions, and, as a c Is 44:22 6051
Who are these that fly as a c Is 60:8 5645
of Zion with a c in his anger Lam 2:1 5743
hast covered thyself with a c Lam 3:44 6051
came out of the north, a great c Eze 1:4 6051
is in the c in the day of rain Eze 1:28 6051
a thick c of incense went up Eze 8:11 6051
the c filled the inner court Eze 10:3 6051
the house was filled with the c Eze 10:4 6051
a c shall cover her, and her Eze 30:18 6051
I will cover the sun with a c Eze 32:7 6051
be like a c to cover the land Eze 38:9 6051
Israel, as a c to cover the land Eze 38:16 6051
your goodness is as a morning c Hos 6:4 6051
they shall be as the morning c Hos 13:3 6051
a bright c overshadowed them Mt 17:5 *3507*
and behold a voice out of the c Mt 17:5 *3507*
there was a c that overshadowed Mk 9:7 *3507*
and a voice came out of the c Mk 9:7 *3507*
he thus spake, there came a c Lk 9:34 *3507*
feared as they entered into the c Lk 9:34 *3507*
there came a voice out of the c Lk 9:35 *3507*
When ye see a c rise out of the Lk 12:54 *3507*
of man coming in a c with power Lk 21:27 *3507*
a c received him out of their Acts 1:9 *3507*
all our fathers were under the c 1Cor 10:1 *3507*
all baptized unto Moses in the c 1Cor 10:2 *3507*
with so great a c of witnesses Heb 12:1 *3509*
from heaven, clothed with a c Rev 10:1 *3507*
they ascended up to heaven in a c Rev 11:12 *3507*
And I looked, and behold a white c Rev 14:14 *3507*
upon the c one sat like unto the Rev 14:14 *3507*
voice to him that sat on the c Rev 14:15 *3507*
he that sat on the c thrust in Rev 14:16 *3507*

CLOUDS
midst of heaven, with darkness, c Deut 4:11 6051
dropped, the c also dropped water Judg 5:4 5645
waters, and thick c of the skies 2Sa 22:12 5645
riseth, even a morning without c 2Sa 23:4 5645
that the heaven was black with c 1Kin 18:45 5645
and his head reach unto the c Job 20:6 5645
Thick c are a covering to him, Job 22:14 5645
up the waters in his thick c Job 26:8 5645
behold the c which are higher Job 35:5 7834
Which the c do drop and distil Job 36:28 7834
the spreadings of the c, or the Job 36:29 5645
With c he covereth the light Job 36:32 3709
thou know the balancings of the c Job 37:16 5645
bright light which is in the c Job 37:21 7834
thou lift up thy voice to the c Job 38:34 5645
Who can number the c in wisdom Job 38:37 7834
waters and thick c of the skies Ps 18:11 5645
was before him his thick c passed Ps 18:12 5645
faithfulness reacheth unto the c Ps 36:5 7834
heavens, and thy truth unto the c Ps 57:10 7834
and his strength is in the c Ps 68:34 7834
The c poured out water Ps 77:17 5645
he had commanded the c from above Ps 78:23 7834
C and darkness are round about him Ps 97:2 6051
who maketh the c his chariot Ps 104:3 5645
and thy truth reacheth unto the c Ps 108:4 7834
Who covereth the heaven with c Ps 147:8 5645
up, and the c drop down the dew Prov 3:20 7834
When he established the c above Prov 8:28 7834
himself of a false gift is like c Prov 25:14 5387
If the c be full of rain, they Eccl 11:3 5645
regardeth the c shall not reap Eccl 11:4 5645
nor the c return after the rain Eccl 12:2 5645
I will also command the c that Is 5:6 5645
ascend above the heights of the c Is 14:14 5645
Behold, he shall come up as c Jer 4:13 6053
of man came with the c of heaven Dan 7:13 6050
and of gloominess, a day of c Joel 2:2 6051
the c are the dust of his feet Nah 1:3 6051
and gloominess, a day of c Zeph 1:15 6051
so the LORD shall make bright c Zec 10:1 2385
in the c of heaven with power Mt 24:30 *3507*
and coming in the c of heaven Mt 26:64 *3507*
coming in the c with great power Mk 13:26 *3507*
and coming in the c of heaven Mk 14:62 *3507*
up together with them in the c 1Th 4:17 *3507*
c that are carried with a tempest 2Pet 2:17 *3507*
c they are without water, carried Jude 12 *3507*
Behold, he cometh with c Rev 1:7 *3507*

CLOUDY
the c pillar descended, and stood Ex 33:9 6051
all the people saw the c pillar Ex 33:10 6051
them in the day by a c pillar Neh 9:12 6051
spake unto them in the c pillar Ps 99:7 6051
day of the LORD is near, a c day Eze 30:3 6051
they have been scattered in the c Eze 34:12 6051

CLOUTED
c upon their feet, and old Josh 9:5 2921

CLOUTS
and took thence old cast c Jer 38:11 5499
Put now these old cast c Jer 38:12 5499

CLOVEN
or of them that divide the c hoof Deut 14:7 8156
them c tongues like as of fire Acts 2:3 *1266*

CLOVENFOOTED
parteth the hoof, and is c Lev 11:3
he divide the hoof, and be c Lev 11:7
divideth the hoof, and is not c Lev 11:26

CLUSTER
a branch with one c of grapes Num 13:23 811
because of the c of grapes which Num 13:24 811
My beloved is unto me as a c of Song 1:14 811
As the new wine is found in the c Is 65:8 811
there is no c to eat Mic 7:1 811

CLUSTERS
the c thereof brought forth ripe Gen 40:10 811
of gall, their c are bitter Deut 32:32 811
corn, and an hundred c of raisins 1Sa 25:18 6778
cake of figs, and two c of raisins 1Sa 30:12 6778
and thy breasts to c of grapes Song 7:7 811
breasts shall be as c of the vine Song 7:8 811
gather the c of the vine of the Rev 14:18 *1009*

CNIDUS (*ni'-dus*) *A port town in southwestern Asia Minor.*
scarce were come over against C Acts 27:7 *2834*

COAL
shall quench my c which is left 2Sa 14:7 1513
me, having a live c in his hand Is 6:6 7531
there shall not be a c to warm at Is 47:14 1513
Their visage is blacker than a c Lam 4:8 7815

COALS
c of fire from off the altar Lev 16:12 1513
c were kindled by it 2Sa 22:9 1513
before him were c of fire kindled 2Sa 22:13 1513
there was a cake baken on the c 1Kin 19:6 7529
His breath kindleth c, and a flame Job 41:21 1513
c were kindled by it Ps 18:8 1513
passed, hail stones and c of fire Ps 18:12 1513
hail stones and c of fire Ps 18:13 1513
of the mighty, with c of juniper Ps 120:4 1513
Let burning c fall upon them Ps 140:10 1513
Can one go upon hot c, and his Prov 6:28 1513
For thou shalt heap c of fire Prov 25:22 1513
As c are to burning c, and Prov 26:21 6352
As c are to burning c Prov 26:21 1513
the c thereof are c of fire Song 8:6 7565
the tongs both worketh in the c Is 44:12 6352
baked bread upon the c thereof Is 44:19 1513
that bloweth the c in the fire Is 54:16 6352
was like burning c of fire Eze 1:13 1513
fill thine hand with c of fire Eze 10:2 1513
set it empty upon the c thereof Eze 24:11 1513
burning c went forth at his feet Hab 3:5 7565
there, who had made a fire of c Jn 18:18 *439*
land, they saw a fire of c there Jn 21:9 *439*
shalt heap c of fire on his head Rom 12:20 *440*

COAST
I bring the locusts into thy c Ex 10:4 1366
by the sea, and by the c of Jordan Num 13:29 3027
by the c of the land of Edom, Num 20:23 1366
Arnon, which is in the utmost c Num 22:36 1366
come from the c of Chittim Num 24:24 3027
of Zin along by the c of Edom Num 34:3 3027
c of the salt sea eastward Num 34:3 7097
the c shall go down from Shepham Num 34:11 1366
Ye are to pass through the c of Deut 2:4 1366
Ar, the c of Moab, this day Deut 2:18 1366
the c thereof, from Chinnereth Deut 3:17 1366
the uttermost sea shall your c be Deut 11:24 1366
with thee in all thy c seven days Deut 16:4 1366
if the LORD thy God enlarge thy c Deut 19:8 1366
down of the sun, shall be your c Josh 1:4 1366
the c of Og king of Bashan, which Josh 12:4 1366
The king of Dor in the c of Dor Josh 12:23 5299
their c was from Aroer, that is Josh 13:16 1366
their c was Jazer, and all the Josh 13:25 1366
their c was from Mahanaim, all Josh 13:30 1366
the uttermost part of the south c Josh 15:1 1366
out of that c were at the sea Josh 15:4 1366
this shall be your south c Josh 15:4 1366
the great sea, and the c thereof Josh 15:12 1366
This is the c of the children of Josh 15:12 1366
children of Judah toward the c of Josh 15:21 1366
westward to the c of Japhleti Josh 16:3 1366
unto the c of Beth-horon the Josh 16:3 1366
the c of Manasseh was from Asher Josh 17:7 1366
the c descended unto the river Josh 17:9 1366
the c of Manasseh also was on the Josh 17:9 1366
abide in their c on the south Josh 18:5 1366
the c of their lot came forth Josh 18:11 1366
this was the south c Josh 18:19 1366
the c reacheth to Tabor, and Josh 19:22 1366
then the c turneth to Ramah, and Josh 19:29 1366
and the c turneth to Hosah Josh 19:29 1366
at the sea from the c to Achzib Josh 19:29 2256
their c was from Heleph, from Josh 19:33 1366
then the c turneth westward to Josh 19:34 1366
the c of their inheritance was Josh 19:41 1366
the c of the children of Dan went Josh 19:47 1366
took Gaza with the c thereof Judg 1:18 1366
and Askelon with the c thereof Judg 1:18 1366
and Ekron with the c thereof Judg 1:18 1366
the c of the Amorites was from Judg 1:36 1366
not Israel to pass through his c Judg 11:20 1366
way of his own c to Beth-shemesh 1Sa 6:9 1366

came no more into the c of Israel 1Sa 7:13 1366
me any more in any c of Israel 1Sa 27:1 1366
upon the c which belongeth to 1Sa 30:14 1366
He restored the c of Israel from 2Kin 14:25 1366
bless me indeed, and enlarge my c 1Chr 4:10 1366
destroy the remnant of the sea c Eze 25:16 2348
which is by the c of Hauran Eze 47:16 1366
to the c of the way of Hethlon Eze 48:1 3027
northward, to the c of Hamath Eze 48:1 3027
unto the inhabitants of the sea c Zeph 2:5 2256
the sea c shall be dwellings and Zeph 2:6 2256
the c shall be for the remnant of Zeph 2:7 2256
which is upon the sea c, in the Mt 4:13 3864
and from the sea c of Tyre Lk 6:17 3882

COASTS
and rested in all the c of Egypt Ex 10:14 1366
one locust in all the c of Egypt Ex 10:19 1366
out of the c of the Amorites Num 21:13 1366
with the cities thereof in the c Num 32:33 1367
land of Canaan with the c thereof Num 34:2 1367
with the c thereof round about Num 34:12 1367
of Argob unto the c of Geshuri Deut 3:14 1366
divide the c of thy land, which Deut 19:3 1366
olive trees throughout all thy c Deut 28:40 1366
in all the c of the great sea Josh 9:1 2348
abide in their c on the north Josh 18:5 1366
by the c thereof round about, Josh 18:20 1367
land for inheritance by their c Josh 19:49 1367
all the c of the Amorites Judg 11:22 1366
that be along by the c of Arnon Judg 11:26 3027
family five men from their c Judg 18:2 7098
sent her into all the c of Israel Judg 19:29 1366
even Ashdod and the c thereof 1Sa 5:6 1366
the c thereof did Israel deliver 1Sa 7:14 1366
unto all the c of Israel 1Sa 11:3 1366
the c of Israel by the hands of 1Sa 11:7 1366
in any of the c of Israel 2Sa 21:5 1366
throughout all the c of Israel 1Kin 1:3 1366
smote them in all the c of Israel 2Kin 10:32 1366
the c thereof from Tirzah 2Kin 15:16 1366
their castles in their c, of the 1Chr 6:54 1366
c out of the tribe of Ephraim 1Chr 6:66 1366
throughout all the c of Israel 1Chr 21:12 1366
to him out of all their c 2Chr 11:13 1366
of flies, and lice in all their c Ps 105:31 1366
and brake the trees of their c Ps 105:33 1366
raised up from the c of the earth Jer 25:32 3411
them from the c of the earth Jer 31:8 3411
raised up from the c of the earth Jer 50:41 3411
of the land take a man of their c Eze 33:2 7097
Zidon, and all the c of Palestine Joel 3:4 1552
and in all the c thereof, from Mt 2:16 3725
he would depart out of their c Mt 8:34 3725
and departed into the c of Tyre Mt 15:21 3313
of Canaan came out of the same c Mt 15:22 3725
and came into the c of Magdala Mt 15:39 3725
into the c of Caesarea Philippi Mt 16:13 3313
came into the c of Judaea beyond Mt 19:1 3725
pray him to depart out of their c Mk 5:17 3725
departing from the c of Tyre Mk 7:31 3725
the midst of the c of Decapolis Mk 7:31 3725
cometh into the c of Judaea by Mk 10:1 3725
and expelled them out of their c Acts 13:50 3725
the upper c came to Ephesus Acts 19:1 3313
and throughout all the c of Judaea Acts 26:20 5561
meaning to sail by the c of Asia Acts 27:2 5117

COAT
he made him a c of many colours Gen 37:3 3801
they stript Joseph out of his c Gen 37:23 3801
his c of many colours that was on Gen 37:23 3801
And they took Joseph's c, and Gen 37:31 3801
dipped the c in the blood Gen 37:31 3801
they sent the c of many colours, Gen 37:32 3801
whether it be thy son's c or no Gen 37:32 3801
it, and said, It is my son's c Gen 37:33 3801
and a robe, and a broidered c Ex 28:4 3801
embroider the c of fine linen Ex 28:39 3801
garments, and put upon Aaron the c Ex 29:5 3801
And he put upon him the c, and Lev 8:7 3801
He shall put on the holy linen c Lev 16:4 3801
his mother made him a little c 1Sa 2:19 4598
and he was armed with a c of mail 1Sa 17:5 8302
the weight of the c was five 1Sa 17:5 8302
he armed him with a c of mail 1Sa 17:38 8302
came to meet him with his c rent 2Sa 15:32 3801
me about as the collar of my c Job 30:18 3801
I have put off my c Song 5:3 3801
at the law, and take away thy c Mt 5:40 5509
forbid not to take thy c also Lk 6:29 5509
and also his c Jn 19:23 5509
now the c was without seam, woven Jn 19:23 5509
he girt his fisher's c unto him Jn 21:7 1903

COATS
did the LORD God make c of skins Gen 3:21 3801
Aaron's sons thou shalt make c Ex 28:40 3801
his sons, and put c upon them Ex 29:8 3801
they made c of fine linen of Ex 39:27 3801
his sons, and clothe them with c Ex 40:14 3801
put c upon them, and girded them Lev 8:13 3801
them in their c out of the camp Lev 10:5 3801
these men were bound in their c Dan 3:21 5622
neither were their c changed Dan 3:27 5622
for your journey, neither two c Mt 10:10 5509
and not put on two c Mk 6:9 5509
unto them, He that hath two c Lk 3:11 5509
neither have two c apiece Lk 9:3 5509
by him weeping, and shewing the c Acts 9:39 5509

COCK
this night, before the c crow Mt 26:34 220
And immediately the c crew Mt 26:74 220
said unto him, Before the c crow Mt 26:75 220
night, before the c crow twice Mk 14:30 220
and the c crew Mk 14:68 220
And the second time the c crew Mk 14:72 220
unto him, Before the c crow twice Mk 14:72 220
the c shall not crow this day, Lk 22:34 220
while he yet spake, the c crew Lk 22:60 220
said unto him, Before the c crow Lk 22:61 220
The c shall not crow, till thou Jn 13:38 220
and immediately the c crew Jn 18:27 220

COCKATRICE
root shall come forth a c Is 14:29 6848

COCKATRICE'
shall put his hand on the c den Is 11:8 6848
They hatch c eggs, and weave the Is 59:5 6848

COCKATRICES
behold, I will send serpents, c Jer 8:17 6848

COCKCROWING
even, or at midnight, or at the c Mk 13:35 219

COCKLE
of wheat, and c instead of barley Job 31:40 890

COFFER
in a c by the side thereof 1Sa 6:8 712
the c with the mice of gold and 1Sa 6:11 712
the c that was with it, wherein 1Sa 6:15 712

COFFIN
and he was put in a c in Egypt Gen 50:26 727

COGITATIONS
my c much troubled me, and my Dan 7:28 7476

COLD
seedtime and harvest, and c Gen 8:22 7120
they have no covering in the c Job 24:7 7135
and c out of the north Job 37:9 7135
who can stand before his c Ps 147:17 7135
will not plow by reason of the c Prov 20:4 2779
As the c of snow in the time of Prov 25:13 6793
away a garment in c weather Prov 25:20 7135
As c waters to a thirsty soul, so Prov 25:25 7119
or shall the c flowing waters Jer 18:14 7119
camp in the hedges in the c day Nah 3:17 7135
of c water only in the name of a Mt 10:42 5593
the love of many shall wax c Mt 24:12 5594
for it was c Jn 18:18 5592
present rain, and because of the c Acts 28:2 5592
thirst, in fastings often, in c 2Cor 11:27 5592
that thou art neither c nor hot Rev 3:15 5593
I would thou wert c or hot Rev 3:15 5593
lukewarm, and neither c nor hot Rev 3:16 5593

COLHOZEH
repaired Shallun the son of C Neh 3:15 3626
the son of Baruch, the son of C Neh 11:5 3626

COLLAR
me about as the c of my coat Job 30:18 6310

COLLARS
beside ornaments, and c, and purple Judg 8:26 5188

COLLECTION
Judah and out of Jerusalem the c 2Chr 24:6 4864
to bring in to the LORD the c 2Chr 24:9 4864
concerning the c for the saints 1Cor 16:1 3048

COLLEGE
she dwelt in Jerusalem in the c 2Kin 22:14 4932
she dwelt in Jerusalem in the c 2Chr 34:22 4932

COLLOPS
maketh c of fat on his flanks Job 15:27 6371

COLONY
of that part of Macedonia, and a c Acts 16:12 2862

COLORS
I will lay thy stones with fair c Is 54:11 6320

COLOSSE (*co-los'-see*) See COLOSSIANS. *A city in Phrygia.*
brethren in Christ which are at C Col 1:2 2857

COLOSSIANS (*co-los'-yans*) *Residents of Colosse.*
from Rome to the C by Tychicus Col *s* 2858

COLOUR
the plague have not changed his c Lev 13:55 5869
the c thereof as the c of Num 11:7 5869
when it giveth his c in the cup Prov 23:31 5869
midst thereof as the c of amber Eze 1:4 5869
like the c of burnished brass Eze 1:7 5869
was like unto the c of a beryl Eze 1:16 5869
as the c of the terrible crystal Eze 1:22 5869
And I saw as the c of amber Eze 1:27 5869
of brightness, as the c of amber Eze 8:2 5869
was as the c of a beryl stone Eze 10:9 5869
his feet like in c to polished Dan 10:6 5869
under c as though they would have Acts 27:30 4392
arrayed in purple and scarlet c Rev 17:4

COLOURED
woman sit upon a scarlet c beast Rev 17:3

COLOURS
and he made him a coat of many c Gen 37:3 6446
coat of many c that was on him Gen 37:23 6446
And they sent the coat of many c Gen 37:32 6446
to Sisera a prey of divers c Judg 5:30 6648
a prey of divers c of needlework Judg 5:30 6648
of divers c of needlework on both Judg 5:30 6648
a garment of divers c upon her 2Sa 13:18 6446
of divers c that was on her 2Sa 13:19 6446
glistering stones, and of divers c 1Chr 29:2 7553
thy high places with divers c Eze 16:16 2921
of feathers, which had divers c Eze 17:3 7553

COLT
his ass's c unto the choice vine Gen 49:11 1121
man be born like a wild ass's c Job 11:12 5895
upon a c the foal of an ass Zec 9:9 5895
find an ass tied, and a c with her Mt 21:2 4454
an ass, and a c the foal of an ass Mt 21:5 4454
And brought the ass, and the c Mt 21:7 4454
into it, ye shall find a c tied Mk 11:2 4454
found the c tied by the door Mk 11:4 4454
them, What do ye, loosing the c Mk 11:5 4454
And they brought the c to Jesus Mk 11:7 4454
entering ye shall find a c tied Lk 19:30 4454
And as they were loosing the c Lk 19:33 4454
unto them, Why loose ye the c Lk 19:33 4454
cast their garments upon the c Lk 19:35 4454
cometh, sitting on an ass's c Jn 12:15 4454

COLTS
Thirty milch camels with their c Gen 32:15 1121
sons that rode on thirty ass c Judg 10:4 5895
rode on threescore and ten ass c Judg 12:14 5895

COME
and it shall c to pass, that every Gen 4:14 1961
end of all flesh is c before me Gen 6:13 935
thou shalt c into the ark, thou, Gen 6:18 935
of every sort shall c unto thee Gen 6:20 935
C thou and all thy house into the Gen 7:1 935
And it shall c to pass, when I Gen 9:14 935
when he was c near to enter into Gen 12:11 7126
Therefore it shall c to pass Gen 12:12 935
that, when Abram was c into Egypt Gen 12:14 935
but he that shall c forth out of Gen 15:4 3318
afterward shall they c out with Gen 15:14 3318
they shall c hither again Gen 15:16 7725
and kings shall c out of thee Gen 17:6 3318
are ye c to your servant Gen 18:5 5674
the cry of it, which is c unto me Gen 18:21 935
any thing till thou be c thither Gen 19:22 935
is not a man in the earth to c in Gen 19:31 935
C, let us make our father drink Gen 19:32 3212
But Abimelech had not c near her Gen 20:4 7126
at every place whither we shall c Gen 20:13 935
and worship, and c again to you Gen 22:5 7725
of the city c out to draw water Gen 24:13 3318
let it c to pass, that the damsel Gen 24:14 935
C in, thou blessed of the LORD Gen 24:31 935
and it shall c to pass, that when Gen 24:43 1961
unto them, Wherefore c ye to me Gen 26:27 935
C near, I pray thee, that I may Gen 27:21 5066
C near now, and kiss me, my son Gen 27:26 5066
it shall c to pass when thou Gen 27:40 1961
So that I c again to my father's Gen 28:21 7725
and said, Thou must c in unto me Gen 30:16 935
answer for me in time to c Gen 30:33 4279
when it shall c for my hire Gen 30:33 935
Now therefore c thou, let us make Gen 31:44 3212
If Esau c to the one company, and Gen 32:8 935
for I fear him, lest he will c Gen 32:11 935
until I c unto my lord unto Seir Gen 33:14 935
held his peace until they were c Gen 34:5 935
kings shall c out of thy loins Gen 35:11 3318
but a little way to c to Ephrath Gen 35:16 935
thy brethren indeed c to bow down Gen 37:10 935
c, and I will send thee unto them Gen 37:13 3212
C now therefore, and let us slay Gen 37:20 3212
when Joseph was c unto his Gen 37:23 935
C, and let us sell him to the Gen 37:27 3212
pray thee, let me c in unto thee Gen 38:16 935
me, that thou mayest c in unto me Gen 38:16 935
there c seven years of great Gen 41:29 935
food of those good years that c Gen 41:35 935
seven years of dearth began to c Gen 41:54 935
and he said unto them, Whence c ye Gen 42:7 935
nakedness of the land ye are c Gen 42:9 935
to buy food are thy servants c Gen 42:10 935
nakedness of the land ye are c Gen 42:12 935
your youngest brother c hither Gen 42:15 935
is this distress c upon us Gen 42:21 935
youngest brother c down with you Gen 44:23 3381
Now therefore when I c to thy Gen 44:30 935
It shall c to pass, when he seeth Gen 44:31 1961
evil that shall c on my father Gen 44:34 4672
C near to me, I pray you Gen 45:4 5066
c down unto me, tarry not Gen 45:9 3381
all that thou hast, c to poverty Gen 45:11
saying, Joseph's brethren are c Gen 45:16 935
and your households, and c unto me Gen 45:18 935
wives, and bring your father, and c Gen 45:19 935
the land of Canaan, are c unto me Gen 46:31 935
And it shall c to pass, when Gen 46:33 1961
are c out of the land of Canaan Gen 47:1 935
to sojourn in the land are we c Gen 47:4 935
and thy brethren are c unto thee Gen 47:5 935
it shall c to pass in the Gen 47:24 1961
a little way to c unto Ephrath Gen 48:7 935
c not thou into their secret Gen 49:6 935
between his feet, until Shiloh c Gen 49:10 935
bury my father, and I will c again Gen 50:5 7725
C on, let us deal wisely with Ex 1:10 3051
it c to pass, that, when there Ex 1:10 1961
ere the midwives c in unto them Ex 1:19 935
it that ye are c so soon to day Ex 2:18 935
I am c down to deliver them out Ex 3:8 3381
children of Israel is c unto me Ex 3:9 935
C now therefore, and I will send Ex 3:10 3212
when I c unto the children of Ex 3:13 935
and thou shalt c, thou and the Ex 3:18 935
and it shall c to pass, that, when Ex 3:21 1961
And it shall c to pass, if they Ex 4:8 1961
And it shall c to pass, if they Ex 4:9 1961
by the river's brink against he c Ex 7:15 7125
c into thine house, and into thy Ex 8:3 935
the frogs shall c up both on thee Ex 8:4 5927
cause frogs to c up upon the land Ex 8:5 5927

C

Context	Reference	No.
the hail shall c down upon them	Ex 9:19	3381
that they may c up upon the land	Ex 10:12	5927
the LORD, until we c thither	Ex 10:26	935
thy servants shall c down unto me	Ex 11:8	3381
not suffer the destroyer to c in	Ex 12:23	935
And it shall c to pass	Ex 12:25	1961
when ye be c to the land which	Ex 12:25	935
And it shall c to pass, when your	Ex 12:26	1961
and then let him c near and keep	Ex 12:48	7126
thy son asketh thee in time to c	Ex 13:14	4279
that the waters may c again upon	Ex 14:26	7725
And it shall c to pass, that on	Ex 16:5	1961
of Israel, C near before the LORD	Ex 16:9	7126
there shall c water out of it,	Ex 17:6	3318
in law Jethro am c unto thee	Ex 18:6	935
that had c upon them by the way	Ex 18:8	4672
Because the people c unto me to	Ex 18:15	935
have a matter, they c unto me	Ex 18:16	935
were c to the desert of Sinai, and	Ex 19:2	935
I c unto thee in a thick cloud,	Ex 19:9	935
c down in the sight of all the	Ex 19:11	3381
they shall c up to the mount	Ex 19:13	5927
c not at your wives	Ex 19:15	5066
which c near to the LORD,	Ex 19:22	5066
people cannot c up to mount Sinai	Ex 19:23	5927
get thee down, and thou shalt c up	Ex 19:24	5927
through to c up unto the LORD	Ex 19:24	5927
for God is c to prove you, and	Ex 20:20	935
record my name I will c unto thee	Ex 20:24	935
But if a man c presumptuously	Ex 21:14	
parties shall c before the judges	Ex 22:9	935
and it shall c to pass, when he	Ex 22:27	1961
the people to whom thou shalt c	Ex 23:27	935
C up unto the LORD, thou, and	Ex 24:1	5927
Moses alone shall c near the LORD	Ex 24:2	5066
but they shall not c nigh	Ex 24:2	5066
C up to me into the mount, and be	Ex 24:12	5927
until we c again unto you	Ex 24:14	7725
to do, let him c unto them	Ex 24:14	5066
six branches shall c out of the	Ex 25:32	3318
that c out of the candlestick	Ex 25:33	3318
his sons, when they c in unto the	Ex 28:43	935
or when they c near unto the	Ex 28:43	5066
or when they c near to the altar	Ex 30:20	5066
to c down out of the mount	Ex 32:1	3381
let him c unto me	Ex 32:26	
I will c up into the midst of	Ex 33:5	5927
And it shall c to pass, while my	Ex 33:22	1961
c up in the morning unto mount	Ex 34:2	5927
And no man shall c up with thee	Ex 34:3	5927
and they were afraid to c nigh him	Ex 34:30	5066
wise hearted among you shall c	Ex 35:10	935
up to c unto the work to do it	Ex 36:2	7126
hath sinned, c to his knowledge	Lev 4:23	3045
hath sinned, c to his knowledge	Lev 4:28	3045
sanctified in them that c nigh me	Lev 10:3	7138
C near, carry your brethren from	Lev 10:4	935
lest wrath c upon all the people	Lev 10:6	
nor c into the sanctuary, until	Lev 12:4	935
he shall c unto the priest	Lev 13:16	935
that he shall c into the camp	Lev 14:8	935
When ye be c into the land of	Lev 14:34	935
he that owneth the house shall c	Lev 14:35	935
the priest shall c again the	Lev 14:39	7725
And if the plague c again, and	Lev 14:43	7725
Then the priest shall c and look,	Lev 14:44	935
And if the priest shall c in	Lev 14:48	935
c before the LORD unto the door	Lev 15:14	935
that he c not at all times into	Lev 16:2	935
Thus shall Aaron c into the holy	Lev 16:3	935
in the holy place, until he c out	Lev 16:17	3318
Aaron shall c into the tabernacle	Lev 16:23	935
c forth, and offer his burnt	Lev 16:24	3318
afterward c into the camp	Lev 16:26	935
he shall c into the camp	Lev 16:28	935
of linen and woollen c upon thee	Lev 19:19	5927
And when ye shall c into the land	Lev 19:23	935
c nigh to offer the offerings of	Lev 21:21	5066
he shall not c nigh to offer the	Lev 21:21	5066
nor c nigh unto the altar,	Lev 21:23	5066
When ye be c into the land which	Lev 23:10	935
When ye c into the land which I	Lev 25:2	935
until her fruits c in ye shall	Lev 25:22	935
if any of his kin c to redeem it	Lev 25:25	935
were c out of the land of Egypt	Num 1:1	3318
setteth forward, Aaron shall c	Num 4:5	935
sons of Kohath shall c to bear it	Num 4:15	935
the spirit of jealousy c upon him	Num 5:14	5674
the spirit of jealousy c upon him	Num 5:14	5674
water, then it shall c to pass	Num 5:27	1961
shall no razor c upon his head	Num 6:5	5674
LORD he shall c at no dead body	Num 6:6	935
Israel c nigh unto the sanctuary	Num 8:19	5066
were c out of the land of Egypt	Num 9:1	3318
c thou with us, and we will do	Num 10:29	3212
And I will c down and talk with	Num 11:17	3381
until it c out at your nostrils,	Num 11:20	3318
shall c to pass unto thee or not	Num 11:23	7136
Miriam, C out ye three unto the	Num 12:4	3318
unto Rehob, as men c to Hamath	Num 13:21	935
of Anak, which c of the giants	Num 13:33	
ye shall not c into the land	Num 14:30	935
When ye be c into the land of	Num 15:2	935
When ye c into the land whither I	Num 15:18	935
will cause him to c near unto him	Num 16:5	7126
will he cause to c near unto him	Num 16:5	7126
which said, We will not c up	Num 16:12	5927
we will not c up	Num 16:14	5927
c near to offer incense before	Num 16:40	7126
And it shall c to pass, that the	Num 17:5	1961
only they shall not c nigh the	Num 18:3	7126
shall not c nigh unto you	Num 18:4	7126
c nigh the tabernacle of the	Num 18:22	7126
he shall c into the camp, and the	Num 19:7	935
all that c into the tent, and all	Num 19:14	935
ye made us to c up out of Egypt	Num 20:5	5927
lest I c out against thee with	Num 20:18	3318
and it shall c to pass, that every	Num 21:8	1961
C into Heshbon, let the city of	Num 21:27	935
is a people c out from Egypt	Num 22:5	3318
C now therefore, I pray thee,	Num 22:6	3212
there is a people c out of Egypt	Num 22:11	3318
c now, curse me them	Num 22:11	3212
Balaam refuseth to c with us	Num 22:14	1980
c therefore, I pray thee, curse	Num 22:17	3212
If the men c to call thee, rise	Num 22:20	935
Balak heard that Balaam was c	Num 22:36	935
unto Balak, Lo, I am c unto thee	Num 22:38	935
the LORD will c to meet me	Num 23:3	7136
C, curse me Jacob, and c	Num 23:7	3212
And Balak said unto him, C	Num 23:13	3212
And Balak said unto Balaam, C	Num 23:27	3212
c therefore, and I will advertise	Num 24:14	3212
there shall c a Star out of Jacob	Num 24:17	1869
Out of Jacob shall c he that	Num 24:19	3381
ships shall c c from the coast	Num 24:24	
of Gilead c the family of the	Num 26:29	
and at his word they shall c in	Num 27:21	935
ye shall c into the camp	Num 31:24	935
were c out of the land of Egypt	Num 33:38	3318
then it shall c to pass, that	Num 33:55	1961
Moreover it shall c to pass	Num 33:56	1961
When ye c into the land of Canaan	Num 34:2	935
When ye be c over Jordan into the	Num 35:10	5674
c without the border of the city	Num 35:26	3318
that he should c again to dwell	Num 35:32	7725
Ye are c unto the mountain of the	Deut 1:20	935
and into what cities we shall c	Deut 1:22	935
until we were c over the brook	Deut 2:14	5674
all these things are c upon thee	Deut 4:30	4672
after they were c forth out of	Deut 4:46	3318
thy son asketh thee in time to c	Deut 6:20	4279
Wherefore it shall c to pass	Deut 7:12	1961
c up unto me into the mount, and	Deut 10:1	5927
And it shall c to pass, if ye	Deut 11:13	1961
And it shall c to pass, when the	Deut 11:29	1961
ye seek, and thither thou shalt c	Deut 12:5	935
ye are not as yet c to the rest	Deut 12:9	935
the sign or the wonder c to pass	Deut 13:2	935
are within thy gates, shall c	Deut 14:29	935
males that c of thy herd and of	Deut 15:19	3205
thou shalt c unto the priests the	Deut 17:9	935
When thou art c unto the land	Deut 17:14	935
if a Levite c from any of thy	Deut 18:6	935
c with all the desire of his mind	Deut 18:6	935
When thou art c into the land	Deut 18:9	935
And it shall c to pass, that	Deut 18:19	1961
nor c to pass, that is the thing	Deut 18:22	935
when ye are c nigh unto the	Deut 20:2	7126
and thy judges shall c forth	Deut 21:2	3318
the sons of Levi shall c near	Deut 21:5	5506
he shall not c within the camp	Deut 23:10	935
he shall c into the camp again	Deut 23:11	935
it c to pass that she find no	Deut 24:1	1961
that ye were c forth out of Egypt	Deut 24:9	3318
they c unto judgment, that the	Deut 25:1	5066
Then shall his brother's wife c	Deut 25:9	5066
when ye were c forth out of Egypt	Deut 25:17	3318
when thou art c in unto the land	Deut 26:1	935
that I am c unto the country	Deut 26:3	935
people, when ye are c over Jordan	Deut 27:12	5674
And it shall c to pass, if thou	Deut 28:1	1961
these blessings shall c on thee	Deut 28:2	935
they shall c out against thee one	Deut 28:7	3318
But it shall c to pass, if thou	Deut 28:15	1961
these curses shall c upon thee	Deut 28:15	935
heaven shall it c down upon thee	Deut 28:24	3381
thou shalt c down very low	Deut 28:43	3381
these curses shall c upon thee	Deut 28:45	935
thy high and fenced walls c down	Deut 28:52	3381
And it shall c to pass, that as	Deut 28:63	1961
it c to pass, when he heareth the	Deut 29:19	1961
So that the generation to c of	Deut 29:22	314
that shall c from a far land	Deut 29:22	935
And it shall c to pass, when all	Deut 30:1	1961
all these things are c upon thee	Deut 30:1	935
I can no more go out and c in	Deut 31:2	935
When all Israel is c to appear	Deut 31:11	935
Are not these evils c upon us	Deut 31:17	4672
And it shall c to pass, when many	Deut 31:21	1961
that shall c upon them make haste	Deut 32:35	6264
let the blessing c upon the head	Deut 33:16	935
forth the men that are c to thee	Josh 2:3	935
for they be c to search out all	Josh 2:3	935
when we c into the land, thou	Josh 2:18	935
c not near unto it, that ye may	Josh 3:4	7126
When ye are c to the brink of the	Josh 3:8	935
C hither, and hear the words of	Josh 3:9	5066
And it shall c to pass, as soon as	Josh 3:13	1961
the waters that c down from above	Josh 3:13	3381
bare the ark were c unto Jordan	Josh 3:15	935
ask their fathers in time to c	Josh 4:6	4279
that they c up out of Jordan	Josh 4:16	5927
saying, C ye up out of Jordan	Josh 4:17	5927
c up out of the midst of Jordan	Josh 4:18	5927
ask their fathers in time to c	Josh 4:21	4279
the host of the LORD am I now c	Josh 5:14	935
And it shall c to pass, that when	Josh 6:5	1961
they shall c into the treasury of	Josh 6:19	935
shall c according to the families	Josh 7:14	7126
shall take shall c by households	Josh 7:14	7126
shall take shall c man by man	Josh 7:14	7126
and it shall c to pass, when they	Josh 8:5	1961
when they c out against us, as at	Josh 8:5	3318
(For they will c out after us)	Josh 8:6	3318
We be c from a far country	Josh 9:6	935
and from whence c ye	Josh 9:8	935
far country thy servants are c	Josh 9:9	935
C up unto me, and help me, that we	Josh 10:4	5927
c up to us quickly, and save us,	Josh 10:6	5927
C near, put your feet upon the	Josh 10:24	7126
that they should c against Israel	Josh 11:20	7122
war, both to go out, and to c in	Josh 14:11	935
and they shall c again to me	Josh 18:4	935
c again to me, that I may here	Josh 18:8	7725
c unto his own city, and unto his	Josh 20:6	935
In time to c your children might	Josh 22:24	4279
say to our children in time to c	Josh 22:27	4279
to our generations in time to c	Josh 22:28	4279
That ye c not among these nations	Josh 23:7	935
all are c to pass unto you, and	Josh 23:14	935
Therefore it shall c to pass	Josh 23:15	1961
as all good things are c upon you	Josh 23:15	935
C up with me into my lot, that we	Judg 1:3	5927
the spies saw a man c forth out	Judg 1:24	3318
them to c down to the valley	Judg 1:34	3381
And it came to pass, when he was c	Judg 3:27	935
it shall be, when any man doth c	Judg 4:20	935
to meet him, and said unto him, C	Judg 4:22	3212
the earth, till thou c unto Gaza	Judg 6:4	935
until I c unto thee, and bring	Judg 6:18	935
I will tarry until thou c again	Judg 6:18	7725
And when Gideon was c, behold,	Judg 7:13	935
when I c to the outside of the	Judg 7:17	935
C down against the Midianites, and	Judg 7:24	3381
When I c again in peace, I will	Judg 8:9	7725
tree, C thou, and reign over us	Judg 9:10	3212
vine, C thou, and reign over us	Judg 9:12	3212
bramble, C thou, and reign over us	Judg 9:14	3212
anoint me king over you, then c	Judg 9:15	935
let fire c out of the bramble, and	Judg 9:15	3318
let fire c out from Abimelech, and	Judg 9:20	3318
let fire c out from the men of	Judg 9:20	3318
and ten sons of Jerubbaal might c	Judg 9:24	935
Increase thine army, and c out	Judg 9:29	3318
and his brethren be c to Shechem	Judg 9:31	935
is with him c out against thee	Judg 9:33	3318
there c people down from the top	Judg 9:36	3381
See there c people down by the	Judg 9:37	3381
another company c along by the	Judg 9:37	935
the people were c forth out of	Judg 9:43	3318
And they said unto Jephthah, C	Judg 11:6	3212
why are ye c unto me now when ye	Judg 11:7	935
that thou art c against me to	Judg 11:12	935
even till thou c to Minnith	Judg 11:33	935
then are ye c up unto me this day	Judg 12:3	5927
and no razor shall c on his head	Judg 13:5	5927
thou didst send c again unto us	Judg 13:8	935
said, Now let thy words c to pass	Judg 13:12	935
that when thy sayings c to pass	Judg 13:17	935
Why are ye c up against us	Judg 15:10	5927
To bind Samson are we c up	Judg 15:10	5927
We are c down to bind thee, that	Judg 15:12	3381
saying, Samson is c hither	Judg 16:2	935
There hath not c a razor upon	Judg 16:17	5927
C up this once, for he hath	Judg 16:18	5927
ye shall c unto a people secure,	Judg 18:10	935
servant said unto his master, C	Judg 19:11	3212
And he said unto his servant, C	Judg 19:13	3212
this man is c into mine house	Judg 19:23	935
when he was c into his house, he	Judg 19:29	935
when they c to Gibeah of Benjamin	Judg 20:10	935
saw that evil was c upon them	Judg 20:41	5060
why is this c to pass in Israel,	Judg 21:3	1961
Shiloh c out to dance in dances	Judg 21:21	3318
then c ye out of the vineyards,	Judg 21:21	3318
brethren c unto us to complain	Judg 21:22	935
when they were c to Beth-lehem	Ruth 1:19	935
art c unto a people which thou	Ruth 2:11	1980
whose wings thou art c to trust	Ruth 2:12	935
her, At mealtime c thou hither	Ruth 2:14	5060
that is c again out of the	Ruth 4:3	7725
is c into thine house like Rachel	Ruth 4:11	935
shall no razor c upon his head	1Sa 1:11	5927
when the time was c about after	1Sa 1:20	8622
not arrogancy c out of your mouth	1Sa 2:3	3318
Behold, the days c, that I will	1Sa 2:31	935
that shall c upon thy two sons,	1Sa 2:34	935
And it shall c to pass, that every	1Sa 2:36	1961
is left in thine house shall c	1Sa 2:36	935
the people were c into the camp	1Sa 4:3	935
of the LORD was c into the camp	1Sa 4:6	935
they said, God is c into the camp	1Sa 4:7	935
nor any that c into Dagon's house	1Sa 5:5	935
on which there hath c no yoke	1Sa 6:7	5927
c ye down, and fetch it up to you	1Sa 6:21	3381
when they were c to the land of	1Sa 9:5	935
his servant that was with him, C	1Sa 9:5	3212
enquire of God, thus he spake, C	1Sa 9:9	3212
c, let us go	1Sa 9:10	3212
As soon as ye be c into the city	1Sa 9:13	935
people will not eat until he c	1Sa 9:13	935
and when they were c into the city	1Sa 9:14	935
because their cry is c unto me	1Sa 9:16	935
when they were c down from the	1Sa 9:25	3381
thou shalt c to the plain of	1Sa 10:3	935
thou shalt c to the hill of God	1Sa 10:5	935
and it shall c to pass	1Sa 10:5	1961
when thou art c thither to the	1Sa 10:5	835
of the LORD will c upon thee	1Sa 10:6	6743
when these signs are c unto thee	1Sa 10:7	935
I will c down unto thee, to offer	1Sa 10:8	3381
till I c to thee, and shew thee	1Sa 10:8	935
that is c unto the son of Kish	1Sa 10:11	1961
the tribes of Israel to c near	1Sa 10:20	7126
to c near by their families	1Sa 10:21	7126
if the man should yet c thither	1Sa 10:22	935
to save us, we will c out to thee	1Sa 11:3	3318
To morrow we will c out unto you	1Sa 11:10	3318
Then said Samuel to the people, C	1Sa 11:14	3212
When Jacob was c into Egypt	1Sa 12:8	935
The Philistines will c down now	1Sa 13:12	3381

Context	Reference	Number
young man that bare his armour, C	1Sa 14:1	3212
young man that bare his armour, C	1Sa 14:6	3212
unto us, Tarry until we c to you	1Sa 14:9	5060
if they say thus, C up unto us	1Sa 14:10	5927
the Hebrews c forth out of the	1Sa 14:11	3318
C up to us, and we will shew you a	1Sa 14:12	5927
his armourbearer, C up after me	1Sa 14:12	5927
the people were c into the wood	1Sa 14:26	935
I am c to sacrifice to the LORD	1Sa 16:2	935
I am c to sacrifice unto the LORD	1Sa 16:5	935
c with me to the sacrifice	1Sa 16:5	935
it came to pass, when they were c	1Sa 16:6	935
not sit down till he c hither	1Sa 16:11	935
and it shall c to pass, when the	1Sa 16:16	1961
Why are ye c out to set your	1Sa 17:8	3318
for you, and let him c down to me	1Sa 17:8	3381
ye seen this man that is c up	1Sa 17:25	5927
surely to defy Israel is he c up	1Sa 17:25	5927
for thou art c down that thou	1Sa 17:28	3381
C to me, and I will give thy flesh	1Sa 17:44	3212
but I c to thee in the name of	1Sa 17:45	935
until thou c to the valley, and to	1Sa 17:52	935
And when the messengers were c in	1Sa 19:16	935
by my father to c upon thee	1Sa 20:9	935
And Jonathan said unto David, C	1Sa 20:11	3212
c to the place where thou didst	1Sa 20:19	935
then c thou	1Sa 20:21	935
and when the new moon was c	1Sa 20:24	1961
when the lad was c to the place	1Sa 20:37	935
shall this fellow c into my house	1Sa 21:15	935
c forth, and be with you, till I	1Sa 22:3	3318
how much more then if we c to	1Sa 23:3	3212
Saul that David was c to Keilah	1Sa 23:7	935
that Saul seeketh to c to Keilah	1Sa 23:10	935
will Saul c down, as thy servant	1Sa 23:11	3381
And the LORD said, He will c down	1Sa 23:11	3381
Saul was c out to seek his life	1Sa 23:15	3318
c down according to all the	1Sa 23:20	3381
the desire of thy soul to c down	1Sa 23:20	3381
c ye again to me with the	1Sa 23:23	7725
and it shall c to pass, if he be	1Sa 23:23	1961
Saul, saying, Haste thee, and c	1Sa 23:27	3212
whom is the king of Israel c out	1Sa 24:14	3318
for we c in a good day	1Sa 25:8	935
behold, I c after you	1Sa 25:19	935
And it shall c to pass, when the	1Sa 25:30	1961
c to meet me, surely there had	1Sa 25:34	935
David were c to Abigail to Carmel	1Sa 25:40	935
that Saul was c in very deed	1Sa 26:4	935
or his day shall c to die	1Sa 26:10	935
of Israel is c out to seek a flea	1Sa 26:20	3318
let one of the young men c over	1Sa 26:22	5674
servants that are c with thee	1Sa 29:10	935
his men were c to Ziklag on the	1Sa 30:1	935
lest these uncircumcised c	1Sa 31:4	935
for anguish is c upon me, because	2Sa 1:9	270
they were c to the hill of Ammah	2Sa 2:24	935
the host that was with him were c	2Sa 3:23	935
when Joab was c out from David,	2Sa 3:26	3318
lame, thou shalt not c in hither	2Sa 5:6	935
thinking, David cannot c in	2Sa 5:6	935
lame shall not c into the house	2Sa 5:8	935
after he was c from Hebron	2Sa 5:13	935
c upon them over against the	2Sa 5:23	935
from Geba until thou c to Gazer	2Sa 5:25	935
shall the ark of the LORD c to me	2Sa 6:9	935
house for a great while to c	2Sa 7:19	
was c unto David, he fell on his	2Sa 9:6	935
strong for thee, then I will c	2Sa 10:11	1980
And when Uriah was c unto him	2Sa 11:7	935
wayfaring man that was c unto him	2Sa 12:4	935
it for the man that was c to him	2Sa 12:4	935
pray thee, let my sister Tamar c	2Sa 13:5	935
and when the king was c to see him	2Sa 13:6	935
pray thee, let Tamar my sister c	2Sa 13:6	935
her, C lie with me, my sister	2Sa 13:11	935
king, Behold, the king's sons c	2Sa 13:35	935
c to the king, and speak on this	2Sa 14:3	935
Now therefore that I am c to	2Sa 14:15	935
but he would not c to him	2Sa 14:29	935
the second time, he would not c	2Sa 14:29	935
C hither, that I may send thee to	2Sa 14:32	935
say, Wherefore am I c from Geshur	2Sa 14:32	935
any suit or cause might c unto me	2Sa 15:4	935
until there c word from you to	2Sa 15:28	935
that when David was c to the top	2Sa 15:32	935
C out, c out, thou bloody man,	2Sa 16:7	3318
was c unto Absalom, that Hushai	2Sa 16:16	935
I will c upon him while he is	2Sa 17:2	935
And when Hushai was c to Absalom	2Sa 17:6	935
and it will c to pass, when some	2Sa 17:9	1961
So shall we c upon him in some	2Sa 17:12	935
not be seen to c into the city	2Sa 17:17	935
when David was c to Mahanaim	2Sa 17:27	935
of all Israel is c to the king	2Sa 19:11	935
the king, as he was c over Jordan	2Sa 19:18	5674
I am c the first this day of all	2Sa 19:20	935
when he was c to Jerusalem to	2Sa 19:25	935
as my lord the king is c again in	2Sa 19:30	935
C thou over with me, and I will	2Sa 19:33	5674
And when the king was c over	2Sa 19:39	5674
C near hither, that I may speak	2Sa 20:16	7126
when he was c near unto her, the	2Sa 20:17	7126
of famine c unto thee in thy land	2Sa 24:13	935
my lord the king c to his servant	2Sa 24:21	935
Now therefore c, let me, I pray	1Kin 1:12	3212
I also will c in after thee, and	1Kin 1:14	935
Otherwise it shall c to pass	1Kin 1:21	1961
when he was c in before the king,	1Kin 1:23	935
Then ye shall c up after him	1Kin 1:35	5927
that he may c	1Kin 1:35	935
and Adonijah said unto him, C in	1Kin 1:42	935
they are c up from thence	1Kin 1:45	5927
him, Thus saith the king, C forth	1Kin 2:30	3318
Jerusalem to Gath, and was c again	1Kin 2:41	7725
I know not how to go out or c in	1Kin 3:7	935
were c out of the land of Egypt	1Kin 6:1	3318
were c out of the holy place	1Kin 8:10	3318
shall c forth out of thy loins	1Kin 8:19	3318
the oath c before thine altar in	1Kin 8:31	935
when he shall c and pray toward	1Kin 8:42	935
and when she was c to Solomon	1Kin 10:2	935
neither shall they c in unto you	1Kin 11:2	935
for all Israel were c to Shechem	1Kin 12:1	935
three days, then c again to me	1Kin 12:5	7725
C to me again the third day	1Kin 12:12	7725
heard that Jeroboam was c again	1Kin 12:20	7725
when Rehoboam was c to Jerusalem	1Kin 12:21	935
C home with me, and refresh	1Kin 13:7	935
C home with me, and eat bread	1Kin 13:15	3212
thy carcase shall not c unto the	1Kin 13:22	935
Samaria, shall surely c to pass	1Kin 13:32	1961
C in, thou wife of Jeroboam	1Kin 14:6	935
of Jeroboam shall c to the grave	1Kin 14:13	935
out or c in to Asa king of Judah	1Kin 15:17	935
c and break thy league with Baasha	1Kin 15:19	3212
art thou c unto me to call my sin	1Kin 17:18	935
child's soul c into him again	1Kin 17:21	7725
And it shall c to pass, as soon as	1Kin 18:12	1961
and so when I c and tell Ahab, and	1Kin 18:12	935
all the people, C near unto me	1Kin 18:30	5066
And it shall c to pass, that him	1Kin 19:17	1961
There are men c out of Samaria	1Kin 20:17	3318
Whether they be c out for peace	1Kin 20:18	3318
or whether they be c out for war	1Kin 20:18	3318
of Syria will c up against thee	1Kin 20:22	5927
any thing would c from him	1Kin 20:33	
he caused him to c up into the	1Kin 20:33	5927
of affliction, until I c in peace	1Kin 22:27	935
Thou shalt not c down from that	2Kin 1:4	3381
therefore thou shalt not c down	2Kin 1:6	3381
God, the king hath said, C down	2Kin 1:9	3381
then let fire c down from heaven,	2Kin 1:10	3381
C down quickly	2Kin 1:11	3381
let fire c down from heaven, and	2Kin 1:12	3381
therefore thou shalt not c down	2Kin 1:16	3381
were c up to fight against them	2Kin 3:21	5927
the creditor is c to take unto	2Kin 4:1	935
And when thou art c in, thou shalt	2Kin 4:4	935
run to the man of God, and c again	2Kin 4:22	7725
when Elisha was c into the house	2Kin 4:32	935
And when she was c in unto him	2Kin 4:36	935
when this letter is c unto thee	2Kin 5:6	935
let him c now to me, and he shall	2Kin 5:8	935
thy flesh shall c again to thee	2Kin 5:10	7725
He will surely c out to me	2Kin 5:11	3318
even now there be c to me from	2Kin 5:22	935
thither the Syrians are c down	2Kin 6:9	5185
when they were c into Samaria	2Kin 6:20	935
Now therefore c, and let us fall	2Kin 7:4	3212
when they were c to the uttermost	2Kin 7:5	935
of the Egyptians, to c upon us	2Kin 7:6	935
some mischief will c upon us	2Kin 7:9	4672
now therefore c, that we may go	2Kin 7:9	3212
When they c out of the city, we	2Kin 7:12	3318
it shall also c upon the land	2Kin 8:1	935
The man of God is c hither	2Kin 8:7	935
of Judah was c down to see Joram	2Kin 9:16	3381
And when Jehu was c to Jezreel	2Kin 9:30	935
And when he was c in, he did eat	2Kin 9:34	935
c to me to Jezreel by to morrow	2Kin 10:6	935
C with me, and see my zeal for the	2Kin 10:16	3212
let none c forth	2Kin 10:25	3381
that were to c in on the sabbath	2Kin 11:9	935
Jehu, king of Israel, saying, C	2Kin 14:8	3212
c up, and save me out of the hand	2Kin 16:7	5927
when the king was c from Damascus	2Kin 16:12	935
c up against all the fenced	2Kin 18:13	5927
And when they were c up, they came	2Kin 18:17	5927
Am I now c up without the LORD	2Kin 18:25	5927
c out to me, and then eat ye every	2Kin 18:31	3318
Until I c and take you away to a	2Kin 18:32	935
the children are c to the birth	2Kin 19:3	935
he is c out to fight against thee	2Kin 19:9	3318
I am c up to the height of the	2Kin 19:23	5927
thy tumult is c up into mine ears	2Kin 19:28	5927
He shall not c into this city,	2Kin 19:32	935
nor c before it with shield, nor	2Kin 19:32	6923
shall not c into this city, saith	2Kin 19:33	935
They are c from a far country,	2Kin 20:14	935
Behold, the days c, that all that	2Kin 20:17	935
were to c after seven days from	1Chr 9:25	935
lest these uncircumcised c	1Chr 10:4	935
to David, Thou shalt not c hither	1Chr 11:5	935
If ye be c peaceably unto me to	1Chr 12:17	935
but if ye be c to betray me to	1Chr 12:17	
were expressed by name, to c	1Chr 12:31	935
c upon them over against the	1Chr 14:14	935
an offering, and c before him	1Chr 16:29	935
And it shall c to pass, when thy	1Chr 17:11	1961
house for a great while to c	1Chr 17:17	
are not his servants c unto thee	1Chr 19:3	935
the kings that were c were by	1Chr 19:9	935
to c into the house of the LORD	1Chr 24:19	935
honour c of thee, and thou	1Chr 29:12	
for all things c of thee, and of	1Chr 29:14	
go out and c in before this people	2Chr 1:10	935
were c out of the holy place	2Chr 5:11	3318
shall c forth out of thy loins	2Chr 6:9	3318
the oath c before thine altar in	2Chr 6:22	935
but is c from a far country for	2Chr 6:32	935
if they c and pray in this house	2Chr 6:32	935
the ark of the LORD hath c	2Chr 8:11	935
and when she was c to Solomon	2Chr 9:1	935
all Israel c to make him king	2Chr 10:1	935
C again unto me after three days	2Chr 10:5	7725
C again to me on the third day	2Chr 10:12	7725
when Rehoboam was c to Jerusalem	2Chr 11:1	935
ambushment to c about behind them	2Chr 13:13	935
out or c in to Asa king of Judah	2Chr 16:1	935
And when he was c to the king	2Chr 18:14	935
what cause soever shall c to you	2Chr 19:10	935
the LORD, and so wrath c upon you	2Chr 19:10	1961
to c to cast us out of thy	2Chr 20:11	935
they c up by the cliff of Ziz	2Chr 20:16	5927
which were c against Judah	2Chr 20:22	935
for when he was c, he went out	2Chr 22:7	935
But let none c into the house of	2Chr 23:6	935
that were to c in on the sabbath	2Chr 23:8	935
when she was c to the entering of	2Chr 23:15	935
the army that was c to him out of	2Chr 25:10	935
after that Amaziah was c from the	2Chr 25:14	935
Jehu, king of Israel, saying, C	2Chr 25:17	3212
For again the Edomites had c	2Chr 28:17	935
c near and bring sacrifices and	2Chr 29:31	5066
that they should c to the house	2Chr 30:1	935
that they should c to keep the	2Chr 30:5	935
so that they shall c again into	2Chr 30:9	7725
saw that Sennacherib was c	2Chr 32:2	935
Why should the kings of Assyria c	2Chr 32:4	935
when he was c into the house of	2Chr 32:21	935
I c not against thee this day,	2Chr 35:21	
And when the seventh month was c	Ezr 3:1	5060
all they that were c out of the	Ezr 3:8	935
thee to us are c unto Jerusalem	Ezr 4:12	858
which were c again out of	Ezr 6:21	7725
which were c out of the captivity	Ezr 8:35	935
after all that is c upon us for	Ezr 9:13	935
would not c within three days	Ezr 10:8	935
our cities c at appointed times	Ezr 10:14	935
me over till I c into Judah	Neh 2:7	935
c a man to seek the welfare of	Neh 2:10	935
c, and let us build up the wall of	Neh 2:17	3212
all of them together to c	Neh 4:8	935
till we c in the midst among them	Neh 4:11	935
and Geshem sent unto me, saying, C	Neh 6:2	3212
work, so that I cannot c down	Neh 6:3	3381
I leave it, and c down to you	Neh 6:3	3381
C now therefore, and let us take	Neh 6:7	3212
for they will c to slay thee	Neh 6:10	935
night will they c to slay thee	Neh 6:10	935
congregation of them that were c	Neh 8:17	7725
before thee, that hath c upon us	Neh 9:32	4672
the Moabite should not c into the	Neh 13:1	935
themselves, and that they should c	Neh 13:22	935
to c at the king's commandment by	Est 1:12	935
shall c abroad unto all women	Est 1:17	3318
That Vashti c no more before king	Est 1:19	935
was c to go in to king Ahasuerus	Est 2:12	5060
was c to go in unto the king, she	Est 2:15	5060
shall c unto the king into the	Est 4:11	935
c in unto the king these thirty	Est 4:11	935
who knoweth whether thou art c to	Est 4:14	5060
Haman c this day unto the banquet	Est 5:4	935
Haman c to the banquet that I	Est 5:8	935
man c in with the king unto the	Est 5:12	935
Now Haman was c into the outward	Est 6:4	935
And the king said, Let him c in	Est 6:5	935
evil that shall c unto my people	Est 8:6	4672
matter, and which had c unto them	Est 9:26	5060
all this evil that was c upon him	Job 2:11	935
together to c to mourn with him	Job 2:11	935
let it not c into the number of	Job 3:6	935
let no joyful voice c therein	Job 3:7	935
I greatly feared is c upon me	Job 3:25	857
I was afraid of is c unto me	Job 3:25	935
But now it is c upon thee	Job 4:5	935
Thou shalt c to thy grave in a	Job 5:26	935
to the grave shall c up no more	Job 7:9	5927
of the wicked shall c to nought	Job 8:22	
we should c together in judgment	Job 9:32	935
speak, and let c on me what will	Job 13:13	5674
hypocrite shall not c before him	Job 13:16	935
will I wait, till my change c	Job 14:14	935
His sons c to honour, and he	Job 14:21	
the destroyer shall c upon him	Job 15:21	935
When a few years are c, then I	Job 16:22	857
you all, do ye return, and c now	Job 17:10	935
They that c after him shall be	Job 18:20	
His troops c together, and raise	Job 19:12	935
of the wicked shall c upon him	Job 20:22	935
thereby good shall c unto thee	Job 22:21	935
that I might c even to his seat	Job 23:3	935
tried me, I shall c forth as gold	Job 23:10	3318
the day and night c to an end	Job 26:10	
the cry of the poor to c unto him	Job 34:28	935
He causeth it to c, whether for	Job 37:13	4672
And said, Hitherto shalt thou c	Job 38:11	935
or who can c to him with his	Job 41:13	935
that no air can c between them	Job 41:16	935
I will c into thy house in the	Ps 5:7	935
of the wicked c to an end	Ps 7:9	
shall c down upon his own pate	Ps 7:16	3381
destructions are c to a perpetual	Ps 9:6	
of Israel were c out of Zion	Ps 14:7	
Let my sentence c forth from thy	Ps 17:2	3318
They shall c, and shall declare	Ps 22:31	935
and the King of glory shall c in	Ps 24:7	935
and the King of glory shall c in	Ps 24:9	935
they shall not c nigh unto him	Ps 32:6	5060
lest they c near unto thee	Ps 32:9	7126
C, ye children, hearken unto me	Ps 34:11	3212
Let destruction c upon him at	Ps 35:8	935
the foot of pride c against me	Ps 36:11	935
Then said I, Lo, I c	Ps 40:7	935
if he c to see me, he speaketh	Ps 41:6	935
when shall I c and appear before	Ps 42:2	935
All this is c upon us	Ps 44:17	935
C, behold the works of the LORD,	Ps 46:8	3212
Our God shall c, and shall not	Ps 50:3	935
David is c to the house of	Ps 52:t	935
of Israel were c out of Zion	Ps 53:6	

and trembling are c upon me Ps 55:5 935
unto thee shall all flesh c Ps 65:2 935
C and see the works of God Ps 66:5 3212
C and hear, all ye that fear God, Ps 66:16 3212
Princes shall c out of Egypt Ps 68:31 857
the waters are c in unto my soul Ps 69:1 935
I am c into deep waters, where Ps 69:2 935
and let them not c into thy Ps 69:27 935
power to every one that is to c Ps 71:18 935
He shall c down like rain upon Ps 72:6 3381
to c the praises of the LORD Ps 78:4 314
generation to c might know them Ps 78:6 314
the heathen are c into thine Ps 79:1 935
of the prisoner c before thee Ps 79:11 935
stir up thy strength, and c Ps 80:2 3212
They have said, C, and let us cut Ps 83:4 3212
whom thou hast made shall c Ps 86:9 935
Let my prayer c before thee Ps 88:2 935
I am shut up, and I cannot c forth Ps 88:8 3318
but it shall not c nigh thee Ps 91:7 5066
any plague c nigh thy dwelling Ps 91:10 7126
O c, let us sing unto the LORD Ps 95:1 3212
Let us c before his presence with Ps 95:2 6923
O c, let us worship and bow down Ps 95:6 935
an offering, and c into his courts Ps 96:8 935
c before his presence with Ps 100:2 935
O when wilt thou c unto me Ps 101:2 935
O LORD, and let my cry c unto thee Ps 102:1 935
her, yea, the set time, is c Ps 102:13 935
written for the generation to c Ps 102:18 314
cursing, so let it c unto him Ps 109:17 935
so let it c into his bowels like Ps 109:18 935
Let thy mercies c also unto me Ps 119:41 935
Let thy tender mercies c unto me Ps 119:77 935
Let my cry c near before thee, O Ps 119:169 7126
Let my supplication c before thee Ps 119:170 935
shall doubtless c again with Ps 126:6 935
Surely I will not c into the Ps 132:3 935
thy heavens, O LORD, and c down Ps 144:5 3381
C with us, let us lay wait for Prov 1:11 3212
c again, and to morrow I will give Prov 3:28 7725
c not nigh the door of her house Prov 5:8 7126
when thou art c into the hand of Prov 6:3 935
So shall thy poverty c as one Prov 6:11 935
shall his calamity c suddenly Prov 6:15 935
C, let us take our fill of love Prov 7:18 3212
will c home at the day appointed Prov 7:20 935
C, eat of my bread, and drink of Prov 9:5 3212
the wicked, it shall c upon him Prov 10:24 935
mischief, it shall c unto him Prov 11:27 935
the just shall c out of trouble Prov 12:13 3318
not sleep, lest thou c to poverty Prov 20:13
the rich, shall surely c to want Prov 22:16
and the glutton shall c to poverty Prov 23:21
a good blessing shall c upon them Prov 24:25 935
So shall thy poverty c as one Prov 24:34 935
there shall c forth a vessel for Prov 25:4 3318
it be said unto thee, C up hither Prov 25:7 5927
the curse causeless shall not c Prov 26:2 935
not that poverty shall c upon him Prov 28:22 935
and she shall rejoice in time to c Prov 31:25 314
place from whence the rivers c Eccl 1:7 1980
of things that are to c with Eccl 1:11 314
with those that shall c after Eccl 1:11 1961
I am c to great estate, and have Eccl 1:16
days to c shall all be forgotten Eccl 2:16 935
they also that c after shall not Eccl 4:16 314
God shall c forth of them all Eccl 7:18 3318
saw the wicked buried, who had c Eccl 8:10 935
All things c alike to all Eccl 9:2
youth, while the evil days c not Eccl 12:1 935
my love, my fair one, and c away Song 2:10 3212
time of the singing of birds is c Song 2:12 5060
my love, my fair one, and c away Song 2:13 3212
C with me from Lebanon, my spouse Song 4:8 935
and c, thou south Song 4:16 935
Let my beloved c into his garden, Song 4:16 935
I am c into my garden, my sister, Song 5:1 935
C, my beloved, let us go forth Song 7:11 3212
When ye c to appear before me, Is 1:12 935
C now, and let us reason together, Is 1:18 3212
cause of the widow c unto them Is 1:23 935
it shall c to pass in the last Is 2:2 1961
C ye, and let us go up to the Is 2:3 3212
c ye, and let us walk in the light Is 2:5 3212
And it shall c to pass, that Is 3:24 1961
And it shall c to pass, that he Is 4:3 1961
but there shall c up briers Is 5:6 5927
Holy One of Israel draw nigh and c Is 5:19 935
they shall c with speed swiftly Is 5:26 935
stand, neither shall it c to pass Is 7:7 1961
house, days that have not c Is 7:17 935
it shall c to pass in that day, Is 7:18 1961
And they shall c, and shall rest Is 7:19 935
it shall c to pass in that day, Is 7:21 1961
And it shall c to pass, for the Is 7:22 1961
it shall c to pass in that day, Is 7:23 1961
and with bows shall men c thither Is 7:24 935
there shall not c thither the Is 7:25 935
he shall c up over all his Is 8:7 5927
together, and it shall c to nought Is 8:10
and it shall c to pass, that when Is 8:21 1961
desolation which shall c from far Is 10:3 935
Wherefore it shall c to pass Is 10:12 1961
it shall c to pass in that day, Is 10:20 1961
it shall c to pass in that day, Is 10:27 1961
He is c to Aiath, he is passed to Is 10:28 935
there shall c forth a rod out of Is 11:1 3318
it shall c to pass in that day, Is 11:11 1961
They c from a far country, from Is 13:5 935
it shall c as a destruction from Is 13:6 935
and her time is near to c, and her Is 13:22 935
it shall c to pass in the day Is 14:3 1961
no feller is c up against us Is 14:8 5927

thought, so shall it c to pass Is 14:24 1961
root shall c forth a cockatrice Is 14:29 3318
for there shall c from the north Is 14:31 935
they are c even unto Jazer, they Is 16:8 5060
And it shall c to pass, when it is Is 16:12 1961
that he shall c to his sanctuary Is 16:12 935
And in that day it shall c to pass Is 17:4 1961
cloud, and shall c into Egypt Is 19:1 935
the Assyrian shall c into Egypt Is 19:23 935
enquire ye: return, c Is 21:12 857
And it shall c to pass, that thy Is 22:7 1961
it shall c to pass in that day, Is 22:20 1961
it shall c to pass in that day, Is 23:15 1961
it shall c to pass after the end Is 23:17 1961
is shut up, that no man may c in Is 24:10 935
And it shall c to pass, that he Is 24:18 1961
it shall c to pass in that day, Is 24:21 1961
C, my people, enter thou into thy Is 26:20 3212
them that c of Jacob to take root Is 27:6 935
the women c, and set them on fire Is 27:11 935
it shall c to pass in that day, Is 27:12 1961
it shall c to pass in that day, Is 27:13 1961
they shall c which were ready to Is 27:13 935
through, it shall not c unto us Is 28:15 935
spirit shall c to understanding Is 29:24 3045
anguish, from whence c the young Is 30:6
may be for the time to c for ever Is 30:8 314
c into the mountain of the LORD Is 30:29 935
so shall the LORD of hosts c down Is 31:4 3381
fail, the gathering shall not c Is 32:10 935
of my people shall c up thorns Is 32:13 5927
C near, ye nations, to hear Is 34:1 7126
and all things that c forth of it Is 34:1 6631
their stink shall c up out of Is 34:3 5927
it shall c down upon Idumea, and Is 34:5 3381
unicorns shall c down with them Is 34:7 3381
thorns shall c up in her palaces, Is 34:13 5927
your God will c with vengeance, Is 35:4 935
he will c and save you Is 35:4 935
and c to Zion with songs and Is 35:10 935
am I now c up without the LORD Is 36:10 5927
me by a present, and c out to me Is 36:16 3318
Until I c and take you away to a Is 36:17 935
the children are c to the birth Is 37:3 935
He is c forth to make war with Is 37:9 3318
am I c up to the height of the Is 37:24 5927
is c up into mine ears, therefore Is 37:29 5927
He shall not c into this city, Is 37:33 935
nor c before it with shields, nor Is 37:33 6923
shall not c into this city, saith Is 37:34 935
They are c from a far country Is 39:3 935
Behold, the days c, that all that Is 39:6 935
Lord GOD will c with strong hand Is 40:10 935
let them c near Is 41:1 5066
let us c near together to Is 41:1 7126
or declare us things for to c Is 41:22 935
things that are to c hereafter Is 41:23 857
one from the north, and he shall c Is 41:25 857
he shall c upon princes as upon Is 41:25 935
the former things are c to pass Is 42:9 935
hearken and hear for the time to c Is 42:23
that are coming, and shall c Is 44:7 935
of things to c concerning my sons Is 45:11 857
shall c over unto thee, and they Is 45:14 5674
they shall c after thee Is 45:14 3212
in chains they shall c over Is 45:14 5674
Assemble yourselves and c Is 45:20 935
even to him shall men c Is 45:24 935
C down, and sit in the dust, O Is 47:1 3381
But these two things shall c to Is 47:9 935
they shall c upon thee in their Is 47:9 935
Therefore shall evil c upon thee Is 47:11 935
desolation shall c upon thee Is 47:11 935
things that shall c upon thee Is 47:13 935
are c forth out of the waters of Is 48:1 3318
C ye near unto me, hear ye this Is 48:16 7126
Behold, these shall c from far Is 49:12 935
themselves together, and c to thee Is 49:18 935
let him c near to me Is 50:8 5066
and c with singing unto Zion Is 51:11 935
These two things are c unto thee Is 51:19 7122
c into thee the uncircumcised Is 52:1 935
for it shall not c near thee Is 54:14 7126
c ye to the waters, and he that Is 55:1 3212
c ye, buy, and eat Is 55:1 3212
yea, c, buy wine and milk without Is 55:1 3212
Incline your ear, and c unto me Is 55:3 3212
the thorn shall c up the fir tree Is 55:13 5927
brier shall c up the myrtle tree Is 55:13 5927
for my salvation is near to c Is 56:1 935
c to devour, yea, all ye beasts Is 56:9 857
C ye, say they, I will fetch wine Is 56:12 857
is taken away from the evil to c Is 57:1
the enemy shall c in like a flood Is 59:19 935
And the Redeemer shall c to Zion Is 59:20 935
for thy light is c, and the glory Is 60:1 935
the Gentiles shall c to thy light Is 60:3 1980
together, they c to thee Is 60:4 935
thy sons shall c from far Is 60:4 935
of the Gentiles shall c unto thee Is 60:5 935
all they from Sheba shall c Is 60:6 935
they shall c up with acceptance Is 60:7 5927
of Lebanon shall c unto thee Is 60:13 935
thee shall c bending unto thee Is 60:14 1980
and the year of my redeemed is c Is 63:4 935
that thou wouldest c down Is 64:1 3381
by thyself, c not near to me Is 65:5 5066
be remembered, nor c into mind Is 65:17 5927
And it shall c to pass, that Is 65:24 1961
behold, the LORD will c with fire Is 66:15 935
it shall c, that I will gather Is 66:18 935
and they shall c, and see my glory Is 66:18 935
And it shall c to pass, that from Is 66:23 1961
shall all flesh c to worship Is 66:23 935

and they shall c, and they shall Jer 1:15 935
evil shall c upon them, saith the Jer 2:3 935
we will c no more unto thee Jer 2:31 935
And it shall c to pass, when ye be Jer 3:16 1961
neither shall it c to mind Jer 3:16 5927
they shall c together out of the Jer 3:18 935
Behold, we c unto thee Jer 3:22 857
lest my fury c forth like fire, Jer 4:4 3318
The lion is c up from his thicket Jer 4:7 5927
it shall c to pass at that day, Jer 4:9 1961
from those places shall c unto me Jer 4:12 935
he shall c up as clouds, and his Jer 4:13 5927
that watchers c from a far Jer 4:16 935
neither shall evil c upon us Jer 5:12 935
And it shall c to pass, when ye Jer 5:19 1961
their flocks shall c unto her Jer 6:3 935
spoiler shall suddenly c upon us Jer 6:26 935
And c and stand before me in this Jer 7:10 935
Therefore, behold, the days c Jer 7:32 935
for they are c, and have devoured Jer 8:16 935
mourning women, that they may c Jer 9:17 935
cunning women, that they may c Jer 9:17 935
For death is c up into our Jer 9:21 5927
Behold, the days c, saith the Jer 9:25 935
the noise of the bruit is c Jer 10:22 935
c ye, assemble all the beasts of Jer 12:9 3212
beasts of the field, c to devour Jer 12:9 857
The spoilers are c upon all high Jer 12:12 935
And it shall c to pass, after that Jer 12:15
And it shall c to pass, if they Jer 12:16
your principalities shall c down Jer 13:18 3381
behold them that c from the north Jer 13:20 935
Wherefore c these things upon me Jer 13:22 7122
And it shall c to pass, if they Jer 15:2 1961
And it shall c to pass, when thou Jer 16:10 1961
Therefore, behold, the days c Jer 16:14 935
the Gentiles shall c unto thee Jer 16:19 935
let it c now Jer 17:15 935
whereby the kings of Judah c in Jer 17:19 935
And it shall c to pass, if ye Jer 17:24 1961
they shall c from the cities of Jer 17:26 935
the cold flowing waters that c Jer 18:14
Then said they, C, and let us Jer 18:18 3212
C, and let us smite him with the Jer 18:18 3212
Therefore, behold, the days c Jer 19:6 935
and thou shalt c to Babylon Jer 20:6 935
Who shall c down against us Jer 21:13 5181
thou be when pangs c upon thee Jer 22:23 935
Behold, the days c, saith the Jer 23:5 935
Therefore, behold, the days c Jer 23:7 935
heart, No evil shall c upon you Jer 23:17 935
word of the LORD hath c unto me Jer 25:3 1961
And it shall c to pass, when Jer 25:12 1961
A noise shall c even to the ends Jer 25:31 935
which c to worship in the LORD's Jer 26:2 935
hand of the messengers which c to Jer 27:3 935
until the very time of his land c Jer 27:7 935
And it shall c to pass, that the Jer 27:8 1961
of the prophet shall c to pass Jer 28:9 935
For, lo, the days c, saith the Jer 30:3 935
For it shall c to pass in that Jer 30:8 1961
They shall c with weeping, and Jer 31:9 935
Therefore they shall c and sing in Jer 31:12 935
they shall c again from the land Jer 31:16 7725
that thy children shall c again Jer 31:17 7725
Behold, the days c, saith the Jer 31:27 935
And it shall c to pass, that like Jer 31:28 1961
Behold, the days c, saith the Jer 31:31 935
Behold, the days c, saith the Jer 31:38 935
thine uncle shall c unto thee Jer 32:7 935
all this evil to c upon them Jer 32:23 7122
they are c unto the city to take Jer 32:24 935
thou hast spoken is c to pass Jer 32:24 1961
fight against this city, shall c Jer 32:29 935
They c to fight with the Jer 33:5 935
Behold, the days c, saith the Jer 33:14 935
up into the land, that we said, C Jer 35:11 935
Judah that c out of their cities Jer 36:6 935
in the ears of the people, and c Jer 36:14 3212
king of Babylon shall certainly c Jer 36:29 935
army was c forth out of Egypt Jer 37:5 3318
which is c forth to help you, Jer 37:7 3318
And the Chaldeans shall c again Jer 37:8 7725
Babylon shall not c against you Jer 37:19 935
they c unto thee, and say unto Jer 38:25 935
this thing is c upon you Jer 40:3 1961
to c with me into Babylon, c Jer 40:4 935
thee to c with me into Babylon Jer 40:4 935
Chaldeans, which will c unto us Jer 40:10 935
C to Gedaliah the son of Ahikam Jer 41:6 935
and it shall c to pass, that Jer 42:4 1961
Then it shall c to pass, that the Jer 42:16 1961
C up, ye horses Jer 46:9 5927
and let the mighty men c forth Jer 46:9 3318
king of Babylon should c and smite Jer 46:13 935
Carmel by the sea, so shall he c Jer 46:18 935
of their calamity was c upon them Jer 46:21 935
c against her with axes, as Jer 46:22 935
Baldness is c upon Gaza Jer 47:5 935
c, and let us cut it off from Jer 48:2 3212
spoiler shall c upon every city Jer 48:8 935
Therefore, behold, the days c Jer 48:12 935
The calamity of Moab is near to c Jer 48:16 935
c down from thy glory, and sit in Jer 48:18 3381
spoiler of Moab shall c upon thee Jer 48:18 5927
judgment is c upon the plain Jer 48:21 935
but a fire shall c forth out of Jer 48:45 3318
Therefore, behold, the days c Jer 49:2 935
saying, Who shall c unto me Jer 49:4 935
If grapegatherers c to thee Jer 49:9 935
c against her, and rise up to the Jer 49:14 935
he shall c up like a lion from Jer 49:19 5927
Behold, he shall c up and fly as Jer 49:22 5927
the outcasts of Elam shall not c Jer 49:36 935

But it shall c to pass in the	Jer 49:39	1961
the children of Israel shall c	Jer 50:4	935
faces thitherward, saying, C	Jer 50:5	935
cause to c up against Babylon an	Jer 50:9	5927
C against her from the utmost	Jer 50:26	935
for their day is c, the time of	Jer 50:27	935
for thy day is c, the time that I	Jer 50:31	935
a people shall c from the north	Jer 50:41	935
he shall c up like a lion from	Jer 50:44	5927
c, and let us declare in Zion the	Jer 51:10	935
in treasures, thine end is c	Jer 51:13	935
cause the horses to c up as the	Jer 51:27	5927
the time of her harvest shall c	Jer 51:33	935
The sea is c up upon Babylon	Jer 51:42	5927
a rumour shall both c one year	Jer 51:46	935
in another year shall c a rumour	Jer 51:46	
Therefore, behold, the days c	Jer 51:47	935
for the spoilers shall c unto her	Jer 51:48	935
let Jerusalem c into your mind	Jer 51:50	5927
for strangers are c into the	Jer 51:51	935
Wherefore, behold, the days c	Jer 51:52	935
from me shall spoilers c unto her	Jer 51:53	935
Because the spoiler is c upon her	Jer 51:56	935
evil that should c upon Babylon	Jer 51:60	935
because none c to the solemn	Lam 1:4	935
wreathed, and c up upon my neck	Lam 1:14	5927
their wickedness c before thee	Lam 1:22	935
Fear and a snare is c upon us	Lam 3:47	1961
for our end is c	Lam 4:18	935
O LORD, what is c upon us	Lam 5:1	1961
for thereof shall a fire c forth	Eze 5:4	3318
the end is c upon the four	Eze 7:2	935
Now is the end c upon thee	Eze 7:3	
evil, an only evil, behold, is c	Eze 7:5	935
An end is c, the end is c	Eze 7:6	935
behold, it is c	Eze 7:6	935
The morning is c unto thee	Eze 7:7	935
the time is c, the day of trouble	Eze 7:7	935
Behold the day, behold, it is c	Eze 7:10	935
The time is c, the day draweth	Eze 7:12	935
Mischief shall c upon mischief	Eze 7:26	935
but c not near any man upon whom	Eze 9:6	5066
the things that c into your mind	Eze 11:5	4609
the countries where they shall c	Eze 11:16	935
And they shall c thither, and they	Eze 11:18	935
among the heathen whither they c	Eze 12:16	935
I shall speak shall c to pass	Eze 12:25	6213
he seeth is for many days to c	Eze 12:27	
the souls alive that c unto you	Eze 13:18	
they shall c forth unto you, and	Eze 14:22	3318
thou art c to excellent ornaments	Eze 16:7	935
the like things shall not c	Eze 16:16	935
that they may c unto thee on	Eze 16:33	935
king of Babylon is c to Jerusalem	Eze 17:12	935
wife, neither hath c near to a	Eze 18:6	7126
Are ye c to enquire of me	Eze 20:3	935
of the king of Babylon may c	Eze 21:19	935
both twain shall c forth out of	Eze 21:19	3318
that the sword may c to Rabbath	Eze 21:20	935
that ye are c to remembrance, ye	Eze 21:24	
prince of Israel, whose day is c	Eze 21:25	935
until he c whose right it is	Eze 21:27	935
of the wicked, whose day is c	Eze 21:29	935
midst of it, that her time may c	Eze 22:3	935
art c even unto thy years	Eze 22:4	935
they shall c against thee with	Eze 23:24	935
have sent for men to c from far	Eze 23:40	935
fury to c up to take vengeance	Eze 24:8	5927
it shall c to pass, and I will do	Eze 24:14	835
in that day shall c unto thee	Eze 24:26	835
many nations to c up against thee	Eze 26:3	5927
the sea causeth his waves to c up	Eze 26:3	5927
shall c down from their thrones	Eze 26:16	3381
shall c down from their ships,	Eze 27:29	3381
And the sword shall c upon Egypt	Eze 30:4	935
pride of her power shall c down	Eze 30:6	3381
and great pain shall c upon them	Eze 30:9	1961
king of Babylon shall c upon thee	Eze 32:11	935
seeth the sword c upon the land	Eze 33:3	935
if the sword c, and take him away,	Eze 33:4	935
if the watchman see the sword c	Eze 33:6	935
if the sword c, and take any	Eze 33:6	935
one to his brother, saying, C	Eze 33:30	935
they c unto thee as the people	Eze 33:31	935
cometh to pass, (lo, it will c	Eze 33:33	935
shower to c down in his season	Eze 34:26	3381
for they are at hand to c	Eze 36:8	935
C from the four winds, O breath,	Eze 37:9	935
cause you to c up out of your	Eze 37:12	5927
c into the land that is brought	Eze 38:8	935
c like a storm, thou shalt be	Eze 38:9	935
It shall also c to pass, that at	Eze 38:10	1961
time shall things c into thy mind	Eze 38:10	5927
Art thou c to take a spoil	Eze 38:13	935
thou shalt c from thy place out	Eze 38:15	935
thou shalt c up against my people	Eze 38:16	5927
it shall c to pass at the same	Eze 38:18	1961
c against the land of Israel	Eze 38:18	935
my fury shall c up in my face	Eze 38:18	5927
will cause thee to c up from the	Eze 39:2	5927
Behold, it is c, and it is done,	Eze 39:8	935
it shall c to pass in that day,	Eze 39:11	1961
field, Assemble yourselves, and c	Eze 39:17	935
which c near to the LORD to	Eze 40:46	7131
And they shall not c near unto me	Eze 44:13	5066
nor to c near to any of my holy	Eze 44:13	5066
they shall c near to me to	Eze 44:15	7126
they shall c near to my table, to	Eze 44:16	7126
And it shall c to pass, that when	Eze 44:17	1961
and no wool shall c upon them	Eze 44:17	5927
they shall c at no dead person to	Eze 44:25	935
which shall c near to minister	Eze 45:4	7131
the people of the land shall c	Eze 46:9	935
And it shall c to pass, that every	Eze 47:9	1961
whithersoever the rivers shall c	Eze 47:9	935
these waters shall c thither	Eze 47:9	935
And it shall c to pass, that the	Eze 47:10	1961
till a man c over against Hamath	Eze 47:20	935
And it shall c to pass, that ye	Eze 47:22	1961
And it shall c to pass, that in	Eze 47:23	1961
what should c to pass hereafter	Dan 2:29	1934
to thee what shall c to pass	Dan 2:29	1934
what shall c to pass hereafter	Dan 2:45	1934
to c to the dedication of the	Dan 3:2	858
high God, c forth	Dan 3:26	5312
and c hither	Dan 3:26	858
which is c upon my lord the king	Dan 4:24	4291
I saw him c close unto the ram,	Dan 8:7	5060
transgressors are c to the full	Dan 8:23	
Moses, all this evil is c upon us	Dan 9:13	935
I am now c forth to give thee	Dan 9:22	3318
forth, and I am c to shew thee	Dan 9:23	935
shall c shall destroy the city	Dan 9:26	935
heard, and I am c for thy words	Dan 10:12	935
Now I am c to make thee	Dan 10:14	935
thou wherefore I c unto thee	Dan 10:20	935
lo, the prince of Grecia shall c	Dan 10:20	935
c to the king of the north to	Dan 11:6	935
which shall c with an army, and	Dan 11:7	935
south shall c into his kingdom	Dan 11:9	935
and one shall certainly c, and	Dan 11:10	935
with choler, and shall c forth	Dan 11:11	3318
shall certainly c after certain	Dan 11:13	935
So the king of the north shall c	Dan 11:15	935
but he shall c in peaceably	Dan 11:21	935
for he shall c up, and shall	Dan 11:23	5927
return, and c toward the south	Dan 11:29	935
of Chittim shall c against him	Dan 11:30	935
the king of the north shall c	Dan 11:40	8175
yet he shall c to his end	Dan 11:45	935
it shall c to pass at that day,	Hos 1:5	1961
and it shall c to pass, that in	Hos 1:10	1961
they shall c up out of the land	Hos 1:11	5927
it shall c to pass in that day, I	Hos 2:21	1961
c not ye unto Gilgal, neither go	Hos 4:15	935
C, and let us return unto the LORD	Hos 6:1	3212
he shall c unto us as the rain,	Hos 6:3	935
He shall c as an eagle against	Hos 8:1	
not c into the house of the LORD	Hos 9:4	935
The days of visitation are c	Hos 9:7	935
the days of recompence are c	Hos 9:7	935
the thistle shall c up on their	Hos 10:8	5927
time to seek the LORD, till he c	Hos 10:12	935
travailing woman shall c upon him	Hos 13:13	935
brethren, an east wind shall c	Hos 13:15	935
shall c up from the wilderness	Hos 13:15	5927
For a nation is c up upon my land	Joel 1:6	5927
c, lie all night in sackcloth, ye	Joel 1:13	935
from the Almighty shall it c	Joel 1:15	935
sea, and his stink shall c up	Joel 2:20	5927
and his ill savour shall c up	Joel 2:20	5927
he will cause to c down for you	Joel 2:23	3381
it shall c to pass afterward,	Joel 2:28	1961
and the terrible day of the LORD c	Joel 2:31	635
And it shall c to pass, that	Joel 2:32	1961
let them c up	Joel 3:9	5927
Assemble yourselves, and c	Joel 3:11	935
cause thy mighty ones to c down	Joel 3:11	5181
c up to the valley of Jehoshaphat	Joel 3:12	5927
c, get you down	Joel 3:13	935
it shall c to pass in that day,	Joel 3:18	1961
a fountain shall c forth of the	Joel 3:18	3318
lo, the days shall c upon you	Amos 4:2	935
C to Beth-el, and transgress	Amos 4:4	935
camps to c up unto your nostrils	Amos 4:10	5927
and Beth-el shall c to nought	Amos 5:5	1961
shall c against the fortress	Amos 5:9	935
the seat of violence to c near	Amos 6:3	5066
And it shall c to pass, if there	Amos 6:9	1961
The end is c upon my people of	Amos 8:2	935
it shall c to pass in that day,	Amos 8:9	1961
Behold, the days c, saith the	Amos 8:11	935
Behold, the days c, saith the	Amos 9:13	935
saviours shall c up on mount Zion	Obad 21	5927
wickedness is c up before me	Jonah 1:2	5927
said every one to his fellow, C	Jonah 1:7	3212
made it to c up over Jonah, that	Jonah 4:6	5927
out of his place, and will c down	Mic 1:3	3381
for it is c unto Judah	Mic 1:9	935
he is c unto the gate of my	Mic 1:9	5060
he shall c unto Adullam the glory	Mic 1:15	935
The breaker is c up before them	Mic 2:13	5927
none evil can c upon us	Mic 3:11	935
the last days it shall c to pass	Mic 4:1	1961
And many nations shall c, and say,	Mic 4:2	1980
C, and let us go up	Mic 4:2	3212
of Zion, unto thee shall it c	Mic 4:8	857
the kingdom shall c to the	Mic 4:8	935
yet out of thee shall he c forth	Mic 5:2	3318
Assyrian shall c into our land	Mic 5:5	935
it shall c to pass in that day,	Mic 5:10	1961
shall I c before the LORD	Mic 6:6	6923
shall I c before him with burnt	Mic 6:6	6923
shall c even to thee from Assyria	Mic 7:12	935
There is one c out of thee	Nah 1:11	3318
in pieces is c up before thy face	Nah 2:1	5927
And it shall c to pass, that all	Nah 3:7	1961
their horsemen shall c from far	Hab 1:8	935
They shall c all for violence	Hab 1:9	935
because it will surely c, it will	Hab 2:3	935
it shall c to pass in the day of	Zeph 1:8	1961
it shall c to pass in that day,	Zeph 1:10	1961
it shall c to pass at that time,	Zeph 1:12	1961
anger of the LORD c upon you	Zeph 2:2	935
of the LORD's anger c upon you	Zeph 2:2	935
people say, The time is not c	Hag 1:2	935
the desire of all nations shall c	Hag 2:7	935
and their riders shall c down	Hag 2:22	3381
Then said I, What c these to do	Zec 1:21	935
but these are c to fray them	Zec 1:21	935
c forth, and flee from the land of	Zec 2:6	
for, lo, I c, and I will dwell in	Zec 2:10	935
which are c from Babylon, and c	Zec 6:10	935
And they that are far off shall c	Zec 6:15	935
And this shall c to pass, if ye	Zec 6:15	1961
Therefore it is c to pass	Zec 7:13	1961
And it shall c to pass, that as ye	Zec 8:13	1961
It shall yet c to pass	Zec 8:20	
that there shall c people	Zec 8:20	935
strong nations shall c to seek	Zec 8:22	935
In those days it shall c to pass	Zec 8:23	
forest of the vintage is c down	Zec 11:2	3381
it shall c to pass in that day,	Zec 12:9	1961
nations that c against Jerusalem	Zec 12:9	935
it shall c to pass in that day,	Zec 13:2	1961
And it shall c to pass, that when	Zec 13:3	1961
it shall c to pass in that day,	Zec 13:4	1961
And it shall c to pass, that in	Zec 13:8	1961
and the LORD my God shall c	Zec 14:5	935
it shall c to pass in that day,	Zec 14:6	1961
but it shall c to pass, that at	Zec 14:7	
it shall c to pass in that day,	Zec 14:13	1961
And it shall c to pass, that every	Zec 14:16	1961
that whoso will not c up of all	Zec 14:17	5927
up, and c not, that have no rain	Zec 14:18	935
c not up to keep the feast of	Zec 14:18	5927
c not up to keep the feast of	Zec 14:19	5927
all they that sacrifice shall c	Zec 14:21	935
shall suddenly c to his temple	Mal 3:1	935
behold, he shall c, saith the	Mal 3:1	935
I will c near to you to judgment	Mal 3:5	7126
to their fathers, lest I c	Mal 4:6	935
the east, and are c to worship him	Mt 2:2	*2064*
out of thee shall c a Governor	Mt 2:6	*1831*
bring me word again, that I may c	Mt 2:8	*2064*
when they were c into the house	Mt 2:11	*2064*
Sadducees c to his baptism, he	Mt 3:7	*2064*
you to flee from the wrath to c	Mt 3:7	*3195*
that I am c to destroy the law	Mt 5:17	*2064*
I am not c to destroy, but to	Mt 5:17	*2064*
to thy brother, and then c	Mt 5:24	*2064*
shalt by no means c out thence	Mt 5:26	*1831*
Thy kingdom c	Mt 6:10	*2064*
which c to you in sheep's	Mt 7:15	*2064*
When he was c down from the	Mt 8:1	*2597*
And Jesus saith unto him, I will c	Mt 8:7	*2064*
thou shouldest c under my roof	Mt 8:8	*1525*
and to another, C, and he cometh	Mt 8:9	*2064*
That many shall c from the east	Mt 8:11	*2240*
when Jesus was c into Peter's	Mt 8:14	*2064*
When the even was c, they brought	Mt 8:16	*1096*
when he was c to the other side	Mt 8:28	*2064*
art thou c hither to torment us	Mt 8:29	*2064*
And when they were c out, they	Mt 8:32	*1831*
for I am not c to call the	Mt 9:13	*2064*
but the days will c, when the	Mt 9:15	*2064*
but c and lay thy hand upon her,	Mt 9:18	*2064*
when he was c into the house, the	Mt 9:28	*2064*
when ye c into an house, salute	Mt 10:12	*1525*
worthy, let your peace c upon it	Mt 10:13	*2064*
Israel, till the Son of man be c	Mt 10:23	*2064*
Think not that I am c to send	Mt 10:34	*2064*
For I am c to set a man at	Mt 10:35	*2064*
him, Art thou he that should c	Mt 11:3	*2064*
this is Elias, which was for to c	Mt 11:14	*2064*
C unto me, all ye that labour and	Mt 11:28	*1205*
the kingdom of God is c unto you	Mt 12:28	*5348*
world, neither in the world to c	Mt 12:32	*3195*
and when he is c, he findeth it	Mt 12:44	*2064*
so that the birds of the air c	Mt 13:32	*2064*
the angels shall c forth, and	Mt 13:49	*1831*
when he was c into his own	Mt 13:54	*2064*
and when the evening was c	Mt 14:23	*1096*
bid me c unto thee on the water	Mt 14:28	*2064*
And he said, C	Mt 14:29	*2064*
when Peter was c down out of the	Mt 14:29	*2597*
And when they were c into the ship	Mt 14:32	*1684*
the mouth c forth from the heart	Mt 15:18	*1831*
were c to the other side, they	Mt 16:5	*2064*
If any man will c after me	Mt 16:24	*2064*
For the Son of man shall c in the	Mt 16:27	*2064*
scribes that Elias must first c	Mt 17:10	*2064*
them, Elias truly shall first c	Mt 17:11	*2064*
unto you, That Elias is c already	Mt 17:12	*2064*
when they were c to the multitude	Mt 17:14	*2064*
And when they were c to Capernaum	Mt 17:24	*2064*
when he was c into the house,	Mt 17:25	*1525*
it must needs be that offences c	Mt 18:7	*2064*
For the Son of man is c to save	Mt 18:11	*2064*
and forbid them not, to c unto me	Mt 19:14	*2064*
and c and follow me	Mt 19:21	*1204*
So when even was c, the lord of	Mt 20:8	*1096*
were c to Bethphage, unto the	Mt 21:1	*2064*
when he was c into Jerusalem, all	Mt 21:10	*1525*
when he was c into the temple,	Mt 21:23	*2064*
c, let us kill him, and let us	Mt 21:38	*1205*
and they would not c	Mt 22:3	*2064*
c unto the marriage	Mt 22:4	*1205*
That upon you may c all the	Mt 23:35	*2064*
shall c upon this generation	Mt 23:36	*2240*
For many shall c in my name	Mt 24:5	*2064*
all these things must c to pass	Mt 24:6	*1096*
and then shall the end c	Mt 24:14	*2240*
which is on the housetop not c	Mt 24:17	*2597*
not what hour your Lord doth c	Mt 24:42	*2064*
in what watch the thief would c	Mt 24:43	*2064*
c in a day when he looketh not	Mt 24:50	*2240*
Son of man shall c in his glory	Mt 25:31	*2064*
unto them on his right hand, C	Mt 25:34	*1205*
Now when the even was c, he sat	Mt 26:20	*1096*
him, Friend, wherefore art thou c	Mt 26:50	*3918*
Are ye c out as against a thief	Mt 26:55	*1831*

Context	Reference	Strong's
When the morning was c, all the	Mt 27:1	1096
when they were c unto a place	Mt 27:33	2064
Son of God, c down from the cross	Mt 27:40	2597
let him now c down from the cross	Mt 27:42	2597
whether Elias will c to save him	Mt 27:49	2064
When the even was c, there came a	Mt 27:57	1096
lest his disciples c by night	Mt 27:64	2064
C, see the place where the Lord	Mt 28:6	1205
if this c to the governor's ears,	Mt 28:14	191
C ye after me, and I will make you	Mk 1:17	1205
art thou c to destroy us	Mk 1:24	2064
Hold thy peace, and c out of him	Mk 1:25	1831
when they were c out of the	Mk 1:29	1831
they c unto him, bringing one	Mk 2:3	2064
when they could not c nigh unto	Mk 2:4	4331
and they c and say unto him, Why do	Mk 2:18	2064
But the days will c, when the	Mk 2:20	2064
but that it should c abroad	Mk 4:22	2064
sickle, because the harvest is c	Mk 4:29	3936
the same day, when the even was c	Mk 4:35	1096
when he was c out of the ship,	Mk 5:2	1831
C out of the man, thou unclean	Mk 5:8	1831
they c to Jesus, and see him that	Mk 5:15	2064
when he was c into the ship, he	Mk 5:18	1684
I pray thee, c and lay thy hands	Mk 5:23	2064
And when he was c in, he saith	Mk 5:39	1525
And when the sabbath day was c	Mk 6:2	1096
And when a convenient day was c	Mk 6:21	1096
C ye yourselves apart into a	Mk 6:31	1205
And when even was c, the ship was	Mk 6:47	1096
when they were c out of the ship,	Mk 6:54	1831
when they c from the market,	Mk 7:4	
but the things which c out of him	Mk 7:15	1607
these evil things c from within	Mk 7:23	1607
And when she was c to her house	Mk 7:30	565
them, Whosoever will c after me	Mk 8:34	2064
the kingdom of God c with power	Mk 9:1	2064
scribes that Elias must first c	Mk 9:11	2064
unto you, That Elias is indeed c	Mk 9:13	2064
c out of him, and enter no more	Mk 9:25	1831
when he was c into the house, his	Mk 9:28	1525
This kind can c forth by nothing,	Mk 9:29	1831
the little children to c unto me	Mk 10:14	2064
and c, take up the cross, and	Mk 10:21	1204
and in the world to c eternal life	Mk 10:30	2064
c unto him, saying, Master, we	Mk 10:35	4365
things, and now the eventide was c	Mk 11:11	1511
when they were c from Bethany	Mk 11:12	1831
And they c to Jerusalem	Mk 11:15	2064
And when even was c, he went out	Mk 11:19	1096
which he saith shall c to pass	Mk 11:23	1096
they c again to Jerusalem	Mk 11:27	2064
there c to him the chief priests,	Mk 11:27	2064
c, let us kill him, and the	Mk 12:7	1205
he will c and destroy the	Mk 12:9	2064
And when they were c, they say	Mk 12:14	2064
Then c unto him the Sadducees,	Mk 12:18	2064
For many shall c in my name	Mk 13:6	2064
shall see these things c to pass	Mk 13:29	1096
she is c aforehand to anoint my	Mk 14:8	4301
it is enough, the hour is c	Mk 14:41	2064
And as soon as he was c, he goeth	Mk 14:45	2064
and said unto them, Are ye c out	Mk 14:48	1831
thyself, and c down from the cross	Mk 15:30	2597
And when the sixth hour was c	Mk 15:33	1096
Elias will c to take him down	Mk 15:36	2064
And now when the even was c	Mk 15:42	1096
sweet spices, that they might c	Mk 16:1	2064
The Holy Ghost shall c upon thee	Lk 1:35	1904
mother of my Lord should c to me	Lk 1:43	2064
see this thing which is c to pass	Lk 2:15	1096
you to flee from the wrath to c	Lk 3:7	3195
art thou c to destroy us	Lk 4:34	2064
Hold thy peace, and c out of him	Lk 4:35	1831
unclean spirits, and they c out	Lk 4:36	1831
other ship, that they should c	Lk 5:7	2064
which were c out of every town of	Lk 5:17	2064
But the days will c, when the	Lk 5:35	2064
beseeching him that he would c	Lk 7:3	2064
I myself worthy to c unto thee	Lk 7:7	2064
and to another, C, and he cometh	Lk 7:8	2064
saying, Art thou he that should c	Lk 7:19	2064
When the men were c unto him	Lk 7:20	3854
saying, Art thou he that should c	Lk 7:20	2064
The Son of man is c eating	Lk 7:34	2064
were c to him out of every city,	Lk 8:4	1975
shall not be known and c abroad	Lk 8:17	2064
could not c at him for the press	Lk 8:19	4940
spirit to c out of the man	Lk 8:29	1831
that he would c into his house	Lk 8:41	1525
all, If any man will c after me	Lk 9:23	2064
when he shall c in his own glory,	Lk 9:26	2064
when they were c down from the	Lk 9:37	2718
when the time was c that he	Lk 9:51	4845
fire to c down from heaven	Lk 9:54	2597
is not c to destroy men's lives	Lk 9:56	2064
place, whither he himself would c	Lk 10:1	2064
kingdom of God is c nigh unto you	Lk 10:9	1448
kingdom of God is c nigh unto you	Lk 10:11	1448
spendest more, when I c again	Lk 10:35	1880
Thy kingdom c	Lk 11:2	2064
of mine in his journey is c to me	Lk 11:6	3854
the kingdom of God is c upon you	Lk 11:20	5348
stronger than he shall c upon him	Lk 11:22	1904
that they which c in may see the	Lk 11:33	1531
will c forth and serve them	Lk 12:37	3928
if he shall c in the second watch	Lk 12:38	2064
or c in the third watch, and find	Lk 12:38	2064
known what hour the thief would c	Lk 12:39	2064
c in a day when he looketh not	Lk 12:46	2240
I am c to send fire on the earth	Lk 12:49	2064
Suppose ye that I am c to give	Lk 12:51	3854
these three years I c seeking	Lk 13:7	2064
in them therefore c and be healed,	Lk 13:14	2064
they shall c from the east, and	Lk 13:29	2240
until the time c when ye shall	Lk 13:35	2240
And he that bade thee and him c	Lk 14:9	2064
say to them that were bidden, C	Lk 14:17	2064
a wife, and therefore I cannot c	Lk 14:20	2064
and hedges, and compel them to c in	Lk 14:23	1525
If any man c to me, and hate not	Lk 14:26	2064
c after me, cannot be my disciple	Lk 14:27	2064
said unto him, Thy brother is c	Lk 15:27	2240
But as soon as this thy son was c	Lk 15:30	2064
to us, that would c from thence	Lk 16:26	
lest they also c into this place	Lk 16:28	2064
but that offences will c	Lk 17:1	2064
woe unto him, through whom they c	Lk 17:1	2064
when he is c from the field, Go	Lk 17:7	1525
when the kingdom of God should c	Lk 17:20	2064
the disciples, The days will c	Lk 17:22	2064
let him not c down to take it	Lk 17:31	2597
little children to c unto me	Lk 18:16	2064
and c, follow me	Lk 18:22	1204
time, and in the world to c life	Lk 18:30	2064
that as he was c nigh unto	Lk 18:35	1448
and when he was c near, he asked	Lk 18:40	1448
Zacchaeus, make haste, and c down	Lk 19:5	2597
day is salvation c to this house	Lk 19:9	1096
For the Son of man is c to seek	Lk 19:10	2064
said unto them, Occupy till I c	Lk 19:13	2064
when he was c nigh to Bethphage	Lk 19:29	1448
And when he was c nigh, even now	Lk 19:37	1448
And when he was c near, he beheld	Lk 19:41	1448
For the days shall c upon thee	Lk 19:43	2240
c, let us kill him, that the	Lk 20:14	1205
He shall c and destroy these	Lk 20:16	2064
which ye behold, the days will c	Lk 21:6	2064
when these things shall c to pass	Lk 21:7	1096
for many shall c in my name	Lk 21:8	2064
these things must first c to pass	Lk 21:9	1096
these things begin to c to pass	Lk 21:28	1096
ye see these things c to pass	Lk 21:31	1096
so that day c upon you unawares	Lk 21:34	2186
For as a snare shall it c on all	Lk 21:35	1904
these things that shall c to pass	Lk 21:36	1096
And when the hour was c, he sat	Lk 22:14	1096
until the kingdom of God shall c	Lk 22:18	2064
was c to his disciples, he found	Lk 22:45	2064
the elders, which were c to him	Lk 22:52	3854
Be ye c out	Lk 22:52	1831
And when they were c to the place	Lk 23:33	565
at that which was c to pass	Lk 24:12	1096
are c to pass there in these days	Lk 24:18	1096
therefore am I c baptizing with	Jn 1:31	2064
He saith unto them, C and see	Jn 1:39	2064
any good thing c out of Nazareth	Jn 1:46	1511
Philip saith unto him, C and see	Jn 1:46	2064
mine hour is not yet c	Jn 2:4	2240
thou art a teacher c from God	Jn 3:2	2064
that light is c into the world,	Jn 3:19	2064
baptizeth, and all men c to him	Jn 3:26	2064
not, neither c hither to draw	Jn 4:15	2064
Go, call thy husband, and c hither	Jn 4:16	2064
when he is c, he will tell us all	Jn 4:25	2064
C, see a man, which told me all	Jn 4:29	1205
the Samaritans were c unto him	Jn 4:40	2064
Then when he was c into Galilee	Jn 4:45	2064
was c out of Judaea into Galilee	Jn 4:47	2240
besought him that he would c down	Jn 4:47	2597
him, Sir, c down ere my child die	Jn 4:49	2597
when he was c out of Judaea into	Jn 4:54	2064
lest a worse thing c unto thee	Jn 5:14	1096
shall not c into condemnation	Jn 5:24	2064
And shall c forth	Jn 5:29	1607
And ye will not c to me, that ye	Jn 5:40	2064
I am c in my Father's name, and ye	Jn 5:43	2064
another shall c in his own name	Jn 5:43	2064
and saw a great company c unto him	Jn 6:5	2064
that should c into the world	Jn 6:14	2064
perceived that they would c	Jn 6:15	2064
And when even was now c, his	Jn 6:16	1096
dark, and Jesus was not c to them	Jn 6:17	2064
Father giveth me shall c to me	Jn 6:37	2240
No man can c to me, except the	Jn 6:44	2064
you, that no man can c unto me	Jn 6:65	2064
unto them, My time is not yet c	Jn 7:6	3918
for my time is not yet full c	Jn 7:8	4137
I am not c of myself, but he that	Jn 7:28	2064
because his hour was not yet c	Jn 7:30	2064
where I am, thither ye cannot c	Jn 7:34	2064
where I am, thither ye cannot c	Jn 7:36	2064
any man thirst, let him c unto me	Jn 7:37	2064
Shall Christ c out of Galilee	Jn 7:41	2064
but ye cannot tell whence I c	Jn 8:14	2064
for his hour was not yet c	Jn 8:20	2064
whither I go, ye cannot c	Jn 8:21	2064
saith, Whither I go, ye cannot c	Jn 8:22	2064
judgment I am c into this world	Jn 9:39	2064
I am c that they might have life,	Jn 10:10	2064
which should c into the world	Jn 11:27	2064
secretly, saying, The Master is c	Jn 11:28	3918
Jesus was not yet c into the town	Jn 11:30	2064
when Mary was c where Jesus was	Jn 11:32	2064
They said unto him, Lord, c	Jn 11:34	2064
a loud voice, Lazarus, c forth	Jn 11:43	1204
and the Romans shall c and take	Jn 11:48	2064
that he will not c to the feast	Jn 11:56	2064
people that were c to the feast	Jn 12:12	2064
them, saying, The hour is c	Jn 12:23	2064
light, lest darkness c upon you	Jn 12:35	2638
I am c a light into the world,	Jn 12:46	2064
c that he should depart out of	Jn 13:1	2064
hands, and that he was c from God	Jn 13:3	1831
c, that, when it is c to pass	Jn 13:19	1096
Jews, Whither I go, ye cannot c	Jn 13:33	2064
a place for you, I will c again	Jn 14:3	2064
I will c to you	Jn 14:18	2064
we will c unto him, and make our	Jn 14:23	2064
I go away, and c again unto you	Jn 14:28	2064
have told you before it c to pass	Jn 14:29	1096
that, when it is c to pass	Jn 14:29	1096
If I had not c and spoken unto	Jn 15:22	2064
But when the Comforter is c	Jn 15:26	2064
you, that when the time shall c	Jn 16:4	2064
the Comforter will not c unto you	Jn 16:7	2064
And when he is c, he will reprove	Jn 16:8	2064
he, the Spirit of truth, is c	Jn 16:13	2064
and he will shew you things to c	Jn 16:13	2064
sorrow, because her hour is c	Jn 16:21	2064
Father, and am c into the world	Jn 16:28	2064
the hour cometh, yea, is now c	Jn 16:32	2064
and said, Father, the hour is c	Jn 17:1	2064
are in the world, and I c to thee	Jn 17:11	2064
And now c I to thee	Jn 17:13	2064
all things that should c upon him	Jn 18:4	2064
But when the morning was now c	Jn 21:4	1096
soon then as they were c to land	Jn 21:9	576
Jesus saith unto them, C and dine	Jn 21:12	1205
If I will that he tarry till I c	Jn 21:22	2064
If I will that he tarry till I c	Jn 21:23	2064
they therefore were c together	Acts 1:6	4905
that the Holy Ghost is c upon you	Acts 1:8	1904
shall so c in like manner as ye	Acts 1:11	2064
And when they were c in, they went	Acts 1:13	1525
the day of Pentecost was fully c	Acts 2:1	4845
it shall c to pass in the last	Acts 2:17	1511
and notable day of the Lord c	Acts 2:20	2064
And it shall c to pass, that	Acts 2:21	1511
c from the presence of the Lord	Acts 3:19	2064
And it shall c to pass, that every	Acts 3:23	1511
be of men, it will c to nought	Acts 5:38	2647
c into the land which I shall	Acts 7:3	1204
and after that shall they c forth	Acts 7:7	1834
am c down to deliver them	Acts 7:34	2597
And now c, I will send thee into	Acts 7:34	1204
Who, when they were c down	Acts 8:15	2597
which ye have spoken c upon me	Acts 8:24	1904
had c to Jerusalem for to worship	Acts 8:27	2064
desired Philip that he would c up	Acts 8:31	305
when they were c up out of the	Acts 8:39	305
And when Saul was c to Jerusalem	Acts 9:26	3854
he would not delay to c to them	Acts 9:38	1330
When he was c, they brought him	Acts 9:39	3854
thine alms are c up for a	Acts 10:4	305
is the cause wherefore ye are c	Acts 10:21	3918
found many that were c together	Acts 10:27	4905
or c unto one of another nation	Acts 10:28	4334
hast well done that thou art c	Acts 10:33	3854
when Peter was c up to Jerusalem,	Acts 11:2	305
c unto the house where I was	Acts 11:11	2186
when they were c to Antioch	Acts 11:20	1525
And when Peter was c to himself	Acts 12:11	1096
therefore, lest that c upon you	Acts 13:40	1904
The gods are c down to us in the	Acts 14:11	2597
And when they were c, and had	Acts 14:27	3854
And when they were c to Jerusalem	Acts 15:4	3854
After they were c to Mysia	Acts 16:7	2064
C over into Macedonia, and help us	Acts 16:9	1224
c into my house, and abide there	Acts 16:15	1525
of Jesus Christ to c out of her	Acts 16:18	1831
but let them c themselves	Acts 16:37	2064
upside down are c hither also	Acts 17:6	3918
Timotheus for to c to him with	Acts 17:15	2064
lately c from Italy, with his	Acts 18:2	2064
Timotheus were c from Macedonia	Acts 18:5	2718
who, when he was c, helped them	Acts 18:27	3854
on him which should c after him	Acts 19:4	2064
wherefore they were c together	Acts 19:32	4905
When he therefore was c up again	Acts 20:11	305
And when they were c to him	Acts 20:18	3854
And when he was c unto us, he took	Acts 21:11	2064
And when we were c to Jerusalem	Acts 21:17	1096
multitude must needs c together	Acts 21:22	4905
they will hear that thou art c	Acts 21:22	2064
was c nigh unto Damascus about	Acts 22:6	1448
when I was c again to Jerusalem,	Acts 22:17	5290
and we, or ever he c near, are	Acts 23:15	1448
when thine accusers are also c	Acts 23:35	3854
his accusers to c unto thee	Acts 24:8	2064
the chief captain shall c down	Acts 24:22	2597
to minister or c unto him	Acts 24:23	4334
temperance, and judgment to c	Acts 24:25	1511
Festus was c into the province	Acts 25:1	1910
And when he was c, the Jews which	Acts 25:7	3854
when they were c hither, without	Acts 25:17	4905
on the morrow, when Agrippa was c	Acts 25:23	2064
God day and night, hope to c	Acts 26:7	2658
and Moses did say should c	Acts 26:22	1096
scarce were c over against Cnidus	Acts 27:7	1096
we had much work to c by the boat	Acts 27:16	1096
when the fourteenth night was c	Acts 27:27	1096
while, and saw no harm c to him	Acts 28:6	1096
and when they were c together	Acts 28:17	4905
by the will of God to c unto you	Rom 1:10	2064
I purposed to c unto you, (but	Rom 1:13	2064
Let us do evil, that good may c	Rom 3:8	2064
c short of the glory of God	Rom 3:23	5302
the figure of him that was to c	Rom 5:14	3195
things present, nor things to c	Rom 8:38	3195
of promise, At this time will I c	Rom 9:9	2064
And it shall c to pass, that in	Rom 9:26	1511
salvation is c unto the Gentiles	Rom 11:11	
fulness of the Gentiles be c in	Rom 11:25	1525
There shall c out of Sion the	Rom 11:26	2240
these many years to c unto you	Rom 15:23	2064
into Spain, I will c to you	Rom 15:24	2064
I will c by you into Spain	Rom 15:28	565
when I c unto you, I shall c	Rom 15:29	2064
That I may c unto you with joy by	Rom 15:32	2064
is c abroad unto all men	Rom 16:19	864
So that ye c behind in no gift	1Cor 1:7	5302

of this world, that c to nought ... 1Cor 2:6 2673
or things present, or things to c ... 1Cor 3:22 3195
before the time, until the Lord c ... 1Cor 4:5 2064
as though I would not c to you ... 1Cor 4:18 2064
But I will c to you shortly, if ... 1Cor 4:19 2064
shall I c unto you with a rod, or ... 1Cor 4:21 2064
c together again, that Satan ... 1Cor 7:5 4905
whom the ends of the world are c ... 1Cor 10:11 2658
that ye c together not for the ... 1Cor 11:17 4905
when ye c together in the church, ... 1Cor 11:18 4905
When ye c together therefore into ... 1Cor 11:20 4905
shew the Lord's death till he c ... 1Cor 11:26 2064
when ye c together to eat, tarry ... 1Cor 11:33 4905
that ye c not together unto ... 1Cor 11:34 4905
rest will I set in order when I c ... 1Cor 11:34 2064
when that which is perfect is c ... 1Cor 13:10 2064
if I c unto you speaking with ... 1Cor 14:6 2064
be c together into one place ... 1Cor 14:23 4905
there c in those that are ... 1Cor 14:23 1525
there c in one that believeth not ... 1Cor 14:24 1525
when ye c together, every one of ... 1Cor 14:26 4905
and with what body do they c ... 1Cor 15:35 2064
there be no gatherings when I c ... 1Cor 16:2 2064
And when I c, whomsoever ye shall ... 1Cor 16:3 3854
Now I will c unto you, when I ... 1Cor 16:5 2064
Now if Timotheus c, see that he ... 1Cor 16:10 2064
in peace, that he may c unto me ... 1Cor 16:11 2064
I greatly desired him to c unto ... 1Cor 16:12 2064
was not at all to c at this time ... 1Cor 16:12 2064
but he will c when he shall have ... 1Cor 16:12 2064
I was minded to c unto you before ... 2Cor 1:15 2064
to c again out of Macedonia unto ... 2Cor 1:16 2064
that I would not c again to you ... 2Cor 2:1 2064
Wherefore c out from among them, ... 2Cor 6:17 1831
when we were c into Macedonia, ... 2Cor 7:5 2064
if they of Macedonia c with me ... 2Cor 9:4 2064
for we are c as far as to you ... 2Cor 10:14 5348
I will c to visions and ... 2Cor 12:1 2064
third time I am ready to c to you ... 2Cor 12:14 2064
For I fear, lest, when I c ... 2Cor 12:20 2064
And lest, when I c again, my God ... 2Cor 12:21 2064
if I c again, I will not spare ... 2Cor 13:2 2064
But when Peter was c to Antioch ... Gal 2:11 2064
but when they were c, he withdrew ... Gal 2:12 2064
for if righteousness c by the law ... Gal 2:21
c on the Gentiles through Jesus ... Gal 3:14 1096
till the seed should c to whom ... Gal 3:19 2064
But after that faith is c ... Gal 3:25 2064
the fulness of the time was c ... Gal 4:4 2064
but also in that which is to c ... Eph 1:21 3195
That in the ages to c he might ... Eph 2:7 1904
Till we all c in the unity of the ... Eph 4:13 2658
that whether I c and see you, or ... Phil 1:27 2064
I also myself shall c shortly ... Phil 2:24 2064
Which is c unto you, as it is in ... Col 1:6 3918
Which are a shadow of things to c ... Col 2:17 3195
if he c unto you, receive him ... Col 4:10 2064
delivered us from the wrath to c ... 1Th 1:10 2064
for the wrath is c upon them to ... 1Th 2:16 5348
we would have c unto you, even I ... 1Th 2:18 2064
When he shall c to be glorified ... 2Th 1:10 2064
for that day shall not c ... 2Th 2:3 2064
except there c a falling away ... 2Th 2:3 2064
to c unto the knowledge of the ... 1Ti 2:4 2064
hoping to c unto thee shortly ... 1Ti 3:14 2064
now is, and of that which is to c ... 1Ti 4:8 3195
Till I c, give attendance to ... 1Ti 4:13 2064
foundation against the time to c ... 1Ti 6:19 3195
last days perilous times shall c ... 2Ti 3:1 1764
never able to c to the knowledge ... 2Ti 3:7 2064
For the time will c when they ... 2Ti 4:3 1511
diligence to c shortly unto me ... 2Ti 4:9 2064
thy diligence to c before winter ... 2Ti 4:21 2064
be diligent to c unto me to ... Titus 3:12 2064
put in subjection the world to c ... Heb 2:5 3195
you should seem to c short of it ... Heb 4:1 5302
Let us therefore c boldly unto ... Heb 4:16 4334
and the powers of the world to c ... Heb 6:5 3195
though they c out of the loins of ... Heb 7:5 1831
uttermost that c unto God by him ... Heb 7:25 4334
he saith, Behold, the days c ... Heb 8:8 2064
But Christ being c an high priest ... Heb 9:11 3854
high priest of good things to c ... Heb 9:11 3195
a shadow of good things to c ... Heb 10:1 3195
I c (in the volume of the book it ... Heb 10:7 2240
I c to do thy will, O God ... Heb 10:9 2240
and he that shall c ... Heb 10:37 2064
will c, and will not tarry ... Heb 10:37 2240
and Esau concerning things to c ... Heb 11:20 3195
Moses, when he was c to years ... Heb 11:24 1096
For ye are not c unto the mount ... Heb 12:18 4334
But ye are c unto mount Sion, and ... Heb 12:22 4334
city, but we seek one to c ... Heb 13:14 3195
if he c shortly, I will see you ... Heb 13:23 2064
For if there c unto your assembly ... Jas 2:2 1525
there c in also a poor man in ... Jas 2:2 1525
From whence c wars and fightings ... Jas 4:1
c they not hence, even of your ... Jas 4:1
miseries that shall c upon you ... Jas 5:1 1904
the grace that should c unto you ... 1Pet 1:10
For the time is c that judgment ... 1Pet 4:17
that there shall c in the last ... 2Pet 3:3 2064
that all should c to repentance ... 2Pet 3:9 5562
will c as a thief in the night ... 2Pet 3:10 2240
heard that antichrist shall c ... 1Jn 2:18 2064
is c in the flesh is of God ... 1Jn 4:2 2064
not that Jesus Christ is c in the ... 1Jn 4:3 2064
ye have heard that it should c ... 1Jn 4:3 2064
we know that the Son of God is c ... 1Jn 5:20 2240
Jesus Christ is c in the flesh ... 2Jn 7 2064
If there c any unto you, and bring ... 2Jn 10 2064
but I trust to c unto you ... 2Jn 12 2064
Wherefore, if I c, I will ... 3Jn 10 2064
which must shortly c to pass ... Rev 1:1 1096
and which was, and which is to c ... Rev 1:4 2064
and which was, and which is to c ... Rev 1:8 2064
or else I will c unto thee ... Rev 2:5 2064
or else I will c unto thee ... Rev 2:16 2064
have already hold fast till I c ... Rev 2:25 2240
I will c on thee as a thief, and ... Rev 3:3 2240
know what hour I will c upon thee ... Rev 3:3 2240
behold, I will make them to c ... Rev 3:9 2240
which shall c upon all the world, ... Rev 3:10 2064
Behold, I c quickly ... Rev 3:11 2064
I will c in to him, and will sup ... Rev 3:20 1525
C up hither, and I will shew thee ... Rev 4:1 305
which was, and is, and is to c ... Rev 4:8 2064
one of the four beasts saying, C ... Rev 6:1 2064
I heard the second beast say, C ... Rev 6:3 2064
I heard the third beast say, C ... Rev 6:5 2064
voice of the fourth beast say, C ... Rev 6:7 2064
the great day of his wrath is c ... Rev 6:17 2064
there c two woes more hereafter ... Rev 9:12 2064
mighty angel c down from heaven ... Rev 10:1 2597
saying unto them, C up hither ... Rev 11:12 305
which art, and wast, and art to c ... Rev 11:17 2064
were angry, and thy wrath is c ... Rev 11:18 2064
Now is c salvation, and strength, ... Rev 12:10 1096
for the devil is c down unto you ... Rev 12:12 2597
so that he maketh fire c down ... Rev 13:13 2597
for the hour of his judgment is c ... Rev 14:7 2064
for the time is c for thee to ... Rev 14:15 2064
for all nations shall c and ... Rev 15:4 2240
unclean spirits like frogs c out ... Rev 16:13
Behold, I c as a thief ... Rev 16:15 2064
with me, saying unto me, C hither ... Rev 17:1 1204
one is, and the other is not yet c ... Rev 17:10 2064
another angel c down from heaven ... Rev 18:1 2597
C out of her, my people, that ye ... Rev 18:4 1831
shall her plagues c in one day ... Rev 18:8 2240
for in one hour is thy judgment c ... Rev 18:10 2064
so great riches is c to nought ... Rev 18:17 2049
for the marriage of the Lamb is c ... Rev 19:7 2064
fly in the midst of heaven, C ... Rev 19:17 1205
I saw an angel c down from heaven ... Rev 20:1 2597
C hither, I will shew thee the ... Rev 21:9 1204
Behold, I c quickly ... Rev 22:7 2064
And, behold, I c quickly ... Rev 22:12 2064
And the Spirit and the bride say, C ... Rev 22:17 2064
And let him that heareth say, C ... Rev 22:17 2064
And let him that is athirst c ... Rev 22:17 2064
things saith, Surely I c quickly ... Rev 22:20 2064
Even so, c, Lord Jesus ... Rev 22:20 2064

COMELINESS

he hath no form nor c ... Is 53:2 1926
for it was perfect through my c ... Eze 16:14 1926
they set forth thy c ... Eze 27:10 1926
for my c was turned in me into ... Dan 10:8 1935
parts have more abundant c ... 1Cor 12:23 2157

COMELY

a c person, and the LORD is with ... 1Sa 16:18 8389
his power, nor his c proportion ... Job 41:12 2433
for praise is c for the upright ... Ps 33:1 5000
and praise is c ... Ps 147:1 5000
go well, yea, four are c in going ... Prov 30:29 3190
c for one to eat and to drink, and ... Eccl 5:18 3303
I am black, but c, O ye daughters ... Song 1:5 5000
Thy cheeks are c with rows of ... Song 1:10 4998
voice, and thy countenance is c ... Song 2:14 5000
of scarlet, and thy speech is c ... Song 4:3 5000
c as Jerusalem, terrible as an ... Song 6:4 5000
c for them that are escaped of ... Is 4:2 8597
the daughter of Zion to a c ... Jer 6:2 5000
upon you, but for that which is c ... 1Cor 7:35 2158
is it c that a woman pray unto ... 1Cor 11:13 4241
For our c parts have no need ... 1Cor 12:24 2158

COMERS

make the c thereunto perfect ... Heb 10:1 4334

COMEST

as thou c to Gerar, unto Gaza ... Gen 10:19 935
of Egypt, as thou c unto Zoar ... Gen 13:10 935
when thou c to my kindred ... Gen 24:41 935
when thou c nigh over against the ... Deut 2:19 7126
When thou c nigh unto a city to ... Deut 20:10 7126
When thou c into thy neighbour's ... Deut 23:24 935
When thou c into the standing ... Deut 23:25 935
shalt thou be when thou c in ... Deut 28:6 935
shalt thou be when thou c in ... Deut 28:19 935
said unto him, Whence c thou ... Judg 17:9 935
that thou c with such a company ... Judg 18:23 2199
and whence c thou ... Judg 19:17 935
from Havilah until thou c to Shur ... 1Sa 15:7 935
coming, and said, C thou peaceably ... 1Sa 16:4 935
that thou c to me with staves ... 1Sa 17:43 935
Thou c to me with a sword, and ... 1Sa 17:45 935
said unto him, From whence c thou ... 2Sa 1:3 935
when thou c to see my face ... 2Sa 3:13 935
And she said, C thou peaceably ... 1Kin 2:13 935
and when thou c, anoint Hazael to ... 1Kin 19:15 935
said unto him, Whence c thou ... 2Kin 5:25
And when thou c thither, look out ... 2Kin 9:2 935
said unto Satan, Whence c thou ... Job 1:7 935
unto Satan, From whence c thou ... Job 2:2 935
When thou c to Babylon, and shalt ... Jer 51:61 935
and whence c thou ... Jonah 1:8 935
baptized of thee, and c thou to me ... Mt 3:14 2064
me when thou c into thy kingdom ... Lk 23:42 2064
at Troas with Carpus, when thou c ... 2Ti 4:13 2064

COMETH

the virgin c forth to draw water ... Gen 24:43 3318
his daughter c with the sheep ... Gen 29:6 935
And Leah said, A troop c ... Gen 30:11 935
also he c to meet thee, and four ... Gen 32:6 1980
another, Behold, this dreamer c ... Gen 37:19 935
thy son Joseph c unto thee ... Gen 48:2 935
behold, he c forth to meet thee ... Ex 4:14 3318
lo, he c forth to the water ... Ex 8:20 3318
every firstling that c of a beast ... Ex 13:12 7698
before the LORD, and when he c out ... Ex 28:35 3318
when he c into the tabernacle of ... Ex 29:30 935
such water c shall be unclean ... Lev 11:34 935
the stranger that c nigh shall be ... Num 1:51 7131
the stranger that c nigh shall be ... Num 3:10 7131
the stranger that c nigh shall be ... Num 3:38 7131
the spirit of jealousy c upon him ... Num 5:30 5674
he c out of his mother's womb ... Num 12:12 3318
Whosoever c any thing near unto ... Num 17:13 7131
the stranger that c nigh shall be ... Num 18:7 7131
that c out of the coasts of the ... Num 21:13 3318
of whom c the family of the ... Num 26:5
beside that which c of the sale ... Deut 18:8
it shall be, when evening c on ... Deut 23:11 6437
and cover that which c from thee ... Deut 23:13 6627
that c out from between her feet ... Deut 28:57 3318
that whatsoever c forth of the ... Judg 11:31 3318
of any thing that c of the vine ... Judg 13:14 3318
when it c among us, it may save ... 1Sa 4:3 935
that he saith c surely to pass ... 1Sa 9:6 935
Whosoever c not forth after Saul ... 1Sa 11:7 3318
Wherefore c not the son of Jesse ... 1Sa 20:27 935
Therefore he c not unto the ... 1Sa 20:29 935
whatsoever c to thine hand unto ... 1Sa 25:8 4672
And she said, An old man c up ... 1Sa 28:14 5927
and when thy father c to see thee ... 2Sa 13:5 935
good man, and c with good tidings ... 2Sa 18:27 935
but c out of a far country for ... 1Kin 8:41 935
the wife of Jeroboam c to ask a ... 1Kin 14:5 935
for it shall be, when she c in ... 1Kin 14:5 935
and it shall be, when he c to us ... 2Kin 4:10 935
look, when the messenger c ... 2Kin 6:32 935
came to them, but he c not again ... 2Kin 9:18 7725
even unto them, and c not again ... 2Kin 9:20 7725
as soon as this letter c to you ... 2Kin 10:2 935
he that c within the ranges, let ... 2Kin 11:8 935
as he goeth out and as he c in ... 2Kin 11:8 935
all the money that c into any ... 2Kin 12:4 5927
on the right side as one c into ... 2Kin 12:9 935
because he c to judge the earth ... 1Chr 16:33 935
thine holy name c of thine hand ... 1Chr 29:16
so that whosoever c to consecrate ... 2Chr 13:9 935
There c a great multitude against ... 2Chr 20:2 935
If, when evil c upon us, as the ... 2Chr 20:9 935
great company that c against us ... 2Chr 20:12 935
whosoever else c into the house ... 2Chr 23:7 935
be ye with the king when he c in ... 2Chr 23:7 935
long for death, but it c not ... Job 3:21
For my sighing c before I eat ... Job 3:24 935
Although affliction c not forth ... Job 5:6 3318
afraid of destruction when it c ... Job 5:21 935
shock of corn c in in his season ... Job 5:26 5927
He c forth like a flower, and is ... Job 14:2 3318
the mountain falling c to nought ... Job 14:18 5034
It is drawn, and c out of the body ... Job 20:25 3318
sword c out of his gall ... Job 20:25 1980
how oft c their destruction upon ... Job 21:17 935
his cry when trouble c upon him ... Job 27:9 935
for the earth, out of it c bread ... Job 28:5 3318
Whence then c wisdom ... Job 28:20 935
shine by the cloud that c betwixt ... Job 36:32 6293
Out of the south c the whirlwind ... Job 37:9 935
Fair weather c out of the north ... Job 37:22 857
a night, but joy c in the morning ... Ps 30:5
from him c my salvation ... Ps 62:1
For promotion c neither from the ... Ps 75:6
that passeth away, and c not again ... Ps 78:39 7725
for he c, for he c to judge ... Ps 96:13 935
for he c to judge the earth ... Ps 98:9 935
Blessed be he that c in the name ... Ps 118:26 935
the hills, from whence c my help ... Ps 121:1 935
My help c from the LORD, which ... Ps 121:2
I will mock when your fear c ... Prov 1:26 935
When your fear c as desolation ... Prov 1:27 935
your destruction c as a whirlwind ... Prov 1:27 857
distress and anguish c upon you ... Prov 1:27 935
out of his mouth c knowledge ... Prov 2:6
of the wicked, when it c ... Prov 3:25 935
When pride c, then c shame ... Prov 11:2 935
the wicked c in his stead ... Prov 11:8 935
man is loathsome, and c to shame ... Prov 13:5
Only by pride c contention ... Prov 13:10 5414
heart sick, but when the desire c ... Prov 13:12 935
When the wicked c, then c ... Prov 18:3 935
but his neighbour c and searcheth ... Prov 18:17 935
man's judgment c from the LORD ... Prov 29:26
away, and another generation c ... Eccl 1:4 935
the man do that c after the king ... Eccl 2:12 935
For out of prison he c to reign ... Eccl 4:14 3318
For a dream c through the ... Eccl 5:3 935
For he c in with vanity, and ... Eccl 6:4 935
All that c is vanity ... Eccl 11:8 935
he c leaping upon the mountains, ... Song 2:8 935
Who is this that c out of the ... Song 3:6 5927
Who is this that c up from the ... Song 8:5 5927
Behold, the day of the LORD c ... Is 13:9 935
so it c from the desert, from a ... Is 21:1 935
here c a chariot of men, with a ... Is 21:9 935
The watchman said, The morning c ... Is 21:12 857
he that c up out of the midst of ... Is 24:18 5927
the LORD c out of his place to ... Is 26:21 3318
This also c forth from the LORD ... Is 28:29 3318
whose breaking c suddenly at an ... Is 30:13 935
the name of the LORD c from far ... Is 30:27 935
earth, and that which c out of it ... Is 42:5 6631
For as the rain c down, and the ... Is 55:10 3381
of Zion, Behold, thy salvation c ... Is 62:11 935
Who is this that c from Edom ... Is 63:1 935
To what purpose c there to me ... Jer 6:20 935
a people c from the north country ... Jer 6:22 935
and shall not see when good c ... Jer 17:6 935

and shall not see when heat c Jer 17:8 935
c from the rock of the field Jer 18:14
And when he c, he shall smite the Jer 43:11 935
Who is this that c up as a flood Jer 46:7 5927
fair heifer, but destruction c Jer 46:20 935
it c out of the north Jer 46:20 935
Because of the day that c to Jer 47:4 935
there c up a nation against her Jer 50:3 5927
A sound of a cry c from Babylon Jer 51:54 935
it c to pass, when the Lord Lam 3:37 1961
it with dung that c out of man Eze 4:12 6627
Destruction c; and they shall seek Eze 7:25 935
his face, and c to the prophet Eze 14:4 935
c according to the multitude of Eze 14:4 935
c to a prophet to enquire of him Eze 14:7 935
that which c into your mind shall Eze 20:32 5927
because it c: and every heart shall Eze 21:7 935
behold, it c, and shall be brought Eze 21:7 935
and when this c, ye shall know Eze 24:24 935
for, lo, it c Eze 30:9 935
word that c forth from the LORD Eze 33:30 3318
come unto thee as the people c Eze 33:31 935
And when this c to pass, (lo, it Eze 33:33 935
shall live whither the river c Eze 47:9 935
But he that c against him shall Dan 11:16 935
c to the thousand three hundred Dan 12:12 5060
and the thief c in, and the troop Hos 7:1 935
for the day of the LORD c Joel 2:1 935
the LORD c forth out of his place Mic 1:3 3318
when he c into our land, and when Mic 5:6 935
thy watchmen and thy visitation c Mic 7:4 935
when he c up unto the people, he Hab 3:16 5927
behold, thy King c unto thee Zec 9:9 935
Behold, the day of the LORD c Zec 14:1 935
For, behold, the day c, that Mal 4:1 935
the day that c shall burn them up Mal 4:1 935
but he that c after me is Mt 3:11 2064
Then c Jesus from Galilee to Mt 3:13 3854
is more than these c of evil Mt 5:37 1511
and to another, Come, and he c Mt 8:9 2064
then c the wicked one, and Mt 13:19 2064
but that which c out of the mouth Mt 15:11 1607
take up the fish that first c up Mt 17:27 305
to that man by whom the offence c Mt 18:7 2064
thy King c unto thee, meek, and Mt 21:5 2064
Blessed is he that c in the name Mt 21:9 2064
lord therefore of the vineyard c Mt 21:40 2064
Blessed is he that c in the name Mt 23:39 2064
the lightning c out of the east Mt 24:27 1831
as ye think not the Son of man c Mt 24:44 2064
when he c shall find so doing Mt 24:46 2064
made, Behold, the bridegroom c Mt 25:6 2064
the hour wherein the Son of man c Mt 25:13 2064
time the lord of those servants c Mt 25:19 2064
Then c Jesus with them unto a Mt 26:36 2064
he c unto the disciples, and Mt 26:40 2064
Then c he to his disciples, and Mt 26:45 2064
There c one mightier than I after Mk 1:7 2064
the multitude c together again, Mk 3:20 4905
Satan c immediately, and taketh Mk 4:15 2064
there c one of the rulers of the Mk 5:22 2064
he c to the house of the ruler of Mk 5:38 2064
watch of the night he c unto them Mk 6:48 2064
That which c out of the man, that Mk 7:20 1607
And he c to Bethsaida Mk 8:22 2064
when he c in the glory of his Mk 8:38 2064
told them, Elias verily c first Mk 9:12 2064
c into the coasts of Judaea by Mk 10:1 2064
Blessed is he that c in the name Mk 11:9 2064
that c in the name of the Lord Mk 11:10 2064
when the master of the house c Mk 13:35 2064
the evening he c with the twelve Mk 14:17 2064
And he c, and findeth them sleeping Mk 14:37 2064
he c the third time, and saith Mk 14:41 2064
c Judas, one of the twelve, and Mk 14:43 3854
there c one of the maids of the Mk 14:66 2064
but one mightier than I c Lk 3:16 2064
Whosoever c to me, and heareth my Lk 6:47 2064
and to another, Come, and he c Lk 7:8 2064
then c the devil, and taketh away Lk 8:12 2064
there c one from the ruler of the Lk 8:49 2064
And when he c, he findeth it swept Lk 11:25 2064
that when he c and knocketh, they Lk 12:36 2064
when he c shall find watching Lk 12:37 2064
for the Son of man c at an hour Lk 12:40 2064
when he c shall find so doing Lk 12:43 2064
ye say, There c a shower Lk 12:54 2064
and it c to pass Lk 12:55 1096
Blessed is he that c in the name Lk 13:35 2064
that when he that bade thee c Lk 14:10 2064
that c against him with twenty Lk 14:31 2064
And when he c home, he calleth Lk 15:6 2064
The kingdom of God c not with Lk 17:20 2064
when the Son of man c, shall he Lk 18:8 2064
that c in the name of the Lord Lk 19:38 2064
every man that c into the world Jn 1:9 2064
He that c after me is preferred Jn 1:15 2064
After me c a man which is Jn 1:30 2064
but canst not tell whence it c Jn 3:8 2064
neither c to the light, lest his Jn 3:20 2064
that doeth truth c to the light Jn 3:21 2064
He that c from above is above all Jn 3:31 2064
he that c from heaven is above Jn 3:31 2064
Then c he to a city of Samaria, Jn 4:5 2064
There c a woman of Samaria to Jn 4:7 2064
Woman, believe me, the hour c Jn 4:21 2064
But the hour c, and now is, when Jn 4:23 2064
unto him, I know that Messias c Jn 4:25 2064
four months, and then c harvest Jn 4:35 2064
the honour that c from God only Jn 5:44
is he which c down from heaven Jn 6:33 2597
he that c to me shall never Jn 6:35 2064
him that c to me I will in no Jn 6:37 2064
learned of the Father, c unto me Jn 6:45 2064
bread which c down from heaven Jn 6:50 2597
but when Christ c, no man knoweth Jn 7:27 2064
on him, and said, When Christ c Jn 7:31 2064
That Christ c of the seed of Jn 7:42 2064
the night c, when no man can work Jn 9:4 2064
The thief c not, but for to steal Jn 10:10
in himself c to the grave Jn 11:38 2064
that c in the name of the Lord Jn 12:13 2064
behold, thy King c, sitting on an Jn 12:15 2064
Philip c and telleth Andrew Jn 12:22 2064
Then c he to Simon Peter Jn 13:6 2064
no man c unto the Father, but by Jn 14:6 2064
for the prince of this world c Jn 14:30 2064
But this c to pass, that the word Jn 15:25
yea, the time c, that whosoever Jn 16:2 2064
but the time c, when I shall no Jn 16:25 2064
Behold, the hour c, yea, is now Jn 16:32 2064
c thither with lanterns and Jn 18:3 2064
the week c Mary Magdalene early Jn 20:1 2064
c to Simon Peter, and to the other Jn 20:2 2064
Then c Simon Peter following him, Jn 20:6 2064
Jesus then c, and taketh bread, and Jn 21:13 2064
who, when he c, shall speak unto Acts 10:32 3854
there c one after me, whose shoes Acts 13:25 2064
this feast that c in Jerusalem Acts 18:21 2064
C this blessedness then upon the Rom 4:9
So then faith c by hearing Rom 10:17
Then c the end, when he shall 1Cor 15:24
For if he that c preacheth 2Cor 11:4 2064
that which c upon me daily, the 2Cor 11:28 1999
This persuasion c not of him that Gal 5:8
c the wrath of God upon the Eph 5:6 2064
things' sake the wrath of God c Col 3:6 2064
Lord so c as a thief in the night 1Th 5:2 2064
sudden destruction c upon them 1Th 5:3 2186
strifes of words, whereof c envy 1Ti 6:4 1096
in the rain that c oft upon it Heb 6:7 2064
when he c into the world, he Heb 10:5
for he that c to God must believe Heb 11:6 4334
c down from the Father of lights, Jas 1:17 2591
the Lord c with ten thousands of Jude 14 2064
Behold, he c with clouds Rev 1:7 2064
which c down out of heaven from Rev 3:12 2597
behold, the third woe c quickly Rev 11:14 2064
and when he c, he must continue a Rev 17:10 2064

COMFORT
This same shall c us concerning Gen 5:29 5162
of bread, and c ye your hearts Gen 18:5 5582
doth c himself, purposing to kill Gen 27:42 5162
his daughters rose up to c him Gen 37:35 5162
C thine heart with a morsel of Judg 19:5 5582
C thine heart, I pray thee Judg 19:8 5582
David sent to c him by the hand 2Sa 10:2 5162
and his brethren came to c him 1Chr 7:22 5162
David sent messengers to c him 1Chr 19:2 5162
of Ammon to Hanun, to c him 1Chr 19:2 5162
to mourn with him and to c him Job 2:11 5162
Then should I yet have c Job 6:10 5165
When I say, My bed shall c me Job 7:13 5162
off my heaviness, and c myself Job 9:27 1082
alone, that I may take c a little Job 10:20 1082
How then c ye me in vain, seeing Job 21:34 5162
thy rod and thy staff they c me Ps 23:4 5162
greatness, and c me on every side Ps 71:21 5162
This is my c in my affliction Ps 119:50 5162
thy merciful kindness be for my c Ps 119:76 5162
word, saying, When wilt thou c me Ps 119:82 5162
me with flagons, c me with apples Song 2:5 7502
weep bitterly, labour not to c me Is 22:4 5162
C ye, c ye my people, saith Is 40:1 5162
For the LORD shall c Zion Is 51:3 5162
he will c all her waste places Is 51:3 5162
by whom shall I c thee Is 51:19 5162
Should I receive c in these Is 57:6 5162
to c all that mourn Is 61:2 5162
comforteth, so will I c you Is 66:13 5162
When I would c myself against Jer 8:18 4010
mourning, to c them for the dead Jer 16:7 5162
mourning into joy, and will c them Jer 31:13 5162
her lovers she hath none to c her Lam 1:2 5162
hands, and there is none to c her Lam 1:17 5162
there is none to c me Lam 1:21 5162
equal to thee, that I may c thee Lam 2:13 5162
And they shall c you, when ye see Eze 14:23 5162
in that thou art a c unto them Eze 16:54 5162
and the LORD shall yet c Zion Zec 1:17 5162
they c in vain Zec 10:2 5162
he said, Daughter, be of good c Mt 9:22 2293
saying unto him, Be of good c Mk 10:49 2293
unto her, Daughter, be of good c Lk 8:48 2293
to c them concerning their Jn 11:19 3888
in the c of the Holy Ghost, were Acts 9:31 3874
c of the scriptures might have Rom 15:4 3874
edification, and exhortation, and c 1Cor 14:3 3889
of mercies, and the God of all c 2Cor 1:3 3874
that we may be able to c them 2Cor 1:4 3870
by the c wherewith we ourselves 2Cor 1:4 3874
c him, lest perhaps such a one 2Cor 2:7 3870
I am filled with c, I am 2Cor 7:4 3874
we were comforted in your c 2Cor 7:13 3874
Be perfect, be of good c, be of 2Cor 13:11 3870
and that he might c your hearts Eph 6:22 3870
Christ, if any c of love, if any Phil 2:1 3890
you, that I also may be of good c Phil 2:19 2174
your estate, and c your hearts Col 4:8 3870
God, which have been a c unto me Col 4:11 3931
to c you concerning your faith 1Th 3:2 3870
Wherefore c one another with 1Th 4:18 3870
Wherefore c yourselves together, 1Th 5:11 3870
c the feebleminded, support the 1Th 5:14 3888
C your hearts, and stablish you in 2Th 2:17 3870

COMFORTABLE
my lord the king shall now be c 2Sa 14:17 4496
me with good words and c words Zec 1:13 5150

COMFORTABLY
speak c unto thy servants 2Sa 19:7
Hezekiah spake c unto all the 2Chr 30:22
city, and spake c to them, saying, 2Chr 32:6
Speak ye c to Jerusalem, and cry Is 40:2
wilderness, and speak c unto her Hos 2:14

COMFORTED
Isaac was c after his mother's Gen 24:67 5162
but he refused to be c Gen 37:35 5162
and Judah was c, and went up unto Gen 38:12 5162
he c them, and spake kindly unto Gen 50:21 5162
for that thou hast c me, and for Ruth 2:13 5162
David c Bath-sheba his wife, and 2Sa 12:24 5162
for he was c concerning Amnon, 2Sa 13:39 5162
c him over all the evil that the Job 42:11 5162
my soul refused to be c Ps 77:2 5162
LORD, hast holpen me, and c me Ps 86:17 5162
and have c myself Ps 119:52 5162
for the LORD hath c his people Is 49:13 5162
for the LORD hath c his people Is 52:9 5162
tossed with tempest, and not c Is 54:11 5162
ye shall be c in Jerusalem Is 66:13 5162
refused to be c for her children Jer 31:15 5162
to rest upon them, and I will be c Eze 5:13 5162
ye shall be c concerning the evil Eze 14:22 5162
shall be c in the nether parts of Eze 31:16 5162
shall be c over all his multitude Eze 32:31 5162
her children, and would not be c Mt 2:18 3870
for they shall be c Mt 5:4 3870
but now he is c, and thou art Lk 16:25 3870
c her, when they saw Mary, that Jn 11:31 3888
seen the brethren, they c them Acts 16:40 3870
man alive, and were not a little c Acts 20:12 3870
that I may be c together with you Rom 1:12 4837
all may learn, and all may be c 1Cor 14:31 3870
we ourselves are c of God 2Cor 1:4 3870
or whether we be c, it is for 2Cor 1:6 3870
c us by the coming of Titus 2Cor 7:6 3870
wherewith he was c in you 2Cor 7:7 3870
we were c in your comfort 2Cor 7:13 3870
That their hearts might be c Col 2:2 3870
As ye know how we exhorted and c 1Th 2:11 3888
we were c over you in all our 1Th 3:7 3870

COMFORTEDST
is turned away, and thou c me Is 12:1 5162

COMFORTER
were oppressed, and they had no c Eccl 4:1 5162
but they had no c Eccl 4:1
she had no c Lam 1:9 5162
because the c that should relieve Lam 1:16 5162
and he shall give you another C Jn 14:16 3875
But the C, which is the Holy Jn 14:26 3875
But when the C is come, whom I Jn 15:26 3875
the C will not come unto you Jn 16:7 3875

COMFORTERS
that he hath sent c unto thee 2Sa 10:3 5162
that he hath sent c unto thee 1Chr 19:3 5162
miserable c are ye all Job 16:2 5162
and for c, but I found none Ps 69:20 5162
whence shall I seek c for thee Nah 3:7 5162

COMFORTETH
as one that c the mourners Job 29:25 5162
I, even I, am he that c you Is 51:12 5162
As one whom his mother c, so will Is 66:13 5162
Who c us in all our tribulation, 2Cor 1:4 3870
that c those that are cast down, 2Cor 7:6 3870

COMFORTLESS
I will not leave you c Jn 14:18 3737

COMFORTS
within me thy c delight my soul Ps 94:19 8575
restore c unto him and to his Is 57:18 5150

COMING
and, behold, the camels were c Gen 24:63 935
LORD hath blessed thee since my c Gen 30:30 7272
thee, hinder thee from c unto me Num 22:16 1980
heard of the c of the children of Num 33:40 935
Why is his chariot so long in c Judg 5:28 935
meet a company of prophets c down 1Sa 10:5 3381
of the town trembled at his c 1Sa 16:4 7122
I saw the son of Jesse c to Nob 1Sa 22:9 935
thee from c to shed blood 1Sa 25:26 935
me this day from c to shed blood 1Sa 25:33 935
thy c in with me in the host is 1Sa 29:6 935
of thy c unto me unto this day 1Sa 29:6 935
to know thy going out and thy c in 2Sa 3:25 4126
his servants c on toward him 2Sa 24:20 5674
the son of Rechab c to meet him 2Kin 10:15
the land at the c in of the year 2Kin 13:20 935
and thy going out, and thy c in 2Kin 19:27 935
Ahaziah was of God by c to Joram 2Chr 22:7 935
their c unto the house of God at Ezr 3:8 935
a bridegroom c out of his chamber Ps 19:5 3318
for he seeth that his day is c Ps 37:13 935
thy c in from this time forth, and Ps 121:8 935
city, at the c in at the doors Prov 8:3 3996
for thee to meet thee at thy c Is 14:9 935
shall hail, c down on the forest Is 32:19 3381
and thy going out, and thy c in Is 37:28 935
and the things that are c, and Is 44:7 857
observe the time of their c Jer 8:7 935
an holy one c down from heaven, Dan 4:23 5182
According to the days of thy c Mic 7:15 3318
he had horns c out of his hand Hab 3:4
who may abide the day of his c Mal 3:2 935
prophet before the c of the great Mal 4:5 935
c out of the tombs, exceeding Mt 8:28 1831

the Son of man c in his kingdom	Mt 16:28	*2064*
what shall be the sign of thy c	Mt 24:3	*3952*
so shall also the c of the Son of	Mt 24:27	*3952*
c in the clouds of heaven with	Mt 24:30	*2064*
so shall also the c of the Son of	Mt 24:37	*3952*
so shall also the c of the Son of	Mt 24:39	*3952*
his heart, My lord delayeth his c	Mt 24:48	*2064*
then at my c I should have	Mt 25:27	*2064*
c in the clouds of heaven	Mt 26:64	*2064*
straightway c up out of the water	Mk 1:10	*305*
for there were many c and going,	Mk 6:31	*2064*
shall they see the Son of man c	Mk 13:26	*2064*
Lest c suddenly he find you	Mk 13:36	*2064*
c in the clouds of heaven	Mk 14:62	*2064*
c out of the country, the father	Mk 15:21	*2064*
she c in that instant gave thanks	Lk 2:38	*2186*
And as he was yet a c, the devil	Lk 9:42	*4334*
his heart, My lord delayeth his c	Lk 12:45	*2064*
by her continual c she weary me	Lk 18:5	*2064*
that at my c I might have	Lk 19:23	*2064*
things which are c on the earth	Lk 21:26	*1904*
of man c in a cloud with power	Lk 21:27	*2064*
c out of the country, and on him	Lk 23:26	*2064*
For, behold, the days are c	Lk 23:29	*2064*
c to him, and offering him vinegar	Lk 23:36	*4334*
who c after me is preferred	Jn 1:27	*2064*
day John seeth Jesus c unto him	Jn 1:29	*2064*
Jesus saw Nathanael c to him	Jn 1:47	*2064*
but while I am c, another	Jn 5:7	*2064*
I say unto you, The hour is c	Jn 5:25	*2064*
for the hour is c, in the which	Jn 5:28	*2064*
sheep are not, seeth the wolf c	Jn 10:12	*2064*
as she heard that Jesus was c	Jn 11:20	*2064*
that Jesus was c to Jerusalem	Jn 12:12	*2064*
before of the c of the Just One	Acts 7:52	*1660*
a vision a man named Ananias c in	Acts 9:12	*1525*
And he was with them c in and going	Acts 9:28	*1531*
day an angel of God c in to him	Acts 10:3	*1525*
And as Peter was c in, Cornelius	Acts 10:25	*1525*
c the baptism of repentance to	Acts 13:24	*1529*
who c thither went into the	Acts 17:10	*3854*
And while the day was c on	Acts 27:33	
been much hindered from c to you	Rom 15:22	*2064*
waiting for the c of our Lord	1Cor 1:7	*602*
they that are Christ's at his c	1Cor 15:23	*3952*
I am glad of the c of Stephanas	1Cor 16:17	*3952*
comforted us by the c of Titus	2Cor 7:6	*3952*
And not by his c only, but by the	2Cor 7:7	*3952*
is the third time I am c to you	2Cor 13:1	*2064*
for me by my c to you again	Phil 1:26	*3952*
of our Lord Jesus Christ at his c	1Th 2:19	*3952*
at the c of our Lord Jesus Christ	1Th 3:13	*3952*
remain unto the c of the Lord	1Th 4:15	*3952*
the c of our Lord Jesus Christ	1Th 5:23	*3952*
by the c of our Lord Jesus Christ	2Th 2:1	*3952*
with the brightness of his c	2Th 2:8	*3952*
whose c is after the working of	2Th 2:9	*3952*
brethren, unto the c of the Lord	Jas 5:7	*3952*
for the c of the Lord draweth	Jas 5:8	*3952*
To whom c, as unto a living stone	1Pet 2:4	*4334*
c of our Lord Jesus Christ, but	2Pet 1:16	*3952*
Where is the promise of his c	2Pet 3:4	*3952*
hasting unto the c of the day of	2Pet 3:12	*3952*
be ashamed before him at his c	1Jn 2:28	*3952*
beast c up out of the earth	Rev 13:11	*305*
c down from God out of heaven,	Rev 21:2	*2597*

COMINGS

the c in thereof, and all the	Eze 43:11	4126

COMMAND

him, that he will c his children	Gen 18:19	6680
according to that which I c thee	Gen 27:8	6680
Thy father did c before he died	Gen 50:16	6680
shalt speak all that I c thee	Ex 7:2	6680
LORD our God, as he shall c us	Ex 8:27	559
God c thee so, then thou shalt be	Ex 18:23	6680
thou shalt c the children of	Ex 27:20	6680
thou that which I c thee this day	Ex 34:11	6680
C Aaron and his sons, saying, This	Lev 6:9	6680
Then the priest shall c that they	Lev 13:54	6680
Then shall the priest c to take	Lev 14:4	6680
the priest shall c that one of	Lev 14:5	6680
Then the priest shall c that they	Lev 14:36	6680
Then the priest shall c that they	Lev 14:40	6680
C the children of Israel, that	Lev 24:2	6680
Then I will c my blessing upon	Lev 25:21	6680
C the children of Israel, that	Num 5:2	6680
the LORD will c concerning you	Num 9:8	6680
C the children of Israel, and say	Num 28:2	6680
C the children of Israel, and say	Num 34:2	6680
C the children of Israel, that	Num 35:2	6680
c concerning the daughters of	Num 36:6	6680
c thou the people, saying, Ye are	Deut 2:4	6680
add unto the word which I c you	Deut 4:2	6680
the LORD your God which I c you	Deut 4:2	6680
which I c thee this day, that it	Deut 4:40	6680
his commandments, which I c thee	Deut 6:2	6680
which I c thee this day, shall be	Deut 6:6	6680
which I c thee this day, to do	Deut 7:11	6680
All the commandments which I c	Deut 8:1	6680
statutes, which I c thee this day	Deut 8:11	6680
which I c thee this day for thy	Deut 10:13	6680
which I c you this day, that ye	Deut 11:8	6680
which I c you this day, to love	Deut 11:13	6680
these commandments which I c you	Deut 11:22	6680
your God, which I c you this day	Deut 11:27	6680
of the way which I c you this day	Deut 11:28	6680
shall ye bring all that I c you	Deut 12:11	6680
thou shalt do all that I c thee	Deut 12:14	6680
all these words which I c thee	Deut 12:28	6680
What thing soever I c you	Deut 12:32	6680
which I c thee this day, to do	Deut 13:18	6680
which I c thee this day	Deut 15:5	6680
therefore I c thee, saying, Thou	Deut 15:11	6680
therefore I c thee this thing to	Deut 15:15	6680
unto them all that I shall c him	Deut 18:18	6680
Wherefore I c thee, saying, Thou	Deut 19:7	6680
which I c thee this day, to love	Deut 19:9	6680
therefore I c thee to do this	Deut 24:18	6680
therefore I c thee to do this	Deut 24:22	6680
which I c you this day	Deut 27:1	6680
which I c you this day, in mount	Deut 27:4	6680
statutes, which I c thee this day	Deut 27:10	6680
which I c thee this day, that the	Deut 28:1	6680
The LORD shall c the blessing	Deut 28:8	6680
which I c thee this day, to	Deut 28:13	6680
the words which I c thee this day	Deut 28:14	6680
statutes which I c thee this day	Deut 28:15	6680
to all that I c thee this day	Deut 30:2	6680
which I c thee this day	Deut 30:8	6680
which I c thee this day, it is	Deut 30:11	6680
In that I c thee this day to love	Deut 30:16	6680
which ye shall c your children to	Deut 32:46	6680
c the people, saying, Prepare you	Josh 1:11	6680
thou shalt c the priests that	Josh 3:8	6680
c ye them, saying, Take you hence	Josh 4:3	6680
C the priests that bear the ark	Josh 4:16	6680
servant, so did Moses c Joshua	Josh 11:15	6680
Let our lord now c thy servants	1Sa 16:16	559
Now therefore c thou that they	1Kin 5:6	6680
hearken unto all that I c thee	1Kin 11:38	6680
or if I c the locusts to devour	2Chr 7:13	6680
Doth the eagle mount up at thy c	Job 39:27	6310
Yet the LORD will c his	Ps 42:8	6680
c deliverances for Jacob	Ps 44:4	6680
I will also c the clouds that	Is 5:6	6680
the work of my hands c ye me	Is 45:11	6680
whatsoever I c thee thou shalt	Jer 1:7	6680
speak unto them all that I c thee	Jer 1:17	6680
according to all which I c you	Jer 11:4	6680
all the words that I c thee to	Jer 26:2	6680
c them to say unto their masters,	Jer 27:4	6680
Behold, I will c, saith the LORD,	Jer 34:22	6680
whom thou didst c that they	Lam 1:10	6680
sea, thence will I c the serpent	Amos 9:3	6680
thence will I c the sword	Amos 9:4	6680
For, lo, I will c, and I will sift	Amos 9:9	6680
c that these stones be made bread	Mt 4:3	*2036*
Why did Moses then c to give a	Mt 19:7	*1781*
C therefore that the sepulchre be	Mt 27:64	*2753*
unto them, What did Moses c you	Mk 10:3	*1781*
c this stone that it be made	Lk 4:3	*2036*
c them to go out into the deep	Lk 8:31	*2004*
wilt thou that we c fire to come	Lk 9:54	*2036*
if ye do whatsoever I c you	Jn 15:14	*1781*
These things I c you, that ye	Jn 15:17	*1781*
Did not we straitly c you that ye	Acts 5:28	*3853*
to c them to keep the law of	Acts 15:5	*3853*
I c thee in the name of Jesus	Acts 16:18	*3853*
And unto the married I c, yet not	1Cor 7:10	*3853*
will do the things which we c you	2Th 3:4	*3853*
Now we c you, brethren, in the	2Th 3:6	*3853*
Now them that are such we c	2Th 3:12	*3853*
These things c and teach	1Ti 4:11	*3853*

COMMANDED

And the LORD God c the man	Gen 2:16	6680
whereof I c thee that thou	Gen 3:11	6680
of the tree, of which I c thee	Gen 3:17	6680
according to all that God c him	Gen 6:22	6680
unto all that the LORD c him	Gen 7:5	6680
and the female, as God had c Noah	Gen 7:9	6680
of all flesh, as God had c him	Gen 7:16	6680
Pharaoh c his men concerning him	Gen 12:20	6680
eight days old, as God had c him	Gen 21:4	6680
he c them, saying, Thus shall ye	Gen 32:4	6680
he c the foremost, saying, When	Gen 32:17	6680
so c he the second, and the third,	Gen 32:19	6680
Then Joseph c to fill their sacks	Gen 42:25	6680
he c the steward of his house,	Gen 44:1	6680
Now thou art c, this do ye	Gen 45:19	6680
land of Rameses, as Pharaoh had c	Gen 47:11	6680
Joseph c his servants the	Gen 50:2	6680
unto him according as he c them	Gen 50:12	6680
not as the king of Egypt c them	Ex 1:17	1696
all the signs which he had c him	Ex 4:28	6680
Pharaoh c the same day the	Ex 5:6	6680
and Aaron did as the LORD c them	Ex 7:6	6680
and they did so as the LORD had c	Ex 7:10	6680
and Aaron did so, as the LORD c	Ex 7:20	6680
and did as the LORD had c Moses	Ex 12:28	6680
as the LORD c Moses and Aaron, so	Ex 12:50	6680
the thing which the LORD hath c	Ex 16:16	6680
As the LORD c Moses, so Aaron	Ex 16:34	6680
these words which the LORD c him	Ex 19:7	6680
bread seven days, as I c thee	Ex 23:15	6680
to all things which I have c thee	Ex 29:35	6680
may make all that I have c thee	Ex 31:6	6680
that I have c thee shall they do	Ex 31:11	6680
out of the way which I c them	Ex 32:8	6680
Sinai, as the LORD had c him	Ex 34:4	6680
eat unleavened bread, as I c thee	Ex 34:18	6680
of Israel that which he was c	Ex 34:34	6680
the words which the LORD hath c	Ex 35:1	6680
is the thing which the LORD c	Ex 35:4	6680
and make all that the LORD hath c	Ex 35:10	6680
which the LORD had c to be made	Ex 35:29	6680
to all that the LORD had c	Ex 36:1	6680
work, which the LORD c to make	Ex 36:5	6680
made all that the LORD c Moses	Ex 38:22	6680
as the LORD c Moses	Ex 39:1	6680
as the LORD c Moses	Ex 39:5	6680
as the LORD c Moses	Ex 39:7	6680
as the LORD c Moses	Ex 39:21	6680
as the LORD c Moses	Ex 39:26	6680
as the LORD c Moses	Ex 39:29	6680
as the LORD c Moses	Ex 39:31	6680
to all that the LORD c Moses	Ex 39:32	6680
to all that the LORD c Moses	Ex 39:42	6680
had done it as the LORD had c	Ex 39:43	6680
to all that the LORD c him	Ex 40:16	6680
as the LORD c Moses	Ex 40:19	6680
as the LORD c Moses	Ex 40:21	6680
as the LORD had c Moses	Ex 40:23	6680
as the LORD c Moses	Ex 40:25	6680
as the LORD c Moses	Ex 40:27	6680
as the LORD c Moses	Ex 40:29	6680
as the LORD c Moses	Ex 40:32	6680
Which the LORD c to be given them	Lev 7:36	6680
Which the LORD c Moses in mount	Lev 7:38	6680
in the day that he c the children	Lev 7:38	6680
And Moses did as the LORD c him	Lev 8:4	6680
thing which the LORD c to be done	Lev 8:5	6680
as the LORD c Moses	Lev 8:9	6680
as the LORD c Moses	Lev 8:13	6680
as the LORD c Moses	Lev 8:17	6680
as the LORD c Moses	Lev 8:21	6680
as the LORD c Moses	Lev 8:29	6680
basket of consecrations, as I c	Lev 8:31	6680
day, so the LORD hath c to do	Lev 8:34	6680
for so I am c	Lev 8:35	6680
the LORD c by the hand of Moses	Lev 8:36	6680
c before the tabernacle of the	Lev 9:5	6680
the LORD c that ye should do	Lev 9:6	6680
as the LORD c	Lev 9:7	6680
as the LORD c Moses	Lev 9:10	6680
before the LORD; as Moses c	Lev 9:21	6680
the LORD, which he c them not	Lev 10:1	6680
for so I am c	Lev 10:13	6680
as the LORD hath c	Lev 10:15	6680
it in the holy place, as I c	Lev 10:18	6680
And he did as the LORD c Moses	Lev 16:34	6680
the thing which the LORD hath c	Lev 17:2	6680
of Israel did as the LORD c Moses	Lev 24:23	6680
which the LORD c Moses for the	Lev 27:34	6680
As the LORD c Moses, so he	Num 1:19	6680
to all that the LORD c Moses	Num 1:54	6680
as the LORD c Moses	Num 2:33	6680
to all that the LORD c Moses	Num 2:34	6680
the word of the LORD, as he was c	Num 3:16	6680
Moses numbered, as the LORD c him	Num 3:42	6680
of the LORD, as the LORD c Moses	Num 3:51	6680
of him, as the LORD c Moses	Num 4:49	6680
candlestick, as the LORD c Moses	Num 8:3	6680
unto all that the LORD c Moses	Num 8:20	6680
as the LORD had c Moses	Num 8:22	6680
to all that the LORD c Moses	Num 9:5	6680
hath c you by the hand of Moses	Num 15:23	6680
the day that the LORD c Moses	Num 15:23	6680
as the LORD c Moses	Num 15:36	6680
And Aaron took as Moses c, and ran	Num 16:47	1696
as the LORD c him, so did he	Num 17:11	6680
of the law which the LORD hath c	Num 19:2	6680
from before the LORD, as he c him	Num 20:9	6680
And Moses did as the LORD c	Num 20:27	6680
as the LORD c Moses and the	Num 26:4	6680
of judgment, as the LORD c Moses	Num 27:11	6680
And Moses did as the LORD c him	Num 27:22	6680
as the LORD c by the hand of	Num 27:23	1696
to all that the LORD c Moses	Num 29:40	6680
the thing which the LORD hath c	Num 30:1	6680
statutes, which the LORD c Moses	Num 30:16	6680
Midianites, as the LORD c Moses	Num 31:7	6680
of the law which the LORD c Moses	Num 31:21	6680
priest did as the LORD c Moses	Num 31:31	6680
the priest, as the LORD c Moses	Num 31:41	6680
as the LORD c Moses	Num 31:47	6680
them Moses c Eleazar the priest	Num 32:28	6680
Moses c the children of Israel,	Num 34:13	6680
which the LORD c to give unto the	Num 34:13	6680
These are they whom the LORD c to	Num 34:29	6680
The LORD c my lord to give the	Num 36:2	6680
my lord was c by the LORD to give	Num 36:2	6680
Moses c the children of Israel	Num 36:5	6680
Even as the LORD c Moses, so did	Num 36:10	6680
which the LORD c by the hand of	Num 36:13	6680
I c you at that time all the	Deut 1:18	6680
as the LORD our God c us	Deut 1:19	6680
to all that the LORD our God c us	Deut 1:41	6680
I c you at that time, saying, The	Deut 3:18	6680
I c Joshua at that time, saying,	Deut 3:21	6680
even as the LORD my God c me	Deut 4:5	6680
which he c you to perform, even	Deut 4:13	6680
the LORD c me at that time to	Deut 4:14	6680
as the LORD thy God hath c thee	Deut 5:12	6680
therefore the LORD thy God c thee	Deut 5:15	6680
as the LORD thy God hath c thee	Deut 5:16	6680
as the LORD your God hath c you	Deut 5:32	6680
the LORD your God hath c you	Deut 5:33	6680
the LORD your God c to teach you	Deut 6:1	6680
statutes, which he hath c thee	Deut 6:17	6680
which the LORD our God hath c you	Deut 6:20	6680
the LORD c us to do all these	Deut 6:24	6680
the LORD our God, as he hath c us	Deut 6:25	6680
out of the way which I c them	Deut 9:12	6680
the way which the LORD had c you	Deut 9:16	6680
there they be, as the LORD c me	Deut 10:5	6680
hath given thee, as I have c thee	Deut 12:21	6680
LORD thy God c thee to walk in	Deut 13:5	6680
of heaven, which I have not c	Deut 17:3	6680
which I have not c him to speak	Deut 18:20	6680
as the LORD thy God hath c thee	Deut 20:17	6680
as I c them, so ye shall observe	Deut 24:8	6680
commandments which thou hast c me	Deut 26:13	6680
to all that thou hast c me	Deut 26:14	6680
hath c thee to do these statutes	Deut 26:16	6680
the elders of Israel c the people	Deut 27:1	6680
and his statutes which he c thee	Deut 28:45	6680
which the LORD c Moses to make	Deut 29:1	6680
commandments which I have c you	Deut 31:5	6680
And Moses c them, saying, At the	Deut 31:10	6680
That Moses c the Levites, which	Deut 31:25	6680

from the way which I have c you ... Deut 31:29 6680
Moses c us a law, even the ... Deut 33:4 6680
him, and did as the LORD c Moses ... Deut 34:9 6680
which Moses my servant c thee ... Josh 1:7 6680
Have not I c thee ... Josh 1:9 6680
Then Joshua c the officers of the ... Josh 1:10 6680
the servant of the LORD c you ... Josh 1:13 6680
they c the people, saying, When ... Josh 3:3 6680
of Israel did so as Joshua c ... Josh 4:8 6680
was finished that the LORD c ... Josh 4:10 6680
to all that Moses c Joshua ... Josh 4:10 6680
Joshua therefore c the priests ... Josh 4:17 6680
And Joshua had c the people ... Josh 6:10 6680
my covenant which I c them ... Josh 7:11 6680
he c them, saying, Behold, ye ... Josh 8:4 6680
See, I have c you ... Josh 8:8 6680
of the LORD which he c Joshua ... Josh 8:27 6680
Joshua c that they should take ... Josh 8:29 6680
the LORD c the children of Israel ... Josh 8:31 6680
servant of the LORD had c before ... Josh 8:33 6680
not a word of all that Moses c ... Josh 8:35 6680
how that the LORD thy God c his ... Josh 9:24 6680
down of the sun, that Joshua c ... Josh 10:27 6680
as the LORD God of Israel c ... Josh 10:40 6680
Moses the servant of the LORD c ... Josh 11:12 6680
As the LORD c Moses his servant, ... Josh 11:15 6680
of all that the LORD c Moses ... Josh 11:15 6680
destroy them, as the LORD c Moses ... Josh 11:20 6680
an inheritance, as I have c thee ... Josh 13:6 6680
as the LORD c by the hand of ... Josh 14:2 6680
As the LORD c Moses, so the ... Josh 14:5 6680
The LORD c Moses to give us an ... Josh 17:4 6680
The LORD c by the hand of Moses ... Josh 21:2 6680
as the LORD c by the hand of ... Josh 21:8 6680
the servant of the LORD c you ... Josh 22:2 6680
my voice in all that I c you ... Josh 22:2 6680
the LORD your God, which he c you ... Josh 23:16 6680
covenant which I c their fathers ... Judg 2:20 6680
which he c their fathers by the ... Judg 3:4 6680
Hath not the LORD God of Israel c ... Judg 4:6 6680
all that I c her let her observe ... Judg 13:14 6680
c them, saying, Go and smite the ... Judg 21:10 6680
Therefore they c the children of ... Judg 21:20 6680
Boaz c his young men, saying, Let ... Ruth 2:15 6680
which I have c in my habitation ... 1Sa 2:29 6680
the LORD thy God, which he c thee ... 1Sa 13:13 6680
the LORD hath c him to be captain ... 1Sa 13:14 6680
kept that which the LORD c thee ... 1Sa 13:14 6680
took, and went, as Jesse had c him ... 1Sa 17:20 6680
Saul c his servants, saying, ... 1Sa 18:22 6680
brother, he hath c me to be there ... 1Sa 20:29 6680
The king hath c me a business ... 1Sa 21:2 6680
send thee, and what I have c thee ... 1Sa 21:2 6680
David c his young men, and they ... 2Sa 4:12 6680
did so, as the LORD had c him ... 2Sa 5:25 6680
whom I c to feed my people Israel ... 2Sa 7:7 6680
as since the time that I c judges ... 2Sa 7:11 6680
lord the king hath c his servant ... 2Sa 9:11 6680
Now Absalom had c his servants ... 2Sa 13:28 6680
have not I c you ... 2Sa 13:28 6680
did unto Amnon as Absalom had c ... 2Sa 13:29 6680
And the king c Joab and Abishai and ... 2Sa 18:5 6680
performed all that the king c ... 2Sa 21:14 6680
of Gad, went up as the LORD c ... 2Sa 24:19 6680
So the king c Benaiah the son of ... 1Kin 2:46 6680
And the king c, and they brought ... 1Kin 5:17 6680
judgments, which he c our fathers ... 1Kin 8:58 6680
to all that I have c thee ... 1Kin 9:4 6680
had c him concerning this thing, ... 1Kin 11:10 6680
he kept not that which the LORD c ... 1Kin 11:10 6680
my statutes, which I have c thee ... 1Kin 11:11 6680
which the LORD thy God c thee ... 1Kin 13:21 6680
he c him all the days of his life ... 1Kin 15:5 6680
I have c the ravens to feed thee ... 1Kin 17:4 6680
I have c a widow woman there to ... 1Kin 17:9 6680
the king of Syria c his thirty ... 1Kin 22:31 6680
he c them, saying, This is the ... 2Kin 11:5 6680
things that Jehoiada the priest c ... 2Kin 11:9 6680
But Jehoiada the priest c the ... 2Kin 11:15 6680
law of Moses, wherein the LORD c ... 2Kin 14:6 6680
king Ahaz c Urijah the priest, ... 2Kin 16:15 6680
according to all that king Ahaz c ... 2Kin 16:16 6680
the law which I c your fathers ... 2Kin 17:13 6680
Then the king of Assyria c ... 2Kin 17:27 6680
the LORD c the children of Jacob ... 2Kin 17:34 6680
which the LORD c Moses ... 2Kin 18:6 6680
Moses the servant of the LORD c ... 2Kin 18:12 6680
to all that I have c them ... 2Kin 21:8 6680
law that my servant Moses c them ... 2Kin 21:8 6680
the king c Hilkiah the priest, and ... 2Kin 22:12 6680
the king c Hilkiah the high ... 2Kin 23:4 6680
the king c all the people, saying ... 2Kin 23:21 6680
Moses the servant of God had c ... 1Chr 6:49 6680
David therefore did as God c him ... 1Chr 14:16 6680
as Moses c according to the word ... 1Chr 15:15 6680
the word which he c to a thousand ... 1Chr 16:15 6680
of the LORD, which he c Israel ... 1Chr 16:40 6680
whom I c to feed my people, ... 1Chr 17:6 6680
since the time that I c judges to ... 1Chr 17:10 6680
Is it not I that c the people to ... 1Chr 21:17 559
of the LORD c Gad to say to David ... 1Chr 21:18 559
And the LORD c the angel ... 1Chr 21:27 559
David c to gather together the ... 1Chr 22:2 559
David also c all the princes of ... 1Chr 22:17 6680
to the order c unto them, ... 1Chr 23:31
the LORD God of Israel had c him ... 1Chr 24:19 6680
to all that I have c thee ... 2Chr 7:17 6680
for so had David the man of God c ... 2Chr 8:14 4687
c Judah to seek the LORD God of ... 2Chr 14:4 559
Now the king of Syria had c the ... 2Chr 18:30 6680
that Jehoiada the priest had c ... 2Chr 23:8 6680
book of Moses, where the LORD c ... 2Chr 25:4 6680
he c the priests the sons of ... 2Chr 29:21 559
for the king c that the burnt ... 2Chr 29:24 559
Hezekiah c to offer the burnt ... 2Chr 29:27 559
the princes c the Levites to sing ... 2Chr 29:30 559
Moreover he c the people that ... 2Chr 31:4 559
Then Hezekiah c to prepare ... 2Chr 31:11 559
c Judah and Jerusalem, saying, Ye ... 2Chr 32:12 559
heed to do all that I have c them ... 2Chr 33:8 6680
c Judah to serve the LORD God of ... 2Chr 33:16 559
And the king c Hilkiah, and Ahikam ... 2Chr 34:20 6680
for God c me to make haste ... 2Chr 35:21 559
the king of Persia hath c us ... Ezr 4:3 6680
And I c, and search hath been made, ... Ezr 4:19
Who hath c you to build this ... Ezr 5:3
Who c you to build this house, and ... Ezr 5:9
Whatsoever is c by the God of ... Ezr 7:23
Which thou hast c by thy servants ... Ezr 9:11 6680
which the LORD had c to Israel ... Neh 8:1 6680
law which the LORD had c by Moses ... Neh 8:14 6680
which was c to be given to the ... Neh 13:5 4687
Then I c, and they cleansed the ... Neh 13:9 559
I c that the gates should be shut ... Neh 13:19 559
I c the Levites that they should ... Neh 13:22 559
he c Mehuman, Biztha, Harbona, ... Est 1:10 559
The king Ahasuerus c Vashti the ... Est 1:17 559
the king had so c concerning him ... Est 3:2 6680
had c unto the king's lieutenants ... Est 3:12 6680
Then Mordecai c to answer Esther, ... Est 4:13 559
to all that Esther had c him ... Est 4:17 6680
he c to bring the book of records ... Est 6:1 559
all that Mordecai c unto the Jews ... Est 8:9 6680
the king c it so to be done ... Est 9:14 559
he c by letters that his wicked ... Est 9:25 559
Hast thou c the morning since thy ... Job 38:12 6680
did according as the LORD c them ... Job 42:9 1696
to the judgment that thou hast c ... Ps 7:6 6680
he c, and it stood fast ... Ps 33:9 6680
Thy God hath c thy strength ... Ps 68:28 6680
which he c our fathers, that they ... Ps 78:5 6680
Though he had c the clouds from ... Ps 78:23 6680
the word which he c to a thousand ... Ps 105:8 6680
concerning whom the LORD c them ... Ps 106:34 559
he hath c his covenant for ever ... Ps 111:9 6680
Thou hast c us to keep thy ... Ps 119:4 6680
that thou hast c are righteous ... Ps 119:138 6680
for there the LORD c the blessing ... Ps 133:3 6680
for he c, and they were created ... Ps 148:5 6680
I have c my sanctified ones, I ... Is 13:3 6680
for my mouth it hath c, and his ... Is 34:16 6680
and all their host have I c ... Is 45:12 6680
and my molten image, hath c them ... Is 48:5 6680
nor c them in the day that I ... Jer 7:22 6680
But this thing c I them, saying, ... Jer 7:23 6680
in all the ways that I have c you ... Jer 7:23 6680
which I c them not, neither came ... Jer 7:31 6680
Which I c your fathers in the day ... Jer 11:4 6680
covenant, which I c them to do ... Jer 11:8 6680
it by Euphrates, as the LORD c me ... Jer 13:5 6680
which I c thee to hide there ... Jer 13:6 6680
them not, neither have I c them ... Jer 14:14 6680
sabbath day, as I c your fathers ... Jer 17:22 6680
unto Baal, which I c not, nor ... Jer 19:5 6680
yet I sent them not, nor c them ... Jer 23:32 6680
had c him to speak unto all the ... Jer 26:8 6680
my name, which I have not c them ... Jer 29:23 6680
which I c them not, neither came ... Jer 32:35 6680
the son of Rechab our father c us ... Jer 35:6 6680
all that Jonadab our father c us ... Jer 35:10 6680
that he c his sons not to drink ... Jer 35:14 6680
of their father, which he c them ... Jer 35:16 6680
unto all that he hath c you ... Jer 35:18 6680
And Jeremiah c Baruch, saying, I ... Jer 36:5 6680
that Jeremiah the prophet c him ... Jer 36:8 6680
But the king c Jerahmeel the son ... Jer 36:26 6680
Then Zedekiah the king c that ... Jer 37:21 6680
Then the king c Ebed-melech the ... Jer 38:10 6680
these words that the king had c ... Jer 38:27 6680
to all that I have c thee ... Jer 50:21 6680
c Seraiah the son of Neriah ... Jer 51:59 6680
the LORD hath c concerning Jacob, ... Lam 1:17 6680
that he had c in the days of old ... Lam 2:17 6680
I have done as thou hast c me ... Eze 9:11 6680
that when he had c the man ... Eze 10:6 6680
And I did so as I was c ... Eze 12:7 6680
I did in the morning as I was c ... Eze 24:18 6680
So I prophesied as I was c ... Eze 37:7 6680
So I prophesied as he c me ... Eze 37:10 6680
Then the king c to call the ... Dan 2:2 559
c to destroy all the wise men of ... Dan 2:12 560
c that they should offer an ... Dan 2:46 560
cried aloud, To you it is c ... Dan 3:4 560
fury c to bring Shadrach, Meshach ... Dan 3:13 560
c that they should heat the ... Dan 3:19 560
he c the most mighty men that ... Dan 3:20 560
whereas they c to leave the stump ... Dan 4:26 560
c to bring the golden and silver ... Dan 5:2 560
Then c Belshazzar, and they ... Dan 5:29 560
Then the king c, and they brought ... Dan 6:16 560
c that they should take Daniel up ... Dan 6:23 560
And the king c, and they brought ... Dan 6:24 560
c the prophets, saying, Prophesy ... Amos 2:12 6680
which I c my servants the ... Zec 1:6 6680
which I c unto him in Horeb for ... Mal 4:4 6680
and offer the gift that Moses c ... Mt 8:4 *4367*
c them, saying, Go not into the ... Mt 10:5 *3853*
at meat, he c it to be given her ... Mt 14:9 *2753*
he c the multitude to sit down on ... Mt 14:19 *2753*
For God c, saying, Honour thy ... Mt 15:4 *1781*
he c the multitude to sit down on ... Mt 15:35 *2753*
his lord c him to be sold, and his ... Mt 18:25 *2753*
went, and did as Jesus c them ... Mt 21:6 *4367*
Then Pilate c the body to be ... Mt 27:58 *2753*
things whatsoever I have c you ... Mt 28:20 *1781*
those things which Moses c ... Mk 1:44 *4367*
c that something should be given ... Mk 5:43 *2036*
c them that they should take ... Mk 6:8 *3853*
and c his head to be brought ... Mk 6:27 *2004*
he c them to make all sit down by ... Mk 6:39 *2004*
he c the people to sit down on ... Mk 8:6 *3853*
c to set them also before them ... Mk 8:7 *2036*
still, and c him to be called ... Mk 10:49 *2036*
unto them even as Jesus had c ... Mk 11:6 *1781*
work, and c the porter to watch ... Mk 13:34 *1781*
cleansing, according as Moses c ... Lk 5:14 *4367*
(For he had c the unclean spirit ... Lk 8:29 *3853*
and he c to give her meat ... Lk 8:55 *1299*
c them to tell no man that thing ... Lk 9:21 *3853*
Lord, it is done as thou hast c ... Lk 14:22 *2004*
he did the things that were c him ... Lk 17:9 *1299*
all those things which are c you ... Lk 17:10 *1299*
c him to be brought unto him ... Lk 18:40 *2750*
then he c these servants to be ... Lk 19:15 *2036*
Now Moses in the law c us ... Jn 8:5 *1781*
c them that they should not ... Acts 1:4 *3853*
But when they had c them to go ... Acts 4:15 *2753*
c them not to speak at all nor ... Acts 4:18 *3853*
c to put the apostles forth a ... Acts 5:34 *2753*
they c that they should not speak ... Acts 5:40 *3853*
he c the chariot to stand still ... Acts 8:38 *2753*
all things that are c thee of God ... Acts 10:33 *4367*
he c us to preach unto the people ... Acts 10:42 *3853*
he c them to be baptized in the ... Acts 10:48 *4367*
c that they should be put to ... Acts 12:19 *2753*
For so hath the Lord c us ... Acts 13:47 *1781*
their clothes, and c to beat them ... Acts 16:22 *2753*
(because that Claudius had c all ... Acts 18:2 *1299*
c him to be bound with two chains ... Acts 21:33 *2753*
he c him to be carried into the ... Acts 21:34 *2753*
The chief captain c him to be ... Acts 22:24 *2753*
c the chief priests and all their ... Acts 22:30 *2753*
the high priest Ananias c them ... Acts 23:2 *2004*
c the soldiers to go down, and to ... Acts 23:10 *2753*
the soldiers, as it was c them ... Acts 23:31 *1299*
he c him to be kept in Herod's ... Acts 23:35 *2753*
he c a centurion to keep Paul, and ... Acts 24:23 *1299*
seat c Paul to be brought ... Acts 25:6 *2753*
c the man to be brought forth ... Acts 25:17 *2753*
I c him to be kept till I might ... Acts 25:21 *2753*
c that they which could swim ... Acts 27:43 *2753*
but they are c to be under ... 1Cor 14:34
who c the light to shine out of ... 2Cor 4:6 *2036*
with your own hands, as we c you ... 1Th 4:11 *3853*
we were with you, this we c you ... 2Th 3:10 *3853*
could not endure that which was c ... Heb 12:20 *1291*
it was c them that they should ... Rev 9:4 *4483*

COMMANDEDST

which thou c thy servant Moses ... Neh 1:7 6680
that thou c thy servant Moses ... Neh 1:8 6680
c them precepts, statutes, and ... Neh 9:14 6680
of all that thou c them to do ... Jer 32:23 6680

COMMANDER

a leader and c to the people ... Is 55:4 6680

COMMANDEST

All that thou c us we will do ... Josh 1:16 6680
thy words in all that thou c him ... Josh 1:18 6680
c me to be smitten contrary to ... Acts 23:3 *2753*

COMMANDETH

is the thing which the LORD c ... Ex 16:32 6680
Thy servants will do as my lord c ... Num 32:25 6680
Which c the sun, and it riseth not ... Job 9:7 559
c that they return from iniquity ... Job 36:10 559
c it not to shine by the cloud ... Job 36:32 6680
that they may do whatsoever he c ... Job 37:12 6680
For he c, and raiseth the stormy ... Ps 107:25 559
to pass, when the Lord c it not ... Lam 3:37 6680
For, behold, the LORD c, and he ... Amos 6:11 6680
for with authority c he even the ... Mk 1:27 *2004*
power he c the unclean spirits, ... Lk 4:36 *2004*
for he c even the winds and water, ... Lk 8:25 *2004*
but now c all men every where to ... Acts 17:30 *3853*

COMMANDING

had made an end of c his sons ... Gen 49:33 6680
an end of c his twelve disciples ... Mt 11:1 *1299*
C his accusers to come unto thee ... Acts 24:8 *2753*
c to abstain from meats, which ... 1Ti 4:3

COMMANDMENT

according to the c of Pharaoh ... Gen 45:21 6310
according to the c of the LORD ... Ex 17:1 6310
which I will give thee in c unto ... Ex 25:22 6680
he gave them in c all that the ... Ex 34:32 6680
And Moses gave c, and they caused ... Ex 36:6 6680
according to the c of Moses ... Ex 38:21 6310
numbered at the c of the LORD ... Num 3:39 6310
the c of the LORD by the hand of ... Num 4:37 6310
according to the c of the LORD ... Num 4:41 6310
According to the c of the LORD ... Num 4:49 6310
At the c of the LORD the children ... Num 9:18 6310
at the c of the LORD they pitched ... Num 9:18 6310
according to the c of the LORD ... Num 9:20 6310
according to the c of the LORD ... Num 9:20 6310
At the c of the LORD they rested ... Num 9:23 6310
at the c of the LORD they ... Num 9:23 6310
at the c of the LORD by the hand ... Num 9:23 6310
the c of the LORD by the hand of ... Num 10:13 6310
Moses by the c of the LORD sent ... Num 13:3 6310
ye transgress the c of the LORD ... Num 14:41 6310
of the LORD, and hath broken his c ... Num 15:31 4687
I have received c to bless ... Num 23:20
go beyond the c of the LORD ... Num 24:13 6310
against my c in the desert of Zin ... Num 27:14 6310
journeys by the c of the LORD ... Num 33:2 6310
mount Hor at the c of the LORD ... Num 33:38 6310
LORD had given him in c unto them ... Deut 1:3 6680
the c of the LORD your God ... Deut 1:26 6310
against the c of the LORD ... Deut 1:43 6310
the c of the LORD your God ... Deut 9:23 6310
that he turn not aside from the c ... Deut 17:20 4687

For this c which I command thee ... Deut 30:11 4687
be that doth rebel against thy c ... Josh 1:18 6310
according to the c of the LORD ... Josh 8:8 1697
according to the c of the LORD to ... Josh 15:13 6310
Therefore according to the c of ... Josh 17:4 6310
at the c of the LORD, these ... Josh 21:3 6310
of the c of the LORD your God ... Josh 22:3 4687
take diligent heed to do the c ... Josh 22:5 4687
not rebel against the c of the ... 1Sa 12:14 6310
rebel against the c of the LORD ... 1Sa 12:15 6310
kept the c of the LORD thy God ... 1Sa 13:13 4687
have performed the c of the LORD ... 1Sa 15:13 1697
transgressed the c of the LORD ... 1Sa 15:24 6310
thou despised the c of the LORD ... 2Sa 12:9 1697
the c that I have charged thee ... 1Kin 2:43 4687
hast not kept the c which the ... 1Kin 13:21 4687
c which the LORD commanded the ... 2Kin 17:34 4687
ordinances, and the law, and the c ... 2Kin 17:37 4687
for the king's c was, saying, ... 2Kin 18:36 4687
according to the c of Pharaoh ... 2Kin 23:35 6310
Surely at the c of the LORD came ... 2Kin 24:3 6310
their brethren were at their c ... 1Chr 12:32 6310
their gods there, David gave a c ... 1Chr 14:12 559
people will be wholly at thy c ... 1Chr 28:21 1697
according to the c of Moses ... 2Chr 8:13 4687
they departed not from the c of ... 2Chr 8:15 4687
and to do the law and the c ... 2Chr 14:4 4687
blood and blood, between law and c ... 2Chr 19:10 4687
according to the c of Moses the ... 2Chr 24:6
at the king's c they made a chest ... 2Chr 24:8 559
stoned him with stones at the c ... 2Chr 24:21 4687
according to the c of the king ... 2Chr 29:15 4687
according to the c of David ... 2Chr 29:25 4687
for so was the c of the LORD by ... 2Chr 29:25 4687
and according to the c of the king ... 2Chr 30:6 4687
one heart to do the c of the king ... 2Chr 30:12 4687
And as soon as the c came abroad ... 2Chr 31:5 1697
at the c of Hezekiah the king, and ... 2Chr 31:13 4662
according to the king's c ... 2Chr 35:10 4687
according to the c of David ... 2Chr 35:15 4687
according to the c of king Josiah ... 2Chr 35:16 4687
Give ye now c to cause these men ... Ezr 4:21 2942
until another c shall be given ... Ezr 4:21 2941
according to the c of the God of ... Ezr 6:14 2941
and according to the c of Cyrus ... Ezr 6:14 2942
I sent them with c unto Iddo the ... Ezr 8:17 3318
that tremble at the c of our God ... Ezr 10:3 4687
was the king's c concerning them ... Neh 11:23 4687
according to the c of David the ... Neh 12:24 4687
according to the c of David ... Neh 12:45 4687
the king's c by his chamberlains ... Est 1:12 1697
she hath not performed the c of ... Est 1:15 3982
let there go a royal c from him ... Est 1:19 1697
came to pass, when the king's c ... Est 2:8 1697
for Esther did the c of Mordecai ... Est 2:20 3982
transgressest thou the king's c ... Est 3:3 4687
a c to be given in every province ... Est 3:14 1881
being hastened by the king's c ... Est 3:15 1697
whithersoever the king's c ... Est 4:3 1697
gave him a c to Mordecai, to know ... Est 4:5 6680
and gave him c unto Mordecai ... Est 4:10 6680
a c to be given in every province ... Est 8:13 1881
and pressed on by the king's c ... Est 8:14 1697
city, whithersoever the king's c ... Est 8:17 1697
of the same, when the king's c ... Est 9:1 1697
gone back from the c of his lips ... Job 23:12 4687
the c of the LORD is pure, ... Ps 19:8 4687
thou hast given c to save me ... Ps 71:3 6680
but thy c is exceeding broad ... Ps 119:96 4687
He sendeth forth his c upon earth ... Ps 147:15 565
My son, keep thy father's c ... Prov 6:20 4687
For the c is a lamp ... Prov 6:23 4687
the waters should not pass his c ... Prov 8:29 6310
feareth the c shall be rewarded ... Prov 13:13 4687
He that keepeth the c keepeth his ... Prov 19:16 4687
counsel thee to keep the king's c ... Eccl 8:2 6310
Whoso keepeth the c shall feel no ... Eccl 8:5 4687
the LORD hath given a c against ... Is 23:11 6680
for the king's c was, saying, ... Is 36:21 4687
none, but obey their father's c ... Jer 35:14 4687
performed the c of their father ... Jer 35:16 4687
the c of Jonadab your father ... Jer 35:18 4687
for I have rebelled against his c ... Lam 1:18 6310
because the king's c was urgent ... Dan 3:22 4406
supplications the c came forth ... Dan 9:23 1697
going forth of the c to restore ... Dan 9:25 1697
he willingly walked after the c ... Hos 5:11 6673
hath given a c concerning thee ... Nah 1:14 6680
O ye priests, this c is for you ... Mal 2:1 4687
that I have sent this c unto you ... Mal 2:4 4687
he gave c to depart unto the ... Mt 8:18 *2753*
the c of God by your tradition ... Mt 15:3 *1785*
Thus have ye made the c of God of ... Mt 15:6 *1785*
which is the great c in the law ... Mt 22:36 *1785*
This is the first and great c ... Mt 22:38 *1785*
For laying aside the c of God ... Mk 7:8 *1785*
Full well ye reject the c of God ... Mk 7:9 *1785*
him, Which is the first c of all ... Mk 12:28 *1785*
this is the first c ... Mk 12:30 *1785*
none other c greater than these ... Mk 12:31 *1785*
transgressed I at any time thy c ... Lk 15:29 *1785*
sabbath day according to the c ... Lk 23:56 *1785*
This c have I received of my ... Jn 10:18 *1785*
and the Pharisees had given a c ... Jn 11:57 *1785*
which sent me, he gave me a c ... Jn 12:49 *1785*
I know that his c is life ... Jn 12:50 *1785*
A new c I give unto you, That ye ... Jn 13:34 *1785*
and as the Father gave me c ... Jn 14:31 *1781*
This is my c, That ye love one ... Jn 15:12 *1785*
to whom we gave no such c ... Acts 15:24 *1291*
and receiving a c unto Silas ... Acts 17:15 *1785*
gave c to his accusers also to ... Acts 23:30 *3853*
at Festus' c Paul was brought ... Acts 25:23 *2753*
But sin, taking occasion by the c ... Rom 7:8 *1785*
but when the c came, sin revived, ... Rom 7:9 *1785*
And the c, which was ordained to ... Rom 7:10 *1785*
For sin, taking occasion by the c ... Rom 7:11 *1785*
the c holy, and just, and good ... Rom 7:12 *1785*
that sin by the c might become ... Rom 7:13 *1785*
and if there be any other c ... Rom 13:9 *1785*
according to the c of the ... Rom 16:26 *2003*
this by permission, and not of c ... 1Cor 7:6 *2003*
virgins I have no c of the Lord ... 1Cor 7:25 *2003*
I speak not by c, but by occasion ... 2Cor 8:8 *2003*
which is the first c with promise ... Eph 6:2 *1785*
by the c of God our Saviour ... 1Ti 1:1 *2003*
Now the end of the c is charity ... 1Ti 1:5 *3852*
thou keep this c without spot ... 1Ti 6:14 *1785*
to the c of God our Saviour ... Titus 1:3 *2003*
have a c to take tithes of the ... Heb 7:5 *1785*
not after the law of a carnal c ... Heb 7:16 *1785*
c going before for the weakness ... Heb 7:18 *1785*
gave c concerning his bones ... Heb 11:22 *1781*
were not afraid of the king's c ... Heb 11:23 *1297*
the holy c delivered unto them ... 2Pet 2:21 *1785*
of the c of us the apostles of ... 2Pet 3:2 *1785*
I write no new c unto you ... 1Jn 2:7 *1785*
but an old c which ye had from ... 1Jn 2:7 *1785*
The old c is the word which ye ... 1Jn 2:7 *1785*
a new c I write unto you, which ... 1Jn 2:8 *1785*
And this is his c, That we should ... 1Jn 3:23 *1785*
love one another, as he gave us c ... 1Jn 3:23 *1785*
this c have we from him, That he ... 1Jn 4:21 *1785*
have received a c from the Father ... 2Jn 4 *1785*
though I wrote a new c unto thee ... 2Jn 5 *1785*
This is the c, That, as ye have ... 2Jn 6 *1785*

COMMANDMENTS

my voice, and kept my charge, my c ... Gen 26:5 4687
sight, and wilt give ear to his c ... Ex 15:26 4687
How long refuse ye to keep my c ... Ex 16:28 4687
them that love me, and keep my c ... Ex 20:6 4687
a law, and c which I have written ... Ex 24:12 4687
words of the covenant, the ten c ... Ex 34:28 1697
ignorance against any of the c of ... Lev 4:2 4687
somewhat against any of the c of ... Lev 4:13 4687
ignorance against any of the c of ... Lev 4:22 4687
somewhat against any of the c of ... Lev 4:27 4687
to be done by the c of the LORD ... Lev 5:17 4687
Therefore shall ye keep my c ... Lev 22:31 4687
walk in my statutes, and keep my c ... Lev 26:3 4687
me, and will not do all these c ... Lev 26:14 4687
so that ye will not do all my c ... Lev 26:15 4687
These are the c, which the LORD ... Lev 27:34 4687
and not observed all these c ... Num 15:22 4687
and remember all the c of the LORD ... Num 15:39 4687
ye may remember, and do all my c ... Num 15:40 4687
These are the c and the judgments, ... Num 36:13 4687
that ye may keep the c of the ... Deut 4:2 4687
you to perform, even ten c ... Deut 4:13 1697
therefore his statutes, and his c ... Deut 4:40 4687
of them that love me and keep my c ... Deut 5:10 4687
fear me, and keep all my c always ... Deut 5:29 4687
I will speak unto thee all the c ... Deut 5:31 4687
Now these are the c, the statutes ... Deut 6:1 4687
to keep all his statutes and his c ... Deut 6:2 4687
keep the c of the LORD your God ... Deut 6:17 4687
these c before the LORD our God ... Deut 6:25 4687
him and keep his c to a thousand ... Deut 7:9 4687
Thou shalt therefore keep the c ... Deut 7:11 4687
All the c which I command thee ... Deut 8:1 4687
whether thou wouldest keep his c ... Deut 8:2 4687
keep the c of the LORD thy God ... Deut 8:6 4687
thy God, in not keeping his c ... Deut 8:11 4687
to the first writing, the ten c ... Deut 10:4 1697
To keep the c of the LORD ... Deut 10:13 4687
and his judgments, and his c ... Deut 11:1 4687
c which I command you this day ... Deut 11:8 4687
hearken diligently unto my c ... Deut 11:13 4687
all these c which I command you ... Deut 11:22 4687
if ye obey the c of the LORD your ... Deut 11:27 4687
obey the c of the LORD your God ... Deut 11:28 4687
God, and fear him, and keep his c ... Deut 13:4 4687
to keep all his c which I command ... Deut 13:18 4687
to observe to do all these c ... Deut 15:5 4687
shalt keep all these c to do them ... Deut 19:9 4687
according to all thy c which thou ... Deut 26:13 4687
I have not transgressed thy c ... Deut 26:13 4687
and to keep his statutes, and his c ... Deut 26:17 4687
thou shouldest keep all his c ... Deut 26:18 4687
Keep all the c which I command ... Deut 27:1 4687
of the LORD thy God, and do his c ... Deut 27:10 4687
to do all his c which I command ... Deut 28:1 4687
keep the c of the LORD thy God ... Deut 28:9 4687
unto the c of the LORD thy God ... Deut 28:13 4687
God, to observe to do all his c ... Deut 28:15 4687
the LORD thy God, to keep his c ... Deut 28:45 4687
do all his c which I command thee ... Deut 30:8 4687
the LORD thy God, to keep his c ... Deut 30:10 4687
in his ways, and to keep his c ... Deut 30:16 4687
the c which I have commanded you ... Deut 31:5 4687
in all his ways, and to keep his c ... Josh 22:5 4687
in, obeying the c of the LORD ... Judg 2:17 4687
hearken unto the c of the LORD ... Judg 3:4 4687
me, and hath not performed my c ... 1Sa 15:11 1697
to keep his statutes, and his c ... 1Kin 2:3 4687
ways, to keep my statutes and my c ... 1Kin 3:14 4687
keep all my c to walk in them ... 1Kin 6:12 4687
in all his ways, and to keep his c ... 1Kin 8:58 4687
in his statutes, and to keep his c ... 1Kin 8:61 4687
children, and will not keep my c ... 1Kin 9:6 4687
I chose, because he kept my c ... 1Kin 11:34 4687
to keep my statutes and my c ... 1Kin 11:38 4687
my servant David, who kept my c ... 1Kin 14:8 4687
have forsaken the c of the LORD ... 1Kin 18:18 4687
from your evil ways, and keep my c ... 2Kin 17:13 4687
they left all the c of the LORD ... 2Kin 17:16 4687
not the c of the LORD their God ... 2Kin 17:19 4687
following him, but kept his c ... 2Kin 18:6 4687
after the LORD, and to keep his c ... 2Kin 23:3 4687
if he be constant to do my c ... 1Chr 28:7 4687
seek for all the c of the LORD ... 1Chr 28:8 4687
a perfect heart, to keep thy c ... 1Chr 29:19 4687
and forsake my statutes and my c ... 2Chr 7:19 4687
of his father, and walked in his c ... 2Chr 17:4 4687
transgress ye the c of the LORD ... 2Chr 24:20 4687
God, and in the law, and in the c ... 2Chr 31:21 4687
after the LORD, and to keep his c ... 2Chr 34:31 4687
of the words of the c of the LORD ... Ezr 7:11 4687
for we have forsaken thy c ... Ezr 9:10 4687
Should we again break thy c ... Ezr 9:14 4687
that love him and observe his c ... Neh 1:5 4687
thee, and have not kept the c ... Neh 1:7 4687
if ye turn unto me, and keep my c ... Neh 1:9 4687
and true laws, good statutes and c ... Neh 9:13 4687
necks, and hearkened not to thy c ... Neh 9:16 4687
and hearkened not unto thy c ... Neh 9:29 4687
thy law, nor hearkened unto thy c ... Neh 9:34 4687
do all the c of the LORD our Lord ... Neh 10:29 4687
the works of God, but keep his c ... Ps 78:7 4687
my statutes, and keep not my c ... Ps 89:31 4687
that remember his c to do them ... Ps 103:18 6490
excel in strength, that do his c ... Ps 103:20 1697
all his c are sure ... Ps 111:7 6490
have all they that do his c ... Ps 111:10
that delighteth greatly in his c ... Ps 112:1 4687
I have respect unto all thy c ... Ps 119:6 4687
O let me not wander from thy c ... Ps 119:10 4687
hide not thy c from me ... Ps 119:19 4687
cursed, which do err from thy c ... Ps 119:21 4687
I will run the way of thy c ... Ps 119:32 4687
me to go in the path of thy c ... Ps 119:35 4687
And I will delight myself in thy c ... Ps 119:47 4687
also will I lift up unto thy c ... Ps 119:48 4687
and delayed not to keep thy c ... Ps 119:60 4687
for I have believed thy c ... Ps 119:66 4687
that I may learn thy c ... Ps 119:73 4687
All thy c are faithful ... Ps 119:86 4687
Thou through thy c hast made me ... Ps 119:98 4687
for I will keep the c of my God ... Ps 119:115 4687
Therefore I love thy c above gold ... Ps 119:127 4687
for I longed for thy c ... Ps 119:131 4687
yet thy c are my delights ... Ps 119:143 4687
and all thy c are truth ... Ps 119:151 4687
for thy salvation, and done thy c ... Ps 119:166 4687
for all thy c are righteousness ... Ps 119:172 4687
for I do not forget thy c ... Ps 119:176 4687
my words, and hide my c with thee ... Prov 2:1 4687
but let thine heart keep my c ... Prov 3:1 4687
keep my c, and live ... Prov 4:4 4687
words, and lay up my c with thee ... Prov 7:1 4687
Keep my c, and live ... Prov 7:2 4687
The wise in heart will receive c ... Prov 10:8 4687
Fear God, and keep his c ... Eccl 12:13 4687
that thou hadst hearkened to my c ... Is 48:18 4687
him, and to them that keep his c ... Dan 9:4 4687
the LORD, and have not kept his c ... Amos 2:4 2706
shall break one of these least c ... Mt 5:19 *1785*
for doctrines the c of men ... Mt 15:9 *1778*
wilt enter into life, keep the c ... Mt 19:17 *1785*
On these two c hang all the law ... Mt 22:40 *1785*
for doctrines the c of men ... Mk 7:7 *1778*
Thou knowest the c, Do not commit ... Mk 10:19 *1785*
him, The first of all the c is ... Mk 12:29 *1785*
before God, walking in all the c ... Lk 1:6 *1785*
Thou knowest the c, Do not commit ... Lk 18:20 *1785*
If ye love me, keep my c ... Jn 14:15 *1785*
He that hath my c, and keepeth ... Jn 14:21 *1785*
If ye keep my c, ye shall abide ... Jn 15:10 *1785*
even as I have kept my Father's c ... Jn 15:10 *1785*
the Holy Ghost had given c unto ... Acts 1:2 *1781*
but the keeping of the c of God ... 1Cor 7:19 *1785*
unto you are the c of the Lord ... 1Cor 14:37 *1785*
even the law of c contained in ... Eph 2:15 *1785*
after the c and doctrines of men ... Col 2:22 *1778*
(touching whom ye received c ... Col 4:10 *1785*
For ye know what c we gave you by ... 1Th 4:2 *3852*
c of men, that turn from the ... Titus 1:14 *1785*
we know him, if we keep his c ... 1Jn 2:3 *1785*
I know him, and keepeth not his c ... 1Jn 2:4 *1785*
of him, because we keep his c ... 1Jn 3:22 *1785*
keepeth his c dwelleth in him ... 1Jn 3:24 *1785*
when we love God, and keep his c ... 1Jn 5:2 *1785*
love of God, that we keep his c ... 1Jn 5:3 *1785*
and his c are not grievous ... 1Jn 5:3 *1785*
is love, that we walk after his c ... 2Jn 6 *1785*
her seed, which keep the c of God ... Rev 12:17 *1785*
are they that keep the c of God ... Rev 14:12 *1785*
Blessed are they that do his c ... Rev 22:14 *1785*

COMMEND

into thy hands I c my spirit ... Lk 23:46 *3908*
I c you to God, and to the word of ... Acts 20:32 *3908*
c the righteousness of God ... Rom 3:5 *4921*
I c unto you Phebe our sister, ... Rom 16:1 *4921*
Do we begin again to c ourselves ... 2Cor 3:1 *4921*
For we c not ourselves again unto ... 2Cor 5:12 *4921*
with some that c themselves ... 2Cor 10:12 *4921*

COMMENDATION

some others, epistles of c to you ... 2Cor 3:1 *4956*
to you, or letters of c from you ... 2Cor 3:1 *4956*

COMMENDED

saw her, and c her before Pharaoh ... Gen 12:15 1984
A man shall be c according to his ... Prov 12:8 1984
Then I c mirth, because a man ... Eccl 8:15 7623
the lord c the unjust steward, ... Lk 16:8 *1867*
they c them to the Lord, on whom ... Acts 14:23 *3908*
for I ought to have been c of you ... 2Cor 12:11 *4921*

COMMENDETH

But God c his love toward us, in ... Rom 5:8 *4921*
But meat c us not to God ... 1Cor 8:8 *3936*

C

For not he that c himself is ... 2Cor 10:18 *4921*
is approved, but whom the Lord c ... 2Cor 10:18 *4921*

COMMENDING
truth c ourselves to every man's ... 2Cor 4:2 *4921*

COMMISSION
c from the chief priests, ... Acts 26:12 *2011*

COMMISSIONS
they delivered the king's c unto ... Ezr 8:36 1881

COMMIT
Thou shalt not c adultery ... Ex 20:14 5003
If a soul c a trespass, and sin ... Lev 5:15 4603
c any of these things which are ... Lev 5:17 6213
c a trespass against the LORD, and ... Lev 6:2 4603
and shall not c any of these ... Lev 18:26 6213
For whosoever shall c any of ... Lev 18:29 6213
even the souls that c them shall ... Lev 18:29 6213
that ye c not any one of these ... Lev 18:30 6213
to c whoredom with Molech, from ... Lev 20:5 2181
When a man or woman shall c ... Num 5:6 6213
any sin that men c, to do ... Num 5:6
c a trespass against him, ... Num 5:12 4603
the people began to c whoredom ... Num 25:1 2181
to c trespass against the LORD in ... Num 31:16 4560
Neither shalt thou c adultery ... Deut 5:18 5003
shall henceforth c no more any ... Deut 19:20 6213
c a trespass in the accursed ... Josh 22:20 4603
If he c iniquity, I will chasten ... 2Sa 7:14 5753
of Jerusalem to c fornication ... 2Chr 21:11 2181
and unto God would I c my cause ... Job 5:8 7760
that he should c iniquity ... Job 34:10
Into thine hand I c my spirit ... Ps 31:5 6485
C thy way unto the LORD ... Ps 37:5 1556
C thy works unto the LORD, and thy ... Prov 16:3 1556
to kings to c wickedness ... Prov 16:12 6213
I will c thy government into his ... Is 22:21 5414
shall c fornication with all the ... Is 23:17 2181
c adultery, and swear falsely, and ... Jer 7:9 5003
and weary themselves to c iniquity ... Jer 9:5 5753
they c adultery, and walk in lies ... Jer 23:14 5003
c Jeremiah into the court of the ... Jer 37:21 6485
Wherefore c ye this great evil ... Jer 44:7 6213
and c iniquity, and I lay a ... Eze 3:20 6213
c the abominations which they c ... Eze 8:17 6213
didst c whoredom with them, ... Eze 16:17 2181
followeth thee to c whoredoms ... Eze 16:34 2181
thou shalt not c this lewdness ... Eze 16:43 6213
c ye whoredom after their ... Eze 20:30 2181
the midst of thee they c lewdness ... Eze 22:9 6213
Will they now c whoredoms with ... Eze 23:43 2181
and c iniquity, all his ... Eze 33:13 6213
they shall c whoredom, and shall ... Hos 4:10 2181
your daughters shall c whoredom ... Hos 4:13 2181
and your spouses shall c adultery ... Hos 4:13 5003
daughters when they c whoredom ... Hos 4:14 2181
your spouses when they c adultery ... Hos 4:14 5003
for they c lewdness ... Hos 6:9 6313
for they c falsehood ... Hos 7:1 6466
time, Thou shalt not c adultery ... Mt 5:27 *3431*
causeth her to c adultery ... Mt 5:32 *3429*
which is put away doth c adultery ... Mt 19:9 *3429*
murder, Thou shalt not c adultery ... Mt 19:18 *3431*
Do not c adultery, Do not kill, ... Mk 10:19 *3431*
did c things worthy of stripes, ... Lk 12:48 *4160*
who will c to your trust the true ... Lk 16:11 *4100*
Do not c adultery, Do not kill, ... Lk 18:20 *3431*
Jesus did not c himself unto them ... Jn 2:24 *4100*
that they which c such things are ... Rom 1:32 *4238*
against them which c such things ... Rom 2:2 *4238*
a man should not c adultery ... Rom 2:22 *3431*
dost thou c adultery ... Rom 2:22 *3431*
idols, dost thou c sacrilege ... Rom 2:22 *2416*
this, Thou shalt not c adultery ... Rom 13:9 *3431*
Neither let us c fornication ... 1Cor 10:8 *4203*
This charge I c unto thee ... 1Ti 1:18 *3908*
the same c thou to faithful men, ... 2Ti 2:2 *3908*
ye c sin, and are convinced of the ... Jas 2:9 *2038*
Do not c adultery, said also, Do ... Jas 2:11 *3431*
Now if thou c no adultery ... Jas 2:11 *3431*
according to the will of God c ... 1Pet 4:19 *3908*
is born of God doth not c sin ... 1Jn 3:9 *4160*
unto idols, and to c fornication ... Rev 2:14 *4203*
my servants to c fornication ... Rev 2:20 *4203*
them that c adultery with her ... Rev 2:22 *3431*

COMMITTED
he hath c all that he hath to my ... Gen 39:8 5414
prison c to Joseph's hand all the ... Gen 39:22 5414
for his sin that he hath c ... Lev 4:35 2398
for his trespass, which he hath c ... Lev 5:7 2398
customs, which were c before you ... Lev 18:30 6213
of them have c an abomination ... Lev 20:13 6213
for they c all these things, and ... Lev 20:23 6213
if ought be c by ignorance ... Num 15:24 6213
which have c that wicked thing, ... Deut 17:5 6213
if a man have c a sin worthy of ... Deut 21:22 1961
c a trespass in the accursed ... Josh 7:1 4600
have c against the God of Israel ... Josh 22:16 4600
because ye have not c this ... Josh 22:31 4600
for they have c lewdness and folly ... Judg 20:6 6213
perversely, we have c wickedness ... 1Kin 8:47 7561
with their sins which they had c ... 1Kin 14:22 2398
c them unto the hands of the ... 1Kin 14:27 6485
which he c against the LORD ... 1Chr 10:13 4600
c them to the hands of the chief ... 2Chr 12:10 6485
All that was c to thy servants, ... 2Chr 34:16 5414
we have c iniquity, we have done ... Ps 106:6 5753
For my people have c two evils ... Jer 2:13 6213
whereby backsliding Israel c ... Jer 3:8 5003
c adultery with stones and with ... Jer 3:9 5003
to the full, they then c adultery ... Jer 5:7 5003
horrible thing is c in the land ... Jer 5:30 1961
when they had c abomination ... Jer 6:15 6213
when they had c abomination ... Jer 8:12 6213
have c against the LORD our God ... Jer 16:10 2398
they have c villany in Israel ... Jer 29:23 6213
have c adultery with their ... Jer 29:23 6213
c him unto Gedaliah the son of ... Jer 39:14 5414
had c unto him men, and women, and. Jer 40:7 6485
the captain of the guard had c to ... Jer 41:10 6485
have c to provoke me to anger ... Jer 44:3 6213
which they have c in the land of ... Jer 44:9 6213
the abominations which ye have c ... Jer 44:22 6213
have c in all their abominations ... Eze 6:9 6213
because they have c a trespass ... Eze 15:8 4600
Thou hast also c fornication with ... Eze 16:26 2181
and c abomination before me ... Eze 16:50 6213
hath Samaria c half of thy sins ... Eze 16:51 2398
hast c more abominable than they ... Eze 16:52 8581
to the idols, hath c abomination, ... Eze 18:12 6213
from all his sins that he hath c ... Eze 18:21 6213
his transgressions that he hath c ... Eze 18:22 6213
his wickedness that he hath c ... Eze 18:27 6213
his transgressions that he hath c ... Eze 18:28 6213
in that they have c a trespass ... Eze 20:27 4600
for all your evils that ye have c ... Eze 20:43 6213
one hath c abomination with his ... Eze 22:11 6213
they c whoredoms in Egypt ... Eze 23:3 2181
they c whoredoms in their youth ... Eze 23:3 2181
Thus she c her whoredoms with ... Eze 23:7 5414
That they have c adultery ... Eze 23:37 5003
their idols have they c adultery ... Eze 23:37 5003
for his iniquity that he hath c ... Eze 33:13 6213
c shall be mentioned unto him ... Eze 33:16 2398
abominations which they have c ... Eze 33:29 6213
abominations that they have c ... Eze 43:8 6213
abominations which they have c ... Eze 44:13 6213
have c iniquity, and have done ... Dan 9:5 5753
the land hath c great whoredom ... Hos 1:2 2181
they have c whoredom continually ... Hos 4:18 2181
and an abomination is c in Israel ... Mal 2:11 6213
c adultery with her already in ... Mt 5:28 *3431*
with him, who had c murder in the ... Mk 15:7 *4160*
and to whom men have c much ... Lk 12:48 *3908*
but hath c all judgment unto the ... Jn 5:22 *1325*
men and women c them to prison ... Acts 8:3 *3860*
or have c any thing worthy of ... Acts 25:11 *4238*
he had c nothing worthy of death ... Acts 25:25 *4238*
they c themselves unto the sea, ... Acts 27:40 *1439*
though I have c nothing against ... Acts 28:17 *4160*
them were c the oracles of God ... Rom 3:2 *4100*
of the gospel is c unto me ... 1Cor 9:17 *4100*
fornication, as some of them c ... 1Cor 10:8 *4203*
hath c unto us the word of ... 2Cor 5:19 *5087*
Have I c an offence in abasing ... 2Cor 11:7 *4160*
lasciviousness which they have c ... 2Cor 12:21 *4238*
the uncircumcision was c unto me ... Gal 2:7 *4100*
God, which was c to my trust ... 1Ti 1:11 *4100*
keep that which is c to thy trust ... 1Ti 6:20 *3872*
have c unto him against that day ... 2Ti 1:12 *3866*
That good thing which was c unto ... 2Ti 1:14 *3872*
which is c unto me according to ... Titus 1:3 *4100*
and if he have c sins, they shall ... Jas 5:15 *4160*
but c himself to him that judgeth ... 1Pet 2:23 *3860*
deeds which they have ungodly c ... Jude 15 *764*
of the earth have c fornication ... Rev 17:2 *4203*
earth have c fornication with her ... Rev 18:3 *4203*
who have c fornication and lived ... Rev 18:9 *4203*

COMMITTEST
thou c whoredom, and Israel is ... Hos 5:3 2181

COMMITTETH
the man that c adultery with ... Lev 20:10 5003
even he that c adultery with his ... Lev 20:10 5003
the poor c himself unto thee ... Ps 10:14 5800
But whoso c adultery with a woman ... Prov 6:32 5003
that the house of Israel c here ... Eze 8:6 6213
But as a wife that c adultery ... Eze 16:32 5003
c iniquity, and doeth according to ... Eze 18:24 6213
c iniquity, and dieth in them ... Eze 18:26 6213
c iniquity, he shall even die ... Eze 33:18 6213
her that is divorced c adultery ... Mt 5:32 *3429*
shall marry another, c adultery ... Mt 19:9 *3429*
another, c adultery against her ... Mk 10:11 *3429*
to another, she c adultery ... Mk 10:12 *3429*
and marrieth another, c adultery ... Lk 16:18 *3431*
away from her husband c adultery ... Lk 16:18 *3431*
Whosoever c sin is the servant of ... Jn 8:34 *4160*
but he that c fornication sinneth ... 1Cor 6:18 *4203*
Whosoever c sin transgresseth ... 1Jn 3:4 *4160*
He that c sin is of the devil ... 1Jn 3:8 *4160*

COMMITTING
of life, without c iniquity ... Eze 33:15 6213
c adultery, they break out, and ... Hos 4:2 5003

COMMODIOUS
the haven was not c to winter in ... Acts 27:12 *428*

COMMON
if any one of the c people sin ... Lev 4:27 776
men die the c death of all men ... Num 16:29
There is no c bread under mine ... 1Sa 21:4 2455
and the bread is in a manner c ... 1Sa 21:5 2455
the sun, and it is c among men ... Eccl 6:1 7227
into the graves of the c people ... Jer 26:23 1121
and shall eat them as c things ... Jer 31:5 2490
with the men of the c sort were ... Eze 23:42 7230
took Jesus into the c hall ... Mt 27:27 *4232*
the c people heard him gladly ... Mk 12:37 *4183*
together, and had all things c ... Acts 2:44 *2839*
but they had all things c ... Acts 4:32 *2839*
and put them in the c prison ... Acts 5:18 *1219*
any thing that is c or unclean ... Acts 10:14 *2839*
cleansed, that call not thou c ... Acts 10:15 *2840*
not call any man c or unclean ... Acts 10:28 *2839*
for nothing c or unclean hath at ... Acts 11:8 *2839*
cleansed, that call not thou c ... Acts 11:9 *2839*
taken you but such as is c to man ... 1Cor 10:13 *442*
mine own son after the c faith ... Titus 1:4 *2839*
write unto you of the c salvation ... Jude 3 *2839*

COMMONLY
this saying is c reported among ... Mt 28:15 *1310*
It is reported c that there is ... 1Cor 5:1 *3654*

COMMONWEALTH
being aliens from the c of Israel ... Eph 2:12 *4174*

COMMOTION
a great c out of the north ... Jer 10:22 7494

COMMOTIONS
when ye shall hear of wars and c ... Lk 21:9 *181*

COMMUNE
went out unto Jacob to c with him ... Gen 34:6 1696
I will c with thee from above the ... Ex 25:22 1696
C with David secretly, and say, ... 1Sa 18:22 1696
I will c with my father of thee ... 1Sa 19:3 1696
If we assay to c with thee ... Job 4:2 1697
c with your own heart upon your ... Ps 4:4 559
they c of laying snares privily ... Ps 64:5 5608
I c with mine own heart ... Ps 77:6 7878

COMMUNED
he c with them, saying, If it be ... Gen 23:8 1696
Hamor c with them, saying, The ... Gen 34:8 1696
c with the men of their city, ... Gen 34:20 1696
c with them, and took from them ... Gen 42:24 1696
they c with him at the door of ... Gen 43:19 1696
c with them, and with all the ... Judg 9:1 1696
Samuel c with Saul upon the top ... 1Sa 9:25 1696
c with Abigail, to take her to ... 1Sa 25:39 1696
she c with him of all that was in ... 1Kin 10:2 1696
and they c with her ... 2Kin 22:14 1696
she c with him of all that was in ... 2Chr 9:1 1696
I c with mine own heart, saying, ... Eccl 1:16 1696
And the king c with them ... Dan 1:19 1696
So the angel that c with me said ... Zec 1:14 1696
c one with another what they ... Lk 6:11 *1255*
c with the chief priests and ... Lk 22:4 *4814*
pass, that, while they c together ... Lk 24:15 *3656*
him the oftener, and c with him ... Acts 24:26 *3656*

COMMUNICATE
c unto him that teacheth in all ... Gal 6:6 *2841*
that ye did c with my affliction ... Phil 4:14 *4790*
ready to distribute, willing to c ... 1Ti 6:18 *2843*
But to do good and to c forget not ... Heb 13:16 *2842*

COMMUNICATED
c unto them that gospel which I ... Gal 2:2 *394*
no church c with me as concerning ... Phil 4:15 *2841*

COMMUNICATION
Abner had c with the elders of ... 2Sa 3:17 1697
them, Ye know the man, and his c ... 2Kin 9:11 7879
But let your c be, Yea, yea ... Mt 5:37 *3056*
Let no corrupt c proceed out of ... Eph 4:29 *3056*
filthy c out of your mouth ... Col 3:8 *148*
That the c of thy faith may ... Philem 6 *2842*

COMMUNICATIONS
What manner of c are these that ... Lk 24:17 *3056*
evil c corrupt good manners ... 1Cor 15:33 *3657*

COMMUNING
as he had left c with Abraham ... Gen 18:33 1696
of c with him upon mount Sinai ... Ex 31:18 1696

COMMUNION
is it not the c of the blood of ... 1Cor 10:16 *2842*
is it not the c of the body of ... 1Cor 10:16 *2842*
what c hath light with darkness ... 2Cor 6:14 *2842*
the c of the Holy Ghost, be with ... 2Cor 13:14 *2842*

COMPACT
as a city that is c together ... Ps 122:3 2266

COMPACTED
c by that which every joint ... Eph 4:16 *4822*

COMPANIED
of these men which have c with us ... Acts 1:21 *4905*

COMPANIES
three hundred men into three c ... Judg 7:16 7218
the three c blew the trumpets, and ... Judg 7:20 7218
wait against Shechem in four c ... Judg 9:34 7218
and divided them into three c ... Judg 9:43 7218
the two other c ran upon all the ... Judg 9:44 7218
Saul put the people in three c ... 1Sa 11:11 7218
of the Philistines in three c ... 1Sa 13:17 7218
And the Syrians had gone out by c ... 2Kin 5:2 1416
in the c of the children of Levi ... 1Chr 9:18 4264
the captains of the c that ... 1Chr 28:1 4256
appointed two great c of them ... Neh 12:31
So stood the two c of them that ... Neh 12:40
the c of Sheba waited for them ... Job 6:19 1979
O ye travelling c of Dedanim ... Is 21:13 736
criest, let thy c deliver thee ... Is 57:13
chariots, and with horsemen, and c ... Eze 26:7 6951
down by c upon the green grass ... Mk 6:39 *4849*

COMPANION
his brother, and every man his c ... Ex 32:27 7453
Samson's wife was given to his c ... Judg 14:20 4828
therefore I gave her to thy c ... Judg 15:2 4828
his wife, and given her to his c ... Judg 15:6 4828
the Archite was the king's c ... 1Chr 27:33 7453
to dragons, and a c to owls ... Job 30:29 7453
I am a c of all them that fear ... Ps 119:63 2270
but a c of fools shall be ... Prov 13:20 7462
but he that is a c of riotous men ... Prov 28:7 7462
the same is the c of a destroyer ... Prov 28:24 2270
yet is she thy c, and the wife of ... Mal 2:14 2278
c in labour, and fellow soldier, ... Phil 2:25 *4904*
c in tribulation, and in the ... Rev 1:9 *4791*

C

COMPANIONS
and she went with her c, and ... Judg 11:38 7464
brought thirty c to be with him ... Judg 14:11 4828
Tabeel, and the rest of their c ... Ezr 4:7 3675
scribe, and the rest of their c ... Ezr 4:9 3675
to the rest of their c that dwell ... Ezr 4:17 3675
Shimshai the scribe, and their c ... Ezr 4:23 3675
and Shethar-boznai, and their c ... Ezr 5:3 3675
his c the Apharsachites, which ... Ezr 5:6 3675
your c the Apharsachites, which ... Ezr 6:6 3675
river, Shethar-boznai, and their c ... Ezr 6:13 3675
answer thee, and thy c with thee ... Job 35:4 7453
Shall the c make a banquet of him ... Job 41:6 2271
the virgins her c that follow her ... Ps 45:14 7464
aside by the flocks of thy c ... Song 1:7 2270
the c hearken to thy voice ... Song 8:13 2270
are rebellious, and c of thieves ... Is 1:23 2270
for the children of Israel his c ... Eze 37:16 2270
for all the house of Israel his c ... Eze 37:16 2270
Mishael, and Azariah, his c ... Dan 2:17 2269
Paul's c in travel, they rushed ... Acts 19:29 *4898*
whilst ye became c of them that ... Heb 10:33 *2844*

COMPANIONS'
c sakes, I will now say, Peace be ... Ps 122:8 7453

COMPANY
said, If Esau come to the one c ... Gen 32:8 4264
then the other c which is left ... Gen 32:8 4264
lodged that night in the c ... Gen 32:21 4264
a c of nations shall be of thee, ... Gen 35:11 6951
a c of Ishmeelites came from ... Gen 37:25 736
and it was a very great c ... Gen 50:9 4264
they spake unto all the c of the ... Num 14:7 5712
unto Korah and unto all his c ... Num 16:5 5712
you censers, Korah, and all his c ... Num 16:6 5712
all thy c are gathered together ... Num 16:11 5712
all thy c before the LORD, thou, ... Num 16:16 5712
he be not as Korah, and as his c ... Num 16:40 5712
Now shall this c lick up all that ... Num 22:4 6951
against Aaron in the c of Korah ... Num 26:9 5712
with Korah, when that c died ... Num 26:10 5712
he was not in the c of them that ... Num 27:3 5712
the LORD in the c of Korah ... Num 27:3 5712
another c come along by the plain ... Judg 9:37 7218
the c that was with him, rushed ... Judg 9:44 7218
that thou comest with such a c ... Judg 18:23 2199
that thou shalt meet a c of ... 1Sa 10:5 2256
behold, a c of prophets met him ... 1Sa 10:10 2256
one c turned unto the way that ... 1Sa 13:17 7218
another c turned the way to ... 1Sa 13:18 7218
another c turned to the way of ... 1Sa 13:18 7218
when they saw the c of the ... 1Sa 19:20 3862
thou bring me down to this c ... 1Sa 30:15 1416
I will bring thee down to this c ... 1Sa 30:15 1416
delivered the c that came against ... 1Sa 30:23 1416
the man of God, he and all his c ... 2Kin 5:15 4264
he spied the c of Jehu as he came ... 2Kin 9:17 8229
and said, I see a c ... 2Kin 9:17 8229
at Jerusalem, with a very great c ... 2Chr 9:1 2428
great c that cometh against us ... 2Chr 20:12 1995
came with a small c of men ... 2Chr 24:24
the other c of them that gave ... Neh 12:38
thou hast made desolate all my c ... Job 16:7 5712
Which goeth in c with the workers ... Job 34:8 2274
walked unto the house of God in c ... Ps 55:14 7285
great was the c of those that ... Ps 68:11 6635
Rebuke the c of spearmen, the ... Ps 68:30 2416
and covered the c of Abiram ... Ps 106:17 5712
And a fire was kindled in their c ... Ps 106:18 5712
but he that keepeth c with ... Prov 29:3 7462
to a c of horses in Pharaoh's ... Song 1:9
As it were the c of two armies ... Song 6:13 4246
a great c shall return thither ... Jer 31:8 6951
also bring up a c against thee ... Eze 16:40 6951
great c make for him in the war, ... Eze 17:17 6951
I will bring up a c upon them ... Eze 23:46 6951
the c shall stone them with ... Eze 23:47 6951
the c of the Ashurites have made ... Eze 27:6 1323
in all thy c which is in the ... Eze 27:27 6951
all thy c in the midst of thee ... Eze 27:34 6951
over thee with a c of many people ... Eze 32:3 6951
Asshur is there and all her c ... Eze 32:22 6951
her c is round about her grave ... Eze 32:23 6951
even a great c with bucklers and ... Eze 38:4 6951
all thy c that are assembled unto ... Eze 38:7 6951
gathered thy c to take a prey ... Eze 38:13 6951
riding upon horses, a great c ... Eze 38:15 6951
so the c of priests murder in the ... Hos 6:9 2267
him to have been in the c ... Lk 2:44 *4923*
there was a great c of publicans ... Lk 5:29 *3793*
the c of his disciples, and a ... Lk 6:17 *3793*
shall separate you from their c ... Lk 6:22
them sit down by fifties in a c ... Lk 9:14 *2828*
behold, a man of the c cried out ... Lk 9:38 *3793*
of the c lifted up her voice ... Lk 11:27 *3793*
one of the c said unto him, ... Lk 12:13 *3793*
followed him a great c of people ... Lk 23:27 *4128*
also of our c made us astonished ... Lk 24:22
saw a great c come unto him, he ... Jn 6:5 *3793*
let go, they went to their own c ... Acts 4:23 *2398*
a great c of the priests were ... Acts 6:7 *3793*
for a man that is a Jew to keep c ... Acts 10:28 *2853*
his c loosed from Paphos, they ... Acts 13:13
their own c to Antioch with Paul ... Acts 15:22
the baser sort, and gathered a c ... Acts 17:5 *3792*
we that were of Paul's c departed ... Acts 21:8 *4012*
I be somewhat filled with your c ... Rom 15:24
epistle not to c with fornicators ... 1Cor 5:9 *4874*
written unto you not to keep c ... 1Cor 5:11 *4874*
have no c with him, that he may ... 2Th 3:14 *4874*
and to an innumerable c of angels ... Heb 12:22 *3461*
all the c in ships, and sailors, ... Rev 18:17 *3658*

COMPARABLE
c to fine gold, how are they ... Lam 4:2 5577

COMPARE
what likeness will ye c unto him ... Is 40:18 6186
c me, that we may be like ... Is 46:5 4911
what comparison shall we c it ... Mk 4:30 *3846*
or c ourselves with some that ... 2Cor 10:12 *4793*

COMPARED
the heaven can be c unto the LORD ... Ps 89:6 6186
desire are not to be c unto her ... Prov 3:15 7737
be desired are not to be c to it ... Prov 8:11 7737
I have c thee, O my love, to a ... Song 1:9 1819
time are not worthy to be c with ... Rom 8:18

COMPARING
c spiritual things with spiritual ... 1Cor 2:13 *4793*
c themselves among themselves, ... 2Cor 10:12 *4793*

COMPARISON
What have I done now in c of you ... Judg 8:2
what was I able to do in c of you ... Judg 8:3
your eyes in c of it as nothing ... Hag 2:3 3644
or with what c shall we compare ... Mk 4:30 *3850*

COMPASS
under the c of the altar beneath ... Ex 27:5 3749
grate of network under the c ... Ex 38:4 3749
Red sea, to c the land of Edom ... Num 21:4 5437
the border shall fetch a c from ... Num 34:5 5437
And ye shall c the city, all ye ... Josh 6:3 5437
ye shall c the city seven times ... Josh 6:4 5437
c the city, and let him that is ... Josh 6:7 5437
to Adar, and fetched a c to Karkaa ... Josh 15:3 5437
but fetch a c behind them ... 2Sa 5:23 5437
cubits did c either of them about ... 1Kin 7:15 5437
cubits did c it round about ... 1Kin 7:23 5437
a round c of half a cubit high ... 1Kin 7:35 5439
they fetched a c of seven days' ... 2Kin 3:9 5437
ye shall c the king round about, ... 2Kin 11:8 5362
from brim to brim, round in c ... 2Chr 4:2 5439
cubits did c it round about ... 2Chr 4:2 5437
which did c it round about ... 2Chr 4:3 5437
the Levites shall c the king ... 2Chr 23:7 5362
His archers c me round about, he ... Job 16:13 5437
willows of the brook c him about ... Job 40:22 5437
wilt thou c him as with a shield ... Ps 5:12 5849
of the people c thee about ... Ps 7:7 5437
my deadly enemies, who c me about ... Ps 17:9 5362
so will I c thine altar, O LORD ... Ps 26:6 5437
thou shalt c me about with songs ... Ps 32:7 5437
the LORD, mercy shall c him about ... Ps 32:10 5437
of my heels shall c me about ... Ps 49:5 5437
the head of those that c me about ... Ps 140:9 4524
the righteous shall c me about ... Ps 142:7 3803
when he set a c upon the face of ... Prov 8:27 2329
and he marketh it out with the c ... Is 44:13 4230
that c yourselves about with ... Is 50:11 247
the earth, A woman shall c a man ... Jer 31:22 5437
Gareb, and shall c about to Goath ... Jer 31:39 5437
fillet of twelve cubits did c it ... Jer 52:21 5437
wicked doth c about the righteous ... Hab 1:4 3803
for ye c sea and land to make one ... Mt 23:15 *4013*
c thee round, and keep thee in on ... Lk 19:43 *4033*
And from thence we fetched a c ... Acts 28:13 *4022*

COMPASSED
c the house round, both old and ... Gen 19:4 5437
we c mount Seir many days ... Deut 2:1 5437
Ye have c this mountain long ... Deut 2:3 5437
So the ark of the LORD c the city ... Josh 6:11 5437
second day they c the city once ... Josh 6:14 5437
c the city after the same manner ... Josh 6:15 5437
day they c the city seven times ... Josh 6:15 5437
the border c from Baalah westward ... Josh 15:10 5437
c the corner of the sea southward ... Josh 18:14 5437
c the land of Edom, and the land ... Judg 11:18 5437
they c him in, and laid wait for ... Judg 16:2 5437
for Saul and his men c David ... 1Sa 23:26 5849
that bare Joab's armour c about ... 2Sa 18:15 5437
When the waves of death c me ... 2Sa 22:5 661
The sorrows of hell c me about ... 2Sa 22:6 5437
by night, and c the city about ... 2Kin 6:14 5362
an host c the city both with ... 2Kin 6:15 5437
the Edomites which c him about ... 2Kin 8:21 5437
Therefore they c about him to ... 2Chr 18:31 5437
smote the Edomites which c him in ... 2Chr 21:9 5437
c about Ophel, and raised it up a ... 2Chr 33:14 5437
me, and hath c me with his net ... Job 19:6 5362
He hath c the waters with bounds, ... Job 26:10 2328
They have now c us in our steps ... Ps 17:11 5437
The sorrows of death c me ... Ps 18:4 661
The sorrows of hell c me about ... Ps 18:5 5437
Many bulls have c me ... Ps 22:12 5437
For dogs have c me ... Ps 22:16 5437
innumerable evils have c me about ... Ps 40:12 661
they c me about together ... Ps 88:17 5362
They c me about also with words ... Ps 109:3 5437
The sorrows of death c me ... Ps 116:3 661
All nations c me about ... Ps 118:10 5437
They c me about ... Ps 118:11 5437
yea, they c me about ... Ps 118:11 5437
They c me about like bees ... Ps 118:12 5437
me, and c me with gall and travel ... Lam 3:5 5362
and the floods c me about ... Jonah 2:3 5437
The waters c me about, even to ... Jonah 2:5 661
shall see Jerusalem c with armies ... Lk 21:20 *2944*
himself also is c with infirmity ... Heb 5:2 *4029*
after they were c about seven ... Heb 11:30 *2944*
Wherefore seeing we also are c ... Heb 12:1 *4029*
c the camp of the saints about, ... Rev 20:9 *2944*

COMPASSEST
Thou c my path and my lying down, ... Ps 139:3 2219

COMPASSETH
that is it which c the whole land ... Gen 2:11 5437
the same is it that c the whole ... Gen 2:13 5437
the border c it on the north side ... Josh 19:14 5437
Therefore pride c them about as a ... Ps 73:6 6059
Ephraim c me about with lies, and ... Hos 11:12 5437

COMPASSING
round about there were knops c it ... 1Kin 7:24 5437
in a cubit, c the sea round about ... 1Kin 7:24 5362
in a cubit, c the sea round about ... 2Chr 4:3 5362

COMPASSION
And she had c on him, and said, ... Ex 2:6 2550
have c upon thee, and multiply ... Deut 13:17 7355
have c upon thee, and will return ... Deut 30:3 7355
for ye have c on me ... 1Sa 23:21 2550
give them c before them who ... 1Kin 8:50 7356
that they may have c on them ... 1Kin 8:50 7355
had c on them, and had respect ... 2Kin 13:23 7355
your children shall find c before ... 2Chr 30:9 7356
because he had c on his people ... 2Chr 36:15 2550
had no c upon young man or maiden .. 2Chr 36:17 2550
But he, being full of c, forgave ... Ps 78:38 7349
thou, O Lord, art a God full of c ... Ps 86:15 7349
the LORD is gracious and full of c ... Ps 111:4 7349
he is gracious, and full of c ... Ps 112:4 7349
LORD is gracious, and full of c ... Ps 145:8 7349
not have c on the son of her womb ... Is 49:15 7355
have c on them, and will bring ... Jer 12:15 7355
yet will he have c according to ... Lam 3:32 7355
unto thee, to have c upon thee ... Eze 16:5 2550
again, he will have c upon us ... Mic 7:19 7355
he was moved with c on them ... Mt 9:36 *4697*
and was moved with c toward them ... Mt 14:14 *4697*
I have c on the multitude, ... Mt 15:32 *4697*
of that servant was moved with c ... Mt 18:27 *4697*
have had c on thy fellowservant ... Mt 18:33 *1653*
So Jesus had c on them, and ... Mt 20:34 *4697*
And Jesus, moved with c, put forth ... Mk 1:41 *4697*
for thee, and hath had c on thee ... Mk 5:19 *1653*
and was moved with c toward them ... Mk 6:34 *4697*
I have c on the multitude, ... Mk 8:2 *4697*
thing, have c on us, and help us ... Mk 9:22 *4697*
the Lord saw her, he had c on her ... Lk 7:13 *4697*
when he saw him, he had c on him ... Lk 10:33 *4697*
off, his father saw him, and had c ... Lk 15:20 *4697*
have c on whom I will have c ... Rom 9:15 *3627*
Who can have c on the ignorant, ... Heb 5:2 *3356*
For ye had c of me in my bonds, ... Heb 10:34 *4834*
having c one of another, love as ... 1Pet 3:8 *4835*
up his bowels of c from him ... 1Jn 3:17
And of some have c, making a ... Jude 22 *1653*

COMPASSIONS
consumed, because his c fail not ... Lam 3:22 7355
c every man to his brother ... Zec 7:9 7356

COMPEL
thou shalt not c him to serve as ... Lev 25:39 5647
none did c ... Est 1:8 597
whosoever shall c thee to go a ... Mt 5:41 *29*
they c one Simon a Cyrenian, who ... Mk 15:21 *29*
c them to come in, that my house ... Lk 14:23 *315*

COMPELLED
together with the woman, c him ... 1Sa 28:23 6555
fornication, and c Judah thereto ... 2Chr 21:11 5080
him they c to bear his cross ... Mt 27:32 *29*
synagogue, and c them to blaspheme ... Acts 26:11 *315*
ye have c me ... 2Cor 12:11 *315*
a Greek, was c to be circumcised ... Gal 2:3 *315*

COMPELLEST
why c thou the Gentiles to live ... Gal 2:14 *315*

COMPLAIN
their brethren come unto us to c ... Judg 21:22 7378
I will c in the bitterness of my ... Job 7:11 7878
the furrows likewise thereof c ... Job 31:38 1058
Wherefore doth a living man c ... Lam 3:39 596

COMPLAINED
And when the people c, it ... Num 11:1 596
I c, and my spirit was overwhelmed ... Ps 77:3 7878

COMPLAINERS
These are murmurers, c, walking ... Jude 16 *3202*

COMPLAINING
that there be no c in our streets ... Ps 144:14 6682

COMPLAINT
for out of the abundance of my c ... 1Sa 1:16 7878
me, my couch shall ease my c ... Job 7:13 7878
If I say, I will forget my c ... Job 9:27 7878
I will leave my c upon myself ... Job 10:1 7878
As for me, is my c to man ... Job 21:4 7878
Even to day is my c bitter ... Job 23:2 7878
I mourn in my c, and make a noise ... Ps 55:2 7878
poureth out his c before the LORD ... Ps 102:t 7878
I poured out my c before him ... Ps 142:2 7878

COMPLAINTS
grievous c against Paul, which ... Acts 25:7 *157*

COMPLETE
seven sabbaths shall be c ... Lev 23:15 8549
And ye are c in him, which is the ... Col 2:10 *4137*
and c in all the will of God ... Col 4:12 *4137*

COMPOSITION
other like it, after the c of it ... Ex 30:32 4971
according to the c thereof ... Ex 30:37 4971

COMPOUND
an ointment *c* after the art of ... Ex 30:25 4842

COMPOUNDETH
Whosoever *c* any like it, or ... Ex 30:33 7543

COMPREHEND
doeth he, which we cannot *c* ... Job 37:5 3045
May be able to *c* with all saints ... Eph 3:18 *2638*

COMPREHENDED
c the dust of the earth in a ... Is 40:12 3557
and the darkness *c* it not ... Jn 1:5 *2638*
it is briefly *c* in this saying, ... Rom 13:9 *346*

CONANIAH (*co-na-ni'-ah*) See CONONIAH. *A chief Levite during Josiah's time.*
C also, and Shemaiah and Nethaneel, .. 2Chr 35:9 3562

CONCEAL
slay our brother, and *c* his blood ... Gen 37:26 3680
spare, neither shalt thou *c* him ... Deut 13:8 3680
is with the Almighty will I not *c* ... Job 27:11 3582
I will not *c* his parts, nor his ... Job 41:12 2790
is the glory of God to *c* a thing ... Prov 25:2 5641
publish, and *c* not ... Jer 50:2 3582

CONCEALED
for I have not *c* the words of the ... Job 6:10 3582
I have not *c* thy lovingkindness ... Ps 40:10 3582

CONCEALETH
of a faithful spirit *c* the matter ... Prov 11:13 3680
A prudent man *c* knowledge ... Prov 12:23 3680

CONCEIT
and as an high wall in his own *c* ... Prov 18:11 4906
lest he be wise in his own *c* ... Prov 26:5 5869
thou a man wise in his own *c* ... Prov 26:12 5869
sluggard is wiser in his own *c* ... Prov 26:16 5869
The rich man is wise in his own *c* ... Prov 28:11 5869

CONCEITS
ye should be wise in your own *c* ... Rom 11:25
Be not wise in your own *c* ... Rom 12:16

CONCEIVE
that they should *c* when they came ... Gen 30:38 3179
the stronger cattle did *c* ... Gen 30:41 3179
that they might *c* among the rods ... Gen 30:41 3179
shall be free, and shall *c* seed ... Num 5:28 2232
but thou shalt *c*, and bear a son ... Judg 13:3 2030
For, lo, thou shalt *c*, and bear a ... Judg 13:5 2030
unto me, Behold, thou shalt *c* ... Judg 13:7 2030
They *c* mischief, and bring forth ... Job 15:35 2029
and in sin did my mother *c* me ... Ps 51:5 3179
Behold, a virgin shall *c*, and bear ... Is 7:14 2030
Ye shall *c* chaff, ye shall bring ... Is 33:11 2029
they *c* mischief, and bring forth ... Is 59:4 2029
thou shalt *c* in thy womb, and ... Lk 1:31 *4815*
received strength to *c* seed ... Heb 11:11 *2602*

CONCEIVED
and she *c*, and bare Cain, and said, ... Gen 4:1 2030
and she *c*, and bare Enoch ... Gen 4:17 2030
he went in unto Hagar, and she *c* ... Gen 16:4 2030
and when she saw that she had *c* ... Gen 16:4 2030
and when she saw that she had *c* ... Gen 16:5 2030
For Sarah *c*, and bare Abraham a ... Gen 21:2 2030
of him, and Rebekah his wife *c* ... Gen 25:21 2030
And Leah *c*, and bare a son, and she ... Gen 29:32 2030
she *c* again, and bare a son ... Gen 29:33 2030
she *c* again, and bare a son ... Gen 29:34 2030
she *c* again, and bare a son ... Gen 29:35 2030
And Bilhah *c*, and bare Jacob a son ... Gen 30:5 2030
And Bilhah Rachel's maid *c* again ... Gen 30:7 2030
God hearkened unto Leah, and she *c* ... Gen 30:17 2030
Leah *c* again, and bare Jacob the ... Gen 30:19 2030
And she *c*, and bare a son ... Gen 30:23 2030
the flocks *c* before the rods, and ... Gen 30:39 3179
at the time that the cattle *c* ... Gen 31:10 3179
And she *c*, and bare a son ... Gen 38:3 2029
she *c* again, and bare a son ... Gen 38:4 2030
And she yet again *c*, and bare a son ... Gen 38:5 3254
came in unto her, and she *c* by him ... Gen 38:18 2030
And the woman *c*, and bare a son ... Ex 2:2 2030
saying, If a woman have *c* seed ... Lev 12:2 2232
Have I *c* all this people ... Num 11:12 2030
was come about after Hannah had *c* ... 1Sa 1:20 2030
visited Hannah, so that she *c* ... 1Sa 2:21 2030
And the woman *c*, and sent and told ... 2Sa 11:5 2030
And the woman *c*, and bare a son at ... 2Kin 4:17 2030
he went in to his wife, she *c* ... 1Chr 7:23 2030
was said, There is a man child *c* ... Job 3:3 2030
hath *c* mischief, and brought forth ... Ps 7:14 2030
into the chamber of her that *c* me ... Song 3:4 2030
and she *c*, and bare a son ... Is 8:3 2030
hath *c* a purpose against you ... Jer 49:30 2803
which *c*, and bare him a son ... Hos 1:3 2030
she *c* again, and bare a daughter ... Hos 1:6 2030
she had weaned Lo-ruhamah, she *c* ... Hos 1:8 2030
she that *c* them hath done ... Hos 2:5 2030
for that which is *c* in her is of ... Mt 1:20 *1080*
those days his wife Elisabeth *c* ... Lk 1:24 *4815*
she hath also *c* a son in her old ... Lk 1:36 *4815*
angel before he was *c* in the womb ... Lk 2:21 *4815*
why hast thou *c* this thing in ... Acts 5:4 *5087*
when Rebecca also had *c* by one ... Rom 9:10
Then when lust hath *c*, it ... Jas 1:15 *4815*

CONCEIVING
speaking oppression and revolt, *c* ... Is 59:13 2030

CONCEPTION
multiply thy sorrow and thy *c* ... Gen 3:16 2032
in unto her, the LORD gave her *c* ... Ruth 4:13 2032
and from the womb, and from the *c* ... Hos 9:11 2032

CONCERN
which *c* the Lord Jesus Christ ... Acts 28:31 *4012*
things which *c* mine infirmities ... 2Cor 11:30 *4012*

CONCERNETH
LORD will perfect that which *c* me ... Ps 138:8 1157
This burden *c* the prince in ... Eze 12:10

CONCERNING
same shall comfort us *c* our work ... Gen 5:29
Pharaoh commanded his men *c* him ... Gen 12:20
accepted thee *c* this thing also ... Gen 19:21
and sware to him *c* that matter ... Gen 24:9 5921
told him *c* the well which they ... Gen 26:32
are verily guilty *c* our brother ... Gen 42:21 5921
c the which I did swear to give ... Ex 6:8
made with you *c* all these words ... Ex 24:8 5921
c things which ought not to be ... Lev 4:2
c things which should not be done ... Lev 4:13
of the LORD his God *c* things ... Lev 4:22
an atonement for him as *c* his sin ... Lev 4:26
c things which ought not to be ... Lev 4:27
an atonement for him *c* his sin ... Lev 5:6
c his ignorance wherein he erred ... Lev 5:18 5921
which was lost, and lieth *c* it ... Lev 6:3
for ever in your generations *c* ... Lev 6:18
C the feasts of the LORD, which ... Lev 23:2
c the tithe of the herd, or of ... Lev 27:32
commanded Moses *c* the Levites ... Num 8:20
had commanded Moses *c* the Levites ... Num 8:22 5921
what the LORD will command *c* you ... Num 9:8
LORD hath spoken good *c* Israel ... Num 10:29 5921
c which I sware to make you dwell ... Num 14:30
tribes *c* the children of Israel ... Num 30:1
out of her lips *c* her vows ... Num 30:12
or *c* the bond of her soul, shall ... Num 30:12
So *c* them Moses commanded Eleazar. Num 32:28
c the daughters of Zelophehad ... Num 36:6
unto Moses the man of God *c* me ... Josh 14:6
the LORD your God spake *c* you ... Josh 23:14 5921
And Samson said *c* them, Now shall ... Judg 15:3
c him that came not up to the ... Judg 21:5
former time in Israel *c* redeeming ... Ruth 4:7 5921
c changing, for to confirm all ... Ruth 4:7 5921
which I have spoken *c* his house ... 1Sa 3:12 413
good that he hath spoken *c* thee ... 1Sa 25:30 5921
to day with a fault *c* this woman ... 2Sa 3:8
thou hast spoken *c* thy servant ... 2Sa 7:25 5921
c his house, establish it for ... 2Sa 7:25 5921
David all the things *c* the war ... 2Sa 11:18
for he was comforted *c* Amnon ... 2Sa 13:39 5921
and I will give charge *c* thee ... 2Sa 14:8 5921
all the captains charge *c* Absalom ... 2Sa 18:5
his word which he spake *c* me ... 1Kin 2:4 5921
which he spake *c* the house of Eli ... 1Kin 2:27 5921
all thy desire *c* timber of cedar ... 1Kin 5:8
and *c* timber of fir ... 1Kin 5:8
C this house which thou art in ... 1Kin 6:12
Moreover *c* a stranger, that is ... 1Kin 8:41 413
of Solomon *c* the name of the LORD ... 1Kin 10:1
Of the nations *c* which the LORD ... 1Kin 11:2
And had commanded him *c* this thing. 1Kin 11:10 5921
he doth not prophesy good *c* me ... 1Kin 22:8 5921
he would prophesy no good *c* me ... 1Kin 22:18 5921
the LORD hath spoken evil *c* thee ... 1Kin 22:23 5921
LORD spake *c* the house of Ahab ... 2Kin 10:10 5921
c whom the LORD had charged them, .. 2Kin 17:15
that the LORD hath spoken *c* him ... 2Kin 19:21 5921
the LORD *c* the king of Assyria ... 2Kin 19:32 413
c the words of this book that is ... 2Kin 22:13 5921
all that which is written *c* us ... 2Kin 22:13 5921
to the word of the LORD *c* Israel ... 1Chr 11:10 5921
thou hast spoken *c* thy servant ... 1Chr 17:23 5921
c his house be established for ... 1Chr 17:23 5921
to comfort him *c* his father ... 1Chr 19:2 5921
and give thee charge *c* Israel ... 1Chr 22:12 5921
LORD charged Moses with *c* Israel ... 1Chr 22:13 5921
Now *c* Moses the man of God, his ... 1Chr 23:14
C Rehabiah ... 1Chr 24:21
C Kish ... 1Chr 24:29
C the divisions of the porters ... 1Chr 26:1
As *c* the sons of Laadan ... 1Chr 26:21
Moreover *c* the stranger, which is ... 2Chr 6:32 413
c any matter, or *c* the treasures ... 2Chr 8:15
and of Iddo the seer *c* genealogies ... 2Chr 12:15
also *c* Maachah the mother of Asa ... 2Chr 15:16
Now *c* his sons, and the greatness ... 2Chr 24:27
c the children of Israel and Judah ... 2Chr 31:6
and the Levites *c* the heaps ... 2Chr 31:9 5921
c the words of the book that is ... 2Chr 34:21 5921
saith the LORD God of Israel *c* ... 2Chr 34:26
answer by letter *c* this matter ... Ezr 5:5 5922
his pleasure to us *c* this matter ... Ezr 5:17 5922
Cyrus the king made a decree *c* ... Ezr 6:3
counsellors, to enquire *c* Judah ... Ezr 7:14 5922
is hope in Israel *c* this thing ... Ezr 10:2 5921
I asked them *c* the Jews that had ... Neh 1:2 5921
of the captivity, and *c* Jerusalem ... Neh 1:2 5921
c which thou hadst promised to ... Neh 9:23
was the king's commandment *c* them .. Neh 11:23 5921
hand in all matters *c* the people ... Neh 11:24
c this, and wipe not out my good ... Neh 13:14 5921
my God, *c* this also, and spare me ... Neh 13:22
the king had so commanded *c* him ... Est 3:2
which they had seen *c* this matter ... Est 9:26 5921
The noise thereof sheweth *c* it ... Job 36:33 5921
it, the cattle also *c* the vapour ... Job 36:33 5921
c the words of Cush the Benjamite ... Ps 7:*t* 5921
C the words of men, by the word ... Ps 17:4
and speak wickedly *c* oppression ... Ps 73:8
let it repent thee *c* thy servants ... Ps 90:13 5921
c whom the LORD commanded them ... Ps 106:34
precepts *c* all things to be right ... Ps 119:128
C thy testimonies, I have known ... Ps 119:152
repent himself *c* his servants ... Ps 135:14 5921
search out by wisdom *c* all things ... Eccl 1:13 5921
I said in mine heart *c* the estate ... Eccl 3:18 5921
dost not enquire wisely *c* this ... Eccl 7:10 5921
son of Amoz, which he saw *c* Judah ... Is 1:1 5921
the son of Amoz saw *c* Judah ... Is 2:1 5921
man's pen *c* Maher-shalal-hash-baz ... Is 8:1
spoken *c* Moab since that time ... Is 16:13 413
As at the report *c* Egypt, so ... Is 23:5
c the house of Jacob, Jacob shall ... Is 29:22 413
therefore have I cried *c* this ... Is 30:7
he heard say *c* Tirhakah king of ... Is 37:9 5921
which the LORD hath spoken *c* him ... Is 37:22 5921
the LORD *c* the king of Assyria ... Is 37:33 413
me of things to come *c* my sons ... Is 45:11 5921
c the work of my hands command ye .. Is 45:11 5921
c burnt offerings or sacrifices ... Jer 7:22
came to Jeremiah *c* the dearth ... Jer 14:1
c the prophets that prophesy in ... Jer 14:15 5921
thus saith the LORD *c* the sons ... Jer 16:3 5921
c the daughters that are born in ... Jer 16:3 5921
c their mothers that bare them, ... Jer 16:3 5921
c their fathers that begat them ... Jer 16:3 5921
instant I shall speak *c* a nation ... Jer 18:7 5921
c a kingdom, to pluck up, and to ... Jer 18:7 5921
instant I shall speak *c* a nation ... Jer 18:9 5921
c a kingdom, to build and to plant ... Jer 18:9 5921
c Jehoiakim the son of Josiah ... Jer 22:18 413
the LORD of hosts *c* the prophets ... Jer 23:15 5921
c all the people of Judah in the ... Jer 25:1 5921
the LORD of hosts *c* the pillars ... Jer 27:19 5921
c the sea, and *c* the bases ... Jer 27:19 5921
c the residue of the vessels that ... Jer 27:19 5921
c the vessels that remain in the ... Jer 27:21 5921
Thus saith the LORD *c* Shemaiah ... Jer 29:31 413
c Israel and *c* Judah ... Jer 30:4 413
c this city, whereof ye say, It ... Jer 32:36 413
c the houses of this city, and ... Jer 33:4 5921
c the houses of the kings of ... Jer 33:4 5921
king of Babylon gave charge *c* ... Jer 39:11 5921
The LORD hath said *c* you, O ye ... Jer 42:19 5921
The word that came to Jeremiah *c* ... Jer 44:1 413
C The Ammonites, thus saith the ... Jer 49:1
C Edom, thus saith the LORD of ... Jer 49:7
C Damascus ... Jer 49:23
C Kedar, and *c* the kingdoms ... Jer 49:28
c the pillars, the height of one ... Jer 52:21
the LORD hath commanded *c* Jacob ... Lam 1:17
Israel which prophesy *c* Jerusalem ... Eze 13:16 413
a prophet to enquire of him *c* me ... Eze 14:7
ye shall be comforted *c* the evil ... Eze 14:22 5921
even *c* all that I have brought ... Eze 14:22 854
this proverb *c* the land of Israel ... Eze 18:2 5921
the Lord GOD *c* the Ammonites ... Eze 21:28 413
and *c* their reproach ... Eze 21:28 413
therefore *c* the land of Israel ... Eze 36:6 5921
ears all that I say unto thee *c* ... Eze 44:5
C the ordinance of oil, the bath ... Eze 45:14
c the which I lifted up mine hand ... Eze 47:14
the God of heaven *c* this secret ... Dan 2:18 5922
and made a proclamation *c* him ... Dan 5:29 5922
against Daniel *c* the kingdom ... Dan 6:4 6655
against him *c* the law of his God ... Dan 6:5
the king *c* the king's decree ... Dan 6:12 5922
might not be changed *c* Daniel ... Dan 6:17
As *c* the rest of the beasts, they ... Dan 7:12
the vision *c* the daily sacrifice ... Dan 8:13
which he saw *c* Israel in the days ... Amos 1:1 5921
Thus saith the Lord GOD *c* Edom ... Obad 1
of Judah, which he saw *c* Samaria ... Mic 1:1 5921
Thus saith the LORD *c* the ... Mic 3:5 5921
hath given a commandment *c* thee ... Nah 1:14 5921
Ask now the priests *c* the law ... Hag 2:11
give his angels charge *c* thee ... Mt 4:6 *4012*
to say unto the multitudes *c* John ... Mt 11:7 *4012*
I spake it not to you *c* bread ... Mt 16:11 *4012*
the devil, and also *c* the swine ... Mk 5:16 *4012*
disciples asked him *c* the parable ... Mk 7:17 *4012*
which was told them *c* this child ... Lk 2:17 *4012*
to speak unto the people *c* John ... Lk 7:24 *4012*
c the Son of man shall be ... Lk 18:31
for the things *c* me have an end ... Lk 22:37 *4012*
C Jesus of Nazareth, which was a ... Lk 24:19 *4012*
scriptures the things *c* himself ... Lk 24:27 *4012*
prophets, and in the psalms, *c* me ... Lk 24:44 *4012*
murmuring among the people *c* him ... Jn 7:12 *4012*
people murmured such things *c* him ... Jn 7:32 *4012*
the Jews did not believe *c* him ... Jn 9:18 *4012*
to comfort them *c* their brother ... Jn 11:19 *4012*
of David spake before *c* Judas ... Acts 1:16 *4012*
For David speaketh *c* him, I ... Acts 2:25 *1519*
the things *c* the kingdom of God ... Acts 8:12 *4012*
as *c* that he raised him up from ... Acts 13:34 *3754*
the things *c* the kingdom of God ... Acts 19:8 *4012*
enquire any thing *c* other matters ... Acts 19:39 *4012*
whereof they were informed *c* thee ... Acts 21:24 *4012*
not receive thy testimony *c* me ... Acts 22:18 *4012*
something more perfectly *c* him ... Acts 23:15 *4012*
heard him *c* the faith in Christ ... Acts 24:24 *4012*
c the crime laid against him ... Acts 25:16 *4012*
letters out of Judaea *c* thee ... Acts 28:21 *4012*
for as *c* this sect, we know that ... Acts 28:22 *4012*
of God, persuading them *c* Jesus ... Acts 28:23 *4012*
C his Son Jesus Christ our Lord, ... Rom 1:3 *4012*
of whom as *c* the flesh Christ ... Rom 9:5 *2596*
Esaias also crieth *c* Israel ... Rom 9:27 *5228*
As *c* the gospel, they are enemies ... Rom 11:28 *2596*
which is good, and simple *c* evil ... Rom 16:19 *1519*
c him that hath so done this deed ... 1Cor 5:3
Now *c* the things whereof ye wrote ... 1Cor 7:1 *4012*
Now *c* virgins I have no ... 1Cor 7:25 *4012*
As *c* therefore the eating of ... 1Cor 8:4 *4012*
Now *c* spiritual gifts, brethren, ... 1Cor 12:1 *4012*
Now *c* the collection for the ... 1Cor 16:1 *4012*
my partner and fellowhelper *c* you ... 2Cor 8:23 *1519*
I speak as *c* reproach, as though ... 2Cor 11:21 *2596*
That ye put off *c* the former ... Eph 4:22 *2596*
but I speak *c* Christ and the ... Eph 5:32 *1519*

C zeal, persecuting the church Phil 3:6 2596
communicated with me as c giving Phil 4:15
and to comfort you c your faith 1Th 3:2 4012
c them which are asleep, that ye 1Th 4:13 4012
will of God in Christ Jesus c you 1Th 5:18 1519
away c faith have made shipwreck 1Ti 1:19 4012
professing have erred c the faith 1Ti 6:21 4012
Who c the truth have erred, 2Ti 2:18 4012
minds, reprobate c the faith 2Ti 3:8 4012
Moses spake nothing c priesthood Heb 7:14 4012
Jacob and Esau c things to come Heb 11:20 4012
and gave commandment c his bones Heb 11:22 4012
think it not strange c the fiery 1Pet 4:12 4012
Lord is not slack c his promise 2Pet 3:9 4314
unto you c them that seduce you 1Jn 2:26 4012

CONCISION
of evil workers, beware of the c Phil 3:2 2699

CONCLUDE
Therefore we c that a man is Rom 3:28 3049

CONCLUDED
c that they observe no such thing Acts 21:25 2919
For God hath c them all in Rom 11:32 4788
scripture hath c all under sin Gal 3:22 4788

CONCLUSION
Let us hear the c of the whole Eccl 12:13 5490

CONCORD
what c hath Christ with Belial 2Cor 6:15 4857

CONCOURSE
crieth in the chief place of c Prov 1:21 1993
we may give an account of this c Acts 19:40 4963

CONCUBINE
And his c, whose name was Reumah, Gen 22:24 6370
and lay with Bilhah his father's c Gen 35:22 6370
Timna was c to Eliphaz Esau's son Gen 36:12 6370
his c that was in Shechem, she Judg 8:31 6370
who took to him a c out of Judg 19:1 6370
his c played the whore against Judg 19:2 6370
rose up to depart, he, and his c Judg 19:9 6370
saddled, his c also was with him Judg 19:10 6370
is my daughter a maiden, and his c Judg 19:24 6370
so the man took his c, and brought Judg 19:25 6370
the woman his c was fallen down Judg 19:27 6370
a knife, and laid hold on his c Judg 19:29 6370
belongeth to Benjamin, I and my c Judg 20:4 6370
my c have they forced, that she Judg 20:5 6370
And I took my c, and cut her in Judg 20:6 6370
And Saul had a c, whose name was 2Sa 3:7 6370
thou gone in unto my father's c 2Sa 3:7 6370
of Aiah, the c of Saul, had done 2Sa 21:11 6370
the sons of Keturah, Abraham's c 1Chr 1:32 6370
And Ephah, Caleb's c, bare Haran, 1Chr 2:46 6370
Maachah, Caleb's c, bare Sheber, 1Chr 2:48 6370
(but his c the Aramitess bare 1Chr 7:14 6370

CONCUBINES
But unto the sons of the c Gen 25:6 6370
And David took him more c 2Sa 5:13 6370
king left ten women, which were c 2Sa 15:16 6370
Go in unto thy father's c 2Sa 16:21 6370
went in unto his father's c in 2Sa 16:22 6370
thy wives, and the lives of thy c 2Sa 19:5 6370
the king took the ten women his c 2Sa 20:3 6370
princesses, and three hundred c 1Kin 11:3 6370
David, beside the sons of the c 1Chr 3:9 6370
above all his wives and his c 2Chr 11:21 6370
eighteen wives, and threescore c 2Chr 11:21 6370
chamberlain, which kept the c Est 2:14 6370
threescore queens, and fourscore c Song 6:8 6370
yea, the queens and the c, and they Song 6:9 6370
his princes, his wives, and his c Dan 5:2 3904
his princes, his wives, and his c Dan 5:3 3904
and thy lords, thy wives, and thy c Dan 5:23 3904

CONCUPISCENCE
wrought in me all manner of c Rom 7:8 1939
inordinate affection, evil c Col 3:5 1939
Not in the lust of c, even as the 1Th 4:5 1939

CONDEMN
and whom the judges shall c Ex 22:9 7561
the righteous, and c the wicked Deut 25:1 7561
myself, mine own mouth shall c me Job 9:20 7561
I will say unto God, Do not c me Job 10:2 7561
wilt thou c him that is most just Job 34:17 7561
wilt thou c me, that thou mayest Job 40:8 7561
nor c him when he is judged Ps 37:33 7561
and c the innocent blood Ps 94:21 7561
him from those that c his soul Ps 109:31 8199
a man of wicked devices will he c Prov 12:2 7561
who is he that shall c me Is 50:9 7561
thee in judgment thou shalt c Is 54:17 7561
this generation, and shall c it Mt 12:41 2632
this generation, and shall c it Mt 12:42 2632
they shall c him to death, Mt 20:18 2632
they shall c him to death, and Mk 10:33 2632
c not, and ye shall not be Lk 6:37 2618
men of this generation, and c them Lk 11:31 2632
this generation, and shall c it Lk 11:32 2632
Son into the world to c the world Jn 3:17 2919
unto her, Neither do I c thee Jn 8:11 2632
I speak not this to c you 2Cor 7:3 2633
For if our heart c us, God is 1Jn 3:20 2607
Beloved, if our heart c us not 1Jn 3:21 2607

CONDEMNATION
seeing thou art in the same c Lk 23:40 2917
And this is the c, that light is Jn 3:19 2920
life, and shall not come into c Jn 5:24 2920
for the judgment was by one to c Rom 5:16 2631
judgment came upon all men to c Rom 5:18 2631
There is therefore now no c to Rom 8:1 2631
that ye come not together unto c 1Cor 11:34 2917
if the ministration of c be glory 2Cor 3:9 2633
he fall into the c of the devil 1Ti 3:6 2917
we shall receive the greater c Jas 3:1 2917
lest ye fall into c Jas 5:12 5272
before of old ordained to this c Jude 4 2917

CONDEMNED
c the land in an hundred talents 2Chr 36:3 6064
found no answer, and yet had c Job Job 32:3 7561
he shall be judged, let him be c Ps 109:7
the c in the house of their god Amos 2:8 6064
ye would not have c the guiltless Mt 12:7 2613
and by thy words thou shalt be c Mt 12:37 2613
him, when he saw that he was c Mt 27:3 2632
they all c him to be guilty of Mk 14:64 2632
condemn not, and ye shall not be c Lk 6:37 2613
delivered him to be c to death Lk 24:20
He that believeth on him is not c Jn 3:18 2919
that believeth not is c already Jn 3:18 2919
hath no man c thee Jn 8:10 2632
and for sin, c sin in the flesh Rom 8:3 2632
we should not be c with the world 1Cor 11:32 2632
Sound speech, that cannot be c Titus 2:8 176
and sinneth, being c of himself Titus 3:11 843
by the which he c the world Heb 11:7 2632
Ye have c and killed the just Jas 5:6 2613
another, brethren, lest ye be c Jas 5:9 2632
Gomorrah into ashes c them with 2Pet 2:6 2632

CONDEMNEST
judgest another, thou c thyself Rom 2:1 2632

CONDEMNETH
Thine own mouth c thee, and not I Job 15:6 7561
he that c the just, even they Prov 17:15 7561
Who is he that c Rom 8:34 2632
Happy is he that c not himself in Rom 14:22 4314

CONDEMNING
c the wicked, to bring his way 1Kin 8:32 7561
they have fulfilled them in c him Acts 13:27 2919

CONDESCEND
but c to men of low estate Rom 12:16 4879

CONDITION
On this c will I make a covenant 1Sa 11:2

CONDITIONS
ambassage, and desireth c of peace Lk 14:32 4314

CONDUCT
to c the king over Jordan 2Sa 19:15 5674
the king, to c him over Jordan 2Sa 19:31 7971
but c him forth in peace, that he 1Cor 16:11 4311

CONDUCTED
the people of Judah c the king 2Sa 19:40 5674
they that c Paul brought him unto Acts 17:15 2525

CONDUIT
stood by the c of the upper pool, 2Kin 18:17 8585
and how he made a pool, and a c 2Kin 20:20 8585
at the end of the c of the upper Is 7:3 8585
he stood by the c of the upper Is 36:2 8585

CONEY
And the c, because he cheweth the Lev 11:5 8227
the camel, and the hare, and the c Deut 14:7 8227

CONFECTION
perfume, a c after the art of the Ex 30:35 7545

CONFECTIONARIES
will take your daughters to be c 1Sa 8:13 7543

CONFEDERACY
Say ye not, A c, to all them to Is 8:12 7195
whom this people shall say, A c Is 8:12 7195
All the men of thy c have brought Obad 7 1285

CONFEDERATE
and these were c with Abram Gen 14:13
they are c against thee Ps 83:5
saying, Syria is c with Ephraim Is 7:2 5117

CONFERENCE
somewhat in c added nothing to me Gal 2:6 4323

CONFERRED
he c with Joab the son of Zeruiah 1Kin 1:7
council, they c among themselves, Acts 4:15 4820
when he had c with the council, Acts 25:12 4814
immediately I c not with flesh and Gal 1:16 4323

CONFESS
that he shall c that he hath Lev 5:5 3034
c over him all the iniquities of Lev 16:21 3034
If they shall c their iniquity, Lev 26:40 3034
Then they shall c their sin which Num 5:7 3034
c thy name, and pray, and make 1Kin 8:33 3034
c thy name, and turn from their 1Kin 8:35 3034
c thy name, and pray and make 2Chr 6:24 3034
c thy name, and turn from their 2Chr 6:26 3034
c the sins of the children of Neh 1:6 3034
Then will I also c unto thee that Job 40:14 3034
I will c my transgressions unto Ps 32:5 3034
therefore shall c me before men Mt 10:32 3670
him will I c also before my Mt 10:32 3670
Whosoever shall c me before men Lk 12:8 3670
also c before the angels of God Lk 12:8 3670
any man did c that he was Christ Jn 9:22 3670
the Pharisees they did not c him Jn 12:42 3670
but the Pharisees c both Acts 23:8 3670
But this I c unto thee, that Acts 24:14 3670
That if thou shalt c with thy Rom 10:9 3670
and every tongue shall c to God Rom 14:11 1843
For this cause I will c to thee Rom 15:9 1843
that every tongue should c that Phil 2:11 1843
C your faults one to another, and Jas 5:16 1843
If we c our sins, he is faithful 1Jn 1:9 3670
Whosoever shall c that Jesus is 1Jn 4:15 3670
who c not that Jesus Christ is 2Jn 7 3670
but I will c his name before my Rev 3:5 1843

CONFESSED
Ezra had prayed, and when he had c Ezr 10:1 3034
c their sins, and the iniquities Neh 9:2 3034
and another fourth part they c Neh 9:3 3034
And he c, and denied not Jn 1:20 3670
but c, I am not the Christ Jn 1:20 3670
And many that believed came, and c Acts 19:18 1843
c that they were strangers and Heb 11:13 3670

CONFESSETH
but whoso c and forsaketh them Prov 28:13 3034
Every spirit that c that Jesus 1Jn 4:2 3670
every spirit that c not that 1Jn 4:3 3670

CONFESSING
c my sin and the sin of my people Dan 9:20 3034
of him in Jordan, c their sins Mt 3:6 1843
the river of Jordan, c their sins Mk 1:5 1843

CONFESSION
God of Israel, and make c unto him Josh 7:19 8426
making c to the LORD God of their 2Chr 30:22 3034
Now therefore make c unto the Ezr 10:11 8426
the LORD my God, and made my c Dan 9:4 3034
with the mouth c is made unto Rom 10:10 3670
Pontius Pilate witnessed a good c 1Ti 6:13 3671

CONFIDENCE
men of Shechem put their c in him Judg 9:26 982
What c is this wherein thou 2Kin 18:19 986
Is not this thy fear, thy c Job 4:6 3690
His c shall be rooted out of his Job 18:14 4009
to the fine gold, Thou art my c Job 31:24 4009
who art the c of all the ends of Ps 65:5 4009
in the LORD than to put c in man Ps 118:8 982
the LORD than to put c in princes Ps 118:9 982
For the LORD shall be thy c Prov 3:26 3689
the fear of the LORD is strong c Prov 14:26 4009
the strength of the c thereof Prov 21:22 4009
C in an unfaithful man in time of Prov 25:19 4009
in c shall be your strength Is 30:15 985
What c is this wherein thou Is 36:4 986
was ashamed of Beth-el their c Jer 48:13 4009
yea, they shall dwell with c Eze 28:26 983
more the c of the house of Israel Eze 29:16 4009
a friend, put ye not c in a guide Mic 7:5 982
the Lord Jesus Christ, with all c Acts 28:31 3954
in this c I was minded to come 2Cor 1:15 4006
having c in you all, that my joy 2Cor 2:3 3982
I have c in you in all things 2Cor 7:16 2292
upon the great c which I have in 2Cor 8:22 4006
when I am present with that c 2Cor 10:2 4006
foolishly, in this c of boasting 2Cor 11:17 5287
I have c in you through the Lord, Gal 5:10 3982
access with c by the faith of him Eph 3:12 4006
And having this c, I know that I Phil 1:25 3982
Jesus, and have no c in the flesh Phil 3:3 3982
I might also have c in the flesh Phil 3:4 4006
we have c in the Lord touching 2Th 3:4 3982
Having c in thy obedience I wrote Philem 21 3982
are we, if we hold fast the c Heb 3:6 3954
of our c stedfast unto the end Heb 3:14 5287
Cast not away therefore your c Heb 10:35 3954
he shall appear, we may have c 1Jn 2:28 3954
us not, then have we c toward God 1Jn 3:21 3954
this is the c that we have in him 1Jn 5:14 3954

CONFIDENCES
for the LORD hath rejected thy c Jer 2:37 4009

CONFIDENT
against me, in this will I be c Ps 27:3 982
but the fool rageth, and is c Prov 14:16 982
art c that thou thyself art a Rom 2:19 3982
Therefore we are always c 2Cor 5:6 2292
We are c, I say, and willing 2Cor 5:8 2292
ashamed in this same c boasting 2Cor 9:4 5287
Being c of this very thing, that Phil 1:6 3982
waxing c by my bonds, are much Phil 1:14 3982

CONFIDENTLY
one hour after another c affirmed Lk 22:59 1340

CONFIRM
changing, for to c all things Ruth 4:7 6965
in after thee, and c thy words 1Kin 1:14 4390
him to c the kingdom in his hand 2Kin 15:19 2388
to c this second letter of Purim Est 9:29 6965
To c these days of Purim in their Est 9:31 6965
thou didst c thine inheritance Ps 68:9 3559
weak hands, and c the feeble knees Is 35:3 553
hope that they would c the word Eze 13:6 6965
he shall c the covenant with many Dan 9:27 1396
the Mede, even I, stood to c Dan 11:1 2388
to c the promises made unto the Rom 15:8 950
Who shall also c you unto the end 1Cor 1:8 950
ye would c your love toward him 2Cor 2:8 2964

CONFIRMATION
c of the gospel, ye all are Phil 1:7 951
an oath for c is to them an end Heb 6:16 951

CONFIRMED
For thou hast c to thyself thy 2Sa 7:24 3559
as the kingdom was c in his hand 2Kin 14:5 2388
LORD had c him king over Israel 1Chr 14:2 3559
hath c the same to Jacob for a 1Chr 16:17 5975
the decree of Esther c these Est 9:32 6965
c the same unto Jacob for a law, Ps 105:10 5975
he hath c his words, which he Dan 9:12 6965
with many words, and c them Acts 15:32 1991
testimony of Christ was c in you 1Cor 1:6 950
a man's covenant, yet if it be c Gal 3:15 2964
that was c before of God in Gal 3:17 4300
was c unto us by them that heard Heb 2:3 950
of his counsel, c it by an oath Heb 6:17 3315

CONFIRMETH
he c them, because he held his Num 30:14 6965
Cursed be he that c not all the Deut 27:26 6965
That c the word of his servant, Is 44:26 6965

CONFIRMING
c the word with signs following Mk 16:20 *950*
C the souls of the disciples, and Acts 14:22 *1991*
Syria and Cilicia, c the churches Acts 15:41 *1991*

CONFISCATION
or to c of goods, or to Ezr 7:26 6065

CONFLICT
Having the same c which ye saw in Phil 1:30 *73*
knew what great c I have for you Col 2:1 *73*

CONFORMABLE
being made c unto his death Phil 3:10 *4832*

CONFORMED
to be c to the image of his Son Rom 8:29 *4832*
And be not c to this world Rom 12:2 *4964*

CONFOUND
there c their language, that they Gen 11:7 1101
because the LORD did there c the Gen 11:9 1101
lest I c thee before them Jer 1:17 2865
things of the world to c the wise 1Cor 1:27 *2617*
to c the things which are mighty 1Cor 1:27 *2617*

CONFOUNDED
power, they were dismayed and c 2Kin 19:26 954
They were c because they had Job 6:20 954
trusted in thee, and were not c Ps 22:5 954
Let them be c and put to shame Ps 35:4 954
c together that seek after my Ps 40:14 2659
that seek thee be c for my sake Ps 69:6 3637
c that seek after my soul Ps 70:2 2659
Let them be c and consumed that Ps 71:13 954
for they are c, for they are Ps 71:24 954
Let them be c and troubled for Ps 83:17 954
C be all they that serve graven Ps 97:7 954
Let them all be c and turned back Ps 129:5 954
ye shall be c for the gardens Is 1:29 2659
that weave networks, shall be c Is 19:9 954
Then the moon shall be c, and the Is 24:23 2659
power, they were dismayed and c Is 37:27 954
thee shall be ashamed and c Is 41:11 3637
They shall be ashamed, and also c Is 45:16 3637
ashamed nor c world without end Is 45:17 3637
therefore shall I not be c Is 50:7 3637
neither be thou c Is 54:4 3637
we are greatly c, because we have Jer 9:19 954
every founder is c by the graven Jer 10:14 3001
they were ashamed and c, and Jer 14:3 3637
she hath been ashamed and c Jer 15:9 2659
Let them be c that persecute me, Jer 17:18 954
but let not me be c Jer 17:18 954
and c for all thy wickedness Jer 22:22 3637
I was ashamed, yea, even c Jer 31:19 3637
The daughter of Egypt shall be c Jer 46:24 3001
Kiriathaim is c and taken Jer 48:1 3001
Misgab is c and dismayed Jer 48:1 3001
Moab is c Jer 48:20 3001
Hamath is c, and Arpad Jer 49:23 954
say, Babylon is taken, Bel is c Jer 50:2 3001
her idols are c, her images are Jer 50:2 3001
Your mother shall be sore c Jer 50:12 954
every founder is c by the graven Jer 51:17 3001
and her whole land shall be c Jer 51:47 954
We are c, because we have heard Jer 51:51 954
yea, be thou c also, and bear thy Eze 16:52 954
mayest be c in all that thou hast Eze 16:54 3637
thou mayest remember, and be c Eze 16:63 954
c for your own ways, O house of Eze 36:32 3637
be ashamed, and the diviners c Mic 3:7 2659
see and be c at all their might Mic 7:16 954
the riders on horses shall be c Zec 10:5 3001
came together, and were c, because Acts 2:6 *4797*
c the Jews which dwelt at Acts 9:22 *4797*
believeth on him shall not be c 1Pet 2:6 *2617*

CONFUSED
of the warrior is with c noise Is 9:5 7494
for the assembly was c Acts 19:32 *4797*

CONFUSION
it is c Lev 18:23 8397
they have wrought c Lev 20:12 8397
the son of Jesse to thine own c 1Sa 20:30 1322
unto the c of thy mother's 1Sa 20:30 1322
to c of face, as it is this day Ezr 9:7 1322
I am full of c Job 10:15 7036
brought to c that devise my hurt Ps 35:4 2659
brought to c together that Ps 35:26 2659
My c is continually before me, and Ps 44:15 3639
be turned backward, and put to c Ps 70:2 3637
let me never be put to c Ps 71:1 954
cover themselves with their own c Ps 109:29 1322
The city of c is broken down Is 24:10 8414
in the shadow of Egypt your c Is 30:3 3639
stretch out upon it the line of c Is 34:11 8414
their molten images are wind and c Is 41:29 8414
they shall go to c together that Is 45:16 3639
for c they shall rejoice in their Is 61:7 3639
our shame, and our c covereth us Jer 3:25 3639
to the c of their own faces Jer 7:19 1322
their everlasting c shall never Jer 20:11 3639
unto thee, but unto us c of faces Dan 9:7 1322
O Lord, to us belongeth c of face Dan 9:8 1322
the whole city was filled with c Acts 19:29 *4799*
For God is not the author of c 1Cor 14:33 *181*
envying and strife is, there is c Jas 3:16 *181*

CONGEALED
the depths were c in the heart of Ex 15:8 7087

CONGRATULATE
to c him, because he had fought 1Chr 18:10 1288

CONGREGATION
Speak ye unto all the c of Israel Ex 12:3 5712
the whole assembly of the c of Ex 12:6 5712
be cut off from the c of Israel Ex 12:19 5712
All the c of Israel shall keep it Ex 12:47 5712
all the c of the children of Ex 16:1 5712
the whole c of the children of Ex 16:2 5712
Say unto all the c of the Ex 16:9 5712
whole c of the children of Israel Ex 16:10 5712
and all the rulers of the c came Ex 16:22 5712
all the c of the children of Ex 17:1 5712
of the c without the vail Ex 27:21 4150
in unto the tabernacle of the c Ex 28:43 4150
door of the tabernacle of the c Ex 29:4 4150
before the tabernacle of the c Ex 29:10 4150
door of the tabernacle of the c Ex 29:11 4150
into the tabernacle of the c to Ex 29:30 4150
door of the tabernacle of the c Ex 29:32 4150
of the c before the LORD Ex 29:42 4150
sanctify the tabernacle of the c Ex 29:44 4150
of the tabernacle of the c Ex 30:16 4150
between the tabernacle of the c Ex 30:18 4150
go into the tabernacle of the c Ex 30:20 4150
the tabernacle of the c therewith Ex 30:26 4150
in the tabernacle of the c Ex 30:36 4150
The tabernacle of the c, and the Ex 31:7 4150
called it the Tabernacle of the c Ex 33:7 4150
out unto the tabernacle of the c Ex 33:7 4150
rulers of the c returned unto him Ex 34:31 5712
Moses gathered all the c of the Ex 35:1 5712
Moses spake unto all the c of the Ex 35:4 5712
all the c of the children of Ex 35:20 5712
work of the tabernacle of the c Ex 35:21 4150
door of the tabernacle of the c Ex 38:8 4150
of the c was an hundred talents Ex 38:25 5712
door of the tabernacle of the c Ex 38:30 4150
of the tent of the c finished Ex 39:32 4150
tabernacle, for the tent of the c Ex 39:40 4150
tabernacle of the tent of the c Ex 40:2 4150
tabernacle of the tent of the c Ex 40:6 4150
laver between the tent of the c Ex 40:7 4150
door of the tabernacle of the c Ex 40:12 4150
the table in the tent of the c Ex 40:22 4150
candlestick in the tent of the c Ex 40:24 4150
the tent of the c before the vail Ex 40:26 4150
tabernacle of the tent of the c Ex 40:29 4150
laver between the tent of the c Ex 40:30 4150
they went into the tent of the c Ex 40:32 4150
a cloud covered the tent of the c Ex 40:34 4150
to enter into the tent of the c Ex 40:35 4150
out of the tabernacle of the c Lev 1:1 4150
of the c before the LORD Lev 1:3 4150
door of the tabernacle of the c Lev 1:5 4150
door of the tabernacle of the c Lev 3:2 4150
it before the tabernacle of the c Lev 3:8 4150
it before the tabernacle of the c Lev 3:13 4150
of the c before the LORD Lev 4:4 4150
it to the tabernacle of the c Lev 4:5 4150
is in the tabernacle of the c Lev 4:7 4150
door of the tabernacle of the c Lev 4:7 4150
if the whole c of Israel sin Lev 4:13 5712
then the c shall offer a young Lev 4:14 6951
before the tabernacle of the c Lev 4:14 4150
the elders of the c shall lay Lev 4:15 5712
blood to the tabernacle of the c Lev 4:16 4150
is in the tabernacle of the c Lev 4:18 4150
door of the tabernacle of the c Lev 4:18 4150
it is a sin offering for the c Lev 4:21 6951
of the c they shall eat it Lev 6:16 4150
court of the tabernacle of the c Lev 6:26 4150
into the tabernacle of the c to Lev 6:30 4150
gather thou all the c together Lev 8:3 5712
door of the tabernacle of the c Lev 8:3 4150
door of the tabernacle of the c Lev 8:4 4150
And Moses said unto the c, This is Lev 8:5 5712
door of the tabernacle of the c Lev 8:31 4150
tabernacle of the c in seven days Lev 8:33 4150
of the tabernacle of the c day Lev 8:35 4150
before the tabernacle of the c Lev 9:5 4150
all the c drew near and stood Lev 9:5 5712
went into the tabernacle of the c Lev 9:23 4150
door of the tabernacle of the c Lev 10:7 4150
go into the tabernacle of the c Lev 10:9 4150
you to bear the iniquity of the c Lev 10:17 5712
door of the tabernacle of the c Lev 12:6 4150
door of the tabernacle of the c Lev 14:11 4150
door of the tabernacle of the c Lev 14:23 4150
door of the tabernacle of the c Lev 15:14 4150
door of the tabernacle of the c Lev 15:29 4150
he shall take of the c of the Lev 16:5 5712
door of the tabernacle of the c Lev 16:7 4150
he do for the tabernacle of the c Lev 16:16 4150
the c when he goeth in to make an Lev 16:17 4150
and for all the c of Israel Lev 16:17 6951
place, and the tabernacle of the c Lev 16:20 4150
come into the tabernacle of the c Lev 16:23 4150
for the tabernacle of the c Lev 16:33 4150
and for all the people of the c Lev 16:33 6951
door of the tabernacle of the c Lev 17:4 4150
door of the tabernacle of the c Lev 17:5 4150
door of the tabernacle of the c Lev 17:6 4150
door of the tabernacle of the c Lev 17:9 4150
Speak unto all the c of the Lev 19:2 5712
door of the tabernacle of the c Lev 19:21 4150
in the tabernacle of the c Lev 24:3 4150
head, and let all the c stone him Lev 24:14 5712
all the c shall certainly stone Lev 24:16 5712
Sinai, in the tabernacle of the c Num 1:1 4150
the c of the children of Israel Num 1:2 5712
These were the renowned of the c Num 1:16 5712
they assembled all the c together Num 1:18 5712
the c of the children of Israel Num 1:53 5712
of the c shall they pitch Num 2:2 4150
Then the tabernacle of the c Num 2:17 4150
the charge of the whole c before Num 3:7 5712
before the tabernacle of the c Num 3:7 4150
of the tabernacle of the c Num 3:8 4150
of the c shall be the tabernacle Num 3:25 4150
door of the tabernacle of the c Num 3:25 4150
the tabernacle of the c eastward Num 3:38 4150
work in the tabernacle of the c Num 4:3 4150
Kohath in the tabernacle of the c Num 4:4 4150
Kohath in the tabernacle of the c Num 4:15 4150
work in the tabernacle of the c Num 4:23 4150
and the tabernacle of the c Num 4:25 4150
door of the tabernacle of the c Num 4:25 4150
in the tabernacle of the c Num 4:28 4150
work of the tabernacle of the c Num 4:30 4150
in the tabernacle of the c Num 4:31 4150
in the tabernacle of the c Num 4:33 4150
the chief of the c numbered the Num 4:34 5712
work in the tabernacle of the c Num 4:35 4150
in the tabernacle of the c Num 4:37 4150
work in the tabernacle of the c Num 4:39 4150
in the tabernacle of the c Num 4:41 4150
work in the tabernacle of the c Num 4:43 4150
burden in the tabernacle of the c Num 4:47 4150
door of the tabernacle of the c Num 6:10 4150
door of the tabernacle of the c Num 6:13 4150
door of the tabernacle of the c Num 6:18 4150
of the tabernacle of the c Num 7:5 4150
of the c to speak with him Num 7:89 4150
before the tabernacle of the c Num 8:9 4150
of the tabernacle of the c Num 8:15 4150
Israel in the tabernacle of the c Num 8:19 4150
all the c of the children of Num 8:20 5712
tabernacle of the c before Aaron Num 8:22 4150
of the tabernacle of the c Num 8:24 4150
in the tabernacle of the c Num 8:26 4150
door of the tabernacle of the c Num 10:3 4150
But when the c is to be gathered Num 10:7 6951
them unto the tabernacle of the c Num 11:16 4150
unto the tabernacle of the c Num 12:4 4150
to all the c of the children of Num 13:26 5712
word unto them, and unto all the c Num 13:26 5712
all the c lifted up their voice Num 14:1 5712
the whole c said unto them, Would Num 14:2 5712
the c of the children of Israel Num 14:5 5712
But all the c bade stone them Num 14:10 5712
in the tabernacle of the c before Num 14:10 4150
shall I bear with this evil c Num 14:27 5712
surely do it unto all this evil c Num 14:35 5712
made all the c to murmur against Num 14:36 5712
shall be both for you of the c Num 15:15 6951
without the knowledge of the c Num 15:24 5712
that all the c shall offer one Num 15:24 5712
the c of the children of Israel Num 15:25 5712
the c of the children of Israel Num 15:26 5712
Moses and Aaron, and unto all the c Num 15:33 5712
all the c shall stone him with Num 15:35
all the c brought him without the Num 15:36 5712
of the assembly, famous in the c Num 16:2 4150
you, seeing all the c are holy Num 16:3 5712
above the c of the LORD Num 16:3 6951
you from the c of Israel Num 16:9 5712
to stand before the c to minister Num 16:9 5712
tabernacle of the c with Moses Num 16:18 4150
Korah gathered all the c against Num 16:19 5712
door of the tabernacle of the c Num 16:19 4150
the LORD appeared unto all the c Num 16:19 5712
yourselves from among this c Num 16:21 5712
wilt thou be wroth with all the c Num 16:22 5712
Speak unto the c, saying, Get you Num 16:24 5712
And he spake unto the c, saying, Num 16:26 5712
and they perished from among the c Num 16:33 6951
the c of the children of Israel Num 16:41 5712
when the c was gathered against Num 16:42 5712
toward the tabernacle of the c Num 16:42 4150
before the tabernacle of the c Num 16:43 4150
Get you up from among this c Num 16:45 5712
incense, and go quickly unto the c Num 16:46 5712
and ran into the midst of the c Num 16:47 6951
door of the tabernacle of the c Num 16:50 4150
of the c before the testimony Num 17:4 4150
charge of the tabernacle of the c Num 18:4 4150
of the tabernacle of the c Num 18:6 4150
of the tabernacle of the c Num 18:21 4150
come nigh the tabernacle of the c Num 18:22 4150
of the tabernacle of the c Num 18:23 4150
in the tabernacle of the c Num 18:31 4150
tabernacle of the c seven times Num 19:4 4150
it shall be kept for the c of the Num 19:9 5712
shall be cut off from among the c Num 19:20 6951
of Israel, even the whole c Num 20:1 5712
And there was no water for the c Num 20:2 5712
up the c of the LORD into this Num 20:4 6951
door of the tabernacle of the c Num 20:6 4150
so thou shalt give the c and their Num 20:8 5712
Aaron gathered the c together Num 20:10 6951
the c drank, and their beasts also Num 20:11 5712
ye shall not bring this c into Num 20:12 6951
of Israel, even the whole c Num 20:22 5712
Hor in the sight of all the c Num 20:27 5712
when all the c saw that Aaron was Num 20:29 5712
in the sight of all the c of the Num 25:6 5712
door of the tabernacle of the c Num 25:6 4150
it, he rose up from among the c Num 25:7 5712
Take the sum of all the c of the Num 26:2 5712
which were famous in the c Num 26:9 5712
before the princes and all the c Num 27:2 5712
door of the tabernacle of the c Num 27:2 4150
of Zin, in the strife of the c Num 27:14 5712
all flesh, set a man over the c Num 27:16 5712

that the c of the LORD be not as Num 27:17 5712
the priest, and before all the c Num 27:19 5712
that all the c of the children of Num 27:20 5712
Israel with him, even all the c Num 27:21 5712
the priest, and before all the c Num 27:22 5712
unto the c of the children of Num 31:12 5712
and all the princes of the c Num 31:13 5712
a plague among the c of the LORD Num 31:16 5712
and the chief fathers of the c Num 31:26 5712
to battle, and between all the c Num 31:27 5712
the c was three hundred thousand Num 31:43 5712
it into the tabernacle of the c Num 31:54 4150
and unto the princes of the c Num 32:2 5712
LORD smote before the c of Israel Num 32:4 5712
he stand before the c in judgment Num 35:12 5712
Then the c shall judge between Num 35:24 5712
the c shall deliver the slayer Num 35:25 5712
the c shall restore him to the Num 35:25 5712
not enter into the c of the LORD Deut 23:1 6951
not enter into the c of the LORD Deut 23:2 6951
not enter into the c of the LORD Deut 23:2 6951
not enter into the c of the LORD Deut 23:3 6951
into the c of the LORD for ever Deut 23:3 6951
the c of the LORD in their third Deut 23:8 6951
in the tabernacle of the c Deut 31:14 4150
in the tabernacle of the c Deut 31:14 4150
the c of Israel the words of this Deut 31:30 4150
the inheritance of the c of Jacob Deut 33:4 6952
not before all the c of Israel Josh 8:35 6951
princes of the c sware unto them Josh 9:15 5712
because the princes of the c had Josh 9:18 5712
all the c murmured against the Josh 9:18 5712
the princes said unto all the c Josh 9:19 5712
drawers of water unto all the c Josh 9:21 5712
and drawers of water for the c Josh 9:27 5712
the whole c of the children of Josh 18:1 5712
up the tabernacle of the c there Josh 18:1 4150
door of the tabernacle of the c Josh 19:51 4150
stand before the c for judgment Josh 20:6 5712
until he stood before the c Josh 20:9 5712
the whole c of the children of Josh 22:12 5712
saith the whole c of the LORD Josh 22:16 5712
was a plague in the c of the LORD Josh 22:17 5712
wroth with the whole c of Israel Josh 22:18 5712
wrath fell on all the c of Israel Josh 22:20 5712
priest, and the princes of the c Josh 22:30 5712
the c was gathered together as Judg 20:1 5712
not up with the c unto the LORD Judg 21:5 6951
the c sent thither twelve Judg 21:10 5712
the whole c sent some to speak to Judg 21:13 5712
Then the elders of the c said Judg 21:16 5712
door of the tabernacle of the c 1Sa 2:22 4150
LORD, and the tabernacle of the c 1Kin 8:4 4150
all the c of Israel, that were 1Kin 8:5 5712
and blessed all the c of Israel 1Kin 8:14 6951
all the c of Israel stood 1Kin 8:14 6951
presence of all the c of Israel 1Kin 8:22 6951
blessed all the c of Israel with 1Kin 8:55 6951
and all Israel with him, a great c 1Kin 8:65 6951
all the c of Israel came, and 1Kin 12:3 6951
sent and called him unto the c 1Kin 12:20 5712
tabernacle of the c with singing 1Chr 6:32 4150
door of the tabernacle of the c 1Chr 9:21 4150
said unto all the c of Israel 1Chr 13:2 6951
all the c said that they would do 1Chr 13:4 6951
charge of the tabernacle of the c 1Chr 23:32 4150
of all Israel the c of the LORD 1Chr 28:8 6951
the king said unto all the c 1Chr 29:1 6951
blessed the LORD before all the c 1Chr 29:10 6951
And David said to all the c 1Chr 29:20 6951
all the c blessed the LORD God of 1Chr 29:20 6951
all the c with him, went to the 2Chr 1:3 6951
the tabernacle of the c of God 2Chr 1:3 4150
Solomon and the c sought unto it 2Chr 1:5 6951
was at the tabernacle of the c 2Chr 1:6 4150
before the tabernacle of the c 2Chr 1:13 4150
ark, and the tabernacle of the c 2Chr 5:5 4150
all the c of Israel that were 2Chr 5:6 5712
and blessed the whole c of Israel 2Chr 6:3 6951
all the c of Israel stood 2Chr 6:3 6951
presence of all the c of Israel 2Chr 6:12 6951
knees before all the c of Israel 2Chr 6:13 6951
Israel with him, a very great c 2Chr 7:8 6951
stood in the c of Judah and 2Chr 20:5 6951
of the LORD in the midst of the c 2Chr 20:14 6951
all the c made a covenant with 2Chr 23:3 6951
of the c of Israel, for the 2Chr 24:6 6951
before the princes and all the c 2Chr 28:14 6951
offering before the king and the c 2Chr 29:23 6951
all the c worshipped, and the 2Chr 29:28 6951
the c brought in sacrifices and 2Chr 29:31 6951
offerings, which the c brought 2Chr 29:32 6951
all the c in Jerusalem, to keep 2Chr 30:2 6951
pleased the king and all the c 2Chr 30:4 6951
the second month, a very great c 2Chr 30:13 6951
in the c that were not sanctified 2Chr 30:17 6951
give to the c a thousand bullocks 2Chr 30:24 6951
gave to the c a thousand bullocks 2Chr 30:24 6951
all the c of Judah, with the 2Chr 30:25 6951
all the c that came out of Israel 2Chr 30:25 6951
daughters, through all the c 2Chr 31:18 6951
The whole c together was forty and Ezr 2:64 6951
of Israel a very great c of men Ezr 10:1 6951
himself separated from the c of Ezr 10:8 6951
Then all the c answered and said Ezr 10:12 6951
now our rulers of all the c stand Ezr 10:14 6951
And all the c said, Amen, and Neh 5:13 6951
The whole c together was forty and Neh 7:66 6951
the law before the c both of men Neh 8:2 6951
all the c of them that were come Neh 8:17 6951
come into the c of God for ever Neh 13:1 6951
For the c of hypocrites shall be Job 15:34 5712
I stood up, and I cried in the c Job 30:28 6951
sinners in the c of the righteous Ps 1:5 5712
So shall the c of the people Ps 7:7 5712
midst of the c will I praise thee Ps 22:22 6951
shall be of thee in the great c Ps 22:25 6951
I have hated the c of evildoers Ps 26:5 6951
give thee thanks in the great c Ps 35:18 6951
righteousness in the great c Ps 40:9 6951
and thy truth from the great c Ps 40:10 6951
indeed speak righteousness, O c Ps 58:1 482
Thy c hath dwelt therein Ps 68:10 2416
Remember thy c, which thou hast Ps 74:2 5712
forget not the c of thy poor for Ps 74:19 2416
the c I will judge uprightly Ps 75:2 4150
standeth in the c of the mighty Ps 82:1 5712
also in the c of the saints Ps 89:5 6951
him also in the c of the people Ps 107:32 6951
of the upright, and in the c Ps 111:1 5712
and his praise in the c of saints Ps 149:1 6951
in all evil in the midst of the c Prov 5:14 6951
shall remain in the c of the dead Prov 21:16 6951
be shewed before the whole c Prov 26:26 6951
sit also upon the mount of the c Is 14:13 4150
hear, ye nations, and know, O c Jer 6:18 5712
their c shall be established Jer 30:20 5712
they should not enter into thy c Lam 1:10 6951
them, as their c hath heard Hos 7:12 5712
Gather the people, sanctify the c Joel 2:16 6951
cord by lot in the c of the LORD Mic 2:5 6951
Now when the c was broken up, Acts 13:43 *4865*

CONGREGATIONS
in the c will I bless the LORD Ps 26:12 4721
Bless ye God in the c, even the Ps 68:26 4721
roar in the midst of thy c Ps 74:4 4150

CONIAH (*co-ni'-ah*) See JEHOIACHIN. *Another name for Jehoiachin.*
though C the son of Jehoiakim Jer 22:24 3659
Is this man C a despised broken Jer 22:28 3659
instead of C the son of Jehoiakim Jer 37:1 3659

CONIES
and the rocks for the c Ps 104:18 8226
The c are but a feeble folk, yet Prov 30:26 8226

CONONIAH (*co-no-ni'-ah*) See CONANIAH. *A Levite during Hezekiah's time.*
over which C the Levite was ruler 2Chr 31:12 3562
overseers under the hand of C 2Chr 31:13 3562

CONQUER
he went forth conquering, and to c Rev 6:2 *3528*

CONQUERING
and he went forth c, and to conquer Rev 6:2 *3528*

CONQUERORS
than c through him that loved us Rom 8:37 *5245*

CONSCIENCE
being convicted by their own c Jn 8:9 *4893*
I have lived in all good c before Acts 23:1 *4893*
to have always a c void of Acts 24:16 *4893*
their c also bearing witness, and Rom 2:15 *4893*
my c also bearing me witness in Rom 9:1 *4893*
for wrath, but also for c sake Rom 13:5 *4893*
for some with c of the idol unto 1Cor 8:7 *4893*
their c being weak is defiled 1Cor 8:7 *4893*
shall not the c of him which is 1Cor 8:10 *4893*
brethren, and wound their weak c 1Cor 8:12 *4893*
asking no question for c sake 1Cor 10:25 *4893*
asking no question for c sake 1Cor 10:27 *4893*
that shewed it, and for c sake 1Cor 10:28 *4893*
C, I say, not thine own, but of 1Cor 10:29 *4893*
liberty judged of another man's c 1Cor 10:29 *4893*
is this, the testimony of our c 2Cor 1:12 *4893*
every man's c in the sight of God 2Cor 4:2 *4893*
of a pure heart, and of a good c 1Ti 1:5 *4893*
Holding faith, and a good c 1Ti 1:19 *4893*
mystery of the faith in a pure c 1Ti 3:9 *4893*
having their c seared with a hot 1Ti 4:2 *4893*
from my forefathers with pure c 2Ti 1:3 *4893*
even their mind and c is defiled Titus 1:15 *4893*
perfect, as pertaining to the c Heb 9:9 *4893*
purge your c from dead works to Heb 9:14 *4893*
should have had no more c of sins Heb 10:2 *4893*
hearts sprinkled from an evil c Heb 10:22 *4893*
for we trust we have a good c Heb 13:18 *4893*
if a man for c toward God endure 1Pet 2:19 *4893*
Having a good c 1Pet 3:16 *4893*
the answer of a good c toward God 1Pet 3:21 *4893*

CONSCIENCES
also are made manifest in your c 2Cor 5:11 *4893*

CONSECRATE
make Aaron's garments to c him Ex 28:3 6942
c them, and sanctify them, that Ex 28:41
and thou shalt c Aaron and his sons Ex 29:9
the atonement was made, to c Ex 29:33
seven days shalt thou c them Ex 29:35
c them, that they may minister Ex 30:30 6942
C yourselves to day to the LORD, Ex 32:29
for seven days shall he c you Lev 8:33
whom he shall c to minister in Lev 16:32
he shall c unto the LORD the days Num 6:12 5144
who then is willing to c his 1Chr 29:5
so that whosoever cometh to c 2Chr 13:9
and they shall c themselves Eze 43:26
I will c their gain unto the LORD Mic 4:13 2763

CONSECRATED
therein, and to be c in them Ex 29:29
that is c to put on the garments, Lev 21:10
whom he c to minister in the Num 3:3
and iron, are c unto the LORD Josh 6:19 6944
c one of his sons, who became his Judg 17:5
And Micah c the Levite Judg 17:12
he c him, and he became one of the 1Kin 13:33
that are c to burn incense 2Chr 26:18 6942
Now ye have c yourselves unto the 2Chr 29:31
the c things were six hundred 2Chr 29:33 6942
were c unto the LORD their God 2Chr 31:6 6942
feasts of the LORD that were c Ezr 3:5 6942
the Son, who is c for evermore Heb 7:28 *5048*
way, which he hath c for us Heb 10:20 *1457*

CONSECRATION
for it is a ram of c Ex 29:22 4394
breast of the ram of Aaron's c Ex 29:26 4394
is heaved up, of the ram of the c Ex 29:27 4394
thou shalt take the ram of the c Ex 29:31 4394
the other ram, the ram of c Lev 8:22 4394
for of the ram of c it was Moses' Lev 8:29 4394
the days of your c be at an end Lev 8:33 4394
because the c of his God is upon Num 6:7 5145
he hath defiled the head of his c Num 6:9 5145

CONSECRATIONS
And if ought of the flesh of the c Ex 29:34 4394
trespass offering, and of the c Lev 7:37 4394
they were c for a sweet savour Lev 8:28 4394
bread that is in the basket of c Lev 8:31 4394

CONSENT
But in this will we c unto you Gen 34:15 225
Only herein will the men c unto Gen 34:22 225
only let us c unto them, and they Gen 34:23 225
Thou shalt not c unto him Deut 13:8 14
but he would not c Judg 11:17 14
and they came out with one c 1Sa 11:7 376
him, Hearken not unto him, nor c 1Kin 20:8 14
consulted together with one c Ps 83:5 3820
sinners entice thee, c thou not Prov 1:10 14
of priests murder in the way by c Hos 6:9 7926
the LORD, to serve him with one c Zeph 3:9 7926
they all with one c began to make Lk 14:18
I c unto the law that it is good Rom 7:16 *4852*
except it be with c for a time 1Cor 7:5 *4859*
c not to wholesome words, even 1Ti 6:3 *4334*

CONSENTED
the priests c to receive no more 2Kin 12:8 225
So he c to them in this matter, Dan 1:14 8085
The same had not c to the counsel Lk 23:51 *4784*
longer time with them, he c not Acts 18:20 *1962*

CONSENTEDST
a thief, then thou c with him Ps 50:18 7521

CONSENTING
Saul was c unto his death Acts 8:1 *4909*
c unto his death, and kept the Acts 22:20 *4909*

CONSIDER
c that this nation is thy people Ex 33:13 7200
Then the priest shall c Lev 13:13 7200
c it in thine heart, that the Deut 4:39 7725
Thou shalt also c in thine heart Deut 8:5 3045
c the years of many generations Deut 32:7 995
that they would c their latter Deut 32:29 995
now therefore c what ye have to Judg 18:14 3045
c of it, take advice, and speak Judg 19:30 7760
for c how great things he hath 1Sa 12:24 7200
know and c what thou wilt do 1Sa 25:17 7200
wherefore c, I pray you, and see 2Kin 5:7 3045
will he not then c it Job 11:11 995
when I c, I am afraid of him Job 23:15 995
would not c any of his ways Job 34:27 7919
c the wondrous works of God Job 37:14 995
c my meditation Ps 5:1 995
When I c thy heavens, the work of Ps 8:3 7200
c my trouble which I suffer of Ps 9:13 7200
C and hear me, O LORD my God Ps 13:3 5027
C mine enemies Ps 25:19 7200
thou shalt diligently c his place Ps 37:10 995
Hearken, O daughter, and c Ps 45:10 7200
well her bulwarks, c her palaces Ps 48:13 6448
Now c this, ye that forget God, Ps 50:22 995
they shall wisely c of his doing Ps 64:9 7919
but I will c thy testimonies Ps 119:95 995
C mine affliction, and deliver me Ps 119:153 7200
C how I love thy precepts Ps 119:159 7200
c her ways, and be wise Prov 6:6 7200
c diligently what is before thee Prov 23:1 995
he that pondereth the heart c it Prov 24:12 995
for they c not that they do evil Eccl 5:1 3045
C the work of God Eccl 7:13 7200
but in the day of adversity c Eccl 7:14 7200
not know, my people doth not c Is 1:3 995
neither c the operation of his Is 5:12 7200
c thee, saying, Is this the man Is 14:16 995
I will c in my dwelling place Is 18:4 5027
That they may see, and know, and c Is 41:20 7760
what they be, that we may c them Is 41:22
neither c the things of old Is 43:18 995
they had not heard shall they c Is 52:15 995
c diligently, and see if there be Jer 2:10 995
C ye, and call for the mourning Jer 9:17 995
days ye shall c it perfectly Jer 23:20 995
in the latter days ye shall c it Jer 30:24 995
see, O LORD, and c Lam 1:11 5027
c to whom thou hast done this Lam 2:20 5027
c, and behold our reproach Lam 5:1 5027
it may be they will c, though Eze 12:3 7200
the matter, and c the vision Dan 9:23 995
they c not in their hearts that I Hos 7:2 559
C your ways Hag 1:5
C your ways Hag 1:7
c from this day and upward, from Hag 2:15
C now from this day and upward, Hag 2:18
the LORD's temple was laid, c it Hag 2:18
C the lilies of the field, how Mt 6:28 *2648*
C the ravens Lk 12:24 *2657*
C the lilies how they grow Lk 12:27 *2657*
Nor c that it is expedient for us Jn 11:50 *1260*
together for to c of this matter Acts 15:6 *1492*

C what I say 2Ti 2:7 *3539*
c the Apostle and High Priest of Heb 3:1 *2657*
Now c how great this man was, Heb 7:4 *2334*
let us c one another to provoke Heb 10:24 *2657*
For c him that endured such Heb 12:3 *357*

CONSIDERED
but when I had c it in the 1Kin 3:21 995
I have c the things which thou 1Kin 5:8 8085
Hast thou c my servant Job, that Job 1:8
Hast thou c my servant Job, that Job 2:3
for thou hast c my trouble Ps 31:7 7200
I have c the days of old, the Ps 77:5 2803
Then I saw, and c it well Prov 24:32
c all the oppressions that are Eccl 4:1 7200
I c all travail, and every right Eccl 4:4 7200
I c all the living which walk Eccl 4:15 7200
For all this I c in my heart even Eccl 9:1 5414
I c the horns, and, behold, there Dan 7:8 7920
For they c not the miracle of the Mk 6:52 *4920*
I had fastened mine eyes, I c Acts 11:6 *2657*
And when he had c the thing Acts 12:12 *4894*
he c not his own body now dead, Rom 4:19 *2657*

CONSIDEREST
C thou not what this people have Jer 33:24 7200
but c not the beam that is in Mt 7:3 *2657*

CONSIDERETH
he c all their works Ps 33:15 995
Blessed is he that c the poor Ps 41:1 7919
wisely c the house of the wicked Prov 21:12 7919
c not that poverty shall come Prov 28:22 3045
The righteous c the cause of the Prov 29:7 3045
She c a field, and buyeth it Prov 31:16 2161
none c in his heart, neither is Is 44:19 7725
sins which he hath done, and c Eze 18:14 7200
Because he c, and turneth away Eze 18:28 7200

CONSIDERING
none c that the righteous is Is 57:1 995
And as I was c, behold, an he goat Dan 8:5 995
c thyself, lest thou also be Gal 6:1 *4648*
c the end of their conversation Heb 13:7 *333*

CONSIST
things, and by him all things c Col 1:17 *4921*

CONSISTETH
for a man's life c not in the Lk 12:15 *2076*

CONSOLATION
of c to drink for their father or Jer 16:7 8575
waiting for the c of Israel Lk 2:25 *3874*
for ye have received your c Lk 6:24 *3874*
being interpreted, The son of c Acts 4:36 *3874*
had read, they rejoiced for the c Acts 15:31 *3874*
c grant you to be likeminded one Rom 15:5 *3874*
so our c also aboundeth by Christ 2Cor 1:5 *3874*
we be afflicted, it is for your c 2Cor 1:6 *3874*
we be comforted, it is for your c 2Cor 1:6 *3874*
so shall ye be also of the c 2Cor 1:7 *3874*
but by the c wherewith he was 2Cor 7:7 *3874*
be therefore any c in Christ Phil 2:1 *3874*
and hath given us everlasting c 2Th 2:16 *3874*
c in thy love, because the bowels Philem 7 *3874*
to lie, we might have a strong c Heb 6:18 *3874*

CONSOLATIONS
Are the c of God small with thee Job 15:11 8575
my speech, and let this be your c Job 21:2 8575
with the breasts of her c Is 66:11 8575

CONSORTED
believed, and c with Paul and Silas Acts 17:4 *4345*

CONSPIRACY
And the c was strong 2Sa 15:12 7195
his servants arose, and made a c 2Kin 12:20 7195
Now they made a c against him in 2Kin 14:19 7195
his c which he made, behold, they 2Kin 15:15 7195
made a c against Pekah the son of 2Kin 15:30 7195
king of Assyria found c in Hoshea 2Kin 17:4 7195
made a c against him in Jerusalem 2Chr 25:27 7195
A c is found among the men of Jer 11:9 7195
There is a c of her prophets in Eze 22:25 7195
than forty which had made this c Acts 23:13 *4945*

CONSPIRATORS
is among the c with Absalom 2Sa 15:31 7194

CONSPIRED
they c against him to slay him Gen 37:18 5320
That all of you have c against me 1Sa 22:8 7194
him, Why have ye c against me 1Sa 22:13 7194
house of Issachar, c against him 1Kin 15:27 7194
c against him, as he was in 1Kin 16:9 7194
encamped heard say, Zimri hath c 1Kin 16:16 7194
the son of Nimshi c against Joram 2Kin 9:14 7194
I c against my master, and slew 2Kin 10:9 7194
the son of Jabesh c against him 2Kin 15:10 7194
c against him, and smote him in 2Kin 15:25 7194
servants of Amon c against him 2Kin 21:23 7194
them that had c against king Amon 2Kin 21:24 7194
they c against him, and stoned him 2Chr 24:21 7194
his own servants c against him 2Chr 24:25 7194
these are they that c against him 2Chr 24:26 7194
And his servants c against him 2Chr 33:24 7194
them that had c against king Amon 2Chr 33:25 7194
c all of them together to come and Neh 4:8 7194
Amos hath c against thee in the Amos 7:10 7194

CONSTANT
if he be c to do my commandments 1Chr 28:7 2388

CONSTANTLY
the man that heareth speaketh c Prov 21:28 5331
But she c affirmed that it was Acts 12:15 *1340*
things I will that thou affirm c Titus 3:8 *1226*

CONSTELLATIONS
the c thereof shall not give Is 13:10 3685

CONSTRAIN
they c you to be circumcised Gal 6:12 *315*

CONSTRAINED
and she c him to eat bread 2Kin 4:8 2388
straightway Jesus c his disciples Mt 14:22 *315*
straightway he c his disciples to Mk 6:45 *315*
But they c him, saying, Abide Lk 24:29 *3849*
And she c us Acts 16:15 *3849*
I was c to appeal unto Caesar Acts 28:19 *315*

CONSTRAINETH
the spirit within me c me Job 32:18 6693
For the love of Christ c us 2Cor 5:14 *4912*

CONSTRAINT
the oversight thereof, not by c 1Pet 5:2 *317*

CONSULT
They only c to cast him down from Ps 62:4 3289

CONSULTATION
priests held a c with the elders Mk 15:1 *4824*

CONSULTED
king Rehoboam c with the old men, 1Kin 12:6 3289
c with the young men that were 1Kin 12:8 3289
David c with the captains of 1Chr 13:1 3289
when he had c with the people, he 2Chr 20:21 3289
Then I c with myself, and I Neh 5:7 4427
c against thy hidden ones Ps 83:3 3289
For they have c together with one Ps 83:5 3289
he c with images, he looked in Eze 21:21 7592
have c together to establish a Dan 6:7 3272
now what Balak king of Moab c Mic 6:5 3289
Thou hast c shame to thy house by Hab 2:10 3289
c that they might take Jesus by Mt 26:4 *4823*
But the chief priests c that they Jn 12:10 *1011*

CONSULTER
or a c with familiar spirits, or Deut 18:11 7592

CONSULTETH
c whether he be able with ten Lk 14:31 *1011*

CONSUME
and the famine shall c the land Gen 41:30 3615
them, and that I may c them Ex 32:10 3615
to c them from the face of the Ex 32:12 3615
lest I c thee in the way Ex 33:3 3615
of thee in a moment, and c thee Ex 33:5 3615
ague, that shall c the eyes Lev 26:16 3615
that I may c them in a moment Num 16:21 3615
that I may c them as in a moment Num 16:45 3615
for this great fire will c us Deut 5:25 398
thou shalt c all the people which Deut 7:16 398
thou mayest not c them at once Deut 7:22 3615
for the locust shall c it Deut 28:38 2628
of thy land shall the locust c Deut 28:42 3423
shall c the earth with her Deut 32:22 398
c you, after that he hath done Josh 24:20 3615
altar, shall be to c thine eyes 1Sa 2:33 3615
heaven, and c thee and thy fifty 2Kin 1:10 398
heaven, and c thee and thy fifty 2Kin 1:12 398
thou didst not utterly c them Neh 9:31 3615
to c them, and to destroy them Est 9:24 2000
fire shall c the tabernacles of Job 15:34 398
a fire not blown shall c him Job 20:26 398
Drought and heat c the snow waters Job 24:19 1497
they shall c Ps 37:20 3615
into smoke shall they c away Ps 37:20 3615
his beauty to c away like a moth Ps 39:11 4529
their beauty shall c in the grave Ps 49:14 1086
C them in wrath, c them, Ps 59:13 3615
their days did he c in vanity Ps 78:33 3615
and it shall also c the beard Is 7:20 5595
shall c the glory of his forest, Is 10:18 3615
down, and c the branches thereof Is 27:10 3615
I will surely c them, saith the Jer 8:13 5486
but I will c them by the sword, Jer 14:12 3615
it shall c the palaces of Jer 49:27 398
c away for their iniquity Eze 4:17 4743
hailstones in my fury to c it Eze 13:13 3615
them in the wilderness, to c them Eze 20:13 3615
to c because of the glittering Eze 21:28 398
will c thy filthiness out of thee Eze 22:15 8552
c the flesh, and spice it well, and Eze 24:10 8552
desolate, they are given us to c Eze 35:12 402
c all these kingdoms, and it shall Dan 2:44 5487
take away his dominion, to c Dan 7:26 8046
shall c his branches, and devour Hos 11:6 3615
I will utterly c all things from Zeph 1:2 5486
I will c man and beast Zeph 1:3 5486
I will c the fowls of the heaven, Zeph 1:3 5486
shall c it with the timber Zec 5:4 3615
Their flesh shall c away while Zec 14:12 4743
their eyes shall c away in their Zec 14:12 4743
their tongue shall c away in Zec 14:12 4743
c them, even as Elias did Lk 9:54 *355*
whom the Lord shall c with the 2Th 2:8 *355*
that ye may c it upon your lusts Jas 4:3 *1159*

CONSUMED
lest thou be c in the iniquity of Gen 19:15 5595
to the mountain, lest thou be c Gen 19:17 5595
in the day the drought c me Gen 31:40 398
with fire, and the bush was not c Ex 3:2 398
wrath, which c them as stubble Ex 15:7 398
or the field, be c therewith Ex 22:6 398
the ashes which the fire hath c Lev 6:10 398
c upon the altar the burnt Lev 9:24 398
c them that were in the uttermost Num 11:1 398
half c when he cometh out of his Num 12:12 398
this wilderness they shall be c Num 14:35 8552
lest ye be c in all their sins Num 16:26 5595
c the two hundred and fifty men Num 16:35 398
shall we be c with dying Num 17:13 8552
it hath c Ar of Moab, and the Num 21:28 398
that I c not the children of Num 25:11 3615
in the sight of the LORD, was c Num 32:13 8552
among the host, until they were c Deut 2:15 8552
when all the men of war were c Deut 2:16 8552
until he have c thee from off the Deut 28:21 3615
which came out of Egypt, were c Josh 5:6 8552
of the sword, until they were c Josh 8:24 8552
great slaughter, till they were c Josh 10:20 8552
c the flesh and the unleavened Judg 6:21 398
still do wickedly, ye shall be c 1Sa 12:25 5595
against them until they be c 1Sa 15:18 3615
the king, The man that c us 2Sa 21:5 3615
not again until I had c them 2Sa 22:38 3615
I have c them, and wounded 2Sa 22:39 3615
c the burnt sacrifice, and the 1Kin 18:38 398
Syrians, until thou have c them 1Kin 22:11 3615
heaven, and c him and his fifty 2Kin 1:10 398
heaven, and c him and his fifty 2Kin 1:12 398
of the Israelites that are c 2Kin 7:13 8552
in Aphek, till thou have c them 2Kin 13:17 3615
Syria till thou hadst c it 2Kin 13:19 3615
c the burnt offering and the 2Chr 7:1 398
whom the children of Israel c not 2Chr 8:8 3615
shalt push Syria until they be c 2Chr 18:10 3615
with us till thou hadst c us Ezr 9:14 3615
the gates thereof are c with fire Neh 2:3 398
gates thereof were c with fire Neh 2:13 398
sheep, and the servants, and c them Job 1:16 398
breath of his nostrils are they c Job 4:9 3615
they are c out of their place Job 6:17 1846
As the cloud is c and vanisheth Job 7:9 3615
though my reins be c within me Job 19:27 3615
His flesh is c away, that it Job 33:21 3615
Mine eye is c because of grief Ps 6:7 6244
did I turn again till they were c Ps 18:37 3615
mine eye is c with grief, yea, my Ps 31:9 6244
mine iniquity, and my bones are c Ps 31:10 6244
I am c by the blow of thine hand Ps 39:10 3615
c that are adversaries to my soul Ps 71:13 3615
they are utterly c with terrors Ps 73:19 8552
The fire c their young men Ps 78:63 398
For we are c by thine anger, and Ps 90:7 3615
For my days are c like smoke Ps 102:3 3615
the sinners be c out of the earth Ps 104:35 8552
They had almost c me upon earth Ps 119:87 3615
My zeal hath c me, because mine Ps 119:139 6789
when thy flesh and thy body are c Prov 5:11 3615
that forsake the LORD shall be c Is 1:28 3615
oppressors are c out of the land Is 16:4 8552
to nought, and the scorner is c Is 29:20 3615
thy face from us, and hast c us Is 64:7 4127
and the mouse, shall be c together Is 66:17 5486
thou hast c them, but they have Jer 5:3 3615
burned, the lead is c of the fire Jer 6:29 8552
after them, till I have c them Jer 9:16 3615
him, and c him, and have made his Jer 10:25 3615
the beasts are c, and the birds Jer 12:4 5595
famine shall those prophets be c Jer 14:15 8552
and they shall be c by the sword Jer 16:4 3615
my days should be c with shame Jer 20:18 3615
till they be c from off the land Jer 24:10 8552
until I have c them by his hand Jer 27:8 8552
until all the roll was c in the Jer 36:23 8552
there, and they shall all be c Jer 44:12 8552
they shall even be c by the sword Jer 44:12 8552
have been c by the sword and by Jer 44:18 8552
of Egypt shall be c by the sword Jer 44:27 8552
after them, till I have c them Jer 49:37 3615
and brought up hath mine enemy c Lam 2:22 3615
LORD's mercies that we are not c Lam 3:22 8552
they be c in the midst of thee Eze 5:12 3615
ye shall be c in the midst Eze 13:14 3615
the fire c them Eze 19:12 398
I have c them with the fire of my Eze 22:31 3615
it, that the scum of it may be c Eze 24:11 8552
they shall be no more c with Eze 34:29 622
wherefore I have c them in mine Eze 43:8 398
shall the fruit thereof be c Eze 47:12 8552
which by his hand shall be c Dan 11:16 3615
ye sons of Jacob are not c Mal 3:6 3615
that ye be not c one of another Gal 5:15 *355*

CONSUMETH
And he, as a rotten thing, c Job 13:28 1086
the remnant of them the fire c Job 22:20 398
is a fire that c to destruction Job 31:12 398
stubble, and the flame c the chaff Is 5:24 7503

CONSUMING
For the LORD thy God is a c fire Deut 4:24 398
as a c fire he shall destroy them Deut 9:3 398
For our God is a c fire Heb 12:29 *2654*

CONSUMMATION
it desolate, even until the c Dan 9:27 3617

CONSUMPTION
even appoint over you terror, c Lev 26:16 7829
LORD shall smite thee with a c Deut 28:22 7829
the c decreed shall overflow with Is 10:22 3631
Lord GOD of hosts shall make a c Is 10:23 3617
from the Lord GOD of hosts a c Is 28:22 3617

CONTAIN
heaven of heavens cannot c thee 1Kin 8:27 3557
as great as would c two measures 1Kin 18:32 1004
and heaven of heavens cannot c him 2Chr 2:6 3557
heaven of heavens cannot c thee 2Chr 6:18 3557
that the bath may c the tenth Eze 45:11 5375
not c the books that should be Jn 21:25 *5562*
But if they cannot c, let them 1Cor 7:9 *1467*

CONTAINED
it c two thousand baths 1Kin 7:26 3557
one laver c forty baths 1Kin 7:38 3557

by nature the things c in the law .... Rom 2:14
of commandments c in ordinances .... Eph 2:15
also it is c in the scripture 1Pet 2:6 4023

CONTAINETH
it c much .... Eze 23:32 3557

CONTAINING
c two or three firkins apiece .... Jn 2:6 5562

CONTEMN
Wherefore doth the wicked c God .... Ps 10:13 5006
what if the sword c even the rod .... Eze 21:13 3988

CONTEMNED
In whose eyes a vile person is c .... Ps 15:4 959
c the counsel of the most High .... Ps 107:11 5006
for love, it would utterly be c .... Song 8:7 936
and the glory of Moab shall be c .... Is 16:14 7034

CONTEMNETH
it c the rod of my son, as every .... Eze 21:10 3988

CONTEMPT
Thus shall there arise too much c .... Est 1:18 963
He poureth c upon princes, and .... Job 12:21 937
or did the c of families terrify .... Job 31:34 937
He poureth c upon princes, and .... Ps 107:40 937
Remove from me reproach and c .... Ps 119:22 937
we are exceedingly filled with c .... Ps 123:3 937
ease, and with the c of the proud .... Ps 123:4 937
wicked cometh, then cometh also c .... Prov 18:3 937
glory, and to bring into c all the .... Is 23:9 7043
and some to shame and everlasting c .... Dan 12:2 1860

CONTEMPTIBLE
say, The table of the LORD is c .... Mal 1:7 959
thereof, even his meat, is c .... Mal 1:12 959
Therefore have I also made you c .... Mal 2:9 959
presence is weak, and his speech c 2Cor 10:10 1848

CONTEMPTUOUSLY
and c against the righteous .... Ps 31:18 937

CONTEND
neither c with them in battle .... Deut 2:9 1624
it, and c with him in battle .... Deut 2:24 1624
If he will c with him, he cannot .... Job 9:3 7378
will ye c for God .... Job 13:8 7378
such as keep the law c with them .... Prov 28:4 1624
neither may he c with him that is .... Eccl 6:10 1777
for I will c with him that .... Is 49:25 7378
who will c with me .... Is 50:8 7378
For I will not c for ever .... Is 57:16 7378
then how canst thou c with horses .... Jer 12:5 8474
the voice of them that c with me .... Jer 18:19 3401
the Lord GOD called to c by fire .... Amos 7:4 7378
c thou before the mountains, and .... Mic 6:1 7378
c for the faith which was once .... Jude 3 1864

CONTENDED
Then c I with the rulers, and said .... Neh 13:11 7378
Then I c with the nobles of Judah .... Neh 13:17 7378
I c with them, and cursed them, and .... Neh 13:25 7378
maidservant, when they c with me .... Job 31:13 7378
them, even them that c with thee .... Is 41:12 4695
of the circumcision c with him .... Acts 11:2 1252

CONTENDEST
shew me wherefore thou c with me .... Job 10:2 7378

CONTENDETH
Shall he that c with the Almighty .... Job 40:2 7378
If a wise man c with a foolish .... Prov 29:9 8199
contend with him that c with thee .... Is 49:25 3401

CONTENDING
when c with the devil he disputed .... Jude 9 1252

CONTENT
And his brethren were c .... Gen 37:27 8085
Moses was c to dwell with the man .... Ex 2:21 2974
when Moses heard that, he was c .... Lev 10:20
would to God we had been c .... Josh 7:7 2974
the Levite was c to dwell with .... Judg 17:11 2974
had said unto the man, Be c .... Judg 19:6 2974
And Naaman said, Be c, take two 2Kin 5:23 2974
And one said, Be c, I pray thee, ... 2Kin 6:3 2974
Now therefore be c, look upon me .... Job 6:28 2974
neither will he rest c, though .... Prov 6:35 14
Pilate, willing to c the people .... Mk 15:15
and be c with your wages .... Lk 3:14 714
state I am, therewith to be c .... Phil 4:11 842
and raiment let us be therewith c 1Ti 6:8 714
be c with such things as ye have .... Heb 13:5 714
not c therewith, neither doth he 3Jn 10 714

CONTENTION
Only by pride cometh c .... Prov 13:10 4683
therefore leave off c, before it .... Prov 17:14 7379
A fool's lips enter into c .... Prov 18:6 7379
the scorner, and c shall go out .... Prov 22:10 4066
a man of c to the whole earth .... Jer 15:10 4066
are that raise up strife and c .... Hab 1:3 4066
the c was so sharp between them, ... Acts 15:39 3948
The one preach Christ of c .... Phil 1:16 2052
you the gospel of God with much c 1Th 2:2 73

CONTENTIONS
The lot causeth c to cease .... Prov 18:18 4079
their c are like the bars of a .... Prov 18:19 4079
the c of a wife are a continual .... Prov 19:13 4079
who hath c .... Prov 23:29 4079
Chloe, that there are c among you 1Cor 1:11 2054
questions, and genealogies, and c .... Titus 3:9 2054

CONTENTIOUS
in the wilderness, than with a c .... Prov 21:19 4066
so is a c man to kindle strife .... Prov 26:21 4066
rainy day and a c woman are alike .... Prov 27:15 4066
But unto them that are c, and do .... Rom 2:8
But if any man seem to be c 1Cor 11:16 5380

CONTENTMENT
godliness with c is great gain 1Ti 6:6 841

CONTINUAL
This shall be a c burnt offering .... Ex 29:42 8548
the c bread shall be thereon .... Num 4:7 8548
by day, for a c burnt offering .... Num 28:3 8548
It is a c burnt offering, which .... Num 28:6 8548
beside the c burnt offering, and .... Num 28:10 8548
beside the c burnt offering, and .... Num 28:15 8548
which is for a c burnt offering .... Num 28:23 8548
beside the c burnt offering .... Num 28:24 8548
them beside the c burnt offering .... Num 28:31 8548
the c burnt offering, and the meat .... Num 29:11 8548
beside the c burnt offering, his .... Num 29:16 8548
beside the c burnt offering, and .... Num 29:19 8548
beside the c burnt offering, and .... Num 29:22 8548
beside the c burnt offering, his .... Num 29:25 8548
beside the c burnt offering, and .... Num 29:28 8548
beside the c burnt offering, his .... Num 29:31 8548
beside the c burnt offering, his .... Num 29:34 8548
beside the c burnt offering, and .... Num 29:38 8548
his allowance was a c allowance 2Kin 25:30 8548
for the c shewbread, and for the 2Chr 2:4 8548
offered the c burnt offering .... Ezr 3:5 8548
for the c meat offering, and for .... Neh 10:33 8548
for the c burnt offering, of the .... Neh 10:33 8548
of a merry heart hath a c feast .... Prov 15:15 8548
of a wife are a c dropping .... Prov 19:13 2956
A c dropping in a very rainy day .... Prov 27:15 2956
people in wrath with a c stroke .... Is 14:6
of Luhith c weeping shall go up .... Jer 48:5
there was a c diet given him of .... Jer 52:34 8548
sever out men of c employment .... Eze 39:14 8548
morning for a c burnt offering .... Eze 46:15 8548
lest by her c coming she weary me .... Lk 18:5
heaviness and c sorrow in my heart .... Rom 9:2 88

CONTINUALLY
of his heart was only evil c .... Gen 6:5
returned from off the earth c .... Gen 8:3
the waters decreased c until the .... Gen 8:5 1980
for a memorial before the LORD c .... Ex 28:29 8548
upon his heart before the LORD c .... Ex 28:30 8548
of the first year day by day c .... Ex 29:38 8548
to cause the lamps to burn c .... Lev 24:2 8548
the morning before the LORD c .... Lev 24:3 8548
candlestick before the LORD c .... Lev 24:4 8548
set it in order before the LORD c .... Lev 24:8 8548
the ark of the LORD went on c .... Josh 6:13 1980
and Saul became David's enemy c 1Sa 18:29
shalt eat bread at my table c 2Sa 9:7 8548
for he did eat c at the king's 2Sa 9:13 8548
people increased c with Absalom 2Sa 15:12 1980
before me c in the room of Joab 2Sa 19:13
which stand c before thee 1Kin 10:8 8548
man of God, which passeth by us c 2Kin 4:9 8548
he did eat bread c before him all 2Kin 25:29 8548
the priests with trumpets c 1Chr 16:6 8548
and his strength, seek his face c 1Chr 16:11 8548
to minister before the ark c 1Chr 16:37 8548
of the burnt offering c morning 1Chr 16:40 8548
unto them, c before the LORD 1Chr 23:31 8548
which stand c before thee 2Chr 9:7 8548
between Rehoboam and Jeroboam c 2Chr 12:15
LORD c all the days of Jehoiada 2Chr 24:14 8548
Thus did Job c .... Job 1:5
his praise shall c be in my mouth .... Ps 34:1 8548
yea, let them say c, Let the LORD .... Ps 35:27 8548
halt, and my sorrow is c before me .... Ps 38:17 8548
and thy truth c preserve me .... Ps 40:11 8548
such as love thy salvation say c .... Ps 40:16 8548
while they c say unto me, Where .... Ps 42:3
My confusion is c before me .... Ps 44:15
to have been c before me .... Ps 50:8 8548
the goodness of God endureth c .... Ps 52:1
melt away as waters which run c .... Ps 58:7
and make their loins c to shake .... Ps 69:23 8548
such as love thy salvation say c .... Ps 70:4 8548
whereunto I may c resort .... Ps 71:3 8548
my praise shall be c of thee .... Ps 71:6 8548
But I will hope c, and will yet .... Ps 71:14 8548
also shall be made for him c .... Ps 72:15 8548
Nevertheless I am c with thee .... Ps 73:23 8548
rise up against thee increaseth c .... Ps 74:23 8548
Let his children be c vagabonds .... Ps 109:10
Let them be before the LORD c .... Ps 109:15 8548
a girdle wherewith he is girded c .... Ps 109:19 8548
shall I keep thy law c for ever .... Ps 119:44 8548
My soul is c in my hand .... Ps 119:109 8548
have respect unto thy statutes c .... Ps 119:117 8548
c are they gathered together for .... Ps 140:2
his heart, he deviseth mischief c .... Prov 6:14
Bind them c upon thine heart, and .... Prov 6:21 8548
it whirleth about c, and the wind .... Eccl 1:6
I stand c upon the watchtower in .... Is 21:8 8548
thy walls are c before me .... Is 49:16 8548
hast feared c every day because .... Is 51:13 8548
my name c every day is blasphemed .... Is 52:5 8548
And the LORD shall guide thee c .... Is 58:11 8548
thy gates shall be open c .... Is 60:11 8548
me to anger c to my face .... Is 65:3 8548
before me c is grief and wounds .... Jer 6:7 8548
offerings, and to do sacrifice c .... Jer 33:18
he did c eat bread before him all .... Jer 52:33 8548
a meat offering c by a perpetual .... Eze 46:14 8548
Thy God whom thou servest c .... Dan 6:16 8411
is thy God, whom thou servest c .... Dan 6:20 8411
they have committed whoredom c .... Hos 4:18
and judgment, and wait on thy God c .... Hos 12:6
so shall all the heathen drink c .... Obad 16 8548
hath not thy wickedness passed c .... Nah 3:19 8548
not spare c to slay the nations .... Hab 1:17 8548
were c in the temple, praising and .... Lk 24:53 1725
will give ourselves c to prayer .... Acts 6:4 4342
of them that waited on him c .... Acts 10:7 4342
attending c upon this very thing .... Rom 13:6
abideth a priest c .... Heb 7:3
year c make the comers thereunto .... Heb 10:1
the sacrifice of praise to God c .... Heb 13:15 1275

CONTINUANCE
even great plagues, and of long c .... Deut 28:59 539
and sore sicknesses, and of long c .... Deut 28:59 539
which in c were fashioned, when .... Ps 139:16 3117
in those is c, and we shall be .... Is 64:5 5769
To them who by patient c in well .... Rom 2:7 5281

CONTINUE
if he c a day or two, he shall .... Ex 21:21 5975
she shall then c in the blood of .... Lev 12:4 3427
she shall c in the blood of her .... Lev 12:5 3427
you c following the LORD your God 1Sa 12:14 1961
But now thy kingdom shall not c 1Sa 13:14 6965
that it may c for ever before 2Sa 7:29 1961
That the LORD may c his word 1Kin 2:4 6965
neither shall his substance c .... Job 15:29 6965
doth not mine eye c in their .... Job 17:2 3885
O c thy lovingkindness unto them .... Ps 36:10 4900
their houses shall c for ever .... Ps 49:11
children of thy servants shall c .... Ps 102:28 7931
They c this day according to .... Ps 119:91 5975
that c until night, till wine .... Is 5:11 309
vessel, that they may c many days .... Jer 32:14 5975
he shall c more years than the .... Dan 11:8 5975
because they c with me now three .... Mt 15:32 4357
If ye c in my word, then are ye .... Jn 8:31 3306
c ye in my love .... Jn 15:9 3306
persuaded them to c in the grace .... Acts 13:43 1961
exhorting them to c in the faith .... Acts 14:22 1696
I c unto this day, witnessing .... Acts 26:22 2476
Shall we c in sin, that grace may .... Rom 6:1 1961
if thou c in his goodness .... Rom 11:22 1961
of the gospel might c with you .... Gal 2:5 1265
abide and c with you all for your .... Phil 1:25 4839
If ye c in the faith grounded and .... Col 1:23 1961
C in prayer, and watch in the same .... Col 4:2 4342
if they c in faith and charity and 1Ti 2:15 3306
c in them 1Ti 4:16 1961
But c thou in the things which 2Ti 3:14 3306
suffered to c by reason of death .... Heb 7:23 3887
Let brotherly love c .... Heb 13:1 3306
c there a year, and buy and sell, ... Jas 4:13 4160
all things c as they were from 2Pet 3:4 1265
you, ye also shall c in the Son 1Jn 2:24 3306
was given unto him to c forty .... Rev 13:5 4160
cometh, he must c a short space .... Rev 17:10 3306

CONTINUED
and they c a season in ward .... Gen 40:4 1961
Asher c on the sea shore, and .... Judg 5:17 3427
the country of Moab, and c there .... Ruth 1:2 1961
hath c even from the morning .... Ruth 2:7 5975
as she c praying before the LORD, ... 1Sa 1:12 7235
the ark of the LORD c in the 2Sa 6:11 3427
they c three years without war 1Kin 22:1 3427
all this c until the burnt 2Chr 29:28
also I c in the work of this wall .... Neh 5:16 2388
Moreover Job c his parable .... Job 27:1 3254
Moreover Job c his parable .... Job 29:1 3254
his name shall be c as long as .... Ps 72:17 5125
Daniel c even unto the first year .... Dan 1:21 1961
c all night in prayer to God .... Lk 6:12 1273
Ye are they which have c with me .... Lk 22:28 1265
they c there not many days .... Jn 2:12 3306
So when they c asking him .... Jn 8:7 1961
there c with his disciples .... Jn 11:54 1304
These all c with one accord in .... Acts 1:14 4342
And they c stedfastly in the .... Acts 2:42 4342
he c with Philip, and wondered, ... Acts 8:13 4342
But Peter c knocking .... Acts 12:16 1961
Barnabas c in Antioch, teaching .... Acts 15:35 1304
he c there a year and six months, ... Acts 18:11 2523
this c by the space of two years .... Acts 19:10 1096
c his speech until midnight .... Acts 20:7 3905
c fasting, having taken nothing .... Acts 27:33 1300
because they c not in my covenant .... Heb 8:9 1696
would no doubt have c with us 1Jn 2:19 3306

CONTINUETH
fleeth also as a shadow, and c not .... Job 14:2 5975
Cursed is every one that c not in .... Gal 3:10 1696
c in supplications and prayers 1Ti 5:5 4357
But this man, because he c ever .... Heb 7:24 3306
c therein, he being not a .... Jas 1:25 3887

CONTINUING
forth with fury, a c whirlwind .... Jer 30:23 1641
c daily with one accord in the .... Acts 2:46 4342
c instant in prayer .... Rom 12:12 4342
For here have we no c city .... Heb 13:14 3306

CONTRADICTING
which were spoken by Paul, c .... Acts 13:45 483

CONTRADICTION
without all c the less is blessed .... Heb 7:7 485
such c of sinners against himself .... Heb 12:3 485

CONTRARIWISE
So that c ye ought rather to 2Cor 2:7 5121
But c, when they saw that the .... Gal 2:7 5121
but c blessing 1Pet 3:9 5121

CONTRARY
And if ye walk c unto me, and will .... Lev 26:21 7147
things, but will walk c unto me .... Lev 26:23 7147
Then will I also walk c unto you .... Lev 26:24 7147
unto me, but walk c unto me .... Lev 26:27 7147
Then I will walk c unto you also .... Lev 26:28 7147
also they have walked c unto me .... Lev 26:40 7147
I also have walked c unto them .... Lev 26:41 7147
(though it was turned to the c .... Est 9:1

the *c* is in thee from other women... Eze 16:34 2016
unto thee, therefore thou art *c*... Eze 16:34 2016
for the wind was *c*... Mt 14:24 *1727*
for the wind was *c* unto them... Mk 6:48 *1727*
these all do *c* to the decrees of... Acts 17:7 *561*
men to worship God *c* to the law... Acts 18:13 *3844*
me to be smitten *c* to the law... Acts 23:3 *3891*
things *c* to the name of Jesus of... Acts 26:9 *1727*
Cyprus, because the winds were *c*... Acts 27:4 *1727*
wert graffed *c* to nature into a... Rom 11:24 *3844*
offences *c* to the doctrine which... Rom 16:17 *3844*
these are *c* the one to the other... Gal 5:17 *480*
was against us, which was *c* to us... Col 2:14 *5227*
not God, and are *c* to all men... 1Th 2:15 *1727*
thing that is *c* to sound doctrine... 1Ti 1:10 *480*
is of the *c* part may be ashamed... Titus 2:8 *1727*

CONTRIBUTION
Achaia to make a certain *c* for... Rom 15:26 *2842*

CONTRITE
saveth such as be of a *c* spirit... Ps 34:18 1793
a *c* heart, O God, thou wilt not... Ps 51:17 1794
with him also that is of a *c*... Is 57:15 1793
to revive the heart of the *c* ones... Is 57:15 1792
of a *c* spirit, and trembleth at my... Is 66:2 5223

CONTROVERSIES
judgment of the LORD, and for *c*... 2Chr 19:8 7379

CONTROVERSY
matters of *c* within thy gates... Deut 17:8 7379
the men, between whom the *c* is... Deut 19:17 7379
and by their word shall every *c*... Deut 21:5 7379
If there be a *c* between men... Deut 25:1 7379
that when any man that had a *c*... 2Sa 15:2 7379
of recompences for the *c* of Zion... Is 34:8 7379
LORD hath a *c* with the nations... Jer 25:31 7379
in *c* they shall stand in judgment... Eze 44:24 7379
for the LORD hath a *c* with the... Hos 4:1 7379
The LORD hath also a *c* with Judah... Hos 12:2 7379
ye, O mountains, the LORD's *c*... Mic 6:2 7379
the LORD hath a *c* with his people... Mic 6:2 7379
without *c* great is the mystery of... 1Ti 3:16 *3672*

CONVENIENT
feed me with food *c* for me... Prov 30:8 2706
c for thee to go, thither go... Jer 40:4 3477
it seemeth *c* unto thee to go... Jer 40:5 3477
when a *c* day was come, that Herod... Mk 6:21 *2121*
when I have a *c* season, I will... Acts 24:25 *2540*
do those things which are not *c*... Rom 1:28 *2520*
come when he shall have *c* time... 1Cor 16:12 *2119*
nor jesting, which are not *c*... Eph 5:4 *433*
to enjoin thee that which is *c*... Philem 8 *433*

CONVENIENTLY
sought how he might *c* betray him... Mk 14:11 *2122*

CONVERSANT
strangers that were *c* among them... Josh 8:35 1980
as long as we were *c* with them... 1Sa 25:15 1980

CONVERSATION
to slay such as be of upright *c*... Ps 37:14 1870
his *c* aright will I shew the... Ps 50:23 1870
we have had our *c* in the world... 2Cor 1:12 *390*
For ye have heard of my *c* in time... Gal 1:13 *391*
c in times past in the lusts of... Eph 2:3 *390*
the former *c* the old man, which... Eph 4:22 *391*
Only let your *c* be as it becometh... Phil 1:27 *4176*
For our *c* is in heaven... Phil 3:20 *4175*
of the believers, in word, in *c*... 1Ti 4:12 *391*
Let your *c* be without... Heb 13:5 *5158*
considering the end of their *c*... Heb 13:7 *391*
good *c* his works with meekness of... Jas 3:13 *391*
so be ye holy in all manner of *c*... 1Pet 1:15 *391*
from your vain *c* received by... 1Pet 1:18 *391*
Having your *c* honest among the... 1Pet 2:12 *391*
word be won by the *c* of the wives... 1Pet 3:1 *391*
your chaste *c* coupled with fear... 1Pet 3:2 *391*
accuse your good *c* in Christ... 1Pet 3:16 *391*
with the filthy *c* of the wicked... 2Pet 2:7 *391*
ought ye to be in all holy *c*... 2Pet 3:11 *391*

CONVERSION
declaring the *c* of the Gentiles... Acts 15:3 *1995*

CONVERT
understand with their heart, and *c*... Is 6:10 7725
err from the truth, and one *c* him... Jas 5:19 *1994*

CONVERTED
and sinners shall be *c* unto thee... Ps 51:13 7725
of the sea shall be *c* unto thee... Is 60:5 2015
with their heart, and should be *c*... Mt 13:15 *1994*
I say unto you, Except ye be *c*... Mt 18:3 *4762*
lest at any time they should be *c*... Mk 4:12 *1994*
and when thou art *c*, strengthen... Lk 22:32 *1994*
with their heart, and be *c*... Jn 12:40 *1994*
Repent ye therefore, and be *c*... Acts 3:19 *1994*
with their heart, and should be *c*... Acts 28:27 *1994*

CONVERTETH
that he which *c* the sinner from... Jas 5:20 *1994*

CONVERTING
the LORD is perfect, *c* the soul... Ps 19:7 7725

CONVERTS
and her *c* with righteousness... Is 1:27 7725

CONVEY
I will *c* them by sea in floats... 1Kin 5:9 7760
that they may *c* me over till I... Neh 2:7 5674

CONVEYED
for Jesus had *c* himself away... Jn 5:13 *1593*

CONVICTED
being *c* by their own conscience,... Jn 8:9 *1651*

CONVINCE
to exhort and to *c* the gainsayers... Titus 1:9 *1651*
to *c* all that are ungodly among... Jude 15 *1827*

CONVINCED
there was none of you that *c* Job... Job 32:12 3198
For he mightily *c* the Jews... Acts 18:28 *1246*
he is *c* of all, he is judged of... 1Cor 14:24 *1651*
are *c* of the law as transgressors... Jas 2:9 *1651*

CONVINCETH
Which of you *c* me of sin... Jn 8:46 *1651*

CONVOCATION
day there shall be an holy *c*... Ex 12:16 4744
there shall be an holy *c* to you... Ex 12:16 4744
is the sabbath of rest, an holy *c*... Lev 23:3 4744
first day ye shall have an holy *c*... Lev 23:7 4744
in the seventh day is an holy *c*... Lev 23:8 4744
that it may be an holy *c* unto you... Lev 23:21 4744
of blowing of trumpets, an holy *c*... Lev 23:24 4744
it shall be an holy *c* unto you... Lev 23:27 4744
the first day shall be an holy *c*... Lev 23:35 4744
day shall be an holy *c* unto you... Lev 23:36 4744
the first day shall be an holy *c*... Num 28:18 4744
day ye shall have an holy *c*... Num 28:25 4744
be out, ye shall have an holy *c*... Num 28:26 4744
month, ye shall have an holy *c*... Num 29:1 4744
of this seventh month an holy *c*... Num 29:7 4744

CONVOCATIONS
ye shall proclaim to be holy *c*... Lev 23:2 4744
feasts of the LORD, even holy *c*... Lev 23:4 4744
ye shall proclaim to be holy *c*... Lev 23:37 4744

COOK
And Samuel said unto the *c*... 1Sa 9:23 2876
the *c* took up the shoulder, and... 1Sa 9:24 2876

COOKS
to be confectionaries, and to be *c*... 1Sa 8:13 2876

COOL
in the garden in the *c* of the day... Gen 3:8 7307
finger in water, and *c* my tongue... Lk 16:24 *2711*

COOS (*co'-os*) *An island near Cnidus.*
with a straight course unto C... Acts 21:1 *2972*

COPIED
of Hezekiah king of Judah *c* out... Prov 25:1 6275

COPING
from the foundation unto the *c*... 1Kin 7:9 2947

COPPER
and two vessels of fine *c*,... Ezr 8:27 5178

COPPERSMITH
Alexander the *c* did me much evil... 2Ti 4:14 *5471*

COPULATION
man's seed of *c* go out from him... Lev 15:16 7902
skin, whereon is the seed of *c*... Lev 15:17 7902
whom man shall lie with seed of *c*... Lev 15:18 7902

COPY
that he shall write him a *c* of... Deut 17:18 4932
stones a *c* of the law of Moses... Josh 8:32 4932
This is the *c* of the letter that... Ezr 4:11 6573
Now when the *c* of king... Ezr 4:23 6573
The *c* of the letter that Tatnai,... Ezr 5:6 6573
Now this is the *c* of the letter... Ezr 7:11 6573
The *c* of the writing for a... Est 3:14 6572
Also he gave him the *c* of the... Est 4:8 6572
The *c* of the writing for a... Est 8:13 6572

COR
tenth part of a bath out of the *c*... Eze 45:14 3734

CORAL
No mention shall be made of *c*... Job 28:18 7215
work, and fine linen, and *c*... Eze 27:16 7215

CORBAN (*cor'-ban*) *A sacred gift.*
to his father or mother, It is C... Mk 7:11 *2878*

CORD
down by a *c* through the window... Josh 2:15 2256
Because he hath loosed my *c*... Job 30:11 3499
or his tongue with a *c* which thou... Job 41:1 2256
a threefold *c* is not quickly... Eccl 4:12 2339
Or ever the silver *c* be loosed... Eccl 12:6 2256
have none that shall cast a *c* by... Mic 2:5 2256

CORDS
the pins of the court, and their *c*... Ex 35:18 4340
hanging for the court gate, his *c*... Ex 39:40 4340
the *c* of it for all the service... Num 3:26 4340
and their pins, and their *c*... Num 3:37 4340
the altar round about, and their *c*... Num 4:26 4340
and their pins, and their *c*... Num 4:32 4340
And they bound him with two new *c*... Judg 15:13 5688
the *c* that were upon his arms... Judg 15:14 5688
fastened with *c* of fine linen... Est 1:6 2256
be holden in *c* of affliction... Job 36:8 2256
and cast away their *c* from us... Ps 2:3 5688
bind the sacrifice with *c*... Ps 118:27 5688
cut asunder the *c* of the wicked... Ps 129:4 5688
have hid a snare for me, and *c*... Ps 140:5 2256
be holden with the *c* of his sins... Prov 5:22 2256
draw iniquity with *c* of vanity... Is 5:18 2256
any of the *c* thereof be broken... Is 33:20 2256
spare not, lengthen thy *c*... Is 54:2 4340
spoiled, and all my *c* are broken... Jer 10:20 4340
and they let down Jeremiah with *c*... Jer 38:6 2256
let them down by *c* into the... Jer 38:11 2256
under thine armholes under the *c*... Jer 38:12 2256
So they drew up Jeremiah with *c*... Jer 38:13 2256
of rich apparel, bound with *c*... Eze 27:24 2256
I drew them with *c* of a man... Hos 11:4 2256
he had made a scourge of small *c*... Jn 2:15 *4979*

CORE (*co'-ree*) See KORAH. *Greek form of Korah.*
perished in the gainsaying of C... Jude 11 *2879*

CORIANDER
and it was like *c* seed, white... Ex 16:31 1407
And the manna was as *c* seed... Num 11:7 1407

CORINTH (*cor'-inth*) See CORINTHIANS, CORINTHUS. *Capital of Achaia.*
from Athens, and came to C... Acts 18:1 *2882*
that, while Apollos was at C... Acts 19:1 *2882*
the church of God which is at C... 1Cor 1:2 *2882*
the church of God which is at C... 2Cor 1:1 *2882*
you I came not as yet unto C... 2Cor 1:23 *2882*
Erastus abode at C... 2Ti 4:20 *2882*

CORINTHIANS (*co-rin'-the-uns*) *Residents of Corinth.*
many of the C hearing believed,... Acts 18:8 *2881*
The first epistle to the C was... 1Cor *s* *2881*
O ye C, our mouth is open unto... 2Cor 6:11 *2881*
the C was written from Philippi... 2Cor *s* *2881*

CORINTHUS (*co-rin'-thus*) See CORINTH. *Same as Corinth.*
Written to the Romans from C... Rom *s* *2882*

CORMORANT
And the little owl, and the *c*... Lev 11:17 7994
and the gier eagle, and the *c*... Deut 14:17 7994
But the *c* and the bittern shall... Is 34:11 6893
both the *c* and the bittern shall... Zeph 2:14 6893

CORN
of the earth, and plenty of *c*... Gen 27:28 1715
and with *c* and wine have I... Gen 27:37 1715
seven ears of *c* came up upon one... Gen 41:5
lay up *c* under the hand of... Gen 41:35 1250
Joseph gathered *c* as the sand of... Gen 41:49 1250
into Egypt to Joseph for to buy *c*... Gen 41:57
saw that there was *c* in Egypt... Gen 42:1 7668
heard that there is *c* in Egypt... Gen 42:2 7668
went down to buy *c* in Egypt... Gen 42:3 1250
to buy *c* among those that came... Gen 42:5
carry *c* for the famine of your... Gen 42:19 7668
to fill their sacks with *c*... Gen 42:25 1250
they laded their asses with the *c*... Gen 42:26 7668
when they had eaten up the *c*... Gen 43:2 7668
of the youngest, and his *c* money... Gen 44:2 7668
and ten she asses laden with *c*... Gen 45:23 1250
for the *c* which they bought... Gen 47:14 7668
thorns, so that the stacks of *c*... Ex 22:6
or the standing *c*, or the field... Ex 22:6 7054
green ears of *c* dried by the fire... Lev 2:14
even *c* beaten out of full ears... Lev 2:14 1643
it, part of the beaten *c* thereof... Lev 2:16 1643
eat neither bread, nor parched *c*... Lev 23:14
were the *c* of the threshingfloor... Num 18:27 1715
and the fruit of thy land, thy *c*... Deut 7:13 1715
that thou mayest gather in thy *c*... Deut 11:14 1715
thy gates the tithe of thy *c*... Deut 12:17 1715
name there, the tithe of thy *c*... Deut 14:23 1715
to put the sickle to the *c*... Deut 16:9 7054
that thou hast gathered in thy *c*... Deut 16:13 1637
The firstfruit also of thy *c*... Deut 18:4 1715
the standing *c* of thy neighbour... Deut 23:25 7054
unto thy neighbour's standing *c*... Deut 23:25 7054
the ox when he treadeth out the *c*... Deut 25:4
shall not leave thee either *c*... Deut 28:51 1715
Jacob shall be upon a land of *c*... Deut 33:28 1715
they did eat of the old *c* of the... Josh 5:11 5669
parched *c* in the selfsame day... Josh 5:11
eaten of the old *c* of the land... Josh 5:12 5669
the standing *c* of the Philistines... Judg 15:5 7054
shocks, and also the standing *c*... Judg 15:5 7054
glean ears of *c* after him in... Ruth 2:2
and he reached her parched *c*... Ruth 2:14
down at the end of the heap of *c*... Ruth 3:7 6194
an ephah of this parched *c*... 1Sa 17:17
and five measures of parched *c*... 1Sa 25:18
mouth, and spread ground *c* thereon... 2Sa 17:19 7383
and barley, and flour, and parched *c*... 2Sa 17:28
full ears of *c* in the husk... 2Kin 4:42 3759
like your own land, a land of *c*... 2Kin 18:32 1715
as *c* blasted before it be grown... 2Kin 19:26
in abundance the firstfruits of *c*... 2Chr 31:5 1715
also for the increase of *c*... 2Chr 32:28 1715
therefore we take up *c* for them... Neh 5:2 1715
and houses, that we might buy *c*... Neh 5:3 1715
might exact of them money and *c*... Neh 5:10 1715
part of the money, and of the *c*... Neh 5:11 1715
shall bring the offering of the *c*... Neh 10:39 1715
vessels, and the tithes of the *c*... Neh 13:5 1715
all Judah the tithe of the *c*... Neh 13:12 1715
like as a shock of *c* cometh in in... Job 5:26
reap every one his *c* in the field... Job 24:6 1098
off as the tops of the ears of *c*... Job 24:24
good liking, they grow up with *c*... Job 39:4 1250
than in the time that their *c*... Ps 4:7 1715
thou preparest them *c*, when thou... Ps 65:9 1715
also are covered over with *c*... Ps 65:13 1250
of *c* in the earth upon the top of... Ps 72:16 1250
had given them of the *c* of heaven... Ps 78:24 1715
He that withholdeth *c*, the people... Prov 11:26 1250
the harvestman gathereth the *c*... Is 17:5 7054
threshing, and the *c* of my floor... Is 21:10 1121
Bread *c* is bruised... Is 28:28
like your own land, a land of *c*... Is 36:17 1715
as *c* blasted before it be grown... Is 37:27
c to be meat for thine enemies... Is 62:8 1715
say to their mothers, Where is *c*... Lam 2:12 1715

and I will call for the c, and will ... Eze 36:29 1715
did not know that I gave her c ... Hos 2:8 1715
take away my c in the time ... Hos 2:9 1715
And the earth shall hear the c ... Hos 2:22 1715
they assemble themselves for c ... Hos 7:14 1715
and loveth to tread out the c ... Hos 10:11
they shall revive as the c ... Hos 14:7 1715
for the c is wasted ... Joel 1:10 1715
for the c is withered ... Joel 1:17 1715
people, Behold, I will send you c ... Joel 2:19 1715
moon be gone, that we may sell c ... Amos 8:5 7668
like as c is sifted in a sieve, ... Amos 9:9
upon the mountains, and upon the c ... Hag 1:11 1715
c shall make the young men ... Zec 9:17 1715
on the sabbath day through the c ... Mt 12:1 *4702*
and began to pluck the ears of c ... Mt 12:1 *4719*
that he went through the c fields ... Mk 2:23 *4702*
they went, to pluck the ears of c ... Mk 2:23 *4719*
after that the full c in the ear ... Mk 4:28 *4621*
that he went through the c fields ... Lk 6:1 *4702*
disciples plucked the ears of c ... Lk 6:1 *4719*
Except a c of wheat fall into the ... Jn 12:24 *2848*
heard that there was c in Egypt ... Acts 7:12 *4621*
of the ox that treadeth out the c ... 1Cor 9:9
the ox that treadeth out the c ... 1Ti 5:18

CORNELIUS (*cor-ne'-le-us*) *A Roman centurion converted by Peter.*
certain man in Caesarea called C ... Acts 10:1 *2883*
in to him, and saying unto him, C ... Acts 10:3 *2883*
which spake unto C was departed ... Acts 10:7 *2883*
C had made enquiry for Simon's ... Acts 10:17 *2883*
which were sent unto him from C ... Acts 10:21 *2883*
C the centurion, a just man, and ... Acts 10:22 *2883*
C waited for them, and had called ... Acts 10:24 *2883*
C met him, and fell down at his ... Acts 10:25 *2883*
C said, Four days ago I was ... Acts 10:30 *2883*
And said, C, thy prayer is heard, ... Acts 10:31 *2883*

CORNER
which is toward the north c ... Ex 36:25 6285
shave off the c of their beard ... Lev 21:5 6285
compassed the c of the sea ... Josh 18:14 6285
from the right c of the temple to ... 2Kin 11:11 3802
to the left c of the temple ... 2Kin 11:11 3802
gate of Ephraim unto the c gate ... 2Kin 14:13 6438
the gate of Ephraim to the c gate ... 2Chr 25:23 6437
towers in Jerusalem at the c gate ... 2Chr 26:9 6438
altars in every c of Jerusalem ... 2Chr 28:24 6438
of the wall, even unto the c ... Neh 3:24 6438
and to the going up of the c ... Neh 3:31 6438
between the going up of the c ... Neh 3:32 6438
or who laid the c stone thereof ... Job 38:6 6438
is become the head stone of the c ... Ps 118:22 6438
our daughters may be as c stones ... Ps 144:12 2106
through the street near her c ... Prov 7:8 6438
and lieth in wait at every c ... Prov 7:12 6438
to dwell in a c of the housetop ... Prov 21:9 6438
to dwell in the c of the housetop ... Prov 25:24 6438
a tried stone, a precious c stone ... Is 28:16 6438
be removed into a c any more ... Is 30:20 3671
Hananeel unto the gate of the c ... Jer 31:38 6438
unto the c of the horse gate ... Jer 31:40 6438
and shall devour the c of Moab ... Jer 48:45 6285
not take of thee a stone for a c ... Jer 51:26 6438
in every c of the court there was ... Eze 46:21 4742
in Samaria in the c of a bed ... Amos 3:12 6285
Out of him came forth the c ... Zec 10:4 6438
the first gate, unto the c gate ... Zec 14:10 6434
same is become the head of the c ... Mt 21:42 *1137*
is become the head of the c ... Mk 12:10 *1137*
same is become the head of the c ... Lk 20:17 *1137*
which is become the head of the c ... Acts 4:11 *1137*
this thing was not done in a c ... Acts 26:26 *1137*
himself being the chief c stone ... Eph 2:20 *204*
I lay in Sion a chief c stone ... 1Pet 2:6 *204*
same is made the head of the c ... 1Pet 2:7 *1137*

CORNERS
and put them in the four c thereof ... Ex 25:12 6471
four c that are on the four feet ... Ex 25:26 6285
c of the tabernacle in the two ... Ex 26:23 4742
they shall be for the two c ... Ex 26:24 4742
of it upon the four c thereof ... Ex 27:2 6438
rings in the four c thereof ... Ex 27:4 7098
crown of it, by the two c thereof ... Ex 30:4 6763
two boards made he for the c of ... Ex 36:28 4742
did to both of them in both the c ... Ex 36:29 4742
to be set by the four c of it ... Ex 37:3 6471
four c that were in the four feet ... Ex 37:13 6285
crown thereof, by the two c of it ... Ex 37:27 6763
horns thereof on the four c of it ... Ex 38:2 6438
wholly reap the c of thy field ... Lev 19:9 6285
not round the c of your heads ... Lev 19:27 6285
shalt thou mar the c of thy beard ... Lev 19:27 6285
c of thy field when thou reapest ... Lev 23:22 6285
and shall smite the c of Moab ... Num 24:17 6285
said, I would scatter them into c ... Deut 32:26 6284
and the four c thereof had ... 1Kin 7:30 6471
to the four c of one base ... 1Kin 7:34 6438
and didst divide them into c ... Neh 9:22 6285
and smote the four c of the house ... Job 1:19 6438
from the four c of the earth ... Is 11:12 3671
and all that are in the utmost c ... Jer 9:26 6285
and all that are in the utmost c ... Jer 25:23 6285
them that are in the utmost c ... Jer 49:32 6285
come upon the four c of the land ... Eze 7:2 3671
the c thereof, and the length ... Eze 41:22 4740
on the four c of the settle, and ... Eze 43:20 6438
upon the four c of the settle of ... Eze 45:19 6438
pass by the four c of the court ... Eze 46:21 4742
In the four c of the court there ... Eze 46:22 4742
these four c were of one measure ... Eze 46:22 7106
bowls, and as the c of the altar ... Zec 9:15 2106
in the c of the streets, that ... Mt 6:5 *1137*

a great sheet knit at the four c ... Acts 10:11 *746*
let down from heaven by four c ... Acts 11:5 *746*
on the four c of the earth ... Rev 7:1 *1137*

CORNET
shouting, and with sound of the c ... 1Chr 15:28 7782
sound of c make a joyful noise ... Ps 98:6 7782
time ye hear the sound of the c ... Dan 3:5 7162
people heard the sound of the c ... Dan 3:7 7162
shall hear the sound of the c ... Dan 3:10 7162
time ye hear the sound of the c ... Dan 3:15 7162
Blow ye the c in Gibeah, and the ... Hos 5:8 7782

CORNETS
and on timbrels, and on c, and on ... 2Sa 6:5 4517
and with trumpets, and with c ... 2Chr 15:14 7782

CORNFLOOR
hast loved a reward upon every c ... Hos 9:1

CORPSE
of it, they came and took up his c ... Mk 6:29 *4430*

CORPSES
behold, they were all dead c ... 2Kin 19:35 6297
behold, they were all dead c ... Is 37:36 6297
and there is none end of their c ... Nah 3:3 1472
they stumble upon their c ... Nah 3:3 1472

CORRECT
rebukes dost c man for iniquity ... Ps 39:11 3256
the heathen, shall not he c ... Ps 94:10 3198
C thy son, and he shall give thee ... Prov 29:17 3256
Thine own wickedness shall c thee ... Jer 2:19 3256
O LORD, c me, but with judgment ... Jer 10:24 3256
but I will c thee in measure, and ... Jer 30:11 3256
of thee, but c thee in measure ... Jer 46:28 3256

CORRECTED
A servant will not be c by words ... Prov 29:19 3256
fathers of our flesh which c us ... Heb 12:9 *3810*

CORRECTETH
happy is the man whom God c ... Job 5:17 3198
For whom the LORD loveth he c ... Prov 3:12 3198

CORRECTION
causeth it to come, whether for c ... Job 37:13 7626
neither be weary of his c ... Prov 3:11 8433
as a fool to the c of the stocks ... Prov 7:22 4148
C is grievous unto him that ... Prov 15:10 4148
but the rod of c shall drive it ... Prov 22:15 4148
Withhold not c from the child ... Prov 23:13 4148
they received no c ... Jer 2:30 4148
they have refused to receive c ... Jer 5:3 4148
LORD their God, nor receiveth c ... Jer 7:28 4148
thou hast established them for c ... Hab 1:12 3198
she received not c ... Zeph 3:2 4148
for doctrine, for reproof, for c ... 2Ti 3:16 *1882*

CORRUPT
The earth also was c before God ... Gen 6:11 7843
the earth, and, behold, it was c ... Gen 6:12 7843
Lest ye c yourselves, and make you ... Deut 4:16 7843
shall c yourselves, and make a ... Deut 4:25 7843
ye will utterly c yourselves ... Deut 31:29 7843
My breath is c, my days are ... Job 17:1 2254
They are c, they have done ... Ps 14:1 7843
are c because of my foolishness ... Ps 38:5 4743
C are they, and have done ... Ps 53:1 7843
They are c, and speak wickedly ... Ps 73:8 4167
troubled fountain, and a c spring ... Prov 25:26 7843
nor according to your c doings ... Eze 20:44 7843
she was more c in her inordinate ... Eze 23:11 7843
c words to speak before me, till ... Dan 2:9 7844
covenant shall he c by flatteries ... Dan 11:32 2610
unto the Lord a c thing ... Mal 1:14 7843
I will c your seed, and spread ... Mal 2:3 1605
earth, where moth and rust doth c ... Mt 6:19 *853*
neither moth nor rust doth c ... Mt 6:20 *853*
but a c tree bringeth forth evil ... Mt 7:17 *4550*
neither can a c tree bring forth ... Mt 7:18 *4550*
the tree c, and his fruit c ... Mt 12:33 *4550*
tree bringeth not forth c fruit ... Lk 6:43 *4550*
neither doth a c tree bring forth ... Lk 6:43 *4550*
communications c good manners ... 1Cor 15:33 *5351*
as many, which c the word of God ... 2Cor 2:17 *2585*
which is c according to the ... Eph 4:22 *5351*
Let no c communication proceed ... Eph 4:29 *4550*
disputings of men of c minds ... 1Ti 6:5 *1311*
men of c minds, reprobate ... 2Ti 3:8 *2704*
in those things they c themselves ... Jude 10 *5351*
which did c the earth with her ... Rev 19:2 *5351*

CORRUPTED
for all flesh had c his way upon ... Gen 6:12 7843
the land was c by reason of the ... Ex 8:24 7843
land of Egypt, have c themselves ... Ex 32:7 7843
out of Egypt have c themselves ... Deut 9:12 7843
They have c themselves, their ... Deut 32:5 7843
c themselves more than their ... Judg 2:19 7843
thou wast c more than they in all ... Eze 16:47 7843
thou hast c thy wisdom by reason ... Eze 28:17 7843
They have deeply c themselves ... Hos 9:9 7843
rose early, and c all their doings ... Zeph 3:7 7843
ye have c the covenant of Levi, ... Mal 2:8 7843
wronged no man, we have c no man ... 2Cor 7:2 *5351*
so your minds should be c from ... 2Cor 11:3 *5351*
Your riches are c, and your ... Jas 5:2 *4595*

CORRUPTERS
of evildoers, children that are c ... Is 1:4 7843
they are all c ... Jer 6:28 7843

CORRUPTETH
thief approacheth, neither moth c ... Lk 12:33 *1311*

CORRUPTIBLE
into an image made like to c man ... Rom 1:23 *5349*
they do it to obtain a c crown ... 1Cor 9:25 *5349*
For this c must put on ... 1Cor 15:53 *5349*

So when this c shall have put on ... 1Cor 15:54 *5349*
were not redeemed with c things ... 1Pet 1:18 *5349*
Being born again, not of c seed ... 1Pet 1:23 *5349*
the heart, in that which is not c ... 1Pet 3:4 *862*

CORRUPTING
him the daughter of women, c her ... Dan 11:17 7843

C

CORRUPTION
because their c is in them ... Lev 22:25 4893
the right hand of the mount of c ... 2Kin 23:13 4889
I have said to c, Thou art my ... Job 17:14 7845
suffer thine Holy One to see c ... Ps 16:10 7845
still live for ever, and not see c ... Ps 49:9 7845
delivered it from the pit of c ... Is 38:17 1097
was turned in me into c, and I ... Dan 10:8 4889
thou brought up my life from c ... Jonah 2:6 7845
suffer thine Holy One to see c ... Acts 2:27 *1312*
hell, neither his flesh did see c ... Acts 2:31 *1312*
dead, now no more to return to c ... Acts 13:34 *1312*
suffer thine Holy One to see c ... Acts 13:35 *1312*
laid unto his fathers, and saw c ... Acts 13:36 *1312*
whom God raised again, saw no c ... Acts 13:37 *1312*
of c into the glorious liberty of ... Rom 8:21 *5356*
It is sown in c ... 1Cor 15:42 *5356*
neither doth c inherit ... 1Cor 15:50 *5356*
flesh shall of the flesh reap c ... Gal 6:8 *5356*
having escaped the c that is in ... 2Pet 1:4 *5356*
utterly perish in their own c ... 2Pet 2:12 *5356*
themselves are the servants of c ... 2Pet 2:19 *5356*

CORRUPTLY
And the people did yet c ... 2Chr 27:2 7843
We have dealt very c against thee ... Neh 1:7 2254

COSAM (*co'-sam*) *Son of Elmodam; ancestor of Jesus*
of Addi, which was the son of C ... Lk 3:28 *2973*

COST
we eaten at all of the king's c ... 2Sa 19:42
of that which doth c me nothing ... 2Sa 24:24 2600
offer burnt offerings without c ... 1Chr 21:24 2600
not down first, and counteth the c ... Lk 14:28 *1160*

COSTLINESS
in the sea by reason of her c ... Rev 18:19 *5094*

COSTLY
c stones, and hewed stones, to lay ... 1Kin 5:17 3368
All these were of c stones ... 1Kin 7:9 3368
And the foundation was of c stones ... 1Kin 7:10 3368
And above were c stones, after the ... 1Kin 7:11 3368
of ointment of spikenard, very c ... Jn 12:3 *4186*
or gold, or pearls, or c array ... 1Ti 2:9 *4185*

COTES
manner of beasts, and c for flocks ... 2Chr 32:28 220

COTTAGE
Zion is left as a c in a vineyard ... Is 1:8 5521
and shall be removed like a c ... Is 24:20 4412

COTTAGES
c for shepherds, and folds for ... Zeph 2:6 3741

COUCH
he went up to my c ... Gen 49:4 3326
my c shall ease my complaint ... Job 7:13 4904
When they c in their dens, and ... Job 38:40 7742
I water my c with my tears ... Ps 6:6 6210
of a bed, and in Damascus in a c ... Amos 3:12 6210
his c into the midst before Jesus ... Lk 5:19 *2826*
thee, Arise, and take up thy c ... Lk 5:24 *2826*

COUCHED
he c as a lion, and as an old lion ... Gen 49:9 7257
He c, he lay down as a lion, and ... Num 24:9 3766

COUCHES
stretch themselves upon their c ... Amos 6:4 6210
and laid them on beds and c ... Acts 5:15 *2895*

COUCHETH
and for the deep that c beneath ... Deut 33:13 7257

COUCHING
ass c down between two burdens ... Gen 49:14 7257

COUCHINGPLACE
and the Ammonites a c for flocks ... Eze 25:5 4769

COULD
so that they c not dwell together ... Gen 13:6 3201
were dim, so that he c not see ... Gen 27:1
wherein they were strangers c not ... Gen 36:7 3201
c not speak peaceably unto him ... Gen 37:4 3201
but there was none that c ... Gen 41:8
it c not be known that they had ... Gen 41:21
was none that c declare it to me ... Gen 41:24
c we certainly know that he would ... Gen 43:7
Then Joseph c not refrain himself ... Gen 45:1 3201
his brethren c not answer him ... Gen 45:3 3201
dim for age, so that he c not see ... Gen 48:10 3201
when she c not longer hide him, ... Ex 2:3 3201
the Egyptians c not drink of the ... Ex 7:21 3201
for they c not drink of the water ... Ex 7:24 3201
bring forth lice, but they c not ... Ex 8:18 3201
the magicians c not stand before ... Ex 9:11 3201
c not tarry, neither had they ... Ex 12:39 3201
they c not drink of the waters of ... Ex 15:23 3201
that they c not keep the passover ... Num 9:6 3201
the children of Israel c not ... Josh 7:12 3201
of Judah c not drive them out ... Josh 15:63 3201
Yet the children of Manasseh c ... Josh 17:12 3201
but c not drive out the ... Judg 1:19
so that they c not any longer ... Judg 2:14 3201
so that he c not draw the dagger ... Judg 3:22
that he c not do it by day, that ... Judg 6:27
for he c not frame to pronounce ... Judg 12:6
they c not in three days expound ... Judg 14:14 3201
sojourn where he c find a place ... Judg 17:8

every one c sling stones at an ... Judg 20:16
rose up before one c know another ... Ruth 3:14
to wax dim, that he c not see ... 1Sa 3:2 3201
eyes were dim, that he c not see ... 1Sa 4:15 3201
sought him, he c not be found ... 1Sa 10:21
and went whithersoever they c go ... 1Sa 23:13
c not go over the brook Besor ... 1Sa 30:10
that they c not follow David ... 1Sa 30:21
he c not live after that he was ... 2Sa 1:10
he c not answer Abner a word ... 2Sa 3:11 3201
c not find them, they returned to ... 2Sa 17:20
them, that they c not arise ... 2Sa 22:39
how that David my father c not ... 1Kin 5:3 3201
that c not be told nor numbered ... 1Kin 8:5
So that the priests c not stand ... 1Kin 8:11 3201
so that he c not pull it in again ... 1Kin 13:4 3201
But Ahijah c not see ... 1Kin 14:4 3201
king of Edom: but they c not ... 2Kin 3:26 3201
And they c not eat thereof ... 2Kin 4:40 3201
Ahaz, but c not overcome him ... 2Kin 16:5 3201
c use both the right hand and the ... 1Chr 12:2
that c handle shield and buckler, ... 1Chr 12:8
fifty thousand, which c keep rank ... 1Chr 12:33
that c keep rank, came with a ... 1Chr 12:38
But David c not go before it to ... 1Chr 21:30 3201
of the brass c not be found out ... 2Chr 4:18
which c not be told nor numbered ... 2Chr 5:6
So that the priests c not stand ... 2Chr 5:14 3201
the priests c not enter into the ... 2Chr 7:2 3201
and c not withstand them ... 2Chr 13:7
that they c not recover ... 2Chr 14:13
more than they c carry away ... 2Chr 20:25
that c handle spear and shield ... 2Chr 25:5
which c not deliver their own ... 2Chr 25:15
so that they c not flay all the ... 2Chr 29:34 3201
For they c not keep it at that ... 2Chr 30:3 3201
that c deliver his people out of ... 2Chr 32:14 3201
all that c skill of instruments ... 2Chr 34:12
but they c not shew their ... Ezr 2:59 3201
So that the people c not discern ... Ezr 3:13
that they c not cause them to ... Ezr 5:5
but they c not shew their ... Neh 7:61 3201
and women, and all that c hear with ... Neh 8:2
women, and those that c understand ... Neh 8:3
c not speak in the Jews' language ... Neh 13:24 5234
On that night c not the king ... Est 6:1 5074
tongue, although the enemy c not ... Est 7:4
and no man c withstand them ... Est 9:2
but I c not discern the form ... Job 4:16
I also c speak as ye do ... Job 16:4
I c heap up words against you, and ... Job 16:4
of his highness I c not endure ... Job 31:23 3201
sought him, but he c not be found ... Ps 37:36
then I c have borne it ... Ps 55:12
they have more than heart c wish ... Ps 73:7
floods, that they c not drink ... Ps 78:44
sought him, but I c not find him ... Song 5:6
What c have been done more to my ... Is 5:4
but c not prevail against it ... Is 7:1 3201
a people that c not profit them ... Is 30:5
they c not well strengthen their ... Is 33:23
they c not spread the sail ... Is 33:23
I asked of them, c answer a word ... Is 41:28
they c not deliver the burden, ... Is 46:2 3201
all ashamed, neither c they blush ... Jer 6:15 3045
all ashamed, neither c they blush ... Jer 8:12 3045
yet my mind c not be toward this ... Jer 15:1
with forbearing, and I c not stay ... Jer 20:9 3201
which c not be eaten, they were ... Jer 24:2
So that the LORD c no longer bear ... Jer 44:22 3201
so that men c not touch their ... Lam 4:14 3201
for a nation that c not save us ... Lam 4:17
the garden of God c not hide him ... Eze 31:8
a river that I c not pass over ... Eze 47:5 3201
a river that c not be passed over ... Eze 47:5
but they c not read the writing, ... Dan 5:8 3546
but they c not shew the ... Dan 5:15 5346
but they c find none occasion nor ... Dan 6:4 3202
that c deliver out of his hand ... Dan 8:4
there was none that c deliver the ... Dan 8:7
yet c he not heal you, nor cure ... Hos 5:13 3201
but they c not ... Jonah 1:13 3201
disciples, and they c not cure him ... Mt 17:16 *1410*
Why c not we cast him out ... Mt 17:19 *1410*
c ye not watch with me one hour ... Mt 26:40 *2480*
saw that he c prevail nothing ... Mt 27:24
insomuch that Jesus c no more ... Mk 1:45 *1410*
when they c not come nigh unto ... Mk 2:4 *1410*
so that they c not so much as eat ... Mk 3:20 *1410*
no man c bind him, no, not with ... Mk 5:3 *1410*
neither c any man tame him ... Mk 5:4 *2480*
he c there do no mighty work, ... Mk 6:5 *1410*
but she c not ... Mk 6:19 *1410*
but he c not be hid ... Mk 7:24 *1410*
and they c not ... Mk 9:18 *2489*
Why c not we cast him out ... Mk 9:28 *1410*
She hath done what she c ... Mk 14:8 *2192*
out, he c not speak unto them ... Lk 1:22 *1410*
when they c not find by what way ... Lk 5:19
that house, and c not shake it ... Lk 6:48 *2480*
c not come at him for the press ... Lk 8:19 *1410*
neither c be healed of any, ... Lk 8:43 *2480*
and they c not ... Lk 9:40 *1410*
c in no wise lift up herself ... Lk 13:11 *1410*
they c not answer him again to ... Lk 14:6 *2480*
c not for the press, because he ... Lk 19:3 *1410*
c not find what they might do ... Lk 19:48
that they c not tell whence it ... Lk 20:7 *5342*
they c not take hold of his words ... Lk 20:26 *2480*
were not of God, he c do nothing ... Jn 9:33 *1410*
C not this man, which opened the ... Jn 11:37 *1410*
Therefore they c not believe ... Jn 12:39 *1410*
c not contain the books that ... Jn 21:25
they c say nothing against it ... Acts 4:14 *2192*
was I, that I c withstand God ... Acts 11:17 *1415*
from which ye c not be justified ... Acts 13:39 *1410*
when he c not know the certainty ... Acts 21:34 *1410*
when I c not see for the glory of ... Acts 22:11
Paul, which they c not prove ... Acts 25:7 *2480*
c not bear up into the wind, we ... Acts 27:15 *1410*
commanded that they which c swim ... Acts 27:43 *1410*
For what the law c not do ... Rom 8:3 *102*
For I c wish that myself were ... Rom 9:3
c not speak unto you as unto ... 1Cor 3:1 *1410*
so that I c remove mountains, and ... 1Cor 13:2
c not stedfastly behold the face ... 2Cor 3:7 *1410*
that the children of Israel c not ... 2Cor 3:13
Would to God ye c bear with me a ... 2Cor 11:1
law given which c have given life ... Gal 3:21 *1410*
when we c no longer forbear ... 1Th 3:1
when I c no longer forbear, I ... 1Th 3:5
So we see that they c not enter ... Heb 3:19 *1410*
because he c swear by no greater, ... Heb 6:13 *2192*
that c not make him that did the ... Heb 9:9 *1410*
(For they c not endure that which ... Heb 12:20
multitude, which no man c number ... Rev 7:9 *1410*
no man c learn that song but the ... Rev 14:3 *1410*

COULDEST

and done evil things as thou c ... Jer 3:5 3201
them, and yet c not be satisfied ... Eze 16:28
c not thou watch one hour ... Mk 14:37 *2480*
Thou c have no power at all ... Jn 19:11

COULDST

seeing thou c reveal this secret ... Dan 2:47 3202

COULTER

every man his share, and his c ... 1Sa 13:20 855

COULTERS

for the mattocks, and for the c ... 1Sa 13:21 855

COUNCIL

the princes of Judah and their c ... Ps 68:27 7277
Raca, shall be in danger of the c ... Mt 5:22 *4892*
held a c against him, how they ... Mt 12:14 *4824*
priests, and elders, and all the c ... Mt 26:59 *4892*
all the c sought for witness ... Mk 14:55 *4892*
elders and scribes and the whole c ... Mk 15:1 *4892*
together, and led him into their c ... Lk 22:66 *4892*
priests and the Pharisees a c ... Jn 11:47 *4892*
them to go aside out of the c ... Acts 4:15 *4892*
him, and called the c together ... Acts 5:21 *4892*
them, they set them before the c ... Acts 5:27 *4892*
Then stood there up one in the c ... Acts 5:34 *4892*
from the presence of the c ... Acts 5:41 *4892*
him, and brought him to the c ... Acts 6:12 *4892*
And all that sat in the c, looking ... Acts 6:15 *4892*
priests and all their c to appear ... Acts 22:30 *4892*
Paul, earnestly beholding the c ... Acts 23:1 *4892*
Pharisees, he cried out in the c ... Acts 23:6 *4892*
Now therefore ye with the c ... Acts 23:15 *4892*
down Paul to morrow into the c ... Acts 23:20 *4892*
I brought him forth into their c ... Acts 23:28 *4892*
in me, while I stood before the c ... Acts 24:20 *4892*
when he had conferred with the c ... Acts 25:12 *4824*

COUNCILS

they will deliver you up to the c ... Mt 10:17 *4891*
they shall deliver you up to c ... Mk 13:9 *4891*

COUNSEL

unto my voice, I will give thee c ... Ex 18:19 3289
who shall ask c for him after the ... Num 27:21
Israel, through the c of Balaam ... Num 31:16 1697
For they are a nation void of c ... Deut 32:28 6098
asked not c at the mouth of the ... Josh 9:14
And they said unto him, Ask c ... Judg 18:5
give here your advice and c ... Judg 20:7 6098
asked c of God, and said, Which of ... Judg 20:18
asked c of the LORD, saying, ... Judg 20:23
And Saul asked c of God, Shall I ... 1Sa 14:37
turn the c of Ahithophel into ... 2Sa 15:31 6098
for me defeat the c of Ahithophel ... 2Sa 15:34 6098
Give c among you what we shall do ... 2Sa 16:20 6098
the c of Ahithophel, which he ... 2Sa 16:23 6098
so was all the c of Ahithophel ... 2Sa 16:23 6098
The c that Ahithophel hath given ... 2Sa 17:7 6098
Therefore I c that all Israel be ... 2Sa 17:11 3289
The c of Hushai the Archite is ... 2Sa 17:14 6098
better than the c of Ahithophel ... 2Sa 17:14 6098
defeat the good c of Ahithophel ... 2Sa 17:14 6098
and thus did Ahithophel c Absalom ... 2Sa 17:15 3289
saw that his c was not followed ... 2Sa 17:23 6098
They shall surely ask c at Abel ... 2Sa 20:18
let me, I pray thee, give thee c ... 1Kin 1:12 6098
he forsook the c of the old men ... 1Kin 12:8 6098
What c give ye that we may answer ... 1Kin 12:9 3289
old men's c that they gave him ... 1Kin 12:13 6098
them after the c of the young men ... 1Kin 12:14 6098
Whereupon the king took c ... 1Kin 12:28 3289
took c with his servants, saying, ... 2Kin 6:8 3289
are but vain words,) I have c ... 2Kin 18:20 6098
also for asking c of one that had ... 1Chr 10:13
king Rehoboam took c with the old ... 2Chr 10:6 3289
What c give ye me to return ... 2Chr 10:6 3289
But he forsook the c which the ... 2Chr 10:8 6098
took c with the young men that ... 2Chr 10:8 3289
forsook the c of the old men ... 2Chr 10:13 6098
He walked also after their c ... 2Chr 22:5 6098
Art thou made of the king's c ... 2Chr 25:16 3289
and hast not hearkened unto my c ... 2Chr 25:16 6098
For the king had taken c, and his ... 2Chr 30:2 3289
the whole assembly took c to keep ... 2Chr 30:23 3289
He took c with his princes and his ... 2Chr 32:3 3289
according to the c of my lord ... Ezr 10:3 6098
according to the c of the princes ... Ezr 10:8 6098
God had brought their c to nought ... Neh 4:15 6098
and let us take c together ... Neh 6:7 3289
the c of the froward is carried ... Job 5:13 6098
and shine upon the c of the wicked ... Job 10:3 6098
is wisdom and strength, he hath c ... Job 12:13 6098
his own c shall cast him down ... Job 18:7 6098
the c of the wicked is far from ... Job 21:16 6098
but the c of the wicked is far ... Job 22:18 6098
waited, and kept silence at my c ... Job 29:21 6098
c by words without knowledge ... Job 38:2 6098
that hideth c without knowledge ... Job 42:3 6098
not in the c of the ungodly ... Ps 1:1 6098
and the rulers take c together ... Ps 2:2 3245
long shall I take c in my soul ... Ps 13:2 6098
Ye have shamed the c of the poor ... Ps 14:6 6098
the LORD, who hath given me c ... Ps 16:7 3289
own heart, and fulfil all thy c ... Ps 20:4 6098
while they took c together ... Ps 31:13 3245
The LORD bringeth the c of the ... Ps 33:10 6098
The c of the LORD standeth for ... Ps 33:11 6098
We took sweet c together, and ... Ps 55:14 5475
from the secret c of the wicked ... Ps 64:2 5475
wait for my soul take c together ... Ps 71:10 3289
Thou shalt guide me with thy c ... Ps 73:24 6098
taken crafty c against thy people ... Ps 83:3 5475
they waited not for his c ... Ps 106:13 6098
they provoked him with their c ... Ps 106:43 6098
contemned the c of the most High ... Ps 107:11 6098
ye have set at nought all my c ... Prov 1:25 6098
They would none of my c ... Prov 1:30 6098
C is mine, and sound wisdom ... Prov 8:14 6098
Where no c is, the people fall ... Prov 11:14 8458
he that hearkeneth unto c is wise ... Prov 12:15 6098
Without c purposes are ... Prov 15:22 5475
Hear c, and receive instruction, ... Prov 19:20 6098
nevertheless the c of the LORD ... Prov 19:21 6098
C in the heart of man is like ... Prov 20:5 6098
Every purpose is established by c ... Prov 20:18 6098
nor c against the LORD ... Prov 21:30 6098
For by wise c thou shalt make thy ... Prov 24:6 8458
of a man's friend by hearty c ... Prov 27:9 6098
I c thee to keep the king's ... Eccl 8:2
let the c of the Holy One of ... Is 5:19 6098
have taken evil c against thee ... Is 7:5 3289
Take c together, and it shall come ... Is 8:10 6098
and understanding, the spirit of c ... Is 11:2 6098
Take c, execute judgment ... Is 16:3 6098
and I will destroy the c thereof ... Is 19:3 6098
the c of the wise counsellors of ... Is 19:11 6098
because of the c of the LORD of ... Is 19:17 6098
hath taken this c against Tyre ... Is 23:8 3289
of hosts, which is wonderful in c ... Is 28:29 6098
to hide their c from the LORD ... Is 29:15 6098
saith the LORD, that take c ... Is 30:1 6098
they are but vain words) I have c ... Is 36:5 6098
With whom took he c, and who ... Is 40:14 3289
and performeth the c of his ... Is 44:26 6098
yea, let them take c together ... Is 45:21 3289
My c shall stand, and I will do ... Is 46:10 6098
executeth my c from a far country ... Is 46:11 6098
nor c from the wise, nor the word ... Jer 18:18 6098
all their c against me to slay me ... Jer 18:23 6098
I will make void the c of Judah ... Jer 19:7 6098
hath stood in the c of the LORD ... Jer 23:18 5475
But if they had stood in my c ... Jer 23:22 5475
Great in c, and mighty in work ... Jer 32:19 6098
and if I give thee c, wilt thou ... Jer 38:15 3289
is c perished from the prudent ... Jer 49:7 6098
Therefore hear the c of the LORD ... Jer 49:20 6098
Babylon hath taken c against you ... Jer 49:30 6098
hear ye the c of the LORD ... Jer 50:45 6098
priest, and c from the ancients ... Eze 7:26 6098
give wicked c in this city ... Eze 11:2 6098
Then Daniel answered with c ... Dan 2:14 5843
let my c be acceptable unto thee, ... Dan 4:27 4431
My people ask c at their stocks, ... Hos 4:12
shall be ashamed of his own c ... Hos 10:6 6098
neither understand they his c ... Mic 4:12 6098
the c of peace shall be between ... Zec 6:13 6098
took c how they might entangle ... Mt 22:15 *4824*
elders of the people took c ... Mt 27:1 *4824*
And they took c, and bought with ... Mt 27:7 *4824*
with the elders, and had taken c ... Mt 28:12 *4824*
straightway took c with the ... Mk 3:6 *4824*
lawyers rejected the c of God ... Lk 7:30 *1012*
same had not consented to the c ... Lk 23:51 *1012*
took c together for to put him to ... Jn 11:53 *4823*
which gave c to the Jews, that it ... Jn 18:14 *4823*
delivered by the determinate c ... Acts 2:23 *1012*
thy c determined before to be ... Acts 4:28 *1012*
the heart, and took c to slay them ... Acts 5:33 *1011*
for if this c or this work be of ... Acts 5:38 *1012*
the Jews took c to kill him ... Acts 9:23 *4823*
declare unto you all the c of God ... Acts 20:27 *1012*
the soldiers' c was to kill the ... Acts 27:42 *1012*
after the c of his own will ... Eph 1:11 *1012*
promise the immutability of his c ... Heb 6:17 *1012*
I c thee to buy of me gold tried ... Rev 3:18 *4823*

COUNSELED

How hast thou c him that hath no ... Job 26:3 3289

COUNSELLED

which he c in those days, was as ... 2Sa 16:23 3289
and thus and thus have I c ... 2Sa 17:15 3289
hath Ahithophel c against you ... 2Sa 17:21 3289

COUNSELLOR

the Gilonite, David's c, from his ... 2Sa 15:12 3289
for Zechariah his son, a wise c ... 1Chr 26:14 3289
Jonathan David's uncle was a c ... 1Chr 27:32 3289
And Ahithophel was the king's c ... 1Chr 27:33 3289
mother was his c to do wickedly ... 2Chr 22:3 3289
and the honourable man, and the c ... Is 3:3 3289
name shall be called Wonderful, C ... Is 9:6 3289
or being his c hath taught him ... Is 40:13 6098
among them, and there was no c ... Is 41:28 3289
is thy c perished? ... Mic 4:9 3289

evil against the LORD, a wicked c.......... Nah 1:11 3289
of Arimathaea, an honourable c.......... Mk 15:43 *1010*
there was a man named Joseph, a c..... Lk 23:50 *1010*
or who hath been his c.......... Rom 11:34 *4825*

COUNSELLORS

for they were his c after the.......... 2Chr 22:4 3289
And hired c against them, to.......... Ezr 4:5 3289
of the king, and of his seven c.......... Ezr 7:14 3272
his c have freely offered unto.......... Ezr 7:15 3272
unto me before the king, and his c.......... Ezr 7:28 3289
our God, which the king, and his c.......... Ezr 8:25 3289
c of the earth, which built.......... Job 3:14 3289
He leadeth c away spoiled, and.......... Job 12:17 3289
also are my delight, and my c.......... Ps 119:24 6098
multitude of c there is safety.......... Prov 11:14 3289
but to the c of peace is joy.......... Prov 12:20 3289
of c they are established.......... Prov 15:22 3289
in multitude of c there is safety.......... Prov 24:6 3289
thy c as at the beginning.......... Is 1:26 3289
the counsel of the wise c of.......... Is 19:11 3289
the judges, the treasurers, the c.......... Dan 3:2 1884
the judges, the treasurers, the c.......... Dan 3:3 1884
and spake, and said unto his c.......... Dan 3:24 1907
and captains, and the king's c.......... Dan 3:27 1907
and my c and my lords sought unto.......... Dan 4:36 1907
governors, and the princes, the c.......... Dan 6:7 1907

COUNSELS

it is turned round about by his c.......... Job 37:12 8458
let them fall by their own c.......... Ps 5:10 4156
and they walked in their own c.......... Ps 81:12 4156
shall attain unto wise c.......... Prov 1:5 8458
but the c of the wicked are.......... Prov 12:5 8458
to thee excellent things in c.......... Prov 22:20 4156
thy c of old are faithfulness and.......... Is 25:1 6098
wearied in the multitude of thy c.......... Is 47:13 6098
their ear, but walked in the c.......... Jer 7:24 4156
them, because of their own c.......... Hos 11:6 4156
of Ahab, and ye walk in their c.......... Mic 6:16 4156
make manifest the c of the hearts.......... 1Cor 4:5 *1012*

COUNT

shall make your c for the lamb.......... Ex 12:4 3699
then ye shall c the fruit thereof.......... Lev 19:23
ye shall c unto you from the.......... Lev 23:15 5608
Then let him c the years of the.......... Lev 25:27 2803
jubile, then he shall c with him.......... Lev 25:52 2803
Who can c the dust of Jacob, and.......... Num 23:10 4487
C not thine handmaid for a.......... 1Sa 1:16 5414
and my maids, c me for a stranger.......... Job 19:15 2803
he see my ways, and c all my steps.......... Job 31:4 5608
The LORD shall c, when he writeth.......... Ps 87:6 5608
If I should c them, they are more.......... Ps 139:18 5608
I c them mine enemies.......... Ps 139:22 1961
Shall I c them pure with the.......... Mic 6:11
neither c I my life dear unto.......... Acts 20:24 *2192*
I c all things but loss for the.......... Phil 3:8 *2233*
do c them but dung, that I may.......... Phil 3:8 *2233*
Brethren, I c not myself to have.......... Phil 3:13 *3049*
that our God would c you worthy.......... 2Th 1:11 *515*
Yet c him not as an enemy, but.......... 2Th 3:15 *2233*
servants as are under the yoke c.......... 1Ti 6:1 *2233*
If thou c me therefore a partner,.......... Philem 17 *2192*
c it all joy when ye fall into.......... Jas 1:2 *2233*
we c them happy which endure.......... Jas 5:11 *3106*
as they that c it pleasure to.......... 2Pet 2:13 *2233*
promise, as some men c slackness.......... 2Pet 3:9 *2233*
c the number of the beast.......... Rev 13:18 *5585*

COUNTED

he c it to him for righteousness.......... Gen 15:6 2803
that shall be c stolen with me.......... Gen 30:33
Are we not c of him strangers.......... Gen 31:15 2803
of testimony, as it was c.......... Ex 38:21 6485
be c as the fields of the country.......... Lev 25:31 2803
then it shall be c unto the.......... Num 18:30 2803
which is c to the Canaanite.......... Josh 13:3 2803
son Solomon shall be c offenders.......... 1Kin 1:21
be numbered nor c for multitude.......... 1Kin 3:8 5608
Benjamin c he not among them.......... 1Chr 21:6 6485
as they were c by number of names.......... 1Chr 23:24 6485
for they were c faithful, and.......... Neh 13:13 2803
Wherefore are we c as beasts.......... Job 18:3 2803
Darts are c as stubble.......... Job 41:29 2803
we are c as sheep for the.......... Ps 44:22 2803
I am c with them that go down.......... Ps 88:4 2803
And that was c unto him for.......... Ps 106:31 2803
he holdeth his peace, is c wise.......... Prov 17:28 2803
it shall be c a curse to him.......... Prov 27:14 2803
hoofs shall be c like flint.......... Is 5:28 2803
fruitful field be c for a forest.......... Is 32:15 2803
where is he that c the towers.......... Is 33:18 5608
are c as the small dust of the.......... Is 40:15 2803
they are c to him less than.......... Is 40:17 2803
but they were c as a strange.......... Hos 8:12 2803
because they c him as a prophet.......... Mt 14:5 *2192*
for all men c John, that he was a.......... Mk 11:32 *2192*
rejoicing that they were c worthy.......... Acts 5:41 *2661*
they c the price of them, and.......... Acts 19:19 *4860*
be c for circumcision.......... Rom 2:26 *3049*
God, and it was c unto him for.......... Rom 4:3 *3049*
his faith is c for righteousness.......... Rom 4:5 *3049*
of the promise are c for the seed.......... Rom 9:8 *3049*
those I c loss for Christ.......... Phil 3:7 *2233*
that ye may be c worthy of the.......... 2Th 1:5 *2661*
me, for that he c me faithful.......... 1Ti 1:12 *2233*
well be c worthy of double honour.......... 1Ti 5:17 *515*
For this man was c worthy of more.......... Heb 3:3 *515*
But he whose descent is not c.......... Heb 7:6 *1075*
hath c the blood of the covenant,.......... Heb 10:29 *2233*

COUNTENANCE

was very wroth, and his c fell.......... Gen 4:5 6440
and why is thy c fallen.......... Gen 4:6 6440
And Jacob beheld the c of Laban.......... Gen 31:2 6440
unto them, I see your father's c.......... Gen 31:5 6440
Neither shalt thou c a poor man.......... Ex 23:3 1921
The LORD lift up his c upon thee.......... Num 6:26 6440
A nation of fierce c, which shall.......... Deut 28:50 6440
his c was like the c of.......... Judg 13:6 4758
did eat, and her c was no more sad.......... 1Sa 1:18 6440
unto Samuel, Look not on his c.......... 1Sa 16:7 4758
ruddy, and withal of a beautiful c.......... 1Sa 16:12 5869
a youth, and ruddy, and of a fair c.......... 1Sa 17:42 4758
and of a beautiful c.......... 1Sa 25:3 8389
she was a woman of a fair c.......... 2Sa 14:27 4758
And he settled his c stedfastly.......... 2Kin 8:11 6440
said unto me, Why is thy c sad.......... Neh 2:2 6440
why should not my c be sad.......... Neh 2:3 6440
thou changest his c, and sendest.......... Job 14:20 6440
the light of my c they cast not.......... Job 29:24 6440
up the light of thy c upon us.......... Ps 4:6 6440
through the pride of his c.......... Ps 10:4 639
his c doth behold the upright.......... Ps 11:7 6440
him exceeding glad with thy c.......... Ps 21:6 6440
praise him for the help of his c.......... Ps 42:5 6440
him, who is the health of my c.......... Ps 42:11 6440
him, who is the health of my c.......... Ps 43:5 6440
thine arm, and the light of thy c.......... Ps 44:3 6440
perish at the rebuke of thy c.......... Ps 80:16 6440
O LORD, in the light of thy c.......... Ps 89:15 6440
secret sins in the light of thy c.......... Ps 90:8 6440
A merry heart maketh a cheerful c.......... Prov 15:13 6440
the light of the king's c is life.......... Prov 16:15 6440
so doth an angry c a backbiting.......... Prov 25:23 6440
sharpeneth the c of his friend.......... Prov 27:17 6440
of the c the heart is made better.......... Eccl 7:3 6440
of the stairs, let me see thy c.......... Song 2:14 4758
is thy voice, and thy c is comely.......... Song 2:14 4758
his c is as Lebanon, excellent as.......... Song 5:15 4758
The shew of their c doth witness.......... Is 3:9 6440
they shall be troubled in their c.......... Eze 27:35 6440
the c of the children that eat of.......... Dan 1:13 4758
Then the king's c was changed.......... Dan 5:6 2122
his c was changed in him, and his.......... Dan 5:9 2122
thee, nor let thy c be changed.......... Dan 5:10 2122
me, and my c changed in me.......... Dan 7:28 2122
to the full, a king of fierce c.......... Dan 8:23 6440
as the hypocrites, of a sad c.......... Mt 6:16 *4659*
His c was like lightning, and his.......... Mt 28:3 *2397*
the fashion of his c was altered.......... Lk 9:29 *4383*
make me full of joy with thy c.......... Acts 2:28 *4383*
of Moses for the glory of his c.......... 2Cor 3:7 *4383*
his c was as the sun shineth in.......... Rev 1:16 *3799*

COUNTENANCES

Then let our c be looked upon.......... Dan 1:13 4758
ten days their c appeared fairer.......... Dan 1:15 4758

COUNTERVAIL

could not c the king's damage.......... Est 7:4 7737

COUNTETH

he c me unto him as one of his.......... Job 19:11 2803
me, he c me for his enemy,.......... Job 33:10 2803
c the cost, whether he have.......... Lk 14:28 *5585*

COUNTING

c one by one, to find out the.......... Eccl 7:27

COUNTRIES

after their tongues, in their c.......... Gen 10:20 776
thy seed, I will give all these c.......... Gen 26:3 776
give unto thy seed all these c.......... Gen 26:4 776
all c came into Egypt to Joseph.......... Gen 41:57 776
These are the c which Moses did.......... Josh 13:32
these are the c which the.......... Josh 14:1
and her towns, even three c.......... Josh 17:11 5316
they among all the gods of the c.......... 2Kin 18:35 776
fame and of glory throughout all c.......... 1Chr 22:5 776
and over all the kingdoms of the c.......... 1Chr 29:30 776
throughout all the c of Judah.......... 2Chr 11:23 776
service of the kingdoms of the c.......... 2Chr 12:8 776
upon all the inhabitants of the c.......... 2Chr 15:5 776
on all the kingdoms of those c.......... 2Chr 20:29 776
c that pertained to the children.......... 2Chr 34:33 776
because of the people of those c.......... Ezr 3:3 776
ruled over all c beyond the river.......... Ezr 4:20
shall wound the heads over many c.......... Ps 110:6 776
and give ear, all ye of far c.......... Is 8:9 776
waste all the nations, and their c.......... Is 37:18 776
all c whither I have driven them.......... Jer 23:3 776
from all c whither I had driven.......... Jer 23:8 776
prophesied both against many c.......... Jer 28:8 776
I will gather them out of all c.......... Jer 32:37 776
Edom, and that were in all the c.......... Jer 40:11 776
c that are round about her.......... Eze 5:5 776
the c that are round about her.......... Eze 5:6 776
shall be scattered through the c.......... Eze 6:8 776
I have scattered them among the c.......... Eze 11:16 776
in the c where they shall come.......... Eze 11:16 776
assemble you out of the c where.......... Eze 11:17 776
and disperse them in the c.......... Eze 12:15 776
and disperse them through the c.......... Eze 20:23 776
heathen, as the families of the c.......... Eze 20:32 776
of the c wherein ye are scattered.......... Eze 20:34 776
gather you out of the c wherein.......... Eze 20:41 776
heathen, and a mocking to all c.......... Eze 22:4 776
and disperse thee in the c.......... Eze 22:15 776
cause thee to perish out of the c.......... Eze 25:7 776
midst of the c that are desolate.......... Eze 29:12 776
will disperse them through the c.......... Eze 29:12 776
midst of the c that are desolate.......... Eze 30:7 776
will disperse them through the c.......... Eze 30:23 776
and disperse them among the c.......... Eze 30:26 776
into the c which thou hast not.......... Eze 32:9 776
people, and gather them from the c.......... Eze 34:13 776
these two c shall be mine, and we.......... Eze 35:10 776
they were dispersed through the c.......... Eze 36:19 776
and gather you out of all c.......... Eze 36:24 776
through all the c whither thou.......... Dan 9:7 776
and he shall enter into the c.......... Dan 11:40 776
many c shall be overthrown.......... Dan 11:41
forth his hand also upon the c.......... Dan 11:42 776
they shall remember me in far c.......... Zec 10:9
that are in the c enter thereinto.......... Lk 21:21 *5561*

COUNTRY

unto Abram, Get thee out of thy c.......... Gen 12:1 776
smote all the c of the Amalekites.......... Gen 14:7 7704
the smoke of the c went up as the.......... Gen 19:28 776
from thence toward the south c.......... Gen 20:1 776
But thou shalt go unto my c.......... Gen 24:4 776
for he dwelt in the south c.......... Gen 24:62 776
lived, eastward, unto the east c.......... Gen 25:6 776
It must not be so done in our c.......... Gen 29:26 4725
unto mine own place, and to my c.......... Gen 30:25 776
the land of Seir, the c of Edom.......... Gen 32:3 7704
saidst unto me, Return unto thy c.......... Gen 32:9 776
Hamor the Hivite, prince of the c.......... Gen 34:2 776
went into the c from the face of.......... Gen 36:6 776
us, and took us for spies of the c.......... Gen 42:30 776
And the man, the lord of the c.......... Gen 42:33 776
land of Egypt, in the c of Goshen.......... Gen 47:27 776
whether it be one of your own c.......... Lev 16:29 249
whether it be one of your own c.......... Lev 17:15 249
as for one of your own c.......... Lev 24:22 249
be counted as the fields of the c.......... Lev 25:31 776
All that are born of the c shall.......... Num 15:13 249
pass, I pray thee, through thy c.......... Num 20:17 776
valley, that is in the c of Moab.......... Num 21:20 7704
Even the c which the LORD smote.......... Num 32:4 776
the cities of the c round about.......... Num 32:33 776
the c of Argob unto the coasts of.......... Deut 3:14 2256
in the wilderness, in the plain c.......... Deut 4:43 776
that I am come unto the c which.......... Deut 26:3 776
of Israel to search out the c.......... Josh 2:2 776
be come to search out all the c.......... Josh 2:3 776
of the c do faint because of us.......... Josh 2:24 776
two men that had spied out the c.......... Josh 6:22 776
was noised throughout all the c.......... Josh 6:27 776
them, saying, Go up and view the c.......... Josh 7:2 776
Israel, We be come from a far c.......... Josh 9:6 776
From a very far c thy servants.......... Josh 9:9 776
inhabitants of our c spake to us.......... Josh 9:11 776
smote all the c of the hills.......... Josh 10:40 776
all the c of Goshen, even unto.......... Josh 10:41 776
the hills, and all the south c.......... Josh 11:16
the kings of the c which Joshua.......... Josh 12:7 776
the wilderness, and in the south c.......... Josh 12:8
of the hill c from Lebanon unto.......... Josh 13:6
dukes of Sihon, dwelling in the c.......... Josh 13:21 776
then get thee up to the wood c.......... Josh 17:15
made an end of dividing the c.......... Josh 19:51 776
is Hebron, in the hill c of Judah.......... Josh 21:11
to go unto the c of Gilead.......... Josh 22:9 776
the c was in quietness forty.......... Judg 8:28 776
the inhabitants of that c.......... Judg 11:21 776
in Aijalon in the c of Zebulun.......... Judg 12:12 776
enemy, and the destroyer of our c.......... Judg 16:24 776
went to spy out the c of Laish.......... Judg 18:14 776
sent her throughout all the c of.......... Judg 20:6 7704
went to sojourn in the c of Moab.......... Ruth 1:1 7704
And they came into the c of Moab.......... Ruth 1:2 7704
might return from the c of Moab.......... Ruth 1:6 7704
for she had heard in the c of.......... Ruth 1:6 7704
returned out of the c of Moab.......... Ruth 1:22 7704
with Naomi out of the c of Moab.......... Ruth 2:6 7704
come again out of the c of Moab.......... Ruth 4:3 7704
the ark of the LORD was in the c.......... 1Sa 6:1 7704
of c villages, even unto the.......... 1Sa 6:18 6521
the camp from the c round about.......... 1Sa 14:21
me a place in some town in the c.......... 1Sa 27:5 7704
time that David dwelt in the c of.......... 1Sa 27:7 7704
in the c of the Philistines.......... 1Sa 27:11 7704
all the c wept with a loud voice,.......... 2Sa 15:23 776
over the face of all the c.......... 2Sa 18:8 776
in the c of Benjamin in Zelah.......... 2Sa 21:14 776
son of Uri was in the c of Gilead.......... 1Kin 4:19 776
in the c of Sihon king of the.......... 1Kin 4:19 776
of all the children of the east c.......... 1Kin 4:30
of a far c for thy name's sake.......... 1Kin 8:41 776
she turned and went to her own c.......... 1Kin 10:13 776
and of the governors of the c.......... 1Kin 10:15 776
that I may go to mine own c.......... 1Kin 11:21 776
thou seekest to go to thine own c.......... 1Kin 11:22 776
but the Syrians filled the c.......... 1Kin 20:27 776
city, and every man to his own c.......... 1Kin 22:36 776
the c was filled with water.......... 2Kin 3:20 776
the Moabites, even in their c.......... 2Kin 3:24
their c out of mine hand, that.......... 2Kin 18:35 776
said, They are come from a far c.......... 2Kin 20:14 776
begat children in the c of Moab.......... 1Chr 8:8 7704
wasted the c of the children of.......... 1Chr 20:1 776
but is come from a far c for thy.......... 2Chr 6:32 776
governors of the c brought gold.......... 2Chr 9:14 776
much cattle, both in the low c.......... 2Chr 26:10
invaded the cities of the low c.......... 2Chr 28:18
to city through the c of Ephraim.......... 2Chr 30:10 776
the plain c round about Jerusalem.......... Neh 12:28
so is good news from a far c.......... Prov 25:25 776
Your c is desolate, your cities.......... Is 1:7 776
They come from a far c, from the.......... Is 13:5 776
thee like a ball into a large c.......... Is 22:18 776
are come from a far c unto me.......... Is 39:3 776
executeth my counsel from a far c.......... Is 46:11 776
I brought you into a plentiful c.......... Jer 2:7 776
that watchers come from a far c.......... Jer 4:16 776
and the sweet cane from a far c.......... Jer 6:20 776
a people cometh from the north c.......... Jer 6:22 776
of them that dwell in a far c.......... Jer 8:19 776
commotion out of the north c.......... Jer 10:22 776
no more, nor see his native c.......... Jer 22:10 776
that bare thee, into another c.......... Jer 22:26 776
of Israel out of the north c.......... Jer 23:8 776

C

will bring them from the north c	Jer 31:8	776
which is in the c of Benjamin	Jer 32:8	776
in the c of Pathros, saying,	Jer 44:1	776
north c by the river Euphrates	Jer 46:10	776
the remnant of the c of Caphtor	Jer 47:4	339
judgment is come upon the plain c	Jer 48:21	776
of great nations from the north c	Jer 50:9	776
us go every one into his own c	Jer 51:9	776
out of the c where they sojourn	Eze 20:38	776
into the c for the which I lifted	Eze 20:42	776
his frontiers, the glory of the c	Eze 25:9	776
the c shall be destitute of that	Eze 32:15	776
all the inhabited places of the c	Eze 34:13	776
issue out toward the east c	Eze 47:8	1552
be unto you as born in the c	Eze 47:22	249
And Jacob fled into the c of Syria	Hos 12:12	7704
what is thy c?	Jonah 1:8	776
my saying, when I was yet in my c	Jonah 4:2	127
therein go forth into the north c	Zec 6:6	776
go forth toward the south c	Zec 6:6	776
c have quieted my spirit in the	Zec 6:8	776
quieted my spirit in the north c	Zec 6:8	776
east c, and from the west c	Zec 8:7	776
into their own c another way	Mt 2:12	*5561*
side into the c of the Gergesenes	Mt 8:28	*5561*
abroad his fame in all that c	Mt 9:31	*1093*
when he was come into his own c	Mt 13:54	*3968*
without honour, save in his own c	Mt 13:57	*3968*
out into all that c round about	Mt 14:35	*4066*
husbandmen, and went into a far c	Mt 21:33	*589*
as a man travelling into a far c	Mt 25:14	*589*
into the c of the Gadarenes	Mk 5:1	*5561*
not send them away out of the c	Mk 5:10	*5561*
told it in the city, and in the c	Mk 5:14	*68*
thence, and came into his own c	Mk 6:1	*3968*
without honour, but in his own c	Mk 6:4	*3968*
may go into the c round about	Mk 6:36	*68*
into villages, or cities, or c	Mk 6:56	*68*
husbandmen, and went into a far c	Mk 12:1	*589*
passed by, coming out of the c	Mk 15:21	*68*
they walked, and went into the c	Mk 16:12	*68*
went into the hill c with haste	Lk 1:39	
all the hill c of Judaea	Lk 1:65	
And there were in the same c	Lk 2:8	*5561*
came into all the c about Jordan	Lk 3:3	*4066*
Capernaum, do also here in thy c	Lk 4:23	*3968*
prophet is accepted in his own c	Lk 4:24	*3968*
every place of the c round about	Lk 4:37	*4066*
arrived at the c of the Gadarenes	Lk 8:26	*5561*
told it in the city and in the c	Lk 8:34	*68*
c of the Gadarenes round about	Lk 8:37	*4066*
c round about, and lodge, and get	Lk 9:12	*68*
and took his journey into a far c	Lk 15:13	*5561*
himself to a citizen of that c	Lk 15:15	*5561*
a far c to receive for himself a	Lk 19:12	*5561*
went into a far c for a long time	Lk 20:9	*589*
a Cyrenian, coming out of the c	Lk 23:26	*68*
hath no honour in his own c	Jn 4:44	*3968*
unto a c near to the wilderness	Jn 11:54	*5561*
many went out of the c up to	Jn 11:55	*5561*
a Levite, and of the c of Cyprus	Acts 4:36	*1085*
unto him, Get thee out of thy c	Acts 7:3	*1093*
because their c was nourished by	Acts 12:20	*5561*
was nourished by the king's c	Acts 12:20	*5561*
was with the deputy of the c	Acts 13:7	
and went over all the c of Galatia	Acts 18:23	*5561*
that they drew near to some c	Acts 27:27	*5561*
of promise, as in a strange c	Heb 11:9	
plainly that they seek a c	Heb 11:14	*3968*
that c from whence they came out	Heb 11:15	
But now they desire a better c	Heb 11:16	

COUNTRYMEN

robbers, in perils by mine own c	2Cor 11:26	*1085*
like things of your own c	1Th 2:14	*4853*

COUPLE

c the curtains together with the	Ex 26:6	2266
thou shalt c five curtains by	Ex 26:9	2266
c the tent together, that it may	Ex 26:11	2266
of brass to c the tent together	Ex 36:18	2266
for it, to c it together	Ex 39:4	2266
servant with him, and a c of asses	Judg 19:3	6776
make me a c of cakes in my sight,	2Sa 13:6	8147
with a c of asses saddled, and	2Sa 16:1	6776
a chariot with a c of horsemen	Is 21:7	6776
of men, with a c of horsemen	Is 21:9	6776

COUPLED

be c together one to another	Ex 26:3	2266
shall be c one to another	Ex 26:3	2266
they shall be c together beneath,	Ex 26:24	8382
they shall be c together above	Ex 26:24	8535
he c the five curtains one unto	Ex 36:10	2266
curtains he c one unto another	Ex 36:10	2266
c the curtains one unto another	Ex 36:13	2266
he c five curtains by themselves,	Ex 36:16	2266
And they were c beneath, and	Ex 36:29	8382
c together at the head thereof,	Ex 36:29	8535
the two edges was it c together	Ex 39:4	2266
chaste conversation c with fear	1Pet 3:2	

COUPLETH

of the curtain which c the second	Ex 26:10	2279
of the curtain which c the second	Ex 36:17	2279

COUPLING

from the selvedge in the c	Ex 26:4	2279
curtain, in the c of the second	Ex 26:4	4225
that is in the c of the second	Ex 26:5	4225
curtain that is outmost in the c	Ex 26:10	2279
over against the other c thereof	Ex 28:27	4225
from the selvedge in the c	Ex 36:11	4225
curtain, in the c of the second	Ex 36:11	4225
which was in the c of the second	Ex 36:12	4225
edge of the curtain in the c	Ex 36:17	4225
over against the other c thereof	Ex 39:20	4225

COUPLINGS

buy hewn stone, and timber for c	2Chr 34:11	4226

COURAGE

And be ye of good c, and bring of	Num 13:20	2388
Be strong and of a good c, fear	Deut 31:6	553
Israel, Be strong and of a good c	Deut 31:7	553
and said, Be strong and of a good c	Deut 31:23	553
Be strong and of a good c	Josh 1:6	553
Be strong and of a good c	Josh 1:9	553
only be strong and of a good c	Josh 1:18	553
remain any more c in any man	Josh 2:11	7307
dismayed, be strong and of good c	Josh 10:25	553
Be of good c, and let us play the	2Sa 10:12	2388
Be of good c, and let us behave	1Chr 19:13	2388
be strong, and of good c	1Chr 22:13	553
his son, Be strong and of good c	1Chr 28:20	553
of Oded the prophet, he took c	2Chr 15:8	2388
be of good c, and do it	Ezr 10:4	2388
be of good c, and he shall	Ps 27:14	2388
Be of good c, and he shall	Ps 31:24	2388
said to his brother, Be of good c	Is 41:6	2388
his c against the king of the	Dan 11:25	3824
saw, he thanked God, and took c	Acts 28:15	*2294*

COURAGEOUS

Only be thou strong and very c	Josh 1:7	553
Be ye therefore very c to keep	Josh 23:6	2388
be c, and be valiant	2Sa 13:28	2388
Be strong and c, be not afraid nor	2Chr 32:7	553
he that is c among the mighty	Amos 2:16	

COURAGEOUSLY

Deal c, and the LORD shall be with	2Chr 19:11	2388

COURSE

of every c were twenty and four	1Chr 27:1	4256
Over the first c for the first	1Chr 27:2	4256
in his c were twenty and four	1Chr 27:2	4256
over the c of the second month	1Chr 27:4	4256
of his c was Mikloth also the	1Chr 27:4	4256
in his c likewise were twenty and	1Chr 27:4	4256
in his c were twenty and four	1Chr 27:5	4256
in his c was Ammizabad his son	1Chr 27:6	4256
in his c were twenty and four	1Chr 27:7	4256
in his c were twenty and four	1Chr 27:8	4256
in his c were twenty and four	1Chr 27:9	4256
in his c were twenty and four	1Chr 27:10	4256
in his c were twenty and four	1Chr 27:11	4256
in his c were twenty and four	1Chr 27:12	4256
in his c were twenty and four	1Chr 27:13	4256
in his c were twenty and four	1Chr 27:14	4256
in his c were twenty and four	1Chr 27:15	4256
that ministered to the king by c	1Chr 28:1	4256
and did not then wait by c	2Chr 5:11	4256
sang together by c in praising	Ezr 3:11	
of the earth are out of c	Ps 82:5	4131
every one turned to his c	Jer 8:6	4794
their c is evil, and their force	Jer 23:10	4794
named Zacharias, of the c of Abia	Lk 1:5	*2183*
before God in the order of his c	Lk 1:8	*2183*
And as John fulfilled his c	Acts 13:25	*1408*
with a straight c to Samothracia	Acts 16:11	*2113*
that I might finish my c with joy	Acts 20:24	*1408*
came with a straight c unto Coos	Acts 21:1	*4144*
we had finished our c from Tyre	Acts 21:7	*4144*
the most by three, and that by c	1Cor 14:27	*3313*
according to the c of this world	Eph 2:2	*165*
word of the Lord may have free c	2Th 3:1	*5143*
good fight, I have finished my c	2Ti 4:7	*1408*
setteth on fire the c of nature	Jas 3:6	*5164*

COURSES

the stars in their c fought	Judg 5:20	4546
ten thousand a month by c	1Kin 5:14	2487
into c among the sons of Levi	1Chr 23:6	4256
the king in any matter of the c	1Chr 27:1	4256
Also for the c of the priests and	1Chr 28:13	4256
the c of the priests and the	1Chr 28:21	4256
the c of the priests to their	2Chr 8:14	4256
also by their c at every gate	2Chr 8:14	4256
the priest dismissed not the c	2Chr 23:8	4256
appointed the c of the priests	2Chr 31:2	4256
and the Levites after their c	2Chr 31:2	4256
to give to their brethren by c	2Chr 31:15	4256
charges according to their c	2Chr 31:16	4256
in their charges by their c	2Chr 31:17	4256
of your fathers, after your c	2Chr 35:4	4256
place, and the Levites in their c	2Chr 35:10	4256
and the Levites in their c	Ezr 6:18	4255
grass, as willows by the water c	Is 44:4	2988

COURT

make the c of the tabernacle	Ex 27:9	2691
the c of fine twined linen of an	Ex 27:9	2691
for the breadth of the c on the	Ex 27:12	2691
the breadth of the c on the east	Ex 27:13	2691
for the gate of the c shall be an	Ex 27:16	2691
c shall be filleted with silver	Ex 27:17	2691
The length of the c shall be an	Ex 27:18	2691
thereof, and all the pins of the c	Ex 27:19	2691
The hangings of the c, his	Ex 35:17	2691
the hanging for the door of the c	Ex 35:17	2691
tabernacle, and the pins of the c	Ex 35:18	2691
And he made the c	Ex 38:9	2691
the c were of fine twined linen	Ex 38:9	2691
for the other side of the c gate	Ex 38:15	2691
All the hangings of the c round	Ex 38:16	2691
all the pillars of the c were	Ex 38:17	2691
the gate of the c was needlework	Ex 38:18	2691
to the hangings of the c	Ex 38:18	2691
of the c round about, were of	Ex 38:20	2691
the sockets of the c round about	Ex 38:31	2691
and the sockets of the c gate	Ex 38:31	2691
all the pins of the c round about	Ex 38:31	2691
The hangings of the c, his	Ex 39:40	2691
and the hanging for the c gate	Ex 39:40	2691
shalt set up the c round about	Ex 40:8	2691
hang up the hanging at the c gate	Ex 40:8	2691
he reared up the c round about	Ex 40:33	2691
set up the hanging of the c gate	Ex 40:33	2691
in the c of the tabernacle of the	Lev 6:16	2691
in the c of the tabernacle of the	Lev 6:26	2691
And the hangings of the c, and the	Num 3:26	2691
the curtain for the door of the c	Num 3:26	2691
the pillars of the c round about	Num 3:37	2691
And the hangings of the c, and the	Num 4:26	2691
for the door of the gate of the c	Num 4:26	2691
the pillars of the c round about	Num 4:32	2691
which had a well in his c	2Sa 17:18	2691
he built the inner c with three	1Kin 6:36	2691
had another c within the porch	1Kin 7:8	2691
on the outside toward the great c	1Kin 7:9	2691
the great c round about was with	1Kin 7:12	2691
both for the inner c of the house	1Kin 7:12	2691
c that was before the house of	1Kin 8:64	2691
was gone out into the middle c	2Kin 20:4	5892
he made the c of the priests	2Chr 4:9	2691
great c, and doors for the c	2Chr 4:9	5835
had set it in the midst of the c	2Chr 6:13	5835
hallowed the middle of the c that	2Chr 7:7	2691
of the LORD, before the new c	2Chr 20:5	2691
in the c of the house of the LORD	2Chr 24:21	2691
the c of the house of the LORD	2Chr 29:16	2691
that was by the c of the prison	Neh 3:25	2691
in the c of the garden of the	Est 1:5	2691
before the c of the women's house	Est 2:11	2691
unto the king into the inner c	Est 4:11	2691
stood in the inner c of the	Est 5:1	2691
the queen standing in the c	Est 5:2	2691
And the king said, Who is in the c	Est 6:4	2691
the outward c of the king's house	Est 6:4	2691
Behold, Haman standeth in the c	Est 6:5	2691
of dragons, and a c for owls	Is 34:13	2681
he stood in the c of the LORD's	Jer 19:14	2691
Stand in the c of the LORD's	Jer 26:2	2691
shut up in the c of the prison	Jer 32:2	2691
uncle's son came to me in the c	Jer 32:8	2691
that sat in the c of the prison	Jer 32:12	2691
shut up in the c of the prison	Jer 33:1	2691
the scribe, in the higher c	Jer 36:10	2691
went in to the king into the c	Jer 36:20	2691
Jeremiah into the c of the prison	Jer 37:21	2691
remained in the c of the prison	Jer 37:21	2691
that was in the c of the prison	Jer 38:6	2691
remained in the c of the prison	Jer 38:13	2691
So Jeremiah abode in the c of the	Jer 38:28	2691
out of the c of the prison	Jer 39:14	2691
shut up in the c of the prison	Jer 39:15	2691
brought me to the door of the c	Eze 8:7	2691
the inner c of the LORD's house	Eze 8:16	2691
and the cloud filled the inner c	Eze 10:3	2691
the c was full of the brightness	Eze 10:4	2691
was heard even to the outer c	Eze 10:5	2691
of the c round about the gate	Eze 40:14	2691
brought he me into the outward c	Eze 40:17	2691
made for the c round about	Eze 40:17	2691
forefront of the inner c without	Eze 40:19	2691
the gate of the outward c that	Eze 40:20	2691
the gate of the inner c was over	Eze 40:23	2691
in the inner c toward the south	Eze 40:27	2691
to the inner c by the south gate	Eze 40:28	2691
thereof were toward the utter c	Eze 40:31	2691
into the inner c toward the east	Eze 40:32	2691
thereof were toward the outward c	Eze 40:34	2691
thereof were toward the utter c	Eze 40:37	2691
of the singers in the inner c	Eze 40:44	2691
So he measured the c, an hundred	Eze 40:47	2691
temple, and the porches of the c	Eze 41:15	2691
brought me forth into the utter c	Eze 42:1	2691
cubits which were for the inner c	Eze 42:3	2691
which was for the utter c	Eze 42:3	2691
toward the utter c on the	Eze 42:7	2691
in the utter c was fifty cubits	Eze 42:8	2691
goeth into them from the utter c	Eze 42:9	2691
the wall of the c toward the east	Eze 42:10	2691
the holy place into the utter c	Eze 42:14	2691
and brought me into the inner c	Eze 43:5	2691
in at the gates of the inner c	Eze 44:17	2691
in the gates of the inner c	Eze 44:17	2691
they go forth into the utter c	Eze 44:19	2691
into the utter c to the people	Eze 44:19	2691
when they enter into the inner c	Eze 44:21	2691
the sanctuary, unto the inner c	Eze 44:27	2691
posts of the gate of the inner c	Eze 45:19	2691
The gate of the inner c that	Eze 46:1	2691
them not out into the utter c	Eze 46:20	2691
brought me forth into the utter c	Eze 46:21	2691
pass by the four corners of the c	Eze 46:21	2691
corner of the c there was a c	Eze 46:21	2691
In the four corners of the c	Eze 46:22	2691
chapel, and it is the king's c	Amos 7:13	1004
But the c which is without the	Rev 11:2	*833*

COURTEOUS

as brethren, be pitiful, be c	1Pet 3:8	*5391*

COURTEOUSLY

Julius c entreated Paul, and gave	Acts 27:3	*5364*
us, and lodged us three days c	Acts 28:7	*5390*

COURTS

two c of the house of the LORD	2Kin 21:5	2691
two c of the house of the LORD	2Kin 23:12	2691
the house of the LORD, in the c	1Chr 23:28	2691
he shall build my house and my c	1Chr 28:6	2691
of the c of the house of the LORD	1Chr 28:12	2691
in the c of the house of the LORD	2Chr 23:5	2691
two c of the house of the LORD	2Chr 33:5	2691
roof of his house, and in their c	Neh 8:16	2691

in the c of the house of God, and ... Neh 8:16 2691
in the c of the house of God ... Neh 13:7 2691
thee, that he may dwell in thy c ... Ps 65:4 2691
fainteth for the c of the LORD ... Ps 84:2 2691
For a day in thy c is better than ... Ps 84:10 2691
flourish in the c of our God ... Ps 92:13 2691
an offering, and come into his c ... Ps 96:8 2691
and into his c with praise ... Ps 100:4 2691
In the c of the LORD's house, in ... Ps 116:19 2691
in the c of the house of our God, ... Ps 135:2 2691
this at your hand, to tread my c ... Is 1:12 2691
drink it in the c of my holiness ... Is 62:9 2691
fill the c with the slain ... Eze 9:7 2691
pillars as the pillars of the c ... Eze 42:6 2691
c joined of forty cubits long ... Eze 46:22 2691
my house, and shalt also keep my c ... Zec 3:7 2691
live delicately, are in kings' c ... Lk 7:25

COUSIN
thy c Elisabeth, she hath also ... Lk 1:36 4773

COUSINS
her c heard how the Lord had ... Lk 1:58 4773

COVENANT
with thee will I establish my c ... Gen 6:18 1285
behold, I establish my c with you ... Gen 9:9 1285
And I will establish my c with you ... Gen 9:11 1285
of the c which I make between me ... Gen 9:12 1285
be for a token of a c between me ... Gen 9:13 1285
And I will remember my c, which is ... Gen 9:15 1285
the everlasting c between God ... Gen 9:16 1285
Noah, This is the token of the c ... Gen 9:17 1285
day the LORD made a c with Abram ... Gen 15:18 1285
And I will make my c between me ... Gen 17:2 1285
my c is with thee, and thou shalt ... Gen 17:4 1285
I will establish my c between me ... Gen 17:7 1285
generations for an everlasting c ... Gen 17:7 1285
Thou shalt keep my c therefore ... Gen 17:9 1285
This is my c, which ye shall keep ... Gen 17:10 1285
be a token of the c betwixt me ... Gen 17:11 1285
my c shall be in your flesh for ... Gen 17:13 1285
your flesh for an everlasting c ... Gen 17:13 1285
he hath broken my c ... Gen 17:14 1285
I will establish my c with him ... Gen 17:19 1285
with him for an everlasting c ... Gen 17:19 1285
But my c will I establish with ... Gen 17:21 1285
and both of them made a c ... Gen 21:27 1285
Thus they made a c at Beer-sheba ... Gen 21:32 1285
and let us make a c with thee ... Gen 26:28 1285
come thou, let us make a c ... Gen 31:44 1285
God remembered his c with Abraham ... Ex 2:24 1285
also established my c with them ... Ex 6:4 1285
and I have remembered my c ... Ex 6:5 1285
my voice indeed, and keep my c ... Ex 19:5 1285
Thou shalt make no c with them ... Ex 23:32 1285
And he took the book of the c ... Ex 24:7 1285
said, Behold the blood of the c ... Ex 24:8 1285
generations, for a perpetual c ... Ex 31:16 1285
And he said, Behold, I make a c ... Ex 34:10 1285
lest thou make a c with the ... Ex 34:12 1285
Lest thou make a c with the ... Ex 34:15 1285
words I have made a c with thee ... Ex 34:27 1285
the tables the words of the c ... Ex 34:28 1285
thou suffer the salt of the c of ... Lev 2:13 1285
of Israel by an everlasting c ... Lev 24:8 1285
you, and establish my c with you ... Lev 26:9 1285
but that ye break my c ... Lev 26:15 1285
shall avenge the quarrel of my c ... Lev 26:25 1285
will I remember my c with Jacob ... Lev 26:42 1285
also my c with Isaac ... Lev 26:42 1285
also my c with Abraham will I ... Lev 26:42 1285
and to break my c with them ... Lev 26:44 1285
remember the c of their ancestors ... Lev 26:45 1285
the ark of the c of the LORD went ... Num 10:33 1285
the ark of the c of the LORD ... Num 14:44 1285
it is a c of salt for ever before ... Num 18:19 1285
I give unto him my c of peace ... Num 25:12 1285
even the c of an everlasting ... Num 25:13 1285
And he declared unto you his c ... Deut 4:13 1285
lest ye forget the c of the LORD ... Deut 4:23 1285
nor forget the c of thy fathers ... Deut 4:31 1285
our God made a c with us in Horeb ... Deut 5:2 1285
made not this c with our fathers ... Deut 5:3 1285
thou shalt make no c with them ... Deut 7:2 1285
the faithful God, which keepeth c ... Deut 7:9 1285
God shall keep unto thee the c ... Deut 7:12 1285
that he may establish his c which ... Deut 8:18 1285
even the tables of the c which ... Deut 9:9 1285
stone, even the tables of the c ... Deut 9:11 1285
of the c were in my two hands ... Deut 9:15 1285
bear the ark of the c of the LORD ... Deut 10:8 1285
thy God, in transgressing his c ... Deut 17:2 1285
These are the words of the c ... Deut 29:1 1285
beside the c which he made with ... Deut 29:1 1285
therefore the words of this c ... Deut 29:9 1285
into c with the LORD thy God ... Deut 29:12 1285
with you only do I make this c ... Deut 29:14 1285
to all the curses of the c that ... Deut 29:21 1285
the c of the LORD God of their ... Deut 29:25 1285
bare the ark of the c of the LORD ... Deut 31:9 1285
break my c which I have made with ... Deut 31:16 1285
and provoke me, and break my c ... Deut 31:20 1285
bare the ark of the c of the LORD ... Deut 31:25 1285
ark of the c of the LORD your God ... Deut 31:26 1285
observed thy word, and kept thy c ... Deut 33:9 1285
ark of the c of the LORD your God ... Josh 3:3 1285
saying, Take up the ark of the c ... Josh 3:6 1285
And they took up the ark of the c ... Josh 3:6 1285
that bear the ark of the c ... Josh 3:8 1285
the ark of the c of the Lord of ... Josh 3:11 1285
ark of the c before the people ... Josh 3:14 1285
that bare the ark of the c of the ... Josh 3:17 1285
the ark of the c of the LORD ... Josh 4:7 1285
which bare the ark of the c stood ... Josh 4:9 1285
that bare the ark of the c of the ... Josh 4:18 1285
them, Take up the ark of the c ... Josh 6:6 1285
the ark of the c of the LORD ... Josh 6:8 1285
my c which I commanded them ... Josh 7:11 1285
transgressed the c of the LORD ... Josh 7:15 1285
bare the ark of the c of the LORD ... Josh 8:33 1285
the c of the LORD your God ... Josh 23:16 1285
So Joshua made a c with the ... Josh 24:25 1285
I will never break my c with you ... Judg 2:1 1285
people hath transgressed my c ... Judg 2:20 1285
(for the ark of the c of God was ... Judg 20:27 1285
Let us fetch the ark of the c of ... 1Sa 4:3 1285
ark of the c of the LORD of hosts ... 1Sa 4:4 1285
with the ark of the c of God ... 1Sa 4:4 1285
when the ark of the c of the LORD ... 1Sa 4:5 1285
Make a c with us, and we will ... 1Sa 11:1 1285
will I make a c with you, that I ... 1Sa 11:2
Then Jonathan and David made a c ... 1Sa 18:3 1285
into a c of the LORD with thee ... 1Sa 20:8 1285
So Jonathan made a c with the ... 1Sa 20:16
they two made a c before the LORD ... 1Sa 23:18 1285
bearing the ark of the c of God ... 2Sa 15:24 1285
made with me an everlasting c ... 2Sa 23:5 1285
the ark of the c of the LORD ... 1Kin 3:15 1285
the ark of the c of the LORD ... 1Kin 6:19 1285
might bring up the ark of the c ... 1Kin 8:1 1285
brought in the ark of the c of ... 1Kin 8:6 1285
when the LORD made a c with the ... 1Kin 8:9
ark, wherein is the c of the LORD ... 1Kin 8:21 1285
on earth beneath, who keepest c ... 1Kin 8:23 1285
thee, and thou hast not kept my c ... 1Kin 11:11 1285
of Israel have forsaken thy c ... 1Kin 19:10 1285
of Israel have forsaken thy c ... 1Kin 19:14 1285
I will send thee away with this c ... 1Kin 20:34 1285
So he made a c with him, and sent ... 1Kin 20:34 1285
made a c with them, and took an ... 2Kin 11:4 1285
Jehoiada made a c between the ... 2Kin 11:17 1285
because of his c with Abraham ... 2Kin 13:23 1285
his c that he made with their ... 2Kin 17:15 1285
With whom the LORD had made a c ... 2Kin 17:35 1285
the c that I have made with you ... 2Kin 17:38 1285
their God, but transgressed his c ... 2Kin 18:12 1285
the words of the book of the c ... 2Kin 23:2 1285
made a c before the LORD, to walk ... 2Kin 23:3 1285
to perform the words of this c ... 2Kin 23:3 1285
And all the people stood to the c ... 2Kin 23:3 1285
is written in the book of this c ... 2Kin 23:21 1285
David made a c with them in ... 1Chr 11:3 1285
c of the LORD out of the house of ... 1Chr 15:25 1285
bare the ark of the c of the LORD ... 1Chr 15:26 1285
the c of the LORD with shouting ... 1Chr 15:28 1285
as the ark of the c of the LORD ... 1Chr 15:29 1285
before the ark of the c of God ... 1Chr 16:6 1285
Be ye mindful always of his c ... 1Chr 16:15 1285
Even of the c which he made with ... 1Chr 16:16 1285
and to Israel for an everlasting c ... 1Chr 16:17 1285
ark of the c of the LORD Asaph ... 1Chr 16:37 1285
but the ark of the c of the LORD ... 1Chr 17:1 1285
the ark of the c of the LORD ... 1Chr 22:19 1285
for the ark of the c of the LORD ... 1Chr 28:2 1285
the ark of the c of the LORD ... 1Chr 28:18
to bring up the ark of the c of ... 2Chr 5:2 1285
brought in the ark of the c of ... 2Chr 5:7 1285
when the LORD made a c with the ... 2Chr 5:10
ark, wherein is the c of the LORD ... 2Chr 6:11 1285
which keepest c, and shewest mercy ... 2Chr 6:14 1285
him and to his sons by a c of salt ... 2Chr 13:5 1285
they entered into a c to seek the ... 2Chr 15:12 1285
because of the c that he had made ... 2Chr 21:7 1285
son of Zichri, into c with him ... 2Chr 23:1 1285
all the congregation made a c ... 2Chr 23:3 1285
And Jehoiada made a c between him ... 2Chr 23:16 1285
a c with the LORD God of Israel ... 2Chr 29:10 1285
the words of the book of the c ... 2Chr 34:30 1285
made a c before the LORD, to walk ... 2Chr 34:31 1285
to perform the words of the c ... 2Chr 34:31 1285
did according to the c of God ... 2Chr 34:32 1285
Now therefore let us make a c ... Ezr 10:3 1285
and terrible God, that keepeth c ... Neh 1:5 1285
madest a c with him to give the ... Neh 9:8 1285
the terrible God, who keepest c ... Neh 9:32 1285
of all this we make a sure c ... Neh 9:38
the c of the priesthood, and of ... Neh 13:29 1285
I made a c with mine eyes ... Job 31:1 1285
Will he make a c with thee ... Job 41:4 1285
and truth unto such as keep his c ... Ps 25:10 1285
and he will shew them his c ... Ps 25:14 1285
have we dealt falsely in thy c ... Ps 44:17 1285
made a c with me by sacrifice ... Ps 50:5 1285
shouldest take my c in thy mouth ... Ps 50:16 1285
he hath broken his c ... Ps 55:20 1285
Have respect unto the c ... Ps 74:20 1285
They kept not the c of God ... Ps 78:10 1285
were they stedfast in his c ... Ps 78:37 1285
I have made a c with my chosen, I ... Ps 89:3 1285
my c shall stand fast with him ... Ps 89:28 1285
My c will I not break, nor alter ... Ps 89:34 1285
made void the c of thy servant ... Ps 89:39 1285
To such as keep his c, and to ... Ps 103:18 1285
He hath remembered his c for ever ... Ps 105:8 1285
Which c he made with Abraham, and ... Ps 105:9
and to Israel for an everlasting c ... Ps 105:10 1285
And he remembered for them his c ... Ps 106:45 1285
he will ever be mindful of his c ... Ps 111:5 1285
he hath commanded his c for ever ... Ps 111:9 1285
If thy children will keep my c ... Ps 132:12 1285
and forgetteth the c of her God ... Prov 2:17 1285
broken the everlasting c ... Is 24:5 1285
said, We have made a c with death ... Is 28:15 1285
your c with death shall be ... Is 28:18 1285
he hath broken the c, he hath ... Is 33:8 1285
give thee for a c of the people ... Is 42:6 1285
give thee for a c of the people ... Is 49:8 1285
neither shall the c of my peace ... Is 54:10 1285
make an everlasting c with you ... Is 55:3 1285
please me, and take hold of my c ... Is 56:4 1285
it, and taketh hold of my c ... Is 56:6 1285
bed, and made thee a c with them ... Is 57:8
As for me, this is my c with them ... Is 59:21 1285
make an everlasting c with them ... Is 61:8 1285
The ark of the c of the LORD ... Jer 3:16 1285
Hear ye the words of this c ... Jer 11:2 1285
obeyeth not the words of this c ... Jer 11:3 1285
Hear ye the words of this c ... Jer 11:6 1285
upon them all the words of this c ... Jer 11:8 1285
house of Judah have broken my c ... Jer 11:10 1285
remember, break not thy c with us ... Jer 14:21 1285
the c of the LORD their God ... Jer 22:9 1285
that I will make a new c with the ... Jer 31:31 1285
Not according to the c that I ... Jer 31:32 1285
which my c they brake, although I ... Jer 31:32 1285
But this shall be the c that I ... Jer 31:33 1285
make an everlasting c with them ... Jer 32:40 1285
If ye can break my c of the day ... Jer 33:20 1285
my c of the night, and that there ... Jer 33:20 1285
Then may also my c be broken with ... Jer 33:21 1285
If my c be not with day and night, ... Jer 33:25 1285
the king Zedekiah had made a c ... Jer 34:8 1285
which had entered into the c ... Jer 34:10 1285
I made a c with your fathers in ... Jer 34:13 1285
ye had made a c before me in the ... Jer 34:15 1285
men that have transgressed my c ... Jer 34:18 1285
c which they had made before me ... Jer 34:18 1285
to the LORD in a perpetual c that ... Jer 50:5 1285
and entered into a c with thee ... Eze 16:8 1285
the oath in breaking the c ... Eze 16:59 1285
my c with thee in the days of thy ... Eze 16:60 1285
unto thee an everlasting c ... Eze 16:60 1285
for daughters, but not by thy c ... Eze 16:61 1285
I will establish my c with thee ... Eze 16:62 1285
made a c with him, and hath taken ... Eze 17:13 1285
keeping of his c it might stand ... Eze 17:14 1285
or shall he break the c, and be ... Eze 17:15 1285
whose c he brake, even with him ... Eze 17:16 1285
the oath by breaking the c ... Eze 17:18 1285
my c that he hath broken, even it ... Eze 17:19 1285
bring you into the bond of the c ... Eze 20:37 1285
will make with them a c of peace ... Eze 34:25 1285
will make a c of peace with them ... Eze 37:26 1285
be an everlasting c with them ... Eze 37:26 1285
broken my c because of all your ... Eze 44:7 1285
and dreadful God, keeping the c ... Dan 9:4 1285
he shall confirm the c with many ... Dan 9:27 1285
yea, also the prince of the c ... Dan 11:22 1285
heart shall be against the holy c ... Dan 11:28 1285
indignation against the holy c ... Dan 11:30 1285
with them that forsake the holy c ... Dan 11:30 1285
c shall he corrupt by flatteries ... Dan 11:32 1285
in that day will I make a c for ... Hos 2:18 1285
like men have transgressed the c ... Hos 6:7 1285
they have transgressed my c ... Hos 8:1 1285
swearing falsely in making a c ... Hos 10:4 1285
they do make a c with the ... Hos 12:1 1285
and remembered not the brotherly c ... Amos 1:9 1285
by the blood of thy c I have sent ... Zec 9:11 1285
that I might break my c which I ... Zec 11:10 1285
that my c might be with Levi, ... Mal 2:4 1285
My c was with him of life and ... Mal 2:5 1285
ye have corrupted the c of Levi ... Mal 2:8 1285
by profaning the c of our fathers ... Mal 2:10 1285
companion, and the wife of thy c ... Mal 2:14 1285
even the messenger of the c ... Mal 3:1 1285
and to remember his holy c ... Lk 1:72 *1242*
of the c which God made with our ... Acts 3:25 *1242*
he gave him the c of circumcision ... Acts 7:8 *1242*
For this is my c unto them ... Rom 11:27 *1242*
Though it be but a man's c ... Gal 3:15 *1242*
And this I say, that the c ... Gal 3:17 *1242*
he is the mediator of a better c ... Heb 8:6 *1242*
For if that first c had been ... Heb 8:7
when I will make a new c with the ... Heb 8:8 *1242*
Not according to the c that I ... Heb 8:9 *1242*
they continued not in my c ... Heb 8:9 *1242*
For this is the c that I will ... Heb 8:10 *1242*
In that he saith, A new c ... Heb 8:13
Then verily the first c had also ... Heb 9:1
the ark of the c overlaid round ... Heb 9:4 *1242*
budded, and the tables of the c ... Heb 9:4 *1242*
This is the c that I will make ... Heb 10:16 *1242*
hath counted the blood of the c ... Heb 10:29 *1242*
Jesus the mediator of the new c ... Heb 12:24 *1242*
the blood of the everlasting c ... Heb 13:20 *1242*

COVENANTBREAKERS
Without understanding, c, without ... Rom 1:31 *802*

COVENANTED
according as I have c with David ... 2Chr 7:18 3772
I c with you when ye came out of ... Hag 2:5 3772
they c with him for thirty pieces ... Mt 26:15 *2476*
were glad, and c to give him money ... Lk 22:5 *4934*

COVENANTS
adoption, and the glory, and the c ... Rom 9:4 *1242*
for these are the two c ... Gal 4:24 *1242*
strangers from the c of promise ... Eph 2:12 *1242*

COVER
they shall c the face of the ... Ex 10:5 3680
man shall dig a pit, and not c it ... Ex 21:33 3680
and bowls thereof, to c withal ... Ex 25:29 5258
side and on that side, to c it ... Ex 26:13 3680
breeches to c their nakedness ... Ex 28:42 3680
will c thee with my hand while I ... Ex 33:22 5526
bowls, and his covers to c withal ... Ex 37:16 5258
and c the ark with the vail ... Ex 40:3 5526
the leprosy c all the skin of him ... Lev 13:12 3680
the cloud of the incense may c ... Lev 16:13 3680
blood thereof, and c it with dust ... Lev 17:13 3680
c the ark of testimony with it ... Num 4:5 3680

the bowls, and covers to c withal ... Num 4:7 5258
c the same with a covering of ... Num 4:8 3680
c the candlestick of the light, ... Num 4:9 3680
c it with a covering of badgers' ... Num 4:11 3680
c them with a covering of ... Num 4:12 3680
they c the face of the earth, and ... Num 22:5 3680
c that which cometh from thee ... Deut 23:13 3680
the LORD shall c him all the day ... Deut 33:12 2645
and Saul went in to c his feet ... 1Sa 24:3 5526
to c the chapiters that were upon ... 1Kin 7:18 3680
to c the two bowls of the ... 1Kin 7:41 3680
to c the two bowls of the ... 1Kin 7:42 3680
the two wreaths to c the two ... 2Chr 4:12 3680
to c the two pommels of the ... 2Chr 4:13 3680
c not their iniquity, and let not ... Neh 4:5 3680
c not thou my blood, and let my ... Job 16:18 3680
dust, and the worms shall c them ... Job 21:26 3680
and abundance of waters c thee ... Job 22:11 3680
abundance of waters may c thee ... Job 38:34 3680
The shady trees c him with their ... Job 40:22 5526
He shall c thee with his feathers ... Ps 91:4 5526
turn not again to c the earth ... Ps 104:9 3680
let them c themselves with their ... Ps 109:29 5844
Surely the darkness shall c me ... Ps 139:11 7779
mischief of their own lips c them ... Ps 140:9 3680
the LORD, as the waters c the sea ... Is 11:9 3680
under thee, and the worms c thee ... Is 14:11 4374
captivity, and will surely c thee ... Is 22:17 5844
and shall no more c her slain ... Is 26:21 3680
that c with a covering, but not ... Is 30:1 5258
seest the naked, that thou c him ... Is 58:7 3680
neither shall they c themselves ... Is 59:6 3680
the darkness shall c the earth ... Is 60:2 3680
multitude of camels shall c thee ... Is 60:6 3680
I will go up, and will c the earth ... Jer 46:8 3680
sackcloth, and horror shall c them ... Eze 7:18 3680
thou shalt c thy face, that thou ... Eze 12:6 3680
he shall c his face, that he see ... Eze 12:12 3680
the ground, to c it with dust ... Eze 24:7 3680
c not thy lips, and eat not the ... Eze 24:17 5844
ye shall not c your lips, nor eat ... Eze 24:22 5844
horses their dust shall c thee ... Eze 26:10 3680
and great waters shall c thee ... Eze 26:19 3680
as for her, a cloud shall c her ... Eze 30:18 3680
I will c the heaven, and make the ... Eze 32:7 3680
I will c the sun with a cloud, and ... Eze 32:7 3680
c you with skin, and put breath in ... Eze 37:6 7159
be like a cloud to c the land ... Eze 38:9 3680
Israel, as a cloud to c the land ... Eze 38:16 3680
my flax given to c her nakedness ... Hos 2:9 3680
shall say to the mountains, C us ... Hos 10:8 3680
brother Jacob shame shall c thee ... Obad 10 3680
yea, they shall all c their lips ... Mic 3:7 5844
shame shall c her which said unto ... Mic 7:10 3680
the LORD, as the waters c the sea ... Hab 2:14 3680
violence of Lebanon shall c thee ... Hab 2:17 3680
to c his face, and to buffet him, ... Mk 14:65 *4028*
and to the hills, C us ... Lk 23:30 *2572*
indeed ought not to c his head ... 1Cor 11:7 *2619*
for charity shall c the multitude ... 1Pet 4:8 *2572*

COVERED
under the whole heaven, were c ... Gen 7:19 3680
and the mountains were c ... Gen 7:20 3680
c the nakedness of their father ... Gen 9:23 3680
she took a vail, and c herself ... Gen 24:65 3680
c her with a vail, and wrapped ... Gen 38:14 3680
because she had c her face ... Gen 38:15 3680
came up, and c the land of Egypt ... Ex 8:6 3680
For they c the face of the whole ... Ex 10:15 3680
c the chariots, and the horsemen, ... Ex 14:28 3680
The depths have c them ... Ex 15:5 3680
with thy wind, the sea c them ... Ex 15:10 3680
the quails came up, and c the camp ... Ex 16:13 3680
the mount, and a cloud c the mount ... Ex 24:15 3680
Sinai, and the cloud c it six days ... Ex 24:16 3680
c with their wings over the mercy ... Ex 37:9 5526
c the ark of the testimony ... Ex 40:21 5526
Then a cloud c the tent of the ... Ex 40:34 3680
the leprosy have c all his flesh ... Lev 13:13 3680
to see when the holy things are c ... Num 4:20 1104
six c wagons, and twelve oxen ... Num 7:3 6632
up the cloud c the tabernacle ... Num 9:15 3680
the cloud c it by day, and the ... Num 9:16 3680
and, behold, the cloud c it ... Num 16:42 3680
thick, thou art c with fatness ... Deut 32:15 3780
the sea upon them, and c them ... Josh 24:7 3680
the tent, she c him with a mantle ... Judg 4:18 3680
milk, and gave him drink, and c him ... Judg 4:19 3680
his bolster, and c it with a cloth ... 1Sa 19:13 3680
and he is c with a mantle ... 1Sa 28:14 5844
as he went up, and had his head c ... 2Sa 15:30 2645
was with him c every man his head ... 2Sa 15:30 2645
But the king c his face, and the ... 2Sa 19:4 3813
they c him with clothes, but he ... 1Kin 1:1 3680
c the house with beams and boards ... 1Kin 6:9 5603
he c them on the inside with wood ... 1Kin 6:15 6823
c the floor of the house with ... 1Kin 6:15 6823
so c the altar which was of cedar ... 1Kin 6:20 6823
c them with gold fitted upon the ... 1Kin 6:35 6823
it was c with cedar above upon ... 1Kin 7:3 5603
it was c with cedar from one side ... 1Kin 7:7 5603
ark, and the cherubims c the ark ... 1Kin 8:7 5526
c himself with sackcloth, and went ... 2Kin 19:1 3680
c with sackcloth, to Isaiah the ... 2Kin 19:2 3680
c the ark of the covenant of the ... 1Chr 28:18 5526
ark, and the cherubims c the ark ... 2Chr 5:8 3680
c it, and set up the doors thereof ... Neh 3:15 2926
mourning, and having his head c ... Est 6:12 2645
king's mouth, they c Haman's face ... Est 7:8 2645
neither hath he c the darkness ... Job 23:17 3680
If I c my transgressions as Adam, ... Job 31:33 3680
is forgiven, whose sin is c ... Ps 32:1 3680
and the shame of my face hath c me ... Ps 44:15 3680
c us with the shadow of death ... Ps 44:19 3680
valleys also are c over with corn ... Ps 65:13 5848
the wings of a dove c with silver ... Ps 68:13 2645
shame hath c my face ... Ps 69:7 3680
let them be c with reproach and ... Ps 71:13 5844
The hills were c with the shadow ... Ps 80:10 3680
thou hast c all their sin ... Ps 85:2 3680
thou hast c him with shame ... Ps 89:45 5844
the waters c their enemies ... Ps 106:11 3680
and c the company of Abiram ... Ps 106:17 3680
thou hast c me in my mother's ... Ps 139:13 5526
thou hast c my head in the day of ... Ps 140:7 5526
nettles had c the face thereof, ... Prov 24:31 3680
a potsherd c with silver dross ... Prov 26:23 6823
Whose hatred is c by deceit ... Prov 26:26 3680
his name shall be c with darkness ... Eccl 6:4 3680
with twain he c his face ... Is 6:2 3680
and with twain he c his feet ... Is 6:2 3680
your rulers, the seers hath he c ... Is 29:10 3680
c himself with sackcloth, and went ... Is 37:1 3680
of the priests c with sackcloth ... Is 37:2 3680
I have c thee in the shadow of ... Is 51:16 3680
he hath c me with the robe of ... Is 61:10 3271
and confounded, and c their heads ... Jer 14:3 2645
were ashamed, they c their heads ... Jer 14:4 2645
she is c with the multitude of ... Jer 51:42 3680
shame hath c our faces ... Jer 51:51 3680
How hath the Lord c the daughter ... Lam 2:1 5743
stones, he hath c me with ashes ... Lam 3:16 3728
Thou hast c with anger, and ... Lam 3:43 5526
Thou hast c thyself with a cloud, ... Lam 3:44 5526
to another, and two c their bodies ... Eze 1:11 3680
which c on this side, and every ... Eze 1:23 3680
which c on that side, their ... Eze 1:23 3680
over thee, and c thy nakedness ... Eze 16:8 3680
fine linen, and I c thee with silk ... Eze 16:10 3680
hath c the naked with a garment ... Eze 18:7 3680
hath c the naked with a garment, ... Eze 18:16 3680
a rock, that it should not be c ... Eze 24:8 3680
of Elishah was that which c thee ... Eze 27:7 4374
I c the deep for him, and I ... Eze 31:15 3680
them, and the skin c them above ... Eze 37:8 7159
windows, and the windows were c ... Eze 41:16 3680
c him with sackcloth, and sat in ... Jonah 3:6 3680
beast be c with sackcloth, and cry ... Jonah 3:8 3680
His glory c the heavens, and the ... Hab 3:3 3680
the ship was c with the waves ... Mt 8:24 *2572*
for there is nothing c, that ... Mt 10:26 *2572*
For there is nothing c, that ... Lk 12:2 *4780*
are forgiven, and whose sins are c ... Rom 4:7 *1943*
or prophesying, having his head c ... 1Cor 11:4 *2596*
For if the woman be not c ... 1Cor 11:6 *2619*
be shorn or shaven, let her be c ... 1Cor 11:6 *2619*

COVEREDST
Thou c it with the deep as with a ... Ps 104:6 3680
thy broidered garments, and c them ... Eze 16:18

COVEREST
vesture, wherewith thou c thyself ... Deut 22:12 3680
Who c thyself with light as with ... Ps 104:2 5844

COVERETH
all the fat that c the inwards ... Ex 29:13 3680
and the fat that c the inwards ... Ex 29:22 3680
the fat that c the inwards ... Lev 3:3 3680
and the fat that c the inwards ... Lev 3:9 3680
the fat that c the inwards ... Lev 3:14 3680
the fat that c the inwards ... Lev 4:8 3680
and the fat that c the inwards ... Lev 7:3 3680
that which c the inwards, and the ... Lev 9:19 4374
which c the face of the earth ... Num 22:11 3680
Surely he c his feet in his ... Judg 3:24 5526
he c the faces of the judges ... Job 9:24 1371
Because he c his face with his ... Job 15:27 3680
it, and c the bottom of the sea ... Job 36:30 3680
With clouds he c the light ... Job 36:32 3680
violence c them as a garment ... Ps 73:6 5848
him as the garment which c him ... Ps 109:19 5844
Who c the heaven with clouds, who ... Ps 147:8 3680
but violence c the mouth of the ... Prov 10:6 3680
but violence c the mouth of the ... Prov 10:11 3680
but love c all sins ... Prov 10:12 3680
but a prudent man c shame ... Prov 12:16 3680
He that c a transgression seeketh ... Prov 17:9 3680
He that c his sins shall not ... Prov 28:13 3680
our shame, and our confusion c us ... Jer 3:25 3680
art the anointed cherub that c ... Eze 28:14 5526
for one c violence with his ... Mal 2:16 3680
c it with a vessel, or putteth it ... Lk 8:16 *2572*

COVERING
and Noah removed the c of the ark ... Gen 8:13 4372
he is to thee a c of the eyes ... Gen 20:16 3682
For that is his c only, it is his ... Ex 22:27 3682
c the mercy seat with their wings ... Ex 25:20 5526
to be a c upon the tabernacle ... Ex 26:7 168
thou shalt make a c for the tent ... Ex 26:14 4372
a c above of badgers' skins ... Ex 26:14 4372
tabernacle, his tent, and his c ... Ex 35:11 4372
mercy seat, and the vail of the c ... Ex 35:12 4539
he made a c for the tent of rams' ... Ex 36:19 4372
a c of badgers' skins above that ... Ex 36:19 4372
the c of rams' skins dyed red, and ... Ex 39:34 4372
the c of badgers' skins ... Ex 39:34 4372
and the vail of the c ... Ex 39:34 4539
put the c of the tent above upon ... Ex 40:19 4372
and set up the vail of the c ... Ex 40:21 4539
he shall put a c upon his upper ... Lev 13:45 5844
the c thereof, and the hanging for ... Num 3:25 4372
they shall take down the c vail ... Num 4:5 4539
thereon the c of badgers' skins ... Num 4:6 3681
same with a c of badgers' skins ... Num 4:8 4372
within a c of badgers' skins ... Num 4:10 4372
cover it with a c of badgers' ... Num 4:11 4372
them with a c of badgers' skins ... Num 4:12 4372
upon it a c of badgers' skins ... Num 4:14 3681
made an end of c the sanctuary ... Num 4:15 3680
of the congregation, his c ... Num 4:25 4372
the c of the badgers' skins that ... Num 4:25 4372
broad plates for a c of the altar ... Num 16:38 6826
broad plates for a c of the altar ... Num 16:39 6826
which hath no c bound upon it ... Num 19:15 6781
spread a c over the well's mouth, ... 2Sa 17:19 4539
Thick clouds are a c to him ... Job 22:14 5643
that they have no c in the cold ... Job 24:7 3682
him, and destruction hath no c ... Job 26:6 3682
clothing, or any poor without c ... Job 31:19 3682
He spread a cloud for a c ... Ps 105:39 4539
the c of it of purple, the midst ... Song 3:10 4817
And he discovered the c of Judah ... Is 22:8 4539
of the c cast over all people ... Is 25:7 3875
the c narrower than that he can ... Is 28:20 4541
and that cover with a c, but not ... Is 30:1 4541
Ye shall defile also the c of thy ... Is 30:22 6826
and I make sackcloth their c ... Is 50:3 3682
every precious stone was thy c ... Eze 28:13 4540
O c cherub, from the midst of the ... Eze 28:16 5526
c the altar of the LORD with ... Mal 2:13 3680
for her hair is given her for a c ... 1Cor 11:15 *4018*

COVERINGS
decked my bed with c of tapestry ... Prov 7:16 4765
She maketh herself c of tapestry ... Prov 31:22 4765

COVERS
c thereof, and bowls thereof, to ... Ex 25:29 7184
his c to cover withal, of pure ... Ex 37:16 7184
the bowls, and c to cover withal ... Num 4:7 7184

COVERT
came down by the c of the hill ... 1Sa 25:20 5643
the c for the sabbath that they ... 2Kin 16:18 4329
abide in the c to lie in wait ... Job 38:40 5521
in the c of the reed, and fens ... Job 40:21 5643
will trust in the c of thy wings ... Ps 61:4 5643
for a c from storm and from rain ... Is 4:6 4563
be thou a c to them from the face ... Is 16:4 5643
the wind, and a c from the tempest ... Is 32:2 5643
He hath forsaken his c, as the ... Jer 25:38 5520

COVET
Thou shalt not c thy neighbour's ... Ex 20:17 2530
thou shalt not c thy neighbour's ... Ex 20:17 2530
wife, neither shalt thou c thy ... Deut 5:21 183
they c fields, and take them by ... Mic 2:2 2530
law had said, Thou shalt not c ... Rom 7:7 *1937*
false witness, Thou shalt not c ... Rom 13:9 *1937*
But c earnestly the best gifts ... 1Cor 12:31 *2206*
c to prophesy, and forbid not to ... 1Cor 14:39 *2206*

COVETED
shekels weight, then I c them ... Josh 7:21 2530
I have c no man's silver, or gold ... Acts 20:33 *1937*
which while some c after, they ... 1Ti 6:10 *3713*

COVETETH
He c greedily all the day long ... Prov 21:26 183
Woe to him that c an evil ... Hab 2:9 1214

COVETOUS
heart's desire, and blesseth the c ... Ps 10:3 1214
And the Pharisees also, who were c ... Lk 16:14 *5366*
of this world, or with the c ... 1Cor 5:10 *4123*
a brother be a fornicator, or c ... 1Cor 5:11 *4123*
Nor thieves, nor c, nor drunkards ... 1Cor 6:10 *4123*
nor unclean person, nor c man ... Eph 5:5 *4123*
but patient, not a brawler, not c ... 1Ti 3:3 *866*
be lovers of their own selves, c ... 2Ti 3:2 *5366*
have exercised with c practices ... 2Pet 2:14 *4124*

COVETOUSNESS
fear God, men of truth, hating c ... Ex 18:21 1215
unto thy testimonies, and not to c ... Ps 119:36 1215
but he that hateth c shall ... Prov 28:16 1215
the iniquity of his c was I wroth ... Is 57:17 1215
of them every one is given to c ... Jer 6:13 1215
unto the greatest is given to c ... Jer 8:10 1215
thine heart are not but for thy c ... Jer 22:17 1215
is come, and the measure of thy c ... Jer 51:13 1215
their heart goeth after their c ... Eze 33:31 1215
coveteth an evil c to his house ... Hab 2:9 1215
Thefts, c, wickedness, deceit, ... Mk 7:22 *4124*
them, Take heed, and beware of c ... Lk 12:15 *4124*
fornication, wickedness, c ... Rom 1:29 *4124*
matter of bounty, and not as of c ... 2Cor 9:5 *4124*
and all uncleanness, or c ... Eph 5:3 *4124*
evil concupiscence, and c ... Col 3:5 *4124*
as ye know, nor a cloke of c ... 1Th 2:5 *4124*
your conversation be without c ... Heb 13:5 *866*
through c shall they with feigned ... 2Pet 2:3 *4124*

COVOCATION
month ye shall have an holy c ... Num 29:12

COW
And whether it be c or ewe ... Lev 22:28 7794
But the firstling of a c, or the ... Num 18:17 7794
their c calveth, and casteth not ... Job 21:10 6510
a man shall nourish a young c ... Is 7:21 5697
And the c and the bear shall feed ... Is 11:7 6510
every c at that which is before ... Amos 4:3

COW'S
I have given thee c dung for ... Eze 4:15 1241

COZ (coz) *A descendant of Caleb.*
C begat Anub, and Zobebah, and the ... 1Chr 4:8 6976

COZBI (coz'-bi) *A Midianite woman.*
woman that was slain was C ... Num 25:15 3579
of Peor, and in the matter of C ... Num 25:18 3579

COZEBA See CHOZEBA.

CRACKLING
For as the c of thorns under a ... Eccl 7:6 6963

CRACKNELS
take with thee ten loaves, and c ... 1Kin 14:3 5350

CRAFT
cause c to prosper in his hand ... Dan 8:25 4820
how they might take him by c ... Mk 14:1 *1388*
And because he was of the same c ... Acts 18:3 *3673*
that by this c we have our wealth ... Acts 19:25 *2039*
our c is in danger to be set at ... Acts 19:27 *3313*
craftsman, of whatsoever c he be ... Rev 18:22 *5078*

CRAFTINESS
He taketh the wise in their own c ... Job 5:13 6193
But he perceived their c, and said ... Lk 20:23 *3834*
He taketh the wise in their own c ... 1Cor 3:19 *3834*
of dishonesty, not walking in c ... 2Cor 4:2 *3834*
the sleight of men, and cunning c ... Eph 4:14 *3834*

CRAFTSMAN
the work of the hands of the c ... Deut 27:15 2976
and no c, of whatsoever craft he ... Rev 18:22 *5079*

CRAFTSMEN
thousand captives, and all the c ... 2Kin 24:14 2796
might, even seven thousand, and c ... 2Kin 24:16 2796
for they were c ... 1Chr 4:14 2796
Lod, and Ono, the valley of c ... Neh 11:35 2796
all of it the work of the c ... Hos 13:2 2796
brought no small gain unto the c ... Acts 19:24 *5079*
the c which are with him, have a ... Acts 19:38 *5079*

CRAFTY
the devices of the c, so that ... Job 5:12 6175
thou choosest the tongue of the c ... Job 15:5 6175
They have taken c counsel against ... Ps 83:3 6191
nevertheless, being c, I caught ... 2Cor 12:16 *3835*

CRAG
upon the c of the rock, and the ... Job 39:28 8127

CRANE
Like a c or a swallow, so did I ... Is 38:14 5483
and the turtle and the c and the ... Jer 8:7 5483

CRASHING
and a great c from the hills ... Zeph 1:10 7667

CRAVED
Pilate, and c the body of Jesus ... Mk 15:43 *154*

CRAVETH
for his mouth c it of him ... Prov 16:26 404

CREATE
C in me a clean heart, O God ... Ps 51:10 1254
the LORD will c upon every ... Is 4:5 1254
I form the light, and c darkness ... Is 45:7 1254
I make peace, and c evil ... Is 45:7 1254
I c the fruit of the lips ... Is 57:19 1254
I c new heavens and a new earth ... Is 65:17 1254
for ever in that which I c ... Is 65:18 1254
I c Jerusalem a rejoicing, and her ... Is 65:18 1254

CREATED
In the beginning God c the heaven ... Gen 1:1 1254
God c great whales, and every ... Gen 1:21 1254
So God c man in his own image ... Gen 1:27 1254
in the image of God c he him ... Gen 1:27 1254
male and female c he them ... Gen 1:27 1254
from all his work which God c ... Gen 2:3 1254
and of the earth when they were c ... Gen 2:4 1254
In the day that God c man ... Gen 5:1 1254
Male and female c he them ... Gen 5:2 1254
Adam, in the day when they were c ... Gen 5:2 1254
have c from the face of the earth ... Gen 6:7 1254
day that God c man upon the earth ... Deut 4:32 1254
and the south thou hast c them ... Ps 89:12 1254
shall be c shall praise the LORD ... Ps 102:18 1254
forth thy spirit, they are c ... Ps 104:30 1254
for he commanded, and they were c ... Ps 148:5 1254
and behold who hath c these things ... Is 40:26 1254
the Holy One of Israel hath c it ... Is 41:20 1254
he that c the heavens, and ... Is 42:5 1254
thus saith the LORD that c thee ... Is 43:1 1254
for I have c him for my glory, I ... Is 43:7 1254
I the LORD have c it ... Is 45:8 1254
made the earth, and c man upon it ... Is 45:12 1254
saith the LORD that c the heavens ... Is 45:18 1254
he c it not in vain, he formed it ... Is 45:18 1254
They are c now, and not from the ... Is 48:7 1254
I have c the smith that bloweth ... Is 54:16 1254
I have c the waster to destroy ... Is 54:16 1254
for the LORD hath c a new thing ... Jer 31:22 1254
in the place where thou wast c ... Eze 21:30 1254
thee in the day that thou wast c ... Eze 28:13 1254
from the day that thou wast c ... Eze 28:15 1254
hath not one God c us ... Mal 2:10 1254
which God c unto this time ... Mk 13:19 *2936*
was the man c for the woman ... 1Cor 11:9 *2936*
c in Christ Jesus unto good works ... Eph 2:10 *2936*
who c all things by Jesus Christ ... Eph 3:9 *2936*
after God is c in righteousness ... Eph 4:24 *2936*
For by him were all things c ... Col 1:16 *2936*
all things were c by him, and for ... Col 1:16 *2936*
after the image of him that c him ... Col 3:10 *2936*
which God hath c to be received ... 1Ti 4:3 *2936*
for thou hast c all things ... Rev 4:11 *2936*
thy pleasure they are and were c ... Rev 4:11 *2936*
who c heaven, and the things that ... Rev 10:6 *2936*

CREATETH
c the wind, and declareth unto man ... Amos 4:13 1254

CREATION
of the c God made them male ... Mk 10:6 *2937*
the c which God created unto this ... Mk 13:19 *2937*
things of him from the c of the ... Rom 1:20 *2937*
we know that the whole c groaneth ... Rom 8:22 *2937*
were from the beginning of the c ... 2Pet 3:4 *2937*
the beginning of the c of God ... Rev 3:14 *2937*

CREATOR
Remember now thy C in the days of ... Eccl 12:1 1254
the C of the ends of the earth, ... Is 40:28 1254
the c of Israel, your King ... Is 43:15 1254
the creature more than the C ... Rom 1:25 *2936*
well doing, as unto a faithful C ... 1Pet 4:19 *2939*

CREATURE
the moving c that hath life ... Gen 1:20 8318
and every living c that moveth ... Gen 1:21 5315
forth the living c after his kind ... Gen 1:24 5315
Adam called every living c ... Gen 2:19 5315
every living c that is with you ... Gen 9:10 5315
every living c that is with you, ... Gen 9:12 5315
and every living c of all flesh ... Gen 9:15 5315
every living c of all flesh that ... Gen 9:16 5315
of every living c that moveth in ... Lev 11:46 5315
of every c that creepeth upon the ... Lev 11:46 5315
of the living c was in the wheels ... Eze 1:20 2416
of the living c was in the wheels ... Eze 1:21 2416
living c was as the colour of the ... Eze 1:22 2416
This is the living c that I saw ... Eze 10:15 2416
of the living c was in them ... Eze 10:17 2416
This is the living c that I saw ... Eze 10:20 2416
and preach the gospel to every c ... Mk 16:15 *2937*
served the c more than the ... Rom 1:25 *2937*
c waiteth for the manifestation ... Rom 8:19 *2937*
For the c was made subject to ... Rom 8:20 *2937*
Because the c itself also shall ... Rom 8:21 *2937*
nor depth, nor any other c ... Rom 8:39 *2937*
man be in Christ, he is a new c ... 2Cor 5:17 *2937*
nor uncircumcision, but a new c ... Gal 6:15 *2937*
God, the firstborn of every c ... Col 1:15 *2937*
to every c which is under heaven ... Col 1:23 *2937*
For every c of God is good, and ... 1Ti 4:4 *2938*
Neither is there any c that is ... Heb 4:13 *2937*
every c which is in heaven, and on ... Rev 5:13 *2938*

CREATURES
houses shall be full of doleful c ... Is 13:21 255
the likeness of four living c ... Eze 1:5 2416
for the likeness of the living c ... Eze 1:13 2416
up and down among the living c ... Eze 1:13 2416
And the living c ran and returned ... Eze 1:14 2416
Now as I beheld the living c ... Eze 1:15 2416
upon the earth by the living c ... Eze 1:15 2416
And when the living c went ... Eze 1:19 2416
when the living c were lifted up ... Eze 1:19 2416
living c that touched one another ... Eze 3:13 2416
be a kind of firstfruits of his c ... Jas 1:18 *2938*
of the c which were in the sea ... Rev 8:9 *2938*

CREDITOR
Every c that lendeth ought unto ... Deut 15:2
the c is come to take unto him my ... 2Kin 4:1 5383
There was a certain c which had ... Lk 7:41 *1157*

CREDITORS
or which of my c is it to whom I ... Is 50:1 5383

CREEK
a certain c with a shore, into ... Acts 27:39 *2859*

CREEP
All fowls that c, going upon all ... Lev 11:20 8318
things that c upon the earth ... Lev 11:29 8317
unclean to you among all that c ... Lev 11:31 8318
things that c upon the earth ... Lev 11:42 8317
beasts of the forest do c forth ... Ps 104:20 7430
things that c upon the earth ... Eze 38:20 7430
sort are they which c into houses ... 2Ti 3:6

CREEPETH
every thing that c upon the earth ... Gen 1:25 7431
thing that c upon the earth ... Gen 1:26 7430
every thing that c upon the earth ... Gen 1:30 7430
every thing that c upon the earth ... Gen 7:8 7430
every creeping thing that c upon ... Gen 7:14 7430
thing that c upon the earth ... Gen 7:21 8317
thing that c upon the earth ... Gen 8:17 7430
whatsoever c upon the earth, ... Gen 8:19 7430
every creeping thing that c upon ... Lev 11:41 8317
with any creeping thing that c ... Lev 11:43 8317
thing that c upon the earth ... Lev 11:44 7430
creature that c upon the earth ... Lev 11:46 8317
living thing that c on the ground ... Lev 20:25 7430
of any thing that c on the ground ... Deut 4:18 7430

CREEPING
c thing, and beast of the earth ... Gen 1:24 7431
over every c thing that creepeth ... Gen 1:26 7431
the c thing, and the fowls of the ... Gen 6:7 7431
of every c thing of the earth ... Gen 6:20 7431
every c thing that creepeth upon ... Gen 7:14 7431
of every c thing that creepeth ... Gen 7:21 8318
the c things, and the fowl of the ... Gen 7:23 7431
of every c thing that creepeth ... Gen 8:17 7431
Every beast, every c thing ... Gen 8:19 7431
the carcase of unclean c things ... Lev 5:2 8318
may ye eat of every flying c ... Lev 11:21 8318
But all other flying c things ... Lev 11:23 8318
the c things that creep upon the ... Lev 11:29 8318
every c thing that creepeth upon ... Lev 11:41 8318
hath more feet among all c things ... Lev 11:42 8318
with any c thing that creepeth ... Lev 11:43 8318
of c thing that creepeth upon the ... Lev 11:44 8318
Or whosoever toucheth any c thing ... Lev 22:5 8318
every c thing that flieth is ... Deut 14:19 8318
of c things, and of fishes ... 1Kin 4:33 7431
wherein are things c innumerable ... Ps 104:25 7431
c things, and flying fowl ... Ps 148:10 7431
and behold every form of c things ... Eze 8:10 7431
all c things that creep upon the ... Eze 38:20 7431
with the c things of the ground ... Hos 2:18 7431
of the sea, as the c things ... Hab 1:14 7431
c things, and fowls of the air ... Acts 10:12 *2062*
c things, and fowls of the air ... Acts 11:6 *2062*
and fourfooted beasts, and c things ... Rom 1:23 *2062*

CREPT
are certain men c in unawares ... Jude 4 *3921*

CRESCENS (*cres'-sens*) *A companion of Paul.*
C to Galatia, Titus unto Dalmatia ... 2Ti 4:10 *2913*

CRETE (*creet*) See CRETES. *An island south of Greece.*
suffering us, we sailed under C ... Acts 27:7 *2914*
which is an haven of C, and lieth ... Acts 27:12 *2914*
thence, they sailed close by C ... Acts 27:13 *2914*
me, and not have loosed from C ... Acts 27:21 *2914*
For this cause left I thee in C ... Titus 1:5 *2914*

CRETES (*creets*) See CRETIANS. *Inhabitants of Crete.*
C and Arabians, we do hear them ... Acts 2:11 *2912*

CRETIANS (*cre'-shuns*) See CRETES. *Same as Cretes.*
The C are alway liars, evil ... Titus 1:12 *2912*
bishop of the church of the C ... Titus *s* *2912*

CREW
And immediately the cock c ... Mt 26:74 *5455*
and the cock c ... Mk 14:68 *5455*
And the second time the cock c ... Mk 14:72 *5455*
while he yet spake, the cock c ... Lk 22:60 *5455*
and immediately the cock c ... Jn 18:27 *5455*

CRIB
to serve thee, or abide by thy c ... Job 39:9 18
Where no oxen are, the c is clean ... Prov 14:4 18
owner, and the ass his master's c ... Is 1:3 18

CRIED
he c with a great and exceeding ... Gen 27:34 6817
with me, and I c with a loud voice ... Gen 39:14 7121
that I lifted up my voice and c ... Gen 39:15 7121
as I lifted up my voice and c ... Gen 39:18 7121
they c before him, Bow the knee ... Gen 41:43 7121
the people c to Pharaoh for bread ... Gen 41:55 6817
and he c, Cause every man to go ... Gen 45:1 7121
reason of the bondage, and they c ... Ex 2:23 2199
c unto Pharaoh, saying, Wherefore ... Ex 5:15 6817
Moses c unto the LORD because of ... Ex 8:12 6817
of Israel c out unto the LORD ... Ex 14:10 6817
And he c unto the LORD ... Ex 15:25 6817
Moses c unto the LORD, saying, ... Ex 17:4 6817
And the people c unto Moses ... Num 11:2 6817
Moses c unto the LORD, saying, ... Num 12:13 6817
lifted up their voice, and c ... Num 14:1 5414
when we c unto the LORD, he heard ... Num 20:16 6817
the damsel, because she c not ... Deut 22:24 6817
field, and the betrothed damsel c ... Deut 22:27 6817
when we c unto the LORD God of ... Deut 26:7 6817
when they c unto the LORD, he put ... Josh 24:7 6817
of Israel c unto the LORD ... Judg 3:9 2199
of Israel c unto the LORD ... Judg 3:15 2199
of Israel c unto the LORD ... Judg 4:3 6817
c through the lattice, Why is his ... Judg 5:28 2980
of Israel c unto the LORD ... Judg 6:6 2199
when the children of Israel c ... Judg 6:7 2199
and they c, The sword of the LORD, ... Judg 7:20 7121
and all the host ran, and c ... Judg 7:21 7321
and lifted up his voice, and c ... Judg 9:7 7121
of Israel c unto the LORD ... Judg 10:10 2199
ye c to me, and I delivered you ... Judg 10:12 6817
they c unto the children of Dan ... Judg 18:23 7121
and told it, all the city c out ... 1Sa 4:13 2199
Ekron, that the Ekronites c out ... 1Sa 5:10 2199
Samuel c unto the LORD for Israel ... 1Sa 7:9 2199
your fathers c unto the LORD, ... 1Sa 12:8 2199
they c unto the LORD, and said, We ... 1Sa 12:10 2199
he c unto the LORD all night ... 1Sa 15:11 2199
c unto the armies of Israel, and ... 1Sa 17:8 7121
Jonathan c after the lad, and said ... 1Sa 20:37 7121
Jonathan c after the lad, Make ... 1Sa 20:38 7121
c after Saul, saying, My lord the ... 1Sa 24:8 7121
David c to the people, and to ... 1Sa 26:14 7121
Samuel, she c with a loud voice ... 1Sa 28:12 2199
And the watchman c, and told the ... 2Sa 18:25 7121
the king c with a loud voice, O ... 2Sa 19:4 2199
Then c a wise woman out of the ... 2Sa 20:16 7121
upon the LORD, and c to my God ... 2Sa 22:7 7121
he c against the altar in the ... 1Kin 13:2 7121
which had c against the altar in ... 1Kin 13:4 7121
he c unto the man of God that ... 1Kin 13:21 7121
For the saying which he c by the ... 1Kin 13:32 7121
he c unto the LORD, and said, O ... 1Kin 17:20 7121
c unto the LORD, and said, O LORD ... 1Kin 17:21 7121
they c aloud, and cut themselves ... 1Kin 18:28 7121
passed by, he c unto the king ... 1Kin 20:39 6817
and Jehoshaphat c out ... 1Kin 22:32 2199
And Elisha saw it, and he c ... 2Kin 2:12 6817
Now there c a certain woman of ... 2Kin 4:1 6817
of the pottage, that they c out ... 2Kin 4:40 6817
and he c, and said, Alas, master ... 2Kin 6:5 6817
there c a woman unto him, saying, ... 2Kin 6:26 6817
c to the king for her house and ... 2Kin 8:5 6817
Athaliah rent her clothes, and c ... 2Kin 11:14 7121
c with a loud voice in the Jews' ... 2Kin 18:28 7121
the prophet c unto the LORD ... 2Kin 20:11 7121
for they c to God in the battle, ... 1Chr 5:20 2199
they c unto the LORD, and the ... 2Chr 13:14 6817
Asa c unto the LORD his God, and ... 2Chr 14:11 7121
but Jehoshaphat c out, and the ... 2Chr 18:31 2199
Then they c with a loud voice in ... 2Chr 32:18 7121
of Amoz, prayed and c to heaven ... 2Chr 32:20 2199
c with a loud voice unto the LORD ... Neh 9:4 2199
trouble, when they c unto thee ... Neh 9:27 6817
c unto thee, thou heardest them ... Neh 9:28 2199
c with a loud and a bitter cry ... Est 4:1 2199

I delivered the poor that c ... Job 29:12 7768
(they c after them as after a... Job 30:5 7321
up, and I c in the congregation ... Job 30:28 7768
I c unto the LORD with my voice, ... Ps 3:4 7121
upon the LORD, and c unto my God ... Ps 18:6 7768
They c, but there was none to ... Ps 18:41 7768
They c unto thee, and were ... Ps 22:5 2199
but when he c unto him, he heard... Ps 22:24 7768
I c unto thee, and thou hast... Ps 30:2 7768
I c to thee, O LORD ... Ps 30:8 7121
supplications when I c unto thee ... Ps 31:22 7768
This poor man c, and the LORD... Ps 34:6 7121
I c unto him with my mouth, and he... Ps 66:17 7121
I c unto God with my voice, even... Ps 77:1 6817
God of my salvation, I have c day ... Ps 88:1 6817
But unto thee have I c, O LORD... Ps 88:13 7768
Then they c unto the LORD in... Ps 107:6 6817
Then they c unto the LORD in... Ps 107:13 2199
I c with my whole heart... Ps 119:145 7121
I c unto thee... Ps 119:146 7121
the dawning of the morning, and c... Ps 119:147 7768
In my distress I c unto the LORD... Ps 120:1 7121
of the depths have I c unto thee ... Ps 130:1 7121
In the day when I c thou ... Ps 138:3 7121
I c unto the LORD with my voice ... Ps 142:1 2199
I c unto thee, O LORD... Ps 142:5 2199
one c unto another, and said, Holy... Is 6:3 7121
moved at the voice of him that c ... Is 6:4 7121
And he c, A lion... Is 21:8 7121
have I c concerning this, Their... Is 30:7 7121
c with a loud voice in the Jews' ... Is 36:13 7121
Destruction upon destruction is c ... Jer 4:20 7121
I c out, I c violence and... Jer 20:8 2199
c out, I c violence and spoil... Jer 20:8 7121
Their heart c unto the Lord, O... Lam 2:18 6817
They c unto them, Depart ye ... Lam 4:15 7121
He c also in mine ears with a... Eze 9:1 7121
that I fell upon my face, and c... Eze 9:8 2199
it was c unto them in my hearing,... Eze 10:13 7121
c with a loud voice, and said, Ah ... Eze 11:13 2199
Then an herald c aloud, To you it... Dan 3:4 7123
He c aloud, and said thus, Hew ... Dan 4:14 7123
The king c aloud to bring in the... Dan 5:7 7123
he c with a lamentable voice unto... Dan 6:20 2200
they have not c unto me with... Hos 7:14 2199
c every man unto his god, and cast... Jonah 1:5 2199
Wherefore they c unto the LORD... Jonah 1:14 7121
I c by reason of mine affliction ... Jonah 2:2 7121
out of the belly of hell c I ... Jonah 2:2 7768
the city a day's journey, and he c... Jonah 3:4 7121
whom the former prophets have c ... Zec 1:4 7121
Then c he upon me, and spake unto ... Zec 6:8 2199
hath c by the former prophets... Zec 7:7 7121
it is come to pass, that as he c... Zec 7:13 7121
so they c, and I would not hear,... Zec 7:13 7121
And, behold, they c out, saying, ... Mt 8:29 2896
and they c out for fear... Mt 14:26 2896
and beginning to sink, he c... Mt 14:30 2896
c unto him, saying, Have mercy on ... Mt 15:22 2905
c out, saying, Have mercy on us, ... Mt 20:30 2896
but they c the more, saying, Have ... Mt 20:31 2896
went before, and that followed, c... Mt 21:9 2896
But they c out the more, saying, ... Mt 27:23 2896
hour Jesus c with a loud voice... Mt 27:46 310
when he had c again with a loud ... Mt 27:50 2896
an unclean spirit; and he c out ... Mk 1:23 349
c with a loud voice, he came out... Mk 1:26 2896
him, fell down before him, and c... Mk 3:11 2896
c with a loud voice, and said, ... Mk 5:7 2896
it had been a spirit, and c out ... Mk 6:49 349
the father of the child c out... Mk 9:24 2896
And the spirit c, and rent him sore... Mk 9:26 2896
but he c the more a great deal,... Mk 10:48 2896
before, and they that followed, c... Mk 11:9 2896
they c out again, Crucify him ... Mk 15:13 2896
they c out the more exceedingly, ... Mk 15:14 2896
hour Jesus c with a loud voice... Mk 15:34 994
Jesus c with a loud voice, and... Mk 15:37 863
against him, saw that he so c out ... Mk 15:39 2896
and c out with a loud voice, ... Lk 4:33 349
he had said these things, he c... Lk 8:8 5455
he c out, and fell down before him ... Lk 8:28 349
a man of the company c out ... Lk 9:38 310
And he c and said, Father Abraham,... Lk 16:24 5455
And he c, saying, Jesus, thou son... Lk 18:38 994
but he c so much the more, Thou... Lk 18:39 2896
they c out all at once, saying,... Lk 23:18 349
But they c, saying, Crucify him,... Lk 23:21 2019
when Jesus had c with a loud... Lk 23:46 5455
John bare witness of him, and c... Jn 1:15 2896
Then c Jesus in the temple as he ... Jn 7:28 2896
of the feast, Jesus stood and c... Jn 7:37 2896
he c with a loud voice, Lazarus,... Jn 11:43 2905
and went forth to meet him, and c... Jn 12:13 2896
Jesus c and said, He that... Jn 12:44 2896
Then c they all again, saying,... Jn 18:40 2905
and officers saw him, they c out... Jn 19:6 2905
but the Jews c out, saying, If... Jn 19:12 2896
But they c out, Away with him, ... Jn 19:15 2905
Then they c out with a loud voice ... Acts 7:57 2896
c with a loud voice, Lord, lay... Acts 7:60 2896
same followed Paul and us, and c ... Acts 16:17 2896
But Paul c with a loud voice, ... Acts 16:28 5455
c out, saying, Great is Diana of ... Acts 19:28 2896
Some therefore c one thing ... Acts 19:32 2896
the space of two hours c out... Acts 19:34 2896
some c one thing, some another,... Acts 21:34 994
And as they c out, and cast off... Acts 22:23 2905
wherefore they c so against him... Acts 22:24 2019
he c out in the council, Men and... Acts 23:6 2896
that I c standing among them,... Acts 24:21 2896
they c with a loud voice, saying, ... Rev 6:10 2896
he c with a loud voice to the... Rev 7:2 2896
c with a loud voice, saying,... Rev 7:10 2896
c with a loud voice, as when a... Rev 10:3 2896
and when he had c, seven thunders ... Rev 10:3 2896
And she being with child c ... Rev 12:2 2896
c with a loud cry to him that had... Rev 14:18 5455
he c mightily with a strong voice... Rev 18:2 2896
c when they saw the smoke of her... Rev 18:18 2896
cast dust on their heads, and c ... Rev 18:19 2896
he c with a loud voice, saying to... Rev 19:17 2896

CRIES
the c of them which have reaped... Jas 5:4 995

CRIEST
Moses, Wherefore c thou unto me... Ex 14:15 6817
Who art thou that c to the king... 1Sa 26:14 7121
if thou c after knowledge, and... Prov 2:3 7121
When thou c, let thy companies... Is 57:13 2199
Why c thou for thine affliction ... Jer 30:15 2199

CRIETH
blood c unto me from the ground... Gen 4:10 6817
come to pass, when he c unto me... Ex 22:27 6817
and the soul of the wounded c out... Job 24:12 7768
shall deliver the needy when he c... Ps 72:12 7768
my flesh c out for the living God ... Ps 84:2 7442
Wisdom c without... Prov 1:20 7442
She c in the chief place of... Prov 1:21 7121
She c at the gates, at the entry ... Prov 8:3 7442
she c upon the highest places of... Prov 9:3 7121
is in pain, and c out in her pangs... Is 26:17 2199
of him that c in the wilderness... Is 40:3 7121
it c out against me... Jer 12:8 7121
The LORD's voice c unto the city... Mic 6:9 7121
for she c after us ... Mt 15:23 2896
taketh him, and he suddenly c out ... Lk 9:39 2896
Esaias also c concerning Israel, ... Rom 9:27 2896
is of you kept back by fraud, c ... Jas 5:4 2896

CRIME
For this is an heinous c... Job 31:11 2154
concerning the c laid against him... Acts 25:16 1462

CRIMES
for the land is full of bloody c... Eze 7:23 4941
to signify the c laid against him ... Acts 25:27 156

CRIMSON
and in iron, and in purple, and c ... 2Chr 2:7 3758
blue, and in fine linen, and in c... 2Chr 2:14 3758
the vail of blue, and purple, and c... 2Chr 3:14 3758
though they be red like c... Is 1:18 8438
thou clothest thyself with c... Jer 4:30 8144

CRIPPLE
being a c from his mother's womb,... Acts 14:8 5560

CRISPING
and the wimples, and the c pins, ... Is 3:22 2754

CRISPUS (*cris'-pus*) *A convert of Paul.*
And C, the chief ruler of the... Acts 18:8 2921
I baptized none of you, but C... 1Cor 1:14 2921

CROOKBACKT
Or c, or a dwarf, or that hath a ... Lev 21:20 1384

CROOKED
are a perverse and c generation... Deut 32:5 6618
hand hath formed the c serpent ... Job 26:13 1281
as turn aside unto their c ways... Ps 125:5 6128
Whose ways are c, and they froward... Prov 2:15 6141
That which is c cannot be made... Eccl 1:15 5791
straight, which he hath made c ... Eccl 7:13 5791
even leviathan that c serpent... Is 27:1 6129
the c shall be made straight, and... Is 40:4 6121
before them, and c things straight ... Is 42:16 4625
make the c places straight ... Is 45:2 1921
they have made them c paths... Is 59:8 6140
stone, he hath made my paths c... Lam 3:9 5753
the c shall be made straight, and... Lk 3:5 4646
rebuke, in the midst of a c... Phil 2:15 4646

CROP
away his c with his feathers... Lev 1:16 4760
I will c off from the top of his... Eze 17:22 6998

CROPPED
He c off the top of his young ... Eze 17:4 6998

CROSS
And he that taketh not his c... Mt 10:38 4716
deny himself, and take up his c ... Mt 16:24 4716
him they compelled to bear his c ... Mt 27:32 4716
Son of God, come down from the c... Mt 27:40 4716
let him now come down from the c... Mt 27:42 4716
deny himself, and take up his c... Mk 8:34 4716
and come, take up the c, and follow... Mk 10:21 4716
Alexander and Rufus, to bear his c... Mk 15:21 4716
thyself, and come down from the c ... Mk 15:30 4716
of Israel descend now from the c... Mk 15:32 4716
himself, and take up his c daily ... Lk 9:23 4716
And whosoever doth not bear his c... Lk 14:27 4716
and on him they laid the c... Lk 23:26 4716
he bearing his c went forth into... Jn 19:17 4716
wrote a title, and put it on the c ... Jn 19:19 4716
by the c of Jesus his mother... Jn 19:25 4716
upon the c on the sabbath day ... Jn 19:31 4716
lest the c of Christ should be... 1Cor 1:17 4716
of the c is to them that perish... 1Cor 1:18 4716
is the offence of the c ceased ... Gal 5:11 4716
persecution for the c of Christ... Gal 6:12 4716
save in the c of our Lord Jesus... Gal 6:14 4716
unto God in one body by the c... Eph 2:16 4716
death, even the death of the c ... Phil 2:8 4716
the enemies of the c of Christ... Phil 3:18 4716
peace through the blood of his c... Col 1:20 4716
of the way, nailing it to his c ... Col 2:14 4716
was set before him endured the c ... Heb 12:2 4716

CROSSWAY
thou have stood in the c, to cut ... Obad 14 6563

CROUCH
c to him for a piece of silver and... 1Sa 2:36 7812

CROUCHETH
He c, and humbleth himself, that... Ps 10:10 1794

CROW
this night, before the cock c... Mt 26:34 5455
said unto him, Before the cock c... Mt 26:75 5455
night, before the cock c twice... Mk 14:30 5455
unto him, Before the cock c twice ... Mk 14:72 5455
the cock shall not c this day... Lk 22:34 5455
said unto him, Before the cock c ... Lk 22:61 5455
unto thee, The cock shall not c ... Jn 13:38 5455

CROWN
on the c of the head of him that ... Gen 49:26 6936
upon it a c of gold round about... Ex 25:11 2213
make thereto a c of gold round ... Ex 25:24 2213
thou shalt make a golden c to the ... Ex 25:25 2213
put the holy c upon the mitre... Ex 29:6 5145
unto it a c of gold round about... Ex 30:3 2213
thou make to it under the c of it... Ex 30:4 2213
made a c of gold to it round... Ex 37:2 2213
made thereunto a c of gold round... Ex 37:11 2213
made a c of gold for the border ... Ex 37:12 2213
unto it a c of gold round about... Ex 37:26 2213
gold for it under the c thereof... Ex 37:27 2213
plate of the holy c of pure gold... Ex 39:30 5145
put the golden plate, the holy c... Lev 8:9 5145
for the c of the anointing oil of ... Lev 21:12 5145
the arm with the c of the head ... Deut 33:20 6936
I took the c that was upon his... 2Sa 1:10 5145
their king's c from off his head... 2Sa 12:30 5850
to the c of his head there was no... 2Sa 14:25 6936
put the c upon him, and gave him... 2Kin 11:12 5145
David took the c of their king... 1Chr 20:2 5850
king's son, and put upon him the c ... 2Chr 23:11 5145
before the king with the c royal ... Est 1:11 3804
he set the royal c upon her head... Est 2:17 3804
the c royal which is set upon his... Est 6:8 3804
white, and with a great c of gold ... Est 8:15 5850
the sole of his foot unto his c... Job 2:7 6936
and taken the c from my head... Job 19:9 5850
shoulder, and bind it as a c to me ... Job 31:36 5850
thou settest a c of pure gold on... Ps 21:3 5850
thou hast profaned his c by ... Ps 89:39 5145
upon himself shall his c flourish ... Ps 132:18 5145
a c of glory shall she deliver to... Prov 4:9 5850
woman is a c to her husband ... Prov 12:4 5850
The c of the wise is their riches... Prov 14:24 5850
The hoary head is a c of glory ... Prov 16:31 5850
children are the c of old men ... Prov 17:6 5850
doth the c endure to every... Prov 27:24 5145
c wherewith his mother crowned... Song 3:11 5850
c of the head of the daughters of... Is 3:17 6936
Woe to the c of pride, to the... Is 28:1 5850
The c of pride, the drunkards of... Is 28:3 5850
LORD of hosts be for a c of glory... Is 28:5 5850
Thou shalt also be a c of glory... Is 62:3 5850
have broken the c of thy head... Jer 2:16 6936
down, even the c of your glory... Jer 13:18 5850
Moab, and the c of the head of the... Jer 48:45 6936
The c is fallen from our head ... Lam 5:16 5850
a beautiful c upon thine head... Eze 16:12 5850
the diadem, and take off the c ... Eze 21:26 5850
shall be as the stones of a c... Zec 9:16 5145
they had platted a c of thorns... Mt 27:29 4735
purple, and platted a c of thorns ... Mk 15:17 4735
soldiers platted a c of thorns ... Jn 19:2 4735
forth, wearing the c of thorns... Jn 19:5 4735
do it to obtain a corruptible c ... 1Cor 9:25 4735
and longed for, my joy and c ... Phil 4:1 4735
hope, or joy, or c of rejoicing... 1Th 2:19 4735
up for me a c of righteousness... 2Ti 4:8 4735
he shall receive the c of life... Jas 1:12 4735
ye shall receive a c of glory ... 1Pet 5:4 4735
and I will give thee a c of life ... Rev 2:10 4735
thou hast, that no man take thy c... Rev 3:11 4735
and a c was given unto him... Rev 6:2 4735
upon her head a c of twelve stars... Rev 12:1 4735
having on his head a golden c... Rev 14:14 4735

CROWNED
hast c him with glory and honour... Ps 8:5 5849
the prudent are c with knowledge ... Prov 14:18 3803
the crown wherewith his mother c... Song 3:11 5849
Thy c are as the locusts, and thy ... Nah 3:17 4502
for masteries, yet is he not c ... 2Ti 2:5 4737
of death, c with glory and honour ... Heb 2:9 4737

CROWNEDST
thou c him with glory and honour,... Heb 2:7 4737

CROWNEST
Thou c the year with thy goodness ... Ps 65:11 5849

CROWNETH
who c thee with lovingkindness and ... Ps 103:4 5849

CROWNING
the c city, whose merchants are... Is 23:8 5849

CROWNS
beautiful c upon their heads... Eze 23:42 5850
take silver and gold, and make c... Zec 6:11 5850
the c shall be to Helem, and to... Zec 6:14 5850
they had on their heads c of gold... Rev 4:4 4735
cast their c before the throne,... Rev 4:10 4735
heads were as it were c like gold... Rev 9:7 4735
horns, and seven c upon his heads... Rev 12:3 1238
horns, and upon his horns ten c... Rev 13:1 1238
fire, and on his head were many c ... Rev 19:12 1238

CRUCIFIED
Son of man is betrayed to be c Mt 26:2 4717
all say unto him, Let him be c Mt 27:22 4717
the more, saying, Let him be c Mt 27:23 4717
Jesus, he delivered him to be c Mt 27:26 4717
And they c him, and parted his Mt 27:35 4717
were there two thieves c with him Mt 27:38 4717
also, which were c with him Mt 27:44 4957
that ye seek Jesus, which was c Mt 28:5 4717
when he had scourged him, to be c Mk 15:15 4717
And when they had c him, they Mk 15:24 4717
was the third hour, and they c him Mk 15:25 4717
they that were c with him reviled Mk 15:32 4957
Jesus of Nazareth, which was c Mk 16:6 4717
requiring that he might be c Lk 23:23 4717
called Calvary, there they c him Lk 23:33 4717
the hands of sinful men, and be c Lk 24:7 4717
condemned to death, and have c him Lk 24:20 4717
him therefore unto them to be c Jn 19:16 4717
Where they c him, and two others Jn 19:18 4717
Jesus was c was nigh to the city Jn 19:20 4717
soldiers, when they had c Jesus Jn 19:23 4717
of the other which was c with him Jn 19:32 4957
where he was c there was a garden Jn 19:41 4717
taken, and by wicked hands have c Acts 2:23 4362
that same Jesus, whom ye have c Acts 2:36 4717
Christ of Nazareth, whom ye c Acts 4:10 4717
that our old man is c with him Rom 6:6 4957
was Paul c for you? 1Cor 1:13 4717
But we preach Christ c, unto the 1Cor 1:23 4717
you, save Jesus Christ, and him c 1Cor 2:2 4717
not have c the Lord of glory 1Cor 2:8 4717
though he was c through weakness 2Cor 13:4 4717
I am c with Christ Gal 2:20 4957
evidently set forth, c among you Gal 3:1 4717
they that are Christ's have c the Gal 5:24 4717
by whom the world is c unto me Gal 6:14 4717
Egypt, where also our Lord was c Rev 11:8 4717

CRUCIFY
mock, and to scourge, and to c him Mt 20:19 4717
some of them ye shall kill and c Mt 23:34 4717
on him, and led him away to c him Mt 27:31 4717
And they cried out again, C him Mk 15:13 4717
out the more exceedingly, C him Mk 15:14 4717
on him, and led him out to c him Mk 15:20 4717
And with him they c two thieves Mk 15:27 4717
cried, saying, C him, c him Lk 23:21 4717
out, saying, C him, c him Jn 19:6 4717
unto them, Take ye him, and c him Jn 19:6 4717
not that I have power to c thee Jn 19:10 4717
with him, away with him, c him Jn 19:15 4717
unto them, Shall I c your King Jn 19:15 4717
seeing they c to themselves the Heb 6:6 388

CRUEL
and their wrath, for it was c Gen 49:7 7185
of spirit, and for c bondage Ex 6:9 7185
dragons, and the c venom of asps Deut 32:33 393
Thou art become c to me Job 30:21 393
and they hate me with c hatred Ps 25:19 2555
hand of the unrighteous and c man Ps 71:4 2556
others, and thy years unto the c Prov 5:9 394
but he that is c troubleth his Prov 11:17 394
mercies of the wicked are c Prov 12:10 394
therefore a c messenger shall be Prov 17:11 394
Wrath is c, and anger is Prov 27:4 395
jealousy is c as the grave Song 8:6
c both with wrath and fierce anger Is 13:9 394
over into the hand of a c lord Is 19:4 7186
they are c, and have no mercy Jer 6:23 394
with the chastisement of a c one Jer 30:14 394
they are c, and will not shew Jer 50:42 394
daughter of my people is become c Lam 4:3 393
And others had trial of c mockings Heb 11:36

CRUELLY
father, because he c oppressed Eze 18:18 6233

CRUELTY
instruments of c are in their Gen 49:5 2555
That the c done to the threescore Judg 9:24 2555
me, and such as breathe out c Ps 27:12 2555
are full of the habitations of c Ps 74:20 2555
with c have ye ruled them Eze 34:4 6531

CRUMBS
yet the dogs eat of the c which Mt 15:27 5589
the table eat of the children's c Mk 7:28 5589
desiring to be fed with the c Lk 16:21 5589

CRUSE
the c of water, and let us go 1Sa 26:11 6835
the c of water from Saul's 1Sa 26:12 6835
the c of water that was at his 1Sa 26:16 6835
a c of honey, and go to him 1Kin 14:3 1228
a barrel, and a little oil in a c 1Kin 17:12 6835
neither shall the c of oil fail 1Kin 17:14 6835
neither did the c of oil fail 1Kin 17:16 6835
and a c of water at his head 1Kin 19:6 6835
And he said, Bring me a new c 2Kin 2:20 6746

CRUSH
that the foot may c them, or that Job 39:15 2115
against me to c my young men Lam 1:15 7665
To c under his feet all the Lam 3:34 1792
which c the needy, which say to Amos 4:1 7533

CRUSHED
LORD that which is bruised, or c Lev 22:24 3807
c Balaam's foot against the wall Num 22:25 3905
be only oppressed and c alway Deut 28:33 7533
which are c before the moth Job 4:19 1792
they are c in the gate, neither Job 5:4 1792
that which is c breaketh out into Is 59:5 2116
hath devoured me, he hath c me Jer 51:34 2000

CRY
LORD said, Because the c of Sodom Gen 18:20 2201
according to the c of it, which Gen 18:21 6818
because the c of them is waxen Gen 19:13 6818
a great and exceeding bitter c Gen 27:34 6818
their c came up unto God by Ex 2:23 7775
have heard their c by reason of Ex 3:7 6818
the c of the children of Israel Ex 3:9 6818
therefore they c, saying, Let us Ex 5:8 6817
And there shall be a great c Ex 11:6 6818
and there was a great c in Egypt Ex 12:30 6818
they c at all unto me Ex 22:23 6817
I will surely hear their c Ex 22:23 6818
of them that c for being overcome Ex 32:18 6030
upon his upper lip, and shall c Lev 13:45 7121
about them fled at the c of them Num 16:34 6963
he c unto the LORD against thee Deut 15:9 7121
lest he c against thee unto the Deut 24:15 7121
c unto the gods which ye have Judg 10:14 2199
the c of the city went up to 1Sa 5:12 7775
Cease not to c unto the LORD our 1Sa 7:8 2199
ye shall c out in that day 1Sa 8:18 2199
because their c is come unto me 1Sa 9:16 6818
I yet to c any more unto the king 2Sa 19:28 2199
my c did enter into his ears 2Sa 22:7 7775
my God, to hearken unto the c 1Kin 8:28 7440
mocked them, and said, C aloud 1Kin 18:27 7121
she went forth to c unto the king 2Kin 8:3 6817
my God, to hearken unto the c 2Chr 6:19 7440
trumpets to c alarm against you 2Chr 13:12 7321
c unto thee in our affliction, 2Chr 20:9 2199
there was a great c of the people Neh 5:1 6818
very angry when I heard their c Neh 5:6 2201
heardest their c by the Red sea Neh 9:9 2201
cried with a loud and a bitter c Est 4:1 2201
of the fastings and their c Est 9:31 2201
blood, and let my c have no place Job 16:18 2201
I c out of wrong, but I am not Job 19:7 6817
I c aloud, but there is no Job 19:7 7768
Will God hear his c when trouble Job 27:9 6818
I c unto thee, and thou dost not Job 30:20 7768
though they c in his destruction Job 30:24 7769
If my land c against me, or that Job 31:38 2199
So that they cause the c of the Job 34:28 6818
he heareth the c of the afflicted Job 34:28 6818
they make the oppressed to c Job 35:9 2199
they c out by reason of the arm Job 35:9 7768
There they c, but none giveth Job 35:12 6817
they c not when he bindeth them Job 36:13 7768
when his young ones c unto God Job 38:41 7768
Hearken unto the voice of my c Ps 5:2 7773
not the c of the humble Ps 9:12 6818
right, O LORD, attend unto my c Ps 17:1 7440
my c came before him, even into Ps 18:6 7775
I c in the daytime, but thou Ps 22:2 7121
O LORD, when I c with my voice Ps 27:7 7121
Unto thee will I c, O LORD my Ps 28:1 7121
when I c unto thee, when I lift Ps 28:2 7768
and his ears are open unto their c Ps 34:15 7775
The righteous c, and the LORD Ps 34:17 6817
O LORD, and give ear unto my c Ps 39:12 7775
inclined unto me, and heard my c Ps 40:1 7775
at noon, will I pray, and c aloud Ps 55:17 1993
When I c unto thee, then shall Ps 56:9 7121
I will c unto God most high Ps 57:2 7121
Hear my c, O God Ps 61:1 7440
of the earth will I c unto thee Ps 61:2 7121
for I c unto thee daily Ps 86:3 7121
incline thine ear unto my c Ps 88:2 7440
He shall c unto me, Thou art my Ps 89:26 7121
LORD, and let my c come unto thee Ps 102:1 7775
affliction, when he heard their c Ps 106:44 7440
Then they c unto the LORD in Ps 107:19 2199
Then they c unto the LORD in Ps 107:28 6817
Let my c come near before thee, O Ps 119:169 7440
Lord, I c unto thee Ps 141:1 7121
unto my voice, when I c unto thee Ps 141:1 7121
Attend unto my c Ps 142:6 7440
he also will hear their c Ps 145:19 7775
and to the young ravens which c Ps 147:9 7121
Doth not wisdom c Prov 8:1 7121
his ears at the c of the poor Prov 21:13 2201
he also shall c himself Prov 21:13 7121
heard in quiet more than the c of Eccl 9:17 2201
for righteousness, but behold a c Is 5:7 6818
child shall have knowledge to c Is 8:4 7121
C out and shout, thou inhabitant Is 12:6 6670
shall c in their desolate houses Is 13:22 6030
c, O city Is 14:31 2199
And Heshbon shall c, and Elealeh Is 15:4 2199
soldiers of Moab shall c out Is 15:4 7321
My heart shall c out for Moab Is 15:5 2199
shall raise up a c of destruction Is 15:5 2201
For the c is gone round about the Is 15:8 2201
for they shall c unto the LORD Is 19:20 6817
they shall c aloud from the sea Is 24:14 6670
c ye out, and c Is 29:9 8173
unto thee at the voice of thy c Is 30:19 2201
valiant ones shall c without Is 33:7 6817
the satyr shall c to his fellow Is 34:14 7121
c unto her, that her warfare is Is 40:2 7121
The voice said, C Is 40:6 7121
And he said, What shall I c Is 40:6 7121
He shall not c, nor lift up, nor Is 42:2 6817
he shall c, yea, roar Is 42:13 7321
now will I c like a travailing Is 42:14 6463
whose c is in the ships Is 43:14 7440
yea, one shall c unto him Is 46:7 6817
c aloud, thou that didst not Is 54:1 6670
C aloud, spare not, lift up thy Is 58:1 7121
thou shalt c, and he shall say, Is 58:9 7768
but ye shall c for sorrow of Is 65:14 6817
c in the ears of Jerusalem, Jer 2:2 7121
thou not from this time c unto me Jer 3:4 7121
c, gather together, and say, Jer 4:5 7121
neither lift up c nor prayer for Jer 7:16 7440
Behold the voice of the c of the Jer 8:19 7775
and though they shall c unto me Jer 11:11 2199
c unto the gods unto whom they Jer 11:12 2199
neither lift up a c or prayer for Jer 11:14 7440
they c unto me for their trouble Jer 11:14 7121
the c of Jerusalem is gone up Jer 14:2 6682
fast, I will not hear their c Jer 14:12 7440
Let a c be heard from their Jer 18:22 2201
let him hear the c in the morning Jer 20:16 2201
Go up to Lebanon, and c Jer 22:20 6817
in Bashan, and c from the passages Jer 22:20 6817
Howl, ye shepherds, and c Jer 25:34 2199
A voice of the c of the shepherds Jer 25:36 6818
upon the mount Ephraim shall c Jer 31:6 7121
thy c hath filled the land Jer 46:12 6682
They did c there, Pharaoh king of Jer 46:17 7121
then the men shall c, and all the Jer 47:2 2199
ones have caused a c to be heard Jer 48:4 2201
have heard a c of destruction Jer 48:5 6818
howl and c; tell ye it in Arnon Jer 48:20 2199
I will c out for all Moab Jer 48:31 2199
From the c of Heshbon even unto Jer 48:34 2201
c, ye daughters of Rabbah, gird Jer 49:3 6817
at the c the noise thereof was Jer 49:21 6818
and they shall c unto them Jer 49:29 7121
the c is heard among the nations Jer 50:46 2201
A sound of a c cometh from Jer 51:54 2201
Arise, c out in the night Lam 2:19 7442
Also when I c and shout, he Lam 3:8 2199
ear at my breathing, at my c Lam 3:56 7775
though they c in mine ears with a Eze 8:18 7121
that c for all the abominations Eze 9:4 602
C and howl, son of man Eze 21:12 2199
Forbear to c, make no mourning Eze 24:17 602
of thy fall, when the wounded c Eze 26:15 602
the sound of the c of thy pilots Eze 27:28 2201
shall c bitterly, and shall cast Eze 27:30 2199
c aloud at Beth-aven, after thee, Hos 5:8 7321
Israel shall c unto me, My God, Hos 8:2 2199
your God, and c unto the LORD, Joel 1:14 2199
O LORD, to thee will I c Joel 1:19 7121
of the field c also unto thee Joel 1:20 6165
a young lion c out of his den Amos 3:4
that great city, and c against it Jonah 1:2 7121
sackcloth, and c mightily unto God Jonah 3:8 7121
Then shall they c unto the LORD Mic 3:4 2199
that bite with their teeth, and c Mic 3:5 7121
Now why dost thou c out aloud Mic 4:9 7321
Stand, stand, shall they c Nah 2:8
O LORD, how long shall I c Hab 1:2 7768
even c out unto thee of violence, Hab 1:2 2199
the stone shall c out of the wall Hab 2:11 2199
noise of a c from the fish gate Zeph 1:10 6818
mighty man shall c there bitterly Zeph 1:14 6873
C thou, saying, Thus saith the Zec 1:14 7121
C yet, saying, Thus saith the Zec 1:17 7121
He shall not strive, nor c Mt 12:19 2905
And at midnight there was a c made Mt 25:6 2906
of Nazareth, he began to c out Mk 10:47 2896
avenge his own elect, which c day Lk 18:7 994
stones would immediately c out Lk 19:40 2896
And there arose a great c Acts 23:9 2906
Spirit of adoption, whereby we c Rom 8:15 2896
break forth and c, thou that Gal 4:27 994
cried with a loud c to him that Rev 14:18 2906

CRYING
when Eli heard the noise of the c 1Sa 4:14 6818
hand on her head, and went on c 2Sa 13:19 2201
regardeth he the c of the driver Job 39:7 8663
I am weary of my c Ps 69:3 7121
let not thy soul spare for his c Prov 19:18 4191
horseleach hath two daughters, c Prov 30:15
walls, and of c to the mountains Is 22:5 7771
There is a c for wine in the Is 24:11 6682
heard in her, nor the voice of c Is 65:19 2201
A voice of c shall be from Jer 48:3 6818
thereof with shoutings, c Zec 4:7
with weeping, and with c out Mal 2:13 603
The voice of one c in the Mt 3:3 994
two blind men followed him, c Mt 9:27 2896
the children c in the temple, and Mt 21:15 2896
The voice of one c in the Mk 1:3 994
the mountains, and in the tombs, c Mk 5:5 2896
the multitude c aloud began to Mk 15:8 310
The voice of one c in the Lk 3:4 994
c out, and saying, Thou art Christ Lk 4:41 2896
voice of one c in the wilderness Jn 1:23 994
c with loud voice, came out of Acts 8:7 994
ran in among the people, c out, Acts 14:14 2896
unto the rulers of the city, c Acts 17:6 994
C out, Men of Israel, help Acts 21:28 2896
of the people followed after, c Acts 21:36 2896
c that he ought not to live any Acts 25:24 1916
of his Son into your hearts, c Gal 4:6 2896
and supplications with strong c Heb 5:7 2906
c with a loud voice to him that Rev 14:15 2896
more death, neither sorrow, nor c Rev 21:4 2906

CRYSTAL
The gold and the c cannot equal it Job 28:17 2137
as the colour of the terrible c Eze 1:22 7140
was a sea of glass like unto c Rev 4:6 2930
like a jasper stone, clear as c Rev 21:11 2929
of water of life, clear as c Rev 22:1 2930

CUBIT
in a c shalt thou finish it above Gen 6:16 520
be the length thereof, and a c Ex 25:10 520
half the breadth thereof, and a c Ex 25:10 520
be the length thereof, and a c Ex 25:17 520
c the breadth thereof, and a c Ex 25:23 520
a c on the one side, and a c Ex 26:13 520

be the length of a board, and a *c*	Ex 26:16	520
A *c* shall be the length thereof,	Ex 30:2	520
and a *c* the breadth thereof	Ex 30:2	520
and the breadth of a board one *c*	Ex 36:21	520
half was the length of it, and a *c*	Ex 37:1	520
a half the breadth of it, and a *c*	Ex 37:1	520
was the length thereof, and one *c*	Ex 37:6	520
c the breadth thereof, and a *c*	Ex 37:10	520
a *c*, and the breadth of it a *c*	Ex 37:25	520
of it, after the *c* of a man	Deut 3:11	520
had two edges, of a *c* length	Judg 3:16	1574
knops compassing it, ten in a *c*	1Kin 7:24	520
the chapiter and above was a *c*	1Kin 7:31	520
after the work of the base, a *c*	1Kin 7:31	520
a wheel was a *c* and half a *c*	1Kin 7:32	520
a round compass of half a *c* high	1Kin 7:35	520
ten in a *c*, compassing the sea	2Chr 4:3	520
reed of six cubits long by the *c*	Eze 40:5	520
chambers was one *c* on this side	Eze 40:12	520
the space was one *c* on that side	Eze 40:12	520
a *c* and an half long, and a *c*	Eze 40:42	520
and an half broad, and one *c* high	Eze 40:42	520
breadth inward, a way of one *c*	Eze 42:4	520
The *c* is a *c* and an hand	Eze 43:13	520
The *c* is a *c* and an hand	Eze 43:13	520
be a *c*, and the breadth a *c*	Eze 43:13	520
two cubits, and the breadth one *c*	Eze 43:14	520
four cubits, and the breadth one *c*	Eze 43:14	520
border about it shall be half a *c*	Eze 43:17	520
bottom thereof shall be a *c* about	Eze 43:17	520
can add one *c* unto his stature	Mt 6:27	*4083*
can add to his stature one *c*	Lk 12:25	*4083*

CUBITS

the ark shall be three hundred *c*	Gen 6:15	520
c, the breadth of it fifty *c*	Gen 6:15	520
and the height of it thirty *c*	Gen 6:15	520
Fifteen *c* upward did the waters	Gen 7:20	520
two *c* and a half shall be the	Ex 25:10	520
two *c* and a half shall be the	Ex 25:17	520
two *c* shall be the length thereof	Ex 25:23	520
shall be eight and twenty *c*	Ex 26:2	520
the breadth of one curtain four *c*	Ex 26:2	520
of one curtain shall be thirty *c*	Ex 26:8	520
the breadth of one curtain four *c*	Ex 26:8	520
Ten *c* shall be the length of a	Ex 26:16	520
five *c* long, and five *c* broad	Ex 27:1	520
height thereof shall be three *c*	Ex 27:1	520
of an hundred *c* long for one side	Ex 27:9	520
be hangings of an hundred *c* long	Ex 27:11	
side shall be hangings of fifty *c*	Ex 27:12	520
side eastward shall be fifty *c*	Ex 27:13	520
of the gate shall be fifteen *c*	Ex 27:14	520
side shall be hangings fifteen *c*	Ex 27:15	
shall be an hanging of twenty *c*	Ex 27:16	520
the court shall be an hundred *c*	Ex 27:18	520
the height five *c* of fine twined	Ex 27:18	520
two *c* shall be the height thereof	Ex 30:2	520
one curtain was twenty and eight *c*	Ex 36:9	520
the breadth of one curtain four *c*	Ex 36:9	520
of one curtain was thirty *c*	Ex 36:15	520
four *c* was the breadth of one	Ex 36:15	520
The length of a board was ten *c*	Ex 36:21	520
two *c* and a half was the length of	Ex 37:1	520
two *c* and a half was the length	Ex 37:6	520
two *c* was the length thereof, and	Ex 37:10	520
two *c* was the height of it	Ex 37:25	520
five *c* was the length thereof, and	Ex 38:1	520
five *c* the breadth thereof	Ex 38:1	520
three *c* the height thereof	Ex 38:1	520
fine twined linen, an hundred *c*	Ex 38:9	520
the hangings were an hundred *c*	Ex 38:11	520
side were hangings of fifty *c*	Ex 38:12	520
the east side eastward fifty *c*	Ex 38:13	520
side of the gate were fifteen *c*	Ex 38:14	520
hand, were hangings of fifteen *c*	Ex 38:15	520
twenty *c* was the length, and the	Ex 38:18	520
height in the breadth was five *c*	Ex 38:18	520
as it were two *c* high upon the	Num 11:31	520
outward a thousand *c* round about	Num 35:4	520
on the east side two thousand *c*	Num 35:5	520
on the south side two thousand *c*	Num 35:5	520
on the west side two thousand *c*	Num 35:5	520
on the north side two thousand *c*	Num 35:5	520
nine *c* was the length thereof, and	Deut 3:11	520
four *c* the breadth of it, after	Deut 3:11	520
about two thousand *c* by measure	Josh 3:4	520
of Gath, whose height was six *c*	1Sa 17:4	520
length thereof was threescore *c*	1Kin 6:2	520
and the breadth thereof twenty *c*	1Kin 6:2	
and the height thereof thirty *c*	1Kin 6:2	520
twenty *c* was the length thereof,	1Kin 6:3	520
ten *c* was the breadth thereof	1Kin 6:3	520
chamber was five *c* broad	1Kin 6:6	520
and the middle was six *c* broad	1Kin 6:6	520
and the third was seven *c* broad	1Kin 6:6	520
all the house, five *c* high	1Kin 6:10	520
he built twenty *c* on the sides of	1Kin 6:16	520
before it, was forty *c* long	1Kin 6:17	520
forepart was twenty *c* in length	1Kin 6:20	520
twenty *c* in breadth	1Kin 6:20	520
twenty *c* in the height thereof	1Kin 6:20	520
of olive tree, each ten *c* high	1Kin 6:23	520
five *c* was the one wing of the	1Kin 6:24	520
five *c* the other wing of the	1Kin 6:24	520
part of the other were ten *c*	1Kin 6:24	520
And the other cherub was ten *c*	1Kin 6:25	520
of the one cherub was ten *c*	1Kin 6:26	520
length thereof was an hundred *c*	1Kin 7:2	520
and the breadth thereof fifty *c*	1Kin 7:2	520
and the height thereof thirty *c*	1Kin 7:2	520
the length thereof was fifty *c*	1Kin 7:6	520
and the breadth thereof thirty *c*	1Kin 7:6	520
ten *c*, and stones of eight *c*	1Kin 7:10	520
brass, of eighteen *c* high apiece	1Kin 7:15	520
a line of twelve *c* did compass	1Kin 7:15	520
of the one chapiter was five *c*	1Kin 7:16	520
of the other chapiter was five *c*	1Kin 7:16	520
of lily work in the porch, four *c*	1Kin 7:19	520
ten *c* from the one brim to the	1Kin 7:23	520
about, and his height was five *c*	1Kin 7:23	520
a line of thirty *c* did compass it	1Kin 7:23	520
four *c* was the length of one base	1Kin 7:27	520
four *c* the breadth thereof, and	1Kin 7:27	520
and three *c* the height of it	1Kin 7:27	520
and every laver was four *c*	1Kin 7:38	520
the corner gate, four hundred *c*	2Kin 14:13	520
of the one pillar was eighteen *c*	2Kin 25:17	520
height of the chapiter three *c*	2Kin 25:17	520
man of great stature, five *c* high	1Chr 11:23	520
The length by *c* after the first	2Chr 3:3	520
first measure was threescore *c*	2Chr 3:3	520
c, and the breadth twenty *c*	2Chr 3:3	520
breadth of the house, twenty *c*	2Chr 3:4	520
breadth of the house, twenty *c*	2Chr 3:8	520
and the breadth thereof twenty *c*	2Chr 3:8	520
the cherubims were twenty *c* long	2Chr 3:11	520
wing of the one cherub was five *c*	2Chr 3:11	520
other wing was likewise five *c*	2Chr 3:11	520
of the other cherub was five *c*	2Chr 3:12	520
and the other wing was five *c* also	2Chr 3:12	520
spread themselves forth twenty *c*	2Chr 3:13	520
pillars of thirty and five *c* high	2Chr 3:15	520
top of each of them was five *c*	2Chr 3:15	520
twenty *c* the length thereof, and	2Chr 4:1	520
twenty *c* the breadth thereof, and	2Chr 4:1	520
and ten *c* the height thereof	2Chr 4:1	520
sea of ten *c* from brim to brim	2Chr 4:2	520
five *c* the height thereof	2Chr 4:2	520
a line of thirty *c* did compass it	2Chr 4:2	520
a brasen scaffold, of five *c* long	2Chr 6:13	520
five *c* broad, and three *c*	2Chr 6:13	520
the corner gate, four hundred *c*	2Chr 25:23	520
the height thereof threescore *c*	Ezr 6:3	521
the breadth thereof threescore *c*	Ezr 6:3	521
a thousand *c* on the wall unto the	Neh 3:13	520
a gallows be made of fifty *c* high	Est 5:14	520
also, the gallows fifty *c* high	Est 7:9	520
of one pillar was eighteen *c*	Jer 52:21	520
fillet of twelve *c* did compass it	Jer 52:21	520
height of one chapiter was five *c*	Jer 52:22	520
reed of six *c* long by the cubit	Eze 40:5	520
the little chambers were five *c*	Eze 40:7	520
he the porch of the gate, eight *c*	Eze 40:9	520
and the posts thereof, two *c*	Eze 40:9	520
of the entry of the gate, ten *c*	Eze 40:11	520
length of the gate, thirteen *c*	Eze 40:11	520
chambers were six *c* on this side	Eze 40:12	520
and six *c* on that side	Eze 40:12	520
the breadth was five and twenty *c*	Eze 40:13	520
made also posts of threescore *c*	Eze 40:14	520
of the inner gate were fifty *c*	Eze 40:15	520
without, an hundred *c* eastward	Eze 40:19	520
the length thereof was fifty *c*	Eze 40:21	520
and the breadth five and twenty *c*	Eze 40:21	520
from gate to gate an hundred *c*	Eze 40:23	520
the length was fifty *c*	Eze 40:25	520
and the breadth five and twenty *c*	Eze 40:25	520
toward the south an hundred *c*	Eze 40:27	520
it was fifty *c* long	Eze 40:29	520
and five and twenty *c* broad	Eze 40:29	520
about were five and twenty *c* long	Eze 40:30	520
and five *c* broad	Eze 40:30	520
it was fifty *c* long	Eze 40:33	520
and five and twenty *c* broad	Eze 40:33	520
the length was fifty *c*, and the	Eze 40:36	520
and the breadth five and twenty *c*	Eze 40:36	520
the court, an hundred *c* long	Eze 40:47	520
and an hundred *c* broad	Eze 40:47	520
five *c* on this side	Eze 40:48	520
and five *c* on that side	Eze 40:48	520
the gate was three *c* on this side	Eze 40:48	520
and three *c* on that side	Eze 40:48	520
length of the porch was twenty *c*	Eze 40:49	520
and the breadth eleven *c*	Eze 40:49	520
six *c* broad on the one side, and	Eze 41:1	520
six *c* broad on the other side,	Eze 41:1	520
the breadth of the door was ten *c*	Eze 41:2	520
door were five *c* on the one side	Eze 41:2	520
and five *c* on the other side	Eze 41:2	520
the length thereof, forty *c*	Eze 41:2	520
and the breadth, twenty *c*	Eze 41:2	520
the post of the door, two *c*	Eze 41:3	520
and the door, six *c*	Eze 41:3	520
the breadth of the door, seven *c*	Eze 41:3	520
the length thereof, twenty *c*	Eze 41:4	520
and the breadth, twenty *c*, before	Eze 41:4	520
the wall of the house, six *c*	Eze 41:5	520
of every side chamber, four *c*	Eze 41:5	520
were a full reed of six great *c*	Eze 41:8	520
side chamber without, was five *c*	Eze 41:9	520
was the wideness of twenty *c*	Eze 41:10	520
was left was five *c* round about	Eze 41:11	520
the west was seventy *c* broad	Eze 41:12	520
was five *c* thick round about	Eze 41:12	520
and the length thereof ninety *c*	Eze 41:12	520
the house, an hundred *c* long	Eze 41:13	520
walls thereof, an hundred *c* long	Eze 41:13	520
toward the east, an hundred *c*	Eze 41:14	520
on the other side, an hundred *c*	Eze 41:15	520
altar of wood was three *c* high	Eze 41:22	520
and the length thereof two *c*	Eze 41:22	520
an hundred *c* was the north door	Eze 42:2	520
and the breadth was fifty *c*	Eze 42:2	520
Over against the twenty *c* which	Eze 42:3	520
a walk of ten *c* breadth inward	Eze 42:4	520
the length thereof was fifty *c*	Eze 42:7	520
in the utter court was fifty *c*	Eze 42:8	520
the temple were an hundred *c*	Eze 42:8	520
measures of the altar after the *c*	Eze 43:13	520
the lower settle shall be two *c*	Eze 43:14	520
greater settle shall be four *c*	Eze 43:14	520
So the altar shall be four *c*	Eze 43:15	520
the altar shall be twelve *c* long	Eze 43:16	
settle shall be fourteen *c* long	Eze 43:17	
fifty *c* round about for the	Eze 45:2	520
courts joined of forty *c* long	Eze 46:22	
he measured a thousand *c*	Eze 47:3	520
whose height was threescore *c*	Dan 3:1	521
and the breadth thereof six *c*	Dan 3:1	521
the length thereof is twenty *c*	Zec 5:2	520
and the breadth thereof ten *c*	Zec 5:2	520
but as it were two hundred *c*	Jn 21:8	*4088*
an hundred and forty and four *c*	Rev 21:17	*4088*

CUCKOW

owl, and the night hawk, and the *c*	Lev 11:16	7828
owl, and the night hawk, and the *c*	Deut 14:15	7828

CUCUMBERS

the *c*, and the melons, and the	Num 11:5	7180
as a lodge in a garden of *c*	Is 1:8	4750

CUD

is clovenfooted, and cheweth the *c*	Lev 11:3	1625
not eat of them that chew the *c*	Lev 11:4	1625
camel, because he cheweth the *c*	Lev 11:4	1625
coney, because he cheweth the *c*	Lev 11:5	1625
hare, because he cheweth the *c*	Lev 11:6	1625
yet he cheweth not the *c*	Lev 11:7	1625
clovenfooted, nor cheweth the *c*	Lev 11:26	1625
cheweth the *c* among the beasts,	Deut 14:6	1625
not eat of them that chew the *c*	Deut 14:7	1625
for they chew the *c*, but divide	Deut 14:7	1625
the hoof, yet cheweth not the *c*	Deut 14:8	1625

CUMBERED

But Martha was *c* about much	Lk 10:40	*4049*

CUMBERETH

why *c* it the ground	Lk 13:7	*2673*

CUMBRANCE

can I myself alone bear your *c*	Deut 1:12	2960

CUMI

hand, and said unto her, Talitha *c*	Mk 5:41	*2891*

CUMMIN

the fitches, and scatter the *c*	Is 28:25	3646
wheel turned about upon the *c*	Is 28:27	3646
with a staff, and the *c* with a rod	Is 28:27	3646
pay tithe of mint and anise and *c*	Mt 23:23	*2951*

CUN See CHUN.

CUNNING

and Esau was a *c* hunter, a man of	Gen 25:27	3045
with cherubims of *c* work shalt	Ex 26:1	2803
and fine twined linen of *c* work	Ex 26:31	2803
and fine twined linen, with *c* work	Ex 28:6	2803
of judgment with *c* work	Ex 28:15	2803
To devise *c* works, to work in	Ex 31:4	4284
to make any manner of *c* work	Ex 35:33	4284
of the *c* workman, and of the	Ex 35:35	2803
and of those that devise *c* work	Ex 35:35	4284
cherubims of *c* work made he them	Ex 36:8	2803
cherubims made he it of *c* work	Ex 36:35	2803
a *c* workman, and an embroiderer in	Ex 38:23	2803
and in the fine linen, with *c* work	Ex 39:3	2803
he made the breastplate of *c* work	Ex 39:8	2803
who is a *c* player on an harp	1Sa 16:16	3045
that is *c* in playing, and a mighty	1Sa 16:18	3045
c to work all works in brass	1Kin 7:14	1847
all manner of *c* men for every	1Chr 22:15	2450
of the LORD, even all that were *c*	1Chr 25:7	995
therefore a man *c* to work in gold	2Chr 2:7	2450
can skill to grave with the *c* men	2Chr 2:7	2450
And now I have sent a *c* man	2Chr 2:13	2450
be put to him, with thy *c* men	2Chr 2:14	2450
with the *c* men of my lord David	2Chr 2:14	2450
engines, invented by *c* men	2Chr 26:15	2803
let my right hand forget her *c*	Ps 137:5	
work of the hands of a *c* workman	Song 7:1	542
the *c* artificer, and the eloquent	Is 3:3	2450
he seeketh unto him a *c* workman	Is 40:20	2450
and send for *c* women, that they	Jer 9:17	2450
they are all the work of *c* men	Jer 10:9	2450
c in knowledge, and understanding	Dan 1:4	3045
c craftiness, whereby they lie in	Eph 4:14	

CUNNINGLY

not followed *c* devised fables	2Pet 1:16	

CUP

Pharaoh's *c* was in my hand	Gen 40:11	3563
and pressed them into Pharaoh's *c*	Gen 40:11	3563
I gave the *c* into Pharaoh's hand	Gen 40:11	3563
deliver Pharaoh's *c* into his hand	Gen 40:13	3563
he gave the *c* into Pharaoh's hand	Gen 40:21	3563
And put my *c*, the silver *c*	Gen 44:2	1375
the *c* was found in Benjamin's	Gen 44:12	1375
he also with whom the *c* is found	Gen 44:16	1375
man in whose hand the *c* is found	Gen 44:17	1375
own meat, and drank of his own *c*	2Sa 12:3	3563
was wrought like the brim of a *c*	1Kin 7:26	3563
like the work of the brim of a *c*	2Chr 4:5	3563
shall be the portion of their *c*	Ps 11:6	3563
of mine inheritance and of my *c*	Ps 16:5	3563
my *c* runneth over	Ps 23:5	3563
waters of a full *c* are wrung out	Ps 73:10	
the hand of the LORD there is a *c*	Ps 75:8	3563
I will take the *c* of salvation	Ps 116:13	3563
it giveth his colour in the *c*	Prov 23:31	3599
of the LORD the *c* of his fury	Is 51:17	3563
the dregs of the *c* of trembling	Is 51:17	3563
of thine hand the *c* of trembling	Is 51:22	3563
the dregs of the *c* of my fury	Is 51:22	3563

the c of consolation to drink for ... Jer 16:7 3563
Take the wine c of this fury at ... Jer 25:15 3563
Then took I the c at the LORD's ... Jer 25:17 3563
take the c at thine hand to drink ... Jer 25:28 3563
of the c have assuredly drunken ... Jer 49:12 3563
a golden c in the LORD's hand ... Jer 51:7 3563
the c also shall pass through ... Lam 4:21 3563
will I give her c into thine hand ... Eze 23:31 3563
drink of thy sister's c deep ... Eze 23:32 3563
with the c of astonishment and ... Eze 23:33 3563
with the c of thy sister Samaria ... Eze 23:33 3563
the c of the LORD's right hand ... Hab 2:16 3563
I will make Jerusalem a c of ... Zec 12:2 5592
c of cold water only in the name ... Mt 10:42 *4221*
of the c that I shall drink of ... Mt 20:22 *4221*
Ye shall drink indeed of my c ... Mt 20:23 *4221*
make clean the outside of the c ... Mt 23:25 *4221*
first that which is within the c ... Mt 23:26 *4221*
And he took the c, and gave thanks, ... Mt 26:27 *4221*
possible, let this c pass from me ... Mt 26:39 *4221*
if this c may not pass away from ... Mt 26:42 *4221*
a c of water to drink in my name ... Mk 9:41 *4221*
ye drink of the c that I drink of ... Mk 10:38 *4221*
drink of the c that I drink of ... Mk 10:39 *4221*
And he took the c, and when he had ... Mk 14:23 *4221*
take away this c from me ... Mk 14:36 *4221*
make clean the outside of the c ... Lk 11:39 *4221*
And he took the c, and gave thanks, ... Lk 22:17 *4221*
Likewise also the c after supper ... Lk 22:20 *4221*
This c is the new testament in my ... Lk 22:20 *4221*
be willing, remove this c from me ... Lk 22:42 *4221*
the c which my Father hath given ... Jn 18:11 *4221*
The c of blessing which we bless, ... 1Cor 10:16 *4221*
Ye cannot drink the c of the Lord ... 1Cor 10:21 *4221*
and the c of devils ... 1Cor 10:21 *4221*
same manner also he took the c ... 1Cor 11:25 *4221*
This c is the new testament in my ... 1Cor 11:25 *4221*
eat this bread, and drink this c ... 1Cor 11:26 *4221*
drink this c of the Lord, ... 1Cor 11:27 *4221*
of that bread, and drink of that c ... 1Cor 11:28 *4221*
into the c of his indignation ... Rev 14:10 *4221*
to give unto her the c of the ... Rev 16:19 *4221*
having a golden c in her hand ... Rev 17:4 *4221*
in the c which she hath filled ... Rev 18:6 *4221*

CUPBEARER
For I was the king's c ... Neh 1:11 4945

CUPBEARERS
and their apparel, and his c ... 1Kin 10:5 4945
his c also, and their apparel ... 2Chr 9:4 4945

CUPS
and the bowls, and the c ... 1Chr 28:17 7184
quantity, from the vessels of c ... Is 22:24 101
pots full of wine, and c, and I ... Jer 35:5 3563
and the spoons, and the c ... Jer 52:19 4518
to hold, as the washing of c ... Mk 7:4 *4221*
men, as the washing of pots and c ... Mk 7:8 *4221*

CURDLED
out as milk, and c me like cheese ... Job 10:10 7087

CURE
health and c, and I will c them ... Jer 33:6 7495
heal you, nor c you of your wound ... Hos 5:13 1455
and they could not c him ... Mt 17:16 *2323*
over all devils, and to c diseases ... Lk 9:1 *2323*

CURED
for thou shalt not be c ... Jer 46:11 8585
the child was c from that very ... Mt 17:18 *2323*
in that same hour he c many of ... Lk 7:21 *2323*
said unto him that was c, It is ... Jn 5:10 *2323*

CURES
I do c to day and to morrow, and ... Lk 13:32 *2392*

CURIOUS
the c girdle of the ephod, which ... Ex 28:8
above the c girdle of the ephod ... Ex 28:27
above the c girdle of the ephod ... Ex 28:28
gird him with the c girdle of the ... Ex 29:5
And to devise c works, to work in ... Ex 35:32 4284
the c girdle of his ephod, that ... Ex 39:5
above the c girdle of the ephod ... Ex 39:20
above the c girdle of the ephod ... Ex 39:21
with the c girdle of the ephod ... Lev 8:7
used c arts brought their books ... Acts 19:19 *4021*

CURIOUSLY
c wrought in the lowest parts of ... Ps 139:15 7551

CURRENT
c money with the merchant ... Gen 23:16 5674

CURSE
I will not again c the ground any ... Gen 8:21 7043
thee, and c him that curseth thee ... Gen 12:3 779
and I shall bring a c upon me ... Gen 27:12 7045
said unto him, Upon me be thy c ... Gen 27:13 7045
nor c the ruler of thy people ... Ex 22:28 779
Thou shalt not c the deaf ... Lev 19:14 7043
bitter water that causeth the c ... Num 5:18 779
bitter water that causeth the c ... Num 5:19 779
the woman, The LORD make thee a c ... Num 5:21 423
the c shall go into thy bowels ... Num 5:22 779
bitter water that causeth the c ... Num 5:24 779
the c shall enter into her ... Num 5:24 779
the c shall enter into her ... Num 5:27 779
shall be a c among her people ... Num 5:27 423
I pray thee, c me this people ... Num 22:6 779
come now, c me them ... Num 22:11 6895
thou shalt not c the people ... Num 22:12 779
I pray thee, c me this people ... Num 22:17 6895
c me Jacob, and come, defy Israel ... Num 23:7 779
How shall I c, whom God hath not ... Num 23:8 5344
I took thee to c mine enemies ... Num 23:11 6895
and c me them from thence ... Num 23:13 6895
Neither c them at all, nor bless ... Num 23:25 6895
thou mayest c me them from thence ... Num 23:27 6895
I called thee to c mine enemies ... Num 24:10 6895
you this day a blessing and a c ... Deut 11:26 7045
And a c, if ye will not obey the ... Deut 11:28 7045
Gerizim, and the c upon mount Ebal ... Deut 11:29 7045
Pethor of Mesopotamia, to c thee ... Deut 23:4 7043
the c into a blessing unto thee ... Deut 23:5 7045
shall stand upon mount Ebal to c ... Deut 27:13 7045
he heareth the words of this c ... Deut 29:19 423
upon thee, the blessing and the c ... Deut 30:1 7045
and make the camp of Israel a c ... Josh 6:18 2764
Balaam the son of Beor to c you ... Josh 24:9 7043
C ye Meroz, said the angel of the ... Judg 5:23 779
c ye bitterly the inhabitants ... Judg 5:23 779
upon them came the c of Jotham ... Judg 9:57 7045
this dead dog c my lord the king ... 2Sa 16:9 7043
so let him c, because the LORD ... 2Sa 16:10 7043
LORD hath said unto him, C David ... 2Sa 16:10 7043
let him alone, and let him c ... 2Sa 16:11 7043
c in the day when I went to ... 1Kin 2:8 7045
should become a desolation and a c ... 2Kin 22:19 7045
their nobles, and entered into a c ... Neh 10:29 423
them, that he should c them ... Neh 13:2 7043
God turned the c into a blessing ... Neh 13:2 7045
he will c thee to thy face ... Job 1:11 1288
he will c thee to thy face ... Job 2:5 1288
c God, and die ... Job 2:9 1288
Let them c it ... Job 3:8 5344
that c the day, who are ready ... Job 3:8 779
to sin by wishing a c to his soul ... Job 31:30 423
their mouth, but they c inwardly ... Ps 62:4 7043
Let them c, but bless thou ... Ps 109:28 7043
The c of the LORD is in the house ... Prov 3:33 3994
corn, the people shall c him ... Prov 11:26 5344
him shall the people c, nations ... Prov 24:24 5344
so the c causeless shall not come ... Prov 26:2 7045
it shall be counted a c to him ... Prov 27:14 7045
his eyes shall have many a c ... Prov 28:27 3994
unto his master, lest he c thee ... Prov 30:10 7043
lest thou hear thy servant c thee ... Eccl 7:21 7043
C not the king, no not in thy ... Eccl 10:20 7043
c not the rich in thy bedchamber ... Eccl 10:20 7043
c their king and their God, and ... Is 8:21 7043
hath the c devoured the earth ... Is 24:6 423
and upon the people of my c ... Is 34:5 2764
and have given Jacob to the c ... Is 43:28 2764
your name for a c unto my chosen ... Is 65:15 7621
yet every one of them doth c me ... Jer 15:10 7043
and a proverb, a taunt and a c ... Jer 24:9 7045
astonishment, an hissing, and a c ... Jer 25:18 7045
will make this city a c to all ... Jer 26:6 7045
kingdoms of the earth, to be a c ... Jer 29:18 423
of them shall be taken up a c by ... Jer 29:22 7045
and an astonishment, and a c ... Jer 42:18 7045
off, and that ye might be a c ... Jer 44:8 7045
and an astonishment, and a c ... Jer 44:12 7045
and an astonishment, and a c ... Jer 44:22 7045
a reproach, a waste, and a c ... Jer 49:13 7045
sorrow of heart, thy c unto them ... Lam 3:65 8381
therefore the c is poured upon us ... Dan 9:11 423
This is the c that goeth forth ... Zec 5:3 423
as ye were a c among the heathen ... Zec 8:13 7045
I will even send a c upon you ... Mal 2:2 3994
and I will c your blessings ... Mal 2:2 779
Ye are cursed with a c ... Mal 3:9 3994
come and smite the earth with a c ... Mal 4:6 2764
enemies, bless them that c you ... Mt 5:44 *2672*
Then began he to c and to swear ... Mt 26:74 *2653*
But he began to c and to swear, ... Mk 14:71 *332*
Bless them that c you, and pray ... Lk 6:28 *2672*
and bound themselves under a c ... Acts 23:12 *332*
bound ourselves under a great c ... Acts 23:14 *332*
bless, and c not ... Rom 12:14 *2672*
works of the law are under the c ... Gal 3:10 *2671*
redeemed us from the c of the law ... Gal 3:13 *2671*
being made a c for us ... Gal 3:13 *2671*
and therewith c we men, which are ... Jas 3:9 *2672*
And there shall be no more c ... Rev 22:3 *2652*

CURSED
thou art c above all cattle, and ... Gen 3:14 779
c is the ground for thy sake ... Gen 3:17 779
now art thou c from the earth, ... Gen 4:11 779
the ground which the LORD hath c ... Gen 5:29 779
And he said, C be Canaan ... Gen 9:25 779
c be every one that curseth thee, ... Gen 27:29 779
C be their anger, for it was ... Gen 49:7 779
he hath c his father or his ... Lev 20:9 7043
the name of the LORD, and c ... Lev 24:11 7043
him that hath c without the camp ... Lev 24:14 7043
him that had c out of the camp ... Lev 24:23 7043
and he whom thou cursest is c ... Num 22:6 779
I curse, whom God hath not c ... Num 23:8 6895
c is he that curseth thee ... Num 24:9 779
lest thou be a c thing like it ... Deut 7:26 2764
for it is a c thing ... Deut 7:26 2764
of the c thing to thine hand ... Deut 13:17 2764
C be the man that maketh any ... Deut 27:15 779
C be he that setteth light by his ... Deut 27:16 779
C be he that removeth his ... Deut 27:17 779
C be he that maketh the blind to ... Deut 27:18 779
C be he that perverteth the ... Deut 27:19 779
C be he that lieth with his ... Deut 27:20 779
C be he that lieth with any ... Deut 27:21 779
C be he that lieth with his ... Deut 27:22 779
C be he that lieth with his ... Deut 27:23 779
C be he that smiteth his ... Deut 27:24 779
C be he that taketh reward to ... Deut 27:25 779
C be he that confirmeth not all ... Deut 27:26 779
C shalt thou be in the city, and ... Deut 28:16 779
c shalt thou be in the field ... Deut 28:16 779
C shall be thy basket and thy ... Deut 28:17 779
C shall be the fruit of thy body, ... Deut 28:18 779
C shalt thou be when thou comest ... Deut 28:19 779
c shalt thou be when thou goest ... Deut 28:19 779
C be the man before the LORD, ... Josh 6:26 779
Now therefore ye are c, and there ... Josh 9:23 779
did eat and drink, and c Abimelech ... Judg 9:27 7043
C be he that giveth a wife to ... Judg 21:18 779
C be the man that eateth any food ... 1Sa 14:24 779
C be the man that eateth any food ... 1Sa 14:28 779
the Philistine c David by his ... 1Sa 17:43 7043
c be they before the LORD ... 1Sa 26:19 779
came forth, and c still as he came ... 2Sa 16:5 7043
And thus said Shimei when he c ... 2Sa 16:7 7043
c as he went, and threw stones at ... 2Sa 16:13 7043
because he c the LORD's anointed ... 2Sa 19:21 7043
which c me with a grievous curse ... 1Kin 2:8 7043
c them in the name of the LORD ... 2Kin 2:24 7043
and said, Go, see now this c woman ... 2Kin 9:34 779
c them, and smote certain of them, ... Neh 13:25 7043
sinned, and c God in their hearts ... Job 1:5 1288
Job his mouth, and c his day ... Job 3:1 7043
but suddenly I c his habitation ... Job 5:3 5344
their portion is c in the earth ... Job 24:18 7043
they that be c of him shall be ... Ps 37:22 7043
hast rebuked the proud that are c ... Ps 119:21 779
thyself likewise hast c others ... Eccl 7:22 7043
C be the man that obeyeth not the ... Jer 11:3 779
C be the man that trusteth in man ... Jer 17:5 779
C be the day wherein I was born ... Jer 20:14 779
C be the man who brought tidings ... Jer 20:15 779
C be he that doeth the work of ... Jer 48:10 779
c be he that keepeth back his ... Jer 48:10 779
But c be the deceiver, which hath ... Mal 1:14 779
I have c them already, because ye ... Mal 2:2 779
Ye are c with a curse ... Mal 3:9 779
left hand, Depart from me, ye c ... Mt 25:41 *2672*
who knoweth not the law are c ... Jn 7:49 *1944*
C is every one that continueth ... Gal 3:10 *1944*
C is every one that hangeth on a ... Gal 3:13 *1944*
with covetous practices; c children ... 2Pet 2:14 *2671*

CURSEDST
from thee, about which thou c ... Judg 17:2 422
which thou c is withered away ... Mk 11:21 *2672*

CURSES
shall write these c in a book ... Num 5:23 423
that all these c shall come upon ... Deut 28:15 7045
Moreover all these c shall come ... Deut 28:45 7045
all the c that are written in ... Deut 29:20 423
according to all the c of the ... Deut 29:21 423
to bring upon it all the c that ... Deut 29:27 7045
all these c upon thine enemies ... Deut 30:7 423
even all the c that are written ... 2Chr 34:24 423

CURSEST
and he whom thou c is cursed ... Num 22:6 779

CURSETH
thee, and curse him that c thee ... Gen 12:3 7043
cursed be every one that c thee ... Gen 27:29 779
he that c his father, or his ... Ex 21:17 7043
For every one that c his father ... Lev 20:9 7043
Whosoever c his God shall bear ... Lev 24:15 7043
thee, and cursed is he that c thee ... Num 24:9 779
Whoso c his father or his mother, ... Prov 20:20 7043
a generation that c their father ... Prov 30:11 7043
He that c father or mother, let ... Mt 15:4 *2551*
Whoso c father or mother, let him ... Mk 7:10 *2551*

CURSING
the woman with an oath of c ... Num 5:21 423
The LORD shall send upon thee c ... Deut 28:20 3994
you life and death, blessing and c ... Deut 30:19 7045
me good for his c this day ... 2Sa 16:12 7045
His mouth is full of c and deceit ... Ps 10:7 423
and for c and lying which they ... Ps 59:12 423
As he loved c, so let it come ... Ps 109:17 7045
with c like as with his garment ... Ps 109:18 7045
he heareth c, and bewrayeth it not ... Prov 29:24 423
Whose mouth is full of c and ... Rom 3:14 *685*
is rejected, and is nigh unto c ... Heb 6:8 *2671*
mouth proceedeth blessing and c ... Jas 3:10 *2671*

CURSINGS
of the law, the blessings and c ... Josh 8:34 7045

CURTAIN
length of one c shall be eight ... Ex 26:2 3407
the breadth of one c four cubits ... Ex 26:2 3407
one c from the selvedge in the ... Ex 26:4 3407
the uttermost edge of another c ... Ex 26:4 3407
shalt thou make in the one c ... Ex 26:5 3407
thou make in the edge of the c ... Ex 26:5 3407
The length of one c shall be ... Ex 26:8 3407
the breadth of one c four cubits ... Ex 26:8 3407
shalt double the sixth c in the ... Ex 26:9 3407
loops on the edge of the one c ... Ex 26:10 3407
the c which coupleth the second ... Ex 26:10 3407
the half c that remaineth, shall ... Ex 26:12 3407
The length of one c was twenty ... Ex 36:9 3407
the breadth of one c four cubits ... Ex 36:9 3407
of one c from the selvedge in the ... Ex 36:11 3407
the uttermost side of another c ... Ex 36:11 3407
Fifty loops made he in one c ... Ex 36:12 3407
made he in the edge of the c ... Ex 36:12 3407
the loops held one c to another ... Ex 36:12
length of one c was thirty cubits ... Ex 36:15 3407
cubits was the breadth of one c ... Ex 36:15 3407
edge of the c in the coupling ... Ex 36:17 3407
the c which coupleth the second ... Ex 36:17 3407
the c for the door of the court, ... Num 3:26 4539
out the heavens like a c ... Ps 104:2 3407
stretcheth out the heavens as a c ... Is 40:22 1852

CURTAINS
with ten c of fine twined linen ... Ex 26:1 3407
every one of the c shall have one ... Ex 26:2 3407
The five c shall be coupled ... Ex 26:3 3407

other five c shall be coupled one Ex 26:3 3407
couple the c together with the Ex 26:6 3407
thou shalt make c of goats' hair Ex 26:7 3407
eleven c shalt thou make Ex 26:7 3407
the eleven c shall be all of one Ex 26:8 3407
shalt couple five c by themselves Ex 26:9 3407
six c by themselves, and shalt Ex 26:9 3407
remaineth of the c of the tent Ex 26:12 3407
the length of the c of the tent Ex 26:13 3407
made ten c of fine twined linen Ex 36:8 3407
the c were all of one size Ex 36:9 3407
the five c one unto another Ex 36:10 3407
the other five c he coupled one Ex 36:10 3407
coupled the c one unto another Ex 36:13 3407
he made c of goats' hair for the Ex 36:14 3407
eleven c he made them Ex 36:14 3407
the eleven c were of one size Ex 36:15 3407
he coupled five c by themselves Ex 36:16 3407
and six c by themselves Ex 36:16 3407
bear the c of the tabernacle Num 4:25 3407
the ark of God dwelleth within c 2Sa 7:2 3407
of the LORD remaineth under c 1Chr 17:1 3407
of Kedar, as the c of Solomon Song 1:5 3407
forth the c of thine habitations Is 54:2 3407
spoiled, and my c in a moment Jer 4:20 3407
tent any more, and to set up my c Jer 10:20 3407
shall take to themselves their c Jer 49:29 3407
the c of the land of Midian did Hab 3:7 3407

CUSH (*cush*) See ETHIOPIA.
1. A son of Ham.
C, and Mizraim, and Phut, Gen 10:6 3568
the sons of C; Seba, and Havilah Gen 10:7 3568
And C begat Nimrod Gen 10:8 3568
C, and Mizraim, Put, and Canaan 1Chr 1:8 3568
the sons of C; Seba, and Havilah 1Chr 1:9 3568
And C begat Nimrod 1Chr 1:10 3568
2. A Benjaminite.
the words of C the Benjamite Ps 7:*t* 3568
3. Land of descendants of Cush.
Egypt, and from Pathros, and from C Is 11:11 3568

CUSHAN (*cu'-shan*) See CHUSHAN-RISHATHAIM.
Same as Chushan-rishathaim.
saw the tents of C in affliction Hab 3:7 3572

CUSHAN-RISHATHIAM

CUSHI (*cu'-shi*)
1. Messenger of David.
Then said Joab to C, Go tell the 2Sa 18:21 3569
C bowed himself unto Joab, and ran 2Sa 18:21 3569
me, I pray thee, also run after C 2Sa 18:22 3569
way of the plain, and overran C 2Sa 18:23 3569
And, behold, C came 2Sa 18:31 3569
C said, Tidings, my lord the king 2Sa 18:31 3569
And the king said unto C, Is the 2Sa 18:32 3569
C answered, The enemies of my 2Sa 18:32 3569
2. Ancestor of Jehudi.
son of Shelemiah, the son of C Jer 36:14 3569
3. Father of Zephaniah.
came unto Zephaniah the son of C Zeph 1:1 3569

CUSTODY
And under the c and charge of the Num 3:36 6486
unto the c of Hege the king's Est 2:3 3027
to the c of Hegai, that Esther Est 2:8 3027
to the c of Hegai, keeper of the Est 2:8 3027
to the c of Shaashgaz, the king's Est 2:14 3027

CUSTOM
for the c of women is upon me Gen 31:35 1870
And it was a c in Israel, Judg 11:39 2706
the priest's c with the people 1Sa 2:13 4941
by number, according to the c Ezr 3:4 4941
they not pay toll, tribute, and c Ezr 4:13 1983
and toll, tribute, and c, was paid Ezr 4:20 1983
to impose toll, tribute, or c Ezr 7:24 1983
sealed according to the law and c Jer 32:11 2706
sitting at the receipt of c Mt 9:9 *5058*
of the earth take c or tribute Mt 17:25 *5056*
sitting at the receipt of c Mk 2:14 *5058*
According to the c of the Lk 1:9 *1485*
do for him after the c of the law Lk 2:27 *1480*
after the c of the feast Lk 2:42 *1485*
and, as his c was, he went into Lk 4:16
Levi, sitting at the receipt of c Lk 5:27 *5058*
But ye have a c, that I should Jn 18:39 *4914*
c to whom c; fear to whom fear Rom 13:7 *5056*
be contentious, we have no such c 1Cor 11:16 *4914*

CUSTOMS
not any one of these abominable c Lev 18:30 2708
For the c of the people are vain Jer 10:3 2708
shall change the c which Moses Acts 6:14 *1485*
And teach c, which are not lawful Acts 16:21 *1485*
neither to walk after the c Acts 21:21 *1485*
I know thee to be expert in all c Acts 26:3 *1485*
or c of our fathers, yet was I Acts 28:17 *1485*

CUT
neither shall all flesh be c off Gen 9:11 3772
that soul shall be c off from his Gen 17:14 3772
c off the foreskin of her son, and Ex 4:25 3772
thou shalt be c off from the Ex 9:15 3582
soul shall be c off from Israel Ex 12:15 3772
even that soul shall be c off Ex 12:19 3772
and I will c them off Ex 23:23 3582
thou shalt c the ram in pieces, Ex 29:17 5408
shall even be c off from his Ex 30:33 3772
shall even be c off from his Ex 30:38 3772
that soul shall be c off from Ex 31:14 3772
images, and c down their groves Ex 34:13 3772
c it into wires, to work it in Ex 39:3 7112
offering, and c it into his pieces Lev 1:6 5408
he shall c it into his pieces, Lev 1:12 5408
shall be c off from his people Lev 7:20 3772
shall be c off from his people Lev 7:21 3772
it shall be c off from his people Lev 7:25 3772
shall be c off from his people Lev 7:27 3772
And he c the ram into pieces Lev 8:20 5408
that man shall be c off from Lev 17:4 3772
even that man shall be c off from Lev 17:9 3772
will c him off from among his Lev 17:10 3772
eateth it shall be c off Lev 17:14 3772
be c off from among their people Lev 18:29 3772
that soul shall be c off from Lev 19:8 3772
will c him off from among his Lev 20:3 3772
will c him off, and all that go a Lev 20:5 3772
will c him off from among his Lev 20:6 3772
they shall be c off in the sight Lev 20:17 3772
both of them shall be c off from Lev 20:18 3772
that soul shall be c off from my Lev 22:3 3772
or crushed, or broken, or c Lev 22:24 3772
he shall be c off from among his Lev 23:29 3772
c down your images, and cast your Lev 26:30 3772
C ye not off the tribe of the Num 4:18 3772
be c off from among his people Num 9:13 3772
c down from thence a branch with Num 13:23 3772
of Israel c down from thence Num 13:24 3772
that soul shall be c off from Num 15:30 3772
that soul shall utterly be c off Num 15:31 3772
soul shall be c off from Israel Num 19:13 3772
that soul shall be c off from Num 19:20 3772
c down their groves, and burn Deut 7:5 1438
c off the nations from before Deut 12:29 3772
ye shall not c yourselves Deut 14:1 1413
thy God hath c off the nations Deut 19:1 3772
with the axe to c down the tree Deut 19:5 3772
thou shalt not c them down (for Deut 20:19 3772
thou shalt destroy and c them down Deut 20:20 3772
or hath his privy member c off Deut 23:1 3772
Then thou shalt c off her hand Deut 25:12 7112
c off from the waters that come Josh 3:13 3772
salt sea, failed, and were c off Josh 3:16 3772
were c off before the ark of the Josh 4:7 3772
the waters of Jordan were c off Josh 4:7 3772
c off our name from the earth Josh 7:9 3772
c off the Anakims from the Josh 11:21 3772
c down for thyself there in the Josh 17:15 1254
a wood, and thou shalt c it down Josh 17:18 1254
all the nations that I have c off Josh 23:4 3772
c off his thumbs and his great Judg 1:6 7112
thumbs and their great toes c off Judg 1:7 7112
c down the grove that is by it Judg 6:25 3772
the grove which thou shalt c down Judg 6:26 3772
the grove was c down that was by Judg 6:28 3772
because he hath c down the grove Judg 6:30 3772
c down a bough from the trees, and Judg 9:48 3772
all the people likewise c down Judg 9:49 3772
c her in pieces, and sent her Judg 20:6 5408
There is one tribe c off from Judg 21:6 1438
not c off from among his brethren Ruth 4:10 3772
that I will c off thine arm, and 1Sa 2:31 1438
whom I shall not c off from mine 1Sa 2:33 3772
were c off upon the threshold 1Sa 5:4 3772
him, and c off his head therewith 1Sa 17:51 3772
But also thou shalt not c off thy 1Sa 20:15 3772
not when the LORD hath c off the 1Sa 20:15 3772
c off the skirt of Saul's robe 1Sa 24:4 3772
because he had c off Saul's skirt 1Sa 24:5 3772
for in that I c off the skirt of 1Sa 24:11 3772
that thou wilt not c off my seed 1Sa 24:21 3772
how he hath c off those that have 1Sa 28:9 3772
they c off his head, and stripped 1Sa 31:9 3772
c off their hands and their feet, 2Sa 4:12 7112
have c off all thine enemies out 2Sa 7:9 3772
c off their garments in the 2Sa 10:4 3772
they c off the head of Sheba the 2Sa 20:22 3772
Then will I c off Israel out of 1Kin 9:7 3772
until he had c off every male in 1Kin 11:16 3772
of Jeroboam, even to c it off 1Kin 13:34 3582
will c off from Jeroboam him that 1Kin 14:10 3772
who shall c off the house of 1Kin 14:14 3772
when Jezebel c off the prophets 1Kin 18:4 3772
c it in pieces, and lay it on wood 1Kin 18:23 5408
c themselves after their manner 1Kin 18:28 1413
c the bullock in pieces, and laid 1Kin 18:33 5408
will c off from Ahab him that 1Kin 21:21 3772
came to Jordan, they c down wood 2Kin 6:4 1504
he c down a stick, and cast it in 2Kin 6:6 7094
I will c off from Ahab him that 2Kin 9:8 3772
the LORD began to c Israel short 2Kin 10:32 7096
king Ahaz c off the borders of 2Kin 16:17 7112
c down the groves, and brake in 2Kin 18:4 3772
At that time did Hezekiah c off 2Kin 18:16 7112
will c down the tall cedar trees 2Kin 19:23 3772
c down the groves, and filled 2Kin 23:14 3772
c in pieces all the vessels of 2Kin 24:13 7112
have c off all thine enemies from 1Chr 17:8 3772
c off their garments in the midst 1Chr 19:4 3772
c them with saws, and with harrows 1Chr 20:3 7787
can skill to c timber in Lebanon 2Chr 2:8 3772
the hewers that c timber 2Chr 2:10 3772
we will c wood out of Lebanon, as 2Chr 2:16 3772
the images, and c down the groves 2Chr 14:3 1438
Asa c down her idol, and stamped 2Chr 15:16 3772
to c off the house of Ahab 2Chr 22:7 3772
for he was c off from the house 2Chr 26:21 1504
c in pieces the vessels of the 2Chr 28:24 7112
c down the groves, and threw down 2Chr 31:1 1438
which c off all the mighty men of 2Chr 32:21 3582
on high above them, he c down 2Chr 34:4 1438
c down all the idols throughout 2Chr 34:7 1438
or where were the righteous c off Job 4:7 3582
let loose his hand, and c me off Job 6:9 1214
not c down, it withereth before Job 8:12 6998
Whose hope shall be c off Job 8:14 6990
If he c off, and shut up, or Job 11:10 2498
forth like a flower, and is c down Job 14:2 5243
hope of a tree, if it be c down Job 14:7 3772
above shall his branch be c off Job 18:16 5243
his months is c off in the midst Job 21:21 2686
Which were c down out of time, Job 22:16 7059
our substance is not c down Job 22:20 3582
Because I was not c off before Job 23:17 6780
c off as the tops of the ears of Job 24:24 5243
Who c up mallows by the bushes, Job 30:4 6998
when people are c off in their Job 36:20 5927
The LORD shall c off all Ps 12:3 3772
I am c off from before thine eyes Ps 31:22 1629
to c off the remembrance of them Ps 34:16 3772
soon be c down like the grass Ps 37:2 5243
For evildoers shall be c off Ps 37:9 3772
be cursed of him shall be c off Ps 37:22 3772
seed of the wicked shall be c off Ps 37:28 3772
when the wicked are c off Ps 37:34 3772
end of the wicked shall be c off Ps 37:38 3772
c them off in thy truth Ps 54:5 6789
let them be as c in pieces Ps 58:7 4135
of the wicked also will I c off Ps 75:10 1438
He shall c off the spirit of Ps 76:12 1219
is burned with fire, it is c down Ps 80:16 3683
let us c them off from being a Ps 83:4 3582
they are c off from thy hand Ps 88:5 1504
thy terrors have c me off Ps 88:16 6789
in the evening it is c down Ps 90:6 4135
for it is soon c off, and we fly Ps 90:10 1504
shall c them off in their own Ps 94:23 6789
the LORD our God shall c them off Ps 94:23 6789
his neighbour, him will I c off Ps 101:5 6789
that I may c off all wicked doers Ps 101:8 3772
c the bars of iron in sunder Ps 107:16 1438
Let his posterity be c off Ps 109:13 3772
that he may c off the memory of Ps 109:15 3772
he hath c asunder the cords of Ps 129:4 7112
of thy mercy c off mine enemies, Ps 143:12 6789
shall be c off from the earth Prov 2:22 3772
the froward tongue shall be c out Prov 10:31 3772
expectation shall not be c off Prov 23:18 3772
expectation shall not be c off Prov 24:14 3772
the sycomores are c down, but we Is 9:10 1438
LORD will c off from Israel head Is 9:14 3772
and c off nations not a few Is 10:7 3772
he shall c down the thickets of Is 10:34 5362
of Judah shall be c off Is 11:13 3772
how art thou c down to the ground Is 14:12 1438
c off from Babylon the name, and Is 14:22 3772
be baldness, and every beard c off Is 15:2 1438
he shall both c off the sprigs Is 18:5 3772
take away and c down the branches Is 18:5 8456
be removed, and be c down, and fall Is 22:25 1438
that was upon it shall be c off Is 22:25 3772
that watch for iniquity are c off Is 29:20 3772
as thorns c up shall they be Is 33:12 3683
I will c down the tall cedars Is 37:24 3772
I have c off like a weaver my Is 38:12 7088
he will c me off with pining Is 38:12 1214
c in sunder the bars of iron Is 45:2 1438
for thee, that I c thee not off Is 48:9 3772
c off nor destroyed from before Is 48:19 3772
Art thou not it that hath c Rahab Is 51:9 2672
for he was c off out of the land Is 53:8 1504
sign that shall not be c off Is 55:13 3772
name, that shall not be c off Is 56:5 3772
as if he c off a dog's neck Is 66:3
is c off from their mouth Jer 7:28 3772
C off thine hair, O Jerusalem, and Jer 7:29 1494
to c off the children from Jer 9:21 3772
let us c him off from the land of Jer 11:19 3772
nor c themselves, nor make Jer 16:6 1413
they shall c down thy choice Jer 22:7 3772
are c down because of the fierce Jer 25:37 1826
when they c the calf in twain, and Jer 34:18 3772
he c it with the penknife, and Jer 36:23 7167
having c themselves, with Jer 41:5 1413
to c off from you man and woman, Jer 44:7 3772
that ye might c yourselves off, Jer 44:8 3772
for evil, and to c off all Judah Jer 44:11 3772
They shall c down her forest, Jer 46:23 3772
to c off from Tyrus and Zidon Jer 47:4 3772
Ashkelon is c off with the Jer 47:5 1820
how long wilt thou c thyself Jer 47:5 1413
let us c it off from being a Jer 48:2 3772
Also thou shalt be c down Jer 48:2 1826
The horn of Moab is c off Jer 48:25 1438
of war shall be c off in that day Jer 49:26 1826
C off the sower from Babylon, and Jer 50:16 3772
of the whole earth c in asunder Jer 50:23 1438
of war shall be c off in that day Jer 50:30 1826
be not c off in her iniquity Jer 51:6 1826
to c it off, that none shall Jer 51:62 3772
He hath c off in his fierce anger Lam 2:3 1438
They have c off my life in the Lam 3:53 6789
then I said, I am c off Lam 3:54 1504
and your images may be c down Eze 6:6 1438
I will c him off from the midst Eze 14:8 3772
will c off man and beast from it Eze 14:13 3772
so that I c off man and beast from Eze 14:17 3772
to c off from it man and beast Eze 14:19 3772
to c off from it man and beast Eze 14:21 3772
wast born thy navel was not c Eze 16:4 3772
c off the fruit thereof, that it Eze 17:9 7082
forts, to c off many persons Eze 17:17 3772
and will c off from thee the Eze 21:3 3772
Seeing then that I will c off Eze 21:4 3772
I will c thee off from the people Eze 25:7 3772
will c off man and beast from it Eze 25:13 3772
I will c off the Cherethims, and Eze 25:16 3772
c off man and beast out of thee Eze 29:8 3772
I will c off the multitude of No Eze 30:15 3772
have c him off, and have left him Eze 31:12 3772
c off from it him that passeth Eze 35:7 3772
we are c off for our parts Eze 37:11 1504
neither c down any out of the Eze 39:10 2404
thereof, ye shall be c in pieces Dan 2:5 5648

a stone was *c* out without hands... Dan 2:34 1505
was *c* out of the mountain without... Dan 2:45 1505
shall be *c* in pieces, and their... Dan 3:29 5648
c off his branches, shake off his... Dan 4:14 7113
two weeks shall Messiah be *c* off... Dan 9:26 3772
idols, that they may be *c* off... Hos 8:4 3772
her king is *c* off as the foam... Hos 10:7 1820
king of Israel utterly be *c* off... Hos 10:15 1820
for it is *c* off from your mouth... Joel 1:5 3772
the drink offering is *c* off from... Joel 1:9 3772
Is not the meat *c* off before our... Joel 1:16 3772
c off the inhabitant from the... Amos 1:5 3772
I will *c* off the inhabitant from... Amos 1:8 3772
I will *c* off the judge from the... Amos 2:3 3772
horns of the altar shall be *c* off... Amos 3:14 1438
c them in the head, all of them... Amos 9:1 1214
by night, (how art thou *c* off... Obad 5 1820
of Esau may be *c* off by slaughter... Obad 9 3772
and thou shalt be *c* off for ever... Obad 10 3772
to *c* off those of his that did... Obad 14 3772
all thine enemies shall be *c* off... Mic 5:9 3772
that I will *c* off thy horses out... Mic 5:10 3772
I will *c* off the cities of thy... Mic 5:11 3772
I will *c* off witchcrafts out of... Mic 5:12 3772
graven images also will I *c* off... Mic 5:13 3772
yet thus shall they be *c* down... Nah 1:12 1494
will I *c* off the graven image... Nah 1:14 3772
he is utterly *c* off... Nah 1:15 3772
I will *c* off thy prey from the... Nah 2:13 3772
the sword shall *c* thee off... Nah 3:15 3772
shall be *c* off from the fold... Hab 3:17 1504
I will *c* off man from off the... Zeph 1:3 3772
I will *c* off the remnant of Baal... Zeph 1:4 3772
the merchant people are *c* down... Zeph 1:11 1820
they that bear silver are *c* off... Zeph 1:11 3772
I have *c* off the nations... Zeph 3:6 3772
dwelling should not be *c* off... Zeph 3:7 3772
one that stealeth shall be *c* off... Zec 5:3 5352
one that sweareth shall be *c* off... Zec 5:3 5352
I will *c* off the pride of the... Zec 9:6 3772
I will *c* off the chariot from... Zec 9:10 3772
and the battle bow shall be *c* off... Zec 9:10 3772
also I *c* off in one month... Zec 11:8 3582
is to be *c* off, let it be *c* off... Zec 11:9 3582
c it asunder, that I might break... Zec 11:10 1438
Then I *c* asunder mine other staff... Zec 11:14 1438
not visit those that be *c* off... Zec 11:16 3582
with it shall be *c* in pieces... Zec 12:3 8295
that I will *c* off the names of... Zec 13:2 3772
two parts therein shall be *c* off... Zec 13:8 3772
shall not be *c* off from the city... Zec 14:2 3772
The LORD will *c* off the man that... Mal 2:12 3772
c it off, and cast it from thee... Mt 5:30 1581
c them off, and cast them from... Mt 18:8 1581
others *c* down branches from the... Mt 21:8 2875
shall *c* him asunder, and appoint... Mt 24:51 1371
if thy hand offend thee, *c* it off... Mk 9:43 609
if thy foot offend thee, *c* it off... Mk 9:45 609
others *c* down branches off the... Mk 11:8 2875
the high priest, and *c* off his ear... Mk 14:47 581
will *c* him in sunder, and will... Lk 12:46 1371
c it down... Lk 13:7 1581
after that thou shalt *c* it down... Lk 13:9 1581
priest, and *c* off his right ear... Lk 22:50 851
servant, and *c* off his right ear... Jn 18:10 609
his kinsman whose ear Peter *c* off... Jn 18:26 609
they were *c* to the heart, and took... Acts 5:33 1282
they were *c* to the heart, and they... Acts 7:54 1282
Then the soldiers *c* off the ropes... Acts 27:32 609
c it short in righteousness... Rom 9:28 4932
thou also shalt be *c* off... Rom 11:22 1581
For if thou wert *c* out of the... Rom 11:24 1581
that I may *c* off occasion from... 2Cor 11:12 1581
were even *c* off which trouble you... Gal 5:12 609

CUTH (*cuth*) See CUTHAH. *A Babylonian city.*
the men of *C* made Nergal, and the... 2Kin 17:30 3575

CUTHAH (*cu'-thah*) See CUTH. *Same as Cuth.*
men from Babylon, and from *C*... 2Kin 17:24 3575

CUTTEST
When thou *c* down thine harvest in... Deut 24:19 7114

CUTTETH
He *c* out rivers among the rocks... Job 28:10 1234
the bow, and *c* the spear in sunder... Ps 46:9 7112
the grave's mouth, as when one *c*... Ps 141:7 6398
the hand of a fool *c* off the feet... Prov 26:6 7096
for one *c* a tree out of the... Jer 10:3 3772
chambers, and *c* him out windows... Jer 22:14 7167

CUTTING
in *c* of stones, to set them, and... Ex 31:5 2799
in the *c* of stones, to set them,... Ex 35:33 2799
I said in the *c* off of my days, I... Is 38:10 1824
to thy house by *c* off many people... Hab 2:10 7096
crying, and *c* himself with stones... Mk 5:5 2629

CUTTINGS
Ye shall not make any *c* in your... Lev 19:28 8296
nor make any *c* in their flesh... Lev 21:5 8296
upon all the hands shall be *c*... Jer 48:37 1417

CUZA See CHUZA.

CYMBAL
sounding brass, or a tinkling *c*... 1Cor 13:1 2950

CYMBALS
timbrels, and on cornets, and on *c*... 2Sa 6:5 6767
and with timbrels, and with *c*... 1Chr 13:8 4700
musick, psalteries and harps and *c*... 1Chr 15:16 4700
to sound with *c* of brass... 1Chr 15:19 4700
and with trumpets, and with *c*... 1Chr 15:28 4700
but Asaph made a sound with *c*... 1Chr 16:5 4700
c for those that should make a... 1Chr 16:42 4700
harps, with psalteries, and with *c*... 1Chr 25:1 4700
in the house of the LORD, with *c*... 1Chr 25:6 4700
arrayed in white linen, having *c*... 2Chr 5:12 4700
voice with the trumpets and *c*... 2Chr 5:13 4700
in the house of the LORD with *c*... 2Chr 29:25 4700
Levites the sons of Asaph with *c*... Ezr 3:10 4700
and with singing, with *c*,... Neh 12:27 4700
Praise him upon the loud *c*... Ps 150:5 6767
him upon the high sounding *c*... Ps 150:5 6767

CYPRESS
him down cedars, and taketh the *c*... Is 44:14 8645

CYPRUS (*si'-prus*) *An island off the Syrian coast.*
a Levite, and of the country of *C*... Acts 4:36 2954
travelled as far as Phenice, and *C*... Acts 11:19 2954
And some of them were men of *C*... Acts 11:20 2954
and from thence they sailed to *C*... Acts 13:4 2954
took Mark, and sailed unto *C*... Acts 15:39 2954
Now when we had discovered *C*... Acts 21:3 2954
brought with them one Mnason of *C*... Acts 21:16 2954
from thence, we sailed under *C*... Acts 27:4 2954

CYRENE (*si-re'-ne*) See CYRENIAN. *A Libyan city.*
came out, they found a man of *C*... Mt 27:32 2957
and in the parts of Libya about *C*... Acts 2:10 2957
of them were men of Cyprus and *C*... Acts 11:20 2957
was called Niger, and Lucius of *C*... Acts 13:1 2957

CYRENIAN (*si-re'-ne-an*) See CYRENIANS. *A native of Cyrene.*
And they compel one Simon a *C*... Mk 15:21 2956
laid hold upon one Simon, a *C*... Lk 23:26 2956

CYRENIANS (*si-re'-ne-ans*)
synagogue of the Libertines, and *C*... Acts 6:9 2956

CYRENIUS (*si-re'-ne-us*) *A Roman governor of Syria.*
made when *C* was governor of Syria... Lk 2:2 2958

CYRUS (*si'-rus*) *Founder of the Persian Empire.*
first year of *C* king of Persia... 2Chr 36:22 3566
up the spirit of *C* king of Persia... 2Chr 36:22 3566
Thus saith *C* king of Persia, All... 2Chr 36:23 3566
first year of *C* king of Persia... Ezr 1:1 3566
up the spirit of *C* king of Persia... Ezr 1:1 3566
Thus saith *C* king of Persia, The... Ezr 1:2 3566
Also *C* the king brought forth the... Ezr 1:7 3566
Even those did *C* king of Persia... Ezr 1:8 3566
that they had of *C* king of Persia... Ezr 3:7 3566
as king *C* the king of Persia hath... Ezr 4:3 3566
all the days of *C* king of Persia... Ezr 4:5 3566
But in the first year of *C* the... Ezr 5:13 3567
C made a decree to build this... Ezr 5:13 3567
those did *C* the king take out of... Ezr 5:14 3567
that a decree was made of *C* the... Ezr 5:17 3567
In the first year of *C* the king... Ezr 6:3 3567
the same *C* the king made a decree... Ezr 6:3 3567
according to the commandment of *C*... Ezr 6:14 3567
That saith of *C*, He is my... Is 44:28 3566
the LORD to his anointed, to *C*... Is 45:1 3566
unto the first year of king *C*... Dan 1:21 3566
and in the reign of *C* the Persian... Dan 6:28 3567
In the third year of *C* king of... Dan 10:1 3566

D

DABAREH (*dab'-a-reh*) See DABARETH. *A Levitical city in Issachar.*
her suburbs, *D* with her suburbs,... Josh 21:28 1705

DABBASHETH (*dab'-ba-sheth*) *A border city of Issachar.*
sea, and Maralah, and reached to *D*... Josh 19:11 1708

DABBESHETH See DABBASHETH.

DABERATH (*dab'-e-rath*) See DABAREH. *Same as Dabareh.*
and then goeth out to *D*, and goeth... Josh 19:12 1705
her suburbs, *D* with her suburbs,... 1Chr 6:72 1705

DAGGER
made him a *d* which had two edges... Judg 3:16 2719
took the *d* from his right thigh,... Judg 3:21 2719
not draw the *d* out of his belly... Judg 3:22 2719

DAGON See BETH-DAGON, DAGON'S. *A Philistine god.*
great sacrifice unto *D* their god... Judg 16:23 1712
house of *D*, and set it by *D*... 1Sa 5:2 1712
D was fallen upon his face to the... 1Sa 5:3 1712
And they took *D*, and set him in his... 1Sa 5:3 1712
D was fallen upon his face to the... 1Sa 5:4 1712
and the head of *D* and both the... 1Sa 5:4 1712
the stump of *D* was left to him... 1Sa 5:4 1712
neither the priests of *D*, nor any... 1Sa 5:5 1712
of *D* in Ashdod unto this day... 1Sa 5:5 1712
sore upon us, and upon *D* our god... 1Sa 5:7 1712
his head in the temple of *D*... 1Chr 10:10 1712

DAGON'S
nor any that come into *D* house... 1Sa 5:5 1712

DAILY
your *d* tasks, as when there was... Ex 5:13 3117
from your bricks of your *d* task... Ex 5:19 3117
be twice as much as they gather *d*... Ex 16:5 3117
the *d* meat offering, and the... Num 4:16 8548
this manner ye shall offer *d*... Num 28:24 3117
the *d* burnt offering, and his meat... Num 29:6 8548
she pressed him *d* with her words... Judg 16:16 3117
a *d* rate for every day, all the... 2Kin 25:30 3117
his *d* portion for their service... 2Chr 31:16 3117
offered the *d* burnt offerings by... Ezr 3:4 3117
was prepared for me *d* was one ox... Neh 5:18
pass, when they spake *d* unto him... Est 3:4 3117
soul, having sorrow in my heart *d*... Ps 13:2 3119
while they say *d* unto me, Where... Ps 42:10
he fighting *d* oppresseth me... Ps 56:1
enemies would *d* swallow me up... Ps 56:2
that I may *d* perform my vows... Ps 61:8 3117
who *d* loadeth us with benefits,... Ps 68:19 3117
and *d* shall he be praised... Ps 72:15
foolish man reproacheth thee *d*... Ps 74:22
for I cry unto thee *d*... Ps 86:3
LORD, I have called *d* upon thee... Ps 88:9
came round about me *d* like water... Ps 88:17
I was *d* his delight, rejoicing... Prov 8:30 3117
watching *d* at my gates, waiting... Prov 8:34 3117
Yet they seek me *d*, and delight to... Is 58:2 3117
d rising up early and sending them... Jer 7:25 3117
I am in derision *d*, every one... Jer 20:7
unto me, and a derision, *d*... Jer 20:8
that they should give him *d* a... Jer 37:21 3117
and Noph shall have distresses *d*... Eze 30:16 3119
without blemish *d* the seven days... Eze 45:23 3117
of the goats *d* for a sin offering... Eze 45:23 3117
Thou shalt *d* prepare a burnt... Eze 46:13 3117
the king appointed them a *d*... Dan 1:5 3117
by him the *d* sacrifice was taken... Dan 8:11 8548
the *d* sacrifice by reason of... Dan 8:12 8548
vision concerning the *d* sacrifice... Dan 8:13 8548
shall take away the *d* sacrifice... Dan 11:31 8548
And from the time that the *d*... Dan 12:11 8548
he *d* increaseth lies and... Hos 12:1
Give us this day our *d* bread... Mt 6:11 1967
I sat *d* with you teaching in the... Mt 26:55
I was *d* with you in the temple... Mk 14:49
himself, and take up his cross *d*... Lk 9:23
Give us day by day our *d* bread... Lk 11:3 1967
he taught *d* in the temple... Lk 19:47
When I was *d* with you in the... Lk 22:53
continuing *d* with one accord in... Acts 2:46
church *d* such as should be saved... Acts 2:47
whom they laid *d* at the gate of... Acts 3:2
d in the temple, and in every... Acts 5:42
neglected in the *d* ministration... Acts 6:1 2522
faith, and increased in number *d*... Acts 16:5
and searched the scriptures *d*... Acts 17:11
in the market *d* with them that... Acts 17:17
disputing *d* in the school of one... Acts 19:9
in Christ Jesus our Lord, I die *d*... 1Cor 15:31
that which cometh upon me *d*... 2Cor 11:28
But exhort one another *d*, while... Heb 3:13
Who needeth not *d*, as those high... Heb 7:27
priest standeth *d* ministering... Heb 10:11
be naked, and destitute of *d* food... Jas 2:15 2184

DAINTIES
be fat, and he shall yield royal *d*... Gen 49:20 4574
and let me not eat of their *d*... Ps 141:4 4516
Be not desirous of his *d*... Prov 23:3 4303

DAINTY
bread, and his soul *d* meat... Job 33:20 8378
neither desire thou his *d* meats... Prov 23:6 4303
thee, and all things which were *d*... Rev 18:14 3045

DALAIAH (*dal-a-i'-ah*) See DELAIAH. *A descendant of Judah.*
and Akkub, and Johanan, and *D*... 1Chr 3:24 1806

DALE
of Shaveh, which is the king's *d*... Gen 14:17 6010
pillar, which is in the king's *d*... 2Sa 18:18 6010

DALMANUTHA (*dal-ma-nu'-thah*) *A village in Galilee.*
and came into the parts of *D*... Mk 8:10 1148

DALMATIA (*dal-ma'-she-ah*) *A Roman province west of Macedonia.*
Crescens to Galatia, Titus unto *D*... 2Ti 4:10 1149

DALPHON (*dal'-fon*) *A son of Haman.*
And Parshandatha, and *D*... Est 9:7 1813

DAM
seven days it shall be with his *d*... Ex 22:30 517
shall be seven days under the *d*... Lev 22:27 517
the *d* sitting upon the young, or... Deut 22:6 517
not take the *d* with the young... Deut 22:6 517
shalt in any wise let the *d* go... Deut 22:7 517

DAMAGE
why should *d* grow to the hurt of... Ezr 4:22 2257
not countervail the king's *d*... Est 7:4 5143
off the feet, and drinketh *d*... Prov 26:6 2555
and the king should have no *d*... Dan 6:2 5142

will be with hurt and much *d*	Acts 27:10	*2209*
might receive *d* by us in nothing	2Cor 7:9	*2210*

DAMARIS (*dam'-a-ris*) *An Athenian convert of Paul.*

Areopagite, and a woman named *D*	Acts 17:34	*1152*

DAMASCENES (*dam-as-senes'*) *Inhabitants of Damascus.*

the city of the *D* with a garrison	2Cor 11:32	*1159*

DAMASCUS (*da-mas'-cus*) See DAMASCENES, SYRIA-DAMASCUS. *A city in Syria.*

which is on the left hand of *D*	Gen 14:15	1834
of my house is this Eliezer of *D*	Gen 15:2	1834
when the Syrians of *D* came to	2Sa 8:5	1834
David put garrisons in Syria of *D*	2Sa 8:6	1834
and they went to *D*, and dwelt	1Kin 11:24	1834
and dwelt therein, and reigned in *D*	1Kin 11:24	1834
king of Syria, that dwelt at *D*	1Kin 15:18	1834
on thy way to the wilderness of *D*	1Kin 19:15	1834
shalt make streets for thee in *D*	1Kin 20:34	1834
not Abana and Pharpar, rivers of *D*	2Kin 5:12	1834
And Elisha came to *D*	2Kin 8:7	1834
even of every good thing of *D*	2Kin 8:9	1834
he warred, and how he recovered *D*	2Kin 14:28	1834
king of Assyria went up against *D*	2Kin 16:9	1834
king Ahaz went to *D* to meet	2Kin 16:10	1834
and saw an altar that was at *D*	2Kin 16:10	1834
that king Ahaz had sent from *D*	2Kin 16:11	1834
it against king Ahaz came from *D*	2Kin 16:11	1834
And when the king was come from *D*	2Kin 16:12	1834
when the Syrians of *D* came to	1Chr 18:5	1834
king of Syria, that dwelt at *D*	2Chr 16:2	1834
spoil of them unto the king of *D*	2Chr 24:23	1834
captives, and brought them to *D*	2Chr 28:5	1834
he sacrificed unto the gods of *D*	2Chr 28:23	1834
of Lebanon which looketh toward *D*	Song 7:4	1834
For the head of Syria is *D*	Is 7:8	1834
and the head of *D* is Rezin	Is 7:8	1834
and my mother, the riches of *D*	Is 8:4	1834
is not Samaria as *D*	Is 10:9	1834
The burden of *D*	Is 17:1	1834
D is taken away from being a city	Is 17:1	1834
Ephraim, and the kingdom from *D*	Is 17:3	1834
Concerning *D*. Hamath is confounded	Jer 49:23	1834
D is waxed feeble, and turneth	Jer 49:24	1834
kindle a fire in the wall of *D*	Jer 49:27	1834
D was thy merchant in the	Eze 27:18	1834
which is between the border of *D*	Eze 47:16	1834
be Hazar-enan, the border of *D*	Eze 47:17	1834
measure from Hauran, and from *D*	Eze 47:18	1834
the border of *D* northward	Eze 48:1	1834
For three transgressions of *D*	Amos 1:3	1834
I will break also the bar of *D*	Amos 1:5	1834
of a bed, and in *D* in a couch	Amos 3:12	1833
you to go into captivity beyond *D*	Amos 5:27	1834
D shall be the rest thereof	Zec 9:1	1834
letters to *D* to the synagogues	Acts 9:2	*1154*
as he journeyed, he came near *D*	Acts 9:3	*1154*
the hand, and brought him into *D*	Acts 9:8	*1154*
there was a certain disciple at *D*	Acts 9:10	*1154*
the disciples which were at *D*	Acts 9:19	*1154*
the Jews which dwelt at *D*	Acts 9:22	*1154*
boldly at *D* in the name of Jesus	Acts 9:27	*1154*
unto the brethren, and went to *D*	Acts 22:5	*1154*
was come nigh unto *D* about noon	Acts 22:6	*1154*
said unto me, Arise, and go into *D*	Acts 22:10	*1154*
that were with me, I came into *D*	Acts 22:11	*1154*
as I went to *D* with authority	Acts 26:12	*1154*
But shewed first unto them of *D*	Acts 26:20	*1154*
In *D* the governor under Aretas	2Cor 11:32	*1154*
Arabia, and returned again unto *D*	Gal 1:17	*1154*

DAMNABLE

privily shall bring in *d* heresies	2Pet 2:1	*684*

DAMNATION

ye shall receive the greater *d*	Mt 23:14	*2917*
how can ye escape the *d* of hell	Mt 23:33	*2920*
but is in danger of eternal *d*	Mk 3:29	*2920*
these shall receive greater *d*	Mk 12:40	*2917*
the same shall receive greater *d*	Lk 20:47	*2917*
evil, unto the resurrection of *d*	Jn 5:29	*2920*
whose *d* is just	Rom 3:8	*2917*
shall receive to themselves *d*	Rom 13:2	*2917*
drinketh *d* to himself, not	1Cor 11:29	*2917*
Having *d*, because they have cast	1Ti 5:12	*2917*
not, and their *d* slumbereth not	2Pet 2:3	*684*

DAMNED

he that believeth not shall be *d*	Mk 16:16	*2632*
he that doubteth is *d* if he eat	Rom 14:23	*2632*
That they all might be *d* who	2Th 2:12	*2919*

DAMSEL

that the *d* to whom I shall say,	Gen 24:14	5291
the *d* was very fair to look upon,	Gen 24:16	5291
And the *d* ran, and told them of her	Gen 24:28	5291
Let the *d* abide with us a few	Gen 24:55	5291
And they said, We will call the *d*	Gen 24:57	5291
of Jacob, and he loved the *d*	Gen 34:3	5291
and spake kindly unto the *d*	Gen 34:3	5291
saying, Get me this *d* to wife	Gen 34:4	3207
but give me the *d* to wife	Gen 34:12	5291
Then shall the father of the *d*	Deut 22:15	5291
them unto the father of the *d*	Deut 22:19	5291
virginity be not found for the *d*	Deut 22:20	5291
the *d* to the door of her father's	Deut 22:21	5291
If a *d* that is a virgin be	Deut 22:23	5291
the *d*, because she cried not,	Deut 22:24	5291
find a betrothed *d* in the field	Deut 22:25	5291
But unto the *d* thou shalt do	Deut 22:26	5291
there is in the *d* no sin worthy	Deut 22:26	5291
field, and the betrothed *d* cried	Deut 22:27	5291
If a man find a *d* that is a	Deut 22:28	5291
to every man a *d* or two	Judg 5:30	7356
when the father of the *d* saw him	Judg 19:3	5291
over the reapers, Whose *d* is this	Ruth 2:5	5291
It is the Moabitish *d* that came	Ruth 2:6	5291
So they sought for a fair *d*	1Kin 1:3	5291
the *d* was very fair, and cherished	1Kin 1:4	5291
in a charger, and given to the *d*	Mt 14:11	*2877*
a *d* came unto him, saying, Thou	Mt 26:69	*3814*
the *d* is not dead, but sleepeth	Mk 5:39	*3813*
the father and the mother of the *d*	Mk 5:40	*3813*
entereth in where the *d* was lying	Mk 5:40	*3813*
And he took the *d* by the hand	Mk 5:41	*3813*
which is, being interpreted, *D*	Mk 5:41	*2877*
And straightway the *d* arose	Mk 5:42	*2877*
him, the king said unto the *d*	Mk 6:22	*2877*
in a charger, and gave it to the *d*	Mk 6:28	*2877*
the *d* gave it to her mother	Mk 6:28	*2877*
Then saith the *d* that kept the	Jn 18:17	*3814*
a *d* came to hearken, named Rhoda	Acts 12:13	*3814*
a certain *d* possessed with a	Acts 16:16	*3814*

DAMSEL'S

d virginity unto the elders of	Deut 22:15	5291
the *d* father shall say unto the	Deut 22:16	5291
with her shall give unto the *d*	Deut 22:29	5291
the *d* father, retained him	Judg 19:4	5291
the *d* father said unto his son in	Judg 19:5	5291
for the *d* father had said unto	Judg 19:6	5291
the *d* father said, Comfort thine	Judg 19:8	5291
the *d* father, said unto him,	Judg 19:9	5291

DAMSELS

And Rebekah arose, and her *d*	Gen 24:61	5291
with five *d* of hers that went	1Sa 25:42	5291
among them were the *d* playing	Ps 68:25	5959

DAN (*dan*) See DANITES, DAN-JAAN, LAISH, MAHANEH-DAN.

1. A son of Jacob.

therefore called she his name *D*	Gen 30:6	1835
D, and Naphtali	Gen 35:25	1835
And the sons of *D*	Gen 46:23	1835
D shall judge his people, as one	Gen 49:16	1835
D shall be a serpent by the way,	Gen 49:17	1835
D, and Naphtali, Gad, and Asher	Ex 1:4	1835
therein, and called Leshem, *D*	Josh 19:47	1835
after the name of *D* their father	Josh 19:47	1835
after the name of *D* their father	Judg 18:29	1835
D, Joseph, and Benjamin, Naphtali,	1Chr 2:2	1835
D also and Javan going to and fro	Eze 27:19	1835

2. A city and tribal territory in northern Canaan.

eighteen, and pursued them unto *D*	Gen 14:14	1835
all the land of Gilead, unto *D*	Deut 34:1	1835
called the name of the city *D*	Judg 18:29	1835
from *D* even to Beer-sheba, with	Judg 20:1	1835
all Israel from *D* even to	1Sa 3:20	1835
from *D* even to Beer-sheba	2Sa 3:10	1835
from *D* even to Beer-sheba, as the	2Sa 17:11	1835
from *D* even to Beer-sheba, and	2Sa 24:2	1835
from *D* even to Beer-sheba seventy	2Sa 24:15	1835
from *D* even to Beer-sheba, all	1Kin 4:25	1835
Beth-el, and the other put he in *D*	1Kin 12:29	1835
before the one, even unto *D*	1Kin 12:30	1835
of Israel, and smote Ijon, and *D*	1Kin 15:20	1835
in Beth-el, and that were in *D*	2Kin 10:29	1835
Israel from Beer-sheba even to *D*	1Chr 21:2	1835
and they smote Ijon, and *D*, and	2Chr 16:4	1835
Israel, from Beer-sheba even to *D*	2Chr 30:5	1835
For a voice declareth from *D*	Jer 4:15	1835
of his horses was heard from *D*	Jer 8:16	1835
a portion for *D*	Eze 48:1	1835
And by the border of *D*, from the	Eze 48:2	1835
gate of Benjamin, one gate of *D*	Eze 48:32	1835
of Samaria, and say, Thy god, O *D*	Amos 8:14	1835

3. Tribe descended from Dan 1.

of Ahisamach, of the tribe of *D*	Ex 31:6	1835
of Ahisamach, of the tribe of *D*	Ex 35:34	1835
of Ahisamach, of the tribe of *D*	Ex 38:23	1835
of Dibri, of the tribe of *D*	Lev 24:11	1835
Of *D*; Ahiezer the son	Num 1:12	1835
Of the children of *D*, by their	Num 1:38	1835
of them, even of the tribe of *D*	Num 1:39	1835
The standard of the camp of *D*	Num 2:25	1835
of *D* shall be Ahiezer the son of	Num 2:25	1835
of *D* were an hundred thousand	Num 2:31	1835
prince of the children of *D*	Num 7:66	1835
of the children of *D* set forward	Num 10:25	1835
Of the tribe of *D*, Ammiel the son	Num 13:12	1835
sons of *D* after their families	Num 26:42	1835
of *D* after their families	Num 26:42	1835
of the tribe of the children of *D*	Num 34:22	1835
Gad, and Asher, and Zebulun, *D*	Deut 27:13	1835
Dan he said, *D* is a lion's whelp	Deut 33:22	1835
of *D* according to their families	Josh 19:40	1835
of *D* went out too little for them	Josh 19:47	1835
therefore the children of *D* went	Josh 19:47	1835
of *D* according to their families	Josh 19:48	1835
Ephraim, and out of the tribe of *D*	Josh 21:5	1835
And out of the tribe of *D*, Eltekeh	Josh 21:23	1835
children of *D* into the mountain	Judg 1:34	1835
why did *D* remain in ships	Judg 5:17	1835
in the camp of *D* between Zorah	Judg 13:25	1835
the children of *D* sent of their	Judg 18:2	1835
which were of the children of *D*	Judg 18:16	1835
and overtook the children of *D*	Judg 18:22	1835
they cried unto the children of *D*	Judg 18:23	1835
the children of *D* said unto him	Judg 18:25	1835
the children of *D* went their way	Judg 18:26	1835
the children of *D* set up the	Judg 18:30	1835
were priests to the tribe of *D*	Judg 18:30	1835
Of *D*, Azareel the son of Jeroham	1Chr 27:22	1835
of a woman of the daughters of *D*	2Chr 2:14	1835

DANCE

of Shiloh come out to *d* in dances	Judg 21:21	2342
like a flock, and their children *d*	Job 21:11	7540
Let them praise his name in the *d*	Ps 149:3	4234
Praise him with the timbrel and *d*	Ps 150:4	4234
a time to mourn, and a time to *d*	Eccl 3:4	7540
there, and satyrs shall *d* there	Is 13:21	7540
shall the virgin rejoice in the *d*	Jer 31:13	4234
our *d* is turned into mourning	Lam 5:15	4234

DANCED

to their number, of them that *d*	Judg 21:23	2342
David *d* before the LORD with all	2Sa 6:14	3769
piped unto you, and ye have not *d*	Mt 11:17	*3738*
of Herodias *d* before them	Mt 14:6	*3738*
the said Herodias came in, and *d*	Mk 6:22	*3738*
piped unto you, and ye have not *d*	Lk 7:32	*3738*

DANCES

after her with timbrels and with *d*	Ex 15:20	4246
meet him with timbrels and with *d*	Judg 11:34	4246
of Shiloh come out to dance in *d*	Judg 21:21	4246
sing one to another of him in *d*	1Sa 21:11	4246
they sang one to another in *d*	1Sa 29:5	4246
shalt go forth in the *d* of them	Jer 31:4	

DANCING

that he saw the calf, and the *d*	Ex 32:19	4246
cities of Israel, singing and *d*	1Sa 18:6	4246
earth, eating and drinking, and *d*	1Sa 30:16	2287
leaping and *d* before the LORD	2Sa 6:16	3769
out at a window saw king David *d*	1Chr 15:29	7540
turned for me my mourning into *d*	Ps 30:11	4234
the house, he heard musick and *d*	Lk 15:25	*5525*

DANDLED

her sides, and be *d* upon her knees	Is 66:12	8173

DANGER

shall be in *d* of the judgment	Mt 5:21	*1777*
shall be in *d* of the judgment	Mt 5:22	*1777*
shall be in *d* of the council	Mt 5:22	*1777*
shall be in *d* of hell fire	Mt 5:22	*1777*
but is in *d* of eternal damnation	Mk 3:29	*1777*
craft is in *d* to be set at nought	Acts 19:27	*2793*
For we are in *d* to be called in	Acts 19:40	*2793*

DANGEROUS

spent, and when sailing was now *d*	Acts 27:9	*2000*

DANIEL See BELTESHAZZAR.

1. A son of David.

the second *D*, of Abigail the	1Chr 3:1	1840

2. An Israelite who renewed the covenant.

of the sons of Ithamar; *D*	Ezr 8:2	1840
D, Ginnethon, Baruch,	Neh 10:6	1840

3. A major prophet.

Though these three men, Noah, *D*	Eze 14:14	1840
Though Noah, *D*, and Job, were in	Eze 14:20	1840
Behold, thou art wiser than *D*	Eze 28:3	1840
were of the children of Judah, *D*	Dan 1:6	1840
for he gave unto *D* the name of	Dan 1:7	1840
But *D* purposed in his heart that	Dan 1:8	1840
Now God had brought *D* into favour	Dan 1:9	1840
prince of the eunuchs said unto *D*	Dan 1:10	1840
Then said *D* to Melzar, whom the	Dan 1:11	1840
of the eunuchs had set over *D*	Dan 1:11	1840
D had understanding in all	Dan 1:17	1840
them all was found none like *D*	Dan 1:19	1840
D continued even unto the first	Dan 1:21	1840
and they sought *D* and his fellows	Dan 2:13	1841
Then *D* answered with counsel and	Dan 2:14	1841
Arioch made the thing known to *D*	Dan 2:15	1841
Then *D* went in, and desired of the	Dan 2:16	1841
Then *D* went to his house, and made	Dan 2:17	1841
that *D* and his fellows should not	Dan 2:18	1841
revealed unto *D* in a night vision	Dan 2:19	1841
Then *D* blessed the God of heaven	Dan 2:19	1841
D answered and said, Blessed be	Dan 2:20	1841
Therefore *D* went in unto Arioch,	Dan 2:24	1841
Then Arioch brought in *D* before	Dan 2:25	1841
The king answered and said to *D*	Dan 2:26	1841
D answered in the presence of the	Dan 2:27	1841
upon his face, and worshipped *D*	Dan 2:46	1841
The king answered unto *D*, and said	Dan 2:47	1841
Then the king made *D* a great man	Dan 2:48	1841
Then *D* requested of the king, and	Dan 2:49	1841
but *D* sat in the gate of the king	Dan 2:49	1841
But at the last *D* came in before	Dan 4:8	1841
Then *D*, whose name was	Dan 4:19	1841
doubts, were found in the same *D*	Dan 5:12	1841
now let *D* be called, and he will	Dan 5:12	1841
Then was *D* brought in before the	Dan 5:13	1841
said unto Daniel, Art thou that *D*	Dan 5:13	1841
Then *D* answered and said before	Dan 5:17	1841
and they clothed *D* with scarlet	Dan 5:29	1841
of whom *D* was first	Dan 6:2	1841
Then this *D* was preferred above	Dan 6:3	1841
against *D* concerning the kingdom	Dan 6:4	1841
find any occasion against this *D*	Dan 6:5	1841
Now when *D* knew that the writing	Dan 6:10	1841
found *D* praying and making	Dan 6:11	1841
and said before the king, That *D*	Dan 6:13	1841
set his heart on *D* to deliver him	Dan 6:14	1841
king commanded, and they brought *D*	Dan 6:16	1841
Now the king spake and said unto *D*	Dan 6:16	1841
might not be changed concerning *D*	Dan 6:17	1841
with a lamentable voice unto *D*	Dan 6:20	1841
king spake and said to Daniel, O *D*	Dan 6:20	1841
Then said *D* unto the king, O king	Dan 6:21	1841
should take *D* up out of the den	Dan 6:23	1841
So *D* was taken up out of the den,	Dan 6:23	1841
those men which had accused *D*	Dan 6:24	1841
and fear before the God of *D*	Dan 6:26	1841
who hath delivered *D* from the	Dan 6:27	1841
So this *D* prospered in the reign	Dan 6:28	1841
king of Babylon *D* had a dream	Dan 7:1	1841
D spake and said, I saw in my	Dan 7:2	1841
I *D* was grieved in my spirit in	Dan 7:15	1841
As for me *D*, my cogitations much	Dan 7:28	1841

appeared unto me, even unto me D...... Dan 8:1 1840
it came to pass, when I, even I D........ Dan 8:15 1840
I D fainted, and was sick certain........... Dan 8:27 1840
the first year of his reign I D................... Dan 9:2 1840
and talked with me, and said, O D........ Dan 9:22 1840
a thing was revealed unto D................. Dan 10:1 1840
In those days I D was mourning........... Dan 10:2 1840
And I D alone saw the vision................ Dan 10:7 1840
And he said unto me, O D, a man........... Dan 10:11 1840
Then said he unto me, Fear not, D......... Dan 10:12 1840
But thou, O D, shut up the words,......... Dan 12:4 1840
Then I D looked, and, behold,............... Dan 12:5 1840
And he said, Go thy way, D.................. Dan 12:9 1840
spoken of by D the prophet..................... Mt 24:15 1158
spoken of by D the prophet..................... Mk 13:14 1158

DANITES (dan'-ites) *Descendants of Dan 1.*
of Zorah, of the family of the D............ Judg 13:2 1839
D sought them an inheritance to............ Judg 18:1 1839
thence of the family of the D................ Judg 18:11 1839
of the D expert in war twenty and......... 1Chr 12:35 1839

DAN-JAAN (dan-ja'-an) *A place between Gilead and Zidon.*
and they came to D, and about to......... 2Sa 24:6 1842

DANNAH (dan'-nah) *A city in Judah.*
And D, and Kirjath-sannah, which is... Josh 15:49 1837

DARA (da'-rah) See DARDA. *A son of Zerah.*
Ethan, and Heman, and Calcol, and D. 1Chr 2:6 1873

DARDA (dar'-dah) See DARA. *A wise man.*
and Heman, and Chalcol, and D............ 1Kin 4:31 1862

DARE
is so fierce that d stir him up............... Job 41:10
good man some would even d to die.... Rom 5:7 5111
For I will not d to speak of any............ Rom 15:18 5111
D any of you, having a matter............... 1Cor 6:1 5111
For we d not make ourselves of............ 2Cor 10:12 5111

DARIUS (da-ri'-us)
1. Darius Hystaspes, king of Persia.
the reign of D king of Persia................. Ezr 4:5 1867
of the reign of D king of Persia............ Ezr 4:24 1868
cease, till the matter came to D............. Ezr 5:5 1868
the river, sent unto D the king.............. Ezr 5:6 1868
Unto D the king, all peace..................... Ezr 5:7 1868
Then D the king made a decree, and.... Ezr 6:1 1868
I D have made a decree........................ Ezr 6:12 1868
to that which D the king had sent......... Ezr 6:13 1868
to the commandment of Cyrus, and D. Ezr 6:14 1868
year of the reign of D the king............. Ezr 6:15 1868
In the second year of D the king........... Hag 1:1 1867
in the second year of D the king........... Hag 1:15 1867
month, in the second year of D............. Hag 2:10 1867
month, in the second year of D............. Zec 1:1 1867
Sebat, in the second year of D.............. Zec 1:7 1867
pass in the fourth year of king D.......... Zec 7:1 1867
2. Darius Nothus, king of Persia.
to the reign of D the Persian................ Neh 12:22 1867
3. Cyaxares, king of Media.
D the Median took the kingdom,............ Dan 5:31 1868
It pleased D to set over the.................. Dan 6:1 1868
and said thus unto him, King D............. Dan 6:6 1868
Wherefore king D signed the................ Dan 6:9 1868
Then king D wrote unto all people........ Dan 6:25 1868
prospered in the reign of D.................. Dan 6:28 1868
year of D the son of Ahasuerus............ Dan 9:1 1867
I in the first year of D the Mede........... Dan 11:1 1867

DARK
the sun went down, and it was d.......... Gen 15:17 5939
if the plague be somewhat d................ Lev 13:6 3544
than the skin, but be somewhat d......... Lev 13:21 3544
the other skin, but be somewhat d........ Lev 13:26 3544
in the skin, but it be somewhat d......... Lev 13:28 3544
the plague be somewhat d after........... Lev 13:56 3544
apparently, and not in d speeches......... Num 12:8 2420
of the gate, when it was d.................... Josh 2:5 2822
d waters, and thick clouds of the......... 2Sa 22:12 2841
began to be d before the sabbath......... Neh 13:19 6751
of the twilight thereof be d................. Job 3:9 2821
They grope in the d without light......... Job 12:25 2822
shall be d in his tabernacle................. Job 18:6 2821
can he judge through the d cloud......... Job 22:13 6205
In the d they dig through houses,........ Job 24:16 2822
round about him were d waters............. Ps 18:11 2824
Let their way be d and slippery............ Ps 35:6 2822
I will open my d saying upon the.......... Ps 49:4 2420
for the d places of the earth are........... Ps 74:20 4285
I will utter d sayings of old.................. Ps 78:2 2420
thy wonders be known in the d............. Ps 88:12 2822
He sent darkness, and made it d............ Ps 105:28 2821
of the wise, and their d sayings............ Prov 1:6 2420
evening, in the black and d night.......... Prov 7:9 653
LORD, and their works are in the d........ Is 29:15 4285
in a d place of the earth....................... Is 45:19 2822
feet stumble upon the d mountains........ Jer 13:16 5399
He hath set me in d places.................... Lam 3:6 4285
the house of Israel do in the d.............. Eze 8:12 2822
and make the stars thereof d................. Eze 32:7 6937
of heaven will I make d over thee......... Eze 32:8 6937
scattered in the cloudy and d day......... Eze 34:12 6205
and understanding d sentences............. Dan 8:23 2420
the sun and the moon shall be d........... Joel 2:10 6937
and maketh the day d with night........... Amos 5:8 2821
even very d, and no brightness in......... Amos 5:20 651
and it shall be d unto you..................... Mic 3:6 2821
and the day shall be d over them......... Mic 3:6 6937
light shall not be clear, nor d............... Zec 14:6 7087
full of light, having no part d.............. Lk 11:36 4652
And it was now d, and Jesus was not.. Jn 6:17 4653
early, when it was yet d, unto............... Jn 20:1 4653
a light that shineth in a d place............ 2Pet 1:19 850

DARKEN
I will d the earth in the clear.............. Amos 8:9 2821

DARKENED
earth, so that the land was d............... Ex 10:15 2821
Let their eyes be d, that they............... Ps 69:23 2821
the moon, or the stars, be not d........... Eccl 12:2 2821
that look out of the windows be d........ Eccl 12:3 2821
the light is d in the heavens................ Is 5:30 2821
the LORD of hosts is the land d............. Is 9:19 6272
the sun shall be d in his going.............. Is 13:10 2821
all joy is d, the mirth of the.................. Is 24:11 6150
also the day shall be d, when I............. Eze 30:18 2821
The sun and the moon shall be d.......... Joel 3:15 6937
his right eye shall be utterly d.............. Zec 11:17 3543
of those days shall the sun be d............ Mt 24:29 4654
tribulation, the sun shall be d............... Mk 13:24 4654
And the sun was d, and the veil of....... Lk 23:45 4654
and their foolish heart was d.............. Rom 1:21 4654
Let their eyes be d, that they............... Rom 11:10 4654
Having the understanding d.................. Eph 4:18 4654
as the third part of them was d............ Rev 8:12 4654
the air were d by reason of the............ Rev 9:2 4654

DARKENETH
Who is this that d counsel by............... Job 38:2 2821

DARKISH
skin of their flesh be d white................ Lev 13:39 3544

DARKLY
For now we see through a glass, d........ 1Cor 13:12

DARKNESS
d was upon the face of the deep.......... Gen 1:2 2822
God divided the light from the d.......... Gen 1:4 2822
Day, and the d he called Night............ Gen 1:5 2822
and to divide the light from the d........ Gen 1:18 2822
horror of great d fell upon him............ Gen 15:12 2825
that there may be d over the land......... Ex 10:21 2822
Egypt, even d which may be felt.......... Ex 10:21 2822
there was a thick d in all the................ Ex 10:22 2822
d to them, but it gave light by............. Ex 14:20 2822
unto the thick d where God was........... Ex 20:21 6205
with d, clouds, and thick d.................. Deut 4:11 6205
of the cloud, and of the thick d........... Deut 5:22 6205
voice out of the midst of the d............. Deut 5:23 2822
as the blind gropeth in d..................... Deut 28:29 653
he put d between you and the............... Josh 24:7 3990
the wicked shall be silent in d............. 1Sa 2:9 2822
and d was under his feet..................... 2Sa 22:10 6205
he made d pavilions round about.......... 2Sa 22:12 2822
and the LORD will lighten my d............. 2Sa 22:29 2822
he would dwell in the thick d............... 1Kin 8:12 6205
he would dwell in the thick d............... 2Chr 6:1 6205
Let that day be d................................. Job 3:4 2822
Let d and the shadow of death............. Job 3:5 2822
that night, let d seize upon it.............. Job 3:6 652
They meet with d in the daytime......... Job 5:14 2822
not return, even to the land of d.......... Job 10:21 2822
A land of d, as d itself......................... Job 10:22 5890
order, and where the light is as d........ Job 10:22 652
discovereth deep things out of d.......... Job 12:22 2822
not that he shall return out of d........... Job 15:22 2822
the day of d is ready at his hand......... Job 15:23 2822
He shall not depart out of d................. Job 15:30 2822
the light is short because of d............. Job 17:12 2822
I have made my bed in the d................ Job 17:13 2822
shall be driven from light into d.......... Job 18:18 2822
and he hath set d in my paths.............. Job 19:8 2822
All d shall be hid in his secret............ Job 20:26 2822
Or d, that thou canst not see.............. Job 22:11 2822
I was not cut off before the d............. Job 23:17 2822
he covered the d from my face............. Job 23:17 652
He setteth an end to d, and................. Job 28:3 2822
the stones of d, and the shadow of....... Job 28:3 652
by his light I walked through d............. Job 29:3 2822
I waited for light, there came d........... Job 30:26 652
There is no d, nor shadow of............... Job 34:22 2822
order our speech by reason of d.......... Job 37:19 2822
thick d a swaddlingband for it,............ Job 38:9 6205
and as for d, where is the place.......... Job 38:19 2822
and d was under his feet..................... Ps 18:9 6205
He made d his secret place.................. Ps 18:11 2822
LORD my God will enlighten my d.......... Ps 18:28 2822
they walk on in d................................ Ps 82:5 2825
laid me in the lowest pit, in d.............. Ps 88:6 4285
me, and mine acquaintance into d........ Ps 88:18 4285
the pestilence that walketh in d........... Ps 91:6 652
Clouds and d are round about him........ Ps 97:2 6205
Thou makest d, and it is night.............. Ps 104:20 2822
He sent d, and made it dark................. Ps 105:28 2822
Such as sit in d and in the shadow....... Ps 107:10 2822
He brought them out of d and the......... Ps 107:14 2822
there ariseth light in the d.................. Ps 112:4 2822
Surely the d shall cover me................. Ps 139:11 2822
the d hideth not from thee.................. Ps 139:12 2822
the d and the light are both alike......... Ps 139:12 2825
he hath made me to dwell in d............. Ps 143:3 4285
to walk in the ways of d...................... Prov 2:13 2822
The way of the wicked is as d.............. Prov 4:19 653
shall be put out in obscure d............... Prov 20:20 2822
as far as light excelleth d.................... Eccl 2:13 2822
but the fool walketh in d..................... Eccl 2:14 2822
All his days also he eateth in d............ Eccl 5:17 2822
in with vanity, and departeth in d........ Eccl 6:4 2822
his name shall be covered with d......... Eccl 6:4 2822
let him remember the days of d............ Eccl 11:8 2822
that put d for light, and light............... Is 5:20 2822
for light, and light for d...................... Is 5:20 2822
one look unto the land, behold d.......... Is 5:30 2822
and behold trouble and d, dimness........ Is 8:22 2825
and they shall be driven to d................ Is 8:22 653
in d have seen a great light................. Is 9:2 2822
see out of obscurity, and out of d........ Is 29:18 2822
them that sit in d out of the................. Is 42:7 2822
I will make d light before them,........... Is 42:16 4285
will give thee the treasures of d.......... Is 45:3 2822
I form the light, and create d.............. Is 45:7 2822
thou silent, and get thee into d........... Is 47:5 2822
to them that are in d, Shew.................. Is 49:9 2822
of his servant, that walketh in d.......... Is 50:10 2825
and thy d be as the noonday............... Is 58:10 653
for brightness, but we walk in d.......... Is 59:9 653
the d shall cover the earth, and.......... Is 60:2 2822
the earth, and gross d the people......... Is 60:2 6205
a land of d....................................... Jer 2:31 3991
LORD your God, before he cause d........ Jer 13:16 2821
of death, and make it gross d.............. Jer 13:16 6205
them as slippery ways in the d............. Jer 23:12 653
hath led me, and brought me into d...... Lam 3:2 2822
set d upon thy land, saith the............... Eze 32:8 2822
he knoweth what is in the d................. Dan 2:22 2816
A day of d and of gloominess, a........... Joel 2:2 2822
a day of clouds and of thick d.............. Joel 2:2 6205
The sun shall be turned into d............. Joel 2:31 2822
that maketh the morning d................... Amos 4:13 5890
the day of the LORD is d, and not......... Amos 5:18 2822
not the day of the LORD be d................ Amos 5:20 2822
when I sit in d, the LORD shall............. Mic 7:8 2822
d shall pursue his enemies.................. Nah 1:8 2822
and desolation, a day of d.................. Zeph 1:15 2822
a day of clouds and thick d.................. Zeph 1:15 6205
which sat in d saw great light.............. Mt 4:16 4655
thy whole body shall be full of d.......... Mt 6:23 4652
be d, how great is that d..................... Mt 6:23 4655
shall be cast out into outer d.............. Mt 8:12 4655
What I tell you in d, that speak........... Mt 10:27 4653
away, and cast him into outer d........... Mt 22:13 4655
unprofitable servant into outer d.......... Mt 25:30 4655
was d over all the land unto the........... Mt 27:45 4655
there was d over the whole land.......... Mk 15:33 4655
give light to them that sit in d............. Lk 1:79 4655
evil, thy body also is full of d.............. Lk 11:34 4652
light which is in thee be not d............. Lk 11:35 4655
in d shall be heard in the light............. Lk 12:3 4653
is your hour, and the power of d........... Lk 22:53 4655
there was a d over all the earth........... Lk 23:44 4655
And the light shineth in d.................... Jn 1:5 4653
the d comprehended it not.................... Jn 1:5 4653
men loved d rather than light,.............. Jn 3:19 4655
followeth me shall not walk in d........... Jn 8:12 4653
the light, lest d come upon you............ Jn 12:35 4653
for he that walketh in d knoweth.......... Jn 12:35 4653
on me should not abide in d................. Jn 12:46 4653
The sun shall be turned into d............. Acts 2:20 4655
there fell on him a mist and a d............ Acts 13:11 4655
and to turn them from d to light............ Acts 26:18 4655
a light of them which are in d.............. Rom 2:19 4655
therefore cast off the works of d........... Rom 13:12 4655
to light the hidden things of d.............. 1Cor 4:5 4655
the light to shine out of d.................... 2Cor 4:6 4655
what communion hath light with d......... 2Cor 6:14 4655
For ye were sometimes d, but now......... Eph 5:8 4655
with the unfruitful works of d.............. Eph 5:11 4655
the rulers of the d of this world........... Eph 6:12 4655
delivered us from the power of d.......... Col 1:13 4655
But ye, brethren, are not in d.............. 1Th 5:4 4655
we are not of the night, nor of d.......... 1Th 5:5 4655
fire, nor unto blackness, and d............. Heb 12:18 4655
of d into his marvellous light................ 1Pet 2:9 4655
delivered them into chains of d............. 2Pet 2:4 2217
to whom the mist of d is reserved......... 2Pet 2:17 4655
light, and in him is no d at all............... 1Jn 1:5 4653
fellowship with him, and walk in d........ 1Jn 1:6 4655
because the d is past, and the............. 1Jn 2:8 4653
brother, is in d even until now............. 1Jn 2:9 4653
is in d, and walketh in d..................... 1Jn 2:11 4653
because that d hath blinded his........... 1Jn 2:11 4653
in everlasting chains under d............... Jude 6 2217
the blackness of d for ever.................. Jude 13 4655
and his kingdom was full of d.............. Rev 16:10 4656

DARKON (dar'-kon) *A family of exiles.*
of Jaalah, the children of D.................. Ezr 2:56 1874
of Jaala, the children of D.................... Neh 7:58 1874

DARLING
my d from the power of the dog........... Ps 22:20 3173
destructions, my d from the lions......... Ps 35:17 3173

DART
the spear, the d, nor the..................... Job 41:26 4551
Till a d strike through his liver............. Prov 7:23 2671
or thrust through with a d.................... Heb 12:20 1002

DARTS
And he took three d in his hand........... 2Sa 18:14 7626
in the city of David, and made d........... 2Chr 32:5 7973
D are counted as stubble..................... Job 41:29 8455
all the fiery d of the wicked................. Eph 6:16 956

DASH
wilt d their children, and rip up........... 2Kin 8:12 7376
thou shalt d them in pieces like........... Ps 2:9 5310
lest thou d thy foot against a.............. Ps 91:12 5062
Their bows also shall d the young......... Is 13:18 7376
I will d them one against another......... Jer 13:14 5310
lest at any time thou d thy foot............ Mt 4:6 4350
lest at any time thou d thy foot............ Lk 4:11 4350

DASHED
hath d in pieces the enemy.................. Ex 15:6 7492
be d to pieces before their eyes........... Is 13:16 7376
the mother was d in pieces upon.......... Hos 10:14 7376
infants shall be d in pieces................. Hos 13:16 7376
her young children also were d in......... Nah 3:10 7376

DASHETH
d thy little ones against the................ Ps 137:9 5310
He that d in pieces is come up............ Nah 2:1 6327

D

DATHAN (*da'-than*) *A conspirator against Moses.*

of Kohath, the son of Levi, and *D*	Num 16:1	1885
And Moses sent to call *D* and Abiram	Num 16:12	1885
about the tabernacle of Korah, *D*	Num 16:24	1885
And Moses rose up and went unto *D*	Num 16:25	1885
from the tabernacle of Korah, *D*	Num 16:27	1885
and *D* and Abiram came out	Num 16:27	1885
Nemuel, and *D*, and Abiram	Num 26:9	1885
This is that *D* and Abiram, which	Num 26:9	1885
And what he did unto *D* and Abiram,	Deut 11:6	1885
earth opened and swallowed up *D*	Ps 106:17	1885

DAUB

Say unto them which *d* it with	Eze 13:11	2902

DAUBED

d it with slime and with pitch, and	Ex 2:3	2560
others *d* it with untempered	Eze 13:10	2902
daubing wherewith ye have *d* it	Eze 13:12	2902
ye have *d* with untempered morter	Eze 13:14	2902
upon them that have *d* it with	Eze 13:15	2902
no more, neither they that *d* it	Eze 13:15	2902
her prophets have *d* them with	Eze 22:28	2902

DAUBING

Where is the *d* wherewith ye have	Eze 13:12	2915

DAUGHTER

the *d* of Haran, the father of	Gen 11:29	1323
son's son, and Sarai his *d* in law	Gen 11:31	3618
she is the *d* of my father, but	Gen 20:12	1323
but not the *d* of my mother	Gen 20:12	1323
And said, Whose *d* art thou	Gen 24:23	1323
I am the *d* of Bethuel the son of	Gen 24:24	1323
her, and said, Whose *d* art thou	Gen 24:47	1323
The *d* of Bethuel, Nahor's son,	Gen 24:47	1323
master's brother's *d* unto his son	Gen 24:48	1323
the *d* of Bethuel the Syrian of	Gen 25:20	1323
Judith the *d* of Beeri the Hittite	Gen 26:34	1323
Bashemath the *d* of Elon the	Gen 26:34	1323
the *d* of Ishmael Abraham's son	Gen 28:9	1323
Rachel his *d* cometh with the	Gen 29:6	1323
when Jacob saw Rachel the *d* of	Gen 29:10	1323
years for Rachel thy younger *d*	Gen 29:18	1323
evening, that he took Leah his *d*	Gen 29:23	1323
Laban gave unto his *d* Leah Zilpah	Gen 29:24	1323
him Rachel his *d* to wife also	Gen 29:28	1323
Laban gave to Rachel his *d* Bilhah	Gen 29:29	1323
And afterwards she bare a *d*	Gen 30:21	1323
And Dinah the *d* of Leah, which she	Gen 34:1	1323
clave unto Dinah the *d* of Jacob	Gen 34:3	1323
that he had defiled Dinah his *d*	Gen 34:5	1323
in Israel in lying with Jacob's *d*	Gen 34:7	1323
my son Shechem longeth for your *d*	Gen 34:8	1323
then will we take our *d*, and we	Gen 34:17	1323
he had delight in Jacob's *d*	Gen 34:19	1323
Adah the *d* of Elon the Hittite,	Gen 36:2	1323
Aholibamah the *d* of Anah the	Gen 36:2	1323
Anah the *d* of Zibeon the Hivite	Gen 36:2	1323
And Bashemath Ishmael's *d*, sister	Gen 36:3	1323
d of Anah the *d* of Zibeon	Gen 36:14	1323
came of Aholibamah the *d* of Anah	Gen 36:18	1323
and Aholibamah the *d* of Anah	Gen 36:25	1323
the *d* of Matred, the *d* of	Gen 36:39	1323
Judah saw there a *d* of a certain	Gen 38:2	1323
said Judah to Tamar his *d* in law	Gen 38:11	3618
in process of time the *d* of Shuah	Gen 38:12	1323
not that she was his *d* in law	Gen 38:16	3618
Tamar thy *d* in law hath played	Gen 38:24	3618
the *d* of Poti-pherah priest of On	Gen 41:45	1323
came, which Asenath the *d* of	Gen 41:50	1323
in Padan-aram, with his *d* Dinah	Gen 46:15	1323
whom Laban gave to Leah his *d*	Gen 46:18	1323
Ephraim, which Asenath the *d* of	Gen 46:20	1323
Laban gave unto Rachel his *d*	Gen 46:25	1323
but if it be a *d*, then she shall	Ex 1:16	1323
every *d* ye shall save alive	Ex 1:22	1323
Levi, and took to wife a *d* of Levi	Ex 2:1	1323
the *d* of Pharaoh came down to	Ex 2:5	1323
said his sister to Pharaoh's *d*	Ex 2:7	1323
Pharaoh's *d* said to her, Go	Ex 2:8	1323
Pharaoh's *d* said unto her, Take	Ex 2:9	1323
she brought him unto Pharaoh's *d*	Ex 2:10	1323
and he gave Moses Zipporah his *d*	Ex 2:21	1323
d of Amminadab, sister of Naashon	Ex 6:23	1323
thou, nor thy son, nor thy *d*	Ex 20:10	1323
if a man sell his *d* to be a	Ex 21:7	1323
gored a son, or have gored a *d*	Ex 21:31	1323
fulfilled, for a son, or for a *d*	Lev 12:6	1323
the *d* of thy father, or *d*	Lev 18:9	1323
d, or of thy daughter's *d*	Lev 18:10	1323
of thy father's wife's *d*	Lev 18:11	1323
the nakedness of thy *d* in law	Lev 18:15	3618
the nakedness of a woman and her *d*	Lev 18:17	1323
son's *d*, or her daughter's *d*	Lev 18:17	1323
Do not prostitute thy *d*, to cause	Lev 19:29	1323
And if a man lie with his *d* in law	Lev 20:12	3618
father's *d*, or his mother's *d*	Lev 20:17	1323
and for his son, and for his *d*	Lev 21:2	1323
the *d* of any priest, if she	Lev 21:9	1323
If the priest's *d* also be married	Lev 22:12	1323
But if the priest's *d* be a widow	Lev 22:13	1323
the *d* of Dibri, of the tribe of	Lev 24:11	1323
was slain was Cozbi, the *d* of Zur	Num 25:15	1323
the *d* of a prince of Midian,	Num 25:18	1323
the name of the *d* of Asher was	Num 26:46	1323
the *d* of Levi, whom her mother	Num 26:59	1323
inheritance to pass unto his *d*	Num 27:8	1323
And if he have no *d*, then ye shall	Num 27:9	1323
wife, between the father and his *d*	Num 30:16	1323
And every *d*, that possesseth an	Num 36:8	1323
thou, nor thy son, nor thy *d*	Deut 5:14	1323
thy *d* thou shalt not give unto	Deut 7:3	1323
nor his *d* shalt thou take unto	Deut 7:3	1323
thou, and thy son, and thy *d*	Deut 12:18	1323
thy mother, or thy son, or thy *d*	Deut 13:6	1323
God, thou, and thy son, and thy *d*	Deut 16:11	1323
feast, thou, and thy son, and thy *d*	Deut 16:14	1323
or his *d* to pass through the fire	Deut 18:10	1323
I gave my *d* unto this man to wife	Deut 22:16	1323
saying, I found not thy *d* a maid	Deut 22:17	1323
the *d* of his father, or the	Deut 27:22	1323
father, or the *d* of his mother	Deut 27:22	1323
toward her son, and toward her *d*	Deut 28:56	1323
will I give Achsah my *d* to wife	Josh 15:16	1323
he gave him Achsah his *d* to wife	Josh 15:17	1323
will I give Achsah my *d* to wife	Judg 1:12	1323
he gave him Achsah his *d* to wife	Judg 1:13	1323
his *d* came out to meet him with	Judg 11:34	1323
her he had neither son nor *d*	Judg 11:34	1323
his clothes, and said, Alas, my *d*	Judg 11:35	1323
went yearly to lament the *d* of	Judg 11:40	1323
Behold, here is my *d* a maiden	Judg 19:24	1323
give his *d* unto Benjamin to wife	Judg 21:1	1323
her *d* in law, with her, which	Ruth 1:22	3618
And she said unto her, Go, my *d*	Ruth 2:2	1323
unto Ruth, Hearest thou not, my *d*	Ruth 2:8	1323
And Naomi said unto her *d* in law	Ruth 2:20	3618
d in law, It is good, my *d*	Ruth 2:22	1323
mother in law said unto her, My *d*	Ruth 3:1	1323
Blessed be thou of the LORD, my *d*	Ruth 3:10	1323
And now, my *d*, fear not	Ruth 3:11	1323
law, she said, Who art thou, my *d*	Ruth 3:16	1323
Then said she, Sit still, my *d*	Ruth 3:18	1323
for thy *d* in law, which loveth	Ruth 4:15	3618
thine handmaid for a *d* of Belial	1Sa 1:16	1323
his *d* in law, Phinehas' wife, was	1Sa 4:19	3618
was Ahinoam, the *d* of Ahimaaz	1Sa 14:50	1323
riches, and will give him his *d*	1Sa 17:25	1323
to David, Behold my elder *d* Merab	1Sa 18:17	1323
at the time when Merab Saul's *d*	1Sa 18:19	1323
And Michal Saul's *d* loved David	1Sa 18:20	1323
gave him Michal his *d* to wife	1Sa 18:27	1323
and that Michal Saul's *d* loved him	1Sa 18:28	1323
But Saul had given Michal his *d*	1Sa 25:44	1323
the *d* of Talmai king of Geshur	2Sa 3:3	1323
name was Rizpah, the *d* of Aiah	2Sa 3:7	1323
thou first bring Michal Saul's *d*	2Sa 3:13	1323
Michal Saul's *d* looked through a	2Sa 6:16	1323
Michal the *d* of Saul came out to	2Sa 6:20	1323
Therefore Michal the *d* of Saul	2Sa 6:23	1323
the *d* of Eliam, the wife of Uriah	2Sa 11:3	1323
his bosom, and was unto him as a *d*	2Sa 12:3	1323
were born three sons, and one *d*	2Sa 14:27	1323
in to Abigail the *d* of Nahash	2Sa 17:25	1323
two sons of Rizpah the *d* of Aiah	2Sa 21:8	1323
five sons of Michal the *d* of Saul	2Sa 21:8	1323
Rizpah the *d* of Aiah took	2Sa 21:10	1323
David what Rizpah the *d* of Aiah	2Sa 21:11	1323
of Egypt, and took Pharaoh's *d*	1Kin 3:1	1323
Taphath the *d* of Solomon to wife	1Kin 4:11	1323
Basmath the *d* of Solomon to wife	1Kin 4:15	1323
also an house for Pharaoh's *d*	1Kin 7:8	1323
given it for a present unto his *d*	1Kin 9:16	1323
But Pharaoh's *d* came up out of	1Kin 9:24	1323
together with the *d* of Pharaoh	1Kin 11:1	1323
was Maachah, the *d* of Abishalom	1Kin 15:2	1323
was Maachah, the *d* of Abishalom	1Kin 15:10	1323
the *d* of Ethbaal king of the	1Kin 16:31	1323
name was Azubah the *d* of Shilhi	1Kin 22:42	1323
for the *d* of Ahab was his wife	2Kin 8:18	1323
the *d* of Omri king of Israel	2Kin 8:26	1323
for she is a king's *d*	2Kin 9:34	1323
the *d* of king Joram, sister of	2Kin 11:2	1323
Give thy *d* to my son to wife	2Kin 14:9	1323
name was Jerusha, the *d* of Zadok	2Kin 15:33	1323
also was Abi, the *d* of Zachariah	2Kin 18:2	1323
The virgin the *d* of Zion hath	2Kin 19:21	1323
the *d* of Jerusalem hath shaken	2Kin 19:21	1323
the *d* of Haruz of Jotbah	2Kin 21:19	1323
the *d* of Adaiah of Boscath	2Kin 22:1	1323
his *d* to pass through the fire to	2Kin 23:10	1323
the *d* of Jeremiah of Libnah	2Kin 23:31	1323
the *d* of Pedaiah of Rumah	2Kin 23:36	1323
the *d* of Elnathan of Jerusalem	2Kin 24:8	1323
the *d* of Jeremiah of Libnah	2Kin 24:18	1323
the *d* of Matred, the *d* of	1Chr 1:50	1323
of the *d* of Shua the Canaanitess	1Chr 2:3	1323
Tamar his *d* in law bare him	1Chr 2:4	3618
d of Machir the father of Gilead	1Chr 2:21	1323
Sheshan gave his *d* to Jarha his	1Chr 2:35	1323
and the *d* of Caleb was Achsa	1Chr 2:49	1323
the *d* of Talmai king of Geshur	1Chr 3:2	1323
of Bath-shua the *d* of Ammiel	1Chr 3:5	1323
sons of Bithiah the *d* of Pharaoh	1Chr 4:18	1323
his *d* was Sherah, who built	1Chr 7:24	1323
that Michal the *d* of Saul looking	1Chr 15:29	1323
Solomon brought up the *d* of	2Chr 8:11	1323
Rehoboam took him Mahalath the *d*	2Chr 11:18	1121
Abihail the *d* of Eliab the son of	2Chr 11:18	1323
he took Maachah the *d* of Absalom	2Chr 11:20	1323
Rehoboam loved Maachah the *d* of	2Chr 11:21	1323
Michaiah the *d* of Uriel of Gibeah	2Chr 13:2	1323
name was Azubah the *d* of Shilhi	2Chr 20:31	1323
for he had the *d* of Ahab to wife	2Chr 21:6	1323
also was Athaliah the *d* of Omri	2Chr 22:2	1323
the *d* of the king, took Joash the	2Chr 22:11	
the *d* of king Jehoram, the wife	2Chr 22:11	1323
Give thy *d* to my son to wife	2Chr 25:18	1323
also was Jerushah, the *d* of Zadok	2Chr 27:1	1323
was Abijah, the *d* of Zechariah	2Chr 29:1	1323
the *d* of Meshullam the son of	Neh 6:18	1323
that is, Esther, his uncle's *d*	Est 2:7	1323
were dead, took for his own *d*	Est 2:7	1323
the *d* of Abihail the uncle of	Est 2:15	1323
who had taken her for his *d*	Est 2:15	1323
the *d* of Abihail, and Mordecai the	Est 9:29	1323
in the gates of the *d* of Zion	Ps 9:14	1323
Hearken, O *d*, and consider, and	Ps 45:10	1323
the *d* of Tyre shall be there with	Ps 45:12	1323
The king's *d* is all glorious	Ps 45:13	1323
O *d* of Babylon, who art to be	Ps 137:8	1323
thy feet with shoes, O prince's *d*	Song 7:1	1323
the *d* of Zion is left as a	Is 1:8	1323
Lift up thy voice, O *d* of Gallim	Is 10:30	1323
the mount of the *d* of Zion	Is 10:32	1004
unto the mount of the *d* of Zion	Is 16:1	1323
spoiling of the *d* of my people	Is 22:4	1323
land as a river, O *d* of Tarshish	Is 23:10	1323
thou oppressed virgin, *d* of Zidon	Is 23:12	1323
the *d* of Zion, hath despised thee	Is 37:22	1323
the *d* of Jerusalem hath shaken	Is 37:22	1323
O virgin *d* of Babylon, sit on the	Is 47:1	1323
no throne, O *d* of the Chaldeans	Is 47:1	1323
darkness, O *d* of the Chaldeans	Is 47:5	1323
of thy neck, O captive *d* of Zion	Is 52:2	1323
world, Say ye to the *d* of Zion	Is 62:11	1323
toward the *d* of my people	Jer 4:11	1323
child, the voice of the *d* of Zion	Jer 4:31	1323
I have likened the *d* of Zion to a	Jer 6:2	1323
of the *d* of my people slightly	Jer 6:14	
for war against thee, O *d* of Zion	Jer 6:23	1323
O *d* of my people, gird thee with	Jer 6:26	1323
of the *d* of my people slightly	Jer 8:11	1323
the voice of the cry of the *d* of	Jer 8:19	1323
For the hurt of the *d* of my	Jer 8:21	1323
of the *d* of my people recovered	Jer 8:22	1323
the slain of the *d* of my people	Jer 9:1	1323
shall I do for the *d* of my people	Jer 9:7	1323
for the virgin *d* of my people is	Jer 14:17	1323
go about, O thou backsliding *d*	Jer 31:22	1323
balm, O virgin, the *d* of Egypt	Jer 46:11	1323
O thou *d* dwelling in Egypt,	Jer 46:19	1323
The *d* of Egypt shall be	Jer 46:24	1323
Thou *d* that dost inhabit Dibon,	Jer 48:18	1323
flowing valley, O backsliding *d*	Jer 49:4	1323
against thee, O *d* of Babylon	Jer 50:42	1323
The *d* of Babylon is like a	Jer 51:33	1323
the *d* of Jeremiah of Libnah	Jer 52:1	1323
from the *d* of Zion all her beauty	Lam 1:6	1323
the *d* of Judah, as in a winepress	Lam 1:15	1323
the *d* of Zion with a cloud in his	Lam 2:1	1323
strong holds of the *d* of Judah	Lam 2:2	1323
the tabernacle of the *d* of Zion	Lam 2:4	1323
in the *d* of Judah mourning	Lam 2:5	1323
destroy the wall of the *d* of Zion	Lam 2:8	1323
The elders of the *d* of Zion sit	Lam 2:10	1323
destruction of the *d* of my people	Lam 2:11	1323
I liken to thee, O *d* of Jerusalem	Lam 2:13	1323
comfort thee, O virgin *d* of Zion	Lam 2:13	1323
their head at the *d* of Jerusalem	Lam 2:15	1323
the Lord, O wall of the *d* of Zion	Lam 2:18	1323
destruction of the *d* of my people	Lam 3:48	1323
the *d* of my people is become	Lam 4:3	1323
of the iniquity of the *d* of my	Lam 4:6	1323
destruction of the *d* of my people	Lam 4:10	1323
O *d* of Edom, that dwellest in the	Lam 4:21	1323
is accomplished, O *d* of Zion	Lam 4:22	1323
visit thine iniquity, O *d* of Edom	Lam 4:22	1323
shall deliver neither son nor *d*	Eze 14:20	1323
As is the mother, so is her *d*	Eze 16:44	1323
Thou art thy mother's *d*, that	Eze 16:45	1323
hath lewdly defiled his *d* in law	Eze 22:11	3618
his sister, his father's *d*	Eze 22:11	1323
for mother, or for son, or for *d*	Eze 44:25	1323
for the king's *d* of the south	Dan 11:6	1323
he shall give him the *d* of women	Dan 11:17	1323
and took Gomer the *d* of Diblaim	Hos 1:3	1323
she conceived again, and bare a *d*	Hos 1:6	1323
of the sin to the *d* of Zion	Mic 1:13	1323
the strong hold of the *d* of Zion	Mic 4:8	1323
shall come to the *d* of Jerusalem	Mic 4:8	1323
O *d* of Zion, like a woman in	Mic 4:10	1323
Arise and thresh, O *d* of Zion	Mic 4:13	1323
thyself in troops, O *d* of troops	Mic 5:1	1323
the *d* riseth up against her	Mic 7:6	1323
the *d* in law against her mother	Mic 7:6	3618
even the *d* of my dispersed, shall	Zeph 3:10	1323
Sing, O *d* of Zion	Zeph 3:14	1323
all the heart, O *d* of Jerusalem	Zeph 3:14	1323
dwellest with the *d* of Babylon	Zec 2:7	1323
Sing and rejoice, O *d* of Zion	Zec 2:10	1323
Rejoice greatly, O *d* of Zion	Zec 9:9	1323
shout, O *d* of Jerusalem	Zec 9:9	1323
married the *d* of a strange god	Mal 2:11	1323
saying, My *d* is even now dead	Mt 9:18	*2364*
and when he saw her, he said, *D*	Mt 9:22	*2364*
the *d* against her mother, and the	Mt 10:35	*2364*
the *d* in law against her mother	Mt 10:35	*3565*
he that loveth son or *d* more than	Mt 10:37	*2364*
the *d* of Herodias danced before	Mt 14:6	*2364*
my *d* is grievously vexed with a	Mt 15:22	*2364*
her *d* was made whole from that	Mt 15:28	*2364*
Tell ye the *d* of Sion, Behold,	Mt 21:5	*2364*
My little *d* lieth at the point of	Mk 5:23	*2365*
And he said unto her, *D*, thy faith	Mk 5:34	*2364*
certain which said, Thy *d* is dead	Mk 5:35	*2364*
when the *d* of the said Herodias	Mk 6:22	*2364*
whose young *d* had an unclean	Mk 7:25	*2365*
cast forth the devil out of her *d*	Mk 7:26	*2364*
the devil is gone out of thy *d*	Mk 7:29	*2364*
out, and her *d* laid upon the bed	Mk 7:30	*2364*
the *d* of Phanuel, of the tribe of	Lk 2:36	*2364*
For he had one only *d*, about	Lk 8:42	*2364*
And he said unto her, *D*, be of	Lk 8:48	*2364*
saying to him, Thy *d* is dead	Lk 8:49	*2364*
the mother against the *d*	Lk 12:53	*2364*
and the *d* against the mother	Lk 12:53	*2364*
in law against her *d* in law	Lk 12:53	*3565*
the *d* in law against her mother	Lk 12:53	*3565*
being a *d* of Abraham, whom Satan	Lk 13:16	*2364*
Fear not, *d* of Sion	Jn 12:15	*2364*
Pharaoh's *d* took him up, and	Acts 7:21	*2364*

be called the son of Pharaoh's *d* Heb 11:24 *2364*

DAUGHTER'S

daughter, or of thy *d* daughter Lev 18:10 1323
or her *d* daughter, to uncover her Lev 18:17 1323
are the tokens of my *d* virginity Deut 22:17 1323

DAUGHTERS

and he begat sons and *d* Gen 5:4 1121
seven years, and begat sons and *d* Gen 5:7 1121
fifteen years, and begat sons and *d* Gen 5:10 1121
forty years, and begat sons and *d* Gen 5:13 1121
thirty years, and begat sons and *d* Gen 5:16 1121
hundred years, and begat sons and *d* Gen 5:19 1121
hundred years, and begat sons and *d* Gen 5:22 1121
and two years, and begat sons and *d* Gen 5:26 1121
and five years, and begat sons and *d* Gen 5:30 1121
earth, and *d* were born unto them, Gen 6:1 1121
the *d* of men that they were fair Gen 6:2 1121
of God came in unto the *d* of men Gen 6:4 1121
hundred years, and begat sons and *d* Gen 11:11 1121
three years, and begat sons and *d* Gen 11:13 1121
three years, and begat sons and *d* Gen 11:15 1121
thirty years, and begat sons and *d* Gen 11:17 1121
and nine years, and begat sons and *d* Gen 11:19 1121
seven years, and begat sons and *d* Gen 11:21 1121
hundred years, and begat sons and *d* Gen 11:23 1121
years, and begat sons and *d* Gen 11:25 1121
I have two *d* which have not known Gen 19:8 1121
son in law, and thy sons, and thy *d* Gen 19:12 1121
sons in law, which married his *d* Gen 19:14 1121
take thy wife, and thy two *d* Gen 19:15 1121
and upon the hand of his two *d* Gen 19:16 1121
mountain, and his two *d* with him Gen 19:30 1121
dwelt in a cave, he and his two *d* Gen 19:30 1121
Thus were both the *d* of Lot with Gen 19:36 1121
my son of the *d* of the Canaanites Gen 24:3 1121
the *d* of the men of the city come Gen 24:13 1121
my son of the *d* of the Canaanites Gen 24:37 1121
my life because of the *d* of Heth Gen 27:46 1121
take a wife of the *d* of Heth Gen 27:46 1121
which are of the *d* of the land Gen 27:46 1121
take a wife of the *d* of Canaan Gen 28:1 1121
d of Laban thy mother's brother Gen 28:2 1121
take a wife of the *d* of Canaan Gen 28:6 1121
Esau seeing that the *d* of Canaan Gen 28:8 1121
And Laban had two *d* Gen 29:16 1121
for the *d* will call me blessed Gen 30:13 1121
to me, and carried away my *d* Gen 31:26 1121
me to kiss my sons and my *d* Gen 31:28 1121
take by force thy *d* from me Gen 31:31 1121
thee fourteen years for thy two *d* Gen 31:41 1121
These *d* are my *d*, and Gen 31:43 1121
Jacob, These *d* are my *d* Gen 31:43 1121
can I do this day unto these my *d* Gen 31:43 1121
If thou shalt afflict my *d* Gen 31:50 1121
take other wives beside my *d* Gen 31:50 1121
up, and kissed his sons and his *d* Gen 31:55 1121
went out to see the *d* of the land Gen 34:1 1121
with us, and give your *d* unto us Gen 34:9 1121
unto us, and take our *d* unto you Gen 34:9 1121
Then will we give our *d* unto you Gen 34:16 1121
and we will take your *d* to us Gen 34:16 1121
us take their *d* to us for wives Gen 34:21 1121
and let us give them our *d* Gen 34:21 1121
took his wives of the *d* of Canaan Gen 36:2 1121
his wives, and his sons, and his *d* Gen 36:6 1121
all his *d* rose up to comfort him Gen 37:35 1121
his *d*, and his sons' *d* Gen 46:7 1121
his *d* were thirty and three Gen 46:15 1121
the priest of Midian had seven *d* Ex 2:16 1121
And he said unto his *d*, And where Ex 2:20 1121
upon your sons, and upon your *d* Ex 3:22 1121
one of the *d* of Putiel to wife Ex 6:25 1121
old, with our sons and with our *d* Ex 10:9 1121
and she have born him sons or *d* Ex 21:4 1121
with her after the manner of *d* Ex 21:9 1121
wives, of your sons, and of your *d* Ex 32:2 1121
take of their *d* unto thy sons Ex 34:16 1121
their *d* go a whoring after their Ex 34:16 1121
and thy sons, and thy *d* with thee Lev 10:14 1121
the flesh of your *d* shall ye eat Lev 26:29 1121
to thy *d* with thee, by a statute Num 18:11 1121
thy *d* with thee, by a statute for Num 18:19 1121
his sons that escaped, and his *d* Num 21:29 1121
whoredom with the *d* of Moab Num 25:1 1121
son of Hepher had no sons, but *d* Num 26:33 1121
the names of the *d* of Zelophehad Num 26:33 1121
Then came the *d* of Zelophehad Num 27:1 1121
and these are the names of his *d* Num 27:1 1121
The *d* of Zelophehad speak right Num 27:7 1121
Zelophehad our brother unto his *d* Num 36:2 1121
concerning the *d* of Zelophehad Num 36:6 1121
so did the *d* of Zelophehad Num 36:10 1121
the *d* of Zelophehad, were married Num 36:11 1121
God, ye, and your sons, and your *d* Deut 12:12 1121
their *d* they have burnt in the Deut 12:31 1121
be no whore of the *d* of Israel Deut 23:17 1121
thy *d* shall be given unto another Deut 28:32 1121
Thou shalt beget sons and *d* Deut 28:41 1121
the flesh of thy sons and of thy *d* Deut 28:53 1121
of his sons, and of his *d* Deut 32:19 1121
of gold, and his sons, and his *d* Josh 7:24 1121
of Manasseh, had no sons, but *d* Josh 17:3 1121
and these are the names of his *d* Josh 17:3 1121
Because the *d* of Manasseh had an Josh 17:6 1121
they took their *d* to be their Judg 3:6 1121
gave their *d* to their sons, and Judg 3:6 1121
That the *d* of Israel went yearly Judg 11:40 1121
he had thirty sons, and thirty *d* Judg 12:9 1121
took in thirty *d* from abroad for Judg 12:9 1121
of the *d* of the Philistines Judg 14:1 1121
of the *d* of the Philistines Judg 14:2 1121
woman among the *d* of thy brethren Judg 14:3 1121
not give them of our *d* to wives Judg 21:7 1121
may not give them wives of our *d* Judg 21:18 1121
if the *d* of Shiloh come out to Judg 21:21 1121
man his wife of the *d* of Shiloh Judg 21:21 1121
Then she arose with her *d* in law Ruth 1:6 3618
her two *d* in law with her Ruth 1:7 3618
Naomi said unto her two *d* in law Ruth 1:8 3618
And Naomi said, Turn again, my *d* Ruth 1:11 1121
Turn again, my *d*, go your way Ruth 1:12 1121
nay, my *d* Ruth 1:13 1121
wife, and to all her sons and her *d* 1Sa 1:4 1121
and bare three sons and two *d* 1Sa 2:21 1121
he will take your *d* to be 1Sa 8:13 1121
the names of his two *d* were these 1Sa 14:49 1121
wives, and their sons, and their *d* 1Sa 30:3 1121
man for his sons and for his *d* 1Sa 30:6 1121
nor great, neither sons nor *d* 1Sa 30:19 1121
lest the *d* of the Philistines 2Sa 1:20 1121
lest the *d* of the uncircumcised 2Sa 1:20 1121
Ye *d* of Israel, weep over Saul, 2Sa 1:24 1121
were yet sons and *d* born to David 2Sa 5:13 1121
d that were virgins apparelled 2Sa 13:18 1121
the lives of thy sons and of thy *d* 2Sa 19:5 1121
their *d* to pass through the fire, 2Kin 17:17 1121
Now Sheshan had no sons, but *d* 1Chr 2:34 1121
Shimei had sixteen sons and six *d* 1Chr 4:27 1121
and Zelophehad had *d* 1Chr 7:15 1121
and David begat more sons and *d* 1Chr 14:3 1121
died, and had no sons, but *d* 1Chr 23:22 1121
to Heman fourteen sons and three *d* 1Chr 25:5 1121
son of a woman of the *d* of Dan 2Chr 2:14 1121
and eight sons, and threescore *d* 2Chr 11:21 1121
twenty and two sons, and sixteen *d* 2Chr 13:21 1121
and he begat sons and *d* 2Chr 24:3 1121
thousand, women, sons, and *d* 2Chr 28:8 1121
the sword, and our sons and our *d* 2Chr 29:9 1121
wives, and their sons, and their *d* 2Chr 31:18 1121
which took a wife of the *d* of Ezr 2:61 1121
taken of their *d* for themselves Ezr 9:2 1121
give not your *d* unto their sons Ezr 9:12 1121
take their *d* unto your sons Ezr 9:12 1121
part of Jerusalem, he and his *d* Neh 3:12 1121
brethren, your sons, and your *d* Neh 4:14 1121
that said, We, our sons, and our *d* Neh 5:2 1121
our *d* to be servants Neh 5:5 1121
some of our *d* are brought unto Neh 5:5 1121
which took one of the *d* of Neh 7:63 1121
wives, their sons, and their *d* Neh 10:28 1121
that we would not give our *d* unto Neh 10:30 1121
nor take their *d* for our sons Neh 10:30 1121
not give your *d* unto their sons Neh 13:25 1121
nor take their *d* unto your sons Neh 13:25 1121
unto him seven sons and three *d* Job 1:2 1121
his *d* were eating and drinking Job 1:13 1121
thy *d* were eating and drinking Job 1:18 1121
He had also seven sons and three *d* Job 42:13 1121
found so fair as the *d* of Job Job 42:15 1121
Kings' *d* were among thy Ps 45:9 1121
let the *d* of Judah be glad, Ps 48:11 1121
the *d* of Judah rejoiced because Ps 97:8 1121
sons and their *d* unto devils, Ps 106:37 1121
blood of their sons and of their *d* Ps 106:38 1121
that our *d* may be as corner Ps 144:12 1121
The horseleach hath two *d* Prov 30:15 1121
Many *d* have done virtuously, but Prov 31:29 1121
all the *d* of musick shall be Eccl 12:4 1121
O ye *d* of Jerusalem, as the tents Song 1:5 1121
thorns, so is my love among the *d* Song 2:2 1121
O ye *d* of Jerusalem, by the roes, Song 2:7 1121
O ye *d* of Jerusalem, by the roes, Song 3:5 1121
with love, for the *d* of Jerusalem Song 3:10 1121
O ye *d* of Zion, and behold king Song 3:11 1121
O *d* of Jerusalem, if ye find my Song 5:8 1121
is my friend, O *d* of Jerusalem Song 5:16 1121
The *d* saw her, and blessed her Song 6:9 1121
O *d* of Jerusalem, that ye stir Song 8:4 1121
Because the *d* of Zion are haughty Is 3:16 1121
of the head of the *d* of Zion Is 3:17 1121
away the filth of the *d* of Zion Is 4:4 1121
so the *d* of Moab shall be at the Is 16:2 1121
hear my voice, ye careless *d* Is 32:9 1121
my *d* from the ends of the earth Is 43:6 1121
thy *d* shall be carried upon their Is 49:22 1121
name better than of sons and of *d* Is 56:5 1121
thy *d* shall be nursed at thy side Is 60:4 1121
herds, their sons and their *d* Jer 3:24 1121
thy sons and thy *d* should eat Jer 5:17 1121
their sons and their *d* in the fire Jer 7:31 1121
mouth, and teach your *d* wailing Jer 9:20 1121
their *d* shall die by famine Jer 11:22 1121
nor their sons, nor their *d* Jer 14:16 1121
thou have sons or *d* in this place Jer 16:2 1121
concerning the *d* that are born in Jer 16:3 1121
sons and the flesh of their *d* Jer 19:9 1121
Take ye wives, and beget sons and *d* Jer 29:6 1121
give your *d* to husbands Jer 29:6 1121
that they may bear sons and *d* Jer 29:6 1121
their *d* to pass through the fire Jer 32:35 1121
our wives, our sons, nor our *d* Jer 35:8 1121
were in Mizpah, even the king's *d* Jer 41:10 1121
and children, and the king's *d* Jer 43:6 1121
taken captives, and thy *d* captives Jer 48:46 1121
her *d* shall be burned with fire Jer 49:2 1121
ye *d* of Rabbah, gird you with Jer 49:3 1121
because of all the *d* of my city Lam 3:51 1121
face against the *d* of thy people Eze 13:17 1121
shall deliver neither sons nor *d* Eze 14:16 1121
shall deliver neither sons nor *d* Eze 14:18 1121
be brought forth, both sons and *d* Eze 14:22 1121
thou hast taken thy sons and thy *d* Eze 16:20 1121
the *d* of the Philistines, which Eze 16:27 1121
her *d* that dwell at thy left hand Eze 16:46 1121
thy right hand, is Sodom and her *d* Eze 16:46 1121
hath not done, she nor her *d* Eze 16:48 1121
as thou hast done, thou and thy *d* Eze 16:48 1121
idleness was in her and in her *d* Eze 16:49 1121
the captivity of Sodom and her *d* Eze 16:53 1121
the captivity of Samaria and her *d* Eze 16:53 1121
When thy sisters, Sodom and her *d* Eze 16:55 1121
her *d* shall return to their Eze 16:55 1121
thy *d* shall return to your former Eze 16:55 1121
of thy reproach of the *d* of Syria Eze 16:57 1121
the *d* of the Philistines, which Eze 16:57 1121
I will give them unto thee for *d* Eze 16:61 1121
two women, the *d* of one mother Eze 23:2 1121
were mine, and they bare sons and *d* Eze 23:4 1121
they took her sons and her *d* Eze 23:10 1121
they shall take thy sons and thy *d* Eze 23:25 1121
shall slay their sons and their *d* Eze 23:47 1121
your *d* whom ye have left shall Eze 24:21 1121
minds, their sons and their *d* Eze 24:25 1121
her *d* which are in the field Eze 26:6 1121
with the sword thy *d* in the field Eze 26:8 1121
her *d* shall go into captivity Eze 30:18 1121
the *d* of the nations shall lament Eze 32:16 1121
the *d* of the famous nations, unto Eze 32:18 1121
therefore your *d* shall commit Hos 4:13 1121
I will not punish your *d* when Hos 4:14 1121
your *d* shall prophesy, your old Joel 2:28 1121
your *d* into the hand of the Joel 3:8 1121
thy *d* shall fall by the sword, and Amos 7:17 1121
and his wife was of the *d* of Aaron Lk 1:5 *2364*
D of Jerusalem, weep not for me, Lk 23:28 *2364*
your *d* shall prophesy, and your Acts 2:17 *2364*
And the same man had four *d* Acts 21:9 *2364*
you, and ye shall be my sons and *d* 2Cor 6:18 *2364*
whose *d* ye are, as long as ye do 1Pet 3:6 *5043*

DAVID See DAVID'S. *Second king of Israel.*

father of Jesse, the father of *D* Ruth 4:17 1732
begat Jesse, and Jesse begat *D* Ruth 4:22 1732
came upon *D* from that day forward 1Sa 16:13 1732
Jesse, and said, Send me *D* thy son 1Sa 16:19 1732
sent them by *D* his son unto Saul 1Sa 16:20 1732
D came to Saul, and stood before 1Sa 16:21 1732
Saul sent to Jesse, saying, Let *D* 1Sa 16:22 1732
that *D* took an harp, and played 1Sa 16:23 1732
Now *D* was the son of that 1Sa 17:12 1732
And *D* was the youngest 1Sa 17:14 1732
But *D* went and returned from Saul 1Sa 17:15 1732
And Jesse said unto *D* his son 1Sa 17:17 1732
D rose up early in the morning, 1Sa 17:20 1732
D left his carriage in the hand 1Sa 17:22 1732
and *D* heard them 1Sa 17:23 1732
D spake to the men that stood by 1Sa 17:26 1732
anger was kindled against *D* 1Sa 17:28 1732
D said, What have I now done 1Sa 17:29 1732
words were heard which *D* spake 1Sa 17:31 1732
D said to Saul, Let no man's 1Sa 17:32 1732
And Saul said to *D*, Thou art not 1Sa 17:33 1732
D said unto Saul, Thy servant 1Sa 17:34 1732
D said moreover, The LORD that 1Sa 17:37 1732
And Saul said unto *D*, Go, and the 1Sa 17:37 1732
Saul armed *D* with his armour, and 1Sa 17:38 1732
D girded his sword upon his 1Sa 17:39 1732
D said unto Saul, I cannot go 1Sa 17:39 1732
And *D* put them off him 1Sa 17:39 1732
came on and drew near unto *D* 1Sa 17:41 1732
Philistine looked about, and saw *D* 1Sa 17:42 1732
And the Philistine said unto *D* 1Sa 17:43 1732
Philistine cursed *D* by his gods 1Sa 17:43 1732
And the Philistine said to *D* 1Sa 17:44 1732
Then said *D* to the Philistine, 1Sa 17:45 1732
and came and drew nigh to meet *D* 1Sa 17:48 1732
that *D* hasted, and ran toward the 1Sa 17:48 1732
D put his hand in his bag, and 1Sa 17:49 1732
So *D* prevailed over the 1Sa 17:50 1732
was no sword in the hand of *D* 1Sa 17:50 1732
Therefore *D* ran, and stood upon 1Sa 17:51 1732
D took the head of the Philistine 1Sa 17:54 1732
when Saul saw *D* go forth against 1Sa 17:55 1732
as *D* returned from the slaughter 1Sa 17:57 1732
D answered, I am the son of thy 1Sa 17:58 1732
was knit with the soul of *D* 1Sa 18:1 1732
D made a covenant, because he 1Sa 18:3 1732
was upon him, and gave it to *D* 1Sa 18:4 1732
D went out whithersoever Saul 1Sa 18:5 1732
when *D* was returned from the 1Sa 18:6 1732
thousands, and *D* his ten thousands 1Sa 18:7 1732
ascribed unto *D* ten thousands 1Sa 18:8 1732
Saul eyed *D* from that day and 1Sa 18:9 1732
D played with his hand, as at 1Sa 18:10 1732
I will smite *D* even to the wall 1Sa 18:11 1732
D avoided out of his presence 1Sa 18:11 1732
And Saul was afraid of *D*, because 1Sa 18:12 1732
D behaved himself wisely in all 1Sa 18:14 1732
But all Israel and Judah loved *D* 1Sa 18:16 1732
And Saul said to *D*, Behold my 1Sa 18:17 1732
D said unto Saul, Who am I 1Sa 18:18 1732
should have been given to *D* 1Sa 18:19 1732
And Michal Saul's daughter loved *D* 1Sa 18:20 1732
Wherefore Saul said to *D*, Thou 1Sa 18:21 1732
saying, Commune with *D* secretly 1Sa 18:22 1732
those words in the ears of *D* 1Sa 18:23 1732
D said, Seemeth it to you a light 1Sa 18:23 1732
saying, On this manner spake *D* 1Sa 18:24 1732
Saul said, Thus shall ye say to *D* 1Sa 18:25 1732
to make *D* fall by the hand of the 1Sa 18:25 1732
his servants told *D* these words 1Sa 18:26 1732
it pleased *D* well to be the 1Sa 18:26 1732
Wherefore *D* arose and went, he and 1Sa 18:27 1732
D brought their foreskins, and 1Sa 18:27 1732
and knew that the LORD was with *D* 1Sa 18:28 1732
Saul was yet the more afraid of *D* 1Sa 18:29 1732
that *D* behaved himself more 1Sa 18:30 1732
servants, that they should kill *D* 1Sa 19:1 1732
Saul's son delighted much in *D* 1Sa 19:2 1732
and Jonathan told *D*, saying, Saul 1Sa 19:2 1732
good of *D* unto Saul his father 1Sa 19:4 1732

against his servant, against *D*	1Sa 19:4	1732
to slay *D* without a cause	1Sa 19:5	1732
And Jonathan called *D*	1Sa 19:7	1732
And Jonathan brought *D* to Saul	1Sa 19:7	1732
D went out, and fought with the	1Sa 19:8	1732
and *D* played with his hand	1Sa 19:9	1732
Saul sought to smite *D* even to	1Sa 19:10	1732
D fled, and escaped that night	1Sa 19:10	1732
So Michal let *D* down through a	1Sa 19:12	1732
Saul sent messengers to take *D*	1Sa 19:14	1732
the messengers again to see *D*	1Sa 19:15	1732
So *D* fled, and escaped, and came to	1Sa 19:18	1732
Behold, *D* is at Naioth in Ramah	1Sa 19:19	1732
And Saul sent messengers to take *D*	1Sa 19:20	1732
and said, Where are Samuel and *D*	1Sa 19:22	1732
D fled from Naioth in Ramah, and	1Sa 20:1	1732
D sware moreover, and said, Thy	1Sa 20:3	1732
Then said Jonathan unto *D*	1Sa 20:4	1732
D said unto Jonathan, Behold, to	1Sa 20:5	1732
D earnestly asked leave of me	1Sa 20:6	1732
Then said *D* to Jonathan, Who	1Sa 20:10	1732
And Jonathan said unto *D*, Come, and	1Sa 20:11	1732
And Jonathan said unto *D*, O LORD	1Sa 20:12	1732
behold, if there be good toward *D*	1Sa 20:12	1732
hath cut off the enemies of *D*	1Sa 20:15	1732
a covenant with the house of *D*	1Sa 20:16	1732
Jonathan caused *D* to swear again	1Sa 20:17	1732
Then Jonathan said to *D*, To	1Sa 20:18	1732
So *D* hid himself in the field	1Sa 20:24	1732
D earnestly asked leave of me to	1Sa 20:28	1732
of his father to slay *D*	1Sa 20:33	1732
for he was grieved for *D*, because	1Sa 20:34	1732
at the time appointed with *D*	1Sa 20:35	1732
Jonathan and *D* knew the matter	1Sa 20:39	1732
D arose out of a place toward the	1Sa 20:41	1732
with another, until *D* exceeded	1Sa 20:41	1732
And Jonathan said to *D*, Go in	1Sa 20:42	1732
Then came *D* to Nob to Ahimelech	1Sa 21:1	1732
was afraid at the meeting of *D*	1Sa 21:1	1732
D said unto Ahimelech the priest,	1Sa 21:2	1732
And the priest answered *D*, and said	1Sa 21:4	1732
D answered the priest, and said	1Sa 21:5	1732
D said unto Ahimelech, And is	1Sa 21:8	1732
D said, There is none like that	1Sa 21:9	1732
D arose, and fled that day for	1Sa 21:10	1732
Is not this *D* the king of the	1Sa 21:11	1732
thousands, and *D* his ten thousands	1Sa 21:11	1732
D laid up these words in his	1Sa 21:12	1732
D therefore departed thence, and	1Sa 22:1	1732
D went thence to Mizpeh of Moab	1Sa 22:3	1732
the while that *D* was in the hold	1Sa 22:4	1732
And the prophet Gad said unto *D*	1Sa 22:5	1732
Then *D* departed, and came into the	1Sa 22:5	1732
Saul heard that *D* was discovered	1Sa 22:6	1732
among all thy servants as *D*	1Sa 22:14	1732
because their hand also is with *D*	1Sa 22:17	1732
escaped, and fled after *D*	1Sa 22:20	1732
Abiathar shewed *D* that Saul had	1Sa 22:21	1732
D said unto Abiathar, I knew it	1Sa 22:22	1732
Then they told *D*, saying, Behold,	1Sa 23:1	1732
Therefore *D* enquired of the LORD,	1Sa 23:2	1732
And the LORD said unto *D*, Go, and	1Sa 23:2	1732
Then *D* enquired of the LORD yet	1Sa 23:4	1732
So *D* and his men went to Keilah,	1Sa 23:5	1732
So *D* saved the inhabitants of	1Sa 23:5	1732
of Ahimelech fled to *D* to Keilah	1Sa 23:6	1732
Saul that *D* was come to Keilah	1Sa 23:7	1732
go down to Keilah, to besiege *D*	1Sa 23:8	1732
D knew that Saul secretly	1Sa 23:9	1732
Then said *D*, O LORD God of Israel	1Sa 23:10	1732
Then said *D*, Will the men of	1Sa 23:12	1732
Then *D* and his men, which were	1Sa 23:13	1732
it was told Saul that *D* was	1Sa 23:13	1732
D abode in the wilderness in	1Sa 23:14	1732
D saw that Saul was come out to	1Sa 23:15	1732
D was in the wilderness of Ziph	1Sa 23:15	1732
went to *D* into the wood, and	1Sa 23:16	1732
D abode in the wood, and Jonathan	1Sa 23:18	1732
Doth not *D* hide himself with us	1Sa 23:19	1732
but *D* and his men were in the	1Sa 23:24	1732
And they told *D*	1Sa 23:25	1732
he pursued after *D* in the	1Sa 23:25	1732
this side of the mountain, and *D*	1Sa 23:26	1732
D made haste to get away for fear	1Sa 23:26	1732
for Saul and his men compassed *D*	1Sa 23:26	1732
returned from pursuing after *D*	1Sa 23:28	1732
D went up from thence, and dwelt	1Sa 23:29	1732
D is in the wilderness of En-gedi	1Sa 24:1	1732
of all Israel, and went to seek *D*	1Sa 24:2	1732
and *D* and his men remained in the	1Sa 24:3	1732
the men of *D* said unto him,	1Sa 24:4	1732
Then *D* arose, and cut off the	1Sa 24:4	1732
So *D* stayed his servants with	1Sa 24:7	1732
D also arose afterward, and went	1Sa 24:8	1732
D stooped with his face to the	1Sa 24:8	1732
D said to Saul, Wherefore hearest	1Sa 24:9	1732
Behold, *D* seeketh thy hurt	1Sa 24:9	1732
when *D* had made an end of	1Sa 24:16	1732
said, Is this thy voice, my son *D*	1Sa 24:16	1732
And he said to *D*, Thou art more	1Sa 24:17	1732
And *D* sware unto Saul	1Sa 24:22	1732
but *D* and his men gat them up unto	1Sa 24:22	1732
D arose, and went down to the	1Sa 25:1	1732
D heard in the wilderness that	1Sa 25:4	1732
D sent out ten young men, and	1Sa 25:5	1732
D said unto the young men, Get	1Sa 25:5	1732
thy servants, and to thy son *D*	1Sa 25:8	1732
all those words in the name of *D*	1Sa 25:9	1732
servants, and said, Who is *D*	1Sa 25:10	1732
D said unto his men, Gird ye on	1Sa 25:13	1732
D also girded on his sword	1Sa 25:13	1732
there went up after *D* about four	1Sa 25:13	1732
D sent messengers out of the	1Sa 25:14	1732
covert of the hill, and, behold, *D*	1Sa 25:20	1732
Now *D* had said, Surely in vain	1Sa 25:21	1732
also do God unto the enemies of *D*	1Sa 25:22	1732
And when Abigail saw *D*, she hasted	1Sa 25:23	1732
ass, and fell before *D* on her face	1Sa 25:23	1732
D said to Abigail, Blessed be the	1Sa 25:32	1732
So *D* received of her hand that	1Sa 25:35	1732
when *D* heard that Nabal was dead,	1Sa 25:39	1732
D sent and communed with Abigail,	1Sa 25:39	1732
when the servants of *D* were come	1Sa 25:40	1732
D sent us unto thee, to take thee	1Sa 25:40	1732
went after the messengers of *D*	1Sa 25:42	1732
D also took Ahinoam of Jezreel	1Sa 25:43	1732
Doth not *D* hide himself in the	1Sa 26:1	1732
to seek *D* in the wilderness of	1Sa 26:2	1732
But *D* abode in the wilderness, and	1Sa 26:3	1732
D therefore sent out spies, and	1Sa 26:4	1732
D arose, and came to the place	1Sa 26:5	1732
D beheld the place where Saul lay	1Sa 26:5	1732
Then answered *D* and said to	1Sa 26:6	1732
So *D* and Abishai came to the	1Sa 26:7	1732
Then said Abishai to *D*, God hath	1Sa 26:8	1732
D said to Abishai, Destroy him	1Sa 26:9	1732
D said furthermore, As the LORD	1Sa 26:10	1732
So *D* took the spear and the cruse	1Sa 26:12	1732
Then *D* went over to the other	1Sa 26:13	1732
D cried to the people, and to	1Sa 26:14	1732
D said to Abner, Art not thou a	1Sa 26:15	1732
said, Is this thy voice, my son *D*	1Sa 26:17	1732
D said, It is my voice, my lord,	1Sa 26:17	1732
return, my son *D*	1Sa 26:21	1732
D answered and said, Behold the	1Sa 26:22	1732
D, Blessed be thou, my son *D*	1Sa 26:25	1732
So *D* went on his way, and Saul	1Sa 26:25	1732
D said in his heart, I shall now	1Sa 27:1	1732
D arose, and he passed over with	1Sa 27:2	1732
D dwelt with Achish at Gath, he	1Sa 27:3	1732
even *D* with his two wives,	1Sa 27:3	1732
told Saul that *D* was fled to Gath	1Sa 27:4	1732
D said unto Achish, If I have now	1Sa 27:5	1732
the time that *D* dwelt in the	1Sa 27:7	1732
And *D* and his men went up, and	1Sa 27:8	1732
D smote the land, and left neither	1Sa 27:9	1732
D said, Against the south of	1Sa 27:10	1732
D saved neither man nor woman	1Sa 27:11	1732
tell on us, saying, So did *D*	1Sa 27:11	1732
And Achish believed *D*, saying, He	1Sa 27:12	1732
And Achish said unto *D*, Know thou	1Sa 28:1	1732
D said to Achish, Surely thou	1Sa 28:2	1732
And Achish said to *D*, Therefore	1Sa 28:2	1732
it to thy neighbour, even to *D*	1Sa 28:17	1732
but *D* and his men passed on in the	1Sa 29:2	1732
of the Philistines, Is not this *D*	1Sa 29:3	1732
Is not this *D*, of whom they sang	1Sa 29:5	1732
thousands, and *D* his ten thousands	1Sa 29:5	1732
Then Achish called *D*, and said	1Sa 29:6	1732
D said unto Achish, But what have	1Sa 29:8	1732
And Achish answered and said to *D*	1Sa 29:9	1732
So *D* and his men rose up early to	1Sa 29:11	1732
And it came to pass, when *D*	1Sa 30:1	1732
So *D* and his men came to the city,	1Sa 30:3	1732
Then *D* and the people that were	1Sa 30:4	1732
And *D* was greatly distressed	1Sa 30:6	1732
but *D* encouraged himself in the	1Sa 30:6	1732
D said to Abiathar the priest,	1Sa 30:7	1732
brought thither the ephod to *D*	1Sa 30:7	1732
D enquired at the LORD, saying,	1Sa 30:8	1732
So *D* went, he and the six hundred	1Sa 30:9	1732
But *D* pursued, he and four hundred	1Sa 30:10	1732
in the field, and brought him to *D*	1Sa 30:11	1732
And *D* said unto him, To whom	1Sa 30:13	1732
D said to him, Canst thou bring	1Sa 30:15	1732
D smote them from the twilight	1Sa 30:17	1732
And *D* recovered all that the	1Sa 30:18	1732
and *D* rescued his two wives	1Sa 30:18	1732
D recovered all	1Sa 30:19	1732
D took all the flocks and the	1Sa 30:20	1732
D came to the two hundred men,	1Sa 30:21	1732
that they could not follow *D*	1Sa 30:21	1732
and they went forth to meet *D*	1Sa 30:21	1732
when *D* came near to the people,	1Sa 30:21	1732
Belial, of those that went with *D*	1Sa 30:22	1732
Then said *D*, Ye shall not do so,	1Sa 30:23	1732
when *D* came to Ziklag, he sent of	1Sa 30:26	1732
to all the places where *D* himself	1Sa 30:31	1732
when *D* was returned from the	2Sa 1:1	1732
D had abode two days in Ziklag	2Sa 1:1	1732
and so it was, when he came to *D*	2Sa 1:2	1732
D said unto him, From whence	2Sa 1:3	1732
D said unto him, How went the	2Sa 1:4	1732
D said unto the young man that	2Sa 1:5	1732
Then *D* took hold on his clothes,	2Sa 1:11	1732
D said unto the young man that	2Sa 1:13	1732
D said unto him, How wast thou	2Sa 1:14	1732
D called one of the young men, and	2Sa 1:15	1732
D said unto him, Thy blood be	2Sa 1:16	1732
D lamented with this lamentation	2Sa 1:17	1732
that *D* enquired of the LORD,	2Sa 2:1	1732
D said, Whither shall I go up	2Sa 2:1	1732
So *D* went up thither, and his two	2Sa 2:2	1732
that were with him did *D* bring up	2Sa 2:3	1732
there they anointed *D* king over	2Sa 2:4	1732
And they told *D*, saying, That the	2Sa 2:4	1732
D sent messengers unto the men of	2Sa 2:5	1732
But the house of Judah followed *D*	2Sa 2:10	1732
the time that *D* was king in	2Sa 2:11	1732
of Zeruiah, and the servants of *D*	2Sa 2:13	1732
and twelve of the servants of *D*	2Sa 2:15	1732
Israel, before the servants of *D*	2Sa 2:17	1732
But the servants of *D* had smitten	2Sa 2:31	1732
house of Saul and the house of *D*	2Sa 3:1	1732
but *D* waxed stronger and stronger,	2Sa 3:1	1732
unto *D* were sons born in Hebron	2Sa 3:2	1732
These were born to *D* in Hebron	2Sa 3:5	1732
house of Saul and the house of *D*	2Sa 3:6	1732
delivered thee into the hand of *D*	2Sa 3:8	1732
as the LORD hath sworn to *D*	2Sa 3:9	1732
up the throne of *D* over Israel	2Sa 3:10	1732
messengers to *D* on his behalf	2Sa 3:12	1732
D sent messengers to Ish-bosheth	2Sa 3:14	1732
Ye sought for *D* in times past to	2Sa 3:17	1732
for the LORD hath spoken of *D*	2Sa 3:18	1732
By the hand of my servant *D* I	2Sa 3:18	1732
also to speak in the ears of *D* in	2Sa 3:19	1732
So Abner came to *D* to Hebron	2Sa 3:20	1732
D made Abner and the men that were	2Sa 3:20	1732
And Abner said unto *D*, I will	2Sa 3:21	1732
And *D* sent Abner away	2Sa 3:21	1732
And, behold, the servants of *D*	2Sa 3:22	1732
Abner was not with *D* in Hebron	2Sa 3:22	1732
And when Joab was come out from *D*	2Sa 3:26	1732
but *D* knew it not	2Sa 3:26	1732
And afterward when *D* heard it	2Sa 3:28	1732
D said to Joab, and to all the	2Sa 3:31	1732
king *D* himself followed the bier	2Sa 3:31	1732
D to eat meat while it was yet	2Sa 3:35	1732
D sware, saying, So do God to me,	2Sa 3:35	1732
of Ish-bosheth unto *D* to Hebron	2Sa 4:8	1732
D answered Rechab and Baanah his	2Sa 4:9	1732
D commanded his young men, and	2Sa 4:12	1732
tribes of Israel to *D* unto Hebron	2Sa 5:1	1732
king *D* made a league with them in	2Sa 5:3	1732
they anointed *D* king over Israel	2Sa 5:3	1732
D was thirty years old when he	2Sa 5:4	1732
which spake unto *D*, saying,	2Sa 5:6	1732
thinking, *D* cannot come in	2Sa 5:6	1732
Nevertheless *D* took the strong	2Sa 5:7	1732
the same is the city of *D*	2Sa 5:7	1732
D said on that day, Whosoever	2Sa 5:8	1732
So *D* dwelt in the fort	2Sa 5:9	1732
and called it the city of *D*	2Sa 5:9	1732
D built round about from Millo and	2Sa 5:9	1732
D went on, and grew great, and the	2Sa 5:10	1732
king of Tyre sent messengers to *D*	2Sa 5:11	1732
and they built *D* an house	2Sa 5:11	1732
D perceived that the LORD had	2Sa 5:12	1732
D took him more concubines and	2Sa 5:13	1732
yet sons and daughters born to *D*	2Sa 5:13	1732
had anointed *D* king over Israel	2Sa 5:17	1732
the Philistines came up to seek *D*	2Sa 5:17	1732
D heard of it, and went down to	2Sa 5:17	1732
D enquired of the LORD, saying,	2Sa 5:19	1732
And the LORD said unto *D*, Go up	2Sa 5:19	1732
D came to Baal-perazim	2Sa 5:20	1732
D smote them there, and said, The	2Sa 5:20	1732
they left their images, and *D*	2Sa 5:21	1732
when *D* enquired of the LORD, he	2Sa 5:23	1732
D did so, as the LORD had	2Sa 5:25	1732
D gathered together all the	2Sa 6:1	1732
D arose, and went with all the	2Sa 6:2	1732
And *D* and all the house of Israel	2Sa 6:5	1732
D was displeased, because the	2Sa 6:8	1732
D was afraid of the LORD that day	2Sa 6:9	1732
So *D* would not remove the ark of	2Sa 6:10	1732
LORD unto him into the city of *D*	2Sa 6:10	1732
but *D* carried it aside into the	2Sa 6:10	1732
And it was told king *D*, saying,	2Sa 6:12	1732
So *D* went and brought up the ark	2Sa 6:12	1732
into the city of *D* with gladness	2Sa 6:12	1732
D danced before the LORD with all	2Sa 6:14	1732
D was girded with a linen ephod	2Sa 6:14	1732
So *D* and all the house of Israel	2Sa 6:15	1732
the LORD came into the city of *D*	2Sa 6:16	1732
a window, and saw king *D* leaping	2Sa 6:16	1732
that *D* had pitched for it	2Sa 6:17	
D offered burnt offerings and	2Sa 6:17	1732
as soon as *D* had made an end of	2Sa 6:18	1732
Then *D* returned to bless his	2Sa 6:20	1732
of Saul came out to meet *D*	2Sa 6:20	1732
D said unto Michal, It was before	2Sa 6:21	1732
Go and tell my servant *D*, Thus	2Sa 7:5	1732
shalt thou say unto my servant *D*	2Sa 7:8	1732
so did Nathan speak unto *D*	2Sa 7:17	1732
Then went king *D* in, and sat	2Sa 7:18	1732
what can *D* say more unto thee	2Sa 7:20	1732
D be established before thee	2Sa 7:26	1732
that *D* smote the Philistines, and	2Sa 8:1	1732
D took Metheg-ammah out of the	2Sa 8:1	1732
D smote also Hadadezer, the son	2Sa 8:3	1732
D took from him a thousand	2Sa 8:4	1732
D houghed all the chariot horses,	2Sa 8:4	1732
D slew of the Syrians two and	2Sa 8:5	1732
Then *D* put garrisons in Syria of	2Sa 8:6	1732
the Syrians became servants to *D*	2Sa 8:6	1732
And the LORD preserved *D*	2Sa 8:6	1732
D took the shields of gold that	2Sa 8:7	1732
king *D* took exceeding much brass	2Sa 8:8	1732
D had smitten all the host of	2Sa 8:9	1732
sent Joram his son unto king *D*	2Sa 8:10	1732
Which also king *D* did dedicate	2Sa 8:11	1732
D gat him a name when he returned	2Sa 8:13	1732
And the LORD preserved *D*	2Sa 8:14	1732
D reigned over all Israel	2Sa 8:15	1732
D executed judgment and justice	2Sa 8:15	1732
D said, Is there yet any that is	2Sa 9:1	1732
when they had called him unto *D*	2Sa 9:2	1732
Then king *D* sent, and fetched him	2Sa 9:5	1732
the son of Saul, was come unto *D*	2Sa 9:6	1732
And *D* said, Mephibosheth	2Sa 9:6	1732
D said unto him, Fear not	2Sa 9:7	1732
Then said *D*, I will shew kindness	2Sa 10:2	1732
D sent to comfort him by the hand	2Sa 10:2	1732
Thinkest thou that *D* doth honour	2Sa 10:3	1732
hath not *D* rather sent his	2Sa 10:3	1732
When they told it unto *D*, he sent	2Sa 10:5	1732
saw that they stank before *D*	2Sa 10:6	1732
when *D* heard of it, he sent Joab,	2Sa 10:7	1732
And when it was told *D*, he	2Sa 10:17	1732
set themselves in array against *D*	2Sa 10:17	1732

D slew the men of seven hundred 2Sa 10:18 1732
that D sent Joab, and his servants 2Sa 11:1 1732
But D tarried still at Jerusalem 2Sa 11:1 1732
that D arose from off his bed, and 2Sa 11:2 1732
D sent and enquired after the 2Sa 11:3 1732
D sent messengers, and took her 2Sa 11:4 1732
conceived, and sent and told D 2Sa 11:5 1732
D sent to Joab, saying, Send me 2Sa 11:6 1732
And Joab sent Uriah to D 2Sa 11:6 1732
D demanded of him how Joab did, 2Sa 11:7 1732
D said to Uriah, Go down to thy 2Sa 11:8 1732
And when they had told D, saying, 2Sa 11:10 1732
D said unto Uriah, Camest thou 2Sa 11:10 1732
And Uriah said unto D, The ark, and 2Sa 11:11 1732
D said to Uriah, Tarry here to 2Sa 11:12 1732
when D had called him, he did eat 2Sa 11:13 1732
that D wrote a letter to Joab, and 2Sa 11:14 1732
the people of the servants of D 2Sa 11:17 1732
told D all the things concerning 2Sa 11:18 1732
shewed D all that Joab had sent 2Sa 11:22 1732
And the messenger said unto D 2Sa 11:23 1732
Then D said unto the messenger, 2Sa 11:25 1732
D sent and fetched her to his 2Sa 11:27 1732
But the thing that D had done 2Sa 11:27 1732
And the LORD sent Nathan unto D 2Sa 12:1 1732
And Nathan said to D, Thou art the 2Sa 12:7 1732
D said unto Nathan, I have sinned 2Sa 12:13 1732
And Nathan said unto D, The LORD 2Sa 12:13 1732
that Uriah's wife bare unto D 2Sa 12:15 1732
D therefore besought God for the 2Sa 12:16 1732
D fasted, and went in, and lay all 2Sa 12:16 1732
the servants of D feared to tell 2Sa 12:18 1732
But when D saw that his servants 2Sa 12:19 1732
D perceived that the child was 2Sa 12:19 1732
therefore D said unto his 2Sa 12:19 1732
Then D arose from the earth, and 2Sa 12:20 1732
D comforted Bath-sheba his wife, 2Sa 12:24 1732
And Joab sent messengers to D 2Sa 12:27 1732
D gathered all the people 2Sa 12:29 1732
So D and all the people returned 2Sa 12:31 1732
the son of D had a fair sister 2Sa 13:1 1732
and Amnon the son of D loved her 2Sa 13:1 1732
Then D sent home to Tamar, saying 2Sa 13:7 1732
But when king D heard of all 2Sa 13:21 1732
the way, that tidings came to D 2Sa 13:30 1732
D mourned for his son every day 2Sa 13:37
the soul of king D longed to go 2Sa 13:39 1732
And there came a messenger to D 2Sa 15:13 1732
D said unto all his servants that 2Sa 15:14 1732
D said to Ittai, Go and pass over 2Sa 15:22 1732
D went up by the ascent of mount 2Sa 15:30 1732
And one told D, saying, Ahithophel 2Sa 15:31 1732
D said, O LORD, I pray thee, turn 2Sa 15:31 1732
that when D was come to the top 2Sa 15:32 1732
Unto whom D said, If thou passest 2Sa 15:33 1732
when D was a little past the top 2Sa 16:1 1732
when king D came to Bahurim, 2Sa 16:5 1732
And he cast stones at D, and at all 2Sa 16:6 1732
and at all the servants of king D 2Sa 16:6 1732
LORD hath said unto him, Curse D 2Sa 16:10 1732
D said to Abishai, and to all his 2Sa 16:11 1732
And as D and his men went by the 2Sa 16:13 1732
counsel of Ahithophel both with D 2Sa 16:23 1732
and pursue after D this night 2Sa 17:1 1732
therefore send quickly, and tell D 2Sa 17:16 1732
and they went and told king D 2Sa 17:17 1732
told king D, and said unto D 2Sa 17:21 1732
Then D arose, and all the people 2Sa 17:22 1732
Then D came to Mahanaim 2Sa 17:24 1732
when D was come to Mahanaim, that 2Sa 17:27 1732
sheep, and cheese of kine, for D 2Sa 17:29 1732
D numbered the people that were 2Sa 18:1 1732
D sent forth a third part of the 2Sa 18:2 1732
slain before the servants of D 2Sa 18:7 1732
And Absalom met the servants of D 2Sa 18:9 1732
D sat between the two gates 2Sa 18:24 1732
king D sent to Zadok and to 2Sa 19:11 1732
the men of Judah to meet king D 2Sa 19:16 1732
D said, What have I to do with 2Sa 19:22 1732
have also more right in D than ye 2Sa 19:43 1732
and said, We have no part in D 2Sa 20:1 1732
of Israel went up from after D 2Sa 20:2 1732
D came to his house at Jerusalem 2Sa 20:3 1732
D said to Abishai, Now shall 2Sa 20:6 1732
Joab, and he that is for D 2Sa 20:11 1732
against the king, even against D 2Sa 20:21 1732
Jairite was a chief ruler about D 2Sa 20:26 1732
in the days of D three years 2Sa 21:1 1732
and D enquired of the LORD 2Sa 21:1 1732
Wherefore D said unto the 2Sa 21:3 1732
that was between them, between D 2Sa 21:7 1732
it was told D what Rizpah the 2Sa 21:11 1732
D went and took the bones of Saul 2Sa 21:12 1732
D went down, and his servants with 2Sa 21:15 1732
and D waxed faint 2Sa 21:15 1732
sword, thought to have slain D 2Sa 21:16 1732
Then the men of D sware unto him 2Sa 21:17 1732
Shimeah the brother of D slew him 2Sa 21:21 1732
in Gath, and fell by the hand of D 2Sa 21:22 1732
D spake unto the LORD the words 2Sa 22:1 1732
mercy to his anointed, unto D 2Sa 22:51 1732
Now these be the last words of D 2Sa 23:1 1732
D the son of Jesse said, and the 2Sa 23:1 1732
of the mighty men whom D had 2Sa 23:8 1732
of the three mighty men with D 2Sa 23:9 1732
came to D in the harvest time 2Sa 23:13 1732
D was then in an hold, and the 2Sa 23:14 1732
D longed, and said, Oh that one 2Sa 23:15 1732
and took it, and brought it to D 2Sa 23:16 1732
And D set him over his guard 2Sa 23:23 1732
he moved D against them to say, 2Sa 24:1 1732
D said unto the LORD, I have 2Sa 24:10 1732
For when D was up in the morning, 2Sa 24:11 1732
Go and say unto D, Thus saith the 2Sa 24:12 1732
So Gad came to D, and told him, and 2Sa 24:13 1732
D said unto Gad, I am in a great 2Sa 24:14 1732
D spake unto the LORD when he saw 2Sa 24:17 1732
And Gad came that day to D 2Sa 24:18 1732
And D, according to the saying of 2Sa 24:19 1732
D said, To buy the threshingfloor 2Sa 24:21 1732
And Araunah said unto D, Let my 2Sa 24:22 1732
So D bought the threshingfloor and 2Sa 24:24 1732
D built there an altar unto the 2Sa 24:25 1732
Now king D was old and stricken in 1Kin 1:1 1732
mighty men which belonged to D 1Kin 1:8 1732
D our lord knoweth it not 1Kin 1:11 1732
Go and get thee in unto king D 1Kin 1:13 1732
Then king D answered and said, 1Kin 1:28 1732
Let my lord king D live for ever 1Kin 1:31 1732
And king D said, Call me Zadok the 1Kin 1:32 1732
than the throne of my lord king D 1Kin 1:37 1732
Verily our lord king D hath made 1Kin 1:43 1732
came to bless our lord king D 1Kin 1:47 1732
Now the days of D drew nigh that 1Kin 2:1 1732
So D slept with his fathers 1Kin 2:10 1732
and was buried in the city of D 1Kin 2:10 1732
the days that D reigned over 1Kin 2:11 1732
upon the throne of D his father 1Kin 2:12 1732
me on the throne of D my father 1Kin 2:24 1732
the Lord GOD before D my father 1Kin 2:26 1732
my father D not knowing thereof, 1Kin 2:32 1732
but upon D, and upon his seed, and 1Kin 2:33 1732
that thou didst to D my father 1Kin 2:44 1732
and the throne of D shall be 1Kin 2:45 1732
and brought her into the city of D 1Kin 3:1 1732
in the statutes of D his father 1Kin 3:3 1732
servant D my father great mercy 1Kin 3:6 1732
king instead of D my father 1Kin 3:7 1732
as thy father D did walk 1Kin 3:14 1732
for Hiram was ever a lover of D 1Kin 5:1 1732
Thou knowest how that D my father 1Kin 5:3 1732
the LORD spake unto D my father 1Kin 5:5 1732
which hath given unto D a wise 1Kin 5:7 1732
which I spake unto D thy father 1Kin 6:12 1732
which D his father had dedicated 1Kin 7:51 1732
of the LORD out of the city of D 1Kin 8:1 1732
with his mouth unto D my father 1Kin 8:15 1732
but I chose D to be over my 1Kin 8:16 1732
it was in the heart of D my 1Kin 8:17 1732
And the LORD said unto D my father 1Kin 8:18 1732
up in the room of D my father 1Kin 8:20 1732
D my father that thou promisedst 1Kin 8:24 1732
keep with thy servant D my father 1Kin 8:25 1732
unto thy servant D my father 1Kin 8:26 1732
LORD had done for D his servant 1Kin 8:66 1732
as D thy father walked, in 1Kin 9:4 1732
as I promised to D thy father 1Kin 9:5 1732
came up out of the city of D unto 1Kin 9:24 1732
as was the heart of D his father 1Kin 11:4 1732
the LORD, as did D his father 1Kin 11:6 1732
not do it for D thy father's sake 1Kin 11:12 1732
thy son for D my servant's sake 1Kin 11:13 1732
when D was in Edom, and Joab the 1Kin 11:15 1732
that D slept with his fathers 1Kin 11:21 1732
when D slew them of Zobah 1Kin 11:24 1732
of the city of D his father 1Kin 11:27 1732
my judgments, as did D his father 1Kin 11:33 1732
his life for D my servant's sake 1Kin 11:34
that D my servant may have a 1Kin 11:36 1732
commandments, as D my servant did 1Kin 11:38 1732
a sure house, as I built for D 1Kin 11:38 1732
for this afflict the seed of D 1Kin 11:39 1732
in the city of D his father 1Kin 11:43 1732
saying, What portion have we in D 1Kin 12:16 1732
now see to thine own house, D 1Kin 12:16 1732
the house of D unto this day 1Kin 12:19 1732
none that followed the house of D 1Kin 12:20 1732
kingdom return to the house of D 1Kin 12:26 1732
shall be born unto the house of D 1Kin 13:2 1732
kingdom away from the house of D 1Kin 14:8 1732
hast not been as my servant D 1Kin 14:8 1732
with his fathers in the city of D 1Kin 14:31 1732
God, as the heart of D his father 1Kin 15:3 1732
Because D did that which was 1Kin 15:5 1732
they buried him in the city of D 1Kin 15:8 1732
of the LORD, as did D his father 1Kin 15:11 1732
in the city of D his father 1Kin 15:24 1732
in the city of D his father 1Kin 22:50 1732
Judah for D his servant's sake 2Kin 8:19 1732
with his fathers in the city of D 2Kin 8:24 1732
with his fathers in the city of D 2Kin 9:28 1732
with his fathers in the city of D 2Kin 12:21 1732
LORD, yet not like D his father 2Kin 14:3 1732
with his fathers in the city of D 2Kin 14:20 1732
with his fathers in the city of D 2Kin 15:7 1732
in the city of D his father 2Kin 15:38 1732
LORD his God, like D his father 2Kin 16:2 1732
with his fathers in the city of D 2Kin 16:20 1732
rent Israel from the house of D 2Kin 17:21 1732
to all that D his father did 2Kin 18:3 1732
the LORD, the God of D thy father 2Kin 20:5 1732
of which the LORD said to D 2Kin 21:7 1732
in all the way of D his father 2Kin 22:2 1732
Ozem the sixth, D the seventh 1Chr 2:15 1732
Now these were the sons of D 1Chr 3:1 1732
These were all the sons of D 1Chr 3:9 1732
their cities unto the reign of D 1Chr 4:31 1732
these are they whom D set over 1Chr 6:31 1732
number was in the days of D two 1Chr 7:2 1732
in their villages, whom D 1Chr 9:22 1732
kingdom unto D the son of Jesse 1Chr 10:14 1732
themselves to D unto Hebron 1Chr 11:1 1732
D made a covenant with them in 1Chr 11:3 1732
they anointed D king over Israel, 1Chr 11:3 1732
And D and all Israel went to 1Chr 11:4 1732
inhabitants of Jebus said to D 1Chr 11:5 1732
Nevertheless D took the castle of 1Chr 11:5 1732
of Zion, which is the city of D 1Chr 11:5 1732
D said, Whosoever smiteth the 1Chr 11:6 1732
And D dwelt in the castle 1Chr 11:7 1732
they called it the city of D 1Chr 11:7 1732
So D waxed greater and greater 1Chr 11:9 1732
of the mighty men whom D had 1Chr 11:10 1732
of the mighty men whom D had 1Chr 11:11
He was with D at Pas-dammim, and 1Chr 11:13 1732
went down to the rock to D 1Chr 11:15 1732
D was then in the hold, and the 1Chr 11:16 1732
D longed, and said, Oh that one 1Chr 11:17 1732
and took it, and brought it to D 1Chr 11:18 1732
but D would not drink of it, but 1Chr 11:18 1732
and D set him over his guard 1Chr 11:25 1732
are they that came to D to Ziklag 1Chr 12:1 1732
D into the hold to the wilderness 1Chr 12:8 1732
and Judah to the hold unto D 1Chr 12:16 1732
D went out to meet them, and 1Chr 12:17 1732
and he said, Thine are we, D 1Chr 12:18 1732
Then D received them, and made 1Chr 12:18 1732
there fell some of Manasseh to D 1Chr 12:19 1732
they helped D against the band of 1Chr 12:21 1732
day there came to D to help him 1Chr 12:22 1732
came to D to Hebron, to turn the 1Chr 12:23 1732
by name, to come and make D king 1Chr 12:31 1732
to make D king over all Israel 1Chr 12:38 1732
were of one heart to make D king 1Chr 12:38 1732
there they were with D three days 1Chr 12:39 1732
D consulted with the captains of 1Chr 13:1 1732
D said unto all the congregation 1Chr 13:2 1732
So D gathered all Israel together 1Chr 13:5 1732
D went up, and all Israel, to 1Chr 13:6 1732
And D and all Israel played before 1Chr 13:8 1732
D was displeased, because the 1Chr 13:11 1732
D was afraid of God that day, 1Chr 13:12 1732
So D brought not the ark home to 1Chr 13:13 1732
home to himself to the city of D 1Chr 13:13 1732
king of Tyre sent messengers to D 1Chr 14:1 1732
D perceived that the LORD had 1Chr 14:2 1732
D took more wives at Jerusalem 1Chr 14:3 1732
D begat more sons and daughters 1Chr 14:3 1732
that D was anointed king over all 1Chr 14:8 1732
the Philistines went up to seek D 1Chr 14:8 1732
D heard of it, and went out 1Chr 14:8 1732
D enquired of God, saying, Shall 1Chr 14:10 1732
and D smote them there 1Chr 14:11 1732
Then D said, God hath broken in 1Chr 14:11 1732
D gave a commandment, and they 1Chr 14:12 1732
Therefore D enquired again of God 1Chr 14:14 1732
D therefore did as God commanded 1Chr 14:16 1732
the fame of D went out into all 1Chr 14:17 1732
D made him houses in the city of 1Chr 15:1
made him houses in the city of D 1Chr 15:1 1732
Then D said, None ought to carry 1Chr 15:2 1732
D gathered all Israel together to 1Chr 15:3 1732
D assembled the children of Aaron 1Chr 15:4 1732
D called for Zadok and Abiathar 1Chr 15:11 1732
D spake to the chief of the 1Chr 15:16 1732
So D, and the elders of Israel, and 1Chr 15:25 1732
D was clothed with a robe of fine 1Chr 15:27 1732
D also had upon him an ephod of 1Chr 15:27 1732
of the LORD came to the city of D 1Chr 15:29 1732
at a window saw king D dancing 1Chr 15:29 1732
tent that D had pitched for it 1Chr 16:1 1732
when D had made an end of 1Chr 16:2 1732
Then on that day D delivered 1Chr 16:7 1732
D returned to bless his house 1Chr 16:43 1732
as D sat in his house 1Chr 17:1 1732
that D said to Nathan the prophet 1Chr 17:1 1732
Then Nathan said unto D, Do all 1Chr 17:2 1732
tell D my servant, Thus saith the 1Chr 17:4 1732
shalt thou say unto my servant D 1Chr 17:7 1732
so did Nathan speak unto D 1Chr 17:15 1732
D the king came and sat before the 1Chr 17:16 1732
What can D speak more to thee for 1Chr 17:18 1732
let the house of D thy servant be 1Chr 17:24 1732
that D smote the Philistines, and 1Chr 18:1 1732
D smote Hadarezer king of Zobah 1Chr 18:3 1732
D took from him a thousand 1Chr 18:4 1732
D also houghed all the chariot 1Chr 18:4 1732
D slew of the Syrians two and 1Chr 18:5 1732
Then D put garrisons in 1Chr 18:6 1732
preserved D whithersoever he went 1Chr 18:6 1732
D took the shields of gold that 1Chr 18:7 1732
brought D very much brass, 1Chr 18:8 1732
how D had smitten all the host of 1Chr 18:9 1732
He sent Hadoram his son to king D 1Chr 18:10 1732
Them also king D dedicated unto 1Chr 18:11 1732
preserved D whithersoever he went 1Chr 18:13 1732
So D reigned over all Israel, and 1Chr 18:14 1732
the sons of D were chief about 1Chr 18:17 1732
D said, I will shew kindness unto 1Chr 19:2 1732
D sent messengers to comfort him 1Chr 19:2 1732
So the servants of D came into 1Chr 19:2 1732
Thinkest thou that D doth honour 1Chr 19:3 1732
told D how the men were served 1Chr 19:5 1732
had made themselves odious to D 1Chr 19:6 1732
when D heard of it, he sent Joab, 1Chr 19:8 1732
And it was told D 1Chr 19:17 1732
So when D had put the battle in 1Chr 19:17 1732
D slew of the Syrians seven 1Chr 19:18 1732
Israel, they made peace with D 1Chr 19:19 1732
But D tarried at Jerusalem 1Chr 20:1 1732
D took the crown of their king 1Chr 20:2 1732
Even so dealt D with all the 1Chr 20:3 1732
And D and all the people returned 1Chr 20:3 1732
and they fell by the hand of D 1Chr 20:8 1732
provoked D to number Israel 1Chr 21:1 1732
D said to Joab and to the rulers 1Chr 21:2 1732
the number of the people unto D 1Chr 21:5 1732
D said unto God, I have sinned 1Chr 21:8 1732
Go and tell D, saying, Thus saith 1Chr 21:10 1732
So Gad came to D, and said unto 1Chr 21:11 1732
D said unto Gad, I am in a great 1Chr 21:13 1732
D lifted up his eyes, and saw the 1Chr 21:16 1732

Then *D* and the elders of Israel,	1Chr 21:16	1732
D said unto God, Is it not I that	1Chr 21:17	1732
LORD commanded Gad to say to *D*	1Chr 21:18	1732
that *D* should go up, and set up an	1Chr 21:18	1732
D went up at the saying of Gad,	1Chr 21:19	1732
as *D* came to Ornan	1Chr 21:21	1732
Ornan looked and saw *D*	1Chr 21:21	1732
bowed himself to *D* with his face	1Chr 21:21	1732
Then *D* said to Ornan, Grant me	1Chr 21:22	1732
And Ornan said unto *D*, Take it to	1Chr 21:23	1732
king *D* said to Ornan, Nay	1Chr 21:24	1732
So *D* gave to Ornan for the place	1Chr 21:25	1732
D built there an altar unto the	1Chr 21:26	1732
At that time when *D* saw that the	1Chr 21:28	1732
But *D* could not go before it to	1Chr 21:30	1732
Then *D* said, This is the house of	1Chr 22:1	1732
D commanded to gather together	1Chr 22:2	1732
D prepared iron in abundance for	1Chr 22:3	1732
Tyre brought much cedar wood to *D*	1Chr 22:4	1732
D said, Solomon my son is young	1Chr 22:5	1732
So *D* prepared abundantly before	1Chr 22:5	1732
D said to Solomon, My son, as for	1Chr 22:7	1732
D also commanded all the princes	1Chr 22:17	1732
So when *D* was old and full of days	1Chr 23:1	1732
instruments which I made, said *D*	1Chr 23:5	1732
D divided them into courses among	1Chr 23:6	1732
For *D* said, The LORD God of	1Chr 23:25	1732
For by the last words of *D* the	1Chr 23:27	1732
D distributed them, both Zadok of	1Chr 24:3	1732
in the presence of *D* the king	1Chr 24:31	1732
Moreover *D* and the captains of the	1Chr 25:1	1732
which *D* the king, and the chief	1Chr 26:26	1732
reign of *D* they were sought for	1Chr 26:31	1732
whom king *D* made rulers over the	1Chr 26:32	1732
Elihu, one of the brethren of *D*	1Chr 27:18	1732
But *D* took not the number of them	1Chr 27:23	1732
of the Chronicles of king *D*	1Chr 27:24	1732
D assembled all the princes of	1Chr 28:1	1732
Then *D* the king stood up upon his	1Chr 28:2	1732
Then *D* gave to Solomon his son	1Chr 28:11	1732
All this, said *D*, the LORD made	1Chr 28:19	1732
D said to Solomon his son, Be	1Chr 28:20	1732
Furthermore *D* the king said unto	1Chr 29:1	1732
D the king also rejoiced with	1Chr 29:9	1732
Wherefore *D* blessed the LORD	1Chr 29:10	1732
D said, Blessed be thou, LORD God	1Chr 29:10	1732
D said to all the congregation,	1Chr 29:20	1732
the son of *D* king the second time	1Chr 29:22	1732
as king instead of *D* his father	1Chr 29:23	1732
all the sons likewise of king *D*	1Chr 29:24	1732
Thus *D* the son of Jesse reigned	1Chr 29:26	1732
Now the acts of *D* the king	1Chr 29:29	1732
And Solomon the son of *D* was	2Chr 1:1	1732
But the ark of God had *D* brought	2Chr 1:4	1732
to the place which *D* had prepared	2Chr 1:4	1732
great mercy unto *D* my father	2Chr 1:8	1732
let thy promise unto *D* my father	2Chr 1:9	1732
thou didst deal with *D* my father	2Chr 2:3	1732
whom *D* my father did provide	2Chr 2:7	1732
who hath given to *D* the king a	2Chr 2:12	1732
men of my lord *D* thy father	2Chr 2:14	1732
D his father had numbered them	2Chr 2:17	1732
LORD appeared unto *D* his father	2Chr 3:1	1732
in the place that *D* had prepared	2Chr 3:1	1732
that *D* his father had dedicated	2Chr 5:1	1732
of the LORD out of the city of *D*	2Chr 5:2	1732
with his mouth to my father *D*	2Chr 6:4	1732
have chosen *D* to be over my	2Chr 6:6	1732
Now it was in the heart of *D* my	2Chr 6:7	1732
But the LORD said to *D* my father	2Chr 6:8	1732
up in the room of *D* my father	2Chr 6:10	1732
hast kept with thy servant *D* my	2Chr 6:15	1732
keep with thy servant *D* my father	2Chr 6:16	1732
hast spoken unto thy servant *D*	2Chr 6:17	1732
the mercies of *D* thy servant	2Chr 6:42	1732
which *D* the king had made to	2Chr 7:6	1732
when *D* praised by their ministry	2Chr 7:6	1732
that the LORD had shewed unto *D*	2Chr 7:10	1732
as *D* thy father walked, and do	2Chr 7:17	1732
have covenanted with *D* thy father	2Chr 7:18	1732
of *D* unto the house that he had	2Chr 8:11	1732
in the house of *D* king of Israel	2Chr 8:11	1732
to the order of *D* his father	2Chr 8:14	1732
for so had *D* the man of God	2Chr 8:14	1732
in the city of *D* his father	2Chr 9:31	1732
saying, What portion have we in *D*	2Chr 10:16	1732
your tents, O Israel, and now, *D*	2Chr 10:16	1732
the house of *D* unto this day	2Chr 10:19	1732
years they walked in the way of *D*	2Chr 11:17	1732
of Jerimoth the son of *D* to wife	2Chr 11:18	1732
and was buried in the city of *D*	2Chr 12:16	1732
kingdom over Israel to *D* for ever	2Chr 13:5	1732
servant of Solomon the son of *D*	2Chr 13:6	1732
LORD in the hand of the sons of *D*	2Chr 13:8	1732
they buried him in the city of *D*	2Chr 14:1	1732
made for himself in the city of *D*	2Chr 16:14	1732
in the first ways of his father *D*	2Chr 17:3	1732
with his fathers in the city of *D*	2Chr 21:1	1732
would not destroy the house of *D*	2Chr 21:7	1732
covenant that he had made with *D*	2Chr 21:7	1732
the LORD God of *D* thy father	2Chr 21:12	1732
they buried him in the city of *D*	2Chr 21:20	1732
LORD hath said of the sons of *D*	2Chr 23:3	1732
whom *D* had distributed in the	2Chr 23:18	1732
singing, as it was ordained by *D*	2Chr 23:18	1732
in the city of *D* among the kings	2Chr 24:16	1732
they buried him in the city of *D*	2Chr 24:25	1732
they buried him in the city of *D*	2Chr 27:9	1732
of the LORD, like *D* his father	2Chr 28:1	1732
to all that *D* his father had done	2Chr 29:2	1732
according to the commandment of *D*	2Chr 29:25	1732
stood with the instruments of *D*	2Chr 29:26	1732
ordained by *D* king of Israel	2Chr 29:27	1732
unto the LORD with the words of *D*	2Chr 29:30	1732
of *D* king of Israel there was not	2Chr 30:26	1732
repaired Millo in the city of *D*	2Chr 32:5	1732
to the west side of the city of *D*	2Chr 32:30	1732
the sepulchres of the sons of *D*	2Chr 32:33	1732
God, of which God had said to *D*	2Chr 33:7	1732
a wall without the city of *D*	2Chr 33:14	1732
in the ways of *D* his father	2Chr 34:2	1732
after the God of *D* his father	2Chr 34:3	1732
son of *D* king of Israel did build	2Chr 35:3	1732
the writing of *D* king of Israel	2Chr 35:4	1732
according to the commandment of *D*	2Chr 35:15	1732
the ordinance of *D* king of Israel	Ezr 3:10	1732
of the sons of *D*	Ezr 8:2	1732
Also of the Nethinims, whom *D*	Ezr 8:20	1732
that go down from the city of *D*	Neh 3:15	1732
over against the sepulchres of *D*	Neh 3:16	1732
commandment of *D* the man of God	Neh 12:24	1732
instruments of *D* the man of God	Neh 12:36	1732
up by the stairs of the city of *D*	Neh 12:37	1732
of the wall, above the house of *D*	Neh 12:37	1732
according to the commandment of *D*	Neh 12:45	1732
For in the days of *D* and Asaph of	Neh 12:46	1732
A Psalm of *D*, when he fled from	Ps 3:*t*	1732
on Neginoth, A Psalm of *D*	Ps 4:*t*	1732
upon Nehiloth, A Psalm of *D*	Ps 5:*t*	1732
upon Sheminith, A Psalm of *D*	Ps 6:*t*	1732
Shiggaion of *D*, which he sang	Ps 7:*t*	1732
upon Gittith, A Psalm of *D*	Ps 8:*t*	1732
upon Muth-labben, A Psalm of *D*	Ps 9:*t*	1732
the chief Musician, A Psalm of *D*	Ps 11:*t*	1732
upon Sheminith, A Psalm of *D*	Ps 12:*t*	1732
the chief Musician, A Psalm of *D*	Ps 13:*t*	1732
the chief Musician, A Psalm of *D*	Ps 14:*t*	1732
A Psalm of *D*	Ps 15:*t*	1732
Michtam of *D*	Ps 16:*t*	1732
A Prayer of *D*	Ps 17:*t*	1732
the chief Musician, A Psalm of *D*	Ps 18:*t*	1732
mercy to his anointed, to *D*	Ps 18:50	1732
the chief Musician, A Psalm of *D*	Ps 19:*t*	1732
the chief Musician, A Psalm of *D*	Ps 20:*t*	1732
the chief Musician, A Psalm of *D*	Ps 21:*t*	1732
Aijeleth Shahar, A Psalm of *D*	Ps 22:*t*	1732
A Psalm of *D*	Ps 23:*t*	1732
A Psalm of *D*	Ps 24:*t*	1732
A Psalm of *D*	Ps 25:*t*	1732
A Psalm of *D*	Ps 26:*t*	1732
A Psalm of *D*	Ps 27:*t*	1732
A Psalm of *D*	Ps 28:*t*	1732
A Psalm of *D*	Ps 29:*t*	1732
the dedication of the house of *D*	Ps 30:*t*	1732
the chief Musician, A Psalm of *D*	Ps 31:*t*	1732
A Psalm of *D*, A Maschil	Ps 32:*t*	1732
A Psalm of *D*, when he changed his	Ps 34:*t*	1732
A Psalm of *D*	Ps 35:*t*	1732
the chief Musician, A Psalm of *D*	Ps 36:*t*	1732
A Psalm of *D*	Ps 37:*t*	1732
A Psalm of *D*, to bring to	Ps 38:*t*	1732
even to Jeduthun, A Psalm of *D*	Ps 39:*t*	1732
the chief Musician, A Psalm of *D*	Ps 40:*t*	1732
the chief Musician, A Psalm of *D*	Ps 41:*t*	1732
the chief Musician, A Psalm of *D*	Ps 51:*t*	1732
Musician, Maschil, A Psalm of *D*	Ps 52:*t*	1732
D is come to the house of	Ps 52:*t*	1732
Mahalath, Maschil, A Psalm of *D*	Ps 53:*t*	1732
Neginoth, Maschil, A Psalm of *D*	Ps 54:*t*	1732
Doth not *D* hide himself with us	Ps 54:*t*	1732
Neginoth, Maschil, A Psalm of *D*	Ps 55:*t*	1732
a Michtam of *D*, when the	Ps 56:*t*	1732
Altaschith, Michtam of *D*	Ps 57:*t*	1732
Altaschith, Michtam of *D*	Ps 58:*t*	1732
Altaschith, Michtam of *D*	Ps 59:*t*	1732
upon Shushan-eduth, Michtam of *D*	Ps 60:*t*	1732
upon Neginah, A Psalm of *D*	Ps 61:*t*	1732
to Jeduthun, A Psalm of *D*	Ps 62:*t*	1732
A Psalm of *D*, when he was in the	Ps 63:*t*	1732
the chief Musician, A Psalm of *D*	Ps 64:*t*	1732
Musician, A Psalm and Song of *D*	Ps 65:*t*	1732
Musician, A Psalm or Song of *D*	Ps 68:*t*	1732
upon Shoshannim, A Psalm of *D*	Ps 69:*t*	1732
the chief Musician, A Psalm of *D*	Ps 70:*t*	1732
The prayers of *D* the son of Jesse	Ps 72:20	1732
He chose *D* also his servant, and	Ps 78:70	1732
A Prayer of *D*	Ps 86:*t*	1732
I have sworn unto *D* my servant	Ps 89:3	1732
I have found *D* my servant	Ps 89:20	1732
that I will not lie unto *D*	Ps 89:35	1732
thou swarest unto *D* in thy truth	Ps 89:49	1732
A Psalm of *D*	Ps 101:*t*	1732
A Psalm of *D*	Ps 103:*t*	1732
A Song or Psalm of *D*	Ps 108:*t*	1732
the chief Musician, A Psalm of *D*	Ps 109:*t*	1732
A Psalm of *D*	Ps 110:*t*	1732
A Song of degrees of *D*	Ps 122:*t*	1732
the thrones of the house of *D*	Ps 122:5	1732
A Song of degrees of *D*	Ps 124:*t*	1732
A Song of degrees of *D*	Ps 131:*t*	1732
Lord, remember *D*, and all his	Ps 132:1	1732
LORD hath sworn in truth unto *D*	Ps 132:11	1732
will I make the horn of *D* to bud	Ps 132:17	1732
A Song of degrees of *D*	Ps 133:*t*	1732
A Psalm of *D*	Ps 138:*t*	1732
the chief Musician, A Psalm of *D*	Ps 139:*t*	1732
the chief Musician, A Psalm of *D*	Ps 140:*t*	1732
A Psalm of *D*	Ps 141:*t*	1732
Maschil of *D*	Ps 142:*t*	1732
A Psalm of *D*	Ps 143:*t*	1732
A Psalm of *D*	Ps 144:*t*	1732
who delivereth *D* his servant from	Ps 144:10	1732
Proverbs of Solomon the son of *D*	Prov 1:1	1732
of the Preacher, the son of *D*	Eccl 1:1	1732
tower of *D* builded for an armoury	Song 4:4	1732
And it was told the house of *D*	Is 7:2	1732
said, Hear ye now, O house of *D*	Is 7:13	1732
be no end, upon the throne of *D*	Is 9:7	1732
in truth in the tabernacle of *D*	Is 16:5	1732
the breaches of the city of *D*	Is 22:9	1732
the key of the house of *D* will I	Is 22:22	1732
to Ariel, the city where *D* dwelt	Is 29:1	1732
the LORD, the God of *D* thy father	Is 38:5	1732
you, even the sure mercies of *D*	Is 55:3	1732
sitting upon the throne of *D*	Jer 17:25	1732
O house of *D*, thus saith the LORD	Jer 21:12	1732
that sittest upon the throne of *D*	Jer 22:2	1732
sitting upon the throne of *D*	Jer 22:4	1732
sitting upon the throne of *D*	Jer 22:30	1732
raise unto *D* a righteous Branch	Jer 23:5	1732
that sitteth upon the throne of *D*	Jer 29:16	1732
D their king, whom I will raise	Jer 30:9	1732
righteousness to grow up unto *D*	Jer 33:15	1732
D shall never want a man to sit	Jer 33:17	1732
be broken with *D* my servant	Jer 33:21	1732
multiply the seed of *D* my servant	Jer 33:22	1732
D my servant, so that I will not	Jer 33:26	1732
none to sit upon the throne of *D*	Jer 36:30	1732
feed them, even my servant *D*	Eze 34:23	1732
my servant *D* a prince among them	Eze 34:24	1732
D my servant shall be king over	Eze 37:24	1732
my servant *D* shall be their	Eze 37:25	1732
LORD their God, and *D* their king	Hos 3:5	1732
instruments of musick, like *D*	Amos 6:5	1732
tabernacle of *D* that is fallen	Amos 9:11	1732
that the glory of the house of *D*	Zec 12:7	1732
them at that day shall be as *D*	Zec 12:8	1732
the house of *D* shall be as God,	Zec 12:8	1732
I will pour upon the house of *D*	Zec 12:10	1732
family of the house of *D* apart	Zec 12:12	1732
fountain opened to the house of *D*	Zec 13:1	1732
of Jesus Christ, the son of *D*	Mt 1:1	*1138*
And Jesse begat *D* the king	Mt 1:6	*1138*
D the king begat Solomon of her	Mt 1:6	*1138*
to *D* are fourteen generations	Mt 1:17	*1138*
from *D* until the carrying away	Mt 1:17	*1138*
saying, Joseph, thou son of *D*	Mt 1:20	*1138*
crying, and saying, Thou son of *D*	Mt 9:27	*1138*
them, Have ye not read what *D* did	Mt 12:3	*1138*
and said, Is not this the son of *D*	Mt 12:23	*1138*
on me, O Lord, thou son of *D*	Mt 15:22	*1138*
on us, O Lord, thou son of *D*	Mt 20:30	*1138*
on us, O Lord, thou son of *D*	Mt 20:31	*1138*
saying, Hosanna to the son of *D*	Mt 21:9	*1138*
saying, Hosanna to the son of *D*	Mt 21:15	*1138*
They say unto him, The son of *D*	Mt 22:42	*1138*
How then doth *D* in spirit call	Mt 22:43	*1138*
If *D* then call him Lord	Mt 22:45	*1138*
Have ye never read what *D* did	Mk 2:25	*1138*
out, and say, Jesus, thou son of *D*	Mk 10:47	*1138*
more a great deal, Thou son of *D*	Mk 10:48	*1138*
be the kingdom of our father *D*	Mk 11:10	*1138*
that Christ is the son of *D*	Mk 12:35	*1138*
For *D* himself said by the Holy	Mk 12:36	*1138*
D therefore himself calleth him	Mk 12:37	*1138*
was Joseph, of the house of *D*	Lk 1:27	*1138*
him the throne of his father *D*	Lk 1:32	*1138*
us in the house of his servant *D*	Lk 1:69	*1138*
into Judaea, unto the city of *D*	Lk 2:4	*1138*
was of the house and lineage of *D*	Lk 2:4	*1138*
day in the city of *D* a Saviour	Lk 2:11	*1138*
of Nathan, which was the son of *D*	Lk 3:31	*1138*
read so much as this, what *D* did	Lk 6:3	*1138*
saying, Jesus, thou son of *D*	Lk 18:38	*1138*
so much the more, Thou son of *D*	Lk 18:39	*1138*
D himself saith in the book of	Lk 20:42	*1138*
D therefore calleth him Lord, how	Lk 20:44	*1138*
Christ cometh of the seed of *D*	Jn 7:42	*1138*
town of Bethlehem, where *D* was	Jn 7:42	*1138*
D spake before concerning Judas	Acts 1:16	*1138*
For *D* speaketh concerning him, I	Acts 2:25	*1138*
speak unto you of the patriarch *D*	Acts 2:29	*1138*
For *D* is not ascended into the	Acts 2:34	*1138*
mouth of thy servant *D* hast said	Acts 4:25	*1138*
our fathers, unto the days of *D*	Acts 7:45	*1138*
up unto them *D* to be their king	Acts 13:22	*1138*
I have found *D* the son of Jesse,	Acts 13:22	*1138*
give you the sure mercies of *D*	Acts 13:34	*1138*
For *D*, after he had served his	Acts 13:36	*1138*
build again the tabernacle of *D*	Acts 15:16	*1138*
seed of *D* according to the flesh	Rom 1:3	*1138*
Even as *D* also describeth the	Rom 4:6	*1138*
D saith, Let their table be made	Rom 11:9	*1138*
of *D* was raised from the dead	2Ti 2:8	*1138*
a certain day, saying in *D*	Heb 4:7	*1138*
of *D* also, and Samuel, and of the	Heb 11:32	*1138*
true, he that hath the key of *D*	Rev 3:7	*1138*
the tribe of Juda, the Root of *D*	Rev 5:5	*1138*
am the root and the offspring of *D*	Rev 22:16	*1138*

DAVID'S

Saul became *D* enemy continually	1Sa 18:29	1732
also sent messengers unto *D* house	1Sa 19:11	1732
Michal *D* wife told him, saying,	1Sa 19:11	1732
it at the hand of *D* enemies	1Sa 20:16	1732
Saul's side, and *D* place was empty	1Sa 20:25	1732
the month, that *D* place was empty	1Sa 20:27	1732
D men said unto him, Behold, we	1Sa 23:3	1732
that *D* heart smote him, because	1Sa 24:5	1732
when *D* young men came, they spake	1Sa 25:9	1732
And Nabal answered *D* servants	1Sa 25:10	1732
So *D* young men turned their way,	1Sa 25:12	1732
D wife, to Phalti the son of	1Sa 25:44	1732
And Saul knew *D* voice, and said, Is	1Sa 26:17	1732
D two wives were taken captives,	1Sa 30:5	1732
cattle, and said, This is *D* spoil	1Sa 30:20	1732
there lacked of *D* servants	2Sa 2:30	1732
sixth, Ithream, by Eglah *D* wife	2Sa 3:5	1732
blind, that are hated of *D* soul	2Sa 5:8	1732
so the Moabites became *D* servants	2Sa 8:2	1732
they of Edom became *D* servants	2Sa 8:14	1732
and *D* sons were chief rulers	2Sa 8:18	1732

D servants came into the land of 2Sa 10:2 1732
Wherefore Hanun took *D* servants 2Sa 10:4 1732
D anger was greatly kindled 2Sa 12:5 1732
and it was set on *D* head 2Sa 12:30 1732
the son of Shimeah *D* brother 2Sa 13:3 1732
the son of Shimeah *D* brother 2Sa 13:32 1732
D counsellor, from his city, even 2Sa 15:12 1732
So Hushai *D* friend came into the 2Sa 15:37 1732
D friend, was come unto Absalom, 2Sa 16:16 1732
all *D* men with him, over Jordan 2Sa 19:41 1732
D heart smote him after that he 2Sa 24:10 1732
the prophet Gad, *D* seer, saying, 2Sa 24:11 1732
Solomon to ride upon king *D* mule 1Kin 1:38 1732
one tribe for my servant *D* sake 1Kin 11:32 1732
Nevertheless for *D* sake did the 1Kin 15:4 1732
did the priest give king *D* spears 2Kin 11:10 1732
sake, and for my servant *D* sake 2Kin 19:34 1732
sake, and for my servant *D* sake 2Kin 20:6 1732
and the Moabites became *D* servants 1Chr 18:2 1732
and the Syrians became *D* servants 1Chr 18:6 1732
the Edomites became *D* servants 1Chr 18:13 1732
Wherefore Hanun took *D* servants 1Chr 19:4 1732
and it was set upon *D* head 1Chr 20:2 1732
son of Shimea *D* brother slew him 1Chr 20:7 1732
spake unto Gad, *D* seer, saying, 1Chr 21:9 1732
of the substance which was king *D* 1Chr 27:31 1732
Also Jonathan *D* uncle was a 1Chr 27:32 1732
and shields, that had been king *D* 2Chr 23:9 1732
For thy servant *D* sake turn not Ps 132:10 1732
D Psalm of praise Ps 145:*t* 1732
sake, and for my servant *D* sake Is 37:35 1732
the kings that sit upon *D* throne Jer 13:13 1732
How say they that Christ is *D* son Lk 20:41 *1138*

DAWN
as it began to *d* toward the first Mt 28:1 *2020*
in a dark place, until the day *d* 2Pet 1:19 *1306*

DAWNING
rose early about the *d* of the day Josh 6:15 5927
the woman in the *d* of the day Judg 19:26 6437
let it see the *d* of the day Job 3:9 6079
to and fro unto the *d* of the day Job 7:4 5399
I prevented the *d* of the morning Ps 119:147 5399

DAY
And God called the light *D* Gen 1:5 3117
and the morning were the first *d* Gen 1:5 3117
and the morning were the second *d* Gen 1:8 3117
and the morning were the third *d* Gen 1:13 3117
to divide the *d* from the night Gen 1:14 3117
the greater light to rule the *d* Gen 1:16 3117
And to rule over the *d* and over the Gen 1:18 3117
and the morning were the fourth *d* Gen 1:19 3117
and the morning were the fifth *d* Gen 1:23 3117
and the morning were the sixth *d* Gen 1:31 3117
on the seventh *d* God ended his Gen 2:2 3117
he rested on the seventh *d* from Gen 2:2 3117
And God blessed the seventh *d* Gen 2:3 3117
in the *d* that the LORD God made Gen 2:4 3117
for in the *d* that thou eatest Gen 2:17 3117
know that in the *d* ye eat thereof Gen 3:5 3117
the garden in the cool of the *d* Gen 3:8 3117
this *d* from the face of the earth Gen 4:14 3117
In the *d* that God created man, in Gen 5:1 3117
in the *d* when they were created Gen 5:2 3117
the seventeenth *d* of the month Gen 7:11 3117
the same *d* were all the fountains Gen 7:11 3117
In the selfsame *d* entered Noah Gen 7:13 3117
on the seventeenth *d* of the month Gen 8:4 3117
on the first *d* of the month Gen 8:5 3117
the first *d* of the month, the Gen 8:13 3117
twentieth *d* of the month, was the Gen 8:14 3117
heat, and summer and winter, and *d* Gen 8:22 3117
In the same *d* the LORD made a Gen 15:18 3117
their foreskin in the selfsame *d* Gen 17:23 3117
In the selfsame *d* was Abraham Gen 17:26 3117
tent door in the heat of the *d* Gen 18:1 3117
of the Moabites unto this *d* Gen 19:37 3117
the children of Ammon unto this *d* Gen 19:38 3117
the same *d* that Isaac was weaned Gen 21:8 3117
yet heard I of it, but to *d* Gen 21:26 3117
Then on the third *d* Abraham Gen 22:4 3117
as it is said to this *d*, In the Gen 22:14 3117
thee, send me good speed this *d* Gen 24:12 3117
I came this *d* unto the well, and Gen 24:42 3117
Sell me this *d* thy birthright Gen 25:31 3117
And Jacob said, Swear to me this *d* Gen 25:33 3117
And it came to pass the same *d* Gen 26:32 3117
city is Beer-sheba unto this *d* Gen 26:33 3117
old, I know not the *d* of my death Gen 27:2 3117
also of you both in one *d* Gen 27:45 3117
And he said, Lo, it is yet high *d* Gen 29:7 3117
pass through all thy flock to *d* Gen 30:32 3117
he removed that *d* the he goats Gen 30:35 3117
the third *d* that Jacob was fled Gen 31:22 3117
require it, whether stolen by *d* Gen 31:39 3117
in the *d* the drought consumed me, Gen 31:40 3117
what can I do this *d* unto these Gen 31:43 3117
witness between me and thee this *d* Gen 31:48 3117
him until the breaking of the *d* Gen 32:24 7837
Let me go, for the *d* breaketh Gen 32:26 7837
hollow of the thigh, unto this *d* Gen 32:32 3117
men should overdrive them one *d* Gen 33:13 3117
that *d* on his way unto Seir Gen 33:16 3117
And it came to pass on the third *d* Gen 34:25 3117
me in the *d* of my distress Gen 35:3 3117
of Rachel's grave unto this *d* Gen 35:20 3117
as she spake to Joseph *d* by *d* Gen 39:10 3117
Wherefore look ye so sadly to *d* Gen 40:7 3117
And it came to pass the third *d* Gen 40:20 3117
I do remember my faults this *d* Gen 41:9 3117
is this *d* with our father Gen 42:13 3117
Joseph said unto them the third *d* Gen 42:18 3117
the youngest is this *d* with our Gen 42:32 3117
Behold, I have bought you this *d* Gen 47:23 3117
the land of Egypt unto this *d* Gen 47:26 3117
me all my life long unto this *d* Gen 48:15 3117
And he blessed them that *d* Gen 48:20 3117
to bring to pass, as it is this *d* Gen 50:20 3117
And when he went out the second *d* Ex 2:13 3117
it that ye are come so soon to *d* Ex 2:18 3117
Pharaoh commanded the same *d* the Ex 5:6 3117
brick both yesterday and to *d* Ex 5:14 3117
it came to pass on the *d* when the Ex 6:28 3117
in that *d* the land of Goshen Ex 8:22 3117
since the *d* that they were upon Ex 10:6 3117
were upon the earth unto this *d* Ex 10:6 3117
wind upon the land all that *d* Ex 10:13 3117
for in that *d* thou seest my face Ex 10:28 3117
In the tenth *d* of this month they Ex 12:3
fourteenth *d* of the same month Ex 12:6 3117
this *d* shall be unto you for a Ex 12:14 3117
even the first *d* ye shall put Ex 12:15 3117
the first *d* until the seventh *d* Ex 12:15 3117
in the first *d* there shall be an Ex 12:16 3117
in the seventh *d* there shall be Ex 12:16 3117
for in this selfsame *d* have I Ex 12:17 3117
this *d* in your generations by an Ex 12:17 3117
on the fourteenth *d* of the month Ex 12:18 3117
twentieth *d* of the month at even Ex 12:18 3117
the selfsame *d* it came to pass Ex 12:41 3117
And it came to pass the selfsame *d* Ex 12:51 3117
unto the people, Remember this *d* Ex 13:3 3117
This *d* came ye out in the month Ex 13:4 3117
in the seventh *d* shall be a feast Ex 13:6 3117
thou shalt shew thy son in that *d* Ex 13:8 3117
them by *d* in a pillar of a cloud Ex 13:21 3119
to go by *d* and night Ex 13:21 3119
away the pillar of the cloud by *d* Ex 13:22 3119
which he will shew to you to *d* Ex 14:13 3117
Egyptians whom ye have seen to *d* Ex 14:13 3117
that *d* out of the hand of the Ex 14:30 3117
on the fifteenth *d* of the second Ex 16:1 3117
and gather a certain rate every *d* Ex 16:4 3117
that on the sixth *d* they shall Ex 16:5 3117
that on the sixth *d* they gathered Ex 16:22 3117
bake that which ye will bake to *d* Ex 16:23
And Moses said, Eat that to *d* Ex 16:25 3117
for to *d* is a sabbath unto the Ex 16:25 3117
to *d* ye shall not find it in the Ex 16:25 3117
but on the seventh *d*, which is Ex 16:26 3117
on the seventh *d* for to gather Ex 16:27 3117
the sixth *d* the bread of two days Ex 16:29 3117
out of his place on the seventh *d* Ex 16:29 3117
people rested on the seventh *d* Ex 16:30 3117
the same *d* came they into the Ex 19:1 3117
the people, and sanctify them to *d* Ex 19:10 3117
And be ready against the third *d* Ex 19:11 3117
for the third *d* the LORD will Ex 19:11 3117
Be ready against the third *d* Ex 19:15 3117
on the third *d* in the morning Ex 19:16 3117
Remember the sabbath *d*, to keep Ex 20:8 3117
But the seventh *d* is the sabbath Ex 20:10 3117
them is, and rested the seventh *d* Ex 20:11 3117
the LORD blessed the sabbath *d* Ex 20:11 3117
if he continue a *d* or two Ex 21:21 3117
on the eighth *d* thou shalt give Ex 22:30 3117
on the seventh *d* thou shalt rest Ex 23:12 3117
the seventh *d* he called unto Ex 24:16 3117
thou shalt offer every *d* a Ex 29:36 3117
first year *d* by *d* continually Ex 29:38 3117
doeth any work in the sabbath *d* Ex 31:15 3117
and on the seventh *d* he rested Ex 31:17 3117
that *d* about three thousand men Ex 32:28 3117
yourselves to *d* to the LORD Ex 32:29 3117
bestow upon you a blessing this *d* Ex 32:29 3117
nevertheless in the *d* when I Ex 32:34 3117
that which I command thee this *d* Ex 34:11 3117
on the seventh *d* thou shalt rest Ex 34:21 3117
but on the seventh *d* there shall Ex 35:2 3117
there shall be to you an holy *d* Ex 35:2
habitations upon the sabbath *d* Ex 35:3 3117
On the first *d* of the first month Ex 40:2 3117
year, on the first *d* of the month Ex 40:17
till the *d* that it was taken up Ex 40:37 3117
LORD was upon the tabernacle by *d* Ex 40:38 3119
in the *d* of his trespass offering Lev 6:5 3119
LORD in the *d* when he is anointed Lev 6:20 3119
the same *d* that it is offered Lev 7:15 3119
it shall be eaten the same *d* that Lev 7:16 3119
third *d* shall be burnt with fire Lev 7:17 3119
be eaten at all on the third *d* Lev 7:18 3119
in the *d* when he presented them Lev 7:35 3119
in the *d* that he anointed them, Lev 7:36 3119
in the *d* that he commanded the Lev 7:38 3119
As he hath done this *d*, so the Lev 8:34 3117
tabernacle of the congregation *d* Lev 8:35 3119
it came to pass on the eighth *d* Lev 9:1 3117
for to *d* the LORD will appear Lev 9:4 3117
this *d* have they offered their Lev 10:19 3117
I had eaten the sin offering to *d* Lev 10:19 3117
in the eighth *d* the flesh of his Lev 12:3 3117
shall look on him the seventh *d* Lev 13:5 3117
look on him again the seventh *d* Lev 13:6 3117
shall look upon him the seventh *d* Lev 13:27 3117
in the seventh *d* the priest shall Lev 13:32 3117
in the seventh *d* the priest shall Lev 13:34 3117
on the plague on the seventh *d* Lev 13:51 3117
leper in the *d* of his cleansing Lev 14:2 3117
But it shall be on the seventh *d* Lev 14:9 3117
on the eighth *d* he shall take two Lev 14:10 3117
d for his cleansing unto the Lev 14:23 3117
shall come again the seventh *d* Lev 14:39 3117
on the eighth *d* he shall take to Lev 15:14 3117
on the eighth *d* she shall take Lev 15:29 3117
on the tenth *d* of the month Lev 16:29
For on that *d* shall the priest Lev 16:30 3117
be eaten the same *d* ye offer it Lev 19:6 3117
if ought remain until the third *d* Lev 19:6 3117
it be eaten at all on the third *d* Lev 19:7 3117
and from the eighth *d* and Lev 22:27 3117
it and her young both in one *d* Lev 22:28 3117
On the same *d* it shall be eaten Lev 22:30 3117
but the seventh *d* is the sabbath Lev 23:3 3117
In the fourteenth *d* of the first Lev 23:5
on the fifteenth *d* of the same Lev 23:6 3117
In the first *d* ye shall have an Lev 23:7 3117
in the seventh *d* is an holy Lev 23:8 3117
ye shall offer that *d* when ye Lev 23:12 3117
until the selfsame *d* that ye have Lev 23:14 3117
from the *d* that ye brought the Lev 23:15 3117
shall proclaim on the selfsame *d* Lev 23:21 3117
in the first *d* of the month Lev 23:24
Also on the tenth *d* of this Lev 23:27
there shall be a *d* of atonement Lev 23:27 3117
shall do no work in that same *d* Lev 23:28 3117
for it is a *d* of atonement, to Lev 23:28 3117
not be afflicted in that same *d* Lev 23:29 3117
doeth any work in that same *d* Lev 23:30 3117
in the ninth *d* of the month at Lev 23:32
The fifteenth *d* of this seventh Lev 23:34 3117
On the first *d* shall be an holy Lev 23:35 3117
on the eighth *d* shall be an holy Lev 23:36 3117
offerings, every thing upon his *d* Lev 23:37 3117
fifteenth *d* of the seventh month Lev 23:39 3117
on the first *d* shall be a sabbath Lev 23:39 3117
on the eighth *d* shall be a Lev 23:39 3117
d the boughs of goodly trees Lev 23:40 3117
the tenth *d* of the seventh month Lev 25:9
in the *d* of atonement shall ye Lev 25:9 3117
give thine estimation in that *d* Lev 27:23 3117
on the first *d* of the second Num 1:1
the first *d* of the second month Num 1:18
Moses in the *d* that the LORD Num 3:1 3117
for on the *d* that I smote all the Num 3:13 3117
head in the *d* of his cleansing Num 6:9 3117
on the seventh *d* shall he shave Num 6:9 3117
on the eighth *d* he shall bring Num 6:10 3117
shall hallow his head that same *d* Num 6:11 3117
it came to pass on the *d* that Num 7:1 3117
in the *d* that it was anointed Num 7:10 3117
offering, each prince on his *d* Num 7:11 3117
first *d* was Nahshon the son of Num 7:12 3117
On the second *d* Nethaneel the son Num 7:18 3117
On the third *d* Eliab the son of Num 7:24 3117
On the fourth *d* Elizur the son of Num 7:30 3117
On the fifth *d* Shelumiel the son Num 7:36 3117
On the sixth *d* Eliasaph the son Num 7:42 3117
On the seventh *d* Elishama the son Num 7:48 3117
On the eighth *d* offered Gamaliel Num 7:54 3117
On the ninth *d* Abidan the son of Num 7:60 3117
On the tenth *d* Ahiezer the son of Num 7:66 3117
On the eleventh *d* Pagiel the son Num 7:72 3117
On the twelfth *d* Ahira the son of Num 7:78 3117
in the *d* when it was anointed, by Num 7:84 3117
on the *d* that I smote every Num 8:17 3117
In the fourteenth *d* of this month Num 9:3 3117
d of the first month at even in Num 9:5 3117
not keep the passover on that *d* Num 9:6 3117
Moses and before Aaron on that *d* Num 9:6 3117
The fourteenth *d* of the second Num 9:11 3117
on the *d* that the tabernacle was Num 9:15 3117
the cloud covered it by *d* Num 9:16
whether it was by *d* or by night Num 9:21 3119
Also in the *d* of your gladness, Num 10:10 3117
twentieth *d* of the second month Num 10:11
of the LORD was upon them by *d* Num 10:34 3119
Ye shall not eat one *d*, nor two Num 11:19 3117
And the people stood up all that *d* Num 11:32 3117
all that night, and all the next *d* Num 11:32 3117
each *d* for a year, shall ye bear Num 14:34 3117
Moses, from the *d* that the LORD Num 15:23 3117
sticks upon the sabbath *d* Num 15:32 3117
himself with it on the third *d* Num 19:12 3117
on the seventh *d* he shall be Num 19:12 3117
he purify not himself the third *d* Num 19:12 3117
then the seventh *d* he shall not Num 19:12 3117
third *d*, and on the seventh *d* Num 19:19 3117
on the seventh *d* he shall purify Num 19:19 3117
since I was thine unto this *d* Num 22:30 3117
which was slain in the *d* of the Num 25:18 3117
first year without spot *d* by *d* Num 28:3 3117
on the sabbath *d* two lambs of the Num 28:9 3117
in the fourteenth *d* of the first Num 28:16 3117
in the fifteenth *d* of this month Num 28:17 3117
In the first *d* shall be an holy Num 28:18 3117
on the seventh *d* ye shall have an Num 28:25 3117
Also in the *d* of the firstfruits, Num 28:26 3117
on the first *d* of the month Num 29:1
it is a *d* of blowing the trumpets Num 29:1 3117
ye shall have on the tenth *d* of Num 29:7
on the fifteenth *d* of the seventh Num 29:12 3117
on the second *d* ye shall offer Num 29:17 3117
on the third *d* eleven bullocks, Num 29:20 3117
And on the fourth *d* ten bullocks Num 29:23 3117
on the fifth *d* nine bullocks, two Num 29:26 3117
on the sixth *d* eight bullocks, Num 29:29 3117
on the seventh *d* seven bullocks Num 29:32 3117
On the eighth *d* ye shall have a Num 29:35 3117
her in the *d* that he heareth Num 30:5 3117
at her in the *d* that he heard it Num 30:7 3117
her on the *d* that he heard it Num 30:8 3117
them void on the *d* he heard them Num 30:12 3117
his peace at her from *d* to *d* Num 30:14 3117
her in the *d* that he heard them Num 30:14 3117
third *d*, and on the seventh *d* Num 31:19 3117
your clothes on the seventh *d* Num 31:24 3117
on the fifteenth *d* of the first Num 33:3 3117
in the first *d* of the fifth month Num 33:38
on the first *d* of the month Deut 1:3
ye are this *d* as the stars of Deut 1:10 3117
ye should go, and in a cloud by *d* Deut 1:33 3119

D

which in that *d* had no knowledge	Deut 1:39	3117
Ar, the coast of Moab, this *d*	Deut 2:18	3117
in their stead even unto this *d*	Deut 2:22	3117
This *d* will I begin to put the	Deut 2:25	3117
thy hand, as appeareth this *d*	Deut 2:30	3117
Bashan-havoth-jair, unto this *d*	Deut 3:14	3117
are alive every one of you this *d*	Deut 4:4	3117
which I set before you this *d*	Deut 4:8	3117
Specially the *d* that thou	Deut 4:10	3117
no manner of similitude on the *d*	Deut 4:15	3117
of inheritance, as ye are this *d*	Deut 4:20	3117
to witness against you this *d*	Deut 4:26	3117
since the *d* that God created man	Deut 4:32	3117
an inheritance, as it is this *d*	Deut 4:38	3117
Know therefore this *d*, and	Deut 4:39	3117
which I command thee this *d*	Deut 4:40	3117
which I speak in your ears this *d*	Deut 5:1	3117
are all of us here alive this *d*	Deut 5:3	3117
Keep the sabbath *d* to sanctify it	Deut 5:12	3117
But the seventh *d* is the sabbath	Deut 5:14	3117
thee to keep the sabbath *d*	Deut 5:15	3117
we have seen this *d* that God doth	Deut 5:24	3117
which I command thee this *d*	Deut 6:6	3117
us alive, as it is at this *d*	Deut 6:24	3117
which I command thee this *d*	Deut 7:11	3117
this *d* shall ye observe to do	Deut 8:1	3117
which I command thee this *d*	Deut 8:11	3117
unto thy fathers, as it is this *d*	Deut 8:18	3117
I testify against you this *d* that	Deut 8:19	3117
art to pass over Jordan this *d*	Deut 9:1	3117
Understand therefore this *d*	Deut 9:3	3117
from the *d* that thou didst depart	Deut 9:7	3117
the fire in the *d* of the assembly	Deut 9:10	3117
LORD from the *d* that I knew you	Deut 9:24	3117
the fire in the *d* of the assembly	Deut 10:4	3117
to bless in his name, unto this *d*	Deut 10:8	3117
command thee this *d* for thy good	Deut 10:13	3117
above all people, as it is this *d*	Deut 10:15	3117
And know ye this *d*	Deut 11:2	3117
hath destroyed them unto this *d*	Deut 11:4	3117
which I command you this *d*	Deut 11:8	3117
which I command you this *d*	Deut 11:13	3117
set before you this *d* a blessing	Deut 11:26	3117
God, which I command you this *d*	Deut 11:27	3117
way which I command you this *d*	Deut 11:28	3117
which I set before you this *d*	Deut 11:32	3117
the things that we do here this *d*	Deut 12:8	3117
which I command thee this *d*	Deut 13:18	3117
which I command thee this *d*	Deut 15:5	3117
I command thee this thing to *d*	Deut 15:15	3117
d when thou camest forth out of	Deut 16:3	3117
sacrificedst the first *d* at even	Deut 16:4	3117
on the seventh *d* shall be a	Deut 16:8	3117
in Horeb in the *d* of the assembly	Deut 18:16	3117
them, which I command thee this *d*	Deut 19:9	3117
ye approach this *d* unto battle	Deut 20:3	3117
shalt in any wise bury him that *d*	Deut 21:23	3117
At his *d* thou shalt give him his	Deut 24:15	3117
I profess this *d* unto the LORD	Deut 26:3	3117
This *d* the LORD thy God hath	Deut 26:16	3117
the LORD this *d* to be thy God	Deut 26:17	3117
this *d* to be his peculiar people	Deut 26:18	3117
which I command you this *d*	Deut 27:1	3117
it shall be on the *d* when ye	Deut 27:2	3117
which I command you this *d*	Deut 27:4	3117
this *d* thou art become the people	Deut 27:9	3117
which I command thee this *d*	Deut 27:10	3117
charged the people the same *d*	Deut 27:11	3117
which I command thee this *d*	Deut 28:1	3117
God, which I command thee this *d*	Deut 28:13	3117
words which I command thee this *d*	Deut 28:14	3117
which I command thee this *d*	Deut 28:15	3117
longing for them all the *d* long	Deut 28:32	3117
and thou shalt fear *d* and night, and	Deut 28:66	3119
see, and ears to hear, unto this *d*	Deut 29:4	3117
Ye stand this *d* all of you before	Deut 29:10	3117
thy God maketh with thee this *d*	Deut 29:12	3117
to *d* for a people unto himself	Deut 29:13	3117
us this *d* before the LORD our God	Deut 29:15	3117
that is not here with us this *d*	Deut 29:15	3117
away this *d* from the LORD our God	Deut 29:18	3117
another land, as it is this *d*	Deut 29:28	3117
to all that I command thee this *d*	Deut 30:2	3117
which I command thee this *d*	Deut 30:8	3117
which I command thee this *d*	Deut 30:11	3117
have set before thee this *d* life	Deut 30:15	3117
this *d* to love the LORD thy God	Deut 30:16	3117
I denounce unto you this *d*	Deut 30:18	3117
to record this *d* against you	Deut 30:19	3117
and twenty years old this *d*	Deut 31:2	3117
be kindled against them in that *d*	Deut 31:17	3117
so that they will say in that *d*	Deut 31:17	3117
surely hide my face in that *d* for	Deut 31:18	3117
wrote this song the same *d*	Deut 31:22	3117
I am yet alive with you this *d*	Deut 31:27	3117
for the *d* of their calamity is at	Deut 32:35	3117
which I testify among you this *d*	Deut 32:46	3117
spake unto Moses that selfsame *d*	Deut 32:48	3117
shall cover him all the *d* long	Deut 33:12	3117
of his sepulchre unto this *d*	Deut 34:6	3117
but thou shalt meditate therein *d*	Josh 1:8	3119
This *d* will I begin to magnify	Josh 3:7	3117
and they are there unto this *d*	Josh 4:9	3117
On that *d* the LORD magnified	Josh 4:14	3117
on the tenth *d* of the first month	Josh 4:19	
This *d* have I rolled away the	Josh 5:9	3117
is called Gilgal unto this *d*	Josh 5:9	3117
d of the month at even in the	Josh 5:10	3117
and parched corn in the selfsame *d*	Josh 5:11	3117
the seventh *d* ye shall compass	Josh 6:4	3117
until the *d* I bid you shout	Josh 6:10	3117
the second *d* they compassed the	Josh 6:14	3117
it came to pass on the seventh *d*	Josh 6:15	3117
early about the dawning of the *d*	Josh 6:15	7837
only on that *d* they compassed the	Josh 6:15	3117
in Israel even unto this *d*	Josh 6:25	3117
LORD shall trouble thee this *d*	Josh 7:25	3117
great heap of stones unto this *d*	Josh 7:26	3117
The valley of Achor, unto this *d*	Josh 7:26	3117
it was, that all that fell that *d*	Josh 8:25	3117
even a desolation unto this *d*	Josh 8:28	3117
that remaineth unto this *d*	Josh 8:29	3117
out of our houses on the *d* we	Josh 9:12	3117
unto their cities on the third *d*	Josh 9:17	3117
made them that *d* hewers of wood	Josh 9:27	3117
of the LORD, even unto this *d*	Josh 9:27	3117
d when the LORD delivered up the	Josh 10:12	3117
not to go down about a whole *d*	Josh 10:13	3117
there was no *d* like that before	Josh 10:14	3117
which remain until this very *d*	Josh 10:27	3117
that *d* Joshua took Makkedah, and	Josh 10:28	3117
which took it on the second *d*	Josh 10:32	3117
And they took it on that *d*	Josh 10:35	3117
he utterly destroyed that *d*	Josh 10:35	3117
among the Israelites until this *d*	Josh 13:13	3117
And Moses sware on that *d*, saying,	Josh 14:9	3117
and now, lo, I am this *d* fourscore	Josh 14:10	3117
As yet I am as strong this *d* as I	Josh 14:11	3117
I was in the *d* that Moses sent me	Josh 14:11	3117
whereof the LORD spake in that *d*	Josh 14:12	3117
for thou heardest in that *d* how	Josh 14:12	3117
the Kenezite unto this *d*, because	Josh 14:14	3117
of Judah at Jerusalem unto this *d*	Josh 15:63	3117
among the Ephraimites unto this *d*	Josh 16:10	3117
these many days unto this *d*	Josh 22:3	3117
Israel, to turn away this *d* from	Josh 22:16	3117
rebel this *d* against the LORD	Josh 22:16	3117
we are not cleansed until this *d*	Josh 22:17	3117
this *d* from following the LORD	Josh 22:18	3117
ye rebel to *d* against the LORD	Josh 22:18	3117
the LORD, (save us not this *d*	Josh 22:22	3117
turn this *d* from following the	Josh 22:29	3117
This *d* we perceive that the LORD	Josh 22:31	3117
God, as ye have done unto this *d*	Josh 23:8	3117
to stand before you unto this *d*	Josh 23:9	3117
this *d* I am going the way of all	Josh 23:14	3117
choose you this *d* whom ye will	Josh 24:15	3117
a covenant with the people that *d*	Josh 24:25	3117
Benjamin in Jerusalem unto this *d*	Judg 1:21	3117
is the name thereof unto this *d*	Judg 1:26	3117
that *d* under the hand of Israel	Judg 3:30	3117
for this is the *d* in which the	Judg 4:14	3117
So God subdued on that *d* Jabin	Judg 4:23	3117
the son of Abinoam on that *d*	Judg 5:1	3117
unto this *d* it is yet in Ophrah	Judg 6:24	3117
that he could not do it by *d*	Judg 6:27	3119
Therefore on that *d* he called him	Judg 6:32	3117
against my father's house this *d*	Judg 9:18	3117
and with his house this *d*, then	Judg 9:19	3117
against the city all that *d*	Judg 9:45	3117
called Havoth-jair unto this *d*	Judg 10:4	3117
us only, we pray thee, this *d*	Judg 10:15	3117
LORD the Judge be judge this *d*	Judg 11:27	3117
are ye come up unto me this *d*	Judg 12:3	3117
the womb to the *d* of his death	Judg 13:7	3117
me, that came unto me the other *d*	Judg 13:10	3117
it came to pass on the seventh *d*	Judg 14:15	3117
it came to pass on the seventh *d*	Judg 14:17	3117
d before the sun went down	Judg 14:18	3117
which is in Lehi unto this *d*	Judg 15:19	3117
In the morning, when it is *d*	Judg 16:2	1242
for unto that *d* all their	Judg 18:1	3117
place Mahaneh-dan unto this *d*	Judg 18:12	3117
d of the captivity of the land	Judg 18:30	3117
it came to pass on the fourth *d*	Judg 19:5	3117
morning on the fifth *d* to depart	Judg 19:8	3117
now the *d* draweth toward evening,	Judg 19:9	3117
the *d* groweth to an end, lodge	Judg 19:9	3117
by Jebus, the *d* was far spent	Judg 19:11	3117
when the *d* began to spring, they	Judg 19:25	7837
the woman in the dawning of the *d*	Judg 19:26	1242
the *d* that the children of Israel	Judg 19:30	3117
of the land of Egypt unto this *d*	Judg 19:30	3117
of the Israelites that *d* twenty	Judg 20:21	3117
themselves in array the first *d*	Judg 20:22	3117
children of Benjamin the second *d*	Judg 20:24	3117
them out of Gibeah the second *d*	Judg 20:25	3117
LORD, and fasted that *d* until even	Judg 20:26	3117
of Benjamin on the third *d*	Judg 20:30	3117
of the Benjamites that *d* twenty	Judg 20:35	3117
that *d* of Benjamin were twenty	Judg 20:46	3117
that there should be to *d* one	Judg 21:3	3117
tribe cut off from Israel this *d*	Judg 21:6	3117
her, Where hast thou gleaned to *d*	Ruth 2:19	3117
with whom I wrought to *d* is Boaz	Ruth 2:19	3117
he have finished the thing this *d*	Ruth 3:18	3117
What *d* thou buyest the field of	Ruth 4:5	3117
people, Ye are witnesses this *d*	Ruth 4:9	3117
ye are witnesses this *d*	Ruth 4:10	3117
thee this *d* without a kinsman	Ruth 4:14	3117
in one *d* they shall die both of	1Sa 2:34	3117
In that *d* I will perform against	1Sa 3:12	3117
us to *d* before the Philistines	1Sa 4:3	3117
the same *d* with his clothes rent	1Sa 4:12	3117
I fled to *d* out of the army	1Sa 4:16	3117
of Dagon in Ashdod unto this *d*	1Sa 5:5	3117
the same *d* unto the LORD	1Sa 6:15	3117
they returned to Ekron the same *d*	1Sa 6:16	3117
this *d* in the field of Joshua	1Sa 6:18	3117
the LORD, and fasted on that *d*	1Sa 7:6	3117
on that *d* upon the Philistines	1Sa 7:10	3117
d that I brought them up out of	1Sa 8:8	3117
up out of Egypt even unto this *d*	1Sa 8:8	3117
ye shall cry out in that *d*	1Sa 8:18	3117
LORD will not hear you in that *d*	1Sa 8:18	3117
now, for he came to *d* to the city	1Sa 9:12	3117
the people to *d* in the high place	1Sa 9:12	3117
in his ear a *d* before Saul came	1Sa 9:15	3117
for ye shall eat with me to *d*	1Sa 9:19	3117
Saul did eat with Samuel that *d*	1Sa 9:24	3117
to pass about the spring of the *d*	1Sa 9:26	7837
thou art departed from me to *d*	1Sa 10:2	3117
those signs came to pass that *d*	1Sa 10:9	3117
ye have this *d* rejected your God,	1Sa 10:19	3117
Ammonites until the heat of the *d*	1Sa 11:11	3117
not a man be put to death this *d*	1Sa 11:13	3117
for to *d* the LORD hath wrought	1Sa 11:13	3117
you from my childhood unto this *d*	1Sa 12:2	3117
and his anointed is witness this *d*	1Sa 12:5	3117
Is it not wheat harvest to *d*	1Sa 12:17	3117
LORD sent thunder and rain that *d*	1Sa 12:18	3117
came to pass in the *d* of battle	1Sa 13:22	3117
Now it came to pass upon a *d*	1Sa 14:1	3117
So the LORD saved Israel that *d*	1Sa 14:23	3117
of Israel were distressed that *d*	1Sa 14:24	3117
man that eateth any food this *d*	1Sa 14:28	3117
d of the spoil of their enemies	1Sa 14:30	3117
that *d* from Michmash to Aijalon	1Sa 14:31	3117
roll a great stone unto me this *d*	1Sa 14:33	3117
But he answered him not that *d*	1Sa 14:37	3117
wherein this sin hath been this *d*	1Sa 14:38	3117
he hath wrought with God this *d*	1Sa 14:45	3117
of Israel from thee this *d*	1Sa 15:28	3117
see Saul until the *d* of his death	1Sa 15:35	3117
upon David from that *d* forward	1Sa 16:13	3117
defy the armies of Israel this *d*	1Sa 17:10	3117
This *d* will the LORD deliver thee	1Sa 17:46	3117
this *d* unto the fowls of the air	1Sa 17:46	3117
And Saul took him that *d*, and would	1Sa 18:2	3117
And Saul eyed David from that *d*	1Sa 18:9	3117
Thou shalt this *d* be my son in	1Sa 18:21	3117
and lay down naked all that *d*	1Sa 19:24	3117
field unto the third *d* at even	1Sa 20:5	
morrow any time, or the third *d*	1Sa 20:12	
Saul spake not any thing that *d*	1Sa 20:26	3117
was the second *d* of the month	1Sa 20:27	
meat, neither yesterday, nor to *d*	1Sa 20:27	3117
no meat the second *d* of the month	1Sa 20:34	3117
sanctified this *d* in the vessel	1Sa 21:5	3117
in the *d* when it was taken away	1Sa 21:6	3117
servants of Saul was there that *d*	1Sa 21:7	3117
fled that *d* for fear of Saul, and	1Sa 21:10	3117
me, to lie in wait, as at this *d*	1Sa 22:8	3117
me, to lie in wait, as at this *d*	1Sa 22:13	3117
and slew on that *d* fourscore	1Sa 22:18	3117
unto Abiathar, I knew it that *d*	1Sa 22:22	3117
And Saul sought him every *d*	1Sa 23:14	3117
Behold the *d* of which the LORD	1Sa 24:4	3117
this *d* thine eyes have seen how	1Sa 24:10	3117
to *d* into mine hand in the cave	1Sa 24:10	3117
thou hast shewed this *d* how that	1Sa 24:18	3117
thou hast done unto me this *d*	1Sa 24:19	3117
for we come in a good *d*	1Sa 25:8	3117
a wall unto us both by night and *d*	1Sa 25:16	3119
which sent thee this *d* to meet me	1Sa 25:32	3117
which hast kept me this *d* from	1Sa 25:33	3117
enemy into thine hand this *d*	1Sa 26:8	3117
or his *d* shall come to die	1Sa 26:10	3117
they have driven me out this *d*	1Sa 26:19	3117
was precious in thine eyes this *d*	1Sa 26:21	3117
delivered thee into my hand to *d*	1Sa 26:23	3117
much set by this *d* in mine eyes	1Sa 26:24	3117
perish one *d* by the hand of Saul	1Sa 27:1	3117
Achish gave him Ziklag that *d*	1Sa 27:6	3117
the kings of Judah unto this *d*	1Sa 27:6	3117
Whither have ye made a road to *d*	1Sa 27:10	3117
done this thing unto thee this *d*	1Sa 28:18	3117
he had eaten no bread all the *d*	1Sa 28:20	3117
since he fell unto me unto this *d*	1Sa 29:3	3117
found evil in thee since the *d* of	1Sa 29:6	3117
of thy coming unto me unto this *d*	1Sa 29:6	3117
I have been with thee unto this *d*	1Sa 29:8	3117
come to Ziklag on the third *d*	1Sa 30:1	3117
unto the evening of the next *d*	1Sa 30:17	4283
And it was so from that *d* forward	1Sa 30:25	3117
ordinance for Israel unto this *d*	1Sa 30:25	3117
all his men, that same *d* together	1Sa 31:6	3117
came even to pass on the third *d*	2Sa 1:2	3117
was a very sore battle that *d*	2Sa 2:17	3117
they came to Hebron at break of *d*	2Sa 2:32	215
this *d* unto the house of Saul thy	2Sa 3:8	3117
that thou chargest me to *d* with a	2Sa 3:8	3117
to eat meat while it was yet *d*	2Sa 3:35	3117
all Israel understood that *d* that	2Sa 3:37	3117
great man fallen this *d* in Israel	2Sa 3:38	3117
And I am this *d* weak, though	2Sa 3:39	3117
sojourners there until this *d*	2Sa 4:3	3117
came about the heat of the *d* to	2Sa 4:5	3117
my lord the king this *d* of Saul	2Sa 4:8	3117
And David said on that *d*,	2Sa 5:8	3117
the place Perez-uzzah to this *d*	2Sa 6:8	3117
was afraid of the LORD that *d*	2Sa 6:9	3117
to *d* in the eyes of the handmaids	2Sa 6:20	3117
no child unto the *d* of her death	2Sa 6:23	3117
out of Egypt, even to this *d*	2Sa 7:6	3117
to Uriah, Tarry here to *d* also	2Sa 11:12	3117
Uriah abode in Jerusalem that *d*	2Sa 11:12	3117
it came to pass on the seventh *d*	2Sa 12:18	3117
king's son, lean from *d* to *d*	2Sa 13:4	1242
king's son, lean from *d* to *d*	2Sa 13:4	1242
hath been determined from the *d*	2Sa 13:32	3117
David mourned for his son every *d*	2Sa 13:37	3117
should I this *d* make thee go up	2Sa 15:20	3117
me good for his cursing this *d*	2Sa 16:12	3117
that *d* of twenty thousand men	2Sa 18:7	3117
that *d* than the sword devoured	2Sa 18:8	3117
and it is called unto this *d*	2Sa 18:18	3117
shalt not bear tidings this *d*	2Sa 18:20	3117
thou shalt bear tidings another *d*	2Sa 18:20	3117
but this *d* thou shalt bear no	2Sa 18:20	3117
this *d* of all them that rose up	2Sa 18:31	3117
the victory that *d* was turned	2Sa 19:2	3117

d how the king was grieved for 2Sa 19:2 3117
by stealth that *d* into the city 2Sa 19:3 3117
said Thou hast shamed this *d* the 2Sa 19:5 3117
which this *d* have saved thy life, 2Sa 19:5 3117
For thou hast declared this *d* 2Sa 19:6 3117
for this *d* I perceive, that if 2Sa 19:6 3117
lived, and all we had died this *d* 2Sa 19:6 3117
d that my lord the king went out 2Sa 19:19 3117
I am come the first this *d* of all 2Sa 19:20 3117
Zeruiah, that ye should this *d* be 2Sa 19:22 3117
be put to death this *d* in Israel 2Sa 19:22 3117
that I am this *d* king over Israel 2Sa 19:22 3117
from the *d* the king departed 2Sa 19:24 3117
the *d* he came again in peace 2Sa 19:24 3117
I am this *d* fourscore years old 2Sa 19:35 3117
shut up unto the *d* of their death 2Sa 20:3 3117
of the air to rest on them by *d* 2Sa 21:10 3119
in the *d* that the LORD had 2Sa 22:1 3117
me in the *d* of my calamity 2Sa 22:19 3117
wrought a great victory that *d* 2Sa 23:10 3117
And Gad came that *d* to David 2Sa 24:18 3117
For he is gone down this *d* 1Kin 1:25 3117
so will I certainly do this *d* 1Kin 1:30 3117
one to sit on my throne this *d* 1Kin 1:48 3117
me to *d* that he will not slay his 1Kin 1:51 3117
in the *d* when I went to Mahanaim 1Kin 2:8 3117
shall be put to death this *d* 1Kin 2:24 3117
that on the *d* thou goest out, and 1Kin 2:37 3117
on the *d* thou goest out, and 1Kin 2:42 3117
on his throne, as it is this *d* 1Kin 3:6 3117
it came to pass the third *d* after 1Kin 3:18 3117
one *d* was thirty measures of fine 1Kin 4:22 3117
said, Blessed be the LORD this *d* 1Kin 5:7 3117
and there they are unto this *d* 1Kin 8:8 3117
Since the *d* that I brought forth 1Kin 8:16 3117
with thine hand, as it is this *d* 1Kin 8:24 3117
servant prayeth before thee to *d* 1Kin 8:28 3117
open toward this house night and *d* 1Kin 8:29 3117
be nigh unto the LORD our God *d* 1Kin 8:59 3119
his commandments, as at this *d* 1Kin 8:61 3117
The same *d* did the king hallow 1Kin 8:64 3117
On the eighth *d* he sent the 1Kin 8:66 3117
the land of Cabul unto this *d* 1Kin 9:13 3117
of bondservice unto this *d* 1Kin 9:21 3117
trees, nor were seen unto this *d* 1Kin 10:12 3117
a servant unto this people this *d* 1Kin 12:7 3117
came to Rehoboam the third *d* 1Kin 12:12 3117
Come to me again the third *d* 1Kin 12:12 3117
the house of David unto this *d* 1Kin 12:19 3117
on the fifteenth *d* of the month 1Kin 12:32 3117
fifteenth *d* of the eighth month 1Kin 12:33 3117
And he gave a sign the same *d* 1Kin 13:3 3117
of God had done that *d* in Beth-el 1Kin 13:11 3117
off the house of Jeroboam that *d* 1Kin 14:14 3117
over Israel that *d* in the camp 1Kin 16:16 3117
until the *d* that the LORD sendeth 1Kin 17:14 3117
surely shew myself unto him to *d* 1Kin 18:15 3117
let it be known this *d* that thou 1Kin 18:36 3117
deliver it into thine hand this *d* 1Kin 20:13 3117
that in the seventh *d* the battle 1Kin 20:29 3117
hundred thousand footmen in one *d* 1Kin 20:29 3117
at the word of the LORD to *d* 1Kin 22:5 3117
Behold, thou shalt see in that *d* 1Kin 22:25 3117
And the battle increased that *d* 1Kin 22:35 3117
thy master from thy head to *d* 2Kin 2:3 3117
thy master from thy head to *d* 2Kin 2:5 3117
waters were healed unto this *d* 2Kin 2:22 3117
And it fell on a *d*, that Elisha 2Kin 4:8 3117
And it fell on a *d*, that he came 2Kin 4:11 3117
child was grown, it fell on a *d* 2Kin 4:18 3117
wilt thou go to him to *d* 2Kin 4:23 3117
thy son, that we may eat him to *d* 2Kin 6:28 3117
and I said unto her on the next *d* 2Kin 6:29 3117
Shaphat shall stand on him this *d* 2Kin 6:31 3117
this *d* is a *d* of good tidings, 2Kin 7:9 3117
this *d* is a *d* of good tidings, 2Kin 7:9 3117
the *d* that she left the land 2Kin 8:6 3117
the hand of Judah unto this *d* 2Kin 8:22 3117
it a draught house unto this *d* 2Kin 10:27 3117
name of it Joktheel unto this *d* 2Kin 14:7 3117
a leper unto the *d* of his death 2Kin 15:5 3117
Elath, and dwelt there unto this *d* 2Kin 16:6 3117
own land to Assyria unto this *d* 2Kin 17:23 3117
Unto this *d* they do after the 2Kin 17:34 3117
fathers, so do they unto this *d* 2Kin 17:41 3117
This *d* is a *d* of trouble 2Kin 19:3 3117
on the third *d* thou shalt go up 2Kin 20:5 3117
the house of the LORD the third *d* 2Kin 20:8 3117
have laid up in store unto this *d* 2Kin 20:17 3117
since the *d* their fathers came 2Kin 21:15 3117
out of Egypt, even unto this *d* 2Kin 21:15 3117
in the tenth *d* of the month 2Kin 25:1 3117
on the ninth *d* of the fourth 2Kin 25:3
on the seventh *d* of the month 2Kin 25:8
twentieth *d* of the month, that 2Kin 25:27
king, a daily rate for every *d* 2Kin 25:30 3117
them utterly unto this *d*, and 1Chr 4:41 3117
and dwelt there unto this *d* 1Chr 4:43 3117
to the river Gozan, unto this *d* 1Chr 5:26 3117
they were employed in that work *d* 1Chr 9:33 3119
slew a lion in a pit in a snowy *d* 1Chr 11:22 3117
For at that time *d* by *d* there 1Chr 12:22 3117
is called Perez-uzza to this *d* 1Chr 13:11 3117
And David was afraid of God that *d* 1Chr 13:12 3117
Then on that *d* David delivered 1Chr 16:7 3117
shew forth from *d* to *d* his 1Chr 16:23 3117
forth from *d* to *d* his salvation 1Chr 16:23 3117
d that I brought up Israel unto 1Chr 17:5 3117
I brought up Israel unto this *d* 1Chr 17:5 3117
four a *d*, southward four a *d* 1Chr 26:17 3117
and my judgments, as at this *d* 1Chr 28:7 3117
his service this *d* unto the LORD 1Chr 29:5 3117
LORD, on the morrow after that *d* 1Chr 29:21 3117
on that *d* with great gladness 1Chr 29:22 3117
the second *d* of the second month 2Chr 3:2
And there it is unto this *d* 2Chr 5:9 3117
Since the *d* that I brought forth 2Chr 6:5 3117
with thine hand, as it is this *d* 2Chr 6:15 3117
may be open upon this house *d* 2Chr 6:20 3119
in the eighth *d* they made a 2Chr 7:9 3117
twentieth *d* of the seventh month 2Chr 7:10 3117
make to pay tribute until this *d* 2Chr 8:8 3117
Even after a certain rate every *d* 2Chr 8:13 3117
as the duty of every *d* required 2Chr 8:14 3117
Solomon was prepared unto the *d* 2Chr 8:16 3117
came to Rehoboam on the third *d* 2Chr 10:12 3117
Come again to me on the third *d* 2Chr 10:12 3117
the house of David unto this *d* 2Chr 10:19 3117
at the word of the LORD to *d* 2Chr 18:4 3117
thou shalt see on that *d* when 2Chr 18:24 3117
And the battle increased that *d* 2Chr 18:34 3117
on the fourth *d* they assembled 2Chr 20:26 3117
valley of Berachah, unto this *d* 2Chr 20:26 3117
the hand of Judah unto this *d* 2Chr 21:10 3117
reason of the sickness *d* by *d* 2Chr 21:15 3117
Thus they did *d* by *d*, and 2Chr 24:11 3117
a leper unto the *d* of his death 2Chr 26:21 3117
and twenty thousand in one *d* 2Chr 28:6 3117
Now they began on the first *d* of 2Chr 29:17
on the eighth *d* of the month came 2Chr 29:17
in the sixteenth *d* of the first 2Chr 29:17
fourteenth *d* of the second month 2Chr 30:15
priests praised the LORD *d* by *d* 2Chr 30:21 3117
fourteenth *d* of the first month 2Chr 35:1
the LORD was prepared the same *d* 2Chr 35:16 3117
I come not against thee this *d* 2Chr 35:21 3117
in their lamentations to this *d* 2Chr 35:25 3117
as the duty of every *d* required Ezr 3:4 3117
From the first *d* of the seventh Ezr 3:6 3117
given them *d* by *d* without fail Ezr 6:9 3118
on the third *d* of the month Adar Ezr 6:15 3118
fourteenth *d* of the first month Ezr 6:19
For upon the first *d* of the first Ezr 7:9
on the first *d* of the fifth month Ezr 7:9
the twelfth *d* of the first month Ezr 8:31
on the fourth *d* was the silver Ezr 8:33 3117
in a great trespass unto this *d* Ezr 9:7 3117
of face, as it is this *d* Ezr 9:7 3117
yet escaped, as it is this *d* Ezr 9:15 3117
on the twentieth *d* of the month Ezr 10:9
is this a work of one *d* or two Ezr 10:13 3117
sat down in the first *d* of the Ezr 10:16 3117
by the first *d* of the first month Ezr 10:17 3117
which I pray before thee now, *d* Neh 1:6 3119
I pray thee, thy servant this *d* Neh 1:11 3117
will they make an end in a *d* Neh 4:2 3117
and set a watch against them *d* Neh 4:9 3119
a guard to us, and labour on the *d* Neh 4:22 3117
I pray you, to them, even this *d* Neh 5:11 3117
fifth *d* of the month Elul, in Neh 6:15
upon the first *d* of the seventh Neh 8:2 3117
This *d* is holy unto the LORD your Neh 8:9 3117
for this *d* is holy unto our Lord Neh 8:10 3117
your peace, for the *d* is holy Neh 8:11 3117
on the second *d* were gathered Neh 8:13 3117
d had not the children of Israel Neh 8:17 3117
Also *d* by *d*, from the first *d* Neh 8:18 3117
the first *d* unto the last *d* Neh 8:18 3117
on the eighth *d* was a solemn Neh 8:18 3117
fourth *d* of this month the Neh 9:1 3117
God one fourth part of the *d* Neh 9:3 3117
get thee a name, as it is this *d* Neh 9:10 3117
them in the *d* by a cloudy pillar Neh 9:12 3119
cloud departed not from them by *d* Neh 9:19 3119
the kings of Assyria unto this *d* Neh 9:32 3117
Behold, we are servants this *d* Neh 9:36 3117
victuals on the sabbath *d* to sell Neh 10:31 3117
on the sabbath, or on the holy *d* Neh 10:31 3117
for the singers, due for every *d* Neh 11:23 3117
Also that *d* they offered great Neh 12:43 3117
the porters, every *d* his portion Neh 12:47 3117
On that *d* they read in the book Neh 13:1 3117
into Jerusalem on the sabbath *d* Neh 13:15 3117
the *d* wherein they sold victuals Neh 13:15 3117
ye do, and profane the sabbath *d* Neh 13:17 3117
be brought in on the sabbath *d* Neh 13:19 3117
gates, to sanctify the sabbath *d* Neh 13:22 3117
On the seventh *d*, when the heart Est 1:10 3117
Media say this *d* unto all the Est 1:18 3117
Mordecai walked every *d* before Est 2:11 3117
lot, before Haman from *d* to *d* Est 3:7 3117
lot, before Haman from *d* to *d* Est 3:7 3117
thirteenth *d* of the first month Est 3:12 3117
children and women, in one *d* Est 3:13 3117
thirteenth *d* of the twelfth month Est 3:13 3117
should be ready against that *d* Est 3:14 3117
nor drink three days, night or *d* Est 4:16 3117
it came to pass on the third *d* Est 5:1 3117
Haman come this *d* unto the Est 5:4 3117
went Haman forth that *d* joyful Est 5:9 3117
second *d* at the banquet of wine Est 7:2 3117
On that *d* did the king Ahasuerus Est 8:1 3117
the three and twentieth *d* thereof Est 8:9
Upon one *d* in all the provinces Est 8:12 3117
upon the thirteenth *d* of the Est 8:12
should be ready against that *d* to Est 8:13 3117
and gladness, a feast and a good *d* Est 8:17 3117
on the thirteenth *d* of the same Est 9:1 3117
in the *d* that the enemies of the Est 9:1 3117
On that *d* the number of those Est 9:11 3117
d also of the month Adar, and slew Est 9:15 3117
thirteenth *d* of the month Adar Est 9:17 3117
on the fourteenth *d* of the same Est 9:17
made it a *d* of feasting and Est 9:17 3117
on the thirteenth *d* thereof Est 9:18
on the fifteenth *d* of the same Est 9:18
made it a *d* of feasting and Est 9:18 3117
made the fourteenth *d* of the Est 9:19 3117
of the month Adar a *d* of gladness Est 9:19
gladness and feasting, and a good *d* Est 9:19 3117
fourteenth *d* of the month Adar Est 9:21
and the fifteenth *d* of the same Est 9:21 3117
and from mourning into a good *d* Est 9:22 3117
in their houses, every one his *d* Job 1:4 3117
Now there was a *d* when the sons Job 1:6 3117
there was a *d* when his sons and Job 1:13 3117
Again there was a *d* when the sons Job 2:1 3117
Job his mouth, and cursed his *d* Job 3:1 3117
Let the *d* perish wherein I was Job 3:3 3117
Let that *d* be darkness Job 3:4 3117
the blackness of the *d* terrify it Job 3:5 3117
them curse it that curse the *d* Job 3:8 3117
let it see the dawning of the *d* Job 3:9 7837
and fro unto the dawning of the *d* Job 7:4 5399
accomplish, as an hireling, his *d* Job 14:6 3117
he knoweth that the *d* of darkness Job 15:23 3117
They change the night into *d* Job 17:12 3117
him shall be astonied at his *d* Job 18:20 3117
at the latter *d* upon the earth Job 19:25
flow away in the *d* of his wrath Job 20:28 3117
reserved to the *d* of destruction Job 21:30 3117
brought forth to the *d* of wrath Job 21:30 3117
Even to *d* is my complaint bitter Job 23:2 3117
waters with bounds, until the *d* Job 26:10 216
trouble, against the *d* of battle Job 38:23 3117
and in his law doth he meditate *d* Ps 1:2 3119
this *d* have I begotten thee Ps 2:7 3117
is angry with the wicked every *d* Ps 7:11 3117
the *d* that the LORD delivered him Ps 18:*t* 3117
me in the *d* of my calamity Ps 18:18 3117
D unto *d* uttereth speech, and Ps 19:2 3117
D unto *d* uttereth speech, and Ps 19:2 3117
hear thee in the *d* of trouble Ps 20:1 3117
on thee do I wait all the *d* Ps 25:5 3117
through my roaring all the *d* long Ps 32:3 3117
For *d* and night thy hand was heavy Ps 32:4 3119
and of thy praise all the *d* long Ps 35:28 3117
for he seeth that his *d* is coming Ps 37:13 3117
I go mourning all the *d* long Ps 38:6 3117
and imagine deceits all the *d* long Ps 38:12 3117
My tears have been my meat *d* Ps 42:3 3119
In God we boast all the *d* long Ps 44:8 3117
sake are we killed all the *d* long Ps 44:22 3117
call upon me in the *d* of trouble Ps 50:15 3117
D and night they go about it upon Ps 55:10 3119
Every *d* they wrest my words Ps 56:5 3117
and refuge in the *d* of my trouble Ps 59:16 3117
and with thy honour all the *d* Ps 71:8 3117
and thy salvation all the *d* Ps 71:15 3117
thy righteousness all the *d* long Ps 71:24 3117
For all the *d* long have I been Ps 73:14 3117
The *d* is thine, the night also is Ps 74:16 3117
In the *d* of my trouble I sought Ps 77:2 3117
turned back in the *d* of battle Ps 78:9 3117
nor the *d* when he delivered them Ps 78:42 3117
appointed, on our solemn feast *d* Ps 81:3 3117
For a *d* in thy courts is better Ps 84:10 3117
In the *d* of my trouble I will Ps 86:7 3117
of my salvation, I have cried *d* Ps 88:1 3117
name shall they rejoice all the *d* Ps 89:16 3117
for the arrow that flieth by *d* Ps 91:5 3119
A Psalm or Song for the sabbath *d* Ps 92:*t* 3117
To *d* if ye will hear his voice, Ps 95:7 3117
as in the *d* of temptation in the Ps 95:8 3117
forth his salvation from *d* to *d* Ps 96:2 3117
me in the *d* when I am in trouble Ps 102:2 3117
in the *d* when I call answer me Ps 102:2 3117
enemies reproach me all the *d* Ps 102:8 3117
be willing in the *d* of thy power Ps 110:3 3117
kings in the *d* of his wrath Ps 110:5 3117
This is the *d* which the LORD hath Ps 118:24 3117
They continue this *d* according to Ps 119:91 3117
it is my meditation all the *d* Ps 119:97 3117
Seven times a *d* do I praise thee Ps 119:164 3117
The sun shall not smite thee by *d* Ps 121:6 3119
The sun to rule by *d* Ps 136:8 3117
of Edom in the *d* of Jerusalem Ps 137:7 3117
In the *d* when I cried thou Ps 138:3 3117
but the night shineth as the *d* Ps 139:12 3117
my head in the *d* of battle Ps 140:7 3117
Every *d* will I bless thee Ps 145:2 3117
in that very *d* his thoughts Ps 146:4 3117
more and more unto the perfect *d* Prov 4:18 3117
not spare in the *d* of vengeance Prov 6:34 3117
this *d* have I payed my vows Prov 7:14 3117
will come home at the *d* appointed Prov 7:20 3117
profit not in the *d* of wrath Prov 11:4 3117
even the wicked for the *d* of evil Prov 16:4 3117
coveteth greedily all the *d* long Prov 21:26 3117
prepared against the *d* of battle Prov 21:31 3117
I have made known to thee this *d* Prov 22:19 3117
fear of the LORD all the *d* long Prov 23:17 3117
thou faint in the *d* of adversity Prov 24:10 3117
not what a *d* may bring forth Prov 27:1 3117
house in the *d* of thy calamity Prov 27:10 3117
dropping in a very rainy *d* Prov 27:15 3117
the *d* of death than the *d* of Eccl 7:1 3117
death than the *d* of one's birth Eccl 7:1 3117
In the *d* of prosperity be joyful, Eccl 7:14 3117
but in the *d* of adversity Eccl 7:14 3117
hath he power in the *d* of death Eccl 8:8 3117
d nor night seeth sleep with his Eccl 8:16 3117
In the *d* when the keepers of the Eccl 12:3 3117
Until the *d* break, and the shadows Song 2:17 3117
him in the *d* of his espousals Song 3:11 3117
in the *d* of the gladness of his Song 3:11 3117
Until the *d* break, and the shadows Song 4:6 3117
we do for our sister in the *d* Song 8:8 3117
alone shall be exalted in that *d* Is 2:11 3117
For the *d* of the LORD of hosts Is 2:12 3117
alone shall be exalted in that *d* Is 2:17 3117
In that *d* a man shall cast his Is 2:20 3117

In that *d* shall he swear, saying, Is 3:7 3117
In that *d* the Lord will take away Is 3:18 3117
in that *d* seven women shall take Is 4:1 3117
In that *d* shall the branch of the Is 4:2 3117
assemblies, a cloud and smoke by *d* Is 4:5 3119
in that *d* they shall roar against Is 5:30 3117
from the *d* that Ephraim departed Is 7:17 3117
it shall come to pass in that *d* Is 7:18 3117
In the same *d* shall the Lord Is 7:20 3117
it shall come to pass in that *d* Is 7:21 3117
it shall come to pass in that *d* Is 7:23 3117
oppressor, as in the *d* of Midian Is 9:4 3117
and tail, branch and rush, in one *d* Is 9:14 3117
will ye do in the *d* of visitation Is 10:3 3117
his thorns and his briers in one *d* Is 10:17 3117
it shall come to pass in that *d* Is 10:20 3117
it shall come to pass in that *d* Is 10:27 3117
yet shall he remain at Nob that *d* Is 10:32 3117
in that *d* there shall be a root Is 11:10 3117
it shall come to pass in that *d* Is 11:11 3117
d that he came up out of the land Is 11:16 3117
in that *d* thou shalt say, O LORD, Is 12:1 3117
in that *d* shall ye say, Praise Is 12:4 3117
for the *d* of the LORD is at hand Is 13:6 3117
the *d* of the LORD cometh, cruel Is 13:9 3117
in the *d* of his fierce anger Is 13:13 3117
it shall come to pass in the *d* Is 14:3 3117
in that *d* it shall come to pass Is 17:4 3117
At that *d* shall a man look to his Is 17:7 3117
In that *d* shall his strong cities Is 17:9 3117
In the *d* shalt thou make thy Is 17:11 3117
shall be a heap in the *d* of grief Is 17:11 3117
In that *d* shall Egypt be like Is 19:16 3117
In that *d* shall five cities in Is 19:18 3117
In that *d* shall there be an altar Is 19:19 3117
shall know the LORD in that *d* Is 19:21 3117
In that *d* shall there be a Is 19:23 3117
In that *d* shall Israel be the Is 19:24 3117
of this isle shall say in that *d* Is 20:6 3117
For it is a *d* of trouble, and of Is 22:5 3117
thou didst look in that *d* to the Is 22:8 3117
in that *d* did the Lord GOD of Is 22:12 3117
it shall come to pass in that *d* Is 22:20 3117
In that *d*, saith the LORD of Is 22:25 3117
it shall come to pass in that *d* Is 23:15 3117
it shall come to pass in that *d* Is 24:21 3117
And it shall be said in that *d* Is 25:9 3117
In that *d* shall this song be sung Is 26:1 3117
In that *d* the LORD with his sore Is 27:1 3117
In that *d* sing ye unto her, A Is 27:2 3117
it, I will keep it night and *d* Is 27:3 3117
wind in the *d* of the east wind Is 27:8 3117
it shall come to pass in that *d* Is 27:12 3117
it shall come to pass in that *d* Is 27:13 3117
In that *d* shall the LORD of hosts Is 28:5 3117
morning shall it pass over, by *d* Is 28:19 3117
the plowman plow all *d* to sow Is 28:24 3117
in that *d* shall the deaf hear the Is 29:18 3117
in that *d* shall thy cattle feed Is 30:23 3117
in the *d* of the great slaughter Is 30:25 3117
in the *d* that the LORD bindeth up Is 30:26 3117
For in that *d* every man shall Is 31:7 3117
For it is the *d* of the LORD's Is 34:8 3117
shall not be quenched night nor *d* Is 34:10 3119
This *d* is a *d* of trouble, and of Is 37:3 3117
This *d* is a *d* of trouble Is 37:3 3117
from *d* even to night wilt thou Is 38:12 3117
from *d* even to night wilt thou Is 38:13 3117
shall praise thee, as I do this *d* Is 38:19 3117
laid up in store until this *d* Is 39:6 3117
Yea, before the *d* was I am he Is 43:13 3117
come to thee in a moment in one *d* Is 47:9 3117
even before the *d* when thou Is 48:7 3117
in a *d* of salvation have I helped Is 49:8 3117
d because of the fury of the Is 51:13 3117
continually every *d* is blasphemed Is 52:5 3117
they shall know in that *d* that I Is 52:6 3117
and to morrow shall be as this *d* Is 56:12 3117
in the *d* of your fast ye find Is 58:3 3117
ye shall not fast as ye do this *d* Is 58:4 3117
a *d* for a man to afflict his soul Is 58:5 3117
and an acceptable *d* to the LORD Is 58:5 3117
doing thy pleasure on my holy *d* Is 58:13 3117
shall not be shut *d* nor night Is 60:11 3119
shall be no more thy light by *d* Is 60:19 3119
the *d* of vengeance of our God Is 61:2 3117
hold their peace *d* nor night Is 62:6 3117
For the *d* of vengeance is in mine Is 63:4 3117
the *d* unto a rebellious people Is 65:2 3117
a fire that burneth all the *d* Is 65:5 3117
be made to bring forth in one *d* Is 66:8 3117
I have this *d* set thee over the Jer 1:10 3117
made thee this *d* a defenced city Jer 1:18 3117
from our youth even unto this *d* Jer 3:25 3117
it shall come to pass at that *d* Jer 4:9 3117
for the *d* goeth away, for the Jer 6:4 3117
nor commanded them in the *d* that Jer 7:22 3117
Since the *d* that your fathers Jer 7:25 3117
d I have even sent unto you all Jer 7:25 3117
of tears, that I might weep *d* Jer 9:1 3119
d that I brought them forth out Jer 11:4 3117
milk and honey, as it is this *d* Jer 11:5 3117
unto your fathers in the *d* that I Jer 11:7 3117
land of Egypt, even unto this *d* Jer 11:7 3117
them for the *d* of slaughter Jer 12:3 3117
run down with tears night and *d* Jer 14:17 3119
is gone down while it was yet *d* Jer 15:9 3119
there shall ye serve other gods *d* Jer 16:13 3119
my refuge in the *d* of affliction Jer 16:19 3117
have I desired the woeful *d* Jer 17:16 3117
thou art my hope in the *d* of evil Jer 17:17 3117
bring upon them the *d* of evil Jer 17:18 3117
bear no burden on the sabbath *d* Jer 17:21 3117
of your houses on the sabbath *d* Jer 17:22 3117
work, but hallow ye the sabbath *d* Jer 17:22 3117
of this city on the sabbath *d* Jer 17:24 3117
but hallow the sabbath *d* Jer 17:24 3117
unto me to hallow the sabbath *d* Jer 17:27 3117
of Jerusalem on the sabbath *d* Jer 17:27 3117
in the *d* of their calamity Jer 18:17 3117
Cursed be the *d* wherein I was Jer 20:14 3117
let not the *d* wherein my mother Jer 20:14 3117
king of Judah, even unto this *d* Jer 25:3 3117
as it is this *d* Jer 25:18 3117
of the LORD shall be at that *d* Jer 25:33 3117
be until the *d* that I visit them Jer 27:22 3117
for that *d* is great, so that none Jer 30:7 3117
it shall come to pass in that *d* Jer 30:8 3117
For there shall be a *d*, that the Jer 31:6 3117
made with their fathers in the *d* Jer 31:32 3117
giveth the sun for a light by *d* Jer 31:35 3119
land of Egypt, even unto this *d* Jer 32:20 3119
made thee a name, as at this *d* Jer 32:20 3119
of my fury from the *d* that they Jer 32:31 3119
they built it even unto this *d* Jer 32:31 3119
ye can break my covenant of the *d* Jer 33:20 3117
and that there should not be *d* Jer 33:20 3119
If my covenant be not with *d* Jer 33:25 3119
with your fathers in the *d* that I Jer 34:13 3117
for unto this *d* they drink none, Jer 35:14 3117
from the *d* I spake unto thee, Jer 36:2 3117
days of Josiah, even into this *d* Jer 36:2 3117
LORD's house upon the fasting *d* Jer 36:6 3117
be cast out in the *d* to the heat Jer 36:30 3117
the *d* that Jerusalem was taken Jer 38:28 3117
the ninth *d* of the month, the Jer 39:2 3117
in that *d* before thee Jer 39:16 3117
But I will deliver thee in that *d* Jer 39:17 3117
I loose thee this *d* from the Jer 40:4 3117
it came to pass the second *d* Jer 41:4 3117
that I have admonished you this *d* Jer 42:19 3117
now I have this *d* declared it to Jer 42:21 3117
this *d* they are a desolation, and Jer 44:2 3117
wasted and desolate, as at this *d* Jer 44:6 3117
are not humbled even unto this *d* Jer 44:10 3117
an inhabitant, as at this *d* Jer 44:22 3117
happened unto you, as at this *d* Jer 44:23 3117
For this is the *d* of the Lord GOD Jer 46:10 3117
a *d* of vengeance, that he may Jer 46:10 3117
because the *d* of their calamity Jer 46:21 3117
Because of the *d* that cometh to Jer 47:4 3117
that *d* shall be as the heart of a Jer 48:41 3117
at that *d* shall the heart of the Jer 49:22 3117
of war shall be cut off in that *d* Jer 49:26 3117
for their *d* is come, the time of Jer 50:27 3117
of war shall be cut off in that *d* Jer 50:30 3117
for thy *d* is come, the time that Jer 50:31 3117
for in the *d* of trouble they Jer 51:2 3117
in the tenth *d* of the month Jer 52:4
in the ninth *d* of the month Jer 52:6
in prison till the *d* of his death Jer 52:11 3117
in the tenth *d* of the month Jer 52:12
twentieth *d* of the month, that Jer 52:31
every *d* a portion until the *d* Jer 52:34 3117
me in the *d* of his fierce anger Lam 1:12 3117
me desolate and faint all the *d* Lam 1:13 3117
thou wilt bring the *d* that thou Lam 1:21 3117
footstool in the *d* of his anger Lam 2:1 3117
as in the *d* of a solemn feast Lam 2:7 3117
this is the *d* that we looked for Lam 2:16 3117
let tears run down like a river *d* Lam 2:18 3119
them in the *d* of thine anger Lam 2:21 3117
a solemn *d* my terrors round about Lam 2:22 3117
so that in the *d* of the LORD's Lam 2:22 3117
his hand against me all the *d* Lam 3:3 3117
and their song all the *d* Lam 3:14 3117
in the *d* that I called upon thee Lam 3:57 3117
their device against me all the *d* Lam 3:62 3117
in the fifth *d* of the month Eze 1:1
In the fifth *d* of the month Eze 1:2
is in the cloud in the *d* of rain Eze 1:28 3117
against me, even unto this very *d* Eze 2:3 3117
appointed thee each *d* for a year Eze 4:6 3117
be by weight, twenty shekels a *d* Eze 4:10 3117
the *d* of trouble is near, and not Eze 7:7 3117
Behold the *d*, behold, it is come Eze 7:10 3117
time is come, the *d* draweth near Eze 7:12 3117
in the *d* of the wrath of the LORD Eze 7:19 3117
in the fifth *d* of the month Eze 8:1
remove by *d* in their sight Eze 12:3 3119
thy stuff by *d* in their sight Eze 12:4 3119
I brought forth my stuff by *d* Eze 12:7 3119
the battle in the *d* of the LORD Eze 13:5 3117
in the *d* thou wast born thy navel Eze 16:4 3117
in the *d* that thou wast born Eze 16:5 3117
thy mouth in the *d* of thy pride Eze 16:56 3117
the tenth *d* of the month, that Eze 20:1
In the *d* when I chose Israel, and Eze 20:5 3117
In the *d* that I lifted up mine Eze 20:6 3117
is called Bamah unto this *d* Eze 20:29 3117
all your idols, even unto this *d* Eze 20:31 3117
whose *d* is come, when iniquity Eze 21:25 3117
whose *d* is come, when their Eze 21:29 3117
upon in the *d* of indignation Eze 22:24 3117
my sanctuary in the same *d* Eze 23:38 3117
then they came the same *d* into my Eze 23:39 3117
in the tenth *d* of the month Eze 24:1
man, write thee the name of the *d* Eze 24:2 3117
of the *d*, even of this same *d* Eze 24:2 3117
against Jerusalem this same *d* Eze 24:2 3117
shall it not be in the *d* when I Eze 24:25 3117
in that *d* shall come unto thee Eze 24:26 3117
In that *d* shall thy mouth be Eze 24:27 3117
year, in the first *d* of the month Eze 26:1
tremble in the *d* of thy fall Eze 26:18 3117
of the seas in the *d* of thy ruin Eze 27:27 3117
in the *d* that thou wast created Eze 28:13 3117
from the *d* that thou wast created Eze 28:15 3117
in the twelfth *d* of the month Eze 29:1
in the first *d* of the month Eze 29:17
In that *d* will I cause the horn Eze 29:21 3117
Howl ye, Woe worth the *d* Eze 30:2 3117
even the *d* of the LORD is near, a Eze 30:3 3117
of the LORD is near, a cloudy *d* Eze 30:3 3117
In that *d* shall messengers go Eze 30:9 3117
upon them, as in the *d* of Egypt Eze 30:9 3117
also the *d* shall be darkened Eze 30:18 3117
in the seventh *d* of the month Eze 30:20
in the first *d* of the month Eze 31:1
In the *d* when he went down to the Eze 31:15 3117
in the first *d* of the month Eze 32:1
own life, in the *d* of thy fall Eze 32:10 3117
in the fifteenth *d* of the month Eze 32:17
him in the *d* of his transgression Eze 33:12 3117
in the *d* that he turneth from his Eze 33:12 3117
in the *d* that he sinneth Eze 33:12 3117
in the fifth *d* of the month Eze 33:21
seeketh out his flock in the *d* Eze 34:12 3117
scattered in the cloudy and dark *d* Eze 34:12 3117
In the *d* that I shall have Eze 36:33 3117
In that *d* when my people of Eze 38:14 3117
Surely in that *d* there shall be a Eze 38:19 3117
this is the *d* whereof I have Eze 39:8 3117
it shall come to pass in that *d* Eze 39:11 3117
the *d* that I shall be glorified Eze 39:13 3117
am the LORD their God from that *d* Eze 39:22 3117
year, in the tenth *d* of the month Eze 40:1
in the selfsame *d* the hand of the Eze 40:1 3117
in the *d* when they shall make it Eze 43:18 3117
on the second *d* thou shalt offer Eze 43:22 3117
every *d* a goat for a sin offering Eze 43:25 3117
shall be, that upon the eighth *d* Eze 43:27 3117
in the *d* that he goeth into the Eze 44:27 3117
in the first *d* of the month Eze 45:18
so thou shalt do the seventh *d* of Eze 45:20
in the fourteenth *d* of the month Eze 45:21 3117
upon that *d* shall the prince Eze 45:22 3117
in the fifteenth *d* of the month Eze 45:25 3117
in the *d* of the new moon it shall Eze 46:1 3117
d shall be six lambs without Eze 46:4 3117
in the *d* of the new moon it shall Eze 46:6 3117
as he did on the sabbath *d* Eze 46:12 3117
of the city from that *d* shall be Eze 48:35 3117
upon his knees three times a *d* Dan 6:10 3118
his petition three times a *d* Dan 6:13 3118
confusion of faces, as at this *d* Dan 9:7 3117
gotten thee renown, as at this *d* Dan 9:15 3117
twentieth *d* of the first month, Dan 10:4 3117
for from the first *d* that thou Dan 10:12 3117
it shall come to pass at that *d* Hos 1:5 3117
great shall be the *d* of Jezreel Hos 1:11 3117
her as in the *d* that she was born Hos 2:3 3117
as in the *d* when she came up out Hos 2:15 3117
And it shall be at that *d*, saith Hos 2:16 3117
in that *d* will I make a covenant Hos 2:18 3117
it shall come to pass in that *d* Hos 2:21 3117
shalt thou fall in the *d*, and the Hos 4:5 3117
be desolate in the *d* of rebuke Hos 5:9 3117
in the third *d* he will raise us Hos 6:2 3117
In the *d* of our king the princes Hos 7:5 3117
What will ye do in the solemn *d* Hos 9:5 3117
in the *d* of the feast of the LORD Hos 9:5 3117
Beth-arbel in the *d* of battle Hos 10:14 3117
Alas for the *d* Joel 1:15 3117
for the *d* of the LORD is at hand, Joel 1:15 3117
for the *d* of the LORD cometh, for Joel 2:1 3117
A *d* of darkness and of gloominess, Joel 2:2 3117
a *d* of clouds and of thick Joel 2:2 3117
for the *d* of the LORD is great and Joel 2:11 3117
the terrible *d* of the LORD come Joel 2:31 3117
for the *d* of the LORD is near in Joel 3:14 3117
it shall come to pass in that *d* Joel 3:18 3117
with shouting in the *d* of battle Amos 1:14 3117
tempest in the *d* of the whirlwind Amos 1:14 3117
shall flee away naked in that *d* Amos 2:16 3117
That in the *d* that I shall visit Amos 3:14 3117
maketh the *d* dark with night Amos 5:8 3117
you that desire the *d* of the LORD Amos 5:18 3117
the *d* of the LORD is darkness, and Amos 5:18 3117
Shall not the *d* of the LORD be Amos 5:20 3117
Ye that put far away the evil *d* Amos 6:3 3117
shall be howlings in that *d* Amos 8:3 3117
it shall come to pass in that *d* Amos 8:9 3117
darken the earth in the clear *d* Amos 8:9 3117
and the end thereof as a bitter *d* Amos 8:10 3117
In that *d* shall the fair virgins Amos 8:13 3117
In that *d* will I raise up the Amos 9:11 3117
Shall I not in that *d*, saith the Obad 8 3117
In the *d* that thou stoodest on Obad 11 3117
in the *d* that the strangers Obad 11 3117
not have looked on the *d* of thy Obad 12 3117
the *d* that he became a stranger Obad 12 3117
in the *d* of their destruction Obad 12 3117
proudly in the *d* of distress Obad 12 3117
people in the *d* of their calamity Obad 13 3117
in the *d* of their calamity Obad 13 3117
in the *d* of their calamity Obad 13 3117
did remain in the *d* of distress Obad 14 3117
For the *d* of the LORD is near Obad 15 3117
when the morning rose the next *d* Jonah 4:7 4283
In that *d* shall one take up a Mic 2:4 3117
the *d* shall be dark over them Mic 3:6 3117
In that *d*, saith the LORD, will I Mic 4:6 3117
it shall come to pass in that *d* Mic 5:10 3117
the *d* of thy watchmen and thy Mic 7:4 3117
In the *d* that thy walls are to be Mic 7:11 3117
in that *d* shall the decree be far Mic 7:11 3117
In that *d* also he shall come even Mic 7:12 3117
a strong hold in the *d* of trouble Nah 1:7 3117
in the *d* of his preparation Nah 2:3 3117
camp in the hedges in the cold *d* Nah 3:17 3117
I might rest in the *d* of trouble Hab 3:16 3117

for the *d* of the LORD is at hand ... Zeph 1:7 3117
in the *d* of the LORD's sacrifice ... Zeph 1:8 3117
In the same *d* also will I punish ... Zeph 1:9 3117
it shall come to pass in that *d* ... Zeph 1:10 3117
The great *d* of the LORD is near, ... Zeph 1:14 3117
the voice of the *d* of the LORD ... Zeph 1:14 3117
That *d* is a *d* of wrath, a *d* ... Zeph 1:15 3117
a *d* of trouble and distress, a *d* ... Zeph 1:15 3117
a *d* of wasteness and desolation, a ... Zeph 1:15 3117
a *d* of darkness and gloominess, a ... Zeph 1:15 3117
a *d* of clouds and thick darkness, ... Zeph 1:15 3117
A *d* of the trumpet and alarm ... Zeph 1:16 3117
them in the *d* of the LORD's wrath ... Zeph 1:18 3117
before the *d* pass as the chaff, ... Zeph 2:2 3117
before the *d* of the LORD's anger ... Zeph 2:2 3117
hid in the *d* of the LORD's anger ... Zeph 2:3 3117
until the *d* that I rise up to the ... Zeph 3:8 3117
In that *d* shalt thou not be ... Zeph 3:11 3117
In that *d* it shall be said to ... Zeph 3:16 3117
in the first *d* of the month ... Hag 1:1 3117
twentieth *d* of the sixth month, ... Hag 1:15 3117
twentieth *d* of the month, came ... Hag 2:1
twentieth *d* of the ninth month, ... Hag 2:10
I pray you, consider from this *d* ... Hag 2:15 3117
Consider now from this *d* and ... Hag 2:18 3117
twentieth *d* of the ninth month, ... Hag 2:18 3117
even from the *d* that the ... Hag 2:18 3117
from this *d* will I bless you ... Hag 2:19 3117
twentieth *d* of the month, saying, ... Hag 2:20
In that *d*, saith the LORD of ... Hag 2:23 3117
twentieth *d* of the eleventh month ... Zec 1:7 3117
be joined to the LORD in that *d* ... Zec 2:11 3117
iniquity of that land in one *d* ... Zec 3:9 3117
In that *d*, saith the LORD of ... Zec 3:10 3117
despised the *d* of small things ... Zec 4:10 3117
Babylon, and come thou the same *d* ... Zec 6:10 3117
the fourth *d* of the ninth month ... Zec 7:1
which were in the *d* that the ... Zec 8:9 3117
even to *d* do I declare that I ... Zec 9:12 3117
that *d* as the flock of his people ... Zec 9:16 3117
And it was broken in that *d* ... Zec 11:11 3117
in that *d* will I make Jerusalem a ... Zec 12:3 3117
In that *d*, saith the LORD, I will ... Zec 12:4 3117
In that *d* will I make the ... Zec 12:6 3117
In that *d* shall the LORD defend ... Zec 12:8 3117
them at that *d* shall be as David ... Zec 12:8 3117
it shall come to pass in that *d* ... Zec 12:9 3117
In that *d* shall there be a great ... Zec 12:11 3117
In that *d* there shall be a ... Zec 13:1 3117
it shall come to pass in that *d* ... Zec 13:2 3117
it shall come to pass in that *d* ... Zec 13:4 3117
the *d* of the LORD cometh, and thy ... Zec 14:1 3117
when he fought in the *d* of battle ... Zec 14:3 3117
that *d* upon the mount of Olives ... Zec 14:4 3117
it shall come to pass in that *d* ... Zec 14:6 3117
But it shall be one *d* which shall ... Zec 14:7 3117
shall be known to the LORD, not *d* ... Zec 14:7 3117
And it shall be in that *d*, that ... Zec 14:8 3117
in that *d* shall there be one LORD ... Zec 14:9 3117
it shall come to pass in that *d* ... Zec 14:13 3117
In that *d* shall there be upon the ... Zec 14:20 3117
in that *d* there shall be no more ... Zec 14:21 3117
who may abide the *d* of his coming ... Mal 3:2 3117
in that *d* when I make up my ... Mal 3:17 3117
the *d* cometh, that shall burn as ... Mal 4:1 3117
the *d* that cometh shall burn them ... Mal 4:1 3117
in the *d* that I shall do this ... Mal 4:3 3117
great and dreadful *d* of the LORD ... Mal 4:5 3117
Give us this *d* our daily bread ... Mt 6:11 *4594*
grass of the field, which to *d* is ... Mt 6:30 *4594*
unto the *d* is the evil thereof ... Mt 6:34 *2250*
Many will say to me in that *d* ... Mt 7:22 *2250*
and Gomorrha in the *d* of judgment ... Mt 10:15 *2250*
and Sidon at the *d* of judgment ... Mt 11:22 *2250*
would have remained until this *d* ... Mt 11:23 *4594*
of Sodom in the *d* of judgment ... Mt 11:24 *2250*
on the sabbath *d* through the corn ... Mt 12:1
lawful to do upon the sabbath *d* ... Mt 12:2
man is Lord even of the sabbath *d* ... Mt 12:8
fall into a pit on the sabbath *d* ... Mt 12:11
thereof in the *d* of judgment ... Mt 12:36 *2250*
The same *d* went Jesus out of the ... Mt 13:1 *2250*
It will be foul weather to *d* ... Mt 16:3 *4594*
and be raised again the third *d* ... Mt 16:21 *2250*
the third *d* he shall be raised ... Mt 17:23 *2250*
the labourers for a penny a *d* ... Mt 20:2 *2250*
Why stand ye here all the *d* idle ... Mt 20:6 *2250*
borne the burden and heat of the *d* ... Mt 20:12 *2250*
the third *d* he shall rise again ... Mt 20:19 *2250*
go work to *d* in my vineyard ... Mt 21:28 *4594*
The same *d* came to him the ... Mt 22:23 *2250*
that *d* forth ask him any more ... Mt 22:46 *2250*
winter, neither on the sabbath *d* ... Mt 24:20
But of that *d* and hour knoweth no ... Mt 24:36 *2250*
until the *d* that Noe entered into ... Mt 24:38 *2250*
a *d* when he looketh not for him ... Mt 24:50 *2250*
for ye know neither the *d* nor the ... Mt 25:13 *2250*
But they said, Not on the feast *d* ... Mt 26:5
Now the first *d* of the feast of ... Mt 26:17
until that *d* when I drink it new ... Mt 26:29 *2250*
The field of blood, unto this *d* ... Mt 27:8 *4594*
this *d* in a dream because of him ... Mt 27:19 *4594*
Now the next *d*, that followed the ... Mt 27:62 *1887*
that followed the *d* of the ... Mt 27:62
be made sure until the third *d* ... Mt 27:64 *2250*
toward the first *d* of the week ... Mt 28:1
among the Jews until this *d* ... Mt 28:15 *4595*
straightway on the sabbath *d* he ... Mk 1:21
rising up a great while before *d* ... Mk 1:35 *1773*
the corn fields on the sabbath *d* ... Mk 2:23
d that which is not lawful ... Mk 2:24
would heal him on the sabbath *d* ... Mk 3:2
should sleep, and rise night and *d* ... Mk 4:27 *2250*
And the same *d*, when the even was ... Mk 4:35 *2250*

And always, night and *d*, he was in ... Mk 5:5 *2250*
And when the sabbath *d* was come ... Mk 6:2
and Gomorrha in the *d* of judgment ... Mk 6:11 *2250*
And when a convenient *d* was come ... Mk 6:21 *2250*
when the *d* was now far spent, his ... Mk 6:35 *5610*
killed, he shall rise the third *d* ... Mk 9:31 *2250*
the third *d* he shall rise again ... Mk 10:34 *2250*
But of that *d* and that hour ... Mk 13:32 *2250*
But they said, Not on the feast *d* ... Mk 14:2
the first *d* of unleavened bread, ... Mk 14:12 *2250*
until that *d* that I drink it new ... Mk 14:25 *2250*
I say unto thee, That this *d* ... Mk 14:30 *4594*
the *d* before the sabbath, ... Mk 15:42
morning the first *d* of the week ... Mk 16:2
early the first *d* of the week ... Mk 16:9
until the *d* that these things ... Lk 1:20 *2250*
that on the eighth *d* they came to ... Lk 1:59 *2250*
the *d* of his shewing unto Israel ... Lk 1:80 *2250*
For unto you is born this *d* in ... Lk 2:11 *4594*
fastings and prayers night and *d* ... Lk 2:37 *2250*
the synagogue on the sabbath *d* ... Lk 4:16 *2250*
them, This *d* is this scripture ... Lk 4:21 *4594*
And when it was *d*, he departed and ... Lk 4:42 *2250*
And it came to pass on a certain *d* ... Lk 5:17 *2250*
We have seen strange things to *d* ... Lk 5:26 *4594*
he would heal on the sabbath *d* ... Lk 6:7
And when it was *d*, he called unto ... Lk 6:13 *2250*
Rejoice ye in that *d*, and leap for ... Lk 6:23 *2250*
And it came to pass the *d* after ... Lk 7:11 *2250*
it came to pass on a certain *d* ... Lk 8:22 *2250*
when the *d* began to wear away, ... Lk 9:12 *2250*
slain, and be raised the third *d* ... Lk 9:22 *2250*
came to pass, that on the next *d* ... Lk 9:37 *2250*
tolerable in that *d* for Sodom ... Lk 10:12 *2250*
Give us *d* by *d* our daily bread ... Lk 11:3
Give us *d* by *d* our daily bread ... Lk 11:3
which is to *d* in the field, and to ... Lk 12:28 *4594*
a *d* when he looketh not for him ... Lk 12:46 *2250*
Jesus had healed on the sabbath *d* ... Lk 13:14
healed, and not on the sabbath *d* ... Lk 13:14 *2250*
from this bond on the sabbath *d* ... Lk 13:16 *2250*
The same *d* there came certain of ... Lk 13:31 *2250*
out devils, and I do cures to *d* ... Lk 13:32 *4594*
the third *d* I shall be perfected ... Lk 13:32
Nevertheless I must walk to *d* ... Lk 13:33 *4594*
and to morrow, and the *d* following ... Lk 13:33
to eat bread on the sabbath *d* ... Lk 14:1
lawful to heal on the sabbath *d* ... Lk 14:3
pull him out on the sabbath *d* ... Lk 14:5 *2250*
and fared sumptuously every *d* ... Lk 16:19 *2250*
against thee seven times in a *d* ... Lk 17:4 *2250*
seven times in a *d* turn again to ... Lk 17:4 *2250*
also the Son of man be in his *d* ... Lk 17:24 *2250*
until the *d* that Noe entered into ... Lk 17:27 *2250*
But the same *d* that Lot went out ... Lk 17:29 *2250*
Even thus shall it be in the *d* ... Lk 17:30 *2250*
In that *d*, he which shall be upon ... Lk 17:31 *2250*
avenge his own elect, which cry *d* ... Lk 18:7 *2250*
the third *d* he shall rise again ... Lk 18:33 *2250*
for to *d* I must abide at thy ... Lk 19:5 *4594*
This *d* is salvation come to this ... Lk 19:9 *4594*
even thou, at least in this thy *d* ... Lk 19:42 *2250*
so that *d* come upon you unawares ... Lk 21:34 *2250*
in the *d* time he was teaching in ... Lk 21:37 *2250*
Then came the *d* of unleavened ... Lk 22:7 *2250*
the cock shall not crow this *d* ... Lk 22:34 *4594*
And as soon as it was *d*, the ... Lk 22:66 *2250*
And the same *d* Pilate and Herod ... Lk 23:12 *2250*
To *d* shalt thou be with me in ... Lk 23:43 *4594*
that *d* was the preparation, and ... Lk 23:54 *2250*
rested the sabbath *d* according to ... Lk 23:56
Now upon the first *d* of the week ... Lk 24:1
and the third *d* rise again ... Lk 24:7 *2250*
same *d* to a village called Emmaus ... Lk 24:13 *2250*
to *d* is the third *d* since these ... Lk 24:21 *4594*
to *d* is the third *d* since these ... Lk 24:21 *2250*
evening, and the *d* is far spent ... Lk 24:29 *2250*
to rise from the dead the third *d* ... Lk 24:46 *2250*
The next *d* John seeth Jesus ... Jn 1:29 *1887*
Again the next *d* after John stood ... Jn 1:35 *1887*
dwelt, and abode with him that *d* ... Jn 1:39 *2250*
The *d* following Jesus would go ... Jn 1:43 *1887*
the third *d* there was a marriage ... Jn 2:1 *2250*
at the passover, in the feast *d* ... Jn 2:23
on the same *d* was the sabbath ... Jn 5:9 *2250*
was cured, It is the sabbath *d* ... Jn 5:10
these things on the sabbath *d* ... Jn 5:16
The *d* following, when the people ... Jn 6:22 *1887*
raise it up again at the last *d* ... Jn 6:39 *2250*
I will raise him up at the last *d* ... Jn 6:40 *2250*
I will raise him up at the last *d* ... Jn 6:44 *2250*
I will raise him up at the last *d* ... Jn 6:54 *2250*
on the sabbath *d* circumcise a man ... Jn 7:22
sabbath *d* receive circumcision ... Jn 7:23
every whit whole on the sabbath *d* ... Jn 7:23
In the last *d*, that great *d* of ... Jn 7:37 *2250*
Abraham rejoiced to see my *d* ... Jn 8:56 *2250*
him that sent me, while it is *d* ... Jn 9:4 *2250*
it was the sabbath *d* when Jesus ... Jn 9:14
he keepeth not the sabbath *d* ... Jn 9:16
there not twelve hours in the *d* ... Jn 11:9 *2250*
If any man walk in the *d*, he ... Jn 11:9 *2250*
in the resurrection at the last *d* ... Jn 11:24 *2250*
Then from that *d* forth they took ... Jn 11:53 *2250*
against the *d* of my burying hath ... Jn 12:7 *2250*
On the next *d* much people that ... Jn 12:12 *1887*
shall judge him in the last *d* ... Jn 12:48 *2250*
At that *d* ye shall know that I am ... Jn 14:20 *2250*
in that *d* ye shall ask me nothing ... Jn 16:23 *2250*
At that *d* ye shall ask in my name ... Jn 16:26 *2250*
upon the cross on the sabbath *d* ... Jn 19:31
that sabbath *d* was an high *d* ... Jn 19:31
of the Jews' preparation *d* ... Jn 19:42
The first *d* of the week cometh ... Jn 20:1

Then the same *d* at evening ... Jn 20:19 *2250*
being the first *d* of the week ... Jn 20:19 *2250*
Until the *d* in which he was taken ... Acts 1:2 *2250*
unto that same *d* that he was ... Acts 1:22 *2250*
when the *d* of Pentecost was fully ... Acts 2:1 *2250*
it is but the third hour of the *d* ... Acts 2:15 *2250*
notable *d* of the Lord come ... Acts 2:20 *2250*
sepulchre is with us unto this *d* ... Acts 2:29 *2250*
the same *d* there were added unto ... Acts 2:41 *2250*
put them in hold unto the next *d* ... Acts 4:3 *839*
If we this *d* be examined of the ... Acts 4:9 *4594*
and circumcised him the eighth *d* ... Acts 7:8 *2250*
the next *d* he shewed himself unto ... Acts 7:26 *2250*
And they watched the gates *d* ... Acts 9:24 *2250*
about the ninth hour of the *d* an ... Acts 10:3 *2250*
Him God raised up the third *d* ... Acts 10:40 *2250*
Now as soon as it was *d*, there ... Acts 12:18 *2250*
And upon a set *d* Herod, arrayed in ... Acts 12:21 *2250*
the synagogue on the sabbath *d* ... Acts 13:14 *2250*
which are read every sabbath *d* ... Acts 13:27
this *d* have I begotten thee ... Acts 13:33 *4594*
the next sabbath *d* came almost ... Acts 13:44
the next *d* he departed with ... Acts 14:20 *1887*
in the synagogues every sabbath *d* ... Acts 15:21
and the next *d* to Neapolis ... Acts 16:11
And when it was *d*, the magistrates ... Acts 16:35 *2250*
Because he hath appointed a *d* ... Acts 17:31 *2250*
And upon the first *d* of the week ... Acts 20:7
long while, even till break of *d* ... Acts 20:11 *827*
came the next *d* over against ... Acts 20:15
the next *d* we arrived at Samos, ... Acts 20:15
the next *d* we came to Miletus ... Acts 20:15
at Jerusalem the *d* of Pentecost ... Acts 20:16 *2250*
from the first *d* that I came into ... Acts 20:18 *2250*
I take you to record this *d* ... Acts 20:26 *4594*
every one night and *d* with tears ... Acts 20:31 *2250*
the *d* following unto Rhodes, and ... Acts 21:1
and abode with them one *d* ... Acts 21:7 *2250*
the next *d* we that were of Paul's ... Acts 21:8
the *d* following Paul went in with ... Acts 21:18
the next *d* purifying himself with ... Acts 21:26 *2250*
toward God, as ye all are this *d* ... Acts 22:3 *4594*
before God until this *d* ... Acts 23:1 *2250*
And when it was *d*, certain of the ... Acts 23:12 *2250*
called in question by you this *d* ... Acts 24:21 *4594*
the next *d* sitting on the ... Acts 25:6 *1887*
d before thee touching all the ... Acts 26:2 *4594*
tribes, instantly serving God *d* ... Acts 26:7 *2250*
of God, I continue unto this *d* ... Acts 26:22 *2250*
but also all that hear me this *d* ... Acts 26:29 *4594*
the next *d* we touched at Sidon ... Acts 27:3
the next *d* they lightened the ... Acts 27:18
the third *d* we cast out with our ... Acts 27:19
of the stern, and wished for the *d* ... Acts 27:29 *2250*
while the *d* was coming on, Paul ... Acts 27:33 *2250*
meat, saying, This *d* ... Acts 27:33 *4594*
fourteenth *d* that ye have tarried ... Acts 27:33 *2250*
And when it was *d*, they knew not ... Acts 27:39 *2250*
after one *d* the south wind blew, ... Acts 28:13 *2250*
and we came the next *d* to Puteoli ... Acts 28:13 *2250*
when they had appointed him a *d* ... Acts 28:23 *2250*
wrath against the *d* of wrath ... Rom 2:5 *2250*
In the *d* when God shall judge the ... Rom 2:16 *2250*
sake we are killed all the *d* long ... Rom 8:36 *2250*
All *d* long I have stretched forth ... Rom 10:21 *2250*
should not hear;) unto this *d* ... Rom 11:8
is far spent, the *d* is at hand ... Rom 13:12 *2250*
Let us walk honestly, as in the *d* ... Rom 13:13 *2250*
man esteemeth one *d* above another ... Rom 14:5 *2250*
another esteemeth every *d* alike ... Rom 14:5 *2250*
He that regardeth the *d*, ... Rom 14:6 *2250*
and he that regardeth not the *d* ... Rom 14:6 *2250*
in the *d* of our Lord Jesus Christ ... 1Cor 1:8 *2250*
for the *d* shall declare it, ... 1Cor 3:13 *2250*
of all things unto this *d* ... 1Cor 4:13 *737*
saved in the *d* of the Lord Jesus ... 1Cor 5:5 *2250*
committed, and fell in one *d* three ... 1Cor 10:8 *2250*
d according to the scriptures ... 1Cor 15:4 *2250*
Upon the first *d* of the week let ... 1Cor 16:2
ours in the *d* of the Lord Jesus ... 2Cor 1:14 *2250*
for until this *d* remaineth the ... 2Cor 3:14 *4594*
But even unto this *d*, when Moses ... 2Cor 3:15 *4594*
inward man is renewed *d* by *d* ... 2Cor 4:16 *2250*
in the *d* of salvation have I ... 2Cor 6:2 *2250*
now is the *d* of salvation ... 2Cor 6:2 *2250*
a *d* I have been in the deep ... 2Cor 11:25 *3574*
sealed unto the *d* of redemption ... Eph 4:30 *2250*
able to withstand in the evil *d* ... Eph 6:13 *2250*
gospel from the first *d* until now ... Phil 1:5 *2250*
it until the *d* of Jesus Christ ... Phil 1:6 *2250*
offence till the *d* of Christ ... Phil 1:10 *2250*
I may rejoice in the *d* of Christ ... Phil 2:16 *2250*
Circumcised the eighth *d*, of the ... Phil 3:5 *2250*
since the *d* ye heard of it, and ... Col 1:6 *2250*
since the *d* we heard it, do not ... Col 1:9 *2250*
for labouring night and *d*, because ... 1Th 2:9 *2250*
d praying exceedingly that we ... 1Th 3:10 *2250*
know perfectly that the *d* of the ... 1Th 5:2 *2250*
that that *d* should overtake you ... 1Th 5:4 *2250*
light, and the children of the *d* ... 1Th 5:5 *2250*
But let us, who are of the *d* ... 1Th 5:8 *2250*
among you was believed) in that *d* ... 2Th 1:10 *2250*
as that the *d* of Christ is at ... 2Th 2:2 *2250*
for that *d* shall not come, except ... 2Th 2:3
with labour and travail night and *d* ... 2Th 3:8 *2250*
and prayers night and *d* ... 1Ti 5:5 *2250*
of thee in my prayers night and *d* ... 2Ti 1:3 *2250*
committed unto him against that *d* ... 2Ti 1:12 *2250*
find mercy of the Lord in that *d* ... 2Ti 1:18 *2250*
judge, shall give me at that *d* ... 2Ti 4:8 *2250*
this *d* have I begotten thee ... Heb 1:5 *4594*
To *d* if ye will hear his voice, ... Heb 3:7 *4594*
in the *d* of temptation in the ... Heb 3:8 *2250*
daily, while it is called To *d* ... Heb 3:13 *4594*

To *d* if ye will hear his voice, Heb 3:15 4594
of the seventh *d* on this wise Heb 4:4
the seventh *d* from all his works Heb 4:4 2250
Again, he limiteth a certain *d* Heb 4:7 2250
saying in David, To *d* Heb 4:7 4594
To *d* if ye will hear his voice, Heb 4:7 4594
have spoken of another *d* Heb 4:8 2250
to *d* have I begotten thee Heb 5:5 4594
in the *d* when I took them by the Heb 8:9 2250
more, as ye see the *d* approaching Heb 10:25 2250
the same yesterday, and to *d* Heb 13:8 4594
To *d* or to morrow we will go into Jas 4:13 4594
hearts, as in a *d* of slaughter Jas 5:5 2250
God in the *d* of visitation 1Pet 2:12 2250
in a dark place, until the *d* dawn 2Pet 1:19 2250
the *d* star arise in your hearts 2Pet 1:19 5459
from *d* to *d* with their unlawful 2Pet 2:8 2250
to *d* with their unlawful deeds 2Pet 2:8 2250
the *d* of judgment to be punished 2Pet 2:9 2250
fire against the *d* of judgment 2Pet 3:7 2250
that one *d* is with the Lord as a 2Pet 3:8 2250
and a thousand years as one *d* 2Pet 3:8 2250
But the *d* of the Lord will come 2Pet 3:10 2250
unto the coming of the *d* of God 2Pet 3:12 2250
boldness in the *d* of judgment 1Jn 4:17 2250
unto the judgment of the great *d* Jude 6 2250
was in the Spirit on the Lord's *d* Rev 1:10 2250
and they rest not *d* and night, Rev 4:8 2250
For the great *d* of his wrath is Rev 6:17 2250
the throne of God, and serve him *d* Rev 7:15 2250
the *d* shone not for a third part Rev 8:12 2250
were prepared for an hour, and a *d* Rev 9:15 2250
accused them before our God *d* Rev 12:10 2250
and they have no rest *d* nor night Rev 14:11 2250
of that great *d* of God Almighty Rev 16:14 2250
shall her plagues come in one *d* Rev 18:8 2250
are, and shall be tormented *d* Rev 20:10 2250
it shall not be shut at all by *d* Rev 21:25 2250

DAY'S

as it were a *d* journey on this Num 11:31 3117
as it were a *d* journey on the Num 11:31 3117
But he himself went a *d* journey 1Kin 19:4 3117
as every *d* work required 1Chr 16:37 3117
also according unto this *d* decree Est 9:13 3117
enter into the city a *d* journey Jonah 3:4 3117
in the company, went a *d* journey Lk 2:44 2250
Jerusalem a sabbath *d* journey Acts 1:12
in question for this *d* uproar Acts 19:40 4594

DAYS

signs, and for seasons, and for *d* Gen 1:14 3117
thou eat all the *d* of thy life Gen 3:14 3117
eat of it all the *d* of thy life Gen 3:17 3117
the *d* of Adam after he had Gen 5:4 3117
all the *d* that Adam lived were Gen 5:5 3117
all the *d* of Seth were nine Gen 5:8 3117
all the *d* of Enos were nine Gen 5:11 3117
all the *d* of Cainan were nine Gen 5:14 3117
all the *d* of Mahalaleel were Gen 5:17 3117
all the *d* of Jared were nine Gen 5:20 3117
all the *d* of Enoch were three Gen 5:23 3117
all the *d* of Methuselah were nine Gen 5:27 3117
all the *d* of Lamech were seven Gen 5:31 3117
yet his *d* shall be an hundred and Gen 6:3 3117
giants in the earth in those *d* Gen 6:4 3117
For yet seven *d*, and I will cause Gen 7:4 3117
it to rain upon the earth forty *d* Gen 7:4 3117
And it came to pass after seven *d* Gen 7:10 3117
rain was upon the earth forty *d* Gen 7:12 3117
flood was forty *d* upon the earth Gen 7:17 3117
the earth an hundred and fifty *d* Gen 7:24 3117
fifty *d* the waters were abated Gen 8:3 3117
to pass at the end of forty *d* Gen 8:6 3117
And he stayed yet other seven *d* Gen 8:10 3117
And he stayed yet other seven *d* Gen 8:12 3117
all the *d* of Noah were nine Gen 9:29 3117
for in his *d* was the earth Gen 10:25 3117
the *d* of Terah were two hundred Gen 11:32 3117
it came to pass in the *d* of Gen 14:1 3117
he that is eight *d* old shall be Gen 17:12 3117
his son Isaac being eight *d* old Gen 21:4 3117
in the Philistines' land many *d* Gen 21:34 3117
the damsel abide with us a few *d* Gen 24:55 3117
these are the *d* of the years of Gen 25:7 3117
when her *d* to be delivered were Gen 25:24 3117
that was in the *d* of Abraham Gen 26:1 3117
in the *d* of Abraham his father Gen 26:15 3117
in the *d* of Abraham his father Gen 26:18 3117
The *d* of mourning for my father Gen 27:41 3117
And tarry with him a few *d* Gen 27:44 3117
they seemed unto him but a few *d* Gen 29:20 3117
for my *d* are fulfilled, that I Gen 29:21 3117
went in the *d* of wheat harvest Gen 30:14 3117
the *d* of Isaac were an hundred and Gen 35:28 3117
people, being old and full of *d* Gen 35:29 3117
and mourned for his son many *d* Gen 37:34 3117
The three branches are three *d* Gen 40:12 3117
Yet within three *d* shall Pharaoh Gen 40:13 3117
The three baskets are three *d* Gen 40:18 3117
Yet within three *d* shall Pharaoh Gen 40:19 3117
all together into ward three *d* Gen 42:17 3117
Pharaoh, The *d* of the years of my Gen 47:9 3117
evil have the *d* of the years of Gen 47:9 3117
have not attained unto the *d* of Gen 47:9 3117
in the *d* of their pilgrimage Gen 47:9 3117
shall befall you in the last *d* Gen 49:1 3117
forty *d* were fulfilled for him Gen 50:3 3117
for so are fulfilled the *d* of Gen 50:3 3117
for him threescore and ten *d* Gen 50:3 3117
when the *d* of his mourning were Gen 50:4 3117
a mourning for his father seven *d* Gen 50:10 3117
And it came to pass in those *d* Ex 2:11 3117
seven *d* were fulfilled, after Ex 7:25 3117
in all the land of Egypt three *d* Ex 10:22 3117
any from his place for three *d* Ex 10:23 3117
Seven *d* shall ye eat unleavened Ex 12:15 3117
Seven *d* shall there be no leaven Ex 12:19 3117
Seven *d* thou shalt eat unleavened Ex 13:6 3117
bread shall be eaten seven *d* Ex 13:7 3117
and they went three *d* in the Ex 15:22 3117
Six *d* ye shall gather it Ex 16:26 3117
the sixth day the bread of two *d* Ex 16:29 3117
Six *d* shalt thou labour, and do Ex 20:9 3117
For in six *d* the LORD made heaven Ex 20:11 3117
that thy *d* may be long upon the Ex 20:12 3117
seven *d* it shall be with his dam Ex 22:30 3117
Six *d* thou shalt do thy work, and Ex 23:12 3117
eat unleavened bread seven *d* Ex 23:15 3117
the number of thy *d* I will fulfil Ex 23:26 3117
and the cloud covered it six *d* Ex 24:16 3117
and Moses was in the mount forty *d* Ex 24:18 3117
stead shall put them on seven *d* Ex 29:30 3117
seven *d* shalt thou consecrate Ex 29:35 3117
Seven *d* thou shalt make an Ex 29:37 3117
Six *d* may work be done Ex 31:15 3117
for in six *d* the LORD made heaven Ex 31:17 3117
Seven *d* thou shalt eat unleavened Ex 34:18 3117
Six *d* thou shalt work, but on the Ex 34:21 3117
was there with the LORD forty *d* Ex 34:28 3117
Six *d* shall work be done, but on Ex 35:2 3117
of the congregation in seven *d* Lev 8:33 3117
until the *d* of your consecration Lev 8:33 3117
for seven *d* shall he consecrate Lev 8:33 3117
congregation day and night seven *d* Lev 8:35 3117
then she shall be unclean seven *d* Lev 12:2 3117
according to the *d* of the Lev 12:2 3117
her purifying three and thirty *d* Lev 12:4 3117
until the *d* of her purifying be Lev 12:4 3117
her purifying threescore and six *d* Lev 12:5 3117
when the *d* of her purifying are Lev 12:6 3117
him that hath the plague seven *d* Lev 13:4 3117
shall shut him up seven *d* more Lev 13:5 3117
priest shall shut him up seven *d* Lev 13:21 3117
priest shall shut him up seven *d* Lev 13:26 3117
the plague of the scall seven *d* Lev 13:31 3117
that hath the scall seven *d* more Lev 13:33 3117
All the *d* wherein the plague Lev 13:46 3117
it that hath the plague seven *d* Lev 13:50 3117
he shall shut it up seven *d* more Lev 13:54 3117
abroad out of his tent seven *d* Lev 14:8 3117
and shut up the house seven *d* Lev 14:38 3117
himself seven *d* for his cleansing Lev 15:13 3117
she shall be put apart seven *d* Lev 15:19 3117
him, he shall be unclean seven *d* Lev 15:24 3117
many *d* out of the time of her Lev 15:25 3117
all the *d* of the issue of her Lev 15:25 3117
be as the *d* of her separation Lev 15:25 3117
bed whereon she lieth all the *d* Lev 15:26 3117
shall number to herself seven *d* Lev 15:28 3117
it shall be seven *d* under the dam Lev 22:27 3117
Six *d* shall work be done Lev 23:3 3117
seven *d* ye must eat unleavened Lev 23:6 3117
by fire unto the LORD seven *d* Lev 23:8 3117
sabbath shall ye number fifty *d* Lev 23:16 3117
for seven *d* unto the LORD Lev 23:34 3117
Seven *d* ye shall offer an Lev 23:36 3117
a feast unto the LORD seven *d* Lev 23:39 3117
before the LORD your God seven *d* Lev 23:40 3117
unto the LORD seven *d* in the year Lev 23:41 3117
Ye shall dwell in booths seven *d* Lev 23:42 3117
All the *d* of his separation shall Num 6:4 3117
All the *d* of the vow of his Num 6:5 3117
until the *d* be fulfilled, in the Num 6:5 3117
All the *d* that he separateth Num 6:6 3117
All the *d* of his separation he is Num 6:8 3117
the LORD the *d* of his separation Num 6:12 3117
but the *d* that were before shall Num 6:12 3117
when the *d* of his separation are Num 6:13 3117
long upon the tabernacle many *d* Num 9:19 3117
was a few *d* upon the tabernacle Num 9:20 3117
Or whether it were two *d*, or a Num 9:22 3117
gladness, and in your solemn *d* Num 10:10
one day, nor two *d*, nor five *d* Num 11:19 3117
neither ten *d*, nor twenty *d* Num 11:19 3117
should she not be ashamed seven *d* Num 12:14 3117
be shut out from the camp seven *d* Num 12:14 3117
shut out from the camp seven *d* Num 12:15 3117
of the land after forty *d* Num 13:25 3117
After the number of the *d* in Num 14:34 3117
searched the land, even forty *d* Num 14:34 3117
any man shall be unclean seven *d* Num 19:11 3117
tent, shall be unclean seven *d* Num 19:14 3117
a grave, shall be unclean seven *d* Num 19:16 3117
they mourned for Aaron thirty *d* Num 20:29 3117
do to thy people in the latter *d* Num 24:14 3117
seven *d* shall unleavened bread be Num 28:17 3117
daily, throughout the seven *d* Num 28:24 3117
a feast unto the LORD seven *d* Num 29:12 3117
ye abide without the camp seven *d* Num 31:19 3117
So ye abode in Kadesh many *d* Deut 1:46 3117
according unto the *d* that ye Deut 1:46 3117
and we compassed mount Seir many *d* Deut 2:1 3117
thy heart all the *d* of thy life Deut 4:9 3117
may learn to fear me all the *d* Deut 4:10 3117
shall not prolong your *d* upon it Deut 4:26 3117
upon thee, even in the latter *d* Deut 4:30 3117
ask now of the *d* that are past Deut 4:32 3117
prolong thy *d* upon the earth Deut 4:40 3117
Six *d* thou shalt labour, and do Deut 5:13 3117
that thy *d* may be prolonged, and Deut 5:16 3117
that ye may prolong your *d* in the Deut 5:33 3117
son's son, all the *d* of thy life Deut 6:2 3117
that thy *d* may be prolonged Deut 6:2 3117
then I abode in the mount forty *d* Deut 9:9 3117
to pass at the end of forty *d* Deut 9:11 3117
LORD, as at the first, forty *d* Deut 9:18 3117
fell down before the LORD forty *d* Deut 9:25 3117
to the first time, forty *d* Deut 10:10 3117
ye may prolong your *d* in the land Deut 11:9 3117
That your *d* may be multiplied, and Deut 11:21 3117
the *d* of your children, in the Deut 11:21 3117
as the *d* of heaven upon the earth Deut 11:21 3117
all the *d* that ye live upon the Deut 12:1 3117
seven *d* shalt thou eat unleavened Deut 16:3 3117
of Egypt all the *d* of thy life Deut 16:3 3117
thee in all thy coast seven *d* Deut 16:4 3117
Six *d* thou shalt eat unleavened Deut 16:8 3117
the feast of tabernacles seven *d* Deut 16:13 3117
Seven *d* shalt thou keep a solemn Deut 16:15 3117
judge that shall be in those *d* Deut 17:9 3117
therein all the *d* of his life Deut 17:19 3117
may prolong his *d* in his kingdom Deut 17:20 3117
judges, which shall be in those *d* Deut 19:17 3117
and that thou mayest prolong thy *d* Deut 22:7 3117
he may not put her away all his *d* Deut 22:19 3117
he may not put her away all his *d* Deut 22:29 3117
prosperity all thy *d* for ever Deut 23:6 3117
that thy *d* may be lengthened in Deut 25:15 3117
priest that shall be in those *d* Deut 26:3 3117
not prolong your *d* upon the land Deut 30:18 3117
thy life, and the length of thy *d* Deut 30:20 3117
thy *d* approach that thou must die Deut 31:14 3117
will befall you in the latter *d* Deut 31:29 3117
Remember the *d* of old, consider Deut 32:7 3117
shall prolong your *d* in the land Deut 32:47 3117
and as thy *d*, so shall thy Deut 33:25 3117
in the plains of Moab thirty *d* Deut 34:8 3117
so the *d* of weeping and mourning Deut 34:8 3117
before thee all the *d* of thy life Josh 1:5 3117
for within three *d* ye shall pass Josh 1:11 3117
and hide yourselves there three *d* Josh 2:16 3117
mountain, and abode there three *d* Josh 2:22 3117
And it came to pass after three *d* Josh 3:2 3117
Moses, all the *d* of his life Josh 4:14 3117
Thus shalt thou do six *d* Josh 6:3 3117
so they did six *d* Josh 6:14 3117
to pass at the end of three *d* Josh 9:16 3117
priest that shall be in those *d* Josh 20:6 3117
these many *d* unto this day Josh 22:3 3117
the LORD all the *d* of Joshua Josh 24:31 3117
all the *d* of the elders that Josh 24:31 3117
the LORD all the *d* of Joshua Judg 2:7 3117
all the *d* of the elders that Judg 2:7 3117
enemies all the *d* of the judge Judg 2:18 3117
In the *d* of Shamgar the son of Judg 5:6 3117
in the *d* of Jael, the highways Judg 5:6 3117
forty years in the *d* of Gideon Judg 8:28 3117
the Gileadite four *d* in a year Judg 11:40 3117
within the seven *d* of the feast Judg 14:12 3117
not in three *d* expound the riddle Judg 14:14 3117
she wept before him the seven *d* Judg 14:17 3117
he judged Israel in the *d* of the Judg 15:20 3117
In those *d* there was no king in Judg 17:6 3117
In those *d* there was no king in Judg 18:1 3117
in those *d* the tribe of the Judg 18:1 3117
And it came to pass in those *d* Judg 19:1 3117
and he abode with him three *d* Judg 19:4 3117
of God was there in those *d* Judg 20:27 3117
Aaron, stood before it in those *d* Judg 20:28 3117
In those *d* there was no king in Judg 21:25 3117
in the *d* when the judges ruled Ruth 1:1 3117
the LORD all the *d* of his life 1Sa 1:11 3117
the *d* come, that I will cut off 1Sa 2:31 3117
the LORD was precious in those *d* 1Sa 3:1 3117
Philistines all the *d* of Samuel 1Sa 7:13 3117
Israel all the *d* of his life 1Sa 7:15 3117
asses that were lost three *d* ago 1Sa 9:20 3117
seven *d* shalt thou tarry, till I 1Sa 10:8 3117
And he tarried seven *d*, according 1Sa 13:8 3117
camest not within the *d* appointed 1Sa 13:11 3117
the Philistines all the *d* of Saul 1Sa 14:52 3117
for an old man in the *d* of Saul 1Sa 17:12 3117
and presented himself forty *d* 1Sa 17:16 3117
and the *d* were not expired 1Sa 18:26 3117
And when thou hast stayed three *d* 1Sa 20:19
kept from us about these three *d* 1Sa 21:5 8543
there be many servants now a *d* 1Sa 25:10 3117
not been found in thee all thy *d* 1Sa 25:28 3117
it came to pass about ten *d* after 1Sa 25:38 3117
And it came to pass in those *d* 1Sa 28:1 3117
which hath been with me these *d* 1Sa 29:3 3117
nor drunk any water, three *d* 1Sa 30:12 3117
because three *d* agone I fell sick 1Sa 30:13
tree at Jabesh, and fasted seven *d* 1Sa 31:13 3117
David had abode two *d* in Ziklag 2Sa 1:1 3117
when thy *d* be fulfilled, and thou 2Sa 7:12 3117
which he counselled in those *d* 2Sa 16:23 3117
the men of Judah within three *d* 2Sa 20:4 3117
in the *d* of David three years 2Sa 21:1 3117
d of harvest, in the first *d* 2Sa 21:9
end of nine months and twenty *d* 2Sa 24:8 3117
Now the *d* of David drew nigh that 1Kin 2:1 3117
the *d* that David reigned over 1Kin 2:11 3117
Shimei dwelt in Jerusalem many *d* 1Kin 2:38 3117
name of the LORD, until those *d* 1Kin 3:2 3117
kings like unto thee all thy *d* 1Kin 3:13 3117
walk, then I will lengthen thy *d* 1Kin 3:14 3117
Solomon all the *d* of his life 1Kin 4:21 3117
Beer-sheba, all the *d* of Solomon 1Kin 4:25 3117
the *d* that they live in the land 1Kin 8:40 3117
before the LORD our God, seven *d* 1Kin 8:65 3117
and seven *d*, even fourteen *d* 1Kin 8:65 3117
accounted of in the *d* of Solomon 1Kin 10:21 3117
Notwithstanding in thy *d* I will 1Kin 11:12 3117
to Israel all the *d* of Solomon 1Kin 11:25 3117
the *d* of his life for David my 1Kin 11:34 3117
unto them, Depart yet for three *d* 1Kin 12:5 3117
the *d* which Jeroboam reigned were 1Kin 14:20 3117
Rehoboam and Jeroboam all their *d* 1Kin 14:30 3117
him all the *d* of his life 1Kin 15:5 3117
and Jeroboam all the *d* of his life 1Kin 15:6 3117
perfect with the LORD all his *d* 1Kin 15:14 3117

Baasha king of Israel all their *d* 1Kin 15:16 3117
Baasha king of Israel all their *d* 1Kin 15:32 3117
did Zimri reign seven *d* in Tirzah 1Kin 16:15 3117
In his *d* did Hiel the Beth-elite 1Kin 16:34 3117
he, and her house, did eat many *d* 1Kin 17:15 3117
And it came to pass after many *d* 1Kin 18:1 3117
the strength of that meat forty *d* 1Kin 19:8 3117
over against the other seven *d* 1Kin 20:29 3117
will not bring the evil in his *d* 1Kin 21:29 3117
but in his son's *d* will I bring 1Kin 21:29 3117
in the *d* of his father Asa 1Kin 22:46 3117
and they sought three *d*, but found 2Kin 2:17 3117
In his *d* Edom revolted from under 2Kin 8:20 3117
In those *d* the LORD began to cut 2Kin 10:32 3117
his *d* wherein Jehoiada the priest 2Kin 12:2 3117
the son of Hazael, all their *d* 2Kin 13:3 3117
Israel all the *d* of Jehoahaz 2Kin 13:22 3117
he departed not all his *d* from 2Kin 15:18 3117
In the *d* of Pekah king of Israel 2Kin 15:29 3117
In those *d* the LORD began to send 2Kin 15:37 3117
for unto those *d* the children of 2Kin 18:4 3117
In those *d* was Hezekiah sick unto 2Kin 20:1 3117
will add unto thy *d* fifteen years 2Kin 20:6 3117
the *d* come, that all that is in 2Kin 20:17 3117
if peace and truth be in my *d* 2Kin 20:19 3117
the *d* of the judges that judged 2Kin 23:22 3117
nor in all the *d* of the kings of 2Kin 23:22 3117
In his *d* Pharaoh-nechoh king of 2Kin 23:29 3117
In his *d* Nebuchadnezzar king of 2Kin 24:1 3117
before him all the *d* of his life 2Kin 25:29 3117
every day, all the *d* of his life 2Kin 25:30 3117
because in his *d* the earth was 1Chr 1:19 3117
the *d* of Hezekiah king of Judah 1Chr 4:41 3117
in the *d* of Saul they made war 1Chr 5:10 3117
in the *d* of Jotham king of Judah 1Chr 5:17 3117
in the *d* of Jeroboam king of 1Chr 5:17 3117
number was in the *d* of David two 1Chr 7:2 3117
their father mourned many *d* 1Chr 7:22 3117
were to come after seven *d* from 1Chr 9:25 3117
oak in Jabesh, and fasted seven *d* 1Chr 10:12 3117
they were with David three *d* 1Chr 12:39 3117
not at it in the *d* of Saul 1Chr 13:3 3117
when thy *d* be expired that thou 1Chr 17:11 3117
or else three *d* the sword of the 1Chr 21:12 3117
and quietness unto Israel in his *d* 1Chr 22:9 3117
when David was old and full of *d* 1Chr 23:1 3117
our *d* on the earth are as a 1Chr 29:15 3117
died in a good old age, full of *d* 1Chr 29:28 3117
Solomon kept the feast seven *d* 2Chr 7:8 3117
dedication of the altar seven *d* 2Chr 7:9 3117
seven *d*, and the feast seven *d* 2Chr 7:9 3117
accounted of in the *d* of Solomon 2Chr 9:20 3117
Come again unto me after three *d* 2Chr 10:5 3117
strength again in the *d* of Abijah 2Chr 13:20 3117
In his *d* the land was quiet ten 2Chr 14:1 3117
of Asa was perfect all his *d* 2Chr 15:17 3117
they were three *d* in gathering of 2Chr 20:25 3117
In his *d* the Edomites revolted 2Chr 21:8 3117
all the *d* of Jehoiada the priest 2Chr 24:2 3117
continually all the *d* of Jehoiada 2Chr 24:14 3117
was full of *d* when he died 2Chr 24:15 3117
sought God in the *d* of Zechariah 2Chr 26:5 3117
the house of the LORD in eight *d* 2Chr 29:17 3117
bread seven *d* with great gladness 2Chr 30:21 3117
eat throughout the feast seven *d* 2Chr 30:22 3117
counsel to keep other seven *d* 2Chr 30:23 3117
kept other seven *d* with gladness 2Chr 30:23 3117
In those *d* Hezekiah was sick to 2Chr 32:24 3117
upon them in the *d* of Hezekiah 2Chr 32:26 3117
all his *d* they departed not from 2Chr 34:33 3117
feast of unleavened bread seven *d* 2Chr 35:17 3117
from the *d* of Samuel the prophet 2Chr 35:18 3117
months and ten *d* in Jerusalem 2Chr 36:9 3117
d of Esar-haddon king of Assur Ezr 4:2 3117
all the *d* of Cyrus king of Persia Ezr 4:5 3117
in the *d* of Artaxerxes wrote Ezr 4:7 3117
unleavened bread seven *d* with joy Ezr 6:22 3117
there abode we in tents three *d* Ezr 8:15 3117
Jerusalem, and abode there three *d* Ezr 8:32 3117
Since the *d* of our fathers have Ezr 9:7 3117
would not come within three *d* Ezr 10:8 3117
unto Jerusalem within three *d* Ezr 10:9 3117
and wept, and mourned certain *d* Neh 1:4 3117
Jerusalem, and was there three *d* Neh 2:11 3117
once in ten *d* store of all sorts Neh 5:18 3117
the month Elul, in fifty and two *d* Neh 6:15 3117
Moreover in those *d* the nobles of Neh 6:17 3117
for since the *d* of Jeshua the son Neh 8:17 3117
And they kept the feast seven *d* Neh 8:18 3117
their brethren in the *d* of Jeshua Neh 12:7 3117
in the *d* of Joiakim were priests, Neh 12:12 3117
The Levites in the *d* of Eliashib Neh 12:22 3117
even until the *d* of Johanan the Neh 12:23 3117
These were in the *d* of Joiakim Neh 12:26 3117
in the *d* of Nehemiah the governor Neh 12:26 3117
For in the *d* of David and Asaph of Neh 12:46 3117
all Israel in the *d* of Zerubbabel Neh 12:47 3117
in the *d* of Nehemiah, gave the Neh 12:47 3117
after certain *d* obtained I leave Neh 13:6 3117
In those *d* saw I in Judah some Neh 13:15 3117
In those *d* also saw I Jews that Neh 13:23 3117
to pass in the *d* of Ahasuerus Est 1:1 3117
That in those *d*, when the king Est 1:2 3117
of his excellent majesty many *d* Est 1:4 3117
even an hundred and fourscore *d* Est 1:4 3117
when these *d* were expired, the Est 1:5 3117
both unto great and small, seven *d* Est 1:5 3117
(for so were the *d* of their Est 2:12 3117
In those *d*, while Mordecai sat in Est 2:21 3117
in unto the king these thirty *d* Est 4:11 3117
and neither eat nor drink three *d* Est 4:16 3117
As the *d* wherein the Jews rested Est 9:22 3117
should make them *d* of feasting Est 9:22 3117
d Purim after the name of Pur Est 9:26 3117
two *d* according to their writing Est 9:27 3117
that these *d* should be remembered Est 9:28 3117
that these *d* of Purim should not Est 9:28 3117
To confirm these *d* of Purim in Est 9:31 3117
when the *d* of their feasting were Job 1:5 3117
with him upon the ground seven *d* Job 2:13 3117
be joined unto the *d* of the year Job 3:6 3117
are not his *d* also like the *d* Job 7:1 3117
also like the *d* of a hireling Job 7:1 3117
My *d* are swifter than a weaver's Job 7:6 3117
for my *d* are vanity Job 7:16 3117
because our *d* upon earth are a Job 8:9 3117
Now my *d* are swifter than a post Job 9:25 3117
Are thy *d* as the *d* of man Job 10:5 3117
are thy years as man's *d*, Job 10:5 3117
Are not my *d* few Job 10:20 3117
in length of *d* understanding Job 12:12 3117
is born of a woman is of few *d* Job 14:1 3117
Seeing his *d* are determined, the Job 14:5 3117
all the *d* of my appointed time Job 14:14 3117
travaileth with pain all his *d* Job 15:20 3117
my *d* are extinct, the graves are Job 17:1 3117
My *d* are past, my purposes are Job 17:11 3117
They spend their *d* in wealth Job 21:13 3117
they that know him not see his *d* Job 24:1 3117
as in the *d* when God preserved me Job 29:2 3117
As I was in the *d* of my youth Job 29:4 3117
I shall multiply my *d* as the sand Job 29:18 3117
the *d* of affliction have taken Job 30:16 3117
the *d* of affliction prevented me Job 30:27 3117
D should speak, and multitude of Job 32:7 3117
return to the *d* of his youth Job 33:25 3117
shall spend their *d* in prosperity Job 36:11 3117
commanded the morning since thy *d* Job 38:12 3117
the number of thy *d* is great Job 38:21 3117
Job died, being old and full of *d* Job 42:17 3117
it him, even length of *d* for ever Ps 21:4 3117
follow me all the *d* of my life Ps 23:6 3117
of the LORD all the *d* of my life Ps 27:4 3117
desireth life, and loveth many *d* Ps 34:12 3117
LORD knoweth the *d* of the upright Ps 37:18 3117
in the *d* of famine they shall be Ps 37:19 3117
mine end, and the measure of my *d* Ps 39:4 3117
hast made my *d* as an handbreadth Ps 39:5 3117
what work thou didst in their *d* Ps 44:1 3117
should I fear in the *d* of evil Ps 49:5 3117
shall not live out half their *d* Ps 55:23 3117
In his *d* shall the righteous Ps 72:7 3117
I have considered the *d* of old Ps 77:5 3117
Therefore their *d* did he consume Ps 78:33 3117
and his throne as the *d* of heaven Ps 89:29 3117
The *d* of his youth hast thou Ps 89:45 3117
For all our *d* are passed away in Ps 90:9 3117
The *d* of our years are threescore Ps 90:10 3117
So teach us to number our *d* Ps 90:12 3117
may rejoice and be glad all our *d* Ps 90:14 3117
Make us glad according to the *d* Ps 90:15 3117
him rest from the *d* of adversity Ps 94:13 3117
For my *d* are consumed like smoke, Ps 102:3 3117
My *d* are like a shadow that Ps 102:11 3117
he shortened my *d* Ps 102:23 3117
me not away in the midst of my *d* Ps 102:24 3117
As for man, his *d* are as grass Ps 103:15 3117
Let his *d* be few Ps 109:8 3117
How many are the *d* of thy servant Ps 119:84 3117
Jerusalem all the *d* of thy life Ps 128:5 3117
I remember the *d* of old Ps 143:5 3117
his *d* are as a shadow that Ps 144:4 3117
For length of *d*, and long life, and Prov 3:2 3117
Length of *d* is in her right hand Prov 3:16 3117
For by me thy *d* shall be Prov 9:11 3117
The fear of the LORD prolongeth *d* Prov 10:27 3117
All the *d* of the afflicted are Prov 15:15 3117
covetousness shall prolong his *d* Prov 28:16 3117
and not evil all the *d* of her life Prov 31:12 3117
heaven all the *d* of their life Eccl 2:3 3117
d to come shall all be forgotten Eccl 2:16 3117
For all his *d* are sorrows Eccl 2:23 3117
All his *d* also he eateth in Eccl 5:17 3117
the sun all the *d* of his life Eccl 5:18 3117
much remember the *d* of his life Eccl 5:20 3117
so that the *d* of his years be Eccl 6:3 3117
all the *d* of his vain life which Eccl 6:12 3117
former *d* were better than these Eccl 7:10 3117
have I seen in the *d* of my vanity Eccl 7:15 3117
his *d* be prolonged, yet surely I Eccl 8:12
neither shall he prolong his *d* Eccl 8:13 3117
of his labour the *d* of his life Eccl 8:15 3117
the *d* of the life of thy vanity Eccl 9:9 3117
the sun, all the *d* of thy vanity Eccl 9:9 3117
thou shalt find it after many *d* Eccl 11:1 3117
him remember the *d* of darkness Eccl 11:8 3117
cheer thee in the *d* of thy youth Eccl 11:9 3117
thy Creator in the *d* of thy youth Eccl 12:1 3117
youth, while the evil *d* come not Eccl 12:1 3117
and Jerusalem in the *d* of Uzziah Is 1:1 3117
shall come to pass in the last *d* Is 2:2 3117
it came to pass in the *d* of Ahaz Is 7:1 3117
d that have not come, from the Is 7:17 3117
her *d* shall not be prolonged Is 13:22 3117
whose antiquity is of ancient *d* Is 23:7 3117
according to the *d* of one king Is 23:15 3117
after many *d* shall they be Is 24:22 3117
as the light of seven *d*, in the Is 30:26 3117
Many *d* and years shall ye be Is 32:10 3117
In those *d* was Hezekiah sick unto Is 38:1 3117
will add unto thy *d* fifteen years Is 38:5 3117
I said in the cutting off of my *d* Is 38:10 3117
stringed instruments all the *d* of Is 38:20 3117
the *d* come, that all that is in Is 39:6 3117
shall be peace and truth in my *d* Is 39:8 3117
awake, as in the ancient *d* Is 51:9 3117
his seed, he shall prolong his *d* Is 53:10 3117
the *d* of thy mourning shall be Is 60:20 3117
and carried them all the *d* of old Is 63:9 3117
Then he remembered the *d* of old Is 63:11 3117
be no more thence an infant of *d* Is 65:20 3117
man that hath not filled his *d* Is 65:20 3117
for as the *d* of a tree are the Is 65:22 3117
of a tree are the *d* of my people Is 65:22 3117
word of the LORD came in the *d* of Jer 1:2 3117
It came also in the *d* of Jer 1:3 3117
forgotten me *d* without number Jer 2:32 3117
me in the *d* of Josiah the king Jer 3:6 3117
increased in the land, in those *d* Jer 3:16 3117
In those *d* the house of Judah Jer 3:18 3117
Nevertheless in those *d*, saith Jer 5:18 3117
aged with him that is full of *d* Jer 6:11 3117
the *d* come, saith the LORD, that Jer 7:32 3117
the *d* come, saith the LORD, that Jer 9:25 3117
And it came to pass after many *d* Jer 13:6 3117
place in your eyes, and in your *d* Jer 16:9 3117
the *d* come, saith the LORD, that Jer 16:14 3117
leave them in the midst of his *d* Jer 17:11 3117
the *d* come, saith the LORD, that Jer 19:6 3117
that my *d* should be consumed with Jer 20:18 3117
that shall not prosper in his *d* Jer 22:30 3117
the *d* come, saith the LORD, that Jer 23:5 3117
In his *d* Judah shall be saved, and Jer 23:6 3117
the *d* come, saith the LORD, that Jer 23:7 3117
in the latter *d* ye shall consider Jer 23:20 3117
for the *d* of your slaughter and of Jer 25:34 3117
the *d* of Hezekiah king of Judah Jer 26:18 3117
the *d* come, saith the LORD, that Jer 30:3 3117
in the latter *d* ye shall consider Jer 30:24 3117
the *d* come, saith the LORD, that Jer 31:27 3117
In those *d* they shall say no more Jer 31:29 3117
the *d* come, saith the LORD, that Jer 31:31 3117
After those *d*, saith the LORD, I Jer 31:33 3117
the *d* come, saith the LORD, that Jer 31:38 3117
that they may continue many *d* Jer 32:14 3117
the *d* come, saith the LORD, that Jer 33:14 3117
In those *d*, and at that time, will Jer 33:15 3117
In those *d* shall Judah be saved, Jer 33:16 3117
Jeremiah from the LORD in the *d* Jer 35:1 3117
but all your *d* ye shall dwell in Jer 35:7 3117
that ye may live many *d* in the Jer 35:7 3117
us, to drink no wine all our *d* Jer 35:8 3117
from the *d* of Josiah, even into Jer 36:2 3117
had remained there many *d* Jer 37:16 3117
And it came to pass after ten *d* Jer 42:7 3117
be inhabited, as in the *d* of old Jer 46:26 3117
the *d* come, saith the LORD, that Jer 48:12 3117
captivity of Moab in the latter *d* Jer 48:47 3117
the *d* come, saith the LORD, that Jer 49:2 3117
come to pass in the latter *d* Jer 49:39 3117
In those *d*, and in that time, Jer 50:4 3117
In those *d*, and in that time, Jer 50:20 3117
the *d* come, that I will do Jer 51:47 3117
the *d* come, saith the LORD, that Jer 51:52 3117
before him all the *d* of his life Jer 52:33 3117
his death, all the *d* of his life Jer 52:34 3117
in the *d* of her affliction Lam 1:7 3117
that she had in the *d* of old Lam 1:7 3117
he had commanded in the *d* of old Lam 2:17 3117
end is near, our *d* are fulfilled Lam 4:18 3117
renew our *d* as of old Lam 5:21 3117
astonished among them seven *d* Eze 3:15 3117
to pass at the end of seven *d* Eze 3:16 3117
the *d* that thou shalt lie upon it Eze 4:4 3117
according to the number of the *d* Eze 4:5 3117
d, three hundred and ninety *d* Eze 4:5 3117
of the house of Judah forty *d* Eze 4:6 3117
hast ended the *d* of thy siege Eze 4:8 3117
d that thou shalt lie upon thy Eze 4:9 3117
ninety *d* shalt thou eat thereof Eze 4:9 3117
when the *d* of the siege are Eze 5:2 3117
The *d* are prolonged, and every Eze 12:22 3117
The *d* are at hand, and the effect Eze 12:23 3117
for in your *d*, O rebellious house Eze 12:25 3117
he seeth is for many *d* to come Eze 12:27 3117
not remembered the *d* of thy youth Eze 16:22 3117
not remembered the *d* of thy youth Eze 16:43 3117
with thee in the *d* of thy youth Eze 16:60 3117
hast caused thy *d* to draw near Eze 22:4 3117
in the *d* that I shall deal with Eze 22:14 3117
to remembrance the *d* of her youth Eze 23:19 3117
After many *d* thou shalt be Eze 38:8 3117
it shall be in the latter *d* Eze 38:16 3117
which prophesied in those *d* many Eze 38:17 3117
Seven *d* shalt thou prepare every Eze 43:25 3117
Seven *d* shall they purge the Eze 43:26 3117
when these *d* are expired, it Eze 43:27 3117
shall reckon unto him seven *d* Eze 44:26 3117
the passover, a feast of seven *d* Eze 45:21 3117
seven *d* of the feast he shall Eze 45:23 3117
without blemish daily the seven *d* Eze 45:23 3117
like in the feast of the seven *d* Eze 45:25 3117
shall be shut the six working *d* Eze 46:1 3117
servants, I beseech thee, ten *d* Dan 1:12 3117
this matter, and proved them ten *d* Dan 1:14 3117
at the end of ten *d* their Dan 1:15 3117
Now at the end of the *d* that the Dan 1:18 3117
what shall be in the latter *d* Dan 2:28 3118
in the *d* of these kings shall the Dan 2:44 3118
And at the end of the *d* I Dan 4:34 3118
in the *d* of thy father light and Dan 5:11 3118
of any God or man for thirty *d* Dan 6:7 3118
of any God or man within thirty *d* Dan 6:12 3118
down, and the Ancient of *d* did sit Dan 7:9 3118
and came to the Ancient of *d* Dan 7:13 3118
Until the Ancient of *d* came Dan 7:22 3118
two thousand and three hundred *d* Dan 8:14 3117
for it shall be for many *d* Dan 8:26 3117
fainted, and was sick certain *d* Dan 8:27 3117
In those *d* I Daniel was mourning Dan 10:2 3117
withstood me one and twenty *d* Dan 10:13 3117
befall thy people in the latter *d* Dan 10:14 3117

for yet the vision is for many *d* Dan 10:14 3117
but within few *d* he shall be Dan 11:20 3117
by captivity, and by spoil, many *d* Dan 11:33 3117
thousand two hundred and ninety *d* Dan 12:11 3117
three hundred and five and thirty *d* Dan 12:12 3117
in thy lot at the end of the *d* Dan 12:13 3117
in the *d* of Uzziah, Jotham, Ahaz, Hos 1:1 3117
in the *d* of Jeroboam the son of Hos 1:1 3117
her mirth to cease, her feast *d* Hos 2:11
visit upon her the *d* of Baalim Hos 2:13 3117
as in the *d* of her youth, and as Hos 2:15 3117
Thou shalt abide for me many *d* Hos 3:3 3117
shall abide many *d* without a king Hos 3:4 3117
and his goodness in the latter *d* Hos 3:5 3117
After two *d* will he revive us Hos 6:2 3117
The *d* of visitation are come, the Hos 9:7 3117
the *d* of recompence are come Hos 9:7 3117
themselves, as in the *d* of Gibeah Hos 9:9 3117
hast sinned from the *d* of Gibeah Hos 10:9 3117
as in the *d* of the solemn feast Hos 12:9 3117
Hath this been in your *d*, or even Joel 1:2 3117
or even in the *d* of your fathers Joel 1:2 3117
those *d* will I pour out my spirit Joel 2:29 3117
For, behold, in those *d*, and in Joel 3:1 3117
in the *d* of Uzziah king of Judah Amos 1:1 3117
in the *d* of Jeroboam the son of Amos 1:1 3117
the *d* shall come upon you, that Amos 4:2 3117
I hate, I despise your feast *d* Amos 5:21
the *d* come, saith the Lord GOD, Amos 8:11 3117
will build it as in the *d* of old Amos 9:11 3117
the *d* come, saith the LORD, that Amos 9:13 3117
in the belly of the fish three *d* Jonah 1:17 3117
and he cried, and said, Yet forty *d* Jonah 3:4 3117
the Morasthite in the *d* of Jotham Mic 1:1 3117
But in the last *d* it shall come Mic 4:1 3117
and Gilead, as in the *d* of old Mic 7:14 3117
According to the *d* of thy coming Mic 7:15 3117
our fathers from the *d* of old Mic 7:20 3117
for I will work a work in your *d* Hab 1:5 3117
in the *d* of Josiah the son of Zeph 1:1 3117
Since those *d* were, when one came Hag 2:16
remnant of this people in these *d* Zec 8:6 3117
ye that hear in these *d* these Zec 8:9 3117
For before these *d* there was no Zec 8:10 3117
of this people as in the former *d* Zec 8:11 3117
these *d* to do well unto Jerusalem Zec 8:15 3117
In those *d* it shall come to pass, Zec 8:23 3117
in the *d* of Uzziah king of Judah Zec 14:5 3117
unto the LORD, as in the *d* of old Mal 3:4 3117
Even from the *d* of your fathers Mal 3:7 3117
Judaea in the *d* of Herod the king Mt 2:1 2250
In those *d* came John the Baptist, Mt 3:1 2250
And when he had fasted forty *d* Mt 4:2 2250
but the *d* will come, when the Mt 9:15 2250
from the *d* of John the Baptist Mt 11:12 2250
how that on the sabbath *d* the Mt 12:5
lawful to heal on the sabbath *d* Mt 12:10
to do well on the sabbath *d* Mt 12:12
For as Jonas was three *d* and three Mt 12:40 2250
shall the Son of man be three *d* Mt 12:40 2250
they continue with me now three *d* Mt 15:32 2250
after six *d* Jesus taketh Peter, Mt 17:1 2250
had been in the *d* of our fathers Mt 23:30 2250
to them that give suck in those *d* Mt 24:19 2250
And except those *d* should be Mt 24:22 2250
sake those *d* shall be shortened Mt 24:22 2250
those *d* shall the sun be darkened Mt 24:29 2250
But as the *d* of Noe were, so Mt 24:37 2250
For as in the *d* that were before Mt 24:38 2250
Ye know that after two *d* is the Mt 26:2 2250
of God, and to build it in three *d* Mt 26:61 2250
temple, and buildest it in three *d* Mt 27:40 2250
After three *d* I will rise again Mt 27:63 2250
And it came to pass in those *d* Mk 1:9 2250
there in the wilderness forty *d* Mk 1:13 2250
into Capernaum after some *d* Mk 2:1 2250
But the *d* will come, when the Mk 2:20 2250
then shall they fast in those *d* Mk 2:20 2250
the *d* of Abiathar the high priest Mk 2:26 1909
to do good on the sabbath *d* Mk 3:4
In those *d* the multitude being Mk 8:1 2250
have now been with me three *d* Mk 8:2 2250
and after three *d* rise again Mk 8:31 2250
after six *d* Jesus taketh with him Mk 9:2 2250
to them that give suck in those *d* Mk 13:17 2250
For in those *d* shall be Mk 13:19 2250
the Lord had shortened those *d* Mk 13:20 2250
chosen, he hath shortened the *d* Mk 13:20 2250
But in those *d*, after that Mk 13:24 2250
After two *d* was the feast of the Mk 14:1 2250
within three *d* I will build Mk 14:58 2250
temple, and buildest it in three *d* Mk 15:29 2250
There was in the *d* of Herod Lk 1:5 2250
that, as soon as the *d* of his Lk 1:23 2250
after those *d* his wife Elisabeth Lk 1:24 2250
in the *d* wherein he looked on me Lk 1:25 2250
And Mary arose in those *d*, and went Lk 1:39 2250
before him, all the *d* of our life Lk 1:75 2250
And it came to pass in those *d* Lk 2:1 2250
the *d* were accomplished that she Lk 2:6 2250
when eight *d* were accomplished Lk 2:21 2250
when the *d* of her purification Lk 2:22 2250
And when they had fulfilled the *d* Lk 2:43 2250
that after three *d* they found him Lk 2:46 2250
Being forty *d* tempted of the Lk 4:2 2250
in those *d* he did eat nothing Lk 4:2 2250
were in Israel in the *d* of Elias Lk 4:25 2250
and taught them on the sabbath *d* Lk 4:31
But the *d* will come, when the Lk 5:35 2250
then shall they fast in those *d* Lk 5:35 2250
not lawful to do on the sabbath *d* Lk 6:2
on the sabbath *d* to do good Lk 6:9
And it came to pass in those *d* Lk 6:12 2250
an eight *d* after these sayings Lk 9:28 2250
told no man in those *d* any of Lk 9:36 2250
There are six *d* in which men Lk 13:14 2250
not many *d* after the younger son Lk 15:13 2250
The *d* will come, when ye shall Lk 17:22 2250
one of the *d* of the Son of man Lk 17:22 2250
And as it was in the *d* of Noe Lk 17:26 2250
also in the *d* of the Son of man Lk 17:26 2250
also as it was in the *d* of Lot Lk 17:28 2250
For the *d* shall come upon thee, Lk 19:43 2250
to pass, that on one of those *d* Lk 20:1 2250
the *d* will come, in the which Lk 21:6 2250
For these be the *d* of vengeance Lk 21:22 2250
them that give suck, in those *d* Lk 21:23 2250
the *d* are coming, in the which Lk 23:29 2250
are come to pass there in these *d* Lk 24:18 2250
they continued there not many *d* Jn 2:12 2250
in three *d* I will raise it up Jn 2:19 2250
wilt thou rear it up in three *d* Jn 2:20 2250
and he abode there two *d* Jn 4:40 2250
Now after two *d* he departed Jn 4:43 2250
he abode two *d* still in the same Jn 11:6 2250
lain in the grave four *d* already Jn 11:17 2250
for he hath been dead four *d* Jn 11:39 5066
Then Jesus six *d* before the Jn 12:1 2250
after eight *d* again his disciples Jn 20:26 2250
being seen of them forty *d* Acts 1:3 2250
the Holy Ghost not many *d* hence Acts 1:5 2250
in those *d* Peter stood up in the Acts 1:15 2250
shall come to pass in the last *d* Acts 2:17 2250
pour out in those *d* of my Spirit Acts 2:18 2250
have likewise foretold of these *d* Acts 3:24 2250
before these *d* rose up Theudas Acts 5:36 2250
of Galilee in the *d* of the taxing Acts 5:37 2250
And in those *d*, when the number of Acts 6:1 2250
And they made a calf in those *d* Acts 7:41 2250
our fathers, unto the *d* of David Acts 7:45 2250
he was three *d* without sight, and Acts 9:9 2250
Then was Saul certain *d* with the Acts 9:19 2250
after that many *d* were fulfilled Acts 9:23 2250
And it came to pass in those *d* Acts 9:37 2250
that he tarried many *d* in Joppa Acts 9:43 2250
Four *d* ago I was fasting until Acts 10:30 2250
they him to tarry certain *d* Acts 10:48 2250
in these *d* came prophets from Acts 11:27 2250
pass in the *d* of Claudius Caesar Acts 11:28 1909
(Then were the *d* of unleavened Acts 12:3 2250
he was seen many *d* of them which Acts 13:31 2250
for I work a work in your *d* Acts 13:41 2250
some *d* after Paul said unto Acts 15:36 2250
in that city abiding certain *d* Acts 16:12 2250
And this did she many *d* Acts 16:18 2250
three sabbath *d* reasoned with Acts 17:2
after the *d* of unleavened bread Acts 20:6 2250
came unto them to Troas in five *d* Acts 20:6 2250
where we abode seven *d* Acts 20:6 2250
we tarried there seven *d* Acts 21:4 2250
when we had accomplished those *d* Acts 21:5 2250
And as we tarried there many *d* Acts 21:10 2250
after those *d* we took up our Acts 21:15 2250
of the *d* of purification, until Acts 21:26 2250
when the seven *d* were almost Acts 21:27 2250
before these *d* madest an uproar Acts 21:38 2250
after five *d* Ananias the high Acts 24:1 2250
d since I went up to Jerusalem Acts 24:11 2250
And after certain *d*, when Felix Acts 24:24 2250
after three *d* he ascended from Acts 25:1 2250
among them more than ten *d* Acts 25:6 2250
And after certain *d* king Agrippa Acts 25:13 2250
when they had been there many *d* Acts 25:14 2250
when we had sailed slowly many *d* Acts 27:7 2250
sun nor stars in many *d* appeared Acts 27:20 2250
and lodged us three *d* courteously Acts 28:7 2250
we tarried there three *d* Acts 28:12 2250
to tarry with them seven *d* Acts 28:14 2250
that after three *d* Paul called Acts 28:17 2250
and abode with him fifteen *d* Gal 1:18 2250
Ye observe *d*, and months, and times Gal 4:10 2250
the time, because the *d* are evil Eph 5:16 2250
the new moon, or of the sabbath *d* Col 2:16
that in the last *d* perilous times 2Ti 3:1 2250
Hath in these last *d* spoken unto Heb 1:2 2250
Who in the *d* of his flesh, when Heb 5:7 2250
having neither beginning of *d* Heb 7:3 2250
the *d* come, saith the Lord, when Heb 8:8 2250
the house of Israel after those *d* Heb 8:10 2250
will make with them after those *d* Heb 10:16 2250
call to remembrance the former *d* Heb 10:32 2250
they were compassed about seven *d* Heb 11:30 2250
For they verily for a few *d* Heb 12:10 2250
treasure together for the last *d* Jas 5:3 2250
will love life, and see good *d* 1Pet 3:10 2250
of God waited in the *d* of Noah 1Pet 3:20 2250
shall come in the last *d* scoffers 2Pet 3:3 2250
ye shall have tribulation ten *d* Rev 2:10 2250
even in those *d* wherein Antipas Rev 2:13 2250
in those *d* shall men seek death, Rev 9:6 2250
But in the *d* of the voice of the Rev 10:7 2250
two hundred and threescore *d* Rev 11:3 2250
not in the *d* of their prophecy Rev 11:6 2250
see their dead bodies three *d* Rev 11:9 2250
And after three *d* and an half the Rev 11:11 2250
two hundred and threescore *d* Rev 12:6 2250

DAYS'

he set three *d* journey betwixt Gen 30:36 3117
pursued after him seven *d* journey Gen 31:23 3117
thee, three *d* journey into the Ex 3:18 3117
three *d* journey into the desert, Ex 5:3 3117
We will go three *d* journey into Ex 8:27 3117
mount of the LORD three *d* journey Num 10:33 3117
them in the three *d* journey Num 10:33 3117
went three *d* journey in the Num 33:8 3117
(There are eleven *d* journey from Deut 1:2 3117
unto him, Give us seven *d* respite 1Sa 11:3 3117
be three *d* pestilence in thy land 2Sa 24:13 3117
a compass of seven *d* journey 2Kin 3:9 3117
great city of three *d* journey Jonah 3:3 3117

DAYSMAN

Neither is there any *d* betwixt us Job 9:33 3198

DAYSPRING

caused the *d* to know his place Job 38:12 7837
whereby the *d* from on high hath Lk 1:78 395

DAYTIME

by *d* in a pillar of a cloud, and Num 14:14 3119
They meet with darkness in the *d* Job 5:14 3119
marked for themselves in the *d* Job 24:16 3119
O my God, I cry in the *d*, but Ps 22:2 3119
his lovingkindness in the *d* Ps 42:8 3119
In the *d* also he led them with a Ps 78:14 3119
a shadow in the *d* from the heat Is 4:6 3119
upon the watchtower in the *d* Is 21:8 3119
it pleasure to riot in the *d* 2Pet 2:13

DEACON

let them use the office of a *d* 1Ti 3:10 1247
a *d* well purchase to themselves a 1Ti 3:13 1247

DEACONS

Philippi, with the bishops and *d* Phil 1:1 1249
Likewise must the *d* be grave 1Ti 3:8 1249
Let the *d* be the husbands of one 1Ti 3:12 1249

DEAD

him, Behold, thou art but a *d* man Gen 20:3 4191
stood up from before his *d* Gen 23:3 4191
I may bury my *d* out of my sight Gen 23:4 4191
of our sepulchres bury thy *d* Gen 23:6 4191
but that thou mayest bury thy *d* Gen 23:6 4191
should bury my *d* out of my sight Gen 23:8 4191
bury thy *d* Gen 23:11 4191
of me, and I will bury my *d* there Gen 23:13 4191
bury therefore thy *d* Gen 23:15 4191
for his brother is *d*, and he is Gen 42:38 4191
and his brother is *d*, and he alone Gen 44:20 4191
saw that their father was *d* Gen 50:15 4191
for all the men are *d* which Ex 4:19 4191
of the cattle of the Israelites *d* Ex 9:7 4191
a house where there was not one *d* Ex 12:30 4191
for they said, We be all *d* men Ex 12:33 4191
Egyptians *d* upon the sea shore Ex 14:30 4191
and the *d* beast shall be his Ex 21:34 4191
the *d* ox also they shall divide Ex 21:35 4191
and the *d* shall be his own Ex 21:36 4191
doth touch them, when they be *d* Lev 11:31 4194
any of them, when they are *d* Lev 11:32 4194
cuttings in your flesh for the *d* Lev 19:28 5315
for the *d* among his people Lev 21:1 5315
shall he go in to any *d* body Lev 21:11 4191
thing that is unclean by the *d* Lev 22:4 5315
and whosoever is defiled by the *d* Num 5:2 5315
LORD he shall come at no *d* body Num 6:6 4191
him, for that he sinned by the *d* Num 6:11 5315
defiled by the *d* body of a man Num 9:6 5315
defiled by the *d* body of a man Num 9:7 5315
be unclean by reason of a *d* body Num 9:10 5315
Let her not be as one *d*, of whom Num 12:12 4191
And he stood between the *d* Num 16:48 4191
He that toucheth the *d* body of Num 19:11 4191
Whosoever toucheth the *d* body of Num 19:13 4191
d body of any man that is *d* Num 19:13 4191
in the open fields, or a *d* body Num 19:16 4191
a bone, or one slain, or one *d* Num 19:18 4191
congregation saw that Aaron was *d* Num 20:29 1478
and *d* from among the people, Deut 2:16 4191
between your eyes for the *d* Deut 14:1 4191
flesh, nor touch their *d* carcase Deut 14:8 5038
the wife of the *d* shall not marry Deut 25:5 1101
name of his brother which is *d* Deut 25:6 4191
nor given ought thereof for the *d* Deut 26:14 4191
Moses my servant is *d* Josh 1:2 4191
to pass, when the judge was *d* Judg 2:19 4191
was fallen down *d* on the earth Judg 3:25 4191
of the LORD, when Ehud was *d* Judg 4:1 4191
her tent, behold, Sisera lay *d* Judg 4:22 4191
he bowed, there he fell down *d* Judg 5:27 7703
to pass, as soon as Gideon was *d* Judg 8:33 4191
Israel saw that Abimelech was *d* Judg 9:55 4191
So the *d* which he slew at his Judg 16:30 4191
have they forced, that she is *d* Judg 20:5 4191
you, as ye have dealt with the *d* Ruth 1:8 4191
to the living and to the *d* Ruth 2:20 4191
the Moabitess, the wife of the *d* Ruth 4:5 4191
of the *d* upon his inheritance Ruth 4:5 4191
of the *d* upon his inheritance Ruth 4:10 4191
that the name of the *d* be not cut Ruth 4:10 4191
also, Hophni and Phinehas, are *d* 1Sa 4:17 4191
in law and her husband were *d* 1Sa 4:19 4191
saw their champion was *d*, they 1Sa 17:51 4191
after a *d* dog, after a flea 1Sa 24:14 4191
when David heard that Nabal was *d* 1Sa 25:39 4191
Now Samuel was *d*, and all Israel 1Sa 28:3 4191
armourbearer saw that Saul was *d* 1Sa 31:5 4191
and that Saul and his sons were *d* 1Sa 31:7 4191
the people also are fallen and *d* 2Sa 1:4 4191
and Jonathan his son are *d* also 2Sa 1:4 4191
Saul and Jonathan his son be *d* 2Sa 1:5 4191
for your master Saul is *d* 2Sa 2:7 4191
heard that Abner was *d* in Hebron 2Sa 4:1 4191
me, saying, Behold, Saul is *d* 2Sa 4:10 4191
look upon such a *d* dog as I am 2Sa 9:8 4191
Uriah the Hittite is *d* also 2Sa 11:21 4191
some of the king's servants be *d* 2Sa 11:24 4191
Uriah the Hittite is *d* also 2Sa 11:24 4191
that Uriah her husband was *d* 2Sa 11:26 4191
to tell him that the child was *d* 2Sa 12:18 4191
we tell him that the child is *d* 2Sa 12:18 4191
perceived that the child was *d* 2Sa 12:19 4191
unto his servants, Is the child *d* 2Sa 12:19 4191

And they said, He is *d*	2Sa 12:19	4191
but when the child was *d*, thou	2Sa 12:21	4191
But now he is *d*, wherefore should	2Sa 12:23	4191
for Amnon only is *d*	2Sa 13:32	4191
that all the king's sons are *d*	2Sa 13:33	4191
for Amnon only is *d*	2Sa 13:33	4191
concerning Amnon, seeing he was *d*	2Sa 13:39	4191
had a long time mourned for the *d*	2Sa 14:2	4191
widow woman, and mine husband is *d*	2Sa 14:5	4191
Why should this *d* dog curse my	2Sa 16:9	4191
because the king's son is *d*	2Sa 18:20	4191
anointed over us, is *d* in battle	2Sa 19:10	4191
but *d* men before my lord the king	2Sa 19:28	4194
laid her *d* child in my bosom	1Kin 3:20	4191
my child suck, behold, it was *d*	1Kin 3:21	4191
is my son, and the *d* is thy son	1Kin 3:22	4191
but the *d* is thy son, and the	1Kin 3:22	4191
that liveth, and thy son is the *d*	1Kin 3:23	4191
but thy son is the *d*, and my son	1Kin 3:23	4191
the captain of the host was *d*	1Kin 11:21	4191
to his sons, saying, When I am *d*	1Kin 13:31	4191
saying, Naboth is stoned, and is *d*	1Kin 21:14	4191
that Naboth was stoned, and was *d*	1Kin 21:15	4191
for Naboth is not alive, but *d*	1Kin 21:15	4191
when Ahab heard that Naboth was *d*	1Kin 21:16	4191
it came to pass, when Ahab was *d*	2Kin 3:5	4194
Thy servant my husband is *d*	2Kin 4:1	4191
house, behold, the child was *d*	2Kin 4:32	4191
he had restored a *d* body to life	2Kin 8:5	4191
of Ahaziah saw that her son was *d*	2Kin 11:1	4191
behold, they were all *d* corpses	2Kin 19:35	4191
him in a chariot *d* from Megiddo	2Kin 23:30	4191
And when Bela was *d*, Jobab the son	1Chr 1:44	4191
And when Jobab was *d*, Husham of	1Chr 1:45	4191
And when Husham was *d*, Hadad the	1Chr 1:46	4191
And when Hadad was *d*, Samlah of	1Chr 1:47	4191
And when Samlah was *d*, Shaul of	1Chr 1:48	4191
And when Shaul was *d*, Baal-hanan	1Chr 1:49	4191
And when Baal-hanan was *d*, Hadad	1Chr 1:50	4191
And when Azubah was *d*, Caleb took	1Chr 2:19	4191
Hezron was *d* in Caleb-ephratah	1Chr 2:24	4194
armourbearer saw that Saul was *d*	1Chr 10:5	4191
and that Saul and his sons were *d*	1Chr 10:7	4191
they were *d* bodies fallen to the	2Chr 20:24	6297
both riches with the *d* bodies	2Chr 20:25	6297
of Ahaziah saw that her son was *d*	2Chr 22:10	4191
when her father and mother were *d*	Est 2:7	4194
upon the young men, and they are *d*	Job 1:19	4191
D things are formed from under	Job 26:5	7496
forgotten as a *d* man out of mind	Ps 31:12	4191
and horse are cast into a *d* sleep	Ps 76:6	
The *d* bodies of thy servants have	Ps 79:2	5038
Free among the *d*, like the slain	Ps 88:5	4191
Wilt thou shew wonders to the *d*	Ps 88:10	4191
shall the *d* arise and praise thee	Ps 88:10	7496
and ate the sacrifices of the *d*	Ps 106:28	4191
fill the places with the *d* bodies	Ps 110:6	1472
The *d* praise not the LORD,	Ps 115:17	4191
as those that have been long *d*	Ps 143:3	4191
death, and her paths unto the *d*	Prov 2:18	7496
knoweth not that the *d* are there	Prov 9:18	7496
in the congregation of the *d*	Prov 21:16	7496
Wherefore I praised the *d* which	Eccl 4:2	4191
the *d* which are already *d* more	Eccl 4:2	4191
and after that they go to the *d*	Eccl 9:3	4191
dog is better than a *d* lion	Eccl 9:4	4191
but the *d* know not any thing,	Eccl 9:5	4191
D flies cause the ointment of the	Eccl 10:1	4194
for the living to the *d*	Is 8:19	4191
it stirreth up the *d* for thee	Is 14:9	7496
with the sword, nor *d* in battle	Is 22:2	4191
They are *d*, they shall not live	Is 26:14	4191
Thy *d* men shall live, together	Is 26:19	4191
together with my *d* body shall	Is 26:19	5038
and the earth shall cast out the *d*	Is 26:19	7496
behold, they were all *d* corpses	Is 37:36	4191
are in desolate places as *d* men	Is 59:10	4191
to comfort them for the *d*	Jer 16:7	4191
Weep ye not for the *d*, neither	Jer 22:10	4191
cast his *d* body into the graves	Jer 26:23	5038
the whole valley of the *d* bodies	Jer 31:40	6297
them with the *d* bodies of men	Jer 33:5	6297
their *d* bodies shall be for meat	Jer 34:20	5038
his *d* body shall be cast out in	Jer 36:30	5038
cast all the *d* bodies of the men	Jer 41:9	6297
places, as they that be of old	Lam 3:6	4191
I will lay the *d* carcases of the	Eze 6:5	
cry, make no mourning for the *d*	Eze 24:17	4191
they shall come at no *d* person to	Eze 44:25	4191
of any thing that is *d* of itself	Eze 44:31	5038
there shall be many *d* bodies in	Amos 8:3	6297
by a *d* body touch any of these	Hag 2:13	
But when Herod was *d*, behold, an	Mt 2:19	5053
for they are *d* which sought the	Mt 2:20	2348
and let the *d* bury their *d*	Mt 8:22	3498
saying, My daughter is even now *d*	Mt 9:18	5053
for the maid is not *d*, but	Mt 9:24	599
cleanse the lepers, raise the *d*	Mt 10:8	3498
the *d* are raised up, and the poor	Mt 11:5	3498
he is risen from the *d*	Mt 14:2	3498
of man be risen again from the *d*	Mt 17:9	3498
the resurrection of the *d*	Mt 22:31	3498
God is not the God of the *d*	Mt 22:32	3498
are within full of *d* men's bones	Mt 23:27	3498
people, He is risen from the *d*	Mt 27:64	3498
did shake, and became as *d* men	Mt 28:4	3498
that he is risen from the *d*	Mt 28:7	3498
which said, Thy daughter is *d*	Mk 5:35	599
the damsel is not *d*, but sleepeth	Mk 5:39	599
the Baptist was risen from the *d*	Mk 6:14	3498
he is risen from the *d*	Mk 6:16	3498
Son of man were risen from the *d*	Mk 9:9	3498
the rising from the *d* should mean	Mk 9:10	3498
and he was as one *d*	Mk 9:26	3498
insomuch that many said, He is *d*	Mk 9:26	599
when they shall rise from the *d*	Mk 12:25	3498
And as touching the *d*, that they	Mk 12:26	3498
He is not the God of the *d*	Mk 12:27	3498
marvelled if he were already *d*	Mk 15:44	2348
whether he had been any while *d*	Mk 15:44	599
there was a *d* man carried out,	Lk 7:12	2348
And he that was *d* sat up, and began	Lk 7:15	3498
the *d* are raised, to the poor the	Lk 7:22	3498
saying to him, Thy daughter is *d*	Lk 8:49	2348
she is not *d*, but sleepeth	Lk 8:52	599
to scorn, knowing that she was *d*	Lk 8:53	599
that John was risen from the *d*	Lk 9:7	3498
Let the *d* bury their *d*	Lk 9:60	3498
and departed, leaving him half *d*	Lk 10:30	2258
For this my son was *d*, and is	Lk 15:24	3498
for this thy brother was *d*	Lk 15:32	3498
if one went unto them from the *d*	Lk 16:30	3498
though one rose from the *d*	Lk 16:31	3498
and the resurrection from the *d*	Lk 20:35	3498
Now that the *d* are raised	Lk 20:37	3498
For he is not a God of the *d*	Lk 20:38	3498
seek ye the living among the *d*	Lk 24:5	3498
to rise from the *d* the third day	Lk 24:46	3498
therefore he was risen from the *d*	Jn 2:22	3498
as the Father raiseth up the *d*	Jn 5:21	3498
when the *d* shall hear the voice	Jn 5:25	3498
manna in the wilderness, and are *d*	Jn 6:49	599
fathers did eat manna, and are *d*	Jn 6:58	599
Abraham is *d*, and the prophets	Jn 8:52	599
our father Abraham, which is *d*	Jn 8:53	599
and the prophets are *d*	Jn 8:53	599
unto them plainly, Lazarus is *d*	Jn 11:14	599
believeth in me, though he were *d*	Jn 11:25	599
the sister of him that was *d*	Jn 11:39	2348
for he hath been *d* four days	Jn 11:39	
the place where the *d* was laid	Jn 11:41	2348
And he that was *d* came forth	Jn 11:44	2348
Lazarus was which had been *d*	Jn 12:1	2348
d, whom he raised from the *d*	Jn 12:1	3498
whom he had raised from the *d*	Jn 12:9	3498
grave, and raised him from the *d*	Jn 12:17	3498
and saw that he was *d* already	Jn 19:33	2348
he must rise again from the *d*	Jn 20:9	3498
that he was risen from the *d*	Jn 21:14	3498
David, that he is both *d* and	Acts 2:29	5053
whom God hath raised from the *d*	Acts 3:15	3498
Jesus the resurrection from the *d*	Acts 4:2	3498
whom God raised from the *d*	Acts 4:10	3498
young men came in, and found her *d*	Acts 5:10	3498
thence, when his father was *d*	Acts 7:4	599
with him after he rose from the *d*	Acts 10:41	3498
God to be the Judge of quick and *d*	Acts 10:42	3498
But God raised him from the *d*	Acts 13:30	3498
that he raised him up from the *d*	Acts 13:34	3498
the city, supposing he had been *d*	Acts 14:19	2348
and risen again from the *d*	Acts 17:3	3498
he hath raised him from the *d*	Acts 17:31	3498
of the resurrection of the *d*	Acts 17:32	3498
the third loft, and was taken up *d*	Acts 20:9	3498
resurrection of the *d* I am called	Acts 23:6	3498
shall be a resurrection of the *d*	Acts 24:15	3498
the resurrection of the *d* I am	Acts 24:21	3498
and of one Jesus, which was *d*	Acts 25:19	2348
you, that God should raise the *d*	Acts 26:8	3498
first that should rise from the *d*	Acts 26:23	3498
or fallen down *d* suddenly	Acts 28:6	3498
by the resurrection from the *d*	Rom 1:4	3498
even God, who quickeneth the *d*	Rom 4:17	3498
considered not his own body now *d*	Rom 4:19	3499
up Jesus our Lord from the *d*	Rom 4:24	3498
the offence of one many be *d*	Rom 5:15	599
How shall we, that are *d* to sin	Rom 6:2	599
the *d* by the glory of the Father	Rom 6:4	3498
For he that is *d* is freed from	Rom 6:7	599
Now if we be *d* with Christ	Rom 6:8	599
raised from the *d* dieth no more	Rom 6:9	3498
to be *d* indeed unto sin, but	Rom 6:11	3498
those that are alive from the *d*	Rom 6:13	3498
but if the husband be *d*, she is	Rom 7:2	599
but if her husband be *d*, she is	Rom 7:3	599
ye also are become *d* to the law	Rom 7:4	2289
to him who is raised from the *d*	Rom 7:4	3498
that being *d* wherein we were held	Rom 7:6	599
For without the law sin was *d*	Rom 7:8	3498
the body is *d* because of sin	Rom 8:10	3498
up Jesus from the *d* dwell in you	Rom 8:11	3498
d shall also quicken your mortal	Rom 8:11	3498
bring up Christ again from the *d*	Rom 10:7	3498
God hath raised him from the *d*	Rom 10:9	3498
of them be, but life from the *d*	Rom 11:15	3498
he might be Lord both of the *d*	Rom 14:9	3498
but if her husband be *d*, she is	1Cor 7:39	2837
preached that he rose from the *d*	1Cor 15:12	3498
there is no resurrection of the *d*	1Cor 15:12	3498
there be no resurrection of the *d*	1Cor 15:13	3498
up, if so be that the *d* rise not	1Cor 15:15	3498
For if the *d* rise not, then is	1Cor 15:16	3498
now is Christ risen from the *d*	1Cor 15:20	3498
also the resurrection of the *d*	1Cor 15:21	3498
do which are baptized for the *d*	1Cor 15:29	3498
if the *d* rise not at all	1Cor 15:29	3498
are they then baptized for the *d*	1Cor 15:29	3498
it me, if the *d* rise not	1Cor 15:32	3498
will say, How are the *d* raised up	1Cor 15:35	3498
also is the resurrection of the *d*	1Cor 15:42	3498
sound, and the *d* shall be raised	1Cor 15:52	3498
but in God which raiseth the *d*	2Cor 1:9	3498
one died for all, then were all *d*	2Cor 5:14	599
Father, who raised him from the *d*	Gal 1:1	3498
I through the law am *d* to the law	Gal 2:19	599
the law, then Christ is *d* in vain	Gal 2:21	599
when he raised him from the *d*	Eph 1:20	3498
who were *d* in trespasses and sins	Eph 2:1	3498
Even when we were *d* in sins	Eph 2:5	3498
sleepest, and arise from the *d*	Eph 5:14	3498
unto the resurrection of the *d*	Phil 3:11	3498
the firstborn from the *d*	Col 1:18	3498
who hath raised him from the *d*	Col 2:12	3498
being *d* in your sins and the	Col 2:13	3498
Wherefore if ye be *d* with Christ	Col 2:20	599
For ye are *d*, and your life is hid	Col 3:3	599
heaven, whom he raised from the *d*	1Th 1:10	3498
the *d* in Christ shall rise first	1Th 4:16	3498
in pleasure is *d* while she liveth	1Ti 5:6	2348
from the *d* according to my gospel	2Ti 2:8	3498
For if we be *d* with him, we shall	2Ti 2:11	4880
the *d* at his appearing and his	2Ti 4:1	3498
of repentance from *d* works	Heb 6:1	3498
and of resurrection of the *d*	Heb 6:2	3498
purge your conscience from *d*	Heb 9:14	3498
is of force after men are *d*	Heb 9:17	3498
and by it he being *d* yet speaketh	Heb 11:4	599
even of one, and him as good as *d*	Heb 11:12	3499
to raise him up, even from the *d*	Heb 11:19	3498
their *d* raised to life again	Heb 11:35	3498
again from the *d* our Lord Jesus	Heb 13:20	3498
faith, if it hath not works, is *d*	Jas 2:17	3498
that faith without works is *d*	Jas 2:20	3498
the body without the spirit is *d*	Jas 2:26	3498
so faith without works is *d* also	Jas 2:26	3498
of Jesus Christ from the *d*	1Pet 1:3	3498
that raised him up from the *d*	1Pet 1:21	3498
being *d* to sins, should live unto	1Pet 2:24	581
ready to judge the quick and the *d*	1Pet 4:5	3498
preached also to them that are *d*	1Pet 4:6	3498
withereth, without fruit, twice *d*	Jude 12	599
and the first begotten of the *d*	Rev 1:5	3498
saw him, I fell at his feet as *d*	Rev 1:17	3498
I am he that liveth, and was *d*	Rev 1:18	3498
first and the last, which was *d*	Rev 2:8	3498
a name that thou livest, and art *d*	Rev 3:1	3498
their *d* bodies shall lie in the	Rev 11:8	4430
see their *d* bodies three days	Rev 11:9	4430
shall not suffer their *d* bodies	Rev 11:9	4430
is come, and the time of the *d*	Rev 11:18	3498
Blessed are the *d* which die in	Rev 14:13	3498
it became as the blood of a *d* man	Rev 16:3	3498
But the rest of the *d* lived not	Rev 20:5	3498
And I saw the *d*, small and great,	Rev 20:12	3498
the *d* were judged out of those	Rev 20:12	3498
gave up the *d* which were in it	Rev 20:13	3498
up the *d* which were in them	Rev 20:13	3498

DEADLY

for there was a *d* destruction	1Sa 5:11	4194
oppress me, from my *d* enemies	Ps 17:9	5315
the groanings of a *d* wounded man	Eze 30:24	
and if they drink any *d* thing	Mk 16:18	2286
an unruly evil, full of *d* poison	Jas 3:8	2287
and his *d* wound was healed	Rev 13:3	2288
beast, whose *d* wound was healed	Rev 13:12	2288

DEADNESS

neither yet the *d* of Sarah's womb	Rom 4:19	3500

DEAF

or who maketh the dumb, or *d*	Ex 4:11	2795
Thou shalt not curse the *d*	Lev 19:14	2795
But I, as a *d* man, heard not	Ps 38:13	2795
they are like the *d* adder that	Ps 58:4	2795
in that day shall the *d* hear the	Is 29:18	2795
the ears of the *d* shall be	Is 35:5	2795
Hear, ye *d*	Is 42:18	2795
or *d*, as my messenger that I sent	Is 42:19	2795
eyes, and the *d* that have ears	Is 43:8	2795
mouth, their ears shall be *d*	Mic 7:16	2790
the *d* hear, the dead are raised	Mt 11:5	2974
bring unto him one that was *d*	Mk 7:32	2974
he maketh both the *d* to hear	Mk 7:37	2974
d spirit, I charge thee, come out	Mk 9:25	2974
the *d* hear, the dead are raised,	Lk 7:22	2974

DEAL

now will we *d* worse with thee,	Gen 19:9	
thou wilt not *d* falsely with me	Gen 21:23	
And now if ye will *d* kindly	Gen 24:49	6213
and I will *d* well with thee	Gen 32:9	
Should he *d* with our sister as	Gen 34:31	6213
d kindly and truly with me	Gen 47:29	6213
let us *d* wisely with them	Ex 1:10	
but let not Pharaoh *d* deceitfully	Ex 8:29	
he shall *d* with her after the	Ex 21:9	6213
thou shalt *d* with thy vineyard	Ex 23:11	6213
tenth *d* of flour mingled with the	Ex 29:40	
one tenth *d* of fine flour mingled	Lev 14:21	
not steal, neither *d* falsely	Lev 19:11	
if thou *d* thus with me, kill me,	Num 11:15	6213
tenth *d* of flour mingled with the	Num 15:4	
a several tenth *d* of flour	Num 28:13	
A several tenth *d* shalt thou	Num 28:21	
A several tenth *d* unto one lamb	Num 28:29	
one tenth *d* for one lamb,	Num 29:4	
A several tenth *d* for one lamb	Num 29:10	
a several tenth *d* to each lamb of	Num 29:15	
But thus shall ye *d* with them	Deut 7:5	6213
the land, that we will *d* kindly	Josh 2:14	6213
the LORD *d* kindly with you, as ye	Ruth 1:8	6213
Therefore thou shalt *d* kindly	1Sa 20:8	6213
D gently for my sake with the	2Sa 18:5	
As thou didst *d* with David my	2Chr 2:3	6213
dwell therein, even so *d* with me	2Chr 2:3	
D courageously, and the LORD shall	2Chr 19:11	6213
lest I *d* with you after your	Job 42:8	6213
unto the fools, *D* not foolishly	Ps 75:4	
to *d* subtilly with his servants	Ps 105:25	
D bountifully with thy servant,	Ps 119:17	1580
D with thy servant according unto	Ps 119:124	6213
for thou shalt *d* bountifully with	Ps 142:7	1580
but they that *d* truly are his	Prov 12:22	6213

of uprightness will he *d* unjustly Is 26:10
make an end to *d* treacherously Is 33:1
they shall *d* treacherously with Is 33:1
wouldest *d* very treacherously Is 48:8
my servant shall *d* prudently Is 52:13
Is it not to *d* thy bread to the Is 58:7 6536
happy that *d* very treacherously Jer 12:1
d thus with them in the time of Jer 18:23 6213
if so be that the LORD will *d* Jer 21:2 6213
Therefore will I also *d* in fury Eze 8:18 6213
I will even *d* with thee as thou Eze 16:59 6213
kept my judgments, to *d* truly Eze 18:9 6213
the days that I shall *d* with thee Eze 22:14 6213
they shall *d* furiously with thee Eze 23:25 6213
they shall *d* with thee hatefully, Eze 23:29 6213
he shall surely *d* with him Eze 31:11 6213
thou seest, *d* with thy servants Dan 1:13 6213
shall *d* against them, and shall Dan 11:7 6213
upon them that *d* treacherously Hab 1:13
why do we *d* treacherously every Mal 2:10
let none *d* treacherously against Mal 2:15
that ye *d* not treacherously Mal 2:16
more a great *d* they published it Mk 7:36 *4054*
but he cried the more a great *d* Mk 10:48

DEALER
the treacherous *d* dealeth Is 21:2

DEALERS
the treacherous *d* have dealt Is 24:16
the treacherous *d* have dealt very Is 24:16

DEALEST
Wherefore *d* thou thus with thy Ex 5:15 6213
d treacherously, and they dealt Is 33:1

DEALETH
thus *d* Micah with me, and hath Judg 18:4 6213
told me that he *d* very subtilly 1Sa 23:22
poor that *d* with a slack hand Prov 10:4 6213
prudent man *d* with knowledge Prov 13:16 6213
He that is soon angry *d* foolishly Prov 14:17 6213
is his name, who *d* in proud wrath Prov 21:24 6213
dealer *d* treacherously, and the Is 21:2
the priest every one *d* falsely Jer 6:13 6213
the priest every one *d* falsely Jer 8:10 6213
God *d* with you as with sons Heb 12:7 4374

DEALING
his violent *d* shall come down Ps 7:16

DEALINGS
of your evil *d* by all this people 1Sa 2:23 1697
have no *d* with the Samaritans Jn 4:9 *4798*

DEALS
three tenth *d* of fine flour for a Lev 14:10
thereof shall be two tenth *d* of Lev 23:13
two wave loaves of two tenth *d* Lev 23:17
two tenth *d* shall be in one cake Lev 24:5
for a meat offering two tenth *d* Num 15:6
d of flour mingled with half an Num 15:9
two tenth *d* of flour for a meat Num 28:9
three tenth *d* of flour for a meat Num 28:12
two tenth *d* of flour for a meat Num 28:12
three tenth *d* shall ye offer for Num 28:20
bullock, and two tenth *d* for a ram Num 28:20
three tenth *d* unto one bullock, Num 28:28
two tenth *d* unto one ram, Num 28:28
three tenth *d* for a bullock Num 29:3
and two tenth *d* for a ram Num 29:3
three tenth *d* to a bullock Num 29:9
and two tenth *d* to one ram, Num 29:9
three tenth *d* unto every bullock Num 29:14
two tenth *d* to each ram of the Num 29:14

DEALT
when Sarai *d* hardly with her, she Gen 16:6
because God hath *d* graciously Gen 33:11
Wherefore *d* ye so ill with me, as Gen 43:6
Therefore God *d* well with the Ex 1:20
hast thou *d* thus with us, to Ex 14:11 6213
they *d* proudly he was above them Ex 18:11
seeing he hath *d* deceitfully with Ex 21:8
if ye have *d* well with Jerubbaal Judg 9:16 6213
If ye then have *d* truly and Judg 9:19 6213
and the men of Shechem *d* Judg 9:23
as ye have *d* with the dead, and Ruth 1:8 6213
hath *d* very bitterly with me Ruth 1:20
how that thou hast *d* well with me 1Sa 24:18 6213
shall have *d* well with my lord 1Sa 25:31
he *d* among all the people, even 2Sa 6:19 2505
for they *d* faithfully 2Kin 12:15 6213
d with familiar spirits and 2Kin 21:6 6213
hand, because they *d* faithfully 2Kin 22:7 6213
he *d* to every one of Israel, both 1Chr 16:3 2505
Even so *d* David with all the 1Chr 20:3 6213
done amiss, and have *d* wickedly 2Chr 6:37
he *d* wisely, and dispersed of all 2Chr 11:23
d with a familiar spirit, and with 2Chr 33:6 6213
We have *d* very corruptly against Neh 1:7
that they *d* proudly against them Neh 9:10
But they and our fathers *d* proudly Neh 9:16
yet they *d* proudly, and hearkened Neh 9:29
My brethren have *d* deceitfully as Job 6:15
because he hath *d* bountifully Ps 13:6 1580
neither have we *d* falsely in thy Ps 44:17
d unfaithfully like their fathers Ps 78:57
He hath not *d* with us after our Ps 103:10 6213
for the LORD hath *d* bountifully Ps 116:7 1580
Thou hast *d* well with thy servant Ps 119:65 6213
for they *d* perversely with me Ps 119:78
He hath not *d* so with any nation Ps 147:20 6213
dealers have *d* treacherously Is 24:16
dealers have *d* very treacherously Is 24:16
they *d* not treacherously with Is 33:1
so have ye *d* treacherously with Jer 3:20
the house of Judah have *d* very Jer 5:11
even they have *d* treacherously Jer 12:6
all her friends have *d* Lam 1:2
in the midst of thee have they *d* Eze 22:7 6213
Because that Edom hath *d* against Eze 25:12 6213
the Philistines have *d* by revenge Eze 25:15 6213
They have *d* treacherously against Hos 5:7
there have they *d* treacherously Hos 6:7
that hath *d* wondrously with you Joel 2:26 6213
our doings, so hath he *d* with us Zec 1:6 6213
Judah hath *d* treacherously, and an Mal 2:11
whom thou hast *d* treacherously Mal 2:14
Thus hath the Lord *d* with me in Lk 1:25 *4160*
Son, why hast thou thus *d* with us Lk 2:48 *4160*
The same *d* subtilly with our Acts 7:19 *2686*
of the Jews have *d* with me Acts 25:24 *1793*
according as God hath *d* to every Rom 12:3 *3307*

DEAR
Is Ephraim my *d* son Jer 31:20 3357
who was *d* unto him, was sick, and Lk 7:2 *1784*
count I my life *d* unto myself Acts 20:24 *5093*
followers of God, as *d* children Eph 5:1 *27*
of Epaphras our *d* fellowservant Col 1:7 *27*
us into the kingdom of his *d* Son Col 1:13 *26*
souls, because ye were *d* unto us 1Th 2:8 *27*

DEARLY
I have given the *d* beloved of my Jer 12:7
D beloved, avenge not yourselves, Rom 12:19
my *d* beloved, flee from idolatry 1Cor 10:14
these promises *d* beloved, let us 2Cor 7:1
d beloved, for your edifying 2Cor 12:19
Therefore, my brethren *d* beloved Phil 4:1
fast in the Lord, my *d* beloved Phil 4:1
To Timothy, my *d* beloved son 2Ti 1:2
unto Philemon our *d* beloved Philem 1
D beloved, I beseech you as 1Pet 2:11

DEARTH
seven years of *d* began to come Gen 41:54 7458
and the *d* was in all lands Gen 41:54 7458
and there was a *d* in the land 2Kin 4:38 7458
If there be *d* in the land 2Chr 6:28 7458
might buy corn, because of the *d* Neh 5:3 7458
came to Jeremiah concerning the *d* Jer 14:1 1226
Now there came a *d* over all the Acts 7:11 *3042*
great *d* throughout all the world Acts 11:28 *3042*

DEATH
Let me not see the *d* of the child Gen 21:16 4194
comforted after his mother's *d* Gen 24:67
to pass after the *d* of Abraham Gen 25:11 4194
his wife shall surely be put to *d* Gen 26:11 4191
them after the *d* of Abraham Gen 26:18 4194
old, I know not the day of my *d* Gen 27:2 4194
thee before the LORD before my *d* Gen 27:7 4194
he may bless thee before his *d* Gen 27:10 4194
may take away from me this *d* only Ex 10:17 4194
mount shall be surely put to *d* Ex 19:12 4191
he die, shall be surely put to *d* Ex 21:12 4191
mother, shall be surely put to *d* Ex 21:15 4191
hand, he shall surely be put to *d* Ex 21:16 4191
mother, shall surely be put to *d* Ex 21:17 4191
his owner also shall be put to *d* Ex 21:29 4191
a beast shall surely be put to *d* Ex 22:19 4191
it shall surely be put to *d* Ex 31:14 4191
day, he shall surely be put to *d* Ex 31:15 4191
work therein shall be put to *d* Ex 35:2 4191
the *d* of the two sons of Aaron Lev 16:1 4194
they shall not be put to *d* Lev 19:20 4191
he shall surely be put to *d* Lev 20:2 4191
mother shall be surely put to *d* Lev 20:9 4191
shall surely be put to *d* Lev 20:10 4191
of them shall surely be put to *d* Lev 20:11 4191
of them shall surely be put to *d* Lev 20:12 4191
they shall surely be put to *d* Lev 20:13 4191
he shall surely be put to *d* Lev 20:15 4191
they shall surely be put to *d* Lev 20:16 4191
wizard, shall surely be put to *d* Lev 20:27 4191
LORD, he shall surely be put to *d* Lev 24:16 4191
of the LORD, shall be put to *d* Lev 24:16 4191
any man shall surely be put to *d* Lev 24:17 4191
a man, he shall be put to *d* Lev 24:21 4191
but shall surely be put to *d* Lev 27:29 4191
cometh nigh shall be put to *d* Num 1:51 4191
cometh nigh shall be put to *d* Num 3:10 4191
cometh nigh shall be put to *d* Num 3:38 4191
The man shall be surely put to *d* Num 15:35 4191
men die the common *d* of all men Num 16:29 4194
cometh nigh shall be put to *d* Num 18:7 4191
Let me die the *d* of the righteous Num 23:10 4194
murderer shall surely be put to *d* Num 35:16 4191
murderer shall surely be put to *d* Num 35:17 4191
murderer shall surely be put to *d* Num 35:18 4191
him shall surely be put to *d* Num 35:21 4191
it unto the *d* of the high priest Num 35:25 4194
until the *d* of the high priest Num 35:28 4194
but after the *d* of the high Num 35:28 4194
to *d* by the mouth of witnesses Num 35:30 7523
a murderer, which is guilty of *d* Num 35:31 4191
but he shall be surely put to *d* Num 35:31 4191
until the *d* of the priest Num 35:32 4194
of dreams, shall be put to *d* Deut 13:5 4191
be first upon him to put him to *d* Deut 13:9 4191
is worthy of *d* be put to *d* Deut 17:6 4191
witness he shall not be put to *d* Deut 17:6 4191
be first upon him to put him to *d* Deut 17:7 4191
whereas he was not worthy of *d* Deut 19:6 4194
have committed a sin worthy of *d* Deut 21:22 4194
and he be to be put to *d* Deut 21:22 4191
in the damsel no sin worthy of *d* Deut 22:26 4194
not be put to *d* for the children Deut 24:16 4191
be put to *d* for the fathers Deut 24:16 4191
shall be put to *d* for his own sin Deut 24:16 4191
thee this day life and good, and *d* Deut 30:15 4194
I have set before you life and *d* Deut 30:19 4194
and how much more after my *d* Deut 31:27 4194
my *d* ye will utterly corrupt Deut 31:29 4194
children of Israel before his *d* Deut 33:1 4194
Now after the *d* of Moses the Josh 1:1 4194
him, he shall be put to *d* Josh 1:18 4191
have, and deliver our lives from *d* Josh 2:13 4194
until the *d* of the high priest Josh 20:6 4194
Now after the *d* of Joshua it came Judg 1:1 4194
jeoparded their lives unto the *d* Judg 5:18 4191
let him be put to *d* whilst it is Judg 6:31 4191
from the womb to the day of his *d* Judg 13:7 4194
so that his soul was vexed unto *d* Judg 16:16 4191
d were more than they which he Judg 16:30 4194
Gibeah, that we may put them to *d* Judg 20:13 4191
He shall surely be put to *d* Judg 21:5 4191
also, if ought but *d* part thee Ruth 1:17 4194
law since the *d* of thine husband Ruth 2:11 4194
about the time of her *d* the women 1Sa 4:20 4191
men, that we may put them to *d* 1Sa 11:12 4191
not a man be put to *d* this day 1Sa 11:13 4191
the bitterness of *d* is past 1Sa 15:32 4194
see Saul until the day of his *d* 1Sa 15:35 4194
is but a step between me and *d* 1Sa 20:3 4194
I have occasioned the *d* of all 1Sa 22:22
came to pass after the *d* of Saul 2Sa 1:1 4194
in their *d* they were not divided 2Sa 1:23 4194
no child unto the day of her *d* 2Sa 6:23 4194
two lines measured he to put to *d* 2Sa 8:2 4191
shall be, whether in *d* or life 2Sa 15:21 4194
not Shimei be put to *d* for this 2Sa 19:21 4191
be put to *d* this day in Israel 2Sa 19:22 4191
shut up unto the day of their *d* 2Sa 20:3 4194
were put to *d* in the days of 2Sa 21:9 4191
When the waves of *d* compassed me 2Sa 22:5 4194
the snares of *d* prevented me 2Sa 22:6 4194
not put thee to *d* with the sword 1Kin 2:8 4191
shall be put to *d* this day 1Kin 2:24 4191
for thou art worthy of *d* 1Kin 2:26 4194
not at this time put thee to *d* 1Kin 2:26 4191
in Egypt until the *d* of Solomon 1Kin 11:40 4194
Israel after the *d* of Ahab 2Kin 1:1 4194
thence any more *d* or barren land 2Kin 2:21 4194
man of God, there is *d* in the pot 2Kin 4:40 4194
not be put to *d* for the children 2Kin 14:6 4191
be put to *d* for the fathers 2Kin 14:6 4191
shall be put to *d* for his own sin 2Kin 14:6 4191
king of Judah lived after the *d* 2Kin 14:17 4194
was a leper unto the day of his *d* 2Kin 15:5 4194
days was Hezekiah sick unto *d* 2Kin 20:1 4191
prepared abundantly before his *d* 1Chr 22:5 4194
God of Israel should be put to *d* 2Chr 15:13 4191
after the *d* of his father to his 2Chr 22:4 4194
the house, he shall be put to *d* 2Chr 23:7 4191
Now after the *d* of Jehoiada came 2Chr 24:17 4194
d of Joash son of Jehoahaz king 2Chr 25:25 4194
was a leper unto the day of his *d* 2Chr 26:21 4194
days Hezekiah was sick to the *d* 2Chr 32:24 4191
Jerusalem did him honour at his *d* 2Chr 32:33 4194
upon him, whether it be unto *d* Ezr 7:26 4193
is one law of his to put him to *d* Est 4:11 4191
and the shadow of *d* stain it Job 3:5 6757
Which long for *d*, but it cometh Job 3:21 4194
he shall redeem thee from *d* Job 5:20 4194
and *d* rather than my life Job 7:15 4194
of darkness and the shadow of *d* Job 10:21 6757
and of the shadow of *d*, without Job 10:22 6757
out to light the shadow of *d* Job 12:22 6757
on my eyelids is the shadow of *d* Job 16:16 6757
even the firstborn of *d* shall Job 18:13 4194
to them even as the shadow of *d* Job 24:17 6757
in the terrors of the shadow of *d* Job 24:17 6757
of him shall be buried in *d* Job 27:15 4194
of darkness, and the shadow of *d* Job 28:3 6757
d say, We have heard the fame Job 28:22 4194
know that thou wilt bring me to *d* Job 30:23 4194
is no darkness, nor shadow of *d* Job 34:22 6757
Have the gates of *d* been opened Job 38:17 4194
seen the doors of the shadow of *d* Job 38:17 6757
For in *d* there is no remembrance Ps 6:5 4194
for him the instruments of *d* Ps 7:13 4194
liftest me up from the gates of *d* Ps 9:13 4194
eyes, lest I sleep the sleep of *d* Ps 13:3 4194
The sorrows of *d* compassed me Ps 18:4 4194
the snares of *d* prevented me Ps 18:5 4194
brought me into the dust of *d* Ps 22:15 4194
the valley of the shadow of *d* Ps 23:4 6757
To deliver their soul from *d* Ps 33:19 4194
covered us with the shadow of *d* Ps 44:19 6757
he will be our guide even unto *d* Ps 48:14 4192
d shall feed on them Ps 49:14 4194
the terrors of *d* are fallen upon Ps 55:4 4194
Let *d* seize upon them, and let Ps 55:15 4194
hast delivered my soul from *d* Ps 56:13 4194
the Lord belong the issues from *d* Ps 68:20 4194
For there are no bands in their *d* Ps 73:4 4194
he spared not their soul from *d* Ps 78:50 4194
that liveth, and shall not see *d* Ps 89:48 4194
those that are appointed to *d* Ps 102:20 8546
in darkness and in the shadow of *d* Ps 107:10 6757
of darkness and the shadow of *d* Ps 107:14 6757
draw near unto the gates of *d* Ps 107:18 4194
The sorrows of *d* compassed me Ps 116:3 4194
hast delivered my soul from *d* Ps 116:8 4194
the LORD is the *d* of his saints Ps 116:15 4194
he hath not given me over unto *d* Ps 118:18 4194
For her house inclineth unto *d* Prov 2:18 4194
Her feet go down to *d* Prov 5:5 4194
going down to the chambers of *d* Prov 7:27 4194
all they that hate me love *d* Prov 8:36 4194
righteousness delivereth from *d* Prov 10:2 4194
righteousness delivereth from *d* Prov 11:4 4194
evil pursueth it to his own *d* Prov 11:19 4194
the pathway thereof there is no *d* Prov 12:28 4194
to depart from the snares of *d* Prov 13:14 4194

the end thereof are the ways of d ..... Prov 14:12 4194
to depart from the snares of d ..... Prov 14:27 4194
the righteous hath hope in his d ..... Prov 14:32 4194
of a king is as messengers of d ..... Prov 16:14 4194
the end thereof are the ways of d ..... Prov 16:25 4194
D and life are in the power of the ..... Prov 18:21 4194
to and fro of them that seek d ..... Prov 21:6 4194
them that are drawn unto d ..... Prov 24:11 4194
casteth firebrands, arrows, and d ..... Prov 26:18 4194
the day of d than the day of ..... Eccl 7:1 4194
find more bitter than d the woman ..... Eccl 7:26 4194
hath he power in the day of d ..... Eccl 8:8 4194
for love is strong as d ..... Song 8:6 4194
in the land of the shadow of d ..... Is 9:2 6757
He will swallow up d in victory ..... Is 25:8 4194
We have made a covenant with d ..... Is 28:15 4194
your covenant with d shall be ..... Is 28:18 4194
days was Hezekiah sick unto d ..... Is 38:1 4191
thee, d can not celebrate thee ..... Is 38:18 4194
wicked, and with the rich in his d ..... Is 53:9 4194
hath poured out his soul unto d ..... Is 53:12 4194
of drought, and of the shadow of d ..... Jer 2:6 6757
d shall be chosen rather than ..... Jer 8:3 4194
For d is come up into our windows ..... Jer 9:21 4194
he turn it into the shadow of d ..... Jer 13:16 6757
Such as are for d, to d ..... Jer 15:2 4194
Such as are for d, to d ..... Jer 15:2 4194
and let their men be put to d ..... Jer 18:21 4194
the way of life, and the way of d ..... Jer 21:8 4194
certain, that if ye put me to d ..... Jer 26:15 4191
and all Judah put him at all to d ..... Jer 26:19 4191
the king sought to put him to d ..... Jer 26:21 4191
of the people to put him to d ..... Jer 26:24 4191
thee, let this man be put to d ..... Jer 38:4 4191
wilt thou not surely put me to d ..... Jer 38:15 4191
soul, I will not put thee to d ..... Jer 38:16 4191
us, and we will not put thee to d ..... Jer 38:25 4191
that they might put us to d ..... Jer 43:3 4191
such as are for d to d ..... Jer 43:11 4194
in prison till the day of his d ..... Jer 52:11 4194
put them to d in Riblah in the ..... Jer 52:27 4191
a portion until the day of his d ..... Jer 52:34 4194
bereaveth, at home there is as d ..... Lam 1:20 4194
in the d of him that dieth ..... Eze 18:32 4194
for they are all delivered unto d ..... Eze 31:14 4194
pleasure in the d of the wicked ..... Eze 33:11 4194
I will redeem them from d ..... Hos 13:14 4194
O d, I will be thy plagues ..... Hos 13:14 4194
the shadow of d into the morning ..... Amos 5:8 6757
do well to be angry, even unto d ..... Jonah 4:9 4194
his desire as hell, and is as d ..... Hab 2:5 4194
And was there until the d of Herod ..... Mt 2:15 5054
shadow of d light is sprung up ..... Mt 4:16 2288
shall deliver up the brother to d ..... Mt 10:21 2288
and cause them to be put to d ..... Mt 10:21 2289
when he would have put him to d ..... Mt 14:5 615
or mother, let him die the d ..... Mt 15:4 2288
here, which shall not taste of d ..... Mt 16:28 2288
and they shall condemn him to d ..... Mt 20:18 2288
exceeding sorrowful, even unto d ..... Mt 26:38 2288
against Jesus, to put him to d ..... Mt 26:59 2289
and said, He is guilty of d ..... Mt 26:66 2288
against Jesus to put him to d ..... Mt 27:1 2289
daughter lieth at the point of d ..... Mk 5:23 2079
or mother, let him die the d ..... Mk 7:10 2288
here, which shall not taste of d ..... Mk 9:1 2288
and they shall condemn him to d ..... Mk 10:33 2288
shall betray the brother to d ..... Mk 13:12 2288
shall cause them to be put to d ..... Mk 13:12 2289
him by craft, and put him to d ..... Mk 14:1 615
is exceeding sorrowful unto d ..... Mk 14:34 2288
against Jesus to put him to d ..... Mk 14:55 2289
condemned him to be guilty of d ..... Mk 14:64 2288
in darkness and in the shadow of d ..... Lk 1:79 2288
Ghost, that he should not see d ..... Lk 2:26 2288
here, which shall not taste of d ..... Lk 9:27 2288
scourge him, and put him to d ..... Lk 18:33 615
shall they cause to be put to d ..... Lk 21:16 2289
thee, both into prison, and to d ..... Lk 22:33 2288
worthy of d is done unto him ..... Lk 23:15 2288
I have found no cause of d in him ..... Lk 23:22 2288
led with him to be put to d ..... Lk 23:32 337
him to be condemned to d, and have ..... Lk 24:20 2288
for he was at the point of d ..... Jn 4:47 599
but is passed from d unto life ..... Jn 5:24 2288
my saying, he shall never see d ..... Jn 8:51 2288
saying, he shall never taste of d ..... Jn 8:52 2288
said, This sickness is not unto d ..... Jn 11:4 2288
Howbeit Jesus spake of his d ..... Jn 11:13 2288
together for to put him to d ..... Jn 11:53 615
they might put Lazarus also to d ..... Jn 12:10 615
signifying what d he should die ..... Jn 12:33 2288
lawful for us to put any man to d ..... Jn 18:31 615
signifying what d he should die ..... Jn 18:32 2288
signifying by what d he should ..... Jn 21:19 2288
up, having loosed the pains of d ..... Acts 2:24 2288
And Saul was consenting unto his d ..... Acts 8:1 336
that they should be put to d ..... Acts 12:19 520
they found no cause of d in him ..... Acts 13:28 2288
I persecuted this way unto the d ..... Acts 22:4 2288
by, and consenting unto his d ..... Acts 22:20 336
charge worthy of d or of bonds ..... Acts 23:29 336
committed any thing worthy of d ..... Acts 25:11 336
had committed nothing worthy of d ..... Acts 25:25 336
and when they were put to d ..... Acts 26:10 337
nothing worthy of d or of bonds ..... Acts 26:31 2288
there was no cause of d in me ..... Acts 28:18 2288
such things are worthy of d ..... Rom 1:32 2288
to God by the d of his Son ..... Rom 5:10 2288
into the world, and d by sin ..... Rom 5:12 2288
so d passed upon all men, for ..... Rom 5:12 2288
Nevertheless d reigned from Adam ..... Rom 5:14 2288
man's offence d reigned by one ..... Rom 5:17 2288
That as sin hath reigned unto d ..... Rom 5:21 2288
Christ were baptized into his d ..... Rom 6:3 2288
buried with him by baptism into d ..... Rom 6:4 2288
together in the likeness of his d ..... Rom 6:5 2288
d hath no more dominion over him ..... Rom 6:9 2288
whether of sin unto d, or of ..... Rom 6:16 2288
for the end of those things is d ..... Rom 6:21 2288
For the wages of sin is d ..... Rom 6:23 2288
to bring forth fruit unto d ..... Rom 7:5 2288
to life, I found to be unto d ..... Rom 7:10 2288
that which is good made d unto me ..... Rom 7:13 2288
working d in me by that which is ..... Rom 7:13 2288
me from the body of this d ..... Rom 7:24 2288
me free from the law of sin and d ..... Rom 8:2 2288
For to be carnally minded is d ..... Rom 8:6 2288
I am persuaded, that neither d ..... Rom 8:38 2288
or the world, or life, or d 1Cor 3:22 2288
last, as it were appointed to d 1Cor 4:9 1935
do shew the Lord's d till he come 1Cor 11:26 2288
For since by man came d, by man 1Cor 15:21 2288
that shall be destroyed is d 1Cor 15:26 2288
D is swallowed up in victory 1Cor 15:54 2288
O d, where is thy sting 1Cor 15:55 2288
The sting of d is sin 1Cor 15:56 2288
the sentence of d in ourselves 2Cor 1:9 2288
delivered us from so great a d 2Cor 1:10 2288
we are the savour of d unto d 2Cor 2:16 2288
we are the savour of d unto d 2Cor 2:16 2288
But if the ministration of d 2Cor 3:7 2288
delivered unto d for Jesus' sake 2Cor 4:11 2288
So then d worketh in us, but life 2Cor 4:12 2288
the sorrow of the world worketh d 2Cor 7:10 2288
whether it be by life, or by d ..... Phil 1:20 2288
and became obedient unto d ..... Phil 2:8 2288
even the d of the cross ..... Phil 2:8 2288
indeed he was sick nigh unto d ..... Phil 2:27 2288
work of Christ he was nigh unto d ..... Phil 2:30 2288
being made conformable unto his d ..... Phil 3:10 2288
the body of his flesh through d ..... Col 1:22 2288
Christ, who hath abolished d 2Ti 1:10 2288
the angels for the suffering of d ..... Heb 2:9 2288
God should taste d for every man ..... Heb 2:9 2288
that through d he might destroy ..... Heb 2:14 2288
him that had the power of d ..... Heb 2:14 2288
them who through fear of d were ..... Heb 2:15 2288
that was able to save him from d ..... Heb 5:7 2288
to continue by reason of d ..... Heb 7:23 2288
new testament, that by means of d ..... Heb 9:15 2288
be the d of the testator ..... Heb 9:16 2288
that he should not see d ..... Heb 11:5 2288
it is finished, bringeth forth d ..... Jas 1:15 2288
his way shall save a soul from d ..... Jas 5:20 2288
God, being put to d in the flesh 1Pet 3:18 2289
we have passed from d unto life 1Jn 3:14 2288
not his brother abideth in d 1Jn 3:14 2288
sin a sin which is not unto d 1Jn 5:16 2288
life for them that sin not unto d 1Jn 5:16 2288
There is a sin unto d 1Jn 5:16 2288
and there is a sin not unto d 1Jn 5:17 2288
and have the keys of hell and of d ..... Rev 1:18 2288
be thou faithful unto d, and I ..... Rev 2:10 2288
shall not be hurt of the second d ..... Rev 2:11 2288
I will kill her children with d ..... Rev 2:23 2288
and his name that sat on him was D ..... Rev 6:8 2288
sword, and with hunger, and with d ..... Rev 6:8 2288
And in those days shall men seek d ..... Rev 9:6 2288
to die, and d shall flee from them ..... Rev 9:6 2288
loved not their lives unto the d ..... Rev 12:11 2288
his heads as it were wounded to d ..... Rev 13:3 2288
her plagues come in one day, d ..... Rev 18:8 2288
such the second d hath no power ..... Rev 20:6 2288
and d and hell delivered up the ..... Rev 20:13 2288
And d and hell were cast into the ..... Rev 20:14 2288
This is the second d ..... Rev 20:14 2288
and there shall be no more d ..... Rev 21:4 2288
which is the second d ..... Rev 21:8 2288

DEATHS
They shall die of grievous d ..... Jer 16:4 4463
thou shalt die the d of them that ..... Eze 28:8 4463
Thou shalt die the d of the ..... Eze 28:10 4194
prisons more frequent, in d oft 2Cor 11:23 2288

DEBASE
didst d thyself even unto hell ..... Is 57:9 8213

DEBATE
D thy cause with thy neighbour ..... Prov 25:9 7378
forth, thou wilt d with it ..... Is 27:8 7378
Behold, ye fast for strife and d ..... Is 58:4 4683
full of envy, murder, d, deceit, ... Rom 1:29 2054

DEBATES
lest there be d, envyings, wraths 2Cor 12:20 2054

DEBIR (de'-bur) See KIRJATH-SANNAH, KIRJATH-SEPHER.
1. An Amorite king.
unto D king of Eglon, saying, ... Josh 10:3 1688
2. A city in Judah.
and all Israel with him, to D ..... Josh 10:38 1688
done to Hebron, so he did to D ..... Josh 10:39 1688
mountains, from Hebron, from D ..... Josh 11:21 1688
The king of D, one ..... Josh 12:13 1688
toward D from the valley of Achor ..... Josh 15:7 1688
up thence to the inhabitants of D ..... Josh 15:15 1688
and the name of D before was ..... Josh 15:15 1688
and Kirjath-sannah, which is D ..... Josh 15:49 1688
suburbs, and D with her suburbs, ... Josh 21:15 1688
went against the inhabitants of D ..... Judg 1:11 1688
and the name of D before was ..... Judg 1:11 1688
her suburbs, D with her suburbs, ... 1Chr 6:58 1688
3. The boundary of Gad.
Mahanaim unto the border of D ..... Josh 13:26 1688

DEBORAH (deb'-o-rah)
1. Rebekah's nurse.
But D Rebekah's nurse died, and ..... Gen 35:8 1683
2. A judge of Israel.
And D, a prophetess, the wife of ..... Judg 4:4 1683
the palm tree of D between Ramah ..... Judg 4:5 1683
D arose, and went with Barak to ..... Judg 4:9 1683
and D went up with him ..... Judg 4:10 1683
And D said unto Barak, Up ..... Judg 4:14 1683
Then sang D and Barak the son of ..... Judg 5:1 1683
in Israel, until that I D arose ..... Judg 5:7 1683
Awake, awake, D ..... Judg 5:12 1683
princes of Issachar were with D ..... Judg 5:15 1683

DEBT
and every one that was in d 1Sa 22:2 5378
Go, sell the oil, and pay thy d 2Kin 4:7 5386
year, and the exaction of every d ..... Neh 10:31 3027
loosed him, and forgave him the d ..... Mt 18:27 1156
prison, till he should pay the d ..... Mt 18:30 3784
I forgave thee all that d ..... Mt 18:32 3782
not reckoned of grace, but of d ..... Rom 4:4 3783

DEBTOR
hath restored to the d his pledge ..... Eze 18:7 2326
the gold of the temple, he is a d ..... Mt 23:16 3784
I am d both to the Greeks, and to ..... Rom 1:14 3781
that he is a d to do the whole ..... Gal 5:3 3781

DEBTORS
us our debts, as we forgive our d ..... Mt 6:12 3781
certain creditor which had two d ..... Lk 7:41 5533
one of his lord's d unto him ..... Lk 16:5 5533
Therefore, brethren, we are d ..... Rom 8:12 3781
and their d they are ..... Rom 15:27 3781

DEBTS
of them that are sureties for d ..... Prov 22:26 4859
And forgive us our d, as we ..... Mt 6:12 3783

DECAPOLIS (de-cap'-o-lis) *A district east of the Jordan River.*
of people from Galilee, and from D ..... Mt 4:25 1179
began to publish in D how great ..... Mk 5:20 1179
the midst of the coasts of D ..... Mk 7:31 1179

DECAY
poor, and fallen in d with thee ..... Lev 25:35 4131

DECAYED
of the bearers of burdens is d ..... Neh 4:10 3782
raise up the d places thereof ..... Is 44:26 2723

DECAYETH
fail from the sea, and the flood d ..... Job 14:11 2717
much slothfulness the building d ..... Eccl 10:18 4355
Now that which d and waxeth old is ..... Heb 8:13 3822

DECEASE
spake of his d which he should ..... Lk 9:31 1841
that ye may be able after my d to 2Pet 1:15 1841

DECEASED
they are d, they shall not rise ..... Is 26:14 7496
when he had married a wife, d ..... Mt 22:25 5053

DECEIT
and their belly prepareth d ..... Job 15:35 4820
wickedness, nor my tongue utter d ..... Job 27:4 7423
or if my foot hath hasted to d ..... Job 31:5 4820
His mouth is full of cursing and d ..... Ps 10:7 4820
of his mouth are iniquity and d ..... Ps 36:3 4820
to evil, and thy tongue frameth d ..... Ps 50:19 4820
d and guile depart not from her ..... Ps 55:11 8496
He shall redeem their soul from d ..... Ps 72:14 8496
He that worketh d shall not dwell ..... Ps 101:7 7423
for their d is falsehood ..... Ps 119:118 8649
the counsels of the wicked are d ..... Prov 12:5 4820
but a false witness d ..... Prov 12:17 4820
D is in the heart of them that ..... Prov 12:20 4820
but the folly of fools is d ..... Prov 14:8 4820
Bread of d is sweet to a man ..... Prov 20:17 8267
lips, and layeth up d within him ..... Prov 26:24 4820
Whose hatred is covered by d ..... Prov 26:26 4860
neither was any d in his mouth ..... Is 53:9 4820
so are their houses full of d ..... Jer 5:27 4820
they hold fast d, they refuse to ..... Jer 8:5 8649
habitation is in the midst of d ..... Jer 9:6 4820
through d they refuse to know me, ... Jer 9:6 4820
it speaketh d ..... Jer 9:8 4820
nought, and the d of their heart ..... Jer 14:14 8649
of the d of their own heart ..... Jer 23:26 8649
and the house of Israel with d ..... Hos 11:12 4820
the balances of d are in his hand ..... Hos 12:7 4820
and falsifying the balances by d ..... Amos 8:5 4820
houses with violence and d ..... Zeph 1:9 4820
covetousness, wickedness, d ..... Mk 7:22 1388
full of envy, murder, debate, d ..... Rom 1:29 1388
their tongues they have used d ..... Rom 3:13 1387
you through philosophy and vain d ..... Col 2:8 539
For our exhortation was not of d 1Th 2:3 4106

DECEITFUL
will abhor the bloody and d man ..... Ps 5:6 4820
but they devise d matters against ..... Ps 35:20 4820
O deliver me from the d and unjust ..... Ps 43:1 4820
devouring words, O thou d tongue ..... Ps 52:4 4820
d men shall not live out half ..... Ps 55:23 4820
were turned aside like a d bow ..... Ps 78:57 7423
the mouth of the d are opened ..... Ps 109:2 4820
lying lips, and from a d tongue ..... Ps 120:2 7423
The wicked worketh a d work ..... Prov 11:18 8267
but a d witness speaketh lies ..... Prov 14:25 4820
for they are d meat ..... Prov 23:3 3577
but the kisses of an enemy are d ..... Prov 27:6 6280
poor and the d man meet together ..... Prov 29:13 8501
Favour is d, and beauty is vain ..... Prov 31:30 8267
The heart is d above all things, ... Jer 17:9 6121
they are like a d bow ..... Hos 7:16 7423
and with the bag of d weights ..... Mic 6:11 4820
their tongue is d in their mouth ..... Mic 6:12 7423
neither shall a d tongue be found ..... Zeph 3:13 8649
apostles, d workers, transforming 2Cor 11:13 1386
corrupt according to the d lusts ..... Eph 4:22 539

D

DECEITFULLY
Shechem and Hamor his father *d* Gen 34:13 4820
but let not Pharaoh deal *d* any Ex 8:29 2048
seeing he hath dealt *d* with her Ex 21:8 898
the thing which he hath *d* gotten Lev 6:4 6231
brethren have dealt *d* as a brook Job 6:15 898
and talk *d* for him Job 13:7 7423
his soul unto vanity, nor sworn *d* Ps 24:4 4820
like a sharp rasor, working *d* Ps 52:2 7423
that doeth the work of the LORD *d* Jer 48:10 7423
made with him he shall work *d* Dan 11:23 4820
nor handling the word of God *d* 2Cor 4:2 *1389*

DECEITFULNESS
the *d* of riches, choke the word, Mt 13:22 *539*
the *d* of riches, and the lusts of Mk 4:19 *539*
be hardened through the *d* of sin Heb 3:13 *539*

DECEITS
imagine *d* all the day long Ps 38:12 4820
unto us smooth things, prophesy *d* Is 30:10 4123

DECEIVABLENESS
with all *d* of unrighteousness in 2Th 2:10 *539*

DECEIVE
of Ner, that he came to *d* thee 2Sa 3:25 6601
did I not say, Do not *d* me 2Kin 4:28 7952
the king, Let not Hezekiah *d* you 2Kin 18:29 5377
God in whom thou trustest *d* thee 2Kin 19:10 5377
therefore let not Hezekiah *d* you 2Chr 32:15 5377
and *d* not with thy lips Prov 24:28 6601
the king, Let not Hezekiah *d* you Is 36:14 5377
d thee, saying, Jerusalem shall Is 37:10 5377
they will *d* every one his Jer 9:5 2048
d you, neither hearken to your Jer 29:8 5377
D not yourselves, saying, The Jer 37:9 5377
they wear a rough garment to *d* Zec 13:4 3884
them, Take heed that no man *d* you Mt 24:4 *4105*
and shall *d* many Mt 24:5 *4105*
shall rise, and shall *d* many Mt 24:11 *4105*
they shall *d* the very elect Mt 24:24 *4105*
say, Take heed lest any man *d* you Mk 13:5 *4105*
and shall *d* many Mk 13:6 *4105*
fair speeches *d* the hearts of the Rom 16:18 *1818*
Let no man *d* himself 1Cor 3:18 *1818*
whereby they lie in wait to *d* Eph 4:14 *4106*
Let no man *d* you with vain words Eph 5:6 *538*
Let no man *d* you by any means 2Th 2:3 *1818*
we *d* ourselves, and the truth is 1Jn 1:8 *4105*
Little children, let no man *d* you 1Jn 3:7 *4105*
that he should *d* the nations no Rev 20:3 *4105*
shall go out to *d* the nations Rev 20:8 *4105*

DECEIVED
And your father hath *d* me, and Gen 31:7 2048
violence, or hath *d* his neighbour Lev 6:2 6231
that your heart be not *d* Deut 11:16 6601
Michal, Why hast thou *d* me so 1Sa 19:17 7411
Saul, saying, Why hast thou *d* me 1Sa 28:12 7411
My lord, O king, my servant *d* me 2Sa 19:26 7411
the *d* and the deceiver are his Job 12:16 7683
not him that is *d* trust in vanity Job 15:31 8582
mine heart have been *d* by a woman Job 31:9 6601
whosoever is *d* thereby is not Prov 20:1 7686
fools, the princes of Noph are *d* Is 19:13 5377
a *d* heart hath turned him aside, Is 44:20 2048
thou hast greatly *d* this people Jer 4:10 5377
O LORD, thou hast *d* me, and I was Jer 20:7 6601
thou hast *d* me, and I was *d* Jer 20:7 6601
Thy terribleness hath *d* thee Jer 49:16 5377
for my lovers, but they *d* me Lam 1:19 7411
if the prophet be *d* when he hath Eze 14:9 6601
I the LORD have *d* that prophet Eze 14:9 6601
pride of thine heart hath *d* thee Obad 3 5377
at peace with thee have *d* thee Obad 7 5377
said, Take heed that ye be not *d* Lk 21:8 *4105*
them the Pharisees, Are ye also *d* Jn 7:47 *4105*
d me, and by it slew me Rom 7:11 *1818*
Be not *d*: neither fornicators 1Cor 6:9 *4105*
Be not *d*: evil communications 1Cor 15:33 *4105*
Be not *d*; God is not Gal 6:7 *4105*
And Adam was not *d*, but the woman 1Ti 2:14 *538*
but the woman being *d* was in the 1Ti 2:14 *538*
and worse, deceiving, and being *d* 2Ti 3:13 *4105*
sometimes foolish, disobedient, *d* Titus 3:3 *4105*
thy sorceries were all nations *d* Rev 18:23 *4105*
with which he *d* them that had Rev 19:20 *4105*
the devil that *d* them was cast Rev 20:10 *4105*

DECEIVER
me, and I shall seem to him as a *d* Gen 27:12 8591
the deceived and the *d* are his Job 12:16 7686
But cursed be the *d*, which hath Mal 1:14 5230
Sir, we remember that that *d* said Mt 27:63 *4108*
This is a *d* and an antichrist 2Jn 7 *4108*

DECEIVERS
as *d*, and yet true 2Cor 6:8 *4108*
many unruly and vain talkers and *d* Titus 1:10 *5423*
For many *d* are entered into the 2Jn 7 *4108*

DECEIVETH
is the man that *d* his neighbour Prov 26:19 7411
but he *d* the people Jn 7:12 *4105*
when he is nothing, he *d* himself Gal 6:3 *5422*
but *d* his own heart, this man's Jas 1:26 *538*
and Satan, which *d* the whole world Rev 12:9 *4105*
d them that dwell on the earth by Rev 13:14 *4105*

DECEIVING
shall wax worse and worse, *d* 2Ti 3:13 *4105*
hearers only, *d* your own selves Jas 1:22 *3884*

DECEIVINGS
own *d* while they feast with you 2Pet 2:13 *539*

DECENTLY
Let all things be done *d* and in 1Cor 14:40 *2156*

DECIDED
thyself hast *d* it 1Kin 20:40 2782

DECISION
multitudes in the valley of *d* Joel 3:14 2742
LORD is near in the valley of *d* Joel 3:14 2742

DECK
D thyself now with majesty and Job 40:10 5710
They *d* it with silver and with Jer 10:4 3302

DECKED
I have *d* my bed with coverings of Prov 7:16 7234
I *d* thee also with ornaments, and Eze 16:11 5710
Thus wast thou *d* with gold Eze 16:13 5710
she *d* herself with her earrings Hos 2:13 5710
d with gold and precious stones and Rev 17:4 *5558*
d with gold, and precious stones, Rev 18:16 *5558*

DECKEDST
d thy high places with divers Eze 16:16 6213
d thyself with ornaments, Eze 23:40 5710

DECKEST
though thou *d* thee with ornaments Jer 4:30 5710

DECKETH
as a bridegroom *d* himself with Is 61:10 3547

DECLARATION
the *d* of the greatness of Est 10:2 6575
my speech, and my *d* with your ears Job 13:17 262
d of those things which are most Lk 1:1 *1335*
Lord, and *d* of your ready mind 2Cor 8:19

DECLARE
was none that could *d* it to me Gen 41:24 5046
Moab, began Moses to *d* this law Deut 1:5 874
shall *d* his cause in the ears of Josh 20:4 1696
if ye can certainly *d* it me Judg 14:12 5046
But if ye cannot *d* it me, then Judg 14:13 5046
that he may *d* unto us the riddle, Judg 14:15 5046
the words of the prophets *d* good 1Kin 22:13
D his glory among the heathen 1Chr 16:24 5608
d good to the king with one 2Chr 18:12
to *d* it unto her, and to charge Est 4:8 5046
of the sea shall *d* unto thee Job 12:8 5608
that which I have seen I will *d* Job 15:17 5608
Who shall *d* his way to his face Job 21:31 5046
Then did he see it, and *d* it Job 28:27 5608
I would *d* unto him the number of Job 31:37 5046
d, if thou hast understanding Job 38:4 5046
d if thou knowest it all Job 38:18 5046
demand of thee, and *d* thou unto me Job 40:7 3045
demand of thee, and *d* thou unto me Job 42:4 3045
I will *d* the decree Ps 2:7 5608
d among the people his doings Ps 9:11 5046
The heavens *d* the glory of God Ps 19:1 5608
I will *d* thy name unto my Ps 22:22 5608
shall *d* his righteousness unto a Ps 22:31 5046
shall it *d* thy truth Ps 30:9 5046
For I will *d* mine iniquity Ps 38:18 5046
if I would *d* and speak of them, Ps 40:5 5046
heavens shall *d* his righteousness Ps 50:6 5046
hast thou to do to *d* my statutes Ps 50:16 5608
fear, and shall *d* the work of God Ps 64:9 5046
I will *d* what he hath done for my Ps 66:16 5608
that I may *d* all thy works Ps 73:28 5608
name is near thy wondrous works *d* Ps 75:1 5608
But I will *d* for ever Ps 75:9 5046
arise and *d* them to their children Ps 78:6 5608
D his glory among the heathen, Ps 96:3 5608
The heavens *d* his righteousness, Ps 97:6 5046
To *d* the name of the LORD in Zion Ps 102:21 5608
d his works with rejoicing Ps 107:22 5608
live, and *d* the works of the LORD Ps 118:17 5608
and shall *d* thy mighty acts Ps 145:4 5046
and I will *d* thy greatness Ps 145:6 5608
in my heart even to *d* all this Eccl 9:1 952
they *d* their sin as Sodom, they Is 3:9 5046
d his doings among the people, Is 12:4 3045
watchman, let him *d* what he seeth Is 21:6 5046
or *d* us things for to come Is 41:22 8085
to pass, and new things do I *d* Is 42:9 5046
d his praise in the islands Is 42:12 5046
who among them can *d* this Is 43:9 5046
d thou, that thou mayest be Is 43:26 5608
as I, shall call, and shall *d* it Is 44:7 5046
I *d* things that are right Is 45:19 5046
and will not ye *d* it Is 48:6 5046
with a voice of singing *d* ye Is 48:20 5046
who shall *d* his generation Is 53:8 7878
I will *d* thy righteousness, and Is 57:12 5046
they shall *d* my glory among the Is 66:19 5046
D ye in Judah, and publish in Jer 4:5 5046
D this in the house of Jacob, and Jer 5:20 5046
hath spoken, that he may *d* it Jer 9:12 5046
d it in the isles afar off, and Jer 31:10 5046
If I *d* it unto thee, wilt thou Jer 38:15 5046
D unto us now what thou hast said Jer 38:25 5046
answer you, I will *d* it unto you Jer 42:4 5046
so *d* unto us, and we will do it Jer 42:20 5046
D ye in Egypt, and publish in Jer 46:14 5046
D ye among the nations, and Jer 50:2 5046
to *d* in Zion the vengeance of the Jer 50:28 5046
let us *d* in Zion the work of the Jer 51:10 5608
that they may *d* all their Eze 12:16 5608
d unto them their abominations Eze 23:36 5046
d all that thou seest to the Eze 40:4 5046
d the interpretation thereof, Dan 4:18 560
D ye it not at Gath, weep ye not Mic 1:10 5046
to *d* unto Jacob his transgression Mic 3:8 5046
even to day do I *d* that I will Zec 9:12 5046
D unto us the parable of the Mt 13:36 *5419*
unto him, *D* unto us this parable Mt 15:15 *5419*
unto them thy name, and will *d* it Jn 17:26 *1107*
who shall *d* his generation Acts 8:33 *1334*
we *d* unto you glad tidings, how Acts 13:32 *2097*
though a man *d* it unto you Acts 13:41 *1555*
worship, him *d* I unto you Acts 17:23 *2605*
For I have not shunned to *d* unto Acts 20:27 *312*
to *d* his righteousness for the Rom 3:25 *1732*
To *d*, I say, at this time his Rom 3:26 *1732*
for the day shall *d* it, because 1Cor 3:13 *1213*
Now in this that I *d* unto you I 1Cor 11:17 *3853*
I *d* unto you the gospel which I 1Cor 15:1 *1107*
state shall Tychicus *d* unto you Col 4:7 *1107*
I will *d* thy name unto my Heb 2:12 *518*
things *d* plainly that they seek a Heb 11:14 *1718*
heard *d* we unto you, that ye also 1Jn 1:3 *518*
d unto you, that God is light, and 1Jn 1:5 *312*

DECLARED
that my name may be *d* throughout Ex 9:16 5608
Moses *d* unto the children of Lev 23:44 1696
they *d* their pedigrees after Num 1:18
because it was not *d* what should Num 15:34 6567
he *d* unto you his covenant, which Deut 4:13 5046
For thou hast *d* this day, that 2Sa 19:6 5046
the words that were *d* unto them Neh 8:12 3045
plentifully *d* the thing as it is Job 26:3 3045
I have *d* thy faithfulness and thy Ps 40:10 559
hitherto have I *d* thy wondrous Ps 71:17 5046
thou hast *d* thy strength among Ps 77:14 3045
lovingkindness be *d* in the grave Ps 88:11 5608
With my lips have I *d* all the Ps 119:13 5608
I have *d* my ways, and thou Ps 119:26 5608
A grievous vision is *d* unto me Is 21:2 5046
God of Israel, have I *d* unto you Is 21:10 5046
Who hath *d* from the beginning, Is 41:26 5046
I have *d*, and have saved, and I Is 43:12 5046
thee from that time, and have *d* it Is 44:8 5046
who hath *d* this from ancient time Is 45:21 8085
I have *d* the former things from Is 48:3 5046
from the beginning *d* it to thee Is 48:5 5046
among them hath *d* these things Is 48:14 5046
Then Michaiah *d* unto them all the Jer 36:13 5046
now I have this day *d* it to you Jer 42:21 5046
she *d* unto him before all the Lk 8:47 *518*
of the Father, he hath *d* him Jn 1:18 *1834*
I have *d* unto them thy name, and Jn 17:26 *1107*
d unto them how he had seen the Acts 9:27 *1334*
when he had *d* all these things Acts 10:8 *1834*
d unto them how the Lord had Acts 12:17 *1334*
they *d* all things that God had Acts 15:4 *312*
Simeon hath *d* how God at the Acts 15:14 *1834*
he *d* particularly what things God Acts 21:19 *1834*
Festus *d* Paul's cause unto the Acts 25:14 *394*
d to be the Son of God with power Rom 1:4 *3724*
thee, and that my name might be *d* Rom 9:17 *1229*
For it hath been *d* unto me of you 1Cor 1:11 *1213*
d to be the epistle of Christ 2Cor 3:3 *5319*
Who also *d* unto us your love in Col 1:8 *1213*
as he hath *d* to his servants the Rev 10:7 *2097*

DECLARETH
yea, there is none that *d* Is 41:26 5046
For a voice *d* from Dan, and Jer 4:15 5046
and their staff *d* unto them Hos 4:12 5046
d unto man what is his thought, Amos 4:13 5046

DECLARING
D the end from the beginning, and Is 46:10 5046
d the conversion of the Gentiles Acts 15:3 *1555*
d what miracles and wonders God Acts 15:12 *1834*
d unto you the testimony of God 1Cor 2:1 *2605*

DECLINE
to *d* after many to wrest judgment Ex 23:2 5186
thou shalt not *d* from the Deut 17:11 5493
yet do I not *d* from thy Ps 119:157 5186
neither *d* from the words of my Prov 4:5 5186
Let not thine heart *d* to her ways Prov 7:25 7847

DECLINED
d neither to the right hand, nor 2Chr 34:2 5493
his way have I kept, and not *d* Job 23:11 5186
have our steps *d* from thy way Ps 44:18 5186
yet have I not *d* from thy law Ps 119:51 5186

DECLINETH
My days are like a shadow that *d* Ps 102:11 5186
am gone like the shadow when it *d* Ps 109:23 5186

DECREASE
suffereth not their cattle to *d* Ps 107:38 4591
He must increase, but I must *d* Jn 3:30 *1642*

DECREASED
the waters *d* continually until Gen 8:5 2637

DECREE
So they established a *d* to make 2Chr 30:5 1697
a *d* to build this house of God Ezr 5:13 2942
that a *d* was made of Cyrus the Ezr 5:17 2942
Then Darius the king made a *d* Ezr 6:1 2942
d concerning the house of God at Ezr 6:3 2942
Moreover I make a *d* what ye shall Ezr 6:8 2942
Also I have made a *d*, that Ezr 6:11 2942
I Darius have made a *d* Ezr 6:12 2942
I make a *d*, that all they of the Ezr 7:13 2942
do make a *d* to all the treasurers Ezr 7:21 2942
when the king's *d* which he shall Est 1:20 6599
his *d* was heard, and when many Est 2:8 1881
the *d* was given in Shushan the Est 3:15 1881
his *d* came, there was great Est 4:3 1881
d that was given at Shushan to Est 4:8 1881
the *d* was given at Shushan the Est 8:14 1881
his *d* came, the Jews had joy and Est 8:17 1881
his *d* drew near to be put in Est 9:1 1881
also according unto this day's *d* Est 9:13 1881

the *d* was given at Shushan Est 9:14 1881
the *d* of Esther confirmed these Est 9:32 3982
Thou shalt also *d* a thing Job 22:28 1504
When he made a *d* for the rain Job 28:26 2706
I will declare the *d* Ps 2:7 2706
he hath made a *d* which shall not Ps 148:6 2706
kings reign, and princes *d* justice Prov 8:15 2710
When he gave to the sea his *d* Prov 8:29 2706
Woe unto them that *d* unrighteous Is 10:1 2710
bound of the sea by a perpetual *d* Jer 5:22 2706
dream, there is but one *d* for you Dan 2:9 1882
the *d* went forth that the wise Dan 2:13 1882
Why is the *d* so hasty from the Dan 2:15 1882
Thou, O king, hast made a *d* Dan 3:10 2942
Therefore I make a *d*, That every Dan 3:29 2942
Therefore made I a *d* to bring in Dan 4:6 2942
is by the *d* of the watchers Dan 4:17 1510
this is the *d* of the most High, Dan 4:24 1510
statute, and to make a firm *d* Dan 6:7 633
Now, O king, establish the *d* Dan 6:8 633
signed the writing and the *d* Dan 6:9 633
the king concerning the king's *d* Dan 6:12 633
Hast thou not signed a *d*, that Dan 6:12 633
nor the *d* that thou hast signed, Dan 6:13 633
That no *d* nor statute which the Dan 6:15 633
I make a *d*, That in every Dan 6:26 2942
Nineveh by the *d* of the king Jonah 3:7 2940
day shall the *d* be far removed Mic 7:11 2706
Before the *d* bring forth, before Zeph 2:2 2706
went out a *d* from Caesar Augustus Lk 2:1 *1378*

DECREED
done, and what was *d* against her Est 2:1 1504
as they had *d* for themselves and Est 9:31 6965
And brake up for it my *d* place Job 38:10 2706
the consumption *d* shall overflow Is 10:22 2782
hath so *d* in his heart that he 1Cor 7:37 *2919*

DECREES
them that decree unrighteous *d* Is 10:1 2711
delivered them the *d* for to keep Acts 16:4 *1378*
do contrary to the *d* of Caesar Acts 17:7 *1378*

DEDAN (*de'-dan*) See DEDANIM.
1. A grandson of Cush.
sons of Raamah; Sheba, and *D* Gen 10:7 1719
sons of Raamah; Sheba, and *D* 1Chr 1:9 1719
2. A son of Jokshan.
And Jokshan begat Sheba, and *D* Gen 25:3 1719
the sons of *D* were Asshurim, and Gen 25:3 1719
sons of Jokshan; Sheba, and *D* 1Chr 1:32 1719
3. A district between Sela and the Salt Sea.
D, and Tema, and Buz, and all that Jer 25:23 1719
dwell deep, O inhabitants of *D* Jer 49:8 1719
they of *D* shall fall by the sword Eze 25:13 1719
The men of *D* were thy merchants Eze 27:15 1719
D was thy merchant in precious Eze 27:20 1719
Sheba, and *D*, and the merchants of Eze 38:13 1719

DEDANIM (*ded'-a-nim*) See DODANIM. *Descendants of Raamah.*
O ye travelling companies of *D* Is 21:13 1720

DEDANITES See DEDANIM.

DEDICATE
the battle, and another man *d* it Deut 20:5 2596
king David did *d* unto the LORD 2Sa 8:11 6942
d to maintain the house of the 1Chr 26:27 6942
to *d* it to him, and to burn before 2Chr 2:4 6942

DEDICATED
a new house, and hath not *d* it Deut 20:5 2596
I had wholly *d* the silver unto Judg 17:3 6942
gold that he had *d* of all nations 2Sa 8:11 6942
which David his father had *d* 1Kin 7:51 6944
of Israel *d* the house of the LORD 1Kin 8:63 2596
the things which his father had *d* 1Kin 15:15 6944
and the things which himself had *d* 1Kin 15:15 6944
All the money of the *d* things 2Kin 12:4 6944
fathers, kings of Judah, had *d* 2Kin 12:18 6942
also king David *d* unto the LORD 1Chr 18:11 6942
the treasures of the *d* things 1Chr 26:20 6944
all the treasures of the *d* things 1Chr 26:26 6944
the captains of the host, had *d* 1Chr 26:26 6942
and Joab the son of Zeruiah, had *d* 1Chr 26:28 6942
and whosoever had *d* any thing 1Chr 26:28 6942
of the treasuries of the *d* things 1Chr 28:12 6944
that David his father had *d* 2Chr 5:1 6944
all the people *d* the house of God 2Chr 7:5 2596
the things that his father had *d* 2Chr 15:18 6944
and that he himself had *d* 2Chr 15:18 6944
also all the *d* things of the 2Chr 24:7 6944
tithes and the *d* things faithfully 2Chr 31:12 6944
every *d* thing in Israel shall be Eze 44:29 2764
testament was *d* without blood Heb 9:18 *1457*

DEDICATING
the princes offered for *d* of the Num 7:10 2598
his day, for the *d* of the altar Num 7:11 2598

DEDICATION
This was the *d* of the altar Num 7:84 2598
This was the *d* of the altar Num 7:88 2598
for they kept the *d* of the altar 2Chr 7:9 2598
kept the *d* of this house of God Ezr 6:16 2597
offered at the *d* of this house of Ezr 6:17 2597
at the *d* of the wall of Jerusalem Neh 12:27 2598
to keep the *d* with gladness, both Neh 12:27 2598
Song at the *d* of the house of Ps 30:*t* 2598
to come to the *d* of the image Dan 3:2 2597
unto the *d* of the image that Dan 3:3 2597
at Jerusalem the feast of the *d* Jn 10:22 *1456*

DEED
What *d* is this that ye have done Gen 44:15 4639
in very *d* for this cause have I Ex 9:16 199
There was no such *d* done nor seen Judg 19:30
For in very *d*, as the LORD God of 1Sa 25:34 199
that Saul was come in very *d* 1Sa 26:4 3559
because by this *d* thou hast given 2Sa 12:14 1697
But will God in very *d* dwell with 2Chr 6:18
For this *d* of the queen shall Est 1:17 1697
have heard of the *d* of the queen Est 1:18 1697
to the counsel and *d* of them Lk 23:51 *4334*
which was a prophet mighty in *d* Lk 24:19 *2041*
good *d* done to the impotent man Acts 4:9 *2108*
Gentiles obedient, by word and *d* Rom 15:18 *2041*
that he that hath done this *d* 1Cor 5:2 *2041*
him that hath so done this *d* 1Cor 5:3
be also in *d* when we are present 2Cor 10:11 *2041*
And whatsoever ye do in word or *d* Col 3:17 *2041*
man shall be blessed in his *d* Jas 1:25 *4162*
but in *d* and in truth 1Jn 3:18 *2041*

DEEDS
thou hast done *d* unto me that Gen 20:9 4639
make known his *d* among the people 1Chr 16:8 5949
And his *d*, first and last, behold, 2Chr 35:27 1697
is come upon us for our evil *d* Ezr 9:13 4639
reported his good *d* before me Neh 6:19
wipe not out my good *d* that I Neh 13:14
Give them according to their *d* Ps 28:4 6467
make known his *d* among the people Ps 105:1 5949
According to their *d*, accordingly Is 59:18 1578
they overpass the *d* of the wicked Jer 5:28 1697
them according to their *d* Jer 25:14 6467
ye allow the *d* of your fathers Lk 11:48 *2041*
receive the due reward of our *d* Lk 23:41
light, because their *d* were evil Jn 3:19 *2041*
lest his *d* should be reproved Jn 3:20 *2041*
that his *d* may be made manifest, Jn 3:21 *2041*
Ye do the *d* of your father Jn 8:41 *2041*
and was mighty in words and in *d* Acts 7:22 *2041*
and confessed, and shewed their *d* Acts 19:18 *4234*
that very worthy *d* are done unto Acts 24:2 *2735*
to every man according to his *d* Rom 2:6 *2041*
Therefore by the *d* of the law Rom 3:20 *2041*
by faith without the *d* of the law Rom 3:28 *2041*
do mortify the *d* of the body Rom 8:13 *4234*
in signs, and wonders, and mighty *d* 2Cor 12:12 *1411*
put off the old man with his *d* Col 3:9 *4234*
day to day with their unlawful *d* 2Pet 2:8 *2041*
speed is partaker of his evil *d* 2Jn 11 *2041*
remember his *d* which he doeth 3Jn 10 *2041*
ungodly *d* which they have ungodly Jude 15 *2041*
hatest the *d* of the Nicolaitanes Rev 2:6 *2041*
except they repent of their *d* Rev 2:22 *2041*
sores, and repented not of their *d* Rev 16:11 *2041*

DEEMED
about midnight the shipmen *d* that Acts 27:27 *5282*

DEEP
was upon the face of the *d* Gen 1:2 8415
the LORD God caused a *d* sleep to Gen 2:21 8639
of the great *d* broken up, and the Gen 7:11 8415
The fountains also of the *d* Gen 8:2 8415
a *d* sleep fell upon Abram Gen 15:12 8639
of the *d* that lieth under Gen 49:25 8415
for the *d* that coucheth beneath, Deut 33:13 8415
because a *d* sleep from the LORD 1Sa 26:12 8639
when *d* sleep falleth on men, Job 4:13 8639
He discovereth *d* things out of Job 12:22 6013
when *d* sleep falleth upon men, in Job 33:15 8639
and the face of the *d* is frozen Job 38:30 8415
He maketh the *d* to boil like a Job 41:31 4688
one would think the *d* to be hoary Job 41:32 8415
thy judgments are a great *d* Ps 36:6 8415
D calleth unto *d* at the noise Ps 42:7 8415
D calleth unto *d* at the noise Ps 42:7 8415
one of them, and the heart, is *d* Ps 64:6 6013
I sink in *d* mire, where there is Ps 69:2 4688
I am come into *d* waters, where Ps 69:2 4615
hate me, and out of the *d* waters Ps 69:14 4615
neither let the *d* swallow me up Ps 69:15 4688
and didst cause it to take *d* root Ps 80:9 8328
and thy thoughts are very *d* Ps 92:5 6009
are the *d* places of the earth Ps 95:4 4278
it with the *d* as with a garment Ps 104:6 8415
the LORD, and his wonders in the *d* Ps 107:24 4688
in the seas, and all *d* places Ps 135:6 8415
into *d* pits, that they rise not Ps 140:10 4113
the fountains of the *d* Prov 8:28 8415
of a man's mouth are as *d* waters Prov 18:4 6013
casteth into a *d* sleep Prov 19:15 8639
the heart of man is like *d* water Prov 20:5 6013
mouth of strange women is a *d* pit Prov 22:14 6013
For a whore is a *d* ditch Prov 23:27 6013
which is far off, and exceeding *d* Eccl 7:24 6013
upon you the spirit of *d* sleep Is 29:10 8639
Woe unto them that seek *d* to hide Is 29:15 6009
he hath made it *d* and large Is 30:33 6009
That saith to the *d*, Be dry, and I Is 44:27 6683
sea, the waters of the great *d* Is 51:10 8415
That led them through the *d* Is 63:13 8415
Flee ye, turn back, dwell *d* Jer 49:8 6009
Flee, get you far off, dwell *d* Jer 49:30 6009
shalt drink of thy sister's cup *d* Eze 23:32 6013
I shall bring up the *d* upon thee Eze 26:19 8415
the *d* set him up on high with her Eze 31:4 8415
I covered the *d* for him, and I Eze 31:15 8415
Then will I make their waters *d* Eze 32:14 8257
and to have drunk of the *d* waters Eze 34:18 4950
He revealeth the *d* and secret Dan 2:22 5994
I was in a *d* sleep on my face Dan 8:18 7290
then was I in a *d* sleep on my Dan 10:9 7290
fire, and it devoured the great *d* Amos 7:4 8415
For thou hadst cast me into the *d* Jonah 2:3 4688
the *d* uttered his voice, and Hab 3:10 8415
unto Simon, Launch out into the *d* Lk 5:4 *899*
which built an house, and digged *d* Lk 6:48
command them to go out into the *d* Lk 8:31 *12*
to draw with, and the well is *d* Jn 4:11 *901*
being fallen into a *d* sleep Acts 20:9 *901*
Or, Who shall descend into the *d* Rom 10:7 *12*
things, yea, the *d* things of God 1Cor 2:10 *899*
their *d* poverty abounded unto the 2Cor 8:2 *899*
and a day I have been in the *d* 2Cor 11:25 *1037*

DEEPER
the plague in sight be *d* than the Lev 13:3 6013
in sight be not *d* than the skin Lev 13:4 6013
and it be in sight *d* than the skin Lev 13:25 6013
if it be in sight *d* than the skin Lev 13:30 6013
be not in sight *d* than the skin Lev 13:31 6013
be not in sight *d* than the skin Lev 13:32 6013
nor be in sight *d* than the skin Lev 13:34 6013
d than hell; what canst thou know? Job 11:8 6013
a people of a *d* speech than thou Is 33:19 6012

DEEPLY
of Israel have *d* revolted Is 31:6 6009
They have *d* corrupted themselves, Hos 9:9 6009
he sighed *d* in his spirit, and Mk 8:12 *389*

DEEPNESS
because they had no *d* of earth Mt 13:5 *899*

DEEPS
thou threwest into the *d*, as a Neh 9:11 4688
lowest pit, in darkness, in the *d* Ps 88:6 4688
the earth, ye dragons, and all *d* Ps 148:7 8415
all the *d* of the river shall dry Zec 10:11 4688

DEER
and the roebuck, and the fallow *d* Deut 14:5 3180

DEFAMED
Being *d*, we intreat 1Cor 4:13 *987*

DEFAMING
For I heard the *d* of many Jer 20:10 1681

DEFEAT
then mayest thou for me *d* the 2Sa 15:34 6565
For the LORD had appointed to *d* 2Sa 17:14 6565

DEFENCE
their *d* is departed from them, and Num 14:9 6738
and built cities for *d* in Judah 2Chr 11:5 4692
Yea, the Almighty shall be thy *d* Job 22:25 1220
My *d* is of God, which saveth the Ps 7:10 4043
for an house of *d* to save me Ps 31:2 4686
for God is my *d* Ps 59:9 4869
for thou hast been my *d* and refuge Ps 59:16 4869
for God is my *d*, and the God of my Ps 59:17 4869
he is my *d* Ps 62:2 4869
he is my *d* Ps 62:6 4869
For the LORD is our *d* Ps 89:18 4043
But the LORD is my *d* Ps 94:22 4869
For wisdom is a *d* Eccl 7:12 6738
and money is a *d* Eccl 7:12 6738
upon all the glory shall be a *d* Is 4:5 2646
the brooks of *d* shall be emptied Is 19:6 4692
his place of *d* shall be the Is 33:16 4869
and the *d* shall be prepared Nah 2:5 5526
have made his *d* unto the people Acts 19:33 *626*
hear ye my *d* which I make now Acts 22:1 *627*
as both in my bonds, and in the *d* Phil 1:7 *627*
I am set for the *d* of the gospel Phil 1:17 *627*

DEFENCED
of a *d* city a ruin Is 25:2 1219
Yet the *d* city shall be desolate, Is 27:10 1219
against all the *d* cities of Judah Is 36:1 1219
waste *d* cities into ruinous heaps Is 37:26 1219
have made thee this day a *d* city Jer 1:18 4013
and let us go into the *d* cities Jer 4:5 4013
and let us enter into the *d* cities Jer 8:14 4013
for these *d* cities remained of Jer 34:7 4013
and to Judah in Jerusalem the *d* Eze 21:20 1219

DEFEND
to *d* Israel Tola the son of Puah Judg 10:1 3467
For I will *d* this city, to save 2Kin 19:34 1598
I will *d* this city for mine own 2Kin 20:6 1598
name of the God of Jacob *d* thee Ps 20:1 7682
d me from them that rise up Ps 59:1 7682
D the poor and fatherless Ps 82:3 8199
the LORD of hosts *d* Jerusalem Is 31:5 1598
For I will *d* this city to save it Is 37:35 1598
and I will *d* this city Is 38:6 1598
The LORD of hosts shall *d* them Zec 9:15 1598
In that day shall the LORD *d* the Zec 12:8 1598

DEFENDED
d it, and slew the Philistines 2Sa 23:12 5337
he *d* him, and avenged him that was Acts 7:24 *292*

DEFENDEST
for joy, because thou *d* them Ps 5:11 5526

DEFENDING
d also he will deliver it Is 31:5 1598

DEFER
a vow unto God, *d* not to pay it Eccl 5:4 309
name's sake will I *d* mine anger Is 48:9 748
d not, for thine own sake, O my Dan 9:19 309

DEFERRED
the young man *d* not to do the Gen 34:19 309
Hope *d* maketh the heart sick, but Prov 13:12 4900
he *d* them, and said, When Lysias Acts 24:22 *306*

DEFERRETH
discretion of a man *d* his anger Prov 19:11 748

DEFIED
I defy, whom the LORD hath not *d* Num 23:8 2194
seeing he hath *d* the armies of 1Sa 17:36 2778
of Israel, whom thou hast *d* 1Sa 17:45 2778
And when he *d* Israel, Jonathan the 2Sa 21:21 2778
when they *d* the Philistines that 2Sa 23:9 2778
But when he *d* Israel, Jonathan 1Chr 20:7 2778

DEFILE
neither shall ye *d* yourselves Lev 11:44 2930
when they *d* my tabernacle that is Lev 15:31 2930
wife, to *d* thyself with her Lev 18:20 2930
any beast to *d* thyself therewith Lev 18:23 2930
D not ye yourselves in any of Lev 18:24 2930
not you out also, when ye *d* it Lev 18:28 2930
that ye *d* not yourselves therein Lev 18:30 2930
to *d* my sanctuary, and to profane Lev 20:3 2930
But he shall not *d* himself Lev 21:4 2930
nor *d* himself for his father, or Lev 21:11 2930
not eat to *d* himself therewith Lev 22:8 2930
that they *d* not their camps, in Num 5:3 2930
D not therefore the land which ye Num 35:34 2930
children of Ammon, did the king *d* 2Kin 23:13 2930
how shall I *d* them? Song 5:3 2936
Ye shall *d* also the covering of Is 30:22 2930
is called by my name, to *d* it Jer 32:34 2930
shall enter into it, and *d* it Eze 7:22 2490
D the house, and fill the courts Eze 9:7 2930
d not yourselves with the idols Eze 20:7 2930
nor *d* yourselves with their idols Eze 20:18 2930
against herself to *d* herself Eze 22:3 2930
they shall *d* thy brightness Eze 28:7 2490
ye *d* every one his neighbour's Eze 33:26 2930
Neither shall they *d* themselves Eze 37:23 2930
the house of Israel no more *d* Eze 43:7 2930
at no dead person to *d* themselves Eze 44:25 2930
no husband, they may *d* themselves Eze 44:25 2930
in his heart that he would not *d* Dan 1:8 1351
that he might not *d* himself Dan 1:8 1351
and they *d* the man Mt 15:18 *2840*
are the things which *d* a man Mt 15:20 *2840*
that entering into him can *d* him Mk 7:15 *2840*
those are they that *d* the man Mk 7:15 *2840*
into the man, it cannot *d* him Mk 7:18 *2840*
come from within, and *d* the man Mk 7:23 *2840*
If any man *d* the temple of God, 1Cor 3:17 *5351*
for them that *d* themselves with 1Ti 1:10 *733*
these filthy dreamers *d* the flesh Jude 8 *3392*

DEFILED
her, and lay with her, and *d* her Gen 34:2 6031
that he had *d* Dinah his daughter Gen 34:5 2930
because he had *d* Dinah their Gen 34:13 2930
because they had *d* their sister Gen 34:27 2930
be that a man shall be *d* withal Lev 5:3 2930
them, that ye should be *d* thereby Lev 11:43 2933
shall be in him he shall be *d* Lev 13:46 2930
goeth from him, and is *d* therewith Lev 15:32 2930
are *d* which I cast out before you Lev 18:24 2930
And the land is *d* Lev 18:25 2930
were before you, and the land is *d* Lev 18:27 2930
after wizards, to be *d* by them Lev 19:31 2930
There shall none be *d* for the Lev 21:1 2930
for her may he be *d* Lev 21:3 2930
and whosoever is *d* by the dead Num 5:2 2931
and be kept close, and she be *d* Num 5:13 2930
jealous of his wife, and she be *d* Num 5:14 2930
of his wife, and she be not *d* Num 5:14 2930
of thy husband, and if thou be *d* Num 5:20 2930
come to pass, that, if she be *d* Num 5:27 2930
And if the woman be not *d*, but be Num 5:28 2930
instead of her husband, and is *d* Num 5:29 2930
he hath *d* the head of his Num 6:9 2930
because his separation was *d* Num 6:12 2930
who were *d* by the dead body of a Num 9:6 2931
We are *d* by the dead body of a Num 9:7 2931
because he hath *d* the sanctuary Num 19:20 2930
that thy land be not *d*, which Deut 21:23 2930
the fruit of thy vineyard, be *d* Deut 22:9 6942
be his wife, after that she is *d* Deut 24:4 2930
d the high places where the 2Kin 23:8 2930
he *d* Topheth, which is in the 2Kin 23:10 2930
forasmuch as he *d* his father's 1Chr 5:1 2490
they have *d* the priesthood Neh 13:29 1351
my skin, and *d* my horn in the dust Job 16:15 5953
they have *d* by casting down the Ps 74:7 2490
thy holy temple have they *d* Ps 79:1 2930
Thus were they *d* with their own Ps 106:39 2930
The earth also is *d* under the Is 24:5 2610
For your hands are *d* with blood Is 59:3 1351
ye *d* my land, and made mine Jer 2:7 2930
her whoredom, that she *d* the land Jer 3:9 2610
because they have *d* my land Jer 16:18 2490
shall be *d* as the place of Tophet Jer 19:13 2931
their *d* bread among the Gentiles Eze 4:13 2931
because thou hast *d* my sanctuary Eze 5:11 2930
and their holy places shall be *d* Eze 7:24 2490
neither hath *d* his neighbour's Eze 18:6 2930
and *d* his neighbour's wife, Eze 18:11 2930
hath not *d* his neighbour's wife, Eze 18:15 2930
doings, wherein ye have been *d* Eze 20:43 2930
hast *d* thyself in thine idols Eze 22:4 2930
hath lewdly *d* his daughter in law Eze 22:11 2930
all their idols she *d* herself Eze 23:7 2930
Then I saw that she was *d* Eze 23:13 2930
they *d* her with their whoredom, Eze 23:17 2930
they have *d* my sanctuary in the Eze 23:38 2930
Thou hast *d* thy sanctuaries by Eze 28:18 2490
they *d* it by their own way and by Eze 36:17 2930
they have even *d* my holy name by Eze 43:8 2930
whoredom, and Israel is *d* Hos 5:3 2930
whoredom of Ephraim, Israel is *d* Hos 6:10 2930
thee, that say, Let her be *d* Mic 4:11 2610
of his disciples eat bread with *d* Mk 7:2 2839
hall, lest they should be *d* Jn 18:28 3392
their conscience being weak is *d* 1Cor 8:7 3435
but unto them that are *d* and Titus 1:15 3392
their mind and conscience is *d* Titus 1:15 3392
trouble you, and thereby many be *d* Heb 12:15 3392
which have not *d* their garments Rev 3:4 3435
they which were not *d* with women Rev 14:4 3435

DEFILEDST
then *d* thou it Gen 49:4 2490

DEFILETH
every one that *d* it shall surely Ex 31:14 2490
d the tabernacle of the LORD Num 19:13 2930
for blood it *d* the land Num 35:33 2610
goeth into the mouth *d* a man Mt 15:11 *2840*
out of the mouth, this *d* a man Mt 15:11 *2840*
with unwashen hands *d* not a man Mt 15:20 *2840*
out of the man, that *d* the man Mk 7:20 *2840*
that it *d* the whole body, and Jas 3:6 *4695*
enter into it any thing that *d* Rev 21:27 *2840*

DEFRAUD
Thou shalt not *d* thy neighbour Lev 19:13 6231
D not, Honour thy father and Mk 10:19 *650*
Nay, ye do wrong, and *d*, and that 1Cor 6:8 *650*
D ye not one the other, except it 1Cor 7:5 *650*
d his brother in any matter 1Th 4:6 *4122*

DEFRAUDED
or whom have I *d*? 1Sa 12:3 6231
And they said, Thou hast not *d* us 1Sa 12:4 6231
rather suffer yourselves to be *d* 1Cor 6:7 *650*
no man, we have *d* no man 2Cor 7:2 *4122*

DEFY
curse me Jacob, and come, *d* Israel Num 23:7 2194
or how shall I *d*, whom the LORD Num 23:8 2194
I *d* the armies of Israel this day 1Sa 17:10 2778
surely to *d* Israel is he come up 1Sa 17:25 2778
that he should *d* the armies of 1Sa 17:26 2778

DEGENERATE
then art thou turned into the *d* Jer 2:21 5494

DEGREE
their brethren of the second *d* 1Chr 15:18
to the estate of a man of high *d* 1Chr 17:17
Surely men of low *d* are vanity Ps 62:9
and men of high *d* are a lie Ps 62:9
seats, and exalted them of low *d* Lk 1:52 *5011*
purchase to themselves a good *d* 1Ti 3:13 *898*
Let the brother of low *d* rejoice Jas 1:9 *5011*

DEGREES
shall the shadow go forward ten *d* 2Kin 20:9 4609
or go back ten *d* 2Kin 20:9 4609
for the shadow to go down ten *d* 2Kin 20:10 4609
the shadow return backward ten *d* 2Kin 20:10 4609
brought the shadow ten *d* backward 2Kin 20:11 4609
A Song of *d* Ps 120:t 4609
A Song of *d* Ps 121:t 4609
A Song of *d* of David Ps 122:t 4609
A Song of *d* Ps 123:t 4609
A Song of *d* of David Ps 124:t 4609
A Song of *d* Ps 125:t 4609
A Song of *d* Ps 126:t 4609
A Song of *d* for Solomon Ps 127:t 4609
A Song of *d* Ps 128:t 4609
A Song of *d* Ps 129:t 4609
A Song of *d* Ps 130:t 4609
A Song of *d* of David Ps 131:t 4609
A Song of *d* Ps 132:t 4609
A Song of *d* of David Ps 133:t 4609
A Song of *d* Ps 134:t 4609
bring again the shadow of the *d* Is 38:8 4609
sun dial of Ahaz, ten *d* backward Is 38:8 4609
So the sun returned ten *d* Is 38:8 4609
by which *d* it was gone down Is 38:8 4609

DEHAVITES (*de-ha'-vites*) *Foreign settlers in Samaria.*
the Susanchites, the *D*, and the Ezr 4:9 1723

DEKAR (*de'-kar*) *Father of an officer of Solomon.*
The son of *D*, in Makaz, and in 1Kin 4:9 1857

DELAIAH (*del-a-i'-ah*) See DALAIAH.
1. A priest of David.
The three and twentieth to *D* 1Chr 24:18 1806
2. A family with a lost genealogy.
The children of *D*, the children Ezr 2:60 1806
The children of *D*, the children Neh 7:62 1806
3. An opponent of Nehemiah.
son of *D* the son of Mehetabeel Neh 6:10 1806
4. A prince of Judah.
D the son of Shemaiah, and Jer 36:12 1806
Nevertheless Elnathan and *D* Jer 36:25 1806

DELAY
Thou shalt not *d* to offer the Ex 22:29 309
he would not *d* to come to them Acts 9:38 *3635*
without any *d* on the morrow I sat Acts 25:17 *311*

DELAYED
d to come down out of the mount Ex 32:1 954
d not to keep thy commandments Ps 119:60 4102

DELAYETH
his heart, My lord *d* his coming Mt 24:48 *5549*
his heart, My lord *d* his coming Lk 12:45 *5549*

DELECTABLE
their *d* things shall not profit Is 44:9 2530

DELICACIES
through the abundance of her *d* Rev 18:3 *4764*

DELICATE
is tender among you, and very *d* Deut 28:54 6028
d woman among you, which would Deut 28:56 6028
no more be called tender and *d* Is 47:1 6028
of Zion to a comely and *d* woman Jer 6:2 6026
and poll thee for thy *d* children Mic 1:16 8588

DELICATELY
And Agag came unto him *d* 1Sa 15:32 4574
He that *d* bringeth up his servant Prov 29:21 6445
They that did feed *d* are desolate Lam 4:5 4574
gorgeously apparelled, and live *d* Lk 7:25 *5172*

DELICATENESS
of her foot upon the ground for *d* Deut 28:56 6026

DELICATES
hath filled his belly with my *d* Jer 51:34 5730

DELICIOUSLY
glorified herself, and lived *d* Rev 18:7 *4763*
lived *d* with her, shall bewail Rev 18:9 *4763*

DELIGHT
because he had *d* in Jacob's Gen 34:19 2654
If the LORD *d* in us, then he will Num 14:8 2654
Only the LORD had a *d* in thy Deut 10:15 2836
be, if thou have no *d* in her Deut 21:14 2654
as great *d* in burnt offerings 1Sa 15:22 2656
Behold, the king hath *d* in thee 1Sa 18:22 2654
he thus say, I have no *d* in thee 2Sa 15:26 2654
my lord the king *d* in this thing 2Sa 24:3 2654
To whom would the king *d* to do Est 6:6 2654
thou have thy *d* in the Almighty Job 22:26 6026
Will he *d* himself in the Almighty Job 27:10 6026
that he should *d* himself with God Job 34:9 7521
But his *d* is in the law of the Ps 1:2 2656
excellent, in whom is all my *d* Ps 16:3 2656
D thyself also in the LORD Ps 37:4 6026
shall *d* themselves in the Ps 37:11 6026
I *d* to do thy will, O my God Ps 40:8 2654
they *d* in lies Ps 62:4 7521
thou the people that *d* in war Ps 68:30 2654
within me thy comforts *d* my soul Ps 94:19 8173
I will *d* myself in thy statutes Ps 119:16 8173
Thy testimonies also are my *d* Ps 119:24 8191
for therein do I *d* Ps 119:35 2654
And I will *d* myself in thy Ps 119:47 8173
but I *d* in thy law Ps 119:70 8173
for thy law is my *d* Ps 119:77 8191
and thy law is my *d* Ps 119:174 8191
the scorners *d* in their scorning Prov 1:22 2531
d in the frowardness of the Prov 2:14 1523
and I was daily his *d*, rejoicing Prov 8:30 8191
but a just weight is his *d* Prov 11:1 7522
upright in their way are his *d* Prov 11:20 7522
they that deal truly are his *d* Prov 12:22 7522
prayer of the upright is his *d* Prov 15:8 7522
Righteous lips are the *d* of kings Prov 16:13 7522
A fool hath no *d* in understanding Prov 18:2 2654
D is not seemly for a fool Prov 19:10 8588
them that rebuke him shall be *d* Prov 24:25 5276
he shall give *d* unto thy soul Prov 29:17 4574
under his shadow with great *d* Song 2:3 2530
I *d* not in the blood of bullocks, Is 1:11 2654
for gold, they shall not *d* in it Is 13:17 2654
let your soul *d* itself in fatness Is 55:2 6026
d to know my ways, as a nation Is 58:2 2654
they take *d* in approaching to God Is 58:2 2654
and call the sabbath a *d*, the holy Is 58:13 6027
Then shalt thou *d* thyself in the Is 58:14 6026
they have no *d* in it Jer 6:10 2654
for in these things I *d*, saith Jer 9:24 2654
of the covenant, whom ye *d* in Mal 3:1 2655
For I *d* in the law of God after Rom 7:22 *4913*

DELIGHTED
Saul's son *d* much in David 1Sa 19:2 2654
delivered me, because he *d* in me 2Sa 22:20 2654
which *d* in thee, to set thee on 1Kin 10:9 2654
which *d* in thee to set thee on 2Chr 9:8 2654
d themselves in thy great Neh 9:25 5727
no more, except the king *d* in her Est 2:14 2654
delivered me, because he *d* in me Ps 18:19 2654
deliver him, seeing he *d* in him Ps 22:8 2654
as he *d* not in blessing, so let Ps 109:17 2654
did choose that wherein I *d* not Is 65:12 2654
and chose that in which I *d* not Is 66:4 2654
be *d* with the abundance of her Is 66:11 6026

DELIGHTEST
thou *d* not in burnt offering Ps 51:16 7521

DELIGHTETH
the man whom the king *d* to honour Est 6:6 2654
the man whom the king *d* to honour Est 6:7 2654
withal whom the king *d* to honour Est 6:9 2654
the man whom the king *d* to honour Est 6:9 2654
the man whom the king *d* to honour Est 6:11 2654
and he *d* in his way Ps 37:23 2654
the LORD, that *d* greatly in his Ps 112:1 2654
He *d* not in the strength of the Ps 147:10 2654
as a father the son in whom he *d* Prov 3:12 7521
mine elect, in whom my soul *d* Is 42:1 7521
for the LORD *d* in thee, and thy Is 62:4 2654
ways, and their soul *d* in their Is 66:3 2654
for ever, because he *d* in mercy Mic 7:18 2654
of the LORD, and he *d* in them Mal 2:17 2654

DELIGHTS
you in scarlet, with other *d* 2Sa 1:24 5730
Unless thy law had been my *d* Ps 119:92 8191
yet thy commandments are my *d* Ps 119:143 8191
my *d* were with the sons of men Prov 8:31 8191
the *d* of the sons of men, as Eccl 2:8 8588
pleasant art thou, O love, for *d* Song 7:6 8588

DELIGHTSOME
for ye shall be a *d* land, saith Mal 3:12 2656

DELILAH (*de-li'-lah*) *Woman who betrayed Samson.*
valley of Sorek, whose name was *D* Judg 16:4 1807
D said to Samson, Tell me, I pray Judg 16:6 1807
D said unto Samson, Behold, thou Judg 16:10 1807
D therefore took new ropes, and Judg 16:12 1807
D said unto Samson, Hitherto thou Judg 16:13 1807
when *D* saw that he had told her Judg 16:18 1807

DELIVER

D me, I pray thee, from the hand	Gen 32:11	5337
to *d* him to his father again	Gen 37:22	7725
thou shalt *d* Pharaoh's cup into	Gen 40:13	5414
so will I *d* you your brother, and	Gen 42:34	5414
d him into my hand, and I will	Gen 42:37	5414
I am come down to *d* them out of	Ex 3:8	5337
yet shall ye *d* the tale of bricks	Ex 5:18	5414
but God *d* him into his hand	Ex 21:13	579
If a man shall *d* unto his	Ex 22:7	5414
If a man *d* unto his neighbour an	Ex 22:10	5414
thou shalt *d* it unto him by that	Ex 22:26	7725
for I will *d* the inhabitants of	Ex 23:31	5414
they shall *d* you your bread again	Lev 26:26	7725
If thou wilt indeed *d* this people	Num 21:2	5414
the congregation shall *d* the	Num 35:25	5337
to *d* us into the hand of the	Deut 1:27	5414
that he might *d* him into thy hand	Deut 2:30	5414
for I will *d* him, and all his	Deut 3:2	5414
thy God shall *d* them before thee	Deut 7:2	5414
the LORD thy God shall *d* thee	Deut 7:16	5414
thy God shall *d* them unto thee	Deut 7:23	5414
he shall *d* their kings into thine	Deut 7:24	5414
d him into the hand of the	Deut 19:12	5414
to *d* thee, and to give up thine	Deut 23:14	5337
Thou shalt not *d* unto his master	Deut 23:15	5462
In any case thou shalt *d* him the	Deut 24:13	7725
d her husband out of the hand of	Deut 25:11	5337
any that can *d* out of my hand	Deut 32:39	5337
have, and *d* our lives from death	Josh 2:13	5337
to *d* us into the hand of the	Josh 7:7	5414
your God will *d* it into your hand	Josh 8:7	5414
morrow about this time will I *d*	Josh 11:6	5414
then they shall not *d* the slayer	Josh 20:5	5462
I will *d* him into thine hand	Judg 4:7	5414
d the Midianites into thine hand	Judg 7:7	5414
Israel, Did not I *d* you from the	Judg 10:11	
wherefore I will *d* you no more	Judg 10:13	3467
let them *d* you in the time of	Judg 10:14	3467
d us only, we pray thee, this day	Judg 10:15	5337
the LORD *d* them before me, shall	Judg 11:9	5414
If thou shalt without fail *d* the	Judg 11:30	5414
he shall begin to *d* Israel out of	Judg 13:5	3467
that we may *d* thee into the hand	Judg 15:12	5414
fast, and *d* thee into their hand	Judg 15:13	5414
Now therefore *d* us the men	Judg 20:13	5414
I will *d* them into thine hand	Judg 20:28	5414
who shall *d* us out of the hand of	1Sa 4:8	5337
he will *d* you out of the hand of	1Sa 7:3	5337
Israel *d* out of the hands of the	1Sa 7:14	5337
but now *d* us out of the hand of	1Sa 12:10	5337
things, which cannot profit nor *d*	1Sa 12:21	5337
wilt thou *d* them into the hand of	1Sa 14:37	5414
he will *d* me out of the hand of	1Sa 17:37	5337
the LORD *d* thee into mine hand	1Sa 17:46	5462
for I will *d* the Philistines into	1Sa 23:4	5414
of Keilah *d* me up into his hand	1Sa 23:11	5462
Will the men of Keilah *d* me	1Sa 23:12	5462
LORD said, They will *d* thee up	1Sa 23:12	5462
our part shall be to *d* him into	1Sa 23:20	5462
I will *d* thine enemy into thine	1Sa 24:4	5414
cause, and *d* me out of thine hand	1Sa 24:15	8199
LORD, and let him *d* me out of all	1Sa 26:24	5337
Moreover the LORD will also *d*	1Sa 28:19	5414
the LORD also shall *d* the host of	1Sa 28:19	5414
nor *d* me into the hands of my	1Sa 30:15	5462
D me my wife Michal, which I	2Sa 3:14	5414
wilt thou *d* them into mine hand	2Sa 5:19	5414
for I will doubtless *d* the	2Sa 5:19	5414
D him that smote his brother,	2Sa 14:7	5414
to *d* his handmaid out of the hand	2Sa 14:16	5337
d him only, and I will depart from	2Sa 20:21	5414
d them to the enemy, so that they	1Kin 8:46	5414
that thou wouldest *d* thy servant	1Kin 18:9	5414
Thou shalt *d* me thy silver, and	1Kin 20:5	5414
I will *d* it into thine hand this	1Kin 20:13	5414
therefore will I *d* all this great	1Kin 20:28	5414
for the Lord shall *d* it into the	1Kin 22:6	5414
for the LORD shall *d* it into the	1Kin 22:12	5414
for the LORD shall *d* it into the	1Kin 22:15	5414
to *d* them into the hand of Moab	2Kin 3:10	5414
to *d* them into the hand of Moab	2Kin 3:13	5414
he will *d* the Moabites also into	2Kin 3:18	5414
but *d* it for the breaches of the	2Kin 12:7	5414
he shall *d* you out of the hand of	2Kin 17:39	5337
I will *d* thee two thousand horses	2Kin 18:23	5414
be able to *d* you out of his hand	2Kin 18:29	5337
saying, The LORD will surely *d* us	2Kin 18:30	5337
you, saying, The LORD will *d* us	2Kin 18:32	5337
that the LORD should *d* Jerusalem	2Kin 18:35	5337
and I will *d* thee and this city out	2Kin 20:6	5337
d them into the hand of their	2Kin 21:14	5414
let them *d* it into the hand of	2Kin 22:5	5414
wilt thou *d* them into mine hand	1Chr 14:10	5414
for I will *d* them into thine hand	1Chr 14:10	5414
d us from the heathen, that we	1Chr 16:35	5337
d them over before their enemies,	2Chr 6:36	5414
for God will *d* it into the king's	2Chr 18:5	5414
for the LORD shall *d* it into the	2Chr 18:11	5414
which could not *d* their own	2Chr 25:15	5337
that he might *d* them into the	2Chr 25:20	5414
d the captives again, which ye	2Chr 28:11	7725
The LORD our God shall *d* us out	2Chr 32:11	5337
to *d* their lands out of mine hand	2Chr 32:13	5337
that could *d* his people out of	2Chr 32:14	5337
be able to *d* you out of mine hand	2Chr 32:14	5337
to *d* his people out of mine hand	2Chr 32:15	5337
your God *d* you out of mine hand	2Chr 32:15	5337
d his people out of mine hand	2Chr 32:17	5337
those *d* thou before the God of	Ezr 7:19	8000
many times didst thou *d* them	Neh 9:28	5337
neither is there any to *d* them	Job 5:4	5337
He shall *d* thee in six troubles	Job 5:19	5337
D me from the enemy's hand	Job 6:23	4422
none that can *d* out of thine hand	Job 10:7	5337
He shall *d* the island of the	Job 22:30	4422
D him from going down to the pit	Job 33:24	6308
He will *d* his soul from going	Job 33:28	6299
then a great ransom cannot *d* thee	Job 36:18	5186
Return, O LORD, *d* my soul	Ps 6:4	2502
them that persecute me, and *d* me	Ps 7:1	5337
pieces, while there is none to *d*	Ps 7:2	5337
d my soul from the wicked, which	Ps 17:13	6403
trusted, and thou didst *d* them	Ps 22:4	6403
on the LORD that he would *d* him	Ps 22:8	6403
let him *d* him, seeing he	Ps 22:8	5337
D my soul from the sword	Ps 22:20	5337
O keep my soul, and *d* me	Ps 25:20	5337
D me not over unto the will of	Ps 27:12	5414
d me in thy righteousness	Ps 31:1	6403
d me speedily	Ps 31:2	5337
d me from the hand of mine	Ps 31:15	5337
neither shall he *d* any by his	Ps 33:17	4422
To *d* their soul from death, and to	Ps 33:19	5337
LORD shall help them, and *d* them	Ps 37:40	6403
he shall *d* them from the wicked,	Ps 37:40	6403
D me from all my transgressions	Ps 39:8	5337
Be pleased, O LORD, to *d* me	Ps 40:13	5337
the LORD will *d* him in time of	Ps 41:1	4422
thou wilt not *d* him unto the will	Ps 41:2	5414
O *d* me from the deceitful and	Ps 43:1	6403
I will *d* thee, and thou shalt	Ps 50:15	2502
in pieces, and there be none to *d*	Ps 50:22	5337
D me from bloodguiltiness, O God,	Ps 51:14	5337
wilt not thou *d* my feet from	Ps 56:13	5337
D me from mine enemies, O my God	Ps 59:1	5337
D me from the workers of iniquity	Ps 59:2	5337
D me out of the mire, and let me	Ps 69:14	5337
d me because of mine enemies	Ps 69:18	6299
Make haste, O God, to *d* me	Ps 70:1	5337
D me in thy righteousness, and	Ps 71:2	5337
D me, O my God, out of the hand	Ps 71:4	6403
for there is none to *d* him	Ps 71:11	5337
For he shall *d* the needy when he	Ps 72:12	5337
O *d* not the soul of thy	Ps 74:19	5414
d us, and purge away our sins, for	Ps 79:9	5337
D the poor and needy	Ps 82:4	6403
shall he *d* his soul from the hand	Ps 89:48	4422
Surely he shall *d* thee from the	Ps 91:3	5337
upon me, therefore will I *d* him	Ps 91:14	6403
I will *d* him, and honour him	Ps 91:15	2502
Many times did he *d* them	Ps 106:43	5337
thy mercy is good, *d* thou me	Ps 109:21	5337
O LORD, I beseech thee, *d* my soul	Ps 116:4	4422
D me from the oppression of man	Ps 119:134	6299
Consider mine affliction, and *d* me	Ps 119:153	2502
Plead my cause, and *d* me	Ps 119:154	1350
d me according to thy word	Ps 119:170	5337
D my soul, O LORD, from lying	Ps 120:2	5337
D me, O LORD, from the evil man	Ps 140:1	2502
d me from my persecutors	Ps 142:6	5337
D me, O LORD, from mine enemies	Ps 143:9	5337
d me out of great waters, from	Ps 144:7	5337
d me from the hand of strange	Ps 144:11	5337
To *d* thee from the way of the	Prov 2:12	5337
To *d* thee from the strange woman,	Prov 2:16	5337
of glory shall she *d* to thee	Prov 4:9	4042
d thyself, when thou art come	Prov 6:3	5337
D thyself as a roe from the hand	Prov 6:5	5337
of the upright shall *d* them	Prov 11:6	5337
mouth of the upright shall *d* them	Prov 12:6	5337
for if thou *d* him, yet thou must	Prov 19:19	5337
shalt *d* his soul from hell	Prov 23:14	5337
If thou forbear to *d* them that	Prov 24:11	5337
neither shall wickedness *d* those	Eccl 8:8	4422
it away safe, and none shall *d* it	Is 5:29	5337
a great one, and he shall *d* them	Is 19:20	5337
which men *d* to one that is	Is 29:11	5414
defending also he will *d* it	Is 31:5	5337
for he shall not be able to *d* you	Is 36:14	5337
saying, The LORD will surely *d* us	Is 36:15	5337
you, saying, The LORD will *d* us	Is 36:18	5337
that the LORD should *d* Jerusalem	Is 36:20	5337
And I will *d* thee and this city out	Is 38:6	5337
is none that can *d* out of my hand	Is 43:13	5337
prayeth unto it, and saith, *D* me	Is 44:17	5337
aside, that he cannot *d* his soul	Is 44:20	5337
they could not *d* the burden	Is 46:2	4422
even I will carry, and will *d* you	Is 46:4	4422
they shall not *d* themselves from	Is 47:14	5337
or have I no power to *d*	Is 50:2	5337
criest, let thy companies *d* thee	Is 57:13	5337
for I am with thee to *d* thee	Jer 1:8	5337
thee, saith the LORD, to *d* thee	Jer 1:19	5337
I *d* to the sword before their	Jer 15:9	5414
to *d* thee, saith the LORD	Jer 15:20	5337
I will *d* thee out of the hand of	Jer 15:21	5337
Therefore *d* up their children to	Jer 18:21	5414
Moreover I will *d* all the	Jer 20:5	5414
I will *d* Zedekiah king of Judah,	Jer 21:7	5414
d him that is spoiled out of the	Jer 21:12	5337
d the spoiled out of the hand of	Jer 22:3	5337
I will *d* them to be removed into	Jer 24:9	5414
will *d* them to be removed to all	Jer 29:18	5414
I will *d* them into the hand of	Jer 29:21	5414
lest they *d* me into their hand,	Jer 38:19	5414
said, They shall not *d* thee	Jer 38:20	5414
But I will *d* thee in that day,	Jer 39:17	5337
For I will surely *d* thee, and thou	Jer 39:18	4422
you, and to *d* you from his hand	Jer 42:11	5337
for to *d* us into the hand of the	Jer 43:3	5414
d such as are for death to death	Jer 43:11	
I will *d* them into the hand of	Jer 46:26	5414
Babylon, and *d* every man his soul	Jer 51:6	4422
d ye every man his soul from the	Jer 51:45	4422
that doth *d* us out of their hand	Lam 5:8	6561
d them in the day of the wrath of	Eze 7:19	5337
d you into the hands of strangers	Eze 11:9	5414
d my people out of your hand, and	Eze 13:21	5337
for I will *d* my people out of	Eze 13:23	5337
they should *d* but their own souls	Eze 14:14	5337
they shall *d* neither sons nor	Eze 14:16	5337
they shall *d* neither sons nor	Eze 14:18	5337
they shall *d* neither son nor	Eze 14:20	5337
they shall but *d* their own souls	Eze 14:20	5337
d thee into the hand of brutish	Eze 21:31	5414
I will *d* thee into the hand of	Eze 23:28	5414
therefore I will *d* thee to the	Eze 25:4	5414
will *d* thee for a spoil to the	Eze 25:7	5414
taketh warning shall *d* his soul	Eze 33:5	4422
shall not *d* him in the day of his	Eze 33:12	5337
for I will *d* my flock from their	Eze 34:10	5337
will *d* them out of all places	Eze 34:12	5337
that shall *d* you out of my hands	Dan 3:15	7804
to *d* us from the burning fiery	Dan 3:17	7804
he will *d* us out of thine hand, O	Dan 3:17	7804
God that can *d* after this sort	Dan 3:29	5338
set his heart on Daniel to *d* him	Dan 6:14	7804
going down of the sun to *d* him	Dan 6:14	5338
continually, he will *d* thee	Dan 6:16	7804
able to *d* thee from the lions	Dan 6:20	7804
any that could *d* out of his hand	Dan 8:4	5337
could *d* the ram out of his hand	Dan 8:7	5337
none shall *d* her out of mine hand	Hos 2:10	5337
how shall I *d* thee, Israel	Hos 11:8	4042
captivity, to *d* them up to Edom	Amos 1:6	5462
shall the mighty *d* himself	Amos 2:14	4422
swift of foot shall not *d* himself	Amos 2:15	4422
that rideth the horse *d* himself	Amos 2:15	4422
therefore will I *d* up the city	Amos 6:8	5462
his head, to *d* him from his grief	Jonah 4:6	5337
thus shall he *d* us from the	Mic 5:6	5337
teareth in pieces, and none can *d*	Mic 5:8	5337
shalt take hold, but shalt not *d*	Mic 6:14	6403
d them in the day of the LORD's	Zeph 1:18	5337
D thyself, O Zion, that dwellest	Zec 2:7	4422
I will *d* the men every one into	Zec 11:6	4672
of their hand I will not *d* them	Zec 11:6	5337
the adversary *d* thee to the judge	Mt 5:25	*3860*
the judge *d* thee to the officer,	Mt 5:25	*3860*
temptation, but *d* us from evil	Mt 6:13	*4506*
for they will *d* you up to the	Mt 10:17	*3860*
But when they *d* you up, take no	Mt 10:19	*3860*
the brother shall *d* up the	Mt 10:21	*3860*
shall *d* him to the Gentiles to	Mt 20:19	*3860*
Then shall they *d* you up to be	Mt 24:9	*3860*
give me, and I will *d* him unto you	Mt 26:15	*3860*
let him *d* him now, if he will	Mt 27:43	*4506*
shall *d* him to the Gentiles	Mk 10:33	*3860*
for they shall *d* you up to	Mk 13:9	*3860*
d you up, take no thought	Mk 13:11	*3860*
but *d* us from evil	Lk 11:4	*4506*
the judge *d* thee to the officer,	Lk 12:58	*3860*
they might *d* him unto the power	Lk 20:20	*3860*
that God by his hand would *d* them	Acts 7:25	*1325*
and am come down to *d* them	Acts 7:34	*1807*
shall *d* him into the hands of the	Acts 21:11	*3860*
no man may *d* me unto them	Acts 25:11	*5483*
of the Romans to *d* any man to die	Acts 25:16	*5483*
who shall *d* me from the body of	Rom 7:24	*4506*
To *d* such a one unto Satan for	1Cor 5:5	*3860*
from so great a death, and doth *d*	2Cor 1:10	*4506*
we trust that he will yet *d* us	2Cor 1:10	*4506*
that he might *d* us from this	Gal 1:4	*1807*
the Lord shall *d* me from every	2Ti 4:18	*4506*
d them who through fear of death	Heb 2:15	*525*
The Lord knoweth how to *d* the	2Pet 2:9	*4506*

DELIVERANCE

to save your lives by a great *d*	Gen 45:7	6413
Thou hast given this great *d* into	Judg 15:18	8668
the LORD had given *d* unto Syria	2Kin 5:1	8668
said, The arrow of the LORD'S *d*	2Kin 13:17	8668
and the arrow of *d* from Syria	2Kin 13:17	8668
the LORD saved them by a great *d*	1Chr 11:14	8668
but I will grant them some *d*	2Chr 12:7	6413
and hast given us such *d* as this	Ezr 9:13	6413
d arise to the Jews from another	Est 4:14	2020
Great *d* giveth he to his king	Ps 18:50	3444
compass me about with songs of *d*	Ps 32:7	6405
not wrought any *d* in the earth	Is 26:18	3444
Zion and in Jerusalem shall be *d*	Joel 2:32	6413
But upon mount Zion shall be *d*	Obad 17	6413
to preach *d* to the captives, and	Lk 4:18	*859*
were tortured, not accepting *d*	Heb 11:35	*629*

DELIVERANCES

command *d* for Jacob	Ps 44:4	3444

DELIVERED

into your hand are they *d*	Gen 9:2	5414
which hath *d* thine enemies into	Gen 14:20	4042
her days to be *d* were fulfilled	Gen 25:24	3205
he *d* them into the hand of his	Gen 32:16	5414
he *d* him out of their hands	Gen 37:21	5337
are *d* ere the midwives come in	Ex 1:19	3205
An Egyptian *d* us out of the hand	Ex 2:19	5337
hast thou *d* thy people at all	Ex 5:23	5337
the Egyptians, and *d* our houses	Ex 12:27	5337
d me from the sword of Pharaoh	Ex 18:4	5337
the way, and how the LORD *d* them	Ex 18:8	5337
whom he had *d* out of the hand of	Ex 18:9	5337
who hath *d* you out of the hand of	Ex 18:10	5337
who hath *d* the people from under	Ex 18:10	5337
in that which was *d* him to keep	Lev 6:2	6487
or that which was *d* him to keep	Lev 6:4	6487
ye shall be *d* into the hand of	Lev 26:25	5414
of Israel, and *d* up the Canaanites	Num 21:3	5414
for I have *d* him into thy hand,	Num 21:34	5414
So there were *d* out of the	Num 31:5	4560
the LORD our God *d* him before us	Deut 2:33	5414
the LORD our God *d* all unto us	Deut 2:36	5414
So the LORD our God *d* into our	Deut 3:3	5414

of stone, and *d* them unto me Deut 5:22 5414
the LORD *d* unto me two tables of Deut 9:10 5414
God hath *d* it into thine hands Deut 20:13 5414
God hath *d* them into thine hands Deut 21:10 5414
d it unto the priests the sons of Deut 31:9 5414
Truly the LORD hath *d* into our Josh 2:24 5414
d them out of the hand of the Josh 9:26 5337
for I have *d* them into thine hand Josh 10:8 5414
LORD *d* up the Amorites before the Josh 10:12 5414
God hath *d* them into your hand Josh 10:19 5414
And the LORD *d* it also, and the Josh 10:30 5414
the LORD *d* Lachish into the hand Josh 10:32 5414
the LORD *d* them into the hand of Josh 11:8 5414
the LORD *d* all their enemies into Josh 21:44 5414
now ye have *d* the children of Josh 22:31 5337
so I *d* you out of his hand Josh 24:10 5337
and I *d* them into your hand Josh 24:11 5414
I have *d* the land into his hand Judg 1:2 5414
the LORD *d* the Canaanites and the Judg 1:4 5414
he *d* them into the hands of Judg 2:14 5414
which *d* them out of the hand of Judg 2:16 3467
d them out of the hand of their Judg 2:18 3467
neither *d* he them into the hand Judg 2:23 5414
who *d* them, even Othniel the son Judg 3:9 3467
the LORD *d* Chushan-rishathaim Judg 3:10 5414
for the LORD hath *d* your enemies Judg 3:28 5414
and he also *d* Israel Judg 3:31 3467
hath *d* Sisera into thine hand Judg 4:14 5414
They that are *d* from the noise of Judg 5:11
the LORD *d* them into the hand of Judg 6:1 5414
I *d* you out of the hand of the Judg 6:9 5337
d us into the hands of the Judg 6:13 5414
for I have *d* it into thine hand Judg 7:9 5414
into his hand hath God *d* Midian Judg 7:14 5414
for the LORD hath *d* into your Judg 7:15 5414
God hath *d* into your hands the Judg 8:3 5414
when the LORD hath *d* Zebah Judg 8:7 5414
for thou hast *d* us from the hand Judg 8:22 3467
who had *d* them out of the hands Judg 8:34 5337
d you out of the hand of Midian Judg 9:17 5337
I *d* you out of their hand Judg 10:12 3467
And the LORD God of Israel *d* Sihon Judg 11:21 5414
the LORD *d* them into his hands Judg 11:32 5414
ye *d* me not out of their hands Judg 12:2 3467
And when I saw that ye *d* me not Judg 12:3 3467
the LORD *d* them into my hand Judg 12:3 5414
the LORD *d* them into the hand of Judg 13:1 5414
Our god hath *d* Samson our enemy Judg 16:23 5414
Our god hath *d* into our hands our Judg 16:24 5414
was with child, near to be *d* 1Sa 4:19 3205
d you out of the hand of the 1Sa 10:18 5337
d you out of the hand of your 1Sa 12:11 5337
for the LORD hath *d* them into our 1Sa 14:10 5414
for the LORD hath *d* them into the 1Sa 14:12 5414
d Israel out of the hands of them 1Sa 14:48 5337
him, and *d* it out of his mouth 1Sa 17:35 5337
The LORD that *d* me out of the paw 1Sa 17:37 5337
God hath *d* him into mine hand 1Sa 23:7 5234
but God *d* him not into his hand 1Sa 23:14 5414
d thee to day into mine hand in 1Sa 24:10 5414
the LORD had *d* me into thine hand 1Sa 24:18 5462
God hath *d* thine enemy into thine 1Sa 26:8 5462
for the LORD *d* thee into my hand 1Sa 26:23 5414
d the company that came against 1Sa 30:23 5414
have not *d* thee into the hand of 2Sa 3:8 4672
the rest of the people he *d* into 2Sa 10:10 5414
I *d* thee out of the hand of Saul 2Sa 12:7 5337
the LORD hath *d* the kingdom into 2Sa 16:8 5414
which hath *d* up the men that 2Sa 18:28 5462
he *d* us out of the hand of the 2Sa 19:9 4422
men of his sons be *d* unto us 2Sa 21:6 5414
he *d* them into the hands of the 2Sa 21:9 5414
in the day that the LORD had *d* 2Sa 22:1 5337
He *d* me from my strong enemy, and 2Sa 22:18 5337
he *d* me, because he delighted in 2Sa 22:20 2502
Thou also hast *d* me from the 2Sa 22:44 6403
thou hast *d* me from the violent 2Sa 22:49 5337
I was *d* of a child with her in 1Kin 3:17 3205
the third day after that I was *d* 1Kin 3:18 3205
that this woman was *d* also 1Kin 3:18 3205
the LORD hath *d* him unto the lion 1Kin 13:26 5414
d them into the hand of his 1Kin 15:18 5414
house, and *d* him unto his mother 1Kin 17:23 5414
into whose hand they *d* the money 2Kin 12:15 5414
he *d* them into the hand of Hazael 2Kin 13:3 5414
d them into the hand of spoilers 2Kin 17:20 5414
this city shall not be *d* into the 2Kin 18:30 5414
any of the gods of the nations *d* 2Kin 18:33 5337
have they *d* Samaria out of mine 2Kin 18:34 5337
that have *d* their country out of 2Kin 18:35 5337
Jerusalem shall not be *d* into the 2Kin 19:10 5414
and shalt thou be *d* 2Kin 19:11 5337
d them which my fathers have 2Kin 19:12 5337
money that was *d* into their hand 2Kin 22:7 5414
have *d* it into the hand of them 2Kin 22:9 5414
the priest hath *d* me a book 2Kin 22:10 5414
Hagarites were *d* into their hand 1Chr 5:20 5414
d it, and slew the Philistines 1Chr 11:14 5337
Then on that day David *d* first 1Chr 16:7 5414
the rest of the people he *d* unto 1Chr 19:11 5414
God *d* them into their hand 2Chr 13:16 5414
he *d* them into thine hand 2Chr 16:8 5414
they shall be *d* into your hand 2Chr 18:14 5414
d to the captains of hundreds 2Chr 23:9 5414
the LORD *d* a very great host into 2Chr 24:24 5414
Wherefore the LORD his God *d* him 2Chr 28:5 5414
he was also *d* into the hand of 2Chr 28:5 5414
he hath *d* them into your hand, and 2Chr 28:9 5414
he hath *d* them to trouble, to 2Chr 29:8 5414
d their people out of mine hand 2Chr 32:17 5337
they *d* the money that was brought 2Chr 34:9 5414
Hilkiah *d* the book to Shaphan 2Chr 34:15 5414
have *d* it into the hand of the 2Chr 34:17 5414
Babylon, and they were *d* unto one Ezr 5:14 3052
he *d* us from the hand of the Ezr 8:31 5337
they *d* the king's commissions Ezr 8:36 5414
been *d* into the hand of the kings Ezr 9:7 5414
horse be *d* to the hand of one of Est 6:9 5414
God hath *d* me to the ungodly, and Job 16:11 5462
it is *d* by the pureness of thine Job 22:30 4422
so should I be *d* for ever from my Job 23:7 6403
Because I *d* the poor that cried Job 29:12 4422
I have *d* him that without cause Ps 7:4 2502
d him from the hand of all his Ps 18:*t* 5337
He *d* me from my strong enemy, and Ps 18:17 5337
he *d* me, because he delighted in Ps 18:19 2502
Thou hast *d* me from the strivings Ps 18:43 6403
thou hast *d* me from the violent Ps 18:48 5337
They cried unto thee, and were *d* Ps 22:5 4422
man is not *d* by much strength Ps 33:16 5337
me, and *d* me from all my fears Ps 34:4 5337
For he hath *d* me out of all Ps 54:7 5337
He hath *d* my soul in peace from Ps 55:18 6299
For thou hast *d* my soul from Ps 56:13 5337
That thy beloved may be *d* Ps 60:5 2502
let me be *d* from them that hate Ps 69:14 5337
day when he *d* them from the enemy Ps 78:42 6299
d his strength into captivity, and Ps 78:61 5414
his hands were *d* from the pots Ps 81:6 5674
calledst in trouble, and I *d* thee Ps 81:7 2502
thou hast *d* my soul from the Ps 86:13 5337
he *d* them out of their distresses Ps 107:6 5337
d them from their destructions Ps 107:20 4422
That thy beloved may be *d* Ps 108:6 2502
For thou hast *d* my soul from Ps 116:8 2502
The righteous is *d* out of trouble Prov 11:8 2502
knowledge shall the just be *d* Prov 11:9 2502
seed of the righteous shall be *d* Prov 11:21 4422
walketh wisely, he shall be *d* Prov 28:26 4422
and he by his wisdom *d* the city Eccl 9:15 4422
to be *d* from the king of Assyria Is 20:6 5337
the book is *d* to him that is not Is 29:12 5414
he hath *d* them to the slaughter Is 34:2 5414
this city shall not be *d* into the Is 36:15 5414
any of the gods of the nations *d* Is 36:18 5337
have they *d* Samaria out of my Is 36:19 5337
that have *d* their land out of my Is 36:20 5337
and shalt thou be *d* Is 37:11 5337
d them which my fathers have Is 37:12 5337
thou hast in love to my soul *d* it Is 38:17
mighty, or the lawful captive *d* Is 49:24 4422
prey of the terrible shall be *d* Is 49:25 4422
came, she was *d* of a man child Is 66:7 4422
and say, We are *d* to do all these Jer 7:10 5337
for he hath *d* the soul of the Jer 20:13 5337
but shall surely be *d* into the Jer 32:4 5414
Now when I had *d* the evidence of Jer 32:16 5414
It shall be *d* into the hand of Jer 32:36 5414
be taken, and *d* into his hand Jer 34:3 5414
thou shalt be *d* into the hand of Jer 37:17 5414
she shall be *d* into the hand of Jer 46:24 5414
the Lord hath *d* me into their Lam 1:14 5414
but thou hast *d* thy soul Eze 3:19 5337
also thou hast *d* thy soul Eze 3:21 5337
they only shall be *d*, but the Eze 14:16 5337
they only shall be *d* themselves Eze 14:18 5337
d them to cause them to pass Eze 16:21 5414
d thee unto the will of them that Eze 16:27 5414
he break the covenant, and be *d* Eze 17:15 4422
Wherefore I have *d* her into the Eze 23:9 5414
I have therefore *d* him into the Eze 31:11 5414
for they are all *d* unto death Eze 31:14 5414
she is *d* to the sword Eze 32:20 5414
but thou hast *d* thy soul Eze 33:9 5337
d them out of the hand of those Eze 34:27 5337
d his servants that trusted in Dan 3:28 7804
who hath *d* Daniel from the power Dan 6:27 7804
that time thy people shall be *d* Dan 12:1 4422
the name of the LORD shall be *d* Joel 2:32 4422
because they *d* up the whole Amos 1:9 5462
escapeth of them shall not be *d* Amos 9:1 4422
neither shouldest thou have *d* up Obad 14 5462
there shalt thou be *d* Mic 4:10 5337
that he may be *d* from the power Hab 2:9 5337
they that tempt God are even *d* Mal 3:15 4422
All things are *d* unto me of my Mt 11:27 *3860*
d him to the tormentors, till he Mt 18:34 *3860*
and *d* unto them his goods Mt 25:14 *3860*
d him to Pontius Pilate the Mt 27:2 *3860*
knew that for envy they had *d* him Mt 27:18 *3860*
Jesus, he *d* him to be crucified Mt 27:26 *3860*
Pilate commanded the body to be *d* Mt 27:58 *591*
your tradition, which ye have *d* Mk 7:13 *3860*
The Son of man is *d* into the Mk 9:31 *3860*
shall be *d* unto the chief priests Mk 10:33 *3860*
him away, and *d* him to Pilate Mk 15:1 *3860*
chief priests had *d* him for envy Mk 15:10 *3860*
d Jesus, when he had scourged him Mk 15:15 *3860*
Even as they *d* them unto us Lk 1:2 *3860*
time came that she should be *d* Lk 1:57 *5088*
being *d* out of the hand of our Lk 1:74 *4506*
accomplished that she should be *d* Lk 2:6 *5088*
for that is *d* unto me Lk 4:6 *3860*
there was *d* unto him the book of Lk 4:17 *1929*
And he *d* him to his mother Lk 7:15 *1325*
d him again to his father Lk 9:42 *591*
shall be *d* into the hands of men Lk 9:44 *3860*
All things are *d* to me of my Lk 10:22 *3860*
that thou mayest be *d* from him Lk 12:58 *525*
For he shall be *d* unto the Lk 18:32 *3860*
d them ten pounds, and said unto Lk 19:13 *1825*
but he *d* Jesus to their will Lk 23:25 *3860*
The Son of man must be *d* into the Lk 24:7 *3860*
our rulers *d* him to be condemned Lk 24:20 *3860*
as soon as she is *d* of the child Jn 16:21 *1080*
would not have *d* him up unto thee Jn 18:30 *3860*
chief priests have *d* thee unto me Jn 18:35 *3860*
I should not be *d* to the Jews Jn 18:36 *3860*
therefore he that *d* me unto thee Jn 19:11 *3860*
Then *d* he him therefore unto them Jn 19:16 *3860*
being *d* by the determinate Acts 2:23 *1560*
whom ye *d* up, and denied him in Acts 3:13 *3860*
the customs which Moses *d* us Acts 6:14 *3860*
d him out of all his afflictions, Acts 7:10 *1807*
d him to four quaternions of Acts 12:4 *3860*
hath *d* me out of the hand of Acts 12:11 *1807*
together, they *d* the epistle Acts 15:30 *1929*
they *d* them the decrees for to Acts 16:4 *3860*
d the epistle to the governor, Acts 23:33 *325*
sail into Italy, they *d* Paul Acts 27:1 *3860*
the centurion *d* the prisoners to Acts 28:16 *3860*
yet was I *d* prisoner from Acts 28:17 *3860*
Who was *d* for our offences, and Rom 4:25 *3860*
form of doctrine which was *d* you Rom 6:17 *3860*
But now we are *d* from the law Rom 7:6 *2673*
creature itself also shall be *d* Rom 8:21 *1659*
but *d* him up for us all, how Rom 8:32 *3860*
That I may be *d* from them that do Rom 15:31 *4506*
ordinances, as I *d* them to you 1Cor 11:2 *3860*
Lord that which also I *d* unto you 1Cor 11:23 *3860*
For I *d* unto you first of all 1Cor 15:3 *3860*
when he shall have *d* up the 1Cor 15:24 *3860*
Who *d* us from so great a death, 2Cor 1:10 *4506*
d unto death for Jesus' sake 2Cor 4:11 *3860*
Who hath *d* us from the power of Col 1:13 *4506*
which *d* us from the wrath to come 1Th 1:10 *4506*
And that we may be *d* from 2Th 3:2 *4506*
whom I have *d* unto Satan, that 1Ti 1:20 *3860*
but out of them all the Lord *d* me 2Ti 3:11 *4506*
I was *d* out of the mouth of the 2Ti 4:17 *4506*
was *d* of a child when she was Heb 11:11 *5088*
d them into chains of darkness, 2Pet 2:4 *3860*
d just Lot, vexed with the filthy 2Pet 2:7 *4506*
the holy commandment *d* unto them 2Pet 2:21 *3860*
which was once *d* unto the saints Jude 3 *3860*
in birth, and pained to be *d* Rev 12:2 *5088*
the woman which was ready to be *d* Rev 12:4 *5088*
hell *d* up the dead which were in Rev 20:13 *1325*

DELIVEREDST
Therefore thou *d* them into the Neh 9:27 5414
thou *d* unto me five talents Mt 25:20 *3860*
thou *d* unto me two talents Mt 25:22 *3860*

DELIVERER
the LORD raised up a *d* to the Judg 3:9 3467
LORD, the LORD raised them up a *d* Judg 3:15 3467
And there was no *d*, because it was Judg 18:28 5337
my rock, and my fortress, and my *d* 2Sa 22:2 6403
my rock, and my fortress, and my *d* Ps 18:2 6403
thou art my help and my *d* Ps 40:17 6403
thou art my help and my *d* Ps 70:5 6403
my high tower, and my *d* Ps 144:2 6403
a *d* by the hand of the angel Acts 7:35 *3086*
shall come out of Sion the *D* Rom 11:26 *4506*

DELIVEREST
which *d* the poor from him that is Ps 35:10 5337
that which thou *d* will I give up Mic 6:14 6403

DELIVERETH
He *d* the poor in his affliction, Job 36:15 2502
He *d* me from mine enemies Ps 18:48 6403
them that fear him, and *d* them Ps 34:7 2502
d them out of all their troubles Ps 34:17 5337
but the LORD *d* him out of them Ps 34:19 5337
he *d* them out of the hand of the Ps 97:10 5337
who *d* David his servant from the Ps 144:10 6475
but righteousness *d* from death Prov 10:2 5337
but righteousness *d* from death Prov 11:4 5337
A true witness *d* souls Prov 14:25 5337
d girdles unto the merchant Prov 31:24 5414
they are for a prey, and none *d* Is 42:22 5337
He *d* and rescueth, and he worketh Dan 6:27 7804

DELIVERING
d you up to the synagogues, and Lk 21:12 *3860*
d into prisons both men and women Acts 22:4 *3860*
D thee from the people, and from Acts 26:17 *1807*

DELIVERY
draweth near the time of her *d* Is 26:17 3205

DELUSION
God shall send them strong *d* 2Th 2:11 *4106*

DELUSIONS
I also will choose their *d* Is 66:4 8586

DEMAND
for I will *d* of thee, and answer Job 38:3 7592
I will *d* of thee, and declare thou Job 40:7 7592
I will *d* of thee, and declare thou Job 42:4 7592
the *d* by the word of the holy Dan 4:17 7595

DEMANDED
set over them, were beaten, and *d* Ex 5:14 559
David *d* of him how Joab did, and 2Sa 11:7 7592
king hath *d* cannot the wise men Dan 2:27 7593
he *d* of them where Christ should Mt 2:4 *4441*
And the soldiers likewise *d* of him Lk 3:14 *1905*
when he was *d* of the Pharisees, Lk 17:20 *1905*
d who he was, and what he had done Acts 21:33 *4441*

DEMAS (*de'-mas*) *A companion of Paul.*
Luke, the beloved physician, and *D* Col 4:14 *1214*
For *D* hath forsaken me, having 2Ti 4:10 *1214*
Marcus, Aristarchus, *D*, Lucas, my Philem 24 *1214*

DEMETRIUS (*de-me'-tre-us*)
1. An opponent of Paul.
For a certain man named *D* Acts 19:24 *1216*
Wherefore if *D*, and the craftsmen Acts 19:38 *1216*
2. Disciple commended by John.
D hath good report of all men, and 3Jn 12 *1216*

D

DEMONSTRATION
- but in *d* of the Spirit and of ... 1Cor 2:4 585

DEN
- wait secretly as a lion in his *d* ... Ps 10:9 5520
- put his hand on the cockatrice' *d* ... Is 11:8 3975
- become a *d* of robbers in your ... Jer 7:11 4631
- heaps, and a *d* of dragons ... Jer 9:11 4583
- Judah desolate, and a *d* of dragons ... Jer 10:22 4583
- shall be cast into the *d* of lions ... Dan 6:7 1358
- shall be cast into the *d* of lions ... Dan 6:12 1358
- and cast him into the *d* of lions ... Dan 6:16 1358
- and laid upon the mouth of the *d* ... Dan 6:17 1358
- went in haste unto the *d* of lions ... Dan 6:19 1358
- And when he came to the *d*, he ... Dan 6:20 1358
- take Daniel up out of the *d* ... Dan 6:23 1358
- Daniel was taken up out of the *d* ... Dan 6:23 1358
- cast them into the *d* of lions ... Dan 6:24 1358
- they came at the bottom of the *d* ... Dan 6:24 1358
- a young lion cry out of his *d* ... Amos 3:4 4585
- ye have made it a *d* of thieves ... Mt 21:13 *4693*
- ye have made it a *d* of thieves ... Mk 11:17 *4693*
- ye have made it a *d* of thieves ... Lk 19:46 *4693*

DENIED
- Then Sarah *d*, saying, I laughed ... Gen 18:15 3584
- and I *d* him not ... 1Kin 20:7 4513
- for I should have *d* the God that ... Job 31:28 3584
- But he *d* before them all, saying, ... Mt 26:70 *720*
- again he *d* with an oath, I do not ... Mt 26:72 *720*
- But he *d*, saying, I know not, ... Mk 14:68 *720*
- And he *d* it again ... Mk 14:70 *720*
- When all *d*, Peter and they that ... Lk 8:45 *720*
- be *d* before the angels of God ... Lk 12:9 *533*
- he *d* him, saying, Woman, I know ... Lk 22:57 *720*
- And he confessed, and *d* not ... Jn 1:20 *720*
- crow, till thou hast *d* me thrice ... Jn 13:38 *533*
- He *d* it, and said, I am not ... Jn 18:25 *720*
- Peter then *d* again ... Jn 18:27 *720*
- *d* him in the presence of Pilate, ... Acts 3:13 *720*
- But ye *d* the Holy One and the Just ... Acts 3:14 *720*
- he hath *d* the faith, and is worse ... 1Ti 5:8 *720*
- my name, and hast not *d* my faith ... Rev 2:13 *720*
- my word, and hast not *d* my name ... Rev 3:8 *720*

DENIETH
- But he that *d* me before men shall ... Lk 12:9 *720*
- that *d* that Jesus is the Christ ... 1Jn 2:22 *720*
- that *d* the Father and the Son ... 1Jn 2:22 *720*
- Whosoever *d* the Son, the same ... 1Jn 2:23 *720*

DENOUNCE
- I *d* unto you this day, that ye ... Deut 30:18 5046

DENS
- of Israel made them the *d* which ... Judg 6:2 4492
- Then the beasts go into *d* ... Job 37:8 695
- When they couch in their *d* ... Job 38:40 4585
- and lay them down in their *d* ... Ps 104:22 4585
- and Hermon, from the lions' *d* ... Song 4:8 4585
- and towers shall be for *d* for ever ... Is 32:14 4631
- with prey, and his *d* with ravin ... Nah 2:12 4585
- deserts, and in mountains, and in *d* ... Heb 11:38 *4693*
- free man, hid themselves in the *d* ... Rev 6:15 *4693*

DENY
- unto you, lest ye *d* your God ... Josh 24:27 3584
- one petition of thee, *d* me not ... 1Kin 2:16 7725
- his place, then it shall *d* him ... Job 8:18 3584
- *d* me them not before I die ... Prov 30:7 4513
- *d* thee, and say, Who is the LORD ... Prov 30:9 3584
- whosoever shall *d* me before men ... Mt 10:33 *720*
- him will I also *d* before my ... Mt 10:33 *720*
- come after me, let him *d* himself ... Mt 16:24 *533*
- cock crow, thou shalt *d* me thrice ... Mt 26:34 *533*
- with thee, yet will I not *d* thee ... Mt 26:35 *533*
- cock crow, thou shalt *d* me thrice ... Mt 26:75 *533*
- come after me, let him *d* himself ... Mk 8:34 *533*
- twice, thou shalt *d* me thrice ... Mk 14:30 *533*
- I will not *d* thee in any wise ... Mk 14:31 *533*
- twice, thou shalt *d* me thrice ... Mk 14:72 *533*
- come after me, let him *d* himself ... Lk 9:23 *533*
- which *d* that there is any ... Lk 20:27 *483*
- thrice *d* that thou knowest me ... Lk 22:34 *533*
- cock crow, thou shalt *d* me thrice ... Lk 22:61 *533*
- and we cannot *d* it ... Acts 4:16 *720*
- if we *d* him, he also will *d* us ... 2Ti 2:12 *720*
- if we *d* him, he also will *d* us ... 2Ti 2:12 *720*
- he cannot *d* himself ... 2Ti 2:13 *720*
- but in works they *d* him, being ... Titus 1:16 *720*

DENYING
- but *d* the power thereof ... 2Ti 3:5 *720*
- *d* ungodliness and worldly lusts, ... Titus 2:12 *720*
- even *d* the Lord that bought them, ... 2Pet 2:1 *720*
- *d* the only Lord God, and our Lord ... Jude 4 *720*

DEPART
- or if thou *d* to the right hand, ... Gen 13:9
- sceptre shall not *d* from Judah ... Gen 49:10 5493
- And the frogs shall *d* from thee ... Ex 8:11 5493
- of flies may *d* from Pharaoh ... Ex 8:29 5493
- And Moses let his father in law *d* ... Ex 18:27 7971
- so that her fruit *d* from her ... Ex 21:22 3318
- And the LORD said unto Moses, *D* ... Ex 33:1 3212
- And then shall he *d* from thee ... Lev 25:41 3318
- but I will *d* to mine own land, and ... Num 10:30 3212
- unto the congregation, saying, *D* ... Num 16:26 5493
- lest they *d* from thy heart all ... Deut 4:9 5493
- didst *d* out of the land of Egypt ... Deut 9:7 3318
- law shall not *d* out of thy mouth ... Josh 1:8 4185
- So Joshua let the people *d* ... Josh 24:28 7971
- *D* not hence, I pray thee, until I ... Judg 6:18 4185
- *d* early from mount Gilead ... Judg 7:3 6852
- the morning, that he rose up to *d* ... Judg 19:5 3212
- And when the man rose up to *d* ... Judg 19:7 3212
- the morning on the fifth day to *d* ... Judg 19:8 3212
- And when the man rose up to *d* ... Judg 19:9 3212
- Saul said unto the Kenites, Go, *d* ... 1Sa 15:6 5493
- *d*, and get thee into the land of ... 1Sa 22:5 3212
- in the morning, and have light, *d* ... 1Sa 29:10 3212
- rose up early to *d* in the morning ... 1Sa 29:11 3212
- they may lead them away, and *d* ... 1Sa 30:22 3212
- mercy shall not *d* away from him ... 2Sa 7:15 5493
- and to morrow I will let thee *d* ... 2Sa 11:12 7971
- shall never *d* from thine house ... 2Sa 12:10 5493
- make speed to *d*, lest he overtake ... 2Sa 15:14 3212
- only, and I will *d* from the city ... 2Sa 20:21 3212
- statutes, I did not *d* from them ... 2Sa 22:23 5493
- Hadad said to Pharaoh, Let me *d* ... 1Kin 11:21 7971
- *D* yet for three days, then come ... 1Kin 12:5 3212
- of the LORD, and returned to *d* ... 1Kin 12:24 3212
- of Israel, that he may *d* from me ... 1Kin 15:19 5927
- of Israel, that he may *d* from me ... 2Chr 16:3 5927
- and God moved them to *d* from him ... 2Chr 18:31
- they might not *d* from their ... 2Chr 35:15 5493
- How long wilt thou not *d* from me ... Job 7:19 8159
- He shall not *d* out of darkness ... Job 15:30 5493
- The increase of his house shall *d* ... Job 20:28 1540
- they say unto God, *D* from us ... Job 21:14 5493
- Which said unto God, *D* from us ... Job 22:17 5493
- to *d* from evil is understanding ... Job 28:28 5493
- *D* from me, all ye workers of ... Ps 6:8 5493
- *D* from evil, and do good ... Ps 34:14 5493
- *D* from evil, and do good ... Ps 37:27 5493
- guile *d* not from her streets ... Ps 55:11 4185
- A froward heart shall *d* from me ... Ps 101:4 5493
- *D* from me, ye evildoers ... Ps 119:115 5493
- *d* from me therefore, ye bloody ... Ps 139:19 5493
- fear the LORD, and *d* from evil ... Prov 3:7 5493
- let not them *d* from thine eyes ... Prov 3:21 3868
- Let them not *d* from thine eyes ... Prov 4:21 3868
- *d* not from the words of my mouth ... Prov 5:7 5493
- to *d* from the snares of death ... Prov 13:14 5493
- to fools to *d* from evil ... Prov 13:19 5493
- to *d* from the snares of death ... Prov 14:27 5493
- that he may *d* from hell beneath ... Prov 15:24 5493
- fear of the LORD men *d* from evil ... Prov 16:6 5493
- of the upright is to *d* from evil ... Prov 16:17 5493
- evil shall not *d* from his house ... Prov 17:13 4185
- he is old, he will not *d* from it ... Prov 22:6 5493
- not his foolishness *d* from him ... Prov 27:22 5493
- The envy also of Ephraim shall *d* ... Is 11:13 5493
- shall his yoke *d* from off them ... Is 14:25 5493
- his burden *d* from off their ... Is 14:25 5493
- *D* ye, *d* ye, go ye out from ... Is 52:11 5493
- *d* ye, go ye out from thence, ... Is 52:11 5493
- For the mountains shall *d* ... Is 54:10 4185
- my kindness shall not *d* from thee ... Is 54:10 4185
- shall not *d* out of thy mouth, nor ... Is 59:21 4185
- lest my soul *d* from thee ... Jer 6:8 3363
- they that *d* from me shall be ... Jer 17:13 3249
- those ordinances *d* from before me ... Jer 31:36 4185
- that they shall not *d* from me ... Jer 32:40 5493
- Chaldeans shall surely *d* from us ... Jer 37:9 1980
- for they shall not *d* ... Jer 37:9 1980
- they shall remove, they shall *d* ... Jer 50:3 1980
- They cried unto them, *D* ye ... Lam 4:15 5493
- *d*, *d*, touch not ... Lam 4:15 5493
- *d*, *d*, touch not ... Lam 4:15 5493
- and my jealousy shall *d* from thee ... Eze 16:42 5493
- also to them when I *d* from them ... Hos 9:12 5493
- Arise ye, and *d* ... Mic 2:10 3212
- the sceptre of Egypt shall *d* away ... Zec 10:11 5493
- *d* from me, ye that work iniquity ... Mt 7:23 *672*
- to *d* unto the other side ... Mt 8:18 *565*
- he would *d* out of their coasts ... Mt 8:34 *3327*
- when ye *d* out of that house or ... Mt 10:14 *1831*
- said unto them, They need not *d* ... Mt 14:16 *565*
- *D* from me, ye cursed, into ... Mt 25:41 *4198*
- pray him to *d* out of their coasts ... Mk 5:17 *565*
- abide till ye *d* from that place ... Mk 6:10 *1831*
- nor hear you, when ye *d* thence ... Mk 6:11 *1607*
- thou thy servant *d* in peace ... Lk 2:29 *630*
- that he should not *d* from them ... Lk 4:42 *4198*
- Jesus' knees, saying, *D* from me ... Lk 5:8 *1831*
- about besought him to *d* from them ... Lk 8:37 *565*
- into, there abide, and thence *d* ... Lk 9:4 *1831*
- thee, thou shalt not *d* thence ... Lk 12:59 *1831*
- *d* from me, all ye workers of ... Lk 13:27 *868*
- him, Get thee out, and *d* hence ... Lk 13:31 *4198*
- are in the midst of it *d* out ... Lk 21:21 *1633*
- *D* hence, and go into Judaea, that ... Jn 7:3 *3327*
- *d* out of this world unto the ... Jn 13:1 *3327*
- but if I *d*, I will send him unto ... Jn 16:7 *4198*
- they should not *d* from Jerusalem ... Acts 1:4 *5562*
- now therefore *d*, and go in peace ... Acts 16:36 *1831*
- desired them to *d* out of the city ... Acts 16:39 *1831*
- commanded all Jews to *d* from Rome ... Acts 18:2 *5562*
- them, ready to *d* on the morrow ... Acts 20:7 *1826*
- And he said unto me, *D* ... Acts 22:21 *4198*
- captain then let the young man *d* ... Acts 23:22 *630*
- himself would *d* shortly thither ... Acts 25:4 *1607*
- part advised to *d* thence also ... Acts 27:12 *321*
- not the wife *d* from her husband ... 1Cor 7:10 *5562*
- But and if she *d*, let her remain ... 1Cor 7:11 *5562*
- But if the unbelieving *d*, let him ... 1Cor 7:15 *5562*
- the unbelieving *d*, let him *d* ... 1Cor 7:15 *5562*
- thrice, that it might *d* from me ... 2Cor 12:8 *868*
- betwixt two, having a desire to *d* ... Phil 1:23 *360*
- times some shall *d* from the faith ... 1Ti 4:1 *868*
- name of Christ *d* from iniquity ... 2Ti 2:19 *868*
- *D* in peace, be ye warmed and ... Jas 2:16 *5217*

DEPARTED
- So Abram *d*, as the LORD had ... Gen 12:4 3212
- years old when he *d* out of Haran ... Gen 12:4 3318
- in Sodom, and his goods, and *d* ... Gen 14:12 3212
- and she *d*, and wandered in the ... Gen 21:14 3212
- of the camels of his master, and *d* ... Gen 24:10 3212
- Isaac *d* thence, and pitched his ... Gen 26:17 3212
- away, and they *d* from him in peace ... Gen 26:31 3212
- my sleep *d* from mine eyes ... Gen 31:40 5074
- and Laban *d*, and returned unto his ... Gen 31:55 3212
- And the man said, They are *d* hence ... Gen 37:17 5265
- asses with the corn, and *d* thence ... Gen 42:26 3212
- sent his brethren away, and they *d* ... Gen 45:24 3212
- For they were *d* from Rephidim ... Ex 19:2 5265
- *d* not out of the tabernacle ... Ex 33:11 4185
- of the children of Israel *d* from ... Ex 35:20 3318
- if the plague be *d* from them ... Lev 13:58 5493
- they *d* from the mount of the LORD ... Num 10:33 5265
- kindled against them; and he *d* ... Num 12:9 3212
- And the cloud *d* from off the ... Num 12:10 5493
- their defence is *d* from them ... Num 14:9 5493
- and Moses, *d* not out of the camp ... Num 14:44 4185
- the elders of Midian *d* with the ... Num 22:7 3212
- they *d* from Rameses in the first ... Num 33:3 5265
- they *d* from Succoth, and pitched ... Num 33:6 5265
- they *d* from before Pi-hahiroth, ... Num 33:8 5265
- they *d* from Dophkah, and encamped ... Num 33:13 5265
- they *d* from Rephidim, and pitched ... Num 33:15 5265
- they *d* from Kibroth-hattaavah, and ... Num 33:17 5265
- they *d* from Hazeroth, and pitched ... Num 33:18 5265
- they *d* from Rithmah, and pitched ... Num 33:19 5265
- they *d* from Rimmon-parez, and ... Num 33:20 5265
- they *d* from Tahath, and pitched at ... Num 33:27 5265
- they *d* from Hashmonah, and ... Num 33:30 5265
- they *d* from Moseroth, and pitched ... Num 33:31 5265
- they *d* from Ebronah, and encamped ... Num 33:35 5265
- they *d* from mount Hor, and pitched ... Num 33:41 5265
- they *d* from Zalmonah, and pitched ... Num 33:42 5265
- they *d* from Punon, and pitched in ... Num 33:43 5265
- they *d* from Oboth, and pitched in ... Num 33:44 5265
- they *d* from Iim, and pitched in ... Num 33:45 5265
- they *d* from the mountains of ... Num 33:48 5265
- when we *d* from Horeb, we went ... Deut 1:19 5265
- when she is *d* out of his house, ... Deut 24:2 3318
- And she sent them away, and they *d* ... Josh 2:21 3212
- *d* from the children of Israel out ... Josh 22:9 3212
- of the LORD *d* out of his sight ... Judg 6:21 1980
- they *d* every man unto his place ... Judg 9:55 3212
- not that the LORD was *d* from him ... Judg 16:20 5493
- the man *d* out of the city from ... Judg 17:8 3212
- Then the five men *d*, and came to ... Judg 18:7 3212
- So they turned and *d*, and put the ... Judg 18:21 3212
- that night, but he rose up and *d* ... Judg 19:10 3212
- of Israel *d* thence at that time ... Judg 21:24 1980
- The glory is *d* from Israel ... 1Sa 4:21 1540
- said, The glory is *d* from Israel ... 1Sa 4:22 1540
- not let the people go, and they *d* ... 1Sa 6:6 3212
- When thou art *d* from me to day, ... 1Sa 10:2 3212
- So the Kenites *d* from among the ... 1Sa 15:6 5493
- Spirit of the LORD *d* from Saul ... 1Sa 16:14 5493
- and the evil spirit *d* from him ... 1Sa 16:23 5493
- was with him, and was *d* from Saul ... 1Sa 18:12 5493
- And he arose and *d* ... 1Sa 20:42 3212
- David therefore *d* thence, and ... 1Sa 22:1 3212
- Then David *d*, and came into the ... 1Sa 22:5 3212
- arose and *d* out of Keilah, and went ... 1Sa 23:13 3318
- God is *d* from me, and answereth me ... 1Sa 28:15 5493
- seeing the LORD is *d* from thee ... 1Sa 28:16 5493
- So all the people *d* every one to ... 2Sa 6:19 3212
- Uriah *d* out of the king's house, ... 2Sa 11:8 3318
- And Nathan *d* unto his house ... 2Sa 12:15 3212
- came to pass, after they were *d* ... 2Sa 17:21 3212
- from the day the king *d* until the ... 2Sa 19:24 3212
- have not wickedly *d* from my God ... 2Sa 22:22
- And the people *d* ... 1Kin 12:5 3212
- So Israel *d* unto their tents ... 1Kin 12:16 3212
- And Jeroboam's wife arose, and *d* ... 1Kin 14:17 3212
- So he *d* thence, and found Elisha ... 1Kin 19:19 3212
- And the messengers *d*, and brought ... 1Kin 20:9 3212
- as soon as thou art *d* from me ... 1Kin 20:36 1980
- And as soon as he was *d* from him ... 1Kin 20:36 3212
- So the prophet *d*, and waited for ... 1Kin 20:38 3212
- And Elijah *d* ... 2Kin 1:4 3212
- he *d* not therefrom ... 2Kin 3:3 5493
- they *d* from him, and returned to ... 2Kin 3:27 5265
- And he *d*, and took with him ten ... 2Kin 5:5 3212
- So he *d* from him a little way ... 2Kin 5:19 3212
- and he let the men go, and they *d* ... 2Kin 5:24 3212
- So he *d* from Elisha, and came to ... 2Kin 8:14 3212
- And he arose and *d*, and came to ... 2Kin 10:12 935
- And when he was *d* thence, he ... 2Kin 10:15 3212
- Jehu *d* not from after them, to ... 2Kin 10:29 5493
- for he *d* not from the sins of ... 2Kin 10:31 5493
- he *d* not therefrom ... 2Kin 13:2 5493
- Nevertheless they *d* not from the ... 2Kin 13:6 5493
- he *d* not from all the sins of ... 2Kin 13:11 5493
- he *d* not from all the sins of ... 2Kin 14:24 5493
- he *d* not from the sins of ... 2Kin 15:9 5493
- he *d* not all his days from the ... 2Kin 15:18 5493
- he *d* not from the sins of ... 2Kin 15:24 5493
- he *d* not from the sins of ... 2Kin 15:28 5493
- they *d* not from them ... 2Kin 17:22 5493
- *d* not from following him, but ... 2Kin 18:6 5493
- heard that he was *d* from Lachish ... 2Kin 19:8 5265
- So Sennacherib king of Assyria *d* ... 2Kin 19:36 5265
- all the people *d* every man to his ... 1Chr 16:43 3212
- Wherefore Joab *d*, and went ... 1Chr 21:4 3318
- they *d* not from the commandment ... 2Chr 8:15 5493
- And the people *d* ... 2Chr 10:5 3212
- *d* not from it, doing that which ... 2Chr 20:32 5493
- years, and *d* without being desired ... 2Chr 21:20 3212
- And when they were *d* from him ... 2Chr 24:25 3212
- all his days they *d* not from ... 2Chr 34:33 5493
- Then we *d* from the river of Ahava ... Ezr 8:31 5265
- the cloud *d* not from them by day ... Neh 9:19 5493
- have not wickedly *d* from my God ... Ps 18:21
- who drove him away, and he *d* ... Ps 34:*t* 3212
- Egypt was glad when they *d* ... Ps 105:38 3318
- I have not *d* from thy judgments ... Ps 119:102 5493
- the day that Ephraim *d* from Judah ... Is 7:17 5493
- heard that he was *d* from Lachish ... Is 37:8 5265
- So Sennacherib king of Assyria *d* ... Is 37:37 5265

Mine age is *d*, and is removed from...... Is 38:12 5265
the smiths, were *d* from Jerusalem...... Jer 29:2 3318
of them, they *d* from Jerusalem...... Jer 37:5 5927
d to go over to the Ammonites...... Jer 41:10 3212
And they *d*, and dwelt in the...... Jer 41:17 3212
of Zion all her beauty is *d*...... Lam 1:6 3318
heart, which hath *d* from me...... Eze 6:9 5493
Then the glory of the LORD *d* from...... Eze 10:18 3318
The kingdom is *d* from thee...... Dan 4:31 5709
thereof, because it is *d* from it...... Hos 10:5 1540
But ye are *d* out of the way...... Mal 2:8 5493
they had heard the king, they *d*...... Mt 2:9 *4198*
they *d* into their own country...... Mt 2:12 *402*
And when they were *d*, behold, the...... Mt 2:13 *402*
mother by night, and *d* into Egypt...... Mt 2:14 *402*
into prison, he *d* into Galilee...... Mt 4:12 *402*
And he arose, and *d* to his house...... Mt 9:7 *565*
And when Jesus *d* thence, two blind...... Mt 9:27 *3855*
But they, when they were *d*...... Mt 9:31 *1831*
he *d* thence to teach and to preach...... Mt 11:1 *3327*
And as they *d*, Jesus began to say...... Mt 11:7 *4198*
And when he was *d* thence, he went...... Mt 12:9 *3327*
these parables, he *d* thence...... Mt 13:53 *3332*
he *d* thence by ship into a desert...... Mt 14:13 *402*
d into the coasts of Tyre and...... Mt 15:21 *402*
Jesus *d* from thence, and came nigh...... Mt 15:29 *3327*
And he left them, and *d*...... Mt 16:4 *565*
and he *d* out of him...... Mt 17:18 *1831*
he *d* from Galilee, and came into...... Mt 19:1 *3332*
his hands on them, and *d* thence...... Mt 19:15 *4198*
as they *d* from Jericho, a great...... Mt 20:29 *1607*
went out, and *d* from the temple...... Mt 24:1 *4198*
of silver in the temple, and *d*...... Mt 27:5 *402*
the door of the sepulchre, and *d*...... Mt 27:60 *565*
they *d* quickly from the sepulchre...... Mt 28:8 *1831*
d into a solitary place, and there...... Mk 1:35 *565*
the leprosy *d* from him, and he was...... Mk 1:42 *565*
And he *d*, and began to publish in...... Mk 5:20 *565*
they *d* into a desert place by...... Mk 6:32 *565*
he *d* into a mountain to pray...... Mk 6:46 *565*
ship again *d* to the other side...... Mk 8:13 *565*
they *d* thence, and passed through...... Mk 9:30 *1831*
he *d* to his own house...... Lk 1:23 *565*
And the angel *d* from her...... Lk 1:38 *565*
which *d* not from the temple, but...... Lk 2:37 *868*
he *d* from him for a season...... Lk 4:13 *868*
And when it was day, he *d* and went...... Lk 4:42 *1831*
the leprosy *d* from him...... Lk 5:13 *565*
d to his own house, glorifying...... Lk 5:25 *565*
the messengers of John were *d*...... Lk 7:24 *565*
out of whom the devils were *d*...... Lk 8:35 *1831*
d besought him that he might be...... Lk 8:38 *1831*
And they *d*, and went through the...... Lk 9:6 *1831*
as they *d* from him, Peter said...... Lk 9:33 *1316*
his raiment, and wounded him, and *d*...... Lk 10:30 *565*
And on the morrow when he *d*...... Lk 10:35 *1831*
clothes laid by themselves, and *d*...... Lk 24:12 *565*
Judaea, and *d* again into Galilee...... Jn 4:3 *565*
Now after two days he *d* thence...... Jn 4:43 *565*
The man *d*, and told the Jews that...... Jn 5:15 *565*
he *d* again into a mountain...... Jn 6:15 *402*
These things spake Jesus, and *d*...... Jn 12:36 *565*
they *d* from the presence of the...... Acts 5:41 *4198*
which spake unto Cornelius was *d*...... Acts 10:7 *565*
Then *d* Barnabas to Tarsus, for to...... Acts 11:25 *1831*
and forthwith the angel *d* from him...... Acts 12:10 *868*
And he *d*, and went into another...... Acts 12:17 *1831*
the Holy Ghost, *d* unto Seleucia...... Acts 13:4 *2718*
But when they *d* from Perga...... Acts 13:14 *1330*
the next day he *d* with Barnabas...... Acts 14:20 *1831*
who *d* from them from Pamphylia,...... Acts 15:38 *868*
that they *d* in asunder one from...... Acts 15:39 *673*
And Paul chose Silas, and *d*...... Acts 15:40 *1831*
they comforted them, and *d*...... Acts 16:40 *1831*
to him with all speed, they *d*...... Acts 17:15 *1826*
So Paul *d* from among them...... Acts 17:33 *1831*
these things Paul *d* from Athens...... Acts 18:1 *5562*
he *d* thence, and entered into a...... Acts 18:7 *1831*
had spent some time there, he *d*...... Acts 18:23 *1831*
he *d* from them, and separated the...... Acts 19:9 *868*
and the diseases *d* from them...... Acts 19:12 *525*
d for to go into Macedonia...... Acts 20:1 *1831*
even till break of day, so he *d*...... Acts 20:11 *1831*
had accomplished those days, we *d*...... Acts 21:5 *1831*
we that were of Paul's company *d*...... Acts 21:8 *1831*
Then straightway they *d* from him...... Acts 22:29 *868*
and when we *d*, they laded us with...... Acts 28:10 *321*
after three months we *d* in a ship...... Acts 28:11 *321*
not among themselves, they *d*...... Acts 28:25 *630*
had said these words, the Jews *d*...... Acts 28:29 *565*
when I *d* from Macedonia, no...... Phil 4:15 *1831*
world, and is *d* unto Thessalonica...... 2Ti 4:10 *4198*
he therefore *d* for a season...... Philem 15 *5563*
the heaven *d* as a scroll when it...... Rev 6:14 *673*
soul lusted after are *d* from thee...... Rev 18:14 *565*
dainty and goodly are *d* from thee...... Rev 18:14 *565*

DEPARTETH

wind carrieth him away, and he *d*...... Job 27:21 3212
wise man feareth, and *d* from evil...... Prov 14:16 5493
d in darkness, and his name shall...... Eccl 6:4 3212
he that *d* from evil maketh...... Is 59:15 5493
treacherously *d* from her husband...... Jer 3:20
whose heart *d* from the LORD...... Jer 17:5 5493
the prey *d* not...... Nah 3:1 4185
and bruising him hardly *d* from him...... Lk 9:39 *672*

DEPARTING

to pass, as her soul was in *d*...... Gen 35:18 3318
their *d* out of the land of Egypt...... Ex 16:1 3318
d away from our God, speaking...... Is 59:13 5253
even by *d* from thy precepts and...... Dan 9:5 5493
transgressed thy law, even by *d*...... Dan 9:11 5493
great whoredom, *d* from the LORD...... Hos 1:2
And the people saw them *d*, and many...... Mk 6:33 *5217*
d from the coasts of Tyre and...... Mk 7:31 *1831*
John *d* from them returned to...... Acts 13:13 *672*
that after my *d* shall grievous...... Acts 20:29 *867*
in *d* from the living God...... Heb 3:12 *868*
made mention of the *d* of the...... Heb 11:22 *1841*

DEPARTURE

sea shall be troubled at thy *d*...... Eze 26:18 3318
and the time of my *d* is at hand...... 2Ti 4:6 *359*

DEPOSED

he was *d* from his kingly throne,...... Dan 5:20 5182

DEPRIVED

why should I be *d* also of you...... Gen 27:45 7921
Because God hath *d* her of wisdom...... Job 39:17 5382
I am *d* of the residue of my years...... Is 38:10 6485

DEPTH

The *d* saith, It is not in me...... Job 28:14 8415
walked in the search of the *d*...... Job 38:16 8415
he layeth up the *d* in storehouses...... Ps 33:7 8415
a compass upon the face of the *d*...... Prov 8:27 8415
for height, and the earth for *d*...... Prov 25:3 6012
ask it either in the *d*, or in the...... Is 7:11 6009
the *d* closed me round about, the...... Jonah 2:5 8415
were drowned in the *d* of the sea...... Mt 18:6 *3989*
up, because it had no *d* of earth...... Mk 4:5 *899*
Nor height, nor *d*, nor any other...... Rom 8:39 *899*
O the *d* of the riches both of the...... Rom 11:33 *899*
is the breadth, and length, and *d*...... Eph 3:18 *899*

DEPTHS

The *d* have covered them...... Ex 15:5 8415
the *d* were congealed in the heart...... Ex 15:8 8415
d that spring out of valleys and...... Deut 8:7 8415
again from the *d* of the sea...... Ps 68:22 4688
up again from the *d* of the earth...... Ps 71:20 8415
the *d* also were troubled...... Ps 77:16 8415
them drink as out of the great *d*...... Ps 78:15 8415
so he led them through the *d*...... Ps 106:9 8415
they go down again to the *d*...... Ps 107:26 8415
Out of the *d* have I cried unto...... Ps 130:1 4615
his knowledge the *d* are broken up...... Prov 3:20 8415
When there were no *d*, I was...... Prov 8:24 8415
her guests are in the *d* of hell...... Prov 9:18 6010
that hath made the *d* of the sea a...... Is 51:10 4615
be broken by the seas in the *d* of...... Eze 27:34 4615
their sins into the *d* of the sea...... Mic 7:19 4688
have not known the *d* of Satan...... Rev 2:24 *899*

DEPUTED

but there is no man *d* of the king...... 2Sa 15:3

DEPUTIES

and to the lieutenants, and the *d*...... Est 8:9 6346
and the lieutenants, and the *d*...... Est 9:3 6346
the law is open, and there are *d*...... Acts 19:38 *446*

DEPUTY

a *d* was king...... 1Kin 22:47 5324
was with the *d* of the country...... Acts 13:7 *446*
to turn away the *d* from the faith...... Acts 13:8 *446*
Then the *d*, when he saw what was...... Acts 13:12 *446*
when Gallio was the *d* of Achaia...... Acts 18:12 *446*

DERBE *(der'-by) A south Galatian town.*

of it, and fled unto Lystra and *D*...... Acts 14:6 *1191*
he departed with Barnabas to *D*...... Acts 14:20 *1191*
Then came he to *D* and Lystra...... Acts 16:1 *1191*
and Gaius of *D*, and Timotheus...... Acts 20:4 *1191*

DERIDE

they shall *d* every strong hold...... Hab 1:10 7832

DERIDED

and they *d* him...... Lk 16:14 *1592*
the rulers also with them *d* him...... Lk 23:35 *1592*

DERISION

are younger than I have me in *d*...... Job 30:1 7832
the Lord shall have them in *d*...... Ps 2:4 3932
a *d* to them that are round about...... Ps 44:13 7047
shalt have all the heathen in *d*...... Ps 59:8 3932
d to them that are round about us...... Ps 79:4 7047
proud have had me greatly in *d*...... Ps 119:51 3887
I am in *d* daily, every one...... Jer 20:7 7814
made a reproach unto me, and a *d*...... Jer 20:8 7047
vomit, and he also shall be in *d*...... Jer 48:26 7814
For was not Israel a *d* unto thee...... Jer 48:27 7814
so shall Moab be a *d* and a...... Jer 48:39 7814
I was a *d* to all my people...... Lam 3:14 7814
be laughed to scorn and had in *d*...... Eze 23:32 3932
d to the residue of the heathen...... Eze 36:4 3932
this shall be their *d* in the land...... Hos 7:16 3932

DESCEND

and the border shall *d*, and shall...... Num 34:11 3381
or he shall *d* into battle...... 1Sa 26:10 3381
his glory shall not *d* after him...... Ps 49:17 3381
that rejoiceth, shall *d* into it...... Is 5:14 3381
with them that *d* into the pit...... Eze 26:20 3381
with them that *d* into the pit...... Eze 31:16 3381
of Israel *d* now from the cross...... Mk 15:32 *2597*
saw a vision, A certain vessel *d*...... Acts 11:5 *2597*
Who shall *d* into the deep...... Rom 10:7 *2597*
shall *d* from heaven with a shout...... 1Th 4:16 *2597*

DESCENDED

the LORD *d* upon it in fire...... Ex 19:18 3381
tabernacle, the cloudy pillar *d*...... Ex 33:9 3381
the LORD *d* in the cloud, and stood...... Ex 34:5 3381
the brook that *d* out of the mount...... Deut 9:21 3381
d from the mountain, and passed...... Josh 2:23 3381
the coast *d* unto the river Kanah,...... Josh 17:9 3381
the border *d* to Ataroth-adar,...... Josh 18:13 3381
d to the valley of Hinnom, to the...... Josh 18:16 3381
on the south, and *d* to En-rogel,...... Josh 18:16 3381
d to the stone of Bohan the son...... Josh 18:17 3381
as the dew that *d* upon the...... Ps 133:3 3381
ascended up into heaven, or *d*...... Prov 30:4 3381
And the rain *d*, and the floods came...... Mt 7:25 *2597*
And the rain *d*, and the floods came...... Mt 7:27 *2597*
angel of the Lord *d* from heaven...... Mt 28:2 *2597*
the Holy Ghost *d* in a bodily...... Lk 3:22 *2597*
the high priest *d* with the elders...... Acts 24:1 *2597*
what is it but that he also *d*...... Eph 4:9 *2597*
He that *d* is the same also that...... Eph 4:10 *2597*

DESCENDETH

This wisdom *d* not from above, but...... Jas 3:15 *2718*

DESCENDING

of God ascending and *d* on it...... Gen 28:12 3381
the Spirit of God *d* like a dove...... Mt 3:16 *2597*
the Spirit like a dove *d* upon him...... Mk 1:10 *2597*
I saw the Spirit *d* from heaven...... Jn 1:32 *2597*
whom thou shalt see the Spirit *d*...... Jn 1:33 *2597*
and *d* upon the Son of man...... Jn 1:51 *2597*
and a certain vessel *d* unto him...... Acts 10:11 *2597*
d out of heaven from God,...... Rev 21:10 *2597*

DESCENT

even now at the *d* of the mount of...... Lk 19:37 *2600*
father, without mother, without *d*...... Heb 7:3 *35*
But he whose *d* is not counted...... Heb 7:6 *1075*

DESCRIBE

d it according to the inheritance...... Josh 18:4 3789
Ye shall therefore *d* the land...... Josh 18:6 3789
them that went to *d* the land...... Josh 18:8 3789
d it, and come again to me, that I...... Josh 18:8 3789

DESCRIBED

d it by cities into seven parts...... Josh 18:9 3789
he *d* unto him the princes of...... Judg 8:14 3789

DESCRIBETH

Even as David also *d* the...... Rom 4:6 *3004*
For Moses *d* the righteousness...... Rom 10:5 *1125*

DESCRIPTION

bring the *d* hither to me, that I...... Josh 18:6

DESCRY

house of Joseph sent to *d* Beth-el...... Judg 1:23 8446

DESERT

flock to the backside of the *d*...... Ex 3:1 4057
three days' journey into the *d*...... Ex 5:3 4057
and were come to the *d* of Sinai...... Ex 19:2 4057
from the *d* unto the river...... Ex 23:31 4057
into the *d* of Zin in the first...... Num 20:1 4057
my commandment in the *d* of Zin...... Num 27:14 4057
they removed from the *d* of Sinai...... Num 33:16 4057
He found him in a *d* land, and in...... Deut 32:10 4057
Also he built towers in the *d*...... 2Chr 26:10 4057
Behold, as wild asses in the *d*...... Job 24:5 4057
render to them their *d*...... Ps 28:4 1576
and grieve him in the *d*...... Ps 78:40 3452
I am like an owl of the *d*...... Ps 102:6 2723
and tempted God in the *d*...... Ps 106:14 3452
beasts of the *d* shall lie there...... Is 13:21 6728
The burden of the *d* of the sea...... Is 21:1 4057
so it cometh from the *d*, from a...... Is 21:1 4057
The wild beasts of the *d* shall...... Is 34:14 6728
the *d* shall rejoice, and blossom...... Is 35:1 6160
break out, and streams in the *d*...... Is 35:6 6160
make straight in the *d* a highway...... Is 40:3 6160
I will set in the *d* the fir tree...... Is 41:19 6160
wilderness, and rivers in the *d*...... Is 43:19 3452
wilderness, and rivers in the *d*...... Is 43:20 3452
her *d* like the garden of the LORD...... Is 51:3 6160
shall be like the heath in the *d*...... Jer 17:6 6160
people that dwell in the *d*...... Jer 25:24 4057
a wilderness, a dry land, and a *d*...... Jer 50:12 6160
the wild beasts of the *d* with the...... Jer 50:39 6728
country, and go down into the *d*...... Eze 47:8 6160
by ship into a *d* place apart...... Mt 14:13 *2048*
to him, saying, This is a *d* place...... Mt 14:15 *2048*
unto you, Behold, he is in the *d*...... Mt 24:26 *2048*
city, but was without in *d* places...... Mk 1:45 *2048*
yourselves apart into a *d* place...... Mk 6:31 *2048*
they departed into a *d* place by...... Mk 6:32 *2048*
him, and said, This is a *d* place...... Mk 6:35 *2048*
departed and went into a *d* place...... Lk 4:42 *2048*
a *d* place belonging to the city...... Lk 9:10 *2048*
for we are here in a *d* place...... Lk 9:12 *2048*
fathers did eat manna in the *d*...... Jn 6:31 *2048*
Jerusalem unto Gaza, which is *d*...... Acts 8:26 *2048*

DESERTS

when he led them through the *d*...... Is 48:21 2723
wilderness, through a land of *d*...... Jer 2:6 6160
to their *d* will I judge them...... Eze 7:27 4941
are like the foxes in the *d*...... Eze 13:4 2723
was in the *d* till the day of his...... Lk 1:80 *2048*
they wandered in *d*, and in...... Heb 11:38 *2047*

DESERVE

us less than our iniquities *d*...... Ezr 9:13

DESERVETH

thee less than thine iniquity *d*...... Job 11:6

DESERVING

according to the *d* of his hands...... Judg 9:16 1576

DESIRABLE

rulers, all of them *d* young men...... Eze 23:6 2531
horses, all of them *d* young men...... Eze 23:12 2531
all of them *d* young men, captains...... Eze 23:23 2531

DESIRE

thy *d* shall be to thy husband, and...... Gen 3:16 8669
And unto thee shall be his *d*...... Gen 4:7 8669
for that ye did *d*...... Ex 10:11 1245
neither shall any man *d* thy land...... Ex 34:24 2530
Neither shalt thou *d* thy...... Deut 5:21 2530
thou shalt not *d* the silver or...... Deut 7:25 2530
come with all the *d* of his mind...... Deut 18:6 183
hast a *d* unto her, that thou...... Deut 21:11 2836

I would *d* a request of you, that Judg 8:24 7592
And on whom is all the *d* of Israel 1Sa 9:20 2532
the *d* of thy soul to come down 1Sa 23:20 183
is all my salvation, and all my *d* 2Sa 23:5 2656
I *d* one small petition of thee 1Kin 2:20 7592
I will do all thy *d* concerning 1Kin 5:8 2656
and thou shalt accomplish my *d* 1Kin 5:9 2656
fir trees according to all his *d* 1Kin 5:10 2656
all Solomon's *d* which he was 1Kin 9:1 2837
with gold, according to all his *d* 1Kin 9:11 2656
unto the queen of Sheba all her *d* 1Kin 10:13 2656
said, Did I *d* a son of my lord 2Kin 4:28 7592
to the queen of Sheba all her *d* 2Chr 9:12 2656
and sought him with their whole *d* 2Chr 15:15 7522
servants, who *d* to fear thy name Neh 1:11 2655
and I *d* to reason with God Job 13:3 2654
thou wilt have a *d* to the work of Job 14:15 3700
for we *d* not the knowledge of thy Job 21:14 2654
withheld the poor from their *d* Job 31:16 2656
behold, my *d* is, that the Job 31:35 8420
speak, for I *d* to justify thee Job 33:32 2654
My *d* is that Job may be tried Job 34:36 15
D not the night, when people are Job 36:20 7602
wicked boasteth of his heart's *d* Ps 10:3 8378
hast heard the *d* of the humble Ps 10:17 8378
Thou hast given him his heart's *d* Ps 21:2 8378
Lord, all my *d* is before thee Ps 38:9 8378
and offering thou didst not *d* Ps 40:6 2654
the king greatly *d* thy beauty Ps 45:11 183
hath seen his *d* upon mine enemies Ps 54:7
let me see my *d* upon mine enemies Ps 59:10
put to confusion, that *d* my hurt Ps 70:2 2655
upon earth that I *d* beside thee Ps 73:25 2654
for he gave them their own *d* Ps 78:29 8378
shall see my *d* on mine enemies Ps 92:11
mine ears shall hear my *d* of the Ps 92:11
he see his *d* upon his enemies Ps 112:8
the *d* of the wicked shall perish Ps 112:10 8378
I see my *d* upon them that hate me Ps 118:7
satisfiest the *d* of every living Ps 145:16 7522
He will fulfil the *d* of them that Ps 145:19 7522
all the things thou canst *d* are Prov 3:15 2656
but the *d* of the righteous shall Prov 10:24 8378
The *d* of the righteous is only Prov 11:23 8378
heart sick, but when the *d* cometh Prov 13:12 8378
The *d* accomplished is sweet to Prov 13:19 8378
Through *d* a man, having separated Prov 18:1 8378
The *d* of a man is his kindness Prov 19:22 8378
The *d* of the slothful killeth him Prov 21:25 8378
neither *d* thou his dainty meats Prov 23:6 183
neither *d* to be with them Prov 24:1 183
eyes than the wandering of the *d* Eccl 6:9 5315
be a burden, and *d* shall fail Eccl 12:5 35
beloved's, and his *d* is toward me Song 7:10 8669
the *d* of our soul is to thy name Is 26:8 8378
is no beauty that we should *d* him Is 53:2 2530
land whereunto they *d* to return Jer 22:27
in the place whither ye *d* to go Jer 42:22 2654
have a *d* to return to dwell there Jer 44:14
I take away from thee the *d* of Eze 24:16 4261
the *d* of your eyes, and that which Eze 24:21 4261
the *d* of their eyes, and that Eze 24:25 4261
That they would *d* mercies of the Dan 2:18 1156
nor the *d* of women, nor regard Dan 11:37 2532
It is in my *d* that I should Hos 10:10 183
Woe unto you that *d* the day of Amos 5:18 183
he uttereth his mischievous *d* Mic 7:3 5315
home, who enlargeth his *d* as hell Hab 2:5 5315
the *d* of all nations shall come Hag 2:7 2532
If any man *d* to be first, the Mk 9:35 2309
do for us whatsoever we shall *d* Mk 10:35 154
unto you, What things soever ye *d* Mk 11:24 154
d him to do as he had ever done Mk 15:8 154
when ye shall *d* to see one of the Lk 17:22 1937
which *d* to walk in long robes, and Lk 20:46 2309
With *d* I have desired to eat this Lk 22:15 1939
The Jews have agreed to *d* thee Acts 23:20 2065
But we *d* to hear of thee what Acts 28:22 515
Brethren, my heart's *d* and prayer Rom 10:1 2107
having a great *d* these many years Rom 15:23 1974
d spiritual gifts, but rather 1Cor 14:1 2206
when he told us your earnest *d* 2Cor 7:7 1972
what fear, yea, what vehement *d* 2Cor 7:11 1972
from them which *d* occasion 2Cor 11:12 2309
For though I would *d* to glory 2Cor 12:6 2309
whereunto ye *d* again to be in Gal 4:9 2309
I *d* to be present with you now Gal 4:20 2309
ye that *d* to be under the law, do Gal 4:21 2309
As many as *d* to make a fair shew Gal 6:12 2309
but *d* to have you circumcised Gal 6:13 2309
Wherefore I *d* that ye faint not Eph 3:13 154
having a *d* to depart, and to be Phil 1:23 1939
Not because I *d* a gift Phil 4:17 1934
but I *d* fruit that may abound to Phil 4:17 1934
to *d* that ye might be filled with Col 1:9 154
to see your face with great *d* 1Th 2:17 1939
If a man *d* the office of a bishop 1Ti 3:1 3713
we *d* that every one of you do Heb 6:11 1937
But now they *d* a better country Heb 11:16 3713
d to have, and cannot obtain Jas 4:2 2206
things the angels *d* to look into 1Pet 1:12 1937
d the sincere milk of the word 1Pet 2:2 1971
shall *d* to die, and death shall Rev 9:6 1937

DESIRED

a tree to be *d* to make one wise Gen 3:6 2530
ye have chosen, and whom ye have *d* 1Sa 12:13 7592
that which Solomon *d* to build in 1Kin 9:19 2836
all that Solomon *d* to build in 2Chr 8:6 2836
And he *d* many wives 2Chr 11:23 7592
and departed without being *d* 2Chr 21:20 2532
whatsoever she *d* was given her to Est 2:13 559
shall not save of that which he *d* Job 20:20 2530
More to be *d* are they than gold Ps 19:10 2530
One thing have I *d* of the LORD Ps 27:4 7592
bringeth them unto their *d* haven Ps 107:30 2656
he hath *d* it for his habitation Ps 132:13 183
for I have *d* it Ps 132:14 183
all the things that may be *d* are Prov 8:11 2656
There is treasure to be *d* Prov 21:20 2530
mine eyes *d* I kept not from them Eccl 2:10 7592
of the oaks which ye have *d* Is 1:29 2530
soul have I *d* thee in the night Is 26:9 183
neither have I *d* the woeful day Jer 17:16 183
d of the king that he would give Dan 2:16 1156
unto me now what we *d* of thee Dan 2:23 1156
For I *d* mercy, and not sacrifice Hos 6:6 2654
my soul *d* the firstripe fruit Mic 7:1 183
gather together, O nation not *d* Zeph 2:1 3700
righteous men have *d* to see those Mt 13:17 1939
tempting *d* him that he would shew Mt 16:1 1905
one prisoner, whomsoever they *d* Mk 15:6 154
one of the Pharisees *d* him that Lk 7:36 2065
And he *d* to see him Lk 9:9 2212
kings have *d* to see those things Lk 10:24 2309
With desire I have *d* to eat this Lk 22:15 1937
Satan hath *d* to have you, that he Lk 22:31 1809
cast into prison, whom they had *d* Lk 23:25 154
d him, saying, Sir, we would see Jn 12:21 2065
d a murderer to be granted unto Acts 3:14 154
d to find a tabernacle for the Acts 7:46 154
he *d* Philip that he would come up Acts 8:31 3870
d of him letters to Damascus to Acts 9:2 154
chamberlain their friend, *d* peace Acts 12:20 154
d to hear the word of God Acts 13:7 1934
And afterward they *d* a king Acts 13:21 154
yet *d* they Pilate that he should Acts 13:28 154
d them to depart out of the city Acts 16:39 2065
When they *d* him to tarry longer Acts 18:20 2065
d favour against him, that he Acts 25:3 154
were *d* to tarry with them seven Acts 28:14 3870
I greatly *d* him to come unto you 1Cor 16:12 3870
Insomuch that we *d* Titus, that as 2Cor 8:6 3870
I *d* Titus, and with him I sent a 2Cor 12:18 3870
the petitions that we *d* of him 1Jn 5:15 154

DESIREDST

According to all that thou *d* of Deut 18:16 7592
all that debt, because thou *d* me Mt 18:32 3870

DESIRES

give thee the *d* of thine heart Ps 37:4 4862
not, O LORD, the *d* of the wicked Ps 140:8 3970
fulfilling the *d* of the flesh Eph 2:3 2307

DESIREST

thou *d* truth in the inward parts Ps 51:6 2654
For thou *d* not sacrifice Ps 51:16 2654

DESIRETH

or for whatsoever thy soul *d* Deut 14:26 7592
then take as much as thy soul *d* 1Sa 2:16 8378
The king *d* not any dowry, but an 1Sa 18:25 2656
unto David, Whatsoever thy soul *d* 1Sa 20:4 559
reign over all that thine heart *d* 2Sa 3:21 8378
according to all that thy soul *d* 1Kin 11:37 8378
a servant earnestly *d* the shadow Job 7:2 7602
And what his soul *d*, even that he Job 23:13 183
What man is he that *d* life Ps 34:12 2655
the hill which God *d* to dwell in Ps 68:16 2530
The wicked *d* the net of evil men Prov 12:12 2530
The soul of the sluggard *d* Prov 13:4 183
The soul of the wicked *d* evil Prov 21:10 183
for his soul of all that he *d* Eccl 6:2 183
drunk old wine straightway *d* new Lk 5:39 2309
and *d* conditions of peace Lk 14:32 2065
of a bishop, he *d* a good work 1Ti 3:1 1937

DESIRING

without, *d* to speak with him Mt 12:46 2212
without, *d* to speak with thee Mt 12:47 2212
him, and *d* a certain thing of him Mt 20:20 154
stand without, *d* to see thee Lk 8:20 2309
d to be fed with the crumbs which Lk 16:21 1937
d him that he would not delay to Acts 9:38 3870
d him that he would not adventure Acts 19:31 3870
d to have judgment against him Acts 25:15 154
earnestly *d* to be clothed upon 2Cor 5:2 1971
d greatly to see us, as we also 1Th 3:6 1971
D to be teachers of the law 1Ti 1:7 2309
Greatly *d* to see thee, being 2Ti 1:4 1971

DESIROUS

Be not *d* of his dainties Prov 23:3 183
for he was *d* to see him of a long Lk 23:8 2309
knew that they were *d* to ask him Jn 16:19 2309
a garrison, *d* to apprehend me 2Cor 11:32 2309
Let us not be *d* of vain glory Gal 5:26 2755
So being affectionately *d* of you 1Th 2:8 2442

DESOLATE

not die, that the land be not *d* Gen 47:19 3456
lest the land become *d*, and the Ex 23:29 8077
and your high ways shall be *d* Lev 26:22 8074
and your land shall be *d*, and your Lev 26:33 8077
sabbaths, as long as it lieth *d* Lev 26:34 8074
long as it lieth *d* it shall rest Lev 26:35 8074
while she lieth *d* without them Lev 26:43 8074
So Tamar remained *d* in her 2Sa 13:20 8076
as she lay *d* she kept sabbath 2Chr 36:21 8074
earth, which built *d* places for Job 3:14 2723
And he dwelleth in *d* cities Job 15:28 3582
of hypocrites shall be *d*, and fire Job 15:34 1565
thou hast made *d* all my company Job 16:7 8074
the wilderness in former time *d* Job 30:3 7722
To satisfy the *d* and waste ground Job 38:27 7722
for I am *d* and afflicted Ps 25:16 3173
hate the righteous shall be *d* Ps 34:21 816
them that trust in him shall be *d* Ps 34:22 816
Let them be *d* for a reward of Ps 40:15 8074
Let their habitation be *d* Ps 69:25 8074
bread also out of their *d* places Ps 109:10 2723
my heart within me is *d* Ps 143:4 8074
Your country is *d*, your cities Is 1:7 8077
it in your presence, and it is *d* Is 1:7 8077
she being *d* shall sit upon the Is 3:26 5352
Of a truth many houses shall be *d* Is 5:9 8047
man, and the land be utterly *d* Is 6:11 8077
rest all of them in the *d* valleys Is 7:19 1327
fierce anger, to lay the land *d* Is 13:9 8047
shall cry in their *d* houses Is 13:22 490
the waters of Nimrim shall be *d* Is 15:6 4923
and they that dwell therein are *d* Is 24:6 816
Yet the defenced city shall be *d* Is 27:10 910
cause to inherit the *d* heritages Is 49:8 8076
thy *d* places, and the land of thy Is 49:19 8074
I have lost my children, and am *d* Is 49:21 1565
of the *d* than the children of the Is 54:1 8074
make the *d* cities to be inhabited Is 54:3 8077
we are in *d* places as dead men Is 59:10 820
thy land any more be termed *D* Is 62:4 8077
be horribly afraid, be ye very *d* Jer 2:12 2717
from his place to make thy land *d* Jer 4:7 8047
said, The whole land shall be *d* Jer 4:27 8077
lest I make thee *d*, a land not Jer 6:8 8077
for the land shall be *d* Jer 7:34 2723
I will make the cities of Judah *d* Jer 9:11 8077
to make the cities of Judah *d* Jer 10:22 8077
and have made his habitation *d* Jer 10:25 8074
pleasant portion a *d* wilderness Jer 12:10 8077
They have made it *d* Jer 12:11 8077
being *d* it mourneth unto me Jer 12:11 8077
the whole land is made *d*, because Jer 12:11 8074
To make their land *d*, and a Jer 18:16 8047
And I will make this city *d* Jer 19:8 8047
for their land is *d* because of Jer 25:38 8047
this city shall be *d* without an Jer 26:9 2717
It is *d* without man or beast Jer 32:43 8077
ye say shall be *d* without man Jer 33:10 2717
streets of Jerusalem, that are *d* Jer 33:10 8074
which is *d* without man and without Jer 33:12 2717
and they are wasted and *d*, as at Jer 44:6 8077
waste and *d* without an inhabitant Jer 46:19 3341
for the cities thereof shall be *d* Jer 48:9 8047
waters also of Nimrim shall be *d* Jer 48:34 4923
and it shall be a *d* heap, and her Jer 49:2 8077
their habitations *d* with them Jer 49:20 8074
her, which shall make her land *d* Jer 50:3 8047
but it shall be wholly *d* Jer 50:13 8077
make their habitation *d* with them Jer 50:45 8074
but thou shalt be *d* for ever Jer 51:26 8077
but that it shall be *d* for ever Jer 51:62 8077
all her gates are *d* Lam 1:4 8076
he hath made me *d* and faint all Lam 1:13 8076
my children are *d*, because the Lam 1:16 8076
he hath made me *d* Lam 3:11 8076
delicately are *d* in the streets Lam 4:5 8074
the mountain of Zion, which is *d* Lam 5:18 8074
And your altars shall be *d* Eze 6:4 8074
and the high places shall be *d* Eze 6:6 3456
may be laid waste and made *d* Eze 6:6 816
upon them, and make the land *d* Eze 6:14 8077
more *d* than the wilderness toward Eze 6:14 8047
that her land may be *d* from all Eze 12:19 3456
waste, and the land shall be *d* Eze 12:20 8077
and they spoil it, so that it be *d* Eze 14:15 8077
but the land shall be *d* Eze 14:16 8077
And I will make the land *d* Eze 15:8 8077
And he knew their *d* palaces Eze 19:7 490
and the land was *d*, and the fulness Eze 19:7 3456
womb, that I might make them *d* Eze 20:26 8074
the land of Israel, when it was *d* Eze 25:3 8074
and I will make it *d* from Teman Eze 25:13 2723
When I shall make thee a *d* city Eze 26:19 2717
of the earth, in places *d* of old Eze 26:20 2723
And the land of Egypt shall be *d* Eze 29:9 8077
land of Egypt utterly waste and *d* Eze 29:10 8077
d in the midst of the countries Eze 29:12 8077
midst of the countries that are *d* Eze 29:12 8074
laid waste shall be *d* forty years Eze 29:12 8077
they shall be *d* in the midst of Eze 30:7 8074
midst of the countries that are *d* Eze 30:7 8074
And I will make Pathros *d*, and will Eze 30:14 8074
I shall make the land of Egypt *d* Eze 32:15 8077
For I will lay the land most *d* Eze 33:28 8077
mountains of Israel shall be *d* Eze 33:28 8074
land most *d* because of all their Eze 33:29 8077
thee, and I will make thee most *d* Eze 35:3 8077
cities waste, and thou shalt be *d* Eze 35:4 8077
will I make mount Seir most *d* Eze 35:7 8077
Israel, saying, They are laid *d* Eze 35:12 8074
rejoiceth, I will make thee *d* Eze 35:14 8077
house of Israel, because it was *d* Eze 35:15 8074
thou shalt be *d*, O mount Seir, and Eze 35:15 8077
Because they have made you *d* Eze 36:3 8074
to the valleys, to the *d* wastes Eze 36:4 8076
the *d* land shall be tilled Eze 36:34 8074
whereas it lay *d* in the sight of Eze 36:34 8077
This land that was *d* is become Eze 36:35 8074
and the waste and *d* and ruined Eze 36:35 8074
places, and plant that that was *d* Eze 36:36 8074
to turn thine hand upon the *d* Eze 38:12 2723
upon thy sanctuary that is *d* Dan 9:17 8074
abominations he shall make it *d* Dan 9:27 8074
shall be poured upon the *d* Dan 9:27 8076
the abomination that maketh *d* Dan 11:31 8074
abomination that maketh *d* set up Dan 12:11 8074
Ephraim shall be *d* in the day of Hos 5:9 8047
Samaria shall become *d* Hos 13:16 816
clods, the garners are laid *d* Joel 1:17 8074
the flocks of sheep are made *d* Joel 1:18 816
and behind them a *d* wilderness Joel 2:3 8077
drive him into a land barren and *d* Joel 2:20 8077
and Edom shall be a *d* wilderness Joel 3:19 8077
high places of Isaac shall be *d* Amos 7:9 8074

the idols thereof will I lay *d* Mic 1:7 8077
in making thee *d* because of thy Mic 6:13 8074
the land shall be *d* because of Mic 7:13 8077
their towers are *d* Zeph 3:6 8074
Thus the land was *d* after them Zec 7:14 8074
for they laid the pleasant land *d* Zec 7:14 8047
will return and build the *d* places Mal 1:4 2723
your house is left unto you *d* Mt 23:38 *2048*
your house is left unto you *d* Lk 13:35 *2048*
Psalms, Let his habitation be *d* Acts 1:20 *2048*
for the *d* hath many more children Gal 4:27 *2048*
she that is a widow indeed, and *d* 1Ti 5:5 *3443*
the whore, and shall make her *d* Rev 17:16 *2049*
for in one hour is she made *d* Rev 18:19 *2049*

DESOLATION
and bring your sanctuaries unto *d* Lev 26:31 8074
And I will bring the land into *d* Lev 26:32 8074
for ever, even a *d* unto this day Josh 8:28 8077
that they should become a *d* 2Kin 22:19 8047
who therefore gave them up to *d* 2Chr 30:7 8047
in the *d* they rolled themselves Job 30:14 7722
How are they brought into *d* Ps 73:19 8047
When your fear cometh as *d* Prov 1:27 7584
neither of the *d* of the wicked Prov 3:25 7722
in the *d* which shall come from Is 10:3 7722
and there shall be *d* Is 17:9 8077
In the city is left *d*, and the Is 24:12 8047
d shall come upon thee suddenly, Is 47:11 7722
d, and destruction, and the famine, Is 51:19 7701
is a wilderness, Jerusalem a *d* Is 64:10 8077
that this house shall become a *d* Jer 22:5 2723
And this whole land shall be a *d* Jer 25:11 2723
princes thereof, to make them a *d* Jer 25:18 2723
Judah a *d* without an inhabitant Jer 34:22 8077
and, behold, this day they are a *d* Jer 44:2 2723
therefore is your land a *d* Jer 44:22 2723
that Bozrah shall become a *d* Jer 49:13 8047
Also Edom shall be a *d* Jer 49:17 8047
for dragons, and a *d* for ever Jer 49:33 8077
become a *d* among the nations Jer 50:23 8047
Babylon a *d* without an inhabitant Jer 51:29 8047
Her cities are a *d*, a dry land, Jer 51:43 8047
and a snare is come upon us, *d*, Lam 3:47 7612
prince shall be clothed with *d* Eze 7:27 8077
with the cup of astonishment and *d* Eze 23:33 8077
and the transgression of *d* Dan 8:13 8074
he daily increaseth lies and *d* Hos 12:1 7701
Egypt shall be a *d*, and Edom shall Joel 3:19 8077
that I should make thee a *d* Mic 6:16 8047
a booty, and their houses a *d* Zeph 1:13 8047
distress, a day of wasteness and *d* Zeph 1:15 4875
be forsaken, and Ashkelon a *d* Zeph 2:4 8077
and saltpits, and a perpetual *d* Zeph 2:9 8077
and will make Nineveh a *d*, and dry Zeph 2:13 8077
d shall be in the thresholds Zeph 2:14 2721
how is she become a *d*, a place Zeph 2:15 8047
against itself is brought to *d* Mt 12:25 *2049*
shall see the abomination of *d* Mt 24:15 *2050*
ye shall see the abomination of *d* Mk 13:14 *2050*
against itself is brought to *d* Lk 11:17 *2049*
know that the *d* thereof is nigh Lk 21:20 *2050*

DESOLATIONS
God, and to repair the *d* thereof Ezr 9:9 2723
what *d* he hath made in the earth Ps 46:8 8047
up thy feet unto the perpetual *d* Ps 74:3 4876
they shall raise up the former *d* Is 61:4 8074
the *d* of many generations Is 61:4 8074
and an hissing, and perpetual *d* Jer 25:9 2723
and will make it perpetual *d* Jer 25:12 8077
I will make thee perpetual *d* Eze 35:9 8077
years in the *d* of Jerusalem Dan 9:2 2723
open thine eyes, and behold our *d* Dan 9:18 8074
end of the war *d* are determined Dan 9:26 8074

DESPAIR
and Saul shall *d* of me, to seek me 1Sa 27:1 2976
d of all the labour which I took Eccl 2:20 2976
we are perplexed, but not in *d* 2Cor 4:8 *1820*

DESPAIRED
insomuch that we *d* even of life 2Cor 1:8 *1820*

DESPERATE
and the speeches of one that is *d* Job 6:26 2976
the day of grief and of *d* sorrow Is 17:11 605

DESPERATELY
above all things, and *d* wicked Jer 17:9 605

DESPISE
And if ye shall *d* my statutes Lev 26:15 3988
they that *d* me shall be lightly 1Sa 2:30 959
why then did ye *d* us, that our 2Sa 19:43 7043
so that they shall *d* their Est 1:17 959
therefore *d* not thou the Job 5:17 3988
I would *d* my life Job 9:21 3988
that thou shouldest *d* the work of Job 10:3 3988
If I did *d* the cause of my Job 31:13 3988
heart, O God, thou wilt not *d* Ps 51:17 959
awakest, thou shalt *d* their image Ps 73:20 959
destitute, and not *d* their prayer Ps 102:17 959
but fools *d* wisdom and instruction Prov 1:7 936
d not the chastening of the LORD Prov 3:11 3988
Men do not *d* a thief, if he steal Prov 6:30 936
for he will *d* the wisdom of thy Prov 23:9 936
d not thy mother when she is old Prov 23:22 936
of Israel, Because ye *d* this word Is 30:12 3988
thy lovers will *d* thee, they will Jer 4:30 3988
say still unto them that *d* me Jer 23:17 5006
all that honoured her *d* her Lam 1:8 2107
which *d* thee round about Eze 16:57 7590
that *d* them round about them Eze 28:26 7590
I *d* your feast days, and I will Amos 5:21 3988
you, O priests, that *d* my name Mal 1:6 959
hold to the one, and *d* the other Mt 6:24 *2706*
Take heed that ye *d* not one of Mt 18:10 *2706*
hold to the one, and *d* the other Lk 16:13 *2706*
that eateth *d* him that eateth not Rom 14:3 *1848*
or *d* ye the church of God, and 1Cor 11:22 *2706*
Let no man therefore *d* him 1Cor 16:11 *1848*
D not prophesyings 1Th 5:20 *1848*
Let no man *d* thy youth 1Ti 4:12 *2706*
masters, let them not *d* them 1Ti 6:2 *2706*
Let no man *d* thee Titus 2:15 *4065*
d not thou the chastening of the Heb 12:5 *3643*
of uncleanness, and *d* government 2Pet 2:10 *2706*
d dominion, and speak evil of Jude 8 *114*

DESPISED
her mistress was *d* in her eyes Gen 16:4 7043
conceived, I was *d* in her eyes Gen 16:5 7043
thus Esau *d* his birthright Gen 25:34 959
even because they *d* my judgments Lev 26:43 3988
because that ye have *d* the LORD Num 11:20 3988
know the land which ye have *d* Num 14:31 3988
Because he hath *d* the word of the Num 15:31 959
this the people that thou hast *d* Judg 9:38 3988
And they *d* him, and brought him no 1Sa 10:27 959
and she *d* him in her heart 2Sa 6:16 959
Wherefore hast thou *d* the 2Sa 12:9 959
because thou hast *d* me, and hast 2Sa 12:10 959
the daughter of Zion hath *d* thee 2Kin 19:21 959
and she *d* him in her heart 1Chr 15:29 959
d his words, and misused his 2Chr 36:16 959
d us, and said, What is this thing Neh 2:19 959
for we are *d* Neh 4:4 939
d in the thought of him that is Job 12:5 937
Yea, young children *d* me Job 19:18 3988
of men, and *d* of the people Ps 22:6 959
For he hath not *d* nor abhorred Ps 22:24 959
to shame, because God hath *d* them Ps 53:5 3988
they *d* the pleasant land, they Ps 106:24 3988
I am small and *d* Ps 119:141 959
they *d* all my reproof Prov 1:30 5006
and my heart *d* reproof Prov 5:12 5006
is of a perverse heart shall be *d* Prov 12:8 937
He that is *d*, and hath a servant, Prov 12:9 7034
the poor man's wisdom is *d* Eccl 9:16 959
yea, I should not be *d* Song 8:1 937
d the word of the Holy One of Is 5:24 5006
he hath *d* the cities, he Is 33:8 3988
the daughter of Zion, hath *d* thee Is 37:22 959
He is *d* and rejected of men Is 53:3 959
he was *d*, and we esteemed him not Is 53:3 959
all they that *d* thee shall bow Is 60:14 5006
this man Coniah a *d* broken idol Jer 22:28 959
thus they have *d* my people Jer 33:24 5006
the heathen, and *d* among men Jer 49:15 959
hath *d* in the indignation of his Lam 2:6 5006
which hast *d* the oath in breaking Eze 16:59 959
made him king, whose oath he *d* Eze 17:16 959
Seeing he *d* the oath by breaking Eze 17:18 959
surely mine oath that he hath *d* Eze 17:19 959
they *d* my judgments, which if a Eze 20:13 3988
Because they *d* my judgments Eze 20:16 3988
but had *d* my statutes, and had Eze 20:24 3988
Thou hast *d* mine holy things, and Eze 22:8 959
are round about them, that *d* them Eze 28:24 7590
because they have *d* the law of Amos 2:4 3988
thou art greatly *d* Obad 2 959
For who hath *d* the day of small Zec 4:10 937
say, Wherein have we *d* thy name Mal 1:6 959
they were righteous, and *d* others Lk 18:9 *1848*
great goddess Diana should be *d* Acts 19:27
the world, and things which are *d* 1Cor 1:28 *1848*
ye are honourable, but we are *d* 1Cor 4:10 *820*
which was in my flesh ye *d* not Gal 4:14 *1848*
He that *d* Moses' law died without Heb 10:28 *114*
But ye have *d* the poor Jas 2:6 *818*

DESPISERS
Behold, ye *d*, and wonder, and Acts 13:41 *2707*
d of those that are good, 2Ti 3:3 *865*

DESPISEST
Or *d* thou the riches of his Rom 2:4 *2706*

DESPISETH
God is mighty, and *d* not any Job 36:5 3988
the poor, and *d* not his prisoners Ps 69:33 959
is void of wisdom *d* his neighbour Prov 11:12 936
Whoso *d* the word shall be Prov 13:13 936
is perverse in his ways *d* him Prov 14:2 959
He that *d* his neighbour sinneth Prov 14:21 936
A fool *d* his father's instruction Prov 15:5 5006
but a foolish man *d* his mother Prov 15:20 959
instruction *d* his own soul Prov 15:32 3988
but he that *d* his ways shall die Prov 19:16 959
d to obey his mother, the ravens Prov 30:17 936
he that *d* the gain of oppressions Is 33:15 3988
his Holy One, to him whom man *d* Is 49:7 960
he that *d* you *d* me Lk 10:16 *114*
d me *d* him that sent me Lk 10:16 *114*
He therefore that *d*, *d* not man 1Th 4:8 *114*

DESPISING
d the shame, and is set down at Heb 12:2 *2706*

DESPITE
thy *d* against the land of Israel Eze 25:6 7589
hath done *d* unto the Spirit of Heb 10:29 *1796*

DESPITEFUL
taken vengeance with a *d* heart Eze 25:15 7589
with *d* minds, to cast it out for Eze 36:5 7589
Backbiters, haters of God, *d* Rom 1:30 *5197*

DESPITEFULLY
and pray for them which *d* use you Mt 5:44 *1908*
and pray for them which *d* use you Lk 6:28 *1908*
with their rulers, to use them *d* Acts 14:5 *5195*

DESTITUTE
who hath not left *d* my master of Gen 24:27 5800
will regard the prayer of the *d* Ps 102:17 6199
leave not my soul *d* Ps 141:8 6168
is joy to him that is *d* of wisdom Prov 15:21 2638
the country shall be *d* of that Eze 32:15 8047
d of the truth, supposing that 1Ti 6:5 *650*
being *d*, afflicted, tormented Heb 11:37 *5302*
be naked, and *d* of daily food, Jas 2:15 *3007*

DESTROY
I will *d* man whom I have created Gen 6:7 4229
I will *d* them with the earth Gen 6:13 7843
to *d* all flesh, wherein is the Gen 6:17 7843
that I have made will I *d* from Gen 7:4 4229
more be a flood to *d* the earth Gen 9:11 7843
become a flood to *d* all flesh Gen 9:15 7843
Wilt thou also *d* the righteous Gen 18:23 5595
wilt thou also *d* and not spare the Gen 18:24 5595
wilt thou *d* all the city for lack Gen 18:28 7843
forty and five, I will not *d* it Gen 18:28 7843
I will not *d* it for twenty's sake Gen 18:31 7843
I will not *d* it for ten's sake Gen 18:32 7843
For we will *d* this place, because Gen 19:13 7843
and the LORD hath sent us to *d* it Gen 19:13 7843
for the LORD will *d* this city Gen 19:14 7843
to *d* the frogs from thee and thy Ex 8:9 3772
shall not be upon you to *d* you Ex 12:13 4889
my sword, my hand shall *d* them Ex 15:9 3423
will *d* all the people to whom Ex 23:27 2000
But ye shall *d* their altars Ex 34:13 5422
the same soul will I *d* from among Lev 23:30 6
d your cattle, and make you few in Lev 26:22 3772
I will *d* your high places, and cut Lev 26:30 8045
to *d* them utterly, and to break my Lev 26:44 3615
I will utterly *d* their cities Num 21:2 2763
d all the children of Sheth Num 24:17 6979
shall *d* him that remaineth of the Num 24:19 6
ye shall *d* all this people Num 32:15 7843
d all their pictures, and *d* Num 33:52 6
the hand of the Amorites, to *d* us Deut 1:27 8045
to *d* them from among the host, Deut 2:15 2000
not forsake thee, neither *d* thee Deut 4:31 7843
d thee from off the face of the Deut 6:15 8045
smite them, and utterly *d* them Deut 7:2 2763
against you, and *d* thee suddenly Deut 7:4 8045
ye shall *d* their altars, and break Deut 7:5 5422
hate him to their face, to *d* them Deut 7:10 6
shall *d* them with a mighty Deut 7:23 2000
thou shalt *d* their name from Deut 7:24 6
a consuming fire he shall *d* them Deut 9:3 8045
d them quickly, as the LORD hath Deut 9:3 6
Let me alone, that I may *d* them Deut 9:14 8045
was wroth against you to *d* you Deut 9:19 8045
the LORD had said he would *d* you Deut 9:25 8045
d not thy people and thine Deut 9:26 7843
and the LORD would not *d* thee Deut 10:10 7843
Ye shall utterly *d* all the places Deut 12:2 6
d the names of them out of that Deut 12:3 6
But thou shalt utterly *d* them Deut 20:17 2763
thou shalt not *d* the trees Deut 20:19 7843
not trees for meat, thou shalt *d* Deut 20:20 7843
will rejoice over you to *d* you Deut 28:63 6
he will *d* these nations from Deut 31:3 8045
shall *d* both the young man and the Deut 32:25 7921
and shall say, *D* them Deut 33:27 8045
the hand of the Amorites, to *d* us Josh 7:7 6
except ye *d* the accursed from Josh 7:12 8045
to *d* all the inhabitants of the Josh 9:24 8045
that he might *d* them utterly Josh 11:20 2763
favour, but that he might *d* them Josh 11:20 8045
to *d* the land wherein the Josh 22:33 7843
entered into the land to *d* it Judg 6:5 7843
do, Ye shall utterly *d* every male Judg 21:11 2763
utterly *d* all that they have, and 1Sa 15:3 2763
lest I *d* you with them 1Sa 15:6 622
good, and would not utterly *d* them 1Sa 15:9 2763
utterly *d* the sinners the 1Sa 15:18 2763
to *d* the city for my sake 1Sa 23:10 7843
that thou wilt not *d* my name out 1Sa 24:21 8045
David said to Abishai, *D* him not 1Sa 26:9 7843
people in to *d* the king thy lord 1Sa 26:15 7843
hand to *d* the LORD's anointed 2Sa 1:14 7843
and we will *d* the heir also 2Sa 14:7 8045
revengers of blood to *d* any more 2Sa 14:11 7843
lest they *d* my son 2Sa 14:11 8045
hand of the man that would *d* me 2Sa 14:16 8045
thou seekest to *d* a city and a 2Sa 20:19 4191
me, that I should swallow up or *d* 2Sa 20:20 7843
that I might *d* them that hate me 2Sa 22:41 6789
his hand upon Jerusalem to *d* it 2Sa 24:16 7843
also were not able utterly to *d* 1Kin 9:21 2763
to *d* it from off the face of the 1Kin 13:34 8045
Thus did Zimri *d* all the house of 1Kin 16:12 8045
Yet the LORD would not *d* Judah 2Kin 8:19 7843
might *d* the worshippers of Baal 2Kin 10:19 6
and Jacob, and would not *d* them 2Kin 13:23 7843
LORD against this place to *d* it 2Kin 18:25 7843
Go up against this land, and *d* it 2Kin 18:25 7843
sent them against Judah to *d* it 2Kin 24:2 6
an angel unto Jerusalem to *d* it 1Chr 21:15 7843
therefore I will not *d* them 2Chr 12:7 7843
he would not *d* him altogether 2Chr 12:12 7843
Seir, utterly to slay and *d* them 2Chr 20:23 8045
every one helped to *d* another 2Chr 20:23 4889
would not *d* the house of David 2Chr 21:7 7843
God hath determined to *d* thee 2Chr 25:16 7843
is with me, that he *d* thee not 2Chr 35:21 7843
name to dwell there *d* all kings Ezr 6:12 4049
to *d* this house of God which is Ezr 6:12 2255
to *d* all the Jews that were Est 3:6 8045
all the king's provinces, to *d* Est 3:13 8045
for the Jews, to *d* them Est 4:7 6
was given at Shushan to *d* them Est 4:8 8045

which he wrote to d the Jews Est 8:5 6
and to stand for their life, to d Est 8:11 8045
against the Jews to d them Est 9:24 6
to consume them, and to d them Est 9:24 6
him, to d him without cause Job 2:3 1104
that it would please God to d me Job 6:9 1792
If he d him from his place, then Job 8:18 1104
yet thou dost d me Job 10:8 1104
after my skin worms d this body Job 19:26 5362
Thou shalt d them that speak Ps 5:6 6
D thou them, O God Ps 5:10 816
that I might d them that hate me Ps 18:40 6789
fruit shalt thou d from the earth Ps 21:10 6
of his hands, he shall d them Ps 28:5 2040
that seek after my soul to d it Ps 40:14 5595
shall likewise d thee for ever Ps 52:5 5422
D, O Lord, and divide their Ps 55:9 1104
those that seek my soul, to d it Ps 63:9 7722
they that would d me, being mine Ps 69:4 6789
hearts, Let us d them together Ps 74:8 3238
I will early d all the wicked of Ps 101:8 6789
he said that he would d them Ps 106:23 8045
his wrath, lest he should d them Ps 106:23 7843
They did not d the nations Ps 106:34 8045
name of the LORD will I d them Ps 118:10 4135
name of the LORD I will d them Ps 118:11 4135
name of the LORD I will d them Ps 118:12 4135
wicked have waited for me to d me Ps 119:95 6
d all them that afflict my soul Ps 143:12 6
shoot out thine arrows, and d them Ps 144:6 1949
but all the wicked will he d Ps 145:20 8045
prosperity of fools shall d them Prov 1:32 6
of transgressors shall d them Prov 11:3 7703
The LORD will d the house of the Prov 15:25 5255
of the wicked shall d them Prov 21:7 1641
d the work of thine hands Eccl 5:6 2254
why shouldest thou d thyself Eccl 7:16 8074
to err, and d the way of thy paths Is 3:12 1104
but it is in his heart to d Is 10:7 8045
nor d in all my holy mountain Is 11:9 7843
the LORD shall utterly d the Is 11:15 2763
indignation, to d the whole land Is 13:5 2254
he shall d the sinners thereof Is 13:9 8045
I will d the counsel thereof Is 19:3 1104
to d the strong holds thereof Is 23:11 8045
he will d in this mountain the Is 25:7 1104
to d the poor with lying words Is 32:7 2254
LORD against this land to d it Is 36:10 7843
Go up against this land, and d it Is 36:10 7843
I will d and devour at once Is 42:14 5395
as if he were ready to d Is 51:13 7843
and I have created the waster to d Is 54:16 2254
cluster, and one saith, D it not Is 65:8 7843
sakes, that I may not d them all Is 65:8 7843
nor d in all my holy mountain Is 65:25 7843
out, and to pull down, and to d Jer 1:10 6
Go ye up upon her walls, and d Jer 5:10 7843
by night, and let us d her palaces Jer 6:5 7843
Let us d the tree with the fruit Jer 11:19 7843
d that nation, saith the LORD Jer 12:17 6
spare, nor have mercy, but d them Jer 13:14 7843
of the earth, to devour and d Jer 15:3 7843
my hand against thee, and d thee Jer 15:6 7843
I will d my people, since they Jer 15:7 6
d them with double destruction Jer 17:18 7665
up, and to pull down, and to d it Jer 18:7 6
Woe be unto the pastors that d Jer 23:1 6
about, and will utterly d them Jer 25:9 2763
down, and to throw down, and to d Jer 31:28 6
d this land, and shall cause to Jer 36:29 7843
I will d the city and the Jer 46:8 6
he shall d thy strong holds Jer 48:18 7843
they will d till they have enough Jer 49:9 7843
will d from thence the king and Jer 49:38 6
utterly d after them, saith the Jer 50:21 2763
her up as heaps, and d her utterly Jer 50:26 2763
d ye utterly all her host Jer 51:3 2763
is against Babylon, to d it Jer 51:11 7843
and with thee will I d kingdoms Jer 51:20 7843
The LORD hath purposed to d the Lam 2:8 7843
d them in anger from under the Lam 3:66 8045
and which I will send to d you Eze 5:16 7843
I will d your high places Eze 6:3 6
wilt thou d all the residue of Eze 9:8 7843
will d him from the midst of my Eze 14:9 8045
of brutish men, and skilful to d Eze 21:31 4889
to d souls, to get dishonest gain Eze 22:27 6
the land, that I should not d it Eze 22:30 7843
I will d thee Eze 25:7 8045
to d it for the old hatred Eze 25:15 4889
d the remnant of the sea coast Eze 25:16 9
they shall d the walls of Tyrus Eze 26:4 7843
walls, and d thy pleasant houses Eze 26:12 5422
and I will d thee, O covering Eze 28:16 6
shall be brought to d the land Eze 30:11 7843
I will also d the idols, and I Eze 30:13 6
I will d also all the beasts Eze 32:13 6
but I will d the fat and the Eze 34:16 8045
I saw when I came to d the city Eze 43:3 7843
commanded to d all the wise men Dan 2:12 7
to d the wise men of Babylon Dan 2:24 7
D not the wise men of Babylon Dan 2:24 7
Hew the tree down, and d it Dan 4:23 2255
consume and to d it unto the end Dan 7:26 7
he shall d wonderfully, and shall Dan 8:24 7843
shall d the mighty and the holy Dan 8:24 7843
heart, and by peace shall d many Dan 8:25 7843
that shall come shall d the city Dan 9:26 7843
portion of his meat shall d him Dan 11:26 7665
go forth with great fury to d Dan 11:44 8045
I will d her vines and her fig Hos 2:12 8074
the night, and I will d thy mother Hos 4:5 1820
I will not return to d Ephraim Hos 11:9 7843
I will d it from off the face of Amos 9:8 8045
not utterly d the house of Jacob Amos 9:8 8045
even d the wise men out of Edom Obad 8 6
it is polluted, it shall d you Mic 2:10 2254
of thee, and I will d thy chariots Mic 5:10 6
so will I d thy cities Mic 5:14 8045
Philistines, I will even d thee Zeph 2:5 6
against the north, and d Assyria Zeph 2:13 6
I will d the strength of the Hag 2:22 8045
that I will seek to d all the Zec 12:9 8045
he shall not d the fruits of your Mal 3:11 7843
seek the young child to d him Mt 2:13 622
not that I am come to d the law Mt 5:17 2647
I am not come to d, but to fulfil Mt 5:17 2647
him which is able to d both soul Mt 10:28 622
against him, how they might d him Mt 12:14 622
will miserably d those wicked men Mt 21:41 622
I am able to d the temple of God Mt 26:61 2647
should ask Barabbas, and d Jesus Mt 27:20 622
art thou come to d us Mk 1:24 622
against him, how they might d him Mk 3:6 622
and into the waters, to d him Mk 9:22 622
and sought how they might d him Mk 11:18 622
d the husbandmen, and will give Mk 12:9 622
I will d this temple that is made Mk 14:58 2647
art thou come to d us Lk 4:34 622
to save life, or to d it Lk 6:9 622
man is not come to d men's lives Lk 9:56 622
of the people sought to d him Lk 19:47 622
d these husbandmen, and shall give Lk 20:16 622
D this temple, and in three days I Jn 2:19 3089
for to steal, and to kill, and to d Jn 10:10 622
of Nazareth shall d this place Acts 6:14 2647
D not him with thy meat, for whom Rom 14:15 622
For meat d not the work of God Rom 14:20 2647
I will d the wisdom of the wise 1Cor 1:19 622
temple of God, him shall God d 1Cor 3:17 5351
but God shall d both it and them 1Cor 6:13 2673
shall d with the brightness of 2Th 2:8 2673
that through death he might d him Heb 2:14 2673
who is able to save and to d Jas 4:12 622
that he might d the works of the 1Jn 3:8 3089
d them which d the earth Rev 11:18 1311

DESTROYED

every living substance was d Gen 7:23 4229
they were d from the earth Gen 7:23 4229
where, before the LORD d Sodom Gen 13:10 7843
when God d the cities of the Gen 19:29 7843
and I shall be d, I and my house Gen 34:30 8045
thou not yet that Egypt is d Ex 10:7 6
LORD only, he shall be utterly d Ex 22:20 2763
and they utterly d them and their Num 21:3 2763
d you in Seir, even unto Hormah Deut 1:44 3807
when they had d them from before Deut 2:12 8045
but the LORD d them before them Deut 2:21 8045
when he d the Horims from before Deut 2:22 8045
d them, and dwelt in their stead Deut 2:23 8045
that time, and utterly d the men Deut 2:34 2763
And we utterly d them, as we did Deut 3:6 2763
God hath d them from among you Deut 4:3 8045
upon it, but shall utterly be d Deut 4:26 8045
hide themselves from thee, be d Deut 7:20 6
destruction, until they be d Deut 7:23 8045
thee, until thou have d them Deut 7:24 8045
was angry with you to have d you Deut 9:8 8045
angry with Aaron to have d him Deut 9:20 8045
how the LORD hath d them unto Deut 11:4 6
that they be d from before thee Deut 12:30 8045
unto for to do, until thou be d Deut 28:20 8045
down upon thee, until thou be d Deut 28:24 8045
and overtake thee, till thou be d Deut 28:45 8045
thy neck, until he have d thee Deut 28:48 8045
of thy land, until thou be d Deut 28:51 8045
thy sheep, until he have d thee Deut 28:51 6
bring upon thee, until thou be d Deut 28:61 8045
unto the land of them, whom he d Deut 31:4 8045
Sihon and Og, whom ye utterly d Josh 2:10 2763
they utterly d all that was in Josh 6:21 2763
until he had utterly d all the Josh 8:26 2763
had taken Ai, and had utterly d it Josh 10:1 2763
and the king thereof he utterly d Josh 10:28 2763
therein he utterly d that day Josh 10:35 2763
but d it utterly, and all the Josh 10:37 2763
utterly d all the souls that were Josh 10:39 2763
but utterly d all that breathed Josh 10:40 2763
the sword, and he utterly d them Josh 11:12 2763
the sword, until they had d them Josh 11:14 8045
Joshua d them utterly with their Josh 11:21 2763
until he have d you from off this Josh 23:15 8045
and I d them from before you Josh 24:8 8045
Zephath, and utterly d it Judg 1:17 2763
until they had d Jabin king of Judg 4:24 3772
d the increase of the earth, till Judg 6:4 7843
d down to the ground of the Judg 20:21 7843
d down to the ground of the Judg 20:25 7843
the children of Israel d of the Judg 20:35 7843
they d in the midst of them Judg 20:42 7843
the women are d out of Benjamin Judg 21:16 8045
a tribe be not d out of Israel Judg 21:17 4229
he d them, and smote them with 1Sa 5:6 8074
utterly d all the people with the 1Sa 15:8 2763
and refuse, that they d utterly 1Sa 15:9 2763
and the rest we have utterly d 1Sa 15:15 2763
have utterly d the Amalekites 1Sa 15:20 2763
which should have been utterly d 1Sa 15:21 2764
they d the children of Ammon, and 2Sa 11:1 7843
be d from remaining in any of the 2Sa 21:5 8045
pursued mine enemies, and d them 2Sa 22:38 8045
to the angel that d the people 2Sa 24:16 7843
Asa d her idol, and burnt it by 1Kin 15:13 3772
that breathed, until he had d him 1Kin 15:29 8045
in Samaria, till he had d him 2Kin 10:17 8045
Thus Jehu d Baal out of Israel 2Kin 10:28 8045
she arose and d all the seed royal 2Kin 11:1 6
for the king of Syria had d them 2Kin 13:7 6
them which my fathers have d 2Kin 19:12 843
of Assyria have d the nations 2Kin 19:17 2717
therefore they have d them 2Kin 19:18 6
which Hezekiah his father had d 2Kin 21:3 6
d before the children of Israel 2Kin 21:9 8045
d them utterly unto this day, and 1Chr 4:41 2763
the land, whom God d before them 1Chr 5:25 8045
And Joab smote Rabbah, and d it 1Chr 20:1 2040
months to be d before thy foes 1Chr 21:12 5595
evil, and said to the angel that d 1Chr 21:15 7843
for they were d before the LORD 2Chr 14:13 7665
And nation was d of nation 2Chr 15:6 3807
turned from them, and d them not 2Chr 20:10 8045
d all the seed royal of the house 2Chr 22:10 1696
d all the princes of the people 2Chr 24:23 7843
until they had utterly d them all 2Chr 31:1 3615
nations that my fathers utterly d 2Chr 32:14 2763
whom the LORD had d before the 2Chr 33:9 8045
which the kings of Judah had d 2Chr 34:11 7843
d all the goodly vessels thereof 2Chr 36:19 7843
for which cause was this city d Ezr 4:15 2718
who d this house, and carried the Ezr 5:12 5642
it be written that they may be d Est 3:9 6
and thy father's house shall be d Est 4:14 6
are sold, I and my people, to be d Est 7:4 8045
Jews slew and d five hundred men Est 9:6 6
d five hundred men in Shushan the Est 9:12 6
They are d from morning to Job 4:20 3807
He hath d me on every side, and I Job 19:10 5422
in the night, so that they are d Job 34:25 1792
thou hast d the wicked, thou hast Ps 9:5 6
and thou hast d cities Ps 9:6 5428
If the foundations be d, what can Ps 11:3 2040
transgressors shall be d together Ps 37:38 8045
thou hast d all them that go a Ps 73:27 6789
their iniquity, and d them not Ps 78:38 7843
and frogs, which d them Ps 78:45 7843
He d their vines with hail, and Ps 78:47 2026
is that they shall be d for ever Ps 92:7 8045
of Babylon, who art to be d Ps 137:8 7703
despiseth the word shall be d Prov 13:13 2254
a companion of fools shall be d Prov 13:20 7321
is that is d for want of judgment Prov 13:23 5595
his neck, shall suddenly be d Prov 29:1 7665
they that are led of them are d Is 9:16 1104
the yoke shall be d because of Is 10:27 2254
and d the cities thereof Is 14:17 2040
because thou hast d thy land Is 14:20 7843
d them, and made all their memory Is 26:14 8045
he hath utterly d them, he hath Is 34:2 2763
them which my fathers have d Is 37:12 7843
therefore they have d them Is 37:19 6
been cut off nor d from before me Is 48:19 8045
Many pastors have d my vineyard Jer 12:10 7843
for all thy lovers are d Jer 22:20 7665
Moab is d Jer 48:4 7665
perish, and the plain shall be d Jer 48:8 8045
Moab shall be d from being a Jer 48:42 8045
Babylon is suddenly fallen and d Jer 51:8 7665
d out of her the great voice Jer 51:55 6
he hath d his strong holds, and Lam 2:5 7843
he hath d his places of the Lam 2:6 7843
he hath d and broken her bars Lam 2:9 6
and say to thee, How art thou d Eze 26:17 6
like the d in the midst of the Eze 27:32 1822
when all her helpers shall be d Eze 30:8 7665
the multitude thereof shall be d Eze 32:12 8045
a kingdom, which shall never be d Dan 2:44 2255
kingdom that which shall not be d Dan 6:26 2255
beast was slain, and his body d Dan 7:11 7
kingdom that which shall not be d Dan 7:14 2255
but within few days he shall be d Dan 11:20 7665
My people are d for lack of Hos 4:6 1820
the sin of Israel, shall be d Hos 10:8 8045
O Israel, thou hast d thyself Hos 13:9 7843
Yet d I the Amorite before them Amos 2:9 8045
yet I d his fruit from above, and Amos 2:9 8045
their cities are d, so that there Zeph 3:6 6658
d those murderers, and burned up Mt 22:7 622
and the flood came, and d them all Lk 17:27 622
from heaven, and d them all Lk 17:29 622
shall be d from among the people Acts 3:23 1842
Is not this he that d them which Acts 9:21 4199
when he had d seven nations in Acts 13:19 2507
and her magnificence should be d Acts 19:27 2507
that the body of sin might be d Rom 6:6 2673
tempted, and were d of serpents 1Cor 10:9 622
and were d of the destroyer 1Cor 10:10 622
enemy that shall be d is death 1Cor 15:26 2673
cast down, but not d 2Cor 4:9 622
the faith which once he d Gal 1:23 4199
build again the things which I d Gal 2:18 2647
lest he that d the firstborn Heb 11:28 3645
beasts, made to be taken and d 2Pet 2:12 5356
afterward d them that believed Jude 5 622
third part of the ships were d Rev 8:9 1311

DESTROYER

will not suffer the d to come in Ex 12:23 7843
the d of our country, which slew Judg 16:24 2717
in prosperity the d shall come Job 15:21 7703
kept me from the paths of the d Ps 17:4 6530
the same is the companion of a d Prov 28:24 7843
the d of the Gentiles is on his Jer 4:7 7843
and were destroyed of the d 1Cor 10:10 3644

DESTROYERS

the grave, and his life to the d Job 33:22 4191
thy d and they that made thee Is 49:17 2040
And I will prepare d against thee Jer 22:7 7843
O ye d of mine heritage, because Jer 50:11 8154

DESTROYEST
and thou *d* the hope of man ... Job 14:19 6
the LORD, which *d* all the earth ... Jer 51:25 7843
Thou that *d* the temple, and ... Mt 27:40 *2647*
thou that *d* the temple, and ... Mk 15:29 *2647*

DESTROYETH
which the LORD *d* before your face ... Deut 8:20 6
He *d* the perfect and the wicked ... Job 9:22 3615
increaseth the nations, and *d* them ... Job 12:23 6
he that doeth it *d* his own soul ... Prov 6:32 7843
with his mouth *d* his neighbour ... Prov 11:9 7843
thy ways to that which *d* kings ... Prov 31:3 4229
and a gift *d* the heart ... Eccl 7:7 6
but one sinner *d* much good ... Eccl 9:18 6

DESTROYING
of Heshbon, utterly *d* the men ... Deut 3:6 2763
d it utterly, and all that is ... Deut 13:15 2763
edge of the sword, utterly *d* them ... Josh 11:11 2763
to all lands, by *d* them utterly ... 2Kin 19:11 2763
land, and the angel of the LORD *d* ... 1Chr 21:12 7843
and as he was *d*, the LORD beheld, ... 1Chr 21:15 7843
a *d* storm, as a flood of mighty ... Is 28:2 6986
to all lands by *d* them utterly ... Is 37:11 2763
your prophets, like a *d* lion ... Jer 2:30 7843
that rise up against me, a *d* wind ... Jer 51:1 7843
O *d* mountain, saith the LORD, ... Jer 51:25 4889
not withdrawn his hand from *d* ... Lam 2:8 1104
man with his *d* weapon in his hand ... Eze 9:1 4892
mine eye spared them from *d* them ... Eze 20:17 7843

DESTRUCTION
destroy them with a mighty *d* ... Deut 7:23 4103
burning heat, and with bitter *d* ... Deut 32:24 6986
the city with a very great *d* ... 1Sa 5:9 4103
for there was a deadly *d* ... 1Sa 5:11 4103
a man whom I appointed to utter *d* ... 1Kin 20:42 2764
the death of his father to his *d* ... 2Chr 22:4 4889
the *d* of Ahaziah was of God by ... 2Chr 22:7 8395
his heart was lifted up to his *d* ... 2Chr 26:16 7843
endure to see the *d* of my kindred ... Est 8:6 13
of the sword, and slaughter, and *d* ... Est 9:5 12
be afraid of *d* when it cometh ... Job 5:21 7701
At *d* and famine thou shalt laugh ... Job 5:22 7701
d shall be ready at his side ... Job 18:12 343
how oft cometh their *d* upon them ... Job 21:17 343
His eyes shall see his *d*, and he ... Job 21:20 3589
is reserved to the day of *d* ... Job 21:30 343
before him, and *d* hath no covering ... Job 26:6 11
D and death say, We have heard the ... Job 28:22 11
up against me the ways of their *d* ... Job 30:12 343
grave, though they cry in his *d* ... Job 30:24 6365
Is not *d* to the wicked ... Job 31:3 343
it is a fire that consumeth to *d* ... Job 31:12 11
For *d* from God was a terror to me ... Job 31:23 343
at the *d* of him that hated me ... Job 31:29 6365
Let *d* come upon him at unawares ... Ps 35:8 7722
into that very *d* let him fall ... Ps 35:8 7722
bring them down into the pit of *d* ... Ps 55:23 7845
thou castedst them down into *d* ... Ps 73:18 4876
or thy faithfulness in *d* ... Ps 88:11 11
Thou turnest man to *d* ... Ps 90:3 1793
nor for the *d* that wasteth at ... Ps 91:6 6986
Who redeemeth thy life from *d* ... Ps 103:4 7845
your *d* cometh as a whirlwind ... Prov 1:27 343
mouth of the foolish is near *d* ... Prov 10:14 4288
the *d* of the poor is their ... Prov 10:15 4288
but *d* shall be to the workers of ... Prov 10:29 4288
wide his lips shall have *d* ... Prov 13:3 4288
of people is the *d* of the prince ... Prov 14:28 4288
Hell and *d* are before the LORD ... Prov 15:11 11
Pride goeth before *d*, and an ... Prov 16:18 7667
that exalteth his gate seeketh *d* ... Prov 17:19 7667
A fool's mouth is his *d*, and his ... Prov 18:7 4288
Before *d* the heart of man is ... Prov 18:12 7667
but *d* shall be to the workers of ... Prov 21:15 4288
For their heart studieth *d* ... Prov 24:2 7701
Hell and *d* are never full ... Prov 27:20 10
of all such as are appointed to *d* ... Prov 31:8 2475
the *d* of the transgressors and of ... Is 1:28 7667
cease, and mine anger in their *d* ... Is 10:25 8399
come as a *d* from the Almighty ... Is 13:6 7701
will sweep it with the besom of *d* ... Is 14:23 8045
they shall raise up a cry of *d* ... Is 15:5 7667
shall be called, The city of *d* ... Is 19:18 2041
and the gate is smitten with *d* ... Is 24:12 7591
places, and the land of thy *d* ... Is 49:19 2035
desolation, and *d*, and the famine, ... Is 51:19 7667
wasting and *d* are in their paths ... Is 59:7 7667
wasting nor *d* within thy borders ... Is 60:18 7667
evil from the north, and a great *d* ... Jer 4:6 7667
D upon *d* is cried ... Jer 4:20 7667
out of the north, and great *d* ... Jer 6:1 7667
and destroy them with double *d* ... Jer 17:18 7670
a very fair heifer, but *d* cometh ... Jer 46:20 7171
Horonaim, spoiling and great *d* ... Jer 48:3 7667
the enemies have heard a cry of *d* ... Jer 48:5 7667
is in the land, and of great *d* ... Jer 50:22 7667
great *d* from the land of the ... Jer 51:54 7667
for the *d* of the daughter of my ... Lam 2:11 7667
is come upon us, desolation and *d* ... Lam 3:47 7667
d of the daughter of my people ... Lam 3:48 7667
they were their meat in the *d* of ... Lam 4:10 7667
which shall be for their *d* ... Eze 5:16 4889
D cometh; and they shall seek ... Eze 7:25 7089
bring thy *d* among the nations ... Eze 32:9 7667
fled from me: *d* unto them ... Hos 7:13 7701
lo, they are gone because of *d* ... Hos 9:6 7701
O grave, I will be thy *d* ... Hos 13:14 6987
as a *d* from the Almighty shall it ... Joel 1:15 7701
of Judah in the day of their *d* ... Obad 12 6
destroy you, even with a sore *d* ... Mic 2:10 2256
and there shall be no more utter *d* ... Zec 14:11 2764
is the way, that leadeth to *d* ... Mt 7:13 *684*
D and misery are in their ways ... Rom 3:16 *4938*
the vessels of wrath fitted to *d* ... Rom 9:22 *684*
unto Satan for the *d* of the flesh ... 1Cor 5:5 *3639*
edification, and not for your *d* ... 2Cor 10:8 *2506*
me to edification, and not to *d* ... 2Cor 13:10 *2506*
Whose end is *d*, whose God is ... Phil 3:19 *684*
then sudden *d* cometh upon them, ... 1Th 5:3 *3639*
be punished with everlasting *d* ... 2Th 1:9 *3639*
lusts, which drown men in *d* ... 1Ti 6:9 *3639*
and bring upon themselves swift *d* ... 2Pet 2:1 *684*
scriptures, unto their own *d* ... 2Pet 3:16 *684*

DESTRUCTIONS
d are come to a perpetual end ... Ps 9:6 2723
rescue my soul from their *d* ... Ps 35:17 7722
and delivered them from their *d* ... Ps 107:20 7825

DETAIN
LORD, I pray thee, let us *d* thee ... Judg 13:15 6113
unto Manoah, Though thou *d* me ... Judg 13:16 6113

DETAINED
there that day, *d* before the LORD ... 1Sa 21:7 6113

DETERMINATE
being delivered by the *d* counsel ... Acts 2:23 *3724*

DETERMINATION
for my *d* is to gather the nations ... Zeph 3:8 4941

DETERMINE
and he shall pay as the judges *d* ... Ex 21:22

DETERMINED
be sure that evil is *d* by him ... 1Sa 20:7 3615
d by my father to come upon thee ... 1Sa 20:9 3615
Jonathan knew that it was *d* of ... 1Sa 20:33 3615
for evil is *d* against our master, ... 1Sa 25:17 3615
of Absalom this hath been *d* from ... 2Sa 13:32 7760
Solomon *d* to build an house for ... 2Chr 2:1 559
that God hath *d* to destroy thee ... 2Chr 25:16 3289
evil *d* against him by the king ... Est 7:7 3615
Seeing his days are *d*, the number ... Job 14:5 2782
shall make a consumption, even *d* ... Is 10:23 2782
hosts, which he hath *d* against it ... Is 19:17 3289
even *d* upon the whole earth ... Is 28:22 2782
weeks are *d* upon thy people ... Dan 9:24 2852
end of the war desolations are *d* ... Dan 9:26 2782
that *d* shall be poured upon the ... Dan 9:27 2782
for that that is *d* shall be done ... Dan 11:36 2782
the Son of man goeth, as it was *d* ... Lk 22:22 *3724*
when he was *d* to let him go ... Acts 3:13 *2919*
thy counsel *d* before to be done ... Acts 4:28 *4309*
d to send relief unto the ... Acts 11:29 *3724*
they *d* that Paul and Barnabas, and ... Acts 15:2 *5021*
Barnabas *d* to take with them John ... Acts 15:37 *1011*
hath *d* the times before appointed ... Acts 17:26 *3724*
it shall be *d* in a lawful ... Acts 19:39 *1956*
For Paul had *d* to sail by Ephesus ... Acts 20:16 *2919*
to Augustus, I have *d* to send him ... Acts 25:25 *2919*
when it was *d* that we should sail ... Acts 27:1 *2919*
For I *d* not to know any thing ... 1Cor 2:2 *2919*
But I *d* this with myself, that I ... 2Cor 2:1 *2919*
for I have *d* there to winter ... Titus 3:12 *2919*

DETEST
but thou shalt utterly *d* it ... Deut 7:26 8262

DETESTABLE
with the carcases of their *d* ... Jer 16:18 8251
sanctuary with all thy *d* things ... Eze 5:11 8251
of their *d* things therein ... Eze 7:20 8251
away all the *d* things thereof ... Eze 11:18 8251
after the heart of their *d* things ... Eze 11:21 8251
idols, nor with their *d* things ... Eze 37:23 8251

DEUEL (de-u'-el) See REUEL. *Father of Eliasaph.*
Eliasaph the son of *D* ... Num 1:14 1845
sixth day Eliasaph the son of *D* ... Num 7:42 1845
offering of Eliasaph the son of *D* ... Num 7:47 1845
of Gad was Eliasaph the son of *D* ... Num 10:20 1845

DEVICE
to find out every *d* which shall ... 2Chr 2:14 4284
his *d* that he had devised against ... Est 8:3 4284
by letters that his wicked *d* ... Est 9:25 4284
they imagined a mischievous *d* ... Ps 21:11
further not his wicked *d* ... Ps 140:8
for there is no work, nor *d* ... Eccl 9:10 2808
you, and devise a *d* against you ... Jer 18:11 4284
for his *d* is against Babylon, to ... Jer 51:11 4209
their *d* against me all the day ... Lam 3:62 1902
stone, graven by art and man's *d* ... Acts 17:29 *1761*

DEVICES
disappointeth the *d* of the crafty ... Job 5:12 4284
the *d* which ye wrongfully imagine ... Job 21:27 4209
in the *d* that they have imagined ... Ps 10:2 4209
he maketh the *d* of the people of ... Ps 33:10 4284
man who bringeth wicked *d* to pass ... Ps 37:7 4209
and be filled with their own *d* ... Prov 1:31 4156
a man of wicked *d* will he condemn ... Prov 12:2 4209
and a man of wicked *d* is hated ... Prov 14:17 4209
There are many *d* in a man's heart ... Prov 19:21 4284
he deviseth wicked *d* to destroy ... Is 32:7 2154
they had devised *d* against me ... Jer 11:19 4284
but we will walk after our own *d* ... Jer 18:12 4284
let us devise *d* against Jeremiah ... Jer 18:18 4284
he shall forecast his *d* against ... Dan 11:24 4284
they shall forecast *d* against him ... Dan 11:25 4284
for we are not ignorant of his *d* ... 2Cor 2:11 *3540*

DEVIL
wilderness to be tempted of the *d* ... Mt 4:1 *1228*
Then the *d* taketh him up into the ... Mt 4:5 *1228*
the *d* taketh him up into an ... Mt 4:8 *1228*
Then the *d* leaveth him, and ... Mt 4:11 *1228*
him a dumb man possessed with a *d* ... Mt 9:32 *1139*
when the *d* was cast out, the dumb ... Mt 9:33 *1140*
and they say, He hath a *d* ... Mt 11:18 *1140*
unto him one possessed with a *d* ... Mt 12:22 *1139*
enemy that sowed them is the *d* ... Mt 13:39 *1228*
is grievously vexed with a *d* ... Mt 15:22 *1139*
And Jesus rebuked the *d* ... Mt 17:18 *1140*
fire, prepared for the *d* and his ... Mt 25:41 *1228*
him that was possessed with the *d* ... Mk 5:15 *1139*
him that was possessed with the *d* ... Mk 5:16 *1139*
the *d* prayed him that he might be ... Mk 5:18 *1139*
forth the *d* out of her daughter ... Mk 7:26 *1140*
the *d* is gone out of thy daughter ... Mk 7:29 *1140*
house, she found the *d* gone out ... Mk 7:30 *1140*
Being forty days tempted of the *d* ... Lk 4:2 *1228*
the *d* said unto him, If thou be ... Lk 4:3 *1228*
And the *d*, taking him up into an ... Lk 4:5 *1228*
the *d* said unto him, All this ... Lk 4:6 *1228*
when the *d* had ended all the ... Lk 4:13 *1228*
had a spirit of an unclean *d* ... Lk 4:33 *1140*
when the *d* had thrown him in the ... Lk 4:35 *1140*
and ye say, He hath a *d* ... Lk 7:33 *1140*
then cometh the *d*, and taketh away ... Lk 8:12 *1228*
was driven of the *d* into the ... Lk 8:29 *1142*
the *d* threw him down, and tare him ... Lk 9:42 *1140*
And he was casting out a *d* ... Lk 11:14 *1140*
when the *d* was gone out, the dumb ... Lk 11:14 *1140*
you twelve, and one of you is a *d* ... Jn 6:70 *1228*
answered and said, Thou hast a *d* ... Jn 7:20 *1140*
Ye are of your father the *d* ... Jn 8:44 *1228*
thou art a Samaritan, and hast a *d* ... Jn 8:48 *1140*
Jesus answered, I have not a *d* ... Jn 8:49 *1140*
Now we know that thou hast a *d* ... Jn 8:52 *1140*
And many of them said, He hath a *d* ... Jn 10:20 *1140*
the words of him that hath a *d* ... Jn 10:21 *1139*
Can a *d* open the eyes of the ... Jn 10:21 *1140*
the *d* having now put into the ... Jn 13:2 *1228*
all that were oppressed of the *d* ... Acts 10:38 *1228*
all mischief, thou child of the *d* ... Acts 13:10 *1228*
Neither give place to the *d* ... Eph 4:27 *1228*
stand against the wiles of the *d* ... Eph 6:11 *1228*
into the condemnation of the *d* ... 1Ti 3:6 *1228*
reproach and the snare of the *d* ... 1Ti 3:7 *1228*
out of the snare of the *d* ... 2Ti 2:26 *1228*
power of death, that is, the *d* ... Heb 2:14 *1228*
Resist the *d*, and he will flee ... Jas 4:7 *1228*
because your adversary the *d* ... 1Pet 5:8 *1228*
that committeth sin is of the *d* ... 1Jn 3:8 *1228*
for the *d* sinneth from the ... 1Jn 3:8 *1228*
might destroy the works of the *d* ... 1Jn 3:8 *1228*
and the children of the *d* ... 1Jn 3:10 *1228*
when contending with the *d* he ... Jude 9 *1228*
the *d* shall cast some of you into ... Rev 2:10 *1228*
that old serpent, called the *D* ... Rev 12:9 *1228*
for the *d* is come down unto you, ... Rev 12:12 *1228*
that old serpent, which is the *D* ... Rev 20:2 *1228*
the *d* that deceived them was cast ... Rev 20:10 *1228*

DEVILISH
above, but is earthly, sensual, *d* ... Jas 3:15 *1141*

DEVILS
offer their sacrifices unto *d* ... Lev 17:7 8163
They sacrificed unto *d*, not to ... Deut 32:17 7700
for the high places, and for the *d* ... 2Chr 11:15 8163
sons and their daughters unto *d* ... Ps 106:37 7700
those which were possessed with *d* ... Mt 4:24 *1139*
and in thy name have cast out *d* ... Mt 7:22 *1140*
many that were possessed with *d* ... Mt 8:16 *1139*
met him two possessed with *d* ... Mt 8:28 *1139*
So the *d* besought him, saying, If ... Mt 8:31 *1142*
to the possessed of the *d* ... Mt 8:33 *1139*
He casteth out *d* through the ... Mt 9:34 *1140*
through the prince of the *d* ... Mt 9:34 *1140*
raise the dead, cast out *d* ... Mt 10:8 *1140*
This fellow doth not cast out *d* ... Mt 12:24 *1140*
by Beelzebub the prince of the *d* ... Mt 12:24 *1140*
And if I by Beelzebub cast out *d* ... Mt 12:27 *1140*
But if I cast out *d* by the Spirit ... Mt 12:28 *1140*
them that were possessed with *d* ... Mk 1:32 *1139*
diseases, and cast out many *d* ... Mk 1:34 *1140*
and suffered not the *d* to speak ... Mk 1:34 *1140*
all Galilee, and cast out *d* ... Mk 1:39 *1140*
heal sicknesses, and to cast out *d* ... Mk 3:15 *1140*
of the *d* casteth he out *d* ... Mk 3:22 *1140*
all the *d* besought him, saying, ... Mk 5:12 *1142*
And they cast out many *d*, and ... Mk 6:13 *1140*
saw one casting out *d* in thy name ... Mk 9:38 *1140*
out of whom he had cast seven *d* ... Mk 16:9 *1140*
In my name shall they cast out *d* ... Mk 16:17 *1140*
d also came out of many, crying ... Lk 4:41 *1140*
out of whom went seven *d* ... Lk 8:2 *1140*
man, which had *d* long time ... Lk 8:27 *1140*
because many *d* were entered into ... Lk 8:30 *1140*
Then went the *d* out of the man, ... Lk 8:33 *1140*
out of whom the *d* were departed ... Lk 8:35 *1140*
was possessed of the *d* was healed ... Lk 8:36 *1139*
Now the man out of whom the *d* ... Lk 8:38 *1140*
power and authority over all *d* ... Lk 9:1 *1140*
saw one casting out *d* in thy name ... Lk 9:49 *1140*
even the *d* are subject unto us ... Lk 10:17 *1140*
said, He casteth out *d* through ... Lk 11:15 *1140*
Beelzebub the chief of the *d* ... Lk 11:15 *1140*
I cast out *d* through Beelzebub ... Lk 11:18 *1140*
And if I by Beelzebub cast out *d* ... Lk 11:19 *1140*
with the finger of God cast out *d* ... Lk 11:20 *1140*
that fox, Behold, I cast out *d* ... Lk 13:32 *1140*
sacrifice, they sacrifice to *d* ... 1Cor 10:20 *1140*
ye should have fellowship with *d* ... 1Cor 10:20 *1140*
cup of the Lord, and the cup of *d* ... 1Cor 10:21 *1140*
table, and of the table of *d* ... 1Cor 10:21 *1140*
spirits, and doctrines of *d* ... 1Ti 4:1 *1140*
the *d* also believe, and tremble ... Jas 2:19 *1140*
that they should not worship *d* ... Rev 9:20 *1140*
For they are the spirits of *d* ... Rev 16:14 *1142*
and is become the habitation of *d* ... Rev 18:2 *1142*

DEVISE
To *d* cunning works, to work in Ex 31:4 2803
to *d* curious works, to work in Ex 35:32 2803
and of those that *d* cunning work Ex 35:35 2803
yet doth he *d* means, that his 2Sa 14:14 2803
to confusion that *d* my hurt Ps 35:4 2803
but they *d* deceitful matters Ps 35:20 2803
against me do they *d* my hurt Ps 41:7 2803
D not evil against thy neighbour, Prov 3:29 2790
Do they not err that *d* evil Prov 14:22 2790
shall be to them that *d* good Prov 14:22 2790
his eyes to *d* froward things Prov 16:30 2803
you, and *d* a device against you Jer 18:11 2803
let us *d* devices against Jeremiah Jer 18:18 2803
these are the men that *d* mischief Eze 11:2 2803
Woe to them that *d* iniquity Mic 2:1 2803
this family do I *d* an evil Mic 2:3 2803

DEVISED
that *d* against us that we should 2Sa 21:5 1819
which he had *d* of his own heart 1Kin 12:33 908
that he had *d* against the Jews Est 8:3 2803
d by Haman the son of Hammedatha Est 8:5 4284
had *d* against the Jews to destroy Est 9:24 2803
which he *d* against the Jews, Est 9:25 2803
they *d* to take away my life Ps 31:13 2161
they had *d* devices against me Jer 11:19 2803
they have *d* evil against it Jer 48:2 2803
for the LORD hath both *d* and done Jer 51:12 2161
hath done that which he had *d* Lam 2:17 2161
not followed cunningly *d* fables 2Pet 1:16 *4679*

DEVISETH
He *d* mischief upon his bed Ps 36:4 2803
Thy tongue *d* mischiefs Ps 52:2 2803
he *d* mischief continually Prov 6:14 2790
An heart that *d* wicked Prov 6:18 2790
A man's heart *d* his way Prov 16:9 2803
He that *d* to do evil shall be Prov 24:8 2803
he *d* wicked devices to destroy Is 32:7 3289
But the liberal *d* liberal things Is 32:8 3289

DEVOTE
that a man shall *d* unto the LORD Lev 27:28 2763

DEVOTED
holy unto the LORD, as a field *d* Lev 27:21 2764
Notwithstanding no *d* thing Lev 27:28 2764
every *d* thing is most holy unto Lev 27:28 2764
None *d*, which shall be Lev 27:29 2764
which shall be *d* of men Lev 27:29 2763
Every thing *d* in Israel shall be Num 18:14 2764
thy servant, who is *d* to thy fear Ps 119:38

DEVOTIONS
as I passed by, and beheld your *d* Acts 17:23 *4574*

DEVOUR
the morning he shall *d* the prey Gen 49:27 398
blood, and my sword shall *d* flesh Deut 32:42 398
and *d* the cedars of Lebanon Judg 9:15 398
d the men of Shechem, and the Judg 9:20 398
house of Millo, and *d* Abimelech Judg 9:20 398
said, Shall the sword *d* for ever 2Sa 2:26 398
command the locusts to *d* the land 2Chr 7:13 398
It shall *d* the strength of his Job 18:13 398
of death shall *d* his strength Job 18:13 398
wrath, and the fire shall *d* them Ps 21:9 398
a fire shall *d* before him Ps 50:3 398
wild beast of the field doth *d* it Ps 80:13 7462
to *d* the poor from off the earth, Prov 30:14 398
strangers *d* it in your presence, Is 1:7 398
they shall *d* Israel with open Is 9:12 398
it shall *d* the briers and thorns, Is 9:18 398
d his thorns and his briers in one Is 10:17 398
of thine enemies shall *d* them Is 26:11 398
not of a mean man, shall *d* him Is 31:8 398
your breath, as fire, shall *d* you Is 33:11 398
I will destroy and *d* at once Is 42:14 7602
ye beasts of the field, come to *d* Is 56:9 398
all that *d* him shall offend Jer 2:3 398
people wood, and it shall *d* them Jer 5:14 398
beasts of the field, come to *d* Jer 12:9 402
d from the one end of the land Jer 12:12 398
and the beasts of the earth, to *d* Jer 15:3 398
it shall *d* the palaces of Jer 17:27 398
it shall *d* all things round about Jer 21:14 398
that *d* thee shall be devoured Jer 30:16 398
and the sword shall *d*, and it shall Jer 46:10 398
sword shall *d* round about thee Jer 46:14 398
shall *d* the corner of Moab, and Jer 48:45 398
it shall *d* all round about him Jer 50:32 398
famine and pestilence shall *d* him Eze 7:15 398
and another fire shall *d* them Eze 15:7 398
it shall *d* every green tree in Eze 20:47 398
them through the fire, to *d* them Eze 23:37 402
midst of thee, it shall *d* thee Eze 28:18 398
the beast of the land *d* them Eze 34:28 398
thou shalt *d* men no more, neither Eze 36:14 398
thus unto it, Arise, *d* much flesh Dan 7:5 399
shall *d* the whole earth, and shall Dan 7:23 399
now shall a month *d* them with Hos 5:7 398
it shall *d* the palaces thereof Hos 8:14 398
d them, because of their own Hos 11:6 398
there will I *d* them like a lion Hos 13:8 398
which shall *d* the palaces of Amos 1:4 398
which shall *d* the palaces thereof Amos 1:7 398
which shall *d* the palaces thereof Amos 1:10 398
which shall *d* the palaces of Amos 1:12 398
it shall *d* the palaces thereof, Amos 1:14 398
it shall *d* the palaces of Kirioth Amos 2:2 398
it shall *d* the palaces of Amos 2:5 398
d it, and there be none to quench Amos 5:6 398
shall kindle in them, and *d* them Obad 18 398
the sword shall *d* thy young lions Nah 2:13 398
the fire shall *d* thy bars Nah 3:13 398
There shall the fire *d* thee Nah 3:15 398
was as to *d* the poor secretly Hab 3:14 398
and they shall *d*, and subdue with Zec 9:15 398
that the fire may *d* thy cedars Zec 11:1 398
they shall *d* all the people round Zec 12:6 398
for ye *d* widows' houses, and for a Mt 23:14 *2719*
Which *d* widows' houses, and for a Mk 12:40 *2719*
Which *d* widows' houses, and for a Lk 20:47 *2719*
you into bondage, if a man *d* you 2Cor 11:20 *2719*
d one another, take heed that ye Gal 5:15 *2719*
which shall *d* the adversaries Heb 10:27 *2068*
about, seeking whom he may *d* 1Pet 5:8 *2666*
for to *d* her child as soon as it Rev 12:4 *2719*

DEVOURED
hath quite *d* also our money Gen 31:15 398
say, Some evil beast hath *d* him Gen 37:20 398
an evil beast hath *d* him Gen 37:33 398
seven thin ears *d* the seven rank Gen 41:7 1104
the thin ears *d* the seven good Gen 41:24 1104
d them, and they died before the Lev 10:2 398
what time the fire *d* two hundred Num 26:10 398
from them, and they shall be *d* Deut 31:17 398
d with burning heat, and with Deut 32:24 3898
the wood *d* more people that day 2Sa 18:8 398
people that day than the sword *d* 2Sa 18:8 398
and fire out of his mouth *d* 2Sa 22:9 398
and fire out of his mouth *d* Ps 18:8 398
of flies among them, which *d* them Ps 78:45 398
For they have *d* Jacob, and laid Ps 79:7 398
d the fruit of their ground Ps 105:35 398
ye shall be *d* with the sword Is 1:20 398
hath the curse *d* the earth Is 24:6 398
own sword hath *d* your prophets Jer 2:30 398
For shame hath *d* the labour of Jer 3:24 398
have *d* the land, and all that is Jer 8:16 398
d him, and consumed him, and have Jer 10:25 398
they that devour thee shall be *d* Jer 30:16 398
All that found them have *d* them Jer 50:7 398
the king of Assyria hath *d* him Jer 50:17 398
the king of Babylon hath *d* me Jer 51:34 398
it hath *d* the foundations thereof Lam 4:11 398
any work, when the fire hath *d* it Eze 15:5 398
thou sacrificed unto them to be *d* Eze 16:20 398
to catch the prey; it *d* men Eze 19:3 398
to catch the prey, and *d* men Eze 19:6 398
branches, which hath *d* her fruit Eze 19:14 398
they have *d* souls Eze 22:25 398
residue shall be *d* by the fire Eze 23:25 398
will I give to the beasts to be *d* Eze 33:27 398
the beasts of the field to be *d* Eze 39:4 402
it *d* and brake in pieces, and Dan 7:7 399
which *d*, brake in pieces, and Dan 7:19 399
an oven, and have *d* their judges Hos 7:7 398
Strangers have *d* his strength Hos 7:9 398
for the fire hath *d* the pastures Joel 1:19 398
the fire hath *d* the pastures of Joel 1:20 398
increased, the palmerworm *d* them Amos 4:9 398
it *d* the great deep, and did eat Amos 7:4 398
they shall be *d* as stubble fully Nah 1:10 398
be *d* by the fire of his jealousy Zeph 1:18 398
for all the earth shall be *d* with Zeph 3:8 398
and she shall be *d* with fire Zec 9:4 398
and the fowls came and *d* them up Mt 13:4 *2719*
fowls of the air came and *d* it up Mk 4:4 *2719*
and the fowls of the air *d* it Lk 8:5 *2719*
which hath *d* thy living with Lk 15:30 *2719*
from God out of heaven, and *d* them Rev 20:9 *2719*

DEVOURER
will rebuke the *d* for your sakes Mal 3:11 398

DEVOUREST
say unto you, Thou land *d* up men Eze 36:13 398

DEVOURETH
for the sword *d* one as well as 2Sa 11:25 398
mouth of the wicked *d* iniquity Prov 19:28 1104
the man who *d* that which is holy Prov 20:25 3216
as the fire *d* the stubble Is 5:24 398
flaming fire, which *d* round about Lam 2:3 398
the fire *d* both the ends of it, Eze 15:4 398
A fire *d* before them Joel 2:3 398
flame of fire that *d* the stubble Joel 2:5 398
thy tongue when the wicked *d* the Hab 1:13 1104
their mouth, and *d* their enemies Rev 11:5 *2719*

DEVOURING
the glory of the LORD was like *d* Ex 24:17 398
Thou lovest all *d* words, O thou Ps 52:4 1105
tempest, and the flame of *d* fire Is 29:6 398
and his tongue as a *d* fire Is 30:27 398
and with the flame of a *d* fire Is 30:30 398
us shall dwell with the *d* fire Is 33:14 398

DEVOUT
and the same man was just and *d* Lk 2:25 *2126*
d men, out of every nation under Acts 2:5 *2126*
d men carried Stephen to his Acts 8:2 *2126*
A *d* man, and one that feared God Acts 10:2 *2152*
a *d* soldier of them that waited Acts 10:7 *2152*
But the Jews stirred up the *d* Acts 13:50 *4576*
of the *d* Greeks a great multitude Acts 17:4 *4576*
the Jews, and with the *d* persons Acts 17:17 *4576*
a *d* man according to the law, Acts 22:12 *2152*

DEW
God give thee of the *d* of heaven Gen 27:28 2919
of the *d* of heaven from above Gen 27:39 2919
in the morning the *d* lay round Ex 16:13 2919
when the *d* that lay was gone up, Ex 16:14 2919
when the *d* fell upon the camp in Num 11:9 2919
my speech shall distil as the *d* Deut 32:2 2919
things of heaven, for the *d* Deut 33:13 2919
his heavens shall drop down *d* Deut 33:28 2919
if the *d* be on the fleece only, Judg 6:37 2919
wringed the *d* out of the fleece, Judg 6:38 2919
all the ground let there be *d* Judg 6:39 2919
there was *d* on all the ground Judg 6:40 2919
of Gilboa, let there be no *d* 2Sa 1:21 2919
as the *d* falleth on the ground 2Sa 17:12 2919
there shall not be *d* nor rain 1Kin 17:1 2919
the *d* lay all night upon my Job 29:19 2919
who hath begotten the drops of *d* Job 38:28 2919
thou hast the *d* of thy youth Ps 110:3 2919
As the *d* of Hermon, and as the *d* Ps 133:3 2919
up, and the clouds drop down the *d* Prov 3:20 2919
his favour is as *d* upon the grass Prov 19:12 2919
for my head is filled with *d* Song 5:2 2919
like a cloud of *d* in the heat of Is 18:4 2919
for thy *d* is as the *d* of herbs, Is 26:19 2919
it be wet with the *d* of heaven Dan 4:15 2920
it be wet with the *d* of heaven Dan 4:23 2920
wet thee with the *d* of heaven Dan 4:25 2920
body was wet with the *d* of heaven Dan 4:33 2920
body was wet with the *d* of heaven Dan 5:21 2920
as the early *d* it goeth away Hos 6:4 2919
as the early *d* that passeth away, Hos 13:3 2919
I will be as the *d* unto Israel Hos 14:5 2919
many people as a *d* from the LORD Mic 5:7 2919
heaven over you is stayed from *d* Hag 1:10 2919
and the heavens shall give their *d* Zec 8:12 2919

DIADEM
my judgment was as a robe and a *d* Job 29:14 6797
for a *d* of beauty, unto the Is 28:5 6843
a royal *d* in the hand of thy God Is 62:3 6797
Remove the *d*, and take off the Eze 21:26 4701

DIAL
it had gone down in the *d* of Ahaz 2Kin 20:11 4609
is gone down in the sun *d* of Ahaz Is 38:8 4609

DIAMOND
be an emerald, a sapphire, and a *d* Ex 28:18 3095
an emerald, a sapphire, and a *d* Ex 39:11 3095
of iron, and with the point of a *d* Jer 17:1 8068
the sardius, topaz, and the *d* Eze 28:13 3095

DIANA (*di-an'-ah*) *A Greek goddess.*
which made silver shrines for *D* Acts 19:24 *735*
goddess *D* should be despised Acts 19:27 *735*
Great is *D* of the Ephesians Acts 19:28 *735*
Great is *D* of the Ephesians Acts 19:34 *735*
worshipper of the great goddess *D* Acts 19:35 *735*

DIBLAH See DIBLATH.

DIBLAIM (*dib'-la-im*) *Father of Gomer.*
and took Gomer the daughter of *D* Hos 1:3 1691

DIBLATH (*dib'-lath*) *A place in northern Canaan.*
than the wilderness toward *D* Eze 6:14 1689

DIBON (*di'-bon*) See DIBON-GAD, DIMON.
1. A Moabite city.
Heshbon is perished even unto *D* Num 21:30 1769
Ataroth, and *D*, and Jazer, and Num 32:3 1769
And the children of Gad built *D* Num 32:34 1769
He is gone up to Bajith, and to *D* Is 15:2 1769
2. An undefined city.
and all the plain of Medeba unto *D* Josh 13:9 1769
D, and Bamoth-baal, and Josh 13:17 1769
Thou daughter that dost inhabit *D* Jer 48:18 1769
And upon *D*, and upon Nebo Jer 48:22 1769
3. A town in Judah.
in the villages thereof, and at *D* Neh 11:25 1769

DIBON-GAD (*di'-bon-gad'*) *An encampment during the Exodus.*
from Iim, and pitched in *D* Num 33:45 1769
And they removed from *D*, and Num 33:46 1769

DIBRI (*dib'-ri*) *Father of Shelomith.*
was Shelomith, the daughter of *D* Lev 24:11 1704

DID
d eat, and gave also unto her Gen 3:6
and he *d* eat Gen 3:6
gave me of the tree, and I *d* eat Gen 3:12
serpent beguiled me, and I *d* eat Gen 3:13
to his wife *d* the LORD God make Gen 3:21
Thus *d* Noah Gen 6:22 6213
that God commanded him, so *d* he Gen 6:22 6213
Noah *d* according unto all that Gen 7:5 6213
upward *d* the waters prevail Gen 7:20
because the LORD *d* there confound Gen 11:9
from thence *d* the LORD scatter Gen 11:9
under the tree, and they *d* eat Gen 18:8
Wherefore *d* Sarah laugh, saying, Gen 18:13
d bake unleavened bread, and they Gen 19:3
unleavened bread, and they *d* eat Gen 19:3
the LORD *d* unto Sarah as he had Gen 21:1 6213
that God *d* tempt Abraham, and said Gen 22:1
eight Milcah *d* bear to Nahor Gen 22:23
And they *d* eat and drink, he and the Gen 24:54
because he *d* eat of his venison Gen 25:28
he *d* eat and drink, and rose up, and Gen 25:34
the herdmen of Gerar *d* strive Gen 26:20
made them a feast, and they *d* eat Gen 26:30
it near to him, and he *d* eat Gen 27:25
d not I serve with thee for Gen 29:25
And Jacob *d* so, and fulfilled her Gen 29:28 6213
Jacob *d* separate the lambs, and Gen 30:40
the stronger cattle *d* conceive Gen 30:41
they *d* eat there upon the heap Gen 31:46
they *d* eat bread, and tarried all Gen 31:54
they *d* not pursue after the sons Gen 35:5
the thing which he *d* displeased Gen 38:10 6213
he die also, as his brethren *d* Gen 38:11
that he *d* to prosper in his hand Gen 39:3 6213
save the bread which he *d* eat Gen 39:6
this manner *d* thy servant to me Gen 39:19 6213
and whatsoever they *d* there Gen 39:22 6213
was with him, and that which he *d* Gen 39:23 6213
the birds *d* eat them out of the Gen 40:17

Context	Reference	Strong's
Yet *d* not the chief butler	Gen 40:23	
leanfleshed kine *d* eat up the	Gen 41:4	
to his dream he *d* interpret	Gen 41:12	
the ill favoured kine *d* eat up	Gen 41:20	
And they *d* so	Gen 42:20	6213
and thus *d* he unto them	Gen 42:25	6213
The man *d* solemnly protest unto	Gen 43:3	
And the man *d* as Joseph bade	Gen 43:17	6213
for his bowels *d* yearn upon his	Gen 43:30	
which *d* eat with him, by	Gen 43:32	
he *d* according to the word that	Gen 44:2	6213
for God *d* send me before you to	Gen 45:5	
And the children of Israel *d* so	Gen 45:21	6213
d eat their portion which Pharaoh	Gen 47:22	
fathers Abraham and Isaac *d* walk	Gen 48:15	
his sons *d* unto him according as	Gen 50:12	6213
all the evil which we *d* unto him	Gen 50:15	1580
Thy father *d* command before he	Gen 50:16	
for they *d* unto thee evil	Gen 50:17	1580
Therefore they *d* set over them	Ex 1:11	
d not as the king of Egypt	Ex 1:17	6213
he said to him that *d* the wrong	Ex 2:13	
d the signs in the sight of the	Ex 4:30	6213
which they *d* make heretofore, ye	Ex 5:8	
of the children of Israel *d* see	Ex 5:19	
concerning the which I *d* swear to	Ex 6:8	
Aaron *d* as the LORD commanded	Ex 7:6	6213
LORD commanded them, so *d* they	Ex 7:6	6213
they *d* so as the LORD had	Ex 7:10	6213
they also *d* in like manner with	Ex 7:11	6213
And Moses and Aaron *d* so, as the	Ex 7:20	6213
the magicians of Egypt *d* so with	Ex 7:22	6213
neither *d* he hearken unto them	Ex 7:22	6213
neither *d* he set his heart to	Ex 7:23	
the magicians *d* so with their	Ex 8:7	6213
the LORD *d* according to the word	Ex 8:13	6213
And they *d* so	Ex 8:17	6213
the magicians *d* so with their	Ex 8:18	6213
And the LORD *d* so	Ex 8:24	6213
the LORD *d* according to the word	Ex 8:31	6213
the LORD *d* that thing on the	Ex 9:6	6213
he *d* not let the people go	Ex 9:7	
for that ye *d* desire	Ex 10:11	
they *d* eat every herb of the land	Ex 10:15	
Aaron *d* all these wonders before	Ex 11:10	6213
d as the LORD had commanded Moses	Ex 12:28	6213
Moses and Aaron, so *d* they	Ex 12:28	6213
And the children of Israel *d*	Ex 12:35	6213
Thus *d* all the children of Israel	Ex 12:50	6213
Moses and Aaron, so *d* they	Ex 12:50	6213
that the LORD *d* bring the	Ex 12:51	
d unto me when I came forth out	Ex 13:8	6213
And they *d* so	Ex 14:4	6213
word that we *d* tell thee in Egypt	Ex 14:12	
the LORD *d* upon the Egyptians	Ex 14:31	6313
when we *d* eat bread to the full	Ex 16:3	
And the children of Israel *d* so	Ex 16:17	6213
when they *d* mete it with an omer,	Ex 16:18	
it *d* not stink, neither was there	Ex 16:24	
of Israel *d* eat manna forty years	Ex 16:35	
they *d* eat manna, until they came	Ex 16:35	
the people *d* chide with Moses	Ex 17:2	
Moses *d* so in the sight of the	Ex 17:6	6213
So Joshua *d* as Moses had said to	Ex 17:10	6213
d obeisance, and kissed him	Ex 18:7	
saw all that he *d* to the people	Ex 18:14	6213
in law, and *d* all that he had said	Ex 18:24	6213
seen what I *d* unto the Egyptians	Ex 19:4	6213
they saw God, and *d* eat and drink	Ex 24:11	
For mischief *d* he bring them out,	Ex 32:12	
What *d* this people unto thee,	Ex 32:21	6213
the children of Levi *d* according	Ex 32:28	6213
no man *d* put on him his ornaments	Ex 33:4	
he *d* neither eat bread, nor drink	Ex 34:28	
Every one that *d* offer an	Ex 35:24	
hearted *d* spin with their hands	Ex 35:25	
thus *d* he make for all the boards	Ex 36:22	
thus he *d* to both of them in both	Ex 36:29	6213
they *d* beat the gold into thin	Ex 39:3	
they *d* bind the breastplate by	Ex 39:21	
and the children of Israel *d*	Ex 39:32	6213
LORD commanded Moses, so *d* they	Ex 39:32	6213
Moses *d* look upon all the work,	Ex 39:43	
Thus *d* Moses: according to all	Ex 40:16	6213
the LORD commanded him, so *d* he	Ex 40:16	6213
he *d* with the bullock for a sin	Lev 4:20	6213
Moses *d* as the LORD commanded him	Lev 8:4	6213
d he put the golden plate, the	Lev 8:9	
his sons *d* all things which the	Lev 8:36	6213
he *d* wash the inwards and the legs	Lev 9:14	
they *d* according to the word of	Lev 10:7	6213
do with that blood as he *d* with	Lev 16:15	6213
he *d* as the LORD commanded Moses	Lev 16:34	6213
the children of Israel *d* as the	Lev 24:23	6213
because it *d* not rest in your	Lev 26:35	
possession of the land *d* belong	Lev 27:24	
And the children of Israel *d*	Num 1:54	6213
LORD commanded Moses, so *d* they	Num 1:54	6213
And the children of Israel *d*	Num 2:34	6213
Aaron *d* number according to the	Num 4:37	
Aaron *d* number according to the	Num 4:41	
And the children of Israel *d* so	Num 5:4	6213
so *d* the children of Israel	Num 5:4	6213
Zuar, prince of Issachar, *d* offer	Num 7:18	
the children of Zebulun, *d* offer	Num 7:24	
the children of Reuben, *d* offer	Num 7:30	
the children of Simeon, *d* offer	Num 7:36	
And Aaron *d* so; he lighted	Num 8:3	6213
d to the Levites according unto	Num 8:20	6213
so *d* the children of Israel unto	Num 8:20	6213
the Levites, so *d* they unto them	Num 8:22	6213
so *d* the children of Israel	Num 9:5	6213
the other *d* set up the tabernacle	Num 10:21	
which we *d* eat in Egypt freely	Num 11:5	
they prophesied, and *d* not cease	Num 11:25	
which I *d* in Egypt and in the	Num 14:22	6213
Even those men that *d* bring up	Num 14:37	
And Moses *d* so: as the LORD	Num 17:11	6213
the LORD commanded him, so *d* he	Num 17:11	6213
Moses *d* as the LORD commanded	Num 20:27	6213
What he *d* in the Red sea, and in	Num 21:14	2052
D I not earnestly send unto thee	Num 22:37	6213
Balak *d* as Balaam had spoken	Num 23:2	6213
Balak *d* as Balaam had said, and	Num 23:30	6213
and the people *d* eat, and bowed	Num 25:2	
Moses *d* as the LORD commanded him	Num 27:22	6213
Eleazar the priest *d* as the LORD	Num 31:31	6213
Thus *d* your fathers, when I sent	Num 32:8	6213
so *d* the daughters of Zelophehad	Num 36:10	6213
according to all that he *d* for	Deut 1:30	6213
Yet in this thing ye *d* not	Deut 1:32	
as Israel *d* unto the land of his	Deut 2:12	6213
As he *d* to the children of Esau,	Deut 2:22	6213
which dwell in Ar, *d* unto me	Deut 2:29	6213
as we *d* unto Sihon king of	Deut 3:6	6213
the LORD *d* because of Baal-peor	Deut 4:3	6213
But ye that *d* cleave unto the	Deut 4:4	
D ever people hear the voice of	Deut 4:33	
d for you in Egypt before your	Deut 4:34	6213
for the mountain *d* burn with fire	Deut 5:23	
The LORD *d* not set his love upon	Deut 7:7	6213
the LORD thy God *d* unto Pharaoh	Deut 7:18	6213
neither *d* thy fathers know	Deut 8:3	
neither *d* thy foot swell, these	Deut 8:4	
I neither *d* eat bread nor drink	Deut 9:9	
I *d* neither eat bread, nor drink	Deut 9:18	
which he *d* in the midst of Egypt	Deut 11:3	6213
what he *d* unto the army of Egypt,	Deut 11:4	6213
what he *d* unto you in the	Deut 11:5	6213
what he *d* unto Dathan and Abiram,	Deut 11:6	6213
great acts of the LORD which he *d*	Deut 11:7	6213
How *d* these nations serve their	Deut 12:30	
thy God *d* unto Miriam by the way	Deut 24:9	6213
Amalek *d* unto thee by the way	Deut 25:17	6213
Ye have seen all that the LORD *d*	Deut 29:2	6213
do unto them as he *d* to Sihon	Deut 31:4	6213
So the LORD alone *d* lead him	Deut 32:12	
Which *d* eat the fat of their	Deut 32:38	
neither *d* he acknowledge his	Deut 33:9	
d as the LORD commanded Moses	Deut 34:9	6213
what ye *d* unto the two kings of	Josh 2:10	6213
these things, our hearts *d* melt	Josh 2:11	
neither *d* there remain any more	Josh 2:11	
Israel *d* so as Joshua commanded	Josh 4:8	6213
all his banks, as they *d* before	Josh 4:18	
Jordan, *d* Joshua pitch in Gilgal	Josh 4:20	
LORD your God *d* to the Red sea	Josh 4:23	6213
the cause why Joshua *d* circumcise	Josh 5:4	
they *d* eat of the old corn of the	Josh 5:11	
but they *d* eat of the fruit of	Josh 5:12	
d worship, and said unto him, What	Josh 5:14	
And Joshua *d* so	Josh 5:15	6213
so they *d* six days	Josh 6:14	6213
They *d* work wilily, and went and	Josh 9:4	6213
of him, and all that he *d* in Egypt	Josh 9:9	6213
all that he *d* to the two kings of	Josh 9:10	6213
so *d* he unto them, and delivered	Josh 9:26	6213
And they *d* so, and brought forth	Josh 10:23	6213
he *d* to the king of Makkedah as	Josh 10:28	6213
as he *d* unto the king of Jericho	Josh 10:28	6213
but *d* unto the king thereof as he	Josh 10:30	6213
as he *d* unto the king of Jericho	Josh 10:30	6213
so he *d* to Debir, and to the king	Josh 10:39	6213
their land *d* Joshua take at one	Josh 10:42	
Joshua *d* unto them as the LORD	Josh 11:9	6213
d Joshua take, and smote them with	Josh 11:12	
that *d* Joshua burn	Josh 11:13	
so *d* Moses command Joshua, and so	Josh 11:15	6213
command Joshua, and so *d* Joshua	Josh 11:15	6213
Them *d* Moses the servant of the	Josh 12:6	
for these *d* Moses smite, and cast	Josh 13:12	
d the children of Israel slay	Josh 13:22	
d distribute for inheritance in	Josh 13:32	
so the children of Israel *d*	Josh 14:5	6213
but *d* not utterly drive them out	Josh 17:13	
D not Achan the son of Zerah	Josh 22:20	
d not intend to go up against	Josh 22:33	
to that which I *d* among them	Josh 24:5	6213
a land for which ye *d* not labour	Josh 24:13	
which *d* those great signs in our	Josh 24:17	6213
the children of Benjamin *d* not	Judg 1:21	
Neither *d* Manasseh drive out the	Judg 1:27	
d not utterly drive them out	Judg 1:28	
Neither *d* Ephraim drive out the	Judg 1:29	
Neither *d* Zebulun drive out the	Judg 1:30	
Neither *d* Asher drive out the	Judg 1:31	
for they *d* not drive them out	Judg 1:32	
Neither *d* Naphtali drive out the	Judg 1:33	
of the LORD, that he *d* for Israel	Judg 2:7	6213
the children of Israel *d* evil in	Judg 2:11	6213
but they *d* not so	Judg 2:17	6213
as their fathers *d* keep it	Judg 2:22	
the children of Israel *d* evil in	Judg 3:7	6213
the children of Israel *d* evil	Judg 3:12	6213
he *d* gird it under his raiment	Judg 3:16	
the children of Israel again *d*	Judg 4:1	6213
why *d* Dan remain in ships	Judg 5:17	
the children of Israel *d* evil in	Judg 6:1	6213
D not the LORD bring us up from	Judg 6:13	6213
And he *d* so	Judg 6:20	6213
d as the LORD had said unto him	Judg 6:27	6213
it by day, that he *d* it by night	Judg 6:27	6213
And God *d* so that night	Judg 6:40	6213
they *d* chide with him sharply	Judg 8:1	
with whom ye *d* upbraid me	Judg 8:15	
d cast therein every man the	Judg 8:25	
d eat and drink, and cursed	Judg 9:27	
which he *d* unto his father, in	Judg 9:56	6213
d God render upon their heads	Judg 9:57	
the children of Israel *d* evil	Judg 10:6	6213
D not I deliver you from the	Judg 10:11	
and the Maonites, *d* oppress you	Judg 10:12	
D not ye hate me, and expel me out	Judg 11:7	
d he ever strive against Israel,	Judg 11:25	
or *d* he ever fight against them,	Judg 11:25	
why therefore *d* ye not recover	Judg 11:26	
who *d* with her according to his	Judg 11:39	6213
the children of Israel *d* evil	Judg 13:1	6213
and the angel *d* wonderously	Judg 13:19	6213
LORD *d* no more appear to Manoah	Judg 13:21	
and gave them, and they *d* eat	Judg 14:9	
said unto them, As they *d* unto me	Judg 15:11	6213
he *d* grind in the prison house	Judg 16:21	
but every man *d* that which was	Judg 17:6	6213
so they *d* eat and drink, and lodged	Judg 19:4	
d eat and drink both of them	Judg 19:6	
and they *d* eat both of them	Judg 19:8	
their feet, and *d* eat and drink	Judg 19:21	
for ye *d* not give unto them at	Judg 21:22	
And the children of Benjamin *d* so	Judg 21:23	6213
every man *d* that which was right	Judg 21:25	6213
her parched corn, and she *d* eat	Ruth 2:14	
blessed be he that *d* take	Ruth 2:19	
d according to all that her	Ruth 3:6	6213
which two *d* build the house of	Ruth 4:11	
as he *d* so year by year, when she	1Sa 1:7	6213
therefore she wept, and *d* not eat	1Sa 1:7	6213
d eat, and her countenance was no	1Sa 1:18	
the child *d* minister unto the	1Sa 2:11	1961
So they *d* in Shiloh unto all the	1Sa 2:14	6213
that his sons *d* unto all Israel	1Sa 2:22	6213
D I plainly appear unto the house	1Sa 2:27	
d I choose him out of all the	1Sa 2:28	
d I give unto the house of thy	1Sa 2:28	
Now Samuel *d* not yet know the	1Sa 3:7	
d let none of his words fall to	1Sa 3:19	
not, neither *d* she regard it	1Sa 4:20	
d they not let the people go, and	1Sa 6:6	
And the men *d* so	1Sa 6:10	6213
of Israel *d* put away Baalim	1Sa 7:4	
the coasts thereof *d* Israel	1Sa 7:14	
So Saul *d* eat with Samuel that	1Sa 9:24	
of the LORD, which he *d* to you	1Sa 12:7	6213
then the people *d* hide	1Sa 13:6	
the people *d* eat them with the	1Sa 14:32	
I *d* but taste a little honey with	1Sa 14:43	
that which Amalek *d* to Israel	1Sa 15:2	6213
Samuel *d* that which the LORD	1Sa 16:4	6213
For he *d* put his life in his hand	1Sa 19:5	
d eat no meat the second day of	1Sa 20:34	
d they not sing one to another of	1Sa 21:11	
D I then begin to enquire of God	1Sa 22:15	
he fled, and *d* not shew it to me	1Sa 22:17	
five persons that *d* wear a linen	1Sa 22:18	
that Nabal *d* shear his sheep	1Sa 25:4	
So *d* David, and so will be his	1Sa 27:11	6213
d bake unleavened bread thereof	1Sa 28:24	
and they *d* eat	1Sa 28:25	
and gave him bread, and he *d* eat	1Sa 30:11	
fell to the earth, and *d* obeisance	2Sa 1:2	
were with him *d* David bring up	2Sa 2:3	
the king *d* pleased all the people	2Sa 3:36	6213
And David *d* so, as the LORD had	2Sa 5:25	6213
so *d* Nathan speak unto David	2Sa 7:17	
Which also king David *d* dedicate	2Sa 8:11	
fell on his face, and *d* reverence	2Sa 9:6	
for he *d* eat continually at the	2Sa 9:13	
how Joab *d*, and how the people *d*	2Sa 11:7	7965
he *d* eat and drink before him	2Sa 11:13	
unto the city when ye *d* fight	2Sa 11:20	
d not a woman cast a piece of a	2Sa 11:21	
it *d* eat of his own meat, and	2Sa 12:3	
fourfold, because he *d* this thing	2Sa 12:6	6213
neither *d* he eat bread with them	2Sa 12:17	
set bread before him, and he *d* eat	2Sa 12:20	
thus *d* he unto all the cities of	2Sa 12:31	6213
in his sight, and *d* bake the cakes	2Sa 13:8	
the servants of Absalom *d* unto	2Sa 13:29	6213
d obeisance, and said, Help, O	2Sa 14:4	
on this manner *d* Absalom to all	2Sa 15:6	6213
thus *d* Ahithophel counsel Absalom	2Sa 17:15	
d perversely the day that my lord	2Sa 19:19	
that *d* eat at thine own table	2Sa 19:28	
why then *d* ye despise us, that	2Sa 19:43	
do us more harm than *d* Absalom	2Sa 20:6	
of Saul, whom the LORD *d* choose	2Sa 21:6	
he *d* hear my voice out of his	2Sa 22:7	
my cry *d* enter into his ears	2Sa 22:7	
he rode upon a cherub, and *d* fly	2Sa 22:11	
I *d* not depart from them	2Sa 22:23	
so that my feet *d* not slip	2Sa 22:37	
Then *d* I beat them as small as	2Sa 22:43	
I *d* stamp them as the mire of the	2Sa 22:43	
street, and *d* spread them abroad	2Sa 22:43	
These things *d* these three mighty	2Sa 23:17	6213
These things *d* Benaiah the son of	2Sa 23:22	6213
All these things *d* Araunah	2Sa 24:23	
d obeisance unto the king	1Kin 1:16	
d reverence to the king, and said,	1Kin 1:31	
Joab the son of Zeruiah *d* to me	1Kin 2:5	6213
what he *d* to the two captains of	1Kin 2:5	6213
Zadok the priest *d* the king put	1Kin 2:35	
D I not make thee to swear by the	1Kin 2:42	
a thousand burnt offerings *d*	1Kin 3:4	
as thy father David *d* walk	1Kin 3:14	
it was not my son, which I *d* bear	1Kin 3:21	
and Hiram's builders *d* hew them	1Kin 5:18	
a line of twelve cubits *d* compass	1Kin 7:15	
so *d* he for the other chapiter	1Kin 7:18	6213
cubits *d* compass it round about	1Kin 7:23	
of Jordan *d* the king cast them	1Kin 7:46	
d he put among the treasures of	1Kin 7:51	

even those *d* the priests and the	1Kin 8:4	
The same day *d* the king hallow	1Kin 8:64	
upon those *d* Solomon levy a	1Kin 9:21	
Israel *d* Solomon make no bondmen	1Kin 9:22	
then *d* he build Millo	1Kin 9:24	
three times in a year *d* Solomon	1Kin 9:25	
d they bring them out by their	1Kin 10:29	
Solomon *d* evil in the sight of	1Kin 11:6	6213
the LORD, as *d* David his father	1Kin 11:6	
Then *d* Solomon build an high	1Kin 11:7	
likewise *d* he for all his strange	1Kin 11:8	6213
(For six months *d* Joab remain	1Kin 11:16	
beside the mischief that Hadad *d*	1Kin 11:25	
judgments, as *d* David his father	1Kin 11:33	
as David my servant *d*	1Kin 11:38	6213
acts of Solomon, and all that he *d*	1Kin 11:41	6213
thy father *d* put upon us lighter	1Kin 12:9	
now whereas my father *d* lade you	1Kin 12:11	
So *d* he in Beth-el, sacrificing	1Kin 12:32	6213
d eat bread in his house, and	1Kin 13:19	
the which the LORD *d* say to thee	1Kin 13:22	
And Jeroboam's wife *d* so, and arose	1Kin 14:4	6213
the sins of Jeroboam, who *d* sin	1Kin 14:16	
the city which the LORD *d* choose	1Kin 14:21	
Judah *d* evil in the sight of the	1Kin 14:22	6213
they *d* according to all the	1Kin 14:24	6213
of Rehoboam, and all that he *d*	1Kin 14:29	6213
d the LORD his God give him a	1Kin 15:4	
Because David *d* that which was	1Kin 15:5	6213
acts of Abijam, and all that he *d*	1Kin 15:7	6213
Asa *d* that which was right in the	1Kin 15:11	6213
the LORD, as *d* David his father	1Kin 15:11	
all his might, and all that he *d*	1Kin 15:23	6213
he *d* evil in the sight of the	1Kin 15:26	6213
king of Judah *d* Baasha slay him	1Kin 15:28	
acts of Nadab, and all that he *d*	1Kin 15:31	6213
he *d* evil in the sight of the	1Kin 15:34	6213
the acts of Baasha, and what he *d*	1Kin 16:5	6213
he *d* in the sight of the LORD	1Kin 16:7	6213
Thus *d* Zimri destroy all the	1Kin 16:12	
acts of Elah, and all that he *d*	1Kin 16:14	6213
Judah *d* Zimri reign seven days in	1Kin 16:15	
and in his sin which he *d*	1Kin 16:19	6213
d worse than all that were before	1Kin 16:25	
of the acts of Omri which he *d*	1Kin 16:27	6213
Ahab the son of Omri *d* evil in	1Kin 16:30	6213
Ahab *d* more to provoke the LORD	1Kin 16:33	6213
In his days *d* Hiel the Beth-elite	1Kin 16:34	
d according unto the word of the	1Kin 17:5	6213
d according to the saying of	1Kin 17:15	6213
he, and her house, *d* eat many days	1Kin 17:15	6213
neither *d* the cruse of oil fail,	1Kin 17:16	
d when Jezebel slew the prophets	1Kin 18:13	6213
they *d* it the second time	1Kin 18:34	
And they *d* it the third time	1Kin 18:34	
he *d* eat and drink, and laid him	1Kin 19:6	
d eat and drink, and went in the	1Kin 19:8	
unto the people, and they *d* eat	1Kin 19:21	
unto their voice, and *d* so	1Kin 20:25	6213
Now the men *d* diligently observe	1Kin 20:33	
from him, and *d* hastily catch it	1Kin 20:33	
d as Jezebel had sent unto them,	1Kin 21:11	6213
Naboth *d* blaspheme God and the	1Kin 21:13	
which *d* sell himself to work	1Kin 21:25	
he *d* very abominably in following	1Kin 21:26	
to all things as *d* the Amorites	1Kin 21:26	6213
D I not tell thee that he would	1Kin 22:18	
acts of Ahab, and all that he *d*	1Kin 22:39	6213
he *d* evil in the sight of the	1Kin 22:52	6213
of the acts of Ahaziah which he *d*	2Kin 1:18	6213
D I not say unto you, Go not	2Kin 2:18	
that thy servant *d* fear the LORD	2Kin 4:1	
D I desire a son of my lord	2Kin 4:28	
d I not say, Do not deceive me	2Kin 4:28	
set it before them, and they *d* eat	2Kin 4:44	
and the iron *d* swim	2Kin 6:6	
So we boiled my son, and *d* eat him	2Kin 6:29	
d eat and drink, and carried thence	2Kin 7:8	
d after the saying of the man of	2Kin 8:2	6213
of Israel, as *d* the house of Ahab	2Kin 8:18	6213
he *d* evil in the sight of the	2Kin 8:18	
acts of Joram, and all that he *d*	2Kin 8:23	
the son of Ahab king of Israel *d*	2Kin 8:25	
d evil in the sight of the LORD,	2Kin 8:27	6213
as *d* the house of Ahab	2Kin 8:27	
they *d* so at the going up to Gur,	2Kin 9:27	
he *d* eat and drink, and said, Go,	2Kin 9:34	
But Jehu *d* it in subtilty, to the	2Kin 10:19	6213
acts of Jehu, and all that he *d*	2Kin 10:34	6213
Athaliah *d* reign over the land	2Kin 11:3	
d according to all things that	2Kin 11:9	6213
d the priest give king David's	2Kin 11:10	
Jehoash *d* that which was right in	2Kin 12:2	6213
the hands of them that *d* the work	2Kin 12:11	6213
acts of Joash, and all that he *d*	2Kin 12:19	6213
he *d* that which was evil in the	2Kin 13:2	6213
Neither *d* he leave of the people	2Kin 13:7	
of Jehoahaz, and all that he *d*	2Kin 13:8	6213
he *d* that which was evil in the	2Kin 13:11	6213
acts of Joash, and all that he *d*	2Kin 13:12	
Three times *d* Joash beat him, and	2Kin 13:25	
he *d* that which was right in the	2Kin 14:3	6213
he *d* according to all things as	2Kin 14:3	6213
all things as Joash his father *d*	2Kin 14:3	6213
as yet the people *d* sacrifice	2Kin 14:4	
of the acts of Jehoash which he *d*	2Kin 14:15	6213
he *d* that which was evil in the	2Kin 14:24	6213
of Jeroboam, and all that he *d*	2Kin 14:28	6213
he *d* that which was right in the	2Kin 15:3	6213
acts of Azariah, and all that he *d*	2Kin 15:6	6213
d Zachariah the son of Jeroboam	2Kin 15:8	
he *d* that which was evil in the	2Kin 15:9	6213
he *d* that which was evil in the	2Kin 15:18	6213
acts of Menahem, and all that he *d*	2Kin 15:21	6213
he *d* that which was evil in the	2Kin 15:24	6213
of Pekahiah, and all that he *d*	2Kin 15:26	6213
he *d* that which was evil in the	2Kin 15:28	6213
acts of Pekah, and all that he *d*	2Kin 15:31	6213
he *d* that which was right in the	2Kin 15:34	6213
he *d* according to all that his	2Kin 15:34	6213
acts of Jotham, and all that he *d*	2Kin 15:36	6213
d not that which was right in the	2Kin 16:2	6213
Thus *d* Urijah the priest,	2Kin 16:16	6213
of the acts of Ahaz which he *d*	2Kin 16:19	6213
he *d* that which was evil in the	2Kin 17:2	6213
the children of Israel *d* secretly	2Kin 17:9	
as *d* the heathen whom the LORD	2Kin 17:11	
that *d* not believe in the LORD	2Kin 17:14	
the sins of Jeroboam which he *d*	2Kin 17:22	6213
Howbeit they *d* not hearken	2Kin 17:40	
but they *d* after their former	2Kin 17:40	6213
as *d* their fathers, so do they	2Kin 17:41	6213
he *d* that which was right in the	2Kin 18:3	6213
to all that David his father *d*	2Kin 18:3	6213
of Israel *d* burn incense to it	2Kin 18:4	
the king of Assyria *d* carry away	2Kin 18:11	
year of king Hezekiah *d*	2Kin 18:13	
At that time *d* Hezekiah cut off	2Kin 18:16	
he *d* that which was evil in the	2Kin 21:2	6213
a grove, as *d* Ahab king of Israel	2Kin 21:3	6213
than *d* the nations whom the LORD	2Kin 21:9	
above all that the Amorites *d*	2Kin 21:11	6213
of Manasseh, and all that he *d*	2Kin 21:17	6213
he *d* that which was evil in the	2Kin 21:20	6213
LORD, as his father Manasseh *d*	2Kin 21:20	6213
of the acts of Amon which he *d*	2Kin 21:25	6213
he *d* that which was right in the	2Kin 22:2	6213
but they *d* eat of the unleavened	2Kin 23:9	
d the king beat down, and brake	2Kin 23:12	6213
of Ammon, *d* the king defile	2Kin 23:13	
d to them according to all the	2Kin 23:19	6213
d Josiah put away, that he might	2Kin 23:24	
acts of Josiah, and all that he *d*	2Kin 23:28	6213
he *d* that which was evil in the	2Kin 23:32	6213
he *d* that which was evil in the	2Kin 23:37	6213
according to all that he *d*	2Kin 24:3	6213
of Jehoiakim, and all that he *d*	2Kin 24:5	6213
he *d* that which was evil in the	2Kin 24:9	6213
and his servants *d* besiege it	2Kin 24:11	
he *d* that which was evil in the	2Kin 24:19	6213
d Nebuzar-adan the captain of the	2Kin 25:11	
d the Chaldees break in pieces,	2Kin 25:13	
d lift up the head of Jehoiachin	2Kin 25:27	
he *d* eat bread continually before	2Kin 25:29	
neither *d* all their family	1Chr 4:27	
Samuel the seer *d* ordain in their	1Chr 9:22	
These things *d* these three	1Chr 11:19	6213
These things *d* Benaiah the son of	1Chr 11:24	6213
David therefore *d* as God	1Chr 14:16	6213
For because ye *d* it not at the	1Chr 15:13	
d blow with the trumpets before	1Chr 15:24	
so *d* Nathan speak unto David	1Chr 17:15	
that *d* the work for the service	1Chr 23:24	6213
of the spoils won in battles *d*	1Chr 26:27	
over them that *d* the work of the	1Chr 27:26	6213
d eat and drink before the LORD on	1Chr 29:22	
In that night *d* God appear unto	2Chr 1:7	
whom David my father *d* provide	2Chr 2:7	
cubits *d* compass it round about	2Chr 4:2	
which *d* compass it round about	2Chr 4:3	
d Huram his father make to king	2Chr 4:16	
of Jordan *d* the king cast them	2Chr 4:17	
these *d* the priests and the	2Chr 5:5	
d not then wait by course	2Chr 5:11	
them *d* Solomon make to pay	2Chr 8:8	
d Solomon make no servants for	2Chr 8:9	
that thy father *d* put upon us	2Chr 10:9	
he *d* evil, because he prepared	2Chr 12:14	6213
Neither *d* Jeroboam recover	2Chr 13:20	
Asa *d* that which was good and	2Chr 14:2	6213
d turn unto the LORD God of	2Chr 15:4	
for God *d* vex them with all	2Chr 15:6	
I *d* see all Israel scattered upon	2Chr 18:16	
D I not tell thee that he would	2Chr 18:17	
Moreover in Jerusalem *d*	2Chr 19:8	
after this *d* Jehoshaphat king of	2Chr 20:35	
of Israel, who *d* very wickedly	2Chr 20:35	6213
like as *d* the house of Ahab	2Chr 21:6	6213
The same time also *d* Libnah	2Chr 21:10	
Wherefore he *d* evil in the sight	2Chr 22:4	6213
all Judah *d* according to all	2Chr 23:8	6213
Joash *d* that which was right in	2Chr 24:2	6213
LORD *d* they bestow upon Baalim	2Chr 24:7	
Thus they *d* day by day, and	2Chr 24:11	6213
Jehoiada gave it to such as *d* the	2Chr 24:12	6213
he *d* that which was right in the	2Chr 25:2	6213
but *d* as it is written in the law	2Chr 25:4	
d the children of Judah carry	2Chr 25:12	
d turn away from following the	2Chr 25:27	
he *d* that which was right in the	2Chr 26:4	6213
to all that his father Amaziah *d*	2Chr 26:4	6213
d Isaiah the prophet, the son of	2Chr 26:22	
he *d* that which was right in the	2Chr 27:2	6213
to all that his father Uzziah *d*	2Chr 27:2	6213
the people *d* yet corruptly	2Chr 27:2	
So much *d* the children of Ammon	2Chr 27:5	
but he *d* not that which was right	2Chr 28:1	6213
At that time *d* king Ahaz send	2Chr 28:16	
in the time of his distress *d* he	2Chr 28:22	
he *d* that which was right in the	2Chr 29:2	6213
which king Ahaz in his reign *d*	2Chr 29:19	
brethren the Levites *d* help them	2Chr 29:34	
yet *d* they eat the passover	2Chr 30:18	
they *d* eat throughout the feast	2Chr 30:22	
d give to the congregation a	2Chr 30:24	
thus *d* Hezekiah throughout all	2Chr 31:20	6213
he *d* it with all his heart, and	2Chr 31:21	6213
and they *d* help him	2Chr 32:3	
After this *d* Sennacherib king of	2Chr 32:9	
d him honour at his death	2Chr 32:33	6213
But *d* that which was evil in the	2Chr 33:2	6213
Nevertheless the people *d*	2Chr 33:17	
But he *d* that which was evil in	2Chr 33:22	6213
LORD, as *d* Manasseh his father	2Chr 33:22	6213
he *d* that which was right in the	2Chr 34:2	6213
so *d* he in the cities of Manasseh	2Chr 34:6	
the men *d* the work faithfully	2Chr 34:12	6213
d according to the covenant of	2Chr 34:32	6213
of David king of Israel *d* build	2Chr 35:3	
And so *d* they with the oxen	2Chr 35:12	
neither *d* all the kings of Israel	2Chr 35:18	6213
he *d* that which was evil in the	2Chr 36:5	6213
and his abominations which he *d*	2Chr 36:8	6213
he *d* that which was evil in the	2Chr 36:9	6213
he *d* that which was evil in the	2Chr 36:12	6213
Even those *d* Cyrus king of Persia	Ezr 1:8	
All these *d* Sheshbazzar bring up	Ezr 1:11	
those *d* Cyrus the king take out	Ezr 5:14	
king had sent, so they *d* speedily	Ezr 6:13	
the LORD God of Israel, *d* eat,	Ezr 6:21	
he *d* eat no bread, nor drink	Ezr 10:6	
children of the captivity *d* so	Ezr 10:16	6213
not whither I went, or what I *d*	Neh 2:16	6213
nor to the rest that *d* the work	Neh 2:16	6213
But the fish gate *d* the sons of	Neh 3:3	
the people *d* according to this	Neh 5:13	6213
but so *d* not I, because of the	Neh 5:15	6213
so they *d* eat, and were filled, and	Neh 9:25	
they *d* evil again before thee	Neh 9:28	6213
their brethren that *d* the work of	Neh 11:12	6213
evil that Eliashib *d* for Tobiah	Neh 13:7	6213
that *d* the work, were fled every	Neh 13:10	6213
D not your fathers thus, and *d*	Neh 13:18	6213
D not Solomon king of Israel sin	Neh 13:26	
nevertheless even him *d*	Neh 13:26	
none *d* compel	Est 1:8	
the king *d* according to the word	Est 1:21	6213
and he *d* so	Est 2:4	6213
house, to know how Esther *d*	Est 2:11	7965
for Esther *d* the commandment of	Est 2:20	6213
After these things *d* king	Est 3:1	
bowed not, nor *d* him reverence	Est 3:2	
nor *d* him reverence, then was	Est 3:5	
d according to all that Esther	Est 4:17	6213
Esther the queen *d* let no man	Est 5:12	
On that day *d* the king Ahasuerus	Est 8:1	
d what they would unto those that	Est 9:5	6213
Thus *d* Job continually	Job 1:5	6213
In all this *d* not Job sin with	Job 2:10	
why *d* I not give up the ghost	Job 3:11	
Why *d* the knees prevent me	Job 3:12	
D I say, Bring unto me	Job 6:22	
Then *d* he see it, and declare it	Job 28:27	
D not I weep for him that was in	Job 30:25	
If I *d* despise the cause of my	Job 31:13	
D not he that made me in the womb	Job 31:15	
d not one fashion us in the womb	Job 31:15	
The stranger *d* not lodge in the	Job 31:32	
D I fear a great multitude	Job 31:34	
or *d* the contempt of families	Job 31:34	
d according as the LORD commanded	Job 42:9	6213
d eat bread with him in his house	Job 42:11	
there were any that *d* understand	Ps 14:2	
he rode upon a cherub, and *d* fly	Ps 18:10	
he *d* fly upon the wings of the	Ps 18:10	
I *d* not put away his statutes	Ps 18:22	
under me, that my feet *d* not slip	Ps 18:36	
neither *d* I turn again till they	Ps 18:37	
Then *d* I beat them small as the	Ps 18:42	
I *d* cast them out as the dirt in	Ps 18:42	
they that *d* see me without fled	Ps 31:11	
False witnesses *d* rise up	Ps 35:11	
they *d* tear me, and ceased not	Ps 35:15	
which *d* eat of my bread, hath	Ps 41:9	
neither *d* their own arm save them	Ps 44:3	
upon thy right hand *d* stand the	Ps 45:9	
in sin *d* my mother conceive me	Ps 51:5	
d understand, that *d* seek God	Ps 53:2	
that *d* magnify himself against me	Ps 55:12	
there *d* we rejoice in him	Ps 66:6	
Kings of armies *d* flee apace	Ps 68:12	
Marvellous things *d* he in the	Ps 78:12	6213
Man *d* eat angels' food	Ps 78:25	
So they *d* eat, and were well	Ps 78:29	
their days *d* he consume in vanity	Ps 78:33	
Nevertheless they *d* flatter him	Ps 78:36	
d not stir up all his wrath	Ps 78:38	
How oft *d* they provoke him in the	Ps 78:40	
from heaven *d* the LORD behold the	Ps 102:19	
d eat up all the herbs in their	Ps 105:35	
They *d* not destroy the nations,	Ps 106:34	
Many times *d* he deliver them	Ps 106:43	
Princes also *d* sit and speak	Ps 119:23	
but thy servant *d* meditate in thy	Ps 119:23	
that *d* he in heaven, and in earth,	Ps 135:6	6213
Thine eyes *d* see my substance,	Ps 139:16	
the LORD *d* I make my supplication	Ps 142:1	
d not choose the fear of the LORD	Prov 1:29	
and the hills *d* tremble, and their	Is 5:25	
his feet, and with twain he *d* fly	Is 6:2	
afterward *d* more grievously	Is 9:1	
whose graven images *d* excel them	Is 10:10	
Isaiah the son of Amoz *d* see	Is 13:1	
to tremble, that *d* shake kingdoms	Is 14:16	
And he *d* so, walking naked and	Is 20:2	6213
in that day *d* the Lord GOD of	Is 22:12	
or a swallow, so *d* I chatter	Is 38:14	
I *d* mourn as a dove	Is 38:14	
d not the LORD, he against whom	Is 42:24	
I *d* them suddenly, and they came	Is 48:3	6213
yet we *d* esteem him stricken,	Is 53:4	
as a nation that *d* righteousness	Is 58:2	6213

when I called, ye *d* not answer Is 65:12
when I spake, ye *d* not hear Is 65:12 6213
but *d* evil before mine eyes, and Is 65:12
d choose that wherein I delighted Is 65:12 6213
when I called, none *d* answer Is 66:4
when I spake, they *d* not hear Is 66:4
but they *d* evil before mine eyes, Is 66:4 6213
see what I *d* to it for the Jer 7:12 6213
they *d* worse than their fathers Jer 7:26
but they *d* them not Jer 11:8 6213
the wild asses *d* stand in the Jer 14:6
their eyes *d* fail, because there Jer 14:6
for that which he *d* in Jerusalem Jer 15:4 6213
words were found, and I *d* eat them Jer 15:16
d not thy father eat and drink, and Jer 22:15
D Hezekiah king of Judah and all Jer 26:19
d he not fear the LORD, and Jer 26:19
because I *d* bear the reproach of Jer 31:19
Baruch the son of Neriah *d* Jer 36:8 6213
d hearken unto the words of the Jer 37:2
And Jeremiah *d* so Jer 38:12 6213
there they *d* eat bread together Jer 41:1 6213
d we make her cakes to worship Jer 44:19
d not the LORD remember them, and Jer 44:21
because the LORD *d* drive them Jer 46:15
They *d* cry there, Pharaoh king of Jer 46:17
they *d* not stand, because the day Jer 46:21
he *d* that which was evil in the Jer 52:2 6213
of twelve cubits *d* compass it Jer 52:21
he *d* continually eat bread before Jer 52:33
of the enemy, and none *d* help her Lam 1:7
her, and *d* mock at her sabbaths Lam 1:7
They that *d* feed delicately are Lam 4:5
Then *d* I eat it Eze 3:3
the place where they *d* offer Eze 6:13
Then *d* the cherubims lift up Eze 11:22
I *d* so as I was commanded Eze 12:7 6213
neither *d* she strengthen the hand Eze 16:49
this vine *d* bend her roots toward Eze 17:7
d that which is not good among Eze 18:18 6213
they *d* not every man cast away Eze 20:8
neither *d* they forsake the idols Eze 20:8
neither *d* I make an end of them Eze 20:17
I *d* in the morning as I was Eze 24:18 6213
The ships of Tarshish *d* sing of Eze 27:25
under his branches *d* all the Eze 31:6
none *d* search or seek after them Eze 34:6
neither *d* my shepherds search for Eze 34:8
as they *d* cleanse it with the Eze 43:22
as he *d* on the sabbath day Eze 46:12 6213
than all the children which *d* eat Dan 1:15
D not we cast three men bound Dan 3:24
but they *d* not make known unto me Dan 4:7
d eat grass as oxen, and his body Dan 4:33
before his God, as he *d* aforetime Dan 6:10 5648
and the Ancient of days *d* sit Dan 7:9
but he *d* according to his will, Dan 8:4 6213
rose up, and *d* the king's business Dan 8:27 6213
neither *d* I anoint myself at all, Dan 10:3
For she *d* not know that I gave Hos 2:8
because they *d* not hearken unto Hos 9:17
of iniquity *d* not overtake them Hos 10:9
I *d* know thee in the wilderness, Hos 13:5
because he *d* pursue his brother Amos 1:11
d cast off all pity Amos 1:11
his anger *d* tear perpetually, and Amos 1:11
As if a man *d* flee from a lion, Amos 5:19
great deep, and *d* eat up a part Amos 7:4
off those of his that *d* escape Obad 14
d remain in the day of distress Obad 14
and he *d* it not Jonah 3:10 6213
to pass, when the sun *d* arise Jonah 4:8
The lion *d* tear in pieces enough Nah 2:12
which Habakkuk the prophet *d* see Hab 1:1
the perpetual hills *d* bow Hab 3:6
of the land of Midian *d* tremble Hab 3:7
brought it home, I *d* blow upon it Hag 1:9
the people *d* fear before the LORD Hag 1:12
d work in the house of the LORD Hag 1:14 6213
but they *d* not hear, nor hearken Zec 1:4
d they not take hold of your Zec 1:6
so that no man *d* lift up his head Zec 1:21
d ye at all fast unto me, even to Zec 7:5
And when ye *d* eat, and when ye *d* Zec 7:6
d not ye eat for yourselves, and Zec 7:6
Tyrus *d* build herself a strong Zec 9:3
d turn many away from iniquity Mal 2:6
And *d* not he make one Mal 2:15
d as the angel of the Lord had Mt 1:24 4160
when he heard that Archelaus *d* Mt 2:22
him, and so *d* his disciples Mt 9:19
Have ye not read what David *d* Mt 12:3 4160
d eat the shewbread, which was Mt 12:4
he *d* not many mighty works there Mt 13:58 4160
they *d* all eat, and were filled Mt 14:20
well *d* Esaias prophesy of you, Mt 15:7
they *d* all eat, and were filled Mt 15:37
they that *d* eat were four Mt 15:38
his face *d* shine as the sun, and Mt 17:2
Why *d* Moses then command to give Mt 19:7
and ninth hour, and *d* likewise Mt 20:5 4160
d as Jesus commanded them, Mt 21:6 4160
the wonderful things that he *d* Mt 21:15 4160
Why *d* ye not then believe him Mt 21:25
Whether of them twain *d* the will Mt 21:31 4160
they *d* unto them likewise Mt 21:36 4160
D ye never read in the scriptures Mt 21:42
and *d* not minister unto thee Mt 25:44
Inasmuch as ye *d* it not to one of Mt 25:45 4160
least of these, ye *d* it not to me Mt 25:45 4160
my body, she *d* it for my burial Mt 26:12 4160
the disciples *d* as Jesus had Mt 26:19 4160
And as they *d* eat, he said, Verily Mt 26:21
Then *d* they spit in his face, and Mt 26:67

of the children of Israel *d* value Mt 27:9
upon my vesture *d* they cast lots Mt 27:35
and the earth *d* quake, and the Mt 27:51
fear of him the keepers *d* shake Mt 28:4
d run to bring his disciples word Mt 28:8
money, and *d* as they were taught Mt 28:15 4160
John *d* baptize in the wilderness, Mk 1:4
he *d* eat locusts and wild honey Mk 1:6
And at even, when the sun *d* set Mk 1:32
Have ye never read what David *d* Mk 2:25 4160
d eat the shewbread, which is not Mk 2:26
had heard what great things he *d* Mk 3:8 4160
d yield fruit that sprang up and Mk 4:8
and all men *d* marvel Mk 5:20
he *d* many things, and heard him Mk 6:20 4160
they *d* all eat, and were filled Mk 6:42
they that *d* eat of the loaves Mk 6:44
they *d* set them before the people Mk 8:6
So they *d* eat, and were filled Mk 8:8
them, What *d* Moses command you Mk 10:3
Why then *d* ye not believe him Mk 11:31
For all they *d* cast in of their Mk 12:44
but she of her want *d* cast in all Mk 12:44
d eat, Jesus said, Verily I say Mk 14:18
And as they *d* eat, Jesus took Mk 14:22
But neither so *d* their witness Mk 14:59
the servants *d* strike him with Mk 14:65
d spit upon him, and bowing their Mk 15:19
And in those days he *d* eat nothing Lk 4:2
d eat, rubbing them in their Lk 6:1
so much as this, what David *d* Lk 6:3 4160
d take and eat the shewbread, and Lk 6:4
And he *d* so Lk 6:10 4160
for in the like manner *d* their Lk 6:23 4160
for so *d* their fathers to the Lk 6:26 4160
the stream *d* beat vehemently Lk 6:49
d wipe them with the hairs of her Lk 7:38
And they *d* so, and made them all Lk 9:15 4160
And they *d* eat, and were all filled Lk 9:17
one at all things which Jesus *d* Lk 9:43 4160
they *d* not receive him, because Lk 9:53
and consume them, even as Elias *d* Lk 9:54 4160
d not he that made that which is Lk 11:40
neither *d* according to his will, Lk 12:47 4160
d commit things worthy of stripes Lk 12:48
the husks that the swine *d* eat Lk 15:16
thank that servant because he *d* Lk 17:9 4160
They *d* eat, they drank, they Lk 17:27
they *d* eat, they drank, they Lk 17:28
down, and reaping that I *d* not sow Lk 19:22
D not our heart burn within us, Lk 24:32
he took it, and *d* eat before them Lk 24:43
d write, Jesus of Nazareth, the Jn 1:45
d Jesus in Cana of Galilee Jn 2:11 4160
they saw the miracles which he *d* Jn 2:23 4160
But Jesus *d* not commit himself Jn 2:24
told me all things that ever I *d* Jn 4:29 4160
He told me all that ever I *d* Jn 4:39 4160
he *d* at Jerusalem at the feast Jn 4:45 4160
the second miracle that Jesus *d* Jn 4:54 4160
therefore *d* the Jews persecute Jn 5:16
he *d* on them that were diseased Jn 6:2 4160
had seen the miracle that Jesus *d* Jn 6:14 4160
the place where they *d* eat bread Jn 6:23
but because ye *d* eat of the Jn 6:26
Our fathers *d* eat manna in the Jn 6:31
Your fathers *d* eat manna in the Jn 6:49
not as your fathers *d* eat manna Jn 6:58
For neither *d* his brethren Jn 7:5
D not Moses give you the law, and Jn 7:19
this *d* not Abraham Jn 8:40 4160
him, saying, Master, who *d* sin Jn 9:2
But the Jews *d* not believe Jn 9:18
that if any man *d* confess that he Jn 9:22
to him again, What *d* he to thee Jn 9:26 4160
you already, and ye *d* not hear Jn 9:27
but the sheep *d* not hear them Jn 10:8
him, and said, John *d* no miracle Jn 10:41 4160
had seen the things which Jesus *d* Jn 11:45 4160
and *d* hide himself from them Jn 12:36
Pharisees they *d* not confess him Jn 12:42
the works which none other man *d* Jn 15:24 4160
Jesus, and so *d* another disciple Jn 18:15
D not I see thee in the garden Jn 18:26
or *d* others tell it thee of me Jn 18:34
for my vesture they *d* cast lots Jn 19:24
things therefore the soldiers *d* Jn 19:24 4160
the other disciple *d* outrun Peter Jn 20:4
many other signs truly *d* Jesus in Jn 20:30 4160
d cast himself into the sea Jn 21:7
many other things which Jesus *d* Jn 21:25 4160
which God *d* by him in the midst Acts 2:22 4160
Therefore *d* my heart rejoice, and Acts 2:26
his flesh *d* see corruption Acts 2:31
many other words *d* he testify Acts 2:40
d eat their meat with gladness and Acts 2:46
that through ignorance ye *d* it Acts 3:17 4238
as *d* also your rulers Acts 3:17
Why *d* the heathen rage, and the Acts 4:25
D not we straitly command you Acts 5:28
d great wonders and miracles among Acts 6:8 4160
But he that *d* his neighbour wrong Acts 7:27 91
the same *d* God send to be a ruler Acts 7:35
as your fathers *d*, so do ye Acts 7:51
and seeing the miracles which he *d* Acts 8:6 4160
sight, and neither *d* eat nor drink Acts 9:9
works and almsdeeds which she *d* Acts 9:36 4160
of all things which he *d* both in Acts 10:39 4160
of God, even to us, who *d* eat Acts 10:41
the like gift as he *d* unto us Acts 11:17
Which also they *d*, and sent it to Acts 11:30 4160
And so he *d* Acts 12:8 4160
witness, in that he *d* good Acts 14:17 15
Holy Ghost, even as he *d* unto us Acts 15:8

at the first *d* visit the Gentiles Acts 15:14
And this *d* she many days Acts 16:18 4160
chief of the priests, which *d* so Acts 19:14 4160
virgins, which *d* prophesy Acts 21:9
Which thing I also *d* in Jerusalem Acts 26:10 4160
many of the saints *d* I shut up in Acts 26:10 4160
and Moses *d* say should come Acts 26:22
for even their women *d* change the Rom 1:26
even as they *d* not like to retain Rom 1:28
For what if some *d* not believe Rom 3:3
grace *d* much more abound Rom 5:20
d work in our members to bring Rom 7:5
For whom he *d* foreknow Rom 8:29
he also *d* predestinate to be Rom 8:29
Moreover whom he *d* predestinate Rom 8:30
But I say, *D* not Israel know Rom 10:19
and I would to God ye *d* reign 1Cor 4:8
d all eat the same spiritual meat 1Cor 10:3
d all drink the same spiritual 1Cor 10:4
which *d* put all things under him 1Cor 15:27
thus minded, *d* I use lightness 2Cor 1:17
For to this end also *d* I write 2Cor 2:9
as though God *d* beseech you by us 2Cor 5:20
do not repent, though I *d* repent 2Cor 7:8
I *d* it not for his cause that had 2Cor 7:12
And this they *d*, not as we hoped, 2Cor 8:5
But be it so, I *d* not burden you 2Cor 12:16
D I make a gain of you by any of 2Cor 12:17
D Titus make a gain of you 2Cor 12:18
he *d* eat with the Gentiles Gal 2:12
ye *d* service unto them which by Gal 4:8
Ye *d* run well Gal 5:7
who *d* hinder you that ye should Gal 5:7
that ye *d* communicate with my Phil 4:14
Neither *d* we eat any man's bread 2Th 3:8
because I *d* it ignorantly in 1Ti 1:13
the coppersmith *d* me much evil 2Ti 4:14 1731
when they had heard, *d* provoke Heb 3:16
word preached *d* not profit them Heb 4:2
God *d* rest the seventh day from Heb 4:4
his own works, as God *d* from his Heb 4:10
bringing in of a better hope *d* Heb 7:19
for this he *d* once, when he Heb 7:27 4160
him that *d* the service perfect Heb 9:9 3000
which was in them *d* signify 1Pet 1:11
but unto us they *d* minister the 1Pet 1:12
Who *d* no sin, neither was guile 1Pet 2:22 4160
and *d* cast them to the earth Rev 12:4
the wound by a sword, and *d* live Rev 13:14
which *d* corrupt the earth with Rev 19:2
for the glory of God *d* lighten it Rev 21:23

DIDDEST

as thou *d* the Egyptian yesterday Acts 7:28 387

DIDST

why *d* thou not tell me that she Gen 12:18
but thou *d* laugh Gen 18:15
I know that thou *d* this in the Gen 20:6 6213
neither *d* thou tell me, neither Gen 21:26
Wherefore *d* thou flee away Gen 31:27
d not tell me, that I might have Gen 31:27
of my hand *d* thou require it, Gen 31:39
Thou *d* blow with thy wind, the Ex 15:10
as thou *d* anoint their father, Ex 40:15
thou shalt do to him as thou *d* Num 21:34 6213
thou shalt do unto him as thou *d* Deut 3:2 6213
from the day that thou *d* depart Deut 9:7
thou *d* drink the pure blood of Deut 32:14
whom thou *d* prove at Massah, and Deut 33:8
with whom thou *d* strive at the Deut 33:8
which thou *d* let us down by Josh 2:18
her king as thou *d* unto Jericho Josh 8:2 6213
d not call us to go with thee Judg 12:1 6213
thou *d* send come again unto us Judg 13:8 6213
for thou *d* call me 1Sa 3:6
for thou *d* call me 1Sa 3:8
Wherefore then *d* thou not obey 1Sa 15:19
but *d* fly upon the spoil, and 1Sa 15:19
d evil in the sight of the LORD 1Sa 15:19 6213
thou sawest it, and *d* rejoice 1Sa 19:5
come to the place where thou *d* 1Sa 20:19
men of my lord, whom thou *d* send 1Sa 25:25
why then *d* thou not go down unto 2Sa 11:10
For thou *d* it secretly 2Sa 12:12 6213
thou *d* fast and weep for the child 2Sa 12:21
the child was dead, thou *d* rise 2Sa 12:21
the other that thou *d* unto me 2Sa 13:16 6213
why *d* thou not smite him there to 2Sa 18:11
yet *d* thou set thy servant among 2Sa 19:28
D not thou, my lord, O king, 1Kin 1:13
that thou *d* to David my father 1Kin 2:44 6213
thou *d* well that it was in thine 1Kin 8:18
For thou *d* separate them from 1Kin 8:53 6213
All that thou *d* send for to thy 1Kin 20:9
Thou *d* blaspheme God and the king 1Kin 21:10
For thy people Israel *d* thou make 1Chr 17:22
As thou *d* deal with David my 2Chr 2:3
d send him cedars to build him an 2Chr 2:3
thou *d* well in that it was in 2Chr 6:8
because thou *d* rely on the LORD, 2Chr 16:8
who *d* drive out the inhabitants 2Chr 20:7
thou *d* humble thyself before God, 2Chr 34:27
d rend thy clothes, and weep 2Chr 34:27
who *d* choose Abram, and broughtest Neh 9:7
d see the affliction of our Neh 9:9
So *d* thou get thee a name, as it Neh 9:10
thou *d* divide the sea before them Neh 9:11
wonders that thou *d* among them Neh 9:17 6213
forty years *d* thou sustain them Neh 9:21
d divide them into corners Neh 9:22
many times *d* thou deliver them Neh 9:28
Yet many years *d* thou forbear Neh 9:30
thou *d* not utterly consume them Neh 9:31
wherewith thou *d* testify against Neh 9:34

trusted, and thou *d* deliver them Ps 22:4
thou *d* make me hope when I was Ps 22:9
thou *d* hide thy face, and I was Ps 30:7
because thou *d* it Ps 39:9 6213
and offering thou *d* not desire Ps 40:6
what work thou *d* in their days Ps 44:1 6466
How thou *d* drive out the heathen Ps 44:2
how thou *d* afflict the people, and Ps 44:2
which *d* not go out with our Ps 60:10
when thou *d* march through the Ps 68:7
d send a plentiful rain Ps 68:9
whereby thou *d* confirm thine Ps 68:9
Surely thou *d* set them in Ps 73:18
Thou *d* divide the sea by thy Ps 74:13
Thou *d* cleave the fountain and the Ps 74:15
Thou *d* cause judgment to be heard Ps 76:8
d cause it to take deep root, and Ps 80:9
which *d* weaken the nations Is 14:12
thou *d* look in that day to the Is 22:8
thou *d* shew them no mercy Is 47:6
so that thou *d* not lay these Is 47:7
neither *d* remember the latter end Is 47:7
things, and thou *d* not know them Is 48:6
O barren, thou that *d* not bear Is 54:1
thou that *d* not travail with Is 54:1
d increase thy perfumes, and *d* Is 57:9
d debase thyself even unto hell Is 57:9
so *d* thou lead thy people, to Is 63:14
When thou *d* terrible things which Is 64:3 6213
which thou *d* swear to their Jer 32:22
How *d* thou write all these words Jer 36:17
Thou *d* say, Woe is me now Jer 45:3
whom thou *d* command that they Lam 1:10
thou *d* eat fine flour, and honey, Eze 16:13
thou *d* prosper into a kingdom Eze 16:13
But thou *d* trust in thine own Eze 16:15
And of thy garments thou *d* take Eze 16:16
d commit whoredom with them, Eze 16:17
which thou *d* give unto them Eze 16:36
for whom thou *d* wash thyself Eze 23:40
thou *d* enrich the kings of the Eze 27:33
thou *d* break, and rend all their Eze 29:7
As thou *d* rejoice at the Eze 35:15
from the first day that thou *d* Dan 10:12
because thou *d* trust in thy way, Hos 10:13
that thou *d* ride upon thine Hab 3:8
Thou *d* cleave the earth with Hab 3:9
Thou *d* march through the land in Hab 3:12
thou *d* thresh the heathen in Hab 3:12
Thou *d* strike through with his Hab 3:14
Thou *d* walk through the sea with Hab 3:15
d not thou sow good seed in thy Mt 13:27
faith, wherefore *d* thou doubt Mt 14:31
d not thou agree with me for a Mt 20:13
head with oil thou *d* not anoint Lk 7:46
and reapest that thou *d* not sow Lk 19:21
have believed that thou *d* send me Jn 17:8
uncircumcised, and *d* eat with them Acts 11:3
hast thou that thou *d* not receive 1Cor 4:7
now if thou *d* receive it, why 1Cor 4:7
d set him over the works of thy Heb 2:7
unto me, Wherefore *d* thou marvel Rev 17:7

DIDYMUS (*did'-i-mus*) See **THOMAS**. *Another name for Thomas the apostle.*
said Thomas, which is called *D* Jn 11:16 *1324*
one of the twelve, called *D* Jn 20:24 *1324*
Simon Peter, and Thomas called *D* Jn 21:2 *1324*

DIE
thereof thou shalt surely *d* Gen 2:17 4191
shall ye touch it, lest ye *d* Gen 3:3 4191
the woman, Ye shall not surely *d* Gen 3:4 4191
that is in the earth shall *d* Gen 6:17 1478
lest some evil take me, and I *d* Gen 19:19 4191
thou that thou shalt surely *d* Gen 20:7 4191
Behold, I am at the point to *d* Gen 25:32 4191
Because I said, Lest I *d* for her Gen 26:9 4191
my soul may bless thee before I *d* Gen 27:4 4191
Give me children, or else I *d* Gen 30:1 4191
one day, all the flock will *d* Gen 33:13 4191
said, Lest peradventure he *d* also Gen 38:11 4191
that we may live, and not *d* Gen 42:2 4191
be verified, and ye shall not *d* Gen 42:20 4191
that we may live, and not *d* Gen 43:8 4191
it be found, both let him *d* Gen 44:9 4191
his father, his father would *d* Gen 44:22 4191
is not with us, that he will *d* Gen 44:31 4191
I will go and see him before I *d* Gen 45:28 4191
said unto Joseph, Now let me *d* Gen 46:30 4191
why should we *d* in thy presence Gen 47:15 4191
shall we *d* before thine eyes Gen 47:19 4191
seed, that we may live, and not *d* Gen 47:19 4191
time drew nigh that Israel must *d* Gen 47:29 4191
said unto Joseph, Behold, I *d* Gen 48:21 4191
made me swear, saying, Lo, I *d* Gen 50:5 4191
said unto his brethren, I *d* Gen 50:24 4191
fish that is in the river shall *d* Ex 7:18 4191
there shall nothing *d* of all that Ex 9:4 4191
down upon them, and they shall *d* Ex 9:19 4191
thou seest my face thou shalt *d* Ex 10:28 4191
in the land of Egypt shall *d* Ex 11:5 4191
us away to *d* in the wilderness Ex 14:11 4191
we should *d* in the wilderness Ex 14:12 4191
not God speak with us, lest we *d* Ex 20:19 4191
that smiteth a man, so that he *d* Ex 21:12 4191
from mine altar, that he may *d* Ex 21:14 4191
he *d* not, but keepeth his bed Ex 21:18 4191
a rod, and he *d* under his hand Ex 21:20 4191
a man or a woman, that they *d* Ex 21:28 4191
ox hurt another's, that he *d* Ex 21:35 4191
up, and be smitten that he *d* Ex 22:2 4191
and it *d*, or be hurt, or driven Ex 22:10 4191
neighbour, and it be hurt, or *d* Ex 22:14 4191
when he cometh out, that he *d* not Ex 28:35 4191
that they bear not iniquity, and *d* Ex 28:43 4191
wash with water, that they *d* not Ex 30:20 4191
and their feet, that they *d* not Ex 30:21 4191
charge of the LORD, that ye *d* not Lev 8:35 4191
lest ye *d*, and lest wrath come Lev 10:6 4191
of the congregation, lest ye *d* Lev 10:7 4191
of the congregation, lest ye *d* Lev 10:9 4191
any beast, of which ye may eat, *d* Lev 11:39 4191
that they *d* not in their Lev 15:31 4191
that he *d* not Lev 16:2 4191
upon the testimony, that he *d* not Lev 16:13 4191
they shall *d* childless Lev 20:20 4191
d therefore, if they profane it Lev 22:9 4191
touch any holy thing, lest they *d* Num 4:15 4191
that they may live, and not *d* Num 4:19 4191
things are covered, lest they *d* Num 4:20 4191
or for his sister, when they *d* Num 6:7 4194
if any man *d* very suddenly by him Num 6:9 4191
consumed, and there they shall *d* Num 14:35 4191
If these men *d* the common death Num 16:29 4191
from me, that they *d* not Num 17:10 4191
unto Moses, saying, Behold, we *d* Num 17:12 1478
tabernacle of the LORD shall *d* Num 17:13 4191
that neither they, nor ye also, *d* Num 18:3 4191
lest they bear sin, and *d* Num 18:22 4191
the children of Israel, lest ye *d* Num 18:32 4191
we and our cattle should *d* there Num 20:4 4191
unto his people, and shall *d* there Num 20:26 4191
of Egypt to *d* in the wilderness Num 21:5 4191
Let me *d* the death of the Num 23:10 4191
shall surely *d* in the wilderness Num 26:65 4191
of Israel, saying, If a man *d* Num 27:8 4191
that the manslayer *d* not, until Num 35:12 4191
instrument of iron, so that he *d* Num 35:16 4191
wherewith he may *d*, and he *d* Num 35:17 4191
wherewith he may *d*, and he *d* Num 35:18 4191
him by laying of wait, that he *d* Num 35:20 4191
him with his hand, that he *d* Num 35:21 4191
any stone, wherewith a man may *d* Num 35:23 4191
and cast it upon him, that he *d* Num 35:23 4191
any person to cause him to *d* Num 35:30 4191
But I must *d* in this land, I must Deut 4:22 4191
Now therefore why should we *d* Deut 5:25 4191
our God any more, then we shall *d* Deut 5:25 4191
stone him with stones, that he *d* Deut 13:10 4191
them with stones, till they *d* Deut 17:5 4191
the judge, even that man shall *d* Deut 17:12 4191
great fire any more, that I *d* not Deut 18:16 4191
gods, even that prophet shall *d* Deut 18:20 4191
upon his neighbour, that he *d* Deut 19:5 4191
and smite him mortally that he *d* Deut 19:11 4191
avenger of blood, that he may *d* Deut 19:12 4191
lest he *d* in the battle, and Deut 20:5 4191
lest he *d* in the battle, and Deut 20:6 4191
lest he *d* in the battle, and Deut 20:7 4191
stone him with stones, that he *d* Deut 21:21 4191
stone her with stones that she *d* Deut 22:21 4191
then they shall both of them *d* Deut 22:22 4191
them with stones that they *d* Deut 22:24 4191
only that lay with her shall *d* Deut 22:25 4191
or if the latter husband *d* Deut 24:3 4191
then that thief shall *d* Deut 24:7 4191
dwell together, and one of them *d* Deut 25:5 4191
days approach that thou must *d* Deut 31:14 4191
d in the mount whither thou goest Deut 32:50 4191
Let Reuben live, and not *d* Deut 33:6 4191
not *d* by the hand of the avenger Josh 20:9 4191
thou shalt not *d* Judg 6:23 4191
Bring out thy son, that he may *d* Judg 6:30 4191
unto his wife, We shall surely *d* Judg 13:22 4191
and now shall I *d* for thirst Judg 15:18 4191
Let me *d* with the Philistines Judg 16:30 4191
Where thou diest, will I *d* Ruth 1:17 4191
d in the flower of their age 1Sa 2:33 4191
one day they shall *d* both of them 1Sa 2:34 4191
the LORD thy God, that we *d* not 1Sa 12:19 4191
my son, he shall surely *d* 1Sa 14:39 4191
in mine hand, and, lo, I must *d* 1Sa 14:43 4191
for thou shalt surely *d*, Jonathan 1Sa 14:44 4191
said unto Saul, Shall Jonathan *d* 1Sa 14:45 4191
thou shalt not *d* 1Sa 20:2 4191
of the LORD, that I *d* not 1Sa 20:14 4191
unto me, for he shall surely *d* 1Sa 20:31 4191
king said, Thou shalt surely *d* 1Sa 22:16 4191
or his day shall come to *d* 1Sa 26:10 4191
LORD liveth, ye are worthy to *d* 1Sa 26:16 4194
for my life, to cause me to *d* 1Sa 28:9 4191
him, that he may be smitten, and *d* 2Sa 11:15 4191
done this thing shall surely *d* 2Sa 12:5 4194
thou shalt not *d* 2Sa 12:13 4191
is born unto thee shall surely *d* 2Sa 12:14 4191
For we must needs *d*, and are as 2Sa 14:14 4191
neither if half of us *d*, will 2Sa 18:3 4191
unto Shimei, Thou shalt not *d* 2Sa 19:23 4191
that I may *d* in mine own city, and 2Sa 19:37 4191
shall be found in him, he shall *d* 1Kin 1:52 4191
David drew nigh that he should *d* 1Kin 2:1 4191
but I will *d* here 1Kin 2:30 4191
certain that thou shalt surely *d* 1Kin 2:37 4191
whither, that thou shalt surely *d* 1Kin 2:42 4191
into the city, the child shall *d* 1Kin 14:12 4191
my son, that we may eat it, and *d* 1Kin 17:12 4191
for himself that he might *d* 1Kin 19:4 4191
out, and stone him, that he may *d* 1Kin 21:10 4191
art gone up, but shalt surely *d* 2Kin 1:4 4191
art gone up, but shalt surely *d* 2Kin 1:6 4191
art gone up, but shalt surely *d* 2Kin 1:16 4191
Why sit we here until we *d* 2Kin 7:3 4191
in the city, and we shall *d* there 2Kin 7:4 4191
if we sit still here, we *d* also 2Kin 7:4 4191
if they kill us, we shall but *d* 2Kin 7:4 4191
shewed me that he shall surely *d* 2Kin 8:10 4191
honey, that ye may live, and not *d* 2Kin 18:32 4191
for thou shalt *d*, and not live 2Kin 20:1 4191
shall not *d* for the children 2Chr 25:4 4191
the children *d* for the fathers 2Chr 25:4 4191
every man shall *d* for his own sin 2Chr 25:4 4191
over yourselves to *d* by famine 2Chr 32:11 4191
curse God, and *d* Job 2:9 4191
they *d*, even without wisdom Job 4:21 4191
and wisdom shall *d* with you Job 12:2 4191
the stock thereof *d* in the ground Job 14:8 4191
If a man *d*, shall he live again Job 14:14 4191
till I *d* I will not remove mine Job 27:5 1478
I shall *d* in my nest, and I shall Job 29:18 1478
In a moment shall they *d*, and the Job 34:20 4191
they shall *d* without knowledge Job 36:12 1478
They *d* in youth, and their life is Job 36:14 4191
speak evil of me, When shall he *d* Ps 41:5 4191
For he seeth that wise men *d* Ps 49:10 4191
those that are appointed to *d* Ps 79:11 8546
But ye shall *d* like men, and fall Ps 82:7 4191
ready to *d* from my youth up Ps 88:15 1478
takest away their breath, they *d* Ps 104:29 1478
I shall not *d*, but live, and Ps 118:17 4191
He shall *d* without instruction Prov 5:23 4191
but fools *d* for want of wisdom Prov 10:21 4191
and he that hateth reproof shall *d* Prov 15:10 4191
that despiseth his ways shall *d* Prov 19:16 4191
him with the rod, he shall not *d* Prov 23:13 4191
deny me them not before I *d* Prov 30:7 4191
A time to be born, and a time to *d* Eccl 3:2 4191
shouldest thou *d* before thy time Eccl 7:17 4191
the living know that they shall *d* Eccl 9:5 4191
for to morrow we shall *d* Is 22:13 4191
not be purged from you till ye *d* Is 22:14 4191
there shalt thou *d*, and there the Is 22:18 4191
for thou shalt *d*, and not live Is 38:1 4191
therein shall *d* in like manner Is 51:6 4191
be afraid of a man that shall *d* Is 51:12 4191
that he should not *d* in the pit Is 51:14 4191
for the child shall *d* an hundred Is 65:20 4191
for their worm shall not *d* Is 66:24 4191
that thou *d* not by our hand Jer 11:21 4191
young men shall *d* by the sword Jer 11:22 4191
their daughters shall *d* by famine Jer 11:22 4191
They shall *d* of grievous deaths Jer 16:4 4191
and the small shall *d* in this land Jer 16:6 4191
to Babylon, and there thou shalt *d* Jer 20:6 4191
they shall *d* of a great Jer 21:6 4191
in this city shall *d* by the sword Jer 21:9 4191
But he shall *d* in the place Jer 22:12 4191
and there shall ye *d* Jer 22:26 4191
him, saying, Thou shalt surely *d* Jer 26:8 4191
saying, This man is worthy to *d* Jer 26:11 4194
This man is not worthy to *d* Jer 26:16 4194
Why will ye *d*, thou and thy people Jer 27:13 4191
this year thou shalt *d*, because Jer 28:16 4191
But every one shall *d* for his own Jer 31:30 4191
Thou shalt not *d* by the sword Jer 34:4 4191
But thou shalt *d* in peace Jer 34:5 4191
the scribe, lest I *d* there Jer 37:20 4191
in this city shall *d* by the sword Jer 38:2 4191
he is like to *d* for hunger in the Jer 38:9 4191
out of the dungeon, before he *d* Jer 38:10 4191
these words, and thou shalt not *d* Jer 38:24 4191
to Jonathan's house, to *d* there Jer 38:26 4191
and there ye shall *d* Jer 42:16 4191
they shall *d* by the sword, by the Jer 42:17 4191
that ye shall *d* by the sword Jer 42:22 4191
they shall *d*, from the least even Jer 44:12 4191
the wicked, Thou shalt surely *d* Eze 3:18 4191
man shall *d* in his iniquity Eze 3:18 4191
he shall *d* in his iniquity Eze 3:19 4191
before him, he shall *d* Eze 3:20 4191
he shall *d* in his sin, and his Eze 3:20 4191
thee shall *d* with the pestilence Eze 5:12 4191
far off shall *d* of the pestilence Eze 6:12 4191
is besieged shall *d* by the famine Eze 6:12 4191
the field shall *d* with the sword Eze 7:15 4191
see it, though he shall *d* there Eze 12:13 4191
slay the souls that should not *d* Eze 13:19 4191
the midst of Babylon he shall *d* Eze 17:16 4191
the soul that sinneth, it shall *d* Eze 18:4 4191
he shall surely *d* Eze 18:13 4191
he shall not *d* for the iniquity Eze 18:17 4191
even he shall *d* in his iniquity Eze 18:18 4191
The soul that sinneth, it shall *d* Eze 18:20 4191
shall surely live, he shall not *d* Eze 18:21 4191
at all that the wicked should *d* Eze 18:23 4194
hath sinned, in them shall he *d* Eze 18:24 4191
that he hath done shall he *d* Eze 18:26 4191
shall surely live, he shall not *d* Eze 18:28 4191
for why will ye *d*, O house of Eze 18:31 4191
thou shalt *d* the deaths of them Eze 28:8 4191
Thou shalt *d* the deaths of the Eze 28:10 4191
O wicked man, thou shalt surely *d* Eze 33:8 4191
man shall *d* in his iniquity Eze 33:8 4191
he shall *d* in his iniquity Eze 33:9 4191
for why will ye *d*, O house of Eze 33:11 4191
hath committed, he shall *d* for it Eze 33:13 4191
the wicked, Thou shalt surely *d* Eze 33:14 4191
shall surely live, he shall not *d* Eze 33:15 4191
iniquity, he shall even *d* thereby Eze 33:18 4191
caves shall *d* of the pestilence Eze 33:27 4191
Moab shall *d* with tumult, with Amos 2:2 4191
in one house, that they shall *d* Amos 6:9 4191
Jeroboam shall *d* by the sword Amos 7:11 4191
thou shalt *d* in a polluted land Amos 7:17 4191
of my people shall *d* by the sword Amos 9:10 4191
better for me to *d* than to live Jonah 4:3 4194
and wished in himself to *d* Jonah 4:8 4191
better for me to *d* than to live Jonah 4:8 4191
we shall not *d* Hab 1:12 4191
that that dieth, let it *d* Zec 11:9 4191
therein shall be cut off and *d* Zec 13:8 1478
or mother, let him *d* the death Mt 15:4 *5053*
Master, Moses said, If a man *d* Mt 22:24 *599*

D

him, Though I should *d* with thee Mt 26:35 *599*
or mother, let him *d* the death Mk 7:10 *5053*
unto us, If a man's brother *d* Mk 12:19 *599*
If I should *d* with thee, I will Mk 14:31 *4880*
unto him, was sick, and ready to *d* Lk 7:2 *5053*
unto us, If any man's brother *d* Lk 20:28 *599*
he *d* without children, that his Lk 20:28 *599*
Neither can they *d* any more Lk 20:36 *599*
Sir, come down ere my child *d* Jn 4:49 *599*
a man may eat thereof, and not *d* Jn 6:50 *599*
seek me, and shall *d* in your sins Jn 8:21 *599*
you, that ye shall *d* in your sins Jn 8:24 *599*
I am he, ye shall *d* in your sins Jn 8:24 *599*
also go, that we may *d* with him Jn 11:16 *599*
and believeth in me shall never *d* Jn 11:26 *599*
one man should *d* for the people Jn 11:50 *599*
Jesus should *d* for that nation Jn 11:51 *599*
wheat fall into the ground and *d* Jn 12:24 *599*
but if it *d*, it bringeth forth Jn 12:24 *599*
signifying what death he should *d* Jn 12:33 *599*
one man should *d* for the people Jn 18:14 *622*
signifying what death he should *d* Jn 18:32 *599*
law, and by our law he ought to *d* Jn 19:7 *599*
that that disciple should not *d* Jn 21:23 *599*
said not unto him, He shall not *d* Jn 21:23 *599*
but also to *d* at Jerusalem for Acts 21:13 *599*
of death, I refuse not to *d* Acts 25:11 *599*
Romans to deliver any man to *d* Acts 25:16 *684*
for a righteous man will one *d* Rom 5:7 *599*
man some would even dare to *d* Rom 5:7 *599*
live after the flesh, ye shall *d* Rom 8:13 *599*
we *d*, we *d* unto the Lord Rom 14:8 *599*
whether we live therefore, or *d* Rom 14:8 *599*
for it were better for me to *d* 1Cor 9:15 *599*
For as in Adam all *d*, even so in 1Cor 15:22 *599*
Christ Jesus our Lord, I *d* daily 1Cor 15:31 *599*
for to morrow we *d* 1Cor 15:32 *599*
is not quickened, except it *d* 1Cor 15:36 *599*
that ye are in our hearts to *d* 2Cor 7:3 *4880*
live is Christ, and to *d* is gain Phil 1:21 *599*
here men that *d* receive tithes Heb 7:8 *599*
is appointed unto men once to *d* Heb 9:27 *599*
which remain, that are ready to *d* Rev 3:2 *599*
and shall desire to *d*, and death Rev 9:6 *599*
Blessed are the dead which *d* in Rev 14:13 *599*

DIED
and thirty years: and he *d* Gen 5:5 4191
and twelve years: and he *d* Gen 5:8 4191
and five years: and he *d* Gen 5:11 4191
and ten years: and he *d* Gen 5:14 4191
and five years: and he *d* Gen 5:17 4191
and two years: and he *d* Gen 5:20 4191
and nine years: and he *d* Gen 5:27 4191
and seven years: and he *d* Gen 5:31 4191
all flesh *d* that moved upon the Gen 7:21 1478
all that was in the dry land, *d* Gen 7:22 4191
and fifty years: and he *d* Gen 9:29 4191
Haran *d* before his father Terah Gen 11:28 4191
and Terah *d* in Haran Gen 11:32 4191
And Sarah *d* in Kirjath-arba Gen 23:2 4191
d in a good old age, an old man, Gen 25:8 4191
and he gave up the ghost and *d* Gen 25:17 4191
he *d* in the presence of all his Gen 25:18 5307
But Deborah Rebekah's nurse *d* Gen 35:8 4191
(for she *d*) that she called his Gen 35:18 4191
And Rachel *d*, and was buried in the ... Gen 35:19 4191
And Isaac gave up the ghost, and *d* Gen 35:29 4191
And Bela *d*, and Jobab the son of Gen 36:33 4191
And Jobab *d*, and Husham of the land. Gen 36:34 4191
And Husham *d*, and Hadad the son of. Gen 36:35 4191
Hadad *d*, and Samlah of Gen 36:36 4191
And Samlah *d*, and Saul of Rehoboth .. Gen 36:37 4191
And Saul *d*, and Baal-hanan the son Gen 36:38 4191
And Baal-hanan the son of Achbor *d* Gen 36:39 4191
daughter of Shuah Judah's wife *d* Gen 38:12 4191
Onan *d* in the land of Canaan Gen 46:12 4191
Rachel *d* by me in the land of Gen 48:7 4191
father did command before he *d* Gen 50:16 4194
So Joseph *d*, being an hundred and Gen 50:26 4191
And Joseph *d*, and all his brethren, Ex 1:6 4191
of time, that the king of Egypt *d* Ex 2:23 4191
the fish that was in the river *d* Ex 7:21 4191
the frogs *d* out of the houses, Ex 8:13 4191
and all the cattle of Egypt *d* Ex 9:6 4191
the children of Israel *d* not one Ex 9:6 4191
Would to God we had *d* by the hand ... Ex 16:3 4191
them, and they *d* before the LORD Lev 10:2 4191
offered before the LORD, and *d* Lev 16:1 4191
eateth that which *d* of itself Lev 17:15 5038
Abihu *d* before the LORD, when Num 3:4 4191
we had *d* in the land of Egypt Num 14:2 4191
God we had *d* in this wilderness Num 14:2 4191
d by the plague before the LORD Num 14:37 4191
stoned him with stones, and he *d* Num 15:36 4191
Now they that *d* in the plague Num 16:49 4191
beside them that *d* about the Num 16:49 4191
and Miriam *d* there, and was buried Num 20:1 4191
Would God that we had *d* when our Num 20:3 1478
our brethren *d* before the LORD Num 20:3 1478
Aaron *d* there in the top of the Num 20:28 4191
and much people of Israel *d* Num 21:6 4191
those that *d* in the plague were Num 25:9 4191
with Korah, when that company *d* Num 26:10 4194
the children of Korah *d* not Num 26:11 4191
Onan *d* in the land of Canaan Num 26:19 4191
And Nadab and Abihu *d*, when they Num 26:61 4191
Our father *d* in the wilderness, Num 27:3 4191
but *d* in his own sin, and had no Num 27:3 4191
d there, in the fortieth year Num 33:38 4191
years old when he *d* in mount Hor Num 33:39 4194
there Aaron *d*, and there he was Deut 10:6 4191
Aaron thy brother *d* in mount Hor Deut 32:50 4191
LORD *d* there in the land of Moab Deut 34:5 4191
and twenty years old when he *d* Deut 34:7 4194
d in the wilderness by the way, Josh 5:4 4191
upon them unto Azekah, and they *d* Josh 10:11 4191
they were more which *d* with Josh 10:11 4191
Nun, the servant of the LORD, *d* Josh 24:29 4191
And Eleazar the son of Aaron *d* Josh 24:33 4191
him to Jerusalem, and there he *d* Judg 1:7 4191
Nun, the servant of the LORD, *d* Judg 2:8 4191
which Joshua left when he *d* Judg 2:21 4191
And Othniel the son of Kenaz *d* Judg 3:11 4191
asleep and weary. So he *d* Judg 4:21 4191
son of Joash *d* in a good old age Judg 8:32 4191
of the tower of Shechem *d* also Judg 9:49 4191
man thrust him through, and he *d* Judg 9:54 4191
twenty and three years, and *d* Judg 10:2 4191
And Jair *d*, and was buried in Camon.. Judg 10:5 4191
Then *d* Jephthah the Gileadite, and Judg 12:7 4191
Then *d* Ibzan, and was buried at Judg 12:10 4191
And Elon the Zebulonite *d*, and was Judg 12:12 4191
son of Hillel the Pirathonite *d* Judg 12:15 4191
And Elimelech Naomi's husband *d* Ruth 1:3 4191
Chilion *d* also both of them Ruth 1:5 4191
gate, and his neck brake, and he *d* 1Sa 4:18 4191
the men that *d* not were smitten 1Sa 5:12 4191
rescued Jonathan, that he *d* not 1Sa 14:45 4191
And Samuel *d*; and all the Israelites 1Sa 25:1 4191
that his heart *d* within him 1Sa 25:37 4191
the LORD smote Nabal, that he *d* 1Sa 25:38 4191
upon his sword, and *d* with him 1Sa 31:5 4191
So Saul *d*, and his three sons, and 1Sa 31:6 4191
And he smote him that he *d* 2Sa 1:15 4191
there, and *d* in the same place 2Sa 2:23 4191
Asahel fell down and *d* stood still 2Sa 2:23 4191
three hundred and threescore men *d* 2Sa 2:31 4191
under the fifth rib, that he *d* 2Sa 3:27 4191
and said, *D* Abner as a fool dieth 2Sa 3:33 4191
there he *d* by the ark of God 2Sa 6:7 4191
king of the children of Ammon *d* 2Sa 10:1 4191
of their host, who *d* there 2Sa 10:18 4191
and Uriah the Hittite *d* also 2Sa 11:17 4191
the wall, that he *d* in Thebez 2Sa 11:21 4191
the seventh day, that the child *d* 2Sa 12:18 4191
in order, and hanged himself, and *d* 2Sa 17:23 4191
would God I had *d* for thee 2Sa 18:33 4191
lived, and all we had *d* this day 2Sa 19:6 4191
him not again; and he *d* 2Sa 20:10 4191
there *d* of the people from Dan 2Sa 24:15 4191
and he fell upon him that he *d* 1Kin 2:25 4191
out, and fell upon him, that he *d* 1Kin 2:46 4191
this woman's child *d* in the night 1Kin 3:19 4191
stoned him with stones, that he *d* 1Kin 12:18 4191
of the door, the child *d* 1Kin 14:17 4191
house over him with fire, and *d* 1Kin 16:18 4191
so Tibni *d*, and Omri reigned 1Kin 16:22 4191
stoned him with stones, that he *d* 1Kin 21:13 4191
against the Syrians, and *d* at even 1Kin 22:35 4191
So the king *d*, and was brought to 1Kin 22:37 4191
So he *d* according to the word of 2Kin 1:17 4191
on her knees till noon, and then *d* 2Kin 4:20 4191
upon him in the gate, and he *d* 2Kin 7:17 4191
upon him in the gate, and he *d* 2Kin 7:20 4191
it on his face, so that he *d* 2Kin 8:15 4191
And he fled to Megiddo, and *d* there 2Kin 9:27 4191
his servants, smote him, and he *d* 2Kin 12:21 4191
sick of his sickness whereof he *d* 2Kin 13:14 4191
And Elisha *d*, and they buried him 2Kin 13:20 4191
So Hazael king of Syria *d* 2Kin 13:24 4191
and he came to Egypt, and *d* there 2Kin 23:34 4191
him, and smote Gedaliah, that he *d* 2Kin 25:25 4191
Hadad *d* also. And the dukes 1Chr 1:51 4191
but Seled *d* without children 1Chr 2:30 4191
Jether *d* without children 1Chr 2:32 4191
fell likewise on the sword, and *d* 1Chr 10:5 4191
So Saul *d*, and his three sons 1Chr 10:6 4191
and all his house *d* together 1Chr 10:6 4191
So Saul *d* for his transgression 1Chr 10:13 4191
and there he *d* before God 1Chr 13:10 4191
king of the children of Ammon *d* 1Chr 19:1 4191
And Eleazar *d*, and had no sons, but 1Chr 23:22 4191
Abihu *d* before their father, and 1Chr 24:2 4191
he *d* in a good old age, full of 1Chr 29:28 4191
stoned him with stones, that he *d* 2Chr 10:18 4191
and the LORD struck him, and he *d* 2Chr 13:20 4191
d in the one and fortieth year of 2Chr 16:13 4191
time of the sun going down he *d* 2Chr 18:34 4191
so he *d* of sore diseases 2Chr 21:19 4191
and was full of days when he *d* 2Chr 24:15 4191
thirty years old was he when he *d* 2Chr 24:15 4194
And when he *d*, he said, The LORD 2Chr 24:22 4191
and slew him on his bed, and he *d* 2Chr 24:25 4191
brought him to Jerusalem, and he *d* 2Chr 35:24 4191
Why *d* I not from the womb Job 3:11 4191
So Job *d*, being old and full of Job 42:17 4191
d I saw also the Lord sitting Is 6:1 4194
that king Ahaz *d* was this burden Is 14:28 4194
So Hananiah the prophet *d* the Jer 28:17 4191
Pelatiah the son of Benaiah *d* Eze 11:13 4191
and at even my wife *d* Eze 24:18 4191
when he offended in Baal, he *d* Hos 13:1 4191
And last of all the woman *d* also Mt 22:27 *599*
And the second took her, and *d* Mk 12:21 *599*
last of all the woman *d* also Mk 12:22 *599*
came to pass, that the beggar *d* Lk 16:22 *599*
the rich man also *d*, and was Lk 16:22 *599*
a wife, and *d* without children Lk 20:29 *599*
her to wife, and he *d* childless Lk 20:30 *599*
and they left no children, and *d* Lk 20:31 *599*
Last of all the woman *d* also Lk 20:32 *599*
been here, my brother had not *d* Jn 11:21 *599*
been here, my brother had not *d* Jn 11:32 *599*
even this man should not have *d* Jn 11:37 *599*
Jacob went down into Egypt, and *d* Acts 7:15 *5053*
days, that she was sick, and *d* Acts 9:37 *599*
due time Christ *d* for the ungodly Rom 5:6 *599*
were yet sinners, Christ *d* for us Rom 5:8 *599*
that he *d*, he *d* unto sin once Rom 6:10 *599*
came, sin revived, and I *d* Rom 7:9 *599*
It is Christ that *d*, yea rather, Rom 8:34 *599*
For to this end Christ both *d* Rom 14:9 *599*
with thy meat, for whom Christ *d* Rom 14:15 *599*
brother perish, for whom Christ *d* 1Cor 8:11 *599*
how that Christ *d* for our sins 1Cor 15:3 *599*
thus judge, that if one *d* for all 2Cor 5:14 *599*
And that he *d* for all, that they 2Cor 5:15 *599*
but unto him which *d* for them 2Cor 5:15 *599*
For if we believe that Jesus *d* 1Th 4:14 *599*
Who *d* for us, that, whether we 1Th 5:10 *599*
law *d* without mercy under two or Heb 10:28 *599*
These all *d* in faith, not having Heb 11:13 *599*
By faith Joseph, when he *d* Heb 11:22 *5053*
were in the sea, and had life, *d* Rev 8:9 *599*
many men *d* of the waters, because Rev 8:11 *599*
and every living soul *d* in the sea Rev 16:3 *599*

DIEST
Where thou *d*, will I die, and Ruth 1:17 4191

DIET
And for his *d*, there was a Jer 52:34 737
there was a continual *d* given him Jer 52:34 737

DIETH
fat of the beast that *d* of itself Lev 7:24 5038
That which *d* of itself, or is Lev 22:8 5038
the law, when a man *d* in a tent Num 19:14 4191
eat of any thing that *d* of itself Deut 14:21 5038
and said, Died Abner as a fool *d* 2Sa 3:33 4194
Him that *d* of Jeroboam in the 1Kin 14:11 4191
him that *d* in the field shall the 1Kin 14:11 4191
Him that *d* of Baasha in the city 1Kin 16:4 4191
him that *d* of his in the fields 1Kin 16:4 4191
Him that *d* of Ahab in the city 1Kin 21:24 4191
him that *d* in the field shall the 1Kin 21:24 4191
But man *d*, and wasteth away Job 14:10 4191
One *d* in his full strength, being Job 21:23 4191
another *d* in the bitterness of Job 21:25 4191
For when he *d* he shall carry Ps 49:17 4194
When a wicked man *d*, his Prov 11:7 4194
And how *d* the wise man Eccl 2:16 4191
as the one *d*, so *d* the other Eccl 3:19 4194
is no water, and *d* for thirst Is 50:2 4191
he that eateth of their eggs *d* Is 59:5 4191
eaten of that which *d* of itself Eze 4:14 5038
committeth iniquity, and *d* in them Eze 18:26 4191
in the death of him that *d* Eze 18:32 4191
that that *d*, let it die Zec 11:9 4191
Where their worm *d* not, and the Mk 9:44 *5053*
Where their worm *d* not, and the Mk 9:46 *5053*
Where their worm *d* not, and the Mk 9:48 *5053*
raised from the dead *d* no more Rom 6:9 *599*
himself, and no man *d* to himself Rom 14:7 *599*

DIFFER
who maketh thee to *d* from another 1Cor 4:7 *1252*

DIFFERENCE
put a *d* between the Egyptians Ex 11:7 6395
And that ye may put *d* between holy Lev 10:10 914
To make a *d* between the unclean Lev 11:47 914
put *d* between clean beasts Lev 20:25 914
have put no *d* between the holy Eze 22:26
they shewed *d* between the unclean Eze 22:26
my people the *d* between the holy Eze 44:23
put no *d* between us and them, Acts 15:9 *1252*
for there is no *d* Rom 3:22 *1293*
For there is no *d* between the Jew Rom 10:12 *1293*
There is *d* also between a wife and 1Cor 7:34 *3307*
some have compassion, making a *d* Jude 22 *1252*

DIFFERENCES
there are *d* of administrations, 1Cor 12:5 *1243*

DIFFERETH
for one star *d* from another star 1Cor 15:41 *1308*
d nothing from a servant, though Gal 4:1 *1308*

DIFFERING
Having then gifts *d* according to Rom 12:6 *1313*

DIG
a pit, or if a man shall *d* a pit Ex 21:33 3738
whose hills thou mayest *d* brass Deut 8:9 2672
abroad, thou shalt *d* therewith Deut 23:13 2658
d for it more than for hid Job 3:21 2658
ye *d* a pit for your friend Job 6:27 3738
yea, thou shalt *d* about thee Job 11:18 2658
In the dark they *d* through houses Job 24:16 2864
me, Son of man, *d* now in the wall Eze 8:8 2864
D thou through the wall in their Eze 12:5 2864
they shall *d* through the wall to Eze 12:12 2864
Though they *d* into hell, thence Amos 9:2 2864
also, till I shall *d* about it Lk 13:8 *4626*
I cannot *d* Lk 16:3 *4626*

DIGGED
unto me, that I have *d* this well Gen 21:30 2658
had *d* in the days of Abraham his Gen 26:15 2658
Isaac *d* again the wells of water, Gen 26:18 2658
which they had *d* in the days of Gen 26:18 2658
Isaac's servants *d* in the valley Gen 26:19 2658
they *d* another well, and strove Gen 26:21 2658
from thence, and *d* another well Gen 26:22 2658
there Isaac's servants *d* a well Gen 26:25 3738
the well which they had *d* Gen 26:32 2658
their selfwill they *d* down a wall Gen 49:6 6131
in my grave which I have *d* for me Gen 50:5 3738
all the Egyptians *d* round about Ex 7:24 2658
The princes *d* the well Num 21:18 2658
the nobles of the people *d* it Num 21:18 3738
thou filledst not, and wells *d* Deut 6:11 2672
I have *d* and drunk strange waters, 2Kin 19:24 5365
in the desert, and *d* many wells 2Chr 26:10 2672
houses full of all goods, wells *d* Neh 9:25 2672

d it, and is fallen into the ditch Ps 7:15 2658
cause they have *d* for my soul Ps 35:7 2658
they have *d* a pit before me, into Ps 57:6 3738
until the pit be *d* for the wicked Ps 94:13 3738
The proud have *d* pits for me Ps 119:85 3738
it shall not be pruned, nor *d* Is 5:6 5737
that shall be *d* with the mattock Is 7:25 5737
I have *d*, and drunk water Is 37:25 5365
hole of the pit whence ye are *d* Is 51:1 5365
Then I went to Euphrates, and *d* Jer 13:7 2658
for they have *d* a pit for my soul Jer 18:20 3738
for they have *d* a pit to take me Jer 18:22 3738
when I had *d* in the wall, behold Eze 8:8 2864
in the even I *d* through the wall Eze 12:7 2864
d a winepress in it, and built a Mt 21:33 *3736*
d in the earth, and hid his lord's Mt 25:18 *3736*
d a place for the winefat, and Mk 12:1 *3736*
d deep, and laid the foundation on Lk 6:48 *4626*
prophets, and *d* down thine altars Rom 11:3 *2679*

DIGGEDST
and wells digged, which thou *d* not Deut 6:11 2672

DIGGETH
An ungodly man *d* up evil Prov 16:27 3738
Whoso *d* a pit shall fall therein Prov 26:27 3738
He that *d* a pit shall fall into Eccl 10:8 2658

DIGNITIES
are not afraid to speak evil of *d* 2Pet 2:10 *1891*
dominion, and speak evil of *d* Jude 8 *1891*

DIGNITY
my strength, the excellency of *d* Gen 49:3 7613
d hath been done to Mordecai for Est 6:3 1420
Folly is set in great *d*, and the Eccl 10:6 4791
and their *d* shall proceed of Hab 1:7 7613

DIKLAH (*dik'-lah*) *A son of Joktan.*
And Hadoram, and Uzal, and *D* Gen 10:27 1853
Hadoram also, and Uzal, and *D* 1Chr 1:21 1853

DILEAN (*dil'-e-an*) *A city in Judah.*
And *D*, and Mizpeh, and Joktheel, Josh 15:38 1810

DILIGENCE
Keep thy heart with all *d* Prov 4:23 4929
give *d* that thou mayest be Lk 12:58 *2039*
he that ruleth, with *d* Rom 12:8 *4710*
and knowledge, and in all *d* 2Cor 8:7 *4710*
Do thy *d* to come shortly unto me 2Ti 4:9 *4704*
Do thy *d* to come before winter 2Ti 4:21 *4704*
one of you do shew the same *d* to Heb 6:11 *4710*
And beside this, giving all *d* 2Pet 1:5 *4710*
give *d* to make your calling and 2Pet 1:10 *4704*
when I gave all *d* to write unto Jude 3 *4710*

DILIGENT
judges shall make *d* inquisition Deut 19:18 3190
But take *d* heed to do the Josh 22:5 3966
they accomplish a *d* search Ps 64:6
and my spirit made *d* search Ps 77:6
but the hand of the *d* maketh rich Prov 10:4 2742
The hand of the *d* shall bear rule Prov 12:24 2742
substance of a *d* man is precious Prov 12:27 2742
soul of the *d* shall be made fat Prov 13:4 2742
The thoughts of the *d* tend only Prov 21:5 2742
thou a man *d* in his business Prov 22:29 4106
Be thou *d* to know the state of Prov 27:23
proved *d* in many things 2Cor 8:22 *4705*
but now much more *d* 2Cor 8:22 *4707*
be *d* to come unto me to Nicopolis Titus 3:12 *4704*
be *d* that ye may be found of him 2Pet 3:14 *4704*

DILIGENTLY
If thou wilt *d* hearken to the Ex 15:26
Moses *d* sought the goat of the Lev 10:16
to thyself, and keep thy soul *d* Deut 4:9 3966
teach them *d* unto thy children Deut 6:7 8150
Ye shall *d* keep the commandments Deut 6:17
if ye shall hearken *d* unto my Deut 11:13
For if ye shall *d* keep all these Deut 11:22
enquire, and make search, and ask *d* Deut 13:14 3190
hast heard of it, and enquired *d* Deut 17:4 3190
of leprosy, that thou observe *d* Deut 24:8 3966
if thou shalt hearken *d* unto the Deut 28:1
Now the men did *d* observe whether 1Kin 20:33 5172
let it be *d* done for the house of Ezr 7:23 149
Hear *d* my speech, and my Job 13:17
Hear *d* my speech, and let this be Job 21:2
thou shalt *d* consider his place Ps 37:10 995
us to keep thy precepts *d* Ps 119:4 3966
d to seek thy face, and I have Prov 7:15 7836
He that *d* seeketh good procureth Prov 11:27 7836
consider *d* what is before thee Prov 23:1
he hearkened *d* with much heed Is 21:7 7182
hearken *d* unto me, and eat ye that Is 55:2
and send unto Kedar, and consider *d* Jer 2:10 3966
if they will *d* learn the ways of Jer 12:16
if ye *d* hearken unto me, saith Jer 17:24
if ye will *d* obey the voice of Zec 6:15
enquired of them *d* what time the Mt 2:7
search *d* for the young child Mt 2:8 *199*
he had *d* enquired of the wise men Mt 2:16
house, and seek *d* till she find it Lk 15:8 *1960*
taught *d* the things of the Lord, Acts 18:25 *199*
if she have *d* followed every good 1Ti 5:10
in Rome, he sought me out very *d* 2Ti 1:17 *4706*
and Apollos on their journey *d* Titus 3:13 *4709*
rewarder of them that *d* seek him Heb 11:6 *1567*
Looking *d* lest any man fail of Heb 12:15
have enquired and searched *d* 1Pet 1:10

DIM
Isaac was old, and his eyes were *d* Gen 27:1 3543
the eyes of Israel were *d* for age Gen 48:10 3513
his eye was not *d*, nor his Deut 34:7 3543
place, and his eyes began to wax *d* 1Sa 3:2 3544
and his eyes were *d*, that he could 1Sa 4:15 6965

Mine eye also is *d* by reason of Job 17:7 3543
of them that see shall not be *d* Is 32:3 8159
How is the gold become *d* Lam 4:1 6004
for these things our eyes are *d* Lam 5:17 2821

DIMINISH
ye shall not *d* ought thereof Ex 5:8 1639
duty of marriage, shall he not *d* Ex 21:10 1639
thou shalt *d* the price of it Lev 25:16 4591
neither shall ye *d* ought from it Deut 4:2 1639
not add thereto, nor *d* from it Deut 12:32 1639
d not a word Jer 26:2 1639
therefore will I also *d* thee Eze 5:11 1639
for I will *d* them, that they Eze 29:15 4591

DIMINISHED
not ought of your work shall be *d* Ex 5:11 1639
gotten by vanity shall be *d* Prov 13:11 4591
the children of Kedar, shall be *d* Is 21:17 4591
may be increased there, and not *d* Jer 29:6 4591
have *d* thine ordinary food, and Eze 16:27 1639

DIMINISHING
the *d* of them the riches of the Rom 11:12 *2275*

DIMNAH (*dim'-nah*) *A Levitical city in Zebulun.*
D with her suburbs, Nahalal with Josh 21:35 1829

DIMNESS
trouble and darkness, *d* of anguish Is 8:22 4588
Nevertheless the *d* shall not be Is 9:1 4155

DIMON (*di'-mon*) See DIBON, DIMONAH. *A Moabite city.*
For the waters of *D* shall be full Is 15:9 1775
for I will bring more upon *D* Is 15:9 1775

DIMONAH (*di-mo'-nah*) See DIMON. *A city in Judah.*
And Kinah, and *D*, and Adadah, Josh 15:22 1776

DINAH See DINAH'S. *A daughter of Jacob.*
a daughter, and called her name *D* Gen 30:21 1783
D the daughter of Leah, which she Gen 34:1 1783
his soul clave unto *D* the Gen 34:3 1783
he had defiled *D* his daughter Gen 34:5 1783
he had defiled *D* their sister Gen 34:13 1783
took *D* out of Shechem's house, and Gen 34:26 1783
Padan-aram, with his daughter *D* Gen 46:15 1783

DINAH'S
D brethren, took each man his Gen 34:25 1783

DINAITES (*di'-na-ites*) *Foreign settlers in Samaria.*
the *D*, the Apharsathchites, the Ezr 4:9 1784

DINE
these men shall *d* with me at noon Gen 43:16 398
besought him to *d* with him Lk 11:37 *709*
Jesus saith unto them, Come and *d* Jn 21:12 *709*

DINED
So when they had *d*, Jesus saith Jn 21:15 *709*

DINHABAH (*din'-ha-bah*) *Capital of Edom.*
and the name of his city was *D* Gen 36:32 1838
and the name of his city was *D* 1Chr 1:43 1838

DINNER
Better is a *d* of herbs where love Prov 15:17 737
Behold, I have prepared my *d* Mt 22:4 *712*
he had not first washed before *d* Lk 11:38 *712*
When thou makest a *d* or a supper Lk 14:12 *712*

DIONYSIUS (*di-on-ish'-yus*) *An Athenian convert of Paul.*
the which was *D* the Areopagite Acts 17:34 *1354*

DIOTREPHES (*di-ot'-re-feez*) *A believer condemned by John.*
but *D*, who loveth to have the 3Jn 9 *1361*

DIP
d it in the blood that is in the Ex 12:22 2881
the priest shall *d* his finger in Lev 4:6 2881
the priest shall *d* his finger in Lev 4:17 2881
and the hyssop, and shall *d* them Lev 14:6 2881
the priest shall *d* his right Lev 14:16 2881
d them in the blood of the slain Lev 14:51 2881
d it in the water, and sprinkle it Num 19:18 2881
let him *d* his foot in oil Deut 33:24 2881
d thy morsel in the vinegar Ruth 2:14 2881
that he may *d* the tip of his Lk 16:24 *911*

DIPPED
goats, and *d* the coat in the blood Gen 37:31 2881
he *d* his finger in the blood, and Lev 9:9 2881
were *d* in the brim of the water Josh 3:15 2881
d it in an honeycomb, and put his 1Sa 14:27 2881
d himself seven times in Jordan, 2Kin 5:14 2881
d it in water, and spread it on 2Kin 8:15 2881
That thy foot may be *d* in the Ps 68:23 4272
give a sop, when I have *d* it Jn 13:26 *911*
And when he had *d* the sop, he gave Jn 13:26 *1686*
clothed with a vesture *d* in blood Rev 19:13 *911*

DIPPETH
He that *d* his hand with me in the Mt 26:23 *1686*
that *d* with me in the dish Mk 14:20 *1686*

DIRECT
to *d* his face unto Goshen Gen 46:28 3384
will I *d* my prayer unto thee Ps 5:3 6186
him, and he shall *d* thy paths Prov 3:6 3474
of the perfect shall *d* his way Prov 11:5 3474
but wisdom is profitable to *d* Eccl 10:10 3787
and I will *d* all his ways Is 45:13 3474
I will *d* their work in truth, and Is 61:8 5414
man that walketh to *d* his steps Jer 10:23 3559
Jesus Christ, *d* our way unto you 1Th 3:11 *2720*
the Lord *d* your hearts into the 2Th 3:5 *2720*

DIRECTED
Now he hath not *d* his words Job 32:14 6186
O that my ways were *d* to keep thy Ps 119:5 3559
Who hath *d* the Spirit of the LORD Is 40:13 8505

DIRECTETH
He *d* it under the whole heaven, Job 37:3 3474
but the LORD *d* his steps Prov 16:9 3559
as for the upright, he *d* his way Prov 21:29 3559

DIRECTION
by the *d* of the lawgiver, with Num 21:18

DIRECTLY
sprinkle of her blood *d* before Num 19:4
even the way *d* before the wall Eze 42:12 1903

DIRT
and the *d* came out Judg 3:22 6574
them out as the *d* in the streets Ps 18:42 2916
whose waters cast up mire and *d* Is 57:20 2916

DISALLOW
But if her father *d* her in the Num 30:5 5106

DISALLOWED
her, because her father *d* her Num 30:5 5106
But if her husband *d* her on the Num 30:8 5106
his peace at her, and *d* her not Num 30:11 5106
d indeed of men, but chosen of 1Pet 2:4 *593*
the stone which the builders *d* 1Pet 2:7 *593*

DISANNUL
Wilt thou also *d* my judgment Job 40:8 6565
hath purposed, and who shall *d* it Is 14:27 6565
and thirty years after, cannot *d* Gal 3:17 *208*

DISANNULLED
covenant with death shall be *d* Is 28:18 3722

DISANNULLETH
yet if it be confirmed, no man *d* Gal 3:15 *114*

DISANNULLING
For there is verily a *d* of the Heb 7:18 *115*

DISAPPOINT
O LORD, *d* him, cast him down Ps 17:13 6923

DISAPPOINTED
Without counsel purposes are *d* Prov 15:22 6565

DISAPPOINTETH
He *d* the devices of the crafty, Job 5:12 6565

DISCERN
before our brethren *d* thou what Gen 31:32 5234
and she said, *D*, I pray thee, Gen 38:25 5234
so is my lord the king to *d* good 2Sa 14:17 8085
can I *d* between good and evil 2Sa 19:35 3045
that I may *d* between good and bad 1Kin 3:9 995
understanding to *d* judgment 1Kin 3:11 8085
So that the people could not *d* Ezr 3:13 5234
but I could not *d* the form Job 4:16 5234
cannot my taste *d* perverse things Job 6:30 995
cause them to *d* between the Eze 44:23 3045
cannot *d* between their right hand Jonah 4:11 3045
d between the righteous and the Mal 3:18 7200
ye can *d* the face of the sky Mt 16:3 *1252*
but can ye not *d* the signs of the Mt 16:3
ye can *d* the face of the sky and Lk 12:56 *1381*
is it that ye do not *d* this time Lk 12:56
senses exercised to *d* both good Heb 5:14 *1253*

DISCERNED
he *d* him not, because his hands Gen 27:23 5234
the king of Israel *d* him that he 1Kin 20:41 5234
I *d* among the youths, a young man Prov 7:7 995
because they are spiritually *d* 1Cor 2:14 *350*

DISCERNER
is a *d* of the thoughts and intents Heb 4:12 *2924*

DISCERNETH
and a wise man's heart *d* both time Eccl 8:5 3045

DISCERNING
to himself, not *d* the Lord's body 1Cor 11:29 *1252*
to another *d* of spirits 1Cor 12:10 *1253*

DISCHARGE
and there is no *d* in that war Eccl 8:8 4917

DISCHARGED
and will cause them to be *d* there 1Kin 5:9 5310

DISCIPLE
The *d* is not above his master, Mt 10:24 *3101*
It is enough for the *d* that he be Mt 10:25 *3101*
water only in the name of a *d* Mt 10:42 *3101*
who also himself was Jesus' *d* Mt 27:57 *3100*
The *d* is not above his master Lk 6:40 *3101*
own life also, he cannot be my *d* Lk 14:26 *3101*
and come after me, cannot be my *d* Lk 14:27 *3101*
that he hath, he cannot be my *d* Lk 14:33 *3101*
him, and said, Thou art his *d* Jn 9:28 *3101*
Jesus, and so did another *d* Jn 18:15 *3101*
that *d* was known unto the high Jn 18:15 *3101*
Then went out that other *d* Jn 18:16 *3101*
the *d* standing by, whom he loved, Jn 19:26 *3101*
Then saith he to the *d*, Behold Jn 19:27 *3101*
from that hour that *d* took her Jn 19:27 *3101*
being a *d* of Jesus, but secretly Jn 19:38 *3101*
to Simon Peter, and to the other *d* Jn 20:2 *3101*
went forth, and that other *d* Jn 20:3 *3101*
the other *d* did outrun Peter, and Jn 20:4 *3101*
Then went in also that other *d* Jn 20:8 *3101*
Therefore that *d* whom Jesus loved Jn 21:7 *3101*
seeth the *d* whom Jesus loved Jn 21:20 *3101*
that that *d* should not die Jn 21:23 *3101*
This is the *d* which testifieth of Jn 21:24 *3101*
there was a certain *d* at Damascus Acts 9:10 *3101*
and believed not that he was a *d* Acts 9:26 *3101*
Joppa a certain *d* named Tabitha Acts 9:36 *3102*

D

and, behold, a certain *d* was there ... Acts 16:1 *3101*
one Mnason of Cyprus, an old *d* ... Acts 21:16 *3101*

DISCIPLES
seal the law among my *d* ... Is 8:16 3928
he was set, his *d* came unto him ... Mt 5:1 *3101*
And another of his *d* said unto him ... Mt 8:21 *3101*
into a ship, his *d* followed him ... Mt 8:23 *3101*
his *d* came to him, and awoke him, ... Mt 8:25 *3101*
and sat down with him and his *d* ... Mt 9:10 *3101*
saw it, they said unto his *d* ... Mt 9:11 *3101*
Then came to him the *d* of John ... Mt 9:14 *3101*
fast oft, but thy *d* fast not ... Mt 9:14 *3101*
and followed him, and so did his *d* ... Mt 9:19 *3101*
Then saith he unto his *d*, The ... Mt 9:37 *3101*
had called unto him his twelve *d* ... Mt 10:1 *3101*
an end of commanding his twelve *d* ... Mt 11:1 *3101*
of Christ, he sent two of his *d* ... Mt 11:2 *3101*
his *d* were an hungred, and began ... Mt 12:1 *3101*
thy *d* do that which is not lawful ... Mt 12:2 *3101*
forth his hand toward his *d* ... Mt 12:49 *3101*
the *d* came, and said unto him, Why ... Mt 13:10 *3101*
his *d* came unto him, saying, ... Mt 13:36 *3101*
his *d* came, and took up the body, ... Mt 14:12 *3101*
his *d* came to him, saying, This ... Mt 14:15 *3101*
and gave the loaves to his *d* ... Mt 14:19 *3101*
and the *d* to the multitude ... Mt 14:19 *3101*
his *d* to get into a ship, and to ... Mt 14:22 *3101*
when the *d* saw him walking on the ... Mt 14:26 *3101*
Why do thy *d* transgress the ... Mt 15:2 *3101*
Then came his *d*, and said unto him ... Mt 15:12 *3101*
his *d* came and besought him, ... Mt 15:23 *3101*
Then Jesus called his *d* unto him ... Mt 15:32 *3101*
his *d* say unto him, Whence should ... Mt 15:33 *3101*
and brake them, and gave to his *d* ... Mt 15:36 *3101*
and the *d* to the multitude ... Mt 15:36 *3101*
when his *d* were come to the other ... Mt 16:5 *3101*
Caesarea Philippi, he asked his *d* ... Mt 16:13 *3101*
Then charged he his *d* that they ... Mt 16:20 *3101*
began Jesus to shew unto his *d* ... Mt 16:21 *3101*
Then said Jesus unto his *d* ... Mt 16:24 *3101*
And when the *d* heard it, they fell ... Mt 17:6 *3101*
his *d* asked him, saying, Why then ... Mt 17:10 *3101*
Then the *d* understood that he ... Mt 17:13 *3101*
And I brought him to thy *d* ... Mt 17:16 *3101*
Then came the *d* to Jesus apart, ... Mt 17:19 *3101*
same time came the *d* unto Jesus ... Mt 18:1 *3101*
His *d* say unto him, If the case ... Mt 19:10 *3101*
and the *d* rebuked them ... Mt 19:13 *3101*
Then said Jesus unto his *d* ... Mt 19:23 *3101*
When his *d* heard it, they were ... Mt 19:25 *3101*
the twelve *d* apart in the way ... Mt 20:17 *3101*
of Olives, then sent Jesus two *d* ... Mt 21:1 *3101*
the *d* went, and did as Jesus ... Mt 21:6 *3101*
And when the *d* saw it, they ... Mt 21:20 *3101*
him their *d* with the Herodians ... Mt 22:16 *3101*
to the multitude, and to his *d* ... Mt 23:1 *3101*
his *d* came to him for to shew him ... Mt 24:1 *3101*
the *d* came unto him privately, ... Mt 24:3 *3101*
these sayings, he said unto his *d* ... Mt 26:1 *3101*
But when his *d* saw it, they had ... Mt 26:8 *3101*
bread the *d* came to Jesus ... Mt 26:17 *3101*
passover at thy house with my *d* ... Mt 26:18 *3101*
the *d* did as Jesus had appointed ... Mt 26:19 *3101*
and brake it, and gave it to the *d* ... Mt 26:26 *3101*
Likewise also said all the *d* ... Mt 26:35 *3101*
Gethsemane, and saith unto the *d* ... Mt 26:36 *3101*
And he cometh unto the *d*, and ... Mt 26:40 *3101*
Then cometh he to his *d*, and saith ... Mt 26:45 *3101*
Then all the *d* forsook him ... Mt 26:56 *3101*
lest his *d* come by night, and ... Mt 27:64 *3101*
tell his *d* that he is risen from ... Mt 28:7 *3101*
and did run to bring his *d* word ... Mt 28:8 *3101*
And as they went to tell his *d* ... Mt 28:9 *3101*
His *d* came by night, and stole him ... Mt 28:13 *3101*
Then the eleven *d* went away into ... Mt 28:16 *3101*
also together with Jesus and his *d* ... Mk 2:15 *3101*
and sinners, they said unto his *d* ... Mk 2:16 *3101*
the *d* of John and of the Pharisees ... Mk 2:18 *3101*
unto him, Why do the *d* of John ... Mk 2:18 *3101*
fast, but thy *d* fast not ... Mk 2:18 *3101*
his *d* began, as they went, to ... Mk 2:23 *3101*
himself with his *d* to the sea ... Mk 3:7 *3101*
And he spake to his *d*, that a ... Mk 3:9 *3101*
he expounded all things to his *d* ... Mk 4:34 *3101*
his *d* said unto him, Thou seest ... Mk 5:31 *3101*
and his *d* follow him ... Mk 6:1 *3101*
when his *d* heard of it, they came ... Mk 6:29 *3101*
his *d* came unto him, and said, ... Mk 6:35 *3101*
gave them to his *d* to set before ... Mk 6:41 *3101*
his *d* to get into the ship ... Mk 6:45 *3101*
of his *d* eat bread with defiled ... Mk 7:2 *3101*
Why walk not thy *d* according to ... Mk 7:5 *3101*
his *d* asked him concerning the ... Mk 7:17 *3101*
eat, Jesus called his *d* unto him ... Mk 8:1 *3101*
his *d* answered him, From whence ... Mk 8:4 *3101*
gave to his *d* to set before them ... Mk 8:6 *3101*
he entered into a ship with his *d* ... Mk 8:10 *3101*
Now the *d* had forgotten to take ... Mk 8:14
And Jesus went out, and his *d* ... Mk 8:27 *3101*
and by the way he asked his *d* ... Mk 8:27 *3101*
turned about and looked on his *d* ... Mk 8:33 *3101*
people unto him with his *d* also ... Mk 8:34 *3101*
And when he came to his *d*, he saw ... Mk 9:14 *3101*
I spake to thy *d* that they should ... Mk 9:18 *3101*
his *d* asked him privately, Why ... Mk 9:28 *3101*
For he taught his *d*, and said unto ... Mk 9:31 *3101*
in the house his *d* asked him ... Mk 10:10 *3101*
his *d* rebuked those that brought ... Mk 10:13 *3101*
round about, and saith unto his *d* ... Mk 10:23 *3101*
the *d* were astonished at his ... Mk 10:24 *3101*
he went out of Jericho with his *d* ... Mk 10:46 *3101*
he sendeth forth two of his *d* ... Mk 11:1 *3101*
And his *d* heard it ... Mk 11:14 *3101*
And he called unto him his *d* ... Mk 12:43 *3101*
one of his *d* saith unto him, ... Mk 13:1 *3101*
his *d* said unto him, Where wilt ... Mk 14:12 *3101*
And he sendeth forth two of his *d* ... Mk 14:13 *3101*
shall eat the passover with my *d* ... Mk 14:14 *3101*
his *d* went forth, and came into ... Mk 14:16 *3101*
and he saith to his *d*, Sit ye here ... Mk 14:32 *3101*
But go your way, tell his *d* ... Mk 16:7 *3101*
Pharisees murmured against his *d* ... Lk 5:30 *3101*
Why do the *d* of John fast often, ... Lk 5:33 *3101*
likewise the *d* of the Pharisees ... Lk 5:33
his *d* plucked the ears of corn, ... Lk 6:1 *3101*
was day, he called unto him his *d* ... Lk 6:13 *3101*
plain, and the company of his *d* ... Lk 6:17 *3101*
And he lifted up his eyes on his *d* ... Lk 6:20 *3101*
many of his *d* went with him, and ... Lk 7:11 *3101*
the *d* of John shewed him of all ... Lk 7:18 *3101*
two of his *d* sent them to Jesus ... Lk 7:19 *3101*
his *d* asked him, saying, What ... Lk 8:9 *3101*
he went into a ship with his *d* ... Lk 8:22 *3101*
he called his twelve *d* together ... Lk 9:1 *3101*
And he said to his *d*, Make them ... Lk 9:14 *3101*
gave to the *d* to set before the ... Lk 9:16 *3101*
praying, his *d* were with him ... Lk 9:18 *3101*
I besought thy *d* to cast him out ... Lk 9:40 *3101*
Jesus did, he said unto his *d* ... Lk 9:43 *3101*
And when his *d* James and John saw ... Lk 9:54 *3101*
And he turned him unto his *d* ... Lk 10:23 *3101*
one of his *d* said unto him, Lord, ... Lk 11:1 *3101*
pray, as John also taught his *d* ... Lk 11:1 *3101*
to say unto his *d* first of all ... Lk 12:1 *3101*
And he said unto his *d*, Therefore ... Lk 12:22 *3101*
And he said also unto his *d* ... Lk 16:1 *3101*
Then said he unto the *d*, It is ... Lk 17:1 *3101*
And he said unto the *d*, The days ... Lk 17:22 *3101*
but when his *d* saw it, they ... Lk 18:15 *3101*
of Olives, he sent two of his *d* ... Lk 19:29 *3101*
of the *d* began to rejoice ... Lk 19:37 *3101*
unto him, Master, rebuke thy *d* ... Lk 19:39 *3101*
all the people he said unto his *d* ... Lk 20:45 *3101*
shall eat the passover with my *d* ... Lk 22:11 *3101*
and his *d* also followed him ... Lk 22:39 *3101*
from prayer, and was come to his *d* ... Lk 22:45 *3101*
after John stood, and two of his *d* ... Jn 1:35 *3101*
the two *d* heard him speak, and ... Jn 1:37 *3101*
both Jesus was called, and his *d* ... Jn 2:2 *3101*
and his *d* believed on him ... Jn 2:11 *3101*
mother, and his brethren, and his *d* ... Jn 2:12 *3101*
his *d* remembered that it was ... Jn 2:17 *3101*
his *d* remembered that he had said ... Jn 2:22 *3101*
his *d* into the land of Judaea ... Jn 3:22 *3101*
question between some of John's *d* ... Jn 3:25 *3101*
made and baptized more *d* than John ... Jn 4:1 *3101*
himself baptized not, but his *d* ... Jn 4:2 *3101*
(For his *d* were gone away unto ... Jn 4:8 *3101*
And upon this came his *d*, and ... Jn 4:27 *3101*
the mean while his *d* prayed him ... Jn 4:31 *3101*
said the *d* one to another ... Jn 4:33 *3101*
and there he sat with his *d* ... Jn 6:3 *3101*
One of his *d*, Andrew, Simon ... Jn 6:8 *3101*
thanks, he distributed to the *d* ... Jn 6:11 *3101*
the *d* to them that were set down ... Jn 6:11 *3101*
were filled, he said unto his *d* ... Jn 6:12 *3101*
his *d* went down unto the sea, ... Jn 6:16 *3101*
one whereinto his *d* were entered ... Jn 6:22 *3101*
went not with his *d* into the boat ... Jn 6:22 *3101*
but that his *d* were gone away ... Jn 6:22 *3101*
was not there, neither his *d* ... Jn 6:24 *3101*
Many therefore of his *d*, when ... Jn 6:60 *3101*
himself that his *d* murmured at it ... Jn 6:61 *3101*
that time many of his *d* went back ... Jn 6:66 *3101*
that thy *d* also may see the works ... Jn 7:3 *3101*
my word, then are ye my *d* indeed ... Jn 8:31 *3101*
his *d* asked him, saying, Master, ... Jn 9:2 *3101*
will ye also be his *d* ... Jn 9:27 *3101*
but we are Moses' *d* ... Jn 9:28 *3101*
Then after that saith he to his *d* ... Jn 11:7 *3101*
His *d* say unto him, Master, the ... Jn 11:8 *3101*
Then said his *d*, Lord, if he ... Jn 11:12 *3101*
and there continued with his *d* ... Jn 11:54 *3101*
Then saith one of his *d*, Judas ... Jn 12:4 *3101*
understood not his *d* at the first ... Jn 12:16 *3101*
Then the *d* looked one on another, ... Jn 13:22 *3101*
on Jesus' bosom one of his *d* ... Jn 13:23 *3101*
all men know that ye are my *d* ... Jn 13:35 *3101*
so shall ye be my *d* ... Jn 15:8 *3101*
some of his *d* among themselves ... Jn 16:17 *3101*
His *d* said unto him, Lo, now ... Jn 16:29 *3101*
with his *d* over the brook Cedron ... Jn 18:1 *3101*
the which he entered, and his *d* ... Jn 18:1 *3101*
resorted thither with his *d* ... Jn 18:2 *3101*
not thou also one of this man's *d* ... Jn 18:17 *3101*
priest then asked Jesus of his *d* ... Jn 18:19 *3101*
Art not thou also one of his *d* ... Jn 18:25 *3101*
Then the *d* went away again unto ... Jn 20:10 *3101*
told the *d* that she had seen the ... Jn 20:18 *3101*
the doors were shut where the *d* ... Jn 20:19 *3101*
Then were the *d* glad, when they ... Jn 20:20 *3101*
The other *d* therefore said unto ... Jn 20:25 *3101*
days again his *d* were within ... Jn 20:26 *3101*
Jesus in the presence of his *d* ... Jn 20:30 *3101*
to the *d* at the sea of Tiberias ... Jn 21:1 *3101*
of Zebedee, and two other of his *d* ... Jn 21:2 *3101*
but the *d* knew not that it was ... Jn 21:4 *3101*
the other *d* came in a little ship ... Jn 21:8 *3101*
none of the *d* durst ask him, Who ... Jn 21:12 *3101*
Jesus shewed himself to his *d* ... Jn 21:14 *3101*
stood up in the midst of the *d* ... Acts 1:15 *3101*
number of the *d* was multiplied ... Acts 6:1 *3101*
the multitude of the *d* unto them ... Acts 6:2 *3101*
the number of the *d* multiplied in ... Acts 6:7 *3101*
against the *d* of the Lord ... Acts 9:1 *3101*
with the *d* which were at Damascus ... Acts 9:19 *3101*
Then the *d* took him by night, and ... Acts 9:25 *3101*
assayed to join himself to the *d* ... Acts 9:26 *3101*
the *d* had heard that Peter was ... Acts 9:38 *3101*
the *d* were called Christians ... Acts 11:26 *3101*
Then the *d*, every man according ... Acts 11:29 *3101*
the *d* were filled with joy, and ... Acts 13:52 *3101*
as the *d* stood round about him, ... Acts 14:20 *3101*
Confirming the souls of the *d* ... Acts 14:22 *3101*
they abode long time with the *d* ... Acts 14:28 *3101*
put a yoke upon the neck of the *d* ... Acts 15:10 *3101*
in order, strengthening all the *d* ... Acts 18:23 *3101*
exhorting the *d* to receive him ... Acts 18:27 *3101*
and finding certain *d*, ... Acts 19:1 *3101*
from them, and separated the *d* ... Acts 19:9 *3101*
people, the *d* suffered him not ... Acts 19:30 *3101*
Paul called unto him the *d* ... Acts 20:1 *3101*
when the *d* came together to break ... Acts 20:7 *3101*
things, to draw away *d* after them ... Acts 20:30 *3101*
And finding *d*, we tarried there ... Acts 21:4 *3101*
also certain of the *d* of Caesarea ... Acts 21:16 *3101*

DISCIPLES'
and began to wash the *d* feet ... Jn 13:5 *3101*

DISCIPLINE
He openeth also their ear to *d* ... Job 36:10 4148

DISCLOSE
the earth also shall *d* her blood ... Is 26:21 1540

DISCOMFITED
And Joshua *d* Amalek and his people .. Ex 17:13 2522
them, and *d* them, even unto Hormah. Num 14:45 3807
the LORD *d* them before Israel, and ... Josh 10:10 1949
And the LORD *d* Sisera, and all his ... Judg 4:15 2000
and Zalmunna, and *d* all the host ... Judg 8:12 2729
upon the Philistines, and *d* them ... 1Sa 7:10 1949
lightning, and *d* them ... 2Sa 22:15 2000
he shot out lightnings, and *d* them ... Ps 18:14 1949
and his young men shall be *d* ... Is 31:8 4522

DISCOMFITURE
and there was a very great *d* ... 1Sa 14:20 4103

DISCONTENTED
in debt, and every one that was *d* ... 1Sa 22:2

DISCONTINUE
shalt *d* from thine heritage that ... Jer 17:4 8058

DISCORD
he soweth *d* ... Prov 6:14 4066
he that soweth *d* among brethren ... Prov 6:19 4090

DISCOURAGE
wherefore *d* ye the heart of the ... Num 32:7 5106

DISCOURAGED
was much *d* because of the way ... Num 21:4 7114
they *d* the heart of the children ... Num 32:9 5106
fear not, neither be *d* ... Deut 1:21 2865
our brethren have *d* our heart ... Deut 1:28 4549
He shall not fail nor be *d* ... Is 42:4 7533
children to anger, lest they be *d* ... Col 3:21 *120*

DISCOVER
wife, nor *d* his father's skirt ... Deut 22:30 1540
we will *d* ourselves unto them ... 1Sa 14:8 1540
Who can *d* the face of his garment ... Job 41:13 1540
but that his heart may *d* itself ... Prov 18:2 1540
d not a secret to another ... Prov 25:9 1540
the LORD will *d* their secret ... Is 3:17 6168
Therefore will I *d* thy skirts ... Jer 13:26 2834
he will *d* thy sins ... Lam 4:22 1540
will *d* thy nakedness unto them, ... Eze 16:37 1540
now will I *d* her lewdness in the ... Hos 2:10 1540
I will *d* the foundations thereof ... Mic 1:6 1540
I will *d* thy skirts upon thy face ... Nah 3:5 1540

DISCOVERED
thy nakedness be not *d* thereon ... Ex 20:26 1540
he hath *d* her fountain, and she ... Lev 20:18 6168
both of them *d* themselves unto ... 1Sa 14:11 1540
When Saul heard that David was *d* ... 1Sa 22:6 3045
foundations of the world were *d* ... 2Sa 22:16 1540
of the world were *d* at thy rebuke ... Ps 18:15 1540
he *d* the covering of Judah, and ... Is 22:8 1540
for thou hast *d* thyself to ... Is 57:8 1540
thine iniquity are thy skirts *d* ... Jer 13:22 1540
they have not *d* thine iniquity, ... Lam 2:14 1540
the foundation thereof shall be *d* ... Eze 13:14 1540
thy nakedness *d* through thy ... Eze 16:36 1540
Before thy wickedness was *d* ... Eze 16:57 1540
in that your transgressions are *d* ... Eze 21:24 1540
In thee have they *d* their ... Eze 22:10 1540
These *d* her nakedness ... Eze 23:10 1540
So she *d* her whoredoms, and ... Eze 23:18 1540
her whoredoms, and *d* her nakedness .. Eze 23:18 1540
of thy whoredoms shall be *d* ... Eze 23:29 1540
the iniquity of Ephraim was *d* ... Hos 7:1 1540
Now when we had *d* Cyprus, we left ... Acts 21:3 *398*
but they *d* a certain creek with a ... Acts 27:39 *2657*

DISCOVERETH
He *d* deep things out of darkness, ... Job 12:22 1540
hinds to calve, and *d* the forests ... Ps 29:9 2834

DISCOVERING
by *d* the foundation unto the neck ... Hab 3:13 6168

DISCREET
let Pharaoh look out a man *d* ... Gen 41:33 995
thee all this, there is none so *d* ... Gen 41:39 995
To be *d*, chaste, keepers at home, ... Titus 2:5 *4998*

DISCREETLY
when Jesus saw that he answered *d* ... Mk 12:34 *3562*

DISCRETION
he will guide his affairs with *d* ... Ps 112:5 4941
to the young man knowledge and *d* ... Prov 1:4 4209
D shall preserve thee, ... Prov 2:11 4209
keep sound wisdom and *d* ... Prov 3:21 4209

That thou mayest regard *d* Prov 5:2 4209
a fair woman which is without *d* Prov 11:22 2940
The *d* of a man deferreth his Prov 19:11 7922
his God doth instruct him to *d* Is 28:26 4941
out the heavens by his *d* Jer 10:12 8394

DISDAINED
about, and saw David, he *d* him 1Sa 17:42 959
whose fathers I would have *d* to Job 30:1 3988

DISEASE
whether I shall recover of this *d* 2Kin 1:2 2483
saying, Shall I recover of this *d* 2Kin 8:8 2483
saying, Shall I recover of this *d* 2Kin 8:9 2483
until his *d* was exceeding great 2Chr 16:12 2483
yet in his *d* he sought not to the 2Chr 16:12 2483
great sickness by *d* of thy bowels 2Chr 21:15 4245
in his bowels with an incurable *d* 2Chr 21:18 2483
of my *d* is my garment changed Job 30:18
are filled with a loathsome *d* Ps 38:7
An evil *d*, say they, cleaveth Ps 41:8 1697
is vanity, and it is an evil *d* Eccl 6:2 2483
all manner of *d* among the people Mt 4:23 *3119*
and every *d* among the people Mt 9:35 *3119*
of sickness and all manner of *d* Mt 10:1 *3119*
made whole of whatsoever *d* he had Jn 5:4 *3553*

DISEASED
his old age he was *d* in his feet 1Kin 15:23 2470
of his reign was *d* in his feet 2Chr 16:12 2470
The *d* have ye not strengthened, Eze 34:4 2456
pushed all the *d* with your horns, Eze 34:21 2456
which was *d* with an issue of Mt 9:20
brought unto him all that were *d* Mt 14:35
brought unto him all that were *d* Mk 1:32
which he did on them that were *d* Jn 6:2 *770*

DISEASES
put none of these *d* upon thee Ex 15:26 4245
put none of the evil *d* of Egypt Deut 7:15 4064
upon thee all the *d* of Egypt Deut 28:60 4064
so he died of sore *d* 2Chr 21:19 8463
(for they left him in great *d* 2Chr 24:25 4251
who healeth all thy *d* Ps 103:3 8463
that were taken with divers *d* Mt 4:24 *3554*
many that were sick of divers *d* Mk 1:34 *3554*
divers *d* brought them unto him Lk 4:40 *3554*
him, and to be healed of their *d* Lk 6:17 *3554*
over all devils, and to cure *d* Lk 9:1 *3554*
the *d* departed from them, and the Acts 19:12 *3554*
which had *d* in the island, came, Acts 28:9 *769*

DISFIGURE
for they *d* their faces, that they Mt 6:16 *853*

DISGRACE
do not *d* the throne of thy glory Jer 14:21 5034

DISGUISE
d thyself, that thou be not known 1Kin 14:2 8138
unto Jehoshaphat, I will *d* myself 1Kin 22:30 2664
unto Jehoshaphat, I will *d* myself 2Chr 18:29 2664

DISGUISED
Saul *d* himself, and put on other 1Sa 28:8 2664
d himself with ashes upon his 1Kin 20:38 2664
And the king of Israel *d* himself 1Kin 22:30 2664
So the king of Israel *d* himself 2Chr 18:29 2664
but *d* himself, that he might 2Chr 35:22 2664

DISGUISETH
and *d* his face Job 24:15 5643

DISH
forth butter in a lordly *d* Judg 5:25 5602
Jerusalem as a man wipeth a *d* 2Kin 21:13 6747
dippeth his hand with me in the *d* Mt 26:23 *5165*
that dippeth with me in the *d* Mk 14:20 *5165*

DISHAN (*di'-shan*) See DISHON. *A son of Seir.*
And Dishon, and Ezer, and *D* Gen 36:21 1789
The children of *D* are these Gen 36:28 1789
Duke Dishon, duke Ezer, duke *D* Gen 36:30 1789
Anah, and Dishon, and Ezar *D* 1Chr 1:38 1789
The sons of *D* 1Chr 1:42 1789

DISHES
And thou shalt make the *d* thereof Ex 25:29 7086
which were upon the table, his *d* Ex 37:16 7086
of blue, and put thereon the *d* Num 4:7 7086

DISHON (*di'-shon*) See DISHAN.
1. A son of Seir.
And *D*, and Ezer, and Dishan Gen 36:21 1788
And these are the children of *D* Gen 36:26 1788
Duke *D*, duke Ezer, duke Dishan Gen 36:30 1788
Shobal, and Zibeon, and Anah, and *D*. 1Chr 1:38 1788
2. A son of Anah.
D, and Aholibamah the daughter of Gen 36:25 1788
The sons of Anah; *D* 1Chr 1:41 1788
And the sons of *D* 1Chr 1:41 1788

DISHONEST
thy *d* gain which thou hast made Eze 22:13 1215
to destroy souls, to get *d* gain Eze 22:27 1215

DISHONESTY
renounced the hidden things of *d* 2Cor 4:2 *152*

DISHONOUR
meet for us to see the king's *d* Ezr 4:14 6173
d that magnify themselves against Ps 35:26 3639
and my shame, and my *d* Ps 69:19 3639
reproach and *d* that seek my hurt Ps 71:13 3639
A wound and *d* shall he get Prov 6:33 7036
I honour my Father, and ye do *d* me Jn 8:49 *818*
to *d* their own bodies between Rom 1:24 *818*
unto honour, and another unto *d* Rom 9:21 *819*
It is sown in *d* 1Cor 15:43 *819*
By honour and *d*, by evil report and 2Cor 6:8 *819*
and some to honour, and some to *d* 2Ti 2:20 *819*

DISHONOUREST
breaking the law *d* thou God Rom 2:23 *818*

DISHONOURETH
For the son *d* the father, the Mic 7:6 5034
his head covered, *d* his head 1Cor 11:4 *2617*
her head uncovered *d* her head 1Cor 11:5 *2617*

DISINHERIT
d them, and will make of thee a Num 14:12 3423

DISMAYED
fear not, neither be *d* Deut 31:8 2865
be not afraid, neither be thou *d* Josh 1:9 2865
Fear not, neither be thou *d* Josh 8:1 2865
unto them, Fear not, nor be *d* Josh 10:25 2865
of the Philistine, they were *d* 1Sa 17:11 2865
were of small power, they were *d* 2Kin 19:26 2865
dread not, nor be *d* 1Chr 22:13 2865
fear not, nor be *d* 1Chr 28:20 2865
Be not afraid nor *d* by reason of 2Chr 20:15 2865
fear not, nor be *d* 2Chr 20:17 2865
be not afraid nor *d* for the king 2Chr 32:7 2865
I was *d* at the seeing of it Is 21:3 926
were of small power, they were *d* Is 37:27 2865
be not *d* Is 41:10 8159
or do evil, that we may be *d* Is 41:23 8159
be not *d* at their faces, lest I Jer 1:17 2865
wise men are ashamed, they are *d* Jer 8:9 2865
be not *d* at the signs of heaven Jer 10:2 2865
for the heathen are *d* at them Jer 10:2 2865
be *d*, but let not me be *d* Jer 17:18 2865
they shall fear no more, nor be *d* Jer 23:4 2865
neither be *d*, O Israel Jer 30:10 2865
Wherefore have I seen them *d* Jer 46:5 2844
O my servant Jacob, and be not *d* Jer 46:27 2865
Misgab is confounded and *d* Jer 48:1 2865
Elam to be *d* before their enemies Jer 49:37 2865
and they shall be *d* Jer 50:36 2865
nor be *d* at their looks, though Eze 2:6 2865
neither be *d* at their looks, Eze 3:9 2865
mighty men, O Teman, shall be *d* Obad 9 2865

DISMAYING
a *d* to all them about him Jer 48:39 4288

DISMISSED
the priest *d* not the courses 2Chr 23:8 6362
So when they were *d*, they came to Acts 15:30 *630*
thus spoken, he *d* the assembly Acts 19:41 *630*

DISOBEDIENCE
For as by one man's *d* many were Rom 5:19 *3876*
in a readiness to revenge all *d* 2Cor 10:6 *3876*
now worketh in the children of *d* Eph 2:2 *543*
of God upon the children of *d* Eph 5:6 *543*
God cometh on the children of *d* Col 3:6 *543*
d received a just recompence of Heb 2:2 *3876*

DISOBEDIENT
who was *d* unto the word of the 1Kin 13:26 4784
Nevertheless they were *d*, and Neh 9:26 4784
the *d* to the wisdom of the just Lk 1:17 *545*
I was not *d* unto the heavenly Acts 26:19 *545*
of evil things, *d* to parents, Rom 1:30 *545*
stretched forth my hands unto a *d* Rom 10:21 *544*
man, but for the lawless and *d* 1Ti 1:9 *506*
d to parents, unthankful, unholy, 2Ti 3:2 *545*
deny him, being abominable, and *d* Titus 1:16 *545*
also were sometimes foolish, *d* Titus 3:3 *545*
but unto them which be *d*, the 1Pet 2:7 *544*
stumble at the word, being *d* 1Pet 2:8 *544*
Which sometime were *d*, when once 1Pet 3:20 *544*

DISOBEYED
thou hast *d* the mouth of the LORD 1Kin 13:21 4784

DISORDERLY
from every brother that walketh *d* 2Th 3:6 *814*
behaved not ourselves *d* among you 2Th 3:7 *812*
are some which walk among you *d* 2Th 3:11 *814*

DISPATCH
and *d* them with their swords Eze 23:47 1254

DISPENSATION
a *d* of the gospel is committed 1Cor 9:17 *3622*
That in the *d* of the fulness of Eph 1:10 *3622*
If ye have heard of the *d* of the Eph 3:2 *3622*
according to the *d* of God which Col 1:25 *3622*

DISPERSE
D yourselves among the people, and 1Sa 14:34 6327
The lips of the wise *d* knowledge Prov 15:7 2219
and *d* them in the countries Eze 12:15 2219
d them through the countries Eze 20:23 2219
d thee in the countries, and will Eze 22:15 2219
will *d* them through the countries Eze 29:12 2219
will *d* them through the countries Eze 30:23 2219
d them among the countries Eze 30:26 2219

DISPERSED
d of all his children throughout 2Chr 11:23 6555
d among the people in all the Est 3:8 6504
He hath *d*, he hath given to the Ps 112:9 6340
Let thy fountains be *d* abroad Prov 5:16 6327
gather together the *d* of Judah Is 11:12 5310
they were *d* through the countries Eze 36:19 2219
even the daughter of my *d* Zeph 3:10 6327
go unto the *d* among the Gentiles Jn 7:35 *1290*
as many as obeyed him, were *d* Acts 5:37 *1287*
it is written, He hath *d* abroad 2Cor 9:9 *4650*

DISPERSIONS
of your *d* are accomplished Jer 25:34 8600

DISPLAYED
that it may be *d* because of the Ps 60:4 5127

DISPLEASE
Let it not *d* my lord that I Gen 31:35 2734
now therefore, if it *d* thee Num 22:34
that thou *d* not the lords of the 1Sa 29:7
Joab, Let not this thing *d* thee 2Sa 11:25
it *d* him, and he turn away his Prov 24:18

DISPLEASED
the thing which he did *d* the LORD Gen 38:10
the head of Ephraim, it *d* him Gen 48:17
people complained, it *d* the LORD Num 11:1
Moses also was *d* Num 11:10
But the thing *d* Samuel, when they 1Sa 8:6
very wroth, and the saying *d* him 1Sa 18:8
And David was *d*, because the LORD 2Sa 6:8 2734
that David had done *d* the LORD 2Sa 11:27
his father had not *d* him at any 1Kin 1:6 6087
went to his house heavy and *d* 1Kin 20:43 2198
d because of the word which 1Kin 21:4 2198
And David was *d*, because the LORD 1Chr 13:11 2734
God was *d* with this thing 1Chr 21:7
scattered us, thou hast been *d* Ps 60:1 599
it *d* him that there was no Is 59:15
was sore *d* with himself, and set Dan 6:14 888
But it *d* Jonah exceedingly, and he Jonah 4:1
Was the LORD *d* against the rivers Hab 3:8 2734
been sore *d* with your fathers Zec 1:2 7107
I am very sore *d* with the heathen Zec 1:15 7107
for I was but a little *d*, and they Zec 1:15 7107
they were sore *d*, Mt 21:15 *23*
when Jesus saw it, he was much *d* Mk 10:14 *23*
began to be much *d* with James Mk 10:41 *23*
Herod was highly *d* with them of Acts 12:20 *2371*

DISPLEASURE
was afraid of the anger and hot *d* Deut 9:19 2534
Philistines, though I do them a *d* Judg 15:3 7451
wrath, and vex them in his sore *d* Ps 2:5 2740
neither chasten me in thy hot *d* Ps 6:1 2534
neither chasten me in thy hot *d* Ps 38:1 2534

DISPOSED
Or who hath *d* the whole world Job 34:13 7760
Dost thou know when God *d* them Job 37:15 7760
when he was *d* to pass into Achaia Acts 18:27 *1014*
you to a feast, and ye be *d* to go 1Cor 10:27 *2309*

DISPOSING
but the whole *d* thereof is of the Prov 16:33 4941

DISPOSITION
the law by the *d* of angels Acts 7:53 *1296*

DISPOSSESS
ye shall *d* the inhabitants of the Num 33:53 3423
how can I *d* them Deut 7:17 3423

DISPOSSESSED
d the Amorite which was in it Num 32:39 3423
d the Amorites from before his Judg 11:23 3423

DISPUTATION
d with them, they determined that Acts 15:2 *4803*

DISPUTATIONS
receive ye, but not to doubtful *d* Rom 14:1 *1253*

DISPUTE
the righteous might *d* with him Job 23:7 3198

DISPUTED
What was it that ye *d* among Mk 9:33 *1260*
way they had *d* among themselves Mk 9:34 *1256*
Jesus, and *d* against the Grecians Acts 9:29 *4802*
Therefore *d* he in the synagogue Acts 17:17 *1256*
he *d* about the body of Moses Jude 9 *1256*

DISPUTER
where is the *d* of this world 1Cor 1:20 *4804*

DISPUTING
and of Asia, *d* with Stephen Acts 6:9 *4802*
And when there had been much *d* Acts 15:7 *4803*
for the space of three months, *d* Acts 19:8 *1256*
d daily in the school of one Acts 19:9 *1256*
me in the temple *d* with any man Acts 24:12 *1256*

DISPUTINGS
things without murmurings and *d* Phil 2:14 *1261*
Perverse *d* of men of corrupt 1Ti 6:5 *3859*

DISQUIET
d the inhabitants of Babylon Jer 50:34 7264

DISQUIETED
said to Saul, Why hast thou *d* me 1Sa 28:15 7264
surely they are *d* in vain Ps 39:6 1993
and why art thou *d* in me Ps 42:5 1993
and why art thou *d* within me Ps 42:11 1993
and why art thou *d* within me Ps 43:5 1993
For three things the earth is *d* Prov 30:21 7264

DISQUIETNESS
by reason of the *d* of my heart Ps 38:8 5100

DISSEMBLED
d also, and they have put it even Josh 7:11 3584
For ye *d* in your hearts, when ye Jer 42:20 8582
the other Jews *d* likewise with Gal 2:13 *4942*

DISSEMBLERS
neither will I go in with *d* Ps 26:4 5956

DISSEMBLETH
He that hateth *d* with his lips Prov 26:24 5234

DISSENSION
Paul and Barnabas had no small *d* Acts 15:2 *4714*
there arose a *d* between the Acts 23:7 *4714*
And when there arose a great *d* Acts 23:10 *4714*

DISSIMULATION
Let love be without *d* Rom 12:9 *505*
was carried away with their *d* Gal 2:13 *5272*

D

DISSOLVE
make interpretations, and *d* doubts Dan 5:16 8271

DISSOLVED
all the inhabitants thereof are *d* Ps 75:3 4127
thou, whole Palestina, art *d* Is 14:31 4127
broken down, the earth is clean *d* Is 24:19 6565
all the host of heaven shall be *d* Is 34:4 4743
opened, and the palace shall be *d* Nah 2:6 4127
house of this tabernacle were *d* 2Cor 5:1 2647
that all these things shall be *d* 2Pet 3:11 3089
heavens being on fire shall be *d* 2Pet 3:12 3089

DISSOLVEST
ride upon it, and *d* my substance Job 30:22 4127

DISSOLVING
d of doubts, were found in the Dan 5:12 8271

DISTAFF
spindle, and her hands hold the *d* Prov 31:19 6418

DISTANT
equally *d* one from another Ex 36:22 7947

DISTIL
my speech shall *d* as the dew Deut 32:2 5140
do drop and *d* upon man abundantly Job 36:28 7491

DISTINCTION
they give a *d* in the sounds 1Cor 14:7 1293

DISTINCTLY
in the book in the law of God *d* Neh 8:8 6567

DISTRACTED
while I suffer thy terrors I am *d* Ps 88:15 6323

DISTRACTION
attend upon the Lord without *d* 1Cor 7:35 563

DISTRESS
answered me in the day of my *d* Gen 35:3 6869
therefore is this *d* come upon us Gen 42:21 6869
D not the Moabites, neither Deut 2:9 6696
d them not, nor meddle with them Deut 2:19 6696
thine enemies shall *d* thee Deut 28:53 6693
shall *d* thee in all thy gates Deut 28:55 6693
enemy shall *d* thee in thy gates Deut 28:57 6693
come unto me now when ye are in *d* Judg 11:7 6887
And every one that was in *d* 1Sa 22:2 4689
In my *d* I called upon the LORD, 2Sa 22:7 6862
redeemed my soul out of all *d* 1Kin 1:29 6869
in the time of his *d* did he 2Chr 28:22 6887
Ye see the *d* that we are in, how Neh 2:17 7451
pleasure, and we are in great *d* Neh 9:37 6869
hast enlarged me when I was in *d* Ps 4:1 6862
In my *d* I called upon the LORD, Ps 18:6 6862
I called upon the LORD in *d* Ps 118:5 4712
In my *d* I cried unto the LORD, and Ps 120:1 6869
when *d* and anguish cometh upon you Prov 1:27 6869
a strength to the needy in his *d* Is 25:4 6862
Yet I will *d* Ariel, and there Is 29:2 6693
and her munition, and that *d* her Is 29:7 6693
land at this once, and will *d* them Jer 10:18 6887
for I am in *d* Lam 1:20 6887
spoken proudly in the day of *d* Obad 12 6869
that did remain in the day of *d* Obad 14 6869
of wrath, a day of trouble and *d* Zeph 1:15 4691
And I will bring *d* upon men Zeph 1:17 6887
shall be great *d* in the land Lk 21:23 318
and upon the earth *d* of nations Lk 21:25 4928
shall tribulation, or *d*, or Rom 8:35 4730
this is good for the present *d* 1Cor 7:26 318
our affliction and *d* by your faith 1Th 3:7 318

DISTRESSED
Jacob was greatly afraid and *d* Gen 32:7 3334
Moab was *d* because of the Num 22:3 6973
and they were greatly *d* Judg 2:15 3334
so that Israel was sore *d* Judg 10:9 3334
a strait, (for the people were *d* 1Sa 13:6 5065
the men of Israel were *d* that day 1Sa 14:24 5065
And Saul answered, I am sore *d* 1Sa 28:15 6887
And David was greatly *d* 1Sa 30:6 3334
I am *d* for thee, my brother 2Sa 1:26 6887
d him, but strengthened him not 2Chr 28:20 6696
troubled on every side, yet not *d* 2Cor 4:8 4729

DISTRESSES
O bring thou me out of my *d* Ps 25:17 4691
he delivered them out of their *d* Ps 107:6 4691
and he saved them out of their *d* Ps 107:13 4691
and he saveth them out of their *d* Ps 107:19 4691
he bringeth them out of their *d* Ps 107:28 4691
and Noph shall have *d* daily Eze 30:16 6862
afflictions, in necessities, in *d* 2Cor 6:4 4730
in *d* for Christ's sake 2Cor 12:10 4730

DISTRIBUTE
d for inheritance in the plains Josh 13:32 5157
to *d* the oblations of the LORD, 2Chr 31:14 5414
was to *d* unto their brethren Neh 13:13 2505
d unto the poor, and thou shalt Lk 18:22 1239
be rich in good works, ready to *d* 1Ti 6:18 2130

DISTRIBUTED
d for inheritance to them Josh 14:1 5157
And David *d* them, both Zadok of 1Chr 24:3 2505
whom David had *d* in the house of 2Chr 23:18 2505
he *d* to the disciples, and the Jn 6:11 1239
But as God hath *d* to every man 1Cor 7:17 3307
the rule which God hath *d* to us 2Cor 10:13 3307

DISTRIBUTETH
God *d* sorrows in his anger Job 21:17 2505

DISTRIBUTING
D to the necessity of saints Rom 12:13 2841

DISTRIBUTION
d was made unto every man Acts 4:35 1239
and for your liberal *d* unto them 2Cor 9:13 2842

DITCH
Yet shalt thou plunge me in the *d* Job 9:31 7845
fallen into the *d* which he made Ps 7:15 7845
For a whore is a deep *d* Prov 23:27 7745
Ye made also a *d* between the two Is 22:11 4724
blind, both shall fall into the *d* Mt 15:14 999
they not both fall into the *d* Lk 6:39 999

DITCHES
LORD, Make this valley full of *d* 2Kin 3:16 1356

DIVERS
not sow thy vineyard with *d* seeds Deut 22:9 3610
not wear a garment of *d* sorts Deut 22:11 8162
not have in thy bag *d* weights Deut 25:13
have in thine house *d* measures Deut 25:14
to Sisera a prey of *d* colours Judg 5:30 6648
a prey of *d* colours of needlework Judg 5:30 6648
of *d* colours of needlework on Judg 5:30 6648
a garment of *d* colours upon her 2Sa 13:18 6446
rent her garment of *d* colours 2Sa 13:19 6446
of *d* colours, and all manner of 1Chr 29:2 7553
d kinds of spices prepared by the 2Chr 16:14
d also of the princes of Israel 2Chr 21:4
Nevertheless *d* of Asher and 2Chr 30:11 582
He sent *d* sorts of flies among Ps 78:45
there came *d* sorts of flies, and Ps 105:31
D weights, and *d* measures, Prov 20:10
D weights are an abomination unto Prov 20:23
words there are also *d* vanities Eccl 5:7
thy high places with *d* colours Eze 16:16 2921
of feathers, which had *d* colours Eze 17:3 7553
that were taken with *d* diseases Mt 4:24 4164
and earthquakes, in *d* places Mt 24:7
many that were sick of *d* diseases Mk 1:34 4164
for *d* of them came from far Mk 8:3 5100
shall be earthquakes in *d* places Mk 13:8
d diseases brought them unto him Lk 4:40 4164
earthquakes shall be in *d* places Lk 21:11
But when *d* were hardened, and Acts 19:9 5100
to another *d* kinds of tongues 1Cor 12:10
with sins, led away with *d* lusts 2Ti 3:6 4164
deceived, serving *d* lusts Titus 3:3 4164
in *d* manners spake in time past Heb 1:1 4187
with *d* miracles, and gifts of the Heb 2:4 4164
d washings, and carnal ordinances, Heb 9:10 1313
Be not carried about with *d* Heb 13:9 4164
when ye fall into *d* temptations Jas 1:2 4164

DIVERSE
thy cattle gender with a *d* kind Lev 19:19 3610
vessels being *d* one from another Est 1:7 8138
their laws are *d* from all people Est 3:8 8138
from the sea, *d* one from another Dan 7:3 8133
it was *d* from all the beasts that Dan 7:7 8133
which was *d* from all the others, Dan 7:19 8133
which shall be *d* from all Dan 7:23 8133
he shall be *d* from the first, and Dan 7:24 8133

DIVERSITIES
Now there are *d* of gifts, but the 1Cor 12:4 1243
there are *d* of operations, but it 1Cor 12:6 1243
helps, governments, *d* of tongues 1Cor 12:28 1085

DIVIDE
let it *d* the waters from the Gen 1:6 914
to *d* the day from the night Gen 1:14 914
to *d* the light from the darkness Gen 1:18 914
I will *d* them in Jacob, and Gen 49:7 2505
and at night he shall *d* the spoil Gen 49:27 2505
thine hand over the sea, and *d* it Ex 14:16 1234
will overtake, I will *d* the spoil Ex 15:9 2505
the live ox, and *d* the money of it Ex 21:35 2673
and the dead ox also they shall *d* Ex 21:35 2673
the vail shall *d* unto you between Ex 26:33 914
but shall not *d* it asunder Lev 1:17 914
neck, but shall not *d* it asunder Lev 5:8 2505
cud, or of them that *d* the hoof Lev 11:4 6536
the swine, though he *d* the hoof Lev 11:7 6536
d the prey into two parts Num 31:27 2673
ye shall *d* the land by lot for an Num 33:54 5157
which shall *d* the land unto you Num 34:17 5157
to *d* the land by inheritance Num 34:18 5157
to *d* the inheritance unto the Num 34:29
or of them that *d* the cloven hoof Deut 14:7 6536
chew the cud, but *d* not the hoof Deut 14:7 6536
d the coasts of thy land, which Deut 19:3
d for an inheritance the land Josh 1:6
only *d* thou it by lot unto the Josh 13:6 5307
Now therefore *d* this land for an Josh 13:7 2505
they shall *d* it into seven parts Josh 18:5 2505
d the spoil of your enemies with Josh 22:8 2505
said, Thou and Ziba *d* the land 2Sa 19:29 2505
D the living child in two, and 1Kin 3:25 1504
neither mine nor thine, but *d* it 1Kin 3:26 1504
thou didst *d* the sea before them, Neh 9:11 1234
didst *d* them into corners Neh 9:22 2505
the innocent shall *d* the silver Job 27:17 2505
O Lord, and *d* their tongues Ps 55:9 6385
I will *d* Shechem, and mete out the Ps 60:6 2505
Thou didst *d* the sea by thy Ps 74:13 6565
I will *d* Shechem, and mete out the Ps 108:7 2505
than to *d* the spoil with the Prov 16:19 2505
men rejoice when they *d* the spoil Is 9:3 2505
Therefore will I *d* him a portion Is 53:12 5312
he shall *d* the spoil with the Is 53:12 5312
balances to weigh, and *d* the hair Eze 5:1 2505
when ye shall *d* by lot the land Eze 45:1 5307
So shall ye *d* this land unto you Eze 47:21 2505
that ye shall *d* it by lot for an Eze 47:22 5307
shall *d* by lot unto the tribes of Eze 48:29 5307
shall *d* the land for gain Dan 11:39 2505
that he *d* the inheritance with me Lk 12:13 3307
this, and *d* it among yourselves Lk 22:17 1266

DIVIDED
God *d* the light from the darkness Gen 1:4 914
d the waters which were under the Gen 1:7 914
of the Gentiles *d* in their lands Gen 10:5 6504
for in his days was the earth *d* Gen 10:25 6385
by these were the nations *d* in Gen 10:32 5504
he *d* himself against them, he and Gen 14:15 2505
d them in the midst, and laid each Gen 15:10 1334
but the birds *d* he not Gen 15:10 1334
he *d* the people that was with him Gen 32:7 2673
he *d* the children unto Leah, and Gen 33:1 2673
dry land, and the waters were *d* Ex 14:21 1234
Unto these the land shall be *d* Num 26:53 2505
the land shall be *d* by lot Num 26:55 2505
thereof be *d* between many Num 26:56 2505
which Moses *d* from the men that Num 31:42 2673
hath *d* unto all nations under the Deut 4:19 2505
When the Most High *d* to the Deut 32:8
of Israel did, and they *d* the land Josh 14:5 2505
there Joshua *d* the land unto the Josh 18:10 2505
d for an inheritance by lot in Josh 19:51
I have *d* unto you by lot these Josh 23:4 5307
have they not *d* the prey Judg 5:30 2505
he *d* the three hundred men into Judg 7:16 2673
d them into three companies, and Judg 9:43 2673
d her, together with her bones, Judg 19:29 5408
and in their death they were not *d* 2Sa 1:23 6504
people of Israel *d* into two parts 1Kin 16:21 2505
So they *d* the land between them 1Kin 18:6 2505
the waters, and they were *d* hither 2Kin 2:8 2673
in his days the earth was *d* 1Chr 1:19 6385
David *d* them into courses among 1Chr 23:6 2505
and thus were they *d* 1Chr 24:4 2505
Thus were they *d* by lot, one sort 1Chr 24:5 2505
d them speedily among all the 2Chr 35:13 7323
Who hath *d* a watercourse for the Job 38:25 6385
that tarried at home *d* the spoil Ps 68:12 2505
He *d* the sea, and caused them to Ps 78:13 1234
d them an inheritance by line, and Ps 78:55 5307
To him which *d* the Red sea into Ps 136:13 1504
is the prey of a great spoil *d* Is 33:23 2505
his hand hath *d* it unto them by Is 34:17 2505
that *d* the sea, whose waves Is 51:15 7280
The anger of the LORD hath *d* them Lam 4:16 2505
neither shall they be *d* into two Eze 37:22 2673
of iron, the kingdom shall be *d* Dan 2:41 6386
Thy kingdom is *d*, and given to the Dan 5:28 6537
shall be *d* toward the four winds Dan 11:4 2673
Their heart is *d* Hos 10:2 2505
and thy land shall be *d* by line Amos 7:17 2505
turning away he hath *d* our fields Mic 2:4 2505
thy spoil shall be *d* in the midst Zec 14:1 2505
Every kingdom *d* against itself is Mt 12:25 3307
every city or house *d* against Mt 12:25 3307
Satan, he is *d* against himself Mt 12:26 3307
if a kingdom be *d* against itself Mk 3:24 3307
if a house be *d* against itself, Mk 3:25 3307
rise up against himself, and be *d* Mk 3:26 3307
the two fishes *d* he among them Mk 6:41 3307
Every kingdom *d* against itself is Lk 11:17 1266
a house *d* against a house falleth Lk 11:17
Satan also be *d* against himself Lk 11:18 1266
shall be five in one house *d* Lk 12:52 1266
father shall be *d* against the son Lk 12:53 1266
he *d* unto them his living Lk 15:12 1244
he *d* their land to them by lot Acts 13:19 2624
the multitude of the city was *d* Acts 14:4 4977
and the multitude was *d* Acts 23:7 4977
Is Christ *d*? 1Cor 1:13 3307
great city was *d* into three parts Rev 16:19 1096

DIVIDER
made me a judge or a *d* over you Lk 12:14 3312

DIVIDETH
the cud, but *d* not the hoof Lev 11:4 6536
the cud, but *d* not the hoof Lev 11:5 6536
the cud, but *d* not the hoof Lev 11:6 6536
of every beast which *d* the hoof Lev 11:26 6536
the swine, because it *d* the hoof Deut 14:8 6536
He *d* the sea with his power, and Job 26:12 7280
of the LORD *d* the flames of fire Ps 29:7 2672
which *d* the sea when the waves Jer 31:35 7280
as a shepherd *d* his sheep from Mt 25:32 873
he trusted, and *d* his spoils Lk 11:22 1239

DIVIDING
of *d* the land for inheritance by Josh 19:49
they made an end of *d* the country Josh 19:51 2505
d the water before them, to make Is 63:12 1234
a time and times and the *d* of time Dan 7:25 6387
d to every man severally as he 1Cor 12:11 1244
rightly *d* the word of truth 2Ti 2:15 3718
even to the *d* asunder of soul Heb 4:12 3311

DIVINATION
the rewards of *d* in their hand Num 22:7 7081
is there any *d* against Israel Num 23:23 7081
through the fire, or that useth *d* Deut 18:10 7081
pass through the fire, and used *d* 2Kin 17:17 7081
unto you a false vision and *d* Jer 14:14 7081
d within the house of Israel Eze 12:24 4738
They have seen vanity and lying *d* Eze 13:6 7081
and have ye not spoken a lying *d* Eze 13:7 4738
head of the two ways, to use *d* Eze 21:21 7081
hand was the *d* for Jerusalem Eze 21:22 7081
them as a false *d* in their sight Eze 21:23 7080
with a spirit of *d* met us Acts 16:16 4436

DIVINATIONS
see no more vanity, nor divine *d* Eze 13:23 7081

DIVINE
such a man as I can certainly *d* Gen 44:15 5172
d unto me by the familiar spirit, 1Sa 28:8 7080
A *d* sentence is in the lips of Prov 16:10 7081
that see vanity, and that *d* lies Eze 13:9 7080

no more vanity, nor *d* divinations Eze 13:23 7181
whiles they *d* a lie unto thee, to Eze 21:29 7080
unto you, that ye shall not *d* Mic 3:6 7080
the prophets thereof *d* for money Mic 3:11 7080
had also ordinances of *d* service Heb 9:1 *2999*
According as his *d* power hath 2Pet 1:3 *2304*
be partakers of the *d* nature 2Pet 1:4 *2304*

DIVINERS
observers of times, and unto *d* Deut 18:14 7080
called for the priests and the *d* 1Sa 6:2 7080
of the liars, and maketh *d* mad Is 44:25 7080
to your prophets, nor to your *d* Jer 27:9 7080
Let not your prophets and your *d* Jer 29:8 7080
be ashamed, and the *d* confounded Mic 3:7 7080
the *d* have seen a lie, and have Zec 10:2 7080

DIVINETH
drinketh, and whereby indeed he *d* Gen 44:5 5172

DIVINING
d lies unto them, saying, Thus Eze 22:28 7080

DIVISION
I will put a *d* between my people Ex 8:23 6304
after the *d* of the families of 2Chr 35:5 2515
you, Nay; but rather *d* Lk 12:51 *1267*
So there was a *d* among the people Jn 7:43 *4978*
And there was a *d* among them Jn 9:16 *4978*
There was a *d* therefore again Jn 10:19 *4978*

DIVISIONS
to their *d* by their tribes Josh 11:23 4256
a possession according to their *d* Josh 12:7 4256
of Israel according to their *d* Josh 18:10 4256
For the *d* of Reuben there were Judg 5:15 6391
For the *d* of Reuben there were Judg 5:16 6391
Now these are the *d* of the sons 1Chr 24:1 4256
Concerning the *d* of the porters 1Chr 26:1 4256
these were the *d* of the porters 1Chr 26:12 4256
These are the *d* of the porters 1Chr 26:19 4256
d of the families of the fathers 2Chr 35:5 6391
might give according to the *d* of 2Chr 35:12 4653
they set the priests in their *d* Ezr 6:18 6392
And of the Levites were *d* in Judah Neh 11:36 4256
brethren, mark them which cause *d* Rom 16:17 *1370*
and that there be no *d* among you 1Cor 1:10 *4978*
you envying, and strife, and *d* 1Cor 3:3 *1370*
I hear that there be *d* among you 1Cor 11:18 *4978*

DIVORCE
away, and given her a bill of *d* Jer 3:8 3748

DIVORCED
or a *d* woman, or profane, or an Lev 21:14 1644
daughter be a widow, or *d* Lev 22:13 1644
of a widow, and of her that is *d* Num 30:9 1644
her that is *d* committeth adultery Mt 5:32 *630*

DIVORCEMENT
let him write her a bill of *d* Deut 24:1 3748
her, and write her a bill of *d* Deut 24:3 3748
is the bill of your mother's *d* Is 50:1 3748
let him give her a writing of *d* Mt 5:31 *647*
command to give a writing of *d* Mt 19:7 *647*
suffered to write a bill of *d* Mk 10:4 *647*

DIZAHAB *(diz'-a-hab) A place in the Sinai wilderness.*
and Laban, and Hazeroth, and *D* Deut 1:1 1774

DO
d bring a flood of waters upon Gen 6:17
I *d* set my bow in the cloud, and Gen 9:13
and this they begin to *d* Gen 11:6 6213
which they have imagined to *d* Gen 11:6 6213
d to her as it pleaseth thee Gen 16:6 6213
And they said, So *d*, as thou hast Gen 18:5 6213
from Abraham that thing which I *d* Gen 18:17 6213
LORD, to *d* justice and judgment Gen 18:19 6213
from thee to *d* after this manner Gen 18:25 6213
Judge of all the earth *d* right Gen 18:25 6213
I will not *d* it for forty's sake Gen 18:29 6213
And he said, I will not *d* it Gen 18:30 6213
you, brethren, *d* not so wickedly Gen 19:7
d ye to them as is good in your Gen 19:8 6213
only unto these men *d* nothing Gen 19:8 6213
for I cannot *d* any thing till Gen 19:22 6213
unto thee, thou shalt *d* unto me Gen 21:23 6213
neither *d* thou any thing unto him Gen 22:12 6213
if now thou *d* prosper my way Gen 24:42
shall this birthright *d* to me Gen 25:32
That thou wilt *d* us no hurt Gen 26:29 6213
what shall I *d* now unto thee, my Gen 27:37 6213
what good shall my life *d* me Gen 27:46
if thou wilt *d* this thing for me, Gen 30:31 6213
God hath said unto thee, *d* Gen 31:16 6213
power of my hand to *d* you hurt Gen 31:29 6213
what can I *d* this day unto these Gen 31:43 6213
saidst, I will surely *d* thee good Gen 32:12
We cannot *d* this thing, to give Gen 34:14 6213
man deferred not to *d* the thing Gen 34:19 6213
D not thy brethren feed the flock Gen 37:13
how then can I *d* this great Gen 39:9 6213
into the house to *d* his business Gen 39:11 6213
D not interpretations belong to Gen 40:8
I *d* remember my faults this day Gen 41:9
Pharaoh what he is about to *d* Gen 41:25 6213
What God is about to *d* he sheweth Gen 41:28 6213
Let Pharaoh *d* this, and let him Gen 41:34 6213
what he saith to you, *d* Gen 41:55 6213
Why *d* ye look one upon another Gen 42:1
unto them the third day, This *d* Gen 42:18 6213
D not sin against the child Gen 42:22
If it must be so now, *d* this Gen 43:11 6213
should *d* according to this thing Gen 44:7 6213
God forbid that I should *d* so Gen 44:17 6213
Say unto thy brethren, This *d* ye Gen 45:17 6213
Now thou art commanded, this *d* ye Gen 45:19 6213
I will *d* as thou hast said Gen 47:30 6213
When ye *d* the office of a midwife Ex 1:16
I will *d* in the midst thereof Ex 3:20 6213
and will teach you what ye shall *d* Ex 4:15 6213
wherewith thou shalt *d* signs Ex 4:17 6213
see that thou *d* all those wonders Ex 4:21 6213
said unto them, Wherefore *d* ye Ex 5:4
us go and *d* sacrifice to the LORD Ex 5:17
thou see what I will *d* to Pharaoh Ex 6:1 6213
that they may *d* sacrifice unto Ex 8:8
said, It is not meet so to *d* Ex 8:26 6213
shall *d* this thing in the land Ex 9:5 6213
wilt *d* that which is right in his Ex 15:26 6213
wherefore *d* ye tempt the LORD Ex 17:2
What shall I *d* unto this people Ex 17:4 6213
I *d* make them know the statutes Ex 18:16
and the work that they must *d* Ex 18:20 6213
If thou shalt *d* this thing Ex 18:23 6213
the LORD hath spoken we will *d* Ex 19:8 6213
thou labour, and *d* all thy work Ex 20:9 6213
in it thou shalt not *d* any work Ex 20:10 6213
not go out as the menservants *d* Ex 21:7 3318
if he *d* not these three unto her, Ex 21:11 6213
shalt thou *d* with thine oxen Ex 22:30 6213
not follow a multitude to *d* evil Ex 23:2
Six days thou shalt *d* thy work Ex 23:12 6213
his voice, and *d* all that I speak Ex 23:22 6213
them, nor *d* after their works Ex 23:24 6213
the LORD hath said will we *d* Ex 24:3 6213
that the LORD hath said will we *d* Ex 24:7 6213
if any man have any matters to *d* Ex 24:14 1167
shalt *d* unto them to hallow them Ex 29:1 6213
And thus shalt thou *d* unto Aaron Ex 29:35 6213
shalt *d* thereto according to the Ex 29:41 6213
have commanded thee shall they *d* Ex 31:11 6213
he thought to *d* unto his people Ex 32:14 6213
noise of them that sing *d* I hear Ex 32:18
I may know what to *d* unto thee Ex 33:5 6213
I will *d* this thing also that Ex 33:17 6213
all thy people I will *d* marvels Ex 34:10 6213
thing that I will *d* with thee Ex 34:10 6213
d sacrifice unto their gods, and Ex 34:15
commanded, that ye should *d* them Ex 35:1 6213
to *d* service in the holy place, Ex 35:19
even of them that *d* any work Ex 35:35 6213
up to come unto the work to *d* it Ex 36:2 6213
to *d* service in the holy place, Ex 39:1
The cloths of service to *d* Ex 39:41
shall *d* against any of them Lev 4:2 6213
If the priest that is anointed *d* Lev 4:3
he shall *d* with the bullock as he Lev 4:20 6213
offering, so shall he *d* with this Lev 4:20 6213
if he *d* not utter it, then he Lev 5:1
his lips to *d* evil, or to *d* good Lev 5:4
so the LORD hath commanded to *d* Lev 8:34 6213
LORD commanded that ye should *d* Lev 9:6 6213
D not drink wine nor strong drink Lev 10:9
d with that blood as he did with Lev 16:15 6213
so shall he *d* for the tabernacle Lev 16:16 6213
d no work at all, whether it be Lev 16:29 6213
wherein ye dwelt, shall ye not *d* Lev 18:3 6213
I bring you, shall ye not *d* Lev 18:3 6213
Ye shall *d* my judgments, and keep Lev 18:4 6213
which if a man *d*, he shall live Lev 18:5 6213
therefore I *d* visit the iniquity Lev 18:25
Ye shall *d* no unrighteousness in Lev 19:15 6213
D not prostitute thy daughter, to Lev 19:29
Ye shall *d* no unrighteousness in Lev 19:35 6213
and all my judgments, and *d* them Lev 19:37 6213
if the people of the land *d* any Lev 20:4
shall keep my statutes, and *d* them Lev 20:8 6213
and all my judgments, and *d* them Lev 20:22 6213
bread of their God, they *d* offer Lev 21:6
for I the LORD *d* sanctify him Lev 21:15
for I the LORD *d* sanctify them Lev 21:23
I the LORD *d* sanctify them Lev 22:9
for I the LORD *d* sanctify them Lev 22:16
keep my commandments, and *d* them Lev 22:31 6213
ye shall *d* no work therein Lev 23:3 6213
ye shall *d* no servile work Lev 23:7 6213
ye shall *d* no servile work Lev 23:8 6213
ye shall *d* no servile work Lev 23:21 6213
Ye shall *d* no servile work Lev 23:25 6213
ye shall *d* no work in that same Lev 23:28 6213
Ye shall *d* no manner of work Lev 23:31 6213
ye shall *d* no servile work Lev 23:35 6213
ye shall *d* no servile work Lev 23:36 6213
Wherefore ye shall *d* my statutes Lev 25:18 6213
and keep my judgments, and *d* them Lev 25:18 6213
that *d* sojourn among you, of them Lev 25:45
keep my commandments, and *d* them Lev 26:3 6213
will not *d* all these commandments Lev 26:14 6213
ye will not *d* all my commandments Lev 26:15 6213
I also will *d* this unto you Lev 26:16 6213
of which they *d* not offer a Lev 27:11
those that *d* pitch next unto him Num 2:5
to *d* the service of the Num 3:7 5647
Israel, to *d* the service of the Num 3:8 5647
to *d* the work in the tabernacle Num 4:3 6213
But thus *d* unto them, that they Num 4:19 6213
to *d* the work in the tabernacle Num 4:23 5647
to *d* the work of the tabernacle Num 4:30 5647
all that might *d* service in the Num 4:37 5647
of all that might *d* service in Num 4:41 5647
every one that came to *d* the Num 4:47 5647
to *d* a trespass against the LORD, Num 5:6 6213
so he must *d* after the law of his Num 6:21 6213
that they may be to *d* the service Num 7:5 5647
And thus shalt thou *d* unto them Num 8:7 6213
d the service of the tabernacle Num 8:15 5647
to *d* the service of the children Num 8:19 5647
that went the Levites in to *d* Num 8:22 5647
the charge, and shall *d* no service Num 8:26 5647
Thus shalt thou *d* unto the Num 8:26 6213
the manner thereof, so shall he *d* Num 9:14 6213
with us, and we will *d* thee good Num 10:29
goodness the LORD shall *d* unto us Num 10:32 3190
the same will we *d* unto thee Num 10:32 3190
Medad *d* prophesy in the camp Num 11:27
in mine ears, so will I *d* to you Num 14:28 6213
I will surely *d* it unto all this Num 14:35 6213
Wherefore now *d* ye transgress the Num 14:41
so shall ye *d* to every one Num 15:12 6213
are born of the country shall *d* Num 15:13 6213
as ye *d*, so he shall *d* Num 15:14 6213
as ye *d* the heave offering of the Num 15:20
of the LORD, and *d* them Num 15:39 6213
d all my commandments, and be holy Num 15:40 6213
This *d*; Take you censers Num 16:6 6213
d the service of the tabernacle Num 16:9 5647
hath sent me to *d* all these works Num 16:28 6213
the LORD, to *d* the service of the Num 18:6 5647
But the Levites shall *d* the Num 18:23 5647
thou shalt *d* to him as thou didst Num 21:34 6213
I will *d* whatsoever thou sayest Num 22:17 6213
LORD my God, to *d* less or more Num 22:18 6213
say unto thee, that shalt thou *d* Num 22:20 6213
was I ever wont to *d* so unto thee Num 22:30 6213
he said, and shall he not *d* it Num 23:19 6213
the LORD speaketh, that I must *d* Num 23:26 6213
to *d* either good or bad of mine Num 24:13 6213
d to thy people in the latter Num 24:14 6213
and Israel shall *d* valiantly Num 24:18 6213
ye shall *d* no manner of servile Num 28:18 6213
ye shall *d* no servile work Num 28:25 6213
ye shall *d* no servile work Num 28:26 6213
ye shall *d* no servile work Num 29:1 6213
ye shall not *d* any work therein Num 29:7 6213
ye shall *d* no servile work, and ye Num 29:12 6213
ye shall *d* no servile work Num 29:35 6213
These things ye shall *d* unto the Num 29:39 6213
he shall *d* according to all that Num 30:2 6213
d ye abide without the camp seven Num 31:19 6213
them, If ye will *d* this thing Num 32:20 6213
But if ye will not *d* so, behold, Num 32:23 6213
d that which hath proceeded out Num 32:24 6213
Thy servants will *d* as my lord Num 32:25 6213
unto thy servants, so will we *d* Num 32:31 6213
to pass, that I shall *d* unto you Num 33:56 6213
as I thought to *d* unto them Num 33:56 6213
hast spoken is good for us to *d* Deut 1:14 6213
all the things which ye should *d* Deut 1:18 6213
you, and chased you, as bees *d* Deut 1:44 6213
thou shalt *d* unto him as thou Deut 3:2 6213
so shall the LORD *d* unto all the Deut 3:21 6213
that can *d* according to thy works Deut 3:24 6213
which I teach you, for to *d* them Deut 4:1 6213
that ye should *d* so in the land Deut 4:5 6213
Keep therefore and *d* them Deut 4:6 6213
that ye might *d* them in the land Deut 4:14 6213
shall *d* evil in the sight of the Deut 4:25 6213
learn them, and keep, and *d* them Deut 5:1 6213
shalt labour, and *d* all thy work Deut 5:13 6213
in it thou shalt not *d* any work Deut 5:14 6213
and we will hear it, and *d* it Deut 5:27 6213
that they may *d* them in the land Deut 5:31 6213
Ye shall observe to *d* therefore Deut 5:32 6213
that ye might *d* them in the land Deut 6:1 6213
O Israel, and observe to *d* it Deut 6:3 6213
thou shalt *d* that which is right Deut 6:18 6213
us to *d* all these statutes Deut 6:24 6213
if we observe to *d* all these Deut 6:25 6213
command thee this day, to *d* them Deut 7:11 6213
d them, that the LORD thy God Deut 7:12 6213
so shall the LORD thy God *d* unto Deut 7:19 6213
this day shall ye observe to *d* Deut 8:1 6213
to *d* thee good at thy latter end Deut 8:16
if thou *d* at all forget the LORD Deut 8:19
to *d* them, to love the LORD your Deut 11:22 6213
observe to *d* all the statutes Deut 11:32 6213
ye shall observe to *d* in the land Deut 12:1 6213
Ye shall not *d* so unto the LORD Deut 12:4 6213
Ye shall not *d* after all the Deut 12:8 6213
things that we *d* here this day Deut 12:8 6213
there thou shalt *d* all that I Deut 12:14 6213
when thou shalt *d* that which is Deut 12:25 6213
even so will I *d* likewise Deut 12:30 6213
Thou shalt not *d* so unto the LORD Deut 12:31 6213
I command you, observe to *d* it Deut 12:32 6213
fear, and shall *d* no more any such Deut 13:11 6213
to *d* that which is right in the Deut 13:18 6213
to observe to *d* all these Deut 15:5 6213
maidservant thou shalt *d* likewise Deut 15:17 6213
thou shalt *d* no work with the Deut 15:19
thou shalt *d* no work therein Deut 16:8 6213
shalt observe and *d* these statutes Deut 16:12 6213
thou shalt *d* according to the Deut 17:10 6213
thou shalt observe to *d* according Deut 17:10 6213
shall tell thee, thou shalt *d* Deut 17:11 6213
man that will *d* presumptuously Deut 17:12 6213
fear, and *d* no more presumptuously Deut 17:13
law and these statutes, to *d* them Deut 17:19 6213
as all his brethren the Levites *d* Deut 18:7
thou shalt not learn to *d* after Deut 18:9 6213
For all that *d* these things are Deut 18:12 6213
hath not suffered thee so to *d* Deut 18:14
all these commandments to *d* them Deut 19:9 6213
Then shall ye *d* unto him, as he Deut 19:19 6213
d not tremble, neither be ye Deut 20:3
Thus shalt thou *d* unto all the Deut 20:15 6213
That they teach you not to *d* Deut 20:18 6213
when thou shalt *d* that which is Deut 21:9 6213
manner shalt thou *d* with his ass Deut 22:3 6213
so shalt thou *d* with his raiment Deut 22:3 6213
hast found, shalt thou *d* likewise Deut 22:3 6213
for all that *d* so are abomination Deut 22:5 6213
the damsel thou shalt *d* nothing Deut 22:26 6213
d according to all that the Deut 24:8 6213

them, so ye shall observe to *d*	Deut 24:8	6213
I command thee to *d* this thing	Deut 24:18	6213
I command thee to *d* this thing	Deut 24:22	6213
For all that *d* such things	Deut 25:16	6213
all that *d* unrighteously, are an	Deut 25:16	6213
thee to *d* these statutes and	Deut 26:16	6213
d them with all thine heart, and	Deut 26:16	6213
d his commandments and his	Deut 27:10	6213
the words of this law to *d* them	Deut 27:26	6213
to *d* all his commandments which I	Deut 28:1	6213
this day, to observe and to *d* them	Deut 28:13	6213
thy God, to observe to *d* all his	Deut 28:15	6213
settest thine hand unto for to *d*	Deut 28:20	6213
If thou wilt not observe to *d* all	Deut 28:58	6213
rejoiced over you to *d* you good	Deut 28:63	
d them, that ye may prosper in	Deut 29:9	6213
ye may prosper in all that ye *d*	Deut 29:9	6213
you only *d* I make this covenant	Deut 29:14	
that we may *d* all the words of	Deut 29:29	6213
he will *d* thee good, and multiply	Deut 30:5	
d all his commandments which I	Deut 30:8	6213
us, that we may hear it, and *d* it	Deut 30:12	6213
us, that we may hear it, and *d* it	Deut 30:13	6213
thy heart, that thou mayest *d* it	Deut 30:14	6213
the LORD shall *d* unto them as he	Deut 31:4	6213
that ye may *d* unto them according	Deut 31:5	6213
observe to *d* all the words of	Deut 31:12	6213
because ye will *d* evil in the	Deut 31:29	6213
D ye thus requite the LORD, O	Deut 32:6	
your children to observe to *d*	Deut 32:46	6213
which the LORD sent him to *d* in	Deut 34:11	6213
the land which I *d* give to them	Josh 1:2	
to *d* according to all the law	Josh 1:7	6213
to *d* according to all that is	Josh 1:8	6213
that thou commandest us we will *d*	Josh 1:16	6213
the country *d* faint because of us	Josh 2:24	
the LORD will *d* wonders among you	Josh 3:5	6213
Thus shalt thou *d* six days	Josh 6:3	6213
what wilt thou *d* unto thy great	Josh 7:9	6213
And thou shalt *d* to Ai and her king	Josh 8:2	6213
of the LORD shall ye *d*	Josh 8:8	6213
This we will *d* to them	Josh 9:20	6213
and right unto thee to *d* unto us	Josh 9:25	6213
right unto thee to *d* unto us, *d*	Josh 9:25	6213
for thus shall the LORD *d* to all	Josh 10:25	6213
heed to *d* the commandment	Josh 22:5	6213
What have ye to *d* with the LORD	Josh 22:24	
that we might *d* the service of	Josh 22:27	5647
to *d* all that is written in the	Josh 23:6	6213
Else if ye *d* in any wise go back,	Josh 23:12	
which ye planted not *d* ye eat	Josh 24:13	
d you hurt, and consume you, after	Josh 24:20	
that he could not *d* it by day	Judg 6:27	6213
them, Look on me, and *d* likewise	Judg 7:17	6213
be that, as I *d*, so shall ye *d*	Judg 7:17	6213
and what was I able to *d* in	Judg 8:3	6213
then mayest thou *d* to them as	Judg 9:33	6213
with him, What ye have seen me *d*	Judg 9:48	6213
make haste, and *d* as I have done	Judg 9:48	6213
d thou unto us whatsoever seemeth	Judg 10:15	6213
if we *d* not so according to thy	Judg 11:10	6213
What hast thou to *d* with me	Judg 11:12	
d to me according to that which	Judg 11:36	6213
teach us what we shall *d* unto the	Judg 13:8	6213
child, and how shall we *d* unto him	Judg 13:12	4640
come to pass we may *d* thee honour	Judg 13:17	
for so used the young men to *d*	Judg 14:10	6213
though I *d* them a displeasure	Judg 15:3	6213
to *d* to him as he hath done to us	Judg 15:10	6213
I that the LORD will *d* me good	Judg 17:13	
D ye know that there is in these	Judg 18:14	
consider what ye have to *d*	Judg 18:14	6213
the priest unto them, What *d* ye	Judg 18:18	6213
I pray you, *d* not so wickedly	Judg 19:23	
into mine house, *d* not this folly	Judg 19:23	6213
d with them what seemeth good	Judg 19:24	6213
but unto this man *d* not so vile a	Judg 19:24	6213
thing which we will *d* to Gibeah	Judg 20:9	6213
for the people, that they may *d*	Judg 20:10	6213
How shall we *d* for wives for them	Judg 21:7	6213
this is the thing that ye shall *d*	Judg 21:11	6213
How shall we *d* for wives for them	Judg 21:16	6213
the LORD *d* so to me, and more also	Ruth 1:17	6213
be on the field that they *d* reap	Ruth 2:9	
will tell thee what thou shalt *d*	Ruth 3:4	6213
that thou sayest unto me I will *d*	Ruth 3:5	6213
I will *d* to thee all that thou	Ruth 3:11	6213
let him *d* the kinsman's part	Ruth 3:13	
but if he will not *d* the part of	Ruth 3:13	
then will I *d* the part of a	Ruth 3:13	
d thou worthily in Ephratah, and	Ruth 4:11	6213
her, *D* what seemeth thee good	1Sa 1:23	6213
unto them, Why *d* ye such things	1Sa 2:23	6213
that shall *d* according to that	1Sa 2:35	6213
I will *d* a thing in Israel, at	1Sa 3:11	6213
God *d* so to thee, and more also,	1Sa 3:17	6213
let him *d* what seemeth him good	1Sa 3:18	6213
What shall we *d* with the ark of	1Sa 5:8	6213
What shall we *d* to the ark of the	1Sa 6:2	6213
Wherefore then *d* ye harden your	1Sa 6:6	
If ye *d* return unto the LORD with	1Sa 7:3	
gods, so *d* they also unto thee	1Sa 8:8	6213
saying, What shall I *d* for my son	1Sa 10:2	6213
that thou *d* as occasion serve	1Sa 10:7	6213
and shew thee what thou shalt *d*	1Sa 10:8	6213
ye shall *d* with us all that	1Sa 11:10	6213
the LORD will *d* before your eyes	1Sa 12:16	6213
But if ye shall still *d* wickedly	1Sa 12:25	
D all that is in thine heart	1Sa 14:7	6213
D whatsoever seemeth good unto	1Sa 14:36	6213
D what seemeth good unto thee	1Sa 14:40	6213
And Saul answered, God *d* so	1Sa 14:44	6213
will shew thee what thou shalt *d*	1Sa 16:3	6213
my father will *d* nothing either	1Sa 20:2	6213
I will even *d* it for thee	1Sa 20:4	6213
The LORD *d* so and much more to	1Sa 20:13	6213
please my father to *d* thee evil	1Sa 20:13	
d not I know that thou hast	1Sa 20:30	
I know what God will *d* for me	1Sa 22:3	6213
that thou mayest *d* to him as it	1Sa 24:4	6213
d this thing unto my master	1Sa 24:6	6213
know and consider what thou wilt *d*	1Sa 25:17	6213
more also *d* God unto the enemies	1Sa 25:22	6213
for I will no more *d* thee harm	1Sa 26:21	
thou shalt both *d* great things	1Sa 26:25	6213
shalt know what thy servant can *d*	1Sa 28:2	6213
make known unto me what I shall *d*	1Sa 28:15	6213
What *d* these Hebrews here	1Sa 29:3	
said David, Ye shall not *d* so	1Sa 30:23	6213
which against Judah *d* shew	2Sa 3:8	6213
So *d* God to Abner, and more also,	2Sa 3:9	6213
to David, even so I *d* to him	2Sa 3:9	6213
Now then *d* it	2Sa 3:18	6213
So *d* God to me, and more also, if	2Sa 3:35	6213
d all that is in thine heart	2Sa 7:3	6213
to *d* for you great things and	2Sa 7:23	6213
for ever, and *d* as thou hast said	2Sa 7:25	6213
servant, so shall thy servant *d*	2Sa 9:11	6213
the LORD *d* that which seemeth him	2Sa 10:12	6213
liveth, I will not *d* this thing	2Sa 11:11	6213
the LORD, to *d* evil in his sight	2Sa 12:9	6213
but I will *d* this thing before	2Sa 12:12	6213
for him to *d* any thing to her	2Sa 13:2	6213
Nay, my brother, *d* not force me	2Sa 13:12	6213
d not thou this folly	2Sa 13:12	6213
unto me, and I would *d* him justice	2Sa 15:4	
nigh to him to *d* him obeisance	2Sa 15:5	
thy servants are ready to *d*	2Sa 15:15	
let him *d* to me as seemeth good	2Sa 15:26	6213
said, What have I to *d* with you	2Sa 16:10	
more now may this Benjamite *d* it	2Sa 16:11	
counsel among you what we shall *d*	2Sa 16:20	6213
shall we *d* after his saying	2Sa 17:6	6213
What seemeth you best I will *d*	2Sa 18:4	6213
rise against thee to *d* thee hurt	2Sa 18:32	
God *d* so to me, and more also, if	2Sa 19:13	6213
to *d* what he thought good	2Sa 19:18	6213
neither *d* thou remember that	2Sa 19:19	
said, What have I to *d* with you	2Sa 19:22	
for *d* not I know that I am this	2Sa 19:22	
d therefore what is good in thine	2Sa 19:27	6213
d to him what shall seem good	2Sa 19:37	6213
I will *d* to him that which shall	2Sa 19:38	6213
of me, that will I *d* for thee	2Sa 19:38	6213
d us more harm than did Absalom	2Sa 20:6	
And he answered, I *d* hear	2Sa 20:17	
What shall I *d* for you	2Sa 21:3	6213
shall say, that will I *d* for you	2Sa 21:4	6213
me, O LORD, that I should *d* this	2Sa 23:17	6213
that I may *d* it unto thee	2Sa 24:12	6213
so will I certainly *d* this day	1Kin 1:30	6213
D therefore according to thy	1Kin 2:6	6213
what thou oughtest to *d* unto him	1Kin 2:9	6213
God *d* so to me, and more also, if	1Kin 2:23	6213
D as he hath said, and fall upon	1Kin 2:31	6213
hath said, so will thy servant *d*	1Kin 2:38	6213
of God was in him, to *d* judgment	1Kin 3:28	6213
and I will *d* all thy desire	1Kin 5:8	6213
Then hear thou in heaven, and *d*	1Kin 8:32	6213
dwelling place, and forgive, and *d*	1Kin 8:39	6213
d according to all that the	1Kin 8:43	6213
fear thee, as *d* thy people Israel	1Kin 8:43	
desire which he was pleased to *d*	1Kin 9:1	6213
to *d* according to all that I have	1Kin 9:4	6213
king, to *d* judgment and justice	1Kin 10:9	6213
in thy days I will not *d* it for	1Kin 11:12	6213
to *d* that which is right in mine	1Kin 11:33	6213
d that is right in my sight, to	1Kin 11:38	6213
How *d* ye advise that I may answer	1Kin 12:6	
If this people go up to *d*	1Kin 12:27	6213
to *d* that only which was right in	1Kin 14:8	6213
go and *d* as thou hast said	1Kin 17:13	6213
What have I to *d* with thee	1Kin 17:18	
And he said, *D* it the second time	1Kin 18:34	
And he said, *D* it the third time	1Kin 18:34	
saying, So let the gods *d* to me	1Kin 19:2	6213
thy servant at the first I will *d*	1Kin 20:9	6213
but this thing I may not *d*	1Kin 20:9	6213
The gods *d* so unto me, and more	1Kin 20:10	6213
d this thing, Take the kings away	1Kin 20:24	6213
go forth, and *d* so	1Kin 22:22	6213
Ask what I shall *d* for thee	2Kin 2:9	6213
What have I to *d* with thee	2Kin 3:13	
unto her, What shall I *d* for thee	2Kin 4:2	6213
d not lie unto thine handmaid	2Kin 4:16	
did I not say, *D* not deceive me	2Kin 4:28	
had bid thee *d* some great thing	2Kin 5:13	
how shall we *d*?	2Kin 6:15	6213
If the LORD *d* not help thee,	2Kin 6:27	
Then he said, God *d* so and more	2Kin 6:31	6213
one to another, We *d* not well	2Kin 7:9	6213
d unto the children of Israel	2Kin 8:12	6213
that he should *d* this great thing	2Kin 8:13	6213
What hast thou to *d* with peace	2Kin 9:18	
What hast thou to *d* with peace	2Kin 9:19	
will *d* all that thou shalt bid us	2Kin 10:5	6213
d thou that which is good in	2Kin 10:5	6213
a great sacrifice to *d* to Baal	2Kin 10:19	
This is the thing that ye shall *d*	2Kin 11:5	6213
them, Ye shall not *d* this thing	2Kin 17:12	6213
that they should not *d* like them	2Kin 17:15	6213
sold themselves to *d* evil in the	2Kin 17:17	6213
Unto this day they *d* after the	2Kin 17:34	6213
neither *d* they after their	2Kin 17:34	6213
and to him shall ye *d* sacrifice	2Kin 17:36	
shall observe to *d* for evermore	2Kin 17:37	6213
fathers, so *d* they unto this day	2Kin 17:41	6213
would not hear them, nor *d* them	2Kin 18:12	6213
of the LORD of hosts shall *d* this	2Kin 19:31	6213
that the LORD will *d* the thing	2Kin 20:9	6213
to *d* according to all that I have	2Kin 21:8	6213
Manasseh seduced them to *d* more	2Kin 21:9	6213
the hand of them that *d* the work	2Kin 22:9	6213
to *d* according unto all that	2Kin 22:13	6213
it me, that I should *d* this thing	1Chr 11:19	6213
to know what Israel ought to *d*	1Chr 12:32	6213
said that they would *d* so	1Chr 13:4	6213
suffered no man to *d* them wrong	1Chr 16:21	
and *d* my prophets no harm	1Chr 16:22	
to *d* according to all that is	1Chr 16:40	
D all that is in thine heart	1Chr 17:2	6213
for ever, and *d* as thou hast said	1Chr 17:23	6213
let the LORD *d* that which is good	1Chr 19:13	6213
d away the iniquity of thy	1Chr 21:8	5674
that I may *d* it unto thee	1Chr 21:10	6213
let my lord the king *d* that which	1Chr 21:23	6213
be constant to *d* my commandments	1Chr 28:7	6213
be strong, and *d* it	1Chr 28:10	6213
and of good courage, and *d* it	1Chr 28:20	6213
to *d* all these things, and to	1Chr 29:19	6213
Then hear thou from heaven, and *d*	2Chr 6:23	6213
d according to all that the	2Chr 6:33	6213
d according to all that I have	2Chr 7:17	6213
them, to *d* judgment and justice	2Chr 9:8	6213
to *d* the law and the commandment	2Chr 14:4	6213
go out, and *d* even so	2Chr 18:21	6213
the judges, Take heed what ye *d*	2Chr 19:6	6213
take heed and *d* it	2Chr 19:7	6213
Thus shall ye *d* in the fear of	2Chr 19:9	6213
this *d*, and ye shall not trespass	2Chr 19:10	6213
neither know we what to *d*	2Chr 20:12	6213
was his counsellor to *d* wickedly	2Chr 22:3	
This is the thing that ye shall *d*	2Chr 23:4	6213
d it, be strong for the battle	2Chr 25:8	6213
But what shall we *d* for the	2Chr 25:9	6213
to *d* the commandment of the king	2Chr 30:12	6213
Whereon *d* ye trust, that ye abide	2Chr 32:10	
d all that I have commanded them	2Chr 33:8	6213
to *d* worse than the heathen, whom	2Chr 33:9	6213
to thy servants, they *d* it	2Chr 34:16	6213
to *d* after all that is written in	2Chr 34:21	6213
that they may *d* according to the	2Chr 35:6	6213
What have I to *d* with thee	2Chr 35:21	
for we seek your God, as ye *d*	Ezr 4:2	
we *d* sacrifice unto him since the	Ezr 4:2	
Ye have nothing to *d* with us to	Ezr 4:3	
now that ye fail not to *d* this	Ezr 4:22	5648
I make a decree what ye shall *d*	Ezr 6:8	5648
the law of the LORD, and to *d* it	Ezr 7:10	6213
to *d* with the rest of the silver	Ezr 7:18	5648
that *d* after the will of your God	Ezr 7:18	5648
d make a decree to all the	Ezr 7:21	
will not *d* the law of thy God	Ezr 7:26	5648
be of good courage, and *d* it	Ezr 10:4	6213
should *d* according to this word	Ezr 10:5	6213
your fathers, and *d* his pleasure	Ezr 10:11	6213
As thou hast said, so must we *d*	Ezr 10:12	6213
keep my commandments, and *d* them	Neh 1:9	6213
put in my heart to *d* at Jerusalem	Neh 2:12	6213
What is this thing that ye *d*	Neh 2:19	6213
and said, What *d* these feeble Jews	Neh 4:2	6213
I said, It is not good that ye *d*	Neh 5:9	6213
so will we *d* as thou sayest	Neh 5:12	6213
that they should *d* according to	Neh 5:12	6213
But they thought to *d* me mischief	Neh 6:2	6213
d so, and sin, and that they might	Neh 6:13	6213
that they might *d* with them as	Neh 9:24	6213
thy judgments, (which if a man *d*	Neh 9:29	6213
d all the commandments of the	Neh 10:29	6213
What evil thing is this that ye *d*	Neh 13:17	6213
if ye *d* so again, I will lay	Neh 13:21	
unto you to *d* all this great evil	Neh 13:27	6213
that they should *d* according to	Est 1:8	6213
What shall we *d* unto the queen	Est 1:15	6213
to *d* with them as it seemeth good	Est 3:11	6213
d know, that whosoever, whether	Est 4:11	
that he may *d* as Esther hath said	Est 5:5	6213
I will *d* to morrow as the king	Est 5:8	6213
to *d* honour more than to myself	Est 6:6	6213
d even so to Mordecai the Jew,	Est 6:10	6213
presume in his heart to *d* so	Est 7:5	6213
Jews which are in Shushan to *d* to	Est 9:13	6213
undertook to *d* as they had begun	Est 9:23	6213
the terrors of God *d* set	Job 6:4	
D ye imagine to reprove words, and	Job 6:26	
what shall I *d* unto thee, O thou	Job 7:20	6466
proud helpers *d* stoop under him	Job 9:13	
say unto God, *D* not condemn me	Job 10:2	
what canst thou *d*?	Job 11:8	6466
ye know, the same *d* I know also	Job 13:2	
mocketh another, *d* ye so mock him	Job 13:9	
if ye *d* secretly accept persons	Job 13:10	
Wherefore *d* I take my flesh in my	Job 13:14	
Only *d* not two things unto me	Job 13:20	6213
wherewith he can *d* no good	Job 15:3	5953
and what *d* thy eyes wink at,	Job 15:12	
I also could speak as ye *d*	Job 16:4	
you all, *d* ye return, and come now	Job 17:10	
Why *d* ye persecute me as God, and	Job 19:22	
Therefore *d* my thoughts cause me	Job 20:2	
Wherefore *d* the wicked live,	Job 21:7	
d ye not know their tokens,	Job 21:29	
what can the Almighty *d* for them	Job 22:17	6466
d they that know him not see his	Job 24:1	
What then shall I *d* when God	Job 31:14	
neither *d* the aged understand	Job 32:9	
God, that he should *d* wickedness	Job 34:10	
surely God will not *d* wickedly	Job 34:12	
done iniquity, I will *d* no more	Job 34:32	6466
Which the clouds *d* drop and distil	Job 36:28	
that they may *d* whatsoever he	Job 37:12	6467
Men *d* therefore fear him	Job 37:24	6213

thou mark when the hinds *d* calve ...... Job 39:1
remember the battle, *d* no more ...... Job 41:8
that thou canst *d* every thing ...... Job 42:2
Why *d* the heathen rage, and the ...... Ps 2:1
my God, in thee *d* I put my trust ...... Ps 7:1
what can the righteous *d* ...... Ps 11:3 6466
with a double heart *d* they speak ...... Ps 12:2
for in thee *d* I put my trust ...... Ps 16:1
thee, O LORD, *d* I lift up my soul ...... Ps 25:1
on thee *d* I wait all the day ...... Ps 25:5
IN thee, O LORD, *d* I put my trust ...... Ps 31:1 6213
The young lions *d* lack, and suffer ...... Ps 34:10 6213
Depart from evil, and *d* good ...... Ps 34:14 6213
LORD is against them that *d* evil ...... Ps 34:16 6213
left off to be wise, and to *d* good ...... Ps 36:3
Trust in the LORD, and *d* good ...... Ps 37:3 6213
not thyself in any wise to *d* evil ...... Ps 37:8
Depart from evil, and *d* good ...... Ps 37:27 6213
For in thee, O LORD, *d* I hope ...... Ps 38:15
I delight to *d* thy will, O my God ...... Ps 40:8 6213
against me *d* they devise my hurt ...... Ps 41:7
What hast thou to *d* to declare my ...... Ps 50:16
D good in thy good pleasure unto ...... Ps 51:18
not fear what flesh can *d* unto me ...... Ps 56:4 6213
be afraid what man can *d* unto me ...... Ps 56:11 6213
D ye indeed speak righteousness, ... Ps 58:1
d ye judge uprightly, O ye sons ...... Ps 58:1
Through God we shall *d* valiantly ...... Ps 60:12 6213
suddenly *d* they shoot at him, and ...... Ps 64:4
In thee, O LORD, *d* I put my trust ...... Ps 71:1
d we give thanks, unto thee *d* we ...... Ps 75:1 6213
which pass by the way *d* pluck her ...... Ps 80:12 6213
d justice to the afflicted and ...... Ps 82:3
D unto them as unto the ...... Ps 83:9 6213
thee, O Lord, *d* I lift up my soul ...... Ps 86:4
how I *d* bear in my bosom the ...... Ps 89:50
workers of iniquity *d* flourish ...... Ps 92:7
people that *d* err in their heart ...... Ps 95:10
his commandments to *d* them ...... Ps 103:18 6213
that *d* his commandments, ... Ps 103:20 6213
of his, that *d* his pleasure ...... Ps 103:21 6213
of the forest *d* creep forth ...... Ps 104:20
suffered no man to *d* them wrong ...... Ps 105:14
and *d* my prophets no harm ...... Ps 105:15
that *d* business in great waters ...... Ps 107:23 6213
Through God we shall *d* valiantly ...... Ps 108:13 6213
But *d* thou for me, O GOD the Lord ...... Ps 109:21 6213
all they that *d* his commandments ...... Ps 111:10 6213
what can man *d* unto me ...... Ps 118:6 6213
They also *d* no iniquity ...... Ps 119:3 6466
which *d* err from thy commandments.. Ps 119:21
for therein *d* I delight ...... Ps 119:35
yet *d* I not forget thy statutes ...... Ps 119:83
yet *d* I not forget thy law ...... Ps 119:109
but thy law *d* I love ...... Ps 119:113
as thou usest to *d* unto those ...... Ps 119:132
yet *d* not I forget thy precepts ...... Ps 119:141
for I *d* not forget thy law ...... Ps 119:153
yet *d* I not decline from thy ...... Ps 119:157
but thy law *d* I love ...... Ps 119:163
Seven times a day *d* I praise thee ...... Ps 119:164
for I *d* not forget thy ...... Ps 119:176
D good, O LORD, unto those that ...... Ps 125:4
Neither *d* they which go by say, ... Ps 129:8
wait, and in his word *d* I hope ...... Ps 130:5
neither *d* I exercise myself in ...... Ps 131:1
If I *d* not remember thee, let my ...... Ps 137:6
D not I hate them, O LORD, that ...... Ps 139:21
for in thee *d* I trust ...... Ps 143:8
Teach me to *d* thy will ...... Ps 143:10 6213
Who rejoice to *d* evil, and delight ...... Prov 2:14 6213
the power of thine hand to *d* it ...... Prov 3:27 6213
D this now, my son, and deliver ...... Prov 6:3 6213
Men *d* not despise a thief, if he ...... Prov 6:30
and the froward mouth, *d* I hate ...... Prov 8:13
as sport to a fool to *d* mischief ...... Prov 10:23 6213
D they not err that devise evil ...... Prov 14:22
much less *d* lying lips a prince ...... Prov 17:7
brethren of the poor *d* hate him ...... Prov 19:7
how much more *d* his friends go ...... Prov 19:7
him, yet thou must *d* it again ...... Prov 19:19
so *d* stripes the inward parts of ...... Prov 20:30
To *d* justice and judgment is more ...... Prov 21:3 6213
because they refuse to *d* judgment ...... Prov 21:7 6213
is joy to the just to *d* judgment ...... Prov 21:15 6213
He that deviseth to *d* evil shall ...... Prov 24:8
I will *d* so to him as he hath ...... Prov 24:29 6213
not what to *d* in the end thereof ...... Prov 25:8 6213
When righteous men *d* rejoice ...... Prov 28:12
She will *d* him good and not evil ...... Prov 31:12 1580
which they should *d* under the ...... Eccl 2:3 6213
labour that I had laboured to *d* ...... Eccl 2:11 6213
for what can the man *d* that ...... Eccl 2:12
rejoice, and to *d* good in his life ...... Eccl 3:12 6213
saith he, For whom *d* I labour ...... Eccl 4:8
consider not that they *d* evil ...... Eccl 5:1 6213
d not all go to one place ...... Eccl 6:6
is fully set in them to *d* evil ...... Eccl 8:11 6213
Though a sinner *d* evil an hundred ...... Eccl 8:12 6213
to *d*, *d* it with thy might ...... Eccl 9:10 6213
he *d* not whet the edge, then must ...... Eccl 10:10
nor how the bones *d* grow in the ...... Eccl 11:5
therefore *d* the virgins love thee ...... Song 1:3
what shall we *d* for our sister in ...... Song 8:8 6213
cease to *d* evil ...... Is 1:16
Learn to *d* well ...... Is 1:17
you what I will *d* to my vineyard ...... Is 5:5 6213
neither *d* they seek the LORD of ...... Is 9:13
what will ye *d* in the day of ...... Is 10:3 6213
so *d* to Jerusalem and her idols ...... Is 10:11 6213
that they *d* not rise, nor possess ...... Is 14:21
or tail, branch or rush, may *d* ...... Is 19:15 6213
shall *d* sacrifice and oblation ...... Is 19:21 5647
neither *d* I nourish up young men, ... Is 23:4

people of the earth *d* languish ...... Is 24:4
all the merryhearted *d* sigh ...... Is 24:7
foundations of the earth *d* shake ...... Is 24:18
I the LORD *d* keep it ...... Is 27:3
of Gibeon, that he may *d* his work ...... Is 28:21 6213
and with their lips *d* honour me ...... Is 29:13
I will proceed to *d* a marvellous ...... Is 29:14
of the LORD of hosts shall *d* this ...... Is 37:32 6213
that the LORD will *d* this thing ...... Is 38:7 6213
praise thee, as I *d* this day ...... Is 38:19
d good, or *d* evil, that we may ...... Is 41:23
pass, and new things *d* I declare ...... Is 42:9
These things will I *d* unto them ...... Is 42:16 6213
Behold, I will *d* a new thing ...... Is 43:19 6213
I the LORD *d* all these things ...... Is 45:7 6213
and I will *d* all my pleasure ...... Is 46:10 6213
purposed it, I will also *d* it ...... Is 46:11 6213
for mine own sake, will I *d* it ...... Is 48:11 6213
he will *d* his pleasure on Babylon ...... Is 48:14 6213
Wherefore *d* ye spend money for ...... Is 55:2
Keep ye judgment, and *d* justice ...... Is 56:1 6213
Against whom *d* ye sport ...... Is 57:4
shall not fast as ye *d* this day ...... Is 58:4
and we all *d* fade as a leaf ...... Is 64:6
so will I *d* for my servants' ...... Is 65:8 6213
after things that *d* not profit ...... Jer 2:8
thou to *d* in the way of Egypt ...... Jer 2:18
or what hast thou to *d* in the way ...... Jer 2:18
they are wise to *d* evil ...... Jer 4:22
but to *d* good they have no ...... Jer 4:22
art spoiled, what wilt thou *d* ...... Jer 4:30 6213
of the needy *d* they not judge ...... Jer 5:28
what will ye *d* in the end thereof ...... Jer 5:31 6213
We are delivered to *d* all these ...... Jer 7:10 6213
will I *d* unto this house, which ...... Jer 7:14 6213
they *d* in the cities of Judah ...... Jer 7:17 6213
D they provoke me to anger ...... Jer 7:19
d they not provoke themselves to ...... Jer 7:19
How *d* ye say, We are wise, and the ...... Jer 8:8
Why *d* we sit still ...... Jer 8:14
for how shall I *d* for the ...... Jer 9:7 6213
for they cannot *d* evil, neither ...... Jer 10:5
also is it in them to *d* good ...... Jer 10:5
d them, according to all which I ...... Jer 11:4 6213
words of this covenant, and *d* them ...... Jer 11:6 6213
which I commanded them to *d* ...... Jer 11:8 6213
my beloved to *d* in mine house ...... Jer 11:15
then how wilt thou *d* in the ...... Jer 12:5 6213
D we not certainly know that ...... Jer 13:12
then may ye also *d* good ...... Jer 13:23
that are accustomed to *d* evil ...... Jer 13:23
d thou it for thy name's sake ...... Jer 14:7 6213
D not abhor us, for thy name's ...... Jer 14:21
d not disgrace the throne of thy ...... Jer 14:21
neither *d* ye any work, but hallow ...... Jer 17:22 6213
sabbath day, to *d* no work therein ...... Jer 17:24 6213
cannot I *d* with you as this ...... Jer 18:6 6213
that I thought to *d* unto them ...... Jer 18:8 6213
If it *d* evil in my sight, that it ...... Jer 18:10 6213
and we will every one *d* the ...... Jer 18:12 6213
Thus will I *d* unto this place, ... Jer 19:12 6213
d no wrong, *d* no violence to the ...... Jer 22:3
For if ye *d* this thing indeed, ... Jer 22:4 6213
d judgment and justice, and then it ...... Jer 22:15 6213
and for violence, to *d* it ...... Jer 22:17 6213
D not I fill heaven and earth ...... Jer 23:24
d tell them, and cause my people ...... Jer 23:32 6213
and I will *d* you no hurt ...... Jer 25:6
which I purpose to *d* unto them ...... Jer 26:3 6213
d with me as seemeth good and meet.. Jer 26:14 6213
the LORD *d* so ...... Jer 28:6 6213
good that I will *d* for my people ...... Jer 29:32 6213
wherefore *d* I see every man with ...... Jer 30:6
I *d* earnestly remember him still ...... Jer 31:20
that thou commandedst them to *d* ...... Jer 32:23 6213
they should *d* this abomination ...... Jer 32:35 6213
away from them, to *d* them good ...... Jer 32:40
rejoice over them to *d* them good ...... Jer 32:41
all the good that I *d* unto them ...... Jer 33:9 6213
to *d* sacrifice continually ...... Jer 33:18 6213
which I purpose to *d* unto them ...... Jer 36:3 6213
that can *d* any thing against you ...... Jer 38:5
well to him, and *d* him no harm ...... Jer 39:12 6213
but *d* unto him even as he shall ...... Jer 39:12 6213
Thou shalt not *d* this thing ...... Jer 40:16 6213
many, as thine eyes *d* behold us ...... Jer 42:2
walk, and the thing that we may *d* ...... Jer 42:3 6213
if we *d* not even according to all ...... Jer 42:5 6213
declare unto us, and we will *d* it ...... Jer 42:20 6213
d not this abominable thing that ...... Jer 44:4 6213
But we will certainly *d* ...... Jer 44:17 6213
as she hath done, *d* unto her ...... Jer 50:15 6213
d according to all that I have ...... Jer 50:21 6213
that she hath done, *d* unto her ...... Jer 50:29 6213
that I will *d* judgment upon the ...... Jer 51:47
that I will *d* judgment upon her ...... Jer 51:52
when her waves *d* roar like great ...... Jer 51:55
The ways of Zion *d* mourn, because ...... Lam 1:4
d unto them, as thou hast done ...... Lam 1:22 5953
Mine eyes *d* fail with tears, my ...... Lam 2:11
I *d* send thee unto them ...... Eze 2:4
I will *d* in thee that which I ...... Eze 5:9 6213
I will not *d* any more the like ...... Eze 5:9 6213
I would *d* this evil unto them ...... Eze 6:10 6213
I will *d* unto them after their ...... Eze 7:27 6213
of man, seest thou what they *d* ...... Eze 8:6 6213
abominations that they *d* here ...... Eze 8:9 6213
the house of Israel *d* in the dark ...... Eze 8:12 6213
greater abominations that they *d* ...... Eze 8:13 6213
keep mine ordinances, and *d* them ...... Eze 11:20 6213
be taken thereof to *d* any work ...... Eze 15:3 6213
to *d* any of these unto thee, to ...... Eze 16:5 6213
d that which is lawful and right, ... Eze 18:5 6213
d that which is lawful and right, ... Eze 18:21 6213

my judgments, which if a man *d* ...... Eze 20:11 6213
my judgments, which if a man *d* ...... Eze 20:13 6213
and keep my judgments, and *d* them... Eze 20:19 6213
to *d* them, which if a man *d* ...... Eze 20:21 6213
your doings your sins *d* appear ...... Eze 21:24
LORD have spoken it, and will *d* it ...... Eze 22:14 6213
I will *d* these things unto thee, ... Eze 23:30 6213
not to *d* after your lewdness ...... Eze 23:48 6213
come to pass, and I will *d* it ...... Eze 24:14 6213
ye shall *d* as I have done ...... Eze 24:22 6213
all that he hath done shall ye *d* ...... Eze 24:24 6213
Because that Moab and Seir *d* say ...... Eze 25:8
they shall *d* in Edom according to ...... Eze 25:14 6213
if he *d* not turn from his way, he ...... Eze 33:9
d that which is lawful and right ...... Eze 33:14 6213
d that which is lawful and right, ... Eze 33:19 6213
words, but they will not *d* them ...... Eze 33:31 6213
thy words, but they *d* them not ...... Eze 33:32 6213
of Israel that *d* feed themselves ...... Eze 34:2
I will even *d* according to thine ...... Eze 35:11 6213
desolate, so will I *d* unto thee ...... Eze 35:15 6213
will *d* better unto you than at ...... Eze 36:11
I *d* not this for your sakes, O ...... Eze 36:22 6213
keep my judgments, and *d* them ...... Eze 36:27 6213
Not for your sakes *d* I this ...... Eze 36:32 6213
have spoken it, and I will *d* it ...... Eze 36:36 6213
house of Israel, to *d* it for them ...... Eze 36:37 6213
and observe my statutes, and *d* them... Eze 37:24 6213
that I the LORD *d* sanctify Israel ...... Eze 37:28
that I *d* sacrifice for you ...... Eze 39:17
the ordinances thereof, and *d* them ...... Eze 43:11 6213
to *d* the office of a priest unto ...... Eze 44:13
so thou shalt *d* the seventh day ...... Eze 45:20 6213
shall he *d* the like in the feast ...... Eze 45:25 6213
d not ye serve my gods, nor ...... Dan 3:14
known that the heavens *d* rule ...... Dan 4:26
for we *d* not present our ...... Dan 9:18
O Lord, hearken and *d* ...... Dan 9:19 6213
and *d* according to his will ...... Dan 11:3 6213
shall *d* according to his own will ...... Dan 11:16 6213
thus shall he *d* ...... Dan 11:17 6213
he shall *d* that which his fathers ...... Dan 11:24 6213
hearts shall be to *d* mischief ...... Dan 11:27
and he shall *d* exploits, and return ...... Dan 11:28 6213
so shall he *d* ...... Dan 11:30 6213
such as *d* wickedly against the ...... Dan 11:32
but the people that *d* know their ...... Dan 11:32
shall be strong, and *d* exploits ...... Dan 11:32 6213
the king shall *d* according to his ...... Dan 11:36 6213
Thus shall he *d* in the most ...... Dan 11:39 6213
but the wicked shall *d* wickedly ...... Dan 12:10
her rulers with shame *d* love ...... Hos 4:18
Ephraim, what shall I *d* unto thee ...... Hos 6:4 6213
O Judah, what shall I *d* unto thee ...... Hos 6:4 6213
they *d* not return to the LORD ...... Hos 7:10
yet *d* they imagine mischief ...... Hos 7:15
What will ye *d* in the solemn day, ... Hos 9:5 6213
what then should a king *d* to us ...... Hos 10:3 6213
So shall Beth-el *d* unto you ...... Hos 10:15 6213
they *d* make a covenant with the ...... Hos 12:1
What have I to *d* any more with ...... Hos 14:8
How *d* the beasts groan ...... Joel 1:18
for the LORD will *d* great things ...... Joel 2:21 6213
of the wilderness *d* spring ...... Joel 2:22
the vine *d* yield their strength ...... Joel 2:22 6213
Yea, and what have ye to *d* with me... Joel 3:4
the Lord GOD will *d* nothing ...... Amos 3:7 6213
For they know not to *d* right ...... Amos 3:10 6213
Therefore thus will I *d* unto thee ...... Amos 4:12 6213
because I will *d* this unto thee ...... Amos 4:12 6213
him, What shall we *d* unto thee ...... Jonah 1:11 6213
said that he would *d* unto them ...... Jonah 3:10 6213
I *d* well to be angry, even unto ...... Jonah 4:9
this family *d* I devise an evil ...... Mic 2:3
d not my words *d* good to him ...... Mic 2:7
in the spirit and falsehood *d* lie ...... Mic 2:11
require of thee, but to *d* justly ...... Mic 6:8 6213
That they may *d* evil with both ...... Mic 7:3
What *d* ye imagine against the ...... Nah 1:9
heart, The LORD will not *d* good ...... Zeph 1:12
neither will he *d* evil ...... Zeph 1:12
he will not *d* iniquity ...... Zeph 3:5 6213
of Israel shall not *d* iniquity ...... Zeph 3:13 6213
and how *d* ye see it now ...... Hag 2:3
and with his skirt *d* touch bread ...... Hag 2:12
prophets, *d* they live for ever ...... Zec 1:5
of hosts thought to *d* unto us ...... Zec 1:6 6213
Then said I, What come these to *d* ...... Zec 1:21 6213
Whither *d* these bear the ephah ...... Zec 5:10
days to *d* well unto Jerusalem ...... Zec 8:15
are the things that ye shall *d* ...... Zec 8:16 6213
even to day *d* I declare that I ...... Zec 9:12
d not magnify themselves against ...... Zec 12:7
neither *d* ye kindle fire on mine ...... Mal 1:10
because ye *d* not lay it to heart ...... Mal 2:2
why *d* we deal treacherously every ...... Mal 2:10
yea, and all that *d* wickedly ...... Mal 4:1 6213
in the day that I shall *d* this ...... Mal 4:3 6213
Blessed are they which *d* hunger ...... Mt 5:6
Neither *d* men light a candle, and ...... Mt 5:15
but whosoever shall *d* and teach ...... Mt 5:19 *4160*
d good to them that hate you, and ...... Mt 5:44 *4160*
d not even the publicans the same ...... Mt 5:46 *4160*
what *d* ye more than others ...... Mt 5:47 *4160*
d not even the publicans so ...... Mt 5:47 *4160*
Take heed that ye *d* not your alms ...... Mt 6:1 *4160*
d not sound a trumpet before thee ...... Mt 6:2
hypocrites *d* in the synagogues ...... Mt 6:2 *4160*
repetitions, as the heathen *d* ...... Mt 6:7
where thieves *d* not break through ...... Mt 6:20
neither *d* they reap, nor gather ...... Mt 6:26
toil not, neither *d* they spin ...... Mt 6:28
these things *d* the Gentiles seek ...... Mt 6:32
ye would that men should *d* to you ...... Mt 7:12 *4160*

d ye even so to them	Mt 7:12	4160
D men gather grapes of thorns, or	Mt 7:16	
servant, *D* this, and he doeth it	Mt 8:9	4160
What have we to *d* with thee	Mt 8:29	4160
of John, saying, Why *d* we	Mt 9:14	
Neither *d* men put new wine into	Mt 9:17	
ye that I am able to *d* this	Mt 9:28	4160
come, or *d* we look for another	Mt 11:3	
those things which ye *d* hear	Mt 11:4	
thy disciples *d* that which is not	Mt 12:2	4160
lawful to *d* upon the sabbath day	Mt 12:2	4160
to *d* well on the sabbath days	Mt 12:12	4160
by whom *d* your children cast them	Mt 12:27	
For whosoever shall *d* the will of	Mt 12:50	4160
neither *d* they understand	Mt 13:13	
offend, and them which *d* iniquity	Mt 13:41	4160
therefore mighty works *d* shew	Mt 14:2	
Why *d* thy disciples transgress	Mt 15:2	
Why *d* ye also transgress the	Mt 15:3	
But in vain they *d* worship me	Mt 15:9	4160
D not ye yet understand, that	Mt 15:17	
D ye not yet understand, neither	Mt 16:9	
How is it that ye *d* not	Mt 16:11	
Whom *d* men say that I the Son of	Mt 16:13	
of whom *d* the kings of the earth	Mt 17:25	
That in heaven their angels *d*	Mt 18:10	
heavenly Father *d* also unto you	Mt 18:35	4160
Master, what good thing shall I *d*	Mt 19:16	4160
said, Thou shalt *d* no murder	Mt 19:18	
said, Friend, I *d* thee no wrong	Mt 20:13	91
me to *d* what I will with mine own	Mt 20:15	4160
will ye that I shall *d* unto you	Mt 20:32	4160
ye shall not only *d* this which is	Mt 21:21	4160
what authority I *d* these things	Mt 21:24	4160
what authority I *d* these things	Mt 21:27	4160
what will he *d* unto those	Mt 21:40	4160
Ye *d* err, not knowing the	Mt 22:29	
you observe, that observe and *d*	Mt 23:3	4160
but *d* not ye after their works	Mt 23:3	4160
for they say, and *d* not	Mt 23:3	4160
they *d* for to be seen of men	Mt 23:5	4160
an oath, I *d* not know the man	Mt 26:72	
nothing to *d* with that just man	Mt 27:19	
What shall I *d* then with Jesus	Mt 27:22	4160
what have we to *d* with thee	Mk 1:24	
spirits, and they *d* obey him	Mk 1:27	
Why *d* the disciples of John and of	Mk 2:18	
why *d* they on the sabbath day	Mk 2:24	4160
Is it lawful to *d* good on the	Mk 3:4	15
on the sabbath days, or to *d* evil	Mk 3:4	2554
whosoever shall *d* the will of God	Mk 3:35	
said, What have I to *d* with thee	Mk 5:7	
he could there *d* no mighty work	Mk 6:5	4160
therefore mighty works *d* shew	Mk 6:14	
Howbeit in vain *d* they worship me	Mk 7:7	
many other such like things ye *d*	Mk 7:8	4160
ye suffer him no more to *d* ought	Mk 7:12	4160
and many such like things *d* ye	Mk 7:13	4160
D ye not perceive, that	Mk 7:18	
and *d* ye not remember	Mk 8:18	
is it that ye *d* not understand	Mk 8:21	
them, Whom *d* men say that I am	Mk 8:27	
but if thou canst *d* any thing	Mk 9:22	
shall *d* a miracle in my name	Mk 9:39	4160
what shall I *d* that I may inherit	Mk 10:17	4160
D not commit adultery, *D* not	Mk 10:19	
D not kill, *D* not steal	Mk 10:19	
D not bear false witness, Defraud	Mk 10:19	
d for us whatsoever we shall	Mk 10:35	4160
would ye that I should *d* for you	Mk 10:36	4160
thou that I should *d* unto thee	Mk 10:51	4160
man say unto you, Why *d* ye this	Mk 11:3	4160
there said unto them, What *d* ye	Mk 11:5	4160
But if ye *d* not forgive, neither	Mk 11:26	
this authority to *d* these things	Mk 11:28	4160
what authority I *d* these things	Mk 11:29	4160
Neither *d* I tell you by what	Mk 11:33	4160
what authority I *d* these things	Mk 11:33	4160
the lord of the vineyard *d*	Mk 12:9	4160
D ye not therefore err, because	Mk 12:24	
ye therefore *d* greatly err	Mk 12:27	
speak, neither *d* ye premeditate	Mk 13:11	
ye will ye may *d* them good	Mk 14:7	4160
aloud began to desire him to *d* as	Mk 15:8	
d unto him whom ye call the King	Mk 15:12	4160
to *d* for him after the custom of	Lk 2:27	4160
him, saying, What shall we *d* then	Lk 3:10	4160
hath meat, let him *d* likewise	Lk 3:11	4160
unto him, Master, what shall we *d*	Lk 3:12	4160
him, saying, And what shall we *d*	Lk 3:14	4160
D violence to no man, neither	Lk 3:14	1286
d also here in thy country	Lk 4:23	4160
what have we to *d* with thee	Lk 4:34	
Why *d* ye eat and drink with	Lk 5:30	
Why *d* the disciples of John fast	Lk 5:33	
Why *d* ye that which is not lawful	Lk 6:2	4160
lawful to *d* on the sabbath days	Lk 6:2	4160
on the sabbath days to *d* good	Lk 6:9	15
or to *d* evil?	Lk 6:9	2554
what they might *d* to Jesus	Lk 6:11	4160
d good to them which hate you,	Lk 6:27	4160
ye would that men should *d* to you	Lk 6:31	4160
d ye also to them likewise	Lk 6:31	4160
if ye *d* good to them which	Lk 6:33	
good to them which *d* good to you	Lk 6:33	15
for sinners also *d* even the same	Lk 6:33	4160
d good, and lend, hoping for	Lk 6:35	15
of thorns men *d* not gather figs	Lk 6:44	
d not the things which I say	Lk 6:46	4160
worthy for whom he should *d* this	Lk 7:4	3930
servant, *D* this, and he doeth it	Lk 7:8	4160
hear the word of God, and *d* it	Lk 8:21	4160
said, What have I to *d* with thee	Lk 8:28	
we *d* wipe off against you	Lk 10:11	
what shall I *d* to inherit eternal	Lk 10:25	4160
this *d*, and thou shalt live	Lk 10:28	4160
unto him, Go, and *d* thou likewise	Lk 10:37	4160
by whom *d* your sons cast them out	Lk 11:19	
Now *d* ye Pharisees make clean the	Lk 11:39	
that have no more that they can *d*	Lk 12:4	4160
himself, saying, What shall I *d*	Lk 12:17	4160
And he said, This will I *d*	Lk 12:18	4160
to *d* that thing which is least	Lk 12:26	
For all these things *d* the	Lk 12:30	
that ye *d* not discern this time	Lk 12:56	
I *d* cures to day and to morrow, and	Lk 13:32	2005
these many years *d* I serve thee	Lk 15:29	
within himself, What shall I *d*	Lk 16:3	4160
I am resolved what to *d*, that,	Lk 16:4	4160
done that which was our duty to *d*	Lk 17:10	4160
what shall I *d* to inherit eternal	Lk 18:18	4160
D not commit adultery	Lk 18:20	
D not kill, *D* not steal	Lk 18:20	
D not steal, *D* not bear false	Lk 18:20	
thou that I shall *d* unto thee	Lk 18:41	4160
man ask you, Why *d* ye loose him	Lk 19:31	
could not find what they might *d*	Lk 19:48	4160
what authority I *d* these things	Lk 20:8	4160
of the vineyard, What shall I *d*	Lk 20:13	4160
lord of the vineyard *d* unto them	Lk 20:15	4160
this *d* in remembrance of me	Lk 22:19	4160
it was that should *d* this thing	Lk 22:23	4238
For if they *d* these things in a	Lk 23:31	4160
for they know not what they *d*	Lk 23:34	4160
why *d* thoughts arise in your	Lk 24:38	
Woman, what have I to *d* with thee	Jn 2:4	
he saith unto you, *d* it	Jn 2:5	4160
for no man can *d* these miracles	Jn 3:2	4160
thee, We speak that we *d* know	Jn 3:11	
My meat is to *d* the will of him	Jn 4:34	4160
The Son can *d* nothing of himself,	Jn 5:19	4160
but what he seeth the Father *d*	Jn 5:19	4160
I can of mine own self *d* nothing	Jn 5:30	4160
finish, the same works that I *d*	Jn 5:36	4160
D not think that I will accuse	Jn 5:45	
he himself knew what he would *d*	Jn 6:6	4160
they unto him, What shall we *d*	Jn 6:28	4160
not to *d* mine own will, but the	Jn 6:38	4160
If thou *d* these things, shew	Jn 7:4	4160
If any man will *d* his will	Jn 7:17	4160
D the rulers know indeed that	Jn 7:26	
will he *d* more miracles than	Jn 7:31	4160
her, Neither *d* I condemn thee	Jn 8:11	
that I *d* nothing of myself	Jn 8:28	4160
for I *d* always those things that	Jn 8:29	4160
ye *d* that which ye have seen with	Jn 8:38	4160
ye would *d* the works of Abraham	Jn 8:39	4160
Ye *d* the deeds of your father	Jn 8:41	4160
Why *d* ye not understand my speech	Jn 8:43	
lusts of your father ye will *d*	Jn 8:44	4160
truth, why *d* ye not believe me	Jn 8:46	
my Father, and ye *d* dishonour me	Jn 8:49	
mine eyes, and I washed, and *d* see	Jn 9:15	
that is a sinner *d* such miracles	Jn 9:16	4160
not of God, he could *d* nothing	Jn 9:33	4160
the works that I *d* in my Father's	Jn 10:25	4160
of those works *d* ye stone me	Jn 10:32	
If I *d* not the works of my Father	Jn 10:37	4160
But if I *d*, though ye believe not	Jn 10:38	4160
if he sleep, he shall *d* well	Jn 11:12	4982
a council, and said, What *d* we	Jn 11:47	4160
What I *d* thou knowest not now	Jn 13:7	4160
that ye should *d* as I have done	Jn 13:15	4160
things, happy are ye if ye *d* them	Jn 13:17	4160
him, That thou doest, *d* quickly	Jn 13:27	4160
works that I *d* shall he *d* also	Jn 14:12	4160
works than these shall he *d*	Jn 14:12	4160
ask in my name, that will I *d*	Jn 14:13	4160
any thing in my name, I will *d* it	Jn 14:14	4160
gave me commandment, even so I *d*	Jn 14:31	4160
for without me ye can *d* nothing	Jn 15:5	4160
if ye *d* whatsoever I command you	Jn 15:14	4160
d unto you for my name's sake	Jn 15:21	4160
these things will they *d* unto you	Jn 16:3	4160
D ye enquire among yourselves of	Jn 16:19	
answered them, *D* ye now believe	Jn 16:31	
work which thou gavest me to *d*	Jn 17:4	4160
Lord, and what shall this man *d*	Jn 21:21	
of all that Jesus began both to *d*	Acts 1:1	4160
we *d* hear them speak in our	Acts 2:11	
Men and brethren, what shall we *d*	Acts 2:37	4160
What shall we *d* to these men	Acts 4:16	4160
For to *d* whatsoever thy hand and	Acts 4:28	4160
intend to *d* as touching these men	Acts 5:35	4238
why *d* ye wrong one to another	Acts 7:26	91
ye *d* always resist the Holy Ghost	Acts 7:51	
as your fathers did, so *d* ye	Acts 7:51	
Lord, what wilt thou have me to *d*	Acts 9:6	4160
be told thee what thou must *d*	Acts 9:6	4160
tell thee what thou oughtest to *d*	Acts 10:6	4160
Sirs, why *d* ye these things	Acts 14:15	4160
keep yourselves, ye shall *d* well	Acts 15:29	4238
of the Lord, and see how they *d*	Acts 15:36	2192
d exceedingly trouble our city,	Acts 16:20	
voice, saying, *D* thyself no harm	Acts 16:28	4238
Sirs, what must I *d* to be saved	Acts 16:30	4160
now *d* they thrust us out privily	Acts 16:37	
these all *d* contrary to the	Acts 17:7	4160
be quiet, and to *d* nothing rashly	Acts 19:36	4160
D therefore this that we say to	Acts 21:23	4160
And I said, What shall I *d*	Acts 22:10	4160
which are appointed for thee to *d*	Acts 22:10	4160
But *d* not thou yield unto them	Acts 23:21	
I *d* the more cheerfully answer	Acts 24:10	
herein *d* I exercise myself, to	Acts 24:16	
willing to *d* the Jews a pleasure,	Acts 25:9	2698
that I ought to *d* many things	Acts 26:9	4238
d works meet for repentance	Acts 26:20	4238
to *d* those things which are not	Rom 1:28	4160
of death, not only *d* the same	Rom 1:32	
have pleasure in them that *d* them	Rom 1:32	4238
judgest them which *d* such things	Rom 2:3	4238
d not obey the truth, but obey	Rom 2:8	
d by nature the things contained	Rom 2:14	4160
that we say,) Let us *d* evil	Rom 3:8	4160
D we then make void the law	Rom 3:31	
For that which I *d* I allow not	Rom 7:15	2716
for what I would, that *d* I not	Rom 7:15	4238
but what I hate, that *d* I	Rom 7:15	4160
If then I *d* that which I would	Rom 7:16	4160
then it is no more I that *d* it	Rom 7:17	2716
For the good that I would I *d* not	Rom 7:19	4160
evil which I would not, that I *d*	Rom 7:19	4238
Now if I *d* that I would not	Rom 7:20	4160
it is no more I that *d* it	Rom 7:20	2716
a law, that, when I would *d* good	Rom 7:21	4160
For what the law could not *d*	Rom 8:3	
d mind the things of the flesh	Rom 8:5	
but if ye through the Spirit *d*	Rom 8:13	
then *d* we with patience wait for	Rom 8:25	
let him *d* it with simplicity	Rom 12:8	
Rejoice with them that *d* rejoice	Rom 12:15	
d that which is good, and thou	Rom 13:3	4160
But if thou *d* that which is evil,	Rom 13:4	4160
them that *d* not believe in Judaea	Rom 15:31	
For what have I to *d* to judge	1Cor 5:12	
d not ye judge them that are	1Cor 5:12	
D ye not know that the saints	1Cor 6:2	
Why *d* ye not rather take wrong	1Cor 6:7	
why *d* ye not rather suffer	1Cor 6:7	
ye *d* wrong, and defraud, and that	1Cor 6:8	
let him *d* what he will, he	1Cor 7:36	4160
to them that *d* examine me is this	1Cor 9:3	
D ye not know that they which	1Cor 9:13	
For if I *d* this thing willingly,	1Cor 9:17	4238
this I *d* for the gospel's sake,	1Cor 9:23	4160
Now they *d* it to obtain a	1Cor 9:25	
D we provoke the Lord to jealousy	1Cor 10:22	
eat, or drink, or whatsoever ye *d*	1Cor 10:31	4160
d all to the glory of God	1Cor 10:31	4160
this *d* in remembrance of me	1Cor 11:24	4160
this *d* ye, as oft as ye drink it,	1Cor 11:25	4160
ye *d* shew the Lord's death till	1Cor 11:26	
d all speak with tongues	1Cor 12:30	
d all interpret?	1Cor 12:30	
Else what shall they *d* which are	1Cor 15:29	4160
and with what body *d* they come	1Cor 15:35	
churches of Galatia, even so *d* ye	1Cor 16:1	4160
for I *d* pass through Macedonia	1Cor 16:5	
the work of the Lord, as I also *d*	1Cor 16:10	
d I purpose according to the	2Cor 1:17	
D we begin again to commend	2Cor 3:1	
are in this tabernacle *d* groan	2Cor 5:4	
I *d* not repent, though I did	2Cor 7:8	
we *d* you to wit of the grace of	2Cor 8:1	1107
have begun before, not only to *d*	2Cor 8:10	4160
Whether any *d* enquire of Titus,	2Cor 8:23	
we *d* not war after the flesh	2Cor 10:3	
D ye look on things after the	2Cor 10:7	
wages of them, to *d* you service	2Cor 11:8	
But what I *d*, that I will *d*,	2Cor 11:12	4160
But what I *d*, that I will *d*	2Cor 11:12	4160
but we *d* all things, dearly	2Cor 12:19	
I pray to God that ye *d* no evil	2Cor 13:7	4160
but that ye should *d* that which	2Cor 13:7	4160
For we can *d* nothing against the	2Cor 13:8	
For *d* I now persuade men, or God	Gal 1:10	
or *d* I seek to please men	Gal 1:10	
which I also was forward to *d*	Gal 2:10	4160
not as *d* the Jews, why compellest	Gal 2:14	
Gentiles to live as *d* the Jews	Gal 2:14	
I *d* not frustrate the grace of	Gal 2:21	
in the book of the law to *d* them	Gal 3:10	4160
the law, *d* ye not hear the law	Gal 4:21	
he is a debtor to *d* the whole law	Gal 5:3	4160
why *d* I yet suffer persecution	Gal 5:11	
so that ye cannot *d* the things	Gal 5:17	4160
that they which *d* such things	Gal 5:21	4238
let us *d* good unto all men,	Gal 6:10	2038
Now unto him that is able to *d*	Eph 3:20	4160
d the same things unto them,	Eph 6:9	4160
may know my affairs, and how I *d*	Eph 6:21	4238
and I therein *d* rejoice, yea, and	Phil 1:18	
to *d* of his good pleasure	Phil 2:13	1754
D all things without murmurings	Phil 2:14	4160
For the same cause also *d* ye joy	Phil 2:18	
d count them but dung, that I may	Phil 3:8	
but this one thing I *d*,	Phil 3:13	
and heard, and seen in me, *d*	Phil 4:9	4238
I can *d* all things through Christ	Phil 4:13	2480
d not cease to pray for you, and	Col 1:9	
Christ forgave you, so also *d* ye	Col 3:13	
whatsoever ye *d* in word or deed,	Col 3:17	4160
d all in the name of the Lord	Col 3:17	4160
And whatsoever ye *d*	Col 3:23	4160
d it heartily, as to the Lord, and	Col 3:23	2038
all men, even as we *d* toward you	1Th 3:12	
indeed ye *d* it toward all the	1Th 4:10	4160
to *d* your own business, and to	1Th 4:11	4238
let us not sleep, as *d* others	1Th 5:6	
one another, even as also ye *d*	1Th 5:11	4160
calleth you, who also will *d* it	1Th 5:24	4160
Lord touching you, that ye both *d*	2Th 3:4	4160
will *d* the things which we	2Th 3:4	4160
which is in faith: so *d*	1Ti 1:4	
but rather *d* them service,	1Ti 6:2	1398
That they *d* good, that they be	1Ti 6:18	14
that they *d* gender strifes	2Ti 2:23	
so *d* these also resist the truth	2Ti 3:8	
d the work of an evangelist, make	2Ti 4:5	4160
D thy diligence to come shortly	2Ti 4:9	4704
D thy diligence to come before	2Ti 4:21	4704

thy mind would I *d* nothing Philem 14 4160
albeit I *d* not say to thee how Philem 19 4160
thou wilt also *d* more than I say Philem 21 4160
They *d* alway err in their heart Heb 3:10
have believed *d* enter into rest Heb 4:3
of him with whom we have to *d* Heb 4:13
And this will we *d*, if God permit Heb 6:3 4160
to the saints, and *d* minister Heb 6:10
d shew the same diligence to the Heb 6:11
of me,) to *d* thy will, O God Heb 10:7 4160
said he, Lo, I come to *d* thy will Heb 10:9 4160
not made of things which *d* appear Heb 11:3
assaying to *d* were drowned Heb 11:29
not fear what man shall *d* unto me Heb 13:6
But to *d* good and to communicate Heb 13:16 2140
that they may *d* it with joy Heb 13:17 4160
beseech you the rather to *d* this Heb 13:19 4160
in every good work to *d* his will Heb 13:21 4160
D not err, my beloved brethren Jas 1:16
D not rich men oppress you, and Jas 2:6
D not they blaspheme that worthy Jas 2:7
neighbour as thyself, ye *d* well Jas 2:8 4160
D not commit adultery, said also, Jas 2:11
adultery, said also, *D* not kill Jas 2:11
So speak ye, and so *d*, as they Jas 2:12 4160
D ye think that the scripture Jas 4:5
we shall live, and *d* this, or that Jas 4:15 4160
to him that knoweth to *d* good Jas 4:17 4160
if any of you *d* err from the Jas 5:19
Who by him *d* believe in God, that 1Pet 1:21
the praise of them that *d* well 1Pet 2:14 17
but if, when ye *d* well, and suffer 1Pet 2:20 15
ye are, as long as ye *d* well 1Pet 3:6 15
Let him eschew evil, and *d* good 1Pet 3:11 4160
Lord is against them that *d* evil 1Pet 3:12 4160
let him *d* it as of the ability 1Pet 4:11
for if ye *d* these things, ye 2Pet 1:10 4160
whereunto ye *d* well that ye take 2Pet 1:19 4160
wrest, as they *d* also the other 2Pet 3:16
we lie, and *d* not the truth 1Jn 1:6 4160
hereby we *d* know that we know him 1Jn 2:3
d those things that are pleasing 1Jn 3:22 4160
d testify that the Father sent 1Jn 4:14
I *d* not say that he shall pray 1Jn 5:16
a godly sort, thou shalt *d* well 3Jn 6 4160
and repent, and *d* the first works Rev 2:5 4160
are Jews, and are not, but *d* lie Rev 3:9
of thy nakedness *d* not appear Rev 3:18
heads, and with them they *d* hurt Rev 9:19
to *d* in the sight of the beast Rev 13:14 4160
and their works *d* follow them Rev 14:13
said unto me, See thou *d* it not Rev 19:10
of the earth *d* bring their glory Rev 21:24
he unto me, See thou *d* it not Rev 22:9
are they that *d* his commandments Rev 22:14 4160

DOCTOR
a *d* of the law, had in reputation Acts 5:34 3547

DOCTORS
sitting in the midst of the *d* Lk 2:46 1320
d of the law sitting by, which Lk 5:17 3547

DOCTRINE
My *d* shall drop as the rain, my Deut 32:2 3948
My *d* is pure, and I am clean in Job 11:4 3948
For I give you good *d*, forsake ye Prov 4:2 3948
shall he make to understand *d* Is 28:9 8052
they that murmured shall learn *d* Is 29:24 3948
the stock is a *d* of vanities Jer 10:8 4148
people were astonished at his *d* Mt 7:28 1322
but of the *d* of the Pharisees and Mt 16:12 1322
they were astonished at his *d* Mt 22:33 1322
And they were astonished at his *d* Mk 1:22 1322
what new *d* is this Mk 1:27 1322
and said unto them in his *d* Mk 4:2 1322
people was astonished at his *d* Mk 11:18 1322
And he said unto them in his *d* Mk 12:38 1322
And they were astonished at his *d* Lk 4:32 1322
My *d* is not mine, but his that Jn 7:16 1322
his will, he shall know of the *d* Jn 7:17 1322
of his disciples, and of his *d* Jn 18:19 1322
stedfastly in the apostles' *d* Acts 2:42 1322
have filled Jerusalem with your *d* Acts 5:28 1322
astonished at the *d* of the Lord Acts 13:12 1322
May we know what this new *d* Acts 17:19 1322
form of *d* which was delivered you Rom 6:17 1322
to the *d* which ye have learned Rom 16:17 1322
or by prophesying, or by *d* 1Cor 14:6 1322
one of you hath a psalm, hath a *d* 1Cor 14:26 1322
about with every wind of *d* Eph 4:14 1319
some that they teach no other *d* 1Ti 1:3
thing that is contrary to sound *d* 1Ti 1:10 1319
the words of faith and of good *d* 1Ti 4:6 1319
to reading, to exhortation, to *d* 1Ti 4:13 1319
heed unto thyself, and unto the *d* 1Ti 4:16 1319
they who labour in the word and *d* 1Ti 5:17 1319
of God and his *d* be not blasphemed 1Ti 6:1 1319
to the *d* which is according to 1Ti 6:3 1319
But thou hast fully known my *d* 2Ti 3:10 1319
of God, and is profitable for *d* 2Ti 3:16 1319
with all longsuffering and *d* 2Ti 4:2 1322
when they will not endure sound *d* 2Ti 4:3 1319
be able by sound *d* both to exhort Titus 1:9 1319
the things which become sound *d* Titus 2:1 1319
in *d* shewing uncorruptness, Titus 2:7 1319
that they may adorn the *d* of God Titus 2:10 1319
the principles of the *d* of Christ Heb 6:1 3056
Of the *d* of baptisms, and of Heb 6:2 1322
and abideth not in the *d* of Christ 2Jn 9 1322
that abideth in the *d* of Christ 2Jn 9 1322
any unto you, and bring not this *d* 2Jn 10 1322
them that hold the *d* of Balaam Rev 2:14 1322
hold the *d* of the Nicolaitanes Rev 2:15 1322
as many as have not this *d* Rev 2:24 1322

DOCTRINES
teaching for *d* the commandments Mt 15:9 1319
teaching for *d* the commandments Mk 7:7 1319
the commandments and *d* of men Col 2:22 1319
seducing spirits, and *d* of devils 1Ti 4:1 1319
about with divers and strange *d* Heb 13:9 1322

DODAI (*do'-dahee*) See DODO. *A captain in David's army.*
the second month was *D* an Ahohite 1Chr 27:4 1739

DODANIM (*do'-da-nim*) See RODANIM. *Descendants of Javan.*
and Tarshish, Kittim, and *D* Gen 10:4 1721
and Tarshish, Kittim, and *D* 1Chr 1:7 1721

DODAVAH (*do'-da-vah*) *Father of Eliezer.*
Then Eliezer the son of *D* of 2Chr 20:37 1735

DODAVAHU See DODAVAH.

DODO (*do'-do*) See DODAI.
1. Grandfather of Tola.
the son of Puah, the son of *D* Judg 10:1 1734
2. Father of Eleazar.
Eleazar the son of *D* the Ahohite 2Sa 23:9 1734
him was Eleazar the son of *D* 1Chr 11:12 1734
3. Father of Elhanan.
the son of *D* of Beth-lehem 2Sa 23:24 1734
the son of *D* of Beth-lehem 1Chr 11:26 1734

DOEG (*do'-eg*) *Chief herdsman of King Saul.*
and his name was *D*, an Edomite, 1Sa 21:7 1673
Then answered *D* the Edomite 1Sa 22:9 1673
And the king said to *D*, Turn thou, 1Sa 22:18 1673
D the Edomite turned, and he fell 1Sa 22:18 1673
when *D* the Edomite was there, 1Sa 22:22 1673
when *D* the Edomite came and told Ps 52:t 1673

DOER
did there, he was the *d* of it Gen 39:22 6218
the *d* of evil according to his 2Sa 3:39 6218
plentifully rewardeth the proud *d* Ps 31:23 6218
A wicked *d* giveth heed to false Prov 17:4
I suffer trouble, as an evil *d* 2Ti 2:9 2557
a hearer of the word, and not a *d* Jas 1:23 4163
but a *d* of the work, this man Jas 1:25 4163
law, thou art not a *d* of the law Jas 4:11 4163

DOERS
the hand of the *d* of the work 2Kin 22:5 6213
let them give it to the *d* of the 2Kin 22:5 6213
neither will he help the evil *d* Job 8:20
d from the city of the LORD Ps 101:8 6466
but the *d* of the law shall be Rom 2:13 4163
But be ye *d* of the word, and not Jas 1:22 4163

DOEST
If thou *d* well, shalt thou not be Gen 4:7
if thou *d* not well, sin lieth at Gen 4:7
is with thee in all that thou *d* Gen 21:22 6213
thing that thou *d* to the people Ex 18:14 6213
The thing that thou *d* is not good Ex 18:17 6213
when thou *d* that which is good and Deut 12:28 6213
work of thine hand which thou *d* Deut 14:29 6213
bless thee in all that thou *d* Deut 15:18 6213
but thou *d* me wrong to war Judg 11:27 6213
in, and to know all that thou *d* 2Sa 3:25 6213
mayest prosper in all that thou *d* 1Kin 2:3 6213
him, What *d* thou here, Elijah 1Kin 19:9
and said, What *d* thou here, Elijah 1Kin 19:13
and mark, and see what thou *d* 1Kin 20:22 6213
will say unto him, What *d* thou Job 9:12 6213
sinnest, what *d* thou against him Job 35:6 6466
multiplied, what *d* thou unto him Job 35:6 6213
when thou *d* well to thyself Ps 49:18
Thou art the God that *d* wonders Ps 77:14 6213
art great, and *d* wondrous things Ps 86:10 6213
Thou art good, and *d* good Ps 119:68
who may say unto him, What *d* thou Eccl 8:4 6213
when thou *d* evil, then thou Jer 11:15
shall go aside to ask how thou *d* Jer 15:5 7965
said unto thee, What *d* thou Eze 12:9 6213
seeing thou *d* all these things, Eze 16:30 6213
things are to us, that thou *d* so Eze 24:19 6213
or say unto him, What *d* thou Dan 4:35 5648
the LORD, *D* thou well to be angry Jonah 4:4
D thou well to be angry for the Jonah 4:9
Therefore when thou *d* thine alms Mt 6:2 4160
But when thou *d* alms, let not thy Mt 6:3 4160
authority *d* thou these things Mt 21:23 4160
authority *d* thou these things Mk 11:28 4160
authority *d* thou these things Lk 20:2 4160
seeing that thou *d* these things Jn 2:18 4160
can do these miracles that thou *d* Jn 3:2 4160
may see the works that thou *d* Jn 7:3 4160
said Jesus unto him, That thou *d* Jn 13:27 4160
saying, Take heed what thou *d* Acts 22:26 4160
that judgest *d* the same things Rom 2:1 4238
d the same, that thou shalt Rom 2:3 4160
there is one God; thou *d* well Jas 2:19 4160
thou *d* faithfully whatsoever thou 3Jn 5 4160
whatsoever thou *d* to the brethren 3Jn 5 4160

DOETH
seen all that Laban *d* unto thee Gen 31:12 6213
for whosoever *d* any work therein, Ex 31:14 6213
whosoever *d* any work in the Ex 31:15 6213
whosoever *d* work therein shall be Ex 35:2 6213
while he *d* somewhat against any Lev 4:27 6213
in any of all these that a man *d* Lev 6:3 6213
that *d* any work in that same day Lev 23:30 6213
But the soul that *d* ought Num 15:30 6213
who shall live when God *d* this Num 24:23 7760
Which *d* great things and Job 5:9 6213
Which *d* great things past finding Job 9:10 6213
his soul desireth, even that he *d* Job 23:13 6213
and *d* not good to the widow Job 24:21
great things *d* he, which we Job 37:5 6213
and whatsoever he *d* shall prosper Ps 1:3 6213
works, there is none that *d* good Ps 14:1 6213
there is none that *d* good Ps 14:3 6213
nor *d* evil to his neighbour, nor Ps 15:3 6213
He that *d* these things shall Ps 15:5 6213
there is none that *d* good Ps 53:1 6213
there is none that *d* good Ps 53:3 6213
who only *d* wondrous things Ps 72:18 6213
he that *d* righteousness at all Ps 106:3 6213
hand of the LORD *d* valiantly Ps 118:15 6213
hand of the LORD *d* valiantly Ps 118:16 6213
To him who alone *d* great wonders Ps 136:4 6213
he that *d* it destroyeth his own Prov 6:32 6213
The merciful man *d* good to his Prov 11:17 1580
the heart of the foolish *d* not so Prov 15:7
a fool *d* it to his sorrow Prov 17:21
A merry heart *d* good like a Prov 17:22
A man that *d* violence to the Prov 28:17
and of mirth, What *d* it Eccl 2:2 6213
I know that, whatsoever God *d* Eccl 3:14 6213
and God *d* it, that men should fear Eccl 3:14 6213
just man upon earth, that *d* good Eccl 7:20 6213
for he *d* whatsoever pleaseth him Eccl 8:3 6213
bind them on thee, as a bride *d* Is 49:18
Blessed is the man that *d* this Is 56:2 6213
Wherefore *d* the LORD our God all Jer 5:19 6213
Cursed be he that *d* the work of Jer 48:10 6213
he escape that *d* such things Eze 17:15 6213
that *d* the like to any one of Eze 18:10 6213
that *d* not any of those duties, Eze 18:11 6213
considereth, and *d* not such like, Eze 18:14 6213
and *d* according to all the Eze 18:24 6213
that the wicked man *d*, shall he Eze 18:24 6213
d that which is lawful and right, Eze 18:27 6213
he *d* according to his will in the Dan 4:35 5648
in all his works which he *d* Dan 9:14 6213
name, saith the LORD that *d* this Amos 9:12 6213
will cut off the man that *d* this Mal 2:12 6213
Every one that *d* evil is good in Mal 2:17 6213
hand know what thy right hand *d* Mt 6:3 4160
but he that *d* the will of my Mt 7:21 4160
d them, I will liken him unto a Mt 7:24 4160
d them not, shall be likened unto Mt 7:26 4160
my servant, Do this, and he *d* it Mt 8:9 4160
d them, I will shew you to whom Lk 6:47 4160
d not, is like a man that without Lk 6:49 4160
my servant, Do this, and he *d* it Lk 7:8 4238
For every one that *d* evil hateth Jn 3:20 4160
But he that *d* truth cometh to the Jn 3:21 4160
for what things soever he *d* Jn 5:19 4160
these also *d* the Son likewise Jn 5:19 4160
him all things that himself *d* Jn 5:20 4160
no man that *d* any thing in secret Jn 7:4 4160
it hear him, and know what he *d* Jn 7:51 4160
d his will, him he heareth Jn 9:31 4160
for this man *d* many miracles Jn 11:47 4160
dwelleth in me, he *d* the works Jn 14:10 4160
knoweth not what his lord *d* Jn 15:15 4160
will think that he *d* God service Jn 16:2 4374
the Lord, who *d* all these things Acts 15:17 4160
This man *d* nothing worthy of Acts 26:31 4238
every soul of man that *d* evil Rom 2:9
there is none that *d* good Rom 3:12 4160
That the man which *d* those things Rom 10:5 4160
wrath upon him that *d* evil Rom 13:4 4238
that a man *d* is without the body 1Cor 6:18 4160
he will keep his virgin, *d* well 1Cor 7:37 4160
giveth her in marriage *d* well 1Cor 7:38 4160
her not in marriage *d* better 1Cor 7:38 4160
d he it by the works of the law, Gal 3:5
The man that *d* them shall live in Gal 3:12 4160
whatsoever good thing any man *d* Eph 6:8 4160
But he that *d* wrong shall receive Col 3:25 91
d it not, to him it is sin Jas 4:17 4160
but he that *d* the will of God 1Jn 2:17 4160
ye know that every one that *d* 1Jn 2:29 4160
he that *d* righteousness is 1Jn 3:7 4160
whosoever *d* not righteousness is 1Jn 3:10 4160
remember his deeds which he *d* 3Jn 10 4160
He that *d* good is of God 3Jn 11 15
but he that *d* evil hath not seen 3Jn 11 2554
he *d* great wonders, so that he Rev 13:13 4160

DOG
shall not a *d* move his tongue Ex 11:7 3611
of a whore, or the price of a *d* Deut 23:18 3611
as a *d* lappeth, him shalt thou Judg 7:5 3611
said unto David, Am I a *d* 1Sa 17:43 3611
after a dead *d*, after a flea 1Sa 24:14 3611
look upon such a dead *d* as I am 2Sa 9:8 3611
Why should this dead *d* curse my 2Sa 16:9 3611
But what, is thy servant a *d* 2Kin 8:13 3611
darling from the power of the *d* Ps 22:20 3611
they make a noise like a *d* Ps 59:6 3611
and let them make a noise like a *d* Ps 59:14 3611
As a *d* returneth to his vomit, so Prov 26:11 3611
one that taketh a *d* by the ears Prov 26:17 3611
for a living *d* is better than a Eccl 9:4 3611
The *d* is turned to his own vomit 2Pet 2:22 2965

DOG'S
and said, Am I a *d* head, which 2Sa 3:8 3611
a lamb, as if he cut off a *d* neck Is 66:3 3611

DOGS
ye shall cast it to the *d* Ex 22:31 3611
in the city shall the *d* eat 1Kin 14:11 3611
in the city shall the *d* eat 1Kin 16:4 3611
In the place where *d* licked the 1Kin 21:19 3611
of Naboth shall *d* lick thy blood 1Kin 21:19 3611
The *d* shall eat Jezebel by the 1Kin 21:23 3611
Ahab in the city the *d* shall eat 1Kin 21:24 3611
the *d* licked up his blood 1Kin 22:38 3611
the *d* shall eat Jezebel in the 2Kin 9:10 3611
shall *d* eat the flesh of Jezebel 2Kin 9:36 3611

have set with the *d* of my flock Job 30:1 3611
For *d* have compassed me Ps 22:16 3611
the tongue of thy *d* in the same Ps 68:23 3611
all ignorant, they are all dumb *d* Is 56:10 3611
they are greedy *d* which can never Is 56:11 3611
the *d* to tear, and the fowls of Jer 15:3 3611
not that which is holy unto the *d* Mt 7:6 2965
bread, and to cast it to *d* Mt 15:26 2952
yet the *d* eat of the crumbs which Mt 15:27 2952
bread, and to cast it unto the *d* Mk 7:27 2952
yet the *d* under the table eat of Mk 7:28 2952
moreover the *d* came and licked his Lk 16:21 2965
Beware of *d*, beware of evil Phil 3:2 2965
For without are *d*, and sorcerers, Rev 22:15 2965

DOING

hast now done foolishly in so *d* Gen 31:28 6213
ye have done evil in so *d* Gen 44:5 6213
fearful in praises, *d* wonders Ex 15:11 6213
without *d* any thing else, go Num 20:19
in *d* wickedly in the sight of the Deut 9:18 6213
So Hiram made an end of *d* all the 1Kin 7:40 6213
d evil in the sight of the LORD 1Kin 16:19 6213
d that which was right in the 1Kin 22:43 6213
in *d* that which was evil in the 2Kin 21:16 6213
Arise therefore, and be *d*, and the 1Chr 22:16 6213
d that which was right in the 2Chr 20:32 6213
d according to their abominations Ezr 9:1
I am *d* a great work, so that I Neh 6:3 6213
in so *d* my maker would soon take Job 32:22
shall wisely consider of his *d* Ps 64:9 4640
he is terrible in his *d* toward Ps 66:5 5949
This is the LORD's *d* Ps 118:23 854
keepeth his hand from *d* any evil Is 56:2 6213
from *d* thy pleasure on my holy Is 58:13 6213
not *d* thine own ways, nor finding Is 58:13 6213
this is the Lord's *d*, and it is Mt 21:42 1096
when he cometh shall find so *d* Mt 24:46 4160
This was the Lord's *d*, and it is Mk 12:11 1096
when he cometh shall find so *d* Lk 12:43 4160
who went about *d* good, and healing Acts 10:38 2109
they have found any evil *d* in me Acts 24:20 92
in well *d* seek for glory and Rom 2:7 2041
for in so *d* thou shalt heap coals Rom 12:20 4160
Now therefore perform the *d* of it 2Cor 8:11 4160
And let us not be weary in well *d* Gal 6:9 4160
d the will of God from the heart Eph 6:6 4160
With good will *d* service, as to Eph 6:7 1398
brethren, be not weary in well *d* 2Th 3:13 2569
for in *d* this thou shalt both 1Ti 4:16 4160
another, *d* nothing by partiality 1Ti 5:21 4160
that with well *d* ye may put to 1Pet 2:15 15
be so, that ye suffer for well *d* 1Pet 3:17 15
for well *d*, than for evil *d* 1Pet 3:17 2554
of their souls to him in well *d* 1Pet 4:19 16

DOINGS

After the *d* of the land of Egypt, Lev 18:3 4640
after the *d* of the land of Canaan Lev 18:3 4640
of the wickedness of thy *d* Deut 28:20 4611
they ceased not from their own *d* Judg 2:19 4611
man was churlish and evil in his *d* 1Sa 25:3 4611
and not after the *d* of Israel 2Chr 17:4 4640
declare among the people his *d* Ps 9:11 5949
of all thy work, and talk of thy *d* Ps 77:12 5949
Even a child is known by his *d* Prov 20:11 4611
of your *d* from before mine eyes Is 1:16 4611
their *d* are against the LORD, to Is 3:8 4611
shall eat the fruit of their *d* Is 3:10 4611
declare his *d* among the people, Is 12:4 5949
it because of the evil of your *d* Jer 4:4 4611
thy *d* have procured these things Jer 4:18 4611
Israel, Amend your ways and your *d* Jer 7:3 4611
amend your ways and your *d* Jer 7:5 4611
then thou shewedst me their *d* Jer 11:18 4611
according to the fruit of his *d* Jer 17:10 4611
and make your ways and your *d* good. Jer 18:11 4611
it, because of the evil of your *d* Jer 21:12 4611
according to the fruit of your *d* Jer 21:14 4611
visit upon you the evil of your *d* Jer 23:2 4611
way, and from the evil of their *d* Jer 23:22 4611
way, and from the evil of your *d* Jer 25:5 4611
because of the evil of their *d* Jer 26:3 4611
now amend your ways and your *d* Jer 26:13 4611
according to the fruit of his *d* Jer 32:19 4611
his evil way, and amend your *d* Jer 35:15 4611
because of the evil of your *d* Jer 44:22 4611
ye shall see their way and their *d* Eze 14:22 5949
when ye see their ways and their *d* Eze 14:23 5949
remember your ways, and all your *d* Eze 20:43 5949
nor according to your corrupt *d* Eze 20:44 5949
in all your *d* your sins do appear Eze 21:24 5949
thy ways, and according to thy *d* Eze 24:14 5949
it by their own way and by their *d* Eze 36:17 5949
to their *d* I judged them Eze 36:19 5949
your *d* that were not good, and Eze 36:31 4611
ways, and reward them their *d* Hos 4:9 4611
their *d* to turn unto their God Hos 5:4 4611
now their own *d* have beset them Hos 7:2 4611
for the wickedness of their *d* I Hos 9:15 4611
according to his *d* will he Hos 12:2 4611
are these his *d* Mic 2:7 4611
behaved themselves ill in their *d* Mic 3:4 4611
therein, for the fruit of their *d* Mic 7:13 4611
early, and corrupted all their *d* Zeph 3:7 5949
thou not be ashamed for all thy *d* Zeph 3:11 5949
evil ways, and from your evil *d* Zec 1:4 4611
our ways, and according to our *d* Zec 1:6 4611

DOLEFUL

shall be full of *d* creatures Is 13:21 255
and lament with a *d* lamentation Mic 2:4 5093

DOMINION

let them have *d* over the fish of Gen 1:26 7287
have *d* over the fish of the sea, Gen 1:28 7287
pass when thou shalt have the *d* Gen 27:40 7300
shalt thou indeed have *d* over us Gen 37:8 4910
shall come he that shall have *d* Num 24:19 7287
have *d* over the nobles among the Judg 5:13 7287
made me have *d* over the mighty Judg 5:13 7287
the Philistines had *d* over Israel Judg 14:4 4910
For he had *d* over all the region 1Kin 4:24 7287
and in all the land of his *d* 1Kin 9:19 4475
in his house, nor in all his *d* 2Kin 20:13 4475
and Saraph, who had the *d* in Moab 1Chr 4:22 1166
his *d* by the river Euphrates 1Chr 18:3 3027
throughout all the land of his *d* 2Chr 8:6 4475
from under the *d* of Judah 2Chr 21:8 3027
so that they had the *d* over them Neh 9:28 7287
also they have *d* over our bodies, Neh 9:37 4910
D and fear are with him Job 25:2 4910
canst thou set the *d* thereof in Job 38:33 4896
Thou madest him to have *d* over Ps 8:6 4910
let them not have *d* over me Ps 19:13 4910
the upright shall have *d* over Ps 49:14 7287
He shall have *d* also from sea to Ps 72:8 7287
his works in all places of his *d* Ps 103:22 4475
his sanctuary, and Israel his *d* Ps 114:2 4475
not any iniquity have *d* over me Ps 119:133 7980
thy *d* endureth throughout all Ps 145:13 4475
besides thee have had *d* over us Is 26:13 1196
in his house, nor in all his *d* Is 39:2 4475
kingdoms of the earth of his *d* Jer 34:1 4475
thereof, and all the land of his *d* Jer 51:28 4475
his *d* is from generation to Dan 4:3 7985
thy *d* to the end of the earth Dan 4:22 7985
whose *d* is an everlasting *d* Dan 4:34 7985
That in every *d* of my kingdom men Dan 6:26 7985
his *d* shall be even unto the end Dan 6:26 7985
and *d* was given to it Dan 7:6 7985
they had their *d* taken away Dan 7:12 7985
And there was given him *d*, and Dan 7:14 7985
his *d* is an everlasting *d*, Dan 7:14 7985
and they shall take away his *d* Dan 7:26 7985
And the kingdom and *d*, and the Dan 7:27 7985
up, that shall rule with great *d* Dan 11:3 4474
according to his *d* which he ruled Dan 11:4 4915
be strong above him, and have *d* Dan 11:5 4910
his *d* shall be a great *d* Dan 11:5 4474
shall it come, even the first *d* Mic 4:8 4475
his *d* shall be from sea even to Zec 9:10 4915
the Gentiles exercise *d* over them Mt 20:25 2634
death hath no more *d* over him Rom 6:9 2961
For sin shall not have *d* over you Rom 6:14 2961
how that the law hath *d* over a Rom 7:1 2961
that we have *d* over your faith 2Cor 1:24 2961
and power, and might, and *d* Eph 1:21 2963
be praise and *d* for ever and ever 1Pet 4:11 2904
be glory and *d* for ever and ever 1Pet 5:11 2904
defile the flesh, despise *d* Jude 8 2963
Saviour, be glory and majesty, *d* Jude 25 2904
be glory and *d* for ever and ever Rev 1:6 2904

DOMINIONS

all *d* shall serve and obey him Dan 7:27 7985
whether they be thrones, or *d* Col 1:16 2963

DONE

What is this that thou hast *d* Gen 3:13 6213
serpent, Because thou hast *d* this Gen 3:14 6213
And he said, What hast thou *d* Gen 4:10 6213
every thing living, as I have *d* Gen 8:21 6213
his younger son had *d* unto him Gen 9:24 6213
is this that thou hast *d* unto me Gen 12:18 6213
now, and see whether they have *d* Gen 18:21 6213
of my hands have I *d* this Gen 20:5 6213
him, What hast thou *d* unto us Gen 20:9 6213
thou hast *d* deeds unto me that Gen 20:9 6213
unto me that ought not to be *d* Gen 20:9 6213
thou, that thou hast *d* this thing Gen 20:10 6213
kindness that I have *d* unto thee Gen 21:23 6213
I wot not who hath *d* this thing Gen 21:26 6213
because thou hast *d* this thing Gen 22:16 6213
to pass, before he had *d* speaking Gen 24:15 3615
when she had *d* giving him drink, Gen 24:19 3615
also, until they have *d* drinking Gen 24:19 3615
as the camels had *d* drinking Gen 24:22 3615
before I had *d* speaking in mine Gen 24:45 3615
Isaac all things that he had *d* Gen 24:66 6213
What is this thou hast *d* unto us Gen 26:10 6213
as we have *d* unto thee nothing Gen 26:29 6213
I have *d* according as thou badest Gen 27:19 6213
that which thou hast *d* to him Gen 27:45 6213
until I have *d* that which I have Gen 28:15 6213
What is this thou hast *d* unto me Gen 29:25 6213
must not be so *d* in our country Gen 29:26 6213
my service which I have *d* thee Gen 30:26 5647
said to Jacob, What hast thou *d* Gen 31:26 6213
thou hast now *d* foolishly in so Gen 31:28
which thing ought not to be *d* Gen 34:7 6213
here also have I *d* nothing that Gen 40:15 6213
is this that God hath *d* unto us Gen 42:28 6213
ye have *d* evil in so doing Gen 44:5
What deed is this that ye have *d* Gen 44:15 6213
them, Why have ye *d* this thing Ex 1:18 6213
to wit what would be *d* to him Ex 2:4 6213
that which is *d* to you in Egypt Ex 3:16 6213
he hath *d* evil to this people Ex 5:23
signs which I have *d* among them Ex 10:2 7760
manner of work shall be *d* in them Ex 12:16 6213
eat, that only may be *d* of you Ex 12:16 6213
This is *d* because of that which Ex 13:8
and they said, Why have we *d* this Ex 14:5 6213
of all that God had *d* for Moses Ex 18:1 6213
that the LORD had *d* unto Pharaoh Ex 18:8 6213
which the LORD had *d* to Israel Ex 18:9 6213
judgment shall it be *d* unto him Ex 21:31 6213
Six days may work be *d* Ex 31:15 6213
have not been *d* in all the earth Ex 34:10 1254
till Moses had *d* speaking with Ex 34:33 3615
Six days shall work be *d*, but on Ex 35:2 6213
they had *d* it as the LORD had Ex 39:43 6213
commanded, even so had they *d* it Ex 39:43 6213
things which ought not to be *d* Lev 4:2 6213
they have *d* somewhat against any Lev 4:13 6213
things which should not be *d* Lev 4:13 6213
d somewhat through ignorance Lev 4:22 6213
things which should not be *d* Lev 4:22 6213
things which ought not to be *d* Lev 4:27 6213
that he hath *d* in the holy thing Lev 5:16
which are forbidden to be *d* by Lev 5:17 6213
he hath *d* in trespassing therein Lev 6:7 6213
which the LORD commanded to be *d* Lev 8:5 6213
As he hath *d* this day, so the Lev 8:34 6213
it be, wherein any work is *d* Lev 11:32 6213
have the men of the land *d* Lev 18:27 6213
LORD for his sin which he hath *d* Lev 19:22
he hath *d* shall be forgiven him Lev 19:22
Six days shall work be *d* Lev 23:3 6213
as he hath *d*, so shall it be *d* Lev 24:19 6213
so shall it be *d* to him again Lev 24:20 5414
their sin which they have *d* Num 5:7 6213
have *d* trespass against her Num 5:27
us, wherein we have *d* foolishly Num 12:11
shall it be *d* for one bullock Num 15:11 6213
declared what should be *d* to him Num 15:34 6213
for I have not *d* them of mine own Num 16:28
that Israel had *d* to the Amorites Num 22:2 6213
Balaam, What have I *d* unto thee Num 22:28 6213
Balaam, What hast thou *d* unto me Num 23:11 6213
the name of our father be *d* away Num 27:4 1639
that had *d* evil in the sight of Num 32:13 6213
God hath *d* unto these two kings Deut 3:21 6213
that hath *d* for thee these great Deut 10:21 6213
have they *d* unto their gods Deut 12:31 6213
to have *d* unto his brother Deut 19:19 6213
which they have *d* unto their gods Deut 20:18 6213
So shall it be *d* unto that man Deut 25:9 6213
have *d* according to all that thou Deut 26:14 6213
the LORD *d* thus unto this land Deut 29:24 6213
and the LORD hath not *d* all this Deut 32:27 6466
when they had *d* circumcising all Josh 5:8 8552
and tell me now what thou hast *d* Josh 7:19 6213
Israel, and thus and thus have I *d* Josh 7:20 6213
what Joshua had *d* unto Jericho Josh 9:3 6213
of you, and have *d* this thing Josh 9:24 6213
as he had *d* to Jericho and her Josh 10:1 6213
and her king, so he had *d* to Ai Josh 10:1 6213
to all that he had *d* to Libnah Josh 10:32 6213
to all that he had *d* to Lachish Josh 10:35 6213
to all that he had *d* to Eglon Josh 10:37 6213
as he had *d* to Hebron, so he did Josh 10:39 6213
as he had *d* also to Libnah, and to Josh 10:39 6213
if we have not rather *d* it for Josh 22:24 6213
d unto all these nations because Josh 23:3 6213
as ye have *d* unto this day Josh 23:8 6213
have seen what I have *d* in Egypt Josh 24:7 6213
after that he hath *d* you good Josh 24:20
LORD, that he had *d* for Israel Josh 24:31 6213
as I have *d*, so God hath requited Judg 1:7 6213
why have ye *d* this Judg 2:2 6213
works which he had *d* for Israel Judg 2:10 6213
because they had *d* evil in the Judg 3:12 6213
to another, Who hath *d* this thing Judg 6:29 6213
son of Joash hath *d* this thing Judg 6:29 6213
What have I *d* now in comparison Judg 8:2 6213
Now therefore, if ye have *d* truly Judg 9:16 6213
have *d* unto him according to the Judg 9:16 6213
That the cruelty *d* to the Judg 9:24
do, make haste, and do as I have *d* Judg 9:48
Let this thing be *d* for me Judg 11:37 6213
or his mother what he had *d* Judg 14:6 6213
Philistines said, Who hath *d* this Judg 15:6 6213
unto them, Though ye have *d* this Judg 15:7 6213
to do to him as he hath *d* to us Judg 15:10 6213
is this that thou hast *d* unto us Judg 15:11 6213
unto me, so have I *d* unto them Judg 15:11 6213
There was no such deed *d* nor seen Judg 19:30 1961
is this that is *d* among you Judg 20:12 1961
all that thou hast *d* unto thy Ruth 2:11 6213
man, until he shall have *d* eating Ruth 3:3 3615
her all that the man had *d* to her Ruth 3:16 6213
And he said, What is there *d* 1Sa 4:16 1697
then he hath *d* us this great evil 1Sa 6:9 6213
d since the day that I brought 1Sa 8:8 6213
so shall it be *d* unto his oxen 1Sa 11:7 6213
which ye have *d* in the sight of 1Sa 12:17 6213
ye have *d* all this wickedness 1Sa 12:20 6213
great things he hath *d* for you 1Sa 12:24
And Samuel said, What hast thou *d* 1Sa 13:11 6213
to Saul, Thou hast *d* foolishly 1Sa 13:13
Tell me what thou hast *d* 1Sa 14:43 6213
What shall be *d* to the man that 1Sa 17:26 6213
So shall it be *d* to the man that 1Sa 17:27 6213
And David said, What have I now *d* 1Sa 17:29 6213
him all that Saul had *d* to him 1Sa 19:18 6213
before Jonathan, What have I *d* 1Sa 20:1 6213
what hath he *d*? 1Sa 20:32 6213
his father had *d* him shame 1Sa 20:34
that thou hast *d* unto me this day 1Sa 24:19 6213
when the LORD shall have *d* to my 1Sa 25:30 6213
is not good that thou hast *d* 1Sa 26:16 6213
for what have I *d* 1Sa 26:18 6213
thou knowest what Saul hath *d* 1Sa 28:9 6213
And the LORD hath *d* to him 1Sa 28:17 6213
therefore hath the LORD *d* this 1Sa 28:18 6213
unto Achish, But what have I *d* 1Sa 29:8 6213
the Philistines had *d* to Saul 1Sa 31:11 6213
because ye have *d* this thing 2Sa 2:6 6213
king, and said, What hast thou *d* 2Sa 3:24 6213
hast thou *d* all these great 2Sa 7:21 6213
David had *d* displeased the LORD 2Sa 11:27 6213
the man that hath *d* this thing 2Sa 12:5 6213
thing is this that thou hast *d* 2Sa 12:21 6213

thing ought to be *d* in Israel 2Sa 13:12 6213
thy servant Joab *d* this thing 2Sa 14:20 6213
Behold now, I have *d* this thing 2Sa 14:21 6213
had *d* passing out of the city 2Sa 15:24 8552
say, Wherefore hast thou *d* so 2Sa 16:10 6213
the concubine of Saul, had *d* 2Sa 21:11 6213
who had *d* many acts, he slew two 2Sa 23:20 6213
sinned greatly in that I have *d* 2Sa 24:10 6213
for I have *d* very foolishly 2Sa 24:10
have sinned, and I have *d* wickedly 2Sa 24:17
but these sheep, what have they *d* 2Sa 24:17 6213
in saying, Why hast thou *d* so 1Kin 1:6 6213
Is this thing *d* by my lord the 1Kin 1:27
I have *d* according to thy words 1Kin 3:12 6213
have *d* perversely, we have 1Kin 8:47
LORD had *d* for David his servant 1Kin 8:66 6213
Why hath the LORD *d* thus unto 1Kin 9:8 6213
Forasmuch as this is *d* of thee 1Kin 11:11
of God had *d* that day in Beth-el 1Kin 13:11 6213
But hast *d* evil above all that 1Kin 14:9 6213
all that their fathers had *d* 1Kin 14:22 6213
father, which he had *d* before him 1Kin 15:3 6213
that I have *d* all these things at 1Kin 18:36 6213
Jezebel all that Elijah had *d* 1Kin 19:1 6213
for what have I *d* to thee 1Kin 19:20 6213
to all that his father had *d* 1Kin 22:53 6213
what is to be *d* for thee 2Kin 4:13 6213
What then is to be *d* for her 2Kin 4:14 6213
wouldest thou not have *d* it 2Kin 5:13 6213
you what the Syrians have *d* to us 2Kin 7:12 6213
great things that Elisha hath *d* 2Kin 8:4 6213
for the LORD hath *d* that which he 2Kin 10:10 6213
Because thou hast *d* well in 2Kin 10:30
hast *d* unto the house of Ahab 2Kin 10:30 6213
all that his father Amaziah had *d* 2Kin 15:3 6213
of the LORD, as his fathers had *d* 2Kin 15:9 6213
all that his father Uzziah had *d* 2Kin 15:34 6213
Assyria, as he had *d* year by year 2Kin 17:4
of Assyria have *d* to all lands 2Kin 19:11 6213
heard long ago how I have *d* it 2Kin 19:25 6213
have *d* that which is good in thy 2Kin 20:3 6213
Judah hath *d* these abominations 2Kin 21:11 6213
hath *d* wickedly above all that 2Kin 21:11 6213
Because they have *d* that which 2Kin 21:15 6213
these things that thou hast *d* 2Kin 23:17 6213
the acts that he had *d* in Beth-el 2Kin 23:19 6213
to all that his fathers had *d* 2Kin 23:32 6213
to all that his fathers had *d* 2Kin 23:37 6213
to all that his father had *d* 2Kin 24:9 6213
to all that Jehoiakim had *d* 2Kin 24:19 6213
the Philistines had *d* to Saul 1Chr 10:11 6213
of Kabzeel, who had *d* many acts 1Chr 11:22
marvellous works that he hath *d* 1Chr 16:12 6213
hast thou *d* all this greatness, 1Chr 17:19 6213
because I have *d* this thing 1Chr 21:8 6213
for I have *d* very foolishly 1Chr 21:8
that have sinned and *d* evil indeed 1Chr 21:17
for these sheep, what have they *d* 1Chr 21:17 6213
We have sinned, we have *d* amiss 2Chr 6:37
Why hath the LORD *d* thus unto 2Chr 7:21 6213
for this thing is *d* of me 2Chr 11:4
Herein thou hast *d* foolishly 2Chr 16:9
because he had *d* good in Israel 2Chr 24:16 6213
Jehoiada his father had *d* to him 2Chr 24:22 6213
thee, because thou hast *d* this 2Chr 25:16 6213
all that David his father had *d* 2Chr 29:2 6213
d that which was evil in the eyes 2Chr 29:6 6213
for the thing was *d* suddenly 2Chr 29:36
for they had not *d* it of a long 2Chr 30:5 6213
my fathers have *d* unto all the 2Chr 32:13 6213
to the benefit *d* unto him 2Chr 32:25
the wonder that was *d* in the land 2Chr 32:31
let it be *d* with speed Ezr 6:12 5648
require of you, it be *d* speedily, Ezr 7:21 5648
let it be diligently *d* for the Ezr 7:23 5648
Now when these things were *d* Ezr 9:1 3615
let it be *d* according to the law Ezr 10:3 6213
all that I have *d* for this people Neh 5:19 6213
no such things *d* as thou sayest Neh 6:8
from the work, that it be not *d* Neh 6:9 6213
not the children of Israel *d* so Neh 8:17 6213
for thou hast *d* right Neh 9:33 6213
but we have *d* wickedly Neh 9:33
I have *d* for the house of my God Neh 13:14 6213
hath not *d* wrong to the king only Est 1:16
Vashti, and what she had *d* Est 2:1 6213
Mordecai perceived all that was *d* Est 4:1 6213
dignity hath been *d* to Mordecai Est 6:3 6213
him, There is nothing *d* for him Est 6:3 6213
What shall be *d* unto the man whom Est 6:6 6213
Thus shall it be *d* to the man Est 6:9 6213
Thus shall it be *d* unto the man Est 6:11 6213
what have they *d* in the rest of Est 9:12 6213
and it shall be *d* Est 9:12 6213
the king commanded it so to be *d* Est 9:14 6213
shall repay him what he hath *d* Job 21:31 6213
whether it be *d* against a nation, Job 34:29
if I have *d* iniquity, I will do Job 34:32 6466
O LORD my God, if I have *d* this Ps 7:3 6213
they have *d* abominable works, Ps 14:1
be born, that he hath *d* this Ps 22:31 6213
and all his works are *d* in truth Ps 33:4
For he spake, and it was *d* Ps 33:9
wonderful works which thou hast *d* Ps 40:5 6213
These things hast thou *d*, and I Ps 50:21 6213
and *d* this evil in thy sight Ps 51:4 6213
for ever, because thou hast *d* it Ps 52:9 6213
have *d* abominable iniquity Ps 53:1
what he hath *d* for my soul Ps 66:16 6213
high, who hast *d* great things Ps 71:19 6213
hath *d* wickedly in the sanctuary Ps 74:3
wonderful works that he hath *d* Ps 78:4 6213
for he hath *d* marvellous things Ps 98:1 6213
marvellous works that he hath *d* Ps 105:5 6213

iniquity, we have *d* wickedly Ps 106:6 6213
which had *d* great things in Egypt Ps 106:21
that thou, LORD, hast *d* it Ps 109:27 6213
are *d* in truth and uprightness Ps 111:8 6213
he hath *d* whatsoever he hath Ps 115:3 6213
I have *d* judgment and justice Ps 119:121 6213
salvation, and *d* thy commandments Ps 119:166 6213
or what shall be *d* unto thee Ps 120:3 3254
The LORD hath *d* great things for Ps 126:2 6213
The LORD hath *d* great things for Ps 126:3 6213
if he have *d* thee no harm Prov 3:30 1580
not, except they have *d* mischief Prov 4:16
do so to him as he hath *d* to me Prov 24:29 6213
and saith, I have *d* no wickedness Prov 30:20 466
If thou hast *d* foolishly in Prov 30:32
Many daughters have *d* virtuously Prov 31:29 6466
is *d* is that which shall be *d* Eccl 1:9 6466
things that are *d* under heaven Eccl 1:13 6466
works that are *d* under the sun Eccl 1:14 6466
that which hath been already *d* Eccl 2:12 6466
that are *d* under the sun Eccl 4:1 6466
evil work that is *d* under the sun Eccl 4:3 6466
work that is *d* under the sun Eccl 8:9 6466
in the city where they had so *d* Eccl 8:10 6466
vanity which is *d* upon the earth Eccl 8:14 6466
business that is *d* upon the earth Eccl 8:16 6466
the work that is *d* under the sun Eccl 8:17 6466
things that are *d* under the sun Eccl 9:3 6466
any thing that is *d* under the sun Eccl 9:6 6466
have been *d* more to my vineyard Is 5:4 6466
that I have not *d* in it Is 5:4 6466
as I have *d* unto Samaria and her Is 10:11 6466
strength of my hand I have *d* it Is 10:13 6466
for he hath *d* excellent things Is 12:5 6466
grapes when the vintage is *d* Is 24:13 3615
for thou hast *d* wonderful things Is 25:1 6213
that are far off, what I have *d* Is 33:13 6213
what the kings of Assyria have *d* Is 37:11 6213
heard long ago, how I have *d* it Is 37:26 6213
have *d* that which is good in thy Is 38:3 6213
unto me, and himself hath *d* it Is 38:15 6213
d it, calling the generations Is 41:4 6213
the hand of the LORD hath *d* this Is 41:20 6213
for the LORD hath *d* it Is 44:23 6213
the things that are not yet *d* Is 46:10 6213
say, Mine idol hath *d* them Is 48:5 6213
because he had *d* no violence Is 53:9 6213
the valley, know what thou hast *d* Jer 2:23 6213
d evil things as thou couldest Jer 3:5 6213
which backsliding Israel hath *d* Jer 3:6 6213
after she had *d* all these things Jer 3:7 6213
neither shall that be *d* any more Jer 3:16 6213
thus shall it be *d* unto them Jer 5:13 6213
because ye have *d* all these works Jer 7:13 6213
fathers, as I have *d* to Shiloh Jer 7:14 6213
of Judah have *d* evil in my sight Jer 7:30 6213
wickedness, saying, What have I *d* Jer 8:6 6213
which they have *d* against Jer 11:17 6213
ye have *d* worse than your fathers Jer 16:12 6213
hath *d* a very horrible thing Jer 18:13 6213
Wherefore hath the LORD *d* thus Jer 22:8 6213
I have *d* these things unto thee Jer 30:15 6213
not return, until he have *d* it Jer 30:24 6213
Israel for all that they have *d* Jer 31:37 6213
they have *d* nothing of all that Jer 32:23 6213
d evil before me from their youth Jer 32:30 6213
which they have *d* to provoke me Jer 32:32 6213
had *d* right in my sight, in Jer 34:15 6213
d according to all that Jonadab Jer 35:10 6213
d according unto all that he hath Jer 35:18 6213
these men have *d* evil in all that Jer 38:9
have *d* to Jeremiah the prophet Jer 38:9 6213
d according as he hath said Jer 40:3 6213
the son of Nethaniah had *d* Jer 41:11 6213
the evil that I have *d* unto you Jer 42:10 6213
offerings unto her, as we have *d* Jer 44:17 6213
that escapeth, and say, What is *d* Jer 48:19
as she hath *d*, do unto her Jer 50:15 6213
according to all that she hath *d* Jer 50:29 6213
d that which he spake against the Jer 51:12 6213
they have *d* in Zion in your sight Jer 51:24 6213
The violence *d* to me and to my Jer 51:35 6213
to all that Jehoiakim had *d* Jer 52:2 6213
my sorrow, which is *d* unto me Lam 1:12 5953
they are glad that thou hast *d* it Lam 1:21 6213
as thou hast *d* unto me for all my Lam 1:22 5953
The LORD hath *d* that which he had Lam 2:17 6213
consider to whom thou hast *d* this Lam 2:20 5953
he hath *d* shall not be remembered Eze 3:20 6213
neither have *d* according to the Eze 5:7 6213
in thee that which I have not *d* Eze 5:9 6213
that be *d* in the midst thereof Eze 9:4 6213
I have *d* as thou hast commanded Eze 9:11 6213
but have *d* after the manners of Eze 11:12 6213
d, so shall it be *d* unto them Eze 12:11 6213
which I have spoken shall be *d* Eze 12:28 6213
d without cause all that I have Eze 14:23 6213
cause all that I have *d* in it Eze 14:23 6213
nor *d* after their abominations Eze 16:47 6213
GOD, Sodom thy sister hath not *d* Eze 16:48 6213
nor her daughters, as thou hast *d* Eze 16:48 6213
abominations which they have *d* Eze 16:51 6213
in all that thou hast *d*, in that Eze 16:54 6213
deal with thee as thou hast *d* Eze 16:59 6213
thee for all that thou hast *d* Eze 16:63 6213
hath *d* all these things, he shall Eze 17:18 6213
the LORD have spoken and have *d* it Eze 17:24 6213
he hath *d* all these abominations Eze 18:13 6213
his father's sins which he hath *d* Eze 18:14 6213
When the son hath *d* that which is Eze 18:19 6213
all my statutes, and hath *d* them Eze 18:19 6213
that he hath *d* he shall live Eze 18:22 6213
he hath *d* shall not be mentioned Eze 18:24 6213
that he hath *d* shall he die Eze 18:26 6213

Moreover this they have *d* unto me Eze 23:38 6213
thus have they *d* in the midst of Eze 23:39 6213
And ye shall do as I have *d* Eze 24:22 6213
to all that he hath *d* shall ye do Eze 24:24 6213
he hath *d* that which is lawful and Eze 33:16 6213
Behold, it is come, and it is *d* Eze 39:8
transgressions have I *d* unto them Eze 39:24 6213
ashamed of all that they have *d* Eze 43:11 6213
for all that shall be *d* therein Eze 44:14 6213
thee, O king, have I *d* no hurt Dan 6:22 5648
have *d* wickedly, and have rebelled Dan 9:5
as hath been *d* upon Jerusalem Dan 9:12 6213
have sinned, we have *d* wickedly Dan 9:15
that which his fathers have not *d* Dan 11:24 6213
that is determined shall be *d* Dan 11:36 6213
conceived them hath *d* shamefully Hos 2:5
because he hath *d* great things Joel 2:20 6213
a city, and the LORD hath not *d* it Amos 3:6 6213
d, it shall be *d* unto thee Obad 15 6213
unto him, Why hast thou *d* this Jonah 1:10 6213
hast *d* as it pleased thee Jonah 1:14 6213
people, what have I *d* unto thee Mic 6:3 6213
they have *d* violence to the law Zeph 3:4
as I have *d* these so many years Zec 7:3 6213
And this have ye *d* again, covering Mal 2:13 6213
Now all this was *d*, that it might Mt 1:22 *1096*
Thy will be *d* in earth, as it is Mt 6:10 *1096*
in thy name *d* many wonderful Mt 7:22 *4160*
believed, so be it *d* unto thee Mt 8:13 *1096*
most of his mighty works were *d* Mt 11:20 *1096*
d in you, had been *d* in Tyre Mt 11:21 *1096*
d in thee, had been *d* in Sodom Mt 11:23 *1096*
unto them, An enemy hath *d* this Mt 13:28 *4160*
but have *d* unto him whatsoever Mt 17:12 *4160*
it shall be *d* for them of my Mt 18:19 *1096*
his fellowservants saw what was *d* Mt 18:31 *1096*
unto their lord all that was *d* Mt 18:31 *1096*
All this was *d*, that it might be Mt 21:4 *1096*
this which is *d* to the fig tree Mt 21:21
into the sea; it shall be *d* Mt 21:21 *1096*
these ought ye to have *d*, and not Mt 23:23 *4160*
His lord said unto him, Well *d* Mt 25:21
His lord said unto him, Well *d* Mt 25:23
Inasmuch as ye have *d* it unto one Mt 25:40 *4160*
my brethren, ye have *d* it unto me Mt 25:40 *4160*
also this, that this woman hath *d* Mt 26:13 *4160*
except I drink it, thy will be *d* Mt 26:42 *1096*
But all this was *d*, that the Mt 26:56 *1096*
said, Why, what evil hath he *d* Mt 27:23 *4160*
and those things that were *d* Mt 27:54 *1096*
all the things that were *d* Mt 28:11 *1096*
these things are *d* in parables Mk 4:11 *1096*
out to see what it was that was *d* Mk 5:14 *1096*
things the Lord hath *d* for thee Mk 5:19 *4160*
great things Jesus had *d* for him Mk 5:20 *4160*
to see her that had *d* this thing Mk 5:32 *4160*
knowing what was *d* in her Mk 5:33 *1096*
all things, both what they had *d* Mk 6:30 *4160*
He hath *d* all things well Mk 7:37 *4160*
they have *d* unto him whatsoever Mk 9:13 *4160*
pass, till all these things be *d* Mk 13:30 *1096*
She hath *d* what she could Mk 14:8 *4160*
this also that she hath *d* shall Mk 14:9 *4160*
to do as he had ever *d* unto them Mk 15:8 *4160*
them, Why, what evil hath he *d* Mk 15:14 *4160*
mighty hath *d* to me great things Lk 1:49 *4160*
all the evils which Herod had *d* Lk 3:19 *4160*
we have heard *d* in Capernaum Lk 4:23 *1096*
And when they had this *d*, they Lk 5:6 *4160*
they that fed them saw what was *d* Lk 8:34 *1096*
they went out to see what was *d* Lk 8:35 *1096*
great things God hath *d* unto thee Lk 8:39 *4160*
great things Jesus had *d* unto him Lk 8:39 *4160*
should tell no man what was *d* Lk 8:56 *1096*
heard of all that was *d* by him Lk 9:7 *1096*
told him all that they had *d* Lk 9:10 *4160*
mighty works had been *d* in Tyre Lk 10:13 *1096*
Sidon, which have been *d* in you Lk 10:13 *1096*
Thy will be *d*, as in heaven, so Lk 11:2 *1096*
these ought ye to have *d*, and not Lk 11:42 *4160*
things that were *d* by him Lk 13:17 *1096*
it is *d* as thou hast commanded Lk 14:22 *1096*
steward, because he had *d* wisely Lk 16:8 *4160*
when ye shall have *d* all those Lk 17:10 *4160*
we have *d* that which was our duty Lk 17:10 *4160*
not my will, but thine, be *d* Lk 22:42 *1096*
have seen some miracle *d* by him Lk 23:8 *1096*
worthy of death is *d* unto him Lk 23:15 *4238*
time, Why, what evil hath he *d* Lk 23:22 *4160*
tree, what shall be *d* in the dry Lk 23:31 *1096*
but this man hath *d* nothing amiss Lk 23:41 4238
when the centurion saw what was *d* Lk 23:47 *1096*
beholding the things which were *d* Lk 23:48 *1096*
day since these things were *d* Lk 24:21 *1096*
what things were *d* in the way Lk 24:35
These things were *d* in Bethabara Jn 1:28 *1096*
because he had *d* these things on Jn 5:16 *4160*
they that have *d* good, unto the Jn 5:29 *4160*
and they that have *d* evil, unto Jn 5:29 *4238*
I have *d* one work, and ye all Jn 7:21 *4160*
than these which this man hath *d* Jn 7:31 *4160*
told them what things Jesus had *d* Jn 11:46 *4160*
that they had *d* these things unto Jn 12:16 *4160*
heard that he had *d* this miracle Jn 12:18 *4160*
But though he had *d* so many Jn 12:37 *4160*
Know ye what I have *d* to you Jn 13:12 *4160*
ye should do as I have *d* to you Jn 13:15 *4160*
will, and it shall be *d* unto you Jn 15:7 *1096*
If I had not *d* among them the Jn 15:24 *4160*
what hast thou *d*? Jn 18:35 *4160*
For these things were *d*, that the Jn 19:36 *1096*
signs were *d* by the apostles Acts 2:43 *1096*
or by what name, have ye *d* this Acts 4:7 *4160*
good deed *d* to the impotent man Acts 4:9

D

a notable miracle hath been *d* by ...... Acts 4:16 *1096*
God for that which was *d* ...... Acts 4:21 *1096*
counsel determined before to be *d* ...... Acts 4:28 *1096*
wonders may be *d* by the name of ...... Acts 4:30 *1096*
his wife, not knowing what was *d* ...... Acts 5:7 *1096*
miracles and signs which were *d* ...... Acts 8:13 *1096*
how much evil he hath *d* to thy ...... Acts 9:13 *4160*
This was *d* thrice ...... Acts 10:16 *1096*
thou hast well *d* that thou art ...... Acts 10:33 *4160*
And this was *d* three times ...... Acts 11:10 *1096*
was true which was *d* by the angel ...... Acts 12:9 *1096*
deputy, when he saw what was *d* ...... Acts 13:12 *1096*
wonders to be *d* by their hands ...... Acts 14:3 *1096*
the people saw what Paul had *d* ...... Acts 14:11 *4160*
would have *d* sacrifice with the ...... Acts 14:13
that they had not *d* sacrifice ...... Acts 14:18
all that God had *d* with them ...... Acts 14:27 *4160*
things that God had *d* with them ...... Acts 15:4 *4160*
saying, The will of the Lord be *d* ...... Acts 21:14 *1096*
who he was, and what he had *d* ...... Acts 21:33 *4160*
are *d* unto this nation by thy ...... Acts 24:2 *1096*
to the Jews have I *d* no wrong ...... Acts 25:10 *91*
this thing was not *d* in a corner ...... Acts 26:26 *4238*
So when this was *d*, others also, ... Acts 28:9 *1096*
neither having *d* any good or evil ...... Rom 9:11 *4238*
that he that hath *d* this deed 1Cor 5:2 *4160*
him that hath so *d* this deed 1Cor 5:3 *2716*
that it should be so *d* unto me 1Cor 9:15 *1096*
which is in part shall be *d* away 1Cor 13:10 *2673*
Let all things be *d* unto edifying 1Cor 14:26 *1096*
Let all things be *d* decently 1Cor 14:40 *1096*
all your things be *d* with charity 1Cor 16:14 *1096*
which glory was to be *d* away 2Cor 3:7 *2673*
that which is *d* away was glorious 2Cor 3:11 *2673*
which vail is *d* away in Christ 2Cor 3:14 *2673*
receive the things *d* in his body 2Cor 5:10
according to that he hath *d* 2Cor 5:10 *4238*
his cause that had *d* the wrong 2Cor 7:12 *91*
which are *d* of them in secret ...... Eph 5:12 *1096*
in the evil day, and having *d* all ...... Eph 6:13 *2716*
Let nothing be *d* through strife ...... Phil 2:3
Notwithstanding ye have well *d* ...... Phil 4:14 *4160*
for the wrong which he hath *d* ...... Col 3:25 *91*
you all things which are *d* here ...... Col 4:9
of righteousness which we have *d* ...... Titus 3:5 *4160*
hath *d* despite unto the Spirit of ...... Heb 10:29 *1796*
after ye have *d* the will of God, ... Heb 10:36 *4160*
from the throne, saying, It is *d* ...... Rev 16:17 *1096*
And he said unto me, It is *d* ...... Rev 21:6 *1096*
things which must shortly be *d* ...... Rev 22:6 *1096*

DOOR
not well, sin lieth at the *d* ...... Gen 4:7 6607
the *d* of the ark shalt thou set ...... Gen 6:16 6607
he sat in the tent *d* in the heat ...... Gen 18:1 6607
ran to meet them from the tent *d* ...... Gen 18:2 6607
And Sarah heard it in the tent *d* ...... Gen 18:10 6607
Lot went out at the *d* unto them ...... Gen 19:6 6607
and shut the *d* after him ...... Gen 19:6 1817
Lot, and came near to break the *d* ...... Gen 19:9 1817
house to them, and shut to the *d* ...... Gen 19:10 1817
the *d* of the house with blindness ...... Gen 19:11 6607
wearied themselves to find the *d* ...... Gen 19:11 6607
with him at the *d* of the house ...... Gen 43:19 6607
on the upper *d* post of the houses ...... Ex 12:7 4947
d of his house until the morning ...... Ex 12:22 6607
the LORD will pass over the *d* ...... Ex 12:23 6607
he shall also bring him to the *d* ...... Ex 21:6 1817
or unto the *d* post ...... Ex 21:6 4201
an hanging for the *d* of the tent ...... Ex 26:36 6607
the *d* of the tabernacle of the ...... Ex 29:4 6607
by the *d* of the tabernacle of the ...... Ex 29:11 6607
by the *d* of the tabernacle of the ...... Ex 29:32 6607
your generations at the *d* of the ...... Ex 29:42 6607
and stood every man at his tent *d* ...... Ex 33:8 6607
stood at the *d* of the tabernacle, ... Ex 33:9 6607
pillar stand at the tabernacle *d* ...... Ex 33:10 6607
every man in his tent *d* ...... Ex 33:10 6607
the hanging for the *d* at the ...... Ex 35:15 6607
hanging for the *d* of the court ...... Ex 35:17 8179
for the tabernacle *d* of blue ...... Ex 36:37 6607
which assembled at the *d* of the ...... Ex 38:8 6607
to the *d* of the tabernacle of the ...... Ex 38:30 6607
the hanging for the tabernacle *d* ...... Ex 39:38 6607
of the *d* to the tabernacle ...... Ex 40:5 6607
d of the tabernacle of the tent ...... Ex 40:6 6607
his sons unto the *d* of the ...... Ex 40:12 6607
at the *d* of the tabernacle ...... Ex 40:28 6607
d of the tabernacle of the tent ...... Ex 40:29 6607
at the *d* of the tabernacle of the ...... Lev 1:3 6607
by the *d* of the tabernacle of the ...... Lev 1:5 6607
and kill it at the *d* of the ...... Lev 3:2 6607
the *d* of the tabernacle of the ...... Lev 4:4 6607
which is at the *d* of the ...... Lev 4:7 6607
which is at the *d* of the ...... Lev 4:18 6607
the *d* of the tabernacle of the ...... Lev 8:3 6607
the *d* of the tabernacle of the ...... Lev 8:4 6607
Boil the flesh at the *d* of the ...... Lev 8:31 6607
of the *d* of the tabernacle of the ...... Lev 8:33 6607
at the *d* of the tabernacle of the ...... Lev 8:35 6607
the *d* of the tabernacle of the ...... Lev 10:7 6607
unto the *d* of the tabernacle of ...... Lev 12:6 6607
at the *d* of the tabernacle of the ...... Lev 14:11 6607
unto the *d* of the tabernacle of ...... Lev 14:23 6607
the house to the *d* of the house ...... Lev 14:38 6607
the *d* of the tabernacle of the ...... Lev 15:14 6607
to the *d* of the tabernacle of the ...... Lev 15:29 6607
at the *d* of the tabernacle of the ...... Lev 16:7 6607
the *d* of the tabernacle of the ...... Lev 17:4 6607
unto the *d* of the tabernacle of ...... Lev 17:5 6607
at the *d* of the tabernacle of the ...... Lev 17:6 6607
the *d* of the tabernacle of the ...... Lev 17:9 6607
unto the *d* of the tabernacle of ...... Lev 19:21 6607
the hanging for the *d* of the ...... Num 3:25 6607
curtain for the *d* of the court ...... Num 3:26 6607
the hanging for the *d* of the ...... Num 4:25 6607
the hanging for the *d* of the gate ...... Num 4:26 6607
to the *d* of the tabernacle of the ...... Num 6:10 6607
the *d* of the tabernacle of the ...... Num 6:13 6607
at the *d* of the tabernacle of the ...... Num 6:18 6607
at the *d* of the tabernacle of the ...... Num 10:3 6607
every man in the *d* of his tent ...... Num 11:10 6607
stood in the *d* of the tabernacle, ... Num 12:5 6607
stood in the *d* of the tabernacle ...... Num 16:18 6607
against them unto the *d* of the ...... Num 16:19 6607
stood in the *d* of their tents, and ...... Num 16:27 6607
the *d* of the tabernacle of the ...... Num 16:50 6607
the *d* of the tabernacle of the ...... Num 20:6 6607
the *d* of the tabernacle of the ...... Num 25:6 6607
by the *d* of the tabernacle of the ...... Num 27:2 6607
upon the *d* posts of thine house ...... Deut 11:20 4201
it through his ear unto the *d* ...... Deut 15:17 1817
to the *d* of her father's house ...... Deut 22:21 6607
over the *d* of the tabernacle ...... Deut 31:15 6607
at the *d* of the tabernacle of the ...... Josh 19:51 6607
her, Stand in the *d* of the tent ...... Judg 4:20 6607
went hard unto the *d* of the tower ...... Judg 9:52 6607
round about, and beat at the *d* ...... Judg 19:22 1817
fell down at the *d* of the man's ...... Judg 19:26 6607
fallen down at the *d* of the house ...... Judg 19:27 6607
at the *d* of the tabernacle of the 1Sa 2:22 6607
But Uriah slept at the *d* of the 2Sa 11:9 6607
from me, and bolt the *d* after her 2Sa 13:17 1817
out, and bolted the *d* after her 2Sa 13:18 1817
The *d* for the middle chamber was 1Kin 6:8 6907
So also made he for the *d* of the 1Kin 6:33 6907
leaves of the one *d* were folding 1Kin 6:34 1817
of the other *d* were folding 1Kin 6:34 1817
her feet, as she came in at the *d* 1Kin 14:6 6607
came to the threshold of the *d* 1Kin 14:17 1004
which kept the *d* of the king's 1Kin 14:27 6607
thou shalt shut the *d* upon thee 2Kin 4:4 1817
from him, and shut the *d* upon her 2Kin 4:5 1817
called her, she stood in the *d* 2Kin 4:15 6607
of God, and shut the *d* upon him 2Kin 4:21
shut the *d* upon them twain, and 2Kin 4:33 1817
stood at the *d* of the house of 2Kin 5:9 6607
d, and hold him fast at the *d* 2Kin 6:32 1817
Then open the *d*, and flee, and 2Kin 9:3 1817
And he opened the *d*, and fled 2Kin 9:10 1817
the priests that kept the *d* put 2Kin 12:9 5592
which the keepers of the *d* have 2Kin 22:4 5592
order, and the keepers of the *d* 2Kin 23:4 5592
and the three keepers of the *d* 2Kin 25:18 5592
of the *d* of the tabernacle of the 1Chr 9:21 6607
d of the house of Eliashib the ...... Neh 3:20 6607
from the *d* of the house of ...... Neh 3:21 6607
Teresh, of those which kept the *d* ...... Est 2:21 5592
the keepers of the *d*, who sought ...... Est 6:2 5592
laid wait at my neighbour's *d* ...... Job 31:9 6607
silence, and went not out of the *d* ...... Job 31:34 6607
Keep the *d* of my lips ...... Ps 141:3 1817
come not nigh the *d* of her house ...... Prov 5:8 6607
she sitteth at the *d* of her house ...... Prov 9:14 6607
As the *d* turneth upon his hinges, ... Prov 26:14 1817
in his hand by the hole of the *d* ...... Song 5:4 6607
and if she be a *d*, we will inclose ...... Song 8:9 1817
the posts of the *d* moved at the ...... Is 6:4 5592
of Shallum, the keeper of the *d* ...... Jer 35:4 5592
and the three keepers of the *d* ...... Jer 52:24 5592
to the *d* of the inner gate, that ...... Eze 8:3 6607
brought me to the *d* of the court ...... Eze 8:7 6607
digged in the wall, behold a *d* ...... Eze 8:8 6607
Then he brought me to the *d* of ...... Eze 8:14 6607
at the *d* of the temple of the ...... Eze 8:16 6607
every one stood at the *d* of the ...... Eze 10:19 6607
behold at the *d* of the gate five ...... Eze 11:1 6607
and twenty cubits, *d* against *d* ...... Eze 40:13 6607
breadth of the *d* was ten cubits ...... Eze 41:2 6607
the sides of the *d* were five ...... Eze 41:2 6607
and measured the post of the *d* ...... Eze 41:3 6607
and the *d*, six cubits ...... Eze 41:3 6607
and the breadth of the *d*, seven ...... Eze 41:3 6607
one *d* toward the north, and ...... Eze 41:11 6607
another *d* toward the south ...... Eze 41:11 6607
The *d* posts, and the narrow ...... Eze 41:16 5592
three stories, over against the *d* ...... Eze 41:16 5592
To that above the *d*, even unto ...... Eze 41:17 6607
unto above the *d* were cherubims ...... Eze 41:20 6607
two leaves for the one *d* ...... Eze 41:24 1817
and two leaves for the other *d* ...... Eze 41:24 1817
an hundred cubits was the north *d* ...... Eze 42:2 6607
was a *d* in the head of the way ...... Eze 42:12 6607
the land shall worship at the *d* ...... Eze 46:3 6607
me again unto the *d* of the house ...... Eze 47:1 6607
valley of Achor for a *d* of hope ...... Hos 2:15 6607
said, Smite the lintel of the *d* ...... Amos 9:1
and when thou hast shut thy *d* ...... Mt 6:6 *2374*
and the *d* was shut ...... Mt 25:10 *2374*
stone to the *d* of the sepulchre ...... Mt 27:60 *2374*
rolled back the stone from the *d* ...... Mt 28:2 *2374*
was gathered together at the *d* ...... Mk 1:33 *2374*
no, not so much as about the *d* ...... Mk 2:2 *2374*
found the colt tied by the *d* ...... Mk 11:4 *2374*
stone unto the *d* of the sepulchre ...... Mk 15:46 *2374*
stone from the *d* of the sepulchre ...... Mk 16:3 *2374*
the *d* is now shut, and my children ...... Lk 11:7 *2374*
risen up, and hath shut to the *d* ...... Lk 13:25 *2374*
without, and to knock at the *d* ...... Lk 13:25 *2374*
not by the *d* into the sheepfold ...... Jn 10:1 *2374*
d is the shepherd of the sheep ...... Jn 10:2 *2374*
unto you, I am the *d* of the sheep ...... Jn 10:7 *2374*
I am the *d* ...... Jn 10:9 *2374*
But Peter stood at the *d* without ...... Jn 18:16 *2374*
and spake unto her that kept the *d* ...... Jn 18:16 *2377*
damsel that kept the *d* unto Peter ...... Jn 18:17 *2377*
buried thy husband are at the *d* ...... Acts 5:9 *2374*
before the *d* kept the prison ...... Acts 12:6 *2374*
knocked at the *d* of the gate ...... Acts 12:13
and when they had opened the *d* ...... Acts 12:16
how he had opened the *d* of faith ...... Acts 14:27 *2374*
For a great *d* and effectual is 1Cor 16:9 *2374*
a *d* was opened unto me of the 2Cor 2:12 *2374*
open unto us a *d* of utterance ...... Col 4:3 *2374*
the judge standeth before the *d* ...... Jas 5:9 *2374*
I have set before thee an open *d* ...... Rev 3:8 *2374*
Behold, I stand at the *d*, and ...... Rev 3:20 *2374*
man hear my voice, and open the *d* ...... Rev 3:20 *2374*
behold, a *d* was opened in heaven ...... Rev 4:1 *2374*

DOORKEEPER
I had rather be a *d* in the house ...... Ps 84:10 5605

DOORKEEPERS
and Elkanah were *d* for the ark 1Chr 15:23 7778
and Jehiah were *d* for the ark 1Chr 15:24 7778

DOORS
d of thy house into the street ...... Josh 2:19 1817
shut the *d* of the parlour upon ...... Judg 3:23 1817
the *d* of the parlour were locked, ... Judg 3:24 1817
opened not the *d* of the parlour ...... Judg 3:25 1817
of the *d* of my house to meet me ...... Judg 11:31 1817
took the *d* of the gate of the ...... Judg 16:3 1817
opened the *d* of the house, and ...... Judg 19:27 1817
opened the *d* of the house of the 1Sa 3:15 1817
and scrabbled on the *d* of the gate 1Sa 21:13 1817
oracle he made *d* of olive tree 1Kin 6:31 1817
The two *d* also were of olive tree 1Kin 6:32 1817
the two *d* were of fir tree 1Kin 6:34 1817
And all the *d* and posts were square 1Kin 7:5 6607
both for the *d* of the inner house 1Kin 7:50 1817
for the *d* of the house, to wit, ... 1Kin 7:50 1817
the *d* of the temple of the LORD 2Kin 18:16 1817
the nails for the *d* of the gates 1Chr 22:3 1817
and the *d* thereof, with gold 2Chr 3:7 1817
great court, and *d* for the court 2Chr 4:9 1817
overlaid the *d* of them with brass 2Chr 4:9 1817
the inner *d* thereof for the most 2Chr 4:22 1817
the *d* of the house of the temple, ... 2Chr 4:22 1817
shall be porters of the *d* 2Chr 23:4 5592
shut up the *d* of the house of the 2Chr 28:24 1817
opened the *d* of the house of the 2Chr 29:3 1817
have shut up the *d* of the porch 2Chr 29:7 1817
the *d* had gathered of the hand of 2Chr 34:9 5592
it, and set up the *d* of it ...... Neh 3:1 1817
thereof, and set up the *d* thereof ...... Neh 3:3 1817
thereof, and set up the *d* thereof ...... Neh 3:6 1817
built it, and set up the *d* thereof ...... Neh 3:13 1817
build it, and set up the *d* thereof ...... Neh 3:14 1817
it, and set up the *d* thereof ...... Neh 3:15 1817
not set up the *d* upon the gates ...... Neh 6:1 1817
let us shut the *d* of the temple ...... Neh 6:10 1817
was built, and I had set up the *d* ...... Neh 7:1 1817
stand by, let them shut the *d* ...... Neh 7:3 1817
not up the *d* of my mother's womb ...... Job 3:10 1817
but I opened my *d* to the ...... Job 31:32 1817
Or who shut up the sea with *d* ...... Job 38:8 1817
decreed place, and set bars and *d* ...... Job 38:10 1817
or hast thou seen the *d* of the ...... Job 38:17 8179
Who can open the *d* of his face ...... Job 41:14 1817
be ye lifted up, ye everlasting *d* ...... Ps 24:7 6607
lift them up, ye everlasting *d* ...... Ps 24:9 6607
above, and opened the *d* of heaven ...... Ps 78:23 1817
city, at the coming in at the *d* ...... Prov 8:3 6607
waiting at the posts of my *d* ...... Prov 8:34 6607
the *d* shall be shut in the ...... Eccl 12:4 1817
and shut thy *d* about thee ...... Is 26:20 1817
Behind the *d* also and the posts ...... Is 57:8 1817
in the *d* of the houses, and speak ...... Eze 33:30 6607
the *d* of the side chambers were ...... Eze 41:11 6607
temple and the sanctuary had two *d* ...... Eze 41:23 1817
the *d* had two leaves apiece, two ...... Eze 41:24 1817
on the *d* of the temple, cherubims ...... Eze 41:25 1817
and their *d* toward the north ...... Eze 42:4 6607
fashions, and according to their *d* ...... Eze 42:11 6607
according to the *d* of the ...... Eze 42:12 6607
keep the *d* of thy mouth from her ...... Mic 7:5 6607
Open thy *d*, O Lebanon, that the ...... Zec 11:1 1817
that would shut the *d* for nought ...... Mal 1:10 1817
that it is near, even at the *d* ...... Mt 24:33 *2374*
that it is nigh, even at the *d* ...... Mk 13:29 *2374*
when the *d* were shut where the ...... Jn 20:19 *2374*
the *d* being shut, and stood in the ...... Jn 20:26 *2374*
Lord by night opened the prison *d* ...... Acts 5:19 *2374*
standing without before the *d* ...... Acts 5:23 *2374*
immediately all the *d* were opened ...... Acts 16:26 *2374*
and seeing the prison *d* open ...... Acts 16:27 *2374*
and forthwith the *d* were shut ...... Acts 21:30 *2374*

DOPHKAH (*dof'-kah*) *An encampment during the Exodus.*
of Sin, and encamped in *D* ...... Num 33:12 1850
And they departed from *D*, and ...... Num 33:13 1850

DOR (*dor*) See EN-DOR. *A Canaanite city.*
in the borders of *D* on the west ...... Josh 11:2 1756
The king of *D* in the coast of *D* ...... Josh 12:23 1756
towns, and the inhabitants of *D* ...... Josh 17:11 1756
towns, nor the inhabitants of *D* ...... Judg 1:27 1756
Abinadab, in all the region of *D* 1Kin 4:11 1756
towns, Megiddo and her towns, *D* 1Chr 7:29 1756

DORCAS (*dor'-cas*) See TABITHA. *Disciple raised from the dead by Peter.*
by interpretation is called *D* ...... Acts 9:36 *1393*
coats and garments which *D* made ...... Acts 9:39 *1393*

DOST
it that thou *d* ask after my name ...... Gen 32:29
when thou *d* overtake them, say ...... Gen 44:4
d thou go to possess their land ...... Deut 9:5
When thou *d* lend thy brother any ...... Deut 24:10
the man to whom thou *d* lend shall ...... Deut 24:11
Thou *d* but hate me, and lovest me ...... Judg 14:16

after whom *d* thou pursue 1Sa 24:14
Wherefore then *d* thou ask of me 1Sa 28:16
why *d* thou ask Abishag the 1Kin 2:22
D thou now govern the kingdom of 1Kin 21:7
Now on whom *d* thou trust, that 2Kin 18:20
sin, when thou *d* afflict them 2Chr 6:26
For what *d* thou make request Neh 2:4
D thou still retain thine Job 2:9
And why *d* thou not pardon my Job 7:21
yet thou *d* destroy me Job 10:8
d thou open thine eyes upon such Job 14:3
d thou not watch over my sin Job 14:16
d thou restrain wisdom to thyself Job 15:8
unto thee, and thou *d* not hear me Job 30:20
Why *d* thou strive against him Job 33:13
D thou know when God disposed Job 37:15
D thou know the balancings of the Job 37:16
When thou with rebukes *d* correct Ps 39:11
why *d* thou cast me off Ps 43:2
d not increase thy wealth by Ps 44:12
thou *d* establish equity, thou Ps 99:4
honour, when thou *d* embrace her Prov 4:8
for thou *d* not enquire wisely Eccl 7:10
beloved, that thou *d* so charge us Song 5:9
d weigh the path of the just Is 26:7
now on whom *d* thou trust, that Is 36:5
Wherefore *d* thou prophesy, and say Jer 32:3
D thou certainly know that Baalis Jer 40:14
daughter that *d* inhabit Dibon Jer 48:18
Wherefore *d* thou forget us for Lam 5:20
thou *d* dwell among scorpions Eze 2:6
Whom *d* thou pass in beauty Eze 32:19
if thou *d* not speak to warn the Eze 33:8
Now why *d* thou cry out aloud Mic 4:9
Why *d* thou shew me iniquity, and Hab 1:3
d thou not care that my sister Lk 10:40
D not thou fear God, seeing thou Lk 23:40
what *d* thou work? Jn 6:30
born in sins, and *d* thou teach us Jn 9:34
D thou believe on the Son of God Jn 9:35
How long *d* thou make us to doubt Jn 10:24
him, Lord, *d* thou wash my feet Jn 13:6
should not steal, *d* thou steal Rom 2:21
adultery, *d* thou commit adultery Rom 2:22
idols, *d* thou commit sacrilege Rom 2:22
circumcision *d* transgress the law Rom 2:27
But why *d* thou judge thy brother Rom 14:10
or why *d* thou set at nought thy Rom 14:10
why *d* thou glory, as if thou 1Cor 4:7
d thou not judge and avenge our Rev 6:10

DOTE
and they shall *d*: a sword is Jer 50:36 2973

DOTED
she *d* on her lovers, on the Eze 23:5 5689
and with all on whom she *d* Eze 23:7 5689
of the Assyrians, upon whom she *d* Eze 23:9 5689
She *d* upon the Assyrians her Eze 23:12 5689
eyes, she *d* upon them, and sent Eze 23:16 5689
For she *d* upon their paramours, Eze 23:20 5689

DOTH
For God *d* know that in the day ye Gen 3:5
d comfort himself, purposing to Gen 27:42
d my father yet live Gen 45:3
d put a difference between the Ex 11:7
I am the LORD that *d* sanctify you Ex 31:13
why *d* thy wrath wax hot against Ex 32:11
whosoever *d* touch them, when they Lev 11:31
d fall, it shall be unclean Lev 11:32
of the fruits *d* he sell unto thee Lev 25:16
when the LORD *d* make thy thigh to Num 5:21
the man whom the LORD *d* choose Num 16:7
the LORD *d* command concerning the Num 36:6
the LORD our God *d* give unto us Deut 1:20
which the LORD our God *d* give us Deut 1:25
as a man *d* bear his son, in all Deut 1:31
this day that God *d* talk with man Deut 5:24
that man *d* not live by bread only Deut 8:3
the mouth of the LORD *d* man live Deut 8:3
of these nations the LORD *d* drive Deut 9:4
these nations the LORD thy God *d* Deut 9:5
what *d* the LORD thy God require Deut 10:12
He *d* execute the judgment of the Deut 10:18
for a gift *d* blind the eyes of Deut 16:19
abominations the LORD thy God *d* Deut 18:12
which the LORD thy God *d* give Deut 20:16
God, he it is that *d* go with thee Deut 31:6
he it is that *d* go before thee Deut 31:8
Whosoever he be that *d* rebel Josh 1:18
when he that *d* flee unto one of Josh 20:4
it shall be, when any man *d* come Judg 4:20
d know that thou art a virtuous Ruth 3:11
because he *d* bless the sacrifice 1Sa 9:13
D not David hide himself with us 1Sa 23:19
D not David hide himself in the 1Sa 26:1
Wherefore *d* my lord thus pursue 1Sa 26:18
as when one *d* hunt a partridge in 1Sa 26:20
that David *d* honour thy father 2Sa 10:3
for the king *d* speak this thing 2Sa 14:13
in that the king *d* not fetch home 2Sa 14:13
neither *d* God respect any person 2Sa 14:14
yet *d* he devise means, that his 2Sa 14:14
the king *d* sit in the gate 2Sa 19:8
For thy servant *d* know that I 2Sa 19:20
but why *d* my lord the king 2Sa 24:3
of that which *d* cost me nothing 2Sa 24:24
the son of Haggith *d* reign 1Kin 1:11
why then *d* Adonijah reign 1Kin 1:13
for he *d* not prophesy good 1Kin 22:8
spirit of Elijah *d* rest on Elisha 2Kin 2:15
that this man *d* send unto me to 2Kin 5:7
that David *d* honour thy father 1Chr 19:3
why then *d* my lord require this 1Chr 21:3
as *d* thy people Israel, and may 2Chr 6:33
D not Hezekiah persuade you to 2Chr 32:11
D Job fear God for nought Job 1:9
D not their excellency which is Job 4:21
neither *d* trouble spring out of Job 5:6
D the wild ass bray when he hath Job 6:5
but what *d* your arguing reprove Job 6:25
D God pervert judgment Job 8:3
or *d* the Almighty pervert justice Job 8:3
D not the ear try words Job 12:11
Why *d* thine heart carry thee away Job 15:12
my reins asunder, and *d* not spare Job 16:13
d not mine eye continue in their Job 17:2
And thou sayest, How *d* God know Job 22:13
On the left hand, where he *d* work Job 23:9
so *d* the grave those which have Job 24:19
upon whom *d* not his light arise Job 25:3
D not he see my ways, and count Job 31:4
Therefore *d* Job open his mouth in Job 35:16
he *d* establish them for ever, and Job 36:7
D the hawk fly by thy wisdom, and Job 39:26
D the eagle mount up at thy Job 39:27
By his neesings a light *d* shine Job 41:18
in his law *d* he meditate day and Ps 1:2
in his pride *d* persecute the poor Ps 10:2
in the secret places *d* he murder Ps 10:8
he *d* catch the poor, when he Ps 10:9
Wherefore *d* the wicked contemn Ps 10:13
his countenance *d* behold the Ps 11:7
in his temple *d* every one speak Ps 29:9
because mine enemy *d* not triumph Ps 41:11
D not David hide himself with us Ps 54:*t*
for who, say they, *d* hear Ps 59:7
he *d* send out his voice, and that Ps 68:33
And they say, How *d* God know Ps 73:11
why *d* thine anger smoke against Ps 74:1
d his promise fail for evermore Ps 77:8
boar out of the wood *d* waste it Ps 80:13
beast of the field *d* devour it Ps 80:13
neither *d* a fool understand this Ps 92:6
therefore *d* my soul keep them Ps 119:129
wait for the LORD, my soul *d* wait Ps 130:5
The LORD *d* build up Jerusalem Ps 147:2
These six things *d* the LORD hate Prov 6:16
D not wisdom cry? Prov 8:1
a stranger *d* not intermeddle with Prov 14:10
he that *d* keep his soul shall be Prov 22:5
d not he that pondereth the heart Prov 24:12
thy soul, *d* not he know it Prov 24:12
so *d* an angry countenance a Prov 25:23
so *d* the slothful upon his bed Prov 26:14
so *d* the sweetness of a man's Prov 27:9
d the crown endure to every Prov 27:24
but the righteous *d* sing and Prov 29:6
and *d* not bless their mother Prov 30:11
her husband *d* safely trust in her Prov 31:11
so *d* a little folly him that is Eccl 10:1
and his right hand *d* embrace me Song 2:6
but Israel *d* not know Is 1:3
my people *d* not consider Is 1:3
neither *d* the cause of the widow Is 1:23
d take away from Jerusalem and Is 3:1
d witness against them Is 3:9
neither *d* his heart think so Is 10:7
D the plowman plow all day to sow Is 28:24
d he open and break the clods of Is 28:24
d he not cast abroad the fitches, Is 28:25
For his God *d* instruct him to Is 28:26
him to discretion, and *d* teach him Is 28:26
stream of brimstone, *d* kindle it Is 30:33
the villages that Kedar *d* inhabit Is 42:11
an ash, and the rain *d* nourish it Is 44:14
day that I am he that *d* speak Is 52:6
neither *d* justice overtake us Is 59:9
glory for that which *d* not profit Jer 2:11
for to thee *d* it appertain Jer 10:7
Wherefore *d* the way of the wicked Jer 12:1
the LORD *d* not accept them Jer 14:10
yet every one of them *d* curse me Jer 15:10
that none *d* return from his Jer 23:14
see whether a man *d* travail with Jer 30:6
him, as a shepherd *d* his flock Jer 31:10
why then *d* their king inherit Gad Jer 49:1
neither *d* any son of man pass Jer 51:43
How *d* the city sit solitary, that Lam 1:1
For he *d* not afflict willingly Lam 3:33
Wherefore *d* a living man complain Lam 3:39
there is none that *d* deliver us Lam 5:8
When a righteous man *d* turn from Eze 3:20
he *d* not sin, he shall surely Eze 3:21
d not the son bear the iniquity Eze 18:19
of me, *D* he not speak parables Eze 20:49
that *d* not understand shall fall Hos 4:14
of Israel *d* testify to his face Hos 5:5
what *d* the LORD require of thee, Mic 6:8
judgment *d* never go forth Hab 1:4
for the wicked *d* compass about Hab 1:4
every morning *d* he bring his Zeph 3:5
rust *d* corrupt, and where thieves Mt 6:19
neither moth nor rust *d* corrupt Mt 6:20
This fellow *d* not cast out devils Mt 12:24
D not your master pay tribute Mt 17:24
d he not leave the ninety and nine Mt 18:12
is put away *d* commit adultery Mt 19:9
How then *d* David in spirit call Mt 22:43
not what hour your Lord *d* come Mt 24:42
he is at hand that *d* betray me Mt 26:46
Why *d* this man thus speak Mk 2:7
the new wine *d* burst the bottles Mk 2:22
Why *d* this generation seek after Mk 8:12
My soul *d* magnify the Lord, Lk 1:46
neither *d* a corrupt tree bring Lk 6:43
of a candle *d* give thee light Lk 11:36
d not each one of you on the Lk 13:15
as a hen *d* gather her brood under Lk 13:34
whosoever *d* not bear his cross, Lk 14:27
d not leave the ninety and nine in Lk 15:4
d not light a candle, and sweep Lk 15:8
D he thank that servant because Lk 17:9
that is chief, as he that *d* serve Lk 22:26
beginning *d* set forth good wine Jn 2:10
said unto them, *D* this offend you Jn 6:61
D our law judge any man, before Jn 7:51
how then *d* he now see Jn 9:19
Therefore *d* my Father love me, Jn 10:17
even by him *d* this man stand here Acts 4:10
what *d* hinder me to be baptized Acts 8:36
the high priest *d* bear me witness Acts 22:5
much learning *d* make thee mad Acts 26:24
man seeth, why *d* he yet hope for Rom 8:24
unto me, Why *d* he yet find fault Rom 9:19
to the Lord he *d* not regard it Rom 14:6
D God take care for oxen 1Cor 9:9
D not even nature itself teach 1Cor 11:14
D not behave itself unseemly, 1Cor 13:5
neither *d* corruption inherit 1Cor 15:50
so great a death, and *d* deliver 2Cor 1:10
much more *d* the ministration of 2Cor 3:9
for whatsoever *d* make manifest is Eph 5:13
as it *d* also in you, since the Col 1:6
as a father *d* his children, 1Th 2:11
of iniquity *d* already work 2Th 2:7
their word will eat as *d* a canker 2Ti 2:17
all shall wax old as *d* a garment Heb 1:11
the sin which *d* so easily beset Heb 12:1
What *d* it profit, my brethren, Jas 2:14
to the body; what *d* it profit? Jas 2:16
D a fountain send forth at the Jas 3:11
and he *d* not resist you Jas 5:6
d also now save us (not the 1Pet 3:21
and so *d* Marcus my son 1Pet 5:13
it *d* not yet appear what we shall 1Jn 3:2
is born of God *d* not commit sin 1Jn 3:9
neither *d* he himself receive the 3Jn 10
and in righteousness he *d* judge Rev 19:11

DOTHAN (*do'-than*) *A city in Manasseh.*
I heard them say, Let us go to *D* Gen 37:17 1886
his brethren, and found them in *D* Gen 37:17 1886
him, saying, Behold, he is in *D* 2Kin 6:13 1886

DOTING
but *d* about questions and strifes 1Ti 6:4 *3552*

DOUBLE
take *d* money in your hand Gen 43:12 4932
they took *d* money in their hand, Gen 43:15 4932
he shall restore *d* Ex 22:4 8147
the thief be found, let him pay *d* Ex 22:7 8147
he shall pay *d* unto his neighbour Ex 22:9 8147
shalt *d* the sixth curtain in the Ex 26:9 3717
they made the breastplate *d* Ex 39:9 3717
worth a *d* hired servant to thee Deut 15:18 4932
by giving him a *d* portion of all Deut 21:17 8147
let a *d* portion of thy spirit be 2Kin 2:9 8147
they were not of *d* heart 1Chr 12:33
that they are *d* to that which is Job 11:6 3718
can come to him with his *d* bridle Job 41:13 3718
with a *d* heart do they speak Ps 12:2
LORD's hand *d* for all her sins Is 40:2 3718
For your shame ye shall have *d* Is 61:7 4932
land they shall possess the *d* Is 61:7 4932
their iniquity and their sin *d* Jer 16:18 4932
destroy them with *d* destruction Jer 17:18 4932
that I will render *d* unto thee Zec 9:12 4932
be counted worthy of *d* honour 1Ti 5:17 *1362*
A *d* minded man is unstable in all Jas 1:8 *1374*
purify your hearts, ye *d* minded Jas 4:8 *1374*
d unto her *d* according to Rev 18:6 *1363*
she hath filled fill to her *d* Rev 18:6 *1362*

DOUBLED
dream was *d* unto Pharaoh twice Gen 41:32 8138
Foursquare it shall be being *d* Ex 28:16 3717
span the breadth thereof, being *d* Ex 39:9 3717
let the sword be *d* the third time Eze 21:14 3717

DOUBLETONGUED
must the deacons be grave, not *d* 1Ti 3:8 *1351*

DOUBT
is without *d* rent in pieces Gen 37:33
life shall hang in *d* before thee Deut 28:66
No *d* but ye are the people, and Job 12:2 551
faith, wherefore didst thou *d* Mt 14:31 *1365*
d not, ye shall not only do this Mt 21:21 *1252*
shall not *d* in his heart, but Mk 11:23 *1252*
no *d* the kingdom of God is come Lk 11:20 *686*
How long dost thou make us to *d* Jn 10:24
were all amazed, and were in *d* Acts 2:12 *1280*
No *d* this man is a murderer, whom Acts 28:4 *3843*
For our sakes, no *d*, this is 1Cor 9:10 *1063*
for I stand in *d* of you Gal 4:20 *639*
they would no *d* have continued 1Jn 2:19

DOUBTED
but some *d* Mt 28:17 *1365*
they *d* of them whereunto this Acts 5:24 *1280*
Now while Peter *d* in himself what Acts 10:17 *1280*
because I *d* of such manner of Acts 25:20 *639*

DOUBTETH
he that *d* is damned if he eat, Rom 14:23 *1252*

DOUBTFUL
drink, neither be ye of *d* mind Lk 12:29 *3349*
but not to *d* disputations Rom 14:1 *1261*

DOUBTING
on another, *d* of whom he spake Jn 13:22 639
down, and go with them, *d* nothing Acts 10:20 *1252*
bade me go with them, nothing *d* Acts 11:12 *1252*
up holy hands, without wrath and *d* 1Ti 2:8 *1261*

DOUBTLESS
D ye shall not come into the land ... Num 14:30 518
for I will *d* deliver the ... 2Sa 5:19
shall *d* come again with rejoicing ... Ps 126:6
D thou art our father, though ... Is 63:16 3588
unto others, yet *d* I am to you ... 1Cor 9:2 *1065*
not expedient for me *d* to glory ... 2Cor 12:1 *1211*
Yea *d*, and I count all things but ... Phil 3:8 *3304*

DOUBTS
sentences, and dissolving of *d* ... Dan 5:12 7001
interpretations, and dissolve *d* ... Dan 5:16 7001

DOUGH
the people took their *d* before it ... Ex 12:34 1217
baked unleavened cakes of the *d* ... Ex 12:39 1217
of your *d* for an heave offering ... Num 15:20 6182
Of the first of your *d* ye shall ... Num 15:21 6182
bring the firstfruits of our *d* ... Neh 10:37 6182
fire, and the women knead their *d* ... Jer 7:18 1217
the priest the first of your *d* ... Eze 44:30 6182
after he hath kneaded the *d* ... Hos 7:4 1217

DOVE
Also he sent forth a *d* from him ... Gen 8:8 3123
But the *d* found no rest for the ... Gen 8:9 3123
sent forth the *d* out of the ark ... Gen 8:10 3123
the *d* came in to him in the ... Gen 8:11 3123
and sent forth the *d* ... Gen 8:12 3123
Oh that I had wings like a *d* ... Ps 55:6 3123
wings of a *d* covered with silver ... Ps 68:13 3123
O my *d*, that art in the clefts of ... Song 2:14 3123
to me, my sister, my love, my *d* ... Song 5:2 3123
My *d*, my undefiled is but one ... Song 6:9 3123
I did mourn as a *d* ... Is 38:14 3123
be like the *d* that maketh her ... Jer 48:28 3123
is like a silly *d* without heart ... Hos 7:11 3123
as a *d* out of the land of Assyria ... Hos 11:11 3123
Spirit of God descending like a *d* ... Mt 3:16 *4058*
the Spirit like a *d* descending ... Mk 1:10 *4058*
a bodily shape like a *d* upon him ... Lk 3:22 *4058*
descending from heaven like a *d* ... Jn 1:32 *4058*

DOVE'S
the fourth part of a cab of *d* ... 2Kin 6:25 1686

DOVES
eyes of *d* by the rivers of waters ... Song 5:12 3123
like bears, and mourn sore like *d* ... Is 59:11 3123
as the *d* to their windows ... Is 60:8 3123
mountains like *d* of the valleys ... Eze 7:16 3123
lead her as with the voice of *d* ... Nah 2:7 3123
as serpents, and harmless as *d* ... Mt 10:16 *4058*
and the seats of them that sold *d* ... Mt 21:12 *4058*
and the seats of them that sold *d* ... Mk 11:15 *4058*
that sold oxen and sheep and *d* ... Jn 2:14 *4058*
And said unto them that sold *d* ... Jn 2:16 *4058*

DOVES'
thou art fair; thou hast *d* eyes. ... Song 1:15 3123
thou hast *d* eyes within thy locks ... Song 4:1 3123

DOWN
the LORD came *d* to see the city ... Gen 11:5 3381
Go to, let us go *d*, and there ... Gen 11:7 3381
Abram went *d* into Egypt to ... Gen 12:10 3381
fowls came *d* upon the carcases ... Gen 15:11 3381
And when the sun was going *d* ... Gen 15:12 935
pass, that, when the sun went *d* ... Gen 15:17 935
I will go *d* now, and see whether ... Gen 18:21 3381
But before they lay *d*, the men of ... Gen 19:4
he perceived not when she lay *d* ... Gen 19:33
he perceived not when she lay *d* ... Gen 19:35
sat her *d* over against him a good ... Gen 21:16
Abraham bowed *d* himself before ... Gen 23:12 7812
he made his camels to kneel *d* ... Gen 24:11 1288
Let *d* thy pitcher, I pray thee ... Gen 24:14 5186
she went *d* to the well, and filled ... Gen 24:16 3381
let *d* her pitcher upon her hand ... Gen 24:18 3381
And the man bowed *d* his head ... Gen 24:26 6915
she went *d* unto the well, and drew ... Gen 24:45 3381
let *d* her pitcher from her ... Gen 24:46 3381
And I bowed *d* my head, and ... Gen 24:48 6915
him, and said, Go not *d* into Egypt ... Gen 26:2 3381
thee, and nations bow *d* to thee ... Gen 27:29 7812
thy mother's sons bow *d* to thee ... Gen 27:29 7812
lay *d* in that place to sleep ... Gen 28:11
d ourselves to thee to the earth ... Gen 37:10 7812
And they sat *d* to eat bread ... Gen 37:25
going to carry it *d* to Egypt ... Gen 37:25 3381
For I will go *d* into the grave ... Gen 37:35 3381
that Judah went *d* from his ... Gen 38:1 3381
And Joseph was brought *d* to Egypt ... Gen 39:1 3381
which had brought him *d* thither ... Gen 39:1 3381
get you *d* thither, and buy for us ... Gen 42:2 3381
went *d* to buy corn in Egypt ... Gen 42:3 3381
bowed *d* themselves before him ... Gen 42:6 7812
My son shall not go *d* with you ... Gen 42:38 3381
then shall ye bring *d* my gray ... Gen 42:38 3381
our brother with us, we will go *d* ... Gen 43:4 3381
not send him, we will not go *d* ... Gen 43:5 3381
would say, Bring your brother *d* ... Gen 43:7 3381
carry *d* the man a present, a ... Gen 43:11 3381
went *d* to Egypt, and stood before ... Gen 43:15 3381
we came indeed *d* at the first ... Gen 43:20 3381
d in our hands to buy food ... Gen 43:22 3381
they bowed *d* their heads, and made ... Gen 43:28 6915
Then they speedily took *d* every ... Gen 44:11 3381
thy servants, Bring him *d* unto me ... Gen 44:21 3381
youngest brother come *d* with you ... Gen 44:23 3381
And we said, We cannot go *d* ... Gen 44:26 3381
be with us, then will we go *d* ... Gen 44:26 3381
ye shall bring *d* my gray hairs ... Gen 44:29 3381
thy servants shall bring *d* the ... Gen 44:31 3381
come *d* unto me, tarry not ... Gen 45:9 3381
haste and bring *d* my father hither ... Gen 45:13 3381
fear not to go *d* into Egypt ... Gen 46:3 3381
I will go *d* with thee into Egypt ... Gen 46:4 3381
selfwill they digged *d* a wall ... Gen 49:6 6131
children shall bow *d* before thee ... Gen 49:8 7812
he stooped *d*, he couched as a ... Gen 49:9
couching *d* between two burdens ... Gen 49:14
went and fell *d* before his face ... Gen 50:18
d to wash herself at the river ... Ex 2:5 3381
and he sat *d* by a well ... Ex 2:15
I am come *d* to deliver them out ... Ex 3:8 3381
Aaron cast *d* his rod before ... Ex 7:10
For they cast *d* every man his rod ... Ex 7:12
the hail shall come *d* upon them ... Ex 9:19 3381
thy servants shall come *d* unto me ... Ex 11:8 3381
bow *d* themselves unto me, saying ... Ex 11:8 7812
and when he let *d* his hand ... Ex 17:11 5117
until the going *d* of the sun ... Ex 17:12 935
third day the LORD will come *d* in ... Ex 19:11 3381
Moses went *d* from the mount unto ... Ex 19:14 3381
the LORD came *d* upon mount Sinai ... Ex 19:20 3381
And the LORD said unto Moses, Go *d* ... Ex 19:21 3381
said unto him, Away, get thee *d* ... Ex 19:24 3381
So Moses went *d* unto the people ... Ex 19:25 3381
shalt not bow *d* thyself to them ... Ex 20:5 7812
unto him by that the sun goeth *d* ... Ex 22:26 935
shalt not bow *d* to their gods ... Ex 23:24 7812
quite break *d* their images ... Ex 23:24 7665
to come *d* out of the mount ... Ex 32:1 3381
and the people sat *d* to eat ... Ex 32:6
said unto Moses, Go, get thee *d* ... Ex 32:7 3381
went *d* from the mount, and the two ... Ex 32:15 3381
images, and cut *d* their groves ... Ex 34:13
when Moses came *d* from mount ... Ex 34:29 3381
when he came *d* from the mount ... Ex 34:29 3381
came *d* from offering of the sin ... Lev 9:22 3381
for pots, they shall be broken *d* ... Lev 11:35 5422
And he shall break *d* the house ... Lev 14:45 5422
before a beast to lie *d* thereto ... Lev 18:23 7250
d as a talebearer among thy ... Lev 19:16
lie *d* thereto, thou shalt kill ... Lev 20:16 7250
And when the sun is *d*, he shall be ... Lev 22:7 935
in your land, to bow *d* unto it ... Lev 26:1 7812
in the land, and ye shall lie *d* ... Lev 26:6
cut *d* your images, and cast your ... Lev 26:30
the Levites shall take it *d* ... Num 1:51 3381
they shall take *d* the covering ... Num 4:5 3381
And the tabernacle was taken *d* ... Num 10:17 3381
And I will come *d* and talk with ... Num 11:17 3381
And the LORD came *d* in a cloud ... Num 11:25 3381
the LORD came *d* in the pillar of ... Num 12:5 3381
cut *d* from thence a branch with ... Num 13:23
of Israel cut *d* from thence ... Num 13:24
Then the Amalekites came *d* ... Num 14:45 3381
they go *d* quick into the pit ... Num 16:30 3381
went *d* alive into the pit, and the ... Num 16:33 3381
How our fathers went *d* into Egypt ... Num 20:15 3381
Eleazar came *d* from the mount ... Num 20:28 3381
goeth *d* to the dwelling of Ar ... Num 21:15 5186
the LORD, she fell *d* under Balaam ... Num 22:27 7257
and he bowed *d* his head, and fell ... Num 22:31 6915
he shall not lie *d* until he eat ... Num 23:24 7901
he lay *d* as a lion, and as a great ... Num 24:9 7901
did eat, and bowed *d* to their gods ... Num 25:2 7812
quite pluck *d* all their high ... Num 33:52 8045
the coast shall go *d* from Shepham ... Num 34:11 3381
the border shall go *d* to Jordan ... Num 34:12 3381
hands, and brought it *d* unto us ... Deut 1:25 3381
shalt not bow *d* thyself unto them ... Deut 5:9 7812
by the way, and when thou liest *d* ... Deut 6:7 7901
break *d* their images, and cut *d* ... Deut 7:5
bring them *d* before thy face ... Deut 9:3 3665
get thee *d* quickly from hence ... Deut 9:12 3381
came *d* from the mount, and the ... Deut 9:15 3381
I fell *d* before the LORD, as at ... Deut 9:18
Thus I fell *d* before the LORD ... Deut 9:25
nights, as I fell *d* at the first ... Deut 9:25
came *d* from the mount, and put the ... Deut 10:5 3381
Thy fathers went *d* into Egypt ... Deut 10:22 3381
by the way, when thou liest *d* ... Deut 11:19
by the way where the sun goeth *d* ... Deut 11:30 3996
ye shall hew *d* the graven images ... Deut 12:3 1438
even, at the going *d* of the sun ... Deut 16:6 935
with the axe to cut *d* the tree ... Deut 19:5
thou shalt not cut them *d* (for ... Deut 20:19
thou shalt destroy and cut them *d* ... Deut 20:20
d the heifer unto a rough valley ... Deut 21:4 3381
ass or his ox fall *d* by the way ... Deut 22:4
and when the sun is *d*, he shall ... Deut 23:11 935
pledge again when the sun goeth *d* ... Deut 24:13 935
shall the sun go *d* upon it ... Deut 24:15 935
When thou cuttest *d* thine harvest ... Deut 24:19
judge shall cause him to lie *d* ... Deut 25:2
set it *d* before the altar of the ... Deut 26:4
and he went *d* into Egypt, and ... Deut 26:5 3381
Look *d* from thy holy habitation ... Deut 26:15
heaven shall it come *d* upon thee ... Deut 28:24 3381
and thou shalt come *d* very low ... Deut 28:43 3381
thy high and fenced walls come *d* ... Deut 28:52 3381
and they sat *d* at thy feet ... Deut 33:3 8497
also his heavens shall drop *d* dew ... Deut 33:28 6201
sea toward the going *d* of the sun ... Josh 1:4 3996
And before they were laid *d* ... Josh 2:8 7901
Then she let them *d* by a cord ... Josh 2:15 3381
which thou didst let us *d* by ... Josh 2:18 3381
the waters that come *d* from above ... Josh 3:13 3381
which came *d* from above stood ... Josh 3:16 3381
those that came *d* toward the sea ... Josh 3:16 3381
they lodged, and laid them *d* there ... Josh 4:8
of the city shall fall *d* flat ... Josh 6:5
shout, that the wall fell *d* flat ... Josh 6:20
and smote them in the going *d* ... Josh 7:5 4174
and as soon as the sun was *d* ... Josh 8:29 935
take his carcase *d* from the tree ... Josh 8:29 3381
were in the going *d* to Beth-horon ... Josh 10:11 4174
that the LORD cast *d* great stones ... Josh 10:11
hasted not to go *d* about a whole ... Josh 10:13
time of the going *d* of the sun ... Josh 10:27
and they took them *d* off the trees ... Josh 10:27 3381
went *d* to Beth-shemesh, and passed ... Josh 15:10 3381
goeth *d* westward to the coast of ... Josh 16:3 3381
it went *d* from Janohah to Ataroth ... Josh 16:7 3381
cut *d* for thyself there in the ... Josh 17:15
is a wood, and thou shalt cut it *d* ... Josh 17:18
the border came *d* to the end of ... Josh 18:16 3381
northward, and went *d* unto Arabah ... Josh 18:18 3381
and his children went *d* into Egypt ... Josh 24:4 3381
the children of Judah went *d* to ... Judg 1:9 3381
them to come *d* to the valley ... Judg 1:34 3381
ye shall throw *d* their altars ... Judg 2:2 5422
serve them, and to bow *d* unto them ... Judg 2:19 7812
was fallen *d* dead on the earth ... Judg 3:25
went *d* with him from the mount ... Judg 3:27 3381
And they went *d* after him, and took ... Judg 3:28 3381
So Barak went *d* from mount Tabor ... Judg 4:14 3381
Sisera lighted *d* off his chariot ... Judg 4:15 3381
of the LORD go *d* to the gates ... Judg 5:11 3381
out of Machir came *d* governors ... Judg 5:14 3381
thou hast trodden *d* strength ... Judg 5:21
feet he bowed, he fell, he lay *d* ... Judg 5:27 7901
he bowed, there he fell *d* dead ... Judg 5:27
throw *d* the altar of Baal that ... Judg 6:25 2040
cut *d* the grove that is by it ... Judg 6:25
the grove which thou shalt cut *d* ... Judg 6:26
the altar of Baal was cast *d* ... Judg 6:28 5422
grove was cut *d* that was by it ... Judg 6:28
he hath cast *d* the altar of Baal ... Judg 6:30
because he hath cut *d* the grove ... Judg 6:30
because one hath cast *d* his altar ... Judg 6:31 5422
he hath thrown *d* his altar ... Judg 6:32 5422
bring them *d* unto the water, and I ... Judg 7:4 3381
So he brought *d* the people unto ... Judg 7:5 3381
boweth *d* upon his knees to drink ... Judg 7:5
the rest of the people bowed *d* ... Judg 7:6
Arise, get thee *d* unto the host ... Judg 7:9 3381
But if thou fear to go *d*, go thou ... Judg 7:10 3381
Phurah thy servant *d* to the host ... Judg 7:10 3381
to go *d* unto the host ... Judg 7:11 3381
Then went he *d* with Phurah his ... Judg 7:11 3381
Come *d* against the Midianites, and ... Judg 7:24 3381
peace, I will break *d* this tower ... Judg 8:9 5242
he beat *d* the tower of Penuel, and ... Judg 8:17 5242
there come people *d* from the top ... Judg 9:36 3381
See there come people *d* by the ... Judg 9:37 3381
beat *d* the city, and sowed it with ... Judg 9:45 5422
cut *d* a bough from the trees, and ... Judg 9:48 3381
cut *d* every man his bough ... Judg 9:49 3381
d upon the mountains, and bewail ... Judg 11:37 3381
And Samson went *d* to Timnath ... Judg 14:1 3381
Then went Samson *d*, and his father ... Judg 14:5 3381
And he went *d*, and talked with the ... Judg 14:7 3381
his father went *d* unto the woman ... Judg 14:10 3381
seventh day before the sun went *d* ... Judg 14:18
he went *d* to Ashkelon, and slew ... Judg 14:19 3381
and he went *d* and dwelt in the top ... Judg 15:8 3381
We are come *d* to bind thee, that ... Judg 15:12 3381
eyes, and brought him *d* to Gaza ... Judg 16:21 3381
the house of his father came *d* ... Judg 16:31 3381
And they sat *d*, and did eat and ... Judg 19:6
the sun went *d* upon them when ... Judg 19:14
he sat him *d* in a street of the ... Judg 19:15
fell *d* at the door of the man's ... Judg 19:26
fallen *d* at the door of the house ... Judg 19:27
destroyed *d* to the ground of the ... Judg 20:21
destroyed *d* to the ground of the ... Judg 20:25
They are smitten *d* before us ... Judg 20:32
they are smitten *d* before us ... Judg 20:39
trode them *d* with ease over ... Judg 20:43
thee, and get thee *d* to the floor ... Ruth 3:3 3381
And it shall be, when he lieth *d* ... Ruth 3:4 7901
uncover his feet, and lay thee *d* ... Ruth 3:4 7901
she went *d* unto the floor, and did ... Ruth 3:6 3381
he went to lie *d* at the end of ... Ruth 3:7 7901
uncovered his feet, and laid her *d* ... Ruth 3:7 7901
lie *d* until the morning ... Ruth 3:13 7901
to the gate, and sat him *d* there ... Ruth 4:1
turn aside, sit *d* here ... Ruth 4:1
And he turned aside, and sat *d* ... Ruth 4:1
the city, and said, Sit ye *d* here ... Ruth 4:2
And they sat *d* ... Ruth 4:2
he bringeth *d* to the grave, and ... 1Sa 2:6 3381
when Eli was laid *d* in his place ... 1Sa 3:2 7901
and Samuel was laid *d* to sleep ... 1Sa 3:3 7901
I called not; lie *d* again ... 1Sa 3:5 7901
And he went and lay *d* ... 1Sa 3:5 7901
called not, my son; lie *d* again ... 1Sa 3:6 7901
Eli said unto Samuel, Go, lie *d* ... 1Sa 3:9 7901
Samuel went and lay *d* in his place ... 1Sa 3:9 7901
the Levites took *d* the ark of the ... 1Sa 6:15 3381
whereon they set *d* the ark of the ... 1Sa 6:18
come ye *d*, and fetch it up to you ... 1Sa 6:21 3381
when they were come *d* from the ... 1Sa 9:25 3381
as they were going *d* to the end ... 1Sa 9:27 3381
d from the high place with a ... 1Sa 10:5 3381
thou shalt go *d* before me to ... 1Sa 10:8 3381
behold, I will come *d* unto thee ... 1Sa 10:8 3381
will come *d* now upon me to Gilgal ... 1Sa 13:12 3381
went *d* to the Philistines ... 1Sa 13:20 3381
went on beating *d* one another ... 1Sa 14:16
Let us go *d* after the Philistines ... 1Sa 14:36 3381
of God, Shall I go *d* after the ... 1Sa 14:37 3381
depart, get you *d* from among the ... 1Sa 15:6 3381
and passed on, and gone *d* to Gilgal ... 1Sa 15:12 3381
not sit *d* till he come hither ... 1Sa 16:11
for you, and let him come *d* to me ... 1Sa 17:8 3381
he said, Why camest thou *d* hither ... 1Sa 17:28 3381
for thou art come *d* that thou ... 1Sa 17:28 3381
fell *d* by the way to Shaaraim ... 1Sa 17:52
let David *d* through a window ... 1Sa 19:12 3381
lay *d* naked all that day and all ... 1Sa 19:24

then thou shalt go *d* quickly	1Sa 20:19	3381
the king sat him *d* to eat meat	1Sa 20:24	
his spittle fall *d* upon his beard	1Sa 21:13	3381
they went *d* thither to him	1Sa 22:1	3381
and said, Arise, go *d* to Keilah	1Sa 23:4	3381
that he came *d* with an ephod in	1Sa 23:6	3381
to go *d* to Keilah, to besiege	1Sa 23:8	3381
will Saul come *d*, as thy servant	1Sa 23:11	3381
And the LORD said, He will come *d*	1Sa 23:11	3381
come *d* according to all the	1Sa 23:20	3381
the desire of thy soul to come *d*	1Sa 23:20	3381
wherefore he came *d* into a rock	1Sa 23:25	3381
went *d* to the wilderness of Paran	1Sa 25:1	3381
that she came *d* by the covert of	1Sa 25:20	3381
and his men came *d* against her	1Sa 25:20	3381
went *d* to the wilderness of Ziph,	1Sa 26:2	3381
Who will go *d* with me to Saul to	1Sa 26:6	3381
said, I will go *d* with thee	1Sa 26:6	3381
let him not go *d* with us to	1Sa 29:4	3381
thou bring me *d* to this company	1Sa 30:15	3381
will bring thee *d* to this company	1Sa 30:15	3381
And when he had brought him *d*	1Sa 30:16	3381
is that goeth *d* to the battle	1Sa 30:24	3381
fell *d* slain in mount Gilboa	1Sa 31:1	
and they sat *d*, the one on the one	2Sa 2:13	
so they fell *d* together	2Sa 2:16	
and he fell *d* there, and died in	2Sa 2:23	
to the place where Asahel fell *d*	2Sa 2:23	
the sun went *d* when they were	2Sa 2:24	
or ought else, till the sun be *d*	2Sa 3:35	935
of it, and went *d* to the hold	2Sa 5:17	3381
casting them *d* to the ground	2Sa 8:2	7901
Go *d* to thy house, and wash thy	2Sa 11:8	3381
lord, and went not *d* to his house	2Sa 11:9	3381
Uriah went not *d* unto his house	2Sa 11:10	3381
thou not go *d* unto thine house	2Sa 11:10	3381
lord, but went not *d* to his house	2Sa 11:13	3381
Lay thee *d* on thy bed, and make	2Sa 13:5	7901
So Amnon lay *d*, and made himself	2Sa 13:6	7901
and he was laid *d*	2Sa 13:8	7901
day make thee go up and *d* with us	2Sa 15:20	5128
they set *d* the ark of God	2Sa 15:24	3332
whither they went *d*	2Sa 17:18	3381
he fell *d* to the earth upon his	2Sa 18:28	7821
came *d* with the men of Judah to	2Sa 19:16	3381
of Gera fell *d* before the king	2Sa 19:18	
to go *d* to meet my lord the king	2Sa 19:20	3381
of Saul came *d* to meet the king	2Sa 19:24	3381
the Gileadite came *d* from Rogelim	2Sa 19:31	3381
battered the wall, to throw it *d*	2Sa 20:15	5307
and David went *d*, and his servants	2Sa 21:15	3381
bowed the heavens also, and came *d*	2Sa 22:10	3381
that thou mayest bring them *d*	2Sa 22:28	3381
that bringeth *d* the people under	2Sa 22:48	8213
three of the thirty chief went *d*	2Sa 23:13	3381
he went *d* also and slew a lion in	2Sa 23:20	3381
but he went *d* to him with a staff	2Sa 23:21	3381
For he is gone *d* this day	1Kin 1:25	3381
own mule, and bring him *d* to Gihon	1Kin 1:33	3381
and the Pelethites, went *d*	1Kin 1:38	3381
they brought him *d* from the altar	1Kin 1:53	3381
head go *d* to the grave in peace	1Kin 2:6	3381
but he came *d* to meet me at	1Kin 2:8	3381
thou *d* to the grave with blood	1Kin 2:9	3381
sat *d* on his throne, and caused a	1Kin 2:19	
them *d* from Lebanon unto the sea	1Kin 5:9	3381
be smitten *d* before the enemy	1Kin 8:33	
brought him *d* out of the chamber	1Kin 17:23	3381
of the LORD that was broken *d*	1Kin 18:30	
them *d* to the brook Kishon	1Kin 18:40	3281
he cast himself *d* upon the earth	1Kin 18:42	1457
thy chariot, and get thee *d*	1Kin 18:44	3381
sat *d* under a juniper tree	1Kin 19:4	
eat and drink, and laid him *d* again	1Kin 19:6	7901
thrown *d* thine altars, and slain	1Kin 19:10	2040
thrown *d* thine altars, and slain	1Kin 19:14	2040
he laid him *d* upon his bed, and	1Kin 21:4	7901
that Ahab rose up to go *d* to the	1Kin 21:16	3381
go *d* to meet Ahab king of Israel,	1Kin 21:18	3381
he is gone *d* to possess it	1Kin 21:18	3381
came *d* to the king of Israel	1Kin 22:2	3381
host about the going *d* of the sun	1Kin 22:36	
Ahaziah fell *d* through a lattice	2Kin 1:2	
Thou shalt not come *d* from that	2Kin 1:4	3381
therefore thou shalt not come *d*	2Kin 1:6	3381
God, the king hath said, Come *d*	2Kin 1:9	3381
then let fire come *d* from heaven	2Kin 1:10	3381
there came *d* fire from heaven, and	2Kin 1:10	3381
Come *d* quickly	2Kin 1:11	3381
God, let fire come *d* from heaven	2Kin 1:12	3381
fire of God came *d* from heaven	2Kin 1:12	3381
there came fire *d* from heaven	2Kin 1:14	3381
said unto Elijah, Go *d* with him	2Kin 1:15	3381
went *d* with him unto the king	2Kin 1:15	3381
therefore thou shalt not come *d*	2Kin 1:16	3381
So they went *d* to Beth-el	2Kin 2:2	3381
and the king of Edom went *d* to him	2Kin 3:12	3381
they beat *d* the cities, and on	2Kin 3:25	2040
Then went he *d*, and dipped himself	2Kin 5:14	3381
when I bow *d* myself in the house	2Kin 5:18	7812
he lighted *d* from the chariot to	2Kin 5:21	
came to Jordan, they cut *d* wood	2Kin 6:4	
he cut *d* a stick, and cast it in	2Kin 6:6	
thither the Syrians are come *d*	2Kin 6:9	5181
And when they came *d* to him	2Kin 6:18	3381
the messenger came *d* unto him	2Kin 6:33	3381
spake when the king came *d* to him	2Kin 7:17	3381
of Jehoram king of Judah went *d*	2Kin 8:29	3381
of Judah was come *d* to see Joram	2Kin 9:16	3381
and he sunk *d* in his chariot	2Kin 9:24	
And he said, Throw her *d*	2Kin 9:33	8058
So they threw her *d*	2Kin 9:33	8058
we go *d* to salute the children of	2Kin 10:13	3381
they brake *d* the image of Baal,	2Kin 10:27	5422
brake *d* the house of Baal, and	2Kin 10:27	5422
house, that it be not broken *d*	2Kin 11:6	4535
the house of Baal, and brake it *d*	2Kin 11:18	5422
they brought *d* the king from the	2Kin 11:19	3381
of Millo, which goeth *d* to Silla	2Kin 12:20	3381
king of Israel came *d* unto him	2Kin 13:14	3381
and when the man was let *d*	2Kin 13:21	3212
Lebanon, and trode *d* the thistle	2Kin 14:9	
brake *d* the wall of Jerusalem	2Kin 14:13	
took *d* the sea from off the	2Kin 16:17	3381
cut *d* the groves, and brake in	2Kin 18:4	
LORD, bow *d* thine ear, and hear	2Kin 19:16	5186
will cut *d* the tall cedar trees	2Kin 19:23	
the shadow to go *d* ten degrees	2Kin 20:10	5186
it had gone *d* in the dial of Ahaz	2Kin 20:11	3381
wiping it, and turning it upside *d*	2Kin 21:13	
he put *d* the idolatrous priests,	2Kin 23:5	7673
he brake *d* the houses of the	2Kin 23:7	5422
brake *d* the high places of the	2Kin 23:8	
of the LORD, did the king beat *d*	2Kin 23:12	5422
brake them *d* from thence, and cast	2Kin 23:12	7323
cut *d* the groves, and filled their	2Kin 23:14	
and the high place he brake *d*	2Kin 23:15	5422
brake *d* the walls of Jerusalem	2Kin 25:10	5422
For there fell *d* many slain	1Chr 5:22	
because they came *d* to take away	1Chr 7:21	3381
fell *d* slain in mount Gilboa	1Chr 10:1	
went *d* to the rock to David	1Chr 11:15	3381
also he went *d* and slew a lion in	1Chr 11:22	3381
he went *d* to him with a staff, and	1Chr 11:23	3381
and bowed *d* their heads, and	1Chr 29:20	6915
kneeled *d* upon his knees before	2Chr 6:13	
the fire came *d* from heaven	2Chr 7:1	3381
of Israel saw how the fire came *d*	2Chr 7:3	3381
so there fell *d* slain of Israel	2Chr 13:17	
brake *d* the images, and cut *d*	2Chr 14:3	
Asa cut *d* her idol, and stamped it	2Chr 15:16	
he went *d* to Ahab to Samaria	2Chr 18:2	3381
time of the sun going *d* he died	2Chr 18:34	
To morrow go ye *d* against them	2Chr 20:16	3381
of Jehoram king of Judah went *d*	2Chr 22:6	3381
the house of Baal, and brake it *d*	2Chr 23:17	5422
brought *d* the king from the house	2Chr 23:20	3381
hath power to help, and to cast *d*	2Chr 25:8	3782
cast them *d* from the top of the	2Chr 25:12	
bowed *d* himself before them, and	2Chr 25:14	7812
Lebanon, and trode *d* the thistle	2Chr 25:18	
brake *d* the wall of Jerusalem	2Chr 25:23	
brake *d* the wall of Gath, and the	2Chr 26:6	
in pieces, and cut *d* the groves	2Chr 31:1	1438
threw *d* the high places and the	2Chr 31:1	5422
brought it straight *d* to the west	2Chr 32:30	4295
Hezekiah his father had broken *d*	2Chr 33:3	5422
they brake *d* the altars of Baalim	2Chr 34:4	5422
were on high above them, he cut *d*	2Chr 34:4	1438
when he had broken *d* the altars	2Chr 34:7	5422
cut *d* all the idols throughout	2Chr 34:7	1438
of Egypt put him *d* at Jerusalem	2Chr 36:3	5493
brake *d* the wall of Jerusalem, and	2Chr 36:19	5422
timber be pulled *d* from his house	Ezr 6:11	
and of my beard, and sat *d* astonied	Ezr 9:3	
casting himself *d* before the	Ezr 10:1	5307
sat *d* in the first day of the	Ezr 10:16	
of Jerusalem also is broken *d*	Neh 1:3	
I heard these words, that I sat *d*	Neh 1:4	
of Jerusalem, which were broken *d*	Neh 2:13	
that go *d* from the city of David	Neh 3:15	3381
even break *d* their stone wall	Neh 4:3	
work, so that I cannot come *d*	Neh 6:3	3381
I leave it, and come *d* to you	Neh 6:3	3381
much cast *d* in their own eyes	Neh 6:16	5307
Thou camest *d* also upon mount	Neh 9:13	3381
the king and Haman sat *d* to drink	Est 3:15	
fell *d* at his feet, and besought	Est 8:3	
and from walking up and *d* in it	Job 1:7	
fell *d* upon the ground, and	Job 1:20	
and from walking up and *d* in it	Job 2:2	
and he sat *d* among the ashes	Job 2:8	
So they sat *d* with him upon the	Job 2:13	
ye see my casting *d*, and are	Job 6:21	
When I lie *d*, I say, When shall I	Job 7:4	7901
so he that goeth *d* to the grave	Job 7:9	3381
alone till I swallow *d* my spittle	Job 7:19	
in his greenness, and not cut *d*	Job 8:12	
Also thou shalt lie *d*, and none	Job 11:19	7257
Behold, he breaketh *d*, and it	Job 12:14	2040
forth like a flower, and is cut *d*	Job 14:2	
is hope of a tree, if it be cut *d*	Job 14:7	
So man lieth *d*, and riseth not	Job 14:12	7901
Lay *d* now, put me in a surety	Job 17:3	
They shall go *d* to the bars of	Job 17:16	3381
his own counsel shall cast him *d*	Job 18:7	
which shall lie *d* with him in the	Job 20:11	7901
He hath swallowed *d* riches	Job 20:15	
and shall not swallow it *d*	Job 20:18	
and in a moment go *d* to the grave	Job 21:13	5181
They shall lie *d* alike in the	Job 21:26	7901
Which were cut *d* out of time	Job 22:16	
our substance is not cut *d*	Job 22:20	
When men are cast *d*, then thou	Job 22:29	8213
The rich man shall lie *d*, but he	Job 27:19	7901
of my countenance they cast not *d*	Job 29:24	5307
and let others bow *d* upon her	Job 31:10	3766
God thrusteth him *d*, not man	Job 32:13	
him from going *d* to the pit	Job 33:24	3381
they pour *d* rain according to the	Job 36:27	
tread *d* the wicked in their place	Job 40:12	
with a cord which thou lettest *d*	Job 41:1	8257
shall not one be cast *d* even at	Job 41:9	2904
I laid me *d* and slept	Ps 3:5	7901
I will both lay me *d* in peace	Ps 4:8	7901
let him tread *d* my life upon the	Ps 7:5	
shall come *d* upon his own pate	Ps 7:16	3381
The heathen are sunk *d* in the pit	Ps 9:15	
The LORD looked *d* from heaven	Ps 14:2	3381
their eyes bowing *d* to the earth	Ps 17:11	5186
LORD, disappoint him, cast him *d*	Ps 17:13	3766
bowed the heavens also, and came *d*	Ps 18:9	3381
but wilt bring *d* high looks	Ps 18:27	8213
They are brought *d* and fallen	Ps 20:8	3766
all they that go *d* to the dust	Ps 22:29	3381
me to lie *d* in green pastures	Ps 23:2	7257
like them that go *d* into the pit	Ps 28:1	3381
that I should not go *d* to the pit	Ps 30:3	3381
my blood, when I go *d* to the pit	Ps 30:9	3381
Bow *d* thine ear to me	Ps 31:2	5186
I bowed *d* heavily, as one that	Ps 35:14	7817
they are cast *d*, and shall not be	Ps 36:12	1760
soon be cut *d* like the grass	Ps 37:2	5243
to cast *d* the poor and needy, and	Ps 37:14	5307
he shall not be utterly cast *d*	Ps 37:24	2904
I am bowed *d* greatly	Ps 38:6	7817
Why art thou cast *d*, O my soul	Ps 42:5	7817
God, my soul is cast *d* within me	Ps 42:6	7817
Why art thou cast *d*, O my soul	Ps 42:11	7817
Why art thou cast *d*, O my soul	Ps 43:5	7817
thee will we push *d* our enemies	Ps 44:5	
our soul is bowed *d* to the dust	Ps 44:25	7743
the sun unto the going *d* thereof	Ps 50:1	
God looked *d* from heaven upon the	Ps 53:2	
let them go *d* quick into hell	Ps 55:15	3381
shalt bring them *d* into the pit	Ps 55:23	3381
in thine anger cast *d* the people	Ps 56:7	
my soul is bowed *d*	Ps 57:6	
and bring them *d*, O Lord our	Ps 59:11	3381
d for meat, and grudge if they be	Ps 59:15	
is that shall tread *d* our enemies	Ps 60:12	
to cast him *d* from his excellency	Ps 62:4	
He shall come *d* like rain upon	Ps 72:6	3381
all kings shall fall *d* before him	Ps 72:11	7812
castedst them *d* into destruction	Ps 73:18	5307
But now they break *d* the carved	Ps 74:6	
they have defiled by casting *d*	Ps 74:7	
he putteth *d* one, and setteth up	Ps 75:7	8231
waters to run *d* like rivers	Ps 78:16	
had rained *d* manna upon them to	Ps 78:24	
smote *d* the chosen men of Israel	Ps 78:31	3766
thou then broken *d* her hedges	Ps 80:12	
look *d* from heaven, and behold, and	Ps 80:14	
is burned with fire, it is cut *d*	Ps 80:16	
shall look *d* from heaven	Ps 85:11	
Bow *d* thine ear, O LORD, hear me	Ps 86:1	5186
with them that go *d* into the pit	Ps 88:4	3381
I will beat *d* his foes before his	Ps 89:23	
Thou hast broken *d* all his hedges	Ps 89:40	
cast his throne *d* to the ground	Ps 89:44	
in the evening it is cut *d*	Ps 90:6	
O come, let us worship and bow *d*	Ps 95:6	3766
hast lifted me up, and cast me *d*	Ps 102:10	
For he hath looked *d* from the	Ps 102:19	
they go *d* by the valleys unto the	Ps 104:8	3381
the sun knoweth his going *d*	Ps 104:19	
and lay them *d* in their dens	Ps 104:22	7257
Therefore he brought *d* their	Ps 107:12	3665
they fell *d*, and there was none to	Ps 107:12	3782
They that go *d* to the sea in	Ps 107:23	3381
they go *d* again to the depths	Ps 107:26	3381
is that shall tread *d* our enemies	Ps 108:13	
I am tossed up and *d* as the locust	Ps 109:23	
of the sun unto the going *d* of	Ps 113:3	
any that go *d* into silence	Ps 115:17	3381
Thou hast trodden *d* all them that	Ps 119:118	
Rivers of waters run *d* mine eyes	Ps 119:136	
that ran *d* upon the beard, even	Ps 133:2	3381
that went *d* to the skirts of his	Ps 133:2	3381
rivers of Babylon, there we sat *d*	Ps 137:1	
compassest my path and my lying *d*	Ps 139:3	7252
smitten my life *d* to the ground	Ps 143:3	
unto them that go *d* into the pit	Ps 143:7	3381
thy heavens, O LORD, and come *d*	Ps 144:5	3381
up all those that be bowed *d*	Ps 145:14	
raiseth them that are bowed *d*	Ps 146:8	
of the wicked he turneth upside *d*	Ps 146:9	
the wicked *d* to the ground	Ps 147:6	8213
as those that go *d* into the pit	Prov 1:12	3381
up, and the clouds drop *d* the dew	Prov 3:20	7491
When thou liest *d*, thou shalt not	Prov 3:24	7901
yea, thou shalt lie *d*, and thy	Prov 3:24	7901
Her feet go *d* to death	Prov 5:5	3381
For she hath cast *d* many wounded	Prov 7:26	
going *d* to the chambers of death	Prov 7:27	3381
plucketh it *d* with her hands	Prov 14:1	8045
they go *d* into the innermost	Prov 18:8	3381
casteth *d* the strength of the	Prov 21:22	3381
Bow *d* thine ear, and hear the	Prov 22:17	5186
lieth *d* in the midst of the sea	Prov 23:34	7901
stone wall thereof was broken *d*	Prov 24:31	2040
A righteous man falling *d* before	Prov 25:26	
is like a city that is broken *d*	Prov 25:28	
they go *d* into the innermost	Prov 26:22	3381
also ariseth, and the sun goeth *d*	Eccl 1:5	
a time to break *d*, and a time to	Eccl 3:3	
I sat *d* under his shadow with	Song 2:3	
beloved is gone *d* into his garden	Song 6:2	3381
I went *d* into the garden of nuts	Song 6:11	3381
my beloved, that goeth *d* sweetly	Song 7:9	
And the mean man boweth *d*, and the	Is 2:9	7817
of men shall be bowed *d*, and the	Is 2:11	7817
loftiness of man shall be bowed *d*	Is 2:17	7817
break *d* the wall thereof	Is 5:5	
and it shall be trodden *d*	Is 5:5	
the mean man shall be brought *d*	Is 5:15	7817
The bricks are fallen *d*, but we	Is 9:10	
the sycomores are cut *d*, but we	Is 9:10	1438
shall bow *d* under the prisoners	Is 10:4	3766
to tread them *d* like the mire of	Is 10:6	
I have put *d* the inhabitants like	Is 10:13	3381
ones of stature shall be hewn *d*	Is 10:33	1438

he shall cut *d* the thickets of ... Is 10:34
leopard shall lie *d* with the kid ... Is 11:6 7257
young ones shall lie *d* together ... Is 11:7 7257
saying, Since thou art laid *d* ... Is 14:8 7901
pomp is brought *d* to the grave ... Is 14:11 3381
how art thou cut *d* to the ground ... Is 14:12 1438
thou shalt be brought *d* to hell ... Is 14:15 3381
that go *d* to the stones of the ... Is 14:19 3381
the needy shall lie *d* in safety ... Is 14:30 7257
of the heathen have broken *d* the ... Is 16:8
be for flocks, which shall lie *d* ... Is 17:2 7257
a nation meted out and trodden *d* ... Is 18:2
take away and cut *d* the branches ... Is 18:5
I was bowed *d* at the hearing of ... Is 21:3
day of trouble, and of treading *d* ... Is 22:5
breaking *d* the walls, and of ... Is 22:5
ye broken *d* to fortify the wall ... Is 22:10 5422
thy state shall he pull thee *d* ... Is 22:19
place be removed, and be cut *d* ... Is 22:25 1438
it waste, and turneth it upside *d* ... Is 24:1
The city of confusion is broken *d* ... Is 24:10
The earth is utterly broken *d* ... Is 24:19
Thou shalt bring *d* the noise of ... Is 25:5 3665
Moab shall be trodden *d* under him ... Is 25:10
is trodden *d* for the dunghill ... Is 25:10
he shall bring *d* their pride ... Is 25:11 8213
of thy walls shall he bring *d* ... Is 25:12 7817
For he bringeth *d* them that dwell ... Is 26:5 7817
The foot shall tread it *d* ... Is 26:6
feed, and there shall he lie *d* ... Is 27:10 7257
shall cast *d* to the earth with ... Is 28:2
then ye shall be trodden *d* by it ... Is 28:18
And thou shalt be brought *d* ... Is 29:4 8213
upside *d* shall be esteemed as the ... Is 29:16
That walk to go *d* into Egypt ... Is 30:2 3381
shew the lighting *d* of his arm ... Is 30:30 5183
shall the Assyrian be beaten *d* ... Is 30:31
them that go *d* to Egypt for help ... Is 31:1 3381
and he that is holpen shall fall *d* ... Is 31:3
come *d* to fight for mount Zion ... Is 31:4 3381
hail, coming *d* on the forest ... Is 32:19 3381
Lebanon is ashamed and hewn *d* ... Is 33:9
that shall not be taken *d* ... Is 33:20
and all their host shall fall *d* ... Is 34:4
it shall come *d* upon Idumea ... Is 34:5 3381
unicorns shall come *d* with them ... Is 34:7 3381
I will cut *d* the tall cedars ... Is 37:24
which is gone *d* in the sun dial ... Is 38:8
by which degrees it was gone *d* ... Is 38:8
they that go *d* into the pit ... Is 38:18 3381
earth, ye that go *d* to the sea ... Is 42:10 3381
have brought *d* all their nobles, ... Is 43:14 3381
they shall lie *d* together ... Is 43:17 3381
He heweth him *d* cedars, and taketh ... Is 44:14
image, and falleth *d* thereto ... Is 44:15 5456
he falleth *d* unto it, and ... Is 44:17 5456
shall I fall *d* to the stock of a ... Is 44:19 5456
Drop *d*, ye heavens, from above, ... Is 45:8
the skies pour *d* righteousness ... Is 45:8
and they shall fall *d* unto thee ... Is 45:14 7812
Bel boweth *d*, Nebo stoopeth, ... Is 46:1 3766
They stoop, they bow *d* together ... Is 46:2 3766
they fall *d*, yea, they worship ... Is 46:6 5456
Come *d*, and sit in the dust, O ... Is 47:1 3381
they shall bow *d* to thee with ... Is 49:23 7812
ye shall lie *d* in sorrow ... Is 50:11 7901
have said to thy soul, Bow *d* ... Is 51:23 7812
arise, and sit *d*, O Jerusalem ... Is 52:2
My people went *d* aforetime into ... Is 52:4 3381
For as the rain cometh *d*, and the ... Is 55:10 3381
sleeping, lying *d*, loving to ... Is 56:10 7901
is it to bow *d* his head as a ... Is 58:5
d at the soles of thy feet ... Is 60:14 7812
Thy sun shall no more go *d* ... Is 60:20
I will tread *d* the people in mine ... Is 63:6
I will bring *d* their strength to ... Is 63:6
a beast goeth *d* into the valley ... Is 63:14 3381
Look *d* from heaven, and behold ... Is 63:15
have trodden *d* thy sanctuary ... Is 63:18
that thou wouldest come *d* ... Is 64:1 3381
might flow *d* at thy presence ... Is 64:1
we looked not for, thou camest *d* ... Is 64:3 3381
flowed *d* at thy presence ... Is 64:3
a place for the herds to lie *d* in ... Is 65:10 7257
shall all bow *d* to the slaughter ... Is 65:12 3766
to root out, and to pull *d* ... Jer 1:10
and to destroy, and to throw *d* ... Jer 1:10 2040
We lie *d* in our shame, and our ... Jer 3:25 7901
d at the presence of the LORD ... Jer 4:26 5422
of hosts said, Hew ye *d* trees ... Jer 6:6
I visit them they shall be cast *d* ... Jer 6:15 3782
visitation they shall be cast *d* ... Jer 8:12 3782
our eyes may run *d* with tears ... Jer 9:18
run *d* with tears, because the ... Jer 13:17
queen, Humble yourselves, sit *d* ... Jer 13:18
your principalities shall come *d* ... Jer 13:18 3381
mine eyes run *d* with tears night ... Jer 14:17
her sun is gone *d* while it was ... Jer 15:9
go *d* to the potter's house, and ... Jer 18:2 3381
Then I went *d* to the potter's ... Jer 18:3 3381
to pluck up, and to pull *d* ... Jer 18:7
say, Who shall come *d* against us ... Jer 21:13 5181
Go *d* to the house of the king of ... Jer 22:1 3381
they shall cut *d* thy choice ... Jer 22:7
build them, and not pull them *d* ... Jer 24:6
peaceable habitations are cut *d* ... Jer 25:37
sat *d* in the entry of the new ... Jer 26:10
them, to pluck up, and to break *d* ... Jer 31:28 5422
and to break *d*, and to throw *d* ... Jer 31:28 2040
nor thrown *d* any more for ever ... Jer 31:40 2040
which are thrown *d* by the mounts ... Jer 33:4 5422
causing their flocks to lie *d* ... Jer 33:12 7901
Then he went *d* into the king's ... Jer 36:12 3381
And they said unto him, Sit *d* now ... Jer 36:15
they let *d* Jeremiah with cords ... Jer 38:6 7971
let them *d* by cords into the ... Jer 38:11 7971
brake *d* the walls of Jerusalem ... Jer 39:8 5422
I build you, and not pull you *d* ... Jer 42:10
which I have built will I break *d* ... Jer 45:4 2040
and their mighty ones are beaten *d* ... Jer 46:5
They shall cut *d* her forest ... Jer 46:23
Also thou shalt be cut *d*, O ... Jer 48:2
for in the going *d* of Horonaim ... Jer 48:5 4174
men are gone *d* to the slaughter ... Jer 48:15 3381
come *d* from thy glory, and sit in ... Jer 48:18 3381
for it is broken *d* ... Jer 48:20
howl, saying, How is it broken *d* ... Jer 48:39
I will bring thee *d* from thence ... Jer 49:16 3381
fallen, her walls are thrown *d* ... Jer 50:15 2040
let them go *d* to the slaughter ... Jer 50:27 3381
roll thee *d* from the rocks, and ... Jer 51:25
I will bring them *d* like lambs to ... Jer 51:40 3381
guard, brake *d* all the walls of ... Jer 52:14 5422
therefore she came *d* wonderfully ... Lam 1:9 3381
mine eye runneth *d* with water ... Lam 1:16
cast *d* from heaven unto the earth ... Lam 2:1
he hath thrown *d* in his wrath the ... Lam 2:2 2040
hath brought them *d* to the ground ... Lam 2:2
hang *d* their heads to the ground ... Lam 2:10 3381
he hath thrown *d*, and hath not ... Lam 2:17 2040
let tears run *d* like a river day ... Lam 2:18
Mine eye runneth *d* with rivers of ... Lam 3:48
Mine eye trickleth *d*, and ceaseth ... Lam 3:49
Till the LORD look *d*, and behold ... Lam 3:50
Behold their sitting *d*, and their ... Lam 3:63
d among the living creatures ... Eze 1:13
stood, they let *d* their wings ... Eze 1:24 7503
stood, and had let *d* their wings ... Eze 1:25 7503
I will cast *d* your slain men ... Eze 6:4 5307
and your images may be cut *d* ... Eze 6:6 1438
Then fell I *d* upon my face, and ... Eze 11:13
So will I break *d* the wall that ... Eze 13:14 2040
bring it *d* to the ground, so that ... Eze 13:14
they shall throw *d* thine eminent ... Eze 16:39 2040
shall break *d* thy high places ... Eze 16:39 5422
LORD have brought *d* the high tree ... Eze 17:24 8213
she lay *d* among lions, she ... Eze 19:2 7257
d among the lions, he became a ... Eze 19:6
she was cast *d* to the ground, and ... Eze 19:12
neither shall thy tears run *d* ... Eze 24:16
of Tyrus, and break *d* her towers ... Eze 26:4 2040
axes he shall break *d* thy towers ... Eze 26:9 5422
shall he tread *d* all thy streets ... Eze 26:11
shall go *d* to the ground ... Eze 26:11 3381
and they shall break *d* thy walls ... Eze 26:12 2040
shall come *d* from their thrones ... Eze 26:16 3381
When I shall bring thee *d* with ... Eze 26:20 3381
with them that go *d* to the pit ... Eze 26:20 3381
shall come *d* from their ships, ... Eze 27:29 3381
shall bring thee *d* to the pit ... Eze 28:8 3381
d in the midst of the stones of ... Eze 28:14
her foundations shall be broken *d* ... Eze 30:4 2040
pride of her power shall come *d* ... Eze 30:6 3381
the arms of Pharaoh shall fall *d* ... Eze 30:25
earth are gone *d* from his shadow ... Eze 31:12
with them that go *d* to the pit ... Eze 31:14 3381
he went *d* to the grave I caused a ... Eze 31:15 3381
when I cast him *d* to hell with ... Eze 31:16 3381
They also went *d* into hell with ... Eze 31:17 3381
yet shalt thou be brought *d* with ... Eze 31:18 3381
of Egypt, and cast them *d*, even ... Eze 32:18 3381
with them that go *d* into the pit ... Eze 32:18 3381
go *d*, and be thou laid with the ... Eze 32:19 3381
they are gone *d*, they lie ... Eze 32:21 3381
which are gone *d* uncircumcised ... Eze 32:24 3381
with them that go *d* to the pit ... Eze 32:24 3381
with them that go *d* to the pit ... Eze 32:25 3381
which are gone *d* to hell with ... Eze 32:27 3381
and with them that go *d* to the pit ... Eze 32:29 3381
which are gone *d* with the slain ... Eze 32:30 3381
with them that go *d* to the pit ... Eze 32:30 3381
and I will cause them to lie *d* ... Eze 34:15 7901
but ye must tread *d* with your ... Eze 34:18
shower to come *d* in his season ... Eze 34:26 3381
set me *d* in the midst of the ... Eze 37:1
the mountains shall be thrown *d* ... Eze 38:20 2040
neither cut *d* any out of the ... Eze 39:10
the waters came *d* from under from ... Eze 47:1 3381
go *d* into the desert, and go into ... Eze 47:8 3381
and all kinds of musick, ye fall *d* ... Dan 3:5
And whoso falleth not *d* and ... Dan 3:6
nations, and the languages, fell *d* ... Dan 3:7
all kinds of musick, shall fall *d* ... Dan 3:10
And whoso falleth not *d* and ... Dan 3:11
and all kinds of musick, ye fall *d* ... Dan 3:15
fell *d* bound into the midst of ... Dan 3:23
and an holy one came *d* from heaven ... Dan 4:13 5182
Hew *d* the tree, and cut off his ... Dan 4:14
an holy one coming *d* from heaven ... Dan 4:23 5182
heaven, and saying, Hew the tree *d* ... Dan 4:23
and whom he would he put *d* ... Dan 5:19 8214
going *d* of the sun to deliver him ... Dan 6:14 4606
till the thrones were cast *d* ... Dan 7:9
whole earth, and shall tread it *d* ... Dan 7:23
but he cast him *d* to the ground ... Dan 8:7
it cast *d* some of the host and of ... Dan 8:10 5307
place of his sanctuary was cast *d* ... Dan 8:11
it cast *d* the truth to the ground ... Dan 8:12
and he shall cast *d* many ten ... Dan 11:12 5307
and many shall fall *d* slain ... Dan 11:26
and will make them to lie *d* safely ... Hos 2:18 7901
I will bring them *d* as the fowls ... Hos 7:12 3381
he shall break *d* their altars ... Hos 10:2
desolate, the barns are broken *d* ... Joel 1:17 2040
cause to come *d* for you the rain ... Joel 2:23 3381
will bring them *d* into the valley ... Joel 3:2 3381
cause thy mighty ones to come *d* ... Joel 3:11 5181
come, get you *d*; for the press ... Joel 3:13 3381
mountains shall drop *d* new wine ... Joel 3:18
they lay themselves *d* upon ... Amos 2:8
he shall bring *d* thy strength ... Amos 3:11 3381
But let judgment run *d* as waters ... Amos 5:24
then go *d* to Gath of the ... Amos 6:2 3381
cause the sun to go *d* at noon ... Amos 8:9
thence will I bring them *d* ... Amos 9:2 3381
shall bring me *d* to the ground ... Obad 3 3381
stars, thence will I bring thee *d* ... Obad 4 3381
drink, and they shall swallow *d* ... Obad 16
of the LORD, and went *d* to Joppa ... Jonah 1:3 3381
went *d* into it, to go with them ... Jonah 1:3 3381
But Jonah was gone *d* into the ... Jonah 1:5 3381
I went *d* to the bottoms of the ... Jonah 2:6 3381
out of his place, and will come *d* ... Mic 1:3 3381
that are poured *d* a steep place ... Mic 1:4
I will pour *d* the stones thereof ... Mic 1:6
but evil came *d* from the LORD ... Mic 1:12 3381
the sun shall go *d* over the ... Mic 3:6
if he go through, both treadeth *d* ... Mic 5:8
throw *d* all thy strong holds ... Mic 5:11 2040
thy casting *d* shall be in the ... Mic 6:14
now shall she be trodden *d* as the ... Mic 7:10
and the rocks are thrown *d* by him ... Nah 1:6 5422
yet thus shall they be cut *d* ... Nah 1:12
all the merchant people are cut *d* ... Zeph 1:11
shall they lie *d* in the evening ... Zeph 2:7 7257
flocks shall lie *d* in the midst ... Zeph 2:14 7257
a place for beasts to lie *d* in ... Zeph 2:15 4769
for they shall feed and lie *d* ... Zeph 3:13 4769
and their riders shall come *d* ... Hag 2:22 3381
which tread *d* their enemies in ... Zec 10:5
of Assyria shall be brought *d* ... Zec 10:11 3381
d in his name, saith the LORD ... Zec 10:12
forest of the vintage is come *d* ... Zec 11:2 3381
shall build, but I will throw *d* ... Mal 1:4 2040
d of the same my name shall be ... Mal 1:11
And ye shall tread *d* the wicked ... Mal 4:3
with Mary his mother, and fell *d* ... Mt 2:11 *4098*
not forth good fruit is hewn *d* ... Mt 3:10 *1581*
be the Son of God, cast thyself *d* ... Mt 4:6 *2736*
I give thee, if thou wilt fall *d* ... Mt 4:9 *4098*
not forth good fruit is hewn *d* ... Mt 7:19 *1581*
When he was come *d* from the ... Mt 8:1 *2597*
shall sit *d* with Abraham, and ... Mt 8:11 *347*
d a steep place into the sea ... Mt 8:32 *2596*
sat *d* with him and his disciples ... Mt 9:10 *347*
shalt be brought *d* to hell ... Mt 11:23 *2601*
they drew to shore, and sat *d* ... Mt 13:48 *2523*
multitude to sit *d* on the grass ... Mt 14:19 *2597*
Peter was come *d* out of the ship ... Mt 14:29 *2597*
into a mountain, and sat *d* there ... Mt 15:29 *2521*
cast them *d* at Jesus' feet ... Mt 15:30 *4496*
multitude to sit *d* on the ground ... Mt 15:35 *377*
as they came *d* from the mountain, ... Mt 17:9 *2597*
a certain man, kneeling *d* to him ... Mt 17:14
The servant therefore fell *d* ... Mt 18:26
fellowservant fell *d* at his feet ... Mt 18:29
others cut *d* branches from the ... Mt 21:8 *2875*
that shall not be thrown *d* ... Mt 24:2 *2647*
is on the housetop not come *d* to ... Mt 24:17 *2597*
come, he sat *d* with the twelve ... Mt 26:20 *345*
he cast *d* the pieces of silver in ... Mt 27:5 *4496*
When he was set *d* on the judgment ... Mt 27:19 *2521*
sitting *d* they watched him there ... Mt 27:36 *2521*
Son of God, come *d* from the cross ... Mt 27:40 *2597*
let him now come *d* from the cross ... Mt 27:42 *2597*
shoes I am not worthy to stoop *d* ... Mk 1:7
him, and kneeling *d* to him ... Mk 1:40
they let *d* the bed wherein the ... Mk 2:4 *5465*
fell *d* before him, and cried, ... Mk 3:11
which came *d* from Jerusalem said ... Mk 3:22 *2597*
the herd ran violently *d* a steep ... Mk 5:13 *2596*
fell *d* before him, and told him ... Mk 5:33
sit *d* by companies upon the green ... Mk 6:39 *347*
And they sat *d* in ranks, by ... Mk 6:40 *377*
the people to sit *d* on the ground ... Mk 8:6 *377*
as they came *d* from the mountain, ... Mk 9:9 *2597*
And he sat *d*, and called the twelve ... Mk 9:35 *2523*
others cut *d* branches off the ... Mk 11:8 *2875*
that shall not be thrown *d* ... Mk 13:2 *2647*
housetop not go *d* into the house ... Mk 13:15 *2597*
thyself, and come *d* from the cross ... Mk 15:30 *2597*
Elias will come to take him *d* ... Mk 15:36 *2507*
bought fine linen, and took him *d* ... Mk 15:46 *2507*
He hath put *d* the mighty from ... Lk 1:52 *2507*
he went *d* with them, and came to ... Lk 2:51 *2597*
not forth good fruit is hewn *d* ... Lk 3:9 *1581*
of God, cast thyself *d* from hence ... Lk 4:9 *2736*
again to the minister, and sat *d* ... Lk 4:20 *2523*
they might cast him *d* headlong ... Lk 4:29 *2630*
came *d* to Capernaum, a city of ... Lk 4:31 *2718*
And he sat *d*, and taught the people ... Lk 5:3 *2523*
let *d* your nets for a draught ... Lk 5:4 *5465*
at thy word I will let *d* the net ... Lk 5:5 *5465*
he fell *d* at Jesus' knees, saying ... Lk 5:8
let him *d* through the tiling with ... Lk 5:19 *2524*
and of others that sat *d* with them ... Lk 5:29 *2621*
he came *d* with them, and stood in ... Lk 6:17 *2597*
good measure, pressed *d*, and ... Lk 6:38
house, and sat *d* to meat ... Lk 7:36 *347*
and it was trodden *d*, and the fowls ... Lk 8:5 *2662*
there came *d* a storm of wind on ... Lk 8:23 *2597*
fell *d* before him, and with a loud ... Lk 8:28
the herd ran violently *d* a steep ... Lk 8:33 *2596*
he fell *d* at Jesus' feet, and ... Lk 8:41
falling *d* before him, she ... Lk 8:47
Make them sit *d* by fifties in a ... Lk 9:14 *2625*
did so, and made them all sit *d* ... Lk 9:15 *347*
they were come *d* from the hill ... Lk 9:37 *2778*
a coming, the devil threw him *d* ... Lk 9:42
sayings sink *d* into your ears ... Lk 9:44
fire to come *d* from heaven ... Lk 9:54 *2597*
heaven, shalt be thrust *d* to hell ... Lk 10:15 *2601*

A certain man went *d* from ... Lk 10:30 2597
by chance there came *d* a certain ... Lk 10:31 2597
and he went in, and sat *d* to meat ... Lk 11:37 377
I will pull *d* my barns, and build ... Lk 12:18 2507
and make them to sit *d* to meat ... Lk 12:37 347
cut it *d*; why cumbereth it ... Lk 13:7 1581
after that thou shalt cut it *d* ... Lk 13:9 1581
shall sit *d* in the kingdom of God ... Lk 13:29 347
sit not *d* in the highest room ... Lk 14:8 2625
go and sit *d* in the lowest room ... Lk 14:10 377
a tower, sitteth not *d* first ... Lk 14:28 2523
another king, sitteth not *d* first ... Lk 14:31 2523
sit *d* quickly, and write fifty ... Lk 16:6 2523
the field, Go and sit *d* to meat ... Lk 17:7 377
fell *d* on his face at his feet, ... Lk 17:16
him not come *d* to take it away ... Lk 17:31 2597
this man went *d* to his house ... Lk 18:14 2597
Zacchaeus, make haste, and come *d* ... Lk 19:5 2597
And he made haste, and came *d* ... Lk 19:6 2597
takest up that thou layedst not *d* ... Lk 19:21
man, taking up that I laid not *d* ... Lk 19:22
that shall not be thrown *d* ... Lk 21:6 2647
be trodden *d* of the Gentiles ... Lk 21:24
when the hour was come, he sat *d* ... Lk 22:14 377
a stone's cast, and kneeled *d* ... Lk 22:41
of blood falling *d* to the ground ... Lk 22:44 2597
the hall, and were set *d* together ... Lk 22:55 4776
Peter sat *d* among them ... Lk 22:55 2521
And he took it *d*, and wrapped it in ... Lk 23:53 2507
bowed *d* their faces to the earth, ... Lk 24:5
and stooping *d*, he beheld the ... Lk 24:12 3879
After this he went *d* to Capernaum ... Jn 2:12 2597
but he that came *d* from heaven ... Jn 3:13 2597
besought him that he would come *d* ... Jn 4:47 2597
him, Sir, come *d* ere my child die ... Jn 4:49 2597
And as he was now going *d*, his ... Jn 4:51 2597
For an angel went *d* at a certain ... Jn 5:4 2597
another steppeth *d* before me ... Jn 5:7 2597
And Jesus said, Make the men sit *d* ... Jn 6:10 377
So the men sat *d*, in number about ... Jn 6:10 377
disciples to them that were set *d* ... Jn 6:11 345
his disciples went *d* unto the sea ... Jn 6:16 2597
is he which cometh *d* from heaven ... Jn 6:33 2597
For I came *d* from heaven, not to ... Jn 6:38 2597
bread which came *d* from heaven ... Jn 6:41 2597
he saith, I came *d* from heaven ... Jn 6:42 2597
bread which cometh *d* from heaven ... Jn 6:50 2597
bread which came *d* from heaven ... Jn 6:51 2597
bread which came *d* from heaven ... Jn 6:58 2597
and he sat *d*, and taught them ... Jn 8:2 2523
But Jesus stooped *d*, and with his ... Jn 8:6 2736
And again he stooped *d*, and wrote ... Jn 8:8 2736
I lay *d* my life for the sheep ... Jn 10:15
love me, because I lay *d* my life ... Jn 10:17
from me, but I lay it *d* of myself ... Jn 10:18
I have power to lay it *d*, and I ... Jn 10:18
she fell *d* at his feet, saying ... Jn 11:32
his garments, and was set *d* again ... Jn 13:12 377
I will lay *d* my life for thy sake ... Jn 13:37
Wilt thou lay *d* thy life for my ... Jn 13:38
that a man lay *d* his life for his ... Jn 15:13
sat *d* in the judgment seat in a ... Jn 19:13 2523
And he stooping *d*, and looking in, ... Jn 20:5 3879
and as she wept, she stooped *d* ... Jn 20:11 3879
laid them *d* at the apostles' feet ... Acts 4:35
hearing these words fell *d* ... Acts 5:5
Then fell she *d* straightway at ... Acts 5:10
So Jacob went *d* into Egypt ... Acts 7:15 2597
am come *d* to deliver them ... Acts 7:34 2597
the witnesses laid *d* their ... Acts 7:58
And he kneeled *d*, and cried with a ... Acts 7:60
Then Philip went *d* to the city of ... Acts 8:5 2718
Who, when they were come *d* ... Acts 8:15 2597
goeth *d* from Jerusalem unto Gaza ... Acts 8:26 2597
they went *d* both into the water, ... Acts 8:38 2597
let him *d* by the wall in a basket ... Acts 9:25 2524
they brought him *d* to Caesarea ... Acts 9:30 2609
he came *d* also to the saints ... Acts 9:32 2718
put them all forth, and kneeled *d* ... Acts 9:40
corners, and let *d* to the earth ... Acts 10:11 2524
Arise therefore, and get thee *d* ... Acts 10:20 2597
Then Peter went *d* to the men ... Acts 10:21 2597
fell *d* at his feet, and worshipped ... Acts 10:25
let *d* from heaven by four corners ... Acts 11:5 2524
he went *d* from Judaea to Caesarea ... Acts 12:19 2718
on the sabbath day, and sat *d* ... Acts 13:14 2523
they took him *d* from the tree ... Acts 13:29 2507
The gods are come *d* to us in the ... Acts 14:11 2597
Perga, they went *d* into Attalia ... Acts 14:25 2597
certain men which came *d* from ... Acts 15:1 2718
of David, which is fallen *d* ... Acts 15:16
passing by Mysia came *d* to Troas ... Acts 16:8 2597
and we sat *d*, and spake unto the ... Acts 16:13 2523
fell *d* before Paul and Silas, ... Acts 16:29
upside *d* are come hither also ... Acts 17:6 387
the church, he went *d* to Antioch ... Acts 18:22 2597
image which fell *d* from Jupiter ... Acts 19:35
he sunk *d* with sleep ... Acts 20:9 2736
fell *d* from the third loft, and ... Acts 20:9
And Paul went *d*, and fell on him, ... Acts 20:10 2597
he had thus spoken, he kneeled *d* ... Acts 20:36
we kneeled *d* on the shore, and ... Acts 21:5
there came *d* from Judaea a ... Acts 21:10 2718
and centurions, and ran *d* unto them ... Acts 21:32 2701
to appear, and brought Paul *d* ... Acts 22:30 2609
commanded the soldiers to go *d* ... Acts 23:10 2597
he bring him *d* unto you to morrow ... Acts 23:15 2609
thee that thou wouldest bring *d* ... Acts 23:20 2609
the chief captain shall come *d* ... Acts 24:22 2597
go *d* with me, and accuse this man, ... Acts 25:5 4782
ten days, he went *d* unto Caesarea ... Acts 25:6 2597
the Jews which came *d* from ... Acts 25:7 2597
d in Adria, about midnight the ... Acts 27:27 1308
when they had let *d* the boat into ... Acts 27:30 5465
or fallen *d* dead suddenly ... Acts 28:6 2667
is, to bring Christ *d* from above ... Rom 10:6 2609
and digged *d* thine altars ... Rom 11:3 2679
see, and bow *d* their back alway ... Rom 11:10 4781
my life laid *d* their own necks ... Rom 16:4 5294
written, The people sat *d* to eat ... 1Cor 10:7 2523
so falling *d* on his face he will ... 1Cor 14:25
when he shall have put *d* all rule ... 1Cor 15:24 2673
cast *d*, but not destroyed ... 2Cor 4:9 2598
comforteth those that are cast *d* ... 2Cor 7:6 5011
to the pulling *d* of strong holds ... 2Cor 10:4 2506
Casting *d* imaginations, and every ... 2Cor 10:5 2504
a basket was I let *d* by the wall ... 2Cor 11:33 5465
hath broken *d* the middle wall of ... Eph 2:14
not the sun go *d* upon your wrath ... Eph 4:26 1931
sat *d* on the right hand of the ... Heb 1:3 2523
sat *d* on the right hand of God ... Heb 10:12 2597
faith the walls of Jericho fell *d* ... Heb 11:30
is set *d* at the right hand of the ... Heb 12:2
lift up the hands which hang *d* ... Heb 12:12 3935
cometh *d* from the Father of ... Jas 1:17 2597
who have reaped *d* your fields ... Jas 5:4
the Holy Ghost sent *d* from heaven ... 1Pet 1:12
sinned, but cast them *d* to hell ... 2Pet 2:4
because he laid *d* his life for us ... 1Jn 3:16
we ought to lay *d* our lives for ... 1Jn 3:16 2597
with a garment *d* to the foot ... Rev 1:13
which cometh *d* out of heaven from ... Rev 3:12 2597
am set *d* with my Father in his ... Rev 3:21 2523
twenty elders fall *d* before him ... Rev 4:10
elders fell *d* before the Lamb ... Rev 5:8
the four and twenty elders fell *d* ... Rev 5:14
mighty angel come *d* from heaven ... Rev 10:1 2597
accuser of our brethren is cast *d* ... Rev 12:10 2598
for the devil is come *d* unto you ... Rev 12:12 2597
so that he maketh fire come *d* ... Rev 13:13 2597
another angel come *d* from heaven ... Rev 18:1 2597
great city Babylon be thrown *d* ... Rev 18:21
elders and the four beasts fell *d* ... Rev 19:4
I saw an angel come *d* from heaven ... Rev 20:1 2597
fire came *d* from God out of ... Rev 20:9 2597
coming *d* from God out of heaven, ... Rev 21:2 2597
I fell *d* to worship before the ... Rev 22:8

DOWNSITTING

Thou knowest my *d* and mine ... Ps 139:2 3427

DOWNWARD

Judah shall yet again take root *d* ... 2Kin 19:30 4295
beast that goeth *d* to the earth ... Eccl 3:21 4295
of Judah shall again take root *d* ... Is 37:31 4295
appearance of his loins even *d* ... Eze 1:27 4295
appearance of his loins even *d* ... Eze 8:2 4295

DOWRY

God hath endued me with a good *d* ... Gen 30:20 2065
Ask me never so much *d* and gift, ... Gen 34:12 4119
according to the *d* of virgins ... Ex 22:17 4119
The king desireth not any *d* ... 1Sa 18:25 4119

DRAG

net, and gather them in their *d* ... Hab 1:15 4365
net, and burn incense unto their *d* ... Hab 1:16 4365

DRAGGING

cubits,) *d* the net with fishes ... Jn 21:8 4951

DRAGON

valley, even before the *d* well ... Neh 2:13 8577
the *d* shalt thou trample under ... Ps 91:13 8577
he shall slay the *d* that is in ... Is 27:1 8577
hath cut Rahab, and wounded the *d* ... Is 51:9 8577
he hath swallowed me up like a *d* ... Jer 51:34 8577
the great *d* that lieth in the ... Eze 29:3 8577
and behold a great red *d*, having ... Rev 12:3 1404
the *d* stood before the woman ... Rev 12:4 1404
his angels fought against the *d* ... Rev 12:7 1404
the *d* fought and his angels, ... Rev 12:7 1404
the great *d* was cast out, that ... Rev 12:9 1404
when the *d* saw that he was cast ... Rev 12:13 1404
which the *d* cast out of his mouth ... Rev 12:16 1404
the *d* was wroth with the woman, ... Rev 12:17 1404
the *d* gave him his power, and his ... Rev 13:2 1404
they worshipped the *d* which gave ... Rev 13:4 1404
like a lamb, and he spake as a *d* ... Rev 13:11 1404
come out of the mouth of the *d* ... Rev 16:13 1404
And he laid hold on the *d*, that ... Rev 20:2 1404

DRAGONS

Their wine is the poison of *d* ... Deut 32:33 8577
I am a brother to *d*, and a ... Job 30:29 8577
sore broken us in the place of *d* ... Ps 44:19 8577
the heads of the *d* in the waters ... Ps 74:13 8577
the LORD from the earth, ye *d* ... Ps 148:7 8577
d in their pleasant palaces ... Is 13:22 8577
and it shall be an habitation of *d* ... Is 34:13 8577
in the habitation of *d*, where ... Is 35:7 8577
the field shall honour me, the *d* ... Is 43:20 8577
Jerusalem heaps, and a den of *d* ... Jer 9:11 8577
of Judah desolate, and a den of *d* ... Jer 10:22 8577
they snuffed up the wind like *d* ... Jer 14:6 8577
Hazor shall be a dwelling for *d* ... Jer 49:33 8577
heaps, a dwelling place for *d* ... Jer 51:37 8577
I will make a wailing like the *d* ... Mic 1:8 8577
waste for the *d* of the wilderness ... Mal 1:3 8568

DRAMS

talents and ten thousand *d* ... 1Chr 29:7 150
and one thousand *d* of gold ... Ezr 2:69 1871
basons of gold, of a thousand *d* ... Ezr 8:27 150
the treasure a thousand *d* of gold ... Neh 7:70 1871
work twenty thousand *d* of gold ... Neh 7:71 1871
was twenty thousand *d* of gold ... Neh 7:72 1871

DRANK

he *d* of the wine, and was drunken ... Gen 9:21 8354
so I *d*, and she made the camels ... Gen 24:46 8354
and he brought him wine, and he *d* ... Gen 27:25 8354
And they *d*, and were merry with him. Gen 43:34 8354
abundantly, and the congregation *d* ... Num 20:11 8354
d the wine of their drink ... Deut 32:38 8354
d of his own cup, and lay in his ... 2Sa 12:3 8354
bread in his house, and *d* water ... 1Kin 13:19 8354
and he *d* of the brook ... 1Kin 17:6
meat, and of the wine which he *d* ... Dan 1:5 4960
nor with the wine which he *d* ... Dan 1:8 4960
d wine before the thousand ... Dan 5:1 8355
and his concubines, *d* in them ... Dan 5:3 8355
They *d* wine, and praised the gods ... Dan 5:4 8355
and they all *d* of it ... Mk 14:23 4095
They did eat, they *d*, they ... Lk 17:27 4095
they did eat, they *d*, they bought ... Lk 17:28 4095
d thereof himself, and his ... Jn 4:12 4095
for they *d* of that spiritual Rock ... 1Cor 10:4 4095

DRAUGHT

made it a *d* house unto this day ... 2Kin 10:27 4280
belly, and is cast out into the *d* ... Mt 15:17 856
belly, and goeth out into the *d* ... Mk 7:19 856
and let down your nets for a *d* ... Lk 5:4 61
at the *d* of the fishes which they ... Lk 5:9 61

DRAVE

wheels, that they *d* them heavily ... Ex 14:25 5090
they *d* not out the Canaanites ... Josh 16:10 3423
which *d* them out from before you, ... Josh 24:12 1644
the LORD *d* out from before us all ... Josh 24:18 1644
he *d* out the inhabitants of the ... Judg 1:19 3423
d them out from before you, and ... Judg 6:9 1644
which they *d* before those other ... 1Sa 30:20 5090
sons of Abinadab, *d* the new cart ... 2Sa 6:3 5090
Syria, and *d* the Jews from Elath ... 2Kin 16:6 5394
Jeroboam *d* Israel from following ... 2Kin 17:21 5071
and Uzza and Ahio *d* the cart ... 1Chr 13:7 5090
whom God *d* out before the face of ... Acts 7:45 1856
he *d* them from the judgment seat ... Acts 18:16 556

DRAW

time that women go out to *d* water ... Gen 24:11 7579
of the city come out to *d* water ... Gen 24:13 7579
I will *d* water for thy camels ... Gen 24:19 7579
again unto the well to *d* water ... Gen 24:20 7579
virgin cometh forth to *d* water ... Gen 24:43 7579
I will also *d* for thy camels ... Gen 24:44 7579
And he said, *D* not nigh hither ... Ex 3:5
them, *D* out and take you a lamb ... Ex 12:21 4900
I will *d* my sword, my hand shall ... Ex 15:9 7324
will *d* out a sword after you ... Lev 26:33 7324
so that he could not *d* the dagger ... Judg 3:22 8025
d toward mount Tabor, and take ... Judg 4:6 4900
I will *d* unto thee to the river ... Judg 4:7 4900
D thy sword, and slay me, that men ... Judg 9:54 8025
let us *d* near to one of these ... Judg 19:13
d them from the city unto the ... Judg 20:32 5423
maidens going out to *d* water ... 1Sa 9:11 7579
Let us *d* near hither unto God ... 1Sa 14:36
D ye near hither, all the chief ... 1Sa 14:38
D thy sword, and thrust me through ... 1Sa 31:4 8025
we will *d* it into the river, ... 2Sa 17:13 5498
D thy sword, and thrust me through ... 1Chr 10:4 8025
and every man shall *d* after him ... Job 21:33 4900
he trusteth that he can *d* up ... Job 40:23 1518
Canst thou *d* out leviathan with ... Job 41:1 4900
D me not away with the wicked, and ... Ps 28:3 4900
D out also the spear, and stop the ... Ps 35:3 7324
D nigh unto my soul, and redeem it ... Ps 69:18
is good for me to *d* near to God ... Ps 73:28
wilt thou *d* out thine anger to ... Ps 85:5 4900
they *d* near unto the gates of ... Ps 107:18
They *d* nigh that follow after ... Ps 119:150
of understanding will *d* it out ... Prov 20:5 1802
come not, nor the years *d* nigh ... Eccl 12:1
D me, we will run after thee ... Song 1:4 4900
Woe unto them that *d* iniquity ... Is 5:18 4900
of the Holy One of Israel *d* nigh ... Is 5:19
ye *d* water out of the wells of ... Is 12:3 7579
people *d* near me with their mouth ... Is 29:13
d near together, ye that are ... Is 45:20
But *d* near hither, ye sons of the ... Is 57:3
a wide mouth, and *d* out the tongue ... Is 57:4 748
if thou *d* out thy soul to the ... Is 58:10 6329
that *d* the bow, to Tubal, and ... Is 66:19 4900
and I will cause him to *d* near ... Jer 30:21
and shield, and *d* near to battle ... Jer 46:3
of the flock shall *d* them out ... Jer 49:20 5498
of the flock shall *d* them out ... Jer 50:45 5498
the sea monsters *d* out the breast ... Lam 4:3 2502
I will *d* out a sword after them ... Eze 5:2 7324
I will *d* out a sword after them ... Eze 5:12 7324
charge over the city to *d* near ... Eze 9:1
I will *d* out the sword after them ... Eze 12:14 7324
will *d* forth my sword out of his ... Eze 21:3 3318
hast caused thy days to *d* near ... Eze 22:4
they shall *d* their swords against ... Eze 28:7 7324
they shall *d* their swords against ... Eze 30:11 7324
d her and all her multitudes ... Eze 32:20 4900
let all the men of war *d* near ... Joel 3:9
D thee waters for the siege, ... Nah 3:14 7579
to *d* out fifty vessels out of the ... Hag 2:16 2834
D out now, and bear unto the ... Jn 2:8 501
a woman of Samaria to *d* water ... Jn 4:7 501
Sir, thou hast nothing to *d* with ... Jn 4:11 502
not, neither come hither to *d* ... Jn 4:15 501
Father which hath sent me *d* him ... Jn 6:44 1670
the earth, will *d* all men unto me ... Jn 12:32 1670
now they were not able to *d* it ... Jn 21:6 1670
to *d* away disciples after them ... Acts 20:30 645
by the which we *d* nigh unto God ... Heb 7:19
Let us *d* near with a true heart ... Heb 10:22 4334
but if any man *d* back, my soul ... Heb 10:38 5288
of them who *d* back unto perdition ... Heb 10:39 5289
d you before the judgment seats ... Jas 2:6 1670
D nigh to God, and he will *d* ... Jas 4:8

DRAWER
thy wood unto the *d* of thy water Deut 29:11 7579

DRAWERS
wood and *d* of water unto all the Josh 9:21 7579
d of water for the house of my Josh 9:23 7579
d of water for the congregation, Josh 9:27 7579

DRAWETH
the wife of the one *d* near for to Deut 25:11
now the day *d* toward evening, I Judg 19:9 7503
He *d* also the mighty with his Job 24:22 4900
his soul *d* near unto the grave, Job 33:22
when he *d* him into his net Ps 10:9 4900
my life *d* nigh unto the grave Ps 88:3
that *d* near the time of her Is 26:17
The time is come, the day *d* near Eze 7:12
This people *d* nigh unto me with Mt 15:8
and the time *d* near Lk 21:8
for your redemption *d* nigh Lk 21:28
for the coming of the Lord *d* nigh Jas 5:8

DRAWING
archers in the places of *d* water Judg 5:11 4857
the sea, and *d* nigh unto the ship Jn 6:19 *1096*

DRAWN
way, and his sword *d* in his hand Num 22:23 8025
way, and his sword *d* in his hand Num 22:31 8025
and which hath not *d* in the yoke Deut 21:3 4900
not hear, but shalt be *d* away Deut 30:17 5080
him with his sword *d* in his hand Josh 5:13 8025
till we have *d* them from the city Josh 8:6 5423
were *d* away from the city Josh 8:16 5423
the border was *d* from the top of Josh 15:9 8388
and the border was *d* to Baalah Josh 15:9 8388
and the border was *d* to Shicron Josh 15:11 8388
And the border was *d* thence Josh 18:14 8388
was *d* from the north, and went Josh 18:17 8388
were *d* away from the city Judg 20:31 5423
that which the young men have *d* Ruth 2:9 7579
having a *d* sword in his hand 1Chr 21:16 8025
It is *d*, and cometh out of the Job 20:25 8025
The wicked have *d* out the sword Ps 37:14 6605
than oil, yet were they *d* swords Ps 55:21 6609
them that are *d* unto death Prov 24:11 3947
from the swords, from the *d* sword Is 21:15 5203
the milk, and *d* from the breasts Is 28:9 6267
with the burial of an ass, *d* Jer 22:19 5498
with lovingkindness have I *d* thee Jer 31:3 4900
he hath *d* back his right hand Lam 2:3 7725
have *d* forth my sword out of his Eze 21:5 3318
thou, The sword, the sword is *d* Eze 21:28 6605
all were *d* up again into heaven Acts 11:10 *385*
when he is *d* away of his own lust Jas 1:14 *1828*

DREAD
the *d* of you shall be upon every Gen 9:2 2844
Fear and *d* shall fall upon them Ex 15:16 6343
D not, neither be afraid of them Deut 1:29 6206
will I begin to put the *d* of thee Deut 2:25 6343
the *d* of you upon all the land Deut 11:25 4172
d not, nor be dismayed 1Chr 22:13 3372
and his *d* fall upon you Job 13:11 6343
let not thy *d* make me afraid Job 13:21 367
your fear, and let him be your *d* Is 8:13 6206

DREADFUL
and said, How *d* is this place Gen 28:17 3372
A *d* sound is in his ears Job 15:21 6343
were so high that they were *d* Eze 1:18 3374
and behold a fourth beast, *d* Dan 7:7 1763
from all the others, exceeding *d* Dan 7:19 1763
d God, keeping the covenant and Dan 9:4 3372
They are terrible and *d* Hab 1:7 3372
my name is *d* among the heathen Mal 1:14 3372
of the great and *d* day of the LORD Mal 4:5 3372

DREAM
came to Abimelech in a *d* by night Gen 20:3 2472
And God said unto him in a *d* Gen 20:6 2472
up mine eyes, and saw in a *d* Gen 31:10 2472
angel of God spake unto me in a *d* Gen 31:11 2472
Laban the Syrian in a *d* by night Gen 31:24 2472
And Joseph dreamed a *d*, and he told Gen 37:5 2472
this *d* which I have dreamed Gen 37:6 2472
And he dreamed yet another *d* Gen 37:9 2472
Behold, I have dreamed a *d* more Gen 37:9 2472
What is this *d* that thou hast Gen 37:10 2472
And they dreamed a *d* both of them Gen 40:5 2472
each man his *d* in one night Gen 40:5 2472
to the interpretation of his *d* Gen 40:5 2472
unto him, We have dreamed a *d* Gen 40:8 2472
chief butler told his *d* to Joseph Gen 40:9 2472
and said to him, In my *d* Gen 40:9 2472
unto Joseph, I also was in my *d* Gen 40:16 2472
awoke, and, behold, it was a *d* Gen 41:7 2472
and Pharaoh told them his *d* Gen 41:8 2472
And we dreamed a *d* in one night Gen 41:11 2472
to the interpretation of his *d* Gen 41:11 2472
to his *d* he did interpret Gen 41:12 2472
unto Joseph, I have dreamed a *d* Gen 41:15 2472
understand a *d* to interpret it Gen 41:15 2472
Pharaoh said unto Joseph, In my *d* Gen 41:17 2472
And I saw in my *d*, and, behold, Gen 41:22 2472
Pharaoh, The *d* of Pharaoh is one Gen 41:25 2472
are seven years: the *d* is one Gen 41:26 2472
for that the *d* was doubled unto Gen 41:32 2472
and will speak unto him in a *d* Num 12:6 2472
man that told a *d* unto his fellow Judg 7:13 2472
and said, Behold, I dreamed a *d* Judg 7:13 2472
Gideon heard the telling of the *d* Judg 7:15 2472
to Solomon in a *d* by night 1Kin 3:5 2472
and, behold, it was a *d* 1Kin 3:15 2472
He shall fly away as a *d*, and Job 20:8 2472
In a *d*, in a vision of the night, Job 33:15 2472
As a *d* when one awaketh Ps 73:20 2472
of Zion, we were like them that *d* Ps 126:1 2472
For a *d* cometh through the Eccl 5:3 2472
shall be as a *d* of a night vision Is 29:7 2472
hath a *d*, let him tell a *d* Jer 23:28 2472
unto them, I have dreamed a *d* Dan 2:3 2472
spirit was troubled to know the *d* Dan 2:3 2472
tell thy servants the *d*, and we Dan 2:4 2493
will not make known unto me the *d* Dan 2:5 2493
But if ye shew the *d*, and the Dan 2:6 2493
therefore shew me the *d*, and the Dan 2:6 2493
the king tell his servants the *d* Dan 2:7 2493
will not make known unto me the *d* Dan 2:9 2493
therefore tell me the *d*, and I Dan 2:9 2493
unto me the *d* which I have seen Dan 2:26 2493
Thy *d*, and the visions of thy head Dan 2:28 2493
This is the *d*; and we will Dan 2:36 2493
and the *d* is certain, and the Dan 2:45 2493
I saw a *d* which made me afraid, Dan 4:5 2493
me the interpretation of the *d* Dan 4:6 2493
and I told the *d* before them Dan 4:7 2493
and before him I told the *d* Dan 4:8 2493
visions of my *d* that I have seen Dan 4:9 2493
This *d* I king Nebuchadnezzar have Dan 4:18 2493
said, Belteshazzar, let not the *d* Dan 4:19 2493
the *d* be to them that hate thee, Dan 4:19 2493
king of Babylon Daniel had a *d* Dan 7:1 2493
then he wrote the *d*, and told the Dan 7:1 2493
your old men shall *d* dreams Joel 2:28 2492
the Lord appeared unto him in a *d* Mt 1:20 *3677*
being warned of God in a *d* that Mt 2:12 *3677*
Lord appeareth to Joseph in a *d* Mt 2:13 *3677*
in a *d* to Joseph in Egypt Mt 2:19 *3677*
being warned of God in a *d* Mt 2:22 *3677*
this day in a *d* because of him Mt 27:19 *3677*
and your old men shall *d* dreams Acts 2:17 *1798*

DREAMED
And he *d*, and behold a ladder set Gen 28:12 2492
Joseph *d* a dream, and he told it Gen 37:5 2492
you, this dream which I have *d* Gen 37:6 2492
he *d* yet another dream, and told Gen 37:9 2492
Behold, I have *d* a dream more Gen 37:9 2492
is this dream that thou hast *d* Gen 37:10 2492
they *d* a dream both of them, each Gen 40:5 2492
said unto him, We have *d* a dream Gen 40:8 2492
of two full years, that Pharaoh *d* Gen 41:1 2492
And he slept and *d* the second time Gen 41:5 2492
we *d* a dream in one night, I and Gen 41:11 2492
we *d* each man according to the Gen 41:11 2492
I have *d* a dream, and there is Gen 41:15 2492
the dreams which he *d* of them Gen 42:9 2492
I *d* a dream, and, lo, a cake of Judg 7:13 2492
saying, I have *d*, I have *d* Jer 23:25 2492
dreams which ye cause to be *d* Jer 29:8 2492
Nebuchadnezzar *d* dreams, Dan 2:1 2492
I have *d* a dream, and my spirit Dan 2:3 2492

DREAMER
to another, Behold, this *d* cometh Gen 37:19
or a *d* of dreams, and giveth thee Deut 13:1 2492
that prophet, or that *d* of dreams Deut 13:3 2492
or that *d* of dreams, shall be put Deut 13:5 2492

DREAMERS
to your diviners, nor to your *d* Jer 27:9 2492
these filthy *d* defile the flesh Jude 8 *1797*

DREAMETH
even be as when an hungry man *d* Is 29:8 2492
or as when a thirsty man *d* Is 29:8 2492

DREAMS
hated him yet the more for his *d* Gen 37:8 2472
see what will become of his *d* Gen 37:20 2472
and he interpreted to us our *d* Gen 41:12 2472
Joseph remembered the *d* which he Gen 42:9 2472
you a prophet, or a dreamer of *d* Deut 13:1 2472
prophet, or that dreamer of *d* Deut 13:3 2472
prophet, or that dreamer of *d* Deut 13:5 2472
answered him not, neither by *d* 1Sa 28:6 2472
neither by prophets, nor by *d* 1Sa 28:15 2472
Then thou scarest me with *d* Job 7:14 2472
For in the multitude of *d* Eccl 5:7 2472
to forget my name by their *d* Jer 23:27 2472
them that prophesy false *d* Jer 23:32 2472
neither hearken to your *d* which Jer 29:8 2472
understanding in all visions and *d* Dan 1:17 2472
Nebuchadnezzar dreamed *d* Dan 2:1 2472
for to shew the king his *d* Dan 2:2 2472
understanding, interpreting of *d* Dan 5:12 2493
your old men shall dream *d* Joel 2:28 2472
seen a lie, and have told false *d* Zec 10:2 2472
and your old men shall dream *d* Acts 2:17 *1797*

DREGS
but the *d* thereof, all the wicked Ps 75:8 8105
thou hast drunken the *d* of the Is 51:17 6907
even the *d* of the cup of my fury Is 51:22 6907

DRESS
into the garden of Eden to *d* it Gen 2:15 5647
and he hasted to *d* it Gen 18:7 6213
d them, but shalt neither drink Deut 28:39 5647
to *d* for the wayfaring man that 2Sa 12:4 6213
d the meat in my sight, that I 2Sa 13:5 6213
Amnon's house, and *d* him meat 2Sa 13:7 6213
d it for me and my son, that we 1Kin 17:12 6213
I will *d* the other bullock, and 1Kin 18:23 6213
for yourselves, and *d* it first 1Kin 18:25 6213

DRESSED
milk, and the calf which he had *d* Gen 18:8 6213
all that is *d* in the fryingpan, Lev 7:9 6213
of wine, and five sheep ready *d* 1Sa 25:18 6213
d it for the man that was come to 2Sa 12:4 6213
king, and had neither *d* his feet 2Sa 19:24 6213
was given them, and they *d* it 1Kin 18:26 6213
meet for them by whom it is *d* Heb 6:7 *1090*

DRESSER
he unto the *d* of his vineyard Lk 13:7 *289*

DRESSERS
vine *d* in the mountains, and in 2Chr 26:10 3755

DRESSETH
when he *d* the lamps, he shall Ex 30:7 3190

DREW
And Abraham *d* near, and said, Wilt Gen 18:23
water, and *d* for all his camels Gen 24:20 8025
down unto the well, and *d* water Gen 24:45 7579
and they *d* and lifted up Joseph out Gen 37:28 4900
as he *d* back his hand, that, Gen 38:29 7725
the time *d* nigh that Israel must Gen 47:29
Because I *d* him out of the water Ex 2:10 4871
d water, and filled the troughs to Ex 2:16 1802
also *d* water enough for us, and Ex 2:19 1802
And when Pharaoh *d* nigh, the Ex 14:10
Moses *d* near unto the thick Ex 20:21
and all the congregation *d* near Lev 9:5
d nigh, and came before the city, Josh 8:11
For Joshua *d* not his hand back, Josh 8:26 7725
twenty thousand men that *d* sword Judg 8:10 8025
But the youth *d* not his sword Judg 8:20 8025
thousand footmen that *d* sword Judg 20:2 8025
and six thousand men that *d* sword Judg 20:15 8025
hundred thousand men that *d* sword Judg 20:17 8025
all these *d* the sword Judg 20:25 8025
all these *d* the sword Judg 20:35 8025
liers in wait *d* themselves along Judg 20:37 4900
thousand men that *d* the sword Judg 20:46 8025
So he *d* off his shoe Ruth 4:8 8025
d water, and poured it out before 1Sa 7:6 7579
the Philistines *d* near to battle 1Sa 7:10
Then Saul *d* near to Samuel in the 1Sa 9:18
And the Philistine *d* near morning 1Sa 17:16
he *d* near to the Philistine 1Sa 17:40
came on and *d* near unto David 1Sa 17:41
d nigh to meet David, that David 1Sa 17:48
d it out of the sheath thereof, 1Sa 17:51 8025
And Joab *d* nigh, and the people 2Sa 10:13
And he came apace, and *d* near 2Sa 18:25
he *d* me out of many waters 2Sa 22:17 4871
d water out of the well of 2Sa 23:16 7579
valiant men that *d* the sword 2Sa 24:9 8025
Now the days of David *d* nigh that 1Kin 2:1
they *d* out the staves, that the 1Kin 8:8 748
a certain man *d* a bow at a 1Kin 22:34 4900
seven hundred men that *d* swords 2Kin 3:26 8025
Jehu *d* a bow with his full 2Kin 9:24
d water out of the well of 1Chr 11:18 7579
d nigh before the Syrians unto 1Chr 19:14
d forth the Syrians that were 1Chr 19:16 3318
hundred thousand men that *d* sword 1Chr 21:5 8025
and ten thousand men that *d* sword 1Chr 21:5 8025
they *d* out the staves of the ark, 2Chr 5:9 748
d bows, two hundred and fourscore 2Chr 14:8 1869
a certain man *d* a bow at a 2Chr 18:33 4900
So Esther *d* near, and touched the Est 5:2
his decree *d* near to be put in Est 9:1
he *d* me out of many waters Ps 18:16 4871
were afraid, *d* near, and came Is 41:5
So they *d* up Jeremiah with cords, Jer 38:13 4900
I *d* them with cords of a man, Hos 11:4 4900
she *d* not near to her God Zeph 3:2
they *d* to shore, and sat down, and Mt 13:48 *307*
when they *d* nigh unto Jerusalem, Mt 21:1
when the time of the fruit *d* near Mt 21:34
d his sword, and struck a servant Mt 26:51 *645*
of Gennesaret, and *d* to the shore Mk 6:53 *4358*
of them that stood by *d* a sword Mk 14:47 *4685*
Then *d* near unto him all the Lk 15:1
d nigh to the house, he heard Lk 15:25
feast of unleavened bread *d* nigh Lk 22:1
d near unto Jesus to kiss him Lk 22:47
preparation, and the sabbath *d* on Lk 23:54 *2020*
and reasoned, Jesus himself *d* near Lk 24:15
they *d* nigh unto the village, Lk 24:28
servants which *d* the water knew Jn 2:9 *501*
Simon Peter having a sword *d* it Jn 18:10 *1670*
d the net to land full of great Jn 21:11 *1670*
d away much people after him Acts 5:37 *868*
the time of the promise *d* nigh Acts 7:17
as he *d* near to behold it, the Acts 7:31 *4334*
d nigh unto the city, Peter went Acts 10:9
d him out of the city, supposing Acts 14:19 *4951*
d them into the marketplace unto Acts 16:19 *1670*
he *d* out his sword, and would have Acts 16:27 *4685*
they *d* Jason and certain brethren Acts 17:6 *4951*
they *d* Alexander out of the Acts 19:33 *4264*
Paul, and *d* him out of the temple Acts 21:30 *1670*
that they *d* near to some country Acts 27:27 *4317*
his tail *d* the third part of the Rev 12:4 *4951*

DREWEST
Thou *d* near in the day that I Lam 3:57

DRIED
were *d* up from off the earth Gen 8:7 3001
the waters were *d* up from off the Gen 8:13 2717
day of the month, was the earth *d* Gen 8:14 3001
green ears of corn *d* by the fire Lev 2:14 7033
nor eat moist grapes, or *d* Num 6:3 3002
But now our soul is *d* away Num 11:6 3001
For we have heard how the LORD *d* Josh 2:10 3001
For the LORD your God *d* up the Josh 4:23 3001
which he *d* up from before us, Josh 4:23 3001
heard that the LORD had *d* up the Josh 5:1 3001
green withs that were never *d* Judg 16:7 2717
green withs which had not been *d* Judg 16:8 2717
d up, so that he could not pull 1Kin 13:4 3001
a while, that the brook *d* up 1Kin 17:7 3001
I *d* up all the rivers of besieged 2Kin 19:24 2717
His roots shall be *d* up beneath Job 18:16 3001

they are *d* up, they are gone away Job 28:4 1809
My strength is *d* up like a Ps 22:15 3001
my throat is *d* Ps 69:3 2787
the Red sea also, and it was *d* up Ps 106:9 2717
their multitude *d* up with thirst Is 5:13 6704
the river shall be wasted and *d* up Is 19:5 3001
defence shall be emptied and *d* up Is 19:6 2717
have I *d* up all the rivers of the Is 37:25 2717
thou not it which hath *d* the sea Is 51:10 2717
places of the wilderness are *d* up Jer 23:10 3001
and they shall be *d* up Jer 50:38 3001
have *d* up the green tree, and have Eze 17:24 3001
and the east wind *d* up her fruit Eze 19:12 3001
behold, they say, Our bones are *d* Eze 37:11 3001
is smitten, their root is *d* up Hos 9:16 3001
and his fountain shall be *d* up Hos 13:15 2717
the new wine is *d* up, the oil Joel 1:10 3001
The vine is *d* up, and the fig tree Joel 1:12 3001
for the rivers of waters are *d* up Joel 1:20 3001
his arm shall be clean *d* up Zec 11:17 3001
fountain of her blood was *d* up Mk 5:29 3583
the fig tree *d* up from the roots Mk 11:20 3583
and the water thereof was *d* up Rev 16:12 3583

DRIEDST

thou *d* up mighty rivers Ps 74:15 3001

DRIETH

and the flood decayeth and *d* up Job 14:11 3001
but a broken spirit *d* the bones Prov 17:22 3001
it dry, and *d* up all the rivers Nah 1:4 3001

DRINK

let us make our father *d* wine Gen 19:32 8248
their father *d* wine that night Gen 19:33 8248
let us make him *d* wine this night Gen 19:34 8248
father *d* wine that night also Gen 19:35 8248
with water, and gave the lad *d* Gen 21:19 8248
I pray thee, that I may *d* Gen 24:14 8354
and she shall say, *D* Gen 24:14 8354
and I will give thy camels *d* also Gen 24:14 8248
d a little water of thy pitcher Gen 24:17 1572
And she said, *D*, my lord Gen 24:18 8354
upon her hand, and gave him *d* Gen 24:18 8248
And when she had done giving him *d* Gen 24:19 8248
little water of thy pitcher to *d* Gen 24:43 8248
And she say to me, Both *d* thou Gen 24:44 8354
and I said unto her, Let me *d* Gen 24:45 8248
from her shoulder, and said, *D* Gen 24:46 8354
and I will give thy camels *d* also Gen 24:46 8248
and she made the camels *d* also Gen 24:46 8354
And they did eat and *d*, he and the Gen 24:54 8354
and he did eat and *d*, and rose up, Gen 25:34 8354
a feast, and they did eat and *d* Gen 26:30 8354
troughs when the flocks came to *d* Gen 30:38 8354
conceive when they came to *d* Gen 30:38 8354
he poured a *d* offering thereon, Gen 35:14 5262
to *d* of the water of the river Ex 7:18 8354
the Egyptians could not *d* of the Ex 7:21 8354
about the river for water to *d* Ex 7:24 8354
for they could not *d* of the water Ex 7:24 8354
they could not *d* of the waters of Ex 15:23 8354
Moses, saying, What shall we *d* Ex 15:24 8354
was no water for the people to *d* Ex 17:1 8354
said, Give us water that we may *d* Ex 17:2 8354
out of it, that the people may *d* Ex 17:6 8354
they saw God, and did eat and *d* Ex 24:11 8354
an hin of wine for a *d* offering Ex 29:40 5262
to the *d* offering thereof Ex 29:41 5262
shall ye pour *d* offering thereon Ex 30:9 5262
people sat down to eat and to *d* Ex 32:6 8354
the children of Israel *d* of it Ex 32:20 8248
neither eat bread, nor *d* water Ex 34:28 8354
Do not *d* wine nor strong *d*, Lev 10:9 8354
Do not *d* wine nor strong *d* Lev 10:9 7941
all *d* that may be drunk in every Lev 11:34 4945
the *d* offering thereof shall be Lev 23:13 5262
their *d* offerings, even an Lev 23:18 5262
d offerings, every thing upon his Lev 23:37 5262
he shall cause the woman to *d* the Num 5:24 8248
cause the woman to *d* the water Num 5:26 8248
he hath made her to *d* the water Num 5:27 8248
himself from wine and strong *d* Num 6:3 7941
shall *d* no vinegar of wine, or Num 6:3 8354
of wine, or vinegar of strong *d* Num 6:3 7941
neither shall he *d* any liquor of Num 6:3 8354
offering, and their *d* offerings Num 6:15 5262
meat offering, and his *d* offering Num 6:17 5262
that the Nazarite may *d* wine Num 6:20 8354
a *d* offering shalt thou prepare Num 15:5 5262
for a *d* offering thou shalt offer Num 15:7 5262
thou shalt bring for a *d* offering Num 15:10 5262
his *d* offering, according to the Num 15:24 5262
neither is there any water to *d* Num 20:5 8354
congregation and their beasts *d* Num 20:8 8248
neither will we *d* of the water of Num 20:17 8354
my cattle *d* of thy water, then I Num 20:19 8354
we will not *d* of the waters of Num 21:22 8354
prey, and *d* the blood of the slain Num 23:24 8354
the *d* offering thereof shall be Num 28:7 5262
unto the LORD for a *d* offering Num 28:7 5262
as the *d* offering thereof, thou Num 28:8 5262
oil, and the *d* offering thereof Num 28:9 5262
burnt offering, and his *d* offering Num 28:10 5262
their *d* offerings shall be half Num 28:14 5262
burnt offering, and his *d* offering Num 28:15 5262
burnt offering, and his *d* offering Num 28:24 5262
blemish) and their *d* offerings Num 28:31 5262
their *d* offerings, according unto Num 29:6 5262
of it, and their *d* offerings Num 29:11 5262
meat offering, and his *d* offering Num 29:16 5262
their *d* offerings for the Num 29:18 5262
thereof, and their *d* offerings Num 29:19 5262
their *d* offerings for the Num 29:21 5262
meat offering, and his *d* offering Num 29:22 5262
their *d* offerings for the Num 29:24 5262
meat offering, and his *d* offering Num 29:25 5262
their *d* offerings for the Num 29:27 5262
meat offering, and his *d* offering Num 29:28 5262
their *d* offerings for the Num 29:30 5262
meat offering, and his *d* offering Num 29:31 5262
their *d* offerings for the Num 29:33 5262
meat offering, and his *d* offering Num 29:34 5262
their *d* offerings for the bullock Num 29:37 5262
meat offering, and his *d* offering Num 29:38 5262
for your *d* offerings, and for your Num 29:39 5262
was no water for the people to *d* Num 33:14 8354
of them for money, that ye may *d* Deut 2:6 8354
me water for money, that I may *d* Deut 2:28 8354
neither did eat bread nor *d* water Deut 9:9 8354
nor *d* water, because of all your Deut 9:18 8354
or for wine, or for strong *d* Deut 14:26 7941
but shalt neither *d* of the wine Deut 28:39 8354
have ye drunk wine or strong *d* Deut 29:6 7941
thou didst *d* the pure blood of Deut 32:14 8354
the wine of their *d* offerings Deut 32:38 5257
I pray thee, a little water to *d* Judg 4:19 8248
a bottle of milk, and gave him *d* Judg 4:19 8248
boweth down upon his knees to *d* Judg 7:5 8354
down upon their knees to *d* water Judg 7:6 8354
of their god, and did eat and *d* Judg 9:27 8354
d not wine nor strong *d* Judg 13:4 8354
and *d* not wine nor strong *d* Judg 13:4 7941
now *d* no wine nor strong Judg 13:7 7941
no wine nor strong *d* Judg 13:7 8354
neither let her *d* wine or strong Judg 13:14 8354
let her *d* wine or strong *d* Judg 13:14 7941
so they did eat and *d*, and lodged Judg 19:4 8354
eat and *d* both of them together Judg 19:6 8354
their feet, and did eat and *d* Judg 19:21 8354
d of that which the young men Ruth 2:9 8354
drunken neither wine nor strong *d* 1Sa 1:15 7941
and they made him *d* water 1Sa 30:11 8248
into mine house, to eat and to *d* 2Sa 11:11 8354
him, he did eat and *d* before him 2Sa 11:13 8354
be faint in the wilderness may *d* 2Sa 16:2 8354
taste what I eat or what I *d* 2Sa 19:35 8354
Oh that one would give me *d* of 2Sa 23:15 8248
he would not *d* thereof, but 2Sa 23:16 8354
therefore he would not *d* it 2Sa 23:17 8354
d before him, and say, God save 1Kin 1:25 8354
bread nor *d* water in this place 1Kin 13:8 8354
nor *d* water, nor turn again by 1Kin 13:9 8354
neither will I eat bread nor *d* 1Kin 13:16 8354
eat no bread nor *d* water there 1Kin 13:17 8354
that he may eat bread and *d* water 1Kin 13:18 8354
thee, Eat no bread, and *d* no water 1Kin 13:22 8354
that thou shalt *d* of the brook 1Kin 17:4 8354
water in a vessel, that I may *d* 1Kin 17:10 8354
unto Ahab, Get thee up, eat and *d* 1Kin 18:41 8354
So Ahab went up to eat and to *d* 1Kin 18:42 8354
And he did eat and *d*, and laid him 1Kin 19:6 8354
And he arose, and did eat and *d* 1Kin 19:8 8354
filled with water, that ye may *d* 2Kin 3:17 8354
them, that they may eat and *d* 2Kin 6:22 8354
into one tent, and did eat and *d* 2Kin 7:8 8354
he was come in, he did eat and *d* 2Kin 9:34 8354
and poured his *d* offering 2Kin 16:13 5262
offering, and their *d* offerings 2Kin 16:15 5262
d their own piss with you 2Kin 18:27 8354
d ye every one the waters of his 2Kin 18:31 8354
Oh that one would give me *d* of 1Chr 11:17 8248
but David would not *d* of it 1Chr 11:18 8354
shall I *d* the blood of these men 1Chr 11:19 8354
Therefore he would not *d* it 1Chr 11:19 8354
lambs, with their *d* offerings 1Chr 29:21 5262
d before the LORD on that day 1Chr 29:22 8353
them, and gave them to eat and to *d* 2Chr 28:15 8248
the *d* offerings for every burnt 2Chr 29:35 5262
and meat, and *d*, and oil, unto them Ezr 3:7 4960
their *d* offerings, and offer them Ezr 7:17 5261
he did eat no bread, nor *d* water Ezr 10:6 8354
d the sweet, and send portions Neh 8:10 8354
went their way to eat, and to *d* Neh 8:12 8354
they gave them *d* in vessels of Est 1:7 8248
the king and Haman sat down to *d* Est 3:15 8354
and neither eat nor *d* three days Est 4:16 8354
sisters to eat and to *d* with them Job 1:4 8354
he shall *d* of the wrath of the Job 21:20 8354
not given water to the weary to *d* Job 22:7 8248
their *d* offerings of blood will I Ps 16:4 5262
thou shalt make them *d* of the Ps 36:8 8248
of bulls, or *d* the blood of goats Ps 50:13 8354
thou hast made us to *d* the wine Ps 60:3 8248
thirst they gave me vinegar to *d* Ps 69:21 8248
shall wring them out, and *d* them Ps 75:8 8354
gave them *d* as out of the great Ps 78:15 8248
floods, that they could not *d* Ps 78:44 8354
them tears to *d* in great measure Ps 80:5 8248
mingled my *d* with weeping, Ps 102:9 8249
They give *d* to every beast of the Ps 104:11 8248
He shall *d* of the brook in the Ps 110:7 8354
and *d* the wine of violence Prov 4:17 8354
D waters out of thine own cistern Prov 5:15 8354
d of the wine which I have Prov 9:5 8354
is a mocker, strong *d* is raging Prov 20:1 7941
Eat and *d*, saith he to thee Prov 23:7 8354
be thirsty, give him water to *d* Prov 25:21 8248
it is not for kings to *d* wine Prov 31:4 8354
nor for princes strong *d* Prov 31:4 7941
Lest they *d*, and forget the law, Prov 31:5 8354
Give strong *d* unto him that is Prov 31:6 7941
Let him *d*, and forget his poverty, Prov 31:7 8354
man, than that he should eat and *d* Eccl 2:24 8354
that every man should eat and *d* Eccl 3:13 8354
and comely for one to eat and to *d* Eccl 5:18 8354
the sun, than to eat, and to *d* Eccl 8:15 8354
d thy wine with a merry heart Eccl 9:7 8354
d, yea, *d* abundantly, O Song 5:1 8354
yea, *d* abundantly, O beloved Song 5:1 7937
I would cause thee to *d* of spiced Song 8:2 8248
that they may follow strong *d* Is 5:11 7941
them that are mighty to *d* wine Is 5:22 8354
of strength to mingle strong *d* Is 5:22 7941
watch in the watchtower, eat, *d* Is 21:5 8354
let us eat and *d* Is 22:13 8354
They shall not *d* wine with a song Is 24:9 8354
strong *d* shall be bitter to them Is 24:9 7941
shall be bitter to them that *d* it Is 24:9 8354
through strong *d* are out of the Is 28:7 7941
have erred through strong *d* Is 28:7 7941
out of the way through strong *d* Is 28:7 7941
stagger, but not with strong *d* Is 29:9 7941
he will cause the *d* of the Is 32:6 4945
d their own piss with you Is 36:12 8354
d ye every one the waters of his Is 36:16 8354
to give *d* to my people, my chosen Is 43:20 8248
thou shalt no more *d* it again Is 51:22 8354
will fill ourselves with strong *d* Is 56:12 7941
hast thou poured a *d* offering Is 57:6 5262
the stranger shall not *d* thy wine Is 62:8 8354
have brought it together shall *d* Is 62:9 8354
that furnish the *d* offering unto Is 65:11 4469
behold, my servants shall *d* Is 65:13 8354
Egypt, to *d* the waters of Sihor Jer 2:18 8354
to *d* the waters of the river Jer 2:18 8354
to pour out *d* offerings unto Jer 7:18 5262
and given us water of gall to *d* Jer 8:14 8248
and give them water of gall to *d* Jer 9:15 8248
d for their father or for their Jer 16:7 8248
to sit with them to eat and to *d* Jer 16:8 8354
have poured out *d* offerings unto Jer 19:13 5262
did not thy father eat and *d* Jer 22:15 8354
make them *d* the water of gall Jer 23:15 8248
to whom I send thee, to *d* it Jer 25:15 8248
And they shall *d*, and be moved, and Jer 25:16 8354
and made all the nations to *d* Jer 25:17 8248
of Sheshach shall *d* after them Jer 25:26 8354
D ye, and be drunken, and spue, and Jer 25:27 8354
take the cup at thine hand to *d* Jer 25:28 8354
Ye shall certainly *d* Jer 25:28 8354
poured out *d* offerings unto other Jer 32:29 5262
chambers, and give them wine to *d* Jer 35:2 8248
and I said unto them, *D* ye wine Jer 35:5 8354
But they said, We will *d* no wine Jer 35:6 8354
us, saying, Ye shall *d* no wine Jer 35:6 8354
to *d* no wine all our days, we Jer 35:8 8354
commanded his sons not to *d* wine Jer 35:14 8354
for unto this day they *d* none Jer 35:14 8354
to pour out *d* offerings unto her, Jer 44:17 5262
to pour out *d* offerings unto her, Jer 44:18 5262
poured out *d* offerings unto her, Jer 44:19 5262
pour out *d* offerings unto her, Jer 44:19 5262
to pour out *d* offerings unto her Jer 44:25 5262
to *d* of the cup have assuredly Jer 49:12 8354
but thou shalt surely *d* of it Jer 49:12 8354
Thou shalt *d* also water by Eze 4:11 8354
from time to time shalt thou *d* Eze 4:11 8354
they shall *d* water by measure, and Eze 4:16 8354
d thy water with trembling and Eze 12:18 8354
d their water with astonishment, Eze 12:19 8354
out there their *d* offerings Eze 20:28 5262
Thou shalt *d* of thy sister's cup Eze 23:32 8354
Thou shalt even *d* it and suck it Eze 23:34 8354
fruit, and they shall *d* thy milk Eze 25:4 8354
in their height, all that *d* water Eze 31:14 8354
best of Lebanon, all that *d* water Eze 31:16 8354
they *d* that which ye have fouled Eze 34:19 8354
that ye may eat flesh, and *d* blood Eze 39:17 8354
d the blood of the princes of the Eze 39:18 8354
d blood till ye be drunken, of my Eze 39:19 8354
Neither shall any priest *d* wine Eze 44:21 8354
d offerings, in the feasts, and in Eze 45:17 5262
appointed your meat and your *d* Dan 1:10 4960
us pulse to eat, and water to *d* Dan 1:12 8354
and the wine that they should *d* Dan 1:16 4960
his concubines, might *d* therein Dan 5:2 8355
wool and my flax, mine oil and my *d* Hos 2:5 8250
Their *d* is sour Hos 4:18 5435
the *d* offering is cut off from Joel 1:9 5262
the *d* offering is withholden from Joel 1:13 5262
a *d* offering unto the LORD your Joel 2:14 5262
girl for wine, that they might *d* Joel 3:3 8354
they *d* the wine of the condemned Amos 2:8 8354
ye gave the Nazarites wine to *d* Amos 2:12 8248
their masters, Bring, and let us *d* Amos 4:1 8354
unto one city, to *d* water Amos 4:8 8354
but ye shall not *d* wine of them Amos 5:11 8354
That *d* wine in bowls, and anoint Amos 6:6 8354
vineyards, and *d* the wine thereof Amos 9:14 8354
d continually, yea, they shall *d* Obad 16 8354
let them not feed, nor *d* water Jonah 3:7 8354
unto thee of wine and of strong *d* Mic 2:11 7941
sweet wine, but shalt not *d* wine Mic 6:15 8354
him that giveth his neighbour *d* Hab 2:15 8248
d thou also, and let thy foreskin Hab 2:16 8354
but not *d* the wine thereof Zeph 1:13 8354
ye *d*, but ye are not filled with Hag 1:6 8354
but ye are not filled with *d* Hag 1:6 7937
when ye did eat, and when ye did *d* Zec 7:6 8354
yourselves, and *d* for yourselves Zec 7:6 8354
and they shall *d*, and make a noise Zec 9:15 8354
ye shall eat, or what ye shall *d* Mt 6:25 4095
or, What shall we *d* Mt 6:31 4095
whosoever shall give to *d* unto Mt 10:42 4222
d of the cup that I shall *d* Mt 20:22 4095
Ye shall *d* indeed of my cup, and Mt 20:23 4095
and to eat and *d* with the drunken Mt 24:49 4095
I was thirsty, and ye gave me *d* Mt 25:35 4222
or thirsty, and gave thee *d* Mt 25:37 4222
I was thirsty, and ye gave me no *d* Mt 25:42 4222
to them, saying, *D* ye all of it Mt 26:27 4095
I will not *d* henceforth of this Mt 26:29 4095

until that day when I *d* it new Mt 26:29 4095
pass away from me, except I *d* it Mt 26:42 4095
vinegar to *d* mingled with gall Mt 27:34 4095
tasted thereof, he would not *d* Mt 27:34 4095
it on a reed, and gave him to *d* Mt 27:48 4095
a cup of water to *d* in my name Mk 9:41 4222
can ye *d* of the cup that I *d* Mk 10:38 4095
d of the cup that I *d* of Mk 10:39 4095
I will *d* no more of the fruit of Mk 14:25 4095
until that day that I *d* it new in Mk 14:25 4095
they gave him to *d* wine mingled Mk 15:23 4095
it on a reed, and gave him to *d* Mk 15:36 4222
if they *d* any deadly thing, it Mk 16:18 4095
shall *d* neither wine nor strong Lk 1:15 4095
neither wine nor strong *d* Lk 1:15 4608
d with publicans and sinners Lk 5:30 4095
but thine eat and *d* Lk 5:33 4095
take thine ease, eat, *d*, and be Lk 12:19 4095
ye shall eat, or what ye shall *d* Lk 12:29 4095
and maidens, and to eat and *d* Lk 12:45 4095
and afterward thou shalt eat and *d* Lk 17:8 4095
I will not *d* of the fruit of the Lk 22:18 4095
d at my table in my kingdom, and Lk 22:30 4095
saith unto her, Give me to *d* Jn 4:7 4095
thou, being a Jew, askest *d* of me Jn 4:9 4095
that saith to thee, Give me to *d* Jn 4:10 4095
d his blood, ye have no life in Jn 6:53 4095
indeed, and my blood is *d* indeed Jn 6:55 4213
let him come unto me, and *d* Jn 7:37 4095
hath given me, shall I not *d* it Jn 18:11 4095
sight, and neither did eat nor *d* Acts 9:9 4095
d with him after he rose from the Acts 10:41 4844
nor *d* till they had killed Paul Acts 23:12 4095
nor *d* till they have killed him Acts 23:21 4095
if he thirst, give him *d* Rom 12:20 4222
kingdom of God is not meat and *d* Rom 14:17 4213
to eat flesh, nor to *d* wine Rom 14:21 4095
Have we not power to eat and to *d* 1Cor 9:4 4095
all *d* the same spiritual *d* 1Cor 10:4 4095
all *d* the same spiritual *d* 1Cor 10:4 4188
The people sat down to eat and *d* 1Cor 10:7 4095
Ye cannot *d* the cup of the Lord, 1Cor 10:21 4095
Whether therefore ye eat, or *d* 1Cor 10:31 4095
ye not houses to eat and to *d* in 1Cor 11:22 4095
this do ye, as oft as ye *d* it 1Cor 11:25 4095
d this cup, ye do shew the Lord's 1Cor 11:26 4095
bread, and *d* this cup of the Lord, 1Cor 11:27 4095
of that bread, and *d* of that cup 1Cor 11:28 4095
all made to *d* into one Spirit 1Cor 12:13 4222
let us eat and *d* 1Cor 15:32 4095
judge you in meat, or in *d* Col 2:16 4213
D no longer water, but use a 1Ti 5:23 5202
because she made all nations of *d* Rev 14:8 4222
The same shall *d* of the wine of Rev 14:10 4095
thou hast given them blood to *d* Rev 16:6 4095

DRINKERS
all ye *d* of wine, because of the Joel 1:5 8354

DRINKETH
Is not this it in which my lord *d* Gen 44:5 8354
d water of the rain of heaven Deut 11:11 8354
the poison whereof *d* up my spirit Job 6:4 8354
which *d* iniquity like water Job 15:16 8354
who *d* up scorning like water Job 34:7 8354
he *d* up a river, and hasteth not Job 40:23 6231
cutteth off the feet, and *d* damage Prov 26:6 8354
man dreameth, and, behold, he *d* Is 29:8 8354
he *d* no water, and is faint Is 44:12 8354
d with publicans and sinners Mk 2:16 4095
Whosoever *d* of this water shall Jn 4:13 4095
But whosoever *d* of the water that Jn 4:14 4095
d my blood, hath eternal life Jn 6:54 4095
d my blood, dwelleth in me, and I Jn 6:56 4095
d unworthily, eateth and *d* 1Cor 11:29 4095
For the earth which *d* in the rain Heb 6:7 4095

DRINKING
also, until they have done *d* Gen 24:19 8354
to pass, as the camels had done *d* Gen 24:22 8354
he shall have done eating and *d* Ruth 3:3 8354
upon all the earth, eating and *d* 1Sa 30:16 8354
the sea in multitude, eating and *d* 1Kin 4:20 8354
all king Solomon's *d* vessels were 1Kin 10:21 4945
d himself drunk in the house of 1Kin 16:9 8354
heard this message, as he was *d* 1Kin 20:12 8354
But Ben-hadad was *d* himself drunk 1Kin 20:16 8354
David three days, eating and *d* 1Chr 12:39 8354
all the *d* vessels of king Solomon 2Chr 9:20 4945
the *d* was according to the law Est 1:8 8360
d wine in their eldest brother's Job 1:13 8354
d wine in their eldest brother's Job 1:18 8354
sheep, eating flesh, and *d* wine Is 22:13 8354
John came neither eating nor *d* Mt 11:18 4095
The Son of man came eating and *d* Mt 11:19 4095
the flood they were eating and *d* Mt 24:38 4095
neither eating bread nor *d* wine Lk 7:33 4095
Son of man is come eating and *d* Lk 7:34 4095
d such things as they give Lk 10:7 4095

DRINKS
Which stood only in meats and *d* Heb 9:10 4188

DRIVE
shall he *d* them out of his land Ex 6:1 1644
which shall *d* out the Hivite, the Ex 23:28 1644
I will not *d* them out from before Ex 23:29 1644
little I will *d* them out from Ex 23:30 1644
thou shalt *d* them out before thee Ex 23:31 1644
I will *d* out the Canaanite, the Ex 33:2 1644
I *d* out before thee the Amorite, Ex 34:11 1644
that I may *d* them out of the land Num 22:6 1644
to overcome them, and *d* them out Num 22:11 1644
Then ye shall *d* out all the Num 33:52 3423
But if ye will not *d* out the Num 33:55 3423
To *d* out nations from before thee Deut 4:38 3423
so shalt thou *d* them out, and Deut 9:3 3423
doth *d* them out from before thee Deut 9:4 3423
doth *d* them out from before thee Deut 9:5 3423
Then will the LORD *d* out all Deut 11:23 3423
the LORD thy God doth *d* them out Deut 18:12 3423
fail *d* out from before you the Josh 3:10 3423
them will I *d* out from before the Josh 13:6 3423
I shall be able to *d* them out Josh 14:12 3423
of Judah could not *d* them out Josh 15:63 3423
d out the inhabitants of those Josh 17:12 3423
but did not utterly *d* them out Josh 17:13 3423
for thou shalt *d* out the Josh 17:18 3423
d them from out of your sight Josh 23:5 3423
d out any of these nations from Josh 23:13 3423
but could not *d* out the Judg 1:19 3423
did not *d* out the Jebusites that Judg 1:21 3423
Neither did Manasseh *d* out the Judg 1:27 3423
and did not utterly *d* them out Judg 1:28 3423
Neither did Ephraim *d* out the Judg 1:29 3423
Neither did Zebulun *d* out the Judg 1:30 3423
Neither did Asher *d* out the Judg 1:31 3423
for they did not *d* them out Judg 1:32 3423
Neither did Naphtali *d* out the Judg 1:33 3423
I will not *d* them out from before Judg 2:3 1644
I also will not henceforth *d* out Judg 2:21 3423
God shall *d* out from before us Judg 11:24 3423
an ass, and said to her servant, *D* 2Kin 4:24 5090
who didst *d* out the inhabitants 2Chr 20:7 3423
side, and shall *d* him to his feet Job 18:11 6327
They *d* away the ass of the Job 24:3 5090
How thou didst *d* out the heathen Ps 44:2 3423
is driven away, so *d* them away Ps 68:2 5086
shall *d* it far from him Prov 22:15
I will *d* thee from thy station, Is 22:19 1920
all places whither I shall *d* them Jer 24:9 5080
and that I should *d* you out Jer 27:10 5080
that I might *d* you out, and that Jer 27:15 5080
not, because the LORD did *d* them Jer 46:15 1920
Gentiles, whither I will *d* them Eze 4:13 5080
That they shall *d* thee from men Dan 4:25 2957
they shall *d* thee from men, and Dan 4:32 2957
I will *d* them out of mine house Hos 9:15 1644
will *d* him into a land barren and Joel 2:20 5080
they shall *d* out Ashdod at the Zeph 2:4 1644
up into the wind, we let her *d* Acts 27:15 1929

DRIVEN
thou hast *d* me out this day from Gen 4:14 1644
they were *d* out from Pharaoh's Ex 10:11 1644
or *d* away, no man seeing it Ex 22:10 7617
until he hath *d* out his enemies Num 32:21 3423
shouldest be *d* to worship them, Deut 4:19 5080
the LORD thy God hath *d* thee Deut 30:1 5080
If any of thine be *d* out unto the Deut 30:4 5080
For the LORD hath *d* out from Josh 23:9 3423
for they have *d* me out this day 1Sa 26:19 1644
is wisdom *d* quite from me Job 6:13 5080
Wilt thou break a leaf *d* to Job 13:25 5086
He shall be *d* from light into Job 18:18 1920
They were *d* forth from among men, Job 30:5 1644
let them be *d* backward and put to Ps 40:14 5472
As smoke is *d* away, so drive them Ps 68:2 5086
Jordan was *d* back Ps 114:3 5437
Jordan, that thou wast *d* back Ps 114:5 5437
The wicked is *d* away in his Prov 14:32 1760
and they shall be *d* to darkness Is 8:22 5080
wither, be *d* away, and be no more Is 19:7 5086
sword, and as *d* stubble to his bow Is 41:2 5086
the places whither I have *d* them Jer 8:3 5080
the lands whither he had *d* them Jer 16:15 5080
d them away, and have not visited Jer 23:2 5080
countries whither I have *d* them Jer 23:3 5080
countries whither I had *d* them Jer 23:8 5080
they shall be *d* on, and fall Jer 23:12 1760
the places whither I have *d* you Jer 29:14 5080
the nations whither I have *d* them Jer 29:18 5080
whither I have *d* them in mine Jer 32:37 5080
of all places whither they were *d* Jer 40:12 5080
nations, whither they had been *d* Jer 43:5 5080
the nations whither I have *d* thee Jer 46:28 5080
ye shall be *d* out every man right Jer 49:5 5080
the lions have *d* him away Jer 50:17 5080
I have *d* him out for his Eze 31:11 1644
again that which was *d* away Eze 34:4 5080
bring again that which was *d* away Eze 34:16 5080
he was *d* from men, and did eat Dan 4:33 2957
he was *d* from the sons of men Dan 5:21 2957
whither thou hast *d* them, because Dan 9:7 5080
as the chaff that is *d* with the Hos 13:3 5590
I will gather her that is *d* out Mic 4:6 5080
and gather her that was *d* out Zeph 3:19 5080
was *d* of the devil into the Lk 8:29 1643
strake sail, and so were *d* Acts 27:17 5342
night was come, as we were *d* up Acts 27:27 1308
a wave of the sea *d* with the wind Jas 1:6 416
are *d* of fierce winds, yet are Jas 3:4 1643

DRIVER
he said unto the *d* of his chariot 1Kin 22:34 7395
regardeth he the crying of the *d* Job 39:7 5065

DRIVETH
for he *d* furiously 2Kin 9:20 5090
the chaff which the wind *d* away Ps 1:4 5086
The north wind *d* away rain Prov 25:23 2342
immediately the spirit *d* him into Mk 1:12 1544

DRIVING
without *d* them out hastily Judg 2:23 3423
the *d* is like the *d* of Jehu 2Kin 9:20 4491
the *d* is like the *d* of Jehu 2Kin 9:20 4491
by *d* out nations from before thy 1Chr 17:21 1644

DROMEDARIES
d brought they unto the place 1Kin 4:28 7409
on mules, camels, and young *d* Est 8:10 7424
thee, the *d* of Midian and Ephah Is 60:6 1070

DROMEDARY
thou art a swift *d* traversing her Jer 2:23 1072

DROP
My doctrine shall *d* as the rain Deut 32:2 6201
also his heavens shall *d* down dew Deut 33:28 6201
Which the clouds do *d* and distil Job 36:28 5140
and thy paths *d* fatness Ps 65:11 7491
They *d* upon the pastures of the Ps 65:12 7491
the clouds *d* down the dew Prov 3:20 7491
a strange woman *d* as an honeycomb Prov 5:3 5197
O my spouse, *d* as the honeycomb Song 4:11 5197
nations are as a *d* of a bucket Is 40:15 4752
D down, ye heavens, from above, Is 45:8 7491
d thy word toward the south, and Eze 20:46 5197
d thy word toward the holy places Eze 21:2 5197
mountains shall *d* down new wine Joel 3:18 5197
d not thy word against the house Amos 7:16 5197
the mountains shall *d* sweet wine Amos 9:13 5197

DROPPED
earth trembled, and the heavens *d* Judg 5:4 5197
the clouds also *d* water Judg 5:4 5197
the wood, behold, the honey *d* 1Sa 14:26 1982
of harvest until water *d* upon 2Sa 21:10 5413
and my speech *d* upon them Job 29:22 5197
the heavens also *d* at the Ps 68:8 5197
my hands *d* with myrrh, and my Song 5:5 5197

DROPPETH
of the hands the house *d* through Eccl 10:18 1811

DROPPING
of a wife are a continual *d* Prov 19:13 1812
A continual *d* in a very rainy day Prov 27:15 1812
lilies, *d* sweet smelling myrrh Song 5:13 5197

DROPS
he maketh small the *d* of water Job 36:27 5197
or who hath begotten the *d* of dew Job 38:28 96
my locks with the *d* of the night Song 5:2 7447
d of blood falling down to the Lk 22:44 2361

DROPSY
man before him which had the *d* Lk 14:2 5203

DROSS
the wicked of the earth like *d* Ps 119:119 5509
Take away the *d* from the silver, Prov 25:4 5509
a potsherd covered with silver *d* Prov 26:23 5509
Thy silver is become *d*, thy wine Is 1:22 5509
thee, and purely purge away thy *d* Is 1:25 5509
house of Israel is to me become *d* Eze 22:18 5509
they are even the *d* of silver Eze 22:18 5509
Because ye are all become *d* Eze 22:19 5509

DROUGHT
in the day the *d* consumed me Gen 31:40 2721
serpents, and scorpions, and *d* Deut 8:15 6774
D and heat consume the snow waters Job 24:19 6723
is turned into the *d* of summer Ps 32:4 2725
and satisfy thy soul in *d* Is 58:11 6710
and of pits, through a land of *d* Jer 2:6 6723
not be careful in the year of *d* Jer 17:8 1226
A *d* is upon her waters Jer 50:38 2721
in the land of great *d* Hos 13:5 8514
And I called for a *d* upon the land Hag 1:11 2721

DROVE
So he *d* out the man Gen 3:24 1644
the carcases, Abram *d* them away Gen 15:11 5380
servants, every *d* by themselves Gen 32:16 5739
me, and put a space betwixt *d* Gen 32:16 5739
and put a space betwixt *d* and *d* Gen 32:16 5739
thou by all this *d* which I met Gen 33:8 4264
the shepherds came and *d* them away Ex 2:17 1644
d out the Amorites that were Num 21:32 3423
Caleb *d* thence the three sons of Josh 15:14 3423
who *d* away the inhabitants of 1Chr 8:13 1272
who *d* him away, and he departed Ps 34:t 1644
beheld, and *d* asunder the nations Hab 3:6 5425
he *d* them all out of the temple, Jn 2:15 1544

DROVES
third, and all that followed the *d* Gen 32:19 5739

DROWN
love, neither can the floods *d* it Song 8:7 7857
which *d* men in destruction and 1Ti 6:9 1036

DROWNED
also are *d* in the Red sea Ex 15:4 2823
and it shall be cast out and *d* Amos 8:8 8248
and shall be *d*, as by the flood of Amos 9:5 8248
that he were *d* in the depth of Mt 18:6 2670
Egyptians assaying to do were *d* Heb 11:29 2666

DROWSINESS
d shall clothe a man with rags Prov 23:21 5124

DRUNK
all drink that may be *d* in every Lev 11:34 8354
neither have ye *d* wine or strong Deut 29:6 8354
make mine arrows *d* with blood Deut 32:42 7937
and when he had *d*, his spirit came Judg 15:19 8354
And when Boaz had eaten and *d* Ruth 3:7 8354
in Shiloh, and after they had *d* 1Sa 1:9 8354
nor *d* any water, three days and 1Sa 30:12 8354
and he made him *d* 2Sa 11:13 7937
d water in the place, of the 1Kin 13:22 8354
eaten bread, and after he had *d* 1Kin 13:23 8354
drinking himself *d* in the house 1Kin 16:9 7910
himself *d* in the pavilions 1Kin 20:16 7910
and when they had eaten and *d* 2Kin 6:23 8354
d strange waters, and with the 2Kin 19:24 8354
I have *d* my wine with my milk Song 5:1 8354
I have digged, and *d* water Is 37:25 8354
which hast *d* at the hand of the Is 51:17 8354
make them *d* in my fury, and I will Is 63:6 7937

and made *d* with their blood ... Jer 46:10 7301
And I will make *d* her princes ... Jer 51:57 7937
to have *d* of the deep waters, but ... Eze 34:18 8354
concubines, have *d* wine in them ... Dan 5:23 8355
For as ye have *d* upon my holy ... Obad 16 8354
No man also having *d* old wine ... Lk 5:39 *4095*
d in thy presence, and thou hast ... Lk 13:26 *4095*
and when men have well *d*, then ... Jn 2:10 *3184*
be not *d* with wine, wherein is ... Eph 5:18 *3182*
been made *d* with the wine of her ... Rev 17:2 *3182*
For all nations have *d* of the ... Rev 18:3

DRUNKARD
he is a glutton, and a *d* ... Deut 21:20 5435
For the *d* and the glutton shall ... Prov 23:21 5435
goeth up into the hand of a *d* ... Prov 26:9 7910
shall reel to and fro like a *d* ... Is 24:20 7910
an idolater, or a railer, or a *d* ... 1Cor 5:11 *3183*

DRUNKARDS
and I was the song of the *d* ... Ps 69:12
to the *d* of Ephraim, whose ... Is 28:1 7910
the *d* of Ephraim, shall be ... Is 28:3 7910
Awake, ye *d*, and weep ... Joel 1:5 7910
and while they are drunken as *d* ... Nah 1:10 5435
Nor thieves, nor covetous, nor *d* ... 1Cor 6:10 *3183*

DRUNKEN
And he drank of the wine, and was *d* .. Gen 9:21 7943
Eli thought she had been *d* ... 1Sa 1:13 7910
unto her, How long wilt thou be *d* ... 1Sa 1:14 7937
I have *d* neither wine nor strong ... 1Sa 1:15 7937
within him for he was very *d* ... 1Sa 25:36 7910
them to stagger like a *d* man ... Job 12:25 7910
and fro, and stagger like a *d* man ... Ps 107:27 7910
as a *d* man staggereth in his ... Is 19:14 7910
they are *d*, but not with wine ... Is 29:9 7937
they shall be *d* with their own ... Is 49:26 7937
thou hast *d* the dregs of the cup ... Is 51:17 8354
now this, thou afflicted, and *d* ... Is 51:21 7937
I am like a *d* man, and like a man ... Jer 23:9 7910
Drink ye, and be *d*, and spue, and ... Jer 25:27 7937
Make ye him *d*: for he magnified ... Jer 48:26 7937
drink of the cup have assuredly *d* ... Jer 49:12 7937
hand, that made all the earth *d* ... Jer 51:7 7937
the nations have *d* of her wine ... Jer 51:7 8354
feasts, and I will make them *d* ... Jer 51:39 7937
he hath made me *d* with wormwood ... Lam 3:15 7301
thou shalt be *d*, and shalt make ... Lam 4:21 7937
We have *d* our water for money ... Lam 5:4 8354
full, and drink blood till ye be *d* ... Eze 39:19 7943
and while they are *d* as drunkards ... Nah 1:10 5435
Thou also shalt be *d* ... Nah 3:11 7937
to him, and makest him *d* also ... Hab 2:15 7937
and to eat and drink with the *d* ... Mt 24:49 *3184*
and to eat and drink, and to be *d* ... Lk 12:45 *3182*
serve me, till I have eaten and *d* ... Lk 17:8 *4095*
For these are not *d*, as ye ... Acts 2:15 *3184*
and one is hungry, and another is *d* ... 1Cor 11:21 *3184*
be *d* are *d* in the night ... 1Th 5:7 *3184*
I saw the woman *d* with the blood ... Rev 17:6 *3184*

DRUNKENNESS
of mine heart, to add *d* to thirst ... Deut 29:19 7302
for strength, and not for *d* ... Eccl 10:17 8358
inhabitants of Jerusalem, with *d* ... Jer 13:13 7943
Thou shalt be filled with *d* ... Eze 23:33 7943
overcharged with surfeiting, and *d* ... Lk 21:34 *3178*
not in rioting and *d*, not in ... Rom 13:13 *3178*
Envyings, murders, *d*, revellings, ... Gal 5:21 *3178*

DRUSILLA (*dru-sil'-lah*) *Wife of Felix.*
when Felix came with his wife *D* ... Acts 24:24 *1409*

DRY
place, and let the *d* land appear ... Gen 1:9 3004
And God called the *d* land Earth ... Gen 1:10 3004
of all that was in the *d* land ... Gen 7:22 2724
the face of the ground was *d* ... Gen 8:13 2720
river, and pour it upon the *d* land ... Ex 4:9 3004
become blood upon the *d* land ... Ex 4:9 3006
children of Israel shall go on *d* ... Ex 14:16 3004
night, and made the sea *d* land ... Ex 14:21 2724
of the sea upon the *d* ground ... Ex 14:22 3004
d land in the midst of the sea ... Ex 14:29 3004
on *d* land in the midst of the sea ... Ex 15:19 3004
offering, mingled with oil, and *d* ... Lev 7:10 2720
it is a *d* scall, even a leprosy ... Lev 13:30 5424
of the LORD stood firm on *d* ... Josh 3:17 2724
passed over on *d* ground, until ... Josh 3:17 2724
were lifted up unto the *d* land ... Josh 4:18 2724
came over this Jordan on *d* land ... Josh 4:22 3004
bread of their provision was *d* ... Josh 9:5 3004
but now, behold, it is *d*, and it ... Josh 9:12 3001
it be *d* upon all the earth beside ... Judg 6:37 2721
let it now be *d* only upon the ... Judg 6:39 2721
for it was *d* upon the fleece only ... Judg 6:40 2721
they two went over on *d* ground ... 2Kin 2:8 2724
midst of the sea on the *d* land ... Neh 9:11 3004
the waters, and they *d* up ... Job 12:15 3001
and wilt thou pursue the *d* stubble ... Job 13:25 3002
the flame shall *d* up his branches ... Job 15:30 3001
my flesh longeth for thee in a *d* ... Ps 63:1 6723
He turned the sea into *d* land ... Ps 66:6 3004
the rebellious dwell in a *d* land ... Ps 68:6 6707
and his hands formed the *d* land ... Ps 95:5 3006
they ran in the *d* places like a ... Ps 105:41 6723
and the watersprings into *d* ground ... Ps 107:33 6774
d ground into watersprings ... Ps 107:35 6723
Better is a *d* morsel, and ... Prov 17:1 2720
as the heat in a *d* place ... Is 25:5 6724
as rivers of water in a *d* place ... Is 32:2 6724
the *d* land springs of water ... Is 41:18 6723
and hills, and *d* up all their herbs ... Is 42:15 3001
islands, and I will *d* up the pools ... Is 42:15 3001
and floods upon the *d* ground ... Is 44:3 3004
That saith to the deep, Be *d* ... Is 44:27 2717
and I will *d* up thy rivers ... Is 44:27 3001
at my rebuke I *d* up the sea ... Is 50:2 2717
and as a root out of a *d* ground ... Is 53:2 6723
eunuch say, Behold, I am a *d* tree ... Is 56:3 3002
A *d* wind of the high places in ... Jer 4:11 6703
wilderness, a *d* land, and a desert ... Jer 50:12 6723
I will *d* up her sea ... Jer 51:36 2717
and make her springs *d* ... Jer 51:36 3001
a *d* land, and a wilderness, a land ... Jer 51:43 6723
have made the *d* tree to flourish ... Eze 17:24 3002
planted in the wilderness, in a *d* ... Eze 19:13 6723
tree in thee, and every *d* tree ... Eze 20:47 3002
And I will make the rivers *d* ... Eze 30:12 2724
and, lo, they were very *d* ... Eze 37:2 3002
O ye *d* bones, hear the word of ... Eze 37:4 3002
and set her like a *d* land ... Hos 2:3 6723
a miscarrying womb and *d* breasts ... Hos 9:14 6784
and his spring shall become *d* ... Hos 13:15 954
hath made the sea and the *d* land ... Jonah 1:9 3004
vomited out Jonah upon the *d* land ... Jonah 2:10 3004
rebuketh the sea, and maketh it *d* ... Nah 1:4 3001
be devoured as stubble fully *d* ... Nah 1:10 3002
and *d* like a wilderness ... Zeph 2:13 6723
earth, and the sea, and the *d* land ... Hag 2:6 2724
the deeps of the river shall *d* up ... Zec 10:11 3001
man, he walketh through *d* places ... Mt 12:43 *504*
man, he walketh through *d* places ... Lk 11:24 *504*
tree, what shall be done in the *d* ... Lk 23:31 *3584*
through the Red sea as by *d* land ... Heb 11:29 *3584*

DRYSHOD
streams, and make men go over *d* ... Is 11:15 5275

DUE
it is thy *d*, and thy sons' *d* ... Lev 10:13 2706
they be thy *d*, and thy sons' *d* ... Lev 10:14 2706
I will give you rain in *d* season ... Lev 26:4
offer unto me in their *d* season ... Num 28:2
rain of your land in his *d* season ... Deut 11:14
be the priest's *d* from the people ... Deut 18:3 4941
their foot shall slide in *d* time ... Deut 32:35
sought him not after the *d* order ... 1Chr 15:13
LORD the glory *d* unto his name ... 1Chr 16:29
for the singers, *d* for every day ... Neh 11:23 1697
LORD the glory *d* unto his name ... Ps 29:2
LORD the glory *d* unto his name ... Ps 96:8
give them their meat in *d* season ... Ps 104:27
them their meat in *d* season ... Ps 145:15
good from them to whom it is *d* ... Prov 3:27 1167
and a word spoken in *d* season ... Prov 15:23
and thy princes eat in *d* season ... Eccl 10:17
pay all that was *d* unto him ... Mt 18:34 *3784*
to give them meat in *d* season ... Mt 24:45
their portion of meat in *d* season ... Lk 12:42
for we receive the *d* reward of ... Lk 23:41 *514*
in *d* time Christ died for the ... Rom 5:6
tribute to whom tribute is *d* ... Rom 13:7
unto the wife *d* benevolence ... 1Cor 7:3 *3784*
as of one born out of *d* time ... 1Cor 15:8
for in *d* season we shall reap, if ... Gal 6:9 *2398*
all, to be testified in *d* time ... 1Ti 2:6 *2398*
But hath in *d* times manifested ... Titus 1:3 *2398*
that he may exalt you in *d* time ... 1Pet 5:6

DUES
Render therefore to all their *d* ... Rom 13:7 *3782*

DUKE
firstborn son of Esau; *d* Teman ... Gen 36:15 441
d Omar, *d* Zepho, *d* Kenaz, ... Gen 36:15 441
D Korah, *d* Gatam, and *d* ... Gen 36:16 441
D Korah, *d* Gatam, and *d* Amalek ... Gen 36:16 441
d Nahath, *d* Zerah ... Gen 36:17 441
d Shammah, *d* ... Gen 36:17 441
d Jeush, *d* Jaalam, *d* Korah ... Gen 36:18 441
came of the Horites; *d* Lotan ... Gen 36:29 441
d Shobal, *d* Zibeon, *d* Anah, ... Gen 36:29 441
D Dishon, *d* Ezer, *d* Dishan ... Gen 36:30 441
by their names; *d* Timnah ... Gen 36:40 441
d Alvah, *d* Jetheth ... Gen 36:40 441
D Aholibamah, *d* Elah, *d* Pinon ... Gen 36:41 441
D Kenaz, *d* Teman, *d* Mibzar, ... Gen 36:42 441
D Magdiel, *d* Iram ... Gen 36:43 441
of Edom were; *d* Timnah ... 1Chr 1:51 441
d Aliah, *d* Jetheth ... 1Chr 1:51 441
D Aholibamah, *d* Elah, *d* Pinon ... 1Chr 1:52 441
D Kenaz, *d* Teman, *d* Mibzar, ... 1Chr 1:53 441
D Magdiel, *d* Iram ... 1Chr 1:54 441

DUKES
These were *d* of the sons of Esau ... Gen 36:15 441
these are the *d* that came of ... Gen 36:16 441
these are the *d* that came of ... Gen 36:17 441
these were the *d* that came of ... Gen 36:18 441
who is Edom, and these are their *d* ... Gen 36:19 441
these are the *d* of the Horites, ... Gen 36:21 441
These are the *d* that came of the ... Gen 36:29 441
these are the *d* that came of Hori ... Gen 36:30 441
among their *d* in the land of Seir ... Gen 36:30 441
names of the *d* that came of Esau ... Gen 36:40 441
these be the *d* of Edom, according ... Gen 36:43 441
Then the *d* of Edom shall be ... Ex 15:15 441
and Reba, which were *d* of Sihon ... Josh 13:21 5257
And the *d* of Edom were ... 1Chr 1:51 441
These are the *d* of Edom ... 1Chr 1:54

DULCIMER
flute, harp, sackbut, psaltery, *d* ... Dan 3:5 5481
harp, sackbut, psaltery, and *d* ... Dan 3:10 5481
harp, sackbut, psaltery, and *d* ... Dan 3:15 5481

DULL
and their ears are *d* of hearing ... Mt 13:15 *917*
and their ears are *d* of hearing ... Acts 28:27 *917*
seeing ye are *d* of hearing ... Heb 5:11 *3576*

DUMAH (*doo'-mah*)
1. Son of Ishmael.
And Mishma, and *D*, and Massa, ... Gen 25:14 1746
Mishma, and *D*, Massa, Hadad, and ... 1Chr 1:30 1746
2. A city in Judah.
Arab, and *D*, and Eshean, ... Josh 15:52 1746
3. An undetermined city.
The burden of *D*. He calleth to ... Is 21:11 1746

DUMB
or who maketh the *d*, or deaf, or ... Ex 4:11 483
I was as a *d* man that openeth not ... Ps 38:13 483
I was *d* with silence, I held my ... Ps 39:2 481
I was *d*, I opened not my mouth ... Ps 39:9 481
Open thy mouth for the *d* in the ... Prov 31:8 483
hart, and the tongue of the *d* sing ... Is 35:6 483
a sheep before her shearers is *d* ... Is 53:7 481
all ignorant, they are all *d* dogs ... Is 56:10 483
thy mouth, that thou shalt be *d* ... Eze 3:26 481
thou shalt speak, and be no more *d* ... Eze 24:27 481
was opened, and I was no more *d* ... Eze 33:22 481
toward the ground, and I became *d* ... Dan 10:15 481
trusteth therein, to make *d* idols ... Hab 2:18 483
to the *d* stone, Arise, it shall ... Hab 2:19 1748
they brought to him a *d* man ... Mt 9:32 *2974*
devil was cast out, the *d* spake ... Mt 9:33 *2974*
with a devil, blind, and *d* ... Mt 12:22 *2974*
the blind and *d* both spake and saw ... Mt 12:22 *2974*
those that were lame, blind, *d* ... Mt 15:30 *2974*
when they saw the *d* to speak ... Mt 15:31 *2974*
deaf to hear, and the *d* to speak ... Mk 7:37 *216*
my son, which hath a *d* spirit ... Mk 9:17 *216*
spirit, saying unto him, Thou *d* ... Mk 9:25 *216*
And, behold, thou shalt be *d* ... Lk 1:20 *4623*
casting out a devil, and it was *d* ... Lk 11:14 *2974*
devil was gone out, the *d* spake ... Lk 11:14 *2974*
like a lamb *d* before his shearer, ... Acts 8:32 *880*
carried away unto these *d* idols ... 1Cor 12:2 *880*
the *d* ass speaking with man's ... 2Pet 2:16 *880*

DUNG
bullock, and his skin, and his *d* ... Ex 29:14 6569
legs, and his inwards, and his *d* ... Lev 4:11 6569
and his hide, his flesh, and his *d* ... Lev 8:17 6569
skins, and their flesh, and their *d* ... Lev 16:27 6569
flesh, and her blood, with her *d* ... Num 19:5 6569
Jeroboam, as a man taketh away *d* ... 1Kin 14:10 1557
d for five pieces of silver ... 2Kin 6:25 2755
d upon the face of the field in ... 2Kin 9:37 1828
that they may eat their own *d* ... 2Kin 18:27
the dragon well, and to the *d* port ... Neh 2:13 830
on the wall unto the *d* gate ... Neh 3:13 830
But the *d* gate repaired Malchiah ... Neh 3:14 830
upon the wall toward the *d* gate ... Neh 12:31 830
perish for ever like his own *d* ... Job 20:7 1561
they became as *d* for the earth ... Ps 83:10 1828
that they may eat their own *d* ... Is 36:12
they shall be for *d* upon the face ... Jer 8:2 1828
fall as *d* upon the open field ... Jer 9:22 1828
but they shall be as *d* upon the ... Jer 16:4 1828
they shall be *d* upon the ground ... Jer 25:33 1828
it with *d* that cometh out of man ... Eze 4:12 1561
given thee cow's *d* for man's *d* ... Eze 4:15 6832
given thee cow's *d* for man's *d* ... Eze 4:15 1561
as dust, and their flesh as the *d* ... Zeph 1:17 1561
spread *d* upon your faces ... Mal 2:3 6569
even the *d* of your solemn feasts ... Mal 2:3 6569
I shall dig about it, and *d* it ... Lk 13:8
things, and do count them but *d* ... Phil 3:8 *4657*

DUNGEON
they should put me into the *d* ... Gen 40:15 953
brought him hastily out of the *d* ... Gen 41:14 953
of the captive that was in the *d* ... Ex 12:29 953
Jeremiah was entered into the *d* ... Jer 37:16 953
cast him into the *d* of Malchiah ... Jer 38:6 953
in the *d* there was no water, but ... Jer 38:6 953
they had put Jeremiah in the *d* ... Jer 38:7 953
whom they have cast into the *d* ... Jer 38:9 953
Jeremiah the prophet out of the *d* ... Jer 38:10 953
by cords into the *d* to Jeremiah ... Jer 38:11 953
and took him up out of the *d* ... Jer 38:13 953
have cut off my life in the *d* ... Lam 3:53 953
name, O LORD, out of the low *d* ... Lam 3:55 953

DUNGHILL
lifteth up the beggar from the *d* ... 1Sa 2:8 830
his house be made a *d* for this ... Ezr 6:11 5122
and lifteth the needy out of the *d* ... Ps 113:7 830
straw is trodden down for the *d* ... Is 25:10 4087
and your houses shall be made a *d* ... Dan 2:5 5122
and their houses shall be made a *d* ... Dan 3:29 5122
for the land, nor yet for the *d* ... Lk 14:35 *2874*

DUNGHILLS
brought up in scarlet embrace *d* ... Lam 4:5 830

DURA (*doo'-rah*) *A plain in Babylonia.*
he set it up in the plain of *D* ... Dan 3:1 1757

DURABLE
d riches and righteousness ... Prov 8:18 6276
sufficiently, and for *d* clothing ... Is 23:18 6266

DURETH
in himself, but *d* for a while ... Mt 13:21 *2076*

DURST
that *d* presume in his heart to do ... Est 7:5
d not shew you mine opinion ... Job 32:6 3372
neither *d* any man from that day ... Mt 22:46 *5111*
no man after that *d* ask him any ... Mk 12:34 *5111*
after that they *d* not ask him any ... Lk 20:40 *5111*
none of the disciples *d* ask him ... Jn 21:12 *5111*
of the rest *d* no man join himself ... Acts 5:13 *5111*
Moses trembled, and *d* not behold ... Acts 7:32 *5111*
d not bring against him a railing ... Jude 9 *5111*

DUST

formed man of the *d* of the ground	Gen 2:7	6083
d shalt thou eat all the days of	Gen 3:14	6083
for *d* thou art, and unto *d*	Gen 3:19	6083
thy seed as the *d* of the earth	Gen 13:16	6083
man can number the *d* of the earth	Gen 13:16	6083
unto the Lord, which am but *d*	Gen 18:27	6083
shall be as the *d* of the earth	Gen 28:14	6083
smite the *d* of the land, that it	Ex 8:16	6083
smote the *d* of the earth, and it	Ex 8:17	6083
all the *d* of the land became lice	Ex 8:17	6083
it shall become small *d* in all	Ex 9:9	80
they shall pour out the *d* that	Lev 14:41	6083
blood thereof, and cover it with *d*	Lev 17:13	6083
of the *d* that is in the floor of	Num 5:17	6083
Who can count the *d* of Jacob	Num 23:10	6083
even until it was as small as *d*	Deut 9:21	6083
I cast the *d* thereof into the	Deut 9:21	6083
the rain of thy land powder and *d*	Deut 28:24	6083
the poison of serpents of the *d*	Deut 32:24	6083
Israel, and put *d* upon their heads	Josh 7:6	6083
raiseth up the poor out of the *d*	1Sa 2:8	6083
and threw stones at him, and cast *d*	2Sa 16:13	6083
as small as the *d* of the earth	2Sa 22:43	6083
as I exalted thee out of the *d*	1Kin 16:2	6083
the wood, and the stones, and the *d*	1Kin 18:38	6083
if the *d* of Samaria shall suffice	1Kin 20:10	6083
made them like the *d* by threshing	2Kin 13:7	6083
cast the *d* of them into the brook	2Kin 23:12	6083
the *d* of the earth in multitude	2Chr 1:9	6083
made *d* of them, and strowed it	2Chr 34:4	1854
sprinkled *d* upon their heads	Job 2:12	6083
whose foundation is in the *d*	Job 4:19	6083
cometh not forth of the *d*	Job 5:6	6083
clothed with worms and clods of *d*	Job 7:5	6083
for now shall I sleep in the *d*	Job 7:21	6083
wilt thou bring me into *d* again	Job 10:9	6083
grow out of the *d* of the earth	Job 14:19	6083
skin, and defiled my horn in the *d*	Job 16:15	6083
our rest together is in the *d*	Job 17:16	6083
shall lie down with him in the *d*	Job 20:11	6083
shall lie down alike in the *d*	Job 21:26	6083
Then shalt thou lay up gold as *d*	Job 22:24	6083
Though he heap up silver as the *d*	Job 27:16	6083
and it hath *d* of gold	Job 28:6	6083
the mire, and I am become like *d*	Job 30:19	6083
and man shall turn again unto *d*	Job 34:15	6083
When the *d* groweth into hardness	Job 38:38	6083
earth, and warmeth them in the *d*	Job 39:14	6083
Hide them in the *d* together	Job 40:13	6083
I abhor myself, and repent in *d*	Job 42:6	6083
and lay mine honour in the *d*	Ps 7:5	6083
small as the *d* before the wind	Ps 18:42	6083
brought me into the *d* of death	Ps 22:15	6083
to the *d* shall bow before him	Ps 22:29	6083
shall the *d* praise thee	Ps 30:9	6083
our soul is bowed down to the *d*	Ps 44:25	6083
and his enemies shall lick the *d*	Ps 72:9	6083
rained flesh also upon them as *d*	Ps 78:27	6083
stones, and favour the *d* thereof	Ps 102:14	6083
he remembereth that we are *d*	Ps 103:14	6083
they die, and return to their *d*	Ps 104:29	6083
raiseth up the poor out of the *d*	Ps 113:7	6083
My soul cleaveth unto the *d*	Ps 119:25	6083
part of the *d* of the world	Prov 8:26	6083
the *d*, and all turn to *d* again	Eccl 3:20	6083
Then shall the *d* return to the	Eccl 12:7	6083
the rock, and hide thee in the *d*	Is 2:10	6083
and their blossom shall go up as *d*	Is 5:24	80
to the ground, even to the *d*	Is 25:12	6083
he bringeth it even to the *d*	Is 26:5	6083
Awake and sing, ye that dwell in *d*	Is 26:19	6083
speech shall be low out of the *d*	Is 29:4	6083
speech shall whisper out of the *d*	Is 29:4	6083
strangers shall be like small *d*	Is 29:5	80
their *d* made fat with fatness	Is 34:7	6083
the *d* thereof into brimstone, and	Is 34:9	6083
comprehended the *d* of the earth	Is 40:12	6083
as the small *d* of the balance	Is 40:15	7834
gave them as the *d* to his sword	Is 41:2	6083
Come down, and sit in the *d*	Is 47:1	6083
and lick up the *d* of thy feet	Is 49:23	6083
Shake thyself from the *d*	Is 52:2	6083
d shall be the serpent's meat	Is 65:25	6083
have cast up *d* upon their heads	Lam 2:10	6083
He putteth his mouth in the *d*	Lam 3:29	6083
the ground, to cover it with *d*	Eze 24:7	6083
I will also scrape her *d* from her	Eze 26:4	6083
horses their *d* shall cover thee	Eze 26:10	80
thy *d* in the midst of the water	Eze 26:12	6083
shall cast up *d* upon their heads	Eze 27:30	6083
in the *d* of the earth shall awake	Dan 12:2	6083
That pant after the *d* of the	Amos 2:7	6083
of Aphrah roll thyself in the *d*	Mic 1:10	6083
shall lick the *d* like a serpent	Mic 7:17	6083
the clouds are the *d* of his feet	Nah 1:3	80
thy nobles shall dwell in the *d*	Nah 3:18	
for they shall heap *d*, and take it	Hab 1:10	6083
blood shall be poured out as *d*	Zeph 1:17	6083
and heaped up silver as the *d*	Zec 9:3	6083
shake off the *d* of your feet	Mt 10:14	*2868*
shake off the *d* under your feet	Mk 6:11	*5522*
shake off the very *d* from your	Lk 9:5	*2868*
Even the very *d* of your city	Lk 10:11	*2868*
But they shook off the *d* of their	Acts 13:51	*2868*
clothes, and threw *d* into the air	Acts 22:23	*2868*
they cast *d* on their heads, and	Rev 18:19	*5522*

DUTIES

And that doeth not any of those *d*	Eze 18:11	

DUTY

her *d* of marriage, shall he not	Ex 21:10	
perform the *d* of an husband's	Deut 25:5	
the *d* of my husband's brother	Deut 25:7	
as the *d* of every day required	2Chr 8:14	1697
as the *d* of every day required	Ezr 3:4	1697
for this is the whole *d* of man	Eccl 12:13	
done that which was our *d* to do	Lk 17:10	*3784*
their *d* is also to minister unto	Rom 15:27	*3784*

DWARF

Or crookbackt, or a *d*, or that	Lev 21:20	1851

DWELL

the father of such as *d* in tents	Gen 4:20	3427
he shall *d* in the tents of Shem	Gen 9:27	7931
them, that they might *d* together	Gen 13:6	3427
so that they could not *d* together	Gen 13:6	3427
he shall *d* in the presence of all	Gen 16:12	7931
for he feared to *d* in Zoar	Gen 19:30	3427
d where it pleaseth thee	Gen 20:15	3427
of the Canaanites, among whom I *d*	Gen 24:3	3427
the Canaanites, in whose land I *d*	Gen 24:37	3427
d in the land which I shall tell	Gen 26:2	7931
now will my husband *d* with me	Gen 30:20	2082
And ye shall *d* with us	Gen 34:10	3427
d and trade ye therein, and get you	Gen 34:10	3427
we will *d* with you, and we will	Gen 34:16	3427
therefore let them *d* in the land	Gen 34:21	3427
consent unto us for to *d* with us	Gen 34:22	3427
unto them, and they will *d* with us	Gen 34:23	3427
go up to Beth-el, and *d* there	Gen 35:1	3427
than that they might *d* together	Gen 36:7	3427
thou shalt *d* in the land of	Gen 45:10	3427
that ye may *d* in the land of	Gen 46:34	3427
let thy servants *d* in the land of	Gen 47:4	3427
make thy father and brethren to *d*	Gen 47:6	3427
in the land of Goshen let them *d*	Gen 47:6	3427
Zebulun shall *d* at the haven of	Gen 49:13	7931
was content to *d* with the man	Ex 2:21	3427
of Goshen, in which my people *d*	Ex 8:22	5975
thou hast made for thee to *d* in	Ex 15:17	3427
They shall not *d* in thy land	Ex 23:33	3427
that I may *d* among them	Ex 25:8	7931
I will *d* among the children of	Ex 29:45	7931
of Egypt, that I may *d* among them	Ex 29:46	7931
he shall *d* alone	Lev 13:46	3427
whither I bring you to *d* therein	Lev 20:22	3427
Ye shall *d* in booths seven days	Lev 23:42	3427
Israelites born shall *d* in booths	Lev 23:42	3427
children of Israel to *d* in booths	Lev 23:43	3427
ye shall *d* in the land in safety	Lev 25:18	3427
your fill, and *d* therein in safety	Lev 25:19	3427
full, and *d* in your land safely	Lev 26:5	3427
your enemies which *d* therein	Lev 26:32	3427
camps, in the midst whereof I *d*	Num 5:3	7931
what the land is that they *d* in	Num 13:19	3427
cities they be that they *d* in	Num 13:19	3427
be strong that *d* in the land	Num 13:28	3427
The Amalekites *d* in the land of	Num 13:29	3427
the Amorites, *d* in the mountains	Num 13:29	3427
and the Canaanites *d* by the sea	Num 13:29	3427
I sware to make you *d* therein	Num 14:30	7931
lo, the people shall *d* alone	Num 23:9	7931
our little ones shall *d* in the	Num 32:17	3427
of the land, and *d* therein	Num 33:53	3427
vex you in the land wherein ye *d*	Num 33:55	3427
their possession cities to *d* in	Num 35:2	3427
cities shall they have to *d* in	Num 35:3	3427
come again to *d* in the land	Num 35:32	3427
ye shall inhabit, wherein I *d*	Num 35:34	7931
for I the LORD *d* among the	Num 35:34	7931
children of Esau, which *d* in Seir	Deut 2:4	3427
children of Esau which *d* in Seir	Deut 2:29	3427
and the Moabites which *d* in Ar	Deut 2:29	3427
which *d* in the champaign over	Deut 11:30	3427
ye shall possess it, and *d* therein	Deut 11:31	3427
d in the land which the LORD your	Deut 12:10	3427
about, so that ye *d* in safety	Deut 12:10	3427
to cause his name to *d* there	Deut 12:11	7931
God hath given thee to *d* there	Deut 13:12	3427
shalt *d* therein, and shalt say, I	Deut 17:14	3427
He shall *d* with thee, even among	Deut 23:16	3427
If brethren *d* together, and one of	Deut 25:5	3427
and thou shalt not *d* therein	Deut 28:30	3427
that thou mayest *d* in the land	Deut 30:20	3427
the LORD shall *d* in safety by him	Deut 33:12	7931
he shall *d* between his shoulders	Deut 33:12	7931
then shall *d* in safety alone	Deut 33:28	7931
Peradventure ye *d* among us	Josh 9:7	3427
when ye *d* among us	Josh 9:22	3427
d in the mountains are gathered	Josh 10:6	3427
the Maachathites *d* among the	Josh 13:13	3427
in the land, save cities to *d* in	Josh 14:4	3427
but the Jebusites *d* with the	Josh 15:63	3427
but the Canaanites *d* among the	Josh 16:10	3427
Canaanites would *d* in that land	Josh 17:12	3427
all the Canaanites that *d* in the	Josh 17:16	3427
a place, that he may *d* among them	Josh 20:4	3427
he shall *d* in that city, until he	Josh 20:6	3427
Moses to give us cities to *d* in	Josh 21:2	3427
ye built not, and ye *d* in them	Josh 24:13	3427
the Amorites, in whose land ye *d*	Josh 24:15	3427
but the Jebusites *d* with the	Judg 1:21	3427
Canaanites would *d* in that land	Judg 1:27	3427
But the Amorites would *d* in mount	Judg 1:35	3427
the Amorites, in whose land ye *d*	Judg 6:10	3427
that they should not *d* in Shechem	Judg 9:41	3427
D with me, and be unto me a father	Judg 17:10	3427
was content to *d* with the man	Judg 17:11	3427
them an inheritance to *d* in	Judg 18:1	3427
made them *d* in this place	1Sa 12:8	3427
the country, that I may *d* there	1Sa 27:5	3427
for why should thy servant *d* in	1Sa 27:5	3427
I *d* in an house of cedar, but the	2Sa 7:2	3427
build me an house for me to *d* in	2Sa 7:5	3427
that they may *d* in a place of	2Sa 7:10	7931
d there, and go not forth thence	1Kin 2:36	3427
this woman *d* in one house	1Kin 3:17	3427
I will *d* among the children of	1Kin 6:13	7931
he would *d* in the thick darkness	1Kin 8:12	7931
built thee an house to *d* in	1Kin 8:13	2073
will God indeed *d* on the earth	1Kin 8:27	3427
belongeth to Zidon, and *d* there	1Kin 17:9	3427
I *d* among mine own people	2Kin 4:13	3427
the place where we *d* with thee is	2Kin 6:1	3427
us a place there, where we may *d*	2Kin 6:2	3427
d there, and let him teach them	2Kin 17:27	3427
d in the land, and serve the king	2Kin 25:24	3427
I *d* in an house of cedars, but	1Chr 17:1	3427
not build me an house to *d* in	1Chr 17:4	3427
they shall *d* in their place, and	1Chr 17:9	7931
that they may *d* in Jerusalem for	1Chr 23:25	7931
build him an house to *d* therein	2Chr 2:3	3427
he would *d* in the thick darkness	2Chr 6:1	7931
very deed *d* with men on the earth	2Chr 6:18	3427
the children of Israel to *d* there	2Chr 8:2	3427
My wife shall not *d* in the house	2Chr 8:11	3427
brethren that *d* in their cities	2Chr 19:10	3427
companions that *d* in Samaria	Ezr 4:17	3488
name to *d* there destroy all kings	Ezr 6:12	7932
d in booths in the feast of the	Neh 8:14	3427
to bring one of ten to *d* in	Neh 11:1	3427
nine parts to *d* in other cities	Neh 11:1	3427
themselves to *d* at Jerusalem	Neh 11:2	3427
let a cloud *d* upon it	Job 3:5	7931
in them that *d* in houses of clay	Job 4:19	7931
wickedness *d* in thy tabernacles	Job 11:14	7931
It shall *d* in his tabernacle,	Job 18:15	7931
They that *d* in mine house, and my	Job 19:15	1481
To *d* in the cliffs of the valleys	Job 30:6	7931
LORD, only makest me *d* in safety	Ps 4:8	3427
neither shall evil *d* with thee	Ps 5:4	1481
who shall *d* in thy holy hill	Ps 15:1	7931
I will *d* in the house of the LORD	Ps 23:6	3427
the world, and they that *d* therein	Ps 24:1	3427
His soul shall *d* at ease	Ps 25:13	3885
that I may *d* in the house of the	Ps 27:4	3427
so shalt thou *d* in the land	Ps 37:3	7931
and *d* for evermore	Ps 37:27	7931
the land, and *d* therein for ever	Ps 37:29	7931
that he may *d* in thy courts	Ps 65:4	7931
They also that *d* in the uttermost	Ps 65:8	3427
the rebellious *d* in a dry land	Ps 68:6	7931
hill which God desireth to *d* in	Ps 68:16	3427
the LORD will *d* in it for ever	Ps 68:16	7931
the LORD God might *d* among them	Ps 68:18	7931
let none *d* in their tents	Ps 69:25	3427
that they may *d* there, and have it	Ps 69:35	3427
love his name shall *d* therein	Ps 69:36	7931
They that *d* in the wilderness	Ps 72:9	
of Israel to *d* in their tents	Ps 78:55	7931
are they that *d* in thy house	Ps 84:4	3427
than to *d* in the tents of	Ps 84:10	1752
that glory may *d* in our land	Ps 85:9	7931
the world, and they that *d* therein	Ps 98:7	3427
the land, that they may *d* with me	Ps 101:6	3427
shall not *d* within my house	Ps 101:7	3427
they found no city to *d* in	Ps 107:4	4186
wickedness of them that *d* therein	Ps 107:34	3427
there he maketh the hungry to *d*	Ps 107:36	3427
that I *d* in the tents of Kedar	Ps 120:5	7931
here will I *d*; for I have	Ps 132:14	3427
brethren to *d* together in unity	Ps 133:1	3427
d in the uttermost parts of the	Ps 139:9	7931
upright shall *d* in thy presence	Ps 140:13	3427
he hath made me to *d* in darkness	Ps 143:3	3427
hearkeneth unto me shall *d* safely	Prov 1:33	7931
the upright shall *d* in the land	Prov 2:21	7931
I wisdom *d* with prudence, and find	Prov 8:12	7931
It is better to *d* in a corner of	Prov 21:9	3427
It is better to *d* in the	Prov 21:19	3427
It is better to *d* in the corner	Prov 25:24	3427
I *d* in the midst of a people of	Is 6:5	3427
they that *d* in the land of the	Is 9:2	3427
wolf also shall *d* with the lamb	Is 11:6	1481
and owls shall *d* there, and satyrs	Is 13:21	7931
Let mine outcasts *d* with thee	Is 16:4	1481
for them that *d* in the wilderness	Is 23:13	
for them that *d* before the LORD	Is 23:18	3427
they that *d* therein are desolate	Is 24:6	3427
bringeth down them that *d* on high	Is 26:5	3427
Awake and sing, ye that *d* in dust	Is 26:19	7931
shall *d* in Zion at Jerusalem	Is 30:19	3427
shall *d* in the wilderness	Is 32:16	7931
my people shall *d* in a peaceable	Is 32:18	3427
Who among us shall *d* with the	Is 33:14	1481
who among us shall *d* with	Is 33:14	1481
He shall *d* on high	Is 33:16	7931
the people that *d* therein shall	Is 33:24	3427
also and the raven shall *d* in it	Is 34:11	7931
generation shall they *d* therein	Is 34:17	7931
them out as a tent to *d* in	Is 40:22	3427
give place to me that I may *d*	Is 49:20	3427
they that *d* therein shall die in	Is 51:6	3427
I *d* in the high and holy place,	Is 57:15	7931
The restorer of paths to *d* in	Is 58:12	3427
it, and my servants shall *d* there	Is 65:9	7931
forsaken, and not a man *d* therein	Jer 4:29	3427
will cause you to *d* in this place	Jer 7:3	7931
I cause you to *d* in this place	Jer 7:7	7931
the city, and those that *d* therein	Jer 8:16	3427
of them that *d* in a far country	Jer 8:19	
corners, that *d* in the wilderness	Jer 9:26	3427
wickedness of them that *d* therein	Jer 12:4	3427
all that *d* in thine house shall	Jer 20:6	3427
saved, and Israel shall *d* safely	Jer 23:6	7931
they shall *d* in their own land	Jer 23:8	3427
them that *d* in the land of Egypt	Jer 24:8	3427
d in the land that the LORD hath	Jer 25:5	3427
people that *d* in the desert	Jer 25:24	7931
they shall till it, and *d* therein	Jer 27:11	3427
Build ye houses, and *d* in them	Jer 29:5	3427

build ye houses, and *d* in them .... Jer 29:28 3427
have a man to *d* among this people...... Jer 29:32 3427
there shall *d* in Judah itself, and........ Jer 31:24 3427
and I will cause them to *d* safely .... Jer 32:37 3427
and Jerusalem shall *d* safely .... Jer 33:16 7931
all your days ye shall *d* in tents............ Jer 35:7 3427
to build houses for us to *d* in.............. Jer 35:9 3427
so we *d* at Jerusalem .... Jer 35:11 3427
ye shall *d* in the land which I.............. Jer 35:15 3427
d with him among the people............... Jer 40:5 3427
d in the land, and serve the king.......... Jer 40:9 3427
I will *d* at Mizpah to serve the............. Jer 40:10 3427
d in your cities that ye have................. Jer 40:10 3427
We will not *d* in this land,..................... Jer 42:13 3427
and there will we *d*................................ Jer 42:14 3427
to *d* in the land of Judah...................... Jer 43:4 3427
to *d* in the land of Judah...................... Jer 43:5 1481
Jews which *d* in the land of Egypt......... Jer 44:1 3427
which *d* at Migdol, and at.................... Jer 44:1 3427
of Egypt, whither ye be gone to *d*.......... Jer 44:8 1481
them that *d* in the land of Egypt........... Jer 44:13 3427
a desire to return to *d* there .... Jer 44:14 3427
all Judah that *d* in the land of.............. Jer 44:26 3427
the city, and them that *d* therein .... Jer 47:2 3427
without any to *d* therein....................... Jer 48:9 3427
O ye that *d* in Moab, leave the.............. Jer 48:28 3427
d in the rock, and be like the................ Jer 48:28 7931
his people *d* in his cities........................ Jer 49:1 3427
d deep, O inhabitants of Dedan............. Jer 49:8 3427
shall a son of man *d* in it........................ Jer 49:18 1481
d deep, O ye inhabitants of Hazor......... Jer 49:30 3427
gates nor bars, which *d* alone.............. Jer 49:31 7931
there, nor any son of man *d* in it .... Jer 49:33 1481
desolate, and none shall *d* therein......... Jer 50:3 3427
of the islands shall *d* there .... Jer 50:39 3427
and the owls shall *d* therein.................. Jer 50:39 3427
shall any son of man *d* therein............... Jer 50:40 1481
against them that *d* in the midst .... Jer 51:1 3427
thou dost *d* among scorpions .... Eze 2:6 3427
of all them that *d* therein .... Eze 12:19 3427
daughters that *d* at thy left hand .... Eze 16:46 3427
under it shall *d* all fowl of.................... Eze 17:23 7931
the branches thereof shall they *d*.......... Eze 17:23 7931
then shall they *d* in their land.............. Eze 28:25 3427
they shall *d* safely therein, and............ Eze 28:26 3427
they shall *d* with confidence,................ Eze 28:26 3427
smite all them that *d* therein................. Eze 32:15 3427
they shall *d* safely in the .... Eze 34:25 3427
but they shall *d* safely, and none.......... Eze 34:28 3427
ye shall *d* in the land that I.................. Eze 36:28 3427
also cause you to *d* in the cities............ Eze 36:33 3427
they shall *d* in the land that I............... Eze 37:25 3427
and they shall *d* therein, even............... Eze 37:25 3427
they shall *d* safely all of them .... Eze 38:8 3427
that *d* safely, all of them....................... Eze 38:11 3427
that *d* in the midst of the land............... Eze 38:12 3427
among them that *d* carelessly in........... Eze 39:6 3427
they that *d* in the cities of...................... Eze 39:9 3427
where I will *d* in the midst of................ Eze 43:7 7931
I will *d* in the midst of them for........... Eze 43:9 7931
wheresoever the children of men *d*........ Dan 2:38 1753
that *d* in all the earth .... Dan 4:1 1753
that *d* in all the earth .... Dan 6:25 1753
They shall not *d* in the LORD'S............... Hos 9:3 3427
yet make thee to *d* in tabernacles......... Hos 12:9 3427
They that *d* under his shadow............... Hos 14:7 3427
But Judah shall *d* for ever .... Joel 3:20 3427
of Israel be taken out that *d* in.............. Amos 3:12 3427
stone, but ye shall not *d* in them........... Amos 5:11 3427
all that *d* therein shall mourn................ Amos 9:5
thou shalt *d* in the field, and .... Mic 4:10 7931
because of them that *d* therein .... Mic 7:13 3427
which *d* solitarily in the wood,.............. Mic 7:14 7931
the world, and all that *d* therein........... Nah 1:5 3427
thy nobles shall *d* in the dust .... Nah 3:18 7931
city, and of all that *d* therein................. Hab 2:8 3427
city, and of all that *d* therein................. Hab 2:17 3427
of all them that *d* in the land .... Zeph 1:18 3427
to *d* in your cieled houses, and .... Hag 1:4 3427
I will *d* in the midst of thee,................. Zec 2:10 7931
I will *d* in the midst of thee, and.......... Zec 2:11 7931
will *d* in the midst of Jerusalem........... Zec 8:3 7931
old women *d* in the streets of................ Zec 8:4 3427
they shall *d* in the midst of................... Zec 8:8 7931
And a bastard shall *d* in Ashdod............ Zec 9:6 3427
And men shall *d* in it, and there .... Zec 14:11 3427
And they enter in and *d* there................ Mt 12:45 *2730*
and they enter in, and *d* there.............. Lk 11:26 *2730*
d on the face of the whole earth............ Lk 21:35 *2521*
desolate, and let no man *d* therein......... Acts 1:20 *2730*
all ye that *d* at Jerusalem, be .... Acts 2:14 *2730*
to all them that *d* in Jerusalem.............. Acts 4:16 *2730*
into this land, wherein ye now *d*........... Acts 7:4 *2730*
For they that *d* at Jerusalem................. Acts 13:27 *2730*
to *d* on all the face of the earth............ Acts 17:26 *2730*
but Paul was suffered to *d* by................ Acts 28:16 *3306*
that the Spirit of God *d* in you .... Rom 8:9 *3611*
up Jesus from the dead *d* in you .... Rom 8:11 *3611*
and she be pleased to *d* with him.......... 1Cor 7:12 *3611*
and if he be pleased to *d* with her......... 1Cor 7:13 *3611*
I will *d* in them, and walk in them 2Cor 6:16 *1774*
That Christ may *d* in your hearts........... Eph 3:17 *2730*
that in him should all fulness *d*............. Col 1:19 *2730*
Let the word of Christ *d* in you .... Col 3:16 *1774*
d with them according to........................ 1Pet 3:7 *4924*
Hereby know we that we *d* in him 1Jn 4:13 *3306*
to try them that *d* upon the earth........... Rev 3:10 *2730*
blood on them that *d* on the earth.......... Rev 6:10 *2730*
on the throne shall *d* among them.......... Rev 7:15 *4637*
they that *d* upon the earth shall............ Rev 11:10 *2730*
ye heavens, and ye that *d* in them .... Rev 12:12 *4637*
and them that *d* in heaven...................... Rev 13:6 *4637*
all that *d* upon the earth shall............... Rev 13:8 *2730*
them which *d* therein to worship .... Rev 13:12 *2730*
deceiveth them that *d* on the................ Rev 13:14 *2730*
to them that *d* on the earth .... Rev 13:14 *2730*
unto them that *d* on the earth .... Rev 14:6 *2730*
they that *d* on the earth shall .... Rev 17:8 *2730*
he will *d* with them, and they .... Rev 21:3 *4637*

DWELLED

the Perizzite *d* then in the land .... Gen 13:7 3427
Abram *d* in the land of Canaan, and .... Gen 13:12 3427
Lot *d* in the cities of the plain,............... Gen 13:12 3427
d between Kadesh and Shur, and .... Gen 20:1 3427
they *d* there about ten years .... Ruth 1:4 3427
on every side, and ye *d* safe.................. 1Sa 12:11 3427

DWELLERS

d on the earth, see ye, when he............. Is 18:3 7931
known unto all the *d* at Jerusalem .... Acts 1:19 *2730*
the *d* in Mesopotamia, and in................. Acts 2:9 *2730*

DWELLEST

them, and *d* in their land........................ Deut 12:29 3427
d in their cities, and in their .... Deut 19:1 3427
and possessest it, and *d* therein .... Deut 26:1 3427
which *d* between the cherubims............. 2Kin 19:15 3427
thou that *d* between the cherubims...... Ps 80:1 3427
O thou that *d* in the heavens .... Ps 123:1 3427
Thou that *d* in the gardens, the............ Song 8:13 3427
hosts, O my people that *d* in Zion.......... Is 10:24 3427
that *d* between the cherubims,.............. Is 37:16 3427
that *d* carelessly, that sayest in............ Is 47:8 3427
O thou that *d* in the clefts of................. Jer 49:16 7931
O thou that *d* upon many waters,........... Jer 51:13 7931
of Edom, that *d* in the land of Uz .... Lam 4:21 3427
thee, O thou that *d* in the land .... Eze 7:7 3427
of man, thou *d* in the midst of a............. Eze 12:2 3427
thou that *d* in the clefts of the.............. Obad 3 7931
that *d* with the daughter of .... Zec 2:7 3427
Master,) where *d* thou........................... Jn 1:38 *3306*
I know thy works, and where thou *d*....... Rev 2:13 *2730*

DWELLETH

But the stranger that *d* with you........... Lev 19:34 1481
if thy brother that *d* by thee be .... Lev 25:39
brother that *d* by him wax poor .... Lev 25:47
and the people that *d* therein .... Num 13:18 3427
he *d* as a lion, and teareth the .... Deut 33:20 7931
she *d* in Israel even unto this............... Josh 6:25 3427
wherein the LORD's tabernacle *d*........... Josh 22:19 7931
which *d* between the cherubims............ 1Sa 4:4 3427
while he *d* in the country of the............ 1Sa 27:11 3427
that *d* between the cherubims............... 2Sa 6:2 3427
the ark of God *d* within curtains............ 2Sa 7:2 3427
that *d* between the cherubims,.............. 1Chr 13:6 3427
he *d* in desolate cities, and in .... Job 15:28 7931
Where is the way where light *d*............. Job 38:19 7931
She *d* and abideth on the rock,.............. Job 39:28 7931
to the LORD, which *d* in Zion .... Ps 9:11 3427
and the place where thine honour *d*....... Ps 26:8 4908
He that *d* in the secret place of .... Ps 91:1 3427
the LORD our God, who *d* on high,.......... Ps 113:5 3427
out of Zion, which *d* at Jerusalem .... Ps 135:21 7931
seeing he *d* securely by thee................. Prov 3:29 3427
of hosts, which *d* in mount Zion .... Is 8:18 7931
for he *d* on high...................................... Is 33:5 7931
the people that *d* in this city .... Jer 29:16 3427
desolation, and no man *d* therein,.......... Jer 44:2 3427
that *d* without care, saith the................ Jer 49:31 3427
a land wherein no man *d*, neither .... Jer 51:43 3427
she *d* among the heathen, she............... Lam 1:3 3427
that *d* at thy right hand, is.................... Eze 16:46 3427
the king *d* that made him king............... Eze 17:16
when my people of Israel *d* safely.......... Eze 38:14 3427
darkness, and the light *d* with him .... Dan 2:22 8271
every one that *d* therein shall .... Hos 4:3 3427
for the LORD *d* in Zion .... Joel 3:21 7931
and every one mourn that *d* therein...... Amos 8:8 3427
by it, and by him that *d* therein............. Mt 23:21 *2730*
my blood, *d* in me, and I in him .... Jn 6:56 *3306*
but the Father that *d* in me .... Jn 14:10 *3306*
for he *d* with you, and shall be in .... Jn 14:17 *3306*
Howbeit the most High *d* not in .... Acts 7:48 *2730*
d not in temples made with hands......... Acts 17:24 *2730*
that do it, but sin that *d* in me............. Rom 7:17 *3611*
is, in my flesh,) *d* no good thing .... Rom 7:18 *3611*
that do it, but sin that *d* in me............. Rom 7:20 *3611*
by his Spirit that *d* in you .... Rom 8:11 *1774*
that the Spirit of God *d* in you 1Cor 3:16 *3611*
For in him *d* all the fulness of.............. Col 2:9 *2730*
by the Holy Ghost which *d* in us........... 2Ti 1:14 *1774*
The spirit that *d* in us lusteth .... Jas 4:5 *2730*
earth, wherein *d* righteousness 2Pet 3:13 *2730*
how *d* the love of God in him 1Jn 3:17 *3306*
keepeth his commandments *d* in him... 1Jn 3:24 *3306*
God *d* in us, and his love is.................. 1Jn 4:12 *3306*
God *d* in him, and he in God................. 1Jn 4:15 *3306*
he that *d* in love *d* in God.................... 1Jn 4:16 *3306*
the truth's sake, which *d* in us.............. 2Jn 2 *3306*
slain among you, where Satan *d*............ Rev 2:13 *2730*

DWELLING

their *d* was from Mesha, as thou .... Gen 10:30 4186
Jacob was a plain man, *d* in tents.......... Gen 25:27 3427
thy *d* shall be the fatness of the .... Gen 27:39 4186
if a man sell a *d* house in a.................. Lev 25:29 4186
that goeth down to the *d* of Ar............... Num 21:15 3427
dukes of Sihon, *d* in the country........... Josh 13:21 3427
hear thou in heaven thy *d* place.......... 1Kin 8:30 3427
hear thou in heaven thy *d* place.......... 1Kin 8:39 3427
Hear thou in heaven thy *d* place 1Kin 8:43 3427
in heaven thy *d* place, and................... 1Kin 8:49 3427
were in his city, *d* with Naboth 1Kin 21:8 3427
at the beginning of their *d* there 2Kin 17:25 3427
they ministered before the *d*................ 1Chr 6:32 4908
Now these are their *d* places 1Chr 6:54 4186
and a place for thy *d* for ever.............. 2Chr 6:2 3427
hear thou from thy *d* place.................. 2Chr 6:21 3427
hear thou from heaven thy *d* place........ 2Chr 6:30 3427
heavens, even from thy *d* place............ 2Chr 6:33 3427
heavens, even from thy *d* place 2Chr 6:39 3427
came up to his holy *d* place................. 2Chr 30:27 4583
on his people, and on his *d* place........... 2Chr 36:15 4583
the *d* place of the wicked shall .... Job 8:22 168
where are the *d* places of the................ Job 21:28 4908
their *d* places to all generations........... Ps 49:11 4908
consume in the grave from their *d*......... Ps 49:14 2073
and pluck thee out of thy *d* place .... Ps 52:5 168
defiled by casting down the *d*.............. Ps 74:7 4908
and his *d* place in Zion.......................... Ps 76:2 4585
Jacob, and laid waste his *d* place.......... Ps 79:7 5116
thou hast been our *d* place in all........... Ps 90:1 4583
shall any plague come nigh thy *d* .... Ps 91:10 168
and oil in the *d* of the wise .... Prov 21:20 5116
against the *d* of the righteous.............. Prov 24:15 5116
upon every *d* place of mount Zion......... Is 4:5 4349
I will consider in my *d* place .... Is 18:4 4349
O thou daughter *d* in Egypt................... Jer 46:19 3427
And Hazor shall be a *d* for dragons....... Jer 49:33 4583
a *d* place for dragons, an .... Jer 51:37 4583
all of them *d* without walls, and........... Eze 38:11 3427
profane place for the city, for *d*........... Eze 48:15 4186
whose *d* is not with flesh....................... Dan 2:11 4070
thy *d* shall be with the beasts of.......... Dan 4:25 4070
thy *d* shall be with the beasts of.......... Dan 4:32 4070
his *d* was with the wild asses .... Dan 5:21 4070
I am the LORD your God *d* in Zion .... Joel 3:17 7931
Where is the *d* of the lions.................... Nah 2:11 4583
so their *d* should not be cut off,............ Zeph 3:7 4583
Who had his *d* among the tombs .... Mk 5:3 *2731*
there were *d* at Jerusalem Jews,............ Acts 2:5 *2730*
Jews and Greeks also *d* at Ephesus .... Acts 19:17 *2730*
d in the light which no man can 1Ti 6:16 *3611*
d in tabernacles with Isaac and............ Heb 11:9 *2730*
that righteous man *d* among them 2Pet 2:8 *1460*

DWELLINGPLACE

parable, and said, Strong is thy *d*......... Num 24:21 4186
and have no certain *d* place.................. 1Cor 4:11 *790*

DWELLINGPLACES

tents, and have mercy on his *d*.............. Jer 30:18 4908
they have burned her *d*......................... Jer 51:30 4908
In all your *d* the cities shall be .... Eze 6:6 4186
will save them out of all their *d*........... Eze 37:23 4186
to possess the *d* that are not .... Hab 1:6 4908

DWELLINGS

of Israel had light in their *d*.................. Ex 10:23 4186
generations throughout all your *d* .... Lev 3:17 4186
or of beast, in any of your *d*.................. Lev 7:26 4186
sabbath of the LORD in all your *d*.......... Lev 23:3 4186
your generations in all your *d*.............. Lev 23:14 4186
d throughout your generations .... Lev 23:21 4186
your generations in all your *d*.............. Lev 23:31 4186
your generations in all your *d*.............. Num 35:29 4186
nor any remaining in his *d*.................... Job 18:19 4033
such are the *d* of the wicked .... Job 18:21 4908
and the barren land his *d*.................... Job 39:6 4908
for wickedness is in their *d*.................. Ps 55:15 4033
Zion more than all the *d* of Jacob.......... Ps 87:2 4908
habitation, and in sure *d*, and in........... Is 32:18 4908
because our *d* have cast us out............. Jer 9:19 4908
in thee, and make their *d* in thee .... Eze 25:4 4908
And the sea coast shall be *d*................. Zeph 2:6 5116

DWELT

d in the land of Nod, on the east........... Gen 4:16 3427
and they *d* there .... Gen 11:2 3427
they came unto Haran, and *d* there........ Gen 11:31 3427
d in the plain of Mamre, which is .... Gen 13:18 3427
Amorites, that *d* in Hazezon-tamar........ Gen 14:7 3427
who *d* in Sodom, and his goods, and..... Gen 14:12 3427
for he *d* in the plain of Mamre.............. Gen 14:13 7931
after Abram had *d* ten years in............. Gen 16:3 3427
the cities in the which Lot *d*.................. Gen 19:29 3427
d in the mountain, and his two............... Gen 19:30 3427
he *d* in a cave, he and his two .... Gen 19:30 3427
d in the wilderness, and became an ...... Gen 21:20 3427
he *d* in the wilderness of Paran .... Gen 21:21 3427
and Abraham *d* at Beer-sheba .... Gen 22:19 3427
Ephron *d* among the children of............. Gen 23:10 3427
for he *d* in the south country .... Gen 24:62 3427
Isaac *d* by the well Lahai-roi .... Gen 25:11 3427
they *d* from Havilah unto Shur,............. Gen 25:18 7931
And Isaac *d* in Gerar .... Gen 26:6 3427
the valley of Gerar, and *d* there............. Gen 26:17 3427
when Israel *d* in that land, that .... Gen 35:22 7931
Thus *d* Esau in mount Seir .... Gen 36:8 3427
Jacob *d* in the land wherein his.............. Gen 37:1 3427
went and *d* in her father's house........... Gen 38:11 3427
Israel *d* in the land of Egypt, in .... Gen 47:27 3427
Joseph *d* in Egypt, he, and his.............. Gen 50:22 3427
and *d* in the land of Midian .... Ex 2:15 3427
who *d* in Egypt, was four hundred.......... Ex 12:40 3427
the land of Egypt, wherein ye *d*............. Lev 18:3 3427
your sabbaths, when ye *d* upon it .... Lev 26:35 3427
and the Canaanites *d* in the valley......... Num 14:25 3427
Canaanites which *d* in that hill.............. Num 14:45 3427
we have *d* in Egypt a long time............. Num 20:15 3427
which *d* in the south, heard tell............ Num 21:1 3427
Israel *d* in all the cities of the .... Num 21:25 3427
Thus Israel *d* in the land of the .... Num 21:31 3427
the Amorites, which *d* at Heshbon.......... Num 21:34 3427
all their cities wherein they *d*............... Num 31:10 4186
and he *d* therein................................... Num 32:40 3427
which *d* in the south in the land .... Num 33:40 3427
which *d* in Heshbon, and Og the............ Deut 1:4 3427
which *d* at Astaroth in Edrei .... Deut 1:4 3427
Ye have *d* long enough in this............... Deut 1:6 3427
which *d* in that mountain, came............ Deut 1:44 3427
which *d* in Seir, through the way........... Deut 2:8 3427
The Emims *d* therein in times past .... Deut 2:10 3427
The Horims also *d* in Seir..................... Deut 2:12 3427

before them, and *d* in their stead — Deut 2:12 3427
giants *d* therein in old time — Deut 2:20 3427
them, and *d* in their stead — Deut 2:21 3427
of Esau, which *d* in Seir, when he — Deut 2:22 3427
d in their stead even unto this — Deut 2:22 3427
And the Avims which *d* in Hazerim — Deut 2:23 3427
them, and *d* in their stead — Deut 2:23 3427
the Amorites, which *d* at Heshbon — Deut 3:2 3427
who *d* at Heshbon, whom Moses and — Deut 4:46 3427
built goodly houses, and *d* therein — Deut 8:12 3427
we have *d* in the land of Egypt — Deut 29:16 3427
will of him that *d* in the bush — Deut 33:16 7931
town wall, and she *d* upon the wall — Josh 2:15 3427
d on the other side Jordan — Josh 7:7 3427
and that they *d* among them — Josh 9:16 3427
who *d* in Heshbon, and ruled from — Josh 12:2 3427
that *d* at Ashtaroth and at Edrei, — Josh 12:4 3427
the Canaanites that *d* in Gezer — Josh 16:10 3427
d therein, and called Leshem, Dan, — Josh 19:47 3427
he built the city, and *d* therein — Josh 19:50 3427
they possessed it, and *d* therein — Josh 21:43 3427
the children of Reuben and Gad *d* — Josh 22:33 3427
Your fathers *d* on the other side — Josh 24:2 3427
ye *d* in the wilderness a long — Josh 24:7 3427
which *d* on the other side Jordan — Josh 24:8 3427
the Amorites which *d* in the land — Josh 24:18 3427
that *d* in the mountain, and in the — Judg 1:9 3427
the Canaanites that *d* in Hebron — Judg 1:10 3427
they went and *d* among the people — Judg 1:16 3427
the Canaanites that *d* in Gezer — Judg 1:29 3427
but the Canaanites *d* in Gezer — Judg 1:29 3427
but the Canaanites *d* among them — Judg 1:30 3427
But the Asherites *d* among the — Judg 1:32 3427
but he *d* among the Canaanites, — Judg 1:33 3427
Hivites that *d* in mount Lebanon — Judg 3:3 3427
of Israel *d* among the Canaanites — Judg 3:5 3427
which *d* in Harosheth of the — Judg 4:2 3427
she *d* under the palm tree of — Judg 4:5 3427
d in tents on the east of Nobah — Judg 8:11 7931
Joash went and *d* in his own house — Judg 8:29 3427
d there, for fear of Abimelech — Judg 9:21 3427
And Abimelech *d* at Arumah — Judg 9:41 3427
he *d* in Shamir in mount Ephraim — Judg 10:1 3427
brethren, and *d* in the land of Tob — Judg 11:3 3427
While Israel *d* in Heshbon — Judg 11:26 3427
d in the top of the rock Etam — Judg 15:8 3427
were therein, how they *d* careless — Judg 18:7 3427
they built a city, and *d* therein — Judg 18:28 3427
repaired the cities, and *d* in them — Judg 21:23 3427
and *d* with her mother in law — Ruth 2:23 3427
he and Samuel went and *d* in Naioth — 1Sa 19:18 3427
they *d* with him all the while — 1Sa 22:4 3427
d in strong holds at En-gedi — 1Sa 23:29 3427
David *d* with Achish at Gath, he — 1Sa 27:3 3427
the time that David *d* in the — 1Sa 27:7 3427
the Philistines came and *d* in them — 1Sa 31:7 3427
they *d* in the cities of Hebron — 2Sa 2:3 3427
So David *d* in the fort, and called — 2Sa 5:9 3427
Whereas I have not *d* in any house — 2Sa 7:6 3427
all that *d* in the house of Ziba — 2Sa 9:12 4186
So Mephibosheth *d* in Jerusalem — 2Sa 9:13 3427
So Absalom *d* two full years in — 2Sa 14:28 3427
Shimei *d* in Jerusalem many days — 1Kin 2:38 3427
And Judah and Israel *d* safely — 1Kin 4:25 3427
his house where he *d* had another — 1Kin 7:8 3427
the Canaanites that *d* in the city — 1Kin 9:16 3427
d therein, and reigned in Damascus — 1Kin 11:24 3427
Solomon, and Jeroboam *d* in Egypt — 1Kin 12:2 3427
which *d* in the cities of Judah — 1Kin 12:17 3427
in mount Ephraim, and *d* therein — 1Kin 12:25 3427
Now there *d* an old prophet in — 1Kin 13:11 3427
the city where the old prophet *d* — 1Kin 13:25 3427
that *d* at Damascus, saying, — 1Kin 15:18 3427
building of Ramah, and *d* in Tirzah — 1Kin 15:21 3427
d by the brook Cherith, that is — 1Kin 17:5 3427
of Israel *d* in their tents — 2Kin 13:5 3427
death, and *d* in a several house — 2Kin 15:5 3427
Elath, and *d* there unto this day — 2Kin 16:6 3427
and *d* in the cities thereof — 2Kin 17:24 3427
d in Beth-el, and taught them how — 2Kin 17:28 3427
in their cities wherein they *d* — 2Kin 17:29 3427
went and returned, and *d* at Nineveh — 2Kin 19:36 3427
(now she *d* in Jerusalem in the — 2Kin 22:14 3427
of the scribes which *d* at Jabez — 1Chr 2:55 3427
those that *d* among plants and — 1Chr 4:23 3427
there they *d* with the king for — 1Chr 4:23 3427
they *d* at Beer-sheba, and Moladah, — 1Chr 4:28 3427
they of Ham had *d* there of old — 1Chr 4:40 3427
this day, and *d* in their rooms — 1Chr 4:41 3427
escaped, and *d* there unto this day — 1Chr 4:43 3427
who *d* in Aroer, even unto Nebo and — 1Chr 5:8 3427
they *d* in their tents throughout — 1Chr 5:10 3427
of Gad *d* over against them — 1Chr 5:11 3427
they *d* in Gilead in Bashan, and in — 1Chr 5:16 3427
they *d* in their steads until the — 1Chr 5:22 3427
tribe of Manasseh *d* in the land — 1Chr 5:23 3427
In these *d* the children of Joseph — 1Chr 7:29 3427
These *d* in Jerusalem — 1Chr 8:28 3427
at Gibeon *d* the father of Gibeon — 1Chr 8:29 3427
these also *d* with their brethren — 1Chr 8:32 3427
d in their possessions in their — 1Chr 9:2
in Jerusalem *d* of the children of — 1Chr 9:3 3427
that *d* in the villages of the — 1Chr 9:16 3427
these *d* at Jerusalem — 1Chr 9:34 3427
in Gibeon *d* the father of Gibeon, — 1Chr 9:35 3427
they also *d* with their brethren — 1Chr 9:38 3427
the Philistines came and *d* in them — 1Chr 10:7 3427
And David *d* in the castle — 1Chr 11:7 3427
For I have not *d* in an house — 1Chr 17:5 3427
that *d* in the cities of Judah — 2Chr 10:17 3427
Rehoboam *d* in Jerusalem, and built — 2Chr 11:5 3427
that *d* at Damascus, saying, — 2Chr 16:2 3427
Jehoshaphat *d* at Jerusalem — 2Chr 19:4 3427
they *d* therein, and have built — 2Chr 20:8 3427
the Arabians that *d* in Gur-baal — 2Chr 26:7 3427
d in a several house, being a — 2Chr 26:21 3427
and they *d* there — 2Chr 28:18 3427
that *d* in Judah, rejoiced — 2Chr 30:25 3427
that *d* in Jerusalem to give the — 2Chr 31:4 3427
that *d* in the cities of Judah, — 2Chr 31:6 3427
(now she *d* in Jerusalem in the — 2Chr 34:22 3427
d in their cities, and all Israel — Ezr 2:70 3427
Moreover the Nethinims *d* in Ophel — Neh 3:26 3427
the Jews which *d* by them came — Neh 4:12 3427
and all Israel, *d* in their cities — Neh 7:73 3427
of the people *d* at Jerusalem — Neh 11:1 3427
the province that *d* in Jerusalem — Neh 11:3 3427
but in the cities of Judah *d* — Neh 11:3 3427
at Jerusalem *d* certain of the — Neh 11:4 3427
All the sons of Perez that *d* at — Neh 11:6 3427
But the Nethinims *d* in Ophel — Neh 11:21 3427
of Judah *d* at Kirjath-arba — Neh 11:25 3427
they *d* from Beer-sheba unto the — Neh 11:30 2583
Benjamin from Geba *d* at Michmash — Neh 11:31
There *d* men of Tyre also therein, — Neh 13:16 3427
that *d* in the unwalled towns, — Est 9:19 3427
and the honourable man *d* in it — Job 22:8 3427
d as a king in the army, as one — Job 29:25 7931
Thy congregation hath *d* therein — Ps 68:10 3427
mount Zion, wherein thou hast *d* — Ps 74:2 7931
my soul had almost *d* in silence — Ps 94:17 7931
My soul hath long *d* with him that — Ps 120:6 7931
neither shall it be *d* in from — Is 13:20 7931
to Ariel, the city where David *d* — Is 29:1 2583
went and returned, and *d* at Nineveh — Is 37:37 3427
passed through, and where no man *d* — Jer 2:6 3427
But we have *d* in tents, and have — Jer 35:10 3427
so he *d* among the people — Jer 39:14 3427
d with him among the people that — Jer 40:6 3427
d in the habitation of Chimham, — Jer 41:17 3427
that *d* in the land of Egypt — Jer 44:15 3427
neither shall it be *d* in from — Jer 50:39 7931
that *d* by the river of Chebar, and — Eze 3:15 3427
under his shadow *d* all great — Eze 31:6 3427
that *d* under his shadow in the — Eze 31:17 3427
of Israel *d* in their own land — Eze 36:17 3427
wherein your fathers have *d* — Eze 37:25 3427
when they *d* safely in their land, — Eze 39:26 3427
heaven *d* in the boughs thereof — Dan 4:12 1753
which the beasts of the field *d* — Dan 4:21 1753
rejoicing city that *d* carelessly — Zeph 2:15 3427
d in a city called Nazareth — Mt 2:23 *2730*
d in Capernaum, which is upon the — Mt 4:13 *2730*
on all that *d* round about them — Lk 1:65 *4039*
above all men that *d* in Jerusalem — Lk 13:4 *2730*
d among us, (and we beheld his — Jn 1:14 *4637*
They came and saw where he *d* — Jn 1:39 *3306*
before he *d* in Charran, — Acts 7:2 *2730*
the Chaldaeans, and *d* in Charran — Acts 7:4 *2730*
the Jews which *d* at Damascus — Acts 9:22 *2730*
to the saints which *d* at Lydda — Acts 9:32 *2730*
And all that *d* at Lydda and Saron — Acts 9:35 *2730*
the brethren which *d* in Judaea — Acts 11:29 *2730*
d as strangers in the land of — Acts 13:17 *3940*
so that all they which *d* in Asia — Acts 19:10 *2730*
of all the Jews which *d* there — Acts 22:12 *2730*
Paul *d* two whole years in his own — Acts 28:30 *3306*
which *d* first in thy grandmother — 2Ti 1:5 *1774*
them that *d* on the earth — Rev 11:10 *2730*

DYED
And rams' skins *d* red, and badgers' — Ex 25:5
for the tent of rams' skins *d* red — Ex 26:14
And rams' skins *d* red, and badgers' — Ex 35:7
for the tent of rams' skins *d* red — Ex 36:19
the covering of rams' skins *d* red — Ex 39:34
with *d* garments from Bozrah — Is 63:1 2556
exceeding in *d* attire upon their — Eze 23:15 2871

DYING
shall we be consumed with *d* — Num 17:13 1478
took a wife, and *d* left no seed — Mk 12:20 *599*
years of age, and she lay a *d* — Lk 8:42 *599*
the body the *d* of the Lord Jesus — 2Cor 4:10 *3500*
as *d*, and, behold, we live — 2Cor 6:9 *599*
By faith Jacob, when he was a *d* — Heb 11:21 *599*

E

EACH
laid *e* piece one against another — Gen 15:10 376
took *e* man his sword, and came — Gen 34:25
e man his dream in one night, — Gen 40:5
e man according to the interpretation — Gen 40:5
we dreamed *e* man according to the — Gen 41:11
to *e* man according to his dream — Gen 41:12
he gave *e* man changes of raiment — Gen 45:22
they asked *e* other of their — Ex 18:7
of *e* shall there be a like weight — Ex 30:34 905
put pure frankincense upon *e* row — Lev 24:7
e one was for the house of his — Num 1:44 376
the princes, and for *e* one an ox — Num 7:3
e prince on his day, for the — Num 7:11 259
E charger of silver weighing an — Num 7:85 259
and thirty shekels, *e* bowl seventy — Num 7:85 259
e day for a year, shall ye bear — Num 14:34
and Aaron, *e* of you his censer — Num 16:17 376
for *e* prince one, according to — Num 17:6
two tenth deals to *e* ram of the — Num 29:14 259
a several tenth deal to *e* lamb of — Num 29:15 259
among you three men for *e* tribe — Josh 18:4
of *e* chief house a prince — Josh 22:14 259
e one was an head of the house of — Josh 22:14
e one resembled the children of a — Judg 8:18
not to *e* man his wife in the war — Judg 21:22
return *e* to her mother's house — Ruth 1:8 802
e of you in the house of her — Ruth 1:9 802
e man his month in a year made — 1Kin 4:7 259
of olive tree, *e* ten cubits high — 1Kin 6:23
king of Judah sat *e* on his throne — 1Kin 22:10 376
e in his chariot, and they went — 2Kin 9:21 376
of *e* man fifty shekels of silver, — 2Kin 15:20 259
on *e* hand, and six on *e* foot — 1Chr 20:6
top of *e* of them was five cubits — 2Chr 3:15
rows of pomegranates on *e* wreath — 2Chr 4:13 259
stays on *e* side of the sitting — 2Chr 9:18
to the language of *e* people — Neh 13:24
and peace have kissed *e* other — Ps 85:10
which they made *e* one for himself — Is 2:20
e one had six wings — Is 6:2 259
of dragons, where *e* lay, shall be — Is 35:7
e one walking in his uprightness — Is 57:2
appointed thee *e* day for a year — Eze 4:6
upon *e* post were palm trees — Eze 40:16
measured *e* post of the porch, — Eze 40:48
doth not *e* one of you on the — Lk 13:15 *1538*
of fire, and it sat upon *e* of them — Acts 2:3 *1538*
let *e* esteem other better than — Phil 2:3 *240*
you all toward *e* other aboundeth — 2Th 1:3 *240*
the four beasts had *e* of them six — Rev 4:8 *303*

EAGLE
the *e*, and the ossifrage, and the — Lev 11:13 5404
and the pelican, and the gier *e* — Lev 11:18 7360
the *e*, and the ossifrage, and the — Deut 14:12 5404
And the pelican, and the gier *e* — Deut 14:17 7360
earth, as swift as the *e* flieth — Deut 28:49 5404
As an *e* stirreth up her nest, — Deut 32:11 5404
as the *e* that hasteth to the prey — Job 9:26 5404
Doth the *e* mount up at thy — Job 39:27 5404
fly away as an *e* toward heaven — Prov 23:5 5404
The way of an *e* in the air — Prov 30:19 5404
Behold, he shall fly as an *e* — Jer 48:40 5404
make thy nest as high as the *e* — Jer 49:16 5404
he shall come up and fly as the *e* — Jer 49:22 5404
four also had the face of an *e* — Eze 1:10 5404
and the fourth the face of an *e* — Eze 10:14 5404
A great *e* with great wings, — Eze 17:3 5404
another great *e* with great wings — Eze 17:7 5404
He shall come as an *e* against the — Hos 8:1 5404
thou exalt thyself as the *e* — Obad 4 5404
enlarge thy baldness as the *e* — Mic 1:16 5404
fly as the *e* that hasteth to eat — Hab 1:8 5404
fourth beast was like a flying *e* — Rev 4:7 *105*
were given two wings of a great *e* — Rev 12:14 *105*

EAGLE'S
thy youth is renewed like the *e* — Ps 103:5 5404
was like a lion, and had *e* wings — Dan 7:4 5403

EAGLES
they were swifter than *e*, they — 2Sa 1:23 5404
out, and the young *e* shall eat it — Prov 30:17 5404
shall mount up with wings as *e* — Is 40:31 5404
his horses are swifter than *e* — Jer 4:13 5404
swifter than the *e* of the heaven — Lam 4:19 5404
there will the *e* be gathered — Mt 24:28 *105*
thither will the *e* be gathered — Lk 17:37 *105*

EAGLES'
and how I bare you on *e* wings — Ex 19:4 5404
hairs were grown like *e* feathers — Dan 4:33 5403

EAR
for the barley was in the *e* — Ex 9:31 24
wilt give *e* to his commandments, — Ex 15:26 238
bore his *e* through with an aul — Ex 21:6 241
the tip of the right *e* of Aaron — Ex 29:20 241
tip of the right *e* of his sons — Ex 29:20 241
upon the tip of Aaron's right *e* — Lev 8:23 241
upon the tip of their right *e* — Lev 8:24 241
it upon the tip of the right *e* of — Lev 14:14 241
e of him that is to be cleansed — Lev 14:17 241
it upon the tip of the right *e* of — Lev 14:25 241
e of him that is to be cleansed — Lev 14:28 241
your voice, nor give *e* unto you — Deut 1:45 238
it through his *e* unto the door — Deut 15:17 241
Give *e*, O ye heavens, and I will — Deut 32:1 238
give *e*, O ye princes — Judg 5:3 238
and will set them to *e* his ground — 1Sa 8:12 2790
in his *e* a day before Saul came — 1Sa 9:15 241
LORD, bow down thine *e*, and hear — 2Kin 19:16 241
but they would not give *e* — 2Chr 24:19 238
Let thine *e* now be attentive, and — Neh 1:6 241
let now thine *e* be attentive to — Neh 1:11 241

yet would they not give e	Neh 9:30	238
mine e received a little thereof	Job 4:12	241
Doth not the e try words	Job 12:11	241
mine e hath heard and understood	Job 13:1	241
When the e heard me, then it	Job 29:11	241
Unto me men gave e, and waited, and	Job 29:21	8085
I gave e to your reasons, whilst	Job 32:11	238
give e unto me, ye that have	Job 34:2	238
For the e trieth words, as the	Job 34:3	241
also their e to discipline	Job 36:10	241
of thee by the hearing of the e	Job 42:5	241
Give e to my words, O LORD	Ps 5:1	238
thou wilt cause thine e to hear	Ps 10:17	241
give e unto my prayer, that goeth	Ps 17:1	238
incline thine e unto me, and hear	Ps 17:6	241
Bow down thine e to me	Ps 31:2	241
O LORD, and give e unto my cry	Ps 39:12	238
and consider, and incline thine e	Ps 45:10	241
give e, all ye inhabitants of the	Ps 49:1	238
will incline mine e to a parable	Ps 49:4	241
give e to the words of my mouth	Ps 54:2	238
Give e to my prayer, O God	Ps 55:1	238
deaf adder that stoppeth her e	Ps 58:4	241
incline thine e unto me, and save	Ps 71:2	241
and he gave e unto me	Ps 77:1	238
Give e, O my people, to my law	Ps 78:1	238
Give e, O Shepherd of Israel,	Ps 80:1	238
give e, O God of Jacob	Ps 84:8	238
Bow down thine e, O LORD, hear me	Ps 86:1	241
Give e, O LORD, unto my prayer	Ps 86:6	238
incline thine e unto my cry	Ps 88:2	241
He that planted the e, shall he	Ps 94:9	241
incline thine e unto me	Ps 102:2	241
he hath inclined his e unto me	Ps 116:2	241
give e unto my voice, when I cry	Ps 141:1	238
give e to my supplications	Ps 143:1	238
thou incline thine e unto wisdom	Prov 2:2	241
incline thine e unto my sayings	Prov 4:20	241
bow thine e to my understanding	Prov 5:1	241
nor inclined mine e to them that	Prov 5:13	241
The e that heareth the reproof of	Prov 15:31	241
a liar giveth e to a naughty	Prov 17:4	238
the e of the wise seeketh	Prov 18:15	241
The hearing e, and the seeing eye,	Prov 20:12	241
Bow down thine e, and hear the	Prov 22:17	241
wise reprover upon an obedient e	Prov 25:12	241
away his e from hearing the law	Prov 28:9	241
nor the e filled with hearing	Eccl 1:8	241
Hear, O heavens, and give e	Is 1:2	238
give e unto the law of our God,	Is 1:10	238
and give e, all ye of far	Is 8:9	238
Give ye e, and hear my voice	Is 28:23	238
the young asses that e the ground	Is 30:24	5647
give e unto my speech	Is 32:9	238
Incline thine e, O LORD, and hear	Is 37:17	241
Who among you will give e to this	Is 42:23	238
time that thine e was not opened	Is 48:8	241
he wakeneth mine e to hear as the	Is 50:4	241
The Lord GOD hath opened mine e	Is 50:5	241
give e unto me, O my nation	Is 51:4	238
Incline your e, and come unto me	Is 55:3	241
neither his e heavy, that it	Is 59:1	241
not heard, nor perceived by the e	Is 64:4	238
their e is uncircumcised, and they	Jer 6:10	241
not, nor inclined their e	Jer 7:24	241
not unto me, nor inclined their e	Jer 7:26	241
let your e receive the word of	Jer 9:20	241
obeyed not, nor inclined their e	Jer 11:8	241
Hear ye, and give e	Jer 13:15	238
not, neither inclined their e	Jer 17:23	241
nor inclined your e to hear	Jer 25:4	241
unto me, neither inclined their e	Jer 34:14	241
but ye have not inclined your e	Jer 35:15	241
nor inclined their e to turn from	Jer 44:5	241
hide not thine e at my breathing,	Lam 3:56	241
O my God, incline thine e	Dan 9:18	241
and give ye e, O house of the king	Hos 5:1	238
Hear this, ye old men, and give e	Joel 1:2	238
lion two legs, or a piece of an e	Amos 3:12	241
and what ye hear in the e, that	Mt 10:27	3775
high priest's, and smote off his e	Mt 26:51	5621
first the blade, then the e	Mk 4:28	4719
after that the full corn in the e	Mk 4:28	4719
the high priest, and cut off his e	Mk 14:47	5621
which ye have spoken in the e in	Lk 12:3	3775
priest, and cut off his right e	Lk 22:50	3775
And he touched his e, and healed	Lk 22:51	5621
servant, and cut off his right e	Jn 18:10	5621
his kinsman whose e Peter cut off	Jn 18:26	5621
nor e heard, neither have entered	1Cor 2:9	3775
if the e shall say, Because I am	1Cor 12:16	3775
He that hath an e, let him hear	Rev 2:7	3775
He that hath an e, let him hear	Rev 2:11	3775
He that hath an e, let him hear	Rev 2:17	3775
He that hath an e, let him hear	Rev 2:29	3775
He that hath an e, let him hear	Rev 3:6	3775
He that hath an e, let him hear	Rev 3:13	3775
He that hath an e, let him hear	Rev 3:22	3775
If any man have an e, let him	Rev 13:9	3775

EARED

which is neither e nor sown	Deut 21:4	5647

EARING

shall neither be e nor harvest	Gen 45:6	2758
in e time and in harvest thou	Ex 34:21	2758

EARLY

your feet, and ye shall rise up e	Gen 19:2	7925
Abraham gat up e in the morning	Gen 19:27	7925
Abimelech rose e in the morning	Gen 20:8	7925
Abraham rose up e in the morning	Gen 21:14	7925
Abraham rose up e in the morning	Gen 22:3	7925
Jacob rose up e in the morning,	Gen 28:18	7925
e in the morning Laban rose up,	Gen 31:55	7925
Rise up e in the morning, and	Ex 8:20	7925
Rise up e in the morning, and	Ex 9:13	7925
rose up e in the morning, and	Ex 24:4	7925
they rose up e on the morrow, and	Ex 32:6	7925
Moses rose up e in the morning,	Ex 34:4	7925
they rose up e in the morning, and	Num 14:40	7925
Joshua rose e in the morning	Josh 3:1	7925
Joshua rose e in the morning, and	Josh 6:12	7925
that they rose e about the	Josh 6:15	7925
Joshua rose up e in the morning	Josh 7:16	7925
Joshua rose up e in the morning	Josh 8:10	7925
it, that they hasted and rose up e	Josh 8:14	7925
the city arose e in the morning	Judg 6:28	7925
for he rose up e on the morrow	Judg 6:38	7925
that were with him, rose up e	Judg 7:1	7925
depart e from mount Gilead	Judg 7:3	6852
the sun is up, thou shalt rise e	Judg 9:33	7925
when they arose e in the morning	Judg 19:5	7925
he arose e in the morning on the	Judg 19:8	7925
to morrow get you e on your way	Judg 19:9	7925
morrow, that the people rose e	Judg 21:4	7925
And they rose up in the morning e	1Sa 1:19	7925
of Ashdod arose e on the morrow	1Sa 5:3	7925
when they arose e on the morrow	1Sa 5:4	7925
And they arose e	1Sa 9:26	7925
when Samuel rose e to meet Saul	1Sa 15:12	7925
David rose up e in the morning,	1Sa 17:20	7925
Wherefore now rise up e in the	1Sa 29:10	7925
soon as ye be up e in the morning	1Sa 29:10	7925
his men rose up e to depart in	1Sa 29:11	7925
And Absalom rose up e, and stood	2Sa 15:2	7925
they rose up e in the morning, and	2Kin 3:22	7925
of the man of God was risen e	2Kin 6:15	7925
when they arose e in the morning	2Kin 19:35	7925
they rose e in the morning, and	2Chr 20:20	7925
Then Hezekiah the king rose e	2Chr 29:20	7925
rose up e in the morning, and	Job 1:5	7925
shall help her, and that right e	Ps 46:5	1242
I myself will awake e	Ps 57:8	7837
e will I seek thee	Ps 63:1	7836
returned and enquired e after God	Ps 78:34	7836
O satisfy us e with thy mercy	Ps 90:14	1242
I will e destroy all the wicked	Ps 101:8	1242
I myself will awake e	Ps 108:2	7837
It is vain for you to rise up e	Ps 127:2	7925
they shall seek me e, but they	Prov 1:28	7836
that seek me e shall find me	Prov 8:17	7836
rising e in the morning, it shall	Prov 27:14	7925
Let us get up e to the vineyards	Song 7:12	7925
that rise up e in the morning	Is 5:11	7925
within me will I seek thee e	Is 26:9	7836
when they arose e in the morning	Is 37:36	7925
and I spake unto you, rising up e	Jer 7:13	7925
the prophets, daily rising up e	Jer 7:25	7925
even unto this day, rising e	Jer 11:7	7925
I have spoken unto you, rising e	Jer 25:3	7925
servants the prophets, rising e	Jer 25:4	7925
I sent unto you, both rising up e	Jer 26:5	7925
the prophets, rising up e	Jer 29:19	7925
though I taught them, rising up e	Jer 32:33	7925
I have spoken unto you, rising e	Jer 35:14	7925
the prophets, rising up e	Jer 35:15	7925
servants the prophets, rising e	Jer 44:4	7925
king arose very e in the morning	Dan 6:19	8238
affliction they will seek me e	Hos 5:15	7836
as the e dew it goeth away	Hos 6:4	7925
as the e dew that passeth away,	Hos 13:3	7925
but they rose e, and corrupted all	Zeph 3:7	7925
which went out e in the morning	Mt 20:1	
very e in the morning the first	Mk 16:2	4404
Now when Jesus was risen e the	Mk 16:9	4404
all the people came e in the	Lk 21:38	3719
very e in the morning, they came	Lk 24:1	3722
which were e at the sepulchre	Lk 24:22	3721
And And e in the morning he came	Jn 8:1	3719
e in the morning he came again	Jn 8:2	3722
of judgment: and it was e	Jn 18:28	4405
the week cometh Mary Magdalene e	Jn 20:1	4404
into the temple e in the morning	Acts 5:21	3722
for it, until he receive the e	Jas 5:7	4406

EARNEST

For the e expectation of the	Rom 8:19	603
given the e of the Spirit in our	2Cor 1:22	728
given unto us the e of the Spirit	2Cor 5:5	728
when he told us your e desire	2Cor 7:7	1972
which put the same e care into	2Cor 8:16	4710
Which is the e of our inheritance	Eph 1:14	728
According to my e expectation	Phil 1:20	603
we ought to give the more e heed	Heb 2:1	4056

EARNESTLY

Did I not e send unto thee to	Num 22:37	
David e asked leave of me that he	1Sa 20:6	
David e asked leave of me to go	1Sa 20:28	
Zabbai e repaired the other piece	Neh 3:20	2734
As a servant e desireth the	Job 7:2	
For I e protested unto your	Jer 11:7	
I do e remember him still	Jer 31:20	
may do evil with both hands e	Mic 7:3	3190
in an agony he prayed more e	Lk 22:44	1617
e looked upon him, and said, This	Lk 22:56	816
or why look ye so e on us	Acts 3:12	816
e beholding the council, said,	Acts 23:1	816
But covet e the best gifts	1Cor 12:31	2206
e desiring to be clothed upon	2Cor 5:2	1971
he prayed e that it might not	Jas 5:17	4335
exhort you that ye should e	Jude 3	1864

EARNETH

he that e wages e wages to	Hag 1:6	7936

EARRING

golden e of half a shekel weight	Gen 24:22	5141
came to pass, when he saw the e	Gen 24:30	5141
I put the e upon her face, and the	Gen 24:47	5141
money, and every one an e of gold	Job 42:11	5141
As an e of gold, and an ornament	Prov 25:12	5141

EARRINGS

all their e which were in their	Gen 35:4	5141
unto them, Break off the golden e	Ex 32:2	5141
golden e which were in their ears	Ex 32:3	5141
and brought bracelets, and e	Ex 35:22	5141
chains, and bracelets, rings, e	Num 31:50	5694
me every man the e of his prey	Judg 8:24	5141
(For they had golden e, because	Judg 8:24	5141
every man the e of his prey	Judg 8:25	5141
golden e that he requested was a	Judg 8:26	5141
and the tablets, and the e	Is 3:20	3908
e in thine ears, and a beautiful	Eze 16:12	5694
and she decked herself with her e	Hos 2:13	5141

EARS

told all these things in their e	Gen 20:8	241
earrings which were in their e	Gen 35:4	241
seven e of corn came up upon one	Gen 41:5	7641
And, behold, seven thin e and	Gen 41:6	7641
the seven thin e devoured the	Gen 41:7	7641
devoured the seven rank and full e	Gen 41:7	7641
seven e came up in one stalk,	Gen 41:22	7641
And, behold, seven e, withered,	Gen 41:23	7641
e devoured the seven good e	Gen 41:24	7641
the seven good e are seven years	Gen 41:26	7641
the seven empty e blasted with	Gen 41:27	7641
thee, speak a word in my lord's e	Gen 44:18	241
in the e of Pharaoh, saying,	Gen 50:4	241
mayest tell in the e of thy son	Ex 10:2	241
Speak now in the e of the people	Ex 11:2	241
and rehearse it in the e of Joshua	Ex 17:14	241
which are in the e of your wives	Ex 32:2	241
earrings which were in their e	Ex 32:3	241
of thy firstfruits green e of	Lev 2:14	24
even corn beaten out of full e	Lev 2:14	3759
nor parched corn, nor green e	Lev 23:14	3759
ye have wept in the e of the LORD	Num 11:18	241
LORD, as ye have spoken in mine e	Num 14:28	241
which I speak in your e this day	Deut 5:1	241
pluck the e with thine hand	Deut 23:25	4425
see, and e to hear, unto this day	Deut 29:4	241
may speak these words in their e	Deut 31:28	241
Moses spake in the e of all the	Deut 31:30	241
this song in the e of the people	Deut 32:44	241
the e of the elders of that city	Josh 20:4	241
proclaim in the e of the people	Judg 7:3	241
in the e of all the men of	Judg 9:2	241
brethren spake of him in the e of	Judg 9:3	241
and spakest of also in mine e	Judg 17:2	241
glean e of corn after him in	Ruth 2:2	7641
at which both the e of every one	1Sa 3:11	241
them in the e of the LORD	1Sa 8:21	241
tidings in the e of the people	1Sa 11:4	241
bleating of the sheep in mine e	1Sa 15:14	241
those words in the e of David	1Sa 18:23	241
also spake in the e of Benjamin	2Sa 3:19	241
the e of David in Hebron all that	2Sa 3:19	241
all that we have heard with our e	2Sa 7:22	241
and my cry did enter into his e	2Sa 22:7	241
full e of corn in the husk	2Kin 4:42	3759
e of the people that are on the	2Kin 18:26	241
thy tumult is come up into mine e	2Kin 19:28	241
of it, both his e shall tingle	2Kin 21:12	241
he read in their e all the words	2Kin 23:2	241
all that we have heard with our e	1Chr 17:20	241
let thine e be attent unto the	2Chr 6:40	241
mine e attent unto the prayer	2Chr 7:15	241
he read in their e all the words	2Chr 34:30	241
the e of all the people were	Neh 8:3	241
and my declaration with your e	Job 13:17	241
A dreadful sound is in his e	Job 15:21	241
off as the tops of the e of corn	Job 24:24	7641
heard the fame thereof with our e	Job 28:22	241
Then he openeth the e of men	Job 33:16	241
and openeth their e in oppression	Job 36:15	241
came before him, even into his e	Ps 18:6	241
his e are open unto their cry	Ps 34:15	241
mine e hast thou opened	Ps 40:6	241
We have heard with our e, O God,	Ps 44:1	241
incline your e to the words of my	Ps 78:1	241
mine e shall hear my desire of	Ps 92:11	241
They have e, but they hear not	Ps 115:6	241
let thine e be attentive to the	Ps 130:2	241
They have e, but they hear not	Ps 135:17	241
Whoso stoppeth his e at the cry	Prov 21:13	241
Speak not in the e of a fool	Prov 23:9	241
thine e to the words of knowledge	Prov 23:12	241
one that taketh a dog by the e	Prov 26:17	241
In mine e said the LORD of hosts,	Is 5:9	241
people fat, and make their e heavy	Is 6:10	241
their eyes, and hear with their e	Is 6:10	241
after the hearing of his e	Is 11:3	241
reapeth the e with his arm	Is 17:5	7641
e in the valley of Rephaim	Is 17:5	7641
in mine e by the LORD of hosts	Is 22:14	241
thine e shall hear a word behind	Is 30:21	241
the e of them that hear shall	Is 32:3	241
that stoppeth his e from hearing	Is 33:15	241
the e of the deaf shall be	Is 35:5	241
in the e of the people that are	Is 36:11	241
tumult, is come up into mine e	Is 37:29	241
opening the e, but he heareth not	Is 42:20	241
eyes, and the deaf that have e	Is 43:8	241
other, shall say again in thine e	Is 49:20	241
cry in the e of Jerusalem, saying	Jer 2:2	241
which have e, and hear not	Jer 5:21	241
heareth, his e shall tingle	Jer 19:3	241
as ye have heard with your e	Jer 26:11	241
speak all these words in your e	Jer 26:15	241
this word that I speak in thine e	Jer 28:7	241
in the e of all the people	Jer 28:7	241
in the e of Jeremiah the prophet	Jer 29:29	241

the e of the people in the LORD's Jer 36:6 241
thou shalt read them in the e of Jer 36:6 241
in the e of all the people Jer 36:10 241
the book in the e of the people Jer 36:13 241
hast read in the e of the people Jer 36:14 241
Sit down now, and read it in our e Jer 36:15 241
So Baruch read it in their e Jer 36:15 241
the words in the e of the king Jer 36:20 241
read it in the e of the king Jer 36:21 241
in the e of all the princes which Jer 36:21 241
thine heart, and hear with thine e Eze 3:10 241
cry in mine e with a loud voice Eze 8:18 241
also in mine e with a loud voice Eze 9:1 241
they have e to hear, and hear not Eze 12:2 241
forehead, and earrings in thine e Eze 16:12 241
take away thy nose and thine e Eze 23:25 241
thee to hear it with thine e Eze 24:26 241
thine eyes, and hear with thine e Eze 40:4 241
hear with thine e all that I say Eze 44:5 241
mouth, their e shall be deaf Mic 7:16 241
the shoulder, and stopped their e Zec 7:11 241
He that hath e to hear, let him Mt 11:15 3775
and began to pluck the e of corn Mt 12:1 4719
Who hath e to hear, let him hear Mt 13:9 3775
their e are dull of hearing, and Mt 13:15 3775
their eyes, and hear with their e Mt 13:15 3775
and your e, for they hear Mt 13:16 3775
Who hath e to hear, let him hear Mt 13:43 3775
if this come to the governor's e Mt 28:14 191
they went, to pluck the e of corn Mk 2:23 4719
unto them, He that hath e to hear Mk 4:9 3775
If any man have e to hear Mk 4:23 3775
If any man have e to hear Mk 7:16 3775
and put his fingers into his e Mk 7:33 3775
And straightway his e were opened Mk 7:35 189
and having e, hear ye not Mk 8:18 3775
thy salutation sounded in mine e Lk 1:44 3775
scripture fulfilled in your e Lk 4:21 3775
disciples plucked the e of corn Lk 6:1 4719
he cried, He that hath e to hear Lk 8:8 3775
sayings sink down into your e Lk 9:44 3775
He that hath e to hear, let him Lk 14:35 3775
and uncircumcised in heart and e Acts 7:51 3775
a loud voice, and stopped their e Acts 7:57 3775
the e of the church which was in Acts 11:22 3775
certain strange things to our e Acts 17:20 189
their e are dull of hearing, and Acts 28:27 3775
their eyes, and hear with their e Acts 28:27 3775
e that they should not hear Rom 11:8 3775
teachers, having itching e 2Ti 4:3 189
turn away their e from the truth 2Ti 4:4 189
into the e of the Lord of Sabaoth Jas 5:4 3775
his e are open unto their prayers 1Pet 3:12 3775

EARTH

God created the heaven and the e Gen 1:1 776
the e was without form, and void Gen 1:2 776
And God called the dry land E Gen 1:10 776
Let the e bring forth grass, the Gen 1:11 776
seed is in itself, upon the e Gen 1:11 776
the e brought forth grass, and Gen 1:12 776
heaven to give light upon the e Gen 1:15 776
heaven to give light upon the e Gen 1:17 776
fowl that may fly above the e in Gen 1:20 776
and let fowl multiply in the e Gen 1:22 776
Let the e bring forth the living Gen 1:24 776
beast of the e after his kind Gen 1:24 776
the beast of the e after his kind Gen 1:25 776
upon the e after his kind Gen 1:25 127
the cattle, and over all the e Gen 1:26 776
thing that creepeth upon the e Gen 1:26 776
and multiply, and replenish the e Gen 1:28 776
thing that moveth upon the e Gen 1:28 776
is upon the face of all the e Gen 1:29 776
And to every beast of the e Gen 1:30 776
thing that creepeth upon the e Gen 1:30 776
the e were finished, and all the Gen 2:1 776
of the e when they were created, Gen 2:4 776
day that the LORD God made the e Gen 2:4 776
the field before it was in the e Gen 2:5 776
not caused it to rain upon the e Gen 2:5 776
there went up a mist from the e Gen 2:6 776
And now art thou cursed from the e Gen 4:11 127
a vagabond shalt thou be in the e Gen 4:12 776
this day from the face of the e Gen 4:14 127
a fugitive and a vagabond in the e Gen 4:14 776
to multiply on the face of the e Gen 6:1 127
giants in the e in those days Gen 6:4 776
of man was great in the e Gen 6:5 776
that he had made man on the e Gen 6:6 776
created from the face of the e Gen 6:7 127
The e also was corrupt before God Gen 6:11 776
the e was filled with violence Gen 6:11 776
And God looked upon the e, and, Gen 6:12 776
had corrupted his way upon the e Gen 6:12 776
for the e is filled with violence Gen 6:13 776
I will destroy them with the e Gen 6:13 776
a flood of waters upon the e Gen 6:17 776
thing that is in the e shall die Gen 6:17 776
thing of the e after his kind Gen 6:20 127
alive upon the face of all the e Gen 7:3 776
it to rain upon the e forty days Gen 7:4 776
from off the face of the e Gen 7:4 127
flood of waters was upon the e Gen 7:6 776
thing that creepeth upon the e Gen 7:8 127
of the flood were upon the e Gen 7:10 776
rain was upon the e forty days Gen 7:12 776
upon the e after his kind Gen 7:14 776
flood was forty days upon the e Gen 7:17 776
and it was lift up above the e Gen 7:17 776
were increased greatly upon the e Gen 7:18 776
prevailed exceedingly upon the e Gen 7:19 776
flesh died that moved upon the e Gen 7:21 776
thing that creepeth upon the e Gen 7:21 776
and they were destroyed from the e Gen 7:23 776
prevailed upon the e an hundred Gen 7:24 776
made a wind to pass over the e Gen 8:1 776
from off the e continually Gen 8:3 776
were dried up from off the e Gen 8:7 776
were on the face of the whole e Gen 8:9 776
waters were abated from off the e Gen 8:11 776
were dried up from off the e Gen 8:13 776
day of the month, was the e dried Gen 8:14 776
thing that creepeth upon the e Gen 8:17 776
may breed abundantly in the e Gen 8:17 776
fruitful, and multiply upon the e Gen 8:17 776
and whatsoever creepeth upon the e Gen 8:19 776
While the e remaineth, seedtime Gen 8:22 776
and multiply, and replenish the e Gen 9:1 776
be upon every beast of the e Gen 9:2 776
upon all that moveth upon the e Gen 9:2 127
bring forth abundantly in the e Gen 9:7 776
of every beast of the e with you Gen 9:10 776
the ark, to every beast of the e Gen 9:10 776
more be a flood to destroy the e Gen 9:11 776
of a covenant between me and the e Gen 9:13 776
when I bring a cloud over the e Gen 9:14 776
of all flesh that is upon the e Gen 9:16 776
and all flesh that is upon the e Gen 9:17 776
them was the whole e overspread Gen 9:19 776
began to be a mighty one in the e Gen 10:8 776
for in his days was the e divided Gen 10:25 776
divided in the e after the flood Gen 10:32 776
the whole e was of one language, Gen 11:1 776
upon the face of the whole e Gen 11:4 776
thence upon the face of all the e Gen 11:8 776
the language of all the e Gen 11:9 776
abroad upon the face of all the e Gen 11:9 776
all families of the e be blessed Gen 12:3 127
thy seed as the dust of the e Gen 13:16 776
man can number the dust of the e Gen 13:16 776
God, possessor of heaven and e Gen 14:19 776
God, the possessor of heaven and e Gen 14:22 776
all the nations of the e shall be Gen 18:18 776
the Judge of all the e do right Gen 18:25 776
the e when Lot entered into Zoar Gen 19:23 776
there is not a man in the e to Gen 19:31 776
us after the manner of all the e Gen 19:31 776
the nations of the e be blessed Gen 22:18 776
of heaven, and the God of the e Gen 24:3 776
the LORD, bowing himself to the e Gen 24:52 776
the nations of the e be blessed Gen 26:4 776
them, and filled them with e Gen 26:15 6083
heaven, and the fatness of the e Gen 27:28 776
shall be the fatness of the e Gen 27:39 776
behold a ladder set up on the e Gen 28:12 776
shall be as the dust of the e Gen 28:14 776
the families of the e be blessed Gen 28:14 127
down ourselves to thee to the e Gen 37:10 776
the e brought forth by handfuls Gen 41:47 776
was over all the face of the e Gen 41:56 776
him with their faces to the e Gen 42:6 776
bowed themselves to him to the e Gen 43:26 776
preserve you a posterity in the e Gen 45:7 776
himself with his face to the e Gen 48:12 776
a multitude in the midst of the e Gen 48:16 776
rod, and smote the dust of the e Ex 8:17 776
am the LORD in the midst of the e Ex 8:22 776
is none like me in all the e Ex 9:14 776
thou shalt be cut off from the e Ex 9:15 776
be declared throughout all the e Ex 9:16 776
know how that the e is the LORD's Ex 9:29 776
rain was not poured upon the e Ex 9:33 776
shall cover the face of the e Ex 10:5 776
one cannot be able to see the e Ex 10:5 776
were upon the e unto this day Ex 10:6 127
covered the face of the whole e Ex 10:15 776
right hand, the e swallowed them Ex 15:12 776
for all the e is mine Ex 19:5 776
or that is in the e beneath Ex 20:4 776
that is in the water under the e Ex 20:4 776
days the LORD made heaven and e Ex 20:11 776
An altar of e thou shalt make Ex 20:24 127
days the LORD made heaven and e Ex 31:17 776
them from the face of the e Ex 32:12 127
that are upon the face of the e Ex 33:16 127
and bowed his head toward the e Ex 34:8 776
have not been done in all the e Ex 34:10 776
all the beasts that are on the e Lev 11:2 776
feet, to leap withal upon the e Lev 11:21 776
things that creep upon the e Lev 11:29 776
the e shall be an abomination Lev 11:41 776
things that creep upon the e Lev 11:42 776
thing that creepeth upon the e Lev 11:44 776
creature that creepeth upon the e Lev 11:46 776
And the vessel of e, that he Lev 15:12 2789
as iron, and your e as brass Lev 26:19 776
high upon the face of the e Num 11:31 776
which were upon the face of the e Num 12:3 127
all the e shall be filled with Num 14:21 776
the e open her mouth, and swallow Num 16:30 127
the e opened her mouth, and Num 16:32 776
pit, and the e closed upon them Num 16:33 776
Lest the e swallow us up also Num 16:34 776
they cover the face of the e Num 22:5 776
which covereth the face of the e Num 22:11 776
the e opened her mouth, and Num 26:10 776
God is there in heaven or in e Deut 3:24 776
that they shall live upon the e Deut 4:10 127
of any beast that is on the e Deut 4:17 776
is in the waters beneath the e Deut 4:18 776
e to witness against you this day Deut 4:26 776
that God created man upon the e Deut 4:32 776
upon e he shewed thee his great Deut 4:36 776
above, and upon the e beneath Deut 4:39 776
prolong thy days upon the e Deut 4:40 127
or that is in the e beneath Deut 5:8 776
is in the waters beneath the e Deut 5:8 776
thee from off the face of the e Deut 6:15 127
that are upon the face of the e Deut 7:6 127
the e also, with all that therein Deut 10:14 776
how the e opened her mouth, and Deut 11:6 776
as the days of heaven upon the e Deut 11:21 776
the days that ye live upon the e Deut 12:1 127
shall pour it upon the e as water Deut 12:16 776
as long as thou livest upon the e Deut 12:19 127
shalt pour it upon the e as water Deut 12:24 776
from the one end of the e even Deut 13:7 776
even unto the other end of the e Deut 13:7 776
the nations that are upon the e Deut 14:2 127
first of all the fruit of the e Deut 26:2 127
high above all nations of the e Deut 28:1 776
all people of the e shall see Deut 28:10 776
the e that is under thee shall be Deut 28:23 776
into all the kingdoms of the e Deut 28:25 776
air, and unto the beasts of the e Deut 28:26 776
from far, from the end of the e Deut 28:49 776
end of the e even unto the other Deut 28:64 776
e to record this day against you, Deut 30:19 776
and e to record against them Deut 31:28 776
and hear, O e, the words of my Deut 32:1 776
ride on the high places of the e Deut 32:13 776
consume the e with her increase Deut 32:22 776
for the precious things of the e Deut 33:16 776
together to the ends of the e Deut 33:17 776
in heaven above, and in e beneath Josh 2:11 776
e passeth over before you into Josh 3:11 776
the LORD, the Lord of all the e Josh 3:13 776
That all the people of the e Josh 4:24 776
Joshua fell on his face to the e Josh 5:14 776
fell to the e upon his face Josh 7:6 776
and cut off our name from the e Josh 7:9 776
they are hid in the e in the Josh 7:21 776
I am going the way of all the e Josh 23:14 776
was fallen down dead on the e Judg 3:25 776
the e trembled, and the heavens Judg 5:4 776
destroyed the increase of the e Judg 6:4 776
it be dry upon all the e beside Judg 6:37 776
of any thing that is in the e Judg 18:10 776
pillars of the e are the LORD's 1Sa 2:8 776
shall judge the ends of the e 1Sa 2:10 776
shout, so that the e rang again 1Sa 4:5 776
rent, and with e upon his head 1Sa 4:12 127
the e before the ark of the LORD 1Sa 5:3 776
also trembled, and the e quaked 1Sa 14:15 776
and to the wild beasts of the e 1Sa 17:46 776
that all the e may know that 1Sa 17:46 776
and he fell upon his face to the e 1Sa 17:49 776
every one from the face of the e 1Sa 20:15 127
stooped with his face to the e 1Sa 24:8 776
herself on her face to the e 1Sa 25:41 776
the spear even to the e at once 1Sa 26:8 776
the e before the face of the LORD 1Sa 26:20 776
I saw gods ascending out of the e 1Sa 28:13 776
straightway all along on the e 1Sa 28:20 776
So he arose from the e, and sat 1Sa 28:23 776
were spread abroad upon all the e 1Sa 30:16 776
clothes rent, and e upon his head 2Sa 1:2 127
to David, that he fell to the e 2Sa 1:2 776
hand, and take you away from the e 2Sa 4:11 776
the great men that are in the e 2Sa 7:9 776
in the e is like thy people 2Sa 7:23 776
in, and lay all night upon the e 2Sa 12:16 776
him, to raise him up from the e 2Sa 12:17 776
Then David arose from the e 2Sa 12:20 776
his garments, and lay on the e 2Sa 13:31 776
name nor remainder upon the e 2Sa 14:7 127
one hair of thy son fall to the e 2Sa 14:11 776
know all things that are in the e 2Sa 14:20 776
his coat rent, and e upon his head 2Sa 15:32 127
up between the heaven and the e 2Sa 18:9 776
he fell down to the e upon his 2Sa 18:28 776
Then the e shook and trembled 2Sa 22:8 776
as small as the dust of the e 2Sa 22:43 776
grass springing out of the e by 2Sa 23:4 776
bowed with her face to the e 1Kin 1:31 776
so that the e rent with the sound 1Kin 1:40 776
not an hair of him fall to the e 1Kin 1:52 776
I go the way of all the e 1Kin 2:2 776
Solomon, from all kings of the e 1Kin 4:34 776
or on e beneath, who keepest 1Kin 8:23 776
will God indeed dwell on the e 1Kin 8:27 776
people of the e may know thy name 1Kin 8:43 776
among all the people of the e 1Kin 8:53 776
That all the people of the e may 1Kin 8:60 776
all the kings of the e for riches 1Kin 10:23 776
all the e sought to Solomon, to 1Kin 10:24 776
it from off the face of the e 1Kin 13:34 127
the LORD sendeth rain upon the e 1Kin 17:14 127
and I will send rain upon the e 1Kin 18:1 127
he cast himself down upon the e 1Kin 18:42 776
that there is no God in all the e 2Kin 5:15 776
servant two mules' burden of e 2Kin 5:17 127
that there shall fall unto the e 2Kin 10:10 776
of all the kingdoms of the e 2Kin 19:15 776
thou hast made heaven and e 2Kin 19:15 776
that all the kingdoms of the e 2Kin 19:19 776
he began to be mighty upon the e 1Chr 1:10 776
in his days the e was divided 1Chr 1:19 776
his judgments are in all the e 1Chr 16:14 776
Sing unto the LORD, all the e 1Chr 16:23 776
Fear before him, all the e 1Chr 16:30 776
be glad, and let the e rejoice 1Chr 16:31 776
because he cometh to judge the e 1Chr 16:33 776
the great men that are in the e 1Chr 17:8 776
what one nation in the e is like 1Chr 17:21 776
of the LORD stand between the e 1Chr 21:16 776
much blood upon the e in my sight 1Chr 22:8 776
the heaven and the e is thine 1Chr 29:11 776
our days on the e are as a shadow 1Chr 29:15 776
the dust of the e in multitude 2Chr 1:9 776
of Israel, that made heaven and e 2Chr 2:12 776

thee in the heaven, nor in the e	2Chr 6:14	776
very deed dwell with men on the e	2Chr 6:18	776
people of the e may know thy name	2Chr 6:33	776
all the kings of the e in riches	2Chr 9:22	776
all the kings of the e sought the	2Chr 9:23	776
to and fro throughout the whole e	2Chr 16:9	776
were dead bodies fallen to the e	2Chr 20:24	776
the gods of the people of the e	2Chr 32:19	776
All the kingdoms of the e hath	2Chr 36:23	776
me all the kingdoms of the e	Ezr 1:2	776
of the God of heaven and e	Ezr 5:11	772
with sackclothes, and e upon them	Neh 9:1	127
with all their host, the e	Neh 9:6	776
From going to and fro in the e	Job 1:7	776
there is none like him in the e	Job 1:8	776
From going to and fro in the e	Job 2:2	776
there is none like him in the e	Job 2:3	776
kings and counsellors of the e	Job 3:14	776
Who giveth rain upon the e	Job 5:10	776
be afraid of the beasts of the e	Job 5:22	776
offspring as the grass of the e	Job 5:25	776
an appointed time to man upon e	Job 7:1	776
our days upon e are a shadow	Job 8:9	776
out of the e shall others grow	Job 8:19	6083
shaketh the e out of her place	Job 9:6	776
The e is given into the hand of	Job 9:24	776
thereof is longer than the e	Job 11:9	776
Or speak to the e, and it shall	Job 12:8	776
them out, and they overturn the e	Job 12:15	776
the chief of the people of the e	Job 12:24	776
the root thereof wax old in the e	Job 14:8	776
grow out of the dust of the e	Job 14:19	776
Unto whom alone the e was given	Job 15:19	776
the perfection thereof upon the e	Job 15:29	776
O e, cover not thou my blood, and	Job 16:18	776
shall the e be forsaken for thee	Job 18:4	776
shall perish from the e, and he	Job 18:17	776
at the latter day upon the e	Job 19:25	6083
old, since man was placed upon e	Job 20:4	776
the e shall rise up against him	Job 20:27	776
for the mighty man, he had the e	Job 22:8	776
the poor of the e hide themselves	Job 24:4	776
their portion is cursed in the e	Job 24:18	776
hangeth the e upon nothing	Job 26:7	776
Iron is taken out of the e	Job 28:2	6083
As for the e, out of it cometh	Job 28:5	776
he looketh to the ends of the e	Job 28:24	776
of the valleys, in caves of the e	Job 30:6	6083
they were viler than the e	Job 30:8	776
given him a charge over the e	Job 34:13	776
us more than the beasts of the e	Job 35:11	776
lightning unto the ends of the e	Job 37:3	776
to the snow, Be thou on the e	Job 37:6	776
the face of the world in the e	Job 37:12	776
quieteth the e by the south wind	Job 37:17	776
I laid the foundations of the e	Job 38:4	776
take hold of the ends of the e	Job 38:13	776
perceived the breadth of the e	Job 38:18	776
the east wind upon the e	Job 38:24	776
To cause it to rain on the e	Job 38:26	776
set the dominion thereof in the e	Job 38:33	776
Which leaveth her eggs in the e	Job 39:14	776
Upon e there is not his like, who	Job 41:33	6083
The kings of the e set themselves	Ps 2:2	776
parts of the e for thy possession	Ps 2:8	776
be instructed, ye judges of the e	Ps 2:10	776
him tread down my life upon the e	Ps 7:5	776
is thy name in all the e	Ps 8:1	776
is thy name in all the e	Ps 8:9	776
man of the e may no more oppress	Ps 10:18	776
as silver tried in a furnace of e	Ps 12:6	776
to the saints that are in the e	Ps 16:3	776
their eyes bowing down to the e	Ps 17:11	776
Then the e shook and trembled	Ps 18:7	776
is gone out through all the e	Ps 19:4	776
shalt thou destroy from the e	Ps 21:10	776
they that be fat upon e shall eat	Ps 22:29	776
The e is the LORD's, and the	Ps 24:1	776
and his seed shall inherit the e	Ps 25:13	776
the e is full of the goodness of	Ps 33:5	776
Let all the e fear the LORD	Ps 33:8	776
upon all the inhabitants of the e	Ps 33:14	776
remembrance of them from the e	Ps 34:16	776
LORD, they shall inherit the e	Ps 37:9	776
But the meek shall inherit the e	Ps 37:11	776
of him shall inherit the e	Ps 37:22	776
and he shall be blessed upon the e	Ps 41:2	776
our belly cleaveth unto the e	Ps 44:25	776
mayest make princes in all the e	Ps 45:16	776
we fear, though the e be removed	Ps 46:2	776
uttered his voice, the e melted	Ps 46:6	776
desolations he hath made in the e	Ps 46:8	776
to cease unto the end of the e	Ps 46:9	776
I will be exalted in the e	Ps 46:10	776
he is a great King over all the e	Ps 47:2	776
For God is the King of all the e	Ps 47:7	776
shields of the e belong unto God	Ps 47:9	776
situation, the joy of the whole e	Ps 48:2	776
thy praise unto the ends of the e	Ps 48:10	776
called the e from the rising of	Ps 50:1	776
heavens from above, and to the e	Ps 50:4	776
let thy glory be above all the e	Ps 57:5	776
let thy glory be above all the e	Ps 57:11	776
violence of your hands in the e	Ps 58:2	776
he is a God that judgeth in the e	Ps 58:11	776
in Jacob unto the ends of the e	Ps 59:13	776
Thou hast made the e to tremble	Ps 60:2	776
From the end of the e will I cry	Ps 61:2	776
go into the lower parts of the e	Ps 63:9	776
of all the ends of the e, and of	Ps 65:5	776
Thou visitest the e, and waterest	Ps 65:9	776
All the e shall worship thee, and	Ps 66:4	776
That thy way may be known upon e	Ps 67:2	776
and govern the nations upon e	Ps 67:4	776
Then shall the e yield her	Ps 67:6	776
the ends of the e shall fear him	Ps 67:7	776
The e shook, the heavens also	Ps 68:8	776
unto God, ye kingdoms of the e	Ps 68:32	776
e praise him, the seas, and every	Ps 69:34	776
up again from the depths of the e	Ps 71:20	776
as showers that water the e	Ps 72:6	776
the river unto the ends of the e	Ps 72:8	776
be an handful of corn in the e	Ps 72:16	776
flourish like grass of the e	Ps 72:16	776
let the whole e be filled with	Ps 72:19	776
tongue walketh through the e	Ps 73:9	776
there is none upon e that I	Ps 73:25	776
salvation in the midst of the e	Ps 74:12	776
hast set all the borders of the e	Ps 74:17	776
for the dark places of the e are	Ps 74:20	776
The e and all the inhabitants	Ps 75:3	776
of the e shall wring them out	Ps 75:8	776
the e feared, and was still	Ps 76:8	776
to save all the meek of the e	Ps 76:9	776
is terrible to the kings of the e	Ps 76:12	776
the e trembled and shook	Ps 77:18	776
palaces, like the e which he hath	Ps 78:69	776
saints unto the beasts of the e	Ps 79:2	776
of the e are out of course	Ps 82:5	776
Arise, O God, judge the e	Ps 82:8	776
they became as dung for the e	Ps 83:10	127
art the most high over all the e	Ps 83:18	776
Truth shall spring out of the e	Ps 85:11	776
are thine, the e also is thine	Ps 89:11	776
higher than the kings of the e	Ps 89:27	776
or ever thou hadst formed the e	Ps 90:2	776
up thyself, thou judge of the e	Ps 94:2	776
hand are the deep places of the e	Ps 95:4	776
sing unto the LORD, all the e	Ps 96:1	776
fear before him, all the e	Ps 96:9	776
rejoice, and let the e be glad	Ps 96:11	776
for he cometh to judge the e	Ps 96:13	776
let the e rejoice	Ps 97:1	776
the e saw, and trembled	Ps 97:4	776
of the LORD of the whole e	Ps 97:5	776
LORD, art high above all the e	Ps 97:9	776
all the ends of the e have seen	Ps 98:3	776
noise unto the LORD, all the e	Ps 98:4	776
for he cometh to judge the e	Ps 98:9	776
let the e be moved	Ps 99:1	776
all the kings of the e thy glory	Ps 102:15	776
heaven did the LORD behold the e	Ps 102:19	776
thou laid the foundation of the e	Ps 102:25	776
as the heaven is high above the e	Ps 103:11	776
Who laid the foundations of the e	Ps 104:5	776
turn not again to cover the e	Ps 104:9	776
the e is satisfied with the fruit	Ps 104:13	776
may bring forth food out of the e	Ps 104:14	776
the e is full of thy riches	Ps 104:24	776
thou renewest the face of the e	Ps 104:30	127
He looketh on the e, and it	Ps 104:32	776
sinners be consumed out of the e	Ps 104:35	776
his judgments are in all the e	Ps 105:7	776
The e opened and swallowed up	Ps 106:17	776
and thy glory above all the e	Ps 108:5	776
off the memory of them from the e	Ps 109:15	776
His seed shall be mighty upon e	Ps 112:2	776
that are in heaven, and in the e	Ps 113:6	776
Tremble, thou e, at the presence	Ps 114:7	776
the LORD which made heaven and e	Ps 115:15	776
but the e hath he given to the	Ps 115:16	776
I am a stranger in the e	Ps 119:19	776
The e, O LORD, is full of thy	Ps 119:64	776
had almost consumed me upon e	Ps 119:87	776
thou hast established the e	Ps 119:90	776
the wicked of the e like dross	Ps 119:119	776
the LORD, which made heaven and e	Ps 121:2	776
of the LORD, who made heaven and e	Ps 124:8	776
and e bless thee out of Zion	Ps 134:3	776
that did he in heaven, and in e	Ps 135:6	776
to ascend from the ends of the e	Ps 135:7	776
out the e above the waters	Ps 136:6	776
kings of the e shall praise thee	Ps 138:4	776
in the lowest parts of the e	Ps 139:15	776
speaker be established in the e	Ps 140:11	776
and cleaveth wood upon the e	Ps 141:7	776
forth, he returneth to his e	Ps 146:4	127
Which made heaven, and e, the sea,	Ps 146:6	776
who prepareth rain for the e	Ps 147:8	776
forth his commandment upon e	Ps 147:15	776
Praise the LORD from the e	Ps 148:7	776
Kings of the e, and all people	Ps 148:11	776
princes, and all judges of the e	Ps 148:11	776
his glory is above the e and	Ps 148:13	776
shall be cut off from the e	Prov 2:22	776
LORD by wisdom hath founded the e	Prov 3:19	776
even all the judges of the e	Prov 8:16	776
the beginning, or ever the e was	Prov 8:23	776
as yet he had not made the e	Prov 8:26	776
the foundations of the e	Prov 8:29	776
in the habitable part of his e	Prov 8:31	776
wicked shall not inhabit the e	Prov 10:30	776
shall be recompensed in the e	Prov 11:31	776
a fool are in the ends of the e	Prov 17:24	776
the e for depth, and the heart of	Prov 25:3	776
established all the ends of the e	Prov 30:4	776
to devour the poor from off the e	Prov 30:14	776
the e that is not filled with	Prov 30:16	776
three things the e is disquieted	Prov 30:21	776
which are little upon the e	Prov 30:24	776
but the e abideth for ever	Eccl 1:4	776
that goeth downward to the e	Eccl 3:21	776
God is in heaven, and thou upon e	Eccl 5:2	776
the profit of the e is for all	Eccl 5:9	776
there is not a just man upon e	Eccl 7:20	776
a vanity which is done upon the e	Eccl 8:14	776
business that is done upon the e	Eccl 8:16	776
walking as servants upon the e	Eccl 10:7	776
not what evil shall be upon the e	Eccl 11:2	776
they empty themselves upon the e	Eccl 11:3	776
dust return to the e as it was	Eccl 12:7	776
The flowers appear on the e	Song 2:12	776
Hear, O heavens, and give ear, O e	Is 1:2	776
rocks, and into the caves of the e	Is 2:19	6083
ariseth to shake terribly the e	Is 2:19	776
ariseth to shake terribly the e	Is 2:21	776
the fruit of the e shall be	Is 4:2	776
alone in the midst of the e	Is 5:8	776
unto them from the end of the e	Is 5:26	776
the whole e is full of his glory	Is 6:3	776
And they shall look unto the e	Is 8:22	776
left, have I gathered all the e	Is 10:14	776
with equity for the meek of the e	Is 11:4	776
he shall smite the e with the rod	Is 11:4	776
for the e shall be full of the	Is 11:9	776
from the four corners of the e	Is 11:12	776
this is known in all the e	Is 12:5	776
the e shall remove out of her	Is 13:13	776
The whole e is at rest, and is	Is 14:7	776
even all the chief ones of the e	Is 14:9	776
man that made the e to tremble	Is 14:16	776
that is purposed upon the whole e	Is 14:26	776
the world, and dwellers on the e	Is 18:3	776
and to the beasts of the e	Is 18:6	776
all the beasts of the e shall	Is 18:6	776
are the honourable of the e	Is 23:8	776
all the honourable of the e	Is 23:9	776
the world upon the face of the e	Is 23:17	127
the LORD maketh the e empty	Is 24:1	776
The e mourneth and fadeth away,	Is 24:4	776
people of the e do languish	Is 24:4	776
The e also is defiled under the	Is 24:5	776
hath the curse devoured the e	Is 24:6	776
inhabitants of the e are burned	Is 24:6	776
part of the e have we heard songs	Is 24:16	776
upon thee, O inhabitant of the e	Is 24:17	776
the foundations of the e do shake	Is 24:18	776
The e is utterly broken down	Is 24:19	776
the e is clean dissolved, the	Is 24:19	776
the e is moved exceedingly	Is 24:19	776
The e shall reel to and fro like a	Is 24:20	776
the kings of the e upon the e	Is 24:21	127
he take away from off all the e	Is 25:8	776
when thy judgments are in the e	Is 26:9	776
it far unto all the ends of the e	Is 26:15	776
wrought any deliverance in the e	Is 26:18	776
the e shall cast out the dead	Is 26:19	776
of the e for their iniquity	Is 26:21	776
the e also shall disclose her	Is 26:21	776
cast down to the e with the hand	Is 28:2	776
even determined upon the whole e	Is 28:22	776
and bread of the increase of the e	Is 30:23	127
The e mourneth and languisheth	Is 33:9	776
let the e hear, and all that is	Is 34:1	776
of all the kingdoms of the e	Is 37:16	776
thou hast made heaven and e	Is 37:16	776
that all the kingdoms of the e	Is 37:20	776
the dust of the e in a measure	Is 40:12	776
from the foundations of the e	Is 40:21	776
sitteth upon the circle of the e	Is 40:22	776
the judges of the e as vanity	Is 40:23	776
shall not take root in the e	Is 40:24	776
the Creator of the ends of the e	Is 40:28	776
the ends of the e were afraid	Is 41:5	776
have taken from the ends of the e	Is 41:9	776
he have set judgment in the e	Is 42:4	776
he that spread forth the e	Is 42:5	776
his praise from the end of the e	Is 42:10	776
daughters from the ends of the e	Is 43:6	776
shout, ye lower parts of the e	Is 44:23	776
spreadeth abroad the e by myself	Is 44:24	776
let the e open, and let them bring	Is 45:8	776
with the potsherds of the e	Is 45:9	127
I have made the e, and created man	Is 45:12	776
God himself that formed the e	Is 45:18	776
secret, in a dark place of the e	Is 45:19	776
ye saved, all the ends of the e	Is 45:22	776
hath laid the foundation of the e	Is 48:13	776
utter it even to the end of the e	Is 48:20	776
salvation unto the end of the e	Is 49:6	776
of the people, to establish the e	Is 49:8	776
and be joyful, O e	Is 49:13	776
thee with their face toward the e	Is 49:23	776
and look upon the e beneath	Is 51:6	776
and the e shall wax old like a	Is 51:6	776
and laid the foundations of the e	Is 51:13	776
and lay the foundations of the e	Is 51:16	776
all the ends of the e shall see	Is 52:10	776
of the whole e shall he be called	Is 54:5	776
Noah should no more go over the e	Is 54:9	776
the heavens are higher than the e	Is 55:9	776
not thither, but watereth the e	Is 55:10	776
upon the high places of the e	Is 58:14	776
the darkness shall cover the e	Is 60:2	776
For as the e bringeth forth her	Is 61:11	776
make Jerusalem a praise in the e	Is 62:7	776
down their strength to the e	Is 63:6	776
e shall bless himself in the God	Is 65:16	776
he that sweareth in the e shall	Is 65:16	776
I create new heavens and a new e	Is 65:17	776
throne, and the e is my footstool	Is 66:1	776
Shall the e be made to bring	Is 66:8	776
as the new heavens and the new e	Is 66:22	776
I beheld the e, and, lo, it was	Jer 4:23	776
For this shall the e mourn	Jer 4:28	776
Hear, O e:	Jer 6:19	776
be raised from the sides of the e	Jer 6:22	776
and for the beasts of the e	Jer 7:33	776
for dung upon the face of the e	Jer 8:2	127
valiant for the truth upon the e	Jer 9:3	776
and righteousness, in the e	Jer 9:24	776
at his wrath the e shall tremble	Jer 10:10	776

not made the heavens and the *e*	Jer 10:11	778
even they shall perish from the *e*	Jer 10:11	772
He hath made the *e* by his power	Jer 10:12	776
to ascend from the ends of the *e*	Jer 10:13	776
for there was no rain in the *e*	Jer 14:4	776
heaven, and the beasts of the *e*	Jer 15:3	776
into all kingdoms of the *e*	Jer 15:4	776
man of contention to the whole *e*	Jer 15:10	776
be as dung upon the face of the *e*	Jer 16:4	127
and for the beasts of the *e*	Jer 16:4	776
unto thee from the ends of the *e*	Jer 16:19	776
from me shall be written in the *e*	Jer 17:13	776
and for the beasts of the *e*	Jer 19:7	776
O *e*, *e*, *e*, hear the word	Jer 22:29	776
judgment and justice in the *e*	Jer 23:5	776
Do not I fill heaven and *e*	Jer 23:24	776
kingdoms of the *e* for their hurt	Jer 24:9	776
which are upon the face of the *e*	Jer 25:26	127
upon all the inhabitants of the *e*	Jer 25:29	776
all the inhabitants of the *e*	Jer 25:30	776
come even to the ends of the *e*	Jer 25:31	776
up from the coasts of the *e*	Jer 25:32	776
day from one end of the *e*	Jer 25:33	776
even unto the other end of the *e*	Jer 25:33	776
curse to all the nations of the *e*	Jer 26:6	776
I have made the *e*, the man and the	Jer 27:5	776
thee from off the face of the *e*	Jer 28:16	127
to all the kingdoms of the *e*	Jer 29:18	776
them from the coasts of the *e*	Jer 31:8	776
hath created a new thing in the *e*	Jer 31:22	776
of the *e* searched out beneath	Jer 31:37	776
the *e* by thy great power and	Jer 32:17	776
before all the nations of the *e*	Jer 33:9	776
the ordinances of heaven and *e*	Jer 33:25	776
kingdoms of the *e* of his dominion	Jer 34:1	776
into all the kingdoms of the *e*	Jer 34:17	776
heaven, and to the beasts of the *e*	Jer 34:20	776
among all the nations of the *e*	Jer 44:8	776
I will go up, and will cover the *e*	Jer 46:8	776
The *e* is moved at the noise of	Jer 49:21	776
of the whole *e* cut in asunder	Jer 50:23	776
up from the coasts of the *e*	Jer 50:41	776
taking of Babylon the *e* is moved	Jer 50:46	776
hand, that made all the *e* drunken	Jer 51:7	776
He hath made the *e* by his power	Jer 51:15	776
to ascend from the ends of the *e*	Jer 51:16	776
LORD, which destroyest all the *e*	Jer 51:25	776
praise of the whole *e* surprised	Jer 51:41	776
Then the heaven and the *e*, and all	Jer 51:48	776
shall fall the slain of all the *e*	Jer 51:49	776
unto the *e* the beauty of Israel	Lam 2:1	776
my liver is poured upon the *e*	Lam 2:11	776
of beauty, The joy of the whole *e*	Lam 2:15	776
feet all the prisoners of the *e*	Lam 3:34	776
The kings of the *e*, and all the	Lam 4:12	776
the *e* by the living creatures	Eze 1:15	776
were lifted up from the *e*	Eze 1:19	776
those were lifted up from the *e*	Eze 1:21	776
the wicked of the *e* for a spoil	Eze 7:21	776
spirit lifted me up between the *e*	Eze 8:3	776
the LORD hath forsaken the *e*	Eze 8:12	776
say, The LORD hath forsaken the *e*	Eze 9:9	776
wings to mount up from the *e*	Eze 10:16	776
mounted up from the *e* in my sight	Eze 10:19	776
thee in the low parts of the *e*	Eze 26:20	776
the *e* with the multitude of thy	Eze 27:33	776
bring thee to ashes upon the *e* in	Eze 28:18	776
all the people of the *e* are gone	Eze 31:12	776
to the nether parts of the *e*	Eze 31:14	776
in the nether parts of the *e*	Eze 31:16	776
unto the nether parts of the *e*	Eze 31:18	776
beasts of the whole *e* with thee	Eze 32:4	776
unto the nether parts of the *e*	Eze 32:18	776
into the nether parts of the *e*	Eze 32:24	776
upon all the face of the *e*	Eze 34:6	776
the *e* shall yield her increase,	Eze 34:27	776
When the whole *e* rejoiceth	Eze 35:14	776
things that creep upon the *e*	Eze 38:20	127
that are upon the face of the *e*	Eze 38:20	127
remain upon the face of the *e*	Eze 39:14	776
the blood of the princes of the *e*	Eze 39:18	776
the *e* shined with his glory	Eze 43:2	776
There is not a man upon the *e*	Dan 2:10	3007
mountain, and filled the whole *e*	Dan 2:35	772
shall bear rule over all the *e*	Dan 2:39	772
that dwell in all the *e*	Dan 4:1	772
a tree in the midst of the *e*	Dan 4:10	772
thereof to the end of all the *e*	Dan 4:11	772
the stump of his roots in the *e*	Dan 4:15	772
the beasts in the grass of the *e*	Dan 4:15	772
and the sight thereof to all the *e*	Dan 4:20	772
thy dominion to the end of the *e*	Dan 4:22	772
of the roots thereof in the *e*	Dan 4:23	772
of the *e* are reputed as nothing	Dan 4:35	772
and among the inhabitants of the *e*	Dan 4:35	772
that dwell in all the *e*	Dan 6:25	772
and wonders in heaven and in *e*	Dan 6:27	772
and it was lifted up from the *e*	Dan 7:4	772
which shall arise out of the *e*	Dan 7:17	772
be the fourth kingdom upon *e*	Dan 7:23	772
and shall devour the whole *e*	Dan 7:23	772
west on the face of the whole *e*	Dan 8:5	776
in the dust of the *e* shall awake	Dan 12:2	127
sword and the battle out of the *e*	Hos 2:18	776
heavens, and they shall hear the *e*	Hos 2:21	776
the *e* shall hear the corn, and the	Hos 2:22	776
I will sow her unto me in the *e*	Hos 2:23	776
latter and former rain unto the *e*	Hos 6:3	776
The *e* shall quake before them	Joel 2:10	776
in the heavens and in the *e*	Joel 2:30	776
the heavens and the *e* shall shake	Joel 3:16	776
of the *e* on the head of the poor	Amos 2:7	776
of all the families of the *e*	Amos 3:2	127
a bird fall in a snare upon the *e*	Amos 3:5	776
one take up a snare from the *e*	Amos 3:5	127
upon the high places of the *e*	Amos 4:13	776
leave off righteousness in the *e*	Amos 5:7	776
them out upon the face of the *e*	Amos 5:8	776
darken the *e* in the clear day	Amos 8:9	776
hath founded his troop in the *e*	Amos 9:6	776
them out upon the face of the *e*	Amos 9:6	776
it from off the face of the *e*	Amos 9:8	127
the least grain fall upon the *e*	Amos 9:9	776
the *e* with her bars was about me	Jonah 2:6	776
hearken, O *e*, and all that therein	Mic 1:2	776
upon the high places of the *e*	Mic 1:3	776
unto the Lord of the whole *e*	Mic 4:13	776
be great unto the ends of the *e*	Mic 5:4	776
and ye strong foundations of the *e*	Mic 6:2	776
good man is perished out of the *e*	Mic 7:2	776
their holes like worms of the *e*	Mic 7:17	776
the *e* is burned at his presence,	Nah 1:5	776
will cut off thy prey from the *e*	Nah 2:13	776
For the *e* shall be filled with	Hab 2:14	776
let all the *e* keep silence before	Hab 2:20	776
the *e* was full of his praise	Hab 3:3	776
He stood, and measured the *e*	Hab 3:6	776
didst cleave the *e* with rivers	Hab 3:9	776
ye the LORD, all ye meek of the *e*	Zeph 2:3	776
will famish all the gods of the *e*	Zeph 2:11	776
for all the *e* shall be devoured	Zeph 3:8	776
praise among all people of the *e*	Zeph 3:20	776
the *e* is stayed from her fruit	Hag 1:10	776
will shake the heavens, and the *e*	Hag 2:6	776
I will shake the heavens and the *e*	Hag 2:21	776
to walk to and fro through the *e*	Zec 1:10	776
walked to and fro through the *e*	Zec 1:11	776
all the *e* sitteth still, and is at	Zec 1:11	776
run to and fro through the whole *e*	Zec 4:10	776
stand by the Lord of the whole *e*	Zec 4:14	776
over the face of the whole *e*	Zec 5:3	776
resemblance through all the *e*	Zec 5:6	776
lifted up the ephah between the *e*	Zec 5:9	776
before the Lord of all the *e*	Zec 6:5	776
walk to and fro through the *e*	Zec 6:7	776
walk to and fro through the *e*	Zec 6:7	776
walked to and fro through the *e*	Zec 6:7	776
river even to the ends of the *e*	Zec 9:10	776
and layeth the foundation of the *e*	Zec 12:1	776
though all the people of the *e* be	Zec 12:3	776
LORD shall be king over all the *e*	Zec 14:9	776
e unto Jerusalem to worship the	Zec 14:17	776
come and smite the *e* with a curse	Mal 4:6	776
for they shall inherit the *e*	Mt 5:5	1093
Ye are the salt of the *e*	Mt 5:13	1093
e pass, one jot or one tittle	Mt 5:18	1093
Nor by the *e*; for it is	Mt 5:35	1093
Thy will be done in *e*, as it is	Mt 6:10	1093
for yourselves treasures upon *e*	Mt 6:19	1093
hath power on *e* to forgive sins	Mt 9:6	1093
that I am come to send peace on *e*	Mt 10:34	1093
O Father, Lord of heaven and *e*	Mt 11:25	1093
nights in the heart of the *e*	Mt 12:40	1093
e to hear the wisdom of Solomon	Mt 12:42	1093
places, where they had not much *e*	Mt 13:5	1093
because they had no deepness of *e*	Mt 13:5	1093
on *e* shall be bound in heaven	Mt 16:19	1093
on *e* shall be loosed in heaven	Mt 16:19	1093
of the *e* take custom or tribute	Mt 17:25	1093
on *e* shall be bound in heaven	Mt 18:18	1093
on *e* shall be loosed in heaven	Mt 18:18	1093
if two of you shall agree on *e* as	Mt 18:19	1093
no man your father upon the *e*	Mt 23:9	1093
righteous blood shed upon the *e*	Mt 23:35	1093
all the tribes of the *e* mourn	Mt 24:30	1093
e shall pass away, but my words	Mt 24:35	1093
one went and digged in the *e*	Mt 25:18	1093
went and hid thy talent in the *e*	Mt 25:25	1093
the *e* did quake, and the rocks	Mt 27:51	1093
given unto me in heaven and in *e*	Mt 28:18	1093
hath power on *e* to forgive sins	Mk 2:10	1093
ground, where it had not much *e*	Mk 4:5	1093
up, because it had no depth of *e*	Mk 4:5	1093
For the *e* bringeth forth fruit of	Mk 4:28	1093
which, when it is sown in the *e*	Mk 4:31	1093
all the seeds that be in the *e*	Mk 4:31	1093
as no fuller on *e* can white them	Mk 9:3	1093
from the uttermost part of the *e*	Mk 13:27	1093
Heaven and *e* shall pass away	Mk 13:31	1093
on *e* peace, good will toward men	Lk 2:14	1093
hath power upon *e* to forgive sins	Lk 5:24	1093
built an house upon the *e*	Lk 6:49	1093
O Father, Lord of heaven and *e*	Lk 10:21	1093
be done, as in heaven, so in *e*	Lk 11:2	1093
from the utmost parts of the *e* to	Lk 11:31	1093
I am come to send fire on the *e*	Lk 12:49	1093
that I am come to give peace on *e*	Lk 12:51	1093
the face of the sky and of the *e*	Lk 12:56	1093
e to pass, than one tittle of the	Lk 16:17	1093
shall he find faith on the *e*	Lk 18:8	1093
upon the *e* distress of nations,	Lk 21:25	1093
things which are coming on the *e*	Lk 21:26	3625
Heaven and *e* shall pass away	Lk 21:33	1093
dwell on the face of the whole *e*	Lk 21:35	1093
all the *e* until the ninth hour	Lk 23:44	1093
bowed down their faces to the *e*	Lk 24:5	1093
he that is of the *e* is earthly	Jn 3:31	1093
is earthly, and speaketh of the *e*	Jn 3:31	1093
I, if I be lifted up from the *e*	Jn 12:32	1093
I have glorified thee on the *e*	Jn 17:4	1093
unto the uttermost part of the *e*	Acts 1:8	1093
above, and signs in the *e* beneath	Acts 2:19	1093
the kindreds of the *e* be blessed	Acts 3:25	1093
God, which hast made heaven, and *e*	Acts 4:24	1093
The kings of the *e* stood up	Acts 4:26	1093
my throne, and *e* is my footstool	Acts 7:49	1093
for his life is taken from the *e*	Acts 8:33	1093
And he fell to the *e*, and heard a	Acts 9:4	1093
And Saul arose from the *e*	Acts 9:8	1093
corners, and let down to the *e*	Acts 10:11	1093
of fourfooted beasts of the *e*	Acts 10:12	1093
and saw fourfooted beasts of the *e*	Acts 11:6	1093
salvation unto the ends of the *e*	Acts 13:47	1093
God, which made heaven, and *e*	Acts 14:15	1093
that he is Lord of heaven and *e*	Acts 17:24	1093
to dwell on all the face of the *e*	Acts 17:26	1093
with such a fellow from the *e*	Acts 22:22	1093
when we were all fallen to the *e*	Acts 26:14	1093
be declared throughout all the *e*	Rom 9:17	1093
will the Lord make upon the *e*	Rom 9:28	1093
their sound went into all the *e*	Rom 10:18	1093
gods, whether in heaven or in *e*	1Cor 8:5	1093
For the *e* is the Lord's, and the	1Cor 10:26	1093
for the *e* is the Lord's, and the	1Cor 10:28	1093
The first man is of the *e*	1Cor 15:47	1093
are in heaven, and which are on *e*	Eph 1:10	1093
family in heaven and *e* is named,	Eph 3:15	1093
into the lower parts of the *e*	Eph 4:9	1093
and thou mayest live long on the *e*	Eph 6:3	1093
things in heaven, and things in *e*	Phil 2:10	1919
and things under the *e*	Phil 2:10	2709
are in heaven, and that are in *e*	Col 1:16	1093
say, whether they be things in *e*	Col 1:20	1093
above, not on things on the *e*	Col 3:2	1093
your members which are upon the *e*	Col 3:5	1093
silver, but also of wood and of *e*	2Ti 2:20	3749
hast laid the foundation of the *e*	Heb 1:10	1093
For the *e* which drinketh in the	Heb 6:7	1093
For if he were on *e*, he should	Heb 8:4	1093
strangers and pilgrims on the *e*	Heb 11:13	1093
and in dens and caves of the *e*	Heb 11:38	1093
who refused him that spake on *e*	Heb 12:25	1093
Whose voice then shook the *e*	Heb 12:26	1093
once more I shake not the *e* only	Heb 12:26	1093
have lived in pleasure on the *e*	Jas 5:5	1093
for the precious fruit of the *e*	Jas 5:7	1093
by heaven, neither by the *e*	Jas 5:12	1093
it rained not on the *e* by the	Jas 5:17	1093
the *e* brought forth her fruit	Jas 5:18	1093
the *e* standing out of the water	2Pet 3:5	1093
But the heavens and the *e*, which	2Pet 3:7	1093
the *e* also and the works that are	2Pet 3:10	1093
look for new heavens and a new *e*	2Pet 3:13	1093
are three that bear witness in *e*	1Jn 5:8	1093
the prince of the kings of the *e*	Rev 1:5	1093
all kindreds of the *e* shall wail	Rev 1:7	1093
to try them that dwell upon the *e*	Rev 3:10	1093
nor in *e*, neither under the *e*	Rev 5:3	1093
of God sent forth into all the *e*	Rev 5:6	1093
and we shall reign on the *e*	Rev 5:10	1093
and on the *e*, and under the *e*	Rev 5:13	1093
thereon to take peace from the *e*	Rev 6:4	1093
over the fourth part of the *e*	Rev 6:8	1093
and with the beasts of the *e*	Rev 6:8	1093
blood on them that dwell on the *e*	Rev 6:10	1093
stars of heaven fell unto the *e*	Rev 6:13	1093
And the kings of the *e*, and the	Rev 6:15	1093
on the four corners of the *e*	Rev 7:1	1093
holding the four winds of the *e*	Rev 7:1	1093
the wind should not blow on the *e*	Rev 7:1	1093
whom it was given to hurt the *e*	Rev 7:2	1093
Saying, Hurt not the *e*, neither	Rev 7:3	1093
the altar, and cast it into the *e*	Rev 8:5	1093
and they were cast upon the *e*	Rev 8:7	1093
to the inhabiters of the *e* by	Rev 8:13	1093
star fall from heaven unto the *e*	Rev 9:1	1093
of the smoke locusts upon the *e*	Rev 9:3	1093
the scorpions of the *e* have power	Rev 9:3	1093
not hurt the grass of the *e*	Rev 9:4	1093
sea, and his left foot on the *e*	Rev 10:2	1093
upon the *e* lifted up his hand to	Rev 10:5	1093
things that therein are, and the *e*	Rev 10:6	1093
upon the sea and upon the *e*	Rev 10:8	1093
standing before the God of the *e*	Rev 11:4	1093
to smite the *e* with all plagues,	Rev 11:6	1093
the *e* shall rejoice over them	Rev 11:10	1093
them that dwelt on the *e*	Rev 11:10	1093
destroy them which destroy the *e*	Rev 11:18	1093
heaven, and did cast them to the *e*	Rev 12:4	1093
he was cast out into the *e*	Rev 12:9	1093
Woe to the inhabiters of the *e*	Rev 12:12	1093
saw that he was cast unto the *e*	Rev 12:13	1093
the *e* helped the woman	Rev 12:16	1093
the *e* opened her mouth, and	Rev 12:16	1093
upon the *e* shall worship him	Rev 13:8	1093
beast coming up out of the *e*	Rev 13:11	1093
before him, and causeth the *e*	Rev 13:12	1093
on the *e* in the sight of men	Rev 13:13	1093
them that dwell on the *e* by the	Rev 13:14	1093
to them that dwell on the *e*	Rev 13:14	1093
which were redeemed from the *e*	Rev 14:3	1093
unto them that dwell on the *e*	Rev 14:6	1093
him that made heaven, and *e*	Rev 14:7	1093
for the harvest of the *e* is ripe	Rev 14:15	1093
thrust in his sickle on the *e*	Rev 14:16	1093
and the *e* was reaped	Rev 14:16	1093
the clusters of the vine of the *e*	Rev 14:18	1093
thrust in his sickle into the *e*	Rev 14:19	1093
and gathered the vine of the *e*	Rev 14:19	1093
of the wrath of God upon the *e*	Rev 16:1	1093
and poured out his vial upon the *e*	Rev 16:2	1093
go forth unto the kings of the *e*	Rev 16:14	1093
was not since men were upon the *e*	Rev 16:18	1093
the *e* have committed fornication	Rev 17:2	1093
the inhabitants of the *e* have	Rev 17:2	1093
OF THE *E*	Rev 17:5	1093
that dwell on the *e* shall wonder	Rev 17:8	1093
reigneth over the kings of the *e*	Rev 17:18	1093
the *e* was lightened with his	Rev 18:1	1093
the kings of the *e* have committed	Rev 18:3	1093
the merchants of the *e* are waxed	Rev 18:3	1093
And the kings of the *e*, who have	Rev 18:9	1093

the merchants of the e shall weep Rev 18:11 1093
were the great men of the e Rev 18:23 1093
of all that were slain upon the e Rev 18:24 1093
the e with her fornication Rev 19:2 1093
the beast, and the kings of the e Rev 19:19 1093
are in the four quarters of the e Rev 20:8 1093
went up on the breadth of the e Rev 20:9 1093
sat on it, from whose face the e Rev 20:11 1093
And I saw a new heaven and a new e. Rev 21:1 1093
the first e were passed away Rev 21:1 1093
the kings of the e do bring their Rev 21:24 1093

EARTHEN
But the e vessel wherein it is Lev 6:28 2789
every e vessel, whereinto any of Lev 11:33 2789
in an e vessel over running water Lev 14:5 2789
in an e vessel over running water Lev 14:50 2789
take holy water in an e vessel Num 5:17 2789
e vessels, and wheat, and barley, 2Sa 17:28 3335
Go and get a potter's e bottle Jer 19:1 2789
and put them in an e vessel Jer 32:14 2789
are they esteemed as e pitchers Lam 4:2 2789
have this treasure in e vessels 2Cor 4:7 3749

EARTHLY
If I have told you e things Jn 3:12 1919
he that is of the earth is e Jn 3:31
For we know that if our e house 2Cor 5:1 1919
in their shame, who mind e things Phil 3:19 1919
not from above, but is e, sensual Jas 3:15 1919

EARTHQUAKE
and after the wind an e 1Kin 19:11 7494
but the LORD was not in the e 1Kin 19:11 7494
And after the e a fire 1Kin 19:12 7494
of hosts with thunder, and with e Is 29:6 7494
of Israel, two years before the e Amos 1:1 7494
e in the days of Uzziah king of Zec 14:5 7494
him, watching Jesus, saw the e Mt 27:54 4578
And, behold, there was a great e Mt 28:2 4578
And suddenly there was a great e Acts 16:26 4578
seal, and, lo, there was a great e Rev 6:12 4578
and lightnings, and an e Rev 8:5 4578
the same hour was there a great e Rev 11:13 4578
in the e were slain of men seven Rev 11:13 4578
voices, and thunderings, and an e Rev 11:19 4578
and there was a great e, such as Rev 16:18 4578
upon the earth, so mighty an e Rev 16:18 4578

EARTHQUAKES
be famines, and pestilences, and e Mt 24:7 4578
there shall be e in divers places Mk 13:8 4578
great e shall be in divers places Lk 21:11 4578

EARTHY
The first man is of the earth, e 1Cor 15:47 5517
As is the e, such are they also 1Cor 15:48 5517
such are they also that are e 1Cor 15:48 5517
we have borne the image of the e 1Cor 15:49 5517

EASE
when thou wilt e thyself abroad Deut 23:13 3427
nations shalt thou find no e Deut 28:65 7280
trode them down with e over Judg 20:43 4496
now therefore e thou somewhat the 2Chr 10:4 7043
E somewhat the yoke that thy 2Chr 10:9 7043
me, my couch shall e my complaint Job 7:13 5375
the thought of him that is at e Job 12:5 7600
I was at e, but he hath broken me Job 16:12 7961
full strength, being wholly at e Job 21:23 7946
His soul shall dwell at e Ps 25:13 2896
scorning of those that are at e Ps 123:4 7600
I will e me of mine adversaries, Is 1:24 5162
Rise up, ye women that are at e Is 32:9 7600
Tremble, ye women that are at e Is 32:11 7600
return, and be in rest and at e Jer 46:27 7599
hath been at e from his youth Jer 48:11 7599
multitude being at e was with her Eze 23:42 7961
Woe to them that are at e in Zion Amos 6:1 7600
with the heathen that are at e Zec 1:15 7600
take thine e, eat, drink, and be Lk 12:19 373

EASED
and though I forbear, what am I e Job 16:6 1980
I mean not that other men be e 2Cor 8:13 425

EASIER
so shall it be e for thyself Ex 18:22 7043
For whether is e, to say, Thy Mt 9:5 2123
It is e for a camel to go through Mt 19:24 2123
Whether is it e to say to the Mk 2:9 2123
It is e for a camel to go through Mk 10:25 2123
Whether is e, to say, Thy sins be Lk 5:23 2123
it is e for heaven and earth to Lk 16:17 2123
For it is e for a camel to go Lk 18:25 2123

EASILY
is not e provoked, thinketh no 1Cor 13:5
the sin which doth so e beset us Heb 12:1

EAST
goeth toward the e of Assyria Gen 2:14 6926
he placed at the e of the garden Gen 3:24 6924
the land of Nod, on the e of Eden Gen 4:16 6926
unto Sephar a mount of the e Gen 10:30 6924
as they journeyed from the e Gen 11:2 6924
a mountain on the e of Beth-el Gen 12:8 6924
on the west, and Hai on the e Gen 12:8 6924
and Lot journeyed e Gen 13:11 6924
eastward, unto the e country Gen 25:6 6924
abroad to the west, and to the e Gen 28:14 6924
the land of the people of the e Gen 29:1 6924
blasted with the e wind sprung up Gen 41:6 6921
thin, and blasted with the e wind Gen 41:23 6921
empty ears blasted with the e Gen 41:27 6921
the LORD brought an e wind upon Ex 10:13 6921
the e wind brought the locusts Ex 10:13 6921
by a strong e wind all that night Ex 14:21 6921
e side eastward shall be fifty Ex 27:13 6924
for the e side eastward fifty Ex 38:13 6924
it beside the altar on the e part Lev 1:16 6924
on the e side toward the rising Num 2:3 6924
the tabernacle toward the e Num 3:38 6924
on the e parts shall go forward Num 10:5 6924
out of the mountains of the e Num 23:7 6924
ye shall point out your e border Num 34:10 6924
to Riblah, on the e side of Ain Num 34:11 6924
on the e side two thousand cubits Num 35:5 6924
in the e border of Jericho Josh 4:19 4217
on the e side of Beth-el, and Josh 7:2 6924
And to the Canaanite on the e Josh 11:3 4217
Hermon, and all the plain on the e Josh 12:1 4217
to the sea of Chinneroth on the e Josh 12:3 4217
plain, even the salt sea on the e Josh 12:3 4217
the e border was the salt sea, Josh 15:5 6924
the water of Jericho on the e Josh 16:1 4217
on the e side was Ataroth-addar Josh 16:5 4217
passed by it on the e to Janohah Josh 16:6 4217
north, and in Issachar on the e Josh 17:10 4217
beyond Jordan on the e, which Josh 18:7 4217
the border of it on the e side Josh 18:20 6924
along on the e to Gittah-hepher Josh 19:13 6924
and the children of the e Judg 6:3 6924
the children of the e were Judg 6:33 6924
all the children of the e lay Judg 7:12 6924
hosts of the children of the e Judg 8:10 6924
dwelt in tents on the e of Nobah Judg 8:11 6924
came by the e side of the land of Judg 11:18
on the e side of the highway that Judg 21:19
all the children of the e country 1Kin 4:30 6924
and three looking toward the e 1Kin 7:25 4217
even unto the e side of the 1Chr 4:39 4217
all the e land of Gilead 1Chr 5:10 4217
on the e side of Jordan, were 1Chr 6:78 4217
were the porters, toward the e 1Chr 9:24 4217
of the valleys, both toward the e 1Chr 12:15 4217
and three looking toward the e 2Chr 4:4 4217
on the right side of the e end 2Chr 4:10 6924
stood at the e end of the altar, 2Chr 5:12 4217
them together into the e street 2Chr 29:4 4217
Levite, the porter toward the e 2Chr 31:14 4217
the water gate toward the e Neh 3:26 4217
the keeper of the e gate Neh 3:29 4217
greatest of all the men of the e Job 1:3 6924
and fill his belly with the e wind Job 15:2 6921
The e wind carrieth him away, and Job 27:21 6921
the e wind upon the earth Job 38:24 6921
ships of Tarshish with an e wind Ps 48:7 6921
cometh neither from the e Ps 75:6 4161
He caused an e wind to blow in Ps 78:26 6921
As far as the e is from the west, Ps 103:12 4217
them out of the lands, from the e Ps 107:3 4217
they be replenished from the e Is 2:6 6924
spoil them of the e together Is 11:14 6924
wind in the day of the e wind Is 27:8 6921
up the righteous man from the e Is 41:2 4217
I will bring thy seed from the e Is 43:5 4217
a ravenous bird from the e Is 46:11 4217
with an e wind before the enemy Jer 18:17 6921
is by the entry of the e gate Jer 19:2 2777
of the horse gate toward the e Jer 31:40 4217
Kedar, and spoil the men of the e Jer 49:28 6924
LORD, and their faces toward the e Eze 8:16 6924
worshipped the sun toward the e Eze 8:16 6924
of the e gate of the LORD's house Eze 10:19 6931
brought me unto the e gate of the Eze 11:1 6931
is on the e side of the city Eze 11:23 6924
when the e wind toucheth it Eze 17:10 6921
the e wind dried up her fruit Eze 19:12 6921
the men of the e for a possession Eze 25:4 6924
men of the e with the Ammonites Eze 25:10 6924
the e wind hath broken thee in Eze 27:26 6921
passengers on the e of the sea Eze 39:11 6926
gate which looketh toward the e Eze 40:6 6921
gate that looketh toward the e Eze 40:22 6921
toward the north, and toward the e Eze 40:23 6921
into the inner court toward the e Eze 40:32 6921
one at the side of the e gate Eze 40:44 6921
the separate place toward the e Eze 41:14 6921
was the entry on the e side Eze 42:9 6921
wall of the court toward the e Eze 42:10 6921
before the wall toward the e Eze 42:12 6921
whose prospect is toward the e Eze 42:15 6921
He measured the e side with the Eze 42:16 6921
gate that looketh toward the e Eze 43:1 6921
Israel came from the way of the e Eze 43:2 6921
whose prospect is toward the e Eze 43:4 6921
stairs shall look toward the e Eze 43:17 6921
which looketh toward the e Eze 44:1 6921
and from the e side eastward Eze 45:7 6924
the west border unto the e border Eze 45:7 6921
e shall be shut the six working Eze 46:1 6921
gate that looketh toward the e Eze 46:12 6921
of the house stood toward the e Eze 47:1 6921
issue out toward the e country Eze 47:8 6930
the e side ye shall measure from Eze 47:18 6921
from the border unto the e sea Eze 47:18 6931
And this is the e side Eze 47:18 6921
for these are his sides e Eze 48:1 6921
from the e side unto the west Eze 48:2 6921
from the e side even unto the Eze 48:3 6921
from the e side unto the west Eze 48:4 6921
from the e side unto the west Eze 48:5 6921
from the e side even unto the Eze 48:6 6921
from the e side unto the west Eze 48:7 6921
from the e side unto the west Eze 48:8 6921
from the e side unto the west Eze 48:8 6921
toward the e ten thousand in Eze 48:10 6921
on the e side four thousand and Eze 48:16 6921
toward the e two hundred and fifty Eze 48:17 6921
the oblation toward the e border Eze 48:21 6921
from the e side unto the west Eze 48:23 6921
from the e side unto the west Eze 48:24 6921
from the e side unto the west Eze 48:25 6921
from the e side unto the west Eze 48:26 6921
from the e side unto the west Eze 48:27 6921
at the e side four thousand and Eze 48:32 6921
toward the south, and toward the e Dan 8:9 4217
But tidings out of the e and out Dan 11:44 4217
and followeth after the e wind Hos 12:1 6921
an e wind shall come, the wind of Hos 13:15 6921
with his face toward the e sea Joel 2:20 6931
and from the north even to the e Amos 8:12 4217
sat on the e side of the city, and Jonah 4:5 6924
God prepared a vehement e wind Jonah 4:8 6921
faces shall sup up as the e wind Hab 1:9 6921
save my people from the e country Zec 8:7 4217
is before Jerusalem on the e Zec 14:4 6924
in the midst thereof toward the e Zec 14:4 4217
wise men from the e to Jerusalem Mt 2:1 395
we have seen his star in the e Mt 2:2 395
the star, which they saw in the e Mt 2:9 395
That many shall come from the e Mt 8:11 395
the lightning cometh out of the e Mt 24:27 395
And they shall come from the e Lk 13:29 395
angel ascending from the e Rev 7:2 395
kings of the e might be prepared Rev 16:12 395
On the e three gates Rev 21:13 395

EASTER *Passover.*
intending after E to bring him Acts 12:4 3957

EASTWARD
God planted a garden e in Eden Gen 2:8 6924
art northward, and southward, and e Gen 13:14 6924
his son, while he yet lived, e Gen 25:6 6924
east side e shall be fifty cubits Ex 27:13 4217
for the east side e fifty cubits Ex 38:13 4217
his finger upon the mercy seat e Lev 16:14 6924
tabernacle of the congregation e Num 3:38 4217
to us on this side Jordan e Num 32:19 4217
outmost coast of the salt sea e Num 34:3 6924
side of the sea of Chinnereth e Num 34:11 6924
this side Jordan near Jericho e Num 34:15 6924
salt sea, under Ashdoth-pisgah e Deut 3:17 4217
and northward, and southward, and e. Deut 3:27 4217
the plain on this side Jordan e Deut 4:49 4217
and unto the valley of Mizpeh e Josh 11:8 4217
Moses gave them, beyond Jordan e Josh 13:8 4217
on the other side Jordan e Josh 13:27 4217
other side Jordan, by Jericho, e Josh 13:32 4217
went about e unto Taanath-shiloh Josh 16:6 4217
turned from Sarid e toward the Josh 19:12 6924
other side Jordan by Jericho e Josh 20:8 4217
in Michmash, e from Beth-aven 1Sa 13:5 6926
house e over against the south 1Kin 7:39 6924
Get thee hence, and turn thee e 1Kin 17:3 6924
From Jordan e, all the land of 2Kin 10:33
And he said, Open the window e 2Kin 13:17 6924
e he inhabited unto the entering 1Chr 5:9 4217
e Naaran, and westward Gezer, with 1Chr 7:28 4217
waited in the king's gate e 1Chr 9:18 4217
the lot e fell to Shelemiah 1Chr 26:14 4217
E were six Levites, northward 1Chr 26:17 4217
David, even unto the water gate e Neh 12:37 4217
the LORD's house, which looketh e Eze 11:1 6921
gate e were three on this side Eze 40:10
without, an hundred cubits e Eze 40:19 6921
westward, and from the east side e Eze 45:7 6921
the threshold of the house e Eze 47:1 6921
gate by the way that looketh e Eze 47:2 6921
the line in his hand went forth e Eze 47:3 6921
portion shall be ten thousand e Eze 48:18 6921

EASY
but knowledge is e unto him that Prov 14:6 7043
For my yoke is e, and my burden is Mt 11:30 5543
tongue words e to be understood 1Cor 14:9 2154
e to be intreated, full of mercy Jas 3:17 2138

EAT
the garden thou mayest freely e Gen 2:16 398
and evil, thou shalt not e of it Gen 2:17 398
Ye shall not e of every tree of Gen 3:1 398
We may e of the fruit of the Gen 3:2 398
hath said, Ye shall not e of it Gen 3:3 398
know that in the day ye e thereof Gen 3:5 398
of the fruit thereof, and did e Gen 3:6 398
and he did e Gen 3:6 398
thee that thou shouldest not e Gen 3:11 398
gave me of the tree, and I did e Gen 3:12 398
serpent beguiled me, and I did e Gen 3:13 398
dust shalt thou e all the days of Gen 3:14 398
saying, Thou shalt not e of it Gen 3:17 398
in sorrow shalt thou e of it all Gen 3:17 398
thou shalt e the herb of the Gen 3:18 398
of thy face shalt thou e bread Gen 3:19 398
also of the tree of life, and e Gen 3:22 398
the blood thereof, shall ye not e Gen 9:4 398
under the tree, and they did e Gen 18:8 398
unleavened bread, and they did e Gen 19:3 398
was set meat before him to e Gen 24:33 398
but he said, I will not e Gen 24:33 398
And they did e and drink, he and the Gen 24:54 398
because he did e of his venison Gen 25:28 6310
and he did e and drink, and rose up, Gen 25:34 398
made them a feast, and they did e Gen 26:30 398
and bring it to me, that I may e Gen 27:4 398
me savoury meat, that I may e Gen 27:7 398
it to thy father, that he may e Gen 27:10 398
e of my venison, that thy soul Gen 27:19 398
I will e of my son's venison, Gen 27:25 398
it near to him, and he did e Gen 27:25 398
e of his son's venison, that thy Gen 27:31 398
I go, and will give me bread to e Gen 28:20 398
they did e there upon the heap Gen 31:46 398
and called his brethren to e bread Gen 31:54 398
and they did e bread, and tarried Gen 31:54 398
the children of Israel e not of Gen 32:32 398

And they sat down to e bread Gen 37:25 398
save the bread which he did e Gen 39:6 398
the birds did e them out of the Gen 40:17 398
the birds shall e thy flesh from Gen 40:19 398
leanfleshed kine did e up the Gen 41:4 398
the ill favoured kine did e up Gen 41:20 398
that they should e bread there Gen 43:25 398
Egyptians, which did e with him Gen 43:32 398
not e bread with the Hebrews Gen 43:32 398
ye shall e the fat of the land Gen 45:18 398
did e their portion which Pharaoh Gen 47:22 398
call him, that he may e bread Ex 2:20 398
they shall e the residue of that Ex 10:5 398
shall e every tree which groweth Ex 10:5 398
e every herb of the land, even Ex 10:12 398
they did e every herb of the land Ex 10:15 398
houses, wherein they shall e it Ex 12:7 398
they shall e the flesh in that Ex 12:8 398
with bitter herbs they shall e it Ex 12:8 398
E not of it raw, nor sodden at Ex 12:9 398
And thus shall ye e it Ex 12:11 398
and ye shall e it in haste Ex 12:11 398
days shall ye e unleavened bread Ex 12:15 398
save that which every man must e Ex 12:16 398
ye shall e unleavened bread, Ex 12:18 398
Ye shall e nothing leavened Ex 12:20 398
shall ye e unleavened bread Ex 12:20 398
There shall no stranger e thereof Ex 12:43 398
him, then shall he e thereof Ex 12:44 398
hired servant shall not e thereof Ex 12:45 398
person shall e thereof Ex 12:48 398
thou shalt e unleavened bread Ex 13:6 398
when we did e bread to the full Ex 16:3 398
you in the evening flesh to e Ex 16:8 398
saying, At even ye shall e flesh Ex 16:12 398
the LORD hath given you to e Ex 16:15 402
And Moses said, E that to day Ex 16:25 398
of Israel did e manna forty years Ex 16:35 398
they did e manna, until they came Ex 16:35 398
to e bread with Moses' father in Ex 18:12 398
neither shall ye e any flesh that Ex 22:31 398
that the poor of thy people may e Ex 23:11 398
the beasts of the field shall e Ex 23:11 398
(thou shalt e unleavened bread Ex 23:15 398
also they saw God, and did e Ex 24:11 398
his sons shall e the flesh of the Ex 29:32 398
they shall e those things Ex 29:33 398
a stranger shall not e thereof Ex 29:33 398
and the people sat down to e Ex 32:6 398
thee, and thou e of his sacrifice Ex 34:15 398
thou shalt e unleavened bread Ex 34:18 398
he did neither e bread, nor drink Ex 34:28 398
that ye e neither fat nor blood Lev 3:17 398
thereof shall Aaron and his sons e Lev 6:16 398
the congregation they shall e it Lev 6:16 398
children of Aaron shall e of it Lev 6:18 398
offereth it for sin shall e it Lev 6:26 398
among the priests shall e thereof Lev 6:29 398
among the priests shall e thereof Lev 7:6 398
all that be clean shall e thereof Lev 7:19 398
e of the flesh of the sacrifice Lev 7:21 398
Ye shall e no manner of fat, of Lev 7:23 398
but ye shall in no wise e of it Lev 7:24 398
Moreover ye shall e no manner of Lev 7:26 398
there e it with the bread that is Lev 8:31 398
Aaron and his sons shall e it Lev 8:31 398
e it without leaven beside the Lev 10:12 398
ye shall e it in the holy place, Lev 10:13 398
shall ye e in a clean place Lev 10:14 398
e among all the beasts that are Lev 11:2 398
among the beasts, that shall ye e Lev 11:3 398
not e of them that chew the cud Lev 11:4 398
Of their flesh shall ye not e Lev 11:8 398
These shall ye e of all that are Lev 11:9 398
and in the rivers, them shall ye e Lev 11:9 398
ye shall not e of their flesh, Lev 11:11 398
Yet these may ye e of every Lev 11:21 398
Even these of them ye may e Lev 11:22 398
if any beast, of which ye may e Lev 11:39 402
the earth, them ye shall not e Lev 11:42 398
No soul of you shall e blood Lev 17:12 398
that sojourneth among you e blood Lev 17:12 398
Ye shall e the blood of no manner Lev 17:14 398
shall ye e of the fruit thereof Lev 19:25 398
Ye shall not e any thing with the Lev 19:26 398
He shall e the bread of his God, Lev 21:22 398
he shall not e of the holy things Lev 22:4 398
shall not e of the holy things, Lev 22:6 398
shall afterward e of the holy Lev 22:7 398
he shall not e to defile himself Lev 22:8 398
no stranger e of the holy thing Lev 22:10 398
shall not e of the holy thing Lev 22:10 398
with his money, he shall e of it Lev 22:11 398
they shall e of his meat Lev 22:11 398
she may not e of an offering of Lev 22:12 398
she shall e of her father's meat Lev 22:13 398
there shall no stranger e thereof Lev 22:13 398
if a man e of the holy thing Lev 22:14 398
when they e their holy things Lev 22:16 398
days ye must e unleavened bread Lev 23:6 398
ye shall e neither bread, nor Lev 23:14 398
they shall e it in the holy place Lev 24:9 398
ye shall e the increase thereof Lev 25:12 398
ye shall e your fill, and dwell Lev 25:19 398
What shall we e the seventh year Lev 25:20 398
e yet of old fruit until the Lev 25:22 398
in ye shall e of the old store Lev 25:22 398
ye shall e your bread to the full Lev 26:5 398
ye shall e old store, and bring Lev 26:10 398
vain, for your enemies shall e it Lev 26:16 398
and ye shall e, and not be Lev 26:26 398
ye shall e the flesh of your sons Lev 26:29 398
of your daughters shall ye e Lev 26:29 398
of your enemies shall e you up Lev 26:38 398
nor e moist grapes, or dried Num 6:3 398
he e nothing that is made of the Num 6:4 398
e it with unleavened bread and Num 9:11 398
Who shall give us flesh to e Num 11:4 398
which we did e in Egypt freely Num 11:5 398
Give us flesh, that we may e Num 11:13 398
to morrow, and ye shall e flesh Num 11:18 398
Who shall give us flesh to e Num 11:18 398
give you flesh, and ye shall e Num 11:18 398
Ye shall not e one day, nor two Num 11:19 398
that they may e a whole month Num 11:21 398
when ye e of the bread of the Num 15:19 398
most holy place shalt thou e it Num 18:10 398
every male shall e it Num 18:10 398
clean in thy house shall e of it Num 18:11 398
in thine house shall e of it Num 18:13 398
ye shall e it in every place, ye Num 18:31 398
lie down until he e of the prey Num 23:24 398
he shall e up the nations his Num 24:8 398
and the people did e, and bowed Num 25:2 398
of them for money, that ye may e Deut 2:6 398
me meat for money, that I may e Deut 2:28 398
neither see, nor hear, nor e Deut 4:28 398
shalt e bread without scarceness Deut 8:9 398
I neither did e bread nor drink Deut 9:9 398
I did neither e bread, nor drink Deut 9:18 398
thy cattle, that thou mayest e Deut 11:15 398
there ye shall e before the LORD Deut 12:7 398
e flesh in all thy gates, Deut 12:15 398
and the clean may e thereof Deut 12:15 398
Only ye shall not e the blood Deut 12:16 398
Thou mayest not e within thy Deut 12:17 398
But thou must e them before the Deut 12:18 398
and thou shalt say, I will e flesh Deut 12:20 398
thy soul longeth to e flesh Deut 12:20 398
thou mayest e flesh, whatsoever Deut 12:20 398
thou shalt e in thy gates Deut 12:21 398
is eaten, so thou shalt e them Deut 12:22 398
the clean shall e of them alike Deut 12:22 398
be sure that thou e not the blood Deut 12:23 398
thou mayest not e the life with Deut 12:23 398
Thou shalt not e it Deut 12:24 398
Thou shalt not e it Deut 12:25 398
God, and thou shalt e the flesh Deut 12:27 398
Thou shalt not e any abominable Deut 14:3 398
are the beasts which ye shall e Deut 14:4 398
among the beasts, that ye shall e Deut 14:6 398
not e of them that chew the cud Deut 14:7 398
ye shall not e of their flesh, Deut 14:8 398
These ye shall e of all that are Deut 14:9 398
have fins and scales shall ye e Deut 14:9 398
not fins and scales ye may not e Deut 14:10 398
Of all clean birds ye shall e Deut 14:11 398
are they of which ye shall not e Deut 14:12 398
But of all clean fowls ye may e Deut 14:20 398
Ye shall not e of any thing that Deut 14:21 398
is in thy gates, that he may e it Deut 14:21 398
thou shalt e before the LORD thy Deut 14:23 398
thou shalt e there before the Deut 14:26 398
thy gates, shall come, and shall e Deut 14:29 398
Thou shalt e it before the LORD Deut 15:20 398
Thou shalt e it within thy gates Deut 15:22 398
the clean person shall e it alike Deut 15:22
shalt not e the blood thereof Deut 15:23 398
Thou shalt e no leavened bread Deut 16:3 398
seven days shalt thou e Deut 16:3 398
e it in the place which the LORD Deut 16:7 398
thou shalt e unleavened bread Deut 16:8 398
they shall e the offerings of the Deut 18:1 398
shall have like portions to e Deut 18:8 398
battle, and another man e of it Deut 20:6 2490
thou shalt e the spoil of thine Deut 20:14 398
for thou mayest e of them Deut 20:19 398
then thou mayest e grapes thy Deut 23:24 398
that they may e within thy gates, Deut 26:12 398
peace offerings, and shalt e there Deut 27:7 398
eyes, and thou shalt not e thereof Deut 28:31 398
which thou knowest not e up Deut 28:33 398
for the worms shall e them Deut 28:39 398
he shall e the fruit of thy Deut 28:51 398
thou shalt e the fruit of thine Deut 28:53 398
of his children whom he shall e Deut 28:55 398
for she shall e them for want of Deut 28:57 398
that he might e the increase of Deut 32:13 398
Which did e the fat of their Deut 32:38 398
they did e of the old corn of the Josh 5:11 398
but they did e of the fruit of Josh 5:12 398
which ye planted not do ye e Josh 24:13 398
the house of their god, and did e Judg 9:27 398
drink, and e not any unclean thing Judg 13:4 398
neither e any unclean thing Judg 13:7 398
She may not e of any thing that Judg 13:14 398
drink, nor e any unclean thing Judg 13:14 398
I will not e of thy bread Judg 13:16 398
and gave them, and they did e Judg 14:9 398
so they did e and drink, and lodged Judg 19:4 398
And they sat down, and did e Judg 19:6 398
and they did e both of them Judg 19:8 398
they washed their feet, and did e Judg 19:21 398
e of the bread, and dip thy morsel Ruth 2:14 398
her parched corn, and she did e Ruth 2:14 398
therefore she wept, and did not e 1Sa 1:7 398
the woman went her way, and did e 1Sa 1:18 398
that I may e a piece of bread 1Sa 2:36 398
he go up to the high place to e 1Sa 9:13 398
people will not e until he come 1Sa 9:13 398
afterwards they e that be bidden 1Sa 9:13 398
for ye shall e with me to day, and 1Sa 9:19 398
set it before thee, and e 1Sa 9:24 398
So Saul did e with Samuel that 1Sa 9:24 398
the people did e them with the 1Sa 14:32 398
in that they e with the blood 1Sa 14:33 398
sheep, and slay them here, and e 1Sa 14:34 398
the king sat him down to e meat 1Sa 20:24 398
did e no meat the second day of 1Sa 20:34 398
and e, that thou mayest have 1Sa 28:22 398
he refused, and said, I will not e 1Sa 28:23 398
and they did e 1Sa 28:25 398
and gave him bread, and he did e 1Sa 30:11 398
to e meat while it was yet day 2Sa 3:35 1262
thou shalt e bread at my table 2Sa 9:7 398
master's son may have food to e 2Sa 9:10 398
thy master's son shall e bread 2Sa 9:10 398
he shall e at my table, as one of 2Sa 9:11 398
for he did e continually at the 2Sa 9:13 398
I then go into mine house, to e 2Sa 11:11 398
David had called him, he did e 2Sa 11:13 398
it did e of his own meat, and 2Sa 12:3 398
neither did he e bread with them 2Sa 12:17 1262
set bread before him, and he did e 2Sa 12:20 398
dead, thou didst rise and e bread 2Sa 12:21 398
I may see it, and e it at her hand 2Sa 13:5 398
sight, that I may e at her hand 2Sa 13:6 1262
but he refused to e 2Sa 13:9 398
that I may e of thine hand 2Sa 13:10 1262
had brought them unto him to e 2Sa 13:11 398
fruit for the young men to e 2Sa 16:2 398
people that were with him, to e 2Sa 17:29 398
that did e at thine own table 2Sa 19:28 398
taste what I e or what I drink 2Sa 19:35 398
and, behold, they e and drink 1Kin 1:25 398
be of those that e at thy table 1Kin 2:7 398
neither will I e bread nor drink 1Kin 13:8 398
E no bread, nor drink water, nor 1Kin 13:9 398
Come home with me, and e bread 1Kin 13:15 398
neither will I e bread nor drink 1Kin 13:16 398
Thou shalt e no bread nor drink 1Kin 13:17 398
thine house, that he may e bread 1Kin 13:18 398
did e bread in his house, and 1Kin 13:19 398
E no bread, and drink no water 1Kin 13:22 398
in the city shall the dogs e 1Kin 14:11 398
shall the fowls of the air e 1Kin 14:11 398
in the city shall the dogs e 1Kin 16:4 398
shall the fowls of the air e 1Kin 16:4 398
me and my son, that we may e it 1Kin 17:12 398
he, and her house, did e many days 1Kin 17:15 398
which e at Jezebel's table 1Kin 18:19 398
said unto Ahab, Get thee up, e 1Kin 18:41 398
So Ahab went up to e and to drink 1Kin 18:42 398
him, and said unto him, Arise and e 1Kin 19:5 398
And he did e and drink, and laid him 1Kin 19:6 398
touched him, and said, Arise and e 1Kin 19:7 398
And he arose, and did e and drink, 1Kin 19:8 398
unto the people, and they did e 1Kin 19:21 398
his face, and would e no bread 1Kin 21:4 398
e bread, and let thine heart be 1Kin 21:7 398
The dogs shall e Jezebel by the 1Kin 21:23 398
Ahab in the city the dogs shall e 1Kin 21:24 398
shall the fowls of the air e 1Kin 21:24 398
and she constrained him to e bread 2Kin 4:8 398
he turned in thither to e bread 2Kin 4:8 398
they poured out for the men to e 2Kin 4:40 398
And they could not e thereof 2Kin 4:40 398
for the people, that they may e 2Kin 4:41 398
unto the people, that they may e 2Kin 4:42 398
Give the people, that they may e 2Kin 4:43 398
thus saith the LORD, They shall e 2Kin 4:43 398
set it before them, and they did e 2Kin 4:44 398
before them, that they may e 2Kin 6:22 398
thy son, that we may e him to day 2Kin 6:28 398
we will e my son to morrow 2Kin 6:28 398
So we boiled my son, and did e him 2Kin 6:29 398
Give thy son, that we may e him 2Kin 6:29 398
eyes, but shalt not e thereof 2Kin 7:2 398
they went into one tent, and did e 2Kin 7:8 398
eyes, but shalt not e thereof 2Kin 7:19 398
the dogs shall e Jezebel in the 2Kin 9:10 398
And when he was come in, he did e 2Kin 9:34 398
shall dogs e the flesh of Jezebel 2Kin 9:36 398
that they may e their own dung, 2Kin 18:27 398
then e ye every man of his own 2Kin 18:31 398
Ye shall e this year such things 2Kin 19:29 398
and e the fruits thereof 2Kin 19:29 398
but they did e of the unleavened 2Kin 23:9 398
he did e bread continually before 2Kin 25:29 398
And did e and drink before the LORD 1Chr 29:22 398
and shod them, and gave them to e 2Chr 28:15 398
yet did they e the passover 2Chr 30:18 398
they did e throughout the feast 2Chr 30:22 398
the LORD, we have had enough to e 2Chr 31:10 398
that they should not e of the Ezr 2:63 398
the LORD God of Israel, did e Ezr 6:21 398
e the good of the land, and leave Ezr 9:12 398
he did e no bread, nor drink Ezr 10:6 398
up corn for them, that we may e Neh 5:2 398
that they should not e of the Neh 7:65 398
e the fat, and drink the sweet, and Neh 8:10 398
the people went their way to e Neh 8:12 398
so they did e, and were filled, and Neh 9:25 398
fathers to e the fruit thereof Neh 9:36 398
neither e nor drink three days, Est 4:16 398
for their three sisters to e Job 1:4 398
For my sighing cometh before I e Job 3:24 3899
Then let me sow, and let another e Job 31:8 398
did e bread with him in his house Job 42:11 398
e up my people as they e bread Ps 14:4 398
The meek shall e and be satisfied Ps 22:26 398
that be fat upon earth shall e Ps 22:29 398
came upon me to e up my flesh Ps 27:2 398
which did e of my bread, hath Ps 41:9 398
Will I e the flesh of bulls, or Ps 50:13 398
e up my people as they e bread Ps 53:4 398
rained down manna upon them to e Ps 78:24 398
Man did e angels' food Ps 78:25 398
So they did e, and were well Ps 78:29 398
so that I forget to e my bread Ps 102:4 398
did e up all the herbs in their Ps 105:35 398
to e the bread of sorrows Ps 127:2 398

For thou shalt e the labour of	Ps 128:2	398
let me not e of their dainties	Ps 141:4	3898
Therefore shall they e of the	Prov 1:31	398
For they e the bread of	Prov 4:17	3898
e of my bread, and drink of the	Prov 9:5	3898
A man shall e good by the fruit	Prov 13:2	398
transgressors shall e violence	Prov 13:2	
love it shall e the fruit thereof	Prov 18:21	398
thou sittest to e with a ruler	Prov 23:1	3898
E thou not the bread of him that	Prov 23:6	3898
E and drink, saith he to thee	Prov 23:7	398
e thou honey, because it is good	Prov 24:13	398
e so much as is sufficient for	Prov 25:16	398
be hungry, give him bread to e	Prov 25:21	398
It is not good to e much honey	Prov 25:27	398
tree shall e the fruit thereof	Prov 27:18	398
and the young eagles shall e it	Prov 30:17	398
for a man, than that he should e	Eccl 2:24	398
For who can e, or who else can	Eccl 2:25	398
And also that every man should e	Eccl 3:13	398
they are increased that e them	Eccl 5:11	398
whether he e little or much	Eccl 5:12	398
it is good and comely for one to e	Eccl 5:18	398
hath given him power to e thereof	Eccl 5:19	398
giveth him not power to e thereof	Eccl 6:2	398
thing under the sun, than to e	Eccl 8:15	398
e thy bread with joy, and drink	Eccl 9:7	398
thy princes e in the morning	Eccl 10:16	398
thy princes e in due season, for	Eccl 10:17	398
garden, and e his pleasant fruits	Song 4:16	398
e, O friends	Song 5:1	398
ye shall e the good of the land	Is 1:19	398
for they shall e the fruit of	Is 3:10	398
We will e our own bread, and wear	Is 4:1	398
of the fat ones shall strangers e	Is 5:17	398
Butter and honey shall he e	Is 7:15	398
shall give, he shall e butter	Is 7:22	398
honey shall every one e that is	Is 7:22	398
he shall e on the left hand, and	Is 9:20	398
they shall e every man the flesh	Is 9:20	398
the lion shall e straw like the	Is 11:7	398
table, watch in the watchtower, e	Is 21:5	398
let us e and drink	Is 22:13	398
to e sufficiently, and for durable	Is 23:18	398
ground shall e clean provender	Is 30:24	398
that they may e their own dung	Is 36:12	398
e ye every one of his vine, and	Is 36:16	398
Ye shall e this year such as	Is 37:30	398
vineyards, and e the fruit thereof	Is 37:30	398
the moth shall e them up	Is 50:9	398
For the moth shall e them up like	Is 51:8	398
the worm shall e them like wool	Is 51:8	398
come ye, buy, and e	Is 55:1	398
e ye that which is good, and let	Is 55:2	398
ye shall e the riches of the	Is 61:6	398
that have gathered it shall e it	Is 62:9	398
which e swine's flesh, and broth	Is 65:4	398
GOD, Behold, my servants shall e	Is 65:13	398
vineyards, and e the fruit of them	Is 65:21	398
shall not plant, and another e	Is 65:22	398
the lion shall e straw like the	Is 65:25	398
to e the fruit thereof and the	Jer 2:7	398
they shall e up thine harvest, and	Jer 5:17	398
sons and thy daughters should e	Jer 5:17	398
they shall e up thy flocks and	Jer 5:17	398
they shall e up thy vines and thy	Jer 5:17	398
unto your sacrifices, and e flesh	Jer 7:21	398
words were found, and I did e them	Jer 15:16	398
feasting, to sit with them to e	Jer 16:8	398
I will cause them to e the flesh	Jer 19:9	398
they shall e every one the flesh	Jer 19:9	398
did not thy father e and drink, and	Jer 22:15	398
The wind shall e up all thy	Jer 22:22	7462
gardens, and e the fruit of them	Jer 29:5	398
gardens, and e the fruit of them	Jer 29:28	398
shall e them as common things	Jer 31:5	
there they did e bread together	Jer 41:1	398
he did continually e bread before	Jer 52:33	398
Shall the women e their fruit	Lam 2:20	398
thy mouth, and e that I give thee	Eze 2:8	398
Son of man, e that thou findest	Eze 3:1	398
e this roll, and go speak unto the	Eze 3:1	398
and he caused me to e that roll	Eze 3:2	398
Son of man, cause thy belly to e	Eze 3:3	398
Then did I e it	Eze 3:3	398
ninety days shalt thou e thereof	Eze 4:9	398
thou shalt e be by weight	Eze 4:10	398
from time to time shalt thou e it	Eze 4:10	398
thou shalt e it as barley cakes	Eze 4:12	398
shall the children of Israel e	Eze 4:13	398
they shall e bread by weight, and	Eze 4:16	398
Therefore the fathers shall e the	Eze 5:10	398
and the sons shall e their fathers	Eze 5:10	398
e thy bread with quaking, and	Eze 12:18	398
They shall e their bread with	Eze 12:19	398
thou didst e fine flour, and honey	Eze 16:13	398
in thee they e upon the mountains	Eze 22:9	398
lips, and e not the bread of men	Eze 24:17	398
your lips, nor e the bread of men	Eze 24:22	398
they shall e thy fruit, and they	Eze 25:4	398
Ye e with the blood, and lift up	Eze 33:25	398
Ye e the fat, and ye clothe you	Eze 34:3	398
they e that which ye have trodden	Eze 34:19	7462
of Israel, that ye may e flesh	Eze 39:17	398
Ye shall e the flesh of the	Eze 39:18	398
ye shall e fat till ye be full	Eze 39:19	398
LORD shall e the most holy things	Eze 42:13	398
in it to e bread before the LORD	Eze 44:3	398
They shall e the meat offering	Eze 44:29	398
The priests shall not e of any	Eze 44:31	398
and let them give us pulse to e	Dan 1:12	398
of the children that e of the	Dan 1:13	398
e the portion of the king's meat	Dan 1:15	398
make thee to e grass as oxen	Dan 4:25	2939
make thee to e grass as oxen	Dan 4:32	2939
did e grass as oxen, and his body	Dan 4:33	399
beasts of the field shall e them	Hos 2:12	398
They e up the sin of my people	Hos 4:8	398
For they shall e, and not have	Hos 4:10	398
of mine offerings, and e it	Hos 8:13	398
they shall e unclean things in	Hos 9:3	398
all that e thereof shall be	Hos 9:4	398
ye shall e in plenty, and be	Joel 2:26	398
e the lambs out of the flock, and	Amos 6:4	398
great deep, and did e up a part	Amos 7:4	398
land of Judah, and there e bread	Amos 7:12	398
gardens, and e the fruit of them	Amos 9:14	398
they that e thy bread have laid a	Obad 7	
Who also e the flesh of my people	Mic 3:3	398
Thou shalt e, but not be	Mic 6:14	398
there is no cluster to e	Mic 7:1	398
it shall e thee up like the	Nah 3:15	398
as the eagle that hasteth to e	Hab 1:8	398
ye e, but ye have not enough	Hag 1:6	398
And when ye did e, and when ye did	Zec 7:6	398
did not ye e for yourselves, and	Zec 7:6	398
let the rest e every one the	Zec 11:9	398
but he shall e the flesh of the	Zec 11:16	398
for your life, what ye shall e	Mt 6:25	*5315*
thought, saying, What shall we e	Mt 6:31	*5315*
pluck the ears of corn, and to e	Mt 12:1	*2068*
did e the shewbread, which was	Mt 12:4	*5315*
which was not lawful for him to e	Mt 12:4	*5315*
give ye them to e	Mt 14:16	*5315*
And they did all e, and were filled	Mt 14:20	*5315*
not their hands when they e bread	Mt 15:2	*2068*
but to e with unwashen hands	Mt 15:20	*5315*
yet the dogs e of the crumbs	Mt 15:27	*2068*
three days, and have nothing to e	Mt 15:32	*5315*
And they did all e, and were filled	Mt 15:37	*5315*
they that did e were four	Mt 15:38	*2068*
smite his fellowservants, and to e	Mt 24:49	*2068*
for thee to e the passover	Mt 26:17	*5315*
And as they did e, he said, Verily	Mt 26:21	*2068*
the disciples, and said, Take, e	Mt 26:26	*5315*
he did e locusts and wild honey	Mk 1:6	*2068*
saw him e with publicans and	Mk 2:16	*2068*
did e the shewbread, which is not	Mk 2:26	*5315*
lawful to e but for the priests	Mk 2:26	*5315*
they could not so much as e bread	Mk 3:20	*5315*
should be given her to e	Mk 5:43	*5315*
had no leisure so much as to e	Mk 6:31	*5315*
for they have nothing to e	Mk 6:36	*5315*
said unto them, Give ye them to e	Mk 6:37	*5315*
of bread, and give them to e	Mk 6:37	*5315*
And they did all e, and were filled	Mk 6:42	*5315*
they that did e of the loaves	Mk 6:44	*5315*
disciples e bread with defiled	Mk 7:2	*2068*
e not, holding the tradition of	Mk 7:3	*2068*
except they wash, they e not	Mk 7:4	*2068*
but e bread with unwashen hands	Mk 7:5	*2068*
table e of the children's crumbs	Mk 7:28	*2068*
great, and having nothing to e	Mk 8:1	*5315*
three days, and have nothing to e	Mk 8:2	*5315*
So they did e, and were filled	Mk 8:8	*5315*
No man e fruit of thee hereafter	Mk 11:14	*5315*
that thou mayest e the passover	Mk 14:12	*5315*
where I shall e the passover with	Mk 14:14	*5315*
And as they sat and did e, Jesus	Mk 14:18	*2068*
And as they did e, Jesus took	Mk 14:22	*2068*
and gave to them, and said, Take, e	Mk 14:22	*5315*
And in those days he did e nothing	Lk 4:2	*5315*
disciples, saying, Why do ye e	Lk 5:30	*2068*
but thine e and drink	Lk 5:33	*2068*
the ears of corn, and did e	Lk 6:1	*2068*
e the shewbread, and gave also to	Lk 6:4	*5315*
to e but for the priests alone	Lk 6:4	*5315*
him that he would e with him	Lk 7:36	*5315*
said unto them, Give ye them to e	Lk 9:13	*5315*
And they did e, and were all filled	Lk 9:17	*5315*
e such things as are set before	Lk 10:8	*2068*
take thine ease, e, drink, and be	Lk 12:19	*5315*
for your life, what ye shall e	Lk 12:22	*5315*
And seek not ye what ye shall e	Lk 12:29	*5315*
menservants and maidens, and to e	Lk 12:45	*2068*
to e bread on the sabbath day	Lk 14:1	*5315*
Blessed is he that shall e bread	Lk 14:15	*5315*
the husks that the swine did e	Lk 15:16	*2068*
and let us e, and be merry	Lk 15:23	*5315*
and afterward thou shalt e	Lk 17:8	*5315*
They did e, they drank, they	Lk 17:27	*2068*
they did e, they drank, they	Lk 17:28	*2068*
us the passover, that we may e	Lk 22:8	*5315*
where I shall e the passover with	Lk 22:11	*5315*
With desire I have desired to e	Lk 22:15	*5315*
I will not any more e thereof	Lk 22:16	*5315*
That ye may e and drink at my	Lk 22:30	*2068*
he took it, and did e before them	Lk 24:43	*5315*
prayed him, saying, Master, e	Jn 4:31	*5315*
I have meat to e that ye know not	Jn 4:32	*5315*
any man brought him ought to e	Jn 4:33	*5315*
we buy bread, that these may e	Jn 6:5	*5315*
the place where they did e bread	Jn 6:23	*5315*
because ye did e of the loaves	Jn 6:26	*5315*
Our fathers did e manna in the	Jn 6:31	*5315*
gave them bread from heaven to e	Jn 6:31	*5315*
Your fathers did e manna in the	Jn 6:49	*5315*
heaven, that a man may e thereof	Jn 6:50	*5315*
if any man e of this bread, he	Jn 6:51	*5315*
this man give us his flesh to e	Jn 6:52	*5315*
Except ye e the flesh of the Son	Jn 6:53	*5315*
not as your fathers did e manna	Jn 6:58	*5315*
that they might e the passover	Jn 18:28	*5315*
did e their meat with gladness and	Acts 2:46	*3335*
sight, and neither did e nor drink	Acts 9:9	*5315*
Rise, Peter; kill, and e	Acts 10:13	*5315*
of God, even to us, who did e	Acts 10:41	*4906*
and didst e with them	Acts 11:3	*4906*
Arise, Peter; slay and e	Acts 11:7	*5315*
e nor drink till they had killed	Acts 23:12	*5315*
that we will e nothing until we	Acts 23:14	*1089*
that they will neither e nor	Acts 23:21	*5315*
he had broken it, he began to e	Acts 27:35	*2068*
that he may e all things	Rom 14:2	*5315*
It is good neither to e flesh	Rom 14:21	*5315*
that doubteth is damned if he e	Rom 14:23	*5315*
with such an one, no not to e	1Cor 5:11	*4906*
of the idol unto this hour e it	1Cor 8:7	*2068*
for neither, if we e, are we the	1Cor 8:8	*5315*
neither, if we e not, are we the	1Cor 8:8	*5315*
e those things which are offered	1Cor 8:10	*2068*
I will e no flesh while the world	1Cor 8:13	*5315*
Have we not power to e and to	1Cor 9:4	*5315*
did all e the same spiritual meat	1Cor 10:3	*5315*
written, The people sat down to e	1Cor 10:7	*5315*
are not they which e of the	1Cor 10:18	*2068*
is sold in the shambles, that e	1Cor 10:25	*2068*
whatsoever is set before you, e	1Cor 10:27	*2068*
e not for his sake that shewed it	1Cor 10:28	*2068*
Whether therefore ye e, or drink	1Cor 10:31	*2068*
this is not to e the Lord's	1Cor 11:20	*5315*
have ye not houses to e and to	1Cor 11:22	*2068*
he brake it, and said, Take, e	1Cor 11:24	*5315*
For as often as ye e this bread	1Cor 11:26	*2068*
whosoever shall e this bread	1Cor 11:27	*2068*
so let him e of that bread, and	1Cor 11:28	*2068*
when ye come together to e	1Cor 11:33	*5315*
any man hunger, let him e at home	1Cor 11:34	*2068*
let us e and drink	1Cor 15:32	*5315*
he did e with the Gentiles	Gal 2:12	*4906*
Neither did we e any man's bread	2Th 3:8	*5315*
not work, neither should he e	2Th 3:10	*2068*
they work, and e their own bread	2Th 3:12	*2068*
their word will e as doth a	2Ti 2:17	
to e which serve the tabernacle	Heb 13:10	*5315*
shall e your flesh as it were	Jas 5:3	*5315*
I give to e of the tree of life	Rev 2:7	*5315*
to e things sacrificed unto idols	Rev 2:14	*5315*
I give to e of the hidden manna	Rev 2:17	*5315*
to e things sacrificed unto idols	Rev 2:20	*5315*
said unto me, Take it, and e it up	Rev 10:9	*2719*
shall e her flesh, and burn her	Rev 17:16	*5315*
That ye may e the flesh of kings	Rev 19:18	*5315*

EATEN

Hast thou e of the tree, whereof	Gen 3:11	398
hast e of the tree, of which I	Gen 3:17	398
unto thee of all food that is e	Gen 6:21	398
that which the young men have e	Gen 14:24	398
I have e of all before thou	Gen 27:33	398
rams of thy flock have I not e	Gen 31:38	398
And when they had e them up	Gen 41:21	
not be known that they had e them	Gen 41:21	
when they had e up the corn which	Gen 43:2	398
In one house shall it be e	Ex 12:46	398
shall no leavened bread be e	Ex 13:3	398
bread shall be e seven days	Ex 13:7	398
and his flesh shall not be e	Ex 21:28	398
cause a field or vineyard to be e	Ex 22:5	1197
it shall not be e, because it is	Ex 29:34	398
shall it be e in the holy place	Lev 6:16	398
it shall not be e	Lev 6:23	398
in the holy place shall it be e	Lev 6:26	398
in the holy place, shall be e	Lev 6:30	398
it shall be e in the holy place	Lev 7:6	398
for thanksgiving shall be e the	Lev 7:15	398
it shall be e the same day that	Lev 7:16	398
the remainder of it shall be e	Lev 7:16	398
be e at all on the third day	Lev 7:18	398
any unclean thing shall not be e	Lev 7:19	398
Wherefore have ye not e the sin	Lev 10:17	398
have e it in the holy place	Lev 10:18	398
if I had e the sin offering to	Lev 10:19	398
they shall not be e, they are an	Lev 11:13	398
Of all meat which may be e	Lev 11:34	398
it shall not be e	Lev 11:41	398
between the beast that may be e	Lev 11:47	398
and the beast that may not be e	Lev 11:47	398
any beast or fowl that may be e	Lev 17:13	398
It shall be e the same day ye	Lev 19:6	398
if it be e at all on the third	Lev 19:7	398
it shall not be e of	Lev 19:23	398
On the same day it shall be e up	Lev 22:30	398
days shall unleavened bread be e	Num 28:17	398
when thou shalt have e and be full	Deut 6:11	398
When thou hast e and art full	Deut 8:10	398
Lest when thou hast e and art full	Deut 8:12	398
as the roebuck and the hart is e	Deut 12:22	398
they shall not be e	Deut 14:19	398
vineyard, and hath not yet e of it	Deut 20:6	2490
I have not e thereof in my	Deut 26:14	398
Ye have not e bread, neither have	Deut 29:6	398
and they shall have e and filled	Deut 31:20	398
had e of the old corn of the land	Josh 5:12	398
And when Boaz had e and drunk, and	Ruth 3:7	398
up after they had e in Shiloh	1Sa 1:9	398
if haply the people had e freely	1Sa 14:30	398
for he had e no bread all the day	1Sa 28:20	398
and when he had e, his spirit came	1Sa 30:12	398
for he had e no bread, nor drunk	1Sa 30:12	398
have we e at all of the king's	2Sa 19:42	398
hast e bread and drunk water in	1Kin 13:22	398
to pass, after he had e bread	1Kin 13:23	398
the lion had not e the carcase	1Kin 13:28	398
and when they had e and drunk, he	2Kin 6:23	398
my brethren have not e the bread	Neh 5:14	398
is unsavoury be e without salt	Job 6:6	398
as a garment that is moth e	Job 13:28	398
Or have e my morsel myself alone	Job 31:17	398
the fatherless hath not e thereof	Job 31:17	398
If I have e the fruits thereof	Job 31:39	398
zeal of thine house hath e me up	Ps 69:9	398

For I have e ashes like bread, and Ps 102:9 398
bread e in secret is pleasant Prov 9:17
thou hast e shalt thou vomit up Prov 23:8 398
I have e my honeycomb with my Song 5:1 398
for ye have e up the vineyard Is 3:14 398
thereof, and it shall be e up Is 5:5 398
and it shall return, and shall be e Is 6:13 1197
I have roasted flesh, and e it Is 44:19 398
for they have e up Jacob, and Jer 10:25 398
figs, which could not be e Jer 24:2 398
evil, very evil, that cannot be e Jer 24:3 398
the evil figs, which cannot be e Jer 24:8 398
like vile figs, that cannot be e Jer 29:17 398
The fathers have e a sour grape Jer 31:29 398
up even till now have I not e of Eze 4:14 398
The fathers have e sour grapes Eze 18:2 398
hath not e upon the mountains, Eze 18:6 398
duties, but even hath e upon the Eze 18:11 398
That hath not e upon the Eze 18:15 398
you to have e up the good pasture Eze 34:18 7462
unleavened bread shall be e Eze 45:21 398
ye have e the fruit of lies Hos 10:13 398
hath left hath the locust e Joel 1:4 398
hath left hath the cankerworm e Joel 1:4 398
hath left hath the caterpiller e Joel 1:4 398
the years that the locust hath e Joel 2:25 398
they that had e were about five Mt 14:21 *2068*
they that had e were about four Mk 8:9 *5315*
shall ye begin to say, We have e Lk 13:26 *5315*
and serve me, till I have e Lk 17:8 *5315*
zeal of thine house hath e me up Jn 2:17 *2719*
and above unto them that had e Jn 6:13 *977*
very hungry, and would have e Acts 10:10 *1089*
for I have never e any thing that Acts 10:14 *5315*
he was e of worms, and gave up the Acts 12:23 *4662*
again, and had broken bread, and e Acts 20:11 *1089*
And when they had e enough Acts 27:38 *2880*
and as soon as I had e it, my Rev 10:10 *5315*

EATER

Out of the e came forth meat, and Judg 14:14 398
to the sower, and bread to the e Is 55:10 398
even fall into the mouth of the e Nah 3:12 398

EATERS

among riotous e of flesh Prov 23:20 2151

EATEST

for in the day that thou e Gen 2:17 398
and why e thou not 1Sa 1:8 398
so sad, that thou e no bread 1Kin 21:5 398

EATETH

for whosoever e leavened bread Ex 12:15 398
for whosoever e that which is Ex 12:19 398
the soul that e of it shall bear Lev 7:18 398
But the soul that e of the flesh Lev 7:20 398
For whosoever e the fat of the Lev 7:25 398
even the soul that e it shall be Lev 7:25 398
it be that e any manner of blood Lev 7:27 398
he that e of the carcase of it Lev 11:40 398
he that e in the house shall wash Lev 14:47 398
that e any manner of blood Lev 17:10 398
against that soul that e blood Lev 17:10 398
whosoever e it shall be cut off Lev 17:14 398
every soul that e that which died Lev 17:15 398
Therefore every one that e it Lev 19:8 398
it, is a land that e up the Num 13:32 398
man that e any food until evening 1Sa 14:24 398
the man that e any food this day 1Sa 14:28 398
Whose harvest the hungry e up Job 5:5 398
soul, and never e with pleasure Job 21:25 398
he e grass as an ox Job 40:15 398
similitude of an ox that e grass Ps 106:20 398
The righteous e to the satisfying Prov 13:25 398
she e, and wipeth her mouth, and Prov 30:20 398
e not the bread of idleness Prov 31:27 398
together, and e his own flesh Eccl 4:5 398
his days also he e in darkness Eccl 5:17 398
eat thereof, but a stranger e it Eccl 6:2 398
it is yet in his hand he e it up Is 28:4 1104
man dreameth, and, behold, he e Is 29:8 398
with part thereof he e flesh Is 44:16 398
he that e of their eggs dieth, and Is 59:5 398
every man that e the sour grape Jer 31:30 398
Why e your Master with publicans Mt 9:11 *2068*
disciples, How is it that he e Mk 2:16 *2068*
One of you which e with me shall Mk 14:18 *2068*
receiveth sinners, and e with them Lk 15:2 *4906*
Whoso e my flesh, and drinketh my Jn 6:54 *5176*
He that e my flesh, and drinketh Jn 6:56 *5176*
so he that e me, even he shall Jn 6:57 *5176*
he that e of this bread shall Jn 6:58 *5176*
He that e bread with me hath Jn 13:18 *5176*
another, who is weak, e herbs Rom 14:2 *2068*
e despise him that e not Rom 14:3 *2068*
which e not judge him that e Rom 14:3 *2068*
He that e, e to the Lord, Rom 14:6 *2068*
e not, to the Lord he e not Rom 14:6 *2068*
for that man who e with offence Rom 14:20 *2068*
because he e not of faith Rom 14:23 *2068*
e not of the fruit thereof 1Cor 9:7 *2068*
e not of the milk of the flock 1Cor 9:7 *2068*
e and drinketh unworthily, e 1Cor 11:29 *2068*

EATING

every man according to his e Ex 12:4 400
it every man according to his e Ex 16:16 400
every man according to his e Ex 16:18 400
every man according to his e Ex 16:21 400
in his hands, and went on e Judg 14:9 398
man, until he shall have done e Ruth 3:3 398
the LORD in e with the blood 1Sa 14:34 398
abroad upon all the earth, e 1Sa 30:16 398
it as they had made an end of e 1Kin 1:41 398
is by the sea in multitude, e 1Kin 4:20 398
as they were e of the pottage, 2Kin 4:40 398
were with David three days, e 1Chr 12:39 398
his sons and his daughters were e Job 1:13 398
Thy sons and thy daughters were e Job 1:18 398
rain it upon him while he is e Job 20:23 3894
e flesh, and drinking wine Is 22:13 398
midst, e swine's flesh, and the Is 66:17 398
an end of e the grass of the land Amos 7:2 398
John came neither e nor drinking Mt 11:18 *2068*
The Son of man came e and drinking Mt 11:19 *2068*
were before the flood they were e Mt 24:38 *5176*
And as they were e, Jesus took Mt 26:26 *2068*
neither e bread nor drinking wine Lk 7:33 *2068*
The Son of man is come e and Lk 7:34 *2068*
And in the same house remain, e Lk 10:7 *2068*
the e of those things that are 1Cor 8:4 *1035*
For in e every one taketh before 1Cor 11:21 *5315*

EBAL (*e'-bal*) *Son of Shobal.*

Alvan, and Manahath, and E, Shepho, Gen 36:23 5858
and the curse upon mount E Deut 11:29 5858
command you this day, in mount E Deut 27:4 5858
shall stand upon mount E to curse Deut 27:13 5858
the LORD God of Israel in mount E Josh 8:30 5858
half of them over against mount E Josh 8:33 5858
And E, and Abimael, and Sheba, 1Chr 1:22 5858
Alian, and Manahath, and E, Shephi, 1Chr 1:40 5858

EBED (*e'-bed*) See EBED-MELECH.

1. Father of Gaal.

Gaal the son of E came with his Judg 9:26 5651
And Gaal the son of E said Judg 9:28 5651
the words of Gaal the son of E Judg 9:30 5651
saying, Behold, Gaal the son of E Judg 9:31 5651
And Gaal the son of E went out Judg 9:35 5651

2. A family of exiles.

E the son of Jonathan, and with Ezr 8:6 5651

EBED-MELECH (*e''-bed-me'-lek*) *An Ethiopian eunuch.*

Now when E the Ethiopian, one of Jer 38:7 5663
E went forth out of the king's Jer 38:8 5663
king commanded E the Ethiopian Jer 38:10 5663
So E took the men with him, and Jer 38:11 5663
E the Ethiopian said unto Jer 38:12 5663
speak to E the Ethiopian, saying, Jer 39:16 5663

EBEN-EZER *A Philistine city.*

to battle, and pitched beside E 1Sa 4:1 72
and brought it from E unto Ashdod 1Sa 5:1 72
Shen, and called the name of it E 1Sa 7:12 72

EBER (*e'-bur*) See HEBER.

1. A great-grandson of Shem.

father of all the children of E Gen 10:21 5677
and Salah begat E Gen 10:24 5677
unto E were born two sons Gen 10:25 5677
lived thirty years, and begat E Gen 11:14 5677
after he begat E four hundred Gen 11:15 5677
E lived four and thirty years, and Gen 11:16 5677
E lived after he begat Peleg four Gen 11:17 5677
begat Shelah, and Shelah begat E 1Chr 1:18 5677
unto E were born two sons 1Chr 1:19 5677
E, Peleg, Reu, 1Chr 1:25 5677

2. Descendants of Eber 1.

Asshur, and shall afflict E Num 24:24 5677

3. Son of Elpaal.

E, and Misham, and Shamed, who 1Chr 8:12 5677

4. A priest of the Amok family.

Kallai; of Amok, E Neh 12:20 5677

EBEZ See ABEZ.

EBIASAPH (*e-bi'-a-saf*) See ABIASAPH. *A great-grandson of Korah.*

E his son, and Assir his son, 1Chr 6:23 43
the son of Assir, the son of E 1Chr 6:37 43
the son of Kore, the son of E 1Chr 9:19 43

EBONY

for a present horns of ivory and e Eze 27:15 1894

EBRONAH (*eb-ro'-nah*) *An encampment during the Exodus.*

from Jotbathah, and encamped at E Num 33:34 5684
And they departed from E, and Num 33:35 5684

ECBATANA See ACHMETHA.

ED (*ed*) *Name of an altar.*

of Gad called the altar E Josh 22:34

EDAR (*e'-dar*) See EDER. *A name of a watchtower.*

his tent beyond the tower of E Gen 35:21 5740

EDEN (*e'-dun*)

1. Original land of Adam and Eve.

planted a garden eastward in E Gen 2:8 5731
went out of E to water the garden Gen 2:10 5731
into the garden of E to dress it Gen 2:15 5731
him forth from the garden of E Gen 3:23 5731
east of the garden of E Cherubim Gen 3:24 5731
the land of Nod, on the east of E Gen 4:16 5731
will make her wilderness like E Is 51:3 5731
hast been in E the garden of God Eze 28:13 5731
so that all the trees of E Eze 31:9 5731
and all the trees of E, the choice Eze 31:16 5731
in greatness among the trees of E Eze 31:18 5731
of E unto the nether parts of the Eze 31:18 5731
is become like the garden of E Eze 36:35 5731
is as the garden of E before them Joel 2:3 5731

2. An undetermined place.

the children of E which were in 2Kin 19:12 5731
the children of E which were in Is 37:12 5731
Haran, and Canneh, and E, the Eze 27:23 5731
the sceptre from the house of E Amos 1:5 5731

3. Son of Joah.

of Zimmah, and E the son of Joah 2Chr 29:12 5731

4. A Levite during Hezekiah's time.

And next him were E, and Miniamin, 2Chr 31:15 5731

EDER (*e'-dur*) See EDAR. *A city in southern Judah.*

Edom southward were Kabzeel, and E. Josh 15:21 5740

2. A grandson of Merari.

Mahli, and E, and Jeremoth, three 1Chr 23:23 5740
Mahli, and E, and Jerimoth 1Chr 24:30 5740

EDGE

his son with the e of the sword Gen 34:26 6310
in the e of the wilderness Ex 13:20 7097
people with the e of the sword Ex 17:13 6310
the e of the one curtain from the Ex 26:4 8193
uttermost e of another curtain Ex 26:4 8193
loops shalt thou make in the e of Ex 26:5 7097
the e of the one curtain that is Ex 26:10 8193
fifty loops in the e of the Ex 26:10 8193
on the e of one curtain from the Ex 36:11 8193
fifty loops made he in the e of Ex 36:12 7097
e of the curtain in the coupling Ex 36:17 7097
fifty loops made he upon the e of Ex 36:17 7097
smote him with the e of the sword Num 21:24 6310
Etham, which is in the e of the Num 33:6 7097
in the e of the land of Edom Num 33:37 7097
that city with the e of the sword Deut 13:15 6310
thereof, with the e of the sword Deut 13:15 6310
thereof with the e of the sword Deut 20:13 6310
and ass, with the e of the sword Josh 6:21 6310
all fallen on the e of the sword Josh 8:24 6310
smote it with the e of the sword Josh 8:24 6310
smote it with the e of the sword Josh 10:28 6310
smote it with the e of the sword Josh 10:30 6310
smote it with the e of the sword Josh 10:32 6310
smote it with the e of the sword Josh 10:35 6310
smote it with the e of the sword Josh 10:37 6310
them with the e of the sword Josh 10:39 6310
therein with the e of the sword Josh 11:11 6310
them with the e of the sword Josh 11:12 6310
smote with the e of the sword Josh 11:14 6310
even unto the e of the sea of Josh 13:27 7097
smote it with the e of the sword Josh 19:47 6310
it with the e of the sword Judg 1:8 6310
the city with the e of the sword Judg 1:25 6310
with the e of the sword before Judg 4:15 6310
fell upon the e of the sword Judg 4:16 6310
them with the e of the sword Judg 18:27 6310
the city with the e of the sword Judg 20:37 6310
them with the e of the sword Judg 20:48 6310
with the e of the sword, with the Judg 21:10 6310
people with the e of the sword 1Sa 15:8 6310
smote he with the e of the sword 1Sa 22:19 6310
and sheep, with the e of the sword 1Sa 22:19 6310
the city with the e of the sword 2Sa 15:14 6310
them with the e of the sword 2Kin 10:25 6310
servants with the e of the sword Job 1:15 6310
servants with the e of the sword Job 1:17 6310
also turned the e of his sword Ps 89:43 6697
be blunt, and he do not whet the e Eccl 10:10 6440
them with the e of the sword Jer 21:7 6310
the children's teeth are set on e Jer 31:29 6949
his teeth shall be set on e Jer 31:30 6949
the children's teeth are set on e Eze 18:2 6949
the border thereof by the e Eze 43:13
shall fall by the e of the sword Lk 21:24 *4750*
escaped the e of the sword, out Heb 11:34 *4750*

EDGES

joined at the two e thereof Ex 28:7 7098
by the two e was it coupled Ex 39:4 7099
made him a dagger which had two e Judg 3:16 6366
hath the sharp sword with two e Rev 2:12 *1366*

EDIFICATION

his neighbour for his good to e Rom 15:2 *3619*
speaketh unto men to e, and 1Cor 14:3 *3619*
the Lord hath given us for e 2Cor 10:8 *3619*
which the Lord hath given me to e 2Cor 13:10 *3619*

EDIFIED

and Galilee and Samaria, and were e Acts 9:31 *3618*
well, but the other is not e 1Cor 14:17 *3618*

EDIFIETH

puffeth up, but charity e 1Cor 8:1 *3618*
in an unknown tongue e himself 1Cor 14:4 *3618*
he that prophesieth e the church 1Cor 14:4 *3618*

EDIFY

wherewith one may e another Rom 14:19 *3619*
for me, but all things e not 1Cor 10:23 *3618*
e one another, even as also ye do 1Th 5:11 *3618*

EDIFYING

that the church may receive e 1Cor 14:5 *3619*
may excel to the e of the church 1Cor 14:12 *3619*
Let all things be done unto e 1Cor 14:26 *3619*
dearly beloved, for your e 2Cor 12:19 *3619*
for the e of the body of Christ Eph 4:12 *3619*
body unto the e of itself in love Eph 4:16 *3619*
which is good to the use of e Eph 4:29 *3619*
than godly e which is in faith 1Ti 1:4 *3618*

EDOM (*e'-dum*) See EDOMITES, ESAU, IDUMEA, OBED-EDOM.

1. Another name for Esau.

children of Seir in the land of E Gen 36:21 123
that reigned in the land of E Gen 36:31 123
Bela the son of Beor reigned in E Gen 36:32 123
these be the dukes of E, Gen 36:43 123
the dukes of E shall be amazed Ex 15:15 123
from Kadesh unto the king of E Num 20:14 123
E said unto him, Thou shalt not Num 20:18 123
E came out against him with much Num 20:20 123
Thus E refused to give Israel Num 20:21 123
by the coast of the land of E Num 20:23 123
Red sea, to compass the land of E Num 21:4 123

E shall be a possession, Seir Num 24:18 123
Hor, in the edge of the land of *E* Num 33:37 123
of Zin along by the coast of *E* Num 34:3 123
even to the border of *E* the Josh 15:1 123
coast of *E* southward were Kabzeel Josh 15:21 123
marchedst out of the field of *E* Judg 5:4 123
messengers unto the king of *E* Judg 11:17 123
but the king of *E* would not Judg 11:17 123
and compassed the land of *E* Judg 11:18 123
children of Ammon, and against *E* 1Sa 14:47 123
And he put garrisons in *E* 2Sa 8:14 123
throughout all *E* put he garrisons 2Sa 8:14 123
all they of *E* became David's 2Sa 8:14 123
of the Red sea, in the land of *E* 1Kin 9:26 123
he was of the king's seed in *E* 1Kin 11:14 123
came to pass, when David was in *E* 1Kin 11:15 123
he had smitten every male in *E* 1Kin 11:15 123
he had cut off every male in *E* 1Kin 11:16 123
There was then no king in *E* 1Kin 22:47 123
way through the wilderness of *E* 2Kin 3:8 123
king of Judah, and the king of *E* 2Kin 3:9 123
the king of *E* went down to him 2Kin 3:12 123
there came water by the way of *E* 2Kin 3:20 123
through even unto the king of *E* 2Kin 3:26 123
In his days *E* revolted from under 2Kin 8:20 123
Yet *E* revolted from under the 2Kin 8:22 123
He slew of *E* in the valley of 2Kin 14:7 123
Thou hast indeed smitten *E* 2Kin 14:10 123
that reigned in the land of *E* 1Chr 1:43 123
And the dukes of *E* were 1Chr 1:51 123
These are the dukes of *E* 1Chr 1:54 123
from *E*, and from Moab, and from the 1Chr 18:11 123
And he put garrisons in *E* 1Chr 18:13 123
at the sea side in the land of *E* 2Chr 8:17 123
they sought after the gods of *E* 2Chr 25:20 123
smote of *E* in the valley of salt Ps 60:*t* 123
over *E* will I cast out my shoe Ps 60:8 123
who will lead me into *E* Ps 60:9 123
The tabernacles of *E*, and the Ps 83:6 123
over *E* will I cast out my shoe Ps 108:9 123
who will lead me into *E* Ps 108:10 123
the children of *E* in the day of Ps 137:7 123
they shall lay their hand upon *E* Is 11:14 123
Who is this that cometh from *E* Is 63:1 123
Egypt, and Judah, and *E*, and the Jer 9:26 123
E, and Moab, and the children of Jer 25:21 123
And send them to the king of *E* Jer 27:3 123
and among the Ammonites, and in *E* Jer 40:11 123
Concerning *E*, thus saith the LORD Jer 49:7 123
Also *E* shall be a desolation Jer 49:17 123
that he hath taken against *E* Jer 49:20 123
E be as the heart of a woman in Jer 49:22 123
and be glad, O daughter of *E* Lam 4:21 123
thine iniquity, O daughter of *E* Lam 4:22 123
Because that *E* hath dealt against Eze 25:12 123
also stretch out mine hand upon *E* Eze 25:13 123
I will lay my vengeance upon *E* by Eze 25:14 123
they shall do in *E* according to Eze 25:14 123
There is *E*, her kings, and all her Eze 32:29 123
escape out of his hand, even *E* Dan 11:41 123
E shall be a desolate wilderness, Joel 3:19 123
to deliver them up to *E* Amos 1:6 123
up the whole captivity to *E* Amos 1:9 123
For three transgressions of *E* Amos 1:11 123
bones of the king of *E* into lime Amos 2:1 123
they may possess the remnant of *E* Amos 9:12 123
saith the Lord GOD concerning *E* Obad 1 123
destroy the wise men out of *E* Obad 8 123
Whereas *E* saith, We are Mal 1:4 123

2. Descendants of Esau.

therefore was his name called *E* Gen 25:30 123
land of Seir, the country of *E* Gen 32:3 123
the generations of Esau, who is *E* Gen 36:1 123
Esau is *E* Gen 36:8 123
came of Eliphaz in the land of *E* Gen 36:16 123
came of Reuel in the land of *E* Gen 36:17 123
are the sons of Esau, who is *E* Gen 36:19 123

EDOMITE (*e'-dum-ite*) See EDOMITES. *A descendant of Esau.*

Thou shalt not abhor an *E* Deut 23:7 130
and his name was Doeg, an *E* 1Sa 21:7 130
Then answered Doeg the *E*, which 1Sa 22:9 130
And Doeg the *E* turned, and he fell 1Sa 22:18 130
day, when Doeg the *E* was there 1Sa 22:22
unto Solomon, Hadad the *E* 1Kin 11:14 130
of David, when Doeg the *E* came Ps 52:*t*

EDOMITES (*e'-dum-ites*)

the father of the *E* in mount Seir Gen 36:9 130
he is Esau the father of the *E* Gen 36:43 130
of the Moabites, Ammonites, *E* 1Kin 11:1 130
certain *E* of his father's 1Kin 11:17
smote the *E* which compassed him 2Kin 8:21 130
the son Zeruiah slew of the *E* in 1Chr 18:12 130
all the *E* became David's servants 1Chr 18:13 130
In his days the *E* revolted from 2Chr 21:8 130
smote the *E* which compassed him 2Chr 21:9 130
So the *E* revolted from under the 2Chr 21:10 130
come from the slaughter of the *E* 2Chr 25:14 130
Lo, thou hast smitten the *E* 2Chr 25:19 130
For again the *E* had come and 2Chr 28:17 130

EDREI (*ed'-re-i*)

1. A city in Bashan.

his people, to the battle at *E* Num 21:33 154
which dwelt at Astaroth in *E* Deut 1:4 154
and all his people, to battle at *E* Deut 3:1 154
and all Bashan, unto Salchah and *E* Deut 3:10 154
that dwelt at Ashtaroth and at *E* Josh 12:4 154
reigned in Ashtaroth and in *E* Josh 13:12 154
half Gilead, and Ashtaroth, and *E* Josh 13:31 154

2. A city in Naphtali

And Kedesh, and *E*, and En-hazor, Josh 19:37 154

EFFECT

she bound her soul, of none *e* Num 30:8 6565
and they spake to her to that *e* 2Chr 34:22
devices of the people of none *e* Ps 33:10 5106
the *e* of righteousness quietness Is 32:17 5656
his lies shall not so *e* it Jer 48:30 6213
at hand, and the *e* of every vision Eze 12:23 1697
God of none *e* by your tradition Mt 15:6 *208*
of none *e* through your tradition Mk 7:13 *208*
make the faith of God without *e* Rom 3:3 *2673*
and the promise made of none *e* Rom 4:14 *2673*
the word of God hath taken none *e* Rom 9:6 *1601*
Christ should be made of none *e* 1Cor 1:17 *2758*
should make the promise of none *e* Gal 3:17 *2673*
Christ is become of no *e* unto you Gal 5:4 *2673*

EFFECTED

his own house, he prosperously *e* 2Chr 7:11 6743

EFFECTUAL

e is opened unto me, and there are 1Cor 16:9 *1756*
which is *e* in the enduring of the 2Cor 1:6 *1754*
me by the *e* working of his power Eph 3:7 *1753*
according to the *e* working in the Eph 4:16 *1753*
of thy faith may become *e* by the Philem 6 *1756*
The *e* fervent prayer of a Jas 5:16 *1754*

EFFECTUALLY

(For he that wrought *e* in Peter Gal 2:8 *1754*
which *e* worketh also in you that 1Th 2:13 *1754*

EFFEMINATE

idolaters, nor adulterers, nor *e* 1Cor 6:9 *3120*

EGG

any taste in the white of an *e* Job 6:6 2495
Or if he shall ask an *e*, will he Lk 11:12 *5609*

EGGS

whether they be young ones, or *e* Deut 22:6 1000
upon the young, or upon the *e* Deut 22:6 1000
Which leaveth her *e* in the earth Job 39:14 1000
as one gathereth *e* that are left Is 10:14 1000
They hatch cockatrice' *e*, and Is 59:5 1000
he that eateth of their *e* dieth Is 59:5 1000
As the partridge sitteth on *e* Jer 17:11

EGLAH (*eg'-lah*) See MICHAL. *A wife of David.*

sixth, Ithream, by *E* David's wife 2Sa 3:5 5698
the sixth, Ithream by *E* his wife 1Chr 3:3 5698

EGLAIM (*eg'-la-im*) See EN-EGLAIM. *A Moabite city.*

the howling thereof unto *E* Is 15:8 97

EGLON (*eg'-lon*)

1. An Amorite city.

Lachish, and unto Debir king of *E* Josh 10:3 5700
king of Lachish, the king of *E* Josh 10:5 5700
king of Lachish, and the king of *E* Josh 10:23 5700
from Lachish Joshua passed unto *E* Josh 10:34 5700
And Joshua went up from *E*, and all Josh 10:36 5700
to all that he had done to *E* Josh 10:37 5700
The king of *E*, one Josh 12:12 5700
Lachish, and Bozkath, and *E* Josh 15:39 5700

2. A Moabite king.

the LORD strengthened *E* the king Judg 3:12 5700
the children of Israel served *E* Judg 3:14 5700
a present unto *E* the king of Moab Judg 3:15 5700
the present unto *E* king of Moab Judg 3:17 5700
and *E* was a very fat man Judg 3:17 5700

EGYPT (*e'-jipt*) See EGYPTIAN, MIZRAIM. *Kingdom in northeast Africa.*

went down into *E* to sojourn there Gen 12:10 4714
he was come near to enter into *E* Gen 12:11 4714
that, when Abram was come into *E* Gen 12:14 4714
And Abram went up out of *E* Gen 13:1 4714
of the LORD, like the land of *E* Gen 13:10 4714
from the river of *E* unto the Gen 15:18 4714
him a wife out of the land of *E* Gen 21:21 4714
unto Shur, that is before *E* Gen 25:18 4714
him, and said, Go not down into *E* Gen 26:2 4714
going to carry it down to *E* Gen 37:25 4714
and they brought Joseph into *E* Gen 37:28 4714
sold him into *E* unto Potiphar Gen 37:36 4714
And Joseph was brought down to *E* Gen 39:1 4714
that the butler of the king of *E* Gen 40:1 4714
offended their lord the king of *E* Gen 40:1 4714
and the baker of the king of *E* Gen 40:5 4714
called for all the magicians of *E* Gen 41:8 4714
in all the land of *E* for badness Gen 41:19 4714
throughout all the land of *E* Gen 41:29 4714
be forgotten in the land of *E* Gen 41:30 4714
and set him over the land of *E* Gen 41:33 4714
of *E* in the seven plenteous years Gen 41:34 4714
which shall be in the land of *E* Gen 41:36 4714
set thee over all the land of *E* Gen 41:41 4714
him ruler over all the land of *E* Gen 41:43 4714
hand or foot in all the land of *E* Gen 41:44 4714
went out over all the land of *E* Gen 41:45 4714
he stood before Pharaoh king of *E* Gen 41:46 4714
went throughout all the land of *E* Gen 41:46 4714
which were in the land of *E* Gen 41:48 4714
that was in the land of *E* Gen 41:53 4714
all the land of *E* there was bread Gen 41:54 4714
all the land of *E* was famished Gen 41:55 4714
waxed sore in the land of *E* Gen 41:56 4714
all countries came into *E* to Gen 41:57 4714
saw that there was corn in *E* Gen 42:1 4714
heard that there is corn in *E* Gen 42:2 4714
went down to buy corn in *E* Gen 42:3 4714
which they had brought out of *E* Gen 43:2 4714
and rose up, and went down to *E* Gen 43:15 4714
your brother, whom ye sold into *E* Gen 45:4 4714
throughout all the land of *E* Gen 45:8 4714
God hath made me lord of all *E* Gen 45:9 4714
my father of all my glory in *E* Gen 45:13 4714
you the good of the land of *E* Gen 45:18 4714
land of *E* for your little ones Gen 45:19 4714
of all the land of *E* is yours Gen 45:20 4714
laden with the good things of *E* Gen 45:23 4714
And they went up out of *E*, and came Gen 45:25 4714
governor over all the land of *E* Gen 45:26 4714
fear not to go down into *E* Gen 46:3 4714
I will go down with thee into *E* Gen 46:4 4714
land of Canaan, and came into *E* Gen 46:6 4714
seed brought he with him into *E* Gen 46:7 4714
of Israel, which came into *E* Gen 46:8 4714
the land of *E* were born Manasseh Gen 46:20 4714
souls that came with Jacob into *E* Gen 46:26 4714
Joseph, which were born him in *E* Gen 46:27 4714
house of Jacob, which came into *E* Gen 46:27 4714
The land of *E* is before thee Gen 47:6 4714
a possession in the land of *E* Gen 47:11 4714
very sore, so that the land of *E* Gen 47:13 4714
that was found in the land of *E* Gen 47:14 4714
money failed in the land of *E* Gen 47:15 4714
all the land of *E* for Pharaoh Gen 47:20 4714
E even to the other end thereof Gen 47:21 4714
over the land of *E* unto this day Gen 47:26 4714
And Israel dwelt in the land of *E* Gen 47:27 4714
in the land of *E* seventeen years Gen 47:28 4714
bury me not, I pray thee, in *E* Gen 47:29 4714
and thou shalt carry me out of *E* Gen 47:30 4714
of *E* before I came unto thee into Gen 48:5 4714
before I came unto thee into *E* Gen 48:5 4714
all the elders of the land of *E* Gen 50:7 4714
And Joseph returned into *E* Gen 50:14 4714
And Joseph dwelt in *E*, he, and his Gen 50:22 4714
and he was put in a coffin in *E* Gen 50:26 4714
of Israel, which came into *E* Ex 1:1 4714
for Joseph was in *E* already Ex 1:5 4714
there arose up a new king over *E* Ex 1:8 4714
the king of *E* spake to the Hebrew Ex 1:15 4714
as the king of *E* commanded them Ex 1:17 4714
the king of *E* called for the Ex 1:18 4714
of time, that the king of *E* died Ex 2:23 4714
of my people which are in *E* Ex 3:7 4714
the children of Israel out of *E* Ex 3:10 4714
the children of Israel out of *E* Ex 3:11 4714
brought forth the people out of *E* Ex 3:12 4714
that which is done to you in *E* Ex 3:16 4714
E unto the land of the Canaanites Ex 3:17 4714
of Israel, unto the king of *E* Ex 3:18 4714
the king of *E* will not let you go Ex 3:19 4714
smite *E* with all my wonders which Ex 3:20 4714
unto my brethren which are in *E* Ex 4:18 4714
in Midian, Go, return into *E* Ex 4:19 4714
and he returned to the land of *E* Ex 4:20 4714
When thou goest to return into *E* Ex 4:21 4714
the king of *E* said unto them, Ex 5:4 4714
throughout all the land of *E* to Ex 5:12 4714
in, speak unto Pharaoh king of *E* Ex 6:11 4714
Israel, and unto Pharaoh king of *E* Ex 6:13 4714
of Israel out of the land of *E* Ex 6:13 4714
of *E* according to their armies Ex 6:26 4714
which spake to Pharaoh king of *E* Ex 6:27 4714
out the children of Israel from *E* Ex 6:27 4714
spake unto Moses in the land of *E* Ex 6:28 4714
of *E* all that I say unto thee Ex 6:29 4714
and my wonders in the land of *E* Ex 7:3 4714
that I may lay my hand upon *E* Ex 7:4 4714
the land of *E* by great judgments Ex 7:4 4714
I stretch forth mine hand upon *E* Ex 7:5 4714
now the magicians of *E*, they also Ex 7:11 4714
thine hand upon the waters of *E* Ex 7:19 4714
throughout all the land of *E* Ex 7:19 4714
throughout all the land of *E* Ex 7:21 4714
the magicians of *E* did so with Ex 7:22 4714
to come up upon the land of *E* Ex 8:5 4714
out his hand over the waters of *E* Ex 8:6 4714
came up, and covered the land of *E* Ex 8:6 4714
up frogs upon the land of *E* Ex 8:7 4714
lice throughout all the land of *E* Ex 8:16 4714
lice throughout all the land of *E* Ex 8:17 4714
houses, and into all the land of *E* Ex 8:24 4714
of Israel and the cattle of *E* Ex 9:4 4714
and all the cattle of *E* died Ex 9:6 4714
small dust in all the land of *E* Ex 9:9 4714
throughout all the land of *E* Ex 9:9 4714
such as hath not been in *E* since Ex 9:18 4714
may be hail in all the land of *E* Ex 9:22 4714
field, throughout the land of *E* Ex 9:22 4714
rained hail upon the land of *E* Ex 9:23 4714
of *E* since it became a nation Ex 9:24 4714
of *E* all that was in the field Ex 9:25 4714
what things I have wrought in *E* Ex 10:2 4714
thou not yet that *E* is destroyed Ex 10:7 4714
the land of *E* for the locusts Ex 10:12 4714
may come up upon the land of *E* Ex 10:12 4714
forth his rod over the land of *E* Ex 10:13 4714
went up over all the land of *E* Ex 10:14 4714
and rested in all the coasts of *E* Ex 10:14 4714
field, through all the land of *E* Ex 10:15 4714
one locust in all the coasts of *E* Ex 10:19 4714
be darkness over the land of *E* Ex 10:21 4714
in all the land of *E* three days Ex 10:22 4714
more upon Pharaoh, and upon *E* Ex 11:1 4714
was very great in the land of *E* Ex 11:3 4714
will I go out into the midst of *E* Ex 11:4 4714
in the land of *E* shall die Ex 11:5 4714
cry throughout all the land of *E* Ex 11:6 4714
be multiplied in the land of *E* Ex 11:9 4714
Moses and Aaron in the land of *E* Ex 12:1 4714
through the land of *E* this night Ex 12:12 4714
the firstborn in the land of *E* Ex 12:12 4714
gods of *E* I will execute judgment Ex 12:12 4714
you, when I smite the land of *E* Ex 12:13 4714
your armies out of the land of *E* Ex 12:17 4714
of the children of Israel in *E* Ex 12:27 4714
the firstborn in the land of *E* Ex 12:29 4714
and there was a great cry in *E* Ex 12:30 4714

E

which they brought forth out of *E*	Ex 12:39	4714
because they were thrust out of *E*	Ex 12:39	4714
of Israel, who dwelt in *E*	Ex 12:40	4714
LORD went out from the land of *E*	Ex 12:41	4714
them out from the land of *E*	Ex 12:42	4714
of the land of *E* by their armies	Ex 12:51	4714
day, in which ye came out from *E*	Ex 13:3	4714
me when I came forth out of *E*	Ex 13:8	4714
the LORD brought thee out of *E*	Ex 13:9	4714
the LORD brought us out from *E*	Ex 13:14	4714
the firstborn in the land of *E*	Ex 13:15	4714
LORD brought us forth out of *E*	Ex 13:16	4714
they see war, and they return to *E*	Ex 13:17	4714
up harnessed out of the land of *E*	Ex 13:18	4714
king of *E* that the people fled	Ex 14:5	4714
and all the chariots of *E*	Ex 14:7	4714
the heart of Pharaoh king of *E*	Ex 14:8	4714
Because there were no graves in *E*	Ex 14:11	4714
us, to carry us forth out of *E*	Ex 14:11	4714
word that we did tell thee in *E*	Ex 14:12	4714
departing out of the land of *E*	Ex 16:1	4714
hand of the LORD in the land of *E*	Ex 16:3	4714
you out from the land of *E*	Ex 16:6	4714
you forth from the land of *E*	Ex 16:32	4714
thou hast brought us up out of *E*	Ex 17:3	4714
LORD had brought Israel out of *E*	Ex 18:1	4714
gone forth out of the land of *E*	Ex 19:1	4714
brought thee out of the land of *E*	Ex 20:2	4714
were strangers in the land of *E*	Ex 22:21	4714
were strangers in the land of *E*	Ex 23:9	4714
for in it thou camest out from *E*	Ex 23:15	4714
them forth out of the land of *E*	Ex 29:46	4714
us up out of the land of *E*	Ex 32:1	4714
thee up out of the land of *E*	Ex 32:4	4714
broughtest out of the land of *E*	Ex 32:7	4714
thee up out of the land of *E*	Ex 32:8	4714
of the land of *E* with great power	Ex 32:11	4714
us up out of the land of *E*	Ex 32:23	4714
brought up out of the land of *E*	Ex 33:1	4714
month Abib thou camest out from *E*	Ex 34:18	4714
you up out of the land of *E*	Lev 11:45	4714
After the doings of the land of *E*	Lev 18:3	4714
were strangers in the land of *E*	Lev 19:34	4714
brought you out of the land of *E*	Lev 19:36	4714
brought you out of the land of *E*	Lev 22:33	4714
brought them out of the land of *E*	Lev 23:43	4714
you forth out of the land of *E*	Lev 25:38	4714
forth out of the land of *E*	Lev 25:42	4714
forth out of the land of *E*	Lev 25:55	4714
you forth out of the land of *E*	Lev 26:13	4714
forth out of the land of *E* in the	Lev 26:45	4714
were come out of the land of *E*	Num 1:1	4714
of *E* I hallowed unto me all the	Num 3:13	4714
of *E* I sanctified them for myself	Num 8:17	4714
were come out of the land of *E*	Num 9:1	4714
which we did eat in *E* freely	Num 11:5	4714
for it was well with us in *E*	Num 11:18	4714
Why came we forth out of *E*	Num 11:20	4714
seven years before Zoan in *E*	Num 13:22	4714
that we had died in the land of *E*	Num 14:2	4714
better for us to return into *E*	Num 14:3	4714
captain, and let us return into *E*	Num 14:4	4714
people, from *E* even until now	Num 14:19	4714
and my miracles, which I did in *E*	Num 14:22	4714
brought you out of the land of *E*	Num 15:41	4714
ye made us to come up out of *E*	Num 20:5	4714
How our fathers went down into *E*	Num 20:15	4714
and we have dwelt in *E* a long time	Num 20:15	4714
and hath brought us forth out of *E*	Num 20:16	4714
out of *E* to die in the wilderness	Num 21:5	4714
there is a people come out from *E*	Num 22:5	4714
there is a people come out of *E*	Num 22:11	4714
God brought them out of *E*	Num 23:22	4714
God brought him forth out of *E*	Num 24:8	4714
went forth out of the land of *E*	Num 26:4	4714
whom her mother bare to Levi in *E*	Num 26:59	4714
of the men that came up out of *E*	Num 32:11	4714
of *E* with their armies under the	Num 33:1	4714
were come out of the land of *E*	Num 33:38	4714
from Azmon unto the river of *E*	Num 34:5	4714
us forth out of the land of *E*	Deut 1:27	4714
did for you in *E* before your eyes	Deut 1:30	4714
the iron furnace, even out of *E*	Deut 4:20	4714
did for you in *E* before your eyes	Deut 4:34	4714
with his mighty power out of *E*	Deut 4:37	4714
after they came forth out of *E*	Deut 4:45	4714
they were come forth out of *E*	Deut 4:46	4714
brought thee out of the land of *E*	Deut 5:6	4714
wast a servant in the land of *E*	Deut 5:15	4714
thee forth out of the land of *E*	Deut 6:12	4714
We were Pharaoh's bondmen in *E*	Deut 6:21	4714
us out of *E* with a mighty hand	Deut 6:21	4714
and wonders, great and sore, upon *E*	Deut 6:22	4714
the hand of Pharaoh king of *E*	Deut 7:8	4714
none of the evil diseases of *E*	Deut 7:15	4714
did unto Pharaoh, and unto all *E*	Deut 7:18	4714
thee forth out of the land of *E*	Deut 8:14	4714
didst depart out of the land of *E*	Deut 9:7	4714
of *E* have corrupted themselves	Deut 9:12	4714
forth out of *E* with a mighty hand	Deut 9:26	4714
were strangers in the land of *E*	Deut 10:19	4714
went down into *E* with threescore	Deut 10:22	4714
which he did in the midst of *E*	Deut 11:3	4714
unto Pharaoh the king of *E*	Deut 11:3	4714
And what he did unto the army of *E*	Deut 11:4	4714
it, is not as the land of *E*	Deut 11:10	4714
brought you out of the land of *E*	Deut 13:5	4714
brought thee out of the land of *E*	Deut 13:10	4714
wast a bondman in the land of *E*	Deut 15:15	4714
thee forth out of *E* by night	Deut 16:1	4714
out of the land of *E* in haste	Deut 16:3	4714
of *E* all the days of thy life	Deut 16:3	4714
that thou camest forth out of *E*	Deut 16:6	4714
that thou wast a bondman in *E*	Deut 16:12	4714
cause the people to return to *E*	Deut 17:16	4714
thee up out of the land of *E*	Deut 20:1	4714
way, when ye came forth out of *E*	Deut 23:4	4714
that ye were come forth out of *E*	Deut 24:9	4714
that thou wast a bondman in *E*	Deut 24:18	4714
wast a bondman in the land of *E*	Deut 24:22	4714
when ye were come forth out of *E*	Deut 25:17	4714
my father, and he went down into *E*	Deut 26:5	4714
forth out of *E* with a mighty hand	Deut 26:8	4714
smite thee with the botch of *E*	Deut 28:27	4714
upon thee all the diseases of *E*	Deut 28:60	4714
thee into *E* again with ships	Deut 28:68	4714
in the land of *E* unto Pharaoh	Deut 29:2	4714
we have dwelt in the land of *E*	Deut 29:16	4714
them forth out of the land of *E*	Deut 29:25	4714
to do in the land of *E* to Pharaoh	Deut 34:11	4714
for you, when ye came out of *E*	Josh 2:10	4714
All the people that came out of *E*	Josh 5:4	4714
the way, after they came out of *E*	Josh 5:4	4714
way as they came forth out of *E*	Josh 5:5	4714
men of war, which came out of *E*	Josh 5:6	4714
the reproach of *E* from off you	Josh 5:9	4714
of him, and all that he did in *E*	Josh 9:9	4714
From Sihor, which is before *E*	Josh 13:3	4714
and went out unto the river of *E*	Josh 15:4	4714
her villages, unto the river of *E*	Josh 15:47	4714
and his children went down into *E*	Josh 24:4	4714
also and Aaron, and I plagued *E*	Josh 24:5	4714
I brought your fathers out of *E*	Josh 24:6	4714
have seen what I have done in *E*	Josh 24:7	4714
other side of the flood, and in *E*	Josh 24:14	4714
our fathers out of the land of *E*	Josh 24:17	4714
of Israel brought up out of *E*	Josh 24:32	4714
I made you to go up out of *E*	Judg 2:1	4714
brought them out of the land of *E*	Judg 2:12	4714
Israel, I brought you up from *E*	Judg 6:8	4714
not the LORD bring us up from *E*	Judg 6:13	4714
land, when they came up out of *E*	Judg 11:13	4714
But when Israel came up from *E*	Judg 11:16	4714
of the land of *E* unto this day	Judg 19:30	4714
when they were in *E* in Pharaoh's	1Sa 2:27	4714
up out of *E* even unto this day	1Sa 8:8	4714
I brought up Israel out of *E*	1Sa 10:18	4714
fathers up out of the land of *E*	1Sa 12:6	4714
When Jacob was come into *E*	1Sa 12:8	4714
forth your fathers out of *E*	1Sa 12:8	4714
the way, when he came up from *E*	1Sa 15:2	4714
when they came up out of *E*	1Sa 15:6	4714
to Shur, that is over against *E*	1Sa 15:7	4714
to Shur, even unto the land of *E*	1Sa 27:8	4714
And he said, I am a young man of *E*	1Sa 30:13	4713
the children of Israel out of *E*	2Sa 7:6	4714
thou redeemedst to thee from *E*	2Sa 7:23	4714
affinity with Pharaoh king of *E*	1Kin 3:1	4714
and unto the border of *E*	1Kin 4:21	4714
country, and all the wisdom of *E*	1Kin 4:30	4714
were come out of the land of *E*	1Kin 6:1	4714
they came out of the land of *E*	1Kin 8:9	4714
forth my people Israel out of *E*	1Kin 8:16	4714
brought them out of the land of *E*	1Kin 8:21	4714
thou broughtest forth out of *E*	1Kin 8:51	4714
broughtest our fathers out of *E*	1Kin 8:53	4714
in of Hamath unto the river of *E*	1Kin 8:65	4714
fathers out of the land of *E*	1Kin 9:9	4714
For Pharaoh king of *E* had gone up	1Kin 9:16	4714
had horses brought out of *E*	1Kin 10:28	4714
went out of *E* for six hundred	1Kin 10:29	4714
servants with him, to go into *E*	1Kin 11:17	4714
to *E*, unto Pharaoh king of *E*	1Kin 11:18	4714
when Hadad heard in *E* that David	1Kin 11:21	4714
And Jeroboam arose, and fled into *E*	1Kin 11:40	4714
unto Shishak king of *E*	1Kin 11:40	4714
was in *E* until the death of	1Kin 11:40	4714
son of Nebat, who was yet in *E*	1Kin 12:2	4714
Solomon, and Jeroboam dwelt in *E*	1Kin 12:2	4714
thee up out of the land of *E*	1Kin 12:28	4714
that Shishak king of *E* came up	1Kin 14:25	4714
sent messengers to So king of *E*	2Kin 17:4	4714
them up out of the land of *E*	2Kin 17:7	4714
the hand of Pharaoh king of *E*	2Kin 17:7	4714
of the land of *E* with great power	2Kin 17:36	4714
of this bruised reed, even upon *E*	2Kin 18:21	4714
so is Pharaoh king of *E* unto all	2Kin 18:21	4714
put thy trust on *E* for chariots	2Kin 18:24	4714
their fathers came forth out of *E*	2Kin 21:15	4714
of *E* went up against the king of	2Kin 23:29	4714
and he came to *E*, and died there	2Kin 23:34	4714
the king of *E* came not again any	2Kin 24:7	4714
had taken from the river of *E*	2Kin 24:7	4714
that pertained to the king of *E*	2Kin 24:7	4714
the armies, arose, and came to *E*	2Kin 25:26	4714
from Shihor of *E* even unto the	1Chr 13:5	4714
whom thou hast redeemed out of *E*	1Chr 17:21	4714
had horses brought out of *E*	2Chr 1:16	4714
brought forth out of *E* a chariot	2Chr 1:17	4714
Israel, when they came out of *E*	2Chr 5:10	4714
my people out of the land of *E* I	2Chr 6:5	4714
in of Hamath unto the river of *E*	2Chr 7:8	4714
them forth out of the land of *E*	2Chr 7:22	4714
and to the border of *E*	2Chr 9:26	4714
unto Solomon horses out of *E*	2Chr 9:28	4714
the son of Nebat, who was in *E*	2Chr 10:2	4714
that Jeroboam returned out of *E*	2Chr 10:2	4714
of *E* came up against Jerusalem	2Chr 12:2	4714
that came with him out of *E*	2Chr 12:3	4714
So Shishak king of *E* came up	2Chr 12:9	4714
they came out of the land of *E*	2Chr 20:10	4714
even to the entering in of *E*	2Chr 26:8	4714
Necho king of *E* came up to fight	2Chr 35:20	4714
the king of *E* put him down at	2Chr 36:3	4714
the king of *E* made Eliakim his	2Chr 36:4	4714
his brother, and carried him to *E*	2Chr 36:4	4714
affliction of our fathers in *E*	Neh 9:9	4714
God that brought thee up out of *E*	Neh 9:18	4714
Princes shall come out of *E*	Ps 68:31	4714
their fathers, in the land of *E*	Ps 78:12	4714
How he had wrought his signs in *E*	Ps 78:43	4714
And smote all the firstborn in *E*	Ps 78:51	4714
Thou hast brought a vine out of *E*	Ps 80:8	4714
he went out through the land of *E*	Ps 81:5	4714
brought thee out of the land of *E*	Ps 81:10	4714
Israel also came into *E*	Ps 105:23	4714
E was glad when they departed	Ps 105:38	4714
understood not thy wonders in *E*	Ps 106:7	4714
which had done great things in *E*	Ps 106:21	4714
When Israel went out of *E*	Ps 114:1	4714
Who smote the firstborn of *E*	Ps 135:8	4714
into the midst of thee, O *E*	Ps 135:9	4714
To him that smote *E* in their	Ps 136:10	4714
works, with fine linen of *E*	Prov 7:16	4714
uttermost part of the rivers of *E*	Is 7:18	4714
thee, after the manner of *E*	Is 10:24	4714
lift it up after the manner of *E*	Is 10:26	4714
be left, from Assyria, and from *E*	Is 11:11	4714
he came up out of the land of *E*	Is 11:16	4714
The burden of *E*	Is 19:1	4714
swift cloud, and shall come into *E*	Is 19:1	4714
the idols of *E* shall be moved at	Is 19:1	4714
the heart of *E* shall melt in the	Is 19:1	4714
the spirit of *E* shall fail in the	Is 19:3	4714
of hosts hath purposed upon *E*	Is 19:12	4714
they have also seduced *E*, even	Is 19:13	4714
they have caused *E* to err in	Is 19:14	4714
shall there be any work for *E*	Is 19:15	4714
In that day shall *E* be like unto	Is 19:16	4714
of Judah shall be a terror unto *E*	Is 19:17	4714
five cities in the land of *E*	Is 19:18	4714
in the midst of the land of *E*	Is 19:19	4714
LORD of hosts in the land of *E*	Is 19:20	4714
And the LORD shall be known to *E*	Is 19:21	4714
And the LORD shall smite *E*	Is 19:22	4714
be a highway out of *E* to Assyria	Is 19:23	4714
and the Assyrian shall come into *E*	Is 19:23	4714
shall Israel be the third with *E*	Is 19:24	4714
saying, Blessed be *E* my people	Is 19:25	4714
years for a sign and wonder upon *E*	Is 20:3	4714
uncovered, to the shame of *E*	Is 20:4	4714
expectation, and of *E* their glory	Is 20:5	4714
As at the report concerning *E*	Is 23:5	4714
of the river unto the stream of *E*	Is 27:12	4714
and the outcasts in the land of *E*	Is 27:13	4714
That walk to go down into *E*	Is 30:2	4714
and to trust in the shadow of *E*	Is 30:2	4714
in the shadow of *E* your confusion	Is 30:3	4714
them that go down to *E* for help	Is 31:1	4714
staff of this broken reed, on *E*	Is 36:6	4714
so is Pharaoh king of *E* to all	Is 36:6	4714
put thy trust on *E* for chariots	Is 36:9	4714
I gave *E* for thy ransom, Ethiopia	Is 43:3	4714
saith the LORD, The labour of *E*	Is 45:14	4714
aforetime into *E* to sojourn there	Is 52:4	4714
us up out of the land of *E*	Jer 2:6	4714
hast thou to do in the way of *E*	Jer 2:18	4714
thou also shalt be ashamed of *E*	Jer 2:36	4714
brought them out of the land of *E*	Jer 7:22	4714
came forth out of the land of *E*	Jer 7:25	4714
E, and Judah, and Edom, and the	Jer 9:26	4714
them forth out of the land of *E*	Jer 11:4	4714
them up out of the land of *E*	Jer 11:7	4714
of Israel out of the land of *E*	Jer 16:14	4714
of Israel out of the land of *E*	Jer 23:7	4714
them that dwell in the land of *E*	Jer 24:8	4714
Pharaoh king of *E*, and his	Jer 25:19	4714
afraid, and fled, and went into *E*	Jer 26:21	4714
the king sent men into *E*, namely,	Jer 26:22	4714
and certain men with him into *E*	Jer 26:22	4714
fetched forth Urijah out of *E*	Jer 26:23	4714
bring them out of the land of *E*	Jer 31:32	4714
signs and wonders in the land of *E*	Jer 32:20	4714
out of the land of *E* with signs	Jer 32:21	4714
them forth out of the land of *E*	Jer 34:13	4714
army was come forth out of *E*	Jer 37:5	4714
shall return to *E* into their own	Jer 37:7	4714
Bethlehem, to go to enter into *E*	Jer 41:17	4714
but we will go into the land of *E*	Jer 42:14	4714
set your faces to enter into *E*	Jer 42:15	4714
you there in the land of *E*	Jer 42:16	4714
follow close after you there in *E*	Jer 42:16	4714
to go into *E* to sojourn there	Jer 42:17	4714
you, when ye shall enter into *E*	Jer 42:18	4714
Go ye not into *E*	Jer 42:19	4714
Go not into *E* to sojourn there	Jer 43:2	4714
So they came into the land of *E*	Jer 43:7	4714
he shall smite the land of *E*	Jer 43:11	4714
in the houses of the gods of *E*	Jer 43:12	4714
array himself with the land of *E*	Jer 43:12	4714
that is in the land of *E*	Jer 43:13	4714
Jews which dwell in the land of *E*	Jer 44:1	4714
unto other gods in the land of *E*	Jer 44:8	4714
the land of *E* to sojourn there	Jer 44:12	4714
and fall in the land of *E*	Jer 44:12	4714
them that dwell in the land of *E*	Jer 44:13	4714
the land of *E* to sojourn there	Jer 44:14	4714
that dwelt in the land of *E*	Jer 44:15	4714
Judah that are in the land of *E*	Jer 44:24	4714
Judah that dwell in the land of *E*	Jer 44:26	4714
man of Judah in all the land of *E*	Jer 44:26	4714
Judah that are in the land of *E*	Jer 44:27	4714
land of *E* into the land of Judah	Jer 44:28	4714
the land of *E* to sojourn there	Jer 44:28	4714
give Pharaoh-hophra king of *E*	Jer 44:30	4714
Against *E*, against the army of	Jer 46:2	4714
army of Pharaoh-necho king of *E*	Jer 46:2	4714
E riseth up like a flood, and his	Jer 46:8	4714
balm, O virgin, the daughter of *E*	Jer 46:11	4714
come and smite the land of *E*	Jer 46:13	4714
Declare ye in *E*, and publish in	Jer 46:14	4714
Pharaoh king of *E* is but a noise	Jer 46:17	4714

O thou daughter dwelling in *E*	Jer 46:19	4714
E is like a very fair heifer, but	Jer 46:20	4714
The daughter of *E* shall be	Jer 46:24	4714
multitude of No, and Pharaoh, and *E*	Jer 46:25	4714
in sending his ambassadors into *E*	Eze 17:15	4714
with chains unto the land of *E*	Eze 19:4	4714
known unto them in the land of *E*	Eze 20:5	4714
E into a land that I had espied	Eze 20:6	4714
yourselves with the idols of *E*	Eze 20:7	4714
did they forsake the idols of *E*	Eze 20:8	4714
in the midst of the land of *E*	Eze 20:8	4714
them forth out of the land of *E*	Eze 20:9	4714
to go forth out of the land of *E*	Eze 20:10	4714
the wilderness of the land of *E*	Eze 20:36	4714
And they committed whoredoms in *E*	Eze 23:3	4714
she her whoredoms brought from *E*	Eze 23:8	4714
the harlot in the land of *E*	Eze 23:19	4714
brought from the land of *E*	Eze 23:27	4714
them, nor remember *E* any more	Eze 23:27	4714
E was that which thou spreadest	Eze 27:7	4714
face against Pharaoh king of *E*	Eze 29:2	4714
against him, and against all *E*	Eze 29:2	4714
against thee, Pharaoh king of *E*	Eze 29:3	4714
all the inhabitants of *E* shall	Eze 29:6	4714
the land of *E* shall be desolate	Eze 29:9	4714
make the land of *E* utterly waste	Eze 29:10	4714
I will make the land of *E*	Eze 29:12	4714
bring again the captivity of *E*	Eze 29:14	4714
I will give the land of *E* unto	Eze 29:19	4714
of *E* for his labour wherewith he	Eze 29:20	4714
And the sword shall come upon *E*	Eze 30:4	4714
when the slain shall fall in *E*	Eze 30:4	4714
also that uphold *E* shall fall	Eze 30:6	4714
LORD, when I have set a fire in *E*	Eze 30:8	4714
upon them, as in the day of *E*	Eze 30:9	4714
of *E* to cease by the hand of	Eze 30:10	4714
shall draw their swords against *E*	Eze 30:11	4714
no more a prince of the land of *E*	Eze 30:13	4714
will put a fear in the land of *E*	Eze 30:13	4714
fury upon Sin, the strength of *E*	Eze 30:15	4714
And I will set fire in *E*	Eze 30:16	4714
shall break there the yokes of *E*	Eze 30:18	4714
will I execute judgments in *E*	Eze 30:19	4714
the arm of Pharaoh king of *E*	Eze 30:21	4714
I am against Pharaoh king of *E*	Eze 30:22	4714
stretch it out upon the land of *E*	Eze 30:25	4714
man, speak unto Pharaoh king of *E*	Eze 31:2	4714
lamentation for Pharaoh king of *E*	Eze 32:2	4714
and they shall spoil the pomp of *E*	Eze 32:12	4714
shall make the land of *E* desolate	Eze 32:15	4714
shall lament for her, even for *E*	Eze 32:16	4714
man, wail for the multitude of *E*	Eze 32:18	4714
the land of *E* with a mighty hand	Dan 9:15	4714
carry captives into *E* their gods	Dan 11:8	4714
the land of *E* shall not escape	Dan 11:42	4714
over all the precious things of *E*	Dan 11:43	4714
she came up out of the land of *E*	Hos 2:15	4714
they call to *E*, they go to	Hos 7:11	4714
their derision in the land of *E*	Hos 7:16	4714
they shall return to *E*	Hos 8:13	4714
but Ephraim shall return to *E*	Hos 9:3	4714
E shall gather them up, Memphis	Hos 9:6	4714
him, and called my son out of *E*	Hos 11:1	4714
not return into the land of *E*	Hos 11:5	4714
shall tremble as a bird out of *E*	Hos 11:11	4714
and oil is carried into *E*	Hos 12:1	4714
LORD thy God from the land of *E*	Hos 12:9	4714
the LORD brought Israel out of *E*	Hos 12:13	4714
LORD thy God from the land of *E*	Hos 13:4	4714
E shall be a desolation, and Edom	Joel 3:19	4714
brought you up from the land of *E*	Amos 2:10	4714
I brought up from the land of *E*	Amos 3:1	4714
in the palaces in the land of *E*	Amos 3:9	4714
pestilence after the manner of *E*	Amos 4:10	4714
and drowned, as by the flood of *E*	Amos 8:8	4714
be drowned, as by the flood of *E*	Amos 9:5	4714
up Israel out of the land of *E*	Amos 9:7	4714
thee up out of the land of *E*	Mic 6:4	4714
thy coming out of the land of *E*	Mic 7:15	4714
E were her strength, and it was	Nah 3:9	4714
with you when ye came out of *E*	Hag 2:5	4714
again also out of the land of *E*	Zec 10:10	4714
the sceptre of *E* shall depart	Zec 10:11	4714
And if the family of *E* go not up	Zec 14:18	4714
This shall be the punishment of *E*	Zec 14:19	4714
and his mother, and flee into *E*	Mt 2:13	*125*
by night, and departed into *E*	Mt 2:14	*125*
Out of *E* have I called my son	Mt 2:15	*125*
in a dream to Joseph in *E*	Mt 2:19	*125*
Phrygia, and Pamphylia, in *E*	Acts 2:10	*125*
with envy, sold Joseph into *E*	Acts 7:9	*125*
in the sight of Pharaoh king of *E*	Acts 7:10	*125*
and he made him governor over *E*	Acts 7:10	*125*
a dearth over all the land of *E*	Acts 7:11	*125*
heard that there was corn in *E*	Acts 7:12	*125*
So Jacob went down into *E*	Acts 7:15	*125*
people grew and multiplied in *E*	Acts 7:17	*125*
of my people which is in *E*	Acts 7:34	*125*
now come, I will send thee into *E*	Acts 7:34	*125*
wonders and signs in the land of *E*	Acts 7:36	*125*
hearts turned back again into *E*	Acts 7:39	*125*
brought us out of the land of *E*	Acts 7:40	*125*
as strangers in the land of *E*	Acts 13:17	*125*
all that came out of *E* by Moses	Heb 3:16	*125*
to lead them out of the land of *E*	Heb 8:9	*125*
riches than the treasures in *E*	Heb 11:26	*125*
By faith he forsook *E*, not	Heb 11:27	*125*
the people out of the land of *E*	Jude 5	*125*
spiritually is called Sodom and *E*	Rev 11:8	*125*

EGYPTIAN (*e-jip'-shun*) See EGYPTIAN'S, EGYPTIANS.

1. An inhabitant of Egypt.

and she had an handmaid, an *E*	Gen 16:1	4713
wife took Hagar her maid the *E*	Gen 16:3	4713
Sarah saw the son of Hagar the *E*	Gen 21:9	4713
Abraham's son, whom Hagar the *E*	Gen 25:12	4713
captain of the guard, an *E*	Gen 39:1	4713
in the house of his master the *E*	Gen 39:2	4713
women are not as the *E* women	Ex 1:19	4713
he spied an *E* smiting an Hebrew,	Ex 2:11	4713
there was no man, he slew the *E*	Ex 2:12	4713
kill me, as thou killedst the *E*	Ex 2:14	4713
An *E* delivered us out of the hand	Ex 2:19	4713
woman, whose father was an *E*	Lev 24:10	4713
thou shalt not abhor an *E*	Deut 23:7	4713
And they found an *E* in the field	1Sa 30:11	4713
And he slew an *E*, a goodly man	2Sa 23:21	4713
the *E* had a spear in his hand	2Sa 23:21	4713
And Sheshan had a servant, an *E*	1Chr 2:34	4713
And he slew an *E*, a man of great	1Chr 11:23	4713
the *E* into Assyria, and the	Is 19:23	4714
was oppressed, and smote the *E*	Acts 7:24	*124*
as thou diddest the *E* yesterday	Acts 7:28	*124*
Art not thou that *E*, which before	Acts 21:38	*124*

2. The Red Sea.

destroy the tongue of the *E* sea	Is 11:15	4714

EGYPTIAN'S (*e-jip'-shuns*)

the *E* house for Joseph's sake	Gen 39:5	4713
the spear out of the *E* hand	2Sa 23:21	4713
in the *E* hand was a spear like a	1Chr 11:23	4713
the spear out of the *E* hand	1Chr 11:23	4713

EGYPTIANS (*e-jip'-shuns*)

when the *E* shall see thee, that	Gen 12:12	4713
the *E* beheld the woman that she	Gen 12:14	4713
and Pharaoh said unto all the *E*	Gen 41:55	4714
storehouses, and sold unto the *E*	Gen 41:56	4714
them by themselves, and for the *E*	Gen 43:32	4713
because the *E* might not eat bread	Gen 43:32	4713
that is an abomination unto the *E*	Gen 43:32	4714
and the *E* and the house of Pharaoh	Gen 45:2	4714
is an abomination unto the *E*	Gen 46:34	4714
all the *E* came unto Joseph, and	Gen 47:15	4714
for the *E* sold every man his	Gen 47:20	4714
the *E* mourned for him threescore	Gen 50:3	4714
is a grievous mourning to the *E*	Gen 50:11	4714
the *E* made the children of Israel	Ex 1:13	4714
them out of the hand of the *E*	Ex 3:8	4714
wherewith the *E* oppress them	Ex 3:9	4714
favour in the sight of the *E*	Ex 3:21	4714
and ye shall spoil the *E*	Ex 3:22	4714
whom the *E* keep in bondage	Ex 6:5	4714
from under the burdens of the *E*	Ex 6:6	4714
from under the burdens of the *E*	Ex 6:7	4714
the *E* shall know that I am the	Ex 7:5	4714
the *E* shall lothe to drink of the	Ex 7:18	4714
the *E* could not drink of the	Ex 7:21	4714
all the *E* digged round about the	Ex 7:24	4714
the houses of the *E* shall be full	Ex 8:21	4714
of the *E* to the LORD our God	Ex 8:26	4714
of the *E* before their eyes	Ex 8:26	4714
the magicians, and upon all the *E*	Ex 9:11	4714
and the houses of all the *E*	Ex 10:6	4714
favour in the sight of the *E*	Ex 11:3	4714
put a difference between the *E*	Ex 11:7	4714
will pass through to smite the *E*	Ex 12:23	4714
in Egypt, when he smote the *E*	Ex 12:27	4714
and all his servants, and all the *E*	Ex 12:30	4714
the *E* were urgent upon the people	Ex 12:33	4714
of the *E* jewels of silver	Ex 12:35	4714
favour in the sight of the *E*	Ex 12:36	4714
And they spoiled the *E*	Ex 12:36	4714
that the *E* may know that I am the	Ex 14:4	4714
But the *E* pursued after them, all	Ex 14:9	4714
behold, the *E* marched after them	Ex 14:10	4714
us alone, that we may serve the *E*	Ex 14:12	4714
been better for us to serve the *E*	Ex 14:12	4714
for the *E* whom ye have seen to	Ex 14:13	4714
I will harden the hearts of the *E*	Ex 14:17	4714
the *E* shall know that I am the	Ex 14:18	4714
it came between the camp of the *E*	Ex 14:20	4714
the *E* pursued, and went in after	Ex 14:23	4714
the *E* through the pillar of fire	Ex 14:24	4714
and troubled the host of the *E*	Ex 14:24	4714
so that the *E* said, Let us flee	Ex 14:25	4714
fighteth for them against the *E*	Ex 14:25	4714
waters may come again upon the *E*	Ex 14:26	4714
and the *E* fled against it	Ex 14:27	4714
the LORD overthrew the *E* in the	Ex 14:27	4714
that day out of the hand of the *E*	Ex 14:30	4714
Israel saw the *E* dead upon the	Ex 14:30	4714
which the LORD did upon the *E*	Ex 14:31	4714
which I have brought upon the *E*	Ex 15:26	4714
to the *E* for Israel's sake, and	Ex 18:8	4714
out of the hand of the *E*	Ex 18:9	4714
you out of the hand of the *E*	Ex 18:10	4714
from under the hand of the *E*	Ex 18:10	4714
have seen what I did unto the *E*	Ex 19:4	4714
Wherefore should the *E* speak	Ex 32:12	4714
Then the *E* shall hear it, (for	Num 14:13	4714
the *E* vexed us, and our fathers	Num 20:15	4714
hand in the sight of all the *E*	Num 33:3	4714
For the *E* buried all their	Num 33:4	4714
the *E* evil entreated us, and	Deut 26:6	4713
the *E* pursued after your fathers	Josh 24:6	4714
put darkness between you and the *E*	Josh 24:7	4713
you out of the hand of the *E*	Judg 6:9	4714
Did not I deliver you from the *E*	Judg 10:11	4714
the *E* with all the plagues in the	1Sa 4:8	4714
ye harden your hearts, as the *E*	1Sa 6:6	4714
you out of the hand of the *E*	1Sa 10:18	4714
Hittites, and the kings of the *E*	2Kin 7:6	4714
Ammonites, the Moabites, the *E*	Ezr 9:1	4713
set the *E* against the *E*	Is 19:2	4714
the *E* will I give over into the	Is 19:4	4714
the *E* shall know the LORD in that	Is 19:21	4714
the *E* shall serve with the	Is 19:23	4714
Assyria lead away the *E* prisoners	Is 20:4	4714
For the *E* shall help in vain, and	Is 30:7	4714
Now the *E* are men, and not God	Is 31:3	4714
of the *E* shall he burn with fire	Jer 43:13	4714
We have given the hand to the *E*	Lam 5:6	4714
with the *E* thy neighbours	Eze 16:26	4714
the *E* for the paps of thy youth	Eze 23:21	4714
scatter the *E* among the nations	Eze 29:12	4714
E from the people whither they	Eze 29:13	4714
scatter the *E* among the nations	Eze 30:23	4714
scatter the *E* among the nations	Eze 30:26	4714
in all the wisdom of the *E*	Acts 7:22	*124*
which the *E* assaying to do were	Heb 11:29	*124*

EHI (*e'-hi*) See AHARAH. *A son of Benjamin.*

and Ashbel, Gera, and Naaman, *E*	Gen 46:21	278

EHUD (*e'-hud*)

1. A son of Gera.

E the son of Gera, a Benjamite, a	Judg 3:15	261
But *E* made him a dagger which had	Judg 3:16	261
And *E* came unto him	Judg 3:20	261
E said, I have a message from God	Judg 3:20	261
E put forth his left hand, and	Judg 3:21	261
Then *E* went forth through the	Judg 3:23	261
E escaped while they tarried, and	Judg 3:26	261
of the LORD, when *E* was dead	Judg 4:1	261

2. A great-grandson of Benjamin.

Jeush, and Benjamin, and *E*, and	1Chr 7:10	261
And these are the sons of *E*	1Chr 8:6	261

EIGHT

Seth were *e* hundred years	Gen 5:4	8083
after he begat Enos *e* hundred	Gen 5:7	8083
after he begat Cainan *e* hundred	Gen 5:10	8083
he begat Mahalaleel *e* hundred	Gen 5:13	8083
after he begat Jared *e* hundred	Gen 5:16	8083
Mahalaleel were *e* hundred ninety	Gen 5:17	8083
he begat Enoch *e* hundred years	Gen 5:19	8083
he that is *e* days old shall be	Gen 17:12	8083
his son Isaac being *e* days old	Gen 21:4	8083
these *e* Milcah did bear to Nahor,	Gen 22:23	8083
length of one curtain shall be *e*	Ex 26:2	8083
And they shall be *e* boards	Ex 26:25	8083
e cubits, and the breadth of one	Ex 36:9	8083
And there were *e* boards	Ex 36:30	8083
e thousand and an hundred,	Num 2:24	8083
were *e* thousand and six hundred,	Num 3:28	8083
were *e* thousand and five hundred	Num 4:48	8083
e oxen he gave unto the sons of	Num 7:8	8083
And on the sixth day *e* bullocks	Num 29:29	8083
shall be forty and *e* cities	Num 35:7	8083
Zered, was thirty and *e* years	Deut 2:14	8083
e cities with their suburbs	Josh 21:41	8083
served Chushan-rishathaim *e* years	Judg 3:8	8083
and he judged Israel *e* years	Judg 12:14	8083
Now Eli was ninety and *e* years old	1Sa 4:15	8083
and he had *e* sons	1Sa 17:12	8083
up his spear against *e* hundred	2Sa 23:8	8083
there were in Israel *e* hundred	2Sa 24:9	8083
ten cubits, and stones of *e* cubits	1Kin 7:10	8083
he reigned *e* years in Jerusalem	2Kin 8:17	8083
in Samaria was twenty and *e* years	2Kin 10:36	8083
Josiah was *e* years old when he	2Kin 22:1	8083
e hundred, ready armed to the war	1Chr 12:24	8083
e hundred, mighty men of valour,	1Chr 12:30	8083
e thousand and six hundred	1Chr 12:35	8083
their brethren, threescore and *e*	1Chr 16:38	8083
by man, was thirty and *e* thousand	1Chr 23:3	8083
e among the sons of Ithamar	1Chr 24:4	8083
was two hundred fourscore and *e*	1Chr 25:7	8083
e sons, and threescore daughters	2Chr 11:21	8083
in array against him with *e*	2Chr 13:3	8083
he reigned *e* years in Jerusalem	2Chr 21:5	8083
he reigned in Jerusalem *e* years	2Chr 21:20	8083
the house of the LORD in *e* days	2Chr 29:17	8083
Josiah was *e* years old when he	2Chr 34:1	8083
Jehoiachin was *e* years old when	2Chr 36:9	8083
and Joab, two thousand *e* hundred	Ezr 2:6	8083
of Ater of Hezekiah, ninety and *e*	Ezr 2:16	8083
Anathoth, an hundred twenty and *e*	Ezr 2:23	8083
of Asaph, an hundred twenty and *e*	Ezr 2:41	8083
and with him twenty and *e* males	Ezr 8:11	8083
thousand and *e* hundred and eighteen	Neh 7:11	8083
of Zattu, *e* hundred forty and five	Neh 7:13	8083
of Binnui, six hundred forty and *e*	Neh 7:15	8083
of Bebai, six hundred twenty and *e*	Neh 7:16	8083
of Ater of Hezekiah, ninety and *e*	Neh 7:21	8083
Hashum, three hundred twenty and *e*	Neh 7:22	8083
an hundred fourscore and *e*	Neh 7:26	8083
Anathoth, an hundred twenty and *e*	Neh 7:27	8083
of Asaph, an hundred forty and *e*	Neh 7:44	8083
of Shobai, an hundred thirty and *e*	Neh 7:45	8083
threescore and *e* valiant men	Neh 11:6	8083
Sallai, nine hundred twenty and *e*	Neh 11:8	8083
the house were *e* hundred twenty	Neh 11:12	8083
of valour, an hundred twenty and *e*	Neh 11:14	8083
a portion to seven, and also to *e*	Eccl 11:2	8083
escaped from Johanan with *e* men	Jer 41:15	8083
from Jerusalem *e* hundred thirty	Jer 52:29	8083
the porch of the gate, *e* cubits	Eze 40:9	8083
and the going up to it had *e* steps	Eze 40:31	8083
and the going up to it had *e* steps	Eze 40:34	8083
and the going up to it had *e* steps	Eze 40:37	8083
e tables, whereupon they slew	Eze 40:41	8083
shepherds, and *e* principal men	Mic 5:5	8083
when *e* days were accomplished for	Lk 2:21	3638
an *e* days after these sayings	Lk 9:28	3638
an infirmity thirty and *e* years	Jn 5:5	3638
after *e* days again his disciples	Jn 20:26	3638
which had kept his bed *e* years	Acts 9:33	3638
e souls were saved by water	1Pet 3:20	3638

EIGHTEEN

his own house, three hundred and *e*	Gen 14:14	
Eglon the king of Moab *e* years	Judg 3:14	

e years, all the children of Judg 10:8
of Israel again e thousand men Judg 20:25
fell of Benjamin e thousand men Judg 20:44
of salt, being e thousand men 2Sa 8:13
of brass, of e cubits high apiece 1Kin 7:15
Jehoiachin was e years old when 2Kin 24:8
of the one pillar was e cubits 2Kin 25:17
half tribe of Manasseh e thousand 1Chr 12:31
in the valley of salt e thousand 1Chr 18:12
sons and brethren, strong men, e 1Chr 26:9
of brass e thousand talents, and 1Chr 29:7
(for he took e wives, and 2Chr 11:21
with him two hundred and e males Ezr 8:9
with his sons and his brethren, e Ezr 8:18
thousand and eight hundred and e Neh 7:11
height of one pillar was e cubits Jer 52:21
round about e thousand measures Eze 48:35
Or those e, upon whom the tower Lk 13:4
had a spirit of infirmity e years Lk 13:11
hath bound, lo, these e years Lk 13:16

EIGHTEENTH
Now in the e year of king 1Kin 15:1
over Israel in Samaria the e year 2Kin 3:1
pass in the e year of king Josiah 2Kin 22:3
But in the e year of king Josiah, 2Kin 23:23
to Hezir, the e to Aphses, 1Chr 24:15
The e to Hanani, he, his sons, and 1Chr 25:25
Now in the e year of king 2Chr 13:1
Now in the e year of his reign, 2Chr 34:8
In the e year of the reign of 2Chr 35:19
of Judah, which was the e year of Jer 32:1
In the e year of Nebuchadrezzar Jer 52:29

EIGHTH
on the e day thou shalt give it Ex 22:30 8066
And it came to pass on the e day Lev 9:1 8066
in the e day the flesh of his Lev 12:3 8066
on the e day he shall take two he Lev 14:10 8066
he shall bring them on the e day Lev 14:23 8066
on the e day he shall take to him Lev 15:14 8066
on the e day she shall take unto Lev 15:29 8066
and from the e day and thenceforth Lev 22:27 8066
on the e day shall be an holy Lev 23:36 8066
on the e day shall be a sabbath Lev 23:39 8066
And ye shall sow the e year Lev 25:22 8066
on the e day he shall bring two Num 6:10 8066
On the e day offered Gamaliel the Num 7:54 8066
On the e day ye shall have a Num 29:35 8066
month Bul, which is the e month 1Kin 6:38 8066
On the e day he sent the people 1Kin 8:66 8066
ordained a feast in the e month 1Kin 12:32 8066
the fifteenth day of the e month 1Kin 12:33 8066
e year of Asa king of Judah began 1Kin 16:29 8083
e year of Azariah king of Judah 2Kin 15:8 8083
him in the e year of his reign 2Kin 24:12 8083
Johanan the e, Elzabad the ninth, 1Chr 12:12 8066
to Hakkoz, the e to Abijah, 1Chr 24:10 8066
The e to Jeshaiah, he, his sons, 1Chr 25:15 8066
the seventh, Peulthai the e 1Chr 26:5 8066
e captain for the e month 1Chr 27:11 8066
in the e day they made a solemn 2Chr 7:9 8066
on the e day of the month came 2Chr 29:17 8066
For in the e year of his reign, 2Chr 34:3 8083
on the e day was a solemn Neh 8:18 8066
it shall be, that upon the e day Eze 43:27 8066
In the e month, in the second Zec 1:1 8066
that on the e day they came to Lk 1:59 *3590*
and circumcised him the e day Acts 7:8 *3590*
Circumcised the e day, of the Phil 3:5 *3637*
but saved Noah the e person 2Pet 2:5 *3590*
was, and is not, even he is the e Rev 17:11 *3590*
the e, beryl Rev 21:20 *3590*

EIGHTIETH
e year after the children of 1Kin 6:1 8084

EIGHTY
And Methuselah lived an hundred e Gen 5:25 8084
he begat Lamech seven hundred e Gen 5:26 8084
And Lamech lived an hundred e Gen 5:28 8084

EITHER
speak not to Jacob e good or bad Gen 31:24
speak not to Jacob e good or bad Gen 31:29
took e of them his censer, and put Lev 10:1 376
e in the warp, or in the woof, or Lev 13:49 176
e in the warp, or in the woof, or Lev 13:51 176
e in the warp, or in the woof, or Lev 13:53 176
e in the warp, or in the woof, or Lev 13:57 176
e warp, or woof, or whatsoever Lev 13:58 176
e in the warp, or woof, or any Lev 13:59 176
E a bullock or a lamb that hath Lev 22:23
E his uncle, or his uncle's son, Lev 25:49 176
When e man or woman shall Num 6:2 376
where was no way to turn e to the Num 22:26
to do e good or bad of mine own Num 24:13
e the sun, or moon, or any of the Deut 17:3
also shall not leave thee e corn Deut 28:51
e that all the sons of Jerubbaal, Judg 9:2
will do nothing e great or small 1Sa 20:2
e that thou hast shed blood 1Sa 25:31
e great or small, but carried 1Sa 30:2
did compass e of them about 1Kin 7:15 8145
there were stays on e side on the 1Kin 10:19
e he is talking, or he is 1Kin 18:27 3588
E three years' famine 1Chr 21:12 518
Judah sat e of them on his throne 2Chr 18:9 376
no man knoweth e love or hatred Eccl 9:1 1571
e this or that, or whether they Eccl 11:6
ask it e in the depth, or in the Is 7:11
e the groves, or the images Is 17:8
e on the right hand, or on the Eze 21:16
for e he will hate the one, and Mt 6:24 *2228*
E make the tree good, and his Mt 12:33 *2228*
E how canst thou say to thy Lk 6:42 *2228*
E what woman having ten pieces of Lk 15:8 *2228*
for e he will hate the one, and Lk 16:13 *2228*
on e side one, and Jesus in the Jn 19:18
but e to tell, or to hear some Acts 17:21 *2228*
speak to you e by revelation 1Cor 14:6 *2228*
attained, e were already perfect Phil 3:12 *2228*
e a vine, figs Jas 3:12 *2228*
on e side of the river, was there Rev 22:2

EKER (*e'-ker*) *Descendant of Judah.*
were, Maaz, and Jamin, and E 1Chr 2:27 6134

EKRON (*ec'-ron*) See EKRONITES. *A Philistine city.*
unto the borders of E northward Josh 13:3 6138
out unto the side of E northward Josh 15:11 6138
E, with her towns and her villages Josh 15:45 6138
From E even unto the sea, all Josh 15:46 6138
And Elon, and Thimnathah, and E Josh 19:43 6138
and E with the coast thereof Judg 1:18 6138
they sent the ark of God to E 1Sa 5:10 6138
pass, as the ark of God came to E 1Sa 5:10 6138
they returned to E the same day 1Sa 6:16 6138
one, for Gath one, for E one 1Sa 6:17 6138
to Israel, from E even unto Gath 1Sa 7:14 6138
the valley, and to the gates of E 1Sa 17:52 6138
even unto Gath, and unto E 1Sa 17:52 6138
of Baal-zebub the god of E 2Kin 1:2 6138
of Baal-zebub the god of E 2Kin 1:3 6138
of Baal-zebub the god of E 2Kin 1:6 6138
of Baal-zebub the god of E 2Kin 1:16 6138
and Ashkelon, and Azzah, and E Jer 25:20 6138
I will turn mine hand against E Amos 1:8 6138
noonday, and E shall be rooted up Zeph 2:4 6138
it, and be very sorrowful, and E Zec 9:5 6138
in Judah, and E as a Jebusite Zec 9:7 6138

EKRONITES (*ek'-ron-ites*) *Inhabitants of Ekron.*
the Gittites, and the E Josh 13:3 6139
that the E cried out, saying, 1Sa 5:10 6139

ELADAH (*el'-a-dah*) *A descendant of Ephraim.*
E his son, and Tahath his son, 1Chr 7:20 497

ELAH (*e'-lah*)
1. An Edomite prince.
Duke Aholibamah, duke E, duke Gen 36:41 425
Duke Aholibamah, duke E, duke 1Chr 1:52 425
2. A valley in Judah.
and pitched by the valley of E 1Sa 17:2 425
Israel, were in the valley of E 1Sa 17:19 425
thou slewest in the valley of E 1Sa 21:9 425
3. Father of Shimei.
Shimei the son of E, in Benjamin 1Kin 4:18 425
4. Son of King Baasha of Israel.
E his son reigned in his stead 1Kin 16:6 425
E the son of Baasha to reign over 1Kin 16:8 425
Baasha, and the sins of E his son 1Kin 16:13 425
Now the rest of the acts of E 1Kin 16:14 425
5. Father of King Hoshea of Israel.
Hoshea the son of E made a 2Kin 15:30 425
Judah began Hoshea the son of E 2Kin 17:1 425
of Hoshea son of E king of Israel 2Kin 18:1 425
of Hoshea son of E king of Israel 2Kin 18:9 425
6. A son of Caleb.
of Jephunneh; Iru, E 1Chr 4:15 425
and the sons of E, even Kenaz 1Chr 4:15 425
7. A Benjamite.
E the son of Uzzi, the son of 1Chr 9:8 425

ELAM (*e'-lam*) See ELAMITES, PERSIA.
1. A son of Shem.
E, and Asshur, and Arphaxad Gen 10:22 5867
E, and Asshur, and Arphaxad 1Chr 1:17 5867
2. Land of the Elamites.
Ellasar, Chedorlaomer king of E Gen 14:1 5867
With Chedorlaomer the king of E Gen 14:9 5867
Pathros, and from Cush, and from E Is 11:11 5867
Go up, O E: Is 21:2 5867
E bare the quiver with chariots Is 22:6 5867
of Zimri, and all the kings of E Jer 25:25 5867
E in the beginning of the reign Jer 49:34 5867
Behold, I will break the bow of E Jer 49:35 5867
upon E will I bring the four Jer 49:36 5867
the outcasts of E shall not come Jer 49:36 5867
For I will cause E to be dismayed Jer 49:37 5867
And I will set my throne in E Jer 49:38 5867
bring again the captivity of E Jer 49:39 5867
There is E and all her multitude Eze 32:24 5867
which is in the province of E Dan 8:2 5867
3. Son of Shashak.
And Hananiah, and E, and Antothijah, 1Chr 8:24 5867
4. A son of Meshelemiah.
E the fifth, Jehohanan the sixth, 1Chr 26:3 5867
5. A family of exiles with Zerubbabel.
The children of E, a thousand two Ezr 2:7 5867
The children of E, a thousand two Neh 7:12 5867
6. A family of exiles with Zerubbabel.
The children of the other E Ezr 2:31 5867
The children of the other E Neh 7:34 5867
7. A family of exiles with Ezra.
And of the sons of E Ezr 8:7 5867
8. An ancestor of Shechaniah.
of Jehiel, one of the sons of E Ezr 10:2 5867
And of the sons of E Ezr 10:26 5867
9. A chief who renewed the covenant.
Parosh, Pahath-moab, E, Zatthu, Neh 10:14 5867
10. A priest who purified the wall.
and Jehohanan, and Malchijah, and E. Neh 12:42 5867

ELAMITES (*e'-lam-ites*) See PERSIANS. *Foreign settlers in Samaria.*
the Dehavites, and the E, Ezr 4:9 5962
Parthians, and Medes, and E Acts 2:9 *1639*

ELASAH (*el'-a-sah*) See ELEASA.
1. Married a foreign wife.
Ishmael, Nethaneel, Jozabad, and E Ezr 10:22 501
2. An ambassador of Hezekiah.
By the hand of E the son of Jer 29:3 501

ELATH (*e'-lath*) See ELOTH. *An Elamite port.*
the way of the plain from E Deut 2:8 359
He built E, and restored it to 2Kin 14:22 359
of Syria recovered E to Syria 2Kin 16:6 359
and drave the Jews from E 2Kin 16:6 359
and the Syrians came to E, and 2Kin 16:6 359

EL-BERITH See BERITH.

EL-BETH-EL *Another name for Bethel.*
an altar, and called the place E Gen 35:7 416

ELDAAH (*el'-da-ah*) *A son of Midian.*
and Hanoch, and Abidah, and E Gen 25:4 420
Epher, and Henoch, and Abida, and E. 1Chr 1:33 420

ELDAD (*el'-dad*) *An elder and prophet with Moses.*
camp, the name of the one was E Num 11:26 419
man, and told Moses, and said, E Num 11:27 419

ELDER
the brother of Japheth the e Gen 10:21 1419
the e shall serve the younger Gen 25:23 7227
these words of Esau her e son Gen 27:42 1419
the name of the e was Leah Gen 29:16 1419
Behold my e daughter Merab, her 1Sa 18:17 1419
for he is mine e brother 1Kin 2:22 1419
aged men, much e than thy father Job 15:10
because they were e than he Job 32:4
thine e sister is Samaria, she and Eze 16:46 1419
receive thy sisters, thine e Eze 16:61 1419
names of them were Aholah the e Eze 23:4 1419
Now his e son was in the field Lk 15:25 *4245*
The e shall serve the younger Rom 9:12 *3187*
Rebuke not an e, but intreat him 1Ti 5:1 *4245*
The e women as mothers 1Ti 5:2 *4245*
Against an e receive not an 1Ti 5:19 *4245*
you I exhort, who am also an e 1Pet 5:1 *4850*
submit yourselves unto the e 1Pet 5:5 *4245*
The e unto the elect lady and her 2Jn 1 *4245*
The e unto the wellbeloved Gaius, 3Jn 1 *4245*

ELDERS
of Pharaoh, the e of his house Gen 50:7 2205
all the e of the land of Egypt, Gen 50:7 2205
gather the e of Israel together, Ex 3:16 2205
the e of Israel, unto the king of Ex 3:18 2205
the e of the children of Israel Ex 4:29 2205
called for all the e of Israel Ex 12:21 2205
take with thee of the e of Israel Ex 17:5 2205
in the sight of the e of Israel Ex 17:6 2205
all the e of Israel, to eat bread Ex 18:12 2205
and called for the e of the people Ex 19:7 2205
and seventy of the e of Israel Ex 24:1 2205
and seventy of the e of Israel Ex 24:9 2205
And he said unto the e, Tarry ye Ex 24:14 2205
the e of the congregation shall Lev 4:15 2205
and his sons, and the e of Israel Lev 9:1 2205
me seventy men of the e of Israel Num 11:16 2205
knowest to be the e of the people Num 11:16 2205
men of the e of the people Num 11:24 2205
and gave it unto the seventy e Num 11:25 2205
the camp, he and the e of Israel Num 11:30 2205
the e of Israel followed him Num 16:25 2205
And Moab said unto the e of Midian Num 22:4 2205
e of Moab and the e of Midian Num 22:7 2205
heads of your tribes, and your e Deut 5:23 2205
Then the e of his city shall send Deut 19:12 2205
Then thy e and thy judges shall Deut 21:2 2205
even the e of that city shall Deut 21:3 2205
the e of that city shall bring Deut 21:4 2205
all the e of that city, that are Deut 21:6 2205
him out unto the e of his city Deut 21:19 2205
shall say unto the e of his city Deut 21:20 2205
the e of the city in the gate Deut 22:15 2205
father shall say unto the e Deut 22:16 2205
cloth before the e of the city Deut 22:17 2205
the e of that city shall take Deut 22:18 2205
wife go up to the gate unto the e Deut 25:7 2205
Then the e of his city shall call Deut 25:8 2205
unto him in the presence of the e Deut 25:9 2205
Moses with the e of Israel Deut 27:1 2205
captains of your tribes, your e Deut 29:10 2205
LORD, and unto all the e of Israel Deut 31:9 2205
unto me all the e of your tribes Deut 31:28 2205
thy e, and they will tell thee Deut 32:7 2205
the e of Israel, and put dust upon Josh 7:6 2205
the e of Israel, before the Josh 8:10 2205
And all Israel, and their e Josh 8:33 2205
Wherefore our e and all the Josh 9:11 2205
in the ears of the e of that city Josh 20:4 2205
for all Israel, and for their e Josh 23:2 2205
and called for the e of Israel Josh 24:1 2205
all the days of the e that Josh 24:31 2205
all the days of the e that Judg 2:7 2205
the e thereof, even threescore and Judg 8:14 2205
And he took the e of the city Judg 8:16 2205
the e of Gilead went to fetch Judg 11:5 2205
said unto the e of Gilead Judg 11:7 2205
the e of Gilead said unto Judg 11:8 2205
said unto the e of Gilead Judg 11:9 2205
the e of Gilead said unto Judg 11:10 2205
went with the e of Gilead Judg 11:11 2205
Then the e of the congregation Judg 21:16 2205
took ten men of the e of the city Ruth 4:2 2205
before the e of my people Ruth 4:4 2205
And Boaz said unto the e, and unto Ruth 4:9 2205
that were in the gate, and the e Ruth 4:11 2205
the e of Israel said, Wherefore 1Sa 4:3 2205
Then all the e of Israel gathered 1Sa 8:4 2205

the e of Jabesh said unto him, 1Sa 11:3 2205
before the e of my people, and 1Sa 15:30 2205
the e of the town trembled at his 1Sa 16:4 2205
of the spoil unto the e of Judah 1Sa 30:26 2205
with the e of Israel, saying, Ye 2Sa 3:17 2205
So all the e of Israel came to 2Sa 5:3 2205
the e of his house arose, and went 2Sa 12:17 2205
well, and all the e of Israel 2Sa 17:4 2205
Absalom and the e of Israel 2Sa 17:15 2205
saying, Speak unto the e of Judah 2Sa 19:11 2205
Solomon assembled the e of Israel 1Kin 8:1 2205
all the e of Israel came, and the 1Kin 8:3 2205
called all the e of the land 1Kin 20:7 2205
And all the e and all the people 1Kin 20:8 2205
and sent the letters unto the e 1Kin 21:8 2205
the men of his city, even the e 1Kin 21:11 2205
his house, and the e sat with him 2Kin 6:32 2205
came to him, he said to the e 2Kin 6:32 2205
the rulers of Jezreel, to the e 2Kin 10:1 2205
the e also, and the bringers up of 2Kin 10:5 2205
the e of the priests, covered 2Kin 19:2 2205
unto him all the e of Judah 2Kin 23:1 2205
Therefore came all the e of 1Chr 11:3 2205
the e of Israel, and the captains 1Chr 15:25 2205
the e of Israel, who were clothed 1Chr 21:16 2205
Solomon assembled the e of Israel 2Chr 5:2 2205
And all the e of Israel came 2Chr 5:4 2205
together all the e of Judah 2Chr 34:29 2205
God was upon the e of the Jews Ezr 5:5 7868
Then asked we those e, and said Ezr 5:9 7868
the e of the Jews build this Ezr 6:7 7868
e of these Jews for the building Ezr 6:8 7868
the e of the Jews builded, and Ezr 6:14 7868
counsel of the princes and the e Ezr 10:8 2205
and with them the e of every city Ezr 10:14 2205
him in the assembly of the e Ps 107:32 2205
sitteth among the e of the land Prov 31:23 2205
the e of the priests covered with Is 37:2 2205
up certain of the e of the land Jer 26:17 2205
of the e which were carried away Jer 29:1 2205
mine e gave up the ghost in the Lam 1:19 2205
The e of the daughter of Zion sit Lam 2:10 2205
priests, they favoured not the e Lam 4:16 2205
the faces of e were not honoured Lam 5:12 2205
The e have ceased from the gate, Lam 5:14 2205
the e of Judah sat before me, Eze 8:1 2205
of the e of Israel unto me Eze 14:1 2205
that certain of the e of Israel Eze 20:1 2205
man, speak unto the e of Israel Eze 20:3 2205
a solemn assembly, gather the e Joel 1:14 2205
the congregation, assemble the e Joel 2:16 2205
transgress the tradition of the e Mt 15:2 4245
and suffer many things of the e Mt 16:21 4245
the e of the people came unto him Mt 21:23 4245
the e of the people, unto the Mt 26:3 4245
chief priests and e of the people Mt 26:47 4245
scribes and the e were assembled Mt 26:57 4245
Now the chief priests, and e Mt 26:59 4245
e of the people took counsel Mt 27:1 4245
silver to the chief priests and e Mt 27:3 4245
accused of the chief priests and e Mt 27:12 4245
e persuaded the multitude that Mt 27:20 4245
him, with the scribes and e Mt 27:41 4245
they were assembled with the e Mt 28:12 4245
holding the tradition of the e Mk 7:3 4245
to the tradition of the e Mk 7:5 4245
things, and be rejected of the e Mk 8:31 4245
priests, and the scribes, and the e Mk 11:27 4245
priest and the scribes and the e Mk 14:43 4245
all the chief priests and the e Mk 14:53 4245
held a consultation with the e Mk 15:1 4245
sent unto him the e of the Jews Lk 7:3 4245
things, and be rejected of the e Lk 9:22 4245
scribes came upon him with the e Lk 20:1 4245
captains of the temple, and the e Lk 22:52 4245
the e of the people and the chief Lk 22:66 4244
morrow, that their rulers, and e Acts 4:5 4245
of the people, and e of Israel, Acts 4:8 4245
priests and e had said unto them Acts 4:23 4245
stirred up the people, and the e Acts 6:12 4245
sent it to the e by the hands of Acts 11:30 4245
ordained them e in every church Acts 14:23 4245
apostles and e about this question Acts 15:2 4245
church, and of the apostles and e Acts 15:4 4245
e came together for to consider Acts 15:6 4245
Then pleased it the apostles and e Acts 15:22 4245
The apostles and e and brethren Acts 15:23 4245
e which were at Jerusalem Acts 16:4 4245
called the e of the church Acts 20:17 4245
and all the e were present Acts 21:18 4245
and all the estate of the e Acts 22:5 4244
came to the chief priests and e Acts 23:14 4245
high priest descended with the e Acts 24:1 4245
the e of the Jews informed me, Acts 25:15 4245
Let the e that rule well be 1Ti 5:17 4245
ordain e in every city, as I had Titus 1:5 4245
For by it the e obtained a good Heb 11:2 4245
him call for the e of the church Jas 5:14 4245
The e which are among you I 1Pet 5:1 4245
twenty e sitting, clothed in Rev 4:4 4245
twenty e fall down before him Rev 4:10 4245
one of the e saith unto me, Weep Rev 5:5 4245
beasts, and in the midst of the e Rev 5:6 4245
twenty e fell down before the Rev 5:8 4245
the throne and the beasts and the e Rev 5:11 4245
twenty e fell down and worshipped Rev 5:14 4245
about the throne, and about the e Rev 7:11 4245
And one of the e answered, saying Rev 7:13 4245
And the four and twenty e, which Rev 11:16 4245
before the four beasts, and the e Rev 14:3 4245
And the four and twenty e and the Rev 19:4 4245

ELDEST

unto his e servant of his house Gen 24:2 2205
not see, he called Esau his e son Gen 27:1 1419
goodly raiment of her e son Esau Gen 27:15 1419
And he searched, and began at the e Gen 44:12 1419
of Reuben, Israel's e son Num 1:20 1060
Reuben, the e son of Israel Num 26:5 1060
the three e sons of Jesse went and 1Sa 17:13 1419
the three e followed Saul 1Sa 17:14 1419
Eliab his e brother heard when he 1Sa 17:28 1419
Then he took his e son that 2Kin 3:27 1060
to the camp had slain all the e 2Chr 22:1 7223
wine in their e brother's house Job 1:13 1060
wine in their e brother's house Job 1:18 1060
one by one, beginning at the e Jn 8:9 4245

ELEAD (e'-le-ad) *A descendant of Ephraim.*

Shuthelah his son, and Ezer, and E 1Chr 7:21 496

ELEADAH See ELADAH.

ELEALEH (el-e-a'-leh) *An Amorite village.*

and Nimrah, and Heshbon, and E Num 32:3 500
of Reuben built Heshbon, and E Num 32:37 500
And Heshbon shall cry, and E Is 15:4 500
with my tears, O Heshbon, and E Is 16:9 500
the cry of Heshbon even unto E Jer 48:34 500

ELEASAH (el-e'-a-sah) See ELASAH.

1. A son of Helez.
begat Helez, and Helez begat E 1Chr 2:39 501
E begat Sisamai, and Sisamai begat 1Chr 2:40 501
2. A descendant of King Saul.
his son, E his son, Azel his son 1Chr 8:37 501
his son, E his son, Azel his son 1Chr 9:43 501

ELEAZAR (el-e-a'-zar)

1. A son of Aaron.
she bare him Nadab, and Abihu, E Ex 6:23 499
E Aaron's son took him one of the Ex 6:25 499
even Aaron, Nadab and Abihu, E Ex 28:1 499
Moses said unto Aaron, and unto E Lev 10:6 499
Moses spake unto Aaron, and unto E Lev 10:12 499
and he was angry with E and Ithamar Lev 10:16 499
Nadab the firstborn, and Abihu, E Num 3:2 499
and E and Ithamar ministered in the Num 3:4 499
E the son of Aaron the priest Num 3:32 499
to the office of E the son of Num 4:16 499
Speak unto E the son of Aaron the Num 16:37 499
E the priest took the brasen Num 16:39 499
shall give her unto E the priest Num 19:3 499
E the priest shall take of her Num 19:4 499
E his son, and bring them up unto Num 20:25 499
and put them upon E his son Num 20:26 499
and put them upon E his son Num 20:28 499
E came down from the mount Num 20:28 499
And when Phinehas, the son of E Num 25:7 499
Phinehas, the son of E, the son Num 25:11 499
unto E the son of Aaron the Num 26:1 499
E the priest spake with them in Num 26:3 499
Aaron was born Nadab, and Abihu, E Num 26:60 499
E the priest, who numbered the Num 26:63 499
before E the priest, and before Num 27:2 499
And set him before E the priest Num 27:19 499
shall stand before E the priest Num 27:21 499
and set him before E the priest Num 27:22 499
Phinehas the son of E the priest Num 31:6 499
E the priest, and unto the Num 31:12 499
E the priest, and all the princes Num 31:13 499
E the priest said unto the men of Num 31:21 499
E the priest, and the chief Num 31:26 499
and give it unto E the priest Num 31:29 499
E the priest did as the LORD Num 31:31 499
unto E the priest, as the LORD Num 31:41 499
E the priest took the gold of Num 31:51 499
E the priest took the gold of the Num 31:54 499
to E the priest, and unto the Num 32:2 499
them Moses commanded E the priest Num 32:28 499
E the priest, and Joshua the son Num 34:17 499
E his son ministered in the Deut 10:6 499
which E the priest, and Joshua the Josh 14:1 499
came near before E the priest Josh 17:4 499
which E the priest, and Joshua the Josh 19:51 499
of the Levites unto E the priest Josh 21:1 499
Phinehas the son of E the priest Josh 22:13 499
Phinehas the son of E the priest Josh 22:31 499
Phinehas the son of E the priest Josh 22:32 499
And E the son of Aaron died Josh 24:33 499
And Phinehas, the son of E Judg 20:28 499
Nadab, and Abihu, E, and Ithamar 1Chr 6:3 499
E begat Phinehas, Phinehas begat 1Chr 6:4 499
E his son, Phinehas his son, 1Chr 6:50 499
Phinehas the son of E was the 1Chr 9:20 499
Nadab, and Abihu, E, and Ithamar 1Chr 24:1 499
therefore E and Ithamar executed 1Chr 24:2 499
them, both Zadok of the sons of E 1Chr 24:3 499
of E than of the sons of Ithamar 1Chr 24:4 499
Among the sons of E there were 1Chr 24:4 499
of God, were of the sons of E 1Chr 24:5 499
household being taken for E 1Chr 24:6 499
the son of Phinehas, the son of E Ezr 7:5 499
2. Son of Abinadab.
sanctified E his son to keep the 1Sa 7:1 499
3. A son of Dodo.
after him was E the son of Dodo 2Sa 23:9 499
after him was E the son of Dodo, 1Chr 11:12 499
4. Son of Mahli.
The sons of Mahli; E, and Kish 1Chr 23:21 499
E died, and had no sons, but 1Chr 23:22 499
Of Mahli came E, who had no sons 1Chr 24:28 499
5. Son of Phinehas.
with him was E the son of Ezr 8:33 499
6. Married a foreign wife.
and Malchiah, and Miamin, and E Ezr 10:25
7. A priest in Nehemiah's time.
And Maaseiah, and Shemaiah, and E Neh 12:42 499

8. Son of Eliud; ancestor of Jesus.
And Eliud begat E Mt 1:15 1648
and E begat Matthan Mt 1:15 1648

ELECT

mine e, in whom my soul Is 42:1 972
servant's sake, and Israel mine e Is 45:4 972
mine e shall inherit it, and my Is 65:9 972
mine e shall long enjoy the work Is 65:22 972
they shall deceive the very e Mt 24:24 1588
his e from the four winds Mt 24:31 1588
if it were possible, even the e Mk 13:22 1588
his e from the four winds Mk 13:27 1588
And shall not God avenge his own e Lk 18:7 1588
thing to the charge of God's e Rom 8:33 1588
Put on therefore, as the e of God Col 3:12 1588
the e angels, that thou observe 1Ti 5:21 1588
according to the faith of God's e Titus 1:1 1588
E according to the foreknowledge 1Pet 1:2 1588
in Sion a chief corner stone, e 1Pet 2:6 1588
The elder unto the e lady 2Jn 1 1588
of thy e sister greet thee 2Jn 13 1588

ELECTED

e together with you, saluteth you 1Pet 5:13 4899

ELECTION

of God according to e might stand Rom 9:11 1589
according to the e of grace Rom 11:5 1589
but the e hath obtained it, and Rom 11:7 1589
but as touching the e, they are Rom 11:28 1589
brethren beloved, your e of God 1Th 1:4 1589
to make your calling and e sure 2Pet 1:10 1589

ELECT'S

but for the e sake those days Mt 24:22 1588
but for the e sake, whom he hath Mk 13:20 1588
endure all things for the e sakes 2Ti 2:10 1588

EL-ELOHE-ISRAEL (el-el-o''-he-iz'-rah-el) *An altar of Jacob near Shechem.*

there an altar, and called it E Gen 33:20 415

ELEMENTS

bondage under the e of the world Gal 4:3 4747
again to the weak and beggarly e Gal 4:9 4747
the e shall melt with fervent 2Pet 3:10 4747
the e shall melt with fervent 2Pet 3:12 4747

ELEPH (e'-lef) *A town in Benjamin.*

And Zelah, E, and Jebusi, which is Josh 18:28 507

ELEVEN

his e sons, and passed over the Gen 32:22
the e stars made obeisance to me Gen 37:9
e curtains shalt thou make Ex 26:7
the e curtains shall be all of Ex 26:8
e curtains he made them Ex 36:14
the e curtains were of one size Ex 36:15
And on the third day e bullocks Num 29:20
(There are e days' journey from Deut 1:2
e cities with their villages Josh 15:51
of us e hundred pieces of silver Judg 16:5
The e hundred shekels of silver Judg 17:2
when he had restored the e Judg 17:3
he reigned e years in Jerusalem 2Kin 23:36
he reigned e years in Jerusalem 2Kin 24:18
he reigned e years in Jerusalem 2Chr 36:5
reigned e years in Jerusalem 2Chr 36:11
he reigned e years in Jerusalem Jer 52:1
cubits, and the breadth e cubits Eze 40:49
Then the e disciples went away Mt 28:16 1733
unto the e as they sat at meat Mk 16:14 1733
told all these things unto the e Lk 24:9 1733
found the e gathered together, and Lk 24:33 1733
was numbered with the e apostles Acts 1:26 1733
But Peter, standing up with the e Acts 2:14 1733

ELEVENTH

On the e day Pagiel the son of Num 7:72
the fortieth year, in the e month Deut 1:3
And in the e year, in the month 1Kin 6:38
in the e year of Joram the son of 2Kin 9:29
unto the e year of king Zedekiah 2Kin 25:2
the tenth, Machbanai the e 1Chr 12:13
The e to Eliashib, the twelfth to 1Chr 24:12
The e to Azareel, he, his sons, 1Chr 25:18
The e captain for the e 1Chr 27:14
unto the end of the e year of Jer 1:3
in the e year of Zedekiah, in the Jer 39:2
unto the e year of king Zedekiah Jer 52:5
And it came to pass in the e year Eze 26:1
And it came to pass in the e year Eze 30:20
And it came to pass in the e year Eze 31:1
and twentieth day of the e month Zec 1:7
about the e hour he went out, and Mt 20:6 1734
that were hired about the e hour Mt 20:9 1734
the e, a jacinth Rev 21:20 1734

ELHANAN (el-ha'-nan)

1. Son of Jair.
where E the son of Jaare-oregim, 2Sa 21:19 445
E the son of Jair slew Lahmi the 1Chr 20:5 445
2. Son of Dodo.
E the son of Dodo of Beth-lehem, 2Sa 23:24 445
E the son of Dodo of Beth-lehem, 1Chr 11:26 445

ELI (e'-li) See ELI'S, ELOI.

1. A High Priest of Israel.
And the two sons of E, Hophni and 1Sa 1:3 5941
Now E the priest sat upon a seat 1Sa 1:9 5941
the LORD, that E marked her mouth 1Sa 1:12 5941
therefore E thought she had been 1Sa 1:13 5941
E said unto her, How long wilt 1Sa 1:14 5941
Then E answered and said, Go in 1Sa 1:17 5941
and brought the child to E 1Sa 1:25 5941
unto the LORD before E the priest 1Sa 2:11 5941
Now the sons of E were sons of 1Sa 2:12 5941
E blessed Elkanah and his wife, and 1Sa 2:20 5941

Now *E* was very old, and heard all 1Sa 2:22 5941
And there came a man of God unto *E*. 1Sa 2:27 5941
ministered unto the LORD before *E*......... 1Sa 3:1 5941
when *E* was laid down in his place....... 1Sa 3:2 5941
And he ran unto *E*, and said, Here....... 1Sa 3:5 5941
And Samuel arose and went to *E*.......... 1Sa 3:6 5941
And he arose and went to *E*, and said . 1Sa 3:8 5941
E perceived that the LORD had............. 1Sa 3:8 5941
Therefore *E* said unto Samuel, Go,........ 1Sa 3:9 5941
E all things which I have spoken 1Sa 3:12 5941
I have sworn unto the house of *E*.......... 1Sa 3:14 5941
feared to shew *E* the vision.................. 1Sa 3:15 5941
Then *E* called Samuel, and said,............ 1Sa 3:16 5941
and the two sons of *E*, Hophni and......... 1Sa 4:4 5941
and the two sons of *E*, Hophni and......... 1Sa 4:11 5941
E sat upon a seat by the wayside......... 1Sa 4:13 5941
when *E* heard the noise of the.............. 1Sa 4:14 5941
man came in hastily, and told *E*........... 1Sa 4:14 5941
Now *E* was ninety and eight years 1Sa 4:15 5941
And the man said unto *E*, I am he......... 1Sa 4:16 5941
the son of Phinehas, the son of *E*.......... 1Sa 14:3 5941
the house of *E* in Shiloh 1Kin 2:27 5941
2. An Aramaic term for God.
with a loud voice, saying, Eli, *E*.............. Mt 27:46 *2241*

ELIAB (*e'-le-ab*) See ELIAB'S, ELIEL.
1. Son of Helon.
E the son of Helon .... Num 1:9 446
E the son of Helon shall be................... Num 2:7 446
the third day *E* the son of Helon........... Num 7:24 446
offering of *E* the son of Helon.............. Num 7:29 446
of Zebulun was *E* the son of Helon .... Num 10:16 446
2. Father of Dathan.
Dathan and Abiram, the sons of *E*........ Num 16:1 446
Dathan and Abiram, the sons of *E*......... Num 16:12 446
the sons of Pallu; *E*.............................. Num 26:8 446
And the sons of *E*.................................. Num 26:9 446
Dathan and Abiram, the sons of *E*......... Deut 11:6 446
3. A son of Jesse.
were come, that he looked on *E*............. 1Sa 16:6 446
the battle were *E* the first born............. 1Sa 17:13 446
E his eldest brother heard when 1Sa 17:28 446
And Jesse begat his firstborn *E*............. 1Chr 2:13 446
daughter of *E* the son of Jesse.............. 2Chr 11:18 446
4. A Levite ancestor of Samuel.
E his son, Jeroham his son,.................... 1Chr 6:27 446
5. A leader in David's army.
Obadiah the second, *E* the third, ... 1Chr 12:9 446
6. A Levite in David's time.
and Jehiel, and Unni, *E*, and................. 1Chr 15:18 446
and Jehiel, and Unni, and *E*................... 1Chr 15:20 446
and Jehiel, and Mattithiah, and *E* 1Chr 16:5 446

ELIAB'S (*e'-le-abs*)
E anger was kindled against David....... 1Sa 17:28 446

ELIADA (*e-li'-a-dah*) See ELIADAH.
1. A son of David.
And Elishama, and *E*, and Eliphalet...... 2Sa 5:16 450
And Elishama, and *E*, and Eliphelet,..... 1Chr 3:8 450
E a mighty man of valour, and with....... 2Chr 17:17 450

ELIADAH (*e-li'-a-dah*) See ELIADA. *An opponent of King Saul.*
adversary, Rezon the son of *E*.............. 1Kin 11:23 450

ELIAH (*e-li'-ah*) See ELIJAH. *A son of Jeroham.*
And Jaresiah, and *E*, and Zichri, the 1Chr 8:27 452
and Abdi, and Jeremoth, and *E*............. Ezr 10:26 452

ELIAHBA (*e-li'-ah-bah*) *A "mighty man" of David.*
E the Shaalbonite, of the sons of........... 2Sa 23:32 455
Baharumite, *E* the Shaalbonite,............. 1Chr 11:33 455

ELIAKIM (*e-li'-a-kim*) See JEHOIAKIM.
1. A son of Hilkiah.
out to them *E* the son of Hilkiah........... 2Kin 18:18 471
Then said *E* the son of Hilkiah............... 2Kin 18:26 471
Then came *E* the son of Hilkiah,............ 2Kin 18:37 471
And he sent *E*, which was over the 2Kin 19:2 471
my servant *E* the son of Hilkiah .... Is 22:20 471
Then came forth unto him *E*................... Is 36:3 471
Then said *E* and Shebna and Joah .... Is 36:11 471
Then came *E*, the son of Hilkiah,.......... Is 36:22 471
And he sent *E*, who was over the .... Is 37:2 471
2. Original name of Jehoiakim.
Pharaoh-nechoh made *E* the son of...... 2Kin 23:34 471
the king of Egypt made *E* his............... 2Chr 36:4 471
3. A priest who dedicated the wall.
E, Maaseiah, Miniamin, Michaiah,......... Neh 12:41 471
4. Son of Abiud; ancestor of Jesus.
and Abiud begat *E*.................................. Mt 1:13 *1662*
and *E* begat Azor...................................... Mt 1:13 *1662*
of Jonan, which was the son of *E* .... Lk 3:30 *1662*

ELIAM (*e'-le-am*)
1. Father of Bathsheba.
Bath-sheba, the daughter of *E*................ 2Sa 11:3 463
2. A "mighty man" of David.
E the son of Ahithophel the................... 2Sa 23:34 463

ELIAS (*e-li'-as*) See ELIJAH. *Greek form of Elijah.*
if ye will receive it, this is *E*................... Mt 11:14 *2243*
some, *E*; and others, Jeremias .... Mt 16:14 *2243*
them Moses and *E* talking with him..... Mt 17:3 *2243*
and one for Moses, and one for *E* .... Mt 17:4 *2243*
scribes that *E* must first come............... Mt 17:10 *2243*
E truly shall first come, and.................. Mt 17:11 *2243*
That *E* is come already, and they.......... Mt 17:12 *2243*
said, This man calleth for *E*.................. Mt 27:47 *2243*
let us see whether *E* will come to .... Mt 27:49 *2243*
Others said, That it is *E*........................ Mk 6:15 *2243*
but some say, *E*...................................... Mk 8:28 *2243*
appeared unto them *E* with Moses......... Mk 9:4 *2243*
and one for Moses, and one for *E* .... Mk 9:5 *2243*
scribes that *E* must first come............... Mk 9:11 *2243*
E verily cometh first, and...................... Mk 9:12 *2243*
That *E* is indeed come, and they .... Mk 9:13 *2243*
it said, Behold, he calleth *E*................. Mk 15:35 *2243*
let us see whether *E* will come to .... Mk 15:36 *2243*
him in the spirit and power of *E*........... Lk 1:17 *2243*
were in Israel in the days of *E*............. Lk 4:25 *2243*
But unto none of them was *E* sent .... Lk 4:26 *2243*
And of some, that *E* had appeared........ Lk 9:8 *2243*
but some say *E*....................................... Lk 9:19 *2243*
two men, which were Moses and *E* .... Lk 9:30 *2243*
and one for Moses, and one for *E*......... Lk 9:33 *2243*
and consume them, even as *E* did......... Lk 9:54 *2243*
Art thou *E*?... Jn 1:21 *2243*
if thou be not that Christ, nor *E*............ Jn 1:25 *2243*
not what the scripture saith of *E*.......... Rom 11:2 *2243*
E was a man subject to like................... Jas 5:17 *2243*

ELIASAPH (*e-li'-a-saf*)
1. A chief of Gad.
E the son of Deuel .... Num 1:14 460
Gad shall be *E* the son of Reuel........... Num 2:14 460
the sixth day *E* the son of Deuel .... Num 7:42 460
offering of *E* the son of Deuel.............. Num 7:47 460
of Gad was *E* the son of Deuel .... Num 10:20 460
2. A Gershonite leader.
shall be *E* the son of Lael..................... Num 3:24 460

ELIASHIB (*e-li'-a-shib*)
1. A descendant of Judah.
of Elioenai were, Hodaiah, and *E* 1Chr 3:24 475
2. A priest in David's time.
The eleventh to *E*, the twelfth to 1Chr 24:12 475
3. Son of Joiakim.
chamber of Johanan the son of *E* .... Ezr 10:6 475
Joiakim, Joiakim also begat *E*.............. Neh 12:10 475
and *E* begat Joiada.............................. Neh 12:10 475
The Levites in the days of *E*................. Neh 12:22 475
the days of Johanan the son of *E*.......... Neh 12:23 475
4. Married a foreign wife.
Of the singers also; *E*............................ Ezr 10:24 475
5. Son of Zotta.
Elioenai, *E*, Mattaniah, and................. Ezr 10:27 475
6. Son of Bani.
Vaniah, Meremoth, *E*,.............................. Ezr 10:36 475
7. High Priest during Nehemiah's time.
Then *E* the high priest rose up............... Neh 3:1 475
of the house of *E* the high priest........... Neh 3:20 475
from the door of the house of *E*............ Neh 3:21 475
even to the end of the house of *E*.......... Neh 3:21 475
this, *E* the priest, having the .... Neh 13:4 475
of the evil that *E* did for Tobiah .... Neh 13:7 475
the son of *E* the high priest, was........... Neh 13:28 475

ELIATHAH (*e-li'-a-thah*) *A son of Heman.*
and Jerimoth, Hananiah, Hanani, *E*....... 1Chr 25:4 448
The twentieth to *E*, he, his sons,........... 1Chr 25:27 448

ELIDAD (*e-li'-dad*) *Son of Chislon.*
of Benjamin, *E* the son of Chislon .... Num 34:21 449

ELIEHOENAI See ELIHOENAI.

ELIEL (*e'-le-el*) See ELIAH.
1. Head of the house of Manasseh.
even Epher, and Ishi, and *E*.................. 1Chr 5:24 447
2. Son of Jeroham.
the son of Jeroham, the son of *E*.......... 1Chr 6:34 447
3. A son of Shimhi.
And Elienai, and Zilthai, and *E*............ 1Chr 8:20 447
4. A son of Shashak.
And Ishpan, and Heber, and *E*.............. 1Chr 8:22 447
5. A captain in David's army.
E the Mahavite, and Jeribai, and.......... 1Chr 11:46 447
6. A "mighty man" of David.
E, and Obed, and Jasiel the................... 1Chr 11:47 447
7. A Gadite ally of David.
Attai the sixth, *E* the seventh,............... 1Chr 12:11 447
8. A chief of Judah.
E the chief, and his brethren 1Chr 15:9 447
9. A chief Levite.
Asaiah, and Joel, Shemaiah, and *E* 1Chr 15:11 447
10. A Levite in Hezekiah's time.
and Jerimoth, and Jozabad, and *E* 2Chr 31:13 447

ELIENAI (*e-li-e'-nahee*) *A son of Shimhi.*
And *E*, and Zilthai, and Eliel,.................. 1Chr 8:20 462

ELIEZER
of my house is this *E* of Damascus....... Gen 15:2 461
And the name of the other was *E*........... Ex 18:4 461
Zemira, and Joash, and *E*, and.............. 1Chr 7:8 461
and Zechariah, and Benaiah, and *E* 1Chr 15:24 461
sons of Moses were, Gershom, and *E*..... 1Chr 23:15 461
And the sons of *E* were, Rehabiah 1Chr 23:17 461
And *E* had none other sons 1Chr 23:17 461
And his brethren by *E*........................... 1Chr 26:25 461
was *E* the son of Zichri.......................... 1Chr 27:16 461
Then *E* the son of Dodavah of................ 2Chr 20:37 461
Then sent I for *E*, for Ariel, for............. Ezr 8:16 461
Maaseiah, and *E*, and Jarib, and .... Ezr 10:18 461
Kelita,) Pethahiah, Judah, and *E* .... Ezr 10:23 461
E, Ishijah, Malchiah, Shemaiah,............. Ezr 10:31 461
of Jose, which was the son of *E* .... Lk 3:29 *1663*

ELIHOENAI (*e-li-ho-e'-nahee*) See ELIOENAI. *A family of exiles.*
E the son of Zerahiah, and with .... Ezr 8:4 454

ELIHOREPH (*e-li-ho'-ref*) *A scribe of Solomon.*
E and Ahiah, the sons of Shisha,............ 1Kin 4:3 456

ELIHU (*e-li'-hew*)
1. Great-grandfather of Samuel.
the son of Jeroham, the son of *E*.......... 1Sa 1:1 453
2. A soldier of David.
and Michael, and Jozabad, and *E* 1Chr 12:20 453
3. A Tabernacle servant.
whose brethren were strong men, *E*..... 1Chr 26:7 453
4. Brother of David.
Of Judah, *E*, one of the brethren 1Chr 27:18 453
5. A friend of Job.
Then was kindled the wrath of *E*............ Job 32:2 453
Now *E* had waited till Job had............... Job 32:4 453
When *E* saw that there was no.............. Job 32:5 453
E the son of Barachel the Buzite............ Job 32:6 453
Furthermore *E* answered and said, ... Job 34:1 453
E spake moreover, and said,................... Job 35:1 453
E also proceeded, and said,.................... Job 36:1 453

ELIJAH (*e-li'-jah*) See ELIAH, ELIAS.
1. The prophet.
E the Tishbite, who was of the 1Kin 17:1 452
E said unto her, Fear not....................... 1Kin 17:13 452
did according to the saying of *E*............. 1Kin 17:15 452
of the LORD, which he spake by *E*........... 1Kin 17:16 452
And she said unto *E*, What have I 1Kin 17:18 452
And the LORD heard the voice of *E*......... 1Kin 17:22 452
E took the child, and brought him......... 1Kin 17:23 452
E said, See, thy son liveth 1Kin 17:23 452
And the woman said to *E*, Now by......... 1Kin 17:24 452
LORD came to *E* in the third year........... 1Kin 18:1 452
E went to shew himself unto Ahab......... 1Kin 18:2 452
was in the way, behold, *E* met him........ 1Kin 18:7 452
and said, Art thou that my lord *E*.......... 1Kin 18:7 452
tell thy lord, Behold, *E* is here............... 1Kin 18:8 452
tell thy lord, Behold, *E* is here............... 1Kin 18:11 452
tell thy lord, Behold, *E* is here............... 1Kin 18:14 452
E said, As the LORD of hosts................... 1Kin 18:15 452
and Ahab went to meet *E*....................... 1Kin 18:16 452
it came to pass, when Ahab saw *E*.......... 1Kin 18:17 452
E came unto all the people, and 1Kin 18:21 452
Then said *E* unto the people, I,............... 1Kin 18:22 452
E said unto the prophets of Baal, ... 1Kin 18:25 452
that *E* mocked them, and said, Cry 1Kin 18:27 452
E said unto all the people, Come 1Kin 18:30 452
E took twelve stones, according 1Kin 18:31 452
that *E* the prophet came near, and 1Kin 18:36 452
E said unto them, Take the..................... 1Kin 18:40 452
E brought them down to the brook 1Kin 18:40 452
E said unto Ahab, Get thee up,............... 1Kin 18:41 452
E went up to the top of Carmel.............. 1Kin 18:42 452
And the hand of the LORD was on *E* 1Kin 18:46 452
told Jezebel all that *E* had done............ 1Kin 19:1 452
Jezebel sent a messenger unto *E*........... 1Kin 19:2 452
unto him, What doest thou here, *E* 1Kin 19:9 452
when *E* heard it, that he wrapped........... 1Kin 19:13 452
and said, What doest thou here, *E*.......... 1Kin 19:13 452
E passed by him, and cast his................ 1Kin 19:19 452
he left the oxen, and ran after *E* 1Kin 19:20 452
Then he arose, and went after *E* 1Kin 19:21 452
the LORD came to *E* the Tishbite.............. 1Kin 21:17 452
And Ahab said to *E*, Hast thou 1Kin 21:20 452
the LORD came to *E* the Tishbite.............. 1Kin 21:28 452
the LORD said to *E* the Tishbite 2Kin 1:3 452
And *E* departed....................................... 2Kin 1:4 452
And he said, It is *E* the Tishbite 2Kin 1:8 452
E answered and said to the captain 2Kin 1:10 452
E answered and said unto them, If 2Kin 1:12 452
and fell on his knees before *E* 2Kin 1:13 452
the angel of the LORD said unto *E*........... 2Kin 1:15 452
of the LORD which *E* had spoken 2Kin 1:17 452
up *E* into heaven by a whirlwind 2Kin 2:1 452
that *E* went with Elisha from.................. 2Kin 2:1 452
E said unto Elisha, Tarry here, I............. 2Kin 2:2 452
E said unto him, Elisha, tarry 2Kin 2:4 452
E said unto him, Tarry, I pray................ 2Kin 2:6 452
E took his mantle, and wrapped it.......... 2Kin 2:8 452
that *E* said unto Elisha, Ask what........... 2Kin 2:9 452
E went up by a whirlwind into 2Kin 2:11 452
mantle of *E* that fell from him 2Kin 2:13 452
mantle of *E* that fell from him 2Kin 2:14 452
said, Where is the LORD God of *E*........... 2Kin 2:14 452
The spirit of *E* doth rest on................... 2Kin 2:15 452
poured water on the hands of *E* 2Kin 3:11 452
by his servant *E* the Tishbite.................. 2Kin 9:36 452
which he spake by his servant *E*............. 2Kin 10:10 452
of the LORD, which he spake to *E* 2Kin 10:17 452
writing to him from *E* the prophet.......... 2Chr 21:12 452
I will send you *E* the prophet.................. Mal 4:5 452
2. Married a foreign wife.
Maaseiah, and *E*, and Shemaiah, and...... Ezr 10:21 452

ELIKA (*e-li'-kah*) *A guard of David.*
the Harodite, *E* the Harodite,...................... 2Sa 23:25 470

ELIM (*e'-lim*) See BEER-ELIM. *An encampment during the Exodus.*
And they came to *E*, where were.......... Ex 15:27 362
And they took their journey from *E*....... Ex 16:1 362
of Sin, which is between *E*..................... Ex 16:1 362
from Marah, and came unto *E*............... Num 33:9 362
in *E* were twelve fountains of .... Num 33:9 362
And they removed from *E*, and.............. Num 33:10 362

ELIMELECH (*e-lim'-e-lek*) See ELIMELECH'S. *Husband of Naomi.*
And the name of the man was *E*........... Ruth 1:2 458
And *E* Naomi's husband died................. Ruth 1:3 458
man of wealth, of the family of *E*.......... Ruth 2:1 458
Boaz, who was of the kindred of *E*........ Ruth 2:3 458

ELIMELECH'S
of land, which was our brother *E*........... Ruth 4:3 458
that I have bought all that was *E*........... Ruth 4:9 458

ELIOENAI (*e-li-o-e'-nahee*) See ELIHOENAI.
1. A son of Neariah.
E, and Hezekiah, and Azrikam, three... 1Chr 3:23 454
And the sons of *E* were, Hodaiah,.......... 1Chr 3:24 454
2. A Simeonite prince.
And *E*, and Jaakobah, and Jeshohaiah, 1Chr 4:36 454
3. A son of Becher.
and Joash, and Eliezer, and *E*................ 1Chr 7:8 454
4. A Temple servant.

the sixth, *E* the seventh ... 1Chr 26:3 454
5. Married a foreign wife.
E, Maaseiah, Ishmael, Nethaneel, ... Ezr 10:22 454
6. A son of Zattu.
E, Eliashib, Mattaniah, and ... Ezr 10:27 454
7. A priest during Nehemiah's time.
Maaseiah, Miniamin, Michaiah, *E* ... Neh 12:41 454

ELIPHAL *(el'-i-fal) A captain in David's army.*
the Hararite, *E* the son of Ur, ... 1Chr 11:35 465

ELIPHALET *(e-lif'-a-let)* See ELIPHELET, ELPALET. *A son of David.*
And Elishama, and Eliada, and *E* ... 2Sa 5:16 467
And Elishama, and Beeliada, and *E* ... 1Chr 14:7 467

ELIPHAZ *(el'-if-az)*
1. A son of Esau.
And Adah bare to Esau *E* ... Gen 36:4 464
E the son of Adah the wife of ... Gen 36:10 464
And the sons of *E* were Teman ... Gen 36:11 464
was concubine to *E* Esau's son ... Gen 36:12 464
and she bare to *E* Amalek ... Gen 36:12 464
the sons of *E* the firstborn son ... Gen 36:15 464
came of *E* in the land of Edom ... Gen 36:16 464
E, Reuel, and Jeush, and Jaalam, and ... 1Chr 1:35 464
The sons of *E*; Teman, and ... 1Chr 1:36 464
2. A friend of Job.
E the Temanite, and Bildad the ... Job 2:11 464
Then *E* the Temanite answered and ... Job 4:1 464
Then answered *E* the Temanite ... Job 15:1 464
Then *E* the Temanite answered and ... Job 22:1 464
the LORD said to *E* the Temanite ... Job 42:7 464
So *E* the Temanite and Bildad the ... Job 42:9 464

ELIPHELEH *(e-lif'-e-leh) A Levite singer.*
and Maaseiah, and Mattithiah, and *E* ... 1Chr 15:18 465
And Mattithiah, and *E*, and Mikneiah, ... 1Chr 15:21 465

ELIPHELEHU See ELIPHELEH.

ELIPHELET *(e-lif'-e-let)* See ELIPHALET.
1. A "mighty man" of David.
E the son of Ahasbai, the son of ... 2Sa 23:34 467
2. A son of David.
Ibhar also, and Elishama, and *E* ... 1Chr 3:6 467
3. Same as Eliphat.
And Elishama, and Eliada, and *E* ... 1Chr 3:8 467
4. A descendant of King Saul.
Jehush the second, and *E* the third ... 1Chr 8:39 467
5. A family of exiles.
whose names are these, *E* ... Ezr 8:13 467
6. A son of Hashum.
Mattenai, Mattathah, Zabad, *E* ... Ezr 10:33 467

ELI'S *(e'-lize) Refers to Eli 1.*
that the iniquity of *E* house ... 1Sa 3:14 5941

ELISABETH *(e-liz'-a-beth)* See ELISABETH'S. *Mother of John the Baptist.*
of Aaron, and her name was *E* ... Lk 1:5 *1665*
child, because that *E* was barren ... Lk 1:7 *1665*
thy wife *E* shall bear thee a son, ... Lk 1:13 *1665*
those days his wife *E* conceived ... Lk 1:24 *1665*
And, behold, thy cousin *E*, she ... Lk 1:36 *1665*
house of Zacharias, and saluted *E* ... Lk 1:40 *1665*
when *E* heard the salutation of ... Lk 1:41 *1665*
E was filled with the Holy Ghost ... Lk 1:41 *1665*

ELISABETH'S *(e-liz'-a-beths)*
Now *E* full time came that she ... Lk 1:57 *1665*

ELISEUS *(el-i-se'-us)* See ELISHA. *Greek form of Elisha.*
in the time of *E* the prophet ... Lk 4:27 *1666*

ELISHA *(e-li'-shah)* See ELISEUS. *A prophet.*
and *E* the son of Shaphat of ... 1Kin 19:16 477
the sword of Jehu shall *E* slay ... 1Kin 19:17 477
found *E* the son of Shaphat, who ... 1Kin 19:19 477
Elijah went with *E* from Gilgal ... 2Kin 2:1 477
And Elijah said unto *E*, Tarry here ... 2Kin 2:2 477
E said unto him, As the LORD ... 2Kin 2:2 477
were at Beth-el came forth to *E* ... 2Kin 2:3 477
And Elijah said unto him, *E* ... 2Kin 2:4 477
that were at Jericho came to *E* ... 2Kin 2:5 477
over, that Elijah said unto *E* ... 2Kin 2:9 477
E said, I pray thee, let a double ... 2Kin 2:9 477
E saw it, and he cried, My father, ... 2Kin 2:12 477
and thither: and *E* went over ... 2Kin 2:14 477
spirit of Elijah doth rest on *E* ... 2Kin 2:15 477
the men of the city said unto *E* ... 2Kin 2:19 477
to the saying of *E* which he spake ... 2Kin 2:22 477
Here is *E* the son of Shaphat, ... 2Kin 3:11 477
E said unto the king of Israel, ... 2Kin 3:13 477
E said, As the LORD of hosts ... 2Kin 3:14 477
the sons of the prophets unto *E* ... 2Kin 4:1 477
E said unto her, What shall I do ... 2Kin 4:2 477
that *E* passed to Shunem, where ... 2Kin 4:8 477
season that *E* had said unto her ... 2Kin 4:17 477
when *E* was come into the house, ... 2Kin 4:32 477
And *E* came again to Gilgal ... 2Kin 4:38 477
when *E* the man of God had heard ... 2Kin 5:8 477
at the door of the house of *E* ... 2Kin 5:9 477
E sent a messenger unto him, ... 2Kin 5:10 477
the servant of *E* the man of God ... 2Kin 5:20 477
E said unto him, Whence comest ... 2Kin 5:25 477
sons of the prophets said unto *E* ... 2Kin 6:1 477
but *E*, the prophet that is in ... 2Kin 6:12 477
E prayed, and said, LORD, I pray ... 2Kin 6:17 477
and chariots of fire round about *E* ... 2Kin 6:17 477
E prayed unto the LORD, and said, ... 2Kin 6:18 477
according to the word of *E* ... 2Kin 6:18 477
E said unto them, This is not the ... 2Kin 6:19 477
come into Samaria, that *E* said ... 2Kin 6:20 477
And the king of Israel said unto *E* ... 2Kin 6:21 477
if the head of *E* the son of ... 2Kin 6:31 477
But *E* sat in his house, and the ... 2Kin 6:32 477
Then *E* said, Hear ye the word of ... 2Kin 7:1 477
Then spake *E* unto the woman, ... 2Kin 8:1 477
the great things that *E* hath done ... 2Kin 8:4 477
her son, whom *E* restored to life ... 2Kin 8:5 477
And *E* came to Damascus ... 2Kin 8:7 477
E said unto him, Go, say unto him ... 2Kin 8:10 477
E answered, The LORD hath shewed ... 2Kin 8:13 477
So he departed from *E*, and came to ... 2Kin 8:14 477
said to him, What said *E* to thee ... 2Kin 8:14 477
E the prophet called one of the ... 2Kin 9:1 477
Now *E* was fallen sick of his ... 2Kin 13:14 477
E said unto him, Take bow and ... 2Kin 13:15 477
E put his hands upon the king's ... 2Kin 13:16 477
Then *E* said, Shoot ... 2Kin 13:17 477
E died, and they buried him ... 2Kin 13:20 477
the man into the sepulchre of *E* ... 2Kin 13:21 477
down, and touched the bones of *E* ... 2Kin 13:21 477

ELISHAH *(e-li'-shah) A son of Javan.*
E, and Tarshish, Kittim, and ... Gen 10:4 473
E, and Tarshish, Kittim, and ... 1Chr 1:7 473
purple from the isles of *E* was ... Eze 27:7 473

ELISHAMA *(e-lish'-a-mah)* See ELISHUA.
1. Grandfather of Joshua.
E the son of Ammihud ... Num 1:10 476
shall be *E* the son of Ammihud ... Num 2:18 476
seventh day *E* the son of Ammihud ... Num 7:48 476
offering of *E* the son of Ammihud ... Num 7:53 476
over his host was *E* the son of ... Num 10:22 476
son, Ammihud his son, *E* his son, ... 1Chr 7:26 476
2. A son of David.
And *E*, and Eliada, and Eliphalet ... 2Sa 5:16 476
Ibhar also, and *E*, and Eliphelet, ... 1Chr 3:6 476
And *E*, and Eliada, and Eliphelet, ... 1Chr 3:8 476
And *E*, and Beeliada, and Eliphalet ... 1Chr 14:7 476
3. A descendant of Judah.
the son of Nethaniah the son of *E* ... Jer 41:1 476
4. Son of Jekamiah.
Jekamiah, and Jekamiah begat *E* ... 1Chr 2:41 476
5. Same as Elishua.
son of Nethaniah, the son of *E* ... 2Kin 25:25 476
6. A priest who taught the law.
and with them *E* and Jehoram, ... 2Chr 17:8 476
7. A scribe of Jehoiakim.
even *E* the scribe, and Delaiah the ... Jer 36:12 476
in the chamber of *E* the scribe ... Jer 36:20 476
he took it out of *E* the scribe's ... Jer 36:21 476

ELISHAPHAT *(e-lish'-a-fat) Assisted in making Joash king.*
E the son of Zichri, into ... 2Chr 23:1 478

ELISHEBA *(e-lish'-e-bah) Daughter of Amminadab.*
And Aaron took him *E*, daughter of ... Ex 6:23 472

ELISHUA *(e-lish'-oo-ah)* See ELISHAMA. *A son of David.*
Ibhar also, and *E*, and Nepheg, and ... 2Sa 5:15 474
And Ibhar, and *E*, and Elpalet, ... 1Chr 14:5 474

ELIUD *(e-li'-ud) Son of Achis; ancestor of Jesus.*
and Achim begat *E* ... Mt 1:14 *1664*
And *E* begat Eleazar ... Mt 1:15 *1664*

ELIZABETH See ELISABETH.

ELIZAPHAN *(e-liz'-a-fan)* See ELZAPHAN.
1. Son of Uzziel.
shall be *E* the son of Uzziel ... Num 3:30 469
Of the sons of *E* ... 1Chr 15:8 469
2. Son of Parnach.
of Zebulun, *E* the son of Parnach ... Num 34:25 469
3. A family of Levites.
And of the sons of *E* ... 2Chr 29:13 469

ELIZUR *(e-li'-zur) Son of Shedeur.*
E the son of Shedeur ... Num 1:5 468
shall be *E* the son of Shedeur ... Num 2:10 468
On the fourth day *E* the son of ... Num 7:30 468
offering of *E* the son of Shedeur ... Num 7:35 468
over his host was *E* the son of ... Num 10:18 468

ELKANAH *(el-ka'-nah)*
1. A grandson of Korah.
Assir, and *E*, and Abiasaph ... Ex 6:24 511
E his son, and Ebiasaph his son, ... 1Chr 6:23 511
2. Father of Samuel.
mount Ephraim, and his name was *E* ... 1Sa 1:1 511
when the time was that *E* offered ... 1Sa 1:4 511
Then said *E* her husband to her, ... 1Sa 1:8 511
and *E* knew Hannah his wife ... 1Sa 1:19 511
And the man *E*, and all his house, ... 1Sa 1:21 511
E her husband said unto her, Do ... 1Sa 1:23 511
E went to Ramah to his house ... 1Sa 2:11 511
And Eli blessed *E* and his wife, and ... 1Sa 2:20 511
son, Jeroham his son, *E* his son ... 1Chr 6:27 511
The son of *E*, the son of Jeroham, ... 1Chr 6:34 511
3. A Levite.
the sons of *E*; Amasai, and ... 1Chr 6:25 511
The son of *E*, the son of Joel, ... 1Chr 6:36 511
4. A descendant of Kohath.
the sons of *E* ... 1Chr 6:26 511
The son of Zuph, the son of *E* ... 1Chr 6:35 511
5. Father of Asa.
the son of Asa, the son of *E* ... 1Chr 9:16 511
6. A soldier in David's army.
E, and Jesiah, and Azareel, and ... 1Chr 12:6 511
7. A Levite doorkeeper.
E were doorkeepers for the ark ... 1Chr 15:23 511
8. An officer of King Ahaz.
E that was next to the king ... 2Chr 28:7 511

ELKOSH See ELKOHSHITE.

ELKOSHITE
book of the vision of Nahum the *E* ... Nah 1:1 512

ELLASAR *(el'-la-sar) A Babylonian city.*
king of Shinar, Arioch king of *E* ... Gen 14:1 495
of Shinar, and Arioch king of *E* ... Gen 14:9 495

ELMODAM *(el-mo'-dam) Son of Er.*
of Cosam, which was the son of *E* ... Lk 3:28 *1678*

ELMS
hills, under oaks and poplars and *e* ... Hos 4:13 424

ELNAAM *(el-na'-am) Father of two of David's "mighty men."*
and Joshaviah, the sons of *E* ... 1Chr 11:46 493

ELNATHAN *(el-na'-than)*
1. Father of Nehushta.
the daughter of *E* of Jerusalem ... 2Kin 24:8 494
E the son of Achbor, and certain ... Jer 26:22 494
E the son of Achbor, and Gemariah ... Jer 36:12 494
Nevertheless *E* and Delaiah and ... Jer 36:25 494
2. Name of three Levites during Ezra's time.
for Ariel, for Shemaiah, and for *E* ... Ezr 8:16 494
and for Jarib, and for *E* ... Ezr 8:16 494
also for Joiarib, and for *E* ... Ezr 8:16 494

ELOI *(e-lo'-ee)* See ELI. *Same as Eli 2.*
a loud voice, saying, *E*, *E* ... Mk 15:34 *1682*

ELON *(e'-lon)* See ELONITES.
1. Esau's father-in-law.
the daughter of *E* the Hittite ... Gen 26:34 356
the daughter of *E* the Hittite ... Gen 36:2 356
2. A son of Zebulun.
Sered, and *E*, and Jahleel ... Gen 46:14 356
of *E*, the family of the Elonites ... Num 26:26 356
3. A Danite town.
And *E*, and Thimnathah, and Ekron, ... Josh 19:43 356
4. A judge of Israel.
And after him *E*, a Zebulonite, ... Judg 12:11 356
E the Zebulonite died, and was ... Judg 12:12 356

ELON-BETH-HANAN *(e'-lon-beth-ha'-nan) A Danite town.*
Shaalbim, and Beth-shemesh, and *E* ... 1Kin 4:9 358

ELONITES *(e'-lon-ites) Descendants of Elon 2.*
of Elon, the family of the *E* ... Num 26:26 440

ELOQUENT
the LORD, O my Lord, I am not *e* ... Ex 4:10 1697
artificer, and the *e* orator ... Is 3:3 995
an *e* man, and mighty in the ... Acts 18:24 *3052*

ELOTH *(e'-loth)* See ELATH. *Same as Elath.*
in Ezion-geber, which is beside *E* ... 1Kin 9:26 359
Solomon to Ezion-geber, and to *E* ... 2Chr 8:17 359
He built *E*, and restored it to ... 2Chr 26:2 359

ELPAAL *(el-pa'-al) A son of Shaharaim.*
of Hushim he begat Abitub, and *E* ... 1Chr 8:11 508
The sons of *E*; Eber, and Misham ... 1Chr 8:12 508
Jezliah, and Jobab, the sons of *E* ... 1Chr 8:18 508

ELPALET *(el-pa'-let)* See ELIPHALET. *A son of David.*
And Ibhar, and Elishua, and *E* ... 1Chr 14:5 467

EL-PARAN *(el-pa'-ran) A place in southern Canaan.*
in their mount Seir, unto *E* ... Gen 14:6 364

ELPELET See ELPALET.

ELSE
Give me children, or *e* I die ... Gen 30:1 369
or *e* by the life of Pharaoh ... Gen 42:16
E, if thou wilt not let my people ... Ex 8:21 3588
E, if thou refuse to let my ... Ex 10:4 3588
only, without doing any thing *e* ... Num 20:19
there is none *e* beside him ... Deut 4:35 5750
the earth beneath: there is none *e* ... Deut 4:39 5750
E if ye do in any wise go back, ... Josh 23:12 3588
This is nothing *e* save the sword ... Judg 7:14
if I taste bread, or ought *e* ... 2Sa 3:35
for we shall not *e* escape from ... 2Sa 15:14
is God, and that there is none *e* ... 1Kin 8:60 5750
or *e* thou shalt pay a talent of ... 1Kin 20:39
or *e*, if it please thee, I will ... 1Kin 21:6
or *e* three days the sword of the ... 1Chr 21:12 518
whosoever *e* cometh into the house ... 2Chr 23:7
this is nothing *e* but sorrow of ... Neh 2:2
e would I give it ... Ps 51:16
or who *e* can hasten hereunto, ... Eccl 2:25
I am the LORD, and there is none *e* ... Is 45:5 5750
I am the LORD, and there is none *e* ... Is 45:6 5750
and there is none *e*, there is no ... Is 45:14 5750
and there is none *e* ... Is 45:18 5750
and there is no God *e* beside me ... Is 45:21 5750
for I am God, and there is none *e* ... Is 45:22 5750
for I am God, and there is none *e* ... Is 46:9 5750
heart, I am, and none *e* beside me ... Is 47:8 5750
heart, I am, and none *e* beside me ... Is 47:10 5750
I am the LORD your God, and none *e* ... Joel 2:27 5750
or *e* he will hold to the one, and ... Mt 6:24
e the bottles break, and the wine ... Mt 9:17 *1490*
Or *e* how can one enter into a ... Mt 12:29
or *e* make the tree corrupt, and ... Mt 12:33
e the new piece that filled it up ... Mk 2:21 *1490*
e the new wine doth burst the ... Mk 2:22 *1490*
e the new wine will burst the ... Lk 5:37 *1490*
Or *e*, while the other is yet a ... Lk 14:32 *1490*
or *e* he will hold to the one, and ... Lk 16:13
or *e* believe me for the very ... Jn 14:11 *1490*
spent their time in nothing *e* ... Acts 17:21 2087
Or *e* let these same here say, if ... Acts 24:20
or *e* excusing one another ... Rom 2:15 *2532*
e were your children unclean ... 1Cor 7:14

E

E when thou shalt bless with the 1Cor 14:16 1893
E what shall they do which are 1Cor 15:29 1893
or e be absent, I may hear of .... Phil 1:27
or e I will come unto thee .... Rev 2:5 1490
or e I will come unto thee .... Rev 2:16 1490

ELTEKE See ELTEKEH.

ELTEKEH (*el'-te-keh*) *A Danite city.*
And E, and Gibbethon, and Baalath, ... Josh 19:44 514
E with her suburbs, Gibbethon .... Josh 21:23 514

ELTEKON (*el'-te-kon*) *A city in Judah.*
And Maarath, and Beth-anoth, and E .. Josh 15:59 515

ELTOLAD (*el-to'-lad*) *A city in Judah.*
And E, and Chesil, and Hormah, ... Josh 15:30 513
And E, and Bethul, and Hormah, ... Josh 19:4 513

ELUL (*e'-lul*) *Sixth month of the Hebrew year.*
and fifth day of the month E .... Neh 6:15 435

ELUZAI (*e-loo'-zahee*) *A soldier in David's army.*
E, and Jerimoth, and Bealiah, and 1Chr 12:5 498

ELYMAS (*el'-i-mas*) See BAR-JESUS. *A sorcerer.*
But E the sorcerer (for so is his .... Acts 13:8 1681

ELZABAD (*el'-za-bad*)
1. A soldier in David's army.
Johanan the eighth, E the ninth, ... 1Chr 12:12 443
2. Son of Shemaiah.
Othni, and Rephael, and Obed, E 1Chr 26:7 443

ELZAPHAN (*el'-za-fan*) See ELIZAPHAN. *A son of Uzziel.*
Mishael, and E, and Zithri .... Ex 6:22 469
And Moses called Mishael and E .... Lev 10:4 469

EMBALM
the physicians to e his father .... Gen 50:2 2590

EMBALMED
and the physicians e Israel .... Gen 50:2 2590
the days of those which are e .... Gen 50:3 2590
and they e him, and he was put in a .... Gen 50:26 2590

EMBOLDENED
of him which is weak be e to eat 1Cor 8:10 3618

EMBOLDENETH
or what e thee that thou .... Job 16:3 4834

EMBRACE
time of life, thou shalt e a son 2Kin 4:16 2263
e the rock for want of a shelter .... Job 24:8 2263
to honour, when thou dost e her .... Prov 4:8 2263
e the bosom of a stranger .... Prov 5:20 2263
a time to e, and a time to refrain .... Eccl 3:5 2263
head, and his right hand doth e me .... Song 2:6 2263
and his right hand should e me .... Song 8:3 2263
brought up in scarlet e dunghills .... Lam 4:5 2263

EMBRACED
e him, and kissed him, and brought .... Gen 29:13 2263
e him, and fell on his neck, and .... Gen 33:4 2263
and he kissed them, and e them .... Gen 48:10 2263
e them, and departed for to go .... Acts 20:1 782
e them, and confessed that they .... Heb 11:13 782

EMBRACING
and a time to refrain from e .... Eccl 3:5 2263
him, and e him said, Trouble not .... Acts 20:10 4843

EMBROIDER
thou shalt e the coat of fine .... Ex 28:39 7660

EMBROIDERER
the cunning workman, and of the e .... Ex 35:35 7551
an e in blue, and in purple, and in .... Ex 38:23 7551

EMEK KEZIZ See KEZIZ.

EMERALD
And the second row shall be an e .... Ex 28:18 5306
And the second row, an e, a .... Ex 39:11 5306
the jasper, the sapphire, the e .... Eze 28:13 5306
throne, in sight like unto an e .... Rev 4:3 4664
a chalcedony; the fourth, an e .... Rev 21:19 4665

EMERALDS
they occupied in thy fairs with e .... Eze 27:16 5306

EMERODS
the botch of Egypt, and with the e .... Deut 28:27 6076
them, and smote them with e 1Sa 5:6 6076
they had e in their secret parts 1Sa 5:9 6076
died not were smitten with the e 1Sa 5:12 6076
They answered, Five golden e 1Sa 6:4 6076
ye shall make images of your e 1Sa 6:5 6076
of gold and the images of their e 1Sa 6:11 2914
these are the golden e which the 1Sa 6:17 2914

EMIM See EMIMS.

EMIMS (*e'-mims*) *A race of giants.*
the E in Shaveh Kiriathaim, ... Gen 14:5 368
The E dwelt therein in times past .... Deut 2:10 368
but the Moabites call them E .... Deut 2:11 368

EMINENT
also built unto thee an e place .... Eze 16:24 1354
In that thou buildest thine e .... Eze 16:31 1354
shall throw down thine e place .... Eze 16:39 1354
it upon an high mountain and e .... Eze 17:22 8524

EMITES See EMIMS.

EMMANUEL (*em-man'-uel*) See IMMANUEL. *A Messianic name.*
and they shall call his name E .... Mt 1:23 1694

EMMAUS (*em'-ma-us*) *A village near Jerusalem.*
same day to a village called E .... Lk 24:13 1695

EMMOR (*em'-mor*) See HAMOR. *Father of Sychem.*
sons of E the father of Sychem .... Acts 7:16 1697

EMPIRE
be published throughout all his e .... Est 1:20 4438

EMPLOY
life) to e them in the siege .... Deut 20:19

EMPLOYED
for they were e in that work day 1Chr 9:33 5921
Tikvah were e about this matter .... Ezr 10:15 5975

EMPLOYMENT
sever out men of continual e .... Eze 39:14

EMPTIED
e her pitcher into the trough, and .... Gen 24:20 6168
to pass as they e their sacks .... Gen 42:35 7324
e the chest, and took it, and 2Chr 24:11 6168
even thus be he shaken out, and e .... Neh 5:13 7386
the brooks of defence shall be e .... Is 19:6 1809
The land shall be utterly e .... Is 24:3 1238
hath not been e from vessel to .... Jer 48:11 7324
for the emptiers have e them out .... Nah 2:2 1238

EMPTIERS
for the e have emptied them out, ... Nah 2:2 1238

EMPTINESS
of confusion, and the stones of e .... Is 34:11 922

EMPTY
thou hadst sent me away now e .... Gen 31:42 7387
and the pit was e, there was no .... Gen 37:24 7386
the seven e ears blasted with the .... Gen 41:27 7386
when ye go, ye shall not go e .... Ex 3:21 7387
and none shall appear before me e .... Ex 23:15 7387
And none shall appear before me e .... Ex 34:20 7387
command that they e the house .... Lev 14:36 6437
thou shalt not let him go away e .... Deut 15:13 7387
not appear before the LORD e .... Deut 16:16 7387
with e pitchers, and lamps within .... Judg 7:16 7385
LORD hath brought me home again e .... Ruth 1:21 7387
Go not e unto thy mother in law .... Ruth 3:17 7387
the God of Israel, send it not e 1Sa 6:3 7387
because thy seat will be e 1Sa 20:18 6485
side, and David's place was e 1Sa 20:25 6485
month, that David's place was e 1Sa 20:27 6485
the sword of Saul returned not e 2Sa 1:22 7387
thy neighbours, even e vessels 2Kin 4:3 7385
Thou hast sent widows away e .... Job 22:9 7387
out the north over the e place .... Job 26:7 8414
they e themselves upon the earth .... Eccl 11:3 7324
the LORD maketh the earth e .... Is 24:1 1238
but he awaketh, and his soul is e .... Is 29:8 7385
to make e the soul of the hungry, ... Is 32:6 7324
returned with their vessels e .... Jer 14:3 7387
shall e his vessels, and break .... Jer 48:12 7324
fan her, and shall e her land .... Jer 51:2 1238
me, he hath made me an e vessel .... Jer 51:34 7385
Then set it e upon the coals .... Eze 24:11 7385
Israel is an e vine, he bringeth .... Hos 10:1 1238
She is e, and void, and waste .... Nah 2:10 950
Shall they therefore e their net .... Hab 1:17 7324
pipes e the golden oil out of .... Zec 4:12 7324
when he is come, he findeth it e .... Mt 12:44 4980
and beat him, and sent him away e .... Mk 12:3 2756
and the rich he hath sent e away .... Lk 1:53 2756
beat him, and sent him away e .... Lk 20:10 2756
shamefully, and sent him away e .... Lk 20:11 2756

EMULATION
to e them which are my flesh .... Rom 11:14 3863

EMULATIONS
witchcraft, hatred, variance, e .... Gal 5:20 2205

EN-MISHPAT *Another name for Kadesh.*
And they returned, and came to E .... Gen 14:7 5880

ENABLED
Jesus our Lord, who hath e me 1Ti 1:12 1743

ENAIM

ENAM (*e'-nam*) *A city in Judah.*
and En-gannim, Tappuah, and E .... Josh 15:34 5879

ENAN (*e'-nan*) See HAZAR-ENAN. *Father of Ahira.*
Ahira the son of E .... Num 1:15 5881
shall be Ahira the son of E .... Num 2:29 5881
twelfth day Ahira the son of E .... Num 7:78 5881
offering of Ahira the son of E .... Num 7:83 5881
Naphtali was Ahira the son of E .... Num 10:27 5881

ENCAMP
e before Pi-hahiroth, between .... Ex 14:2 2583
before it shall ye e by the sea .... Ex 14:2 2583
it, and shall e round about the .... Num 1:50 2583
as they e, so shall they set .... Num 2:17 2583
those that e by him shall be the .... Num 2:27 2583
But those that e before the .... Num 3:38 2583
how we are to e in the wilderness .... Num 10:31 2583
e against the city, and take it 2Sa 12:28 2583
e round about my tabernacle .... Job 19:12 2583
an host should e against me .... Ps 27:3 2583
I will e about mine house because .... Zec 9:8 2583

ENCAMPED
e in Etham, in the edge of the .... Ex 13:20 2583
they e there by the waters .... Ex 15:27 2583
where he e at the mount of God .... Ex 18:5 2583
from Elim, and e by the Red sea .... Num 33:10 2583
e in the wilderness of Sin .... Num 33:11 2583
of Sin, and e in Dophkah .... Num 33:12 2583
from Dophkah, and e in Alush .... Num 33:13 2583
e at Rephidim, where was no water .... Num 33:14 2583
and e at Hazeroth .... Num 33:17 2583
mount Shapher, and e in Haradah .... Num 33:24 2583
from Makheloth, and e at Tahath .... Num 33:26 2583
from Hashmonah, and e at Moseroth .... Num 33:30 2583
Bene-jaakan, and e at Hor-hagidgad .... Num 33:32 2583
from Jotbathah, and e at Ebronah .... Num 33:34 2583
from Ebronah, and e at Ezion-gaber .... Num 33:35 2583
and e in Almon-diblathaim .... Num 33:46 2583
e in Gilgal, in the east border .... Josh 4:19 2583
children of Israel e in Gilgal .... Josh 5:10 2583
e before Gibeon, and made war .... Josh 10:5 2583
e against it, and fought against .... Josh 10:31 2583
they e against it, and fought .... Josh 10:34 2583
they e against them, and destroyed .... Judg 6:4 2583
e against Thebez, and took it .... Judg 9:50 2583
gathered together, and e in Gilead .... Judg 10:17 2583
together, and e in Mizpeh .... Judg 10:17 2583
the morning, and e against Gibeah .... Judg 20:19 2583
up, and e against Jabesh-gilead 1Sa 11:1 2583
but the Philistines e in Michmash 1Sa 13:16 2583
my lord, are e in the open fields 2Sa 11:11 2583
the people were e against 1Kin 16:15 2583
the people that were e heard say 1Kin 16:16 2583
e in the valley of Rephaim 1Chr 11:15 2583
e against the fenced cities, and 2Chr 32:1 2583

ENCAMPETH
The angel of the LORD e round .... Ps 34:7 2583
bones of him that e against thee .... Ps 53:5 2583

ENCAMPING
and overtook them e by the sea .... Ex 14:9 2583

ENCHANTER
or an observer of times, or an e .... Deut 18:10 5172

ENCHANTERS
to your dreamers, nor to your e .... Jer 27:9 6049

ENCHANTMENT
neither shall ye use e, nor .... Lev 19:26 5172
there is no e against Jacob .... Num 23:23 5172
the serpent will bite without e .... Eccl 10:11 3908

ENCHANTMENTS
did in like manner with their e .... Ex 7:11 3858
of Egypt did so with their e .... Ex 7:22 3909
the magicians did so with their e .... Ex 8:7 3909
with their e to bring forth lice .... Ex 8:18 3909
as at other times, to seek for e .... Num 24:1 5172
the fire, and used divination and e 2Kin 17:17 5172
and observed times, and used e 2Kin 21:6 5172
also he observed times, and used e 2Chr 33:6 5172
the great abundance of thine e .... Is 47:9 2267
Stand now with thine e, and with .... Is 47:12 2267

ENCOUNTERED
and of the Stoicks, e him .... Acts 17:18 4820

ENCOURAGE
e him: for he shall cause .... Deut 1:38 2388
and e him, and strengthen him .... Deut 3:28 2388
overthrow it: and e thou him 2Sa 11:25 2388
They e themselves in an evil .... Ps 64:5 2388

ENCOURAGED
the men of Israel e themselves .... Judg 20:22 2388
but David e himself in the LORD 1Sa 30:6 2388
that they might be e in the law 2Chr 31:4 2388
e them to the service of the 2Chr 35:2 2388
So the carpenter e the goldsmith .... Is 41:7 2388

END
The e of all flesh is come before .... Gen 6:13 7093
after the e of the hundred and .... Gen 8:3 7097
to pass at the e of forty days .... Gen 8:6 7093
which is in the e of his field .... Gen 23:9 7097
had made an e of blessing Jacob .... Gen 27:30 3615
pass at the e of two full years .... Gen 41:1 7093
e of the borders of Egypt even to .... Gen 47:21 7097
Egypt even to the other e thereof .... Gen 47:21 7097
made an e of commanding his sons .... Gen 49:33 3615
to the e thou mayest know that I .... Ex 8:22 4616
pass at the e of the four hundred .... Ex 12:41 7093
which is in the e of the year .... Ex 23:16 3318
And make one cherub on the one e .... Ex 25:19 7098
the other cherub on the other e .... Ex 25:19 7098
boards shall reach from e to e .... Ex 26:28 7097
Moses, when he had made an e of .... Ex 31:18 3615
of ingathering at the year's e .... Ex 34:22 8622
from the one e to the other .... Ex 36:33 7097
One cherub on the e on this side .... Ex 37:8 7098
on the other e on that side .... Ex 37:8 7098
of your consecration be at an e .... Lev 8:33 4390
when he hath made an e of .... Lev 16:20 3615
To the e that the children of .... Lev 17:5 4616
his sons have made an e of .... Num 4:15 3615
as he had made an e of speaking .... Num 16:31 3615
and let my last e be like his .... Num 23:10
but his latter e shall be that he .... Num 24:20
to do thee good at thy latter e .... Deut 8:16
to pass at the e of forty days .... Deut 9:11 7093
year even unto the e of the year .... Deut 11:12 319
from the one e of the earth even .... Deut 13:7 7097
unto the other e of the earth .... Deut 13:7 7097
At the e of three years thou .... Deut 14:28 7097
At the e of every seven years .... Deut 15:1 7093
to the e that he should multiply .... Deut 17:16 4616
to the e that he may prolong his .... Deut 17:20 4616
an e of speaking unto the people .... Deut 20:9 3615
When thou hast made an e of .... Deut 26:12 3615
from the e of the earth, as swift .... Deut 28:49 7097
from the one e of the earth even .... Deut 28:64 7097
At the e of every seven years, in .... Deut 31:10 7093
when Moses had made an e of .... Deut 31:24 3615
I will see what their e shall be .... Deut 32:20 319
would consider their latter e .... Deut 32:29
Moses made an e of speaking all .... Deut 32:45 3615
when Israel had made an e of .... Josh 8:24 3615
it came to pass at the e of three .... Josh 9:16 7097
an e of slaying them with a very .... Josh 10:20 3615

sea, even unto the *e* of Jordan Josh 15:5 7097
which is at the *e* of the valley Josh 15:8 7097
was from the *e* of Kirjath-jearim Josh 18:15 7097
the *e* of the mountain that lieth Josh 18:16 7097
salt sea at the south *e* of Jordan Josh 18:19 7097
When they had made an *e* of Josh 19:49 3615
So they made an *e* of dividing the Josh 19:51 3615
when he had made an *e* to offer Judg 3:18 3615
e of the staff that was in his Judg 6:21 7097
to pass at the *e* of two months Judg 11:39 7093
when he had made an *e* of speaking Judg 15:17 3615
behold, the day groweth to an *e* Judg 19:9 2583
unto the *e* of barley harvest Ruth 2:23 3615
down at the *e* of the heap of corn Ruth 3:7 7097
latter *e* than at the beginning Ruth 3:10
I begin, I will also make an *e* 1Sa 3:12 3615
going down to the *e* of the city 1Sa 9:27 7097
he had made an *e* of prophesying 1Sa 10:13 3615
e of offering the burnt offering 1Sa 13:10 3615
wherefore he put forth the *e* of 1Sa 14:27 7097
the *e* of the rod that was in mine 1Sa 14:43 7097
when he had made an *e* of speaking 1Sa 18:1 3615
when David had made an *e* of 1Sa 24:16 3615
e of the spear smote him under 2Sa 2:23
be bitterness in the latter *e* 2Sa 2:26
an *e* of offering burnt offerings 2Sa 6:18 3615
When thou hast made an *e* of 2Sa 11:19 3615
as he had made an *e* of speaking 2Sa 13:36 3615
every year's *e* that he polled it 2Sa 14:26 7093
Jerusalem at the *e* of nine months 2Sa 24:8 7097
as they had made an *e* of eating 1Kin 1:41 3615
to pass at the *e* of three years 1Kin 2:39 7093
until he had made an *e* of 1Kin 3:1 3615
So Hiram made an *e* of doing all 1Kin 7:40 3615
an *e* of praying all this prayer 1Kin 8:54 3615
to pass at the *e* of twenty years 1Kin 9:10 7097
to pass at the seven years' *e* 2Kin 8:3 7097
was full from one *e* to another 2Kin 10:21 6310
as soon as he had made an *e* of 2Kin 10:25 3615
at the *e* of three years they took 2Kin 18:10 7097
Jerusalem from one *e* to another 2Kin 21:16 6310
when David had made an *e* of 1Chr 16:2 3615
on the right side of the east *e* 2Chr 4:10
stood at the east *e* of the altar 2Chr 5:12
Solomon had made an *e* of praying 2Chr 7:1 3615
to pass at the *e* of twenty years 2Chr 8:1 7093
find them at the *e* of the brook 2Chr 20:16 5490
when they had made an *e* of the 2Chr 20:23 3615
after the *e* of two years, his 2Chr 21:19 7093
chest, until they had made an *e* 2Chr 24:10 3615
came to pass at the *e* of the year 2Chr 24:23 8622
of the first month they made an *e* 2Chr 29:17 3615
they had made an *e* of offering 2Chr 29:29 3615
from one *e* to another with their Ezr 9:11 6310
they made an *e* with all the men Ezr 10:17 3615
to the *e* of the house of Eliashib Neh 3:21 8503
will they make an *e* in a day Neh 4:2 3615
and what is mine *e*, that I should Job 6:11 7093
yet thy latter *e* should greatly Job 8:7
Shall vain words have an *e* Job 16:3 7093
it be ere ye make an *e* of words Job 18:2 7078
the day and night come to an *e* Job 26:10 8503
He setteth an *e* to darkness Job 28:3 7093
that Job may be tried unto the *e* Job 34:36 5331
e of Job more than his beginning Job 42:12
of the wicked come to an *e* Ps 7:9 1584
are come to a perpetual *e* Ps 9:6 8552
their words to the *e* of the world Ps 19:4 7097
forth is from the *e* of the heaven Ps 19:6 7097
To the *e* that my glory may sing Ps 30:12 4616
for the *e* of that man is peace Ps 37:37 319
the *e* of the wicked shall be cut Ps 37:38 319
LORD, make me to know mine *e* Ps 39:4 7093
to cease unto the *e* of the earth Ps 46:9 7097
From the *e* of the earth will I Ps 61:2 7097
then understood I their *e* Ps 73:17 319
and thy years shall have no *e* Ps 102:27 8552
man, and are at their wit's *e* Ps 107:27 1104
and I shall keep it unto the *e* Ps 119:33 6118
I have seen an *e* of all Ps 119:96 7093
statutes alway, even unto the *e* Ps 119:112 6118
But her *e* is bitter as wormwood Prov 5:4 319
but the *e* thereof are the ways of Prov 14:12 319
the *e* of that mirth is heaviness Prov 14:13 319
but the *e* thereof are the ways of Prov 16:25 319
mayest be wise in thy latter *e* Prov 19:20
but the *e* thereof shall not be Prov 20:21 319
For surely there is an *e* Prov 23:18 319
not what to do in the *e* thereof Prov 25:8 319
from the beginning to the *e* Eccl 3:11 5490
yet is there no *e* of all his Eccl 4:8 7093
There is no *e* of all the people Eccl 4:16 7093
for that is the *e* of all men Eccl 7:2 5490
Better is the *e* of a thing than Eccl 7:8 319
to the *e* that man should find Eccl 7:14 1700
the *e* of his talk is mischievous Eccl 10:13 319
making many books there is no *e* Eccl 12:12 7093
is there any *e* of their treasures Is 2:7 7097
is there any *e* of their chariots Is 2:7 7097
unto them from the *e* of the earth Is 5:26 7097
at the *e* of the conduit of the Is 7:3 7097
and peace there shall be no *e* Is 9:7 7093
from the *e* of heaven, even the Is 13:5 7093
for the extortioner is at an *e* Is 16:4 657
after the *e* of seventy years Is 23:15 7093
pass after the *e* of seventy years Is 23:17 7093
make an *e* to deal treacherously Is 33:1 5239
night wilt thou make an *e* of me Is 38:12 7999
night wilt thou make an *e* of me Is 38:13 7999
and know the latter *e* of them Is 41:22
praise from the *e* of the earth Is 42:10 7097
nor confounded world without *e* Is 45:17
Declaring the *e* from the Is 46:10 319
didst remember the latter *e* of it Is 47:7

it even to the *e* of the earth Is 48:20 7097
salvation unto the *e* of the earth Is 49:6 7097
unto the *e* of the world, Say ye Is 62:11 7097
unto the *e* of the eleventh year Jer 1:3 8537
will he keep it to the *e* Jer 3:5 5331
yet will I not make a full *e* Jer 4:27 3615
but make not a full *e* Jer 5:10 3615
I will not make a full *e* with you Jer 5:18 3615
will ye do in the *e* thereof Jer 5:31 319
said, He shall not see our last *e* Jer 12:4
e of the land even to the other Jer 12:12 7097
even to the other *e* of the land Jer 12:12 7097
days, and at his *e* shall be a fool Jer 17:11 319
one *e* of the earth even unto the Jer 25:33 7097
unto the other *e* of the earth Jer 25:33 7097
when Jeremiah had made an *e* of Jer 26:8 3615
evil, to give you an expected *e* Jer 29:11 319
though I make a full *e* of all Jer 30:11 3615
will I not make a full *e* of thee Jer 30:11 3615
And there is hope in thine *e* Jer 31:17 319
At the *e* of seven years let ye go Jer 34:14 7093
that when Jeremiah had made an *e* Jer 43:1 3615
until there be an *e* of them Jer 44:27 3615
for I will make a full *e* of all Jer 46:28 3615
I will not make a full *e* of thee Jer 46:28 3615
thine *e* is come, and the measure Jer 51:13 7093
that his city is taken at one *e* Jer 51:31 7097
made an *e* of reading this book Jer 51:63 3615
she remembereth not her last *e* Lam 1:9
our *e* is near, our days are Lam 4:18 7093
for our *e* is come Lam 4:18 7093
to pass at the *e* of seven days Eze 3:16 7097
An *e*, the *e* is come upon the Eze 7:2 7093
Now is the *e* come upon thee, and I Eze 7:3 7093
An *e* is come, the *e* is come Eze 7:6 7093
wilt thou make a full *e* of the Eze 11:13 3615
neither did I make an *e* of them Eze 20:17 3615
to the *e* that they might know Eze 20:26 4616
when iniquity shall have an *e* Eze 21:25 7093
their iniquity shall have an *e* Eze 21:29 7093
At the *e* of forty years will I Eze 29:13 7093
To the *e* that none of all the Eze 31:14 4616
time that their iniquity had an *e* Eze 35:5 7093
after the *e* of seven months shall Eze 39:14 7097
the separate place at the *e* Eze 41:12 6285
Now when he had made an *e* of Eze 42:15 3615
hast made an *e* of cleansing it Eze 43:23 3615
From the north *e* to the coast of Eze 48:1 7097
that at the *e* thereof they might Dan 1:5 7117
at the *e* of ten days their Dan 1:15 7117
Now at the *e* of the days that the Dan 1:18 7117
thereof to the *e* of all the earth Dan 4:11 5491
dominion to the *e* of the earth Dan 4:22 5491
At the *e* of twelve months he Dan 4:29 7118
And at the *e* of the days I Dan 4:34 7118
dominion shall be even unto the *e* Dan 6:26 5491
and to destroy it unto the *e* Dan 7:26 5491
Hitherto is the *e* of the matter Dan 7:28 5491
time of the *e* shall be the vision Dan 8:17 7093
in the last *e* of the indignation Dan 8:19
the time appointed the *e* shall be Dan 8:19 7093
and to make an *e* of sins, and to Dan 9:24 2856
the *e* thereof shall be with a Dan 9:26 7093
unto the *e* of the war desolations Dan 9:26 7093
in the *e* of years they shall join Dan 11:6 7093
for yet the *e* shall be at the Dan 11:27 7093
white, even to the time of the *e* Dan 11:35 7093
at the time of the *e* shall the Dan 11:40 7093
yet he shall come to his *e* Dan 11:45 7093
book, even to the time of the *e* Dan 12:4 7093
it be to the *e* of these wonders Dan 12:6 7093
shall be the *e* of these things Dan 12:8 319
and sealed till the time of the *e* Dan 12:9 7093
But go thou thy way till the *e* be Dan 12:13 7093
in thy lot at the *e* of the days Dan 12:13 7093
the great houses shall have an *e* Amos 3:15 5486
to what *e* is it for you Amos 5:18
that when they had made an *e* of Amos 7:2 3615
The *e* is come upon my people of Amos 8:2 7093
the *e* thereof as a bitter day Amos 8:10 319
to the *e* that every one of the Obad 9 4616
an utter *e* of the place thereof Nah 1:8 3615
he will make an utter *e* Nah 1:9 3615
for there is none *e* of the store Nah 2:9 7097
there is none *e* of their corpses Nah 3:3 7097
but at the *e* it shall speak, and Hab 2:3 7093
endureth to the *e* shall be saved Mt 10:22 *5056*
when Jesus had made an *e* of Mt 11:1 *5055*
the harvest is the *e* of the world Mt 13:39 *4930*
it be in the *e* of this world Mt 13:40 *4930*
shall it be at the *e* of the world Mt 13:49 *4930*
coming, and of the *e* of the world Mt 24:3 *4930*
to pass, but the *e* is not yet Mt 24:6 *5056*
he that shall endure unto the *e* Mt 24:13 *5056*
and then shall the *e* come Mt 24:14 *5056*
from one *e* of heaven to the other Mt 24:31 *206*
with the servants, to see the *e* Mt 26:58 *5056*
In the *e* of the sabbath, as it Mt 28:1 *3796*
even unto the *e* of the world Mt 28:20 *4930*
he cannot stand, but hath an *e* Mk 3:26 *5056*
but the *e* shall not be yet Mk 13:7 *5056*
he that shall endure unto the *e* Mk 13:13 *5056*
his kingdom there shall be no *e* Lk 1:33 *5056*
a parable unto them to this *e* Lk 18:1
but the *e* is not by and by Lk 21:9 *5056*
things concerning me have an *e* Lk 22:37 *5056*
world, he loved them unto the *e* Jn 13:1 *5056*
To this *e* was I born, and for this Jn 18:37
to the *e* they might not live Acts 7:19 *1519*
to the *e* ye may be established Rom 1:11 *1519*
to the *e* the promise might be Rom 4:16 *1519*
for the *e* of those things is Rom 6:21 *5056*
and the *e* everlasting life Rom 6:22 *5056*
For Christ is the *e* of the law Rom 10:4 *5056*

For to this *e* Christ both died Rom 14:9
shall also confirm you unto the *e* 1Cor 1:8 *5056*
Then cometh the *e*, when he shall 1Cor 15:24 *5056*
shall acknowledge even to the *e* 2Cor 1:13 *5056*
For to this *e* also did I write 2Cor 2:9
the *e* of that which is abolished 2Cor 3:13 *5056*
whose *e* shall be according to 2Cor 11:15 *5056*
all ages, world without *e* Eph 3:21
Whose *e* is destruction, whose God Phil 3:19 *5056*
To the *e* he may stablish your 1Th 3:13 *1519*
Now the *e* of the commandment is 1Ti 1:5 *5056*
of the hope firm unto the *e* Heb 3:6 *5056*
confidence stedfast unto the *e* Heb 3:14 *5056*
whose *e* is to be burned Heb 6:8 *5056*
full assurance of hope unto the *e* Heb 6:11 *5056*
is to them an *e* of all strife Heb 6:16 *4009*
beginning of days, nor *e* of life Heb 7:3 *5056*
but now once in the *e* of the Heb 9:26 *4930*
considering the *e* of their Heb 13:7 *1545*
and have seen the *e* of the Lord Jas 5:11 *5056*
Receiving the *e* of your faith 1Pet 1:9 *5056*
hope to the *e* for the grace that 1Pet 1:13 *5049*
But the *e* of all things is at 1Pet 4:7 *5056*
what shall the *e* be of them that 1Pet 4:17 *5056*
the latter *e* is worse with them 2Pet 2:20 *2078*
and keepeth my works unto the *e* Rev 2:26 *5056*
and Omega, the beginning and the *e* Rev 21:6 *5056*
and Omega, the beginning and the *e* Rev 22:13 *5056*

ENDAMAGE
so thou shalt *e* the revenue of Ezr 4:13 5142

ENDANGER
ye make me *e* my head to the king Dan 1:10 2325

ENDANGERED
cleaveth wood shall be *e* thereby Eccl 10:9 5533

ENDEAVOUR
Moreover I will *e* that ye may be 2Pet 1:15 *4704*

ENDEAVOURED
immediately we *e* to go into Acts 16:10 *2212*
e the more abundantly to see your 1Th 2:17 *4704*

ENDEAVOURING
E to keep the unity of the Spirit Eph 4:3 *4704*

ENDEAVOURS
to the wickedness of their *e* Ps 28:4 4611

ENDED
on the seventh day God *e* his work Gen 2:2 3615
was in the land of Egypt, were *e* Gen 41:53 3615
When that year was *e*, they came Gen 47:18 8552
of this song, until they were *e* Deut 31:30 8552
and mourning for Moses were *e* Deut 34:8 8552
until they have *e* all my harvest Ruth 2:21 3615
and so they *e* the matter 2Sa 20:18 8552
So was *e* all the work that king 1Kin 7:51 7999
help them, till the work was *e* 2Chr 29:34 3615
The words of Job are *e* Job 31:40 8552
of David the son of Jesse are *e* Ps 72:20 3615
days of thy mourning shall be *e* Is 60:20 7999
harvest is past, the summer is *e* Jer 8:20 3615
till thou hast *e* the days of thy Eze 4:8 3615
when Jesus had *e* these sayings Mt 7:28 *4931*
and when they were *e*, he afterward Lk 4:2 *4931*
devil had *e* all the temptation Lk 4:13 *4931*
Now when he had *e* all his sayings Lk 7:1 *4137*
And supper being *e*, the devil Jn 13:2 *1096*
After these things were *e* Acts 19:21 *4137*
when the seven days were almost *e* Acts 21:27 *4931*

ENDETH
the noise of them that rejoice *e* Is 24:8 2308

ENDING
and Omega, the beginning and the *e* Rev 1:8 *5056*

ENDLESS
e genealogies, which minister 1Ti 1:4 *562*
but after the power of an *e* life Heb 7:16 *179*

EN-DOR *(en'-dor) A village near Mt. Tabor.*
towns, and the inhabitants of *E* Josh 17:11 5874
that hath a familiar spirit at *E* 1Sa 28:7 5874
Which perished at *E*: they became Ps 83:10 5874

ENDOW
he shall surely *e* her to be his Ex 22:16 4117

ENDS
in the two *e* of the mercy seat Ex 25:18 7098
cherubims on the two *e* thereof Ex 25:19 7098
two chains of pure gold at the *e* Ex 28:14 4020
e of wreathen work of pure gold Ex 28:22 1383
on the two *e* of the breastplate Ex 28:23 7098
are on the *e* of the breastplate Ex 28:24 7098
the other two *e* of the two Ex 28:25 7098
two *e* of the breastplate in the Ex 28:26 7098
on the two *e* of the mercy seat Ex 37:7 7098
cherubims on the two *e* thereof Ex 37:8 7099
the four *e* of the grate of brass Ex 38:5 7099
the breastplate chains at the *e* Ex 39:15 1383
in the two *e* of the breastplate Ex 39:16 7098
rings on the *e* of the breastplate Ex 39:17 7098
the two *e* of the two wreathen Ex 39:18 7098
on the two *e* of the breastplate Ex 39:19 7098
together to the *e* of the earth Deut 33:17 657
shall judge the *e* of the earth 1Sa 2:10 657
that the *e* of the staves were 1Kin 8:8 7218
that the *e* of the staves were 2Chr 5:9 7218
he looketh to the *e* of the earth Job 28:24 7098
lightning unto the *e* of the earth Job 37:3 3671
take hold of the *e* of the earth Job 38:13 3671
and his circuit unto the *e* of it Ps 19:6 7098
All the *e* of the world shall Ps 22:27 657
praise unto the *e* of the earth Ps 48:10 7099
in Jacob unto the *e* of the earth Ps 59:13 657
of all the *e* of the earth Ps 65:5 7099

E

all the *e* of the earth shall fear Ps 67:7 657
the river unto the *e* of the earth Ps 72:8 657
all the *e* of the earth have seen Ps 98:3 657
to ascend from the *e* of the earth Ps 135:7 7097
a fool are in the *e* of the earth Prov 17:24 7097
all the *e* of the earth Prov 30:4 657
far unto all the *e* of the earth Is 26:15 7097
the Creator of the *e* of the earth Is 40:28 7098
the *e* of the earth were afraid, Is 41:5 7098
taken from the *e* of the earth Is 41:9 7098
daughters from the *e* of the earth Is 43:6 7097
ye saved, all the *e* of the earth Is 45:22 657
all the *e* of the earth shall see Is 52:10 657
to ascend from the *e* of the earth Jer 10:13 7097
unto thee from the *e* of the earth Jer 16:19 657
come even to the *e* of the earth Jer 25:31 7097
to ascend from the *e* of the earth Jer 51:16 7097
fire devoureth both the *e* of it Eze 15:4 7098
be great unto the *e* of the earth Mic 5:4 657
river even to the *e* of the earth Zec 9:10 657
salvation unto the *e* of the earth Acts 13:47 *2078*
words unto the *e* of the world Rom 10:18 *4009*
upon whom the *e* of the world are 1Cor 10:11 *5056*

ENDUED

God hath *e* me with a good dowry Gen 30:20 2064
e with prudence and understanding, 2Chr 2:12 3045
e with understanding, of Huram my 2Chr 2:13 3045
until ye be *e* with power from on Lk 24:49 *1746*
e with knowledge among you Jas 3:13 *1990*

ENDURE

me and the children be able to *e* Gen 33:14 7272
so, then thou shalt be able to *e* Ex 18:23 5975
For how can I *e* to see the evil Est 8:6 3201
or how can I *e* to see the Est 8:6 3201
hold it fast, but it shall not *e* Job 8:15 6965
of his highness I could not *e* Job 31:23
But the LORD shall *e* for ever Ps 9:7 3427
weeping may *e* for a night Ps 30:5 3885
thee as long as the sun and moon *e* Ps 72:5 6440
His name shall *e* for ever Ps 72:17 1961
also will I make to *e* for ever Ps 89:29
His seed shall *e* for ever Ps 89:36 1961
thou, O LORD, shalt *e* for ever Ps 102:12 3427
shall perish, but thou shalt *e* Ps 102:26 5975
of the LORD shall *e* for ever Ps 104:31 1961
doth the crown *e* to every Prov 27:24
Can thine heart *e*, or can thine Eze 22:14 5975
But he that shall *e* unto the end Mt 24:13 *5278*
and so *e* but for a time Mk 4:17 *2076*
but he that shall *e* unto the end Mk 13:13 *5278*
and tribulations that ye *e* 2Th 1:4 *430*
Thou therefore *e* hardness 2Ti 2:3 *2553*
Therefore I *e* all things for the 2Ti 2:10 *5278*
they will not *e* sound doctrine 2Ti 4:3 *430*
e afflictions, do the work of an 2Ti 4:5 *2553*
If ye *e* chastening, God dealeth Heb 12:7 *5278*
(For they could not *e* that which Heb 12:20 *5342*
we count them happy which *e* Jas 5:11 *5278*
for conscience toward God *e* grief 1Pet 2:19 *5297*

ENDURED

their time should have *e* for ever Ps 81:15 1961
e with much longsuffering the Rom 9:22 *5342*
what persecutions I *e* 2Ti 3:11 *5297*
And so, after he had patiently *e* Heb 6:15 *3114*
ye *e* a great fight of afflictions Heb 10:32 *5278*
for he *e*, as seeing him who is Heb 11:27 *2594*
was set before him *e* the cross Heb 12:2 *5278*
For consider him that *e* such Heb 12:3 *5278*

ENDURETH

for his mercy *e* for ever 1Chr 16:34
because his mercy *e* for ever 1Chr 16:41
for his mercy *e* for ever 2Chr 5:13
for his mercy *e* for ever 2Chr 7:3
because his mercy *e* for ever 2Chr 7:6
for his mercy *e* for ever 2Chr 20:21
for his mercy *e* for ever toward Ezr 3:11
For his anger *e* but a moment Ps 30:5
the goodness of God *e* continually Ps 52:1
of peace so long as the moon *e* Ps 72:7 1097
his truth *e* to all generations Ps 100:5
for his mercy *e* for ever Ps 106:1
for his mercy *e* for ever Ps 107:1
and his righteousness *e* for ever Ps 111:3 5975
his praise *e* for ever Ps 111:10 5975
and his righteousness *e* for ever Ps 112:3 5975
his righteousness *e* for ever Ps 112:9 5975
the truth of the LORD *e* for ever Ps 117:2
because his mercy *e* for ever Ps 118:1
say, that his mercy *e* for ever Ps 118:2
say, that his mercy *e* for ever Ps 118:3
say, that his mercy *e* for ever Ps 118:4
for his mercy *e* for ever Ps 118:29
righteous judgments *e* for ever Ps 119:160
Thy name, O LORD, *e* for ever Ps 135:13
for his mercy *e* for ever Ps 136:1
for his mercy *e* for ever Ps 136:2
for his mercy *e* for ever Ps 136:3
for his mercy *e* for ever Ps 136:4
for his mercy *e* for ever Ps 136:5
for his mercy *e* for ever Ps 136:6
for his mercy *e* for ever Ps 136:7
for his mercy *e* for ever Ps 136:8
for his mercy *e* for ever Ps 136:9
for his mercy *e* for ever Ps 136:10
for his mercy *e* for ever Ps 136:11
for his mercy *e* for ever Ps 136:12
for his mercy *e* for ever Ps 136:13
for his mercy *e* for ever Ps 136:14
for his mercy *e* for ever Ps 136:15
for his mercy *e* for ever Ps 136:16
for his mercy *e* for ever Ps 136:17
for his mercy *e* for ever Ps 136:18
for his mercy *e* for ever Ps 136:19
for his mercy *e* for ever Ps 136:20
for his mercy *e* for ever Ps 136:21
for his mercy *e* for ever Ps 136:22
for his mercy *e* for ever Ps 136:23
for his mercy *e* for ever Ps 136:24
for his mercy *e* for ever Ps 136:25
for his mercy *e* for ever Ps 136:26
thy mercy, O LORD, *e* for ever Ps 138:8
thy dominion *e* throughout all Ps 145:13
for his mercy *e* for ever Jer 33:11
but he that *e* to the end shall be Mt 10:22 *5278*
which *e* unto everlasting life Jn 6:27 *3306*
hopeth all things, *e* all things 1Cor 13:7 *5278*
is the man that *e* temptation Jas 1:12 *5278*
the word of the Lord *e* for ever 1Pet 1:25 *3306*

ENDURING

of the LORD is clean, *e* for ever Ps 19:9 5975
which is effectual in the *e* of 2Cor 1:6 *5281*
heaven a better and an *e* substance Heb 10:34 *3306*

EN-EGLAIM (*en-eg'-la-im*) *A place near the Salt Sea.*

upon it from En-gedi even unto *E* Eze 47:10 5882

ENEMIES

delivered thine *e* into thy hand Gen 14:20 6862
shall possess the gate of his *e* Gen 22:17 341
shall be in the neck of thine *e* Gen 49:8 341
war, they join also unto our *e* Ex 1:10 8130
I will be an enemy unto thine *e* Ex 23:22 341
I will make all thine *e* turn Ex 23:27 341
unto their shame among their *e* Ex 32:25 6965
And ye shall chase your *e*, and they Lev 26:7 341
your *e* shall fall before you by Lev 26:8 341
in vain, for your *e* shall eat it Lev 26:16 341
ye shall be slain before your *e* Lev 26:17 341
your *e* which dwell therein shall Lev 26:32 341
hearts in the lands of their *e* Lev 26:36 341
no power to stand before your *e* Lev 26:37 341
land of your *e* shall eat you up Lev 26:38 341
them into the land of their *e* Lev 26:41 341
they be in the land of their *e* Lev 26:44 341
and ye shall be saved from your *e* Num 10:9 341
LORD, and let thine *e* be scattered Num 10:35 341
ye be not smitten before your *e* Num 14:42 341
I took thee to curse mine *e* Num 23:11 341
he shall eat up the nations his *e* Num 24:8 6862
I called thee to curse mine *e* Num 24:10 341
shall be a possession for his *e* Num 24:18 341
driven out his *e* from before him Num 32:21 341
lest ye be smitten before your *e* Deut 1:42 341
out all thine *e* from before thee Deut 6:19 341
rest from all your *e* round about Deut 12:10 341
out to battle against thine *e* Deut 20:1 341
day unto battle against your *e* Deut 20:3 341
to fight for you against your *e* Deut 20:4 341
shalt eat the spoil of thine *e* Deut 20:14 341
forth to war against thine *e* Deut 21:10 341
host goeth forth against thine *e* Deut 23:9 341
and to give up thine *e* before thee Deut 23:14 341
rest from all thine *e* round about Deut 25:19 341
The LORD shall cause thine *e* that Deut 28:7 341
thee to be smitten before thine *e* Deut 28:25 341
sheep shall be given unto thine *e* Deut 28:31 341
shalt thou serve thine *e* which Deut 28:48 341
wherewith thine *e* shall distress Deut 28:53 341
wherewith thine *e* shall distress Deut 28:55 341
be sold unto your *e* for bondmen Deut 28:68 341
put all these curses upon thine *e* Deut 30:7 341
even our *e* themselves being Deut 32:31 341
I will render vengeance to mine *e* Deut 32:41 6862
be thou an help to him from his *e* Deut 33:7 6862
thine *e* shall be found liars unto Deut 33:29 341
their backs before their *e* Josh 7:8 341
could not stand before their *e* Josh 7:12 341
turned their backs before their *e* Josh 7:12 341
canst not stand before thine *e* Josh 7:13 341
avenged themselves upon their *e* Josh 10:13 341
ye not, but pursue after your *e* Josh 10:19 341
all your *e* against whom ye fight Josh 10:25 341
a man of all their *e* before them Josh 21:44 341
all their *e* into their hand Josh 21:44 341
of your *e* with your brethren Josh 22:8 341
from all their *e* round about Josh 23:1 341
the hands of their *e* round about Judg 2:14 341
any longer stand before their *e* Judg 2:14 341
their *e* all the days of the judge Judg 2:18 341
e the Moabites into your hand Judg 3:28 341
So let all thine *e* perish Judg 5:31 341
of all their *e* on every side Judg 8:34 341
vengeance for thee of thine *e* Judg 11:36 341
my mouth is enlarged over mine *e* 1Sa 2:1 341
save us out of the hand of our *e* 1Sa 4:3 341
us out of the hand of our *e* 1Sa 12:10 341
the hand of your *e* on every side 1Sa 12:11 341
that I may be avenged on mine *e* 1Sa 14:24 341
spoil of their *e* which they found 1Sa 14:30 341
against all his *e* on every side 1Sa 14:47 341
to be avenged of the king's *e* 1Sa 18:25 341
the *e* of David every one from the 1Sa 20:15 341
it at the hand of David's *e* 1Sa 20:16 341
also do God unto the *e* of David 1Sa 25:22 341
thine own hand, now let thine *e* 1Sa 25:26 341
and the souls of thine *e*, them 1Sa 25:29 341
against the *e* of my lord the king 1Sa 29:8 341
of the spoil of the *e* of the LORD 1Sa 30:26 341
and out of the hand of all their *e* 2Sa 3:18 341
forth upon mine *e* before me 2Sa 5:20 341
rest round about from all his *e* 2Sa 7:1 341
off all thine *e* out of thy sight 2Sa 7:9 341
thee to rest from all thine *e* 2Sa 7:11 341
to the *e* of the LORD to blaspheme 2Sa 12:14 341
LORD hath avenged him of his *e* 2Sa 18:19 341
The *e* of my lord the king, and all 2Sa 18:32 341
In that thou lovest thine *e* 2Sa 19:6 8130
saved us out of the hand of our *e* 2Sa 19:9 341
him out of the hand of all his *e* 2Sa 22:1 341
so shall I be saved from mine *e* 2Sa 22:4 341
I have pursued mine *e*, and 2Sa 22:38 341
also given me the necks of mine *e* 2Sa 22:41 341
bringeth me forth from mine *e* 2Sa 22:49 341
flee three months before thine *e* 2Sa 24:13 6862
hast asked the life of thine *e* 1Kin 3:11 341
soul, in the land of their *e* 1Kin 8:48 341
you out of the hand of all your *e* 2Kin 17:39 341
them into the hand of their *e* 2Kin 21:14 341
a prey and a spoil to all their *e* 2Kin 21:14 341
ye be come to betray me to mine *e* 1Chr 12:17 6862
God hath broken in upon mine *e* by 1Chr 14:11 341
off all thine *e* from before thee 1Chr 17:8 341
I will subdue all thine *e* 1Chr 17:10 341
sword of thine *e* overtaketh thee 1Chr 21:12 341
rest from all his *e* round about 1Chr 22:9 341
honour, nor the life of thine *e* 2Chr 1:11 8130
if their *e* besiege them in the 2Chr 6:28 341
go out to war against their *e* by 2Chr 6:34 341
deliver them over before their *e* 2Chr 6:36 341
made them to rejoice over their *e* 2Chr 20:27 341
fought against the *e* of Israel 2Chr 20:29 341
them into the hand of their *e* 2Chr 25:20
when our *e* heard that it was Neh 4:15 341
the reproach of the heathen our *e* Neh 5:9 341
the Arabian, and the rest of our *e* Neh 6:1 341
that when all our *e* heard thereof Neh 6:16 341
them into the hand of their *e* Neh 9:27 6862
them out of the hand of their *e* Neh 9:27 6862
thou them in the hand of their *e* Neh 9:28 341
to avenge themselves on their *e* Est 8:13 341
in the day that the *e* of the Jews Est 9:1 341
e with the stroke of the sword Est 9:5 341
lives, and had rest from their *e* Est 9:16 341
the Jews rested from their *e* Est 9:22 341
me unto him as one of his *e* Job 19:11 6862
all mine *e* upon the cheek bone Ps 3:7 341
righteousness because of mine *e* Ps 5:8 8324
waxeth old because of all mine *e* Ps 6:7 6887
Let all mine *e* be ashamed Ps 6:10 341
because of the rage of mine *e* Ps 7:6 6887
strength because of thine *e* Ps 8:2 6887
When mine *e* are turned back, they Ps 9:3 341
as for all his *e*, he puffeth at Ps 10:5 6887
that oppress me, from my deadly *e* Ps 17:9 341
him from the hand of all his *e* Ps 18:t 341
so shall I be saved from mine *e* Ps 18:3 341
I have pursued mine *e*, and Ps 18:37 341
also given me the necks of mine *e* Ps 18:40 341
He delivereth me from mine *e* Ps 18:48 341
hand shall find out all thine *e* Ps 21:8 341
me in the presence of mine *e* Ps 23:5 6887
let not mine *e* triumph over me Ps 25:2 341
Consider mine *e*; for they are Ps 25:19 341
When the wicked, even mine *e* Ps 27:2 6862
up above mine *e* round about me Ps 27:6 341
a plain path, because of mine *e* Ps 27:11 8324
not over unto the will of mine *e* Ps 27:12 6862
I was a reproach among all mine *e* Ps 31:11 6887
me from the hand of mine *e* Ps 31:15 341
mine *e* wrongfully rejoice over me Ps 35:19 341
the *e* of the LORD shall be as the Ps 37:20 341
But mine *e* are lively, and they Ps 38:19 341
him unto the will of his *e* Ps 41:2 341
Mine *e* speak evil of me, When Ps 41:5 341
in my bones, mine *e* reproach me Ps 42:10 6887
thee will we push down our *e* Ps 44:5 6862
But thou hast saved us from our *e* Ps 44:7 6862
in the heart of the king's *e* Ps 45:5 341
He shall reward evil unto mine *e* Ps 54:5 8324
hath seen his desire upon mine *e* Ps 54:7 341
Mine *e* would daily swallow me up Ps 56:2 8324
thee, then shall mine *e* turn back Ps 56:9 341
Deliver me from mine *e*, O my God Ps 59:1 341
let me see my desire upon mine *e* Ps 59:10 8324
it is that shall tread down our *e* Ps 60:12 6862
of thy power shall thine *e* submit Ps 66:3 341
God arise, let his *e* be scattered Ps 68:1 341
God shall wound the head of his *e* Ps 68:21 341
be dipped in the blood of thine *e* Ps 68:23 341
me, being mine *e* wrongfully Ps 69:4 341
deliver me because of mine *e* Ps 69:18 341
For mine *e* speak against me Ps 71:10 341
his *e* shall lick the dust Ps 72:9 341
Thine *e* roar in the midst of thy Ps 74:4 6887
Forget not the voice of thine *e* Ps 74:23 6887
but the sea overwhelmed their *e* Ps 78:53 341
he smote his *e* in the hinder Ps 78:66 6862
our *e* laugh among themselves Ps 80:6 341
should soon have subdued their *e* Ps 81:14 341
For, lo, thine *e* make a tumult Ps 83:2 341
thine *e* with thy strong arm Ps 89:10 341
hast made all his *e* to rejoice Ps 89:42 341
Wherewith thine *e* have reproached Ps 89:51 341
For, lo, thine *e*, O LORD, for, lo Ps 92:9 341
for, lo, thine *e* shall perish Ps 92:9 341
shall see my desire on mine *e* Ps 92:11 7790
and burneth up his *e* round about Ps 97:3 6862
Mine *e* reproach me all the day Ps 102:8 341
made them stronger than their *e* Ps 105:24 6862
And the waters covered their *e* Ps 106:11 6862
Their *e* also oppressed them, and Ps 106:42 341
it is that shall tread down our *e* Ps 108:13 6862
I make thine *e* thy footstool Ps 110:1 341
rule thou in the midst of thine *e* Ps 110:2 341
he see his desire upon his *e* Ps 112:8 6862
hast made me wiser than mine *e* Ps 119:98 341
because mine *e* have forgotten thy Ps 119:139 6862
Many are my persecutors and mine *e* Ps 119:157 6862
speak with the *e* in the gate Ps 127:5 341

His e will I clothe with shame ... Ps 132:18 341
And hath redeemed us from our e ... Ps 136:24 6862
hand against the wrath of mine e ... Ps 138:7 341
thine e take thy name in vain ... Ps 139:20 6145
I count them mine e ... Ps 139:22 341
Deliver me, O LORD, from mine e ... Ps 143:9 341
And of thy mercy cut off mine e ... Ps 143:12 341
he maketh even his e to be at ... Prov 16:7 341
and avenge me of mine e ... Is 1:24 341
him, and join his e together ... Is 9:11 341
fire of thine e shall devour them ... Is 26:11 6862
he shall prevail against his e ... Is 42:13 341
adversaries, recompence to his e ... Is 59:18 341
thy corn to be meat for thine e ... Is 62:8 341
rendereth recompence to his e ... Is 66:6 341
and his indignation toward his e ... Is 66:14 341
of my soul into the hand of her e ... Jer 12:7 341
to the sword before their e ... Jer 15:9 341
make thee to pass with thine e ... Jer 15:14 341
e in the land which thou knowest ... Jer 17:4 341
fall by the sword before their e ... Jer 19:7 341
and straitness, wherewith their e ... Jer 19:9 341
fall by the sword of their e ... Jer 20:4 341
I give into the hand of their e ... Jer 20:5 341
and into the hand of their e ... Jer 21:7 341
them into the hand of their e ... Jer 34:20 341
I give into the hand of their e ... Jer 34:21 341
of Egypt into the hand of his e ... Jer 44:30 341
the going down of Horonaim the e ... Jer 48:5 6862
to be dismayed before their e ... Jer 49:37 341
with her, they are become her e ... Lam 1:2 341
are the chief, her e prosper ... Lam 1:5 341
all mine e have heard of my ... Lam 1:21 341
All thine e have opened their ... Lam 2:16 341
All our e have opened their ... Lam 3:46 341
Mine e chased me sore, like a ... Lam 3:52 341
them into the hand of their e ... Eze 39:23 6862
interpretation thereof to thine e ... Dan 4:19 6146
go into captivity before their e ... Amos 9:4 341
thee from the hand of thine e ... Mic 4:10 341
all thine e shall be cut off ... Mic 5:9 341
a man's e are the men of his own ... Mic 7:6 341
and he reserveth wrath for his e ... Nah 1:2 341
and darkness shall pursue his e ... Nah 1:8 341
be set wide open unto thine e ... Nah 3:13 341
which tread down their e in the ... Zec 10:5 341
But I say unto you, Love your e ... Mt 5:44 *2190*
till I make thine e thy footstool ... Mt 22:44 *2190*
till I make thine e thy footstool ... Mk 12:36 *2190*
we should be saved from our e ... Lk 1:71 *2190*
out of the hand of our e might ... Lk 1:74 *2190*
unto you which hear, Love your e ... Lk 6:27 *2190*
But love ye your e, and do good ... Lk 6:35 *2190*
But those mine e, which would not ... Lk 19:27 *2190*
that thine e shall cast a trench ... Lk 19:43 *2190*
Till I make thine e thy footstool ... Lk 20:43 *2190*
For if, when we were e, we were ... Rom 5:10 *2190*
they are e for your sakes ... Rom 11:28 *2190*
he hath put all e under his feet ... 1Cor 15:25 *2190*
that they are the e of the cross ... Phil 3:18 *2190*
e in your mind by wicked works, ... Col 1:21 *2190*
I make thine e thy footstool ... Heb 1:13 *2190*
till his e be made his footstool ... Heb 10:13 *2190*
their mouth, and devoureth their e ... Rev 11:5 *2190*
and their e beheld them ... Rev 11:12 *2190*

ENEMIES'
desolate, and ye be in your e land ... Lev 26:34 341
in their iniquity in your e lands ... Lev 26:39 341
them out of their e lands ... Eze 39:27 341

ENEMY
LORD, hath dashed in pieces the e ... Ex 15:6 341
The e said, I will pursue, I will ... Ex 15:9 341
then I will be an e unto thine ... Ex 23:22 340
delivered into the hand of the e ... Lev 26:25 341
against the e that oppresseth you ... Num 10:9 341
that he die, and was not his e ... Num 35:23 341
wherewith thine e shall distress ... Deut 28:57 341
that I feared the wrath of the e ... Deut 32:27 341
beginning of revenges upon the e ... Deut 32:42 341
thrust out the e from before thee ... Deut 33:27 341
Samson our e into our hand ... Judg 16:23 341
delivered into our hands our e ... Judg 16:24 341
shalt see an e in my habitation ... 1Sa 2:32 6862
Saul became David's e continually ... 1Sa 18:29 341
me so, and sent away mine e ... 1Sa 19:17 341
deliver thine e into thine hand ... 1Sa 24:4 341
For if a man find his e, will he ... 1Sa 24:19 341
thine e into thine hand this day ... 1Sa 26:8 341
from thee, and is become thine e ... 1Sa 28:16 6145
the son of Saul thine e, which ... 2Sa 4:8 341
He delivered me from my strong e ... 2Sa 22:18 341
be smitten down before the e ... 1Kin 8:33 341
if their e besiege them in the ... 1Kin 8:37 341
go out to battle against their e ... 1Kin 8:44 341
them, and deliver them to the e ... 1Kin 8:46 341
captives unto the land of the e ... 1Kin 8:46 341
Hast thou found me, O mine e ... 1Kin 21:20 341
be put to the worse before the e ... 2Chr 6:24 341
shall make thee fall before the e ... 2Chr 25:8 341
to help the king against the e ... 2Chr 26:13 341
help us against the e in the way ... Ezr 8:22 341
us from the hand of the e ... Ezr 8:31 341
the Agagite, the Jews' e ... Est 3:10 6887
tongue, although the e could not ... Est 7:4 6862
and e is this wicked Haman ... Est 7:6 341
the Jews' e unto Esther the queen ... Est 8:1 6887
the e of the Jews, slew they ... Est 9:10 6887
the e of all the Jews, had ... Est 9:24 6887
face, and holdest me for thine e ... Job 13:24 341
mine e sharpeneth his eyes upon ... Job 16:9 6862
Let mine e be as the wicked, and ... Job 27:7 341
me, he counteth me for his e ... Job 33:10 341
him that without cause is mine e ... Ps 7:4 6887
Let the e persecute my soul, and ... Ps 7:5 341
that thou mightest still the e ... Ps 8:2 341
O thou e, destructions are come ... Ps 9:6 341
shall mine e be exalted over me ... Ps 13:2 341
Lest mine e say, I have prevailed ... Ps 13:4 341
He delivered me from my strong e ... Ps 18:17 341
shut me up into the hand of the e ... Ps 31:8 341
because mine e doth not triumph ... Ps 41:11 341
of the oppression of the e ... Ps 42:9 341
of the oppression of the e ... Ps 43:2 341
makest us to turn back from the e ... Ps 44:10 6862
by reason of the e and avenger ... Ps 44:16 341
Because of the voice of the e ... Ps 55:3 341
For it was not an e that ... Ps 55:12 341
me, and a strong tower from the e ... Ps 61:3 341
my life from fear of the e ... Ps 64:1 341
even all that the e hath done ... Ps 74:3 341
shall the e blaspheme thy name ... Ps 74:10 341
that the e hath reproached, O ... Ps 74:18 341
when he delivered them from the e ... Ps 78:42 6862
The e shall not exact upon him ... Ps 89:22 341
them from the hand of the e ... Ps 106:10 341
redeemed from the hand of the e ... Ps 107:2 6862
For the e hath persecuted my soul ... Ps 143:3 341
Rejoice not when thine e falleth ... Prov 24:17 341
If thine e be hungry, give him ... Prov 25:21 8130
the kisses of an e are deceitful ... Prov 27:6 8130
When the e shall come in like a ... Is 59:19 6862
he was turned to be their e ... Is 63:10 341
for the sword of the e and fear is ... Jer 6:25 341
verily I will cause the e to ... Jer 15:11 341
as with an east wind before the e ... Jer 18:17 341
thee with the wound of an e ... Jer 30:14 341
come again from the land of the e ... Jer 31:16 341
king of Babylon, his e, and that ... Jer 44:30 341
gone into captivity before the e ... Lam 1:5 6862
fell into the hand of the e ... Lam 1:7 6862
for the e hath magnified himself ... Lam 1:9 341
desolate, because the e prevailed ... Lam 1:16 341
his right hand from before the e ... Lam 2:3 341
He hath bent his bow like an e ... Lam 2:4 341
The Lord was as an e ... Lam 2:5 341
of the e the walls of her palaces ... Lam 2:7 341
thine e to rejoice over thee ... Lam 2:17 341
brought up hath mine e consumed ... Lam 2:22 341
the e should have entered into ... Lam 4:12 341
Because the e hath said against ... Eze 36:2 341
the e shall pursue him ... Hos 8:3 341
my people is risen up as an e ... Mic 2:8 341
Rejoice not against me, O mine e ... Mic 7:8 341
she that is mine e shall see it ... Mic 7:10 341
seek strength because of the e ... Nah 3:11 341
he hath cast out thine e ... Zeph 3:15 341
thy neighbour, and hate thine e ... Mt 5:43 *2190*
his e came and sowed tares among ... Mt 13:25 *2190*
unto them, An e hath done this ... Mt 13:28 *2190*
The e that sowed them is the ... Mt 13:39 *2190*
and over all the power of the e ... Lk 10:19 *2190*
thou e of all righteousness, wilt ... Acts 13:10 *2190*
Therefore if thine e hunger ... Rom 12:20 *2190*
The last e that shall be ... 1Cor 15:26 *2190*
Am I therefore become your e ... Gal 4:16 *2190*
Yet count him not as an e ... 2Th 3:15 *2190*
of the world is the e of God ... Jas 4:4 *2190*

ENEMY'S
If thou meet thine e ox or his ... Ex 23:4 341
Or, Deliver me from the e hand ... Job 6:23 6862
and his glory into the e hand ... Ps 78:61 6862

ENFLAMING
E yourselves with idols under ... Is 57:5 2552

ENGAGED
for who is this that e his heart ... Jer 30:21 6148

EN-GANNIM (*en-gan'-nim*)
1. A city in Judah.
and E, Tappuah, and Enam ... Josh 15:34 5873
2. A city in Issachar.
Remeth, and E, and En-haddah ... Josh 19:21 5873
her suburbs, E with her suburbs ... Josh 21:29 5873

EN-GEDI (*en-ghe'-di*) See HAZAZON-TAMAR. *A town on the Salt Sea.*
and the city of Salt, and E ... Josh 15:62 5872
and dwelt in strong holds at E ... 1Sa 23:29 5872
David is in the wilderness of E ... 1Sa 24:1 5872
be in Hazazon-tamar, which is E ... 2Chr 20:2 5872
of camphire in the vineyards of E ... Song 1:14 5872
it from E even unto En-eglaim ... Eze 47:10 5872

ENGINES
And he made in Jerusalem e ... 2Chr 26:15 2810
he shall set e of war against thy ... Eze 26:9 4239

ENGRAFTED
receive with meekness the e word ... Jas 1:21 *1721*

ENGRAVE
shalt thou e the two stones with ... Ex 28:11 6605
I will e the graving thereof, ... Zec 3:9 6605

ENGRAVEN
e in stones, was glorious, so ... 2Cor 3:7 *1795*

ENGRAVER
With the work of an e in stone ... Ex 28:11 2796
work all manner of work, of the e ... Ex 35:35 2796
of the tribe of Dan, an e ... Ex 38:23 2796

ENGRAVINGS
like the e of a signet, shalt ... Ex 28:11 6603
names, like the e of a signet ... Ex 28:21 6603
like the e of a signet, HOLINESS ... Ex 28:36 6603
like the e of a signet, every one ... Ex 39:14 6603
like to the e of a signet ... Ex 39:30 6603

EN-HADDAH (*en-had'-dah*) *A city in Issachar.*
And Remeth, and En-gannim, and E ... Josh 19:21 5876

EN-HAKKORE (*en-hak'-ko-re*) *A spring.*
he called the name thereof E ... Judg 15:19 5875

EN-HAZOR (*en-ha'-zor*) *A city in Naphtali.*
And Kedesh, and Edrei, and E ... Josh 19:37 5877

ENJOIN
e thee that which is convenient ... Philem 8 *2004*

ENJOINED
and Esther the queen had e them ... Est 9:31 6965
Who hath e him his way ... Job 36:23 6485
which God hath e unto you ... Heb 9:20 *1781*

ENJOY
shall the land e her sabbaths ... Lev 26:34 7521
the land rest, and e her sabbaths ... Lev 26:34 7521
shall e her sabbaths, while she ... Lev 26:43 7521
e every man the inheritance of ... Num 36:8 3423
but thou shalt not e them ... Deut 28:41 1961
e it, which Moses the LORD's ... Josh 1:15 3423
with mirth, therefore e pleasure ... Eccl 2:1 7200
his soul e good in his labour ... Eccl 2:24 7200
e the good of all his labour, it ... Eccl 3:13 7200
to e the good of all his labour ... Eccl 5:18 7200
mine elect shall long e the work ... Is 65:22 1086
that by thee we e great quietness ... Acts 24:2 *5177*
giveth us richly all things to e ... 1Ti 6:17 *619*
than to e the pleasures of sin ... Heb 11:25 *619*

ENJOYED
until the land had e her sabbaths ... 2Chr 36:21 7521

ENLARGE
God shall e Japheth, and he shall ... Gen 9:27 6601
before thee, and e thy borders ... Ex 34:24 7337
LORD thy God shall e thy border ... Deut 12:20 7337
if the LORD thy God e thy coast ... Deut 19:8 7337
e my coast, and that thine hand ... 1Chr 4:10 7235
when thou shalt e my heart ... Ps 119:32 7337
E the place of thy tent, and let ... Is 54:2 7337
that they might e their border ... Amos 1:13 7337
e thy baldness as the eagle ... Mic 1:16 7337
e the borders of their garments, ... Mt 23:5 *3170*

ENLARGED
my mouth is e over mine enemies ... 1Sa 2:1 7337
Thou hast e my steps under me ... 2Sa 22:37 7337
thou hast e me when I was in ... Ps 4:1 7337
Thou hast e my steps under me, ... Ps 18:36 7337
The troubles of my heart are e ... Ps 25:17 7337
Therefore hell hath e herself ... Is 5:14 7337
thou hast e thy bed, and made thee ... Is 57:8 7337
thine heart shall fear, and be e ... Is 60:5 7337
is open unto you, our heart is e ... 2Cor 6:11 *4115*
unto my children,) be ye also e ... 2Cor 6:13 *4115*
that we shall be e by you ... 2Cor 10:15 *3170*

ENLARGEMENT
at this time, then shall there e ... Est 4:14 7305

ENLARGETH
he said, Blessed be he that e Gad ... Deut 33:20 7337
he e the nations, and straiteneth ... Job 12:23 7849
who e his desire as hell, and is ... Hab 2:5 7337

ENLARGING
And there was an e, and a winding ... Eze 41:7 7337

ENLIGHTEN
LORD my God will e my darkness ... Ps 18:28 5050

ENLIGHTENED
and his eyes were e ... 1Sa 14:27 215
you, how mine eyes have been e ... 1Sa 14:29 215
to be e with the light of the ... Job 33:30 215
His lightnings e the world ... Ps 97:4 215
of your understanding being e ... Eph 1:18 *5461*
for those who were once e ... Heb 6:4 *5461*

ENLIGHTENING
of the LORD is pure, e the eyes ... Ps 19:8 215

ENMITY
I will put e between thee and the ... Gen 3:15 342
Or in e smite him with his hand, ... Num 35:21 342
he thrust him suddenly without e ... Num 35:22
they were at e between themselves ... Lk 23:12 *2189*
the carnal mind is e against God ... Rom 8:7 *2189*
abolished in his flesh the e ... Eph 2:15 *2189*
cross, having slain the e thereby ... Eph 2:16 *2189*
of the world is e with God ... Jas 4:4 *2189*

ENOCH (*e'-nok*) See HENOCH.
1. A son of Cain.
and she conceived, and bare E ... Gen 4:17 2585
And unto E was born Irad ... Gen 4:18 2585
2. A city built by Cain.
after the name of his son, E ... Gen 4:17 2585
3. A son of Jared.
sixty and two years, and he begat E ... Gen 5:18 2585
he begat E eight hundred years ... Gen 5:19 2585
E lived sixty and five years, and ... Gen 5:21 2585
E walked with God after he begat ... Gen 5:22 2585
all the days of E were three ... Gen 5:23 2585
And E walked with God ... Gen 5:24 2585
Mathusala, which was the son of E ... Lk 3:37 *1802*
By faith E was translated that he ... Heb 11:5 *1802*
E also, the seventh from Adam, ... Jude 14 *1802*

ENOS (*e'-nos*) See ENOSH. *Son of Seth.*
and he called his name E ... Gen 4:26 583
hundred and five years, and begat E ... Gen 5:6 583
after he begat E eight hundred ... Gen 5:7 583
E lived ninety years, and begat ... Gen 5:9 583
E lived after he begat Cainan ... Gen 5:10 583
all the days of E were nine ... Gen 5:11 583
Which was the son of E, which was ... Lk 3:38 *1800*

E

ENOSH (*e'-nosh*) See ENOS. *Same as Enos.*
Adam, Sheth, *E*, 1Chr 1:1 583

ENOUGH
We have both straw and provender *e* Gen 24:25 7227
And Esau said, I have *e*, my Gen 33:9 7227
with me, and because I have *e* Gen 33:11 3605
behold, it is large *e* for them Gen 34:21 3027
And Israel said, It is *e* Gen 45:28 7227
and also drew water *e* for us Ex 2:19
Intreat the LORD (for it is *e*) Ex 9:28 7227
e for the service of the work Ex 36:5 1767
have dwelt long *e* in this mount Deut 1:6
compassed this mountain long *e* Deut 2:3
said, The hill is not *e* for us Josh 17:16 4672
destroyed the people, It is *e* 2Sa 24:16 7227
and said, It is *e* 1Kin 19:4 7227
the angel that destroyed, It is *e* 1Chr 21:15 7227
of the LORD, we have had *e* to eat 2Chr 31:10 7644
have goats' milk *e* for thy food Prov 27:27 1767
vain persons shall have poverty *e* Prov 28:19 7644
yea, four things say not, It is *e* Prov 30:15 1952
the fire that saith not, It is *e* Prov 30:16 1952
dogs which can never have *e* Is 56:11 7654
will destroy till they have *e* Jer 49:9 1767
For they shall eat, and not have *e* Hos 4:10 7644
not have stolen till they had *e* Obad 5 1767
tear in pieces *e* for his whelps Nah 2:12 1767
ye eat, but ye have not *e* Hag 1:6 7654
shall not be room *e* to receive it Mal 3:10 1767
It is *e* for the disciple that he Mt 10:25 *713*
lest there be not *e* for us Mt 25:9 *714*
it is *e*, the hour is come Mk 14:41 *566*
of my father's have bread *e* Lk 15:17 *4052*
And he said unto them, It is *e* Lk 22:38 *2425*
And when they had eaten *e*, they Acts 27:38 *2880*

ENQUIRE
the damsel, and *e* at her mouth Gen 24:57 7592
And she went to *e* of the LORD Gen 25:22 1875
people come unto me to *e* of God Ex 18:15 1875
that thou *e* not after their gods, Deut 12:30 1875
Then shalt thou *e*, and make search Deut 13:14 1875
that shall be in those days, and *e* Deut 17:9 1875
e of thee, and say, Is there any Judg 4:20 7592
when a man went to *e* of God 1Sa 9:9 1875
E thou whose son the stripling is 1Sa 17:56 7592
I then begin to *e* of God for him 1Sa 22:15 7592
that I may go to her, and *e* of her 1Sa 28:7 1875
said unto the king of Israel, *E* 1Kin 22:5 1875
besides, that we might *e* of him 1Kin 22:7 1875
by whom we may *e* of the LORD 1Kin 22:8 1875
e of Baal-zebub the god of Ekron 2Kin 1:2 1875
that ye go to *e* of Baal-zebub the 2Kin 1:3 1875
that thou sendest to *e* of 2Kin 1:6 1875
e of Baal-zebub the god of Ekron 2Kin 1:16 1875
no God in Israel to *e* of his word 2Kin 1:16 1875
that we may *e* of the LORD by him 2Kin 3:11 1875
e of the LORD by him, saying, 2Kin 8:8 1875
altar shall be for me to *e* by 2Kin 16:15 1239
e of the LORD for me, and for the 2Kin 22:13 1875
which sent you to *e* of the LORD 2Kin 22:18 1875
had a familiar spirit, to *e* of it 1Chr 10:13 1875
to *e* of his welfare, and to 1Chr 18:10 7592
not go before it to *e* of God 1Chr 21:30 1875
said unto the king of Israel, *E* 2Chr 18:4 1875
besides, that we might *e* of him 2Chr 18:6 1875
man, by whom we may *e* of the LORD 2Chr 18:7 1875
who sent unto him to *e* of the 2Chr 32:31 1875
e of the LORD for me, and for them 2Chr 34:21 1875
who sent you to *e* of the LORD 2Chr 34:26 1875
to *e* concerning Judah and Ezr 7:14 1240
For *e*, I pray thee, of the former Job 8:8 7592
the LORD, and to *e* in his temple Ps 27:4 1239
for thou dost not *e* wisely Eccl 7:10 7592
also the night: if ye will *e* Is 21:12 1158
e ye: return, come Is 21:12 1158
E, I pray thee, of the LORD for Jer 21:2 1875
that sent you unto me to *e* of me Jer 37:7 1875
prophet to *e* of him concerning me Eze 14:7 1875
of Israel came to *e* of the LORD Eze 20:1 1875
Are ye come to *e* of me Eze 20:3 1875
enter, *e* who in it is worthy Mt 10:11 *1833*
they began to *e* among themselves, Lk 22:23 *4802*
Do ye *e* among yourselves of that Jn 16:19 *2212*
e in the house of Judas for one Acts 9:11 *2212*
But if ye *e* any thing concerning Acts 19:39 *1934*
as though ye would *e* something Acts 23:15 *1231*
as though they would *e* somewhat Acts 23:20 *4441*
Whether any do *e* of Titus 2Cor 8:23

ENQUIRED
e diligently, and, behold, it be Deut 17:4 1875
And when they *e* and asked, they Judg 6:29 1875
the men of Succoth, and *e* of him Judg 8:14 7592
children of Israel *e* of the LORD Judg 20:27 7592
Therefore they *e* of the LORD 1Sa 10:22 7592
he *e* of the LORD for him, and gave 1Sa 22:10 7592
hast *e* of God for him, that he 1Sa 22:13 7592
Therefore David *e* of the LORD 1Sa 23:2 7592
Then David *e* of the LORD yet 1Sa 23:4 7592
when Saul *e* of the LORD, the LORD 1Sa 28:6 7592
David *e* at the LORD, saying, 1Sa 30:8 7592
that David *e* of the LORD, saying, 2Sa 2:1 7592
David *e* of the LORD, saying, 2Sa 5:19 7592
when David *e* of the LORD, he said 2Sa 5:23 7592
David sent and *e* after the woman 2Sa 11:3 1875
was as if a man had *e* at the 2Sa 16:23 7592
and David *e* of the LORD 2Sa 21:1 1245
And *e* not of the LORD 1Chr 10:14 1875
for we *e* not at it in the days of 1Chr 13:3 1875
David *e* of God, saying, Shall I 1Chr 14:10 7592
Therefore David *e* again of God 1Chr 14:14 7592
returned and *e* early after God Ps 78:34 7836
should I be *e* of at all by them Eze 14:3 1875
GOD, I will not be *e* of by you Eze 20:3 1875
and shall I be *e* of by you Eze 20:31 1875
GOD, I will not be *e* of by you Eze 20:31
I will yet for this be *e* of by Eze 36:37 1875
that the king *e* of them, he Dan 1:20 1245
sought the LORD, nor *e* for him Zeph 1:6 1875
e of them diligently what time Mt 2:7 *198*
had diligently *e* of the wise men Mt 2:16 *198*
Then *e* he of them the hour when Jn 4:52 *4441*
or our brethren be *e* of, they are 2Cor 8:23
salvation the prophets have *e* 1Pet 1:10 *1567*

ENQUIREST
That thou *e* after mine iniquity, Job 10:6 1245

ENQUIRY
is holy, and after vows to make *e* Prov 20:25 1239
had made *e* for Simon's house Acts 10:17 *1331*

ENRICH
the king will *e* him with great 1Sa 17:25 6238
thou didst *e* the kings of the Eze 27:33 6238

ENRICHED
in every thing ye are *e* by him 1Cor 1:5 *4148*
Being *e* in every thing to all 2Cor 9:11 *4148*

ENRICHEST
thou greatly *e* it with the river Ps 65:9 6238

EN-RIMMON (*en-rim'-mon*) See AIN, RIMMON. *A city in Judah.*
And at *E*, and at Zareah, and at Neh 11:29 5884

EN-ROGEL (*en-ro'-ghel*) *A fountain near Jerusalem.*
the goings out thereof were at *E* Josh 15:7 5883
on the south, and descended to *E* Josh 18:16 5883
Jonathan and Ahimaaz stayed by *E* 2Sa 17:17 5883
stone of Zoheleth, which is by *E* 1Kin 1:9 5883

ENSAMPLE
walk so as ye have us for an *e* Phil 3:17 *5179*
an *e* unto you to follow us 2Th 3:9
making them an *e* unto those that 2Pet 2:6 *5262*

ENSAMPLES
things happened unto them for *e* 1Cor 10:11 *5179*
So that we were *e* to all that 1Th 1:7 *5179*
but being *e* to the flock 1Pet 5:3 *5179*

EN-SHEMESH (*en-she'-mesh*) *A spring.*
passed toward the waters of *E* Josh 15:7 5885
the north, and went forth to *E* Josh 18:17 5885

ENSIGN
with the *e* of their father's Num 2:2 226
he will lift up an *e* to the Is 5:26 5251
stand for an *e* of the people Is 11:10 5251
shall set up an *e* for the nations Is 11:12 5251
lifteth up an *e* on the mountains Is 18:3 5251
a mountain, and as an *e* on an hill Is 30:17 5251
princes shall be afraid of the *e* Is 31:9 5251
lifted up as an *e* upon his land Zec 9:16 5264

ENSIGNS
they set up their *e* for signs Ps 74:4 226

ENSNARED
reign not, lest the people be *e* Job 34:30 4170

ENSUE
let him seek peace, and *e* it 1Pet 3:11 *1377*

ENTANGLE
how they might *e* him in his talk Mt 22:15 *3802*

ENTANGLED
They are *e* in the land, the Ex 14:3 943
be not *e* again with the yoke of Gal 5:1 *1758*
Christ, they are again *e* therein 2Pet 2:20 *1707*

ENTANGLETH
No man that warreth *e* himself 2Ti 2:4 *1707*

EN-TAPPUAH (*en-tap'-poo-ah*) *A town in Manasseh.*
hand unto the inhabitants of *E* Josh 17:7 5887

ENTER
he was come near to *e* into Egypt Gen 12:11 935
able to *e* into the tent of the Ex 40:35 935
all that *e* into the host, to do Num 4:3 935
all that *e* in to perform the Num 4:23 935
the curse shall *e* into her Num 5:24 935
the curse shall *e* into her Num 5:27 935
for he shall not *e* into the land Num 20:24 935
shall not *e* into the congregation Deut 23:1 935
A bastard shall not *e* into the Deut 23:2 935
e into the congregation of the Deut 23:2 935
e into the congregation of the Deut 23:3 935
e into the congregation of the Deut 23:3 935
e into the congregation of the Deut 23:8 935
That thou shouldest *e* into Deut 29:12 5674
them not to *e* into their cities Josh 10:19 935
go, and to *e* to possess the land Judg 18:9 935
my cry did *e* into his ears 2Sa 22:7
and when thy feet *e* into the city 1Kin 14:12 935
myself, and *e* into the battle 1Kin 22:30 935
We will *e* into the city, then the 2Kin 7:4 935
A third part of you that *e* in on 2Kin 11:5 935
I will *e* into the lodgings of his 2Kin 19:23 935
the priests could not *e* into the 2Chr 7:2 935
unclean in any thing should *e* in 2Chr 23:19 935
e into his sanctuary, which he 2Chr 30:8 935
for the house that I shall *e* into Neh 2:8 935
for none might *e* into the king's Est 4:2 935
will he *e* with thee into judgment Job 22:4 935
that he should *e* into judgment Job 34:23 1980
Their sword shall *e* into their Ps 37:15 935
they shall *e* into the king's Ps 45:15 935
they should not *e* into my rest Ps 95:11 935
E into his gates with Ps 100:4 935
into which the righteous shall *e* Ps 118:20 935
e not into judgment with thy Ps 143:2 935
E not into the path of the wicked Prov 4:14 935
A fool's lips *e* into contention, Prov 18:6 935
e not into the fields of the Prov 23:10 935
E into the rock, and hide thee in Is 2:10 935
The LORD will *e* into judgment Is 3:14 935
which keepeth the truth may *e* in Is 26:2 935
e thou into thy chambers, and shut Is 26:20 935
I will *e* into the height of his Is 37:24 935
He shall *e* into peace Is 57:2 935
in the street, and equity cannot *e* Is 59:14 935
that *e* in at these gates to Jer 7:2 935
let us *e* into the defenced cities Jer 8:14 935
if I *e* into the city, then behold Jer 14:18 935
E not into the house of mourning, Jer 16:5 935
that *e* in by these gates Jer 17:20 935
Then shall there *e* into the gates Jer 17:25 935
or who shall *e* into our Jer 21:13 935
thy people that *e* in by these Jer 22:2 935
then shall there *e* in by the Jer 22:4 935
Bethlehem, to go to *e* into Egypt, Jer 41:17 935
set your faces to *e* into Egypt Jer 42:15 935
you, when ye shall *e* into Egypt Jer 42:18 935
not *e* into thy congregation Lam 1:10 935
of his quiver to *e* into my reins Lam 3:13 935
for the robbers shall *e* into it Eze 7:22 935
neither shall they *e* into the Eze 13:9 935
they shall not *e* into the land of Eze 20:38 935
when he shall *e* into thy gates, Eze 26:10 935
as men *e* into a city wherein is Eze 26:10 935
I will cause breath to *e* into you Eze 37:5 935
When the priests *e* therein Eze 42:14 935
and no man shall *e* in by it Eze 44:2 935
he shall *e* by the way of the Eze 44:3 935
shall *e* into my sanctuary, of any Eze 44:9 935
They shall *e* into my sanctuary, Eze 44:16 935
that when they *e* in at the gates Eze 44:17 935
when they *e* into the inner court Eze 44:21 935
the prince shall *e* by the way of Eze 46:2 935
And when the prince shall *e* Eze 46:8 935
shall *e* into the fortress of the Dan 11:7 935
He shall also set his face to *e* Dan 11:17 935
He shall *e* peaceably even upon Dan 11:24 935
he shall *e* into the countries, and Dan 11:40 935
He shall *e* also into the glorious Dan 11:41 935
I will not *e* into the city Hos 11:9 935
they shall *e* in at the windows Joel 2:9 935
nor *e* into Gilgal, and pass not to Amos 5:5 935
Jonah began to *e* into the city a Jonah 3:4 935
it shall *e* into the house of the Zec 5:4 935
ye shall in no case *e* into the Mt 5:20 *1525*
e into thy closet, and when thou Mt 6:6 *1525*
E ye in at the strait gate Mt 7:13 *1525*
shall *e* into the kingdom of Mt 7:21 *1525*
city of the Samaritans *e* ye not Mt 10:5 *1525*
city or town ye shall *e*, enquire Mt 10:11 *1525*
Or else how can one *e* into a Mt 12:29 *1525*
wicked than himself, and they *e* in Mt 12:45 *1525*
ye shall not *e* into the kingdom Mt 18:3 *1525*
to *e* into life halt or maimed Mt 18:8 *1525*
thee to *e* into life with one eye Mt 18:9 *1525*
but if thou wilt *e* into life Mt 19:17 *1525*
e into the kingdom of heaven Mt 19:23 *1525*
than for a rich man to *e* into the Mt 19:24 *1525*
e thou into the joy of thy lord Mt 25:21 *1525*
e thou into the joy of thy lord Mt 25:23 *1525*
that ye *e* not into temptation Mt 26:41 *1525*
no more openly *e* into the city Mk 1:45 *1525*
No man can *e* into a strong man's Mk 3:27 *1525*
swine, that we may *e* into them Mk 5:12 *1525*
place soever ye *e* into a house Mk 6:10 *1525*
out of him, and *e* no more into him Mk 9:25 *1525*
for thee to *e* into life maimed Mk 9:43 *1525*
for thee to *e* halt into life Mk 9:45 *1525*
it is better for thee to *e* into Mk 9:47 *1525*
child, he shall not *e* therein Mk 10:15 *1525*
riches *e* into the kingdom of God Mk 10:23 *1525*
to *e* into the kingdom of God Mk 10:24 *1525*
than for a rich man to *e* into the Mk 10:25 *1525*
into the house, neither *e* therein Mk 13:15 *1525*
lest ye *e* into temptation Mk 14:38 *1525*
thou shouldest *e* under my roof Lk 7:6 *1525*
that they which *e* in may see the Lk 8:16 *1531*
would suffer them to *e* into them Lk 8:32 *1525*
And whatsoever house ye *e* into Lk 9:4 *1525*
And into whatsoever house ye *e* Lk 10:5 *1525*
And into whatsoever city ye *e* Lk 10:8 *1525*
But into whatsoever city ye *e* Lk 10:10 *1525*
and they *e* in, and dwell there Lk 11:26 *1525*
Strive to *e* in at the strait gate Lk 13:24 *1525*
I say unto you, will seek to *e* in Lk 13:24 *1525*
child shall in no wise *e* therein Lk 18:17 *1525*
riches *e* into the kingdom of God Lk 18:24 *1525*
than for a rich man to *e* into the Lk 18:25 *1525*
are in the countries *e* thereinto Lk 21:21 *1525*
them, Pray that ye *e* not into Lk 22:40 *1525*
lest ye *e* into temptation Lk 22:46 *1525*
things, and to *e* into his glory Lk 24:26 *1525*
can he *e* the second time into his Jn 3:4 *1525*
he cannot *e* into the kingdom of Jn 3:5 *1525*
by me if any man *e* in, he shall Jn 10:9 *1525*
e into the kingdom of God Acts 14:22 *1525*
grievous wolves *e* in among you Acts 20:29 *1525*
They shall not *e* into my rest Heb 3:11 *1525*
they should not *e* into his rest Heb 3:18 *1525*
not *e* in because of unbelief Heb 3:19 *1525*
have believed do *e* into rest Heb 4:3 *1525*
if they shall *e* into my rest Heb 4:3 *1525*
If they shall *e* into my rest Heb 4:5 *1525*
that some must *e* therein, and they Heb 4:6 *1525*
therefore to *e* into that rest Heb 4:11 *1525*
boldness to *e* into the holiest by Heb 10:19 *1529*
man was able to *e* into the temple Rev 15:8 *1525*

there shall in no wise e into it ... Rev 21:27 1525
may e in through the gates into ... Rev 22:14 1525

ENTERED

In the selfsame day e Noah ... Gen 7:13 935
in unto him, and e into his house ... Gen 19:3 935
the earth when Lot e into Zoar ... Gen 19:23 935
tent, and e into Rachel's tent ... Gen 31:33 935
he e into his chamber, and wept ... Gen 43:30 935
as Moses e into the tabernacle, ... Ex 33:9 935
which are e into thine house ... Josh 2:3 935
they e into the city, and took it, ... Josh 8:19 935
of them e into fenced cities ... Josh 10:20 935
they e into the land to destroy ... Judg 6:5 935
they e into an hold of the house ... Judg 9:46 935
Abishai, and e into the city ... 2Sa 10:14 935
e into another tent, and carried ... 2Kin 7:8 935
as Jehu e in at the gate, she ... 2Kin 9:31 935
his brother, and e into the city ... 1Chr 19:15 935
when the king e into the house of ... 2Chr 12:11 935
they e into a covenant to seek ... 2Chr 15:12 935
howbeit he e not into the temple ... 2Chr 27:2 935
e into Judah, and encamped against ... 2Chr 32:1 935
e by the gate of the valley, and ... Neh 2:15 935
e into a curse, and into an oath, ... Neh 10:29 935
Hast thou e into the springs of ... Job 38:16 935
Hast thou e into the treasures of ... Job 38:22 935
but when ye e, ye defiled my land ... Jer 2:7 935
is e into our palaces, to cut off ... Jer 9:21 935
which had e into the covenant, ... Jer 34:10 935
Jeremiah was e into the dungeon ... Jer 37:16 935
the heathen e into her sanctuary ... Lam 1:10 935
the enemy should have e into the ... Lam 4:12 935
the spirit e into me when he ... Eze 2:2 935
Then the spirit e into me ... Eze 3:24 935
e into a covenant with thee, ... Eze 16:8 935
when they e unto the heathen, ... Eze 36:20 935
they e into the wall which was of ... Eze 41:6 935
hath e in by it, therefore it ... Eze 44:2 935
foreigners e into his gates, and ... Obad 11 935
Thou shouldest not have e into ... Obad 13 935
rottenness e into my bones, and I ... Hab 3:16 935
when Jesus was e into Capernaum ... Mt 8:5 1525
And when he was e into a ship ... Mt 8:23 1684
he e into a ship, and passed over, ... Mt 9:1 1684
How he e into the house of God, ... Mt 12:4 1525
the day that Noe e into the ark ... Mt 24:38 1525
day he e into the synagogue ... Mk 1:21 1525
they e into the house of Simon and ... Mk 1:29 2064
again he e into Capernaum after ... Mk 2:1 1525
he e again into the synagogue ... Mk 3:1 1525
so that he e into a ship, and sat ... Mk 4:1 1684
went out, and e into the swine ... Mk 5:13 1525
And whithersoever he e, into ... Mk 6:56 1531
when he was e into the house from ... Mk 7:17 1525
e into an house, and would have no ... Mk 7:24 1525
straightway he e into a ship with ... Mk 8:10 1684
and as soon as ye be e into it ... Mk 11:2 1531
Jesus e into Jerusalem, and into ... Mk 11:11 1525
e into the house of Zacharias, and ... Lk 1:40 1525
and e into Simon's house ... Lk 4:38 1525
he e into one of the ships, which ... Lk 5:3 1684
that he e into the synagogue and ... Lk 6:6 1525
the people, he e into Capernaum ... Lk 7:1 1525
I e into thine house, thou gavest ... Lk 7:44 1525
many devils were e into him ... Lk 8:30 1525
of the man, and e into the swine ... Lk 8:33 1525
feared as they e into the cloud ... Lk 9:34 1525
went, and e into a village of the ... Lk 9:52 1525
that he e into a certain village ... Lk 10:38 1525
ye e not in yourselves, and them ... Lk 11:52 1525
as he e into a certain village, ... Lk 17:12 1525
the day that Noe e into the ark ... Lk 17:27 1525
And Jesus e and passed through ... Lk 19:1 1525
Then e Satan into Judas surnamed ... Lk 22:3 1525
when ye are e into the city, ... Lk 22:10 1525
And they e in, and found not the ... Lk 24:3 1525
ye are e into their labours ... Jn 4:38 1525
e into a ship, and went over the ... Jn 6:17 1684
whereinto his disciples were e ... Jn 6:22 1684
And after the sop Satan e into him ... Jn 13:27 1525
was a garden, into the which he e ... Jn 18:1 1525
Then Pilate e into the judgment ... Jn 18:33 1525
e into a ship immediately ... Jn 21:3 305
of them that e into the temple ... Acts 3:2 1531
e with them into the temple, ... Acts 3:8 1525
they e into the temple early in ... Acts 5:21 1525
went his way, and e into the house ... Acts 9:17 1525
morrow after they e into Caesarea ... Acts 10:24 1525
hath at any time e into my mouth ... Acts 11:8 1525
we e into the man's house ... Acts 11:12 1525
e into the house of Lydia ... Acts 16:40 1525
e into a certain man's house, ... Acts 18:7 2064
but he himself e into the ... Acts 18:19 1525
would have e in unto the people ... Acts 19:30 1525
we e into the house of Philip the ... Acts 21:8 1525
with them e into the temple ... Acts 21:26 1524
e into the castle, and told Paul ... Acts 23:16 1525
was e into the place of hearing, ... Acts 25:23 1525
to whom Paul e in, and prayed, and ... Acts 28:8 1525
by one man sin e into the world ... Rom 5:12 1525
Moreover the law e, that the ... Rom 5:20 3922
neither have e into the heart of ... 1Cor 2:9 305
e not in because of unbelief ... Heb 4:6 1525
For he that is e into his rest ... Heb 4:10 1525
the forerunner is for us e ... Heb 6:20 1525
but by his own blood he e in once ... Heb 9:12 1525
For Christ is not e into the holy ... Heb 9:24 1525
e into the ears of the Lord of ... Jas 5:4 1525
deceivers are e into the world ... 2Jn 7 1525
of life from God e into them ... Rev 11:11 1525

ENTERETH

every one that e into the service ... Num 4:30 935
every one that e into the service ... Num 4:35 935
every one that e into the service ... Num 4:39 935
every one that e into the service ... Num 4:43 935
even unto every one that e into ... 2Chr 31:16 935
When wisdom e into thine heart, ... Prov 2:10 935
A reproof e more into a wise man ... Prov 17:10 5181
which e into their privy chambers ... Eze 21:14 935
the east, as one e into them ... Eze 42:12 935
he that e in by the way of the ... Eze 46:9 935
he that e by the way of the south ... Eze 46:9 935
that whatsoever e in at the mouth ... Mt 15:17 1531
e in where the damsel was lying ... Mk 5:40 1531
thing from without e into the man ... Mk 7:18 1531
Because it e not into his heart, ... Mk 7:19 1531
him into the house where he e in ... Lk 22:10 1531
He that e not by the door into ... Jn 10:1 1525
But he that e in by the door is ... Jn 10:2 1525
which e into that within the veil ... Heb 6:19 1525
as the high priest e into the ... Heb 9:25 1525

ENTERING

at the e in of the tabernacle ... Ex 35:15 6607
cast it at the e of the gate of ... Josh 8:29 6607
Hermon unto the e into Hamath ... Josh 13:5 935
at the e of the gate of the city ... Josh 20:4 6607
unto the e in of Hamath ... Judg 3:3 935
stood in the e of the gate of the ... Judg 9:35 6607
even unto the e of the gate ... Judg 9:40 6607
stood in the e of the gate of the ... Judg 9:44 6607
Dan, stood by the e of the gate ... Judg 18:16 6607
the priest stood in the e of the ... Judg 18:17 6607
by e into a town that hath gates ... 1Sa 23:7 935
in array at the e in of the gate ... 2Sa 10:8 6607
them even unto the e of the gate ... 2Sa 11:23 6607
for the e of the oracle he made ... 1Kin 6:31 6607
from the e in of Hamath unto the ... 1Kin 8:65 935
stood in the e in of the cave ... 1Kin 19:13 6607
men at the e in of the gate ... 2Kin 7:3 6607
at the e in of the gate until the ... 2Kin 10:8 6607
the coast of Israel from the e of ... 2Kin 14:25 935
e in of the gate of Joshua the ... 2Kin 23:8 6607
at the e in of the house of the ... 2Kin 23:11 935
e in of the wilderness from the ... 1Chr 5:9 935
Egypt even unto the e of Hemath ... 1Chr 13:5 935
from the e in of Hamath unto the ... 2Chr 7:8 935
the e in of the gate of Samaria ... 2Chr 18:9 6607
part of you e on the sabbath ... 2Chr 23:4 935
stood at his pillar at the e in ... 2Chr 23:13 3996
when she was come to the e of the ... 2Chr 23:15 3996
abroad even to the e in of Egypt ... 2Chr 26:8 935
even to the e in at the fish gate ... 2Chr 33:14 935
that there is no house, no e in ... Is 23:1 935
the e of the gates of Jerusalem ... Jer 1:15 6607
even e in at the gates of ... Jer 17:27 935
mark well the e in of the house, ... Eze 44:5 3996
e in of Hemath unto the river of ... Amos 6:14 935
ye them that are e to go in ... Mt 23:13 1525
and the lusts of other things e in ... Mk 4:19 1531
that e into him can defile him ... Mk 7:15 1531
e into the ship again departed to ... Mk 8:13 1684
e into the sepulchre, they saw a ... Mk 16:5 1525
them that were e in ye hindered ... Lk 11:52 1525
in the which at your e ye shall ... Lk 19:30 1531
e into every house, and haling men ... Acts 8:3 1531
e into a ship of Adramyttium, we ... Acts 27:2 1910
manner of e in we had unto you ... 1Th 1:9 1529
being left us of e into his rest ... Heb 4:1 1525

ENTERPRISE

hands cannot perform their e ... Job 5:12 8454

ENTERTAIN

Be not forgetful to e strangers ... Heb 13:2 5381

ENTERTAINED

some have e angels unawares ... Heb 13:2 3579

ENTICE

if a man e a maid that is not ... Ex 22:16 6601
e thee secretly, saying, Let us ... Deut 13:6 5496
E thy husband, that he may ... Judg 14:15 6601
E him, and see wherein his great ... Judg 16:5 6601
Who shall e Ahab king of Israel, ... 2Chr 18:19 6601
the LORD, and said, I will e him ... 2Chr 18:20 6601
the LORD said, Thou shalt e him ... 2Chr 18:21 6601
My son, if sinners e thee ... Prov 1:10 6601

ENTICED

And my heart hath been secretly e ... Job 31:27 6601
saying, Peradventure he will be e ... Jer 20:10 6601
drawn away of his own lust, and e ... Jas 1:14 1185

ENTICETH

A violent man e his neighbour ... Prov 16:29 6601

ENTICING

not with e words of man's wisdom ... 1Cor 2:4 3981
should beguile you with e words ... Col 2:4 4086

ENTIRE

work, that ye may be perfect and e ... Jas 1:4 3648

ENTRANCE

your border unto the e of Hamath ... Num 34:8 935
the e into the city, and we will ... Judg 1:24 3996
shewed them the e into the city ... Judg 1:25 3996
before Ahab to the e of Jezreel ... 1Kin 18:46 935
in the e of the gate of Samaria ... 1Kin 22:10 6607
And they went to the e of Gedor ... 1Chr 4:39 3996
that kept the e of the king's ... 2Chr 12:10 6607
The e of thy words giveth light ... Ps 119:130 6608
the face of the gate of the e ... Eze 40:15 2978
know our e in unto you, that it ... 1Th 2:1 1529
For so an e shall be ministered ... 2Pet 1:11 1529

ENTRANCES

land of Nimrod in the e thereof ... Mic 5:6 6607

ENTREAT

I will cause the enemy to e thee ... Jer 15:11 6293
e them evil four hundred years ... Acts 7:6 2559

ENTREATED

he e Abram well for her sake ... Gen 12:16
hast thou so evil e this people ... Ex 5:22
And the Egyptians evil e us ... Deut 26:6
e them spitefully, and slew them ... Mt 22:6 5195
shall be mocked, and spitefully e ... Lk 18:32 5195
e him shamefully, and sent him ... Lk 20:11 818
evil e our fathers, so that they ... Acts 7:19 2559
And Julius courteously e Paul ... Acts 27:3 5530
before, and were shamefully e ... 1Th 2:2 5195

ENTREATETH

He evil e the barren that beareth ... Job 24:21

ENTRIES

the e thereof were by the posts ... Eze 40:38 6607

ENTRY

house, and the king's e without ... 2Kin 16:18 3996
the LORD, were keepers of the e ... 1Chr 9:19 3996
the e of the house, the inner ... 2Chr 4:22 6607
at the e of the city, at the ... Prov 8:3 6310
which is by the e of the east ... Jer 19:2 6607
sat down in the e of the new gate ... Jer 26:10 6607
at the e of the new gate of the ... Jer 36:10 6607
e that is in the house of the ... Jer 38:14 3996
which is at the e of Pharaoh's ... Jer 43:9 6607
this image of jealousy in the e ... Eze 8:5 872
art situate at the e of the sea ... Eze 27:3 3996
the breadth of the e of the gate ... Eze 40:11 6607
up to the e of the north gate ... Eze 40:40 6607
was the e on the east side ... Eze 42:9 3996
After he brought me through the e ... Eze 46:19 3996

ENVIED

and the Philistines e him ... Gen 26:14 7065
no children, Rachel e her sister ... Gen 30:1 7065
And his brethren e him ... Gen 37:11 7065
They e Moses also in the camp, and ... Ps 106:16 7065
this a man is e of his neighbour ... Eccl 4:4 7068
were in the garden of God, e him ... Eze 31:9 7065

ENVIES

all guile, and hypocrisies, and e ... 1Pet 2:1 5355

ENVIEST

said unto him, E thou for my sake ... Num 11:29 7065

ENVIETH

charity e not ... 1Cor 13:4 2206

ENVIOUS

neither be thou e against the ... Ps 37:1 7065
For I was e at the foolish, when ... Ps 73:3 7065
Be not thou e against evil men, ... Prov 24:1 7065
neither be thou e at the wicked ... Prov 24:19 7065

ENVIRON

shall e us round, and cut off our ... Josh 7:9 5437

ENVY

man, and e slayeth the silly one ... Job 5:2 7068
E thou not the oppressor, and ... Prov 3:31 7065
but e the rottenness of the bones ... Prov 14:30 7068
Let not thine heart e sinners ... Prov 23:17 7065
but who is able to stand before e ... Prov 27:4 7068
love, and their hatred, and their e ... Eccl 9:6 7068
The e also of Ephraim shall ... Is 11:13 7068
Ephraim shall not e Judah ... Is 11:13 7065
ashamed for their e at the people ... Is 26:11 7068
according to thine e which thou ... Eze 35:11 7068
For he knew that for e they had ... Mt 27:18 5355
priests had delivered him for e ... Mk 15:10 5355
And the patriarchs, moved with e ... Acts 7:9 2206
they were filled with e, and ... Acts 13:45 2205
which believed not, moved with e ... Acts 17:5 2206
full of e, murder, debate, deceit ... Rom 1:29 5355
indeed preach Christ even of e ... Phil 1:15 5355
of words, whereof cometh e ... 1Ti 6:4 5355
pleasures, living in malice and e ... Titus 3:3 5355
that dwelleth in us lusteth to e ... Jas 4:5 5355

ENVYING

and wantonness, not in strife and e ... Rom 13:13 2205
for whereas there is among you e ... 1Cor 3:3 2205
one another, e one another ... Gal 5:26 5354
But if ye have bitter e and strife ... Jas 3:14 2205
For where e and strife is, there ... Jas 3:16 2205

ENVYINGS

lest there be debates, e, wraths, ... 2Cor 12:20 2205
E, murders, drunkenness, ... Gal 5:21 5355

EPAENETUS (*ep-en'-e-tus*) *A Christian acquaintance of Paul.*

Salute my wellbeloved E, who is ... Rom 16:5 1866

EPAPHRAS (*ep'-a-fras*) *A Christian acquaintance of Paul.*

As ye also learned of E our dear ... Col 1:7 1889
E, who is one of you, a servant ... Col 4:12 1889
There salute thee E, my ... Philem 23 1889

EPAPHRODITUS (*e-paf-ro-di'-tus*) *A fellow-worker with Paul.*

it necessary to send to you E ... Phil 2:25 1891
having received of E the things ... Phil 4:18 1891
to the Philippians from Rome by E ... Phil s 1891

EPENETUS See EPAENETUS.

EPHAH (*e'-fah*)

1. A son of Midian; grandson of Abraham.

E, and Epher, and Hanoch, ... Gen 25:4 5891
E, and Epher, and Henoch, and Abida, ... 1Chr 1:33 5891
the dromedaries of Midian and E ... Is 60:6 5891

2. A concubine of Caleb.

And E, Caleb's concubine, bare ... 1Chr 2:46 5891

3. A son of Jahdai.

Jotham, and Gesham, and Pelet, and E ... 1Chr 2:47 5891

4. A grain measure.

an omer is the tenth part of an e ... Ex 16:36 374

of an e of fine flour for a sin ... Lev 5:11 374
the tenth part of an e of fine ... Lev 6:20 374
balances, just weights, a just e ... Lev 19:36 374
tenth part of an e of barley meal ... Num 5:15 374
a tenth part of an e of flour for ... Num 28:5 374
unleavened cakes of an e of flour ... Judg 6:19 374
and it was about an e of barley ... Ruth 2:17 374
one e of flour, and a bottle of ... 1Sa 1:24 374
an e of this parched corn ... 1Sa 17:17 374
seed of an homer shall yield an e ... Is 5:10 374
have just balances, and a just e ... Eze 45:10 374
The e and the bath shall be of one ... Eze 45:11 374
the e the tenth part of an homer ... Eze 45:11 374
part of an e of an homer of wheat ... Eze 45:13 374
of an e of an homer of barley ... Eze 45:13 374
offering of an e for a bullock ... Eze 45:24 374
an e for a ram, and an hin of oil ... Eze 45:24 374
a ram, and an hin of oil for an e ... Eze 45:24 374
offering shall be an e for a ram ... Eze 46:5 374
to give, and an hin of oil to an e ... Eze 46:5 374
an e for a bullock, and ... Eze 46:7 374
an e for a ram, and for the lambs ... Eze 46:7 374
unto, and an hin of oil to an e ... Eze 46:7 374
shall be an e to a bullock ... Eze 46:11 374
an e to a ram, and to the lambs as ... Eze 46:11 374
to give, and an hin of oil to an e ... Eze 46:11 374
morning, the sixth part of an e ... Eze 46:14 374
forth wheat, making the e small ... Amos 8:5 374
This is an e that goeth forth ... Zec 5:6 374
sitteth in the midst of the e ... Zec 5:7 374
cast it into the midst of the e ... Zec 5:8 374
lifted up the e between the earth ... Zec 5:9 374
me, Whither do these bear the e ... Zec 5:10 374

EPHAI (*e'-fahee*) *Family who remained in Jerusalem during captivity.*
the sons of E the Netophathite, ... Jer 40:8 5778

EPHER (*e'-fur*)
1. A son of Midian; grandson of Abraham.
Ephah, and E, and Hanoch ... Gen 25:4 6081
Ephah, and E, and Henoch, and Abida, 1Chr 1:33 6081
2. A descendant of Judah.
Ezra were, Jether, and Mered, and E ... 1Chr 4:17 6081
3. A chief of Manasseh.
house of their fathers, even E ... 1Chr 5:24 6081

EPHES-DAMMIM *A city in Judah.*
between Shochoh and Azekah, in E ... 1Sa 17:1 658

EPHESIAN (*e-fe'-zheun*) See EPHESIANS. *A resident of Ephesus.*
him in the city Trophimus an E ... Acts 21:29 *2180*

EPHESIANS (*e-fe'-zheuns*)
saying, Great is Diana of the E ... Acts 19:28 *2180*
out, Great is Diana of the E ... Acts 19:34 *2180*
E is a worshipper of the great ... Acts 19:35 *2180*
from Rome unto the E by Tychicus ... Eph s *2180*
bishop of the church of the E ... 2Ti s *2180*

EPHESUS (*ef'-e-sus*) See EPHESIAN. *Capital of Roman province of Asia.*
And he came to E, and left them ... Acts 18:19 *2181*
And he sailed from E ... Acts 18:21 *2181*
in the scriptures, came to E ... Acts 18:24 *2181*
the upper coasts came to E ... Acts 19:1 *2181*
Jews and Greeks also dwelling at E ... Acts 19:17 *2181*
see and hear, that not alone at E ... Acts 19:26 *2181*
the people, he said, Ye men of E ... Acts 19:35 *2181*
Paul had determined to sail by E ... Acts 20:16 *2181*
And from Miletus he sent to E ... Acts 20:17 *2181*
I have fought with beasts at E ... 1Cor 15:32 *2181*
I will tarry at E until Pentecost ... 1Cor 16:8 *2181*
God, to the saints which are at E ... Eph 1:1 *2181*
besought thee to abide still at E ... 1Ti 1:3 *2181*
things he ministered unto me at E ... 2Ti 1:18 *2181*
And Tychicus have I sent to E ... 2Ti 4:12 *2181*
unto E, and unto Smyrna, and unto ... Rev 1:11 *2181*
angel of the church of E write ... Rev 2:1 *2181*

EPHLAL (*ef'-lal*) *A descendant of Pharez.*
And Zabad begat E, and E begat ... 1Chr 2:37 654
begat E, and E begat Obed, ... 1Chr 2:37 654

EPHOD (*e'-fod*)
1. Father of Hanniel.
of Manasseh, Hanniel the son of E ... Num 34:23 641
2. A priestly garment.
and stones to be set in the e ... Ex 25:7 646
a breastplate, and an e, and a robe ... Ex 28:4 646
And they shall make the e of gold ... Ex 28:6 646
And the curious girdle of the e ... Ex 28:8 642
upon the shoulders of the e for ... Ex 28:12 646
work of the e thou shalt make it ... Ex 28:15 646
shoulderpieces of the e before it ... Ex 28:25 646
is in the side of the e inward ... Ex 28:26 646
the two sides of the e underneath ... Ex 28:27 646
above the curious girdle of the e ... Ex 28:27 646
of the e with a lace of blue ... Ex 28:28 646
above the curious girdle of the e ... Ex 28:28 646
be not loosed from the e ... Ex 28:28 646
the robe of the e all of blue ... Ex 28:31 646
the coat, and the robe of the e ... Ex 29:5 646
and the e, and the breastplate ... Ex 29:5 646
with the curious girdle of the e ... Ex 29:5 646
and stones to be set for the e ... Ex 35:9 646
and stones to be set, for the e ... Ex 35:27 646
And he made the e of gold, blue, ... Ex 39:2 646
And the curious girdle of his e ... Ex 39:5 642
them on the shoulders of the e ... Ex 39:7 646
work, like the work of the e ... Ex 39:8 646
on the shoulderpieces of the e ... Ex 39:18 646
was on the side of the e inward ... Ex 39:19 646
the two sides of the e underneath ... Ex 39:20 646
above the curious girdle of the e ... Ex 39:20 646
of the e with a lace of blue ... Ex 39:21 646
above the curious girdle of the e ... Ex 39:21 646
might not be loosed from the e ... Ex 39:21 646
the robe of the e of woven work ... Ex 39:22 646
put the e upon him, and he girded ... Lev 8:7 646
with the curious girdle of the e ... Lev 8:7 646
And Gideon made an e thereof ... Judg 8:27 646
an house of gods, and made an e ... Judg 17:5 646
there is in these houses an e ... Judg 18:14 646
took the graven image, and the e ... Judg 18:17 646
fetched the carved image, the e ... Judg 18:18 646
heart was glad, and he took the e ... Judg 18:20 646
a child, girded with a linen e ... 1Sa 2:18 646
incense, to wear an e before me ... 1Sa 2:28 646
priest in Shiloh, wearing an e ... 1Sa 14:3 646
wrapped in a cloth behind the e ... 1Sa 21:9 646
persons that did wear a linen e ... 1Sa 22:18 646
came down with an e in his hand ... 1Sa 23:6 646
the priest, Bring hither the e ... 1Sa 23:9 646
pray thee, bring me hither the e ... 1Sa 30:7 646
brought thither the e to David ... 1Sa 30:7 646
David was girded with a linen e ... 2Sa 6:14 646
also had upon him an e of linen ... 1Chr 15:27 646
without an image, and without an e ... Hos 3:4 646

EPHPHATHA
he sighed, and saith unto him, E ... Mk 7:34 *2188*

EPHRAIM (*e'-fra-im*) See EPHRAIMITE, EPHRAIM'S, EPHRAIN.
1. A son of Joseph.
name of the second called he E ... Gen 41:52 669
of Egypt were born Manasseh and E ... Gen 46:20 669
him his two sons, Manasseh and E ... Gen 48:1 669
And now thy two sons, E and ... Gen 48:5 669
E in his right hand toward ... Gen 48:13 669
his right hand upon the head of E ... Gen 48:17 669
bless, saying, God make thee as E ... Gen 48:20 669
and he set E before Manasseh ... Gen 48:20 669
their families were Manasseh and E ... Num 26:28 669
And the sons of E ... 1Chr 7:20 669
E their father mourned many days, ... 1Chr 7:22 669
2. One of the twelve tribes comprising Israel.
children of Joseph: of E ... Num 1:10 669
namely, of the children of E ... Num 1:32 669
of them, even of the tribe of E ... Num 1:33 669
of E according to their armies ... Num 2:18 669
the captain of the sons of E ... Num 2:18 669
of E were an hundred thousand ... Num 2:24 669
prince of the children of E ... Num 7:48 669
E set forward according to their ... Num 10:22 669
Of the tribe of E, Oshea the son ... Num 13:8 669
sons of E after their families ... Num 26:35 669
of E according to those that were ... Num 26:37 669
of the tribe of the children of E ... Num 34:24 669
they are the ten thousands of E ... Deut 33:17 669
And all Naphtali, and the land of E ... Deut 34:2 669
were two tribes, Manasseh and E ... Josh 14:4 669
children of Joseph, Manasseh and E ... Josh 16:4 669
the border of the children of E ... Josh 16:5 669
children of E by their families ... Josh 16:8 669
cities for the children of E were ... Josh 16:9 669
belonged to the children of E ... Josh 17:8 669
these cities of E are among the ... Josh 17:9 669
the house of Joseph, even to E ... Josh 17:17 669
of the families of the tribe of E ... Josh 21:5 669
their lot out of the tribe of E ... Josh 21:20 669
Neither did E drive out the ... Judg 1:29 669
Out of E was there a root of them ... Judg 5:14 669
Then all the men of E gathered ... Judg 7:24 669
the men of E said unto him, Why ... Judg 8:1 669
of E better than the vintage of ... Judg 8:2 669
and against the house of E ... Judg 10:9 669
the men of E gathered themselves ... Judg 12:1 669
men of Gilead, and fought with E ... Judg 12:4 669
and the men of Gilead smote E ... Judg 12:4 669
of E among the Ephraimites ... Judg 12:4 669
in Pirathon in the land of E ... Judg 12:15 669
and over Jezreel, and over E ... 2Sa 2:9 669
coasts out of the tribe of E ... 1Chr 6:66 669
Benjamin, and of the children of E ... 1Chr 9:3 669
the children of E twenty thousand ... 1Chr 12:30 669
Pelonite, of the children of E ... 1Chr 27:10 669
Pirathonite, of the children of E ... 1Chr 27:14 669
Of the children of E, Hoshea the ... 1Chr 27:20 669
the strangers with them out of E ... 2Chr 15:9 669
of Judah, and in the cities of E ... 2Chr 17:2 669
wit, with all the children of E ... 2Chr 25:7 669
that was come to him out of E ... 2Chr 25:10 669
And Zichri, a mighty man of E ... 2Chr 28:7 669
of the heads of the children of E ... 2Chr 28:12 669
Judah, and wrote letters also to E ... 2Chr 30:1 669
to city through the country of E ... 2Chr 30:10 669
of the people, even many of E ... 2Chr 30:18 669
in E also and Manasseh, until they ... 2Chr 31:1 669
in the cities of Manasseh, and E ... 2Chr 34:6 669
of the hand of Manasseh and E ... 2Chr 34:9 669
E also is the strength of mine ... Ps 60:7 669
The children of E, being armed, ... Ps 78:9 669
and chose not the tribe of E ... Ps 78:67 669
Before E and Benjamin and Manasseh. Ps 80:2 669
E also is the strength of mine ... Ps 108:8 669
Syria is confederate with E ... Is 7:2 669
Because Syria, E, and the son of ... Is 7:5 669
and five years shall E be broken ... Is 7:8 669
And the head of E is Samaria ... Is 7:9 669
from the day that E departed from ... Is 7:17 669
all the people shall know, even E ... Is 9:9 669
Manasseh, E ... Is 9:21 669
and E, Manasseh ... Is 9:21 669
The envy also of E shall depart ... Is 11:13 669
E shall not envy Judah ... Is 11:13 669
and Judah shall not vex E ... Is 11:13 669
fortress also shall cease from E ... Is 17:3 669
of pride, to the drunkards of E ... Is 28:1 669
of pride, the drunkards of E ... Is 28:3 669
even the whole seed of E ... Jer 7:15 669
to Israel, and E is my firstborn ... Jer 31:9 669
I have surely heard E bemoaning ... Jer 31:18 669
Is E my dear son ... Jer 31:20 669
it, For Joseph, the stick of E ... Eze 37:16 669
Joseph, which is in the hand of E ... Eze 37:19 669
the west side, a portion for E ... Eze 48:5 669
And by the border of E, from the ... Eze 48:6 669
E is joined to idols ... Hos 4:17 669
I know E, and Israel is not hid ... Hos 5:3 669
for now, O E, thou committest ... Hos 5:3 669
and E fall in their iniquity ... Hos 5:5 669
E shall be desolate in the day of ... Hos 5:9 669
E is oppressed and broken in ... Hos 5:11 669
will I be unto E as a moth ... Hos 5:12 669
When E saw his sickness, and Judah ... Hos 5:13 669
then went E to the Assyrian, and ... Hos 5:13 669
For I will be unto E as a lion ... Hos 5:14 669
O E, what shall I do unto thee ... Hos 6:4 669
there is the whoredom of E ... Hos 6:10 669
the iniquity of E was discovered ... Hos 7:1 669
E, he hath mixed himself among ... Hos 7:8 669
E is a cake not turned ... Hos 7:8 669
E also is like a silly dove ... Hos 7:11 669
E hath hired lovers ... Hos 8:9 669
Because E hath made many altars ... Hos 8:11 669
but E shall return to Egypt, and ... Hos 9:3 669
The watchman of E was with my God. Hos 9:8 669
As for E, their glory shall fly ... Hos 9:11 669
E, as I saw Tyrus, is planted in ... Hos 9:13 669
but E shall bring forth his ... Hos 9:13 669
E is smitten, their root is dried ... Hos 9:16 669
E shall receive shame, and Israel ... Hos 10:6 669
E is as an heifer that is taught, ... Hos 10:11 669
I will make E to ride ... Hos 10:11 669
I taught E also to go, taking ... Hos 11:3 669
How shall I give thee up, E ... Hos 11:8 669
I will not return to destroy E ... Hos 11:9 669
E compasseth me about with lies, ... Hos 11:12 669
E feedeth on wind, and followeth ... Hos 12:1 669
E said, Yet I am become rich, I ... Hos 12:8 669
E provoked him to anger most ... Hos 12:14 669
When E spake trembling, he ... Hos 13:1 669
The iniquity of E is bound up ... Hos 13:12 669
E shall say, What have I to do ... Hos 14:8 669
shall possess the fields of E ... Obad 19 669
I will cut off the chariot from E ... Zec 9:10 669
for me, filled the bow with E ... Zec 9:13 669
they of E shall be like a mighty ... Zec 10:7 669
3. Mountains in Samaria.
if mount E be too narrow for thee ... Josh 17:15 669
even Timnath-serah in mount E ... Josh 19:50 669
Naphtali, and Shechem in mount E ... Josh 20:7 669
with her suburbs in mount E ... Josh 21:21 669
which is in mount E, on the ... Josh 24:30 669
which was given him in mount E ... Josh 24:33 669
Timnath-heres, in the mount of E ... Judg 2:9 669
a trumpet in the mountain of E ... Judg 3:27 669
Ramah and Beth-el in mount E ... Judg 4:5 669
messengers throughout all mount E ... Judg 7:24 669
and he dwelt in Shamir in mount E ... Judg 10:1 669
And there was a man of mount E ... Judg 17:1 669
he came to mount E to the house ... Judg 17:8 669
who when they came to mount E ... Judg 18:2 669
they passed thence unto mount E ... Judg 18:13 669
sojourning on the side of mount E ... Judg 19:1 669
even, which was also of mount E ... Judg 19:16 669
toward the side of mount E ... Judg 19:18 669
of Ramathaim-zophim, of mount E ... 1Sa 1:1 669
And he passed through mount E ... 1Sa 9:4 669
had hid themselves in mount E ... 1Sa 14:22 669
but a man of mount E, Sheba the ... 2Sa 20:21 669
The son of Hur, in mount E ... 1Kin 4:8 669
Jeroboam built Shechem in mount E ... 1Kin 12:25 669
E two young men of the sons of ... 2Kin 5:22 669
in mount E with her suburbs ... 1Chr 6:67 669
Zemaraim, which is in mount E ... 2Chr 13:4 669
which he had taken from mount E ... 2Chr 15:8 669
people from Beer-sheba to mount E ... 2Chr 19:4 669
affliction from mount E ... Jer 4:15 669
upon the mount E shall cry ... Jer 31:6 669
shall be satisfied upon mount E ... Jer 50:19 669
4. A town near Absalom's farm.
in Baal-hazor, which is beside E ... 2Sa 13:23 669
5. Battle site between David's and Absalom's armies.
the battle was in the wood of E ... 2Sa 18:6 669
6. A northern gate at Jerusalem.
gate of E unto the corner gate ... 2Kin 14:13 669
the gate of E to the corner gate ... 2Chr 25:23 669
and in the street of the gate of E ... Neh 8:16 669
And from above the gate of E ... Neh 12:39 669
7. A city near Jerusalem.
wilderness, into a city called E ... Jn 11:54 *2187*

EPHRAIMITE (*e'-fra-im-ite*) See EPHRAIMITES. *A descendant of Ephraim.*
said unto him, Art thou an E ... Judg 12:5 673

EPHRAIMITES (*e'-fra-im-ites*)
dwell among the E unto this day ... Josh 16:10 669
fugitives of Ephraim among the E ... Judg 12:4 669
passages of Jordan before the E ... Judg 12:5 669
that when those E which were ... Judg 12:5 669
fell at that time of the E forty ... Judg 12:6 669

EPHRAIM'S (*e'-fra-ims*)
1. Refers to Ephraim 1.
hand, and laid it upon E head ... Gen 48:14 669
to remove it from E head unto ... Gen 48:17 669
Joseph saw E children of the ... Gen 50:23 669
2. Refers to Ephraim 2.
Southward it was E, and northward ... Josh 17:10 669

EPHRAIN (*e'-fra-in*) See EPHRAIM, EPHRON. *A city in Benjamin.*
and E with the towns thereof ... 2Chr 13:19 6085

EPHRATAH (ef'-rat-ah) See BETHLEHEM, CALEB-EPHRATAH, EPHRATH, EPHRATHITE.
1. Another name for Bethlehem-judah.
and do thou worthily in E, and be .... Ruth 4:11 672
Lo, we heard of it at E .... Ps 132:6 672
But thou, Beth-lehem E, though .... Mic 5:2 672
2. A wife of Caleb.
son of Hur, the firstborn of E 1Chr 2:50 672
sons of Hur, the firstborn of E 1Chr 4:4 672

EPHRATH (e'-frath) See EPHRATAH.
1. A city in Judah.
was but a little way to come to E .... Gen 35:16 672
and was buried in the way to E .... Gen 35:19 672
but a little way to come unto E .... Gen 48:7 672
buried her there in the way of E .... Gen 48:7 672
2. Same as Ephratah 2.
was dead, Caleb took unto him E 1Chr 2:19 672

EPHRATHAH See EPHRATAH.

EPHRATHITE (ef'-rath-ite) See EPHRATHITES.
An inhabitant of Bethlehem Judah.
of Tohu, the son of Zuph, an E 1Sa 1:1 673
son of that E of Beth-lehem-judah 1Sa 17:12 673
an E of Zereda, Solomon's servant 1Kin 11:26 673

EPHRATHITES (ef'-rath-ites)
and Chilion, E of Beth-lehem-judah .... Ruth 1:2 673

EPHRON (e'-fron) See EPHRAIM, EPHRAIN.
1. Son of Zohar.
for me to E the son of Zohar .... Gen 23:8 6085
E dwelt among the children of .... Gen 23:10 6085
E the Hittite answered Abraham in .... Gen 23:10 6085
he spake unto E in the audience .... Gen 23:13 6085
E answered Abraham, saying unto .... Gen 23:14 6085
And Abraham hearkened unto E .... Gen 23:16 6085
Abraham weighed to E the silver .... Gen 23:16 6085
And the field of E, which was in .... Gen 23:17 6085
in the field of E the son of .... Gen 25:9 6085
is in the field of E the Hittite .... Gen 49:29 6085
bought with the field of E the .... Gen 49:30 6085
a buryingplace of E the Hittite .... Gen 50:13 6085
2. A mountain between Judah and Benjamin.
went out to the cities of mount E .... Josh 15:9 6085

EPICUREANS (ep-i-cu-re'-ans) *Followers of the philosopher Epicurus.*
certain philosophers of the E .... Acts 17:18 1946

EPISTLE
together, they delivered the e .... Acts 15:30 1992
delivered the e to the governor, ... Acts 23:33 1992
I Tertius, who wrote this e .... Rom 16:22 1992
I wrote unto you in an e not to 1Cor 5:9 1992
The first e to the Corinthians .... 1Cor s
Ye are our e written in our 2Cor 3:2 1992
the e of Christ ministered by us 2Cor 3:3 1992
the same e hath made you sorry 2Cor 7:8 1992
The second e to the Corinthians .... 2Cor s
when this e is read among you, ... Col 4:16 1992
likewise read the e from Laodicea .... Col 4:16
this e be read unto all the holy 1Th 5:27 1992
The first e unto the .... 1Th s
taught, whether by word, or our e 2Th 2:15 1992
man obey not our word by this e 2Th 3:14 1992
which is the token in every e 2Th 3:17 1992
The second e to the Thessalonians .... 2Th s
The second e unto Timotheus, ... 2Ti s
This second e, beloved, I now 2Pet 3:1 1992

EPISTLES
e of commendation to you, or 2Cor 3:1 1992
As also in all his e, speaking in 2Pet 3:16 1992

EQUAL
gold and the crystal cannot e it .... Job 28:17 6186
topaz of Ethiopia shall not e it .... Job 28:19 6186
eyes behold the things that are e .... Ps 17:2 4339
But it was thou, a man mine e .... Ps 55:13 6187
The legs of the lame are not e .... Prov 26:7 1809
will ye liken me, or shall I be e .... Is 40:25 7737
will ye liken me, and make me e .... Is 46:5 7737
what shall I e to thee, that I .... Lam 2:13 7737
say, The way of the Lord is not e .... Eze 18:25 8505
Is not my way e .... Eze 18:25 8505
The way of the Lord is not e .... Eze 18:29 8505
of Israel, are not my ways e .... Eze 18:29 8505
say, The way of the Lord is not e .... Eze 33:17 8505
as for them, their way is not e .... Eze 33:17 8505
say, The way of the Lord is not e .... Eze 33:20 8505
and thou hast made them e unto us .... Mt 20:12 2470
for they are e unto the angels .... Lk 20:36 2465
Father, making himself e with God .... Jn 5:18 2470
it not robbery to be e with God .... Phil 2:6 2470
servants that which is just and e .... Col 4:1 2471
breadth and the height of it are e .... Rev 21:16 2470

EQUALITY
But by an e, that now at this 2Cor 8:14 2471
that there may be e 2Cor 8:14 2471

EQUALLY
e distant one from another .... Ex 36:22 7947

EQUALS
many my e in mine own nation .... Gal 1:14 4915

EQUITY
the world, and the people with e .... Ps 98:9 4339
thou dost establish e, thou .... Ps 99:4 4339
justice, and judgment, and e .... Prov 1:3 4339
righteousness, and judgment, and e .... Prov 2:9 4339
good, nor to strike princes for e .... Prov 17:26 3476
wisdom, and in knowledge, and in e .... Eccl 2:21 3788
reprove with e for the meek of .... Is 11:4 4334
in the street, and e cannot enter .... Is 59:14 5229
abhor judgment, and pervert all e .... Mic 3:9 3477
he walked with me in peace and e .... Mal 2:6 4334

ER (ur)
1. A son of Judah.
and he called his name E .... Gen 38:3 6147
took a wife for E his firstborn .... Gen 38:6 6147
And E, Judah's firstborn, was .... Gen 38:7 6147
E, and Onan, and Shelah, and Pharez, ... Gen 46:12 6147
but E and Onan died in the land of .... Gen 46:12 6147
The sons of Judah were E and Onan .... Num 26:19 6147
and E and Onan died in the land of .... Num 26:19 6147
E, and Onan, and Shelah 1Chr 2:3 6147
And E, the firstborn of Judah, was 1Chr 2:3 6147
2. A son of Shelah.
E the father of Lecah, and Laadah 1Chr 4:21 6147
3. Father of Elmodan; ancestor of Jesus.
Elmodam, which was the son of E .... Lk 3:28 2262

ERAN (e'-ran) See ERANITES. *A son of Shathelah.*
of E, the family of the Eranites .... Num 26:36 6197

ERANITES (e'-ran-ites) *Descendants of Eran.*
of Eran, the family of the E .... Num 26:36 6198

ERASTUS (e-ras'-tus)
1. A fellow-worker with Paul.
unto him, Timotheus and E .... Acts 19:22 2037
E abode at Corinth 2Ti 4:20 2037
2. A Corinthian city official.
E the chamberlain of the city .... Rom 16:23 2037

ERE
are delivered e the midwives come .... Ex 1:19 2962
e it was chewed, the wrath of the .... Num 11:33 2962
long will it be e they believe me .... Num 14:11 3808
e the lamp of God went out in the 1Sa 3:3 2962
e thou bid the people return from 2Sa 2:26 3808
but e the messenger came to him, ... 2Kin 6:32 2962
How long will it be e ye make an .... Job 18:2
long will it be e thou be quiet .... Jer 47:6 3808
how long will it be e they attain .... Hos 8:5 3808
Sir, come down e my child die .... Jn 4:49 4250

ERECH (e'-rek) See ARCHEVITES. *A city in Shinar.*
of his kingdom was Babel, and E .... Gen 10:10 751

ERECTED
he e there an altar, and called it .... Gen 33:20 5324

ERI (e'-ri) See ERITES. *A son of Gad.*
and Haggi, Shuni, and Ezbon, E .... Gen 46:16 6179
of E, the family of the Erites .... Num 26:16 6179

ERITES (e'-rites) *Descendants of Eri.*
of Eri, the family of the E .... Num 26:16 6180

ERR
the inhabitants of Jerusalem to e 2Chr 33:9 8582
a people that do e in their heart .... Ps 95:10 8582
which do e from thy commandments .... Ps 119:21 7686
all them that e from thy statutes .... Ps 119:118 7686
Do they not e that devise evil .... Prov 14:22 8582
to e from the words of knowledge .... Prov 19:27 7686
which lead thee cause thee to e .... Is 3:12 8582
of this people cause them to e .... Is 9:16 8582
Egypt to e in every work thereof .... Is 19:14 8582
they e in vision, they stumble in .... Is 28:7 7686
of the people, causing them to e .... Is 30:28 8582
though fools, shall not e therein .... Is 35:8 8582
thou made us to e from thy ways .... Is 63:17 8582
and caused my people Israel to e .... Jer 23:13 8582
my people to e by their lies .... Jer 23:32 8582
whoredoms hath caused them to e .... Hos 4:12 8582
and their lies caused them to e .... Amos 2:4 8582
prophets that make my people e .... Mic 3:5 8582
and said unto them, Ye do e .... Mt 22:29 4105
unto them, Do ye not therefore e .... Mk 12:24 4105
ye therefore do greatly e .... Mk 12:27 4105
They do alway e in their heart .... Heb 3:10 4105
Do not e, my beloved brethren .... Jas 1:16 4105
if any of you do e from the truth .... Jas 5:19 4105

ERRAND
not eat, until I have told mine e .... Gen 24:33 1697
said, I have a secret e unto thee .... Judg 3:19 1697
and he said, I have an e to thee 2Kin 9:5 1697

ERRED
his ignorance wherein he e .... Lev 5:18 7683
And if ye have e, and not observed .... Num 15:22 7683
the fool, and have e exceedingly 1Sa 26:21 7683
me to understand wherein I have e .... Job 6:24 7683
And be it indeed that I have e .... Job 19:4 7683
yet I e not from thy precepts .... Ps 119:110 8582
But they also have e through wine .... Is 28:7 7686
the prophet have e through strong .... Is 28:7 7686
They also that e in spirit shall .... Is 29:24 8582
they have e from the faith, and 1Ti 6:10 635
have e concerning the faith 1Ti 6:21 795
Who concerning the truth have e 2Ti 2:18 795

ERRETH
but he that refuseth reproof e .... Prov 10:17 8582
of the month for every one that e .... Eze 45:20 7686

ERROR
and God smote him there for his e 2Sa 6:7 7944
mine e remaineth with myself .... Job 19:4 4879
the angel, that it was an e .... Eccl 5:6 7684
as an e which proceedeth from the .... Eccl 10:5 7684
to utter e against the LORD, to .... Is 32:6 8432
there any e or fault found in him .... Dan 6:4 7960
so the last e shall be worse than .... Mt 27:64 4106
of their e which was meet .... Rom 1:27 4106
e of his way shall save a soul .... Jas 5:20 4106
escaped from them who live in e 2Pet 2:18 4106
led away with the e of the wicked 2Pet 3:17 4106
of truth, and the spirit of e 1Jn 4:6 4106
after the e of Balaam for reward .... Jude 11 4106

ERRORS
Who can understand his e .... Ps 19:12 7691
They are vanity, and the work of e .... Jer 10:15 8595
They are vanity, the work of e .... Jer 51:18 8595
and for the e of the people .... Heb 9:7 51

ESAIAS (e-sah'-yas) See ISAIAH. *Greek form of Isaiah.*
was spoken of by the prophet E .... Mt 3:3 2268
which was spoken by E the prophet .... Mt 4:14 2268
which was spoken by E the prophet .... Mt 8:17 2268
which was spoken by E the prophet .... Mt 12:17 2268
is fulfilled the prophecy of E .... Mt 13:14 2268
well did E prophesy of you, ... Mt 15:7 2268
Well hath E prophesied of you .... Mk 7:6 2268
of the words of E the prophet .... Lk 3:4 2268
him the book of the prophet E .... Lk 4:17 2268
the Lord, as said the prophet E .... Jn 1:23 2268
That the saying of E the prophet .... Jn 12:38 2268
because that E said again .... Jn 12:39 2268
These things said E, when he saw .... Jn 12:41 2268
in his chariot read E the prophet .... Acts 8:28 2268
and heard him read the prophet E .... Acts 8:30 2268
by E the prophet unto our fathers .... Acts 28:25 2268
E also crieth concerning Israel, ... Rom 9:27 2268
as E said before, Except the Lord .... Rom 9:29 2268
For E saith, Lord, who hath .... Rom 10:16 2268
But E is very bold, and saith, I .... Rom 10:20 2268
E saith, There shall be a root of .... Rom 15:12 2268

ESAR-HADDON (e'-zar-had'-dun) *An Assyrian king.*
E his son reigned in his stead 2Kin 19:37 634
since the days of E king of Assur .... Ezr 4:2 634
E his son reigned in his stead .... Is 37:38 634

ESAU (e'-saw)
1. A son of Isaac.
and they called his name E .... Gen 25:25 6215
E was a cunning hunter, a man of .... Gen 25:27 6215
And Isaac loved E, because he did .... Gen 25:28 6215
E came from the field, and he was .... Gen 25:29 6215
E said to Jacob, Feed me, I pray .... Gen 25:30 6215
E said, Behold, I am at the point .... Gen 25:32 6215
Then Jacob gave E bread and .... Gen 25:34 6215
thus E despised his birthright .... Gen 25:34 6215
E was forty years old when he .... Gen 26:34 6215
he called E his eldest son, and .... Gen 27:1 6215
when Isaac spake to E his son .... Gen 27:5 6215
E went to the field to hunt for .... Gen 27:5 6215
father speak unto E thy brother .... Gen 27:6 6215
E my brother is a hairy man, and I .... Gen 27:11 6215
raiment of her eldest son E .... Gen 27:15 6215
his father, I am E thy firstborn .... Gen 27:19 6215
thou be my very son E or not .... Gen 27:21 6215
but the hands are the hands of E .... Gen 27:22 6215
he said, Art thou my very son E .... Gen 27:24 6215
that E his brother came in from .... Gen 27:30 6215
I am thy son, thy firstborn E .... Gen 27:32 6215
when E heard the words of his .... Gen 27:34 6215
And Isaac answered and said unto E .... Gen 27:37 6215
E said unto his father, Hast thou .... Gen 27:38 6215
E lifted up his voice, and wept .... Gen 27:38 6215
E hated Jacob because of the .... Gen 27:41 6215
E said in his heart, The days of .... Gen 27:41 6215
these words of E her elder son .... Gen 27:42 6215
unto him, Behold, thy brother E .... Gen 27:42 6215
When E saw that Isaac had blessed .... Gen 28:6 6215
E seeing that the daughters of .... Gen 28:8 6215
Then went E unto Ishmael, and took .... Gen 28:9 6215
to E his brother unto the land of .... Gen 32:3 6215
shall ye speak unto my lord E .... Gen 32:4 6215
saying, We came to thy brother E .... Gen 32:6 6215
If E come to the one company, and .... Gen 32:8 6215
of my brother, from the hand of E .... Gen 32:11 6215
hand a present for E his brother .... Gen 32:13 6215
When E my brother meeteth thee, ... Gen 32:17 6215
is a present sent unto my lord E .... Gen 32:18 6215
this manner shall ye speak unto E .... Gen 32:19 6215
E came, and with him four hundred .... Gen 33:1 6215
E ran to meet him, and embraced .... Gen 33:4 6215
E said, I have enough, my brother .... Gen 33:9 6215
E said, Let me now leave with .... Gen 33:15 6215
So E returned that day on his way .... Gen 33:16 6215
from the face of E thy brother .... Gen 35:1 6215
and his sons E and Jacob buried him .... Gen 35:29 6215
these are the generations of E .... Gen 36:1 6215
E took his wives of the daughters .... Gen 36:2 6215
And Adah bare to E Eliphaz .... Gen 36:4 6215
these are the sons of E, which .... Gen 36:5 6215
E took his wives, and his sons, and .... Gen 36:6 6215
E in mount Seir: E is Edom .... Gen 36:8 6215
these are the generations of E .... Gen 36:9 6215
the son of Adah the wife of E .... Gen 36:10 6215
son of Bashemath the wife of E .... Gen 36:10 6215
and she bare to E Jeush, and Jaalam .... Gen 36:14 6215
These were dukes of the sons of E .... Gen 36:15 6215
of Eliphaz the firstborn son of E .... Gen 36:15 6215
These are the sons of E, who is .... Gen 36:19 6215
names of the dukes that came of E .... Gen 36:40 6215
he is E the father of the .... Gen 36:43 6215
And I gave unto Isaac Jacob and E .... Josh 24:4 6215
and I gave unto E mount Seir .... Josh 24:4 6215
sons of Isaac; E and Israel 1Chr 1:34 6215
Was not E Jacob's brother .... Mal 1:2 6215
And I hated E, and laid his .... Mal 1:3 6215
or profane person, as E, who for .... Heb 12:16 2269
2. Descendants of Esau.
your brethren the children of E .... Deut 2:4 6215
Seir unto E for a possession .... Deut 2:5 6215
our brethren the children of E .... Deut 2:8 6215
the children of E succeeded them .... Deut 2:12 6215
As he did to the children of E .... Deut 2:22 6215
children of E which dwell in Seir .... Deut 2:29 6215
The sons of E 1Chr 1:35 6215

E

bring the calamity of *E* upon him ... Jer 49:8 6215
But I have made *E* bare, I have ... Jer 49:10 6215
are the things of *E* searched out ... Obad 6 6215
and the house of *E* for stubble ... Obad 18 6215
any remaining of the house of *E* ... Obad 18 6215
have I loved, but *E* have I hated ... Rom 9:13 *2269*
E concerning things to come ... Heb 11:20 *2269*
3. A mountain.
out of the mount of *E* ... Obad 8 6215
of *E* may be cut off by slaughter ... Obad 9 6215
shall possess the mount of *E* ... Obad 19 6215
Zion to judge the mount of *E* ... Obad 21 6215

ESAU'S (*e'-saws*) *Refers to Esau 1.*
and his hand took hold on *E* heel ... Gen 25:26 6215
hairy, as his brother *E* hands ... Gen 27:23 6215
of Rebekah, Jacob's and *E* mother ... Gen 28:5 6215
These are the names of *E* sons ... Gen 36:10 6215
was concubine to Eliphaz *E* son ... Gen 36:12 6215
were the sons of Adah *E* wife ... Gen 36:12 6215
were the sons of Bashemath *E* wife ... Gen 36:13 6215
the daughter of Zibeon, *E* wife ... Gen 36:14 6215
these are the sons of Reuel *E* son ... Gen 36:17 6215
are the sons of Bashemath *E* wife ... Gen 36:17 6215
are the sons of Aholibamah *E* wife ... Gen 36:18 6215
the daughter of Anah, *E* wife ... Gen 36:18 6215

ESCAPE
that he said, *E* for thy life ... Gen 19:17 4422
e to the mountain, lest thou be ... Gen 19:17 4422
I cannot *e* to the mountain, lest ... Gen 19:19 4422
let me *e* thither, (is it not a ... Gen 19:20 4422
Haste thee, *e* thither ... Gen 19:22 4422
company which is left shall *e* ... Gen 32:8 6413
they let none of them remain or *e* ... Josh 8:22 6412
speedily *e* into the land of the ... 1Sa 27:1 4422
so shall I *e* out of his hand ... 1Sa 27:1 4422
we shall not else *e* from Absalom ... 2Sa 15:14 6413
he get him fenced cities, and *e* us ... 2Sa 20:6 5337
let not one of them *e* ... 1Kin 18:40 4422
then let none go forth nor *e* out ... 2Kin 9:15 6412
I have brought into your hands *e* ... 2Kin 10:24 4422
they that *e* out of mount Zion ... 2Kin 19:31 6413
God, to leave us a remnant to *e* ... Ezr 9:8 6413
thou shalt *e* in the king's house ... Est 4:13 4422
shall fail, and they shall not *e* ... Job 11:20
I would hasten my *e* from the ... Ps 55:8 4655
Shall they *e* by iniquity ... Ps 56:7 6405
righteousness, and cause me to *e* ... Ps 71:2 6403
own nets, whilst that I withal *e* ... Ps 141:10 5674
he that speaketh lies shall not *e* ... Prov 19:5 4422
pleaseth God shall *e* from her ... Eccl 7:26 4422
and how shall we *e* ... Is 20:6 4422
they that *e* out of mount Zion ... Is 37:32 6413
I will send those that *e* of them ... Is 66:19 6412
which they shall not be able to *e* ... Jer 11:11 3318
the principal of the flock to *e* ... Jer 25:35 6413
not *e* out of the hand of the ... Jer 32:4 4422
thou shalt not *e* out of his hand, ... Jer 34:3 4422
thou shalt not *e* out of their ... Jer 38:18 4422
thou shalt not *e* out of their ... Jer 38:23 4422
none of them shall remain or *e* ... Jer 42:17 6412
shall *e* or remain, that they ... Jer 44:14 6412
shall return but such as shall *e* ... Jer 44:14 6412
Yet a small number that *e* the ... Jer 44:28 6412
flee away, nor the mighty man *e* ... Jer 46:6 4422
every city, and no city shall *e* ... Jer 48:8 4422
e out of the land of Babylon, to ... Jer 50:28 6412
let none thereof *e* ... Jer 50:29 6413
e the sword among the nations ... Eze 6:8 6412
they that *e* of you shall remember ... Eze 6:9 6412
But they that *e* of them shall ... Eze 7:16 6403
shall *e*, and shall be on the ... Eze 7:16 6412
shall he *e* that doeth such things ... Eze 17:15 4422
all these things, he shall not *e* ... Eze 17:18 4422
but these shall *e* out of his hand ... Dan 11:41 4422
and the land of Egypt shall not *e* ... Dan 11:42 6413
yea, and nothing shall *e* them ... Joel 2:3 6413
cut off those of his that did *e* ... Obad 14 6412
how can ye *e* the damnation of ... Mt 23:33
to *e* all these things that shall ... Lk 21:36 *1628*
any of them should swim out, and *e* ... Acts 27:42 *1309*
that thou shalt *e* the judgment of ... Rom 2:3 *1628*
temptation also make a way to *e* ... 1Cor 10:13 *1545*
and they shall not *e* ... 1Th 5:3 *1628*
How shall we *e*, if we neglect so ... Heb 2:3 *1628*
earth, much more shall not we *e* ... Heb 12:25 *5343*

ESCAPED
And there came one that had *e* ... Gen 14:13 6412
the residue of that which is *e* ... Ex 10:5 6413
he hath given his sons that *e* ... Num 21:29 6412
is *e* from his master unto thee ... Deut 23:15 5337
Ehud *e* while they tarried, and ... Judg 3:26 4422
the quarries, and *e* unto Seirath ... Judg 3:26 4422
and there *e* not a man ... Judg 3:29 4422
Ephraimites which were *e* said ... Judg 12:5 6412
for them that be *e* of Benjamin ... Judg 21:17 6413
but the people *e* ... 1Sa 14:41 3318
and David fled, and *e* that night ... 1Sa 19:10 4422
and he went, and fled, and *e* ... 1Sa 19:12 4422
away mine enemy, that he is *e* ... 1Sa 19:17 4422
So David fled, and *e*, and came to ... 1Sa 19:18 4422
thence, and *e* to the cave Adullam ... 1Sa 22:1 4422
son of Ahitub, named Abiathar, *e* ... 1Sa 22:20 4422
Saul that David was *e* from Keilah ... 1Sa 23:13 4422
there *e* not a man of them, save ... 1Sa 30:17 4422
Out of the camp of Israel am I *e* ... 2Sa 1:3 4422
and Rechab and Baanah his brother *e* ... 2Sa 4:6 4422
Ben-hadad the king of Syria *e* on ... 1Kin 20:20 4422
the remnant that is *e* of the ... 2Kin 19:30 6413
they *e* into the land of Armenia ... 2Kin 19:37 4422
of the Amalekites that were *e* ... 1Chr 4:43 6413
king of Syria *e* out of thine hand ... 2Chr 16:7 4422
fallen to the earth, and none *e* ... 2Chr 20:24 6413
that are *e* out of the hand of the ... 2Chr 30:6 6413
them that had *e* from the sword ... 2Chr 36:20 7611
for we remain yet *e*, as it is ... Ezr 9:15 6413
concerning the Jews that had *e* ... Neh 1:2 6413
I only am *e* alone to tell thee ... Job 1:15 4422
I only am *e* alone to tell thee ... Job 1:16 4422
I only am *e* alone to tell thee ... Job 1:17 4422
I only am *e* alone to tell thee ... Job 1:19 4422
I am *e* with the skin of my teeth ... Job 19:20 4422
Our soul is *e* as a bird out of ... Ps 124:7 4422
the snare is broken, and we are *e* ... Ps 124:7 4422
for them that are *e* of Israel ... Is 4:2 6413
such as are *e* of the house of ... Is 10:20 6413
the remnant that is *e* of the ... Is 37:31 6413
they *e* into the land of Armenia ... Is 37:38 4422
ye that are *e* of the nations ... Is 45:20 6412
e from Johanan with eight men ... Jer 41:15 4422
Ye that have *e* the sword, go away ... Jer 51:50 6412
LORD's anger none *e* nor remained ... Lam 2:22
mouth be opened to him which is *e* ... Eze 24:27 6412
that one that had *e* out of ... Eze 33:21 6412
evening, afore he that was *e* came ... Eze 33:22 6412
but he *e* out of their hand, ... Jn 10:39 *1831*
that they *e* all safe to land ... Acts 27:44 *1295*
And when they were *e*, then they ... Acts 28:1 *1295*
whom, though he hath *e* the sea ... Acts 28:4 *1295*
down by the wall, and *e* his hands ... 2Cor 11:33 *1628*
e the edge of the sword, out of ... Heb 11:34 *5343*
For if they *e* not who refused him ... Heb 12:25 *5343*
having *e* the corruption that is ... 2Pet 1:4 *668*
those that were clean *e* from them ... 2Pet 2:18 *668*
For if after they have *e* the ... 2Pet 2:20 *668*

ESCAPETH
that him that *e* the sword of ... 1Kin 19:17 4422
him that *e* from the sword of Jehu ... 1Kin 19:17 4422
lions upon him that *e* of Moab ... Is 15:9 6413
him that fleeth, and her that *e* ... Jer 48:19 4422
That he that *e* in that day shall ... Eze 24:26 6412
he that *e* of them shall not be ... Amos 9:1 6412

ESCAPING
there should be no remnant nor *e* ... Ezr 9:14 6413

ESCHEW
Let him *e* evil, and do good ... 1Pet 3:11 *1578*

ESCHEWED
and one that feared God, and *e* evil ... Job 1:1 5493

ESCHEWETH
one that feareth God, and *e* evil ... Job 1:8 5493
one that feareth God, and *e* evil ... Job 2:3 5493

ESEK (*e'-sek*) *A well in the valley of Geran.*
he called the name of the well *E* ... Gen 26:20 6320

ESHAN See ESHEAN.

ESH-BAAL (*esh'-ba-al*) See ISH-BOSHETH. *A son of King Saul.*
and Malchi-shua, and Abinadab, and *E* 1Chr 8:33 792
and Malchi-shua, and Abinadab, and *E* 1Chr 9:39 792

ESHBAN *A son of Dishon.*
Hemdan, and *E*, and Ithran, and ... Gen 36:26 790
Amram, and *E*, and Ithran ... 1Chr 1:41 790

ESHCOL (*esh'-col*)
1. Brother of Mamre and Aner.
Mamre the Amorite, brother of *E* ... Gen 14:13 812
men which went with me, Aner, *E* ... Gen 14:24 812
2. A valley or brook in Hebron.
And they came unto the brook of *E* ... Num 13:23 812
The place was called the brook *E* ... Num 13:24 812
they went up unto the valley of *E* ... Num 32:9 812
and came unto the valley of *E* ... Deut 1:24 812

ESHEAN (*esh'-e-an*) *A city in Judea.*
Arab, and Dumah, and *E*, ... Josh 15:52 824

ESHEK (*e'-shek*) *A descendant of King Saul.*
the sons of *E* his brother were, ... 1Chr 8:39 6232

ESHKALONITES (*esh'-ka-lon-ites*) *Inhabitants of Ashkelon.*
and the Ashdothites, the *E* ... Josh 13:3 832

ESHTAOL (*esh'-ta-ol*) See ESHTAULITES. *A town in Judah.*
And in the valley, *E*, and Zoreah, ... Josh 15:33 847
their inheritance was Zorah, and *E* ... Josh 19:41 847
camp of Dan between Zorah and *E* ... Judg 13:25 847
E in the buryingplace of Manoah ... Judg 16:31 847
of valour, from Zorah, and from *E* ... Judg 18:2 847
unto their brethren to Zorah and *E* ... Judg 18:8 847
Danites, out of Zorah and out of *E* ... Judg 18:11 847

ESHTAOLITES See ESHTAULITES.

ESHTAULITES (*esh'-ta-u-lites*) *Inhabitants of Eshtaol.*
came the Zareathites, and the *E* ... 1Chr 2:53 848

ESHTEMOA (*esh-te-mo'-ah*) See ESHTEMOH.
1. A Levitical town in Judah.
suburbs, and *E* with her suburbs, ... Josh 21:14 851
and to them which were in *E* ... 1Sa 30:28 851
with her suburbs, and Jattir, and *E* ... 1Chr 6:57 851
2. A descendant of Ezra.
and Ishbah the father of *E* ... 1Chr 4:17 851
the Garmite, and *E* the Maachathite ... 1Chr 4:19 851

ESHTEMOH (*esh'-te-moh*) See ESHTEMOA. *Same as Eshtemoa 1.*
And Anab, and *E*, and Anim, ... Josh 15:50 851

ESHTON (*esh'-ton*) *Grandson of Chelub.*
Mehir, which was the father of *E* ... 1Chr 4:11 850
E begat Beth-rapha, and Paseah, and ... 1Chr 4:12 850

ESLI (*es'-li*) *Father of Naum; ancestor of Jesus.*
of Naum, which was the son of *E* ... Lk 3:25 *2069*

ESPECIALLY
but *e* among my neighbours, and a ... Ps 31:11 3966
E because I know thee to be ... Acts 26:3 *3122*
e unto them who are of the ... Gal 6:10 *3122*
e they who labour in the word and ... 1Ti 5:17 *3122*
the books, but *e* the parchments ... 2Ti 4:13 *3122*

ESPIED
in the inn, he *e* his money ... Gen 42:27 7200
into a land that I had *e* for them ... Eze 20:6 8446

ESPOUSALS
crowned him in the day of his *e* ... Song 3:11 2861
of thy youth, the love of thine *e* ... Jer 2:2 3623

ESPOUSED
which I *e* to me for an hundred ... 2Sa 3:14 781
his mother Mary was *e* to Joseph ... Mt 1:18 *3423*
To a virgin *e* to a man whose name ... Lk 1:27 *3423*
To be taxed with Mary his *e* wife ... Lk 2:5 *3423*
for I have *e* you to one husband, ... 2Cor 11:2 *718*

ESPY
Kadesh-barnea to *e* out the land ... Josh 14:7 7270
of Aroer, stand by the way, and *e* ... Jer 48:19 6822

ESROM (*es'-rom*) See HEZRON. *Son of Phares; ancestor of Jesus.*
and Phares begat *E* ... Mt 1:3 *2074*
and *E* begat Aram ... Mt 1:3 *2074*
of Aram, which was the son of *E* ... Lk 3:33 *2074*

ESTABLISH
with thee will I *e* my covenant ... Gen 6:18 6965
I *e* my covenant with you, and with ... Gen 9:9 6965
I will *e* my covenant with you ... Gen 9:11 6965
I will *e* my covenant between me ... Gen 17:7 6965
I will *e* my covenant with him for ... Gen 17:19 6965
my covenant will I *e* with Isaac ... Gen 17:21 6965
you, and *e* my covenant with you ... Lev 26:9 6965
the soul, her husband may *e* it ... Num 30:13 6965
that he may *e* his covenant which ... Deut 8:18 6965
The LORD shall *e* thee an holy ... Deut 28:9 6965
That he may *e* thee to day for a ... Deut 29:13 6965
only the LORD *e* his word ... 1Sa 1:23 6965
bowels, and I will *e* his kingdom ... 2Sa 7:12 3559
e it for ever, and do as thou hast ... 2Sa 7:25 6965
Then I will *e* the throne of thy ... 1Kin 9:5 6965
son after him, and to *e* Jerusalem ... 1Kin 15:4 5975
and I will *e* his kingdom ... 1Chr 17:11 3559
I will *e* the throne of his ... 1Chr 22:10 3559
Moreover I will *e* his kingdom for ... 1Chr 28:7 3559
to *e* them for ever, therefore ... 2Chr 9:8 5975
he doth *e* them for ever, and they ... Job 36:7 3427
but *e* the just: for the righteous ... Ps 7:9 3559
God will *e* it for ever ... Ps 48:8 3559
the highest himself shall *e* her ... Ps 87:5 3559
shalt thou *e* in the very heavens ... Ps 89:2 3559
Thy seed will I *e* for ever ... Ps 89:4 3559
e thou the work of our hands upon ... Ps 90:17 3559
the work of our hands *e* thou it ... Ps 90:17 3559
thou dost *e* equity, thou ... Ps 99:4 3559
but he will *e* the border of the ... Prov 15:25 5324
to *e* it with judgment and with ... Is 9:7 5582
to *e* the earth, to cause to ... Is 49:8 6965
And give him no rest, till he *e* ... Is 62:7 3559
the LORD that formed it, to *e* it ... Jer 33:2 3559
I will *e* unto thee an everlasting ... Eze 16:60 6965
I will *e* my covenant with thee ... Eze 16:62 6965
together to *e* a royal statute ... Dan 6:7 6966
e the decree, and sign the writing ... Dan 6:8 6966
exalt themselves to *e* the vision ... Dan 11:14 5975
good, and *e* judgment in the gate ... Amos 5:15 3322
yea, we *e* the law ... Rom 3:31 *2476*
going about to *e* their own ... Rom 10:3 *2476*
to *e* you, and to comfort you ... 1Th 3:2 *4741*
first, that he may *e* the second ... Heb 10:9 *2476*

ESTABLISHED
which I have *e* between me ... Gen 9:17 6965
is because the thing is *e* by God ... Gen 41:32 3559
I have also *e* my covenant with ... Ex 6:4 6965
O Lord, which thy hands have *e* ... Ex 15:17 3559
e for ever to him that bought it ... Lev 25:30 6965
witnesses, shall the matter be *e* ... Deut 19:15 6965
Hath he not made thee, and *e* thee ... Deut 32:6 3559
was *e* to be a prophet of the LORD ... 1Sa 3:20 539
e thy kingdom upon Israel for ... 1Sa 13:13 3559
the ground, thou shalt not be *e* ... 1Sa 20:31 3559
Israel shall be *e* in thine hand ... 1Sa 24:20 6965
LORD had *e* him king over Israel ... 2Sa 5:12 3559
shall be *e* for ever before thee ... 2Sa 7:16 539
thy throne shall be *e* for ever ... 2Sa 7:16 3559
servant David be *e* before thee ... 2Sa 7:26 3559
and his kingdom was *e* greatly ... 1Kin 2:12 3559
the LORD liveth, which hath *e* me ... 1Kin 2:24 3559
be *e* before the LORD for ever ... 1Kin 2:45 3559
the kingdom was *e* in the hand of ... 1Kin 2:46 3559
throne shall be *e* for evermore ... 1Chr 17:14 3559
his house be *e* for ever, and do as ... 1Chr 17:23 539
Let it even be *e*, that thy name ... 1Chr 17:24 539
thy servant be *e* before thee ... 1Chr 17:24 3559
promise unto David my father be *e* ... 2Chr 1:9 539
when Rehoboam had *e* the kingdom ... 2Chr 12:1 3559
LORD your God, so shall ye be *e* ... 2Chr 20:20 539
when the kingdom was *e* to him ... 2Chr 25:3 2388
So they *e* a decree to make ... 2Chr 30:5 5975
Their seed is *e* in their sight ... Job 21:8 3559
thing, and it shall be *e* unto thee ... Job 22:28 6965
the seas, and *e* it upon the floods ... Ps 24:2 3559
feet upon a rock, and *e* my goings ... Ps 40:2 3559
For he *e* a testimony in Jacob, and ... Ps 78:5 6965
earth which he hath *e* for ever ... Ps 78:69 3245
With whom my hand shall be *e* ... Ps 89:21 3559
It shall be *e* for ever as the ... Ps 89:37 3559

Thy throne is *e* of old Ps 93:2 3559
the world also shall be *e* that it Ps 96:10 3559
their seed shall be *e* before thee Ps 102:28 3559
His heart is *e*, he shall not be Ps 112:8 5564
thou hast *e* the earth, and it Ps 119:90 3559
an evil speaker be *e* in the earth Ps 140:11 3559
hath he *e* the heavens Prov 3:19 3559
feet, and let all thy ways be *e* Prov 4:26 3559
When he *e* the clouds above Prov 8:28 553
man shall not be *e* by wickedness Prov 12:3 3559
lip of truth shall be *e* for ever Prov 12:19 3559
of counsellors they are *e* Prov 15:22 6965
LORD, and thy thoughts shall be *e* Prov 16:3 3559
the throne is *e* by righteousness Prov 16:12 3559
Every purpose is *e* by counsel Prov 20:18 3559
and by understanding it is *e* Prov 24:3 3559
shall be *e* in righteousness Prov 25:5 3559
his throne shall be *e* for ever Prov 29:14 3559
who hath *e* all the ends of the Prov 30:4 6965
be *e* in the top of the mountains Is 2:2 3559
believe, surely ye shall not be *e* Is 7:9 539
And in mercy shall the throne be *e* Is 16:5 3559
he hath *e* it, he created it not Is 45:18 3559
In righteousness shalt thou be *e* Is 54:14 3559
he hath *e* the world by his wisdom Jer 10:12 3559
congregation shall be *e* before me Jer 30:20 3559
he hath *e* the world by his wisdom Jer 51:15 3559
I was *e* in my kingdom, and Dan 4:36 8627
be *e* in the top of the mountains Mic 4:1 3559
thou hast *e* them for correction Hab 1:12 3245
and it shall be *e*, and set there Zec 5:11 3559
witnesses every word may be *e* Mt 18:16 *2476*
were the churches *e* in the faith Acts 16:5 *4732*
gift, to the end ye may be *e* Rom 1:11 *4741*
witnesses shall every word be *e* 2Cor 13:1 *2476*
which was *e* upon better promises Heb 8:6 *3549*
that the heart be *e* with grace Heb 13:9 *950*
be *e* in the present truth 2Pet 1:12 *4741*

ESTABLISHETH
then he *e* all her vows, or all Num 30:14 6965
The king by judgment *e* the land Prov 29:4 5975
which the king *e* may be changed Dan 6:15 6966

ESTABLISHMENT
the *e* thereof, Sennacherib king 2Chr 32:1 571

ESTATE
to the *e* of a man of high degree 1Chr 17:17 8448
e unto another that is better Est 1:19
Who remembered us in our low *e* Ps 136:23
saying, Lo, I am come to great *e* Eccl 1:16
the *e* of the sons of men, that Eccl 3:18 1700
shall return to their former *e* Eze 16:55
shall return to their former *e* Eze 16:55 3653
shall return to your former *e* Eze 16:55
roots shall one stand up in his *e* Dan 11:7 3653
Then shall stand up in his *e* a Dan 11:20 3653
in his *e* shall stand up a vile Dan 11:21 3653
But in his *e* shall he honour the Dan 11:38 3653
the low *e* of his handmaiden Lk 1:48
and all the *e* of the elders Acts 22:5
but condescend to men of low *e* Rom 12:16
that he might know your *e* Col 4:8
which kept not their first *e* Jude 6

ESTATES
will settle you after your old *e* Eze 36:11
captains, and chief *e* of Galilee Mk 6:21

ESTEEM
Will he *e* thy riches Job 36:19 6186
Therefore I *e* all thy precepts Ps 119:128
yet we did *e* him stricken Is 53:4 2803
e other better than themselves Phil 2:3 *2233*
to *e* them very highly in love for 1Th 5:13 *2233*

ESTEEMED
lightly *e* the Rock of his Deut 32:15 5034
despise me shall be lightly *e* 1Sa 2:30 7043
I am a poor man, and lightly *e* 1Sa 18:23 7043
I have *e* the words of his mouth Job 23:12 6845
lips is *e* a man of understanding Prov 17:28
shall be *e* as the potter's clay Is 29:16 2803
field shall be *e* as a forest Is 29:17 2803
he was despised, and we *e* him not Is 53:3
how are they *e* as earthen Lam 4:2 2803
for that which is highly *e* among Lk 16:15
who are least *e* in the church 1Cor 6:4 *1848*

ESTEEMETH
He *e* iron as straw, and brass as Job 41:27 2803
One man *e* one day above another Rom 14:5 *2919*
another *e* every day alike Rom 14:5 *2919*
but to him that *e* any thing to be Rom 14:14 *3049*

ESTEEMING
E the reproach of Christ greater Heb 11:26 *2233*

ESTHER (*est'-thur*) See ESTHER'S, HADASSAH. *A Jewish queen.*
brought up Hadassah, that is, *E* Est 2:7 635
that *E* was brought also unto the Est 2:8 635
E had not shewed her people nor Est 2:10 635
women's house, to know how *E* did Est 2:11 635
Now when the turn of *E*, the Est 2:15 635
E obtained favour in the sight of Est 2:15 635
So *E* was taken unto king Est 2:16 635
the king loved *E* above all the Est 2:17 635
E had not yet shewed her kindred Est 2:20 635
for *E* did the commandment of Est 2:20 635
who told it unto *E* the queen Est 2:22 635
E certified the king thereof in Est 2:22 635
Then called *E* for Hatach, one of Est 4:5 635
destroy them, to shew it unto *E* Est 4:8 635
told *E* the words of Mordecai Est 4:9 635
Again *E* spake unto Hatach, and Est 4:10 635
Mordecai commanded to answer *E* Est 4:13 635
Then *E* bade them return Mordecai Est 4:15 635
to all that *E* had commanded him Est 4:17 635
that *E* put on her royal apparel Est 5:1 635
when the king saw *E* the queen Est 5:2 635
the king held out to *E* the golden Est 5:2 635
So *E* drew near, and touched the Est 5:2 635
unto her, What wilt thou, queen *E* Est 5:3 635
E answered, If it seem good unto Est 5:4 635
that he may do as *E* hath said Est 5:5 635
the banquet that *E* had prepared Est 5:5 635
the king said unto *E* at the Est 5:6 635
Then answered *E*, and said, My Est 5:7 635
E the queen did let no man come Est 5:12 635
the banquet that *E* had prepared Est 6:14 635
came to banquet with *E* the queen Est 7:1 635
unto *E* on the second day at the Est 7:2 635
What is thy petition, queen *E* Est 7:2 635
Then *E* the queen answered and said Est 7:3 635
answered and said unto *E* the queen Est 7:5 635
E said, The adversary and enemy is Est 7:6 635
for his life to *E* the queen Est 7:7 635
fallen upon the bed whereon *E* was Est 7:8 635
the Jews' enemy unto *E* the queen Est 8:1 635
for *E* had told what he was unto Est 8:1 635
E set Mordecai over the house of Est 8:2 635
E spake yet again before the king Est 8:3 635
out the golden sceptre toward *E* Est 8:4 635
So *E* arose, and stood before the Est 8:4 635
Ahasuerus said unto *E* the queen Est 8:7 635
I have given *E* the house of Haman Est 8:7 635
And the king said unto *E* the queen Est 9:12 635
Then said *E*, If it please the Est 9:13 635
But when *E* came before the king Est 9:25
Then *E* the queen, the daughter of Est 9:29 635
E the queen had enjoined them, and Est 9:31 635
the decree of *E* confirmed these Est 9:32 635

ESTHER'S (*es'-thurs*)
and his servants, even *E* feast Est 2:18 635
So *E* maids and her chamberlains Est 4:4 635
And they told to Mordecai *E* words Est 4:12 635

ESTIMATE
LORD, then the priest shall *e* it Lev 27:14 6186
as the priest shall *e* it, so Lev 27:14 6186

ESTIMATION
with thy *e* by shekels of silver Lev 5:15 6187
out of the flock, with thy *e* Lev 5:18 6187
out of the flock, with thy *e* Lev 6:6 6187
shall be for the LORD by thy *e* Lev 27:2 6187
thy *e* shall be of the male from Lev 27:3 6187
even thy *e* shall be fifty shekels Lev 27:3 6187
then thy *e* shall be thirty Lev 27:4 6187
then thy *e* shall be of the male Lev 27:5 6187
then thy *e* shall be of the male Lev 27:6 6187
for the female thy *e* shall be Lev 27:6 6187
then thy *e* shall be fifteen Lev 27:7 6187
But if he be poorer than thy *e* Lev 27:8 6187
a fifth part thereof unto thy *e* Lev 27:13 6187
of the money of thy *e* unto it Lev 27:15 6187
then thy *e* shall be according to Lev 27:16 6187
according to thy *e* it shall stand Lev 27:17 6187
and it shall be abated from thy *e* Lev 27:18 6187
of the money of thy *e* unto it Lev 27:19 6187
unto him the worth of thy *e* Lev 27:23 6187
he shall give thine *e* in that day Lev 27:23 6187
redeem it according to thine *e* Lev 27:27 6187
shall be sold according to thy *e* Lev 27:27 6187
thou redeem, according to thine *e* Num 18:16 6187

ESTIMATIONS
all thy *e* shall be according to Lev 27:25 6187

ESTRANGED
acquaintance are verily *e* from me Job 19:13 2114
The wicked are *e* from the womb Ps 58:3 2114
They were not *e* from their lust Ps 78:30 2114
have *e* this place, and have burned Jer 19:4 5234
because they are all *e* from me Eze 14:5 2114

ETAM (*e'-tam*)
1. An area in western Judah.
and dwelt in the top of the rock *E* Judg 15:8 5862
went to the top of the rock *E* Judg 15:11 5862
2. A descendant of Judah.
And these were of the father of *E* 1Chr 4:3 5862
3. A village in Simeon.
And their villages were, *E* 1Chr 4:32 5862
4. A town in Judah.
He built even Beth-lehem, and *E* 2Chr 11:6 5862

ETERNAL
The *e* God is thy refuge, and Deut 33:27 6924
I will make thee an *e* excellency Is 60:15 5769
I do, that I may have *e* life Mt 19:16 *166*
but the righteous into life *e* Mt 25:46 *166*
but is in danger of *e* damnation Mk 3:29 *166*
I do that I may inherit *e* life Mk 10:17 *166*
and in the world to come *e* life Mk 10:30 *166*
what shall I do to inherit *e* life Lk 10:25 *166*
what shall I do to inherit *e* life Lk 18:18 *166*
not perish, but have *e* life Jn 3:15 *166*
and gathereth fruit unto life *e* Jn 4:36 *166*
in them ye think ye have *e* life Jn 5:39 *166*
and drinketh my blood, hath *e* life Jn 6:54 *166*
thou hast the words of *e* life Jn 6:68 *166*
And I give unto them *e* life Jn 10:28 *166*
world shall keep it unto life *e* Jn 12:25 *166*
that he should give *e* life to as Jn 17:2 *166*
And this is life *e*, that they Jn 17:3 *166*
were ordained to *e* life believed Acts 13:48 *166*
that are made, even his *e* power Rom 1:20 *126*
and honour and immortality, *e* life Rom 2:7 *166*
through righteousness unto *e* life Rom 5:21 *166*
but the gift of God is *e* life Rom 6:23 *166*
exceeding and *e* weight of glory 2Cor 4:17 *166*
things which are not seen are *e* 2Cor 4:18 *166*
made with hands, *e* in the heavens 2Cor 5:1 *166*
According to the *e* purpose which Eph 3:11 *165*
Now unto the King *e*, immortal 1Ti 1:17 *165*
of faith, lay hold on *e* life 1Ti 6:12 *166*
that they may lay hold on *e* life 1Ti 6:19 *166*
is in Christ Jesus with *e* glory 2Ti 2:10 *166*
In hope of *e* life, which God Titus 1:2 *166*
according to the hope of *e* life Titus 3:7 *166*
he became the author of *e* Heb 5:9 *166*
of the dead, and of *e* judgment Heb 6:2 *166*
having obtained *e* redemption for Heb 9:12 *166*
who through the *e* Spirit offered Heb 9:14 *166*
the promise of *e* inheritance Heb 9:15 *166*
unto his *e* glory by Christ Jesus 1Pet 5:10 *166*
and shew unto you that *e* life 1Jn 1:2 *166*
he hath promised us, even *e* life 1Jn 2:25 *166*
hath *e* life abiding in him 1Jn 3:15 *166*
that God hath given to us *e* life 1Jn 5:11 *166*
ye may know that ye have *e* life 1Jn 5:13 *166*
This is the true God, and *e* life 1Jn 5:20 *166*
suffering the vengeance of *e* fire Jude 7 *166*
our Lord Jesus Christ unto *e* life Jude 21 *166*

ETERNITY
and lofty One that inhabiteth *e* Is 57:15 5703

ETHAM (*e'-tham*) *An encampment during the Exodus.*
from Succoth, and encamped in *E* Ex 13:20 864
from Succoth, and pitched in *E* Num 33:6 864
And they removed from *E*, and turned Num 33:7 864
journey in the wilderness of *E* Num 33:8 864

ETHAN (*e'-than*)
1. A wise man in Solomon's time.
than *E* the Ezrahite, and Heman, and 1Kin 4:31 387
Maschil of *E* the Ezrahite Ps 89:*t* 387
2. A son of Zerah.
Zimri, and *E*, and Heman, and Calcol 1Chr 2:6 387
And the sons of *E* 1Chr 2:8 387
3. A descendant of Gershon.
The son of *E*, the son of Zimmah 1Chr 6:42 387
4. A descendant of Merari.
E the son of Kishi, the son of 1Chr 6:44 387
brethren, *E* the son of Kushaiah 1Chr 15:17 387
the singers, Heman, Asaph, and *E* 1Chr 15:19 387

ETHANIM (*eth'-a-nim*) *Seventh month of the Hebrew year.*
at the feast in the month *E* 1Kin 8:2 388

ETHBAAL (*eth'-ba-al*) *Father of Jezebel.*
of *E* king of the Zidonians 1Kin 16:31 856

ETHER (*e'-ther*) *A city in Judah.*
Libnah, and *E*, and Ashan Josh 15:42 6281
Ain, Remmon, and *E*, and Ashan Josh 19:7 6281

ETHIOPIA (*e-the-o'-pe-ah*) See CUSH, ETHIOPIAN.
1. The land south of Egypt.
compasseth the whole land of *E* Gen 2:13 3568
reigned from India even unto *E* Est 1:1 3568
which are from India unto *E* Est 8:9 3568
The topaz of *E* shall not equal it Job 28:19 3568
behold Philistia, and Tyre, with *E* Ps 87:4 3568
which is beyond the rivers of *E* Is 18:1 3568
Syene even unto the border of *E* Eze 29:10 3568
the rivers of *E* my suppliants Zeph 3:10 3568
and, behold, a man of *E*, an eunuch Acts 8:27 *128*
2. Inhabitants of Ethiopia.
heard say of Tirhakah king of *E* 2Kin 19:9 3568
E shall soon stretch out her Ps 68:31 3568
and wonder upon Egypt and upon *E* Is 20:3 3568
ashamed of *E* their expectation Is 20:5 3568
say concerning Tirhakah king of *E* Is 37:9 3568
I gave Egypt for thy ransom, *E* Is 43:3 3568
of Egypt, and merchandise of *E* Is 45:14 3568
and great pain shall be in *E* Eze 30:4 3568
E, and Libya, and Lydia, and all the Eze 30:5 3568
Persia, *E*, and Libya with them Eze 38:5 3568
E and Egypt were her strength, and Nah 3:9 3568

ETHIOPIAN
the *E* woman whom he had married Num 12:1 3569
for he had married an *E* woman Num 12:1 3569
the *E* with an host of a thousand 2Chr 14:9 3569
Can the *E* change his skin, or the Jer 13:23 3569
Now when Ebed-melech the *E* Jer 38:7 3569
king commanded Ebed-melech the *E* Jer 38:10 3569
Ebed-melech the *E* said unto Jer 38:12 3569
Go and speak to Ebed-melech the *E* Jer 39:16 3569

ETHIOPIANS *Inhabitants of Ethiopia.*
the Lubim, the Sukkiims, and the *E* 2Chr 12:3 3569
the LORD smote the *E* before Asa 2Chr 14:12 3569
before Judah; and the *E* fled 2Chr 14:12 3569
the *E* were overthrown, that they 2Chr 14:13 3569
Were not the *E* and the Lubims a 2Chr 16:8 3569
Arabians, that were near the *E* 2Chr 21:16 3569
the *E* captives, young and old Is 20:4 3569
the *E* and the Libyans, that handle Jer 46:9 3569
to make the careless *E* afraid Eze 30:9 3569
the *E* shall be at his steps Dan 11:43 3569
not as children of the *E* unto me Amos 9:7 3569
Ye *E* also, ye shall be slain by Zeph 2:12 3569
under Candace queen of the *E* Acts 8:27 *128*

ETH KAZIN See ITTAH-KAZIN

ETHNAN (*eth'-nan*) *Grandson of Ashur.*
were, Zereth, and Jezoar, and *E* 1Chr 4:7 869

ETHNI (*eth'-ni*) See JEATERAI. *Ancestor of Asaph.*
The son of *E*, the son of Zerah 1Chr 6:41 867

EUBULUS (*yu-bu'-lus*) *A Christian acquaintance of Paul.*
E greeteth thee, and Pudens, and ... 2Ti 4:21 *2103*

EUNICE (*yu-ni'-see*) *Mother of Timothy.*
grandmother Lois, and thy mother *E* ... 2Ti 1:5 *2131*

EUNUCH
neither let the *e* say, Behold, I ... Is 56:3 5631
He took also out of the city an *e* ... Jer 52:25 5631
an *e* of great authority under ... Acts 8:27 *2135*
the *e* answered Philip, and said, I ... Acts 8:34 *2135*
the *e* said, See, here is water ... Acts 8:36 *2135*
the water, both Philip and the *e* ... Acts 8:38 *2135*
that the *e* saw him no more ... Acts 8:39 *2135*

EUNUCHS
looked out to him two or three *e* ... 2Kin 9:32 5631
they shall be *e* in the palace of ... 2Kin 20:18 5631
they shalt be *e* in the palace of ... Is 39:7 5631
unto the *e* that keep my sabbaths ... Is 56:4 5631
the king, and the queen, and the *e* ... Jer 29:2 5631
the princes of Jerusalem, the *e* ... Jer 34:19 5631
one of the *e* which was in the ... Jer 38:7 5631
women, and the children, and the *e* ... Jer 41:16 5631
unto Ashpenaz the master of his *e* ... Dan 1:3 5631
the prince of the *e* gave names ... Dan 1:7 5631
of the *e* that he might not defile ... Dan 1:8 5631
love with the prince of the *e* ... Dan 1:9 5631
prince of the *e* said unto Daniel ... Dan 1:10 5631
of the *e* had set over Daniel ... Dan 1:11 5631
of the *e* brought them in before ... Dan 1:18 5631
For there are some *e*, which were ... Mt 19:12 *2135*
and there are some *e*, which were ... Mt 19:12 *2134*
e, which were made *e* of men ... Mt 19:12 *2134*
and there be *e*, which have made ... Mt 19:12 *2135*
which have made themselves *e* for ... Mt 19:12 *2134*

EUODIAS (*yu-o'-de-as*) *A Christian at Philippi.*
I beseech *E*, and beseech Syntyche, ... Phil 4:2 *2136*

EUPHRATES (*yu-fra'-teze*) *A river in Mesopotamia.*
And the fourth river is *E* ... Gen 2:14 6578
unto the great river, the river *E* ... Gen 15:18 6578
unto the great river, the river *E* ... Deut 1:7 6578
from the river, the river *E* ... Deut 11:24 6578
unto the great river, the river *E* ... Josh 1:4 6578
recover his border at the river *E* ... 2Sa 8:3 6578
king of Assyria to the river *E* ... 2Kin 23:29 6578
river of Egypt unto the river *E* ... 2Kin 24:7 6578
the wilderness from the river *E* ... 1Chr 5:9 6578
his dominion by the river *E* ... 1Chr 18:3 6578
to fight against Charchemish by *E* ... 2Chr 35:20 6578
upon thy loins, and arise, go to *E* ... Jer 13:4 6578
So I went, and hid it by *E* ... Jer 13:5 6578
LORD said unto me, Arise, go to *E* ... Jer 13:6 6578
Then I went to *E*, and digged, and ... Jer 13:7 6578
was by the river *E* in Carchemish ... Jer 46:2 6578
toward the north by the river *E* ... Jer 46:6 6578
the north country by the river *E* ... Jer 46:10 6578
and cast it into the midst of *E* ... Jer 51:63 6578
are bound in the great river *E* ... Rev 9:14 *2166*
his vial upon the great river *E* ... Rev 16:12 *2166*

EURAQUILO See EUROCLYDON.

EUROCLYDON (*yu-roc'-lid-on*) *A Mediterranean wind.*
it a tempestuous wind, called *E* ... Acts 27:14 *2148*

EUTYCHUS (*yu'-tik-us*) *Youth restored to life.*
a certain young man named *E* ... Acts 20:9 *2161*

EVANGELIST
into the house of Philip the *e* ... Acts 21:8 *2099*
afflictions, do the work of an *e* ... 2Ti 4:5 *2099*

EVANGELISTS
and some, *e*; and some, pastors ... Eph 4:11 *2099*

EVE (*eev*) *Wife of Adam.*
And Adam called his wife's name *E* ... Gen 3:20 2332
And Adam knew *E* his wife ... Gen 4:1 2332
beguiled *E* through his subtilty ... 2Cor 11:3 *2096*
For Adam was first formed, then *E* ... 1Ti 2:13 *2096*

EVEN
e I, do bring a flood of waters ... Gen 6:17
e as the green herb have I given ... Gen 9:3
E as Nimrod the mighty hunter ... Gen 10:9
and Zeboim, *e* unto Lasha ... Gen 10:19
e to him were children born ... Gen 10:21 1571
from the south *e* to Beth-el ... Gen 13:3
e as the garden of the LORD, like ... Gen 13:10
from a thread *e* to a shoelatchet ... Gen 14:23 5704
came two angels to Sodom at *e* ... Gen 19:1 6153
e the men of Sodom, compassed the ... Gen 19:4
e Lot, and came near to break the ... Gen 19:9
e she herself said, He is my ... Gen 20:5 1571
be heir with my son, *e* with Isaac ... Gen 21:10
e to the children of Heth ... Gen 23:7
e of all that went in at the gate ... Gen 23:10
e the time that women go out to ... Gen 24:11
e betwixt us and thee, and let us ... Gen 26:28
Bless me, *e* me also, O my father ... Gen 27:34 1571
bless me, *e* me also, O my father ... Gen 27:38 1571
spoiled *e* all that was in the ... Gen 34:29
with him, *e* a pillar of stone ... Gen 35:14
e before he came near unto them, ... Gen 37:18
and, lo, it is *e* in my sack ... Gen 42:28
for thou art *e* as Pharaoh ... Gen 44:18
bare unto Jacob, *e* sixteen souls ... Gen 46:18
cattle from our youth *e* until now ... Gen 46:34
e five men, and presented them ... Gen 47:2
Egypt *e* to the other end thereof ... Gen 47:21
e a fruitful bough by a well ... Gen 49:22
E by the God of thy father, who ... Gen 49:25
the mountain of God, *e* to Horeb ... Ex 3:1
e he shall be to thee instead of ... Ex 4:16
Israel is my son, *e* my firstborn ... Ex 4:22
slay thy son, *e* thy firstborn ... Ex 4:23
foundation thereof *e* until now ... Ex 9:18
e all that the hail hath left ... Ex 10:12 853
e darkness which may be felt ... Ex 10:21
e unto the firstborn of the ... Ex 11:5
e the first day ye shall put away ... Ex 12:15 389
fourteenth day of the month at *e* ... Ex 12:18 6153
twentieth day of the month at *e* ... Ex 12:18 6153
e that soul shall be cut off from ... Ex 12:19
and herds, *e* very much cattle ... Ex 12:38
e the selfsame day it came to ... Ex 12:41
e all Pharaoh's horses, his ... Ex 14:23
all the children of Israel, At *e* ... Ex 16:6 6153
At *e* ye shall eat flesh, and in ... Ex 16:12 6153
that at *e* the quails came up, and ... Ex 16:13 6153
stand by thee from morning unto *e* ... Ex 18:14 6153
e unto the sea of the Philistines ... Ex 23:31
thereof, *e* so shall ye make it ... Ex 25:9
e of the mercy seat shall ye make ... Ex 25:19
that the net may be *e* to the ... Ex 27:5
e Aaron, Nadab and Abihu, Eleazar ... Ex 28:1
e of gold, of blue, and purple, and ... Ex 28:8
of stones, *e* four rows of stones ... Ex 28:17
from the loins *e* unto the thighs ... Ex 28:42
e of that which is for Aaron, and ... Ex 29:27
e their heave offering unto the ... Ex 29:28
other lamb thou shalt offer at *e* ... Ex 29:39 6153
other lamb thou shalt offer at *e* ... Ex 29:41 6153
Aaron lighteth the lamps at *e* ... Ex 30:8 6153
to them, *e* to him and to his seed ... Ex 30:21
e two hundred and fifty shekels, ... Ex 30:23
shall *e* be cut off from his ... Ex 30:33
shall *e* be cut off from his ... Ex 30:38
e every man upon his son, and upon ... Ex 32:29 3588
e of them that do any work, and of ... Ex 35:35
e every one whose heart stirred ... Ex 36:2
e two rings upon the one side of ... Ex 37:3
e to the mercy seatward were the ... Ex 37:9
e of the tabernacle of testimony, ... Ex 38:21
e the gold of the offering, was ... Ex 38:24
e with the lamps to be set in ... Ex 39:37
commanded, *e* so had they done it ... Ex 39:43
e of the herd, and of the flock ... Lev 1:2
e corn beaten out of full ears ... Lev 2:14
e an offering made by fire unto ... Lev 3:14
E the whole bullock shall he ... Lev 4:12
the LORD, *e* before the vail ... Lev 4:17
e a memorial thereof, and burn it ... Lev 5:12 853
he shall *e* restore it in the ... Lev 6:5
e the memorial of it, unto the ... Lev 6:15
e the priest shall have to ... Lev 7:8
e that soul shall be cut off from ... Lev 7:20
e that soul shall be cut off from ... Lev 7:21
e the soul that eateth it shall ... Lev 7:25
e that soul shall be cut off from ... Lev 7:27
e upon his forefront, did he put ... Lev 8:9
They shall be *e* an abomination ... Lev 11:11
E these of them ye may eat ... Lev 11:22
them shall be unclean until the *e* ... Lev 11:24 6153
and be unclean until the *e* ... Lev 11:25 6153
shall be unclean until the *e* ... Lev 11:27 6153
and be unclean until the *e* ... Lev 11:28 6153
shall be unclean until the *e* ... Lev 11:31 6153
it shall be unclean until the *e* ... Lev 11:32 6153
shall be unclean until the *e* ... Lev 11:39 6153
and be unclean until the *e* ... Lev 11:40 6153
and be unclean until the *e* ... Lev 11:40 6153
from his head *e* to his foot ... Lev 13:12
e in the skin thereof, was a boil ... Lev 13:18
e a leprosy upon the head or ... Lev 13:30
spots, *e* white bright spots ... Lev 13:38
e all his hair he shall shave off ... Lev 14:9
E such as he is able to get, the ... Lev 14:31
up shall be unclean until the *e* ... Lev 14:46 6153
water, and be unclean until the *e* ... Lev 15:5 6153
water, and be unclean until the *e* ... Lev 15:6 6153
water, and be unclean until the *e* ... Lev 15:7 6153
water, and be unclean until the *e* ... Lev 15:8 6153
him shall be unclean until the *e* ... Lev 15:10 6153
water, and be unclean until the *e* ... Lev 15:10 6153
water, and be unclean until the *e* ... Lev 15:11 6153
water, and be unclean until the *e* ... Lev 15:16 6153
water, and be unclean until the *e* ... Lev 15:17 6153
water, and be unclean until the *e* ... Lev 15:18 6153
her shall be unclean until the *e* ... Lev 15:19 6153
water, and be unclean until the *e* ... Lev 15:21 6153
water, and be unclean until the *e* ... Lev 15:22 6153
he shall be unclean until the *e* ... Lev 15:23 6153
water, and be unclean until the *e* ... Lev 15:27 6153
clothes, *e* the holy garments ... Lev 16:32
e that they may bring them unto ... Lev 17:5
e that man shall be cut off from ... Lev 17:9
I will *e* set my face against that ... Lev 17:10
he shall *e* pour out the blood ... Lev 17:13
water, and be unclean until the *e* ... Lev 17:15 6153
e their nakedness thou shalt not ... Lev 18:9
e their nakedness thou shalt not ... Lev 18:10
e the souls that commit them ... Lev 18:29
e a ram for a trespass offering ... Lev 19:21
I will *e* set my face against that ... Lev 20:6
e he that committeth adultery ... Lev 20:10
any such shall be unclean until *e* ... Lev 22:6 6153
e these are my feasts ... Lev 23:2
e holy convocations, which ye ... Lev 23:4
month at *e* is the LORD's passover ... Lev 23:5 6153
E unto the morrow after the ... Lev 23:16
e an offering made by fire, of ... Lev 23:18
month at *e*, from *e* unto *e* ... Lev 23:32 6153
e an offering made by fire unto ... Lev 24:7
I will *e* appoint over you terror, ... Lev 26:16
e I, will chastise you seven ... Lev 26:28 637
e then shall the land rest, and ... Lev 26:34
e because they despised my ... Lev 26:43
years old *e* unto sixty years old ... Lev 27:3
e thy estimation shall be fifty ... Lev 27:3
years old *e* unto twenty years old ... Lev 27:5
a month old *e* unto five years old ... Lev 27:6
e unto the year of the jubile, and ... Lev 27:18
e unto the year of the jubile ... Lev 27:23
e to him to whom the possession ... Lev 27:24
e of whatsoever passeth under the ... Lev 27:32
e of the tribe of Reuben, were ... Num 1:21
e of the tribe of Simeon, were ... Num 1:23
e of the tribe of Gad, were forty ... Num 1:25
e of the tribe of Judah, were ... Num 1:27
e of the tribe of Issachar, were ... Num 1:29
e of the tribe of Zebulun, were ... Num 1:31
e of the tribe of Ephraim, were ... Num 1:33
e of the tribe of Manasseh, were ... Num 1:35
e of the tribe of Benjamin, were ... Num 1:37
e of the tribe of Dan, were ... Num 1:39
e of the tribe of Asher, were ... Num 1:41
e of the tribe of Naphtali, were ... Num 1:43
E all they that were numbered ... Num 1:46
e those that were numbered of ... Num 3:22
e before the tabernacle of the ... Num 3:38
Thou shalt *e* take five shekels ... Num 3:47
upward *e* until fifty years old, ... Num 4:3
e the censers, the fleshhooks, and ... Num 4:14
upward *e* unto fifty years old ... Num 4:30
upward *e* unto fifty years old, ... Num 4:35
upward *e* unto fifty years old, ... Num 4:39
E those that were numbered of ... Num 4:40
upward *e* unto fifty years old, ... Num 4:43
E those that were numbered of ... Num 4:44
upward *e* unto fifty years old, ... Num 4:47
E those that were numbered of ... Num 4:48
unto the LORD, *e* to the priest ... Num 5:8
e the memorial thereof, and burn ... Num 5:26
from the kernels *e* to the husk ... Num 6:4
e the princes offered their ... Num 7:10
e fine flour mingled with oil, and ... Num 8:8
e instead of the firstborn of all ... Num 8:16
day of this month, at *e*, ye shall ... Num 9:3 6153
day of the first month at *e* in ... Num 9:5 6153
month at *e* they shall keep it ... Num 9:11 6153
e the same soul shall be cut off ... Num 9:13
and at *e* there was upon the ... Num 9:15 6153
abode from *e* unto the morning ... Num 9:21 6153
But *e* a whole month, until it ... Num 11:20 5704
e apparently, and not in dark ... Num 12:8
people, from Egypt *e* until now ... Num 14:19
e forty days, each day for a year ... Num 14:34
e forty years, and ye shall know ... Num 14:34
E those men that did bring up the ... Num 14:37
discomfited them, *e* unto Hormah ... Num 14:45
E all that the LORD hath ... Num 15:23
E to morrow the LORD will shew ... Num 16:5
e him whom he hath chosen will he ... Num 16:5
fathers' houses, *e* twelve rods ... Num 17:6
e the service of the tabernacle ... Num 18:21
e a tenth part of the tithe ... Num 18:26
e the hallowed part thereof out ... Num 18:29 853
shall be unclean until the *e* ... Num 19:7 6153
and shall be unclean until the *e* ... Num 19:8 6153
and be unclean until the *e* ... Num 19:10 6153
in water, and shall be clean at *e* ... Num 19:19 6153
shall be unclean until *e* ... Num 19:21 6153
it shall be unclean until *e* ... Num 19:22 6153
e the whole congregation, into ... Num 20:1
e the whole congregation, ... Num 20:22
e all the house of Israel ... Num 20:29
e unto the children of Ammon ... Num 21:24
out of his hand, *e* unto Arnon ... Num 21:26
Heshbon is perished *e* unto Dibon ... Num 21:30
laid them waste *e* unto Nophah ... Num 21:30
e the covenant of an everlasting ... Num 25:13
e that was slain with the ... Num 25:14
with him, *e* all the congregation ... Num 27:21
other lamb shalt thou offer at *e* ... Num 28:4 6153
other lamb shalt thou offer at *e* ... Num 28:8 6153
E of the children of Israel's ... Num 31:47
of them, *e* all wrought jewels ... Num 31:51
E the country which the LORD ... Num 32:4
e to the children of Gad, and to ... Num 32:33
e the cities of the country round ... Num 32:33
from Beth-jesimoth *e* unto ... Num 33:49
e the land of Canaan with the ... Num 34:2
ye shall *e* have the great sea for ... Num 34:6
E as the LORD commanded Moses, so ... Num 36:10
you in Seir, *e* unto Hormah ... Deut 1:44
in their stead *e* unto this day ... Deut 2:22
e unto Azzah, the Caphtorims, ... Deut 2:23
e unto Gilead, there was not one ... Deut 2:36
e unto the river Arnon half the ... Deut 3:16
the border *e* unto the river ... Deut 3:16
from Chinnereth *e* unto the sea of ... Deut 3:17
the plain, *e* the salt sea, under ... Deut 3:17
e as the LORD my God ... Deut 4:5
to perform, *e* ten commandments ... Deut 4:13
e all the host of heaven, ... Deut 4:19
e out of Egypt, to be unto him a ... Deut 4:20
a consuming fire, *e* a jealous God ... Deut 4:24
e in the latter days, if thou ... Deut 4:30
e unto mount Sion which is Hermon ... Deut 4:48
e unto the sea of the plain, ... Deut 4:49
e us, who are all of us here ... Deut 5:3
e all the heads of your tribes, ... Deut 5:23
e the tables of the covenant ... Deut 9:9
e the tables of the covenant ... Deut 9:11
e until it was as small as dust ... Deut 9:21
e you above all people, as it is ... Deut 10:15
year *e* unto the end of the year ... Deut 11:12
e unto the uttermost sea shall ... Deut 11:24
e unto his habitation shall ye ... Deut 12:5
E as the roebuck and the hart is ... Deut 12:22 389
e so will I do likewise ... Deut 12:30 1571

for *e* their sons and their ... Deut 12:31 1571
from the one end of the earth *e* ... Deut 13:7
e the bread of affliction ... Deut 16:3
sacrificedst the first day at *e* ... Deut 16:4 6153
shalt sacrifice the passover at *e* ... Deut 16:6 6153
e that man or that woman, and ... Deut 17:5
the judge, *e* that man shall die ... Deut 17:12
gods, *e* that prophet shall die ... Deut 18:20
e all the spoil thereof, shalt ... Deut 20:14
e the elders of that city shall ... Deut 21:3
slayeth him, *e* so is this matter ... Deut 22:26
e to his tenth generation shall ... Deut 23:2 1571
e to their tenth generation shall ... Deut 23:3 1571
e among you, in that place which ... Deut 23:16
for *e* both these are abomination ... Deut 23:18 1571
e a freewill offering, according ... Deut 23:23
e all that were feeble behind ... Deut 25:18
e a land that floweth with milk ... Deut 26:9
e great plagues, and of long ... Deut 28:59
end of the earth *e* unto the other ... Deut 28:64
have known, *e* wood and stone ... Deut 28:64
shalt say, Would God it were *e* ... Deut 28:67 6153
at *e* thou shalt say, Would God it ... Deut 28:67 6153
E all nations shall say, ... Deut 29:24
e now, before I have brought them ... Deut 31:21
e our enemies themselves being ... Deut 32:31
e I, am he, and there is no god ... Deut 32:39
a law, *e* the inheritance of the ... Deut 33:4
e to the children of Israel ... Josh 1:2
this Lebanon *e* unto the great ... Josh 1:4
Go view the land, *e* Jericho ... Josh 2:1
for *e* all the inhabitants of the ... Josh 2:24 1571
e the salt sea, failed, and were ... Josh 3:16
e all the men of war, died in the ... Josh 5:4
at *e* in the plains of Jericho ... Josh 5:10 6153
e it, and all that are therein, to ... Josh 6:17
in Israel *e* unto this day ... Josh 6:25
before the gate *e* unto Shebarim ... Josh 7:5
for they have *e* taken of the ... Josh 7:11 1571
they have put it *e* among their ... Josh 7:11 1571
the city, *e* behind the city ... Josh 8:4
e the people of war that were ... Josh 8:11
e all the host that was on the ... Josh 8:13
thousand, *e* all the men of Ai ... Josh 8:25
e a desolation unto this day ... Josh 8:28
we will *e* let them live, lest ... Josh 9:20
e unto this day, in the place ... Josh 9:27
from Kadesh-barnea *e* unto Gaza ... Josh 10:41
country of Goshen, *e* unto Gibeon ... Josh 10:41
e as the sand that is upon the ... Josh 11:4
E from the mount Halak, that ... Josh 11:17
e unto Baal-gad in the valley of ... Josh 11:17
e unto the river Jabbok, which is ... Josh 12:2
e the salt sea on the east, the ... Josh 12:3
of Lebanon *e* unto the mount Halak ... Josh 12:7
e unto the borders of Ekron ... Josh 13:3
e as Moses the servant of the ... Josh 13:8
e unto the children of Gad ... Josh 13:24
e unto the edge of the sea of ... Josh 13:27
e to the one half of the children ... Josh 13:31
e since the LORD spake this word ... Josh 14:10
e so is my strength now, for war, ... Josh 14:11
e to the border of Edom the ... Josh 15:1
sea, *e* unto the end of Jordan ... Josh 15:5
e the city of Arba the father of ... Josh 15:13
From Ekron *e* unto the sea, all ... Josh 15:46
e the border of their inheritance ... Josh 16:5
and her towns, *e* three countries ... Josh 17:11
e to Ephraim and to Manasseh, ... Josh 17:17
e for the tribe of the children ... Josh 19:1
and Kanah, *e* unto great Zidon ... Josh 19:28
e for the children of Naphtali ... Josh 19:32
e Timnath-serah in mount Ephraim ... Josh 19:50
e they had the cities of their ... Josh 21:20
e unto the great sea westward ... Josh 23:4
e these that remain among you, and ... Josh 23:12
e Terah, the father of Abraham, ... Josh 24:2
e the two kings of the Amorites ... Josh 24:12
e the Amorites which dwelt in the ... Josh 24:18
e as many of Israel as had not ... Judg 3:1
e Othniel the son of Kenaz, ... Judg 3:9 853
e nine hundred chariots of iron, ... Judg 4:13
e I, will sing unto the LORD ... Judg 5:3
e that Sinai from before the LORD ... Judg 5:5
e the righteous acts toward the ... Judg 5:11
e Issachar, and also Barak ... Judg 5:15
e they came up against them ... Judg 6:3
e the second bullock of seven ... Judg 6:25
e throughout all the host ... Judg 7:22
e threescore and seventeen men ... Judg 8:14
brethren, *e* the sons of my mother ... Judg 8:19
put it in his city, *e* in Ophrah ... Judg 8:27
e unto the entering of the gate ... Judg 9:40
from Arnon *e* unto Jabbok, and unto ... Judg 11:13
from Arnon *e* unto Jabbok, and from ... Judg 11:22
from the wilderness *e* unto Jordan ... Judg 11:22
e till thou come to Minnith, *e* ... Judg 11:33
e twenty cities, and unto the ... Judg 11:33
e of the children of Ammon ... Judg 11:36
e unto the house of Micah, and ... Judg 18:15
his work out of the field at *e* ... Judg 19:16 6153
from Dan *e* to Beer-sheba, with ... Judg 20:1
e of all the tribes of Israel, ... Judg 20:2
and wept before the LORD until *e* ... Judg 20:23 6153
LORD, and fasted that day until *e* ... Judg 20:26 6153
e out of the meadows of Gibeah ... Judg 20:33
and abode there till *e* before God ... Judg 21:2 6153
hath continued *e* from the morning ... Ruth 2:7 227
Let her glean *e* among the sheaves ... Ruth 2:15 1571
she gleaned in the field until *e* ... Ruth 2:17 6153
And all Israel from Dan *e* to ... 1Sa 3:20
e Ashdod and the coasts thereof ... 1Sa 5:6 853
e unto the great stone of Abel, ... 1Sa 6:18
e he smote of the people fifty ... 1Sa 6:19
to Israel, from Ekron *e* unto Gath ... 1Sa 7:14
up out of Egypt *e* unto this day ... 1Sa 8:8
e the best of them, and give them ... 1Sa 8:14
e they also turned to be with the ... 1Sa 14:21
e they also followed hard after ... 1Sa 14:22
bag which he had, *e* in a scrip ... 1Sa 17:40
e unto Gath, and unto Ekron ... 1Sa 17:52
e to his sword, and to his bow, and ... 1Sa 18:4
I will smite David *e* to the wall ... 1Sa 18:11
Saul sought to smite David *e* to ... 1Sa 19:10
desireth, I will *e* do it for thee ... 1Sa 20:4
the field unto the third day at *e* ... 1Sa 20:5 6153
Let the LORD *e* require it at the ... 1Sa 20:16
e upon a seat by the wall ... 1Sa 20:25
this man of Belial, *e* Nabal ... 1Sa 25:25
let it *e* be given unto the young ... 1Sa 25:27
with the spear *e* to the earth at ... 1Sa 26:8
e David with his two wives, ... 1Sa 27:3
to Shur, *e* unto the land of Egypt ... 1Sa 27:8
him in Ramah, *e* in his own city ... 1Sa 28:3
it to thy neighbour, *e* to David ... 1Sa 28:17
e unto the evening of the next ... 1Sa 30:17
e to his friends, saying, Behold ... 1Sa 30:26
It came *e* to pass on the third ... 2Sa 1:2
and wept, and fasted until *e* ... 2Sa 1:12 6153
e unto Saul, and have buried him ... 2Sa 2:5
sworn to David, *e* so I do to him ... 2Sa 3:9 3588
Judah, from Dan *e* to Beer-sheba ... 2Sa 3:10
e from Phaltiel the son of Laish ... 2Sa 3:15
e on harps, and on psalteries, and ... 2Sa 6:5
e among the whole multitude of ... 2Sa 6:19
e to this day, but have walked in ... 2Sa 7:6
e like Israel, whom God went to ... 2Sa 7:23
e with two lines measured he to ... 2Sa 8:2
e to their buttocks, and sent them ... 2Sa 10:4
at *e* he went out to lie on his ... 2Sa 11:13 6153
we were upon them *e* unto the ... 2Sa 11:23
from the sole of his foot *e* to ... 2Sa 14:25
e from Giloh, while he offered ... 2Sa 15:12
e there also will thy servant be ... 2Sa 15:21 3588
from Dan *e* to Beer-sheba, as the ... 2Sa 17:11
the young man, *e* with Absalom ... 2Sa 18:5
come to the king, *e* to his house ... 2Sa 19:11
e as the heart of one man ... 2Sa 19:14
aged man, *e* fourscore years old ... 2Sa 19:32
from Jordan *e* to Jerusalem ... 2Sa 20:2
against the king, *e* against David ... 2Sa 20:21
e unto the LORD, but he answered ... 2Sa 22:42
e a morning without clouds ... 2Sa 23:4
from Dan *e* to Beer-sheba, and ... 2Sa 24:2
south of Judah, *e* to Beer-sheba ... 2Sa 24:7
morning *e* to the time appointed ... 2Sa 24:15
died of the people from Dan *e* to ... 2Sa 24:15
e me thy servant, and Zadok the ... 1Kin 1:26
E as I sware unto thee by the ... 1Kin 1:30 3588
e so will I certainly do this day ... 1Kin 1:30 3588
e so be he with Solomon, and make ... 1Kin 1:37
this day, mine eyes *e* seeing it ... 1Kin 1:48
e for him, and for Abiathar the ... 1Kin 2:22
e unto the place that is beyond ... 1Kin 4:12
river, from Tiphsah *e* to Azzah ... 1Kin 4:24
from Dan *e* to Beer-sheba, all the ... 1Kin 4:25
e as the sand that is on the sea ... 1Kin 4:29
cedar tree that is in Lebanon *e* ... 1Kin 4:33
he *e* built them for it within, ... 1Kin 6:16
e for the oracle, *e* for the ... 1Kin 6:16
e for the most holy place ... 1Kin 6:16
judge, *e* the porch of judgment ... 1Kin 7:7
e from the foundation unto the ... 1Kin 7:9
e great stones, stones of ten ... 1Kin 7:10
e two rows of pomegranates for ... 1Kin 7:42
e the silver, and the gold, and the ... 1Kin 7:51 853
e those did the priests and the ... 1Kin 8:4
place, *e* under the wings of the ... 1Kin 8:6
e toward the place of which thou ... 1Kin 8:29
e thou only, knowest the hearts ... 1Kin 8:39
and seven days, *e* fourteen days ... 1Kin 8:65
e he lifted up his hand against ... 1Kin 11:26
give it unto thee, *e* ten tribes ... 1Kin 11:35
e unto Rehoboam king of Judah, and ... 1Kin 12:27
before the one, *e* unto Dan ... 1Kin 12:30
e in the month which he had ... 1Kin 12:33
e to cut it off, and to destroy it ... 1Kin 13:34
that day: but what? *e* now ... 1Kin 14:14 1571
he *e* took away all ... 1Kin 14:26
e her he removed from being queen ... 1Kin 15:13
E in the third year of Asa king ... 1Kin 15:28
e for all the evil that he did in ... 1Kin 16:7
e I only, remain a prophet of the ... 1Kin 18:22
of Baal from morning *e* until noon ... 1Kin 18:26
and I, *e* I only, am left ... 1Kin 19:10
and I, *e* I only, am left ... 1Kin 19:14
e the goodliest, are mine ... 1Kin 20:3
E by the young men of the princes ... 1Kin 20:14
e all the children of Israel, ... 1Kin 20:15
e the elders and the nobles who ... 1Kin 21:11
e against Naboth, in the presence ... 1Kin 21:13
dogs lick thy blood, *e* thine ... 1Kin 21:19 1571
against the Syrians, and died at *e* ... 1Kin 22:35 6153
the Moabites, *e* in their country ... 2Kin 3:24
to break through *e* unto the king ... 2Kin 3:26
thy neighbours, *e* empty vessels ... 2Kin 4:3
e now there be come to me from ... 2Kin 5:22
e the noise of a great host ... 2Kin 7:6
e the camp as it was, and fled for ... 2Kin 7:7
they are *e* as all the multitude ... 2Kin 7:13
she left the land, *e* until now ... 2Kin 8:6
e of every good thing of Damascus ... 2Kin 8:9
e the young man the prophet, went ... 2Kin 9:4
people of the LORD, *e* over Israel ... 2Kin 9:6
He came *e* unto them, and cometh ... 2Kin 9:20
Look *e* out the best and meetest of ... 2Kin 10:3
house, *e* two and forty men ... 2Kin 10:14
river Arnon, *e* Gilead and Bashan ... 2Kin 10:33
e him and his nurse, in the ... 2Kin 11:2
enter in on the sabbath shall *e* ... 2Kin 11:5
e they shall keep the watch of ... 2Kin 11:7
e the money of every one that ... 2Kin 12:4
e thou, and Judah with thee ... 2Kin 14:10
e with the kings of Israel ... 2Kin 14:29
e of all the mighty men of wealth ... 2Kin 15:20
e two calves, and made a grove, and ... 2Kin 17:16
e unto Gaza, and the borders ... 2Kin 18:8
e in the sixth year of Hezekiah, ... 2Kin 18:10
e upon Egypt, on which if a man ... 2Kin 18:21
e thou alone, of all the kingdoms ... 2Kin 19:15
art the LORD God, *e* thou only ... 2Kin 19:19
e against the Holy One of Israel ... 2Kin 19:22
a far country, *e* from Babylon ... 2Kin 20:14
out of Egypt, *e* unto this day ... 2Kin 21:15
e all the words of the book which ... 2Kin 22:16
e ten thousand captives, and all ... 2Kin 24:14
e seven thousand, and craftsmen and ... 2Kin 24:16
e them the king of Babylon ... 2Kin 24:16
e over them he made Gedaliah the ... 2Kin 25:22
e Ishmael the son of Nethaniah, ... 2Kin 25:23
thereof, *e* threescore cities ... 1Chr 2:23
and the sons of Elah, *e* Kenaz ... 1Chr 4:15
e unto the east side of the ... 1Chr 4:39
e of the sons of Simeon, five ... 1Chr 4:42
Aroer, *e* unto Nebo and Baal-meon ... 1Chr 5:8
e Epher, and Ishi, and Eliel, and ... 1Chr 5:24
e the Reubenites, and the Gadites, ... 1Chr 5:26
e Asaph the son of Berachiah, the ... 1Chr 6:39
e against the word of the LORD, ... 1Chr 10:13
e when Saul was king, thou wast ... 1Chr 11:2 1571
about, *e* from Millo round about ... 1Chr 11:8
e of Saul's brethren of Benjamin ... 1Chr 12:2
e unto Issachar and Zebulun and ... 1Chr 12:40
from Shihor of Egypt *e* unto the ... 1Chr 13:5
from Gibeon *e* to Gazer ... 1Chr 14:16
E of the covenant which he made ... 1Chr 16:16
e a few, and strangers in it ... 1Chr 16:19
e from following the sheep, that ... 1Chr 17:7
Let it *e* be established, that thy ... 1Chr 17:24
God of Israel, *e* a God to Israel ... 1Chr 17:24
E so dealt David with all the ... 1Chr 20:3
Israel from Beer-sheba *e* to Dan ... 1Chr 21:2
e the pestilence, in the land, and ... 1Chr 21:12
e I it is that have sinned and ... 1Chr 21:17
e the chief of the fathers, as ... 1Chr 23:24
praise the LORD, and likewise at *e* ... 1Chr 23:30 6153
e the principal fathers over ... 1Chr 24:31
e all that were cunning, was two ... 1Chr 25:7
e among the chief men, having ... 1Chr 26:12
e of Laadan the Gershonite, were ... 1Chr 26:21
e among the Hebronites, according ... 1Chr 26:31
E the weight for the candlesticks ... 1Chr 28:15
e all the works of this pattern ... 1Chr 28:19
e my God, will be with thee ... 1Chr 28:20
e they shall be with thee for all ... 1Chr 28:21
E three thousand talents of gold, ... 1Chr 29:4
e a thousand bullocks, a thousand ... 1Chr 29:21
dwell therein, *e* so deal with me ... 2Chr 2:3
E to prepare me timber in ... 2Chr 2:9
place, *e* under the wings of the ... 2Chr 5:7
It came *e* to pass, as the ... 2Chr 5:13
a cloud, *e* the house of the LORD ... 2Chr 5:13
thy dwelling place, *e* from heaven ... 2Chr 6:21
e from thy dwelling place, and do ... 2Chr 6:33
e from thy dwelling place, their ... 2Chr 6:39
e two hundred and fifty, that bare ... 2Chr 8:10
E after a certain rate every day, ... 2Chr 8:13
e in the feast of unleavened ... 2Chr 8:13
the river *e* unto the land of the ... 2Chr 9:26
He built *e* Beth-lehem, and Etam, ... 2Chr 11:6
e four hundred thousand chosen ... 2Chr 13:3
e to him and to his sons by a ... 2Chr 13:5
e to Ben-hail, and to Obadiah, and ... 2Chr 17:7
e Shemaiah, and Nethaniah, and ... 2Chr 17:8
e what my God saith, that will I ... 2Chr 18:13 3588
go out, and do *e* so ... 2Chr 18:21
against the Syrians until the *e* ... 2Chr 18:34 6153
ye shall *e* warn them that they ... 2Chr 19:10
e out of all the cities of Judah ... 2Chr 20:4 1571
e vessels to minister, and to ... 2Chr 24:14
from Samaria *e* unto Beth-horon, ... 2Chr 25:13
e thou, and Judah with thee ... 2Chr 25:19
his name spread abroad *e* to the ... 2Chr 26:8
the leprosy *e* rose up in his ... 2Chr 26:19
e with you, sins against the LORD ... 2Chr 28:10 7535
him in the city, *e* in Jerusalem ... 2Chr 28:27
Israel, from Beer-sheba *e* to Dan ... 2Chr 30:5
and Manasseh *e* unto Zebulun ... 2Chr 30:10
e many of Ephraim, and Manasseh, ... 2Chr 30:18
dwelling place, *e* unto heaven ... 2Chr 30:27
e unto every one that entereth ... 2Chr 31:16
e to the entering in at the fish ... 2Chr 33:14
e unto Naphtali, with their ... 2Chr 34:6
E to the artificers and builders ... 2Chr 34:11
e all the curses that are written ... 2Chr 34:24
I have *e* heard thee also, saith ... 2Chr 34:27
e to serve the LORD their God ... 2Chr 34:33
E those did Cyrus king of Persia ... Ezr 1:8
e burnt offerings morning and ... Ezr 3:3
e until the reign of Darius king ... Ezr 4:5
e unto Artaxerxes the king ... Ezr 4:11
of the God of Israel, *e* unto them ... Ezr 5:1
since that time *e* until now hath ... Ezr 5:16
e of the tribute beyond the river ... Ezr 6:8
e a scribe of the words of the ... Ezr 7:11
e I Artaxerxes the king, do make ... Ezr 7:21
e the offering of the house of ... Ezr 8:25
I *e* weighed unto their hand six ... Ezr 8:26
e of the Canaanites, the Hittites ... Ezr 9:1
e before the dragon well, and to ... Neh 2:13
e unto the tower of Meah they ... Neh 3:1
e over against his house ... Neh 3:10

e to the end of the house of	Neh 3:21	
of the wall, *e* unto the corner	Neh 3:24	
out, *e* unto the wall of Ophel	Neh 3:27	
E that which they build, if a fox	Neh 4:3	1571
he shall *e* break down their stone	Neh 4:3	
I *e* set the people after their	Neh 4:13	
will ye *e* sell your brethren	Neh 5:8	1571
e this day, their lands, their	Neh 5:11	
e thus be he shaken out, and	Neh 5:13	3602
the twentieth year *e* unto the two	Neh 5:14	
e their servants bare rule over	Neh 5:15	
e to understand the words of the	Neh 8:13	
Thou, *e* thou, art LORD alone	Neh 9:6	
e until the days of Johanan the	Neh 12:23	
e unto the water gate eastward	Neh 12:37	
furnaces *e* unto the broad wall	Neh 12:38	
of Meah, *e* unto the sheep gate	Neh 12:39	
of Jerusalem was heard *e* afar off	Neh 12:43	
nevertheless *e* him did outlandish	Neh 13:26	
from India *e* unto Ethiopia	Est 1:1	
e an hundred and fourscore days	Est 1:4	
and his servants, *e* Esther's feast	Est 2:18	853
e the people of Mordecai	Est 3:6	
e upon the thirteenth day of the	Est 3:13	
came *e* before the king's gate	Est 4:2	5704
it shall be *e* given thee to the	Est 5:3	
e to the half of the kingdom it	Est 5:6	
do *e* so to Mordecai the Jew, that	Est 6:10	
e to the half of the kingdom	Est 7:2	
E as I have seen, they that plow	Job 4:8	
they die, *e* without wisdom	Job 4:21	
taketh it *e* out of the thorns, and	Job 5:5	
E that it would please God to	Job 6:9	
e to the land of darkness and the	Job 10:21	
e on his neck, upon the thick	Job 15:26	
e the eyes of his children shall	Job 17:5	
e the thoughts of my heart	Job 17:11	
e the firstborn of death shall	Job 18:13	
E when I remember I am afraid, and	Job 21:6	
E to day is my complaint bitter	Job 23:2	1571
that I might come *e* to his seat	Job 23:3	
soul desireth, *e* that he doeth	Job 23:13	
to them *e* as the shadow of death	Job 24:17	
Behold *e* to the moon, and it	Job 25:5	
e the waters forgotten of the	Job 28:4	
Let me be weighed in an *e* balance	Job 31:6	6664
Shall *e* he that hateth right	Job 34:17	637
E so would he have removed thee	Job 36:16	
cast down *e* at the sight of him	Job 41:9	1571
sons' sons, *e* four generations	Job 42:16	
came before him, *e* into his ears	Ps 18:6	
e unto the LORD, but he answered	Ps 18:41	
e length of days for ever and ever	Ps 21:4	
e lift them up, ye everlasting	Ps 24:9	
My foot standeth in an *e* place	Ps 26:12	4334
e mine enemies and my foes, came	Ps 27:2	
e unto my cause, my God and my	Ps 35:23	
e to Jeduthun, A Psalm of David	Ps 39:*t*	
I held my peace, *e* from good	Ps 39:2	
my mouth, *e* praise unto our God	Ps 40:3	
e the rich among the people shall	Ps 45:12	
e the people of the God of	Ps 47:9	
he will be our guide *e* unto death	Ps 48:14	
e the LORD, hath spoken, and	Ps 50:1	
I am God, *e* thy God	Ps 50:7	
them, *e* he that abideth of old	Ps 55:19	
I lie *e* among them that are set	Ps 57:4	
e the sons of men, whose teeth	Ps 57:4	
them *e* be taken in their pride	Ps 59:12	
their arrows, *e* bitter words	Ps 64:3	
thy house, *e* of thy holy temple	Ps 65:4	
e our own God, shall bless us	Ps 67:6	
e Sinai itself was moved at the	Ps 68:8	
thousand, *e* thousands of angels	Ps 68:17	
e the God of our salvation	Ps 68:19	
e the goings of my God, my King,	Ps 68:24	
e the Lord, from the fountain of	Ps 68:26	
righteousness, *e* of thine only	Ps 71:16	
psaltery, *e* thy truth, O my God	Ps 71:22	
e to such as are of a clean heart	Ps 73:1	
e all that the enemy hath done	Ps 74:3	
thou thy hand, *e* thy right hand	Ps 74:11	
Thou, *e* thou, art to be feared	Ps 76:7	
voice, *e* unto God with my voice	Ps 77:1	
e the children which should be	Ps 78:6	
e to this mountain, which his	Ps 78:54	
e fainteth for the courts of the	Ps 84:2	1571
e thine altars, O LORD of hosts,	Ps 84:3	853
e from everlasting to everlasting	Ps 90:2	
e according to thy fear, so is	Ps 90:11	
e the most High, thy habitation	Ps 91:9	
e Joseph, who was sold for a	Ps 105:17	
e the ruler of the people, and let	Ps 105:20	
him at the sea, *e* at the Red sea	Ps 106:7	
e the blood of their sons and of	Ps 106:38	
e they shall understand the	Ps 107:43	
and give praise, *e* with my glory	Ps 108:1	637
that he might *e* slay the broken	Ps 109:16	
e with the princes of his people	Ps 113:8	
e the heavens, are the LORD's	Ps 115:16	
e unto the horns of the altar	Ps 118:27	
e thy salvation, according to thy	Ps 119:41	
statutes alway, *e* unto the end	Ps 119:112	
time forth, and *e* for evermore	Ps 121:8	
people from henceforth *e* for ever	Ps 125:2	
my soul is *e* as a weaned child	Ps 131:2	
upon the beard, *e* Aaron's beard	Ps 133:2	
the blessing, *e* life for evermore	Ps 133:3	
E an heritage unto Israel his	Ps 136:22	
e to the foundation thereof	Ps 137:7	
E there shall thy hand lead me,	Ps 139:10	1571
e the night shall be light about	Ps 139:11	
e thy God, O Zion, unto all	Ps 146:10	
e of the children of Israel, a	Ps 148:14	
e from the stranger which	Prov 2:16	
e as a father the son in whom he	Prov 3:12	
e all the judges of the earth	Prov 8:16	
E in laughter the heart is	Prov 14:13	1571
The poor is hated *e* of his own	Prov 14:20	1571
e the wicked for the day of evil	Prov 16:4	1571
he maketh *e* his enemies to be at	Prov 16:7	1571
e they both are abomination to	Prov 17:15	1571
E a fool, when he holdeth his	Prov 17:28	1571
E a child is known by his doings,	Prov 20:11	1571
the LORD hath made *e* both of them	Prov 20:12	1571
known to thee this day, *e* to thee	Prov 22:19	637
my heart shall rejoice, *e* mine	Prov 23:15	1571
e his prayer shall be abomination	Prov 28:9	1571
the son of Jakeh, *e* the prophecy	Prov 30:1	
Ithiel, *e* unto Ithiel and Ucal,	Prov 30:1	
e that which hath been already	Eccl 2:12	853
the fool, so it happeneth *e* to me	Eccl 2:15	1571
e one thing befalleth them	Eccl 3:19	
e of all that have been before	Eccl 4:16	
e of foolishness and madness	Eccl 7:25	
in my heart *e* to declare all this	Eccl 9:1	
e so thou knowest not the works	Eccl 11:5	3602
was upright, *e* words of truth	Eccl 12:10	
a flock of sheep that are *e* shorn	Song 4:2	
foot *e* unto the head there is no	Is 1:6	
is iniquity, *e* the solemn meeting	Is 1:13	
e every one that is written among	Is 4:3	
e great and fair, without	Is 5:9	
midst of it, *e* the son of Tabeal	Is 7:6	
e the king of Assyria	Is 7:17	853
it shall *e* be for briers and	Is 7:23	
e the king of Assyria, and all his	Is 8:7	853
he shall reach *e* to the neck	Is 8:8	
from henceforth *e* for ever	Is 9:7	
e Ephraim and the inhabitant of	Is 9:9	
e the remnant of Jacob, unto the	Is 10:21	
e determined, in the midst of all	Is 10:23	
e them that rejoice in my	Is 13:3	
e the LORD, and the weapons of his	Is 13:5	
e a man than the golden wedge of	Is 13:12	
e all the chief ones of the earth	Is 14:9	
e all of them, lie in glory,	Is 14:18	
voice shall be heard *e* unto Jahaz	Is 15:4	
e of his haughtiness, and his	Is 16:6	
they are come *e* unto Jazer	Is 16:8	
e in vessels of bulrushes upon	Is 18:2	
e they that are the stay of the	Is 19:13	
they shall return *e* to the LORD	Is 19:22	
e a blessing in the midst of the	Is 19:24	
e with their buttocks uncovered,	Is 20:4	
e unto Shebna, which is over the	Is 22:15	
e to all the vessels of flagons	Is 22:24	
e the strength of the sea, saying	Is 23:4	
e the name of the LORD God of	Is 24:15	
songs, *e* glory to the righteous	Is 24:16	
e the heat with the shadow of a	Is 25:5	
e as straw is trodden down for	Is 25:10	
to the ground, *e* to the dust	Is 25:12	
he layeth it low, *e* to the ground	Is 26:5	
he bringeth it *e* to the dust	Is 26:5	
e the feet of the poor, and the	Is 26:6	
e leviathan that crooked serpent	Is 27:1	
e determined upon the whole earth	Is 28:22	
e all that fight against her and	Is 29:7	
It shall *e* be as when an hungry	Is 29:8	
e a marvellous work and a wonder	Is 29:14	
e when the needy speaketh right	Is 32:7	
rejoice *e* with joy and singing	Is 35:2	637
e God with a recompence	Is 35:4	
e thou alone, of all the kingdoms	Is 37:16	
thou art the LORD, *e* thou only	Is 37:20	
e against the Holy One of Israel	Is 37:23	
e the LORD, in the land of the	Is 38:11	
from day *e* to night wilt thou	Is 38:12	
from day *e* to night wilt thou	Is 38:13	
country unto me, *e* from Babylon	Is 39:3	
E the youths shall faint and be	Is 40:30	
e by the way that he had not gone	Is 41:3	
e them that contended with thee	Is 41:12	
e among them, and there was no	Is 41:28	
E every one that is called by my	Is 43:7	
I, *e* I, am the LORD	Is 43:11	
I will *e* make a way in the	Is 43:19	637
e I, am he that blotteth out thy	Is 43:25	
ye are *e* my witnesses	Is 44:8	
maketh a god, *e* his graven image	Is 44:17	
e saying to Jerusalem, Thou shalt	Is 44:28	
I have *e* called thee by thy name	Is 45:4	
e my hands, have stretched out	Is 45:12	
e to him shall men come	Is 45:24	
e to your old age I am he	Is 46:4	
e to hoar hairs will I carry you	Is 46:4	
e I will carry, and will deliver	Is 46:4	
e thy merchants, from thy youth	Is 47:15	
I have *e* from the beginning	Is 48:5	
e hidden things, and thou didst	Is 48:6	
e before the day when thou	Is 48:7	
e for mine own sake, will I do it	Is 48:11	
I, *e* I, have spoken	Is 48:15	
utter it *e* to the end of the	Is 48:20	
e by the springs of water shall	Is 49:10	
shall *e* now be too narrow by	Is 49:19	3588
E the captives of the mighty	Is 49:25	1571
e I, am he that comforteth you	Is 51:12	
e the dregs of the cup of my fury	Is 51:22	
e the sure mercies of David	Is 55:3	
E unto them will I give in mine	Is 56:5	
E them will I bring to my holy	Is 56:7	
e to them hast thou poured a	Is 57:6	1571
e thither wentest thou up to	Is 57:7	1571
didst debase thyself *e* unto hell	Is 57:9	
have not I held my peace *e* of old	Is 57:11	
e recompense into their bosom,	Is 65:6	
e to him that is poor and of a	Is 66:2	
from our youth *e* unto this day	Jer 3:25	
E a full wind from those places	Jer 4:12	
for *e* the husband with the wife	Jer 6:11	1571
For from the least of them *e* unto	Jer 6:13	
from the prophet *e* unto the	Jer 6:13	
e the fruit of their thoughts,	Jer 6:19	
e I have seen it, saith the LORD	Jer 7:11	1571
e the whole seed of Ephraim	Jer 7:15	853
e sent unto you all my servants	Jer 7:25	
for every one from the least *e*	Jer 8:10	
from the prophet *e* unto the	Jer 8:10	
e this people, with wormwood, and	Jer 9:15	
E the carcases of men shall fall	Jer 9:22	
e they shall perish from the	Jer 10:11	
e unto this day, rising early and	Jer 11:7	
e altars to burn incense unto	Jer 11:13	
e the year of their visitation	Jer 11:23	
For *e* thy brethren, and the house	Jer 12:6	1571
e they have dealt treacherously	Jer 12:6	1571
e to the other end of the land	Jer 12:12	
shall *e* be as this girdle, which	Jer 13:10	
e the kings that sit upon David's	Jer 13:13	
e the fathers and the sons	Jer 13:14	
e the crown of your glory	Jer 13:18	
thy sins, *e* in all thy borders	Jer 15:13	
e lovingkindness and mercies	Jer 16:5	853
e thyself, shalt discontinue from	Jer 17:4	
e to give every man according to	Jer 17:10	
e entering in at the gates of	Jer 17:27	
E so will I break this people and	Jer 19:11	3602
e make this city as Tophet	Jer 19:12	
e in anger, and in fury, and in	Jer 21:5	
e into the hand of Nebuchadrezzar	Jer 22:25	
e the year of their visitation,	Jer 23:12	
in fury, *e* a grievous whirlwind	Jer 23:19	
I will *e* forsake you, saith the	Jer 23:33	
I will *e* punish that man and his	Jer 23:34	
e I, will utterly forget you, and	Jer 23:39	
e like the figs that are first	Jer 24:2	
e unto this day, that is the	Jer 25:3	
e all that is written in this	Jer 25:13	
A noise shall come *e* to the ends	Jer 25:31	
day from one end of the earth *e*	Jer 25:33	
E the prophet Jeremiah said, Amen	Jer 28:6	
E so will I break the yoke of	Jer 28:11	3602
e I know, and am a witness, saith	Jer 29:23	
it is *e* the time of Jacob's	Jer 30:7	
e Israel, when I went to cause	Jer 31:2	
e confounded, because I did bear	Jer 31:19	1571
e the way which thou wentest	Jer 31:21	
e seventeen shekels of silver	Jer 32:9	
e unto this day, and in Israel, and	Jer 32:20	
they built it *e* unto this day	Jer 32:31	
e in the cities of Judah, and in	Jer 33:10	
chosen, he hath *e* cast them off	Jer 33:24	
I will *e* give them into the hand	Jer 34:20	
days of Josiah, *e* into this day	Jer 36:2	
e Elishama the scribe, and Delaiah	Jer 36:12	
e Nergal-sharezer, Samgar-nebo,	Jer 39:3	
but do unto him *e* as he shall say	Jer 39:12	3651
E they sent, and took Jeremiah out	Jer 39:14	
e they and their men, heard that	Jer 40:7	
e Ishmael the son of Nethaniah,	Jer 40:8	
E all the Jews returned out of	Jer 40:12	
e ten men with him, came unto	Jer 41:1	
e with Gedaliah, at Mizpah, and	Jer 41:3	
e fourscore men, having their	Jer 41:5	
e the king's daughters, and all	Jer 41:10	853
e mighty men of war, and the women	Jer 41:16	
the least *e* unto the greatest	Jer 42:1	
thy God, *e* for all this remnant	Jer 42:2	
if we do not *e* according to all	Jer 42:5	3651
from the least *e* to the greatest	Jer 42:8	
him to them, *e* all these words,	Jer 43:1	853
E men, and women, and children, and	Jer 43:6	853
thus came they *e* to Tahpanhes	Jer 43:7	
are not humbled *e* unto this day	Jer 44:10	
they shall *e* be consumed by the	Jer 44:12	
from the least *e* unto the	Jer 44:12	
e all the people that dwelt in	Jer 44:15	
will pluck up, *e* this whole land	Jer 45:4	
e Pharaoh, and all them that trust	Jer 46:25	
they reach *e* to the sea of Jazer	Jer 48:32	
the cry of Heshbon *e* unto Elealeh	Jer 48:34	
e unto Jahaz, have they uttered	Jer 48:34	
from Zoar *e* unto Horonaim, as an	Jer 48:34	
e upon Moab, the year of their	Jer 48:44	
e my fierce anger, saith the LORD	Jer 49:37	853
e the LORD, the hope of their	Jer 50:7	
e against it, and against the	Jer 50:21	
and is lifted up *e* to the skies	Jer 51:9	
e upon Babylon, and her mighty men	Jer 51:56	
e all these words that are	Jer 51:60	853
E the sea monsters draw out the	Lam 4:3	1571
appearance of his loins *e* upward	Eze 1:27	
of his loins *e* downward, I saw as	Eze 1:27	
against me, *e* unto this very day	Eze 2:3	
upon it the city, *e* Jerusalem	Eze 4:1	853
E thus shall the children of	Eze 4:13	3602
for from my youth up *e* till now	Eze 4:14	
e I, am against thee, and will	Eze 5:8	1571
e I, will bring a sword upon you,	Eze 6:3	
the trumpet, *e* to make all ready	Eze 7:14	
of his loins *e* downward, fire	Eze 8:2	
and from his loins *e* upward	Eze 8:2	
e the great abominations that the	Eze 8:6	
e every man with his destroying	Eze 9:1	
e under the cherub, and fill thine	Eze 10:2	
was heard *e* to the outer court	Eze 10:5	
e the wheels that they four had	Eze 10:12	
e thy brethren, the men of thy	Eze 11:15	
I will *e* gather you from the	Eze 11:17	
go forth at *e* in their sight	Eze 12:4	6153

Context	Reference	Strong's
in the e I digged through the	Eze 12:7	6153
e because they have seduced my	Eze 13:10	
I will e rend it with a stormy	Eze 13:13	
e the souls that ye hunt to make	Eze 13:20	
of the prophet shall be e as the	Eze 14:10	
e concerning all that I have	Eze 14:22	
thou hast e set it before them	Eze 16:19	
I will e gather them round about	Eze 16:37	
I will e deal with thee as thou	Eze 16:59	
e without great power or many	Eze 17:9	
e with him in the midst of	Eze 17:16	
e it will I recompense upon his	Eze 17:19	
but e hath eaten upon the	Eze 18:11	1571
e he shall die in his iniquity	Eze 18:18	
a man do, he shall e live in them	Eze 20:11	
a man do, he shall e live in them	Eze 20:13	
a man do, he shall e live in them	Eze 20:21	
all your idols, e unto this day	Eze 20:31	
if the sword contemn e the rod	Eze 21:13	1571
e say thou, The sword, the sword	Eze 21:28	
art come e unto thy years	Eze 22:4	
they are e the dross of silver	Eze 22:18	
Thou shalt e drink it and suck it	Eze 23:34	
of the day, e of this same day	Eze 24:2	
e every good piece, the thigh, and	Eze 24:4	
I will e make the pile for fire	Eze 24:9	
and at e my wife died	Eze 24:18	6153
from the tower of Syene e unto	Eze 29:10	
e the day of the LORD is near, a	Eze 30:3	
thou swimmest, e to the mountains	Eze 32:6	
e for Egypt, and for all her	Eze 32:16	
e her, and the daughters of the	Eze 32:18	
e Pharaoh and all his army slain	Eze 32:31	
e Pharaoh and all his multitude,	Eze 32:32	
iniquity, he shall e die thereby	Eze 33:18	
e I, will both search my sheep,	Eze 34:11	
e I, will judge between the fat	Eze 34:20	
feed them, e my servant David	Eze 34:23	853
e the house of Israel, are my	Eze 34:30	
e blood shall pursue thee	Eze 35:6	
I will e do according to thine	Eze 35:11	
Seir, and all Idumea, e all of it	Eze 35:15	
e the ancient high places are	Eze 36:2	
e the house of Israel, e all of it	Eze 36:10	
walk upon you, e my people Israel	Eze 36:12	853
e with the stick of Judah, and	Eze 37:19	853
e they, and their children, and	Eze 37:25	
e a great company with bucklers	Eze 38:4	
e a great sacrifice upon the	Eze 39:17	
e unto the post of the court	Eze 40:14	
e unto the inner house, and	Eze 41:17	
e the way directly before the	Eze 42:12	
e the gate that looketh toward	Eze 43:1	
e according to the vision that I	Eze 43:3	
they have e defiled my holy name	Eze 43:8	
e the bottom shall be a cubit, and	Eze 43:13	
e to the lower settle shall be	Eze 43:14	
from the lesser settle e to the	Eze 43:14	
e to the house of Israel, Thus	Eze 44:6	
e my house, when ye offer my	Eze 44:7	853
they shall e bear their iniquity	Eze 44:10	
e into the utter court to the	Eze 44:19	
it from En-gedi e unto En-eglaim	Eze 47:10	
from Tamar e to the waters of	Eze 47:19	
east side e unto the west side	Eze 48:3	
east side e unto the west side	Eze 48:6	
e for the priests, shall be this	Eze 48:10	
the border shall be e from Tamar	Eze 48:28	
Daniel continued e unto the first	Dan 1:21	
e as iron is not mixed with clay	Dan 2:43	1887
e with a band of iron and brass,	Dan 4:15	
e with a band of iron and brass,	Dan 4:23	
I have e heard of thee, that the	Dan 5:14	
dominion shall be e unto the end	Dan 6:26	
I beheld e till the beast was	Dan 7:11	5705
for ever, e for ever and ever	Dan 7:18	5705
e of that horn that had eyes, and	Dan 7:20	
e unto me Daniel, after that	Dan 8:1	
great, e to the host of heaven	Dan 8:10	
he magnified himself e to the	Dan 8:11	
e I Daniel, had seen the vision,	Dan 8:15	
e by departing from thy precepts	Dan 9:5	
e by departing, that they might	Dan 9:11	
e the man Gabriel, whom I had	Dan 9:21	
and the wall, e in troublous times	Dan 9:25	
e until the consummation, and that	Dan 9:27	
e I, stood to confirm and to	Dan 11:1	
e for others beside those	Dan 11:4	
be stirred up, e to his fortress	Dan 11:10	
e with the king of the north	Dan 11:11	
He shall enter peaceably e upon	Dan 11:24	
the strong holds, e for a time	Dan 11:24	
he shall e return, and have	Dan 11:30	
white, e to the time of the end	Dan 11:35	
e Edom, and Moab, and the chief of	Dan 11:41	
was a nation e to that same time	Dan 12:1	
book, e to the time of the end	Dan 12:4	
I will e betroth thee unto me in	Hos 2:20	
e I, will tear and go away	Hos 5:14	
yet will I slay e the beloved	Hos 9:16	
E the LORD God of hosts	Hos 12:5	
or e in the days of your fathers	Joel 1:2	518
e all the trees of the field, are	Joel 1:12	
after it, e to the years of many	Joel 2:2	
turn ye e to me with all your	Joel 2:12	
e a meat offering and a drink	Joel 2:14	
Is it not e thus, O ye children	Amos 2:11	637
shall be e round about the land	Amos 3:11	
e a lamentation, O house of	Amos 5:1	
e very dark, and no brightness in	Amos 5:20	
e to make the poor of the land to	Amos 8:4	
and from the north e to the east	Amos 8:12	
e they shall fall, and never rise	Amos 8:14	
have brought thee e to the border	Obad 7	
e destroy the wise men out of	Obad 8	
e thou wast as one of them	Obad 11	1571
the Canaanites, e unto Zarephath	Obad 20	
compassed me about, e to the soul	Jonah 2:5	
of them e to the least of them	Jonah 3:5	
do well to be angry, e unto death	Jonah 4:9	
gate of my people, e to Jerusalem	Mic 1:9	
house, e a man and his heritage	Mic 2:2	
E of late my people is risen up	Mic 2:8	
e with a sore destruction	Mic 2:10	
he shall e be the prophet of this	Mic 2:11	
he will e hide his face from them	Mic 3:4	
they e prepare war against him	Mic 3:5	
Zion from henceforth, e for ever	Mic 4:7	
it come, e the first dominion	Mic 4:8	
and thou shalt go e to Babylon	Mic 4:10	
shall come e to thee from Assyria	Mic 7:12	
from the fortress e to the river	Mic 7:12	
e the old lion, walked, and the	Nah 2:11	
they shall e fall into the mouth	Nah 3:12	
e cry out unto thee of violence,	Hab 1:2	
oaths of the tribes, e thy word	Hab 3:9	
e for salvation with thine	Hab 3:13	
e the voice of the day of the	Zeph 1:14	
for he shall make e a speedy	Zeph 1:18	
I will e destroy thee, that there	Zeph 2:5	
e the breeding of nettles, and	Zeph 2:9	
e all the isles of the heathen	Zeph 2:11	
e all my fierce anger	Zeph 3:8	
e the daughter of my dispersed,	Zeph 3:10	
e the LORD, is in the midst of	Zeph 3:15	
e in the time that I gather you	Zeph 3:20	
month, e from the day that the	Hag 2:18	
e the LORD that hath chosen	Zec 3:2	
e of Heldai, of Tobijah, and of	Zec 6:10	
E he shall build the temple of	Zec 6:13	
of the ninth month, e in Chisleu	Zec 7:1	
e those seventy years, did ye at	Zec 7:5	
ye at all fast unto me, e to me	Zec 7:5	
e shall take hold of the skirt of	Zec 8:23	
e he, shall be for our God, and he	Zec 9:7	1571
shall be from sea e to sea	Zec 9:10	
from the river e to the ends of	Zec 9:10	
e to day do I declare that I will	Zec 9:12	1571
e you, O poor of the flock	Zec 11:7	3651
e Beauty, and cut it asunder, that	Zec 11:10	853
e Bands, that I might break the	Zec 11:14	853
in her own place, e in Jerusalem	Zec 12:6	
e go up from year to year to	Zec 14:16	
e upon them shall be no rain	Zec 14:17	
Who is there e among you that	Mal 1:10	1571
For from the rising of the sun e	Mal 1:11	
e his meat, is contemptible	Mal 1:12	
I will e send a curse upon you,	Mal 2:2	
e the dung of your solemn feasts	Mal 2:3	
e the messenger of the covenant,	Mal 3:1	
E from the days of your fathers	Mal 3:7	
robbed me, e this whole nation	Mal 3:9	
that tempt God are e delivered	Mal 3:15	
do not e the publicans the same	Mt 5:46	2532
do not e the publicans so	Mt 5:47	2532
e as your Father which is in	Mt 5:48	5618
That e Solomon in all his glory	Mt 6:29	3761
do to you, do ye e so to them	Mt 7:12	2532
E so every good tree bringeth	Mt 7:17	
When the e was come, they brought	Mt 8:16	3798
that e the winds and the sea obey	Mt 8:27	2532
saying, My daughter is e now dead	Mt 9:18	737
E so, Father	Mt 11:26	
man is Lord e of the sabbath day	Mt 12:8	2532
E so shall it be also unto this	Mt 12:45	
be taken away e that he hath	Mt 13:12	2532
be it unto thee e as thou wilt	Mt 15:28	
E so it is not the will of your	Mt 18:14	
e as I had pity on thee	Mt 18:33	2532
So when e was come, the lord of	Mt 20:8	3798
unto this last, e as unto thee	Mt 20:14	2532
E as the Son of man came not to	Mt 20:28	5618
for one is your Master, e Christ	Mt 23:8	
for one is your Master, e Christ	Mt 23:10	
E so ye also outwardly appear	Mt 23:28	
e as a hen gathereth her chickens	Mt 23:37	
east, and shineth e unto the west	Mt 24:27	
that it is near, e at the doors	Mt 24:33	
taken away e that which he hath	Mt 25:29	2532
Now when the e was come, he sat	Mt 26:20	3798
exceeding sorrowful, e unto death	Mt 26:38	
When the e was come, there came a	Mt 27:57	3798
e unto the end of the world	Mt 28:20	
he e the unclean spirits, and they	Mk 1:27	2532
And at e, when the sun did set,	Mk 1:32	
be taken e that which he hath	Mk 4:25	2532
the same day, when the e was come	Mk 4:35	3798
they took him e as he was in the	Mk 4:36	
that e the wind and the sea obey	Mk 4:41	2532
that e such mighty works are	Mk 6:2	2532
when e was come, the ship was in	Mk 6:47	3798
For e the Son of man came not to	Mk 10:45	2532
they said unto them e as Jesus	Mk 11:6	2531
when e was come, he went out of	Mk 11:19	3796
that she had, e all her living	Mk 12:44	
if it were possible, e the elect	Mk 13:22	2532
that it is nigh, e at the doors	Mk 13:29	
master of the house cometh, at e	Mk 13:35	3796
e in this night, before the cock	Mk 14:30	
e into the palace of the high	Mk 14:54	2193
And now when the e was come	Mk 15:42	3798
E as they delivered them unto us,	Lk 1:2	2531
Ghost, e from his mother's womb	Lk 1:15	2089
Let us now go e unto Bethlehem,	Lk 2:15	
for sinners also do e the same	Lk 6:33	2532
from him shall be taken e that	Lk 8:18	2532
for he commandeth e the winds	Lk 8:25	2532
and consume them, e as Elias did	Lk 9:54	2532
E the very dust of your city,	Lk 10:11	2532
e the devils are subject unto us	Lk 10:17	2532
e so, Father; for so it seemed	Lk 10:21	3483
But e the very hairs of your head	Lk 12:7	2532
this parable unto us, or e to all	Lk 12:41	2532
why e of yourselves judge ye not	Lk 12:57	2532
E thus shall it be in the day	Lk 17:30	
adulterers, or e as this publican	Lk 18:11	2532
e that he hath shall be taken	Lk 19:26	2532
found e as he had said unto them	Lk 19:32	2531
e now at the descent of the mount	Lk 19:37	2536
e thou, at least in this thy day,	Lk 19:42	2532
shall lay thee e with the ground,	Lk 19:44	
e Moses shewed at the bush, when	Lk 20:37	2532
found it e so as the women had	Lk 24:24	3779
e to them that believe on his	Jn 1:12	
e the Son of man which is in	Jn 3:13	
e so must the Son of man be	Jn 3:14	
e so the Son quickeneth whom he	Jn 5:21	2532
e as they honour the Father	Jn 5:23	2531
e Moses, in whom ye trust	Jn 5:45	
And when e was now come, his	Jn 6:16	3798
eateth me, e he shall live by me	Jn 6:57	2548
at the eldest, e unto the last	Jn 8:9	
E the same that I said unto you	Jn 8:25	2532
we have one Father, e God	Jn 8:41	
e because ye cannot hear my word	Jn 8:43	
me, e so know I the Father	Jn 10:15	2504
But I know, that e now,	Jn 11:22	2532
have caused that e this man	Jn 11:37	2532
e as the Father said unto me, so	Jn 12:50	2531
E the Spirit of truth	Jn 14:17	
gave me commandment, e so I do	Jn 14:31	
e as I have kept my Father's	Jn 15:10	2531
e the Spirit of truth, which	Jn 15:26	
e as I am not of the world	Jn 17:14	2531
e as I am not of the world	Jn 17:16	2531
e so have I also sent them into	Jn 17:18	2504
they may be one, e as we are one	Jn 17:22	2531
hath sent me, e so send I you	Jn 20:21	2504
I suppose that e the world itself	Jn 21:25	3761
e as many as the Lord our God	Acts 2:39	
e by him doth this man stand here	Acts 4:10	
e as many as obeyed him, were	Acts 5:37	
be found e to fight against God	Acts 5:39	2532
e Jesus, that appeared unto thee	Acts 9:17	
e to us, who did eat and drink	Acts 10:41	
and it came e to me	Acts 11:5	891
affirmed that it was e so	Acts 12:15	
Holy Ghost, e as he did unto us	Acts 15:8	2532
we shall be saved, e as they	Acts 15:11	2548
e till break of day, so he	Acts 20:11	
e while I prayed in the temple, I	Acts 22:17	
I persecuted them e unto strange	Acts 26:11	2532
that it shall be e as it was told	Acts 27:25	3779
e as among other Gentiles	Rom 1:13	2532
e his eternal power and Godhead	Rom 1:20	
for e their women did change the	Rom 1:26	5037
e as they did not like to retain	Rom 1:28	2531
E the righteousness of God which	Rom 3:22	1161
E as David also describeth the	Rom 4:6	2509
e God, who quickeneth the dead,	Rom 4:17	
good man some would e dare to die	Rom 5:7	
e over them that had not sinned	Rom 5:14	2532
e so by the righteousness of one	Rom 5:18	2532
e so might grace reign through	Rom 5:21	2532
e so we also should walk in	Rom 6:4	
e so now yield your members	Rom 6:19	3779
e to him who is raised from the	Rom 7:4	
e we ourselves groan within	Rom 8:23	2532
who is e at the right hand of God	Rom 8:34	2532
by one, e by our father Isaac	Rom 9:10	
E for this same purpose have I	Rom 9:17	
E us, whom he hath called, not of	Rom 9:24	2532
e the righteousness which is of	Rom 9:30	1161
e in thy mouth, and in thy heart	Rom 10:8	
E so then at this present time	Rom 11:5	2532
E so have these also now not	Rom 11:31	
For e Christ pleased not himself	Rom 15:3	2532
e the Father of our Lord Jesus	Rom 15:6	2532
E as the testimony of Christ was	1Cor 1:6	2531
e the hidden wisdom, which God	1Cor 2:7	
e so the things of God knoweth no	1Cor 2:11	2532
e as unto babes in Christ	1Cor 3:1	
e as the Lord gave to every man	1Cor 3:5	2532
E unto this present hour we both	1Cor 4:11	
For e Christ our passover is	1Cor 5:7	2532
that all men were e as I myself	1Cor 7:7	2532
for them if they abide e as I	1Cor 7:8	2504
E so hath the Lord ordained that	1Cor 9:14	2532
E as I please all men in all	1Cor 10:33	2504
of me, e as I also am of Christ	1Cor 11:1	2531
for that is e all one as if she	1Cor 11:5	2532
e so is the man also by the woman	1Cor 11:12	
Doth not e nature itself teach	1Cor 11:14	3761
dumb idols, e as ye were led	1Cor 12:2	5613
shall I know e as also I am known	1Cor 13:12	2531
e things without life giving	1Cor 14:7	3676
E so ye, forasmuch as ye are	1Cor 14:12	2532
e so in Christ shall all be made	1Cor 15:22	2532
the kingdom to God, e the Father	1Cor 15:24	2532
churches of Galatia, e so do ye	1Cor 16:1	2532
e the Father of our Lord Jesus	2Cor 1:3	2532
that we despaired e of life	2Cor 1:8	2532
ye shall acknowledge e to the end	2Cor 1:13	2532
e as ye also are ours in the day	2Cor 1:14	2509
e by me and Silvanus and Timotheus,	2Cor 1:19	
For e that which was made	2Cor 3:10	2532
But e unto this day, when Moses	2Cor 3:15	2193
e as by the Spirit of the Lord	2Cor 3:18	
e so our boasting, which I made	2Cor 7:14	2532
is Christ's, e so are we Christ's	2Cor 10:7	2532
us, a measure to reach e unto you	2Cor 10:13	2532
glory, they may be found e as we	2Cor 11:12	2532

also we wish, e your perfection	2Cor 13:9	
e we have believed in Jesus	Gal 2:16	2532
E as Abraham believed God, and it	Gal 3:6	2531
E so we, when we were children,	Gal 4:3	2532
angel of God, e as Christ Jesus	Gal 4:14	
after the Spirit, e so it is now	Gal 4:29	2532
I would they were e cut off which	Gal 5:12	2532
fulfilled in one word, e in this	Gal 5:14	
which are on earth; e in him	Eph 1:10	
children of wrath, e as others	Eph 2:3	2532
E when we were dead in sins, hath	Eph 2:5	2532
e the law of commandments	Eph 2:15	
e as ye are called in one hope of	Eph 4:4	2532
which is the head, e Christ	Eph 4:15	
e as God for Christ's sake hath	Eph 4:32	2532
For it is a shame e to speak of	Eph 5:12	2532
e as Christ is the head of the	Eph 5:23	2532
e as Christ also loved the church	Eph 5:25	2531
it, e as the Lord the church	Eph 5:29	2532
so love his wife e as himself	Eph 5:33	5613
E as it is meet for me to think	Phil 1:7	2531
indeed preach Christ e of envy	Phil 1:15	2532
death, e the death of the cross	Phil 2:8	1161
God shall reveal e this unto you	Phil 3:15	2532
often, and now tell you e weeping	Phil 3:18	2532
able e to subdue all things unto	Phil 3:21	2532
For e in Thessalonica ye sent	Phil 4:16	2532
e the forgiveness of sins	Col 1:14	
E the mystery which hath been hid	Col 1:26	
e as Christ forgave you, so also	Col 3:13	2532
e Jesus, which delivered us from	1Th 1:10	
But e after that we had suffered	1Th 2:2	2532
with the gospel, e so we speak	1Th 2:4	
e as a nurse cherisheth her	1Th 2:7	
e as they have of the Jews	1Th 2:14	2532
unto you, e I Paul, once and again	1Th 2:18	3303
Are not e ye in the presence of	1Th 2:19	2532
e as it came to pass, and ye know	1Th 3:4	2532
all men, e as we do toward you	1Th 3:12	2532
e our Father, at the coming of	1Th 3:13	2532
e your sanctification, that ye	1Th 4:3	
e as the Gentiles which know not	1Th 4:5	2532
e as others which have no hope	1Th 4:13	2532
e so them also which sleep in	1Th 4:14	
one another, e as also ye do	1Th 5:11	2531
E him, whose coming is after the	2Th 2:9	
e our Father, which hath loved us	2Th 2:16	2532
be glorified, e as it is with you	2Th 3:1	2532
For e when we were with you, this	2Th 3:10	2532
E so must their wives be grave,	1Ti 3:11	5615
e the words of our Lord Jesus	1Ti 6:3	
as an evil doer, e unto bonds	2Ti 2:9	
e a prophet of their own, said,	Titus 1:12	
but e their mind and conscience is	Titus 1:15	2532
unto me e thine own self besides	Philem 19	2532
e thy God, hath anointed thee	Heb 1:9	
piercing e to the dividing	Heb 4:12	
e those who by reason of use have	Heb 5:14	
e Jesus, made an high priest for	Heb 6:20	
unto whom e the patriarch Abraham	Heb 7:4	2532
Therefore sprang there e of one	Heb 11:12	2532
to raise him up, e from the dead	Heb 11:19	2532
E so faith, if it hath not works,	Jas 2:17	2532
E so the tongue is a little	Jas 3:5	2532
bless we God, e the Father	Jas 3:9	
e of your lusts that war in your	Jas 4:1	
It is e a vapour, that appeareth	Jas 4:14	1063
e the salvation of your souls	1Pet 1:9	
e to them which stumble at the	1Pet 2:8	
For e hereunto were ye called	1Pet 2:21	
e the ornament of a meek and quiet	1Pet 3:4	
E as Sarah obeyed Abraham,	1Pet 3:6	5613
The like figure whereunto e	1Pet 3:21	
e so minister the same one to	1Pet 4:10	
e as our Lord Jesus Christ hath	2Pet 1:14	2532
e as there shall be false	2Pet 2:1	2532
e denying the Lord that bought	2Pet 2:1	2532
e as our beloved brother Paul	2Pet 3:15	2531
also so to walk, e as he walked	1Jn 2:6	2531
is in darkness e until now	1Jn 2:9	
e now are there many antichrists	1Jn 2:18	2532
hath promised us, e eternal life	1Jn 2:25	
e as it hath taught you, ye shall	1Jn 2:27	2531
himself, e as he is pure	1Jn 3:3	2531
righteous, e as he is righteous	1Jn 3:7	2531
e now already is it in the world	1Jn 4:3	2532
overcometh the world, e our faith	1Jn 5:4	
by water and blood, e Jesus Christ	1Jn 5:6	
e in his Son Jesus Christ	1Jn 5:20	
health, e as thy soul prospereth	3Jn 2	2531
e as thou walkest in the truth	3Jn 3	2531
E as Sodom and Gomorrha, and the	Jude 7	5613
hating e the garment spotted by	Jude 23	2532
E so, Amen	Rev 1:7	3483
dwellest, e where Satan's seat is	Rev 2:13	
e in those days wherein Antipas	Rev 2:13	2532
e as I received of my Father	Rev 2:27	2504
Thou hast a few names e in Sardis	Rev 3:4	2532
e as I also overcame, and am set	Rev 3:21	2504
e as a fig tree casteth her	Rev 6:13	
e unto the horse bridles, by the	Rev 14:20	
E so, Lord God Almighty, true and	Rev 16:7	3483
e he is the eighth, and is of the	Rev 17:11	2532
Reward her e as she rewarded you,	Rev 18:6	2532
e like a jasper stone, clear as	Rev 21:11	5613
E so, come, Lord Jesus	Rev 22:20	3483

EVENING

And the e and the morning were the	Gen 1:5	6153
And the e and the morning were the	Gen 1:8	6153
And the e and the morning were the	Gen 1:13	6153
And the e and the morning were the	Gen 1:19	6153
And the e and the morning were the	Gen 1:23	6153
And the e and the morning were the	Gen 1:31	6153
the dove came in to him in the e	Gen 8:11	6153
of water at the time of the e	Gen 24:11	6153
And it came to pass in the e	Gen 29:23	6153
came out of the field in the e	Gen 30:16	6153
of Israel shall kill it in the e	Ex 12:6	6153
give you in the e flesh to eat	Ex 16:8	6153
Moses from the morning unto the e	Ex 18:13	6153
from e to morning before the LORD	Ex 27:21	6153
the e unto the morning before the	Lev 24:3	6153
when e cometh on, he shall wash	Deut 23:11	6153
upon the trees until the e	Josh 10:26	6153
now the day draweth toward e	Judg 19:9	6150
man that eateth any food until e	1Sa 14:24	6153
Philistine drew near morning and e	1Sa 17:16	6150
even unto the e of the next day	1Sa 30:17	6153
and bread and flesh in the e	1Kin 17:6	6153
the offering of the e sacrifice	1Kin 18:29	
the offering of the e sacrifice	1Kin 18:36	
the e meat offering, and the	2Kin 16:15	6153
offering continually morning and e	1Chr 16:40	6153
the burnt offerings morning and e	2Chr 2:4	6153
every e burnt sacrifices and sweet	2Chr 13:11	6153
lamps thereof, to burn every e	2Chr 13:11	6153
e burnt offerings, and the burnt	2Chr 31:3	6153
even burnt offerings morning and e	Ezr 3:3	6153
astonied until the e sacrifice	Ezr 9:4	6153
at the e sacrifice I arose up	Ezr 9:5	6153
In the e she went, and on the	Est 2:14	6153
are destroyed from morning to e	Job 4:20	6153
E, and morning, and at noon, will I	Ps 55:17	6153
They return at e: they make a	Ps 59:6	6153
And at e let them return	Ps 59:14	6153
of the morning and e to rejoice	Ps 65:8	6153
in the e it is cut down, and	Ps 90:6	6153
work and to his labour until the e	Ps 104:23	6153
up of my hands as the e sacrifice	Ps 141:2	6153
In the twilight, in the e	Prov 7:9	6153
in the e withhold not thine hand	Eccl 11:6	6153
of the e are stretched out	Jer 6:4	6153
of the LORD was upon me in the e	Eze 33:22	6153
shall not be shut until the e	Eze 46:2	6153
And the vision of the e and the	Dan 8:26	6153
about the time of the e oblation	Dan 9:21	6153
are more fierce than the e wolves	Hab 1:8	6153
shall they lie down in the e	Zeph 2:7	6153
her judges are e wolves	Zeph 3:3	6153
that at e time it shall be light	Zec 14:7	6153
And when it was e, his disciples	Mt 14:15	3798
and when the e was come, he was	Mt 14:23	3798
and said unto them, When it is e	Mt 16:2	3798
in the e he cometh with the	Mk 14:17	3798
for it is toward e, and the day is	Lk 24:29	2073
Then the same day at e, being the	Jn 20:19	3798
the prophets, from morning till e	Acts 28:23	2073

EVENINGS

a wolf of the e shall spoil them,	Jer 5:6	6160

EVENINGTIDE

And it came to pass in an e	2Sa 11:2	
And behold at e trouble	Is 17:14	

EVENT

that one e happeneth to them all	Eccl 2:14	4745
there is one e to the righteous,	Eccl 9:2	4745
sun, that there is one e unto all	Eccl 9:3	4745

EVENTIDE

to meditate in the field at the e	Gen 24:63	
the ark of the LORD until the e	Josh 7:6	6153
of Ai he hanged on a tree until e	Josh 8:29	
now the e was come, he went out	Mk 11:11	
for it was now e	Acts 4:3	2073

EVER

of life, and eat, and live for e	Gen 3:22	5769
I give it, and to thy seed for e	Gen 13:15	5769
then let me bear the blame for e	Gen 43:9	
bear the blame to my father for e	Gen 44:32	
this is my name for e, and this is	Ex 3:15	5769
it a feast by an ordinance for e	Ex 12:14	5769
generations by an ordinance for e	Ex 12:17	5769
to thee and to thy sons for e	Ex 12:24	5769
see them again no more for e	Ex 14:13	5769
The LORD shall reign for e	Ex 15:18	5769
LORD shall reign for e and e	Ex 15:18	5703
with thee, and believe thee for e	Ex 19:9	5769
and he shall serve him for e	Ex 21:6	5769
it shall be a statute for e unto	Ex 27:21	5769
shall be a statute for e unto him	Ex 28:43	5769
his sons' by a statute for e from	Ex 29:28	5769
shall be a statute for e to them	Ex 30:21	5769
and the children of Israel for e	Ex 31:17	5769
and they shall inherit it for e	Ex 32:13	5769
The fire shall e be burning upon	Lev 6:13	8548
It shall be a statute for e in	Lev 6:18	5769
is a statute for e unto the LORD	Lev 6:22	5769
for e from among the children of	Lev 7:34	5769
by a statute for e throughout	Lev 7:36	5769
it shall be a statute for e	Lev 10:9	5769
with thee, by a statute for e	Lev 10:15	5769
shall be a statute for e unto you	Lev 16:29	5769
your souls, by a statute for e	Lev 16:31	5769
for e unto them throughout their	Lev 17:7	5769
it shall be a statute for e	Lev 23:14	5769
for e in all your dwellings	Lev 23:21	5769
it shall be a statute for e	Lev 23:31	5769
statute for e in your generations	Lev 23:41	5769
statute for e in your generations	Lev 24:3	5769
The land shall not be sold for e	Lev 25:23	6783
for e to him that bought it	Lev 25:30	6783
they shall be your bondmen for e	Lev 25:46	5769
for e throughout your generations	Num 10:8	5769
an ordinance for e in your	Num 15:15	5769
thy sons, by an ordinance for e	Num 18:8	5769
with thee, by a statute for e	Num 18:11	5769
with thee, by a statute for e	Num 18:19	5769
for e before the LORD unto thee	Num 18:19	5769
it shall be a statute for e	Num 18:23	5769
among them, for a statute for e	Num 19:10	5769
upon which thou hast ridden e	Num 22:30	5750
was I e wont to do so unto thee	Num 22:30	
end shall be that he perish for e	Num 24:20	5703
and he also shall perish for e	Num 24:24	5703
Did e people hear the voice of	Deut 4:33	
LORD thy God giveth thee, for e	Deut 4:40	
and with their children for e	Deut 5:29	5769
thy children after thee for e	Deut 12:28	5769
and it shall be an heap for e	Deut 13:16	5769
and he shall be thy servant for e	Deut 15:17	5769
the LORD, him and his sons for e	Deut 18:5	
thy God, and to walk e in his ways	Deut 19:9	
congregation of the LORD for e	Deut 23:3	5769
prosperity all thy days for e	Deut 23:6	5769
a wonder, and upon thy seed for e	Deut 28:46	5769
unto us and to our children for e	Deut 29:29	5769
to heaven, and say, I live for e	Deut 32:40	5769
unto the children of Israel for e	Josh 4:7	5769
fear the LORD your God for e	Josh 4:24	
Ai, and made it an heap for e	Josh 8:28	5769
and thy children's for e, because	Josh 14:9	5769
did he e strive against Israel,	Judg 11:25	
or did he e fight against them,	Judg 11:25	
the LORD, and there abide for e	1Sa 1:22	5769
should walk before me for e	1Sa 2:30	5769
an old man in thine house for e	1Sa 2:32	
walk before mine anointed for e	1Sa 2:35	
for e for the iniquity which he	1Sa 3:13	5769
with sacrifice nor offering for e	1Sa 3:14	5769
thy kingdom upon Israel for e	1Sa 13:13	5769
thy kindness from my house for e	1Sa 20:15	5769
LORD be between thee and me for e	1Sa 20:23	5769
between my seed and thy seed for e	1Sa 20:42	5769
he shall be my servant for e	1Sa 27:12	5769
thee keeper of mine head for e	1Sa 28:2	
Shall the sword devour for e	2Sa 2:26	5331
guiltless before the LORD for e	2Sa 3:28	5769
the throne of his kingdom for e	2Sa 7:13	5769
be established for e before thee	2Sa 7:16	5769
throne shall be established for e	2Sa 7:16	5769
to be a people unto thee for e	2Sa 7:24	5769
his house, establish it for e	2Sa 7:25	5769
let thy name be magnified for e	2Sa 7:26	5769
it may continue for e before thee	2Sa 7:29	5769
of thy servant be blessed for e	2Sa 7:29	5769
Let my lord king David live for e	1Kin 1:31	5769
upon the head of his seed for e	1Kin 2:33	5769
be peace for e from the LORD	1Kin 2:33	5769
established before the LORD for e	1Kin 2:45	
for Hiram was e a lover of David	1Kin 5:1	
place for thee to abide in for e	1Kin 8:13	5769
built, to put my name there for e	1Kin 9:3	5769
of thy kingdom upon Israel for e	1Kin 9:5	5769
the LORD loved Israel for e	1Kin 10:9	5769
the seed of David, but not for e	1Kin 11:39	
they will be thy servants for e	1Kin 12:7	
unto thee, and unto thy seed for e	2Kin 5:27	5769
Israel, will I put my name for e	2Kin 21:7	5769
and to minister unto him for e	1Chr 15:2	5769
for his mercy endureth for e	1Chr 16:34	5769
be the LORD God of Israel for e	1Chr 16:36	5769
LORD God of Israel for e and e	1Chr 16:36	
because his mercy endureth for e	1Chr 16:41	5769
I will stablish his throne for e	1Chr 17:12	5769
mine house and in my kingdom for e	1Chr 17:14	5769
thou make thine own people for e	1Chr 17:22	5769
his house be established for e	1Chr 17:23	5769
thy name may be magnified for e	1Chr 17:24	5769
that it may be before thee for e	1Chr 17:27	5769
and it shall be blessed for e	1Chr 17:27	5769
of his kingdom over Israel for e	1Chr 22:10	5769
holy things, he and his sons for e	1Chr 23:13	5769
and to bless in his name for e	1Chr 23:13	5769
they may dwell in Jerusalem for e	1Chr 23:25	5769
to be king over Israel for e	1Chr 28:4	5769
will establish his kingdom for e	1Chr 28:7	5769
for your children after you for e	1Chr 28:8	5769
him, he will cast thee off for e	1Chr 28:9	5703
Israel our father, for e and e	1Chr 29:10	
fathers, keep this for e in the	1Chr 29:18	5769
is an ordinance for e to Israel	2Chr 2:4	5769
for his mercy endureth for e	2Chr 5:13	5769
and a place for thy dwelling for e	2Chr 6:2	5769
for his mercy endureth for e	2Chr 7:3	5769
because his mercy endureth for e	2Chr 7:6	5769
that my name may be there for e	2Chr 7:16	5769
Israel, to establish them for e	2Chr 9:8	5769
they will be thy servants for e	2Chr 10:7	
over Israel to David for e	2Chr 13:5	5769
seed of Abraham thy friend for e	2Chr 20:7	5769
for his mercy endureth for e	2Chr 20:21	5769
light to him and to his sons for e	2Chr 21:7	
which he hath sanctified for e	2Chr 30:8	5769
Jerusalem shall my name be for e	2Chr 33:4	5769
Israel, will I put my name for e	2Chr 33:7	5865
endureth for e toward Israel	Ezr 3:11	5769
their peace or their wealth for e	Ezr 9:12	5769
to your children for e	Ezr 9:12	5769
the king, Let the king live for e	Neh 2:3	5769
the LORD your God for e and e	Neh 9:5	5769
the congregation of God for e	Neh 13:1	5769
who e perished, being innocent	Job 4:7	
they perish for e without any	Job 4:20	5331
Thou prevailest for e against him	Job 14:20	5331
pen and lead in the rock for e	Job 19:24	5703
perish for e like his own dung	Job 20:7	5331
be delivered for e from my judge	Job 23:7	5331
yea, he doth establish them for e	Job 36:7	5331
thou take him for a servant for e	Job 41:4	5769
let them e shout for joy, because	Ps 5:11	5769

hast put out their name for e	Ps 9:5	5769
put out their name for e and e	Ps 9:5	5703
But the LORD shall endure for e	Ps 9:7	5769
the poor shall not perish for e	Ps 9:18	5703
The LORD is King for e and e	Ps 10:16	5769
The LORD is King for e and e	Ps 10:16	5703
them from this generation for e	Ps 12:7	5769
forget me, O LORD? for e?	Ps 13:1	5331
the LORD is clean, enduring for e	Ps 19:9	5703
it him, even length of days for e	Ps 21:4	5769
even length of days for e and e	Ps 21:4	5703
hast made him most blessed for e	Ps 21:6	5703
your heart shall live for e	Ps 22:26	5703
in the house of the LORD for e	Ps 23:6	
for they have been e of old	Ps 25:6	
Mine eyes are e toward the LORD	Ps 25:15	8548
them also, and lift them up for e	Ps 28:9	5769
yea, the LORD sitteth King for e	Ps 29:10	5769
will give thanks unto thee for e	Ps 30:12	5769
of the LORD standeth for e	Ps 33:11	5769
their inheritance shall be for e	Ps 37:18	5769
He is e merciful, and lendeth	Ps 37:26	
they are preserved for e	Ps 37:28	5769
the land, and dwell therein for e	Ps 37:29	5703
settest me before thy face for e	Ps 41:12	5769
long, and praise thy name for e	Ps 44:8	5769
arise, cast us not off for e	Ps 44:23	5331
God hath blessed thee for e	Ps 45:2	5769
Thy throne, O God, is for e	Ps 45:6	5769
throne, O God, is for e and e	Ps 45:6	5703
the people praise thee for e	Ps 45:17	5769
people praise thee for e and e	Ps 45:17	5703
God will establish it for e	Ps 48:8	5769
For this God is our God for e	Ps 48:14	5769
this God is our God for e and e	Ps 48:14	5703
is precious, and it ceaseth for e	Ps 49:8	5769
That he should still live for e	Ps 49:9	5331
their houses shall continue for e	Ps 49:11	5769
and my sin is e before me	Ps 51:3	8548
shall likewise destroy thee for e	Ps 52:5	5331
I trust in the mercy of God for e	Ps 52:8	5769
in the mercy of God for e and e	Ps 52:8	5703
I will praise thee for e, because	Ps 52:9	5769
abide in thy tabernacle for e	Ps 61:4	5769
He shall abide before God for e	Ps 61:7	5769
I sing praise unto thy name for e	Ps 61:8	5703
He ruleth by his power for e	Ps 66:7	5769
the LORD will dwell in it for e	Ps 68:16	5331
His name shall endure for e	Ps 72:17	5769
be his glorious name for e	Ps 72:19	5769
of my heart, and my portion for e	Ps 73:26	5769
why hast thou cast us off for e	Ps 74:1	5331
enemy blaspheme thy name for e	Ps 74:10	5331
congregation of thy poor for e	Ps 74:19	5331
But I will declare for e	Ps 75:9	5769
Will the Lord cast off for e	Ps 77:7	5769
Is his mercy clean gone for e	Ps 77:8	5331
which he hath established for e	Ps 78:69	5769
wilt thou be angry for e	Ps 79:5	5331
will give thee thanks for e	Ps 79:13	5769
time should have endured for e	Ps 81:15	5769
be confounded and troubled for e	Ps 83:17	5703
Wilt thou be angry with us for e	Ps 85:5	5769
of the mercies of the LORD for e	Ps 89:1	5769
Mercy shall be built up for e	Ps 89:2	5769
Thy seed will I establish for e	Ps 89:4	5769
also will I make to endure for e	Ps 89:29	5703
His seed shall endure for e	Ps 89:36	5769
be established for e as the moon	Ps 89:37	5769
wilt thou hide thyself for e	Ps 89:46	5331
or e thou hadst formed the earth	Ps 90:2	
they shall be destroyed for e	Ps 92:7	5703
thine house, O LORD, for e	Ps 93:5	
thou, O LORD, shalt endure for e	Ps 102:12	5769
will he keep his anger for e	Ps 103:9	5769
it should not be removed for e	Ps 104:5	
of the LORD shall endure for e	Ps 104:31	5769
remembered his covenant for e	Ps 105:8	5769
for his mercy endureth for e	Ps 106:1	5769
for his mercy endureth for e	Ps 107:1	5769
Thou art a priest for e after the	Ps 110:4	5769
his righteousness endureth for e	Ps 111:3	5703
he will e be mindful of his	Ps 111:5	5769
They stand fast for e and e, and	Ps 111:8	5703
They stand fast for e and e	Ps 111:8	5769
hath commanded his covenant for e	Ps 111:9	5769
his praise endureth for e	Ps 111:10	5769
his righteousness endureth for e	Ps 112:3	5703
he shall not be moved for e	Ps 112:6	5769
his righteousness endureth for e	Ps 112:9	5703
truth of the LORD endureth for e	Ps 117:2	5769
because his mercy endureth for e	Ps 118:1	5769
that his mercy endureth for e	Ps 118:2	5769
that his mercy endureth for e	Ps 118:3	5769
that his mercy endureth for e	Ps 118:4	5769
for his mercy endureth for e	Ps 118:29	5769
I keep thy law continually for e	Ps 119:44	5769
thy law continually for e and e	Ps 119:44	5703
For e, O LORD, thy word is	Ps 119:89	5769
for they are e with me	Ps 119:98	5769
have I taken as an heritage for e	Ps 119:111	5769
that thou hast founded them for e	Ps 119:152	5769
judgments endureth for e	Ps 119:160	5769
be removed, but abideth for e	Ps 125:1	5769
people from henceforth even for e	Ps 125:2	5769
the LORD from henceforth and for e	Ps 131:3	5769
This is my rest for e	Ps 132:14	5703
Thy name, O LORD, endureth for e	Ps 135:13	5769
for his mercy endureth for e	Ps 136:1	5769
for his mercy endureth for e	Ps 136:2	5769
for his mercy endureth for e	Ps 136:3	5769
for his mercy endureth for e	Ps 136:4	5769
for his mercy endureth for e	Ps 136:5	5769
for his mercy endureth for e	Ps 136:6	5769
for his mercy endureth for e	Ps 136:7	5769
for his mercy endureth for e	Ps 136:8	5769
for his mercy endureth for e	Ps 136:9	5769
for his mercy endureth for e	Ps 136:10	5769
for his mercy endureth for e	Ps 136:11	5769
for his mercy endureth for e	Ps 136:12	5769
for his mercy endureth for e	Ps 136:13	5769
for his mercy endureth for e	Ps 136:14	5769
for his mercy endureth for e	Ps 136:15	5769
for his mercy endureth for e	Ps 136:16	5769
for his mercy endureth for e	Ps 136:17	5769
for his mercy endureth for e	Ps 136:18	5769
for his mercy endureth for e	Ps 136:19	5769
for his mercy endureth for e	Ps 136:20	5769
for his mercy endureth for e	Ps 136:21	5769
for his mercy endureth for e	Ps 136:22	5769
for his mercy endureth for e	Ps 136:23	5769
for his mercy endureth for e	Ps 136:24	5769
for his mercy endureth for e	Ps 136:25	5769
for his mercy endureth for e	Ps 136:26	5769
thy mercy, O LORD, endureth for e	Ps 138:8	5769
and I will bless thy name for e	Ps 145:1	5769
will bless thy name for e and e	Ps 145:1	5703
and I will praise thy name for e	Ps 145:2	5769
praise thy name for e and e	Ps 145:2	5703
flesh bless his holy name for e	Ps 145:21	5769
bless his holy name for e and e	Ps 145:21	5703
which keepeth truth for e	Ps 146:6	5769
The LORD shall reign for e	Ps 146:10	5769
hath also stablished them for e	Ps 148:6	5703
stablished them for e and e	Ps 148:6	5769
the beginning, or e the earth was	Prov 8:23	6924
truth shall be established for e	Prov 12:19	5703
For riches are not for e	Prov 27:24	5769
throne shall be established for e	Prov 29:14	5703
but the earth abideth for e	Eccl 1:4	5769
wise more than of the fool for e	Eccl 2:16	5769
God doeth, it shall be for e	Eccl 3:14	5769
they any more a portion for e in	Eccl 9:6	5769
Or e the silver cord be loosed,	Eccl 12:6	
Or e I was aware, my soul made me	Song 6:12	3808
from henceforth even for e	Is 9:7	5769
Trust ye in the LORD for e	Is 26:4	5703
he will not e be threshing it	Is 28:28	5331
may be for the time to come for e	Is 30:8	5703
the time to come for e and e	Is 30:8	5769
and towers shall be for dens for e	Is 32:14	5769
quietness and assurance for e	Is 32:17	5769
stakes thereof shall e be removed	Is 33:20	5331
smoke thereof shall go up for e	Is 34:10	5769
none shall pass through it for e	Is 34:10	5331
pass through it for e and e	Is 34:10	5769
they shall possess it for e	Is 34:17	5769
word of our God shall stand for e	Is 40:8	5769
saidst, I shall be a lady for e	Is 47:7	5769
but my salvation shall be for e	Is 51:6	5769
my righteousness shall be for e	Is 51:8	5769
For I will not contend for e	Is 57:16	5769
LORD, from henceforth and for e	Is 59:21	5769
they shall inherit the land for e	Is 60:21	5769
neither remember iniquity for e	Is 64:9	5703
rejoice for e in that which I	Is 65:18	5703
Will he reserve his anger for e	Jer 3:5	5769
and I will not keep anger for e	Jer 3:12	5769
to your fathers, for e and e	Jer 7:7	5769
anger, which shall burn for e	Jer 17:4	5769
and this city shall remain for e	Jer 17:25	5769
and to your fathers for e and e	Jer 25:5	5769
being a nation before me for e	Jer 31:36	
nor thrown down any more for e	Jer 31:40	5769
way, that they may fear me for e	Jer 32:39	
for his mercy endureth for e	Jer 33:11	5769
neither ye, nor your sons for e	Jer 35:6	5769
a man to stand before me for e	Jer 35:19	
dragons, and a desolation for e	Jer 49:33	5769
shall be no more inhabited for e	Jer 50:39	5331
but thou shalt be desolate for e	Jer 51:26	5769
that it shall be desolate for e	Jer 51:62	5769
the Lord will not cast off for e	Lam 3:31	5769
Thou, O LORD, remainest for e	Lam 5:19	5769
dost thou forget us for e	Lam 5:20	5331
their children's children for e	Eze 37:25	5769
David shall be their prince for e	Eze 37:25	5769
of the children of Israel for e	Eze 43:7	5769
dwell in the midst of them for e	Eze 43:9	5769
in Syriack, O king, live for e	Dan 2:4	5957
Blessed be the name of God for e	Dan 2:20	5957
be the name of God for e and e	Dan 2:20	5957
kingdoms, and it shall stand for e	Dan 2:44	5957
O king, live for e	Dan 3:9	5957
and honoured him that liveth for e	Dan 4:34	5957
spake and said, O king, live for e	Dan 5:10	5957
unto him, King Darius, live for e	Dan 6:6	5757
unto the king, O king, live for e	Dan 6:21	5957
all their bones in pieces or e	Dan 6:24	3809
the living God, and stedfast for e	Dan 6:26	5957
the kingdom for e, even for e	Dan 7:18	5957
for e, even for e and e	Dan 7:18	5957
righteousness as the stars for e	Dan 12:3	5769
as the stars for e and e	Dan 12:3	5703
for e that it shall be for a time	Dan 12:7	5769
I will betroth thee unto me for e	Hos 2:19	5769
there hath not been e the like	Joel 2:2	5769
But Judah shall dwell for e	Joel 3:20	5769
and he kept his wrath for e	Amos 1:11	5331
and thou shalt be cut off for e	Obad 10	5769
with her bars was about me for e	Jonah 2:6	5769
have ye taken away my glory for e	Mic 2:9	5769
name of the LORD our God for e	Mic 4:5	5769
of the LORD our God for e and e	Mic 4:5	5703
Zion from henceforth, even for e	Mic 4:7	5769
he retaineth not his anger for e	Mic 7:18	5703
the prophets, do they live for e	Zec 1:5	5769
the LORD hath indignation for e	Mal 1:4	5769
and the power, and the glory, for e	Mt 6:13	*165*
grow on thee henceforward for e	Mt 21:19	*165*
to this time, no, nor e shall be	Mt 24:21	*3364*
eat fruit of thee hereafter for e	Mk 11:14	*165*
to do as he had e done unto them	Mk 15:8	*104*
over the house of Jacob for e	Lk 1:33	*165*
to Abraham, and to his seed for e	Lk 1:55	*165*
unto him, Son, thou art e with me	Lk 15:31	*3842*
told me all things that e I did	Jn 4:29	*3745*
He told me all that e I did	Jn 4:39	*3745*
this bread, he shall live for e	Jn 6:51	*165*
of this bread shall live for e	Jn 6:58	*165*
abideth not in the house for e	Jn 8:35	*165*
but the Son abideth e	Jn 8:35	*165*
All that e came before me are	Jn 10:8	*3745*
the law that Christ abideth for e	Jn 12:34	*165*
that he may abide with you for e	Jn 14:16	*165*
I e taught in the synagogue, and	Jn 18:20	*3842*
or e he come near, are ready to	Acts 23:15	*4253*
the Creator, who is blessed for e	Rom 1:25	*165*
is over all, God blessed for e	Rom 9:5	*165*
to whom be glory for e	Rom 11:36	*165*
glory through Jesus Christ for e	Rom 16:27	*165*
his righteousness remaineth for e	2Cor 9:9	*165*
To whom be glory for e and e	Gal 1:5	*165*
For no man e yet hated his own	Eph 5:29	*4218*
our Father be glory for e and e	Phil 4:20	*165*
so shall we e be with the Lord	1Th 4:17	*3842*
but e follow that which is good,	1Th 5:15	*3842*
be honour and glory for e and e	1Ti 1:17	*165*
E learning, and never able to come	2Ti 3:7	*3842*
to whom be glory for e and e	2Ti 4:18	*165*
thou shouldest receive him for e	Philem 15	*166*
throne, O God, is for e and e	Heb 1:8	*165*
Thou art a priest for e after the	Heb 5:6	*165*
made an high priest for e after	Heb 6:20	*165*
Thou art a priest for e after the	Heb 7:17	*165*
Thou art a priest for e after the	Heb 7:21	*165*
this man, because he continueth e	Heb 7:24	*165*
seeing he e liveth to make	Heb 7:25	*3842*
one sacrifice for sins for e	Heb 10:12	*1336*
for e them that are sanctified	Heb 10:14	*1336*
yesterday, and to day, and for e	Heb 13:8	*165*
to whom be glory for e and e	Heb 13:21	*165*
which liveth and abideth for e	1Pet 1:23	*165*
word of the Lord endureth for e	1Pet 1:25	*165*
praise and dominion for e and e	1Pet 4:11	*165*
glory and dominion for e and e	1Pet 5:11	*165*
of darkness is reserved for e	2Pet 2:17	*165*
To him be glory both now and for e	2Pet 3:18	
the will of God abideth for e	1Jn 2:17	*165*
in us, and shall be with us for e	2Jn 2	*165*
the blackness of darkness for e	Jude 13	*165*
dominion and power, both now and e	Jude 25	
glory and dominion for e and e	Rev 1:6	*165*
throne, who liveth for e and e	Rev 4:9	*165*
him that liveth for e and e	Rev 4:10	*165*
and unto the Lamb for e and e	Rev 5:13	*165*
him that liveth for e and e	Rev 5:14	*165*
be unto our God for e and e	Rev 7:12	*165*
by him that liveth for e and e	Rev 10:6	*165*
and he shall reign for e and e	Rev 11:15	*165*
ascendeth up for e and e	Rev 14:11	*165*
of God, who liveth for e and e	Rev 15:7	*165*
her smoke rose up for e and e	Rev 19:3	*165*
day and night for e and e	Rev 20:10	*165*
and they shall reign for e and e	Rev 22:5	*165*

EVERLASTING

the e covenant between God	Gen 9:16	5769
generations for an e covenant	Gen 17:7	5769
of Canaan, for an e possession	Gen 17:8	5769
in your flesh for an e covenant	Gen 17:13	5769
with him for an e covenant	Gen 17:19	5769
the name of the LORD, the e God	Gen 21:33	5769
after thee for an e possession	Gen 48:4	5769
the utmost bound of the e hills	Gen 49:26	5769
an e priesthood throughout their	Ex 40:15	5769
shall be an e statute unto you	Lev 16:34	5769
of Israel by an e covenant	Lev 24:8	5769
the covenant of an e priesthood	Num 25:13	5769
and underneath are the e arms	Deut 33:27	5769
hath made with me an e covenant	2Sa 23:5	5769
and to Israel for an e covenant	1Chr 16:17	5769
and be ye lifted up, ye e doors	Ps 24:7	5769
even lift them up, ye e doors	Ps 24:9	5769
Israel from e, and to e	Ps 41:13	5769
world, even from e to e	Ps 90:2	5769
thou art from e	Ps 93:2	5769
his mercy is e	Ps 100:5	5769
e to e upon them that	Ps 103:17	5769
and to Israel for an e covenant	Ps 105:10	5769
of Israel from e to e	Ps 106:48	5769
shall be in e remembrance	Ps 112:6	5769
is an e righteousness, and thy law	Ps 119:142	5769
of thy testimonies is e	Ps 119:144	5769
in me, and lead me in the way e	Ps 139:24	5769
Thy kingdom is an e kingdom	Ps 145:13	5769
I was set up from e, from the	Prov 8:23	5769
the righteous is an e foundation	Prov 10:25	5769
The e Father, The Prince of Peace	Is 9:6	5703
ordinance, broken the e covenant	Is 24:5	5769
in the LORD JEHOVAH is e strength	Is 26:4	5769
us shall dwell with e burnings	Is 33:14	5769
songs and e joy upon their heads	Is 35:10	5769
thou not heard, that the e God	Is 40:28	5769
in the LORD with an e salvation	Is 45:17	5769
e joy shall be upon their head	Is 51:11	5769
but with e kindness will I have	Is 54:8	5769
I will make an e covenant with	Is 55:3	5769
for an e sign that shall not be	Is 55:13	5769
I will give them an e name	Is 56:5	5769
shall be unto thee an e light	Is 60:19	5769
the LORD shall be thine e light	Is 60:20	5769

e joy shall be unto them	Is 61:7	5769
I will make an *e* covenant with	Is 61:8	5769
them, to make himself an *e* name	Is 63:12	5769
thy name is from *e*	Is 63:16	5769
is the living God, and an *e* king	Jer 10:10	5769
their *e* confusion shall never be	Jer 20:11	5769
I will bring an *e* reproach upon	Jer 23:40	5769
I have loved thee with an *e* love	Jer 31:3	5769
I will make an *e* covenant with	Jer 32:40	5769
establish unto thee an *e* covenant	Eze 16:60	5769
it shall be an *e* covenant with	Eze 37:26	5769
his kingdom is an *e* kingdom	Dan 4:3	5957
whose dominion is an *e* dominion	Dan 4:34	5957
his dominion is an *e* dominion	Dan 7:14	5957
whose kingdom is an *e* kingdom	Dan 7:27	5957
to bring in *e* righteousness, and	Dan 9:24	5769
earth shall awake, some to *e* life	Dan 12:2	5769
and some to shame and *e* contempt	Dan 12:2	5769
have been from of old, from *e*	Mic 5:2	5769
Art thou not from *e*, O LORD my	Hab 1:12	6924
the *e* mountains were scattered,	Hab 3:6	5703
his ways are *e*	Hab 3:6	5769
two feet to be cast into *e* fire	Mt 18:8	*166*
and shall inherit *e* life	Mt 19:29	*166*
from me, ye cursed, into *e* fire	Mt 25:41	*166*
shall go away into *e* punishment	Mt 25:46	*166*
receive you into *e* habitations	Lk 16:9	*166*
and in the world to come life *e*	Lk 18:30	*166*
not perish, but have *e* life	Jn 3:16	*166*
believeth on the Son hath *e* life	Jn 3:36	*166*
of water springing up into *e* life	Jn 4:14	*166*
on him that sent me, hath *e* life	Jn 5:24	*166*
meat which endureth unto *e* life	Jn 6:27	*166*
believeth on him, may have *e* life	Jn 6:40	*166*
that believeth on me hath *e* life	Jn 6:47	*166*
that his commandment is life *e*	Jn 12:50	*166*
yourselves unworthy of *e* life	Acts 13:46	*166*
unto holiness, and the end *e* life	Rom 6:22	*166*
to the commandment of the *e* God	Rom 16:26	*166*
shall of the Spirit reap life *e*	Gal 6:8	*166*
Who shall be punished with *e*	2Th 1:9	*166*
and hath given us *e* consolation	2Th 2:16	*166*
believe on him to life *e*	1Ti 1:16	*166*
to whom be honour and power *e*	1Ti 6:16	*166*
the blood of the *e* covenant	Heb 13:20	*166*
into the *e* kingdom of our Lord	2Pet 1:11	*166*
he hath reserved in *e* chains	Jude 6	*126*
having the *e* gospel to preach	Rev 14:6	*166*

EVERMORE

be only oppressed and spoiled *e*	Deut 28:29	
unto David, and to his seed for *e*	2Sa 22:51	5769
you, ye shall observe to do for *e*	2Kin 17:37	
throne shall be established for *e*	1Chr 17:14	5769
hand there are pleasures for *e*	Ps 16:11	5331
to David, and to his seed for *e*	Ps 18:50	5769
and dwell for *e*	Ps 37:27	5769
doth his promise fail for *e*	Ps 77:8	1755
and I will glorify thy name for *e*	Ps 86:12	5769
mercy will I keep for him for *e*	Ps 89:28	5769
Blessed be the LORD for *e*	Ps 89:52	5769
thou, LORD, art most high for *e*	Ps 92:8	5769
seek his face *e*	Ps 105:4	8548
unto all generations for *e*	Ps 106:31	5769
from this time forth and for *e*	Ps 113:2	5769
from this time forth and for *e*	Ps 115:18	5769
this time forth, and even for *e*	Ps 121:8	5769
also sit upon thy throne for *e*	Ps 132:12	5703
the blessing, even life for *e*	Ps 133:3	5769
in the midst of them for *e*	Eze 37:26	5769
be in the midst of them for *e*	Eze 37:28	5769
him, Lord, *e* give us this bread	Jn 6:34	*3842*
Christ, which is blessed for *e*	2Cor 11:31	
Rejoice *e*	1Th 5:16	*3842*
the Son, who is consecrated for *e*	Heb 7:28	
and, behold, I am alive for *e*	Rev 1:18	

EVERY

e living creature that moveth,	Gen 1:21	3605
e winged fowl after his kind	Gen 1:21	3605
e thing that creepeth upon the	Gen 1:25	3605
over *e* creeping thing that	Gen 1:26	3605
over *e* living thing that moveth	Gen 1:28	3605
I have given you *e* herb bearing	Gen 1:29	3605
e tree, in the which is the fruit	Gen 1:29	3605
to *e* beast of the earth	Gen 1:30	3605
to *e* fowl of the air	Gen 1:30	3605
to *e* thing that creepeth upon the	Gen 1:30	3605
I have given *e* green herb for	Gen 1:30	3605
God saw *e* thing that he had made,	Gen 1:31	3605
e plant of the field before it	Gen 2:5	3605
e herb of the field before it	Gen 2:5	3605
made the LORD God to grow *e* tree	Gen 2:9	3605
Of *e* tree of the garden thou	Gen 2:16	3605
God formed *e* beast of the field	Gen 2:19	3605
and *e* fowl of the air	Gen 2:19	3605
Adam called *e* living creature	Gen 2:19	
air, and to *e* beast of the field	Gen 2:20	3605
not eat of *e* tree of the garden	Gen 3:1	3605
above *e* beast of the field	Gen 3:14	3605
flaming sword which turned *e* way	Gen 3:24	
that *e* one that findeth me shall	Gen 4:14	3605
an instructer of *e* artificer in	Gen 4:22	3605
that *e* imagination of the	Gen 6:5	3605
e thing that is in the earth	Gen 6:17	3605
of *e* living thing of all flesh,	Gen 6:19	3605
two of *e* sort shalt thou bring	Gen 6:19	3605
of *e* creeping thing of the earth	Gen 6:20	3605
two of *e* sort shall come unto	Gen 6:20	3605
Of *e* clean beast thou shalt take	Gen 7:2	3605
e living substance that I have	Gen 7:4	3605
of *e* thing that creepeth upon the	Gen 7:8	3605
e beast after his kind, and all	Gen 7:14	3605
e creeping thing that creepeth	Gen 7:14	3605
e fowl after his kind	Gen 7:14	3605
his kind, *e* bird of *e* sort	Gen 7:14	3605
of *e* creeping thing that creepeth	Gen 7:21	3605
creepeth upon the earth, and *e* man	Gen 7:21	3605
e living substance was destroyed	Gen 7:23	3605
e living thing, and all the cattle	Gen 8:1	3605
Bring forth with thee *e* living	Gen 8:17	3605
of *e* creeping thing that creepeth	Gen 8:17	3605
E beast, *e* creeping thing, and	Gen 8:19	3605
e fowl, and whatsoever creepeth	Gen 8:19	3605
took of *e* clean beast	Gen 8:20	3605
of *e* clean fowl, and offered burnt	Gen 8:20	3605
smite any more *e* thing living	Gen 8:21	3605
be upon *e* beast of the earth	Gen 9:2	3605
upon *e* fowl of the air, upon all	Gen 9:2	
E moving thing that liveth shall	Gen 9:3	3605
at the hand of *e* beast will I	Gen 9:5	
at the hand of *e* man's brother	Gen 9:5	
with *e* living creature that is	Gen 9:10	3605
of *e* beast of the earth with you	Gen 9:10	3605
the ark, to *e* beast of the earth	Gen 9:10	3605
e living creature that is with	Gen 9:12	3605
e living creature of all flesh	Gen 9:15	3605
e living creature of all flesh	Gen 9:16	3605
e one after his tongue, after	Gen 10:5	376
that it was well watered *e* where	Gen 13:10	3605
his hand will be against *e* man	Gen 16:12	3605
and *e* man's hand against him	Gen 16:12	3605
E man child among you shall be	Gen 17:10	3605
e man child in your generations,	Gen 17:12	3605
e male among the men of Abraham's	Gen 17:23	3605
all the people from *e* quarter	Gen 19:4	
at *e* place whither we shall come,	Gen 20:13	3605
cursed be *e* one that curseth thee	Gen 27:29	
e one that is not speckled and	Gen 30:33	3605
e one that had some white in it,	Gen 30:35	3605
servants, *e* drove by themselves	Gen 32:16	
that *e* male of you be circumcised	Gen 34:15	3605
if *e* male among us be circumcised	Gen 34:22	3605
e beast of theirs be ours	Gen 34:23	3605
e male was circumcised, all that	Gen 34:24	3605
which was round about *e* city	Gen 41:48	
to restore *e* man's money into his	Gen 42:25	
e man's bundle of money was in	Gen 42:35	
e man's money was in the mouth of	Gen 43:21	
put *e* man's money in his sack's	Gen 44:1	
down *e* man his sack to the ground	Gen 44:11	
and opened *e* man his sack	Gen 44:11	
laded *e* man his ass, and returned	Gen 44:13	
Cause *e* man to go out from me	Gen 45:1	3605
for *e* shepherd is an abomination	Gen 46:34	3605
Egyptians sold *e* man his field	Gen 47:20	
e one according to his blessing	Gen 49:28	
e man and his household came with	Ex 1:1	
E son that is born ye shall cast	Ex 1:22	3605
e daughter ye shall save alive	Ex 1:22	3605
But *e* woman shall borrow of her	Ex 3:22	
For they cast down *e* man his rod	Ex 7:12	376
for upon *e* man and beast which	Ex 9:19	3605
upon *e* herb of the field,	Ex 9:22	3605
the hail smote *e* herb of the	Ex 9:25	3605
brake *e* tree of the field	Ex 9:25	3605
shall eat *e* tree which groweth	Ex 10:5	3605
eat *e* herb of the land, even all	Ex 10:12	3605
they did eat *e* herb of the land,	Ex 10:15	3605
let *e* man borrow of his neighbour	Ex 11:2	
e woman of her neighbour, jewels	Ex 11:2	
shall take to them *e* man a lamb	Ex 12:3	
e man according to his eating	Ex 12:4	
save that which *e* man must eat	Ex 12:16	3605
But *e* man's servant that is	Ex 12:44	
e firstling that cometh of a	Ex 13:12	3605
e firstling of an ass thou shalt	Ex 13:13	3605
and captains over *e* one of them	Ex 14:7	3605
and gather a certain rate *e* day	Ex 16:4	
Gather of it *e* man according to	Ex 16:16	
to his eating, an omer for *e* man	Ex 16:16	
take ye *e* man for them which are	Ex 16:16	
they gathered *e* man according to	Ex 16:18	
And they gathered it *e* morning	Ex 16:21	
e man according to his eating	Ex 16:21	
abide ye *e* man in his place, let	Ex 16:29	
that *e* great matter they shall	Ex 18:22	3605
but *e* small matter they shall	Ex 18:22	3605
but *e* small matter they judged	Ex 18:26	3605
of *e* man that giveth it willingly	Ex 25:2	3605
e one of the curtains shall have	Ex 26:2	3605
and the breadth fifty *e* where	Ex 27:18	
e one with his name shall they be	Ex 28:21	376
thou shalt offer *e* day a bullock	Ex 29:36	
thereon sweet incense *e* morning	Ex 30:7	
then shall they give *e* man a	Ex 30:12	
e one that passeth among them	Ex 30:13	3605
E one that passeth among them	Ex 30:14	3605
e one that defileth it shall	Ex 31:14	
Put *e* man his sword by his side,	Ex 32:27	
slay *e* man his brother	Ex 32:27	
e man his companion, and *e* man	Ex 32:27	
even *e* man upon his son, and upon	Ex 32:29	
that *e* one which sought the LORD	Ex 33:7	3605
stood *e* man at his tent door, and	Ex 33:8	376
e man in his tent door	Ex 33:10	
e firstling among thy cattle,	Ex 34:19	3605
e wise hearted among you shall	Ex 35:10	3605
e one whose heart stirred him up,	Ex 35:21	3605
e one whom his spirit made	Ex 35:21	3605
e man that offered offered an	Ex 35:22	3605
e man, with whom was found blue,	Ex 35:23	3605
E one that did offer an offering	Ex 35:24	3605
e man, with whom was found	Ex 35:24	3605
e man and woman, whose heart made	Ex 35:29	3605
e wise hearted man, in whom the	Ex 36:1	3605
e wise hearted man, in whose	Ex 36:2	3605
even *e* one whose heart stirred	Ex 36:2	3605
unto him free offerings *e* morning	Ex 36:3	
came *e* man from his work which	Ex 36:4	
e wise hearted man among them	Ex 36:8	3605
under *e* board two sockets	Ex 36:30	259
A bekah for *e* man, that is, half	Ex 38:26	
for *e* one that went to be	Ex 38:26	3605
e one with his name, according to	Ex 39:14	376
e oblation of thy meat offering	Lev 2:13	3605
shall burn wood on it *e* morning	Lev 6:12	
e one that toucheth them shall be	Lev 6:18	3605
For *e* meat offering for the	Lev 6:23	3605
E male among the priests shall	Lev 7:6	3605
e meat offering, mingled with oil	Lev 7:10	3605
E raven after his kind	Lev 11:15	
Yet these may ye eat of *e* flying	Lev 11:21	3605
The carcases of *e* beast which	Lev 11:26	3605
e one that toucheth them shall be	Lev 11:26	3605
e earthen vessel, whereinto any	Lev 11:33	3605
in *e* such vessel shall be unclean	Lev 11:34	3605
e thing whereupon any part of	Lev 11:35	3605
e creeping thing that creepeth	Lev 11:41	3605
of *e* living creature that moveth	Lev 11:46	3605
of *e* creature that creepeth upon	Lev 11:46	3605
E bed, whereon he lieth that hath	Lev 15:4	3605
e thing, whereon he sitteth,	Lev 15:4	
e vessel of wood shall be rinsed	Lev 15:12	3605
e garment, and *e* skin, whereon	Lev 15:17	3605
e thing that she lieth upon in	Lev 15:20	3605
e thing also that she sitteth	Lev 15:20	3605
E bed whereon she lieth all the	Lev 15:26	3605
e soul that eateth that which	Lev 17:15	3605
Ye shall fear *e* man his mother,	Lev 19:3	
Therefore *e* one that eateth it	Lev 19:8	
gather *e* grape of thy vineyard	Lev 19:10	
For *e* one that curseth his father	Lev 20:9	376
offerings, *e* thing upon his day	Lev 23:37	
E sabbath he shall set it in	Lev 24:8	
ye shall return *e* man unto his	Lev 25:10	
ye shall return *e* man unto his	Lev 25:10	
return *e* man unto his possession	Lev 25:13	
e devoted thing is most holy unto	Lev 27:28	3605
names, *e* male by their polls	Num 1:2	3605
there shall be a man of *e* tribe	Num 1:4	376
e one head of the house of his	Num 1:4	376
e male from twenty years old and	Num 1:20	3605
e male from twenty years old and	Num 1:22	3605
e man by his own camp	Num 1:52	
e man by his own standard,	Num 1:52	
E man of the children of Israel	Num 2:2	
e man in his place by their	Num 2:17	
e one after their families,	Num 2:34	376
e male from a month old and upward	Num 3:15	3605
appoint them *e* one to his service	Num 4:19	376
e one that entereth into the	Num 4:30	3605
e one that entereth into the	Num 4:35	3605
e one that entereth into the	Num 4:39	3605
e one that entereth into the	Num 4:43	3605
e one that came to do the service	Num 4:47	3605
e one according to his service,	Num 4:49	376
they put out of the camp *e* leper	Num 5:2	3605
e one that hath an issue, and	Num 5:2	3605
e offering of all the holy things	Num 5:9	3605
e man's hallowed things shall be	Num 5:10	
to *e* man according to his service	Num 7:5	
instead of such as open *e* womb	Num 8:16	3605
on the day that I smote *e*	Num 8:17	3605
e man in the door of his tent	Num 11:10	
of *e* tribe of their fathers shall	Num 13:2	376
a man, *e* one a ruler among them	Num 13:2	3605
so shall ye do to *e* one according	Num 15:12	
e one of them, and the LORD is	Num 16:3	3605
take *e* man his censer, and put	Num 16:17	
before the LORD *e* man his censer	Num 16:17	
they took *e* man his censer, and	Num 16:18	
Dathan, and Abiram, on *e* side	Num 16:27	376
take of *e* one of them a rod	Num 17:2	
write thou *e* man's name upon his	Num 17:2	
e one of their princes gave him a	Num 17:6	3605
looked, and took *e* man his rod	Num 17:9	
office for *e* thing of the altar	Num 18:7	3605
e oblation of theirs, *e* meat	Num 18:9	3605
e sin offering of theirs, and	Num 18:9	3605
e trespass offering of theirs,	Num 18:9	3605
e male shall eat it	Num 18:10	3605
e one that is clean in thy house	Num 18:11	3605
e one that is clean in thine	Num 18:13	3605
E thing devoted in Israel shall	Num 18:14	3605
E thing that openeth the matrix	Num 18:15	3605
e heave offering of the LORD	Num 18:29	3605
And ye shall eat it in *e* place	Num 18:31	3605
e open vessel, which hath no	Num 19:15	3605
that *e* one that is bitten, when	Num 21:8	3605
offered on *e* altar a bullock	Num 23:2	
offered upon *e* altar a bullock	Num 23:4	
a bullock and a ram on *e* altar	Num 23:14	
a bullock and a ram on *e* altar	Num 23:30	
Slay ye *e* one his men that were	Num 25:5	376
to *e* one shall his inheritance be	Num 26:54	376
the burnt offering of *e* sabbath	Num 28:10	
this is the burnt offering of *e*	Num 28:14	
deal shalt thou offer for *e* lamb	Num 28:21	
three tenth deals unto *e* bullock	Num 29:14	259
e bond wherewith she hath bound	Num 30:4	3605
But *e* vow of a widow, and of her	Num 30:9	
e bond wherewith she bound her	Num 30:11	3605
E vow, and *e* binding oath to	Num 30:13	3605
Of *e* tribe a thousand, throughout	Num 31:4	
of Israel, a thousand of *e* tribe	Num 31:5	
to the war, a thousand of *e* tribe	Num 31:6	
Now therefore kill *e* male among	Num 31:17	3605
kill *e* woman that hath known man	Num 31:17	3605
E thing that may abide the fire,	Num 31:23	3605
what *e* man hath gotten, of jewels	Num 31:50	
taken spoil, *e* man for himself	Num 31:53	
inherited *e* man his inheritance	Num 32:18	

e man armed for war, before the	Num 32:27	3605
e man armed to battle, before the	Num 32:29	3605
e man's inheritance shall be in	Num 33:54	
shall take one prince of e tribe	Num 34:18	
e one shall give of his cities	Num 35:8	376
that e one that killeth any	Num 35:15	3605
for e one of the children of	Num 36:7	376
e daughter, that possesseth an	Num 36:8	
e man the inheritance of his	Num 36:8	
but e one of the tribes of the	Num 36:9	376
judge righteously between e man	Deut 1:16	
ye came near unto me e one of you	Deut 1:22	3605
when ye had girded on e man his	Deut 1:41	376
of e city, we left none to remain	Deut 2:34	3605
women, and children, of e city	Deut 3:6	3605
then shall ye return e man unto	Deut 3:20	
are alive e one of you this day	Deut 4:4	3605
but by e word that proceedeth out	Deut 8:3	3605
E place whereon the soles of your	Deut 11:24	3605
the hills, and under e green tree	Deut 12:2	3605
e man whatsoever is right in his	Deut 12:8	
in e place that thou seest	Deut 12:13	3605
for e abomination to the LORD,	Deut 12:31	3605
and all the spoil thereof e whit	Deut 13:16	3632
e beast that parteth the hoof, and	Deut 14:6	3605
And e raven after his kind,	Deut 14:14	3605
e creeping thing that flieth is	Deut 14:19	3605
At the end of e seven years thou	Deut 15:1	
E creditor that lendeth ought	Deut 15:2	3605
E man shall give as he is able,	Deut 16:17	
that e slayer may flee thither	Deut 19:3	3605
thou shalt smite e male thereof	Deut 20:13	3605
by their word shall e controversy	Deut 21:5	3605
controversy and e stroke be tried	Deut 21:5	3605
keep thee from e wicked thing	Deut 23:9	3605
e man shall be put to death for	Deut 24:16	
thou shalt rejoice in e good	Deut 26:11	3605
Also e sickness, and e plague,	Deut 28:61	3605
plenteous in e work of thine hand	Deut 30:9	3605
At the end of e seven years	Deut 31:10	
e one shall receive of thy words	Deut 33:3	
E place that the sole of your	Josh 1:3	3605
of Israel, out of e tribe a man	Josh 3:12	
the people, out of e tribe a man,	Josh 4:2	
of Israel, out of e tribe a man	Josh 4:4	
take you up e man of you a stone	Josh 4:5	
until e thing was finished that	Josh 4:10	3605
up e man straight before him	Josh 6:5	
e man straight before him, and	Josh 6:20	
but e man they smote with the	Josh 11:14	3605
These cities were e one with	Josh 21:42	
e man unto his inheritance	Josh 24:28	
e man unto his inheritance to	Judg 2:6	
to e man a damsel or two	Judg 5:30	7218
E one that lappeth of the water	Judg 7:5	3605
likewise e one that boweth down	Judg 7:5	3605
people go e man unto his place	Judg 7:7	
of Israel e man unto his tent	Judg 7:8	
he put a trumpet in e man's hand	Judg 7:16	3605
also on e side of all the camp	Judg 7:18	3605
they stood e man in his place	Judg 7:21	
the LORD set e man's sword	Judg 7:22	
that ye would give me e man the	Judg 8:24	
did cast therein e man the	Judg 8:25	
of all their enemies on e side	Judg 8:34	5437
likewise cut down e man his bough	Judg 9:49	
they departed e man unto his	Judg 9:55	
we will give thee e one of us	Judg 16:5	376
but e man did that which was	Judg 17:6	
e one could sling stones at an	Judg 20:16	3605
sword, as well the men of e city	Judg 20:48	
Ye shall utterly destroy e male	Judg 21:11	3605
e woman that hath lain by man	Judg 21:11	3605
catch you e man his wife of the	Judg 21:21	
e man to his tribe and to his	Judg 21:24	
thence e man to his inheritance	Judg 21:24	
e man did that which was right in	Judg 21:25	
that e one that is left in thine	1Sa 2:36	3605
of e one that heareth it shall	1Sa 3:11	3605
And Samuel told him e whit	1Sa 3:18	3605
they fled e man into his tent	1Sa 4:10	
Go ye e man unto his city	1Sa 8:22	
people away, e man to his house	1Sa 10:25	
hand of your enemies on e side	1Sa 12:11	5437
people he sent e man to his tent	1Sa 13:2	
to sharpen e man his share, and	1Sa 13:20	
e man's sword was against his	1Sa 14:20	
Bring me hither e man his ox	1Sa 14:34	
e man his sheep, and slay them	1Sa 14:34	
all the people brought e man his	1Sa 14:34	
against all his enemies on e side	1Sa 14:47	5437
but e thing that was vile and	1Sa 15:9	3605
cut off the enemies of David e	1Sa 20:15	376
e one that was in distress, and	1Sa 22:2	3605
e one that was in debt	1Sa 22:2	3605
e one that was discontented,	1Sa 22:2	3605
of Jesse give e one of you fields	1Sa 22:7	3605
And Saul sought him e day, but God	1Sa 23:14	3605
break away e man from his master	1Sa 25:10	
Gird ye on e man his sword	1Sa 25:13	
And they girded on e man his sword	1Sa 25:13	
The LORD render to e man his	1Sa 26:23	
e man with his household, even	1Sa 27:3	
e man for his sons and for his	1Sa 30:6	
save to e man his wife and his	1Sa 30:22	
up, e man with his household	2Sa 2:3	
they caught e one his fellow by	2Sa 2:16	376
e one from following his brother	2Sa 2:27	376
to e one a cake of bread, and a	2Sa 6:19	376
departed e one to his house	2Sa 6:19	376
And they went out e man from him	2Sa 13:9	
e man gat him up upon his mule,	2Sa 13:29	
David mourned for his son e day	2Sa 13:37	3605
(for it was at e year's end that	2Sa 14:26	
that e man which hath any suit or	2Sa 15:4	3605
with him covered e man his head	2Sa 15:30	
unto me e thing that ye can hear	2Sa 15:36	3605
all Israel fled e one to his tent	2Sa 18:17	376
Israel had fled e man to his tent	2Sa 19:8	
e man to his tents, O Israel	2Sa 20:1	376
So e man of Israel went up from	2Sa 20:2	376
when he saw that e one that came	2Sa 20:12	3605
from the city, e man to his tent	2Sa 20:22	
that had on e hand six fingers,	2Sa 21:20	
on e foot six toes, four and	2Sa 21:20	
and rose up, and went e man his way	1Kin 1:49	
e man under his vine and under his	1Kin 4:25	
table, e man in his month	1Kin 4:27	
e man according to his charge	1Kin 4:28	
which were about him on e side	1Kin 5:3	5437
God hath given me rest on e side	1Kin 5:4	5437
e base had four brasen wheels, and	1Kin 7:30	259
molten, at the side of e addition	1Kin 7:30	376
to the proportion of e one	1Kin 7:36	376
and e laver was four cubits	1Kin 7:38	259
upon e one of the ten bases one	1Kin 7:38	
which shall know e man the plague	1Kin 8:38	
give to e man according to his	1Kin 8:39	
e one that passeth by it shall be	1Kin 9:8	3605
they brought e man his present,	1Kin 10:25	
he had smitten e male in Edom	1Kin 11:15	3605
he had cut off e male in Edom	1Kin 11:16	3605
return e man to his house	1Kin 12:24	
on e high hill, and under e	1Kin 14:23	3605
e mouth which hath not kissed him	1Kin 19:18	3605
And they slew e one his man	1Kin 20:20	376
e man out of his place, and put	1Kin 20:24	376
let them return e man to his	1Kin 22:17	
Hearken, O people, e one of you	1Kin 22:28	3605
E man to his city, and e man	1Kin 22:36	
And ye shall smite e fenced city	2Kin 3:19	3605
e choice city, and shall fell	2Kin 3:19	3605
city, and shall fell e good tree	2Kin 3:19	3605
mar e good piece of land with	2Kin 3:19	3605
on e good piece of land cast	2Kin 3:25	3605
of land cast e man his stone	2Kin 3:25	
and take thence e man a beam	2Kin 6:2	
even of e good thing of Damascus,	2Kin 8:9	3605
took e man his garment, and put it	2Kin 9:13	
e man with his weapons in his	2Kin 11:8	
they took e man his men that were	2Kin 11:9	
e man with his weapons in his	2Kin 11:11	
even the money of e one that	2Kin 12:4	3605
the money that e man is set at	2Kin 12:4	
e man of his acquaintance	2Kin 12:5	
but e man shall be put to death	2Kin 14:6	
they fled e man to their tents	2Kin 14:12	
the hills, and under e green tree	2Kin 16:4	3605
images and groves in e high hill	2Kin 17:10	3605
and under e green tree	2Kin 17:10	3605
Howbeit e nation made gods of	2Kin 17:29	
e nation in their cities wherein	2Kin 17:29	
then eat ye e man of his own vine	2Kin 18:31	
e one of his fig tree	2Kin 18:31	376
drink ye e one the waters of his	2Kin 18:31	376
of e one according to his	2Kin 23:35	376
e great man's house burnt he with	2Kin 25:9	3605
the king, a daily rate for e day	2Kin 25:30	
the opening thereof e morning	1Chr 9:27	
to prepare it e sabbath	1Chr 9:32	
and hundreds, and with e leader	1Chr 13:1	3605
abroad unto our brethren e where	1Chr 13:2	
he dealt to e one of Israel, both	1Chr 16:3	376
to e one a loaf of bread, and a	1Chr 16:3	376
as e day's work required	1Chr 16:37	
departed e man to his house	1Chr 16:43	
cunning men for e manner of work	1Chr 22:15	3605
he not given you rest on e side	1Chr 22:18	5437
to stand e morning to thank and	1Chr 23:30	
of their fathers, for e gate	1Chr 26:13	
for e matter pertaining to God,	1Chr 26:32	3605
of e course were twenty and four	1Chr 27:1	259
instruments of e kind of service	1Chr 28:14	3605
gold, by weight for e candlestick	1Chr 28:15	
to the use of e candlestick	1Chr 28:15	
tables of shewbread, for e table	1Chr 28:16	
gave gold by weight for e bason	1Chr 28:17	
by weight for e bason of silver	1Chr 28:17	
workmanship e willing skilful man	1Chr 28:21	3605
to e governor in all Israel, the	2Chr 1:2	3605
to find out e device which shall	2Chr 2:14	3605
when e one shall know his own	2Chr 6:29	376
render unto e man according unto	2Chr 6:30	
to e one that passeth by it	2Chr 7:21	3605
Even after a certain rate e day	2Chr 8:13	
as the duty of e day required	2Chr 8:14	
also by their courses at e gate	2Chr 8:14	
e three years once came the ships	2Chr 9:21	
they brought e man his present,	2Chr 9:24	
e man to your tents, O Israel, and	2Chr 10:16	
return e man to his house	2Chr 11:4	
in e several city he put shields	2Chr 11:12	3605
and Benjamin, unto e fenced city	2Chr 11:23	3605
they burn unto the LORD e morning	2Chr 13:11	
e evening burnt sacrifices and	2Chr 13:11	
lamps thereof, to burn e evening	2Chr 13:11	
he hath given us rest on e side	2Chr 14:7	5437
e man to his house in peace	2Chr 18:16	
e one helped to destroy another	2Chr 20:23	376
e man of Judah and Jerusalem, and	2Chr 20:27	3605
e man with his weapons in his	2Chr 23:7	
took e man his men that were to	2Chr 23:8	
e man having his weapon in his	2Chr 23:10	
but e man shall die for his own	2Chr 25:4	
they fled e man to his tent	2Chr 25:22	
the hills, and under e green tree	2Chr 28:4	3605
altars in e corner of Jerusalem	2Chr 28:24	3605
in e several city of Judah he	2Chr 28:25	3605
offerings for e burnt offering	2Chr 29:35	
for e one that was not clean	2Chr 30:17	3605
The good LORD pardon e one	2Chr 30:18	3605
e man to his possession, into	2Chr 31:1	
e man according to his service,	2Chr 31:2	
even unto e one that entereth	2Chr 31:16	3605
in e several city, the men that	2Chr 31:19	3605
in e work that he began in the	2Chr 31:21	3605
other, and guided them on e side	2Chr 32:22	5437
and the porters waited at e gate	2Chr 35:15	
and Judah, e one unto his city	Ezr 2:1	376
as the duty of e day required	Ezr 3:4	
of e one that willingly offered a	Ezr 3:5	3605
e one to his place, and place them	Ezr 6:5	
By number and by weight of e one	Ezr 8:34	3605
Then were assembled unto me e one	Ezr 9:4	3605
and with them the elders of e city	Ezr 10:14	
e one over against his house	Neh 3:28	376
to the wall, e one unto his work	Neh 4:15	376
e one with one of his hands	Neh 4:17	376
e one had his sword girded by his	Neh 4:18	376
Let e one with his servant lodge	Neh 4:22	376
saving that e one put them off	Neh 4:23	376
exact usury, e one of his brother	Neh 5:7	376
So God shake out e man from his	Neh 5:13	
e one in his watch, and e one	Neh 7:3	376
and to Judah, e one unto his city	Neh 7:6	376
e one upon the roof of his house,	Neh 8:16	376
e one having knowledge, and having	Neh 10:28	3605
year, and the exaction of e debt	Neh 10:31	3605
in the cities of Judah dwelt e	Neh 11:3	376
Judah, e one in his inheritance	Neh 11:20	376
be for the singers, due for e day	Neh 11:23	
and the porters, e day his portion	Neh 12:47	
were fled e one to his field	Neh 13:10	376
Levites, e one in his business	Neh 13:30	376
do according to e man's pleasure	Est 1:8	
into e province according to the	Est 1:22	
to e people after their language,	Est 1:22	376
that e man should bear rule in	Est 1:22	
to the language of e people	Est 1:22	
Mordecai walked e day before the	Est 2:11	
Now when e maid's turn was come	Est 2:12	
Then thus came e maiden unto the	Est 2:13	
that were over e province	Est 3:12	
to the rulers of e people	Est 3:12	
of e province according to the	Est 3:12	
to e people after their language	Est 3:12	
a commandment to be given in e	Est 3:14	3605
in e province, whithersoever the	Est 4:3	3605
all his friends e thing that had	Est 6:13	3605
unto e province according to the	Est 8:9	
unto e people after their	Est 8:9	
in e city to gather themselves	Est 8:11	3605
a commandment to be given in e	Est 8:13	3605
in e province, and in e city,	Est 8:17	3605
to their appointed time e year	Est 9:27	3605
e generation, e family	Est 9:28	
e province, and e city	Est 9:28	
in their houses, e one his day	Job 1:4	376
about all that he hath on e side	Job 1:10	5437
they came e one from his own	Job 2:11	376
they rent e one his mantle, and	Job 2:12	376
shouldest visit him e morning	Job 7:18	
and try him e moment	Job 7:18	
is the soul of e living thing	Job 12:10	3605
shall make him afraid on e side	Job 18:11	5437
He hath destroyed me on e side	Job 19:10	5437
e hand of the wicked shall come	Job 20:22	3605
e man shall draw after him, as	Job 21:33	3605
They reap e one his corn in the	Job 24:6	
his eye seeth e precious thing	Job 28:10	3605
cause e man to find according to	Job 34:11	
E man may see it	Job 36:25	3605
He sealeth up the hand of e man	Job 37:7	3605
he searcheth after e green thing	Job 39:8	3605
behold e one that is proud, and	Job 40:11	3605
Look on e one that is proud, and	Job 40:12	3605
I know that thou canst do e thing	Job 42:2	3605
e man also gave him a piece of	Job 42:11	
and e one an earring of gold	Job 42:11	376
is angry with the wicked e day	Ps 7:11	3605
They speak vanity e one with his	Ps 12:2	376
The wicked walk on e side	Ps 12:8	5437
in his temple doth e one speak of	Ps 29:9	3605
fear was on e side	Ps 31:13	5437
For this shall e one that is	Ps 32:6	3605
verily e man at his best state is	Ps 39:5	3605
Surely e man walketh in a vain	Ps 39:6	
surely e man is vanity	Ps 39:11	3605
For e beast of the forest is mine	Ps 50:10	3605
E one of them is gone back	Ps 53:3	3605
E day they wrest my words	Ps 56:5	3605
let e one of them pass away	Ps 58:8	
for thou renderest to e man	Ps 62:12	
e one that sweareth by him shall	Ps 63:11	3605
inward thought of e one of them	Ps 64:6	376
little hills rejoice on e side	Ps 65:12	
till e one submit himself with	Ps 68:30	
e thing that moveth therein	Ps 69:34	3605
thy power to e one that is to	Ps 71:18	3605
and comfort me on e side	Ps 71:21	5437
plagued, and chastened e morning	Ps 73:14	
e one of them in Zion appeareth	Ps 84:7	
and thy faithfulness e night	Ps 92:2	
drink to e beast of the field	Ps 104:11	3605
so is e one that trusteth in them	Ps 115:8	3605
refrained my feet from e evil way	Ps 119:101	3605
therefore I hate e false way	Ps 119:104	3605
and I hate e false way	Ps 119:128	3605
e one of thy righteous judgments	Ps 119:160	3605
Blessed is e one that feareth the	Ps 128:1	3605
so is e one that trusteth in them	Ps 135:18	3605
E day will I bless thee	Ps 145:2	3605

the desire of *e* living thing	Ps 145:16	3605
Let *e* thing that hath breath	Ps 150:6	3605
So are the ways of *e* one that is	Prov 1:19	3605
yea, *e* good path	Prov 2:9	3605
happy is *e* one that retaineth her	Prov 3:18	
and lieth in wait at *e* corner	Prov 7:12	3605
E prudent man dealeth with	Prov 13:16	3605
E wise woman buildeth her house	Prov 14:1	
The simple believeth *e* word	Prov 14:15	3605
eyes of the LORD are in *e* place	Prov 15:3	3605
E one that is proud in heart is	Prov 16:5	3605
e man is a friend to him that	Prov 19:6	3605
but *e* fool will be meddling	Prov 20:3	3605
proclaim *e* one his own goodness	Prov 20:6	376
E purpose is established by	Prov 20:18	
E way of a man is right in his	Prov 21:2	3605
but of *e* one that is hasty only	Prov 21:5	3605
shall not he render to *e* man	Prov 24:12	
E man shall kiss his lips that	Prov 24:26	
soul *e* bitter thing is sweet	Prov 27:7	3605
the crown endure to *e* generation	Prov 27:24	
but *e* man's judgment cometh from	Prov 29:26	
E word of God is pure	Prov 30:5	3605
To *e* thing there is a season, and	Eccl 3:1	3605
a time to *e* purpose under the	Eccl 3:1	3605
He hath made *e* thing beautiful in	Eccl 3:11	3605
also that *e* man should eat and	Eccl 3:13	3605
is a time there for *e* purpose	Eccl 3:17	3605
for *e* purpose and for *e* work	Eccl 3:17	3605
e right work, that for this a man	Eccl 4:4	3605
E man also to whom God hath given	Eccl 5:19	3605
Because to *e* purpose there is	Eccl 8:6	3605
applied my heart unto *e* work that	Eccl 8:9	3605
he saith to *e* one that he is a	Eccl 10:3	3605
foolish wearieth *e* one of them	Eccl 10:15	
shall bring *e* work into judgment	Eccl 12:14	3605
with *e* secret thing, whether it	Eccl 12:14	3605
e man hath his sword upon his	Song 3:8	
whereof *e* one bear twins, and none	Song 4:2	3605
whereof *e* one beareth twins, and	Song 6:6	3605
e one for the fruit thereof was	Song 8:11	376
e one loveth gifts, and followeth	Is 1:23	3605
shall be upon *e* one that is proud	Is 2:12	3605
upon *e* one that is lifted up	Is 2:12	3605
upon *e* high tower, and upon *e*	Is 2:15	3605
e one by another, and *e* one by	Is 3:5	376
even *e* one that is written among	Is 4:3	3605
the LORD will create upon *e*	Is 4:5	3605
honey shall *e* one eat that is	Is 7:22	3605
that *e* place shall be, where	Is 7:23	3605
For *e* battle of the warrior is	Is 9:5	3605
for *e* one is an hypocrite and an	Is 9:17	3605
and *e* mouth speaketh folly	Is 9:17	3605
they shall eat *e* man the flesh of	Is 9:20	
and *e* man's heart shall melt	Is 13:7	3605
they shall *e* man turn to his own	Is 13:14	
flee *e* one into his own land	Is 13:14	376
E one that is found shall be	Is 13:15	3605
e one that is joined unto them	Is 13:15	3605
in glory, *e* one in his own house	Is 14:18	376
be baldness, and *e* beard cut off	Is 15:2	3605
e one shall howl, weeping	Is 15:3	3605
howl for Moab, *e* one shall howl	Is 16:7	3605
they shall fight *e* one against	Is 19:2	376
e one against his neighbour	Is 19:2	376
e thing sown by the brooks, shall	Is 19:7	3605
Egypt to err in *e* work thereof	Is 19:14	3605
e one that maketh mention thereof	Is 19:17	3605
e house is shut up, that no man	Is 24:10	3605
I will water it *e* moment	Is 27:3	
shall be upon *e* high mountain	Is 30:25	3605
upon *e* high hill, rivers and	Is 30:25	3605
in *e* place where the grounded	Is 30:32	3605
For in that day *e* man shall cast	Is 31:7	
be thou their arm *e* morning	Is 33:2	
be gathered, *e* one with her mate	Is 34:15	802
eat ye *e* one of his vine, and	Is 36:16	376
e one of his fig tree	Is 36:16	376
drink ye *e* one the waters of his	Is 36:16	376
E valley shall be exalted, and	Is 40:4	3605
e mountain and hill shall be made	Is 40:4	3605
They helped *e* one his neighbour	Is 41:6	376
e one said to his brother, Be of	Is 41:6	376
Even *e* one that is called by my	Is 43:7	3605
O forest, and *e* tree therein	Is 44:23	3605
That unto me *e* knee shall bow,	Is 45:23	3605
e tongue shall swear	Is 45:23	3605
they shall wander *e* one to his	Is 47:15	376
hast feared continually *e* day	Is 51:13	3605
continually *e* day is blasphemed	Is 52:5	3605
we have turned *e* one to his own	Is 53:6	376
e tongue that shall rise against	Is 54:17	3605
e one that thirsteth, come ye to	Is 55:1	3605
e one that keepeth the sabbath	Is 56:6	3605
e one for his gain, from his	Is 56:11	376
with idols under *e* green tree	Is 57:5	3605
go free, and that ye break *e* yoke	Is 58:6	3605
they shall set *e* one his throne	Jer 1:15	376
when upon *e* high hill and under	Jer 2:20	3605
under *e* green tree thou wanderest	Jer 2:20	3605
is gone up upon *e* high mountain	Jer 3:6	3605
under *e* green tree, and there hath	Jer 3:6	3605
the strangers under *e* green tree	Jer 3:13	3605
e city shall be forsaken, and not	Jer 4:29	3605
e one that goeth out thence shall	Jer 5:6	3605
e one neighed after his	Jer 5:8	376
they shall feed *e* one in his	Jer 6:3	376
e one is given to covetousness	Jer 6:13	3605
the priest *e* one dealeth falsely	Jer 6:13	3605
of the enemy and fear is on *e* side	Jer 6:25	5437
e one turned to his course, as	Jer 8:6	3605
for *e* one from the least even	Jer 8:10	3605
the priest *e* one dealeth falsely	Jer 8:10	3605
Take ye heed *e* one of his	Jer 9:4	376
for *e* brother will utterly	Jer 9:4	3605
e neighbour will walk with	Jer 9:4	3605
will deceive *e* one his neighbour	Jer 9:5	376
e one her neighbour lamentation	Jer 9:20	802
E man is brutish in his knowledge	Jer 10:14	3605
e founder is confounded by the	Jer 10:14	3605
ear, but walked *e* one in the	Jer 11:8	376
and the herbs of *e* field wither	Jer 12:4	3605
e man to his heritage	Jer 12:15	
and *e* man to his land	Jer 12:15	
E bottle shall be filled with	Jer 13:12	3605
e bottle shall be filled with	Jer 13:12	3605
yet *e* one of them doth curse me	Jer 15:10	3605
behold, ye walk *e* one after the	Jer 16:12	376
e mountain, and from *e* hill	Jer 16:16	3605
even to give *e* man according to	Jer 17:10	
return ye now *e* one from his evil	Jer 18:11	376
we will *e* one do the imagination	Jer 18:12	376
e one that passeth thereby shall	Jer 18:16	3605
e one that passeth thereby shall	Jer 19:8	3605
they shall eat *e* one the flesh of	Jer 19:9	376
derision daily, *e* one mocketh me	Jer 20:7	3605
defaming of many, fear on *e* side	Jer 20:10	5437
thee, *e* one with his weapons	Jer 22:7	376
they shall say *e* man to his	Jer 22:8	
they say unto *e* one that walketh	Jer 23:17	3605
they tell *e* man to his neighbour	Jer 23:27	
that steal my words *e* one from	Jer 23:30	376
Thus shall ye say *e* one to his	Jer 23:35	376
e one to his brother, What hath	Jer 23:35	376
for *e* man's word shall be his	Jer 23:36	
Turn ye again now *e* one from his	Jer 25:5	376
turn *e* man from his evil way	Jer 26:3	
for *e* man that is mad, and maketh	Jer 29:26	
wherefore do I see *e* man with his	Jer 30:6	3605
e one of them, shall go into	Jer 30:16	3605
have replenished *e* sorrowful soul	Jer 31:25	3605
But *e* one shall die for his own	Jer 31:30	376
e man that eateth the sour grape,	Jer 31:30	
teach no more *e* man his neighbour	Jer 31:34	
e man his brother, saying, Know	Jer 31:34	
to give *e* one according to his	Jer 32:19	376
That *e* man should let his	Jer 34:9	
e man his maidservant, being an	Jer 34:9	
heard that *e* one should let his	Jer 34:10	376
e one his maidservant, go free,	Jer 34:10	376
ye go *e* man his brother an Hebrew	Jer 34:14	
liberty *e* man to his neighbour	Jer 34:15	
caused *e* man his servant, and	Jer 34:16	
e man his handmaid, whom he had	Jer 34:16	
e one to his brother	Jer 34:17	
and *e* man to his neighbour	Jer 34:17	
Return ye now *e* man from his evil	Jer 35:15	
that they may return *e* man from	Jer 36:3	
will return *e* one from his evil	Jer 36:7	376
they rise up *e* man in his tent	Jer 37:10	
e person that Nebuzar-adan the	Jer 43:6	3605
Zidon *e* helper that remaineth	Jer 47:4	3605
spoiler shall come upon *e* city	Jer 48:8	3605
For *e* head shall be bald, and	Jer 48:37	3605
shall be bald, and *e* beard clipped	Jer 48:37	3605
be driven out *e* man right forth	Jer 49:5	
e one that goeth by it shall be	Jer 49:17	3605
cry unto them, Fear is on *e* side	Jer 49:29	5437
e one that goeth by Babylon shall	Jer 50:13	3605
shall turn *e* one to his people	Jer 50:16	376
they shall flee *e* one to his own	Jer 50:16	376
e one put in array, like a man to	Jer 50:42	
and deliver *e* man his soul	Jer 51:6	
let us go *e* one into his own	Jer 51:9	376
E man is brutish by his knowledge	Jer 51:17	3605
e founder is confounded by the	Jer 51:17	3605
for *e* purpose of the LORD shall	Jer 51:29	
deliver ye *e* man his soul from	Jer 51:45	
e one of their bows is broken	Jer 51:56	
e day a portion until the day of	Jer 52:34	
for hunger in the top of *e* street	Lam 2:19	3605
They are new *e* morning	Lam 3:23	
poured out in the top of *e* street	Lam 4:1	3605
e one had four faces	Eze 1:6	
and *e* one had four wings	Eze 1:6	
they went *e* one straight forward	Eze 1:9	376
two wings of *e* one were joined	Eze 1:11	376
they went *e* one straight forward	Eze 1:12	376
e one had two, which covered on	Eze 1:23	376
e one had two, which covered on	Eze 1:23	376
upon *e* high hill, in all the tops	Eze 6:13	3605
under *e* green tree, and under	Eze 6:13	3605
under *e* thick oak, the place	Eze 6:13	3605
mourning, *e* one for his iniquity	Eze 7:16	376
behold *e* form of creeping things,	Eze 8:10	3605
with *e* man his censer in his hand	Eze 8:11	
e man in the chambers of his	Eze 8:12	
even *e* man with his destroying	Eze 9:1	
e man a slaughter weapon in his	Eze 9:2	
And *e* one had four faces	Eze 10:14	
e one stood at the door of the	Eze 10:19	
E one had four faces apiece, and	Eze 10:21	
faces apiece, and *e* one four wings	Eze 10:21	
they went *e* one straight forward	Eze 10:22	376
into your mind, *e* one of them	Eze 11:5	
I will scatter toward *e* wind all	Eze 12:14	3605
prolonged, and *e* vision faileth	Eze 12:22	3605
hand, and the effect of *e* vision	Eze 12:23	3605
head of *e* stature to hunt souls	Eze 13:18	3605
E man of the house of Israel that	Eze 14:4	
For *e* one of the house of Israel,	Eze 14:7	376
on *e* one that passed by	Eze 16:15	3605
thee an high place in *e* street	Eze 16:24	3605
high place at *e* head of the way	Eze 16:25	3605
thy feet to *e* one that passed by	Eze 16:25	3605
place in the head of *e* way	Eze 16:31	3605
thine high place in *e* street	Eze 16:31	3605
thee on *e* side for thy whoredom	Eze 16:33	5437
e one that useth proverbs shall	Eze 16:44	3605
it shall dwell all fowl of *e* wing	Eze 17:23	3605
e one according to his ways,	Eze 18:30	376
him on *e* side from the provinces	Eze 19:8	5437
unto them, Cast ye away *e* man the	Eze 20:7	
they did not *e* man cast away the	Eze 20:8	
them, then they saw *e* high hill	Eze 20:28	3605
serve ye *e* one his idols, and	Eze 20:39	376
it shall devour *e* green tree in	Eze 20:47	3605
green tree in thee, and *e* dry tree	Eze 20:47	3605
e heart shall melt, and all hands	Eze 21:7	3605
e spirit shall faint, and all	Eze 21:7	3605
the rod of my son, as *e* tree	Eze 21:10	3605
e one were in thee to their power	Eze 22:6	376
bring them against thee on *e* side	Eze 23:22	5437
even *e* good piece, the thigh, and	Eze 24:4	3605
and shall tremble at *e* moment	Eze 26:16	
e precious stone was thy covering	Eze 28:13	3605
by the sword upon her on *e* side	Eze 28:23	5437
e head was made bald	Eze 29:18	3605
and *e* shoulder was peeled	Eze 29:18	3605
and they shall tremble at *e* moment	Eze 32:10	
e man for his own life, in the	Eze 32:10	
I will judge you *e* one after his	Eze 33:20	376
ye defile *e* one his neighbour's	Eze 33:26	376
e one to his brother, saying,	Eze 33:30	376
mountains, and upon *e* high hill	Eze 34:6	3605
meat to *e* beast of the field	Eze 34:8	3605
and swallowed you up on *e* side	Eze 36:3	5437
and will gather them on *e* side	Eze 37:21	5437
e wall shall fall to the ground	Eze 38:20	3605
e man's sword shall be against	Eze 38:21	
unto the ravenous birds of *e* sort	Eze 39:4	3605
Speak unto *e* feathered fowl, and	Eze 39:17	3605
to *e* beast of the field, Assemble	Eze 39:17	3605
gather yourselves on *e* side to my	Eze 39:17	5437
e little chamber was one reed	Eze 40:7	
and the breadth of *e* side chamber	Eze 41:5	
round about the house on *e* side	Eze 41:5	5437
round about the house on *e* side	Eze 41:10	5437
and *e* cherub had two faces	Eze 41:18	
e day a goat for a sin offering	Eze 43:25	
with *e* going forth of the	Eze 44:5	3605
e dedicated thing in Israel shall	Eze 44:29	3605
e oblation of all, of *e* sort	Eze 44:30	3605
the month for *e* one that erreth	Eze 45:20	376
thou shalt prepare it *e* morning	Eze 46:13	
a meat offering for it *e* morning	Eze 46:14	
e morning for a continual burnt	Eze 46:15	
e man from his possession	Eze 46:18	
in *e* corner of the court there	Eze 46:21	
that *e* thing that liveth, which	Eze 47:9	3605
e thing shall live whither the	Eze 47:9	3605
that *e* man that shall hear the	Dan 3:10	3606
That *e* people, nation, and	Dan 3:29	3606
that *e* man that shall ask a	Dan 6:12	3606
That in *e* dominion of my kingdom	Dan 6:26	3606
and magnify himself above *e* god	Dan 11:36	3605
e one that shall be found written	Dan 12:1	3605
e one that dwelleth therein shall	Hos 4:3	3605
loved a reward upon *e* cornfloor	Hos 9:1	3605
shall march *e* one on his ways	Joel 2:7	376
they shall walk *e* one in his path	Joel 2:8	1397
clothes laid to pledge by *e* altar	Amos 2:8	3605
e cow at that which is before her	Amos 4:3	802
bring your sacrifices *e* morning	Amos 4:4	
be many dead bodies in *e* place	Amos 8:3	3605
e one mourn that dwelleth therein	Amos 8:8	3605
loins, and baldness upon *e* head	Amos 8:10	3605
to the end that *e* one of the	Obad 9	376
cried *e* man unto his god, and cast	Jonah 1:5	
they said *e* one to his fellow,	Jonah 1:7	376
let them turn *e* one from his evil	Jonah 3:8	376
shall sit *e* man under his vine	Mic 4:4	
For all people will walk *e* one in	Mic 4:5	376
they hunt *e* man his brother with	Mic 7:2	
they shall deride *e* strong hold	Hab 1:10	3605
e one from his place, even all	Zeph 2:11	376
e one that passeth by her shall	Zeph 2:15	3605
e morning doth he bring his	Zeph 3:5	
fame in *e* land where they have	Zeph 3:19	3605
ye run *e* man unto his own house	Hag 1:9	
so is *e* work of their hands	Hag 2:14	3605
e one by the sword of his brother	Hag 2:22	376
shall ye call *e* man his neighbour	Zec 3:10	
for *e* one that stealeth shall be	Zec 5:3	3605
e one that sweareth shall be cut	Zec 5:3	3605
compassions *e* man to his brother	Zec 7:9	
e man with his staff in his hand	Zec 8:4	
for I set all men *e* one against	Zec 8:10	376
Speak ye *e* man the truth to his	Zec 8:16	
to *e* one grass in the field	Zec 10:1	376
out of him *e* oppressor together	Zec 10:4	3605
I will deliver the men *e* one into	Zec 11:6	376
let the rest eat *e* one the flesh	Zec 11:9	802
I will smite *e* horse with	Zec 12:4	3605
will smite *e* horse of the people	Zec 12:4	3605
land shall mourn, *e* family apart	Zec 12:12	
e family apart, and their wives	Zec 12:14	
be ashamed *e* one of his vision	Zec 13:4	376
they shall lay hold *e* one on the	Zec 14:13	376
that *e* one that is left of all	Zec 14:16	3605
e pot in Jerusalem and in Judah	Zec 14:21	3605
in *e* place incense shall be	Mal 1:11	3605
e man against his brother	Mal 2:10	
E one that doeth evil is good in	Mal 2:17	3605
therefore *e* tree which bringeth	Mt 3:10	*3956*
but by *e* word that proceedeth out	Mt 4:4	*3956*
For *e* one that asketh receiveth	Mt 7:8	*3956*
Even so *e* good tree bringeth	Mt 7:17	*3956*
E tree that bringeth not forth	Mt 7:19	*3956*
Not *e* one that saith unto me,	Mt 7:21	*3956*
e one that heareth these sayings	Mt 7:26	*3956*
told *e* thing, and what was	Mt 8:33	*3956*

healing e sickness and e Mt 9:35 3956
e disease among the people Mt 9:35 3956
E kingdom divided against itself Mt 12:25 3956
e city or house divided against Mt 12:25 3956
That e idle word that men shall Mt 12:36 3956
the sea, and gathered of e kind Mt 13:47 3956
Therefore e scribe which is Mt 13:52 3956
E plant, which my heavenly Father Mt 15:13 3956
then he shall reward e man Mt 16:27 1538
e word may be established Mt 18:16 3956
not e one his brother their Mt 18:35 1538
to put away his wife for e cause Mt 19:3 3956
e one that hath forsaken houses, Mt 19:29 3956
hour, they received e man a penny Mt 20:9 303
likewise received e man a penny Mt 20:10 303
to e man according to his several Mt 25:15 1538
For unto e one that hath shall be Mt 25:29 3956
began e one of them to say unto Mt 26:22 1538
they came to him from e quarter Mk 1:45 3836
Hearken unto me e one of you Mk 7:14 3956
restored, and saw e man clearly Mk 8:25 537
For e one shall be salted with Mk 9:49 3956
e sacrifice shall be salted with Mk 9:49 3956
to e man his work, and commanded Mk 13:34 1538
upon them, what e man should take Mk 15:24 5100
preach the gospel to e creature Mk 16:15 3956
went forth, and preached e where Mk 16:20 3837
be taxed, e one into his own city Lk 2:3 1538
E male that openeth the womb Lk 2:23 3956
e year at the feast of the Lk 2:41 2596
E valley shall be filled, and Lk 3:5 3956
e mountain and hill shall be Lk 3:5 3956
e tree therefore which bringeth Lk 3:9 3956
bread alone, but by e word of God Lk 4:4 3956
into e place of the country round Lk 4:37 3956
laid his hands on e one of them Lk 4:40 1538
come out of e town of Galilee Lk 5:17 3956
Give to e man that asketh of thee Lk 6:30 3956
but e one that is perfect shall Lk 6:40 3956
For e tree is known by his own Lk 6:44 1538
that he went throughout e city Lk 8:1 2596
and were come to him out of e city Lk 8:4 2596
the gospel, and healing e where Lk 9:6 3837
But while they wondered e one at Lk 9:43 3956
two before his face into e city Lk 10:1 3956
for we also forgive e one that is Lk 11:4 3956
For e one that asketh receiveth Lk 11:10 3956
E kingdom divided against itself Lk 11:17 3956
So he called e one of his lord's Lk 16:5 1538
and e man presseth into it Lk 16:16 3956
linen, and fared sumptuously e day Lk 16:19 2596
for e one that exalteth himself Lk 18:14 3956
much e man had gained by trading Lk 19:15 5101
That unto e one which hath shall Lk 19:26 3956
round, and keep thee in on e side Lk 19:43 3840
which lighteth e man that cometh Jn 1:9 3956
E man at the beginning doth set Jn 2:10 3956
so is e one that is born of the Jn 3:8 3956
For e one that doeth evil hateth Jn 3:20 3956
that e one of them may take a Jn 6:7 1538
that e one which seeth the Son, Jn 6:40 3956
E man therefore that hath heard, Jn 6:45 3956
because I have made a man e whit Jn 7:23 3650
e man went unto his own house Jn 7:53 1538
his feet, but is clean e whit Jn 13:10 3650
E branch in me that beareth not Jn 15:2 3956
e branch that beareth fruit, he Jn 15:2 3956
e man to his own, and shall leave Jn 16:32 1538
E one that is of the truth Jn 18:37 3956
four parts, to e soldier a part Jn 19:23 1538
if they should be written e one Jn 21:25 2596
out of e nation under heaven Acts 2:5 3956
because that e man heard them Acts 2:6 1538
how hear we e man in our own Acts 2:8 1538
be baptized e one of you in the Acts 2:38 1538
And fear came upon e soul Acts 2:43 3956
to all men, as e man had need Acts 2:45 5100
shall come to pass, that e soul Acts 3:23 3956
in turning away e one of you from Acts 3:26 1538
distribution was made unto e man Acts 4:35 1538
and they were healed e one Acts 5:16 537
in e house, they ceased not to Acts 5:42 2596
the church, entering into e house Acts 8:3 2596
went e where preaching the word Acts 8:4 1330
But in e nation he that feareth Acts 10:35 3956
e man according to his ability, Acts 11:29
which are read e sabbath day Acts 13:27 3956
ordained them elders in e church Acts 14:23 2596
in e city them that preach him Acts 15:21 2596
in the synagogues e sabbath day Acts 15:21 3956
visit our brethren in e city Acts 15:36 3956
e one's bands were loosed Acts 16:26 3956
he be not far from e one of us Acts 17:27 1538
all men e where to repent Acts 17:30 3837
in the synagogue e sabbath Acts 18:4 3956
Holy Ghost witnesseth in e city Acts 20:23 2596
I ceased not to warn e one night Acts 20:31 1538
be offered for e one of them Acts 21:26 1538
that teacheth all men e where Acts 21:28 3837
beat in e synagogue them that Acts 22:19 2596
punished them oft in e synagogue Acts 26:11 3956
a fire, and received us e one Acts 28:2 3956
we know that e where it is spoken Acts 28:22 3837
salvation to e one that believeth Rom 1:16 3956
Who will render to e man Rom 2:6 1538
upon e soul of man that doeth Rom 2:9 3956
to e man that worketh good, to Rom 2:10 3956
Much e way: chiefly, because Rom 3:2 3956
let God be true, but e man a liar Rom 3:4 3956
that e mouth may be stopped, and Rom 3:19 3956
to e one that believeth Rom 10:4 3956
to e man that is among you, not Rom 12:3 3956
to e man the measure of faith Rom 12:3 1538
e one members one of another Rom 12:5 2596
Let e soul be subject unto the Rom 13:1 3956
another esteemeth e day alike Rom 14:5 3956
Let e man be fully persuaded in Rom 14:5 1538
e knee shall bow to me Rom 14:11 3956
e tongue shall confess to God Rom 14:11 3956
So then e one of us shall give Rom 14:12 1538
Let e one of us please his Rom 15:2 1538
with all that in e place call 1Cor 1:2 3956
That in e thing ye are enriched 1Cor 1:5 3956
that e one of you saith, I am of 1Cor 1:12 1538
even as the Lord gave to e man 1Cor 3:5 1538
e man shall receive his own 1Cor 3:8 1538
But let e man take heed how he 1Cor 3:10 1538
E man's work shall be made 1Cor 3:13 1538
the fire shall try e man's work 1Cor 3:13 1538
then shall e man have praise of 1Cor 4:5 1538
as I teach e where in e 1Cor 4:17 3837
I teach e where in e church 1Cor 4:17 3956
E sin that a man doeth is without 1Cor 6:18 3956
let e man have his own wife, and 1Cor 7:2 1538
let e woman have her own husband 1Cor 7:2 1538
But e man hath his proper gift of 1Cor 7:7 1538
as God hath distributed to e man 1Cor 7:17 1538
as the Lord hath called e one 1Cor 7:17 1538
Let e man abide in the same 1Cor 7:20 1538
Brethren, let e man, wherein he 1Cor 7:24 1538
is not in e man that knowledge 1Cor 8:7 3956
e man that striveth for the 1Cor 9:25 3956
but e man another's wealth 1Cor 10:24 1538
that the head of e man is Christ 1Cor 11:3 3956
E man praying or prophesying, 1Cor 11:4 3956
But e woman that prayeth or 1Cor 11:5 3956
For in eating e one taketh before 1Cor 11:21 1538
given to e man to profit withal 1Cor 12:7 1538
dividing to e man severally as he 1Cor 12:11 1538
members e one of them in the body 1Cor 12:18 1538
e one of you hath a psalm, hath a 1Cor 14:26 1538
But e man in his own order 1Cor 15:23 1538
why stand we in jeopardy e hour 1Cor 15:30 3956
him, and to e seed his own body 1Cor 15:38 1538
the first day of the week let e 1Cor 16:2 1538
to e one that helpeth with us, and 1Cor 16:16 3956
of his knowledge by us in e place 2Cor 2:14 3956
e man's conscience in the sight 2Cor 4:2 3956
We are troubled on e side 2Cor 4:8 3956
that e one may receive the things 2Cor 5:10 1538
but we were troubled on e side 2Cor 7:5 3956
as ye abound in e thing, in 2Cor 8:7 376
E man according as he purposeth 2Cor 9:7 1538
things, may abound to e good work 2Cor 9:8 3956
Being enriched in e thing to all 2Cor 9:11 3956
e high thing that exalteth itself 2Cor 10:5 3956
bringing into captivity e thought 2Cor 10:5 3956
shall e word be established 2Cor 13:1 3956
Cursed is e one that continueth Gal 3:10 3956
Cursed is e one that hangeth on a Gal 3:13 3956
For I testify again to e man that Gal 5:3 3956
But let e man prove his own work, Gal 6:4 1538
For e man shall bear his own Gal 6:5 1538
e name that is named, not only in Eph 1:21 3956
But unto e one of us is given Eph 4:7 1538
about with e wind of doctrine Eph 4:14 3596
by that which e joint supplieth Eph 4:16 3596
working in the measure of e part Eph 4:16
speak e man truth with his Eph 4:25 1538
to their own husbands in e thing Eph 5:24 3956
Nevertheless let e one of you in Eph 5:33
my God upon e remembrance of you Phil 1:3 3956
Always in e prayer of mine for Phil 1:4 3956
e way, whether in pretence, or in Phil 1:18 3956
Look not e man on his own things, Phil 2:4 1538
but e man also on the things of Phil 2:4 1538
him a name which is above e name Phil 2:9 3956
name of Jesus e knee should bow Phil 2:10 3956
that e tongue should confess that Phil 2:11 3956
but in e thing by prayer and Phil 4:6 3956
e where and in all things I am Phil 4:12 3956
Salute e saint in Christ Jesus Phil 4:21 3956
being fruitful in e good work Col 1:10 3956
God, the firstborn of e creature Col 1:15 3956
which was preached to e creature Col 1:23 3956
Whom we preach, warning e man Col 1:28 3956
teaching e man in all wisdom Col 1:28 3956
that we may present e man perfect Col 1:28 3956
know how ye ought to answer e man Col 4:6
but also in e place your faith to 1Th 1:8 3956
charged e one of you, as a father 1Th 2:11 1538
That e one of you should know how 1Th 4:4 1538
In e thing give thanks 1Th 5:18 3956
the charity of e one of you all 2Th 1:3 1538
and stablish you in e good word 2Th 2:17 3956
ye withdraw yourselves from e 2Th 3:6 3956
which is the token in e epistle 2Th 3:17 3956
therefore that men pray e where 1Ti 2:8
For e creature of God is good, and 1Ti 4:4 3956
diligently followed e good work 1Ti 5:10 3956
Let e one that nameth the name of 2Ti 2:19 3956
use, and prepared unto e good work 2Ti 2:21 3956
shall deliver me from e evil work 2Ti 4:18 3956
and ordain elders in e city Titus 1:5 2596
unto e good work reprobate Titus 1:16 3956
to be ready to e good work Titus 3:1 3956
by the acknowledging of e good Philem 6 3956
e transgression and disobedience Heb 2:2 3956
God should taste death for e man Heb 2:9 3956
For e house is builded by some Heb 3:4 3956
For e high priest taken from Heb 5:1 3956
For e one that useth milk is Heb 5:13 3956
we desire that e one of you do Heb 6:11 1538
For e high priest is ordained to Heb 8:3 3956
not teach e man his neighbour Heb 8:11 1538
e man his brother, saying, Know Heb 8:11 1538
the high priest alone once e year Heb 9:7
e precept to all the people Heb 9:19 3956
place e year with blood of others Heb 9:25 2596
again made of sins e year Heb 10:3 2596
And e priest standeth daily Heb 10:11 3956
let us lay aside e weight Heb 12:1 3956
scourgeth e son whom he receiveth Heb 12:6 3956
Make you perfect in e good work Heb 13:21 3956
But e man is tempted, when he is Jas 1:14 1538
E good gift and e perfect gift Jas 1:17 3956
let e man be swift to hear, slow Jas 1:19 3956
For e kind of beasts, and of birds Jas 3:7 3956
there is confusion and e evil work Jas 3:16 3956
judgeth according to e man's work 1Pet 1:17 1538
Submit yourselves to e ordinance 1Pet 2:13 3956
always to give an answer to e man 1Pet 3:15 3956
As e man hath received the gift, 1Pet 4:10 1538
ye know that e one that doeth 1Jn 2:29 3956
e man that hath this hope in him 1Jn 3:3 3956
Beloved, believe not e spirit 1Jn 4:1 3956
E spirit that confesseth that 1Jn 4:2 3956
e spirit that confesseth not that 1Jn 4:3 3956
e one that loveth is born of God, 1Jn 4:7 3956
e one that loveth him that begat 1Jn 5:1 3956
e eye shall see him, and they also Rev 1:7 3956
I will give unto e one of you Rev 2:23 1538
having e one of them harps, and Rev 5:8 1538
God by thy blood out of e kindred Rev 5:9 3956
e creature which is in heaven, and Rev 5:13 3956
were given unto e one of them Rev 6:11 1538
e mountain and island were moved Rev 6:14 3956
e bondman, and e free man, hid Rev 6:15 3956
to e nation, and kindred, and Rev 14:6 3956
e living soul died in the sea Rev 16:3 3956
e island fled away, and the Rev 16:20 3956
e stone about the weight of a Rev 16:21
and the hold of e foul spirit Rev 18:2 3956
and a cage of e unclean Rev 18:2 3956
e shipmaster, and all the company Rev 18:17 3956
they were judged e man according Rev 20:13 1538
e several gate was of one pearl Rev 21:21 1538
and yielded her fruit e month Rev 22:2 1538
to give e man according as his Rev 22:12 1538
For I testify unto e man that Rev 22:18 3956

EVI (e'-vi) *A Midian prince.*
namely, E, and Rekem, and Zur, and Num 31:8 189
with the princes of Midian, E Josh 13:21 189

EVIDENCE
And I subscribed the e, and sealed Jer 32:10 5612
So I took the e of the purchase, Jer 32:11 5612
I gave the e of the purchase unto Jer 32:12 5612
this e of the purchase, both Jer 32:14 5612
sealed, and this e which is open Jer 32:14 5612
Now when I had delivered the e of Jer 32:16 5612
for, the e of things not seen Heb 11:1 1650

EVIDENCES
Take these e, this evidence of Jer 32:14 5612
fields for money, and subscribe e Jer 32:44 5612

EVIDENT
for it is e unto you if I lie Job 6:28
law in the sight of God, it is e Gal 3:11 1212
to them an e token of perdition Phil 1:28 1732
For it is e that our Lord sprang Heb 7:14 4271
And it is yet far more e Heb 7:15 2612

EVIDENTLY
He saw in a vision e about the Acts 10:3 5320
Christ hath been e set forth Gal 3:1 4270

EVIL
tree of knowledge of good and e Gen 2:9 7451
of the knowledge of good and e Gen 2:17 7451
be as gods, knowing good and e Gen 3:5 7451
as one of us, to know good and e Gen 3:22 7451
his heart was only e continually Gen 6:5 7451
man's heart is e from his youth Gen 8:21 7451
the mountain, lest some e take me Gen 19:19 7451
unto his father their e report Gen 37:2 7451
Some e beast hath devoured him Gen 37:20 7451
an e beast hath devoured him Gen 37:33 7451
have ye rewarded e for good Gen 44:4 7451
ye have done e in so doing Gen 44:5 7489
lest peradventure I see the e Gen 44:34 7451
e have the days of the years of Gen 47:9 7451
which redeemed me from all e Gen 48:16 7451
all the e which we did unto him Gen 50:15 7451
for they did unto thee e Gen 50:17 7451
for you, ye thought e against me Gen 50:20 7451
did see that they were in e case Ex 5:19 7451
thou so e entreated this people Ex 5:22 7489
he hath done e to this people Ex 5:23 7489
for e is before you Ex 10:10 7451
not follow a multitude to do e Ex 23:2 7451
repent of this e against thy Ex 32:12 7451
the LORD repented of the e which Ex 32:14 7451
the people heard these e tidings Ex 33:4 7451
pronouncing with his lips to do e Lev 5:4 7489
I will rid e beasts out of the Lev 26:6 7451
they brought up an e report of Num 13:32 1681
I bear with this e congregation Num 14:27 7451
it unto all this e congregation Num 14:35 7451
up the e report upon the land Num 14:37 7451
to bring us in unto this e place Num 20:5 7451
that had done e in the sight of Num 32:13 7451
not one of these men of this e Deut 1:35 7451
no knowledge between good and e Deut 1:39 7451
shall do e in the sight of the Deut 4:25 7451
none of the e diseases of Egypt Deut 7:15 7451
So shalt thou put the e away from Deut 13:5 7451
thine eye be e against thy poor Deut 15:9 7489
put the e away from among you Deut 17:7 7451
shalt put away the e from Israel Deut 17:12 7451
put the e away from among you Deut 19:19 7451
no more any such e among you Deut 19:20 7451
so shalt thou put e away from Deut 21:21 7451

bring up an *e* name upon her, and	Deut 22:14	7451
an *e* name upon a virgin of Israel	Deut 22:19	7451
so shalt thou put *e* away from	Deut 22:21	7451
shalt thou put away *e* from Israel	Deut 22:22	7451
shalt put away *e* from among you	Deut 22:24	7451
thou shalt put *e* away from among	Deut 24:7	7451
And the Egyptians *e* entreated us	Deut 26:6	7489
his eye shall be *e* toward his	Deut 28:54	7489
her eye shall be *e* toward the	Deut 28:56	7489
LORD shall separate him unto *e*	Deut 29:21	7451
day life and good, and death and *e*	Deut 30:15	7451
e will befall you in the latter	Deut 31:29	7451
because ye will do *e* in the sight	Deut 31:29	7451
LORD bring upon you all *e* things	Josh 23:15	7451
if it seem *e* unto you to serve	Josh 24:15	7489
did *e* in the sight of the LORD	Judg 2:11	7451
the LORD was against them for *e*	Judg 2:15	7451
did *e* in the sight of the LORD	Judg 3:7	7451
the children of Israel did *e*	Judg 3:12	7451
because they had done *e* in the	Judg 3:12	7451
did *e* in the sight of the LORD	Judg 4:1	7451
did *e* in the sight of the LORD	Judg 6:1	7451
Then God sent an *e* spirit between	Judg 9:23	7451
all the *e* of the men of Shechem	Judg 9:57	7451
the children of Israel did *e*	Judg 10:6	7451
the children of Israel did *e*	Judg 13:1	7451
death, and put away *e* from Israel	Judg 20:13	7451
knew not that *e* was near them	Judg 20:34	7451
for they saw that *e* was come upon	Judg 20:41	7451
for I hear of your *e* dealings by	1Sa 2:23	7451
then he hath done us this great *e*	1Sa 6:9	7451
added unto all our sins this *e*	1Sa 12:19	7451
didst *e* in the sight of the LORD	1Sa 15:19	7451
an *e* spirit from the LORD	1Sa 16:14	7451
an *e* spirit from God troubleth	1Sa 16:15	7451
when the *e* spirit from God is	1Sa 16:16	7451
when the *e* spirit from God was	1Sa 16:23	7451
the *e* spirit departed from him	1Sa 16:23	7451
that the *e* spirit from God came	1Sa 18:10	7451
the *e* spirit from the LORD was	1Sa 19:9	7451
then be sure that *e* is determined	1Sa 20:7	7451
for if I knew certainly that *e*	1Sa 20:9	7451
it please my father to do thee *e*	1Sa 20:13	7451
see that there is neither *e* nor	1Sa 24:11	7451
whereas I have rewarded thee *e*	1Sa 24:17	7451
was churlish and *e* in his doings	1Sa 25:3	7451
for *e* is determined against our	1Sa 25:17	7451
and he hath requited me *e* for good	1Sa 25:21	7451
and they that seek *e* to my lord	1Sa 25:26	7451
e hath not been found in thee all	1Sa 25:28	7451
and hath kept his servant from *e*	1Sa 25:39	7451
or what *e* is in mine hand	1Sa 26:18	7451
for I have not found *e* in thee	1Sa 29:6	7451
of *e* according to his wickedness	2Sa 3:39	7451
of the LORD, to do *e* in his sight	2Sa 12:9	7451
I will raise up *e* against thee	2Sa 12:11	7451
this *e* in sending me away is	2Sa 13:16	7451
bring *e* upon us, and smite the	2Sa 15:14	7451
LORD might bring *e* upon Absalom	2Sa 17:14	7451
e that befell thee from thy youth	2Sa 19:7	7451
can I discern between good and *e*	2Sa 19:35	7451
the LORD repented him of the *e*	2Sa 24:16	7451
neither adversary nor *e* occurrent	1Kin 5:4	7451
LORD brought upon them all this *e*	1Kin 9:9	7451
Solomon did *e* in the sight of the	1Kin 11:6	7451
returned not from his *e* way	1Kin 13:33	7451
But hast done *e* above all that	1Kin 14:9	7489
I will bring *e* upon the house of	1Kin 14:10	7451
Judah did *e* in the sight of the	1Kin 14:22	7451
he did *e* in the sight of the LORD	1Kin 15:26	7451
he did *e* in the sight of the LORD	1Kin 15:34	7451
even for all the *e* that he did in	1Kin 16:7	7451
doing *e* in the sight of the LORD	1Kin 16:19	7451
But Omri wrought *e* in the eyes of	1Kin 16:25	7451
Ahab the son of Omri did *e* in the	1Kin 16:30	7451
hast thou also brought *e* upon the	1Kin 17:20	7489
work *e* in the sight of the LORD	1Kin 21:20	7451
Behold, I will bring *e* upon thee	1Kin 21:21	7451
will not bring the *e* in his days	1Kin 21:29	7451
will I bring the *e* upon his house	1Kin 21:29	7451
good concerning me, but *e*	1Kin 22:8	7451
no good concerning me, but *e*	1Kin 22:18	7451
hath spoken *e* concerning thee	1Kin 22:23	7451
he did *e* in the sight of the LORD	1Kin 22:52	7451
he wrought *e* in the sight of the	2Kin 3:2	7451
Behold, this *e* is of the LORD	2Kin 6:33	7451
Because I know the *e* that thou	2Kin 8:12	7451
he did *e* in the sight of the LORD	2Kin 8:18	7451
did *e* in the sight of the LORD,	2Kin 8:27	7451
he did that which was *e* in the	2Kin 13:2	7451
he did that which was *e* in the	2Kin 13:11	7451
he did that which was *e* in the	2Kin 14:24	7451
he did that which was *e* in the	2Kin 15:9	7451
he did that which was *e* in the	2Kin 15:18	7451
he did that which was *e* in the	2Kin 15:24	7451
he did that which was *e* in the	2Kin 15:28	7451
he did that which was *e* in the	2Kin 17:2	7451
saying, Turn ye from your *e* ways	2Kin 17:13	7451
sold themselves to do *e* in the	2Kin 17:17	7451
he did that which was *e* in the	2Kin 21:2	7451
seduced them to do more *e* than	2Kin 21:9	7451
am bringing such *e* upon Jerusalem	2Kin 21:12	7451
done that which was *e* in my sight	2Kin 21:15	7451
in doing that which was *e* in the	2Kin 21:16	7451
he did that which was *e* in the	2Kin 21:20	7451
I will bring *e* upon this place,	2Kin 22:16	7451
eyes shall not see all the *e*	2Kin 22:20	7451
he did that which was *e* in the	2Kin 23:32	7451
he did that which was *e* in the	2Kin 23:37	7451
he did that which was *e* in the	2Kin 24:9	7451
he did that which was *e* in the	2Kin 24:19	7451
was *e* in the sight of the LORD	1Chr 2:3	7451
that thou wouldest keep me from *e*	1Chr 4:10	7451
because it went *e* with his house	1Chr 7:23	7451
and he repented him of the *e*	1Chr 21:15	7451
that have sinned and done *e* indeed	1Chr 21:17	7489
he brought all this *e* upon them	2Chr 7:22	7451
And he did *e*, because he prepared	2Chr 12:14	7451
good unto me, but always *e*	2Chr 18:7	7451
not prophesy good unto me, but *e*	2Chr 18:17	7451
LORD hath spoken *e* against thee	2Chr 18:22	7451
when *e* cometh upon us, as the	2Chr 20:9	7451
was *e* in the eyes of the LORD	2Chr 21:6	7451
Wherefore he did *e* in the sight	2Chr 22:4	7451
done that which was *e* in the eyes	2Chr 29:6	7451
But did that which was *e* in the	2Chr 33:2	7451
he wrought much *e* in the sight of	2Chr 33:6	7451
was *e* in the sight of the LORD	2Chr 33:22	7451
I will bring *e* upon this place,	2Chr 34:24	7451
the *e* that I will bring upon this	2Chr 34:28	7451
he did that which was *e* in the	2Chr 36:5	7451
he did that which was *e* in the	2Chr 36:9	7451
he did that which was *e* in the	2Chr 36:12	7451
is come upon us for our *e* deeds	Ezr 9:13	7451
might have matter for an *e* report	Neh 6:13	7451
they did *e* again before thee	Neh 9:28	7451
understood of the *e* that Eliashib	Neh 13:7	7451
What *e* thing is this that ye do,	Neh 13:17	7451
our God bring all this *e* upon us	Neh 13:18	7451
unto you to do all this great *e*	Neh 13:27	7451
for he saw that there was *e*	Est 7:7	7451
e that shall come unto my people	Est 8:6	7451
that feared God, and eschewed *e*	Job 1:1	7451
that feareth God, and escheweth *e*	Job 1:8	7451
that feareth God, and escheweth *e*	Job 2:3	7451
of God, and shall we not receive *e*	Job 2:10	7451
all this *e* that was come upon him	Job 2:11	7451
seven there shall no *e* touch thee	Job 5:19	7451
neither will he help the *e* doers	Job 8:20	7489
He *e* entreateth the barren that	Job 24:21	7462
to depart from *e* is understanding	Job 28:28	7451
for good, then *e* came unto me	Job 30:26	7451
lifted up myself when *e* found him	Job 31:29	7451
because of the pride of *e* men	Job 35:12	7451
comforted him over all the *e* that	Job 42:11	7451
neither shall *e* dwell with thee	Ps 5:4	7451
If I have rewarded *e* unto him	Ps 7:4	7451
arm of the wicked and the *e* man	Ps 10:15	7451
nor doeth *e* to his neighbour, nor	Ps 15:3	7451
For they intended *e* against thee	Ps 21:11	7451
shadow of death, I will fear no *e*	Ps 23:4	7451
Keep thy tongue from *e*, and thy	Ps 34:13	7451
Depart from *e*, and do good	Ps 34:14	7451
LORD is against them that do *e*	Ps 34:16	7451
E shall slay the wicked	Ps 34:21	7451
They rewarded me *e* for good to	Ps 35:12	7451
he abhorreth not *e*	Ps 36:4	7451
not thyself in any wise to do *e*	Ps 37:8	7489
not be ashamed in the *e* time	Ps 37:19	7451
Depart from *e*, and do good	Ps 37:27	7451
They also that render *e* for good	Ps 38:20	7451
and put to shame that wish me *e*	Ps 40:14	7451
Mine enemies speak *e* of me	Ps 41:5	7451
An *e* disease, say they, cleaveth	Ps 41:8	1100
should I fear in the days of *e*	Ps 49:5	7451
Thou givest thy mouth to *e*	Ps 50:19	7451
and done this *e* in thy sight	Ps 51:4	7451
Thou lovest *e* more than good	Ps 52:3	7451
He shall reward *e* unto mine	Ps 54:5	7451
thoughts are against me for *e*	Ps 56:5	7451
themselves in an *e* matter	Ps 64:5	7451
by sending *e* angels among them	Ps 78:49	7451
the years wherein we have seen *e*	Ps 90:15	7451
There shall no *e* befall thee	Ps 91:10	7451
Ye that love the LORD, hate *e*	Ps 97:10	7451
they have rewarded me *e* for good	Ps 109:5	7451
them that speak *e* against my soul	Ps 109:20	7451
shall not be afraid of *e* tidings	Ps 112:7	7451
my feet from every *e* way, that I	Ps 119:101	7451
shall preserve thee from all *e*	Ps 121:7	7451
me, O LORD, from the *e* man	Ps 140:1	7451
Let not an *e* speaker be	Ps 140:11	
e shall hunt the violent man to	Ps 140:11	7451
not my heart to any *e* thing	Ps 141:4	7451
For their feet run to *e*, and make	Prov 1:16	7451
and shall be quiet from fear of *e*	Prov 1:33	7451
thee from the way of the *e* man	Prov 2:12	7451
Who rejoice to do *e*, and delight	Prov 2:14	7451
fear the LORD, and depart from *e*	Prov 3:7	7451
Devise not *e* against thy	Prov 3:29	7451
and go not in the way of *e* men	Prov 4:14	7451
remove thy foot from *e*	Prov 4:27	7451
in all *e* in the midst of the	Prov 5:14	7451
To keep thee from the *e* woman	Prov 6:24	7451
The fear of the LORD is to hate *e*	Prov 8:13	7451
pride, and arrogancy, and the *e* way	Prov 8:13	7451
so he that pursueth *e* pursueth it	Prov 11:19	7451
wicked desireth the net of *e* men	Prov 12:12	7451
the heart of them that imagine *e*	Prov 12:20	7451
There shall no *e* happen to the	Prov 12:21	205
to fools to depart from *e*	Prov 13:19	7451
E pursueth sinners	Prov 13:21	7451
man feareth, and departeth from *e*	Prov 14:16	7451
The *e* bow before the good	Prov 14:19	7451
Do they not err that devise *e*	Prov 14:22	7451
in every place, beholding the *e*	Prov 15:3	7451
the days of the afflicted are *e*	Prov 15:15	7451
the wicked poureth out *e* things	Prov 15:28	7451
even the wicked for the day of *e*	Prov 16:4	7451
of the LORD men depart from *e*	Prov 16:6	7451
the upright is to depart from *e*	Prov 16:17	7451
An ungodly man diggeth up *e*	Prov 16:27	7451
his lips he bringeth *e* to pass	Prov 16:30	7451
An *e* man seeketh only rebellion	Prov 17:11	7451
Whoso rewardeth *e* for good	Prov 17:13	7451
e shall not depart from his house	Prov 17:13	7451
he shall not be visited with *e*	Prov 19:23	7451
away all *e* with his eyes	Prov 20:8	7451
Say not thou, I will recompense *e*	Prov 20:22	7451
of a wound cleanseth away *e*	Prov 20:30	7451
The soul of the wicked desireth *e*	Prov 21:10	7451
A prudent man foreseeth the *e*	Prov 22:3	7451
bread of him that hath an *e* eye	Prov 23:6	7451
Be not thou envious against *e* men	Prov 24:1	7451
He that deviseth to do *e* shall be	Prov 24:8	7489
Fret not thyself because of *e* men	Prov 24:19	7489
shall be no reward to the *e* man	Prov 24:20	7451
A prudent man foreseeth the *e*	Prov 27:12	7451
E men understand not judgment	Prov 28:5	7451
to go astray in an *e* way, he	Prov 28:10	7451
hasteth to be rich hath an *e* eye	Prov 28:22	7451
of an *e* man there is a snare	Prov 29:6	7451
or if thou hast thought *e*	Prov 30:32	
not *e* all the days of her life	Prov 31:12	7451
This also is vanity and a great *e*	Eccl 2:21	7451
who hath not seen the *e* work that	Eccl 4:3	7451
they consider not that they do *e*	Eccl 5:1	7451
There is a sore *e* which I have	Eccl 5:13	7451
those riches perish by *e* travail	Eccl 5:14	7451
And this also is a sore *e*, that in	Eccl 5:16	7451
There is an *e* which I have seen	Eccl 6:1	7451
is vanity, and it is an *e* disease	Eccl 6:2	7451
stand not in an *e* thing	Eccl 8:3	7451
commandment shall feel no *e* thing	Eccl 8:5	7451
Because sentence against an *e*	Eccl 8:11	7451
men is fully set in them to do *e*	Eccl 8:11	7451
a sinner do *e* an hundred times	Eccl 8:12	7451
This is an *e* among all things	Eccl 9:3	7451
of the sons of men is full of *e*	Eccl 9:3	7451
fishes that are taken in an *e* net	Eccl 9:12	7451
sons of men snared in an *e* time	Eccl 9:12	7451
There is an *e* which I have seen	Eccl 10:5	7451
what *e* shall be upon the earth	Eccl 11:2	7451
put away *e* from thy flesh	Eccl 11:10	7451
while the *e* days come not, nor	Eccl 12:1	7451
it be good, or whether it be *e*	Eccl 12:14	7451
put away the *e* of your doings	Is 1:16	7455
cease to do *e*	Is 1:16	7489
have rewarded *e* unto themselves	Is 3:9	7451
that call *e* good, and good *e*	Is 5:20	7451
have taken *e* counsel against thee	Is 7:5	7451
that he may know to refuse the *e*	Is 7:15	7451
child shall know to refuse the *e*	Is 7:16	7451
will punish the world for their *e*	Is 13:11	7451
he also is wise, and will bring *e*	Is 31:2	7451
also of the churl are *e*	Is 32:7	7451
shutteth his eyes from seeing *e*	Is 33:15	7451
yea, do good, or do *e*, that we	Is 41:23	7489
I make peace, and create *e*	Is 45:7	7451
Therefore shall *e* come upon thee	Is 47:11	7451
keepeth his hand from doing any *e*	Is 56:2	7451
is taken away from the *e* to come	Is 57:1	7451
Their feet run to *e*, and they make	Is 59:7	7451
from *e* maketh himself a prey	Is 59:15	7451
but did *e* before mine eyes, and	Is 65:12	7451
but they did *e* before mine eyes,	Is 66:4	7451
Out of the north an *e* shall break	Jer 1:14	7451
e shall come upon them, saith the	Jer 2:3	7451
and see that it is an *e* thing	Jer 2:19	7451
done *e* things as thou couldest	Jer 3:5	7451
the imagination of their *e* heart	Jer 3:17	7451
because of the *e* of your doings	Jer 4:4	7455
for I will bring *e* from the north	Jer 4:6	7451
they are wise to do *e*, but to do	Jer 4:22	7489
neither shall *e* come upon us	Jer 5:12	7451
for *e* appeareth out of the north,	Jer 6:1	7451
I will bring *e* upon this people,	Jer 6:19	7451
the imagination of their *e* heart	Jer 7:24	7451
of Judah have done *e* in my sight	Jer 7:30	7451
them that remain of this *e* family	Jer 8:3	7451
for they proceed from *e* to *e*	Jer 9:3	7451
for they cannot do *e*, neither	Jer 10:5	7489
the imagination of their *e* heart	Jer 11:8	7451
Behold, I will bring *e* upon them	Jer 11:11	7451
when thou doest *e*, then thou	Jer 11:15	7451
hath pronounced *e* against thee	Jer 11:17	7451
for the *e* of the house of Israel	Jer 11:17	7451
for I will bring *e* upon the men	Jer 11:23	7451
against all mine *e* neighbours	Jer 12:14	7451
This *e* people, which refuse to	Jer 13:10	7451
good, that are accustomed to do *e*	Jer 13:23	7489
thee well in the time of *e*	Jer 15:11	7451
all this great *e* against us	Jer 16:10	7451
the imagination of his *e* heart	Jer 16:12	7451
thou art my hope in the day of *e*	Jer 17:17	7451
bring upon them the day of *e*	Jer 17:18	7451
pronounced, turn from their *e*	Jer 18:8	7451
I will repent of the *e* that I	Jer 18:8	7451
If it do *e* in my sight, that it	Jer 18:10	7451
I frame *e* against you, and devise	Jer 18:11	7451
ye now every one from his *e* way	Jer 18:11	7451
do the imagination of his *e* heart	Jer 18:12	7451
Shall *e* be recompensed for good	Jer 18:20	7451
I will bring *e* upon this place,	Jer 19:3	7451
upon all her towns all the *e* that	Jer 19:15	7451
my face against this city for *e*	Jer 21:10	7451
because of the *e* of your doings	Jer 21:12	7455
upon you the *e* of your doings	Jer 23:2	7455
dried up, and their course is *e*	Jer 23:10	7451
for I will bring *e* upon them	Jer 23:12	7451
heart, No *e* shall come upon you	Jer 23:17	7451
have turned them from their *e* way	Jer 23:22	7451
from the *e* of their doings	Jer 23:22	7455
and the *e*, very *e*	Jer 24:3	7451
cannot be eaten, they are so *e*	Jer 24:3	7455
And as the *e* figs, which cannot be	Jer 24:8	7451
cannot be eaten, they are so *e*	Jer 24:8	7455
now every one from his *e* way	Jer 25:5	7451
from the *e* of your doings, and	Jer 25:5	7455
I begin to bring *e* on the city	Jer 25:29	7489
e shall go forth from nation to	Jer 25:32	7451
and turn every man from his *e* way	Jer 26:3	7451

that I may repent me of the e Jer 26:3 7451
because of the e of their doings Jer 26:3 7455
e that he hath pronounced against Jer 26:13 7451
the LORD repented him of the e Jer 26:19 7451
procure great e against our souls Jer 26:19 7451
great kingdoms, of war, and of e Jer 28:8 7451
thoughts of peace, and not of e Jer 29:11 7451
cannot be eaten, they are so e Jer 29:17 7455
all this e to come upon them Jer 32:23 7451
of Judah have only done e before Jer 32:30 7451
Because of all the e of the Jer 32:32 7451
all this great e upon this people Jer 32:42 7451
ye now every man from his e way Jer 35:15 7451
of Jerusalem all the e that I Jer 35:17 7451
of Judah will hear all the e Jer 36:3 7451
return every man from his e way Jer 36:3 7451
return every one from his e way Jer 36:7 7451
all the e that I have pronounced Jer 36:31 7451
these men have done e in all that Jer 38:9 7489
my words upon this city for e Jer 39:16 7451
pronounced this e upon this place Jer 40:2 7451
heard of all the e that Ishmael Jer 41:11 7451
it be good, or whether it be e Jer 42:6 7451
for I repent me of the e that I Jer 42:10 7451
the e that I will bring upon them Jer 42:17 7451
Ye have seen all the e that I Jer 44:2 7451
this great e against your souls Jer 44:7 7451
set my face against you for e Jer 44:11 7451
and were well, and saw no e Jer 44:17 7451
because of the e of your doings Jer 44:22 7455
therefore this e is happened unto Jer 44:23 7451
I will watch over them for e Jer 44:27 7451
surely stand against you for e Jer 44:29 7451
I will bring e upon all flesh, Jer 45:5 7451
they have devised e against it Jer 48:2 7451
for they have heard e tidings Jer 49:23 7451
and I will bring e upon them Jer 49:37 7451
of Chaldea all their e that they Jer 51:24 7451
wrote in a book all the e that Jer 51:60 7451
shall not rise from the e that I Jer 51:64 7451
he did that which was e in the Jer 52:2 7451
of the most High proceedeth not e Lam 3:38 7451
upon them the e arrows of famine Eze 5:16 7451
e beasts, and they shall bereave Eze 5:17 7451
that I would do this e unto them Eze 6:10 7451
Alas for all the e abominations Eze 6:11 7451
An e, an only e, behold, is Eze 7:5 7451
the e that I have brought upon Eze 14:22 7451
turn ye, turn ye from your e ways Eze 33:11 7451
will cause the e beasts to cease Eze 34:25 7451
shall ye remember your own e ways Eze 36:31 7451
and thou shalt think an e thought Eze 38:10 7451
us, by bringing upon us a great e Dan 9:12 7451
all this e is come upon us Dan 9:13 7451
hath the LORD watched upon the e Dan 9:14 7451
and repenteth him of the e Joel 2:13 7451
shall there be e in a city Amos 3:6 7451
for it is an e time Amos 5:13 7451
Seek good, and not e, that ye may Amos 5:14 7451
Hate the e, and love the good, and Amos 5:15 7451
Ye that put far away the e day Amos 6:3 7451
set mine eyes upon them for e Amos 9:4 7451
The e shall not overtake nor Amos 9:10 7451
for whose cause this e is upon us Jonah 1:7 7451
for whose cause this e is upon us Jonah 1:8 7451
turn every one from his e way Jonah 3:8 7451
that they turned from their e way Jonah 3:10 7451
and God repented of the e, that he Jonah 3:10 7451
and repentest thee of the e Jonah 4:2 7451
but e came down from the LORD Mic 1:12 7451
and work e upon their beds Mic 2:1 7451
this family do I devise an e Mic 2:3 7451
for this time is e Mic 2:3 7451
Who hate the good, and love the e Mic 3:2 7451
none e can come upon us Mic 3:11 7451
That they may do e with both Mic 7:3 7451
that imagineth e against the LORD Nah 1:11 7451
of purer eyes than to behold e Hab 1:13 7451
an e covetousness to his house Hab 2:9 7451
be delivered from the power of e Hab 2:9 7451
not do good, neither will he do e Zeph 1:12 7489
thou shalt not see e any more Zeph 3:15 7451
e ways, and from your e doings Zec 1:4 7451
let none of you imagine e against Zec 7:10 7451
let none of you imagine e in your Zec 8:17 7451
blind for sacrifice, is it not e Mal 1:8 7451
the lame and sick, is it not e Mal 1:8 7451
Every one that doeth e is good in Mal 2:17 7451
manner of e against you falsely Mt 5:11 4190
is more than these cometh of e Mt 5:37 4190
unto you, That ye resist not e Mt 5:39 4190
maketh his sun to rise on the e Mt 5:45 4190
temptation, but deliver us from e Mt 6:13 4190
But if thine eye be e, thy whole Mt 6:23 4190
unto the day is the e thereof Mt 6:34 2549
If ye then, being e, know how to Mt 7:11 4190
tree bringeth forth e fruit Mt 7:17 4190
tree cannot bring forth e fruit Mt 7:18 4190
think ye e in your hearts Mt 9:4 4190
of vipers, how can ye, being e Mt 12:34 4190
an e man out of the e treasure Mt 12:35 4190
bringeth forth e things Mt 12:35 4190
answered and said unto them, An e Mt 12:39 4190
of the heart proceed e thoughts Mt 15:19 4190
Is thine eye e, because I am good Mt 20:15 4190
if that e servant shall say in Mt 24:48 2556
said, Why, what e hath he done Mt 27:23 2556
on the sabbath days, or to do e Mk 3:4 2554
proceed e thoughts, adulteries, Mk 7:21 2556
an e eye, blasphemy, pride, Mk 7:22 4190
All these e things come from Mk 7:23 4190
that can lightly speak e of me Mk 9:39 2551
them, Why, what e hath he done Mk 15:14 2556
days to do good, or to do e Lk 6:9 2554
you, and cast out your name as e Lk 6:22 4190
unto the unthankful and to the e Lk 6:35 4190
an e man out of the e treasure Lk 6:45 4190
bringeth forth that which is e Lk 6:45 4190
and plagues, and of e spirits Lk 7:21 4190
had been healed of e spirits Lk 8:2 4190
but deliver us from e Lk 11:4 4190
If ye then, being e, know how to Lk 11:13 4190
to say, This is an e generation Lk 11:29 4190
but when thine eye is e, thy body Lk 11:34 4190
and likewise Lazarus e things Lk 16:25 2556
time, Why, what e hath he done Lk 23:22 2556
light, because their deeds were e Jn 3:19 4190
one that doeth e hateth the light Jn 3:20 5337
and they that have done e, unto Jn 5:29 5337
it, that the works thereof are e Jn 7:7 4190
shouldest keep them from the e Jn 17:15 4190
answered him, If I have spoken e Jn 18:23 2560
bear witness of the e Jn 18:23 2556
entreat them e four hundred years Acts 7:6 2559
e entreated our fathers, so that Acts 7:19 2559
how much e he hath done to thy Acts 9:13 2556
made their minds e affected Acts 14:2 2559
but spake e of that way before Acts 19:9
the e spirits went out of them Acts 19:12 4190
to call over them which had e Acts 19:13 4190
the e spirit answered and said, Acts 19:15 4190
the man in whom the e spirit was Acts 19:16 4190
Thou shalt not speak e of the Acts 23:5 2560
saying, We find no e in this man Acts 23:9 2556
they have found any e doing in me Acts 24:20 92
boasters, inventors of e things Rom 1:30 2556
every soul of man that doeth e Rom 2:9 2556
affirm that we say,) Let us do e Rom 3:8 2556
but the e which I would not, that Rom 7:19 2556
do good, e is present with me Rom 7:21 2556
neither having done any good or e Rom 9:11 2556
Abhor that which is e Rom 12:9 4190
Recompense to no man e for e Rom 12:17 2556
Recompense to no man e for e Rom 12:17 2556
Be not overcome of e Rom 12:21 2556
but overcome e with good Rom 12:21 2556
to good works, but to the e Rom 13:3 2556
But if thou do that which is e Rom 13:4 2556
wrath upon him that doeth e Rom 13:4 2556
not then your good be e spoken of Rom 14:16
but it is e for that man who Rom 14:20 2556
is good, and simple concerning e Rom 16:19 2556
we should not lust after e things 1Cor 10:6 2556
why am I e spoken of for that for 1Cor 10:30 987
easily provoked, thinketh no e 1Cor 13:5 2556
e communications corrupt good 1Cor 15:33 2556
by e report and good report 2Cor 6:8 1426
Now I pray to God that ye do no e 2Cor 13:7 2556
us from this present e world Gal 1:4 4190
e speaking, be put away from you, Eph 4:31 988
the time, because the days are e Eph 5:16 4190
be able to withstand in the e day Eph 6:13 4190
of dogs, beware of e workers Phil 3:2 2556
e concupiscence, and covetousness, Col 3:5 2556
See that none render e for e 1Th 5:15 2556
Abstain from all appearance of e 1Th 5:22 4190
stablish you, and keep you from e 2Th 3:3 4190
strife, railings, e surmisings, 1Ti 6:4 4190
of money is the root of all e 1Ti 6:10 2556
I suffer trouble, as an e doer 2Ti 2:9 2557
But e men and seducers shall wax 2Ti 3:13 4190
the coppersmith did me much e 2Ti 4:14 2556
deliver me from every e work 2Ti 4:18 4190
liars, e beasts, slow bellies Titus 1:12 2556
having no e thing to say of you Titus 2:8 5337
To speak e of no man, to be no Titus 3:2 987
any of you an e heart of unbelief Heb 3:12 4190
to discern both good and e Heb 5:14 2556
sprinkled from an e conscience Heb 10:22 4190
for God cannot be tempted with e Jas 1:13 2556
are become judges of e thoughts Jas 2:4 4190
it is an unruly e, full of deadly Jas 3:8 2556
is confusion and every e work Jas 3:16 5337
Speak not e one of another, Jas 4:11 2635
He that speaketh e of his brother Jas 4:11 2635
speaketh e of the law, and judgeth Jas 4:11 2635
all such rejoicing is e Jas 4:16 4190
and envies, and all e speakings, 1Pet 2:1 2636
Not rendering e for e, or 1Pet 3:9 2556
Not rendering e for e, or 1Pet 3:9 2556
let him refrain his tongue from e 1Pet 3:10 2556
Let him eschew e, and do good 1Pet 3:11 2556
Lord is against them that do e 1Pet 3:12 2556
that, whereas they speak e of you 1Pet 3:16 2635
for well doing, than for e doing 1Pet 3:17 2554
excess of riot, speaking e of you 1Pet 4:4 987
on their part he is e spoken of 1Pet 4:14 987
way of truth shall be e spoken of 2Pet 2:2 987
afraid to speak e of dignities 2Pet 2:10 987
speak e of the things that they 2Pet 2:12 987
Because his own works were e 1Jn 3:12 4190
speed is partaker of his e deeds 2Jn 11 4190
follow not that which is e 3Jn 11 2556
he that doeth e hath not seen God 3Jn 11 2554
dominion, and speak e of dignities Jude 8 987
But these speak e of those things Jude 10 987
canst not bear them which are e Rev 2:2 2556

EVILDOER
every one is an hypocrite and an e Is 9:17 7489
or as a thief, or as an e 1Pet 4:15 2555

EVILDOERS
have hated the congregation of e Ps 26:5
Fret not thyself because of e Ps 37:1 7489
For e shall be cut off Ps 37:9 7489
will rise up for me against the e Ps 94:16 7489
Depart from me, ye e Ps 119:115 7489
laden with iniquity, a seed of e Is 1:4 7489
the seed of e shall never be Is 14:20 7489
arise against the house of the e Is 31:2 7489
of the poor from the hand of e Jer 20:13 7489
strengthen also the hands of e Jer 23:14 7489
they speak against you as e 1Pet 2:12 2555
by him for the punishment of e 1Pet 2:14 2555
they speak evil of you, as of e 1Pet 3:16 2555

EVILFAVOUREDNESS
wherein is blemish, or any e Deut 17:1

EVIL-MERODACH (*e'-vil-mer'-o-dak*) *Son of Nebuchadnezzar.*
that E king of Babylon in the 2Kin 25:27 192
that E king of Babylon in the Jer 52:31 192

EVILS
they shall be devoured, and many e Deut 31:17 7451
day, Are not these e come upon us Deut 31:17 7451
e which they shall have wrought Deut 31:18 7451
shall come to pass, when many e Deut 31:21 7451
For innumerable e have compassed Ps 40:12 7451
my people have committed two e Jer 2:13 7451
e which they have committed in Eze 6:9 7451
all your e that ye have committed Eze 20:43 7451
for all the e which Herod had Lk 3:19 4190

EWE
Abraham set seven e lambs of the Gen 21:28 3535
What mean these seven e lambs Gen 21:29 3535
For these seven e lambs shalt Gen 21:30 3535
one e lamb of the first year Lev 14:10 3535
And whether it be cow or e Lev 22:28 7716
one e lamb of the first year Num 6:14 3535
nothing, save one little e lamb 2Sa 12:3 3535

EWES
thy e and thy she goats have not Gen 31:38 7353
and twenty he goats, two hundred e Gen 32:14 7353
From following the e great with Ps 78:71 5763

EXACT
he shall not e it of his Deut 15:2 5065
foreigner thou mayest e it again Deut 15:3 5065
Ye e usury, every one of his Neh 5:7 5378
might e of them money and corn Neh 5:10 5383
and the oil, that ye e of them Neh 5:11 5383
The enemy shall not e upon him Ps 89:22 5378
pleasure, and e all your labours Is 58:3 5065
E no more than that which is Lk 3:13 4238

EXACTED
Menahem e the money of Israel, 2Kin 15:20 3318
he e the silver and the gold of 2Kin 23:35 5065

EXACTETH
God e of thee less than thine Job 11:6 5382

EXACTION
year, and the e of every debt Neh 10:31 4855

EXACTIONS
take away your e from my people Eze 45:9 1646

EXACTORS
peace, and thine e righteousness Is 60:17 5065

EXALT
my father's God, and I will e him Ex 15:2 7311
e the horn of his anointed 1Sa 2:10 7311
therefore shalt thou not e them Job 17:4 7311
let us e his name together Ps 34:3 7311
he shall e thee to inherit the Ps 37:34 7311
not the rebellious e themselves Ps 66:7 7311
But my horn shalt thou e like the Ps 92:10 7311
E ye the LORD our God, and worship Ps 99:5 7311
E the LORD our God, and worship at Ps 99:9 7311
Let them e him also in the Ps 107:32 7311
thou art my God, I will e thee Ps 118:28 7311
lest they e themselves Ps 140:8 7311
E her, and she shall promote thee Prov 4:8 5549
e the voice unto them, shake the Is 13:2 7311
I will e my throne above the Is 14:13 7311
I will e thee, I will praise thy Is 25:1 7311
e him that is low, and abase him Eze 21:26 1361
neither shall it e itself any Eze 29:15 5375
e themselves for their height Eze 31:14 1361
e themselves to establish the Dan 11:14 5375
and he shall e himself, and magnify Dan 11:36 7311
High, none at all would e him Hos 11:7 7311
Though thou e thyself as the Obad 4 1361
whosoever shall e himself shall Mt 23:12 5312
take of you, if a man e himself 2Cor 11:20 1869
that he may e you in due time 1Pet 5:6 5312

EXALTED
Agag, and his kingdom shall be e Num 24:7 5375
LORD, mine horn is e in the LORD 1Sa 2:1 7311
that he had e his kingdom for his 2Sa 5:12 5375
e be the God of the rock of my 2Sa 22:47 7311
the son of Haggith e himself 1Kin 1:5 5375
Forasmuch as I e thee from among 1Kin 14:7 7311
Forasmuch as I e thee out of the 1Kin 16:2 7311
whom hast thou e thy voice 2Kin 19:22 7311
thou art e as head above all 1Chr 29:11 5375
which is e above all blessing and Neh 9:5 7311
which mourn may be e to safety Job 5:11 7682
They are e for a little while, Job 24:24 7426
them for ever, and they are e Job 36:7 1361
side, when the vilest men are e Ps 12:8 7311
shall mine enemy be e over me Ps 13:2 7311
let the God of my salvation be e Ps 18:46 7311
Be thou e, LORD, in thine own Ps 21:13 7311
I will be e among the heathen Ps 46:10 7311
I will be e in the earth Ps 46:10 7311
he is greatly e Ps 47:9 5927
Be thou e, O God, above the Ps 57:5 7311
Be thou e, O God, above the Ps 57:11 7311
horns of the righteous shall be e Ps 75:10 7311
thy righteousness shall they be e Ps 89:16 7311

in thy favour our horn shall be *e* Ps 89:17 7311
I have *e* one chosen out of the Ps 89:19 7311
and in my name shall his horn be *e* Ps 89:24 7311
thou art *e* far above all gods Ps 97:9 5927
Be thou *e*, O God, above the Ps 108:5 7311
his horn shall be *e* with honour Ps 112:9 7311
The right hand of the LORD is *e* Ps 118:16 7426
of the upright the city is *e* Prov 11:11 7311
shall be *e* above the hills Is 2:2 5375
LORD alone shall be *e* in that day Is 2:11 7682
LORD alone shall be *e* in that day Is 2:17 7682
of hosts shall be *e* in judgment Is 5:16 1361
make mention that his name is *e* Is 12:4 7682
you, and therefore will he be *e* Is 30:18 7311
The LORD is *e* Is 33:5 7682
now will I be *e* Is 33:10 7311
whom hast thou *e* thy voice Is 37:23 7311
Every valley shall be *e*, and every Is 40:4 5375
a way, and my highways shall be *e* Is 49:11 7311
deal prudently, he shall be *e* Is 52:13 7311
have *e* the low tree, have dried Eze 17:24 1361
her stature was *e* among the thick Eze 19:11 1361
Therefore his height was *e* above Eze 31:5 1361
trembling, he *e* himself in Israel Hos 13:1 5375
were filled, and their heart was *e* Hos 13:6 7311
it shall be *e* above the hills Mic 4:1 5375
which art *e* unto heaven, shalt be Mt 11:23 *5312*
shall humble himself shall be *e* Mt 23:12 *5312*
seats, and *e* them of low degree Lk 1:52 *5312*
Capernaum, which art *e* to heaven Lk 10:15 *5312*
that humbleth himself shall be *e* Lk 14:11 *5312*
that humbleth himself shall be *e* Lk 18:14 *5312*
being by the right hand of God *e* Acts 2:33 *5312*
Him hath God *e* with his right Acts 5:31 *5312*
e the people when they dwelt as Acts 13:17 *5312*
abasing myself that ye might be *e* 2Cor 11:7 *5312*
lest I should be *e* above measure 2Cor 12:7 *5229*
lest I should be *e* above measure 2Cor 12:7 *5229*
God also hath highly *e* him Phil 2:9 *5251*
degree rejoice in that he is *e* Jas 1:9 *5311*

EXALTEST
As yet *e* thou thyself against my Ex 9:17 5549

EXALTETH
Behold, God *e* by his power Job 36:22 7682
He also *e* the horn of his people, Ps 148:14 7311
that is hasty of spirit *e* folly Prov 14:29 7311
Righteousness *e* a nation Prov 14:34 7311
he that *e* his gate seeketh Prov 17:19 1361
For whosoever *e* himself shall be Lk 14:11 *5312*
for every one that *e* himself Lk 18:14 *5312*
every high thing that *e* itself 2Cor 10:5 *1869*
e himself above all that is 2Th 2:4 *5229*

EXAMINATION
O king Agrippa, that, after *e* had Acts 25:26 *351*

EXAMINE
the tenth month to *e* the matter Ezr 10:16 1875
E me, O LORD, and prove me Ps 26:2 974
to them that do *e* me is this 1Cor 9:3 *350*
But let a man *e* himself, and so 1Cor 11:28 *1381*
E yourselves, whether ye be in 2Cor 13:5 3985

EXAMINED
having *e* him before you, have Lk 23:14 *350*
If we this day be *e* of the good Acts 4:9 *350*
he *e* the keepers, and commanded Acts 12:19 *350*
that he should be *e* by scourging Acts 22:24 *426*
from him which should have *e* him Acts 22:29 *426*
Who, when they had *e* me, would Acts 28:18 *350*

EXAMINING
by *e* of whom thyself mayest take Acts 24:8 *350*

EXAMPLE
willing to make her a publick *e* Mt 1:19 *3856*
For I have given you an *e* Jn 13:15 *5262*
but be thou an *e* of the believers 1Ti 4:12 *5179*
fall after the same *e* of unbelief Heb 4:11 *5262*
Who serve unto the *e* and shadow of Heb 8:5 *5262*
for an *e* of suffering affliction, Jas 5:10 *5262*
suffered for us, leaving us an *e* 1Pet 2:21 *5261*
flesh, are set forth for an *e* Jude 7 *1164*

EXAMPLES
Now these things were our *e* 1Cor 10:6 *5179*

EXCEED
stripes he may give him, and not *e* Deut 25:3 3254
lest, if he should *e*, and beat him Deut 25:3 3254
shall *e* the righteousness of the Mt 5:20 *4052*
of righteousness *e* in glory 2Cor 3:9 *4052*

EXCEEDED
one with another, until David *e* 1Sa 20:41 1431
So king Solomon *e* all the kings 1Kin 10:23 1431
transgressions that they have *e* Job 36:9 1396

EXCEEDEST
for thou *e* the fame that I heard 2Chr 9:6 3254

EXCEEDETH
prosperity *e* the fame which I 1Kin 10:7 3254

EXCEEDING
thy shield, and thy *e* great reward Gen 15:1 3966
And I will make thee *e* fruitful Gen 17:6 3966
e bitter cry, and said unto his Gen 27:34 3966
and multiplied, and waxed *e* mighty Ex 1:7 3966
the voice of the trumpet *e* loud Ex 19:16 3966
to search it, is an *e* good land Num 14:7 3966
Talk no more so *e* proudly 1Sa 2:3
king David took *e* much brass 2Sa 8:8 3966
The rich man had *e* many flocks 2Sa 12:2 3966
wisdom and understanding *e* much 1Kin 4:29 3966
because they were *e* many 1Kin 7:47 3966
he brought also *e* much spoil out 1Chr 20:2 3966
for the LORD must be *e* magnifical 1Chr 22:5 4605
and spears, and made them *e* strong 2Chr 11:12
for there was *e* much spoil in 2Chr 14:14 7235
until his disease was *e* great 2Chr 16:12 4605
And Hezekiah had *e* much riches 2Chr 32:27 3966
thou hast made him *e* glad with Ps 21:6 2302
altar of God, unto God my *e* joy Ps 43:4 8057
but thy commandment is *e* broad Ps 119:96 3966
the earth, but they are *e* wise Prov 30:24
e deep, who can find it out Eccl 7:24
(he is *e* proud) his loftiness, and Jer 48:29 3966
of Israel and Judah is *e* great Eze 9:9 3966
and thou wast *e* beautiful, and thou Eze 16:13 3966
e in dyed attire upon their heads Eze 23:15 5628
upon their feet, an *e* great army Eze 37:10 3966
the fish of the great sea, *e* many Eze 47:10 3966
was urgent, and the furnace *e* hot Dan 3:22 2493
Then was the king *e* glad for him Dan 6:23 7689
e dreadful, whose teeth were of Dan 7:19 3493
little horn, which waxed *e* great Dan 8:9 3499
Now Nineveh was an *e* great city Jonah 3:3 430
So Jonah was *e* glad of the gourd Jonah 4:6 1419
they rejoiced with *e* great joy Mt 2:10 *4970*
was *e* wroth, and sent forth, and Mt 2:16 *3029*
him up into an *e* high mountain Mt 4:8 *3029*
Rejoice, and be *e* glad Mt 5:12
e fierce, so that no man might Mt 8:28 *3029*
And they were *e* sorry Mt 17:23 *4970*
And they were *e* sorrowful, and Mt 26:22 *4970*
unto them, My soul is *e* sorrowful Mt 26:38 *4036*
And the king was *e* sorry Mk 6:26 *4036*
became shining, *e* white as snow Mk 9:3 *3029*
My soul is *e* sorrowful unto death Mk 14:34 *4036*
Herod saw Jesus, he was *e* glad Lk 23:8 *3029*
was *e* fair, and nourished up in Acts 7:20
commandment might become *e* sinful Rom 7:13
worketh for us a far more *e* 2Cor 4:17
comfort, I am *e* joyful in all our 2Cor 7:4 *5248*
you for the *e* grace of God in you 2Cor 9:14 *5235*
what is the *e* greatness of his Eph 1:19 *5235*
the *e* riches of his grace in his Eph 2:7 *5235*
do *e* abundantly above all that we Eph 3:20 *5228*
Lord was *e* abundant with faith 1Ti 1:14 *5250*
ye may be glad also with *e* joy 1Pet 4:13
Whereby are given unto us *e* great 2Pet 1:4
presence of his glory with *e* joy Jude 24
the plague thereof was *e* great Rev 16:21 *4970*

EXCEEDINGLY
waters prevailed *e* upon the earth Gen 7:19 3966
and sinners before the LORD *e* Gen 13:13 3966
her, I will multiply thy seed *e* Gen 16:10 7235
and thee, and will multiply thee *e* Gen 17:2 3966
fruitful, and will multiply him *e* Gen 17:20 3966
And Isaac trembled very *e*, and said Gen 27:33 1419
And the man increased *e*, and had Gen 30:43 3966
therein, and grew, and multiplied *e* Gen 47:27 3966
played the fool, and have erred *e* 1Sa 26:21
Then Amnon hated her *e* 2Sa 13:15
But they were *e* afraid, and said, 2Kin 10:4 3966
e in the sight of all Israel 1Chr 29:25 4605
was with him, and magnified him *e* 2Chr 1:1 4605
And Jehoshaphat waxed great *e* 2Chr 17:12 4605
for he strengthened himself *e* 2Chr 26:8 4605
it grieved them *e* that there was Neh 2:10 1419
Then was the queen *e* grieved Est 4:4 3966
Which rejoice *e*, and are glad, Job 3:22
yea, let them *e* rejoice Ps 68:3 8057
But lusted *e* in the wilderness, Ps 106:14
and I love them *e* Ps 119:167 3966
for we are *e* filled with contempt Ps 123:3 7227
Our soul is *e* filled with the Ps 123:4 7227
dissolved, the earth is moved *e* Is 24:19
dreadful and terrible, and strong *e* Dan 7:7 3493
Then were the men *e* afraid Jonah 1:10 1419
Then the men feared the LORD *e* Jonah 1:16 1419
But it displeased Jonah *e* Jonah 4:1 1419
heard it, they were *e* amazed Mt 19:25 *4970*
And they feared *e*, and said one to Mk 4:41
And they cried out the more *e* Mk 15:14 *4056*
Jews, do *e* trouble our city, Acts 16:20 *1613*
being *e* mad against them, I Acts 26:11 *4057*
we being *e* tossed with a tempest, Acts 27:18 *4971*
e the more joyed we for the joy 2Cor 7:13 *4056*
being more *e* zealous of the Gal 1:14 *4056*
day praying *e* that we might see 1Th 3:10
because that your faith groweth *e* 2Th 1:3
Moses said, I *e* fear and quake Heb 12:21 *1630*

EXCEL
as water, thou shalt not *e* Gen 49:4 3498
with harps on the Sheminith to *e* 1Chr 15:21 5329
that *e* in strength, that do his Ps 103:20 1368
images did *e* them of Jerusalem Is 10:10
seek that ye may *e* to the 1Cor 14:12 *4052*

EXCELLED
Solomon's wisdom *e* the wisdom of 1Kin 4:30 7227

EXCELLENCY
e of dignity, and the *e* of power Gen 49:3 3499
in the greatness of thine *e* thou Ex 15:7 1347
thy help, and in his *e* on the sky Deut 33:26 1346
and who is the sword of thy *e* Deut 33:29 1346
Doth not their *e* which is in them Job 4:21 3499
Shall not his *e* make you afraid Job 13:11 7613
Though his *e* mount up to the Job 20:6 7863
with the voice of his *e* Job 37:4 1347
thyself now with majesty and *e* Job 40:10 1363
the *e* of Jacob whom he loved Ps 47:4 1347
to cast him down from his *e* Ps 62:4 7613
his *e* is over Israel, and his Ps 68:34 1346
but the *e* of knowledge is, that Eccl 7:12 3504
the beauty of the Chaldees' *e* Is 13:19 1347
the *e* of Carmel and Sharon, they Is 35:2 1926
of the LORD, and the *e* of our God Is 35:2 1926
I will make thee an eternal *e* Is 60:15 1347
the *e* of your strength, the Eze 24:21 1347
of hosts, I abhor the *e* of Jacob Amos 6:8 1347
LORD hath sworn by the *e* of Jacob Amos 8:7 1347
hath turned away the *e* of Jacob Nah 2:2 1347
of Jacob, as the *e* of Israel Nah 2:2 1347
came not with *e* of speech or of 1Cor 2:1 *5247*
that the *e* of the power may be of 2Cor 4:7 *5236*
the *e* of the knowledge of Christ Phil 3:8 *5242*

EXCELLENT
honour of his *e* majesty many days Est 1:4 1420
he is *e* in power, and in judgment, Job 37:23 7689
how *e* is thy name in all the Ps 8:1 117
how *e* is thy name in all the Ps 8:9 117
are in the earth, and to the *e* Ps 16:3 117
How *e* is thy lovingkindness, O Ps 36:7 3368
e than the mountains of prey Ps 76:4 117
it shall be an *e* oil, which shall Ps 141:5 7218
for his name alone is *e* Ps 148:13 7682
him according to his *e* greatness Ps 150:2 7230
for I will speak of *e* things Prov 8:6 5057
is more *e* than his neighbour Prov 12:26 8446
E speech becometh not a fool Prov 17:7 3499
understanding is of an *e* spirit Prov 17:27 7119
to thee *e* things in counsels Prov 22:20 7991
is as Lebanon, *e* as the cedars Song 5:15 977
the fruit of the earth shall be *e* Is 4:2 1347
for he hath done *e* things Is 12:5 1348
in counsel, and *e* in working Is 28:29 1431
and thou art come to *e* ornaments Eze 16:7 5716
image, whose brightness was *e* Dan 2:31 3493
e majesty was added unto me Dan 4:36 3493
Forasmuch as an *e* spirit, and Dan 5:12 3493
e wisdom is found in thee Dan 5:14 3493
because an *e* spirit was in him Dan 6:3 3493
thee in order, most *e* Theophilus, Lk 1:3 *2903*
Claudius Lysias unto the most *e* Acts 23:26 *2903*
the things that are more *e* Rom 2:18 *1308*
yet shew I unto you a more *e* way 1Cor 12:31
ye may approve things that are *e* Phil 1:10 *1308*
obtained a more *e* name than they Heb 1:4 *1313*
he obtained a more *e* ministry Heb 8:6 *1313*
God a more *e* sacrifice than Cain Heb 11:4 *4119*
a voice to him from the *e* glory 2Pet 1:17 *3169*

EXCELLEST
virtuously, but thou *e* them all Prov 31:29 5927

EXCELLETH
Then I saw that wisdom *e* folly Eccl 2:13 3504
as far as light *e* darkness Eccl 2:13 3504
by reason of the glory that *e* 2Cor 3:10 *5235*

EXCEPT
E the God of my father, the God Gen 31:42 3884
not let thee go, *e* thou bless me Gen 32:26
e your youngest brother come Gen 42:15
e your brother be with you Gen 43:3 1115
e your brother be with you Gen 43:5 1115
For *e* we had lingered, surely now Gen 43:10 3884
E your youngest brother come down Gen 44:23
e our youngest brother be with us Gen 44:26 369
e the land of the priests only, Gen 47:26 7535
e thou make thyself altogether a Num 16:13 3588
e their Rock had sold them, and Deut 32:30
e ye destroy the accursed from Josh 7:12
e thou hadst hasted and come to 1Sa 25:34
do God to Abner, and more also, *e* 2Sa 3:9 3588
e thou first bring Michal Saul's 2Sa 3:13
E thou take away the blind and the 2Sa 5:6
thy riding for me, *e* I bid thee 2Kin 4:24
e the king delighted in her, and Est 2:14
e such to whom the king shall Est 4:11 905
E the LORD build the house, they Ps 127:1
e the LORD keep the city, the Ps 127:1
e they have done mischief Prov 4:16
E the LORD of hosts had left unto Is 1:9 3884
e the gods, whose dwelling is not Dan 2:11 3861
worship any god, *e* their own God Dan 3:28 3861
Daniel, *e* we find it against him Dan 6:5 3861
walk together, *e* they be agreed Amos 3:3 1115
That *e* your righteousness shall Mt 5:20 *3362*
e he first bind the strong man Mt 12:29 *3362*
E ye be converted, and become as Mt 18:3 *3362*
e it be for fornication, and shall Mt 19:9 *1508*
e those days should be shortened, Mt 24:22 *1508*
e I drink it, thy will be done Mt 26:42 *3362*
e he will first bind the strong Mk 3:27 *3362*
e they wash their hands oft, eat Mk 7:3 *3362*
e they wash, they eat not Mk 7:4 *3362*
e that the Lord had shortened Mk 13:20 *1508*
e we should go and buy meat for Lk 9:13 *1509*
e ye repent, ye shall all Lk 13:3 *3362*
e ye repent, ye shall all Lk 13:5 *3362*
thou doest, *e* God be with him Jn 3:2 *3362*
E a man be born again, he cannot Jn 3:3 *3362*
E a man be born of water and of Jn 3:5 *3362*
e it be given him from heaven Jn 3:27 *3362*
E ye see signs and wonders, ye Jn 4:48 *3362*
e the Father which hath sent me Jn 6:44 *3362*
E ye eat the flesh of the Son of Jn 6:53 *3362*
e it were given unto him of my Jn 6:65 *3362*
E a corn of wheat fall into the Jn 12:24 *3362*
of itself, *e* it abide in the vine Jn 15:4 *3362*
no more can ye, *e* ye abide in me Jn 15:4 *3362*
e it were given thee from above Jn 19:11 *1508*
E I shall see in his hands the Jn 20:25 *3362*
Judaea and Samaria, *e* the apostles Acts 8:1 *4133*
e some man should guide me Acts 8:31 *3362*
E ye be circumcised after the Acts 15:1 *3362*
E it be for this one voice, that Acts 24:21 *2228*
such as I am, *e* these bonds Acts 26:29 *3923*
E these abide in the ship, ye Acts 27:31 *3362*
e the law had said, Thou shalt Rom 7:7 *1508*
E the Lord of Sabaoth had left us Rom 9:29 *1508*
shall they preach, *e* they be sent Rom 10:15 *3362*

e it be with consent for a time, 1Cor 7:5 1509
e he interpret, that the church 1Cor 14:5
e I shall speak to you either by 1Cor 14:6 3362
e they give a distinction in the 1Cor 14:7 3362
e ye utter by the tongue words 1Cor 14:9 3362
sowest is not quickened, e it die 1Cor 15:36 3362
e it be that I myself was not 2Cor 12:13 1508
is in you, e ye be reprobates 2Cor 13:5 1509
e there come a falling away first 2Th 2:3 3362
not crowned, e he strive lawfully 2Ti 2:5 3362
out of his place, e thou repent Rev 2:5 3362
e they repent of their deeds Rev 2:22 3362

EXCEPTED
him, it is manifest that he is e 1Cor 15:27 1622

EXCESS
they are full of extortion and e Mt 23:25 192
not drunk with wine, wherein is e Eph 5:18 810
lusts, e of wine, revellings, 1Pet 4:3 3632
with them to the same e of riot 1Pet 4:4 401

EXCHANGE
gave them bread in e for horses Gen 47:17
the e thereof shall be holy Lev 27:10 8545
the e of it shall not be for Job 28:17 8545
shall not sell of it, neither e Eze 48:14 4171
a man give in e for his soul Mt 16:26 465
a man give in e for his soul Mk 8:37 465

EXCHANGERS
to have put my money to the e Mt 25:27 5133

EXCLUDE
yea, they would e you, that ye Gal 4:17 1576

EXCLUDED
is boasting then? It is e Rom 3:27 1576

EXCUSE
with one consent began to make e Lk 14:18 3868
so that they are without e Rom 1:20 379
think ye that we e ourselves unto 2Cor 12:19 626

EXCUSED
I pray thee have me e Lk 14:18 3868
I pray thee have me e Lk 14:19 3868

EXCUSING
accusing or else e one another Rom 2:15 626

EXECRATION
and ye shall be an e, and an Jer 42:18 423
and they shall be an e, and an Jer 44:12 423

EXECUTE
gods of Egypt I will e judgment Ex 12:12 6213
the priest shall e upon her all Num 5:30 6213
that they may e the service of Num 8:11 5647
He doth e the judgment of the Deut 10:18 6213
e my judgments, and keep all my 1Kin 6:12 6213
when wilt thou e judgment on them Ps 119:84 6213
To e vengeance upon the heathen, Ps 149:7 6213
To e upon them the judgment Ps 149:9 6213
Take counsel, e judgment Is 16:3 6213
if ye throughly e judgment Jer 7:5 6213
E judgment in the morning, and Jer 21:12 1777
E ye judgment and righteousness, Jer 22:3 6213
shall e judgment and justice in Jer 23:5 6213
and he shall e judgment and Jer 33:15 6213
will e judgments in the midst of Eze 5:8 6213
I will e judgments in thee, and Eze 5:10 6213
when I shall e judgments in thee Eze 5:15 6213
will e judgments among you Eze 11:9 6213
e judgments upon thee in the Eze 16:41 6213
I will e judgments upon Moab Eze 25:11 6213
I will e great vengeance upon Eze 25:17 6213
Zoan, and will e judgments in No Eze 30:14 6213
Thus will I e judgments in Egypt Eze 30:19 6213
e judgment and justice, take away Eze 45:9 6213
I will not e the fierceness of Hos 11:9 6213
I will e vengeance in anger and Mic 5:15 6213
my cause, and e judgment for me Mic 7:9 6213
E true judgment, and shew mercy and Zec 7:9 8199
e the judgment of truth and peace Zec 8:16 8199
him authority to e judgment also Jn 5:27 4160
a revenger to e wrath upon him Rom 13:4
To e judgment upon all, and to Jude 15 4160

EXECUTED
gods also the LORD e judgments Num 33:4 6213
he e the justice of the LORD, and Deut 33:21 6213
David e judgment and justice unto 2Sa 8:15 6213
(he it is that e the priest's 1Chr 6:10
e judgment and justice among all 1Chr 18:14 6213
Ithamar e the priest's office 1Chr 24:2
So they e judgment against Joash 2Chr 24:24 6213
let judgment be e speedily upon Ezr 7:26 5648
stood up Phinehas, and e judgment Ps 106:30
an evil work is not e speedily Eccl 8:11 6213
shall not return, until he have e Jer 23:20 6213
neither e my judgments, but have Eze 11:12 6213
hath e true judgment between man Eze 18:8 6213
hath e my judgments, hath walked Eze 18:17 6213
they had not e my judgments Eze 20:24 6213
for they had e judgment upon her Eze 23:10 6213
I shall have e judgments in her Eze 28:22 6213
when I have e judgments upon all Eze 28:26 6213
see my judgment that I have e Eze 39:21 6213
that while he e the priest's Lk 1:8 2407

EXECUTEDST
nor e his fierce wrath upon 1Sa 28:18 6213

EXECUTEST
thou e judgment and righteousness Ps 99:4 6213

EXECUTETH
known by the judgment which he e Ps 9:16 6213
The LORD e righteousness and Ps 103:6 6213
Which e judgment for the Ps 146:7 6213

the man that e my counsel from a Is 46:11
if there be any that e judgment Jer 5:1 6213
for he is strong that e his word Joel 2:11 6213

EXECUTING
in e that which is right in mine 2Kin 10:30 6213
e the priest's office unto the 2Chr 11:14
when Jehu was e judgment upon the 2Chr 22:8

EXECUTION
decree drew near to be put in e Est 9:1 6213

EXECUTIONER
And immediately the king sent an e Mk 6:27 4688

EXEMPTED
throughout all Judah; none was e 1Kin 15:22 5355

EXERCISE
neither do I e myself in great Ps 131:1 1980
the LORD which e lovingkindness Jer 9:24 6213
the Gentiles e dominion over them Mt 20:25 2634
are great e authority upon them Mt 20:25 2715
the Gentiles e lordship over them Mk 10:42 2634
their great ones e authority upon Mk 10:42 2715
the Gentiles e lordship over them Lk 22:25 2961
they that e authority upon them Lk 22:25 1850
And herein do I e myself, to have Acts 24:16 778
e thyself rather unto godliness 1Ti 4:7 1128
For bodily e profiteth little 1Ti 4:8 1129

EXERCISED
the sons of man to be e therewith Eccl 1:13 6031
to the sons of men to be e in it Eccl 3:10 6031
e robbery, and have vexed the poor Eze 22:29
senses e to discern both good Heb 5:14 1128
unto them which are e thereby Heb 12:11 1128
an heart they have e with 2Pet 2:14 1128

EXERCISETH
he e all the power of the first Rev 13:12 4160

EXHORT
other words did he testify and e Acts 2:40 3870
now I e you to be of good cheer Acts 27:22 3867
it necessary to e the brethren 2Cor 9:5 3870
e you by the Lord Jesus, that as 1Th 4:1 3870
Now we e you, brethren, warn them 1Th 5:14 3870
e by our Lord Jesus Christ, that 2Th 3:12 3870
I e therefore, that, first of all 1Ti 2:1 3870
These things teach and e 1Ti 6:2 3870
e with all longsuffering and 2Ti 4:2 3870
able by sound doctrine both to e Titus 1:9 3870
men likewise e to be sober minded Titus 2:6 3870
E servants to be obedient unto Titus 2:9
These things speak, and e, and Titus 2:15 3870
But e one another daily, while it Heb 3:13 3870
elders which are among you I e 1Pet 5:1 3870
e you that ye should earnestly Jude 3 3870

EXHORTATION
many other things in his e Lk 3:18 3870
have any word of e for the people Acts 13:15 3874
parts, and had given them much e Acts 20:2 3870
Or he that exhorteth, on e Rom 12:8 3874
unto men to edification, and e 1Cor 14:3 3874
For indeed he accepted the e 2Cor 8:17 3874
For our e was not of deceit, nor 1Th 2:3 3874
give attendance to reading, to e 1Ti 4:13 3874
ye have forgotten the e which Heb 12:5 3874
brethren, suffer the word of e Heb 13:22 3874

EXHORTED
e them all, that with purpose of Acts 11:23 3870
e the brethren with many words, Acts 15:32 3870
As ye know how we e and comforted 1Th 2:11 3870

EXHORTETH
Or he that e, on exhortation Rom 12:8 3870

EXHORTING
e them to continue in the faith, Acts 14:22 3870
e the disciples to receive him Acts 18:27 4389
but e one another Heb 10:25 3870
I have written briefly, e 1Pet 5:12 3870

EXILE
thou art a stranger, and also an e 2Sa 15:19 1540
The captive e hasteneth that he Is 51:14 6808

EXORCISTS
certain of the vagabond Jews, e Acts 19:13 1845

EXPECTATION
the e of the poor shall not Ps 9:18 8615
for my e is from him Ps 62:5 8615
but the e of the wicked shall Prov 10:28 8615
man dieth, his e shall perish Prov 11:7 8615
but the e of the wicked is wrath Prov 11:23 8615
thine e shall not be cut off Prov 23:18 8615
thy e shall not be cut off Prov 24:14 8615
and ashamed of Ethiopia their e Is 20:5 4007
that day, Behold, such is our e Is 20:6 4007
for her e shall be ashamed Zec 9:5 4007
And as the people were in e Lk 3:15 4328
from all the e of the people of Acts 12:11 4329
For the earnest e of the creature Rom 8:19 603
According to my earnest e Phil 1:20 603

EXPECTED
not of evil, to give you an e end Jer 29:11 8615

EXPECTING
e to receive something of them Acts 3:5 4328
From henceforth e till his Heb 10:13 1551

EXPEDIENT
Nor consider that it is e for us Jn 11:50 4851
It is e for you that I go away Jn 16:7 4851
that it was e that one man should Jn 18:14 4851
unto me, but all things are not e 1Cor 6:12 4851
for me, but all things are not e 1Cor 10:23 4851
for this is e for you, who have 2Cor 8:10 4851
It is not e for me doubtless to 2Cor 12:1 4851

EXPEL
he shall e them from before you, Josh 23:5 1920
e me out of my father's house Judg 11:7 1644

EXPELLED
of Israel e not the Geshurites Josh 13:13 3423
he e thence the three sons of Judg 1:20 3423
his banished be not e from him 2Sa 14:14 5080
e them out of their coasts Acts 13:50 1544

EXPENCES
let the e be given out of the Ezr 6:4 5313
forthwith e be given unto these Ezr 6:8 5313

EXPERIENCE
for I have learned by e that the Gen 30:27 5172
my heart had great e of wisdom Eccl 1:16 7200
And patience, e Rom 5:4 1382
and e, hope Rom 5:4 1382

EXPERIMENT
Whiles by the e of this 2Cor 9:13 1382

EXPERT
e in war, with all instruments of 1Chr 12:33 6186
And of the Danites e in war twenty 1Chr 12:35 6186
battle, e in war, forty thousand 1Chr 12:36 6186
all hold swords, being e in war Song 3:8 3925
shall be as of a mighty e man Jer 50:9 7919
know thee to be e in all customs Acts 26:3 1109

EXPIRED
and the days were not e 1Sa 18:26 4390
to pass, after the year was e 2Sa 11:1 8666
when thy days be e that thou must 1Chr 17:11 4390
pass, that after the year was e 1Chr 20:1 8666
And when the year was e, king 2Chr 36:10 8666
And when these days were e Est 1:5 4390
And when these days are e, it Eze 43:27 3615
And when forty years were e Acts 7:30 4137
And when the thousand years are e Rev 20:7 5055

EXPLOITS
and he shall do e, and return to Dan 11:28
God shall be strong, and do e Dan 11:32

EXPOUND
not in three days e the riddle Judg 14:14 5046

EXPOUNDED
unto them which e the riddle Judg 14:19 5046
he e all things to his disciples Mk 4:34 1956
he e unto them in all the Lk 24:27 1329
e it by order unto them, saying, Acts 11:4 1620
e unto him the way of God more Acts 18:26 1620
to whom he e and testified the Acts 28:23 1620

EXPRESS
the e image of his person, and Heb 1:3 5481

EXPRESSED
men which are e by their names Num 1:17 5344
thousand, which were e by name 1Chr 12:31 5344
were chosen, who were e by name 1Chr 16:41 5344
men which were e by name rose up 2Chr 28:15 5344
city, the men that were e by name 2Chr 31:19 5344
all of them were e by name Ezr 8:20

EXPRESSLY
If I e say unto the lad, Behold, 1Sa 20:21 559
came e unto Ezekiel the priest Eze 1:3
Now the Spirit speaketh e 1Ti 4:1 4490

EXTEND
there be none to e mercy unto him Ps 109:12 4900
I will e peace to her like a Is 66:12 5186

EXTENDED
hath e mercy unto me before the Ezr 7:28 5186
but hath e mercy unto us in the Ezr 9:9 5186

EXTENDETH
my goodness e not to thee Ps 16:2

EXTINCT
breath is corrupt, my days are e Job 17:1 2193
they are e, they are quenched as Is 43:17 1846

EXTOL
I will e thee, O LORD Ps 30:1 7311
e him that rideth upon the Ps 68:4 5549
I will e thee, my God, O king Ps 145:1 7311
Now I Nebuchadnezzar praise and e Dan 4:37 7313

EXTOLLED
mouth, and he was e with my tongue Ps 66:17 7318
he shall be exalted and e Is 52:13 5375

EXTORTION
gained of thy neighbours by e Eze 22:12 6233
but within they are full of e Mt 23:25 724

EXTORTIONER
Let the e catch all that he hath Ps 109:11 5383
for the e is at an end, the Is 16:4 4160
a railer, or a drunkard, or an e 1Cor 5:11 727

EXTORTIONERS
that I am not as other men are, e Lk 18:11 727
world, or with the covetous, or e 1Cor 5:10 727
drunkards, nor revilers, nor e 1Cor 6:10 727

EXTREME
and with an e burning, and with Deut 28:22 2746

EXTREMITY
yet he knoweth it not in great e Job 35:15 6580

EYE
E for e, tooth for tooth, hand Ex 21:24 5869
a man smite the e of his servant Ex 21:26 5869
or the e of his maid, that it Ex 21:26 5869
or that hath a blemish in his e Lev 21:20 5869
e for e, tooth for tooth Lev 24:20 5869

thine *e* shall have no pity upon Deut 7:16 5869
neither shall thine *e* pity him Deut 13:8 5869
thine *e* be evil against thy poor Deut 15:9 5869
Thine *e* shall not pity him, but Deut 19:13 5869
And thine *e* shall not pity Deut 19:21 5869
e for *e*, tooth for tooth, hand Deut 19:21 5869
thine *e* shall not pity her Deut 25:12 5869
his *e* shall be evil toward his Deut 28:54 5869
her *e* shall be evil toward the Deut 28:56 5869
he kept him as the apple of his *e* Deut 32:10 5869
his *e* was not dim, nor his Deut 34:7 5869
but mine *e* spared thee 1Sa 24:10 5869
to my cleanness in his *e* sight 2Sa 22:25 5869
But the *e* of their God was upon Ezr 5:5 5870
mine *e* shall no more see good Job 7:7 5869
The *e* of him that hath seen me Job 7:8 5869
up the ghost, and no *e* had seen me Job 10:18 5869
mine *e* hath seen all this, mine Job 13:1 5869
but mine *e* poureth out tears unto Job 16:20 5869
doth not mine *e* continue in their Job 17:2 5869
Mine *e* also is dim by reason of Job 17:7 5869
The *e* also which saw him shall Job 20:9 5869
The *e* also of the adulterer Job 24:15 5869
saying, No *e* shall see me Job 24:15 5869
the vulture's *e* hath not seen Job 28:7 5869
his *e* seeth every precious thing Job 28:10 5869
and when the *e* saw me, it gave Job 29:11 5869
but now mine *e* seeth thee Job 42:5 5869
Mine *e* is consumed because of Ps 6:7 5869
Keep me as the apple of the *e* Ps 17:8 5869
mine *e* is consumed with grief, Ps 31:9 5869
I will guide thee with mine *e* Ps 32:8 5869
the *e* of the LORD is upon them Ps 33:18 5869
e that hate me without a cause Ps 35:19 5869
Aha, aha, our *e* hath seen it Ps 35:21 5869
mine *e* hath seen his desire upon Ps 54:7 5869
Mine *e* mourneth by reason of Ps 88:9 5869
Mine *e* also shall see my desire Ps 92:11 5869
he that formed the *e*, shall he Ps 94:9 5869
and my law as the apple of thine *e* Prov 7:2 5869
winketh with the *e* causeth sorrow Prov 10:10 5869
The hearing ear, and the seeing *e* Prov 20:12 5869
a bountiful *e* shall be blessed Prov 22:9 5869
bread of him that hath an evil *e* Prov 23:6 5869
hasteth to be rich hath an evil *e* Prov 28:22 5869
The *e* that mocketh at his father, Prov 30:17 5869
the *e* is not satisfied with Eccl 1:8 5869
neither is his *e* satisfied with Eccl 4:8 5869
their *e* shall not spare children Is 13:18 5869
for they shall see *e* to *e* Is 52:8 5869
the ear, neither hath the *e* seen Is 64:4 5869
mine *e* shall weep sore, and run Jer 13:17 5869
mine *e*, mine *e* runneth down Lam 1:16 5869
to the *e* in the tabernacle of the Lam 2:4 5869
not the apple of thine *e* cease Lam 2:18 5869
Mine *e* runneth down with rivers Lam 3:48 5869
Mine *e* trickleth down, and ceaseth Lam 3:49 5869
Mine *e* affecteth mine heart Lam 3:51 5869
neither shall mine *e* spare Eze 5:11 5869
mine *e* shall not spare thee, Eze 7:4 5869
mine *e* shall not spare, neither Eze 7:9 5869
mine *e* shall not spare, neither Eze 8:18 5869
let not your *e* spare, neither Eze 9:5 5869
mine *e* shall not spare, neither Eze 9:10 5869
None *e* pitied thee, to do any of Eze 16:5 5869
Nevertheless mine *e* spared them Eze 20:17 5869
and let our *e* look upon Zion Mic 4:11 5869
you toucheth the apple of his *e* Zec 2:8 5869
upon his arm, and upon his right *e* Zec 11:17 5869
his right *e* shall be utterly Zec 11:17 5869
And if thy right *e* offend thee Mt 5:29 3788
hath been said, An *e* for an *e* Mt 5:38 3788
The light of the body is the *e* Mt 6:22 3788
if therefore thine *e* be single Mt 6:22 3788
But if thine *e* be evil, thy whole Mt 6:23 3788
mote that is in thy brother's *e* Mt 7:3 3788
the beam that is in thine own *e* Mt 7:3 3788
pull out the mote out of thine *e* Mt 7:4 3788
behold, a beam is in thine own *e* Mt 7:4 3788
out the beam out of thine own *e* Mt 7:5 3788
the mote out of thy brother's *e* Mt 7:5 3788
if thine *e* offend thee, pluck it Mt 18:9 3788
to enter into life with one *e* Mt 18:9 3442
to go through the *e* of a needle Mt 19:24 5169
Is thine *e* evil, because I am Mt 20:15 3788
deceit, lasciviousness, an evil *e* Mk 7:22 3788
if thine *e* offend thee, pluck it Mk 9:47 3788
the kingdom of God with one *e* Mk 9:47 3442
to go through the *e* of a needle Mk 10:25 5168
mote that is in thy brother's *e* Lk 6:41 3788
the beam that is in thine own *e* Lk 6:41 3788
out the mote that is in thine *e* Lk 6:42 3788
the beam that is in thine own *e* Lk 6:42 3788
first the beam out of thine own *e* Lk 6:42 3788
mote that is in thy brother's *e* Lk 6:42 3788
The light of the body is the *e* Lk 11:34 3788
therefore when thine *e* is single Lk 11:34 3788
but when thine *e* is evil, thy Lk 11:34
camel to go through a needle's *e* Lk 18:25 5168
E hath not seen, nor ear heard, 1Cor 2:9 3788
shall say, Because I am not the *e* 1Cor 12:16 3788
If the whole body were an *e* 1Cor 12:17 3788
the *e* cannot say unto the hand, I 1Cor 12:21 3788
moment, in the twinkling of an *e* 1Cor 15:52 3788
every *e* shall see him, and they Rev 1:7 3788

EYEBROWS

his head and his beard and his *e* Lev 14:9

EYED

Leah was tender *e* Gen 29:17 5869
Saul *e* David from that day and 1Sa 18:9 5770

EYELIDS

on my *e* is the shadow of death Job 16:16 6079
are like the *e* of the morning Job 41:18 6079
his eyes behold, his *e* try Ps 11:4 6079
mine eyes, or slumber to mine *e* Ps 132:4 6079
let thine *e* look straight before Prov 4:25 6079
eyes, nor slumber to thine *e* Prov 6:4 6079
let her take thee with her *e* Prov 6:25 6079
and their *e* are lifted up Prov 30:13 6079
our *e* gush out with waters Jer 9:18 6079

EYE'S

let him go free for his *e* sake Ex 21:26 5869

EYES

then your *e* shall be opened, and Gen 3:5 5869
and that it was pleasant to the *e* Gen 3:6 5869
the *e* of them both were opened, Gen 3:7 5869
found grace in the *e* of the LORD Gen 6:8 5869
And Lot lifted up his *e*, and beheld Gen 13:10 5869
from him, Lift up now thine *e* Gen 13:14 5869
mistress was despised in her *e* Gen 16:4 5869
I was despised in her *e* Gen 16:5 5869
And he lift up his *e* and looked, and Gen 18:2 5869
ye to them as is good in your *e* Gen 19:8 5869
he is to thee a covering of the *e* Gen 20:16 5869
And God opened her *e*, and she saw a Gen 21:19 5869
third day Abraham lifted up his *e* Gen 22:4 5869
And Abraham lifted up his *e* Gen 22:13 5869
and he lifted up his *e*, and saw, and Gen 24:63 5869
And Rebekah lifted up her *e* Gen 24:64 5869
his *e* were dim, so that he could Gen 27:1 5869
if I have found favour in thine *e* Gen 30:27 5869
e of the cattle in the gutters Gen 30:41 5869
that I lifted up mine *e*, and saw Gen 31:10 5869
And he said, Lift up now thine *e* Gen 31:12 5869
and my sleep departed from mine *e* Gen 31:40 5869
And Jacob lifted up his *e*, and Gen 33:1 5869
And he lifted up his *e*, and saw the Gen 33:5 5869
Let me find grace in your *e* Gen 34:11 5869
and they lifted up their *e* Gen 37:25 5869
wife cast her *e* upon Joseph Gen 39:7 5869
was good in the *e* of Pharaoh Gen 41:37 5869
in the *e* of all his servants Gen 41:37 5869
and bound him before their *e* Gen 42:24 5869
And he lifted up his *e*, and saw his Gen 43:29 5869
that I may set mine *e* upon him Gen 44:21 5869
And, behold, your *e* see, and the Gen 45:12 5869
the *e* of my brother Benjamin, Gen 45:12 5869
shall put his hand upon thine *e* Gen 46:4 5869
shall we die before thine *e* Gen 47:19 5869
Now the *e* of Israel were dim for Gen 48:10 5869
His *e* shall be red with wine, and Gen 49:12 5869
now I have found grace in your *e* Gen 50:4 5869
be abhorred in the *e* of Pharaoh Ex 5:21 5869
in the *e* of his servants, to put Ex 5:21 5869
of the Egyptians before their *e* Ex 8:26 5869
and for a memorial between thine *e* Ex 13:9 5869
and for frontlets between thine *e* Ex 13:16 5869
of Israel lifted up their *e* Ex 14:10 5869
the *e* of the children of Israel Ex 24:17 5869
be hid from the *e* of the assembly Lev 4:13 5869
ways hide their *e* from the man Lev 20:4 5869
ague, that shall consume the *e* Lev 26:16 5869
be hid from the *e* of her husband Num 5:13 5869
thou mayest be to us instead of *e* Num 10:31 5869
beside this manna, before our *e* Num 11:6 5869
your own heart and your own *e* Num 15:39 5869
thou put out the *e* of these men Num 16:14 5869
ye unto the rock before their *e* Num 20:8 5869
to sanctify me in the *e* of the Num 20:12 5869
the LORD opened the *e* of Balaam Num 22:31 5869
And Balaam lifted up his *e* Num 24:2 5869
the man whose *e* are open hath Num 24:3 5869
a trance, but having his *e* open Num 24:4 5869
the man whose *e* are open hath Num 24:15 5869
a trance, but having his *e* open Num 24:16 5869
me at the water before their *e* Num 27:14 5869
of them shall be pricks in your *e* Num 33:55 5869
for you in Egypt before your *e* Deut 1:30 5869
Thine *e* have seen all that the Deut 3:21 5869
and lift up thine *e* westward Deut 3:27 5869
and behold it with thine *e* Deut 3:27 5869
Your *e* have seen what the LORD Deut 4:3 5869
things which thine *e* have seen Deut 4:9 5869
thou lift up thine *e* unto heaven Deut 4:19 5869
for you in Egypt before your *e* Deut 4:34 5869
be as frontlets between thine *e* Deut 6:8 5869
all his household, before our *e* Deut 6:22 5869
temptations which thine *e* saw Deut 7:19 5869
and brake them before your *e* Deut 9:17 5869
things, which thine *e* have seen Deut 10:21 5869
But your *e* have seen all the Deut 11:7 5869
the *e* of the LORD thy God are Deut 11:12 5869
be as frontlets between your *e* Deut 11:18 5869
whatsoever is right in his own *e* Deut 12:8 5869
in the *e* of the LORD thy God Deut 13:18 5869
between your *e* for the dead Deut 14:1 5869
gift doth blind the *e* of the wise Deut 16:19 5869
blood, neither have our *e* seen it Deut 21:7 5869
that she find no favour in his *e* Deut 24:1 5869
ox shall be slain before thine *e* Deut 28:31 5869
thine *e* shall look, and fail with Deut 28:32 5869
of thine *e* which thou shalt see Deut 28:34 5869
trembling heart, and failing of *e* Deut 28:65 5869
of thine *e* which thou shalt see Deut 28:67 5869
your *e* in the land of Egypt unto Deut 29:2 5869
which thine *e* have seen, the Deut 29:3 5869
e to see, and ears to hear, unto Deut 29:4 5869
thee to see it with thine *e* Deut 34:4 5869
Jericho, that he lifted up his *e* Josh 5:13 5869
your sides, and thorns in your *e* Josh 23:13 5869
your *e* have seen what I have done Josh 24:7 5869
took him, and put out his *e* Judg 16:21 5869
of the Philistines for my two *e* Judg 16:28 5869
that which was right in his own *e* Judg 17:6 5869
And when he had lifted up his *e* Judg 19:17 5869
that which was right in his own *e* Judg 21:25 5869
Let thine *e* be on the field that Ruth 2:9 5869
Why have I found grace in thine *e* Ruth 2:10 5869
shall be to consume thine *e* 1Sa 2:33 5869
his *e* began to wax dim, that he 1Sa 3:2 5869
his *e* were dim, that he could not 1Sa 4:15 5869
and they lifted up their *e* 1Sa 6:13 5869
I may thrust out all your right *e* 1Sa 11:2 5869
bribe to blind mine *e* therewith 1Sa 12:3 5869
the LORD will do before your *e* 1Sa 12:16 5869
and his *e* were enlightened 1Sa 14:27 5869
how mine *e* have been enlightened, 1Sa 14:29 5869
I have found grace in thine *e* 1Sa 20:3 5869
if I have found favour in thine *e* 1Sa 20:29 5869
this day thine *e* have seen how 1Sa 24:10 5869
young men find favour in thine *e* 1Sa 25:8 5869
was precious in thine *e* this day 1Sa 26:21 5869
much set by this day in mine *e* 1Sa 26:24 5869
much set by in the *e* of the LORD 1Sa 26:24 5869
I have now found grace in thine *e* 1Sa 27:5 5869
to day in the *e* of the handmaids 2Sa 6:20 5869
take thy wives before thine *e* 2Sa 12:11 5869
kept the watch lifted up his *e* 2Sa 13:34 5869
find favour in the *e* of the LORD 2Sa 15:25 5869
unto the wall, and lifted up his *e* 2Sa 18:24 5869
therefore what is good in thine *e* 2Sa 19:27 5869
but thine *e* are upon the haughty, 2Sa 22:28 5869
that the *e* of my lord the king 2Sa 24:3 5869
the *e* of all Israel are upon thee 1Kin 1:20 5869
this day, mine *e* even seeing it 1Kin 1:48 5869
That thine *e* may be open toward 1Kin 8:29 5869
That thine *e* may be open unto the 1Kin 8:52 5869
and mine *e* and mine heart shall be 1Kin 9:3 5869
I came, and mine *e* had seen it 1Kin 10:7 5869
do that which is right in mine *e* 1Kin 11:33 5869
for his *e* were set by reason of 1Kin 14:4 5869
only which was right in mine *e* 1Kin 14:8 5869
was right in the *e* of the LORD 1Kin 15:5 5869
was right in the *e* of the LORD 1Kin 15:11 5869
wrought evil in the *e* of the LORD 1Kin 16:25 5869
whatsoever is pleasant in thine *e* 1Kin 20:6 5869
was right in the *e* of the LORD 1Kin 22:43 5869
his *e* upon his *e*, and his hands 2Kin 4:34 5869
times, and the child opened his *e* 2Kin 4:35 5869
LORD, I pray thee, open his *e* 2Kin 6:17 5869
opened the *e* of the young man 2Kin 6:17 5869
open the *e* of these men, that 2Kin 6:20 5869
And the LORD opened their *e* 2Kin 6:20 5869
thou shalt see it with thine *e* 2Kin 7:2 5869
thou shalt see it with thine *e* 2Kin 7:19 5869
that which is good in thine *e* 2Kin 10:5 5869
that which is right in mine *e* 2Kin 10:30 5869
open, LORD, thine *e*, and see 2Kin 19:16 5869
and lifted up thine *e* on high 2Kin 19:22 5869
thine *e* shall not see all the 2Kin 22:20 5869
the sons of Zedekiah before his *e* 2Kin 25:7 5869
and put out the *e* of Zedekiah 2Kin 25:7 5869
right in the *e* of all the people 1Chr 13:4 5869
this was a small thing in thine *e* 1Chr 17:17 5869
And David lifted up his *e*, and saw 1Chr 21:16 5869
do that which is good in his *e* 1Chr 21:23 5869
That thine *e* may be open upon 2Chr 6:20 5869
thine *e* be open, and let thine 2Chr 6:40 5869
Now mine *e* shall be open, and mine 2Chr 7:15 5869
and mine *e* and mine heart shall be 2Chr 7:16 5869
I came, and mine *e* had seen it 2Chr 9:6 5869
right in the *e* of the LORD his 2Chr 14:2 5869
For the *e* of the LORD run to and 2Chr 16:9 5869
but our *e* are upon thee 2Chr 20:12 5869
was evil in the *e* of the LORD 2Chr 21:6 5869
evil in the *e* of the LORD our God 2Chr 29:6 5869
to hissing, as ye see with your *e* 2Chr 29:8 5869
neither shall thine *e* see all the 2Chr 34:28 5869
house was laid before their *e* Ezr 3:12 5870
that our God may lighten our *e* Ezr 9:8 5869
now be attentive, and thine *e* open Neh 1:6 5869
much cast down in their own *e* Neh 6:16 5869
despise their husbands in their *e* Est 1:17 5869
king, and I be pleasing in his *e* Est 8:5 5869
they lifted up their *e* afar off Job 2:12 5869
womb, nor hid sorrow from mine *e* Job 3:10 5869
an image was before mine *e* Job 4:16 5869
thine *e* are upon me, and I am not Job 7:8 5869
Hast thou *e* of flesh Job 10:4 5869
is pure, and I am clean in thine *e* Job 11:4 5869
But the *e* of the wicked shall Job 11:20 5869
open thine *e* upon such an one Job 14:3 5869
and what do thy *e* wink at, Job 15:12 5869
enemy sharpeneth his *e* upon me Job 16:9 5869
even the *e* of his children shall Job 17:5 5869
mine *e* shall behold, and not Job 19:27 5869
and their offspring before their *e* Job 21:8 5869
His *e* shall see his destruction, Job 21:20 5869
yet his *e* are upon their ways Job 24:23 5869
he openeth his *e*, and he is not Job 27:19 5869
is hid from the *e* of all living Job 28:21 5869
I was *e* to the blind, and feet was Job 29:15 5869
I made a covenant with mine *e* Job 31:1 5869
and mine heart walked after mine *e* Job 31:7 5869
or have caused the *e* of the widow Job 31:16 5869
he was righteous in his own *e* Job 32:1 5869
For his *e* are upon the ways of Job 34:21 5869
not his *e* from the righteous Job 36:7 5869
prey, and her *e* behold afar off Job 39:29 5869
He taketh it with his *e* Job 40:24 5869
his *e* are like the eyelids of the Job 41:18 5869
his *e* are privily set against the Ps 10:8 5869
his *e* behold, his eyelids try, Ps 11:4 5869
lighten mine *e*, lest I sleep the Ps 13:3 5869
In whose *e* a vile person is Ps 15:4 5869
let thine *e* behold the things Ps 17:2 5869
they have set their *e* bowing down Ps 17:11 5869

LORD is pure, enlightening the e Ps 19:8 5869
Mine e are ever toward the LORD Ps 25:15 5869
lovingkindness is before mine e Ps 26:3 5869
I am cut off from before thine e Ps 31:22 5869
The e of the LORD are upon the Ps 34:15 5869
is no fear of God before his e Ps 36:1 5869
flattereth himself in his own e Ps 36:2 5869
as for the light of mine e Ps 38:10 5869
set them in order before thine e Ps 50:21 5869
his e behold the nations Ps 66:7 5869
mine e fail while I wait for my Ps 69:3 5869
Let their e be darkened, that Ps 69:23 5869
Their e stand out with fatness Ps 73:7 5869
Thou holdest mine e waking Ps 77:4 5869
Only with thine e shalt thou Ps 91:8 5869
set no wicked thing before mine e Ps 101:3 5869
Mine e shall be upon the faithful Ps 101:6 5869
e have they, but they see not Ps 115:5 5869
mine e from tears, and my feet Ps 116:8 5869
it is marvellous in our e Ps 118:23 5869
Open thou mine e, that I may Ps 119:18 5869
Turn away mine e from beholding Ps 119:37 5869
Mine e fail for thy word, saying Ps 119:82 5869
Mine e fail for thy salvation, and Ps 119:123 5869
Rivers of waters run down mine e Ps 119:136 5869
Mine e prevent the night watches Ps 119:148 5869
lift up mine e unto the hills Ps 121:1 5869
Unto thee lift I up mine e Ps 123:1 5869
as the e of servants look unto Ps 123:2 5869
as the e of a maiden unto the Ps 123:2 5869
so our e wait upon the LORD our Ps 123:2 5869
is not haughty, nor mine e lofty Ps 131:1 5869
I will not give sleep to mine e Ps 132:4 5869
e have they, but they see not Ps 135:16 5869
Thine e did see my substance, yet Ps 139:16 5869
But mine e are unto thee, O GOD Ps 141:8 5869
The e of all wait upon thee Ps 145:15 5869
LORD openeth the e of the blind Ps 146:8
Be not wise in thine own e Prov 3:7 5869
let not them depart from thine e Prov 3:21 5869
Let them not depart from thine e Prov 4:21 5869
Let thine e look right on, and let Prov 4:25 5869
man are before the e of the LORD Prov 5:21 5869
Give not sleep to thine e Prov 6:4 5869
He winketh with his e, he Prov 6:13 5869
the teeth, and as smoke to the e Prov 10:26 5869
of a fool is right in his own e Prov 12:15 5869
The e of the LORD are in every Prov 15:3 5869
The light of the e rejoiceth the Prov 15:30 5869
of a man are clean in his own e Prov 16:2 5869
He shutteth his e to devise Prov 16:30 5869
in the e of him that hath it Prov 17:8 5869
but the e of a fool are in the Prov 17:24 5869
away all evil with his e Prov 20:8 5869
open thine e, and thou shalt be Prov 20:13 5869
of a man is right in his own e Prov 21:2 5869
findeth no favour in his e Prov 21:10 5869
The e of the LORD preserve Prov 22:12 5869
Wilt thou set thine e upon that Prov 23:5 5869
let thine e observe my ways Prov 23:26 5869
who hath redness of e Prov 23:29 5869
Thine e shall behold strange Prov 23:33 5869
the prince whom thine e have seen Prov 25:7 5869
so the e of man are never Prov 27:20 5869
but he that hideth his e shall Prov 28:27 5869
the LORD lighteneth both their e Prov 29:13 5869
that are pure in their own e Prov 30:12 5869
O how lofty are their e Prov 30:13 5869
whatsoever mine e desired I kept Eccl 2:10 5869
The wise man's e are in his head Eccl 2:14 5869
beholding of them with their e Eccl 5:11 5869
the e than the wandering of the Eccl 6:9 5869
nor night seeth sleep with his e Eccl 8:16 5869
it is for the e to behold the sun Eccl 11:7 5869
heart, and in the sight of thine e Eccl 11:9 5869
thou hast doves' e Song 1:15 5869
hast doves' e within thy locks Song 4:1 5869
my heart with one of thine e Song 4:9 5869
His e are as the e of doves by Song 5:12 5869
Turn away thine e from me Song 6:5 5869
thine e like the fishpools in Song 7:4 5869
then was I in his e as one that Song 8:10 5869
I will hide mine e from you Is 1:15 5869
of your doings from before mine e Is 1:16 5869
to provoke the e of his glory Is 3:8 5869
stretched forth necks and wanton e Is 3:16 5869
the e of the lofty shall be Is 5:15 5869
them that are wise in their own e Is 5:21 5869
for mine e have seen the King Is 6:5 5869
their ears heavy, and shut their e Is 6:10 5869
lest they see with their e Is 6:10 5869
judge after the sight of his e Is 11:3 5869
dashed to pieces before their e Is 13:16 5869
his e shall have respect to the Is 17:7 5869
deep sleep, and hath closed your e Is 29:10 5869
the e of the blind shall see out Is 29:18 5869
but thine e shall see thy Is 30:20 5869
the e of them that see shall not Is 32:3 5869
shutteth his e from seeing evil Is 33:15 5869
Thine e shall see the king in his Is 33:17 5869
thine e shall see Jerusalem a Is 33:20 5869
Then the e of the blind shall be Is 35:5 5869
open thine e, O LORD, and see Is 37:17 5869
and lifted up thine e on high Is 37:23 5869
mine e fail with looking upward Is 38:14 5869
Lift up your e on high, and behold Is 40:26 5869
To open the blind e, to bring out Is 42:7 5869
the blind people that have e Is 43:8 5869
for he hath shut their e, that Is 44:18 5869
be glorious in the e of the LORD Is 49:5 5869
Lift up thine e round about Is 49:18 5869
Lift up your e to the heavens, and Is 51:6 5869
arm in the e of all the nations Is 52:10 5869
and we grope as if we had no e Is 59:10 5869
Lift up thine e round about Is 60:4 5869
but did evil before mine e Is 65:12 5869
because they are hid from mine e Is 65:16 5869
but they did evil before mine e Is 66:4 5869
Lift up thine e unto the high Jer 3:2 5869
are not thine e upon the truth Jer 5:3 5869
which have e, and see not Jer 5:21 5869
become a den of robbers in your e Jer 7:11 5869
mine e a fountain of tears, that Jer 9:1 5869
that our e may run down with Jer 9:18 5869
Lift up your e, and behold them Jer 13:20 5869
their e did fail, because there Jer 14:6 5869
Let mine e run down with tears Jer 14:17 5869
cease out of this place in your e Jer 16:9 5869
For mine e are upon all their Jer 16:17 5869
is their iniquity hid from mine e Jer 16:17 5869
and thine e shall behold it Jer 20:4 5869
But thine e and thine heart are Jer 22:17 5869
set mine e upon them for good Jer 24:6 5869
he shall slay them before your e Jer 29:21 5869
weeping, and thine e from tears Jer 31:16 5869
his e shall behold his e Jer 32:4 5869
for thine e are open upon all the Jer 32:19 5869
thine e shall behold the e of Jer 34:3 5869
the e of the king of Babylon Jer 34:3 5869
Zedekiah in Riblah before his e Jer 39:6 5869
Moreover he put out Zedekiah's e Jer 39:7 5869
of many, as thine e do behold us Jer 42:2 5869
was evil in the e of the LORD Jer 52:2 5869
the sons of Zedekiah before his e Jer 52:10 5869
Then he put out the e of Zedekiah Jer 52:11 5869
Mine e do fail with tears, my Lam 2:11 5869
our e as yet failed for our vain Lam 4:17 5869
for these things our e are dim Lam 5:17 5869
full of e round about them four Eze 1:18 5869
departed from me, and with their e Eze 6:9 5869
lift up thine e now the way Eze 8:5 5869
So I lifted up mine e the way Eze 8:5 5869
were full of e round about Eze 10:12 5869
house, which have e to see Eze 12:2 5869
he see not the ground with his e Eze 12:12 5869
neither hath lifted up his e to Eze 18:6 5869
hath lifted up his e to the idols Eze 18:12 5869
neither hath lifted up his e to Eze 18:15 5869
man the abominations of his e Eze 20:7 5869
away the abominations of their e Eze 20:8 5869
their e were after their fathers' Eze 20:24 5869
bitterness sigh before their e Eze 21:6 5869
have hid their e from my sabbaths Eze 22:26 5869
soon as she saw them with her e Eze 23:16 5869
not lift up thine e unto them Eze 23:27 5869
wash thyself, paintedst thy e Eze 23:40 5869
desire of thine e with a stroke Eze 24:16 5869
strength, the desire of your e Eze 24:21 5869
glory, the desire of their e Eze 24:25 5869
lift up your e toward your idols Eze 33:25 5869
sanctified in you before their e Eze 36:23 5869
be in thine hand before their e Eze 37:20 5869
in thee, O Gog, before their e Eze 38:16 5869
be known in the e of many nations Eze 38:23 5869
Son of man, behold with thine e Eze 40:4 5869
mark well, and behold with thine e Eze 44:5 5869
lifted up mine e unto heaven Dan 4:34 5870
in this horn were e like the e Dan 7:8 5870
horn were e like the e of man Dan 7:8 5870
even of that horn that had e Dan 7:20 5870
Then I lifted up mine e, and saw Dan 8:3 5869
had a notable horn between his e Dan 8:5 5869
between his e is the first king Dan 8:21 5869
open thine e, and behold our Dan 9:18 5869
Then I lifted up mine e, and Dan 10:5 5869
his e as lamps of fire, and his Dan 10:6 5869
shall be hid from mine e Hos 13:14 5869
not the meat cut off before our e Joel 1:16 5869
I will set mine e upon them for Amos 9:4 5869
the e of the Lord GOD are upon Amos 9:8 5869
mine e shall behold her Mic 7:10 5869
Thou art of purer e than to Hab 1:13 5869
back your captivity before your e Zeph 3:20 5869
is it not in your e in comparison Hag 2:3 5869
Then lifted I up mine e, and saw Zec 1:18 5869
I lifted up mine e again, and Zec 2:1 5869
upon one stone shall be seven e Zec 3:9 5869
they are the e of the LORD Zec 4:10 5869
I turned, and lifted up mine e Zec 5:1 5869
said unto me, Lift up now thine e Zec 5:5 5869
Then lifted I up mine e, and Zec 5:9 5869
And I turned, and lifted up mine e Zec 6:1 5869
If it be marvellous in the e of Zec 8:6 5869
it also be marvellous in mine e Zec 8:6 5869
when the e of man, as of all the Zec 9:1 5869
for now have I seen with mine e Zec 9:8 5869
I will open mine e upon the house Zec 12:4 5869
their e shall consume away in Zec 14:12 5869
your e shall see, and ye shall say Mal 1:5 5869
Then touched he their e, saying Mt 9:29 3788
And their e were opened Mt 9:30 3788
and their e they have closed Mt 13:15 3788
time they should see with their e Mt 13:15 3788
But blessed are your e, for they Mt 13:16 3788
when they had lifted up their e Mt 17:8 3788
rather than having two e to be Mt 18:9 3788
Lord, that our e may be opened Mt 20:33 3788
on them, and touched their e Mt 20:34
their e received sight, and they Mt 20:34 3788
and it is marvellous in our e Mt 21:42 3788
for their e were heavy Mt 26:43 3788
Having e, see ye not Mk 8:18 3788
and when he had spit on his e Mk 8:23 3659
he put his hands again upon his e Mk 8:25 3788
than having two e to be cast into Mk 9:47 3788
and it is marvellous in our e Mk 12:11 3788
again, (for their e were heavy Mk 14:40 3788
For mine e have seen thy Lk 2:30 3788
the e of all them that were in Lk 4:20 3788
lifted up his e on his disciples Lk 6:20 3788
Blessed are the e which see the Lk 10:23 3788
And in hell he lift up his e Lk 16:23 3788
up so much as his e unto heaven Lk 18:13 3788
but now they are hid from thine e Lk 19:42 3788
But their e were holden that they Lk 24:16 3788
their e were opened, and they knew Lk 24:31 3788
I say unto you, Lift up your e Jn 4:35 3788
When Jesus then lifted up his e Jn 6:5 3788
he anointed the e of the blind Jn 9:6 3788
unto him, How were thine e opened Jn 9:10 3788
made clay, and anointed mine e Jn 9:11 3788
made the clay, and opened his e Jn 9:14 3788
them, He put clay upon mine e Jn 9:15 3788
him, that he hath opened thine e Jn 9:17 3788
or who hath opened his e, we know Jn 9:21 3788
how opened he thine e Jn 9:26 3788
is, and yet he hath opened mine e Jn 9:30 3788
the e of one that was born blind Jn 9:32 3788
a devil open the e of the blind Jn 10:21 3788
which opened the e of the blind Jn 11:37 3788
And Jesus lifted up his e, and said Jn 11:41 3788
He hath blinded their e, and Jn 12:40 3788
they should not see with their e Jn 12:40 3788
and lifted up his e to heaven Jn 17:1 3788
fastening his e upon him with Acts 3:4
when his e were opened, he saw no Acts 9:8 3788
from his e as it had been scales Acts 9:18 3788
And she opened her e Acts 9:40 3788
which when I had fastened mine e Acts 11:6
the Holy Ghost, set his e on him Acts 13:9
To open their e, and to turn them Acts 26:18 3788
and their e have they closed Acts 28:27 3788
lest they should see with their e Acts 28:27 3788
is no fear of God before their e Rom 3:18 3788
e that they should not see, and Rom 11:8 3788
Let their e be darkened, that Rom 11:10 3788
before whose e Jesus Christ hath Gal 3:1 3788
would have plucked out your own e Gal 4:15 3788
The e of your understanding being Eph 1:18 3788
opened unto the e of him with Heb 4:13 3788
For the e of the Lord are over 1Pet 3:12 3788
Having e full of adultery, and 2Pet 2:14 3788
which we have seen with our e 1Jn 1:1 3788
that darkness hath blinded his e 1Jn 2:11 3788
the flesh, and the lust of the e 1Jn 2:16 3788
his e were as a flame of fire Rev 1:14 3788
who hath his e like unto a flame Rev 2:18 3788
anoint thine e with eyesalve Rev 3:18 3788
were four beasts full of e before Rev 4:6 3788
and they were full of e within Rev 4:8 3788
having seven horns and seven e Rev 5:6 3788
wipe away all tears from their e Rev 7:17 3788
His e were as a flame of fire, and Rev 19:12 3788
wipe away all tears from their e Rev 21:4 3788

EYESALVE
and anoint thine eyes with e Rev 3:18 2854

EYESERVICE
Not with e, as menpleasers Eph 6:6 3787
not with e, as menpleasers Col 3:22 3787

EYESIGHT
cleanness of my hands in his e Ps 18:24 5869

EYEWITNESSES
which from the beginning were e Lk 1:2 845
but were e of his majesty 2Pet 1:16 2030

EZAR (*e'-zar*) See EZER. *A son of Seir.*
Zibeon, and Anah, and Dishon, and E 1Chr 1:38 687

EZBAI (*ez'-bahee*) *Father of Naarai.*
Carmelite, Naarai the son of E 1Chr 11:37 229

EZBON (*ez'-bon*)
1. Son of Gad.
Ziphion, and Haggi, Shuni, and E Gen 46:16 675
2. Son of Bela.
E, and Uzzi, and Uzziel, and 1Chr 7:7 675

EZEKIAS (*ez-e-ki'-as*) See HEZEKIAH. *Greek form of Hezekiah.*
and Achaz begat E Mt 1:9 1478
And E begat Manasses Mt 1:10 1478

EZEKIEL *A priest and prophet.*
came expressly unto E the priest Eze 1:3 3168
Thus E is unto you a sign Eze 24:24 3168

EZEL *A boundary stone.*
and shalt remain by the stone E 1Sa 20:19 237

EZEM *A city in Judah.*
And at Bilhah, and at E, and at 1Chr 4:29 6107

EZER
1. Son of Seir the Horite.
And Dishon, and E, and Dishan Gen 36:21 687
The children of E are these Gen 36:27 687
Duke Dishon, duke E, duke Dishan Gen 36:30 687
The sons of E; Bilhan 1Chr 1:42 687
2. A descendant of Judah.
Gedor, and E the father of Hushah 1Chr 4:4 5829
3. A son of Ephraim.
son, and Shuthelah his son, and E 1Chr 7:21 5827
4. A Gadite who fought for David.
E the first, Obadiah the second 1Chr 12:9 5829
5. A Levite who repaired the Jerusalem wall.
him repaired E the son of Jeshua Neh 3:19 5829
6. A priest in the time of Nehemiah.
and Malchijah, and Elam, and E Neh 12:42 5829

EZION-GABER *Same as Ezion-geber.*
from Ebronah, and encamped at E Num 33:35 6100
And they removed from E, and Num 33:36 6100
the plain from Elath, and from E Deut 2:8 6100
and they made the ships in E 2Chr 20:36 6100

EZION-GEBER (*e'-ze-on-ghe'-bur*) See EZION-GABER. *An Israelite seaport.*
Solomon made a navy of ships in *E* ... 1Kin 9:26 6100
for the ships were broken at *E* ... 1Kin 22:48 6100
Then went Solomon to *E*, and to ... 2Chr 8:17 6100

EZNITE (*ez'-nite*) *Descendant of Adino.*
the same was Adino the *E* ... 2Sa 23:8 6112

EZRA (*ez'-rah*) See AZARIAH, EZRAHITE.
1. A descendant of Judah.
And the sons of *E* were, Jether, and ... 1Chr 4:17 5830
2. Priest who led exiles back to Jerusalem.
E the son of Seraiah, the son of ... Ezr 7:1 5830
This *E* went up from Babylon ... Ezr 7:6 5830
For *E* had prepared his heart to ... Ezr 7:10 5830
Artaxerxes gave unto *E* the priest ... Ezr 7:11 5830
unto *E* the priest, a scribe of ... Ezr 7:12 5830
that whatsoever *E* the priest ... Ezr 7:21 5830
And thou, *E*, after the wisdom of ... Ezr 7:25 5830
Now when *E* had prayed ... Ezr 10:1 5830
of Elam, answered and said unto *E* ... Ezr 10:2 5830
Then arose *E*, and made the chief ... Ezr 10:5 5830
Then *E* rose up from before the ... Ezr 10:6 5830
E the priest stood up, and said ... Ezr 10:10 5830
E the priest, with certain chief ... Ezr 10:16 5830
they spake unto *E* the scribe to ... Neh 8:1 5830
E the priest brought the law ... Neh 8:2 5830
E the scribe stood upon a pulpit ... Neh 8:4 5830
E opened the book in the sight of ... Neh 8:5 5830
E blessed the LORD, the great God ... Neh 8:6 5830
E the priest the scribe, and the ... Neh 8:9 5830
unto *E* the scribe, even to ... Neh 8:13 5830
Of *E*, Meshullam ... Neh 12:13 5830
of *E* the priest, the scribe ... Neh 12:26 5830
And Azariah, *E*, and Meshullam, ... Neh 12:33 5830
God, and *E* the scribe before them ... Neh 12:36 5830
3. A priest who returned from exile.
Seraiah, Jeremiah, *E*, ... Neh 12:1 5830

EZRAH See EZRA.

EZRAHITE (*ez'-rah-hite*)
than Ethan the *E*, and Heman, and ... 1Kin 4:31 250
Leannoth, Maschil of Heman the *E* ... Ps 88:*t* 250
Maschil of Ethan the *E* ... Ps 89:*t* 250

EZRI (*ez'-ri*) *A superintendent of David.*
ground was *E* the son of Chelub ... 1Chr 27:26 5836

F

FABLES
Neither give heed to *f* and endless ... 1Ti 1:4 *3454*
refuse profane and old wives' *f* ... 1Ti 4:7 *3454*
truth, and shall be turned unto *f* ... 2Ti 4:4 *3454*
Not giving heed to Jewish *f* ... Titus 1:14 *3454*
not followed cunningly devised *f* ... 2Pet 1:16 *3454*

FACE
was upon the *f* of the deep ... Gen 1:2 6440
moved upon the *f* of the waters ... Gen 1:2 6440
is upon the *f* of all the earth ... Gen 1:29 6440
watered the whole *f* of the ground ... Gen 2:6 6440
In the sweat of thy *f* shalt thou ... Gen 3:19 639
this day from the *f* of the earth ... Gen 4:14 6440
from thy *f* shall I be hid ... Gen 4:14 6440
to multiply on the *f* of the earth ... Gen 6:1 6440
created from the *f* of the earth ... Gen 6:7 6440
alive upon the *f* of all the earth ... Gen 7:3 6440
from off the *f* of the earth ... Gen 7:4 6440
ark went upon the *f* of the waters ... Gen 7:18 6440
was upon the *f* of the ground ... Gen 7:23 6440
from off the *f* of the ground ... Gen 8:8 6440
were on the *f* of the whole earth ... Gen 8:9 6440
the *f* of the ground was dry ... Gen 8:13 6440
upon the *f* of the whole earth ... Gen 11:4 6440
upon the *f* of all the earth ... Gen 11:8 6440
upon the *f* of all the earth ... Gen 11:9 6440
with her, she fled from her *f* ... Gen 16:6 6440
I flee from the *f* of my mistress ... Gen 16:8 6440
And Abram fell on his *f* ... Gen 17:3 6440
Then Abraham fell upon his *f* ... Gen 17:17 6440
with his *f* toward the ground ... Gen 19:1 639
great before the *f* of the LORD ... Gen 19:13 6440
and I put the earring upon her *f* ... Gen 24:47 639
come for my hire before thy *f* ... Gen 30:33 6440
set his *f* toward the mount Gilead ... Gen 31:21 6440
me, and afterward I will see his *f* ... Gen 32:20 6440
for I have seen God *f* to *f* ... Gen 32:30 6440
for therefore I have seen thy *f* ... Gen 33:10 6440
as though I had seen the *f* of God ... Gen 33:10 6440
from the *f* of Esau thy brother ... Gen 35:1 6440
he fled from the *f* of his brother ... Gen 35:7 6440
from the *f* of his brother Jacob ... Gen 36:6 6440
because she had covered her *f* ... Gen 38:15 6440
was over all the *f* of the earth ... Gen 41:56 6440
us, saying, Ye shall not see my *f* ... Gen 43:3 6440
unto us, Ye shall not see my *f* ... Gen 43:5 6440
And he washed his *f*, and went out, ... Gen 43:31 6440
you, ye shall see my *f* no more ... Gen 44:23 6440
for we may not see the man's *f* ... Gen 44:26 6440
to direct his *f* unto Goshen ... Gen 46:28 6440
me die, since I have seen thy *f* ... Gen 46:30 6440
I had not thought to see thy *f* ... Gen 48:11 6440
himself with his *f* to the earth ... Gen 48:12 639
Joseph fell upon his father's *f* ... Gen 50:1 6440
went and fell down before his *f* ... Gen 50:18 6440
Moses fled from the *f* of Pharaoh ... Ex 2:15 6440
And Moses hid his *f* ... Ex 3:6 6440
shall cover the *f* of the earth ... Ex 10:5 5869
covered the *f* of the whole earth ... Ex 10:15 5869
heed to thyself, see my *f* no more ... Ex 10:28 6440
thou seest my *f* thou shalt die ... Ex 10:28 6440
I will see thy *f* again no more ... Ex 10:29 6440
cloud went from before their *f* ... Ex 14:19 6440
Let us flee from the *f* of Israel ... Ex 14:25 6440
upon the *f* of the wilderness ... Ex 16:14 6440
them from the *f* of the earth ... Ex 32:12 6440
LORD spake unto Moses *f* to *f* ... Ex 33:11 6440
that are upon the *f* of the earth ... Ex 33:16 6440
he said, Thou canst not see my *f* ... Ex 33:20 6440
but my *f* shall not be seen ... Ex 33:23 6440
wist not that the skin of his *f* ... Ex 34:29 6440
behold, the skin of his *f* shone ... Ex 34:30 6440
with them, he put a vail on his *f* ... Ex 34:33 6440
of Israel saw the *f* of Moses ... Ex 34:35 6440
that the skin of Moses' *f* shone ... Ex 34:35 6440
put the vail upon his *f* again ... Ex 34:35 6440
the part of his head toward his *f* ... Lev 13:41 6440
I will even set my *f* against that ... Lev 17:10 6440
honour the *f* of the old man, and ... Lev 19:32 6440
I will set my *f* against that man, ... Lev 20:3 6440
I will set my *f* against that man ... Lev 20:5 6440
even set my *f* against that soul ... Lev 20:6 6440
And I will set my *f* against you ... Lev 26:17 6440
LORD make his *f* shine upon thee ... Num 6:25 6440
high upon the *f* of the earth ... Num 11:31 6440
were upon the *f* of the earth ... Num 12:3 6440
her father had but spit in her *f* ... Num 12:14 6440
that thou LORD art seen *f* to *f* ... Num 14:14 5869
heard it, he fell upon his *f* ... Num 16:4 6440
one shall slay her before his *f* ... Num 19:3 6440
they cover the *f* of the earth ... Num 22:5 5869
which covereth the *f* of the earth ... Num 22:11 5869
his head, and fell flat on his *f* ... Num 22:31 639
but he set his *f* toward the ... Num 24:1 6440
not be afraid of the *f* of man ... Deut 1:17 6440
LORD talked with you *f* to *f* in ... Deut 5:4 6440
thee from off the *f* of the earth ... Deut 6:15 6440
that are upon the *f* of the earth ... Deut 7:6 6440
them that hate him to their *f* ... Deut 7:10 6440
him, he will repay him to his *f* ... Deut 7:10 6440
the LORD destroyeth before your *f* ... Deut 8:20 6440
bring them down before thy *f* ... Deut 9:3 6440
and to be beaten before his *f* ... Deut 25:2 6440
off his foot, and spit in his *f* ... Deut 25:9 6440
thee to be smitten before thy *f* ... Deut 28:7 6440
taken away from before thy *f* ... Deut 28:31 6440
shall give them up before your *f* ... Deut 31:5 6440
and I will hide my *f* from them ... Deut 31:17 6440
I will surely hide my *f* in that ... Deut 31:18 6440
said, I will hide my *f* from them ... Deut 32:20 6440
whom the LORD knew *f* to *f* ... Deut 34:10 6440
Joshua fell on his *f* to the earth ... Josh 5:14 6440
his *f* before the ark of the LORD ... Josh 7:6 6440
liest thou thus upon thy *f* ... Josh 7:10 6440
an angel of the LORD *f* to *f* ... Judg 6:22 6440
Then she fell on her *f*, and bowed ... Ruth 2:10 6440
Dagon was fallen upon his *f* to ... 1Sa 5:3 6440
Dagon was fallen upon his *f* to ... 1Sa 5:4 6440
he fell upon his *f* to the earth ... 1Sa 17:49 6440
every one from the *f* of the earth ... 1Sa 20:15 6440
fell on his *f* to the ground, and ... 1Sa 20:41 639
stooped with his *f* to the earth ... 1Sa 24:8 639
and fell before David on her *f* ... 1Sa 25:23 6440
herself on her *f* to the earth ... 1Sa 25:41 639
earth before the *f* of the LORD ... 1Sa 26:20 6440
stooped with his *f* to the ground ... 1Sa 28:14 639
hold up my *f* to Joab thy brother ... 2Sa 2:22 6440
that is, Thou shalt not see my *f* ... 2Sa 3:13 6440
when thou comest to see my *f* ... 2Sa 3:13 6440
come unto David, he fell on his *f* ... 2Sa 9:6 6440
she fell on her *f* to the ground ... 2Sa 14:4 639
Joab fell to the ground on his *f* ... 2Sa 14:22 6440
house, and let him not see my *f* ... 2Sa 14:24 6440
house, and saw not the king's *f* ... 2Sa 14:24 6440
and saw not the king's *f* ... 2Sa 14:28 6440
therefore let me see the king's *f* ... 2Sa 14:32 6440
bowed himself on his *f* to the ... 2Sa 14:33 639
over the *f* of all the country ... 2Sa 18:8 6440
earth upon his *f* before the king ... 2Sa 18:28 639
But the king covered his *f* ... 2Sa 19:4 6440
the king on his *f* upon the ground ... 2Sa 24:20 639
the king with his *f* to the ground ... 1Kin 1:23 639
bowed with her *f* to the earth ... 1Kin 1:31 639
And the king turned his *f* about ... 1Kin 8:14 6440
Intreat now the *f* of the LORD thy ... 1Kin 13:6 6440
it from off the *f* of the earth ... 1Kin 13:34 6440
and he knew him, and fell on his *f* ... 1Kin 18:7 6440
put his *f* between his knees, ... 1Kin 18:42 6440
he wrapped his *f* in his mantle ... 1Kin 19:13 6440
himself with ashes upon his *f* ... 1Kin 20:38 5869
and took the ashes away from his *f* ... 1Kin 20:41 5869
his bed, and turned away his *f* ... 1Kin 21:4 6440
my staff upon the *f* of the child ... 2Kin 4:29 6440
the staff upon the *f* of the child ... 2Kin 4:31 6440
in water, and spread it on his *f* ... 2Kin 8:15 6440
and she painted her *f*, and tired ... 2Kin 9:30 5869
he lifted up his *f* to the window ... 2Kin 9:32 6440
shall be as dung upon the *f* of ... 2Kin 9:37 6440
Hazael set his *f* to go up to ... 2Kin 12:17 6440
down unto him, and wept over his *f* ... 2Kin 13:14 6440
let us look one another in the *f* ... 2Kin 14:8 6440
another in the *f* at Beth-shemesh ... 2Kin 14:11 6440
then wilt thou turn away the *f* of ... 2Kin 18:24 6440
Then he turned his *f* to the wall ... 2Kin 20:2 6440
strength, seek his *f* continually ... 1Chr 16:11 6440
to David with his *f* to the ground ... 1Chr 21:21 639
And the king turned his *f*, and ... 2Chr 6:3 6440
not away the *f* of thine anointed ... 2Chr 6:42 6440
themselves, and pray, and seek my *f* ... 2Chr 7:14 6440
his head with his *f* to the ground ... 2Chr 20:18 639
let us see one another in the *f* ... 2Chr 25:17 6440
and they saw one another in the *f* ... 2Chr 25:21 6440
will not turn away his *f* from you ... 2Chr 30:9 6440
with shame of *f* to his own land ... 2Chr 32:21 6440
would not turn his *f* from him ... 2Chr 35:22 6440
and blush to lift up my *f* to thee ... Ezr 9:6 6440
to a spoil, and to confusion of *f* ... Ezr 9:7 6440
and Media, which saw the king's *f* ... Est 1:14 6440
mouth, they covered Haman's *f* ... Est 7:8 6440
and he will curse thee to thy *f* ... Job 1:11 6440
and he will curse thee to thy *f* ... Job 2:5 6440
Then a spirit passed before my *f* ... Job 4:15 6440
thou lift up thy *f* without spot ... Job 11:15 6440
Wherefore hidest thou thy *f* ... Job 13:24 6440
covereth his *f* with his fatness ... Job 15:27 6440
up in me beareth witness to my *f* ... Job 16:8 6440
My *f* is foul with weeping, and on ... Job 16:16 6440
shall declare his way to his *f* ... Job 21:31 6440
and shalt lift up thy *f* unto God ... Job 22:26 6440
he covered the darkness from my *f* ... Job 23:17 6440
and disguiseth his *f* ... Job 24:15 6440
holdeth back the *f* of his throne ... Job 26:9 6440
me, and spare not to spit in my *f* ... Job 30:10 6440
and he shall see his *f* with joy ... Job 33:26 6440
and when he hideth his *f*, who then ... Job 34:29 6440
the *f* of the world in the earth ... Job 37:12 6440
the *f* of the deep is frozen ... Job 38:30 6440
can discover the *f* of his garment ... Job 41:13 6440
Who can open the doors of his *f* ... Job 41:14 6440
make thy way straight before my *f* ... Ps 5:8 6440
he hideth his *f* ... Ps 10:11 6440
long wilt thou hide thy *f* from me ... Ps 13:1 6440
behold thy *f* in righteousness ... Ps 17:15 6440
thy strings against the *f* of them ... Ps 21:12 6440
hath he hid his *f* from him ... Ps 22:24 6440
that seek him, that seek thy *f* ... Ps 24:6 6440
When thou saidst, Seek ye my *f* ... Ps 27:8 6440
my heart said unto thee, Thy *f* ... Ps 27:8 6440
Hide not thy *f* far from me ... Ps 27:9 6440
thou didst hide thy *f*, and I was ... Ps 30:7 6440
Make thy *f* to shine upon thy ... Ps 31:16 6440
The *f* of the LORD is against them ... Ps 34:16 6440
settest me before thy *f* for ever ... Ps 41:12 6440
the shame of my *f* hath covered me ... Ps 44:15 6440
Wherefore hidest thou thy *f* ... Ps 44:24 6440
Hide thy *f* from my sins, and blot ... Ps 51:9 6440
cause his *f* to shine upon us ... Ps 67:1 6440
shame hath covered my *f* ... Ps 69:7 6440
hide not thy *f* from thy servant ... Ps 69:17 6440
O God, and cause thy *f* to shine ... Ps 80:3 6440
of hosts, and cause thy *f* to shine ... Ps 80:7 6440
of hosts, cause thy *f* to shine ... Ps 80:19 6440
look upon the *f* of thine anointed ... Ps 84:9 6440
why hidest thou thy *f* from me ... Ps 88:14 6440
and truth shall go before thy *f* ... Ps 89:14 6440
beat down his foes before his *f* ... Ps 89:23 6440
Hide not thy *f* from me in the day ... Ps 102:2 6440
and oil to make his *f* to shine ... Ps 104:15 6440
Thou hidest thy *f*, they are ... Ps 104:29 6440
thou renewest the *f* of the earth ... Ps 104:30 6440
seek his *f* evermore ... Ps 105:4 6440
Make thy *f* to shine upon thy ... Ps 119:135 6440
not away the *f* of thine anointed ... Ps 132:10 6440
hide not thy *f* from me, lest I be ... Ps 143:7 6440
with an impudent *f* said unto him ... Prov 7:13 6440
thee, diligently to seek thy *f* ... Prov 7:15 6440
a compass upon the *f* of the depth ... Prov 8:27 6440
A wicked man hardeneth his *f* ... Prov 21:29 6440
nettles had covered the *f* thereof ... Prov 24:31 6440
As in water *f* answereth to *f*, ... Prov 27:19 6440
wisdom maketh his *f* to shine ... Eccl 8:1 6440
of his *f* shall be changed ... Eccl 8:1 6440
with twain he covered his *f* ... Is 6:2 6440
that hideth his *f* from the house ... Is 8:17 6440
nor fill the *f* of the world with ... Is 14:21 6440
to them from the *f* of the spoiler ... Is 16:4 6440
the world upon the *f* of the earth ... Is 23:17 6440
destroy in this mountain the *f* of ... Is 25:7 6440
fill the *f* of the world with ... Is 27:6 6440
he hath made plain the *f* thereof ... Is 28:25 6440
neither shall his *f* now wax pale ... Is 29:22 6440
then wilt thou turn away the *f* of ... Is 36:9 6440
turned his *f* toward the wall ... Is 38:2 6440
with their *f* toward the earth ... Is 49:23 639
I hid not my *f* from shame ... Is 50:6 6440
have I set my *f* like a flint ... Is 50:7 6440
I hid my *f* from thee for a moment ... Is 54:8 6440
your sins have hid his *f* from you ... Is 59:2 6440
for thou hast hid thy *f* from us ... Is 64:7 6440
me to anger continually to my *f* ... Is 65:3 6440
the *f* thereof is toward the north ... Jer 1:13 6440
back unto me, and not their *f* ... Jer 2:27 6440

thou rentest thy *f* with painting	Jer 4:30	5869
for dung upon the *f* of the earth	Jer 8:2	6440
I discover thy skirts upon thy *f*	Jer 13:26	6440
as dung upon the *f* of the earth	Jer 16:4	6440
they are not hid from my *f*	Jer 16:17	6440
shew them the back, and not the *f*	Jer 18:17	6440
For I have set my *f* against this	Jer 21:10	6440
hand of them whose *f* thou fearest	Jer 22:25	6440
which are upon the *f* of the earth	Jer 25:26	6440
thee from off the *f* of the earth	Jer 28:16	6440
should remove it from before my *f*	Jer 32:31	6440
unto me the back, and not the *f*	Jer 32:33	6440
I have hid my *f* from this city	Jer 33:5	6440
I will set my *f* against you for	Jer 44:11	6440
water before the *f* of the Lord	Lam 2:19	6440
man before the *f* of the most High	Lam 3:35	6440
they four had the *f* of a man	Eze 1:10	6440
the *f* of a lion, on the right	Eze 1:10	6440
they four had the *f* of an ox on	Eze 1:10	6440
four also had the *f* of an eagle	Eze 1:10	6440
when I saw it, I fell upon my *f*	Eze 1:28	6440
I have made thy *f* strong against	Eze 3:8	6440
and I fell on my *f*	Eze 3:23	6440
set thy *f* against it, and it shall	Eze 4:3	6440
Therefore thou shalt set thy *f*	Eze 4:7	6440
set thy *f* toward the mountains of	Eze 6:2	6440
My *f* will I turn also from them,	Eze 7:22	6440
I was left, that I fell upon my *f*	Eze 9:8	6440
first *f* was the *f* of a cherub	Eze 10:14	6440
second *f* was the *f* of a man	Eze 10:14	6440
and the third the *f* of a lion	Eze 10:14	6440
and the fourth the *f* of an eagle	Eze 10:14	6440
Then fell I down upon my *f*	Eze 11:13	6440
thou shalt cover thy *f*, that thou	Eze 12:6	6440
he shall cover his *f*, that he see	Eze 12:12	6440
set thy *f* against the daughters	Eze 13:17	6440
of their iniquity before their *f*	Eze 14:3	6440
of his iniquity before his *f*	Eze 14:4	6440
of his iniquity before his *f*	Eze 14:7	6440
I will set my *f* against that man,	Eze 14:8	6440
And I will set my *f* against them	Eze 15:7	6440
when I set my *f* against them	Eze 15:7	6440
will I plead with you *f* to *f*	Eze 20:35	6440
will I plead with you *f* to *f*	Eze 20:35	6440
set thy *f* toward the south, and	Eze 20:46	6440
set thy *f* toward Jerusalem, and	Eze 21:2	6440
left, whithersoever thy *f* is set	Eze 21:16	6440
set thy *f* against the Ammonites,	Eze 25:2	6440
set thy *f* against Zidon, and	Eze 28:21	6440
set thy *f* against Pharaoh king of	Eze 29:2	6440
upon all the *f* of the earth	Eze 34:6	6440
set thy *f* against mount Seir, and	Eze 35:2	6440
set thy *f* against Gog, the land	Eze 38:2	6440
my fury shall come up in my *f*	Eze 38:18	639
that are upon the *f* of the earth	Eze 38:20	6440
remain upon the *f* of the earth	Eze 39:14	6440
therefore hid I my *f* from them	Eze 39:23	6440
unto them, and hid my *f* from them	Eze 39:24	6440
I hide my *f* any more from them	Eze 39:29	6440
from the *f* of the gate of the	Eze 40:15	6440
gate of the entrance unto the *f*	Eze 40:15	6440
the breadth of the *f* of the house	Eze 41:14	6440
So that the *f* of a man was toward	Eze 41:19	6440
the *f* of a young lion toward the	Eze 41:19	6440
and the *f* of the sanctuary	Eze 41:21	6440
upon the *f* of the porch without	Eze 41:25	6440
and I fell upon my *f*	Eze 43:3	6440
and I fell upon my *f*	Eze 44:4	6440
Nebuchadnezzar fell upon his *f*	Dan 2:46	600
west on the *f* of the whole earth	Dan 8:5	6440
I was afraid, and fell upon my *f*	Dan 8:17	6440
sleep on my *f* toward the ground	Dan 8:18	6440
I set my *f* unto the Lord God, to	Dan 9:3	6440
to us belongeth confusion of *f*	Dan 9:8	6440
cause thy *f* to shine upon thy	Dan 9:17	6440
his *f* as the appearance of	Dan 10:6	6440
was I in a deep sleep on my *f*	Dan 10:9	6440
and my *f* toward the ground	Dan 10:9	6440
I set my *f* toward the ground, and	Dan 10:15	6440
He shall also set his *f* to enter	Dan 11:17	6440
he turn his *f* unto the isles	Dan 11:18	6440
Then he shall turn his *f* toward	Dan 11:19	6440
of Israel doth testify to his *f*	Hos 5:5	6440
their offence, and seek my *f*	Hos 5:15	6440
they are before my *f*	Hos 7:2	6440
of Israel testifieth to his *f*	Hos 7:10	6440
Before their *f* the people shall	Joel 2:6	6440
with his *f* toward the east sea,	Joel 2:20	6440
them out upon the *f* of the earth	Amos 5:8	6440
them out upon the *f* of the earth	Amos 9:6	6440
it from off the *f* of the earth	Amos 9:8	6440
he will even hide his *f* from them	Mic 3:4	6440
in pieces is come up before thy *f*	Nah 2:1	6440
discover thy skirts upon thy *f*	Nah 3:5	6440
over the *f* of the whole earth	Zec 5:3	6440
anoint thine head, and wash thy *f*	Mt 6:17	*4383*
I send my messenger before thy *f*	Mt 11:10	*4383*
ye can discern the *f* of the sky	Mt 16:3	*4383*
his *f* did shine as the sun, and	Mt 17:2	*4383*
heard it, they fell on their *f*	Mt 17:6	*4383*
angels do always behold the *f* of	Mt 18:10	*4383*
little farther, and fell on his *f*	Mt 26:39	*4383*
Then did they spit in his *f*	Mt 26:67	*4383*
I send my messenger before thy *f*	Mk 1:2	*4383*
to spit on him, and to cover his *f*	Mk 14:65	*4383*
for thou shalt go before the *f* of	Lk 1:76	*4383*
before the *f* of all people	Lk 2:31	*4383*
who seeing Jesus fell on his *f*	Lk 5:12	*4383*
I send my messenger before thy *f*	Lk 7:27	*4383*
set his *f* to go to Jerusalem	Lk 9:51	*4383*
And sent messengers before his *f*	Lk 9:52	*4383*
because his *f* was as though he	Lk 9:53	*4383*
two before his *f* into every city	Lk 10:1	*4383*
ye can discern the *f* of the sky	Lk 12:56	*4383*
And fell down on his *f* at his feet	Lk 17:16	*4383*
dwell on the *f* of the whole earth	Lk 21:35	*4383*
him, they struck him on the *f*	Lk 22:64	*4383*
his *f* was bound about with a	Jn 11:44	*3799*
the Lord always before my *f*	Acts 2:25	*1799*
saw his *f* as it had been the *f*	Acts 6:15	*4383*
out before the *f* of our fathers	Acts 7:45	*4383*
dwell on all the *f* of the earth	Acts 17:26	*4383*
of God, shall see my *f* no more	Acts 20:25	*4383*
they should see his *f* no more	Acts 20:38	*4383*
have the accusers *f* to *f*	Acts 25:16	*4383*
but then *f* to *f*	1Cor 13:12	*4383*
down on his *f* he will worship God	1Cor 14:25	*4383*
f of Moses for the glory of his	2Cor 3:7	*4383*
which put a vail over his *f*	2Cor 3:13	*4383*
with open *f* beholding as in a	2Cor 3:18	*4383*
of God in the *f* of Jesus Christ	2Cor 4:6	*4383*
if a man smite you on the *f*	2Cor 11:20	*4383*
was unknown by *f* unto the	Gal 1:22	*4383*
Antioch, I withstood him to the *f*	Gal 2:11	*4383*
have not seen my *f* in the flesh	Col 2:1	*4383*
to see your *f* with great desire	1Th 2:17	*4383*
that we might see your *f*, and	1Th 3:10	*4383*
his natural *f* in a glass	Jas 1:23	*4383*
but the *f* of the Lord is against	1Pet 3:12	*4383*
speak *f* to *f*, that our joy may	2Jn 12	*4750*
come unto you, and speak *f* to *f*	2Jn 12	*4750*
thee, and we shall speak *f* to *f*	3Jn 14	*4750*
thee, and we shall speak *f* to *f*	3Jn 14	*4750*
the third beast had a *f* as a man	Rev 4:7	*4383*
hide us from the *f* of him that	Rev 6:16	*4383*
his *f* was as it were the sun, and	Rev 10:1	*4383*
from the *f* of the serpent	Rev 12:14	*4383*
sat on it, from whose *f* the earth	Rev 20:11	*4383*
And they shall see his *f*	Rev 22:4	*4383*

FACES

their *f* were backward, and they	Gen 9:23	6440
men turned their *f* from thence	Gen 18:22	
set the *f* of the flocks toward	Gen 30:40	6440
him with their *f* to the earth	Gen 42:6	639
laid before their *f* all these	Ex 19:7	6440
his fear may be before your *f*	Ex 20:20	6440
their *f* shall look one to another	Ex 25:20	6440
shall the *f* of the cherubims be	Ex 25:20	6440
with their *f* one to another	Ex 37:9	6440
were the *f* of the cherubims	Ex 37:9	6440
they shouted, and fell on their *f*	Lev 9:24	6440
Aaron fell on their *f* before all	Num 14:5	6440
And they fell upon their *f*	Num 16:22	6440
And they fell upon their *f*	Num 16:45	6440
and they fell upon their *f*	Num 20:6	6440
and fell on their *f* to the ground	Judg 13:20	6440
And they turned their *f*, and said	Judg 18:23	6440
day the *f* of all thy servants	2Sa 19:5	6440
that all Israel set their *f* on me	1Kin 2:15	6440
saw it, they fell on their *f*	1Kin 18:39	6440
f were like the *f* of lions	1Chr 12:8	6440
in sackcloth, fell upon their *f*	1Chr 21:16	6440
feet, and their *f* were inward	2Chr 3:13	6440
bowed themselves with their *f* to	2Chr 7:3	639
have turned away their *f* from the	2Chr 29:6	6440
LORD with their *f* to the ground	Neh 8:6	639
he covereth the *f* of the judges	Job 9:24	6440
and bind their *f* in secret	Job 40:13	6440
and their *f* were not ashamed	Ps 34:5	6440
Fill their *f* with shame	Ps 83:16	6440
and grind the *f* of the poor	Is 3:15	6440
their *f* shall be as flames	Is 13:8	6440
wipe away tears from off all *f*	Is 25:8	6440
we hid as it were our *f* from him	Is 53:3	6440
Be not afraid of their *f*	Jer 1:8	6440
be not dismayed at their *f*	Jer 1:17	6440
made their *f* harder than a rock	Jer 5:3	6440
to the confusion of their own *f*	Jer 7:19	6440
all *f* are turned into paleness	Jer 30:6	6440
set your *f* to enter into Egypt	Jer 42:15	6440
f to go into Egypt to sojourn	Jer 42:17	6440
that have set their *f* to go into	Jer 44:12	6440
to Zion with their *f* thitherward	Jer 50:5	6440
shame hath covered our *f*	Jer 51:51	6440
the *f* of elders were not honoured	Lam 5:12	6440
And every one had four *f*, and every	Eze 1:6	6440
and they four had their *f* and their	Eze 1:8	6440
As for the likeness of their *f*	Eze 1:10	6440
Thus were their *f*	Eze 1:11	6440
living creatures, with his four *f*	Eze 1:15	6440
thy face strong against their *f*	Eze 3:8	6440
and shame shall be upon all *f*	Eze 7:18	6440
LORD, and their *f* toward the east	Eze 8:16	6440
And every one had four *f*	Eze 10:14	6440
Every one had four *f* apiece	Eze 10:21	6440
the likeness of their *f* was the	Eze 10:22	6440
f which I saw by the river of	Eze 10:22	6440
turn away your *f* from all your	Eze 14:6	6440
all *f* from the south to the north	Eze 20:47	6440
and every cherub had two *f*	Eze 41:18	6440
for why should he see your *f*	Dan 1:10	6440
thee, but unto us confusion of *f*	Dan 9:7	6440
all *f* shall gather blackness	Joel 2:6	6440
and the *f* of them all gather	Nah 2:10	6440
their *f* shall sup up as the east	Hab 1:9	6440
seed, and spread dung upon your *f*	Mal 2:3	6440
for they disfigure their *f*	Mt 6:16	*4383*
bowed down their *f* to the earth	Lk 24:5	*4383*
fell before the throne on their *f*	Rev 7:11	*4383*
their *f* were as the *f* of men	Rev 9:7	*4383*
on their seats, fell upon their *f*	Rev 11:16	*4383*

FADE

Strangers shall *f* away, and they	2Sa 22:46	5034
The strangers shall *f* away	Ps 18:45	5034
and we all do *f* as a leaf	Is 64:6	5034
the fig tree, and the leaf shall *f*	Jer 8:13	5034
for meat, whose leaf shall not *f*	Eze 47:12	5034
the rich man *f* away in his ways	Jas 1:11	*3133*

FADETH

shall be as an oak whose leaf *f*	Is 1:30	5034
f away, the world languisheth and	Is 24:4	5034
f away, the haughty people of the	Is 24:4	5034
The grass withereth, the flower *f*	Is 40:7	5034
The grass withereth, the flower *f*	Is 40:8	5034
that *f* not away, reserved in	1Pet 1:4	*263*
a crown of glory that *f* not away	1Pet 5:4	*262*

FADING

glorious beauty is a *f* flower	Is 28:1	5034
fat valley, shall be a *f* flower	Is 28:4	5034

FAIL

you for your cattle, if money *f*	Gen 47:16	656
f with longing for them all the	Deut 28:32	3615
he will not *f* thee, nor forsake	Deut 31:6	7503
be with thee, he will not *f* thee	Deut 31:8	7503
I will not *f* thee, nor forsake	Josh 1:5	7503
that he will without *f* drive out	Josh 3:10	
If thou shalt without *f* deliver	Judg 11:30	
Let them not *f* to burn the fat	1Sa 2:16	
no man's heart *f* because of him	1Sa 17:32	5307
I should not *f* to sit with the	1Sa 20:5	
them, and without *f* recover all	1Sa 30:8	
let there not *f* from the house of	2Sa 3:29	3772
there shall not *f* thee (said he)	1Kin 2:4	3772
There shall not *f* thee a man in	1Kin 8:25	3772
There shall not *f* thee a man upon	1Kin 9:5	3772
neither shall the cruse of oil *f*	1Kin 17:14	2637
neither did the cruse of oil *f*	1Kin 17:16	2638
he will not *f* thee, nor forsake	1Chr 28:20	7503
There shall not *f* thee a man in	2Chr 6:16	3772
There shall not *f* thee a man to	2Chr 7:18	3772
heed now that ye *f* not to do this	Ezr 4:22	7960
given them day by day without *f*	Ezr 6:9	7960
let nothing *f* of all that thou	Est 6:10	5307
unto them, so as it should not *f*	Est 9:27	5674
should not *f* from among the Jews	Est 9:28	5674
the eyes of the wicked shall *f*	Job 11:20	3615
As the waters *f* from the sea	Job 14:11	235
the eyes of his children shall *f*	Job 17:5	3615
caused the eyes of the widow to *f*	Job 31:16	3615
for the faithful *f* from among the	Ps 12:1	6461
mine eyes *f* while I wait for my	Ps 69:3	3615
doth his promise *f* for evermore	Ps 77:8	1584
nor suffer my faithfulness to *f*	Ps 89:33	8266
Mine eyes *f* for thy word, saying,	Ps 119:82	3615
Mine eyes *f* for thy salvation, and	Ps 119:123	3615
and the rod of his anger shall *f*	Prov 22:8	3615
be a burden, and desire shall *f*	Eccl 12:5	6565
shall *f* in the midst thereof	Is 19:3	1238
the waters shall *f* from the sea	Is 19:5	5405
and all the glory of Kedar shall *f*	Is 21:16	3615
and they all shall *f* together	Is 31:3	3615
the drink of the thirsty to *f*	Is 32:6	2637
for the vintage shall *f*, the	Is 32:10	3615
no one of these shall *f*, none	Is 34:16	5737
mine eyes *f* with looking upward	Is 38:14	1809
He shall not *f* nor be discouraged	Is 42:4	3543
pit, nor that his bread should *f*	Is 51:14	2637
for the spirit should *f* before me	Is 57:16	5848
of water, whose waters *f* not	Is 58:11	3576
their eyes did *f*, because there	Jer 14:6	3615
me as a liar, and as waters that *f*	Jer 15:18	539
wine to *f* from the winepresses	Jer 48:33	7673
Mine eyes do *f* with tears	Lam 2:11	3615
because his compassions *f* not	Lam 3:22	3615
and the new wine shall *f* in her	Hos 9:2	3584
to make the poor of the land to *f*	Amos 8:4	7673
the labour of the olive shall *f*	Hab 3:17	3584
that, when ye *f*, they may receive	Lk 16:9	*1587*
than one tittle of the law to *f*	Lk 16:17	*4098*
for thee, that thy faith *f* not	Lk 22:32	*1587*
there be prophecies, they shall *f*	1Cor 13:8	*2673*
same, and thy years shall not *f*	Heb 1:12	*1587*
for the time would *f* me to tell	Heb 11:32	*1952*
any man *f* of the grace of God	Heb 12:15	*5302*

FAILED

and their heart *f* them, and they	Gen 42:28	3318
when money *f* in the land of Egypt	Gen 47:15	8552
the plain, even the salt sea, *f*	Josh 3:16	8552
There *f* not ought of any good	Josh 21:45	5307
that not one thing hath *f* of all	Josh 23:14	5307
and not one thing hath *f* thereof	Josh 23:14	5307
there hath not *f* one word of all	1Kin 8:56	5307
My kinsfolk have *f*, and my	Job 19:14	2308
refuge *f* me; no man cared	Ps 142:4	6
my soul *f* when he spake	Song 5:6	3318
their might hath *f*	Jer 51:30	5405
our eyes as yet *f* for our vain	Lam 4:17	3615

FAILETH

for the money *f*	Gen 47:15	656
Their bull gendereth, and *f* not	Job 21:10	1602
my strength *f* because of mine	Ps 31:10	3782
heart panteth, my strength *f* me	Ps 38:10	5800
therefore my heart *f* me	Ps 40:12	5800
forsake me not when my strength *f*	Ps 71:9	3615
My flesh and my heart *f*	Ps 73:26	3615
and my flesh *f* of fatness	Ps 109:24	3584
my spirit *f*	Ps 143:7	3615
by the way, his wisdom *f* him	Eccl 10:3	2638
hay is withered away, the grass *f*	Is 15:6	3615
strong in power; not one *f*	Is 40:26	5737
and their tongue *f* for thirst	Is 41:17	5405
he is hungry, and his strength *f*	Is 44:12	369
Yea, truth *f*	Is 59:15	5737
are prolonged, and every vision *f*	Eze 12:22	6
his judgment to light, he *f* not	Zeph 3:5	5737
in the heavens that *f* not	Lk 12:33	*413*
Charity never *f*	1Cor 13:8	*1601*

FAILING
f of eyes, and sorrow of mind Deut 28:65 3631
Men's hearts *f* them for fear, and Lk 21:26 *674*

FAIN
he would *f* flee out of his hand Job 27:22 1272
he would *f* have filled his belly Lk 15:16 *1937*

FAINT
came from the field, and he was *f* Gen 25:29 5889
red pottage; for I am *f* Gen 25:30 5889
let not your hearts *f*, fear not, Deut 20:3 7401
heart *f* as well as his heart Deut 20:8 4549
behind thee, when thou wast *f* Deut 25:18 5889
of the land *f* because of you Josh 2:9 4127
of the country do *f* because of us Josh 2:24 4127
hundred men that were with him, *f* Judg 8:4 5889
for they be *f*, and I am pursuing Judg 8:5 5889
And the people were *f* 1Sa 14:28 5774
and the people were very *f* 1Sa 14:31 5774
which were so *f* that they could 1Sa 30:10 6296
which were so *f* that they could 1Sa 30:21 6296
wine, that such as be *f* in the 2Sa 16:2 3287
and David waxed *f* 2Sa 21:15 5774
If thou *f* in the day of adversity Prov 24:10 7503
is sick, and the whole heart *f* Is 1:5 1742
Therefore shall all hands be *f* Is 13:7 7503
he awaketh, and, behold, he is *f* Is 29:8 5889
He giveth power to the *f* Is 40:29 3287
Even the youths shall *f* and be Is 40:30 3286
and they shall walk, and not *f* Is 40:31 3286
he drinketh no water, and is *f* Is 44:12 3286
sorrow, my heart is *f* in me Jer 8:18 1742
And lest your heart *f*, and ye fear Jer 51:46 7401
made me desolate and *f* all the day Lam 1:13 1738
sighs are many, and my heart is *f* Lam 1:22 1742
that *f* for hunger in the top of Lam 2:19 5848
For this our heart is *f* Lam 5:17 1739
feeble, and every spirit shall *f* Eze 21:7 3543
gates, that their heart may *f* Eze 21:15 4127
virgins and young men *f* for thirst Amos 8:13 5968
fasting, lest they *f* in the way Mt 15:32 *1590*
houses, they will *f* by the way Mk 8:3 *1590*
ought always to pray, and not to *f* Lk 18:1 *1573*
we have received mercy, we *f* not 2Cor 4:1 *1573*
For which cause we *f* not 2Cor 4:16 *1573*
season we shall reap, if we *f* not Gal 6:9 *1590*
Wherefore I desire that ye *f* not Eph 3:13 *1573*
ye be wearied and *f* in your minds Heb 12:3 *1590*
nor *f* when thou art rebuked of Heb 12:5 *1590*

FAINTED
And Jacob's heart *f*, for he Gen 45:26 6313
all the land of Canaan *f* by Gen 47:13 3856
I had *f*, unless I had believed to Ps 27:13
and thirsty, their soul *f* in them Ps 107:5 5848
Thy sons have *f*, they lie at the Is 51:20 5968
I *f* in my sighing, and I find no Jer 45:3 3021
the trees of the field *f* for him Eze 31:15 5969
And I Daniel *f*, and was sick Dan 8:27 1961
When my soul *f* within me I Jonah 2:7 5848
upon the head of Jonah, that he *f* Jonah 4:8 5968
on them, because they *f*, and were Mt 9:36 *1590*
sake hast laboured, and hast not *f* Rev 2:3 *2577*

FAINTEST
it is come upon thee, and thou *f* Job 4:5 3811

FAINTETH
even *f* for the courts of the LORD Ps 84:2 3615
My soul *f* for thy salvation Ps 119:81 3615
be as when a standard-bearer *f* Is 10:18 4549
earth, *f* not, neither is weary Is 40:28 3286

FAINTHEARTED
man is there that is fearful and *f* Deut 20:8 3824
neither be *f* for the two tails of Is 7:4 3824
they are *f* Jer 49:23 4127

FAINTNESS
f into their hearts in the lands Lev 26:36 4816

FAIR
daughters of men that they were *f* Gen 6:2 2896
thou art a *f* woman to look upon Gen 12:11 3303
the woman that she was very *f* Gen 12:14 3303
damsel was very *f* to look upon Gen 24:16 2896
because she was *f* to look upon Gen 26:7 2896
and ruddy, and of a *f* countenance 1Sa 17:42 3303
the son of David had a *f* sister 2Sa 13:1 3303
was a woman of a *f* countenance 2Sa 14:27 3303
So they sought for a *f* damsel 1Kin 1:3 3303
And the damsel was very *f*, and 1Kin 1:4 3303
for she was *f* to look on Est 1:11 2896
Let there be *f* young virgins Est 2:2 2896
may gather together all the *f* Est 2:3 4758
nor mother, and the maid was *f* Est 2:7 3303
F weather cometh out of the north Job 37:22 2091
so *f* as the daughters of Job Job 42:15 3303
With her much *f* speech she caused Prov 7:21 3948
so is a *f* woman which is without Prov 11:22 3303
When he speaketh *f*, believe him Prov 26:25 2603
Behold, thou art *f*, my love Song 1:15 3302
behold, thou art *f* Song 1:15 3302
Behold, thou art *f*, my beloved, Song 1:16 3302
my love, my *f* one, and come away Song 2:10 3302
my love, my *f* one, and come away Song 2:13 3302
Behold, thou art *f*, my love Song 4:1 3302
behold, thou art *f* Song 4:1 3302
Thou art all *f*, my love Song 4:7 3302
How *f* is thy love, my sister, my Song 4:10 3302
f as the moon, clear as the sun, Song 6:10 3303
How *f* and how pleasant art thou, O Song 7:6 3302
be desolate, even great and *f* Is 5:9 2896
will lay thy stones with *f* colors Is 54:11 6320
in vain shalt thou make thyself *f* Jer 4:30 3302
thy name, A green olive tree, *f* Jer 11:16 3303
they speak *f* words unto thee Jer 12:6 2896
Egypt is like a very *f* heifer Jer 46:20 3304
taken thy *f* jewels of my gold Eze 16:17 8597
and shall take thy *f* jewels Eze 16:39 8597
and take away thy *f* jewels Eze 23:26 8597
cedar in Lebanon with *f* branches Eze 31:3 3303
Thus was he *f* in his greatness, Eze 31:7 3302
I have made him *f* by the Eze 31:9 3303
The leaves thereof were *f* Dan 4:12 8209
Whose leaves were *f*, and the fruit Dan 4:21 8209
but I passed over upon her *f* neck Hos 10:11 2898
In that day shall the *f* virgins Amos 8:13 3303
Let them set a *f* mitre upon his Zec 3:5 2889
So they set a *f* mitre upon his Zec 3:5 2889
ye say, It will be *f* weather Mt 16:2 *2105*
was born, and was exceeding *f* Acts 7:20 *791*
which is called The *f* havens Acts 27:8 *2568*
f speeches deceive the hearts of Rom 16:18 *2129*
to make a *f* shew in the flesh Gal 6:12 *2146*

FAIRER
not her younger sister *f* than she Judg 15:2 2896
Thou art *f* than the children of Ps 45:2 3302
their countenances appeared *f* Dan 1:15 2896

FAIREST
O thou *f* among women, go thy way Song 1:8 3303
beloved, O thou *f* among women Song 5:9 3303
gone, O thou *f* among women Song 6:1 3303

FAIRS
and lead, they traded in thy *f* Eze 27:12 5801
traded in thy *f* with horses Eze 27:14 5801
occupied in thy *f* with emeralds Eze 27:16 5801
going to and fro occupied in thy *f* Eze 27:19 5801
they occupied in thy *f* with chief Eze 27:22 5801
Thy riches, and thy *f*, thy Eze 27:27 5801

FAITH
children in whom is no *f* Deut 32:20 529
but the just shall live by his *f* Hab 2:4 530
more clothe you, O ye of little *f* Mt 6:30 *3640*
you, I have not found so great *f* Mt 8:10 *4102*
are ye fearful, O ye of little *f* Mt 8:26 *3640*
Jesus seeing their *f* said unto Mt 9:2 *4102*
thy *f* hath made thee whole Mt 9:22 *4102*
to your *f* be it unto you Mt 9:29 *4102*
said unto him, O thou of little *f* Mt 14:31 *3640*
unto her, O woman, great is thy *f* Mt 15:28 *4102*
said unto them, O ye of little *f* Mt 16:8 *3640*
If ye have *f* as a grain of Mt 17:20 *4102*
I say unto you, If ye have *f* Mt 21:21 *4102*
of the law, judgment, mercy, and *f* Mt 23:23 *4102*
When Jesus saw their *f*, he said Mk 2:5 *4102*
how is it that ye have no *f* Mk 4:40 *4102*
thy *f* hath made thee whole Mk 5:34 *4102*
thy *f* hath made thee whole Mk 10:52 *4102*
saith unto them, Have *f* in God Mk 11:22 *4102*
And when he saw their *f*, he said Lk 5:20 *4102*
you, I have not found so great *f* Lk 7:9 *4102*
the woman, Thy *f* hath saved thee Lk 7:50 *4102*
said unto them, Where is your *f* Lk 8:25 *4102*
thy *f* hath made thee whole Lk 8:48 *4102*
he clothe you, O ye of little *f* Lk 12:28 *3640*
unto the Lord, Increase our *f* Lk 17:5 *4102*
If ye had *f* as a grain of mustard Lk 17:6 *4102*
thy *f* hath made thee whole Lk 17:19 *4102*
shall he find *f* on the earth Lk 18:8 *4102*
thy *f* hath saved thee Lk 18:42 *4102*
for thee, that thy *f* fail not Lk 22:32 *4102*
his name through *f* in his name Acts 3:16 *4102*
the *f* which is by him hath given Acts 3:16 *4102*
chose Stephen, a man full of *f* Acts 6:5 *4102*
priests were obedient to the *f* Acts 6:7 *4102*
And Stephen, full of *f* and power, Acts 6:8 *4102*
and full of the Holy Ghost and of *f* Acts 11:24 *4102*
turn away the deputy from the *f* Acts 13:8 *4102*
that he had *f* to be healed Acts 14:9 *4102*
them to continue in the *f* Acts 14:22 *4102*
the door of *f* unto the Gentiles Acts 14:27 *4102*
them, purifying their hearts by *f* Acts 15:9 *4102*
the churches established in the *f* Acts 16:5 *4102*
f toward our Lord Jesus Christ Acts 20:21 *4102*
him concerning the *f* in Christ Acts 24:24 *4102*
are sanctified by *f* that is in me Acts 26:18 *4102*
to the *f* among all nations Rom 1:5 *4102*
you all, that your *f* is spoken of Rom 1:8 *4102*
you by the mutual *f* both of you Rom 1:12 *4102*
of God revealed from *f* to *f* Rom 1:17 *4102*
written, The just shall live by *f* Rom 1:17 *4102*
make the *f* of God without effect Rom 3:3 *4102*
of God which is by *f* of Jesus Rom 3:22 *4102*
through *f* in his blood, to Rom 3:25 *4102*
but by the law of *f* Rom 3:27 *4102*
that a man is justified by *f* Rom 3:28 *4102*
justify the circumcision by *f* Rom 3:30 *4102*
and uncircumcision through *f* Rom 3:30 *4102*
then make void the law through *f* Rom 3:31 *4102*
the ungodly, his *f* is counted for Rom 4:5 *4102*
for we say that *f* was reckoned to Rom 4:9 *4102*
of the *f* which he had yet being Rom 4:11 *4102*
of that *f* of our father Abraham Rom 4:12 *4102*
through the righteousness of *f* Rom 4:13 *4102*
f is made void, and the promise Rom 4:14 *4102*
Therefore it is of *f*, that it Rom 4:16 *4102*
also which is of the *f* of Abraham Rom 4:16 *4102*
And being not weak in *f*, he Rom 4:19 *4102*
but was strong in *f*, giving glory Rom 4:20 *4102*
Therefore being justified by *f* Rom 5:1 *4102*
by *f* into this grace wherein we Rom 5:2 *4102*
the righteousness which is of *f* Rom 9:30 *4102*
Because they sought it not by *f* Rom 9:32 *4102*
is of *f* speaketh on this wise Rom 10:6 *4102*
that is, the word of *f*, which we Rom 10:8 *4102*
So then *f* cometh by hearing, and Rom 10:17 *4102*
broken off, and thou standest by *f* Rom 11:20 *4102*
to every man the measure of *f* Rom 12:3 *4102*
according to the proportion of *f* Rom 12:6 *4102*
that is weak in the *f* receive ye Rom 14:1 *4102*
Hast thou *f*? Rom 14:22 *4102*
eat, because he eateth not of *f* Rom 14:23 *4102*
for whatsoever is not of *f* is sin Rom 14:23 *4102*
nations for the obedience of *f* Rom 16:26 *4102*
That your *f* should not stand in 1Cor 2:5 *4102*
To another *f* by the same Spirit 1Cor 12:9 *4102*
and though I have all *f*, so that I 1Cor 13:2 *4102*
And now abideth *f*, hope, charity, 1Cor 13:13 *4102*
vain, and your *f* is also vain 1Cor 15:14 *4102*
be not raised, your *f* is vain 1Cor 15:17 *4102*
Watch ye, stand fast in the *f* 1Cor 16:13 *4102*
that we have dominion over your *f* 2Cor 1:24 *4102*
for by *f* ye stand 2Cor 1:24 *4102*
We having the same spirit of *f* 2Cor 4:13 *4102*
(For we walk by *f*, not by sight 2Cor 5:7 *4102*
as ye abound in every thing, in *f* 2Cor 8:7 *4102*
when your *f* is increased, that we 2Cor 10:15 *4102*
whether ye be in the *f* 2Cor 13:5 *4102*
the *f* which once he destroyed Gal 1:23 *4102*
but by the *f* of Jesus Christ, Gal 2:16 *4102*
be justified by the *f* of Christ Gal 2:16 *4102*
I live by the *f* of the Son of God Gal 2:20 *4102*
the law, or by the hearing of *f* Gal 3:2 *4102*
the law, or by the hearing of *f* Gal 3:5 *4102*
that they which are of *f*, the Gal 3:7 *4102*
justify the heathen through *f* Gal 3:8 *4102*
So then they which be of *f* are Gal 3:9 *4102*
for, The just shall live by *f* Gal 3:11 *4102*
And the law is not of *f* Gal 3:12 *4102*
promise of the Spirit through *f* Gal 3:14 *4102*
that the promise by *f* of Jesus Gal 3:22 *4102*
But before *f* came, we were kept Gal 3:23 *4102*
shut up unto the *f* which should Gal 3:23 *4102*
that we might be justified by *f* Gal 3:24 *4102*
But after that *f* is come, we are Gal 3:25 *4102*
of God by *f* in Christ Jesus Gal 3:26 *4102*
the hope of righteousness by *f* Gal 5:5 *4102*
but *f* which worketh by love Gal 5:6 *4102*
gentleness, goodness, *f*, Gal 5:22 *4102*
who are of the household of *f* Gal 6:10 *4102*
heard of your *f* in the Lord Jesus Eph 1:15 *4102*
by grace are ye saved through *f* Eph 2:8 *4102*
with confidence by the *f* of him Eph 3:12 *4102*
may dwell in your hearts by *f* Eph 3:17 *4102*
One Lord, one *f*, one baptism, Eph 4:5 *4102*
we all come in the unity of the *f* Eph 4:13 *4102*
Above all, taking the shield of *f* Eph 6:16 *4102*
to the brethren, and love with *f* Eph 6:23 *4102*
for your furtherance and joy of *f* Phil 1:25 *4102*
together for the *f* of the gospel Phil 1:27 *4102*
sacrifice and service of your *f* Phil 2:17 *4102*
which is through the *f* of Christ Phil 3:9 *4102*
which is of God by *f* Phil 3:9 *4102*
heard of your *f* in Christ Jesus Col 1:4 *4102*
If ye continue in the *f* grounded Col 1:23 *4102*
stedfastness of your *f* in Christ Col 2:5 *4102*
up in him, and stablished in the *f* Col 2:7 *4102*
the *f* of the operation of God Col 2:12 *4102*
without ceasing your work of *f* 1Th 1:3 *4102*
f to God-ward is spread abroad 1Th 1:8 *4102*
to comfort you concerning your *f* 1Th 3:2 *4102*
forbear, I sent to know your *f* 1Th 3:5 *4102*
brought us good tidings of your *f* 1Th 3:6 *4102*
affliction and distress by your *f* 1Th 3:7 *4102*
that which is lacking in your *f* 1Th 3:10 *4102*
putting on the breastplate of *f* 1Th 5:8 *4102*
because that your *f* groweth 2Th 1:3 *4102*
f in all your persecutions and 2Th 1:4 *4102*
and the work of *f* with power 2Th 1:11 *4102*
for all men have not *f* 2Th 3:2 *4102*
Unto Timothy, my own son in the *f* 1Ti 1:2 *4102*
than godly edifying which is in *f* 1Ti 1:4 *4102*
conscience, and of *f* unfeigned 1Ti 1:5 *4102*
was exceeding abundant with *f* 1Ti 1:14 *4102*
Holding *f*, and a good conscience 1Ti 1:19 *4102*
concerning *f* have made shipwreck 1Ti 1:19 *4102*
a teacher of the Gentiles in *f* 1Ti 2:7 *4102*
if they continue in *f* and charity 1Ti 2:15 *4102*
of the *f* in a pure conscience 1Ti 3:9 *4102*
great boldness in the *f* which is 1Ti 3:13 *4102*
some shall depart from the *f* 1Ti 4:1 *4102*
nourished up in the words of *f* 1Ti 4:6 *4102*
in charity, in spirit, in *f* 1Ti 4:12 *4102*
own house, he hath denied the *f* 1Ti 5:8 *4102*
they have cast off their first *f* 1Ti 5:12 *4102*
after, they have erred from the *f* 1Ti 6:10 *4102*
after righteousness, godliness, *f* 1Ti 6:11 *4102*
Fight the good fight of *f* 1Ti 6:12 *4102*
have erred concerning the *f* 1Ti 6:21 *4102*
the unfeigned *f* that is in thee 2Ti 1:5 *4102*
which thou hast heard of me, in *f* 2Ti 1:13 *4102*
and overthrow the *f* of some 2Ti 2:18 *4102*
but follow righteousness, *f* 2Ti 2:22 *4102*
minds, reprobate concerning the *f* 2Ti 3:8 *4102*
manner of life, purpose, *f* 2Ti 3:10 *4102*
f which is in Christ Jesus 2Ti 3:15 *4102*
my course, I have kept the *f* 2Ti 4:7 *4102*
according to the *f* of God's elect Titus 1:1 *4102*
mine own son after the common *f* Titus 1:4 *4102*
that they may be sound in the *f* Titus 1:13 *4102*
grave, temperate, sound in *f* Titus 2:2 *4102*
Greet them that love us in the *f* Titus 3:15 *4102*
Hearing of thy love and *f*, which Philem 5 *4102*
thy *f* may become effectual by the Philem 6 *4102*
not being mixed with *f* in them Heb 4:2 *4102*
dead works, and of *f* toward God, Heb 6:1 *4102*
followers of them who through *f* Heb 6:12 *4102*
true heart in full assurance of *f* Heb 10:22 *4102*
of our *f* without wavering Heb 10:23 *1680*
Now the just shall live by *f* Heb 10:38 *4102*
Now *f* is the substance of things Heb 11:1 *4102*
Through *f* we understand that the Heb 11:3 *4102*

By f Abel offered unto God a more Heb 11:4 4102
By f Enoch was translated that he Heb 11:5 4102
But without f it is impossible to Heb 11:6 4102
By f Noah, being warned of God of Heb 11:7 4102
the righteousness which is by f Heb 11:7 4102
By f Abraham, when he was called Heb 11:8 4102
By f he sojourned in the land of Heb 11:9 4102
Through f also Sara herself Heb 11:11 4102
These all died in f, not having Heb 11:13 4102
By f Abraham, when he was tried, Heb 11:17 4102
By f Isaac blessed Jacob and Esau Heb 11:20 4102
By f Jacob, when he was a dying, Heb 11:21 4102
By f Joseph, when he died, made Heb 11:22 4102
By f Moses, when he was born, was Heb 11:23 4102
By f Moses, when he was come to Heb 11:24 4102
By f he forsook Egypt, not Heb 11:27 4102
Through f he kept the passover, Heb 11:28 4102
By f they passed through the Red Heb 11:29 4102
By f the walls of Jericho fell Heb 11:30 4102
By f the harlot Rahab perished Heb 11:31 4102
Who through f subdued kingdoms, Heb 11:33 4102
obtained a good report through f Heb 11:39 4102
the author and finisher of our f Heb 12:2 4102
whose f follow, considering the Heb 13:7 4102
trying of your f worketh patience Jas 1:3 4102
But let him ask in f, nothing Jas 1:6 4102
have not the f of our Lord Jesus Jas 2:1 4102
the poor of this world rich in f Jas 2:5 4102
though a man say he hath f Jas 2:14 4102
can f save him? Jas 2:14 4102
Even so f, if it hath not works, Jas 2:17 4102
Yea, a man may say, Thou hast f Jas 2:18 4102
shew me thy f without thy works, Jas 2:18 4102
I will shew thee my f by my works Jas 2:18 4102
that f without works is dead Jas 2:20 4102
Seest thou how f wrought with his Jas 2:22 4102
and by works was f made perfect Jas 2:22 4102
is justified, and not by f only Jas 2:24 4102
so f without works is dead also Jas 2:26 4102
the prayer of f shall save the Jas 5:15 4102
f unto salvation ready to be 1Pet 1:5 4102
That the trial of your f, being 1Pet 1:7 4102
Receiving the end of your f 1Pet 1:9 4102
that your f and hope might be in 1Pet 1:21 4102
Whom resist stedfast in the f 1Pet 5:9 4102
precious f with us through the 2Pet 1:1 4102
diligence, add to your f virtue 2Pet 1:5 4102
overcometh the world, even our f 1Jn 5:4 4102
earnestly contend for the f which Jude 3 4102
up yourselves on your most holy f Jude 20 4102
my name, and hast not denied my f Rev 2:13 4102
and charity, and service, and f Rev 2:19 4102
patience and the f of the saints Rev 13:10 4102
of God, and the f of Jesus Rev 14:12 4102

FAITHFUL

who is f in all mine house Num 12:7 539
thy God, he is God, the f God Deut 7:9 539
And I will raise me up a f priest 1Sa 2:35 539
who is so f among all thy 1Sa 22:14 539
that are peaceable and f in Israel 2Sa 20:19 539
for he was a f man, and feared God Neh 7:2 571
foundest his heart f before thee Neh 9:8 539
for they were counted f, and their Neh 13:13 539
for the f fail from among the Ps 12:1 539
for the LORD preserveth the f Ps 31:23 539
moon, and as a f witness in heaven Ps 89:37 539
shall be upon the f of the land Ps 101:6 539
All thy commandments are f Ps 119:86 530
commanded are righteous and very f Ps 119:138 530
but he that is of a f spirit Prov 11:13 539
but a f ambassador is health Prov 13:17 529
A f witness will not lie Prov 14:5 529
but a f man who can find Prov 20:6 529
so is a f messenger to them that Prov 25:13 539
F are the wounds of a friend Prov 27:6 539
A f man shall abound with Prov 28:20 530
How is the f city become an Is 1:21 539
city of righteousness, the f city Is 1:26 539
I took unto me f witnesses to Is 8:2 539
because of the LORD that is f Is 49:7 539
f witness between us, if we do Jer 42:5 539
forasmuch as he was f, neither Dan 6:4 540
with God, and is f with the saints Hos 11:12 539
Who then is a f and wise servant, Mt 24:45 4103
Well done, thou good and f servant Mt 25:21 4103
thou hast been f over a few Mt 25:21 4103
him, Well done, good and f servant Mt 25:23 4103
thou hast been f over a few Mt 25:23 4103
the Lord said, Who then is that f Lk 12:42 4103
He that is f in that which is Lk 16:10 4103
which is least is f also in much Lk 16:10 4103
been f in the unrighteous mammon Lk 16:11 4103
if ye have not been f in that Lk 16:12 4103
thou hast been f in a very little Lk 19:17 4103
judged me to be f to the Lord Acts 16:15 4103
God is f, by whom ye were called 1Cor 1:9 4103
stewards, that a man be found f 1Cor 4:2 4103
f in the Lord, who shall bring 1Cor 4:17 4103
mercy of the Lord to be f 1Cor 7:25 4103
but God is f, who will not suffer 1Cor 10:13 4103
faith are blessed with f Abraham Gal 3:9 4103
and to the f in Christ Jesus Eph 1:1 4103
f minister in the Lord, shall Eph 6:21 4103
f brethren in Christ which are at Col 1:2 4103
who is for you a f minister of Col 1:7 4103
a f minister and fellowservant in Col 4:7 4103
With Onesimus, a f and beloved Col 4:9 4103
F is he that calleth you, who 1Th 5:24 4103
But the Lord is f, who shall 2Th 3:3 4103
me, for that he counted me f 1Ti 1:12 4103
This is a f saying, and worthy of 1Ti 1:15 4103
sober, f in all things 1Ti 3:11 4103
This is a f saying and worthy of 1Ti 4:9 4103
them service, because they are f 1Ti 6:2 4103
the same commit thou to f men 2Ti 2:2 4103
It is a f saying 2Ti 2:11 4103
we believe not, yet he abideth f 2Ti 2:13 4103
having f children not accused of Titus 1:6 4103
Holding fast the f word as he Titus 1:9 4103
This is a f saying, and these Titus 3:8 4103
and f high priest in things Heb 2:17 4103
Who was f to him that appointed Heb 3:2 4103
also Moses was f in all his house Heb 3:2
verily was f in all his house Heb 3:5 4103
(for he is f that promised Heb 10:23 4103
she judged him f who had promised Heb 11:11 4103
well doing, as unto a f Creator 1Pet 4:19 4103
a f brother unto you, as I 1Pet 5:12 4103
If we confess our sins, he is f 1Jn 1:9 4103
Christ, who is the f witness Rev 1:5 4103
be thou f unto death, and I will Rev 2:10 4103
wherein Antipas was my f martyr Rev 2:13 4103
things saith the Amen, the f Rev 3:14 4103
him are called, and chosen, and f Rev 17:14 4103
he that sat upon him was called F Rev 19:11 4103
for these words are true and f Rev 21:5 4103
said unto me, These sayings are f Rev 22:6 4103

FAITHFULLY

for they dealt f 2Kin 12:15 530
their hand, because they dealt f 2Kin 22:7 530
ye do in the fear of the LORD, f 2Chr 19:9 530
tithes and the dedicated things f 2Chr 31:12 530
And the men did the work f 2Chr 34:12 530
The king that f judgeth the poor, Prov 29:14 571
my word, let him speak my word f Jer 23:28 571
thou doest f whatsoever thou 3Jn 5 4103

FAITHFULNESS

man his righteousness and his f 1Sa 26:23 530
For there is no f in their mouth Ps 5:9 3559
thy f reacheth unto the clouds Ps 36:5 530
I have declared thy f and thy Ps 40:10 530
or thy f in destruction Ps 88:11 530
known thy f to all generations Ps 89:1 530
thy f shalt thou establish in the Ps 89:2 530
thy f also in the congregation of Ps 89:5 530
or to thy f round about thee Ps 89:8 530
But my f and my mercy shall be Ps 89:24 530
from him, nor suffer my f to fail Ps 89:33 530
morning, and thy f every night, Ps 92:2 530
that thou in f hast afflicted me Ps 119:75 530
Thy f is unto all generations Ps 119:90 530
in thy f answer me, and in thy Ps 143:1 530
f the girdle of his reins Is 11:5 530
thy counsels of old are f Is 25:1 530
great is thy f Lam 3:23 530
even betroth thee unto me in f Hos 2:20 530

FAITHLESS

Then Jesus answered and said, O f Mt 17:17 571
O f generation, how long shall I Mk 9:19 571
And Jesus answering said, O f Lk 9:41 571
and be not f, but believing Jn 20:27 571

FALL

a deep sleep to f upon Adam Gen 2:21 5307
f upon us, and take us for bondmen Gen 43:18 5307
See that ye f not out by the way Gen 45:24 7264
that his rider shall f backward Gen 49:17 5307
lest he f upon us with pestilence Ex 5:3 6293
Fear and dread shall f upon them Ex 15:16 5307
it, and an ox or an ass f therein Ex 21:33 5307
them, when they are dead, doth f Lev 11:32 5307
if any part of their carcase f Lev 11:37 5307
part of their carcase f thereon Lev 11:38 5307
lest the land f to whoredom Lev 19:29
they shall f before you by the Lev 26:7 5307
your enemies shall f before you Lev 26:8 5307
they shall f when none pursueth Lev 26:36 5307
they shall f one upon another, as Lev 26:37 3782
let them f by the camp, as it Num 11:31 5203
to f by the sword, that our wives Num 14:3 5307
shall f in this wilderness Num 14:29 5307
they shall f in this wilderness Num 14:32 5307
you, and ye shall f by the sword Num 14:43 5307
f unto you for an inheritance Num 34:2 5307
ass or his ox f down by the way Deut 22:4 5307
house, if any man f from thence Deut 22:8 5307
of the city shall f down flat Josh 6:5 5307
said, Rise thou, and f upon us Judg 8:21 6293
that ye will not f upon me Judg 15:12 6293
thirst, and f into the hand of the Judg 15:18 5307
let f also some of the handfuls Ruth 2:16 7997
thou know how the matter will f Ruth 3:18 5307
none of his words f to the ground 1Sa 3:19 5307
hair of his head f to the ground 1Sa 14:45 5307
f by the hand of the Philistines 1Sa 18:25 5307
let his spittle f down upon his 1Sa 21:13 3381
not put forth their hand to f 1Sa 22:17 6293
Turn thou, and f upon the priests 1Sa 22:18 6293
let not my blood f to the earth 1Sa 26:20 5307
and said, Go near, and f upon him 2Sa 1:15 6293
hair of thy son f to the earth 2Sa 14:11 5307
let us f now into the hand of the 2Sa 24:14 5307
let me not f into the hand of man 2Sa 24:14 5307
not an hair of him f to the earth 1Kin 1:52 5307
Jehoiada, saying, Go, f upon him 1Kin 2:29 6293
said, and f upon him, and bury him 1Kin 2:31 6293
may go up and f at Ramoth-gilead 1Kin 22:20 5307
let us f unto the host of the 2Kin 7:4 5307
Know now that there shall f unto 2Kin 10:10 5307
thy hurt, that thou shouldest f 2Kin 14:10 5307
I will cause him to f by the 2Kin 19:7 5307
He will f to his master Saul to 1Chr 12:19 5307
let me f now into the hand of the 1Chr 21:13 5307
but let me not f into the hand of 1Chr 21:13 5307
may go up and f at Ramoth-gilead 2Chr 18:19 5307
until thy bowels f out by reason 2Chr 21:15 3318
make thee f before the enemy 2Chr 25:8 3782
thine hurt, that thou shouldest f 2Chr 25:19 5307
before whom thou hast begun to f Est 6:13 5307
but shalt surely f before him Est 6:13 5307
and his dread f upon you Job 13:11 5307
Then let mine arm f from my Job 31:22 5307
let them f by their own counsels Ps 5:10 5307
are turned back, they shall f Ps 9:3 3782
that the poor may f by his strong Ps 10:10 5307
that very destruction let him f Ps 35:8 5307
Though he f, he shall not be Ps 37:24 5307
whereby the people f under thee Ps 45:5 5307
They shall f by the sword Ps 63:10 5064
own tongue to f upon themselves Ps 64:8 3782
all kings shall f down before him Ps 72:11 7812
he let it f in the midst of their Ps 78:28 5307
f like one of the princes Ps 82:7 5307
A thousand shall f at thy side Ps 91:7 5307
thrust sore at me that I might f Ps 118:13 5307
Let burning coals f upon them Ps 140:10 4131
Let the wicked f into their own Ps 141:10 5307
The LORD upholdeth all that f Ps 145:14 5307
away, unless they cause some to f Prov 4:16 3782
but a prating fool shall f Prov 10:8 3832
but a prating fool shall f Prov 10:10 3832
but the wicked shall f by his own Prov 11:5 5307
Where no counsel is, the people f Prov 11:14 5307
trusteth in his riches shall f Prov 11:28 5307
and an haughty spirit before a f Prov 16:18 3783
of the LORD shall f therein Prov 22:14 5307
the wicked shall f into mischief Prov 24:16 3782
diggeth a pit shall f therein Prov 26:27 5307
he shall f himself into his own Prov 28:10 5307
his heart shall f into mischief Prov 28:14 5307
in his ways shall f at once Prov 28:18 5307
the righteous shall see their f Prov 29:16 4658
For if they f, the one will lift Eccl 4:10 5307
diggeth a pit shall f into it Eccl 10:8 5307
if the tree f toward the south, Eccl 11:3 5307
Thy men shall f by the sword Is 3:25 5307
among them shall stumble, and f Is 8:15 5307
they shall f under the slain Is 10:4 5307
Lebanon shall f by a mighty one Is 10:34 5307
unto them shall f by the sword Is 13:15 5307
be removed, and be cut down, and f Is 22:25 5307
of the fear shall f into the pit Is 24:18 5307
and it shall f, and not rise again Is 24:20 5307
f backward, and be broken, and Is 28:13 3782
be to you as a breach ready to f Is 30:13 5307
slaughter, when the towers f Is 30:25 5307
both he that helpeth shall f Is 31:3 3782
and he that is holpen shall f down Is 31:3 5307
the Assyrian f with the sword Is 31:8 5307
and all their host shall f down Is 34:4 5034
I will cause him to f by the Is 37:7 5307
and the young men shall utterly f Is 40:30 3782
shall I f down to the stock of a Is 44:19 5456
they shall f down unto thee, they Is 45:14 7812
they f down, yea, they worship Is 46:6 5456
and mischief shall f upon thee Is 47:11 5307
against thee shall f for thy sake Is 54:15 5307
cause mine anger to f upon you Jer 3:12 5307
they shall f among them that f Jer 6:15 5307
sons together shall f upon them Jer 6:21 3782
Shall they f, and not arise Jer 8:4 5307
shall they f among them that f Jer 8:12 5307
f as dung upon the open field Jer 9:22 5307
caused him to f upon it suddenly Jer 15:8 5307
I will cause them to f by the Jer 19:7 5307
they shall f by the sword of their Jer 20:4 5307
shall be driven on, and f therein Jer 23:12 5307
it shall f grievously upon the Jer 23:19 2342
ye, and be drunken, and spue, and f Jer 25:27 5307
ye shall f like a pleasant vessel Jer 25:34 5307
it shall f with pain upon the Jer 30:23 2342
I f not away to the Chaldeans Jer 37:14 5307
and thou shalt not f by the sword Jer 39:18 5307
and f in the land of Egypt Jer 44:12 5307
f toward the north by the river Jer 46:6 5307
He made many to f, yea, one fell Jer 46:16 3782
the fear shall f into the pit Jer 48:44 5307
is moved at the noise of their f Jer 49:21 5307
young men shall f in her streets Jer 49:26 5307
her young men f in the streets Jer 50:30 5307
the most proud shall stumble and f Jer 50:32 5307
Thus the slain shall f in the Jer 51:4 5307
yea, the wall of Babylon shall f Jer 51:44 5307
slain shall f in the midst of her Jer 51:47 5307
caused the slain of Israel to f Jer 51:49 5307
so at Babylon shall f the slain Jer 51:49 5307
he hath made my strength to f Lam 1:14 3782
a third part shall f by the sword Eze 5:12 5307
the slain shall f in the midst of Eze 6:7 5307
for they shall f by the sword Eze 6:11 5307
that is near shall f by the sword Eze 6:12 5307
Ye shall f by the sword Eze 11:10 5307
morter, that it shall f Eze 13:11 5307
ye, O great hailstones, shall f Eze 13:11 5307
be discovered, and it shall f Eze 13:14 5307
his bands shall f by the sword Eze 17:21 5307
thy remnant shall f by the sword Eze 23:25 5307
let no lot f upon it Eze 24:6 5307
ye have left shall f by the sword Eze 24:21 5307
of Dedan shall f by the sword Eze 25:13 5307
isles shake at the sound of thy f Eze 26:15 4658
isles tremble in the day of thy f Eze 26:18 4658
shall f into the midst of the Eze 27:27 5307
in the midst of thee shall f Eze 27:34 5307
thou shalt f upon the open fields Eze 29:5 5307
when the slain shall f in Egypt Eze 30:4 5307
shall f with them by the sword Eze 30:5 5307
also that uphold Egypt shall f Eze 30:6 5307
shall they f in it by the sword Eze 30:6 5307
of Pi-beseth shall f by the sword Eze 30:17 5307

the sword to *f* out of his hand — Eze 30:22 — 5307
the arms of Pharaoh shall *f* down — Eze 30:25 — 5307
to shake at the sound of his *f* — Eze 31:16 — 4658
his own life, in the day of thy *f* — Eze 32:10 — 4658
will I cause thy multitude to *f* — Eze 32:12 — 4658
They shall *f* in the midst of them — Eze 32:20 — 4658
he shall not *f* thereby in the day — Eze 33:12 — 3782
the wastes shall *f* by the sword — Eze 33:27 — 5307
shall they *f* that are slain with — Eze 35:8 — 5307
cause thy nations to *f* any more — Eze 36:15 — 3782
down, and the steep places shall *f* — Eze 38:20 — 5307
every wall shall *f* to the ground — Eze 38:20 — 5307
arrows to *f* out of thy right hand — Eze 39:3 — 5307
Thou shalt *f* upon the mountains — Eze 39:4 — 5307
Thou shalt *f* upon the open field — Eze 39:5 — 5307
of Israel to *f* into iniquity — Eze 44:12 — 4383
this land shall *f* unto you for — Eze 47:14 — 5307
ye *f* down and worship the golden — Dan 3:5 — 5308
all kinds of musick, shall *f* down — Dan 3:10 — 5308
ye *f* down and worship the image — Dan 3:15 — 5308
but they shall *f* — Dan 11:14 — 3782
but he shall stumble and *f* — Dan 11:19 — 5307
and many shall *f* down slain — Dan 11:26 — 5307
yet they shall *f* by the sword — Dan 11:33 — 3782
Now when they shall *f*, they shall — Dan 11:34 — 3782
of them of understanding shall *f* — Dan 11:35 — 3782
Therefore shalt thou *f* in the day — Hos 4:5 — 3782
shall *f* with thee in the night — Hos 4:5 — 3782
that doth not understand shall *f* — Hos 4:14 — 3832
Ephraim *f* in their iniquity — Hos 5:5 — 3782
Judah also shall *f* with them — Hos 5:5 — 3782
their princes shall *f* by the — Hos 7:16 — 5307
and to the hills, *F* on us — Hos 10:8 — 5307
they shall *f* by the sword — Hos 13:16 — 5307
the transgressors shall *f* therein — Hos 14:9 — 3872
when they *f* upon the sword, they — Joel 2:8 — 5307
Can a bird *f* in a snare upon the — Amos 3:5 — 5307
be cut off, and *f* to the ground — Amos 3:14 — 5307
daughters shall *f* by the sword — Amos 7:17 — 5307
even they shall *f*, and never rise — Amos 8:14 — 5307
the least grain *f* upon the earth — Amos 9:9 — 5307
when I *f*, I shall arise — Mic 7:8 — 5307
they shall even *f* into the mouth — Nah 3:12 — 5307
I give thee, if thou wilt *f* down — Mt 4:9 — *4098*
and great was the *f* of it — Mt 7:27 — *4431*
one of them shall not *f* on the — Mt 10:29 — *4098*
if it *f* into a pit on the sabbath — Mt 12:11 — *1706*
both shall *f* into the ditch — Mt 15:14 — *4098*
which *f* from their masters' table — Mt 15:27 — *4098*
whosoever shall *f* on this stone — Mt 21:44 — *4098*
but on whomsoever it shall *f* — Mt 21:44 — *4098*
and the stars shall *f* from heaven — Mt 24:29 — *4098*
And the stars of heaven shall *f* — Mk 13:25 — *1601*
this child is set for the *f* — Lk 2:34 — *4431*
they not both *f* into the ditch — Lk 6:39 — *4098*
and in time of temptation *f* away — Lk 8:13 — *868*
Satan as lightning *f* from heaven — Lk 10:18 — *4098*
Whosoever shall *f* upon that stone — Lk 20:18 — *4098*
but on whomsoever it shall *f* — Lk 20:18 — *4098*
they shall *f* by the edge of the — Lk 21:24 — *4098*
to say to the mountains, *F* on us — Lk 23:30 — *4098*
a corn of wheat *f* into the ground — Jn 12:24 — *4098*
they should *f* into the quicksands — Acts 27:17 — *1601*
of the boat, and let her *f* off — Acts 27:32 — *1601*
f from the head of any of you — Acts 27:34 — *4098*
they stumbled that they should *f* — Rom 11:11 — *4098*
but rather through their *f* — Rom 11:11 — *3900*
Now if the *f* of them be the — Rom 11:12 — *3900*
or an occasion to *f* in his — Rom 14:13 — *4625*
he standeth take heed lest he *f* — 1Cor 10:12 — *4098*
he *f* into the condemnation of the — 1Ti 3:6 — *1706*
lest he *f* into reproach and the — 1Ti 3:7
will be rich *f* into temptation — 1Ti 6:9
lest any man *f* after the same — Heb 4:11 — *4098*
If they shall *f* away, to renew — Heb 6:6 — *3895*
It is a fearful thing to *f* into — Heb 10:31 — *1706*
when ye *f* into divers temptations — Jas 1:2 — *4045*
lest ye *f* into condemnation — Jas 5:12 — *4098*
do these things, ye shall never *f* — 2Pet 1:10 — *4417*
f from your own stedfastness — 2Pet 3:17 — *1601*
twenty elders *f* down before him — Rev 4:10 — *4098*
F on us, and hide us from the face — Rev 6:16 — *4098*
I saw a star *f* from heaven unto — Rev 9:1 — *4098*

FALLEN

and why is thy countenance *f* — Gen 4:6 — 5307
man whose hair is *f* off his head — Lev 13:40 — 4803
he that hath his hair *f* off from — Lev 13:41 — 4803
poor, and *f* in decay with thee — Lev 25:35 — 4131
is *f* to us on this side Jordan — Num 32:19 — 935
and that your terror is *f* upon us — Josh 2:9 — 5307
when they were all *f* on the edge — Josh 8:24 — 5307
their lord was *f* down dead on the — Judg 3:25 — 5307
f unto them among the tribes of — Judg 18:1 — 5307
the woman his concubine was *f* — Judg 19:27 — 5307
Dagon was *f* upon his face to the — 1Sa 5:3 — 5307
Dagon was *f* upon his face to the — 1Sa 5:4 — 5307
from the LORD was *f* upon them — 1Sa 26:12 — 5307
his three sons *f* in mount Gilboa — 1Sa 31:8 — 5307
and many of the people also are *f* — 2Sa 1:4 — 5307
not live after that he was *f* — 2Sa 1:10 — 5307
because they were *f* by the sword — 2Sa 1:12 — 5307
how are the mighty *f* — 2Sa 1:19 — 5307
How are the mighty *f* in the midst — 2Sa 1:25 — 5307
How are the mighty *f*, and the — 2Sa 1:27 — 5307
a great man *f* this day in Israel — 2Sa 3:38 — 5307
yea, they are *f* under my feet — 2Sa 22:39 — 5307
Now Elisha was *f* sick of his — 2Kin 13:14
his sons *f* in mount Gilboa — 1Chr 10:8 — 5307
were dead bodies *f* to the earth — 2Chr 20:24 — 5307
our fathers have *f* by the sword — 2Chr 29:9 — 5307
Haman was *f* upon the bed whereon — Est 7:8 — 5307
The fire of God is *f* from heaven — Job 1:16 — 5307
is *f* into the ditch which he made — Ps 7:15 — 5307
The lines are *f* unto me in — Ps 16:6 — 5307
they are *f* under my feet — Ps 18:38 — 5307
They are brought down and *f* — Ps 20:8 — 5307
are the workers of iniquity *f* — Ps 36:12 — 5307
terrors of death are *f* upon me — Ps 55:4 — 5307
whereof they are *f* themselves — Ps 57:6 — 5307
reproached thee are *f* upon me — Ps 69:9 — 5307
is ruined, and Judah is *f* — Is 3:8 — 5307
The bricks are *f* down, but we — Is 9:10 — 5307
How art thou *f* from heaven — Is 14:12 — 5307
fruits and for thy harvest is *f* — Is 16:9 — 5307
he answered and said, Babylon is *f* — Is 21:9 — 5307
and said, Babylon is *f*, is *f* — Is 21:9 — 5307
the inhabitants of the world *f* — Is 26:18 — 5307
for truth is *f* in the street, and — Is 59:14 — 3782
Jews that are *f* to the Chaldeans — Jer 38:19 — 5307
and they are *f* both together — Jer 46:12 — 5307
the spoiler is *f* upon thy summer — Jer 48:32 — 5307
her foundations are *f*, her walls — Jer 50:15 — 5307
Babylon is suddenly *f* and — Jer 51:8 — 5307
my young men are *f* by the sword — Lam 2:21 — 5307
The crown is *f* from our head — Lam 5:16 — 5307
Lo, when the wall is *f*, shall it — Eze 13:12 — 5307
the valleys his branches are *f* — Eze 31:12 — 5307
all of them slain, *f* by the sword — Eze 32:22 — 5307
f by the sword, which caused — Eze 32:23 — 5307
f by the sword, which are gone — Eze 32:24 — 5307
that are *f* of the uncircumcised — Eze 32:27 — 5307
all their kings are *f* — Hos 7:7 — 5307
for thou hast *f* by thine iniquity — Hos 14:1 — 3782
The virgin of Israel is *f* — Amos 5:2 — 5307
the tabernacle of David that is *f* — Amos 9:11 — 5307
for the cedar is *f* — Zec 11:2 — 5307
have an ass or an ox *f* into a pit — Lk 14:5 — *1706*
as yet he was *f* upon none of them — Acts 8:16 — *1968*
of David, which is *f* down — Acts 15:16 — *4098*
being *f* into a deep sleep — Acts 20:9 — *2702*
when we were all *f* to the earth — Acts 26:14 — *2667*
lest we should have *f* upon rocks — Acts 27:29 — *1601*
swollen, or *f* down dead suddenly — Acts 28:6 — *2667*
present, but some are *f* asleep — 1Cor 15:6 — *2837*
Then they also which are *f* asleep — 1Cor 15:18 — *2837*
ye are *f* from grace — Gal 5:4 — *1601*
which happened unto me have *f* out — Phil 1:12 — *2064*
therefore from whence thou art *f* — Rev 2:5 — *1601*
saying, Babylon is *f*, is *f* — Rev 14:8 — *4098*
five are *f*, and one is, and the — Rev 17:10 — *4098*
Babylon the great is *f*, is *f* — Rev 18:2 — *4098*

FALLEST

Thou *f* away to the Chaldeans — Jer 37:13 — 5307

FALLETH

when there *f* out any war, they — Ex 1:10 — 7122
vessel, whereinto any of them *f* — Lev 11:33 — 5307
their carcase *f* shall be unclean — Lev 11:35 — 5307
be in the place where his lot *f* — Num 33:54 — 3918
or that *f* on the sword, or that — 2Sa 3:29 — 5307
as a man *f* before wicked men, so — 2Sa 3:34 — 5307
him as the dew *f* on the ground — 2Sa 17:12 — 5307
night, when deep sleep *f* on men — Job 4:13 — 5307
night, when deep sleep *f* upon men — Job 33:15 — 5307
wicked messenger *f* into mischief — Prov 13:17 — 5307
a perverse tongue *f* into mischief — Prov 17:20 — 5307
For a just man *f* seven times — Prov 24:16 — 5307
Rejoice not when thine enemy *f* — Prov 24:17 — 5307
to him that is alone when he *f* — Eccl 4:10 — 5307
when it *f* suddenly upon them — Eccl 9:12 — 5307
in the place where the tree *f* — Eccl 11:3 — 5307
as the leaf *f* off from the vine — Is 34:4 — 5034
a graven image, and *f* down thereto — Is 44:15 — 5456
he *f* down unto it, and worshippeth — Is 44:17 — 5456
f to the Chaldeans that besiege — Jer 21:9 — 5307
whoso *f* not down and worshippeth — Dan 3:6 — 5308
whoso *f* not down and worshippeth — Dan 3:11 — 5308
for ofttimes he *f* into the fire — Mt 17:15 — *4098*
a house divided against a house *f* — Lk 11:17 — *4098*
the portion of goods that *f* to me — Lk 15:12 — *1911*
his own master he standeth or *f* — Rom 14:4 — *4098*
grass, and the flower thereof *f* — Jas 1:11 — *1601*
and the flower thereof *f* away — 1Pet 1:24 — *1601*

FALLING

f into a trance, but having his — Num 24:4 — 5307
f into a trance, but having his — Num 24:16 — 5307
have upholden him that was *f* — Job 4:4 — 3782
the mountain *f* cometh to nought — Job 14:18 — 5307
not thou deliver my feet from *f* — Ps 56:13 — 1762
from tears, and my feet from *f* — Ps 116:8 — 1762
A righteous man *f* down before the — Prov 25:26 — 4131
as a *f* fig from the fig tree — Is 34:4 — 5034
f down before him, she declared — Lk 8:47 — *4363*
of blood *f* down to the ground — Lk 22:44 — *2597*
f headlong, he burst asunder in — Acts 1:18 — *1096*
f into a place where two seas met — Acts 27:41 — *4045*
so *f* down on his face he will — 1Cor 14:25 — *4098*
except there come a *f* away first — 2Th 2:3 — *646*
that is able to keep you from *f* — Jude 24 — *679*

FALLOW

the *f* deer, and the wild goat, and — Deut 14:5 — 3180
Jerusalem, Break up your *f* ground — Jer 4:3 — 5215
break up your *f* ground — Hos 10:12 — 5215

FALLOWDEER

beside harts, and roebucks, and *f* — 1Kin 4:23 — 3180

FALSE

Thou shalt not bear *f* witness — Ex 20:16 — 8267
Thou shalt not raise a *f* report — Ex 23:1 — 7723
Keep thee far from a *f* matter — Ex 23:7 — 8267
Neither shalt thou bear *f* witness — Deut 5:20 — 7723
If a *f* witness rise up against — Deut 19:16 — 2555
if the witness be a *f* witness — Deut 19:18 — 8267
And they said, It is *f* — 2Kin 9:12 — 8267
For truly my words shall not be *f* — Job 36:4 — 8267
for *f* witnesses are risen up — Ps 27:12 — 8267
F witnesses did rise up — Ps 35:11 — 2555
therefore I hate every *f* way — Ps 119:104 — 8267
and I hate every *f* way — Ps 119:128 — 8267
be done unto thee, thou *f* tongue — Ps 120:3 — 7423
A *f* witness that speaketh lies — Prov 6:19 — 8267
A *f* balance is abomination to the — Prov 11:1 — 4820
but a *f* witness deceit — Prov 12:17 — 8267
but a *f* witness will utter lies — Prov 14:5 — 8267
wicked doer giveth heed to *f* lips — Prov 17:4 — 205
A *f* witness shall not be — Prov 19:5 — 8267
A *f* witness shall not be — Prov 19:9 — 8267
and a *f* balance is not good — Prov 20:23 — 4820
A *f* witness shall perish — Prov 21:28 — 3577
of a *f* gift is like clouds — Prov 25:14 — 8267
A man that beareth *f* witness — Prov 25:18 — 8267
they prophesy unto you a *f* vision — Jer 14:14 — 8267
them that prophesy *f* dreams — Jer 23:32 — 8267
Then said Jeremiah, It is *f* — Jer 37:14 — 8267
but have seen for thee *f* burdens — Lam 2:14 — 7723
as a *f* divination in their sight — Eze 21:23 — 7723
and love no *f* oath — Zec 8:17 — 8267
seen a lie, and have told *f* dreams — Zec 10:2 — 7723
against *f* swearers, and against — Mal 3:5 — 8267
Beware of *f* prophets, which come — Mt 7:15 — *5573*
thefts, *f* witness, blasphemies — Mt 15:19 — *5577*
Thou shalt not bear *f* witness — Mt 19:18 — *5576*
many *f* prophets shall rise, and — Mt 24:11 — *5573*
For there shall arise *f* Christs — Mt 24:24
f prophets, and shall shew great — Mt 24:24 — *5573*
sought *f* witness against Jesus — Mt 26:59 — *5580*
though many *f* witnesses came, yet — Mt 26:60 — *5575*
At the last came two *f* witnesses — Mt 26:60 — *5575*
not steal, Do not bear *f* witness — Mk 10:19 — *5576*
For *f* Christs and *f* prophets — Mk 13:22 — *5580*
For many bare *f* witness against — Mk 14:56 — *5576*
bare *f* witness against him — Mk 14:57 — *5576*
their fathers to the *f* prophets — Lk 6:26 — *5573*
not steal, Do not bear *f* witness — Lk 18:20 — *5576*
from any man by *f* accusation — Lk 19:8 — *4811*
set up *f* witnesses, which said — Acts 6:13 — *5571*
a *f* prophet, a Jew, whose name — Acts 13:6 — *5578*
Thou shalt not bear *f* witness — Rom 13:9 — *5576*
we are found *f* witnesses of God — 1Cor 15:15 — *5575*
For such are *f* apostles — 2Cor 11:13 — *5570*
sea, in perils among *f* brethren — 2Cor 11:26 — *5569*
that because of *f* brethren — Gal 2:4 — *5569*
f accusers, incontinent, fierce — 2Ti 3:3 — *1228*
not *f* accusers, not given to much — Titus 2:3 — *1228*
But there were *f* prophets also — 2Pet 2:1 — *5578*
shall be *f* teachers among you — 2Pet 2:1 — *5572*
because many *f* prophets are gone — 1Jn 4:1 — *5578*
out of the mouth of the *f* prophet — Rev 16:13 — *5578*
with him the *f* prophet that — Rev 19:20 — *5578*
the *f* prophet are, and shall be — Rev 20:10 — *5578*

FALSEHOOD

wrought *f* against mine own life — 2Sa 18:13 — 8267
in your answers there remaineth *f* — Job 21:34 — 4604
mischief, and brought forth *f* — Ps 7:14 — 8267
for their deceit is *f* — Ps 119:118 — 8267
right hand is a right hand of *f* — Ps 144:8 — 8267
right hand is a right hand of *f* — Ps 144:11 — 8267
under *f* have we hid ourselves — Is 28:15 — 8267
of transgression, a seed of *f* — Is 57:4 — 8267
from the heart words of *f* — Is 59:13 — 8267
for his molten image is *f* — Jer 10:14 — 8267
forgotten me, and trusted in *f* — Jer 13:25 — 8267
for his molten image is *f* — Jer 51:17 — 8267
for they commit *f*; and the thief — Hos 7:1 — 8267
f do lie, saying, I will prophesy — Mic 2:11 — 8267

FALSELY

that thou wilt not deal *f* with me — Gen 21:23 — 8266
concerning it, and sweareth *f* — Lev 6:3 — 8267
that about which he hath sworn *f* — Lev 6:5 — 8267
shall not steal, neither deal *f* — Lev 19:11 — 3584
ye shall not swear by my name *f* — Lev 19:12 — 8267
hath testified *f* against his — Deut 19:18 — 8267
have we dealt *f* in thy covenant — Ps 44:17 — 8266
surely they swear *f* — Jer 5:2 — 8267
The prophets prophesy *f*, and the — Jer 5:31 — 8267
the priest every one dealeth *f* — Jer 6:13 — 8267
and commit adultery, and swear *f* — Jer 7:9 — 8267
the priest every one dealeth *f* — Jer 8:10 — 8267
For they prophesy *f* unto you in — Jer 29:9 — 8267
for thou speakest *f* of Ishmael — Jer 40:16 — 8267
unto Jeremiah, Thou speakest *f* — Jer 43:2 — 8267
swearing *f* in making a covenant — Hos 10:4 — 7723
of him that sweareth *f* by my name — Zec 5:4 — 8267
all manner of evil against you *f* — Mt 5:11 — *5574*
to no man, neither accuse any *f* — Lk 3:14
of science *f* so called — 1Ti 6:20 — *5581*
they may be ashamed that *f* accuse — 1Pet 3:16

FALSIFYING

and *f* the balances by deceit — Amos 8:5 — 5791

FAME

the *f* thereof was heard in — Gen 45:16 — 6963
heard the *f* of thee will speak — Num 14:15 — 8088
his *f* was noised throughout all — Josh 6:27 — 8089
for we have heard the *f* of him — Josh 9:9 — 8089
his *f* was in all nations round — 1Kin 4:31 — 8034
f of Solomon concerning the name — 1Kin 10:1 — 8088
exceedeth the *f* which I heard — 1Kin 10:7 — 8052
the *f* of David went out into all — 1Chr 14:17 — 8034
be exceeding magnifical, of *f* — 1Chr 22:5 — 8034
Sheba heard of the *f* of Solomon — 2Chr 9:1 — 8088
thou exceedest the *f* that I heard — 2Chr 9:6 — 8052
his *f* went out throughout all the — Est 9:4 — 8089
We have heard the *f* thereof with — Job 28:22 — 8088
off, that have not heard my *f* — Is 66:19 — 8088
We have heard the *f* thereof — Jer 6:24 — 8089
f in every land where they have — Zeph 3:19 — 8034
his *f* went throughout all Syria — Mt 4:24 — *189*
the *f* hereof went abroad into all — Mt 9:26 — *5345*

spread abroad his *f* in all that Mt 9:31 *1310*
tetrarch heard of the *f* of Jesus Mt 14:1 *189*
immediately his *f* spread abroad Mk 1:28 *189*
there went out a *f* of him through Lk 4:14 *5345*
the *f* of him went out into every Lk 4:37 *2279*
more went there a *f* abroad of him Lk 5:15 *3056*

FAMILIAR
not them that have *f* spirits Lev 19:31
after such as have *f* spirits Lev 20:6
or woman that hath a *f* spirit Lev 20:27
or a consulter with *f* spirits Deut 18:11
put away those that had *f* spirits 1Sa 28:3
me a woman that hath a *f* spirit 1Sa 28:7
that hath a *f* spirit at En-dor 1Sa 28:7
divine unto me by the *f* spirit 1Sa 28:8
cut off those that have *f* spirits 1Sa 28:9
and dealt with *f* spirits and 2Kin 21:6
the workers with *f* spirits 2Kin 23:24
of one that had a *f* spirit 1Chr 10:13
and dealt with a *f* spirit 2Chr 33:6
my *f* friends have forgotten me Job 19:14 3045
Yea, mine own *f* friend, in whom I Ps 41:9 7965
unto them that have *f* spirits Is 8:19
and to them that have *f* spirits Is 19:3
as of one that hath a *f* spirit Is 29:4

FAMILIARS
All my *f* watched for my halting, Jer 20:10 7965

FAMILIES
after his tongue, after their *f* Gen 10:5 4940
afterward were the *f* of the Gen 10:18 4940
the sons of Ham, after their *f* Gen 10:20 4940
the sons of Shem, after their *f* Gen 10:31 4940
These are the *f* of the sons of Gen 10:32 4940
in thee shall all *f* of the earth Gen 12:3 4940
all the *f* of the earth be blessed Gen 28:14 4940
of Esau, according to their *f* Gen 36:40 4940
with bread, according to their *f* Gen 47:12 2945
these be the *f* of Reuben Ex 6:14 4940
these are the *f* of Simeon Ex 6:15 4940
and Shimi, according to their *f* Ex 6:17 4940
these are the *f* of Levi according Ex 6:19 4940
these are the *f* of the Korhites Ex 6:24 4940
the Levites according to their *f* Ex 6:25 4940
you a lamb according to your *f* Ex 12:21 4940
of their *f* that are with you, Lev 25:45 4940
children of Israel, after their *f* Num 1:2 4940
their pedigrees after their *f* Num 1:18 4940
their generations, after their *f* Num 1:20 4940
their generations, after their *f* Num 1:22 4940
their generations, after their *f* Num 1:24 4940
their generations, after their *f* Num 1:26 4940
their generations, after their *f* Num 1:28 4940
their generations, after their *f* Num 1:30 4940
their generations, after their *f* Num 1:32 4940
their generations, after their *f* Num 1:34 4940
their generations, after their *f* Num 1:36 4940
their generations, after their *f* Num 1:38 4940
their generations, after their *f* Num 1:40 4940
their generations, after their *f* Num 1:42 4940
forward, every one after their *f* Num 2:34 4940
of their fathers, by their *f* Num 3:15 4940
of the sons of Gershon by their *f* Num 3:18 4940
And the sons of Kohath by their *f* Num 3:19 4940
And the sons of Merari by their *f* Num 3:20 4940
These are the *f* of the Levites Num 3:20 4940
these are the *f* of the Num 3:21 4940
The *f* of the Gershonites shall Num 3:23 4940
these are the *f* of the Kohathites Num 3:27 4940
The *f* of the sons of Kohath shall Num 3:29 4940
the *f* of the Kohathites shall be Num 3:30 4940
these are the *f* of Merari Num 3:33 4940
the house of the father of the *f* Num 3:35 4940
of the LORD, throughout their *f* Num 3:39 4940
the sons of Levi, after their *f* Num 4:2 4940
f of the Kohathites from among Num 4:18 4940
of their fathers, by their *f* Num 4:22 4940
of the *f* of the Gershonites Num 4:24 4940
This is the service of the *f* of Num 4:28 4940
shalt number them after their *f* Num 4:29 4940
of the *f* of the sons of Merari Num 4:33 4940
of the Kohathites after their *f* Num 4:34 4940
were numbered of them by their *f* Num 4:36 4940
of the *f* of the Kohathites Num 4:37 4940
of Gershon, throughout their *f* Num 4:38 4940
of them, throughout their *f* Num 4:40 4940
of the *f* of the sons of Gershon Num 4:41 4940
of the *f* of the sons of Merari Num 4:42 4940
throughout their *f*, by the house Num 4:42 4940
numbered of them after their *f* Num 4:44 4940
of the *f* of the sons of Merari Num 4:45 4940
of Israel numbered, after their *f* Num 4:46 4940
people weep throughout their *f* Num 11:10 4940
These are the *f* of the Reubenites Num 26:7 4940
The sons of Simeon after their *f* Num 26:12 4940
These are the *f* of the Simeonites Num 26:14 4940
The children of Gad after their *f* Num 26:15 4940
These are the *f* of the children Num 26:18 4940
sons of Judah after their *f* were Num 26:20 4940
These are the *f* of Judah Num 26:22 4940
sons of Issachar after their *f* Num 26:23 4940
These are the *f* of Issachar Num 26:25 4940
the sons of Zebulun after their *f* Num 26:26 4940
These are the *f* of the Num 26:27 4940
after their *f* were Manasseh Num 26:28 4940
These are the *f* of Manasseh Num 26:34 4940
the sons of Ephraim after their *f* Num 26:35 4940
These are the *f* of the sons of Num 26:37 4940
the sons of Joseph after their *f* Num 26:37 4940
sons of Benjamin after their *f* Num 26:38 4940
sons of Benjamin after their *f* Num 26:41 4940
are the sons of Dan after their *f* Num 26:42 4940
These are the *f* of Dan after Num 26:42 4940
the *f* of Dan after their *f* Num 26:42 4940
All the *f* of the Shuhamites, Num 26:43 4940
children of Asher after their *f* Num 26:44 4940
These are the *f* of the sons of Num 26:47 4940
sons of Naphtali after their *f* Num 26:48 4940
These are the *f* of Naphtali Num 26:50 4940
of Naphtali according to their *f* Num 26:50 4940
of the Levites after their *f* Num 26:57 4940
These are the *f* of the Levites Num 26:58 4940
of the *f* of Manasseh the son of Num 27:1 4940
for an inheritance among your *f* Num 33:54 4940
the chief fathers of the *f* of the Num 36:1 4940
of the *f* of the sons of Joseph, Num 36:1 4940
they were married into the *f* of Num 36:12 4940
come according to the *f* thereof Josh 7:14 4940
inheritance according to their *f* Josh 13:15 4940
children of Reuben after their *f* Josh 13:23 4940
children of Gad according their *f* Josh 13:24 4940
the children of Gad after their *f* Josh 13:28 4940
children of Manasseh by their *f* Josh 13:29 4940
the children of Machir by their *f* Josh 13:31 4940
the children of Judah by their *f* Josh 15:1 4940
round about according to their *f* Josh 15:12 4940
of Judah according to their *f* Josh 15:20 4940
according to their *f* was thus Josh 16:5 4940
children of Ephraim by their *f* Josh 16:8 4940
children of Manasseh by their *f* Josh 17:2 4940
the son of Joseph by their *f* Josh 17:2 4940
came up according to their *f* Josh 18:11 4940
round about, according to their *f* Josh 18:20 4940
according to their *f* were Jericho Josh 18:21 4940
of Benjamin according to their *f* Josh 18:28 4940
of Simeon according to their *f* Josh 19:1 4940
of Simeon according to their *f* Josh 19:8 4940
of Zebulun according to their *f* Josh 19:10 4940
of Zebulun according to their *f* Josh 19:16 4940
of Issachar according to their *f* Josh 19:17 4940
of Issachar according to their *f* Josh 19:23 4940
of Asher according to their *f* Josh 19:24 4940
of Asher according to their *f* Josh 19:31 4940
of Naphtali according to their *f* Josh 19:32 4940
of Naphtali according to their *f* Josh 19:39 4940
of Dan according to their *f* Josh 19:40 4940
of Dan according to their *f* Josh 19:48 4940
out for the *f* of the Kohathites Josh 21:4 4940
of the *f* of the tribe of Ephraim Josh 21:5 4940
of the *f* of the tribe of Issachar Josh 21:6 4940
f had out of the tribe of Reuben Josh 21:7 4940
being of the *f* of the Kohathites, Josh 21:10 4940
the *f* of the children of Kohath, Josh 21:20 4940
f of the children of Kohath that Josh 21:26 4940
of the *f* of the Levites, out of Josh 21:27 4940
Gershonites according to their *f* Josh 21:33 4940
unto the *f* of the children of Josh 21:34 4940
the children of Merari by their *f* Josh 21:40 4940
remaining of the *f* of the Levites Josh 21:40 4940
the *f* of the tribe of Benjamin 1Sa 9:21 4940
Benjamin to come near by their *f* 1Sa 10:21 4940
And the *f* of Kirjath-jearim 1Chr 2:53 4940
the *f* of the scribes which dwelt 1Chr 2:55 4940
These are the *f* of the Zorathites 1Chr 4:2 4940
the *f* of Aharhel the son of Harum 1Chr 4:8 4940
the *f* of the house of them that 1Chr 4:21 4940
names were princes in their *f* 1Chr 4:38 4940
And his brethren by their *f* 1Chr 5:7 4940
these are the *f* of the Levites 1Chr 6:19 4940
of the *f* of the Kohathites 1Chr 6:54 4940
their *f* were thirteen cities 1Chr 6:60 4940
of Gershom throughout their *f* out 1Chr 6:62 4940
given by lot, throughout their *f* 1Chr 6:63 4940
the residue of the *f* of the sons 1Chr 6:66 4940
their brethren among all the *f* of 1Chr 7:5 4940
to the divisions of the *f* of the 2Chr 35:5 1004
division of the *f* of the Levites 2Chr 35:5 1004
divisions of the *f* of the people 2Chr 35:12 1004
after their *f* with their swords Neh 4:13 4940
did the contempt of *f* terrify me Job 31:34 4940
God setteth the solitary in *f* Ps 68:6 1004
maketh him *f* like a flock Ps 107:41 4940
I will call all the *f* of the Jer 1:15 4940
all the *f* of the house of Israel Jer 2:4 4940
upon the *f* that call not on thy Jer 10:25 4940
and take all the *f* of the north Jer 25:9 4940
be the God of all the *f* of Israel Jer 31:1 4940
The two *f* which the LORD hath Jer 33:24 4940
as the *f* of the countries, to Eze 20:32 4940
I known of all the *f* of the earth Amos 3:2 4940
f through her witchcrafts Nah 3:4 4940
All the *f* that remain, every Zec 12:14 4940
will not come up of all the *f* of Zec 14:17 4940

FAMILY
that man, and against his *f* Lev 20:5 4940
shall return every man unto his *f* Lev 25:10 4940
and shall return unto his own *f* Lev 25:41 4940
to the stock of the stranger's *f* Lev 25:47 4940
unto him of his *f* may redeem him Lev 25:49 4940
Gershon was the *f* of the Libnites Num 3:21 4940
and the *f* of the Shimites Num 3:21 4940
Kohath was the *f* of the Amramites Num 3:27 4940
the *f* of the Izeharites, and the Num 3:27 4940
the *f* of the Hebronites, and the Num 3:27 4940
and the *f* of the Uzzielites Num 3:27 4940
Merari was the *f* of the Mahlites Num 3:33 4940
and the *f* of the Mushites Num 3:33 4940
cometh the *f* of the Hanochites Num 26:5 4940
of Pallu, the *f* of the Palluites Num 26:5 4940
Hezron, the *f* of the Hezronites Num 26:6 4940
of Carmi, the *f* of the Carmites Num 26:6 4940
Nemuel, the *f* of the Nemuelites Num 26:12 4940
of Jamin, the *f* of the Jaminites Num 26:12 4940
Jachin, the *f* of the Jachinites Num 26:12 4940
Of Zerah, the *f* of the Zarhites Num 26:13 4940
of Shaul, the *f* of the Shaulites Num 26:13 4940
Zephon, the *f* of the Zephonites Num 26:15 4940
of Haggi, the *f* of the Haggites Num 26:15 4940
of Shuni, the *f* of the Shunites Num 26:15 4940
Of Ozni, the *f* of the Oznites Num 26:16 4940
of Eri, the *f* of the Erites Num 26:16 4940
Of Arod, the *f* of the Arodites Num 26:17 4940
of Areli, the *f* of the Arelites Num 26:17 4940
Shelah, the *f* of the Shelanites Num 26:20 4940
of Pharez, the *f* of the Pharzites Num 26:20 4940
of Zerah, the *f* of the Zarhites Num 26:20 4940
Hezron, the *f* of the Hezronites Num 26:21 4940
of Hamul, the *f* of the Hamulites Num 26:21 4940
of Tola, the *f* of the Tolaites Num 26:23 4940
of Pua, the *f* of the Punites Num 26:23 4940
Jashub, the *f* of the Jashubites Num 26:24 4940
Shimron, the *f* of the Shimronites Num 26:24 4940
of Sered, the *f* of the Sardites Num 26:26 4940
of Elon, the *f* of the Elonites Num 26:26 4940
Jahleel, the *f* of the Jahleelites Num 26:26 4940
Machir, the *f* of the Machirites Num 26:29 4940
come the *f* of the Gileadites Num 26:29 4940
Jeezer, the *f* of the Jeezerites Num 26:30 4940
of Helek, the *f* of the Helekites Num 26:30 4940
Asriel, the *f* of the Asrielites Num 26:31 4940
Shechem, the *f* of the Shechemites Num 26:31 4940
Shemida, the *f* of the Shemidaites Num 26:32 4940
Hepher, the *f* of the Hepherites Num 26:32 4940
the *f* of the Shuthalhites Num 26:35 4940
of Becher, the *f* of the Bachrites Num 26:35 4940
of Tahan, the *f* of the Tahanites Num 26:35 4940
of Eran, the *f* of the Eranites Num 26:36 4940
of Bela, the *f* of the Belaites Num 26:38 4940
Ashbel, the *f* of the Ashbelites Num 26:38 4940
Ahiram, the *f* of the Ahiramites Num 26:38 4940
Shupham, the *f* of the Shuphamites Num 26:39 4940
Hupham, the *f* of the Huphamites Num 26:39 4940
of Ard, the *f* of the Ardites Num 26:40 4940
of Naaman, the *f* of the Naamites Num 26:40 4940
Shuham, the *f* of the Shuhamites Num 26:42 4940
of Jimna, the *f* of the Jimnites Num 26:44 4940
of Jesui, the *f* of the Jesuites Num 26:44 4940
of Beriah, the *f* of the Beriites Num 26:44 4940
of Heber, the *f* of the Heberites Num 26:45 4940
the *f* of the Malchielites Num 26:45 4940
Jahzeel, the *f* of the Jahzeelites Num 26:48 4940
of Guni, the *f* of the Gunites Num 26:48 4940
Of Jezer, the *f* of the Jezerites Num 26:49 4940
Shillem, the *f* of the Shillemites Num 26:49 4940
Gershon, the *f* of the Gershonites Num 26:57 4940
Kohath, the *f* of the Kohathites Num 26:57 4940
of Merari, the *f* of the Merarites Num 26:57 4940
the *f* of the Libnites Num 26:58 4940
the *f* of the Hebronites Num 26:58 4940
the *f* of the Mahlites Num 26:58 4940
the *f* of the Mushites Num 26:58 4940
Mushites, the *f* of the Korathites Num 26:58 4940
be done away from among his *f* Num 27:4 4940
that is next to him of his *f* Num 27:11 4940
only to the *f* of the tribe of Num 36:6 4940
the *f* of the tribe of her father Num 36:8 4940
tribe of the *f* of their father Num 36:12 4940
be among you man, or woman, or *f* Deut 29:18 4940
the *f* which the LORD shall take Josh 7:14 4940
And he brought the *f* of Judah Josh 7:17 4940
he took the *f* of the Zarhites Josh 7:17 4940
he brought the *f* of the Zarhites Josh 7:17 4940
they let go the man and all his *f* Judg 1:25 4940
my *f* is poor in Manasseh, and I am Judg 6:15 504
with all the *f* of the house of Judg 9:1 4940
of the *f* of the Danites, whose Judg 13:2 4940
of the *f* of Judah, who was a Judg 17:7 4940
f five men from their coasts Judg 18:2 4940
thence of the *f* of the Danites Judg 18:11 4940
unto a tribe and a *f* in Israel Judg 18:19 4940
man to his tribe and to his *f* Judg 21:24 4940
of wealth, of the *f* of Elimelech Ruth 2:1 4940
my *f* the least of all the 1Sa 9:21 4940
the *f* of Matri was taken, and Saul 1Sa 10:21 4940
life, or my father's *f* in Israel 1Sa 18:18 4940
sacrifice there for all the *f* 1Sa 20:6 4940
for our *f* hath a sacrifice in the 1Sa 20:29 4940
the whole *f* is risen against 2Sa 14:7 4940
man of the *f* of the house of Saul 2Sa 16:5 4940
neither did all their *f* multiply 1Chr 4:27 4940
were left of the *f* of that tribe 1Chr 6:61 4940
for the *f* of the remnant of the 1Chr 6:70 4940
f of the half tribe of Manasseh 1Chr 6:71 4940
ark of God remained with the *f* of 1Chr 13:14 1004
every generation, every *f* Est 9:28 4940
you one of a city, and two of a *f* Jer 3:14 4940
them that remain of this evil *f* Jer 8:3 4940
against the whole *f* which I Amos 3:1 4940
against this *f* do I devise an Mic 2:3 4940
land shall mourn, every *f* apart Zec 12:12 4940
the *f* of the house of David apart Zec 12:12 4940
the *f* of the house of Nathan Zec 12:12 4940
The *f* of the house of Levi apart, Zec 12:13 4940
the *f* of Shimei apart, and their Zec 12:13 4940
that remain, every *f* apart Zec 12:14 4940
if the *f* of Egypt go not up, and Zec 14:18 4940
Of whom the whole *f* in heaven Eph 3:15 *3965*

FAMINE
And there was a *f* in the land Gen 12:10 7458
for the *f* was grievous in the Gen 12:10 7458
And there was a *f* in the land Gen 26:1 7458
beside the first *f* that was in Gen 26:1 7458
wind shall be seven years of *f* Gen 41:27 7458
arise after them seven years of *f* Gen 41:30 7458
the *f* shall consume the land Gen 41:30 7458
by reason of that *f* following Gen 41:31 7458
land against the seven years of *f* Gen 41:36 7458
the land perish not through the *f* Gen 41:36 7458
sons before the years of *f* came Gen 41:50 7458

the *f* was over all the face of Gen 41:56 7458
the *f* waxed sore in the land of Gen 41:56 7458
because that the *f* was so sore in Gen 41:57 7458
for the *f* was in the land of Gen 42:5 7458
corn for the *f* of your houses Gen 42:19 7459
take food for the *f* of your Gen 42:33 7459
the *f* was sore in the land Gen 43:1 7458
years hath the *f* been in the land Gen 45:6 7458
for yet there are five years of *f* Gen 45:11 7458
for the *f* is sore in the land of Gen 47:4 7458
for the *f* was very sore, so that Gen 47:13 7458
Canaan fainted by reason of the *f* Gen 47:13 7458
because the *f* prevailed over them Gen 47:20 7458
that there was a *f* in the land Ruth 1:1 7458
Then there was a *f* in the days of 2Sa 21:1 7458
Shall seven years of *f* come unto 2Sa 24:13 7458
If there be in the land *f* 1Kin 8:37 7458
And there was a sore *f* in Samaria 1Kin 18:2 7458
And there was a great *f* in Samaria 2Kin 6:25 7458
then the *f* is in the city, and we 2Kin 7:4 7458
for the LORD hath called for a *f* 2Kin 8:1 7458
month the *f* prevailed in the city 2Kin 25:3 7458
Either three years' *f* 1Chr 21:12 7458
judgment, or pestilence, or *f* 2Chr 20:9 7458
give over yourselves to die by *f* 2Chr 32:11 7458
In *f* he shall redeem thee from Job 5:20 7458
destruction and *f* thou shalt laugh Job 5:22 3720
For want and *f* they were solitary Job 30:3 3720
death, and to keep them alive in *f* Ps 33:19 7458
in the days of *f* they shall be Ps 37:19 7459
he called for a *f* upon the land Ps 105:16 7458
and I will kill thy root with *f* Is 14:30 7458
and destruction, and the *f* Is 51:19 7458
neither shall we see sword nor *f* Jer 5:12 7458
and their daughters shall die by *f* Jer 11:22 7458
them by the sword, and by the *f* Jer 14:12 7458
sword, neither shall ye have *f* Jer 14:13 7458
f shall not be in this land Jer 14:15 7458
f shall those prophets be Jer 14:15 7458
of Jerusalem because of the *f* Jer 14:16 7458
behold them that are sick with *f* Jer 14:18 7458
as are for the *f*, to the *f* Jer 15:2 7458
be consumed by the sword, and by *f* Jer 16:4 7458
up their children to the *f* Jer 18:21 7458
from the sword, and from the *f* Jer 21:7 7458
die by the sword, and by the *f* Jer 21:9 7458
And I will send the sword, the *f* Jer 24:10 7458
with the sword, and with the *f* Jer 27:8 7458
people, by the sword, by the *f* Jer 27:13 7458
send upon them the sword, the *f* Jer 29:17 7458
them with the sword, with the *f* Jer 29:18 7458
because of the sword, and of the *f* Jer 32:24 7458
Babylon by the sword, and by the *f* Jer 32:36 7458
to the pestilence, and to the *f* Jer 34:17 7458
shall die by the sword, by the *f* Jer 38:2 7458
in the land of Egypt, and the *f* Jer 42:16 7458
shall die by the sword, by the *f* Jer 42:17 7458
shall die by the sword, by the *f* Jer 42:22 7458
consumed by the sword and by the *f* Jer 44:12 7458
by the sword and by the *f* Jer 44:12 7458
Jerusalem, by the sword, by the *f* Jer 44:13 7458
consumed by the sword and by the *f* Jer 44:18 7458
consumed by the sword and by the *f* Jer 44:27 7458
the *f* was sore in the city, so Jer 52:6 7458
an oven because of the terrible *f* Lam 5:10 7458
with *f* shall they be consumed in Eze 5:12 7458
upon them the evil arrows of *f* Eze 5:16 7458
and I will increase the *f* upon you Eze 5:16 7458
So will I send upon you *f* Eze 5:17 7458
shall fall by the sword, by the *f* Eze 6:11 7458
and is besieged shall die by the *f* Eze 6:12 7458
and the pestilence and the *f* within Eze 7:15 7458
and he that is in the city, *f* Eze 7:15 7458
them from the sword, from the *f* Eze 12:16 7458
thereof, and will send *f* upon it Eze 14:13 7458
Jerusalem, the sword, and the *f* Eze 14:21 7458
increase it, and lay no *f* upon you Eze 36:29 7458
reproach of *f* among the heathen Eze 36:30 7458
that I will send a *f* in the land Amos 8:11 7458
not a *f* of bread, nor a thirst Amos 8:11 7458
when great *f* was throughout all Lk 4:25 *3042*
arose a mighty *f* in that land Lk 15:14 *3042*
or distress, or persecution, or *f* Rom 8:35 *3042*
one day, death, and mourning, and *f* Rev 18:8 *3042*

FAMINES
and there shall be *f*, and Mt 24:7 *3042*
places, and there shall be *f* Mk 13:8 *3042*
shall be in divers places, and *f* Lk 21:11 *3042*

FAMISH
the soul of the righteous to *f* Prov 10:3 7456
for he will *f* all the gods of the Zeph 2:11 7329

FAMISHED
when all the land of Egypt was *f* Gen 41:55 7456
and their honourable men are *f* Is 5:13 7458

FAMOUS
f in the congregation, men of Num 16:2 7148
which were *f* in the congregation, Num 26:9 7121
Ephratah, and be *f* in Beth-lehem Ruth 4:11 8034
that his name may be *f* in Israel Ruth 4:14 7121
f men, and heads of the house of 1Chr 5:24 8034
f throughout the house of their 1Chr 12:30 8034
A man was *f* according as he had Ps 74:5 3045
And slew *f* kings Ps 136:18 117
and she became *f* among women Eze 23:10 8034
and the daughters of the *f* nations Eze 32:18 117

FAN
with the shovel and with the *f* Is 30:24 4214
Thou shalt *f* them, and the wind Is 41:16 2219
daughter of my people, not to *f* Jer 4:11 2219
I will *f* them with a *f* in the Jer 15:7 2219
Babylon fanners, that shall *f* her Jer 51:2 2219
Whose *f* is in his hand, and he Mt 3:12 *4425*
Whose *f* is in his hand, and he Lk 3:17 *4425*

FANNERS
And will send unto Babylon *f* Jer 51:2 2114

FAR
That be *f* from thee to do after Gen 18:25 2486
the wicked, that be *f* from thee Gen 18:25 2486
out of the city, and not yet *f* off Gen 44:4 7368
only ye shall not go very *f* away Ex 8:28 7368
Keep thee *f* from a false matter Ex 23:7 7368
f off about the tabernacle of the Num 2:2 5048
his name there be too *f* from thee Deut 12:21 7368
or *f* off from thee, from the one Deut 13:7 7350
if the place be too *f* from thee Deut 14:24 7368
which are very *f* off from thee Deut 20:15 7350
a nation against thee from *f* Deut 28:49 7350
that shall come from a *f* land Deut 29:22 7350
from thee, neither is it *f* off Deut 30:11 7350
an heap very *f* from the city Adam Josh 3:16 7368
go not very *f* from the city, but Josh 8:4 7368
We be come from a *f* country Josh 9:6 7350
From a very *f* country thy Josh 9:9 7350
saying, We are very *f* from you Josh 9:22 7350
for you, and adventured his life *f* Judg 9:17 5048
they were *f* from the Zidonians, Judg 18:7 7350
because it was *f* from Zidon Judg 18:28 7350
by Jebus, the day was *f* spent Judg 19:11 3966
the LORD saith, Be it *f* from me 1Sa 2:30 2486
Jonathan said, *F* be it from thee 1Sa 20:9 2486
be it *f* from me 1Sa 22:15 2486
tarried in a place that was *f* off 2Sa 15:17 4801
F be it, *f* be it from me, that 2Sa 20:20 2486
f be it from me, that I should 2Sa 20:20 2486
Be it *f* from me, O LORD, that I 2Sa 23:17 2486
but cometh out of a *f* country for 1Kin 8:41 7350
the land of the enemy, *f* or near 1Kin 8:46 7350
They are come from a *f* country 2Kin 20:14 7350
but is come from a *f* country for 2Chr 6:32 7350
unto a land *f* off or near 2Chr 6:36 7350
And his name spread *f* abroad 2Chr 26:15 7350
the river, be ye *f* from thence Ezr 6:6 7352
upon the wall, one *f* from another Neh 4:19 7350
king Ahasuerus, both nigh and *f* Est 9:20 7350
His children are *f* from safety Job 5:4 7368
be in thine hand, put it *f* away Job 11:14 7350
Withdraw thine hand *f* from me Job 13:21 7350
He hath put my brethren *f* from me Job 19:13 7350
of the wicked is *f* from me Job 21:16 7350
of the wicked is *f* from me Job 22:18 7350
iniquity *f* from thy tabernacles Job 22:23 7350
abhor me, they flee *f* from me Job 30:10 7350
f be it from God, that he should Job 34:10 2486
thy judgments are *f* above out of Ps 10:5 5048
why art thou so *f* from helping me Ps 22:1 7350
Be not *f* from me Ps 22:11 7368
But be not thou *f* from me Ps 22:19 7368
Hide not thy face *f* from me Ps 27:9
O Lord, be not *f* from me Ps 35:22 7368
O my God, be not *f* from me Ps 38:21 7368
Lo, then would I wander *f* off Ps 55:7 7368
O God, be not *f* from me Ps 71:12 7368
they that are *f* from thee shall Ps 73:27 7369
away mine acquaintance *f* from me Ps 88:8 7368
and friend hast thou put *f* from me Ps 88:18 7368
thou art exalted *f* above all gods Ps 97:9 3966
As *f* as the east is from the west Ps 103:12 7350
so *f* hath he removed our Ps 103:12 7350
blessing, so let it be *f* from him Ps 109:17 7368
they are *f* from thy law Ps 119:150 7368
Salvation is *f* from the wicked Ps 119:155 7350
and perverse lips put *f* from thee Prov 4:24 7368
Remove thy way *f* from her Prov 5:8 7368
The LORD is *f* from the wicked Prov 15:29 7350
more do his friends go *f* from him Prov 19:7 7368
his soul shall be *f* from them Prov 22:5 7368
shall drive it *f* from him Prov 22:15 7368
so is good news from a *f* country Prov 25:25 4801
that is near than a brother *f* off Prov 27:10 7350
Remove *f* from me vanity and lies Prov 30:8 7369
for her price is *f* above rubies Prov 31:10 7350
as *f* as light excelleth darkness Eccl 2:13
but it was *f* from me Eccl 7:23 7350
That which is *f* off, and exceeding Eccl 7:24 7350
an ensign to the nations from *f* Is 5:26 7350
the LORD have removed men *f* away Is 6:12 7368
give ear, all ye of *f* countries Is 8:9 4801
which shall come from *f* Is 10:3 4801
They come from a *f* country Is 13:5 4801
them, and they shall flee *f* off Is 17:13 4801
they shall turn the rivers *f* away Is 19:6
together, which have fled from *f* Is 22:3 7350
thou hadst removed it *f* unto all Is 26:15 7368
removed their heart *f* from me Is 29:13 7368
name of the LORD cometh from *f* Is 30:27 4801
Hear, ye that are *f* off, what I Is 33:13 7350
the land that is very *f* off Is 33:17 4801
are come from a *f* country unto me Is 39:3 7350
bring my sons from *f*, and my Is 43:6 7350
my counsel from a *f* country Is 46:11 4801
that are *f* from righteousness Is 46:12 7350
it shall not be *f* off, and my Is 46:13 7368
and hearken, ye people, from *f* Is 49:1 7350
Behold, these shall come from *f* Is 49:12 7350
swallowed thee up shall be *f* away Is 49:19 7368
thou shalt be *f* from oppression Is 54:14 7368
didst send thy messengers *f* off Is 57:9 7350
Peace, peace to him that is *f* off Is 57:19 7350
Therefore is judgment *f* from us Is 59:9 7368
but it is *f* off from us Is 59:11 7368
thy sons shall come from *f* Is 60:4 7350
first, to bring thy sons from *f* Is 60:9 7350
me, that they are gone *f* from me Jer 2:5 7368
watchers come from a *f* country Jer 4:16 4801
bring a nation upon you from *f* Jer 5:15 4801
the sweet cane from a *f* country Jer 6:20 4801
of them that dwell in a *f* country Jer 8:19 4801
mouth, and *f* from their reins Jer 12:2 7350
And all the kings of the north, *f* Jer 25:26 7350
to remove you *f* from your land Jer 27:10 7368
of the land of Moab, *f* or near Jer 48:24 7350
Thus *f* is the judgment of Moab Jer 48:47 2008
Flee, get you *f* off, dwell deep, Jer 49:30 3966
Thus *f* are the words of Jeremiah Jer 51:64 2008
relieve my soul is *f* from me Lam 1:16 7368
removed my soul *f* off from peace Lam 3:17 2186
He that is *f* off shall die of the Eze 6:12 7350
have I set it *f* from them Eze 7:20 5079
that I should go *f* off from my Eze 8:6 7368
said, Get you *f* from the LORD Eze 11:15 7368
cast them *f* off among the heathen Eze 11:16 7368
of the times that are *f* off Eze 12:27 7350
and those that be *f* from thee Eze 22:5 7350
have sent for men to come from *f* Eze 23:40 4801
f from me, and I will dwell in the Eze 43:9 7350
that are gone away *f* from me Eze 44:10 7350
that are near, and that are *f* off Dan 9:7 7350
the fourth shall be *f* richer than Dan 11:2 1419
But I will remove *f* off from you Joel 2:20 7368
remove them *f* from their border Joel 3:6 7368
to the Sabeans, to a people *f* off Joel 3:8 7350
Ye that put *f* away the evil day, Amos 6:3
her that was cast *f* off a strong Mic 4:7
day shall the decree be *f* removed Mic 7:11 7368
their horsemen shall come from *f* Hab 1:8 7350
they that are *f* off shall come and Zec 6:15 7350
shall remember me in *f* countries Zec 10:9 4801
but their heart is *f* from me Mt 15:8 *4206*
saying, Be it *f* from thee, Lord Mt 16:22 *2436*
and went into a *f* country Mt 21:33
a man travelling into a *f* country Mt 25:14
And when the day was now *f* spent Mk 6:35 *4183*
and now the time is *f* passed Mk 6:35 *4183*
but their heart is *f* from me Mk 7:6 *4206*
for divers of them came from *f* Mk 8:3 *3113*
and went into a *f* country Mk 12:1
Thou art not *f* from the kingdom Mk 12:34 *3112*
is as a man taking a *f* journey Mk 13:34
he was now not *f* from the house Lk 7:6 *3112*
took his journey into a *f* country Lk 15:13 *3117*
f country to receive for himself Lk 19:12 *3117*
went into a *f* country for a long Lk 20:9
and said, Suffer ye thus *f* Lk 22:51 *2193*
evening, and the day is *f* spent Lk 24:29
led them out as *f* as to Bethany Lk 24:50 *2193*
(for they were not *f* from land Jn 21:8 *3112*
Stephen travelled as *f* as Phenice Acts 11:19 *2193*
that he should go as *f* as Antioch Acts 11:22 *2193*
though he be not *f* from every one Acts 17:27 *3112*
for I will send thee *f* hence unto Acts 22:21 *3112*
to meet us as *f* as Appii forum Acts 28:15 *891*
The night is *f* spent, the day is Rom 13:12
worketh for us a *f* more exceeding 2Cor 4:17 *1519*
for we are come as *f* as to you 2Cor 10:14 *891*
F above all principality, and Eph 1:21 *5231*
Jesus ye who sometimes were *f* off Eph 2:13 *3112*
ascended up *f* above all heavens Eph 4:10 *5231*
be with Christ; which is *f* better Phil 1:23 *4183*
And it is yet *f* more evident Heb 7:15 *4054*

FARE
and look how thy brethren *f* 1Sa 17:18 7965
so he paid the *f* thereof, and went Jonah 1:3 7939
shall do well. *F* ye well Acts 15:29 *4517*

FARED
linen, and *f* sumptuously every day Lk 16:19 *2165*

FAREWELL
but let me first go bid them *f* Lk 9:61 *657*
But bade them *f*, saying, I must Acts 18:21 *657*
what they had against him. *F*. Acts 23:30 *4517*
Finally, brethren, *f* 2Cor 13:11 *5463*

FARM
and went their ways, one to his *f* Mt 22:5 *00*

FARTHER
And he went a little *f*, and fell on Mt 26:39 *4281*
he had gone a little *f* thence Mk 1:19 *4260*
of Judaea by the *f* side of Jordan Mk 10:1 *4008*

FARTHING
thou hast paid the uttermost *f* Mt 5:26 *2835*
Are not two sparrows sold for a *f* Mt 10:29 *787*
in two mites, which make a *f* Mk 12:42 *2835*

FARTHINGS
not five sparrows sold for two *f* Lk 12:6 *787*

FASHION
this is the *f* which thou shalt Gen 6:15
f thereof which was shewed thee Ex 26:30 4941
the *f* of almonds in one branch Ex 37:19
and according to all the *f* of it 1Kin 6:38 4941
the priest the *f* of the altar 2Kin 16:10 1823
did not one *f* us in the womb Job 31:15 3559
the *f* thereof, and the goings out Eze 43:11 8498
saying, We never saw it on this *f* Mk 2:12 *3778*
the *f* of his countenance was Lk 9:29 *1491*
to the *f* that he had seen Acts 7:44 *5179*
for the *f* of this world passeth 1Cor 7:31 *4976*
And being found in *f* as a man Phil 2:8 *4976*
grace of the *f* of it perisheth Jas 1:11 *4383*

FASHIONED
f it with a graving tool, after Ex 32:4 3335
f me together round about Job 10:8 6213
Thy hands have made me and *f* me Ps 119:73 3559
which in continuance were *f* Ps 139:16 3335
unto him that *f* it long ago Is 22:11 3335
thy breasts are *f*, and thine hair Eze 16:7 3559

that it may be *f* like unto his ... Phil 3:21 4832

FASHIONETH
He *f* their hearts alike ... Ps 33:15 3335
f it with hammers, and worketh it ... Is 44:12 3335
the clay say to him that *f* it ... Is 45:9 3335

FASHIONING
not *f* yourselves according to the ... 1Pet 1:14 4964

FASHIONS
were both according to their *f* ... Eze 42:11 4941

FAST
For the LORD had *f* closed up all ... Gen 20:18
for he was *f* asleep and weary ... Judg 4:21
but we will bind thee *f*, and ... Judg 15:13
If they bind me *f* with new ropes ... Judg 16:11
but abide here *f* by my maidens ... Ruth 2:8
Thou shalt keep *f* by my young men ... Ruth 2:21
So she kept *f* by the maidens of ... Ruth 2:23
thou didst *f* and weep for the ... 2Sa 12:21 6684
he is dead, wherefore should I *f* ... 2Sa 12:23 6684
the letters, saying, Proclaim a *f* ... 1Kin 21:9 6685
They proclaimed a *f*, and set ... 1Kin 21:12 6685
door, and hold him *f* at the door ... 2Kin 6:32
proclaimed a *f* throughout all ... 2Chr 20:3 6685
walls, and this work goeth *f* on ... Ezr 5:8 629
Then I proclaimed a *f* there ... Ezr 8:21 6685
f ye for me, and neither eat nor ... Est 4:16 6684
and my maidens will *f* likewise ... Est 4:16 6684
still he holdeth *f* his integrity ... Job 2:3
he shall hold it *f*, but it shall ... Job 8:15
My righteousness I hold *f* ... Job 27:6
and the clods cleave *f* together ... Job 38:38
he commanded, and it stood *f* ... Ps 33:9
For thine arrows stick *f* in me ... Ps 38:2
say they, cleaveth *f* unto him ... Ps 41:8
strength setteth *f* the mountains ... Ps 65:6
covenant shall stand *f* with him ... Ps 89:28
They stand *f* for ever and ever, and ... Ps 111:8
Take *f* hold of instruction ... Prov 4:13
day of your *f* ye find pleasure ... Is 58:3 6685
ye *f* for strife and debate, and to ... Is 58:4 6684
ye shall not *f* as ye do this day, ... Is 58:4 6684
Is it such a *f* that I have chosen ... Is 58:5 6685
wilt thou call this a *f*, and an ... Is 58:5 6685
Is not this the *f* that I have ... Is 58:6 6685
they hold *f* deceit, they refuse ... Jer 8:5
When they *f*, I will not hear ... Jer 14:12 6684
that they proclaimed a *f* before ... Jer 36:9 6685
say ye, Stand *f*, and prepare thee ... Jer 46:14
come, and his affliction hasteth *f* ... Jer 48:16 3966
took them captives held them *f* ... Jer 50:33
Sanctify ye a *f*, call a solemn ... Joel 1:14 6685
the trumpet in Zion, sanctify a *f* ... Joel 2:15 6685
and he lay, and was *f* asleep ... Jonah 1:5
believed God, and proclaimed a *f* ... Jonah 3:5 6685
years, did ye at all *f* unto me ... Zec 7:5 6684
The *f* of the fourth month, and the ... Zec 8:19 6685
the *f* of the fifth ... Zec 8:19 6685
the *f* of the seventh ... Zec 8:19 6685
and the *f* of ... Zec 8:19 6685
Moreover when ye *f*, be not, as ... Mt 6:16 3522
they may appear unto men to *f* ... Mt 6:16 3522
thou appear not unto men to *f* ... Mt 6:18 3522
Why do we and the Pharisees *f* oft ... Mt 9:14 3522
f oft, but thy disciples *f* not ... Mt 9:14 3522
from them, and then shall they *f* ... Mt 9:15 3522
hold him *f* ... Mt 26:48
and of the Pharisees used to *f* ... Mk 2:18 3522
of John and of the Pharisees *f* ... Mk 2:18 3522
but thy disciples *f* not ... Mk 2:18 3522
children of the bridechamber *f* ... Mk 2:19 3522
with them, they cannot *f* ... Mk 2:19 3522
then shall they *f* in those days ... Mk 2:20 3522
do the disciples of John *f* often ... Lk 5:33 3522
children of the bridechamber *f* ... Lk 5:34 3522
then shall they *f* in those days ... Lk 5:35 3522
I *f* twice in the week, I give ... Lk 18:12 3522
made their feet *f* in the stocks ... Acts 16:24 805
because the *f* was now already ... Acts 27:9 3521
and the forepart stuck *f*, and ... Acts 27:41
stand *f* in the faith, quit you ... 1Cor 16:13
Stand *f* therefore in the liberty ... Gal 5:1
that ye stand *f* in one spirit ... Phil 1:27
so stand *f* in the Lord, my dearly ... Phil 4:1
live, if ye stand *f* in the Lord ... 1Th 3:8
hold *f* that which is good ... 1Th 5:21 2722
Therefore, brethren, stand *f* ... 2Th 2:15
Hold *f* the form of sound words, ... 2Ti 1:13
Holding *f* the faithful word as he ... Titus 1:9 472
if we hold *f* the confidence and ... Heb 3:6 2722
let us hold *f* our profession ... Heb 4:14
Let us hold *f* the profession of ... Heb 10:23 2722
and thou holdest *f* my name ... Rev 2:13
have already hold *f* till I come ... Rev 2:25
hast received and heard, and hold *f* ... Rev 3:3
hold that *f* which thou hast, that ... Rev 3:11

FASTED
f that day until even, and offered ... Judg 20:26 6684
f on that day, and said there, We ... 1Sa 7:6 6684
a tree at Jabesh, and *f* seven days ... 1Sa 31:13 6684
f until even, for Saul, and for ... 2Sa 1:12 6684
and David *f*, and went in, and lay ... 2Sa 12:16 6684
the child was yet alive, I *f* ... 2Sa 12:22 6684
sackcloth upon his flesh, and *f* ... 1Kin 21:27 6684
oak in Jabesh, and *f* seven days ... 1Chr 10:12 6684
So we *f* and besought our God for ... Ezr 8:23 6684
and mourned certain days, and *f* ... Neh 1:4 6684
Wherefore have we *f*, say they, and ... Is 58:3 6684
to the priests, saying, When ye *f* ... Zec 7:5 6684
And when he had *f* forty days ... Mt 4:2 3522
they ministered to the Lord, and *f* ... Acts 13:2 3522
And when they had *f* and prayed, and. Acts 13:3 3522

FASTEN
f the wreathen chains to the ... Ex 28:14 5414
thou shalt *f* in the two ouches ... Ex 28:25 5414
to *f* it on high upon the mitre ... Ex 39:31 5414
I will *f* him as a nail in a sure ... Is 22:23 8628
they *f* it with nails and with ... Jer 10:4 2388

FASTENED
chains they *f* in the two ouches ... Ex 39:18 5414
f his sockets, and set up the ... Ex 40:18 5414
temples, and *f* it into the ground ... Judg 4:21 6795
she *f* it with the pin, and said ... Judg 16:14 8628
they *f* his body to the wall of ... 1Sa 31:10 8628
f upon his loins in the sheath ... 2Sa 20:8 6775
be *f* in the walls of the house ... 1Kin 6:6 270
f his head in the temple of Dagon ... 1Chr 10:10 8628
which were *f* to the throne, and ... 2Chr 9:18 270
f with cords of fine linen and ... Est 1:6 270
are the foundations thereof *f* ... Job 38:6 2883
as nails *f* by the masters of ... Eccl 12:11 5193
shall the nail that is *f* in the ... Is 22:25 8628
he *f* it with nails, that it ... Is 41:7 2388
an hand broad, *f* round about ... Eze 40:43 3559
in the synagogue were *f* on him ... Lk 4:20 816
the which when I had *f* mine eyes ... Acts 11:6 816
out of the heat, and *f* on his hand ... Acts 28:3 2510

FASTENING
f his eyes upon him with John, ... Acts 3:4 816

FASTEST
But thou, when thou *f*, anoint ... Mt 6:17 2522

FASTING
of Israel were assembled with *f* ... Neh 9:1 6685
mourning among the Jews, and *f* ... Est 4:3 6685
I humbled my soul with *f* ... Ps 35:13 6685
wept, and chastened my soul with *f* ... Ps 69:10 6685
My knees are weak through *f* ... Ps 109:24 6685
the LORD's house upon the *f* day ... Jer 36:6 6685
his palace, and passed the night *f* ... Dan 6:18 2908
prayer and supplications, with *f* ... Dan 9:3 6685
me with all your heart, and with *f* ... Joel 2:12 6685
and I will not send them away *f* ... Mt 15:32 3523
goeth not out but by prayer and *f* ... Mt 17:21 3521
them away *f* to their own houses ... Mk 8:3 3523
by nothing, but by prayer and *f* ... Mk 9:29 3521
days ago I was *f* until this hour ... Acts 10:30 3522
church, and had prayed with *f* ... Acts 14:23 3521
ye have tarried and continued *f* ... Acts 27:33 777
that ye may give yourselves to *f* ... 1Cor 7:5 3521

FASTINGS
their seed, the matters of the *f* ... Est 9:31 6685
the temple, but served God with *f* ... Lk 2:37 3521
in labours, in watchings, in *f* ... 2Cor 6:5 3521
in *f* often, in cold and nakedness ... 2Cor 11:27 3521

FAT
of his flock and of the *f* thereof ... Gen 4:4 2459
the seven well favoured and *f* kine ... Gen 41:4 1277
did eat up the first seven *f* kine ... Gen 41:20 1277
and ye shall eat the *f* of the land ... Gen 45:18 2459
Out of Asher his bread shall be *f* ... Gen 49:20 8082
neither shall the *f* of my ... Ex 23:18 2459
thou shalt take all the *f* that ... Ex 29:13 2459
the *f* that is upon them, and burn ... Ex 29:13 2459
thou shalt take of the ram the *f* ... Ex 29:22 2459
the *f* that covereth the inwards, ... Ex 29:22 2459
the *f* that is upon them, and the ... Ex 29:22 2459
lay the parts, the head, and the *f* ... Lev 1:8 6309
pieces, with his head and his *f* ... Lev 1:12 6309
the *f* that covereth the inwards, ... Lev 3:3 2459
all the *f* that is upon the ... Lev 3:3 2459
the *f* that is on them, which is ... Lev 3:4 2459
the *f* thereof, and the whole rump, ... Lev 3:9 2459
the *f* that covereth the inwards, ... Lev 3:9 2459
all the *f* that is upon the ... Lev 3:9 2459
the *f* that is upon them, which is ... Lev 3:10 2459
the *f* that covereth the inwards, ... Lev 3:14 2459
all the *f* that is upon the ... Lev 3:14 2459
the *f* that is upon them, which is ... Lev 3:15 2459
all the *f* is the LORD's ... Lev 3:16 2459
that ye eat neither *f* nor blood ... Lev 3:17 2459
the *f* of the bullock for the sin ... Lev 4:8 2459
the *f* that covereth the inwards, ... Lev 4:8 2459
all the *f* that is upon the ... Lev 4:8 2459
the *f* that is upon them, which is ... Lev 4:9 2459
he shall take all his *f* from him ... Lev 4:19 2459
burn all his *f* upon the altar ... Lev 4:26 2459
as the *f* of the sacrifice of ... Lev 4:26 2459
shall take away all the *f* thereof ... Lev 4:31 2459
as the *f* is taken away from off ... Lev 4:31 2459
shall take away all the *f* thereof ... Lev 4:35 2459
as the *f* of the lamb is taken ... Lev 4:35 2459
the *f* of the peace offerings ... Lev 6:12 2459
offer of it all the *f* thereof ... Lev 7:3 2459
the *f* that covereth the inwards, ... Lev 7:3 2459
the *f* that is on them, which is ... Lev 7:4 2459
Ye shall eat no manner of *f* ... Lev 7:23 2459
the *f* of the beast that dieth of ... Lev 7:24 2459
the *f* of that which is torn with ... Lev 7:24 2459
eateth the *f* of the beast ... Lev 7:25 2459
the *f* with the breast, it shall ... Lev 7:30 2459
shall burn the *f* upon the altar ... Lev 7:31 2459
of the peace offerings, and the *f* ... Lev 7:33 2459
he took all the *f* that was upon ... Lev 8:16 2459
and the two kidneys, and their *f* ... Lev 8:16 2459
the head, and the pieces, and the *f* ... Lev 8:20 6309
And he took the *f*, and the rump, and . Lev 8:25 2459
all the *f* that was upon the ... Lev 8:25 2459
and the two kidneys, and their *f* ... Lev 8:25 2459
one wafer, and put them on the *f* ... Lev 8:26 2459
But the *f*, and the kidneys, and the ... Lev 9:10 2459
the *f* of the bullock and of the ... Lev 9:19 2459
they put the *f* upon the breasts, ... Lev 9:20 2459
he burnt the *f* upon the altar ... Lev 9:20 2459
altar the burnt offering and the *f* ... Lev 9:24 2459
offerings made by fire of the *f* ... Lev 10:15 2459
the *f* of the sin offering shall ... Lev 16:25 2459
burn the *f* for a sweet savour ... Lev 17:6 2459
land is, whether it be *f* or lean ... Num 13:20 8082
shalt burn their *f* for an ... Num 18:17 2459
and filled themselves, and waxen *f* ... Deut 31:20 1878
with *f* of lambs, and rams of the ... Deut 32:14 2459
with the *f* of kidneys of wheat ... Deut 32:14 2459
But Jeshurun waxed *f*, and kicked ... Deut 32:15 8080
thou art waxen *f*, thou art grown ... Deut 32:15 8080
Which did eat the *f* of their ... Deut 32:38 2459
and Eglon was a very *f* man ... Judg 3:17 1277
the *f* closed upon the blade, so ... Judg 3:22 2459
Also before they burnt the *f* ... 1Sa 2:15 2459
not fail to burn the *f* presently ... 1Sa 2:16 2459
to make yourselves *f* with the ... 1Sa 2:29 1254
and to hearken than the *f* of rams ... 1Sa 15:22 2459
the woman had a *f* calf in the ... 1Sa 28:24 4770
from the *f* of the mighty, the bow ... 2Sa 1:22 2459
f cattle by the stone of Zoheleth ... 1Kin 1:9 4806
f cattle and sheep in abundance, ... 1Kin 1:19 4806
f cattle and sheep in abundance, ... 1Kin 1:25 4806
Ten *f* oxen, and twenty oxen out of ... 1Kin 4:23 1277
the *f* of the peace offerings ... 1Kin 8:64 2459
the *f* of the peace offerings ... 1Kin 8:64 2459
And they found *f* pasture and good, ... 1Chr 4:40 8082
the *f* of the peace offerings, ... 2Chr 7:7 2459
and the meat offerings, and the *f* ... 2Chr 7:7 2459
with the *f* of the peace offerings ... 2Chr 29:35 2459
offerings and the *f* until night ... 2Chr 35:14 2459
unto them, Go your way, eat the *f* ... Neh 8:10 4924
a *f* land, and possessed houses ... Neh 9:25 8082
eat, and were filled, and became *f* ... Neh 9:25 8082
f land which thou gavest before ... Neh 9:35 8082
maketh collops of *f* on his flanks ... Job 15:27 6371
They are inclosed in their own *f* ... Ps 17:10 2459
All they that be *f* upon earth ... Ps 22:29 1879
LORD shall be as the *f* of lambs ... Ps 37:20 3368
they shall be *f* and flourishing ... Ps 92:14 1879
Their heart is as *f* as grease ... Ps 119:70 2954
The liberal soul shall be made *f* ... Prov 11:25 1878
of the diligent shall be made *f* ... Prov 13:4 1878
a good report maketh the bones *f* ... Prov 15:30 1878
trust in the LORD shall be made *f* ... Prov 28:25 1878
of rams, and the *f* of fed beasts ... Is 1:11 2459
the waste places of the *f* ones ... Is 5:17 4220
Make the heart of this people *f* ... Is 6:10 8082
send among his *f* ones leanness ... Is 10:16 4924
all people a feast of *f* things ... Is 25:6 8081
of *f* things full of marrow, of ... Is 25:6 8081
of the *f* valleys of them that are ... Is 28:1 8081
is on the head of the *f* valley ... Is 28:4 8081
of the earth, and it shall be *f* ... Is 30:23 1879
it is made *f* with fatness, and ... Is 34:6 1878
with the *f* of the kidneys of rams ... Is 34:6 2459
and their dust made *f* with fatness ... Is 34:7 1878
me with the *f* of thy sacrifices ... Is 43:24 2459
in drought, and make *f* thy bones ... Is 58:11 2502
They are waxen *f*, they shine ... Jer 5:28 8080
because ye are grown *f* as the ... Jer 50:11 6335
Ye eat the *f*, and ye clothe you ... Eze 34:3 2459
in a *f* pasture shall they feed ... Eze 34:14 8082
but I will destroy the *f* and the ... Eze 34:16 8082
will judge between the *f* cattle ... Eze 34:20 1277
ye shall eat *f* till ye be full, ... Eze 39:19 2459
when ye offer my bread, the *f* ... Eze 44:7 2459
before me to offer unto me the *f* ... Eze 44:15 2459
out of the *f* pastures of Israel ... Eze 45:15 4945
peace offerings of your *f* beasts ... Amos 5:22 4806
by them their portion is *f* ... Hab 1:16 8082
he shall eat the flesh of the *f* ... Zec 11:16 1277

FATFLESHED
seven well favoured kine and *f* ... Gen 41:2 1277
up out of the river seven kine, *f* ... Gen 41:18 1277

FATHER
Therefore shall a man leave his *f* ... Gen 2:24 1
he was the *f* of such as dwell in ... Gen 4:20 1
he was the *f* of all such as ... Gen 4:21 1
and Ham is the *f* of Canaan ... Gen 9:18 1
And Ham, the *f* of Canaan ... Gen 9:22 1
saw the nakedness of his *f* ... Gen 9:22 1
covered the nakedness of their *f* ... Gen 9:23 1
the *f* of all the children of Eber ... Gen 10:21 1
Haran died before his *f* Terah in ... Gen 11:28 1
the *f* of Milcah, and the *f* of ... Gen 11:29 1
thou shalt be a *f* of many nations ... Gen 17:4 1
for a *f* of many nations have I ... Gen 17:5 1
Our *f* is old, and there is not a ... Gen 19:31 1
let us make our *f* drink wine ... Gen 19:32 1
we may preserve seed of our *f* ... Gen 19:32 1
they made their *f* drink wine that ... Gen 19:33 1
went in, and lay with her *f* ... Gen 19:33 1
I lay yesternight with my *f* ... Gen 19:34 1
we may preserve seed of our *f* ... Gen 19:34 1
they made their *f* drink wine that ... Gen 19:35 1
of Lot with child by their *f* ... Gen 19:36 1
the same is the *f* of the Moabites ... Gen 19:37 1
the same is the *f* of the children ... Gen 19:38 1
she is the daughter of my *f* ... Gen 20:12 1
Abraham his *f*, and said, My *f* ... Gen 22:7 1
brother, and Kemuel the *f* of Aram ... Gen 22:21 1
which I sware unto Abraham thy *f* ... Gen 26:3 1
in the days of Abraham his *f* ... Gen 26:15 1
in the days of Abraham his *f* ... Gen 26:18 1
by which his *f* had called them ... Gen 26:18 1
I am the God of Abraham thy *f* ... Gen 26:24 1
I heard thy *f* speak unto Esau thy ... Gen 27:6 1
make them savoury meat for thy *f* ... Gen 27:9 1
And thou shalt bring it to thy *f* ... Gen 27:10 1
My *f* peradventure will feel me, ... Gen 27:12 1
savoury meat, such as his *f* loved ... Gen 27:14 1
unto his *f*, and said, My *f* ... Gen 27:18 1

And Jacob said unto his *f*, I am	Gen 27:19	1
Jacob went near unto Isaac his *f*	Gen 27:22	1
his *f* Isaac said unto him, Come	Gen 27:26	1
from the presence of Isaac his *f*	Gen 27:30	1
his *f*, and said unto his *f*	Gen 27:31	1
unto his *f*, Let my *f* arise	Gen 27:31	1
Isaac his *f* said unto him, Who	Gen 27:32	1
Esau heard the words of his *f*	Gen 27:34	1
bitter cry, and said unto his *f*	Gen 27:34	1
Bless me, even me also, O my *f*	Gen 27:34	1
And Esau said unto his *f*	Gen 27:38	1
Hast thou but one blessing, my *f*	Gen 27:38	1
bless me, even me also, O my *f*	Gen 27:38	1
And Isaac his *f* answered and said	Gen 27:39	1
wherewith his *f* blessed him	Gen 27:41	1
of mourning for my *f* are at hand	Gen 27:41	1
house of Bethuel thy mother's *f*	Gen 28:2	1
And that Jacob obeyed his *f*	Gen 28:7	1
of Canaan pleased not Isaac his *f*	Gen 28:8	1
am the LORD God of Abraham thy *f*	Gen 28:13	1
and she ran and told her *f*	Gen 29:12	1
the God of my *f* hath been with me	Gen 31:5	1
all my power I have served your *f*	Gen 31:6	1
your *f* hath deceived me, and	Gen 31:7	1
taken away the cattle of your *f*	Gen 31:9	1
which God hath taken from our *f*	Gen 31:16	1
Isaac his *f* in the land of Canaan	Gen 31:18	1
but the God of your *f* spake unto	Gen 31:29	1
And she said to her *f*, Let it not	Gen 31:35	1
Except the God of my *f*, the God	Gen 31:42	1
God of Nahor, the God of their *f*	Gen 31:53	1
sware by the fear of his *f* Isaac	Gen 31:53	1
Jacob said, O God of my *f* Abraham	Gen 32:9	1
and God of my *f* Isaac	Gen 32:9	1
children of Hamor, Shechem's *f*	Gen 33:19	1
And Shechem spake unto his *f* Hamor	Gen 34:4	1
Hamor the *f* of Shechem went out	Gen 34:6	1
And Shechem said unto her *f*	Gen 34:11	1
Hamor his *f* deceitfully, and said,	Gen 34:13	1
than all the house of his *f*	Gen 34:19	1
but his *f* called him Benjamin	Gen 35:18	1
came unto Isaac his *f* unto Mamre	Gen 35:27	1
f of the Edomites in mount Seir	Gen 36:9	1
he fed the asses of Zibeon his *f*	Gen 36:24	1
he is Esau the *f* of the Edomites	Gen 36:43	1
land wherein his *f* was a stranger	Gen 37:1	1
unto his *f* their evil report	Gen 37:2	1
f loved him more than all his	Gen 37:4	1
And he told it to his *f*, and to his	Gen 37:10	1
his *f* rebuked him, and said unto	Gen 37:10	1
but his *f* observed the saying	Gen 37:11	1
to deliver him to his *f* again	Gen 37:22	1
and they brought it to their *f*	Gen 37:32	1
Thus his *f* wept for him	Gen 37:35	1
Behold thy *f* in law goeth up to	Gen 38:13	2524
forth, she sent to her *f* in law	Gen 38:25	2524
youngest is this day with our *f*	Gen 42:13	1
their *f* unto the land of Canaan	Gen 42:29	1
be twelve brethren, sons of our *f*	Gen 42:32	1
with our *f* in the land of Canaan	Gen 42:32	1
their *f* saw the bundles of money,	Gen 42:35	1
Jacob their *f* said unto them, Me	Gen 42:36	1
And Reuben spake unto his *f*	Gen 42:37	1
their *f* said unto them, Go again,	Gen 43:2	1
saying, Is your *f* yet alive	Gen 43:7	1
And Judah said unto Israel his *f*	Gen 43:8	1
their *f* Israel said unto them, If	Gen 43:11	1
your God, and the God of your *f*	Gen 43:23	1
welfare, and said, Is your *f* well	Gen 43:27	1
Thy servant our *f* is in good	Gen 43:28	1
get you up in peace unto your *f*	Gen 44:17	1
his servants, saying, Have ye a *f*	Gen 44:19	1
we said unto my lord, We have a *f*	Gen 44:20	1
his mother, and his *f* loveth him	Gen 44:20	1
lord, The lad cannot leave his *f*	Gen 44:22	1
leave his *f*, his *f* would die	Gen 44:22	
we came up unto thy servant my *f*	Gen 44:24	1
our *f* said, Go again, and buy us a	Gen 44:25	1
And thy servant my *f* said unto us	Gen 44:27	1
when I come to thy servant my *f*	Gen 44:30	1
our *f* with sorrow to the grave	Gen 44:31	1
surety for the lad unto my *f*	Gen 44:32	1
bear the blame to my *f* for ever	Gen 44:32	1
For how shall I go up to my *f*	Gen 44:34	1
the evil that shall come on my *f*	Gen 44:34	1
doth my *f* yet live	Gen 45:3	1
and he hath made me a *f* to Pharaoh	Gen 45:8	1
Haste ye, and go up to my *f*	Gen 45:9	1
ye shall tell my *f* of all my	Gen 45:13	1
haste and bring down my *f* hither	Gen 45:13	
And take your *f* and your households	Gen 45:18	1
for your wives, and bring your *f*	Gen 45:19	1
to his *f* he sent after this	Gen 45:23	1
and meat for his *f* by the way	Gen 45:23	1
land of Canaan unto Jacob their *f*	Gen 45:25	1
spirit of Jacob their *f* revived	Gen 45:27	1
unto the God of his *f* Isaac	Gen 46:1	1
said, I am God, the God of thy *f*	Gen 46:3	1
of Israel carried Jacob their *f*	Gen 46:5	1
and went up to meet Israel his *f*	Gen 46:29	1
and told Pharaoh, and said, My *f*	Gen 47:1	1
spake unto Joseph, saying, Thy *f*	Gen 47:5	1
the best of the land make thy *f*	Gen 47:6	1
And Joseph brought in Jacob his *f*	Gen 47:7	1
And Joseph placed his *f* and his	Gen 47:11	1
And Joseph nourished his *f*	Gen 47:12	1
Joseph, Behold, thy *f* is sick	Gen 48:1	1
And Joseph said unto his *f*	Gen 48:9	1
when Joseph saw that his *f* laid	Gen 48:17	1
unto his *f*, Not so, my *f*	Gen 48:18	1
his *f* refused, and said, I know it	Gen 48:19	1
and hearken unto Israel your *f*	Gen 49:2	1
Even by the God of thy *f*, who	Gen 49:25	1
The blessings of thy *f* have	Gen 49:26	1
it that their *f* spake unto them	Gen 49:28	1
the physicians to embalm his *f*	Gen 50:2	1
My *f* made me swear, saying, Lo, I	Gen 50:5	1
go up, I pray thee, and bury my *f*	Gen 50:5	1
said, Go up, and bury thy *f*	Gen 50:6	1
And Joseph went up to bury his *f*	Gen 50:7	1
a mourning for his *f* seven days	Gen 50:10	1
went up with him to bury his *f*	Gen 50:14	1
after he had buried his *f*	Gen 50:14	1
saw that their *f* was dead	Gen 50:15	1
Thy *f* did command before he died,	Gen 50:16	1
the servants of the God of thy *f*	Gen 50:17	1
when they came to Reuel their *f*	Ex 2:18	1
the flock of Jethro his *f* in law	Ex 3:1	2859
he said, I am the God of thy *f*	Ex 3:6	1
returned to Jethro his *f* in law	Ex 4:18	2859
priest of Midian, Moses' *f* in law	Ex 18:1	2859
Then Jethro, Moses' *f* in law	Ex 18:2	2859
for the God of my *f*, said he, was	Ex 18:4	1
And Jethro, Moses' *f* in law	Ex 18:5	2859
I thy *f* in law Jethro am come	Ex 18:6	2859
went out to meet his *f* in law	Ex 18:7	2859
Moses told his *f* in law all that	Ex 18:8	2859
And Jethro, Moses' *f* in law	Ex 18:12	2859
with Moses' *f* in law before God	Ex 18:12	2859
when Moses' *f* in law saw all that	Ex 18:14	2859
And Moses said unto his *f* in law	Ex 18:15	2859
Moses' *f* in law said unto him,	Ex 18:17	2589
to the voice of his *f* in law	Ex 18:24	2859
And Moses let his *f* in law depart	Ex 18:27	2859
Honour thy *f* and thy mother	Ex 20:12	1
And he that smiteth his *f*, or his	Ex 21:15	1
And he that curseth his *f*, or his	Ex 21:17	1
If her *f* utterly refuse to give	Ex 22:17	1
as thou didst anoint their *f*	Ex 40:15	1
The nakedness of thy *f*, or the	Lev 18:7	1
thy sister, the daughter of thy *f*	Lev 18:9	1
daughter, begotten of thy *f*	Lev 18:11	1
every man his mother, and his *f*	Lev 19:3	1
f or his mother shall be surely	Lev 20:9	1
hath cursed his *f* or his mother	Lev 20:9	1
is, for his mother, and for his *f*	Lev 21:2	1
the whore, she profaneth her *f*	Lev 21:9	1
nor defile himself for his *f*	Lev 21:11	1
whose *f* was an Egyptian, went out	Lev 24:10	1121
in the sight of Aaron their *f*	Num 3:4	1
the *f* of the Gershonites shall be	Num 3:24	1
of the *f* of the families of the	Num 3:30	1
f of the families of Merari was	Num 3:35	1
make himself unclean for his *f*	Num 6:7	1
the Midianite, Moses' *f* in law	Num 10:29	2859
as a nursing *f* beareth the	Num 11:12	
If her *f* had but spit in her face	Num 12:14	1
tribe of Levi, the tribe of thy *f*	Num 18:2	1
Our *f* died in the wilderness, and	Num 27:3	1
Why should the name of our *f* be	Num 27:4	1
among the brethren of our *f*	Num 27:4	1
of their *f* to pass unto them	Num 27:7	1
if his *f* have no brethren, then	Num 27:11	1
her *f* hear her vow, and her bond	Num 30:4	1
her *f* shall hold his peace at her	Num 30:4	1
But if her *f* disallow her in the	Num 30:5	1
because her *f* disallowed her	Num 30:5	1
a man and his wife, between the *f*	Num 30:16	1
tribe of their *f* shall they marry	Num 36:6	1
the family of the tribe of her *f*	Num 36:8	1
tribe of the family of their *f*	Num 36:12	1
Honour thy *f* and thy mother, as	Deut 5:16	1
in thine house, and bewail her *f*	Deut 21:13	1
will not obey the voice of his *f*	Deut 21:18	1
Then shall his *f* and his mother	Deut 21:19	1
Then shall the *f* of the damsel	Deut 22:15	1
the damsel's *f* shall say unto the	Deut 22:16	1
them unto the *f* of the damsel	Deut 22:19	1
f fifty shekels of silver	Deut 22:29	1
A Syrian ready to perish was my *f*	Deut 26:5	1
light by his *f* or his mother	Deut 27:16	1
his sister, the daughter of his *f*	Deut 27:22	1
is not he thy *f* that hath bought	Deut 32:6	1
ask thy *f*, and he will shew thee	Deut 32:7	1
Who said unto his *f* and to his	Deut 33:9	1
And that ye will save alive my *f*	Josh 2:13	1
and thou shalt bring thy *f*	Josh 2:18	1
and brought out Rahab, and her *f*	Josh 6:23	1
the city of Arba the *f* of Anak	Josh 15:13	1
moved him to ask of her *f* a field	Josh 15:18	1
of Manasseh, the *f* of Gilead	Josh 17:1	1
among the brethren of their *f*	Josh 17:4	1
after the name of Dan their *f*	Josh 19:47	1
the city of Arba the *f* of Anak	Josh 21:11	1
the *f* of Abraham, and the *f*	Josh 24:2	1
I took your *f* Abraham from the	Josh 24:3	1
the *f* of Shechem for an hundred	Josh 24:32	1
moved him to ask of her *f* a field	Judg 1:14	1
of the Kenite, Moses' *f* in law	Judg 1:16	2859
of Hobab the *f* in law of Moses	Judg 4:11	2859
the altar of Baal that thy *f* hath	Judg 6:25	1
in the sepulchre of Joash his *f*	Judg 8:32	1
of the house of his mother's *f*	Judg 9:1	1
(For my *f* fought for you, and	Judg 9:17	1
the men of Hamor the *f* of Shechem	Judg 9:28	1
which he did unto his *f*, in	Judg 9:56	1
And she said unto him, My *f*	Judg 11:36	1
And she said unto her *f*, Let this	Judg 11:37	1
that she returned unto her *f*	Judg 11:39	1
And he came up, and told his *f*	Judg 14:2	1
Then his *f* and his mother said	Judg 14:3	1
And Samson said unto his *f*	Judg 14:3	1
But his *f* and his mother knew not	Judg 14:4	1
Then went Samson down, and his *f*	Judg 14:5	1
but he told not his *f* or his	Judg 14:6	1
went on eating, and came to his *f*	Judg 14:9	1
So his *f* went down unto the woman	Judg 14:10	1
not told it my *f* nor my mother	Judg 14:16	1
But her *f* would not suffer him to	Judg 15:1	1
her *f* said, I verily thought that	Judg 15:2	1
and burnt her and her *f* with fire	Judg 15:6	1
all the house of his *f* came down	Judg 16:31	1
the buryingplace of Manoah his *f*	Judg 16:31	1
Dwell with me, and be unto me a *f*	Judg 17:10	1
and go with us, and be to us a *f*	Judg 18:19	1
after the name of Dan their *f*	Judg 18:29	1
when the *f* of the damsel saw him,	Judg 19:3	1
his *f* in law, the damsel's *f*	Judg 19:4	2859
his *f* in law, the damsel's *f*	Judg 19:4	1
the damsel's *f* said unto his son	Judg 19:5	1
for the damsel's *f* had said unto	Judg 19:6	1
to depart, his *f* in law urged him	Judg 19:7	2859
and the damsel's *f* said, Comfort	Judg 19:8	1
his *f* in law, the damsel's *f*	Judg 19:9	2859
his *f* in law, the damsel's *f*	Judg 19:9	1
and how thou hast left thy *f*	Ruth 2:11	1
f of Jesse, the *f* of David	Ruth 4:17	1
not unto the voice of their *f*	1Sa 2:25	1
appear unto the house of thy *f*	1Sa 2:27	1
I give unto the house of thy *f*	1Sa 2:28	1
thy house, and the house of thy *f*	1Sa 2:30	1
was taken, and that her *f* in law	1Sa 4:19	2524
taken, and because of her *f* in law	1Sa 4:21	2524
asses of Kish Saul's *f* were lost	1Sa 9:3	1
lest my *f* leave caring for the	1Sa 9:5	1
thy *f* hath left the care of the	1Sa 10:2	1
and said, But who is their *f*	1Sa 10:12	1
But he told not his *f*	1Sa 14:1	1
his *f* charged the people with the	1Sa 14:27	1
Thy *f* straitly charged the people	1Sa 14:28	1
My *f* hath troubled the land	1Sa 14:29	1
And Kish was the *f* of Saul	1Sa 14:51	1
Ner the *f* of Abner was the son of	1Sa 14:51	1
Saul my *f* seeketh to kill thee	1Sa 19:2	1
stand beside my *f* in the field	1Sa 19:3	1
I will commune with my *f* of thee	1Sa 19:3	1
good of David unto Saul his *f*	1Sa 19:4	1
and what is my sin before thy *f*	1Sa 20:1	1
my *f* will do nothing either great	1Sa 20:2	1
why should my *f* hide this thing	1Sa 20:2	1
Thy *f* certainly knoweth that I	1Sa 20:3	1
If thy *f* at all miss me, then say	1Sa 20:6	1
shouldest thou bring me to thy *f*	1Sa 20:8	1
by my *f* to come upon thee	1Sa 20:9	1
or what if thy *f* answer thee	1Sa 20:10	1
when I have sounded my *f* about to	1Sa 20:12	1
if it please my *f* to do thee evil	1Sa 20:13	1
thee, as he hath been with my *f*	1Sa 20:13	1
And Jonathan answered Saul his *f*	1Sa 20:32	1
determined of his *f* to slay David	1Sa 20:33	1
because his *f* had done him shame	1Sa 20:34	1
unto the king of Moab, Let my *f*	1Sa 22:3	1
nor to all the house of my *f*	1Sa 22:15	1
of Saul my *f* shall not find thee	1Sa 23:17	1
and that also Saul my *f* knoweth	1Sa 23:17	1
Moreover, my *f*, see, yea, see the	1Sa 24:11	1
him in the sepulchre of his *f*	2Sa 2:32	1
day unto the house of Saul thy *f*	2Sa 3:8	1
LORD, which chose me before thy *f*	2Sa 6:21	1
I will be his *f*, and he shall be	2Sa 7:14	1
thee all the land of Saul thy *f*	2Sa 9:7	1
as his *f* shewed kindness unto me	2Sa 10:2	1
hand of his servants for his *f*	2Sa 10:2	1
thou that David doth honour thy *f*	2Sa 10:3	1
when thy *f* cometh to see thee,	2Sa 13:5	1
restore me the kingdom of my *f*	2Sa 16:3	1
that thou art abhorred of thy *f*	2Sa 16:21	1
said Hushai, thou knowest thy *f*	2Sa 17:8	1
thy *f* is a man of war, and will	2Sa 17:8	1
that thy *f* is a mighty man	2Sa 17:10	1
buried in the sepulchre of his *f*	2Sa 17:23	1
and be buried by the grave of my *f*	2Sa 19:37	1
in the sepulchre of Kish his *f*	2Sa 21:14	1
his *f* had not displeased him at	1Kin 1:6	1
upon the throne of David his *f*	1Kin 2:12	1
me on the throne of David my *f*	1Kin 2:24	1
of the Lord GOD before David my *f*	1Kin 2:26	1
in all wherein my *f* was afflicted	1Kin 2:26	1
me, and from the house of my *f*	1Kin 2:31	1
my *f* David not knowing thereof,	1Kin 2:32	1
to, that thou didst to David my *f*	1Kin 2:44	1
in the statutes of David his *f*	1Kin 3:3	1
servant David my *f* great mercy	1Kin 3:6	1
king instead of David my *f*	1Kin 3:7	1
as thy *f* David did walk, then I	1Kin 3:14	1
him king in the room of his *f*	1Kin 5:1	1
f could not build an house unto	1Kin 5:3	1
as the LORD spake unto David my *f*	1Kin 5:5	1
which I spake unto David thy *f*	1Kin 6:12	1
his *f* was a man of Tyre, a worker	1Kin 7:14	1
which David his *f* had dedicated	1Kin 7:51	1
with his mouth unto David my *f*	1Kin 8:15	1
f to build an house for the name	1Kin 8:17	1
And the LORD said unto David my *f*	1Kin 8:18	1
up in the room of David my *f*	1Kin 8:20	1
my *f* that thou promisedst him	1Kin 8:24	1
my *f* that thou promisedst him	1Kin 8:25	1
unto thy servant David my *f*	1Kin 8:26	1
before me, as David thy *f* walked	1Kin 9:4	1
as I promised to David thy *f*	1Kin 9:5	1
as was the heart of David his *f*	1Kin 11:4	1
the LORD, as did David his *f*	1Kin 11:6	1
of the city of David his *f*	1Kin 11:27	1
my judgments, as did David his *f*	1Kin 11:33	1
buried in the city of David his *f*	1Kin 11:43	1
Thy *f* made our yoke grievous	1Kin 12:4	1
the grievous service of thy *f*	1Kin 12:4	1
Solomon his *f* while he yet lived	1Kin 12:6	1
thy *f* did put upon us lighter	1Kin 12:9	1
Thy *f* made our yoke heavy, but	1Kin 12:10	1
now whereas my *f* did lade you	1Kin 12:11	1
my *f* hath chastised you with	1Kin 12:11	1

My *f* made your yoke heavy, and I	1Kin 12:14	1
my *f* also chastised you with	1Kin 12:14	1
them they told also to their *f*	1Kin 13:11	1
their *f* said unto them, What way	1Kin 13:12	1
walked in all the sins of his *f*	1Kin 15:3	1
God, as the heart of David his *f*	1Kin 15:3	1
of the LORD, as did David his *f*	1Kin 15:11	1
things which his *f* had dedicated	1Kin 15:15	1
and between my *f* and thy *f*	1Kin 15:19	1
in the city of David his *f*	1Kin 15:24	1
and walked in the way of his *f*	1Kin 15:26	1
Let me, I pray thee, kiss my *f*	1Kin 19:20	1
which my *f* took from thy *f*,	1Kin 20:34	1
Damascus, as my *f* made in Samaria	1Kin 20:34	1
in all the ways of Asa his *f*	1Kin 22:43	1
remained in the days of his *f* Asa	1Kin 22:46	1
in the city of David his *f*	1Kin 22:50	1
and walked in the way of his *f*	1Kin 22:52	1
to all that his *f* had done	1Kin 22:53	1
it, and he cried, My *f*, my *f*	2Kin 2:12	1
but not like his *f*, and like his	2Kin 3:2	1
image of Baal that his *f* had made	2Kin 3:2	1
get thee to the prophets of thy *f*	2Kin 3:13	1
went out to his *f* to the reapers	2Kin 4:18	1
And he said unto his *f*, My head,	2Kin 4:19	1
and spake unto him, and said, My *f*	2Kin 5:13	1
Elisha, when he saw them, My *f*	2Kin 6:21	1
rode together after Ahab his *f*	2Kin 9:25	1
face, and said, O my *f*, my *f*	2Kin 13:14	1
the hand of Jehoahaz his *f* by war	2Kin 13:25	1
LORD, yet not like David his *f*	2Kin 14:3	1
to all things as Joash his *f* did	2Kin 14:3	1
which had slain the king his *f*	2Kin 14:5	1
him king instead of his *f* Amaziah	2Kin 14:21	1
all that his *f* Amaziah had done	2Kin 15:3	1
to all that his *f* Uzziah had done	2Kin 15:34	1
in the city of David his *f*	2Kin 15:38	1
LORD his God, like David his *f*	2Kin 16:2	1
to all that David his *f* did	2Kin 18:3	1
the LORD, the God of David thy *f*	2Kin 20:5	1
Hezekiah his *f* had destroyed	2Kin 21:3	1
the LORD, as his *f* Manasseh did	2Kin 21:20	1
all the way that his *f* walked in	2Kin 21:21	1
the idols that his *f* served	2Kin 21:21	1
in all the way of David his *f*	2Kin 22:2	1
king in the room of Josiah his *f*	2Kin 23:34	1
to all that his *f* had done	2Kin 24:9	1
the *f* of Amasa was Jether the	1Chr 2:17	1
of Machir the *f* of Gilead	1Chr 2:21	1
sons of Machir the *f* of Gilead	1Chr 2:23	1
bare him Ashur the *f* of Tekoa	1Chr 2:24	1
which was the *f* of Ziph	1Chr 2:42	1
sons of Mareshah the *f* of Hebron	1Chr 2:42	1
begat Raham, the *f* of Jorkoam	1Chr 2:44	1
and Maon was the *f* of Beth-zur	1Chr 2:45	1
also Shaaph the *f* of Madmannah	1Chr 2:49	1
Sheva the *f* of Machbenah, and the	1Chr 2:49	1
of Machbenah, and the *f* of Gibea	1Chr 2:49	1
Shobal the *f* of Kirjath-jearim,	1Chr 2:50	1
Salma the *f* of Beth-lehem	1Chr 2:51	1
Hareph the *f* of Beth-gader	1Chr 2:51	1
Shobal the *f* of Kirjath-jearim	1Chr 2:52	1
the *f* of the house of Rechab	1Chr 2:55	1
And these were of the *f* of Etam	1Chr 4:3	1
And Penuel the *f* of Gedor, and Ezer	1Chr 4:4	1
of Gedor, and Ezer the *f* of Hushah	1Chr 4:4	1
of Ephratah, the *f* of Beth-lehem	1Chr 4:4	1
Ashur the *f* of Tekoa had two	1Chr 4:5	1
Mehir, which was the *f* of Eshton	1Chr 4:11	1
and Tehinnah the *f* of Ir-nahash	1Chr 4:12	1
the *f* of the valley of Charashim	1Chr 4:14	1
and Ishbah the *f* of Eshtemoa	1Chr 4:17	1
bare Jered the *f* of Gedor	1Chr 4:18	1
and Heber the *f* of Socho	1Chr 4:18	1
and Jekuthiel the *f* of Zanoah	1Chr 4:18	1
the *f* of Keilah the Garmite, and	1Chr 4:19	1
Er the *f* of Lecah	1Chr 4:21	1
Laadah the *f* of Mareshah, and the	1Chr 4:21	1
bare Machir the *f* of Gilead	1Chr 7:14	1
Ephraim their *f* mourned many days	1Chr 7:22	1
who is the *f* of Birzavith	1Chr 7:31	1
at Gibeon dwelt the *f* of Gibeon	1Chr 8:29	25
brethren, of the house of his *f*	1Chr 9:19	1
in Gibeon dwelt the *f* of Gibeon	1Chr 9:35	25
I will be his *f*, and he shall be	1Chr 17:13	25
because his *f* shewed kindness to	1Chr 19:2	25
to comfort him concerning his *f*	1Chr 19:2	25
thou that David doth honour thy *f*	1Chr 19:3	25
be my son, and I will be his *f*	1Chr 22:10	25
and Abihu died before their *f*	1Chr 24:2	25
their manner, under Aaron their *f*	1Chr 24:19	25
the hands of their *f* Jeduthun	1Chr 25:3	25
f for song in the house of the	1Chr 25:6	25
throughout the house of their *f*	1Chr 26:6	25
yet his *f* made him the chief	1Chr 26:10	25
me before all the house of my *f*	1Chr 28:4	25
house of Judah, the house of my *f*	1Chr 28:4	25
among the sons of my *f* he liked	1Chr 28:4	25
to be my son, and I will be his *f*	1Chr 28:6	25
son, know thou the God of thy *f*	1Chr 28:9	25
be thou, LORD God of Israel our *f*	1Chr 29:10	25
as king instead of David his *f*	1Chr 29:23	25
great mercy unto David my *f*	2Chr 1:8	25
unto David my *f* be established	2Chr 1:9	25
thou didst deal with David my *f*	2Chr 2:3	25
whom David my *f* did provide	2Chr 2:7	25
his *f* was a man of Tyre, skilful	2Chr 2:14	25
men of my lord David thy *f*	2Chr 2:14	25
David his *f* had numbered them	2Chr 2:17	25
LORD appeared unto David his *f*	2Chr 3:1	25
did Huram his *f* make to king	2Chr 4:16	25
that David his *f* had dedicated	2Chr 5:1	25
with his mouth to my *f* David	2Chr 6:4	25
f to build an house for the name	2Chr 6:7	25
But the LORD said to David my *f*	2Chr 6:8	25
up in the room of David my *f*	2Chr 6:10	25
f that which thou hast promised	2Chr 6:15	25
f that which thou hast promised	2Chr 6:16	25
before me, as David thy *f* walked	2Chr 7:17	25
have covenanted with David thy *f*	2Chr 7:18	25
to the order of David his *f*	2Chr 8:14	25
buried in the city of David his *f*	2Chr 9:31	25
Thy *f* made our yoke grievous	2Chr 10:4	25
the grievous servitude of thy *f*	2Chr 10:4	25
Solomon his *f* while he yet lived	2Chr 10:6	25
yoke that thy *f* did put upon us	2Chr 10:9	25
Thy *f* made our yoke heavy, but	2Chr 10:10	25
For whereas my *f* put a heavy yoke	2Chr 10:11	25
my *f* chastised you with whips,	2Chr 10:11	25
My *f* made your yoke heavy, but I	2Chr 10:14	25
my *f* chastised you with whips,	2Chr 10:14	25
things that his *f* had dedicated	2Chr 15:18	25
was between my *f* and thy *f*	2Chr 16:3	25
which Asa his *f* had taken	2Chr 17:2	25
in the first ways of his *f* David	2Chr 17:3	25
sought to the LORD God of his *f*	2Chr 17:4	25
he walked in the way of Asa his *f*	2Chr 20:32	25
their *f* gave them great gifts of	2Chr 21:3	25
risen up to the kingdom of his *f*	2Chr 21:4	25
saith the LORD God of David thy *f*	2Chr 21:12	25
in the ways of Jehoshaphat thy *f*	2Chr 21:12	25
death of his *f* to his destruction	2Chr 22:4	25
Jehoiada his *f* had done to him	2Chr 24:22	25
that had killed the king his *f*	2Chr 25:3	25
king in the room of his *f* Amaziah	2Chr 26:1	25
to all that his *f* Amaziah did	2Chr 26:4	25
to all that his *f* Uzziah did	2Chr 27:2	25
of the LORD, like David his *f*	2Chr 28:1	25
to all that David his *f* had done	2Chr 29:2	25
Hezekiah his *f* had broken down	2Chr 33:3	1
the LORD, as did Manasseh his *f*	2Chr 33:22	1
which Manasseh his *f* had made	2Chr 33:22	1
as Manasseh his *f* had humbled	2Chr 33:23	1
walked in the ways of David his *f*	2Chr 34:2	1
seek after the God of David his *f*	2Chr 34:3	1
for she had neither *f* nor mother	Est 2:7	1
whom Mordecai, when her *f*	Est 2:7	1
aged men, much elder than thy *f*	Job 15:10	1
said to corruption, Thou art my *f*	Job 17:14	1
I was a *f* to the poor	Job 29:16	1
brought up with me, as with a *f*	Job 31:18	1
Hath the rain a *f*	Job 38:28	1
their *f* gave them inheritance	Job 42:15	1
When my *f* and my mother	Ps 27:10	1
A *f* of the fatherless, and a judge	Ps 68:5	1
shall cry unto me, Thou art my *f*	Ps 89:26	1
Like as a *f* pitieth his children,	Ps 103:13	1
hear the instruction of thy *f*	Prov 1:8	1
even as a *f* the son in whom he	Prov 3:12	1
children, the instruction of a *f*	Prov 4:1	1
A wise son maketh a glad *f*	Prov 10:1	1
A wise son maketh a glad *f*	Prov 15:20	1
the *f* of a fool hath no joy	Prov 17:21	1
A foolish son is a grief to his *f*	Prov 17:25	1
son is the calamity of his *f*	Prov 19:13	1
He that wasteth his *f*, and chaseth	Prov 19:26	1
Whoso curseth his *f* or his mother	Prov 20:20	1
unto thy *f* that begat thee	Prov 23:22	1
The *f* of the righteous shall	Prov 23:24	1
Thy *f* and thy mother shall be glad	Prov 23:25	1
of riotous men shameth his *f*	Prov 28:7	1
Whoso robbeth his *f* or his mother	Prov 28:24	1
loveth wisdom rejoiceth his *f*	Prov 29:3	1
a generation that curseth their *f*	Prov 30:11	1
The eye that mocketh at his *f*	Prov 30:17	1
his brother of the house of his *f*	Is 3:6	1
shall have knowledge to cry, My *f*	Is 8:4	1
The mighty God, The everlasting *F*	Is 9:6	1
and he shall be a *f* to the	Is 22:21	1
the LORD, the God of David thy *f*	Is 38:5	1
the *f* to the children shall make	Is 38:19	1
Thy first *f* hath sinned, and thy	Is 43:27	1
unto him that saith unto his *f*	Is 45:10	1
Look unto Abraham your *f*, and unto	Is 51:2	1
with the heritage of Jacob thy *f*	Is 58:14	1
Doubtless thou art our *f*, though	Is 63:16	1
thou, O LORD, art our *f*, our	Is 63:16	1
But now, O LORD, thou art our *f*	Is 64:8	1
Saying to a stock, Thou art my *f*	Jer 2:27	1
from this time cry unto me, My *f*	Jer 3:4	1
I said, Thou shalt call me, My *f*	Jer 3:19	1
brethren, and the house of thy *f*	Jer 12:6	1
for their *f* or for their mother	Jer 16:7	1
man who brought tidings to my *f*	Jer 20:15	1
reigned instead of Josiah his *f*	Jer 22:11	1
did not thy *f* eat and drink, and do	Jer 22:15	1
for I am a *f* to Israel, and	Jer 31:9	1
son of Rechab our *f* commanded us	Jer 35:6	1
Jonadab the son of Rechab our *f*	Jer 35:8	1
that Jonadab our *f* commanded us	Jer 35:10	1
the commandment of their *f*	Jer 35:16	1
the commandment of Jonadab your *f*	Jer 35:18	1
thy *f* was an Amorite, and thy	Eze 16:3	1
an Hittite, and your *f* an Amorite	Eze 16:45	1
as the soul of the *f*, so also the	Eze 18:4	1
not die for the iniquity of his *f*	Eze 18:17	1
As for his *f*, because he cruelly	Eze 18:18	1
son bear the iniquity of the *f*	Eze 18:19	1
not bear the iniquity of the *f*	Eze 18:20	1
neither shall the *f* bear the	Eze 18:20	1
In thee have they set light by *f*	Eze 22:7	1
but for *f*, or for mother, or for	Eze 44:25	1
silver vessels which his *f*	Dan 5:2	2
and in the days of thy *f* light	Dan 5:11	2
the king Nebuchadnezzar thy *f*	Dan 5:11	2
the king, I say, thy *f*	Dan 5:11	2
whom the king my *f* brought out of	Dan 5:13	2
Nebuchadnezzar thy *f* a kingdom	Dan 5:18	2
his *f* will go in unto the same	Amos 2:7	2
For the son dishonoureth the *f*	Mic 7:6	2
shall yet prophesy, then his *f*	Zec 13:3	2
and his *f* and his mother that begat	Zec 13:3	2
A son honoureth his *f*, and a	Mal 1:6	2
if then I be a *f*, where is mine	Mal 1:6	2
Have we not all one *f*	Mal 2:10	2
Judaea in the room of his *f* Herod	Mt 2:22	3962
We have Abraham to our *f*	Mt 3:9	3962
in a ship with Zebedee their *f*	Mt 4:21	3962
left the ship and their *f*, and	Mt 4:22	3962
glorify your *F* which is in heaven	Mt 5:16	3962
of your *F* which is in heaven	Mt 5:45	3962
even as your *F* which is in heaven	Mt 5:48	3962
of your *F* which is in heaven	Mt 6:1	3962
thy *F* which seeth in secret	Mt 6:4	3962
pray to thy *F* which is in secret	Mt 6:6	3962
thy *F* which seeth in secret shall	Mt 6:6	3962
for your *F* knoweth what things ye	Mt 6:8	3962
Our *F* which art in heaven,	Mt 6:9	3962
your heavenly *F* will also forgive	Mt 6:14	3962
neither will your *F* forgive your	Mt 6:15	3962
but unto thy *F* which is in secret	Mt 6:18	3962
and thy *F*, which seeth in secret,	Mt 6:18	3962
yet your heavenly *F* feedeth them	Mt 6:26	3962
for your heavenly *F* knoweth that	Mt 6:32	3962
how much more shall your *F* which	Mt 7:11	3962
will of my *F* which is in heaven	Mt 7:21	3962
me first to go and bury my *f*	Mt 8:21	3962
of your *F* which speaketh in you	Mt 10:20	3962
to death, and the *f* the child	Mt 10:21	3962
fall on the ground without your *F*	Mt 10:29	3962
before my *F* which is in heaven	Mt 10:32	3962
before my *F* which is in heaven	Mt 10:33	3962
a man at variance against his *f*	Mt 10:35	3962
He that loveth *f* or mother more	Mt 10:37	3962
and said, I thank thee, O *F*	Mt 11:25	3962
Even so, *F*: for so it seemed	Mt 11:26	3962
are delivered unto me of my *F*	Mt 11:27	3962
no man knoweth the Son, but the *F*	Mt 11:27	3962
neither knoweth any man the *F*	Mt 11:27	3962
will of my *F* which is in heaven	Mt 12:50	3962
the sun in the kingdom of their *F*	Mt 13:43	3962
commanded, saying, Honour thy *f*	Mt 15:4	3962
and, He that curseth *f* or mother	Mt 15:4	3962
shall say to his *f* or his mother	Mt 15:5	3962
And honour not his *f* or his mother	Mt 15:6	3962
my heavenly *F* hath not planted	Mt 15:13	3962
but my *F* which is in heaven	Mt 16:17	3962
glory of his *F* with his angels	Mt 16:27	3962
face of my *F* which is in heaven	Mt 18:10	3962
will of your *F* which is in heaven	Mt 18:14	3962
them of my *F* which is in heaven	Mt 18:19	3962
my heavenly *F* do also unto you	Mt 18:35	3962
this cause shall a man leave *f*	Mt 19:5	3962
Honour thy *f* and thy mother	Mt 19:19	3962
or brethren, or sisters, or *f*	Mt 19:29	3962
for whom it is prepared of my *F*	Mt 20:23	3962
them twain did the will of his *f*	Mt 21:31	3962
call no man your *f* upon the earth	Mt 23:9	3962
for one is your *F*, which is in	Mt 23:9	3962
angels of heaven, but my *F* only	Mt 24:36	3962
hand, Come, ye blessed of my *F*	Mt 25:34	3962
face, and prayed, saying, O my *F*	Mt 26:39	3962
time, and prayed, saying, O my *F*	Mt 26:42	3962
that I cannot now pray to my *F*	Mt 26:53	3962
them in the name of the *F*	Mt 28:19	3962
they left their *f* Zebedee in the	Mk 1:20	3962
put them all out, he taketh the *f*	Mk 5:40	3962
For Moses said, Honour thy *f*	Mk 7:10	3962
and, Whoso curseth *f* or mother	Mk 7:10	3962
man shall say to his *f* or mother	Mk 7:11	3962
do ought for his *f* or his mother	Mk 7:12	3962
of his *F* with the holy angels	Mk 8:38	3962
And he asked his *f*, How long is it	Mk 9:21	3962
straightway the *f* of the child	Mk 9:24	3962
cause shall a man leave his *f*	Mk 10:7	3962
Defraud not, Honour thy *f*	Mk 10:19	3962
or brethren, or sisters, or *f*	Mk 10:29	3962
be the kingdom of our *f* David	Mk 11:10	3962
that your *F* also which is in	Mk 11:25	3962
neither will your *F* which is in	Mk 11:26	3962
to death, and the *f* the son	Mk 13:12	3962
neither the Son, but the *F*	Mk 13:32	3962
And he said, Abba, *F*, all things	Mk 14:36	3962
the *f* of Alexander and Rufus, to	Mk 15:21	3962
him the throne of his *f* David	Lk 1:32	3962
after the name of his *f*	Lk 1:59	3962
And they made signs to his *f*	Lk 1:62	3962
his *f* Zacharias was filled with	Lk 1:67	3962
which he sware to our *f* Abraham	Lk 1:73	3962
behold, thy *f* and I have sought	Lk 2:48	3962
We have Abraham to our *f*	Lk 3:8	3962
as your *F* also is merciful	Lk 6:36	3962
and James, and John, and the *f*	Lk 8:51	3962
and delivered him again to his *f*	Lk 9:42	3962
me first to go and bury my *f*	Lk 9:59	3962
and said, I thank thee, O *F*	Lk 10:21	3962
even so, *F*; for so it seemed	Lk 10:21	3962
are delivered to me of my *F*	Lk 10:22	3962
knoweth who the Son is, but the *F*	Lk 10:22	3962
and who the *F* is, but the Son, and	Lk 10:22	3962
Our *F* which art in heaven,	Lk 11:2	3962
bread of any of you that is a *f*	Lk 11:11	3962
F give the Holy Spirit to them	Lk 11:13	3962
your *F* knoweth that ye have need	Lk 12:30	3962
The *f* shall be divided against	Lk 12:53	3962
the son, and the son against the *f*	Lk 12:53	3962
man come to me, and hate not his *f*	Lk 14:26	3962
the younger of them said to his *f*	Lk 15:12	3962
of them said to his *f*, *F*	Lk 15:12	3962
I will arise and go to my *f*	Lk 15:18	3962
and will say unto him, *F*	Lk 15:18	3962
And he arose, and came to his *f*	Lk 15:20	3962

his *f* saw him, and had compassion,	Lk 15:20	3962
And the son said unto him, *F*	Lk 15:21	3962
But the *f* said to his servants,	Lk 15:22	3962
thy *f* hath killed the fatted calf	Lk 15:27	3962
therefore came his *f* out, and	Lk 15:28	3962
And he answering said to his *f*	Lk 15:29	3962
F Abraham, have mercy on me, and	Lk 16:24	3962
he said, I pray thee therefore, *f*	Lk 16:27	3962
And he said, Nay, *f* Abraham	Lk 16:30	3962
bear false witness, Honour thy *f*	Lk 18:20	3962
as my *F* hath appointed unto me	Lk 22:29	3962
Saying, *F*, if thou be willing,	Lk 22:42	3962
Then said Jesus, *F*, forgive them	Lk 23:34	3962
with a loud voice, he said, *F*	Lk 23:46	3962
send the promise of my *F* upon you	Lk 24:49	3962
as of the only begotten of the *F*	Jn 1:14	3962
which is in the bosom of the *F*	Jn 1:18	3962
The *F* loveth the Son, and hath	Jn 3:35	3962
Art thou greater than our *f* Jacob	Jn 4:12	3962
yet at Jerusalem, worship the *F*	Jn 4:21	3962
shall worship the *F* in spirit	Jn 4:23	3962
for the *F* seeketh such to worship	Jn 4:23	3962
So the *f* knew that it was at the	Jn 4:53	3962
My *F* worketh hitherto, and I work	Jn 5:17	3962
but said also that God was his *F*	Jn 5:18	3962
but what he seeth the *F* do	Jn 5:19	3962
For the *F* loveth the Son, and	Jn 5:20	3962
For as the *F* raiseth up the dead,	Jn 5:21	3962
For the *F* judgeth no man, but	Jn 5:22	3962
Son, even as they honour the *F*	Jn 5:23	3962
not the *F* which hath sent him	Jn 5:23	3962
For as the *F* hath life in himself	Jn 5:26	3962
will of the *F* which hath sent me	Jn 5:30	3962
the *F* hath given me to finish	Jn 5:36	3962
of me, that the *F* hath sent me	Jn 5:36	3962
the *F* himself, which hath sent me	Jn 5:37	3962
that I will accuse you to the *F*	Jn 5:45	3962
for him hath God the *F* sealed	Jn 6:27	3962
but my *F* giveth you the true	Jn 6:32	3962
All that the *F* giveth me shall	Jn 6:37	3962
Jesus, the son of Joseph, whose *f*	Jn 6:42	3962
except the *F* which hath sent me	Jn 6:44	3962
heard, and hath learned of the *F*	Jn 6:45	3962
Not that any man hath seen the *F*	Jn 6:46	3962
is of God, he hath seen the *F*	Jn 6:46	3962
As the living *F* hath sent me	Jn 6:57	3962
hath sent me, and I live by the *F*	Jn 6:57	3962
it were given unto him of my *F*	Jn 6:65	3962
but I and the *F* that sent me	Jn 8:16	3962
the *F* that sent me beareth	Jn 8:18	3962
they unto him, Where is thy *F*	Jn 8:19	3962
Ye neither know me, nor my *F*	Jn 8:19	3962
ye should have known my *F* also	Jn 8:19	3962
that he spake to them of the *F*	Jn 8:27	3962
but as my *F* hath taught me, I	Jn 8:28	3962
the *F* hath not left me alone	Jn 8:29	3962
that which I have seen with my *F*	Jn 8:38	3962
which ye have seen with your *f*	Jn 8:38	3962
said unto him, Abraham is our *f*	Jn 8:39	3962
Ye do the deeds of your *f*	Jn 8:41	3962
we have one *F*, even God	Jn 8:41	3962
unto them, If God were your *F*	Jn 8:42	3962
Ye are of your *f* the devil	Jn 8:44	3962
and the lusts of your *f* ye will do	Jn 8:44	3962
for he is a liar, and the *f* of it	Jn 8:44	3962
but I honour my *F*, and ye do	Jn 8:49	3962
thou greater than our *f* Abraham	Jn 8:53	3962
it is my *F* that honoureth me	Jn 8:54	3962
Your *f* Abraham rejoiced to see my	Jn 8:56	3962
As the *F* knoweth me, even so know	Jn 10:15	3962
knoweth me, even so know I the *F*	Jn 10:15	3962
Therefore doth my *F* love me	Jn 10:17	3962
have I received of my *F*	Jn 10:18	3962
My *F*, which gave them me, is	Jn 10:29	3962
I and my *F* are one	Jn 10:30	3962
works have I shewed you from my *F*	Jn 10:32	3962
whom the *F* hath sanctified, and	Jn 10:36	3962
If I do not the works of my *F*	Jn 10:37	3962
and believe, that the *F* is in me	Jn 10:38	3962
lifted up his eyes, and said, *F*	Jn 11:41	3962
serve me, him will my *F* honour	Jn 12:26	3962
F, save me from this hour	Jn 12:27	3962
F, glorify thy name	Jn 12:28	3962
but the *F* which sent me, he gave	Jn 12:49	3962
even as the *F* said unto me, so I	Jn 12:50	3962
out of this world unto the *F*	Jn 13:1	3962
Jesus knowing that the *F* had	Jn 13:3	3962
no man cometh unto the *F*, but by	Jn 14:6	3962
ye should have known my *F* also	Jn 14:7	3962
unto him, Lord, shew us the *F*	Jn 14:8	3962
that hath seen me hath seen the *F*	Jn 14:9	3962
sayest thou then, Shew us the *F*	Jn 14:9	3962
am in the *F*, and the *F* in me	Jn 14:10	3962
but the *F* that dwelleth in me, he	Jn 14:10	3962
am in the *F*, and the *F* in me	Jn 14:11	3962
because I go unto my *F*	Jn 14:12	3962
that the *F* may be glorified in	Jn 14:13	3962
And I will pray the *F*, and he shall	Jn 14:16	3962
ye shall know that I am in my *F*	Jn 14:20	3962
loveth me shall be loved of my *F*	Jn 14:21	3962
my *F* will love him, and we will	Jn 14:23	3962
whom the *F* will send in my name,	Jn 14:26	3962
because I said, I go unto the *F*	Jn 14:28	3962
for my *F* is greater than I	Jn 14:28	3962
world may know that I love the *F*	Jn 14:31	3962
as the *F* gave me commandment,	Jn 14:31	3962
vine, and my *F* is the husbandman	Jn 15:1	3962
Herein is my *F* glorified, that ye	Jn 15:8	3962
As the *F* hath loved me, so have I	Jn 15:9	3962
my *F* I have made known unto you	Jn 15:15	3962
ye shall ask of the *F* in my name	Jn 15:16	3962
that hateth me hateth my *F* also	Jn 15:23	3962
seen and hated both me and my *F*	Jn 15:24	3962
I will send unto you from the *F*	Jn 15:26	3962
which proceedeth from the *F*	Jn 15:26	3962
because they have not known the *F*	Jn 16:3	3962
because I go to my *F*, and ye see	Jn 16:10	3962
things that the *F* hath are mine	Jn 16:15	3962
see me, because I go to the *F*	Jn 16:16	3962
and, Because I go to the *F*	Jn 16:17	3962
ye shall ask the *F* in my name	Jn 16:23	3962
I shall shew you plainly of the *F*	Jn 16:25	3962
that I will pray the *F* for you	Jn 16:26	3962
For the *F* himself loveth you,	Jn 16:27	3962
I came forth from the *F*, and am	Jn 16:28	3962
I leave the world, and go to the *F*	Jn 16:28	3962
alone, because the *F* is with me	Jn 16:32	3962
up his eyes to heaven, and said, *F*	Jn 17:1	3962
And now, O *F*, glorify thou me with	Jn 17:5	3962
Holy *F*, keep through thine own	Jn 17:11	3962
as thou, *F*, art in me, and I in	Jn 17:21	3962
F, I will that they also, whom	Jn 17:24	3962
O righteous *F*, the world hath not	Jn 17:25	3962
the cup which my *F* hath given me	Jn 18:11	3962
for he was *f* in law to Caiaphas,	Jn 18:13	3995
for I am not yet ascended to my *F*	Jn 20:17	3962
ascend unto my *F*, and your *F*	Jn 20:17	3962
as my *F* hath sent me, even so	Jn 20:21	3962
but wait for the promise of the *F*	Acts 1:4	3962
which the *F* hath put in his own	Acts 1:7	3962
having received of the *F* the	Acts 2:33	3962
glory appeared unto our *f* Abraham	Acts 7:2	3962
from thence, when his *f* was dead	Acts 7:4	3962
called his *f* Jacob to him, and all	Acts 7:14	3962
the sons of Emmor the *f* of Sychem	Acts 7:16	
but his *f* was a Greek	Acts 16:1	3962
knew all that his *f* was a Greek	Acts 16:3	3962
that the *f* of Publius lay sick of	Acts 28:8	3962
to you and peace from God our *F*	Rom 1:7	3962
we say then that Abraham our *f*	Rom 4:1	3962
that he might be the *f* of all	Rom 4:11	3962
the *f* of circumcision to them who	Rom 4:12	3962
of that faith of our *f* Abraham	Rom 4:12	3962
who is the *f* of us all,	Rom 4:16	3962
made thee a *f* of many nations	Rom 4:17	3962
become the *f* of many nations	Rom 4:18	3962
the dead by the glory of the *F*	Rom 6:4	3962
adoption, whereby we cry, Abba, *F*	Rom 8:15	3962
by one, even by our *f* Isaac	Rom 9:10	3962
even the *F* of our Lord Jesus	Rom 15:6	3962
you, and peace, from God our *F*	1Cor 1:3	3962
to us there is but one God, the *F*	1Cor 8:6	3962
up the kingdom to God, even the *F*	1Cor 15:24	3962
be to you and peace from God our *F*	2Cor 1:2	3962
even the *F* of our Lord Jesus	2Cor 1:3	3962
the *F* of mercies, and the God of	2Cor 1:3	3962
And will be a *F* unto you, and ye	2Cor 6:18	3962
F of our Lord Jesus Christ, which	2Cor 11:31	3962
but by Jesus Christ, and God the *F*	Gal 1:1	3962
be to you and peace from God the *F*	Gal 1:3	3962
to the will of God and our *F*	Gal 1:4	3962
until the time appointed of the *f*	Gal 4:2	3962
into your hearts, crying, Abba, *F*	Gal 4:6	3962
to you, and peace, from God our *F*	Eph 1:2	3962
F of our Lord Jesus Christ, who	Eph 1:3	3962
the *F* of glory, may give unto you	Eph 1:17	3962
access by one Spirit unto the *F*	Eph 2:18	3962
the *F* of our Lord Jesus Christ	Eph 3:14	3962
F of all, who is above all, and	Eph 4:6	3962
the *F* in the name of our Lord	Eph 5:20	3962
cause shall a man leave his *f*	Eph 5:31	3962
Honour thy *f* and mother	Eph 6:2	3962
love with faith, from God the *F*	Eph 6:23	3962
you, and peace, from God our *F*	Phil 1:2	3962
Lord, to the glory of God the *F*	Phil 2:11	3962
of him, that, as a son with the *f*	Phil 2:22	3962
our *F* be glory for ever and ever	Phil 4:20	3962
you, and peace, from God our *F*	Col 1:2	3962
the *F* of our Lord Jesus Christ,	Col 1:3	3962
Giving thanks unto the *F*, which	Col 1:12	3962
For it pleased the *F* that in him	Col 1:19	
the mystery of God, and of the *F*	Col 2:2	3962
thanks to God and the *F* by him	Col 3:17	3962
which is in God the *F* and in the	1Th 1:1	3962
you, and peace, from God our *F*	1Th 1:1	3962
in the sight of God and our *F*	1Th 1:3	3962
as a *f* doth his children,	1Th 2:11	3962
Now God himself and our *F*, and our	1Th 3:11	3962
holiness before God, even our *F*	1Th 3:13	3962
of the Thessalonians in God our *F*	2Th 1:1	3962
you, and peace, from God our *F*	2Th 1:2	3962
himself, and God, even our *F*	2Th 2:16	3962
mercy, and peace, from God our *F*	1Ti 1:2	3962
an elder, but intreat him as a *f*	1Ti 5:1	3962
mercy, and peace, from God the *F*	2Ti 1:2	3962
mercy, and peace, from God the *F*	Titus 1:4	3962
to you, and peace, from God our *F*	Philem 3	3962
And again, I will be to him a *F*	Heb 1:5	3962
Without *f*, without mother,	Heb 7:3	540
he was yet in the loins of his *f*	Heb 7:10	3962
is he whom the *f* chasteneth not	Heb 12:7	3962
subjection unto the *F* of spirits	Heb 12:9	3962
cometh down from the *F* of lights	Jas 1:17	3962
the *F* is this, To visit the	Jas 1:27	3962
Abraham our *f* justified by works	Jas 2:21	3962
bless we God, even the *F*	Jas 3:9	3962
to the foreknowledge of God the *F*	1Pet 1:2	3962
F of our Lord Jesus Christ, which	1Pet 1:3	3962
And if ye call on the *F*, who	1Pet 1:17	3962
he received from God the *F* honour	2Pet 1:17	3962
life, which was with the *F*	1Jn 1:2	3962
our fellowship is with the *F*	1Jn 1:3	3962
we have an advocate with the *F*	1Jn 2:1	3962
because ye have known the *F*	1Jn 2:13	3962
the love of the *F* is not in him	1Jn 2:15	3962
pride of life, is not of the *F*	1Jn 2:16	3962
is antichrist, that denieth the *F*	1Jn 2:22	3962
the Son, the same hath not the *F*	1Jn 2:23	3962
the Son hath the *F* also	1Jn 2:23	
continue in the Son, and in the *F*	1Jn 2:24	3962
love the *F* hath bestowed upon us	1Jn 3:1	3962
do testify that the *F* sent the	1Jn 4:14	3962
that bear record in heaven, the *F*	1Jn 5:7	3962
mercy, and peace, from God the *F*	2Jn 3	3962
Jesus Christ, the Son of the *F*	2Jn 3	3962
received a commandment from the *F*	2Jn 4	3962
of Christ, he hath both the *F*	2Jn 9	3962
that are sanctified by God the *F*	Jude 1	3962
and priests unto God and his *F*	Rev 1:6	3962
even as I received of my *F*	Rev 2:27	3962
will confess his name before my *F*	Rev 3:5	3962
set down with my *F* in his throne	Rev 3:21	3962

FATHERLESS

not afflict any widow, or *f* child	Ex 22:22	3490
be widows, and your children *f*	Ex 22:24	3490
execute the judgment of the *f*	Deut 10:18	3490
thee,) and the stranger, and the *f*	Deut 14:29	3490
gates, and the stranger, and the *f*	Deut 16:11	3490
Levite, the stranger, and the *f*	Deut 16:14	3490
of the stranger, nor of the *f*	Deut 24:17	3490
be for the stranger, for the *f*	Deut 24:19	3490
be for the stranger, for the *f*	Deut 24:20	3490
be for the stranger, for the *f*	Deut 24:21	3490
the Levite, the stranger, the *f*	Deut 26:12	3490
and unto the stranger, to the *f*	Deut 26:13	3490
the judgment of the stranger, *f*	Deut 27:19	3490
Yea, ye overwhelm the *f*, and ye	Job 6:27	3490
the arms of the *f* have been	Job 22:9	3490
They drive away the ass of the *f*	Job 24:3	3490
They pluck the *f* from the breast,	Job 24:9	3490
the poor that cried, and the *f*	Job 29:12	3490
the *f* hath not eaten thereof	Job 31:17	3490
lifted up my hand against the *f*	Job 31:21	3490
thou art the helper of the *f*	Ps 10:14	3490
To judge the *f* and the oppressed,	Ps 10:18	3490
A father of the *f*, and a judge of	Ps 68:5	3490
Defend the poor and *f*	Ps 82:3	3490
and the stranger, and murder the *f*	Ps 94:6	3490
Let his children be *f*, and his	Ps 109:9	3490
be any to favour his *f* children	Ps 109:12	3490
he relieveth the *f* and widow	Ps 146:9	3490
not into the fields of the *f*	Prov 23:10	3490
the oppressed, judge the *f*	Is 1:17	3490
they judge not the *f*, neither	Is 1:23	3490
shall have mercy on their *f*	Is 9:17	3490
prey, and that they may rob the *f*	Is 10:2	3490
not the cause, the cause of the *f*	Jer 5:28	3490
oppress not the stranger, the *f*	Jer 7:6	3490
violence to the stranger, the *f*	Jer 22:3	3490
Leave thy *f* children, I will	Jer 49:11	3490
We are orphans and *f*, our mothers	Lam 5:3	3691
in thee have they vexed the *f*	Eze 22:7	3490
for in thee the *f* findeth mercy	Hos 14:3	3490
oppress not the widow, nor the *f*	Zec 7:10	3490
in his wages, the widow, and the *f*	Mal 3:5	3490
Father is this, To visit the *f*	Jas 1:27	3737

FATHER'S

and they saw not their *f* nakedness	Gen 9:23	1
thy kindred, and from thy *f* house	Gen 12:1	1
me to wander from my *f* house	Gen 20:13	1
which took me from my *f* house	Gen 24:7	1
is there room in thy *f* house for	Gen 24:23	1
But thou shalt go unto my *f* house	Gen 24:38	1
of my kindred, and of my *f* house	Gen 24:40	1
For all the wells which his *f*	Gen 26:15	1
come again to my *f* house in peace	Gen 28:21	1
Rachel came with her *f* sheep	Gen 29:9	1
Rachel that he was her *f* brother	Gen 29:12	1
taken away all that was our *f*	Gen 31:1	1
of that which was our *f* hath he	Gen 31:1	1
I see your *f* countenance, that it	Gen 31:5	1
inheritance for us in our *f* house	Gen 31:14	1
stolen the images that were her *f*	Gen 31:19	1
sore longedst after thy *f* house	Gen 31:30	1
lay with Bilhah his *f* concubine	Gen 35:22	1
the sons of Zilpah, his *f* wives	Gen 37:2	1
to feed their *f* flock in Shechem	Gen 37:12	1
Remain a widow at thy *f* house	Gen 38:11	1
went and dwelt in her *f* house	Gen 38:11	1
all my toil, and all my *f* house	Gen 41:51	1
his brethren, and unto his *f* house	Gen 46:31	1
my *f* house, which were in the	Gen 46:31	1
all his *f* household, with bread,	Gen 47:12	1
and he held up his *f* hand, to	Gen 48:17	1
thou wentest up to thy *f* bed	Gen 49:4	1
thy *f* children shall bow down	Gen 49:8	1
And Joseph fell upon his *f* face	Gen 50:1	1
and his brethren, and his *f* house	Gen 50:8	1
in Egypt, he, and his *f* house	Gen 50:22	1
troughs to water their *f* flock	Ex 2:16	1
him Jochebed his *f* sister to wife	Ex 6:20	1733
my *f* God, and I will exalt him	Ex 15:2	1
priest's office in his *f* stead	Lev 16:32	1
The nakedness of thy *f* wife shalt	Lev 18:8	1
it is thy *f* nakedness	Lev 18:8	1
of thy *f* wife's daughter,	Lev 18:11	1
the nakedness of thy *f* sister	Lev 18:12	1
she is thy *f* near kinswoman	Lev 18:12	1
the nakedness of thy *f* brother	Lev 18:14	1
his *f* wife hath uncovered his	Lev 20:11	1
hath uncovered his *f* nakedness	Lev 20:11	1
his *f* daughter, or his mother's	Lev 20:17	1
sister, nor of thy *f* sister	Lev 20:19	1
and is returned unto her *f* house	Lev 22:13	1
she shall eat of her *f* meat	Lev 22:13	1
with the ensign of their *f* house	Num 2:2	1
thy *f* house with thee shall bear	Num 18:1	1
among their *f* brethren	Num 27:7	1
inheritance unto his *f* brethren	Num 27:10	1
being in her *f* house in her youth	Num 30:3	1
yet in her youth in her *f* house	Num 30:16	1

unto their f brothers' sons	Num 36:11	1730
damsel to the door of her f house	Deut 22:21	1
to play the whore in her f house	Deut 22:21	1
A man shall not take his f wife	Deut 22:30	1
nor discover his f skirt	Deut 22:30	1
be he that lieth with his f wife	Deut 27:20	1
because he uncovereth his f skirt	Deut 27:20	1
shew kindness unto my f house	Josh 2:12	1
all thy f household, home unto	Josh 2:18	1
her f household, and all that she	Josh 6:25	1
and I am the least in my f house	Judg 6:15	1
Take thy f young bullock, even	Judg 6:25	1
because he feared his f household	Judg 6:27	1
went unto his f house at Ophrah	Judg 9:5	1
up against my f house this day	Judg 9:18	1
shalt not inherit in our f house	Judg 11:2	1
me, and expel me out of my f house	Judg 11:7	1
thee and thy f house with fire	Judg 14:15	1
and he went up to his f house	Judg 14:19	1
her f house to Beth-lehem-judah	Judg 19:2	1
she brought him into her f house	Judg 19:3	1
arm, and the arm of thy f house	1Sa 2:31	1
on thee, and on all thy f house	1Sa 9:20	1
to feed his f sheep at Beth-lehem	1Sa 17:15	1
make his f house free in Israel	1Sa 17:25	1
Thy servant kept his f sheep	1Sa 17:34	1
go no more home to his f house	1Sa 18:2	1
or my f family in Israel, that I	1Sa 18:18	1
all his f house heard it, they	1Sa 22:1	1
son of Ahitub, and all his f house	1Sa 22:11	1
thou, and all thy f house	1Sa 22:16	1
of all the persons of thy f house	1Sa 22:22	1
destroy my name out of my f house	1Sa 24:21	1
thou gone in unto my f concubine	2Sa 3:7	1
of Joab, and on all his f house	2Sa 3:29	1
kindness for Jonathan thy f sake	2Sa 9:7	1
be on me, and on my f house	2Sa 14:9	1
have been thy f servant hitherto	2Sa 15:34	1
I have served in thy f presence	2Sa 16:19	1
Go in unto thy f concubines	2Sa 16:21	1
Absalom went in unto his f	2Sa 16:22	1
For all of my f house were but	2Sa 19:28	1
against me, and against my f house	2Sa 24:17	1
not do it for David thy f sake	1Kin 11:12	1
of his f servants with him	1Kin 11:17	1
shall be thicker than my f loins	1Kin 12:10	1
thy f house, in that ye have	1Kin 18:18	1
sons, and set him on his f throne	2Kin 10:3	1
and made him king in his f stead	2Kin 23:30	1
his f brother king in his stead	2Kin 24:17	1730
forasmuch as he defiled his f bed	1Chr 5:1	1
Shemuel, heads of their f house	1Chr 7:2	1
of Asher, heads of their f house	1Chr 7:40	1
of his f house twenty and two	1Chr 12:28	1
God, be on me, and on my f house	1Chr 21:17	1
according to their f house	1Chr 23:11	1
with understanding, of Huram my f	2Chr 2:13	1
shall be thicker than my f loins	2Chr 10:10	1
slain thy brethren of thy f house	2Chr 21:13	1
king in his f stead in Jerusalem	2Chr 36:1	1
they could not shew their f house	Ezr 2:59	1
both I and my f house have sinned	Neh 1:6	1
they could not shew their f house	Neh 7:61	1
thy f house shall be destroyed	Est 4:14	1
thine own people, and thy f house	Ps 45:10	1
For I was my f son, tender and	Prov 4:3	1
keep thy f commandment, and	Prov 6:20	1
son heareth his f instruction	Prov 13:1	1
fool despiseth his f instruction	Prov 15:5	1
thy f friend, forsake not	Prov 27:10	1
thy people, and upon thy f house	Is 7:17	1
a glorious throne to his f house	Is 22:23	1
him all the glory of his f house	Is 22:24	1
but obey their f commandment	Jer 35:14	1
that seeth all his f sins which	Eze 18:14	1
his sister, his f daughter	Eze 22:11	1
it new with you in my F kingdom	Mt 26:29	3962
I must be about my F business	Lk 2:49	3962
in his own glory, and in his F	Lk 9:26	3962
for it is your F good pleasure to	Lk 12:32	3962
of my f have bread enough	Lk 15:17	3962
wouldest send him to my f house	Lk 16:27	3962
make not my F house an house of	Jn 2:16	3962
I am come in my F name, and ye	Jn 5:43	3962
this is the F will which hath	Jn 6:39	3962
the works that I do in my F name	Jn 10:25	3962
to pluck them out of my F hand	Jn 10:29	3962
In my F house are many mansions	Jn 14:2	3962
not mine, but the F which sent me	Jn 14:24	3962
as I have kept my F commandments	Jn 15:10	3962
up in his f house three months	Acts 7:20	3962
that one should have his f wife	1Cor 5:1	3962
having his F name written in	Rev 14:1	3962

FATHERS

thou shalt go to thy f in peace	Gen 15:15	1
Return unto the land of thy f	Gen 31:3	1
until now, both we, and also our f	Gen 46:34	1
shepherds, both we, and also our f	Gen 47:3	1
of the years of the life of my f	Gen 47:9	1
But I will lie with my f, and thou	Gen 47:30	1
God, before whom my f Abraham	Gen 48:15	1
them, and the name of my f Abraham	Gen 48:16	1
you again unto the land of your f	Gen 48:21	1
bury me with my f in the cave	Gen 49:29	1
The God of your f hath sent me	Ex 3:13	1
of Israel, The LORD God of your f	Ex 3:15	1
unto them, The LORD God of your f	Ex 3:16	1
that the LORD God of their f	Ex 4:5	1
these are the heads of the f of	Ex 6:25	1
the Egyptians; which neither thy f	Ex 10:6	1
nor thy fathers' f have seen	Ex 10:6	1
according to the house of their f	Ex 12:3	1
he sware unto thy f to give thee	Ex 13:5	1
as he sware unto thee and to thy f	Ex 13:11	1
the f upon the children unto the	Ex 20:5	1
of the f upon the children	Ex 34:7	1
of his f shall he return	Lev 25:41	1
f shall they pine away with them	Lev 26:39	1
and the iniquity of their f	Lev 26:40	1
families, by the house of their f	Num 1:2	1
one head of the house of his f	Num 1:4	1
princes of the tribes of their f	Num 1:16	1
families, by the house of their f	Num 1:18	1
families, by the house of their f	Num 1:20	1
families, by the house of their f	Num 1:22	1
families, by the house of their f	Num 1:24	1
families, by the house of their f	Num 1:26	1
families, by the house of their f	Num 1:28	1
families, by the house of their f	Num 1:30	1
families, by the house of their f	Num 1:32	1
families, by the house of their f	Num 1:34	1
families, by the house of their f	Num 1:36	1
families, by the house of their f	Num 1:38	1
families, by the house of their f	Num 1:40	1
families, by the house of their f	Num 1:42	1
one was for the house of his f	Num 1:44	1
Israel, by the house of their f	Num 1:45	1
after the tribe of their f were	Num 1:47	1
of Israel by the house of their f	Num 2:32	1
according to the house of their f	Num 2:34	1
Levi after the house of their f	Num 3:15	1
according to the house of their f	Num 3:20	1
families, by the house of their f	Num 4:2	1
throughout the houses of their f	Num 4:22	1
families, by the house of their f	Num 4:29	1
and after the house of their f	Num 4:34	1
and by the house of their f	Num 4:38	1
families, by the house of their f	Num 4:40	1
families, by the house of their f	Num 4:42	1
and after the house of their f	Num 4:46	1
heads of the house of their f	Num 7:2	1
which thou swarest unto their f	Num 11:12	1
of their f shall ye send a man	Num 13:2	1
the f upon the children unto the	Num 14:18	1
land which I sware unto their f	Num 14:23	1
according to the house of their f	Num 17:2	1
the house of their f twelve rods	Num 17:2	1
the head of the house of their f	Num 17:3	1
How our f went down into Egypt	Num 20:15	1
the Egyptians vexed us, and our f	Num 20:15	1
of their f they shall inherit	Num 26:55	1
the chief f of the congregation	Num 31:26	1
Thus did your f, when I sent them	Num 32:8	1
the chief f of the tribes of the	Num 32:28	1
tribes of your f ye shall inherit	Num 33:54	1
according to the house of their f	Num 34:14	1
according to the house of their f	Num 34:14	1
the chief f of the families of	Num 36:1	1
the chief f of the children of	Num 36:1	1
from the inheritance of our f	Num 36:3	1
inheritance of the tribe of our f	Num 36:4	1
inheritance of the tribe of his f	Num 36:7	1
man the inheritance of his f	Num 36:8	1
which the LORD sware unto your f	Deut 1:8	1
(The LORD God of your f make you	Deut 1:11	1
God of thy f hath said unto thee	Deut 1:21	1
which I sware to give unto your f	Deut 1:35	1
the LORD God of your f giveth you	Deut 4:1	1
of thy f which he sware unto them	Deut 4:31	1
And because he loved thy f	Deut 4:37	1
made not this covenant with our f	Deut 5:3	1
the f upon the children unto the	Deut 5:9	1
God of thy f hath promised thee	Deut 6:3	1
land which he sware unto thy f	Deut 6:10	1
which the LORD sware unto thy f	Deut 6:18	1
land which he sware unto our f	Deut 6:23	1
which he had sworn unto your f	Deut 7:8	1
mercy which he sware unto thy f	Deut 7:12	1
he sware unto thy f to give thee	Deut 7:13	1
which the LORD sware unto your f	Deut 8:1	1
not, neither did thy f know	Deut 8:3	1
with manna, which thy f knew not	Deut 8:16	1
which he sware unto thy f	Deut 8:18	1
which the LORD sware unto thy f	Deut 9:5	1
unto their f to give unto them	Deut 10:11	1
a delight in thy f to love them	Deut 10:15	1
Thy f went down into Egypt with	Deut 10:22	1
unto your f to give unto them	Deut 11:9	1
sware unto your f to give them	Deut 11:21	1
thy f giveth thee to possess it	Deut 12:1	1
hast not known, thou, nor thy f	Deut 13:6	1
thee, as he hath sworn unto thy f	Deut 13:17	1
as he hath sworn unto thy f	Deut 19:8	1
he promised to give unto thy f	Deut 19:8	1
The f shall not be put to death	Deut 24:16	1
be put to death for the f	Deut 24:16	1
sware unto our f for to give us	Deut 26:3	1
cried unto the LORD God of our f	Deut 26:7	1
us, as thou swarest unto our f	Deut 26:15	1
God of thy f hath promised thee	Deut 27:3	1
sware unto thy f to give thee	Deut 28:11	1
neither thou nor thy f have known	Deut 28:36	1
neither thou nor thy f have known	Deut 28:64	1
and as he hath sworn unto thy f	Deut 29:13	1
of the LORD God of their f	Deut 29:25	1
the land which thy f possessed	Deut 30:5	1
and multiply thee above thy f	Deut 30:5	1
good, as he rejoiced over thy f	Deut 30:9	1
which the LORD sware unto thy f	Deut 30:20	1
sworn unto their f to give them	Deut 31:7	1
thou shalt sleep with thy f	Deut 31:16	1
land which I sware unto their f	Deut 31:20	1
newly up, whom your f feared not	Deut 32:17	1
I sware unto their f to give them	Josh 1:6	1
ask their f in time to come	Josh 4:6	1
shall ask their f in time to come	Josh 4:21	1
their f that he would give us	Josh 5:6	1
the heads of the f of the tribes	Josh 14:1	1
LORD God of your f hath given you	Josh 18:3	1
the heads of the f of the tribes	Josh 19:51	1
f of the Levites unto Eleazar the	Josh 21:1	1
unto the heads of the f of the	Josh 21:1	1
he sware to give unto their f	Josh 21:43	1
to all that he sware unto their f	Josh 21:44	1
f among the thousands of Israel	Josh 22:14	1
of the LORD, which our f made	Josh 22:28	1
Your f dwelt on the other side of	Josh 24:2	1
And I brought your f out of Egypt	Josh 24:6	1
after your f with chariots	Josh 24:6	1
put away the gods which your f	Josh 24:14	1
whether the gods which your f	Josh 24:15	1
our f out of the land of Egypt,	Josh 24:17	1
land which I sware unto your f	Judg 2:1	1
were gathered unto their f	Judg 2:10	1
forsook the LORD God of their f	Judg 2:12	1
the way which their f walked in	Judg 2:17	1
themselves more than their f	Judg 2:19	1
which I commanded their f	Judg 2:20	1
as their f did keep it, or not	Judg 2:22	1
their f by the hand of Moses	Judg 3:4	1
miracles which our f told us of	Judg 6:13	1
when their f or their brethren	Judg 21:22	1
that brought your f up out of the	1Sa 12:6	1
which he did to you and to your f	1Sa 12:7	1
your f cried unto the LORD, then	1Sa 12:8	1
brought forth your f out of Egypt	1Sa 12:8	1
you, as it was against your f	1Sa 12:15	1
and thou shalt sleep with thy f	2Sa 7:12	1
the king shall sleep with his f	1Kin 1:21	1
So David slept with his f	1Kin 2:10	1
the chief of the f of the	1Kin 8:1	1
LORD, which he made with our f	1Kin 8:21	1
which thou gavest unto their f	1Kin 8:34	1
land which thou gavest unto our f	1Kin 8:40	1
which thou gavest unto their f	1Kin 8:48	1
broughtest our f out of Egypt	1Kin 8:53	1
be with us, as he was with our f	1Kin 8:57	1
which he commanded our f	1Kin 8:58	1
who brought forth their f out of	1Kin 9:9	1
Egypt that David slept with his f	1Kin 11:21	1
And Solomon slept with his f	1Kin 11:43	1
come unto the sepulchre of thy f	1Kin 13:22	1
land, which he gave to their f	1Kin 14:15	1
and he slept with his f, and Nadab	1Kin 14:20	1
above all that their f had done	1Kin 14:22	1
And Rehoboam slept with his f	1Kin 14:31	1
was buried with his f in the city	1Kin 14:31	1
And Abijam slept with his f	1Kin 15:8	1
all the idols that his f had made	1Kin 15:12	1
And Asa slept with his f	1Kin 15:24	1
was buried with his f in the city	1Kin 15:24	1
So Baasha slept with his f	1Kin 16:6	1
So Omri slept with his f, and was	1Kin 16:28	1
for I am not better than my f	1Kin 19:4	1
the inheritance of my f unto thee	1Kin 21:3	1
give thee the inheritance of my f	1Kin 21:4	1
So Ahab slept with his f	1Kin 22:40	1
And Jehoshaphat slept with his f	1Kin 22:50	1
was buried with his f in the city	1Kin 22:50	1
And Joram slept with his f	2Kin 8:24	1
was buried with his f in the city	2Kin 8:24	1
with his f in the city of David	2Kin 9:28	1
And Jehu slept with his f	2Kin 10:35	1
and Jehoram, and Ahaziah, his f	2Kin 12:18	1
with his f in the city of David	2Kin 12:21	1
And Jehoahaz slept with his f	2Kin 13:9	1
And Joash slept with his f	2Kin 13:13	1
The f shall not be put to death	2Kin 14:6	1
be put to death for the f	2Kin 14:6	1
And Jehoash slept with his f	2Kin 14:16	1
with his f in the city of David	2Kin 14:20	1
that the king slept with his f	2Kin 14:22	1
And Jeroboam slept with his f	2Kin 14:29	1
So Azariah slept with his f	2Kin 15:7	1
with his f in the city of David	2Kin 15:7	1
of the LORD, as his f had done	2Kin 15:9	1
And Menahem slept with his f	2Kin 15:22	1
And Jotham slept with his f	2Kin 15:38	1
was buried with his f in the city	2Kin 15:38	1
And Ahaz slept with his f, and was	2Kin 16:20	1
was buried with his f in the city	2Kin 16:20	1
the law which I commanded your f	2Kin 17:13	1
like to the neck of their f	2Kin 17:14	1
that he made with their f	2Kin 17:15	1
as did their f, so do they unto	2Kin 17:41	1
them which my f have destroyed	2Kin 19:12	1
that which thy f have laid up in	2Kin 20:17	1
And Hezekiah slept with his f	2Kin 20:21	1
of the land which I gave their f	2Kin 21:8	1
since the day their f came forth	2Kin 21:15	1
And Manasseh slept with his f	2Kin 21:18	1
he forsook the LORD God of his f	2Kin 21:22	1
because our f have not hearkened	2Kin 22:13	1
I will gather thee unto thy f	2Kin 22:20	1
to all that his f had done	2Kin 23:32	1
to all that his f had done	2Kin 23:37	1
So Jehoiakim slept with his f	2Kin 24:6	1
of their f increased greatly	1Chr 4:38	1
of the house of their f were	1Chr 5:13	1
chief of the house of their f	1Chr 5:15	1
the heads of the house of their f	1Chr 5:24	1
and heads of the house of their f	1Chr 5:24	1
against the God of their f	1Chr 5:25	1
the Levites according to their f	1Chr 6:19	1
after the house of their f	1Chr 7:4	1
heads of the house of their f	1Chr 7:7	1
heads of the house of their f	1Chr 7:9	1
Jediael, by the heads of their f	1Chr 7:11	1
the f of the inhabitants of Geba	1Chr 8:6	1
were his sons, heads of the f	1Chr 8:10	1
who were heads of the f of the	1Chr 8:13	1

These were heads of the *f*	1Chr 8:28	1
f in the house of their *f*	1Chr 9:9	1
f in the house of their *f*	1Chr 9:9	1
heads of the house of their *f*	1Chr 9:13	1
and their *f*, being over the host	1Chr 9:19	1
chief of the *f* of the Levites,	1Chr 9:33	1
These chief *f* of the Levites were	1Chr 9:34	1
the God of our *f* look thereon	1Chr 12:17	1
throughout the house of their *f*	1Chr 12:30	1
the chief of the *f* of the Levites	1Chr 15:12	1
thou must go to be with thy *f*	1Chr 17:11	1
were the chief of the *f* of Laadan	1Chr 23:9	1
Levi after the house of their *f*	1Chr 23:24	1
even the chief of the *f*, as they	1Chr 23:24	1
chief men of the house of their *f*	1Chr 24:4	1
according to the house of their *f*	1Chr 24:4	1
the chief of the *f* of the priests	1Chr 24:6	1
after the house of their *f*	1Chr 24:30	1
the chief of the *f* of the priests	1Chr 24:31	1
even the principal *f* over against	1Chr 24:31	1
according to the house of their *f*	1Chr 26:13	1
of the Gershonite Laadan, chief *f*	1Chr 26:21	1
David the king, and the chief *f*	1Chr 26:26	1
to the generations of his *f*	1Chr 26:31	1
thousand and seven hundred chief *f*	1Chr 26:32	1
their number, to wit, the chief *f*	1Chr 27:1	1
Then the chief of the *f* and	1Chr 29:6	1
and sojourners, as were all our *f*	1Chr 29:15	1
Isaac, and of Israel, our *f*	1Chr 29:18	1
blessed the LORD God of their *f*	1Chr 29:20	1
in all Israel, the chief of the *f*	2Chr 1:2	1
the chief of the *f* of the	2Chr 5:2	1
thou gavest to them and to their *f*	2Chr 6:25	1
land which thou gavest unto our *f*	2Chr 6:31	1
which thou gavest unto their *f*	2Chr 6:38	1
forsook the LORD God of their *f*	2Chr 7:22	1
And Solomon slept with his *f*	2Chr 9:31	1
unto the LORD God of their *f*	2Chr 11:16	1
And Rehoboam slept with his *f*	2Chr 12:16	1
against the LORD God of your *f*	2Chr 13:12	1
upon the LORD God of their *f*	2Chr 13:18	1
So Abijah slept with his *f*	2Chr 14:1	1
to seek the LORD God of their *f*	2Chr 14:4	1
of their *f* with all their heart	2Chr 15:12	1
And Asa slept with his *f*, and died	2Chr 16:13	1
according to the house of their *f*	2Chr 17:14	1
back unto the LORD God of their *f*	2Chr 19:4	1
of the chief of the *f* of Israel	2Chr 19:8	1
And said, O LORD God of our *f*	2Chr 20:6	1
hearts unto the God of their *f*	2Chr 20:33	1
Now Jehoshaphat slept with his *f*	2Chr 21:1	1
was buried with his *f* in the city	2Chr 21:1	1
forsaken the LORD God of his *f*	2Chr 21:10	1
him, like the burning of his *f*	2Chr 21:19	1
and the chief of the *f* of Israel	2Chr 23:2	1
house of the LORD God of their *f*	2Chr 24:18	1
forsaken the LORD God of their *f*	2Chr 24:24	1
The *f* shall not die for the	2Chr 25:4	1
shall the children die for the *f*	2Chr 25:4	1
to the houses of their *f*,	2Chr 25:5	1
buried him with his *f* in the city	2Chr 25:28	1
that the king slept with his *f*	2Chr 26:2	1
number of the chief of the *f* of	2Chr 26:12	1
So Uzziah slept with his *f*	2Chr 26:23	1
they buried him with his *f* in the	2Chr 26:23	1
And Jotham slept with his *f*	2Chr 27:9	1
forsaken the LORD God of their *f*	2Chr 28:6	1
of your *f* was wroth with Judah	2Chr 28:9	1
to anger the LORD God of his *f*	2Chr 28:25	1
And Ahaz slept with his *f*, and they	2Chr 28:27	1
house of the LORD God of your *f*	2Chr 29:5	1
For our *f* have trespassed, and	2Chr 29:6	1
our *f* have fallen by the sword,	2Chr 29:9	1
And be not ye like your *f*, and like	2Chr 30:7	1
against the LORD God of their *f*	2Chr 30:7	1
not stiffnecked, as your *f* were	2Chr 30:8	1
seek God, the LORD God of his *f*	2Chr 30:19	1
to the LORD God of their *f*	2Chr 30:22	1
priests by the house of their *f*	2Chr 31:17	1
my *f* have done unto all the	2Chr 32:13	1
that my *f* utterly destroyed	2Chr 32:14	1
hand, and out of the hand of my *f*	2Chr 32:15	1
And Hezekiah slept with his *f*	2Chr 32:33	1
which I have appointed for your *f*	2Chr 33:8	1
greatly before the God of his *f*	2Chr 33:12	1
So Manasseh slept with his *f*	2Chr 33:20	1
because our *f* have not kept the	2Chr 34:21	1
I will gather thee to thy *f*	2Chr 34:28	1
of God, the God of their *f*	2Chr 34:32	1
the LORD, the God of their *f*	2Chr 34:33	1
by the houses of your *f*, after	2Chr 35:4	1
of the families of the *f* of your	2Chr 35:5	1
in one of the sepulchres of his *f*	2Chr 35:24	1
the LORD God of their *f* sent to	2Chr 36:15	1
up the chief of the *f* of Judah	Ezr 1:5	1
And some of the chief of the *f*	Ezr 2:68	1
and Levites and chief of the *f*	Ezr 3:12	1
and to the chief of the *f*	Ezr 4:2	1
of the chief of the *f* of Israel	Ezr 4:3	1
the book of the records of thy *f*	Ezr 4:15	2
But after that our *f* had provoked	Ezr 5:12	2
Blessed be the LORD God of our *f*	Ezr 7:27	1
are now the chief of their *f*	Ezr 8:1	1
unto the LORD God of your *f*	Ezr 8:28	1
and chief of the *f* of Israel	Ezr 8:29	1
Since the days of our *f* have we	Ezr 9:7	1
unto the LORD God of your *f*	Ezr 10:11	1
with certain chief of the *f*	Ezr 10:16	1
after the house of their *f*	Ezr 10:16	1
chief of the *f* gave unto the work	Neh 7:70	1
some of the chief of the *f* gave	Neh 7:71	1
chief of the *f* of all the people	Neh 8:13	1
and the iniquities of their *f*	Neh 9:2	1
the affliction of our *f* in Egypt	Neh 9:9	1
our *f* dealt proudly, and hardened	Neh 9:16	1
thou hadst promised to their *f*	Neh 9:23	1
and on our prophets, and on our *f*	Neh 9:32	1
princes, our priests, nor our *f*	Neh 9:34	1
our *f* to eat the fruit thereof	Neh 9:36	1
God, after the houses of our *f*	Neh 10:34	1
And his brethren, chief of the *f*	Neh 11:13	1
were priests, the chief of the *f*	Neh 12:12	1
were recorded chief of the *f*	Neh 12:22	1
sons of Levi, the chief of the *f*	Neh 12:23	1
Did not your *f* thus, and did not	Neh 13:18	1
thyself to the search of their *f*	Job 8:8	1
wise men have told from their *f*	Job 15:18	1
whose *f* I would have disdained to	Job 30:1	1
Our *f* trusted in thee	Ps 22:4	1
and a sojourner, as all my *f* were	Ps 39:12	1
our *f* have told us, what work	Ps 44:1	1
Instead of thy *f* shall be thy	Ps 45:16	1
go to the generation of his *f*	Ps 49:19	1
and known, and our *f* have told us	Ps 78:3	1
Israel, which he commanded our *f*	Ps 78:5	1
And might not be as their *f*	Ps 78:8	1
did he in the sight of their *f*	Ps 78:12	1
dealt unfaithfully like their *f*	Ps 78:57	1
When your *f* tempted me, proved me	Ps 95:9	1
We have sinned with our *f*	Ps 106:6	1
Our *f* understood not thy wonders	Ps 106:7	1
Let the iniquity of his *f* be	Ps 109:14	1
the glory of children are their *f*	Prov 17:6	1
riches are the inheritance of *f*	Prov 19:14	1
landmark, which thy *f* have set	Prov 22:28	1
for the iniquity of their *f*	Is 14:21	1
them which my *f* have destroyed	Is 37:12	1
that which thy *f* have laid up in	Is 39:6	1
And kings shall be thy nursing *f*	Is 49:23	
where our *f* praised thee, is	Is 64:11	1
the iniquities of your *f* together	Is 65:7	1
iniquity have your *f* found in me	Jer 2:5	1
for an inheritance unto your *f*	Jer 3:18	1
labour of our *f* from our youth	Jer 3:24	1
the LORD our God, we and our *f*	Jer 3:25	1
before this people, and the *f*	Jer 6:21	1
in the land that I gave to your *f*	Jer 7:7	1
which I gave to you and to your *f*	Jer 7:14	1
the *f* kindle the fire, and the	Jer 7:18	1
For I spake not unto your *f*	Jer 7:22	1
Since the day that your *f* came	Jer 7:25	1
they did worse than their *f*	Jer 7:26	1
Baalim, which their *f* taught them	Jer 9:14	1
they nor their *f* have known	Jer 9:16	1
Which I commanded your *f* in the	Jer 11:4	1
which I have sworn unto your *f*	Jer 11:5	1
f in the day that I brought them	Jer 11:7	1
which I made with their *f*	Jer 11:10	1
one against another, even the *f*	Jer 13:14	1
and the iniquity of our *f*	Jer 14:20	1
concerning their *f* that begat	Jer 16:3	1
Because your *f* have forsaken me,	Jer 16:11	1
And ye have done worse than your *f*	Jer 16:12	1
know not, neither ye nor your *f*	Jer 16:13	1
land that I gave unto their *f*	Jer 16:15	1
Surely our *f* have inherited lies,	Jer 16:19	1
day, as I commanded your *f*	Jer 17:22	1
they nor their *f* have known	Jer 19:4	1
as their *f* have forgotten my name	Jer 23:27	1
city that I gave you and your *f*	Jer 23:39	1
I gave unto them and to their *f*	Jer 24:10	1
to your *f* for ever and ever	Jer 25:5	1
the land that I gave to their *f*	Jer 30:3	1
The *f* have eaten a sour grape, and	Jer 31:29	1
f in the day that I took them by	Jer 31:32	1
the iniquity of the *f* into the	Jer 32:18	1
swear to their *f* to give them	Jer 32:22	1
and with the burnings of thy *f*	Jer 34:5	1
I made a covenant with your *f* in	Jer 34:13	1
but your *f* hearkened not unto me,	Jer 34:14	1
I have given to you and to your *f*	Jer 35:15	1
not, neither they, ye, nor your *f*	Jer 44:3	1
the wickedness of your *f*, and the	Jer 44:9	1
I set before you and before your *f*	Jer 44:10	1
as we have done, we, and our *f*	Jer 44:17	1
of Jerusalem, ye, and your *f*	Jer 44:21	1
the *f* shall not look back to	Jer 47:3	1
the LORD, the hope of their *f*	Jer 50:7	1
Our *f* have sinned, and are not	Lam 5:7	1
their *f* have transgressed against	Eze 2:3	1
Therefore the *f* shall eat the	Eze 5:10	1
and the sons shall eat their *f*	Eze 5:10	1
The *f* have eaten sour grapes, and	Eze 18:2	1
know the abominations of their *f*	Eze 20:4	1
ye not in the statutes of your *f*	Eze 20:18	1
Yet in this your *f* have	Eze 20:27	1
after the manner of your *f*	Eze 20:30	1
Like as I pleaded with your *f* in	Eze 20:36	1
up mine hand to give it to your *f*	Eze 20:42	1
in the land that I gave to your *f*	Eze 36:28	1
wherein your *f* have dwelt	Eze 37:25	1
mine hand to give it unto your *f*	Eze 47:14	1
praise thee, O thou God of my *f*	Dan 2:23	2
our kings, our princes, and our *f*	Dan 9:6	1
to our princes, and to our *f*	Dan 9:8	1
and for the iniquities of our *f*	Dan 9:16	1
do that which his *f* have not done	Dan 11:24	1
have not done, nor his fathers' *f*	Dan 11:24	1
shall he regard the God of his *f*	Dan 11:37	1
a god whom his *f* knew not shall	Dan 11:38	1
I saw your *f* as the firstripe in	Hos 9:10	1
or even in the days of your *f*	Joel 1:2	1
the which their *f* have walked	Amos 2:4	1
unto our *f* from the days of old	Mic 7:20	1
been sore displeased with your *f*	Zec 1:2	1
Be ye not as your *f*, unto whom	Zec 1:4	1
Your *f*, where are they	Zec 1:5	1
did they not take hold of your *f*	Zec 1:6	1
when your *f* provoked me to wrath,	Zec 8:14	1
profaning the covenant of our *f*	Mal 2:10	1
your *f* ye are gone away from mine	Mal 3:7	1
heart of the *f* to the children	Mal 4:6	1
heart of the children to their *f*	Mal 4:6	1
we had been in the days of our *f*	Mt 23:30	*3962*
ye up then the measure of your *f*	Mt 23:32	*3962*
hearts of the *f* to the children	Lk 1:17	*3962*
As he spake to our *f*, to Abraham,	Lk 1:55	*3962*
the mercy promised to our *f*	Lk 1:72	*3962*
did their *f* unto the prophets	Lk 6:23	*3962*
for so did their *f* to the false	Lk 6:26	*3962*
prophets, and your *f* killed them	Lk 11:47	*3962*
that ye allow the deeds of your *f*	Lk 11:48	*3962*
Our *f* worshipped in this mountain	Jn 4:20	*3962*
Our *f* did eat manna in the desert	Jn 6:31	*3962*
Your *f* did eat manna in the	Jn 6:49	*3962*
not as your *f* did eat manna, and	Jn 6:58	*3962*
it is of Moses, but of the *f*	Jn 7:22	*3962*
and of Jacob, the God of our *f*	Acts 3:13	*3962*
For Moses truly said unto the *f*	Acts 3:22	*3962*
which God made with our *f*	Acts 3:25	*3962*
The God of our *f* raised up Jesus,	Acts 5:30	*3962*
And he said, Men, brethren, and *f*	Acts 7:2	*3962*
our *f* found no sustenance	Acts 7:11	*3962*
in Egypt, he sent out our *f* first	Acts 7:12	*3962*
into Egypt, and died, he, and our *f*	Acts 7:15	*3962*
kindred, and evil entreated our *f*	Acts 7:19	*3962*
Saying, I am the God of thy *f*	Acts 7:32	*3962*
in the mount Sina, and with our *f*	Acts 7:38	*3962*
To whom our *f* would not obey, but	Acts 7:39	*3962*
Our *f* had the tabernacle of	Acts 7:44	*3962*
Which also our *f* that came after	Acts 7:45	*3962*
out before the face of our *f*	Acts 7:45	*3962*
as your *f* did, so do ye	Acts 7:51	*3962*
have not your *f* persecuted	Acts 7:52	*3962*
this people of Israel chose our *f*	Acts 13:17	*3962*
promise which was made unto the *f*	Acts 13:32	*3962*
on sleep, and was laid unto his *f*	Acts 13:36	*3962*
which neither our *f* nor we were	Acts 15:10	*3962*
Men, brethren, and *f*, hear ye my	Acts 22:1	*3962*
manner of the law of the *f*	Acts 22:3	*3971*
The God of our *f* hath chosen thee	Acts 22:14	*3962*
so worship I the God of my *f*	Acts 24:14	*3971*
promise made of God unto our *f*	Acts 26:6	*3962*
the people, or customs of our *f*	Acts 28:17	*3971*
by Esaias the prophet unto our *f*	Acts 28:25	*3962*
Whose are the *f*, and of whom as	Rom 9:5	*3962*
the promises made unto the *f*	Rom 15:8	*3962*
in Christ, yet have ye not many *f*	1Cor 4:15	*3962*
how that all our *f* were under the	1Cor 10:1	*3962*
zealous of the traditions of my *f*	Gal 1:14	*3967*
And, ye *f*, provoke not your	Eph 6:4	*3962*
F, provoke not your children to	Col 3:21	*3962*
and profane, for murderers of *f*	1Ti 1:9	*3964*
past unto the *f* by the prophets	Heb 1:1	*3962*
When your *f* tempted me, proved me	Heb 3:9	*3962*
covenant that I made with their *f*	Heb 8:9	*3962*
Furthermore we have had *f* of our	Heb 12:9	*3962*
received by tradition from your *f*	1Pet 1:18	*3970*
for since the *f* fell asleep	2Pet 3:4	*3962*
I write unto you, *f*, because ye	1Jn 2:13	*3962*
I have written unto you, *f*	1Jn 2:14	*3962*

FATHERS'

be the heads of their *f* houses	Ex 6:14	1
nor thy *f* fathers have seen,	Ex 10:6	1
one, according to their *f* houses	Num 17:6	1
upward, throughout their *f* house	Num 26:2	1
ye are risen up in your *f* stead	Num 32:14	1
the place of my *f* sepulchres	Neh 2:3	1
unto the city of my *f* sepulchres	Neh 2:5	1
eyes were after their *f* idols	Eze 20:24	1
they discovered their *f* nakedness	Eze 22:10	1
have not done, nor his *f* fathers	Dan 11:24	1
they are beloved for the *f* sakes	Rom 11:28	*3962*

FATHOMS

And sounded, and found it twenty *f*	Acts 27:28	*3712*
again, and found it fifteen *f*	Acts 27:28	*3712*

FATLING

the young lion and the *f* together	Is 11:6	4806

FATLINGS

and of the oxen, and of the *f*	1Sa 15:9	4932
paces, he sacrificed oxen and *f*	2Sa 6:13	4806
unto thee burnt sacrifices of *f*	Ps 66:15	4220
bullocks, all of them *f* of Bashan	Eze 39:18	4806
my *f* are killed, and all things	Mt 22:4	*4619*

FATNESS

the *f* of the earth, and plenty of	Gen 27:28	4924
shall be the *f* of the earth	Gen 27:39	4924
thick, thou art covered with *f*	Deut 32:15	
unto them, Should I leave my *f*	Judg 9:9	1880
he covereth his face with his *f*	Job 15:27	2459
on thy table should be full of *f*	Job 36:16	1880
satisfied with the *f* of thy house	Ps 36:8	1880
be satisfied as with marrow and *f*	Ps 63:5	1880
and thy paths drop *f*	Ps 65:11	1880
Their eyes stand out with *f*	Ps 73:7	2459
and my flesh faileth of *f*	Ps 109:24	8081
the *f* of his flesh shall wax lean	Is 17:4	4924
with blood, it is made fat with *f*	Is 34:6	2459
and their dust made fat with *f*	Is 34:7	2459
let your soul delight itself in *f*	Is 55:2	1880
the soul of the priests with *f*	Jer 31:14	1880
the root and *f* of the olive tree	Rom 11:17	*4096*

FATS

the *f* shall overflow with wine and	Joel 2:24	3342
the press is full, the *f* overflow	Joel 3:13	3342

FATTED

and fallowdeer, and *f* fowl	1Kin 4:23	75
the midst of her like *f* bullocks	Jer 46:21	4770

And bring hither the *f* calf Lk 15:23 4618
thy father hath killed the *f* calf Lk 15:27 4618
hast killed for him the *f* calf Lk 15:30 4618

FATTER
f in flesh than all the children Dan 1:15 1277

FATTEST
upon them, and slew the *f* of them Ps 78:31 4924
upon the *f* places of the province Dan 11:24 4924

FAULT
but the *f* is in thine own people Ex 5:16 2398
his face, according to his *f* Deut 25:2 7564
I have found no *f* in him since he 1Sa 29:3 3972
with a *f* concerning this woman 2Sa 3:8 5771
prepare themselves without my *f* Ps 59:4 5771
could find none occasion nor *f* Dan 6:4 7844
there any error or *f* found in him Dan 6:4 7844
go and tell him his *f* between thee Mt 18:15 1651
unwashen, hands, they found *f* Mk 7:2 3201
people, I find no *f* in this man Lk 23:4 158
have found no *f* in this man Lk 23:14 158
them, I find in him no *f* at all Jn 18:38 156
may know that I find no *f* in him Jn 19:4 156
for I find no *f* in him Jn 19:6 156
unto me, Why doth he yet find *f* Rom 9:19 3201
there is utterly a *f* among you 1Cor 6:7 2275
if a man be overtaken in a *f* Gal 6:1 3900
For finding *f* with them, he saith Heb 8:8 3201
for they are without *f* before the Rev 14:5 299

FAULTLESS
if that first covenant had been *f* Heb 8:7 278
to present you *f* before the Jude 24 299

FAULTS
I do remember my *f* this day Gen 41:9 2399
cleanse thou me from secret *f* Ps 19:12
Confess your *f* one to another, and Jas 5:16 3900
when ye be buffeted for your *f* 1Pet 2:20 264

FAULTY
this thing as one which is *f* 2Sa 14:13 818
now shall they be found *f* Hos 10:2 816

FAVOUR
now I have found *f* in thy sight Gen 18:3 2580
if I have found *f* in thine eyes Gen 30:27 2580
gave him *f* in the sight of the Gen 39:21 2580
I will give this people *f* in the Ex 3:21 2580
the LORD gave the people *f* in the Ex 11:3 2580
the LORD gave the people *f* in the Ex 12:36 2580
have I not found *f* in thy sight Num 11:11 2580
if I have found *f* in thy sight Num 11:15 2580
that she find no *f* in his eyes Deut 24:1 2580
the old, nor shew *f* to the young Deut 28:50 2603
O Naphtali, satisfied with *f* Deut 33:23 7522
and that they might have no *f* Josh 11:20 8467
Let me find *f* in thy sight, my Ruth 2:13 2580
was in *f* both with the LORD, and 1Sa 2:26 2896
for he hath found *f* in my sight 1Sa 16:22 2580
if I have found *f* in thine eyes 1Sa 20:29 2580
young men find *f* in thine eyes 1Sa 25:8 2580
nevertheless the lords *f* thee not 1Sa 29:6 2896
if I shall find *f* in the eyes of 2Sa 15:25 2580
Hadad found great *f* in the sight 1Kin 11:19 2580
servant have found *f* in thy sight Neh 2:5 3190
Esther obtained *f* in the sight of Est 2:15 2580
f in his sight more than all the Est 2:17 2617
that she obtained *f* in his sight Est 5:2 2580
If I have found *f* in the sight of Est 5:8 2580
If I have found *f* in thy sight Est 7:3 2580
and if I have found *f* in his sight Est 8:5 2580
Thou hast granted me life and *f* Job 10:12 2617
with *f* wilt thou compass him as Ps 5:12 7522
in his *f* is life Ps 30:5 7522
by thy *f* thou hast made my Ps 30:7 7522
that *f* my righteous cause Ps 35:27 2655
because thou hadst a *f* unto them Ps 44:3 7520
the people shall intreat thy *f* Ps 45:12 6440
in thy *f* our horn shall be Ps 89:17 7522
for the time to *f* her, yea, the Ps 102:13 2603
her stones, and *f* the dust thereof Ps 102:14 2603
with the *f* that thou bearest unto Ps 106:4 7522
any to *f* his fatherless children Ps 109:12 2603
A good man sheweth *f*, and lendeth Ps 112:5 2603
I intreated thy *f* with my whole Ps 119:58 6440
So shalt thou find *f* and good Prov 3:4 2580
and shall obtain *f* of the LORD Prov 8:35 7522
seeketh good procureth *f* Prov 11:27 7522
good man obtaineth *f* of the LORD Prov 12:2 7522
Good understanding giveth *f* Prov 13:15 2580
among the righteous there is *f* Prov 14:9 7522
The king's *f* is toward a wise Prov 14:35 7522
his *f* is as a cloud of the latter Prov 16:15 7522
thing, and obtaineth *f* of the LORD Prov 18:22 7522
will intreat the *f* of the prince Prov 19:6 6440
but his *f* is as dew upon the Prov 19:12 7522
findeth no *f* in his eyes Prov 21:10 2603
loving *f* rather than silver and Prov 22:1 2580
f than he that flattereth with Prov 28:23 2580
Many seek the ruler's *f* Prov 29:26 6440
F is deceitful, and beauty is vain Prov 31:30 2580
nor yet *f* to men of skill Eccl 9:11 2580
I in his eyes as one that found *f* Song 8:10 7965
Let *f* be shewed to the wicked Is 26:10 2603
formed them will shew them no *f* Is 27:11 2603
but in my *f* have I had mercy on Is 60:10 7522
where I will not shew you *f* Jer 16:13 2594
Now God had brought Daniel into *f* Dan 1:9 2617
for thou hast found *f* with God Lk 1:30 5485
stature, and in *f* with God and man Lk 2:52 5485
having *f* with all the people Acts 2:47 5485
his afflictions, and gave him *f* Acts 7:10 5485
Who found *f* before God, and Acts 7:46 5485
desired *f* against him, that he Acts 25:3 5485

FAVOURABLE
Be *f* unto them for our sakes Judg 21:22 2603
God, and he will be *f* unto him Job 33:26 7520
and will he be *f* no more Ps 77:7 7520
thou hast been *f* unto thy land Ps 85:1 7520

FAVOURED
Rachel was beautiful and well *f* Gen 29:17 4758
was a goodly person, and well *f* Gen 39:6 4758
of the river seven well *f* kine Gen 41:2 4758
them out of the river, ill *f* Gen 41:3 4758
And the ill *f* and leanfleshed kine Gen 41:4 4758
kine did eat up the seven well *f* Gen 41:4 4758
seven kine, fatfleshed and well *f* Gen 41:18 8389
up after them, poor and very ill *f* Gen 41:19 8389
the ill *f* kine did eat up the Gen 41:20
but they were still ill *f* Gen 41:21
ill *f* kine that came up after Gen 41:27
priests, they *f* not the elders Lam 4:16 2603
whom was no blemish, but well *f* Dan 1:4 4758
Hail, thou that art highly *f* Lk 1:28 5487

FAVOUREST
By this I know that thou *f* me Ps 41:11 2654

FAVOURETH
by him, and said, He that *f* Joab 2Sa 20:11 2654

FEAR
the *f* of you and the dread of you Gen 9:2 4172
in a vision, saying, *F* not, Abram Gen 15:1 3372
Surely the *f* of God is not in Gen 20:11 3374
f not; for God hath heard Gen 21:17 3372
f not, for I am with thee, and Gen 26:24 3372
the *f* of Isaac, had been with me, Gen 31:42 6343
Jacob sware by the *f* of his Gen 31:53 6343
for I *f* him, lest he will come and Gen 32:11 3373
the midwife said unto her, *F* not Gen 35:17 3372
for I *f* God Gen 42:18 3373
he said, Peace be to you, *f* not Gen 43:23 3372
f not to go down into Egypt Gen 46:3 3372
And Joseph said unto them, *F* not Gen 50:19 3372
Now therefore *f* ye not Gen 50:21 3372
ye will not yet *f* the LORD God Ex 9:30 3372
F ye not, stand still, and see the Ex 14:13 3372
F and dread shall fall upon them Ex 15:16 367
people able men, such as *f* God Ex 18:21 3373
Moses said unto the people, *F* not Ex 20:20 3372
that his *f* may be before your Ex 20:20 3374
I will send my *f* before thee Ex 23:27 367
Ye shall *f* every man his mother, Lev 19:3 3372
the blind, but shalt *f* thy God Lev 19:14 3372
face of the old man, and *f* thy God Lev 19:32 3372
but thou shalt *f* thy God Lev 25:17 3372
but *f* thy God Lev 25:36 3372
but shalt *f* thy God Lev 25:43 3372
neither *f* ye the people of the Num 14:9 3372
LORD is with us: *f* them not Num 14:9 3372
LORD said unto Moses, *F* him not Num 21:34 3372
f not, neither be discouraged Deut 1:21 3372
the *f* of thee upon the nations Deut 2:25 3374
the LORD said unto me, *F* him not Deut 3:2 3372
Ye shall not *f* them Deut 3:22 3372
that they may learn to *f* me all Deut 4:10 3372
in them, that they would *f* me Deut 5:29 3372
thou mightest *f* the LORD thy God Deut 6:2 3372
Thou shalt *f* the LORD thy God, and Deut 6:13 3372
to *f* the LORD our God, for our Deut 6:24 3372
to walk in his ways, and to *f* him Deut 8:6 3372
but to *f* the LORD thy God, to Deut 10:12 3372
Thou shalt *f* the LORD thy God Deut 10:20 3372
your God shall lay the *f* of you Deut 11:25 6343
f him, and keep his commandments, Deut 13:4 3372
And all Israel shall hear, and *f* Deut 13:11 3372
to *f* the LORD thy God always Deut 14:23 3372
all the people shall hear, and *f* Deut 17:13 3372
may learn to *f* the LORD his God Deut 17:19 3372
which remain shall hear, and *f* Deut 19:20 3372
f not, and do not tremble, neither Deut 20:3 3372
and all Israel shall hear, and *f* Deut 21:21 3372
that thou mayest *f* this glorious Deut 28:58 3372
and thou shalt *f* day and night, and Deut 28:66 6342
for the *f* of thine heart Deut 28:67 6343
heart wherewith thou shalt *f* Deut 28:67 6342
f not, nor be afraid of them Deut 31:6 3372
f not, neither be dismayed Deut 31:8 3372
f the LORD your God, and observe Deut 31:12 3372
learn to *f* the LORD your God, as Deut 31:13 3372
that ye might *f* the LORD your God Josh 4:24 3372
F not, neither be thou dismayed Josh 8:1 3372
LORD said unto Joshua, *F* them not Josh 10:8 3372
F not, nor be dismayed, be strong Josh 10:25 3372
done it for *f* of this thing Josh 22:24 1674
Now therefore *f* the LORD, and Josh 24:14 3372
turn in to me; *f* not Judg 4:18 3372
f not the gods of the Amorites, Judg 6:10 3372
f not: thou shalt not die Judg 6:23 3372
But if thou *f* to go down, go thou Judg 7:10 3372
for *f* of Abimelech his brother Judg 9:21 6440
And now, my daughter, *f* not Ruth 3:11 3372
stood by her said unto her, *F* not 1Sa 4:20 3372
the *f* of the LORD fell on the 1Sa 11:7 6343
If ye will *f* the LORD, and serve 1Sa 12:14 3372
said unto the people, *F* not 1Sa 12:20 3372
Only *f* the LORD, and serve him in 1Sa 12:24 3372
and fled that day for *f* of Saul 1Sa 21:10 6440
Abide thou with me, *f* not 1Sa 22:23 3372
And he said unto him, *F* not 1Sa 23:17 3372
haste to get away for *f* of Saul 1Sa 23:26 6440
And David said unto him, *F* not 2Sa 9:7 3372
then kill him, *f* not 2Sa 13:28 3372
be just, ruling in the *f* of God 2Sa 23:3 3374
That they may *f* thee all the days 1Kin 8:40 3372
to *f* thee, as do thy people 1Kin 8:43 3372
And Elijah said unto her, *F* not 1Kin 17:13 3372
but I thy servant *f* the LORD from 1Kin 18:12 3372
that thy servant did *f* the LORD 2Kin 4:1 3373
And he answered, *F* not 2Kin 6:16 3372
them how they should *f* the LORD 2Kin 17:28 3372
they *f* not the LORD, neither do 2Kin 17:34 3373
saying, Ye shall not *f* other gods 2Kin 17:35 3372
stretched out arm, him shall ye *f* 2Kin 17:36 3372
and ye shall not *f* other gods 2Kin 17:37 3372
neither shall ye *f* other gods 2Kin 17:38 3372
But the LORD your God ye shall *f* 2Kin 17:39 3372
F not to be the servants of the 2Kin 25:24 3372
the LORD brought the *f* of him 1Chr 14:17 6343
F before him, all the earth 1Chr 16:30 2342
f not, nor be dismayed 1Chr 28:20 3372
That they may *f* thee, to walk in 2Chr 6:31 3372
f thee, as doth thy people Israel 2Chr 6:33 3372
for the *f* of the LORD came upon 2Chr 14:14 6343
the *f* of the LORD fell upon all 2Chr 17:10 6343
Wherefore now let the *f* of the 2Chr 19:7 6343
shall ye do in the *f* of the LORD 2Chr 19:9 3374
f not, nor be dismayed 2Chr 20:17 3372
the *f* of God was on all the 2Chr 20:29 6343
for *f* was upon them because of Ezr 3:3 367
who desire to *f* thy name Neh 1:11 3372
the *f* of our God because of the Neh 5:9 3374
not I, because of the *f* of God Neh 5:15 3374
that would have put me in *f* Neh 6:14 3372
sent letters to put me in *f* Neh 6:19 3372
for the *f* of the Jews fell upon Est 8:17 6343
for the *f* of them fell upon all Est 9:2 6343
because the *f* of Mordecai fell Est 9:3 6343
Doth Job *f* God for nought Job 1:9 3372
Is not this thy *f*, thy confidence Job 4:6 3374
F came upon me, and trembling, Job 4:14 6343
forsaketh the *f* of the Almighty Job 6:14 3374
me, and let not his *f* terrify me Job 9:34 367
Then would I speak, and not *f* him Job 9:35 3372
shalt be stedfast, and shalt not *f* Job 11:15 3372
Yea, thou castest off *f*, and Job 15:4 3374
Their houses are safe from *f* Job 21:9 6343
he reprove thee for *f* of thee Job 22:4 3374
thee, and sudden *f* troubleth thee Job 22:10 6343
Dominion and *f* are with him Job 25:2 6343
the *f* of the LORD, that is wisdom Job 28:28 3374
Did I *f* a great multitude, or did Job 31:34 6206
Men do therefore *f* him Job 37:24 3372
her labour is in vain without *f* Job 39:16 6343
He mocketh at *f*, and is not Job 39:22 6343
his like, who is made without *f* Job 41:33 2844
Serve the LORD with *f*, and rejoice Ps 2:11 3374
in thy *f* will I worship toward Ps 5:7 3374
Put them in *f*, O LORD Ps 9:20 4172
There were they in great *f* Ps 14:5 6342
he honoureth them that *f* the LORD Ps 15:4 3373
The *f* of the LORD is clean, Ps 19:9 3374
Ye that *f* the LORD, praise him Ps 22:23 3373
f him, all ye the seed of Israel Ps 22:23 1481
my vows before them that *f* him Ps 22:25 3373
shadow of death, I will *f* no evil Ps 23:4 3372
the LORD is with them that *f* him Ps 25:14 3373
whom shall I *f*? Ps 27:1 3372
against me, my heart shall not *f* Ps 27:3 3372
and a *f* to mine acquaintance Ps 31:11 6343
f was on every side Ps 31:13 4032
hast laid up for them that *f* thee Ps 31:19 3373
Let all the earth *f* the LORD Ps 33:8 3372
the LORD is upon them that *f* him Ps 33:18 3373
round about them that *f* him Ps 34:7 3373
O *f* the LORD, ye his saints Ps 34:9 3372
is no want to them that *f* him Ps 34:9 3373
will teach you the *f* of the LORD Ps 34:11 3374
that there is no *f* of God before Ps 36:1 6343
many shall see it, and *f*, and shall Ps 40:3 3372
Therefore will not we *f*, though Ps 46:2 3372
F took hold upon them there, and Ps 48:6 7461
Wherefore should I *f* in the days Ps 49:5 3372
righteous also shall see, and *f* Ps 52:6 3372
There were they in great *f* Ps 53:5 6343
in great *f*, where no *f* was Ps 53:5 6343
changes, therefore they *f* not God Ps 55:19 3372
I will not *f* what flesh can do Ps 56:4 3372
a banner to them that *f* thee Ps 60:4 3373
heritage of those that *f* thy name Ps 61:5 3373
my life from *f* of the enemy Ps 64:1 6343
do they shoot at him, and *f* not Ps 64:4 3372
And all men shall *f*, and shall Ps 64:9 3372
Come and hear, all ye that *f* God Ps 66:16 3373
the ends of the earth shall *f* him Ps 67:7 3372
They shall *f* thee as long as the Ps 72:5 3372
salvation is nigh them that *f* him Ps 85:9 3373
unite my heart to *f* thy name Ps 86:11 3372
even according to thy *f*, so is Ps 90:11 3374
f before him, all the earth Ps 96:9 2342
shall *f* the name of the LORD Ps 102:15 3372
his mercy toward them that *f* him Ps 103:11 3373
the LORD pitieth them that *f* him Ps 103:13 3373
everlasting upon them that *f* him Ps 103:17 3373
for the *f* of them fell upon them Ps 105:38 6343
given meat unto them that *f* him Ps 111:5 3373
The *f* of the LORD is the Ps 111:10 3374
Ye that *f* the LORD, trust in the Ps 115:11 3373
will bless them that *f* the LORD Ps 115:13 3373
Let them now that *f* the LORD say Ps 118:4 3373
I will not *f* Ps 118:6 3372
servant, who is devoted to thy *f* Ps 119:38 3374
Turn away my reproach which I *f* Ps 119:39 3025
companion of all them that *f* thee Ps 119:63 3373
They that *f* thee will be glad Ps 119:74 3373
Let those that *f* thee turn unto Ps 119:79 3373
My flesh trembleth for *f* of thee Ps 119:120 6343
ye that *f* the LORD, bless the Ps 135:20 3373
the desire of them that *f* him Ps 145:19 3373
pleasure in them that *f* him Ps 147:11 3373
The *f* of the LORD is the Prov 1:7 3374
I will mock when your *f* cometh Prov 1:26 6343

When your f cometh as desolation, Prov 1:27 6343
did not choose the f of the LORD Prov 1:29 3374
and shall be quiet from f of evil Prov 1:33 6343
thou understand the f of the LORD Prov 2:5 3374
f the LORD, and depart from evil Prov 3:7 3372
Be not afraid of sudden f Prov 3:25 6343
The f of the LORD is to hate evil Prov 8:13 3374
The f of the LORD is the Prov 9:10 3374
The f of the wicked, it shall Prov 10:24 4034
The f of the LORD prolongeth days Prov 10:27 3374
In the f of the LORD is strong Prov 14:26 3374
The f of the LORD is a fountain Prov 14:27 3374
Better is little with the f of Prov 15:16 3374
The f of the LORD is the Prov 15:33 3374
by the f of the LORD men depart Prov 16:6 3374
The f of the LORD tendeth to life Prov 19:23 3374
The f of a king is as the roaring Prov 20:2 367
the f of the LORD are riches, and Prov 22:4 3374
but be thou in the f of the LORD Prov 23:17 3374
f thou the LORD and the king Prov 24:21 3372
The f of man bringeth a snare Prov 29:25 2731
it, that men should f before him Eccl 3:14 3372
but f thou God Eccl 5:7 3372
be well with them that f God Eccl 8:12 3373
that f God, which f before him Eccl 8:12 3372
F God, and keep his commandments Eccl 12:13 3372
thigh because of f in the night Song 3:8 6343
for f of the LORD, and for the Is 2:10 6343
for f of the LORD, and for the Is 2:19 6343
for f of the LORD, and for the Is 2:21 6343
f not, neither be fainthearted Is 7:4 3372
not come thither the f of briers Is 7:25 3374
neither f ye their f, nor be Is 8:12 3372
neither f ye their f, nor be Is 8:12 4172
and let him be your f, and let him Is 8:13 4172
knowledge and of the f of the LORD Is 11:2 3374
in the f of the LORD Is 11:3 3374
from thy sorrow, and from thy f Is 14:3 7267
f because of the shaking of the Is 19:16 6342
hath he turned into f unto me Is 21:4 2731
F, and the pit, and the snare, are Is 24:17 6343
of the f shall fall into the pit Is 24:18 6343
the terrible nations shall f thee Is 25:3 3372
their f toward me is taught by Is 29:13 3374
shall f the God of Israel Is 29:23 6206
over to his strong hold for f Is 31:9 4032
the f of the LORD is his treasure Is 33:6 3374
a fearful heart, Be strong, f not Is 35:4 3372
F thou not; for I am Is 41:10 3372
hand, saying unto thee, F not Is 41:13 3372
F not, thou worm Jacob, and ye men Is 41:14 3372
that formed thee, O Israel, F not Is 43:1 3372
F not: for I am with thee Is 43:5 3372
F not, O Jacob, my servant Is 44:2 3372
F ye not, neither be afraid Is 44:8 6342
yet they shall f, and they shall Is 44:11 6342
f ye not the reproach of men, Is 51:7 3372
F not; for thou shalt not be ashamed Is 54:4 3372
for thou shalt not f Is 54:14 3372
So shall they f the name of the Is 59:19 3372
together, and thine heart shall f Is 60:5 6342
and hardened our heart from thy f Is 63:17 3374
that my f is not in thee, saith Jer 2:19 6345
F ye not me? saith the LORD Jer 5:22 3372
Let us now f the LORD our God, Jer 5:24 3372
the enemy and f is on every side Jer 6:25 4032
Who would not f thee, O King of Jer 10:7 3372
defaming of many, f on every side Jer 20:10 4032
and they shall f no more, nor be Jer 23:4 3372
did he not f the LORD, and Jer 26:19 3373
heard a voice of trembling, of f Jer 30:5 6343
Therefore f thou not, O my Jer 30:10 3372
way, that they may f me for ever Jer 32:39 3372
I will put my f in their hearts Jer 32:40 3374
and they shall f and tremble for Jer 33:9 6342
let us go to Jerusalem for f of Jer 35:11 6440
for f of the army of the Syrians Jer 35:11 6440
Jerusalem for f of Pharaoh's army Jer 37:11 6440
F not to serve the Chaldeans Jer 40:9 3372
for f of Baasha king of Israel Jer 41:9 6440
for f was round about, saith the Jer 46:5 4032
But f not thou, O my servant Jer 46:27 3372
F thou not, O Jacob my servant, Jer 46:28 3372
F, and the pit, and the snare, Jer 48:43 6343
the f shall fall into the pit Jer 48:44 6343
I will bring a f upon thee Jer 49:5 6343
to flee, and f hath seized on her Jer 49:24 7374
cry unto them, F is on every side Jer 49:29 4032
for f of the oppressing sword Jer 50:16 6440
ye f for the rumour that shall be Jer 51:46 3372
F and a snare is come upon us, Lam 3:47 6343
thou saidst, F not Lam 3:57 3372
f them not, neither be dismayed Eze 3:9 3372
I will put a f in the land of Eze 30:13 3374
I f my lord the king, who hath Dan 1:10 3373
f before the God of Daniel Dan 6:26 1763
said he unto me, F not, Daniel Dan 10:12 3372
O man greatly beloved, f not Dan 10:19 3372
shall f the LORD and his goodness Hos 3:5 6342
shall f because of the calves of Hos 10:5 1481
F not, O land Joel 2:21 3372
lion hath roared, who will not f Amos 3:8 3372
I f the LORD, the God of heaven, Jonah 1:9 3373
God, and shall f because of thee Mic 7:17 3372
I said, Surely thou wilt f me Zeph 3:7 3372
be said to Jerusalem, F thou not Zeph 3:16 3372
the people did f before the LORD Hag 1:12 3372
remaineth among you: f ye not Hag 2:5 3372
f not, but let your hands be Zec 8:13 3372
to the house of Judah: f ye not Zec 8:15 3372
Ashkelon shall see it, and f Zec 9:5 3372
if I be a master, where is my f Mal 1:6 4172
for the f wherewith he feared me Mal 2:5 4172
f not me, saith the LORD of hosts Mal 3:5 3372
But unto you that f my name shall Mal 4:2 3373
f not to take unto thee Mary thy Mt 1:20 5399
F them not therefore Mt 10:26 5399
f not them which kill the body, Mt 10:28 5399
but rather f him which is able to Mt 10:28 5399
F ye not therefore, ye are of Mt 10:31 5399
and they cried out for f Mt 14:26 5401
we f the people Mt 21:26 5399
for f of him the keepers did Mt 28:4 5401
and said unto the women, F not ye Mt 28:5 5399
quickly from the sepulchre with f Mt 28:8 5401
was troubled, and f fell upon him Lk 1:12 5401
said unto him, F not, Zacharias Lk 1:13 5399
angel said unto her, F not, Mary Lk 1:30 5399
that f him from generation to Lk 1:50 5399
f came on all that dwelt round Lk 1:65 5401
enemies might serve him without f Lk 1:74 870
the angel said unto them, F not Lk 2:10 5399
And Jesus said unto Simon, F not Lk 5:10 5399
God, and were filled with f Lk 5:26 5401
And there came a f on all Lk 7:16 5401
for they were taken with great f Lk 8:37 5401
he answered him, saying, F not Lk 8:50 5399
will forewarn you whom ye shall f Lk 12:5 5399
F him, which after he hath killed Lk 12:5 5399
yea, I say unto you, F him Lk 12:5 5399
F not therefore Lk 12:7 5399
F not, little flock Lk 12:32 5399
himself, Though I f not God Lk 18:4 5399
Men's hearts failing them for f Lk 21:26 5401
him, saying, Dost not thou f God Lk 23:40 5399
openly of him for f of the Jews Jn 7:13 5401
F not, daughter of Sion Jn 12:15 5399
but secretly for f of the Jews Jn 19:38 5401
were assembled for f of the Jews Jn 20:19 5401
And f came upon every soul Acts 2:43 5401
great f came on all them that Acts 5:5 5401
great f came upon all the church, Acts 5:11 5401
and walking in the f of the Lord Acts 9:31 5401
Men of Israel, and ye that f God Acts 13:16 5399
f fell on them all, and the name Acts 19:17 5401
Saying, F not, Paul Acts 27:24 5399
There is no f of God before their Rom 3:18 5401
the spirit of bondage again to f Rom 8:15 5401
Be not highminded, but f Rom 11:20 5399
to whom custom; f to whom Rom 13:7 5401
to whom f; honour to whom Rom 13:7 5401
was with you in weakness, and in f 1Cor 2:3 5401
that he may be with you without f 1Cor 16:10 820
holiness in the f of God 2Cor 7:1 5401
what indignation, yea, what f 2Cor 7:11 5401
obedience of you all, how with f 2Cor 7:15 5401
But I f, lest by any means, as 2Cor 11:3 5399
For I f, lest, when I come, I 2Cor 12:20 5399
one to another in the f of God Eph 5:21 5401
according to the flesh, with f Eph 6:5 5401
bold to speak the word without f Phil 1:14 870
out your own salvation with f Phil 2:12 5401
all, that others also may f 1Ti 5:20 5401
hath not given us the spirit of f 2Ti 1:7 1167
through f of death were all their Heb 2:15 5401
Let us therefore f, lest, a Heb 4:1 5399
not seen as yet, moved with f Heb 11:7 2125
that Moses said, I exceedingly f Heb 12:21 1630
with reverence and godly f Heb 12:28 2124
I will not f what man shall do Heb 13:6 5399
time of your sojourning here in f 1Pet 1:17 5401
F God. Honour the king 1Pet 2:17 5399
to your masters with all f 1Pet 2:18 5401
conversation coupled with f 1Pet 3:2 5401
that is in you with meekness and f 1Pet 3:15 5401
There is no f in love 1Jn 4:18 5401
but perfect love casteth out f 1Jn 4:18 5401
because f hath torment 1Jn 4:18 5401
you, feeding themselves without f Jude 12 870
And others save with f, pulling Jude 23 5401
upon me, saying unto me, F not Rev 1:17 5399
F none of those things which thou Rev 2:10 5399
great f fell upon them which saw Rev 11:11 5401
saints, and them that f thy name Rev 11:18 5399
F God, and give glory to him Rev 14:7 5399
Who shall not f thee, O Lord, and Rev 15:4 5399
afar off for the f of her torment Rev 18:10 5401
afar off for the f of her torment Rev 18:15 5401
ye his servants, and ye that f him Rev 19:5 5399

FEARED

for he f to dwell in Zoar Gen 19:30 3372
for he f to say, She is my wife Gen 26:7 3372
But the midwives f God, and did Ex 1:17 3372
pass, because the midwives f God Ex 1:21 3372
And Moses f, and said, Surely this Ex 2:14 3372
He that f the word of the LORD Ex 9:20 3373
and the people f the LORD, and Ex 14:31 3372
and he f not God Deut 25:18 3373
newly up, whom your fathers f not Deut 32:17 8175
Were it not that I f the wrath of Deut 32:27 1481
and they f him, as they f Josh 4:14 3372
That they f greatly, because Josh 10:2 3372
because he f his father's Judg 6:27 3372
for he f, because he was yet a Judg 8:20 3372
Samuel f to shew Eli the vision 1Sa 3:15 3372
all the people greatly f the LORD 1Sa 12:18 3372
for the people f the oath 1Sa 14:26 3372
because I f the people, and obeyed 1Sa 15:24 3372
a word again, because he f him 2Sa 3:11 3372
So the Syrians f to help the 2Sa 10:19 3372
the servants of David f to tell 2Sa 12:18 3372
Adonijah f because of Solomon, and 1Kin 1:50 3372
and they f the king 1Kin 3:28 3372
(Now Obadiah f the LORD greatly 1Kin 18:3 3373
of Egypt, and had f other gods, 2Kin 17:7 3372
there, that they f not the LORD 2Kin 17:25 3372
So they f the LORD, and made unto 2Kin 17:32 3373
They f the LORD, and served their 2Kin 17:33 3373
So these nations f the LORD 2Kin 17:41 3373
he also is to be f above all gods 1Chr 16:25 3372
And Jehoshaphat f, and set himself 2Chr 20:3 3372
faithful man, and f God above many Neh 7:2 3372
and upright, and one that f God Job 1:1 3373
which I greatly f is come upon me Job 3:25 6342
Thou, even thou, art to be f Ps 76:7 3372
the earth f, and was still, Ps 76:8 3372
unto him that ought to be f Ps 76:11 4172
on safely, so that they f not Ps 78:53 6342
God is greatly to be f in the Ps 89:7 6206
he is to be f above all gods Ps 96:4 3372
with thee, that thou mayest be f Ps 130:4 3372
The isles saw it, and f Is 41:5 3372
hast f continually every day Is 51:13 6342
whom hast thou been afraid or f Is 57:11 3372
treacherous sister Judah f not Jer 3:8 3372
pass, that the sword, which ye f Jer 42:16 3373
this day, neither have they f Jer 44:10 3372
Ye have f the sword Eze 11:8 3372
trembled and f before him Dan 5:19 1763
because we f not the LORD Hos 10:3 3372
Then the men f the LORD Jonah 1:16 3372
for the fear wherewith he f me Mal 2:5 3372
Then they that f the LORD spake Mal 3:16 3372
him for them that f the LORD Mal 3:16 3372
he f the multitude, because they Mt 14:5 5399
they f the multitude, because Mt 21:46 5399
they f greatly, saying, Truly Mt 27:54 5399
they f exceedingly, and said one Mk 4:41 5401
For Herod f John, knowing that he Mk 6:20 5399
for they f him, because all the Mk 11:18 5399
they f the people Mk 11:32 5399
lay hold on him, but f the people Mk 12:12 5399
they f as they entered into the Lk 9:34 5399
they f to ask him of that saying Lk 9:45 5399
which f not God, neither regarded Lk 18:2 5399
For I f thee, because thou art an Lk 19:21 5399
and they f the people Lk 20:19 5399
for they f the people Lk 22:2 5399
parents, because they f the Jews Jn 9:22 5399
for they f the people, lest they Acts 5:26 5399
one that f God with all his house Acts 10:2 5399
and they f, when they heard that Acts 16:38 5399
death, and was heard in that he f Heb 5:7 2124

FEAREST

for now I know that thou f God Gen 22:12 3373
even of old, and thou f me not Is 57:11 3372
hand of them whose face thou f Jer 22:25 1481

FEARETH

Behold, Adonijah f king Solomon 1Kin 1:51 3372
and an upright man, one that f God Job 1:8 3373
and an upright man, one that f God Job 2:3 3373
What man is he that f the LORD Ps 25:12 3373
is the man that f the LORD Ps 112:1 3372
is every one that f the Lord Ps 128:1 3373
man be blessed that f the LORD Ps 128:4 3373
but he that f the commandment Prov 13:13 3373
in his uprightness f the LORD Prov 14:2 3373
A wise man f, and departeth from Prov 14:16 3373
Happy is the man that f alway Prov 28:14 6342
but a woman that f the LORD Prov 31:30 3373
for he that f God shall come Eccl 7:18 3373
because he f not before God Eccl 8:13 3373
sweareth, as he that f an oath Eccl 9:2 3373
Who is among you that f the LORD Is 50:10 3373
a just man, and one that f God Acts 10:22 5399
But in every nation he that f him Acts 10:35 5399
and whosoever among you f God Acts 13:26 5399
He that f is not made perfect in 1Jn 4:18 5399

FEARFUL

f in praises, doing wonders Ex 15:11 3372
say, What man is there that is f Deut 20:8 3373
and f name, THE LORD THY GOD Deut 28:58 3372
people, saying, Whosoever is f Judg 7:3 3373
Say to them that are of a f heart Is 35:4 4116
he saith unto them, Why are ye f Mt 8:26 1169
said unto them, Why are ye so f Mk 4:40 1169
f sights and great signs shall Lk 21:11 5400
But a certain f looking for of Heb 10:27 5398
It is a f thing to fall into the Heb 10:31 5398
But the f, and unbelieving, and the Rev 21:8 1169

FEARFULLY

for I am f and wonderfully made Ps 139:14 3372

FEARFULNESS

F and trembling are come upon me, Ps 55:5 3374
My heart panted, f affrighted me Is 21:4 6427
f hath surprised the hypocrites Is 33:14 7461

FEARING

children cease from f the LORD Josh 22:25 3372
But the woman f and trembling, Mk 5:33 5399
f lest Paul should have been Acts 23:10 2125
f lest they should fall into the Acts 27:17 5399
Then f lest we should have fallen Acts 27:29 5399
himself, f them which were of the Gal 2:12 5399
but in singleness of heart, f God Col 3:22 5399
not f the wrath of the king Heb 11:27 5399

FEARS

me, and delivered me from all my f Ps 34:4 4035
f shall be in the way, and the Eccl 12:5 2849
and will bring their f upon them Is 66:4 4035
were fightings, within were f 2Cor 7:5 5401

FEAST

and he made them a f, and did bake Gen 19:3 4960
Abraham made a great f the same Gen 21:8 4960
And he made them a f, and they did Gen 26:30 4960
the men of the place, and made a f Gen 29:22 4960
that he made a f unto all his Gen 40:20 4960
that they may hold a f unto me in Ex 5:1 2287

we must hold a *f* unto the LORD Ex 10:9 2282
ye shall keep it a *f* to the LORD Ex 12:14 2282
ye shall keep it a *f* by an Ex 12:14 2287
observe the *f* of unleavened bread Ex 12:17
day shall be a *f* to the LORD Ex 13:6 2282
keep a *f* unto me in the year Ex 23:14 2287
keep the *f* of unleavened bread Ex 23:15 2282
the *f* of harvest, the firstfruits Ex 23:16 2282
the *f* of ingathering, which is in Ex 23:16 2282
To morrow is a *f* to the LORD Ex 32:5 2282
The *f* of unleavened bread shalt Ex 34:18 2282
thou shalt observe the *f* of weeks Ex 34:22 2282
the *f* of ingathering at the Ex 34:22 2282
shall the sacrifice of the *f* of Ex 34:25 2282
f of unleavened bread unto the Lev 23:6 2282
f of tabernacles for seven days Lev 23:34 2282
ye shall keep a *f* unto the LORD Lev 23:39 2282
ye shall keep it a *f* unto the Lev 23:41 2282
day of this month is the *f* Num 28:17 2282
ye shall keep a *f* unto the LORD Num 29:12 2282
thou shalt keep the *f* of weeks Deut 16:10 2282
Thou shalt observe the *f* of Deut 16:13 2282
And thou shalt rejoice in thy *f* Deut 16:14 2282
f unto the LORD thy God in the Deut 16:15 2287
in the *f* of unleavened bread, and Deut 16:16 2282
bread, and in the *f* of weeks Deut 16:16 2282
and in the *f* of tabernacles Deut 16:16 2282
release, in the *f* of tabernacles, Deut 31:10 2282
and Samson made there a *f* Judg 14:10 4960
me within the seven days of the *f* Judg 14:12 4960
seven days, while their *f* lasted Judg 14:17 4960
there is a *f* of the LORD in Judg 21:19 2282
he held a *f* in his house, like 1Sa 25:36 4960
his house, like the *f* of a king 1Sa 25:36 4960
and the men that were with him a *f* 2Sa 3:20 4960
made a *f* to all his servants 1Kin 3:15 4960
at the *f* in the month Ethanim 1Kin 8:2 2282
And at that time Solomon held a *f* 1Kin 8:65 2282
ordained a *f* in the eighth month 1Kin 12:32 2282
like unto the *f* that is in Judah, 1Kin 12:32 2282
ordained a *f* unto the children of 1Kin 12:33 2282
f which was in the seventh month 2Chr 5:3 2282
Solomon kept the *f* seven days 2Chr 7:8 2282
seven days, and the *f* seven days 2Chr 7:9 2282
even in the *f* of unleavened bread 2Chr 8:13 2282
bread, and in the *f* of weeks 2Chr 8:13 2282
and in the *f* of tabernacles 2Chr 8:13 2282
much people to keep the *f* of 2Chr 30:13 2282
present at Jerusalem kept the *f* 2Chr 30:21 2282
eat throughout the *f* seven days 2Chr 30:22 4150
the *f* of unleavened bread seven 2Chr 35:17 2282
kept also the *f* of tabernacles Ezr 3:4 2282
kept the *f* of unleavened bread Ezr 6:22 2282
in the *f* of the seventh month Neh 8:14 2282
And they kept the *f* seven days Neh 8:18 2282
he made a *f* unto all his princes Est 1:3 4960
the king made a *f* unto all the Est 1:5 4960
a *f* for the women in the royal Est 1:9 4960
a great *f* unto all his princes Est 2:18 4960
and his servants, even Esther's *f* Est 2:18 4960
the Jews had joy and gladness, a *f* Est 8:17 4960
appointed, on our solemn *f* day Ps 81:3 2282
a merry heart hath a continual *f* Prov 15:15 4960
A *f* is made for laughter, and wine Eccl 10:19 3899
unto all people a *f* of fat things Is 25:6 4960
a *f* of wines on the lees, of fat Is 25:6 4960
LORD, as in the day of a solemn *f* Lam 2:7 4150
the passover, a *f* of seven days Eze 45:21 2282
seven days of the *f* he shall Eze 45:23 2282
like in the *f* of the seven days Eze 45:25 2282
the king made a great *f* to a Dan 5:1 3900
her *f* days, her new moons, and her Hos 2:11 2282
in the day of the *f* of the LORD Hos 9:5 2282
as in the days of the solemn *f* Hos 12:9 4150
I hate, I despise your *f* days Amos 5:21 2282
to keep the *f* of tabernacles Zec 14:16 2282
up to keep the *f* of tabernacles Zec 14:18 2282
up to keep the *f* of tabernacles Zec 14:19 2282
two days is the *f* of the passover Mt 26:2
But they said, Not on the *f* day Mt 26:5 1859
of the *f* of unleavened bread the Mt 26:17
Now at that *f* the governor was Mt 27:15 1859
days was the *f* of the passover Mk 14:1
But they said, Not on the *f* day Mk 14:2 1859
Now at that *f* he released unto Mk 15:6 1859
year at the *f* of the passover Lk 2:41 1859
after the custom of the *f* Lk 2:42 1859
him a great *f* in his own house Lk 5:29 1408
But when thou makest a *f*, call Lk 14:13 1408
Now the *f* of unleavened bread Lk 22:1 1859
release one unto them at the *f* Lk 23:17 1859
bear unto the governor of the *f* Jn 2:8 755
When the ruler of the *f* had Jn 2:9 755
the governor of the *f* called the Jn 2:9 755
at the passover, in the *f* day Jn 2:23 1859
that he did at Jerusalem at the *f* Jn 4:45 1859
for they also went unto the *f* Jn 4:45 1859
this there was a *f* of the Jews Jn 5:1 1859
a *f* of the Jews, was nigh Jn 6:4 1859
Now the Jews' *f* of tabernacles Jn 7:2 1859
Go ye up unto this *f* Jn 7:8 1859
I go not up yet unto this *f* Jn 7:8 1859
then went he also up unto the *f* Jn 7:10 1859
Then the Jews sought him at the *f* Jn 7:11 1859
Now about the midst of the *f* Jn 7:14 1859
last day, that great day of the *f* Jn 7:37 1859
Jerusalem the *f* of the dedication Jn 10:22 1456
that he will not come to the *f* Jn 11:56 1859
people that were come to the *f* Jn 12:12 1859
that came up to worship at the *f* Jn 12:20 1859
Now before the *f* of the passover, Jn 13:1 1859
we have need of against the *f* Jn 13:29 1859
this *f* that cometh in Jerusalem Acts 18:21 1859
Therefore let us keep the *f* 1Cor 5:8 1858
that believe not bid you to a *f* 1Cor 10:27
deceivings while they *f* with you 2Pet 2:13 4910
of charity, when they *f* with you Jude 12 4910

FEASTED
f in their houses, every one his Job 1:4 4960

FEASTING
they, and made it a day of *f* Est 9:17 4960
rested, and made it a day of *f* Est 9:18 4960
month Adar a day of gladness and *f* Est 9:19 4960
they should make them days of *f* Est 9:22 4960
days of their *f* were gone about Job 1:5 4960
than to go to the house of *f* Eccl 7:2 4960
not also go into the house of *f* Jer 16:8 4960

FEASTS
Concerning the *f* of the LORD Lev 23:2 4150
convocations, even these are my *f* Lev 23:2 4150
These are the *f* of the LORD Lev 23:4 4150
These are the *f* of the LORD Lev 23:37 4150
of Israel the *f* of the LORD Lev 23:44 4150
offering, or in your solemn *f* Num 15:3 4150
do unto the LORD in your set *f* Num 29:39 4150
in the new moons, and on the set *f* 1Chr 23:31 4150
on the solemn *f* of the LORD our 2Chr 2:4 4150
the new moons, and on the solemn *f* 2Chr 8:13 4150
the new moons, and for the set *f* 2Chr 31:3 4150
of all the set *f* of the LORD that Ezr 3:5 4150
of the new moons, for the set *f* Neh 10:33 4150
With hypocritical mockers in *f* Ps 35:16 4580
your appointed *f* my soul hateth Is 1:14
and pipe, and wine, are in their *f* Is 5:12 4960
In their heat I will make their *f* Jer 51:39 4960
because none come to the solemn *f* Lam 1:4 4150
the LORD hath caused the solemn *f* Lam 2:6 4150
of Jerusalem in her solemn *f* Eze 36:38 4150
and drink offerings, in the *f* Eze 45:17 2282
before the LORD in the solemn *f* Eze 46:9 4150
And in the *f* and in the solemnities Eze 46:11 2282
her sabbaths, and all her solemn *f* Hos 2:11 4150
I will turn your *f* into mourning Amos 8:10 2282
O Judah, keep thy solemn *f* Nah 1:15 2282
joy and gladness, and cheerful *f* Zec 8:19 4150
even the dung of your solemn *f* Mal 2:3 2282
And love the uppermost rooms at *f* Mt 23:6 1173
and the uppermost rooms at *f* Mk 12:39 1173
and the chief rooms at *f* Lk 20:46 1173
are spots in your *f* of charity Jude 12

FEATHERED
f fowls like as the sand of the Ps 78:27 3671
Speak unto every *f* fowl, and to Eze 39:17 3671

FEATHERS
pluck away his crop with his *f* Lev 1:16 5133
or wings and *f* unto the ostrich Job 39:13 2624
silver, and her *f* with yellow gold Ps 68:13 84
He shall cover thee with his *f* Ps 91:4 84
wings, longwinged, full of *f* Eze 17:3 5133
eagle with great wings and many *f* Eze 17:7 5133
hairs were grown like eagles' *f* Dan 4:33

FED
Jacob *f* the rest of Laban's Gen 30:36 7462
as he *f* the asses of Zibeon his Gen 36:24 7462
and they *f* in a meadow Gen 41:2 7462
and they *f* in a meadow Gen 41:18 7462
he *f* them with bread for all Gen 47:17 5095
the God which *f* me all my life Gen 48:15 7462
I have *f* you in the wilderness Ex 16:32 398
f thee with manna, which thou Deut 8:3 398
Who *f* thee in the wilderness with Deut 8:16 398
f them, but went not in unto them 2Sa 20:3 3557
f them with bread and water 1Kin 18:4 3557
f them with bread and water 1Kin 18:13 3557
over the herds that *f* in Sharon 1Chr 27:29 7462
land, and verily thou shalt be *f* Ps 37:3 7462
So he *f* them according to the Ps 78:72 7462
He should have *f* them also with Ps 81:16 398
of rams, and the fat of *f* beasts Is 1:11 4806
when I had *f* them to the full, Jer 5:7
They were as *f* horses in the Jer 5:8 2109
oil, and honey, wherewith I *f* thee Eze 16:19 398
the wool, ye kill them that are *f* Eze 34:3 1277
f themselves, and *f* not my flock Eze 34:8 7462
thereof, and all flesh was *f* of it Dan 4:12 2110
they *f* him with grass like oxen, Dan 5:21 2939
and I *f* the flock Zec 11:7 7462
saw we thee an hungred, and *f* thee Mt 25:37 5142
they that *f* the swine fled, and Mk 5:14 1006
When they that *f* them saw what Lk 8:34 1006
desiring to be *f* with the crumbs Lk 16:21 5526
I have *f* you with milk, and not 1Cor 3:2 4222

FEEBLE
But when the cattle were *f* Gen 30:42 5848
even all that were *f* behind thee Deut 25:18 2826
hath many children is waxed *f* 1Sa 2:5 535
dead in Hebron, his hands were *f* 2Sa 4:1 7503
carried all the *f* of them upon 2Chr 28:15 3782
and said, What do these *f* Jews Neh 4:2 537
hast strengthened the *f* knees Job 4:4 3766
I am *f* and sore broken Ps 38:8 6313
there was not one *f* person among Ps 105:37 3782
The conies are but a *f* folk Prov 30:26 3808
remnant shall be very small and *f* Is 16:14 3808
hands, and confirm the *f* knees Is 35:3 3782
our hands wax *f* Jer 6:24 7503
Damascus is waxed *f*, and turneth Jer 49:24 7503
of them, and his hands waxed *f* Jer 50:43 7503
All hands shall be *f*, and all Eze 7:17 7503
melt, and all hands shall be *f* Eze 21:7 7503
he that is *f* among them at that Zec 12:8 3782
the body, which seem to be more *f* 1Cor 12:22 772
which hang down, and the *f* knees Heb 12:12 3886

FEEBLEMINDED
that are unruly, comfort the *f* 1Th 5:14 3642

FEEBLENESS
to their children for *f* of hands Jer 47:3 7510

FEEBLER
so the *f* were Laban's, and the Gen 30:42 5848

FEED
F me, I pray thee, with that same Gen 25:30 3938
ye the sheep, and go and *f* them Gen 29:7 7462
this thing for me, I will again *f* Gen 30:31 7462
his brethren went to *f* their Gen 37:12 7462
Do not thy brethren *f* the flock Gen 37:13 7462
where they *f* their flocks Gen 37:16 7462
their trade hath been to *f* cattle Gen 46:32
shall *f* in another man's field Ex 22:5 1197
nor herds *f* before that mount Ex 34:3 7462
Saul to *f* his father's sheep at 1Sa 17:15 7462
Thou shalt *f* my people Israel, and 2Sa 5:2 7462
I commanded to *f* my people Israel 2Sa 7:7 7462
me, and I will *f* thee with me in 2Sa 19:33 3557
the ravens to *f* thee there 1Kin 17:4 3557
f him with bread of affliction and 1Kin 22:27 398
Thou shalt *f* my people Israel, and 1Chr 11:2 7462
whom I commanded to *f* my people 1Chr 17:6 7462
f him with bread of affliction and 2Chr 18:26 398
take away flocks, and *f* thereof Job 24:2 7462
the worm shall *f* sweetly on him Job 24:20
f them also, and lift them up for Ps 28:9 7462
death shall *f* on them Ps 49:14 7462
brought him to *f* Jacob his people Ps 78:71 7462
The lips of the righteous *f* many Prov 10:21 7462
f me with food convenient for me Prov 30:8 2963
f thy kids beside the shepherds' Song 1:8 7462
twins, which *f* among the lilies Song 4:5 7462
to *f* in the gardens, and to gather Song 6:2 7462
the lambs *f* after their manner Is 5:17 7462
And the cow and the bear shall *f* Is 11:7 7462
the firstborn of the poor shall *f* Is 14:30 7462
there shall the calf *f*, and there Is 27:10 7462
thy cattle *f* in large pastures Is 30:23 7462
He shall *f* his flock like a Is 40:11 7462
They shall *f* in the ways, and Is 49:9 7462
I will *f* them that oppress thee Is 49:26 398
f thee with the heritage of Jacob Is 58:14 398
f your flocks, and the sons of the Is 61:5 7462
wolf and the lamb shall *f* together Is 65:25 7462
which shall *f* you with knowledge Jer 3:15 7462
they shall *f* every one in his Jer 6:3 7462
Behold, I will *f* them, even this Jer 9:15 398
the pastors that *f* my people Jer 23:2 7462
over them which shall *f* them Jer 23:4 7462
I will *f* them with wormwood, and Jer 23:15 398
he shall *f* on Carmel and Bashan, Jer 50:19 7462
They that did *f* delicately are Lam 4:5 398
of Israel that do *f* themselves Eze 34:2 7462
not the shepherds *f* the flocks Eze 34:2 7462
but ye *f* not the flock Eze 34:3 7462
shepherds *f* themselves any more Eze 34:10 7462
f them upon the mountains of Eze 34:13 7462
I will *f* them in a good pasture, Eze 34:14 7462
in a fat pasture shall they *f* Eze 34:14 7462
I will *f* my flock, and I will Eze 34:15 7462
I will *f* them with judgment Eze 34:16 7462
over them, and he shall *f* them Eze 34:23 7462
he shall *f* them, and he shall be Eze 34:23 7462
they that *f* of the portion of his Dan 11:26 398
now the LORD will *f* them as a Hos 4:16 7462
and the winepress shall not *f* them Hos 9:2 7462
let them not *f*, nor drink water Jonah 3:7 7462
f in the strength of the LORD, in Mic 5:4 7462
F thy people with thy rod, the Mic 7:14 7462
let them *f* in Bashan and Gilead, Mic 7:14 7462
they shall *f* thereupon Zeph 2:7 7462
for they shall *f* and lie down, and Zeph 3:13 7462
F the flock of the slaughter Zec 11:4 7462
I will *f* the flock of slaughter, Zec 11:7 7462
Then said I, I will not *f* you Zec 11:9 7462
nor *f* that that standeth still Zec 11:16 3557
him into his fields to *f* swine Lk 15:15 1006
He saith unto him, *F* my lambs Jn 21:15 1006
He saith unto him, *F* my sheep Jn 21:16 4165
Jesus saith unto him, *F* my sheep Jn 21:17 1006
to *f* the church of God, which he Acts 20:28 4165
if thine enemy hunger, *f* him Rom 12:20 5595
bestow all my goods to *f* the poor 1Cor 13:3 5595
F the flock of God which is among 1Pet 5:2 4165
midst of the throne shall *f* them Rev 7:17 4165
that they should *f* her there a Rev 12:6 5142

FEEDEST
Thou *f* them with the bread of Ps 80:5 398
whom my soul loveth, where thou *f* Song 1:7 7462

FEEDETH
mouth of fools *f* on foolishness Prov 15:14 7462
he *f* among the lilies Song 2:16 7462
he *f* among the lilies Song 6:3 7462
He *f* on ashes Is 44:20 7462
Ephraim *f* on wind, and followeth Hos 12:1 7462
yet your heavenly Father *f* them Mt 6:26 5142
and God *f* them Lk 12:24 5142
or who *f* a flock, and eateth not 1Cor 9:7 4165

FEEDING
was *f* the flock with his brethren Gen 37:2 7462
and the asses *f* beside them Job 1:14 7462
them to cease from *f* the flock Eze 34:10 7462
the *f* place of the young lions, Nah 2:11 4829
from them an herd of many swine *f* Mt 8:30 1006
mountains a great herd of swine *f* Mk 5:11 1006
of many swine *f* on the mountain Lk 8:32 1006
a servant plowing or *f* cattle Lk 17:7 4165
f themselves without fear Jude 12 4165

FEEL
My father peradventure will *f* me .... Gen 27:12 4959
I pray thee, that I may *f* thee .... Gen 27:21 4184
Suffer me that I may *f* the .... Judg 16:26 4184
Surely he shall not *f* quietness .... Job 20:20 3045
Before your pots can *f* the thorns .... Ps 58:9 995
commandment shall *f* no evil thing .... Eccl 8:5 3045
if haply they might *f* after him .... Acts 17:27 *5584*

FEELING
Who being past *f* have given .... Eph 4:19 *524*
with the *f* of our infirmities .... Heb 4:15 *4834*

FEET
you, be fetched, and wash your *f* .... Gen 18:4 7272
tarry all night, and wash your *f* .... Gen 19:2 7272
camels, and water to wash his *f* .... Gen 24:32 7272
the men's *f* that were with him .... Gen 24:32 7272
water, and they washed their *f* .... Gen 43:24 7272
nor a lawgiver from between his *f* .... Gen 49:10 7272
he gathered up his *f* into the bed .... Gen 49:33 7272
put off thy shoes from off thy *f* .... Ex 3:5 7272
of her son, and cast it at his *f* .... Ex 4:25 7272
girded, your shoes on your *f* .... Ex 12:11 7272
there was under his *f* as it were .... Ex 24:10 7272
that are on the four *f* thereof .... Ex 25:26 7272
their hands and their *f* thereat .... Ex 30:19 7272
shall wash their hands and their *f* .... Ex 30:21 7272
that were in the four *f* thereof .... Ex 37:13 7272
their hands and their *f* thereat .... Ex 40:31 7272
the great toes of their right *f* .... Lev 8:24 7272
which have legs above their *f* .... Lev 11:21 7272
things, which have four *f* .... Lev 11:23 7272
or whatsoever hath more *f* among .... Lev 11:42 7272
thing else, go through on my *f* .... Num 20:19 7272
only I will pass through on my *f* .... Deut 2:28 7272
your *f* shall tread shall be yours .... Deut 11:24 7272
cometh out from between her *f* .... Deut 28:57 7272
and they sat down at thy *f* .... Deut 33:3 7272
as soon as the soles of the *f* of .... Josh 3:13 7272
the *f* of the priests that bare .... Josh 3:15 7272
where the priests' *f* stood firm .... Josh 4:3 7272
in the place where the *f* of the .... Josh 4:9 7272
the soles of the priests' *f* were .... Josh 4:18 7272
old shoes and clouted upon their *f* .... Josh 9:5 7272
put your *f* upon the necks of .... Josh 10:24 7272
put their *f* upon the necks of .... Josh 10:24 7272
thy *f* have trodden shall be thine .... Josh 14:9 7272
his *f* in his summer chamber .... Judg 3:24 7272
up with ten thousand men at his *f* .... Judg 4:10 7272
chariot, and fled away on his *f* .... Judg 4:15 7272
f to the tent of Jael the wife of .... Judg 4:17 7272
At her *f* he bowed, he fell, he .... Judg 5:27 7272
at her *f* he bowed, he fell .... Judg 5:27 7272
and they washed their *f*, and did .... Judg 19:21 7272
shalt go in, and uncover his *f* .... Ruth 3:4 4772
came softly, and uncovered his *f* .... Ruth 3:7 4772
and, behold, a woman lay at his *f* .... Ruth 3:8 4772
she lay at his *f* until the .... Ruth 3:14 4772
He will keep the *f* of his saints 1Sa 2:9 7272
up upon his hands and upon his *f* 1Sa 14:13 7272
and Saul went in to cover his *f* 1Sa 24:3 7272
And fell at his *f*, and said, Upon 1Sa 25:24 7272
be a servant to wash the *f* of the 1Sa 25:41 7272
nor thy *f* put into fetters 2Sa 3:34 7272
had a son that was lame of his *f* 2Sa 4:4 7272
and cut off their hands and their *f* 2Sa 4:12 7272
yet a son, which is lame on his *f* 2Sa 9:3 7272
and was lame on both his *f* 2Sa 9:13 7272
down to thy house, and wash thy *f* 2Sa 11:8 7272
and had neither dressed his *f* 2Sa 19:24 7272
and darkness was under his *f* 2Sa 22:10 7272
He maketh my *f* like hinds' *f* 2Sa 22:34 7272
so that my *f* did not slip 2Sa 22:37 7166
yea, they are fallen under my *f* 2Sa 22:39 7272
in his shoes that were on his *f* 1Kin 2:5 7272
put them under the soles of his *f* 1Kin 5:3 7272
Ahijah heard the sound of her *f* 1Kin 14:6 7272
when thy *f* enter into the city, ... 1Kin 14:12 7272
old age he was diseased in his *f* 1Kin 15:23 7272
the hill, she caught him by the *f* 2Kin 4:27 7272
she went in, and fell at his *f* 2Kin 4:37 7272
of his master's *f* behind him 2Kin 6:32 7272
of her than the skull, and the *f* 2Kin 9:35 7272
he revived, and stood up on his *f* 2Kin 13:21 7272
with the sole of my *f* have I 2Kin 19:24 6471
Neither will I make the *f* of 2Kin 21:8 7272
the king stood up upon his *f* 1Chr 28:2 7272
and they stood on their *f*, and 2Chr 3:13 7272
his reign was diseased in his *f* 2Chr 16:12 7272
not old, and their *f* swelled not .... Neh 9:21 7272
the king, and fell down at his *f* .... Est 8:3 7272
f is as a lamp despised in the .... Job 12:5 7272
Thou puttest my *f* also in the .... Job 13:27 7272
a print upon the heels of my *f* .... Job 13:27 7272
is cast into a net by his own *f* .... Job 18:8 7272
side, and shall drive him to his *f* .... Job 18:11 7272
the blind, and *f* was I to the lame .... Job 29:15 7272
they push away my *f*, and they .... Job 30:12 7272
He putteth my *f* in the stocks .... Job 33:11 7272
hast put all things under his *f* .... Ps 8:6 7272
and darkness was under his *f* .... Ps 18:9 7272
He maketh my *f* like hinds' *f*, ... Ps 18:33 7272
under me, that my *f* did not slip .... Ps 18:36 7166
they are fallen under my *f* .... Ps 18:38 7272
they pierced my hands and my *f* .... Ps 22:16 7272
shall pluck my *f* out of the net .... Ps 25:15 7272
hast set my *f* in a large room .... Ps 31:8 7272
clay, and set my *f* upon a rock, and .... Ps 40:2 7272
us, and the nations under our *f* .... Ps 47:3 7272
thou deliver my *f* from falling .... Ps 56:13 7272
he shall wash his *f* in the blood .... Ps 58:10 6471
suffereth not our *f* to be moved .... Ps 66:9 7272
as for me, my *f* were almost gone .... Ps 73:2 7272
Lift up thy *f* unto the perpetual .... Ps 74:3 6471
dragon shalt thou trample under *f* .... Ps 91:13
Whose *f* they hurt with fetters .... Ps 105:18 7272
f have they, but they walk not .... Ps 115:7 7272
from tears, and my *f* from falling .... Ps 116:8 7272
turned my *f* unto thy testimonies .... Ps 119:59 7272
my *f* from every evil way, that I .... Ps 119:101 7272
Thy word is a lamp unto my *f* .... Ps 119:105 7272
Our *f* shall stand within thy .... Ps 122:2 7272
For their *f* run to evil, and make .... Prov 1:16 7272
Ponder the path of thy *f*, and let .... Prov 4:26 7272
Her *f* go down to death .... Prov 5:5 7272
his eyes, he speaketh with his *f* .... Prov 6:13 7272
f that be swift in running to .... Prov 6:18 7272
hot coals, and his *f* not be burned .... Prov 6:28 7272
her *f* abide not in her house .... Prov 7:11 7272
that hasteth with his *f* sinneth .... Prov 19:2 7272
hand of a fool cutteth off the *f* .... Prov 26:6 7272
spreadeth a net for his *f* .... Prov 29:5 6471
I have washed my *f* .... Song 5:3 7272
beautiful are thy *f* with shoes .... Song 7:1 6471
and making a tinkling with their *f* .... Is 3:16 7272
tinkling ornaments about their *f* .... Is 3:18
and with twain he covered his *f* .... Is 6:2 7272
the head, and the hair of the *f* .... Is 7:20 7272
as a carcase trodden under *f* .... Is 14:19
her own *f* shall carry her afar .... Is 23:7 7272
even the *f* of the poor, and the .... Is 26:6 7272
Ephraim, shall be trodden under *f* .... Is 28:3 7272
forth thither the *f* of the ox .... Is 32:20 7272
with the sole of my *f* have I .... Is 37:25 6471
that he had not gone with his *f* .... Is 41:3 7272
and lick up the dust of thy *f* .... Is 49:23 7272
the *f* of him that bringeth good .... Is 52:7 7272
Their *f* run to evil, and they make .... Is 59:7 7272
make the place of my *f* glorious .... Is 60:13 7272
down at the soles of thy *f* .... Is 60:14 7272
before your *f* stumble upon the .... Jer 13:16 7272
they have not refrained their *f* .... Jer 14:10 7272
take me, and hid snares for my *f* .... Jer 18:22 7272
thy *f* are sunk in the mire, and .... Jer 38:22 7272
he hath spread a net for my *f* .... Lam 1:13 7272
To crush under his *f* all the .... Lam 3:34 7272
And their *f* were straight *f* .... Eze 1:7 7272
the sole of their *f* was like the .... Eze 1:7 7272
me, Son of man, stand upon thy *f* .... Eze 2:1 7272
unto me, and set me upon my *f* .... Eze 2:2 7272
into me, and set me upon my *f* .... Eze 3:24 7272
hast opened thy *f* to every one .... Eze 16:25 7272
and put on thy shoes upon thy *f* .... Eze 24:17 7272
heads, and your shoes upon your *f* .... Eze 24:23 7272
hands, and stamped with the *f* .... Eze 25:6 7272
troubledst the waters with thy *f* .... Eze 32:2 7272
f the residue of your pastures .... Eze 34:18 7272
must foul the residue with your *f* .... Eze 34:18 7272
which ye have trodden with your *f* .... Eze 34:19 7272
which ye have fouled with your *f* .... Eze 34:19 7272
lived, and stood up upon their *f* .... Eze 37:10 7272
and the place of the soles of my *f* .... Eze 43:7 7272
his *f* part of iron and part of .... Dan 2:33 7271
upon his *f* that were of iron .... Dan 2:34 7271
And whereas thou sawest the *f* .... Dan 2:41 7271
toes of the *f* were part of iron .... Dan 2:42 7271
and made stand upon the *f* as a man ... Dan 7:4 7271
the residue with the *f* of it .... Dan 7:7 7271
and stamped the residue with his *f* .... Dan 7:19 7271
his *f* like in colour to polished .... Dan 10:6 4772
the clouds are the dust of his *f* .... Nah 1:3 7272
the *f* of him that bringeth good .... Nah 1:15 7272
burning coals went forth at his *f* .... Hab 3:5 7272
will make my *f* like hinds' *f* .... Hab 3:19 7272
his *f* shall stand in that day .... Zec 14:4 7272
while they stand upon their *f* .... Zec 14:12 7272
ashes under the soles of your *f* .... Mal 4:3 7272
they trample them under their *f* .... Mt 7:6 4228
shake off the dust of your *f* .... Mt 10:14 4228
and cast them down at Jesus' *f* .... Mt 15:30 4228
two *f* to be cast into everlasting .... Mt 18:8 4228
fellowservant fell down at his *f* .... Mt 18:29 4228
And they came and held him by the *f* .. Mt 28:9 4228
when he saw him, he fell at his *f* .... Mk 5:22 4228
f for a testimony against them .... Mk 6:11 4228
of him, and came and fell at his *f* .... Mk 7:25 4228
than having two *f* to be cast into .... Mk 9:45 4228
to guide our *f* into the way of .... Lk 1:79 4228
stood at his *f* behind him weeping .... Lk 7:38 4228
and began to wash his *f* with tears .... Lk 7:38 4228
of her head, and kissed his *f* .... Lk 7:38 4228
thou gavest me no water for my *f* .... Lk 7:44 4228
she hath washed my *f* with tears .... Lk 7:44 4228
in hath not ceased to kiss my *f* .... Lk 7:45 4228
hath anointed my *f* with ointment .... Lk 7:46 4228
sitting at the *f* of Jesus .... Lk 8:35 4228
and he fell down at Jesus' *f* .... Lk 8:41 4228
off the very dust from your *f* for .... Lk 9:5 4228
Mary, which also sat at Jesus' *f* .... Lk 10:39 4228
on his hand, and shoes on his *f* .... Lk 15:22 4228
And fell down on his face at his *f* .... Lk 17:16 4228
Behold my hands and my *f*, that it .... Lk 24:39 4228
he shewed them his hands and his *f* .... Lk 24:40 4228
wiped his *f* with her hair, whose .... Jn 11:2 4228
saw him, she fell down at his *f* .... Jn 11:32 4228
and anointed the *f* of Jesus .... Jn 12:3 4228
wiped his *f* with her hair .... Jn 12:3 4228
and began to wash the disciples' *f* .... Jn 13:5 4228
him, Lord, dost thou wash my *f* .... Jn 13:6 4228
him, Thou shalt never wash my *f* .... Jn 13:8 4228
unto him, Lord, not my *f* only .... Jn 13:9 4228
needeth not save to wash his *f* .... Jn 13:10 4228
So after he had washed their *f* .... Jn 13:12 4228
and Master, have washed your *f* .... Jn 13:14 4228
ought to wash one another's *f* .... Jn 13:14 4228
the head, and the other at the *f* .... Jn 20:12 4228
and immediately his *f* and ancle .... Acts 3:7 *939*
laid them down at the apostles' *f* .... Acts 4:35 *4228*
and laid it at the apostles' *f* .... Acts 4:37 *4228*
and laid it at the apostles' *f* .... Acts 5:2 *4228*
the *f* of them which have buried .... Acts 5:9 *4228*
she down straightway at his *f* .... Acts 5:10 *4228*
him, Put off thy shoes from thy *f* .... Acts 7:33 *4228*
their clothes at a young man's *f* .... Acts 7:58 *4228*
met him, and fell down at his *f* .... Acts 10:25 *4228*
whose shoes of his *f* I am not .... Acts 13:25 *4228*
the dust of their *f* against them .... Acts 13:51 *4228*
man at Lystra, impotent in his *f* .... Acts 14:8 *4228*
voice, Stand upright on thy *f* .... Acts 14:10 *4228*
made their *f* fast in the stocks .... Acts 16:24 *4228*
and bound his own hands and *f* .... Acts 21:11 *4228*
in this city at the *f* of Gamaliel .... Acts 22:3 *4228*
But rise, and stand upon thy *f* .... Acts 26:16 *4228*
Their *f* are swift to shed blood .... Rom 3:15 *4228*
How beautiful are the *f* of them .... Rom 10:15 *4228*
bruise Satan under your *f* shortly .... Rom 16:20 *4228*
nor again the head to the *f* 1Cor 12:21 *4228*
hath put all enemies under his *f* 1Cor 15:25 *4228*
hath put all things under his *f* 1Cor 15:27 *4228*
hath put all things under his *f* .... Eph 1:22 *4228*
your *f* shod with the preparation .... Eph 6:15 *4228*
if she have washed the saints' *f* 1Ti 5:10 *4228*
things in subjection under his *f* .... Heb 2:8 *4228*
And make straight paths for your *f* .... Heb 12:13 *4228*
his *f* like unto fine brass, as if .... Rev 1:15 *4228*
saw him, I fell at his *f* as dead .... Rev 1:17 *4228*
his *f* are like fine brass .... Rev 2:18 *4228*
to come and worship before thy *f* .... Rev 3:9 *4228*
sun, and his *f* as pillars of fire .... Rev 10:1 *4228*
them, and they stood upon their *f* .... Rev 11:11 *4228*
the sun, and the moon under her *f* .... Rev 12:1 *4228*
his *f* were as the *f* of a bear .... Rev 13:2 *4228*
I fell at his *f* to worship him .... Rev 19:10 *4228*
f of the angel which shewed me .... Rev 22:8 *4228*

FEIGN
f thyself to be a mourner, and put 2Sa 14:2
that she shall *f* herself to be 1Kin 14:5 5234
which should *f* themselves just .... Lk 20:20 *5271*

FEIGNED
f himself mad in their hands, and 1Sa 21:13
that goeth not out of *f* lips .... Ps 17:1 4820
covetousness shall they with *f* 2Pet 2:3 *4112*

FEIGNEDLY
me with her whole heart, but *f* .... Jer 3:10 8267

FEIGNEST
why *f* thou thyself to be another 1Kin 14:6 5234
but thou *f* them out of thine own .... Neh 6:8 908

FELIX (*fe'-lix*) See FELIX'. *A Roman procurator of Judea.*
him safe unto *F* the governor .... Acts 23:24 *5344*
governor *F* sendeth greeting .... Acts 23:26 *5344*
and in all places, most noble *F* .... Acts 24:3 *5344*
when *F* heard these things, having .... Acts 24:22 *5344*
when *F* came with his wife .... Acts 24:24 *5344*
F trembled, and answered, Go thy .... Acts 24:25 *5344*
and *F*, willing to shew the Jews a .... Acts 24:27 *5344*
a certain man left in bonds by *F* .... Acts 25:14 *5344*

FELIX' (*fe'-lix*)
Porcius Festus came into *F* room .... Acts 24:27 *5344*

FELL
very wroth, and his countenance *f* .... Gen 4:5 5307
and Gomorrah fled, and *f* there .... Gen 14:10 5307
down, a deep sleep *f* upon Abram .... Gen 15:12 5307
of great darkness *f* upon him .... Gen 15:12 5307
And Abram *f* on his face .... Gen 17:3 5307
Then Abraham *f* upon his face, and .... Gen 17:17 5307
f on his neck, and kissed him .... Gen 33:4 5307
they *f* before him on the ground .... Gen 44:14 5307
he *f* upon his brother Benjamin's .... Gen 45:14 5307
he *f* on his neck, and wept on his .... Gen 46:29 5307
Joseph *f* upon his father's face, ... Gen 50:1 5307
went and *f* down before his face .... Gen 50:18 5307
there *f* of the people that day .... Ex 32:28 5307
they shouted, and *f* on their faces .... Lev 9:24 5307
goat upon which the LORD's lot *f* .... Lev 16:9 5927
on which the lot *f* to be the .... Lev 16:10 5927
that was among them *f* a lusting .... Num 11:4
when the dew *f* upon the camp in .... Num 11:9 3381
in the night, the manna *f* upon it .... Num 11:9 3381
Aaron *f* on their faces before all .... Num 14:5 5307
heard it, he *f* upon his face .... Num 16:4 5307
they *f* upon their faces, and said, ... Num 16:22 5307
And they *f* upon their faces .... Num 16:45 5307
and they *f* upon their faces .... Num 20:6 5307
the LORD, she *f* down under Balaam .... Num 22:27 7257
his head, and *f* flat on his face .... Num 22:31 7812
I *f* down before the LORD, as at .... Deut 9:18 5307
Thus I *f* down before the LORD .... Deut 9:25 5307
nights, as I *f* down at the first .... Deut 9:25 5307
Joshua *f* on his face to the earth .... Josh 5:14 5307
shout, that the wall *f* down flat .... Josh 6:20 5307
f to the earth upon his face .... Josh 7:6 5307
it was, that all that *f* that day .... Josh 8:25 5307
and they *f* upon them .... Josh 11:7 5307
Joseph *f* from Jordan by Jericho .... Josh 16:1 3318
there *f* ten portions to Manasseh, ... Josh 17:5 5307
wrath *f* on all the congregation .... Josh 22:20 1961
all the host of Sisera *f* upon the .... Judg 4:16 5307
At her feet he bowed, he *f* .... Judg 5:27 5307
at her feet he bowed, he *f* .... Judg 5:27 5307
he bowed, there he *f* down dead, ... Judg 5:27 5307
a tent, and smote it that it *f* .... Judg 7:13 5307
for there *f* an hundred and twenty .... Judg 8:10 5307
there *f* at that time of the .... Judg 12:6 5307
f on their faces to the ground .... Judg 13:20 5307
the house *f* upon the lords, and .... Judg 16:30 5307
f down at the door of the man's .... Judg 19:26 5307
there *f* of Benjamin eighteen .... Judg 20:44 5307

So that all which *f* that day of Judg 20:46 5307
Then she *f* on her face, and bowed Ruth 2:10 5307
for there *f* of Israel thirty 1Sa 4:10 5307
that he *f* from off the seat 1Sa 4:18 5307
fear of the LORD *f* on the people 1Sa 11:7 5307
and they *f* before Jonathan 1Sa 14:13 5307
he *f* upon his face to the earth 1Sa 17:49 5307
f down by the way to Shaaraim 1Sa 17:52 5307
f on his face to the ground, and 1Sa 20:41 5307
he *f* upon the priests, and slew on 1Sa 22:18 6298
f before David on her face, and 1Sa 25:23 5307
f at his feet, and said, Upon me, 1Sa 25:24 5307
Then Saul *f* straightway all along 1Sa 28:20 5307
since he *f* unto me unto this day 1Sa 29:3 5307
because three days agone I *f* sick 1Sa 30:13
f down slain in mount Gilboa 1Sa 31:1 5307
Saul took a sword, and *f* upon it 1Sa 31:4 5307
he *f* likewise upon his sword, and 1Sa 31:5 5307
that he *f* to the earth, and did 2Sa 1:2 5307
so they *f* down together 2Sa 2:16 5307
he *f* down there, and died in the 2Sa 2:23 5307
to the place where Asahel *f* down 2Sa 2:23 5307
she made haste to flee, that he *f* 2Sa 4:4 5307
David, he *f* on his face, and did 2Sa 9:6 5307
there *f* some of the people of the 2Sa 11:17 5307
that he *f* sick for his sister 2Sa 13:2
she *f* on her face to the ground, 2Sa 14:4 5307
Joab *f* to the ground on his face, 2Sa 14:22 5307
he *f* down to the earth upon his 2Sa 18:28 7812
of Gera *f* down before the king 2Sa 19:18 5307
and as he went forth it *f* out 2Sa 20:8 5307
they *f* all seven together, and 2Sa 21:9 5307
f by the hand of David, and by the 2Sa 21:22 5307
he *f* upon him that he died 1Kin 2:25 6293
who *f* upon two men more righteous 1Kin 2:32 6293
up, and *f* upon him, and slew him 1Kin 2:34 6293
out, and *f* upon him, that he died 1Kin 2:46 6293
Abijah the son of Jeroboam *f* sick 1Kin 14:1
the mistress of the house, *f* sick 1Kin 17:17
f on his face, and said, Art thou 1Kin 18:7 5307
Then the fire of the LORD *f* 1Kin 18:38 5307
saw it, they *f* on their faces 1Kin 18:39 5307
and there a wall *f* upon twenty 1Kin 20:30 5307
Ahaziah *f* down through a lattice 2Kin 1:2 5307
f on his knees before Elijah, and 2Kin 1:13 3766
mantle of Elijah that *f* from him 2Kin 2:13 5307
mantle of Elijah that *f* from him 2Kin 2:14 5307
shall *f* every good tree, and stop 2Kin 3:19 5307
it *f* on a day, that Elisha passed 2Kin 4:8 1961
it *f* on a day, that he came 2Kin 4:11 1961
it *f* on a day, that he went out 2Kin 4:18 1961
f at his feet, and bowed herself 2Kin 4:37 5307
the ax head *f* into the water 2Kin 6:5 5307
the man of God said, Where *f* it 2Kin 6:6 5307
And so it *f* out unto him 2Kin 7:20 1961
the fugitives that *f* away to the 2Kin 25:11 5307
Hagarites, who *f* by their hand 1Chr 5:10 5307
For there *f* down many slain, 1Chr 5:22 5307
f down slain in mount Gilboa 1Chr 10:1 5307
Saul took a sword, and *f* upon it 1Chr 10:4 5307
he *f* likewise on the sword, and 1Chr 10:5 5307
there *f* some of Manasseh to David 1Chr 12:19 5307
there *f* to him of Manasseh, Adnah 1Chr 12:20 5307
they *f* by the hand of David, and 1Chr 20:8 5307
there *f* of Israel seventy 1Chr 21:14 5307
in sackcloth, *f* upon their faces 1Chr 21:16 5307
the lot eastward *f* to Shelemiah 1Chr 26:14 5307
because there *f* wrath for it 1Chr 27:24 1961
so there *f* down slain of Israel 2Chr 13:17 5307
for they *f* to him out of Israel 2Chr 15:9 5307
the fear of the LORD *f* upon all 2Chr 17:10 1961
of Jerusalem *f* before the LORD 2Chr 20:18 5307
his bowels *f* out by reason of his 2Chr 21:19 3318
f upon the cities of Judah, from 2Chr 25:13 6584
I *f* upon my knees, and spread out Ezr 9:5 3766
f down at his feet, and besought Est 8:3 5307
the fear of the Jews *f* upon them Est 8:17 5307
fear of them *f* upon all people Est 9:2 5307
the fear of Mordecai *f* upon them Est 9:3 5307
And the Sabeans *f* upon them Job 1:15 5307
f upon the camels, and have Job 1:17 6584
it *f* upon the young men, and they Job 1:19 5307
f down upon the ground, and Job 1:20 5307
up my flesh, they stumbled and *f* Ps 27:2 5307
Their priests *f* by the sword Ps 78:64 5307
for the fear of them *f* upon them Ps 105:38 5307
they *f* down, and there was none to Ps 107:12 3782
in the city, and those that *f* away Jer 39:9 5307
that *f* to him, with the rest of Jer 39:9 5307
to fall, yea, one *f* upon another Jer 46:16 5307
in the city, and those that *f* away Jer 52:15 5307
that *f* to the king of Babylon, and Jer 52:15 5307
when her people *f* into the hand Lam 1:7 5307
the children *f* under the wood Lam 5:13 3782
I *f* upon my face, and I heard a Eze 1:28 5307
and I *f* on my face Eze 3:23 5307
of the Lord GOD *f* there upon me Eze 8:1 5307
that I *f* upon my face, and cried, Eze 9:8 5307
the Spirit of the LORD *f* upon me Eze 11:5 5307
Then *f* I down upon my face, and Eze 11:13 5307
so *f* they all by the sword Eze 39:23 5307
and I *f* upon my face Eze 43:3 5307
and I *f* upon my face Eze 44:4 5307
Nebuchadnezzar *f* upon his face Dan 2:46 5308
f down and worshipped the golden Dan 3:7 5308
f down bound into the midst of Dan 3:23 5308
there *f* a voice from heaven, Dan 4:31 5308
came up, and before whom three *f* Dan 7:20 5308
I was afraid, and *f* upon my face Dan 8:17 5307
but a great quaking *f* upon them Dan 10:7 5307
lots, and the lot *f* upon Jonah Jonah 1:7 5307
f down, and worshipped him Mt 2:11 *4098*
and it *f* not: for it was founded Mt 7:25 *4098*
and it *f*: and great was the fall Mt 7:27 *4098*
some seeds *f* by the way side, and Mt 13:4 *4098*
Some *f* upon stony places, where Mt 13:5 *4098*
And some *f* among thorns Mt 13:7 *4098*
But other *f* into good ground, and Mt 13:8 *4098*
they *f* on their face, and were Mt 17:6 *4098*
The servant therefore *f* down Mt 18:26 *4098*
fellowservant *f* down at his feet Mt 18:29 *4098*
f on his face, and prayed, saying, Mt 26:39 *4098*
f down before him, and cried, Mk 3:11 *4363*
some *f* by the way side, and the Mk 4:4 *4098*
some *f* on stony ground, where it Mk 4:5 *4098*
some *f* among thorns, and the Mk 4:7 *4098*
other *f* on good ground, and did Mk 4:8 *4098*
he saw him, he *f* at his feet, Mk 5:22 *4098*
f down before him, and told him Mk 5:33 *4363*
of him, and came and *f* at his feet Mk 7:25 *4363*
he *f* on the ground, and wallowed Mk 9:20 *4098*
f on the ground, and prayed that, Mk 14:35 *4098*
was troubled, and fear *f* upon him Lk 1:12 *1968*
he *f* down at Jesus' knees, saying Lk 5:8 *4363*
who seeing Jesus *f* on his face Lk 5:12 *4098*
vehemently, and immediately it *f* Lk 6:49 *4098*
he sowed, some *f* by the way side Lk 8:5 *4098*
And some *f* upon a rock Lk 8:6 *4098*
And some *f* among thorns Lk 8:7 *4098*
other *f* on good ground, and sprang Lk 8:8 *4098*
that which *f* among thorns are Lk 8:14 *4098*
But as they sailed he *f* asleep Lk 8:23
f down before him, and with a loud Lk 8:28 *4363*
he *f* down at Jesus' feet, and Lk 8:41 *4098*
f among thieves, which stripped Lk 10:30 *4045*
unto him that *f* among the thieves Lk 10:36 *1706*
upon whom the tower in Siloam *f* Lk 13:4 *4098*
f on his neck, and kissed him Lk 15:20 *1968*
which *f* from the rich man's table Lk 16:21 *4098*
f down on his face at his feet, Lk 17:16 *4098*
she *f* down at his feet, saying Jn 11:32 *4098*
went backward, and *f* to the ground Jn 18:6 *4098*
which Judas by transgression *f* Acts 1:25
and the lot *f* upon Matthias Acts 1:26 *4098*
hearing these words *f* down Acts 5:5 *4098*
Then *f* she down straightway at Acts 5:10 *4098*
he had said this, he *f* asleep Acts 7:60
he *f* to the earth, and heard a Acts 9:4 *4098*
immediately there *f* from his eyes Acts 9:18 *634*
made ready, he *f* into a trance, Acts 10:10 *1968*
f down at his feet, and worshipped Acts 10:25 *4098*
the Holy Ghost *f* on all them Acts 10:44 *1968*
speak, the Holy Ghost *f* on them Acts 11:15 *1968*
his chains *f* off from his hands Acts 12:7 *1601*
immediately there *f* on him a mist Acts 13:11 *1968*
f on sleep, and was laid unto his Acts 13:36
f down before Paul and Silas, Acts 16:29 *4363*
fear *f* on them all, and the name Acts 19:17 *1968*
image which *f* down from Jupiter Acts 19:35 *1356*
f down from the third loft, and Acts 20:9 *4098*
f on him, and embracing him said, Acts 20:10 *1968*
f on Paul's neck, and kissed him, Acts 20:37 *1968*
I *f* unto the ground, and heard a Acts 22:7 *4098*
on them which *f*, severity Rom 11:22 *4098*
them that reproached thee *f* on me Rom 15:3 *1968*
f in one day three and twenty 1Cor 10:8 *4098*
sinned, whose carcases *f* in the Heb 3:17 *4098*
faith the walls of Jericho *f* down Heb 11:30 *4098*
for since the fathers *f* asleep 2Pet 3:4
saw him, I *f* at his feet as dead Rev 1:17 *4098*
twenty elders *f* down before the Rev 5:8 *4098*
the four and twenty elders *f* down Rev 5:14 *4098*
stars of heaven *f* unto the earth Rev 6:13 *4098*
f before the throne on their Rev 7:11 *4098*
there *f* a great star from heaven, Rev 8:10 *4098*
it *f* upon the third part of the Rev 8:10 *4098*
great fear *f* upon them which saw Rev 11:11 *4098*
and the tenth part of the city *f* Rev 11:13 *4098*
f upon their faces, and worshipped Rev 11:16 *4098*
there *f* a noisome and grievous Rev 16:2 *1096*
and the cities of the nations *f* Rev 16:19 *4098*
there *f* upon men a great hail out Rev 16:21 *2597*
elders and the four beasts *f* down Rev 19:4 *4098*
I *f* at his feet to worship him Rev 19:10 *4098*
I *f* down to worship before the Rev 22:8 *4098*

FELLED
of water, and *f* all the good trees 2Kin 3:25 5307

FELLER
no *f* is come up against us Is 14:8 3772

FELLEST
before wicked men, so *f* thou 2Sa 3:34 5307

FELLING
But as one was *f* a beam, the ax 2Kin 6:5 5307

FELLOES
and their naves, and their *f* 1Kin 7:33 2839

FELLOW
This one *f* came in to sojourn, and Gen 19:9 7453
Wherefore smitest thou thy *f* Ex 2:13 7453
man that told a dream unto his *f* Judg 7:13 7453
his *f* answered and said, This is Judg 7:14 7453
every man's sword against his *f* Judg 7:22 7453
man's sword was against his *f* 1Sa 14:20 7453
this *f* to play the mad man in my 1Sa 21:15
shall this *f* come into my house 1Sa 21:15
this *f* hath in the wilderness 1Sa 25:21
said unto him, Make this *f* return 1Sa 29:4 376
every one his *f* by the head 2Sa 2:16 7453
Put this *f* in the prison, and feed 1Kin 22:27
wherefore came this mad *f* to thee 2Kin 9:11
Put this *f* in the prison, and feed 2Chr 18:26
fall, the one will lift up his *f* Eccl 4:10 2270
and the satyr shall cry to his *f* Is 34:14 7453
And they said every one to his *f*, Jonah 1:7 7453
and against the man that is my *f* Zec 13:7 5997
This *f* doth not cast out devils, Mt 12:24
And said, This *f* said, I am able Mt 26:61
This *f* was also with Jesus of Mt 26:71
Of a truth this *f* also was with Lk 22:59
We found this *f* perverting the Lk 23:2
as for this *f*, we know not from Jn 9:29
This *f* persuadeth men to worship Acts 18:13
Away with such a *f* from the earth Acts 22:22
have found this man a pestilent *f* Acts 24:5
f soldier, but your messenger, and Phil 2:25
These only are my *f* workers unto Col 4:11

FELLOWCITIZENS
but *f* with the saints, and of the Eph 2:19 *4847*

FELLOWDISCIPLES
is called Didymus, unto his *f* Jn 11:16 *4827*

FELLOWHEIRS
That the Gentiles should be *f* Eph 3:6 *4789*

FELLOWHELPER
is my partner and *f* concerning you 2Cor 8:23 *4904*

FELLOWHELPERS
that we might be *f* to the truth 3Jn 8 *4904*

FELLOWLABOURER
our *f* in the gospel of Christ, to 1Th 3:2 *4904*
Philemon our dearly beloved, and *f* Philem 1 *4904*

FELLOWLABOURERS
Clement also, and with other my *f* Phil 4:3 *4904*
Aristarchus, Demas, Lucas, my *f* Philem 24 *4904*

FELLOWPRISONER
Aristarchus my *f* saluteth you Col 4:10 *4869*
Epaphras, my *f* in Christ Jesus Philem 23 *4869*

FELLOWPRISONERS
and Junia, my kinsmen, and my *f* Rom 16:7 *4869*

FELLOW'S
and thrust his sword in his *f* side 2Sa 2:16 7453

FELLOWS
and bewail my virginity, I and my *f* Judg 11:37 7464
lest angry *f* run upon thee, and Judg 18:25 582
as one of the vain *f* shamelessly 2Sa 6:20
the oil of gladness above thy *f* Ps 45:7 2270
all his *f* shall be ashamed Is 44:11 2270
and the tribes of Israel his *f* Eze 37:19 2270
Daniel and his *f* to be slain Dan 2:13 2269
his *f* should not perish with the Dan 2:18 2269
look was more stout than his *f* Dan 7:20 2273
thy *f* that sit before thee Zec 3:8 7453
markets, and calling unto their *f* Mt 11:16 *2083*
certain lewd *f* of the baser sort Acts 17:5 *435*
the oil of gladness above thy *f* Heb 1:9 *3353*

FELLOWSERVANT
his *f* fell down at his feet, and Mt 18:29 4889
also have had compassion on thy *f* Mt 18:33 4889
learned of Epaphras our dear *f* Col 1:7 4889
minister and *f* in the Lord Col 4:7 4889
I am thy *f*, and of thy brethren Rev 19:10 4889
for I am thy *f*, and of thy Rev 22:9 4889

FELLOWSERVANTS
went out, and found one of his *f* Mt 18:28 4889
So when his *f* saw what was done, Mt 18:31 4889
And shall begin to smite his *f* Mt 24:49 4889
little season, until their *f* also Rev 6:11 4889

FELLOWSHIP
delivered him to keep, or in *f* Lev 6:2 8667
of iniquity have *f* with thee Ps 94:20 2266
in the apostles' doctrine and *f* Acts 2:42 *2842*
the *f* of his Son Jesus Christ our 1Cor 1:9 *2842*
that ye should have *f* with devils 1Cor 10:20 *2844*
for what *f* hath righteousness 2Cor 6:14 *3352*
take upon us the *f* of the 2Cor 8:4 *2842*
and Barnabas the right hands of *f* Gal 2:9 *2842*
see what is the *f* of the mystery Eph 3:9 *2842*
have no *f* with the unfruitful Eph 5:11 *4790*
For your *f* in the gospel from the Phil 1:5 *2842*
if any *f* of the Spirit, if any Phil 2:1 *2842*
the *f* of his sufferings, being Phil 3:10 *2842*
that ye also may have *f* with us 1Jn 1:3 *2842*
truly our *f* is with the Father, 1Jn 1:3 *2842*
If we say that we have *f* with him 1Jn 1:6 *2842*
we have *f* one with another, and 1Jn 1:7 *2842*

FELLOWSOLDIER
Apphia, and Archippus our *f* Philem 2 *4961*

FELT
he *f* him, and said, The voice is Gen 27:22 4959
even darkness which may be *f* Ex 10:21 4959
have beaten me, and I *f* it not Prov 23:35 3045
she *f* in her body that she was Mk 5:29 *1097*
beast into the fire, and *f* no harm Acts 28:5 *3958*

FEMALE
male and *f* created he them Gen 1:27 5347
Male and *f* created he them Gen 5:2 5347
they shall be male and *f* Gen 6:19 5347
thee by sevens, the male and his *f* Gen 7:2 802
clean by two, the male and his *f* Gen 7:2 802
air by sevens, the male and the *f* Gen 7:3 5347
into the ark, the male and the *f* Gen 7:9 5347
f of all flesh, as God had Gen 7:16 5347
whether it be a male or *f* Lev 3:1 5347
male or *f*, he shall offer it Lev 3:6 5347
a *f* without blemish, for his sin Lev 4:28 5347
bring it a *f* without blemish Lev 4:32 5347
a *f* from the flock, a lamb or a Lev 5:6 5347
her that hath born a male or a *f* Lev 12:7 5347
And if it be a *f*, then thy Lev 27:4 5347
shekels, and for the *f* ten shekels Lev 27:5 5347
for the *f* thy estimation shall be Lev 27:6 5347
shekels, and for the *f* ten shekels Lev 27:7 5347
f shall ye put out, without the Num 5:3 5347

figure, the likeness of male or *f* ... Deut 4:16 5347
not be male or *f* barren among you ... Deut 7:14 5347
the beginning made them male and *f* ... Mt 19:4 *2338*
creation God made them male and *f* ... Mk 10:6 *2338*
free, there is neither male nor *f* ... Gal 3:28 *2338*

FENCE
shall ye be, and as a tottering *f* ... Ps 62:3 1447

FENCED
in the *f* cities because of the ... Num 32:17 4013
and Beth-haran, *f* cities ... Num 32:36 4013
cities were *f* with high walls ... Deut 3:5 1219
cities great and *f* up to heaven ... Deut 9:1 1219
f walls come down, wherein thou ... Deut 28:52 1219
of them entered into *f* cities ... Josh 10:20 4013
that the cities were great and *f* ... Josh 14:12 1219
the *f* cities are Ziddim, Zer, and ... Josh 19:35 4013
the five lords, both of *f* cities ... 1Sa 6:18 4013
him, lest he get him *f* cities ... 2Sa 20:6 1211
touch them must be *f* with iron ... 2Sa 23:7 4390
And ye shall smite every *f* city ... 2Kin 3:19 4013
horses, a *f* city also, and armour ... 2Kin 10:2 4013
of the watchmen to the *f* city ... 2Kin 17:9 4013
of the watchmen to the *f* city ... 2Kin 18:8 4013
against all the *f* cities of Judah ... 2Kin 18:13 1219
waste *f* cities into ruinous heaps ... 2Kin 19:25 1219
f cities, with walls, gates, and ... 2Chr 8:5 4692
in Judah and in Benjamin *f* cities ... 2Chr 11:10 4694
and Benjamin, unto every *f* city ... 2Chr 11:23 4694
he took the *f* cities which ... 2Chr 12:4 4694
he built *f* cities in Judah ... 2Chr 14:6 4694
in all the *f* cities of Judah ... 2Chr 17:2 1219
the *f* cities throughout all Judah ... 2Chr 17:19 4013
all the *f* cities of Judah ... 2Chr 19:5 1219
things, with *f* cities in Judah ... 2Chr 21:3 4694
and encamped against the *f* cities ... 2Chr 32:1 1219
war in all the *f* cities of Judah ... 2Chr 33:14 1219
hast *f* me with bones and sinews ... Job 10:11 7753
He hath *f* up my way that I cannot ... Job 19:8 1443
high tower, and upon every *f* wall ... Is 2:15 1219
And he *f* it, and gathered out the ... Is 5:2 5823
shall impoverish thy *f* cities ... Jer 5:17 4013
unto this people a *f* brasen wall ... Jer 15:20 1219
and ruined cities are become *f* ... Eze 36:35 1219
mount, and take the most *f* cities ... Dan 11:15 4013
and Judah hath multiplied *f* cities ... Hos 8:14 1219
and alarm against the *f* cities ... Zeph 1:16 1219

FENS
in the covert of the reed, and *f* ... Job 40:21 1207

FERRET
And the *f*, and the chameleon, and ... Lev 11:30 604

FERRY
there went over a *f* boat to carry ... 2Sa 19:18 5679

FERVENT
being *f* in the spirit, he spake ... Acts 18:25 *2204*
f in spirit; serving the Lord ... Rom 12:11 *2204*
mourning, your *f* mind toward me ... 2Cor 7:7 *2205*
The effectual *f* prayer of a ... Jas 5:16
above all things have *f* charity ... 1Pet 4:8 *1618*
elements shall melt with *f* heat ... 2Pet 3:10
elements shall melt with *f* heat ... 2Pet 3:12

FERVENTLY
always labouring *f* for you in ... Col 4:12
one another with a pure heart *f* ... 1Pet 1:22 *1619*

FESTUS (*fes'-tus*) See FESTUS'. *A Roman procurator of Judea.*
Porcius *F* came into Felix' room ... Acts 24:27 *5347*
Now when *F* was come into the ... Acts 25:1 *5347*
But *F* answered, that Paul should ... Acts 25:4 *5347*
But *F*, willing to do the Jews a ... Acts 25:9 *5347*
Then *F*, when he had conferred ... Acts 25:12 *5347*
came unto Caesarea to salute *F* ... Acts 25:13 *5347*
F declared Paul's cause unto the ... Acts 25:14 *5347*
Then Agrippa said unto *F*, I would ... Acts 25:22 *5347*
F said, King Agrippa, and all men ... Acts 25:24 *5347*
F said with a loud voice, Paul, ... Acts 26:24 *5347*
said, I am not mad, most noble *F* ... Acts 26:25 *5347*
Then said Agrippa unto *F*, This ... Acts 26:32 *5347*

FESTUS' (*fes'-tus*)
at *F* commandment Paul was brought. Acts 25:23 *5347*

FETCH
I will *f* a morsel of bread, and ... Gen 18:5 3947
f me from thence two good kids of ... Gen 27:9 3947
obey my voice, and go *f* me them ... Gen 27:13 3947
will send, and *f* thee from thence ... Gen 27:45 3947
let him *f* your brother, and ye ... Gen 42:16 3947
flags, she sent her maid to *f* it ... Ex 2:5 3947
must we *f* you water out of this ... Num 20:10 3318
the border shall *f* a compass from ... Num 34:5
f him thence, and deliver him into ... Deut 19:12 3947
go into his house to *f* his pledge ... Deut 24:10 5670
thou shalt not go again to *f* it ... Deut 24:19 3947
and from thence will he *f* thee ... Deut 30:4 3947
the elders of Gilead went to *f* ... Judg 11:5 3947
to *f* victual for the people, that ... Judg 20:10 3947
Let us *f* the ark of the covenant ... 1Sa 4:3 3947
come ye down, and *f* it up to you ... 1Sa 6:21 5927
said unto Jesse, Send and *f* him ... 1Sa 16:11 3947
f him unto me, for he shall ... 1Sa 20:31 3947
the young men come over and *f* it ... 1Sa 26:22 3947
but *f* a compass behind them, and ... 2Sa 5:23
not *f* home again his banished ... 2Sa 14:13 7725
To *f* about this form of speech ... 2Sa 14:20 5437
F me, I pray thee, a little water ... 1Kin 17:10 3947
And as she was going to *f* it ... 1Kin 17:11 3947
he is, that I may send and *f* him ... 2Kin 6:13 3947
F quickly Micaiah the son of Imla ... 2Chr 18:8
f olive branches, and pine ... Neh 8:15 935
I will *f* my knowledge from afar ... Job 36:3 5375
Come ye, say they, I will *f* wine ... Is 56:12 3947
king sent Jehudi to *f* the roll ... Jer 36:21 3947
them come themselves and *f* us out ... Acts 16:37 *1806*

FETCHED
a little water, I pray you, be *f* ... Gen 18:4 3947
And he went, and *f*, and brought them Gen 27:14 3947
to Adar, and *f* a compass to Karkaa ... Josh 15:3
f the carved image, the ephod, and ... Judg 18:18 3947
And they ran and *f* him thence ... 1Sa 10:23 3947
as though they would have *f* wheat ... 2Sa 4:6 3947
f him out of the house of Machir ... 2Sa 9:5 3947
f her to his house, and she became ... 2Sa 11:27 622
f thence a wise woman, and said ... 2Sa 14:2 3947
sent and *f* Hiram out of Tyre ... 1Kin 7:13 3947
f from thence gold, four hundred ... 1Kin 9:28 3947
they *f* a compass of seven days' ... 2Kin 3:9
f the rulers over hundreds, with ... 2Kin 11:4 3947
And they *f* up, and brought forth ... 2Chr 1:17 5927
f them, and brought them again ... 2Chr 12:11 5375
they *f* forth Urijah out of Egypt ... Jer 26:23 3318
And from thence we *f* a compass ... Acts 28:13

FETCHETH
his hand *f* a stroke with the axe ... Deut 19:5 5080

FETCHT
f a calf tender and good, and gave ... Gen 18:7 3947

FETTERS
and bound him with *f* of brass ... Judg 16:21 5178
bound, nor thy feet put into *f* ... 2Sa 3:34 5178
and bound him with *f* of brass ... 2Kin 25:7 5178
the thorns, and bound him with *f* ... 2Chr 33:11 5178
of Babylon, and bound him in *f* ... 2Chr 36:6 5178
And if they be bound in *f*, and be ... Job 36:8 2131
Whose feet they hurt with *f* ... Ps 105:18 3525
and their nobles with *f* of iron ... Ps 149:8 3525
he had been often bound with *f* ... Mk 5:4 *3976*
by him, and the *f* broken in pieces ... Mk 5:4 *3976*
kept bound with chains and in *f* ... Lk 8:29 *3976*

FEVER
with a consumption, and with a *f* ... Deut 28:22 6920
mother laid, and sick of a *f* ... Mt 8:14 *4445*
her hand, and the *f* left her ... Mt 8:15 *4446*
wife's mother lay sick of a *f* ... Mk 1:30 *4445*
and immediately the *f* left her ... Mk 1:31 *4446*
mother was taken with a great *f* ... Lk 4:38 *4446*
stood over her, and rebuked the *f* ... Lk 4:39 *4446*
the seventh hour the *f* left him ... Jn 4:52 *4446*
father of Publius lay sick of a *f* ... Acts 28:8 *4446*

FEW
the damsel abide with us a *f* days ... Gen 24:55
And tarry with him a *f* days ... Gen 27:44 259
they seemed unto him but a *f* days ... Gen 29:20 259
I being *f* in number, they shall ... Gen 34:30 4962
f and evil have the days of the ... Gen 47:9 4592
if there remain but *f* years unto ... Lev 25:52 4592
cattle, and make you *f* in number ... Lev 26:22 4591
when the cloud was a *f* days upon ... Num 9:20 4557
they be strong or weak, *f* or many ... Num 13:18 4592
to *f* thou shalt give the less ... Num 26:54 4592
be divided between many and *f* ... Num 26:56 4592
that have *f* ye shall give *f* ... Num 35:8 4592
that have *f* ye shall give *f* ... Num 35:8 4591
ye shall be left *f* in number ... Deut 4:27 4962
and sojourned there with a *f* ... Deut 26:5 4592
And ye shall be left *f* in number ... Deut 28:62 4592
and let not his men be *f* ... Deut 33:6 4557
for they are but *f* ... Josh 7:3 4592
the LORD to save by many or by *f* ... 1Sa 14:6 4592
those *f* sheep in the wilderness ... 1Sa 17:28 4592
empty vessels; borrow not a *f* ... 2Kin 4:3 4591
When ye were but *f*, even a *f*, ... 1Chr 16:19 4962
When ye were but *f*, even a *f* ... 1Chr 16:19 4592
But the priests were too *f* ... 2Chr 29:34 4592
night, I and some *f* men with me ... Neh 2:12 4592
but the people were *f* therein ... Neh 7:4 4592
Are not my days *f* ... Job 10:20 4592
is born of a woman is of *f* days ... Job 14:1 7116
When a *f* years are come, then I ... Job 16:22 4557
they were but a *f* men in number ... Ps 105:12 4962
yea, very *f*, and strangers in it ... Ps 105:12 4592
Let his days be *f* ... Ps 109:8 4592
therefore let thy words be *f* ... Eccl 5:2 4592
a little city, and *f* men within it ... Eccl 9:14 4592
grinders cease because they are *f* ... Eccl 12:3 4592
and cut off nations not a *f* ... Is 10:7 4592
trees of his forest shall be *f* ... Is 10:19 4557
earth are burned, and *f* men left ... Is 24:6 4213
them, and they shall not be *f* ... Jer 30:19 4591
(for we are left but a *f* of many ... Jer 42:2 4592
also take thereof a *f* in number ... Eze 5:3 4592
But I will leave a *f* men of them ... Eze 12:16 4557
but within *f* days he shall be ... Dan 11:20 259
life, and *f* there be that find it ... Mt 7:14 *3641*
but the labourers are *f* ... Mt 9:37 *3641*
said, Seven, and a *f* little fishes ... Mt 15:34 *3641*
for many be called, but *f* chosen ... Mt 20:16 *3641*
many are called, but *f* are chosen ... Mt 22:14 *3641*
been faithful over a *f* things ... Mt 25:21 *3641*
been faithful over a *f* things ... Mt 25:23 *3641*
laid his hands upon a *f* sick folk ... Mk 6:5 *3641*
they had a *f* small fishes ... Mk 8:7 *3641*
is great, but the labourers are *f* ... Lk 10:2 *3641*
shall be beaten with *f* stripes ... Lk 12:48 *3641*
are there *f* that be saved ... Lk 13:23 *3641*
and of the chief women not a *f* ... Acts 17:4 *3641*
were Greeks, and of men, not a *f* ... Acts 17:12 *3641*
hear us of thy clemency a *f* words ... Acts 24:4 *4935*
(as I wrote afore in *f* words ... Eph 3:3 *3641*
For they verily for a *f* days ... Heb 12:10 *3641*
a letter unto you in *f* words ... Heb 13:22 *1024*
ark was a preparing, wherein *f* ... 1Pet 3:20 *3641*
But I have a *f* things against ... Rev 2:14 *3641*
I have a *f* things against thee ... Rev 2:20 *3641*
Thou hast a *f* names even in ... Rev 3:4 *3641*

FEWER
to the *f* ye shall give the less ... Num 33:54 4592

FEWEST
for ye were the *f* of all people ... Deut 7:7 4592

FEWNESS
according to the *f* of years thou ... Lev 25:16 4591

FIDELITY
but shewing all good *f* ... Titus 2:10 *4102*

FIELD
every plant of the *f* before it ... Gen 2:5 7704
herb of the *f* before it grew ... Gen 2:5 7704
God formed every beast of the *f* ... Gen 2:19 7704
air, and to every beast of the *f* ... Gen 2:20 7704
the *f* which the LORD God had made ... Gen 3:1 7704
and above every beast of the *f* ... Gen 3:14 7704
thou shalt eat the herb of the *f* ... Gen 3:18 7704
to pass, when they were in the *f* ... Gen 4:8 7704
which is in the end of his *f* ... Gen 23:9 7704
the *f* give I thee, and the cave ... Gen 23:11 7704
I will give thee money for the *f* ... Gen 23:13 7704
the *f* of Ephron, which was in ... Gen 23:17 7704
which was before Mamre, the *f* ... Gen 23:17 7704
all the trees that were in the *f* ... Gen 23:17 7704
the *f* of Machpelah before Mamre ... Gen 23:19 7704
And the *f*, and the cave that is ... Gen 23:20 7704
meditate in the *f* at the eventide ... Gen 24:63 7704
that walketh in the *f* to meet us ... Gen 24:65 7704
in the *f* of Ephron the son of ... Gen 25:9 7704
The *f* which Abraham purchased of ... Gen 25:10 7704
a cunning hunter, a man of the *f* ... Gen 25:27 7704
and Esau came from the *f*, and he ... Gen 25:29 7704
and thy bow, and go out to the *f* ... Gen 27:3 7704
Esau went to the *f* to hunt for ... Gen 27:5 7704
a *f* which the LORD hath blessed ... Gen 27:27 7704
looked, and behold a well in the *f* ... Gen 29:2 7704
and found mandrakes in the *f* ... Gen 30:14 7704
came out of the *f* in the evening ... Gen 30:16 7704
Leah to the *f* unto his flock ... Gen 31:4 7704
And he bought a parcel of a *f* ... Gen 33:19 7704
were with his cattle in the *f* ... Gen 34:5 7704
out of the *f* when they heard it ... Gen 34:7 7704
city, and that which was in the *f* ... Gen 34:28 7704
who smote Midian in the *f* of Moab ... Gen 36:35 7704
we were binding sheaves in the *f* ... Gen 37:7 7704
behold, he was wandering in the *f* ... Gen 37:15 7704
he had in the house, and in the *f* ... Gen 39:5 7704
the food of the *f*, which was ... Gen 41:48 7704
Egyptians sold every man his *f* ... Gen 47:20 7704
be your own, for seed of the *f* ... Gen 47:24 7704
is in the *f* of Ephron the Hittite ... Gen 49:29 7704
that is in the *f* of Machpelah ... Gen 49:30 7704
the *f* of Ephron the Hittite for a ... Gen 49:30 7704
The purchase of the *f* and of the ... Gen 49:32 7704
in the cave of the *f* of Machpelah ... Gen 50:13 7704
with the *f* for a possession of a ... Gen 50:13 7704
in all manner of service in the *f* ... Ex 1:14 7704
upon thy cattle which is in the *f* ... Ex 9:3 7704
and all that thou hast in the *f* ... Ex 9:19 7704
which shall be found in the *f* ... Ex 9:19 7704
servants and his cattle in the *f* ... Ex 9:21 7704
and upon every herb of the *f* ... Ex 9:22 7704
of Egypt all that was in the *f* ... Ex 9:25 7704
hail smote every herb of the *f* ... Ex 9:25 7704
and brake every tree of the *f* ... Ex 9:25 7704
groweth for you out of the *f* ... Ex 10:5 7704
trees, or in the herbs of the *f* ... Ex 10:15 7704
day ye shall not find it in the *f* ... Ex 16:25 7704
If a man shall cause a *f* or ... Ex 22:5 7704
and shall feed in another man's *f* ... Ex 22:5 7704
of the best of his own *f*, and of ... Ex 22:5 7704
or the standing corn, or the *f* ... Ex 22:6 7704
that is torn of beasts in the *f* ... Ex 22:31 7704
the beasts of the *f* shall eat ... Ex 23:11 7704
which thou hast sown in the *f* ... Ex 23:16 7704
in thy labours out of the *f* ... Ex 23:16 7704
the beast of the *f* multiply ... Ex 23:29 7704
living bird loose into the open *f* ... Lev 14:7 7704
which they offer in the open *f* ... Lev 17:5 7704
wholly reap the corners of thy *f* ... Lev 19:9 7704
not sow thy *f* with mingled seed ... Lev 19:19 7704
of thy *f* when thou reapest ... Lev 23:22 7704
Six years thou shalt sow thy *f* ... Lev 25:3 7704
thou shalt neither sow thy *f* ... Lev 25:4 7704
the increase thereof out of the *f* ... Lev 25:12 7704
But the *f* of the suburbs of their ... Lev 25:34 7704
the trees of the *f* shall yield ... Lev 26:4 7704
part of a *f* of his possession ... Lev 27:16 7704
If he sanctify his *f* from the ... Lev 27:17 7704
sanctify his *f* after the jubile ... Lev 27:18 7704
if he that sanctified the *f* will ... Lev 27:19 7704
And if he will not redeem the *f* ... Lev 27:20 7704
he have sold the *f* to another man ... Lev 27:20 7704
But the *f*, when it goeth out in ... Lev 27:21 7704
unto the LORD, as a *f* devoted ... Lev 27:21 7704
the LORD a *f* which he hath bought ... Lev 27:22 7704
f shall return unto him of whom ... Lev 27:24 7704
of the *f* of his possession, shall ... Lev 27:28 7704
ox licketh up the grass of the *f* ... Num 22:4 7704
of the way, and went into the *f* ... Num 22:23 7704
brought him into the *f* of Zophim ... Num 23:14 7704
thy neighbour's house, his *f* ... Deut 5:21 7704
of the *f* increase upon thee ... Deut 7:22 7704
that the *f* bringeth forth year by ... Deut 14:22 7704
f is man's life) to employ them ... Deut 20:19 7704
to possess it, lying in the *f* ... Deut 21:1 7704
find a betrothed damsel in the *f* ... Deut 22:25 7704
For he found her in the *f* ... Deut 22:27 7704
down thine harvest in thy *f* ... Deut 24:19 7704
and hast forgot a sheaf in the *f* ... Deut 24:19 7704
and blessed shalt thou be in the *f* ... Deut 28:3 7704

and cursed shalt thou be in the f Deut 28:16 7704
carry much seed out into the f Deut 28:38 7704
the inhabitants of Ai in the f Josh 8:24 7704
him to ask of her father a f Josh 15:18 7704
him to ask of her father a f Judg 1:14 7704
marchedst out of the f of Edom Judg 5:4 7704
death in the high places of the f Judg 5:18 7704
thee, and lie in wait in the f Judg 9:32 7704
the people went out into the f Judg 9:42 7704
companies, and laid wait in the f Judg 9:43 7704
the woman as she sat in the f Judg 13:9 7704
his work out of the f at even Judg 19:16 7704
and the other to Gibeah in the f Judg 20:31 7704
Naomi, Let me now go to the f Ruth 2:2 7704
gleaned in the f after the Ruth 2:3 7704
part of the f belonging unto Boaz Ruth 2:3 7704
Go not to glean in another f Ruth 2:8 7704
be on the f that they do reap Ruth 2:9 7704
she gleaned in the f until even Ruth 2:17 7704
they meet thee not in any other f Ruth 2:22 7704
buyest the f of the hand of Naomi Ruth 4:5 7704
in the f about four thousand men 1Sa 4:2 7704
cart came into the f of Joshua 1Sa 6:14 7704
unto this day in the f of Joshua 1Sa 6:18 7704
came after the herd out of the f 1Sa 11:5 7704
trembling in the host, in the f 1Sa 14:15 7704
air, and to the beasts of the f 1Sa 17:44 7704
my father in the f where thou art 1Sa 19:3 7704
the f unto the third day at even 1Sa 20:5 7704
Come, and let us go out into the f 1Sa 20:11 7704
went out both of them into the f 1Sa 20:11 7704
So David hid himself in the f 1Sa 20:24 7704
the f at the time appointed with 1Sa 20:35 7704
they found an Egyptian in the f 1Sa 30:11 7704
were by themselves in the f 2Sa 10:8 7704
and came out unto us into the f 2Sa 11:23 7704
they two strove together in the f 2Sa 14:6 7704
Joab's f is near mine, and he hath 2Sa 14:30 2513
servants set the f on fire 2Sa 14:30 2513
thy servants set my f on fire 2Sa 14:31 2513
robbed of her whelps in the f 2Sa 17:8 7704
out into the f against Israel 2Sa 18:6 7704
out of the highway into the f 2Sa 20:12 7704
nor the beasts of the f by night 2Sa 21:10 7704
and they two were alone in the f 1Kin 11:29 7704
him that dieth in the f shall the 1Kin 14:11 7704
him that dieth in the f shall the 1Kin 21:24 7704
out into the f to gather herbs 2Kin 4:39 7704
camp to hide themselves in the f 2Kin 7:12 7704
all the fruits of the f since the 2Kin 8:6 7704
of the f of Naboth the Jezreelite 2Kin 9:25 7704
the f in the portion of Jezreel 2Kin 9:37 7704
in the highway of the fuller's f 2Kin 18:17 7704
they were as the grass of the f 2Kin 19:26 7704
smote Midian in the f of Moab 1Chr 1:46 7704
come were by themselves in the f 1Chr 19:9 7704
f for tillage of the ground was 1Chr 27:26 7704
him with his fathers in the f of 2Chr 26:23 7704
and of all the increase of the f 2Chr 31:5 7704
were fled every one to his f Neh 13:10 7704
league with the stones of the f Job 5:23 7704
the beasts of the f shall be at Job 5:23 7704
reap every one his corn in the f Job 24:6 7704
all the beasts of the f play Job 40:20 7704
oxen, yea, and the beasts of the f Ps 8:7 7704
the wild beasts of the f are mine Ps 50:11 7704
land of Egypt, in the f of Zoan Ps 78:12 7704
and his wonders in the f of Zoan Ps 78:43 7704
beast of the f doth devour it Ps 80:13 7704
Let the f be joyful, and all that Ps 96:12 7704
as a flower of the f, so he Ps 103:15 7704
drink to every beast of the f Ps 104:11 7704
make it fit for thyself in the f Prov 24:27 7704
I went by the f of the slothful Prov 24:30 7704
the goats are the price of the f Prov 27:26 7704
She considereth a f, and buyeth it Prov 31:16 7704
king himself is served by the f Eccl 5:9 7704
roes, and by the hinds of the f Song 2:7 7704
roes, and by the hinds of the f Song 3:5 7704
let us go forth into the f Song 7:11 7704
to house, that lay f to f Is 5:8 7704
to house, that lay f to f Is 5:8 7704
in the highway of the fuller's f Is 7:3 7704
his forest, and of his fruitful f Is 10:18
and joy out of the plentiful f Is 16:10
shall be turned into a fruitful f Is 29:17
the fruitful f shall be esteemed Is 29:17
and the wilderness be a fruitful f Is 32:15
the fruitful f be counted for a Is 32:15
remain in the fruitful f Is 32:16
in the highway of the fuller's f Is 36:2 7704
they were as the grass of the f Is 37:27 7704
thereof is as the flower of the f Is 40:6 7704
beast of the f shall honour me Is 43:20 7704
all the trees of the f shall clap Is 55:12 7704
All ye beasts of the f, come to Is 56:9 7704
As keepers of a f, are they Jer 4:17 7704
Go not forth into the f, nor walk Jer 6:25 7704
beast, and upon the trees of the f Jer 7:20 7704
fall as dung upon the open f Jer 9:22 7704
and the herbs of every f wither Jer 12:4 7704
assemble all the beasts of the f Jer 12:9 7704
the hind also calved in the f Jer 14:5 7704
If I go forth into the f, then Jer 14:18 7704
O my mountain in the f, I will Jer 17:3 7704
cometh from the rock of the f Jer 18:14 7704
Zion shall be plowed like a f Jer 26:18 7704
the beasts of the f have I given Jer 27:6 7704
him the beasts of the f also Jer 28:14 7704
Buy thee my f that is in Anathoth Jer 32:7 7704
LORD, and said unto me, Buy my f Jer 32:8 7704
I bought the f of Hanameel my Jer 32:9 7704
GOD, Buy thee the f for money Jer 32:25 7704
neither have we vineyard, nor f Jer 35:9 7704
for we have treasures in the f Jer 41:8 7704
is taken from the plentiful f Jer 48:33
for want of the fruits of the f Lam 4:9 7704
he that is in the f shall die Eze 7:15 7704
thou wast cast out in the open f Eze 16:5 7704
to multiply as the bud of the f Eze 16:7 7704
and planted it in a fruitful f Eze 17:5 7704
all the trees of the f shall know Eze 17:24 7704
against the forest of the south f Eze 20:46 7704
the f shall be slain by the sword Eze 26:6 7704
the sword thy daughters in the f Eze 26:8 7704
for meat to the beasts of the f Eze 29:5 776
unto all the trees of the f Eze 31:4 7704
above all the trees of the f Eze 31:5 7704
of the f bring forth their young Eze 31:6 7704
all the beasts of the f shall be Eze 31:13 7704
trees of the f fainted for him Eze 31:15 7704
cast thee forth upon the open f Eze 32:4 7704
him that is in the open f will I Eze 33:27 7704
meat to all the beasts of the f Eze 34:5 7704
meat to every beast of the f Eze 34:8 7704
the tree of the f shall yield her Eze 34:27 7704
tree, and the increase of the f Eze 36:30 7704
heaven, and the beasts of the f Eze 38:20 7704
beasts of the f to be devoured Eze 39:4 7704
Thou shalt fall upon the open f Eze 39:5 7704
shall take no wood out of the f Eze 39:10 7704
fowl, and to every beast of the f Eze 39:17 7704
of men dwell, the beasts of the f Dan 2:38 1251
the beasts of the f had shadow Dan 4:12 1251
in the tender grass of the f Dan 4:15 1251
which the beasts of the f dwelt Dan 4:21 1251
in the tender grass of the f Dan 4:23 1251
be with the beasts of the f Dan 4:23 1251
shall be with the beasts of the f Dan 4:25 1251
shall be with the beasts of the f Dan 4:32 1251
beasts of the f shall eat them Hos 2:12 7704
for them with the beasts of the f Hos 2:18 7704
with the beasts of the f Hos 4:3 7704
hemlock in the furrows of the f Hos 10:4 7704
The f is wasted, the land Joel 1:10 7704
the harvest of the f is perished Joel 1:11 7704
tree, even all the trees of the f Joel 1:12 7704
burned all the trees of the f Joel 1:19 7704
The beasts of the f cry also unto Joel 1:20 7704
Be not afraid, ye beasts of the f Joel 2:22 7704
make Samaria as an heap of the f Mic 1:6 7704
for your sake be plowed as a f Mic 3:12 7704
and thou shalt dwell in the f Mic 4:10 7704
rain, to every one grass in the f Zec 10:1 7704
fruit before the time in the f Mal 3:11 7704
Consider the lilies of the f Mt 6:28 68
God so clothe the grass of the f Mt 6:30 68
which sowed good seed in his f Mt 13:24 68
not thou sow good seed in thy f Mt 13:27 68
a man took, and sowed in his f Mt 13:31 68
the parable of the tares of the f Mt 13:36 68
The f is the world Mt 13:38 68
is like unto treasure hid in a f Mt 13:44 68
that he hath, and buyeth that f Mt 13:44 68
f return back to take his clothes Mt 24:18 68
Then shall two be in the f Mt 24:40 68
bought with them the potter's f Mt 27:7 68
Wherefore that f was called Mt 27:8 68
The f of blood, unto this day Mt 27:8 68
And gave them for the potter's f Mt 27:10 68
let him that is in the f not turn Mk 13:16 68
shepherds abiding in the f Lk 2:8 68
grass, which is to day in the f Lk 12:28 68
Now his elder son was in the f Lk 15:25 68
and by, when he is come from the f Lk 17:7 68
and he that is in the f, let him Lk 17:31 68
Two men shall be in the f Lk 17:36 68
Now this man purchased a f with Acts 1:18 5564
insomuch as that f is called in Acts 1:19 5564
that is to say, The f of blood Acts 1:19 5564

FIELDS

of the villages, and out of the f Ex 8:13 7704
out of the city into the open f Lev 14:53 7704
counted as the f of the country Lev 25:31 7704
is not of the f of his possession Lev 27:22 7704
or given us inheritance of f Num 16:14 7704
slain with a sword in the open f Num 19:16 7704
we will not pass through the f Num 20:17 7704
we will not turn into the f Num 21:22 7704
grass in thy f for thy cattle Deut 11:15 7704
might eat the increase of the f Deut 32:13 7704
of Sodom, and of the f of Gomorrah Deut 32:32 7709
But the f of the city, and the Josh 21:12 7704
And they went out into the f Judg 9:27 7704
all the people that were in the f Judg 9:44 7704
And he will take your f, and your 1Sa 8:14 7704
of Jesse give every one of you f 1Sa 22:7 7704
with them, when we were in the f 1Sa 25:15 7704
upon you, nor f of offerings 2Sa 1:21 7704
lord, are encamped in the open f 2Sa 11:11 7704
to Anathoth, unto thine own f 1Kin 2:26 7704
him that dieth of his in the f 1Kin 16:4 7704
Jerusalem in the f of Kidron 2Kin 23:4 7709
But the f of the city, and the 1Chr 6:56 7704
let the f rejoice, and all that is 1Chr 16:32 7704
and over the storehouses in the f 1Chr 27:25 7704
which were in the f of the 2Chr 31:19 7704
And for the villages, with their f Neh 11:25 7704
the f thereof, at Azekah, and in Neh 11:30 7704
Gilgal, and out of the f of Geba Neh 12:29 7704
f of the cities the portions of Neh 12:44 7704
and sendeth waters upon the f Job 5:10 2351
And sow the f, and plant vineyards, Ps 107:37 7704
we found it in the f of the wood Ps 132:6 7704
had not made the earth, nor the f Prov 8:26 2351
not into the f of the fatherless Prov 23:10 7704
For the f of Heshbon languish, and Is 16:8 7709
for the teats, for the pleasant f Is 32:12 7704
turned unto others, with their f Jer 6:12 7704
their f to them that shall Jer 8:10 7704
on the hills in the f Jer 13:27 7704
all the f unto the brook of Jer 31:40 8309
Houses and f and vineyards shall be Jer 32:15 7704
f shall be bought in this land, Jer 32:43 7704
Men shall buy f for money Jer 32:44 7704
vineyards and f at the same time Jer 39:10 3010
of the forces which were in the f Jer 40:7 7704
of the forces that were in the f Jer 40:13 7704
thou shalt fall upon the open f Eze 29:5 7704
as heaps in the furrows of the f Hos 12:11 7704
shall possess the f of Ephraim Obad 19 7704
of Ephraim, and the f of Samaria Obad 19 7704
And they covet f, and take them by Mic 2:2 7704
away he hath divided our f Mic 2:4 7704
the f shall yield no meat Hab 3:17 7709
the corn f on the sabbath day Mk 2:23
that he went through the corn f Lk 6:1
sent him into his f to feed swine Lk 15:15 68
up your eyes, and look on the f Jn 4:35 5561
who have reaped down your f Jas 5:4 5561

FIERCE

be their anger, for it was f Gen 49:7 5794
Turn from thy f wrath, and repent Ex 32:12 2740
that the f anger of the LORD may Num 25:4 2740
to augment yet the f anger of the Num 32:14 2740
A nation of f countenance Deut 28:50 5794
arose from the table in f anger 1Sa 20:34 2750
his f wrath upon Amalek, 1Sa 28:18 2740
for the f wrath of the LORD is 2Chr 28:11 2740
there is f wrath against Israel 2Chr 28:13 2740
that his f wrath may turn away 2Chr 29:10 2740
until the f wrath of our God for Ezr 10:14 2740
lion, and the voice of the f lion Job 4:10 7826
Thou huntest me as a f lion Job 10:16 7826
nor the f lion passed by it Job 28:8 7826
None is so f that dare stir him Job 41:10 393
Thy f wrath goeth over me Ps 88:16
for the f anger of Rezin with Is 7:4 2750
f anger, to lay the land desolate Is 13:9 2740
and in the day of his f anger Is 13:13 2740
a f king shall rule over them, Is 19:4 5794
Thou shalt not see a f people Is 33:19 3267
for the f anger of the LORD is Jer 4:8 2740
of the LORD, and by his f anger Jer 4:26 2740
of the f anger of the LORD Jer 12:13 2740
of the f anger of the LORD Jer 25:37 2740
and because of his f anger Jer 25:38 2740
The f anger of the LORD shall not Jer 30:24 2740
evil upon them, even my f anger Jer 49:37 2740
soul from the f anger of the LORD Jer 51:45 2740
me in the day of his f anger Lam 1:12 2740
He hath cut off in his f anger Lam 2:3 2750
he hath poured out his f anger Lam 4:11 2740
a king of f countenance, and Dan 8:23 5794
and turn away from his f anger Jonah 3:9 2740
are more f than the evening Hab 1:8 2300
before the f anger of the LORD Zeph 2:2 2740
indignation, even all my f anger Zeph 3:8 2740
out of the tombs, exceeding f Mt 8:28 5467
And they were the more f, saying, Lk 23:5 2001
false accusers, incontinent, f 2Ti 3:3 434
great, and are driven of f winds Jas 3:4 4642

FIERCENESS

may turn from the f of his anger Deut 13:17 2740
turned from the f of his anger Josh 7:26 2740
not from the f of his great wrath 2Kin 23:26 2740
that the f of his wrath may turn 2Chr 30:8 2740
He swalloweth the ground with f Job 39:24 7494
cast upon them the f of his anger Ps 78:49 2740
thyself from the f of thine anger Ps 85:3 2740
because of the f of the oppressor Jer 25:38 2740
not execute the f of mine anger Hos 11:9 2740
can abide in the f of his anger Nah 1:6 2740
of the wine of the f of his wrath Rev 16:19 2372
treadeth the winepress of the f Rev 19:15 2372

FIERCER

f than the words of the men of 2Sa 19:43 7185

FIERY

the LORD sent f serpents among Num 21:6 8314
unto Moses, Make thee a f serpent Num 21:8 8314
wherein were f serpents, and Deut 8:15 8314
right hand went a f law for them Deut 33:2 799
Thou shalt make them as a f oven Ps 21:9 784
fruit shall be a f flying serpent Is 14:29 8314
f flying serpent, they will carry Is 30:6 8314
the midst of a burning f furnace Dan 3:6 5135
the midst of a burning f furnace Dan 3:11 5135
the midst of a burning f furnace Dan 3:15 5135
us from the burning f furnace Dan 3:17 5135
them into the burning f furnace Dan 3:20 5135
midst of the burning f furnace Dan 3:21 5135
midst of the burning f furnace Dan 3:23 5135
mouth of the burning f furnace Dan 3:26 5135
his throne was like the f flame Dan 7:9 5135
A f stream issued and came forth Dan 7:10 5135
all the f darts of the wicked Eph 6:16 4448
f indignation, which shall devour Heb 10:27 4442
the f trial which is to try you 1Pet 4:12 4451

FIFTEEN

f years, and begat sons and Gen 5:10 6240
F cubits upward did the waters Gen 7:20 6240
an hundred threescore and f years Gen 25:7 2568
of the gate shall be f cubits Ex 27:14 6240
side shall be hangings f cubits Ex 27:15 6240
side of the gate were f cubits Ex 38:14 6240
hand, were hangings of f cubits Ex 38:15 6240
f shekels, after the shekel of Ex 38:25 2568
thy estimation shall be f shekels Lev 27:7 6240

six hundred and threescore and *f* ... Num 31:37 2568
about *f* thousand men, all that ... Judg 8:10 6240
Now Ziba had *f* sons and twenty ... 2Sa 9:10 6240
his *f* sons and his twenty servants ... 2Sa 19:17 6240
on forty five pillars, *f* in a row ... 1Kin 7:3 6240
Jehoahaz king of Israel *f* years ... 2Kin 14:17 6240
I will add unto thy days *f* years ... 2Kin 20:6 6240
Jehoahaz king of Israel *f* years ... 2Chr 25:25 6240
I will add unto thy days *f* years ... Is 38:5 6240
f shekels, shall be your maneh ... Eze 45:12 2568
her to me for *f* pieces of silver ... Hos 3:2 6240
Jerusalem, about *f* furlongs off ... Jn 11:18 *1178*
kindred, threescore and *f* souls ... Acts 7:14 *4002*
again, and found it *f* fathoms ... Acts 27:28 *1178*
Peter, and abode with him *f* days ... Gal 1:18 *1178*

FIFTEENTH

on the *f* day of the second month ... Ex 16:1 6240
on the *f* day of the same month is ... Lev 23:6 6240
The *f* day of this seventh month ... Lev 23:34 6240
Also in the *f* day of the seventh ... Lev 23:39 6240
in the *f* day of this month is the ... Num 28:17 6240
on the *f* day of the seventh month ... Num 29:12 6240
on the *f* day of the first month ... Num 33:3 6240
on the *f* day of the month, like ... 1Kin 12:32 6240
the *f* day of the eighth month ... 1Kin 12:33 6240
In the *f* year of Amaziah the son ... 2Kin 14:23 6240
The *f* to Bilgah, the sixteenth to ... 1Chr 24:14 6240
The *f* to Jeremoth, he, his sons, ... 1Chr 25:22 6240
in the *f* year of the reign of Asa ... 2Chr 15:10 6240
on the *f* day of the same they ... Est 9:18 6240
the *f* day of the same, yearly, ... Est 9:21 6240
in the *f* day of the month, that ... Eze 32:17 6240
in the *f* day of the month, shall ... Eze 45:25 6240
Now in the *f* year of the reign of ... Lk 3:1 *4003*

FIFTH

and the morning were the *f* day ... Gen 1:23 2549
and bare Jacob the *f* son ... Gen 30:17 2549
take up the *f* part of the land of ... Gen 41:34 2567
give the *f* part unto Pharaoh ... Gen 47:24 2549
Pharaoh should have the *f* part ... Gen 47:26 2569
and shall add the *f* part thereto ... Lev 5:16 2549
shall add the *f* part more thereto ... Lev 6:5 2549
in the *f* year shall ye eat of the ... Lev 19:25 2549
put the *f* part thereof unto it ... Lev 22:14 2549
then he shall add a *f* part ... Lev 27:13 2549
then he shall add the *f* part of ... Lev 27:15 2549
then he shall add the *f* part of ... Lev 27:19 2549
shall add a *f* part of it thereto ... Lev 27:27 2549
add thereto the *f* part thereof ... Lev 27:31 2549
and add unto it the *f* part thereof ... Num 5:7 2549
On the *f* day Shelumiel the son of ... Num 7:36 2549
on the *f* day nine bullocks, two ... Num 29:26 2549
in the first day of the *f* month ... Num 33:38 2549
the *f* lot came out for the tribe ... Josh 19:24 2549
morning on the *f* day to depart ... Judg 19:8 2549
spear smote him under the *f* rib ... 2Sa 2:23 2570
and the *f*, Shephatiah the son of ... 2Sa 3:4 2549
smote him there under the *f* rib ... 2Sa 3:27 2570
and they smote him under the *f* rib ... 2Sa 4:6 2570
smote him therewith in the *f* rib ... 2Sa 20:10 2570
posts were a *f* part of the wall ... 1Kin 6:31 2549
in the *f* year of king Rehoboam ... 1Kin 14:25 2549
in the *f* year of Joram the son of ... 2Kin 8:16 2568
And in the *f* month, on the seventh ... 2Kin 25:8 2549
the fourth, Raddai the *f*, ... 1Chr 2:14 2549
The *f*, Shephatiah of Abital ... 1Chr 3:3 2549
Nohah the fourth, and Rapha the *f* ... 1Chr 8:2 2549
the fourth, Jeremiah the *f* ... 1Chr 12:10 2549
The *f* to Malchijah, the sixth to ... 1Chr 24:9 2549
The *f* to Nethaniah, he, his sons, ... 1Chr 25:12 2549
Elam the *f*, Jehohanan the sixth ... 1Chr 26:3 2549
the fourth, and Nethaneel the *f* ... 1Chr 26:4 2549
The *f* captain for the *f* month ... 1Chr 27:8 2549
that in the *f* year of king ... 2Chr 12:2 2549
came to Jerusalem in the *f* month ... Ezr 7:8 2549
on the first day of the *f* month ... Ezr 7:9 2549
unto me in like manner the *f* time ... Neh 6:5 2549
f day of the month Elul, in fifty ... Neh 6:15 2568
Jerusalem captive in the *f* month ... Jer 1:3 2549
fourth year, and in the *f* month ... Jer 28:1 2549
it came to pass in the *f* year of ... Jer 36:9 2549
Now in the *f* month, in the tenth ... Jer 52:12 2549
in the *f* day of the month, as I ... Eze 1:1 2568
In the *f* day of the month ... Eze 1:2 2568
which was the *f* year of king ... Eze 1:2 2549
in the *f* day of the month, as I ... Eze 8:1 2568
the seventh year, in the *f* month ... Eze 20:1 2549
in the *f* day of the month, that ... Eze 33:21 2568
Should I weep in the *f* month ... Zec 7:3 2549
ye fasted and mourned in the *f* ... Zec 7:5 2549
month, and the fast of the *f* ... Zec 8:19 2549
And when he had opened the *f* seal ... Rev 6:9 *3991*
the *f* angel sounded, and I saw a ... Rev 9:1 *3991*
the *f* angel poured out his vial ... Rev 16:10 *3991*
The *f*, sardonyx; the sixth ... Rev 21:20 *3991*

FIFTIES

rulers of hundreds, rulers of *f* ... Ex 18:21 2572
rulers of hundreds, rulers of *f* ... Ex 18:25 2572
over hundreds, and captains over *f* ... Deut 1:15 2572
thousands, and captains over *f* ... 1Sa 8:12 2572
the former *f* with their *f* ... 2Kin 1:14 2572
in ranks, by hundreds, and by *f* ... Mk 6:40 *4004*
them sit down by *f* in a company ... Lk 9:14 *4004*

FIFTIETH

And ye shall hallow the *f* year ... Lev 25:10 2572
shall that *f* year be unto you ... Lev 25:11 2572
In the *f* year of Azariah king of ... 2Kin 15:23 2572
f year of Azariah king of Judah ... 2Kin 15:27 2572

FIFTY

the breadth of it *f* cubits ... Gen 6:15 2572
the earth an hundred and *f* days ... Gen 7:24 2572
f days the waters were abated ... Gen 8:3 2572
flood three hundred and *f* years ... Gen 9:28 2572
Noah were nine hundred and *f* years ... Gen 9:29 2572
Peradventure there be *f* righteous ... Gen 18:24 2572
the *f* righteous that are therein ... Gen 18:24 2572
If I find in Sodom *f* righteous ... Gen 18:26 2572
lack five of the *f* righteous ... Gen 18:28 2572
F loops shalt thou make in the ... Ex 26:5 2572
f loops shalt thou make in the ... Ex 26:5 2572
thou shalt make *f* taches of gold ... Ex 26:6 2572
thou shalt make *f* loops on the ... Ex 26:10 2572
f loops in the edge of the ... Ex 26:10 2572
thou shalt make *f* taches of brass ... Ex 26:11 2572
shall be hangings of *f* cubits ... Ex 27:12 2572
side eastward shall be *f* cubits ... Ex 27:13 2572
and the breadth *f* every where ... Ex 27:18 2572
f shekels, and of sweet calamus ... Ex 30:23 2572
calamus two hundred and *f* shekels, ... Ex 30:23 2572
F loops made he in one curtain, ... Ex 36:12 2572
f loops made he in the edge of ... Ex 36:12 2572
he made *f* taches of gold, and ... Ex 36:13 2572
And he made *f* loops upon the ... Ex 36:17 2572
f loops made he upon the edge of ... Ex 36:17 2572
he made *f* taches of brass to ... Ex 36:18 2572
side were hangings of *f* cubits ... Ex 38:12 2572
the east side eastward *f* cubits ... Ex 38:13 2572
thousand and five hundred and *f* men ... Ex 38:26 2572
sabbath shall ye number *f* days ... Lev 23:16 2572
shall be *f* shekels of silver ... Lev 27:3 2572
be valued at *f* shekels of silver ... Lev 27:16 2572
of the tribe of Simeon, were *f* ... Num 1:23 2572
and five thousand six hundred and *f* ... Num 1:25 2572
of the tribe of Issachar, were *f* ... Num 1:29 2572
of the tribe of Zebulun, were *f* ... Num 1:31 2572
of the tribe of Naphtali, were *f* ... Num 1:43 2572
thousand and five hundred and *f* ... Num 1:46 2572
were numbered thereof, were *f* ... Num 2:6 2572
were numbered thereof, were *f* ... Num 2:8 2572
were numbered of them, were *f* ... Num 2:13 2572
five thousand and six hundred and *f* ... Num 2:15 2572
were an hundred thousand and *f* ... Num 2:16 2572
one thousand and four hundred and *f* ... Num 2:16 2572
were numbered of them, were *f* ... Num 2:30 2572
Dan were an hundred thousand and *f* ... Num 2:31 2572
thousand and five hundred and *f* ... Num 2:32 2572
and upward even until *f* years old ... Num 4:3 2572
upward until *f* years old shalt ... Num 4:23 2572
upward even unto *f* years old ... Num 4:30 2572
and upward even unto *f* years old ... Num 4:35 2572
two thousand seven hundred and *f* ... Num 4:36 2572
and upward even unto *f* years old ... Num 4:39 2572
and upward even unto *f* years old ... Num 4:43 2572
and upward even unto *f* years old ... Num 4:47 2572
from the age of *f* years they ... Num 8:25 2572
f princes of the assembly, famous ... Num 16:2 2572
censer, two hundred and *f* censers ... Num 16:17 2572
f men that offered incense ... Num 16:35 2572
devoured two hundred and *f* men ... Num 26:10 2572
that were numbered of them, *f* ... Num 26:34 2572
who were *f* and three thousand and ... Num 26:47 2572
thou shalt take one portion of *f* ... Num 31:30 2572
half, Moses took one portion of *f* ... Num 31:47 2572
seven hundred and *f* shekels ... Num 31:52 2572
father *f* shekels of silver ... Deut 22:29 2572
wedge of gold of *f* shekels weight ... Josh 7:21 2572
he smote of the people *f* thousand ... 1Sa 6:19 2572
and *f* men to run before him ... 2Sa 15:1 2572
the oxen for *f* shekels of silver ... 2Sa 24:24 2572
and *f* men to run before him ... 1Kin 1:5 2572
and the breadth thereof *f* cubits ... 1Kin 7:2 2572
the length thereof was *f* cubits ... 1Kin 7:6 2572
Solomon's work, five hundred and *f* ... 1Kin 9:23 2572
and an horse for an hundred and *f* ... 1Kin 10:29 2572
and hid them by *f* in a cave ... 1Kin 18:4 2572
Lord's prophets by *f* in a cave ... 1Kin 18:13 2572
of Baal four hundred and *f* ... 1Kin 18:19 2572
are four hundred and *f* men ... 1Kin 18:22 2572
him a captain of *f* with his *f* ... 2Kin 1:9 2572
and said to the captain of *f* ... 2Kin 1:10 2572
heaven, and consume thee and thy *f* ... 2Kin 1:10 2572
heaven, and consumed him and his *f* ... 2Kin 1:10 2572
captain of *f* with his *f* ... 2Kin 1:11 2572
heaven, and consume thee and thy *f* ... 2Kin 1:12 2572
heaven, and consumed him and his *f* ... 2Kin 1:12 2572
of the third *f* with his *f* ... 2Kin 1:13 2572
And the third captain of *f* went up ... 2Kin 1:13 2572
the life of these *f* thy servants ... 2Kin 1:13 2572
f men of the sons of the prophets ... 2Kin 2:7 2572
be with thy servants *f* strong men ... 2Kin 2:16 2572
They sent therefore *f* men ... 2Kin 2:17 2572
people to Jehoahaz but *f* horsemen ... 2Kin 13:7 2572
two and *f* years in Jerusalem ... 2Kin 15:2 2572
of each man *f* shekels of silver, ... 2Kin 15:20 2572
with him *f* men of the Gileadites ... 2Kin 15:25 2572
he began to reign, and reigned *f* ... 2Kin 21:1 2572
of their camels *f* thousand ... 1Chr 5:21 2572
f thousand, and of asses two ... 1Chr 5:21 2572
and sons' sons, an hundred and *f* ... 1Chr 8:40 2572
generations, nine hundred and *f* ... 1Chr 9:9 2572
f thousand, which could keep rank ... 1Chr 12:33 2572
and an horse for an hundred and *f* ... 2Chr 1:17 2572
f thousand and three thousand and ... 2Chr 2:17 2572
the nails was *f* shekels of gold ... 2Chr 3:9 2572
officers, even two hundred and *f* ... 2Chr 8:10 2572
f talents of gold, and brought ... 2Chr 8:18 2572
began to reign, and he reigned *f* ... 2Chr 26:3 2572
began to reign, and he reigned *f* ... 2Chr 33:1 2572
of Elam, a thousand two hundred *f* ... Ezr 2:7 2572
of Bigvai, two thousand *f* ... Ezr 2:14 2572
children of Adin, four hundred *f* ... Ezr 2:15 2572
The men of Netophah, *f* and six ... Ezr 2:22 2572
The children of Nebo, *f* and two ... Ezr 2:29 2572
children of Magbish, an hundred *f* ... Ezr 2:30 2572
Elam, a thousand two hundred *f* ... Ezr 2:31 2572
children of Immer, a thousand *f* ... Ezr 2:37 2572
children of Nekoda, six hundred *f* ... Ezr 2:60 2572
of the males an hundred and *f* ... Ezr 8:3 2572
of Jonathan, and with him *f* males ... Ezr 8:6 2572
f talents of silver, and silver ... Ezr 8:26 2572
f of the Jews and rulers, beside ... Neh 5:17 2572
fifth day of the month Elul, in *f* ... Neh 6:15 2572
children of Arah, six hundred *f* ... Neh 7:10 2572
of Elam, a thousand two hundred *f* ... Neh 7:12 2572
children of Adin, six hundred *f* ... Neh 7:20 2572
The men of the other Nebo, *f* ... Neh 7:33 2572
Elam, a thousand two hundred *f* ... Neh 7:34 2572
children of Immer, a thousand *f* ... Neh 7:40 2572
f basons, five hundred and thirty ... Neh 7:70 2572
gallows be made of *f* cubits high ... Est 5:14 2572
also, the gallows *f* cubits high ... Est 7:9 2572
The captain of *f*, and the ... Is 3:3 2572
of the inner gate were *f* cubits ... Eze 40:15 2572
the length thereof was *f* cubits ... Eze 40:21 2572
the length was *f* cubits, and the ... Eze 40:25 2572
it was *f* cubits long, and five and ... Eze 40:29 2572
it was *f* cubits long, and five and ... Eze 40:33 2572
the length was *f* cubits, and the ... Eze 40:36 2572
door, and the breadth was *f* cubits ... Eze 42:2 2572
the length thereof was *f* cubits ... Eze 42:7 2572
in the utter court was *f* cubits ... Eze 42:8 2572
f cubits round about for the ... Eze 45:2 2572
toward the north two hundred and *f* ... Eze 48:17 2572
toward the south two hundred and *f* ... Eze 48:17 2572
toward the east two hundred and *f* ... Eze 48:17 2572
toward the west two hundred and *f* ... Eze 48:17 2572
out *f* vessels out of the press ... Hag 2:16 2572
hundred pence, and the other *f* ... Lk 7:41 *4004*
and sit down quickly, and write *f* ... Lk 16:6 *4004*
him, Thou art not yet *f* years old ... Jn 8:57 *4004*
of great fishes, an hundred and *f* ... Jn 21:11 *4004*
f years, until Samuel the prophet ... Acts 13:20 *4004*
found it *f* thousand pieces of ... Acts 19:19 *4002*

FIG

they sewed *f* leaves together, and ... Gen 3:7 8384
and *f* trees, and pomegranates ... Deut 8:8 8384
And the trees said to the *f* tree ... Judg 9:10 8384
But the *f* tree said unto them, ... Judg 9:11 8384
his vine and under his *f* tree ... 1Kin 4:25 8384
vine, and every one of his *f* tree ... 2Kin 18:31 8384
their vines also and their *f* trees ... Ps 105:33 8384
Whoso keepeth the *f* tree shall ... Prov 27:18 8384
The *f* tree putteth forth her ... Song 2:13 8384
as a falling *f* from the *f* tree ... Is 34:4 8384
vine, and every one of his *f* tree ... Is 36:16 8384
eat up thy vines and thy *f* trees ... Jer 5:17 8384
the vine, nor figs on the *f* tree ... Jer 8:13 8384
her *f* trees, whereof she hath ... Hos 2:12 8384
in the *f* tree at her first time ... Hos 9:10 8384
vine waste, and barked my *f* tree ... Joel 1:7 8384
up, and the *f* tree languisheth ... Joel 1:12 8384
the *f* tree and the vine do yield ... Joel 2:22 8384
your *f* trees and your olive trees ... Amos 4:9 8384
his vine and under his *f* tree ... Mic 4:4 8384
f trees with the firstripe figs ... Nah 3:12 8384
Although the *f* tree shall not ... Hab 3:17 8384
the *f* tree, and the pomegranate, ... Hag 2:19 8384
the vine and under the *f* tree ... Zec 3:10 8384
when he saw a *f* tree in the way, ... Mt 21:19 *4808*
presently the *f* tree withered ... Mt 21:19 *4808*
How soon is the *f* tree withered ... Mt 21:20 *4808*
this which is done to the *f* tree ... Mt 21:21 *4808*
Now learn a parable of the *f* tree ... Mt 24:32 *4808*
seeing a *f* tree afar off having ... Mk 11:13 *4808*
they saw the *f* tree dried up from ... Mk 11:20 *4808*
the *f* tree which thou cursedst is ... Mk 11:21 *4808*
Now learn a parable of the *f* tree ... Mk 13:28 *4808*
A certain man had a *f* tree ... Lk 13:6 *4808*
come seeking fruit on this *f* tree ... Lk 13:7 *4808*
Behold the *f* tree, and all the ... Lk 21:29 *4808*
when thou wast under the *f* tree ... Jn 1:48 *4808*
thee, I saw thee under the *f* tree ... Jn 1:50 *4808*
Can the *f* tree, my brethren, bear ... Jas 3:12 *4808*
even as a *f* tree casteth her ... Rev 6:13 *4808*

FIGHT

f against us, and so get them up ... Ex 1:10 3898
The Lord shall *f* for you, and ye ... Ex 14:14 3898
out men, and go out, *f* with Amalek ... Ex 17:9 3898
before you, he shall *f* for you ... Deut 1:30 3898
the Lord, we will go up and *f* ... Deut 1:41 3898
unto them, Go not up, neither *f* ... Deut 1:42 3898
and all his people, to *f* at Jahaz ... Deut 2:32 4421
Lord your God he shall *f* for you ... Deut 3:22 3898
to *f* for you against your enemies ... Deut 20:4 3898
nigh unto a city to *f* against it ... Deut 20:10 3898
to *f* with Joshua and with Israel, ... Josh 9:2 3898
your enemies against whom ye *f* ... Josh 10:25 3898
of Merom, to *f* against Israel ... Josh 11:5 3898
Dan went up to *f* against Leshem ... Josh 19:47 3898
first, to *f* against them ... Judg 1:1 3898
that we may *f* against the ... Judg 1:3 3898
down to *f* against the Canaanites ... Judg 1:9 3898
wentest to *f* with the Midianites ... Judg 8:1 3898
out, I pray now, and *f* with them ... Judg 9:38 3898
Jordan to *f* also against Judah ... Judg 10:9 3898
man is he that will begin to *f* ... Judg 10:18 3898
that we may *f* with the children ... Judg 11:6 3898
f against the children of Ammon, ... Judg 11:8 3898
If ye bring me home again to *f* ... Judg 11:9 3898
come against me to *f* in my land ... Judg 11:12 3898
or did he ever *f* against them ... Judg 11:25 3898
of Ammon to *f* against them ... Judg 11:32 3898
f against the children of Ammon ... Judg 12:1 3898
unto me this day, to *f* against me ... Judg 12:3 3898
array to *f* against them at Gibeah ... Judg 20:20 4421
quit yourselves like men, and *f* ... 1Sa 4:9 3898
out before us, and *f* our battles ... 1Sa 8:20 3898
together to *f* with Israel ... 1Sa 13:5 3898

f against them until they be	1Sa 15:18	3898
If he be able to *f* with me	1Sa 17:9	3898
me a man, that we may *f* together	1Sa 17:10	3898
the host was going forth to the *f*	1Sa 17:20	4634
will go and *f* with this Philistine	1Sa 17:32	3898
this Philistine to *f* with him	1Sa 17:33	3898
for me, and *f* the LORD's battles	1Sa 18:17	3898
the Philistines *f* against Keilah	1Sa 23:1	3898
for warfare, to *f* with Israel	1Sa 28:1	3898
that I may not go *f* against the	1Sa 29:8	3898
nigh unto the city when ye did *f*	2Sa 11:20	3898
to *f* against the house of Israel,	1Kin 12:21	3898
nor *f* against your brethren the	1Kin 12:24	3898
but let us *f* against them in the	1Kin 20:23	3898
we will *f* against them in the	1Kin 20:25	3898
up to Aphek, to *f* against Israel	1Kin 20:26	4421
F neither with small nor great,	1Kin 22:31	3898
turned aside to *f* against him	1Kin 22:32	3898
were come up to *f* against them	2Kin 3:21	3898
f for your master's house	2Kin 10:3	3898
he is come out to *f* against thee	2Kin 19:9	3898
to *f* against Israel, that he	2Chr 11:1	3898
nor *f* against your brethren	2Chr 11:4	3898
f ye not against the LORD God of	2Chr 13:12	3898
F ye not with small or great,	2Chr 18:30	3898
they compassed about him to *f*	2Chr 18:31	3898
not need to *f* in this battle	2Chr 20:17	3898
purposed to *f* against Jerusalem	2Chr 32:2	4421
to help us, and to *f* our battles	2Chr 32:8	3898
up to *f* against Charchemish by	2Chr 35:20	3898
himself, that he might *f* with him	2Chr 35:22	3898
came to *f* in the valley of	2Chr 35:22	3898
to *f* against Jerusalem, and to	Neh 4:8	3898
f for your brethren, your sons,	Neh 4:14	3898
our God shall *f* for us	Neh 4:20	3898
f against them that *f* against	Ps 35:1	3898
they be many that *f* against me	Ps 56:2	3898
hands to war, and my fingers to *f*	Ps 144:1	4421
they shall *f* every one against	Is 19:2	3898
the nations that *f* against Ariel	Is 29:7	6633
even all that *f* against her	Is 29:7	6633
that *f* against mount Zion	Is 29:8	6633
of shaking will he *f* with it	Is 30:32	3898
come down to *f* for mount Zion	Is 31:4	6633
they shall *f* against thee	Jer 1:19	3898
they shall *f* against thee, but	Jer 15:20	3898
wherewith ye *f* against the king	Jer 21:4	3898
I myself will *f* against you with	Jer 21:5	3898
though ye *f* with the Chaldeans,	Jer 32:5	3898
that *f* against it, because of the	Jer 32:24	3898
that *f* against this city, shall	Jer 32:29	3898
They come to *f* with the Chaldeans	Jer 33:5	3898
and they shall *f* against it	Jer 34:22	3898
f against this city, and take it,	Jer 37:8	3898
the Chaldeans that *f* against you	Jer 37:10	3898
went to *f* with Ishmael the son of	Jer 41:12	3898
men of Babylon have forborn to *f*	Jer 51:30	3898
now will I return to *f* with the	Dan 10:20	3898
f with him, even with the king of	Dan 11:11	3898
and they shall *f*, because the LORD	Zec 10:5	3898
f against those nations, as when	Zec 14:3	3898
Judah also shall *f* at Jerusalem	Zec 14:14	3898
world, then would my servants *f*	Jn 18:36	*75*
ye be found even to *f* against God	Acts 5:39	*2314*
to him, let us not *f* against God	Acts 23:9	*2313*
so *f* I, not as one that beateth	1Cor 9:26	*4438*
F the good *f* of faith	1Ti 6:12	*73*
I have fought a good *f*, I have	2Ti 4:7	*75*
endured a great *f* of afflictions	Heb 10:32	*119*
made strong, waxed valiant in *f*	Heb 11:34	*4171*
ye *f* and war, yet ye have not,	Jas 4:2	*3164*
will *f* against them with the	Rev 2:16	*4170*

FIGHTETH

for the LORD *f* for them against	Ex 14:25	3898
your God, he it is that *f* for you	Josh 23:10	3898
because my lord *f* the battles of	1Sa 25:28	3898

FIGHTING

of Elah, *f* with the Philistines	1Sa 17:19	3898
Uzziah had an host of *f* men	2Chr 26:11	4421
he *f* daily oppresseth me	Ps 56:1	3898

FIGHTINGS

without were *f*, within were fears	2Cor 7:5	*3163*
whence come wars and *f* among you	Jas 4:1	*3163*

FIGS

of the pomegranates, and of the *f*	Num 13:23	8384
it is no place of seed, or of *f*	Num 20:5	8384
and two hundred cakes of *f*	1Sa 25:18	
gave him a piece of a cake of *f*	1Sa 30:12	
And Isaiah said, Take a lump of *f*	2Kin 20:7	8384
oxen, and meat, meal, cakes of *f*	1Chr 12:40	
as also wine, grapes, and *f*	Neh 13:15	8384
tree putteth forth her green *f*	Song 2:13	6291
said, Let them take a lump of *f*	Is 38:21	8384
nor *f* on the fig tree, and the	Jer 8:13	8384
two baskets of *f* were set before	Jer 24:1	8384
One basket had very good *f*	Jer 24:2	8384
even like the *f* that are first	Jer 24:2	8384
other basket had very naughty *f*	Jer 24:2	8384
And I said, *F*	Jer 24:3	8384
the good *f*, very good	Jer 24:3	8384
Like these good *f*, so will I	Jer 24:5	8384
And as the evil *f*, which cannot be	Jer 24:8	8384
and will make them like vile *f*	Jer 29:17	8384
fig trees with the firstripe *f*	Nah 3:12	
of thorns, or *f* of thistles	Mt 7:16	*4810*
for the time of *f* was not yet	Mk 11:13	*4810*
For of thorns men do not gather *f*	Lk 6:44	*4810*
either a vine, *f*?	Jas 3:12	*4810*
a fig tree casteth her untimely *f*	Rev 6:13	*3653*

FIGURE

image, the similitude of any *f*	Deut 4:16	5566
and maketh it after the *f* of a man	Is 44:13	8403
who is the *f* of him that was to	Rom 5:14	*5179*
I have in a *f* transferred to	1Cor 4:6	*3345*
Which was a *f* for the time then	Heb 9:9	*3850*
also he received him in a *f*	Heb 11:19	*3850*
The like *f* whereunto even baptism	1Pet 3:21	*499*

FIGURES

about with carved *f* of cherubims	1Kin 6:29	4734
f which ye made to worship them	Acts 7:43	*5179*
which are the *f* of the true	Heb 9:24	*499*

FILE

Yet they had a *f* for the mattocks	1Sa 13:21	6477

FILL

f the waters in the seas, and let	Gen 1:22	4390
to *f* their sacks with corn	Gen 42:25	4390
F the men's sacks with food, as	Gen 44:1	4390
And they shall *f* thy houses	Ex 10:6	4390
F an omer of it to be kept for	Ex 16:32	4393
her fruit, and ye shall eat your *f*	Lev 25:19	7648
thy *f* at thine own pleasure	Deut 23:24	7648
f thine horn with oil, and go, I	1Sa 16:1	4390
F four barrels with water, and	1Kin 18:33	4390
Till he *f* thy mouth with laughing	Job 8:21	4390
f his belly with the east wind	Job 15:2	4390
When he is about to *f* his belly	Job 20:23	4390
f my mouth with arguments	Job 23:4	4390
or *f* the appetite of the young	Job 38:39	4390
Canst thou *f* his skin with barbed	Job 41:7	4390
thy mouth wide, and I will *f* it	Ps 81:10	4390
F their faces with shame	Ps 83:16	4390
he shall *f* the places with the	Ps 110:6	4390
we shall *f* our houses with spoil	Prov 1:13	4390
let us take our *f* of love until	Prov 7:18	7301
and I will *f* their treasures	Prov 8:21	4390
out of his wings shall *f* the	Is 8:8	4393
nor *f* the face of the world with	Is 14:21	4390
f the face of the world with	Is 27:6	4390
we will *f* ourselves with strong	Is 56:12	4390
I will *f* all the inhabitants of	Jer 13:13	5433
Do not I *f* heaven and earth	Jer 23:24	4390
but it is to *f* them with the dead	Jer 33:5	4390
Surely I will *f* thee with men	Jer 51:14	4390
f thy bowels with this roll that	Eze 3:3	4390
souls, neither *f* their bowels	Eze 7:19	4390
f the courts with the slain	Eze 9:7	4390
f thine hand with coals of fire	Eze 10:2	4390
f it with the choice bones	Eze 24:4	4390
f the land with the slain	Eze 30:11	4390
I will *f* the beasts of the whole	Eze 32:4	7646
f the valleys with thy height	Eze 32:5	4390
I will *f* his mountains with his	Eze 35:8	4390
which *f* their masters' houses	Zeph 1:9	4390
I will *f* this house with glory,	Hag 2:7	4390
for that which is put in to *f* it	Mt 9:16	*4138*
as to *f* so great a multitude	Mt 15:33	*5526*
F ye up then the measure of your	Mt 23:32	*4137*
F the waterpots with water	Jn 2:7	*1072*
God of hope *f* you with all joy	Rom 15:13	*4137*
that he might *f* all things	Eph 4:10	*4137*
f up that which is behind of the	Col 1:24	*466*
saved, to *f* up their sins alway	1Th 2:16	*878*
she hath filled *f* to her double	Rev 18:6	*2767*

FILLED

and the earth was *f* with violence	Gen 6:11	4390
for the earth is *f* with violence	Gen 6:13	4390
f the bottle with water, and gave	Gen 21:19	4390
f her pitcher, and came up	Gen 24:16	4390
them, and *f* them with earth	Gen 26:15	4390
and the land was *f* with them	Ex 1:7	4390
f the troughs to water their	Ex 2:16	4390
morning ye shall be *f* with bread	Ex 16:12	7646
whom I have *f* with the spirit of	Ex 28:3	4390
I have *f* him with the spirit of	Ex 31:3	4390
he hath *f* him with the spirit of	Ex 35:31	4390
Them hath he *f* with wisdom of	Ex 35:35	4390
of the LORD *f* the tabernacle	Ex 40:34	4390
of the LORD *f* the tabernacle	Ex 40:35	4390
all the earth shall be *f* with the	Num 14:21	4390
may eat within thy gates, and be *f*	Deut 26:12	7646
f themselves, and waxen fat	Deut 31:20	7646
these bottles of wine, which we *f*	Josh 9:13	4390
and he was *f* with wisdom, and	1Kin 7:14	4390
that the cloud *f* the house of the	1Kin 8:10	4390
LORD had *f* the house of the LORD	1Kin 8:11	4390
he *f* the trench also with water	1Kin 18:35	4390
but the Syrians *f* the country	1Kin 20:27	4390
that valley shall be *f* with water	2Kin 3:17	4390
and the country was *f* with water	2Kin 3:20	4390
cast every man his stone, and *f* it	2Kin 3:25	4390
till he had *f* Jerusalem from one	2Kin 21:16	4390
f their places with the bones of	2Kin 23:14	4390
for he *f* Jerusalem with innocent	2Kin 24:4	4390
then the house was *f* with a cloud	2Chr 5:13	4390
the LORD had *f* the house of God	2Chr 5:14	4390
the glory of the LORD *f* the house	2Chr 7:1	4390
the LORD had *f* the LORD's house	2Chr 7:2	4390
bed which was *f* with sweet odours	2Chr 16:14	4390
which have *f* it from one end to	Ezr 9:11	4390
so they did eat, and were *f*	Neh 9:25	7646
who *f* their houses with silver	Job 3:15	4390
thou hast *f* me with wrinkles,	Job 16:8	7059
Yet he *f* their houses with good	Job 22:18	4390
For my loins are *f* with a	Ps 38:7	4390
Let my mouth be *f* with thy praise	Ps 71:8	4390
whole earth be *f* with his glory	Ps 72:19	4390
So they did eat, and were well *f*	Ps 78:29	7646
take deep root, and it *f* the land	Ps 80:9	4390
thine hand, they are *f* with good	Ps 104:28	7646
are exceedingly *f* with contempt	Ps 123:3	7646
Our soul is exceedingly *f* with	Ps 123:4	7646
was our mouth *f* with laughter	Ps 126:2	4390
be *f* with their own devices	Prov 1:31	7646
shall thy barns be *f* with plenty	Prov 3:10	4390
strangers be *f* with thy wealth	Prov 5:10	7646
wicked shall be *f* with mischief	Prov 12:21	4390
shall be *f* with his own ways	Prov 14:14	7646
of his lips shall he be *f*	Prov 18:20	7646
his mouth shall be *f* with gravel	Prov 20:17	4390
chambers be *f* with all precious	Prov 24:4	4390
thee, lest thou be *f* therewith	Prov 25:16	7646
earth that is not *f* with water	Prov 30:16	7646
and a fool when he is *f* with meat	Prov 30:22	7646
nor the ear *f* with hearing	Eccl 1:8	4390
and his soul be not *f* with good	Eccl 6:3	7646
and yet the appetite is not *f*	Eccl 6:7	4390
for my head is *f* with dew	Song 5:2	4390
up, and his train *f* the temple	Is 6:1	4390
and the house was *f* with smoke	Is 6:4	4390
are my loins *f* with pain	Is 21:3	4390
he hath *f* Zion with judgment and	Is 33:5	4390
sword of the LORD is *f* with blood	Is 34:6	4390
neither hast thou *f* me with the	Is 43:24	7301
old man that hath not *f* his days	Is 65:20	4390
Every bottle shall be *f* with wine	Jer 13:12	4390
every bottle shall be *f* with wine	Jer 13:12	4390
for thou hast *f* me with	Jer 15:17	4390
they have *f* mine inheritance with	Jer 16:18	4390
have *f* this place with the blood	Jer 19:4	4390
f it with them that were slain	Jer 41:9	4390
shame, and thy cry hath *f* the land	Jer 46:12	4390
though their land was *f* with sin	Jer 51:5	4390
he hath *f* his belly with my	Jer 51:34	4390
He hath *f* me with bitterness, he	Lam 3:15	7646
he is *f* full with reproach	Lam 3:30	7646
for they have *f* the land with	Eze 8:17	4390
the cloud *f* the inner court	Eze 10:3	4390
the house was *f* with the cloud,	Eze 10:4	4390
ye have *f* the streets thereof	Eze 11:6	4390
Thou shalt be *f* with drunkenness	Eze 23:33	4390
of thy merchandise they have *f*	Eze 28:16	4390
cities be *f* with flocks of men	Eze 36:38	4390
Thus ye shall be *f* at my table	Eze 39:20	7646
the glory of the LORD *f* the house	Eze 43:5	4390
the LORD *f* the house of the LORD	Eze 44:4	4390
mountain, and *f* the whole earth	Dan 2:35	4391
to their pasture, so were they *f*	Hos 13:6	7646
they were *f*, and their heart was	Hos 13:6	7646
f his holes with prey, and his	Nah 2:12	4390
For the earth shall be *f* with the	Hab 2:14	4390
Thou art *f* with shame for glory	Hab 2:16	7646
but ye are not *f* with drink	Hag 1:6	
f the bow with Ephraim, and raised	Zec 9:13	4390
and they shall be *f* like bowls	Zec 9:15	4390
for they shall be *f*	Mt 5:6	*5526*
And they did all eat, and were *f*	Mt 14:20	*5526*
And they did all eat, and were *f*	Mt 15:37	*5526*
f it with vinegar, and put it on a	Mt 27:48	*4130*
else the new piece that *f* it up	Mk 2:21	*4138*
And they did all eat, and were *f*	Mk 6:42	*5526*
her, Let the children first be *f*	Mk 7:27	*5526*
So they did eat, and were *f*	Mk 8:8	*5526*
f a spunge full of vinegar, and	Mk 15:36	*1072*
he shall be *f* with the Holy Ghost	Lk 1:15	*4130*
Elisabeth was *f* with the Holy	Lk 1:41	*4130*
He hath *f* the hungry with good	Lk 1:53	*1705*
was *f* with the Holy Ghost	Lk 1:67	*4130*
strong in spirit, *f* with wisdom	Lk 2:40	*4137*
Every valley shall be *f*, and every	Lk 3:5	*4137*
these things, were *f* with wrath,	Lk 4:28	*4130*
f both the ships, so that they	Lk 5:7	*4130*
were *f* with fear, saying, We have	Lk 5:26	*4130*
And they were *f* with madness	Lk 6:11	*4130*
for ye shall be *f*	Lk 6:21	*5526*
they were *f* with water, and were	Lk 8:23	*4845*
And they did eat, and were all *f*	Lk 9:17	*5526*
come in, that my house may be *f*	Lk 14:23	*1072*
he would fain have *f* his belly	Lk 15:16	*1072*
they *f* them up to the brim	Jn 2:7	*1072*
When they were *f*, he said unto	Jn 6:12	*1705*
f twelve baskets with the	Jn 6:13	*1072*
did eat of the loaves, and were *f*	Jn 6:26	*5526*
the house was *f* with the odour of	Jn 12:3	*4137*
you, sorrow hath *f* your heart	Jn 16:6	*4137*
they *f* a spunge with vinegar, and	Jn 19:29	*4130*
it *f* all the house where they	Acts 2:2	*4137*
they were all *f* with the Holy	Acts 2:4	*4130*
they were *f* with wonder and	Acts 3:10	*4130*
f with the Holy Ghost, said unto	Acts 4:8	*4130*
they were all *f* with the Holy	Acts 4:31	*4130*
why hath Satan *f* thine heart to	Acts 5:3	*4137*
and were *f* with indignation,	Acts 5:17	*4137*
ye have *f* Jerusalem with your	Acts 5:28	*4137*
and be *f* with the Holy Ghost	Acts 9:17	*4130*
f with the Holy Ghost, set his	Acts 13:9	*4130*
multitudes, they were *f* with envy	Acts 13:45	*4130*
And the disciples were *f* with joy	Acts 13:52	*4137*
whole city was *f* with confusion	Acts 19:29	*4130*
Being *f* with all unrighteousness,	Rom 1:29	*4137*
f with all knowledge, able also	Rom 15:14	*4137*
I be somewhat *f* with your company	Rom 15:24	*1705*
I am *f* with comfort, I am	2Cor 7:4	*4137*
that ye might be *f* with all the	Eph 3:19	*4137*
but be *f* with the Spirit	Eph 5:18	*4137*
Being *f* with the fruits of	Phil 1:11	*4137*
to desire that ye might be *f* with	Col 1:9	*4137*
tears, that I may be *f* with joy	2Ti 1:4	*4137*
in peace, be ye warmed and *f*	Jas 2:16	*5526*
f it with fire of the altar, and	Rev 8:5	*1072*
for in them is *f* up the wrath of	Rev 15:1	*5055*
the temple was *f* with smoke from	Rev 15:8	*1072*
she hath *f* fill to her double	Rev 18:6	*2767*
the fowls were *f* with their flesh	Rev 19:21	*5526*

FILLEDST
all good things, which thou *f* not .... Deut 6:11 4390
of the seas, thou *f* many people .... Eze 27:33 7646

FILLEST
whose belly thou *f* with thy hid .... Ps 17:14 4390

FILLET
a *f* of twelve cubits did compass .... Jer 52:21 2339

FILLETED
the court shall be *f* with silver .... Ex 27:17 2836
of the court were *f* with silver .... Ex 38:17 2836
their chapiters, and *f* them .... Ex 38:28 2836

FILLETH
breath, but *f* me with bitterness .... Job 9:18 7646
the rain also *f* the pools .... Ps 84:6 5844
f the hungry soul with goodness .... Ps 107:9 4390
the mower *f* not his hand .... Ps 129:7 4390
f thee with the finest of the .... Ps 147:14 7646
fulness of him that *f* all in all .... Eph 1:23 *4131*

FILLETS
their *f* shall be of silver .... Ex 27:10 2838
the pillars and their *f* of silver .... Ex 27:11 2838
chapiters and their *f* with gold .... Ex 36:38 2838
pillars and their *f* were of silver .... Ex 38:10 2838
the pillars and their *f* of silver .... Ex 38:11 2838
the pillars and their *f* of silver .... Ex 38:12 2838
the pillars and their *f* of silver .... Ex 38:17 2838
chapiters and their *f* of silver .... Ex 38:19 2838

FILLING
f our hearts with food and .... Acts 14:17 *1705*

FILTH
the *f* of the daughters of Zion .... Is 4:4 6675
will cast abominable *f* upon thee .... Nah 3:6
we are made as the *f* of the world 1Cor 4:13 *4027*
away of the *f* of the flesh 1Pet 3:21 4509

FILTHINESS
carry forth the *f* out of the holy 2Chr 29:5 5079
the *f* of the heathen of the land .... Ezr 6:21 2932
the *f* of the people of the lands .... Ezr 9:11 5079
and yet is not washed from their *f* .... Prov 30:12 6675
all tables are full of vomit and *f* .... Is 28:8 6675
Her *f* is in her skirts .... Lam 1:9 2932
Because thy *f* was poured out, and .... Eze 16:36 5178
and will consume thy *f* out of thee .... Eze 22:15 2932
that the *f* of it may be molten in .... Eze 24:11 2932
In thy *f* is lewdness .... Eze 24:13 2932
not be purged from thy *f* any more .... Eze 24:13 2932
from all your *f*, and from all your .... Eze 36:25 2932
ourselves from all *f* of the flesh 2Cor 7:1 *3436*
Neither *f*, nor foolish talking, ... Eph 5:4 *151*
Wherefore lay apart all *f* .... Jas 1:21 *4507*
and *f* of her fornication .... Rev 17:4 *168*

FILTHY
f is man, which drinketh iniquity .... Job 15:16 444
they are all together become *f* .... Ps 14:3 444
they are altogether become *f* .... Ps 53:3 444
our righteousnesses are as *f* rags .... Is 64:6 5708
Woe to her that is *f* and polluted, ... Zeph 3:1 4754
was clothed with *f* garments .... Zec 3:3 6674
Take away the *f* garments from him .... Zec 3:4 6674
f communication out of your mouth .... Col 3:8 *148*
no striker, not greedy of *f* lucre 1Ti 3:3
much wine, not greedy of *f* lucre 1Ti 3:8
no striker, not given to *f* lucre .... Titus 1:7 *150*
ought not, for *f* lucre's sake .... Titus 1:11 *150*
not for *f* lucre, but of a ready 1Pet 5:2 *147*
vexed with the *f* conversation of 2Pet 2:7 *766*
Likewise also these *f* dreamers .... Jude 8
and he which is *f*, let him be .... Rev 22:11 *4510*
let him be *f* still .... Rev 22:11 *4510*

FINALLY
F, brethren, farewell 2Cor 13:11 *3063*
F, my brethren, be strong in the .... Eph 6:10 *3063*
F, my brethren, rejoice in the .... Phil 3:1 *3063*
F, brethren, whatsoever things .... Phil 4:8 *3063*
F, brethren, pray for us, that 2Th 3:1 *3063*
F, be ye all of one mind, having 1Pet 3:8 *5056*

FIND
If I *f* in Sodom fifty righteous .... Gen 18:26 4672
If I *f* there forty and five, I .... Gen 18:28 4672
not do it, if I *f* thirty there .... Gen 18:30 4672
wearied themselves to *f* the door .... Gen 19:11 4672
that I may *f* grace in thy sight .... Gen 32:5 4672
ye speak unto Esau, when ye *f* him .... Gen 32:19 4672
These are to *f* grace in the sight .... Gen 33:8 4672
let me *f* grace in the sight of my .... Gen 33:15 4672
Let me *f* grace in your eyes, and .... Gen 34:11 4672
to Judah, and said, I cannot *f* her .... Gen 38:22 4672
Can we *f* such a one as this is, a .... Gen 41:38 4672
let us *f* grace in the sight of my .... Gen 47:25 4672
get you straw where ye can *f* it .... Ex 5:11 4672
ye shall not *f* it in the field .... Ex 16:25 4672
that I may *f* grace in thy sight .... Ex 33:13 4672
be sure your sin will *f* you out .... Num 32:23 4672
the revenger of blood *f* him .... Num 35:27 4672
LORD thy God, thou shalt *f* him .... Deut 4:29 4672
a man *f* her in the city, and lie .... Deut 22:23 4672
But if a man *f* a betrothed damsel .... Deut 22:25 4672
If a man *f* a damsel that is a .... Deut 22:28 4672
that she *f* no favour in his eyes .... Deut 24:1 4672
nations shalt thou *f* no ease .... Deut 28:65
to them as thou shalt *f* occasion .... Judg 9:33 4672
f it out, then I will give you .... Judg 14:12 4672
sojourn where he could *f* a place .... Judg 17:8 4672
to sojourn where I may *f* a place .... Judg 17:9 4672
LORD grant you that ye may *f* rest .... Ruth 1:9 4672
in whose sight I shall *f* grace .... Ruth 2:2 4672
Let me *f* favour in thy sight, my .... Ruth 2:13 4672
handmaid *f* grace in thy sight 1Sa 1:18 4672
city, ye shall straightway *f* him 1Sa 9:13 4672
about this time ye shall *f* him 1Sa 9:13 4672
then thou shalt *f* two men by 1Sa 10:2 4672
lad, saying, Go, *f* out the arrows 1Sa 20:21 4672
f out now the arrows which I 1Sa 20:36 4672
Saul my father shall not *f* thee 1Sa 23:17 4672
For if a man *f* his enemy, will he 1Sa 24:19 4672
young men *f* favour in thine eyes 1Sa 25:8 4672
if I shall *f* favour in the eyes 2Sa 15:25 4672
that I may *f* grace in thy sight 2Sa 16:4 4672
had sought and could not *f* them 2Sa 17:20 4672
peradventure we may *f* grass to 1Kin 18:5 4672
and tell Ahab, and he cannot *f* thee 1Kin 18:12 4672
to *f* out every device which shall 2Chr 2:14 2803
ye shall *f* them at the end of the 2Chr 20:16 4672
your children shall *f* compassion 2Chr 30:9
of Assyria come, and *f* much water 2Chr 32:4 4672
so shalt thou *f* in the book of .... Ezr 4:15 7912
gold that thou canst *f* in all the .... Ezr 7:16 7912
glad, when they can *f* the grave .... Job 3:22 4672
Canst thou by searching *f* out God .... Job 11:7 4672
canst thou *f* out the Almighty .... Job 11:7 4672
for I cannot *f* one wise man among .... Job 17:10 4672
that I knew where I might *f* him .... Job 23:3 4672
cause every man to *f* according to .... Job 34:11 4672
the Almighty, we cannot *f* him out .... Job 37:23 4672
his wickedness till thou *f* none .... Ps 10:15 4672
hast tried me, and shalt *f* nothing .... Ps 17:3 4672
Thine hand shall *f* out all thine .... Ps 21:8 4672
thy right hand shall *f* out those .... Ps 21:8 4672
Until I *f* out a place for the .... Ps 132:5 4672
We shall *f* all precious substance .... Prov 1:13 4672
me early, but they shall not *f* me .... Prov 1:28 4672
LORD, and *f* the knowledge of God .... Prov 2:5 4672
So shalt thou *f* favour and good .... Prov 3:4 4672
are life unto those that *f* them .... Prov 4:22 4672
and right to them that *f* knowledge .... Prov 8:9 4672
and *f* out knowledge of witty .... Prov 8:12 4672
that seek me early shall *f* me .... Prov 8:17 4672
a matter wisely shall *f* good .... Prov 16:20 4672
understanding shall *f* good .... Prov 19:8 4672
but a faithful man who can *f* .... Prov 20:6 4672
shall *f* more favour than he that .... Prov 28:23 4672
Who can *f* a virtuous woman .... Prov 31:10 4672
so that no man can *f* out the work .... Eccl 3:11 4672
man should *f* nothing after him .... Eccl 7:14 4672
exceeding deep, who can *f* it out .... Eccl 7:24 4672
I *f* more bitter than death the .... Eccl 7:26 4672
one by one, to *f* out the account .... Eccl 7:27 4672
yet my soul seeketh, but I *f* not .... Eccl 7:28 4672
that a man cannot *f* out the work .... Eccl 8:17 4672
it out, yet he shall not *f* it .... Eccl 8:17 4672
yet shall he not be able to *f* it .... Eccl 8:17 4672
for thou shalt *f* it after many .... Eccl 11:1 4672
sought to *f* out acceptable words .... Eccl 12:10 4672
sought him, but I could not *f* him .... Song 5:6 4672
if ye *f* my beloved, that ye tell .... Song 5:8 4672
when I should *f* thee without .... Song 8:1 4672
f for herself a place of rest .... Is 34:14 4672
seek them, and shalt not *f* them .... Is 41:12 4672
day of your fast ye *f* pleasure .... Is 58:3 4672
in her month they shall *f* her .... Jer 2:24 4672
places thereof, if ye can *f* a man .... Jer 5:1 4672
ye shall *f* rest for your souls .... Jer 6:16 4672
them, that they may *f* it so .... Jer 10:18 4672
f me, when ye shall search for me .... Jer 29:13 4672
in my sighing, and I *f* no rest .... Jer 45:3 4672
like harts that *f* no pasture .... Lam 1:6 4672
her prophets also *f* no vision .... Lam 2:9 4672
princes sought to *f* occasion .... Dan 6:4 7912
but they could *f* none occasion .... Dan 6:4 7912
We shall not *f* any occasion .... Dan 6:5 7912
except we *f* it against him .... Dan 6:5 7912
that she shall not *f* her paths .... Hos 2:6 4672
seek them, but shall not *f* them .... Hos 2:7 4672
but they shall not *f* him .... Hos 5:6 4672
in all my labours they shall *f* .... Hos 12:8 4672
of the LORD, and shall not *f* it .... Amos 8:12 4672
seek, and ye shall *f* .... Mt 7:7 *2147*
life, and few there be that *f* it .... Mt 7:14 *2147*
his life for my sake shall *f* it .... Mt 10:39 *2147*
ye shall *f* rest unto your souls .... Mt 11:29 *2147*
his life for my sake shall *f* it .... Mt 16:25 *2147*
thou shalt *f* a piece of money .... Mt 17:27 *2147*
And if so be that he *f* it, verily .... Mt 18:13 *2147*
ye shall *f* an ass tied, and a colt .... Mt 21:2 *2147*
and as many as ye shall *f* .... Mt 22:9 *2147*
when he cometh shall *f* so doing .... Mt 24:46 *2147*
ye shall *f* a colt tied, whereon .... Mk 11:2 *2147*
he might *f* any thing thereon .... Mk 11:13 *2147*
coming suddenly he *f* you sleeping .... Mk 13:36 *2147*
Ye shall *f* the babe wrapped in .... Lk 2:12 *2147*
when they could not *f* by what way .... Lk 5:19 *2147*
that they might *f* an accusation .... Lk 6:7 *2147*
seek, and ye shall *f* .... Lk 11:9 *2147*
when he cometh shall *f* watching .... Lk 12:37 *2147*
f them so, blessed are those .... Lk 12:38 *2147*
when he cometh shall *f* so doing .... Lk 12:43 *2147*
fruit on this fig tree, and *f* none .... Lk 13:7 *2147*
that which is lost, until he *f* it .... Lk 15:4 *2147*
and seek diligently till she *f* it .... Lk 15:8 *2147*
shall he *f* faith on the earth .... Lk 18:8 *2147*
entering ye shall *f* a colt tied .... Lk 19:30 *2147*
could not *f* what they might do .... Lk 19:48 *2147*
people, I *f* no fault in this man .... Lk 23:4 *2147*
shall seek me, and shall not *f* me .... Jn 7:34 *2147*
he go, that we shall not *f* him .... Jn 7:35 *2147*
shall seek me, and shall not *f* me .... Jn 7:36 *2147*
shall go in and out, and *f* pasture .... Jn 10:9 *2147*
I *f* in him no fault at all .... Jn 18:38 *2147*
may know that I *f* no fault in him .... Jn 19:4 *2147*
for I *f* no fault in him .... Jn 19:6 *2147*
side of the ship, and ye shall *f* .... Jn 21:6 *2147*
desired to *f* a tabernacle for the .... Acts 7:46 *2147*
f him, though he be not far from .... Acts 17:27 *2147*
saying, We *f* no evil in this man .... Acts 23:9 *2147*
that which is good I *f* not .... Rom 7:18 *2147*
I *f* then a law, that, when I .... Rom 7:21 *2147*
unto me, Why doth he yet *f* fault .... Rom 9:19
f you unprepared, we (that we say 2Cor 9:4 *2147*
I shall not *f* you such as I would 2Cor 12:20 *2147*
f mercy of the Lord in that day 2Ti 1:18 *2147*
f grace to help in time of need .... Heb 4:16 *2147*
men seek death, and shall not *f* it .... Rev 9:6 *2147*
thou shalt *f* them no more at all .... Rev 18:14 *2147*

FINDEST
With whomsoever thou *f* thy gods .... Gen 31:32 4672
me, Son of man, eat that thou *f* .... Eze 3:1 4672

FINDETH
every one that *f* me shall slay me .... Gen 4:14 4672
he *f* occasions against me, he .... Job 33:10 4672
word, as one that *f* great spoil .... Ps 119:162 4672
Happy is the man that *f* wisdom .... Prov 3:13 4672
For whoso *f* me *f* life .... Prov 8:35 4672
seeketh wisdom, and *f* it not .... Prov 14:6 4672
hath a froward heart *f* no good .... Prov 17:20 4672
Whoso *f* a wife *f* a good .... Prov 18:22 4672
his neighbour *f* no favour in his .... Prov 21:10
righteousness and mercy *f* life .... Prov 21:21 4672
Whatsoever thy hand *f* to do .... Eccl 9:10 4672
among the heathen, she *f* no rest .... Lam 1:3 4672
in thee the fatherless *f* mercy .... Hos 14:3
and he that seeketh *f* .... Mt 7:8 *2147*
He that *f* his life shall lose it .... Mt 10:39 *2147*
places, seeking rest, and *f* none .... Mt 12:43 *2147*
is come, he *f* it empty, swept, and .... Mt 12:44 *2147*
f them asleep, and saith unto .... Mt 26:40 *2147*
f them sleeping, and saith unto .... Mk 14:37 *2147*
and he that seeketh *f* .... Lk 11:10 *2147*
he *f* it swept and garnished .... Lk 11:25 *2147*
He first *f* his own brother Simon, ... Jn 1:41 *2147*
f Philip, and saith unto him, ... Jn 1:43 *2147*
Philip *f* Nathanael, and saith unto .... Jn 1:45 *2147*
Afterward Jesus *f* him in the .... Jn 5:14 *2147*

FINDING
lest any *f* him should kill him .... Gen 4:15 4672
doeth great things past *f* out .... Job 9:10 2714
nor *f* thine own pleasure, nor .... Is 58:13 4672
f none, he saith, I will return .... Lk 11:24 *2147*
f nothing how they might punish .... Acts 4:21 *2147*
and *f* certain disciples, ... Acts 19:1 *2147*
f a ship sailing over unto .... Acts 21:2 *2147*
f disciples, we tarried there .... Acts 21:4 *429*
judgments, and his ways past *f* out .... Rom 11:33 *421*
For *f* fault with them, he saith, ... Heb 8:8

FINE
quickly three measures of *f* meal .... Gen 18:6
him in vestures of *f* linen .... Gen 41:42
and *f* linen, and goats' hair, ... Ex 25:4
ten curtains of *f* twined linen .... Ex 26:1
f twined linen of cunning work .... Ex 26:31
f twined linen, wrought with .... Ex 26:36
of *f* twined linen of an hundred .... Ex 27:9
f twined linen, wrought with .... Ex 27:16
five cubits of *f* twined linen .... Ex 27:18
and purple, and scarlet, and *f* linen .... Ex 28:5
f twined linen, with cunning work .... Ex 28:6
and scarlet, and *f* twined linen .... Ex 28:8
of *f* twined linen, shalt thou .... Ex 28:15
embroider the coat of *f* linen .... Ex 28:39
shalt make the mitre of *f* linen .... Ex 28:39
and *f* linen, and goats' hair, ... Ex 35:6
f linen, and goats' hair, and red .... Ex 35:23
and of scarlet, and of *f* linen .... Ex 35:25
in *f* linen, and of the weaver, ... Ex 35:35
ten curtains of *f* twined linen .... Ex 36:8
and scarlet, and *f* twined linen .... Ex 36:35
f twined linen, of needlework .... Ex 36:37
the court were of *f* twined linen .... Ex 38:9
about were of *f* twined linen .... Ex 38:16
and scarlet, and *f* twined linen .... Ex 38:18
purple, and in scarlet, and *f* linen .... Ex 38:23
and scarlet, and *f* twined linen .... Ex 39:2
in the scarlet, and in the *f* linen .... Ex 39:3
and scarlet, and *f* twined linen .... Ex 39:5
and scarlet, and *f* twined linen .... Ex 39:8
they made coats of *f* linen of .... Ex 39:27
And a mitre of *f* linen .... Ex 39:28
and goodly bonnets of *f* linen .... Ex 39:28
linen breeches of *f* twined linen .... Ex 39:28
a girdle of *f* twined linen, and .... Ex 39:29
his offering shall be of *f* flour .... Lev 2:1
cakes of *f* flour mingled with oil .... Lev 2:4
it shall be of *f* flour unleavened .... Lev 2:5
shall be made of *f* flour with oil .... Lev 2:7
of *f* flour for a sin offering .... Lev 5:11
of *f* flour for a meat offering .... Lev 6:20
with oil, of *f* flour, fried .... Lev 7:12
three tenth deals of *f* flour for .... Lev 14:10
one tenth deal of *f* flour mingled .... Lev 14:21
deals of *f* flour mingled with oil .... Lev 23:13
they shall be of *f* flour .... Lev 23:17
And thou shalt take *f* flour .... Lev 24:5
cakes of *f* flour mingled with oil .... Num 6:15
both of them were full of *f* flour .... Num 7:13
both of them full of *f* flour .... Num 7:19
both of them full of *f* flour .... Num 7:25
both of them full of *f* flour .... Num 7:31
both of them full of *f* flour .... Num 7:37
both of them full of *f* flour .... Num 7:43
both of them full of *f* flour .... Num 7:49
both of them full of *f* flour .... Num 7:55
both of them full of *f* flour .... Num 7:61
both of them full of *f* flour .... Num 7:67
both of them full of *f* flour .... Num 7:73
both of them full of *f* flour .... Num 7:79

even f flour mingled with oil, and Num 8:8
was thirty measures of f flour 1Kin 4:22
of f flour be sold for a shekel 2Kin 7:1
So a measure of f flour was sold 2Kin 7:16
a measure of f flour for a shekel 2Kin 7:18
of them that wrought f linen 1Chr 4:21
the f flour, and the wine, and the 1Chr 9:29
clothed with a robe of f linen 1Chr 15:27
for the f flour for meat offering 1Chr 23:29
in f linen, and in crimson 2Chr 2:14
which he overlaid with f gold 2Chr 3:5 2896
and he overlaid it with f gold 2Chr 3:8 2896
f linen, and wrought cherubims 2Chr 3:14
and two vessels of f copper Ezr 8:27 6668
fastened with cords of f linen Est 1:6
and with a garment of f linen Est 8:15
a place for gold where they f it Job 28:1 2212
shall not be for jewels of f gold Job 28:17
hope, or have said to the f gold Job 31:24
than gold, yea, than much f gold Ps 19:10
yea, above f gold Ps 119:127
and the gain thereof than f gold Prov 3:14
works, with f linen of Egypt Prov 7:16
than gold, yea, than f gold Prov 8:19
of gold, and an ornament of f gold Prov 25:12
She maketh f linen, and selleth it Prov 31:24
His head is as the most f gold Song 5:11
set upon sockets of f gold Song 5:15
the f linen, and the hoods, and the Is 3:23
a man more precious than f gold Is 13:12
Moreover they that work in f flax Is 19:9 8305
how is the most f gold changed Lam 4:1
of Zion, comparable to f gold Lam 4:2
I girded thee about with f linen Eze 16:10
and thy raiment was of f linen Eze 16:13
thou didst eat f flour, and honey, Eze 16:13
f flour, and oil, and honey, Eze 16:19
F linen with broidered work from Eze 27:7
f linen, and coral, and agate Eze 27:16
oil, to temper with the f flour Eze 46:14
This image's head was of f gold Dan 2:32 2869
were girded with f gold of Uphaz Dan 10:5
f gold as the mire of the streets Zec 9:3
And he bought f linen, and took him Mk 15:46
f linen, and fared sumptuously Lk 16:19
And his feet like unto f brass Rev 1:15
and his feet are like f brass Rev 2:18
f linen, and purple, and silk, and Rev 18:12
f flour, and wheat, and beasts, and Rev 18:13 4585
city, that was clothed in f linen Rev 18:16
she should be arrayed in f linen Rev 19:8
for the f linen is the Rev 19:8
white horses, clothed in f linen Rev 19:14

FINER
come forth a vessel for the f Prov 25:4 6884

FINEST
them also with the f of the wheat Ps 81:16 2459
thee with the f of the wheat Ps 147:14 2459

FINGER
Pharaoh, This is the f of God Ex 8:19 676
the horns of the altar with thy f Ex 29:12 676
stone, written with the f of God Ex 31:18 676
shall dip his f in the blood Lev 4:6 676
dip his f in some of the blood Lev 4:17 676
of the sin offering with his f Lev 4:25 676
of the blood thereof with his f Lev 4:30 676
of the sin offering with his f Lev 4:34 676
the altar round about with his f Lev 8:15 676
and he dipped his f in the blood Lev 9:9 676
f in the oil that is in his left Lev 14:16 676
his f seven times before the LORD Lev 14:16 676
shall sprinkle with his right f Lev 14:27 676
sprinkle it with his f upon the Lev 16:14 676
the blood with his f seven times Lev 16:14 676
upon it with his f seven times Lev 16:19 676
take of her blood with his f Num 19:4 676
stone written with the f of God Deut 9:10 676
My little f shall be thicker than 1Kin 12:10
My little f shall be thicker than 2Chr 10:10
yoke, the putting forth of the f Is 58:9 676
But if I with the f of God cast Lk 11:20 1147
may dip the tip of his f in water Lk 16:24 1147
with his f wrote on the ground, Jn 8:6 1147
put my f into the print of the Jn 20:25 1147
he to Thomas, Reach hither thy f Jn 20:27 1147

FINGERS
that had on every hand six f 2Sa 21:20 676
a man of great stature, whose f 1Chr 20:6 676
thy heavens, the work of thy f Ps 8:3 676
my hands to war, and my f to fight Ps 144:1 676
his feet, he teacheth with his f Prov 6:13 676
Bind them upon thy f, write them Prov 7:3 676
my f with sweet smelling myrrh, Song 5:5 676
that which their own f have made Is 2:8 676
that which his f have made Is 17:8 676
blood, and your f with iniquity Is 59:3 676
the thickness thereof was four f Jer 52:21 676
hour came forth f of a man's hand Dan 5:5 677
not move them with one of their f Mt 23:4 1147
put his f into his ears, and he Mk 7:33 1147
the burdens with one of your f Lk 11:46 1147

FINING
The f pot is for silver, and the Prov 17:3 4715
As the f pot for silver, and the Prov 27:21 4715

FINISH
in a cubit shalt thou f it above Gen 6:16 3615
to f the transgression, and to Dan 9:24 3607
his hands shall also f it Zec 4:9 1214
he have sufficient to f it Lk 14:28 535
and is not able to f it, all that Lk 14:29 1615
to build, and was not able to f Lk 14:30 1615
that sent me, and to f his work Jn 4:34 5048
the Father hath given me to f Jn 5:36 5048
so that I might f my course with Acts 20:24 5048
For he will f the work, and cut it Rom 9:28 4931
so he would also f in you the 2Cor 8:6 2005

FINISHED
the heavens and the earth were f Gen 2:1 3615
of the tent of the congregation f Ex 39:32 3615
So Moses f the work Ex 40:33 3615
law in a book, until they were f Deut 31:24 8552
until every thing was f that the Josh 4:10 8552
until he have f the thing this Ruth 3:18 3615
So he built the house, and f it 1Kin 6:9 3615
Solomon built the house, and f it 1Kin 6:14 3615
until he had f all the house 1Kin 6:22 8552
was the house f throughout all 1Kin 6:38 3615
years, and he f all his house 1Kin 7:1 3615
so was the work of the pillars f 1Kin 7:22 8552
when Solomon had f the building 1Kin 9:1 3615
So he f the house 1Kin 9:25 7999
began to number, but he f not 1Chr 27:24 3615
until thou hast f all the work 1Chr 28:20 3615
Huram f the work that he was to 2Chr 4:11 3615
for the house of the LORD was f 2Chr 5:1 7999
Thus Solomon f the house of the 2Chr 7:11 3615
of the LORD, and until it was f 2Chr 8:16 3615
And when they had f it, they 2Chr 24:14 3615
until the burnt offering was f 2Chr 29:28 3615
Now when all this was f, all 2Chr 31:1 3615
f them in the seventh month 2Chr 31:7 3615
in building, and yet it is not f Ezr 5:16 8000
and f it, according to the Ezr 6:14 3635
this house was f on the third day Ezr 6:15 3319
So the wall was f in the twenty Neh 6:15 7999
numbered thy kingdom, and f it Dan 5:26 8000
all these things shall be f Dan 12:7 3615
when Jesus had f these parables Mt 13:53 5055
when Jesus had f these sayings Mt 19:1 5055
when Jesus had f all these Mt 26:1 5055
I have f the work which thou Jn 17:4 5048
the vinegar, he said, It is f Jn 19:30 5055
when we had f our course from Acts 21:7 1274
I have f my course, I have kept 2Ti 4:7 5055
although the works were f from Heb 4:3 1096
and sin, when it is f, bringeth Jas 1:15 658
the mystery of God should be f Rev 10:7 5055
they shall have f their testimony Rev 11:7 5055
until the thousand years were f Rev 20:5 5055

FINISHER
the author and f of our faith Heb 12:2 5047

FINS
whatsoever hath f and scales in Lev 11:9 5579
And all that have not f and scales Lev 11:10 5579
Whatsoever hath no f nor scales Lev 11:12 5579
all that have f and scales shall Deut 14:9 5579
And whatsoever hath not f and Deut 14:10 5579

FIR
of instruments made of f wood 2Sa 6:5 1265
cedar, and concerning timber of f 1Kin 5:8 1265
f trees according to all his 1Kin 5:10 1265
of the house with planks of f 1Kin 6:15 1265
And the two doors were of f tree 1Kin 6:34 1265
f trees, and with gold, according 1Kin 9:11 1265
the choice f trees thereof 2Kin 19:23 1265
f trees, and algum trees, out of 2Chr 2:8 1265
house he cieled with f tree 2Chr 3:5 1265
the f trees are her house Ps 104:17 1265
are cedar, and our rafters of f Song 1:17 1266
the f trees rejoice at thee, and Is 14:8 1265
the choice f trees thereof Is 37:24 1265
will set in the desert the f tree Is 41:19 1265
thorn shall come up the f tree Is 55:13 1265
the f tree, the pine tree, and the Is 60:13 1265
ship boards of f trees of Senir Eze 27:5 1265
the f trees were not like his Eze 31:8 1265
I am like a green f tree Hos 14:8 1265
the f trees shall be terribly Nah 2:3 1265
Howl, f tree Zec 11:2 1265

FIRE
f from the LORD out of heaven Gen 19:24 784
and he took the f in his hand Gen 22:6 784
And he said, Behold the f and the Gen 22:7 784
of f out of the midst of a bush Ex 3:2 784
behold, the bush burned with f Ex 3:2 784
the f ran along upon the ground Ex 9:23 784
f mingled with the hail, very Ex 9:24 784
flesh in that night, roast with f Ex 12:8 784
all with water, but roast with f Ex 12:9 784
the morning ye shall burn with f Ex 12:10 784
and by night in a pillar of f Ex 13:21 784
day, nor the pillar of f by night Ex 13:22 784
Egyptians through the pillar of f Ex 14:24 784
the LORD descended upon it in f Ex 19:18 784
If f break out, and catch in Ex 22:6 784
he that kindled the f shall Ex 22:6 1200
f on the top of the mount in the Ex 24:17 784
thou burn with f without the camp Ex 29:14 784
offering made by f unto the LORD Ex 29:18
offering made by f unto the LORD Ex 29:25
shalt burn the remainder with f Ex 29:34 784
offering made by f unto the LORD Ex 29:41
offering made by f unto the LORD Ex 30:20
had made, and burnt it in the f Ex 32:20 784
then I cast it into the f Ex 32:24 784
Ye shall kindle no f throughout Ex 35:3 784
f was on it by night, in the Ex 40:38 784
priest shall put f upon the altar Lev 1:7 784
lay the wood in order upon the f Lev 1:7 784
on the f which is upon the altar Lev 1:8 784
sacrifice, an offering made by f Lev 1:9
on the f which is upon the altar Lev 1:12 784
sacrifice, an offering made by f Lev 1:13
upon the wood that is upon the f Lev 1:17 784
sacrifice, an offering made by f Lev 1:17
to be an offering made by f Lev 2:2
offerings of the LORD made by f Lev 2:3
it is an offering made by f Lev 2:9
offerings of the LORD made by f Lev 2:10
offering of the LORD made by f Lev 2:11
green ears of corn dried by the f Lev 2:14 784
offering made by f unto the LORD Lev 2:16
offering made by f unto the LORD Lev 3:3
is upon the wood that is on the f Lev 3:5 784
it is an offering made by f Lev 3:5
offering made by f unto the LORD Lev 3:9
offering made by f unto the LORD Lev 3:11
offering made by f unto the LORD Lev 3:14
made by f for a sweet savour Lev 3:16
and burn him on the wood with f Lev 4:12 784
offerings made by f unto the LORD Lev 4:35
offerings made by f unto the LORD Lev 5:12
the f of the altar shall be Lev 6:9 784
take up the ashes which the f Lev 6:10 784
the f upon the altar shall be Lev 6:12 784
The f shall ever be burning upon Lev 6:13 784
portion of my offerings made by f Lev 6:17
offerings of the LORD made by f Lev 6:18
it shall be burnt in the f Lev 6:30 784
offering made by f unto the LORD Lev 7:5
third day shall be burnt with f Lev 7:17 784
it shall be burnt with f Lev 7:19 784
offering made by f unto the LORD Lev 7:25
offerings of the LORD made by f Lev 7:30
offerings of the LORD made by f Lev 7:35
he burnt with f without the camp Lev 8:17 784
offering made by f unto the LORD Lev 8:21
offering made by f unto the LORD Lev 8:28
of the bread shall ye burn with f Lev 8:32 784
he burnt with f without the camp Lev 9:11 784
there came a f out from before Lev 9:24 784
put f therein, and put incense Lev 10:1 784
offered strange f before the LORD Lev 10:1 784
And there went out f from the LORD Lev 10:2 784
offerings of the LORD made by f Lev 10:12
sacrifices of the LORD made by f Lev 10:13
offerings made by f of the fat Lev 10:15
it shall be burnt in the f Lev 13:52 784
thou shalt burn it in the f Lev 13:55 784
that wherein the plague is with f Lev 13:57 784
f from off the altar before the Lev 16:12 784
upon the f before the LORD Lev 16:13 784
shall burn in the f their skins Lev 16:27 784
seed pass through the f to Molech Lev 18:21
day, it shall be burnt in the f Lev 19:6 784
they shall be burnt with f Lev 20:14 784
offerings of the LORD made by f Lev 21:6
she shall be burnt with f Lev 21:9 784
offerings of the LORD made by f Lev 21:21
nor make an offering by f of them Lev 22:22
offering made by f unto the LORD Lev 22:27
by f unto the LORD seven days Lev 23:8 784
an offering made by f unto the Lev 23:13
even an offering made by f Lev 23:18
offering made by f unto the LORD Lev 23:25
offering made by f unto the LORD Lev 23:27 784
offering made by f unto the LORD Lev 23:36
offering made by f unto the LORD Lev 23:36
offering made by f unto the LORD Lev 23:37
offering made by f unto the LORD Lev 24:7
made by f by a perpetual statute Lev 24:9
offered strange f before the LORD Num 3:4 784
put it in the f which is under Num 6:18 784
as it were the appearance of f Num 9:15 784
and the appearance of f by night Num 9:16 784
the f of the LORD burnt among Num 11:1 784
unto the LORD, the f was quenched Num 11:2 784
because the f of the LORD burnt Num 11:3 784
and in a pillar of f by night Num 14:14 784
an offering by f unto the LORD Num 15:3
wine, for an offering made by f Num 15:10
in offering an offering made by f Num 15:13
will offer an offering made by f Num 15:14
sacrifice made by f unto the LORD Num 15:25
put f therein, and put incense in Num 16:7 784
put f in them, and laid incense Num 16:18 784
there came out a f from the LORD Num 16:35 784
and scatter thou the f yonder Num 16:37 784
put f therein from off the altar, Num 16:46 784
holy things, reserved from the f Num 18:9 784
fat for an offering made by f Num 18:17
For there is a f gone out of Num 21:28 784
what time the f devoured two Num 26:10 784
offered strange f before the LORD Num 26:61 784
bread for my sacrifices made by f Num 28:2
This is the offering made by f Num 28:3
sacrifice made by f unto the LORD Num 28:6
offer it, a sacrifice made by f Num 28:8
sacrifice made by f unto the LORD Num 28:13
f for a burnt offering unto the Num 28:19
meat of the sacrifice made by f Num 28:24
sacrifice made by f unto the LORD Num 29:6
offering, a sacrifice made by f Num 29:13
offering, a sacrifice made by f Num 29:36
all their goodly castles, with f Num 31:10 784
Every thing that may abide the f Num 31:23 784
ye shall make it go through the f Num 31:23 784
all that abideth not the f ye Num 31:23 784
in f by night, to shew you by Deut 1:33 784
with f unto the midst of heaven Deut 4:11 784
you out of the midst of the f Deut 4:12 784
Horeb out of the midst of the f Deut 4:15 784
the LORD thy God is a consuming f Deut 4:24 784
out of the midst of the f Deut 4:33 784
earth he shewed thee his great f Deut 4:36 784
words out of the midst of the f Deut 4:36 784

F

mount out of the midst of the f Deut 5:4 784
ye were afraid by reason of the f Deut 5:5 784
mount out of the midst of the f Deut 5:22 784
(for the mountain did burn with f Deut 5:23 784
voice out of the midst of the f Deut 5:24 784
for this great f will consume us Deut 5:25 784
out of the midst of the f Deut 5:26 784
burn their graven images with f Deut 7:5 784
their gods shall ye burn with f Deut 7:25 784
as a consuming f he shall destroy Deut 9:3 784
the f in the day of the assembly Deut 9:10 784
mount, and the mount burned with f Deut 9:15 784
ye had made, and burnt it with f Deut 9:21 784
the f in the day of the assembly Deut 10:4 784
and burn their groves with f Deut 12:3 784
have burnt in the f to their gods Deut 12:31 784
and shalt burn with f the city Deut 13:16 784
offerings of the LORD made by f Deut 18:1
daughter to pass through the f Deut 18:10 784
let me see this great f any more Deut 18:16 784
For a f is kindled in mine anger, Deut 32:22 784
set on f the foundations of the Deut 32:22 3857
And they burnt the city with f Josh 6:24 784
thing shall be burnt with f Josh 7:15 784
stones, and burned them with f Josh 7:25 784
that ye shall set the city on f Josh 8:8 784
and hasted and set the city on f Josh 8:19 784
and burn their chariots with f Josh 11:6 784
and burnt their chariots with f Josh 11:9 784
and he burnt Hazor with f Josh 11:11 784
made by f are their inheritance Josh 13:14
the sword, and set the city on f Judg 1:8 784
there rose up f out of the rock, Judg 6:21 784
let f come out of the bramble, and Judg 9:15 784
let f come out from Abimelech, and Judg 9:20 784
let f come out from the men of Judg 9:20 784
and set the hold on f upon them Judg 9:49 784
of the tower to burn it with f Judg 9:52 784
burn thine house upon thee with f Judg 12:1 784
thee and thy father's house with f Judg 14:15 784
when he had set the brands on f Judg 15:5 784
and burnt her and her father with f Judg 15:6 784
as flax that was burnt with f Judg 15:14 784
is broken when it toucheth the f Judg 16:9 784
sword, and burnt the city with f Judg 18:27 784
also they set on f all the cities Judg 20:48 784
by f of the children of Israel 1Sa 2:28
Ziklag, and burned it with f 1Sa 30:1 784
and, behold, it was burned with f 1Sa 30:3 784
and we burned Ziklag with f 1Sa 30:14 784
go and set it on f 2Sa 14:30 784
servants set the field on f 2Sa 14:30 784
thy servants set my field on f 2Sa 14:31 784
f out of his mouth devoured 2Sa 22:9 784
him were coals of f kindled 2Sa 22:13 784
burned with f in the same place 2Sa 23:7 784
taken Gezer, and burnt it with f 1Kin 9:16 784
the king's house over him with f 1Kin 16:18 784
lay it on wood, and put no f under 1Kin 18:23 784
lay it on wood, and put no f under 1Kin 18:23 784
and the God that answereth by f 1Kin 18:24 784
of your gods, but put no f under 1Kin 18:25 784
Then the f of the LORD fell, and 1Kin 18:38 784
And after the earthquake a f 1Kin 19:12 784
but the LORD was not in the f 1Kin 19:12 784
after the f a still small voice 1Kin 19:12 784
then let f come down from heaven, 2Kin 1:10 784
And there came down f from heaven 2Kin 1:10 784
let f come down from heaven, and 2Kin 1:12 784
the f of God came down from 2Kin 1:12 784
there came f down from heaven, and 2Kin 1:14 784
a chariot of f, and horses of f 2Kin 2:11 784
chariots of f round about Elisha 2Kin 6:17 784
strong holds wilt thou set on f 2Kin 8:12 784
his son to pass through the f 2Kin 16:3 784
daughters to pass through the f 2Kin 17:17 784
children in f to Adrammelech 2Kin 17:31 784
have cast their gods into the f 2Kin 19:18 784
made his son pass through the f 2Kin 21:6 784
to pass through the f to Molech 2Kin 23:10 784
the chariots of the sun with f 2Kin 23:11 784
great man's house burnt he with f 2Kin 25:9 784
and they were burned with f 1Chr 14:12 784
by f upon the altar of burnt 1Chr 21:26 784
the f came down from heaven, and 2Chr 7:1 784
of Israel saw how the f came down 2Chr 7:3 784
and burnt his children in the f 2Chr 28:3 784
the f in the valley of the son of 2Chr 33:6 784
with f according to the ordinance 2Chr 35:13 784
all the palaces thereof with f 2Chr 36:19 784
gates thereof are burned with f Neh 1:3 784
gates thereof are consumed with f Neh 2:3 784
thereof were consumed with f Neh 2:13 784
gates thereof are burned with f Neh 2:17 784
and in the night by a pillar of f Neh 9:12 784
neither the pillar of f by night Neh 9:19 784
The f of God is fallen from Job 1:16 784
f shall consume the tabernacles Job 15:34 784
spark of his f shall not shine Job 18:5 784
a f not blown shall consume him Job 20:26 784
remnant of them the f consumeth Job 22:20 784
it is turned up as it were f Job 28:5 784
For it is a f that consumeth to Job 31:12 784
lamps, and sparks of f leap out Job 41:19 784
wicked he shall rain snares, f Ps 11:6 784
f out of his mouth devoured Ps 18:8 784
passed, hail stones and coals of f Ps 18:12 784
hail stones and coals of f Ps 18:13 784
wrath, and the f shall devour them Ps 21:9 784
the LORD divideth the flames of f Ps 29:7 784
while I was musing the f burned Ps 39:3 784
he burneth the chariot in the f Ps 46:9 784
a f shall devour before him, and Ps 50:3 784
even among them that are set on f Ps 57:4 3857
we went through f and through Ps 66:12 784
as wax melteth before the f Ps 68:2 784
They have cast f into thy Ps 74:7 784
all the night with a light of f Ps 78:14 784
so a f was kindled against Jacob, Ps 78:21 784
The f consumed their young men Ps 78:63 784
shall thy jealousy burn like f Ps 79:5 784
It is burned with f, it is cut Ps 80:16 784
As the f burneth a wood, and as Ps 83:14 784
flame setteth the mountains on f Ps 83:14 3857
shall thy wrath burn like f Ps 89:46 784
A f goeth before him, and burneth Ps 97:3 784
his ministers a flaming f Ps 104:4 784
rain, and flaming f in their land Ps 105:32 784
f to give light in the night Ps 105:39 784
a f was kindled in their company Ps 106:18 784
are quenched as the f of thorns Ps 118:12 784
let them be cast into the f Ps 140:10 784
F, and hail; snow, and Ps 148:8 784
Can a man take f in his bosom Prov 6:27 784
his lips there is as a burning f Prov 16:27 784
heap coals of f upon his head Prov 25:22
no wood is, there the f goeth out Prov 26:20 784
to burning coals, and wood to f Prov 26:21 784
the f that saith not, It is Prov 30:16 784
the coals thereof are coals of f Song 8:6 784
your cities are burned with f Is 1:7 784
shining of a flaming f by night Is 4:5 784
Therefore as the f devoureth the Is 5:24 784
be with burning and fuel of f Is 9:5 784
For wickedness burneth as the f Is 9:18 784
shall be as the fuel of the f Is 9:19 784
a burning like the burning of a f Is 10:16 784
light of Israel shall be for a f Is 10:17 784
the f of thine enemies shall Is 26:11 784
the women come, and set them on f Is 27:11 215
and the flame of devouring f Is 29:6 784
a sherd to take f from the hearth Is 30:14 784
and his tongue as a devouring f Is 30:27 784
with the flame of a devouring f Is 30:30 784
the pile thereof is f and much Is 30:33 784
whose f is in Zion, and his Is 31:9 217
your breath, as f, shall devour Is 33:11 784
up shall they be burned in the f Is 33:12 784
shall dwell with the devouring f Is 33:14 784
have cast their gods into the f Is 37:19 784
it hath set him on f round about Is 42:25 3857
when thou walkest through the f Is 43:2 784
He burneth part thereof in the f Is 44:16 784
Aha, I am warm, I have seen the f Is 44:16 217
I have burned part of it in the f Is 44:19 784
the f shall burn them Is 47:14 784
warm at, nor f to sit before it Is 47:14 217
Behold, all ye that kindle a f Is 50:11 784
walk in the light of your f Is 50:11 784
that bloweth the coals in the f Is 54:16 784
As when the melting f burneth Is 64:2 784
the f causeth the waters to boil, Is 64:2 784
praised thee, is burned up with f Is 64:11 784
a f that burneth all the day Is 65:5 784
behold, the LORD will come with f Is 66:15 784
and his rebuke with flames of f Is 66:15 784
For by f and by his sword will the Is 66:16 784
neither shall their f be quenched Is 66:24 784
lest my fury come forth like f Jer 4:4 784
will make my words in thy mouth f Jer 5:14 784
up a sign of f in Beth-haccerem Jer 6:1
the lead is consumed of the f Jer 6:29 784
wood, and the fathers kindle the f Jer 7:18 784
sons and their daughters in the f Jer 7:31 784
tumult he hath kindled f upon it Jer 11:16 784
for a f is kindled in mine anger, Jer 15:14 784
ye have kindled a f in mine anger Jer 17:4 784
I kindle a f in the gates thereof Jer 17:27 784
to burn their sons with f for Jer 19:5 784
a burning f shut up in my bones Jer 20:9 784
and he shall burn it with f Jer 21:10 784
lest my fury go out like f Jer 21:12 784
I will kindle a f in the forest Jer 21:14 784
cedars, and cast them into the f Jer 22:7 784
Is not my word like as a f Jer 23:29 784
king of Babylon roasted in the f Jer 29:22 784
set f on this city, and burn it Jer 32:29 784
to pass through the f unto Molech Jer 32:35
and he shall burn it with f Jer 34:2 784
and and take it, and burn it with f Jer 34:22 784
there was a f on the hearth Jer 36:22
cast it into the f that was on Jer 36:23 784
in the f that was on the hearth Jer 36:23 784
king of Judah had burned in the f Jer 36:32 784
and take it, and burn it with f Jer 37:8 784
tent, and burn this city with f Jer 37:10 784
city shall not be burned with f Jer 38:17 784
and they shall burn it with f Jer 38:18 784
this city to be burned with f Jer 38:23 784
the houses of the people, with f Jer 39:8 784
I will kindle a f in the houses Jer 43:12 784
Egyptians shall he burn with f Jer 43:13 784
but a f shall come forth out of Jer 48:45 784
daughters shall be burned with f Jer 49:2 784
I will kindle a f in the wall of Jer 49:27 784
I will kindle a f in his cities Jer 50:32 784
the reeds they have burned with f Jer 51:32 784
high gates shall be burned with f Jer 51:58 784
in vain, and the folk in the f Jer 51:58 784
the great men, burned he with f Jer 52:13 784
hath he sent f into my bones Lam 1:13 784
against Jacob like a flaming f Lam 2:3 784
he poured out his fury like f Lam 2:4 784
and hath kindled a f in Zion Lam 4:11 784
a f infolding itself, and a Eze 1:4 784
amber, out of the midst of the f Eze 1:4 784
was like burning coals of f Eze 1:13 784
living creatures; and the f was bright Eze 1:13 784
out of the f went forth lightning Eze 1:13 784
as the appearance of f round Eze 1:27 784
as it were the appearance of f Eze 1:27 784
Thou shalt burn with f a third Eze 5:2 217
cast them into the midst of the f Eze 5:4 784
and burn them in the f Eze 5:4 784
for thereof shall a f come forth Eze 5:4 784
a likeness as the appearance of f Eze 8:2 784
of his loins even downward, f Eze 8:2 784
of f from between the cherubims Eze 10:2 784
Take f from between the wheels, Eze 10:6 784
f that was between the cherubims Eze 10:7 784
it is cast into the f for fuel Eze 15:4 784
the f devoureth both the ends of Eze 15:4 784
when the f hath devoured it, and Eze 15:5 784
I have given to the f for fuel Eze 15:6 784
they shall go out from one f Eze 15:7 784
another f shall devour them Eze 15:7 784
to pass through the f for them Eze 16:21
shall burn thine houses with f Eze 16:41 784
the f consumed them Eze 19:12 784
f is gone out of a rod of her Eze 19:14 784
the f all that openeth the womb Eze 20:26
your sons to pass through the f Eze 20:31 784
Behold, I will kindle a f in thee Eze 20:47 784
against thee in the f of my wrath Eze 21:31 784
Thou shalt be for fuel to the f Eze 21:32 784
furnace, to blow the f upon it Eze 22:20 784
upon you in the f of my wrath Eze 22:21 784
them with the f of my wrath Eze 22:31 784
shall be devoured by the f Eze 23:25 784
to pass for them through the f Eze 23:37
and burn up their houses with f Eze 23:47 784
even make the pile for f great Eze 24:9
Heap on wood, kindle the f Eze 24:10 784
her scum shall be in the f Eze 24:12 784
in the midst of the stones of f Eze 28:14 784
from the midst of the stones of f Eze 28:16 784
forth a f from the midst of thee Eze 28:18 784
when I have set a f in Egypt Eze 30:8 784
desolate, and will set f in Zoan Eze 30:14 784
And I will set f in Egypt Eze 30:16 784
Surely in the f of my jealousy Eze 36:5 784
in the f of my wrath have I Eze 38:19 784
rain, and great hailstones, f Eze 38:22 784
And I will send a f on Magog Eze 39:6 784
shall go forth, and shall set on f Eze 39:9 784
burn them with f seven years Eze 39:9 784
shall burn the weapons with f Eze 39:10 784
the flame of the f slew those men Dan 3:22 5135
men bound into the midst of the f Dan 3:24 5135
walking in the midst of the f Dan 3:25 5135
came forth of the midst of the f Dan 3:26 5135
whose bodies the f had no power Dan 3:27 5135
nor the smell of f had passed on Dan 3:27 5135
flame, and his wheels as burning f Dan 7:9 5135
and his eyes as lamps of f Dan 10:6 784
morning it burneth as a flaming f Hos 7:6 784
I will send a f upon his cities Hos 8:14 784
for the f hath devoured the Joel 1:19 784
the f hath devoured the pastures Joel 1:20 784
A f devoureth before them Joel 2:3 784
of f that devoureth the stubble Joel 2:5 784
and in the earth, blood, and f Joel 2:30 784
But I will send a f into the Amos 1:4 784
But I will send a f on the wall Amos 1:7 784
But I will send a f on the wall Amos 1:10 784
But I will send a f upon Teman Amos 1:12 784
But I will kindle a f in the wall Amos 1:14 784
But I will send a f upon Moab Amos 2:2 784
But I will send a f upon Judah Amos 2:5 784
out like f in the house of Joseph Amos 5:6 784
Lord GOD called to contend by f Amos 7:4 784
the house of Jacob shall be a f Obad 18 784
be cleft, as wax before the f Mic 1:4 784
shall be burned with the f Mic 1:7 784
his fury is poured out like f Nah 1:6 784
the f shall devour thy bars Nah 3:13 701
There shall the f devour thee Nah 3:15 784
people shall labour in the very f Hab 2:13 784
devoured by the f of his jealousy Zeph 1:18 784
with the f of my jealousy Zeph 3:8 784
unto her a wall of f round about Zec 2:5 784
this a brand plucked out of the f Zec 3:2 784
and she shall be devoured with f Zec 9:4 784
that the f may devour thy cedars Zec 11:1 784
an hearth of f among the wood Zec 12:6 784
and like a torch of f in a sheaf Zec 12:6 784
the third part through the f Zec 13:9 784
neither do ye kindle f on mine Mal 1:10
for he is like a refiner's f Mal 3:2 784
is hewn down, and cast into the f Mt 3:10 4442
with the Holy Ghost, and with f Mt 3:11 4442
up the chaff with unquenchable f Mt 3:12 4442
shall be in danger of hell f Mt 5:22 4442
is hewn down, and cast into the f Mt 7:19 4442
are gathered and burned in the f Mt 13:40 4442
cast them into a furnace of f Mt 13:42 4442
cast them into the furnace of f Mt 13:50 4442
ofttimes he falleth into the f Mt 17:15 4442
to be cast into everlasting f Mt 18:8 4442
two eyes to be cast into hell f Mt 18:9 4442
me, ye cursed, into everlasting f Mt 25:41 4442
it hath cast him into the f Mk 9:22 4442
into the f that never shall be Mk 9:43 4442
not, and the f is not quenched Mk 9:44 4442
into the f that never shall be Mk 9:45 4442
not, and the f is not quenched Mk 9:46 4442
two eyes to be cast into hell f Mk 9:47 4442
not, and the f is not quenched Mk 9:48 4442
every one shall be salted with f Mk 9:49 4442
and warmed himself at the f Mk 14:54 5457
is hewn down, and cast into the f Lk 3:9 4442
you with the Holy Ghost and with f Lk 3:16 4442

he will burn with *f* unquenchable	Lk 3:17	4442
f to come down from heaven	Lk 9:54	4442
I am come to send *f* on the earth	Lk 12:49	4442
Lot went out of Sodom it rained *f*	Lk 17:29	4442
when they had kindled a *f* in the	Lk 22:55	4442
beheld him as he sat by the *f*	Lk 22:56	5457
them, and cast them into the *f*	Jn 15:6	4442
there, who had made a *f* of coals	Jn 18:18	
they saw a *f* of coals there, and	Jn 21:9	
them cloven tongues like as of *f*	Acts 2:3	4442
blood, and *f*, and vapour of smoke	Acts 2:19	4442
Lord in a flame of *f* in a bush	Acts 7:30	4442
for they kindled a *f*, and received	Acts 28:2	4443
of sticks, and laid them on the *f*	Acts 28:3	4443
he shook off the beast into the *f*	Acts 28:5	4442
shalt heap coals of *f* on his head	Rom 12:20	4442
because it shall be revealed by *f*	1Cor 3:13	4442
the *f* shall try every man's work	1Cor 3:13	4442
yet so as by *f*	1Cor 3:15	4442
In flaming *f* taking vengeance on	2Th 1:8	4442
and his ministers a flame of *f*	Heb 1:7	4442
Quenched the violence of *f*	Heb 11:34	4442
be touched, and that burned with *f*	Heb 12:18	4442
For our God is a consuming *f*	Heb 12:29	4442
a matter a little *f* kindleth	Jas 3:5	4442
And the tongue is a *f*, a world of	Jas 3:6	4442
setteth on *f* the course of nature	Jas 3:6	5394
and it is set on *f* of hell	Jas 3:6	5394
shall eat your flesh as it were *f*	Jas 5:3	4442
though it be tried with *f*	1Pet 1:7	4442
reserved unto *f* against the day	2Pet 3:7	4442
being on *f* shall be dissolved	2Pet 3:12	4448
the vengeance of eternal *f*	Jude 7	4442
fear, pulling them out of the *f*	Jude 23	4442
and his eyes were as a flame of *f*	Rev 1:14	4442
his eyes like unto a flame of *f*	Rev 2:18	4442
to buy of me gold tried in the *f*	Rev 3:18	4442
of *f* burning before the throne	Rev 4:5	4442
and filled it with *f* of the altar	Rev 8:5	4442
f mingled with blood, and they	Rev 8:7	4442
with *f* was cast into the sea	Rev 8:8	4442
on them, having breastplates of *f*	Rev 9:17	4447
and out of their mouths issued *f*	Rev 9:17	4442
part of men killed, by the *f*	Rev 9:18	4442
sun, and his feet as pillars of *f*	Rev 10:1	4442
f proceedeth out of their mouth,	Rev 11:5	4442
so that he maketh *f* come down	Rev 13:13	4442
and he shall be tormented with *f*	Rev 14:10	4442
the altar, which had power over *f*	Rev 14:18	4442
a sea of glass mingled with *f*	Rev 15:2	4442
unto him to scorch men with *f*	Rev 16:8	4442
eat her flesh, and burn her with *f*	Rev 17:16	4442
shall be utterly burned with *f*	Rev 18:8	4442
His eyes were as a flame of *f*	Rev 19:12	4442
lake of *f* burning with brimstone	Rev 19:20	4442
f came down from God out of	Rev 20:9	4442
them was cast into the lake of *f*	Rev 20:10	4442
hell were cast into the lake of *f*	Rev 20:14	4442
life was cast into the lake of *f*	Rev 20:15	4442
in the lake which burneth with *f*	Rev 21:8	4442

FIREBRAND

put a *f* in the midst between two	Judg 15:4	3940
ye were as a *f* plucked out of the	Amos 4:11	181

FIREBRANDS

three hundred foxes, and took *f*	Judg 15:4	3940
As a mad man who casteth *f*	Prov 26:18	2131
the two tails of these smoking *f*	Is 7:4	181

FIREPANS

and his fleshhooks, and his *f*	Ex 27:3	4289
and the fleshhooks, and the *f*	Ex 38:3	4289
And the *f*, and the bowls, and such	2Kin 25:15	4289
And the basons, and the *f*, and the	Jer 52:19	4289

FIRES

glorify ye the LORD in the *f*	Is 24:15	217

FIRKINS

containing two or three *f* apiece	Jn 2:6	3355

FIRM

f on dry ground in the midst of	Josh 3:17	3559
where the priests' feet stood *f*	Josh 4:3	3559
they are *f* in themselves	Job 41:23	3332
His heart is as *f* as a stone	Job 41:24	3332
but their strength is *f*	Ps 73:4	1277
statute, and to make a *f* decree	Dan 6:7	8631
of the hope *f* unto the end	Heb 3:6	949

FIRMAMENT

Let there be a *f* in the midst of	Gen 1:6	7549
And God made the *f*, and divided the	Gen 1:7	7549
the *f* from the waters which were	Gen 1:7	7549
the waters which were above the *f*	Gen 1:7	7549
And God called the *f* Heaven	Gen 1:8	7549
Let there be lights in the *f* of	Gen 1:14	7549
the *f* of the heaven to give light	Gen 1:15	7549
God set them in the *f* of the	Gen 1:17	7549
the earth in the open *f* of heaven	Gen 1:20	7549
the *f* sheweth his handywork	Ps 19:1	7549
praise him in the *f* of his power	Ps 150:1	7549
the likeness of the *f* upon the	Eze 1:22	7549
under the *f* were their wings	Eze 1:23	7549
the *f* that was over their heads	Eze 1:25	7549
above the *f* that was over their	Eze 1:26	7549
in the *f* that was above the head	Eze 10:1	7549
shine as the brightness of the *f*	Dan 12:3	7549

FIRST

and the morning were the *f* day	Gen 1:5	259
The name of the *f* is Pison	Gen 2:11	259
on the *f* day of the month, were	Gen 8:5	259
and *f* year, in the *f* month	Gen 8:13	7223
the *f* day of the month, the	Gen 8:13	259
which he had made there at the *f*	Gen 13:4	7223
the *f* came out red, all over like	Gen 25:25	7223
beside the *f* famine that was in	Gen 26:1	7223
that city was called Luz at the *f*	Gen 28:19	7223
thread, saying, This came out *f*	Gen 38:28	7223
did eat up the *f* seven fat kine	Gen 41:20	7223
at the *f* time are we brought in	Gen 43:18	8462
down at the *f* time to buy food	Gen 43:20	8462
to the voice of the *f* sign	Ex 4:8	7223
it shall be the *f* month of the	Ex 12:2	7223
blemish, a male of the *f* year	Ex 12:5	1121
even the *f* day ye shall put away	Ex 12:15	7223
the *f* day until the seventh day	Ex 12:15	7223
in the *f* day there shall be an	Ex 12:16	7223
In the *f* month, on the fourteenth	Ex 12:18	7223
to offer the *f* of thy ripe fruits	Ex 22:29	4395
The *f* of the firstfruits of thy	Ex 23:19	7225
the *f* row shall be a sardius, a	Ex 28:17	
this shall be the *f* row	Ex 28:17	259
two lambs of the *f* year day by	Ex 29:38	1121
tables of stone like unto the *f*	Ex 34:1	7223
words that were in the *f* tables	Ex 34:1	7223
tables of stone like unto the *f*	Ex 34:4	7223
The *f* of the firstfruits of thy	Ex 34:26	7225
the *f* row was a sardius, a topaz,	Ex 39:10	
this was the *f* row	Ex 39:10	259
On the *f* day of the *f* month	Ex 40:2	7223
On the *f* day of the *f* month	Ex 40:2	259
it came to pass in the *f* month in	Ex 40:17	7223
on the *f* day of the month, that	Ex 40:17	259
him as he burned the *f* bullock	Lev 4:21	7223
which is for the sin offering *f*	Lev 5:8	7223
and a lamb, both of the *f* year	Lev 9:3	1121
and offered it for sin, as the *f*	Lev 9:15	7223
the *f* year for a burnt offering	Lev 12:6	1121
one ewe lamb of the *f* year	Lev 14:10	1323
the *f* month at even is the LORD's	Lev 23:5	7223
In the *f* day ye shall have an	Lev 23:7	7223
f year for a burnt offering unto	Lev 23:12	1121
without blemish of the *f* year	Lev 23:18	1121
two lambs of the *f* year for a	Lev 23:19	1121
the *f* fruits for a wave offering	Lev 23:20	
in the *f* day of the month, shall	Lev 23:24	259
On the *f* day shall be an holy	Lev 23:35	7223
on the *f* day shall be a sabbath,	Lev 23:39	7223
ye shall take you on the *f* day	Lev 23:40	7223
on the *f* day of the second month,	Num 1:1	259
on the *f* day of the second month	Num 1:18	259
These shall *f* set forth	Num 2:9	7223
shall bring a lamb of the *f* year	Num 6:12	1121
one he lamb of the *f* year without	Num 6:14	1121
one ewe lamb of the *f* year	Num 6:14	1323
the *f* day was Nahshon the son of	Num 7:12	7223
one ram, one lamb of the *f* year	Num 7:15	1121
goats, five lambs of the *f* year	Num 7:17	1121
one ram, one lamb of the *f* year	Num 7:21	1121
goats, five lambs of the *f* year	Num 7:23	1121
one ram, one lamb of the *f* year	Num 7:27	1121
goats, five lambs of the *f* year	Num 7:29	1121
one ram, one lamb of the *f* year	Num 7:33	1121
goats, five lambs of the *f* year	Num 7:35	1121
one ram, one lamb of the *f* year	Num 7:39	1121
goats, five lambs of the *f* year	Num 7:41	1121
one ram, one lamb of the *f* year	Num 7:45	1121
goats, five lambs of the *f* year	Num 7:47	1121
one ram, one lamb of the *f* year	Num 7:51	1121
goats, five lambs of the *f* year	Num 7:53	1121
one ram, one lamb of the *f* year	Num 7:57	1121
goats, five lambs of the *f* year	Num 7:59	1121
one ram, one lamb of the *f* year	Num 7:63	1121
goats, five lambs of the *f* year	Num 7:65	1121
one ram, one lamb of the *f* year	Num 7:69	1121
goats, five lambs of the *f* year	Num 7:71	1121
one ram, one lamb of the *f* year	Num 7:75	1121
goats, five lambs of the *f* year	Num 7:77	1121
one ram, one lamb of the *f* year	Num 7:81	1121
goats, five lambs of the *f* year	Num 7:83	1121
the lambs of the *f* year twelve	Num 7:87	1121
the lambs of the *f* year sixty	Num 7:88	1121
in the *f* month of the second year	Num 9:1	7223
on the fourteenth day of the *f*	Num 9:5	7223
they *f* took their journey	Num 10:13	7223
In the *f* place went the standard	Num 10:14	7223
the *f* of your dough for an heave	Num 15:20	7225
Of the *f* of your dough ye shall	Num 15:21	7225
of the *f* year for a sin offering	Num 15:27	1323
whatsoever is *f* ripe in the land,	Num 18:13	1061
the desert of Zin in the *f* month	Num 20:1	7223
Amalek was the *f* of the nations	Num 24:20	7225
two lambs of the *f* year without	Num 28:3	1121
lambs of the *f* year without spot	Num 28:9	1121
lambs of the *f* year without spot	Num 28:11	1121
f month is the passover of the	Num 28:16	7223
In the *f* day shall be an holy	Num 28:18	7223
ram, and seven lambs of the *f* year	Num 28:19	1121
ram, seven lambs of the *f* year	Num 28:27	1121
on the *f* day of the month, ye	Num 29:1	259
seven lambs of the *f* year without	Num 29:2	1121
ram, and seven lambs of the *f* year	Num 29:8	1121
and fourteen lambs of the *f* year	Num 29:13	1121
lambs of the *f* year without spot	Num 29:17	1121
of the *f* year without blemish	Num 29:20	1121
of the *f* year without blemish	Num 29:23	1121
lambs of the *f* year without spot	Num 29:26	1121
of the *f* year without blemish	Num 29:29	1121
of the *f* year without blemish	Num 29:32	1121
seven lambs of the *f* year without	Num 29:36	1121
from Rameses in the *f* month	Num 33:3	7223
the fifteenth day of the *f* month	Num 33:3	7223
in the *f* day of the fifth month	Num 33:38	259
on the *f* day of the month, that	Deut 1:3	259
down before the LORD, as at the *f*	Deut 9:18	7223
nights, as I fell down at the *f*	Deut 9:25	
tables of stone like unto the *f*	Deut 10:1	7223
the *f* tables which thou brakest	Deut 10:2	7223
tables of stone like unto the *f*	Deut 10:3	7223
according to the *f* writing	Deut 10:4	7223
mount, according to the *f* time	Deut 10:10	7223
the *f* rain and the latter rain,	Deut 11:14	3138
thine hand shall be *f* upon him to	Deut 13:9	7223
sacrificedst the *f* day at even	Deut 16:4	7223
be *f* upon him to put him to death	Deut 17:7	7223
the *f* of the fleece of thy sheep,	Deut 18:4	7225
That thou shalt take of the *f* of	Deut 26:2	7225
he provided the *f* part for	Deut 33:21	7225
on the tenth day of the *f* month	Josh 4:19	7223
come out against us, as at the *f*	Josh 8:5	7223
They flee before us, as at the *f*	Josh 8:6	7223
for theirs was the *f* lot	Josh 21:10	7223
for us against the Canaanites *f*	Judg 1:1	8462
of the city was Laish at the *f*	Judg 18:29	7223
Which of us shall go up *f* to the	Judg 20:18	8462
LORD said, Judah shall go up *f*	Judg 20:18	8462
put themselves in array the *f* day	Judg 20:22	7223
down before us, as at the *f*	Judg 20:32	7223
before us, as in the *f* battle	Judg 20:39	7223
that *f* slaughter, which Jonathan	1Sa 14:14	7223
the same was the *f* altar that he	1Sa 14:35	2490
the battle were Eliab the *f* born	1Sa 17:13	
except thou *f* bring Michal Saul's	2Sa 3:13	6440
of them be overthrown at the *f*	2Sa 17:9	8462
I am come the *f* this day of all	2Sa 19:20	7223
f had in bringing back our king	2Sa 19:43	7223
days of harvest, in the *f* days	2Sa 21:9	7223
he attained not unto the *f* three	2Sa 23:19	
he attained not to the *f* three	2Sa 23:23	
f year of Asa king of Judah began	1Kin 16:23	259
make me thereof a little cake *f*	1Kin 17:13	7223
for yourselves, and dress it *f*	1Kin 18:25	7223
to thy servant at the *f* I will do	1Kin 20:9	7223
of the provinces went out *f*	1Kin 20:17	7223
Now the *f* inhabitants that dwelt	1Chr 9:2	7223
the Jebusites *f* shall be chief	1Chr 11:6	7223
Joab the son of Zeruiah went *f* up	1Chr 11:6	7223
he attained not to the *f* three	1Chr 11:21	
but attained not to the *f* three	1Chr 11:25	
Ezer the *f*, Obadiah the second,	1Chr 12:9	7218
went over Jordan in the *f* month	1Chr 12:15	7223
because ye did it not at the *f*	1Chr 15:13	7223
on that day David delivered *f*	1Chr 16:7	7218
Jeriah the *f*, Amariah the second,	1Chr 23:19	7218
Micah the *f*, and Jesiah the second	1Chr 23:20	7218
Now the *f* lot came forth to	1Chr 24:7	7223
of Rehabiah, the *f* was Isshiah	1Chr 24:21	7218
Jeriah the *f*, Amariah the second,	1Chr 24:23	
Now the *f* lot came forth for	1Chr 25:9	7223
Over the *f* course for the *f*	1Chr 27:2	7223
of the host for the *f* month	1Chr 27:3	7223
Now the acts of David the king, *f*	1Chr 29:29	7223
f measure was threescore cubits	2Chr 3:3	7223
rest of the acts of Solomon, *f*	2Chr 9:29	7223
Now the acts of Rehoboam, *f*	2Chr 12:15	7223
And, behold, the acts of Asa, *f*	2Chr 16:11	7223
in the *f* ways of his father David	2Chr 17:3	7223
of the acts of Jehoshaphat, *f*	2Chr 20:34	7223
rest of the acts of Amaziah, *f*	2Chr 25:26	7223
the rest of the acts of Uzziah, *f*	2Chr 26:22	7223
of his acts and of all his ways, *f*	2Chr 28:26	7223
He in the *f* year of his reign, in	2Chr 29:3	7223
year of his reign, in the *f* month	2Chr 29:3	7223
Now they began on the *f* day of	2Chr 29:17	7223
day of the *f* month to sanctify	2Chr 29:17	7223
of the *f* month they made an end	2Chr 29:17	7223
the fourteenth day of the *f* month	2Chr 35:1	7223
And his deeds, *f* and last, behold,	2Chr 35:27	7223
Now in the *f* year of Cyrus king	2Chr 36:22	259
Now in the *f* year of Cyrus king	Ezr 1:1	259
From the *f* day of the seventh	Ezr 3:6	259
men, that had seen the *f* house	Ezr 3:12	7223
But in the *f* year of Cyrus the	Ezr 5:13	2298
In the *f* year of Cyrus the king	Ezr 6:3	2298
the fourteenth day of the *f* month	Ezr 6:19	7223
For upon the *f* day of the	Ezr 7:9	259
f month began he to go up from	Ezr 7:9	7223
on the *f* day of the fifth month	Ezr 7:9	259
on the twelfth day of the *f* month	Ezr 8:31	7223
sat down in the *f* day of the	Ezr 10:16	259
by the *f* day of the *f* month	Ezr 10:17	259
by the *f* day of the *f* month	Ezr 10:17	7223
of them which came up at the *f*	Neh 7:5	7223
upon the *f* day of the seventh	Neh 8:2	259
from the *f* day unto the last day,	Neh 8:18	7223
which sat the *f* in the kingdom	Est 1:14	7223
In the *f* month, that is, the	Est 3:7	7223
the thirteenth day of the *f* month	Est 3:12	7223
Art thou the *f* man that was born	Job 15:7	7223
And he called the name of the *f*	Job 42:14	7223
He that is *f* in his own cause	Prov 18:17	7223
restore thy judges as at the *f*	Is 1:26	7223
when at the *f* he lightly	Is 9:1	7223
I the LORD, the *f*, and with the	Is 41:4	7223
The *f* shall say to Zion, Behold,	Is 41:27	7223
Thy *f* father hath sinned, and thy	Is 43:27	7223
I am the *f*, and I am the last	Is 44:6	7223
I am the *f*, I also am the last	Is 48:12	7223
me, and the ships of Tarshish *f*	Is 60:9	7223
that bringeth forth her *f* child	Jer 4:31	1069
where I set my name at the *f*	Jer 7:12	7223
f I will recompense their	Jer 16:18	7223
like the figs that are *f* ripe	Jer 24:2	1073
of Judah, that was the *f* year of	Jer 25:1	7224
and will build them, as at the *f*	Jer 33:7	7223
of the land, as at the *f*, saith	Jer 33:11	7223
words that were in the *f* roll	Jer 36:28	7223
f the king of Assyria hath	Jer 50:17	7223
king of Babylon in the *f* year of	Jer 52:31	
the *f* face was the face of a	Eze 10:14	259
in the *f* day of the month, that	Eze 26:1	259
and twentieth year, in the *f* month	Eze 29:17	7223
in the *f* day of the month, the	Eze 29:17	259

F

the eleventh year, in the *f* month Eze 30:20 7223
in the *f* day of the month, that Eze 31:1 259
in the *f* day of the month, that Eze 32:1 259
after the measure of the *f* gate Eze 40:21 7223
the *f* of all the firstfruits of Eze 44:30 7225
the priest the *f* of your dough Eze 44:30 7225
In the *f* month, in the Eze 45:18 7223
in the *f* day of the month, thou Eze 45:18 259
In the *f* month, in the fourteenth Eze 45:21 7223
of the *f* year without blemish Eze 46:13 1121
unto the *f* year of king Cyrus Dan 1:21 259
of whom Daniel was *f* Dan 6:2 2298
In the *f* year of Belshazzar king Dan 7:1 2298
The *f* was like a lion, and had Dan 7:4 6933
whom there were three of the *f* Dan 7:8 6933
and he shall be diverse from the *f* Dan 7:24 6933
which appeared unto me at the *f* Dan 8:1 8462
is between his eyes is the *f* king Dan 8:21 7223
In the *f* year of Darius the son Dan 9:1 259
In the *f* year of his reign I Dan 9:2 259
and twentieth day of the *f* month Dan 10:4 7223
for from the *f* day that thou Dan 10:12 7223
Also I in the *f* year of Darius Dan 11:1 259
will go and return to my *f* husband Hos 2:7 7223
in the fig tree at her *f* time Hos 9:10 7225
and the latter rain in the *f* month Joel 2:23 7223
with the *f* that go captive Amos 6:7 7218
it come, even the *f* dominion Mic 4:8 7223
in the *f* day of the month, came Hag 1:1 259
saw this house in her *f* glory Hag 2:3 7223
In the *f* chariot were red horses Zec 6:2 7223
shall save the tents of Judah *f* Zec 12:7 7223
gate unto the place of the *f* gate Zec 14:10 7223
f be reconciled to thy brother, Mt 5:24 *4412*
But seek ye *f* the kingdom of God, Mt 6:33 *4412*
f cast out the beam out of thine Mt 7:5 *4412*
unto him, Lord, suffer me *f* to go Mt 8:21 *4412*
The *f*, Simon, who is called Peter Mt 10:2 *4413*
except he *f* bind the strong man Mt 12:29 *4412*
of that man is worse than the *f* Mt 12:45 *4413*
Gather ye together *f* the tares Mt 13:30 *4412*
scribes that Elias must *f* come Mt 17:10 *4412*
them, Elias truly shall *f* come Mt 17:11 *4412*
take up the fish that *f* cometh up Mt 17:27 *4413*
But many that are *f* shall be last Mt 19:30 *4413*
and the last shall be *f* Mt 19:30 *4413*
from the last unto the *f* Mt 20:8 *4413*
But when the *f* came, they Mt 20:10 *4413*
shall be *f*, and the *f* last Mt 20:16 *4413*
and he came to the *f*, and said, Son Mt 21:28 *4413*
They say unto him, The *f* Mt 21:31 *4413*
other servants more than the *f* Mt 21:36 *4413*
and the *f*, when he had married a Mt 22:25 *4413*
This is the *f* and great Mt 22:38 *4413*
cleanse *f* that which is within Mt 23:26 *4412*
Now the *f* day of the feast of Mt 26:17 *4413*
error shall be worse than the *f* Mt 27:64 *4413*
dawn toward the *f* day of the week Mt 28:1 *3391*
except he will *f* bind the strong Mk 3:27 *4412*
f the blade, then the ear, after Mk 4:28 *4412*
her, Let the children *f* be filled Mk 7:27 *4412*
scribes that Elias must *f* come Mk 9:11 *4412*
told them, Elias verily cometh *f* Mk 9:12 *4412*
them, If any man desire to be *f* Mk 9:35 *4413*
But many that are *f* shall be last Mk 10:31 *4413*
and the last *f* Mk 10:31 *4413*
the *f* took a wife, and dying left Mk 12:20 *4413*
Which is the *f* commandment of all Mk 12:28 *4413*
The *f* of all the commandments is, Mk 12:29 *4413*
this is the *f* commandment Mk 12:30 *4413*
the gospel must *f* be published Mk 13:10 *4412*
the *f* day of unleavened bread, Mk 14:12 *4413*
the morning the *f* day of the week Mk 16:2 *3391*
risen early the *f* day of the week Mk 16:9 *4413*
he appeared *f* to Mary Magdalene, Mk 16:9 *4412*
of all things from the very *f* Lk 1:3 *509*
this taxing was *f* made when Lk 2:2 *4413*
on the second sabbath after the *f* Lk 6:1 *1207*
cast out *f* the beam out of thine Lk 6:42 *4412*
he said, Lord, suffer me *f* to go Lk 9:59 *4412*
but let me *f* go bid them farewell Lk 9:61 *4412*
f say, Peace be to this house Lk 10:5 *4412*
of that man is worse than the *f* Lk 11:26 *4413*
he had not *f* washed before dinner Lk 11:38 *4412*
say unto his disciples *f* of all Lk 12:1 *4412*
there are last which shall be *f* Lk 13:30 *4413*
there are *f* which shall be last Lk 13:30 *4413*
The *f* said unto him, I have Lk 14:18 *4413*
build a tower, sitteth not down *f* Lk 14:28 *4412*
another king, sitteth not down *f* Lk 14:31 *4412*
unto him, and said unto the *f* Lk 16:5 *4413*
But *f* must he suffer many things, Lk 17:25 *4412*
Then came the *f*, saying, Lord, Lk 19:16 *4413*
the *f* took a wife, and died Lk 20:29 *4413*
these things must *f* come to pass Lk 21:9 *4412*
Now upon the *f* day of the week, Lk 24:1 *3891*
He *f* findeth his own brother Jn 1:41 *4413*
whosoever then *f* after the Jn 5:4 *4413*
let him *f* cast a stone at her Jn 8:7 *4413*
place where John at *f* baptized Jn 10:40 *4412*
not his disciples at the *f* Jn 12:16 *4412*
And led him away to Annas *f* Jn 18:13 *4412*
and brake the legs of the *f* Jn 19:32 *4413*
which at the *f* came to Jesus by Jn 19:39 *4412*
The *f* day of the week cometh Mary Jn 20:1 *3391*
Peter, and came *f* to the sepulchre Jn 20:4 *4413*
which came *f* to the sepulchre, and Jn 20:8 *4413*
being the *f* day of the week, when Jn 20:19 *3391*
Unto you *f* God, having raised up Acts 3:26 *4412*
Egypt, he sent out our fathers *f* Acts 7:12 *4412*
called Christians *f* in Antioch Acts 11:26 *4412*
When they were past the *f* Acts 12:10 *4413*
When John had *f* preached before Acts 13:24
should *f* have been spoken to you Acts 13:46 *4412*
at the *f* did visit the Gentiles Acts 15:14 *4412*
upon the *f* day of the week, when Acts 20:7 *3391*
from the *f* day that I came into Acts 20:18 *4413*
which was at the *f* among mine own Acts 26:4 *746*
But shewed *f* unto them of Acts 26:20 *4412*
that he should be the *f* that Acts 26:23 *4413*
cast themselves *f* into the sea Acts 27:43 *4413*
F, I thank my God through Jesus Rom 1:8 *4412*
to the Jew *f*, and also to the Rom 1:16 *4412*
man that doeth evil, of the Jew *f* Rom 2:9 *4412*
that worketh good, to the Jew *f* Rom 2:10 *4412*
F Moses saith, I will provoke you Rom 10:19 *4413*
Or who hath *f* given to him, and it Rom 11:35 *4272*
if *f* I be somewhat filled with Rom 15:24 *4412*
For *f* of all, when ye come 1Cor 11:18 *4412*
f apostles, secondarily prophets, 1Cor 12:28 *4412*
by, let the *f* hold his peace 1Cor 14:30 *4413*
you *f* of all that which I also 1Cor 15:3 *4413*
The *f* man Adam was made a living 1Cor 15:45 *4413*
that was not *f* which is spiritual 1Cor 15:46 *4412*
The *f* man is of the earth, earthy 1Cor 15:47 *4413*
Upon the *f* day of the week let 1Cor 16:2 *3391*
The *f* epistle to the Corinthians 1Cor *s* *4413*
but *f* gave their own selves to 2Cor 8:5 *4412*
For if there be *f* a willing mind 2Cor 8:12 *4295*
the gospel unto you at the *f* Gal 4:13 *4386*
glory, who *f* trusted in Christ Eph 1:12 *4276*
f into the lower parts of the Eph 4:9 *4412*
which is the *f* commandment with Eph 6:2 *4413*
gospel from the *f* day until now Phil 1:5 *4413*
the dead in Christ shall rise *f* 1Th 4:16 *4412*
The *f* epistle unto the 1Th *s* *4413*
there come a falling away *f* 2Th 2:3 *4412*
that in me *f* Jesus Christ might 1Ti 1:16 *4413*
f of all, supplications, prayers, 1Ti 2:1 *4412*
For Adam was *f* formed, then Eve 1Ti 2:13 *4413*
And let these also *f* be proved 1Ti 3:10 *4412*
let them learn *f* to shew piety at 1Ti 5:4 *4412*
they have cast off their *f* faith 1Ti 5:12 *4413*
The *f* to Timothy was written from 1Ti *s* *4413*
which dwelt *f* in thy grandmother 2Ti 1:5 *4412*
must be *f* partaker of the fruits 2Ti 2:6 *4413*
At my *f* answer no man stood with 2Ti 4:16 *4413*
ordained the *f* bishop of the 2Ti *s* *4413*
that is an heretick after the *f* Titus 3:10 *3391*
ordained the *f* bishop of the Titus *s* *4413*
which at the *f* began to be spoken Heb 2:3 *746*
they to whom it was *f* preached Heb 4:6 *4386*
f principles of the oracles of Heb 5:12 *746*
f being by interpretation King of Heb 7:2 *4412*
f for his own sins, and then for Heb 7:27 *4386*
For if that *f* covenant had been Heb 8:7 *4413*
covenant, he hath made the *f* old Heb 8:13 *4413*
Then verily the *f* covenant had Heb 9:1 *4413*
the *f*, wherein was the Heb 9:2 *4413*
went always into the *f* tabernacle Heb 9:6 *4413*
while as the *f* tabernacle was yet Heb 9:8 *4413*
that were under the *f* testament Heb 9:15 *4413*
Whereupon neither the *f* testament Heb 9:18 *4413*
He taketh away the *f*, that he may Heb 10:9 *4413*
that is from above is *f* pure Jas 3:17 *4412*
if it *f* begin at us, what shall 1Pet 4:17 *4412*
Knowing this *f*, that no prophecy 2Pet 1:20 *4412*
Knowing this *f*, that there shall 2Pet 3:3 *4412*
love him, because he *f* loved us 1Jn 4:19 *4413*
which kept not their *f* estate Jude 6 *746*
the *f* begotten of the dead, and Rev 1:5 *4416*
I am Alpha and Omega, the *f* Rev 1:11 *4413*
I am the *f* and the last Rev 1:17 *4413*
because thou hast left thy *f* love Rev 2:4 *4413*
and repent, and do the *f* works Rev 2:5 *4413*
These things saith the *f* and the Rev 2:8 *4413*
and the last to be more than the *f* Rev 2:19 *4413*
the *f* voice which I heard was as Rev 4:1 *4413*
the *f* beast was like a lion, and Rev 4:7 *4413*
The *f* angel sounded, and there Rev 8:7 *4413*
power of the *f* beast before him Rev 13:12 *4413*
therein to worship the *f* beast Rev 13:12 *4413*
the *f* went, and poured out his Rev 16:2 *4413*
This is the *f* resurrection Rev 20:5 *4413*
hath part in the *f* resurrection Rev 20:6 *4413*
f heaven and the *f* earth Rev 21:1 *4413*
The *f* foundation was jasper Rev 21:19 *4413*
the beginning and the end, the *f* Rev 22:13 *4413*

FIRSTBEGOTTEN

bringeth in the *f* into the world Heb 1:6 *4416*

FIRSTBORN

And Canaan begat Sidon his *f* Gen 10:15 1060
the *f* said unto the younger, Our Gen 19:31 1067
the *f* went in, and lay with her Gen 19:33 1067
that the *f* said unto the younger, Gen 19:34 1067
the *f* bare a son, and called his Gen 19:37 1067
Huz his *f*, and Buz his brother, and Gen 22:21 1060
the *f* of Ishmael, Nebajoth Gen 25:13 1060
unto his father, I am Esau thy *f* Gen 27:19 1060
he said, I am thy son, thy *f* Esau Gen 27:32 1060
to give the younger before the *f* Gen 29:26 1067
Reuben, Jacob's *f*, and Simeon, and Gen 35:23 1060
sons of Eliphaz the *f* son of Esau Gen 36:15 1060
And Judah took a wife for Er his *f* Gen 38:6 1060
And Er, Judah's *f*, was wicked in Gen 38:7 1060
called the name of the *f* Manasseh Gen 41:51 1060
the *f* according to his birthright Gen 43:33 1060
Reuben, Jacob's *f* Gen 46:8 1060
for Manasseh was the *f* Gen 48:14 1060
for this is the *f* Gen 48:18 1060
Reuben, thou art my *f*, my might, Gen 49:3 1060
LORD, Israel is my son, even my *f* Ex 4:22 1060
I will slay thy son, even thy *f* Ex 4:23 1060
sons of Reuben the *f* of Israel Ex 6:14 1060
all the *f* in the land of Egypt Ex 11:5 1060
from the *f* of Pharaoh that Ex 11:5 1060
throne, even unto the *f* of the Ex 11:5 1060
and all the *f* of beasts Ex 11:5 1060
will smite all the *f* in the land Ex 12:12 1060
all the *f* in the land of Egypt Ex 12:29 1060
from the *f* of Pharaoh that sat on Ex 12:29 1060
f of the captive that was in the Ex 12:29 1060
and all the *f* of cattle Ex 12:29 1060
Sanctify unto me all the *f* Ex 13:2 1060
all the *f* of man among thy Ex 13:13 1060
all the *f* in the land of Egypt Ex 13:15 1060
land of Egypt, both the *f* of man Ex 13:15 1060
of man, and the *f* of beast Ex 13:15 1060
but all the *f* of my children I Ex 13:15 1060
the *f* of thy sons shalt thou give Ex 22:29 1060
All the *f* of thy sons thou shalt Ex 34:20 1060
Nadab the *f*, and Abihu, Eleazar, Num 3:2 1060
of Israel instead of all the *f* Num 3:12 1060
Because all the *f* are mine Num 3:13 1060
f in the land of Egypt I hallowed Num 3:13 1060
unto me all the *f* in Israel Num 3:13 1060
Number all the *f* of the males of Num 3:40 1060
f among the children of Israel Num 3:41 1060
all the *f* among the children of Num 3:42 1060
all the *f* males by the number of Num 3:43 1060
f among the children of Israel Num 3:45 1060
thirteen of the *f* of the children Num 3:46 1060
Of the *f* of the children of Num 3:50 1060
even instead of the *f* of all the Num 8:16 1060
For all the *f* of the children of Num 8:17 1060
every *f* in the land of Egypt I Num 8:17 1060
the *f* of the children of Israel Num 8:18 1060
nevertheless the *f* of man shalt Num 18:15 1060
the Egyptians buried all their *f* Num 33:4 1060
if the *f* son be hers that was Deut 21:15 1060
f before the son of the hated Deut 21:16 1069
which is indeed the *f* Deut 21:16 1060
the son of the hated for the *f* Deut 21:17 1060
the right of the *f* is his Deut 21:17 1062
that the *f* which she beareth Deut 25:6 1060
the foundation thereof in his *f* Josh 6:26 1060
for he was the *f* of Joseph Josh 17:1 1060
wit, for Machir the *f* of Manasseh Josh 17:1 1060
And he said unto Jether his *f* Judg 8:20 1060
Now the name of his *f* was Joel 1Sa 8:2 1060
the name of the *f* Merab, and the 1Sa 14:49 1067
his *f* was Amnon, of Ahinoam the 2Sa 3:2 1060
thereof in Abiram his *f*, and set 1Kin 16:34 1060
And Canaan begat Zidon his *f* 1Chr 1:13 1060
The *f* of Ishmael, Nebaioth 1Chr 1:29 1060
the *f* of Judah, was evil in the 1Chr 2:3 1060
And Jesse begat his *f* Eliab 1Chr 2:13 1060
of Jerahmeel the *f* of Hezron were 1Chr 2:25 1060
Ram the *f*, and Bunah 1Chr 2:25 1060
of Ram the *f* of Jerahmeel were 1Chr 2:27 1060
of Jerahmeel were, Mesha his *f* 1Chr 2:42 1060
the son of Hur, the *f* of Ephratah 1Chr 2:50 1060
the *f* Amnon, of Ahinoam the 1Chr 3:1 1060
the *f* Johanan, the second 1Chr 3:15 1060
the *f* of Ephratah, the father of 1Chr 4:4 1060
sons of Reuben the *f* of Israel 1Chr 5:1 1060
(for he was the *f*; 1Chr 5:1 1060
of Reuben the *f* of Israel were, 1Chr 5:3 1060
the *f* Vashni, and Abiah 1Chr 6:28 1060
Now Benjamin begat Bela his *f* 1Chr 8:1 1060
his *f* son Abdon, and Zur, and Kish, 1Chr 8:30 1060
his brother were, Ulam his *f* 1Chr 8:39 1060
Asaiah the *f*, and his sons 1Chr 9:5 1060
who was the *f* of Shallum the 1Chr 9:31 1060
his *f* son Abdon, then Zur, and 1Chr 9:36 1060
Meshelemiah were, Zechariah the *f* 1Chr 26:2 1060
of Obed-edom were, Shemaiah the *f* 1Chr 26:4 1060
(for though he was not the *f* 1Chr 26:10 1060
because he was the *f* 2Chr 21:3 1060
Also the *f* of our sons, and of our Neh 10:36 1060
even the *f* of death shall devour Job 18:13 1060
And smote all the *f* in Egypt Ps 78:51 1060
Also I will make him my *f* Ps 89:27 1060
also all the *f* in their land Ps 105:36 1060
Who smote the *f* of Egypt, both of Ps 135:8 1060
him that smote Egypt in their *f* Ps 136:10 1060
the *f* of the poor shall feed, and Is 14:30 1060
to Israel, and Ephraim is my *f* Jer 31:9 1060
shall I give my *f* for my Mic 6:7 1060
that is in bitterness for his *f* Zec 12:10 1060
she had brought forth her *f* son Mt 1:25 *4416*
And she brought forth her *f* son Lk 2:7 *4416*
be the *f* among many brethren Rom 8:29 *4416*
God, the *f* of every creature Col 1:15 *4416*
beginning, the *f* from the dead Col 1:18 *4416*
destroyed the *f* should touch them Heb 11:28 *4416*
assembly and church of the *f* Heb 12:23 *4416*

FIRSTFRUIT

The *f* also of thy corn, of thy Deut 18:4 7225
For if the *f* be holy, the lump is Rom 11:16 *536*

FIRSTFRUITS

the *f* of thy labours, which thou Ex 23:16 1061
The first of the *f* of thy land Ex 23:19 1061
of the *f* of wheat harvest, and the Ex 34:22 1061
The first of the *f* of thy land Ex 34:26 1061
As for the oblation of the *f* Lev 2:12 7225
offering of thy *f* unto the LORD Lev 2:14 1061
for the meat offering of thy *f* Lev 2:14 1061
ye shall bring a sheaf of the *f* Lev 23:10 7225
they are the *f* unto the LORD Lev 23:17 1061
the *f* of them which they shall Num 18:12 7225
Also in the day of the *f*, when ye Num 28:26 1061
I have brought the *f* of the land Deut 26:10 7225
the man of God bread of the *f* 2Kin 4:42 1061
in abundance the *f* of corn 2Chr 31:5 7225
to bring the *f* of our ground, and Neh 10:35 1061
the *f* of all fruit of all trees, Neh 10:35 1061
should bring the *f* of our dough Neh 10:37 7225
for the offerings, for the *f* Neh 12:44 7225
at times appointed, and for the *f* Neh 13:31 1061

with the *f* of all thine increase Prov 3:9 7225
LORD, and the *f* of his increase Jer 2:3 7225
the *f* of your oblations, with all Eze 20:40 7225
first of all the *f* of all things Eze 44:30 1061
nor alienate the *f* of the land Eze 48:14 7225
which have the *f* of the Spirit Rom 8:23 *536*
who is the *f* of Achaia unto Rom 16:5 *536*
become the *f* of them that slept 1Cor 15:20 *536*
Christ the *f* 1Cor 15:23 *536*
that it is the *f* of Achaia 1Cor 16:15 *536*
be a kind of *f* of his creatures Jas 1:18 *536*
among men, being the *f* unto God Rev 14:4 *536*

FIRSTLING
every *f* that cometh of a beast Ex 13:12 6363
every *f* of an ass thou shalt Ex 13:13 6363
every *f* among thy cattle, whether Ex 34:19 6363
But the *f* of an ass thou shalt Ex 34:20 6363
Only the *f* of the beasts, which Lev 27:26 1060
which should be the LORD's *f* Lev 27:26 1069
the *f* of unclean beasts shalt Num 18:15 1060
f of a cow, or the *f* Num 18:17 1060
or the *f* of a goat, thou shalt Num 18:17 1060
All the *f* males that come of thy Deut 15:19 1060
no work with the *f* of thy bullock Deut 15:19 1060
nor shear the *f* of thy sheep Deut 15:19 1060
is like the *f* of his bullock Deut 33:17 1060

FIRSTLINGS
brought of the *f* of his flock Gen 4:4 1062
all the *f* among the cattle of the Num 3:41 1060
the *f* of your herds and of your Deut 12:6 1062
or the *f* of thy herds or of thy Deut 12:17 1062
the *f* of thy herds and of thy Deut 14:23 1062
the *f* of our herds and of our Neh 10:36 1062

FIRSTRIPE
time was the time of the *f* grapes Num 13:20 1061
I saw your fathers as the *f* in Hos 9:10 1063
my soul desired the *f* fruit Mic 7:1 1063
be like fig trees with the *f* figs Nah 3:12 1063

FISH
dominion over the *f* of the sea Gen 1:26 1710
dominion over the *f* of the sea Gen 1:28 1710
the *f* that is in the river shall Ex 7:18 1710
the *f* that was in the river died Ex 7:21 1710
We remember the *f*, which we did Num 11:5 1710
or shall all the *f* of the sea be Num 11:22 1709
the likeness of any *f* that is in Deut 4:18 1710
to the entering in at the *f* gate 2Chr 33:14 1709
But the *f* gate did the sons of Neh 3:3 1709
the old gate, and above the *f* gate Neh 12:39 1709
also therein, which brought *f* Neh 13:16 1709
or his head with *f* spears Job 41:7 1709
the *f* of the sea, and whatsoever Ps 8:8 1709
into blood, and slew their *f* Ps 105:29 1710
that make sluices and ponds for *f* Is 19:10 5315
their *f* stinketh, because there Is 50:2 1710
the LORD, and they shall *f* them Jer 16:16 1770
I will cause the *f* of thy rivers Eze 29:4 1710
all the *f* of thy rivers shall Eze 29:4 1710
thee and all the *f* of thy rivers Eze 29:5 1710
be a very great multitude of *f* Eze 47:9 1710
their *f* shall be according to Eze 47:10 1710
as the *f* of the great sea, Eze 47:10 1710
a great *f* to swallow up Jonah Jonah 1:17 1709
in the belly of the *f* three days Jonah 1:17 1709
And the LORD spake unto the *f* Jonah 2:10 1709
noise of a cry from the *f* gate Zeph 1:10 1709
Or if he ask a *f*, will he give Mt 7:10 *2486*
take up the *f* that first cometh Mt 17:27 *2486*
or if he ask a *f* Lk 11:11 *2486*
will he for a *f* give him a Lk 11:11 *2486*
gave him a piece of a broiled *f* Lk 24:42 *2486*
and *f* laid thereon, and bread Jn 21:9 *3795*
Bring of the *f* which ye have now Jn 21:10 *3795*
and giveth them, and *f* likewise Jn 21:13 *3795*

FISHERMEN
but the *f* were gone out of them, Lk 5:2 *231*

FISHER'S
he girt his *f* coat unto him, (for Jn 21:7 *1903*

FISHERS
The *f* also shall mourn, and all Is 19:8 1771
Behold, I will send for many *f* Jer 16:16 1728
that the *f* shall stand upon it Eze 47:10 1728
for they were *f* Mt 4:18 *231*
me, and I will make you *f* of men Mt 4:19 *231*
for they were *f* Mk 1:16 *231*
will make you to become *f* of men Mk 1:17 *231*

FISHES
and upon all the *f* of the sea Gen 9:2 1709
and of creeping things, and of *f* 1Kin 4:33 1709
the *f* of the sea shall declare Job 12:8 1709
as the *f* that are taken in an Eccl 9:12 1709
So that the *f* of the sea, and the Eze 38:20 1709
the *f* of the sea also shall be Hos 4:3 1709
And makest men as the *f* of the sea Hab 1:14 1709
and the *f* of the sea, and the Zeph 1:3 1709
here but five loaves, and two *f* Mt 14:17 *2486*
the five loaves, and the two *f* Mt 14:19 *2486*
said, Seven, and a few little *f* Mt 15:34 *2485*
he took the seven loaves and the *f* Mt 15:36 *2486*
knew, they say, Five, and two *f* Mk 6:38 *2486*
the five loaves and the two *f* Mk 6:41 *2486*
the two *f* divided he among them Mk 6:41 *2486*
of the fragments, and of the *f* Mk 6:43 *2486*
And they had a few small *f* Mk 8:7 *2485*
inclosed a great multitude of *f* Lk 5:6 *2486*
of the *f* which they had taken Lk 5:9 *2486*
no more but five loaves and two *f* Lk 9:13 *2486*
took the five loaves and the two *f* Lk 9:16 *2486*
barley loaves, and two small *f* Jn 6:9 *3795*
likewise of the *f* as much as they Jn 6:11 *3795*
to draw it for the multitude of *f* Jn 21:6 *2486*
cubits,) dragging the net with *f* Jn 21:8 *2486*
the net to land full of great *f* Jn 21:11 *2486*
flesh of beasts, another of *f* 1Cor 15:39 *2486*

FISHHOOKS
hooks, and your posterity with *f* Amos 4:2

FISHING
Peter saith unto them, I go a *f* Jn 21:3 *232*

FISHPOOLS
thine eyes like the *f* in Heshbon Song 7:4 1295

FISH'S
LORD his God out of the *f* belly Jonah 2:1 1710

FIST
with a stone, or with his *f* Ex 21:18 106
to smite with the *f* of wickedness Is 58:4 106

FISTS
hath gathered the wind in his *f* Prov 30:4 2651

FIT
of a *f* man into the wilderness Lev 16:21 6261
f to go out for war and battle 1Chr 7:11
men of war *f* for the battle, that 1Chr 12:8
Is it *f* to say to a king, Thou Job 34:18
make it *f* for thyself in the Prov 24:27 6257
is *f* for the kingdom of God Lk 9:62 *2111*
It is neither *f* for the land Lk 14:35 *2111*
for it is not *f* that he should Acts 22:22 *2520*
husbands, as it is *f* in the Lord Col 3:18 *433*

FITCHES
doth he not cast abroad the *f* Is 28:25 7100
For the *f* are not threshed with a Is 28:27 7100
but the *f* are beaten out with a Is 28:27 7100
and lentiles, and millet, and *f* Eze 4:9 3698

FITLY
A word *f* spoken is like apples of Prov 25:11
washed with milk, and *f* set Song 5:12
In whom all the building *f* framed Eph 2:21 *4883*
the whole body *f* joined together Eph 4:16 *4883*

FITTED
with gold *f* upon the carved work 1Kin 6:35 3474
shall withal be *f* in thy lips Prov 22:18 3559
vessels of wrath *f* to destruction Rom 9:22 *2675*

FITTETH
he *f* it with planes, and he Is 44:13 6213

FIVE
hundred and *f* years, and begat Enos Gen 5:6 2568
Enos were nine hundred and *f* years Gen 5:11 2568
sixty and *f* years, and begat Jared Gen 5:15 2568
eight hundred ninety and *f* years Gen 5:17 2568
f years, and begat Methuselah Gen 5:21 2568
three hundred sixty and *f* years Gen 5:23 2568
he begat Noah *f* hundred ninety Gen 5:30 2568
f years, and begat sons and Gen 5:30 2568
Noah was *f* hundred years old Gen 5:32 2568
he begat Arphaxad *f* hundred years Gen 11:11 2568
And Arphaxad lived *f* and thirty Gen 11:12 2568
Terah were two hundred and *f* years Gen 11:32 2568
f years old when he departed out Gen 12:4 2568
Ellasar; four kings with *f* Gen 14:9 2568
lack *f* of the fifty righteous Gen 18:28 2568
all the city for lack of *f* Gen 18:28 2568
said, If I find there forty and *f* Gen 18:28 2568
but Benjamin's mess was *f* times Gen 43:34 2568
and yet there are *f* years, in the Gen 45:6 2568
yet there are *f* years of famine Gen 45:11 2568
silver, and *f* changes of raiment Gen 45:22 2568
some of his brethren, even *f* men Gen 47:2 2568
he shall restore *f* oxen for an ox Ex 22:1 2568
The *f* curtains shall be coupled Ex 26:3 2568
other *f* curtains shall be coupled Ex 26:3 2568
thou shalt couple *f* curtains by Ex 26:9 2568
f for the boards of the one side Ex 26:26 2568
f bars for the boards of the Ex 26:27 2568
f bars for the boards of the side Ex 26:27 2568
hanging *f* pillars of shittim wood Ex 26:37 2568
thou shalt cast *f* sockets of Ex 26:37 2568
f cubits long, and *f* cubits Ex 27:1 2568
the height *f* cubits of fine Ex 27:18 2568
of pure myrrh *f* hundred shekels Ex 30:23 2568
of cassia *f* hundred shekels, Ex 30:24 2568
he coupled the *f* curtains one Ex 36:10 2568
the other *f* curtains he coupled Ex 36:10 2568
And he coupled *f* curtains by Ex 36:16 2568
f for the boards of the one side Ex 36:31 2568
f bars for the boards of the Ex 36:32 2568
f bars for the boards of the Ex 36:32 2568
the *f* pillars of it with their Ex 36:38 2568
but their *f* sockets were of brass Ex 36:38 2568
f cubits was the length thereof, Ex 38:1 2568
f cubits the breadth thereof Ex 38:1 2568
in the breadth was *f* cubits Ex 38:18 2568
and *f* hundred and fifty men Ex 38:26 2568
f shekels he made hooks for the Ex 38:28 2568
f of you shall chase an hundred, Lev 26:8 2568
if it be from *f* years old even Lev 27:5 2568
a month old even unto *f* years old Lev 27:6 2568
of the male *f* shekels of silver Lev 27:6 2568
and six thousand and *f* hundred Num 1:21 2568
f thousand six hundred and fifty Num 1:25 2568
were forty thousand and *f* hundred Num 1:33 2568
f thousand and four hundred Num 1:37 2568
and one thousand and *f* hundred Num 1:41 2568
thousand and *f* hundred and fifty Num 1:46 2568
and six thousand and *f* hundred Num 2:11 2568
f thousand and six hundred and Num 2:15 2568
were forty thousand and *f* hundred Num 2:19 2568
f thousand and four hundred Num 2:23 2568
and one thousand and *f* hundred Num 2:28 2568
thousand and *f* hundred and fifty Num 2:32 2568
were seven thousand and *f* hundred Num 3:22 2568
Thou shalt even take *f* shekels Num 3:47 2568
f shekels, after the shekel of Num 3:50 2568
and *f* hundred and fourscore Num 4:48 2568
f rams, *f* he goats, *f* lambs Num 7:17 2568
f rams, *f* he goats, *f* lambs Num 7:23 2568
f rams, *f* he goats, *f* lambs Num 7:29 2568
f rams, *f* he goats, *f* lambs Num 7:35 2568
f rams, *f* he goats, *f* lambs Num 7:41 2568
f rams, *f* he goats, *f* lambs Num 7:47 2568
f rams, *f* he goats, *f* lambs Num 7:53 2568
f rams, *f* he goats, *f* lambs Num 7:59 2568
f rams, *f* he goats, *f* lambs Num 7:65 2568
f rams, *f* he goats, *f* lambs Num 7:71 2568
f he goats, *f* lambs of the Num 7:71 2568
f rams, *f* he goats, *f* lambs Num 7:77 2568
f rams, *f* he goats, *f* lambs Num 7:83 2568
f years old and upward they shall Num 8:24 2568
nor *f* days, neither ten days, nor Num 11:19 2568
for the money of *f* shekels Num 18:16 2568
them, forty thousand and *f* hundred Num 26:18 2568
and sixteen thousand and *f* hundred Num 26:22 2568
threescore thousand and *f* hundred Num 26:27 2568
and two thousand and *f* hundred Num 26:37 2568
f thousand and six hundred Num 26:41 2568
f thousand and four hundred Num 26:50 2568
Hur, and Reba, *f* kings of Midian Num 31:8 2568
one soul of *f* hundred, both of Num 31:28 2568
thousand and *f* thousand sheep, Num 31:32 2568
thousand and *f* hundred sheep Num 31:36 2568
were thirty thousand and *f* hundred Num 31:39 2568
thousand and *f* hundred sheep, Num 31:43 2568
thousand asses and *f* hundred, Num 31:45 2568
And he took about *f* thousand men Josh 8:12 2568
Therefore the *f* kings of the Josh 10:5 2568
But these *f* kings fled, and hid Josh 10:16 2568
The *f* kings are found hid in a Josh 10:17 2568
bring out those *f* kings unto me Josh 10:22 2568
brought forth those *f* kings unto Josh 10:23 2568
them, and hanged them on *f* trees Josh 10:26 2568
f lords of the Philistines Josh 13:3 2568
f years, even since the LORD Josh 14:10 2568
this day fourscore and *f* years old Josh 14:10 2568
f lords of the Philistines, and Judg 3:3 2568
family *f* men from their coasts Judg 18:2 2568
Then the *f* men departed, and came Judg 18:7 2568
Then answered the *f* men that went Judg 18:14 2568
the *f* men that went to spy out Judg 18:17 2568
f thousand and an hundred men Judg 20:35 2568
in the highways *f* thousand men Judg 20:45 2568
f thousand men that drew the Judg 20:46 2568
F golden emerods, and *f* golden 1Sa 6:4 2568
f golden mice, according to the 1Sa 6:4 2568
And when the *f* lords of the 1Sa 6:16 2568
belonging to the *f* lords, both of 1Sa 6:18 2568
was *f* thousand shekels of brass 1Sa 17:5 2568
chose him *f* smooth stones out of 1Sa 17:40 2568
give me *f* loaves of bread in mine 1Sa 21:3 2568
f persons that did wear a linen 1Sa 22:18 2568
f sheep ready dressed, and 1Sa 25:18 2568
f measures of parched corn, and an 1Sa 25:18 2568
with *f* damsels of hers that went 1Sa 25:42 2568
He was *f* years old when the 2Sa 4:4 2568
the *f* sons of Michal the daughter 2Sa 21:8 2568
Judah were *f* hundred thousand men 2Sa 24:9 2568
and his songs were a thousand and *f* 1Kin 4:32 2568
chamber was *f* cubits broad 1Kin 6:6 2568
all the house, *f* cubits high 1Kin 6:10 2568
f cubits was the one wing of the 1Kin 6:24 2568
f cubits the other wing of the 1Kin 6:24 2568
that lay on forty *f* pillars 1Kin 7:3 2568
of the one chapiter was *f* cubits 1Kin 7:16 2568
the other chapiter was *f* cubits 1Kin 7:16 2568
about, and his height was *f* cubits 1Kin 7:23 2568
he put *f* bases on the right side 1Kin 7:39 2568
f on the left side of the house 1Kin 7:39 2568
f on the right side, and *f* on 1Kin 7:49 2568
f on the left, before the oracle, 1Kin 7:49 2568
f hundred and fifty, which bare 1Kin 9:23 2568
f years old when he began to 1Kin 22:42 2568
twenty and *f* years in Jerusalem 1Kin 22:42 2568
dung for *f* pieces of silver 2Kin 6:25 2568
f of the horses that remain, 2Kin 7:13 2568
have smitten *f* or six times 2Kin 13:19 2568
f years old when he began to 2Kin 14:2 2568
F and twenty years old was he when 2Kin 15:33 2568
f years old was he when he began 2Kin 18:2 2568
hundred fourscore and *f* thousand 2Kin 19:35 2568
fifty and *f* years in Jerusalem 2Kin 21:1 2568
f years old when he began to 2Kin 23:36 2568
f men of them that were in the 2Kin 25:19 2568
All the sons of Judah were *f* 1Chr 2:4 2568
f of them in all 1Chr 2:6 2568
and Hasadiah, Jushab-hesed, *f* 1Chr 3:20 2568
and Tochen, and Ashan, *f* cities 1Chr 4:32 2568
f hundred men, went to mount Seir 1Chr 4:42 2568
and Obadiah, and Joel, Ishiah, *f* 1Chr 7:3 2568
and Uzziel, and Jerimoth, and Iri, *f* 1Chr 7:7 2568
of great stature, *f* cubits high 1Chr 11:23 2568
of God of gold *f* thousand talents 1Chr 29:7 2568
of the one cherub was *f* cubits 2Chr 3:11 2568
other wing was likewise *f* cubits 2Chr 3:11 2568
of the other cherub was *f* cubits 2Chr 3:12 2568
the other wing was *f* cubits also 2Chr 3:12 2568
f cubits high, and the chapiter 2Chr 3:15 2568
top of each of them was *f* cubits 2Chr 3:15 2568
f cubits the height thereof 2Chr 4:2 2568
put *f* on the right hand, and 2Chr 4:6 2568
f on the left, to wash in them 2Chr 4:6 2568
f on the right hand, and *f* on 2Chr 4:7 2568
f on the right side, and *f* on 2Chr 4:8 2568
of *f* cubits long, and *f* cubits 2Chr 6:13 2568
f hundred thousand chosen men 2Chr 13:17 2568
there was no more war unto the *f* 2Chr 15:19 2568

f years old when he began to	2Chr 20:31	2568
twenty and *f* years in Jerusalem	2Chr 20:31	2568
f years old when he began to	2Chr 25:1	2568
f hundred, that made war with	2Chr 26:13	2568
f years old when he began to	2Chr 27:1	2568
He was *f* and twenty years old when	2Chr 27:8	2568
began to reign when he was *f*	2Chr 29:1	2568
fifty and *f* years in Jerusalem	2Chr 33:1	2568
offerings *f* thousand small cattle	2Chr 35:9	2568
small cattle, and *f* hundred oxen	2Chr 35:9	2568
f years old when he began to	2Chr 36:5	2568
gold and of silver were *f* thousand	Ezr 1:11	2568
Arah, seven hundred seventy and *f*	Ezr 2:5	2568
of Zattu, nine hundred forty and *f*	Ezr 2:8	2568
children of Gibbar, ninety and *f*	Ezr 2:20	2568
and Ono, seven hundred twenty and *f*	Ezr 2:33	2568
Jericho, three hundred forty and *f*	Ezr 2:34	2568
mules, two hundred forty and *f*	Ezr 2:66	2568
camels, four hundred thirty and *f*	Ezr 2:67	2568
f thousand pound of silver, and	Ezr 2:69	2568
Zattu, eight hundred forty and *f*	Neh 7:13	2568
of Adin, six hundred fifty and *f*	Neh 7:20	2568
children of Gibeon, ninety and *f*	Neh 7:25	2568
Jericho, three hundred forty and *f*	Neh 7:36	2568
f singing men and singing women	Neh 7:67	2568
mules, two hundred forty and *f*	Neh 7:68	2568
camels, four hundred thirty and *f*	Neh 7:69	2568
f hundred and thirty priests'	Neh 7:70	2568
slew and destroyed *f* hundred men	Est 9:6	2568
destroyed *f* hundred men in	Est 9:12	2568
f thousand, but they laid not	Est 9:16	2568
f hundred yoke of oxen, and *f*	Job 1:3	2568
f hundred she asses, and a very	Job 1:3	2568
f years shall Ephraim be broken,	Is 7:8	2568
four or *f* in the outmost fruitful	Is 17:6	2568
In that day shall *f* cities in the	Is 19:18	2568
at the rebuke of *f* shall ye flee	Is 30:17	2568
and fourscore and *f* thousand	Is 37:36	2568
of one chapiter was *f* cubits	Jer 52:22	2568
seven hundred forty and *f* persons	Jer 52:30	2568
in the twelfth month, in the *f*	Jer 52:31	2568
porch and the altar, were about *f*	Eze 8:16	2568
behold at the door of the gate *f*	Eze 11:1	2568
In the *f* and twentieth year of our	Eze 40:1	2568
the little chambers were *f* cubits	Eze 40:7	2568
the breadth was *f* and twenty	Eze 40:13	2568
fifty cubits, and the breadth *f*	Eze 40:21	2568
fifty cubits, and the breadth *f*	Eze 40:25	2568
it was fifty cubits long, and *f*	Eze 40:29	2568
And the arches round about were *f*	Eze 40:30	2568
cubits long, and *f* cubits broad	Eze 40:30	2568
it was fifty cubits long, and *f*	Eze 40:33	2568
fifty cubits, and the breadth *f*	Eze 40:36	2568
f cubits on this side	Eze 40:48	2568
and *f* cubits on that side	Eze 40:48	2568
were *f* cubits on the one side	Eze 41:2	2568
f cubits on the other side	Eze 41:2	2568
chamber without, was *f* cubits	Eze 41:9	2568
was left was *f* cubits round about	Eze 41:11	2568
was *f* cubits thick round about	Eze 41:12	2568
f hundred reeds, with the	Eze 42:16	2568
f hundred reeds, with the	Eze 42:17	2568
f hundred reeds, with the	Eze 42:18	2568
measured *f* hundred reeds with the	Eze 42:19	2568
f hundred reeds long, and	Eze 42:20	2568
f hundred broad, to make a	Eze 42:20	2568
length shall be the length of *f*	Eze 45:1	2568
the sanctuary *f* hundred in length	Eze 45:2	2568
with *f* hundred in breadth, square	Eze 45:2	2568
thou measure the length of *f*	Eze 45:3	2568
And the *f* and twenty thousand of	Eze 45:5	2568
city *f* thousand broad, and *f*	Eze 45:6	2568
twenty shekels, *f* and twenty	Eze 45:12	2568
which ye shall offer of *f*	Eze 48:8	2568
offer unto the LORD shall be of *f*	Eze 48:9	2568
toward the north *f* and twenty	Eze 48:10	2568
in breadth, and toward the south *f*	Eze 48:10	2568
priests the Levites shall have *f*	Eze 48:13	2568
all the length shall be *f*	Eze 48:13	2568
the *f* thousand, that are left in	Eze 48:15	2568
in the breadth over against the *f*	Eze 48:15	2568
f hundred, and the south side four	Eze 48:16	2568
f hundred, and on the east side	Eze 48:16	2568
f hundred, and the west side four	Eze 48:16	2568
side four thousand and *f* hundred	Eze 48:16	2568
be *f* and twenty thousand by *f*	Eze 48:20	2568
of the city, over against the *f*	Eze 48:21	2568
and westward over against the *f*	Eze 48:21	2568
thousand and *f* hundred measures	Eze 48:30	2568
side four thousand and *f* hundred	Eze 48:32	2568
thousand and *f* hundred measures	Eze 48:33	2568
f hundred, with their three gates	Eze 48:34	2568
the thousand three hundred and *f*	Dan 12:12	2568
him, We have here but *f* loaves	Mt 14:17	*4002*
the grass, and took the *f* loaves	Mt 14:19	*4002*
eaten were about *f* thousand men	Mt 14:21	*4000*
neither remember the *f* loaves of	Mt 16:9	*4002*
f thousand, and how many baskets	Mt 16:9	*4000*
f of them were wise, and *f* were	Mt 25:2	*4000*
And unto one he gave *f* talents	Mt 25:15	*4000*
had received the *f* talents went	Mt 25:16	*4000*
and made them other *f* talents	Mt 25:16	*4000*
that had received *f* talents came	Mt 25:20	*4000*
came and brought other *f* talents	Mt 25:20	*4000*
deliveredst unto me *f* talents	Mt 25:20	*4000*
gained beside them *f* talents more	Mt 25:20	*4000*
And when they knew, they say, *F*	Mk 6:38	*4000*
And when he had taken the *f* loaves	Mk 6:41	*4000*
loaves were about *f* thousand men	Mk 6:44	*4000*
When I brake the *f* loaves among	Mk 8:19	*4002*
f thousand, how many baskets	Mk 8:19	*4000*
and hid herself *f* months, saying,	Lk 1:24	*4002*
the one owed *f* hundred pence, and	Lk 7:41	*4001*
We have no more but *f* loaves	Lk 9:13	*4002*
they were about *f* thousand men	Lk 9:14	*4000*
Then he took the *f* loaves	Lk 9:16	*4002*
Are not *f* sparrows sold for two	Lk 12:6	*4002*
shall be *f* in one house divided	Lk 12:52	*4002*
I have bought *f* yoke of oxen	Lk 14:19	*4002*
For I have *f* brethren	Lk 16:28	*4002*
thy pound hath gained *f* pounds	Lk 19:18	*4002*
him, Be thou also over *f* cities	Lk 19:19	*4002*
For thou hast had *f* husbands	Jn 4:18	*4002*
tongue Bethesda, having *f* porches	Jn 5:2	*4002*
which hath *f* barley loaves, and	Jn 6:9	*4002*
down, in number about *f* thousand	Jn 6:10	*4000*
fragments of the *f* barley loaves	Jn 6:13	*4002*
So when they had rowed about *f*	Jn 6:19	*4002*
of the men was about *f* thousand	Acts 4:4	*4002*
came unto them to Troas in *f* days	Acts 20:6	*4002*
after *f* days Ananias the high	Acts 24:1	*4002*
f words with my understanding	1Cor 14:19	*4002*
he was seen of above *f* hundred	1Cor 15:6	*4001*
Of the Jews *f* times received I	2Cor 11:24	*3999*
they should be tormented *f* months	Rev 9:5	*4002*
power was to hurt men *f* months	Rev 9:10	*4002*
f are fallen, and one is, and the	Rev 17:10	*4002*

FIXED

My heart is *f*, O God, my heart is	Ps 57:7	3559
is *f*, O God, my heart is *f*	Ps 57:7	3559
O God, my heart is *f*	Ps 108:1	3559
his heart is *f*, trusting in the	Ps 112:7	3559
us and you there is a great gulf *f*	Lk 16:26	*4741*

FLAG

can the *f* grow without water	Job 8:11	260

FLAGON

piece of flesh, and a *f* of wine	2Sa 6:19	809
piece of flesh, and a *f* of wine	1Chr 16:3	809

FLAGONS

Stay me with *f*, comfort me with	Song 2:5	809
even to all the vessels of *f*	Is 22:24	5035
to other gods, and love *f* of wine	Hos 3:1	809

FLAGS

she laid it in the *f* by the	Ex 2:3	5488
when she saw the ark among the *f*	Ex 2:5	5488
the reeds and *f* shall wither	Is 19:6	5488

FLAKES

The *f* of his flesh are joined	Job 41:23	4651

FLAME

a *f* of fire out of the midst of a	Ex 3:2	3827
a *f* from the city of Sihon	Num 21:28	3852
when the *f* went up toward heaven	Judg 13:20	3851
ascended in the *f* of the altar	Judg 13:20	3851
f with smoke rise up out of the	Judg 20:38	4864
But when the *f* began to arise up	Judg 20:40	4864
the *f* of the city ascended up to	Judg 20:40	3632
the *f* shall dry up his branches,	Job 15:30	7957
a *f* goeth out of his mouth	Job 41:21	3851
as the *f* setteth the mountains on	Ps 83:14	3852
the *f* burned up the wicked	Ps 106:18	3852
which hath a most vehement *f*	Song 8:6	7957
the *f* consumeth the chaff, so	Is 5:24	3852
a fire, and his Holy One for a *f*	Is 10:17	3852
and the *f* of devouring fire	Is 29:6	3851
with the *f* of a devouring fire,	Is 30:30	3851
shall the *f* kindle upon thee	Is 43:2	3852
from the power of the *f*	Is 47:14	3852
a *f* from the midst of Sihon, and	Jer 48:45	3852
the flaming *f* shall not be	Eze 20:47	7957
the *f* of the fire slew those men	Dan 3:22	7631
his throne was like the fiery *f*	Dan 7:9	7631
and given to the burning *f*	Dan 7:11	785
shall fall by the sword, and by *f*	Dan 11:33	3852
the *f* hath burned all the trees	Joel 1:19	3852
and behind them a *f* burneth	Joel 2:3	3852
like the noise of a *f* of fire	Joel 2:5	3851
fire, and the house of Joseph a *f*	Obad 18	3852
for I am tormented in this *f*	Lk 16:24	*5395*
the Lord in a *f* of fire in a bush	Acts 7:30	*5395*
and his ministers a *f* of fire	Heb 1:7	*5395*
and his eyes were as a *f* of fire	Rev 1:14	*5395*
his eyes like unto a *f* of fire	Rev 2:18	*5395*
His eyes were as a *f* of fire	Rev 19:12	*5395*

FLAMES

the LORD divideth the *f* of fire	Ps 29:7	3852
their faces shall be as *f*	Is 13:8	3851
and his rebuke with *f* of fire	Is 66:15	3851

FLAMING

a *f* sword which turned every way,	Gen 3:24	3858
his ministers a *f* fire	Ps 104:4	3857
for rain, and *f* fire in their land	Ps 105:32	3852
the shining of a *f* fire by night	Is 4:5	3852
against Jacob like a *f* fire	Lam 2:3	3852
the *f* flame shall not be quenched	Eze 20:47	3852
morning it burneth as a *f* fire	Hos 7:6	3852
with *f* torches in the day of his	Nah 2:3	784
In *f* fire taking vengeance on	2Th 1:8	*5395*

FLANKS

is on them, which is by the *f*	Lev 3:4	3689
is upon them, which is by the *f*	Lev 3:10	3689
is upon them, which is by the *f*	Lev 3:15	3689
is upon them, which is by the *f*	Lev 4:9	3689
is on them, which is by the *f*	Lev 7:4	3689
and maketh collops of fat on his *f*	Job 15:27	3689

FLASH

appearance of a *f* of lightning	Eze 1:14	965

FLAT

a lame, or he that hath a *f* nose	Lev 21:18	2763
his head, and fell *f* on his face	Num 22:31	639
of the city shall fall down *f*	Josh 6:5	8478
shout, that the wall fell down *f*	Josh 6:20	8478

FLATTER

they *f* with their tongue	Ps 5:9	2505
they did *f* him with their mouth	Ps 78:36	6601

FLATTERETH

For he *f* himself in his own eyes,	Ps 36:2	2505
stranger which *f* with her words	Prov 2:16	2505
stranger which *f* with her words	Prov 7:5	2505
not with him that *f* with his lips	Prov 20:19	6601
than he that *f* with the tongue	Prov 28:23	2505
A man that *f* his neighbour	Prov 29:5	2505

FLATTERIES

and obtain the kingdom by *f*	Dan 11:21	2519
covenant shall he corrupt by *f*	Dan 11:32	2514
many shall cleave to them with *f*	Dan 11:34	2519

FLATTERING

let me give *f* titles unto man	Job 32:21	3665
For I know not to give *f* titles	Job 32:22	3665
with *f* lips and with a double	Ps 12:2	2513
The LORD shall cut off all *f* lips	Ps 12:3	2513
with the *f* of her lips she forced	Prov 7:21	2506
and a *f* mouth worketh ruin	Prov 26:28	2509
f divination within the house of	Eze 12:24	2509
at any time used we *f* words	1Th 2:5	*2850*

FLATTERY

He that speaketh *f* to his friends	Job 17:5	2506
from the *f* of the tongue of a	Prov 6:24	2513

FLAX

And the *f* and the barley was	Ex 9:31	6594
in the ear, and the *f* was bolled	Ex 9:31	6594
and hid them with the stalks of *f*	Josh 2:6	6593
as *f* that was burnt with fire	Judg 15:14	6593
She seeketh wool, and *f*, and	Prov 31:13	6593
Moreover they that work in fine *f*	Is 19:9	6593
the smoking *f* shall he not quench	Is 42:3	6594
with a line of *f* in his hand	Eze 40:3	6593
and my water, my wool and my *f*	Hos 2:5	6593
my *f* given to cover her nakedness	Hos 2:9	6593
smoking *f* shall he not quench,	Mt 12:20	*3043*

FLAY

he shall *f* the burnt offering, and	Lev 1:6	6584
so that they could not *f* all the	2Chr 29:34	6584
f their skin from off them	Mic 3:3	6584

FLAYED

hands, and the Levites *f* them	2Chr 35:11	6584

FLEA

after a dead dog, after a *f*	1Sa 24:14	6550
of Israel is come out to seek a *f*	1Sa 26:20	6550

FLED

the kings of Sodom and Gomorrah *f*	Gen 14:10	5127
that remained *f* to the mountain	Gen 14:10	5127
with her, she *f* from her face	Gen 16:6	1272
in that he told him not that he *f*	Gen 31:20	1272
So he *f* with all that he had	Gen 31:21	1272
on the third day that Jacob was *f*	Gen 31:22	1272
when he *f* from the face of his	Gen 35:7	1272
his garment in her hand, and *f*	Gen 39:12	5127
in her hand, and was *f* forth,	Gen 39:13	5127
he left his garment with me, and *f*	Gen 39:15	5127
his garment with me, and *f* out	Gen 39:18	5127
But Moses *f* from the face of	Ex 2:15	1272
and Moses *f* from before it	Ex 4:3	5127
king of Egypt that the people *f*	Ex 14:5	1272
and the Egyptians *f* against it	Ex 14:27	5127
about them *f* at the cry of them	Num 16:34	5127
of his refuge, whither he was *f*	Num 35:25	5127
of his refuge, whither he was *f*	Num 35:26	5127
is *f* to the city of his refuge	Num 35:32	5127
they *f* before the men of Ai	Josh 7:4	5127
f by the way of the wilderness	Josh 8:15	5127
and the people that *f* to the	Josh 8:20	5127
as they *f* from before Israel, and	Josh 10:11	5127
But these five kings *f*, and hid	Josh 10:16	5127
unto the city from whence he *f*	Josh 20:6	5127
But Adoni-bezek *f*	Judg 1:6	5127
chariot, and *f* away on his feet	Judg 4:15	5127
Howbeit Sisera *f* away on his feet	Judg 4:17	5127
all the host ran, and cried, and *f*	Judg 7:21	5127
the host *f* to Beth-shittah in	Judg 7:22	5127
And when Zebah and Zalmunna *f*	Judg 8:12	5127
And Jotham ran away, and *f*	Judg 9:21	1272
he *f* before him, and many were	Judg 9:40	5127
thither *f* all the men and women,	Judg 9:51	5127
Then Jephthah *f* from his brethren	Judg 11:3	1272
f toward the wilderness unto the	Judg 20:45	5127
f to the wilderness unto the rock	Judg 20:47	5127
they *f* every man into his tent	1Sa 4:10	5127
I *f* to day out of the army	1Sa 4:16	5127
and said, Israel is *f* before the	1Sa 4:17	5127
they heard that the Philistines *f*	1Sa 14:22	5127
f from him, and were sore afraid	1Sa 17:24	5127
their champion was dead, they *f*	1Sa 17:51	5127
and they *f* from him	1Sa 19:8	5127
and David *f*, and escaped that night	1Sa 19:10	5127
and he went, and *f*, and escaped	1Sa 19:12	1272
So David *f*, and escaped, and came	1Sa 19:18	1272
David *f* from Naioth in Ramah, and	1Sa 20:1	1272
f that day for fear of Saul, and	1Sa 21:10	1272
and because they knew when he *f*	1Sa 22:17	1272
escaped, and *f* after David	1Sa 22:20	1272
of Ahimelech *f* to David to Keilah	1Sa 23:6	1272
Saul that David was *f* to Gath	1Sa 27:4	1272
men, which rode upon camels, and *f*	1Sa 30:17	5127
the men of Israel *f* from before	1Sa 31:1	5127
saw that the men of Israel *f*	1Sa 31:7	5127
they forsook the cities, and *f*	1Sa 31:7	5127
the people are *f* from the battle	2Sa 1:4	5127
And the Beerothites *f* to Gittaim	2Sa 4:3	1272
and his nurse took him up, and *f*	2Sa 4:4	5127
and they *f* before him	2Sa 10:13	5127

Ammon saw that the Syrians were *f* 2Sa 10:14 5127
then *f* they also before Abishai, 2Sa 10:14 5127
the Syrians *f* before Israel 2Sa 10:18 5127
gat him up upon his mule, and *f* 2Sa 13:29 5127
But Absalom *f*. And the young man 2Sa 13:34 1272
But Absalom *f*, and went to Talmai, 2Sa 13:37 1272
So Absalom *f*, and went to Geshur, 2Sa 13:38 1272
all Israel *f* every one to his 2Sa 18:17 5127
for Israel had *f* every man to his 2Sa 19:8 5127
now he is *f* out of the land for 2Sa 19:9 1272
the people *f* from the Philistines 2Sa 23:11 1272
for so they came to me when I *f* 1Kin 2:7 1272
Joab *f* unto the tabernacle of the 1Kin 2:28 5127
f unto the tabernacle of the LORD 1Kin 2:29 5127
That Hadad *f*, he and certain 1Kin 11:17 1272
which *f* from his lord Hadadezer 1Kin 11:23 1272
f into Egypt, unto Shishak king 1Kin 11:40 1272
(for he was *f* from the presence 1Kin 12:2 1272
and the Syrians *f* 1Kin 20:20 5127
But the rest *f* to Aphek, into the 1Kin 20:30 5127
And Ben-hadad *f*, and came into the 1Kin 20:30 5127
so that they *f* before them 2Kin 3:24 5127
f in the twilight, and left their 2Kin 7:7 5127
as it was, and *f* for their life 2Kin 7:7 5127
the people *f* into their tents 2Kin 8:21 5127
And he opened the door, and *f* 2Kin 9:10 5127
And Joram turned his hands, and *f* 2Kin 9:23 5127
he *f* by the way of the garden 2Kin 9:27 5127
he *f* to Megiddo, and died there 2Kin 9:27 5127
they *f* every man to their tents 2Kin 14:12 5127
and he *f* to Lachish 2Kin 14:19 5127
all the men of war *f* by night by 2Kin 25:4
the men of Israel *f* from before 1Chr 10:1 5127
in the valley saw that they *f* 1Chr 10:7 5127
they forsook their cities, and *f* 1Chr 10:7 5127
the people *f* from before the 1Chr 11:13 5127
and they *f* before him 1Chr 19:14 5127
Ammon saw that the Syrians were *f* 1Chr 19:15 5127
they likewise *f* before Abishai 1Chr 19:15 5127
But the Syrians *f* before Israel 1Chr 19:18 5127
whither he had *f* from the 2Chr 10:2 1272
children of Israel *f* before Judah 2Chr 13:16 5127
and the Ethiopians *f* 2Chr 14:12 5127
they *f* every man to his tent 2Chr 25:22 5127
and he *f* to Lachish 2Chr 25:27 5127
were *f* every one to his field Neh 13:10 1272
when he *f* from Absalom his son Ps 3:*t* 1272
that did see me without *f* from me Ps 31:11 5074
when he *f* from Saul in the cave Ps 57:*t* 1272
At thy rebuke they *f* Ps 104:7 5127
The sea saw it, and *f* Ps 114:3 5127
Gibeah of Saul is *f* Is 10:29 5127
with their bread him that *f* Is 21:14 5074
For they *f* from the swords, from Is 21:15 5074
All thy rulers are *f* together Is 22:3 5074
together, which have *f* from far Is 22:3 1272
noise of the tumult the people *f* Is 33:3 5074
the birds of the heavens were *f* Jer 4:25 5074
of the heavens and the beast are *f* Jer 9:10 5074
heard it, he was afraid, and *f* Jer 26:21 1272
all the men of war, then they *f* Jer 39:4 1272
are *f* apace, and look not back Jer 46:5 5127
back, and are *f* away together Jer 46:21 5127
They that *f* stood under the Jer 48:45 5127
up, and all the men of war *f* Jer 52:7 1272
when they *f* away and wandered, Lam 4:15 5132
so that they *f* to hide themselves Dan 10:7 1272
for they have *f* from me Hos 7:13 5074
Jacob *f* into the country of Syria Hos 12:12 1272
For the men knew that he *f* from Jonah 1:10 1272
Therefore I *f* before unto Jonah 4:2 1272
like as ye *f* from before the Zec 14:5 5127
And they that kept them *f*, and went Mt 8:33 *5343*
the disciples forsook him, and *f* Mt 26:56 *5343*
And they that fed the swine *f* Mk 5:14 *5343*
And they all forsook him, and *f* Mk 14:50 *5343*
linen cloth, and *f* from them naked Mk 14:52 *5343*
quickly, and *f* from the sepulchre Mk 16:8 *5343*
them saw what was done, they *f* Lk 8:34 *5343*
Then *f* Moses at this saying, and Acts 7:29 *5343*
f unto Lystra and Derbe, cities of Acts 14:6 *2703*
that the prisoners had been *f* Acts 16:27 *1628*
so that they *f* out of that house Acts 19:16 *1628*
who have *f* for refuge to lay hold Heb 6:18 *2703*
the woman *f* into the wilderness, Rev 12:6 *5343*
And every island *f* away, and the Rev 16:20 *5343*
the earth and the heaven *f* away Rev 20:11 *5343*

FLEDDEST
thou *f* from the face of Esau thy Gen 35:1 1272
thee, O thou sea, that thou *f* Ps 114:5 5127

FLEE
I *f* from the face of my mistress Gen 16:8 1272
now, this city is near to *f* unto Gen 19:20 5127
f thou to Laban my brother to Gen 27:43 1272
didst thou *f* away secretly Gen 31:27 1272
his cattle *f* into the houses Ex 9:20 5127
Let us *f* from the face of Israel Ex 14:25 5127
thee a place whither he shall *f* Ex 21:13 5127
ye shall *f* when none pursueth you Lev 26:17 5127
and they shall *f*, as fleeing from Lev 26:36 5127
them that hate thee *f* before thee Num 10:35 5127
Therefore now *f* thou to thy place Num 24:11 1272
manslayer, that he may *f* thither Num 35:6 5127
that the slayer may *f* thither Num 35:11 5127
any person unawares may *f* thither Num 35:15 5127
That the slayer might *f* thither Deut 4:42 5127
that every slayer may *f* thither Deut 19:3 5127
the slayer, which shall *f* thither Deut 19:4 5127
he shall *f* unto one of those Deut 19:5 5127
way, and *f* before thee seven ways Deut 28:7 5127
them, and *f* seven ways before them Deut 28:25 5127
first, that we will *f* before them Josh 8:5 5127
They *f* before us, as at the first Josh 8:6 5127
therefore we will *f* before them Josh 8:6 5127
power to *f* this way or that way Josh 8:20 5127
and unwittingly may *f* thither Josh 20:3 5127
when he that doth *f* unto one of Josh 20:4 5127
at unawares might *f* thither Josh 20:9 5127
children of Israel said, Let us *f* Judg 20:32 5127
to pass, as she made haste to *f* 2Sa 4:4 5127
at Jerusalem, Arise, and let us *f* 2Sa 15:14 1227
people that are with him shall *f* 2Sa 17:2 5127
for if we *f* away, they will not 2Sa 18:3 5127
steal away when they *f* in battle 2Sa 19:3 5127
or wilt thou *f* three months 2Sa 24:13 5127
to his chariot, to *f* to Jerusalem 1Kin 12:18 5127
Then open the door, and *f*, and 2Kin 9:3 5127
to his chariot, to *f* to Jerusalem 2Chr 10:18 5127
I said, Should such a man as I *f* Neh 6:11 1272
they *f* away, they see no good Job 9:25 1272
He shall *f* from the iron weapon, Job 20:24 1272
he would fain *f* out of his hand Job 27:22 1272
they *f* far from me, and spare not Job 30:10 7368
The arrow cannot make him *f* Job 41:28 1272
F as a bird to your mountain Ps 11:1 5110
all that see them shall *f* away Ps 64:8 5074
also that hate him *f* before him Ps 68:1 5127
Kings of armies did *f* apace Ps 68:12 5074
shall I *f* from thy presence Ps 139:7 1272
I *f* unto thee to hide me Ps 143:9 3680
The wicked *f* when no man pursueth Prov 28:1 5127
of any person shall *f* to the pit Prov 28:17 5127
day break, and the shadows *f* away Song 2:17 5127
day break, and the shadows *f* away Song 4:6 5127
to whom will ye *f* for help Is 10:3 5127
of Gebim gather themselves to *f* Is 10:31
f every one into his own land Is 13:14 5127
his fugitives shall *f* unto Zoar Is 15:5
them, and they shall *f* far off Is 17:13 5127
whither we *f* for help to be Is 20:6 5127
for we will *f* upon horses Is 30:16 5127
therefore shall ye *f* Is 30:16 5127
One thousand shall *f* at the Is 30:17
at the rebuke of five shall ye *f* Is 30:17 5127
but he shall *f* from the sword, and Is 31:8 5127
and sorrow and sighing shall *f* away Is 35:10 5127
f ye from the Chaldeans, with a Is 48:20 1272
sorrow and mourning shall *f* away Is 51:11 5127
The whole city shall *f* for the Jer 4:29 1272
gather yourselves to *f* out of the Jer 6:1 5756
shepherds shall have no way to *f* Jer 25:35 4498
Let not the swift *f* away, nor the Jer 46:6 5127
F, save your lives, and be like Jer 48:6 5127
wings unto Moab, that it may *f* Jer 48:9 5323
F ye, turn back, dwell deep, O Jer 49:8 5127
feeble, and turneth herself to *f* Jer 49:24 5127
F, get you far off, dwell deep, O Jer 49:30 5127
they shall *f* every one to his own Jer 50:16 5127
The voice of them that *f* and Jer 50:28 5127
F out of the midst of Babylon, and Jer 51:6 5127
shall *f* away naked in that day Amos 2:16 5127
As if a man did *f* from a lion Amos 5:19 5127
f thee away into the land of Amos 7:12 1272
fleeth of them shall not *f* away Amos 9:1 5127
But Jonah rose up to *f* unto Jonah 1:3 1272
yet they shall *f* away Nah 2:8 5127
look upon thee shall *f* from thee Nah 3:7 5074
when the sun ariseth they *f* away Nah 3:17 5074
f from the land of the north, Zec 2:6 5127
ye shall *f* to the valley of the Zec 14:5 5127
yea, ye shall *f*, like as ye fled Zec 14:5 5127
f into Egypt, and be thou there Mt 2:13 *5343*
you to *f* from the wrath to come Mt 3:7 *5343*
in this city, *f* ye into another Mt 10:23 *5343*
be in Judaea *f* into the mountains Mt 24:16 *5343*
be in Judaea *f* to the mountains Mk 13:14 *5343*
you to *f* from the wrath to come Lk 3:7 *5343*
are in Judaea *f* to the mountains Lk 21:21 *5343*
not follow, but will *f* from him Jn 10:5 *5343*
were about to *f* out of the ship Acts 27:30 *5343*
F fornication 1Cor 6:18 *5343*
dearly beloved, *f* from idolatry 1Cor 10:14 *5343*
O man of God, *f* these things 1Ti 6:11 *5343*
F also youthful lusts 2Ti 2:22 *5343*
the devil, and he will *f* from you Jas 4:7 *5343*
die, and death shall *f* from them Rev 9:6 *5343*

FLEECE
the first of the *f* of thy sheep Deut 18:4 1488
I will put a *f* of wool in the Judg 6:37 1492
and if the dew be on the *f* only Judg 6:37 1492
morrow, and thrust the *f* together Judg 6:38 1492
and wringed the dew out of the *f* Judg 6:38 1492
thee, but this once with the *f* Judg 6:39 1492
let it now be dry only upon the *f* Judg 6:39 1492
for it was dry upon the *f* only Judg 6:40 1492
not warmed with the *f* of my sheep Job 31:20 1488

FLEEING
shall flee, as *f* from a sword Lev 26:36 4499
that *f* unto one of these cities Deut 4:42 5127
f into the wilderness in former Job 30:3 6207

FLEETH
f into one of these cities Deut 19:11 5127
he *f* also as a shadow, and Job 14:2 1272
that he who *f* from the noise of Is 24:18 5127
ask him that *f*, and her that Jer 48:19 5127
He that *f* from the fear shall Jer 48:44 5211
he that *f* of them shall not flee Amos 9:1 5127
cankerworm spoileth, and *f* away Nah 3:16 5775
and leaveth the sheep, and *f* Jn 10:12 *5343*
The hireling *f*, because he is an Jn 10:13 *5343*

FLESH
closed up the *f* instead thereof Gen 2:21 1320
of my bones, and *f* of my *f* Gen 2:23 1320
and they shall be one *f* Gen 2:24 1320
with man, for that he also is *f* Gen 6:3 1320
for all *f* had corrupted his way Gen 6:12 1320
The end of all *f* is come before Gen 6:13 1320
upon the earth, to destroy all *f* Gen 6:17 1320
And of every living thing of all *f* Gen 6:19 1320
into the ark, two and two of all *f* Gen 7:15 1320
went in male and female of all *f* Gen 7:16 1320
all *f* died that moved upon the Gen 7:21 1320
thing that is with thee, of all *f* Gen 8:17 1320
But *f* with the life thereof, Gen 9:4 1320
neither shall all *f* be cut off Gen 9:11 1320
and every living creature of all *f* Gen 9:15 1320
become a flood to destroy all *f* Gen 9:15 1320
of all *f* that is upon the earth Gen 9:16 1320
all *f* that is upon the earth Gen 9:17 1320
circumcise the *f* of your foreskin Gen 17:11 1320
f for an everlasting covenant Gen 17:13 1320
whose *f* of his foreskin is not Gen 17:14 1320
circumcised the *f* of their Gen 17:23 1320
in the *f* of his foreskin Gen 17:24 1320
in the *f* of his foreskin Gen 17:25 1320
Surely thou art my bone and my *f* Gen 29:14 1320
for he is our brother and our *f* Gen 37:27 1320
shall eat thy *f* from off thee Gen 40:19 1320
was turned again as his other *f* Ex 4:7 1320
shall eat the *f* in that night Ex 12:8 1320
of the *f* abroad out of the house Ex 12:46 1320
Egypt, when we sat by the *f* pots Ex 16:3 1320
give you in the evening *f* to eat Ex 16:8 1320
saying, At even ye shall eat *f* Ex 16:12 1320
and his *f* shall not be eaten Ex 21:28 1320
neither shall ye eat any *f* that Ex 22:31 1320
But the *f* of the bullock, and his Ex 29:14 1320
seethe his *f* in the holy place Ex 29:31 1320
sons shall eat the *f* of the ram Ex 29:32 1320
And if ought of the *f* of the Ex 29:34 1320
Upon man's *f* shall it not be Ex 30:32 1320
skin of the bullock, and all his *f* Lev 4:11 1320
breeches shall he put upon his *f* Lev 6:10 1320
touch the *f* thereof shall be holy Lev 6:27 1320
the *f* of the sacrifice of his Lev 7:15 1320
But the remainder of the *f* of the Lev 7:17 1320
if any of the *f* of the sacrifice Lev 7:18 1320
the *f* that toucheth any unclean Lev 7:19 1320
and as for the *f*, all that be Lev 7:19 1320
the *f* of the sacrifice of peace Lev 7:20 1320
eat of the *f* of the sacrifice of Lev 7:21 1320
the bullock, and his hide, his *f* Lev 8:17 1320
Boil the *f* at the door of the Lev 8:31 1320
And that which remaineth of the *f* Lev 8:32 1320
And the *f* and the hide he burnt Lev 9:11 1320
Of their *f* shall ye not eat, and Lev 11:8 1320
ye shall not eat of their *f* Lev 11:11 1320
in the eighth day the *f* of his Lev 12:3 1320
in the skin of his *f* a rising Lev 13:2 1320
it be in the skin of his *f* like Lev 13:2 1320
the plague in the skin of the *f* Lev 13:3 1320
be deeper than the skin of his *f* Lev 13:3 1320
be white in the skin of his *f* Lev 13:4 1320
be quick raw *f* in the rising Lev 13:10 1320
old leprosy in the skin of his *f* Lev 13:11 1320
leprosy have covered all his *f* Lev 13:13 1320
But when raw *f* appeareth in him, Lev 13:14 1320
And the priest shall see the raw *f* Lev 13:15 1320
for the raw *f* is unclean Lev 13:15 1320
Or if the raw *f* turn again Lev 13:16 1320
The *f* also, in which, even in the Lev 13:18 1320
Or if there be any *f*, in the skin Lev 13:24 1320
the quick *f* that burneth have a Lev 13:24
the skin of their *f* bright spots Lev 13:38 1320
skin of their *f* be darkish white Lev 13:39 1320
appeareth in the skin of the *f* Lev 13:43 1320
also he shall wash his *f* in water Lev 14:9 1320
hath a running issue out of his *f* Lev 15:2 1320
whether his *f* run with his issue, Lev 15:3 1320
or his *f* be stopped from his Lev 15:3 1320
he that toucheth the *f* of him Lev 15:7 1320
bathe his *f* in running water, and Lev 15:13 1320
he shall wash all his *f* in water Lev 15:16 1320
and her issue in her *f* be blood Lev 15:19 1320
the linen breeches upon his *f* Lev 16:4 1320
shall he wash his *f* in water Lev 16:4 1320
he shall wash his *f* with water in Lev 16:24 1320
clothes, and bathe his *f* in water Lev 16:26 1320
the fire their skins, and their *f* Lev 16:27 1320
clothes, and bathe his *f* in water Lev 16:28 1320
the life of the *f* is in the blood Lev 17:11 1320
For it is the life of all *f* Lev 17:14 1320
eat the blood of no manner of *f* Lev 17:14 1320
for the life of all *f* is the Lev 17:14 1320
he wash them not, nor bathe his *f* Lev 17:16 1320
cuttings in your *f* for the dead Lev 19:28 1320
nor make any cuttings in their *f* Lev 21:5 1320
unless he wash his *f* with water Lev 22:6 1320
ye shall eat the *f* of your sons Lev 26:29 1320
the *f* of your daughters shall ye Lev 26:29 1320
and let them shave all their *f* Num 8:7 1320
said, Who shall give us *f* to eat Num 11:4 1320
Whence should I have *f* to give Num 11:13 1320
weep unto me, saying, Give us *f* Num 11:13 1320
to morrow, and ye shall eat *f* Num 11:18 1320
Who shall give us *f* to eat Num 11:18 1320
the LORD will give you *f*, and ye Num 11:18 1320
hast said, I will give them *f* Num 11:21 1320
while the *f* was yet between their Num 11:33 1320
of whom the *f* is half consumed Num 12:12 1320
the God of the spirits of all *f* Num 16:22 1320
that openeth the matrix in all *f* Num 18:15 1320
the *f* of them shall be thine, as Num 18:18 1320
her skin, and her *f*, and her blood, Num 19:5 1320
and he shall bathe his *f* in water Num 19:7 1320
in water, and bathe his *f* in water Num 19:8 1320
the God of the spirits of all *f* Num 27:16 1320
For who is there of all *f* Deut 5:26 1320
kill and eat *f* in all thy gates, Deut 12:15 1320

F

and thou shalt say, I will eat *f* Deut 12:20 1320
because thy soul longeth to eat *f* Deut 12:20 1320
thou mayest eat *f*, whatsoever thy Deut 12:20 1320
not eat the life with the *f* Deut 12:23 1320
offer thy burnt offerings, the *f* Deut 12:27 1320
thy God, and thou shalt eat the *f* Deut 12:27 1320
ye shall not eat of their *f* Deut 14:8 1320
shall there any thing of the *f* Deut 16:4 1320
the *f* of thy sons and of thy Deut 28:53 1320
f of his children whom he shall Deut 28:55 1320
blood, and my sword shall devour *f* Deut 32:42 1320
the *f* he put in a basket, and he Judg 6:19 1320
of God said unto him, Take the *f* Judg 6:20 1320
was in his hand, and touched the *f* Judg 6:21 1320
of the rock, and consumed the *f* Judg 6:21 1320
then I will tear your *f* with the Judg 8:7 1320
that I am your bone and your *f* Judg 9:2 1320
while the *f* was in seething, with 1Sa 2:13 1320
Give *f* to roast for the priest 1Sa 2:15 1320
he will not have sodden *f* of thee 1Sa 2:15 1320
I will give thy *f* unto the fowls 1Sa 17:44 1320
my *f* that I have killed for my 1Sa 25:11 2878
Behold, we are thy bone and thy *f* 2Sa 5:1 1320
of bread, and a good piece of *f* 2Sa 6:19 829
brethren, ye are my bones and my *f* 2Sa 19:12 1320
thou not of my bone, and of my *f* 2Sa 19:13 1320
f in the morning, and bread and 1Kin 17:6 1320
and bread and *f* in the evening 1Kin 17:6 1320
them, and boiled their *f* with the 1Kin 19:21 1320
and put sackcloth upon his *f* 1Kin 21:27 1320
the *f* of the child waxed warm 2Kin 4:34 1320
thy *f* shall come again to thee, 2Kin 5:10 1320
his *f* came again like unto the 2Kin 5:14 1320
like unto the *f* of a little child 2Kin 5:14 1320
had sackcloth within upon his *f* 2Kin 6:30 1320
shall dogs eat the *f* of Jezebel 2Kin 9:36 1320
Behold, we are thy bone and thy *f* 1Chr 11:1 1320
of bread, and a good piece of *f* 1Chr 16:3 829
With him is an arm of *f* 2Chr 32:8 1320
f is as the *f* of our brethren Neh 5:5 1320
now, and touch his bone and his *f* Job 2:5 1320
the hair of my *f* stood up Job 4:15 1320
or is my *f* of brass Job 6:12 1320
My *f* is clothed with worms and Job 7:5 1320
Hast thou eyes of *f* Job 10:4 1320
hast clothed me with skin and *f* Job 10:11 1320
do I take my *f* in my teeth Job 13:14 1320
But his *f* upon him shall have Job 14:22 1320
cleaveth to my skin and to my *f* Job 19:20 1320
and are not satisfied with my *f* Job 19:22 1320
yet in my *f* shall I see God Job 19:26 1320
and trembling taketh hold on my *f* Job 21:6 1320
said not, Oh that we had of his *f* Job 31:31 1320
His *f* is consumed away, that it Job 33:21 1320
His *f* shall be fresher than a Job 33:25 1320
All *f* shall perish together, and Job 34:15 1320
The flakes of his *f* are joined Job 41:23 1320
my *f* also shall rest in hope Ps 16:9 1320
foes, came upon me to eat up my *f* Ps 27:2 1320
in my *f* because of thine anger Ps 38:3 1320
and there is no soundness in my *f* Ps 38:7 1320
Will I eat the *f* of bulls Ps 50:13 1320
not fear what *f* can do unto me Ps 56:4 1320
my *f* longeth for thee in a dry and Ps 63:1 1320
unto thee shall all *f* come Ps 65:2 1320
My *f* and my heart faileth Ps 73:26 7607
can he provide *f* for his people Ps 78:20 7607
He rained *f* also upon them as Ps 78:27 7607
remembered that they were but *f* Ps 78:39 1320
the *f* of thy saints unto the Ps 79:2 1320
my *f* crieth out for the living Ps 84:2 1320
and my *f* faileth of fatness Ps 109:24 1320
My *f* trembleth for fear of thee Ps 119:120 1320
Who giveth food to all *f* Ps 136:25 1320
let all *f* bless his holy name for Ps 145:21 1320
them, and health to all their *f* Prov 4:22 1320
mourn at the last, when thy *f* Prov 5:11 1320
that is cruel troubleth his own *f* Prov 11:17 7607
sound heart is the life of the *f* Prov 14:30 1320
among riotous eaters of *f* Prov 23:20 1320
together, and eateth his own *f* Eccl 4:5 1320
thy mouth to cause thy *f* to sin Eccl 5:6 1320
and put away evil from thy *f* Eccl 11:10 1320
study is a weariness of the *f* Eccl 12:12 1320
every man the *f* of his own arm Is 9:20 1320
fatness of his *f* shall wax lean Is 17:4 1320
oxen, and killing sheep, eating *f* Is 22:13 1320
and their horses *f*, and not spirit Is 31:3 1320
all *f* shall see it together Is 40:5 1320
All *f* is grass, and all the Is 40:6 1320
with part thereof he eateth *f* Is 44:16 1320
I have roasted *f*, and eaten it Is 44:19 1320
oppress thee with their own *f* Is 49:26 1320
all *f* shall know that I the LORD Is 49:26 1320
hide not thyself from thine own *f* Is 58:7 1320
monuments, which eat swine's *f* Is 65:4 1320
will the LORD plead with all *f* Is 66:16 1320
in the midst, eating swine's *f* Is 66:17 1320
shall all *f* come to worship Is 66:23 1320
shall be an abhorring unto all *f* Is 66:24 1320
unto your sacrifices, and eat *f* Jer 7:21 1320
the holy *f* is passed from thee Jer 11:15 1320
no *f* shall have peace Jer 12:12 1320
maketh *f* his arm, and whose heart Jer 17:5 1320
them to eat the *f* of their sons Jer 19:9 1320
the *f* of their daughters, and they Jer 19:9 1320
the *f* of his friend in the siege Jer 19:9 1320
nations, he will plead with all *f* Jer 25:31 1320
I am the LORD, the God of all *f* Jer 32:27 1320
I will bring evil upon all *f* Jer 45:5 1320
to my *f* be upon Babylon, shall Jer 51:35 7607
My *f* and my skin hath he made old Lam 3:4 1320
there abominable *f* into my mouth Eze 4:14 1320
is the caldron, and we be the *f* Eze 11:3 1320
the midst of it, they are the *f* Eze 11:7 1320
ye be the *f* in the midst thereof Eze 11:11 1320
the stony heart out of their *f* Eze 11:19 1320
and will give them an heart of *f* Eze 11:19 1320
thy neighbours, great of *f* Eze 16:26 1320
all *f* shall see that I the LORD Eze 20:48 1320
all *f* from the south to the north Eze 21:4 1320
That all *f* may know that I the Eze 21:5 1320
whose *f* is as the *f* of asses, Eze 23:20 1320
kindle the fire, consume the *f* Eze 24:10 1320
I will lay thy *f* upon the Eze 32:5 1320
the stony heart out of your *f* Eze 36:26 1320
and I will give you an heart of *f* Eze 36:26 1320
you, and will bring up *f* upon you Eze 37:6 1320
the *f* came up upon them, and the Eze 37:8 1320
of Israel, that ye may eat *f* Eze 39:17 1320
Ye shall eat the *f* of the mighty Eze 39:18 1320
tables was the *f* of the offering Eze 40:43 1320
in heart, and uncircumcised in *f* Eze 44:7 1320
in heart, nor uncircumcised in *f* Eze 44:9 1320
fatter in *f* than all the children Dan 1:15 1320
whose dwelling is not with *f* Dan 2:11 1321
thereof, and all *f* was fed of it Dan 4:12 1321
unto it, Arise, devour much *f* Dan 7:5 1321
neither came *f* nor wine in my Dan 10:3 1320
They sacrifice *f* for the Hos 8:13 1320
pour out my spirit upon all *f* Joel 2:28 1320
their *f* from off their bones Mic 3:2 7607
Who also eat the *f* of my people Mic 3:3 7607
pot, and as *f* within the caldron Mic 3:3 1320
as dust, and their *f* as the dung Zeph 1:17 3894
If one bear holy *f* in the skirt Hag 2:12 1320
Be silent, O all *f*, before the Zec 2:13 1320
eat every one the *f* of another Zec 11:9 1320
but he shall eat the *f* of the fat Zec 11:16 1320
Their *f* shall consume away while Zec 14:12 1320
for *f* and blood hath not revealed Mt 16:17 4561
and they twain shall be one *f* Mt 19:5 4561
they are no more twain, but one *f* Mt 19:6 4561
there should no *f* be saved Mt 24:22 4561
is willing, but the *f* is weak Mt 26:41 4561
And they twain shall be one *f* Mk 10:8 4561
they are no more twain, but one *f* Mk 10:8 4561
those days, no *f* should be saved Mk 13:20 4561
truly is ready, but the *f* is weak Mk 14:38 4561
all *f* shall see the salvation of Lk 3:6 4561
for a spirit hath not *f* and bones, Lk 24:39 4561
blood, nor of the will of the *f* Jn 1:13 4561
And the Word was made *f*, and dwelt Jn 1:14 4561
which is born of the *f* is *f* Jn 3:6 4561
which is born of the *f* is *f* Jn 3:6
bread that I will give is my *f* Jn 6:51 4561
can this man give us his *f* to eat Jn 6:52 4561
ye eat the *f* of the Son of man Jn 6:53 4561
Whoso eateth my *f*, and drinketh my Jn 6:54 4561
For my *f* is meat indeed, and my Jn 6:55 4561
He that eateth my *f*, and drinketh Jn 6:56 4561
the *f* profiteth nothing Jn 6:63 4561
Ye judge after the *f* Jn 8:15 4561
hast given him power over all *f* Jn 17:2 4561
pour out of my Spirit upon all *f* Acts 2:17 4561
moreover also my *f* shall rest in Acts 2:26 4561
of his loins, according to the *f* Acts 2:30 4561
neither his *f* did see corruption Acts 2:31 4561
seed of David according to the *f* Rom 1:3 4561
which is outward in the *f* Rom 2:28 4561
no *f* be justified in his sight Rom 3:20 4561
father, as pertaining to the *f* Rom 4:1 4561
of the infirmity of your *f* Rom 6:19 4561
For when we were in the *f* Rom 7:5 4561
know that in me (that is, in my *f* Rom 7:18 4561
but with the *f* the law of sin Rom 7:25 4561
Jesus, who walk not after the *f* Rom 8:1 4561
in that it was weak through the *f* Rom 8:3 4561
Son in the likeness of sinful *f* Rom 8:3 4561
for sin, condemned sin in the *f* Rom 8:3 4561
in us, who walk not after the *f* Rom 8:4 4561
f do mind the things of the *f* Rom 8:5 4561
are in the *f* cannot please God Rom 8:8 4561
But ye are not in the *f*, but in Rom 8:9 4561
to the *f*, to live after the *f* Rom 8:12 4561
For if ye live after the *f* Rom 8:13 4561
my kinsmen according to the *f* Rom 9:3 4561
as concerning the *f* Christ came Rom 9:5 4561
which are the children of the *f* Rom 9:8 4561
to emulation them which are my *f* Rom 11:14 4561
and make not provision for the *f* Rom 13:14 4561
It is good neither to eat *f* Rom 14:21 2907
not many wise men after the *f* 1Cor 1:26 4561
That no *f* should glory in his 1Cor 1:29 4561
for the destruction of the *f* 1Cor 5:5 4561
for two, saith he, shall be one *f* 1Cor 6:16 4561
such shall have trouble in the *f* 1Cor 7:28 4561
I will eat no *f* while the world 1Cor 8:13 2907
Behold Israel after the *f* 1Cor 10:18 4561
All *f* is not the same *f* 1Cor 15:39 4561
but there is one kind of *f* of men 1Cor 15:39 4561
another *f* of beasts, another of 1Cor 15:39 4561
Now this I say, brethren, that *f* 1Cor 15:50 4561
do I purpose according to the *f* 2Cor 1:17 4561
be made manifest in our mortal *f* 2Cor 4:11 4561
know we no man after the *f* 2Cor 5:16 4561
we have known Christ after the *f* 2Cor 5:16 4561
from all filthiness of the *f* 2Cor 7:1 4561
our *f* had no rest, but we were 2Cor 7:5 4561
if we walked according to the *f* 2Cor 10:2 4561
For though we walk in the *f* 2Cor 10:3 4561
we do not war after the *f* 2Cor 10:3 4561
that many glory after the *f* 2Cor 11:18 4561
was given to me a thorn in the *f* 2Cor 12:7 4561
I conferred not with *f* and blood Gal 1:16 4561
the law shall no *f* be justified Gal 2:16 4561
life which I now live in the *f* I Gal 2:20 4561
are ye now made perfect by the *f* Gal 3:3 4561
how through infirmity of the *f* I Gal 4:13 4561
which was in my *f* ye despised not Gal 4:14 4561
bondwoman was born after the *f* Gal 4:23 4561
f persecuted him that was born Gal 4:29 4561
liberty for an occasion to the *f* Gal 5:13 4561
not fulfil the lust of the *f* Gal 5:16 4561
For the *f* lusteth against the Gal 5:17 4561
and the Spirit against the *f* Gal 5:17 4561
the works of the *f* are manifest Gal 5:19 4561
the *f* with the affections Gal 5:24 4561
to his *f* shall of the *f* reap Gal 6:8 4561
to make a fair shew in the *f* Gal 6:12 4561
that they may glory in your *f* Gal 6:13 4561
times past in the lusts of our *f* Eph 2:3 4561
fulfilling the desires of the *f* Eph 2:3 4561
in time past Gentiles in the *f* Eph 2:11 4561
in the *f* made by hands Eph 2:11 4561
abolished in his *f* the enmity Eph 2:15 4561
no man ever yet hated his own *f* Eph 5:29 4561
are members of his body, of his *f* Eph 5:30 4561
wife, and they two shall be one *f* Eph 5:31 4561
your masters according to the *f* Eph 6:5 4561
For we wrestle not against *f* Eph 6:12 4561
But if I live in the *f*, this is Phil 1:22 4561
in the *f* is more needful for you Phil 1:24 4561
and have no confidence in the *f* Phil 3:3 4561
also have confidence in the *f* Phil 3:4 4561
whereof he might trust in the *f* Phil 3:4 4561
the body of his *f* through death Col 1:22 4561
in my *f* for his body's sake Col 1:24 4561
as have not seen my face in the *f* Col 2:1 4561
For though I be absent in the *f* Col 2:5 4561
f by the circumcision of Christ Col 2:11 4561
and the uncircumcision of your *f* Col 2:13 4561
honour to the satisfying of the *f* Col 2:23 4561
your masters according to the *f* Col 3:22 4561
God was manifest in the *f* 1Ti 3:16 4561
more unto thee, both in the *f* Philem 16 4561
the children are partakers of *f* Heb 2:14 4561
Who in the days of his *f*, when he Heb 5:7 4561
to the purifying of the *f* Heb 9:13 4561
the veil, that is to say, his *f* Heb 10:20 4561
of our *f* which corrected us Heb 12:9 4561
shall eat your *f* as it were fire Jas 5:3 4561
For all *f* is as grass, and all the 1Pet 1:24 4561
God, being put to death in the *f* 1Pet 3:18 4561
away of the filth of the *f* 1Pet 3:21 4561
hath suffered for us in the *f* 1Pet 4:1 4561
in the *f* hath ceased from sin 1Pet 4:1 4561
time in the *f* to the lusts of men 1Pet 4:2 4561
judged according to men in the *f* 1Pet 4:6 4561
them that walk after the *f* in the 2Pet 2:10 4561
allure through the lusts of the *f* 2Pet 2:18 4561
in the world, the lust of the *f* 1Jn 2:16 4561
Christ is come in the *f* is of God 1Jn 4:2 4561
is come in the *f* is not of God 1Jn 4:3 4561
Jesus Christ is come in the *f* 2Jn 7 4561
and going after strange *f* Jude 7 4561
filthy dreamers defile the *f* Jude 8 4561
even the garment spotted by the *f* Jude 23 4561
and naked, and shall eat her *f* Rev 17:16 4561
That ye may eat the *f* of kings Rev 19:18 4561
the *f* of captains, and the *f* Rev 19:18 4561
the *f* of mighty men Rev 19:18 4561
the *f* of horses, and of them that Rev 19:18 4561
the *f* of all men, both free and Rev 19:18 4561
fowls were filled with their *f* Rev 19:21 4561

FLESHHOOK

with a *f* of three teeth in his 1Sa 2:13 4207
all that the *f* brought up the 1Sa 2:14 4207

FLESHHOOKS

shovels, and his basons, and his *f* Ex 27:3 4207
shovels, and the basons, and the *f* Ex 38:3 4207
about it, even the censers, the *f* Num 4:14 4207
Also pure gold for the *f*, and the 1Chr 28:17 4207
also, and the shovels, and the *f* 2Chr 4:16 4207

FLESHLY

sincerity, not with *f* wisdom 2Cor 1:12 4559
vainly puffed up by his *f* mind Col 2:18
and pilgrims, abstain from *f* lusts 1Pet 2:11 4559

FLESHY

but in *f* tables of the heart 2Cor 3:3 4560

FLEW

the people *f* upon the spoil, and 1Sa 14:32 6213
Then *f* one of the seraphims unto Is 6:6 5774

FLIES

I will send swarms of *f* upon thee Ex 8:21
shall be full of swarms of *f* Ex 8:21
no swarms of *f* shall be there Ex 8:22
of *f* into the house of Pharaoh Ex 8:24
by reason of the swarm of *f* Ex 8:24
of *f* may depart from Pharaoh Ex 8:29
the swarms of *f* from Pharaoh Ex 8:31
sent divers sorts of *f* among them Ps 78:45 6157
and there came divers sorts of *f* Ps 105:31 6157
Dead *f* cause the ointment of the Eccl 10:1 2070

FLIETH

any winged fowl that *f* in the air Deut 4:17 5774
thing that *f* is unclean unto you Deut 14:19 5775
earth, as swift as the eagle *f* Deut 28:49 1675
nor for the arrow that *f* by day Ps 91:5 5774

FLIGHT

you shall put ten thousand to *f* Lev 26:8 7291
and two put ten thousand to *f* Deut 32:30 5127
they put to *f* all them of the 1Chr 12:15 1272
go out with haste, nor go by *f* Is 52:12 4499
Therefore the *f* shall perish from Amos 2:14 4498
that your *f* be not in the winter Mt 24:20 5437
pray ye that your *f* be not in the Mk 13:18 5437
turned to *f* the armies of the Heb 11:34

FLINT

forth water out of the rock of *f*	Deut 8:15	2496
the *f* into a fountain of waters	Ps 114:8	2496
hoofs shall be counted like *f*	Is 5:28	6864
have I set my face like a *f*	Is 50:7	2496
than *f* have I made thy forehead	Eze 3:9	6864

FLINTY

rock, and oil out of the *f* rock	Deut 32:13	2496

FLOATS

I will convey them by sea in *f*	1Kin 5:9	1702

FLOCK

of the firstlings of his *f*	Gen 4:4	6629
ewe lambs of the *f* by themselves	Gen 21:28	6629
Go now to the *f*, and fetch me from	Gen 27:9	6629
watered the *f* of Laban his	Gen 29:10	6629
I will again feed and keep thy *f*	Gen 30:31	6629
pass through all thy *f* to day	Gen 30:32	6629
all the brown in the *f* of Laban	Gen 30:40	6629
and Leah to the field unto his *f*	Gen 31:4	6629
the rams of thy *f* have I not	Gen 31:38	6629
them one day, all the *f* will die	Gen 33:13	6629
was feeding the *f* with his	Gen 37:2	6629
feed their father's *f* in Shechem	Gen 37:12	6629
brethren feed the *f* in Shechem	Gen 37:13	
I will send thee a kid from the *f*	Gen 38:17	6629
troughs to water their father's *f*	Ex 2:16	6629
helped them, and watered their *f*	Ex 2:17	6629
enough for us, and watered the *f*	Ex 2:19	6629
Now Moses kept the *f* of Jethro	Ex 3:1	6629
he led the *f* to the backside of	Ex 3:1	6629
even of the herd, and of the *f*	Lev 1:2	6629
unto the LORD be of the *f*	Lev 3:6	6629
hath sinned, a female from the *f*	Lev 5:6	6629
ram without blemish out of the *f*	Lev 5:18	6629
ram without blemish out of the *f*	Lev 6:6	6629
tithe of the herd, or of the *f*	Lev 27:32	6629
LORD, of the herd, or of the *f*	Num 15:3	6629
of thy herds or of thy *f*, nor any	Deut 12:17	6629
kill of thy herd and of thy *f*	Deut 12:21	6629
him liberally out of thy *f*	Deut 15:14	6629
of thy *f* thou shalt sanctify unto	Deut 15:19	6629
unto the LORD thy God, of the *f*	Deut 16:2	6629
bear, and took a lamb out of the *f*	1Sa 17:34	5739
and he spared to take of his own *f*	2Sa 12:4	6629
gave to the people, of the *f*	2Chr 35:7	6629
a ram of the *f* for their trespass	Ezr 10:19	6629
forth their little ones like a *f*	Job 21:11	6629
to have set with the dogs of my *f*	Job 30:1	6629
like a *f* by the hand of Moses	Ps 77:20	6629
them in the wilderness like a *f*	Ps 78:52	5739
thou that leadest Joseph like a *f*	Ps 80:1	6629
and maketh him families like a *f*	Ps 107:41	6629
thou makest thy *f* to rest at noon	Song 1:7	
forth by the footsteps of the *f*	Song 1:8	6629
thy hair is as a *f* of goats	Song 4:1	5739
Thy teeth are like a *f* of sheep	Song 4:2	5739
thy hair is as a *f* of goats that	Song 6:5	5739
Thy teeth are as a *f* of sheep	Song 6:6	5739
shall feed his *f* like a shepherd	Is 40:11	5739
sea with the shepherd of his *f*	Is 63:11	6629
because the LORD's *f* is carried	Jer 13:17	5739
where is the *f* that was given	Jer 13:20	5739
was given thee, thy beautiful *f*	Jer 13:20	6629
Ye have scattered my *f*, and driven	Jer 23:2	6629
f out of all countries whither I	Jer 23:3	6629
the ashes, ye principal of the *f*	Jer 25:34	6629
the principal of the *f* to escape	Jer 25:35	6629
howling of the principal of the *f*	Jer 25:36	6629
him, as a shepherd doth his *f*	Jer 31:10	5739
oil, and for the young of the *f*	Jer 31:12	6629
of the *f* shall draw them out	Jer 49:20	6629
of the *f* shall draw them out	Jer 50:45	6629
with thee the shepherd and his *f*	Jer 51:23	5739
Take the choice of the *f*, and burn	Eze 24:5	6629
but ye feed not the *f*	Eze 34:3	6629
my *f* was scattered upon all the	Eze 34:6	6629
surely because my *f* became a prey	Eze 34:8	6629
my *f* became meat to every beast	Eze 34:8	6629
did my shepherds search for my *f*	Eze 34:8	6629
fed themselves, and fed not my *f*	Eze 34:8	6629
I will require my *f* at their hand	Eze 34:10	6629
them to cease from feeding the *f*	Eze 34:10	6629
deliver my *f* from their mouth	Eze 34:10	6629
As a shepherd seeketh out his *f*	Eze 34:12	5739
I will feed my *f*, and I will cause	Eze 34:15	6629
And as for you, O my *f*, thus saith	Eze 34:17	6629
And as for my *f*, they eat that	Eze 34:19	6629
Therefore will I save my *f*	Eze 34:22	6629
And ye my *f*, the *f* of my	Eze 34:31	6629
the *f* of my pasture, are men, and	Eze 34:31	6629
increase them with men like a *f*	Eze 36:37	6629
As the holy *f*, as the *f* of	Eze 36:38	6629
ram out of the *f* without blemish	Eze 43:23	6629
bullock, and a ram out of the *f*	Eze 43:25	6629
And one lamb out of the *f*, out of	Eze 45:15	6629
and eat the lambs out of the *f*	Amos 6:4	6629
LORD took me as I followed the *f*	Amos 7:15	6629
neither man nor beast, herd nor *f*	Jonah 3:7	6629
as the *f* in the midst of their	Mic 2:12	5739
And thou, O tower of the *f*	Mic 4:8	5739
the *f* of thine heritage, which	Mic 7:14	6629
the *f* shall be cut off from the	Hab 3:17	6629
that day as the *f* of his people	Zec 9:16	6629
they went their way as a *f*	Zec 10:2	6629
visited his *f* the house of Judah	Zec 10:3	5739
Feed the *f* of the slaughter	Zec 11:4	6629
And I will feed the *f* of slaughter	Zec 11:7	6629
even you, O poor of the *f*	Zec 11:7	6629
and I fed the *f*	Zec 11:7	6629
so the poor of the *f* that waited	Zec 11:11	6629
idol shepherd that leaveth the *f*	Zec 11:17	6629
which hath in his *f* a male	Mal 1:14	5739
the sheep of the *f* shall be	Mt 26:31	*4167*
watch over their *f* by night	Lk 2:8	*4167*
Fear not, little *f*	Lk 12:32	*4168*
unto yourselves, and to all the *f*	Acts 20:28	*4168*
in among you, not sparing the *f*	Acts 20:29	*4168*
or who feedeth a *f*, and eateth not	1Cor 9:7	*4167*
eateth not of the milk of the *f*	1Cor 9:7	*4167*
Feed the *f* of God which is among	1Pet 5:2	*4168*
but being ensamples to the *f*	1Pet 5:3	*4168*

FLOCKS

which went with Abram, had *f*	Gen 13:5	6629
and he hath given him *f*, and herds,	Gen 24:35	6629
For he had possession of *f*	Gen 26:14	6629
there were three *f* of sheep lying	Gen 29:2	5739
of that well they watered the *f*	Gen 29:2	5739
thither were all the *f* gathered	Gen 29:3	5739
until all the *f* be gathered	Gen 29:8	5739
Jacob fed the rest of Laban's *f*	Gen 30:36	6629
f in the gutters in the watering	Gen 30:38	6629
troughs when the *f* came to drink	Gen 30:38	6629
the *f* conceived before the rods,	Gen 30:39	6629
set the faces of the *f* toward the	Gen 30:40	6629
and he put his own *f* by themselves	Gen 30:40	5739
And I have oxen, and asses, *f*	Gen 32:5	6629
that was with him, and the *f*	Gen 32:7	6629
the children are tender, and the *f*	Gen 33:13	6629
thy brethren, and well with the *f*	Gen 37:14	6629
thee, where they feed their *f*	Gen 37:16	
thy children's children, and thy *f*	Gen 45:10	6629
and they have brought their *f*	Gen 46:32	6629
father and my brethren, and their *f*	Gen 47:1	6629
have no pasture for their *f*	Gen 47:4	6629
exchange for horses, and for the *f*	Gen 47:17	6629
their little ones, and their *f*	Gen 50:8	6629
and with our daughters, with our *f*	Ex 10:9	6629
only let your *f* and your herds be	Ex 10:24	6629
Also take your *f* and your herds,	Ex 12:32	6629
and *f*, and herds, even very much	Ex 12:38	6629
neither let the *f* nor herds feed	Ex 34:3	6629
And if his offering be of the *f*	Lev 1:10	6629
ram without blemish out of the *f*	Lev 5:15	6629
Shall the *f* and the herds be slain	Num 11:22	6629
all their cattle, and all their *f*	Num 31:9	4735
beeves, of the asses, and of the *f*	Num 31:30	6629
Our little ones, our wives, our *f*	Num 32:26	4735
the *f* of thy sheep, in the land	Deut 7:13	6251
thy *f* multiply, and thy silver and	Deut 8:13	6629
of your herds and of your *f*	Deut 12:6	6629
of thy herds and of thy *f*	Deut 14:23	6629
thy kine, and the *f* of thy sheep	Deut 28:4	6251
thy kine, and the *f* of thy sheep	Deut 28:18	6251
or *f* of thy sheep, until he have	Deut 28:51	6251
to hear the bleatings of the *f*	Judg 5:16	5739
And David took all the *f* and the	1Sa 30:20	6629
The rich man had exceeding many *f*	2Sa 12:2	6629
them like two little *f* of kids	1Kin 20:27	2835
to seek pasture for their *f*	1Chr 4:39	6629
was pasture there for their *f*	1Chr 4:41	6629
over the *f* was Jaziz the Hagerite	1Chr 27:31	6629
and the Arabians brought him *f*	2Chr 17:11	6629
manner of beasts, and cotes for *f*	2Chr 32:28	5739
him cities, and possessions of *f*	2Chr 32:29	6629
of our herds and of our *f*, to	Neh 10:36	6629
they violently take away *f*	Job 24:2	5739
The pastures are clothed with *f*	Ps 65:13	6629
their *f* to hot thunderbolts	Ps 78:48	4735
to know the state of thy *f*	Prov 27:23	6629
aside by the *f* of thy companions	Song 1:7	5739
they shall be for *f*, which shall	Is 17:2	5739
joy of wild asses, a pasture of *f*	Is 32:14	5739
All the *f* of Kedar shall be	Is 60:7	6629
shall stand and feed your *f*	Is 61:5	6629
And Sharon shall be a fold of *f*	Is 65:10	6629
their *f* and their herds, their	Jer 3:24	6629
they shall eat up thy *f* and thine	Jer 5:17	6629
with their *f* shall come unto her	Jer 6:3	5739
all their *f* shall be scattered	Jer 10:21	4830
and they that go forth with *f*	Jer 31:24	5739
causing their *f* to lie down	Jer 33:12	6629
shall the *f* pass again under the	Jer 33:13	6629
their *f* shall they take away	Jer 49:29	6629
be as the he goats before the *f*	Jer 50:8	6629
Ammonites a couchingplace for *f*	Eze 25:5	6629
not the shepherds feed the *f*	Eze 34:2	6629
cities be filled with *f* of men	Eze 36:38	6629
They shall go with their *f*	Hos 5:6	6629
the *f* of sheep are made desolate	Joel 1:18	5739
a young lion among the *f* of sheep	Mic 5:8	5739
for shepherds, and folds for *f*	Zeph 2:6	6629
shall lie down in the midst of	Zeph 2:14	5739

FLOOD

do bring a *f* of waters upon the	Gen 6:17	3999
f of waters was upon the earth	Gen 7:6	3999
because of the waters of the *f*	Gen 7:7	3999
of the *f* were upon the earth	Gen 7:10	3999
the *f* was forty days upon the	Gen 7:17	3999
off any more by the waters of a *f*	Gen 9:11	3999
more be a *f* to destroy the earth	Gen 9:11	3999
become a *f* to destroy all flesh	Gen 9:15	3999
lived after the *f* three hundred	Gen 9:28	3999
them were sons born after the *f*	Gen 10:1	3999
divided in the earth after the *f*	Gen 10:32	3999
Arphaxad two years after the *f*	Gen 11:10	3999
other side of the *f* in old time	Josh 24:2	5104
from the other side of the *f*	Josh 24:3	5104
served on the other side of the *f*	Josh 24:14	5104
were on the other side of the *f*	Josh 24:15	5104
the *f* decayeth and drieth up	Job 14:11	5104
foundation was overflown with a *f*	Job 22:16	5104
The *f* breaketh out from the	Job 28:4	5158
The LORD sitteth upon the *f*	Ps 29:10	3999
they went through the *f* on foot	Ps 66:6	5104
cleave the fountain and the *f*	Ps 74:15	5158
carriest them away as with a *f*	Ps 90:5	2229
storm, as a *f* of mighty waters	Is 28:2	2230
the enemy shall come in like a *f*	Is 59:19	5104
Who is this that cometh up as a *f*	Jer 46:7	2975
Egypt riseth up like a *f*, and his	Jer 46:8	2975
and shall be an overflowing *f*	Jer 47:2	5158
the end thereof shall be with a *f*	Dan 9:26	7858
with the arms of a *f* shall they	Dan 11:22	7858
and it shall rise up wholly as a *f*	Amos 8:8	2975
and drowned, as by the *f* of Egypt	Amos 8:8	2975
it shall rise up wholly like a *f*	Amos 9:5	2975
be drowned, as by the *f* of Egypt	Amos 9:5	2975
But with an overrunning *f* he will	Nah 1:8	7858
before the *f* they were eating	Mt 24:38	*2627*
And knew not until the *f* came	Mt 24:39	*2627*
and when the *f* arose, the stream	Lk 6:48	*4182*
the *f* came, and destroyed them all	Lk 17:27	*2627*
bringing in the *f* upon the world	2Pet 2:5	*2627*
water as a *f* after the woman	Rev 12:15	*4215*
her to be carried away of the *f*	Rev 12:15	*4216*
swallowed up the *f* which the	Rev 12:16	*4215*

FLOODS

the *f* stood upright as an heap,	Ex 15:8	5140
the *f* of ungodly men made me	2Sa 22:5	5158
shall not see the rivers, the *f*	Job 20:17	5104
He bindeth the *f* from overflowing	Job 28:11	5104
the *f* of ungodly men made me	Ps 18:4	5158
and established it upon the *f*	Ps 24:2	5104
surely in the *f* of great waters	Ps 32:6	7858
waters, where the *f* overflow me	Ps 69:2	7641
and their *f*, that they could not	Ps 78:44	5140
The *f* have lifted up, O LORD, the	Ps 93:3	5104
the *f* have lifted up their voice	Ps 93:3	5104
the *f* lift up their waves	Ps 93:3	5104
Let the *f* clap their hands	Ps 98:8	5104
love, neither can the *f* drown it	Song 8:7	5104
thirsty, and *f* upon the dry ground	Is 44:3	5140
and I restrained the *f* thereof	Eze 31:15	5104
and the *f* compassed me about	Jonah 2:3	5104
the *f* came, and the winds blew, and	Mt 7:25	*4215*
the *f* came, and the winds blew, and	Mt 7:27	*4215*

FLOOR

saw the mourning in the *f* of Atad	Gen 50:11	1637
of the dust that is in the *f* of	Num 5:17	7172
out of thy flock, and out of thy *f*	Deut 15:14	1637
put a fleece of wool in the *f*	Judg 6:37	1637
thee, and get thee down to the *f*	Ruth 3:3	1637
And she went down unto the *f*	Ruth 3:6	1637
that a woman came into the *f*	Ruth 3:14	1637
both the *f* of the house, and the	1Kin 6:15	7172
covered the *f* of the house with	1Kin 6:15	7172
sides of the house, both the *f*	1Kin 6:16	7172
the *f* of the house he overlaid	1Kin 6:30	7172
one side of the *f* to the other	1Kin 7:7	7172
to *f* the houses which the kings	2Chr 34:11	7136
my threshing, and the corn of my *f*	Is 21:10	1637
The *f* and the winepress shall not	Hos 9:2	1637
with the whirlwind out of the *f*	Hos 13:3	1637
them as the sheaves into the *f*	Mic 4:12	1637
and he will throughly purge his *f*	Mt 3:12	*257*
and he will throughly purge his *f*	Lk 3:17	*257*

FLOORS

the *f* shall be full of wheat, and	Joel 2:24	1637

FLOTES

it to thee in *f* by sea to Joppa	2Chr 2:16	7513

FLOUR

of wheaten *f* shalt thou make them	Ex 29:2	5560
the one lamb a tenth deal of *f*	Ex 29:40	5560
his offering shall be of fine *f*	Lev 2:1	5560
his handful of the *f* thereof	Lev 2:2	5560
cakes of fine *f* mingled with oil	Lev 2:4	5560
it shall be of fine *f* unleavened	Lev 2:5	5560
shall be made of fine *f* with oil	Lev 2:7	5560
of fine *f* for a sin offering	Lev 5:11	5560
of the *f* of the meat offering, and	Lev 6:15	5560
f for a meat offering perpetual	Lev 6:20	5560
cakes mingled with oil, of fine *f*	Lev 7:12	5560
of fine *f* for a meat offering	Lev 14:10	5560
one tenth deal of fine *f* mingled	Lev 14:21	5560
deals of fine *f* mingled with oil	Lev 23:13	5560
they shall be of fine *f*	Lev 23:17	5560
And thou shalt take fine *f*	Lev 24:5	5560
cakes of fine *f* mingled with oil,	Num 6:15	5560
f mingled with oil for a meat	Num 7:13	5560
both of them full of fine *f*	Num 7:19	5560
both of them full of fine *f*	Num 7:25	5560
both of them full of fine *f*	Num 7:31	5560
both of them full of fine *f*	Num 7:37	5560
both of them full of fine *f*	Num 7:43	5560
both of them full of fine *f*	Num 7:49	5560
both of them full of fine *f*	Num 7:55	5560
both of them full of fine *f*	Num 7:61	5560
both of them full of fine *f*	Num 7:67	5560
both of them full of fine *f*	Num 7:73	5560
both of them full of fine *f*	Num 7:79	5560
even fine *f* mingled with oil, and	Num 8:8	5560
offering of a tenth deal of *f*	Num 15:4	5560
offering two tenth deals of *f*	Num 15:6	5560
of three tenth deals of *f* mingled	Num 15:9	5560
an ephah of *f* for a meat offering	Num 28:5	5560
two tenth deals of *f* for a meat	Num 28:9	5560
deals of *f* for a meat offering	Num 28:12	5560
two tenth deals of *f* for a meat	Num 28:12	5560
a several tenth deal of *f* mingled	Num 28:13	5560
shall be of *f* mingled with oil	Num 28:20	5560
offering of *f* mingled with oil	Num 28:28	5560
shall be of *f* mingled with oil	Num 29:3	5560
shall be of *f* mingled with oil	Num 29:9	5560
shall be of *f* mingled with oil	Num 29:14	5560
unleavened cakes of an ephah of *f*	Judg 6:19	7058
three bullocks, and one ephah of *f*	1Sa 1:24	7058

hasted, and killed it, and took *f* 1Sa 28:24 7058
And she took *f*, and kneaded it, and 2Sa 13:8 1217
and wheat, and barley, and *f* 2Sa 17:28 7058
day was thirty measures of fine *f* 1Kin 4:22 5560
of fine *f* be sold for a shekel 2Kin 7:1 5560
So a measure of fine *f* was sold 2Kin 7:16 5560
a measure of fine *f* for a shekel 2Kin 7:18 5560
of the sanctuary, and the fine *f* 1Chr 9:29 5560
for the fine *f* for meat offering, 1Chr 23:29 5560
thou didst eat fine *f*, and honey, Eze 16:13 5560
also which I gave thee, fine *f* Eze 16:19 5560
of oil, to temper with the fine *f* Eze 46:14 5560
and wine, and oil, and fine *f* Rev 18:13 *4585*

FLOURISH
In his days shall the righteous *f* Ps 72:7 6524
they of the city shall *f* like Ps 72:16 6692
all the workers of iniquity do *f* Ps 92:7 6692
shall *f* like the palm tree Ps 92:12 6524
shall *f* in the courts of our God Ps 92:13 6524
upon himself shall his crown *f* Ps 132:18 6692
the righteous shall *f* as a branch Prov 11:28 6524
tabernacle of the upright shall *f* Prov 14:11 6524
way, and the almond tree shall *f* Eccl 12:5 5006
let us see if the vine *f*, whether Song 7:12 6524
shalt thou make thy seed to *f* Is 17:11 6524
your bones shall *f* like an herb Is 66:14 6524
and have made the dry tree to *f* Eze 17:24 6524

FLOURISHED
and to see whether the vine *f* Song 6:11 6524
last your care of me hath *f* again Phil 4:10 *330*

FLOURISHETH
In the morning it *f*, and groweth Ps 90:6 6692
as a flower of the field, so he *f* Ps 103:15 6692

FLOURISHING
they shall be fat and *f* Ps 92:14 7488
in mine house, and *f* in my palace Dan 4:4 7487

FLOW
his goods shall *f* away in the day Job 20:28 5064
his wind to blow, and the waters *f* Ps 147:18 5140
that the spices thereof may *f* out Song 4:16 5140
and all nations shall *f* unto it Is 2:2 5102
he caused the waters to *f* out of Is 48:21 5140
f together, and thine heart shall Is 60:5 5102
might *f* down at thy presence Is 64:1 2151
shall *f* together to the goodness Jer 31:12 5102
the nations shall not *f* together Jer 51:44 5102
and the hills shall *f* with milk Joel 3:18 3212
of Judah shall *f* with waters Joel 3:18 3212
and people shall *f* unto it Mic 4:1 5102
shall *f* rivers of living water Jn 7:38 *4482*

FLOWED
f over all his banks, as they did Josh 4:18 3212
the mountains *f* down at thy Is 64:3 2151
Waters *f* over mine head Lam 3:54 6687

FLOWER
with a knop and a *f* in one branch Ex 25:33 6525
other branch, with a knop and a *f* Ex 25:33 6525
in one branch, a knop and a *f* Ex 37:19 6525
in another branch, a knop and a *f* Ex 37:19 6525
shall die in the *f* of their age 1Sa 2:33 582
He cometh forth like a *f*, and is Job 14:2 6731
shall cast off his *f* as the olive Job 15:33 5328
as a *f* of the field, so he Ps 103:15 6731
sour grape is ripening in the *f* Is 18:5 5328
glorious beauty is a fading *f* Is 28:1 6731
fat valley, shall be a fading *f* Is 28:4 6733
thereof is as the *f* of the field Is 40:6 6731
The grass withereth, the *f* fadeth Is 40:7 6731
The grass withereth, the *f* fadeth Is 40:8 6731
the *f* of Lebanon languisheth Nah 1:4 6525
if she pass the *f* of her age 1Cor 7:36 *5230*
because as the *f* of the grass he Jas 1:10 *438*
the *f* thereof falleth, and the Jas 1:11 *438*
glory of man as the *f* of grass 1Pet 1:24 *438*
the *f* thereof falleth away 1Pet 1:24 *438*

FLOWERS
his bowls, his knops, and his *f* Ex 25:31 6525
with their knops and their *f* Ex 25:34 6525
his bowls, his knops, and his *f* Ex 37:17 6525
like almonds, his knops, and his *f* Ex 37:20 6525
her *f* be upon him, he shall be Lev 15:24 5079
And of her that is sick of her *f* Lev 15:33 5079
shaft thereof, unto the *f* thereof Num 8:4 6525
was carved with knops and open *f* 1Kin 6:18 6731
cherubims and palm trees and open *f* 1Kin 6:29 6731
cherubims and palm trees and open *f* 1Kin 6:32 6731
cherubims and palm trees and open *f* 1Kin 6:35 6731
brim of a cup, with *f* of lilies 1Kin 7:26 6525
before the oracle, with the *f* 1Kin 7:49 6525
brim of a cup, with *f* of lilies 2Chr 4:5 6525
And the *f*, and the lamps, and the 2Chr 4:21 6525
The *f* appear on the earth Song 2:12 5339
as a bed of spices, as sweet *f* Song 5:13 4026

FLOWETH
it, a land that *f* with milk Lev 20:24 2100
us, and surely it *f* with milk Num 13:27 2100
a land which *f* with milk and honey Num 14:8 2100
up out of a land that *f* with milk Num 16:13 2100
us into a land that *f* with milk Num 16:14 2100
in the land that *f* with milk Deut 6:3 2100
seed, a land that *f* with milk Deut 11:9 2100
even a land that *f* with milk Deut 26:9 2100
fathers, a land that *f* with milk Deut 26:15 2100
thee, a land that *f* with milk Deut 27:3 2100
that *f* with milk and honey Deut 31:20 2100
give us, a land that *f* with milk Josh 5:6 2100

FLOWING
a large, unto a land *f* with milk Ex 3:8 2100
unto a land *f* with milk and honey Ex 3:17 2100
a land *f* with milk and honey, that Ex 13:5 2100
Unto a land *f* with milk and honey Ex 33:3 2100
wellspring of wisdom as a *f* brook Prov 18:4 5042
of the Gentiles like a *f* stream Is 66:12 7857
to give them a land *f* with milk Jer 11:5 2100
or shall the cold *f* waters that Jer 18:14 5140
a land *f* with milk and honey Jer 32:22 2100
thy *f* valley, O backsliding Jer 49:4 2100
f with milk and honey, which is Eze 20:6 2100
f with milk and honey, which is Eze 20:15 2100

FLUTE
hear the sound of the cornet, *f* Dan 3:5 4953
heard the sound of the cornet, *f* Dan 3:7 4953
hear the sound of the cornet, *f* Dan 3:10 4953
hear the sound of the cornet, *f* Dan 3:15 4953

FLUTTERETH
f over her young, spreadeth Deut 32:11 7363

FLUX
sick of a fever and of a bloody *f* Acts 28:8 *1420*

FLY
fowl that may *f* above the earth Gen 1:20 5774
but didst *f* upon the spoil, and 1Sa 15:19 5860
he rode upon a cherub, and did *f* 2Sa 22:11 5774
trouble, as the sparks *f* upward Job 5:7 5774
He shall *f* away as a dream, and Job 20:8 5774
Doth the hawk *f* by thy wisdom Job 39:26 82
he rode upon a cherub, and did *f* Ps 18:10 5774
he did *f* upon the wings of the Ps 18:10 1675
for then would I *f* away, and be at Ps 55:6 5774
it is soon cut off, and we *f* away Ps 90:10 5774
they *f* away as an eagle toward Prov 23:5 5774
his feet, and with twain he did *f* Is 6:2 5774
the LORD shall hiss for the *f* Is 7:18 2070
But they shall *f* upon the Is 11:14 5774
Who are these that *f* as a cloud Is 60:8 5774
he shall *f* as an eagle, and shall Jer 48:40 1675
f as the eagle, and spread his Jer 49:22 1675
hunt the souls to make them *f* Eze 13:20 6524
souls that ye hunt to make them *f* Eze 13:20 6524
being caused to *f* swiftly Dan 9:21 3286
glory shall *f* away like a bird Hos 9:11 5774
they shall *f* as the eagle that Hab 1:8 5774
that she might *f* into the Rev 12:14 *4072*
I saw another angel *f* in the Rev 14:6 *4072*
that *f* in the midst of heaven Rev 19:17 *4072*

FLYING
Yet these may ye eat of every *f* Lev 11:21 5775
But all other *f* creeping things, Lev 11:23 5775
creeping things, and *f* fowl Ps 148:10 3671
by wandering, as the swallow by *f* Prov 26:2 5774
fruit shall be a fiery *f* serpent Is 14:29 5774
fiery *f* serpent, they will carry Is 30:6 5774
As birds *f*, so will the LORD of Is 31:5 5774
and looked, and behold a *f* roll Zec 5:1 5774
And I answered, I see a *f* roll Zec 5:2 5774
fourth beast was like a *f* eagle Rev 4:7 *4072*
heard an angel *f* through the Rev 8:13 *4072*

FOAL
Binding his *f* unto the vine, and Gen 49:11 5895
and upon a colt the *f* of an ass Zec 9:9 1121
an ass, and a colt the *f* of an ass Mt 21:5 *5207*

FOALS
bulls, twenty she asses, and ten *f* Gen 32:15 5895

FOAM
cut off as the *f* upon the water Hos 10:7 7110

FOAMETH
and he *f*, and gnasheth with his Mk 9:18 *875*
and it teareth him that he *f* again Lk 9:39 *876*

FOAMING
fell on the ground, and wallowed *f* Mk 9:20 *876*
of the sea, *f* out their own shame Jude 13 *1890*

FODDER
or loweth the ox over his *f* Job 6:5 1098

FOES
to be destroyed before thy *f* 1Chr 21:12 6862
and slew of their *f* seventy Est 9:16 8130
wicked, even mine enemies and my *f* Ps 27:2 341
hast not made my *f* to rejoice Ps 30:1 341
beat down his *f* before his face Ps 89:23 6862
a man's *f* shall be they of his Mt 10:36 *2190*
Until I make thy *f* thy footstool Acts 2:35 *2190*

FOLD
the shepherds make their *f* there Is 13:20 7257
And Sharon shall be a *f* of flocks Is 65:10 5116
of Israel shall their *f* be Eze 34:14 5116
there shall they lie in a good *f* Eze 34:14 5116
the flock in the midst of their *f* Mic 2:12 1699
flock shall be cut off from the *f* Hab 3:17 4356
I have, which are not of this *f* Jn 10:16 *833*
and there shall be one *f*, and one Jn 10:16 *4167*
as a vesture shalt thou *f* them up Heb 1:12 *1667*

FOLDEN
For while they be *f* together as Nah 1:10 5440

FOLDETH
The fool *f* his hands together, and Eccl 4:5 2263

FOLDING
two leaves of the one door were *f* 1Kin 6:34 1550
leaves of the other door were *f* 1Kin 6:34 1550
a little *f* of the hands to sleep Prov 6:10 2264
a little *f* of the hands to sleep Prov 24:33 2264

FOLDS
little ones, and *f* for your sheep Num 32:24 1448
and *f* of sheep Num 32:36 1448
house, nor he goats out of thy *f* Ps 50:9 4356
will bring them again to their *f* Jer 23:3 5116
for shepherds, and *f* for flocks Zeph 2:6 1448

FOLK
some of the *f* that are with me Gen 33:15 5971
The conies are but a feeble *f* Prov 30:26 5971
the *f* in the fire, and they shall Jer 51:58 3816
laid his hands upon a few sick *f* Mk 6:5
a great multitude of impotent *f* Jn 5:3

FOLKS
unto Jerusalem, bringing sick *f* Acts 5:16

FOLLOW
be willing to *f* me unto this land Gen 24:5
will not be willing to *f* thee Gen 24:8
the woman will not *f* me Gen 24:39
his steward, Up, *f* after the men Gen 44:4 7291
and all the people that *f* thee Ex 11:8 7272
heart, that he shall *f* after them Ex 14:4 7291
Egyptians, and they shall *f* them Ex 14:17 310
from her, and yet no mischief *f* Ex 21:22 1961
And if any mischief *f*, then thou Ex 21:23 1961
Thou shalt not *f* a multitude to Ex 23:2
is altogether just shalt thou *f* Deut 16:20 7291
of the LORD, if the thing *f* not Deut 18:22 1961
And he said unto them, *F* after me Judg 3:28 7291
bread unto the people that *f* me Judg 8:5 7272
hearts inclined to *f* Abimelech Judg 9:3
unto the young men that *f* my lord 1Sa 25:27
faint that they could not *f* David 1Sa 30:21
among the people that *f* Absalom 2Sa 17:9 310
if the LORD be God, *f* him 1Kin 18:21
but if Baal, then *f* him 1Kin 18:21
my mother, and then I will *f* thee 1Kin 19:20
for all the people that *f* me 1Kin 20:10 7272
f me, and I will bring you to the 2Kin 6:19
mercy shall *f* me all the days of Ps 23:6 7291
because I *f* the thing that good Ps 38:20 7291
f her shall be brought unto thee Ps 45:14 310
the upright in heart shall *f* it Ps 94:15 310
draw nigh that *f* after mischief Ps 119:150 7291
that they may *f* strong drink Is 5:11 7291
ye that *f* after righteousness, ye Is 51:1 7291
from being a pastor to *f* thee Jer 17:16 310
shall *f* close after you there in Jer 42:16 1692
that *f* their own spirit, and have Eze 13:3
she shall *f* after her lovers, but Hos 2:7 7291
if we *f* on to know the LORD Hos 6:3 7291
F me, and I will make you fishers Mt 4:19
I will *f* thee whithersoever thou Mt 8:19 *190*
But Jesus said unto him, *F* me Mt 8:22 *190*
and he saith unto him, *F* me Mt 9:9 *190*
and take up his cross, and *f* me Mt 16:24 *190*
and come and *f* me Mt 19:21 *190*
of custom, and said unto him, *F* me Mk 2:14 *190*
And he suffered no man to *f* him Mk 5:37 *4870*
and his disciples *f* him Mk 6:1 *190*
and take up his cross, and *f* me Mk 8:34 *190*
come, take up the cross, and *f* me Mk 10:21 *190*
bearing a pitcher of water: *f* him Mk 14:13 *190*
signs shall *f* them that believe Mk 16:17 *3877*
and he said unto him, *F* me Lk 5:27 *190*
take up his cross daily, and *f* me Lk 9:23 *190*
I will *f* thee whithersoever thou Lk 9:57 *190*
And he said unto another, *F* me Lk 9:59 *190*
also said, Lord, I will *f* thee Lk 9:61 *190*
go not after them, nor *f* them Lk 17:23 *1377*
in heaven: and come, *f* me Lk 18:22 *190*
f him into the house where he Lk 22:10 *190*
were about him saw what would *f* Lk 22:49 *2071*
Philip, and saith unto him, *F* me Jn 1:43 *190*
before them, and the sheep *f* him Jn 10:4 *190*
And a stranger will they not *f* Jn 10:5 *190*
and I know them, and they *f* me Jn 10:27 *190*
If any man serve me, let him *f* me Jn 12:26 *190*
I go, thou canst not *f* me now Jn 13:36 *190*
but thou shalt *f* me afterwards Jn 13:36 *190*
Lord, why cannot I *f* thee now Jn 13:37 *190*
this, he saith unto him, *F* me Jn 21:19 *190*
is that to thee? *f* thou me Jn 21:22 *190*
from Samuel and those that *f* after Acts 3:24 *2517*
thy garment about thee, and *f* me Acts 12:8 *190*
Let us therefore *f* after the Rom 14:19 *1377*
F after charity, and desire 1Cor 14:1 *1377*
but I *f* after, if that I may Phil 3:12 *1377*
but ever *f* that which is good, 1Th 5:15 *1377*
know how ye ought to *f* us 2Th 3:7 *3401*
an ensample unto you to *f* us 2Th 3:9 *3401*
and some men they *f* after 1Ti 5:24 *1872*
f after righteousness, godliness, 1Ti 6:11 *1377*
but *f* righteousness, faith, 2Ti 2:22 *1377*
F peace with all men, and holiness Heb 12:14 *1377*
whose faith *f*, considering the Heb 13:7 *3401*
and the glory that should *f* 1Pet 1:11
that ye should *f* his steps 1Pet 2:21 *1872*
many shall *f* their pernicious 2Pet 2:2 *1811*
f not that which is evil, but 3Jn 11 *3401*
These are they which *f* the Lamb Rev 14:4 *190*
and their works do *f* them Rev 14:13 *190*

FOLLOWED
upon the camels, and *f* the man Gen 24:61
all that *f* the droves, saying, On Gen 32:19
hath *f* me fully, him will I bring Num 14:24 310
and the elders of Israel *f* him Num 16:25
because they have not wholly *f* me Num 32:11 310
for they have wholly *f* the LORD Num 32:12 310
because he hath wholly *f* the LORD Deut 1:36 310
for all the men that *f* Baal-peor Deut 4:3
the covenant of the LORD *f* them Josh 6:8
but I wholly *f* the LORD my God Josh 14:8 310
hast wholly *f* the LORD my God Josh 14:9 310
wholly *f* the LORD God of Israel Josh 14:14 310
f other gods, of the gods of the Judg 2:12
and light persons, which *f* him Judg 9:4
f Abimelech, and put them to the Judg 9:49

and all the people *f* him trembling … 1Sa 13:7 310
even they also *f* hard after them … 1Sa 14:22 1692
went and *f* Saul to the battle … 1Sa 17:13
and the three eldest *f* Saul … 1Sa 17:14
the Philistines *f* hard upon Saul … 1Sa 31:2 1692
horsemen *f* hard after him … 2Sa 1:6 1692
But the house of Judah *f* David … 2Sa 2:10
And king David himself *f* the bier … 2Sa 3:31
there *f* him a mess of meat from … 2Sa 11:8
saw that his counsel was not *f* … 2Sa 17:23 6213
f Sheba the son of Bichri … 2Sa 20:2 310
none that *f* the house of David … 1Kin 12:20 310
who *f* me with all his heart, to … 1Kin 14:8
half of the people *f* Tibni the … 1Kin 16:21
and half *f* Omri … 1Kin 16:21 310
But the people that *f* Omri … 1Kin 16:22 310
that *f* Tibni the son of Ginath … 1Kin 16:22 310
the LORD, and thou hast *f* Baalim … 1Kin 18:18
city, and the army which *f* them … 1Kin 20:19 310
and for the cattle that *f* them … 2Kin 3:9 7272
And he arose, and *f* her … 2Kin 4:30
So Gehazi *f* after Naaman … 2Kin 5:21 7291
Jehu *f* after him, and said, Smite … 2Kin 9:27 7291
f the sins of Jeroboam the son of … 2Kin 13:2
they *f* vanity, and became vain, and … 2Kin 17:15
the Philistines *f* hard after Saul … 1Chr 10:2 1692
the men of the guard which *f* me … Neh 4:23 310
players on instruments *f* after … Ps 68:25
whither the head looked they *f* it … Eze 10:11
the LORD took me as I *f* the flock … Amos 7:15 310
left their nets, and *f* him … Mt 4:20 190
ship and their father, and *f* him … Mt 4:22 190
there *f* him great multitudes of … Mt 4:25 190
mountain, great multitudes *f* him … Mt 8:1 190
marvelled, and said to them that *f* … Mt 8:10 190
into a ship, his disciples *f* him … Mt 8:23 190
And he arose, and *f* him … Mt 9:9 190
f him, and so did his disciples … Mt 9:19 190
thence, two blind men *f* him … Mt 9:27 190
and great multitudes *f* him … Mt 12:15 190
they *f* him on foot out of the … Mt 14:13 190
And great multitudes *f* him … Mt 19:2 190
we have forsaken all, and *f* thee … Mt 19:27 190
unto you, That ye which have *f* me … Mt 19:28 190
Jericho, a great multitude *f* him … Mt 20:29 190
received sight, and they *f* him … Mt 20:34 190
that went before, and that *f* … Mt 21:9 190
But Peter *f* him afar off unto the … Mt 26:58 190
which *f* Jesus from Galilee, … Mt 27:55 190
that *f* the day of the preparation … Mt 27:62
they forsook their nets, and *f* him … Mk 1:18 190
that were with him *f* after him … Mk 1:36 2614
And he arose and *f* him … Mk 2:14 190
there were many, and they *f* him … Mk 2:15 190
multitude from Galilee *f* him … Mk 3:7 190
and much people *f* him, and thronged … Mk 5:24 190
we have left all, and have *f* thee … Mk 10:28 190
and as they *f*, they were afraid … Mk 10:32 190
his sight, and *f* Jesus in the way … Mk 10:52 190
that went before, and they that *f* … Mk 11:9 190
there *f* him a certain young man, … Mk 14:51 190
Peter *f* him afar off, even into … Mk 14:54 190
f him, and ministered unto him … Mk 15:41 190
land, they forsook all, and *f* him … Lk 5:11 190
And he left all, rose up, and *f* him … Lk 5:28 190
said unto the people that *f* him … Lk 7:9 190
people, when they knew it, *f* him … Lk 9:11 190
Lo, we have left all, and *f* thee … Lk 18:28 190
sight, and *f* him, glorifying God … Lk 18:43 190
and his disciples also *f* him … Lk 22:39 190
And Peter *f* afar off … Lk 22:54 190
there *f* him a great company of … Lk 23:27 190
the women that *f* him from Galilee … Lk 23:49 4870
f after, and beheld the sepulchre, … Lk 23:55 2628
heard him speak, and they *f* Jesus … Jn 1:37 190
f him, was Andrew, Simon Peter's … Jn 1:40 190
And a great multitude *f* him … Jn 6:2 190
f her, saying, She goeth unto the … Jn 11:31 190
And Simon Peter *f* Jesus, and so did … Jn 18:15 190
And he went out, and *f* him … Acts 12:9 190
and religious proselytes *f* Paul … Acts 13:43 190
The same *f* Paul and us, and cried, … Acts 16:17 2628
multitude of the people *f* after … Acts 21:36 190
which *f* not after righteousness, … Rom 9:30 1377
Israel, which *f* after the law of … Rom 9:31 1377
that spiritual Rock that *f* them … 1Cor 10:4 190
have diligently *f* every good work … 1Ti 5:10 1872
For we have not *f* cunningly … 2Pet 1:16 1811
him was Death, and Hell *f* with him … Rev 6:8 190
angel sounded, and there *f* hail … Rev 8:7 1096
there *f* another angel, saying, … Rev 14:8 190
And the third angel *f* them … Rev 14:9 190
in heaven *f* him upon white horses … Rev 19:14 190

FOLLOWEDST
inasmuch as thou *f* not young men … Ruth 3:10

FOLLOWERS
I beseech you, be ye *f* of me … 1Cor 4:16 3402
Be ye *f* of me, even as I also am … 1Cor 11:1 3402
Be ye therefore *f* of God, as dear … Eph 5:1 3402
be *f* together of me, and mark them … Phil 3:17 4831
And ye became *f* of us, and of the … 1Th 1:6 3402
became *f* of the churches of God … 1Th 2:14 3402
but *f* of them who through faith … Heb 6:12 3402
if ye be *f* of that which is good … 1Pet 3:13 3402

FOLLOWETH
him that *f* her kill with the … 2Kin 11:15
and whoso *f* her, let him be slain … 2Chr 23:14
My soul *f* hard after thee … Ps 63:8 1692
but he that *f* vain persons is … Prov 12:11 7291
him that *f* after righteousness … Prov 15:9 7291
He that *f* after righteousness and … Prov 21:21 7291
but he that *f* after vain persons … Prov 28:19 7291

loveth gifts, and *f* after rewards … Is 1:23 7291
whereas none *f* thee to commit … Eze 16:34 310
on wind, and *f* after the east wind … Hos 12:1 7291
f after me, is not worthy of me … Mt 10:38 190
in thy name, and he *f* not us … Mk 9:38 190
forbad him, because he *f* not us … Mk 9:38 190
him, because he *f* not with us … Lk 9:49 190
he that *f* me shall not walk in … Jn 8:12 190

FOLLOWING
land by reason of that famine *f* … Gen 41:31
will turn away thy son from *f* me … Deut 7:4 310
that thou be not snared by *f* them … Deut 12:30 310
away this day from *f* the LORD … Josh 22:16 310
away this day from *f* the LORD … Josh 22:18 310
an altar to turn from *f* the LORD … Josh 22:23 310
and turn this day from *f* the LORD … Josh 22:29 310
in *f* other gods to serve them, and … Judg 2:19
or to return from *f* after thee … Ruth 1:16
you continue *f* the LORD your God … 1Sa 12:14 310
turn not aside from *f* the LORD … 1Sa 12:20 310
went up from *f* the Philistines … 1Sa 14:46 310
for he is turned back from *f* me … 1Sa 15:11 310
returned from *f* the Philistines … 1Sa 24:1 310
hand nor to the left from *f* Abner … 2Sa 2:19 310
not turn aside from *f* of him … 2Sa 2:21 310
Asahel, Turn thee aside from *f* me … 2Sa 2:22 310
return from *f* their brethren … 2Sa 2:26 310
up every one from *f* his brother … 2Sa 2:27 310
And Joab returned from *f* Abner … 2Sa 2:30 310
from *f* the sheep, to be ruler … 2Sa 7:8 310
they *f* Adonijah helped him … 1Kin 1:7 310
if ye shall at all turn from *f* me … 1Kin 9:6 310
he did very abominably in *f* idols … 1Kin 21:26
drave Israel from *f* the LORD … 2Kin 17:21 310
LORD, and departed not from *f* him … 2Kin 18:6 310
sheepcote, even from *f* the sheep … 1Chr 17:7 310
f the LORD they made a conspiracy … 2Chr 25:27 310
they departed not from *f* the LORD … 2Chr 34:33 310
may tell it to the generation *f* … Ps 48:13 314
From *f* the ewes great with young … Ps 78:71 310
in the generation *f* let their … Ps 109:13 312
confirming the word with signs *f* … Mk 16:20 1872
day, and to morrow, and the day *f* … Lk 13:33 2192
Then Jesus turned, and saw them *f* … Jn 1:38 190
The day *f* Jesus would go forth … Jn 1:43 1887
The day *f*, when the people which … Jn 6:22 1887
Then cometh Simon Peter *f* him … Jn 20:6 190
the disciple whom Jesus loved *f* … Jn 21:20 190
the day *f* unto Rhodes, and from … Acts 21:1 1836
the day *f* Paul went in with us … Acts 21:18 1966
the night *f* the Lord stood by him … Acts 23:11
f the way of Balaam the son of … 2Pet 2:15 1811

FOLLY
because he had wrought *f* in … Gen 34:7 5039
she hath wrought *f* in Israel … Deut 22:21 5039
he hath wrought *f* in Israel … Josh 7:15 5039
into mine house, do not this *f* … Judg 19:23 5039
committed lewdness and *f* in Israel … Judg 20:6 5039
according to all the *f* that they … Judg 20:10 5039
is his name, and *f* is with him … 1Sa 25:25 5039
do not thou this *f* … 2Sa 13:12 5039
and his angels he charged with *f* … Job 4:18 8417
yet God layeth not *f* to them … Job 24:12 8604
lest I deal with you after your *f* … Job 42:8 5039
This their way is their *f* … Ps 49:13 3689
but let them not turn again to *f* … Ps 85:8 3690
of his *f* he shall go astray … Prov 5:23 200
but a fool layeth open his *f* … Prov 13:16 200
but the *f* of fools is deceit … Prov 14:8 200
The simple inherit *f* … Prov 14:18 200
but the foolishness of fools is *f* … Prov 14:24 200
is hasty of spirit exalteth *f* … Prov 14:29 200
F is joy to him that is destitute … Prov 15:21 200
but the instruction of fools is *f* … Prov 16:22 200
man, rather than a fool in his *f* … Prov 17:12 200
before he heareth it, it is *f* … Prov 18:13 200
not a fool according to his *f* … Prov 26:4 200
Answer a fool according to his *f* … Prov 26:5 200
so a fool returneth to his *f* … Prov 26:11 200
wisdom, and to know madness and *f* … Eccl 1:17 5531
and to lay hold on *f*, till I might … Eccl 2:3 5531
behold wisdom, and madness, and *f* … Eccl 2:12 5531
I saw that wisdom excelleth *f* … Eccl 2:13 5531
and to know the wickedness of *f* … Eccl 7:25 3689
so doth a little *f* him that is in … Eccl 10:1 5531
F is set in great dignity, and the … Eccl 10:6 5529
and every mouth speaketh *f* … Is 9:17 5039
I have seen *f* in the prophets of … Jer 23:13 8604
bear with me a little in my *f* … 2Cor 11:1 877
for their *f* shall be manifest … 2Ti 3:9 454

FOOD
to the sight, and good for *f* … Gen 2:9 3978
saw that the tree was good for *f* … Gen 3:6 3978
unto thee of all *f* that is eaten … Gen 6:21 3978
and it shall be for *f* for thee … Gen 6:21 402
let them gather all the *f* of … Gen 41:35 400
and let them keep *f* in the cities … Gen 41:35 400
that *f* shall be for store to the … Gen 41:36 400
up all the *f* of the seven years … Gen 41:48 400
laid up the *f* in the cities … Gen 41:48 400
the *f* of the field, which was … Gen 41:48 400
From the land of Canaan to buy *f* … Gen 42:7 400
but to buy *f* are thy servants … Gen 42:10 400
take *f* for the famine of your … Gen 42:33
them, Go again, buy us a little *f* … Gen 43:2 400
us, we will go down and buy thee *f* … Gen 43:4 400
down at the first time to buy *f* … Gen 43:20 400
down in our hands to buy *f* … Gen 43:22 400
Fill the men's sacks with *f* … Gen 44:1 400
Go again, and buy us a little *f* … Gen 44:25 400
seed of the field, and for your *f* … Gen 47:24 400
for *f* for your little ones … Gen 47:24 398

her *f*, her raiment, and her duty … Ex 21:10 7607
it is the *f* of the offering made … Lev 3:11 3899
it is the *f* of the offering made … Lev 3:16 3899
planted all manner of trees for *f* … Lev 19:23 3978
because it is his *f* … Lev 22:7 3899
the stranger, in giving him *f* … Deut 10:18 3899
that eateth any *f* until evening … 1Sa 14:24 3899
none of the people tasted any *f* … 1Sa 14:24 3899
man that eateth any *f* this day … 1Sa 14:28 3899
master's son may have *f* to eat … 2Sa 9:10 3899
in giving *f* for my household … 1Kin 5:9 3899
of wheat for *f* to his household … 1Kin 5:11 4361
mouth more than my necessary *f* … Job 23:12
wilderness yieldeth *f* for them … Job 24:5 3899
Who provideth for the raven his *f* … Job 38:41 6718
the mountains bring him forth *f* … Job 40:20 944
Man did eat angels' *f* … Ps 78:25 3899
bring forth *f* out of the earth … Ps 104:14 3899
Who giveth *f* to all flesh … Ps 136:25 3899
which giveth *f* to the hungry … Ps 146:7 3899
He giveth to the beast his *f* … Ps 147:9 3899
gathereth her *f* in the harvest … Prov 6:8 3978
Much *f* is in the tillage of the … Prov 13:23 400
have goats' milk enough for thy *f* … Prov 27:27 3899
for the *f* of thy household, and … Prov 27:27 3899
sweeping rain which leaveth no *f* … Prov 28:3 3899
feed me with *f* convenient for me … Prov 30:8 3899
she bringeth her *f* from afar … Prov 31:14 3899
have diminished thine ordinary *f* … Eze 16:27
f unto them that serve the city … Eze 48:18 3899
filling our hearts with *f* … Acts 14:17 5160
both minister bread for your *f* … 2Cor 9:10 1035
And having *f* and raiment let us be … 1Ti 6:8 1304
be naked, and destitute of daily *f* … Jas 2:15 5160

FOOL
behold, I have played the *f* … 1Sa 26:21 5528
and said, Died Abner as a *f* dieth … 2Sa 3:33 5036
The *f* hath said in his heart, … Ps 14:1 5036
that wise men die, likewise the *f* … Ps 49:10 3684
The *f* hath said in his heart, … Ps 53:1 5036
neither doth a *f* understand this … Ps 92:6 3684
or as a *f* to the correction of … Prov 7:22 191
but a prating *f* shall fall … Prov 10:8 191
but a prating *f* shall fall … Prov 10:10 191
that uttereth a slander, is a *f* … Prov 10:18 3684
is as sport to a *f* to do mischief … Prov 10:23 3684
the *f* shall be servant to the … Prov 11:29 191
The way of a *f* is right in his … Prov 12:15 191
but a *f* layeth open his folly … Prov 13:16 3684
but the *f* rageth, and is confident … Prov 14:16 3684
A *f* despiseth his father's … Prov 15:5 191
Excellent speech becometh not a *f* … Prov 17:7 5036
than an hundred stripes into a *f* … Prov 17:10 3684
man, rather than a *f* in his folly … Prov 17:12 3684
in the hand of a *f* to get wisdom … Prov 17:16 3684
He that begetteth a *f* doeth it to … Prov 17:21 3684
and the father of a *f* hath no joy … Prov 17:21 5036
but the eyes of a *f* are in the … Prov 17:24 3684
Even a *f*, when he holdeth his … Prov 17:28 191
A *f* hath no delight in … Prov 18:2 3684
perverse in his lips, and is a *f* … Prov 19:1 3684
Delight is not seemly for a *f* … Prov 19:10 3684
but every *f* will be meddling … Prov 20:3 191
Speak not in the ears of a *f* … Prov 23:9 3684
Wisdom is too high for a *f* … Prov 24:7 191
so honour is not seemly for a *f* … Prov 26:1 3684
Answer not a *f* according to his … Prov 26:4 3684
Answer a *f* according to his folly … Prov 26:5 3684
hand of a *f* cutteth off the feet … Prov 26:6 3684
is he that giveth honour to a *f* … Prov 26:8 3684
all things both rewardeth the *f* … Prov 26:10 3684
so a *f* returneth to his folly … Prov 26:11 3684
is more hope of a *f* than of him … Prov 26:12 3684
Though thou shouldest bray a *f* in … Prov 27:22 191
trusteth in his own heart is a *f* … Prov 28:26 3684
A *f* uttereth all his mind … Prov 29:11 3684
is more hope of a *f* than of him … Prov 29:20 3684
a *f* when he is filled with meat … Prov 30:22 5030
but the *f* walketh in darkness … Eccl 2:14 3684
heart, As it happeneth to the *f* … Eccl 2:15 3684
wise more than of the *f* for ever … Eccl 2:16 3684
the wise man? as the *f* … Eccl 2:16 3684
he shall be a wise man or a *f* … Eccl 2:19 5530
The *f* foldeth his hands together, … Eccl 4:5 3684
hath the wise more than the *f* … Eccl 6:8 3684
pot, so is the laughter of the *f* … Eccl 7:6 3684
when he that is a *f* walketh by … Eccl 10:3 5530
saith to every one that he is a *f* … Eccl 10:3 5530
but the lips of a *f* will swallow … Eccl 10:12 3684
A *f* also is full of words … Eccl 10:14 5536
days, and at his end shall be a *f* … Jer 17:11 5036
the prophet is a *f*, the spiritual … Hos 9:7 191
but whosoever shall say, Thou *f* … Mt 5:22 3474
But God said unto him, Thou *f* … Lk 12:20 876
in this world, let him become a *f* … 1Cor 3:18 3474
Thou *f*, that which thou sowest is … 1Cor 15:36 876
again, Let no man think me a *f* … 2Cor 11:16 876
yet as a *f* receive me, that I may … 2Cor 11:16 876
(I speak as a *f*) I am more … 2Cor 11:23 3912
to glory, I shall not be a *f* … 2Cor 12:6 876
I am become a *f* in glorying … 2Cor 12:11 876

FOOLISH
the LORD, O *f* people and unwise … Deut 32:6 5036
them to anger with a *f* nation … Deut 32:21 5036
as one of the *f* women speaketh … Job 2:10 5039
For wrath killeth the *f* man … Job 5:2 191
I have seen the *f* taking root … Job 5:3 191
The *f* shall not stand in thy … Ps 5:5 1984
make me not the reproach of the *f* … Ps 39:8 5036
For I was envious at the *f* … Ps 73:3 1984
So *f* was I, and ignorant … Ps 73:22 1198
that the *f* people have blasphemed … Ps 74:18 5036
remember how the *f* man … Ps 74:22 5036

Forsake the *f*, and live Prov 9:6 6612
A *f* woman is clamorous Prov 9:13 3687
but a *f* son is the heaviness of Prov 10:1 3684
of the *f* is near destruction Prov 10:14 191
but the *f* plucketh it down with Prov 14:1 200
mouth of the *f* is a rod of pride Prov 14:3 191
Go from the presence of a *f* man Prov 14:7 3684
the heart of the *f* doeth not so Prov 15:7 3684
but a *f* man despiseth his mother Prov 15:20 3684
A *f* son is a grief to his father, Prov 17:25 3684
A *f* son is the calamity of his Prov 19:13 3684
but a *f* man spendeth it up Prov 21:20 3684
wise man contendeth with a *f* man Prov 29:9 191
f king, who will no more be Eccl 4:13 3684
much wicked, neither be thou *f* Eccl 7:17 5530
The labour of the *f* wearieth Eccl 10:15 3684
and maketh their knowledge *f* Is 44:25 5528
For my people is *f*, they have not Jer 4:22 191
these are poor; they are *f* Jer 5:4 2973
now this, O *f* people, and without Jer 5:21 5530
they are altogether brutish and *f* Jer 10:8 3688
seen vain and *f* things for thee Lam 2:14 8602
Woe unto the *f* prophets, that Eze 13:3 5036
the instruments of a *f* shepherd Zec 11:15 196
shall be likened unto a *f* man Mt 7:26 *3474*
of them were wise, and five were *f* Mt 25:2 *3474*
They that were *f* took their lamps Mt 25:3 *3474*
the *f* said unto the wise, Give us Mt 25:8 *3474*
their *f* heart was darkened Rom 1:21 *801*
An instructor of the *f*, a teacher Rom 2:20 *878*
by a *f* nation I will anger you Rom 10:19 *801*
hath not God made *f* the wisdom of 1Cor 1:20 *3471*
But God hath chosen the *f* things 1Cor 1:27 *3474*
O *f* Galatians, who hath bewitched Gal 3:1 *453*
Are ye so *f*? Gal 3:3 *453*
nor *f* talking, nor jesting, which Eph 5:4 *3473*
and a snare, and into many *f* 1Ti 6:9 *453*
But *f* and unlearned questions 2Ti 2:23 *3474*
ourselves also were sometimes *f* Titus 3:3 *453*
But avoid *f* questions, and Titus 3:9 *3474*
to silence the ignorance of *f* men 1Pet 2:15 *878*

FOOLISHLY
thou hast now done *f* in so doing Gen 31:28 5528
upon us, wherein we have done *f* Num 12:11 2973
said to Saul, Thou hast done *f* 1Sa 13:13 5528
for I have done very *f* 2Sa 24:10 5528
for I have done very *f* 1Chr 21:8 5528
Herein thou hast done *f* 2Chr 16:9 5528
Job sinned not, nor charged God *f* Job 1:22 8604
I said unto the fools, Deal not *f* Ps 75:4 1984
He that is soon angry dealeth *f* Prov 14:17 200
If thou hast done *f* in lifting up Prov 30:32 5034
after the Lord, but as it were *f* 2Cor 11:17
any is bold, (I speak *f*,) I am 2Cor 11:21

FOOLISHNESS
the counsel of Ahithophel into *f* 2Sa 15:31 5528
and are corrupt because of my *f* Ps 38:5 200
O God, thou knowest my *f* Ps 69:5 200
the heart of fools proclaimeth *f* Prov 12:23 200
but the *f* of fools is folly Prov 14:24 200
the mouth of fools poureth out *f* Prov 15:2 200
the mouth of fools feedeth on *f* Prov 15:14 200
The *f* of man perverteth his way Prov 19:3 200
F is bound in the heart of a Prov 22:15 200
The thought of *f* is sin Prov 24:9 200
will not his *f* depart from him Prov 27:22 200
wickedness of folly, even of *f* Eccl 7:25 5531
of the words of his mouth is *f* Eccl 10:13 5531
an evil eye, blasphemy, pride, *f* Mk 7:22 *877*
cross is to them that perish *f* 1Cor 1:18 *3472*
it pleased God by the *f* of 1Cor 1:21 *3472*
and unto the Greeks *f* 1Cor 1:23 *3472*
Because the *f* of God is wiser 1Cor 1:25 *3472*
for they are *f* unto him 1Cor 2:14 *3472*
of this world is *f* with God 1Cor 3:19 *3472*

FOOL'S
A *f* wrath is presently known Prov 12:16 191
A *f* lips enter into contention, Prov 18:6 3684
A *f* mouth is his destruction, and Prov 18:7 3684
the ass, and a rod for the *f* back Prov 26:3 3684
but a *f* wrath is heavier than Prov 27:3 191
a *f* voice is known by multitude Eccl 5:3 3684
but a *f* heart at his left Eccl 10:2 3684

FOOLS
be as one of the *f* in Israel 2Sa 13:13 5036
spoiled, and maketh the judges *f* Job 12:17 1984
They were children of *f*, yea, Job 30:8 5036
I said unto the *f*, Deal not Ps 75:4 1984
and ye *f*, when will ye be wise Ps 94:8 3684
F, because of their transgression Ps 107:17 191
but *f* despise wisdom and Prov 1:7 191
scorning, and *f* hate knowledge Prov 1:22 3684
the prosperity of *f* shall destroy Prov 1:32 3684
shame shall be the promotion of *f* Prov 3:35 3684
and, ye *f*, be ye of an Prov 8:5 3684
but *f* die for want of wisdom Prov 10:21 191
but the heart of *f* proclaimeth Prov 12:23 3684
to *f* to depart from evil Prov 13:19 3684
companion of *f* shall be destroyed Prov 13:20 3684
but the folly of *f* is deceit Prov 14:8 3684
F make a mock at sin Prov 14:9 191
but the foolishness of *f* is folly Prov 14:24 3684
in the midst of *f* is made known Prov 14:33 3684
but the mouth of *f* poureth out Prov 15:2 3684
but the mouth of *f* feedeth on Prov 15:14 3684
but the instruction of *f* is folly Prov 16:22 191
and stripes for the back of *f* Prov 19:29 3684
so is a parable in the mouth of *f* Prov 26:7 3684
so is a parable in the mouth of *f* Prov 26:9 3684
than to give the sacrifice of *f* Eccl 5:1 3684
for he hath no pleasure in *f* Eccl 5:4 3684
but the heart of *f* is in the Eccl 7:4 3684
for a man to hear the song of *f* Eccl 7:5 3684
anger resteth in the bosom of *f* Eccl 7:9 3684
cry of him that ruleth among *f* Eccl 9:17 3684
Surely the princes of Zoan are *f* Is 19:11 191
The princes of Zoan are become *f* Is 19:13 2973
the wayfaring men, though *f* Is 35:8 191
Ye *f* and blind Mt 23:17 *3474*
Ye *f* and blind Mt 23:19 *3474*
Ye *f*, did not he that made that Lk 11:40 *878*
Then he said unto them, O *f* Lk 24:25 *453*
to be wise, they became *f* Rom 1:22 *3471*
We are *f* for Christ's sake, but 1Cor 4:10 *3474*
For ye suffer *f* gladly, seeing ye 2Cor 11:19 *878*
ye walk circumspectly, not as *f* Eph 5:15 *781*

FOOT
no rest for the sole of her *f* Gen 8:9 7272
or *f* in all the land of Egypt Gen 41:44 7272
thousand on *f* that were men Ex 12:37 7273
tooth, hand for hand, *f* for *f* Ex 21:24 7272
the great toe of their right *f* Ex 29:20 7272
his *f* also of brass, to wash Ex 30:18 3653
vessels, and the laver and his *f* Ex 30:28 3653
furniture, and the laver and his *f* Ex 31:9 3653
his vessels, the laver and his *f* Ex 35:16 3653
the *f* of it of brass, of the Ex 38:8 3653
his vessels, the laver and his *f* Ex 39:39 3653
shalt anoint the laver and his *f* Ex 40:11 3653
vessels, both the laver and his *f* Lev 8:11 3653
upon the great toe of his right *f* Lev 8:23 7272
from his head even to his *f* Lev 13:12 7272
upon the great toe of his right *f* Lev 14:14 7272
upon the great toe of his right *f* Lev 14:17 7272
upon the great toe of his right *f* Lev 14:25 7272
upon the great toe of his right *f* Lev 14:28 7272
Balaam's *f* against the wall Num 22:25 7272
thee, neither did thy *f* swell Deut 8:4 7272
seed, and wateredst it with thy *f* Deut 11:10 7272
tooth, hand for hand, *f* for *f* Deut 19:21 7272
and loose his shoe from off his *f* Deut 25:9 7272
from the sole of thy *f* unto the Deut 28:35 7272
sole of her *f* upon the ground for Deut 28:56 7272
shall the sole of thy *f* have rest Deut 28:65 7272
shoe is not waxen old upon thy *f* Deut 29:5 7272
their *f* shall slide in due time Deut 32:35 7272
and let him dip his *f* in oil Deut 33:24 7272
sole of your *f* shall tread upon Josh 1:3 7272
Loose thy shoe from off thy *f* Josh 5:15 7272
he was sent on *f* into the valley Judg 5:15 7272
was as light of *f* as a wild roe 2Sa 2:18 7272
from the sole of his *f* even to 2Sa 14:25 7272
fingers, and on every *f* six toes 2Sa 21:20 7272
and he trode her under *f* 2Kin 9:33
on each hand, and six on each *f* 1Chr 20:6
will I any more remove the *f* of 2Chr 33:8 7272
the sole of his *f* unto his crown Job 2:7 7272
My *f* hath held his steps, his way Job 23:11 7272
the waters forgotten of the *f* Job 28:4 7272
or if my *f* hath hasted to deceit Job 31:5 7272
that the *f* may crush them Job 39:15 7272
they hid is their own *f* taken Ps 9:15 7272
My *f* standeth in an even place Ps 26:12 7272
Let not the *f* of pride come Ps 36:11 7272
when my *f* slippeth, they magnify Ps 38:16 7272
they went through the flood on *f* Ps 66:6 7272
That thy *f* may be dipped in the Ps 68:23 7272
thou dash thy *f* against a stone Ps 91:12 7272
When I said, My *f* slippeth Ps 94:18 7272
will not suffer thy *f* to be moved Ps 121:3 7272
refrain thy *f* from their path Prov 1:15 7272
and thy *f* shall not stumble Prov 3:23 7272
shall keep thy *f* from being taken Prov 3:26 7272
remove thy *f* from evil Prov 4:27 7272
Withdraw thy *f* from thy Prov 25:17 7272
broken tooth, and a *f* out of joint Prov 25:19 7272
Keep thy *f* when thou goest to the Eccl 5:1 7272
From the sole of the *f* even unto Is 1:6 7272
my mountains tread him under *f* Is 14:25 947
meted out and trodden under *f* Is 18:7 4001
and put off thy shoe from thy *f* Is 20:2 7272
The *f* shall tread it down, even Is 26:6 7272
the east, called him to his *f* Is 41:2 7272
turn away thy *f* from the sabbath Is 58:13 7272
Withhold thy *f* from being unshod, Jer 2:25 7272
have trodden my portion under *f* Jer 12:10 947
The Lord hath trodden under *f* all Lam 1:15 5541
was like the sole of a calf's *f* Eze 1:7 7272
thine hand, and stamp with thy *f* Eze 6:11 7272
No *f* of man shall pass through it Eze 29:11 7272
nor *f* of beast shall pass through Eze 29:11 7272
neither shall the *f* of man Eze 32:13 7272
and the host to be trodden under *f* Dan 8:13 4823
he that is swift of *f* shall not Amos 2:15 7272
thou dash thy *f* against a stone Mt 4:6 *4228*
and to be trodden under *f* of men Mt 5:13 *2662*
him on *f* out of the cities Mt 14:13 *3979*
if thy hand or thy *f* offend thee Mt 18:8 *4228*
the servants, Bind him hand and *f* Mt 22:13 *4228*
if thy *f* offend thee, cut it off Mk 9:45 *4228*
thou dash thy *f* against a stone Lk 4:11 *4228*
bound hand and *f* with graveclothes Jn 11:44 *4228*
not so much as to set his *f* on Acts 7:5 *4228*
If the *f* shall say, Because I am 1Cor 12:15 *4228*
trodden under *f* the Son of God Heb 10:29 *2662*
with a garment down to the *f* Rev 1:13 *4158*
he set his right *f* upon the sea Rev 10:2 *4228*
and his left *f* on the earth Rev 10:2
shall they tread under *f* forty Rev 11:2

FOOTBREADTH
land, no, not so much as a *f* Deut 2:5

FOOTMEN
I am, are six hundred thousand *f* Num 11:21 7273
thousand *f* that drew sword Judg 20:2
fell of Israel thirty thousand *f* 1Sa 4:10 7273
in Telaim, two hundred thousand *f* 1Sa 15:4 7273
unto the *f* that stood about him 1Sa 22:17 7328
horsemen, and twenty thousand *f* 2Sa 8:4
of Zoba, twenty thousand *f* 2Sa 10:6 7273
an hundred thousand *f* in one day 1Kin 20:29 7273
ten chariots, and ten thousand *f* 2Kin 13:7 7273
horsemen, and twenty thousand *f* 1Chr 18:4
in chariots, and forty thousand *f* 1Chr 19:18
If thou hast run with the *f* Jer 12:5 7273

FOOTSTEPS
in thy paths, that my *f* slip not Ps 17:5 6471
waters, and thy *f* are not known Ps 77:19 6119
the *f* of thine anointed Ps 89:51 6119
way forth by the *f* of the flock Song 1:8 6119

FOOTSTOOL
for the *f* of our God, and had made 1Chr 28:2
with a *f* of gold, which were 2Chr 9:18 3534
LORD our God, and worship at his *f* Ps 99:5
until I make thine enemies thy *f* Ps 110:1
we will worship at his *f* Ps 132:7
my throne, and the earth is my *f* Is 66:1
remembered not his *f* in the day Lam 2:1
for it is his *f* Mt 5:35
till I make thine enemies thy *f* Mt 22:44
till I make thine enemies thy *f* Mk 12:36
Till I make thine enemies thy *f* Lk 20:43
Until I make thy foes thy *f* Acts 2:35
is my throne, and earth is my *f* Acts 7:49
until I make thine enemies thy *f* Heb 1:13
till his enemies be made his *f* Heb 10:13
there, or sit here under my *f* Jas 2:3 *5286*

FOR See PREFACE.

FORASMUCH
F as God hath shewed thee all Gen 41:39 310
f as thou knowest how we are to Num 10:31
f as he hath no part nor Deut 12:12 3588
f as the LORD hath said unto you, Deut 17:16
f as the LORD hath blessed me Josh 17:14 5704
f as the LORD hath taken Judg 11:36
f as we have sworn both of us in 1Sa 20:42
f as when the LORD had delivered 1Sa 24:18
f as my lord the king is come 2Sa 19:30
F as this is done of thee, and 1Kin 11:11
F as thou hast disobeyed the 1Kin 13:21
F as I exalted thee from among 1Kin 14:7
F as I exalted thee out of the 1Kin 16:2
F as thou hast sent messengers to 2Kin 1:16
f as he defiled his father's bed, 1Chr 5:1
F as it was in thine heart to 2Chr 6:8
F as thou art sent of the king, Ezr 7:14
F as this people refuseth the Is 8:6
F as this people draw near me Is 29:13
F as there is none like unto thee Jer 10:6
f as among all the wise men of Jer 10:7
f as iron breaketh in pieces and Dan 2:40
f as thou sawest the iron mixed Dan 2:41
F as thou sawest that the stone Dan 2:45
f as all the wise men of my Dan 4:18
F as an excellent spirit, and Dan 5:12
f as he was faithful, neither was Dan 6:4
f as before him innocency was Dan 6:22
F therefore as your treading is Amos 5:11 3282
But *f* as he had not to pay, his Mt 18:25
F as many have taken in hand to Lk 1:1 *1895*
f as Lydda was nigh to Joppa, and Acts 9:38 *5607*
F then as God gave them the like Acts 11:17 *1487*
F as we have heard, that certain Acts 15:24 *1894*
F then as we are the offspring of Acts 17:29
F as I know that thou hast been Acts 24:10
f as he is the image and glory of 1Cor 11:7
f as ye are zealous of spiritual 1Cor 14:12 *1893*
f as ye know that your labour is 1Cor 15:58
F as ye are manifestly declared 2Cor 3:3
F then as the children are Heb 2:14 *1893*
F as ye know that ye were not 1Pet 1:18
F then as Christ hath suffered 1Pet 4:1

FORBAD
whatsoever the LORD our God *f* us Deut 2:37 6680
But John *f* him, saying, I have Mt 3:14 *1254*
we *f* him, because he followeth Mk 9:38 *2967*
we *f* him, because he followeth Lk 9:49 *2967*
f the madness of the prophet 2Pet 2:16 *2967*

FORBARE
and he *f* to go forth 1Sa 23:13 2308
Then the prophet *f*, and said, I 2Chr 25:16 2308
So he *f*, and slew them not among Jer 41:8 2308

FORBEAR
wouldest *f* to help him, thou Ex 23:5 2308
But if thou shalt *f* to vow Deut 23:22 2308
to battle, or shall I *f* 1Kin 22:6 2308
to battle, or shall we *f* 1Kin 22:15 2308
to battle, or shall I *f* 2Chr 18:5 2308
to battle, or shall I *f* 2Chr 18:14 2308
f; why shouldest thou be smitten 2Chr 25:16 2308
f thee from meddling with God, 2Chr 35:21 2308
Yet many years didst thou *f* them Neh 9:30 4900
and though I *f*, what am I eased Job 16:6 2308
If thou *f* to deliver them that Prov 24:11 2820
to come with me into Babylon, *f* Jer 40:4 2308
will hear, or whether they will *f* Eze 2:5 2308
will hear, or whether they will *f* Eze 2:7 2308
will hear, or whether they will *f* Eze 3:11 2308
and he that forbeareth, let him *f* Eze 3:27 2308
F to cry, make no mourning for Eze 24:17 1826
my price; and if not, *f* Zec 11:12 2308
have not we power to *f* working 1Cor 9:6 *3361*
but now I *f*, lest any man should 2Cor 12:6 *5339*
when we could no longer *f* 1Th 3:1 *4722*
cause, when I could no longer *f* 1Th 3:5 *4722*

FORBEARANCE
the riches of his goodness and *f* ... Rom 2:4 *463*
are past, through the *f* of God ... Rom 3:25 *463*

FORBEARETH
f to keep the passover, even the ... Num 9:13 2308
and he that *f*, let him forbear ... Eze 3:27 2310

FORBEARING
By long *f* is a prince persuaded, ... Prov 25:15 639
my bones, and I was weary with *f* ... Jer 20:9 3557
f one another in love ... Eph 4:2 *430*
things unto them, *f* threatening ... Eph 6:9 *447*
F one another, and forgiving one ... Col 3:13 *430*

FORBID
God *f* that thy servants should do ... Gen 44:7 2486
God *f* that I should do so ... Gen 44:17 2486
and said, My lord Moses, *f* them ... Num 11:28 3607
God *f* that we should rebel ... Josh 22:29 2486
God *f* that we should forsake the ... Josh 24:16 2486
God *f* that I should sin against ... 1Sa 12:23 2486
God *f*: as the LORD liveth ... 1Sa 14:45 2486
And he said unto him, God *f* ... 1Sa 20:2 2486
The LORD *f* that I should do this ... 1Sa 24:6 2486
The LORD *f* that I should stretch ... 1Sa 26:11 2486
said to Ahab, The LORD *f* it me ... 1Kin 21:3 2486
And said, My God *f* it me, that I ... 1Chr 11:19 2486
God *f* that I should justify you ... Job 27:5 2486
f them not, to come unto me ... Mt 19:14 *2967*
But Jesus said, *F* him not ... Mk 9:39 *2967*
to come unto me, and *f* them not ... Mk 10:14 *2967*
cloke *f* not to take thy coat also ... Lk 6:29 *2967*
And Jesus said unto him, *F* him not ... Lk 9:50 *2967*
to come unto me, and *f* them not ... Lk 18:16 *2967*
they heard it, they said, God *f* ... Lk 20:16
Can any man *f* water, that these ... Acts 10:47 *2967*
that he should *f* none of his ... Acts 24:23 *2967*
God *f*: yea, let God be true ... Rom 3:4
God *f*: for then how shall God ... Rom 3:6
God *f*: yea, we establish the law ... Rom 3:31
God *f*. How shall we ... Rom 6:2
but under grace? God *f* ... Rom 6:15
Is the law sin? God *f* ... Rom 7:7
good made death unto me? God *f* ... Rom 7:13
unrighteousness with God? God *f* ... Rom 9:14
God cast away his people? God *f* ... Rom 11:1
that they should fall? God *f* ... Rom 11:11
members of an harlot? God *f* ... 1Cor 6:15
f not to speak with tongues ... 1Cor 14:39 *2967*
the minister of sin? God *f* ... Gal 2:17
the promises of God? God *f* ... Gal 3:21
But God *f* that I should glory, ... Gal 6:14

FORBIDDEN
any of these things which are *f* ... Lev 5:17 3808
the LORD thy God hath *f* thee ... Deut 4:23 6680
were *f* of the Holy Ghost to ... Acts 16:6 *2967*

FORBIDDETH
f them that would, and casteth ... 3Jn 10 *2967*

FORBIDDING
f to give tribute to Caesar, ... Lk 23:2 *2967*
with all confidence, no man *f* him ... Acts 28:31 *209*
F us to speak to the Gentiles ... 1Th 2:16 *2967*
F to marry, and commanding to ... 1Ti 4:3 *2967*

FORBORN
men of Babylon have *f* to fight ... Jer 51:30 2308

FORCE
take by *f* thy daughters from me ... Gen 31:31 1497
in the field, and the man *f* her ... Deut 22:25 2388
not dim, nor his natural *f* abated ... Deut 34:7 3893
and if not, I will take it by *f* ... 1Sa 2:16 2394
him, Nay, my brother, do not *f* me ... 2Sa 13:12 6031
Jews, and made them to cease by *f* ... Ezr 4:23 153
Will he *f* the queen also before ... Est 7:8 3533
By the great *f* of my disease is ... Job 30:18 3581
his *f* is in the navel of his ... Job 40:16 202
their blood by the *f* of the sword ... Jer 18:21 3027
is evil, and their *f* is not right ... Jer 23:10 1369
of Heshbon because of the *f* ... Jer 48:45 3581
but with *f* and with cruelty have ... Eze 34:4 2394
the *f* of the sword in the time of ... Eze 35:5 3027
strong shall not strengthen his *f* ... Amos 2:14 3581
and the violent take it by *f* ... Mt 11:12 *726*
they would come and take him by *f* ... Jn 6:15 *726*
to take him by *f* from among them, ... Acts 23:10 *726*
is of *f* after men are dead ... Heb 9:17 *949*

FORCED
the Amorites *f* the children of ... Judg 1:34 3905
and my concubine have they *f* ... Judg 20:5 6031
I *f* myself therefore, and offered ... 1Sa 13:12 662
than she, *f* her, and lay with her ... 2Sa 13:14 6031
because he had *f* his sister Tamar ... 2Sa 13:22 6031
day that he *f* his sister Tamar ... 2Sa 13:32 6031
flattering of her lips she *f* him ... Prov 7:21 5080

FORCES
he placed *f* in all the fenced ... 2Chr 17:2 2428
gold, nor all the *f* of strength ... Job 36:19 3981
the *f* of the Gentiles shall come ... Is 60:5 2428
unto thee the *f* of the Gentiles ... Is 60:11 2428
of the *f* which were in the fields ... Jer 40:7 2428
of the *f* that were in the fields ... Jer 40:13 2428
of the *f* that were with him ... Jer 41:11 2428
of the *f* that were with him ... Jer 41:13 2428
of the *f* that were with him ... Jer 41:16 2428
Then all the captains of the *f* ... Jer 42:1 2428
of the *f* which were with him ... Jer 42:8 2428
and all the captains of the *f* ... Jer 43:4 2428
and all the captains of the *f* ... Jer 43:5 2428
assemble a multitude of great *f* ... Dan 11:10 2428
shall he honour the God of *f* ... Dan 11:38 4581
carried away captive his *f* ... Obad 11 2428

FORCIBLE
How *f* are right words ... Job 6:25 4834

FORCING
thereof by *f* an ax against them ... Deut 20:19 5080
so the *f* of wrath bringeth forth ... Prov 30:33 4330

FORD
sons, and passed over the *f* Jabbok ... Gen 32:22 4569

FORDS
them the way to Jordan unto the *f* ... Josh 2:7 4569
took the *f* of Jordan toward Moab, ... Judg 3:28 4569
Moab shall be at the *f* of Arnon ... Is 16:2 4569

FORECAST
he shall *f* his devices against ... Dan 11:24 2803
for they shall *f* devices against ... Dan 11:25 2803

FOREFATHERS
back to the iniquities of their *f* ... Jer 11:10
from my *f* with pure conscience ... 2Ti 1:3 *4269*

FOREFRONT
in the *f* of the tabernacle ... Ex 26:9
upon the *f* of the mitre it shall ... Ex 28:37
upon the mitre, even upon his *f* ... Lev 8:9
The *f* of the one was situate ... 1Sa 14:5 8127
Set ye Uriah in the *f* of the ... 2Sa 11:15
from the *f* of the house, from ... 2Kin 16:14 6440
and Jehoshaphat in the *f* of them ... 2Chr 20:27 7218
the *f* of the lower gate unto the ... Eze 40:19 6440
the *f* of the inner court without ... Eze 40:19 6440
for the *f* of the house stood ... Eze 47:1 6440

FOREHEAD
And it shall be upon Aaron's *f* ... Ex 28:38 4696
and it shall be always upon his *f* ... Ex 28:38 4696
toward his face, he is *f* bald ... Lev 13:41 1371
be in the bald head, or bald *f* ... Lev 13:42 1372
in his bald head, or his bald *f* ... Lev 13:42 1372
his bald head, or in his bald *f* ... Lev 13:43 1372
and smote the Philistine in his *f* ... 1Sa 17:49 4696
that the stone sunk into his *f* ... 1Sa 17:49 4696
f before the priests in the house ... 2Chr 26:19 4696
behold, he was leprous in his *f* ... 2Chr 26:20 4696
and thou hadst a whore's *f* ... Jer 3:3 4696
thy *f* strong against their ... Eze 3:8 4696
than flint have I made thy *f* ... Eze 3:9 4696
And I put a jewel on thy *f* ... Eze 16:12 639
and receive his mark in his *f* ... Rev 14:9 *3359*
upon her *f* was a name written, ... Rev 17:5 *3359*

FOREHEADS
forehead strong against their *f* ... Eze 3:8 4696
set a mark upon the *f* of the men ... Eze 9:4 4696
servants of our God in their *f* ... Rev 7:3 *3359*
not the seal of God in their *f* ... Rev 9:4 *3359*
their right hand, or in their *f* ... Rev 13:16 *3359*
Father's name written in their *f* ... Rev 14:1 *3359*
received his mark upon their *f* ... Rev 20:4 *3359*
and his name shall be in their *f* ... Rev 22:4 *3359*

FOREIGNER
A *f* and an hired servant shall not ... Ex 12:45 8453
Of a *f* thou mayest exact it again ... Deut 15:3 5237

FOREIGNERS
f entered into his gates, and cast ... Obad 11 5237
ye are no more strangers and *f* ... Eph 2:19 *3941*

FOREKNEW
cast away his people which he *f* ... Rom 11:2 *4267*

FOREKNOW
For whom he did *f*, he also did ... Rom 8:29 *4267*

FOREKNOWLEDGE
f of God, ye have taken, and by ... Acts 2:23 *4268*
to the *f* of God the Father ... 1Pet 1:2 *4268*

FOREMOST
And he commanded the *f*, saying, ... Gen 32:17 7223
the handmaids and their children *f* ... Gen 33:2 7223
f is like the running of Ahimaaz ... 2Sa 18:27 7223

FOREORDAINED
Who verily was *f* before the ... 1Pet 1:20 *4267*

FOREPART
underneath, toward the *f* thereof ... Ex 28:27 6440
underneath, toward the *f* of it ... Ex 39:20 6440
the oracle in the *f* was twenty ... 1Kin 6:20 6440
court on the *f* of the chambers ... Eze 42:7 6440
the *f* stuck fast, and remained ... Acts 27:41 *4408*

FORERUNNER
Whither the *f* is for us entered, ... Heb 6:20 *4274*

FORESAW
I *f* the Lord always before my ... Acts 2:25 *4308*

FORESEEING
f that God would justify the ... Gal 3:8 *4375*

FORESEETH
A prudent man *f* the evil, and ... Prov 22:3 7200
A prudent man *f* the evil, and ... Prov 27:12 7200

FORESHIP
have cast anchors out of the *f* ... Acts 27:30 *4408*

FORESKIN
circumcise the flesh of your *f* ... Gen 17:11 6190
flesh of his *f* is not circumcised ... Gen 17:14 6190
of their *f* in the selfsame day ... Gen 17:23 6190
circumcised in the flesh of his *f* ... Gen 17:24 6190
circumcised in the flesh of his *f* ... Gen 17:25 6190
and cut off the *f* of her son ... Ex 4:25 6190
of his *f* shall be circumcised ... Lev 12:3 6190
therefore the *f* of your heart ... Deut 10:16 6190
also, and let thy *f* be uncovered ... Hab 2:16 6188

FORESKINS
of Israel at the hill of the *f* ... Josh 5:3 6190
dowry, but an hundred *f* of the ... 1Sa 18:25 6190
and David brought their *f*, and they ... 1Sa 18:27 6190
an hundred *f* of the Philistines ... 2Sa 3:14 6190
and take away the *f* of your heart ... Jer 4:4 6190

FOREST
and came into the *f* of Hareth ... 1Sa 22:5 3293
the house of the *f* of Lebanon ... 1Kin 7:2 3293
in the house of the *f* of Lebanon ... 1Kin 10:17 3293
f of Lebanon were of pure gold ... 1Kin 10:21 3293
and into the *f* of his Carmel ... 2Kin 19:23 3293
in the house of the *f* of Lebanon ... 2Chr 9:16 3293
f of Lebanon were of pure gold ... 2Chr 9:20 3293
Asaph the keeper of the king's *f* ... Neh 2:8 6508
For every beast of the *f* is mine ... Ps 50:10 3293
beasts of the *f* do creep forth ... Ps 104:20 3293
kindle in the thickets of the *f* ... Is 9:18 3293
shall consume the glory of his *f* ... Is 10:18 3293
the trees of his *f* shall be few ... Is 10:19 3293
the thickets of the *f* with iron ... Is 10:34 3293
In the *f* in Arabia shall ye lodge ... Is 21:13 3293
the armour of the house of the *f* ... Is 22:8 3293
field shall be esteemed as a *f* ... Is 29:17 3293
fruitful field be counted for a *f* ... Is 32:15 3293
shall hail, coming down on the *f* ... Is 32:19 3293
border, and the *f* of his Carmel ... Is 37:24 3293
himself among the trees of the *f* ... Is 44:14 3293
into singing, ye mountains, O *f* ... Is 44:23 3293
yea, all ye beasts in the *f* ... Is 56:9 3293
lion out of the *f* shall slay them ... Jer 5:6 3293
one cutteth a tree out of the *f* ... Jer 10:3 3293
is unto me as a lion in the *f* ... Jer 12:8 3293
kindle a fire in the *f* thereof ... Jer 21:14 3293
house as the high places of a *f* ... Jer 26:18 3293
They shall cut down her *f* ... Jer 46:23 3293
which is among the trees of the *f* ... Eze 15:2 3293
tree among the trees of the *f* ... Eze 15:6 3293
against the *f* of the south field ... Eze 20:46 3293
say to the *f* of the south, Hear ... Eze 20:47 3293
and I will make them a *f*, and the ... Hos 2:12 3293
Will a lion roar in the *f* ... Amos 3:4 3293
house as the high places of the *f* ... Mic 3:12 3293
a lion among the beasts of the *f* ... Mic 5:8 3293
for the *f* of the vintage is come ... Zec 11:2 3293

FORESTS
in the *f* he built castles and ... 2Chr 27:4 2793
to calve, and discovereth the *f* ... Ps 29:9 3295
neither cut down any out of the *f* ... Eze 39:10 3293

FORETELL
f you, as if I were present, the ... 2Cor 13:2 *4302*

FORETOLD
behold, I have *f* you all things ... Mk 13:23 *4280*
have likewise *f* of these days ... Acts 3:24 *4293*

FOREWARN
But I will *f* you whom ye shall ... Lk 12:5 *5263*

FOREWARNED
all such, as we also have *f* you ... 1Th 4:6 *4277*

FORFEITED
all his substance should be *f* ... Ezr 10:8 2763

FORGAT
butler remember Joseph, but *f* him ... Gen 40:23 7911
f the LORD their God, and served ... Judg 3:7 7911
when they *f* the LORD their God, ... 1Sa 12:9 7911
f his works, and his wonders that ... Ps 78:11 7911
They soon *f* his works ... Ps 106:13 7911
They *f* God their saviour, which ... Ps 106:21 7911
I *f* prosperity ... Lam 3:17 5382
lovers, and *f* me, saith the LORD ... Hos 2:13 7911

FORGAVE
f their iniquity, and destroyed ... Ps 78:38 3722
and loosed him, and *f* him the debt ... Mt 18:27 *863*
I *f* thee all that debt, because ... Mt 18:32 *863*
to pay, he frankly *f* them both ... Lk 7:42 *5483*
that he, to whom he *f* most ... Lk 7:43 *5483*
f any thing, to whom I *f* it ... 2Cor 2:10 *5483*
for your sakes *f* I it in the ... 2Cor 2:10
even as Christ *f* you, so also do ... Col 3:13 *5483*

FORGAVEST
thou *f* the iniquity of my sin ... Ps 32:5 5375
thou wast a God that *f* them ... Ps 99:8 5375

FORGED
The proud have *f* a lie against me ... Ps 119:69 2950

FORGERS
But ye are *f* of lies, ye are all ... Job 13:4 2950

FORGET
he *f* that which thou hast done to ... Gen 27:45 7911
he, hath made me *f* all my toil ... Gen 41:51 5382
lest thou *f* the things which ... Deut 4:9 7911
lest ye *f* the covenant of the ... Deut 4:23 7911
nor *f* the covenant of thy fathers ... Deut 4:31 7911
Then beware lest thou *f* the LORD ... Deut 6:12 7911
Beware that thou *f* not the LORD ... Deut 8:11 7911
thou *f* the LORD thy God, which ... Deut 8:14 7911
thou do at all *f* the LORD thy God ... Deut 8:19 7911
f not, how thou provokedst the ... Deut 9:7 7911
thou shalt not *f* it ... Deut 25:19 7911
not *f* thine handmaid, but wilt ... 1Sa 1:11 7911
have made with you ye shall not *f* ... 2Kin 17:38 7911
are the paths of all that *f* God ... Job 8:13 7911
I will *f* my complaint, I will ... Job 9:27 7911
Because thou shalt *f* thy misery ... Job 11:16 7911
The womb shall *f* him ... Job 24:20 7911
and all the nations that *f* God ... Ps 9:17 7913
f not the humble ... Ps 10:12 7911
How long wilt thou *f* me, O LORD ... Ps 13:1 7911
f also thine own people, and thy ... Ps 45:10 7911

F

Now consider this, ye that *f* God ... Ps 50:22 7911
Slay them not, lest my people *f* ... Ps 59:11 7911
f not the congregation of thy ... Ps 74:19 7911
F not the voice of thine enemies ... Ps 74:23 7911
not *f* the works of God, but keep ... Ps 78:7 7911
so that I *f* to eat my bread ... Ps 102:4 7911
soul, and *f* not all his benefits ... Ps 103:2 7911
I will not *f* thy word ... Ps 119:16 7911
yet do I not *f* thy statutes ... Ps 119:83 7911
I will never *f* thy precepts ... Ps 119:93 7911
yet do I not *f* thy law ... Ps 119:109 7911
yet do not I *f* thy precepts ... Ps 119:141 7911
for I do not *f* thy law ... Ps 119:153 7911
for I do not *f* thy commandments ... Ps 119:176 7911
If I *f* thee, O Jerusalem ... Ps 137:5 7911
let my right hand *f* her cunning ... Ps 137:5 7911
My son, *f* not my law ... Prov 3:1 7911
get understanding: *f* it not ... Prov 4:5 7911
f the law, and pervert the ... Prov 31:5 7911
f his poverty, and remember his ... Prov 31:7 7911
Can a woman *f* her sucking child, ... Is 49:15 7911
yea, they may *f*, yet will I not ... Is 49:15 7911
may *f*, yet will I not *f* thee ... Is 49:15 7911
for thou shalt *f* the shame of thy ... Is 54:4 7911
that *f* my holy mountain, that ... Is 65:11 7913
Can a maid *f* her ornaments, or a ... Jer 2:32 7911
think to cause my people to *f* my ... Jer 23:27 7911
I, even I, will utterly *f* you ... Jer 23:39 5382
Wherefore dost thou *f* us for ever ... Lam 5:20 7911
I will also *f* thy children ... Hos 4:6 7911
I will never *f* any of their works ... Amos 8:7 7911
is not unrighteous to *f* your work ... Heb 6:10 *1950*
do good and to communicate *f* not ... Heb 13:16 *1950*

FORGETFUL
Be not *f* to entertain strangers ... Heb 13:2 *1950*
therein, he being not a *f* hearer ... Jas 1:25 *1953*

FORGETFULNESS
righteousness in the land of *f* ... Ps 88:12 5388

FORGETTEST
face, and *f* our affliction and our ... Ps 44:24 7911
f the LORD thy maker, that hath ... Is 51:13 7911

FORGETTETH
f that the foot may crush them, ... Job 39:15 7911
he *f* not the cry of the humble ... Ps 9:12 7911
f the covenant of her God ... Prov 2:17 7913
straightway *f* what manner of man ... Jas 1:24 *1950*

FORGETTING
f those things which are behind, ... Phil 3:13 *1950*

FORGIVE
So shall ye say unto Joseph, *F* ... Gen 50:17 5375
f the trespass of the servants of ... Gen 50:17 5375
Now therefore *f*, I pray thee, my ... Ex 10:17 5375
Yet now, if thou wilt *f* their sin ... Ex 32:32 5375
and the LORD shall *f* her, because ... Num 30:5 5545
and the LORD shall *f* her ... Num 30:8 5545
and the LORD shall *f* her ... Num 30:12 5545
he will not *f* your transgressions ... Josh 24:19 5375
f the trespass of thine handmaid ... 1Sa 25:28 5375
and when thou hearest, *f* ... 1Kin 8:30 5545
f the sin of thy people Israel, ... 1Kin 8:34 5545
f the sin of thy servants, and of ... 1Kin 8:36 5545
heaven thy dwelling place, and *f* ... 1Kin 8:39 5545
f thy people that have sinned ... 1Kin 8:50 5545
and when thou hearest, *f* ... 2Chr 6:21 5545
f the sin of thy people Israel, ... 2Chr 6:25 5545
f the sin of thy servants, and of ... 2Chr 6:27 5545
heaven thy dwelling place, and *f* ... 2Chr 6:30 5545
f thy people which have sinned ... 2Chr 6:39 5545
will *f* their sin, and will heal ... 2Chr 7:14 5545
and *f* all my sins ... Ps 25:18 5375
Lord, art good, and ready to *f* ... Ps 86:5 5546
therefore *f* them not ... Is 2:9 5375
f not their iniquity, neither ... Jer 18:23 3722
for I will *f* their iniquity, and I ... Jer 31:34 5545
that I may *f* their iniquity and ... Jer 36:3 5545
O Lord, hear; O Lord, *f* ... Dan 9:19 5545
land, then I said, O Lord GOD, *f* ... Amos 7:2 5545
f us our debts, as we *f* our ... Mt 6:12 *863*
For if ye *f* men their trespasses, ... Mt 6:14 *863*
heavenly Father will also *f* you ... Mt 6:14 *863*
But if ye *f* not men their ... Mt 6:15 *863*
your Father *f* your trespasses ... Mt 6:15 *863*
man hath power on earth to *f* sins ... Mt 9:6 *863*
sin against me, and I *f* him ... Mt 18:21 *863*
if ye from your hearts *f* not ... Mt 18:35 *863*
who can *f* sins but God only ... Mk 2:7 *863*
man hath power on earth to *f* sins ... Mk 2:10 *863*
And when ye stand praying, *f* ... Mk 11:25 *863*
heaven may *f* you your trespasses ... Mk 11:25 *863*
But if ye do not *f*, neither will ... Mk 11:26 *863*
is in heaven *f* your trespasses ... Mk 11:26 *863*
Who can *f* sins, but God alone ... Lk 5:21 *863*
hath power upon earth to *f* sins ... Lk 5:24 *863*
f, and ye shall be forgiven ... Lk 6:37 *630*
And *f* us our sins ... Lk 11:4 *863*
for we also *f* every one that is ... Lk 11:4 *863*
and if he repent, *f* him ... Lk 17:3 *863*
thou shalt *f* him ... Lk 17:4 *863*
Then said Jesus, Father, *f* them ... Lk 23:34 *863*
ye ought rather to *f* him, and ... 2Cor 2:7 *5483*
ye *f* any thing, I *f* also ... 2Cor 2:10 *5483*
f me this wrong ... 2Cor 12:13 *5483*
just to *f* us our sins, and to ... 1Jn 1:9 *863*

FORGIVEN
for them, and it shall be *f* them ... Lev 4:20 5545
his sin, and it shall be *f* him ... Lev 4:26 5545
for him, and it shall be *f* him ... Lev 4:31 5545
committed, and it shall be *f* him ... Lev 4:35 5545
hath sinned, and it shall be *f* him ... Lev 5:10 5545
of these, and it shall be *f* him ... Lev 5:13 5545
offering, and it shall be *f* him ... Lev 5:16 5545
wist it not, and it shall be *f* him ... Lev 5:18 5545
it shall be *f* him for any thing ... Lev 6:7 5545
which he hath done shall be *f* him ... Lev 19:22 5545
and as thou hast *f* this people ... Num 14:19 5375
of Israel, and it shall be *f* them ... Num 15:25 5545
And it shall be *f* all the ... Num 15:26 5545
and it shall be *f* him ... Num 15:28 5545
And the blood shall be *f* them ... Deut 21:8 3722
is he whose transgression is *f* ... Ps 32:1 5375
Thou hast *f* the iniquity of thy ... Ps 85:2 5375
therein shall be *f* their iniquity ... Is 33:24 5375
thy sins be *f* thee ... Mt 9:2 *863*
to say, Thy sins be *f* thee ... Mt 9:5 *863*
and blasphemy shall be *f* unto men ... Mt 12:31 *863*
Ghost shall not be *f* unto men ... Mt 12:31 *863*
the Son of man, it shall be *f* him ... Mt 12:32 *863*
Holy Ghost, it shall not be *f* him ... Mt 12:32 *863*
palsy, Son, thy sins be *f* thee ... Mk 2:5 *863*
of the palsy, Thy sins be *f* thee ... Mk 2:9 *863*
All sins shall be *f* unto the sons ... Mk 3:28 *863*
and their sins should be *f* them ... Mk 4:12 *863*
him, Man, thy sins are *f* thee ... Lk 5:20 *863*
to say, Thy sins be *f* thee ... Lk 5:23 *863*
forgive, and ye shall be *f* ... Lk 6:37 *630*
Her sins, which are many, are *f* ... Lk 7:47 *863*
but to whom little is *f*, the same ... Lk 7:47 *863*
he said unto her, Thy sins are *f* ... Lk 7:48 *863*
the Son of man, it shall be *f* him ... Lk 12:10 *863*
the Holy Ghost it shall not be *f* ... Lk 12:10 *863*
of thine heart may be *f* thee ... Acts 8:22 *863*
are they whose iniquities are *f* ... Rom 4:7 *863*
God for Christ's sake hath *f* you ... Eph 4:32 *5483*
having *f* you all trespasses ... Col 2:13 *5483*
sins, they shall be *f* him ... Jas 5:15 *863*
because your sins are *f* you for ... 1Jn 2:12 *863*

FORGIVENESS
But there is *f* with thee, that ... Ps 130:4 5547
the Holy Ghost hath never *f* ... Mk 3:29 *859*
to Israel, and *f* of sins ... Acts 5:31 *859*
preached unto you the *f* of sins ... Acts 13:38 *859*
that they may receive *f* of sins ... Acts 26:18 *859*
the *f* of sins, according to the ... Eph 1:7 *859*
his blood, even the *f* of sins ... Col 1:14 *859*

FORGIVENESSES
Lord our God belong mercies and *f* ... Dan 9:9 5547

FORGIVETH
Who *f* all thine iniquities ... Ps 103:3 5545
Who is this that *f* sins also ... Lk 7:49 *863*

FORGIVING
f iniquity and transgression and ... Ex 34:7 5375
f iniquity and transgression, and ... Num 14:18 5375
f one another, even as God for ... Eph 4:32 *5483*
f one another, if any man have a ... Col 3:13 *5483*

FORGOT
hast *f* a sheaf in the field, thou ... Deut 24:19 7911

FORGOTTEN
shall be *f* in the land of Egypt ... Gen 41:30 7911
neither have I *f* them ... Deut 26:13 7911
for it shall not be *f* out of the ... Deut 31:21 7911
hast *f* God that formed thee ... Deut 32:18 7911
and my familiar friends have *f* me ... Job 19:14 7911
even the waters *f* of the foot ... Job 28:4 7911
the needy shall not alway be *f* ... Ps 9:18 7911
said in his heart, God hath *f* ... Ps 10:11 7911
I am *f* as a dead man out of mind ... Ps 31:12 7911
God my rock, Why hast thou *f* me ... Ps 42:9 7911
yet have we not *f* thee, neither ... Ps 44:17 7911
If we have *f* the name of our God, ... Ps 44:20 7911
Hath God *f* to be gracious ... Ps 77:9 7911
but I have not *f* thy law ... Ps 119:61 7911
mine enemies have *f* thy words ... Ps 119:139 7911
the days to come shall all be *f* ... Eccl 2:16 7911
they were *f* in the city where ... Eccl 8:10 7911
for the memory of them is *f* ... Eccl 9:5 7911
Because thou hast *f* the God of ... Is 17:10 7911
Tyre shall be *f* seventy years ... Is 23:15 7911
thou harlot that hast been *f* ... Is 23:16 7911
Israel, thou shalt not be *f* of me ... Is 44:21 5382
forsaken me, and my Lord hath *f* me ... Is 49:14 7911
because the former troubles are *f* ... Is 65:16 7911
yet my people have *f* me days ... Jer 2:32 7911
they have *f* the LORD their God ... Jer 3:21 7911
because thou hast *f* me, and ... Jer 13:25 7911
Because my people hath *f* me ... Jer 18:15 7911
confusion shall never be *f* ... Jer 20:11 7911
fathers have *f* my name for Baal ... Jer 23:27 7911
shame, which shall not be *f* ... Jer 23:40 7911
All thy lovers have *f* thee ... Jer 30:14 7911
Have ye *f* the wickedness of your ... Jer 44:9 7911
covenant that shall not be *f* ... Jer 50:5 7911
they have *f* their restingplace ... Jer 50:6 7911
and sabbaths to be *f* in Zion ... Lam 2:6 7911
by extortion, and hast *f* me ... Eze 22:12 7911
Because thou hast *f* me, and cast ... Eze 23:35 7911
seeing thou hast *f* the law of thy ... Hos 4:6 7911
For Israel hath *f* his Maker ... Hos 8:14 7911
therefore have they *f* me ... Hos 13:6 7911
side, they had *f* to take bread ... Mt 16:5 *1950*
the disciples had *f* to take bread ... Mk 8:14 *1950*
not one of them is *f* before God ... Lk 12:6 *1950*
ye have *f* the exhortation which ... Heb 12:5 *1585*
hath *f* that he was purged from ... 2Pet 1:9

FORKS
and for the coulters, and for the *f* ... 1Sa 13:21

FORM
And the earth was without *f* ... Gen 1:2 8414
he said unto her, What *f* is he of ... 1Sa 28:14 8389
To fetch about this *f* of speech ... 2Sa 14:20 6440
of gold according to their *f* ... 2Chr 4:7 4941
I could not discern the *f* thereof ... Job 4:16 4758
I *f* the light, and create darkness ... Is 45:7 3335
his *f* more than the sons of men ... Is 52:14 8389
he hath no *f* nor comeliness ... Is 53:2 8389
earth, and, lo, it was without *f* ... Jer 4:23 8414
And he put forth the *f* of an hand ... Eze 8:3 8403
behold every *f* of creeping things ... Eze 8:10 8403
the *f* of a man's hand under their ... Eze 10:8 8403
shew them the *f* of the house ... Eze 43:11 6699
they may keep the whole *f* thereof ... Eze 43:11 6699
the *f* thereof was terrible ... Dan 2:31 7299
the *f* of his visage was changed ... Dan 3:19 6755
the *f* of the fourth is like the ... Dan 3:25 7299
in another *f* unto two of them ... Mk 16:12 *3444*
which hast the *f* of knowledge ... Rom 2:20 *3446*
f of doctrine which was delivered ... Rom 6:17 *5179*
Who, being in the *f* of God ... Phil 2:6 *3444*
took upon him the *f* of a servant ... Phil 2:7 *3444*
Hold fast the *f* of sound words, ... 2Ti 1:13 *5296*
Having a *f* of godliness, but ... 2Ti 3:5 *3446*

FORMED
the LORD God *f* man of the dust of ... Gen 2:7 3335
he put the man whom he had *f* ... Gen 2:8 3335
God *f* every beast of the field ... Gen 2:19 3335
and hast forgotten God that *f* thee ... Deut 32:18 2342
of ancient times that I have *f* it ... 2Kin 19:25 3335
Dead things are *f* from under the ... Job 26:5 2342
his hand hath *f* the crooked ... Job 26:13 2342
I also am *f* out of the clay ... Job 33:6 7169
or ever thou hadst *f* the earth ... Ps 90:2 2342
he that *f* the eye, shall he not ... Ps 94:9 3335
and his hands *f* the dry land ... Ps 95:5 3335
The great God that *f* all things ... Prov 26:10 2342
he that *f* them will shew them no ... Is 27:11 3335
ancient times, that I have *f* it ... Is 37:26 3335
thee, O Jacob, and he that *f* thee ... Is 43:1 3335
him for my glory, I have *f* him ... Is 43:7 3335
before me there was no God *f* ... Is 43:10 3335
This people have I *f* for myself ... Is 43:21 3335
f thee from the womb, which will ... Is 44:2 3335
Who hath *f* a god, or molten a ... Is 44:10 3335
I have *f* thee ... Is 44:21 3335
he that *f* thee from the womb, I ... Is 44:24 3335
God himself that *f* the earth ... Is 45:18 3335
in vain, he *f* it to be inhabited ... Is 45:18 3335
saith the LORD that *f* me from the ... Is 49:5 3335
No weapon that is *f* against thee ... Is 54:17 3335
Before I *f* thee in the belly I ... Jer 1:5 3335
maker thereof, the LORD that *f* it ... Jer 33:2 3335
behold, he *f* grasshoppers in the ... Amos 7:1 3335
Shall the thing *f* say to him that ... Rom 9:20 *4110*
thing *f* say to him that *f* it ... Rom 9:20 *4110*
again until Christ be *f* in you ... Gal 4:19 *3445*
For Adam was first *f*, then Eve ... 1Ti 2:13 *4111*

FORMER
after the *f* manner when thou wast ... Gen 40:13 7223
fought against the *f* king of Moab ... Num 21:26 7223
Her *f* husband, which sent her ... Deut 24:4 7223
in *f* time in Israel concerning ... Ruth 4:7 6440
him again after the *f* manner ... 1Sa 17:30 7223
the *f* fifties with their fifties ... 2Kin 1:14 7223
day they do after the *f* manners ... 2Kin 17:34 7223
but they did after their *f* manner ... 2Kin 17:40 7223
But the *f* governors that had been ... Neh 5:15 7223
I pray thee, of the *f* age ... Job 8:8 7223
the wilderness in *f* time desolate ... Job 30:3 570
not against us *f* iniquities ... Ps 79:8 7223
where are thy *f* lovingkindnesses, ... Ps 89:49 7223
is no remembrance of *f* things ... Eccl 1:11 7223
What is the cause that the *f* days ... Eccl 7:10 7223
let them shew the *f* things ... Is 41:22 7223
the *f* things are come to pass, and ... Is 42:9 7223
declare this, and shew us *f* things ... Is 43:9 7223
Remember ye not the *f* things ... Is 43:18 7223
Remember the *f* things of old ... Is 46:9 7223
I have declared the *f* things from ... Is 48:3 7223
shall raise up the *f* desolations ... Is 61:4 7223
their *f* work into their bosom ... Is 65:7 7223
because the *f* troubles are ... Is 65:16 7223
the *f* shall not be remembered, ... Is 65:17 7223
God, that giveth rain, both the *f* ... Jer 5:24 3138
for he is the *f* of all things ... Jer 10:16 3335
the *f* kings which were before ... Jer 34:5 7223
write in it all the *f* words that ... Jer 36:28 7223
for he is the *f* of all things ... Jer 51:19 3335
shall return to their *f* estate ... Eze 16:55 6927
shall return to their *f* estate ... Eze 16:55 6927
shall return to your *f* estate ... Eze 16:55 6927
a multitude greater than the *f* ... Dan 11:13 7223
but it shall not be as the *f* ... Dan 11:29 7223
latter and *f* rain unto the earth ... Hos 6:3 3138
given you the *f* rain moderately ... Joel 2:23 4175
the *f* rain, and the latter rain in ... Joel 2:23 4175
shall be greater than of the *f* ... Hag 2:9 7223
unto whom the *f* prophets have ... Zec 1:4 7223
LORD hath cried by the *f* prophets ... Zec 7:7 7223
in his spirit by the *f* prophets ... Zec 7:12 7223
of this people as in the *f* days ... Zec 8:11 7223
half of them toward the *f* sea ... Zec 14:8 6931
the days of old, and as in *f* years ... Mal 3:4 6931
The *f* treatise have I made, O ... Acts 1:1 *4413*
the *f* conversation the old man ... Eph 4:22 *4387*
call to remembrance the *f* days ... Heb 10:32 *4386*
to the *f* lusts in your ignorance ... 1Pet 1:14 *4386*
for the *f* things are passed away ... Rev 21:4 *4413*

FORMETH
he that *f* the mountains, and ... Amos 4:13 3335
f the spirit of man within him ... Zec 12:1 3335

FORMS
in thereof, and all the *f* thereof ... Eze 43:11 6699
thereof, and all the *f* thereof ... Eze 43:11 6699

FORNICATION
of Jerusalem to commit *f*, and 2Chr 21:11 2181
shall commit *f* with all the Is 23:17 2181
f with the Egyptians thy Eze 16:26 2181
thy *f* in the land of Canaan unto Eze 16:29 8457
wife, saving for the cause of *f* Mt 5:32 4202
away his wife, except it be for *f* Mt 19:9 4202
they to him, We be not born of *f* Jn 8:41 4202
pollutions of idols, and from *f* Acts 15:20 4202
from things strangled, and from *f* Acts 15:29 4202
and from strangled, and from *f* Acts 21:25 4202
with all unrighteousness, *f* Rom 1:29 4202
that there is *f* among you 1Cor 5:1 4202
such *f* as is not so much as named 1Cor 5:1 4202
Now the body is not for *f* 1Cor 6:13 4202
Flee *f*. Every sin that 1Cor 6:18 4202
but he that committeth *f* sinneth 1Cor 6:18 4203
Nevertheless, to avoid *f*, let 1Cor 7:2 4202
Neither let us commit *f*, as some 1Cor 10:8 4203
repented of the uncleanness and *f* 2Cor 12:21 4202
Adultery, *f*, uncleanness, Gal 5:19 4202
But *f*, and all uncleanness, or Eph 5:3 4202
f, uncleanness, inordinate Col 3:5 4202
that ye should abstain from *f* 1Th 4:3 4202
giving themselves over to *f* Jude 7 1608
unto idols, and to commit *f* Rev 2:14 4203
to seduce my servants to commit *f* Rev 2:20 4203
gave her space to repent of her *f* Rev 2:21 4202
their sorceries, nor of their *f* Rev 9:21 4202
of the wine of the wrath of her *f* Rev 14:8 4202
of the earth have committed *f* Rev 17:2 4203
made drunk with the wine of her *f* Rev 17:2 4202
and filthiness of her *f* Rev 17:4 4202
of the wine of the wrath of her *f* Rev 18:3 4202
earth have committed *f* with her Rev 18:3 4203
the earth, who have committed *f* Rev 18:9 4203
did corrupt the earth with her *f* Rev 19:2 4202

FORNICATIONS
pouredst out thy *f* on every one Eze 16:15 8457
thoughts, murders, adulteries, *f* Mt 15:19 4202
evil thoughts, adulteries, *f* Mk 7:21 4202

FORNICATOR
that is called a brother be a *f* 1Cor 5:11 4205
Lest there be any *f*, or profane Heb 12:16 4205

FORNICATORS
an epistle not to company with *f* 1Cor 5:9 4205
with the *f* of this world, or with 1Cor 5:10 4205
neither *f*, nor idolaters, nor 1Cor 6:9 4205

FORSAKE
he will not *f* thee, neither Deut 4:31 7503
f not the Levite as long as thou Deut 12:19 5800
thou shalt not *f* him Deut 14:27 5800
he will not fail thee, nor *f* thee Deut 31:6 5800
not fail thee, neither *f* thee Deut 31:8 5800
go to be among them, and will *f* me Deut 31:16 5800
in that day, and I will *f* them Deut 31:17 5800
I will not fail thee, nor *f* thee Josh 1:5 5800
forbid that we should *f* the LORD Josh 24:16 5800
If ye *f* the LORD, and serve Josh 24:20 5800
Should I *f* my sweetness, and my Judg 9:11 2308
For the LORD will not *f* his 1Sa 12:22 5203
will not *f* my people Israel 1Kin 6:13 5800
let him not leave us, nor *f* us 1Kin 8:57 5203
I will *f* the remnant of mine 2Kin 21:14 5203
but if thou *f* him, he will cast 1Chr 28:9 5800
nor *f* thee, until thou hast 1Chr 28:20 5800
f my statutes and my commandments, 2Chr 7:19 5800
if ye *f* him, he will *f* you 2Chr 15:2 5800
is against all them that *f* him Ezr 8:22 5800
utterly consume them, nor *f* them Neh 9:31 5800
we will not *f* the house of our Neh 10:39 5800
f it not, but keep it still Job 20:13 5800
leave me not, neither *f* me Ps 27:9 5800
When my father and my mother *f* me Ps 27:10 5800
Cease from anger, and *f* wrath Ps 37:8 5800
F me not, O LORD Ps 38:21 5800
f me not when my strength faileth Ps 71:9 5800
and greyheaded, O God, *f* me not Ps 71:18 5800
If his children *f* my law, and walk Ps 89:30 5800
neither will he *f* his inheritance Ps 94:14 5800
O *f* me not utterly Ps 119:8 5800
of the wicked that *f* thy law Ps 119:53 5800
f not the works of thine own Ps 138:8 7503
f not the law of thy mother Prov 1:8 5203
Let not mercy and truth *f* thee Prov 3:3 5800
good doctrine, *f* ye not my law Prov 4:2 5800
F her not, and she shall preserve Prov 4:6 5800
f not the law of thy mother Prov 6:20 5203
F the foolish, and live Prov 9:6 5800
and thy father's friend, *f* not Prov 27:10 5800
They that *f* the law praise the Prov 28:4 5800
they that *f* the LORD shall be Is 1:28 5800
the God of Israel will not *f* them Is 41:17 5800
I do unto them, and not *f* them Is 42:16 5800
Let the wicked *f* his way, and the Is 55:7 5800
But ye are they that *f* the LORD Is 65:11 5800
all that *f* thee shall be ashamed, Jer 17:13 5800
I will even *f* you, saith the LORD Jer 23:33 5203
forget you, and I will *f* you Jer 23:39 5203
f her, and let us go every one Jer 51:9 5800
us for ever, and *f* us so long time Lam 5:20 5800
neither did they *f* the idols of Eze 20:8 5800
them that *f* the holy covenant Dan 11:30 5800
lying vanities *f* their own mercy Jonah 2:8 5800
are among the Gentiles to *f* Moses Acts 21:21
will never leave thee, nor *f* thee Heb 13:5 1459

FORSAKEN
doings, whereby thou hast *f* me Deut 28:20 5800
Because they have *f* the covenant Deut 29:25 5800
but now the LORD hath *f* us Judg 6:13 5203
both because we have *f* our God Judg 10:10 5800
Yet ye have *f* me, and served other Judg 10:13 5800
day, wherewith they have *f* me 1Sa 8:8 5800
because we have *f* the LORD 1Sa 12:10 5800
Because that they have *f* me 1Kin 11:33 5800
house, in that ye have *f* the 1Kin 18:18 5800
of Israel have *f* thy covenant 1Kin 19:10 5800
of Israel have *f* thy covenant 1Kin 19:14 5800
Because they have *f* me, and have 2Kin 22:17 5800
Thus saith the LORD, Ye have *f* me 2Chr 12:5 5800
is our God, and we have not *f* him 2Chr 13:10 5800
but ye have *f* him 2Chr 13:11 5800
because he had *f* the LORD God of 2Chr 21:10 5800
because ye have *f* the LORD 2Chr 24:20 5800
he hath also *f* you 2Chr 24:20 5800
because they had *f* the LORD God 2Chr 24:24 5800
because they had *f* the LORD God 2Chr 28:6 5800
the LORD our God, and have *f* him 2Chr 29:6 5800
Because they have *f* me, and have 2Chr 34:25 5800
God hath not *f* us in our bondage Ezr 9:9 5800
for we have *f* thy commandments, Ezr 9:10 5800
said, Why is the house of God *f* Neh 13:11 5800
shall the earth be *f* for thee Job 18:4 5800
hath oppressed and hath *f* the poor Job 20:19 5800
hast not *f* them that seek thee Ps 9:10 5800
God, my God, why hast thou *f* me Ps 22:1 5800
have I not seen the righteous *f* Ps 37:25 5800
Saying, God hath *f* him Ps 71:11 5800
they have *f* the LORD, they have Is 1:4 5800
Therefore thou hast *f* thy people Is 2:6 5203
shall be *f* of both her kings Is 7:16 5800
The cities of Aroer are *f* Is 17:2 5800
his strong cities be as a *f* bough Is 17:9 5800
be desolate, and the habitation *f* Is 27:10 7971
Because the palaces shall be *f* Is 32:14 5203
But Zion said, The LORD hath *f* me Is 49:14 5800
hath called thee as a woman *f* Is 54:6 5800
For a small moment have I *f* thee Is 54:7 5800
Whereas thou hast been *f* and hated Is 60:15 5800
Thou shalt no more be termed *F* Is 62:4 5800
called, Sought out, A city not *f* Is 62:12 5800
their wickedness, who have *f* me Jer 1:16 5800
they have *f* me the fountain of Jer 2:13 5800
that thou hast *f* the LORD thy God Jer 2:17 5800
that thou hast *f* the LORD thy God Jer 2:19 5800
every city shall be *f*, and not a Jer 4:29 5800
thy children have *f* me, and sworn Jer 5:7 5800
answer them, Like as ye have *f* me Jer 5:19 5800
f the generation of his wrath Jer 7:29 5203
Because they have *f* my law which Jer 9:13 5800
because we have *f* the land Jer 9:19 5800
I have *f* mine house, I have left Jer 12:7 5800
Thou hast *f* me, saith the LORD, Jer 15:6 5203
Because your fathers have *f* me Jer 16:11 5800
worshipped them, and have *f* me Jer 16:11 5800
because they have *f* the LORD Jer 17:13 5800
that come from another place be *f* Jer 18:14 5428
Because they have *f* me, and have Jer 19:4 5800
Because they have *f* the covenant Jer 22:9 5800
He hath *f* his covert, as the lion Jer 25:38 5800
For Israel hath not been *f* Jer 51:5 488
the LORD hath *f* the earth Eze 8:12 5800
say, The LORD hath *f* the earth Eze 9:9 5800
and to the cities that are *f* Eze 36:4 5800
she is *f* upon her land Amos 5:2 5203
For Gaza shall be *f*, and Ashkelon Zeph 2:4 5800
unto him, Behold, we have *f* all Mt 19:27 863
And every one that hath *f* houses Mt 19:29 863
God, my God, why hast thou *f* me Mt 27:46 1459
God, my God, why hast thou *f* me Mk 15:34 1459
Persecuted, but not *f* 2Cor 4:9 1459
For Demas hath *f* me, having loved 2Ti 4:10 1459
Which have *f* the right way, and 2Pet 2:15 2641

FORSAKETH
but he *f* the fear of the Almighty Job 6:14 5800
judgment, and *f* not his saints Ps 37:28 5800
Which *f* the guide of her youth, Prov 2:17 5800
grievous unto him that *f* the way Prov 15:10 5800
and *f* them shall have mercy Prov 28:13 5800
you that *f* not all that he hath Lk 14:33 657

FORSAKING
there be a great *f* in the midst Is 6:12 5805
Not *f* the assembling of ourselves Heb 10:25 1459

FORSOMUCH
f as he also is a son of Abraham Lk 19:9 2530

FORSOOK
then he *f* God which made him, and Deut 32:15 5203
they *f* the LORD God of their Judg 2:12 5800
they *f* the LORD, and served Baal Judg 2:13 5800
f the LORD, and served not him Judg 10:6 5800
they *f* the cities, and fled 1Sa 31:7 5800
Because they *f* the LORD their God 1Kin 9:9 5800
But he *f* the counsel of the old 1Kin 12:8 5800
f the old men's counsel that they 1Kin 12:13 5800
he *f* the LORD God of his fathers, 2Kin 21:22 5800
then they *f* their cities, and fled 1Chr 10:7 5800
Because they *f* the LORD God of 2Chr 7:22 5800
But he *f* the counsel which the 2Chr 10:8 5800
king Rehoboam *f* the counsel of 2Chr 10:13 5800
he *f* the law of the LORD, and all 2Chr 12:1 5800
So that he *f* the tabernacle of Ps 78:60 5203
but I *f* not thy precepts Ps 119:87 5800
f not the ordinance of their God Is 58:2 5800
f it, because there was no grass Jer 14:5 5800
Then all the disciples *f* him Mt 26:56 863
And straightway they *f* their nets Mk 1:18 863
And they all *f* him, and fled Mk 14:50 863
their ships to land, they *f* all Lk 5:11 863
stood with me, but all men *f* me 2Ti 4:16 1459
By faith he *f* Egypt, not fearing Heb 11:27 2641

FORSOOKEST
of great kindness, and *f* them not Neh 9:17 5800
f them not in the wilderness Neh 9:19 5800

FORSWEAR
time, Thou shalt not *f* thyself Mt 5:33 1964

FORT
So David dwelt in the *f*, and 2Sa 5:9 4686
the fortress of the high *f* of thy Is 25:12 4869
build a *f* against it, and cast a Eze 4:2 1785
to cast a mount, and to build a *f* Eze 21:22 1785
and he shall make a *f* against thee Eze 26:8 1785
face toward the *f* of his own land Dan 11:19 4581

FORTH
said, Let the earth bring *f* grass Gen 1:11 1876
And the earth brought *f* grass Gen 1:12 3318
Let the waters bring *f* abundantly Gen 1:20 8317
the waters brought *f* abundantly Gen 1:21 8317
Let the earth bring *f* the living Gen 1:24 3318
thou shalt bring *f* children Gen 3:16 3205
thistles shall it bring *f* to thee Gen 3:18 6779
and now, lest he put *f* his hand Gen 3:22 7971
him *f* from the garden of Eden Gen 3:23
And he sent *f* a raven, which went Gen 8:7
f a raven, which went *f* to Gen 8:7 3318
Also he sent *f* a dove from him, Gen 8:8
then he put *f* his hand, and took Gen 8:9 7971
again he sent *f* the dove out of Gen 8:10
and sent *f* the dove Gen 8:12
Go *f* of the ark, thou, and thy Gen 8:16 3318
Bring *f* with thee every living Gen 8:17 3318
And Noah went *f*, and his sons, and Gen 8:18 3318
kinds, went *f* out of the ark Gen 8:19 3318
bring *f* abundantly in the earth, Gen 9:7 8317
that went *f* of the ark, were Shem Gen 9:18 3318
Out of that land went *f* Asshur Gen 10:11 3318
they went *f* with them from Ur of Gen 11:31 3318
they went *f* to go into the land Gen 12:5 3318
king of Salem brought *f* bread Gen 14:18 3318
but he that shall come *f* out of Gen 15:4 3318
And he brought him *f* abroad Gen 15:5 3318
But the men put *f* their hand Gen 19:10 7971
and they brought him *f*, and set him Gen 19:16 3318
they had brought them *f* abroad Gen 19:17 3318
And Abraham stretched *f* his hand Gen 22:10
the virgin cometh *f* to draw water Gen 24:43 3318
Rebekah came *f* with her pitcher Gen 24:45 3318
brought *f* jewels of silver Gen 24:53 3318
brought *f* cattle ringstraked, Gen 30:39 3209
And Judah said, Bring her *f* Gen 38:24 3318
When she was brought *f*, she sent Gen 38:25 3318
she said, How hast thou broken *f* Gen 38:29 6556
in her hand, and was fled *f* Gen 39:13 2315
it budded, and her blossoms shot *f* Gen 40:10
thereof brought *f* ripe grapes Gen 40:10 1310
the earth brought *f* by handfuls Gen 41:47 6213
Pharaoh ye shall not go *f* hence Gen 42:15 3318
that thou mayest bring *f* my Ex 3:10 3318
that I should bring *f* the Ex 3:11 3318
When thou hast brought *f* the Ex 3:12 3318
Put *f* thine hand, and take it by Ex 4:4 7971
he put *f* his hand, and caught it, Ex 4:4 7971
behold, he cometh *f* to meet thee Ex 4:14 3318
way, as they came *f* from Pharaoh Ex 5:20 3318
bring *f* mine armies, and my people Ex 7:4 3318
when I stretch *f* mine hand upon Ex 7:5
shall bring *f* frogs abundantly Ex 8:3 8317
Stretch *f* thine hand with thy rod Ex 8:5
enchantments to bring *f* lice Ex 8:18 3318
lo, he cometh *f* to the water Ex 8:20 3318
breaking *f* with blains upon man Ex 9:9
breaking *f* with blains upon man Ex 9:10
Stretch *f* thine hand toward Ex 9:22
Moses stretched *f* his rod toward Ex 9:23
Moses stretched *f* his rod over Ex 10:13
Moses stretched *f* his hand toward Ex 10:22
get you *f* from among my people, Ex 12:31 3318
which they brought *f* out of Egypt Ex 12:39 3318
thou shalt not carry *f* ought of Ex 12:46 3318
me when I came *f* out of Egypt Ex 13:8 3318
LORD brought us *f* out of Egypt Ex 13:16 3318
to carry us *f* out of Egypt Ex 14:11 3318
Moses stretched *f* his hand over Ex 14:27
thou sentest *f* thy wrath, which Ex 15:7
led *f* the people which thou hast Ex 15:13
brought us *f* into this wilderness Ex 16:3 3318
when I brought you *f* from the Ex 16:32 3318
gone *f* out of the land of Egypt Ex 19:1 3318
Moses brought *f* the people out of Ex 19:17 3318
lest the LORD break *f* upon them Ex 19:22
LORD, lest he break *f* upon them Ex 19:24
stretch *f* their wings on high Ex 25:20
that brought them *f* out of the Ex 29:46 3318
which thou hast brought *f* out of Ex 32:11 3318
whole bullock shall he carry *f* Lev 4:12 3318
he shall carry *f* the bullock Lev 4:21 3318
carry *f* the ashes without the Lev 6:11 3318
priest shall go *f* out of the camp Lev 14:3 3318
he shall carry them *f* out of the Lev 14:45 3318
and put on his garments, and come *f* Lev 16:24 3318
shall one carry *f* without the Lev 16:27 3318
a sheep, or a goat, is brought *f* Lev 22:27 3205
Bring *f* him that hath cursed Lev 24:14 3318
that they should bring *f* him that Lev 24:23 3318
it shall bring *f* fruit for three Lev 25:21 6213
which brought you *f* out of the Lev 25:38 3318
which I brought *f* out of the land Lev 25:42 3318
f out of the land of Egypt Lev 25:55 3318
bring *f* the old because of the Lev 26:10 3318
which brought you *f* out of the Lev 26:13 3318
whom I brought *f* out of the land Lev 26:45 3318
are able to go *f* to war in Israel Num 1:3 3318
all that were able to go *f* to war Num 1:20 3318

F

all that were able to go *f* to war	Num 1:22	3318
all that were able to go *f* to war	Num 1:24	3318
all that were able to go *f* to war	Num 1:26	3318
all that were able to go *f* to war	Num 1:28	3318
all that were able to go *f* to war	Num 1:30	3318
all that were able to go *f* to war	Num 1:32	3318
all that were able to go *f* to war	Num 1:34	3318
all that were able to go *f* to war	Num 1:36	3318
all that were able to go *f* to war	Num 1:38	3318
all that were able to go *f* to war	Num 1:40	3318
all that were able to go *f* to war	Num 1:42	3318
able to go *f* to war in Israel	Num 1:45	3318
These shall first set *f*	Num 2:9	5265
they shall set *f* in the second	Num 2:16	5265
Why came we *f* out of Egypt	Num 11:20	3318
there went *f* a wind from the LORD	Num 11:31	5265
and they both came *f*	Num 12:5	
was budded, and brought *f* buds	Num 17:8	3318
may bring her *f* without the camp	Num 19:3	3318
and it shall give *f* his water	Num 20:8	
thou shalt bring *f* to them water	Num 20:8	3318
and hath brought us *f* out of Egypt	Num 20:16	3318
As the valleys are they spread *f*	Num 24:6	
God brought him *f* out of Egypt	Num 24:8	4161
which went *f* out of the land of	Num 26:4	3318
went *f* to meet them without the	Num 31:13	3318
which went *f* out of the land of	Num 33:1	3318
the going *f* thereof shall be from	Num 34:4	8444
the goings *f* of the border shall	Num 34:8	8444
he hath brought us *f* out of the	Deut 1:27	3318
which came *f* out of Caphtor,	Deut 2:23	3318
brought you *f* out of the iron	Deut 4:20	3318
after they came *f* out of Egypt	Deut 4:45	3318
they were come *f* out of Egypt	Deut 4:46	3318
which brought thee *f* out of the	Deut 6:12	3318
which brought thee *f* out of the	Deut 8:14	4161
who brought thee *f* water out of	Deut 8:15	4161
f out of Egypt have corrupted	Deut 9:12	3318
which thou hast brought *f* out of	Deut 9:26	3318
the field bringeth *f* year by year	Deut 14:22	3318
f all the tithe of thine increase	Deut 14:28	3318
thee *f* out of Egypt by night	Deut 16:1	3318
for thou camest *f* out of the land	Deut 16:3	3318
the day when thou camest *f* out of	Deut 16:3	3318
that thou camest *f* out of Egypt	Deut 16:6	3318
Then shalt thou bring *f* that man	Deut 17:5	3318
elders and thy judges shall come *f*	Deut 21:2	3318
When thou goest *f* to war against	Deut 21:10	3318
bring *f* the tokens of the	Deut 22:15	3318
way, when ye came *f* out of Egypt	Deut 23:4	3318
When the host goeth *f* against	Deut 23:9	3318
whither thou shalt go *f* abroad	Deut 23:12	3318
that ye were come *f* out of Egypt	Deut 24:9	3318
putteth *f* her hand, and taketh him	Deut 25:11	7971
when ye were come *f* out of Egypt	Deut 25:17	3318
the LORD brought us *f* out of	Deut 26:8	3318
them *f* out of the land of Egypt	Deut 29:25	3318
he shined *f* from mount Paran, and	Deut 33:2	
fruits brought *f* by the sun	Deut 33:14	
precious things put *f* by the moon	Deut 33:14	1645
Bring *f* the men that are come to	Josh 2:3	3318
way as they came *f* out of Egypt	Josh 5:5	3318
Joshua therefore sent them *f*	Josh 8:9	
the day we came *f* to go unto you	Josh 9:12	3318
brought *f* those five kings unto	Josh 10:23	3318
the coast of their lot came *f*	Josh 18:11	3318
went *f* to En-shemesh, and went	Josh 18:17	3318
went *f* toward Geliloth, which is	Josh 18:17	3318
the second lot came *f* to Simeon	Josh 19:1	3318
saw a man come *f* out of the city	Judg 1:24	3318
Ehud put *f* his left hand, and took	Judg 3:21	7971
Then Ehud went *f* through the	Judg 3:23	3318
she brought *f* butter in a lordly	Judg 5:25	7126
sun when he goeth *f* in his might	Judg 5:31	3318
brought you *f* out of the house of	Judg 6:8	3318
bring *f* my present, and set it	Judg 6:18	3318
f the end of the staff that was	Judg 6:21	7971
The trees went *f* on a time to	Judg 9:8	
were come *f* out of the city	Judg 9:43	3318
that whatsoever cometh *f* of the	Judg 11:31	3318
I will now put *f* a riddle unto	Judg 14:12	2330
Put *f* thy riddle, that we may	Judg 14:13	2330
Out of the eater came *f* meat	Judg 14:14	3318
of the strong came *f* sweetness	Judg 14:14	3318
thou hast put *f* a riddle unto the	Judg 14:16	2330
put *f* his hand, and took it, and	Judg 15:15	7971
Bring *f* the man that came into	Judg 19:22	3318
and brought her *f* unto them	Judg 19:25	3318
of Benjamin came *f* out of Gibeah	Judg 20:21	3318
Benjamin went *f* against them out	Judg 20:25	3318
Israel came *f* out of their places	Judg 20:33	1518
Wherefore she went *f* out of the	Ruth 1:7	3318
and she brought *f*, and gave to her	Ruth 2:18	3318
Whosoever cometh not *f* after Saul	1Sa 11:7	3318
which brought *f* your fathers out	1Sa 12:8	3318
the Hebrews come *f* out of the	1Sa 14:11	3318
wherefore he put *f* the end of the	1Sa 14:27	7971
the host was going *f* to the fight	1Sa 17:20	3318
David go *f* against the Philistine	1Sa 17:55	3318
princes of the Philistines went *f*	1Sa 18:30	3318
came to pass, after they went *f*	1Sa 18:30	3318
and my mother, I pray thee, come *f*	1Sa 22:3	3318
of the king would not put *f* their	1Sa 22:17	7971
and he forbare to go *f*	1Sa 23:13	3318
to stretch *f* mine hand against	1Sa 24:6	
I will not put *f* mine hand	1Sa 24:10	7971
for who can stretch *f* his hand	1Sa 26:9	
f mine hand against the LORD's	1Sa 26:11	
but I would not stretch *f* mine	1Sa 26:23	
they went *f* to meet David, and to	1Sa 30:21	3318
f thine hand to destroy the	2Sa 1:14	
The LORD hath broken *f* upon mine	2Sa 5:20	
Uzzah put *f* his hand to the ark	2Sa 6:6	7971
time when kings go *f* to battle	2Sa 11:1	3318
he brought *f* the spoil of the	2Sa 12:30	3318
he brought *f* the people that were	2Sa 12:31	3318
David longed to go *f* unto Absalom	2Sa 13:39	3318
he put *f* his hand, and took him,	2Sa 15:5	7971
And the king went *f*, and all his	2Sa 15:16	3318
And the king went *f*, and all the	2Sa 15:17	3318
he came *f*, and cursed still as he	2Sa 16:5	3318
which came *f* of my bowels,	2Sa 16:11	3318
David sent *f* a third part of the	2Sa 18:2	
I will surely go *f* with you	2Sa 18:2	3318
answered, Thou shalt not go *f*	2Sa 18:3	3318
yet would I not put *f* mine hand	2Sa 18:12	7971
Now therefore arise, go *f*	2Sa 19:7	3318
by the LORD, if thou go not *f*	2Sa 19:7	3318
and as he went *f* it fell out	2Sa 20:8	3318
He brought me *f* also into a large	2Sa 22:20	3318
that bringeth me *f* from mine	2Sa 22:49	4161
him, Thus saith the king, Come *f*	1Kin 2:30	3318
go not *f* thence any whither	1Kin 2:36	3318
they stretched *f* the wings of the	1Kin 6:27	
For the cherubims spread *f* their	1Kin 8:7	
Since the day that I brought *f* my	1Kin 8:16	3318
shall come *f* out of thy loins	1Kin 8:19	3318
spread *f* his hands toward heaven	1Kin 8:22	
spread *f* his hands toward this	1Kin 8:38	
thou broughtest *f* out of Egypt	1Kin 8:51	3318
who brought *f* their fathers out	1Kin 9:9	3318
that he put *f* his hand from the	1Kin 13:4	7971
hand, which he put *f* against him	1Kin 13:4	7971
And he said, Go *f*, and stand upon	1Kin 19:11	3318
Then Ben-hadad came *f* to him	1Kin 20:33	3318
carried him *f* out of the city	1Kin 21:13	3318
And there came *f* a spirit, and	1Kin 22:21	3318
And he said, I will go *f*, and I	1Kin 22:22	3318
go *f*, and do so	1Kin 22:22	3318
were at Beth-el came *f* to Elisha	2Kin 2:3	3318
he went *f* unto the spring of the	2Kin 2:21	3318
there came *f* little children out	2Kin 2:23	3318
there came *f* two she bears out of	2Kin 2:24	3318
of God was risen early, and gone *f*	2Kin 6:15	3318
she went *f* to cry unto the king	2Kin 8:3	3318
Then Jehu came *f* to the servants	2Kin 9:11	3318
then let none go *f* nor escape out	2Kin 9:15	3318
Bring *f* vestments for all the	2Kin 10:22	3318
And he brought them *f* vestments	2Kin 10:22	3318
let none come *f*	2Kin 10:25	3318
they brought *f* the images out of	2Kin 10:26	3318
all you that go *f* on the sabbath	2Kin 11:7	3318
he brought *f* the king's son, and	2Kin 11:12	3318
Have her *f* without the ranges	2Kin 11:15	3318
prospered whithersoever he went *f*	2Kin 18:7	3318
there is not strength to bring *f*	2Kin 19:3	3205
of Jerusalem shall go *f* a remnant	2Kin 19:31	3318
their fathers came *f* out of Egypt	2Kin 21:15	3318
to bring *f* out of the temple of	2Kin 23:4	3318
Zebulun, such as went *f* to battle	1Chr 12:33	3318
Asher, such as went *f* to battle	1Chr 12:36	3318
Uzza put *f* his hand to hold the	1Chr 13:9	7971
like the breaking *f* of waters	1Chr 14:11	
for God is gone *f* before thee to	1Chr 14:15	3318
shew *f* from day to day his	1Chr 16:23	1319
drew *f* the Syrians that were	1Chr 19:16	3318
Joab led *f* the power of the army,	1Chr 20:1	
the first lot came *f* to Jehoiarib	1Chr 24:7	3318
lot came *f* for Asaph to Joseph	1Chr 25:9	3318
and Hosah the lot came *f* westward	1Chr 26:16	
brought *f* out of Egypt a chariot	2Chr 1:17	3318
spread themselves *f* twenty cubits	2Chr 3:13	
For the cherubims spread *f* their	2Chr 5:8	
f my people out of the land of	2Chr 6:5	3318
shall come *f* out of thy loins	2Chr 6:9	3318
of Israel, and spread *f* his hands	2Chr 6:12	
spread *f* his hands toward heaven,	2Chr 6:13	
shall spread *f* his hands in this	2Chr 6:29	
which brought them *f* out of the	2Chr 7:22	3318
went *f* into the wilderness of	2Chr 20:20	3318
and as they went *f*, Jehoshaphat	2Chr 20:20	3318
Jehoram went *f* with his princes	2Chr 21:9	5674
them, Have her *f* of the ranges	2Chr 23:14	3318
choice men, able to go *f* to war	2Chr 25:5	3318
led *f* his people, and went to the	2Chr 25:11	
And he went *f* and warred against	2Chr 26:6	3318
carry *f* the filthiness out of the	2Chr 29:5	3318
they brought *f* the he goats for	2Chr 29:23	
they that came *f* of his own	2Chr 32:21	3329
Also Cyrus the king brought *f* the	Ezr 1:7	3318
had brought *f* out of Jerusalem	Ezr 1:7	3318
f by the hand of Mithredath the	Ezr 1:8	3318
which Nebuchadnezzar took *f* out	Ezr 6:5	5312
it came to pass from that time *f*	Neh 4:16	
Go *f* unto the mount, and fetch	Neh 8:15	3318
So the people went *f*, and brought	Neh 8:16	3318
broughtest him *f* out of Ur of the	Neh 9:7	3318
broughtest *f* water for them out	Neh 9:15	3318
therefore I cast *f* all the	Neh 13:8	
From that time *f* came they no	Neh 13:21	
So Hatach went *f* to Mordecai unto	Est 4:6	3318
Then went Haman *f* that day joyful	Est 5:9	3318
But put *f* thine hand now, and	Job 1:11	7971
upon himself put not *f* thine hand	Job 1:12	7971
So Satan went *f* from the presence	Job 1:12	3318
But put *f* thine hand now, and	Job 2:5	7971
So went Satan *f* from the presence	Job 2:7	3318
cometh not *f* of the dust, neither	Job 5:6	3318
branch shooteth *f* in his garden	Job 8:16	3318
thou brought me *f* out of the womb	Job 10:18	3318
thou shalt shine *f*, thou shalt be	Job 11:17	
He cometh *f* like a flower, and is	Job 14:2	3318
bring *f* boughs like a plant	Job 14:9	6213
bring *f* vanity, and their belly	Job 15:35	3205
They send *f* their little ones	Job 21:11	
be brought *f* to the day of wrath	Job 21:30	
tried me, I shall come *f* as gold	Job 23:10	3318
desert, go they *f* to their work	Job 24:5	3318
He putteth *f* his hand upon the	Job 28:9	7971
is hid bringeth he *f* to light	Job 28:11	3318
They were driven *f* from among men	Job 30:5	
sea with doors, when it brake *f*	Job 38:8	1518
of the tender herb to spring *f*	Job 38:27	6779
Canst thou bring *f* Mazzaroth in	Job 38:32	3318
wild goats of the rock bring *f*	Job 39:1	3205
thou the time when they bring *f*	Job 39:2	3205
they bring *f* their young ones,	Job 39:3	6398
they go *f*, and return not unto	Job 39:4	3318
the mountains bring him *f* food	Job 40:20	
that bringeth *f* his fruit in his	Ps 1:3	5414
mischief, and brought *f* falsehood	Ps 7:14	3205
I will shew *f* all thy marvellous	Ps 9:1	
That I may shew *f* all thy praise	Ps 9:14	
sentence come *f* from thy presence	Ps 17:2	3318
He brought me *f* also into a large	Ps 18:19	3318
His going *f* is from the end of	Ps 19:6	4161
And he shall bring *f* thy	Ps 37:6	3318
goest not *f* with our armies	Ps 44:9	3318
my mouth shall shew *f* thy praise	Ps 51:15	
He hath put *f* his hands against	Ps 55:20	7971
God shall send *f* his mercy	Ps 57:3	
Sing *f* the honour of his name	Ps 66:2	
thou wentest *f* before thy people	Ps 68:7	3318
shall shew *f* thy righteousness	Ps 71:15	
his own people to go *f* like sheep	Ps 78:52	5265
we will shew *f* thy praise to all	Ps 79:13	5608
between the cherubims, shine *f*	Ps 80:1	
I am shut up, and I cannot come *f*	Ps 88:8	3318
the mountains were brought *f*	Ps 90:2	3205
To shew *f* thy lovingkindness in	Ps 92:2	
still bring *f* fruit in old age	Ps 92:14	5107
shew *f* his salvation from day to	Ps 96:2	
that he may bring *f* food out of	Ps 104:14	3318
beasts of the forest do creep *f*	Ps 104:20	
Man goeth *f* unto his work and to	Ps 104:23	3318
Thou sendest *f* thy spirit	Ps 104:30	
land brought *f* frogs in abundance	Ps 105:30	8317
He brought them *f* also with	Ps 105:37	3318
he brought *f* his people with joy,	Ps 105:43	3318
who can shew *f* all his praise	Ps 106:2	
he led them *f* by the right way,	Ps 107:7	
thou, O God, go *f* with our hosts	Ps 108:11	3318
name of the LORD from this time *f*	Ps 113:2	
bless the LORD from this time *f*	Ps 115:18	
and thy coming in from this time *f*	Ps 121:8	
lest the righteous put *f* their	Ps 125:3	7971
the LORD shall lead them *f* with	Ps 125:5	
He that goeth *f* and weepeth,	Ps 126:6	
thou shalt stretch *f* thine hand	Ps 138:7	
Let my prayer be set *f* before	Ps 141:2	
I stretch *f* my hands unto thee	Ps 143:6	
Cast *f* lightning, and scatter them	Ps 144:6	
our sheep may bring *f* thousands	Ps 144:13	
His breath goeth *f*, he returneth	Ps 146:4	3318
He sendeth *f* his commandment upon	Ps 147:15	
He casteth *f* his ice like morsels	Ps 147:17	
Therefore came I *f* to meet thee	Prov 7:15	3318
and understanding put *f* her voice	Prov 8:1	
were no depths, I was brought *f*	Prov 8:24	2342
before the hills was I brought *f*	Prov 8:25	2342
She hath sent *f* her maidens	Prov 9:3	
of the just bringeth *f* wisdom	Prov 10:31	5107
truth sheweth *f* righteousness	Prov 12:17	
there shall come *f* a vessel for	Prov 25:4	3318
Put not *f* thyself in the presence	Prov 25:6	1921
Go not *f* hastily to strive, lest	Prov 25:8	3318
not what a day may bring *f*	Prov 27:1	3205
yet go they *f* all of them by	Prov 30:27	3318
of milk bringeth *f* butter	Prov 30:33	3318
of the nose bringeth *f* blood	Prov 30:33	3318
of wrath bringeth *f* strife	Prov 30:33	3318
she reacheth *f* her hands to the	Prov 31:20	6566
the wood that bringeth *f* trees	Eccl 2:6	6779
As he came *f* of his mother's womb	Eccl 5:15	3318
God shall come *f* of them all	Eccl 7:18	3318
to send *f* a stinking savour	Eccl 10:1	
thy name is as ointment poured *f*	Song 1:3	
go thy way *f* by the footsteps of	Song 1:8	3318
sendeth *f* the smell thereof	Song 1:12	
he looketh *f* at the windows,	Song 2:9	
fig tree putteth *f* her green figs	Song 2:13	2590
Go *f*, O ye daughters of Zion, and	Song 3:11	3318
she that looketh *f* as the morning	Song 6:10	
let us go *f* into the field	Song 7:11	3318
appear, and the pomegranates bud *f*	Song 7:12	5132
there thy mother brought thee *f*	Song 8:5	2254
she brought thee *f* that bare thee	Song 8:5	2254
And when ye spread *f* your hands	Is 1:15	
out of Zion shall go *f* the law	Is 2:3	3318
and walk with stretched *f* necks	Is 3:16	
that it should bring *f* grapes	Is 5:2	6213
and it brought *f* wild grapes	Is 5:2	6213
that it should bring *f* grapes	Is 5:4	6213
brought it *f* wild grapes	Is 5:4	6213
he hath stretched *f* his hand	Is 5:25	
Go *f* now to meet Ahaz, thou, and	Is 7:3	3318
be for the sending *f* of oxen	Is 7:25	
there shall come *f* a rod out of	Is 11:1	3318
shall be darkened in his going *f*	Is 13:10	3318
they break *f* into singing	Is 14:7	
root shall come *f* a cockatrice	Is 14:29	3318
travail not, nor bring *f* children	Is 23:4	3205
he shall spread *f* his hands in	Is 25:11	
spreadeth *f* his hands to swim	Is 25:11	
we have as it were brought *f* wind	Is 26:18	3205
In measure, when it shooteth *f*	Is 27:8	
that it goeth *f* it shall take you	Is 28:19	5674
This also cometh *f* from the LORD	Is 28:29	3318
shepherds is called *f* against him	Is 31:4	
that send *f* thither the feet of	Is 32:20	
chaff, ye shall bring *f* stubble	Is 33:11	3205
and all things that come *f* of it	Is 34:1	6631

Then came *f* unto him Eliakim,	Is 36:3	3318
there is not strength to bring *f*	Is 37:3	3205
He is come *f* to make war with	Is 37:9	3318
of Jerusalem shall go *f* a remnant	Is 37:32	3318
Then the angel of the LORD went *f*	Is 37:36	3318
bring *f* your strong reasons,	Is 41:21	5066
Let them bring them *f*, and shew us	Is 41:22	5066
he shall bring *f* judgment to the	Is 42:1	3318
he shall bring *f* judgment unto	Is 42:3	3318
he that spread *f* the earth	Is 42:5	
they spring *f* I tell you of them	Is 42:9	
LORD shall go *f* as a mighty man	Is 42:13	3318
Bring *f* the blind people that	Is 43:8	3318
let them bring *f* their witnesses,	Is 43:9	
Which bringeth *f* the chariot	Is 43:17	4161
now it shall spring *f*	Is 43:19	6779
they shall shew *f* my praise	Is 43:21	
break *f* into singing, ye	Is 44:23	
that stretcheth *f* the heavens	Is 44:24	
and let them bring *f* salvation	Is 45:8	6509
woman, What hast thou brought *f*	Is 45:10	2342
are come *f* out of the waters of	Is 48:1	3318
they went *f* out of my mouth, and I	Is 48:3	3318
Go ye *f* of Babylon, flee ye from	Is 48:20	3318
mayest say to the prisoners, Go *f*	Is 49:9	3318
break *f* into singing, O mountains	Is 49:13	
thee waste shall go *f* of thee	Is 49:17	3318
my salvation is gone *f*, and mine	Is 51:5	3318
that hath stretched *f* the heavens	Is 51:13	
the sons whom she hath brought *f*	Is 51:18	3205
Break *f* into joy, sing together,	Is 52:9	
break *f* into singing, and cry	Is 54:1	
let them stretch *f* the curtains	Is 54:2	
shalt break *f* on the right hand	Is 54:3	
that bringeth *f* an instrument for	Is 54:16	4161
the earth, and maketh it bring *f*	Is 55:10	3205
be that goeth *f* out of my mouth	Is 55:11	3318
with joy, and be led *f* with peace	Is 55:12	2986
the hills shall break *f* before	Is 55:12	
thy light break *f* as the morning	Is 58:8	
health shall spring *f* speedily	Is 58:8	
the putting *f* of the finger, and	Is 58:9	7971
mischief, and bring *f* iniquity	Is 59:4	3205
they shall shew *f* the praises of	Is 60:6	
as the earth bringeth *f* her bud	Is 61:11	3318
that are sown in it to spring *f*	Is 61:11	
praise to spring *f* before all the	Is 61:11	
thereof go *f* as brightness	Is 62:1	3318
I will bring *f* a seed out of	Is 65:9	3318
in vain, nor bring *f* for trouble	Is 65:23	3205
she travailed, she brought *f*	Is 66:7	3205
be made to bring *f* in one day	Is 66:8	2342
she brought *f* her children	Is 66:8	3205
birth, and not cause to bring *f*	Is 66:9	3205
shall I cause to bring *f*, and shut	Is 66:9	3205
And they shall go *f*, and look upon	Is 66:24	3318
before thou camest *f* out of the	Jer 1:5	3318
Then the LORD put *f* his hand	Jer 1:9	7971
the north an evil shall break *f*	Jer 1:14	
a stone, Thou hast brought me *f*	Jer 2:27	3205
Yea, thou shalt go *f* from him	Jer 2:37	3318
lest my fury come *f* like fire	Jer 4:4	3318
he is gone *f* from his place to	Jer 4:7	3318
that bringeth *f* her first child	Jer 4:31	
Go not *f* into the field, nor walk	Jer 6:25	3318
f out of the land of Egypt unto	Jer 7:25	3318
bringeth *f* the wind out of his	Jer 10:13	3318
my children are gone *f* of me	Jer 10:20	3318
to stretch *f* my tent any more	Jer 10:20	
them *f* out of the land of Egypt	Jer 11:4	3318
grow, yea, they bring *f* fruit	Jer 12:2	6213
If I go *f* into the field, then	Jer 14:18	3318
out of my sight, and let them go *f*	Jer 15:1	3318
unto thee, Whither shall we go *f*	Jer 15:2	3318
if thou take *f* the precious from	Jer 15:19	3318
Neither carry *f* a burden out of	Jer 17:22	3318
go *f* unto the valley of the son	Jer 19:2	3318
that Pashur brought *f* Jeremiah	Jer 20:3	3318
Wherefore came I *f* out of the	Jer 20:18	3318
which went *f* out of this place	Jer 22:11	3318
cast *f* beyond the gates of	Jer 22:19	
gone *f* into all the land	Jer 23:15	3318
of the LORD is gone *f* in fury	Jer 23:19	3318
evil shall go *f* from nation to	Jer 25:32	3318
they fetched *f* Urijah out of	Jer 26:23	3318
gone *f* with you into captivity	Jer 29:16	3318
of the LORD goeth *f* with fury	Jer 30:23	3318
shalt go *f* in the dances of them	Jer 31:4	3318
and they that go *f* with flocks	Jer 31:24	5265
f over against it upon the hill	Jer 31:39	3318
hast brought *f* thy people Israel	Jer 32:21	3318
them *f* out of the land of Egypt	Jer 34:13	3318
army was come *f* out of Egypt	Jer 37:5	3318
army, which is come *f* to help you	Jer 37:7	3318
Then Jeremiah went *f* out of	Jer 37:12	3318
but he that goeth *f* to the	Jer 38:2	3318
Ebed-melech went *f* out of the	Jer 38:8	3318
If thou wilt assuredly go *f* unto	Jer 38:17	3318
But if thou wilt not go *f* to the	Jer 38:18	3318
But if thou refuse to go *f*	Jer 38:21	3318
f to the king of Babylon's	Jer 38:22	4163
went *f* out of the city by night,	Jer 39:4	3318
went *f* from Mizpah to meet them	Jer 41:6	3318
poured *f* upon the inhabitants of	Jer 42:18	
my fury be poured *f* upon you	Jer 42:18	
he shall go *f* from thence in	Jer 43:12	3318
fury and mine anger was poured *f*	Jer 44:6	
goeth *f* out of our own mouth	Jer 44:17	3318
stand *f* with your helmets	Jer 46:4	
and let the mighty men come *f*	Jer 46:9	3318
Chemosh shall go *f* into captivity	Jer 48:7	3318
fire shall come *f* out of Heshbon	Jer 48:45	3318
be driven out every man right *f*	Jer 49:5	6440
go *f* out of the land of the	Jer 50:8	3318
hath brought *f* the weapons of his	Jer 50:25	3318
hath brought *f* our righteousness	Jer 51:10	3318
bringeth *f* the wind out of his	Jer 51:16	3318
I will bring *f* out of his mouth	Jer 51:44	3318
went *f* out of the city by night	Jer 52:7	3318
brought him *f* out of prison,	Jer 52:31	3318
Zion spreadeth *f* her hands	Lam 1:17	
out of the fire went *f* lightning	Eze 1:13	3318
stretched *f* over their heads	Eze 1:22	
go *f* into the plain, and I will	Eze 3:22	3318
I arose, and went *f* into the plain	Eze 3:23	3318
f into all the house of Israel	Eze 5:4	3318
the morning is gone *f*	Eze 7:10	3318
he put *f* the form of an hand, and	Eze 8:3	7971
with the slain: go ye *f*	Eze 9:7	3318
And they went *f*, and slew in the	Eze 9:7	3318
one cherub stretched *f* his hand	Eze 10:7	
but I will bring you *f* out of the	Eze 11:7	3318
Then shalt thou bring *f* thy stuff	Eze 12:4	3318
thou shalt go *f* at even in their	Eze 12:4	3318
as they that go *f* into captivity	Eze 12:4	4161
carry it *f* in the twilight	Eze 12:6	3318
I brought *f* my stuff by day, as	Eze 12:7	3318
I brought it *f* in the twilight,	Eze 12:7	3318
in the twilight, and shall go *f*	Eze 12:12	3318
a remnant that shall be brought *f*	Eze 14:22	4163
they shall come *f* unto you	Eze 14:22	3318
thy renown went *f* among the	Eze 16:14	3318
put *f* a riddle, and speak a	Eze 17:2	2330
a vine, and brought *f* branches	Eze 17:6	6213
and shot *f* sprigs.	Eze 17:6	
shot *f* her branches toward him,	Eze 17:7	
that it might bring *f* branches	Eze 17:8	6213
and it shall bring *f* boughs	Eze 17:23	5375
that hath not given *f* upon usury	Eze 18:8	
Hath given *f* upon usury, and hath	Eze 18:13	
to bring them *f* of the land of	Eze 20:6	3318
in bringing them *f* out of the	Eze 20:9	3318
to go *f* out of the land of Egypt	Eze 20:10	3318
in whose sight I brought them *f*	Eze 20:22	3318
I will bring them *f* out of the	Eze 20:38	3318
will draw *f* my sword out of his	Eze 21:3	3318
therefore shall my sword go *f* out	Eze 21:4	3318
f my sword out of his sheath	Eze 21:5	3318
shall come *f* out of one land	Eze 21:19	3318
great scum went not *f* out of her	Eze 24:12	3318
thou spreadest *f* to be thy sail	Eze 27:7	
they set *f* thy comeliness	Eze 27:10	
thy wares went *f* out of the seas	Eze 27:33	3318
therefore will I bring *f* a fire	Eze 28:18	3318
of the house of Israel to bud *f*	Eze 29:21	
go *f* from me in ships to make the	Eze 30:9	3318
of waters, when he shot *f*	Eze 31:5	
of the field bring *f* their young	Eze 31:6	3205
thou camest *f* with thy rivers, and	Eze 32:2	1518
I will cast thee *f* upon the open	Eze 32:4	
word that cometh *f* from the LORD	Eze 33:30	3318
ye shall shoot *f* your branches	Eze 36:8	
are gone *f* out of his land	Eze 36:20	3318
thy jaws, and I will bring thee *f*	Eze 38:4	3318
but it is brought *f* out of the	Eze 38:8	3318
the cities of Israel shall go *f*	Eze 39:9	3318
Then he brought me *f* into the	Eze 42:1	3318
he brought me *f* toward the gate	Eze 42:15	3318
every going *f* of the sanctuary	Eze 44:5	4161
when they go *f* into the utter	Eze 44:19	3318
then he shall go *f*	Eze 46:2	3318
he shall go *f* by the way thereof	Eze 46:8	3318
go *f* by the way of the north gate	Eze 46:9	3318
but shall go *f* over against it	Eze 46:9	3318
and when they go *f*, shall go *f*	Eze 46:10	3318
then he shall go *f*	Eze 46:12	3318
after his going *f* one shall shut	Eze 46:12	3318
Then he brought me *f* into the	Eze 46:21	3318
line in his hand went *f* eastward	Eze 47:3	3318
being brought *f* into the sea	Eze 47:8	3318
shall be a place to spread *f* nets	Eze 47:10	
it shall bring *f* new fruit	Eze 47:12	
the decree went *f* that the wise	Dan 2:13	5312
which was gone *f* to slay the wise	Dan 2:14	5312
of the most high God, come *f*	Dan 3:26	5312
came *f* of the midst of the fire	Dan 3:26	5312
In the same hour came *f* fingers	Dan 5:5	5312
issued and came *f* from before him	Dan 7:10	5312
one of them came *f* a little horn	Dan 8:9	3318
that hast brought thy people *f*	Dan 9:15	3318
I am now come *f* to give thee	Dan 9:22	3318
the commandment came *f*, and I am	Dan 9:23	3318
that from the going *f* of the	Dan 9:25	4161
and when I am gone *f*, lo, the	Dan 10:20	3318
with choler, and shall come *f*	Dan 11:11	3318
he shall set *f* a great multitude	Dan 11:11	5975
shall set *f* a multitude greater	Dan 11:13	
He shall stretch *f* his hand also	Dan 11:42	
therefore he shall go *f* with	Dan 11:44	3318
his going *f* is prepared as the	Hos 6:3	4161
are as the light that goeth *f*	Hos 6:5	3318
but Ephraim shall bring *f* his	Hos 9:13	3318
yea, though they bring *f*, yet	Hos 9:16	3205
he bringeth *f* fruit unto himself	Hos 10:1	7737
of the breaking *f* of children	Hos 13:13	4866
cast *f* his roots as Lebanon	Hos 14:5	5221
bridegroom go *f* of his chamber	Joel 2:16	3318
a fountain shall come *f* of the	Joel 3:18	3318
that which went *f* by an hundred	Amos 5:3	3318
go into captivity *f* of his land	Amos 7:17	
shall cast them *f* with silence	Amos 8:3	
sabbath, that we may set *f* wheat	Amos 8:5	6605
cast *f* the wares that were in the	Jonah 1:5	2904
me up, and cast me *f* into the sea	Jonah 1:12	2904
Jonah, and cast him *f* into the sea	Jonah 1:15	2904
the LORD cometh *f* out of his	Mic 1:3	3318
f in the mourning of Beth-ezel	Mic 1:11	3318
for the law shall go *f* of Zion	Mic 4:2	3318
Be in pain, and labour to bring *f*	Mic 4:10	1518
shalt thou go *f* out of the city	Mic 4:10	3318
yet out of thee shall he come *f*	Mic 5:2	3318
whose goings *f* have been from of	Mic 5:2	4163
which travaileth hath brought *f*	Mic 5:3	3205
he will bring me *f* to the light	Mic 7:9	3318
and judgment doth never go *f*	Hab 1:4	3318
burning coals went *f* at his feet	Hab 3:5	3318
Thou wentest *f* for the salvation	Hab 3:13	3318
Before the decree bring *f*	Zeph 2:2	3205
that which the ground bringeth *f*	Hag 1:11	3318
olive tree, hath not brought *f*	Hag 2:19	5375
be stretched *f* upon Jerusalem	Zec 1:16	
angel that talked with me went *f*	Zec 2:3	3318
Ho, ho, come *f*, and flee from the	Zec 2:6	
I will bring *f* my servant the	Zec 3:8	935
he shall bring *f* the headstone	Zec 4:7	3318
f over the face of the whole	Zec 5:3	3318
I will bring it *f*, saith the LORD	Zec 5:4	3318
angel that talked with me went *f*	Zec 5:5	3318
and see what is this that goeth *f*	Zec 5:5	3318
This is an ephah that goeth *f*	Zec 5:6	3318
which go *f* from standing before	Zec 6:5	3318
go *f* into the north country	Zec 6:6	3318
and the white go *f* after them	Zec 6:6	3318
the grisled go *f* toward the south	Zec 6:6	3318
And the bay went *f*, and sought to	Zec 6:7	3318
of thy covenant I have sent *f* thy	Zec 9:11	
arrow shall go *f* as the lightning	Zec 9:14	3318
Out of him came *f* the corner	Zec 10:4	3318
which stretcheth *f* the heavens	Zec 12:1	
city shall go *f* into captivity	Zec 14:2	3318
Then shall the LORD go *f*, and	Zec 14:3	3318
and ye shall go *f*, and grow up as	Mal 4:2	3318
And she shall bring *f* a son	Mt 1:21	*5088*
child, and shall bring *f* a son	Mt 1:23	*5088*
had brought *f* her firstborn son	Mt 1:25	*5088*
was exceeding wroth, and sent *f*	Mt 2:16	*649*
Bring *f* therefore fruits meet for	Mt 3:8	*4160*
not *f* good fruit is hewn down	Mt 3:10	*4160*
good tree bringeth *f* good fruit	Mt 7:17	*4160*
tree bringeth *f* evil fruit	Mt 7:17	*4160*
tree cannot bring *f* evil fruit	Mt 7:18	*4160*
a corrupt tree bring *f* good fruit	Mt 7:18	*4160*
not *f* good fruit is hewn down	Mt 7:19	*4160*
And Jesus put *f* his hand, and	Mt 8:3	*1614*
And as Jesus passed *f* from thence	Mt 9:9	*3855*
But when the people were put *f*	Mt 9:25	*1544*
that he will send *f* labourers	Mt 9:38	*1544*
These twelve Jesus sent *f*	Mt 10:5	*649*
I send you *f* as sheep in the	Mt 10:16	*649*
to the man, Stretch *f* thine hand	Mt 12:13	*1614*
And he stretched it *f*	Mt 12:13	*1614*
till he send *f* judgment unto	Mt 12:20	*1544*
the heart bringeth *f* good things	Mt 12:35	*1544*
treasure bringeth *f* evil things	Mt 12:35	
he stretched *f* his hand toward	Mt 12:49	*1614*
Behold, a sower went *f* to sow	Mt 13:3	*1831*
good ground, and brought *f* fruit	Mt 13:8	
also beareth fruit, and bringeth *f*	Mt 13:23	*4160*
parable put he *f* unto them	Mt 13:24	*3908*
was sprung up, and brought *f* fruit	Mt 13:26	*4160*
parable put he *f* unto them	Mt 13:31	*3908*
of man shall send *f* his angels	Mt 13:41	*649*
f as the sun in the kingdom of	Mt 13:43	*1584*
the angels shall come *f*, and sever	Mt 13:49	*3318*
which bringeth *f* out of his	Mt 13:52	*1544*
works do shew *f* themselves in him	Mt 14:2	*1754*
And Jesus went *f*, and saw a great	Mt 14:14	*1831*
Jesus stretched *f* his hand	Mt 14:31	*1614*
the mouth come *f* from the heart	Mt 15:18	*3318*
From that time *f* began Jesus to	Mt 16:21	
bringing *f* the fruits thereof	Mt 21:43	*4160*
sent *f* his servants to call them	Mt 22:3	*649*
he sent *f* other servants, saying,	Mt 22:4	*649*
and he sent *f* his armies, and	Mt 22:7	
day *f* ask him any more questions	Mt 22:46	
in the desert; go not *f*	Mt 24:26	*1831*
yet tender, and putteth *f* leaves	Mt 24:32	*1631*
went *f* to meet the bridegroom	Mt 25:1	*1831*
for therefore came I *f*	Mk 1:38	*1831*
put *f* his hand, and touched him,	Mk 1:41	*1614*
bed, and went *f* before them all	Mk 2:12	*1831*
he went *f* again by the sea side	Mk 2:13	*1831*
had the withered hand, Stand *f*	Mk 3:3	
the man, Stretch *f* thine hand	Mk 3:5	*1614*
And the Pharisees went *f*, and	Mk 3:6	*1831*
he might send them *f* to preach	Mk 3:14	*649*
and brought *f*, some thirty, and	Mk 4:8	*5348*
and receive it, and bring *f* fruit	Mk 4:20	*2592*
earth bringeth *f* fruit of herself	Mk 4:28	*2592*
But when the fruit is brought *f*	Mk 4:29	*3860*
and began to send them *f* by two	Mk 6:7	*1614*
works do shew *f* themselves in him	Mk 6:14	*1754*
For Herod himself had sent *f*	Mk 6:17	*1614*
And she went *f*, and said unto her	Mk 6:24	*1831*
f the devil out of her daughter	Mk 7:26	*1544*
And the Pharisees came *f*, and began	Mk 8:11	*1831*
This kind can come *f* by nothing	Mk 9:29	*1831*
when he was gone *f* into the way	Mk 10:17	*1607*
he sendeth *f* two of his disciples	Mk 11:1	*1614*
yet tender, and putteth *f* leaves	Mk 13:28	*1631*
he sendeth *f* two of his disciples	Mk 14:13	*1614*
And his disciples went *f*, and came	Mk 14:16	*1831*
And they went *f*, and preached every	Mk 16:20	*1831*
many have taken in hand to set *f*	Lk 1:1	*392*
in thy womb, and bring *f* a son	Lk 1:31	*5088*
and she brought *f* a son	Lk 1:57	*1080*
she brought *f* her firstborn son,	Lk 2:7	*5088*
that came *f* to be baptized of him	Lk 3:7	*1607*
Bring *f* therefore fruits worthy	Lk 3:8	*4160*
not *f* good fruit is hewn down	Lk 3:9	*4160*
he put *f* his hand, and touched him	Lk 5:13	*1614*
And after these things he went *f*	Lk 5:27	*1831*

Rise up, and stand *f* in the midst Lk 6:8
And he arose and stood *f* Lk 6:8
unto the man, Stretch *f* thy hand Lk 6:10 *1614*
tree bringeth not *f* corrupt fruit Lk 6:43 *4160*
a corrupt tree bring *f* good fruit Lk 6:43 *4160*
bringeth *f* that which is good Lk 6:45 *4393*
bringeth *f* that which is evil Lk 6:45 *4393*
him went *f* throughout all Judaea Lk 7:17 *1831*
which, when they have heard, go *f* Lk 8:14 *4198*
bring *f* fruit with patience Lk 8:15
And they launched *f* Lk 8:22 *321*
And when he went *f* to land Lk 8:27 *1831*
that he would send *f* labourers Lk 10:2 *1544*
I send you *f* as lambs among Lk 10:3 *649*
rich man brought *f* plentifully Lk 12:16 *2164*
sit down to meat, and will come *f* Lk 12:37 *3928*
he put *f* a parable to those which Lk 14:7 *3004*
Bring *f* the best robe, and put it Lk 15:22 *1627*
let it *f* to husbandmen, and went Lk 20:9 *1554*
sent *f* spies, which should feign Lk 20:20 *649*
When they now shoot *f*, ye see and Lk 21:30 *4261*
ye stretched *f* no hands against Lk 22:53 *1614*
Jesus would go *f* into Galilee Jn 1:43 *1831*
beginning doth set *f* good wine Jn 2:10 *5087*
and manifested *f* his glory Jn 2:11 *5319*
And shall come *f*; they that have Jn 5:29 *1607*
for I proceeded *f* and came from Jn 8:42 *1831*
when he putteth *f* his own sheep Jn 10:4 *1554*
a loud voice, Lazarus, come *f* Jn 11:43 *1854*
And he that was dead came *f* Jn 11:44 *1831*
Then from that day *f* they took Jn 11:53
went *f* to meet him, and cried, Jn 12:13 *1831*
it die, it bringeth *f* much fruit Jn 12:24
that it may bring *f* more fruit Jn 15:2
the same bringeth *f* much fruit Jn 15:5
he is cast *f* as a branch, and is Jn 15:6 *1854*
ye should go and bring *f* fruit Jn 15:16
I came *f* from the Father, and am Jn 16:28 *1831*
that thou camest *f* from God Jn 16:30 *1831*
he went *f* with his disciples over Jn 18:1 *1831*
that should come upon him, went *f* Jn 18:4 *1831*
Pilate therefore went *f* again Jn 19:4 *1854*
Behold, I bring him *f* to you Jn 19:4 *1854*
Then came Jesus *f*, wearing the Jn 19:5 *1854*
that saying, he brought Jesus *f* Jn 19:13 *1854*
he bearing his cross went *f* into Jn 19:17 *1831*
Peter therefore went *f*, and that Jn 20:3 *1831*
They went *f*, and entered into a Jn 21:3 *1831*
thou shalt stretch *f* thy hands Jn 21:18 *1614*
And they gave *f* their lots Acts 1:26
Holy Ghost, he hath shed *f* this Acts 2:33 *1632*
By stretching *f* thine hand to Acts 4:30 *1614*
her dead, and, carrying her *f* Acts 5:10 *1627*
f the sick into the streets Acts 5:15 *1627*
prison doors, and brought them *f* Acts 5:19 *1806*
put the apostles *f* a little space Acts 5:34 *1854*
and after that shall they come *f* Acts 7:7 *1831*
Caesarea, and sent him *f* to Tarsus Acts 9:30 *1821*
But Peter put them all *f*, and Acts 9:40 *1854*
and they sent *f* Barnabas, that he Acts 11:22 *1821*
time Herod the king stretched *f* Acts 12:1 *1911*
to bring him *f* to the people Acts 12:4 *321*
Herod would have brought him *f* Acts 12:6 *4254*
being sent *f* by the Holy Ghost, Acts 13:4 *1599*
would Paul have to go *f* with him Acts 16:3 *1831*
to be a setter *f* of strange gods Acts 17:18 *2604*
we went aboard, and set *f* Acts 21:2 *321*
I brought him *f* into their Acts 23:28 *2609*
And when he was called *f*, Acts 24:2 *2564*
commanded the man to be brought *f* Acts 25:17
commandment Paul was brought *f* Acts 25:23
I have brought him *f* before you Acts 25:26 *4254*
Then Paul stretched *f* the hand Acts 26:1 *1614*
but speak *f* the words of truth and Acts 26:25 *669*
Paul stood *f* in the midst of them Acts 27:21
Whom God hath set *f* to be a Rom 3:25 *4388*
we should bring *f* fruit unto God Rom 7:4
to bring *f* fruit unto death Rom 7:5
f my hands unto a disobedient Rom 10:21 *1600*
hath set *f* us the apostles last 1Cor 4:9 *584*
but conduct him *f* in peace 1Cor 16:11 *4311*
Christ hath been evidently set *f* Gal 3:1 *4270*
time was come, God sent *f* his Son Gal 4:4 *1821*
God hath sent *f* the Spirit of his Gal 4:6 *1821*
break *f* and cry, thou that Gal 4:27 *4486*
Holding *f* the word of life Phil 2:16 *1907*
reaching *f* unto those things Phil 3:13 *1901*
and bringeth *f* fruit, as it doth Col 1:6
might shew *f* all longsuffering 1Ti 1:16 *1731*
sent *f* to minister for them who Heb 1:14 *649*
bringeth *f* herbs meet for them by Heb 6:7 *5088*
Let us go *f* therefore unto him Heb 13:13 *1831*
hath conceived, it bringeth *f* sin Jas 1:15 *616*
it is finished, bringeth *f* death Jas 1:15 *5088*
Doth a fountain send *f* at the Jas 3:11 *1032*
and the earth brought *f* her fruit Jas 5:18 *985*
that ye should shew *f* the praises 1Pet 2:9 *1804*
for his name's sake they went *f* 3Jn 7 *1831*
are set *f* for an example, Jude 7 *4295*
of God sent *f* into all the earth Rev 5:6 *649*
he went *f* conquering, and to Rev 6:2 *1831*
And she brought *f* a man child Rev 12:5 *5088*
which brought *f* the man child Rev 12:13 *5088*
which go *f* unto the kings of the Rev 16:14 *1607*

FORTHWITH
f expences be given unto these Ezr 6:8 629
f they sprung up, because they Mt 13:5 *2112*
f he came to Jesus, and said, Hail Mt 26:49 *2112*
f, when they were come out of the Mk 1:29 *2112*
charged him, and *f* sent him away Mk 1:43 *2112*
And *f* Jesus gave them leave Mk 5:13 *2112*
f came there out blood and water Jn 19:34 *2117*
and he received sight *f*, and arose, Acts 9:18 *3916*
f the angel departed from him Acts 12:10 *2112*
and *f* the doors were shut Acts 21:30 *2112*

FORTIETH
in the *f* year after the children Num 33:38 705
And it came to pass in the *f* year Deut 1:3 705
In the *f* year of the reign of 1Chr 26:31 705
in the one and *f* year of his reign 2Chr 16:13 705

FORTIFIED
he *f* the strong holds, and put 2Chr 11:11 2388
turning of the wall, and *f* them 2Chr 26:9 2388
they *f* Jerusalem unto the broad Neh 3:8 5800
Assyria, and from the *f* cities Mic 7:12 4692

FORTIFY
they *f* the city against thee Judg 9:31 6696
will they *f* themselves Neh 4:2 5800
have ye broken down to *f* the wall Is 22:10 1219
though she should *f* the height of Jer 51:53 1219
strong, *f* thy power mightily Nah 2:1 553
for the siege, *f* thy strong holds Nah 3:14 2388

FORTRESS
The LORD is my rock, and my *f* 2Sa 22:2 4686
The LORD is my rock, and my *f* Ps 18:2 4686
For thou art my rock and my *f* Ps 31:3 4686
me, for thou art my rock and my *f* Ps 71:3 4686
the LORD, He is my refuge and my *f* Ps 91:2 4686
My goodness, and my *f* Ps 144:2 4686
The *f* also shall cease from Is 17:3 4013
the *f* of the high fort of thy Is 25:12 4013
a *f* among my people, that thou Jer 6:27 4013
the land, O inhabitant of the *f* Jer 10:17 4693
O LORD, my strength, and my *f* Jer 16:19 4581
shall enter into the *f* of the Dan 11:7 4581
and be stirred up, even to his *f* Dan 11:10 4581
spoiled shall come against the *f* Amos 5:9 4013
from the *f* even to the river, and Mic 7:12 4693

FORTRESSES
and brambles in the *f* thereof Is 34:13 4013
all thy *f* shall be spoiled, as Hos 10:14 4013

FORTS
they built *f* against it round 2Kin 25:1 1785
and I will raise *f* against thee Is 29:3 4694
the *f* and towers shall be for dens Is 32:14 6076
built *f* against it round about Jer 52:4 1785
casting up mounts, and building *f* Eze 17:17 1785
and they that be in the *f* Eze 33:27 4679

FORTUNATUS (*for-chu-na'-tus*) *A Christian acquaintance of Paul.*
of the coming of Stephanas and F 1Cor 16:17 *5415*
from Philippi by Stephanus, and F 1Cor *s* *5415*

FORTY
f years, and begat sons and Gen 5:13 705
it to rain upon the earth *f* days Gen 7:4 705
the earth *f* days and *f* nights Gen 7:4 705
the earth *f* days and *f* nights Gen 7:12 705
the flood was *f* days upon the Gen 7:17 705
came to pass at the end of *f* days Gen 8:6 705
And he said, If I find there *f* Gen 18:28 705
there shall be *f* found there Gen 18:29 705
Isaac was *f* years old when he Gen 25:20 705
Esau was *f* years old when he took Gen 26:34 705
f kine, and ten bulls, twenty she Gen 32:15 705
age of Jacob was an hundred *f* Gen 47:28 705
f days were fulfilled for him Gen 50:3 705
of Israel did eat manna *f* years Ex 16:35 705
the mount *f* days and *f* nights Ex 24:18 705
thou shalt make *f* sockets of Ex 26:19 705
their *f* sockets of silver Ex 26:21 705
the LORD *f* days and *f* nights Ex 34:28 705
f sockets of silver he made under Ex 36:24 705
their *f* sockets of silver Ex 36:26 705
of years shall be unto thee *f* Lev 25:8 705
of the tribe of Reuben, were *f* Num 1:21 705
even of the tribe of Gad, were *f* Num 1:25 705
were *f* thousand and five hundred Num 1:33 705
of the tribe of Asher, were *f* Num 1:41 705
were numbered thereof, were *f* Num 2:11 705
were numbered of them, were *f* Num 2:15 705
were *f* thousand and five hundred Num 2:19 705
were numbered of them, were *f* Num 2:28 705
of the land after *f* days Num 13:25 705
wander in the wilderness *f* years Num 14:33 705
ye searched the land, even *f* days Num 14:34 705
even *f* years, and ye shall know my Num 14:34 705
that were numbered of them were *f* Num 26:7 705
f thousand and five hundred Num 26:18 705
that were numbered of them were *f* Num 26:41 705
that were numbered of them were *f* Num 26:50 705
wander in the wilderness *f* years Num 32:13 705
and to them ye shall add *f* Num 35:6 705
give to the Levites shall be *f* Num 35:7 705
these *f* years the LORD thy God Deut 2:7 705
these *f* years in the wilderness Deut 8:2 705
did thy foot swell, these *f* years Deut 8:4 705
then I abode in the mount *f* days Deut 9:9 705
f nights, I neither did eat bread Deut 9:9 705
came to pass at the end of *f* days Deut 9:11 705
f nights, that the LORD gave me Deut 9:11 705
the first, *f* days and *f* nights Deut 9:18 705
fell down before the LORD *f* days Deut 9:25 705
f nights, as I fell down at the Deut 9:25 705
time, *f* days and *f* nights Deut 10:10 705
F stripes he may give him, and not Deut 25:3 705
I have led you *f* years in the Deut 29:5 705
About *f* thousand prepared for war Josh 4:13 705
walked *f* years in the wilderness Josh 5:6 705
F years old was I when Moses the Josh 14:7 705
me alive, as he said, these *f* Josh 14:10 705
of the children of Israel were *f* Josh 21:41 705
And the land had rest *f* years Judg 3:11 705
seen among *f* thousand in Israel Judg 5:8 705
And the land had rest *f* years Judg 5:31 705
f years in the days of Gideon Judg 8:28 705
at that time of the Ephraimites *f* Judg 12:6 705
And he had *f* sons and thirty Judg 12:14 705
hand of the Philistines *f* years Judg 13:1 705
And he had judged Israel *f* years 1Sa 4:18 705
and presented himself *f* days 1Sa 17:16 705
was *f* years old when he began to 2Sa 2:10 705
to reign, and he reigned *f* years 2Sa 5:4 705
f thousand horsemen, and smote 2Sa 10:18 705
And it came to pass after *f* years 2Sa 15:7 705
reigned over Israel were *f* years 1Kin 2:11 705
Solomon had *f* thousand stalls of 1Kin 4:26 705
before it, was *f* cubits long 1Kin 6:17 705
that lay on *f* five pillars, 1Kin 7:3 705
one laver contained *f* baths 1Kin 7:38 705
over all Israel was *f* years 1Kin 11:42 705
Rehoboam was *f* and one years old 1Kin 14:21 705
And *f* and one years reigned he in 1Kin 15:10 705
the strength of that meat *f* days 1Kin 19:8 705
f nights unto Horeb the mount of 1Kin 19:8 705
bears out of the wood, and tare *f* 2Kin 2:24 705
f camels' burden, and came and 2Kin 8:9 705
shearing house, even two and *f* men 2Kin 10:14 705
f years reigned he in Jerusalem 2Kin 12:1 705
to reign in Samaria, and reigned *f* 2Kin 14:23 705
f thousand seven hundred and 1Chr 5:18 705
battle, expert in war, *f* thousand 1Chr 12:36 705
f thousand footmen, and killed 1Chr 19:18 705
reigned over Israel was *f* years 1Chr 29:27 705
Jerusalem over all Israel *f* years 2Chr 9:30 705
f years old when he began to 2Chr 12:13 705
F and two years old was Ahaziah 2Chr 22:2 705
he reigned *f* years in Jerusalem 2Chr 24:1 705
children of Zattu, nine hundred *f* Ezr 2:8 705
children of Bani, six hundred *f* Ezr 2:10 705
The children of Azmaveth, *f* Ezr 2:24 705
and Beeroth, seven hundred and *f* Ezr 2:25 705
of Jericho, three hundred *f* Ezr 2:34 705
Pashur, a thousand two hundred *f* Ezr 2:38 705
whole congregation together was *f* Ezr 2:64
their mules, two hundred *f* Ezr 2:66 705
beside *f* shekels of silver Neh 5:15 705
of Zattu, eight hundred *f* Neh 7:13 705
children of Binnui, six hundred *f* Neh 7:15 705
The men of Beth-azmaveth, *f* Neh 7:28 705
and Beeroth, seven hundred *f* Neh 7:29 705
of Jericho, three hundred *f* Neh 7:36 705
Pashur, a thousand two hundred *f* Neh 7:41 705
children of Asaph, an hundred *f* Neh 7:44 705
children of Nekoda, six hundred *f* Neh 7:62 705
whole congregation together was *f* Neh 7:66
and they had two hundred *f* Neh 7:67 705
their mules, two hundred *f* Neh 7:68 705
f years didst thou sustain them Neh 9:21 705
of the fathers, two hundred *f* Neh 11:13 705
f years, and saw his sons, and his Job 42:16 705
F years long was I grieved with Ps 95:10 705
of the Jews seven hundred *f* Jer 52:30 705
of the house of Judah *f* days Eze 4:6 705
shall it be inhabited *f* years Eze 29:11 705
waste shall be desolate *f* years Eze 29:12 705
At the end of *f* years will I Eze 29:13 705
the length thereof, *f* cubits Eze 41:2 705
courts joined of *f* cubits long Eze 46:22 705
led you *f* years through the Amos 2:10 705
in the wilderness *f* years Amos 5:25 705
Yet *f* days, and Nineveh shall be Jonah 3:4 705
And when he had fasted *f* days Mt 4:2 *5062*
f nights, he was afterward an Mt 4:2 *5062*
there in the wilderness *f* days Mk 1:13 *5062*
Being *f* days tempted of the devil Lk 4:2 *5062*
Then said the Jews, *F* and six Jn 2:20 *5062*
proofs, being seen of them *f* days Acts 1:3 *5062*
For the man was above *f* years old Acts 4:22 *5062*
And when he was full *f* years old Acts 7:23 *5063*
when *f* years were expired, there Acts 7:30 *5062*
sea, and in the wilderness *f* years Acts 7:36 *5062*
of *f* years in the wilderness Acts 7:42 *5062*
about the time of *f* years Acts 13:18 *5063*
Benjamin, by the space of *f* years Acts 13:21 *5062*
they were more than *f* which had Acts 23:13 *5062*
for him of them more than *f* men Acts 23:21 *5062*
received I *f* stripes save one 2Cor 11:24 *5062*
me, and saw my works *f* years Heb 3:9 *5062*
with whom was he grieved *f* years Heb 3:17 *5062*
there were sealed an hundred and *f* Rev 7:4 *5062*
shall they tread under foot *f* Rev 11:2 *5062*
was given unto him to continue *f* Rev 13:5 *5062*
Sion, and with him an hundred *f* Rev 14:1 *5062*
that song but the hundred and *f* Rev 14:3 *5062*
the wall thereof, an hundred and *f* Rev 21:17 *5062*

FORTY'S
said, I will not do it for *f* sake Gen 18:29 705

FORUM
came to meet us as far as Appii *f* Acts 28:15 675

FORWARD
And the man waxed great, and went *f* Gen 26:13 1980
of Israel, that they go *f* Ex 14:15 5265
And when the tabernacle setteth *f* Num 1:51 5265
of the congregation shall set *f* Num 2:17 5265
they encamp, so shall they set *f* Num 2:17 5265
they shall go *f* in the third rank Num 2:24 5265
their standards, and so they set *f* Num 2:34 5265
And when the camp setteth *f* Num 4:5 5265
as the camp is to set *f* Num 4:15 5265
lie on the east parts shall go *f* Num 10:5 5265
and the sons of Merari set *f* Num 10:17 5265
set *f* according to their armies Num 10:18 5265
And the Kohathites set *f*, bearing Num 10:21 5265
set *f* according to their armies Num 10:22 5265
camp of the children of Dan set *f* Num 10:25 5265

to their armies, when they set *f* Num 10:28 5265
came to pass, when the ark set *f* Num 10:35 5265
And the children of Israel set *f* Num 21:10 5265
And the children of Israel set *f* Num 22:1 5265
them on yonder side Jordan, or *f* Num 32:19 1973
that was with him, rushed *f* Judg 9:44 6584
shalt thou go on *f* from thence 1Sa 10:3 1973
came upon David from that day *f* 1Sa 16:13 4605
eyed David from that day and *f* 1Sa 18:9 1973
And it was so from that day *f* 1Sa 30:25 4605
but they went *f* smiting the 2Kin 3:24
to her servant, Drive, and go *f* 2Kin 4:24
shall the shadow go *f* ten degrees 2Kin 20:9
four thousand were to set *f* the 1Chr 23:4 5921
of the Kohathites, to set it *f* 2Chr 34:12
to set *f* the work of the house of Ezr 3:8 5921
to set *f* the workmen in the house Ezr 3:9 5921
Behold, I go *f*, but he is not Job 23:8 6924
they set *f* my calamity, they have Job 30:13 3276
heart, and went backward, and not *f* Jer 7:24 6440
they went every one straight *f* Eze 1:9 6440
And they went every one straight *f* Eze 1:12 6440
they went every one straight *f* Eze 10:22 6440
LORD their God from that day and *f* Eze 39:22 1973
that upon the eighth day, and so *f* Eze 43:27 1973
they helped *f* the affliction Zec 1:15
he went *f* a little, and fell on Mk 14:35 *4281*
multitude, the Jews putting him *f* Acts 19:33 *4261*
do, but also to be *f* a year ago 2Cor 8:10 *2309*
but being more *f*, of his own 2Cor 8:17 *4707*
the same which I also was *f* to do Gal 2:10 *4704*
whom if thou bring *f* on their 3Jn 6 *4311*

FORWARDNESS

by occasion of the *f* of others 2Cor 8:8 *4710*
For I know the *f* of your mind 2Cor 9:2 *4288*

FOUGHT

f with Israel in Rephidim Ex 17:8 3898
had said to him, and *f* with Amalek Ex 17:10 3898
then he *f* against Israel, and took Num 21:1 3898
to Jahaz, and *f* against Israel Num 21:23 3898
who had *f* against the former king Num 21:26 3898
for the LORD *f* for Israel Josh 10:14 3898
unto Libnah, and *f* against Libnah Josh 10:29 3898
against it, and *f* against it Josh 10:31 3898
against it, and *f* against it Josh 10:34 3898
and they *f* against it Josh 10:36 3898
to Debir; and *f* against it Josh 10:38 3898
LORD God of Israel *f* for Israel Josh 10:42 3898
God is he that hath *f* for you Josh 23:3 3898
and they *f* with you Josh 24:8 3898
the men of Jericho *f* against you Josh 24:11 3898
they *f* against him, and they slew Judg 1:5 3898
of Judah had *f* against Jerusalem Judg 1:8 3898
The kings came and *f* Judg 5:19 3898
then *f* the kings of Canaan in Judg 5:19 3898
They *f* from heaven Judg 5:20 3898
in their courses *f* against Sisera Judg 5:20 3898
(For my father *f* for you, and Judg 9:17 3898
of Shechem, and *f* with Abimelech Judg 9:39 3898
Abimelech *f* against the city all Judg 9:45 3898
f against it, and went hard unto Judg 9:52 3898
in Jahaz, and *f* against Israel Judg 11:20 3898
men of Gilead, and *f* with Ephraim Judg 12:4 3898
And the Philistines *f*, and Israel 1Sa 4:10 3898
of Moab, and they *f* against them 1Sa 12:9 3898
f against all his enemies on 1Sa 14:47 3898
f with the Philistines, and slew 1Sa 19:8 3898
f with the Philistines, and 1Sa 23:5 3898
the Philistines *f* against Israel 1Sa 31:1 3898
no more, neither *f* they any more 2Sa 2:28 3898
him, because he had *f* against 2Sa 8:10 3898
against David, and *f* with him 2Sa 10:17 3898
the city went out, and *f* with Joab 2Sa 11:17 3898
Joab *f* against Rabbah of the 2Sa 12:26 3898
I have *f* against Rabbah, and have 2Sa 12:27 3898
and *f* against it, and took it 2Sa 12:29 3898
f against the Philistines 2Sa 21:15 3898
when he *f* against Hazael king of 2Kin 8:29 3898
when he *f* with Hazael king of 2Kin 9:15 3898
f against Gath, and took it 2Kin 12:17 3898
his might wherewith he *f* against 2Kin 13:12 3898
how he *f* with Amaziah king of 2Kin 14:15 3898
the Philistines *f* against Israel 1Chr 10:1 3898
him, because he had *f* against 1Chr 18:10 3898
the Syrians, they *f* with him 1Chr 19:17 3898
thousand men which *f* in chariots 1Chr 19:18
they had heard that the LORD *f* 2Chr 20:29 3898
when he *f* with Hazael king of 2Chr 22:6 3898
He *f* also with the king of the 2Chr 27:5 3898
f against me without a cause Ps 109:3 3898
f against Ashdod, and took it Is 20:1 3898
their enemy, and he *f* against them Is 63:10 3898
f against Jerusalem, and against Jer 34:1 3898
army *f* against Jerusalem, and Jer 34:7 3898
as when he *f* in the day of battle Zec 14:3 3898
that have *f* against Jerusalem Zec 14:12 6633
I have *f* with beasts at Ephesus 1Cor 15:32 *2341*
I have *f* a good fight, I have 2Ti 4:7 *75*
his angels *f* against the dragon Rev 12:7 *4170*
and the dragon *f* and his angels, Rev 12:7 *4170*

FOUL

My face is *f* with weeping, and on Job 16:16 2560
but ye must *f* the residue with Eze 34:18 7515
It will be *f* weather to day Mt 16:3 *5494*
together, he rebuked the *f* spirit Mk 9:25 *169*
and the hold of every *f* spirit Rev 18:2 *169*

FOULED

which ye have *f* with your feet Eze 34:19 4833

FOULEDST

with thy feet, and *f* their rivers Eze 32:2 7515

FOUND

was not *f* an help meet for him Gen 2:20 4672
But Noah *f* grace in the eyes of Gen 6:8 4672
But the dove *f* no rest for the Gen 8:9 4672
that they *f* a plain in the land Gen 11:2 4672
the angel of the LORD *f* her by a Gen 16:7 4672
if now I have *f* favour in thy Gen 18:3 4672
there shall be forty *f* there Gen 18:29 4672
there shall thirty be *f* there Gen 18:30 4672
there shall be twenty *f* there Gen 18:31 4672
Peradventure ten shall be *f* there Gen 18:32 4672
thy servant hath *f* grace in thy Gen 19:19 4672
f there a well of springing water Gen 26:19 4672
and said unto him, We have *f* water Gen 26:32 4672
it that thou hast *f* it so quickly Gen 27:20 4672
f mandrakes in the field, and Gen 30:14 4672
if I have *f* favour in thine eyes, Gen 30:27 4672
but he *f* them not Gen 31:33 4672
all the tent, but *f* them not Gen 31:34 4672
he searched, but *f* not the images Gen 31:35 4672
what hast thou *f* of all thy Gen 31:37 4672
if now I have *f* grace in thy Gen 33:10 4672
this was that Anah that *f* the Gen 36:24 4672
And a certain man *f* him, and, Gen 37:15 4672
his brethren, and *f* them in Dothan Gen 37:17 4672
and said, This have we *f* Gen 37:32 4672
but he *f* her not Gen 38:20 4672
this kid, and thou hast not *f* her Gen 38:23 4672
Joseph *f* grace in his sight, and Gen 39:4 4672
which we *f* in our sacks' mouths, Gen 44:8 4672
of thy servants it be *f*, both let Gen 44:9 4672
he with whom it is *f* shall be my Gen 44:10 4672
the cup was *f* in Benjamin's sack Gen 44:12 4672
God hath *f* out the iniquity of Gen 44:16 4672
and he also with whom the cup is *f* Gen 44:16 4672
man in whose hand the cup is *f* Gen 44:17 4672
that was *f* in the land of Egypt Gen 47:14 4672
If now I have *f* grace in thy Gen 47:29 4672
If now I have *f* grace in your Gen 50:4 4672
which shall be *f* in the field Ex 9:19 4672
be no leaven *f* in your houses Ex 12:19 4672
in the wilderness, and *f* no water Ex 15:22 4672
day for to gather, and they *f* none Ex 16:27 4672
him, or if he be *f* in his hand Ex 21:16 4672
If a thief be *f* breaking up Ex 22:2 4672
be certainly *f* in his hand alive Ex 22:4 4672
if the thief be *f*, let him pay Ex 22:7 4672
If the thief be not *f*, then the Ex 22:8 4672
thou hast also *f* grace in my Ex 33:12 4672
if I have *f* grace in thy sight, Ex 33:13 4672
thy people have *f* grace in thy Ex 33:16 4672
for thou hast *f* grace in my sight Ex 33:17 4672
If now I have *f* grace in thy Ex 34:9 4672
every man, with whom was *f* blue Ex 35:23 4672
with whom was *f* shittim wood for Ex 35:24 4672
Or have *f* that which was lost, and Lev 6:3 4672
or the lost thing which he *f* Lev 6:4 4672
have I not *f* favour in thy sight Num 11:11 4672
if I have *f* favour in thy sight Num 11:15 4672
they *f* a man that gathered sticks Num 15:32 4672
they that *f* him gathering sticks Num 15:33 4672
if we have *f* grace in thy sight, Num 32:5 4672
If there be *f* among you, within Deut 17:2 4672
There shall not be *f* among you Deut 18:10 4672
that all the people that is *f* Deut 20:11 4672
If one be *f* slain in the land Deut 21:1 4672
he hath lost, and thou hast *f* Deut 22:3 4672
I came to her, I *f* her not a maid Deut 22:14 4672
I *f* not thy daughter a maid Deut 22:17 4672
virginity be not *f* for the damsel Deut 22:20 4672
If a man be *f* lying with a woman Deut 22:22 4672
For he *f* her in the field, and the Deut 22:27 4672
and lie with her, and they be *f* Deut 22:28 4672
his eyes, because he hath *f* some Deut 24:1 4672
If a man be *f* stealing any of his Deut 24:7 4672
He *f* him in a desert land, and in Deut 32:10 4672
shall be *f* liars unto thee Deut 33:29
all the way, but *f* them not Josh 2:22 4672
The five kings are *f* hid in a Josh 10:17 4672
they *f* Adoni-bezek in Bezek Judg 1:5 4672
If now I have *f* grace in thy Judg 6:17 4672
ye had not *f* out my riddle Judg 14:18 4672
he *f* a new jawbone of an ass, and Judg 15:15 4672
they *f* among the inhabitants of Judg 21:12 4672
Why have I *f* grace in thine eyes, Ruth 2:10 4672
of Shalisha, but they *f* them not 1Sa 9:4 4672
Benjamites, but they *f* them not 1Sa 9:4 4672
they *f* young maidens going out to 1Sa 9:11 4672
for they are *f* 1Sa 9:20 4672
which thou wentest to seek are *f* 1Sa 10:2 4672
us plainly that the asses were *f* 1Sa 10:16 4672
sought him, he could not be *f* 1Sa 10:21 4672
ye have not *f* ought in my hand 1Sa 12:5 4672
Now there was no smith *f* 1Sa 13:19 4672
spear *f* in the hand of any of the 1Sa 13:22 4672
with Jonathan his son was there *f* 1Sa 13:22 4672
of their enemies which they *f* 1Sa 14:30 4672
for he hath *f* favour in my sight 1Sa 16:22 4672
that I have *f* grace in thine eyes 1Sa 20:3 4672
if I have *f* favour in thine eyes, 1Sa 20:29 4672
evil hath not been *f* in thee all 1Sa 25:28 4672
If I have now *f* grace in thine 1Sa 27:5 4672
I have *f* no fault in him since he 1Sa 29:3 4672
for I have not *f* evil in thee 1Sa 29:6 4672
what hast thou *f* in thy servant 1Sa 29:8 4672
they *f* an Egyptian in the field, 1Sa 30:11 4672
strip the slain, that they *f* Saul 1Sa 31:8 4672
f in his heart to pray this 2Sa 7:27 4672
that I have *f* grace in thy sight 2Sa 14:22 4672
in some place where he shall be *f* 2Sa 17:12 4672
be not one small stone *f* there 2Sa 17:13
f Abishag a Shunammite, and 1Kin 1:3 4672
if wickedness shall be *f* in him 1Kin 1:52 4672
was the weight of the brass *f* out 1Kin 7:47 2713
Hadad *f* great favour in the sight 1Kin 11:19 4672
the Shilonite *f* him in the way 1Kin 11:29 4672
f him sitting under an oak 1Kin 13:14 4672
f his carcase cast in the way, and 1Kin 13:28 4672
because in him there is *f* some 1Kin 14:13 4672
and nation, that they *f* thee not 1Kin 18:10 4672
f Elisha the son of Shaphat, who 1Kin 19:19 4672
departed from him, a lion *f* him 1Kin 20:36 4672
Then he *f* another man, and said, 1Kin 20:37 4672
said to Elijah, Hast thou *f* me 1Kin 21:20 4672
And he answered, I have *f* thee 1Kin 21:20 4672
sought three days, but *f* him not 2Kin 2:17 4672
f a wild vine, and gathered 2Kin 4:39 4672
but they *f* no more of her than 2Kin 9:35 4672
wheresoever any breach shall be *f* 2Kin 12:5 4672
told the money that was *f* in the 2Kin 12:10 4672
all the gold that was *f* in the 2Kin 12:18 4672
were *f* in the house of the LORD 2Kin 14:14 4672
gold that was *f* in the house of 2Kin 16:8 4672
the king of Assyria *f* conspiracy 2Kin 17:4 4672
was *f* in the house of the LORD 2Kin 18:15 4672
f the king of Assyria warring 2Kin 19:8 4672
all that was *f* in his treasures 2Kin 20:13 4672
I have *f* the book of the law in 2Kin 22:8 4672
the money that was *f* in the house 2Kin 22:9 4672
the words of this book that is *f* 2Kin 22:13 4672
was *f* in the house of the LORD 2Kin 23:2 4672
priest *f* in the house of the LORD 2Kin 23:24 4672
which were *f* in the city, and the 2Kin 25:19 4672
the land that were *f* in the city 2Kin 25:19 4672
they *f* fat pasture and good, and 1Chr 4:40 4672
the habitations that were *f* there 1Chr 4:41 4672
strip the slain, that they *f* Saul 1Chr 10:8 4672
therefore thy servant hath *f* in 1Chr 17:25 4672
f it to weigh a talent of gold, 1Chr 20:2 4672
there were more chief men *f* of 1Chr 24:4 4672
there were *f* among them mighty 1Chr 26:31 4672
seek him, he will be *f* of thee 1Chr 28:9 4672
f gave them to the treasure of 1Chr 29:8 4672
they were *f* an hundred and fifty 2Chr 2:17 4672
of the brass could not be *f* out 2Chr 4:18 2713
ye seek him, he will be *f* of you 2Chr 15:2 4672
and sought him, he was *f* of them 2Chr 15:4 4672
and he was *f* of them 2Chr 15:15 4672
there are good things *f* in thee 2Chr 19:3 4672
they *f* among them in abundance 2Chr 20:25 4672
that was *f* in the king's house 2Chr 21:17 4672
f the princes of Judah, and the 2Chr 22:8 4672
f them three hundred thousand 2Chr 25:5 4672
were *f* in the house of God with 2Chr 25:24 4672
all the uncleanness that they *f* 2Chr 29:16 4672
Hilkiah the priest *f* a book of 2Chr 34:14 4672
I have *f* the book of the law in 2Chr 34:15 4672
was *f* in the house of the LORD 2Chr 34:17 4672
the words of the book that is *f* 2Chr 34:21 4672
was *f* in the house of the LORD 2Chr 34:30 4672
did, and that which was *f* in him 2Chr 36:8 4672
by genealogy, but they were not *f* Ezr 2:62 4672
it is *f* that this city of old Ezr 4:19 7912
there was *f* at Achmetha, in the Ezr 6:2 7912
f there none of the sons of Levi Ezr 8:15 4672
f that had taken strange wives Ezr 10:18 4672
have *f* favour in thy sight Neh 2:5
peace, and *f* nothing to answer Neh 5:8 4672
I *f* a register of the genealogy Neh 7:5 4672
the first, and *f* written therein, Neh 7:5 4672
by genealogy, but it was not *f* Neh 7:64 4672
they *f* written in the law which Neh 8:14 4672
and therein was *f* written, that Neh 13:1 4672
made of the matter, it was *f* out Est 2:23 4672
If I have *f* favour in the sight Est 5:8 4672
it was *f* written, that Mordecai Est 6:2 4672
If I have *f* favour in thy sight, Est 7:3 4672
if I have *f* favour in his sight, Est 8:5 4672
the root of the matter is *f* in me Job 19:28 4672
as a dream, and shall not be *f* Job 20:8 4672
But where shall wisdom be *f* Job 28:12 4672
neither is it *f* in the land of Job 28:13 4672
lifted up myself when evil *f* him Job 31:29 4672
because they had *f* no answer Job 32:3 4672
should say, We have *f* out wisdom Job 32:13 4672
I have *f* a ransom Job 33:24 4672
in all the land were no women *f* Job 42:15 4672
in a time when thou mayest be *f* Ps 32:6 4672
his iniquity be *f* to be hateful Ps 36:2 4672
sought him, but he could not be *f* Ps 37:36 4672
and for comforters, but I *f* none Ps 69:20 4672
men of might have *f* their hands Ps 76:5 4672
Yea, the sparrow hath *f* an house Ps 84:3 4672
I have *f* David my servant Ps 89:20 4672
they *f* no city to dwell in Ps 107:4 4672
I *f* trouble and sorrow Ps 116:3 4672
we *f* it in the fields of the wood Ps 132:6 4672
But if he be *f*, he shall restore Prov 6:31 4672
seek thy face, and I have *f* thee Prov 7:15 4672
hath understanding wisdom is *f* Prov 10:13 4672
glory, if it be *f* in the way of Prov 16:31 4672
when thou hast *f* it, then there Prov 24:14 4672
Hast thou *f* honey Prov 25:16 4672
reprove thee, and thou be *f* a liar Prov 30:6
curse thee, and thou be *f* guilty Prov 30:10
Behold, this have I *f*, saith the Eccl 7:27 4672
one man among a thousand have I *f* Eccl 7:28 4672
among all those have I not *f* Eccl 7:28 4672
Lo, this only have I *f*, that God Eccl 7:29 4672
Now there was *f* in it a poor wise Eccl 9:15 4672
I sought him, but I *f* him not Song 3:1 4672
I sought him, but I *f* him not Song 3:2 4672
that go about the city *f* me Song 3:3 4672

but I *f* him whom my soul loveth	Song 3:4	4672
that went about the city *f* me	Song 5:7	4672
in his eyes as one that *f* favour	Song 8:10	4672
As my hand hath *f* the kingdoms of	Is 10:10	4672
my hand hath *f* as a nest the	Is 10:14	4672
Every one that is *f* shall be	Is 13:15	4672
all that are *f* in thee are bound	Is 22:3	4672
so that there shall not be *f* in	Is 30:14	4672
thereon, it shall not be *f* there	Is 35:9	4672
f the king of Assyria warring	Is 37:8	4672
all that was *f* in his treasures	Is 39:2	4672
and gladness shall be *f* therein	Is 51:3	4672
ye the LORD while he may be *f*	Is 55:6	4672
thou hast *f* the life of thine	Is 57:10	4672
I am *f* of them that sought me not	Is 65:1	4672
the new wine is *f* in the cluster	Is 65:8	4672
have your fathers *f* in me	Jer 2:5	4672
the thief is ashamed when he is *f*	Jer 2:26	4672
Also in thy skirts is *f* the blood	Jer 2:34	4672
I have not *f* it by secret search,	Jer 2:34	4672
among my people are *f* wicked men	Jer 5:26	4672
A conspiracy is *f* among the men	Jer 11:9	4672
came to the pits, and *f* no water	Jer 14:3	4672
Thy words were *f*, and I did eat	Jer 15:16	4672
house have I *f* their wickedness	Jer 23:11	4672
And I will be *f* of you, saith the	Jer 29:14	4672
sword *f* grace in the wilderness	Jer 31:2	4672
the Chaldeans that were *f* there	Jer 41:3	4672
But ten men were *f* among them	Jer 41:8	4672
f him by the great waters that	Jer 41:12	4672
was he *f* among thieves	Jer 48:27	4672
All that *f* them have devoured	Jer 50:7	4672
of Judah, and they shall not be *f*	Jer 50:20	4672
thou art *f*, and also caught,	Jer 50:24	4672
person, which were *f* in the city	Jer 52:25	4672
that were *f* in the midst of the	Jer 52:25	4672
we have *f*, we have seen it	Lam 2:16	4672
not destroy it: but I *f* none	Eze 22:30	4672
yet shalt thou never be *f* again	Eze 26:21	4672
till iniquity was *f* in thee	Eze 28:15	4672
them all was *f* none like Daniel	Dan 1:19	4672
he *f* them ten times better than	Dan 1:20	4672
I have *f* a man of the captives of	Dan 2:25	4672
that no place was *f* for them	Dan 2:35	7912
wisdom of the gods, was *f* in him	Dan 5:11	7912
were *f* in the same Daniel, whom	Dan 5:12	7912
and excellent wisdom is *f* in thee	Dan 5:14	7912
in the balances, and art *f* wanting	Dan 5:27	7912
there any error or fault *f* in him	Dan 6:4	7912
f Daniel praying and making	Dan 6:11	7912
before him innocency was *f* in me	Dan 6:22	7912
no manner of hurt was *f* upon him	Dan 6:23	7912
stumble and fall, and not be *f*	Dan 11:19	4672
shall be *f* written in the book	Dan 12:1	4672
I *f* Israel like grapes in the	Hos 9:10	4672
now shall they be *f* faulty	Hos 10:2	
he *f* him in Beth-el, and there he	Hos 12:4	4672
I have *f* me out substance	Hos 12:8	4672
From me is thy fruit *f*	Hos 14:8	4672
he *f* a ship going to Tarshish	Jonah 1:3	4672
of Israel were *f* in thee	Mic 1:13	4672
tongue be *f* in their mouth	Zeph 3:13	4672
and place shall not be *f* for them	Zec 10:10	4672
and iniquity was not *f* in his lips	Mal 2:6	4672
she was *f* with child of the Holy	Mt 1:18	2147
and when ye have *f* him, bring me	Mt 2:8	2147
I have not *f* so great faith, no,	Mt 8:10	2147
the which when a man hath *f*	Mt 13:44	2147
when he had *f* one pearl of great	Mt 13:46	2147
f one of his fellowservants,	Mt 18:28	2147
f others standing idle, and saith	Mt 20:6	2147
f nothing thereon, but leaves	Mt 21:19	2147
together all as many as they *f*	Mt 22:10	2147
And he came and *f* them asleep again	Mt 26:43	2147
But *f* none: yea, though	Mt 26:60	2147
witnesses came, yet *f* they none	Mt 26:60	
they *f* a man of Cyrene, Simon by	Mt 27:32	2147
And when they had *f* him, they said	Mk 1:37	2147
unwashen, hands, they *f* fault	Mk 7:2	
she *f* the devil gone out, and her	Mk 7:30	2147
f the colt tied by the door	Mk 11:4	2147
to it, he *f* nothing but leaves	Mk 11:13	2147
f as he had said unto them	Mk 14:16	2147
he *f* them asleep again, (for	Mk 14:40	2147
and *f* none.	Mk 14:55	2147
for thou hast *f* favour with God	Lk 1:30	2147
f Mary, and Joseph, and the babe	Lk 2:16	429
And when they *f* him not, they	Lk 2:45	2147
days they *f* him in the temple	Lk 2:46	2147
he *f* the place where it was	Lk 4:17	2147
I have not *f* so great faith, no,	Lk 7:9	2147
f the servant whole that had been	Lk 7:10	2147
f the man, out of whom the devils	Lk 8:35	2147
voice was past, Jesus was *f* alone	Lk 9:36	2147
sought fruit thereon, and *f* none	Lk 13:6	2147
And when he hath *f* it, he layeth	Lk 15:5	2147
for I have *f* my sheep which was	Lk 15:6	2147
And when she hath *f* it, she	Lk 15:9	2147
for I have *f* the piece which I	Lk 15:9	2147
he was lost, and is *f*	Lk 15:24	2147
and was lost, and is *f*	Lk 15:32	2147
There are not *f* that returned to	Lk 17:18	2147
f even as he had said unto them	Lk 19:32	2147
f as he had said unto them	Lk 22:13	2147
he *f* them sleeping for sorrow,	Lk 22:45	2147
We *f* this fellow perverting the	Lk 23:2	2147
have *f* no fault in this man	Lk 23:14	2147
I have *f* no cause of death in him	Lk 23:22	2147
they *f* the stone rolled away from	Lk 24:2	2147
f not the body of the Lord Jesus	Lk 24:3	2147
when they *f* not his body, they	Lk 24:23	2147
f it even so as the women had	Lk 24:24	2147
f the eleven gathered together,	Lk 24:33	2147
We have *f* the Messias, which is,	Jn 1:41	2147
and saith unto him, We have *f* him	Jn 1:45	2147
f in the temple those that sold	Jn 2:14	2147
when they had *f* him on the other	Jn 6:25	2147
and when he had *f* him, he said	Jn 9:35	2147
he *f* that he had lain in the	Jn 11:17	2147
Jesus, when he had *f* a young ass	Jn 12:14	2147
f her dead, and, carrying her	Acts 5:10	2147
f them not in the prison, they	Acts 5:22	2147
The prison truly *f* we shut with	Acts 5:23	2147
we had opened, we *f* no man within	Acts 5:23	2147
lest haply ye be *f* even to fight	Acts 5:39	2147
our fathers *f* no sustenance	Acts 7:11	2147
Who *f* favour before God, and	Acts 7:46	2147
But Philip was *f* at Azotus	Acts 8:40	2147
that if he *f* any of this way,	Acts 9:2	2147
there he *f* a certain man named	Acts 9:33	2147
f many that were come together	Acts 10:27	2147
And when he had *f* him, he brought	Acts 11:26	2147
f him not, he examined the	Acts 12:19	2147
they *f* a certain sorcerer, a	Acts 13:6	2147
I have *f* David the son of Jesse,	Acts 13:22	2147
though they *f* no cause of death	Acts 13:28	2147
And when they *f* them not, they	Acts 17:6	2147
devotions, I *f* an altar with this	Acts 17:23	2147
f a certain Jew named Aquila,	Acts 18:2	2147
f it fifty thousand pieces of	Acts 19:19	2147
For we have *f* this man a	Acts 24:5	2147
they neither *f* me in the temple	Acts 24:12	2147
certain Jews from Asia *f* me	Acts 24:18	2147
if they have *f* any evil doing in	Acts 24:20	2147
But when I *f* that he had	Acts 25:25	2638
there the centurion *f* a ship of	Acts 27:6	2147
sounded, and *f* it twenty fathoms	Acts 27:28	2147
again, and *f* it fifteen fathoms	Acts 27:28	2147
Where we *f* brethren, and were	Acts 28:14	2147
pertaining to the flesh, hath *f*	Rom 4:1	2147
to life, I *f* to be unto death	Rom 7:10	2147
I was *f* of them that sought me	Rom 10:20	2147
that a man be *f* faithful	1Cor 4:2	2147
we are *f* false witnesses of God	1Cor 15:15	2147
because I *f* not Titus my brother	2Cor 2:13	2147
clothed we shall not be *f* naked	2Cor 5:3	2147
I made before Titus, is *f* a truth	2Cor 7:14	1096
glory, they may be *f* even as we	2Cor 11:12	2147
that I shall be *f* unto you such	2Cor 12:20	2147
we ourselves also are *f* sinners	Gal 2:17	2147
being *f* in fashion as a man, he	Phil 2:8	2147
be *f* in him, not having mine own	Phil 3:9	2147
of a deacon, being *f* blameless	1Ti 3:10	
me out very diligently, and *f* me	2Ti 1:17	2147
and was not *f*, because God had	Heb 11:5	2147
for he *f* no place of repentance,	Heb 12:17	2147
might be *f* unto praise and honour	1Pet 1:7	2147
neither was guile *f* in his mouth	1Pet 2:22	2147
that ye may be *f* of him in peace	2Pet 3:14	2147
I rejoiced greatly that I *f* of	2Jn 4	2147
and are not, and hast *f* them liars	Rev 2:2	2147
for I have not *f* thy works	Rev 3:2	2147
no man was *f* worthy to open	Rev 5:4	2147
their place *f* any more in heaven	Rev 12:8	2147
And in their mouth was *f* no guile	Rev 14:5	2147
away, and the mountains were not *f*	Rev 16:20	2147
shall be *f* no more at all	Rev 18:21	2147
shall be *f* any more in thee	Rev 18:22	2147
in her was *f* the blood of	Rev 18:24	2147
there was *f* no place for them	Rev 20:11	2147
whosoever was not *f* written in	Rev 20:15	2147

FOUNDATION

the *f* thereof even until now	Ex 9:18	3245
he shall lay the *f* thereof in his	Josh 6:26	3245
to lay the *f* of the house	1Kin 5:17	3245
In the fourth year was the *f* of	1Kin 6:37	3245
even from the *f* unto the coping,	1Kin 7:9	4527
the *f* was of costly stones, even	1Kin 7:10	3245
he laid the *f* thereof in Abiram	1Kin 16:34	3245
of the *f* of the house of the LORD	2Chr 8:16	4143
a third part at the gate of the *f*	2Chr 23:5	3247
began to lay the *f* of the heaps	2Chr 31:7	3245
But the *f* of the temple of the	Ezr 3:6	3245
the *f* of the temple of the LORD	Ezr 3:10	3245
because the *f* of the house of the	Ezr 3:11	3245
when the *f* of this house was laid	Ezr 3:12	3245
laid the *f* of the house of God	Ezr 5:16	787
whose *f* is in the dust, which are	Job 4:19	3247
whose *f* was overflown with a	Job 22:16	3247
His *f* is in the holy mountains	Ps 87:1	3248
hast thou laid the *f* of the earth	Ps 102:25	3245
rase it, even to the *f* thereof	Ps 137:7	3247
the righteous is an everlasting *f*	Prov 10:25	3247
I lay in Zion for a *f* a stone	Is 28:16	3248
a precious corner stone, a sure *f*	Is 28:16	4143
the temple, Thy *f* shall be laid	Is 44:28	3245
also hath laid the *f* of the earth	Is 48:13	3245
so that the *f* thereof shall be	Eze 13:14	3247
discovering the *f* unto the neck	Hab 3:13	3247
even from the day that the *f* of	Hag 2:18	3245
have laid the *f* of this house	Zec 4:9	3248
the *f* of the house of the LORD of	Zec 8:9	3248
layeth the *f* of the earth, and	Zec 12:1	3248
secret from the *f* of the world	Mt 13:35	2602
for you from the *f* of the world	Mt 25:34	2602
deep, and laid the *f* on a rock	Lk 6:48	2310
is like a man that without a *f*	Lk 6:49	2310
was shed from the *f* of the world	Lk 11:50	2602
haply, after he hath laid the *f*	Lk 14:29	2310
me before the *f* of the world	Jn 17:24	2602
should build upon another man's *f*	Rom 15:20	2310
masterbuilder, I have laid the *f*	1Cor 3:10	2310
For other *f* can no man lay than	1Cor 3:11	2310
if any man build upon this *f* gold	1Cor 3:12	2310
in him before the *f* of the world	Eph 1:4	2602
built upon the *f* of the apostles	Eph 2:20	2310
a good *f* against the time to come	1Ti 6:19	2310
Nevertheless the *f* of God	2Ti 2:19	2310
hast laid the *f* of the earth	Heb 1:10	2311
finished from the *f* of the world	Heb 4:3	2602
not laying again the *f* of	Heb 6:1	2310
suffered since the *f* of the world	Heb 9:26	2602
before the *f* of the world	1Pet 1:20	2602
slain from the *f* of the world	Rev 13:8	2602
of life from the *f* of the world	Rev 17:8	2602
The first *f* was jasper	Rev 21:19	2310

FOUNDATIONS

and set on fire the *f* of the	Deut 32:22	4146
the *f* of heaven moved and shook,	2Sa 22:8	4146
appeared, the *f* of the world were	2Sa 22:16	4146
walls thereof, and joined the *f*	Ezr 4:12	787
let the *f* thereof be strongly	Ezr 6:3	787
when I laid the *f* of the earth	Job 38:4	3245
are the *f* thereof fastened	Job 38:6	134
If the *f* be destroyed, what can	Ps 11:3	8356
the *f* also of the hills moved and	Ps 18:7	4146
seen, and the *f* of the world were	Ps 18:15	4146
all the *f* of the earth are out of	Ps 82:5	4146
Who laid the *f* of the earth	Ps 104:5	4349
he appointed the *f* of the earth	Prov 8:29	4146
for the *f* of Kir-hareseth shall	Is 16:7	808
the *f* of the earth do shake	Is 24:18	4146
from the *f* of the earth	Is 40:21	4146
and laid the *f* of the earth	Is 51:13	3245
lay the *f* of the earth, and say	Is 51:16	3245
and lay thy *f* with sapphires	Is 54:11	3245
up the *f* of many generations	Is 58:12	4146
the *f* of the earth searched out	Jer 31:37	4146
her *f* are fallen, her walls are	Jer 50:15	803
for a corner, nor a stone for *f*	Jer 51:26	4146
and it hath devoured the *f* thereof	Lam 4:11	3247
her *f* shall be broken down	Eze 30:4	3247
the *f* of the side chambers were a	Eze 41:8	4328
and I will discover the *f* thereof	Mic 1:6	3247
and ye strong *f* of the earth	Mic 6:2	4146
so that the *f* of the prison were	Acts 16:26	2310
he looked for a city which hath *f*	Heb 11:10	2310
the wall of the city had twelve *f*	Rev 21:14	2310
the *f* of the wall of the city	Rev 21:19	2310

FOUNDED

For he hath *f* it upon the seas,	Ps 24:2	3245
fulness thereof, thou hast *f* them	Ps 89:11	3245
place which thou hast *f* for them	Ps 104:8	3245
that thou hast *f* them for ever	Ps 119:152	3245
LORD by wisdom hath *f* the earth	Prov 3:19	3245
That the LORD hath *f* Zion	Is 14:32	3245
til the Assyrian *f* it for them	Is 23:13	3245
hath *f* his troop in the earth	Amos 9:6	3245
for it was *f* upon a rock	Mt 7:25	2311
for it was *f* upon a rock	Lk 6:48	2311

FOUNDER

of silver, and gave them to the *f*	Judg 17:4	6884
the *f* melteth in vain	Jer 6:29	6884
workman, and of the hands of the *f*	Jer 10:9	6884
every *f* is confounded by the	Jer 10:14	6884
every *f* is confounded by the	Jer 51:17	6884

FOUNDEST

f his heart faithful before thee,	Neh 9:8	4672

FOUNTAIN

by a *f* of water in the wilderness	Gen 16:7	5869
by the *f* in the way to Shur	Gen 16:7	5869
Nevertheless a *f* or pit, wherein	Lev 11:36	4599
he hath discovered her *f*, and she	Lev 20:18	4726
hath uncovered the *f* of her blood	Lev 20:18	4726
the *f* of Jacob shall be upon a	Deut 33:28	5869
the *f* of the water of Nephtoah	Josh 15:9	4599
by a *f* which is in Jezreel	1Sa 29:1	5869
I went on to the gate of the *f*	Neh 2:14	5869
But the gate of the *f* repaired	Neh 3:15	5869
And at the *f* gate, which was over	Neh 12:37	5869
For with thee is the *f* of life	Ps 36:9	4726
the Lord, from the *f* of Israel	Ps 68:26	4726
Thou didst cleave the *f* and the	Ps 74:15	4599
the flint into a *f* of waters	Ps 114:8	4599
Let thy *f* be blessed	Prov 5:18	4726
law of the wise is a *f* of life	Prov 13:14	4726
fear of the LORD is a *f* of life	Prov 14:27	4726
the wicked is as a troubled *f*	Prov 25:26	4599
or the pitcher be broken at the *f*	Eccl 12:6	4002
a spring shut up, a *f* sealed	Song 4:12	4599
A *f* of gardens, a well of living	Song 4:15	4599
me the *f* of living waters	Jer 2:13	4726
As a *f* casteth out her waters, so	Jer 6:7	953
waters, and mine eyes a *f* of tears	Jer 9:1	4726
the LORD, the *f* of living waters	Jer 17:13	4726
dry, and his *f* shall be dried up	Hos 13:15	4599
a *f* shall come forth of the house	Joel 3:18	4599
a *f* opened to the house of David	Zec 13:1	4726
straightway the *f* of her blood	Mk 5:29	4077
Doth a *f* send forth at the same	Jas 3:11	4077
so can no *f* both yield salt water	Jas 3:12	4077
the *f* of the water of life freely	Rev 21:6	4077

FOUNTAINS

the same day were all the *f* of	Gen 7:11	4599
The *f* also of the deep and the	Gen 8:2	4599
and in Elim were twelve *f* of water	Num 33:9	5869
a land of brooks of water, of *f*	Deut 8:7	5869
the land, unto all *f* of water	1Kin 18:5	4599
the *f* which were without the city	2Chr 32:3	5869
together, who stopped all the *f*	2Chr 32:4	4599
Let thy *f* be dispersed abroad, and	Prov 5:16	4599
when there were no *f* abounding	Prov 8:24	4599
he strengthened the *f* of the deep	Prov 8:28	5869
f in the midst of the valleys	Is 41:18	4599
lead them unto living *f* of waters	Rev 7:17	4077
rivers, and upon the *f* of waters	Rev 8:10	4077
and the sea, and the *f* of waters	Rev 14:7	4077
upon the rivers and *f* of waters	Rev 16:4	4077

FOUR

parted, and became into *f* heads	Gen 2:10	702
after he begat Salah *f* hundred	Gen 11:13	702
after he begat Eber *f* hundred	Gen 11:15	702
And Eber lived *f* and thirty years,	Gen 11:16	702
after he begat Peleg *f* hundred	Gen 11:17	702
f kings with five	Gen 14:9	702
afflict them *f* hundred years	Gen 15:13	702
the land is worth *f* hundred	Gen 23:15	702
f hundred shekels of silver,	Gen 23:16	702
thee, and *f* hundred men with him	Gen 32:6	702
came, and with him *f* hundred men	Gen 33:1	702
f parts shall be your own, for	Gen 47:24	702
was *f* hundred and thirty years	Ex 12:40	702
pass at the end of the *f* hundred	Ex 12:41	702
for an ox, and *f* sheep for a sheep	Ex 22:1	702
thou shalt cast *f* rings of gold	Ex 25:12	702
put them in the *f* corners thereof	Ex 25:12	702
shalt make for it *f* rings of gold	Ex 25:26	702
put the rings in the *f* corners	Ex 25:26	702
that are on the *f* feet thereof	Ex 25:26	702
in the candlestick shall be *f*	Ex 25:34	702
breadth of one curtain *f* cubits	Ex 26:2	702
breadth of one curtain *f* cubits	Ex 26:8	702
it upon *f* pillars of shittim wood	Ex 26:32	702
upon the *f* sockets of silver	Ex 26:32	702
of it upon the *f* corners thereof	Ex 27:2	702
make *f* brasen rings in the *f*	Ex 27:4	702
shall be *f*, and their sockets *f*	Ex 27:16	702
of stones, even *f* rows of stones	Ex 28:17	702
breadth of one curtain *f* cubits	Ex 36:9	702
f cubits was the breadth of one	Ex 36:15	702
he made thereunto *f* pillars of	Ex 36:36	702
he cast for them *f* sockets of	Ex 36:36	702
And he cast for it *f* rings of gold	Ex 37:3	702
to be set by the *f* corners of it	Ex 37:3	702
And he cast for it *f* rings of gold	Ex 37:13	702
put the rings upon the *f* corners	Ex 37:13	702
that were in the *f* feet thereof	Ex 37:13	702
were *f* bowls made like almonds	Ex 37:20	702
thereof on the *f* corners of it	Ex 38:2	702
he cast *f* rings for the *f* ends	Ex 38:5	702
And their pillars were *f*	Ex 38:19	702
and their sockets of brass *f*	Ex 38:19	702
two thousand and *f* hundred shekels	Ex 38:29	702
they set in it *f* rows of stones	Ex 39:10	702
that creep, going upon all *f*	Lev 11:20	702
thing that goeth upon all *f*	Lev 11:21	702
things, which have *f* feet	Lev 11:23	702
manner of beasts that go on all *f*	Lev 11:27	702
and whatsoever goeth upon all *f*	Lev 11:42	702
and *f* thousand and *f* hundred	Num 1:29	702
and seven thousand and *f* hundred	Num 1:31	702
and five thousand and *f* hundred	Num 1:37	702
and three thousand and *f* hundred	Num 1:43	702
and *f* thousand and *f* hundred	Num 2:6	702
and seven thousand and *f* hundred	Num 2:8	702
f hundred, throughout their	Num 2:9	702
f hundred and fifty, throughout	Num 2:16	702
and five thousand and *f* hundred	Num 2:23	702
and three thousand and *f* hundred	Num 2:30	702
f oxen he gave unto the sons of	Num 7:7	702
f wagons and eight oxen he gave	Num 7:8	702
f hundred shekels, after the	Num 7:85	702
f bullocks, the rams sixty, the	Num 7:88	702
plague were twenty and *f* thousand	Num 25:9	702
f thousand and three hundred	Num 26:25	702
and *f* thousand and *f* hundred	Num 26:43	702
and three thousand and *f* hundred	Num 26:47	702
and five thousand and *f* hundred	Num 26:50	702
f cubits the breadth of it, after	Deut 3:11	702
the *f* quarters of thy vesture	Deut 22:12	702
f cities and their villages	Josh 19:7	702
Almon with her suburbs; *f* cities	Josh 21:18	702
Beth-horon with her suburbs; *f* cities	Josh 21:22	702
with her suburbs; *f* cities	Josh 21:24	702
with her suburbs; *f* cities	Josh 21:29	702
Rehob with her suburbs; *f* cities	Josh 21:31	702
with her suburbs; *f* cities	Josh 21:35	702
with her suburbs; *f* cities	Josh 21:37	702
Jazer with her suburbs; *f* cities	Josh 21:39	702
against Shechem in *f* companies	Judg 9:34	702
the Gileadite *f* days in a year	Judg 11:40	702
and was there *f* whole months	Judg 19:2	702
f hundred thousand footmen that	Judg 20:2	702
were numbered *f* hundred thousand	Judg 20:17	702
abode in the rock Rimmon *f* months	Judg 20:47	702
f hundred young virgins, that had	Judg 21:12	702
in the field about *f* thousand men	1Sa 4:2	702
were with him about *f* hundred men	1Sa 22:2	702
after David about *f* hundred men	1Sa 25:13	702
was a full year and *f* months	1Sa 27:7	702
pursued, he and *f* hundred men	1Sa 30:10	702
save *f* hundred young men, which	1Sa 30:17	702
and on every foot six toes, *f*	2Sa 21:20	702
These *f* were born to the giant in	2Sa 21:22	702
it came to pass in the *f* hundred	1Kin 6:1	702
upon *f* rows of cedar pillars,	1Kin 7:2	702
lily work in the porch, *f* cubits	1Kin 7:19	702
f cubits was the length of one	1Kin 7:27	702
f cubits the breadth thereof, and	1Kin 7:27	702
And every base had *f* brasen wheels	1Kin 7:30	702
the *f* corners thereof had	1Kin 7:30	702
under the borders were *f* wheels	1Kin 7:32	702
there were *f* undersetters to the	1Kin 7:34	702
to the *f* corners of one base	1Kin 7:34	702
and every laver was *f* cubits	1Kin 7:38	702
f hundred pomegranates for the	1Kin 7:42	702
f hundred and twenty talents, and	1Kin 9:28	702
f hundred chariots, and twelve	1Kin 10:26	702
in Tirzah, twenty and *f* years	1Kin 15:33	702
and the prophets of Baal *f* hundred	1Kin 18:19	702
prophets of the groves *f* hundred	1Kin 18:19	702
but Baal's prophets are *f* hundred	1Kin 18:22	702
Fill *f* barrels with water, and	1Kin 18:33	702
about *f* hundred men, and said unto	1Kin 22:6	702
there were *f* leprous men at the	2Kin 7:3	702
the corner gate, *f* hundred cubits	2Kin 14:13	702
Shobab, and Nathan, and Solomon, *f*	1Chr 3:5	702
bow, and skilful in war, were *f*	1Chr 5:18	702
and Puah, Jashub, and Shimrom, *f*	1Chr 7:1	702
and two thousand and thirty and *f*	1Chr 7:7	702
In *f* quarters were the porters,	1Chr 9:24	702
the *f* chief porters, were in	1Chr 9:26	702
the children of Levi *f* thousand	1Chr 12:26	702
whose fingers and toes were *f*	1Chr 20:6	702
Judah was *f* hundred threescore and	1Chr 21:5	702
and his *f* sons with him hid	1Chr 21:20	702
f thousand were to set forward	1Chr 23:4	702
Moreover *f* thousand were porters	1Chr 23:5	702
f thousand praised the LORD with	1Chr 23:5	702
These *f* were the sons of Shimei	1Chr 23:10	702
Izhar, Hebron, and Uzziel, *f*	1Chr 23:12	702
and twentieth to Delaiah, the *f*	1Chr 24:18	702
The *f* and twentieth to	1Chr 25:31	702
f a day, southward *f* a day	1Chr 26:17	702
f at the causeway, and two at	1Chr 26:18	702
course were twenty and *f* thousand	1Chr 27:1	702
course were twenty and *f* thousand	1Chr 27:2	702
were twenty and *f* thousand	1Chr 27:4	702
course were twenty and *f* thousand	1Chr 27:5	702
course were twenty and *f* thousand	1Chr 27:7	702
course were twenty and *f* thousand	1Chr 27:8	702
course were twenty and *f* thousand	1Chr 27:9	702
course were twenty and *f* thousand	1Chr 27:10	702
course were twenty and *f* thousand	1Chr 27:11	702
course were twenty and *f* thousand	1Chr 27:12	702
course were twenty and *f* thousand	1Chr 27:13	702
course were twenty and *f* thousand	1Chr 27:14	702
course were twenty and *f* thousand	1Chr 27:15	702
f hundred chariots, and twelve	2Chr 1:14	702
f hundred pomegranates on the two	2Chr 4:13	702
Ophir, and took thence *f* hundred	2Chr 8:18	702
Solomon had *f* thousand stalls for	2Chr 9:25	702
even *f* hundred thousand chosen	2Chr 13:3	702
of prophets *f* hundred men	2Chr 18:5	702
the corner gate, *f* hundred cubits	2Chr 25:23	702
basons of a second sort *f* hundred	Ezr 1:10	702
were five thousand and *f* hundred	Ezr 1:11	702
a thousand two hundred fifty and *f*	Ezr 2:7	702
of Adin, *f* hundred fifty and *f*	Ezr 2:15	702
a thousand two hundred fifty and *f*	Ezr 2:31	702
of Hodaviah, seventy and *f*	Ezr 2:40	702
camels, *f* hundred thirty and five	Ezr 2:67	702
two hundred rams, *f* hundred lambs	Ezr 6:17	703
unto me *f* times after this sort	Neh 6:4	702
a thousand two hundred fifty and *f*	Neh 7:12	702
Bezai, three hundred twenty and *f*	Neh 7:23	702
a thousand two hundred fifty and *f*	Neh 7:34	702
children of Hodevah, seventy and *f*	Neh 7:43	702
camels, *f* hundred thirty and five	Neh 7:69	702
were *f* hundred threescore	Neh 11:6	702
were two hundred fourscore and *f*	Neh 11:18	702
smote the *f* corners of the house,	Job 1:19	702
sons' sons, even *f* generations	Job 42:16	702
f things say not, It is enough	Prov 30:15	702
for me, yea, *f* which I know not	Prov 30:18	702
for *f* which it cannot bear	Prov 30:21	702
There be *f* things which are	Prov 30:24	702
well, yea, *f* are comely in going	Prov 30:29	702
from the *f* corners of the earth	Is 11:12	702
f or five in the outmost fruitful	Is 17:6	702
I will appoint over them *f* kinds	Jer 15:3	702
Jehudi had read three or *f* leaves	Jer 36:23	702
upon Elam will I bring the *f*	Jer 49:36	702
from the *f* quarters of heaven	Jer 49:36	702
thickness thereof was *f* fingers	Jer 52:21	702
all the persons were *f* thousand	Jer 52:30	702
likeness of *f* living creatures	Eze 1:5	702
And every one had *f* faces	Eze 1:6	702
and every one had *f* wings	Eze 1:6	702
their wings on their *f* sides	Eze 1:8	702
they *f* had their faces and their	Eze 1:8	702
they *f* had the face of a man, and	Eze 1:10	702
they *f* had the face of an ox on	Eze 1:10	702
they *f* also had the face of an	Eze 1:10	702
creatures, with his *f* faces	Eze 1:15	702
and they *f* had one likeness	Eze 1:16	702
they went upon their *f* sides	Eze 1:17	702
full of eyes round about them *f*	Eze 1:18	702
upon the *f* corners of the land	Eze 7:2	702
behold the *f* wheels by the	Eze 10:9	702
they *f* had one likeness, as if a	Eze 10:10	702
they went upon their *f* sides	Eze 10:11	702
even the wheels that they *f* had	Eze 10:12	702
And every one had *f* faces	Eze 10:14	702
Every one had *f* faces apiece	Eze 10:21	702
and every one *f* wings	Eze 10:21	702
How much more when I send my *f*	Eze 14:21	702
Come from the *f* winds, O breath,	Eze 37:9	702
F tables were on this side, and	Eze 40:41	702
f tables on that side, by the	Eze 40:41	702
the *f* tables were of hewn stone	Eze 40:42	702
f cubits, round about the house	Eze 41:5	702
He measured it by the *f* sides	Eze 42:20	702
greater settle shall be *f* cubits	Eze 43:14	702
So the altar shall be *f* cubits	Eze 43:15	702
altar and upward shall be *f* horns	Eze 43:15	702
square in the *f* squares thereof	Eze 43:16	702
broad in the *f* squares thereof	Eze 43:17	702
and put it on the *f* horns of it	Eze 43:20	702
on the *f* corners of the settle,	Eze 43:20	702
upon the *f* corners of the settle	Eze 45:19	702
by the *f* corners of the court	Eze 46:21	702
In the *f* corners of the court	Eze 46:22	702
these *f* corners were of one	Eze 46:22	702
about in them, round about them *f*	Eze 46:23	702
the north side *f* thousand	Eze 48:16	702
and the south side *f* thousand	Eze 48:16	702
and on the east side *f* thousand	Eze 48:16	702
and the west side *f* thousand	Eze 48:16	702
f thousand and five hundred	Eze 48:30	702
And at the east side *f* thousand	Eze 48:32	702
And at the south side *f* thousand	Eze 48:33	702
At the west side *f* thousand	Eze 48:34	702
As for these *f* children, God gave	Dan 1:17	702
I see *f* men loose, walking in the	Dan 3:25	703
the *f* winds of the heaven strove	Dan 7:2	703
f great beasts came up from the	Dan 7:3	703
the back of it *f* wings of a fowl	Dan 7:6	703
the beast had also *f* heads	Dan 7:6	703
These great beasts, which are *f*	Dan 7:17	703
are *f* kings, which shall arise	Dan 7:17	703
for it came up *f* notable ones	Dan 8:8	702
ones toward the *f* winds of heaven	Dan 8:8	702
whereas *f* stood up for it	Dan 8:22	702
f kingdoms shall stand up out of	Dan 8:22	702
And in the *f* and twentieth day of	Dan 10:4	702
toward the *f* winds of heaven	Dan 11:4	702
of Damascus, and for *f*, I will not	Amos 1:3	702
transgressions of Gaza, and for *f*	Amos 1:6	702
transgressions of Tyrus, and for *f*	Amos 1:9	702
transgressions of Edom, and for *f*	Amos 1:11	702
the children of Ammon, and for *f*	Amos 1:13	702
transgressions of Moab, and for *f*	Amos 2:1	702
transgressions of Judah, and for *f*	Amos 2:4	702
of Israel, and for *f*, I will not	Amos 2:6	702
In the *f* and twentieth day of the	Hag 1:15	702
In the *f* and twentieth day of the	Hag 2:10	702
this day and upward, from the *f*	Hag 2:18	702
LORD came unto Haggai in the *f*	Hag 2:20	702
Upon the *f* and twentieth day of	Zec 1:7	702
eyes, and saw, and behold *f* horns	Zec 1:18	702
the LORD shewed me *f* carpenters	Zec 1:20	702
as the *f* winds of the heaven	Zec 2:6	702
there came *f* chariots out from	Zec 6:1	702
These are the *f* spirits of the	Zec 6:5	702
that did eat were *f* thousand men	Mt 15:38	5070
seven loaves of the *f* thousand	Mt 16:10	5070
his elect from the *f* winds	Mt 24:31	5064
the palsy, which was borne of *f*	Mk 2:3	5064
had eaten were about *f* thousand	Mk 8:9	5070
when the seven among *f* thousand	Mk 8:20	5070
his elect from the *f* winds	Mk 13:27	5064
f years, which departed not from	Lk 2:37	5064
not ye, There are yet *f* months	Jn 4:35	5072
lain in the grave *f* days already	Jn 11:17	5064
for he hath been dead *f* days	Jn 11:39	5066
made *f* parts, to every soldier a	Jn 19:23	5064
of men, about *f* hundred, joined	Acts 5:36	5064
entreat them evil *f* hundred years	Acts 7:6	5064
great sheet knit at the *f* corners	Acts 10:11	5064
F days ago I was fasting until	Acts 10:30	5067
let down from heaven by *f* corners	Acts 11:5	5064
delivered him to *f* quaternions of	Acts 12:4	5064
about the space of *f* hundred	Acts 13:20	5071
And the same man had *f* daughters	Acts 21:9	5064
We have *f* men which have a vow on	Acts 21:23	5064
f thousand men that were	Acts 21:38	5070
they cast *f* anchors out of the	Acts 27:29	5064
the law, which was *f* hundred	Gal 3:17	5071
And round about the throne were *f*	Rev 4:4	5064
and upon the seats I saw *f*	Rev 4:4	5064
were *f* beasts full of eyes before	Rev 4:6	5064
the *f* beasts had each of them six	Rev 4:8	5064
The *f* and twenty elders fall down	Rev 4:10	5064
of the throne and of the *f* beasts	Rev 5:6	5064
the *f* beasts and *f* and twenty	Rev 5:8	5064
And the *f* beasts said, Amen	Rev 5:14	5064
And the *f* and twenty elders fell	Rev 5:14	5064
one of the *f* beasts saying, Come	Rev 6:1	5064
in the midst of the *f* beasts say	Rev 6:6	5064
after these things I saw *f* angels	Rev 7:1	5064
on the *f* corners of the earth	Rev 7:1	5064
holding the *f* winds of the earth,	Rev 7:1	5064
with a loud voice to the *f* angels	Rev 7:2	5064
f thousand of all the tribes of	Rev 7:4	5064
the *f* beasts, and fell before the	Rev 7:11	5064
I heard a voice from the *f* horns	Rev 9:13	5064
Loose the *f* angels which are	Rev 9:14	5064
the *f* angels were loosed, which	Rev 9:15	5064
And the *f* and twenty elders, which	Rev 11:16	5064
f thousand, having his Father's	Rev 14:1	5064
throne, and before the *f* beasts	Rev 14:3	5064
f thousand, which were redeemed	Rev 14:3	5064
one of the *f* beasts gave unto the	Rev 15:7	5064
And the *f* and twenty elders and the	Rev 19:4	5064
the *f* beasts fell down and	Rev 19:4	5064
in the *f* quarters of the earth	Rev 20:8	5064
f cubits, according to the	Rev 21:17	5064

FOURFOLD

And he shall restore the lamb *f*	2Sa 12:6	706
false accusation, I restore him *f*	Lk 19:8	5073

FOURFOOTED

manner of *f* beasts of the earth	Acts 10:12	5074
saw *f* beasts of the earth, and	Acts 11:6	5074
f beasts, and creeping things	Rom 1:23	5074

FOURSCORE

And Abram was *f* and six years old,	Gen 16:16	8084
Isaac were an hundred and *f* years	Gen 35:28	8084
And Moses was *f* years old, and	Ex 7:7	8084
f years old, and Aaron *f*	Ex 7:7	8084
f thousand and six thousand and	Num 2:9	8084
thousand and five hundred and *f*	Num 4:48	8084
and now, lo, I am this day *f*	Josh 14:10	8084
And the land had rest *f* years	Judg 3:30	8084
priests, and slew on that day *f*	1Sa 22:18	8084
a very aged man, even *f* years old	2Sa 19:32	8084
I am this day *f* years old	2Sa 19:35	8084
and *f* thousand hewers in the	1Kin 5:15	8084

f thousand chosen men, which were	1Kin 12:21	8084
was sold for *f* pieces of silver	2Kin 6:25	8084
Jehu appointed *f* men without	2Kin 10:24	8084
of the Assyrians an hundred *f*	2Kin 19:35	8084
in all by their genealogies *f*	1Chr 7:5	8084
the chief, and his brethren *f*	1Chr 15:9	8084
were cunning, was two hundred *f*	1Chr 25:7	8084
f thousand to hew in the mountain	2Chr 2:2	8084
f thousand to be hewers in the	2Chr 2:18	8084
f thousand chosen men, which were	2Chr 11:1	8084
bows, two hundred and *f* thousand	2Chr 14:8	8084
him two hundred and *f* thousand	2Chr 17:15	8084
f thousand ready prepared for the	2Chr 17:18	8084
with him *f* priests of the LORD,	2Chr 26:17	8084
of Michael, and with him *f* males	Ezr 8:8	8084
and Netophah, an hundred *f*	Neh 7:26	8084
the holy city were two hundred *f*	Neh 11:18	8084
days, even an hundred and *f* days	Est 1:4	8084
of strength they be *f* years	Ps 90:10	8084
f concubines, and virgins without	Song 6:8	8084
of the Assyrians an hundred and *f*	Is 37:36	8084
and from Samaria, even *f* men	Jer 41:5	8084
And she was a widow of about *f*	Lk 2:37	*3589*
him, Take thy bill, and write *f*	Lk 16:7	*3589*

FOURSQUARE

the altar shall be *f*	Ex 27:1	7251
F it shall be being doubled	Ex 28:16	7251
breadth thereof; *f* shall it be	Ex 30:2	7251
of it a cubit; it was *f*	Ex 37:25	7251
the breadth thereof; it was *f*	Ex 38:1	7251
It was *f*; they made the	Ex 39:9	7251
gravings with their borders, *f*	1Kin 7:31	7251
and an hundred cubits broad, *f*	Eze 40:47	7251
shall offer the holy oblation *f*	Eze 48:20	7243
And the city lieth *f*, and the	Rev 21:16	*5068*

FOURTEEN

I served thee *f* years for thy two	Gen 31:41	
all the souls were *f*	Gen 46:22	
f thousand and six hundred	Num 1:27	
f thousand and six hundred	Num 2:4	
in the plague were *f* thousand	Num 16:49	
f lambs of the first year	Num 29:13	
deal to each lamb of the *f* lambs	Num 29:15	
f lambs of the first year without	Num 29:17	
f lambs of the first year without	Num 29:20	
f lambs of the first year without	Num 29:23	
f lambs of the first year without	Num 29:26	
f lambs of the first year without	Num 29:29	
f lambs of the first year without	Num 29:32	
f cities with their villages	Josh 15:36	
f cities with their villages	Josh 18:28	
days and seven days, even *f* days	1Kin 8:65	
And God gave to Heman *f* sons	1Chr 25:5	
waxed mighty, and married *f* wives	2Chr 13:21	
for he had *f* thousand sheep, and	Job 42:12	
the settle shall be *f* cubits long	Eze 43:17	
f broad in the four squares	Eze 43:17	
to David are *f* generations	Mt 1:17	*1180*
into Babylon are *f* generations	Mt 1:17	*1180*
unto Christ are *f* generations	Mt 1:17	*1180*
a man in Christ above *f* years ago	2Cor 12:2	*1180*
Then *f* years after I went up	Gal 2:1	*1180*

FOURTEENTH

in the *f* year came Chedorlaomer,	Gen 14:5	
until the *f* day of the same month	Ex 12:6	
on the *f* day of the month at even	Ex 12:18	
In the *f* day of the first month	Lev 23:5	
In the *f* day of this month, at	Num 9:3	
they kept the passover on the *f*	Num 9:5	
The *f* day of the second month at	Num 9:11	
in the *f* day of the first month	Num 28:16	
kept the passover on the *f* day of	Josh 5:10	
Now in the *f* year of king	2Kin 18:13	
to Huppah, the *f* to Jeshebeab,	1Chr 24:13	
The *f* to Mattithiah, he, his sons	1Chr 25:21	
on the *f* day of the second month	2Chr 30:15	
on the *f* day of the first month	2Chr 35:1	
upon the *f* day of the first month	Ezr 6:19	
the *f* day also of the month Adar	Est 9:15	
on the *f* day of the same rested	Est 9:17	
day thereof, and on the *f* thereof	Est 9:18	
made the *f* day of the month Adar	Est 9:19	
keep the *f* day of the month Adar	Est 9:21	
in the *f* year of king Hezekiah	Is 36:1	
in the *f* year after that the city	Eze 40:1	
in the *f* day of the month, ye	Eze 45:21	
But when the *f* night was come, as	Acts 27:27	*5065*
This day is the *f* day that ye	Acts 27:33	*5065*

FOURTH

and the morning were the *f* day	Gen 1:19	7243
And the *f* river is Euphrates	Gen 2:14	7243
But in the *f* generation they	Gen 15:16	7243
f generation of them that hate me	Ex 20:5	7256
the *f* row a beryl, and an onyx, and	Ex 28:20	7243
f part of an hin of beaten oil	Ex 29:40	7253
the *f* part of an hin of wine for	Ex 29:40	7243
the third and to the *f* generation	Ex 34:7	7256
And the *f* row, a beryl, an onyx,	Ex 39:13	7243
But in the *f* year all the fruit	Lev 19:24	7243
be of wine, the *f* part of a hin	Lev 23:13	7243
On the *f* day Elizur the son of	Num 7:30	7243
unto the third and *f* generation	Num 14:18	7256
with the *f* part of an hin of oil	Num 15:4	7243
the *f* part of an hin of wine for	Num 15:5	7243
number of the *f* part of Israel	Num 23:10	7255
mingled with the *f* part of an hin	Num 28:5	7243
offering thereof shall be the *f*	Num 28:7	7243
a *f* part of an hin unto a lamb	Num 28:14	7243
on the *f* day ten bullocks, two	Num 29:23	7243
f generation of them that hate me	Deut 5:9	7256
the *f* lot came out to Issachar,	Josh 19:17	7243
And it came to pass on the *f* day	Judg 19:5	7243
I have here at hand the *f* part of	1Sa 9:8	7253
And the *f*, Adonijah the son of	2Sa 3:4	7243
in the *f* year of Solomon's reign	1Kin 6:1	7243
olive tree, a *f* part of the wall	1Kin 6:33	7243
In the *f* year was the foundation	1Kin 6:37	7243
to reign over Judah in the *f* year	1Kin 22:41	702
the *f* part of a cab of dove's	2Kin 6:25	7255
thy children of the *f* generation	2Kin 10:30	7243
of Israel unto the *f* generation	2Kin 15:12	7243
in the *f* year of king Hezekiah	2Kin 18:9	7243
on the ninth day of the *f* month	2Kin 25:3	
Nethaneel the *f*, Raddai the fifth	1Chr 2:14	7243
the *f*, Adonijah the son of	1Chr 3:2	7243
the third Zedekiah, the *f* Shallum	1Chr 3:15	7243
Nohah the *f*, and Rapha the fifth	1Chr 8:2	7243
Mishmannah the *f*, Jeremiah the	1Chr 12:10	7243
the third, and Jekameam the *f*	1Chr 23:19	7243
third to Harim, the *f* to Seorim,	1Chr 24:8	7243
the third, Jekameam the *f*	1Chr 24:23	7243
The *f* to Izri, he, his sons, and	1Chr 25:11	7243
the third, Jathniel the *f*	1Chr 26:2	7243
Joah the third, and Sacar the *f*	1Chr 26:4	7243
the third, Zechariah the *f*	1Chr 26:11	7243
The *f* captain for the *f*	1Chr 27:7	7243
The *f* captain for the *f*	1Chr 27:7	7243
in the *f* year of his reign	2Chr 3:2	702
on the *f* day they assembled	2Chr 20:26	7243
Now on the *f* day was the silver	Ezr 8:33	7243
f day of this month the children	Neh 9:1	702
their God one *f* part of the day	Neh 9:3	7243
another *f* part they confessed, and	Neh 9:3	7243
f year of Jehoiakim the son of	Jer 25:1	7243
king of Judah, in the *f* year	Jer 28:1	7243
it came to pass in the *f* year of	Jer 36:1	7243
year of Zedekiah, in the *f* month	Jer 39:2	7243
in the *f* year of Jehoiakim the	Jer 45:1	7243
f year of Jehoiakim the son of	Jer 46:2	7243
in the *f* year of his reign	Jer 51:59	7243
And in the *f* month, in the ninth	Jer 52:6	7243
thirtieth year, in the *f* month	Eze 1:1	7243
the *f* the face of an eagle	Eze 10:14	7243
the *f* kingdom shall be strong as	Dan 2:40	7244
the form of the *f* is like the Son	Dan 3:25	7244
visions, and behold a *f* beast	Dan 7:7	7244
know the truth of the *f* beast	Dan 7:19	7244
The *f* beast shall be the *f*	Dan 7:23	7244
the *f* shall be far richer than	Dan 11:2	7243
in the *f* chariot grisled and bay	Zec 6:3	7243
pass in the *f* year of king Darius	Zec 7:1	702
in the *f* day of the ninth month	Zec 7:1	702
The fast of the *f* month, and the	Zec 8:19	7243
in the *f* watch of the night Jesus	Mt 14:25	*5067*
about the *f* watch of the night he	Mk 6:48	*5067*
the *f* beast was like a flying	Rev 4:7	*5067*
And when he had opened the *f* seal	Rev 6:7	*5067*
the voice of the *f* beast say	Rev 6:7	*5067*
them over the *f* part of the earth	Rev 6:8	*5067*
the *f* angel sounded, and the third	Rev 8:12	*5067*
the *f* angel poured out his vial	Rev 16:8	*5067*
the *f*, an emerald	Rev 21:19	*5067*

FOWL

f that may fly above the earth in	Gen 1:20	5775
every winged *f* after his kind	Gen 1:21	5775
let *f* multiply in the earth	Gen 1:22	5775
over the *f* of the air, and over	Gen 1:26	5775
over the *f* of the air, and over	Gen 1:28	5775
to every *f* of the air, and to	Gen 1:30	5775
the field, and every *f* of the air	Gen 2:19	5775
to the *f* of the air, and to every	Gen 2:20	5775
every *f* after his kind, every	Gen 7:14	5775
moved upon the earth, both of *f*	Gen 7:21	5775
things, and the *f* of the heaven	Gen 7:23	5775
thee, of all flesh, both of *f*	Gen 8:17	5775
every creeping thing, and every *f*	Gen 8:19	5775
clean beast, and of every clean *f*	Gen 8:20	5775
earth, and upon every *f* of the air	Gen 9:2	5775
that is with you, of the *f*	Gen 9:10	5775
whether it be of *f* or of beast	Lev 7:26	5775
law of the beasts, and of the *f*	Lev 11:46	5775
any beast or *f* that may be eaten	Lev 17:13	5775
abominable by beast, or by *f*	Lev 20:25	5775
winged *f* that flieth in the air	Deut 4:17	6833
and fallowdeer, and fatted *f*	1Kin 4:23	1257
he spake also of beasts, and of *f*	1Kin 4:33	5775
is a path which no *f* knoweth	Job 28:7	5861
The *f* of the air, and the fish of	Ps 8:8	6833
creeping things, and flying *f*	Ps 148:10	6833
both the *f* of the heavens and the	Jer 9:10	5775
shall dwell all *f* of every wing	Eze 17:23	6833
Speak unto every feathered *f*	Eze 39:17	6833
or torn, whether it be *f* or beast	Eze 44:31	5775
the back of it four wings of a *f*	Dan 7:6	5776

FOWLER

thee from the snare of the *f*	Ps 91:3	3353
as a bird from the hand of the *f*	Prov 6:5	3353
is a snare of a *f* in all his ways	Hos 9:8	3353

FOWLERS

a bird out of the snare of the *f*	Ps 124:7	3369

FOWLS

thing, and the *f* of the air	Gen 6:7	5775
Of *f* after their kind, and of	Gen 6:20	5775
Of *f* also of the air by sevens,	Gen 7:3	5775
that are not clean, and of *f*	Gen 7:8	5775
when the *f* came down upon the	Gen 15:11	5861
his offering to the LORD be of *f*	Lev 1:14	5775
have in abomination among the *f*	Lev 11:13	5775
All *f* that creep, going upon all	Lev 11:20	5775
and unclean, and between unclean *f*	Lev 20:25	5775
But of all clean *f* ye may eat	Deut 14:20	5775
be meat unto all *f* of the air	Deut 28:26	5775
thy flesh unto the *f* of the air	1Sa 17:44	5775
this day unto the *f* of the air	1Sa 17:46	5775
field shall the *f* of the air eat	1Kin 14:11	5775
fields shall the *f* of the air eat	1Kin 16:4	5775
field shall the *f* of the air eat	1Kin 21:24	5775
also *f* were prepared for me, and	Neh 5:18	6833
the *f* of the air, and they shall	Job 12:7	5775
kept close from the *f* of the air	Job 28:21	5775
us wiser than the *f* of heaven	Job 35:11	5775
I know all the *f* of the mountains	Ps 50:11	5775
feathered *f* like as the sand of	Ps 78:27	5775
be meat unto the *f* of the heaven	Ps 79:2	5775
By them shall the *f* of the heaven	Ps 104:12	5775
unto the *f* of the mountains	Is 18:6	5861
the *f* shall summer upon them, and	Is 18:6	5861
be meat for the *f* of the heaven	Jer 7:33	5775
the *f* of the heaven, and the	Jer 15:3	5775
shall be meat for the *f* of heaven	Jer 16:4	5775
be meat for the *f* of the heaven	Jer 19:7	5775
for meat unto the *f* of the heaven	Jer 34:20	5775
field and to the *f* of the heaven	Eze 29:5	5775
All the *f* of heaven made their	Eze 31:6	5775
all the *f* of the heaven remain	Eze 31:13	5775
will cause all the *f* of the	Eze 32:4	5775
the *f* of the heaven, and the	Eze 38:20	5775
the *f* of the heaven hath he given	Dan 2:38	5776
the *f* of the heaven dwelt in the	Dan 4:12	6853
it, and the *f* from his branches	Dan 4:14	6853
the *f* of the heaven had their	Dan 4:21	6853
with the *f* of heaven, and with the	Hos 2:18	5775
field, and with the *f* of heaven	Hos 4:3	5775
them down as the *f* of the heaven	Hos 7:12	5775
will consume the *f* of the heaven	Zeph 1:3	5775
Behold the *f* of the air	Mt 6:26	*4071*
the *f* came and devoured them up	Mt 13:4	*4071*
the *f* of the air came and devoured	Mk 4:4	*4071*
so that the *f* of the air may	Mk 4:32	*4071*
the *f* of the air devoured it	Lk 8:5	*4071*
more are ye better than the *f*	Lk 12:24	*4071*
the *f* of the air lodged in the	Lk 13:19	*4071*
creeping things, and *f* of the air	Acts 10:12	*4071*
creeping things, and *f* of the air	Acts 11:6	*4071*
saying to all the *f* that fly in	Rev 19:17	*3732*
all the *f* were filled with their	Rev 19:21	*3732*

FOX

if a *f* go up, he shall even break	Neh 4:3	7776
unto them, Go ye, and tell that *f*	Lk 13:32	*258*

FOXES

went and caught three hundred *f*	Judg 15:4	7776
they shall be a portion for *f*	Ps 63:10	7776
Take us the *f*, the little *f*,	Song 2:15	7776
Take us the *f*, the little *f*	Song 2:15	7776
is desolate, the *f* walk upon it	Lam 5:18	7776
are like the *f* in the deserts	Eze 13:4	7776
The *f* have holes, and the birds of	Mt 8:20	*258*
F have holes, and birds of the air	Lk 9:58	*258*

FRAGMENTS

they took up of the *f* that	Mt 14:20	*2801*
up twelve baskets full of the *f*	Mk 6:43	*2801*
many baskets full of *f* took ye up	Mk 8:19	*2801*
many baskets full of *f* took ye up	Mk 8:20	*2801*
there was taken up of *f* that	Lk 9:17	*2801*
Gather up the *f* that remain	Jn 6:12	*2801*
the *f* of the five barley loaves	Jn 6:13	*2801*

FRAIL

that I may know how *f* I am	Ps 39:4	2310

FRAME

for he could not *f* to pronounce	Judg 12:6	3559
For he knoweth our *f*	Ps 103:14	3336
I *f* evil against you, and devise a	Jer 18:11	3335
by which was as the *f* of a city	Eze 40:2	4011
They will not *f* their doings to	Hos 5:4	5414

FRAMED

or shall the thing *f* say of him	Is 29:16	3336
thing *f* say of him that *f* it	Is 29:16	3335
f together groweth unto an holy	Eph 2:21	*4883*
worlds were *f* by the word of God	Heb 11:3	*2675*

FRAMETH

to evil, and thy tongue *f* deceit	Ps 50:19	6775
which *f* mischief by a law	Ps 94:20	3335

FRANKINCENSE

these sweet spices with pure *f*	Ex 30:34	3828
oil upon it, and put *f* thereon	Lev 2:1	3828
thereof, with all the *f* thereof	Lev 2:2	3828
put oil upon it, and lay *f* thereon	Lev 2:15	3828
thereof, with all the *f* thereof	Lev 2:16	3828
shall he put any *f* thereon	Lev 5:11	3828
all the *f* which is upon the meat	Lev 6:15	3828
shalt put pure *f* upon each row	Lev 24:7	3828
no oil upon it, nor put *f* thereon	Num 5:15	3828
and the wine, and the oil, and the *f*	1Chr 9:29	3828
laid the meat offerings, the *f*	Neh 13:5	3828
with the meat offering and the *f*	Neh 13:9	3828
smoke, perfumed with myrrh and *f*	Song 3:6	3828
of myrrh, and to the hill of *f*	Song 4:6	3828
and cinnamon, with all trees of *f*	Song 4:14	3828
gold, and *f*, and myrrh	Mt 2:11	*3030*
and odours, and ointments, and *f*	Rev 18:13	*3030*

FRANKLY

to pay, he *f* forgave them both	Lk 7:42	*5435*

FRAUD

is full of cursing and deceit and *f*	Ps 10:7	8496
which is of you kept back by *f*	Jas 5:4	*650*

FRAY

and no man shall *f* them away	Deut 28:26	2729
and none shall *f* them away	Jer 7:33	2729
but these are come to *f* them	Zec 1:21	2729

FRECKLED
it is a f spot that groweth in ... Lev 13:39 933

FREE
he shall go out f for nothing ... Ex 21:2 2670
I will not go out f ... Ex 21:5 2670
shall she go out f without money ... Ex 21:11 2600
let him go f for his eye's sake ... Ex 21:26 2670
he shall let him go f for his ... Ex 21:27 2670
him f offerings every morning ... Ex 36:3 5071
to death, because she was not f ... Lev 19:20 2666
be thou f from this bitter water ... Num 5:19 5352
then she shall be f, and shall ... Num 5:28 5352
thou shalt let him go f from thee ... Deut 15:12 2670
thou sendest him out f from thee ... Deut 15:13 2670
thou sendest him away f from thee ... Deut 15:18 2670
but he shall be f at home one ... Deut 24:5 5355
his father's house f in Israel ... 1Sa 17:25 2670
remaining in the chambers were f ... 1Chr 9:33 6362
as many as were of a f heart ... 2Chr 29:31 5081
the servant is f from his master ... Job 3:19 2670
Who hath sent out the wild ass f ... Job 39:5 2670
and uphold me with thy f spirit ... Ps 51:12 5082
F among the dead, like the slain ... Ps 88:5 2670
of the people, and let him go f ... Ps 105:20 6605
and to let the oppressed go f ... Is 58:6 2670
an Hebrew or an Hebrewess, go f ... Jer 34:9 2670
every one his maidservant, go f ... Jer 34:10 2670
handmaids, whom they had let go f ... Jer 34:11 2670
thou shalt let him go f from thee ... Jer 34:14 2670
and publish the f offerings ... Amos 4:5 5071
or his mother, he shall be f ... Mt 15:6
unto him, Then are the children f ... Mt 17:26 1658
he shall be f ... Mk 7:11
and the truth shall make you f ... Jn 8:32 1659
sayest thou, Ye shall be made f ... Jn 8:33 1658
Son therefore shall make you f ... Jn 8:36 1659
ye shall be f indeed ... Jn 8:36 1658
And Paul said, But I was f born ... Acts 22:28 1658
offence, so also is the f gift ... Rom 5:15 5486
but the f gift is of many ... Rom 5:16 5486
the f gift came upon all men unto ... Rom 5:18
Being then made f from sin ... Rom 6:18 1659
ye were f from righteousness ... Rom 6:20 1658
But now being made f from sin ... Rom 6:22 1659
be dead, she is f from that law ... Rom 7:3 1658
made me f from the law of sin ... Rom 8:2 1659
but if thou mayest be made f ... 1Cor 7:21 1658
also he that is called, being f ... 1Cor 7:22 1658
am I not f? ... 1Cor 9:1 1658
For though I be f from all men ... 1Cor 9:19 1658
Gentiles, whether we be bond or f ... 1Cor 12:13 1658
there is neither bond nor f ... Gal 3:28 1658
But Jerusalem which is above is f ... Gal 4:26 1658
heir with the son of the f woman ... Gal 4:30 1658
of the bondwoman, but of the f ... Gal 4:31 1658
wherewith Christ hath made us f ... Gal 5:1 1659
the Lord, whether he be bond or f ... Eph 6:8 1658
Barbarian, Scythian, bond nor f ... Col 3:11 1658
of the Lord may have f course ... 2Th 3:1
As f, and not using your liberty ... 1Pet 2:16 1658
and every bondman, and every f man ... Rev 6:15 1658
small and great, rich and poor, f ... Rev 13:16 1658
and the flesh of all men, both f ... Rev 19:18 1658

FREED
of you be f from being bondmen ... Josh 9:23 3772
For he that is dead is f from sin ... Rom 6:7 1344

FREEDMEN See LIBERTINES.

FREEDOM
at all redeemed, nor f given her ... Lev 19:20 2668
a great sum obtained I this f ... Acts 22:28 4174

FREELY
of the garden thou mayest f eat ... Gen 2:16
fish, which we did eat in Egypt f ... Num 11:5 2600
f to day of the spoil of their ... 1Sa 14:30
offered f for the house of God to ... Ezr 2:68
his counsellors have f offered ... Ezr 7:15
I will f sacrifice unto thee ... Ps 54:6 5071
backsliding, I will love them f ... Hos 14:4 5071
f ye have received, f give ... Mt 10:8 1432
f ye have received, f give ... Mt 10:8 1432
let me f speak unto you of the ... Acts 2:29
before whom also I speak f ... Acts 26:26 3955
Being justified f by his grace ... Rom 3:24 1432
him also f give us all things ... Rom 8:32
that are f given to us of God ... 1Cor 2:12
to you the gospel of God f ... 2Cor 11:7 1432
fountain of the water of life f ... Rev 21:6 1432
let him take the water of life f ... Rev 22:17 1432

FREEMAN
being a servant, is the Lord's f ... 1Cor 7:22 558

FREEWILL
vows, and for all his f offerings ... Lev 22:18 5071
or a f offering in beeves or ... Lev 22:21 5071
thou offer for a f offering ... Lev 22:23 5071
and beside all your f offerings ... Lev 23:38 5071
or in a f offering, or in your ... Num 15:3 5071
your f offerings, for your burnt ... Num 29:39 5071
vows, and your f offerings, and the ... Deut 12:6 5071
nor thy f offerings, or heave ... Deut 12:17 5071
of a f offering of thine hand ... Deut 16:10 5071
even a f offering, according as ... Deut 23:23 5071
was over the f offerings of God, ... 2Chr 31:14 5071
beside the f offering for the ... Ezr 1:4 5071
a f offering unto the LORD ... Ezr 3:5 5071
their own f to go up to Jerusalem ... Ezr 7:13 5069
with the f offering of the people ... Ezr 7:16 5069
the gold are a f offering unto ... Ezr 8:28 5071
the f offerings of my mouth, O ... Ps 119:108 5071

FREEWOMAN
by a bondmaid, the other by a f ... Gal 4:22 1658
but he of the f was by promise ... Gal 4:23 1658

FREQUENT
above measure, in prisons more f ... 2Cor 11:23 4056

FRESH
of it was as the taste of f oil ... Num 11:8 3955
My glory was f in me, and my bow ... Job 29:20 2319
I shall be anointed with f oil ... Ps 92:10 7488
both yield salt water and f ... Jas 3:12 1099

FRESHER
flesh shall be f than a child's ... Job 33:25 7375

FRET
it is f inward, whether it be ... Lev 13:55 6356
her sore, for to make her f ... 1Sa 1:6 7481
F not thyself because of ... Ps 37:1 2734
f not thyself because of him who ... Ps 37:7 2734
f not thyself in any wise to do ... Ps 37:8 2734
F not thyself because of evil men ... Prov 24:19 2734
hungry, they shall f themselves ... Is 8:21 7107

FRETTED
but hast f me in all these things ... Eze 16:43 7264

FRETTETH
his heart f against the LORD ... Prov 19:3 2196

FRETTING
the plague is a f leprosy ... Lev 13:51 3992
for it is a f leprosy ... Lev 13:52 3992
it is a f leprosy in the house ... Lev 14:44 3992

FRIED
with oil, of fine flour, f ... Lev 7:12 7246
the pan, and for that which is f ... 1Chr 23:29 7246

FRIEND
his f Hirah the Adullamite ... Gen 38:12 7453
the hand of his f the Adullamite ... Gen 38:20 7453
as a man speaketh unto his f ... Ex 33:11 7453
the wife of thy bosom, or thy f ... Deut 13:6 7453
whom he had used as his f ... Judg 14:20 7462
But Amnon had a f, whose name was ... 2Sa 13:3 7453
So Hushai David's f came into the ... 2Sa 15:37 7463
Hushai the Archite, David's f ... 2Sa 16:16 7463
Is this thy kindness to thy f ... 2Sa 16:17 7453
why wentest thou not with thy f ... 2Sa 16:17 7453
officer, and the king's f ... 1Kin 4:5 7463
seed of Abraham thy f for ever ... 2Chr 20:7 157
pity should be shewed from his f ... Job 6:14 7453
and ye dig a pit for your f ... Job 6:27 7451
he had been my f or brother ... Ps 35:14 7453
Yea, mine own familiar f, in whom ... Ps 41:9
f hast thou put far from me, and ... Ps 88:18 7453
son, if thou be surety for thy f ... Prov 6:1 7453
art come into the hand of thy f ... Prov 6:3 7453
thyself, and make sure thy f ... Prov 6:3 7453
A f loveth at all times, and a ... Prov 17:17 7453
surety in the presence of his f ... Prov 17:18 7453
there is a f that sticketh closer ... Prov 18:24 157
every man is a f to him that ... Prov 19:6 7453
his lips the king shall be his f ... Prov 22:11 7453
Faithful are the wounds of a f ... Prov 27:6 157
of a man's f by hearty counsel ... Prov 27:9 7453
Thine own f, and thy father's ... Prov 27:10 7453
own f, and thy father's f ... Prov 27:10 7453
blesseth his f with a loud voice ... Prov 27:14 7453
the countenance of his f ... Prov 27:17 7453
is my beloved, and this is my f ... Song 5:16 7453
chosen, the seed of Abraham my f ... Is 41:8 157
neighbour and his f shall perish ... Jer 6:21 7453
the flesh of his f in the siege ... Jer 19:9 7453
love a woman beloved of her f ... Hos 3:1 7453
Trust ye not in a f, put ye not ... Mic 7:5 7453
a f of publicans and sinners ... Mt 11:19 5384
answered one of them, and said, F ... Mt 20:13 2083
And he saith unto him, F, how ... Mt 22:12 2083
And Jesus said unto him, F ... Mt 26:50 2083
a f of publicans and sinners ... Lk 7:34 5384
them, Which of you shall have a f ... Lk 11:5 5384
at midnight, and say unto him, F ... Lk 11:5 5384
For a f of mine in his journey is ... Lk 11:6 5384
and give him, because he is his f ... Lk 11:8 5384
cometh, he may say unto thee, F ... Lk 14:10 5384
but the f of the bridegroom ... Jn 3:29 5384
unto them, Our f Lazarus sleepeth ... Jn 11:11 5384
man go, thou art not Caesar's f ... Jn 19:12 5384
the king's chamberlain their f ... Acts 12:20 3982
and he was called the F of God ... Jas 2:23 5384
a f of the world is the enemy of ... Jas 4:4 5384

FRIENDLY
after her, to speak f unto her ... Judg 19:3 3820
hast spoken f unto thine handmaid ... Ruth 2:13 3820
hath friends must shew himself f ... Prov 18:24 7489

FRIENDS
Gerar, and Ahuzzath one of his f ... Gen 26:26 4828
elders of Judah, even to his f ... 1Sa 30:26 7453
to his brethren, and to his f ... 2Sa 3:8 4828
thine enemies, and hatest thy f ... 2Sa 19:6 157
of his kinsfolks, nor of his f ... 1Kin 16:11 7453
home, he sent and called for his f ... Est 5:10 157
all his f unto him, Let a gallows ... Est 5:14 157
all his f every thing that had ... Est 6:13 157
Now when Job's three f heard of ... Job 2:11 7453
My f scorn me ... Job 16:20 7453
that speaketh flattery to his f ... Job 17:5 7453
my familiar f have forgotten me ... Job 19:14
All my inward f abhorred me ... Job 19:19 4962
me, have pity upon me, O ye my f ... Job 19:21 7453
his three f was his wrath kindled ... Job 32:3 7453
thee, and against thy two f ... Job 42:7 7453
of Job, when he prayed for his f ... Job 42:10 7453
my f stand aloof from my sore ... Ps 38:11 7453
but the rich hath many f ... Prov 14:20 157
and a whisperer separateth chief f ... Prov 16:28 441
a matter separateth very f ... Prov 17:9 441
A man that hath f must shew ... Prov 18:24 7453
Wealth maketh many f ... Prov 19:4 7453
more do his f go far from him ... Prov 19:7 4828
eat, O f; drink, yea ... Song 5:1 7453
to thyself, and to all thy f ... Jer 20:4 157
buried there, thou, and all thy f ... Jer 20:6 157
Thy f have set thee on, and have ... Jer 38:22
all her f have dealt ... Lam 1:2 7453
was wounded in the house of my f ... Zec 13:6 157
when his f heard of it, they went ... Mk 3:21
saith unto him, Go home to thy f ... Mk 5:19 4674
the centurion sent f to him ... Lk 7:6 5384
And I say unto you my f, Be not ... Lk 12:4 5384
or a supper, call not thy f ... Lk 14:12 5384
home, he calleth together his f ... Lk 15:6 5384
hath found it, she calleth her f ... Lk 15:9 5384
that I might make merry with my f ... Lk 15:29 5384
to yourselves f of the mammon of ... Lk 16:9 5384
and brethren, and kinsfolks, and f ... Lk 21:16 5384
and Herod were made f together ... Lk 23:12 5384
a man lay down his life for his f ... Jn 15:13 5384
Ye are my f, if ye do whatsoever ... Jn 15:14 5384
but I have called you f ... Jn 15:15 5384
together his kinsmen and near f ... Acts 10:24 5384
chief of Asia, which were his f ... Acts 19:31 5384
go unto his f to refresh himself ... Acts 27:3 5384
Our f salute thee ... 3Jn 14 5384
Greet the f by name ... 3Jn 14 5384

FRIENDSHIP
Make no f with an angry man ... Prov 22:24 7462
know ye not that the f of the ... Jas 4:4 5373

FRINGE
that they put upon the f of the ... Num 15:38 6734
And it shall be unto you for a f ... Num 15:39 6734

FRINGES
them f in the borders of their ... Num 15:38 6734
Thou shalt make thee f upon the ... Deut 22:12 1434

FRO
a raven, which went forth to and f ... Gen 8:7 7725
and walked in the house to and f ... 2Kin 4:35
f throughout the whole earth, to ... 2Chr 16:9 7751
f in the earth, and from walking ... Job 1:7 7751
f in the earth, and from walking ... Job 2:2 7751
f unto the dawning of the day ... Job 7:4
thou break a leaf driven to and f ... Job 13:25
They reel to and f, and stagger ... Ps 107:27
f of them that seek death ... Prov 21:6
f like a drunkard, and shall be ... Is 24:20
f of locusts shall he run upon ... Is 33:4
a captive, and removing to and f ... Is 49:21
ye to and f through the streets of ... Jer 5:1 7751
and run to and f by the hedges ... Jer 49:3 7751
to and f occupied in thy fairs ... Eze 27:19 235
many shall run to and f, and ... Dan 12:4 7751
shall run to and f in the city ... Joel 2:9 8264
f to seek the word of the LORD, ... Amos 8:12 7751
to walk to and f through the earth ... Zec 1:10
f through the earth, and, behold, ... Zec 1:11
f through the whole earth ... Zec 4:10 7751
walk to and f through the earth ... Zec 6:7
walk to and f through the earth ... Zec 6:7
walked to and f through the earth ... Zec 6:7
no more children, tossed to and f ... Eph 4:14 2831

FROGS
will smite all thy borders with f ... Ex 8:2 6854
shall bring forth f abundantly ... Ex 8:3 6854
the f shall come up both on thee, ... Ex 8:4 6854
cause f to come up upon the land ... Ex 8:5 6854
the f came up, and covered the ... Ex 8:6 6854
brought up f upon the land of ... Ex 8:7 6854
he may take away the f from me ... Ex 8:8 6854
to destroy the f from thee ... Ex 8:9 6854
the f shall depart from thee, and ... Ex 8:11 6854
f which he had brought against ... Ex 8:12 6854
the f died out of the houses, out ... Ex 8:13 6854
and f, which destroyed them ... Ps 78:45 6854
land brought forth f in abundance ... Ps 105:30 6854
f come out of the mouth of the ... Rev 16:13 944

FROM See PREFACE.

FRONT
When Joab saw that the f of the ... 2Sa 10:9 6440
that was in the f of the house ... 2Chr 3:4 6440

FRONTIERS
his cities which are on his f ... Eze 25:9 7097

FRONTLETS
hand, and for f between thine eyes ... Ex 13:16 2903
they shall be as f between thine ... Deut 6:8 2903
may be as f between your eyes ... Deut 11:18 2903

FROST
consumed me, and the f by night ... Gen 31:40 7140
small as the hoar f on the ground ... Ex 16:14 3713
By the breath of God f is given ... Job 37:10 7140
and the hoary f of heaven, who ... Job 38:29 3713
and their sycomore trees with f ... Ps 78:47 2602
scattereth the hoar f like ashes ... Ps 147:16 3713
heat, and in the night to the f ... Jer 36:30 7140

FROWARD
for they are a very f generation ... Deut 32:20 8419
with the f thou wilt shew thyself ... 2Sa 22:27 6141
the counsel of the f is carried ... Job 5:13 6617
thyself pure; and with the f ... Ps 18:26 6141
thou wilt shew thyself f ... Ps 18:26 6617
A f heart shall depart from me ... Ps 101:4 6141
the man that speaketh f things ... Prov 2:12 8419
crooked, and they f in their paths ... Prov 2:15 3868

For the f is abomination to the Prov 3:32 3868
Put away from thee a f mouth Prov 4:24 6143
man, walketh with a f mouth Prov 6:12 6143
there is nothing f or perverse in Prov 8:8 6617
way, and the f mouth, do I hate Prov 8:13 8419
but the f tongue shall be cut out Prov 10:31 8419
They that are of a f heart are Prov 11:20 6141
A f man soweth strife Prov 16:28 8419
his eyes to devise f things Prov 16:30 8419
He that hath a f heart findeth no Prov 17:20 6141
The way of man is f and strange Prov 21:8 2019
and snares are in the way of the f Prov 22:5 6141
good and gentle, but also to the f 1Pet 2:18 4646

FROWARDLY
he went on f in the way of his Is 57:17 7726

FROWARDNESS
and delight in the f of the wicked Prov 2:14 8419
F is in his heart, he deviseth Prov 6:14 8419
mouth of the wicked speaketh f Prov 10:32 8419

FROZEN
and the face of the deep is f Job 38:30 3920

FRUIT
the f tree yielding f after Gen 1:11 6529
his kind, and the tree yielding f Gen 1:12 6529
in the which is the f of a tree Gen 1:29 6529
We may eat of the f of the trees Gen 3:2 6529
But of the f of the tree which is Gen 3:3 6529
wise, she took of the f thereof Gen 3:6 6529
that Cain brought of the f of the Gen 4:3 6529
from thee the f of the womb Gen 30:2 6529
all the f of the trees which the Ex 10:15 6529
so that her f depart from her, and Ex 21:22 3206
then ye shall count the f thereof Lev 19:23 6529
But in the fourth year all the f Lev 19:24 6529
shall ye eat of the f thereof Lev 19:25 6529
gathered in the f of the land Lev 23:39 8393
and gather in the f thereof Lev 25:3 8393
And the land shall yield her f Lev 25:19 6529
bring forth f for three years Lev 25:21 8393
eat yet of old f until the ninth Lev 25:22 8393
of the field shall yield their f Lev 26:4 6529
or of the f of the tree, is the Lev 27:30 6529
and bring of the f of the land Num 13:20 6529
and shewed them the f of the land Num 13:26 6529
and this is the f of it Num 13:27 6529
they took of the f of the land in Deut 1:25 6529
will also bless the f of thy womb Deut 7:13 6529
the f of thy land, thy corn, and Deut 7:13 6529
and that the land yield not her f Deut 11:17 2981
lest the f of thy seed which thou Deut 22:9 4395
the f of thy vineyard, be defiled Deut 22:9 8393
first of all the f of the earth Deut 26:2 6529
shall be the f of thy body Deut 28:4 6529
the f of thy ground, and the f Deut 28:4 6529
the f of thy cattle, the increase Deut 28:4 6529
in the f of thy body, and in the Deut 28:11 6529
in the f of thy cattle, and in the Deut 28:11 6529
in the f of thy ground, in the Deut 28:11 6529
Cursed shall be the f of thy body Deut 28:18 6529
the f of thy land, the increase Deut 28:18 6529
The f of thy land, and all thy Deut 28:33 6529
for thine olive shall cast his f Deut 28:40
f of thy land shall the locust Deut 28:42 6529
he shall eat the f of thy cattle Deut 28:51 6529
the f of thy land, until thou be Deut 28:51 6529
shalt eat the f of thine own body Deut 28:53 6529
in the f of thy body Deut 30:9 6529
in the f of thy cattle Deut 30:9 6529
in the f of thy land, for good Deut 30:9 6529
but they did eat of the f of the Josh 5:12 8393
my sweetness, and my good f Judg 9:11 8570
summer f for the young men to eat 2Sa 16:2
root downward, and bear f upward 2Kin 19:30 6529
and f trees in abundance Neh 9:25 3978
our fathers to eat the f thereof Neh 9:36 6529
firstfruits of all f of all trees Neh 10:35 6529
the f of all manner of trees, of Neh 10:37 6529
forth his f in his season Ps 1:3 6529
Their f shalt thou destroy from Ps 21:10 6529
the f thereof shall shake like Ps 72:16 6529
still bring forth f in old age Ps 92:14 5107
satisfied with the f of thy works Ps 104:13 6529
devoured the f of their ground Ps 105:35 6529
the f of the womb is his reward Ps 127:3 6529
Of the f of thy body will I set Ps 132:11 6529
eat of the f of their own way Prov 1:31 6529
My f is better than gold, yea, Prov 8:19 6529
the f of the wicked to sin Prov 10:16 8393
The f of the righteous is a tree Prov 11:30 6529
root of the righteous yieldeth f Prov 12:12
with good by the f of his mouth Prov 12:14 6529
eat good by the f of his mouth Prov 13:2 6529
satisfied with the f of his mouth Prov 18:20 6529
love it shall eat the f thereof Prov 18:21 6529
fig tree shall eat the f thereof Prov 27:18 6529
with the f of her hands she Prov 31:16 6529
Give her of the f of her hands Prov 31:31 6529
his f was sweet to my taste Song 2:3 6529
every one for the f thereof was Song 8:11 6529
keep the f thereof two hundred Song 8:12 6529
shall eat the f of their doings Is 3:10 6529
the f of the earth shall be Is 4:2 6529
I will punish the f of the stout Is 10:12 6529
have no pity on the f of the womb Is 13:18 6529
his f shall be a fiery flying Is 14:29 6529
fill the face of the world with f Is 27:6 8570
this is all the f to take away Is 27:9 6529
as the hasty f before the summer Is 28:4 1061
vineyards, and eat the f thereof Is 37:30 6529
root downward, and bear f upward Is 37:31 6529
I create the f of the lips Is 57:19 5108
vineyards, and eat the f of them Is 65:21 6529
country, to eat the f thereof Jer 2:7 6529
even the f of their thoughts, Jer 6:19 6529
and upon the f of the ground Jer 7:20 6529
olive tree, fair, and of goodly f Jer 11:16 6529
the tree with the f thereof Jer 11:19 3899
grow, yea, they bring forth f Jer 12:2 6529
shall cease from yielding f Jer 17:8 6529
according to the f of his doings Jer 17:10 6529
according to the f of your doings Jer 21:14 6529
gardens, and eat the f of them Jer 29:5 6529
gardens, and eat the f of them Jer 29:28 6529
according to the f of his doings Jer 32:19 6529
Shall the women eat their f Lam 2:20 6529
branches, and that it might bear f Eze 17:8 6529
thereof, and cut off the f thereof Eze 17:9 6529
bring forth boughs, and bear f Eze 17:23 6529
and the east wind dried up her f Eze 19:12 6529
which hath devoured her f Eze 19:14 6529
they shall eat thy f, and they Eze 25:4 6529
of the field shall yield her f Eze 34:27 6529
yield your f to my people of Eze 36:8 6529
and they shall increase and bring f Eze 36:11 6509
I will multiply the f of the tree Eze 36:30 6529
neither shall the f thereof be Eze 47:12 6529
new f according to his months Eze 47:12 1061
the f thereof shall be for meat, Eze 47:12 6529
the f thereof much, and in it was Dan 4:12 4
off his leaves, and scatter his f Dan 4:14 4
the f thereof much, and in it was Dan 4:21 4
is dried up, they shall bear no f Hos 9:16 6529
even the beloved f of their womb Hos 9:16
he bringeth forth f unto himself Hos 10:1 6529
to the multitude of his f he hath Hos 10:1 6529
ye have eaten the f of lies Hos 10:13 6529
From me is thy f found Hos 14:8 6529
for the tree beareth her f Joel 2:22 6529
yet I destroyed his f from above Amos 2:9 6529
the f of righteousness into Amos 6:12 6529
and a gatherer of sycomore f Amos 7:14
and behold a basket of summer f Amos 8:1
And I said, A basket of summer f Amos 8:2
gardens, and eat the f of them Amos 9:14 6529
the f of my body for the sin of Mic 6:7 6529
my soul desired the firstripe f Mic 7:1
for the f of their doings Mic 7:13 6529
neither shall f be in the vines Hab 3:17 2981
and the earth is stayed from her f Hag 1:10 2981
the vine shall give her f Zec 8:12 6529
the f thereof, even his meat, is Mal 1:12 5108
shall your vine cast her f before Mal 3:11 7920
not forth good f is hewn down Mt 3:10 2590
good tree bringeth forth good f Mt 7:17 2590
tree bringeth forth evil f Mt 7:17 2590
tree cannot bring forth evil f Mt 7:18 2590
a corrupt tree bring forth good f Mt 7:18 2590
not forth good f is hewn down Mt 7:19 2590
make the tree good, and his f good Mt 12:33 2590
tree corrupt, and his f corrupt Mt 12:33 2590
for the tree is known by his f Mt 12:33 2590
good ground, and brought forth f Mt 13:8 2590
which also beareth f, and bringeth Mt 13:23 2592
was sprung up, and brought forth f Mt 13:26 2590
unto it, Let no f grow on thee Mt 21:19 2590
when the time of the f drew near Mt 21:34 2590
henceforth of this f of the vine Mt 26:29 1081
and choked it, and it yielded no f Mk 4:7 2590
did yield f that sprang up and Mk 4:8 2590
and receive it, and bring forth f Mk 4:20 2592
earth bringeth forth f of herself Mk 4:28 2592
But when the f is brought forth, Mk 4:29 2590
No man eat f of thee hereafter Mk 11:14 2590
of the f of the vineyard Mk 12:2 2590
no more of the f of the vine Mk 14:25 1081
and blessed is the f of thy womb Lk 1:42 2590
not forth good f is hewn down Lk 3:9 2590
tree bringeth not forth corrupt f Lk 6:43 2590
a corrupt tree bring forth good f Lk 6:43 2590
every tree is known by his own f Lk 6:44 2590
up, and bare f an hundredfold Lk 8:8 2590
life, and bring no f to perfection Lk 8:14 5052
bring forth f with patience Lk 8:15 2592
sought f thereon, and found none Lk 13:6 2590
I come seeking f on this fig tree Lk 13:7 2590
And if it bear f, well Lk 13:9 2590
give him of the f of the vineyard Lk 20:10 2590
not drink of the f of the vine Lk 22:18 1081
gathereth f unto life eternal Jn 4:36 2590
it die, it bringeth forth much f Jn 12:24 2590
that beareth not f he taketh away Jn 15:2 2590
and every branch that beareth f Jn 15:2 2590
that it may bring forth more f Jn 15:2 2590
branch cannot bear f of itself Jn 15:4 2590
the same bringeth forth much f Jn 15:5 2590
glorified, that ye bear much f Jn 15:8 2590
ye should go and bring forth f Jn 15:16 2590
that your f should remain Jn 15:16 2590
that of the f of his loins, Acts 2:30 2590
might have some f among you also Rom 1:13 2590
What f had ye then in those Rom 6:21 2590
ye have your f unto holiness, and Rom 6:22 2590
we should bring forth f unto God Rom 7:4 2592
to bring forth f unto death Rom 7:5 2592
and have sealed to them this f Rom 15:28 2590
and eateth not of the f thereof 1Cor 9:7 2590
But the f of the Spirit is love, Gal 5:22 2590
(For the f of the Spirit is in Eph 5:9 2590
this is the f of my labour Phil 1:22 2590
but I desire f that may abound to Phil 4:17 2590
and bringeth forth f, as it doth Col 1:6 2592
it yieldeth the peaceable f of Heb 12:11 2590
the f of our lips giving thanks Heb 13:15 2590
the f of righteousness is sown in Jas 3:18 2590
for the precious f of the earth Jas 5:7 2590
and the earth brought forth her f Jas 5:18 2590
trees whose f withereth, without Jude 12 5352
whose f withereth, without f Jude 12 175
and yielded her f every month Rev 22:2 2590

FRUITFUL
And God blessed them, saying, Be f Gen 1:22 6509
them, and God said unto them, Be f Gen 1:28 6509
abundantly in the earth, and be f Gen 8:17 6509
his sons, and said unto them, Be f Gen 9:1 6509
And you, be ye f, and multiply Gen 9:7 6509
And I will make thee exceeding f Gen 17:6 6509
blessed him, and will make him f Gen 17:20 6509
us, and we shall be f in the land Gen 26:22 6509
bless thee, and make thee f Gen 28:3 6509
be f and multiply Gen 35:11 6509
be f in the land of my affliction Gen 41:52 6509
me, Behold, I will make thee f Gen 48:4 6509
Joseph is a f bough Gen 49:22 6509
even a f bough by a well Gen 49:22 6509
And the children of Israel were f Ex 1:7 6509
respect unto you, and make you f Lev 26:9 6509
A f land into barrenness, for the Ps 107:34 6529
Thy wife shall be as a f vine by Ps 128:3 6509
f trees, and all cedars Ps 148:9 6529
hath a vineyard in a very f hill Is 5:1
of his forest, and of his f field Is 10:18 3759
in the outmost f branches thereof Is 17:6 6509
shall be turned into a f field Is 29:17 3759
the f field shall be esteemed as Is 29:17 3759
pleasant fields, for the f vine Is 32:12 6509
and the wilderness be a f field Is 32:15 3759
the f field be counted for a Is 32:15 3759
remain in the f field Is 32:16 3759
the f place was a wilderness, and Jer 4:26 3759
and they shall be f and increase Jer 23:3 6509
land, and planted it in a f field Eze 17:5 2233
she was f and full of branches by Eze 19:10 6509
Though he be f among his brethren Hos 13:15 6500
f seasons, filling our hearts Acts 14:17 2593
being f in every good work, and Col 1:10 2592

FRUITS
take of the best f in the land in Gen 43:11 2173
to offer the first of thy ripe f Ex 22:29 4395
and shalt gather in the f thereof Ex 23:10 8393
with the bread of the first f for Lev 23:20 1061
of the f he shall sell unto thee Lev 25:15 8393
of the f doth he sell unto thee Lev 25:16 8393
until her f come in ye shall eat Lev 25:22 8393
trees of the land yield their f Lev 26:20 6529
for the precious f brought forth Deut 33:14 8393
him, and thou shalt bring in the f 2Sa 9:10
and an hundred of summer f 2Sa 16:1
all the f of the field since the 2Kin 8:6 8393
vineyards, and eat the f thereof 2Kin 19:29 6529
If I have eaten the f thereof Job 31:39 3581
which may yield f of increase Ps 107:37 6529
trees in them of all kind of f Eccl 2:5 6529
of pomegranates, with pleasant f Song 4:13 6529
his garden, and eat his pleasant f Song 4:16 6529
nuts to see the f of the valley Song 6:11 3
are all manner of pleasant f Song 7:13
for the shouting for thy summer f Is 16:9
and Carmel shake off their f Is 33:9
ye, gather ye wine, and summer f Jer 40:10
wine and summer f very much Jer 40:12
is fallen upon thy summer f Jer 48:32
for want of the f of the field Lam 4:9 8570
they have gathered the summer f Mic 7:1
not destroy the f of your ground Mal 3:11 6529
therefore f meet for repentance Mt 3:8 2590
Ye shall know them by their f Mt 7:16 2590
by their f ye shall know them Mt 7:20 2590
they might receive the f of it Mt 21:34 2590
render him the f in their seasons Mt 21:41 2590
bringing forth the f thereof Mt 21:43 2590
therefore f worthy of repentance Lk 3:8 2590
have no room where to bestow my f Lk 12:17 2590
and there will I bestow all my f Lk 12:18 1081
sown, and increase the f of your 2Cor 9:10 1081
with the f of righteousness Phil 1:11 2590
must be first partaker of the f 2Ti 2:6 2590
full of mercy and good f, without Jas 3:17 2590
the f that thy soul lusted after Rev 18:14 3703
which bare twelve manner of f Rev 22:2 2590

FRUSTRATE
to f their purpose, all the days Ezr 4:5 656
I do not f the grace of God Gal 2:21 114

FRUSTRATETH
That f the tokens of the liars, Is 44:25 6565

FRYING
meat offering baken in the f pan Lev 2:7 4802

FRYINGPAN
and all that is dressed in the f Lev 7:9 4802

FUEL
be with burning and f of fire Is 9:5 3980
shall be as the f of the fire Is 9:19 3980
it is cast into the fire for f Eze 15:4 402
I have given to the fire for f Eze 15:6 402
Thou shalt be for f to the fire Eze 21:32 402

FUGITIVE
a f and a vagabond shalt thou be Gen 4:12 5128
and I shall be a f and a vagabond Gen 4:14 5128

FUGITIVES
Ye Gileadites are f of Ephraim Judg 12:4 6412
the f that fell away to the king 2Kin 25:11 5307
his f shall flee unto Zoar, an Is 15:5 1280
all his f with all his bands Eze 17:21 4015

FULFIL
F her week, and we will give thee Gen 29:27 4390
F your works, your daily tasks, Ex 5:13 3615

the number of thy days I will *f* Ex 23:26 4390
that he might *f* the word of the 1Kin 2:27 4390
takest heed to *f* the statutes 1Chr 22:13 6213
To *f* the word of the LORD by the 2Chr 36:21 4390
to *f* threescore and ten years 2Chr 36:21 4390
number the months that they *f* Job 39:2
own heart, and *f* all thy counsel Ps 20:4 4390
the LORD *f* all thy petitions Ps 20:5 4390
He will *f* the desire of them that Ps 145:19 6213
us to *f* all righteousness Mt 3:15 4137
am not come to destroy, but to *f* Mt 5:17 4137
heart, which shall *f* all my will Acts 13:22 4160
if it *f* the law, judge thee, who Rom 2:27 5055
the flesh, to *f* the lusts thereof Rom 13:14
ye shall not *f* the lust of the Gal 5:16 5055
and so *f* the law of Christ Gal 6:2 378
F ye my joy, that ye be Phil 2:2 4137
me for you, to *f* the word of God Col 1:25 4137
in the Lord, that thou *f* it Col 4:17 4137
f all the good pleasure of his 2Th 1:11 4137
If ye *f* the royal law according Jas 2:8 5055
put in their hearts to *f* his will Rev 17:17 4160

FULFILLED

her days to be delivered were *f* Gen 25:24 4390
me my wife, for my days are *f* Gen 29:21 4390
And Jacob did so, and *f* her week Gen 29:28 4390
And forty days were *f* for him Gen 50:3 4390
for so are *f* the days of those Gen 50:3 4390
Wherefore have ye not *f* your task Ex 5:14 3615
And seven days were *f*, after that Ex 7:25 4390
the days of her purifying be *f* Lev 12:4 4390
the days of her purifying are *f* Lev 12:6 4390
until the days be *f*, in the which Num 6:5 4390
the days of his separation are *f* Num 6:13 4390
And when thy days be *f*, and thou 2Sa 7:12 4390
in that the king hath *f* the 2Sa 14:22 6213
and hath with his hand *f* it 1Kin 8:15 4390
hast *f* it with thine hand, as it 1Kin 8:24 4390
who hath with his hands *f* that 2Chr 6:4 4390
hast *f* it with thine hand, as it 2Chr 6:15 4390
the mouth of Jeremiah might be *f* Ezr 1:1 3615
But thou hast *f* the judgment of Job 36:17 4390
f with your hand, saying, We will Jer 44:25 4390
he hath *f* his word that he had Lam 2:17 1214
our end is near, our days are *f* Lam 4:18 4390
when the days of the siege are *f* Eze 5:2 4390
the thing *f* upon Nebuchadnezzar Dan 4:33 5487
till three whole weeks were *f* Dan 10:3 4390
that it might be *f* which was Mt 1:22 4137
that it might be *f* which was Mt 2:15 4137
Then was *f* that which was spoken Mt 2:17 4137
that it might be *f* which was Mt 2:23 4137
That it might be *f* which was Mt 4:14 4137
pass from the law, till all be *f* Mt 5:18 1096
That it might be *f* which was Mt 8:17 4137
That it might be *f* which was Mt 12:17 4137
in them is *f* the prophecy of Mt 13:14 378
That it might be *f* which was Mt 13:35 4137
that it might be *f* which was Mt 21:4 4137
pass, till all these things be *f* Mt 24:34 1096
then shall the scriptures be *f* Mt 26:54 4137
of the prophets might be *f* Mt 26:56 4137
Then was *f* that which was spoken Mt 27:9 4137
that it might be *f* which was Mt 27:35 4137
And saying, The time is *f*, and the Mk 1:15 4137
when all these things shall be *f* Mk 13:4 4931
but the scriptures must be *f* Mk 14:49 4137
And the scripture was *f*, which Mk 15:28 4137
which shall be *f* in their season Lk 1:20 4137
And when they had *f* the days Lk 2:43 5048
is this scripture *f* in your ears Lk 4:21 4137
things which are written may be *f* Lk 21:22 4137
the times of the Gentiles be *f* Lk 21:24 4137
not pass away, till all be *f* Lk 21:32 1096
until it be *f* in the kingdom of Lk 22:16 4137
you, that all things must be *f* Lk 24:44 4137
this my joy therefore is *f* Jn 3:29 4137
of Esaias the prophet might be *f* Jn 12:38 4137
but that the scripture may be *f* Jn 13:18 4137
that the word might be *f* that is Jn 15:25 4137
that the scripture might be *f* Jn 17:12 4137
might have my joy *f* in themselves Jn 17:13 4137
That the saying might be *f* Jn 18:9 4137
the saying of Jesus might be *f* Jn 18:32 4137
that the scripture might be *f* Jn 19:24 4137
that the scripture might be *f* Jn 19:28 5048
that the scripture should be *f* Jn 19:36 4137
scripture must needs have been *f* Acts 1:16 4137
should suffer, he hath so *f* Acts 3:18 4137
And after that many days were *f* Acts 9:23 4137
when they had *f* their ministry, Acts 12:25 4137
as John *f* his course, he said, Acts 13:25 4137
they have *f* them in condemning Acts 13:27 4137
when they had *f* all that was Acts 13:29 5055
God hath *f* the same unto us their Acts 13:33 1603
of God for the work which they *f* Acts 14:26 4137
of the law might be *f* in us Rom 8:4 4137
loveth another hath *f* the law Rom 13:8 4137
when your obedience is *f* 2Cor 10:6 4137
For all the law is *f* in one word Gal 5:14 4137
the scripture was *f* which saith Jas 2:23 4137
killed as they were, should be *f* Rev 6:11 4137
of the seven angels were *f* Rev 15:8 5055
until the words of God shall be *f* Rev 17:17 5055
the thousand years should be *f* Rev 20:3 5055

FULFILLING

stormy wind *f* his word Ps 148:8 6213
love is the *f* of the law Rom 13:10 4138
f the desires of the flesh and of Eph 2:3 4160

FULL

vale of Siddim was *f* of slimepits Gen 14:10
of the Amorites is not yet *f* Gen 15:16 8003
age, an old man, and *f* of years Gen 25:8 7649
people, being old and *f* of days Gen 35:29 7649
to pass at the end of two *f* years Gen 41:1 3117
devoured the seven rank and *f* ears Gen 41:7 4392
ears came up in one stalk, *f* Gen 41:22 4392
his sack, our money in *f* weight Gen 43:21
shall be *f* of swarms of flies Ex 8:21 4390
and when we did eat bread to the *f* Ex 16:3 7648
and in the morning bread to the *f* Ex 16:8 7646
put an omer *f* of manna therein, Ex 16:33 4393
for he should make *f* restitution Ex 22:3 7999
even corn beaten out of *f* ears Lev 2:14 3759
he shall take a censer *f* of Lev 16:12 4393
his hands *f* of sweet incense Lev 16:12 4393
the land become *f* of wickedness Lev 19:29 4390
within a *f* year may he redeem it Lev 25:29 3117
within the space of a *f* year Lev 25:30 8549
ye shall eat your bread to the *f* Lev 26:5 7648
both of them were *f* of fine flour Num 7:13 4392
ten shekels of gold, *f* of incense Num 7:14 4392
both of them *f* of fine flour Num 7:19 4392
gold of ten shekels, *f* of incense Num 7:20 4392
both of them *f* of fine flour Num 7:25 4392
of ten shekels, *f* of incense Num 7:26 4392
both of them *f* of fine flour Num 7:31 4392
of ten shekels, *f* of incense Num 7:32 4392
both of them *f* of fine flour Num 7:37 4392
of ten shekels, *f* of incense Num 7:38 4392
both of them *f* of fine flour Num 7:43 4392
of ten shekels, *f* of incense Num 7:44 4392
both of them *f* of fine flour Num 7:49 4392
of ten shekels, *f* of incense Num 7:50 4392
both of them *f* of fine flour Num 7:55 4392
of ten shekels, *f* of incense Num 7:56 4392
both of them *f* of fine flour Num 7:61 4392
of ten shekels, *f* of incense Num 7:62 4392
both of them *f* of fine flour Num 7:67 4392
of ten shekels, *f* of incense Num 7:68 4392
both of them *f* of fine flour Num 7:73 4392
of ten shekels, *f* of incense Num 7:74 4392
both of them *f* of fine flour Num 7:79 4392
of ten shekels, *f* of incense Num 7:80 4392
f of incense, weighing ten Num 7:86 4392
give me his house *f* of silver Num 22:18 4393
give me his house *f* of silver Num 24:13 4393
houses *f* of all good things, Deut 6:11 4392
thou shalt have eaten and be *f* Deut 6:11 7646
When thou hast eaten and art *f* Deut 8:10 7646
when thou hast eaten and art *f* Deut 8:12 7646
that thou mayest eat and be *f* Deut 11:15 7646
father and her mother a *f* month Deut 21:13 3117
f with the blessing of the LORD, Deut 33:23 4392
Nun was *f* of the spirit of wisdom Deut 34:9 4392
of the fleece, a bowl *f* of water Judg 6:38 4392
Now the house was *f* of men Judg 16:27 4390
I went out *f*, and the LORD hath Ruth 1:21 4390
a *f* reward be given thee of the Ruth 2:12 8003
They that were *f* have hired out 1Sa 2:5 7646
gave them in *f* tale to the king 1Sa 18:27 4390
of the Philistines was a *f* year 1Sa 27:7 3117
with one *f* line to keep alive 2Sa 8:2 4393
it came to pass after two *f* years 2Sa 13:23 3117
dwelt two *f* years in Jerusalem 2Sa 14:28 3117
a piece of ground *f* of lentiles 2Sa 23:11 4392
Make this valley *f* of ditches 2Kin 3:16
shalt set aside that which is *f* 2Kin 4:4 4392
to pass, when the vessels were *f* 2Kin 4:6 4390
thereof wild gourds his lap *f* 2Kin 4:39 4393
f ears of corn in the husk 2Kin 4:42
the mountain was *f* of horses 2Kin 6:17 4390
lo, all the way was *f* of garments 2Kin 7:15 4392
drew a bow with his *f* strength 2Kin 9:24 4390
the house of Baal was *f* from one 2Kin 10:21 4390
he reigned a *f* month in Samaria 2Kin 15:13 3117
a parcel of ground *f* of barley 1Chr 11:13 4392
shalt grant it me for the *f* price 1Chr 21:22 4392
verily buy it for the *f* price 1Chr 21:24 4392
f of days, he made Solomon his 1Chr 23:1 7646
f of days, riches, and honour 1Chr 29:28 7646
was *f* of days when he died 2Chr 24:15 7646
possessed houses *f* of all goods Neh 9:25 4392
then was Haman *f* of wrath Est 3:5 4390
he was *f* of indignation against Est 5:9 4390
come to thy grave in a *f* age Job 5:26 3624
I am *f* of tossings to and fro unto Job 7:4 7646
I am *f* of confusion Job 10:15 7646
should a man *f* of talk be Job 11:2
is of few days, and *f* of trouble Job 14:1 7646
His bones are *f* of the sin of his Job 20:11 4390
One dieth in his *f* strength Job 21:23 8537
His breasts are *f* of milk Job 21:24 4390
For I am *f* of matter Job 32:18 4390
thy table should be *f* of fatness Job 36:16 4390
Job died, being old and *f* of days Job 42:17 7646
His mouth is *f* of cursing Ps 10:7 4390
they are *f* of children, and leave Ps 17:14 7646
their right hand is *f* of bribes Ps 26:10 4390
voice of the LORD is *f* of majesty Ps 29:4
the earth is *f* of the goodness of Ps 33:5 4390
right hand is *f* of righteousness Ps 48:10 4390
river of God, which is *f* of water Ps 65:9 4390
and I am *f* of heaviness Ps 69:20
waters of a *f* cup are wrung out Ps 73:10 4392
dark places of the earth are *f* of Ps 74:20 4390
it is *f* of mixture Ps 75:8 4392
he sent them meat to the *f* Ps 78:25 7648
being *f* of compassion, forgave Ps 78:38
art a God *f* of compassion, and Ps 86:15
For my soul is *f* of troubles Ps 88:3 7654
trees of the LORD are *f* of sap Ps 104:16 7654
the earth is *f* of thy riches Ps 104:24 4390
is gracious and *f* of compassion Ps 111:4
f of compassion, and righteous Ps 112:4
earth, O LORD, is *f* of thy mercy Ps 119:64 4390
that hath his quiver *f* of them Ps 127:5 4390
That our garners may be *f* Ps 144:13 4392
is gracious, and *f* of compassion Ps 145:8
than an house *f* of sacrifices Prov 17:1 4392
The *f* soul loatheth an honeycomb Prov 27:7 7646
Hell and destruction are never *f* Prov 27:20 7646
Lest I be *f*, and deny thee, and say Prov 30:9 7646
yet the sea is not *f* Eccl 1:7 4392
All things are *f* of labour Eccl 1:8
both the hands *f* with travail Eccl 4:6 4393
of the sons of men is *f* of evil Eccl 9:3 4390
A fool also is *f* of words Eccl 10:14 7235
If the clouds be *f* of rain Eccl 11:3 4390
I am *f* of the burnt offerings of Is 1:11 7646
your hands are *f* of blood Is 1:15 4390
it was *f* of judgment Is 1:21 4392
Their land also is *f* of silver Is 2:7 4390
their land is also *f* of horses Is 2:7 4390
Their land also is *f* of idols Is 2:8 4390
the whole earth is *f* of his glory Is 6:3 4393
for the earth shall be *f* of the Is 11:9 4390
shall be *f* of doleful creatures Is 13:21 4390
of Dimon shall be *f* of blood Is 15:9 4390
Thou that art *f* of stirs, a Is 22:2 4392
valleys shall be *f* of chariots Is 22:7 4390
lees, of fat things *f* of marrow Is 25:6
For all tables are *f* of vomit Is 28:8 4390
his lips are *f* of indignation, and Is 30:27 4390
they are *f* of the fury of the Is 51:20 4392
Even a *f* wind from those places Jer 4:12 4392
yet will I not make a *f* end Jer 4:27
when I had fed them to the *f* Jer 5:7 7646
but make not a *f* end Jer 5:10
I will not make a *f* end with you Jer 5:18
As a cage is *f* of birds, so are Jer 5:27 4392
so are their houses *f* of deceit Jer 5:27 4392
Therefore I am *f* of the fury of Jer 6:11 4392
aged with him that is *f* of days Jer 6:11 4390
For the land is *f* of adulterers Jer 23:10 4390
Within two *f* years will I bring Jer 28:3 3117
within the space of two *f* years Jer 28:11 3117
though I make a *f* end of all Jer 30:11
will I not make a *f* end of thee Jer 30:11
of the Rechabites pots *f* of wine Jer 35:5 4392
for I will make a *f* end of all Jer 46:28
I will not make a *f* end of thee Jer 46:28
solitary, that was *f* of people Lam 1:1 7227
he is filled *f* with reproach Lam 3:30 7646
their rings were *f* of eyes round Eze 1:18 4392
for the land is *f* of bloody Eze 7:23 4390
and the city is *f* of violence Eze 7:23 4390
great, and the land is *f* of blood Eze 9:9 4390
the city *f* of perverseness Eze 9:9 4390
the court was *f* of the brightness Eze 10:4 4390
were *f* of eyes round about, even Eze 10:12 4392
wilt thou make a *f* end of the Eze 11:13
f of feathers, which had divers Eze 17:3 4392
f of branches by reason of many Eze 19:10
f of wisdom, and perfect in beauty Eze 28:12 4392
and the rivers shall be *f* of thee Eze 32:6 4390
of that whereof it was *f*, when I Eze 32:15 4393
the valley which was *f* of bones Eze 37:1 4392
And ye shall eat fat till ye be *f* Eze 39:19 7654
were a *f* reed of six great cubits Eze 41:8 4393
Then was Nebuchadnezzar *f* of fury Dan 3:19 4391
transgressors are come to the *f* Dan 8:23 8552
Daniel was mourning three *f* weeks Dan 10:2 3117
And the floors shall be *f* of wheat Joel 2:24 4390
for the press is *f*, the fats Joel 3:13 4390
is pressed that is *f* of sheaves Amos 2:13 4392
But truly I am *f* of power by the Mic 3:8 4390
men thereof are *f* of violence Mic 6:12 4390
it is all *f* of lies and robbery Nah 3:1 4392
and the earth was *f* of his praise Hab 3:3 4390
of the city shall be *f* of boys Zec 8:5 4390
whole body shall be *f* of light Mt 6:22 5460
whole body shall be *f* of darkness Mt 6:23
Which, when it was *f*, they drew Mt 13:48 4137
that remained twelve baskets *f* Mt 14:20 4134
that was left seven baskets *f* Mt 15:37 4134
within they are *f* of extortion Mt 23:25 1073
but are within *f* of dead men's Mt 23:27 1073
but within ye are *f* of hypocrisy Mt 23:28 3324
after that the *f* corn in the ear Mk 4:28 4134
the ship, so that it was now *f* Mk 4:37 1072
twelve baskets *f* of the fragments Mk 6:43 4134
F well ye reject the commandment Mk 7:9
how many baskets *f* of fragments Mk 8:19 4134
how many baskets *f* of fragments Mk 8:20 4138
and filled a spunge *f* of vinegar Mk 15:36
Now Elisabeth's *f* time came that Lk 1:57 4130
Jesus being *f* of the Holy Ghost Lk 4:1 4134
city, behold a man *f* of leprosy Lk 5:12 4134
Woe unto you that are *f* Lk 6:25 1705
thy whole body also is *f* of light Lk 11:34 5460
thy body also is *f* of darkness Lk 11:34
body therefore be *f* of light Lk 11:36 5460
the whole shall be *f* of light Lk 11:36 5460
your inward part is *f* of ravening Lk 11:39 1073
was laid at his gate, *f* of sores, Lk 16:20
the Father,) *f* of grace and truth Jn 1:14 4134
for my time is not yet *f* come Jn 7:8 4137
you, and that your joy might be *f* Jn 15:11 4137
receive, that your joy may be *f* Jn 16:24 4137
was set a vessel *f* of vinegar Jn 19:29 3324
the net to land *f* of great fishes Jn 21:11 3324
said, These men are *f* of new wine Acts 2:13 3325
thou shalt make me *f* of joy with Acts 2:28 4137
f of the Holy Ghost and wisdom, Acts 6:3 4134
a man *f* of faith and of the Holy Acts 6:5 4134
f of faith and power, did great Acts 6:8 4134
when he was *f* forty years old, it Acts 7:23 4137
being *f* of the Holy Ghost, looked Acts 7:55 4134
this woman was *f* of good works Acts 9:36 4134

F

- f of the Holy Ghost and of faith ... Acts 11:24 4134
- O f of all subtilty and all ... Acts 13:10 4134
- sayings, they were f of wrath ... Acts 19:28 4134
- f of envy, murder, debate, deceit ... Rom 1:29 3324
- Whose mouth is f of cursing ... Rom 3:14 1073
- that ye also are f of goodness ... Rom 15:14 3324
- Now ye are f, now ye are rich, ye ... 1Cor 4:8 2880
- was f of heaviness, because that ... Phil 2:26
- I am instructed both to be f ... Phil 4:12 5526
- I am f, having received of ... Phil 4:18 4137
- love, and unto all riches of the f ... Col 2:2 4136
- make f proof of thy ministry ... 2Ti 4:5 4135
- to them that are of f age ... Heb 5:14 5046
- f assurance of hope unto the end ... Heb 6:11 4136
- heart in f assurance of faith ... Heb 10:22 4136
- unruly evil, f of deadly poison ... Jas 3:8 3324
- f of mercy and good fruits, ... Jas 3:17 3324
- joy unspeakable and f of glory ... 1Pet 1:8
- Having eyes f of adultery ... 2Pet 2:14 3324
- unto you, that your joy may be f ... 1Jn 1:4 4137
- but that we receive a f reward ... 2Jn 8 4134
- to face, that our joy may be f ... 2Jn 12 4137
- were four beasts f of eyes before ... Rev 4:6 1073
- they were f of eyes within ... Rev 4:8 1073
- and golden vials f of odours ... Rev 5:8 1073
- vials f of the wrath of God ... Rev 15:7 1073
- and his kingdom was f of darkness ... Rev 16:10
- f of names of blasphemy, having ... Rev 17:3 1073
- cup in her hand f of abominations ... Rev 17:4 1073
- vials f of the seven last plagues ... Rev 21:9 1073

FULLER
- so as no f on earth can white ... Mk 9:3 1102

FULLER'S
- is in the highway of the f field ... 2Kin 18:17 3526
- in the highway of the f field ... Is 7:3 3526
- in the highway of the f field ... Is 36:2 3526

FULLERS'
- a refiner's fire, and like f sope ... Mal 3:2 3526

FULLY
- Moses had f set up the tabernacle ... Num 7:1 3615
- with him, and hath followed me f ... Num 14:24 4392
- It hath f been shewed me, all ... Ruth 2:11 5046
- went not f after the LORD, as did ... 1Kin 11:6 4390
- men is f set in them to do evil ... Eccl 8:11 4390
- be devoured as stubble f dry ... Nah 1:10 4390
- the day of Pentecost was f come ... Acts 2:1 4845
- being f persuaded that, what he ... Rom 4:21 4135
- Let every man be f persuaded in ... Rom 14:5 4135
- I have f preached the gospel of ... Rom 15:19 4137
- But thou hast f known my doctrine ... 2Ti 3:10 3877
- me the preaching might be f known ... 2Ti 4:17 4135
- for her grapes are f ripe ... Rev 14:18

FULNESS
- as the f of the winepress ... Num 18:27 4395
- f thereof, and for the good will ... Deut 33:16 4393
- the sea roar, and the f thereof ... 1Chr 16:32 4393
- In the f of his sufficiency he ... Job 20:22 4390
- in thy presence is f of joy ... Ps 16:11 7648
- is the LORD's, and the f thereof ... Ps 24:1 4393
- world is mine, and the f thereof ... Ps 50:12 4393
- the f thereof, thou hast founded ... Ps 89:11 4393
- the sea roar, and the f thereof ... Ps 96:11 4393
- the sea roar, and the f thereof ... Ps 98:7 4393
- f of bread, and abundance of ... Eze 16:49 7653
- the f thereof, by the noise of ... Eze 19:7 4393
- of his f have all we received, and ... Jn 1:16 4138
- how much more their f ... Rom 11:12 4138
- until the f of the Gentiles be ... Rom 11:25 4138
- I shall come in the f of the ... Rom 15:29 4138
- is the Lord's, and the f thereof ... 1Cor 10:26 4138
- is the Lord's, and the f thereof ... 1Cor 10:28 4138
- But when the f of the time was ... Gal 4:4 4138
- of the f of times he might gather ... Eph 1:10 4138
- the f of him that filleth all in ... Eph 1:23 4138
- be filled with all the f of God ... Eph 3:19 4138
- of the stature of the f of Christ ... Eph 4:13 4138
- that in him should all f dwell ... Col 1:19 4138
- all the f of the Godhead bodily ... Col 2:9 4138

FURBISH
- f the spears, and put on the ... Jer 46:4 4838

FURBISHED
- a sword is sharpened, and also f ... Eze 21:9 4803
- it is f that it may glitter ... Eze 21:10 4803
- And he hath given it to be f ... Eze 21:11 4803
- sword is sharpened, and it is f ... Eze 21:11 4803
- for the slaughter it is f ... Eze 21:28 4803

FURIOUS
- with a f man thou shalt not go ... Prov 22:24 2534
- strife, and a f man aboundeth in ... Prov 29:22 2534
- anger and in fury and in f rebukes ... Eze 5:15 2534
- upon them with f rebukes ... Eze 25:17 2534
- the king was angry and very f ... Dan 2:12 7108
- the LORD revengeth, and is f ... Nah 1:2

FURIOUSLY
- for he driveth f ... 2Kin 9:20 7697
- and they shall deal f with thee ... Eze 23:25 2534

FURLONGS
- from Jerusalem about threescore f ... Lk 24:13 4712
- about five and twenty or thirty f ... Jn 6:19 4712
- Jerusalem, about fifteen f off ... Jn 11:18 4712
- of a thousand and six hundred f ... Rev 14:20 4712
- with the reed, twelve thousand f ... Rev 21:16 4712

FURNACE
- it was dark, behold a smoking f ... Gen 15:17 8574
- went up as the smoke of a f ... Gen 19:28 3536
- to you handfuls of ashes of the f ... Ex 9:8 3536
- And they took ashes of the f ... Ex 9:10 3536
- ascended as the smoke of a f ... Ex 19:18 3536
- you forth out of the iron f ... Deut 4:20 3564
- from the midst of the f of iron ... 1Kin 8:51 3564
- as silver tried in a f of earth ... Ps 12:6 5948
- is for silver, and the f for gold ... Prov 17:3 3564
- pot for silver, and the f for gold ... Prov 27:21 3564
- is in Zion, and his f in Jerusalem ... Is 31:9 8574
- thee in the f of affliction ... Is 48:10 3564
- land of Egypt, from the iron f ... Jer 11:4 3564
- and lead, in the midst of the f ... Eze 22:18 3564
- and tin, into the midst of the f ... Eze 22:20 3564
- is melted in the midst of the f ... Eze 22:22 3564
- the midst of a burning fiery f ... Dan 3:6 861
- the midst of a burning fiery f ... Dan 3:11 861
- the midst of a burning fiery f ... Dan 3:15 861
- us from the burning fiery f ... Dan 3:17 861
- that they should heat the f one ... Dan 3:19 861
- them into the burning fiery f ... Dan 3:20 861
- the midst of the burning fiery f ... Dan 3:21 861
- the f exceeding hot, the flame of ... Dan 3:22 861
- the midst of the burning fiery f ... Dan 3:23 861
- the mouth of the burning fiery f ... Dan 3:26 861
- shall cast them into a f of fire ... Mt 13:42 2575
- cast them into the f of fire ... Mt 13:50 2575
- brass, as if they burned in a f ... Rev 1:15 2575
- pit, as the smoke of a great f ... Rev 9:2 2575

FURNACES
- piece, and the tower of the f ... Neh 3:11 8574
- of the f even unto the broad wall ... Neh 12:38 8574

FURNISH
- Thou shalt f him liberally out of ... Deut 15:14 6059
- said, Can God f a table in the ... Ps 78:19 6186
- that f the drink offering unto ... Is 65:11 4390
- f thyself to go into captivity ... Jer 46:19

FURNISHED
- had f Solomon with cedar trees ... 1Kin 9:11 5375
- she hath also f her table ... Prov 9:2 6186
- and the wedding was f with guests ... Mt 22:10 4130
- shew you a large upper room f ... Mk 14:15 4766
- shew you a large upper room f ... Lk 22:12 4766
- throughly f unto all good works ... 2Ti 3:17 1822

FURNITURE
- and put them in the camel's f ... Gen 31:34 3733
- all the f of the tabernacle, ... Ex 31:7 3627
- And the table and his f, and the ... Ex 31:8 3627
- pure candlestick with all his f ... Ex 31:8 3627
- of burnt offering with all his f ... Ex 31:9 3627
- also for the light, and his f ... Ex 35:14 3627
- Moses, the tent, and all his f ... Ex 39:33 3627
- glory out of all the pleasant f ... Nah 2:9 3627

FURROW
- unicorn with his band in the f ... Job 39:10 8525

FURROWS
- or that the f likewise thereof ... Job 31:38 8525
- thou settlest the f thereof ... Ps 65:10 1417
- they made long their f ... Ps 129:3 4618
- it by the f of her plantation ... Eze 17:7 6170
- wither in the f where it grew ... Eze 17:10 6170
- as hemlock in the f of the field ... Hos 10:4 8525
- bind themselves in their two f ... Hos 10:10 5869
- as heaps in the f of the fields ... Hos 12:11 8525

FURTHER
- And the angel of the LORD went f ... Num 22:26 3254
- shall speak f unto the people ... Deut 20:8 3254
- they enquired of the LORD f ... 1Sa 10:22 5750
- or what is thy request f ... Est 9:12 5750
- shalt thou come, but no f ... Job 38:11 3254
- but I will proceed no f ... Job 40:5
- f not his wicked device ... Ps 140:8 6329
- yea f; though a wise man think to ... Eccl 8:17 3254
- And f, by these, my son, be ... Eccl 12:12 3148
- what f need have we of witnesses ... Mt 26:65 2089
- troublest thou the Master any f ... Mk 5:35 2089
- What need we any f witnesses ... Mk 14:63 2089
- said, What need we any f witness ... Lk 22:71 2089
- as though he would have gone f ... Lk 24:28 4206
- it spread no f among the people ... Acts 4:17
- when they had f threatened them ... Acts 4:21
- he proceeded f to take Peter also ... Acts 12:3
- f brought Greeks also into the ... Acts 21:28 2089
- that I be not f tedious unto thee ... Acts 24:4
- and when they had gone a little f ... Acts 27:28 1339
- But they shall proceed no f ... 2Ti 3:9
- what f need was there that ... Heb 7:11 2089

FURTHERANCE
- rather unto the f of the gospel ... Phil 1:12 4297
- continue with you all for your f ... Phil 1:25 4297

FURTHERED
- they f the people, and the house ... Ezr 8:36 5375

FURTHERMORE
- And the LORD said f unto him ... Ex 4:6 5750
- F the LORD was angry with me for ... Deut 4:21
- F the LORD spake unto me, saying, ... Deut 9:13
- David said f, As the LORD liveth, ... 1Sa 26:10
- F I tell thee that the LORD will ... 1Chr 17:10
- F over the tribes of Israel ... 1Chr 27:16
- F David the king said unto all ... 1Chr 29:1
- F he made the court of the ... 2Chr 4:9
- F Elihu answered and said, ... Job 34:1
- He said f unto me, Son of man, ... Eze 8:6
- And f, that ye have sent for men ... Eze 23:40 637
- F, when I came to Troas to preach ... 2Cor 2:12 1161
- F then we beseech you, brethren, ... 1Th 4:1 3063
- F we have had fathers of our ... Heb 12:9 1534

FURY
- until thy brother's f turn away ... Gen 27:44 2534
- walk contrary unto you also in f ... Lev 26:28 2534
- God shall cast the f of his wrath ... Job 20:23 2740
- F is not in me ... Is 27:4 2534
- his f upon all their armies ... Is 34:2 2534
- upon him the f of his anger ... Is 42:25 2534
- because of the f of the oppressor ... Is 51:13 2534
- where is the f of the oppressor ... Is 51:13 2534
- hand of the LORD the cup of his f ... Is 51:17 2534
- are full of the f of the LORD ... Is 51:20 2534
- even the dregs of the cup of my f ... Is 51:22 2534
- f to his adversaries, recompence ... Is 59:18 2534
- anger, and trample them in my f ... Is 63:3 2534
- and my f, it upheld me ... Is 63:5 2534
- anger, and make them drunk in my f .. Is 63:6 2534
- to render his anger with f ... Is 66:15 2534
- lest my f come forth like fire, ... Jer 4:4 2534
- I am full of the f of the LORD ... Jer 6:11 2534
- my f shall be poured out upon ... Jer 7:20 2534
- Pour out thy f upon the heathen ... Jer 10:25 2534
- arm, even in anger, and in f ... Jer 21:5 2534
- lest my f go out like fire, and ... Jer 21:12 2534
- of the LORD is gone forth in f ... Jer 23:19 2534
- the wine cup of this f at my hand ... Jer 25:15 2534
- of the LORD goeth forth with f ... Jer 30:23 2534
- of my f from the day that they ... Jer 32:31 2534
- them in mine anger, and in my f ... Jer 32:37 2534
- slain in mine anger and in my f ... Jer 33:5 2534
- anger and the f that the LORD hath ... Jer 36:7 2534
- my f hath been poured forth upon ... Jer 42:18 2534
- so shall my f be poured forth ... Jer 42:18 2534
- Wherefore my f and mine anger was ... Jer 44:6 2534
- he poured out his f like fire ... Lam 2:4 2534
- The LORD hath accomplished his f ... Lam 4:11 2534
- I will cause my f to rest upon ... Eze 5:13 2534
- I have accomplished my f in them ... Eze 5:13 2534
- in thee in anger and in f and in ... Eze 5:15 2534
- will I accomplish my f upon them ... Eze 6:12 2534
- I shortly pour out my f upon thee ... Eze 7:8 2534
- Therefore will I also deal in f ... Eze 8:18 2534
- out of thy f upon Jerusalem ... Eze 9:8 2534
- it with a stormy wind in my f ... Eze 13:13 2534
- hailstones in my f to consume it ... Eze 13:13 2534
- pour out my f upon it in blood, ... Eze 14:19 2534
- and I will give thee blood in f ... Eze 16:38 2534
- So will I make my f toward thee ... Eze 16:42 2534
- But she was plucked up in f ... Eze 19:12 2534
- I will pour out my f upon them ... Eze 20:8 2534
- I would pour out my f upon them ... Eze 20:13 2534
- I would pour out my f upon them ... Eze 20:21 2534
- with f poured out, will I rule ... Eze 20:33 2534
- out arm, and with f poured out ... Eze 20:34 2534
- and I will cause my f to rest ... Eze 21:17 2534
- you in mine anger and in my f ... Eze 22:20 2534
- have poured out my f upon you ... Eze 22:22 2534
- That it might cause f to come up ... Eze 24:8 2534
- caused my f to rest upon thee ... Eze 24:13 2534
- mine anger and according to my f ... Eze 25:14 2534
- And I will pour my f upon Sin ... Eze 30:15 2534
- spoken in my jealousy and in my f ... Eze 36:6 2534
- Wherefore I poured my f upon them ... Eze 36:18 2534
- that my f shall come up in my ... Eze 38:18 2534
- f commanded to bring Shadrach, ... Dan 3:13 2528
- Then was Nebuchadnezzar full of f ... Dan 3:19 2528
- unto him in the f of his power ... Dan 8:6 2534
- thy f be turned away from thy ... Dan 9:16 2534
- go forth with great f to destroy ... Dan 11:44 2534
- f upon the heathen, such as they ... Mic 5:15 2534
- his f is poured out like fire, and ... Nah 1:6 2534
- was jealous for her with great f ... Zec 8:2 2534

G

GAAL (*ga'-al*) *A son of Ebed.*
G the son of Ebed came with his........... Judg 9:26 1603
G the son of Ebed said, Who is............ Judg 9:28 1603
the words of G the son of Ebed............ Judg 9:30 1603
G the son of Ebed and his brethren....... Judg 9:31 1603
G the son of Ebed went out, and........... Judg 9:35 1603
when G saw the people, he said to......... Judg 9:36 1603
G spake again and said, See there......... Judg 9:37 1603
G went out before the men of.............. Judg 9:39 1603
and Zebul thrust out G and his............ Judg 9:41 1603

GAASH (*ga'-ash*) *A mountain near Mt. Ephraim.*
the north side of the hill of G............ Josh 24:30 1608
on the north side of the hill G............ Judg 2:9 1608
Hiddai of the brooks of G................... 2Sa 23:30 1608
Hurai of the brooks of G, Abiel........... 1Chr 11:32 1608

GABA (*ga'-bah*) See GEBA. *A Levitical city in Benjamin.*
and Ophni, and G............................ Josh 18:24 1387
The children of Ramah and G............... Ezr 2:26 1387
The men of Ramah and G, six............... Neh 7:30 1387

GABBAI (*gab'-bahee*) *A family of exiles.*
And after him G, Sallai, nine............... Neh 11:8 1373

GABBATHA (*gab'-ba-thah*) *Place where Pilate judged.*
Pavement, but in the Hebrew, G........... Jn 19:13 *1042*

GABRIEL (*ga'-bre-el*) *An angel.*
of Ulai, which called, and said, G......... Dan 8:16 1403
in prayer, even the man G.................. Dan 9:21 1403
answering said unto him, I am G........... Lk 1:19 *1043*
in the sixth month the angel G............. Lk 1:26 *1043*

GAD (*gad*)
1. A son of Jacob.
and she called his name G.................. Gen 30:11 1410
Leah's handmaid; G, and Asher............. Gen 35:26 1410
And the sons of G........................... Gen 46:16 1410
G, a troop shall overcome him.............. Gen 49:19 1410
Dan, and Naphtali, G, and Asher........... Ex 1:4 1410
the children of G dwelt over................ 1Chr 5:11 1410
2. The tribe descended from Gad 1.
Of G; Eliasaph the son...................... Num 1:14 1410
Of the children of G, by their.............. Num 1:24 1410
of them, even of the tribe of G............. Num 1:25 1410
Then the tribe of G.......................... Num 2:14 1410
the captain of the sons of G................ Num 2:14 1410
prince of the children of G................. Num 7:42 1410
G was Eliasaph the son of Deuel........... Num 10:20 1410
Of the tribe of G, Geuel the son........... Num 13:15 1410
The children of G after their............... Num 26:15 1410
of G according to those that were......... Num 26:18 1410
the children of G had a very................ Num 32:1 1410
The children of G and the children........ Num 32:2 1410
Moses said unto the children of G......... Num 32:6 1410
And the children of G and the.............. Num 32:25 1410
unto them, If the children of G............ Num 32:29 1410
And the children of G and the.............. Num 32:31 1410
them, even to the children of G............ Num 32:33 1410
And the children of G built Dibon.......... Num 32:34 1410
the tribe of the children of G.............. Num 34:14 1410
Reuben, G, and Asher, and Zebulun,....... Deut 27:13 1410
of G he said, Blessed be he that........... Deut 33:20 1410
Blessed be he that enlargeth G............ Deut 33:20 1410
of Reuben, and the children of G.......... Josh 4:12 1410
inheritance unto the tribe of G............. Josh 13:24 1410
of G according their families............... Josh 13:24 1410
of G after their families..................... Josh 13:28 1410
and G, and Reuben, and half the........... Josh 18:7 1410
in Gilead out of the tribe of G............. Josh 20:8 1410
Reuben, and out of the tribe of G.......... Josh 21:7 1410
And out of the tribe of G, Ramoth.......... Josh 21:38 1410
of Reuben and the children of G........... Josh 22:9 1410
of Reuben and the children of G........... Josh 22:10 1410
of Reuben and the children of G........... Josh 22:11 1410
Reuben, and to the children of G.......... Josh 22:13 1410
Reuben, and to the children of G.......... Josh 22:15 1410
of Reuben and the children of G........... Josh 22:21 1410
of Reuben and children of G................ Josh 22:25 1410
of Reuben and the children of G........... Josh 22:30 1410
Reuben, and to the children of G.......... Josh 22:31 1410
Reuben, and from the children of G....... Josh 22:32 1410
the children of Reuben and G dwelt....... Josh 22:33 1410
the children of G called the................ Josh 22:34 1410
went over Jordan to the land of G......... 1Sa 13:7 1410
in the midst of the river of G............... 2Sa 24:5 1410
Joseph, and Benjamin, Naphtali, G......... 1Chr 2:2 1410
Reuben, and out of the tribe of G.......... 1Chr 6:63 1410
And out of the tribe of G.................... 1Chr 6:80 1410
These were of the sons of G................. 1Chr 12:14 1410
then doth their king inherit G.............. Jer 49:1 1410
unto the west side, G a portion............ Eze 48:27 1410
And by the border of G, at the............... Eze 48:28 1410
one gate of G, one gate of Asher,.......... Eze 48:34 1410
Of the tribe of G were sealed............... Rev 7:5 *1045*
3. A prophet who assisted David.
the prophet G said unto David,.............. 1Sa 22:5 1410
the LORD came unto the prophet G......... 2Sa 24:11 1410
So G came to David, and told him,......... 2Sa 24:13 1410
And David said unto G, I am in a........... 2Sa 24:14 1410
G came that day to David, and said....... 2Sa 24:18 1410
according to the saying of G................ 2Sa 24:19 1410
And the LORD spake unto G, David's....... 1Chr 21:9 1410
So G came to David, and said unto......... 1Chr 21:11 1410
And David said unto G, I am in a........... 1Chr 21:13 1410
LORD commanded G to say to David........ 1Chr 21:18 1410
David went up at the saying of G.......... 1Chr 21:19 1410
and in the book of G the seer............... 1Chr 29:29 1410
of G the king's seer, and Nathan.......... 2Chr 29:25 1410

GADARENES (*gad-a-renes'*) *Inhabitants of Gadara.*
sea, into the country of the G.............. Mk 5:1 *1046*
arrived at the country of the G............. Lk 8:26 *1046*
the G round about besought him to......... Lk 8:37 *1046*

GADDEST
Why g thou about so much to............... Jer 2:36 235

GADDI (*gad'-di*) *One of the twelve spies.*
of Manasseh, G the son of Susi............. Num 13:11 1426

GADDIEL (*gad'-de-el*) *One of the twelve spies.*
of Zebulun, G the son of Sodi.............. Num 13:10 1427

GADI (*ga'-di*) *Father of Menahem.*
the son of G went up from Tirzah.......... 2Kin 15:14 1424
the son of G to reign over Israel.......... 2Kin 15:17 1424

GADITE (*gad'-ite*) See GADITES. *A member of the tribe of Dan.*
of Nathan of Zobah, Bani the G............ 2Sa 23:36 1425

GADITES (*gad'-ites*)
I unto the Reubenites and to the G........ Deut 3:12 1425
unto the G I gave from Gilead.............. Deut 3:16 1425
and Ramoth in Gilead, of the G............. Deut 4:43 1425
unto the Reubenites, and to the G......... Deut 29:8 1425
And to the Reubenites, and to the G....... Josh 1:12 1425
unto the Reubenites, and the G............. Josh 12:6 1425
the G have received their.................... Josh 13:8 1425
called the Reubenites, and the G........... Josh 22:1 1425
all the land of Gilead, the G................. 2Kin 10:33 1425
The sons of Reuben, and the G.............. 1Chr 5:18 1425
even the Reubenites, and the G............. 1Chr 5:26 1425
And of the G there separated................ 1Chr 12:8 1425
of the Reubenites, and the G................. 1Chr 12:37 1425
rulers over the Reubenites, the G........... 1Chr 26:32 1425

GAHAM (*ga'-ham*) *A son of Nahor.*
Reumah, she bare also Tebah, and G....... Gen 22:24 1514

GAHAR (*ga'-har*) *A family of exiles.*
of Giddel, the children of G................. Ezr 2:47 1515
of Giddel, the children of G................. Neh 7:49 1515

GAHER See GAHAR.

GAIN
they took no g of money...................... Judg 5:19 1214
or is it g to him, that thou..................... Job 22:3 1214
of every one that is greedy of g.............. Prov 1:19 1214
the g thereof than fine gold.................. Prov 3:14 8393
He that is greedy of g troubleth.............. Prov 15:27 1214
unjust g increaseth his substance............ Prov 28:8 8636
despiseth the g of oppressions............... Is 33:15 1214
own way, every one for his g................. Is 56:11 1214
dishonest g which thou hast made........... Eze 22:13 1214
destroy souls, to get dishonest g............ Eze 22:27 1214
that ye would g the time, because........... Dan 2:8 2084
and shall divide the land for g............... Dan 11:39 4242
consecrate their g unto the LORD............ Mic 4:13 1214
if he shall g the whole world, and.......... Mt 16:26 *2770*
if he shall g the whole world, and.......... Mk 8:36 *2770*
if he g the whole world, and lose............ Lk 9:25 *2770*
her masters much g by soothsaying......... Acts 16:16 *2039*
brought no small g unto the.................. Acts 19:24 *2039*
unto all, that I might g the more............. 1Cor 9:19 *2770*
as a Jew, that I might g the Jews............ 1Cor 9:20 *2770*
that I might g them that are.................. 1Cor 9:20 *2770*
that I might g them that are.................. 1Cor 9:21 *2770*
as weak, that I might g the weak............. 1Cor 9:22 *2770*
Did I make a g of you by any of............. 2Cor 12:17 *4122*
Did Titus make a g of you..................... 2Cor 12:18 *4122*
to live is Christ, and to die is g............. Phil 1:21 *2771*
But what things were g to me................ Phil 3:7 *2771*
supposing that g is godliness................. 1Ti 6:5 *4200*
with contentment is great g.................. 1Ti 6:6 *4200*
a year, and buy and sell, and get g......... Jas 4:13 *2770*

GAINED
the hypocrite, though he hath g.............. Job 27:8 1214
thou hast greedily g of thy.................... Eze 22:12 1214
thee, thou hast g thy brother................. Mt 18:15 *2770*
received two, he also g other two............ Mt 25:17 *2770*
I have g beside them five talents............. Mt 25:20 *2770*
I have g two other talents beside............. Mt 25:22 *2770*
much every man had g by trading............. Lk 19:15 *1281*
Lord, thy pound hath g ten pounds........... Lk 19:16 *4333*
thy pound hath g five pounds.................. Lk 19:18 *4160*
to have g this harm and loss.................. Acts 27:21 *2770*

GAINS
that the hope of their g was gone........... Acts 16:19 *2039*

GAINSAY
shall not be able to g nor resist.............. Lk 21:15 *471*

GAINSAYERS
to exhort and to convince the g.............. Titus 1:9 *483*

GAINSAYING
came I unto you without g..................... Acts 10:29 *369*
unto a disobedient and g people............. Rom 10:21 *483*
and perished in the g of Core................. Jude 11 *485*

GAIUS (*gah'-yus*)
1. A native of Macedonia.
and having caught G and Aristarchus.. Acts 19:29 *1050*
2. A native of Derbe.
and G of Derbe, and Timotheus.............. Acts 20:4 *1050*
3. A native of Corinth.
G mine host, and of the whole............... Rom 16:23 *1050*
none of you, but Crispus and G.............. 1Cor 1:14 *1050*
4. Addressee of John's third epistle.
The elder unto the wellbeloved G........... 3Jn 1 *1050*

GALAL (*ga'-lal*)
1. Son of Jeduthun.
And Bakbakkar, Heresh, and G............. 1Chr 9:15 1559
2. A Levite exile.
the son of Shemaiah, the son of G.......... 1Chr 9:16 1559
the son of Shammua, the son of G.......... Neh 11:17 1559

GALATIA (*ga-la'-she-ah*) See GALATIANS. *A Roman province in Asia Minor.*
Phrygia and the region of G................... Acts 16:6 *1054*
and went over all the country of G.......... Acts 18:23 *1054*
given order to the churches of G............. 1Cor 16:1 *1053*
with me, unto the churches of G.............. Gal 1:2 *1053*
Crescens to G, Titus unto...................... 2Ti 4:10 *1053*
scattered throughout Pontus, G.............. 1Pet 1:1 *1053*

GALATIANS (*ga-la'-she-uns*) *Inhabitants of Galatia.*
O foolish G, who hath bewitched............. Gal 3:1 *1052*
Unto the G written from Rome................ Gal *s* *1052*

GALBANUM
spices, stacte, and onycha, and g........... Ex 30:34 2464

GALEED (*ga'-le-ed*) See JAGAR-SAHADUTHA. *A memorial mound of stones.*
but Jacob called it G............................ Gen 31:47 1567
was the name of it called G.................. Gen 31:48 1567

GALILAEAN (*gal-i-le'-un*) See GALILAEANS. *An inhabitant of Galilee.*
for thou art a G, and thy speech............. Mk 14:70 *1057*
for he is a G....................................... Lk 22:59 *1057*
he asked whether the man were a G........ Lk 23:6 *1057*

GALILAEANS (*gal-i-le-uns*)
some that told him of the G.................... Lk 13:1 *1057*
Suppose ye that these G were................. Lk 13:2 *1057*
were sinners above all the G.................. Lk 13:2 *1057*
the G received him, having seen............. Jn 4:45 *1057*
are not all these which speak G............... Acts 2:7 *1057*

GALILEE (*gal'-i-lee*) See GALILAEAN. *A district north of Samaria.*
Kedesh in G in mount Naphtali............... Josh 20:7 1551
Kedesh in G with her suburbs, to............ Josh 21:32 1551
twenty cities in the land of G................ 1Kin 9:11 1551
Kedesh, and Hazor, and Gilead, and G. 2Kin 15:29 1551
Kedesh in G with her suburbs, and.......... 1Chr 6:76 1551
Jordan, in G of the nations.................... Is 9:1 1551
turned aside into the parts of G.............. Mt 2:22 *1056*
Jesus from G to Jordan unto John........... Mt 3:13 *1056*
into prison, he departed into G.............. Mt 4:12 *1056*
beyond Jordan, G of the Gentiles............ Mt 4:15 *1056*
And Jesus, walking by the sea of G......... Mt 4:18 *1056*
And Jesus went about all G................... Mt 4:23 *1056*
great multitudes of people from G.......... Mt 4:25 *1056*
and came nigh unto the sea of G............ Mt 15:29 *1056*
And while they abode in G, Jesus........... Mt 17:22 *1056*
these sayings, he departed from G.......... Mt 19:1 *1056*
the prophet of Nazareth of G................. Mt 21:11 *1056*
I will go before you into G.................... Mt 26:32 *1056*
Thou also wast with Jesus of G.............. Mt 26:69 *1056*
off, which followed Jesus from G............ Mt 27:55 *1056*
he goeth before you into G.................... Mt 28:7 *1056*
my brethren that they go into G.............. Mt 28:10 *1056*
eleven disciples went away into G.......... Mt 28:16 *1056*
Jesus came from Nazareth of G.............. Mk 1:9 *1056*
put in prison, Jesus came into G............ Mk 1:14 *1056*
Now as he walked by the sea of G........... Mk 1:16 *1056*
all the region round about G.................. Mk 1:28 *1056*
their synagogues throughout all G.......... Mk 1:39 *1056*
multitude from G followed him............... Mk 3:7 *1056*
captains, and chief estates of G............. Mk 6:21 *1056*
Sidon, he came unto the sea of G........... Mk 7:31 *1056*
thence, and passed through G................ Mk 9:30 *1056*
I will go before you into G.................... Mk 14:28 *1056*
(Who also, when he was in G.................. Mk 15:41 *1056*
that he goeth before you into G.............. Mk 16:7 *1056*
sent from God unto a city of G............... Lk 1:26 *1056*
And Joseph also went up from G............. Lk 2:4 *1056*
of the Lord, they returned into G............ Lk 2:39 *1056*
and Herod being tetrarch of G................ Lk 3:1 *1056*
in the power of the Spirit into G............. Lk 4:14 *1056*
down to Capernaum, a city of G.............. Lk 4:31 *1056*
preached in the synagogues of G............. Lk 4:44 *1056*
were come out of every town of G........... Lk 5:17 *1056*
which is over against G........................ Lk 8:26 *1056*
through the midst of Samaria and G........ Lk 17:11 *1056*
beginning from G to this place................ Lk 23:5 *1056*
When Pilate heard of G, he asked........... Lk 23:6 *1056*
women that followed him from G............ Lk 23:49 *1056*
also, which came with him from G........... Lk 23:55 *1056*
unto you when he was yet in G.............. Lk 24:6 *1056*
Jesus would go forth into G................... Jn 1:43 *1056*
there was a marriage in Cana of G.......... Jn 2:1 *1056*
miracles did Jesus in Cana of G............. Jn 2:11 *1056*
Judaea, and departed again into G.......... Jn 4:3 *1056*
departed thence, and went into G........... Jn 4:43 *1056*
Then when he was come into G................ Jn 4:45 *1056*
Jesus came again into Cana of G............. Jn 4:46 *1056*
was come out of Judaea into G............... Jn 4:47 *1056*
he was come out of Judaea into G........... Jn 4:54 *1056*
Jesus went over the sea of G.................. Jn 6:1 *1056*
these things Jesus walked in G............... Jn 7:1 *1056*
unto them, he abode still in G................ Jn 7:9 *1056*
said, Shall Christ come out of G............. Jn 7:41 *1056*
said unto him, Art thou also of G........... Jn 7:52 *1056*
for out of G ariseth no prophet.............. Jn 7:52 *1056*

G

which was of Bethsaida of G — Jn 12:21 — *1056*
and Nathanael of Cana in G — Jn 21:2 — *1056*
Which also said, Ye men of G — Acts 1:11 — *1056*
of G in the days of the taxing — Acts 5:37 — *1056*
rest throughout all Judaea and G — Acts 9:31 — *1056*
all Judaea, and began from G — Acts 10:37 — *1056*
up with him from G to Jerusalem — Acts 13:31 — *1056*

GALL
among you a root that beareth g — Deut 29:18 — 7219
their grapes are grapes of g — Deut 32:32 — 7219
poureth out my g upon the ground — Job 16:13 — 4845
it is the g of asps within him — Job 20:14 — 4846
sword cometh out of his g — Job 20:25 — 4846
They gave me also g for my meat — Ps 69:21 — 7219
and given us water of g to drink — Jer 8:14 — 7219
and give them water of g to drink — Jer 9:15 — 7219
and make them drink the water of g — Jer 23:15 — 7219
me, and compassed me with g — Lam 3:5 — 7219
my misery, the wormwood and the g — Lam 3:19 — 7219
ye have turned judgment into g — Amos 6:12 — 7219
vinegar to drink mingled with g — Mt 27:34 — *5521*
thou art in the g of bitterness — Acts 8:23 — *5521*

GALLANT
neither shall g ship pass thereby — Is 33:21 — 117

GALLERIES
the king is held in the g — Song 7:5 — 7298
the g thereof on the one side and — Eze 41:15 — 862
the g round about on their three — Eze 41:16 — 862
for the g were higher than these — Eze 42:5 — 862

GALLERY
was g against g in three — Eze 42:3 — 862

GALLEY
wherein shall go no g with oars — Is 33:21 — 590

GALLIM *(gal'-lim) A city in Benjamin.*
the son of Laish, which was of G — 1Sa 25:44 — 1554
up thy voice, O daughter of G — Is 10:30 — 1554

GALLIO *(gal'-le-o) A Roman proconsul of Achaia.*
when G was the deputy of Achaia — Acts 18:12 — *1058*
G said unto the Jews, If it were — Acts 18:14 — *1058*
G cared for none of those things — Acts 18:17 — *1058*

GALLOWS
Let a g be made of fifty cubits — Est 5:14 — 6086
and he caused the g to be made — Est 5:14 — 6086
g that he had prepared for him — Est 6:4 — 6086
the g fifty cubits high, which — Est 7:9 — 6086
on the g that he had prepared for — Est 7:10 — 6086
him they have hanged upon the g — Est 8:7 — 6086
ten sons be hanged upon the g — Est 9:13 — 6086
sons should be hanged on the g — Est 9:25 — 6086

GAMAD See GAMMADIMS.

GAMALIEL *(gam-a'-le-el)*
1. A chief of Manasseh.
G the son of Pedahzur — Num 1:10 — 1583
shall be G the son of Pedahzur — Num 2:20 — 1583
day offered G the son of Pedahzur — Num 7:54 — 1583
offering of G the son of Pedahzur — Num 7:59 — 1583
was G the son of Pedahzur — Num 10:23 — 1583
2. A noted Rabbinic teacher.
the council, a Pharisee, named G — Acts 5:34 — *1059*
up in this city at the feet of G — Acts 22:3 — *1059*

GAMMAD See GAMMADIMS.

GAMMADIM See GAMMADIMS.

GAMMADIMS *(gam'-ma-dims) Defenders of Tyre.*
and the G were in thy towers — Eze 27:11 — 1575

GAMUL *(ga'-mul)* See BETH-GAMUL. *A sanctuary servant in David's time.*
Jachin, the two and twentieth to G — 1Chr 24:17 — 1577

GAP
stand in the g before me for the — Eze 22:30 — 6556

GAPED
They have g upon me with their — Job 16:10 — 6473
They g upon me with their mouths — Ps 22:13 — 6475

GAPS
Ye have not gone up into the g — Eze 13:5 — 6556

GARDEN
God planted a g eastward in Eden — Gen 2:8 — 1588
life also in the midst of the g — Gen 2:9 — 1588
went out of Eden to water the g — Gen 2:10 — 1588
put him into the g of Eden to — Gen 2:15 — 1588
Of every tree of the g thou — Gen 2:16 — 1588
not eat of every tree of the g — Gen 3:1 — 1588
the fruit of the trees of the g — Gen 3:2 — 1588
which is in the midst of the g — Gen 3:3 — 1588
in the g in the cool of the day — Gen 3:8 — 1588
God amongst the trees of the g — Gen 3:8 — 1588
said, I heard thy voice in the g — Gen 3:10 — 1588
sent him forth from the g of Eden — Gen 3:23 — 1588
east of the g of Eden Cherubim — Gen 3:24 — 1588
even as the g of the LORD — Gen 13:10 — 1588
it with thy foot, as a g of herbs — Deut 11:10 — 1588
I may have it for a g of herbs — 1Kin 21:2 — 1588
he fled by the way of the g house — 2Kin 9:27 — 1588
buried in the g of his own house — 2Kin 21:18 — 1588
his own house, in the g of Uzza — 2Kin 21:18 — 1588
in his sepulchre in the g of Uzza — 2Kin 21:26 — 1588
walls, which is by the king's g — 2Kin 25:4 — 1588
pool of Siloah by the king's g — Neh 3:15 — 1588
in the court of the g of the — Est 1:5 — 1594
his wrath went into the palace g — Est 7:7 — 1594
g into the place of the banquet — Est 7:8 — 1594
branch shooteth forth in his g — Job 8:16 — 1593
A g inclosed is my sister, my — Song 4:12 — 1588
blow upon my g, that the spices — Song 4:16 — 1588
Let my beloved come into his g — Song 4:16 — 1588
I am come into my g, my sister — Song 5:1 — 1588
beloved is gone down into his g — Song 6:2 — 1588
I went down into the g of nuts to — Song 6:11 — 1594
as a lodge in a g of cucumbers — Is 1:8
as a g that hath no water — Is 1:30 — 1593
her desert like the g of the LORD — Is 51:3 — 1588
and thou shalt be like a watered g — Is 58:11 — 1588
as the g causeth the things that — Is 61:11 — 1593
soul shall be as a watered g — Jer 31:12 — 1588
night, by the way of the king's g — Jer 39:4 — 1588
walls, which was by the king's g — Jer 52:7 — 1588
tabernacle, as if it were of a g — Lam 2:6 — 1588
hast been in Eden the g of God — Eze 28:13 — 1588
The cedars in the g of God could — Eze 31:8 — 1588
nor any tree in the g of God was — Eze 31:8 — 1588
Eden, that were in the g of God — Eze 31:9 — 1588
is become like the g of Eden — Eze 36:35 — 1588
the land is as the g of Eden — Joel 2:3 — 1588
a man took, and cast into his g — Lk 13:19 — *2779*
the brook Cedron, where was a g — Jn 18:1 — *2779*
not I see thee in the g with him — Jn 18:26 — *2779*
he was crucified there was a g — Jn 19:41 — *2779*
in the g a new sepulchre, wherein — Jn 19:41 — *2779*

GARDENER
She, supposing him to be the g — Jn 20:15 — *2780*

GARDENS
as g by the river's side, as the — Num 24:6 — 1593
I made me g and orchards, and I — Eccl 2:5 — 1593
A fountain of g, a well of living — Song 4:15 — 1588
beds of spices, to feed in the g — Song 6:2 — 1588
Thou that dwellest in the g — Song 8:13 — 1588
for the g that ye have chosen — Is 1:29 — 1593
that sacrificeth in g, and burneth — Is 65:3 — 1593
purify themselves in the g behind — Is 66:17 — 1593
and plant g, and eat the fruit of — Jer 29:5 — 1593
and plant g, and eat the fruit of — Jer 29:28 — 1593
when your g and your vineyards and — Amos 4:9 — 1593
they shall also make g, and eat — Amos 9:14 — 1593

GAREB *(ga'-reb)*
1. A "mighty man" of David.
Ira an Ithrite, G an Ithrite — 2Sa 23:38 — 1619
Ira the Ithrite, G the Ithrite — 1Chr 11:40 — 1619
2. A hill near Jerusalem.
over against it upon the hill G — Jer 31:39 — 1619

GARLANDS
g unto the gates, and would have — Acts 14:13 — *4725*

GARLICK
leeks, and the onions, and the g — Num 11:5 — 7762

GARMENT
And Shem and Japheth took a g — Gen 9:23 — 8071
out red, all over like an hairy g — Gen 25:25 — 155
And she caught him by his g — Gen 39:12 — 899
and he left his g in her hand — Gen 39:12 — 899
he had left his g in her hand — Gen 39:13 — 899
cried, that he left his g with me — Gen 39:15 — 899
And she laid up his g by her — Gen 39:16 — 899
cried, that he left his g with me — Gen 39:18 — 899
priest shall put on his linen g — Lev 6:10 — 4055
of the blood thereof upon any g — Lev 6:27 — 899
The g also that the plague of — Lev 13:47 — 899
a woollen g, or a linen g — Lev 13:47 — 899
be greenish or reddish in the g — Lev 13:49 — 899
if the plague be spread in the g — Lev 13:51 — 899
He shall therefore burn that g — Lev 13:52 — 899
the plague be not spread in the g — Lev 13:53 — 899
he shall rend it out of the g — Lev 13:56 — 899
And if it appear still in the g — Lev 13:57 — 899
And the g, either warp, or woof — Lev 13:58 — 899
in a g of woollen or linen — Lev 13:59 — 899
And for the leprosy of a g — Lev 14:55 — 899
And every g, and every skin — Lev 15:17 — 899
neither shall a g mingled of — Lev 19:19 — 899
shall a man put on a woman's g — Deut 22:5 — 8071
not wear a g of divers sorts — Deut 22:11 — 8162
the spoils a goodly Babylonish g — Josh 7:21 — 155
of Zerah, and the silver, and the g — Josh 7:24 — 155
And they spread a g, and did cast — Judg 8:25 — 8071
she had a g of divers colours — 2Sa 13:18 — 3801
rent her g of divers colours that — 2Sa 13:19 — 3801
Joab's g that he had put on was — 2Sa 20:8 — 4055
he had clad himself with a new g — 1Kin 11:29 — 8008
caught the new g that was on him — 1Kin 11:30 — 8008
hasted, and took every man his g — 2Kin 9:13 — 899
I heard this thing, I rent my g — Ezr 9:3 — 899
and having rent my g and my mantle, — Ezr 9:5 — 899
with a g of fine linen and purple — Est 8:15 — 8509
as a g that is moth eaten — Job 13:28 — 899
of my disease is my g changed — Job 30:18 — 3830
I made the cloud the g thereof — Job 38:9 — 3830
and they stand as a g — Job 38:14 — 3830
can discover the face of his g — Job 41:13 — 3830
I made sackcloth also my g — Ps 69:11 — 3830
violence covereth them as a g — Ps 73:6 — 7897
of them shall wax old like a g — Ps 102:26 — 899
thyself with light as with a g — Ps 104:2 — 8008
it with the deep as with a g — Ps 104:6 — 3830
with cursing like as with his g — Ps 109:18 — 4055
him as the g which covereth him — Ps 109:19 — 899
Take his g that is surety for a — Prov 20:16 — 899
taketh away a g in cold weather — Prov 25:20 — 899
Take his g that is surety for a — Prov 27:13 — 899
who hath bound the waters in a g — Prov 30:4 — 8071
lo, they all shall wax old as a g — Is 50:9 — 899
the earth shall wax old like a g — Is 51:6 — 899
moth shall eat them up like a g — Is 51:8 — 899
the g of praise for the spirit of — Is 61:3 — 4594
as a shepherd putteth on his g — Jer 43:12 — 899
hath covered the naked with a g — Eze 18:7 — 899
hath covered the naked with a g — Eze 18:16 — 899
whose g was white as snow, and the — Dan 7:9 — 3831
ye pull off the robe with the g — Mic 2:8 — 8008
holy flesh in the skirt of his g — Hag 2:12 — 899
they wear a rough g to deceive — Zec 13:4 — 155
one covereth violence with his g — Mal 2:16 — 3830
piece of new cloth unto an old g — Mt 9:16 — *2440*
to fill it up taketh from the g — Mt 9:16 — *2440*
him, and touched the hem of his g — Mt 9:20 — *2440*
herself, If I may but touch his g — Mt 9:21 — *2440*
might only touch the hem of his g — Mt 14:36 — *2440*
man which had not on a wedding g — Mt 22:11 — *1742*
in hither not having a wedding g — Mt 22:12 — *1742*
a piece of new cloth on an old g — Mk 2:21 — *2440*
press behind, and touched his g — Mk 5:27 — *2440*
it were but the border of his g — Mk 6:56 — *2440*
And he, casting away his g — Mk 10:50 — *2440*
back again for to take up his g — Mk 13:16 — *2440*
side, clothed in a long white g — Mk 16:5 — *4749*
a piece of a new g upon an old — Lk 5:36 — *2440*
and touched the border of his g — Lk 8:44 — *2440*
hath no sword, let him sell his g — Lk 22:36 — *2440*
Cast thy g about thee, and follow — Acts 12:8 — *2440*
all shall wax old as doth a g — Heb 1:11 — *2440*
hating even the g spotted by the — Jude 23 — *5509*
clothed with a g down to the foot — Rev 1:13 — *4158*

GARMENTS
and be clean, and change your g — Gen 35:2 — 8071
put her widow's g off from her — Gen 38:14 — 899
put on the g of her widowhood — Gen 38:19 — 899
he washed his g in wine, and his — Gen 49:11 — 3830
thou shalt make holy g for Aaron — Ex 28:2 — 899
make Aaron's g to consecrate him — Ex 28:3 — 899
these are the g which they shall — Ex 28:4 — 899
they shall make holy g for Aaron — Ex 28:4 — 899
And thou shalt take the g, and put — Ex 29:5 — 899
it upon Aaron, and upon his g — Ex 29:21 — 899
upon the g of his sons with him — Ex 29:21 — 899
and he shall be hallowed, and his g — Ex 29:21 — 899
his sons, and his sons' g with him — Ex 29:21 — 899
the holy g of Aaron shall be his — Ex 29:29 — 899
the holy g for Aaron the priest, — Ex 31:10 — 899
the g of his sons, to minister in — Ex 31:10 — 899
the holy g for Aaron the priest, — Ex 35:19 — 899
the g of his sons, to minister in — Ex 35:19 — 899
his service, and for the holy g — Ex 35:21 — 899
and made the holy g for Aaron — Ex 39:1 — 899
the holy g for Aaron the priest, — Ex 39:41 — 899
Aaron the priest, and his sons' g — Ex 39:41 — 899
shalt put upon Aaron the holy g — Ex 40:13 — 899
his g, and put on other g — Lev 6:11 — 899
and his sons with him, and the g — Lev 8:2 — 899
it upon Aaron, and upon his g — Lev 8:30 — 899
and upon his sons' g with him — Lev 8:30 — 899
and sanctified Aaron, and his g — Lev 8:30 — 899
his sons, and his sons' g with him — Lev 8:30 — 899
these are holy g — Lev 16:4 — 899
and shall put off the linen g — Lev 16:23 — 899
the holy place, and put on his g — Lev 16:24 — 899
linen clothes, even the holy g — Lev 16:32 — 899
is consecrated to put on the g — Lev 21:10 — 899
g throughout their generations — Num 15:38 — 899
And strip Aaron of his g, and put — Num 20:26 — 899
And Moses stripped Aaron of his g — Num 20:28 — 899
their feet, and old g upon them — Josh 9:5 — 8008
and these our g and our shoes are — Josh 9:13 — 8008
sheets and thirty change of g — Judg 14:12 — 899
sheets and thirty change of g — Judg 14:13 — 899
gave change of g unto them which — Judg 14:19
and gave it to David, and his g — 1Sa 18:4 — 4055
and cut off their g in the middle — 2Sa 10:4 — 4063
the king arose, and tare his g — 2Sa 13:31 — 899
silver, and vessels of gold, and g — 1Kin 10:25 — 8008
of silver, and two changes of g — 2Kin 5:22 — 899
two bags, with two changes of g — 2Kin 5:23 — 899
to receive money, and to receive g — 2Kin 5:26 — 899
and, lo, all the way was full of g — 2Kin 7:15 — 899
And changed his prison g — 2Kin 25:29 — 899
cut off their g in the midst hard — 1Chr 19:4 — 4063
silver, and one hundred priests' g — Ezr 2:69 — 3801
five hundred and thirty priests' g — Neh 7:70 — 3801
and threescore and seven priests' g — Neh 7:72 — 3801
How thy g are warm, when he — Job 37:17 — 899
They part my g among them — Ps 22:18 — 899
All thy g smell of myrrh, and — Ps 45:8 — 899
went down to the skirts of his g — Ps 133:2 — 4060
Let thy g be always white — Eccl 9:8 — 899
the smell of thy g is like the — Song 4:11 — 8008
noise, and g rolled in blood — Is 9:5 — 8071
put on thy beautiful g, O — Is 52:1 — 899
Their webs shall not become g — Is 59:6 — 899
he put on the g of vengeance for — Is 59:17 — 899
me with the g of salvation — Is 61:10 — 899
Edom, with dyed g from Bozrah — Is 63:1 — 899
thy g like him that treadeth in — Is 63:2 — 899
shall be sprinkled upon my g — Is 63:3 — 899
were not afraid, nor rent their g — Jer 36:24 — 899
And changed his prison g — Jer 52:33 — 899
that men could not touch their g — Lam 4:14 — 3830
of thy g thou didst take, and — Eze 16:16 — 899
And tookest thy broidered g — Eze 16:18 — 899
and put off their broidered g — Eze 26:16 — 899
lay their g wherein they minister — Eze 42:14 — 899
and shall put on other g, and shall — Eze 42:14 — 899
shall be clothed with linen g — Eze 44:17 — 899
their g wherein they ministered — Eze 44:19 — 899
and they shall put on other g — Eze 44:19 — 899
sanctify the people with their g — Eze 44:19 — 899
and their hats, and their other g — Dan 3:21 — 3831
And rend your heart, and not your g — Joel 2:13 — 899
Joshua was clothed with filthy g — Zec 3:3 — 899
Take away the filthy g from him — Zec 3:4 — 899
his head, and clothed him with g — Zec 3:5 — 899
spread their g in the way — Mt 21:8 — *2440*
and enlarge the borders of their g — Mt 23:5 — *2440*

crucified him, and parted his g Mt 27:35 2440
They parted my g among them Mt 27:35 2440
to Jesus, and cast their g on him Mk 11:7 2440
And many spread their g in the way Mk 11:8 2440
crucified him, they parted his g Mk 15:24 2440
they cast their g upon the colt Lk 19:35 2440
men stood by them in shining g Lk 24:4 2067
from supper, and laid aside his g Jn 13:4 2440
their feet, and had taken his g Jn 13:12 2440
had crucified Jesus, took his g Jn 19:23 2440
g which Dorcas made, while she Acts 9:39 2440
and your g are motheaten Jas 5:2 2440
which have not defiled their g Rev 3:4 2440
that watcheth, and keepeth his g Rev 16:15 2440

GARMITE (*gar'-mite*) *A descendant of Judah.*
Naham, the father of Keilah the G 1Chr 4:19 1636

GARNER
and gather his wheat into the g Mt 3:12 596
will gather the wheat into his g Lk 3:17 596

GARNERS
That our g may be full, affording Ps 144:13 4200
the g are laid desolate, the Joel 1:17 214

GARNISH
g the sepulchres of the righteous Mt 23:29 2885

GARNISHED
he g the house with precious 2Chr 3:6 6823
his spirit he hath g the heavens Job 26:13 8235
he findeth it empty, swept, and g Mt 12:44 2885
cometh, he findeth it swept and g Lk 11:25 2885
g with all manner of precious Rev 21:19 2885

GARRISON
where is the g of the Philistines 1Sa 10:5 5333
Jonathan smote the g of the 1Sa 13:3 5333
smitten a g of the Philistines 1Sa 13:4 5333
the g of the Philistines went out 1Sa 13:23 4673
us go over to the Philistines' g 1Sa 14:1 4673
go over unto the Philistines' g 1Sa 14:4 4673
unto the g of these uncircumcised 1Sa 14:6 4673
unto the g of the Philistines 1Sa 14:11 4673
the men of the g answered 1Sa 14:12 4675
the g, and the spoilers, they also 1Sa 14:15 4673
the g of the Philistines was then 2Sa 23:14 4673
the Philistines' g was then at 1Chr 11:16 5333
city of the Damascenes with a g 2Cor 11:32 5432

GARRISONS
Then David put g in Syria of 2Sa 8:6 5333
And he put g in Edom 2Sa 8:14 5333
throughout all Edom put he g 2Sa 8:14 5333
Then David put g in 1Chr 18:6
And he put g in Edom 1Chr 18:13 5333
set g in the land of Judah, and in 2Chr 17:2 5333
thy strong g shall go down to the Eze 26:11 4676

GASHMU (*gash'-mu*) See GESHEM. *A Samaritan in Nehemiah's time.*
G saith it, that thou and the Jews Neh 6:6 1654

GAT
Abraham g up early in the morning Gen 19:27
cloud, and g him up into the mount Ex 24:18 5927
Moses g him into the camp, he and Num 11:30 622
g them up into the top of the Num 14:40 5927
So they g up from the tabernacle Num 16:27 5927
Abimelech g him up to mount Judg 9:48 5927
g them up to the top of the tower Judg 9:51 5927
rose up, and g him unto his place Judg 19:28 3212
g him up from Gilgal unto Gibeah 1Sa 13:15 5927
his men g them up unto the hold 1Sa 24:22 5927
they g them away, and no man saw 1Sa 26:12 3212
g them away through the plain all 2Sa 4:7 3212
David g him a name when he 2Sa 8:13 6213
every man g him up upon his mule, 2Sa 13:29 7392
g him home to his house, to his 2Sa 17:23 3212
the people g them by stealth that 2Sa 19:3 935
with clothes, but he g no heat 1Kin 1:1
the pains of hell g hold upon me Ps 116:3
I g me men singers and women Eccl 2:8 6213
We g our bread with the peril of Lam 5:9 935

GATAM (*ga'-tam*) *A son of Eliphaz.*
were Teman, Omar, Zepho, and G Gen 36:11 1609
Duke Korah, duke G, and duke Gen 36:16 1609
Teman, and Omar, Zephi, and G 1Chr 1:36 1609

GATE
and Lot sat in the g of Sodom Gen 19:1 8179
possess the g of his enemies Gen 22:17 8179
that went in at the g of his city Gen 23:10 8179
that went in at the g of his city Gen 23:18 8179
the g of those which hate them Gen 24:60 8179
God, and this is the g of heaven Gen 28:17 8179
son came unto the g of their city Gen 34:20 8179
went out of the g of his city Gen 34:24 8179
went out of the g of his city Gen 34:24 8179
of the g shall be fifteen cubits Ex 27:14
for the g of the court shall be Ex 27:16 8179
Moses stood in the g of the camp Ex 32:26 8179
out from g to g throughout the Ex 32:27 8179
side of the g were fifteen cubits Ex 38:14
for the other side of the court g Ex 38:15 8179
the hanging for the g of the Ex 38:18 8179
and the sockets of the court g Ex 38:31 8179
and the hanging for the court g Ex 39:40 8179
up the hanging at the court g Ex 40:8 8179
set up the hanging of the court g Ex 40:33 8179
the door of the g of the court Num 4:26 8179
city, and unto the g of his place Deut 21:19 8179
the elders of the city in the g Deut 22:15 8179
both out unto the g of that city Deut 22:24 8179
go up to the g unto the elders Deut 25:7 8179
the time of shutting of the g Josh 2:5 8179
were gone out, they shut the g Josh 2:7 8179
before the g even unto Shebarim Josh 7:5 8179
the entering of the g of the city Josh 8:29 8179
the entering of the g of the city Josh 20:4 8179
the entering of the g of the city Judg 9:35 8179
even unto the entering of the g Judg 9:40 8179
the entering of the g of the city Judg 9:44 8179
all night in the g of the city Judg 16:2 8179
the doors of the g of the city Judg 16:3 8179
stood by the entering of the g Judg 18:16 8179
stood in the entering of the g Judg 18:17 8179
Then went Boaz up to the g Ruth 4:1 8179
and from the g of his place Ruth 4:10 8179
all the people that were in the g Ruth 4:11 8179
backward by the side of the g 1Sa 4:18 8179
Saul drew near to Samuel in the g 1Sa 9:18 8179
scrabbled on the doors of the g 1Sa 21:13 8179
the g to speak with him quietly 2Sa 3:27 8179
array at the entering in of the g 2Sa 10:8 8179
even unto the entering of the g 2Sa 11:23 8179
and stood beside the way of the g 2Sa 15:2 8179
And the king stood by the g side 2Sa 18:4 8179
the roof over the g unto the wall 2Sa 18:24 8179
went up to the chamber over the g 2Sa 18:33 8179
the king arose, and sat in the g 2Sa 19:8 8179
the king doth sit in the g 2Sa 19:8 8179
of Beth-lehem, which is by the g 2Sa 23:15 8179
of Beth-lehem, that was by the g 2Sa 23:16 8179
when he came to the g of the city 1Kin 17:10 6607
the entrance of the g of Samaria 1Kin 22:10 8179
for a shekel, in the g of Samaria 2Kin 7:1 8179
men at the entering in of the g 2Kin 7:3 8179
to have the charge of the g 2Kin 7:17 8179
people trode upon him in the g 2Kin 7:17 8179
this time in the g of Samaria 2Kin 7:18 8179
people trode upon him in the g 2Kin 7:20 8179
And as Jehu entered in at the g 2Kin 9:31 8179
in of the g until the morning 2Kin 10:8 8179
part shall be at the g of Sur 2Kin 11:6 8179
part at the g behind the guard 2Kin 11:6 8179
came by the way of the g of the 2Kin 11:19 8179
g of Ephraim unto the corner g 2Kin 14:13 8179
He built the higher g of the 2Kin 15:35 8179
g of Joshua the governor of the 2Kin 23:8 8179
left hand at the g of the city 2Kin 23:8 8179
way of the g between two walls 2Kin 25:4 8179
waited in the king's g eastward 1Chr 9:18 8179
of Beth-lehem, that is at the g 1Chr 11:17 8179
of Beth-lehem, that was by the g 1Chr 11:18 8179
in array before the g of the city 1Chr 19:9 6607
of their fathers, for every g 1Chr 26:13 8179
with the g Shallecheth, by the 1Chr 26:16 8179
also by their courses at every g 2Chr 8:14 8179
entering in of the g of Samaria 2Chr 18:9 8179
part at the g of the foundation 2Chr 23:5 8179
the horse g by the king's house 2Chr 23:15 8179
the high g into the king's house 2Chr 23:20 8179
set it without at the g of the 2Chr 24:8 8179
g of Ephraim to the corner g 2Chr 25:23 8179
corner g, and at the valley g 2Chr 26:9 8179
He built the high g of the house 2Chr 27:3 8179
the street of the g of the city 2Chr 32:6 8179
to the entering in at the fish g 2Chr 33:14 8179
and the porters waited at every g 2Chr 35:15 8179
by night by the g of the valley Neh 2:13 8179
went on to the g of the fountain Neh 2:14 8179
and entered by the g of the valley Neh 2:15 8179
and they builded the sheep g Neh 3:1 8179
But the fish g did the sons of Neh 3:3 8179
Moreover the old g repaired Neh 3:6 8179
The valley g repaired Hanun, and Neh 3:13 8179
on the wall unto the dung g Neh 3:13 8179
But the dung g repaired Malchiah Neh 3:14 8179
But the g of the fountain Neh 3:15 8179
the water g toward the east Neh 3:26 8179
the horse g repaired the priests Neh 3:28 8179
the keeper of the east g Neh 3:29 8179
over against the g Miphkad Neh 3:31 8179
sheep g repaired the goldsmiths Neh 3:32 8179
that was before the water g Neh 8:1 8179
that was before the water g from Neh 8:3 8179
and in the street of the water g Neh 8:16 8179
in the street of the g of Ephraim Neh 8:16 8179
upon the wall toward the dung g Neh 12:31 8179
And at the fountain g, which was Neh 12:37 8179
even unto the water g eastward Neh 12:37 8179
And from above the g of Ephraim Neh 12:39 8179
the old g, and above the fish g Neh 12:39 8179
of Meah, even unto the sheep g Neh 12:39 8179
they stood still in the prison g Neh 12:39 8179
then Mordecai sat in the king's g Est 2:19 8179
Mordecai sat in the king's g Est 2:21 8179
that were in the king's g Est 3:2 8179
which were in the king's g Est 3:3 8179
And came even before the king's g Est 4:2 8179
king's g clothed with sackcloth Est 4:2 8179
which was before the king's g Est 4:6 8179
over against the g of the house Est 5:1 6607
saw Mordecai in the king's g Est 5:9 8179
the Jew sitting at the king's g Est 5:13 8179
Jew, that sitteth at the king's g Est 6:10 8179
came again to the king's g Est 6:12 8179
and they are crushed in the g Job 5:4 8179
out to the g through the city Job 29:7 8179
when I saw my help in the g Job 31:21 8179
sit in the g speak against me Ps 69:12 8179
This g of the LORD, into which Ps 118:20 8179
speak with the enemies in the g Ps 127:5 8179
his g seeketh destruction Prov 17:19 6607
oppress the afflicted in the g Prov 22:22 8179
he openeth not his mouth in the g Prov 24:7 8179
Heshbon, by the g of Bath-rabbim Song 7:4 8179
Howl, O g; cry, O city Is 14:31 8179
set themselves in array at the g Is 22:7 8179
the g is smitten with destruction Is 24:12 8179
that turn the battle to the g Is 28:6 8179
for him that reproveth in the g Is 29:21 8179
Stand in the g of the LORD's Jer 7:2 8179
stand in the g of the children of Jer 17:19 8179
is by the entry of the east g Jer 19:2 8179
were in the high g of Benjamin Jer 20:2 8179
of the new g of the LORD's house Jer 26:10 8179
Hananeel unto the g of the corner Jer 31:38 8179
of the horse g toward the east Jer 31:40 8179
of the new g of the LORD's house Jer 36:10 8179
when he was in the g of Benjamin Jer 37:13 8179
then sitting in the g of Benjamin Jer 38:7 8179
came in, and sat in the middle g Jer 39:3 8179
by the g betwixt the two walls Jer 39:4 8179
of the g between the two walls Jer 52:7 8179
The elders have ceased from the g Lam 5:14 8179
to the door of the inner g Eze 8:3 8179
behold northward at the g of the Eze 8:5 8179
g of the LORD's house which was Eze 8:14 8179
came from the way of the higher g Eze 9:2 8179
of the east g of the LORD's house Eze 10:19 8179
the east g of the LORD's house Eze 11:1 8179
behold at the door of the g five Eze 11:1 8179
and he stood in the g Eze 40:3 8179
Then came he unto the g which Eze 40:6 8179
measured the threshold of the g Eze 40:6 8179
and the other threshold of the g Eze 40:6
the threshold of the g by the Eze 40:7 8179
of the g within was one reed Eze 40:7 8179
also the porch of the g within Eze 40:8 8179
measured he the porch of the g Eze 40:9 8179
and the porch of the g was inward Eze 40:9 8179
the little chambers of the g Eze 40:10 8179
the breadth of the entry of the g Eze 40:11 8179
and the length of the g, thirteen Eze 40:11 8179
He measured then the g from the Eze 40:13 8179
of the court round about the g Eze 40:14 8179
from the face of the g of the Eze 40:15 8179
of the inner g were fifty cubits Eze 40:15 8179
posts within the g round about Eze 40:16 8179
g unto the forefront of the inner Eze 40:19 8179
the g of the outward court that Eze 40:20 8179
after the measure of the first g Eze 40:21 8179
g that looketh toward the east Eze 40:22 8179
the g of the inner court was over Eze 40:23 8179
against the g toward the north Eze 40:23 8179
from g to g an hundred cubits Eze 40:23 8179
behold a g toward the south Eze 40:24 8179
there was a g in the inner court Eze 40:27 8179
he measured from g to g toward Eze 40:27 8179
to the inner court by the south g Eze 40:28 8179
he measured the south g according Eze 40:28 8179
he measured the g according to Eze 40:32 8179
And he brought me to the north g Eze 40:35 8179
in the porch of the g were two Eze 40:39 8179
up to the entry of the north g Eze 40:40 8179
which was at the porch of the g Eze 40:40 8179
that side, by the side of the g Eze 40:41 8179
without the inner g were the Eze 40:44 8179
was at the side of the north g Eze 40:44 8179
one at the side of the east g Eze 40:44 8179
the breadth of the g was three Eze 40:48 8179
g whose prospect is toward the Eze 42:15 8179
Afterward he brought me to the g Eze 43:1 8179
even the g that looketh toward Eze 43:1 8179
the house by the way of the g Eze 43:4 8179
g of the outward sanctuary which Eze 44:1 8179
This g shall be shut, it shall Eze 44:2 8179
by the way of the porch of that g Eze 44:3 8179
of the north g before the house Eze 44:4 8179
posts of the g of the inner court Eze 45:19 8179
The g of the inner court that Eze 46:1 8179
of the porch of that g without Eze 46:2 8179
shall stand by the post of the g Eze 46:2 8179
worship at the threshold of the g Eze 46:2 8179
but the g shall not be shut until Eze 46:2 8179
worship at the door of this g Eze 46:3 8179
by the way of the porch of that g Eze 46:8 8179
in by the way of the north g to Eze 46:9 8179
go out by the way of the south g Eze 46:9 8179
by the way of the south g shall Eze 46:9 8179
forth by the way of the north g Eze 46:9 8179
way of the g whereby he came in Eze 46:9 8179
one shall then open him the g Eze 46:12 8179
going forth one shall shut the g Eze 46:12 8179
which was at the side of the g Eze 46:19 8179
out of the way of the g northward Eze 47:2 8179
utter g by the way that looketh Eze 47:2 8179
one g of Reuben Eze 48:31 8179
one g of Judah, one g of Levi Eze 48:31 8179
one g of Joseph Eze 48:32 8179
g of Benjamin, one g of Dan Eze 48:32 8179
one g of Simeon Eze 48:33 8179
of Issachar, one g of Zebulun Eze 48:33 8179
one g of Gad Eze 48:34 8179
g of Asher, one g of Naphtali Eze 48:34 8179
Daniel sat in the g of the king Dan 2:49 8651
hate him that rebuketh in the g Amos 5:10 8179
poor in the g from their right Amos 5:12 8179
and establish judgment in the g Amos 5:15 8179
not have entered into the g of my Obad 13 8179
is come unto the g of my people Mic 1:9 8179
the LORD unto the g of Jerusalem Mic 1:12 8179
up, and have passed through the g Mic 2:13 8179
noise of a cry from the fish g Zeph 1:10 8179
from Benjamin's g unto the place Zec 14:10 8179
the first g, unto the corner g Zec 14:10 8179
Enter ye in at the strait g Mt 7:13 4439
for wide is the g, and broad is Mt 7:13 4439
Because strait is the g, and Mt 7:14 4439
he came nigh to the g of the city Lk 7:12 4439
to enter in at the strait g Lk 13:24 4439
Lazarus, which was laid at his g Lk 16:20 4440
whom they laid daily at the g of Acts 3:2 2374

at the Beautiful g of the temple	Acts 3:10	4439
house, and stood before the g	Acts 10:17	4440
they came unto the iron g that	Acts 12:10	4439
knocked at the door of the g	Acts 12:13	4440
she opened not the g for gladness	Acts 12:14	4440
told how Peter stood before the g	Acts 12:14	4440
own blood, suffered without the g	Heb 13:12	4439
every several g was of one pearl	Rev 21:21	

GATES

thy stranger that is within thy g	Ex 20:10	8179
were fenced with high walls, g	Deut 3:5	1817
thy stranger that is within thy g	Deut 5:14	8179
posts of thy house, and on thy g	Deut 6:9	8179
of thine house, and upon thy g	Deut 11:20	8179
the Levite that is within your g	Deut 12:12	8179
kill and eat flesh in all thy g	Deut 12:15	8179
thy g the tithe of thy corn	Deut 12:17	8179
the Levite that is within thy g	Deut 12:18	8179
thee, and thou shalt eat in thy g	Deut 12:21	8179
the stranger that is in thy g	Deut 14:21	8179
the Levite that is within thy g	Deut 14:27	8179
and shalt lay it up within thy g	Deut 14:28	8179
the widow, which are within thy g	Deut 14:29	8179
g in thy land which the LORD thy	Deut 15:7	8179
Thou shalt eat it within thy g	Deut 15:22	8179
the passover within any of thy g	Deut 16:5	8179
the Levite that is within thy g	Deut 16:11	8179
the widow, that are within thy g	Deut 16:14	8179
shalt thou make thee in all thy g	Deut 16:18	8179
within any of thy g which the	Deut 17:2	8179
that wicked thing, unto thy g	Deut 17:5	8179
of controversy within thy g	Deut 17:8	8179
any of thy g out of all Israel	Deut 18:6	8179
he shall choose in one of thy g	Deut 23:16	8179
that are in thy land within thy g	Deut 24:14	8179
that they may eat within thy g	Deut 26:12	8179
shall besiege thee in all thy g	Deut 28:52	8179
all thy g throughout all thy land	Deut 28:52	8179
shall distress thee in all thy g	Deut 28:55	8179
shall distress thee in thy g	Deut 28:57	8179
thy stranger that is within thy g	Deut 31:12	8179
son shall he set up the g of it	Josh 6:26	1817
then was war in the g	Judg 5:8	8179
of the LORD go down to the g	Judg 5:11	8179
the valley, and to the g of Ekron	1Sa 17:52	8179
entering into a town that hath g	1Sa 23:7	1817
And David sat between the two g	2Sa 18:24	8179
set up the g thereof in his	1Kin 16:34	1817
down the high places of the g	2Kin 23:8	8179
service, keepers of the g of the	1Chr 9:19	5592
porters in the g were two hundred	1Chr 9:22	5592
of the g of the house of the LORD	1Chr 9:23	8179
the nails for the doors of the g	1Chr 22:3	8179
fenced cities, with walls, g	2Chr 8:5	1817
about them walls, and towers, g	2Chr 14:7	1817
at the g of the house of the LORD	2Chr 23:19	8179
to praise in the g of the tents	2Chr 31:2	8179
the g thereof are burned with	Neh 1:3	8179
the g thereof are consumed with	Neh 2:3	8179
g of the palace which appertained	Neh 2:8	8179
the g thereof were consumed with	Neh 2:13	8179
the g thereof are burned with	Neh 2:17	8179
not set up the doors upon the g	Neh 6:1	8179
Let not the g of Jerusalem be	Neh 7:3	8179
and their brethren that kept the g	Neh 11:19	8179
ward at the thresholds of the g	Neh 12:25	8179
and purified the people, and the g	Neh 12:30	8179
that when the g of Jerusalem	Neh 13:19	8179
that the g should be shut	Neh 13:19	1817
of my servants set I at the g	Neh 13:19	8179
they should come and keep the g	Neh 13:22	8179
Have the g of death been opened	Job 38:17	8179
liftest me up from the g of death	Ps 9:13	8179
in the g of the daughter of Zion	Ps 9:14	8179
Lift up your heads, O ye g	Ps 24:7	8179
Lift up your heads, O ye g	Ps 24:9	8179
The LORD loveth the g of Zion	Ps 87:2	8179
Enter into his g with	Ps 100:4	8179
For he hath broken the g of brass	Ps 107:16	1817
draw near unto the g of death	Ps 107:18	8179
Open to me the g of righteousness	Ps 118:19	8179
Our feet shall stand within thy g	Ps 122:2	8179
strengthened the bars of thy g	Ps 147:13	8179
in the openings of the g	Prov 1:21	8179
She crieth at the g, at the entry	Prov 8:3	8179
me, watching daily at my g	Prov 8:34	1817
wicked at the g of the righteous	Prov 14:19	8179
Her husband is known in the g	Prov 31:23	8179
her own works praise her in the g	Prov 31:31	8179
at our g are all manner of	Song 7:13	6607
her g shall lament and mourn	Is 3:26	6607
may go into the g of the nobles	Is 13:2	6607
Open ye the g, that the righteous	Is 26:2	8179
I shall go to the g of the grave	Is 38:10	8179
open before him the two leaved g	Is 45:1	1817
and the g shall not be shut	Is 45:1	8179
break in pieces the g of brass	Is 45:2	1817
thy g of carbuncles, and all thy	Is 54:12	8179
Therefore thy g shall be open	Is 60:11	8179
walls Salvation, and thy g Praise	Is 60:18	8179
Go through, go through the g	Is 62:10	8179
entering of the g of Jerusalem	Jer 1:15	8179
in at these g to worship the LORD	Jer 7:2	8179
and the g thereof languish	Jer 14:2	8179
with a fan in the g of the land	Jer 15:7	8179
in all the g of Jerusalem	Jer 17:19	8179
that enter in by these g	Jer 17:20	8179
bring it in by the g of Jerusalem	Jer 17:21	8179
bring in no burden through the g	Jer 17:24	8179
into the g of this city kings	Jer 17:25	8179
even entering in at the g of	Jer 17:27	8179
I kindle a fire in the g thereof	Jer 17:27	8179
people that enter in by these g	Jer 22:2	8179
the g of this house kings sitting	Jer 22:4	8179
forth beyond the g of Jerusalem	Jer 22:19	8179
which have neither g nor bars	Jer 49:31	1817
her high g shall be burned with	Jer 51:58	8179
all her g are desolate	Lam 1:4	8179
Her g are sunk into the ground	Lam 2:9	8179
entered into the g of Jerusalem	Lam 4:12	8179
of the sword against all their g	Eze 21:15	8179
battering rams against the g	Eze 21:22	8179
that was the g of the people	Eze 26:2	1817
when he shall enter into thy g	Eze 26:10	8179
and having neither bars nor g	Eze 38:11	1817
g over against the length of the	Eze 40:18	8179
of the g was the lower pavement	Eze 40:18	8179
were by the posts of the g	Eze 40:38	8179
charge at the g of the house	Eze 44:11	8179
in at the g of the inner court	Eze 44:17	8179
in the g of the inner court	Eze 44:17	8179
the g of the city shall be after	Eze 48:31	8179
three g northward	Eze 48:31	8179
five hundred: and three g	Eze 48:32	8179
measures: and three g	Eze 48:33	8179
five hundred, with their three g	Eze 48:34	8179
and foreigners entered into his g	Obad 11	8179
The g of the rivers shall be	Nah 2:6	8179
the g of thy land shall be set	Nah 3:13	8179
of truth and peace in your g	Zec 8:16	8179
the g of hell shall not prevail	Mt 16:18	4439
And they watched the g day	Acts 9:24	4439
oxen and garlands unto the g	Acts 14:13	4440
great and high, and had twelve g	Rev 21:12	4440
at the g twelve angels, and names	Rev 21:12	4440
On the east three g	Rev 21:13	4440
on the north three g	Rev 21:13	4440
on the south three g	Rev 21:13	4440
and on the west three g	Rev 21:13	4440
the g thereof, and the wall	Rev 21:15	4440
the twelve g were twelve pearls	Rev 21:21	4440
the g of it shall not be shut at	Rev 21:25	4440
in through the g into the city	Rev 22:14	4440

GATH (*gath*) See GATH-HEPHER, GATH-RIMMON, GITTITE, MORESHETH-GATH. *A royal Philistine city.*

only in Gaza, in G, and in Ashdod,	Josh 11:22	1661
of Israel be carried about unto G	1Sa 5:8	1661
one, for Askelon one, for G one	1Sa 6:17	1661
to Israel, from Ekron even unto G	1Sa 7:14	1661
Philistines, named Goliath, of G	1Sa 17:4	1661
the champion, the Philistine of G	1Sa 17:23	1661
the way to Shaaraim, even unto G	1Sa 17:52	1661
and went to Achish the king of G	1Sa 21:10	1661
afraid of Achish the king of G	1Sa 21:12	1661
the son of Maoch, king of G	1Sa 27:2	1661
And David dwelt with Achish at G	1Sa 27:3	1661
Saul that David was fled to G	1Sa 27:4	1661
alive, to bring tidings to G	1Sa 27:11	1661
Tell it not in G, publish it not	2Sa 1:20	1661
men which came after him from G	2Sa 15:18	1661
And there was yet a battle in G	2Sa 21:20	1661
four were born to the giant in G	2Sa 21:22	1661
Achish son of Maachah king of G	1Kin 2:39	1661
Behold, thy servants be in G	1Kin 2:39	1661
went to G to Achish to seek his	1Kin 2:40	1661
and brought his servants from G	1Kin 2:40	1661
had gone from Jerusalem to G	1Kin 2:41	1661
went up, and fought against G	2Kin 12:17	1661
whom the men of G that were born	1Chr 7:21	1661
drove away the inhabitants of G	1Chr 8:13	1661
and subdued them, and took G	1Chr 18:1	1661
And yet again there was war at G	1Chr 20:6	1661
were born unto the giant in G	1Chr 20:8	1661
And G, and Mareshah, and Ziph,	2Chr 11:8	1661
and brake down the wall of G	2Chr 26:6	1661
the Philistines took him in G	Ps 56:t	1661
then go down to G of the	Amos 6:2	1661
Declare ye it not at G, weep ye	Mic 1:10	1661

GATHER

eaten, and thou shalt g it to thee	Gen 6:21	622
said unto his brethren, G stones	Gen 31:46	3950
they shall g themselves together	Gen 34:30	622
let them g all the food of those	Gen 41:35	6908
G yourselves together, that I may	Gen 49:1	622
G yourselves together, and hear,	Gen 49:2	6908
g the elders of Israel together,	Ex 3:16	622
them go and g straw for themselves	Ex 5:7	7197
to g stubble instead of straw	Ex 5:12	7197
g thy cattle, and all that thou	Ex 9:19	5756
g a certain rate every day, that	Ex 16:4	3950
be twice as much as they g daily	Ex 16:5	3950
G of it every man according to	Ex 16:16	3950
Six days ye shall g it	Ex 16:26	3950
on the seventh day for to g	Ex 16:27	3950
shalt g in the fruits thereof	Ex 23:10	622
g thou all the congregation	Lev 8:3	6950
field, neither shalt thou g the	Lev 19:9	3950
neither shalt thou g every grape	Lev 19:10	3950
neither shalt thou g any gleaning	Lev 23:22	3950
and g in the fruit thereof	Lev 25:3	622
neither g the grapes of thy vine	Lev 25:5	1219
nor g the grapes in it of thy	Lev 25:11	1219
not sow, nor g in our increase	Lev 25:20	622
thou shalt g the whole assembly	Num 8:9	6950
shall g themselves unto thee	Num 10:4	3259
G unto me seventy men of the	Num 11:16	622
a man that is clean shall g up	Num 19:9	622
g thou the assembly together,	Num 20:8	6950
G the people together, and I will	Num 21:16	622
G me the people together, and I	Deut 4:10	6950
that thou mayest g in thy corn	Deut 11:14	622
thou shalt g all the spoil of it	Deut 13:16	6908
shalt not g the grapes thereof	Deut 28:30	2490
field, and shalt g but little in	Deut 28:38	622
of the wine, nor g the grapes	Deut 28:39	103
g thee from all the nations,	Deut 30:3	6908
will the LORD thy God g thee	Deut 30:4	6908
G the people together, men, and	Deut 31:12	6950
G unto me all the elders of your	Deut 31:28	6950
g after the reapers among the	Ruth 2:7	622
G all Israel to Mizpeh, and I will	1Sa 7:5	6908
will g all Israel unto my lord	2Sa 3:21	6908
Now therefore g the rest of the	2Sa 12:28	622
g to me all Israel unto mount	1Kin 18:19	6908
out into the field to g herbs	2Kin 4:39	3950
I will g thee unto thy fathers,	2Kin 22:20	622
that they may g themselves unto	1Chr 13:2	6908
g us together, and deliver us from	1Chr 16:35	6908
David commanded to g together the	1Chr 22:2	3664
g of all Israel money to repair	2Chr 24:5	6908
I will g thee to thy fathers, and	2Chr 34:28	622
that they should g themselves	Ezr 10:7	6908
yet will I g them from thence, and	Neh 1:9	6908
heart to g together the nobles	Neh 7:5	6908
to g into them out of the fields	Neh 12:44	3664
that they may g together all the	Est 2:3	6908
g together all the Jews that are	Est 4:16	3664
city to g themselves together	Est 8:11	6950
or g together, then who can	Job 11:10	6950
they g the vintage of the wicked	Job 24:6	3953
if he g unto himself his spirit	Job 34:14	622
thy seed, and g it into thy barn	Job 39:12	622
G not my soul with sinners, nor	Ps 26:9	622
and knoweth not who shall g them	Ps 39:6	622
G my saints together unto me	Ps 50:5	622
They g themselves together, they	Ps 56:6	1481
They g themselves together	Ps 94:21	1413
they g themselves together, and	Ps 104:22	622
That thou givest them they g	Ps 104:28	3950
g us from among the heathen, to	Ps 106:47	6908
he shall g it for him that will	Prov 28:8	6908
sinner he giveth travail, to g	Eccl 2:26	622
a time to g stones together	Eccl 3:5	3664
in the gardens, and to g lilies	Song 6:2	3950
of Gebim g themselves to flee	Is 10:31	5756
g together the dispersed of Judah	Is 11:12	6908
and hatch, and g under her shadow	Is 34:15	1716
he shall g the lambs with his arm	Is 40:11	6908
the east, and g thee from the west	Is 43:5	6908
all these g themselves together,	Is 49:18	6908
with great mercies will I g thee	Is 54:7	6908
they shall surely g together	Is 54:15	1481
whosoever shall g together	Is 54:15	1481
Yet will I g others to him,	Is 56:8	6908
all they g themselves together,	Is 60:4	6908
g out the stones	Is 62:10	5619
come, that I will g all nations	Is 66:18	6908
g together, and say, Assemble	Jer 4:5	4390
g yourselves to flee out of the	Jer 6:1	5756
The children g wood, and the	Jer 7:18	3950
harvestman, and none shall g them	Jer 9:22	622
G up thy wares out of the land, O	Jer 10:17	622
I will g the remnant of my flock	Jer 23:3	6908
I will g you from all the nations	Jer 29:14	6908
g them from the coasts of the	Jer 31:8	6908
that scattered Israel will g him	Jer 31:10	6908
Behold, I will g them out of all	Jer 32:37	6908
g ye wine, and summer fruits, and	Jer 40:10	622
and none shall g up him that	Jer 49:5	6908
G ye together, and come against	Jer 49:14	6908
bright the arrows; g the shields	Jer 51:11	4390
I will even g you from the people	Eze 11:17	6908
therefore I will g all thy lovers	Eze 16:37	6908
I will even g them round about	Eze 16:37	6908
will g you out of the countries	Eze 20:34	6908
g you out of the countries	Eze 20:41	6908
therefore I will g you into the	Eze 22:19	6908
As they g silver, and brass, and	Eze 22:20	6910
so will I g you in mine anger and	Eze 22:20	6908
Yea, I will g you, and blow upon	Eze 22:21	3664
G the pieces thereof into it,	Eze 24:4	622
I g the Egyptians from the people	Eze 29:13	6908
g them from the countries, and	Eze 34:13	6908
g you out of all countries, and	Eze 36:24	6908
will g them on every side, and	Eze 37:21	6908
g yourselves on every side to my	Eze 39:17	622
sent to g together the princes	Dan 3:2	3673
the nations, now will I g them	Hos 8:10	6908
Egypt shall g them up, Memphis	Hos 9:6	6908
assembly, g the elders and all the	Joel 1:14	622
all faces shall g blackness	Joel 2:6	6908
G the people, sanctify the	Joel 2:16	622
g the children, and those that	Joel 2:16	622
I will also g all nations	Joel 3:2	6908
g yourselves together round about	Joel 3:11	6908
I will surely g the remnant of	Mic 2:12	6908
I will g her that is driven out,	Mic 4:6	6908
for he shall g them as the	Mic 4:12	6908
Now g thyself in troops, O	Mic 5:1	1413
the faces of them all g blackness	Nah 2:10	6908
they shall g the captivity as the	Hab 1:9	622
net, and g them in their drag	Hab 1:15	622
G yourselves together, yea,	Zeph 2:1	7197
g together, O nation not desired	Zeph 2:1	7197
determination is to g the nations	Zeph 3:8	622
I will g them that are sorrowful	Zeph 3:18	622
g her that was driven out	Zeph 3:19	6908
even in the time that I g you	Zeph 3:20	6908
I will hiss for them, and g them	Zec 10:8	6908
Egypt, and g them out of Assyria	Zec 10:10	6908
For I will g all nations against	Zec 14:2	622
g his wheat into the garner	Mt 3:12	4863
do they reap, nor g into barns	Mt 6:26	4863
Do men g grapes of thorns, or	Mt 7:16	4816
thou then that we go and g them up	Mt 13:28	4816
lest while ye g up the tares	Mt 13:29	4816
G ye together first the tares, and	Mt 13:30	4816
but g the wheat into my barn	Mt 13:30	4863
they shall g out of his kingdom	Mt 13:41	4816

they shall g together his elect Mt 24:31 *1996*
g where I have not strawed Mt 25:26 *4863*
shall g together his elect from Mk 13:27 *1996*
will g the wheat into his garner Lk 3:17 *4863*
For of thorns men do not g figs Lk 6:44 *4816*
of a bramble bush g they grapes Lk 6:44 *5166*
as a hen doth g her brood under Lk 13:34
G up the fragments that remain, Jn 6:12 *4863*
but that also he should g Jn 11:52 *4863*
men g them, and cast them into the Jn 15:6 *4863*
g together in one all things in Eph 1:10 *346*
g the clusters of the vine of the Rev 14:18 *5166*
to g them to the battle of that Rev 16:14 *4863*
g yourselves together unto the Rev 19:17 *4863*
to g them together to battle Rev 20:8 *4863*

GATHERED

be g together unto one place Gen 1:9 6960
their substance that they had g Gen 12:5 7408
and was g to his people Gen 25:8 622
and was g unto his people Gen 25:17 622
And thither were all the flocks g Gen 29:3 622
the cattle should be g together Gen 29:7 622
all the flocks be g together Gen 29:8 622
Laban g together all the men of Gen 29:22 622
was g unto his people, being old Gen 35:29 622
he g up all the food of the seven Gen 41:48 6908
Joseph g corn as the sand of the Gen 41:49 6651
Joseph g up all the money that Gen 47:14 3950
I am to be g unto my people Gen 49:29 622
he g up his feet into the bed, and Gen 49:33 622
ghost, and was g unto his people Gen 49:33 622
g together all the elders of the Ex 4:29 622
they g them together upon heaps Ex 8:14 6651
the waters were g together Ex 15:8 6192
children of Israel did so, and g Ex 16:17 3950
he that g much had nothing over, Ex 16:18
he that g little had no lack Ex 16:18
they g every man according to his Ex 16:18 3950
they g it every morning, every Ex 16:21 3950
day they g twice as much bread Ex 16:22 3950
when thou hast g in thy labours Ex 23:16 622
the people g themselves together Ex 32:1 6950
all the sons of Levi g themselves Ex 32:26 622
Moses g all the congregation of Ex 35:1 6950
the assembly was g together unto Lev 8:4 6950
when ye have g in the fruit of Lev 23:39 622
when ye are g together within Lev 26:25 622
congregation is to be g together Num 10:7 6950
g it, and ground it in mills, or Num 11:8 3950
of the sea be g together for them Num 11:22 622
g the seventy men of the elders Num 11:24 622
next day, and they g the quails Num 11:32 622
that g least g ten homers Num 11:32 622
that are g together against me Num 14:35 3259
they found a man that g sticks Num 15:32 7197
they g themselves together Num 16:3 6950
all thy company are g together Num 16:11 3259
Korah g all the congregation Num 16:19 6950
congregation was g against Moses Num 16:42 6950
they g themselves together Num 20:2 6950
Aaron g the congregation together Num 20:10 6950
Aaron shall be g unto his people Num 20:24 622
Aaron shall be g unto his people, Num 20:26 622
but Sihon g all his people Num 21:23 622
g themselves together against the Num 27:3 3259
also shalt be g unto thy people Num 27:13 622
as Aaron thy brother was g Num 27:13 622
shalt thou be g unto thy people Num 31:2 622
that thou hast g in thy corn Deut 16:13 622
goest up, and be g unto thy people Deut 32:50 622
Hor, and was g unto his people Deut 32:50 622
tribes of Israel were g together Deut 33:5 622
That they g themselves together, Josh 9:2 6908
g themselves together, and went up Josh 10:5 622
are g together against us Josh 10:6 6908
of the children of Israel g Josh 22:12 6950
Joshua g all the tribes of Israel Josh 24:1 622
g their meat under my table Judg 1:7 3950
were g unto their fathers Judg 2:10 622
he g unto him the children of Judg 3:13 622
Sisera g together all his Judg 4:13 2199
of the east were g together Judg 6:33 622
and Abi-ezer was g after him Judg 6:34 2199
who also was g after him Judg 6:35 2199
the men of Israel g themselves Judg 7:23 6817
of Ephraim g themselves together Judg 7:24 6817
all the men of Shechem g together Judg 9:6 622
g their vineyards, and trode the Judg 9:27 1219
tower of Shechem were g together Judg 9:47 6908
children of Ammon were g together Judg 10:17 6817
there were g vain men to Jephthah Judg 11:3 3950
but Sihon g all his people Judg 11:20 622
the men of Ephraim g themselves Judg 12:1 6817
Then Jephthah g together all the Judg 12:4 6908
g them together for to offer a Judg 16:23 6908
to Micah's house were g together Judg 18:22 2199
was g together as one man Judg 20:1 6950
of Israel were g against the city Judg 20:11 622
But the children of Benjamin g Judg 20:14 622
and g all the lords of the 1Sa 5:8 622
g together all the lords of the 1Sa 5:11 622
they g together to Mizpeh, and 1Sa 7:6 6908
Israel were g together to Mizpeh 1Sa 7:7 6908
of Israel g themselves together 1Sa 8:4 6908
the Philistines g themselves 1Sa 13:5 622
that the Philistines g themselves 1Sa 13:11 622
he g an host, and smote the 1Sa 14:48 6213
Saul g the people together, and 1Sa 15:4 8085
Now the Philistines g together 1Sa 17:1 622
were g together at Shochoh, which 1Sa 17:1 622
the men of Israel were g together 1Sa 17:2 622
And Jonathan's lad g up the arrows 1Sa 20:38 3950
g themselves unto him 1Sa 22:2 6908
the Israelites were g together 1Sa 25:1 6908
that the Philistines g their 1Sa 28:1 6908
the Philistines g themselves 1Sa 28:4 6908
Saul g all Israel together, and 1Sa 28:4 6908
Now the Philistines g together 1Sa 29:1 6908
the children of Benjamin g 2Sa 2:25 6908
when he had g all the people 2Sa 2:30 6908
David g together all the chosen 2Sa 6:1 3254
they g themselves together 2Sa 10:15 622
he g all Israel together, and 2Sa 10:17 622
David g all the people together, 2Sa 12:29 622
which cannot be g up again 2Sa 14:14 622
Israel be generally g unto thee 2Sa 17:11 622
and they were g together, and went 2Sa 20:14 7035
they g the bones of them that 2Sa 21:13 622
were there g together to battle 2Sa 23:9 622
the Philistines were g together 2Sa 23:11 622
Solomon g together chariots and 1Kin 10:26 622
he g men unto him, and became 1Kin 11:24 6908
g the prophets together unto 1Kin 18:20 6908
of Syria g all his host together 1Kin 20:1 6908
of Israel g the prophets together 1Kin 22:6 6908
they g all that were able to put 2Kin 3:21 6817
g thereof wild gourds his lap 2Kin 4:39 3950
king of Syria g all his host 2Kin 6:24 6908
Jehu g all the people together, 2Kin 10:18 6908
of the door have g of the people 2Kin 22:4 622
Thy servants have g the money 2Kin 22:9 5413
thou shalt be g into thy grave in 2Kin 22:20 622
they g unto him all the elders of 2Kin 23:1 622
Then all Israel g themselves to 1Chr 11:1 6908
were g together to battle 1Chr 11:13 622
So David g all Israel together, 1Chr 13:5 6950
David g all Israel together to 1Chr 15:3 6950
And the children of Ammon g 1Chr 19:7 622
he g all Israel, and passed over 1Chr 19:17 622
he g together all the princes of 1Chr 23:2 622
Solomon g chariots and horsemen 2Chr 1:14 622
he g of the house of Judah and 2Chr 11:1 6950
that were g together to Jerusalem 2Chr 12:5 622
there are g unto him vain men, 2Chr 13:7 6908
he g all Judah and Benjamin, and 2Chr 15:9 6908
So they g themselves together at 2Chr 15:10 6908
g together of prophets four 2Chr 18:5 6908
Judah g themselves together, to 2Chr 20:4 6908
g the Levites out of all the 2Chr 23:2 6908
he g together the priests and the 2Chr 24:5 6908
by day, and g money in abundance 2Chr 24:11 622
Moreover Amaziah g Judah together 2Chr 25:5 6908
Ahaz g together the vessels of 2Chr 28:24 622
g them together into the east 2Chr 29:4 622
they g their brethren, and 2Chr 29:15 622
g the rulers of the city, and went 2Chr 29:20 622
people g themselves together to 2Chr 30:3 622
So there was g much people 2Chr 32:4 6908
g them together to him in the 2Chr 32:6 6908
had g of the hand of Manasseh 2Chr 34:9 622
they have g together the money 2Chr 34:17 5413
thou shalt be g to thy grave in 2Chr 34:28 622
g together all the elders of 2Chr 34:29 622
the people g themselves together Ezr 3:1 622
I g together out of Israel chief Ezr 7:28 6908
I g them together to the river Ezr 8:15 6908
Benjamin g themselves together Ezr 10:9 6908
all my servants were g thither Neh 5:16 6908
all the people g themselves Neh 8:1 622
on the second day were g together Neh 8:13 622
the singers g themselves together Neh 12:28 622
I g them together, and set them in Neh 13:11 6908
when many maidens were g together Est 2:8 6908
when the virgins were g together Est 2:19 6908
The Jews g themselves together in Est 9:2 6950
g themselves together on the Est 9:15 6950
provinces g themselves together Est 9:16 6950
they have g themselves together Job 16:10 4390
lie down, but he shall not be g Job 27:19 622
the nettles they were g together Job 30:7 5596
and g themselves together Ps 35:15 622
the abjects g themselves together Ps 35:15 622
of the people are g together Ps 47:9 622
the mighty are g against me Ps 59:3 1481
When the people are g together Ps 102:22 6908
g them out of the lands, from the Ps 107:3 6908
are they g together for war Ps 140:2 1481
and herbs of the mountains are g Prov 27:25 622
who hath g the wind in his fists Prov 30:4 622
I g me also silver and gold, and Eccl 2:8 3664
I have g my myrrh with my spice Song 5:1 717
g out the stones thereof, and Is 5:2
are left, have I g all the earth Is 10:14 622
kingdoms of nations g together Is 13:4 622
ye g together the waters of the Is 22:9 6908
And they shall be g together Is 24:22 622
as prisoners are g in the pit Is 24:22 626
and ye shall be g one by one Is 27:12 3950
your spoil shall be g like the Is 33:4 622
shall the vultures also be g Is 34:15 6908
and his spirit it hath g them Is 34:16 6908
Let all the nations be g together Is 43:9 6908
let them all be g together Is 44:11 6908
to him, Though Israel be not g Is 49:5 622
beside those that are g unto him Is 56:8 6908
shall be g together unto thee Is 60:7 6908
they that have g it shall eat it Is 62:9 622
the nations shall be g unto it Jer 3:17 6960
they shall not be g, nor be Jer 8:2 622
shall not be lamented, neither g Jer 25:33 622
all the people were g against Jer 26:9 6950
g wine and summer fruits very much Jer 40:12 622
that all the Jews which are g Jer 40:15 6908
When I shall have g the house of Eze 28:25 6908
not be brought together, nor g Eze 29:5 6908
is g out of many people, against Eze 38:8 6908
that are g out of the nations Eze 38:12 622
hast thou g thy company to take a Eze 38:13 6950
g them out of their enemies' Eze 39:27 6908
but I have g them unto their own Eze 39:28 3664
were g together unto the Dan 3:3 3673
being g together, saw these men, Dan 3:27 3673
children of Israel be g together Hos 1:11 6908
people shall be g against them Hos 10:10 622
for she g it of the hire of an Mic 1:7 6908
many nations are g against thee Mic 4:11 622
they have g the summer fruits Mic 7:1 622
earth be g together against it Zec 12:3 622
round about shall be g together Zec 14:14 622
when he had g all the chief Mt 2:4 *4863*
were g together unto him, so that Mt 13:2 *4863*
As therefore the tares are g Mt 13:40 *4816*
into the sea, and g of every kind Mt 13:47 *4863*
g the good into vessels, but cast Mt 13:48 *4816*
three are g together in my name Mt 18:20 *4863*
g together all as many as they Mt 22:10 *4863*
to silence, they were g together Mt 22:34 *4863*
the Pharisees were g together Mt 22:41 *4863*
I have g thy children together Mt 23:37 *1996*
will the eagles be g together Mt 24:28 *4863*
before him shall be g all nations Mt 25:32 *4863*
when they were g together Mt 27:17 *4863*
g unto him the whole band of Mt 27:27 *4863*
all the city was g together at Mk 1:33 *1996*
straightway many were g together Mk 2:2 *4863*
there was g unto him a great Mk 4:1 *4863*
side, much people g unto him Mk 5:21 *4863*
the apostles g themselves Mk 6:30 *4863*
when much people were g together Lk 8:4 *4896*
the people were g thick together Lk 11:29 *1865*
when there were g together an Lk 12:1 *1996*
I have g thy children together Lk 13:34 *1996*
the younger son g all together Lk 15:13 *4863*
will the eagles be g together Lk 17:37 *4863*
and found the eleven g together Lk 24:33 *4867*
Therefore they g them together Jn 6:13 *4863*
Then g the chief priests and the Jn 11:47 *4863*
were g together at Jerusalem Acts 4:6 *4863*
the rulers were g together Acts 4:26 *4863*
of Israel, were g together, Acts 4:27 *4863*
where many were g together Acts 12:12 *4863*
had g the church together, they Acts 14:27 *4863*
when they had g the multitude Acts 15:30 *4863*
g a company, and set all the city Acts 17:5 *3792*
where they were g together Acts 20:8 *4863*
when Paul had g a bundle of Acts 28:3 *4962*
Christ, when ye are g together 1Cor 5:4 *4863*
He that had g much had nothing 2Cor 8:15
he that had g little had no lack 2Cor 8:15
g the vine of the earth, and cast Rev 14:19 *5166*
he g them together into a place Rev 16:16 *4863*
g together to make war against Rev 19:19 *4863*

GATHERER

herdman, and a g of sycomore fruit Amos 7:14 1103

GATHEREST

When thou g the grapes of thy Deut 24:21 1219

GATHERETH

he that g the ashes of the heifer Num 19:10 622
He g the waters of the sea Ps 33:7 3664
his heart g iniquity to itself Ps 41:6 6908
he g together the outcasts of Ps 147:2 3664
g her food in the harvest Prov 6:8 103
He that g in summer is a wise son Prov 10:5 103
but he that g by labour shall Prov 13:11 6908
as one g eggs that are left, have Is 10:14 622
as when the harvestman g the corn Is 17:5 622
it shall be as he that g ears in Is 17:5 3950
The Lord God which g the outcasts Is 56:8 6908
the mountains, and no man g them Nah 3:18 6908
but g unto him all nations, and Hab 2:5 622
he that g not with me scattereth Mt 12:30 *4863*
even as a hen g her chickens Mt 23:37 *1996*
he that g not with me scattereth Lk 11:23 *4863*
g fruit unto life eternal Jn 4:36 *4863*

GATHERING

the g together of the waters Gen 1:10 4723
him shall the g of the people be Gen 49:10 3349
they that found him g sticks Num 15:33 7197
widow woman was there g of sticks 1Kin 17:10 7197
I am g two sticks, that I may go 1Kin 17:12 7197
were three days in g of the spoil 2Chr 20:25 962
shall fail, the g shall not come Is 32:10 625
like the g of the caterpiller Is 33:4 625
g where thou hast not strawed Mt 25:24 *4863*
assuredly g that the Lord had Acts 16:10 *4822*
by our g together unto him, 2Th 2:1 *1997*

GATHERINGS

that there be no g when I come 1Cor 16:2 *3048*

GATH-HEPHER (*gath-he'-fer*) See GITTAH-HEPHER. *A town in Zebulun.*

the prophet, which was of G 2Kin 14:25 1662

GATH-RIMMON (*gath-rim'-mon*)

1. A Levitical town in Dan.
And Jehud, and Bene-berak, and G Josh 19:45 1667
2. A Levitical town in Manasseh.
her suburbs, G with her suburbs Josh 21:24 1667
suburbs, and G with her suburbs Josh 21:25 1667
suburbs, and G with her suburbs 1Chr 6:69 1667

GAVE

Adam g names to all cattle, and to Gen 2:20 7121
g also unto her husband with her Gen 3:6 5414
she g me of the tree, and I did Gen 3:12 5414
And he g him tithes of all Gen 14:20 5414
g her to her husband Abram to be Gen 16:3 5414
and good, and g it unto a young man Gen 18:7 5414
g them unto Abraham, and restored Gen 20:14 5414
g it unto Hagar, putting it on Gen 21:14 5414

G

with water, and g the lad drink ... Gen 21:19
and oxen, and g them unto Abimelech Gen 21:27 5414
upon her hand, and g him drink ... Gen 24:18
g straw and provender for the ... Gen 24:32 5414
and raiment, and g them to Rebekah ... Gen 24:53 5414
he g also to her brother and to ... Gen 24:53 5414
Abraham g all that he had unto ... Gen 25:5 5414
Abraham had, Abraham g gifts ... Gen 25:6 5414
Then Abraham g up the ghost ... Gen 25:8
he g up the ghost and died ... Gen 25:17
Then Jacob g Esau bread and ... Gen 25:34 5414
she g the savoury meat and the ... Gen 27:17 5414
which God g unto Abraham ... Gen 28:4 5414
he blessed him he g him a charge ... Gen 28:6
Laban g unto his daughter Leah ... Gen 29:24 5414
he g him Rachel his daughter to ... Gen 29:28 5414
Laban g to Rachel his daughter ... Gen 29:29 5414
she g him Bilhah her handmaid to ... Gen 30:4 5414
her maid, and g her Jacob to wife ... Gen 30:9 5414
g them into the hand of his sons ... Gen 30:35 5414
they g unto Jacob all the strange ... Gen 35:4 5414
And the land which I g Abraham ... Gen 35:12 5414
Isaac g up the ghost, and died, and ... Gen 35:29
he g it her, and came in unto her, ... Gen 38:18 5414
because that I g her not to ... Gen 38:26 5414
g him favour in the sight of the ... Gen 39:21 5414
I g the cup into Pharaoh's hand ... Gen 40:11 5414
he g the cup into Pharaoh's hand ... Gen 40:21 5414
he g him to wife Asenath the ... Gen 41:45 5414
g them water, and they washed ... Gen 43:24 5414
he g their asses provender ... Gen 43:24 5414
Joseph g them wagons, according ... Gen 45:21 5414
g them provision for the way ... Gen 45:21 5414
To all of them he g each man ... Gen 45:22 5414
but to Benjamin he g three ... Gen 45:22 5414
whom Laban g to Leah his daughter ... Gen 46:18 5414
which Laban g unto Rachel his ... Gen 46:25 5414
g them a possession in the land ... Gen 47:11 5414
Joseph g them bread in exchange ... Gen 47:17 5414
portion which Pharaoh g them ... Gen 47:22 5414
he g Moses Zipporah his daughter ... Ex 2:21 5414
g them a charge unto the children ... Ex 6:13
the LORD g the people favour in ... Ex 11:3 5414
the LORD g the people favour in ... Ex 12:36 5414
but it g light by night to these ... Ex 14:20
he g unto Moses, when he had made ... Ex 31:18 5414
So they g it me ... Ex 32:24 5414
he g them in commandment all that ... Ex 34:32
Moses g commandment, and they ... Ex 36:6
Moses g the money of them that ... Num 3:51 5414
oxen, and g them unto the Levites ... Num 7:6 5414
four oxen he g unto the sons of ... Num 7:7 5414
eight oxen he g unto the sons of ... Num 7:8 5414
unto the sons of Kohath he g none ... Num 7:9 5414
g it unto the seventy elders ... Num 11:25 5414
their princes g him a rod apiece ... Num 17:6 5414
g him a charge, as the LORD ... Num 27:23
Moses g the tribute, which was ... Num 31:41 5414
g them unto the Levites, which ... Num 31:47 5414
Moses g unto them, even to the ... Num 32:33 5414
g other names unto the cities ... Num 32:38 7121
Moses g Gilead unto Machir the ... Num 32:40 5414
which the LORD g unto them ... Deut 2:12 5414
g I unto the Reubenites and to the ... Deut 3:12 5414
g I unto the half tribe of ... Deut 3:13 5414
And I g Gilead unto Machir ... Deut 3:15 5414
unto the Gadites I g from Gilead ... Deut 3:16 5414
that the LORD g me the two tables ... Deut 9:11 5414
and the LORD g them unto me ... Deut 10:4 5414
I g my daughter unto this man to ... Deut 22:16 5414
g it for an inheritance unto the ... Deut 29:8 5414
he g Joshua the son of Nun a ... Deut 31:23
Moses g you on this side Jordan ... Josh 1:14 5414
g you on this side Jordan toward ... Josh 1:15 5414
Joshua g it for an inheritance ... Josh 11:23 5414
g it for a possession unto the ... Josh 12:6 5414
which Joshua g unto the tribes of ... Josh 12:7 5414
inheritance, which Moses g them ... Josh 13:8 5414
the servant of the LORD g them ... Josh 13:8 5414
of Levi he g none inheritance ... Josh 13:14 5414
Moses g unto the tribe of the ... Josh 13:15 5414
Moses g inheritance unto the ... Josh 13:24 5414
Moses g inheritance unto the half ... Josh 13:29 5414
Levi Moses g not any inheritance ... Josh 13:33 5414
but unto the Levites he g none ... Josh 14:3 5414
therefore they g no part unto the ... Josh 14:4 5414
g unto Caleb the son of Jephunneh ... Josh 14:13 5414
he g a part among the children of ... Josh 15:13 5414
he g him Achsah his daughter to ... Josh 15:17 5414
he g her the upper springs, and ... Josh 15:19 5414
g them an inheritance among the ... Josh 17:4 5414
the servant of the LORD g them ... Josh 18:7 5414
the children of Israel g an ... Josh 19:49 5414
g him the city which he asked ... Josh 19:50 5414
the children of Israel g unto the ... Josh 21:3 5414
the children of Israel g by lot ... Josh 21:8 5414
they g out of the tribe of the ... Josh 21:9 5414
they g them the city of Arba the ... Josh 21:11 5414
g they to Caleb the son of ... Josh 21:12 5414
Thus they g to the children of ... Josh 21:13 5414
For they g them Shechem with her ... Josh 21:21 5414
they g Golan in Bashan with her ... Josh 21:27
the LORD g unto Israel all the ... Josh 21:43 5414
the LORD g them rest round about, ... Josh 21:44
g you on the other side Jordan ... Josh 22:4 5414
g Joshua among their brethren on ... Josh 22:7 5414
his seed, and g him Isaac ... Josh 24:3 5414
I g unto Isaac Jacob and Esau ... Josh 24:4 5414
I g unto Esau mount Seir, to ... Josh 24:4 5414
I g them into your hand, that ye ... Josh 24:8 5414
he g him Achsah his daughter to ... Judg 1:13 5414
Caleb g her the upper springs and ... Judg 1:15 5414
they g Hebron unto Caleb, as ... Judg 1:20 5414
g their daughters to their sons, ... Judg 3:6 5414

g him drink, and covered him ... Judg 4:19
He asked water, and she g him milk ... Judg 5:25 5414
before you, and g you their land ... Judg 6:9 5414
they g him threescore and ten ... Judg 9:4 5414
and g them, and they did eat ... Judg 14:9 5414
g change of garments unto them ... Judg 14:19 5414
therefore I g her to thy ... Judg 15:2 5414
g them to the founder, who made ... Judg 17:4 5414
g provender unto the asses ... Judg 19:21
for the men of Israel g place to ... Judg 20:36 5414
they g them wives which they had ... Judg 21:14 5414
g to her that she had reserved ... Ruth 2:18 5414
six measures of barley g he me ... Ruth 3:17 5414
shoe, and g it to his neighbour ... Ruth 4:7 5414
the LORD g her conception, and she ... Ruth 4:13 5414
women her neighbours g it a name ... Ruth 4:17 7121
he g to Peninnah his wife, and to ... 1Sa 1:4 5414
unto Hannah he g a worthy portion ... 1Sa 1:5 5414
g her son suck until she weaned ... 1Sa 1:23
Bring the portion which I g thee ... 1Sa 9:23 5414
Samuel, God g him another heart ... 1Sa 10:9
g it to David, and his garments, ... 1Sa 18:4 5414
they g them in full tale to the ... 1Sa 18:27
Saul g him Michal his daughter to ... 1Sa 18:27 5414
Jonathan g his artillery unto his ... 1Sa 20:40 5414
So the priest g him hallowed ... 1Sa 21:6 5414
g him victuals, and g him the ... 1Sa 22:10 5414
Then Achish g him Ziklag that day ... 1Sa 27:6 5414
g him bread, and he did eat ... 1Sa 30:11 5414
they g him a piece of a cake of ... 1Sa 30:12 5414
I g thee thy master's house, and ... 2Sa 12:8 5414
g thee the house of Israel and of ... 2Sa 12:8 5414
king g all the captains charge ... 2Sa 18:5
Joab g up the sum of the number ... 2Sa 24:9 5414
And God g Solomon wisdom and ... 1Kin 4:29 5414
So Hiram g Solomon cedar trees and ... 1Kin 5:10 5414
Solomon g Hiram twenty thousand ... 1Kin 5:11 5414
thus g Solomon to Hiram year by ... 1Kin 5:11 5414
the LORD g Solomon wisdom, as he ... 1Kin 5:12 5414
that then king Solomon g Hiram ... 1Kin 9:11 5414
she g the king an hundred and ... 1Kin 10:10 5414
queen of Sheba g to king Solomon ... 1Kin 10:10 5414
king Solomon g unto the queen of ... 1Kin 10:13 5414
Solomon g her of his royal bounty ... 1Kin 10:13 5414
which g him an house, and ... 1Kin 11:18 5414
him victuals, and g him land ... 1Kin 11:18 5414
so that he g him to wife the ... 1Kin 11:19 5414
old men's counsel that they g him ... 1Kin 12:13 3289
he g a sign the same day, saying, ... 1Kin 13:3 5414
the house of David, and g it thee ... 1Kin 14:8 5414
which he g to their fathers, and ... 1Kin 14:15 5414
g unto the people, and they did ... 1Kin 19:21 5414
And he g him his hand ... 2Kin 10:15 5414
upon him, and g him the testimony ... 2Kin 11:12
they g the money, being told, ... 2Kin 12:11 5414
But they g that to the workmen, ... 2Kin 12:14 5414
the LORD g Israel a saviour, so ... 2Kin 13:5 5414
Menahem g Pul a thousand talents ... 2Kin 15:19 5414
his servant, and g him presents ... 2Kin 17:3 7725
Hezekiah g him all the silver ... 2Kin 18:15 5414
g it to the king of Assyria ... 2Kin 18:16 5414
the land which I g their fathers ... 2Kin 21:8 5414
Hilkiah g the book to Shaphan, and ... 2Kin 22:8 5414
Jehoiakim g the silver and the ... 2Kin 23:35 5414
and they g judgment upon him ... 2Kin 25:6 1696
Sheshan g his daughter to Jarha ... 1Chr 2:35 5414
they g them Hebron in the land of ... 1Chr 6:55 5414
they g to Caleb the son of ... 1Chr 6:56 5414
Aaron they g the cities of Judah ... 1Chr 6:57 5414
the children of Israel g to the ... 1Chr 6:64 5414
they g by lot out of the tribe of ... 1Chr 6:65 5414
they g unto them, of the cities ... 1Chr 6:67 5414
they g also Gezer with her ... 1Chr 6:67
David g a commandment, and they ... 1Chr 14:12
Joab g the sum of the number of ... 1Chr 21:5 5414
So David g to Ornan for the place ... 1Chr 21:25 5414
God g to Heman fourteen sons and ... 1Chr 25:5 5414
Then David g to Solomon his son ... 1Chr 28:11 5414
He g of gold by weight for things ... 1Chr 28:14
by weight he g gold for the ... 1Chr 28:16
for the golden basons he g gold ... 1Chr 28:17
g for the service of the house of ... 1Chr 29:7 5414
g them to the treasure of the ... 1Chr 29:8 5414
she g the king an hundred and ... 2Chr 9:9 5414
the queen of Sheba g king Solomon ... 2Chr 9:9 5414
king Solomon g to the queen of ... 2Chr 9:12 5414
counsel which the old men g him ... 2Chr 10:8 3289
he g them victual in abundance ... 2Chr 11:23 5414
g the kingdom over Israel to ... 2Chr 13:5 5414
Then the men of Judah g a shout ... 2Chr 13:15
the LORD g them rest round about ... 2Chr 15:15
for his God g him rest round ... 2Chr 20:30
their father g them great gifts ... 2Chr 21:3 5414
but the kingdom g he to Jehoram ... 2Chr 21:3 5414
g him the testimony, and made him ... 2Chr 23:11
Jehoiada g it to such as did the ... 2Chr 24:12 5414
the Ammonites g gifts to Uzziah ... 2Chr 26:8 5414
the children of Ammon g him the ... 2Chr 27:5 5414
g them to eat and to drink, and ... 2Chr 28:15
g it unto the king of Assyria ... 2Chr 28:21 5414
who therefore g them up to ... 2Chr 30:7 5414
the princes g to the congregation ... 2Chr 30:24 7311
unto him, and he g him a sign ... 2Chr 32:24 5414
they g it to the workmen that ... 2Chr 34:10 5414
artificers and builders g they it ... 2Chr 34:11 5414
Josiah g to the people, of the ... 2Chr 35:7 7311
his princes g willingly unto the ... 2Chr 35:8 7311
g unto the priests for the ... 2Chr 35:8 5414
g unto the Levites for passover ... 2Chr 35:9 7311
he g them all into his hand ... 2Chr 36:17 5414
They g after their ability unto ... Ezr 2:69 5414
They g money also unto the masons ... Ezr 3:7 5414
he g them into the hand of ... Ezr 5:12 3052
Artaxerxes g unto Ezra the priest ... Ezr 7:11 5414

they g their hands that they ... Ezr 10:19 5414
the wine, and g it unto the king ... Neh 2:1 5414
g them the king's letters ... Neh 2:9 5414
That I g my brother Hanani, and ... Neh 7:2
of the fathers g unto the work ... Neh 7:70 5414
The Tirshatha g to the treasure a ... Neh 7:70 5414
g to the treasure of the work ... Neh 7:71 5414
g was twenty thousand drams of ... Neh 7:72 5414
g the sense, and caused them to ... Neh 8:8 7760
companies of them that g thanks ... Neh 12:31
g thanks went over against them ... Neh 12:38
that g thanks in the house of God ... Neh 12:40
g the portions of the singers and ... Neh 12:47 5414
they g them drink in vessels of ... Est 1:7
he speedily g her her things for ... Est 2:9 5414
g gifts, according to the state ... Est 2:18 5414
g it unto Haman the son of ... Est 3:10 5414
g him a commandment to Mordecai, ... Est 4:5
Also he g him the copy of the ... Est 4:8 5414
g him commandment unto Mordecai ... Est 4:10
from Haman, and g it unto Mordecai ... Est 8:2 5414
the LORD g, and the LORD hath ... Job 1:21 5414
my servant, and he g me no answer ... Job 19:16
eye saw me, it g witness to me ... Job 29:11
Unto me men g ear, and waited, and ... Job 29:21
I g ear to your reasons, whilst ... Job 32:11
also the LORD g Job twice as much ... Job 42:10 3254
every man also g him a piece of ... Job 42:11 5414
their father g them inheritance ... Job 42:15 5414
and the Highest g his voice ... Ps 18:13 5414
The Lord g the word ... Ps 68:11 5414
They g me also gall for my meat ... Ps 69:21 5414
in my thirst they g me vinegar to ... Ps 69:21
and he g ear unto me ... Ps 77:1
g them drink as out of the great ... Ps 78:15
for he g them their own desire ... Ps 78:29 935
He g also their increase unto the ... Ps 78:46 5414
He g up their cattle also to the ... Ps 78:48 5462
but g their life over to the ... Ps 78:50 5462
He g his people over also unto ... Ps 78:62 5462
So I g them up unto their own ... Ps 81:12 7971
and the ordinance that he g them ... Ps 99:7 5414
He g them hail for rain, and ... Ps 105:32 5414
g them the lands of the heathen ... Ps 105:44 5414
And he g them their request ... Ps 106:15 5414
he g them into the hand of the ... Ps 106:41 5414
g their land for an heritage, an ... Ps 135:12 5414
g their land for an heritage ... Ps 136:21 5414
When he g to the sea his decree, ... Prov 8:29 7760
I g my heart to seek and search ... Eccl 1:13 5414
I g my heart to know wisdom, and ... Eccl 1:17 5414
shall return unto God who g it ... Eccl 12:7 5414
he g good heed, and sought out, and ... Eccl 12:9
called him, but he g me no answer ... Song 5:6
g the nations before him, and made ... Is 41:2 5414
he g them as the dust to his ... Is 41:2 5414
Who g Jacob for a spoil, and ... Is 42:24 5414
I g Egypt for thy ransom, ... Is 43:3 5414
I g my back to the smiters, and my ... Is 50:6 5414
the land that I g to your fathers ... Jer 7:7 5414
unto the place which I g to you ... Jer 7:14 5414
land that I g unto their fathers ... Jer 16:15 5414
from thine heritage that I g thee ... Jer 17:4 5414
you, and the city that I g you ... Jer 23:39 5414
off the land that I g unto them ... Jer 24:10 5414
land that I g to their fathers ... Jer 30:3 5414
I g the evidence of the purchase ... Jer 32:12 5414
g it to Baruch the scribe, the ... Jer 36:32 5414
where he g judgment upon him ... Jer 39:5 1696
g them vineyards and fields at the ... Jer 39:10 5414
g charge concerning Jeremiah to ... Jer 39:11
of the guard g him victuals ... Jer 40:5 5414
as I g Zedekiah king of Judah ... Jer 44:30 5414
where he g judgment upon him ... Jer 52:9 1696
mine elders g up the ghost in the ... Lam 1:19
My meat also which I g thee ... Eze 16:19 5414
I g them my statutes, and shewed ... Eze 20:11 5414
Moreover also I g them my ... Eze 20:12 5414
Wherefore I g them also statutes ... Eze 20:25 5414
the land that I g to your fathers ... Eze 36:28 5414
g them into the hand of their ... Eze 39:23 5414
the Lord g Jehoiakim king of ... Dan 1:2 5414
the prince of the eunuchs g names ... Dan 1:7 7760
for he g unto Daniel the name of ... Dan 1:7 7760
and g them pulse ... Dan 1:16 5414
God g them knowledge and skill in ... Dan 1:17 5414
g him many great gifts, and made ... Dan 2:48 3052
O thou king, the most high God g ... Dan 5:18 3052
And for the majesty that he g him ... Dan 5:19 3052
g thanks before his God, as he ... Dan 6:10
did not know that I g her corn ... Hos 2:8 5414
I g thee a king in mine anger, and ... Hos 13:11 5414
But ye g the Nazarites wine to ... Amos 2:12
I g them to him for the fear ... Mal 2:5 5414
he g commandment to depart unto ... Mt 8:18 *2753*
he g them power against unclean ... Mt 10:1 *1325*
g the loaves to his disciples, and ... Mt 14:19 *1325*
g thanks, and brake them ... Mt 15:36 *1325*
g to his disciples, and the ... Mt 15:36 *1325*
who g thee this authority ... Mt 21:23 *1325*
unto one he g five talents, to ... Mt 25:15 *1325*
I was an hungred, and ye g me meat ... Mt 25:35 *1325*
I was thirsty, and ye g me drink ... Mt 25:35 *4222*
or thirsty, and g thee drink ... Mt 25:37 *4222*
an hungred, and ye g me no meat ... Mt 25:42 *1325*
was thirsty, and ye g me no drink ... Mt 25:42 *4222*
g it to the disciples, and said, ... Mt 26:26 *1325*
g thanks, and g it to them, ... Mt 26:27 *1325*
that betrayed him g them a sign ... Mt 26:48 *1325*
g them for the potter's field, as ... Mt 27:10 *1325*
They g him vinegar to drink ... Mt 27:34 *1325*
it on a reed, and g him to drink ... Mt 27:48 *4222*
they g large money unto the ... Mt 28:12 *1325*
g also to them which were with ... Mk 2:26 *1325*

And forthwith Jesus g them leave......... Mk 5:13 2010
g them power over unclean spirits........ Mk 6:7 1325
a charger, and g it to the damsel.......... Mk 6:28 1325
the damsel g it to her mother.............. Mk 6:28 1325
g them to his disciples to set .... Mk 6:41 1325
g thanks, and brake .... Mk 8:6 1325
g to his disciples to set before .... Mk 8:6 1325
who g thee this authority to do .... Mk 11:28 1325
g authority to his servants, and............ Mk 13:34 1325
g to them, and said, Take, eat.............. Mk 14:22 1325
had given thanks, he g it to them .... Mk 14:23 1325
they g him to drink wine mingled.......... Mk 15:23 1325
g him to drink, saying, Let alone........... Mk 15:36 4222
a loud voice, and g up the ghost............ Mk 15:37
g up the ghost, he said, Truly............... Mk 15:39
he g the body to Joseph......................... Mk 15:45 1433
she coming in that instant g.................. Lk 2:38 437
he g it again to the minister, and......... Lk 4:20 591
g also to them that were with him........ Lk 6:4 1325
many that were blind he g sight........... Lk 7:21 5483
g them power and authority over........... Lk 9:1 1325
g to the disciples to set before.............. Lk 9:16 1325
g them to the host, and said unto......... Lk 10:35 1325
and no man g unto him .... Lk 15:16 1325
they saw it, g praise unto God.............. Lk 18:43 1325
or who is he that g thee this .... Lk 20:2 1325
g thanks, and said, Take this, and......... Lk 22:17
g thanks, and brake it............................ Lk 22:19
g unto them, saying, This is my............. Lk 22:19 1325
Pilate g sentence that it should............. Lk 23:24
and the paps which never g suck........... Lk 23:29
said thus, he g up the ghost.................. Lk 23:46
it, and brake, and g to them .... Lk 24:30 1929
they g him a piece of a broiled............... Lk 24:42 1929
to them g he power to become the.......... Jn 1:12 1325
that he g his only begotten Son,............. Jn 3:16 1325
that Jacob g to his son Joseph............... Jn 4:5 1325
which g us the well, and drank.............. Jn 4:12 1325
He g them bread from heaven to............. Jn 6:31 1325
Moses g you not that bread from........... Jn 6:32 1325
Moses therefore g unto you.................... Jn 7:22 1325
which g them me, is greater than .... Jn 10:29 1325
he g me a commandment, what I............ Jn 12:49 1325
he g it to Judas Iscariot, the.................. Jn 13:26 1325
as the Father g me commandment, ... Jn 14:31 1781
which g counsel to the Jews, that........... Jn 18:14 4823
But Jesus g him no answer .... Jn 19:9 1325
bowed his head, and g up the ghost ..... Jn 19:30 3860
and Pilate g him leave........................... Jn 19:38 2010
And they g forth their lots.................... Acts 1:26 1325
as the Spirit g them utterance.............. Acts 2:4 1325
he g heed unto them, expecting to .... Acts 3:5 1907
with great power g the apostles............. Acts 4:33 591
fell down, and g up the ghost................ Acts 5:5
he g him none inheritance in it,............. Acts 7:5 1325
And he g him the covenant of .... Acts 7:8 1325
g him favour and wisdom in the............. Acts 7:10 1325
g them up to worship the host of.......... Acts 7:42 3860
the people with one accord g heed .... Acts 8:6 4337
To whom they all g heed, from the........ Acts 8:10 4337
he g her his hand, and lifted her........... Acts 9:41 1325
which g much alms to the people,.......... Acts 10:2 4160
Forasmuch then as God g them the ...... Acts 11:17 1325
And the people g a shout, saying, ... Acts 12:22
because he g not God the glory............. Acts 12:23 1325
eaten of worms, and g up the ghost ..... Acts 12:23
after that he g unto them judges .... Acts 13:20 1325
God g unto them Saul the son of........... Acts 13:21 1325
to whom also he g testimony .... Acts 13:22 3140
which g testimony unto the word .... Acts 14:3 3140
g us rain from heaven, and.................... Acts 14:17 1325
g audience to Barnabas and Paul, ... Acts 15:12
to whom we g no such commandment Acts 15:24 1291
they g him audience unto this............... Acts 22:22
g commandment to his accusers............. Acts 23:30
I g my voice against them..................... Acts 26:10 2702
g him liberty to go unto his.................. Acts 27:3 2010
g thanks to God in presence of............. Acts 27:35
Wherefore God also g them up to.......... Rom 1:24 3860
For this cause God g them up unto....... Rom 1:26 3860
God g them over to a reprobate .... Rom 1:28 3860
even as the Lord g to every man........... 1Cor 3:5 1325
but God g the increase.......................... 1Cor 3:6
but first g their own selves to 2Cor 8:5 1325
Who g himself for our sins, that............ Gal 1:4 1325
To whom we g place by subjection,........ Gal 2:5 1502
they g to me and Barnabas the.............. Gal 2:9 1325
who loved me, and g himself for me..... Gal 2:20 3860
but God g it to Abraham by .... Gal 3:18 5483
g him to be the head over all .... Eph 1:22 1325
captive, and g gifts unto men............... Eph 4:8 1325
And he g some, apostles .... Eph 4:11 1325
the church, and g himself for it .... Eph 5:25 3860
we g you by the Lord Jesus.................. 1Th 4:2 1325
Who g himself a ransom for all,............ 1Ti 2:6 1325
Who g himself for us, that he............... Titus 2:14 1325
Abraham g a tenth part of all................ Heb 7:2
Abraham g the tenth of the spoils......... Heb 7:4 1325
of which no man g attendance at.......... Heb 7:13 4337
g commandment concerning his............ Heb 11:22
us, and we g them reverence............... Heb 12:9 1788
again, and the heaven g rain .... Jas 5:18 1325
up from the dead, and g him glory........ 1Pet 1:21 1325
another, as he g us commandment 1Jn 3:23 1325
the record that God g of his Son......... 1Jn 5:10 3140
when I g all diligence to write .... Jude 3 4160
Christ, which God g unto him............... Rev 1:1 1325
I g her space to repent of her.............. Rev 2:21 1325
g glory to the God of heaven .... Rev 11:13 1325
the dragon g him his power, and........... Rev 13:2 1325
which g power unto the beast............... Rev 13:4 1325
one of the four beasts g unto the......... Rev 15:7 1325
the sea g up the dead which were......... Rev 20:13 1325

GAVEST
woman whom thou g to be with me .... Gen 3:12 5414
which thou g unto their fathers............ 1Kin 8:34 5414
which thou g unto our fathers.............. 1Kin 8:40 5414
which thou g unto their fathers,........... 1Kin 8:48 5414
the land which thou g to them.............. 2Chr 6:25 5414
which thou g unto our fathers.............. 2Chr 6:31 5414
which thou g unto their fathers,........... 2Chr 6:38 5414
g it to the seed of Abraham thy............ 2Chr 20:7 5414
g him the name of Abraham.................. Neh 9:7 7760
g them right judgments, and true .... Neh 9:13 5414
g them bread from heaven for .... Neh 9:15 5414
Thou g also thy good spirit to .... Neh 9:20 5414
g them water for their thirst................. Neh 9:20 5414
Moreover thou g them kingdoms........... Neh 9:22 5414
g them into their hands, with................ Neh 9:24 5414
mercies thou g them saviours .... Neh 9:27 5414
therefore g thou them into the .... Neh 9:30 5414
great goodness that thou g them.......... Neh 9:35 5414
fat land which thou g before them .... Neh 9:35 5414
for the land that thou g unto our......... Neh 9:36 5414
G thou the goodly wings unto the......... Job 39:13
thou g it him, even length of............... Ps 21:4 5414
g him to be meat to the people............ Ps 74:14 5414
thou g me no water for my feet............ Lk 7:44 1325
Thou g me no kiss................................ Lk 7:45 1325
and yet thou never g me a kid.............. Lk 15:29 1325
Wherefore then g not thou my.............. Lk 19:23 1325
the work which thou g me to do........... Jn 17:4 1325
which thou g me out of the world .... Jn 17:6 1325
they were, and thou g them me............. Jn 17:6 1325
them the words which thou g me .... Jn 17:8 1325
those that thou g me I have kept.......... Jn 17:12 1325
which thou g me I have given them....... Jn 17:22 1325
Of them which thou g me have I .... Jn 18:9 1325

GAY
him that weareth the g clothing............ Jas 2:3 2986

GAZA (*ga'-zah*) See Azzah, Gazites.
1. A royal Philistine city.
as thou comest to Gerar, unto G........... Gen 10:19 5804
from Kadesh-barnea even unto G.......... Josh 10:41 5804
only in G, in Gath, and in Ashdod, ... Josh 11:22 5804
G with her towns and her villages,........ Josh 15:47 5804
Also Judah took G with the coast.......... Judg 1:18 5804
Then went Samson to G, and saw......... Judg 16:1 5804
eyes, and brought him down to G......... Judg 16:21 5804
for Ashdod one, for G one..................... 1Sa 6:17 5804
the Philistines, even unto G................. 2Kin 18:8 5804
before that Pharaoh smote G .... Jer 47:1 5804
Baldness is come upon G...................... Jer 47:5 5804
For three transgressions of G.............. Amos 1:6 5804
will send a fire on the wall of G........... Amos 1:7 5804
For G shall be forsaken, and................ Zeph 2:4 5804
G also shall see it, and be very........... Zec 9:5 5804
and the king shall perish from G.......... Zec 9:5 5804
goeth down from Jerusalem unto G..... Acts 8:26 1048
2. A city in Ephraim.
the earth, till thou come unto G........... Judg 6:4 5804
also and the towns thereof, unto G....... 1Chr 7:28 5804

GAZATHITES (*ga'-zath-ites*) See Gazites. *Inhabitants of Gaza.*
the G, and the Ashdothites, the............ Josh 13:3 5841

GAZE
break through unto the Lord to g......... Ex 19:21 7200

GAZER (*ga'-zur*) See Gezer. *A Canaanite city.*
from Geba until thou come to G........... 2Sa 5:25 1507
Philistines from Gibeon even to G........ 1Chr 14:16 1507

GAZEZ (*ga'-zez*) *A son of Caleb.*
bare Haran, and Moza, and G............... 1Chr 2:46 1495
and Haran begat G............................... 1Chr 2:46 1495

GAZING
why stand ye g up into heaven............. Acts 1:11 1689

GAZINGSTOCK
vile, and will set thee as a g................. Nah 3:6 7210
were made a g both by reproaches....... Heb 10:33 2301

GAZITES (*ga'-zites*) See Gazathites. *Inhabitants of Gaza.*
And it was told the G, saying,............... Judg 16:2 5841

GAZZAM (*gaz'-zam*) *A family of exiles.*
of Nekoda, the children of G................ Ezr 2:48 1502
The children of G, the children............. Neh 7:51 1502

GEBA (*ghe'-bah*) See Gaba, Gibeah, Gibeon. *A Levitical city in Benjamin.*
her suburbs, G with her suburbs, ... Josh 21:17 1387
of the Philistines that was in G............. 1Sa 13:3 1387
from G until thou come to Gazer.......... 2Sa 5:25 1387
Asa built with them G of Benjamin...... 1Kin 15:22 1387
from G to Beer-sheba, and brake......... 2Kin 23:8 1387
G with her suburbs, and Alemeth 1Chr 6:60 1387
fathers of the inhabitants of G............ 1Chr 8:6 1387
and he built therewith G and Mizpah .. 2Chr 16:6 1387
Benjamin from G dwelt at Michmash .. Neh 11:31 1387
Gilgal, and out of the fields of G .... Neh 12:29 1387
have taken up their lodging at G .... Is 10:29 1387
G to Rimmon south of Jerusalem......... Zec 14:10 1387

GEBAL (*ghe'-bal*) See Giblites.
1. An Edomite territory.
G, and Ammon, and Amalek .... Ps 83:7 1381
2. A Phoenician trade city.
The ancients of G and the wise men.... Eze 27:9 1381

GEBALITES See Giblites.

GEBER See Ezion-geber.
1. Father of an officer of Solomon.
The son of G, in Ramoth-gilead............ 1Kin 4:13 1398
2. The son of Uri.
G the son of Uri was in the 1Kin 4:19 1398

GEBIM (*ghe'-bim*) *A city in Benjamin.*
the inhabitants of G gather.................... Is 10:31 1374

GEDALIAH (*ghed-a-li'-ah*)
1. Son of Ahikam.
them he made G the son of Ahikam..... 2Kin 25:22 1436
of Babylon had made G governor.......... 2Kin 25:23 1436
there came to G to Mizpah.................... 2Kin 25:23 1436
G sware to them, and to their men,...... 2Kin 25:24 1436
and ten men with him, and smote G.... 2Kin 25:25 1436
committed him unto G the son of......... Jer 39:14 1436
Go back also to G the son of................. Jer 40:5 1436
Then went Jeremiah unto G the son.... Jer 40:6 1436
the king of Babylon had made G.......... Jer 40:7 1436
Then they came to G to Mizpah............ Jer 40:8 1436
G the son of Ahikam the son of............ Jer 40:9 1436
that he had set over them G the .... Jer 40:11 1436
came to the land of Judah, to G........... Jer 40:12 1436
the fields, came to G to Mizpah,........... Jer 40:13 1436
But G the son of Ahikam believed........ Jer 40:14 1436
spake to G in Mizpah secretly............... Jer 40:15 1436
But G the son of Ahikam said unto...... Jer 40:16 1436
came unto G the son of Ahikam to ...... Jer 41:1 1436
smote G the son of Ahikam the son...... Jer 41:2 1436
that were with him, even with G .... Jer 41:3 1436
second day after he had slain G............ Jer 41:4 1436
Come to G the son of Ahikam .... Jer 41:6 1436
whom he had slain because of G........... Jer 41:9 1436
committed to G the son of Ahikam ...... Jer 41:10 1436
he had slain G the son of Ahikam......... Jer 41:16 1436
had slain G the son of Ahikam .... Jer 41:18 1436
of the guard had left with G the........... Jer 43:6 1436
2. A son of Jeduthun.
G, and Zeri, and Jeshaiah,...................... 1Chr 25:3 1436
the second to G, who with his 1Chr 25:9 1436
3. Priest who married a foreigner.
and Eliezer, and Jarib, and G................. Ezr 10:18 1436
4. Grandfather of Zephaniah.
the son of Cushi, the son of G .... Zeph 1:1 1436
5. A prince who had Jeremiah imprisoned.
G the son of Pashur, and Jucal the....... Jer 38:1 1436

GEDEON (*ghed'-e-on*) See Gideon. *Greek form of Gideon.*
time would fail me to tell of G.............. Heb 11:32 1066

GEDER (*ghe'-dur*) See Beth-gader, Gederite, Gedor. *A Canaanite city.*
the king of G, one.................................. Josh 12:13 1445

GEDERAH (*ghed'-e-rah*) See Gederathite. *A city in Judah.*
And Sharaim, and Adithaim, and G..... Josh 15:36 1449

GEDERATHITE (*ghed'-e-rath-ite*) *An inhabitant of Gederah.*
and Johanan, and Josabad the G.......... 1Chr 12:4 1452

GEDERITE (*ghed'-e-rite*) *An inhabitant of Geder.*
low plains was Baal-hanan the G......... 1Chr 27:28 1451

GEDEROTH (*ghed'-e-roth*) *A town in Judah.*
And G, Beth-dagon, and Naamah, and. Josh 15:41 1450
Beth-shemesh, and Ajalon, and G......... 2Chr 28:18 1450

GEDEROTHAIM (*ghed-e-ro-tha'-im*) *A town in Judah.*
and Adithaim, and Gederah, and G...... Josh 15:36 1453

GEDOR (*ghe'-dor*) See Geder.
1. A city in Judah.
Halhul, Beth-zur, and G,......................... Josh 15:58 1446
2. Hometown of Jeroham.
the sons of Jeroham of G 1Chr 12:7 1446
3. Son of Jehiel.
And G, and Ahio, and Zacher................ 1Chr 8:31 1446
And G, and Ahio, and Zechariah, and.. 1Chr 9:37 1446
4. A descendant of Judah.
And Penuel the father of G.................. 1Chr 4:4 1446
bare Jered the father of G.................... 1Chr 4:18 1446
5. A place in Judah.
And they went to the entrance of G 1Chr 4:39 1446

GE-HARASHIM See Charashim.

GEHAZI (*ghe-ha'-zi*) *A servant of Elijah.*
he said to G his servant, Call.............. 2Kin 4:12 1522
G answered, Verily she hath no........... 2Kin 4:14 1522
that he said to G his servant 2Kin 4:25 1522
but G came near to thrust her 2Kin 4:27 1522
Then he said to G, Gird up thy............. 2Kin 4:29 1522
G passed on before them, and laid........ 2Kin 4:31 1522
And he called G, and said, Call........... 2Kin 4:36 1522
But G, the servant of Elisha the 2Kin 5:20 1522
So G followed after Naaman 2Kin 5:21 1522
unto him, Whence comest thou, G 2Kin 5:25 1522
the king talked with G the.................... 2Kin 8:4 1522
G said, My lord, O king, this is.............. 2Kin 8:5 1522

GELILOTH (*ghel'-il-oth*) *Place on boundary of Benjamin and Judah.*
and went forth toward G, which is....... Josh 18:17 1553

GEMALLI (*ghe-mal'-li*) *One of the twelve spies.*
tribe of Dan, Ammiel the son of G........ Num 13:12 1582

GEMARIAH (*ghem-a-ri'-ah*)
1. Son of Shaphan.
in the chamber of G the son of............. Jer 36:10 1587
When Michaiah the son of G.................. Jer 36:11 1587
G the son of Shaphan, and Zedekiah ... Jer 36:12 1587
G had made intercession to the .... Jer 36:25 1587
2. Son of Hilkiah.
G the son of Hilkiah, (whom .... Jer 29:3 1587

GENDER
thy cattle g with a diverse kind............ Lev 19:19 7250
knowing that they do g strifes.............. 2Ti 2:23 1080

G

GENDERED
frost of heaven, who hath g it ... Job 38:29 3205

GENDERETH
Their bull g, and faileth not ... Job 21:10 5674
which g to bondage, which is Agar ... Gal 4:24 *1080*

GENEALOGIES
All these were reckoned by g in ... 1Chr 5:17 3187
in all by their g fourscore ... 1Chr 7:5 3187
were reckoned by their g twenty ... 1Chr 7:7 3187
So all Israel were reckoned by g ... 1Chr 9:1 3187
and of Iddo the seer concerning g ... 2Chr 12:15 3187
reckoned by g among the Levites ... 2Chr 31:19 3187
give heed to fables and endless g ... 1Ti 1:4 *1076*
But avoid foolish questions, and g ... Titus 3:9 *1076*

GENEALOGY
their habitations, and their g ... 1Chr 4:33 3188
the g is not to be reckoned after ... 1Chr 5:1 3188
when the g of their generations ... 1Chr 5:7 3188
of them, after their g by their ... 1Chr 7:9 3188
the number throughout the g of ... 1Chr 7:40 3188
by their g in their villages ... 1Chr 9:22 3188
Beside their g of males, from ... 2Chr 31:16 3188
Both to the g of the priests by ... 2Chr 31:17 3188
to the g of all their little ones ... 2Chr 31:18 3188
those that were reckoned by g ... Ezr 2:62 3188
this is the g of them that went ... Ezr 8:1 3188
by g of the males an hundred ... Ezr 8:3 3188
that they might be reckoned by g ... Neh 7:5 3188
I found a register of the g of ... Neh 7:5 3188
those that were reckoned by g ... Neh 7:64 3188

GENERAL
the g of the king's army was Joab ... 1Chr 27:34 8269
To the g assembly and church of ... Heb 12:23 *3831*

GENERALLY
Israel be g gathered unto thee ... 2Sa 17:11
There shall be lamentation g upon ... Jer 48:38 3605

GENERATION
righteous before me in this g ... Gen 7:1 1755
But in the fourth g they shall ... Gen 15:16 1755
Ephraim's children of the third g ... Gen 50:23
all his brethren, and all that g ... Ex 1:6 1755
with Amalek from g to g ... Ex 17:16 1755
fourth g of them that hate me ... Ex 20:5
unto the third and to the fourth g ... Ex 34:7
unto the third and fourth g ... Num 14:18
forty years, until all the g ... Num 32:13 1755
of this evil g see that good land ... Deut 1:35 1755
until all the g of the men of war ... Deut 2:14 1755
fourth g of them that hate me, ... Deut 5:9
even to his tenth g shall he not ... Deut 23:2 1755
even to their tenth g shall they ... Deut 23:3 1755
of the LORD in their third g ... Deut 23:8 1755
So that the g to come of your ... Deut 29:22 1755
they are a perverse and crooked g ... Deut 32:5 1755
for they are a very froward g ... Deut 32:20 1755
also all that g were gathered ... Judg 2:10 1755
there arose another g after them ... Judg 2:10 1755
g shall sit on the throne of ... 2Kin 10:30
of Israel unto the fourth g ... 2Kin 15:12
and kept throughout every g ... Est 9:28 1755
them from this g for ever ... Ps 12:7 1755
God is in the g of the righteous ... Ps 14:5 1755
be accounted to the Lord for a g ... Ps 22:30 1755
This is the g of them that seek ... Ps 24:6 1755
ye may tell it to the g following ... Ps 48:13 1755
shall go to the g of his fathers ... Ps 49:19 1755
shewed thy strength unto this g ... Ps 71:18 1755
against the g of thy children ... Ps 73:15 1755
shewing to the g to come the ... Ps 78:4 1755
That the g to come might know ... Ps 78:6 1755
a stubborn and rebellious g ... Ps 78:8 1755
a g that set not their heart ... Ps 78:8 1755
long was I grieved with this g ... Ps 95:10 1755
be written for the g to come ... Ps 102:18 1755
in the g following let their name ... Ps 109:13 1755
the g of the upright shall be ... Ps 112:2 1755
One g shall praise thy works to ... Ps 145:4 1755
doth the crown endure to every g ... Prov 27:24 1755
There is a g that curseth their ... Prov 30:11 1755
There is a g that are pure in ... Prov 30:12 1755
There is a g, O how lofty are ... Prov 30:13 1755
There is a g, whose teeth are as ... Prov 30:14 1755
passeth away, and another g cometh ... Eccl 1:4 1755
be dwelt in from g to g ... Is 13:20 1755
from g to g it shall lie ... Is 34:10 1755
from g to g shall they ... Is 34:17 1755
my salvation from g to g ... Is 51:8 1755
and who shall declare his g ... Is 53:8 1755
O g, see ye the word of the LORD ... Jer 2:31 1755
and forsaken the g of his wrath ... Jer 7:29 1755
be dwelt in from g to g ... Jer 50:39 1755
thy throne from g to g ... Lam 5:19 1755
dominion is from g to g ... Dan 4:3 1859
kingdom is from g to g ... Dan 4:34 1859
and their children another g ... Joel 1:3 1755
and Jerusalem from g to g ... Joel 3:20 1755
The book of the g of Jesus Christ ... Mt 1:1 *1078*
O g of vipers, who hath warned ... Mt 3:7 *1081*
whereunto shall I liken this g ... Mt 11:16 *1074*
O g of vipers, how can ye, being ... Mt 12:34 *1081*
adulterous g seeketh after a sign ... Mt 12:39 *1074*
rise in judgment with this g ... Mt 12:41 *1074*
up in the judgment with this g ... Mt 12:42 *1074*
it be also unto this wicked g ... Mt 12:45 *1074*
adulterous g seeketh after a sign ... Mt 16:4 *1074*
said, O faithless and perverse g ... Mt 17:17 *1074*
ye g of vipers, how can ye escape ... Mt 23:33 *1081*
things shall come upon this g ... Mt 23:36 *1074*
This g shall not pass, till all ... Mt 24:34 *1074*
Why doth this g seek after a sign ... Mk 8:12 *1074*
no sign be given unto this g ... Mk 8:12 *1074*
in this adulterous and sinful g ... Mk 8:38 *1074*
him, and saith, O faithless g ... Mk 9:19 *1074*
that this g shall not pass, till ... Mk 13:30 *1074*
fear him from g to g ... Lk 1:50 *1074*
O g of vipers, who hath warned ... Lk 3:7 *1081*
shall I liken the men of this g ... Lk 7:31 *1074*
said, O faithless and perverse g ... Lk 9:41 *1074*
began to say, This is an evil g ... Lk 11:29 *1074*
also the Son of man be to this g ... Lk 11:30 *1074*
judgment with the men of this g ... Lk 11:31 *1074*
up in the judgment with this g ... Lk 11:32 *1074*
world, may be required of this g ... Lk 11:50 *1074*
It shall be required of this g ... Lk 11:51 *1074*
g wiser than the children of ... Lk 16:8 *1074*
things, and be rejected of this g ... Lk 17:25 *1074*
This g shall not pass away, till ... Lk 21:32 *1074*
yourselves from this untoward g ... Acts 2:40 *1074*
and who shall declare his g ... Acts 8:33 *1074*
his own g by the will of God ... Acts 13:36 *1074*
I was grieved with that g ... Heb 3:10 *1074*
But ye are a chosen g, a royal ... 1Pet 2:9 *1085*

GENERATIONS
These are the g of the heavens and ... Gen 2:4 8435
This is the book of the g of Adam ... Gen 5:1 8435
These are the g of Noah ... Gen 6:9 8435
a just man and perfect in his g ... Gen 6:9 8435
that is with you, for perpetual g ... Gen 9:12 1755
Now these are the g of the sons ... Gen 10:1 8435
the sons of Noah, after their g ... Gen 10:32 8435
These are the g of Shem ... Gen 11:10 8435
Now these are the g of Terah ... Gen 11:27 8435
g for an everlasting covenant ... Gen 17:7 1755
and thy seed after thee in their g ... Gen 17:9 1755
you, every man child in your g ... Gen 17:12 1755
Now these are the g of Ishmael ... Gen 25:12 8435
their names, according to their g ... Gen 25:13 8435
And these are the g of Isaac ... Gen 25:19 8435
Now these are the g of Esau ... Gen 36:1 8435
these are the g of Esau the ... Gen 36:9 8435
These are the g of Jacob ... Gen 37:2 8435
and this is my memorial unto all g ... Ex 3:15 1755
sons of Levi according to their g ... Ex 6:16 8435
of Levi according to their g ... Ex 6:19 8435
to the LORD throughout your g ... Ex 12:14 1755
your g by an ordinance for ever ... Ex 12:17 1755
the children of Israel in their g ... Ex 12:42 1755
omer of it to be kept for your g ... Ex 16:32 1755
the LORD, to be kept for your g ... Ex 16:33 1755
g on the behalf of the children ... Ex 27:21 1755
g at the door of the tabernacle ... Ex 29:42 1755
before the LORD throughout your g ... Ex 30:8 1755
upon it throughout your g ... Ex 30:10 1755
and to his seed throughout their g ... Ex 30:21 1755
oil unto me throughout your g ... Ex 30:31 1755
me and you throughout your g ... Ex 31:13 1755
the sabbath throughout their g ... Ex 31:16 1755
priesthood throughout their g ... Ex 40:15 1755
g throughout all your dwellings ... Lev 3:17 1755
be a statute for ever in your g ... Lev 6:18 1755
for ever throughout their g ... Lev 7:36 1755
for ever throughout your g ... Lev 10:9 1755
ever unto them throughout their g ... Lev 17:7 1755
in their g that hath any blemish ... Lev 21:17 1755
be of all your seed among your g ... Lev 22:3 1755
your g in all your dwellings ... Lev 23:14 1755
your dwellings throughout your g ... Lev 23:21 1755
your g in all your dwellings ... Lev 23:31 1755
be a statute for ever in your g ... Lev 23:41 1755
That your g may know that I made ... Lev 23:43 1755
be a statute for ever in your g ... Lev 24:3 1755
that bought it throughout his g ... Lev 25:30 1755
Israel's eldest son, by their g ... Num 1:20 8435
children of Simeon, by their g ... Num 1:22 8435
the children of Gad, by their g ... Num 1:24 8435
the children of Judah, by their g ... Num 1:26 8435
children of Issachar, by their g ... Num 1:28 8435
children of Zebulun, by their g ... Num 1:30 8435
children of Ephraim, by their g ... Num 1:32 8435
children of Manasseh, by their g ... Num 1:34 8435
children of Benjamin, by their g ... Num 1:36 8435
the children of Dan, by their g ... Num 1:38 8435
the children of Asher, by their g ... Num 1:40 8435
of Naphtali, throughout their g ... Num 1:42 8435
These also are the g of Aaron ... Num 3:1 8435
for ever throughout your g ... Num 10:8 1755
whosoever be among you in your g ... Num 15:14 1755
an ordinance for ever in your g ... Num 15:15 1755
LORD an heave offering in your g ... Num 15:21 1755
and henceforward among your g ... Num 15:23 1755
their garments throughout their g ... Num 15:38 1755
for ever throughout your g ... Num 18:23 1755
your g in all your dwellings ... Num 35:29 1755
his commandments to a thousand g ... Deut 7:9 1755
old, consider the years of many g ... Deut 32:7 1755
our g after us, that we might do ... Josh 22:27 1755
to us or to our g in time to come ... Josh 22:28 1755
Only that the g of the children ... Judg 3:2 1755
Now these are the g of Pharez ... Ruth 4:18 8435
These are their g ... 1Chr 1:29 8435
genealogy of their g was reckoned ... 1Chr 5:7 8435
valiant men of might in their g ... 1Chr 7:2 8435
And with them, by their g, after ... 1Chr 7:4 8435
after their genealogy by their g ... 1Chr 7:9 8435
heads of the fathers, by their g ... 1Chr 8:28 8435
brethren, according to their g ... 1Chr 9:9 8435
were chief throughout their g ... 1Chr 9:34 8435
he commanded to a thousand g ... 1Chr 16:15 1755
according to the g of his fathers ... 1Chr 26:31 8435
and his sons' sons, even four g ... Job 42:16 1755
thoughts of his heart to all g ... Ps 33:11 1755
name to be remembered in all g ... Ps 45:17 1755
and their dwelling places to all g ... Ps 49:11 1755
and his years as many g ... Ps 61:6 1755
and moon endure, throughout all g ... Ps 72:5 1755
shew forth thy praise to all g ... Ps 79:13 1755
draw out thine anger to all g ... Ps 85:5 1755
known thy faithfulness to all g ... Ps 89:1 1755
and build up thy throne to all g ... Ps 89:4 1755
been our dwelling place in all g ... Ps 90:1 1755
and his truth endureth to all g ... Ps 100:5 1755
and thy remembrance unto all g ... Ps 102:12 1755
thy years are throughout all g ... Ps 102:24 1755
he commanded to a thousand g ... Ps 105:8 1755
unto all g for evermore ... Ps 106:31 1755
Thy faithfulness is unto all g ... Ps 119:90 1755
O LORD, throughout all g ... Ps 135:13 1755
endureth throughout all g ... Ps 145:13 1755
even thy God, O Zion, unto all g ... Ps 146:10 1755
calling the g from the beginning ... Is 41:4 1755
the ancient days, in the g of old ... Is 51:9 1755
up the foundations of many g ... Is 58:12 1755
excellency, a joy of many g ... Is 60:15 1755
cities, the desolations of many g ... Is 61:4 1755
it, even to the years of many g ... Joel 2:2 1755
So all the g from Abraham to ... Mt 1:17 *1074*
Abraham to David are fourteen g ... Mt 1:17 *1074*
away into Babylon are fourteen g ... Mt 1:17 *1074*
unto Christ are fourteen g ... Mt 1:17 *1074*
from henceforth all g shall call ... Lk 1:48 *1074*
hath been hid from ages and from g ... Col 1:26 *1074*

GENNESARET (*ghen-nes'-a-ret*) See CHINNERETH. *Same as Galilee.*
they came into the land of G ... Mt 14:34 *1082*
they came into the land of G ... Mk 6:53 *1082*
of God, he stood by the lake of G ... Lk 5:1 *1082*

GENTILE (*jen'-tile*) See GENTILES. *A non-Jew.*
the Jew first, and also of the G ... Rom 2:9 *1672*
the Jew first, and also to the G ... Rom 2:10 *1672*

GENTILES
of the G divided in their lands ... Gen 10:5 1471
which dwelt in Harosheth of the G ... Judg 4:2 1471
from Harosheth of the G unto the ... Judg 4:13 1471
the host, unto Harosheth of the G ... Judg 4:16 1471
to it shall the G seek ... Is 11:10 1471
bring forth judgment to the G ... Is 42:1 1471
the people, for a light of the G ... Is 42:6 1471
give thee for a light to the G ... Is 49:6 1471
I will lift up mine hand to the G ... Is 49:22 1471
and thy seed shall inherit the G ... Is 54:3 1471
the G shall come to thy light, and ... Is 60:3 1471
the forces of the G shall come ... Is 60:5 1471
unto thee the forces of the G ... Is 60:11 1471
shalt also suck the milk of the G ... Is 60:16 1471
ye shall eat the riches of the G ... Is 61:6 1471
seed shall be known among the G ... Is 61:9 1471
the G shall see thy righteousness ... Is 62:2 1471
the glory of the G like a flowing ... Is 66:12 1471
declare my glory among the G ... Is 66:19 1471
destroyer of the G is on his way ... Jer 4:7 1471
of the G that can cause rain ... Jer 14:22 1471
the G shall come unto thee from ... Jer 16:19 1471
the prophet against the G ... Jer 46:1 1471
and her princes are among the G ... Lam 2:9 1471
their defiled bread among the G ... Eze 4:13 1471
the G as a vessel wherein is no ... Hos 8:8 1471
Proclaim ye this among the G ... Joel 3:9 1471
of Jacob shall be among the G in ... Mic 5:8 1471
to cast out the horns of the G ... Zec 1:21 1471
name shall be great among the G ... Mal 1:11 1471
beyond Jordan, Galilee of the G ... Mt 4:15 *1484*
all these things do the G seek ... Mt 6:32 *1484*
Go not into the way of the G ... Mt 10:5 *1484*
a testimony against them and the G ... Mt 10:18 *1484*
he shall shew judgment to the G ... Mt 12:18 *1484*
And in his name shall the G trust ... Mt 12:21 *1484*
deliver him to the G to mock ... Mt 20:19 *1484*
the G exercise dominion over them ... Mt 20:25 *1484*
and shall deliver him to the G ... Mk 10:33 *1484*
the G exercise lordship over them ... Mk 10:42 *1484*
A light to lighten the G, and the ... Lk 2:32 *1484*
he shall be delivered unto the G ... Lk 18:32 *1484*
shall be trodden down of the G ... Lk 21:24 *1484*
the times of the G be fulfilled ... Lk 21:24 *1484*
The kings of the G exercise ... Lk 22:25 *1484*
go unto the dispersed among the G ... Jn 7:35 *1672*
the G, and teach the G ... Jn 7:35 *1672*
and Pontius Pilate, with the G ... Acts 4:27 *1484*
into the possession of the G ... Acts 7:45 *1484*
me, to bear my name before the G ... Acts 9:15 *1484*
because that on the G also was ... Acts 10:45 *1484*
G had also received the word of ... Acts 11:1 *1484*
Then hath God also to the G ... Acts 11:18 *1484*
the G besought that these words ... Acts 13:42 *1484*
life, lo, we turn to the G ... Acts 13:46 *1484*
set thee to be a light of the G ... Acts 13:47 *1484*
when the G heard this, they were ... Acts 13:48 *1484*
unbelieving Jews stirred up the G ... Acts 14:2 *1484*
was an assault made both of the G ... Acts 14:5 *1484*
the door of faith unto the G ... Acts 14:27 *1484*
declaring the conversion of the G ... Acts 15:3 *1484*
that the G by my mouth should ... Acts 15:7 *1484*
had wrought among the G by them ... Acts 15:12 *1484*
God at the first did visit the G ... Acts 15:14 *1484*
seek after the Lord, and all the G ... Acts 15:17 *1484*
among the G are turned to God ... Acts 15:19 *1484*
which are of the G in Antioch ... Acts 15:23 *1484*
henceforth I will go unto the G ... Acts 18:6 *1484*
him into the hands of the G ... Acts 21:11 *1484*
among the G by his ministry ... Acts 21:19 *1484*
are among the G to forsake Moses ... Acts 21:21 *1484*
As touching the G which believe ... Acts 21:25 *1484*
send thee far hence unto the G ... Acts 22:21 *1484*
from the people, and from the G ... Acts 26:17 *1484*
of Judaea, and then to the G ... Acts 26:20 *1484*
unto the people, and to the G ... Acts 26:23 *1484*

of God is sent unto the G...... Acts 28:28 1484
you also, even as among other G...... Rom 1:13 1484
For when the G, which have not...... Rom 2:14 1484
among the G through you, as it is...... Rom 2:24 1484
have before proved both Jews and G... Rom 3:9 1672
is he not also of the G...... Rom 3:29 1484
Yes, of the G also...... Rom 3:29 1484
the Jews only, but also of the G...... Rom 9:24 1484
That the G, which followed not...... Rom 9:30 1484
fall salvation is come unto the G...... Rom 11:11 1484
of them the riches of the G...... Rom 11:12 1484
For I speak to you G, inasmuch as...... Rom 11:13 1484
as I am the apostle of the G...... Rom 11:13 1484
the fulness of the G be come in...... Rom 11:25 1484
that the G might glorify God for...... Rom 15:9 1484
will confess to thee among the G...... Rom 15:9 1484
And again he saith, Rejoice, ye G...... Rom 15:10 1484
again, Praise the Lord, all ye G...... Rom 15:11 1484
shall rise to reign over the G...... Rom 15:12 1484
in him shall the G trust...... Rom 15:12 1484
minister of Jesus Christ to the G...... Rom 15:16 1484
up of the G might be acceptable...... Rom 15:16 1484
by me, to make the G obedient...... Rom 15:18 1484
For if the G have been made...... Rom 15:27 1484
also all the churches of the G...... Rom 16:4 1484
not so much as named among the G... 1Cor 5:1 1484
the things which the G sacrifice...... 1Cor 10:20 1484
neither to the Jews, nor to the G...... 1Cor 10:32 1672
Ye know that ye were G, carried...... 1Cor 12:2 1484
one body, whether we be Jews or G.... 1Cor 12:13 1672
gospel which I preach among the G.... Gal 2:2 1484
was mighty in me toward the G...... Gal 2:8 1484
from James, he did eat with the G...... Gal 2:12 1484
Jew, livest after the manner of G...... Gal 2:14 1483
thou the G to live as do the Jews...... Gal 2:14 1484
nature, and not sinners of the G...... Gal 2:15 1484
on the G through Jesus Christ...... Gal 3:14 1484
being in time past G in the flesh...... Eph 2:11 1484
of Jesus Christ for you G...... Eph 3:1 1484
That the G should be fellowheirs,...... Eph 3:6 1484
the G the unsearchable riches of...... Eph 3:8 1484
walk not as other G walk, in the...... Eph 4:17 1484
glory of this mystery among the G...... Col 1:27 1484
to the G that they might be saved...... 1Th 2:16 1484
even as the G which know not God...... 1Th 4:5 1484
a teacher of the G in faith...... 1Ti 2:7 1484
of angels, preached unto the G...... 1Ti 3:16 1484
an apostle, and a teacher of the G...... 2Ti 1:11 1484
and that all the G might hear...... 2Ti 4:17 1484
conversation honest among the G...... 1Pet 2:12 1484
to have wrought the will of the G...... 1Pet 4:3 1484
forth, taking nothing of the G...... 3Jn 7 1484
for it is given unto the G...... Rev 11:2 1484

GENTLE
But we were *g* among you, even as...... 1Th 2:7 2261
but be *g* unto all men, apt to...... 2Ti 2:24 2261
no man, to be no brawlers, but *g*...... Titus 3:2 1933
is first pure, then peaceable, *g*,...... Jas 3:17 1933
not only to the good and *g*...... 1Pet 2:18 1933

GENTLENESS
and thy *g* hath made me great...... 2Sa 22:36 6031
up, and thy *g* hath made me great...... Ps 18:35 6038
g of Christ, who in presence am...... 2Cor 10:1 1932
joy, peace, longsuffering, *g*,...... Gal 5:22 5544

GENTLY
Deal *g* for my sake with the young...... 2Sa 18:5 3814
shall *g* lead those that are with...... Is 40:11

GENUBATH (*ghen'-u-bath*) *Son of Hadad.*
of Tahpenes bare him G his son...... 1Kin 11:20 1592
G was in Pharaoh's household...... 1Kin 11:20 1592

GERA (*ghe'-rah*) *A son of Bela.*
Belah, and Becher, and Ashbel, G...... Gen 46:21 1617
up a deliverer, Ehud the son of G...... Judg 3:15 1617
name was Shimei, the son of G...... 2Sa 16:5 1617
And Shimei the son of G, a...... 2Sa 19:16 1617
Shimei the son of G fell down...... 2Sa 19:18 1617
with thee Shimei the son of G...... 1Kin 2:8 1617
sons of Bela were, Addar, and G...... 1Chr 8:3 1617
And G, and Shephuphan, and Huram... 1Chr 8:5 1617
And Naaman, and Ahiah, and G...... 1Chr 8:7 1617

GERAHS
(a shekel is twenty *g*...... Ex 30:13 1626
twenty *g* shall be the shekel...... Lev 27:25 1626
(the shekel is twenty *g*...... Num 3:47 1626
the sanctuary, which is twenty *g*...... Num 18:16 1626
And the shekel shall be twenty *g*...... Eze 45:12 1626

GERAR (*ghe'-rar*) *A city in Gaza.*
from Sidon, as thou comest to G...... Gen 10:19 1642
Kadesh and Shur, and sojourned in G. Gen 20:1 1642
and Abimelech king of G sent...... Gen 20:2 1642
king of the Philistines unto G...... Gen 26:1 1642
And Isaac dwelt in G...... Gen 26:6 1642
his tent in the valley of G...... Gen 26:17 1642
the herdmen of G did strive with...... Gen 26:20 1642
Then Abimelech went to him from G... Gen 26:26 1642
were with him pursued them unto G... 2Chr 14:13 1642
all the cities round about G...... 2Chr 14:14 1642

GERGESENES (*ghur'-ghes-enes'*) *Inhabitants of an area near Sea of Galilee.*
side into the country of the G...... Mt 8:28 1086

GERIZIM (*gher'-iz-im*) *A mountain in central Palestine.*
put the blessing upon mount G...... Deut 11:29 1630
upon mount G to bless the people...... Deut 27:12 1630
half of them over against mount G...... Josh 8:33 1630
and stood in the top of mount G...... Judg 9:7 1630

GERSHOM (*ghur'-shom*) See GERSHON.
1. Firstborn son of Moses.
a son, and he called his name G...... Ex 2:22 1648
which the name of the one was G...... Ex 18:3 1648
The sons of Moses were, G...... 1Chr 23:15 1648
Of the sons of G, Shebuel was the...... 1Chr 23:16 1648
And Shebuel the son of G, the son...... 1Chr 26:24 1648
2. A son of Levi.
G, Kohath, and Merari...... 1Chr 6:16 1648
be the names of the sons of G...... 1Chr 6:17 1648
Of G...... 1Chr 6:20 1648
The son of Jahath, the son of G...... 1Chr 6:43 1648
to the sons of G throughout their...... 1Chr 6:62 1648
Unto the sons of G were given out...... 1Chr 6:71 1648
Of the sons of G...... 1Chr 15:7 1648
3. A descendant of Phinehas.
G...... Ezr 8:2 1648
4. Father of Jonathan.
and Jonathan, the son of G...... Judg 18:30 1648

GERSHON (*ghur'-shon*) See GERSHOM, GERSHONITE. *A form of Gershom 2.*
G, Kohath, and Merari...... Gen 46:11 1647
G, and Kohath, and Merari...... Ex 6:16 1647
The sons of G...... Ex 6:17 1647
G, and Kohath, and Merari...... Num 3:17 1647
the sons of G by their families...... Num 3:18 1647
Of G was the family of the...... Num 3:21 1647
of G in the tabernacle of the...... Num 3:25 1647
also the sum of the sons of G...... Num 4:22 1647
of G in the tabernacle of the...... Num 4:28 1647
were numbered of the sons of G...... Num 4:38 1647
of the families of the sons of G...... Num 4:41
oxen he gave unto the sons of G...... Num 7:7 1647
and the sons of G and the sons of...... Num 10:17 1647
of G, the family of the...... Num 26:57 1647
the children of G had by lot out...... Josh 21:6 1647
And unto the children of G...... Josh 21:27 1647
G, Kohath, and Merari...... 1Chr 6:1 1647
among the sons of Levi, namely, G...... 1Chr 23:6 1647

GERSHONITE (*ghur'-shon-ites*) See GERSHONITES. *Descendant of Gershom 2.*
the sons of the G Laadan, chief...... 1Chr 26:21 1649
fathers, even of Laadan the G...... 1Chr 26:21 1649
LORD, by the hand of Jehiel the G...... 1Chr 29:8 1649

GERSHONITES (*ghur'-shon-ites*)
these are the families of the G...... Num 3:21 1649
The families of the G shall pitch...... Num 3:23 1649
G shall be Eliasaph the son of...... Num 3:24 1649
service of the families of the G...... Num 4:24 1649
the service of the sons of the G...... Num 4:27 1649
of Gershon, the family of the G...... Num 26:57 1649
All the cities of the G according...... Josh 21:33 1649
Of the G were, Laadan, and Shimei...... 1Chr 23:7 1649
and of the G...... 2Chr 29:12 1649

GERUTH See CHIMHAM.

GERUTH KIMHAM See CHIMHAM.

GESHAM (*ghe'-sham*) *A son of Jahdai.*
Regem, and Jotham, and G, and Pelet, 1Chr 2:47 1529

GESHAN See GESHAM.

GESHEM (*ghe'-shem*) See GASHMU. *An opponent of Nehemiah.*
G the Arabian, heard it, they...... Neh 2:19 1654
G the Arabian, and the rest of our...... Neh 6:1 1654
G sent unto me, saying, Come, let...... Neh 6:2 1654

GESHUR (*ghe'-shur*) See GESHURITES. *A kingdom in Bashan.*
the daughter of Talmai king of G...... 2Sa 3:3 1650
the son of Ammihud, king of G...... 2Sa 13:37 1650
So Absalom fled, and went to G...... 2Sa 13:38 1650
So Joab arose and went to G...... 2Sa 14:23 1650
say, Wherefore am I come from G...... 2Sa 14:32 1650
a vow while I abode at G in Syria...... 2Sa 15:8 1650
And he took G, and Aram, with the...... 1Chr 2:23 1650
the daughter of Talmai king of G...... 1Chr 3:2 1650

GESHURI (*ghesh'-u-ri*) See GESHURITES.
1. Inhabitants of Geshur.
of Argob unto the coasts of G...... Deut 3:14 1651
2. A people dwelling between Arabia and Philistia.
of the Philistines, and all G...... Josh 13:2 1651

GESHURITES (*ghesh'-u-rites*)
1. Inhabitants of Geshur.
Bashan, unto the border of the G...... Josh 12:5 1651
And Gilead, and the border of the G.... Josh 13:11 1651
of Israel expelled not the G...... Josh 13:13 1651
but the G and the Maachathites...... Josh 13:13 1651
2. Same as Geshuri 2.
his men went up, and invaded the G... 1Sa 27:8 1651

GET
G thee out of thy country, and...... Gen 12:1 3212
said, Up, *g* you out of this place...... Gen 19:14 3318
g thee into the land of Moriah...... Gen 22:2 3212
g thee out from this land, and...... Gen 31:13 3318
saying, G me this damsel to wife...... Gen 34:4 3947
g you possessions therein...... Gen 34:10
g you down thither, and buy for us...... Gen 42:2 3381
g you up in peace unto your...... Gen 44:17 5927
g you unto the land of Canaan...... Gen 45:17 935
so *g* them up out of the land...... Ex 1:10 5927
g you unto your burdens...... Ex 5:4 3212
g you straw where ye can find it...... Ex 5:11 3947
G thee unto Pharaoh in the...... Ex 7:15 3212
G thee from me, take heed to...... Ex 10:28 3212
G thee out, and all the people...... Ex 11:8 3318
g you forth from among my people,...... Ex 12:31 3318
I will *g* me honour upon Pharaoh,...... Ex 14:17 3513
g thee down, and thou shalt come...... Ex 19:24 3381
said unto Moses, Go, *g* thee down...... Ex 32:7 3381
he be poor, and cannot *g* so much...... Lev 14:21 5381
pigeons, such as he is able to *g*...... Lev 14:22 5381
young pigeons, such as he can *g*...... Lev 14:30 5381
Even such as he is able to *g*...... Lev 14:31 5381
whose hand is not able to *g* that...... Lev 14:32 5381
beside that that his hand shall *g*...... Num 6:21 5381
G you up this way southward, and...... Num 13:17 5927
g you into the wilderness by the...... Num 14:25 5265
saying, G you up from about the...... Num 16:24 5927
G you up from among this...... Num 16:45 7426
of Balak, G you into your land...... Num 22:13 3212
thee, I will *g* me back again...... Num 22:34
G thee up into this mount Abarim,...... Num 27:12 5927
g you over the brook Zered...... Deut 2:13 5674
G thee up into the top of Pisgah,...... Deut 3:27 5927
G you into your tents again...... Deut 5:30 7725
giveth thee power to *g* wealth...... Deut 8:18 6213
g thee down quickly from hence...... Deut 9:12 3381
g thee up into the place which...... Deut 17:8 5927
shall *g* up above thee very high...... Deut 28:43 5927
G thee up into this mountain...... Deut 32:49 5927
G you to the mountain, lest the...... Josh 2:16 3212
LORD said unto Joshua, G thee up...... Josh 7:10 6965
then *g* thee up to the wood...... Josh 17:15 5927
g you unto your tents, and unto...... Josh 22:4 3212
g thee down unto the host...... Judg 7:9 3381
now therefore *g* her for me to...... Judg 14:2 3947
unto his father, G her for me...... Judg 14:3 3947
to morrow *g* you early on your way..... Judg 19:9
thee, and *g* thee down to the floor...... Ruth 3:3 3381
Now therefore *g* you up...... 1Sa 9:13 5927
g you down from among the...... 1Sa 15:6 3381
in thine eyes, let me *g* away...... 1Sa 20:29 4422
g thee into the land of Judah...... 1Sa 22:5 935
David made haste to *g* away for...... 1Sa 23:26 3212
G you up to Carmel, and go to...... 1Sa 25:5 5927
lest he *g* him fenced cities, and...... 2Sa 20:6 4672
that my lord the king may *g* heat...... 1Kin 1:2
g thee in unto king David, and say...... 1Kin 1:13 935
G thee to Anathoth, unto thine...... 1Kin 2:26 3212
speed to *g* him up to his chariot...... 1Kin 12:18 5927
and *g* thee to Shiloh...... 1Kin 14:2 1980
g thee to thine own house...... 1Kin 14:12 3212
G thee hence, and turn thee...... 1Kin 17:3 3212
g thee to Zarephath, which...... 1Kin 17:9 3212
Ahab, G thee up, eat and drink...... 1Kin 18:41 5927
g thee down, that the rain stop...... 1Kin 18:44 3381
g thee to the prophets of thy...... 2Kin 3:13 3212
them alive, and *g* into the city...... 2Kin 7:12 935
speed to *g* him up to his chariot...... 2Chr 10:18 5927
So didst thou *g* thee a name...... Neh 9:10 6213
thy precepts I *g* understanding...... Ps 119:104
G wisdom, *g* understanding...... Prov 4:5 7069
therefore *g* wisdom...... Prov 4:7 7069
all thy getting *g* understanding...... Prov 4:7 7069
A wound and dishonour shall he *g*...... Prov 6:33 4672
is it to *g* wisdom than gold...... Prov 16:16 7069
to *g* understanding rather to be...... Prov 16:16 7069
in the hand of a fool to *g* wisdom...... Prov 17:16 7069
ways, and *g* a snare to thy soul...... Prov 22:25 3947
A time to *g*, and a time to lose...... Eccl 3:6 1245
I will *g* me to the mountain of...... Song 4:6 3212
Let us *g* up early to the...... Song 7:12
g thee unto this treasurer, even...... Is 22:15 935
G you out of the way, turn aside...... Is 30:11
shalt say unto it, G thee hence...... Is 30:22 3318
g thee up into the high mountain...... Is 40:9 5927
g thee into darkness, O daughter...... Is 47:5 935
I will *g* me unto the great men,...... Jer 5:5 3212
g thee a linen girdle, and put it...... Jer 13:1 7069
g a potter's earthen bottle, and...... Jer 19:1 7069
g up, ye horsemen, and stand forth...... Jer 46:4 5927
Moab, that it may flee and *g* away...... Jer 48:9 3318
g you far off, dwell deep, O ye...... Jer 49:30 5110
g you up unto the wealthy nation,...... Jer 49:31 5927
me about, that I cannot *g* out...... Lam 3:7 3318
g thee unto the house of Israel,...... Eze 3:4 935
g thee to them of the captivity,...... Eze 3:11 935
said, G you far from the LORD...... Eze 11:15
souls, to *g* dishonest gain...... Eze 22:27 1214
let the beasts *g* away from under...... Dan 4:14 5111
come, *g* you down...... Joel 3:13 3381
I will *g* them praise and fame in...... Zeph 3:19 776
G you hence, walk to and fro...... Zec 6:7 3212
unto him, G thee hence, Satan...... Mt 4:10 5217
his disciples to *g* into a ship...... Mt 14:22 1684
Peter, G thee behind me, Satan...... Mt 16:23 5217
his disciples to *g* into the ship...... Mk 6:45 1684
saying, G thee behind me, Satan...... Mk 8:33 5217
unto him, G thee behind me, Satan...... Lk 4:8 5217
about, and lodge, and *g* victuals...... Lk 9:12 2147
G thee out, and depart hence...... Lk 13:31 1831
G thee out of thy country, and...... Acts 7:3 1831
g thee down, and go with them,...... Acts 10:20 2597
g thee quickly out of Jerusalem...... Acts 22:18 1831
first into the sea, and *g* to land...... Acts 27:43 1826
Lest Satan should *g* an advantage...... 2Cor 2:11 4122
a year, and buy and sell, and *g* gain...... Jas 4:13

GETHER (*ghe'-ther*) *A son of Aram.*
Uz, and Hul, and G, and Mash...... Gen 10:23 1666
Aram, and Uz, and Hul, and G...... 1Chr 1:17 1666

GETHSEMANE (*gheth-sem'-a-ne*) *A garden near Jerusalem.*
with them unto a place called G...... Mt 26:36 1068
came to a place which was named G... Mk 14:32 1068

GETTETH
Whosoever *g* up to the gutter, and...... 2Sa 5:8 5060
the man that *g* understanding...... Prov 3:13 6329
a scorner *g* to himself shame...... Prov 9:7 3947
a wicked man *g* himself a blot...... Prov 9:7
heareth reproof *g* understanding...... Prov 15:32 7069
heart of the prudent *g* knowledge...... Prov 18:15 7069
He that *g* wisdom loveth his own...... Prov 19:8 7069
so he that *g* riches, and not by...... Jer 17:11 6213
he that *g* up out of the pit shall...... Jer 48:44 5927

GETTING

had gotten, the cattle of his g	Gen 31:18	7075
with all thy g get understanding	Prov 4:7	7069
The g of treasures by a lying	Prov 21:6	6467

GEUEL (*ghe-u'-el*) *A son of Machri.*

tribe of Gad, G the son of Machi	Num 13:15	1345

GEZER (*ghe'-zur*) See GAZER, GEZRITES. *A Canaanite city.*

Then Horam king of G came up to	Josh 10:33	1507
the king of G, one	Josh 12:12	1507
of Beth-horon the nether, and to G	Josh 16:3	1507
the Canaanites that dwelt in G	Josh 16:10	1507
and G with her suburbs,	Josh 21:21	1507
the Canaanites that dwelt in G	Judg 1:29	1507
Canaanites dwelt in G among them	Judg 1:29	1507
and Hazor, and Megiddo, and G	1Kin 9:15	1507
of Egypt had gone up, and taken G	1Kin 9:16	1507
And Solomon built G, and Beth-horon.	1Kin 9:17	1507
they gave also G with her suburbs	1Chr 6:67	1507
Naaran, and westward G	1Chr 7:28	1507
war at G with the Philistines	1Chr 20:4	1507

GEZRITES (*ghez'-rites*) *Inhabitants of Gezer.*

invaded the Geshurites, and the G	1Sa 27:8	1511

GHOST

Then Abraham gave up the g	Gen 25:8	1478
and he gave up the g and died	Gen 25:17	1478
And Isaac gave up the g, and died,	Gen 35:29	1478
into the bed, and yielded up the g	Gen 49:33	1478
why did I not give up the g when	Job 3:11	1478
Oh that I had given up the g	Job 10:18	1478
be as the giving up of the g	Job 11:20	5315
my tongue, I shall give up the g	Job 13:19	1478
yea, man giveth up the g, and	Job 14:10	1478
she hath given up the g	Jer 15:9	5315
elders gave up the g in the city	Lam 1:19	1478
found with child of the Holy G	Mt 1:18	*4151*
conceived in her is of the Holy G	Mt 1:20	*4151*
shall baptize you with the Holy G	Mt 3:11	*4151*
G shall not be forgiven unto men	Mt 12:31	*4151*
speaketh against the Holy G	Mt 12:32	*4151*
a loud voice, yielded up the g	Mt 27:50	*4151*
and of the Son, and of the Holy G	Mt 28:19	*4151*
shall baptize you with the Holy G	Mk 1:8	*4151*
the Holy G hath never forgiveness	Mk 3:29	*4151*
David himself said by the Holy G	Mk 12:36	*4151*
not ye that speak, but the Holy G	Mk 13:11	*4151*
a loud voice, and gave up the g	Mk 15:37	*1606*
he so cried out, and gave up the g	Mk 15:39	*1606*
shall be filled with the Holy G	Lk 1:15	*4151*
The Holy G shall come upon thee,	Lk 1:35	*4151*
was filled with the Holy G	Lk 1:41	*4151*
was filled with the Holy G	Lk 1:67	*4151*
and the Holy G was upon him	Lk 2:25	*4151*
revealed unto him by the Holy G	Lk 2:26	*4151*
shall baptize you with the Holy G	Lk 3:16	*4151*
the Holy G descended in a bodily	Lk 3:22	*4151*
the Holy G returned from Jordan	Lk 4:1	*4151*
Holy G it shall not be forgiven	Lk 12:10	*4151*
For the Holy G shall teach you in	Lk 12:12	*4151*
said thus, he gave up the g	Lk 23:46	*1606*
which baptizeth with the Holy G	Jn 1:33	*4151*
for the Holy G was not yet given	Jn 7:39	*4151*
Comforter, which is the Holy G	Jn 14:26	*4151*
bowed his head, and gave up the g	Jn 19:30	*4151*
unto them, Receive ye the Holy G	Jn 20:22	*4151*
after that he through the Holy G	Acts 1:2	*4151*
the Holy G not many days hence	Acts 1:5	*4151*
that the Holy G is come upon you	Acts 1:8	*4151*
which the Holy G by the mouth of	Acts 1:16	*4151*
were all filled with the Holy G	Acts 2:4	*4151*
Father the promise of the Holy G	Acts 2:33	*4151*
receive the gift of the Holy G	Acts 2:38	*4151*
Peter, filled with the Holy G	Acts 4:8	*4151*
were all filled with the Holy G	Acts 4:31	*4151*
thine heart to lie to the Holy G	Acts 5:3	*4151*
words fell down, and gave up the g	Acts 5:5	*1634*
at his feet, and yielded up the g	Acts 5:10	*1634*
and so is also the Holy G, whom	Acts 5:32	*4151*
honest report, full of the Holy G	Acts 6:3	*4151*
full of faith and of the Holy G	Acts 6:5	*4151*
ye do always resist the Holy G	Acts 7:51	*4151*
But he, being full of the Holy G	Acts 7:55	*4151*
they might receive the Holy G	Acts 8:15	*4151*
them, and they received the Holy G	Acts 8:17	*4151*
hands the Holy G was given	Acts 8:18	*4151*
hands, he may receive the Holy G	Acts 8:19	*4151*
and be filled with the Holy G	Acts 9:17	*4151*
and in the comfort of the Holy G	Acts 9:31	*4151*
Jesus of Nazareth with the Holy G	Acts 10:38	*4151*
the Holy G fell on all them which	Acts 10:44	*4151*
poured out the gift of the Holy G	Acts 10:45	*4151*
received the Holy G as well as we	Acts 10:47	*4151*
the Holy G fell on them, as on us	Acts 11:15	*4151*
shall be baptized with the Holy G	Acts 11:16	*4151*
a good man, and full of the Holy G	Acts 11:24	*4151*
eaten of worms, and gave up the g	Acts 12:23	*1634*
Lord, and fasted, the Holy G said	Acts 13:2	*4151*
being sent forth by the Holy G	Acts 13:4	*4151*
Paul,) filled with the Holy G	Acts 13:9	*4151*
with joy, and with the Holy G	Acts 13:52	*4151*
witness, giving them the Holy G	Acts 15:8	*4151*
For it seemed good to the Holy G	Acts 15:28	*4151*
Holy G to preach the word in Asia	Acts 16:6	*4151*
the Holy G since ye believed	Acts 19:2	*4151*
heard whether there be any Holy G	Acts 19:2	*4151*
them, the Holy G came on them	Acts 19:6	*4151*
Save that the Holy G witnesseth	Acts 20:23	*4151*
Holy G hath made you overseers	Acts 20:28	*4151*
and said, Thus saith the Holy G	Acts 21:11	*4151*
Well spake the Holy G by Esaias	Acts 28:25	*4151*
the Holy G which is given unto us	Rom 5:5	*4151*
bearing me witness in the Holy G	Rom 9:1	*4151*
and peace, and joy in the Holy G	Rom 14:17	*4151*
through the power of the Holy G	Rom 15:13	*4151*
being sanctified by the Holy G	Rom 15:16	*4151*
but which the Holy G teacheth	1Cor 2:13	*4151*
of the Holy G which is in you	1Cor 6:19	*4151*
is the Lord, but by the Holy G	1Cor 12:3	*4151*
by kindness, by the Holy G	2Cor 6:6	*4151*
and the communion of the Holy G	2Cor 13:14	*4151*
also in power, and in the Holy G	1Th 1:5	*4151*
with joy of the Holy G	1Th 1:6	*4151*
the Holy G which dwelleth in us	2Ti 1:14	*4151*
and renewing of the Holy G	Titus 3:5	*4151*
miracles, and gifts of the Holy G	Heb 2:4	*4151*
Wherefore (as the Holy G saith	Heb 3:7	*4151*
were made partakers of the Holy G	Heb 6:4	*4151*
The Holy G this signifying, that	Heb 9:8	*4151*
Whereof the Holy G also is a	Heb 10:15	*4151*
the Holy G sent down from heaven	1Pet 1:12	*4151*
as they were moved by the Holy G	2Pet 1:21	*4151*
Father, the Word, and the Holy G	1Jn 5:7	*4151*
holy faith, praying in the Holy G	Jude 20	*4151*

GIAH (*ghi'-ah*) *A place near the wilderness of Gibeon.*

that lieth before G by the way of	2Sa 2:24	1520

GIANT

which was of the sons of the g	2Sa 21:16	7497
which was of the sons of the g	2Sa 21:18	7497
and he also was born to the g	2Sa 21:20	7497
four were born to the g in Gath	2Sa 21:22	7497
that was of the children of the g	1Chr 20:4	7497
and he also was the son of the g	1Chr 20:6	7497
were born unto the g in Gath	1Chr 20:8	7497
he runneth upon me like a g	Job 16:14	1368

GIANTS

There were g in the earth in	Gen 6:4	5303
And there we saw the g	Num 13:33	5303
sons of Anak, which come of the g	Num 13:33	1368
Which also were accounted g	Deut 2:11	7497
also was accounted a land of g	Deut 2:20	7497
g dwelt therein in old time	Deut 2:20	7497
remained of the remnant of g	Deut 3:11	7497
which was called the land of g	Deut 3:13	7497
which was of the remnant of the g	Josh 12:4	7497
remained of the remnant of the g	Josh 13:12	7497
of the valley of the g northward	Josh 15:8	7497
of the Perizzites and of the g	Josh 17:15	7497
the valley of the g on the north	Josh 18:16	7497

GIBALITES See GIBLITES.

GIBBAR (*ghib'-bar*) See GIBEON. *A family of exiles.*

The children of G, ninety and five	Ezr 2:20	1402

GIBBETHON (*ghib'-be-thon*) *A town in Dan.*

And Eltekeh, and G, and Baalath,	Josh 19:44	1405
her suburbs, G with her suburbs,	Josh 21:23	1405
and Baasha smote him at G, which	1Kin 15:27	1405
and all Israel laid siege to G	1Kin 15:27	1405
people were encamped against G	1Kin 16:15	1405
And Omri went up from G, and all	1Kin 16:17	1405

GIBEA (*ghib'-e-ah*) See GIBEAH. *Son of Sheva.*

of Machbenah, and the father of G	1Chr 2:49	1388

GIBEAH (*ghib'-e-ah*) *A city in Judah.*

Cain, G, and Timnah	Josh 15:57	1390
we will pass over to G	Judg 19:12	1390
places to lodge all night, in G	Judg 19:13	1390
upon them when they were by G	Judg 19:14	1390
to go in and to lodge in G	Judg 19:15	1390
and he sojourned in G	Judg 19:16	1390
I came into G that belongeth to	Judg 20:4	1390
the men of G rose against me, and	Judg 20:5	1390
the thing which we will do to G	Judg 20:9	1390
when they come to G of Benjamin	Judg 20:10	1390
of Belial, which are in G	Judg 20:13	1390
together out of the cities unto G	Judg 20:14	1390
beside the inhabitants of G	Judg 20:15	1390
morning, and encamped against G	Judg 20:19	1390
array to fight against them at G	Judg 20:20	1390
of Benjamin came forth out of G	Judg 20:21	1390
them out of G the second day	Judg 20:25	1390
set liers in wait round about G	Judg 20:29	1390
put themselves in array against G	Judg 20:30	1390
and the other to G in the field	Judg 20:31	1390
even out of the meadows of G	Judg 20:33	1390
there came against G ten thousand	Judg 20:34	1390
wait which they had set beside G	Judg 20:36	1390
in wait hasted, and rushed upon G	Judg 20:37	1390
against G toward the sunrising	Judg 20:43	1390
And Saul also went home to G	1Sa 10:26	1390
came the messengers to G of Saul	1Sa 11:4	1390
with Jonathan in G of Benjamin	1Sa 13:2	1390
up from Gilgal unto G of Benjamin	1Sa 13:15	1390
with them, abode in G of Benjamin	1Sa 13:16	1390
in the uttermost part of G under	1Sa 14:2	1390
other southward over against G	1Sa 14:5	1390
of Saul in G of Benjamin looked	1Sa 14:16	1390
went up to his house to G of Saul	1Sa 15:34	1390
(now Saul abode in G under a tree	1Sa 22:6	1390
came up the Ziphites to Saul to G	1Sa 23:19	1390
the Ziphites came unto Saul to G	1Sa 26:1	1390
house of Abinadab that was in G	2Sa 6:3	1390
house of Abinadab which was at G	2Sa 6:4	1390
up unto the LORD in G of Saul	2Sa 21:6	1390
of G of the children of Benjamin	2Sa 23:29	1390
Ithai the son of Ribai of G	1Chr 11:31	1390
the daughter of Uriel of G	2Chr 13:2	1390
G of Saul is fled	Is 10:29	1390
Blow ye the cornet in G, and the	Hos 5:8	1390
themselves, as in the days of G	Hos 9:9	1390
hast sinned from the days of G	Hos 10:9	1390
the battle in G against the	Hos 10:9	1390

GIBEATH (*ghib'-e-ath*) See GIBEAH, GIBEATHITE. *Same as Gibeah.*

and Jebusi, which is Jerusalem, G	Josh 18:28	1394

GIBEATH HAARALOTH See FORESKINS.

GIBEATHITE (*ghib'-e-ath-ite*) *An inhabitant of Gibeah.*

Joash, the sons of Shemaah the G	1Chr 12:3	1395

GIBEON (*ghib'-e-on*) See GEBA, GIBEAH, GIBEONITE.

1. A Hivite city.

when the inhabitants of G heard	Josh 9:3	1391
Now their cities were G, and	Josh 9:17	1391
how the inhabitants of G had made	Josh 10:1	1391
because G was a great city, as	Josh 10:2	1391
and help me, that we may smite G	Josh 10:4	1391
their hosts, and encamped before G	Josh 10:5	1391
the men of G sent unto Joshua to	Josh 10:6	1391
them with a great slaughter at G	Josh 10:10	1391
Sun, stand thou still upon G	Josh 10:12	1391
country of Goshen, even unto G	Josh 10:41	1391
the Hivites the inhabitants of G	Josh 11:19	1391

2. A city in Benjamin.

G, and Ramah, and Beeroth,	Josh 18:25	1391
G with her suburbs, Geba with her	Josh 21:17	1391
Saul, went out from Mahanaim to G	2Sa 2:12	1391
and met together by the pool of G	2Sa 2:13	1391
Helkath-hazzurim, which is in G	2Sa 2:16	1391
by the way of the wilderness of G	2Sa 2:24	1391
brother Asahel at G in the battle	2Sa 3:30	1391
at the great stone which is in G	2Sa 20:8	1391
the king went to G to sacrifice	1Kin 3:4	1391
In G the LORD appeared to Solomon	1Kin 3:5	1391
as he had appeared unto him at G	1Kin 9:2	1391
at G dwelt the father of Gibeon	1Chr 8:29	1391
in G dwelt the father of Gibeon,	1Chr 9:35	1391
Philistines from G even to Gazer	1Chr 14:16	1391
in the high place that was at G	1Chr 16:39	1391
season in the high place at G	1Chr 21:29	1391
to the high place that was at G	2Chr 1:3	1391
place that was at G to Jerusalem	2Chr 1:13	1391
the Meronothite, the men of G	Neh 3:7	1391
The children of G, ninety and five	Neh 7:25	1391
be wroth as in the valley of G	Is 28:21	1391
Azur the prophet, which was of G	Jer 28:1	1391
by the great waters that are in G	Jer 41:12	1391
whom he had brought again from G	Jer 41:16	1391

GIBEONITE (*ghib'-e-on-ite*) See GIBEONITES. *An inhabitant of Gibeon.*

And Ismaiah the G, a mighty man	1Chr 12:4	1393
unto them repaired Melatiah the G	Neh 3:7	1393

GIBEONITES (*ghib'-e-on-ites*)

house, because he slew the G	2Sa 21:1	1393
And the king called the G, and said	2Sa 21:2	1393
(now the G were not of the	2Sa 21:2	1393
Wherefore David said unto the G	2Sa 21:3	1393
the G said unto him, We will have	2Sa 21:4	1393
them into the hands of the G	2Sa 21:9	1393

GIBLITES (*ghib'-lites*) *Inhabitants of Gebal.*

And the land of the G, and all	Josh 13:5	1382

GIDDALTI (*ghid-dal'-ti*) *A son of Heman.*

Hananiah, Hanani, Eliathah, G	1Chr 25:4	1437
The two and twentieth to G	1Chr 25:29	1437

GIDDEL (*ghid'-del*)

1. A family of exiles.

The children of G, the children	Ezr 2:47	1435
of Hanan, the children of G	Neh 7:49	1435

2. Servants of Solomon.

of Darkon, the children of G	Ezr 2:56	1435
of Darkon, the children of G	Neh 7:58	1435

GIDEON (*ghid'-e-on*) See GEDEON, JERUBBAAL. *A judge of Israel.*

his son G threshed wheat by the	Judg 6:11	1439
G said unto him, Oh my Lord, if	Judg 6:13	1439
G went in, and made ready a kid,	Judg 6:19	1439
when G perceived that he was an	Judg 6:22	1439
LORD, G said, Alas, O Lord GOD	Judg 6:22	1439
Then G built an altar there unto	Judg 6:24	1439
Then G took ten men of his	Judg 6:27	1439
G the son of Joash hath done this	Judg 6:29	1439
Spirit of the LORD came upon G	Judg 6:34	1439
G said unto God, If thou wilt	Judg 6:36	1439
G said unto God, Let not thine	Judg 6:39	1439
Then Jerubbaal, who is G, and all	Judg 7:1	1439
And the LORD said unto G, The	Judg 7:2	1439
And the LORD said unto G, The	Judg 7:4	1439
and the LORD said unto G, Every	Judg 7:5	1439
And the LORD said unto G, By the	Judg 7:7	1439
when G was come, behold, there	Judg 7:13	1439
the sword of G the son of Joash	Judg 7:14	1439
when G heard the telling of the	Judg 7:15	1439
The sword of the LORD, and of G	Judg 7:18	1439
So G, and the hundred men that	Judg 7:19	1439
The sword of the LORD, and of G	Judg 7:20	1439
G sent messengers throughout all	Judg 7:24	1439
Zeeb to G on the other side	Judg 7:25	1439
G came to Jordan, and passed over,	Judg 8:4	1439
G said, Therefore when the LORD	Judg 8:7	1439
G went up by the way of them that	Judg 8:11	1439
G the son of Joash returned from	Judg 8:13	1439
G arose, and slew Zebah and	Judg 8:21	1439
the men of Israel said unto G	Judg 8:22	1439
G said unto them, I will not rule	Judg 8:23	1439
G said unto them, I would desire	Judg 8:24	1439
G made an ephod thereof, and put	Judg 8:27	1439
which thing became a snare unto G	Judg 8:27	1439
forty years in the days of G	Judg 8:28	1439
G had threescore and ten sons of	Judg 8:30	1439
G the son of Joash died in a good	Judg 8:32	1439
to pass, as soon as G was dead	Judg 8:33	1439

the house of Jerubbaal, namely, G... Judg 8:35 1439

GIDEONI (ghid-e-o'-ni) *A Benjamite who counted the people.*
Abidan the son of G... Num 1:11 1441
shall be Abidan the son of G... Num 2:22 1441
the ninth day Abidan the son of G... Num 7:60 1441
offering of Abidan the son of G... Num 7:65 1441
Benjamin was Abidan the son of G... Num 10:24 1441

GIDOM (ghi'-dom) *A place near Bethel.*
and pursued hard after them unto G... Judg 20:45 1440

GIER
and the pelican, and the g eagle,... Lev 11:18 7360
the g eagle, and the cormorant,... Deut 14:17 7360

GIFT
Ask me never so much dowry and g... Gen 34:12 4976
And thou shalt take no g... Ex 23:8 7810
for the g blindeth the wise, and... Ex 23:8 7810
given the Levites as a g to Aaron... Num 8:19
are given as a g for the LORD... Num 18:6 4979
office unto you as a service of g... Num 18:7 4979
the heave offering of their g... Num 18:11 4976
respect persons, neither take a g... Deut 16:19 7810
for a g doth blind the eyes of... Deut 16:19 7810
or hath he given us any g... 2Sa 19:42 5379
of Tyre shall be there with a g... Ps 45:12 4503
A g is as a precious stone in the... Prov 17:8 7810
A wicked man taketh a g out of... Prov 17:23 7810
A man's g maketh room for him, and.. Prov 18:16 4976
A g in secret pacifieth anger... Prov 21:14 4976
of a false g is like clouds... Prov 25:14 4991
his labour, it is the g of God... Eccl 3:13 4991
this is the g of God... Eccl 5:19 4991
and a g destroyeth the heart... Eccl 7:7 4979
give a g unto any of his sons... Eze 46:16 4979
But if he give a g of his... Eze 46:17 4979
if thou bring thy g to the altar... Mt 5:23 *1435*
Leave there thy g before the... Mt 5:24 *1435*
and then come and offer thy g... Mt 5:24 *1435*
offer the g that Moses commanded,... Mt 8:4 *1435*
father or his mother, It is a g... Mt 15:5 *1435*
sweareth by the g that is upon it... Mt 23:18 *1435*
for whether is greater, the g... Mt 23:19 *1435*
the altar that sanctifieth the g... Mt 23:19 *1435*
It is Corban, that is to say, a g... Mk 7:11 *1435*
her, If thou knewest the g of God... Jn 4:10 *1431*
receive the g of the Holy Ghost... Acts 2:38 *1431*
thou hast thought that the g of... Acts 8:20 *1431*
out the g of the Holy Ghost... Acts 10:45 *1431*
them the like g as he did unto us... Acts 11:17 *1431*
impart unto you some spiritual g... Rom 1:11 *5486*
offence, so also is the free g... Rom 5:15 *5486*
the g by grace, which is by one... Rom 5:15 *1431*
by one that sinned, so is the g... Rom 5:16 *1434*
but the free g is of many... Rom 5:16 *5486*
of the g of righteousness shall... Rom 5:17 *1431*
the free g came upon all men unto... Rom 5:18
but the g of God is eternal life... Rom 6:23 *5486*
So that ye come behind in no g... 1Cor 1:7 *5486*
man hath his proper g of God... 1Cor 7:7 *5486*
though I have the g of prophecy... 1Cor 13:2
that for the g bestowed upon us... 2Cor 1:11 *5486*
that we would receive the g... 2Cor 8:4 *5485*
be unto God for his unspeakable g... 2Cor 9:15 *1431*
it is the g of God... Eph 2:8 *1435*
according to the g of the grace... Eph 3:7 *1431*
to the measure of the g of Christ... Eph 4:7 *1431*
Not because I desire a g... Phil 4:17 *1390*
Neglect not the g that is in thee... 1Ti 4:14 *5486*
that thou stir up the g of God... 2Ti 1:6 *5486*
and have tasted of the heavenly g... Heb 6:4 *1431*
good g and every perfect g... Jas 1:17 *1394*
As every man hath received the g... 1Pet 4:10 *5486*

GIFTS
which Abraham had, Abraham gave g. Gen 25:6 4979
shall hallow in all their holy g... Ex 28:38 4979
of the LORD, and beside your g... Lev 23:38 4979
Out of all your g ye shall offer... Num 18:29 4979
David's servants, and brought g... 2Sa 8:2 4503
servants to David, and brought g... 2Sa 8:6 4503
David's servants, and brought g... 1Chr 18:2 4503
David's servants, and brought g... 1Chr 18:6 4503
of persons, nor taking of g... 2Chr 19:7 7810
gave them great g of silver... 2Chr 21:3 4979
And the Ammonites gave g to Uzziah. 2Chr 26:8 4503
many brought g unto the LORD to... 2Chr 32:23 4503
to the provinces, and gave g... Est 2:18 4864
one to another, and g to the poor... Est 9:22 4979
thou hast received g for men... Ps 68:18 4979
of Sheba and Seba shall offer g... Ps 72:10 814
though thou givest many g... Prov 6:35 7810
but he that hateth g shall live... Prov 15:27 4979
is a friend to him that giveth g... Prov 19:6 4976
that receiveth g overthroweth it... Prov 29:4 8641
every one loveth g, and followeth... Is 1:23 7810
They give g to all whores... Eze 16:33 5078
givest thy g to all thy lovers... Eze 16:33 5083
And I polluted them in their own g... Eze 20:26 4979
For when ye offer your g, when ye... Eze 20:31 4979
my holy name no more with your g... Eze 20:39 4979
have they taken g to shed blood... Eze 22:12 7810
thereof, ye shall receive of me g... Dan 2:6 4978
man, and gave him many great g... Dan 2:48 4978
Let thy g be to thyself, and give... Dan 5:17 4978
they presented unto him g... Mt 2:11 *1435*
to give good g unto your children... Mt 7:11 *1435*
to give good g unto your children... Lk 11:13 *1390*
casting their g into the treasury... Lk 21:1 *1435*
adorned with goodly stones and g... Lk 21:5 *334*
For the g and calling of God are... Rom 11:29 *5486*
Having then g differing according... Rom 12:6 *5486*
Now concerning spiritual g... 1Cor 12:1
Now there are diversities of g... 1Cor 12:4 *5486*
to another the g of healing by... 1Cor 12:9 *5486*
then g of healings, helps,... 1Cor 12:28 *5486*
Have all the g of healing... 1Cor 12:30 *5486*
But covet earnestly the best g... 1Cor 12:31 *5486*
charity, and desire spiritual g... 1Cor 14:1
as ye are zealous of spiritual g... 1Cor 14:12
captive, and gave g unto men... Eph 4:8 *1390*
g of the Holy Ghost, according to... Heb 2:4 *3311*
to God, that he may offer both g... Heb 5:1 *1435*
priest is ordained to offer g... Heb 8:3 *1435*
that offer g according to the law... Heb 8:4 *1435*
in which were offered both g... Heb 9:9 *1435*
God testifying of his g... Heb 11:4 *1435*
shall send g one to another... Rev 11:10 *1435*

GIHON (ghi'-hon)
1. A river in the Garden of Eden.
the name of the second river is G... Gen 2:13 1521
2. A place near Jerusalem.
own mule, and bring him down to G... 1Kin 1:33 1521
David's mule, and brought him to G... 1Kin 1:38 1521
have anointed him king in G... 1Kin 1:45 1521
the upper watercourse of G... 2Chr 32:30 1521
of David, on the west side of G... 2Chr 33:14 1521

GILALAI (ghil'-a-lahee) *A priest who dedicated the wall.*
Shemaiah, and Azarael, Milalai, G... Neh 12:36 1562

GILBOA (ghil-bo'-ah)
1. A district in Manasseh.
together, and they pitched in G... 1Sa 28:4 1533
Philistines had slain Saul in G... 2Sa 21:12 1533
2. A mountain near the valley Jezreel.
and fell down slain in mount G... 1Sa 31:1 1533
his three sons fallen in mount G... 1Sa 31:8 1533
I happened by chance upon mount G.. 2Sa 1:6 1533
Ye mountains of G, let there be... 2Sa 1:21 1533
and fell down slain in mount G... 1Chr 10:1 1533
and his sons fallen in mount G... 1Chr 10:8 1533

GILEAD (ghil'-e-ad) See GILEADITE, GILEAD'S, JABESH-GILEAD, RAMOTH-GILEAD.
1. District east of the Jordan River.
of Ishmeelites came from G with... Gen 37:25 1568
land of Jazer, and the land of G... Num 32:1 1568
shall be there in the cities of G... Num 32:26 1568
the land of G for a possession... Num 32:29 1568
the son of Manasseh went to G... Num 32:39 1568
Moses gave G unto Machir the son... Num 32:40 1568
that is by the river, even unto G... Deut 2:36 1568
the cities of the plain, and all G... Deut 3:10 1568
And the rest of G, and all Bashan,... Deut 3:13 1568
And I gave G unto Machir... Deut 3:15 1568
unto the Gadites I gave from G... Deut 3:16 1568
and Ramoth in G, of the Gadites... Deut 4:43 1568
LORD shewed him all the land of G... Deut 34:1 1568
of the river, and from half G... Josh 12:2 1568
and the Maachathites, and half G... Josh 12:5 1568
And G, and the border of the... Josh 13:11 1568
was Jazer, and all the cities of G... Josh 13:25 1568
And half G, and Ashtaroth, and Edrei.. Josh 13:31 1568
a man of war, therefore he had G... Josh 17:1 1568
to Manasseh, beside the land of G... Josh 17:5 1568
Manasseh's sons had the land of G... Josh 17:6 1568
Ramoth in G out of the tribe of... Josh 20:8 1568
Ramoth in G with her suburbs, to... Josh 21:38 1568
to go unto the country of G... Josh 22:9 1568
of Manasseh, into the land of G... Josh 22:13 1568
of Manasseh, unto the land of G... Josh 22:15 1568
of Gad, out of the land of G... Josh 22:32 1568
G abode beyond Jordan... Judg 5:17 1568
day, which are in the land of G... Judg 10:4 1568
of the Amorites, which is in G... Judg 10:8 1568
together, and encamped in G... Judg 10:17 1568
princes of G said one to another,... Judg 10:18 1568
over all the inhabitants of G... Judg 10:18 1568
the elders of G went to fetch... Judg 11:5 1568
said unto the elders of G... Judg 11:7 1568
the elders of G said unto... Judg 11:8 1568
over all the inhabitants of G... Judg 11:8 1568
said unto the elders of G... Judg 11:9 1568
the elders of G said unto... Judg 11:10 1568
went with the elders of G... Judg 11:11 1568
Jephthah, and he passed over G... Judg 11:29 1568
and passed over Mizpeh of G... Judg 11:29 1568
from Mizpeh of G he passed over... Judg 11:29 1568
together all the men of G... Judg 12:4 1568
the men of G smote Ephraim,... Judg 12:4 1568
that the men of G said unto him... Judg 12:5 1568
buried in one of the cities of G... Judg 12:7 1568
to Beer-sheba, with the land of G... Judg 20:1 1568
Jordan to the land of Gad and G... 1Sa 13:7 1568
And made him king over G, and over.. 2Sa 2:9 1568
Absalom pitched in the land of G... 2Sa 17:26 1568
Then they came to G, and to the... 2Sa 24:6 1568
son of Manasseh, which are in G... 1Kin 4:13 1568
of Uri was in the country of G... 1Kin 4:19 1568
who was of the inhabitants of G... 1Kin 17:1 1568
Know ye that Ramoth in G is ours... 1Kin 22:3 1568
eastward, all the land of G... 2Kin 10:33 1568
is by the river Arnon, even G... 2Kin 10:33 1568
and Kedesh, and Hazor, and G... 2Kin 15:29 1568
and twenty cities in the land of G... 1Chr 2:22 1568
were multiplied in the land of G... 1Chr 5:9 1568
throughout all the east land of G... 1Chr 5:10 1568
And they dwelt in G in Bashan... 1Chr 5:16 1568
Ramoth in G with her suburbs, and... 1Chr 6:80 1568
men of valour at Jazer of G... 1Chr 26:31 1568
the half tribe of Manasseh in G... 1Chr 27:21 1568
G is mine, and Manasseh is mine... Ps 60:7 1568
G is mine... Ps 108:8 1568
flock of goats that appear from G... Song 6:5 1568
Is there no balm in G... Jer 8:22 1568
Thou art G unto me, and the head... Jer 22:6 1568
Go up into G, and take balm, O... Jer 46:11 1568
satisfied upon mount Ephraim and G... Jer 50:19 1568
and from Damascus, and from G... Eze 47:18 1568
G is a city of them that work... Hos 6:8 1568
Is there iniquity in G... Hos 12:11 1568
because they have threshed G with... Amos 1:3 1568
up the women with child of G... Amos 1:13 1568
and Benjamin shall possess G... Obad 19 1568
let them feed in Bashan and G... Mic 7:14 1568
bring them into the land of G... Zec 10:10 1568
2. A mountain range in Gilead 1.
set his face toward the mount G... Gen 31:21 1568
they overtook him in the mount G... Gen 31:23 1568
pitched in the mount of G... Gen 31:25 1568
the river Arnon, and half mount G... Deut 3:12 1568
and depart early from mount G... Judg 7:3 1568
goats, that appear from mount G... Song 4:1 1568
3. Son of Machir.
and Machir begat G... Num 26:29 1568
of G come the family of the... Num 26:29 1568
These are the sons of G... Num 26:30 1568
the son of Hepher, the son of G... Num 27:1 1568
the families of the children of G... Num 36:1 1568
of Manasseh, the father of G... Josh 17:1 1568
the son of Hepher, the son of G... Josh 17:3 1568
of Machir the father of G... 1Chr 2:21 1568
sons of Machir the father of G... 1Chr 2:23 1568
bare Machir the father of G... 1Chr 7:14 1568
These were the sons of G, the son... 1Chr 7:17 1568
4. Father of Jephthah.
and G begat Jephthah... Judg 11:1 1568
5. A chief of Gad.
the son of Jaroah, the son of G... 1Chr 5:14 1568

GILEADITE (ghil'-e-ad-ite) See GILEADITES. *A descendant of Gilead.*
And after him arose Jair, a G... Judg 10:3 1569
Now Jephthah the G was a mighty... Judg 11:1 1569
the G four days in a year... Judg 11:40 1569
Then died Jephthah the G, and was... Judg 12:7 1569
and Barzillai the G of Rogelim... 2Sa 17:27 1569
Barzillai the G came down from... 2Sa 19:31 1569
unto the sons of Barzillai the G... 1Kin 2:7 1569
the daughters of Barzillai the G... Ezr 2:61 1569
of Barzillai the G to wife... Neh 7:63 1569

GILEADITES (ghil'-e-ad-ites)
Gilead come the family of the G... Num 26:29 1569
Ye G are fugitives of Ephraim... Judg 12:4 1569
the G took the passages of Jordan... Judg 12:5 1569
and with him fifty men of the G... 2Kin 15:25 1569

GILEAD'S (ghil'-e-ads) *Refers to Gilead 4.*
And G wife bare him sons... Judg 11:2 1568

GILGAL (ghil'-gal)
1. A place near Jericho.
in the champaign over against G... Deut 11:30 1537
the first month, and encamped in G... Josh 4:19 1537
of Jordan, did Joshua pitch in G... Josh 4:20 1537
place is called G unto this day... Josh 5:9 1537
children of Israel encamped in G... Josh 5:10 1537
sent unto Joshua to the camp to G... Josh 10:6 1537
So Joshua ascended from G... Josh 10:7 1537
and went up from G all night... Josh 10:9 1537
with him, unto the camp to G... Josh 10:15 1537
with him, unto the camp to G... Josh 10:43 1537
of Judah came unto Joshua in G... Josh 14:6 1537
and so northward, looking toward G... Josh 15:7 1537
the LORD came up from G to Bochim... Judg 2:1 1537
from the quarries that were by G... Judg 3:19 1537
year in circuit to Beth-el, and G... 1Sa 7:16 1537
thou shalt go down before me to G... 1Sa 10:8
people, Come, and let us go to G... 1Sa 11:14 1537
And all the people went to G... 1Sa 11:15 1537
Saul king before the LORD in G... 1Sa 11:15 1537
called together after Saul to G... 1Sa 13:4 1537
As for Saul, he was yet in G... 1Sa 13:7 1537
but Samuel came not to G... 1Sa 13:8 1537
will come down now upon me to G... 1Sa 13:12 1537
gat him up from G unto Gibeah of... 1Sa 13:15 1537
and passed on, and gone down to G... 1Sa 15:12 1537
unto the LORD thy God in G... 1Sa 15:21 1537
in pieces before the LORD in G... 1Sa 15:33 1537
And Judah came to G, to go to meet... 2Sa 19:15 1537
Then the king went on to G... 2Sa 19:40 1537
Also from the house of G, and out... Neh 12:29 1537
and come not ye unto G, neither go... Hos 4:15 1537
All their wickedness is in G... Hos 9:15 1537
they sacrifice bullocks in G... Hos 12:11 1537
at G multiply transgression... Amos 4:4 1537
not Beth-el, nor enter into G... Amos 5:5 1537
for G shall surely go into... Amos 5:5 1537
answered him from Shittim unto G... Mic 6:5 1537
2. A city between Dor and Tirsa.
the king of the nations of G... Josh 12:23 1537
3. A city north of Joppa.
went to Joshua unto the camp at G... Josh 9:6 1537
4. A place south of Ebal and Gerizim.
Elijah went with Elisha from G... 2Kin 2:1 1537
And Elisha came again to G... 2Kin 4:38 1537

GILO See GILOH.

GILOH (ghi'-loh) See GILONITE. *A town in Judah.*
And Goshen, and Holon, and G... Josh 15:51 1542
from his city, even from G... 2Sa 15:12 1542

GILONITE (ghi'-lo-nite) *An inhabitant of Giloh.*
Absalom sent for Ahithophel the G... 2Sa 15:12 1526
Eliam the son of Ahithophel the G... 2Sa 23:34 1526

GIMZO (*ghim'-zo*) *A city in Judah.*
G also and the villages thereof ... 2Chr 28:18 1579

GIN
The *g* shall take him by the heel, ... Job 18:9 6341
the houses of Israel, for a *g* ... Is 8:14 6341
the earth, where no *g* is for him ... Amos 3:5 4170

GINATH (*ghi'-nath*) *Father of Tibni.*
followed Tibni the son of G ... 1Kin 16:21 1527
that followed Tibni the son of G ... 1Kin 16:22 1527

GINNETHO (*ghin'-ne-tho*) See GINNETHON. *A priest who renewed the covenant.*
Iddo, G, Abijah, ... Neh 12:4 1599

GINNETHOI See GINNETHO.

GINNETHON (*ghin'-ne-thon*) See GINNETHO. *Same as Ginnetho.*
Daniel, G, Baruch, ... Neh 10:6 1599
of G, Meshullam ... Neh 12:16 1599

GINS
they have set *g* for me ... Ps 140:5 4170
the *g* of the workers of iniquity ... Ps 141:9 4170

GIRD
g him with the curious girdle of ... Ex 29:5 640
thou shalt *g* them with girdles, ... Ex 29:9 2296
he did *g* it under his raiment ... Judg 3:16 2296
G ye on every man his sword ... 1Sa 25:13 2296
g you with sackcloth, and mourn ... 2Sa 3:31 2296
G up thy loins, and take my staff ... 2Kin 4:29 2296
G up thy loins, and take this box ... 2Kin 9:1 2296
G up now thy loins like a man ... Job 38:3 247
G up thy loins now like a man ... Job 40:7 247
G thy sword upon thy thigh, O ... Ps 45:3 2296
g yourselves, and ye shall be ... Is 8:9 247
g yourselves, and ye shall be ... Is 8:9 247
shall *g* themselves with sackcloth ... Is 15:3 2296
g sackcloth upon your loins ... Is 32:11 2290
Thou therefore *g* up thy loins ... Jer 1:17 2296
For this *g* you with sackcloth, ... Jer 4:8 2296
g thee with sackcloth, and wallow ... Jer 6:26 2296
of Rabbah, *g* you with sackcloth ... Jer 49:3 2296
They shall also *g* themselves with ... Eze 7:18 2296
g them with sackcloth, and they ... Eze 27:31 2296
they shall not *g* themselves with ... Eze 44:18 2296
G yourselves, and lament, ye ... Joel 1:13 2296
unto you, that he shall *g* himself ... Lk 12:37 *4024*
g thyself, and serve me, till I ... Lk 17:8 *4024*
hands, and another shall *g* thee ... Jn 21:18 *2224*
G thyself, and bind on thy sandals ... Acts 12:8 *2224*
Wherefore *g* up the loins of your ... 1Pet 1:13 *328*

GIRDED
with your loins *g*, your shoes on ... Ex 12:11 2296
g him with the girdle, and clothed ... Lev 8:7 2296
he *g* him with the curious girdle ... Lev 8:7 2296
g them with girdles, and put ... Lev 8:13 2296
shall be *g* with a linen girdle, ... Lev 16:4 2296
when ye had *g* on every man his ... Deut 1:41 2296
that stumbled are *g* with strength ... 1Sa 2:4 247
a child, *g* with a linen ephod ... 1Sa 2:18 2296
David *g* his sword upon his armour ... 1Sa 17:39 2296
they *g* on every man his sword ... 1Sa 25:13 2296
David also *g* on his sword ... 1Sa 25:13 2296
David was *g* with a linen ephod ... 2Sa 6:14 2296
that he had put on was *g* unto him ... 2Sa 20:8 2296
he being *g* with a new sword, ... 2Sa 21:16 2296
For thou hast *g* me with strength ... 2Sa 22:40 247
he *g* up his loins, and ran before ... 1Kin 18:46 8151
So they *g* sackcloth on their ... 1Kin 20:32 2296
one had his sword *g* by his side ... Neh 4:18 631
For thou hast *g* me with strength ... Ps 18:39 247
sackcloth, and *g* me with gladness ... Ps 30:11 247
being *g* with power ... Ps 65:6 247
wherewith he hath *g* himself ... Ps 93:1 247
wherewith he is *g* continually ... Ps 109:19 2296
I *g* thee, though thou hast not ... Is 45:5 247
they have *g* themselves with ... Lam 2:10 2296
I *g* thee about with fine linen, ... Eze 16:10 2280
G with girdles upon their loins, ... Eze 23:15 2289
whose loins were *g* with fine gold ... Dan 10:5 2296
Lament like a virgin *g* with ... Joel 1:8 2296
Let your loins be *g* about ... Lk 12:35 *4024*
and took a towel, and *g* himself ... Jn 13:4 *1241*
with the towel wherewith he was *g* ... Jn 13:5 *1241*
breasts *g* with golden girdles ... Rev 15:6 *4024*

GIRDEDST
thou *g* thyself, and walkedst ... Jn 21:18 *2224*

GIRDETH
Let not him that *g* on his harness ... 1Kin 20:11 2296
g their loins with a girdle ... Job 12:18 631
It is God that *g* me with strength ... Ps 18:32 247
She *g* her loins with strength, and ... Prov 31:17 2296

GIRDING
of a stomacher a *g* of sackcloth ... Is 3:24 4228
baldness, and to *g* with sackcloth ... Is 22:12 2296

GIRDLE
a broidered coat, a mitre, and a *g* ... Ex 28:4 73
the curious *g* of the ephod, which ... Ex 28:8 2805
above the curious *g* of the ephod ... Ex 28:27 2805
above the curious *g* of the ephod ... Ex 28:28 2805
shalt make the *g* of needlework ... Ex 28:39 73
with the curious *g* of the ephod ... Ex 29:5 2805
the curious *g* of his ephod, that ... Ex 39:5 2805
above the curious *g* of the ephod ... Ex 39:20 2805
above the curious *g* of the ephod ... Ex 39:21 2805
a *g* of fine twined linen, and blue ... Ex 39:29 73
coat, and girded him with the *g* ... Lev 8:7 73
with the curious *g* of the ephod ... Lev 8:7 2805
and shall be girded with a linen *g* ... Lev 16:4 73
sword, and to his bow, and to his *g* ... 1Sa 18:4 2290
ten shekels of silver, and a *g* ... 2Sa 18:11 2290
upon it a *g* with a sword fastened ... 2Sa 20:8 2290
his *g* that was about his loins ... 1Kin 2:5 2290
girt with a *g* of leather about ... 2Kin 1:8 232
and girdeth their loins with a *g* ... Job 12:18 232
for a *g* wherewith he is girded ... Ps 109:19 4206
and instead of a *g* a rent ... Is 3:24 2290
neither shall the *g* of their ... Is 5:27 232
shall be the *g* of his loins ... Is 11:5 232
faithfulness the *g* of his reins ... Is 11:5 232
and strengthen him with thy *g* ... Is 22:21 73
unto me, Go and get thee a linen *g* ... Jer 13:1 232
So I got a *g* according to the ... Jer 13:2 232
Take the *g* that thou hast got, ... Jer 13:4 232
take the *g* from thence, which I ... Jer 13:6 232
took the *g* from the place where I ... Jer 13:7 232
behold, the *g* was marred, it was ... Jer 13:7 232
them, shall even be as this *g* ... Jer 13:10 232
For as the *g* cleaveth to the ... Jer 13:11 232
a leathern *g* about his loins ... Mt 3:4 *2223*
with a *g* of a skin about his ... Mk 1:6 *2223*
come unto us, he took Paul's *g* ... Acts 21:11 *2223*
bind the man that owneth this *g* ... Acts 21:11 *2223*
about the paps with a golden *g* ... Rev 1:13 *2223*

GIRDLES
and thou shalt make for them *g* ... Ex 28:40 73
And thou shalt gird them with *g* ... Ex 29:9 73
upon them, and girded them with *g* ... Lev 8:13 73
delivereth *g* unto the merchant ... Prov 31:24 2289
Girded with *g* upon their loins, ... Eze 23:15 232
breasts girded with golden *g* ... Rev 15:6 *2223*

GIRGASHITE (*ghur'-gash-ite*) See GIRGASHITES, GIRGASITE. *A Canaanite tribe.*
also, and the Amorite, and the G ... 1Chr 1:14 1622

GIRGASHITES (*ghur'-gash-ites*)
and the Canaanites, and the G ... Gen 15:21 1622
thee, the Hittites, and the G ... Deut 7:1 1622
and the Perizzites, and the G ... Josh 3:10 1622
and the Hittites, and the G ... Josh 24:11 1622
and the Jebusites, and the G ... Neh 9:8 1622

GIRGASITE (*ghur'-ga-site*) See GIRGASHITE. *Same as Girgashite.*
and the Amorite, and the G ... Gen 10:16 1622

GIRL
sold a *g* for wine, that they ... Joel 3:3 3207

GIRLS
g playing in the streets thereof ... Zec 8:5 3207

GIRT
g with a girdle of leather about ... 2Kin 1:8 247
he *g* his fisher's coat unto him, ... Jn 21:7 *1241*
your loins *g* about with truth ... Eph 6:14 *4024*
g about the paps with a golden ... Rev 1:13 *4024*

GIRZITES See GEZRITES.

GISHPA See GISPA.

GISPA (*ghis'-pah*) *An overseer of the Nethinim.*
G were over the Nethinims ... Neh 11:21 1658

GISPHA See GISPA.

GITTAH-HEPHER (*ghit''-tah-he'-fer*) See GATH-HEPHER. *A town in Zebulun.*
passeth on along on the east to G ... Josh 19:13 1662

GITTAIM (*ghit-ta'-im*)
1. A city of refuge.
And the Beerothites fled to G ... 2Sa 4:3 1664
2. A Benjamite city.
Hazor, Ramah, G, ... Neh 11:33 1664

GITTITE (*ghit'-tite*) See GITTITES, GITTITH. *An inhabitant of Gath.*
into the house of Obed-edom the G ... 2Sa 6:10 1663
of Obed-edom the G three months ... 2Sa 6:11 1663
Then said the king to Ittai the G ... 2Sa 15:19 1663
Ittai the G passed over, and all ... 2Sa 15:22 1663
under the hand of Ittai the G ... 2Sa 18:2 1663
slew the brother of Goliath the G ... 2Sa 21:19 1663
into the house of Obed-edom the G ... 1Chr 13:13 1663
the brother of Goliath the G ... 1Chr 20:5 1663

GITTITES
the Eshkalonites, the G, and the ... Josh 13:3 1663
all the Pelethites, and all the G ... 2Sa 15:18 1663

GITTITH (*ghit'-tith*) *A musical instrument.*
To the chief Musician upon G ... Ps 8:*t* 1665
To the chief Musician upon G ... Ps 81:*t* 1665
To the chief Musician upon G ... Ps 84:*t* 1665

GIVE
heaven to *g* light upon the earth ... Gen 1:15
heaven to *g* light upon the earth ... Gen 1:17
Unto thy seed will I *g* this land ... Gen 12:7 5414
thou seest, to thee will I *g* it ... Gen 13:15 5414
for I will *g* it unto thee ... Gen 13:17 5414
G me the persons, and take the ... Gen 14:21 5414
Lord GOD, what wilt thou *g* me ... Gen 15:2 5414
to *g* thee this land to inherit it ... Gen 15:7 5414
I will *g* unto thee, and to thy ... Gen 17:8 5414
her, and *g* thee a son also of her ... Gen 17:16 5414
g me a possession of a ... Gen 23:4 5414
That he may *g* me the cave of ... Gen 23:9 5414
g it me for a possession of a ... Gen 23:9 5414
the field *g* I thee, and the cave ... Gen 23:11 5414
cave that is therein, I *g* it thee ... Gen 23:11 5414
the sons of my people *g* I it thee ... Gen 23:11 5414
saying, But if thou wilt *g* it ... Gen 23:13
I will *g* thee money for the field ... Gen 23:13 5414
Unto thy seed will I *g* this land ... Gen 24:7 5414
I will *g* thy camels drink also ... Gen 24:14
if they *g* not thee one, thou ... Gen 24:41 5414
G me, I pray thee, a little water ... Gen 24:43
I will *g* thy camels drink also ... Gen 24:46
I will *g* all these countries, and ... Gen 26:3 5414
will *g* unto thy seed all these ... Gen 26:4 5414
Therefore God *g* thee of the dew ... Gen 27:28 5414
g thee the blessing of Abraham, ... Gen 28:4 5414
thou liest, to thee will I *g* it ... Gen 28:13 5414
will *g* me bread to eat, and ... Gen 28:20 5414
of all that thou shalt *g* me I ... Gen 28:22 5414
will surely *g* the tenth unto thee ... Gen 28:22
It is better that I *g* her to thee ... Gen 29:19 5414
I should *g* her to another man ... Gen 29:19 5414
G me my wife, for my days are ... Gen 29:21 3051
to *g* the younger before the ... Gen 29:26 5414
we will *g* thee this also for the ... Gen 29:27 5414
G me children, or else I die ... Gen 30:1 3051
G me, I pray thee, of thy son's ... Gen 30:14 5414
G me my wives and my children, for ... Gen 30:26 5414
me thy wages, and I will *g* it ... Gen 30:28 5414
And he said, What shall I *g* thee ... Gen 30:31 5414
Thou shalt not *g* me any thing ... Gen 30:31 5414
I pray you *g* her him to wife ... Gen 34:8 5414
g your daughters unto us, and take ... Gen 34:9 5414
ye shall say unto me I will *g* ... Gen 34:11 5414
I will *g* according as ye shall ... Gen 34:12 5414
but *g* me the damsel to wife ... Gen 34:12 5414
to *g* our sister to one that is ... Gen 34:14 5414
Then will we *g* our daughters unto ... Gen 34:16 5414
let us *g* them our daughters ... Gen 34:21 5414
and Isaac, to thee I will *g* it ... Gen 35:12 5414
seed after thee will I *g* the land ... Gen 35:12 5414
he should *g* seed to his brother ... Gen 38:9 5414
And she said, What wilt thou *g* me ... Gen 38:16 5414
Wilt thou *g* me a pledge, till ... Gen 38:17 5414
said, What pledge shall I *g* thee ... Gen 38:18 5414
God shall *g* Pharaoh an answer of ... Gen 41:16
to *g* them provision for the way ... Gen 42:25 5414
to *g* his ass provender in the inn ... Gen 42:27 5414
God Almighty *g* you mercy before ... Gen 43:14 5414
I will *g* you the good of the land ... Gen 45:18 5414
unto Joseph, and said, G us bread ... Gen 47:15 3051
And Joseph said, G your cattle ... Gen 47:16 3051
I will *g* you for your cattle, if ... Gen 47:16 5414
g us seed, that we may live, and ... Gen 47:19 5414
that ye shall *g* the fifth part ... Gen 47:24 5414
will *g* this land to thy seed ... Gen 48:4 5414
me, and I will *g* thee thy wages ... Ex 2:9 5414
I will *g* this people favour in ... Ex 3:21 5414
Ye shall no more *g* the people ... Ex 5:7 5414
Pharaoh, I will not *g* you straw ... Ex 5:10 5414
to *g* them the land of Canaan, the ... Ex 6:4 5414
I did swear to *g* it to Abraham ... Ex 6:8 5414
I will *g* it you for an heritage ... Ex 6:8 5414
Thou must *g* us also sacrifices and ... Ex 10:25 5414
land which the LORD will *g* you ... Ex 12:25 5414
sware unto thy fathers to *g* thee ... Ex 13:5 5414
thy fathers, and shall *g* it thee, ... Ex 13:11 5414
a pillar of fire, to *g* them light ... Ex 13:21
wilt *g* ear to his commandments, ... Ex 15:26
when the LORD shall *g* you in the ... Ex 16:8 5414
G us water that we may drink ... Ex 17:2 5414
I will *g* thee counsel, and God ... Ex 18:19
then thou shalt *g* life for life ... Ex 21:23 5414
then he shall *g* for the ransom of ... Ex 21:30 5414
he shall *g* unto their master ... Ex 21:32 5414
g money unto the owner of them ... Ex 21:34 7725
utterly refuse to *g* her unto him ... Ex 22:17 5414
of thy sons shalt thou *g* unto me ... Ex 22:29 5414
the eighth day thou shalt *g* it me ... Ex 22:30 5414
I will *g* thee tables of stone, and ... Ex 24:12 5414
testimony which I shall *g* thee ... Ex 25:16 5414
the testimony that I shall *g* thee ... Ex 25:21 5414
of all things which I will *g* thee ... Ex 25:22
that they may *g* light over ... Ex 25:37
then shall they *g* every man a ... Ex 30:12 5414
This they shall *g*, every one that ... Ex 30:13 5414
shall *g* an offering unto the LORD ... Ex 30:14 5414
The rich shall not *g* more ... Ex 30:15
the poor shall not *g* less than ... Ex 30:15
when they *g* an offering unto the ... Ex 30:15 5414
spoken of will I *g* unto your seed ... Ex 32:13 5414
saying, Unto thy seed will I *g* it ... Ex 33:1 5414
with thee, and I will *g* thee rest ... Ex 33:14
thereto, and *g* it unto the priest ... Lev 5:16 5414
and *g* it unto him to whom it ... Lev 6:5 5414
the right shoulder shall ye *g* ... Lev 7:32 5414
which I *g* to you for a possession ... Lev 14:34 5414
and *g* them unto the priest ... Lev 15:14 5414
I will *g* it unto you to possess ... Lev 20:24 5414
shall *g* it unto the priest with ... Lev 22:14 5414
into the land which I *g* unto you ... Lev 23:10 5414
which ye *g* unto the LORD ... Lev 23:38 5414
come into the land which I *g* you ... Lev 25:2 5414
Thou shalt not *g* him thy money ... Lev 25:37 5414
to *g* you the land of Canaan, and ... Lev 25:38 5414
he shall *g* again the price of his ... Lev 25:51 7725
unto his years shall he *g* him ... Lev 25:52 7725
Then I will *g* you rain in due ... Lev 26:4 5414
I will *g* peace in the land, and ye ... Lev 26:6 5414
he shall *g* thine estimation in ... Lev 27:23 5414
thou shalt *g* the Levites unto ... Num 3:9 5414
And thou shalt *g* the money ... Num 3:48 5414
g it unto him against whom he ... Num 5:7 5414
upon thee, and *g* thee peace ... Num 6:26 7760
thou shalt *g* them unto the ... Num 7:5 5414
the seven lamps shall *g* light ... Num 8:2
the LORD said, I will *g* it you ... Num 10:29 5414
Who shall *g* us flesh to eat ... Num 11:4
flesh to *g* unto all this people ... Num 11:13 5414
G us flesh, that we may eat ... Num 11:13 5414
Who shall *g* us flesh to eat ... Num 11:18
the LORD will *g* you flesh ... Num 11:18 5414
I will *g* them flesh, that they ... Num 11:21 5414
which I *g* unto the children of ... Num 13:2 5414
us into this land, and *g* it us ... Num 14:8 5414
habitations, which I *g* unto you, ... Num 15:2 5414

first of your dough ye shall g ... Num 15:21 5414
ye shall g thereof the LORD's ... Num 18:28 5414
ye shall g her unto Eleazar the ... Num 19:3 5414
it shall g forth his water, and ... Num 20:8 5414
so thou shalt g the congregation ... Num 20:8
Thus Edom refused to g Israel ... Num 20:21 5414
together, and I will g them water ... Num 21:16 5414
to g me leave to go with you ... Num 22:13 5414
If Balak would g me his house ... Num 22:18 5414
If Balak would g me his house ... Num 24:13 5414
I g unto him my covenant of peace ... Num 25:12 5414
To many thou shalt g the more ... Num 26:54
to few thou shalt g the less ... Num 26:54
G unto us therefore a possession ... Num 27:4 5414
thou shalt surely g them a ... Num 27:7 5414
then ye shall g his inheritance ... Num 27:9 5414
then ye shall g his inheritance ... Num 27:10 5414
then ye shall g his inheritance ... Num 27:11 5414
g him a charge in their sight ... Num 27:19
g it unto Eleazar the priest, for ... Num 31:29 5414
g them unto the Levites, which ... Num 31:30 5414
then ye shall g them the land of ... Num 32:29 5414
ye shall g the more inheritance ... Num 33:54
ye shall g the less inheritance ... Num 33:54
to g unto the nine tribes ... Num 34:13 5414
that they g unto the Levites of ... Num 35:2 5414
ye shall g also unto the Levites ... Num 35:2 5414
which ye shall g unto the Levites ... Num 35:4 5414
g unto the Levites there shall be ... Num 35:6 5414
g to the Levites shall be forty ... Num 35:7 5414
them shall ye g with their ... Num 35:7
the cities which ye shall g shall ... Num 35:8 5414
that have many ye shall g many ... Num 35:8
them that have few ye shall g few ... Num 35:8
every one shall g of his cities ... Num 35:8 5414
g six cities shall ye have for ... Num 35:13 5414
Ye shall g three cities on this ... Num 35:14 5414
shall ye g in the land of Canaan ... Num 35:14 5414
The LORD commanded my lord to g ... Num 36:2 5414
was commanded by the LORD to g ... Num 36:2 5414
to g unto them and to their seed ... Deut 1:8 5414
the LORD our God doth g unto us ... Deut 1:20 5414
which the LORD our God doth g us ... Deut 1:25 5414
which I sware to g unto your ... Deut 1:35 5414
to him will I g the land that he ... Deut 1:36 5414
thither, and unto them will I g it ... Deut 1:39 5414
to your voice, nor g ear unto you ... Deut 1:45
for I will not g you of their ... Deut 2:5 5414
for I will not g thee of their ... Deut 2:9 5414
for I will not g thee of the land ... Deut 2:19 5414
g me water for money, that I may ... Deut 2:28 5414
Behold, I have begun to g Sihon ... Deut 2:31 5414
to g thee their land for an ... Deut 4:38 5414
land which I g them to possess it ... Deut 5:31 5414
to g thee great and goodly cities, ... Deut 6:10 5414
to g us the land which he sware ... Deut 6:23 5414
thou shalt not g unto his son ... Deut 7:3 5414
sware unto thy fathers to g thee ... Deut 7:13 5414
unto their fathers to g unto them ... Deut 10:11 5414
unto your fathers to g unto them ... Deut 11:9 5414
That I will g you the rain of ... Deut 11:14 5414
sware unto your fathers to g them ... Deut 11:21 5414
thou shalt g it unto the stranger ... Deut 14:21 5414
Thou shalt surely g him, and thine ... Deut 15:10 5414
thee thou shalt g unto him ... Deut 15:14 5414
which thou shalt g unto the LORD ... Deut 16:10 5414
Every man shall g as he is able ... Deut 16:17
they shall g unto the priest the ... Deut 18:3 5414
of thy sheep, shalt thou g him ... Deut 18:4 5414
g thee all the land which he ... Deut 19:8 5414
he promised to g unto thy fathers ... Deut 19:8 5414
doth g thee for an inheritance ... Deut 20:16 5414
g occasions of speech against her ... Deut 22:14 7760
g them unto the father of the ... Deut 22:19 5414
g unto the damsel's father fifty ... Deut 22:29 5414
to g up thine enemies before thee ... Deut 23:14 5414
g it in her hand, and send her out ... Deut 24:1 5414
his day thou shalt g him his hire ... Deut 24:15 5414
Forty stripes he may g him ... Deut 25:3
unto our fathers for to g us ... Deut 26:3 5414
sware unto thy fathers to g thee ... Deut 28:11 5414
the heaven to g the rain unto thy ... Deut 28:12 5414
So that he will not g to any of ... Deut 28:55 5414
but the LORD shall g thee there a ... Deut 28:65 5414
to Isaac, and to Jacob, to g them ... Deut 30:20 5414
the LORD shall g them up before ... Deut 31:5 5414
unto their fathers to g them ... Deut 31:7 5414
that I may g him a charge ... Deut 31:14
G ear, O ye heavens, and I will ... Deut 32:1
which I g unto the children of ... Deut 32:49 5414
which I g the children of Israel ... Deut 32:52 5414
I will g it unto thy seed ... Deut 34:4 5414
the land which I do g to them ... Josh 1:2 5414
unto their fathers to g them ... Josh 1:6 5414
house, and g me a true token ... Josh 2:12 5414
their fathers that he would g us ... Josh 5:6 5414
Joshua said unto Achan, My son, g ... Josh 7:19 7760
for I will g it into thine hand ... Josh 8:18 5414
Moses to g you all the land ... Josh 9:24 5414
Now therefore g me this mountain, ... Josh 14:12 5414
to him will I g Achsah my ... Josh 15:16 5414
Who answered, G me a blessing ... Josh 15:19 5414
g me also springs of water ... Josh 15:19 5414
to g us an inheritance among our ... Josh 17:4 5414
G out from among you three men ... Josh 18:4 3051
g him a place, that he may dwell ... Josh 20:4 5414
Moses to g us cities to dwell in ... Josh 21:2 5414
he sware to g unto their fathers ... Josh 21:43 5414
to him will I g Achsah my ... Judg 1:12 5414
said unto him, G me a blessing ... Judg 1:15 3051
g me also springs of water ... Judg 1:15 5414
G me, I pray thee, a little water ... Judg 4:19
g ear, O ye princes ... Judg 5:3
thee are too many for me to g the ... Judg 7:2 5414

said unto the men of Succoth, G ... Judg 8:5 5414
that we should g bread unto thine ... Judg 8:6 5414
that we should g bread unto thy ... Judg 8:15 5414
that ye would g me every man the ... Judg 8:24 5414
We will willingly g them ... Judg 8:25 5414
then I will g you thirty sheets ... Judg 14:12 5414
then shall ye g me thirty sheets ... Judg 14:13 5414
we will g thee every one of us ... Judg 16:5 5414
I will g thee ten shekels of ... Judg 17:10 5414
g here your advice and counsel ... Judg 20:7 3051
There shall not any of us g his ... Judg 21:1 5414
by the LORD that we will not g ... Judg 21:7 5414
Howbeit we may not g them wives ... Judg 21:18 5414
for ye did not g unto them at ... Judg 21:22 5414
shall g thee of this young woman ... Ruth 4:12 5414
but wilt g unto thine handmaid a ... 1Sa 1:11 5414
then I will g him unto the LORD ... 1Sa 1:11 5414
he shall g strength unto his king ... 1Sa 2:10 5414
G flesh to roast for the priest ... 1Sa 2:15 5414
but thou shalt g it me now ... 1Sa 2:16 5414
The LORD g thee seed of this ... 1Sa 2:20 7760
did I g unto the house of thy ... 1Sa 2:28 5414
wealth which God shall g Israel ... 1Sa 2:32 3190
ye shall g glory unto the God of ... 1Sa 6:5 5414
said, G us a king to judge us ... 1Sa 8:6 5414
them, and g them to his servants ... 1Sa 8:14 5414
g to his officers, and to his ... 1Sa 8:15 5414
that will I g to the man of God, ... 1Sa 9:8 5414
g thee two loaves of bread ... 1Sa 10:4 5414
G us seven days' respite, that we ... 1Sa 11:3
God of Israel, G a perfect lot ... 1Sa 14:41 3051
g me a man, that we may fight ... 1Sa 17:10 5414
will g him his daughter, and make ... 1Sa 17:25 5414
I will g thy flesh unto the fowls ... 1Sa 17:44 5414
I will g the carcases of the host ... 1Sa 17:46 5414
he will g you into our hands ... 1Sa 17:47 5414
her will I g thee to wife ... 1Sa 18:17 5414
I will g him her, that she may be ... 1Sa 18:21 5414
g me five loaves of bread in mine ... 1Sa 21:3 5414
none like that; g it me ... 1Sa 21:9 5414
will the son of Jesse g every one ... 1Sa 22:7 5414
g, I pray thee, whatsoever cometh ... 1Sa 25:8 5414
g it unto men, whom I know not ... 1Sa 25:11 5414
let them g me a place in some ... 1Sa 27:5 5414
we will not g them ought of the ... 1Sa 30:22 5414
g them unto thy neighbour, and he ... 2Sa 12:11 5414
g me meat, and dress the meat in ... 2Sa 13:5 1262
I will g charge concerning thee ... 2Sa 14:8
G counsel among you what we shall ... 2Sa 16:20 3051
And the king said, I will g them ... 2Sa 21:6 5414
I will g thanks unto thee ... 2Sa 22:50
Oh that one would g me drink of ... 2Sa 23:15
as a king, g unto the king ... 2Sa 24:23 5414
g thee counsel, that thou mayest ... 1Kin 1:12
that he g me Abishag the ... 1Kin 2:17 5414
God said, Ask what I shall g thee ... 1Kin 3:5 5414
G therefore thy servant an ... 1Kin 3:9 5414
in the morning to g my child suck ... 1Kin 3:21
g half to the one, and half to the ... 1Kin 3:25 5414
g her the living child, and in no ... 1Kin 3:26 5414
G her the living child, and in no ... 1Kin 3:27 5414
unto thee will I g hire for thy ... 1Kin 5:6 5414
to g him according to his ... 1Kin 8:32 5414
g rain upon thy land, which thou ... 1Kin 8:36 5414
g to every man according to his ... 1Kin 8:39 5414
g them compassion before them who ... 1Kin 8:50 5414
thee, and will g it to thy servant ... 1Kin 11:11 5414
but will g one tribe to thy son ... 1Kin 11:13 5414
will g ten tribes to thee ... 1Kin 11:31 5414
will g it unto thee, even ten ... 1Kin 11:35 5414
unto his son will I g one tribe ... 1Kin 11:36 5414
David, and will g Israel unto thee ... 1Kin 11:38 5414
What counsel g ye that we may ... 1Kin 12:9
and I will g thee a reward ... 1Kin 13:7 5414
If thou wilt g me half thine ... 1Kin 13:8 5414
he shall g Israel up because of ... 1Kin 14:16 5414
his God g him a lamp in Jerusalem ... 1Kin 15:4 5414
And he said unto her, G me thy son ... 1Kin 17:19 5414
them therefore g us two bullocks ... 1Kin 18:23 5414
G me thy vineyard, that I may ... 1Kin 21:2 5414
I will g thee for it a better ... 1Kin 21:2 5414
I will g thee the worth of it in ... 1Kin 21:2 5414
that I should g the inheritance ... 1Kin 21:3 5414
I will not g thee the inheritance ... 1Kin 21:4 5414
G me thy vineyard for money ... 1Kin 21:6 5414
I will g thee another vineyard ... 1Kin 21:6 5414
I will not g thee my vineyard ... 1Kin 21:6 5414
I will g thee the vineyard of ... 1Kin 21:7 5414
he refused to g thee for money ... 1Kin 21:15 5414
G unto the people, that they may ... 2Kin 4:42 5414
G the people, that they may eat ... 2Kin 4:43 5414
g them, I pray thee, a talent of ... 2Kin 5:22 5414
G thy son, that we may eat him to ... 2Kin 6:28 5414
G thy son, that we may eat him ... 2Kin 6:29 5414
him to g him alway a light ... 2Kin 8:19 5414
If it be, g me thine hand ... 2Kin 10:15 5414
the priest g king David's spears ... 2Kin 11:10 5414
G thy daughter to my son to wife ... 2Kin 14:9 5414
to g to the king of Assyria ... 2Kin 15:20 5414
g pledges to my lord the king of ... 2Kin 18:23
let them g it to the doers of the ... 2Kin 22:5 5414
but he taxed the land to g the ... 2Kin 23:35 5414
to g it unto Pharaoh-nechoh ... 2Kin 23:35 5414
Oh that one would g me drink of ... 1Chr 11:17
G thanks unto the LORD, call upon ... 1Chr 16:8
Unto thee will I g the land of ... 1Chr 16:18 5414
G unto the LORD, ye kindreds of ... 1Chr 16:28 3051
g unto the LORD glory and strength ... 1Chr 16:28 3051
G unto the LORD the glory due ... 1Chr 16:29 3051
O g thanks unto the LORD ... 1Chr 16:34
that we may g thanks to thy holy ... 1Chr 16:35
to g thanks to the LORD, because ... 1Chr 16:41
I g thee the oxen also for burnt ... 1Chr 21:23 5414
meat offering; I g it all ... 1Chr 21:23 5414

I will g him rest from all his ... 1Chr 22:9
be Solomon, and I will g peace ... 1Chr 22:9 5414
Only the LORD g thee wisdom ... 1Chr 22:12 5414
g thee charge concerning Israel, ... 1Chr 22:12
to g thanks and to praise the LORD ... 1Chr 25:3
great, and to g strength unto all ... 1Chr 29:12
g unto Solomon my son a perfect ... 1Chr 29:19 5414
unto him, Ask what I shall g thee ... 2Chr 1:7 5414
G me now wisdom and knowledge, ... 2Chr 1:10 5414
I will g thee riches, and wealth, ... 2Chr 1:12 5414
I will g to thy servants, the ... 2Chr 2:10 5414
What counsel g ye me to return ... 2Chr 10:6
What advice g ye that we may ... 2Chr 10:9
he promised to g a light to him ... 2Chr 21:7 5414
but they would not g ear ... 2Chr 24:19
The LORD is able to g thee much ... 2Chr 25:9 5414
G thy daughter to my son to wife ... 2Chr 25:18 5414
was to g them one heart to do the ... 2Chr 30:12 5414
g to the congregation a thousand ... 2Chr 30:24 7311
to g thanks, and to praise in the ... 2Chr 31:2
to g the portion of the priests ... 2Chr 31:4 5414
to g to their brethren by courses ... 2Chr 31:15 5414
to g portions to all the males ... 2Chr 31:19 5414
to g over yourselves to die by ... 2Chr 32:11 5414
that they might g according to ... 2Chr 35:12 5414
G ye now commandment to cause ... Ezr 4:21 7761
to g us a nail in his holy place, ... Ezr 9:8 5414
g us a little reviving in our ... Ezr 9:8 5414
to g us a reviving, to set up the ... Ezr 9:9 5414
to g us a wall in Judah and in ... Ezr 9:9 5414
Now therefore g not your ... Ezr 9:12 5414
that he may g me timber to make ... Neh 2:8 5414
g them for a prey in the land of ... Neh 4:4 5414
to g the land of the Canaanites ... Neh 9:8 5414
and the Girgashites, to g it ... Neh 9:8 5414
to g them light in the way ... Neh 9:12
which thou hadst sworn to g them ... Neh 9:15 5414
yet would they not g ear ... Neh 9:30
that we would not g our daughters ... Neh 10:30 5414
to g thanks, according to the ... Neh 12:24
Ye shall not g your daughters ... Neh 13:25 5414
let the king g her royal estate ... Est 1:19 5414
all the wives shall g to their ... Est 1:20 5414
g the house of Haman the Jews' ... Est 8:1 5414
a man hath will he g for his life ... Job 2:4 5414
why did I not g up the ghost when ... Job 3:11 1478
G a reward for me of your ... Job 6:22
my tongue, I shall g up the ghost ... Job 13:19 1478
neither let me g flattering ... Job 32:21 1478
I know not to g flattering titles ... Job 32:22
g ear unto me, ye that have ... Job 34:2
I shall g thee the heathen for ... Ps 2:8 5415
G ear to my words, O LORD ... Ps 5:1
the grave who shall g thee thanks ... Ps 6:5
g ear unto my prayer, that goeth ... Ps 17:1
will I g thanks unto thee ... Ps 18:49
G them according to their deeds, ... Ps 28:4 5414
g them after the work of their ... Ps 28:4 5414
G unto the LORD, O ye mighty, ... Ps 29:1 3051
g unto the LORD glory and strength ... Ps 29:1 3051
G unto the LORD the glory due ... Ps 29:2 3051
The LORD will g strength unto his ... Ps 29:11 5414
g thanks at the remembrance of ... Ps 30:4
I will g thanks unto thee for ... Ps 30:12
I will g thee thanks in the great ... Ps 35:18
he shall g thee the desires of ... Ps 37:4 5414
O LORD, and g ear unto my cry ... Ps 39:12
g ear, all ye inhabitants of the ... Ps 49:1
nor g to God a ransom for him ... Ps 49:7 5414
else would I g it ... Ps 51:16 5414
g ear to the words of my mouth ... Ps 54:2
G ear to my prayer, O God ... Ps 55:1
I will sing and g praise ... Ps 57:7
G us help from trouble ... Ps 60:11 3051
G the king thy judgments, O God, ... Ps 72:1 5414
O God, do we g ... Ps 75:1
unto thee do we g thanks ... Ps 75:1
G ear, O my people, to my law ... Ps 78:1
can he g bread also ... Ps 78:20 5414
will g thee thanks for ever ... Ps 79:13
G ear, O Shepherd of Israel, thou ... Ps 80:1
g ear, O God of Jacob ... Ps 84:8
the LORD will g grace and glory ... Ps 84:11 5414
the LORD shall g that which is ... Ps 85:12 5414
G ear, O LORD, unto my prayer ... Ps 86:6
g thy strength unto thy servant, ... Ps 86:16 5414
For he shall g his angels charge ... Ps 91:11
thing to g thanks unto the LORD ... Ps 92:1
That thou mayest g him rest from ... Ps 94:13
G unto the LORD, O ye kindreds of ... Ps 96:7 3051
g unto the LORD glory and strength ... Ps 96:7 3051
G unto the LORD the glory due ... Ps 96:8 3051
g thanks at the remembrance of ... Ps 97:12
They g drink to every beast of ... Ps 104:11
that thou mayest g them their ... Ps 104:27 5414
O g thanks unto the LORD ... Ps 105:1
Unto thee will I g the land of ... Ps 105:11 5414
fire to g light in the night ... Ps 105:39
O g thanks unto the LORD ... Ps 106:1
to g thanks unto thy holy name, ... Ps 106:47
O g thanks unto the LORD, for he ... Ps 107:1
g praise, even with my glory ... Ps 108:1
G us help from trouble ... Ps 108:12 3051
but I g myself unto prayer ... Ps 109:4
that he may g them the heritage ... Ps 111:6 5441
us, but unto thy name g glory ... Ps 115:1
O g thanks unto the LORD ... Ps 118:1
O g thanks unto the LORD ... Ps 118:29
G me understanding, and I shall ... Ps 119:34
At midnight I will rise to g ... Ps 119:62
g me understanding, that I may ... Ps 119:73
g me understanding, that I may ... Ps 119:125
g me understanding, and I shall ... Ps 119:144
g me understanding according to ... Ps 119:169

to g thanks unto the name of the	Ps 122:4	
I will not g sleep to mine eyes,	Ps 132:4	5414
O G thanks unto the LORD	Ps 136:1	
O g thanks unto the God of gods	Ps 136:2	
O g thanks to the Lord of lords	Ps 136:3	
O g thanks unto the God of heaven	Ps 136:26	
shall g thanks unto thy name	Ps 140:13	
g ear unto my voice, when I cry	Ps 141:1	
g ear to my supplications	Ps 143:1	
To g subtilty to the simple, to	Prov 1:4	5414
come again, and to morrow I will g	Prov 3:28	5414
For I g you good doctrine,	Prov 4:2	5414
She shall g to thine head an	Prov 4:9	5414
Lest thou g thine honour unto	Prov 5:9	5414
G not sleep to thine eyes, nor	Prov 6:4	5414
he shall g all the substance of	Prov 6:31	5414
G instruction to a wise man, and	Prov 9:9	5414
g me thine heart, and let thine	Prov 23:26	5414
be hungry, g him bread to eat	Prov 25:21	
be thirsty, g him water to drink	Prov 25:21	
The rod and reproof g wisdom	Prov 29:15	5414
thy son, and he shall g thee rest	Prov 29:17	
he shall g delight unto thy soul	Prov 29:17	5414
g me neither poverty nor riches	Prov 30:8	5414
two daughters, crying, G, g	Prov 30:15	3051
two daughters, crying, G, g	Prov 30:15	3051
G not thy strength unto women,	Prov 31:3	5414
G strong drink unto him that is	Prov 31:6	5414
G her of the fruit of her hands	Prov 31:31	5414
mine heart to g myself unto wine	Eccl 2:3	4900
that he may g to him that is good	Eccl 2:26	5414
than to g the sacrifice of fools	Eccl 5:1	5414
G a portion to seven, and also to	Eccl 11:2	5414
the tender grape g a good smell	Song 2:13	5414
there will I g thee my loves	Song 7:12	5414
The mandrakes g a smell, and at	Song 7:13	5414
if a man would g all the	Song 8:7	5414
O heavens, and g ear, O earth	Is 1:2	
g ear unto the law of our God, ye	Is 1:10	
I will g children to be their	Is 3:4	5414
Lord himself shall g you a sign	Is 7:14	5414
of milk that they shall g	Is 7:22	6213
g ear, all ye of far countries	Is 8:9	
of my wrath will I g him a charge	Is 10:6	
thereof shall not g their light	Is 13:10	
shall g thee rest from thy sorrow	Is 14:3	
the Egyptians will I g over into	Is 19:4	5534
G ye ear, and hear my voice	Is 28:23	
though the Lord g you the bread	Is 30:20	5414
Then shall he g the rain of thy	Is 30:23	5414
g ear unto my speech	Is 32:9	
Now therefore g pledges, I pray	Is 36:8	
I will g thee two thousand horses	Is 36:8	5414
I will g to Jerusalem one that	Is 41:27	5414
g thee for a covenant of the	Is 42:6	5414
my glory will I not g to another	Is 42:8	5414
Let them g glory unto the LORD,	Is 42:12	7760
Who among you will g ear to this	Is 42:23	
therefore will I g men for thee	Is 43:4	5414
I will say to the north, G up	Is 43:6	5414
because I g waters in the	Is 43:20	5414
to g drink to my people, my	Is 43:20	
I will g thee the treasures of	Is 45:3	5414
I will not g my glory unto	Is 48:11	5414
I will also g thee for a light to	Is 49:6	5414
g thee for a covenant of the	Is 49:8	5414
g place to me that I may dwell	Is 49:20	5066
g ear unto me, O my nation	Is 51:4	
that it may g seed to the sower,	Is 55:10	5414
unto them will I g in mine house	Is 56:5	5414
I will g them an everlasting name	Is 56:5	5414
shall the moon g light unto thee	Is 60:19	5414
to g unto them beauty for ashes,	Is 61:3	5414
g him no rest, till he establish,	Is 62:7	5414
Surely I will no more g thy corn	Is 62:8	5414
I will g you pastors according to	Jer 3:15	5414
g thee a pleasant land, a goodly	Jer 3:19	5414
now also will I g sentence	Jer 4:12	1696
g out their voice against the	Jer 4:16	5414
g warning, that they may hear	Jer 6:10	
Therefore will I g their wives	Jer 8:10	5414
g them water of gall to drink	Jer 9:15	
to g them a land flowing with	Jer 11:5	5414
Hear ye, and g ear	Jer 13:15	
G glory to the LORD your God,	Jer 13:16	5414
but I will g you assured peace in	Jer 14:13	5414
or can the heavens g showers	Jer 14:22	5414
thy treasures will I g to the	Jer 15:13	5414
neither shall men g them the cup	Jer 16:7	
I will g thy substance and all thy	Jer 17:3	5414
even to g every man according to	Jer 17:10	5414
let us not g heed to any of his	Jer 18:18	
G heed to me, O LORD, and hearken	Jer 18:19	
their carcases will I g to be	Jer 19:7	5414
I will g all Judah into the hand	Jer 20:4	5414
of the kings of Judah will I g	Jer 20:5	5414
I will g thee into the hand of	Jer 22:25	5414
I will g them an heart to know me	Jer 24:7	5414
So will I g Zedekiah the king of	Jer 24:8	5414
he shall g a shout, as they that	Jer 25:30	
he will g them that are wicked to	Jer 25:31	5414
that they should not g him into	Jer 26:24	5414
g your daughters to husbands,	Jer 29:6	5414
of evil, to g you an expected end	Jer 29:11	5414
upon thee will I g for a prey	Jer 30:16	5414
I will g this city into the hand	Jer 32:3	5414
to g every one according to his	Jer 32:19	5414
swear to their fathers to g them	Jer 32:22	5414
I will g this city into the hand	Jer 32:28	5414
I will g them one heart, and one	Jer 32:39	5414
I will g this city into the hand	Jer 34:2	5414
I will g the men that have	Jer 34:18	5414
I will even g them into the hand	Jer 34:20	5414
his princes will I g into the	Jer 34:21	5414
chambers, and g them wine to drink	Jer 35:2	
that they should g him daily a	Jer 37:21	5414
if I g thee counsel, wilt thou	Jer 38:15	
neither will I g thee into the	Jer 38:16	5414
I will g Pharaoh-hophra king of	Jer 44:30	5414
but thy life will I g unto thee	Jer 45:5	5414
G wings unto Moab, that it may	Jer 48:9	5414
that he may g rest to the land,	Jer 50:34	
g thyself no rest	Lam 2:18	5414
G them sorrow of heart, thy curse	Lam 3:65	5414
they g suck to their young ones	Lam 4:3	
thy mouth, and eat that I g thee	Eze 2:8	5414
with this roll that I g thee	Eze 3:3	5414
mouth, and g them warning from me	Eze 3:17	
I will g it into the hands of the	Eze 7:21	5414
g wicked counsel in this city	Eze 11:2	
I will g you the land of Israel	Eze 11:17	5414
I will g them one heart, and I	Eze 11:19	5414
will g them an heart of flesh	Eze 11:19	5414
so will I g the inhabitants of	Eze 15:6	5414
They g gifts to all whores	Eze 16:33	5414
which thou didst g unto them	Eze 16:36	5414
I will g thee blood in fury and	Eze 16:38	5414
I will also g thee into their	Eze 16:39	5414
thou also shalt g no hire any	Eze 16:41	5414
I will g them unto thee for	Eze 16:61	5414
that they might g him horses	Eze 17:15	5414
up mine hand to g it to them	Eze 20:28	5414
mine hand to g it to your fathers	Eze 20:42	5414
to g it into the hand of the	Eze 21:11	5414
and I will g it him	Eze 21:27	5414
therefore will I g her cup into	Eze 23:31	5414
will g them to be removed and	Eze 23:46	5414
will g them in possession, that	Eze 25:10	5414
I will g the land of Egypt unto	Eze 29:19	5414
I will g thee the opening of the	Eze 29:21	5414
and the moon shall not g her light	Eze 32:7	
g again that he had robbed, walk	Eze 33:15	7999
is in the open field will I g to	Eze 33:27	5414
A new heart also will I g you	Eze 36:26	5414
I will g you an heart of flesh	Eze 36:26	5414
I will g thee unto the ravenous	Eze 39:4	5414
that I will g unto Gog a place	Eze 39:11	5414
thou shalt g to the priests the	Eze 43:19	5414
ye shall g them no possession in	Eze 44:28	5414
ye shall also g unto the priest	Eze 44:30	5414
they g to the house of Israel	Eze 45:8	5414
ye shall g the sixth part of an	Eze 45:13	
the people of the land shall g	Eze 45:16	
part to g burnt offerings	Eze 45:17	
lambs as he shall be able to g	Eze 46:5	4991
to the lambs as he is able to g	Eze 46:11	4991
If the prince g a gift unto any	Eze 46:16	5414
But if he g a gift of his	Eze 46:17	5414
but he shall g his sons	Eze 46:18	
hand to g it unto your fathers	Eze 47:14	5414
there shall ye g him his	Eze 47:23	5414
let them g us pulse to eat, and	Dan 1:12	5414
the king that he would g him time	Dan 2:16	5415
and g thy rewards to another	Dan 5:17	3052
might g accounts unto them	Dan 6:2	3052
to g both the sanctuary and the	Dan 8:13	5414
am now come forth to g thee skill	Dan 9:22	
he shall g him the daughter of	Dan 11:17	5414
to whom they shall not g the	Dan 11:21	5414
that g me my bread and my water,	Hos 2:5	5414
I will g her her vineyards from	Hos 2:15	5414
rulers with shame do love, G ye	Hos 4:18	3051
g ye ear, O house of the king	Hos 5:1	
G them, O LORD	Hos 9:14	5414
what wilt thou g	Hos 9:14	5414
g them a miscarrying womb and dry	Hos 9:14	5414
How shall I g thee up, Ephraim	Hos 11:8	5414
saidst, G me a king and princes	Hos 13:10	5414
g ear, all ye inhabitants of the	Joel 1:2	
g not thine heritage to reproach,	Joel 2:17	5414
Therefore shalt thou g presents	Mic 1:14	5414
Therefore will he g them up	Mic 5:3	5414
shall I g my firstborn for my	Mic 6:7	5414
will I g up to the sword	Mic 6:14	5414
and in this place will I g peace	Hag 2:9	5414
I will g thee places to walk	Zec 3:7	5414
the vine shall g her fruit	Zec 8:12	5414
the ground shall g her increase	Zec 8:12	5414
and the heavens shall g their dew	Zec 8:12	5414
g them showers of rain, to every	Zec 10:1	5414
If ye think good, g me my price	Zec 11:12	3051
to g glory unto my name, saith	Mal 2:2	5414
He shall g his angels charge	Mt 4:6	
All these things will I g thee	Mt 4:9	*1325*
let him g her a writing of	Mt 5:31	*1325*
G to him that asketh thee, and	Mt 5:42	*1325*
G us this day our daily bread	Mt 6:11	*1325*
G not that which is holy unto the	Mt 7:6	*1325*
ask bread, will he g him a stone	Mt 7:9	*1929*
a fish, will he g him a serpent	Mt 7:10	*1929*
know how to g good gifts unto	Mt 7:11	*1325*
g good things to them that ask	Mt 7:11	*1325*
He said unto them, G place	Mt 9:24	*402*
freely ye have received, freely g	Mt 10:8	*1325*
whosoever shall g to drink unto	Mt 10:42	*4222*
heavy laden, and I will g you rest	Mt 11:28	
they shall g account thereof in	Mt 12:36	*591*
he promised with an oath to g her	Mt 14:7	*1325*
G me here John Baptist's head in	Mt 14:8	*1325*
g ye them to eat	Mt 14:16	*1325*
I will g unto thee the keys of	Mt 16:19	*1325*
or what shall a man g in exchange	Mt 16:26	*1325*
g unto them for me and thee	Mt 17:27	*1325*
to g a writing of divorcement	Mt 19:7	*1325*
g to the poor, and thou shalt have	Mt 19:21	*1325*
whatsoever is right I will g you	Mt 20:4	
g them their hire, beginning from	Mt 20:8	*591*
I will g unto this last, even as	Mt 20:14	*1325*
and on my left, is not mine to g	Mt 20:23	*1325*
to g his life a ransom for many	Mt 20:28	*1325*
Is it lawful to g tribute unto	Mt 22:17	*1325*
to them that g suck in those days	Mt 24:19	
and the moon shall not g her light	Mt 24:29	*1325*
to g them meat in due season	Mt 24:45	*1325*
unto the wise, G us of your oil	Mt 25:8	*1325*
g it unto him which hath ten	Mt 25:28	*1325*
said unto them, What will ye g me	Mt 26:15	*1325*
he shall presently g me more than	Mt 26:53	*3936*
thou wilt, and I will g it thee	Mk 6:22	*1325*
I will g it thee, unto the half	Mk 6:23	*1325*
saying, I will that thou g me by	Mk 6:25	*1325*
said unto them, G ye them to eat	Mk 6:37	*1325*
of bread, and g them to eat	Mk 6:37	*1325*
Or what shall a man g in exchange	Mk 8:37	*1325*
For whosoever shall g you a cup	Mk 9:41	*4222*
g to the poor, and thou shalt have	Mk 10:21	*1325*
on my left hand is not mine to g	Mk 10:40	*1325*
to g his life a ransom for many	Mk 10:45	*1325*
will g the vineyard unto others	Mk 12:9	*1325*
Is it lawful to g tribute to	Mk 12:14	*1325*
Shall we g, or shall we not g	Mk 12:15	*1325*
to them that g suck in those days	Mk 13:17	
and the moon shall not g her light	Mk 13:24	*1325*
glad, and promised to g him money	Mk 14:11	*1325*
the Lord God shall g unto him the	Lk 1:32	*1325*
To g knowledge of salvation unto	Lk 1:77	*1325*
To g light to them that sit in	Lk 1:79	*2014*
him, All this power will I g thee	Lk 4:6	*1325*
and to whomsoever I will I g it	Lk 4:6	*1325*
He shall g his angels charge over	Lk 4:10	
G to every man that asketh of	Lk 6:30	*1325*
G, and it shall be given unto you	Lk 6:38	*1325*
shall men g into your bosom	Lk 6:38	*1325*
and he commanded to g her meat	Lk 8:55	*1325*
said unto them, G ye them to eat	Lk 9:13	*1325*
and drinking such things as they g	Lk 10:7	*3844*
I g unto you power to tread on	Lk 10:19	*1325*
G us day by day our daily bread	Lk 11:3	*1325*
I cannot rise and g thee	Lk 11:7	*1325*
g him, because he is his friend,	Lk 11:8	*1325*
g him as many as he needeth	Lk 11:8	*1325*
a father, will he g him a stone	Lk 11:11	*1929*
he for a fish g him a serpent	Lk 11:11	*1929*
know how to g good gifts unto	Lk 11:13	*1325*
g the Holy Spirit to them that	Lk 11:13	*1325*
of a candle doth g thee light	Lk 11:36	*5461*
But rather g alms of such things	Lk 11:41	*1325*
pleasure to g you the kingdom	Lk 12:32	*1325*
Sell that ye have, and g alms	Lk 12:33	*1325*
to g them their portion of meat	Lk 12:42	*1325*
I am come to g peace on earth	Lk 12:51	*1325*
g diligence that thou mayest be	Lk 12:58	*1325*
and say to thee, G this man place	Lk 14:9	*1325*
g me the portion of goods that	Lk 15:12	*1325*
g an account of thy stewardship	Lk 16:2	*591*
who shall g you that which is	Lk 16:12	*1325*
that returned to g glory to God	Lk 17:18	*1325*
I g tithes of all that I possess	Lk 18:12	
half of my goods I g to the poor	Lk 19:8	*1325*
g it to him that hath ten pounds	Lk 19:24	*1325*
that they should g him of the	Lk 20:10	*1325*
shall g the vineyard to others	Lk 20:16	*1325*
for us to g tribute unto Caesar	Lk 20:22	*1325*
For I will g you a mouth and	Lk 21:15	*1325*
child, and to them that g suck	Lk 21:23	
and covenanted to g him money	Lk 22:5	*1325*
forbidding to g tribute to Caesar	Lk 23:2	*1325*
that we may g an answer to them	Jn 1:22	*1325*
saith unto her, G me to drink	Jn 4:7	*1325*
that saith to thee, G me to drink	Jn 4:10	*1325*
I shall g him shall never thirst	Jn 4:14	*1325*
but the water that I shall g him	Jn 4:14	*1325*
g me this water, that I thirst	Jn 4:15	*1325*
the Son of man shall g unto you	Jn 6:27	*1325*
Lord, evermore g us this bread	Jn 6:34	*1325*
bread that I will g is my flesh	Jn 6:51	*1325*
which I will g for the life of	Jn 6:51	*1325*
How can this man g us his flesh	Jn 6:52	*1325*
Did not Moses g you the law	Jn 7:19	*1325*
said unto him, G God the praise	Jn 9:24	*1325*
I g unto them eternal life	Jn 10:28	*1325*
ask of God, God will g it thee	Jn 11:22	*1325*
He it is, to whom I shall g a sop	Jn 13:26	*1929*
that he should g something to the	Jn 13:29	*1325*
A new commandment I g unto you	Jn 13:34	*1325*
he shall g you another Comforter,	Jn 14:16	*1325*
with you, my peace I g unto you	Jn 14:27	*1325*
as the world giveth, g I unto you	Jn 14:27	*1325*
in my name, he may g it you	Jn 15:16	*1325*
in my name, he will g it you	Jn 16:23	*1325*
that he should g eternal life to	Jn 17:2	*1325*
but such as I have g I thee	Acts 3:6	*1325*
for to g repentance to Israel, and	Acts 5:31	*1325*
But we will g ourselves	Acts 6:4	*4342*
g it to him for a possession	Acts 7:5	*1325*
the lively oracles to g unto us	Acts 7:38	*1325*
G me also this power, that on	Acts 8:19	*1325*
To him g all the prophets witness	Acts 10:43	
and ye that fear God, g audience	Acts 13:16	
I will g you the sure mercies of	Acts 13:34	*1325*
g an account of this concourse	Acts 19:40	*591*
to g you an inheritance among all	Acts 20:32	*1325*
more blessed to g than to receive	Acts 20:35	*1325*
him also freely g us all things	Rom 8:32	*5483*
but rather g place unto wrath	Rom 12:19	*1325*
if he thirst, g him drink	Rom 12:20	*4222*
shall g account of himself to God	Rom 14:12	*1325*
unto whom not only I g thanks	Rom 16:4	
that ye may g yourselves to	1Cor 7:5	*4980*
yet I g my judgment, as one that	1Cor 7:25	*1325*
of for that for which I g thanks	1Cor 10:30	
G none offence, neither to the	1Cor 10:32	*1096*

Wherefore I g you to understand,	1Cor 12:3	
though I g my body to be burned,	1Cor 13:3	*3860*
except they g a distinction in	1Cor 14:7	*1325*
the trumpet g an uncertain sound	1Cor 14:8	*1325*
to g the light of the knowledge	2Cor 4:6	
but g you occasion to glory on	2Cor 5:12	*1325*
And herein I g my advice	2Cor 8:10	*1325*
in his heart, so let him g	2Cor 9:7	
Cease not to g thanks for you,	Eph 1:16	
may g unto you the spirit of	Eph 1:17	*1325*
Neither g place to the devil	Eph 4:27	*1325*
may have to g to him that needeth	Eph 4:28	*3330*
and Christ shall g thee light	Eph 5:14	
We g thanks to God and the Father	Col 1:3	
g unto your servants that which	Col 4:1	*3930*
We g thanks to God always for you	1Th 1:2	
In every thing g thanks	1Th 5:18	
But we are bound to g thanks	2Th 2:13	
g you peace always by all means	2Th 3:16	*1325*
Neither g heed to fables and	1Ti 1:4	
g attendance to reading, to	1Ti 4:13	
g thyself wholly to them	1Ti 4:15	*2468*
And these things g in charge	1Ti 5:7	
g none occasion to the adversary	1Ti 5:14	*1325*
I g thee charge in the sight of	1Ti 6:13	
The Lord g mercy unto the house	2Ti 1:16	*1325*
the Lord g thee understanding in	2Ti 2:7	*1325*
will g them repentance to the	2Ti 2:25	*1325*
judge, shall g me at that day	2Ti 4:8	*591*
Therefore we ought to g the more	Heb 2:1	
as they that must g account	Heb 13:17	*591*
notwithstanding ye g them not	Jas 2:16	*1325*
be ready always to g an answer to	1Pet 3:15	
Who shall g account to him that	1Pet 4:5	*591*
g diligence to make your calling	2Pet 1:10	
he shall g him life for them that	1Jn 5:16	*1325*
I g to eat of the tree of life	Rev 2:7	*1325*
I will g thee a crown of life	Rev 2:10	*1325*
I g to eat of the hidden manna	Rev 2:17	*1325*
will g him a white stone, and in	Rev 2:17	*1325*
I will g unto every one of you	Rev 2:23	*1325*
to him will I g power over the	Rev 2:26	*1325*
I will g him the morning star	Rev 2:28	*1325*
And when those beasts g glory	Rev 4:9	*1325*
unto him, G me the little book	Rev 10:9	*1325*
I will g power unto my two	Rev 11:3	*1325*
We g thee thanks, O Lord God	Rev 11:17	
that thou shouldest g reward unto	Rev 11:18	*1325*
he had power to g life unto the	Rev 13:15	*1325*
Fear God, and g glory to him	Rev 14:7	*1325*
they repented not to g him glory	Rev 16:9	*1325*
to g unto her the cup of the wine	Rev 16:19	*1325*
shall g their power and strength	Rev 17:13	*1239*
g their kingdom unto the beast,	Rev 17:17	*1325*
so much torment and sorrow g her	Rev 18:7	*1325*
and rejoice, and g honour to him	Rev 19:7	*1325*
I will g unto him that is athirst	Rev 21:6	*1325*
to g every man according as his	Rev 22:12	*591*

GIVEN

I have g you every herb bearing	Gen 1:29	5414
I have g every green herb for	Gen 1:30	
herb have I g you all things	Gen 9:3	5414
Behold, to me thou hast g no seed	Gen 15:3	5414
Unto thy seed have I g this land	Gen 15:18	5414
I have g my maid into thy bosom	Gen 16:5	5414
I have g thy brother a thousand	Gen 20:16	5414
Sarah should have g children suck	Gen 21:7	
he hath g him flocks, and herds,	Gen 24:35	5414
him hath he g all that he hath	Gen 24:36	5414
have I g to him for servants	Gen 27:37	5414
hath therefore g me this son also	Gen 29:33	5414
my voice, and hath g me a son	Gen 30:6	5414
God hath g me my hire	Gen 30:18	5414
because I have g my maiden to my	Gen 30:18	5414
of your father, and g them to me	Gen 31:9	5414
God hath graciously g thy servant	Gen 33:5	2603
she was not g unto him to wife	Gen 38:14	5414
hath g you treasure in your sacks	Gen 43:23	5414
whom God hath g me in this place	Gen 48:9	5414
Moreover I have g to thee one	Gen 48:22	5414
is no straw g unto thy servants	Ex 5:16	5414
for there shall no straw be g you	Ex 5:18	5414
which the LORD hath g you to eat	Ex 16:15	5414
the LORD hath g you the sabbath	Ex 16:29	5414
If his master have g him a wife	Ex 21:4	5414
I have g with him Aholiab, the	Ex 31:6	5414
I have g it unto them for their	Lev 6:17	5414
have g them unto Aaron the priest	Lev 7:34	5414
g them of the children of Israel	Lev 7:36	5414
which are g out of the sacrifices	Lev 10:14	5414
God hath g it you to bear the	Lev 10:17	5414
I have g it to you upon the altar	Lev 17:11	5414
all redeemed, nor freedom g her	Lev 19:20	5414
because he hath g of his seed	Lev 20:3	5414
they are wholly g unto him out of	Num 3:9	5414
For they are wholly g unto me	Num 8:16	5414
I have g the Levites as a gift to	Num 8:19	5414
or g us inheritance of fields and	Num 16:14	5414
to you they are g as a gift for	Num 18:6	5414
I have g your priest's office	Num 18:7	5414
I also have g thee the charge of	Num 18:8	5414
unto thee have I g them by reason	Num 18:8	5414
I have g them unto thee, and to	Num 18:11	5414
unto the LORD, them have I g thee	Num 18:12	5414
unto the LORD, have I g thee	Num 18:19	5414
I have g the children of Levi all	Num 18:21	5414
I have g to the Levites to	Num 18:24	5414
I have g you from them for your	Num 18:26	5414
into the land which I have g them	Num 20:12	5414
into the land which I have g unto	Num 20:24	5414
he hath g his sons that escaped,	Num 21:29	5414
be g according to those that were	Num 26:54	5414
there was no inheritance g them	Num 26:62	5414
see the land which I have g unto	Num 27:12	5414
let this land be g unto thy	Num 32:5	5414
land which the LORD hath g them	Num 32:7	5414
land which the LORD had g them	Num 32:9	5414
for I have g you the land to	Num 33:53	5414
unto all that the LORD had g him	Deut 1:3	
because I have g mount Seir unto	Deut 2:5	5414
because I have g Ar unto the	Deut 2:9	5414
because I have g it unto the	Deut 2:19	5414
I have g into thine hand Sihon	Deut 2:24	5414
The LORD your God hath g you this	Deut 3:18	5414
in your cities which I have g you	Deut 3:19	5414
Until the LORD have g rest unto	Deut 3:20	
God hath g them beyond Jordan	Deut 3:20	5414
possession, which I have g you	Deut 3:20	5414
good land which he hath g thee	Deut 8:10	5414
the land which I have g you	Deut 9:23	5414
LORD thy God which he hath g thee	Deut 12:15	5414
flock, which the LORD hath g thee	Deut 12:21	5414
God hath g thee to dwell there	Deut 13:12	5414
LORD thy God which he hath g thee	Deut 16:17	5414
the LORD thy God hath g thee	Deut 20:14	5414
he hath g occasions of speech	Deut 22:17	7760
hath g thee rest from all thine	Deut 25:19	
hath g us this land, even a land	Deut 26:9	5414
which thou, O LORD, hast g me	Deut 26:10	5414
the LORD thy God hath g unto thee	Deut 26:11	5414
hast g it unto the Levite, the	Deut 26:12	5414
also have g them unto the Levite,	Deut 26:13	5414
nor g ought thereof for the dead	Deut 26:14	5414
and the land which thou hast g us	Deut 26:15	5414
shall be g unto thine enemies	Deut 28:31	5414
shall be g unto another people	Deut 28:32	5414
the LORD thy God hath g thee	Deut 28:52	5414
the LORD thy God hath g thee	Deut 28:53	5414
Yet the LORD hath not g you an	Deut 29:4	5414
and whom he had not g unto them	Deut 29:26	2505
upon, that have I g unto you	Josh 1:3	5414
The LORD your God hath g you rest	Josh 1:13	
and hath g you this land	Josh 1:13	5414
LORD have g your brethren rest	Josh 1:15	
brethren rest, as he hath g you	Josh 1:15	
that the LORD hath g you the land	Josh 2:9	5414
when the LORD hath g us the land	Josh 2:14	5414
I have g into thine hand Jericho,	Josh 6:2	5414
for the LORD hath g you the city	Josh 6:16	5414
I have g into thy hand the king	Josh 8:1	5414
For Moses had g the inheritance	Josh 14:3	5414
for thou hast g me a south land	Josh 15:19	5414
Why hast thou g me but one lot and	Josh 17:14	5414
God of your fathers hath g you	Josh 18:3	5414
hath g rest unto your brethren	Josh 22:4	
Moses had g possession in Bashan	Josh 22:7	5414
time after that the LORD had g	Josh 23:1	
the LORD your God hath g you	Josh 23:13	5414
the LORD your God hath g you	Josh 23:15	5414
land which he hath g unto you	Josh 23:16	5414
I have g you a land for which ye	Josh 24:13	5414
which was g him in mount Ephraim	Josh 24:33	5414
for thou hast g me a south land	Judg 1:15	5414
wife was g to his companion	Judg 14:20	
wife, and g her to his companion	Judg 15:6	5414
and said, Thou hast g this great	Judg 15:18	5414
for God hath g it into your hands	Judg 18:10	5414
a full reward be g thee of the	Ruth 2:12	
the LORD hath g me my petition	1Sa 1:27	5414
hath g it to a neighbour of thine	1Sa 15:28	5414
should have been g to David	1Sa 18:19	5414
that she was g unto Adriel the	1Sa 18:19	5414
in that thou hast g him bread	1Sa 22:13	5414
let it even be g unto the young	1Sa 25:27	5414
But Saul had g Michal his	1Sa 25:44	5414
g it to thy neighbour, even to	1Sa 28:17	5414
that which the LORD hath g us	1Sa 30:23	5414
g him a reward for his tidings	2Sa 4:10	5414
the LORD had g him rest round	2Sa 7:1	
I have g unto thy master's son	2Sa 9:9	5414
moreover have g unto thee such	2Sa 12:8	3254
g great occasion to the enemies	2Sa 12:14	
hath g is not good at this time	2Sa 17:7	3289
I would have g thee ten shekels	2Sa 18:11	5414
or hath he g us any gift	2Sa 19:42	5375
Thou hast also g me the shield of	2Sa 22:36	5414
Thou hast also g me the necks of	2Sa 22:41	5414
which hath g one to sit on my	1Kin 1:48	5414
Let Abishag the Shunammite be g	1Kin 2:21	5414
that thou hast g him a son to sit	1Kin 3:6	5414
I have g thee a wise and an	1Kin 3:12	5414
I have also g thee that which	1Kin 3:13	5414
God hath g me rest on every side	1Kin 5:4	
which hath g unto David a wise	1Kin 5:7	5414
which thou hast g to thy people	1Kin 8:36	5414
that hath g rest unto his people	1Kin 8:56	5414
of the land which I have g them	1Kin 9:7	5414
cities which Solomon had g him	1Kin 9:12	5414
are these which thou hast g me	1Kin 9:13	5414
g it for a present unto his	1Kin 9:16	5414
the old men, which they had g him	1Kin 12:8	3289
God had g by the word of the LORD	1Kin 13:5	5414
took the bullock which was g them	1Kin 18:26	5414
LORD had g deliverance unto Syria	2Kin 5:1	5414
be g to thy servant two mules'	2Kin 5:17	5414
the Syrians had g him at Ramah	2Kin 8:29	5221
which the Syrians had g him	2Kin 9:15	5221
kings of Judah had g to the sun	2Kin 23:11	5414
allowance g him of the king	2Kin 25:30	5414
his birthright was g unto the	1Chr 5:1	5414
were cities g out of the half	1Chr 6:61	
the sons of Merari were g by lot	1Chr 6:63	
g out of the family of the half	1Chr 6:71	
g out of the tribe of Zebulun	1Chr 6:77	
were g them out of the tribe of	1Chr 6:78	
hath he not g you rest on every	1Chr 22:18	
for he hath g the inhabitants of	1Chr 22:18	5414
hath g rest unto his people	1Chr 23:25	
(for the LORD hath g me many sons	1Chr 28:5	5414
which I have g to the house of my	1Chr 29:3	5414
and of thine own have we g thee	1Chr 29:14	5414
who hath g to David the king a	2Chr 2:12	5414
which thou hast g unto thy people	2Chr 6:27	5414
of my land which I have g them	2Chr 7:20	5414
because the LORD had g him rest	2Chr 14:6	
he hath g us rest on every side	2Chr 14:7	
which thou hast g us to inherit	2Chr 20:11	
wounds which were g him at Ramah	2Chr 22:6	5221
I have g to the army of Israel	2Chr 25:9	5414
for God had g him substance very	2Chr 32:29	5414
of the law of the LORD g by Moses	2Chr 34:14	
the priest hath g me a book	2Chr 34:18	5414
hath the LORD God of heaven g me	2Chr 36:23	5414
hath g me all the kingdoms of the	Ezr 1:2	5414
commandment shall be g from me	Ezr 4:21	7761
let the expences be g out of the	Ezr 6:4	3052
expences be g unto these men	Ezr 6:8	3052
let it be g them day by day	Ezr 6:9	3052
the LORD God of Israel had g	Ezr 7:6	5414
The vessels also that are g thee	Ezr 7:19	3052
hast g us such deliverance as	Ezr 9:13	5414
let letters be g me to the	Neh 2:7	5414
which was g by Moses the servant	Neh 10:29	5414
commanded to be g to the Levites	Neh 13:5	
the Levites had not been g them	Neh 13:10	5414
things for purification be g them	Est 2:3	5414
which were meet to be g her	Est 2:9	5414
whatsoever she desired was g her	Est 2:13	5414
Haman, The silver is g to thee	Est 3:11	5414
g in every province was published	Est 3:14	5414
the decree was g in Shushan the	Est 3:15	5414
was g at Shushan to destroy them	Est 4:8	5414
it shall be even g thee to the	Est 5:3	5414
let my life be g me at my	Est 7:3	5414
I have g Esther the house of	Est 8:7	5414
g in every province was published	Est 8:13	5414
the decree was g at Shushan the	Est 8:14	5414
and the decree was g at Shushan	Est 9:14	5414
Wherefore is light g to him that	Job 3:20	5414
Why is light g to a man whose way	Job 3:23	
The earth is g into the hand of	Job 9:24	5414
Oh that I had g up the ghost	Job 10:18	1478
Unto whom alone the earth was g	Job 15:19	5414
Thou hast not g water to the	Job 22:7	
Though it be g him to be in	Job 24:23	5414
of the Almighty hath g me life	Job 33:4	
Who hath g him a charge over the	Job 34:13	
By the breath of God frost is g	Job 37:10	5414
or who hath g understanding to	Job 38:36	5414
Hath thou g the horse strength	Job 39:19	5414
the LORD, who hath g me counsel	Ps 16:7	
Thou hast also g me the shield of	Ps 18:35	5414
Thou hast also g me the necks of	Ps 18:40	5414
Thou hast g him his heart's	Ps 21:2	5414
Thou hast g us like sheep	Ps 44:11	5414
Thou hast g a banner to them that	Ps 60:4	5414
thou hast g me the heritage of	Ps 61:5	5414
thou hast g commandment to save	Ps 71:3	
to him shall be g of the gold of	Ps 72:15	5414
had g them of the corn of heaven	Ps 78:24	5414
maidens were not g to marriage	Ps 78:63	
of thy servants have they g to be	Ps 79:2	5414
He hath g meat unto them that	Ps 111:5	5414
dispersed, he hath g to the poor	Ps 112:9	5414
but the earth hath he g to the	Ps 115:16	5414
but he hath not g me over unto	Ps 118:18	5414
What shall be g unto thee	Ps 120:3	5414
who hath not g us as a prey to	Ps 124:6	5414
that which he hath g will he pay	Prov 19:17	1576
if thou be a man g to appetite	Prov 23:2	1167
with them that are g to change	Prov 24:21	
God g to the sons of man to be	Eccl 1:13	5414
which God hath g to the sons of	Eccl 3:10	5414
also to whom God hath g riches	Eccl 5:19	5414
hath g him power to eat thereof,	Eccl 5:19	
A man to whom God hath g riches	Eccl 6:2	5414
deliver those that are g to it	Eccl 8:8	1167
which he hath g thee under the	Eccl 9:9	5414
which are g from one shepherd	Eccl 12:11	5414
of his hands shall be g him	Is 3:11	6213
the LORD hath g me are for signs	Is 8:18	5414
child is born, unto us a son is g	Is 9:6	5414
the LORD hath g a commandment	Is 23:11	
bread shall be g him	Is 33:16	5414
of Lebanon shall be g unto it	Is 35:2	5414
Jerusalem shall not be g into the	Is 37:10	5414
have g Jacob to the curse, and	Is 43:28	5414
and g them into thine hand	Is 47:6	5414
thou that art g to pleasures	Is 47:8	
The Lord GOD hath g me the tongue	Is 50:4	5414
I have g him for a witness to the	Is 55:4	5414
away, and g her a bill of divorce	Jer 3:8	5414
g for an inheritance unto your	Jer 3:18	
every one is g to covetousness	Jer 6:13	
the greatest is g to covetousness	Jer 8:10	
the things that I have g them	Jer 8:13	5414
g us water of gall to drink	Jer 8:14	
the LORD hath g me knowledge of	Jer 11:18	
I have g the dearly beloved of my	Jer 12:7	5414
is the flock that was g thee	Jer 13:20	5414
she hath g up the ghost	Jer 15:9	5301
it shall be g into the hand of	Jer 21:10	5414
that the LORD hath g unto you	Jer 25:5	5414
have g it unto whom it seemed	Jer 27:5	5414
now have I g all these lands into	Jer 27:6	5414
field have I g also to serve him	Jer 27:6	5414
I have g him the beasts of the	Jer 28:14	5414
hast g them this land, which thou	Jer 32:22	5414
the city is g into the hand of	Jer 32:24	5414
for the city is g into the hand	Jer 32:25	5414
it is g into the hand of the	Jer 32:43	5414

in the land which I have g to you Jer 35:15 5414
This city shall surely be g into Jer 38:3 5414
then shall this city be g into Jer 38:18 5414
thou shalt not be g into the hand Jer 39:17 5414
which had g him that answer Jer 44:20
seeing the LORD hath g it a Jer 47:7
she hath g her hand Jer 50:15 5414
diet g him of the king of Babylon Jer 52:34 5414
they have g their pleasant things Lam 1:11 5414
he hath g up into the hand of the Lam 2:7 5462
We have g the hand to the Lam 5:6 5414
thou hast not g him warning Eze 3:20
I have g thee cow's dung for Eze 4:15 5414
us is this land g in possession Eze 11:15 5414
which I have g to the fire for Eze 15:6 5414
of my silver, which I had g thee Eze 16:17 5414
and no reward is g unto thee Eze 16:34 5414
he had g his hand, and hath done Eze 17:18 5414
hath g his bread to the hungry, Eze 18:7 5414
that hath not g forth upon usury Eze 18:8 5414
Hath g forth upon usury, and hath Eze 18:13 5414
but hath g his bread to the Eze 18:16 5414
into the land which I had g them Eze 20:15 5414
he hath g it to be furbished, Eze 21:11 5414
that I have g to my servant Jacob Eze 28:25 5414
I have g thee for meat to the Eze 29:5 5414
I have g him the land of Egypt Eze 29:20 5414
the land is g us for inheritance Eze 33:24 5414
they are g us to consume Eze 35:12 5414
I have g unto Jacob my servant Eze 37:25 5414
they shall be g to salt Eze 47:11 5414
hast g me wisdom and might Dan 2:23 3052
of heaven hath g thee a kingdom Dan 2:37 3052
heaven hath he g into thine hand Dan 2:38 3052
let a beast's heart be g unto him Dan 4:16 3052
g to the Medes and Persians Dan 5:28 3052
man, and a man's heart was g to it Dan 7:4 3052
and dominion was g to it Dan 7:6 3052
and g to the burning flame Dan 7:11 3052
there was g him dominion, and Dan 7:14 3052
judgment was g to the saints of Dan 7:22 3052
they shall be g into his hand Dan 7:25 3052
shall be g to the people of the Dan 7:27 3052
an host was g him against the Dan 8:12 5414
but she shall be g up, and they Dan 11:6 5414
shall be g into his hand Dan 11:11 5414
my flax g to cover her nakedness Hos 2:9
rewards that my lovers have g me Hos 2:12 5414
for he hath g you the former rain Joel 2:23 5414
have g a boy for an harlot, and Joel 3:3 5414
I also have g you cleanness of Amos 4:6 5414
of their land which I have g them Amos 9:15 5414
the LORD hath g a commandment Nah 1:14
Ask, and it shall be g you Mt 7:7 1325
which had g such power unto men Mt 9:8 1325
for it shall be g you in that Mt 10:19 1325
and there shall no sign be g to it Mt 12:39 1325
Because it is g unto you to know Mt 13:11 1325
heaven, but to them it is not g Mt 13:11 1325
whosoever hath, to him shall be g Mt 13:12 1325
meat, he commanded it to be g her Mt 14:9 1325
in a charger, and g to the damsel Mt 14:11 1325
there shall no sign be g unto it Mt 16:4 1325
saying, save they to whom it is g Mt 19:11 1325
but it shall be g to them for Mt 20:23
g to a nation bringing forth the Mt 21:43 1325
nor are g in marriage, but are as Mt 22:30 1547
every one that hath shall be g Mt 25:29 1325
sold for much, and g to the poor Mt 26:9 1325
All power is g unto me in heaven Mt 28:18 1325
Unto you it is g to know the Mk 4:11 1325
you that hear shall more be g Mk 4:24 4369
he that hath, to him shall be g Mk 4:25 1325
something should be g her to eat Mk 5:43 1325
is this which is g unto him Mk 6:2 1325
no sign be g unto this generation Mk 8:12 1325
but it shall be g to them for Mk 10:40
marry, nor are g in marriage Mk 12:25
shall be g you in that hour Mk 13:11 1325
pence, and have been g to the poor Mk 14:5 1325
the cup, and when he had g thanks Mk 14:23
betrayed him had g them a token Mk 14:44 1325
Give, and it shall be g unto you Lk 6:38 1325
Unto you it is g to know the Lk 8:10 1325
whosoever hath, to him shall be g Lk 8:18 1325
you, Ask, and it shall be g you Lk 11:9 1325
and there shall no sign be g it Lk 11:29 1325
For unto whomsoever much is g Lk 12:48 1325
they were g in marriage, until Lk 17:27
him, to whom he had g the money Lk 19:15 1325
every one which hath shall be g Lk 19:26 1325
world marry, and are g in marriage Lk 20:34
marry, nor are g in marriage Lk 20:35
is my body which is g for you Lk 22:19 1325
For the law was g by Moses Jn 1:17 1325
except it be g him from heaven Jn 3:27 1325
hath g all things into his hand Jn 3:35 1325
he would have g thee living water Jn 4:10 1325
so hath he g to the Son to have Jn 5:26 1325
hath g him authority to execute Jn 5:27 1325
the Father hath g me to finish Jn 5:36 1325
and when he had g thanks, he Jn 6:11
after that the Lord had g thanks Jn 6:23
hath g me I should lose nothing Jn 6:39 1325
except it were g unto him of my Jn 6:65 1325
for the Holy Ghost was not yet g Jn 7:39
the Pharisees had g a commandment Jn 11:57 1325
hundred pence, and g to the poor Jn 12:5 1325
had g all things into his hands Jn 13:3 1325
For I have g you an example, that Jn 13:15 1325
As thou hast g him power over all Jn 17:2 1325
to as many as thou hast g him Jn 17:2 1325
thou hast g me are of thee Jn 17:7 1325
For I have g unto them the words Jn 17:8 1325
but for them which thou hast g me Jn 17:9 1325
name those whom thou hast g me Jn 17:11 1325
I have g them thy word Jn 17:14 1325
thou gavest me I have g them Jn 17:22 1325
they also, whom thou hast g me Jn 17:24 1325
my glory, which thou hast g me Jn 17:24 1325
the cup which my Father hath g me Jn 18:11 1325
except it were g thee from above Jn 19:11 1325
he through the Holy Ghost had g Acts 1:2
g him this perfect soundness in Acts 3:16 1325
name under heaven g among men Acts 4:12 1325
whom God hath g to them that obey Acts 5:32 1325
hands the Holy Ghost was g Acts 8:18 1325
saw the city wholly g to idolatry Acts 17:16
whereof he hath g assurance unto Acts 17:31 3930
had g them much exhortation, he Acts 20:2
And when he had g him licence Acts 21:40
should have been g him of Paul Acts 24:26 1325
God hath g thee all them that Acts 27:24 5483
the Holy Ghost which is g unto us Rom 5:5 1325
God hath g them the spirit of Rom 11:8 1325
Or who hath first g to him Rom 11:35 4272
say, through the grace g unto me Rom 12:3 1325
to the grace that is g to us Rom 12:6 1325
g to hospitality Rom 12:13 1377
the grace that is g to me of God Rom 15:15 1325
which is g you by Jesus Christ 1Cor 1:4 1325
that are freely g to us of God 1Cor 2:12 5483
grace of God which is g unto me 1Cor 3:10 1325
for her hair is g her for a 1Cor 11:15 1325
And when he had g thanks, he brake 1Cor 11:24
g to every man to profit withal 1Cor 12:7 1325
For to one is g by the Spirit the 1Cor 12:8 1325
having g more abundant honour to 1Cor 12:24 1325
as I have g order to the churches 1Cor 16:1
may be g by many on our behalf 2Cor 1:11
g the earnest of the Spirit in 2Cor 1:22 1325
who also hath g unto us the 2Cor 5:5 1325
hath g to us the ministry of 2Cor 5:18 1325
he hath g to the poor 2Cor 9:9 1325
Lord hath g us for edification 2Cor 10:8 1325
there was g to me a thorn in the 2Cor 12:7 1325
the Lord hath g me to edification 2Cor 13:10 1325
the grace that was g unto me Gal 2:9 1325
if there had been a law g Gal 3:21 1325
which could have g life Gal 3:21 2227
might be g to them that believe Gal 3:22 1325
own eyes, and have g them to me Gal 4:15 1325
of God which is g me to you-ward Eph 3:2 1325
of God g unto me by the effectual Eph 3:7 1325
of all saints, is this grace g Eph 3:8 1325
But unto every one of us is g Eph 4:7 1325
have g themselves over unto Eph 4:19 3860
hath g himself for us an offering Eph 5:2 3860
that utterance may be g unto me Eph 6:19 1325
For unto you it is g in the Phil 1:29 5483
g him a name which is above every Phil 2:9 5483
of God which is g to me for you Col 1:25 1325
who hath also g unto us his holy 1Th 4:8 1325
hath g us everlasting consolation 2Th 2:16 1325
g to hospitality, apt to teach 1Ti 3:2
Not g to wine, no striker, not 1Ti 3:3 3943
not g to much wine, not greedy of 1Ti 3:8 4337
which was g thee by prophecy, 1Ti 4:14 1325
For God hath not g us the spirit 2Ti 1:7 1325
which was g us in Christ Jesus 2Ti 1:9 1325
All scripture is g by inspiration 2Ti 3:16
not soon angry, not g to wine Titus 1:7 3943
not g to filthy lucre Titus 1:7
not g to much wine, teachers of Titus 2:3 1402
prayers I shall be g unto you Philem 22 5483
the children which God hath g me Heb 2:13 1325
For if Jesus had g them rest Heb 4:8
and it shall be g him Jas 1:5 1325
as his divine power hath g unto 2Pet 1:3 1433
Whereby are g unto us exceeding 2Pet 1:4 1433
also according to the wisdom g 2Pet 3:15 1325
by the Spirit which he hath g us 1Jn 3:24 1325
because he hath g us of his 1Jn 4:13 1325
that God hath g to us eternal 1Jn 5:11 1325
hath g us an understanding, that 1Jn 5:20 1325
and a crown was g unto him Rev 6:2 1325
power was g to him that sat Rev 6:4 1325
there was g unto him a great Rev 6:4 1325
power was g unto them over the Rev 6:8 1325
white robes were g unto every one Rev 6:11 1325
to whom it was g to hurt the Rev 7:2 1325
to them were g seven trumpets Rev 8:2 1325
there was g unto him much incense Rev 8:3 1325
to him was g the key of the Rev 9:1 1325
and unto them was g power, as the Rev 9:3 1325
to them it was g that they should Rev 9:5 1325
there was g me a reed like unto a Rev 11:1 1325
for it is g unto the Gentiles Rev 11:2 1325
to the woman were g two wings of Rev 12:14 1325
there was g unto him a mouth Rev 13:5 1325
power was g unto him to continue Rev 13:5 1325
it was g unto him to make war Rev 13:7 1325
power was g him over all kindreds Rev 13:7 1325
thou hast g them blood to drink Rev 16:6 1325
power was g unto him to scorch Rev 16:8 1325
them, and judgment was g unto them Rev 20:4 1325

GIVER

so with the g of usury to him Is 24:2
for God loveth a cheerful g 2Cor 9:7 1395

GIVEST

brother, and thou g him nought Deut 15:9 5414
be grieved when thou g unto him Deut 15:10 5414
be righteous, what g thou him Job 35:7 5414
Thou g thy mouth to evil, and thy Ps 50:19 7971
g them tears to drink in great Ps 80:5
That thou g them they gather Ps 104:28 5414
thou g them their meat in due Ps 145:15 5414
content, though thou g many gifts Prov 6:35
thou g him not warning, nor Eze 3:18
but thou g thy gifts to all thy Eze 16:33 5414
and in that thou g a reward Eze 16:34 5414
For thou verily g thanks well 1Cor 14:17

GIVETH

he g goodly words Gen 49:21 5414
therefore he g you on the sixth Ex 16:29 5414
which the LORD thy God g thee Ex 20:12 5414
of every man that g it willingly Ex 25:2
that g any of his seed unto Lev 20:2 5414
when he g of his seed unto Molech Lev 20:4 5414
all that any man g of such unto Lev 27:9 5414
whatsoever any man g the priest Num 5:10 5414
land which the LORD our God g us Deut 2:29 5414
LORD God of your fathers g you Deut 4:1 5414
which the LORD thy God g thee for Deut 4:21 5414
which the LORD thy God g thee Deut 4:40 5414
which the LORD thy God g thee Deut 5:16 5414
for it is he that g thee power to Deut 8:18 5414
that the LORD thy God g thee not Deut 9:6 5414
good land which the LORD g you Deut 11:17 5414
which the LORD your God g you Deut 11:31 5414
thy fathers g thee to possess it Deut 12:1 5414
which the LORD your God g you Deut 12:9 5414
LORD your God g you to inherit Deut 12:10
when he g you rest from all your Deut 12:10
g thee a sign or a wonder, Deut 13:1 5414
God g thee for an inheritance to Deut 15:4 5414
which the LORD thy God g thee Deut 15:7 5414
which the LORD thy God g thee Deut 16:5 5414
which the LORD thy God g thee Deut 16:18 5414
which the LORD thy God g thee Deut 16:20 5414
which the LORD thy God g thee Deut 17:2 5414
which the LORD thy God g thee Deut 17:14 5414
which the LORD thy God g thee Deut 18:9 5414
land the LORD thy God g thee Deut 19:1 5414
LORD thy God g thee to possess it Deut 19:2 5414
LORD thy God g thee to inherit Deut 19:3
which the LORD thy God g thee for Deut 19:10 5414
LORD thy God g thee to possess it Deut 19:14 5414
LORD thy God g thee to possess it Deut 21:1 5414
which the LORD thy God g thee for Deut 21:23 5414
g it in her hand, and sendeth her Deut 24:3 5414
which the LORD thy God g thee for Deut 24:4 5414
which the LORD thy God g thee Deut 25:15 5414
God g thee for an inheritance to Deut 25:19 5414
thy God g thee for an inheritance Deut 26:1 5414
land that the LORD thy God g thee Deut 26:2 5414
which the LORD thy God g thee Deut 27:2 5414
which the LORD thy God g thee Deut 27:3 5414
which the LORD thy God g thee Deut 28:8 5414
LORD your God g you to possess it Josh 1:11 5414
which the LORD your God g them Josh 1:15 5414
Chemosh thy god g thee to possess Judg 11:24
Cursed be he that g a wife to Judg 21:18 5414
Who g rain upon the earth, and Job 5:10 5414
man g up the ghost, and where is Job 14:10 1478
the Almighty g them understanding Job 32:8
for he g not account of any of Job 33:13
When he g quietness, who then can Job 34:29
maker, who g songs in the night Job 35:10 5414
There they cry, but none g answer Job 35:12
but g right to the poor Job 36:6 5414
he g meat in abundance Job 36:31 5414
deliverance g he to his king Ps 18:50
the righteous sheweth mercy, and g Ps 37:21 5414
of Israel is he that g strength Ps 68:35 5414
The entrance of thy words g light Ps 119:130
it g understanding unto the Ps 119:130
for so he g his beloved sleep Ps 127:2 5414
Who g food to all flesh Ps 136:25 5414
It is he that g salvation unto Ps 144:10 5414
which g food to the hungry Ps 146:7 5414
He g to the beast his food, and to Ps 147:9 5414
He g snow like wool Ps 147:16 5414
For the LORD g wisdom Prov 2:6 5414
but he g grace unto the lowly Prov 3:34 5414
Good understanding g favour Prov 13:15 5414
A wicked doer g heed to false Prov 17:4
a liar g ear to a naughty tongue Prov 17:4
is a friend to him that g gifts Prov 19:6
but the righteous g and spareth Prov 21:26 5414
for he g of his bread to the poor Prov 22:9 5414
he that g to the rich, shall Prov 22:16 5414
when it g his colour in the cup, Prov 23:31 5414
his lips that g a right answer Prov 24:26
so is he that g honour to a fool Prov 26:8 5414
He that g unto the poor shall not Prov 28:27 5414
g meat to her household, and a Prov 31:15 5414
For God g to a man that is good Eccl 2:26 5414
but to the sinner he g travail Eccl 2:26 5414
days of his life, which God g him Eccl 5:18 5414
yet God g him not power to eat Eccl 6:2
that wisdom g life to them that Eccl 7:12
which God g him under the sun Eccl 8:15 5414
He g power to the faint Is 40:29 5414
he that g breath unto the people Is 42:5 5414
the LORD our God, that g rain Jer 5:24 5414
wages, and g him not for his work Jer 22:13 5414
which g the sun for a light by Jer 31:35 5414
He g his cheek to him that Lam 3:30 5414
he g wisdom unto the wise, and Dan 2:21 3052
g it to whomsoever he will, and Dan 4:17 5415
g it to whomsoever he will Dan 4:25 5415
g it to whomsoever he will Dan 4:32 5415
Woe unto him that g his neighbour Hab 2:15
it g light unto all that are in Mt 5:15
for God g not the Spirit by Jn 3:34 1325
but my Father g you the true Jn 6:32 1325
heaven, and g life unto the world Jn 6:33 1325
the Father g me shall come to me Jn 6:37 1325
the good shepherd g his life for Jn 10:11 5087

not as the world g, give I unto Jn 14:27 1325
and g them, and fish likewise Jn 21:13 1325
seeing he g to all life, and Acts 17:25 1325
he that g, let him do it with Rom 12:8 3330
to the Lord, for he g God thanks Rom 14:6
he eateth not, and g God thanks Rom 14:6
but God that g the increase 1Cor 3:7
So then he that g her in marriage 1Cor 7:38
but he that g her not in marriage 1Cor 7:38
But God g it a body as it hath 1Cor 15:38 1325
which g us the victory through 1Cor 15:57 1325
killeth, but the spirit g life 2Cor 3:6
who g us richly all things to 1Ti 6:17 3930
that g to all men liberally, and Jas 1:5 1325
But he g more grace Jas 4:6 1325
but g grace unto the humble Jas 4:6 1325
it as of the ability which God g 1Pet 4:11 5524
proud, and g grace to the humble 1Pet 5:5 1325
for the Lord God g them light Rev 22:5

GIVING
And when she had done g him drink Gen 24:19
in g him food and raiment Deut 10:18 5414
by g him a double portion of all Deut 21:17 5414
his people in g them bread Ruth 1:6 5414
in g food for my household 1Kin 5:9 5414
by g him according to his 2Chr 6:23 5414
and g thanks unto the LORD Ezr 3:11
shall be as the g up of the ghost Job 11:20 4646
g in marriage, until the day that Mt 24:38
face at his feet, g him thanks Lk 17:16
g out that himself was some great Acts 8:9 3004
g them the Holy Ghost, even as he Acts 15:8 1325
strong in faith, g glory to God Rom 4:20
the g of the law, and the service Rom 9:4 3548
even things without life g sound 1Cor 14:7 1325
say Amen at thy g of thanks 1Cor 14:16
G no offence in any thing, that 2Cor 6:3 1325
but rather g of thanks Eph 5:4
G thanks always for all things Eph 5:20
with me as concerning g and Phil 4:15 1394
G thanks unto the Father, which Col 1:12
g thanks to God and the Father by Col 3:17
g of thanks, be made for all men 1Ti 2:1
g heed to seducing spirits, and 1Ti 4:1
Not g heed to Jewish fables, and Titus 1:14
of our lips g thanks to his name Heb 13:15
g honour unto the wife, as unto 1Pet 3:7 632
g all diligence, add to your 2Pet 1:5 3923
g themselves over to fornication, Jude 7

GIZONITE (*ghi'-zo-nite*) *A bodyguard of David.*
The sons of Hashem the G, 1Chr 11:34 1493

GLAD
he will be g in his heart Ex 4:14 8056
And the priest's heart was g Judg 18:20 8190
and they were g 1Sa 11:9 8056
g of heart for all the goodness 1Kin 8:66 2896
Let the heavens be g, and let the 1Chr 16:31 8056
people away into their tents, g 2Chr 7:10 8056
that day joyful and with a g heart Est 5:9 2896
city of Shushan rejoiced and was g Est 8:15 8056
rejoice exceedingly, and are g Job 3:22 7797
The righteous see it, and are g Job 22:19 8056
I will be g and rejoice in thee Ps 9:2 8056
rejoice, and Israel shall be g Ps 14:7 8056
Therefore my heart is g, and my Ps 16:9 8056
exceeding g with thy countenance Ps 21:6 2302
I will be g and rejoice in thy Ps 31:7 1523
Be g in the LORD, and rejoice, ye Ps 32:11 8056
shall hear thereof, and be g Ps 34:2 8056
Let them shout for joy, and be g Ps 35:27 8056
seek thee rejoice and be g in thee Ps 40:16 8056
whereby they have made thee g Ps 45:8 8056
shall make g the city of God Ps 46:4 8056
let the daughters of Judah be g Ps 48:11 1528
rejoice, and Israel shall be g Ps 53:6 8056
righteous shall be g in the LORD Ps 64:10 8056
O let the nations be g and sing Ps 67:4 8056
But let the righteous be g Ps 68:3 8056
humble shall see this, and be g Ps 69:32 8056
seek thee rejoice and be g in thee Ps 70:4 8056
may rejoice and be g all our days Ps 90:14 8056
Make us g according to the days Ps 90:15 8056
hast made me g through thy work Ps 92:4 8056
rejoice, and let the earth be g Ps 96:11 1523
multitude of isles be g thereof Ps 97:1 8056
Zion heard, and was g Ps 97:8 8056
that maketh g the heart of man Ps 104:15 8056
I will be g in the LORD Ps 104:34 8056
Egypt was g when they departed Ps 105:38 8056
Then are they g because they be Ps 107:30 8056
we will rejoice and be g in it Ps 118:24 8056
thee will be g when they see me Ps 119:74 8056
I was g when they said unto me, Ps 122:1 8056
whereof we are g Ps 126:3 8056
A wise son maketh a g father Prov 10:1 8056
but a good word maketh it g Prov 12:25 8056
A wise son maketh a g father Prov 15:20 8056
he that is g at calamities shall Prov 17:5 8056
father and thy mother shall be g Prov 23:25 8056
heart be g when he stumbleth Prov 24:17 1523
son, be wise, and make my heart g Prov 27:11 8056
we will be g and rejoice in thee, Song 1:4 1528
have waited for him, we will be g Is 25:9 1528
place shall be g for them Is 35:1 7996
And Hezekiah was g of them Is 39:2 8056
But be ye g and rejoice for ever Is 65:18 7796
be g with her, all ye that love Is 66:10 1528
making him very g Jer 20:15 8056
were with him, then they were g Jer 41:13 8056
Because ye were g, because ye Jer 50:11 8056
they are g that thou hast done it Lam 1:21 7796
Rejoice and be g, O daughter of Lam 4:21 8056
was the king exceeding g for him Dan 6:23 2868
They make the king g with their Hos 7:3 8056
be g and rejoice Joel 2:21 1523
Be g then, ye children of Zion, Joel 2:23 1523
was exceeding g of the gourd Jonah 4:6 8056
therefore they rejoice and are g Hab 1:15 1523
be g and rejoice with all the Zeph 3:14 8056
children shall see it, and be g Zec 10:7 8056
Rejoice, and be exceeding g Mt 5:12 21
when they heard it, they were g Mk 14:11 5463
and to shew thee these g tidings Lk 1:19 2097
shewing the g tidings of the Lk 8:1 2097
we should make merry, and be g Lk 15:32 5463
And they were g, and covenanted to Lk 22:5 5463
saw Jesus, he was exceeding g Lk 23:8 5463
and he saw it, and was g Jn 8:56 5463
I am g for your sakes that I was Jn 11:15 5463
Then were the disciples g Jn 20:20 5463
heart rejoice, and my tongue was g Acts 2:26 21
had seen the grace of God, was g Acts 11:23 5463
And we declare unto you g tidings Acts 13:32 2097
Gentiles heard this, they were g Acts 13:48 5463
bring g tidings of good things Rom 10:15 2097
I am g therefore on your behalf Rom 16:19 5463
I am g of the coming of Stephanas 1Cor 16:17 5463
who is he then that maketh me g 2Cor 2:2 2165
For we are g, when we are weak, 2Cor 13:9 5463
ye may be g also with exceeding 1Pet 4:13 5463
Let us be g and rejoice, and give Rev 19:7 5463

GLADLY
did many things, and heard him g Mk 6:20 2234
And the common people heard him g Mk 12:37 2234
the people g received him Lk 8:40
Then they that g received his Acts 2:41 780
the brethren received us g Acts 21:17 780
For ye suffer fools g, seeing ye 2Cor 11:19 2234
Most g therefore will I rather 2Cor 12:9 2236
And I will very g spend and be 2Cor 12:15 2236

GLADNESS
Also in the day of your g Num 10:10 8057
and with g of heart, for the Deut 28:47 2898
into the city of David with g 2Sa 6:12 8057
strength and g are in his place 1Chr 16:27 2304
the LORD on that day with great g 1Chr 29:22 8057
And they sang praises with g 2Chr 29:30 8057
bread seven days with great g 2Chr 30:21 8057
they kept other seven days with g 2Chr 30:23 8057
And there was very great g Neh 8:17 8057
to keep the dedication with g Neh 12:27 8057
The Jews had light, and g, and joy, Est 8:16 8057
came, the Jews had joy and g Est 8:17 8342
and made it a day of feasting and g Est 9:17 8057
and made it a day of feasting and g Est 9:18 8057
day of the month Adar a day of g Est 9:19 8057
Thou hast put g in my heart Ps 4:7 8057
my sackcloth, and girded me with g Ps 30:11 8057
the oil of g above thy fellows Ps 45:7 8342
With g and rejoicing shall they be Ps 45:15 8057
Make me to hear joy and g Ps 51:8 8057
g for the upright in heart Ps 97:11 8057
Serve the LORD with g Ps 100:2 8057
with joy, and his chosen with g Ps 105:43 7440
rejoice in the g of thy nation Ps 106:5 8057
hope of the righteous shall be g Prov 10:28 8057
in the day of the g of his heart Song 3:11 8057
g is taken away, and joy out of Is 16:10 8057
And behold joy and g, slaying oxen, Is 22:13 8057
g of heart, as when one goeth Is 30:29 8057
they shall obtain joy and g Is 35:10 8057
g shall be found therein, Is 51:3 8057
they shall obtain g and joy Is 51:11 8057
voice of mirth, and the voice of g Jer 7:34 8057
voice of mirth, and the voice of g Jer 16:9 8057
voice of mirth, and the voice of g Jer 25:10 8057
Sing with g for Jacob, and shout Jer 31:7 8057
voice of joy, and the voice of g Jer 33:11 8057
g is taken from the plentiful Jer 48:33 8057
g from the house of our God Joel 1:16 1524
be to the house of Judah joy and g Zec 8:19 8057
immediately receive it with g Mk 4:16 5479
And thou shalt have joy and g Lk 1:14 20
house, did eat their meat with g Acts 2:46 20
she opened not the gate for g Acts 12:14 5479
filling our hearts with food and g Acts 14:17 2167
therefore in the Lord with all g Phil 2:29 5479
the oil of g above thy fellows Heb 1:9 20

GLASS
strong, and as a molten looking g Job 37:18 7209
For now we see through a g 1Cor 13:12 2072
as in a g the glory of the Lord 2Cor 3:18 2734
beholding his natural face in a g Jas 1:23 2072
was a sea of g like unto crystal Rev 4:6 5193
were a sea of g mingled with fire Rev 15:2 5193
his name, stand on the sea of g Rev 15:2 5193
was pure gold, like unto clear g Rev 21:18 5194
gold, as it were transparent g Rev 21:21 5194

GLASSES
The g, and the fine linen, and the Is 3:23 1549

GLEAN
And thou shalt not g thy vineyard Lev 19:10 5953
thou shalt not g it afterward Deut 24:21 5953
g ears of corn after him in whose Ruth 2:2 3950
And she said, I pray you, let me g Ruth 2:7 3950
Go not to g in another field, Ruth 2:8 3950
And when she was risen up to g Ruth 2:15 3950
Let her g even among the sheaves, Ruth 2:15 3950
leave them, that she may g them Ruth 2:16 3950
g unto the end of barley harvest Ruth 2:23 3950
They shall throughly g the Jer 6:9 5953

GLEANED
they g of them in the highways Judg 20:45 5953
g in the field after the reapers Ruth 2:3 3950
So she g in the field until even, Ruth 2:17 3950
even, and beat out that she had g Ruth 2:17 3950
mother in law saw what she had g Ruth 2:18 3950
her, Where hast thou g to day Ruth 2:19 3950

GLEANING
thou gather any g of thy harvest Lev 23:22 3951
Is not the g of the grapes of Judg 8:2 5955
Yet g grapes shall be left in it, Is 17:6 5955
as the g grapes when the vintage Is 24:13 5955
they not leave some g grapes Jer 49:9 5955

GLEANINGS
thou gather the g of thy harvest Lev 19:9 3951

GLEDE
And the g, and the kite, and the Deut 14:13 7201

GLISTERING
g stones, and of divers colours, 1Chr 29:2 6320
and his raiment was white and g Lk 9:29 1823

GLITTER
it is furbished that it may g Eze 21:10 1300

GLITTERING
If I whet my g sword, and mine Deut 32:41 1300
the g sword cometh out of his Job 20:25 1300
the g spear and the shield Job 39:23 3851
to consume because of the g Eze 21:28 1300
the bright sword and the g spear Nah 3:3 1300
and at the shining of thy g spear Hab 3:11 1300

GLOOMINESS
A day of darkness and of g Joel 2:2 653
a day of darkness and g, a day of Zeph 1:15 653

GLORIEST
Wherefore g thou in the valleys, Jer 49:4 1984

GLORIETH
But let him that g glory in this Jer 9:24 1984
as it is written, He that g 1Cor 1:31 2744
But he that g, let him glory in 2Cor 10:17 2744

GLORIFIED
before all the people I will be g Lev 10:3 3513
thou art g Is 26:15 3513
Jacob, and g himself in Israel Is 44:23 6286
O Israel, in whom I will be g Is 49:3 6286
for he hath g thee Is 55:5 6286
of Israel, because he hath g thee Is 60:9 6286
work of my hands, that I may be g Is 60:21 6286
of the LORD, that he might be g Is 61:3 6286
sake, said, Let the LORD be g Is 66:5 3513
I will be g in the midst of thee Eze 28:22 3513
renown the day that I shall be g Eze 39:13 3513
are all thy ways, hast thou not g Dan 5:23 1922
pleasure in it, and I will be g Hag 1:8 3513
g God, which had given such power Mt 9:8 1392
and they g the God of Israel Mt 15:31 1392
g God, saying, We never saw it on Mk 2:12 1392
their synagogues, being g of all Lk 4:15 1392
were all amazed, and they g God Lk 5:26 1392
and they g God, saying, That a Lk 7:16 1392
she was made straight, and g God Lk 13:13 1392
back, and with a loud voice g God Lk 17:15 1392
he g God, saying, Certainly this Lk 23:47 1392
because that Jesus was not yet g Jn 7:39 1392
the Son of God might be g thereby Jn 11:4 1392
but when Jesus was g, then Jn 12:16 1392
that the Son of man should be g Jn 12:23 1392
heaven, saying, I have both g it Jn 12:28 1392
said, Now is the Son of man g Jn 13:31 1392
man g, and God is g in him Jn 13:31 1392
If God be g in him, God shall Jn 13:32 1392
the Father may be g in the Son Jn 14:13 1392
Herein is my Father g, that ye Jn 15:8 1392
I have g thee on the earth Jn 17:4 1392
and I am g in them Jn 17:10 1392
our fathers, hath g his Son Jesus Acts 3:13 1392
for all men g God for that which Acts 4:21 1392
g God, saying, Then hath God also Acts 11:18 1392
glad, and g the word of the Lord Acts 13:48 1392
they g the Lord, and said unto him Acts 21:20 1392
they g him not as God, neither Rom 1:21 1392
that we may be also g together Rom 8:17 4888
whom he justified, them he also g Rom 8:30 1392
And they g God in me Gal 1:24 1392
shall come to be g in his saints 2Th 1:10 1740
Lord Jesus Christ may be g in you 2Th 1:12 1740
may have free course, and be g 2Th 3:1 1392
So also Christ g not himself to Heb 5:5 1392
may be g through Jesus Christ 1Pet 4:11 1392
of, but on your part he is g 1Pet 4:14 1392
How much she hath g herself Rev 18:7 1392

GLORIFIETH
Whoso offereth praise g me Ps 50:23 3513

GLORIFY
all ye the seed of Jacob, g him Ps 22:23 3513
deliver thee, and thou shalt g me Ps 50:15 3513
and shall g thy name Ps 86:9 3513
I will g thy name for evermore Ps 86:12 3513
Wherefore g ye the LORD in the Is 24:15 3513
shall the strong people g thee Is 25:3 3513
I will g the house of my glory Is 60:7 6286
I will also g them, and they shall Jer 30:19 3513
g your Father which is in heaven Mt 5:16 1392
Father, g thy name Jn 12:28 1392
glorified it, and will g it again Jn 12:28 1392
God shall also g him in himself Jn 13:32 1392
and shall straightway g him Jn 13:32 1392
He shall g me Jn 16:14 1392
the hour is come; g thy Son Jn 17:1 1392
that thy Son also may g thee Jn 17:1 1392

g thou me with thine own self — Jn 17:5 *1392*
by what death he should g God — Jn 21:19 *1392*
with one mind and one mouth g God — Rom 15:6 *1392*
might g God for his mercy — Rom 15:9 *1392*
therefore g God in your body, and — 1Cor 6:20 *1392*
they g God for your professed — 2Cor 9:13 *1392*
g God in the day of visitation — 1Pet 2:12 *1392*
but let him g God on this behalf — 1Pet 4:16 *1392*
fear thee, O Lord, and g thy name — Rev 15:4 *1392*

GLORIFYING

And the shepherds returned, g — Lk 2:20 *1392*
departed to his own house, g God — Lk 5:25 *1392*
his sight, and followed him, g God — Lk 18:43 *1392*

GLORIOUS

O LORD, is become g in power — Ex 15:6 142
g in holiness, fearful in praises — Ex 15:11 142
that thou mayest fear this g — Deut 28:58 3513
How g was the king of Israel — 2Sa 6:20 3513
thank thee, and praise thy g name — 1Chr 29:13 8597
and blessed be thy g name, which — Neh 9:5 3519
the riches of his g kingdom — Est 1:4 3519
king's daughter is all g within — Ps 45:13 3520
make his praise g — Ps 66:2 3519
And blessed be his g name for ever — Ps 72:19 3519
Thou art more g and excellent than — Ps 76:4 215
G things are spoken of thee, O — Ps 87:3 3513
His work is honourable and g — Ps 111:3 1926
I will speak of the g honour of — Ps 145:5 3519
the g majesty of his kingdom — Ps 145:12 3519
of the LORD be beautiful and g — Is 4:2 3519
and his rest shall be g — Is 11:10 3519
he shall be for a g throne to his — Is 22:23 3519
whose g beauty is a fading flower — Is 28:1 6643
the g beauty, which is on the — Is 28:4 6643
cause his g voice to be heard — Is 30:30 1935
But there the g LORD will be unto — Is 33:21 117
yet shall I be g in the eyes of — Is 49:5 3513
will make the place of my feet g — Is 60:13 3513
this that is g in his apparel, — Is 63:1 1921
hand of Moses with his g arm — Is 63:12 8597
people, to make thyself a g name — Is 63:14 8597
A g high throne from the — Jer 17:12 3519
made very g in the midst of the — Eze 27:25 3513
and he shall stand in the g land — Dan 11:16 6643
shall enter also into the g land — Dan 11:41 6643
the seas in the g holy mountain — Dan 11:45 6643
g things that were done by him — Lk 13:17 *1741*
g liberty of the children of God — Rom 8:21 *1391*
and engraven in stones, was g — 2Cor 3:7
of the spirit be rather g — 2Cor 3:8
g had no glory in this respect — 2Cor 3:10 *1392*
if that which is done away was g — 2Cor 3:11
more that which remaineth is g — 2Cor 3:11
light of the g gospel of Christ — 2Cor 4:4 *1391*
present it to himself a g church — Eph 5:27 *1741*
be fashioned like unto his g body — Phil 3:21 *1391*
might, according to his g power — Col 1:11 *1391*
According to the g gospel of the — 1Ti 1:11 *1391*
the g appearing of the great God — Titus 2:13 *1391*

GLORIOUSLY

the LORD, for he hath triumphed g — Ex 15:1
the LORD, for he hath triumphed g — Ex 15:21
and before his ancients g — Is 24:23 3519

GLORY

hath he gotten all this g — Gen 31:1 3519
my father of all my g in Egypt — Gen 45:13 3519
said unto Pharaoh, G over me — Ex 8:9 6286
ye shall see the g of the LORD — Ex 16:7 3519
the g of the LORD appeared in the — Ex 16:10 3519
the g of the LORD abode upon — Ex 24:16 3519
the sight of the g of the LORD — Ex 24:17 3519
for Aaron thy brother for g — Ex 28:2 3519
shalt thou make for them, for g — Ex 28:40 3519
shall be sanctified by my g — Ex 29:43 3519
I beseech thee, shew me thy g — Ex 33:18 3519
while my g passeth by, that I — Ex 33:22 3519
the g of the LORD filled the — Ex 40:34 3519
the g of the LORD filled the — Ex 40:35 3519
the g of the LORD shall appear — Lev 9:6 3519
the g of the LORD appeared unto — Lev 9:23 3519
the g of the LORD appeared in the — Num 14:10 3519
be filled with the g of the LORD — Num 14:21 3519
those men which have seen my g — Num 14:22 3519
the g of the LORD appeared unto — Num 16:19 3519
the g of the LORD appeared — Num 16:42 3519
the g of the LORD appeared unto — Num 20:6 3519
LORD our God hath shewed us his g — Deut 5:24 3519
His g is like the firstling of — Deut 33:17 1926
g to the LORD God of Israel, and — Josh 7:19 3519
make them inherit the throne of g — 1Sa 2:8 3519
The g is departed from Israel — 1Sa 4:21 3519
The g is departed from Israel — 1Sa 4:22 3519
ye shall give g unto the God of — 1Sa 6:5 3519
for the g of the LORD had filled — 1Kin 8:11 3519
g of this, and tarry at home — 2Kin 14:10 3513
G ye in his holy name — 1Chr 16:10 1984
Declare his g among the heathen — 1Chr 16:24 3519
G and honour are in his presence — 1Chr 16:27 1935
the people, give unto the LORD g — 1Chr 16:28 3519
the LORD the g due unto his name — 1Chr 16:29 3519
thy holy name, and g in thy praise — 1Chr 16:35 7623
of g throughout all countries — 1Chr 22:5 8597
greatness, and the power, and the g — 1Chr 29:11 8597
for the g of the LORD had filled — 2Chr 5:14 3519
the g of the LORD filled the — 2Chr 7:1 3519
because the g of the LORD had — 2Chr 7:2 3519
the g of the LORD upon the house, — 2Chr 7:3 3519
told them of the g of his riches — Est 5:11 3519
He hath stripped me of my g — Job 19:9 3519
My g was fresh in me, and my bow — Job 29:20 3519
the g of his nostrils is terrible — Job 39:20 1935
and array thyself with g and beauty — Job 40:10 1935
my g, and the lifter up of mine — Ps 3:3 3519
long will ye turn my g into shame — Ps 4:2 3519
who hast set thy g above the — Ps 8:1 1935
and hast crowned him with g — Ps 8:5 3519
heart is glad, and my g rejoiceth — Ps 16:9 3519
The heavens declare the g of God — Ps 19:1 3519
His g is great in thy salvation — Ps 21:5 3519
the King of g shall come in — Ps 24:7 3519
Who is this King of g — Ps 24:8 3519
the King of g shall come in — Ps 24:9 3519
Who is this King of g — Ps 24:10 3519
of hosts, he is the King of g — Ps 24:10 3519
O ye mighty, give unto the LORD g — Ps 29:1 3519
the LORD the g due unto his name — Ps 29:2 3519
the God of g thundereth — Ps 29:3 3519
doth every one speak of his g — Ps 29:9 3519
To the end that my g may sing — Ps 30:12 3519
thigh, O most mighty, with thy g — Ps 45:3 1935
when the g of his house is — Ps 49:16 3519
his g shall not descend after him — Ps 49:17 3519
let thy g be above all the earth — Ps 57:5 3519
Awake up, my g — Ps 57:8 3519
let thy g be above all the earth — Ps 57:11 3519
In God is my salvation and my g — Ps 62:7 3519
To see thy power and thy g — Ps 63:2 3519
one that sweareth by him shall g — Ps 63:11 1984
all the upright in heart shall g — Ps 64:10 1984
whole earth be filled with his g — Ps 72:19 3519
and afterward receive me to g — Ps 73:24 3519
his g into the enemy's hand — Ps 78:61 8597
salvation, for the g of thy name — Ps 79:9 3519
the LORD will give grace and g — Ps 84:11 3519
that g may dwell in our land — Ps 85:9 3519
For thou art the g of their — Ps 89:17 8597
Thou hast made his g to cease — Ps 89:44 2892
thy g unto their children — Ps 90:16 1926
Declare his g among the heathen, — Ps 96:3 3519
the people, give unto the LORD g — Ps 96:7 3519
the LORD the g due unto his name — Ps 96:8 3519
and all the people see his g — Ps 97:6 3519
all the kings of the earth thy g — Ps 102:15 3519
up Zion, he shall appear in his g — Ps 102:16 3519
The g of the LORD shall endure — Ps 104:31 3519
G ye in his holy name — Ps 105:3 1984
nation, that I may g with thine — Ps 106:5 1984
Thus they changed their g into — Ps 106:20 3519
and give praise, even with my g — Ps 108:1 3519
thy g above all the earth — Ps 108:5 3519
and his g above the heavens — Ps 113:4 3519
unto us, but unto thy name give g — Ps 115:1 3519
for great is the g of the LORD — Ps 138:5 3519
speak of the g of thy kingdom — Ps 145:11 3519
his g is above the earth and — Ps 148:13 1935
Let the saints be joyful in g — Ps 149:5 3519
The wise shall inherit g — Prov 3:35 3519
a crown of g shall she deliver to — Prov 4:9 8597
The hoary head is a crown of g — Prov 16:31 8597
the g of children are their — Prov 17:6 8597
it is his g to pass over a — Prov 19:11 8597
The g of young men is their — Prov 20:29 8597
It is the g of God to conceal a — Prov 25:2 3519
search their own g is not g — Prov 25:27 3519
men do rejoice, there is great g — Prov 28:12 8597
LORD, and for the g of his majesty — Is 2:10 1926
for the g of his majesty, when he — Is 2:19 1926
for the g of his majesty, when he — Is 2:21 1926
to provoke the eyes of his g — Is 3:8 3519
for upon all the g shall be a — Is 4:5 3519
and their g, and their multitude, — Is 5:14 1926
the whole earth is full of his g — Is 6:3 3519
the king of Assyria, and all his g — Is 8:7 3519
and where will ye leave your g — Is 10:3 3519
and the g of his high looks — Is 10:12 8597
under his g he shall kindle a — Is 10:16 3519
shall consume the g of his forest — Is 10:18 3519
the g of kingdoms, the beauty of — Is 13:19 6643
even all of them, lie in g — Is 14:18 3519
the g of Moab shall be contemned, — Is 16:14 3519
they shall be as the g of the — Is 17:3 3519
that the g of Jacob shall be made — Is 17:4 3519
expectation, and of Egypt their g — Is 20:5 8597
all the g of Kedar shall fail — Is 21:16 3519
thy g shall be the shame of thy — Is 22:18 3519
all the g of his father's house — Is 22:24 3519
it, to stain the pride of all g — Is 23:9 6643
songs, even g to the righteous — Is 24:16 6643
LORD of hosts be for a crown of g — Is 28:5 6643
the g of Lebanon shall be given — Is 35:2 3519
they shall see the g of the LORD — Is 35:2 3519
the g of the LORD shall be — Is 40:5 3519
shalt g in the Holy One of Israel — Is 41:16 1984
my g will I not give to another, — Is 42:8 3519
Let them give g unto the LORD — Is 42:12 3519
for I have created him for my g — Is 43:7 3519
Israel be justified, and shall g — Is 45:25 1984
salvation in Zion for Israel my g — Is 46:13 8597
I will not give my g unto another — Is 48:11 3519
the g of the LORD shall be thy — Is 58:8 3519
his g from the rising of the sun — Is 59:19 3519
the g of the LORD is risen upon — Is 60:1 3519
his g shall be seen upon thee — Is 60:2 3519
I will glorify the house of my g — Is 60:7 8597
The g of Lebanon shall come unto — Is 60:13 3519
light, and thy God thy g — Is 60:19 8597
in their g shall ye boast — Is 61:6 3519
righteousness, and all kings thy g — Is 62:2 3519
of g in the hand of the LORD — Is 62:3 8597
of thy holiness and of thy g — Is 63:15 8597
with the abundance of her g — Is 66:11 3519
the g of the Gentiles like a — Is 66:12 3519
and they shall come, and see my g — Is 66:18 3519
my fame, neither have seen my g — Is 66:19 3519
declare my g among the Gentiles — Is 66:19 3519
my people have changed their g — Jer 2:11 3519
in him, and in him shall they g — Jer 4:2 1984
not the wise man g in his wisdom — Jer 9:23 1984
let the mighty man g in his might — Jer 9:23 1984
not the rich man g in his riches — Jer 9:23 1984
let him that glorieth g in this — Jer 9:24 1984
name, and for a praise, and for a g — Jer 13:11 8597
Give g to the LORD your God, — Jer 13:16 3519
down, even the crown of your g — Jer 13:18 8597
not disgrace the throne of thy g — Jer 14:21 3519
Ah lord! or, Ah his g! — Jer 22:18 1935
Dibon, come down from thy g — Jer 48:18 3519
the likeness of the g of the LORD — Eze 1:28 3519
Blessed be the g of the LORD from — Eze 3:12 3519
the g of the LORD stood there, as — Eze 3:23 3519
as the g which I saw by the river — Eze 3:23 3519
the g of the God of Israel was — Eze 8:4 3519
the g of the God of Israel was — Eze 9:3 3519
Then the g of the LORD went up — Eze 10:4 3519
of the brightness of the LORD's g — Eze 10:4 3519
Then the g of the LORD departed — Eze 10:18 3519
the g of the God of Israel was — Eze 10:19 3519
the g of the God of Israel was — Eze 11:22 3519
the g of the LORD went up from — Eze 11:23 3519
which is the g of all lands — Eze 20:6 6643
which is the g of all lands — Eze 20:15
strength, the joy of their g — Eze 24:25 8597
frontiers, the g of the country, — Eze 25:9 6643
I shall set g in the land of the — Eze 26:20 6643
To whom art thou thus like in g — Eze 31:18 3519
I will set my g among the heathen — Eze 39:21 3519
the g of the God of Israel came — Eze 43:2 3519
and the earth shined with his g — Eze 43:2 3519
the g of the LORD came into the — Eze 43:4 3519
the g of the LORD filled the — Eze 43:5 3519
the g of the LORD filled the — Eze 44:4 3519
kingdom, power, and strength, and g — Dan 2:37 3367
for the g of my kingdom, mine — Dan 4:36 3367
father a kingdom and majesty, and g — Dan 5:18 3367
and they took his g from him — Dan 5:20 3367
was given him dominion, and g — Dan 7:14 3367
of taxes in the g of the kingdom — Dan 11:20 1925
acknowledge and increase with g — Dan 11:39 3519
will I change their g into shame — Hos 4:7 3519
their g shall fly away like a — Hos 9:11 3519
rejoiced on it, for the g thereof — Hos 10:5 3519
come unto Adullam the g of Israel — Mic 1:15 3519
have ye taken away my g for ever — Mic 2:9 1926
g out of all the pleasant — Nah 2:9 3519
knowledge of the g of the LORD — Hab 2:14 3519
Thou art filled with shame for g — Hab 2:16 3519
spewing shall be on thy g — Hab 2:16 3519
His g covered the heavens, and the — Hab 3:3 1935
saw this house in her first g — Hag 2:3 3519
and I will fill this house with g — Hag 2:7 3519
The g of this latter house shall — Hag 2:9 3519
will be the g in the midst of her — Zec 2:5 3519
After the g hath he sent me unto — Zec 2:8 3519
and he shall bear the g, and shall — Zec 6:13 1935
for their g is spoiled — Zec 11:3 155
that the g of the house of David — Zec 12:7 8597
the g of the inhabitants of — Zec 12:7 8597
to give g unto my name, saith the — Mal 2:2 3519
of the world, and the g of them — Mt 4:8 *1391*
that they may have g of men — Mt 6:2 *1392*
kingdom, and the power, and the g — Mt 6:13 *1391*
his g was not arrayed like one of — Mt 6:29 *1391*
Son of man shall come in the g of — Mt 16:27 *1391*
shall sit in the throne of his g — Mt 19:28 *1391*
of heaven with power and great g — Mt 24:30 *1391*
Son of man shall come in his g — Mt 25:31 *1391*
he sit upon the throne of his g — Mt 25:31 *1391*
when he cometh in the g of his — Mk 8:38 *1391*
other on thy left hand, in thy g — Mk 10:37 *1391*
the clouds with great power and g — Mk 13:26 *1391*
the g of the Lord shone round — Lk 2:9 *1391*
G to God in the highest, and on — Lk 2:14 *1391*
the g of thy people Israel — Lk 2:32 *1391*
I give thee, and the g of them — Lk 4:6 *1391*
when he shall come in his own g — Lk 9:26 *1391*
Who appeared in g, and spake of — Lk 9:31 *1391*
they were awake, they saw his g — Lk 9:32 *1391*
that Solomon in all his g was not — Lk 12:27 *1391*
that returned to give g to God — Lk 17:18 *1391*
in heaven, and g in the highest — Lk 19:38 *1391*
in a cloud with power and great g — Lk 21:27 *1391*
things, and to enter into his g — Lk 24:26 *1391*
among us, (and we beheld his g — Jn 1:14 *1391*
the g as of the only begotten of — Jn 1:14 *1391*
and manifested forth his g — Jn 2:11 *1391*
of himself seeketh his own g — Jn 7:18 *1391*
that seeketh his g that sent him — Jn 7:18 *1391*
And I seek not mine own g — Jn 8:50 *1391*
unto death, but for the g of God — Jn 11:4 *1391*
thou shouldest see the g of God — Jn 11:40 *1391*
said Esaias, when he saw his g — Jn 12:41 *1391*
g which I had with thee before — Jn 17:5 *1391*
the g which thou gavest me I have — Jn 17:22 *1391*
that they may behold my g — Jn 17:24 *1391*
The God of g appeared unto our — Acts 7:2 *1391*
into heaven, and saw the g of God — Acts 7:55 *1391*
because he gave not God the g — Acts 12:23 *1391*
not see for the g of that light — Acts 22:11 *1391*
And changed the g of the — Rom 1:23 *1391*
in well doing seek for g and — Rom 2:7 *1391*
But g, honour, and peace, to every — Rom 2:10 *1391*
through my lie unto his g — Rom 3:7 *1391*
and come short of the g of God — Rom 3:23 *1391*
by works, he hath whereof to g — Rom 4:2 *2745*
strong in faith, giving g to God — Rom 4:20 *1391*
rejoice in hope of the g of God — Rom 5:2 *1391*
but we g in tribulations also — Rom 5:3 *2744*
the dead by the g of the Father — Rom 6:4 *1391*
g which shall be revealed in us — Rom 8:18 *1391*
pertaineth the adoption, and the g — Rom 9:4 *1391*

of his g on the vessels of mercy Rom 9:23 1391
he had afore prepared unto g Rom 9:23 1391
to whom be g for ever Rom 11:36 1391
also received us to the g of God Rom 15:7 1391
g through Jesus Christ in those Rom 15:17 2746
be g through Jesus Christ for Rom 16:27 1391
no flesh should g in his presence 1Cor 1:29 2744
glorieth, let him g in the Lord 1Cor 1:31 2744
before the world unto our g 1Cor 2:7 1391
not have crucified the Lord of g 1Cor 2:8 1391
Therefore let no man g in men 1Cor 3:21 2744
didst receive it, why dost thou g 1Cor 4:7 2744
gospel, I have nothing to g of 1Cor 9:16 2745
ye do, do all to the g of God 1Cor 10:31 1391
as he is the image and g of God 1Cor 11:7 1391
but the woman is the g of the man 1Cor 11:7 1391
have long hair, it is a g to her 1Cor 11:15 1391
but the g of the celestial is one 1Cor 15:40 1391
the g of the terrestrial is 1Cor 15:40 1391
There is one g of the sun 1Cor 15:41 1391
another g of the moon 1Cor 15:41 1391
and another g of the stars 1Cor 15:41 1391
differeth from another star in g 1Cor 15:41 1391
it is raised in g 1Cor 15:43 1391
him Amen, unto the g of God by us 2Cor 1:20 1391
for the g of his countenance 2Cor 3:7 1391
which g was to be done away 2Cor 3:7 1391
ministration of condemnation be g 2Cor 3:9 1391
of righteousness exceed in g 2Cor 3:9 1391
glorious had no g in this respect 2Cor 3:10 1392
by reason of the g that excelleth 2Cor 3:10 1391
as in a glass the g of the Lord 2Cor 3:18 1391
the same image from g to g 2Cor 3:18 1391
the g of God in the face of Jesus 2Cor 4:6 1391
of many redound to the g of God 2Cor 4:15 1391
exceeding and eternal weight of g 2Cor 4:17 1391
you occasion to g on our behalf 2Cor 5:12 2745
answer them which g in appearance 2Cor 5:12 2744
by us to the g of the same Lord 2Cor 8:19 1391
the churches, and the g of Christ 2Cor 8:23 1391
glorieth, let him g in the Lord 2Cor 10:17 2744
that wherein they g, they may be 2Cor 11:12 2744
g after the flesh, I will g also 2Cor 11:18 2744
If I must needs g, I will g 2Cor 11:30 2744
expedient for me doubtless to g 2Cor 12:1 2744
Of such an one will I g 2Cor 12:5 2744
yet of myself I will not g 2Cor 12:5 2744
For though I would desire to g 2Cor 12:6 2744
will I rather g in my infirmities 2Cor 12:9 2744
To whom be g for ever and ever Gal 1:5 1391
Let us not be desirous of vain g Gal 5:26 2755
that they may g in your flesh Gal 6:13 2744
But God forbid that I should g Gal 6:14 2744
the praise of the g of his grace Eph 1:6 1391
should be to the praise of his g Eph 1:12 1391
unto the praise of his g Eph 1:14 1391
Jesus Christ, the Father of g Eph 1:17 1391
what the riches of the g of his Eph 1:18 1391
for you, which is your g Eph 3:13 1391
according to the riches of his g Eph 3:16 1391
Unto him be g in the church by Eph 3:21 1391
are by Jesus Christ, unto the g Phil 1:11 1391
to the g of God the Father Phil 2:11 1391
whose g is in their shame, who Phil 3:19 1391
his riches in g by Christ Jesus Phil 4:19 1391
God and our Father be g for ever Phil 4:20 1391
the g of this mystery among the Col 1:27 1391
is Christ in you, the hope of g Col 1:27 1391
ye also appear with him in g Col 3:4 1391
Nor of men sought we g, neither 1Th 2:6 1391
called you unto his kingdom and g 1Th 2:12 1391
For ye are our g and joy 1Th 2:20 1391
So that we ourselves g in you in 2Th 1:4 2744
Lord, and from the g of his power 2Th 1:9 1391
to the obtaining of the g of our 2Th 2:14 1391
be honour and g for ever and ever 1Ti 1:17 1391
in the world, received up into g 1Ti 3:16 1391
is in Christ Jesus with eternal g 2Ti 2:10 1391
to whom be g for ever and ever 2Ti 4:18 1391
Who being the brightness of his g Heb 1:3 1391
thou crownedst him with g Heb 2:7 1391
of death, crowned with g and Heb 2:9 1391
in bringing many sons unto g Heb 2:10 1391
worthy of more g than Moses Heb 3:3 1391
of g shadowing the mercyseat Heb 9:5 1391
to whom be g for ever and ever Heb 13:21 1391
Lord Jesus Christ, the Lord of g Jas 2:1 1391
g not, and lie not against the Jas 3:14 2620
g at the appearing of Jesus 1Pet 1:7 1391
with joy unspeakable and full of g 1Pet 1:8 1392
and the g that should follow 1Pet 1:11 1391
up from the dead, and gave him g 1Pet 1:21 1391
all the g of man as the flower of 1Pet 1:24 1391
For what g is it, if, when ye be 1Pet 2:20 2811
when his g shall be revealed, ye 1Pet 4:13 1391
for the spirit of g and of God 1Pet 4:14 1391
of the g that shall be revealed 1Pet 5:1 1391
a crown of g that fadeth not away 1Pet 5:4 1391
his eternal g by Christ Jesus 1Pet 5:10 1391
To him be g and dominion for ever 1Pet 5:11 1391
of him that hath called us to g 2Pet 1:3 1391
from God the Father honour and g 2Pet 1:17 1391
voice to him from the excellent g 2Pet 1:17 1391
To him be g both now and for ever 2Pet 3:18 1391
of his g with exceeding joy Jude 24 1391
only wise God our Saviour, be g Jude 25 1391
to him be g and dominion for ever Rev 1:6 1391
And when those beasts give g Rev 4:9 1391
art worthy, O Lord, to receive g Rev 4:11 1391
and strength, and honour, and g Rev 5:12 1391
saying, Blessing, and honour, and g Rev 5:13 1391
Blessing, and g, and wisdom, and Rev 7:12 1391
gave g to the God of heaven Rev 11:13 1391
voice, Fear God, and give g to him Rev 14:7 1391
with smoke from the g of God Rev 15:8 1391
they repented not to give him g Rev 16:9 1391
earth was lightened with his g Rev 18:1 1391
Salvation, and g, and honour, and Rev 19:1 1391
Having the g of God Rev 21:11 1391
for the g of God did lighten it, Rev 21:23 1391
of the earth do bring their g Rev 21:24 1391
And they shall bring the g Rev 21:26 1391

GLORYING
Your g is not good 1Cor 5:6 2745
any man should make my g void 1Cor 9:15 2745
toward you, great is my g of you 2Cor 7:4 2746
I am become a fool in g 2Cor 12:11 2744

GLUTTON
he is a g, and a drunkard Deut 21:20 2151
the g shall come to poverty Prov 23:21 2151

GLUTTONOUS
and they say, Behold a man g Mt 11:19 5314
and ye say, Behold a g man Lk 7:34 5314

GNASH
he shall g with his teeth, and Ps 112:10 2786
they hiss and g the teeth Lam 2:16 2786

GNASHED
they g upon me with their teeth Ps 35:16 2786
they g on him with their teeth Acts 7:54 1031

GNASHETH
he g upon me with his teeth Job 16:9 2786
g upon him with his teeth Ps 37:12 2786
g with his teeth, and pineth away Mk 9:18 5149

GNASHING
shall be weeping and g of teeth Mt 8:12 1030
shall be wailing and g of teeth Mt 13:42 1030
shall be wailing and g of teeth Mt 13:50 1030
shall be weeping and g of teeth Mt 22:13 1030
shall be weeping and g of teeth Mt 24:51 1030
shall be weeping and g of teeth Mt 25:30 1030
g of teeth, when ye shall see Lk 13:28 1030

GNAT
blind guides, which strain at a g Mt 23:24 2971

GNAW
they g not the bones till the Zeph 3:3 1633

GNAWED
they g their tongues for pain, Rev 16:10 3145

GO
upon thy belly shalt thou g Gen 3:14 3212
G forth of the ark, thou, and thy Gen 8:16 3318
from all that g out of the ark, Gen 9:10 3318
G to, let us make brick, and burn Gen 11:3 3051
G to, let us build us a city and a Gen 11:4 3051
G to, let us g down, and there Gen 11:7 3051
G to, let us g down, and there Gen 11:7 3381
to g into the land of Canaan Gen 11:31 3212
they went forth to g into the Gen 12:5 3212
thy wife, take her, and g thy way Gen 12:19 3212
then I will g to the right Gen 13:9
hand, then I will g to the left Gen 13:9
seeing I g childless, and the Gen 15:2 1980
thou shalt g to thy fathers in Gen 15:15 935
I pray thee, g in unto my maid Gen 16:2 935
and whither wilt thou g Gen 16:8 3212
I will g down now, and see whether Gen 18:21 3381
rise up early, and g on your ways Gen 19:2 1980
g thou in, and lie with him, that Gen 19:34 935
and I and the lad will g yonder Gen 22:5 3212
But thou shalt g unto my country, Gen 24:4 3212
that women g out to draw water Gen 24:11 3318
But thou shalt g unto my father's Gen 24:38 3212
thou do prosper my way which I g Gen 24:42 1980
is before thee, take her, and g Gen 24:51 3212
after that she shall g Gen 24:55 3212
me away that I may g to my master Gen 24:56 3212
Wilt thou g with this man Gen 24:58 3212
And she said, I will g Gen 24:58 3212
and said, G not down into Egypt Gen 26:2 3381
said unto Isaac, G from us Gen 26:16 3212
g out to the field, and take me Gen 27:3 3318
G now to the flock, and fetch me Gen 27:9 3212
obey my voice, and g fetch me them Gen 27:13 3212
g to Padan-aram, to the house of Gen 28:2 3212
will keep me in this way that I g Gen 28:20 1980
water ye the sheep, and g and feed Gen 29:7 3212
that I may g in unto her Gen 29:21 935
my maid Bilhah, g in unto her Gen 30:3 935
that I may g unto mine own place, Gen 30:25 3212
I have served thee, and let me g Gen 30:26 3212
for to g to Isaac his father in Gen 31:18 935
And he said, Let me g, for the day Gen 32:26 7971
And he said, I will not let thee g Gen 32:26 7971
us g, and I will g before thee Gen 33:12 3212
g up to Beth-el, and dwell there Gen 35:1 5927
let us arise, and g up to Beth-el Gen 35:3 5927
And he said to him, G, I pray thee Gen 37:14 3212
them say, Let us g to Dothan Gen 37:17 3212
and I, whither shall I g Gen 37:30 935
For I will g down into the grave Gen 37:35 3381
G in unto thy brother's wife, and Gen 38:8 935
G to, I pray thee, let me come in Gen 38:16 3051
all the Egyptians, G unto Joseph Gen 41:55 3212
ye shall not g forth hence Gen 42:15 3318
g ye, carry corn for the famine Gen 42:19 3212
My son shall not g down with you Gen 42:38 3381
him by the way in the which ye g Gen 42:38 3212
G again, buy us a little food Gen 43:2 7725
brother with us, we will g down Gen 43:4 3381
not send him, we will not g down Gen 43:5 3381
with me, and we will arise and g Gen 43:8 3212
and arise, g again unto the man Gen 43:13 7725
G again, and buy us a little food Gen 44:25 7725
And we said, We cannot g down Gen 44:26 3381
be with us, then will we g down Gen 44:26 3381
let the lad g up with his Gen 44:33 5927
For how shall I g up to my father Gen 44:34 5927
Cause every man to g out from me Gen 45:1 3318
g up to my father, and say unto Gen 45:9 5927
lade your beasts, and g, get you Gen 45:17 3212
I will g and see him before I die Gen 45:28 3212
fear not to g down into Egypt Gen 46:3 3381
I will g down with thee into Gen 46:4 3381
his father's house, I will g up Gen 46:31 5927
Now therefore let me g up Gen 50:5 5927
G up, and bury thy father, Gen 50:6 5927
to Pharaoh's daughter, Shall I g Ex 2:7 3212
Pharaoh's daughter said to her, G Ex 2:8 3212
I, that I should g unto Pharaoh Ex 3:11 3212
G, and gather the elders of Israel Ex 3:16 3212
and now let us g, we beseech thee, Ex 3:18 3212
king of Egypt will not let you g Ex 3:19 1980
and after that he will let you g Ex 3:20 7971
when ye g, ye shall not g empty Ex 3:21 3212
Now therefore g, and I will be Ex 4:12 3212
law, and said unto him, Let me g Ex 4:18 3212
Jethro said to Moses, G in peace Ex 4:18 3212
LORD said unto Moses in Midian, G Ex 4:19 3212
he shall not let the people g Ex 4:21 7971
And I say unto thee, Let my son g Ex 4:23 7971
and if thou refuse to let him g Ex 4:23 7971
So he let him g Ex 4:26 7503
G into the wilderness to meet Ex 4:27 3212
God of Israel, Let my people g Ex 5:1 7971
obey his voice to let Israel g Ex 5:2 7971
LORD, neither will I let Israel g Ex 5:2 7971
let us g, we pray thee, three Ex 5:3 3212
let them g and gather straw for Ex 5:7 3212
they cry, saying, Let us g Ex 5:8 3212
G ye, get you straw where ye can Ex 5:11 3212
therefore ye say, Let us g Ex 5:17 3212
G therefore now, and work Ex 5:18 3212
a strong hand shall he let them g Ex 6:1 7971
G in, speak unto Pharaoh king of Ex 6:11 935
of Israel g out of his land Ex 6:11 7971
he refuseth to let the people g Ex 7:14 7971
thee, saying, Let my people g Ex 7:16 7971
G unto Pharaoh, and say unto him, Ex 8:1 935
saith the LORD, Let my people g Ex 8:1 7971
And if thou refuse to let them g Ex 8:2 7971
abundantly, which shall g up Ex 8:3 5927
and I will let the people g Ex 8:8 7971
saith the LORD, Let my people g Ex 8:20 7971
if thou wilt not let my people g Ex 8:21 7971
G ye, sacrifice to your God in Ex 8:25 3212
We will g three days' journey Ex 8:27 3212
And Pharaoh said, I will let you g Ex 8:28 7971
only ye shall not g very far away Ex 8:28 3212
I g out from thee, and I will Ex 8:29 3318
people g to sacrifice to the LORD Ex 8:29 7971
neither would he let the people g Ex 8:32 7971
G in unto Pharaoh, and tell him, Ex 9:1 935
of the Hebrews, Let my people g Ex 9:1 7971
For if thou refuse to let them g Ex 9:2 7971
and he did not let the people g Ex 9:7 7971
of the Hebrews, Let my people g Ex 9:13 7971
that thou wilt not let them g Ex 9:17 7971
and I will let you g, and ye shall Ex 9:28 7971
he let the children of Israel g Ex 9:35 7971
unto Moses, G in unto Pharaoh Ex 10:1 935
let my people g, that they may Ex 10:3 7971
if thou refuse to let my people g Ex 10:4 7971
let the men g, that they may Ex 10:7 7971
and he said unto them, G, serve Ex 10:8 3212
but who are they that shall g Ex 10:8 1980
We will g with our young and with Ex 10:9 3212
and with our herds will we g Ex 10:9 3212
so with you, as I will let you g Ex 10:10 7971
g now ye that are men, and serve Ex 10:11 3212
not let the children of Israel g Ex 10:20 7971
and said, G ye, serve the LORD Ex 10:24 3212
your little ones also g with you Ex 10:24 3212
Our cattle also shall g with us Ex 10:26 3212
heart, and he would not let them g Ex 10:27 7971
he will let you g hence Ex 11:1 7971
when he shall let you g, he shall Ex 11:1 7971
About midnight will I g out into Ex 11:4 3318
and after that I will g out Ex 11:8 3318
of Israel g out of his land Ex 11:10 7971
none of you shall g out at the Ex 12:22 3318
and g, serve the LORD, as ye have Ex 12:31 3212
Pharaoh would hardly let us g Ex 13:15 7971
when Pharaoh had let the people g Ex 13:17 7971
to g by day and night Ex 13:21 3212
have let Israel g from serving us Ex 14:5 7971
of Israel, that they g forward Ex 14:15 5265
the children of Israel shall g on Ex 14:16 935
the LORD caused the sea to g back Ex 14:21 3212
and the people shall g out Ex 16:4 3318
let no man g out of his place on Ex 16:29 3318
G on before the people, and take Ex 17:5 5674
river, take in thine hand, and g Ex 17:5 1980
men, and g out, fight with Amalek Ex 17:9 3318
also g to their place in peace Ex 18:23 935
G unto the people, and sanctify Ex 19:10 3212
that ye g not up into the mount, Ex 19:12 5927
G down, charge the people, lest Ex 19:21 3381
Neither shalt thou g up by steps Ex 20:26 5927
he shall g out free for nothing Ex 21:2 3318
he shall g out by himself Ex 21:3 3318
his wife shall g out with him Ex 21:3 3318
he shall g out by himself Ex 21:4 3318
I will not g out free Ex 21:5 3318
she shall not g out as the Ex 21:7 3318
then shall she g out free without Ex 21:11 3318
he shall let him g free for his Ex 21:26 7971
he shall let him g free for his Ex 21:27 7971

mine Angel shall g before thee Ex 23:23 3212
shall the people g up with him Ex 24:2 5927
When they g into the tabernacle Ex 30:20 935
us gods, which shall g before us Ex 32:1 3212
And the LORD said unto Moses, G Ex 32:7 3212
us gods, which shall g before us Ex 32:23 3212
g in and out from gate to gate Ex 32:27 5674
now I will g up unto the LORD Ex 32:30 5927
Therefore now g, lead the people Ex 32:34 3212
mine Angel shall g before thee Ex 32:34 3212
g up hence, thou and the people Ex 33:1 5927
for I will not g up in the midst Ex 33:3 5927
My presence shall g with thee Ex 33:14 3212
If thy presence g not with me Ex 33:15 1980
my Lord, I pray thee, g among us Ex 34:9 3212
they g a whoring after their gods Ex 34:15
their daughters g a whoring after Ex 34:16
make thy sons g a whoring after Ex 34:16
when thou shalt g up to appear Ex 34:24 5927
it shall never g out Lev 6:13 3518
ye shall not g out of the door of Lev 8:33 3318
G unto the altar, and offer thy Lev 9:7 7126
ye shall not g out from the door Lev 10:7 3318
when ye g into the tabernacle of Lev 10:9 935
of beasts that g on all four Lev 11:27 1980
the priest shall g forth out of Lev 14:3 3318
before the priest g into it to Lev 14:36 935
shall g in to see the house Lev 14:36 935
Then the priest shall g out of Lev 14:38 3318
But he shall let g the living Lev 14:53 7971
seed of copulation g out from him Lev 15:16 3318
to let him g for a scapegoat into Lev 16:10 7971
he shall g out unto the altar Lev 16:18 3318
he shall let g the goat in the Lev 16:22 7971
he that let g the goat for the Lev 16:26 7971
Thou shalt not g up and down as a Lev 19:16 3212
all that g a whoring after him, Lev 20:5
to g a whoring after them, I will Lev 20:6
Neither shall he g in to any dead Lev 21:11 935
Neither shall he g out of the Lev 21:12 3318
he shall not g in unto the vail Lev 21:23 935
and in the jubile it shall g out Lev 25:28 3318
it shall not g out in the jubile Lev 25:30 3318
they shall g out in the jubile Lev 25:31 3318
shall g out in the year of jubile Lev 25:33 3318
then he shall g out in the year Lev 25:54 3318
the sword g through your land Lev 26:6 5674
your yoke, and made you g upright Lev 26:13 3212
all that are able to g forth to Num 1:3 3318
that were able to g forth to war Num 1:20 3318
that were able to g forth to war Num 1:22 3318
that were able to g forth to war Num 1:24 3318
that were able to g forth to war Num 1:26 3318
that were able to g forth to war Num 1:28 3318
that were able to g forth to war Num 1:30 3318
that were able to g forth to war Num 1:32 3318
that were able to g forth to war Num 1:34 3318
that were able to g forth to war Num 1:36 3318
that were able to g forth to war Num 1:38 3318
that were able to g forth to war Num 1:40 3318
that were able to g forth to war Num 1:42 3318
all that were able to g forth to Num 1:45 3318
they shall g forward in the third Num 2:24 5265
They shall g hindmost with their Num 2:31 5265
Aaron and his sons shall g in Num 4:19 935
But they shall not g in to see Num 4:20 935
them, If any man's wife g aside Num 5:12 7847
the curse shall g into thy bowels Num 5:22 935
g in to do the service of the Num 8:15 935
upward they shall g in to wait Num 8:24 935
on the east parts shall g forward Num 10:5 5265
if ye g to war in your land Num 10:9 935
And he said unto him, I will not g Num 10:30 3212
And it shall be, if thou g with us Num 10:32 3212
and g up into the mountain Num 13:17 5927
Let us g up at once, and possess Num 13:30 5927
We be not able to g up against Num 13:31 5927
will g up unto the place which Num 14:40 5927
G not up, for the LORD is not Num 14:42 5927
to g up unto the hill top Num 14:44 5927
after which ye use to g a whoring Num 15:39
they g down quick into the pit Num 16:30 3381
g quickly unto the congregation, Num 16:46 3212
we will g by the king's high way, Num 20:17 3212
We will g by the high way Num 20:19 5927
thing else, g through on my feet Num 20:19 5674
he said, Thou shalt not g through Num 20:20 5674
but we will g along by the king's Num 21:22 3212
Thou shalt not g with them Num 22:12 3212
to give me leave to g with you Num 22:13 1980
I cannot g beyond the word of the Num 22:18 5674
thee, rise up, and g with them Num 22:20 3212
said unto Balaam, G with the men Num 22:35 3212
thy burnt offering, and I will g Num 23:3 3212
G again unto Balak, and say thus Num 23:16 7725
I cannot g beyond the commandment Num 24:13 5674
now, behold, I g unto my people Num 24:14 1980
are able to g to war in Israel Num 26:2 3318
Which may g out before them, and Num 27:17 3318
which may g in before them, and Num 27:17 935
at his word shall they g out Num 27:21 3318
let them g against the Midianites Num 31:3 1961
shall make it g through the fire Num 31:23 5674
ye shall make g through the water Num 31:23 5674
Shall your brethren g to war Num 32:6 935
that they should not g into the Num 32:9 935
But we ourselves will g ready Num 32:17
if ye will g armed before the Num 32:20
will g all of you armed over Num 32:21 5674
shall g on to Hazar-addar, and Num 34:4 3318
the border shall g on to Ziphron Num 34:9 3318
the coast shall g down from Num 34:11 3381
the border shall g down to Jordan Num 34:12 3381
g to the mount of the Amorites, Deut 1:7 935
g in and possess the land which Deut 1:8 935
g up and possess it, as the LORD Deut 1:21 5927
again by what way we must g up Deut 1:22 5927
Notwithstanding ye would not g up Deut 1:26 5927
Whither shall we g up Deut 1:28 5927
shew you by what way ye should g Deut 1:33 3212
Thou also shalt not g in thither Deut 1:37 935
thee, he shall g in thither Deut 1:38 935
and evil, they shall g in thither Deut 1:39 935
against the LORD, we will g up Deut 1:41 5927
were ready to g up into the hill Deut 1:41 5927
them, G not up, neither fight Deut 1:42 5927
I will g along by the high way, I Deut 2:27 3212
I pray thee, let me g over Deut 3:25 5674
thou shalt not g over this Jordan Deut 3:27 5674
for he shall g over before this Deut 3:28 5674
g in and possess the land which Deut 4:1 935
land whither ye g to possess it Deut 4:5 935
whither ye g over to possess it Deut 4:14 5674
that I should not g over Jordan Deut 4:21 5674
that I should not g in unto that Deut 4:21 935
land, I must not g over Jordan Deut 4:22 5674
but ye shall g over, and possess Deut 4:22 5674
ye g over Jordan to possess it Deut 4:26 5674
Or hath God assayed to g and take Deut 4:34 935
that it may g well with thee, and Deut 4:40
that it may g well with thee, in Deut 5:16
G thou near, and hear all that the Deut 5:27 7126
G say to them, Get you into your Deut 5:30 3212
land whither ye g to possess it Deut 6:1 5674
Ye shall not g after other gods, Deut 6:14 3212
thee, and that thou mayest g in Deut 6:18 935
g in and possess the land which Deut 8:1 935
to g in to possess nations Deut 9:1 935
dost thou g to possess their land Deut 9:5 935
G up and possess the land which I Deut 9:23 5927
the people, that they may g in Deut 10:11 935
g in and possess the land Deut 11:8 935
whither ye g to possess it Deut 11:8 5674
whither ye g to possess it, is a Deut 11:11 935
to g after other gods, which ye Deut 11:28 3212
to g in to possess the land which Deut 11:31 935
But when ye g over Jordan Deut 12:10 5674
that it may g well with thee, and Deut 12:25
g unto the place which the LORD Deut 12:26 935
that it may g well with thee, and Deut 12:28
Let us g after other gods, which Deut 13:2 3212
thee secretly, saying, Let us g Deut 13:6 3212
of their city, saying, Let us g Deut 13:13 3212
shalt g unto the place which the Deut 14:25 1980
shalt let him g free from thee Deut 15:12 7971
shalt not let him g away empty Deut 15:13 7971
I will not g away from thee Deut 15:16 3318
the morning, and g unto thy tents Deut 16:7 1980
that it may g well with thee Deut 19:13
but life shall g for life Deut 19:21
let him g and return to his house, Deut 20:5 3212
let him also g and return unto his Deut 20:6 3212
let him g and return unto his Deut 20:7 3212
let him g and return unto his Deut 20:8 3212
that thou shalt g in unto her Deut 21:13 935
shalt let her g whither she will Deut 21:14 7971
ox or his sheep g astray, and hide Deut 22:1
shalt in any wise let the dam g Deut 22:7 7971
g in unto her, and hate her, Deut 22:13 935
then shall he g abroad out of the Deut 23:10 3318
whither thou shalt g forth abroad Deut 23:12 3318
out of his house, she may g Deut 24:2 1980
wife, he shall not g out to war Deut 24:5 3318
thou shalt not g into his house Deut 24:10 935
shall the sun g down upon it Deut 24:15 935
thou shalt not g again to fetch Deut 24:19 7725
thou shalt not g over the boughs Deut 24:20
brother shall g in unto her Deut 25:5 935
then let his brother's wife g up Deut 25:7 5927
shalt g unto the place which the Deut 26:2 1980
thou shalt g unto the priest that Deut 26:3 935
that thou mayest g in unto the Deut 27:3 935
thou shalt not g aside from any Deut 28:14 5493
to g after other gods to serve Deut 28:14 3212
thou shalt g out one way against Deut 28:25 3318
for they shall g into captivity Deut 28:41 3212
day from the LORD our God, to g Deut 29:18 3212
Who shall g up for us to heaven, Deut 30:12 5927
Who shall g over the sea for us, Deut 30:13 5674
over Jordan to g to possess it Deut 30:18 935
I can no more g out and come in Deut 31:2 3318
Thou shalt not g over this Jordan Deut 31:2 5674
he will g over before thee, and he Deut 31:3 5674
he shall g over before thee, as Deut 31:3 5674
he it is that doth g with thee Deut 31:6 1980
for thou must g with this people Deut 31:7 935
he it is that doth g before thee Deut 31:8 1980
ye g over Jordan to possess it Deut 31:13 5674
g a whoring after the gods of the Deut 31:16
whither they g to be among them, Deut 31:16 935
imagination which they g about Deut 31:21 6213
whither ye g over Jordan to Deut 32:47 5674
but thou shalt not g thither unto Deut 32:52 935
but thou shalt not g over thither Deut 34:4 5674
g over this Jordan, thou, and all Josh 1:2 5674
to g in to possess the land, Josh 1:11 935
thou sendest us, we will g Josh 1:16 3212
G view the land, even Jericho Josh 2:1 3212
and afterward may ye g your way Josh 2:16 3212
that whosoever shall g out of the Josh 2:19 3318
from your place, and g after it Josh 3:3 1980
know the way by which ye must g Josh 3:4 3212
g round about the city once Josh 6:3 5362
G into the harlot's house, and Josh 6:22 935
saying, G up and view the country Josh 7:2 5927
him, Let not all the people g up Josh 7:3 5927
two or three thousand men g up Josh 7:3 5927
with thee, and arise, g up to Ai Josh 8:1 5927
people of war, to g up against Ai Josh 8:3 5927
g not very far from the city, but Josh 8:4 7368
g to meet them, and say unto them, Josh 9:11 3212
day we came forth to g unto you Josh 9:12 3212
hasted not to g down about a Josh 10:13 935
now, for war, both to g out Josh 14:11 3318
ye slack to g to possess the land Josh 18:3 935
g through the land, and describe Josh 18:4 1980
to describe the land, saying, G Josh 18:8 3212
to g unto the country of Gilead, Josh 22:9 3212
to g up to war against them Josh 22:12 5927
did not intend to g up against Josh 22:33 5927
Else if ye do in any wise g back Josh 23:12 7725
g in unto them, and they to you Josh 23:12 935
Who shall g up for us against the Judg 1:1 5927
the LORD said, Judah shall g up Judg 1:2 5927
I likewise will g with thee into Judg 1:3 1980
but they let g the man and all his Judg 1:25 7971
I made you to g up out of Egypt, Judg 2:1 5927
when Joshua had let the people g Judg 2:6 7971
of Israel commanded, saying, G Judg 4:6 3212
unto her, If thou wilt g with me Judg 4:8 3212
then I will g Judg 4:8 1982
but if thou wilt not g with me Judg 4:8 3212
then I will not g Judg 4:8 3212
said, I will surely g with thee Judg 4:9 3212
of the LORD g down to the gates Judg 5:11 3381
G in this thy might, and thou Judg 6:14 3212
Now therefore g to, proclaim in Judg 7:3 4994
unto thee, This shall g with thee Judg 7:4 3212
the same shall g with thee Judg 7:4 3212
thee, This shall not g with thee Judg 7:4 3212
the same shall not g Judg 7:4 3212
people g every man unto his place Judg 7:7 3212
But if thou fear to g down Judg 7:10 3381
g thou with Phurah thy servant Judg 7:10 3381
to g down unto the host Judg 7:11 3381
g to be promoted over the trees Judg 9:9 1980
g to be promoted over the trees Judg 9:11 1980
g to be promoted over the trees Judg 9:13 1980
g out, I pray now, and fight with Judg 9:38 3318
G and cry unto the gods which ye Judg 10:14 3212
now, that thou mayest g with us Judg 11:8 1980
unto the LORD, and I cannot g back Judg 11:35 7725
alone two months, that I may g up Judg 11:37 3212
And he said, G Judg 11:38 3212
didst not call us to g with thee Judg 12:1 3212
were escaped said, Let me g over Judg 12:5 5674
I will g in to my wife into the Judg 15:1 935
would not suffer him to g in Judg 15:1 935
he let them g into the standing Judg 15:5 7971
then my strength will g from me Judg 16:17 5493
I will g out as at other times Judg 16:20 3318
I g to sojourn where I may find a Judg 17:9 1980
and they said unto them, G Judg 18:2 3212
which we g shall be prosperous Judg 18:5 1980
priest said unto them, G in peace Judg 18:6 3212
the LORD is your way wherein ye g Judg 18:6 3212
that we may g up against them Judg 18:9 5927
be not slothful to g, and to enter Judg 18:9 3212
When ye g, ye shall come unto a Judg 18:10 935
g with us, and be to us a father Judg 18:19 3212
of bread, and afterward g your way Judg 19:5 3212
your way, that thou mayest g home Judg 19:9 1980
turned aside thither, to g in Judg 19:15 935
began to spring, they let her g Judg 19:25 7971
house, and went out to g his way Judg 19:27 3212
will not any of us g to his tent Judg 20:8 3212
we will g up by lot against it Judg 20:9 3212
to g out to battle against the Judg 20:14 3318
Which of us shall g up first to Judg 20:18 5927
LORD said, Judah shall g up first Judg 20:18 3212
Shall I g up again to battle Judg 20:23 5066
the LORD said, G up against him Judg 20:23 5927
Shall I yet again g out to battle Judg 20:28 3318
And the LORD said, G up Judg 20:28 5927
and commanded them, saying, G Judg 21:10 3212
children of Benjamin, saying, G Judg 21:20 3212
g to the land of Benjamin Judg 21:21 1980
unto her two daughters in law, G Ruth 1:8 3212
why will ye g with me Ruth 1:11 3212
again, my daughters, g your way Ruth 1:12 3212
for whither thou goest, I will g Ruth 1:16 3212
stedfastly minded to g with her Ruth 1:18 3212
Let me now g to the field, and Ruth 2:2 3212
And she said unto her, G, my Ruth 2:2 3212
G not to glean in another field, Ruth 2:8 3212
neither g from hence, but abide Ruth 2:8 5674
do reap, and g thou after them Ruth 2:9 1980
g unto the vessels, and drink of Ruth 2:9 1980
that thou g out with his maidens, Ruth 2:22 3318
he shall lie, and thou shalt g in Ruth 3:4 935
G not empty unto thy mother in Ruth 3:17 935
Eli answered and said, G in peace 1Sa 1:17 3212
I will not g up until the child 1Sa 1:22
Therefore Eli said unto Samuel, G 1Sa 3:9 3212
let it g again to his own place, 1Sa 5:11 7725
did they not let the people g 1Sa 6:6 7971
and send it away, that it may g 1Sa 6:8 1980
and to whom shall he g up from us 1Sa 6:20 5927
g out before us, and fight our 1Sa 8:20 3318
G ye every man unto his city 1Sa 8:22 3212
thee, and arise, g seek the asses 1Sa 9:3 3212
now let us g thither 1Sa 9:6 3212
shew us our way that we should g 1Sa 9:6 1980
his servant, But, behold, if we g 1Sa 9:7 3212
Come, and let us g to the seer 1Sa 9:9 3212
come, let us g 1Sa 9:10 3212
before he g up to the high place 1Sa 9:13 5927
for to g up to the high place 1Sa 9:14 5927
g up before me unto the high 1Sa 9:19 5927
and to morrow I will let thee g 1Sa 9:19 7971
Then shalt thou g on forward from 1Sa 10:3 2498
thou shalt g down before me to 1Sa 10:8 3381

turned his back to g from Samuel 1Sa 10:9 3212
let us g to Gilgal, and renew the 1Sa 11:14 3212
should ye g after vain things 1Sa 12:21 3212
let us g over to the Philistines' 1Sa 14:1 5674
to g over unto the Philistines' 1Sa 14:4 5674
let us g over unto the garrison 1Sa 14:6 5674
place, and will not g up unto them 1Sa 14:9 5927
then we will g up 1Sa 14:10 5927
said, Let us g down after the 1Sa 14:36 3381
of God, Shall I g down after the 1Sa 14:37 3381
Now g and smite Amalek, and utterly 1Sa 15:3 3212
And Saul said unto the Kenites, G 1Sa 15:6 3212
thee on a journey, and said, G 1Sa 15:18 3212
as Samuel turned about to g away 1Sa 15:27 3212
fill thine horn with oil, and g 1Sa 16:1 3212
And Samuel said, How can I g 1Sa 16:2 3212
thy servant will g and fight with 1Sa 17:32 3212
Thou art not able to g against 1Sa 17:33 3212
And Saul said unto David, G 1Sa 17:37 3212
his armour, and he assayed to g 1Sa 17:39 3212
unto Saul, I cannot g with these 1Sa 17:39 3212
when Saul saw David g forth 1Sa 17:55 3318
would let him g no more home to 1Sa 18:2 7725
And I will g out and stand beside 1Sa 19:3 3318
Saul, He said unto me, Let me g 1Sa 19:17 7971
but let me g, that I may hide 1Sa 20:5 7971
let us g out into the field 1Sa 20:11 3318
away, that thou mayest g in peace 1Sa 20:13 1980
then thou shalt g down quickly 1Sa 20:19 3381
I will send a lad, saying, G 1Sa 20:21 3212
g thy way: for the LORD hath 1Sa 20:22 3212
leave of me to g to Beth-lehem 1Sa 20:28
And he said, Let me g, I pray thee 1Sa 20:29 7971
unto his lad, and said unto him, G 1Sa 20:40 3212
G in peace, forasmuch as we have 1Sa 20:42 3212
of the LORD, saying, Shall I g 1Sa 23:2 3212
And the LORD said unto David, G 1Sa 23:2 3212
and said, Arise, g down to Keilah 1Sa 23:4 3381
to g down to Keilah, to besiege 1Sa 23:8 3381
went whithersoever they could g 1Sa 23:13 1980
and he forbare to g forth 1Sa 23:13 3318
G, I pray you, prepare yet, and 1Sa 23:22 3212
certainty, and I will g with you 1Sa 23:23 1980
will he let him g well away 1Sa 24:19 7971
g to Nabal, and greet him in my 1Sa 25:5 935
unto her servants, G on before me 1Sa 25:19 5674
G up in peace to thine house 1Sa 25:35 5927
Who will g down with me to Saul 1Sa 26:6 3381
said, I will g down with thee 1Sa 26:6 3381
the cruse of water, and let us g 1Sa 26:11 3212
of the LORD, saying, G, serve 1Sa 26:19 3212
that thou shalt g out with me to 1Sa 28:1 3318
spirit, that I may g to her 1Sa 28:7 3212
that he may g again to his place 1Sa 29:4 7725
let him not g down with us to 1Sa 29:4 3381
g in peace, that thou displease 1Sa 29:7 3212
that I may not g fight against 1Sa 29:8 3212
He shall not g up with us to the 1Sa 29:9 5927
could not g over the brook Besor 1Sa 30:10 5674
and said, G near, and fall upon him 2Sa 1:15 5066
Shall I g up into any of the 2Sa 2:1 5927
And the LORD said unto him, G up 2Sa 2:1 5927
David said, Whither shall I g up 2Sa 2:1 5927
Then said Abner unto him, G 2Sa 3:16 3212
unto David, I will arise and g 2Sa 3:21 3212
Shall I g up to the Philistines 2Sa 5:19 5927
And the LORD said unto David, G up 2Sa 5:19 5927
he said, Thou shalt not g up 2Sa 5:23 5927
shall the LORD g out before thee 2Sa 5:24 3318
And Nathan said to the king, G 2Sa 7:3 3212
G and tell my servant David, Thus 2Sa 7:5 3212
time when kings g forth to battle 2Sa 11:1 3318
G down to thy house, and wash thy 2Sa 11:8 3381
thou not g down unto thine house 2Sa 11:10 3381
shall I then g into mine house 2Sa 11:11 935
I shall g to him, but he shall 2Sa 12:23 1980
G now to thy brother Amnon's 2Sa 13:7 3212
shall I cause my shame to g 2Sa 13:13 3212
his servants g with thy servant 2Sa 13:24 3212
Nay, my son, let us not all now g 2Sa 13:25 3212
howbeit he would not g, but 2Sa 13:25 3212
let my brother Amnon g with us 2Sa 13:26 3212
him, Why should he g with thee 2Sa 13:26 3212
and all the king's sons g with him 2Sa 13:27 7971
longed to g forth unto Absalom 2Sa 13:39 3318
G to thine house, and I will give 2Sa 14:8 3212
g therefore, bring the young man 2Sa 14:21 3212
g and set it on fire 2Sa 14:30 3212
the king, I pray thee, let me g 2Sa 15:7 3212
king said unto him, G in peace 2Sa 15:9 3212
should I this day make thee g up 2Sa 15:20 3212
seeing I g whither I may, return 2Sa 15:20 1980
And David said to Ittai, G 2Sa 15:22 3212
let me g over, I pray thee, and 2Sa 16:9 5674
G in unto thy father's concubines 2Sa 16:21 935
that thou g to battle in thine 2Sa 17:11 1980
I will surely g forth with you 2Sa 18:2 3318
answered, Thou shalt not g forth 2Sa 18:3 3318
G tell the king what thou hast 2Sa 18:21 3212
g forth, and speak comfortably 2Sa 19:7 3318
if thou g not forth, there will 2Sa 19:7 3318
to g to meet the king, to conduct 2Sa 19:15 3212
g down to meet my lord the king 2Sa 19:20 3381
ride thereon, and g to the king 2Sa 19:26 3212
that I should g up with the king 2Sa 19:34 5927
Thy servant will g a little way 2Sa 19:36 5674
let him g over with my lord the 2Sa 19:37 5674
Chimham shall g over with me 2Sa 19:38 5674
for David, let him g after Joab 2Sa 20:11
Thou shalt g no more out with us 2Sa 21:17 3318
David against them to say, G 2Sa 24:1 3212
G now through all the tribes of 2Sa 24:2 7751
G and say unto David, Thus saith 2Sa 24:12 1980
G up, rear an altar unto the LORD 2Sa 24:18 5927

G and get thee in unto king David, 1Kin 1:13 3212
said unto him, G to thine house 1Kin 1:53 3212
I g the way of all the earth 1Kin 2:2 1980
let not his hoar head g down to 1Kin 2:6 3381
the son of Jehoiada, saying, G 1Kin 2:29 3212
g not forth thence any whither 1Kin 2:36 3318
know not how to g out or come in 1Kin 3:7 3318
If thy people g out to battle 1Kin 8:44 3318
I have set before you, but g 1Kin 9:6 1980
Israel, Ye shall not g in to them 1Kin 11:2 935
he should not g after other gods 1Kin 11:10 3212
with him, to g into Egypt 1Kin 11:17 935
that I may g to mine own country 1Kin 11:21 3212
thou seekest to g to thine own 1Kin 11:22 3212
howbeit let me g in any wise 1Kin 11:22 7971
saith the LORD, Ye shall not g up 1Kin 12:24 5927
If this people g up to do 1Kin 12:27 5927
g again to Rehoboam king of Judah 1Kin 12:27
much for you to g up to Jerusalem 1Kin 12:28 5927
I will not g in with thee, 1Kin 13:8 935
with thee, nor g in with thee 1Kin 13:16 935
nor turn again to g by the way 1Kin 13:17 3212
and a cruse of honey, and g to him 1Kin 14:3 935
G, tell Jeroboam, Thus saith the 1Kin 14:7 3212
g out or come in to Asa king of 1Kin 15:17 3318
two sticks, that I may g in 1Kin 17:12 935
g and do as thou hast said 1Kin 17:13 935
in the third year, saying, G 1Kin 18:1 3212
G into the land, unto all 1Kin 18:5 3212
g, tell thy lord, Behold, Elijah 1Kin 18:8 3212
And now thou sayest, G, tell thy 1Kin 18:11 3212
And now thou sayest, G, tell thy 1Kin 18:14 3212
G up now, look toward the sea 1Kin 18:43 5927
And he said, G again seven times 1Kin 18:43 7725
G up, say unto Ahab, Prepare thy 1Kin 18:44 5927
G forth, and stand upon the mount 1Kin 19:11 3318
And the LORD said unto him, G 1Kin 19:15 3212
And he said unto him, G back again 1Kin 19:20 3212
of Israel, and said unto him, G 1Kin 20:22 3212
g out to the king of Israel 1Kin 20:31 3318
Then he said, G ye, bring him 1Kin 20:33 935
Because thou hast let g out of 1Kin 20:42 7971
thy life shall g for his life 1Kin 20:42 1961
that Ahab rose up to g down to 1Kin 21:16 3381
g down to meet Ahab king of 1Kin 21:18 3381
Wilt thou g with me to battle to 1Kin 22:4 3212
Shall I g against Ramoth-gilead 1Kin 22:6 3212
And they said, G up 1Kin 22:6 5927
G up to Ramoth-gilead, and prosper 1Kin 22:12 5927
shall we g against Ramoth-gilead 1Kin 22:15 3212
And he answered him, G, and prosper 1Kin 22:15 5927
persuade Ahab, that he may g up 1Kin 22:20 5927
And he said, I will g forth 1Kin 22:22 3318
g forth, and do so 1Kin 22:22 3318
when thou shalt g into an inner 1Kin 22:25 935
Tharshish to g to Ophir for gold 1Kin 22:48 3212
Let my servants g with thy 1Kin 22:49 3212
messengers, and said unto them, G 2Kin 1:2 3212
g up to meet the messengers of 2Kin 1:3 5927
Israel, that ye g to enquire of 2Kin 1:3 1980
up to meet us, and said unto us, G 2Kin 1:6 3212
said unto Elijah, G down with him 2Kin 1:15 3381
let them g, we pray thee, and seek 2Kin 2:16 3212
Did I not say unto you, G not 2Kin 2:18 3212
unto him, G up, thou bald head 2Kin 2:23 5927
g up, thou bald head 2Kin 2:23 5927
wilt thou g with me against Moab 2Kin 3:7 3212
And he said, I will g up 2Kin 3:7 5927
he said, Which way shall we g up 2Kin 3:8 5927
Then he said, G, borrow thee 2Kin 4:3 3212
And he said, G, sell the oil, and 2Kin 4:7 3212
wilt thou g to him to day 2Kin 4:23 1980
her servant, Drive, and g forward 2Kin 4:24 3212
staff in thine hand, and g thy way 2Kin 4:29 3212
G to, g, and I will send a letter 2Kin 5:5 3212
the king of Syria said, G to, g 2Kin 5:5 935
a messenger unto him, saying, G 2Kin 5:10 1980
And he said unto him, G in peace 2Kin 5:19 3212
and he let the men g, and they 2Kin 5:24 7971
Let us g, we pray thee, unto 2Kin 6:2 3212
And he answered, G ye 2Kin 6:2 3212
pray thee, and g with thy servants 2Kin 6:3 3212
And he answered, I will g 2Kin 6:3 3212
And he said, G and spy where he is, 2Kin 6:13 3212
and drink, and g to their master 2Kin 6:22 3212
to g unto the camp of the Syrians 2Kin 7:5 935
now therefore come, that we may g 2Kin 7:9 935
host of the Syrians, saying, G 2Kin 7:14 3212
g thou and thine household, and 2Kin 8:1 3212
a present in thine hand, and g 2Kin 8:8 3212
And Elisha said unto him, G 2Kin 8:10 3212
thine hand, and g to Ramoth-gilead 2Kin 9:1 3212
g in, and make him arise up from 2Kin 9:2 935
then let none g forth nor escape 2Kin 9:15 3318
city to g to tell it in Jezreel 2Kin 9:15 3212
he did eat and drink, and said, G 2Kin 9:34 6485
we g down to salute the children 2Kin 10:13 3381
escape, he that letteth him g 2Kin 10:24
the captains, G in, and slay them 2Kin 10:25 935
you that g forth on the sabbath 2Kin 11:7 3318
that should g out on the sabbath 2Kin 11:9 3318
set his face to g up to Jerusalem 2Kin 12:17 5927
and let them g and dwell there, and 2Kin 17:27 3212
it will g into his hand, and 2Kin 18:21 935
G up against this land, and 2Kin 18:25 5927
Jerusalem shall g forth a remnant 2Kin 19:31 3318
on the third day thou shalt g up 2Kin 20:5 5927
that I shall g up into the house 2Kin 20:8 5927
shall the shadow g forward ten 2Kin 20:9 1980
degrees, or g back ten degrees 2Kin 20:9 7725
the shadow to g down ten degrees 2Kin 20:10 5186
G up to Hilkiah the high priest, 2Kin 22:4 5927
G ye, enquire of the LORD for me, 2Kin 22:13 3212
fit to g out for war and battle 1Chr 7:11 3318

saying, Shall I g up against the 1Chr 14:10 5927
And the LORD said unto him, G up 1Chr 14:10 5927
unto him, G not up after them 1Chr 14:14 5927
then thou shalt g out to battle 1Chr 14:15 3318
G and tell David my servant, Thus 1Chr 17:4 3212
must g to be with thy fathers 1Chr 17:11 3212
time that kings g out to battle 1Chr 20:1 3318
and to the rulers of the people, G 1Chr 21:2 3212
G and tell David, saying, Thus 1Chr 21:10 3212
to David, that David should g up 1Chr 21:18 5927
But David could not g before it 1Chr 21:30 3212
and knowledge, that I may g out 2Chr 1:10 3318
If thy people g out to war 2Chr 6:34 3318
I have set before you, and shall g 2Chr 7:19 1980
saith the LORD, Ye shall not g up 2Chr 11:4 5927
in thy name we g against this 2Chr 14:11 935
g out or come in to Asa king of 2Chr 16:1 3318
g, break thy league with Baasha 2Chr 16:3 3212
persuaded him to g up with him to 2Chr 18:2 5927
of Judah, Wilt thou g with me to 2Chr 18:3 3212
Shall we g to Ramoth-gilead to 2Chr 18:5 3212
And they said, G up 2Chr 18:5 5927
G up to Ramoth-gilead, and prosper 2Chr 18:11 5927
shall we g to Ramoth-gilead to 2Chr 18:14 3212
G ye up, and prosper, and they 2Chr 18:14 5927
king of Israel, that he may g up 2Chr 18:19 5927
And he said, I will g out, and be a 2Chr 18:21 3318
g out, and do even so 2Chr 18:21 3318
g into an inner chamber to hide 2Chr 18:24 935
myself, and will g to the battle 2Chr 18:29 935
To morrow g ye down against them 2Chr 20:16 3381
to morrow g out against them 2Chr 20:17 3318
to g again to Jerusalem with joy 2Chr 20:27 7725
to make ships to g to Tarshish 2Chr 20:36 3212
were not able to g to Tarshish 2Chr 20:37 3212
of Jerusalem to g a whoring 2Chr 21:13
they shall g in, for they are 2Chr 23:6 935
that were to g out on the sabbath 2Chr 23:8 3318
G out unto the cities of Judah, 2Chr 24:5 3318
able to g forth to war, that 2Chr 25:5 3318
the army of Israel g with thee 2Chr 25:7 935
But if thou wilt g, do it, be 2Chr 25:8 935
out of Ephraim, to g home again 2Chr 25:10 3212
should not g with him to battle 2Chr 25:13 3212
g out of the sanctuary 2Chr 26:18 3318
yea, himself hasted also to g out 2Chr 26:20 3318
G, enquire of the LORD for me, and 2Chr 34:21 3212
God be with him, and let him g up 2Chr 36:23 5927
let him g up to Jerusalem, which Ezr 1:3 5927
to g up to build the house of the Ezr 1:5 5927
unto him, Take these vessels, g Ezr 5:15 236
began he to g up from Babylon Ezr 7:9 4609
g up to Jerusalem, with thee Ezr 7:13 1946
Israel chief men to g up with me Ezr 7:28 5927
first month, to g unto Jerusalem Ezr 8:31 3212
unto which ye g to possess it Ezr 9:11 935
unto the stairs that g down from Neh 3:15 3381
which they build, if a fox g up Neh 4:3 5927
would g into the temple to save Neh 6:11 935
I will not g in Neh 6:11 935
G your way, eat the fat, and drink Neh 8:10 3212
G forth unto the mount, and fetch Neh 8:15 3318
in the way wherein they should g Neh 9:12 3212
them that they should g in to Neh 9:15 935
and the way wherein they should g Neh 9:19 3212
they should g in to possess it Neh 9:23 935
let there g a royal commandment Est 1:19 3318
come to g in to king Ahasuerus Est 2:12 935
to g with her out of the house of Est 2:13 935
was come to g in unto the king, Est 2:15 935
she should g in unto the king Est 4:8 935
G, gather together all the Jews Est 4:16 3212
so will I g in unto the king, Est 4:16 935
then g thou in merrily with the Est 5:14 935
which is in them g away Job 4:21 5265
they g to nothing, and perish Job 6:18 5927
Before I g whence I shall not Job 10:21 3212
such words g out of thy mouth Job 15:13 3318
of his mouth shall he g away Job 15:30 5493
then I shall g the way whence I Job 16:22 1980
They shall g down to the bars of Job 17:16 3381
it shall g ill with him that is Job 20:26
in a moment g down to the grave Job 21:13 5181
not asked them that g by the way Job 21:29 5674
I g forward, but he is not there Job 23:8 1980
g they forth to their work Job 24:5 3318
They cause him to g naked without Job 24:10 1980
I hold fast, and will not let it g Job 27:6 7503
a prince would I g near unto him Job 31:37 7126
Then the beasts g into dens Job 37:8 935
send lightnings, that they may g Job 38:35 3212
they g forth, and return not unto Job 39:4 3318
Out of his mouth g burning lamps Job 41:19 1980
g to my servant Job, and offer up Job 42:8 3212
all they that g down to the dust Ps 22:29 3381
persons, neither will I g in with Ps 26:4 935
them that g down into the pit Ps 28:1 3381
I should not g down to the pit Ps 30:3 3381
blood, when I g down to the pit Ps 30:9 3381
in the way which thou shalt g Ps 32:8 3212
I g mourning all the day long Ps 38:6 1980
strength, before I g hence Ps 39:13 3212
why g I mourning because of the Ps 42:9 3212
Why g I mourning because of the Ps 43:2 1980
Then will I g unto the altar of Ps 43:4 935
about Zion, and g round about her Ps 48:12 5362
He shall g to the generation of Ps 49:19 935
night they g about it upon the Ps 55:10 5437
let them g down quick into hell Ps 55:15 3381
they g astray as soon as they be Ps 58:3 8582
a dog, and g round about the city Ps 59:6 5437
a dog, and g round about the city Ps 59:14 5437
which didst not g out with our Ps 60:10 3318
shall g into the lower parts of Ps 63:9 935

I will g into thy house with	Ps 66:13	935
I will g in the strength of the	Ps 71:16	935
them that g a whoring from thee	Ps 73:27	
own people to g forth like sheep	Ps 78:52	5265
So will not we g back from thee	Ps 80:18	5472
They g from strength to strength,	Ps 84:7	3212
Righteousness shall g before him	Ps 85:13	1980
them that g down into the pit	Ps 88:4	3381
truth shall g before thy face	Ps 89:14	6923
They g up by the mountains	Ps 104:8	5927
they g down by the valleys unto	Ps 104:8	3381
There g the ships	Ps 104:26	1980
of the people, and let him g free	Ps 105:20	
that they might g to a city of	Ps 107:7	3212
They that g down to the sea in	Ps 107:23	3381
they g down again to the depths	Ps 107:26	3381
O God, g forth with our hosts	Ps 108:11	3318
neither any that g down into	Ps 115:17	3381
I will g into them, and I will	Ps 118:19	935
Make me to g in the path of thy	Ps 119:35	1869
Let us g into the house of the	Ps 122:1	3212
Whither the tribes g up, the	Ps 122:4	5927
Neither do they which g by say	Ps 129:8	5674
of my house, nor g up into my bed	Ps 132:3	5927
We will g into his tabernacles	Ps 132:7	935
Whither shall I g from thy spirit	Ps 139:7	3212
them that g down into the pit	Ps 143:7	3381
as those that g down into the pit	Prov 1:12	3381
None that g unto her return again	Prov 2:19	935
Say not unto thy neighbour, G	Prov 3:28	3212
let her not g	Prov 4:13	7503
g not in the way of evil men	Prov 4:14	833
Her feet g down to death	Prov 5:5	3381
of his folly he shall g astray	Prov 5:23	7686
g, humble thyself, and make sure	Prov 6:3	3212
G to the ant, thou sluggard	Prov 6:6	3212
Can one g upon hot coals, and his	Prov 6:28	1980
g not astray in her paths	Prov 7:25	8582
g in the way of understanding	Prov 9:6	833
who g right on their ways	Prov 9:15	
G from the presence of a foolish	Prov 14:7	3212
neither will he g unto the wise	Prov 15:12	3212
they g down into the innermost	Prov 18:8	3381
do his friends g far from him	Prov 19:7	7368
up a child in the way he should g	Prov 22:6	6310
and contention shall g out	Prov 22:10	3318
a furious man thou shalt not g	Prov 22:24	935
they that g to seek mixed wine	Prov 23:30	935
G not forth hastily to strive,	Prov 25:8	3318
they g down into the innermost	Prov 26:22	3381
neither g into thy brother's	Prov 27:10	935
to g astray in an evil way	Prov 28:10	7686
yet g they forth all of them by	Prov 30:27	3318
be three things which g well	Prov 30:29	6806
G to now, I will prove thee with	Eccl 2:1	3212
All g unto one place	Eccl 3:20	1980
shall he return to g as he came	Eccl 5:15	3212
points as he came, so shall he g	Eccl 5:16	3212
do not all g to one place	Eccl 6:6	1980
It is better to g to the house of	Eccl 7:2	3212
than to g to the house of	Eccl 7:2	3212
Be not hasty to g out of his	Eccl 8:3	3212
and after that they g to the dead	Eccl 9:3	
G thy way, eat thy bread with joy	Eccl 9:7	3212
knoweth not how to g to the city	Eccl 10:15	3212
the mourners g about the streets	Eccl 12:5	5437
g thy way forth by the footsteps	Song 1:8	3318
g about the city in the streets,	Song 3:2	5437
The watchmen that g about the	Song 3:3	5437
held him, and would not let him g	Song 3:4	7503
G forth, O ye daughters of Zion,	Song 3:11	3318
sheep which g up from the washing	Song 6:6	5927
I will g up to the palm tree, I	Song 7:8	5927
let us g forth into the field	Song 7:11	3318
And many people shall g and say,	Is 2:3	1980
let us g up to the mountain of	Is 2:3	5927
out of Zion shall g forth the law	Is 2:3	3318
they shall g into the holes of	Is 2:19	935
To g into the clefts of the rocks	Is 2:21	935
walking and mincing as they g	Is 3:16	3212
And now g to	Is 5:5	
their blossom shall g up as dust	Is 5:24	5927
I send, and who will g for us	Is 6:8	3212
And he said, G, and tell this	Is 6:9	3212
G forth now to meet Ahaz, thou,	Is 7:3	3318
Let us g up against Judah, and vex	Is 7:6	5927
waters of Shiloah that g softly	Is 8:6	1980
channels, and g over all his banks	Is 8:7	1980
g over, he shall reach even to	Is 8:8	5674
and make men g over dryshod	Is 11:15	1869
that they may g into the gates of	Is 13:2	935
that g down to the stones of the	Is 14:19	3381
with weeping shall they g it up	Is 15:5	5927
upon the waters, saying, G	Is 18:2	3212
Isaiah the son of Amoz, saying, G	Is 20:2	3212
G up, O Elam	Is 21:2	5927
hath the Lord said unto me, G	Is 21:6	3212
saith the Lord GOD of hosts, G	Is 22:15	3212
g about the city, thou harlot	Is 23:16	5437
I would g through them, I would	Is 27:4	6585
that they might g, and fall	Is 28:13	3212
That walk to g down into Egypt,	Is 30:2	3381
Now g, write it before them in a	Is 30:8	935
Woe to them that g down to Egypt	Is 31:1	3381
wherein shall g no galley with	Is 33:21	3212
smoke thereof shall g up for ever	Is 34:10	5927
ravenous beast shall g up thereon	Is 35:9	5927
it will g into his hand, and	Is 36:6	935
G up against this land, and	Is 36:10	5927
Jerusalem shall g forth a remnant	Is 37:32	3318
G, and say to Hezekiah, Thus saith	Is 38:5	1980
I shall g to the gates of the	Is 38:10	3212
I shall g softly all my years in	Is 38:15	1718
they that g down into the pit	Is 38:18	3381
g up to the house of the LORD	Is 38:22	5927
ye that g down to the sea, and all	Is 42:10	3381
The LORD shall g forth as a	Is 42:13	3318
I will g before thee, and make the	Is 45:2	3212
and he shall let g my captives	Is 45:13	7971
they shall g to confusion	Is 45:16	1980
by the way that thou shouldest g	Is 48:17	3212
G ye forth of Babylon, flee ye	Is 48:20	3318
say to the prisoners, G forth	Is 49:9	3318
thee waste shall g forth of thee	Is 49:17	3318
Bow down, that we may g over	Is 51:23	5674
g ye out from thence, touch no	Is 52:11	3318
g ye out of the midst of her	Is 52:11	3318
For ye shall not g out with haste	Is 52:12	3318
nor g by flight: for the LORD	Is 52:12	3212
for the LORD will g before you	Is 52:12	1980
should no more g over the earth	Is 54:9	5674
For ye shall g out with joy	Is 55:12	3318
and to let the oppressed g free	Is 58:6	7971
righteousness shall g before thee	Is 58:8	1980
Thy sun shall no more g down	Is 60:20	935
thereof g forth as brightness	Is 62:1	3318
G through, g through the gates	Is 62:10	5674
And they shall g forth, and look	Is 66:24	3318
for thou shalt g to all that I	Jer 1:7	3212
G and cry in the ears of Jerusalem	Jer 2:2	1980
strangers, and after them will I g	Jer 2:25	3212
thou shalt g forth from him, and	Jer 2:37	3318
she g from him, and become another	Jer 3:1	1980
G and proclaim these words toward	Jer 3:12	1980
let us g into the defenced cities	Jer 4:5	935
they shall g into thickets, and	Jer 4:29	935
G ye up upon her walls, and	Jer 5:10	5927
arise, and let us g up at noon	Jer 6:4	5927
let us g by night, and let us	Jer 6:5	5927
G not forth into the field, nor	Jer 6:25	3318
But g ye now unto my place which	Jer 7:12	3212
leave my people, and g from them	Jer 9:2	3212
be borne, because they cannot g	Jer 10:5	6805
and inhabitants of Jerusalem g	Jer 11:12	1980
Thus saith the LORD unto me, G	Jer 13:1	1980
g to Euphrates, and hide it there	Jer 13:4	3212
g to Euphrates, and take the	Jer 13:6	3212
If I g forth into the field, then	Jer 14:18	3318
the priest g about into a land	Jer 14:18	5503
of my sight, and let them g forth	Jer 15:1	3318
thee, Whither shall we g forth	Jer 15:2	3318
or who shall g aside to ask how	Jer 15:5	5493
neither g to lament nor bemoan	Jer 16:5	3212
Thou shalt not also g into the	Jer 16:8	935
G and stand in the gate of the	Jer 17:19	1980
in, and by the which they g out	Jer 17:19	3318
g down to the potter's house, and	Jer 18:2	3381
Now therefore g to, speak to the	Jer 18:11	4994
Thus saith the LORD, G and get a	Jer 19:1	1980
g forth unto the valley of the	Jer 19:2	3318
sight of the men that g with thee	Jer 19:10	1980
house shall g into captivity	Jer 20:6	3212
works, that he may g up from us	Jer 21:2	5927
lest my fury g out like fire, and	Jer 21:12	3318
G down to the house of the king	Jer 22:1	3381
G up to Lebanon, and cry	Jer 22:20	5927
thy lovers shall g into captivity	Jer 22:22	3212
g not after other gods to serve	Jer 25:6	3212
evil shall g forth from nation to	Jer 25:32	3318
and at Jerusalem, g not to Babylon	Jer 27:18	935
G and tell Hananiah, saying, Thus	Jer 28:13	1980
ye call upon me, and ye shall g	Jer 29:12	1980
of them, shall g into captivity	Jer 30:16	3212
shalt g forth in the dances of	Jer 31:4	3318
let us g up to Zion unto the LORD	Jer 31:6	5927
How long wilt thou g about	Jer 31:22	2559
they that g forth with flocks	Jer 31:24	5265
the measuring line shall yet g	Jer 31:39	3318
G and speak to Zedekiah king of	Jer 34:2	1980
mouth, and thou shalt g to Babylon	Jer 34:3	935
an Hebrew or an Hebrewess, g free	Jer 34:9	7971
g free, that none should serve	Jer 34:10	7971
then they obeyed, and let them g	Jer 34:10	7971
whom they had let g free	Jer 34:11	7971
the end of seven years let ye g	Jer 34:14	7971
shalt let him g free from thee	Jer 34:14	7971
G unto the house of the	Jer 35:2	1980
let us g to Jerusalem for fear of	Jer 35:11	935
G and tell the men of Judah and the	Jer 35:13	1980
g not after other gods to serve	Jer 35:15	3212
I cannot g into the house of the	Jer 36:5	935
Therefore g thou, and read in the	Jer 36:6	935
said the princes unto Baruch, G	Jer 36:19	3212
to g into the land of Benjamin	Jer 37:12	3212
g forth unto the king of	Jer 38:17	3318
But if thou wilt not g forth to	Jer 38:18	3318
But if thou refuse to g forth	Jer 38:21	3318
G and speak to Ebed-melech the	Jer 39:16	1980
guard had let him g from Ramah	Jer 40:1	7971
for thee to g, thither g	Jer 40:4	3212
G back also to Gedaliah the son	Jer 40:5	7725
or g wheresoever it seemeth	Jer 40:5	3212
seemeth convenient unto thee to g	Jer 40:5	3212
and a reward, and let him g	Jer 40:5	7971
Mizpah secretly, saying, Let me g	Jer 40:15	3212
departed to g over to the	Jer 41:10	5674
to g to enter into Egypt,	Jer 41:17	3212
but we will g into the land of	Jer 42:14	935
into Egypt, and g to sojourn there	Jer 42:15	935
to g into Egypt to sojourn there	Jer 42:17	935
G ye not into Egypt	Jer 42:19	935
the place whither ye desire to g	Jer 42:22	935
G not into Egypt to sojourn there	Jer 43:2	935
he shall g forth from thence in	Jer 43:12	3318
to g into the land of Egypt to	Jer 44:12	935
and he saith, I will g up, and will	Jer 46:8	5927
G up into Gilead, and take balm, O	Jer 46:11	5927
let us g again to our own people,	Jer 46:16	7725
thyself to g into captivity	Jer 46:19	
thereof shall g like a serpent	Jer 46:22	3212
continual weeping shall g up	Jer 48:5	5927
Chemosh shall g forth into	Jer 48:7	3318
their king shall g into captivity	Jer 49:3	3212
shall altogether g unpunished	Jer 49:12	
thou shalt not g unpunished	Jer 49:12	3212
g up to Kedar, and spoil the men	Jer 49:28	5927
they shall g, and seek the LORD	Jer 50:4	3212
have caused them to g astray	Jer 50:6	8582
g forth out of the land of the	Jer 50:8	3318
G up against the land of	Jer 50:21	5927
let them g down to the slaughter	Jer 50:27	3381
they refused to let them g	Jer 50:33	7971
let us g every one into his own	Jer 51:9	3212
g ye out of the midst of her, and	Jer 51:45	3318
sword, g away, stand not still	Jer 51:50	1980
that we cannot g in our streets	Lam 4:18	3212
whither the spirit was to g	Eze 1:12	3212
Whithersoever the spirit was to g	Eze 1:20	3212
thither was their spirit to g	Eze 1:20	3212
g speak unto the house of Israel	Eze 3:1	3212
And he said unto me, Son of man, g	Eze 3:4	3212
And g, get thee to them of the	Eze 3:11	3212
g forth into the plain, and I will	Eze 3:22	3318
spake with me, and said unto me, G	Eze 3:24	935
thou shalt not g out among them	Eze 3:25	3318
which g a whoring after their	Eze 6:9	
that I should g far off from my	Eze 8:6	7368
G in, and behold the wicked	Eze 8:9	935
G through the midst of the city,	Eze 9:4	5674
G ye after him through the city,	Eze 9:5	5674
with the slain: g ye forth	Eze 9:7	3318
G in between the wheels, even	Eze 10:2	935
thou shalt g forth at even in	Eze 12:4	3318
as they that g forth into	Eze 12:4	4161
shall remove and g into captivity	Eze 12:11	3212
in the twilight, and shall g forth	Eze 12:12	3318
arms, and will let the souls g	Eze 13:20	7971
may g no more astray from me	Eze 14:11	8582
and say, Sword, g through the land	Eze 14:17	5674
they shall g out from one fire,	Eze 15:7	3318
Wherefore I caused them to g	Eze 20:10	3318
is the high place whereunto ye g	Eze 20:29	935
G ye, serve ye every one his	Eze 20:39	3212
therefore shall my sword g forth	Eze 21:4	3318
G thee one way or other, either	Eze 21:16	258
as they g in unto a woman that	Eze 23:44	935
I will not g back, neither will I	Eze 24:14	6544
shall g down to the ground	Eze 26:11	3381
with them that g down to the pit,	Eze 26:20	3381
In that day shall messengers g	Eze 30:9	3318
cities shall g into captivity	Eze 30:17	3212
daughters shall g into captivity	Eze 30:18	3212
with them that g down to the pit	Eze 31:14	3381
with them that g down into the	Eze 32:18	3381
g down, and be thou laid with the	Eze 32:19	3381
with them that g down to the pit	Eze 32:24	3381
with them that g down to the pit	Eze 32:25	3381
with them that g down to the pit	Eze 32:29	3381
with them that g down to the pit	Eze 32:30	3381
I will g up to the land of	Eze 38:11	5927
I will g to them that are at rest	Eze 38:11	935
cities of Israel shall g forth	Eze 39:9	3318
were seven steps to g up to it	Eze 40:26	5930
then shall they not g out of the	Eze 42:14	3318
shall g out by the way of the	Eze 44:3	3318
when they g forth into the utter	Eze 44:19	3318
then he shall g forth	Eze 46:2	3318
he shall g in by the way of the	Eze 46:8	935
he shall g forth by the way	Eze 46:8	3318
g out by the way of the south	Eze 46:9	3318
g forth by the way of the north	Eze 46:9	3318
but shall g forth over against it	Eze 46:9	3318
the midst of them, when they g in	Eze 46:10	935
them, when they g in, shall g in	Eze 46:10	3318
when they g forth, shall g forth	Eze 46:10	3318
then he shall g forth	Eze 46:12	3318
g down into the desert	Eze 47:8	3381
and g into the sea	Eze 47:8	935
way of Hethlon, as men g to Zedad	Eze 47:15	935
therefore he shall g forth with	Dan 11:44	3318
And he said, G thy way, Daniel	Dan 12:9	3212
But g thou thy way till the end	Dan 12:13	3212
And the LORD said to Hosea, G	Hos 1:2	3212
I will g after my lovers, that	Hos 2:5	3212
then shall she say, I will g	Hos 2:7	3212
G yet, love a woman beloved of	Hos 3:1	3212
neither g ye up to Beth-aven, nor	Hos 4:15	5927
They shall g with their flocks and	Hos 5:6	3212
I, even I, will tear and g away	Hos 5:14	3212
I will g and return to my place,	Hos 5:15	3212
call to Egypt, they g to Assyria	Hos 7:11	1980
When they shall g, I will spread	Hos 7:12	3212
I taught Ephraim also to g	Hos 11:3	8637
let the bridegroom g forth of his	Joel 2:16	3318
shall g into captivity unto Kir	Amos 1:5	
their king shall g into captivity	Amos 1:15	1980
his father will g in unto the	Amos 2:7	3212
ye shall g out at the breaches,	Amos 4:3	3318
shall surely g into captivity	Amos 5:5	
Therefore will I cause you to g	Amos 5:27	
from thence g ye to Hamath the	Amos 6:2	3212
then g down to Gath of the	Amos 6:2	3381
Therefore now shall they g	Amos 6:7	
with the first that g captive	Amos 6:7	
said unto Amos, O thou seer, g	Amos 7:12	3212
and the LORD said unto me, G	Amos 7:15	3212
Israel shall surely g into	Amos 7:17	
cause the sun to g down at noon	Amos 8:9	935
though they g into captivity	Amos 9:4	3212
g to Nineveh, that great city, and	Jonah 1:2	3212
to g with them unto Tarshish from	Jonah 1:3	935
g unto Nineveh, that great city,	Jonah 3:2	3312

I will g stripped and naked	Mic 1:8	3212
neither shall ye g haughtily	Mic 2:3	3212
the sun shall g down over the	Mic 3:6	935
let us g up to the mountain of	Mic 4:2	5927
for the law shall g forth of Zion	Mic 4:2	3318
for now shalt thou g forth out of	Mic 4:10	3318
thou shalt g even to Babylon	Mic 4:10	935
if he g through, both treadeth	Mic 5:8	5674
g into clay, and tread the morter,	Nah 3:14	935
and judgment doth never g forth	Hab 1:4	3318
G up to the mountain, and bring	Hag 1:8	5927
which g forth from standing	Zec 6:5	3318
g forth into the north country	Zec 6:6	3318
the white g forth after them	Zec 6:6	3318
the grisled g forth toward the	Zec 6:6	3318
sought to g that they might walk	Zec 6:7	3212
these that g toward the north	Zec 6:8	3318
g into the house of Josiah the	Zec 6:10	935
of one city shall g to another	Zec 8:21	1980
Let us g speedily to pray before	Zec 8:21	3212
I will g also	Zec 8:21	3212
a Jew, saying, We will g with you	Zec 8:23	3212
his arrow shall g forth as the	Zec 9:14	3318
shall g with whirlwinds of the	Zec 9:14	1980
city shall g forth into captivity	Zec 14:2	3318
Then shall the LORD g forth	Zec 14:3	3318
waters shall g out from Jerusalem	Zec 14:8	3318
against Jerusalem shall even g up	Zec 14:16	5927
if the family of Egypt g not up	Zec 14:18	5927
and ye shall g forth, and grow up	Mal 4:2	3318
them to Bethlehem, and said, G	Mt 2:8	*4198*
g into the land of Israel	Mt 2:20	*4198*
Herod, he was afraid to g thither	Mt 2:22	*565*
before the altar, and g thy way	Mt 5:24	*5217*
shall compel thee to g a mile	Mt 5:41	
g with him twain	Mt 5:41	*5217*
many there be which g in thereat	Mt 7:13	*1525*
but g thy way, shew thyself to	Mt 8:4	*5217*
and I say to this man, G, and he	Mt 8:9	*4198*
unto the centurion, G thy way	Mt 8:13	*5217*
him, Lord, suffer me first to g	Mt 8:21	*565*
suffer us to g away into the herd	Mt 8:31	*565*
And he said unto them, G	Mt 8:32	*5217*
up thy bed, and g unto thine house	Mt 9:6	*5217*
But g ye and learn what that	Mt 9:13	*4198*
G not into the way of the	Mt 10:5	*565*
But g rather to the lost sheep of	Mt 10:6	*4198*
And as ye g, preach, saying, The	Mt 10:7	*4198*
and there abide till ye g thence	Mt 10:11	*1831*
answered and said unto them, G	Mt 11:4	*4198*
him, Wilt thou then that we g	Mt 13:28	*565*
that they may g into the villages	Mt 14:15	*565*
to g before him unto the other	Mt 14:22	*4254*
on the water, to g to Jesus	Mt 14:29	*2064*
how that he must g unto Jerusalem	Mt 16:21	*565*
g thou to the sea, and cast an	Mt 17:27	*4198*
shall trespass against thee, g	Mt 18:15	*5217*
him, If thou wilt be perfect, g	Mt 19:21	*5217*
to g through the eye of a needle	Mt 19:24	*1830*
G ye also into the vineyard, and	Mt 20:4	*5217*
G ye also into the vineyard	Mt 20:7	*5217*
Take that thine is, and g thy way	Mt 20:14	*5217*
Behold, we g up to Jerusalem	Mt 20:18	*305*
G into the village over against	Mt 21:2	*4198*
g work to day in my vineyard	Mt 21:28	*5217*
And he answered and said, I g sir	Mt 21:30	*565*
the harlots g into the kingdom of	Mt 21:31	*4254*
G ye therefore into the highways,	Mt 22:9	*4198*
for ye neither g in yourselves	Mt 23:13	*1525*
ye them that are entering to g in	Mt 23:13	*1525*
g not forth	Mt 24:26	*1881*
g ye out to meet him	Mt 25:6	*1881*
but g ye rather to them that sell	Mt 25:9	*4198*
And these shall g away into	Mt 25:46	*565*
G into the city to such a man, and	Mt 26:18	*5217*
I will g before you into Galilee	Mt 26:32	*4254*
disciples, Sit ye here, while I g	Mt 26:36	*565*
g your way, make it as sure as ye	Mt 27:65	*5217*
g quickly, and tell his disciples	Mt 28:7	*4198*
g tell my brethren	Mt 28:10	*565*
that they g into Galilee	Mt 28:10	*5217*
G ye therefore, and teach all	Mt 28:19	*4198*
Let us g into the next towns,	Mk 1:38	*71*
but g thy way, shew thyself to	Mk 1:44	*5217*
g thy way into thine house	Mk 2:11	*5217*
G home to thy friends, and tell	Mk 5:19	*5217*
g in peace, and be whole of thy	Mk 5:34	*5217*
that they may g into the country	Mk 6:36	*565*
And they say unto him, Shall we g	Mk 6:37	*565*
g and see	Mk 6:38	*5217*
to g to the other side before	Mk 6:45	*4254*
her, For this saying g thy way	Mk 7:29	*5217*
Neither g into the town, nor tell	Mk 8:26	*1525*
having two hands to g into hell	Mk 9:43	*565*
g thy way, sell whatsoever thou	Mk 10:21	*5217*
to g through the eye of a needle	Mk 10:25	*1525*
Behold, we g up to Jerusalem	Mk 10:33	*305*
And Jesus said unto him, G thy way	Mk 10:52	*5217*
G your way into the village over	Mk 11:2	*5217*
and they let them g	Mk 11:6	*863*
which love to g in long clothing,	Mk 12:38	*4043*
not g down into the house	Mk 13:15	*2597*
him, Where wilt thou that we g	Mk 14:12	*565*
G ye into the city, and there	Mk 14:13	*5217*
And wheresoever he shall g in	Mk 14:14	*1525*
I will g before you into Galilee	Mk 14:28	*4254*
Rise up, let us g	Mk 14:42	*71*
But g your way, tell his	Mk 16:7	*5217*
G ye into all the world, and	Mk 16:15	*4198*
he shall g before him in the	Lk 1:17	*4281*
for thou shalt g before the face	Lk 1:76	*4313*
Let us now g even unto Bethlehem,	Lk 2:15	*1330*
but g, and shew thyself to the	Lk 5:14	*565*
thy couch, and g into thine house	Lk 5:24	*4198*
me soldiers, and I say unto one, G	Lk 7:8	*4198*
G your way, and tell John what	Lk 7:22	*4198*
faith hath saved thee; g in peace	Lk 7:50	*4198*
g forth, and are choked with cares	Lk 8:14	*4198*
Let us g over unto the other side	Lk 8:22	*1330*
them to g out into the deep	Lk 8:31	*565*
made thee whole; g in peace	Lk 8:48	*4198*
house, he suffered no man to g in	Lk 8:51	*1525*
when ye g out of that city, shake	Lk 9:5	*1831*
that they may g into the towns and	Lk 9:12	*565*
except we should g and buy meat	Lk 9:13	*4198*
set his face to g to Jerusalem	Lk 9:51	*4198*
as though he would g to Jerusalem	Lk 9:53	*4198*
said, Lord, suffer me first to g	Lk 9:59	*565*
but g thou and preach the kingdom	Lk 9:60	*565*
but let me first g bid them	Lk 9:61	
G your ways: behold, I send	Lk 10:3	*5217*
G not from house to house	Lk 10:7	*3327*
g your ways out into the streets	Lk 10:10	*1831*
Then said Jesus unto him, G	Lk 10:37	*4198*
shall g unto him at midnight, and	Lk 11:5	*4198*
G ye, and tell that fox, Behold, I	Lk 13:32	*4198*
him, and healed him, and let him g	Lk 14:4	*630*
But when thou art bidden, g	Lk 14:10	*4198*
unto thee, Friend, g up higher	Lk 14:10	*4320*
of ground, and I must needs g	Lk 14:18	*1831*
of oxen, and I g to prove them	Lk 14:19	*4198*
G out quickly into the streets and	Lk 14:21	*1831*
G out into the highways and hedges	Lk 14:23	*1831*
g after that which is lost, until	Lk 15:4	*4198*
g to my father, and will say unto	Lk 15:18	*4198*
he was angry, and would not g in	Lk 15:28	*1525*
when he is come from the field, G	Lk 17:7	*3928*
G shew yourselves unto the	Lk 17:14	*4198*
said unto him, Arise, g thy way	Lk 17:19	*4198*
g not after them, nor follow them	Lk 17:23	*565*
camel to g through a needle's eye	Lk 18:25	*1525*
we g up to Jerusalem, and all	Lk 18:31	*305*
G ye into the village over	Lk 19:30	*5217*
g ye not therefore after them	Lk 21:8	*4198*
he sent Peter and John, saying, G	Lk 22:8	*4198*
Lord, I am ready to g with thee	Lk 22:33	*4198*
will not answer me, nor let me g	Lk 22:68	*630*
chastise him, and let him g	Lk 23:22	*630*
Jesus would g forth into Galilee	Jn 1:43	*1831*
he must needs g through Samaria	Jn 4:4	*1330*
Jesus saith unto her, G, call thy	Jn 4:16	*5217*
Jesus saith unto him, G thy way	Jn 4:50	*4198*
the twelve, Will ye also g away	Jn 6:67	*5217*
him, Lord, to whom shall we g	Jn 6:68	*565*
g into Judaea, that thy disciples	Jn 7:3	*5217*
G ye up unto this feast	Jn 7:8	*305*
I g not up yet unto this feast	Jn 7:8	*305*
Why g ye about to kill me	Jn 7:19	*2212*
then I g unto him that sent me	Jn 7:33	*5217*
themselves, Whither will he g	Jn 7:35	*4198*
will he g unto the dispersed	Jn 7:35	*4198*
g, and sin no more	Jn 8:11	*4198*
whence I came, and whither I g	Jn 8:14	*5217*
whence I come, and whither I g	Jn 8:14	*5217*
I g my way, and ye shall seek me,	Jn 8:21	*5217*
whither I g, ye cannot come	Jn 8:21	*5217*
because he saith, Whither I g	Jn 8:22	*5217*
And said unto him, G, wash in the	Jn 9:7	*5217*
G to the pool of Siloam, and wash	Jn 9:11	*5217*
he shall be saved, and shall g in	Jn 10:9	*1525*
Let us g into Judaea again	Jn 11:7	*71*
but I g, that I may awake him out	Jn 11:11	*4198*
nevertheless let us g unto him	Jn 11:15	*71*
fellowdisciples, Let us also g	Jn 11:16	*71*
them, Loose him, and let him g	Jn 11:44	*5217*
I said unto the Jews, Whither I g	Jn 13:33	*5217*
Jesus answered him, Whither I g	Jn 13:36	*5217*
I g to prepare a place for you	Jn 14:2	*4198*
And if I g and prepare a place for	Jn 14:3	*4198*
And whither I g ye know, and the	Jn 14:4	*5217*
because I g unto my Father	Jn 14:12	*4198*
I g away, and come again unto you	Jn 14:28	*5217*
I said, I g unto the Father	Jn 14:28	*4198*
Arise, let us g hence	Jn 14:31	*71*
and ordained you, that ye should g	Jn 15:16	*5217*
But now I g my way to him that	Jn 16:5	*5217*
expedient for you that I g away	Jn 16:7	*565*
for if I g not away, the	Jn 16:7	*565*
because I g to my Father, and ye	Jn 16:10	*5217*
because I g to the Father	Jn 16:16	*5217*
Because I g to the Father	Jn 16:17	*5217*
the world, and g to the Father	Jn 16:28	*4198*
ye seek me, let these g their way	Jn 18:8	*5217*
saying, If thou let this man g	Jn 19:12	*630*
but g to my brethren, and say unto	Jn 20:17	*4198*
saith unto them, I g a fishing	Jn 21:3	*5217*
say unto him, We also g with thee	Jn 21:3	*2064*
as ye have seen him g into heaven	Acts 1:11	*4198*
that he might g to his own place	Acts 1:25	*4198*
John about to g into the temple	Acts 3:3	*1524*
he was determined to let him g	Acts 3:13	*630*
to g aside out of the council	Acts 4:15	*565*
threatened them, they let them g	Acts 4:21	*630*
And being let g, they went to	Acts 4:23	*630*
G, stand and speak in the temple	Acts 5:20	*4198*
the name of Jesus, and let them g	Acts 5:40	*630*
Make us gods to g before us	Acts 7:40	*4313*
g toward the south unto the way	Acts 8:26	*4198*
G near, and join thyself to this	Acts 8:29	*4334*
g into the city, and it shall be	Acts 9:6	*1525*
g into the street which is called	Acts 9:11	*4198*
the Lord said unto him, G thy way	Acts 9:15	*4198*
g with them, doubting nothing	Acts 10:20	*4198*
And the Spirit bade me g with them	Acts 11:12	*4905*
that he should g as far as	Acts 11:22	*1330*
G shew these things unto James,	Acts 12:17	
should g up to Jerusalem unto the	Acts 15:2	*305*
they were let g in peace from the	Acts 15:33	*630*
unto Barnabas, Let us g again	Acts 15:36	*1994*
Paul have to g forth with him	Acts 16:3	*1831*
they assayed to g into Bithynia	Acts 16:7	*4198*
endeavoured to g into Macedonia	Acts 16:10	*1831*
saying, Let those men g	Acts 16:35	*630*
have sent to let you g	Acts 16:36	*630*
therefore depart, and g in peace	Acts 16:36	*4198*
and of the other, they let them g	Acts 17:9	*630*
Paul to g as it were to the sea	Acts 17:14	*4198*
I will g unto the Gentiles	Acts 18:6	*4198*
to g to Jerusalem, saying, After	Acts 19:21	*4198*
departed for to g into Macedonia	Acts 20:1	*4198*
minding himself to g afoot	Acts 20:13	
I g bound in the spirit unto	Acts 20:22	*4198*
he should not g up to Jerusalem	Acts 21:4	*305*
him not to g up to Jerusalem	Acts 21:12	*305*
me, Arise, and g into Damascus	Acts 22:10	*4198*
commanded the soldiers to g down	Acts 23:10	*2597*
hundred soldiers to g to Caesarea	Acts 23:23	*4198*
left the horsemen to g with him	Acts 23:32	*4198*
answered, G thy way for this time	Acts 24:25	*4198*
g down with me, and accuse this	Acts 25:5	*4782*
Wilt thou g up to Jerusalem, and	Acts 25:9	*305*
unto Caesar shalt thou g	Acts 25:12	*4198*
whether he would g to Jerusalem	Acts 25:20	*4198*
gave him liberty to g unto his	Acts 27:3	*4198*
examined me, would have let me g	Acts 28:18	*630*
G unto this people, and say,	Acts 28:26	*4198*
But now I g unto Jerusalem to	Rom 15:25	*4198*
must ye needs g out of the world	1Cor 5:10	*1831*
g to law before the unjust, and	1Cor 6:1	
because ye g to law one with	1Cor 6:7	
a feast, and ye be disposed to g	1Cor 10:27	*4198*
I g also, they shall g with me	1Cor 16:4	*4198*
on my journey whithersoever I g	1Cor 16:6	*4198*
that they would g before unto you	2Cor 9:5	*4281*
that we should g unto the heathen	Gal 2:9	
let not the sun g down upon your	Eph 4:26	*1931*
I shall see how it will g with me	Phil 2:23	
That no man g beyond and defraud	1Th 4:6	*5233*
let us g on unto perfection	Heb 6:1	*5342*
when he was called to g out into	Heb 11:8	*1831*
Let us g forth therefore unto him	Heb 13:13	*1831*
G to now, ye that say, To day or	Jas 4:13	*33*
morrow we will g into such a city	Jas 4:13	*4198*
G to now, ye rich men, weep and	Jas 5:1	*33*
my God, and he shall g no more out	Rev 3:12	*1831*
spake unto me again, and said, G	Rev 10:8	*5217*
captivity shall g into captivity	Rev 13:10	*5217*
G your ways, and pour out the	Rev 16:1	*5217*
which g forth unto the kings of	Rev 16:14	*1607*
pit, and g into perdition	Rev 17:8	*5217*
shall g out to deceive the	Rev 20:8	*1831*

GOAD

six hundred men with an ox g	Judg 3:31	4451

GOADS

for the axes, and to sharpen the g	1Sa 13:21	1861
The words of the wise are as g	Eccl 12:11	1861

GOAH See GOATH.

GOAT

a she g of three years old, and a	Gen 15:9	5795
And if his offering be a g	Lev 3:12	5795
his hand upon the head of the g	Lev 4:24	8163
fat, of ox, or of sheep, or of g	Lev 7:23	5795
people's offering, and took the g	Lev 9:15	8163
sought the g of the sin offering	Lev 10:16	8163
Aaron shall bring the g upon	Lev 16:9	8163
But the g, on which the lot fell	Lev 16:10	8163
he kill the g of the sin offering	Lev 16:15	8163
bullock, and of the blood of the g	Lev 16:18	8163
altar, he shall bring the live g	Lev 16:20	8163
hands upon the head of the live g	Lev 16:21	8163
them upon the head of the g	Lev 16:21	8163
the g shall bear upon him all	Lev 16:22	8163
let go the g in the wilderness	Lev 16:22	8163
he that let go the g for the	Lev 16:26	8163
the g for the sin offering, whose	Lev 16:27	8163
that killeth an ox, or lamb, or g	Lev 17:3	5795
a bullock, or a sheep, or a g	Lev 22:27	5795
then he shall bring a she g of	Num 15:27	5795
a sheep, or the firstling of a g	Num 18:17	5795
one g for a sin offering, to make	Num 28:22	8163
And one g for a sin offering	Num 29:22	8163
And one g for a sin offering	Num 29:28	8163
And one g for a sin offering	Num 29:31	8163
And one g for a sin offering	Num 29:34	8163
And one g for a sin offering	Num 29:38	8163
the ox, the sheep, and the g	Deut 14:4	5795
and the fallow deer, and the wild g	Deut 14:5	689
an he g also	Prov 30:31	8495
every day a g for a sin offering	Eze 43:25	8163
an he g came from the west on the	Dan 8:5	5795
the g had a notable horn between	Dan 8:5	6842
the he g waxed very great	Dan 8:8	6842
the rough g is the king of Grecia	Dan 8:21	6842

GOATH *(go'-ath) A place near Jerusalem.*

and shall compass about to G	Jer 31:39	1601

GOATS

thence two good kids of the g	Gen 27:9	5795
the kids of the g upon his hands	Gen 27:16	5795
spotted and speckled among the g	Gen 30:32	5795
speckled and spotted among the g	Gen 30:33	5795
the he g that were ringstraked	Gen 30:35	8495
all the she g that were speckled	Gen 30:35	5795
thy she g have not cast their	Gen 31:38	5795
Two hundred she g	Gen 32:14	5795
and twenty he g	Gen 32:14	8495
coat, and killed a kid of the g	Gen 37:31	5795
out from the sheep, or from the g	Ex 12:5	5795
namely, of the sheep, or of the g	Lev 1:10	5795
his offering, a kid of the g	Lev 4:23	5795

G

his offering, a kid of the g Lev 4:28 5795
flock, a lamb or a kid of the g Lev 5:6 5795
a kid of the g for a sin offering Lev 9:3 5795
kids of the g for a sin offering Lev 16:5 5795
And he shall take the two g Lev 16:7 8163
shall cast lots upon the two g Lev 16:8 8163
beeves, of the sheep, or of the g Lev 22:19 5795
kid of the g for a sin offering Lev 23:19 5795
One kid of the g for a sin Num 7:16 5795
two oxen, five rams, five he g Num 7:17 6260
One kid of the g for a sin Num 7:22 5795
two oxen, five rams, five he g Num 7:23 6260
One kid of the g for a sin Num 7:28 5795
two oxen, five rams, five he g Num 7:29 6260
One kid of the g for a sin Num 7:34 5795
two oxen, five rams, five he g Num 7:35 6260
One kid of the g for a sin Num 7:40 5795
two oxen, five rams, five he g Num 7:41 6260
One kid of the g for a sin Num 7:46 5795
two oxen, five rams, five he g Num 7:47 6260
One kid of the g for a sin Num 7:52 5795
two oxen, five rams, five he g Num 7:53 6260
One kid of the g for a sin Num 7:58 5795
two oxen, five rams, five he g Num 7:59 6260
One kid of the g for a sin Num 7:64 5795
two oxen, five rams, five he g Num 7:65 6260
One kid of the g for a sin Num 7:70 5795
two oxen, five rams, five he g Num 7:71 6260
One kid of the g for a sin Num 7:76 5795
two oxen, five rams, five he g Num 7:77 6260
One kid of the g for a sin Num 7:82 5795
two oxen, five rams, five he g Num 7:83 6260
the kids of the g for sin Num 7:87 5795
the rams sixty, the he g sixty Num 7:88 6260
one kid of the g for a sin Num 15:24 5795
one kid of the g for a sin Num 28:15 5795
And one kid of the g, to make an Num 28:30 5795
one kid of the g for a sin Num 29:5 5795
One kid of the g for a sin Num 29:11 5795
one kid of the g for a sin Num 29:16 5795
one kid of the g for a sin Num 29:19 5795
one kid of the g for a sin Num 29:25 5795
rams of the breed of Bashan, and g Deut 32:14 6260
men upon the rocks of the wild g 1Sa 24:2 3277
thousand sheep, and a thousand g 1Sa 25:2 5795
thousand and seven hundred he g 2Chr 17:11 8495
and seven lambs, and seven he g 2Chr 29:21 5795
they brought forth the he g for 2Chr 29:23 8163
for all Israel, twelve he g Ezr 6:17 5795
twelve he g for a sin offering Ezr 8:35 6842
wild g of the rock bring forth Job 39:1 3277
nor he g out of thy folds Ps 50:9 6260
of bulls, or drink the blood of g Ps 50:13 6260
I will offer bullocks with g Ps 66:15 6260
hills are a refuge for the wild g Ps 104:18 3277
the g are the price of the field Prov 27:26 6260
thy hair is as a flock of g Song 4:1 5795
of g that appear from Gilead Song 6:5 5795
bullocks, or of lambs, or of he g Is 1:11 6260
and with the blood of lambs and g Is 34:6 6260
be as the he g before the flocks Jer 50:8 6260
slaughter, like rams with he g Jer 51:40 6260
with thee in lambs, and rams, and g Eze 27:21 6260
between the rams and the he g Eze 34:17 6260
earth, of rams, of lambs, and of g Eze 39:18 6260
the g without blemish for a sin Eze 43:22 5795
a kid of the g daily for a sin Eze 45:23 5795
shepherds, and I punished the g Zec 10:3 6260
divideth his sheep from the g Mt 25:32 *2056*
right hand, but the g on the left Mt 25:33 *2055*
Neither by the blood of g Heb 9:12 *5131*
For if the blood of bulls and of g Heb 9:13 *5131*
took the blood of calves and of g Heb 9:19 *5131*
of g should take away sins Heb 10:4 *5131*

GOATS'
and fine linen, and g hair, Ex 25:4 5795
thou shalt make curtains of g Ex 26:7 5795
and fine linen, and g hair, Ex 35:6 5795
g hair, and red skins of rams, and Ex 35:23 5795
them up in wisdom spun g hair Ex 35:26 5795
he made curtains of g hair for Ex 36:14 5795
of skins, and all work of g hair Num 31:20 5795
put a pillow of g hair for his 1Sa 19:13 5795
with a pillow of g hair for his 1Sa 19:16 5795
thou shalt have g milk enough for Prov 27:27 5795

GOATSKINS
wandered about in sheepskins and g Heb 11:37

GOB (*gob*) *A place where David battled the Philistines.*
battle with the Philistines at G 2Sa 21:18 1359
battle in G with the Philistines 2Sa 21:19 1359

GOBLET
Thy navel is like a round g Song 7:2 101

GOD (*god*) See GODDESS, GODHEAD, GOD'S, GODS, GOD-WARD.
I. Creator and Ruler of the world, Israel, and the church.
In the beginning G created the Gen 1:1 430
the Spirit of G moved upon the Gen 1:2 430
G said, Let there be light Gen 1:3 430
G saw the light, that it was good Gen 1:4 430
G divided the light from the Gen 1:4 430
G called the light Day, and the Gen 1:5 430
G said, Let there be a firmament Gen 1:6 430
G made the firmament, and divided Gen 1:7 430
G called the firmament Heaven Gen 1:8 430
G said, Let the waters under the Gen 1:9 430
G called the dry land Earth Gen 1:10 430
and G saw that it was good Gen 1:10 430
G said, Let the earth bring forth Gen 1:11 430
and G saw that it was good Gen 1:12 430
G said, Let there be lights in Gen 1:14 430
And G made two great lights Gen 1:16 430
G set them in the firmament of Gen 1:17 430
and G saw that it was good Gen 1:18 430
G said, Let the waters bring Gen 1:20 430
G created great whales, and every Gen 1:21 430
and G saw that it was good Gen 1:21 430
G blessed them, saying, Be Gen 1:22 430
G said, Let the earth bring forth Gen 1:24 430
G made the beast of the earth Gen 1:25 430
and G saw that it was good Gen 1:25 430
G said, Let us make man in our Gen 1:26 430
So G created man in his own image Gen 1:27 430
in the image of G created he him Gen 1:27 430
G blessed them, and G said unto Gen 1:28 430
G said unto them, Be fruitful, and Gen 1:28 430
G said, Behold, I have given you Gen 1:29 430
G saw every thing that he had Gen 1:31 430
on the seventh day G ended his Gen 2:2 430
G blessed the seventh day, and Gen 2:3 430
from all his work which G created Gen 2:3 430
that the LORD G made the earth Gen 2:4 430
for the LORD G had not caused it Gen 2:5 430
the LORD G formed man of the dust Gen 2:7 430
the LORD G planted a garden Gen 2:8 430
LORD G to grow every tree that is Gen 2:9 430
the LORD G took the man, and put Gen 2:15 430
the LORD G commanded the man, Gen 2:16 430
And the LORD G said, It is not Gen 2:18 430
out of the ground the LORD G Gen 2:19 430
the LORD G caused a deep sleep to Gen 2:21 430
which the LORD G had taken from Gen 2:22 430
field which the LORD G had made Gen 3:1 430
unto the woman, Yea, hath G said Gen 3:1 430
G hath said, Ye shall not eat of Gen 3:3 430
For G doth know that in the day Gen 3:5 430
heard the voice of the LORD G Gen 3:8 430
from the presence of the LORD G Gen 3:8 430
the LORD G called unto Adam, and Gen 3:9 430
the LORD G said unto the woman, Gen 3:13 430
the LORD G said unto the serpent, Gen 3:14 430
the LORD G make coats of skins Gen 3:21 430
And the LORD G said, Behold, the Gen 3:22 430
Therefore the LORD G sent him Gen 3:23 430
For G, said she, hath appointed Gen 4:25 430
In the day that G created man Gen 5:1 430
in the likeness of G made he him Gen 5:1 430
Enoch walked with G after he Gen 5:22 430
And Enoch walked with G Gen 5:24 430
for G took him Gen 5:24 430
That the sons of G saw the Gen 6:2 430
when the sons of G came in unto Gen 6:4 430
G saw that the wickedness of man Gen 6:5 3068
and Noah walked with G Gen 6:9 430
earth also was corrupt before G Gen 6:11 430
G looked upon the earth, and, Gen 6:12 430
G said unto Noah, The end of all Gen 6:13 430
to all that G commanded him Gen 6:22 430
female, as G had commanded Noah Gen 7:9 430
all flesh, as G had commanded him Gen 7:16 430
G remembered Noah, and every Gen 8:1 430
G made a wind to pass over the Gen 8:1 430
G spake unto Noah, saying, Gen 8:15 430
G blessed Noah and his sons, and Gen 9:1 430
for in the image of G made he man Gen 9:6 430
G spake unto Noah, and to his sons Gen 9:8 430
G said, This is the token of the Gen 9:12 430
everlasting covenant between G Gen 9:16 430
G said unto Noah, This is the Gen 9:17 430
Blessed be the LORD G of Shem Gen 9:26 430
G shall enlarge Japheth, and he Gen 9:27 430
was the priest of the most high G Gen 14:18 410
be Abram of the most high G Gen 14:19 410
And blessed be the most high G Gen 14:20 410
unto the LORD, the most high G Gen 14:22 410
And Abram said, Lord G, what wilt Gen 15:2 3069
And he said, Lord G, whereby shall Gen 15:8 3069
spake unto her, Thou G seest me Gen 16:13 410
unto him, I am the Almighty G Gen 17:1 410
G talked with him, saying, Gen 17:3 430
to be a G unto thee, and to thy Gen 17:7 430
and I will be their G Gen 17:8 430
G said unto Abraham, Thou shalt Gen 17:9 430
G said unto Abraham, As for Sarai Gen 17:15 430
And Abraham said unto G, O that Gen 17:18 430
G said, Sarah thy wife shall bear Gen 17:19 430
him, and G went up from Abraham Gen 17:22 430
day, as G had said unto him Gen 17:23 430
when G destroyed the cities of Gen 19:29 430
that G remembered Abraham, and Gen 19:29 430
But G came to Abimelech in a Gen 20:3 430
G said unto him in a dream, Yea, Gen 20:6 430
Surely the fear of G is not in Gen 20:11 430
when G caused me to wander from Gen 20:13 430
So Abraham prayed unto G Gen 20:17 430
G healed Abimelech, and his wife, Gen 20:17 430
time of which G had spoken to him Gen 21:2 430
days old, as G had commanded him Gen 21:4 430
G hath made me to laugh, so that Gen 21:6 430
G said unto Abraham, Let it not Gen 21:12 430
G heard the voice of the lad Gen 21:17 430
the angel of G called to Hagar Gen 21:17 430
for G hath heard the voice of the Gen 21:17 430
G opened her eyes, and she saw a Gen 21:19 430
And G was with the lad Gen 21:20 430
G is with thee in all that thou Gen 21:22 430
G that thou wilt not deal falsely Gen 21:23 430
of the LORD, the everlasting G Gen 21:33 410
that G did tempt Abraham, and said Gen 22:1 430
the place of which G had told him Gen 22:3 430
G will provide himself a lamb for Gen 22:8 430
the place which G had told him of Gen 22:9 430
now I know that thou fearest G Gen 22:12 430
the G of heaven Gen 24:3 430
the G of the earth Gen 24:3 430
The LORD G of heaven, which took Gen 24:7 430
O LORD G of my master Abraham, I Gen 24:12 430
Blessed be the LORD G of my Gen 24:27 430
O LORD G of my master Abraham, if Gen 24:42 430
blessed the LORD G of my master Gen 24:48 430
that G blessed his son Isaac Gen 25:11 430
I am the G of Abraham thy father Gen 26:24 430
the LORD thy G brought it to me Gen 27:20 430
Therefore G give thee of the dew Gen 27:28 430
G Almighty bless thee, and make Gen 28:3 410
which G gave unto Abraham Gen 28:4 430
behold the angels of G ascending Gen 28:12 430
I am the LORD G of Abraham thy Gen 28:13 430
thy father, and the G of Isaac Gen 28:13 430
is none other but the house of G Gen 28:17 430
If G will be with me, and will Gen 28:20 430
then shall the LORD be my G Gen 28:21 430
G hath judged me, and hath also Gen 30:6 430
G hearkened unto Leah, and she Gen 30:17 430
G hath given me my hire, because Gen 30:18 430
G hath endued me with a good Gen 30:20 430
G remembered Rachel Gen 30:22 430
G hearkened to her, and opened her Gen 30:22 430
G hath taken away my reproach Gen 30:23 430
but the G of my father hath been Gen 31:5 430
but G suffered him not to hurt me Gen 31:7 430
Thus G hath taken away the cattle Gen 31:9 430
the angel of G spake unto me in a Gen 31:11 430
I am the G of Beth-el, where thou Gen 31:13 410
For all the riches which G hath Gen 31:16 430
whatsoever G hath said unto thee, Gen 31:16 430
G came to Laban the Syrian in a Gen 31:24 430
but the G of your father spake Gen 31:29 430
Except the G of my father Gen 31:42 430
the G of Abraham, and the fear of Gen 31:42 430
G hath seen mine affliction and Gen 31:42 430
G is witness betwixt me and thee Gen 31:50 430
The G of Abraham Gen 31:53 430
the G of Nahor Gen 31:53 430
the G of their father, judge Gen 31:53 430
way, and the angels of G met him Gen 32:1 430
O G of my father Abraham Gen 32:9 430
G of my father Isaac, the LORD Gen 32:9 430
a prince hast thou power with G Gen 32:28 430
for I have seen G face to face Gen 32:30 430
The children which G hath Gen 33:5 430
though I had seen the face of G Gen 33:10 430
because G hath dealt graciously Gen 33:11 430
G said unto Jacob, Arise, go up Gen 35:1 430
and make there an altar unto G Gen 35:1 410
I will make there an altar unto G Gen 35:3 410
the terror of G was upon the Gen 35:5 430
because there G appeared unto him Gen 35:7 430
G appeared unto Jacob again, when Gen 35:9 430
G said unto him, Thy name is Gen 35:10 430
And G said unto him Gen 35:11 430
I am G Almighty Gen 35:11 410
G went up from him in the place Gen 35:13 430
the place where G spake with him Gen 35:15 430
wickedness, and sin against G Gen 39:9 430
not interpretations belong to G Gen 40:8 430
G shall give Pharaoh an answer of Gen 41:16 430
G hath shewed Pharaoh what he is Gen 41:25 430
What G is about to do he sheweth Gen 41:28 430
the thing is established by G Gen 41:32 430
G will shortly bring it to pass Gen 41:32 430
a man in whom the Spirit of G is Gen 41:38 430
Forasmuch as G hath shewed thee Gen 41:39 430
For G, said he, hath made me Gen 41:51 430
For G hath caused me to be Gen 41:52 430
for I fear G Gen 42:18 430
is this that G hath done unto us Gen 42:28 430
G Almighty give you mercy before Gen 43:14 410
your G, and the G of your father Gen 43:23 430
G be gracious unto thee, my son Gen 43:29 430
G forbid that thy servants should Gen 44:7
G hath found out the iniquity of Gen 44:16 430
G forbid that I should do so Gen 44:17
for G did send me before you to Gen 45:5 430
G sent me before you to preserve Gen 45:7 430
you that sent me hither, but G Gen 45:8 430
G hath made me lord of all Egypt Gen 45:9 430
unto the G of his father Isaac Gen 46:1 430
G spake unto Israel in the Gen 46:2 430
I am G, the G of thy father Gen 46:3 430
G Almighty appeared unto me at Gen 48:3 410
whom G hath given me in this Gen 48:9 430
G hath shewed me also thy seed Gen 48:11 430
And he blessed Joseph, and said, G Gen 48:15 430
the G which fed me all my life Gen 48:15 430
G make thee as Ephraim and as Gen 48:20 430
but G shall be with you, and bring Gen 48:21 430
hands of the mighty G of Jacob Gen 49:24
Even by the G of thy father, who Gen 49:25 410
servants of the G of thy father Gen 50:17 430
for am I in the place of G Gen 50:19 430
but G meant it unto good, to Gen 50:20 430
G will surely visit you, and bring Gen 50:24 430
G will surely visit you, and ye Gen 50:25 430
But the midwives feared G Ex 1:17 430
Therefore G dealt well with the Ex 1:20 430
because the midwives feared G Ex 1:21 430
their cry came up unto G by Ex 2:23 430
G heard their groaning Ex 2:24 430
G remembered his covenant with Ex 2:24 430
G looked upon the children of Ex 2:25 430
and G had respect unto them Ex 2:25 430
and came to the mountain of G Ex 3:1 430
G called unto him out of the Ex 3:4 430
I am the G of thy father Ex 3:6 430
the G of Abraham Ex 3:6 430
G of Isaac, and the G of Jacob Ex 3:6 430
for he was afraid to look upon G Ex 3:6 430

And Moses said unto G, Who am I,	Ex 3:11	430
ye shall serve G upon this	Ex 3:12	430
And Moses said unto G, Behold,	Ex 3:13	430
The G of your fathers hath sent	Ex 3:13	430
G said unto Moses, I AM THAT I AM.	Ex 3:14	430
G said moreover unto Moses, Thus	Ex 3:15	430
The LORD G of your fathers	Ex 3:15	430
the G of Abraham	Ex 3:15	430
the G of Isaac	Ex 3:15	430
the G of Jacob	Ex 3:15	430
The LORD G of your fathers	Ex 3:16	430
the G of Abraham, of Isaac, and of	Ex 3:16	430
The LORD G of the Hebrews hath	Ex 3:18	430
may sacrifice to the LORD our G	Ex 3:18	430
that the LORD G of their fathers	Ex 4:5	430
the G of Abraham	Ex 4:5	430
the G of Isaac	Ex 4:5	430
the G of Jacob	Ex 4:5	430
thou shalt be to him instead of G	Ex 4:16	430
took the rod of G in his hand	Ex 4:20	430
and met him in the mount of G	Ex 4:27	430
Thus saith the LORD G of Israel	Ex 5:1	430
The G of the Hebrews hath met	Ex 5:3	430
and sacrifice unto the LORD our G	Ex 5:3	430
Let us go and sacrifice to our G	Ex 5:8	430
G spake unto Moses, and said unto	Ex 6:2	430
Jacob, by the name of G Almighty	Ex 6:3	410
a people, and I will be to you a G	Ex 6:7	430
know that I am the LORD your G	Ex 6:7	430
The LORD G of the Hebrews hath	Ex 7:16	430
is none like unto the LORD our G	Ex 8:10	430
Pharaoh, This is the finger of G	Ex 8:19	430
sacrifice to your G in the land	Ex 8:25	430
the Egyptians to the LORD our G	Ex 8:26	430
and sacrifice to the LORD our G	Ex 8:27	430
the LORD your G in the wilderness	Ex 8:28	430
saith the LORD G of the Hebrews	Ex 9:1	430
saith the LORD G of the Hebrews	Ex 9:13	430
ye will not yet fear the LORD G	Ex 9:30	430
saith the LORD G of the Hebrews	Ex 10:3	430
they may serve the LORD their G	Ex 10:7	430
them, Go, serve the LORD your G	Ex 10:8	430
sinned against the LORD your G	Ex 10:16	430
once, and intreat the LORD your G	Ex 10:17	430
may sacrifice unto the LORD our G	Ex 10:25	430
we take to serve the LORD our G	Ex 10:26	430
that G led them not through the	Ex 13:17	430
for G said, Lest peradventure the	Ex 13:17	430
But G led the people about,	Ex 13:18	430
saying, G will surely visit you	Ex 13:19	430
And the angel of G, which went	Ex 14:19	430
he is my G, and I will prepare him	Ex 15:2	410
my father's G, and I will exalt	Ex 15:2	430
to the voice of the LORD thy G	Ex 15:26	430
Would to G we had died by the	Ex 16:3	
know that I am the LORD your G	Ex 16:12	430
with the rod of G in mine hand	Ex 17:9	430
heard of all that G had done for	Ex 18:1	430
for the G of my father, said he,	Ex 18:4	430
he encamped at the mount of G	Ex 18:5	430
offering and sacrifices for G	Ex 18:12	430
Moses' father in law before G	Ex 18:12	430
come unto me to enquire of G	Ex 18:15	430
make them know the statutes of G	Ex 18:16	430
counsel, and G shall be with thee	Ex 18:19	430
mayest bring the causes unto G	Ex 18:19	430
people able men, such as fear G	Ex 18:21	430
G command thee so, then thou	Ex 18:23	430
And Moses went up unto G, and the	Ex 19:3	430
out of the camp to meet with G	Ex 19:17	430
G answered him by a voice	Ex 19:19	430
G spake all these words, saying,	Ex 20:1	430
I am the LORD thy G, which have	Ex 20:2	430
I the LORD thy G am a jealous G	Ex 20:5	430
I the LORD thy G am a jealous G	Ex 20:5	410
name of the LORD thy G in vain	Ex 20:7	430
is the sabbath of the LORD thy G	Ex 20:10	430
which the LORD thy G giveth thee	Ex 20:12	430
but let not G speak with us, lest	Ex 20:19	430
for G is come to prove you, and	Ex 20:20	430
the thick darkness where G was	Ex 20:21	430
but G deliver him into his hand	Ex 21:13	430
shall appear before the Lord G	Ex 23:17	3068
into the house of the LORD thy G	Ex 23:19	430
And ye shall serve the LORD your G	Ex 23:25	430
And they saw the G of Israel	Ex 24:10	430
also they saw G, and did eat and	Ex 24:11	430
Moses went up into the mount of G	Ex 24:13	430
of Israel, and will be their G	Ex 29:45	430
know that I am the LORD their G	Ex 29:46	430
I am the LORD their G	Ex 29:46	430
filled him with the spirit of G	Ex 31:3	430
written with the finger of G	Ex 31:18	430
And Moses besought the LORD his G	Ex 32:11	430
And the tables were the work of G	Ex 32:16	430
the writing was the writing of G	Ex 32:16	430
Thus saith the LORD G of Israel	Ex 32:27	430
proclaimed, The LORD, The LORD G	Ex 34:6	410
name is Jealous, is a jealous G	Ex 34:14	410
children appear before the Lord G	Ex 34:23	3068
the G of Israel	Ex 34:23	430
the LORD thy G thrice in the year	Ex 34:24	430
unto the house of the LORD thy G	Ex 34:26	430
filled him with the spirit of G	Ex 35:31	430
thy G to be lacking from thy meat	Lev 2:13	430
commandments of the LORD his G	Lev 4:22	430
G hath given it you to bear the	Lev 10:17	
For I am the LORD your G	Lev 11:44	430
the land of Egypt, to be your G	Lev 11:45	430
unto them, I am the LORD your G	Lev 18:2	430
I am the LORD your G	Lev 18:4	430
thou profane the name of thy G	Lev 18:21	430
I am the LORD your G	Lev 18:30	430
for I the LORD your G am holy	Lev 19:2	430
I am the LORD your G	Lev 19:3	430
I am the LORD your G	Lev 19:4	430
I am the LORD your G	Lev 19:10	430
thou profane the name of thy G	Lev 19:12	430
the blind, but shalt fear thy G	Lev 19:14	430
I am the LORD your G	Lev 19:25	430
I am the LORD your G	Lev 19:31	430
of the old man, and fear thy G	Lev 19:32	430
I am the LORD your G	Lev 19:34	430
I am the LORD your G, which	Lev 19:36	430
for I am the LORD your G	Lev 20:7	430
I am the LORD your G, which have	Lev 20:24	430
They shall be holy unto their G	Lev 21:6	430
not profane the name of their G	Lev 21:6	430
by fire, and the bread of their G	Lev 21:6	430
for he is holy unto his G	Lev 21:7	430
he offereth the bread of thy G	Lev 21:8	430
profane the sanctuary of his G	Lev 21:12	430
oil of his G is upon him	Lev 21:12	430
to offer the bread of his G	Lev 21:17	430
nigh to offer the bread of his G	Lev 21:21	430
He shall eat the bread of his G	Lev 21:22	430
bread of your G of any of these	Lev 22:25	430
the land of Egypt, to be your G	Lev 22:33	430
brought an offering unto your G	Lev 23:14	430
I am the LORD your G	Lev 23:22	430
for you before the LORD your G	Lev 23:28	430
before the LORD your G seven days	Lev 23:40	430
I am the LORD your G	Lev 23:43	430
curseth his G shall bear his sin	Lev 24:15	430
for I am the LORD your G	Lev 24:22	430
but thou shalt fear thy G	Lev 25:17	430
for I am the LORD your G	Lev 25:17	430
but fear thy G	Lev 25:36	430
I am the LORD your G, which	Lev 25:38	430
land of Canaan, and to be your G	Lev 25:38	430
but shalt fear thy G	Lev 25:43	430
I am the LORD your G	Lev 25:55	430
for I am the LORD your G	Lev 26:1	430
walk among you, and will be your G	Lev 26:12	430
I am the LORD your G, which	Lev 26:13	430
for I am the LORD their G	Lev 26:44	430
heathen, that I might be their G	Lev 26:45	430
of his G is upon his head	Num 6:7	430
remembered before the LORD your G	Num 10:9	430
you for a memorial before your G	Num 10:10	430
I am the LORD your G	Num 10:10	430
would G that all the LORD's	Num 11:29	
LORD, saying, Heal her now, O G	Num 12:13	410
Would G that we had died in the	Num 14:2	
or would G we had died in this	Num 14:2	
and be holy unto your G	Num 15:40	430
I am the LORD your G, which	Num 15:41	430
the land of Egypt, to be your G	Num 15:41	430
I am the LORD your G	Num 15:41	430
that the G of Israel hath	Num 16:9	430
upon their faces, and said, O G	Num 16:22	410
the G of the spirits of all flesh	Num 16:22	430
Would G that we had died when our	Num 20:3	
And the people spake against G	Num 21:5	430
G came unto Balaam, and said, What	Num 22:9	430
And Balaam said unto G, Balak the	Num 22:10	430
G said unto Balaam, Thou shalt	Num 22:12	430
beyond the word of the LORD my G	Num 22:18	430
G came unto Balaam at night, and	Num 22:20	430
the word that G putteth in my	Num 22:38	430
And G met Balaam	Num 23:4	430
I curse, whom G hath not cursed	Num 23:8	410
G is not a man, that he should	Num 23:19	410
the LORD his G is with him	Num 23:21	430
G brought them out of Egypt	Num 23:22	410
and of Israel, What hath G wrought	Num 23:23	410
peradventure it will please G	Num 23:27	430
and the spirit of G came upon him	Num 24:2	430
said, which heard the words of G	Num 24:4	410
G brought him forth out of Egypt	Num 24:8	410
said, which heard the words of G	Num 24:16	410
who shall live when G doeth this	Num 24:23	410
because he was zealous for his G	Num 25:13	430
the G of the spirits of all flesh	Num 27:16	430
The LORD our G spake unto us in	Deut 1:6	430
The LORD your G hath multiplied	Deut 1:10	430
(The LORD G of your fathers make	Deut 1:11	430
as the LORD our G commanded us	Deut 1:19	430
the LORD our G doth give unto us	Deut 1:20	430
the LORD thy G hath set the land	Deut 1:21	430
as the LORD G of thy fathers hath	Deut 1:21	430
which the LORD our G doth give us	Deut 1:25	430
commandment of the LORD your G	Deut 1:26	430
The LORD your G which goeth	Deut 1:30	430
how that the LORD thy G bare thee	Deut 1:31	430
did not believe the LORD your G	Deut 1:32	430
that the LORD our G commanded us	Deut 1:41	430
For the LORD thy G hath blessed	Deut 2:7	430
LORD thy G hath been with thee	Deut 2:7	430
which the LORD our G giveth us	Deut 2:29	430
for the LORD thy G hardened his	Deut 2:30	430
the LORD our G delivered him	Deut 2:33	430
the LORD our G delivered all unto	Deut 2:36	430
the LORD our G forbad us	Deut 2:37	430
So the LORD our G delivered into	Deut 3:3	430
The LORD your G hath given you	Deut 3:18	430
the land which the LORD your G	Deut 3:20	430
seen all that the LORD your G	Deut 3:21	430
for the LORD your G he shall	Deut 3:22	430
O Lord G, thou hast begun to shew	Deut 3:24	3069
for what G is there in heaven or	Deut 3:24	410
LORD G of your fathers giveth you	Deut 4:1	430
LORD your G which I command you	Deut 4:2	430
the LORD thy G hath destroyed	Deut 4:3	430
did cleave unto the LORD your G	Deut 4:4	430
as the LORD my G commanded me	Deut 4:5	430
who hath G so nigh unto them	Deut 4:7	430
as the LORD our G is in all	Deut 4:7	430
before the LORD thy G in Horeb	Deut 4:10	430
which the LORD thy G hath divided	Deut 4:19	430
which the LORD thy G giveth thee	Deut 4:21	430
the covenant of the LORD your G	Deut 4:23	430
which the LORD thy G hath	Deut 4:23	430
For the LORD thy G is a consuming	Deut 4:24	430
consuming fire, even a jealous G	Deut 4:24	410
in the sight of the LORD thy G	Deut 4:25	430
thou shalt seek the LORD thy G	Deut 4:29	430
if thou turn to the LORD thy G	Deut 4:30	430
the LORD thy G is a merciful G	Deut 4:31	430
the LORD thy G is a merciful G	Deut 4:31	410
since the day that G created man	Deut 4:32	430
of G speaking out of the midst of	Deut 4:33	430
Or hath G assayed to go and take	Deut 4:34	430
to all that the LORD your G did	Deut 4:34	430
know that the LORD he is G	Deut 4:35	430
the LORD he is G in heaven above	Deut 4:39	430
which the LORD thy G giveth thee	Deut 4:40	430
The LORD our G made a covenant	Deut 5:2	430
I am the LORD thy G, which	Deut 5:6	430
I the LORD thy G am a jealous G	Deut 5:9	430
I the LORD thy G am a jealous G	Deut 5:9	410
name of the LORD thy G in vain	Deut 5:11	430
as the LORD thy G hath commanded	Deut 5:12	430
is the sabbath of the LORD thy G	Deut 5:14	430
that the LORD thy G brought thee	Deut 5:15	430
therefore the LORD thy G	Deut 5:15	430
as the LORD thy G hath commanded	Deut 5:16	430
which the LORD thy G giveth thee	Deut 5:16	430
the LORD our G hath shewed us his	Deut 5:24	430
day that G doth talk with man	Deut 5:24	430
voice of the LORD our G any more	Deut 5:25	430
G speaking out of the midst of	Deut 5:26	430
all that the LORD our G shall say	Deut 5:27	430
LORD our G shall speak unto thee	Deut 5:27	430
LORD your G hath commanded you	Deut 5:32	430
LORD your G hath commanded you	Deut 5:33	430
which the LORD your G commanded	Deut 6:1	430
thou mightest fear the LORD thy G	Deut 6:2	430
as the LORD G of thy fathers hath	Deut 6:3	430
The LORD our G is one LORD	Deut 6:4	430
LORD thy G with all thine heart	Deut 6:5	430
when the LORD thy G shall have	Deut 6:10	430
Thou shalt fear the LORD thy G	Deut 6:13	430
(For the LORD thy G is a jealous	Deut 6:15	430
G among you) lest the anger of	Deut 6:15	410
thy G be kindled against thee	Deut 6:15	430
shall not tempt the LORD your G	Deut 6:16	430
commandments of the LORD your G	Deut 6:17	430
the LORD our G hath commanded you.	Deut 6:20	430
statutes, to fear the LORD our G	Deut 6:24	430
before the LORD our G, as he hath	Deut 6:25	430
When the LORD thy G shall bring	Deut 7:1	430
when the LORD thy G shall deliver	Deut 7:2	430
holy people unto the LORD thy G	Deut 7:6	430
the LORD thy G hath chosen thee	Deut 7:6	430
that the LORD thy G, he is G	Deut 7:9	430
the faithful G, which keepeth	Deut 7:9	410
that the LORD thy G shall keep	Deut 7:12	430
the LORD thy G shall deliver thee	Deut 7:16	430
the LORD thy G did unto Pharaoh	Deut 7:18	430
the LORD thy G brought thee out	Deut 7:19	430
so shall the LORD thy G do unto	Deut 7:19	430
Moreover the LORD thy G will send	Deut 7:20	430
for the LORD thy G is among you	Deut 7:21	430
a mighty G and terrible	Deut 7:21	410
the LORD thy G will put out those	Deut 7:22	430
But the LORD thy G shall deliver	Deut 7:23	430
an abomination to the LORD thy G	Deut 7:25	430
G led thee these forty years in	Deut 8:2	430
so the LORD thy G chasteneth thee	Deut 8:5	430
commandments of the LORD thy G	Deut 8:6	430
For the LORD thy G bringeth thee	Deut 8:7	430
thou shalt bless the LORD thy G	Deut 8:10	430
thou forget not the LORD thy G	Deut 8:11	430
up, and thou forget the LORD thy G	Deut 8:14	430
shalt remember the LORD thy G	Deut 8:18	430
do at all forget the LORD thy G	Deut 8:19	430
unto the voice of the LORD your G	Deut 8:20	430
that the LORD thy G is he which	Deut 9:3	430
after that the LORD thy G hath	Deut 9:4	430
of these nations the LORD thy G	Deut 9:5	430
that the LORD thy G giveth thee	Deut 9:6	430
thy G to wrath in the wilderness	Deut 9:7	430
written with the finger of G	Deut 9:10	430
sinned against the LORD your G	Deut 9:16	430
commandment of the LORD your G	Deut 9:23	430
unto the LORD, and said, O Lord G	Deut 9:26	3069
as the LORD thy G promised him	Deut 10:9	430
the LORD thy G require of thee	Deut 10:12	430
but to fear the LORD thy G	Deut 10:12	430
the LORD thy G with all thy heart	Deut 10:12	430
of heavens is the LORD's thy G	Deut 10:14	430
the LORD your G is G of gods	Deut 10:17	430
gods, and Lord of lords, a great G	Deut 10:17	410
Thou shalt fear the LORD thy G	Deut 10:20	430
He is thy praise, and he is thy G	Deut 10:21	430
now the LORD thy G hath made thee	Deut 10:22	430
thou shalt love the LORD thy G	Deut 11:1	430
chastisement of the LORD your G	Deut 11:2	430
which the LORD thy G careth for	Deut 11:12	430
the LORD thy G are always upon it	Deut 11:12	430
this day, to love the LORD your G	Deut 11:13	430
do them, to love the LORD your G	Deut 11:22	430
for the LORD your G shall lay the	Deut 11:25	430
commandments of the LORD your G	Deut 11:27	430
commandments of the LORD your G	Deut 11:28	430
when the LORD thy G hath brought	Deut 11:29	430
which the LORD your G giveth you	Deut 11:31	430
which the LORD G of thy fathers	Deut 12:1	430
not do so unto the LORD your G	Deut 12:4	430
G shall choose out of all your	Deut 12:5	430
shall eat before the LORD your G	Deut 12:7	430

the LORD thy G hath blessed thee	Deut 12:7	430
which the LORD your G giveth you	Deut 12:9	430
LORD your G giveth you to inherit	Deut 12:10	430
G shall choose to cause his name	Deut 12:11	430
rejoice before the LORD your G	Deut 12:12	430
thy G which he hath given thee	Deut 12:15	430
eat them before the LORD thy G in	Deut 12:18	430
which the LORD thy G shall choose	Deut 12:18	430
rejoice before the LORD thy G in	Deut 12:18	430
When the LORD thy G shall enlarge	Deut 12:20	430
thy G hath chosen to put his name	Deut 12:21	430
upon the altar of the LORD thy G	Deut 12:27	430
upon the altar of the LORD thy G	Deut 12:27	430
in the sight of the LORD thy G	Deut 12:28	430
When the LORD thy G shall cut off	Deut 12:29	430
not do so unto the LORD thy G	Deut 12:31	430
for the LORD your G proveth you	Deut 13:3	430
LORD your G with all your heart	Deut 13:3	430
shall walk after the LORD your G	Deut 13:4	430
you away from the LORD your G	Deut 13:5	430
thy G commanded thee to walk in	Deut 13:5	430
thee away from the LORD thy G	Deut 13:10	430
which the LORD thy G hath given	Deut 13:12	430
every whit, for the LORD thy G	Deut 13:16	430
to the voice of the LORD thy G	Deut 13:18	430
in the eyes of the LORD thy G	Deut 13:18	430
the children of the LORD your G	Deut 14:1	430
holy people unto the LORD thy G	Deut 14:2	430
holy people unto the LORD thy G	Deut 14:21	430
shalt eat before the LORD thy G	Deut 14:23	430
to fear the LORD thy G always	Deut 14:23	430
which the LORD thy G shall choose	Deut 14:24	430
the LORD thy G hath blessed thee	Deut 14:24	430
which the LORD thy G shall choose	Deut 14:25	430
eat there before the LORD thy G	Deut 14:26	430
that the LORD thy G may bless	Deut 14:29	430
G giveth thee for an inheritance	Deut 15:4	430
unto the voice of the LORD thy G	Deut 15:5	430
For the LORD thy G blesseth thee	Deut 15:6	430
which the LORD thy G giveth thee	Deut 15:7	430
thy G shall bless thee in all thy	Deut 15:10	430
G hath blessed thee thou shalt	Deut 15:14	430
the LORD thy G redeemed thee	Deut 15:15	430
the LORD thy G shall bless thee	Deut 15:18	430
sanctify unto the LORD thy G	Deut 15:19	430
eat it before the LORD thy G year	Deut 15:20	430
sacrifice it unto the LORD thy G	Deut 15:21	430
the passover unto the LORD thy G	Deut 16:1	430
the month of Abib the LORD thy G	Deut 16:1	430
the passover unto the LORD thy G	Deut 16:2	430
which the LORD thy G giveth thee	Deut 16:5	430
G shall choose to place his name	Deut 16:6	430
which the LORD thy G shall choose	Deut 16:7	430
solemn assembly to the LORD thy G	Deut 16:8	430
of weeks unto the LORD thy G with	Deut 16:10	430
shalt give unto the LORD thy G	Deut 16:10	
the LORD thy G hath blessed thee	Deut 16:10	430
rejoice before the LORD thy G	Deut 16:11	430
G hath chosen to place his name	Deut 16:11	430
thy G in the place which the LORD	Deut 16:15	430
because the LORD thy G shall	Deut 16:15	430
appear before the LORD thy G in	Deut 16:16	430
thy G which he hath given thee	Deut 16:17	430
which the LORD thy G giveth thee	Deut 16:18	430
which the LORD thy G giveth thee	Deut 16:20	430
unto the altar of the LORD thy G	Deut 16:21	430
which the LORD thy G hateth	Deut 16:22	430
unto the LORD thy G any bullock	Deut 17:1	430
abomination unto the LORD thy G	Deut 17:1	430
which the LORD thy G giveth thee	Deut 17:2	430
in the sight of the LORD thy G	Deut 17:2	430
which the LORD thy G shall choose	Deut 17:8	430
there before the LORD thy G	Deut 17:12	430
which the LORD thy G giveth thee	Deut 17:14	430
whom the LORD thy G shall choose	Deut 17:15	430
may learn to fear the LORD his G	Deut 17:19	430
For the LORD thy G hath chosen	Deut 18:5	430
in the name of the LORD his G	Deut 18:7	430
which the LORD thy G giveth thee	Deut 18:9	430
G doth drive them out from before	Deut 18:12	430
be perfect with the LORD thy G	Deut 18:13	430
the LORD thy G hath not suffered	Deut 18:14	430
The LORD thy G will raise up unto	Deut 18:15	430
thy G in Horeb in the day of the	Deut 18:16	430
again the voice of the LORD my G	Deut 18:16	430
When the LORD thy G hath cut off	Deut 19:1	430
land the LORD thy G giveth thee	Deut 19:1	430
which the LORD thy G giveth thee	Deut 19:2	430
which the LORD thy G giveth thee	Deut 19:3	430
if the LORD thy G enlarge thy	Deut 19:8	430
this day, to love the LORD thy G	Deut 19:9	430
which the LORD thy G giveth thee	Deut 19:10	430
thy G giveth thee to possess it	Deut 19:14	430
for the LORD thy G is with thee	Deut 20:1	430
For the LORD your G is he that	Deut 20:4	430
And when the LORD thy G hath	Deut 20:13	430
the LORD thy G hath given thee	Deut 20:14	430
which the LORD thy G doth give	Deut 20:16	430
as the LORD thy G hath commanded	Deut 20:17	430
ye sin against the LORD your G	Deut 20:18	430
thy G giveth thee to possess it	Deut 21:1	430
for them the LORD thy G hath	Deut 21:5	430
the LORD thy G hath delivered	Deut 21:10	430
that is hanged is accursed of G	Deut 21:23	430
which the LORD thy G giveth thee	Deut 21:23	430
abomination unto the LORD thy G	Deut 22:5	430
Nevertheless the LORD thy G would	Deut 23:5	430
but the LORD thy G turned the	Deut 23:5	430
because the LORD thy G loved thee	Deut 23:5	430
For the LORD thy G walketh in the	Deut 23:14	430
of the LORD thy G for any vow	Deut 23:18	430
abomination unto the LORD thy G	Deut 23:18	430
that the LORD thy G may bless	Deut 23:20	430
vow a vow unto the LORD thy G	Deut 23:21	430
for the LORD thy G will surely	Deut 23:21	430
hast vowed unto the LORD thy G	Deut 23:23	430
which the LORD thy G giveth thee	Deut 24:4	430
thy G did unto Miriam by the way	Deut 24:9	430
unto thee before the LORD thy G	Deut 24:13	430
the LORD thy G redeemed thee	Deut 24:18	430
that the LORD thy G may bless	Deut 24:19	430
which the LORD thy G giveth thee	Deut 25:15	430
abomination unto the LORD thy G	Deut 25:16	430
and he feared not G	Deut 25:18	430
when the LORD thy G hath given	Deut 25:19	430
G giveth thee for an inheritance	Deut 25:19	430
the land which the LORD thy G	Deut 26:1	430
that the LORD thy G giveth thee	Deut 26:2	430
the place which the LORD thy G	Deut 26:2	430
this day unto the LORD thy G	Deut 26:3	430
the altar of the LORD thy G	Deut 26:4	430
and say before the LORD thy G	Deut 26:5	430
unto the LORD G of our fathers	Deut 26:7	430
set it before the LORD thy G	Deut 26:10	430
and worship before the LORD thy G	Deut 26:10	430
LORD thy G hath given unto thee	Deut 26:11	430
shalt say before the LORD thy G	Deut 26:13	430
to the voice of the LORD my G	Deut 26:14	430
This day the LORD thy G hath	Deut 26:16	430
the LORD this day to be thy G	Deut 26:17	430
holy people unto the LORD thy G	Deut 26:19	430
which the LORD thy G giveth thee	Deut 27:2	430
which the LORD thy G giveth thee	Deut 27:3	430
as the LORD G of thy fathers hath	Deut 27:3	430
an altar unto the LORD thy G	Deut 27:5	430
of the LORD thy G of whole stones	Deut 27:6	430
thereon unto the LORD thy G	Deut 27:6	430
and rejoice before the LORD thy G	Deut 27:7	430
the people of the LORD thy G	Deut 27:9	430
obey the voice of the LORD thy G	Deut 27:10	430
unto the voice of the LORD thy G	Deut 28:1	430
that the LORD thy G will set thee	Deut 28:1	430
unto the voice of the LORD thy G	Deut 28:2	430
which the LORD thy G giveth thee	Deut 28:8	430
commandments of the LORD thy G	Deut 28:9	430
commandments of the LORD thy G	Deut 28:13	430
unto the voice of the LORD thy G	Deut 28:15	430
unto the voice of the LORD thy G	Deut 28:45	430
the LORD thy G with joyfulness	Deut 28:47	430
the LORD thy G hath given thee	Deut 28:52	430
the LORD thy G hath given thee	Deut 28:53	430
and fearful name, THE LORD THY G	Deut 28:58	430
obey the voice of the LORD thy G	Deut 28:62	430
shalt say, Would G it were even	Deut 28:67	
say, Would G it were morning	Deut 28:67	
know that I am the LORD your G	Deut 29:6	430
all of you before the LORD your G	Deut 29:10	430
into covenant with the LORD thy G	Deut 29:12	430
which the LORD thy G maketh with	Deut 29:12	430
and that he may be unto thee a G	Deut 29:13	430
us this day before the LORD our G	Deut 29:15	430
away this day from the LORD our G	Deut 29:18	430
of the LORD G of their fathers	Deut 29:25	430
things belong unto the LORD our G	Deut 29:29	430
the LORD thy G hath driven thee	Deut 30:1	430
shalt return unto the LORD thy G	Deut 30:2	430
That then the LORD thy G will	Deut 30:3	430
LORD thy G hath scattered thee	Deut 30:3	430
will the LORD thy G gather thee	Deut 30:4	430
the LORD thy G will bring thee	Deut 30:5	430
the LORD thy G will circumcise	Deut 30:6	430
LORD thy G with all thine heart	Deut 30:6	430
the LORD thy G will put all these	Deut 30:7	430
the LORD thy G will make thee	Deut 30:9	430
unto the voice of the LORD thy G	Deut 30:10	430
LORD thy G with all thine heart	Deut 30:10	430
this day to love the LORD thy G	Deut 30:16	430
the LORD thy G shall bless thee	Deut 30:16	430
thou mayest love the LORD thy G	Deut 30:20	430
The LORD thy G, he will go over	Deut 31:3	430
for the LORD thy G, he it is that	Deut 31:6	430
thy G in the place which he shall	Deut 31:11	430
learn, and fear the LORD your G	Deut 31:12	430
and learn to fear the LORD your G	Deut 31:13	430
because our G is not among us	Deut 31:17	430
the covenant of the LORD your G	Deut 31:26	430
ascribe ye greatness unto our G	Deut 32:3	430
a G of truth and without iniquity,	Deut 32:4	410
then he forsook G which made him	Deut 32:15	433
sacrificed unto devils, not to G	Deut 32:17	433
hast forgotten G that formed thee	Deut 32:18	410
jealousy with that which is not G	Deut 32:21	410
wherewith Moses the man of G	Deut 33:1	430
none like unto the G of Jeshurun	Deut 33:26	410
The eternal G is thy refuge, and	Deut 33:27	430
for the LORD thy G is with thee	Josh 1:9	430
which the LORD your G giveth you	Josh 1:11	430
The LORD your G hath given you	Josh 1:13	430
which the LORD your G giveth them	Josh 1:15	430
only the LORD thy G be with thee	Josh 1:17	430
for the LORD your G, he is G in	Josh 2:11	430
the covenant of the LORD your G	Josh 3:3	430
hear the words of the LORD your G	Josh 3:9	430
that the living G is among you	Josh 3:10	410
your G into the midst of Jordan	Josh 4:5	430
For the LORD your G dried up the	Josh 4:23	430
as the LORD your G did to the Red	Josh 4:23	430
fear the LORD your G for ever	Josh 4:24	430
And Joshua said, Alas, O Lord G	Josh 7:7	3069
would to G we had been content,	Josh 7:7	
thus saith the LORD G of Israel	Josh 7:13	430
glory to the LORD G of Israel	Josh 7:19	430
against the LORD G of Israel	Josh 7:20	430
for the LORD your G will deliver	Josh 8:7	430
LORD G of Israel in mount Ebal	Josh 8:30	430
of the name of the LORD thy G	Josh 9:9	430
unto them by the LORD G of Israel	Josh 9:18	430
unto them by the LORD G of Israel	Josh 9:19	430
of water for the house of my G	Josh 9:23	430
how that the LORD thy G commanded.	Josh 9:24	430
for the LORD your G hath	Josh 10:19	430
as the LORD G of Israel commanded	Josh 10:40	430
because the LORD G of Israel	Josh 10:42	430
LORD G of Israel made by fire are	Josh 13:14	430
the LORD G of Israel was their	Josh 13:33	430
Moses the man of G concerning me	Josh 14:6	430
I wholly followed the LORD my G	Josh 14:8	430
wholly followed the LORD my G	Josh 14:9	430
followed the LORD G of Israel	Josh 14:14	430
which the LORD G of your fathers	Josh 18:3	430
you here before the LORD our G	Josh 18:6	430
commandment of the LORD your G	Josh 22:3	430
now the LORD your G hath given	Josh 22:4	430
you, to love the LORD your G	Josh 22:5	430
committed against the G of Israel	Josh 22:16	430
the altar of the LORD our G	Josh 22:19	430
The LORD G of gods, the LORD G	Josh 22:22	410
to do with the LORD G of Israel	Josh 22:24	430
G forbid that we should rebel	Josh 22:29	
the altar of the LORD our G that	Josh 22:29	430
the children of Israel blessed G	Josh 22:33	430
between us that the LORD is G	Josh 22:34	430
your G hath done unto all these	Josh 23:3	430
for the LORD your G is he that	Josh 23:3	430
And the LORD your G, he shall	Josh 23:5	430
as the LORD your G hath promised	Josh 23:5	430
But cleave unto the LORD your G	Josh 23:8	430
for the LORD your G, he it is	Josh 23:10	430
that ye love the LORD your G	Josh 23:11	430
G will no more drive out any of	Josh 23:13	430
the LORD your G hath given you	Josh 23:13	430
LORD your G spake concerning you	Josh 23:14	430
the LORD your G promised you	Josh 23:15	430
the LORD your G hath given you	Josh 23:15	430
the covenant of the LORD your G	Josh 23:16	430
presented themselves before G	Josh 24:1	430
Thus saith the LORD G of Israel	Josh 24:2	430
G forbid that we should forsake	Josh 24:16	
For the LORD our G, he it is that	Josh 24:17	430
for he is our G	Josh 24:18	430
for he is an holy G	Josh 24:19	430
he is a jealous G	Josh 24:19	410
heart unto the LORD G of Israel	Josh 24:23	430
The LORD our G will we serve, and	Josh 24:24	430
words in the book of the law of G	Josh 24:26	430
unto you, lest ye deny your G	Josh 24:27	430
have done, so G hath requited me	Judg 1:7	430
the LORD G of their fathers	Judg 2:12	430
LORD, and forgat the LORD their G	Judg 3:7	430
I have a message from G unto thee	Judg 3:20	430
Hath not the LORD G of Israel	Judg 4:6	430
So G subdued on that day Jabin	Judg 4:23	430
praise to the LORD G of Israel	Judg 5:3	430
from before the LORD G of Israel	Judg 5:5	430
Thus saith the LORD G of Israel	Judg 6:8	430
unto you, I am the LORD your G	Judg 6:10	430
the angel of G said unto him,	Judg 6:20	430
LORD, Gideon said, Alas, O Lord G	Judg 6:22	3069
thy G upon the top of this rock	Judg 6:26	430
And Gideon said unto G, If thou	Judg 6:36	430
And Gideon said unto G, Let not	Judg 6:39	430
And G did so that night	Judg 6:40	430
his hand hath G delivered Midian	Judg 7:14	430
G hath delivered into your hands	Judg 8:3	430
remembered not the LORD their G	Judg 8:34	430
that G may hearken unto you	Judg 9:7	430
wherewith by me they honour G	Judg 9:9	430
I leave my wine, which cheereth G	Judg 9:13	430
Then G sent an evil spirit	Judg 9:23	430
would to G this people were under	Judg 9:29	
Thus G rendered the wickedness of	Judg 9:56	430
did G render upon their heads	Judg 9:57	430
because we have forsaken our G	Judg 10:10	430
the LORD G of Israel delivered	Judg 11:21	430
So now the LORD G of Israel hath	Judg 11:23	430
So whomsoever the LORD our G	Judg 11:24	430
a Nazarite unto G from the womb	Judg 13:5	430
A man of G came unto me, and his	Judg 13:6	430
the countenance of an angel of G	Judg 13:6	430
child shall be a Nazarite to G	Judg 13:7	430
let the man of G which thou didst	Judg 13:8	430
G hearkened to the voice of	Judg 13:9	430
the angel of G came again unto	Judg 13:9	430
die, because we have seen G	Judg 13:22	430
But G clave an hollow place that	Judg 15:19	430
unto G from my mother's womb	Judg 16:17	430
unto the LORD, and said, O Lord G	Judg 16:28	3069
I pray thee, only this once, O G	Judg 16:28	430
Ask counsel, we pray thee, of G	Judg 18:5	430
for G hath given it into your	Judg 18:10	430
that the house of G was in Shiloh	Judg 18:31	430
the assembly of the people of G	Judg 20:2	430
and went up to the house of G	Judg 20:18	1008
and asked counsel of G	Judg 20:18	430
up, and came unto the house of G	Judg 20:26	1008
of G was there in those days	Judg 20:27	430
one goeth up to the house of G	Judg 20:31	1008
the people came to the house of G	Judg 21:2	1008
and abode there till even before G	Judg 21:2	430
O LORD G of Israel, why is this	Judg 21:3	430
thee of the LORD G of Israel	Ruth 2:12	430
the G of Israel grant thee thy	1Sa 1:17	430
is there any rock like our G	1Sa 2:2	430
for the LORD is a G of knowledge	1Sa 2:3	410
And there came a man of G unto Eli	1Sa 2:27	430
the LORD G of Israel saith	1Sa 2:30	430
wealth which G shall give Israel	1Sa 2:32	
ere the lamp of G went out in the	1Sa 3:3	430
the LORD, where the ark of G was	1Sa 3:3	430
G do so to thee, and more also, if	1Sa 3:17	430
with the ark of the covenant of G	1Sa 4:4	430
said, G is come into the camp	1Sa 4:7	430

And the ark of G was taken	1Sa 4:11	430
heart trembled for the ark of G	1Sa 4:13	430
dead, and the ark of G is taken	1Sa 4:17	430
he made mention of the ark of G	1Sa 4:18	430
that the ark of G was taken	1Sa 4:19	430
because the ark of G was taken	1Sa 4:21	430
for the ark of G is taken	1Sa 4:22	430
the Philistines took the ark of G	1Sa 5:1	430
the Philistines took the ark of G	1Sa 5:2	430
The ark of the G of Israel shall	1Sa 5:7	430
with the ark of the G of Israel	1Sa 5:8	430
Let the ark of the G of Israel be	1Sa 5:8	430
of the G of Israel about thither	1Sa 5:8	430
they sent the ark of G to Ekron	1Sa 5:10	430
as the ark of G came to Ekron	1Sa 5:10	430
the ark of the G of Israel to us	1Sa 5:10	430
away the ark of the G of Israel	1Sa 5:11	430
the hand of G was very heavy	1Sa 5:11	430
away the ark of the G of Israel	1Sa 6:3	430
give glory unto the G of Israel	1Sa 6:5	430
to stand before this holy LORD G	1Sa 6:20	430
to cry unto the LORD our G for us	1Sa 7:8	430
there is in this city a man of G	1Sa 9:6	430
present to bring to the man of G	1Sa 9:7	430
that will I give to the man of G	1Sa 9:8	430
when a man went to enquire of G	1Sa 9:9	430
the city where the man of G was	1Sa 9:10	430
I may shew thee the word of G	1Sa 9:27	430
men going up to G to Beth-el	1Sa 10:3	430
thou shalt come to the hill of G	1Sa 10:5	430
for G is with thee	1Sa 10:7	430
Samuel, G gave him another heart	1Sa 10:9	430
and the Spirit of G came upon him	1Sa 10:10	430
Thus saith the LORD G of Israel	1Sa 10:18	430
ye have this day rejected your G	1Sa 10:19	430
shouted, and said, G save the king	1Sa 10:24	
men, whose hearts G had touched	1Sa 10:26	430
the Spirit of G came upon Saul	1Sa 11:6	430
when they forgat the LORD their G	1Sa 12:9	430
the LORD your G was your king	1Sa 12:12	430
following the LORD your G	1Sa 12:14	430
thy servants unto the LORD thy G	1Sa 12:19	430
G forbid that I should sin	1Sa 12:23	
the commandment of the LORD thy G	1Sa 13:13	430
Ahiah, Bring hither the ark of G	1Sa 14:18	430
For the ark of G was at that time	1Sa 14:18	430
Let us draw near hither unto G	1Sa 14:36	430
And Saul asked counsel of G	1Sa 14:37	430
said unto the LORD G of Israel	1Sa 14:41	430
answered, G do so and more also	1Sa 14:44	430
G forbid: as the LORD liveth	1Sa 14:45	
he hath wrought with G this day	1Sa 14:45	430
to sacrifice unto the LORD thy G	1Sa 15:15	430
unto the LORD thy G in Gilgal	1Sa 15:21	430
that I may worship the LORD thy G	1Sa 15:30	430
evil spirit from G troubleth thee	1Sa 16:15	430
evil spirit from G is upon thee	1Sa 16:16	430
evil spirit from G was upon Saul	1Sa 16:23	430
defy the armies of the living G	1Sa 17:26	430
defied the armies of the living G	1Sa 17:36	430
the G of the armies of Israel,	1Sa 17:45	430
know that there is a G in Israel	1Sa 17:46	430
evil spirit from G came upon Saul	1Sa 18:10	430
the Spirit of G was upon the	1Sa 19:20	430
the Spirit of G was upon him also	1Sa 19:23	430
And he said unto him, G forbid	1Sa 20:2	
O LORD G of Israel, when I have	1Sa 20:12	430
till I know what G will do for me	1Sa 22:3	430
and hast enquired of G for him	1Sa 22:13	430
begin to enquire of G for him	1Sa 22:15	430
G hath delivered him into mine	1Sa 23:7	430
O LORD G of Israel, thy servant	1Sa 23:10	430
O LORD G of Israel, I beseech	1Sa 23:11	430
but G delivered him not into his	1Sa 23:14	430
and strengthened his hand in G	1Sa 23:16	430
more also do G unto the enemies	1Sa 25:22	430
of life with the LORD thy G	1Sa 25:29	430
Blessed be the LORD G of Israel	1Sa 25:32	430
as the LORD G of Israel liveth,	1Sa 25:34	430
G hath delivered thine enemy into	1Sa 26:8	430
G is departed from me, and	1Sa 28:15	430
in my sight, as an angel of G	1Sa 29:9	430
himself in the LORD his G	1Sa 30:6	430
And he said, Swear unto me by G	1Sa 30:15	430
As G liveth, unless thou hadst	2Sa 2:27	430
So do G to Abner, and more also,	2Sa 3:9	430
sware, saying, So do G to me	2Sa 3:35	430
the LORD G of hosts was with him	2Sa 5:10	430
bring up from thence the ark of G	2Sa 6:2	430
set the ark of G upon a new cart	2Sa 6:3	430
Gibeah, accompanying the ark of G	2Sa 6:4	430
forth his hand to the ark of G	2Sa 6:6	430
G smote him there for his error	2Sa 6:7	430
and there he died by the ark of G	2Sa 6:7	430
unto him, because of the ark of G	2Sa 6:12	430
brought up the ark of G from the	2Sa 6:12	430
but the ark of G dwelleth within	2Sa 7:2	430
and he said, Who am I, O Lord G	2Sa 7:18	3069
thing in thy sight, O Lord G	2Sa 7:19	3069
this the manner of man, O Lord G	2Sa 7:19	3069
for thou, Lord G, knowest thy	2Sa 7:20	3069
thou art great, O LORD G	2Sa 7:22	430
is there any G beside thee	2Sa 7:22	430
whom G went to redeem for a	2Sa 7:23	430
and thou, LORD, art become their G	2Sa 7:24	430
And now, O LORD G, the word that	2Sa 7:25	430
of hosts is the G over Israel	2Sa 7:26	430
G of Israel, hast revealed to thy	2Sa 7:27	430
And now, O Lord G	2Sa 7:28	3069
thou art that G	2Sa 7:28	430
for thou, O Lord G, hast spoken	2Sa 7:29	3069
shew the kindness of G unto him	2Sa 9:3	430
and for the cities of our G	2Sa 10:12	430
Thus saith the LORD G of Israel	2Sa 12:7	430
besought G for the child	2Sa 12:16	430
Who can tell whether G will be	2Sa 12:22	3068
the king remember the LORD thy G	2Sa 14:11	430
a thing against the people of G	2Sa 14:13	430
neither doth G respect any person	2Sa 14:14	430
out of the inheritance of G	2Sa 14:16	430
for as an angel of G, so is my	2Sa 14:17	430
the LORD thy G will be with thee	2Sa 14:17	430
to the wisdom of an angel of G	2Sa 14:20	430
the ark of the covenant of G	2Sa 15:24	430
and they set down the ark of G	2Sa 15:24	430
back the ark of G into the city	2Sa 15:25	430
the ark of G again to Jerusalem	2Sa 15:29	430
the mount, where he worshipped G	2Sa 15:32	430
G save the king, G save the	2Sa 16:16	
had enquired at the oracle of G	2Sa 16:23	430
said, Blessed be the LORD thy G	2Sa 18:28	430
would G I had died for thee, O	2Sa 18:33	
G do so to me, and more also, if	2Sa 19:13	430
lord the king is as an angel of G	2Sa 19:27	430
after that G was intreated for	2Sa 21:14	430
The G of my rock	2Sa 22:3	430
upon the LORD, and cried to my G	2Sa 22:7	430
not wickedly departed from my G	2Sa 22:22	430
by my G have I leaped over a wall	2Sa 22:30	430
As for G, his way is perfect	2Sa 22:31	410
For who is G, save the LORD	2Sa 22:32	410
and who is a rock, save our G	2Sa 22:32	430
G is my strength and power	2Sa 22:33	410
exalted be the G of the rock of	2Sa 22:47	430
It is G that avengeth me, and that	2Sa 22:48	410
the anointed of the G of Jacob	2Sa 23:1	430
The G of Israel said, the Rock of	2Sa 23:3	430
be just, ruling in the fear of G	2Sa 23:3	430
my house be not so with G	2Sa 23:5	410
Now the LORD thy G add unto the	2Sa 24:3	430
king, The LORD thy G accept thee	2Sa 24:23	430
my G of that which doth cost me	2Sa 24:24	430
LORD thy G unto thine handmaid	1Kin 1:17	430
him, and say, G save king Adonijah	1Kin 1:25	
unto thee by the LORD G of Israel	1Kin 1:30	430
and say, G save king Solomon	1Kin 1:34	
the LORD G of my lord the king	1Kin 1:36	430
people said, G save king Solomon	1Kin 1:39	
G make the name of Solomon better	1Kin 1:47	430
Blessed be the LORD G of Israel	1Kin 1:48	430
keep the charge of the LORD thy G	1Kin 2:3	430
G do so to me, and more also, if	1Kin 2:23	430
the Lord G before David my father	1Kin 2:26	3069
G said, Ask what I shall give	1Kin 3:5	430
And now, O LORD my G, thou hast	1Kin 3:7	430
G said unto him, Because thou	1Kin 3:11	430
that the wisdom of G was in him	1Kin 3:28	430
And G gave Solomon wisdom and	1Kin 4:29	430
G for the wars which were about	1Kin 5:3	430
But now the LORD my G hath given	1Kin 5:4	430
unto the name of the LORD my G	1Kin 5:5	430
Blessed be the LORD G of Israel	1Kin 8:15	430
the name of the LORD G of Israel	1Kin 8:17	430
the name of the LORD G of Israel	1Kin 8:20	430
LORD G of Israel, there is no G	1Kin 8:23	430
LORD G of Israel, keep with thy	1Kin 8:25	430
O G of Israel, let thy word, I	1Kin 8:26	430
But will G indeed dwell on the	1Kin 8:27	430
to his supplication, O LORD my G	1Kin 8:28	430
fathers out of Egypt, O Lord G	1Kin 8:53	3069
The LORD our G be with us	1Kin 8:57	430
be nigh unto the LORD our G day	1Kin 8:59	430
earth may know that the LORD is G	1Kin 8:60	430
be perfect with the LORD our G	1Kin 8:61	430
of Egypt, before the LORD our G	1Kin 8:65	430
they forsook the LORD their G	1Kin 9:9	430
Blessed be the LORD thy G	1Kin 10:9	430
which G had put in his heart	1Kin 10:24	430
not perfect with the LORD his G	1Kin 11:4	430
turned from the LORD G of Israel	1Kin 11:9	430
And G stirred him up another	1Kin 11:23	430
the G of Israel, Behold, I will	1Kin 11:31	430
But the word of G came unto	1Kin 12:22	430
came unto Shemaiah the man of G	1Kin 12:22	430
there came a man of G out of	1Kin 13:1	430
heard the saying of the man of G	1Kin 13:4	430
of G had given by the word of the	1Kin 13:5	430
and said unto the man of G	1Kin 13:6	430
now the face of the LORD thy G	1Kin 13:6	430
the man of G besought the LORD,	1Kin 13:6	430
the king said unto the man of G	1Kin 13:7	430
the man of G said unto the king,	1Kin 13:8	430
of G had done that day in Beth-el	1Kin 13:11	430
seen what way the man of G went	1Kin 13:12	430
And went after the man of G	1Kin 13:14	430
Art thou the man of G that camest	1Kin 13:14	430
the man of G that came from Judah	1Kin 13:21	430
the LORD thy G commanded thee	1Kin 13:21	430
he said, It is the man of G	1Kin 13:26	430
up the carcase of the man of G	1Kin 13:29	430
wherein the man of G is buried	1Kin 13:31	430
Thus saith the LORD G of Israel	1Kin 14:7	430
LORD G of Israel in the house of	1Kin 14:13	430
not perfect with the LORD his G	1Kin 15:3	430
G give him a lamp in Jerusalem	1Kin 15:4	430
the LORD G of Israel to anger	1Kin 15:30	430
in provoking the LORD G of Israel	1Kin 16:13	430
to provoke the LORD G of Israel	1Kin 16:26	430
did more to provoke the LORD G of	1Kin 16:33	430
As the LORD G of Israel liveth,	1Kin 17:1	430
said, As the LORD thy G liveth	1Kin 17:12	430
thus saith the LORD G of Israel	1Kin 17:14	430
to do with thee, O thou man of G	1Kin 17:18	430
the LORD, and said, O LORD my G	1Kin 17:20	430
the LORD, and said, O LORD my G	1Kin 17:21	430
I know that thou art a man of G	1Kin 17:24	430
As the LORD thy G liveth, there	1Kin 18:10	430
if the LORD be G, follow him	1Kin 18:21	430
the G that answereth by fire, let	1Kin 18:24	430
answereth by fire, let him be G	1Kin 18:24	430
LORD G of Abraham, Isaac, and of	1Kin 18:36	430
day that thou art G in Israel	1Kin 18:36	430
may know that thou art the LORD G	1Kin 18:37	430
they said, The LORD, he is the G	1Kin 18:39	430
the LORD, he is the G	1Kin 18:39	430
nights unto Horeb the mount of G	1Kin 19:8	430
jealous for the LORD G of hosts	1Kin 19:10	430
jealous for the LORD G of hosts	1Kin 19:14	430
And there came a man of G, and	1Kin 20:28	430
The LORD is G of the hills	1Kin 20:28	430
but he is not G of the valleys,	1Kin 20:28	430
saying, Thou didst blaspheme G	1Kin 21:10	430
saying, Naboth did blaspheme G	1Kin 21:13	430
to anger the LORD G of Israel	1Kin 22:53	430
there is not a G in Israel	2Kin 1:3	430
there is not a G in Israel	2Kin 1:6	430
he spake unto him, Thou man of G	2Kin 1:9	430
of fifty, If I be a man of G	2Kin 1:10	430
and said unto him, O man of G	2Kin 1:11	430
unto them, If I be a man of G	2Kin 1:12	430
the fire of G came down from	2Kin 1:12	430
him, and said unto him, O man of G	2Kin 1:13	430
no G in Israel to enquire of his	2Kin 1:16	430
Where is the LORD G of Elijah	2Kin 2:14	430
she came and told the man of G	2Kin 4:7	430
that this is an holy man of G	2Kin 4:9	430
said, Nay, my lord, thou man of G	2Kin 4:16	430
him on the bed of the man of G	2Kin 4:21	430
that I may run to the man of G	2Kin 4:22	430
unto the man of G to mount Carmel	2Kin 4:25	430
when the man of G saw her afar	2Kin 4:25	430
came to the man of G to the hill	2Kin 4:27	430
And the man of G said, Let her	2Kin 4:27	430
out, and said, O thou man of G	2Kin 4:40	430
brought the man of G bread of the	2Kin 4:42	430
Would G my lord were with the	2Kin 5:3	
rent his clothes, and said, Am I G	2Kin 5:7	430
when Elisha the man of G had	2Kin 5:8	430
on the name of the LORD his G	2Kin 5:11	430
to the saying of the man of G	2Kin 5:14	430
And he returned to the man of G	2Kin 5:15	430
there is no G in all the earth	2Kin 5:15	430
servant of Elisha the man of G	2Kin 5:20	430
And the man of G said, Where fell	2Kin 6:6	430
the man of G sent unto the king	2Kin 6:9	430
place which the man of G told him	2Kin 6:10	430
of the man of G was risen early	2Kin 6:15	430
G do so and more also to me, if	2Kin 6:31	430
king leaned answered the man of G	2Kin 7:2	430
he died, as the man of G had said	2Kin 7:17	430
man of G had spoken to the king	2Kin 7:18	430
that lord answered the man of G	2Kin 7:19	430
after the saying of the man of G	2Kin 8:2	430
the servant of the man of G	2Kin 8:4	430
The man of G is come hither	2Kin 8:7	430
hand, and go, meet the man of G	2Kin 8:8	430
and the man of G wept	2Kin 8:11	430
Thus saith the LORD G of Israel	2Kin 9:6	430
G of Israel with all his heart	2Kin 10:31	430
hands, and said, G save the king	2Kin 11:12	
the man of G was wroth with him,	2Kin 13:19	430
the word of the LORD G of Israel	2Kin 14:25	430
in the sight of the LORD his G	2Kin 16:2	430
sinned against the LORD their G	2Kin 17:7	430
right against the LORD their G	2Kin 17:9	430
not believe in the LORD their G	2Kin 17:14	430
commandments of the LORD their G	2Kin 17:16	430
commandments of the LORD their G	2Kin 17:19	430
the manner of the G of the land	2Kin 17:26	430
the manner of the G of the land	2Kin 17:26	430
the manner of the G of the land	2Kin 17:27	430
But the LORD your G ye shall fear	2Kin 17:39	430
trusted in the LORD G of Israel	2Kin 18:5	430
not the voice of the LORD their G	2Kin 18:12	430
me, We trust in the LORD our G	2Kin 18:22	430
It may be the LORD thy G will	2Kin 19:4	430
sent to reproach the living G	2Kin 19:4	430
which the LORD thy G hath heard	2Kin 19:4	430
Let not thy G in whom thou	2Kin 19:10	430
O LORD G of Israel, which	2Kin 19:15	430
the cherubims, thou art the G	2Kin 19:15	430
sent him to reproach the living G	2Kin 19:16	430
Now therefore, O LORD our G	2Kin 19:19	430
may know that thou art the LORD G	2Kin 19:19	430
Thus saith the LORD G of Israel	2Kin 19:20	430
the G of David thy father, I have	2Kin 20:5	430
thus saith the LORD G of Israel	2Kin 21:12	430
forsook the LORD G of his fathers	2Kin 21:22	430
Thus saith the LORD G of Israel	2Kin 22:15	430
Thus saith the LORD G of Israel	2Kin 22:18	430
which the man of G proclaimed	2Kin 23:16	430
is the sepulchre of the man of G	2Kin 23:17	430
the passover unto the LORD your G	2Kin 23:21	430
Jabez called on the G of Israel	1Chr 4:10	430
G granted him that which he	1Chr 4:10	430
for they cried to G in the battle	1Chr 5:20	430
slain, because the war was of G	1Chr 5:22	430
against the G of their fathers	1Chr 5:25	430
whom G destroyed before them	1Chr 5:25	430
the G of Israel stirred up the	1Chr 5:26	430
the tabernacle of the house of G	1Chr 6:48	430
the servant of G had commanded	1Chr 6:49	430
the ruler of the house of G	1Chr 9:11	430
of the service of the house of G	1Chr 9:13	430
and treasuries of the house of G	1Chr 9:26	430
lodged round about the house of G	1Chr 9:27	430
the LORD thy G said unto thee,	1Chr 11:2	430
My G forbid it me, that I should	1Chr 11:19	430
the G of our fathers look thereon	1Chr 12:17	430
for thy G helpeth thee	1Chr 12:18	430
a great host, like the host of G	1Chr 12:22	430
and that it be of the LORD our G	1Chr 13:2	430

again the ark of our G to us	1Chr 13:3	430
the ark of G from Kirjath-jearim	1Chr 13:5	430
up thence the ark of G the LORD	1Chr 13:6	430
they carried the ark of G in a	1Chr 13:7	430
before G with all their might	1Chr 13:8	430
and there he died before G	1Chr 13:10	430
And David was afraid of G that day	1Chr 13:12	430
I bring the ark of G home to me	1Chr 13:12	430
the ark of G remained with the	1Chr 13:14	430
And David enquired of G, saying,	1Chr 14:10	430
G hath broken in upon mine	1Chr 14:11	430
David enquired again of G	1Chr 14:14	430
G said unto him, Go not up after	1Chr 14:14	430
for G is gone forth before thee	1Chr 14:15	430
therefore did as G commanded him	1Chr 14:16	430
prepared a place for the ark of G	1Chr 15:1	430
the ark of G but the Levites	1Chr 15:2	430
LORD chosen to carry the ark of G	1Chr 15:2	430
bring up the ark of the LORD G of	1Chr 15:12	430
the LORD our G made a breach upon	1Chr 15:13	430
the ark of the LORD G of Israel	1Chr 15:14	430
G upon their shoulders with the	1Chr 15:15	430
the trumpets before the ark of G	1Chr 15:24	430
when G helped the Levites that	1Chr 15:26	430
So they brought the ark of G	1Chr 16:1	430
and peace offerings before G	1Chr 16:1	430
and praise the LORD G of Israel	1Chr 16:4	430
the ark of the covenant of G	1Chr 16:6	430
He is the LORD our G	1Chr 16:14	430
O G of our salvation, and gather	1Chr 16:35	430
be the LORD G of Israel for ever	1Chr 16:36	430
and with musical instruments of G	1Chr 16:42	430
for G is with thee	1Chr 17:2	430
that the word of G came to Nathan	1Chr 17:3	430
LORD, and said, Who am I, O LORD G	1Chr 17:16	430
a small thing in thine eyes, O G	1Chr 17:17	430
of a man of high degree, O LORD G	1Chr 17:17	430
is there any G beside thee	1Chr 17:20	430
whom G went to redeem to be his	1Chr 17:21	430
and thou, LORD, becamest their G	1Chr 17:22	430
G of Israel, even a G to Israel	1Chr 17:24	430
For thou, O my G, hast told thy	1Chr 17:25	430
And now, LORD, thou art G, and hast	1Chr 17:26	430
and for the cities of our G	1Chr 19:13	430
G was displeased with this thing	1Chr 21:7	430
And David said unto G, I have	1Chr 21:8	430
G sent an angel unto Jerusalem to	1Chr 21:15	430
And David said unto G, Is it not I	1Chr 21:17	430
hand, I pray thee, O LORD my G	1Chr 21:17	430
not go before it to enquire of G	1Chr 21:30	430
This is the house of the LORD G	1Chr 22:1	430
stones to build the house of G	1Chr 22:2	430
an house for the LORD G of Israel	1Chr 22:6	430
unto the name of the LORD my G	1Chr 22:7	430
build the house of the LORD thy G	1Chr 22:11	430
keep the law of the LORD thy G	1Chr 22:12	430
Is not the LORD your G with you	1Chr 22:18	430
your soul to seek the LORD your G	1Chr 22:19	430
ye the sanctuary of the LORD G	1Chr 22:19	430
LORD, and the holy vessels of G	1Chr 22:19	430
Now concerning Moses the man of G	1Chr 23:14	430
The LORD G of Israel hath given	1Chr 23:25	430
of the service of the house of G	1Chr 23:28	430
and governors of the house of G	1Chr 24:5	430
as the LORD G of Israel had	1Chr 24:19	430
the king's seer in the words of G	1Chr 25:5	430
G gave to Heman fourteen sons and	1Chr 25:5	430
for the service of the house of G	1Chr 25:6	430
for G blessed him	1Chr 26:5	430
the treasures of the house of G	1Chr 26:20	430
for every matter pertaining to G	1Chr 26:32	430
and for the footstool of our G	1Chr 28:2	430
But G said unto me, Thou shalt	1Chr 28:3	430
Howbeit the LORD G of Israel	1Chr 28:4	430
LORD, and in the audience of our G	1Chr 28:8	430
commandments of the LORD your G	1Chr 28:8	430
know thou the G of thy father	1Chr 28:9	430
the treasuries of the house of G	1Chr 28:12	430
for the LORD G, even my G	1Chr 28:20	430
all the service of the house of G	1Chr 28:21	430
whom alone G hath chosen, is yet	1Chr 29:1	430
not for man, but for the LORD G	1Chr 29:1	430
my might for the house of my G	1Chr 29:2	430
my affection to the house of my G	1Chr 29:3	430
I have given to the house of my G	1Chr 29:3	430
G of gold five thousand talents	1Chr 29:7	430
LORD G of Israel our father, for	1Chr 29:10	430
Now therefore, our G, we thank	1Chr 29:13	430
O LORD our G, all this store that	1Chr 29:16	430
I know also, my G, that thou	1Chr 29:17	430
O LORD G of Abraham, Isaac, and of	1Chr 29:18	430
Now bless the LORD your G	1Chr 29:20	430
the LORD G of their fathers	1Chr 29:20	430
and the LORD his G was with him	2Chr 1:1	430
of the congregation of G, which	2Chr 1:3	430
But the ark of G had David	2Chr 1:4	430
In that night did G appear unto	2Chr 1:7	430
And Solomon said unto G, Thou hast	2Chr 1:8	430
Now, O LORD G, let thy promise	2Chr 1:9	430
G said to Solomon, Because this	2Chr 1:11	430
to the name of the LORD my G	2Chr 2:4	430
solemn feasts of the LORD our G	2Chr 2:4	430
for great is our G above all gods	2Chr 2:5	430
Blessed be the LORD G of Israel	2Chr 2:12	430
the building of the house of G	2Chr 3:3	430
king Solomon for the house of G	2Chr 4:11	430
that were for the house of G	2Chr 4:19	430
the treasures of the house of G	2Chr 5:1	430
LORD had filled the house of G	2Chr 5:14	430
Blessed be the LORD G of Israel	2Chr 6:4	430
the name of the LORD G of Israel	2Chr 6:7	430
the name of the LORD G of Israel	2Chr 6:10	430
O LORD G of Israel	2Chr 6:14	430
there is no G like thee in the	2Chr 6:14	430
O LORD G of Israel, keep with thy	2Chr 6:16	430
O LORD G of Israel, let thy word	2Chr 6:17	430
But will G in very deed dwell	2Chr 6:18	430
to his supplication, O LORD my G	2Chr 6:19	430
Now, my G, let, I beseech thee,	2Chr 6:40	430
Now therefore arise, O LORD G	2Chr 6:41	430
let thy priests, O LORD G	2Chr 6:41	430
O LORD G, turn not away the face	2Chr 6:42	430
people dedicated the house of G	2Chr 7:5	430
the LORD G of their fathers	2Chr 7:22	430
had David the man of G commanded	2Chr 8:14	430
Blessed be the LORD thy G	2Chr 9:8	430
to be king for the LORD thy G	2Chr 9:8	430
because thy G loved Israel, to	2Chr 9:8	430
that G had put in his heart	2Chr 9:23	430
for the cause was of G, that the	2Chr 10:15	430
came to Shemaiah the man of G	2Chr 11:2	430
G of Israel came to Jerusalem	2Chr 11:16	430
unto the LORD G of their fathers	2Chr 11:16	430
ye not to know that the LORD G of	2Chr 13:5	430
But as for us, the LORD is our G	2Chr 13:10	430
keep the charge of the LORD our G	2Chr 13:11	430
G himself is with us for our	2Chr 13:12	430
the LORD G of your fathers	2Chr 13:12	430
that G smote Jeroboam and all	2Chr 13:15	430
G delivered them into their hand	2Chr 13:16	430
upon the LORD G of their fathers	2Chr 13:18	430
in the eyes of the LORD his G	2Chr 14:2	430
seek the LORD G of their fathers	2Chr 14:4	430
we have sought the LORD our G	2Chr 14:7	430
And Asa cried unto the LORD his G	2Chr 14:11	430
help us, O LORD our G	2Chr 14:11	430
O LORD, thou art our G	2Chr 14:11	430
the Spirit of G came upon Azariah	2Chr 15:1	430
hath been without the true G	2Chr 15:3	430
turn unto the LORD G of Israel	2Chr 15:4	430
for G did vex them with all	2Chr 15:6	430
that the LORD his G was with him	2Chr 15:9	430
a covenant to seek the LORD G of	2Chr 15:12	430
would not seek the LORD G of	2Chr 15:13	430
he brought into the house of G	2Chr 15:18	430
and not relied on the LORD thy G	2Chr 16:7	430
to the LORD G of his father	2Chr 17:4	430
for G will deliver it into the	2Chr 18:5	430
LORD liveth, even what my G saith	2Chr 18:13	430
G moved them to depart from him	2Chr 18:31	430
prepared thine heart to seek G	2Chr 19:3	430
unto the LORD G of their fathers	2Chr 19:4	430
no iniquity with the LORD our G	2Chr 19:7	430
O LORD G of our fathers	2Chr 20:6	430
art not thou G in heaven	2Chr 20:6	430
Art not thou our G, who didst	2Chr 20:7	430
O our G, wilt thou not judge them	2Chr 20:12	430
stood up to praise the LORD G of	2Chr 20:19	430
Believe in the LORD your G	2Chr 20:20	430
the fear of G was on all the	2Chr 20:29	430
for his G gave him rest round	2Chr 20:30	430
unto the G of their fathers	2Chr 20:33	430
the LORD G of his fathers	2Chr 21:10	430
the LORD G of David thy father	2Chr 21:12	430
was of G by coming to Joram	2Chr 22:7	430
hid in the house of G six years	2Chr 22:12	430
with the king in the house of G	2Chr 23:3	430
which were in the house of G	2Chr 23:9	430
him, and said, G save the king	2Chr 23:11	430
house of your G from year to year	2Chr 24:5	430
had broken up the house of G	2Chr 24:7	430
of G laid upon Israel in the	2Chr 24:9	430
set the house of G in his state	2Chr 24:13	430
good in Israel, both toward G	2Chr 24:16	430
of the LORD G of their fathers	2Chr 24:18	430
the Spirit of G came upon	2Chr 24:20	430
and said unto them, Thus saith G	2Chr 24:20	430
the LORD G of their fathers	2Chr 24:24	430
the repairing of the house of G	2Chr 24:27	430
But there came a man of G to him	2Chr 25:7	430
G shall make thee fall before the	2Chr 25:8	430
for G hath power to help, and to	2Chr 25:8	430
And Amaziah said to the man of G	2Chr 25:9	430
And the man of G answered, The	2Chr 25:9	430
I know that G hath determined to	2Chr 25:16	430
for it came of G, that he might	2Chr 25:20	430
in the house of G with Obed-edom	2Chr 25:24	430
he sought G in the days of	2Chr 26:5	430
understanding in the visions of G	2Chr 26:5	430
the LORD, G made him to prosper	2Chr 26:5	430
And G helped him against the	2Chr 26:7	430
against the LORD his G, and went	2Chr 26:16	430
for thine honour from the LORD G	2Chr 26:18	430
his ways before the LORD his G	2Chr 27:6	430
Wherefore the LORD his G	2Chr 28:5	430
the LORD G of their fathers	2Chr 28:6	430
because the LORD G of your	2Chr 28:9	430
you, sins against the LORD your G	2Chr 28:10	430
the vessels of the house of G	2Chr 28:24	430
the vessels of the house of G	2Chr 28:24	430
anger the LORD G of his fathers	2Chr 28:25	430
of the LORD G of your fathers	2Chr 29:5	430
in the eyes of the LORD our G	2Chr 29:6	430
holy place unto the G of Israel	2Chr 29:7	430
with the LORD G of Israel	2Chr 29:10	430
that G had prepared the people	2Chr 29:36	430
unto the LORD G of Israel	2Chr 30:1	430
the LORD G of Israel at Jerusalem	2Chr 30:5	430
again unto the LORD G of Abraham	2Chr 30:6	430
the LORD G of their fathers	2Chr 30:7	430
and serve the LORD your G, that	2Chr 30:8	430
for the LORD your G is gracious	2Chr 30:9	430
Also in Judah the hand of G was	2Chr 30:12	430
to the law of Moses the man of G	2Chr 30:16	430
prepareth his heart to seek G	2Chr 30:19	430
the LORD G of his fathers, though	2Chr 30:19	430
to the LORD G of their fathers	2Chr 30:22	430
consecrated unto the LORD their G	2Chr 31:6	430
the ruler of the house of G	2Chr 31:13	430
over the freewill offerings of G	2Chr 31:14	430
and truth before the LORD his G	2Chr 31:20	430
in the service of the house of G	2Chr 31:21	430
the commandments, to seek his G	2Chr 31:21	430
us is the LORD our G to help us	2Chr 32:8	430
The LORD our G shall deliver us	2Chr 32:11	430
that your G should be able to	2Chr 32:14	430
how much less shall your G	2Chr 32:15	430
spake yet more against the LORD G	2Chr 32:16	430
to rail on the LORD G of Israel	2Chr 32:17	430
so shall not the G of Hezekiah	2Chr 32:17	430
spake against the G of Jerusalem	2Chr 32:19	430
for G had given him substance	2Chr 32:29	430
G left him, to try him, that he	2Chr 32:31	430
he had made, in the house of G	2Chr 33:7	430
of which G had said to David and	2Chr 33:7	430
he besought the LORD his G	2Chr 33:12	430
before the G of his fathers	2Chr 33:12	430
knew that the LORD he was G	2Chr 33:13	430
to serve the LORD G of Israel	2Chr 33:16	430
yet unto the LORD their G only	2Chr 33:17	430
and his prayer unto his G	2Chr 33:18	430
the name of the LORD G of Israel	2Chr 33:18	430
how G was intreated of him, and	2Chr 33:19	
after the G of David his father	2Chr 34:3	430
the house of the LORD his G	2Chr 34:8	430
was brought into the house of G	2Chr 34:9	430
Thus saith the LORD G of Israel	2Chr 34:23	430
Thus saith the LORD G of Israel	2Chr 34:26	430
didst humble thyself before G	2Chr 34:27	430
according to the covenant of G	2Chr 34:32	430
the G of their fathers	2Chr 34:32	430
even to serve the LORD their G	2Chr 34:33	430
the LORD, the G of their fathers	2Chr 34:33	430
serve now the LORD your G	2Chr 35:3	430
Jehiel, rulers of the house of G	2Chr 35:8	430
for G commanded me to make haste	2Chr 35:21	430
forbear thee from meddling with G	2Chr 35:21	430
of Necho from the mouth of G	2Chr 35:22	430
in the sight of the LORD his G	2Chr 36:5	430
in the sight of the LORD his G	2Chr 36:12	430
who had made him swear by G	2Chr 36:13	430
turning unto the LORD G of Israel	2Chr 36:13	430
the LORD G of their fathers sent	2Chr 36:15	430
they mocked the messengers of G	2Chr 36:16	430
all the vessels of the house of G	2Chr 36:18	430
And they burnt the house of G	2Chr 36:19	430
the LORD G of heaven given me	2Chr 36:23	430
The LORD his G be with him	2Chr 36:23	430
The LORD G of heaven hath given	Ezr 1:2	430
his G be with him, and let him go	Ezr 1:3	430
LORD G of Israel, (he is the G	Ezr 1:3	430
house of G that is in Jerusalem	Ezr 1:4	430
them whose spirit G had raised	Ezr 1:5	430
of G to set it up in his place	Ezr 2:68	430
the altar of the G of Israel	Ezr 3:2	430
in the law of Moses the man of G	Ezr 3:2	430
unto the house of G at Jerusalem	Ezr 3:8	430
the workmen in the house of G	Ezr 3:9	430
temple unto the LORD G of Israel	Ezr 4:1	430
for we seek your G, as ye do	Ezr 4:2	430
us to build an house unto our G	Ezr 4:3	430
build unto the LORD G of Israel	Ezr 4:3	430
house of G which is at Jerusalem	Ezr 4:24	426
in the name of the G of Israel	Ezr 5:1	426
house of G which is at Jerusalem	Ezr 5:2	426
the prophets of G helping them	Ezr 5:2	426
But the eye of their G was upon	Ezr 5:5	426
to the house of the great G	Ezr 5:8	426
the servants of the G of heaven	Ezr 5:11	426
the G of heaven unto wrath	Ezr 5:12	426
a decree to build this house of G	Ezr 5:13	426
gold and silver of the house of G	Ezr 5:14	426
let the house of G be builded in	Ezr 5:15	426
house of G which is in Jerusalem	Ezr 5:16	426
this house of G at Jerusalem	Ezr 5:17	426
the house of G at Jerusalem	Ezr 6:3	426
silver vessels of the house of G	Ezr 6:5	426
and place them in the house of G	Ezr 6:5	426
the work of this house of G alone	Ezr 6:7	426
this house of G in his place	Ezr 6:7	426
the building of this house of G	Ezr 6:8	426
offerings of the G of heaven	Ezr 6:9	426
savours unto the G of heaven	Ezr 6:10	426
the G that hath caused his name	Ezr 6:12	426
house of G which is at Jerusalem	Ezr 6:12	426
commandment of the G of Israel	Ezr 6:14	426
of this house of G with joy	Ezr 6:16	426
house of G an hundred bullocks	Ezr 6:17	426
courses, for the service of G	Ezr 6:18	426
to seek the LORD G of Israel	Ezr 6:21	430
the house of G, the G of Israel	Ezr 6:22	430
which the LORD G of Israel had	Ezr 7:6	430
hand of the LORD his G upon him	Ezr 7:6	430
the good hand of his G upon him	Ezr 7:9	430
of the law of the G of heaven	Ezr 7:12	426
of thy G which is in thine hand	Ezr 7:14	426
offered unto the G of Israel	Ezr 7:15	426
of their G which is in Jerusalem	Ezr 7:16	426
of your G which is in Jerusalem	Ezr 7:17	426
that do after the will of your G	Ezr 7:18	426
the service of the house of thy G	Ezr 7:19	426
thou before the G of Jerusalem	Ezr 7:19	426
be needful for the house of thy G	Ezr 7:20	426
of the law of the G of heaven	Ezr 7:21	426
is commanded by the G of heaven	Ezr 7:23	426
for the house of the G of heaven	Ezr 7:23	426
or ministers of this house of G	Ezr 7:24	426
Ezra, after the wisdom of thy G	Ezr 7:25	426
such as know the laws of thy G	Ezr 7:25	426
will not do the law of thy G	Ezr 7:26	426
be the LORD G of our fathers	Ezr 7:27	430
hand of the LORD my G was upon me	Ezr 7:28	430

ministers for the house of our G	Ezr 8:17	430
by the good hand of our G upon us	Ezr 8:18	430
afflict ourselves before our G	Ezr 8:21	430
The hand of our G is upon all	Ezr 8:22	430
fasted and besought our G for this	Ezr 8:23	430
offering of the house of our G	Ezr 8:25	430
unto the LORD G of your fathers	Ezr 8:28	430
Jerusalem unto the house of our G	Ezr 8:30	430
and the hand of our G was upon us	Ezr 8:31	430
weighed in the house of our G by	Ezr 8:33	430
offerings unto the G of Israel	Ezr 8:35	430
the people, and the house of G	Ezr 8:36	430
at the words of the G of Israel	Ezr 9:4	430
out my hands unto the LORD my G	Ezr 9:5	430
And said, O my G, I am ashamed and	Ezr 9:6	430
to lift up my face to thee, my G	Ezr 9:6	430
been shewed from the LORD our G	Ezr 9:8	430
that our G may lighten our eyes,	Ezr 9:8	430
yet our G hath not forsaken us in	Ezr 9:9	430
to set up the house of our G	Ezr 9:9	430
And now, O our G, what shall we	Ezr 9:10	430
seeing that thou our G hast	Ezr 9:13	430
O LORD G of Israel, thou art	Ezr 9:15	430
down before the house of G	Ezr 10:1	430
We have trespassed against our G	Ezr 10:2	430
our G to put away all the wives	Ezr 10:3	430
at the commandment of our G	Ezr 10:3	430
up from before the house of G	Ezr 10:6	430
in the street of the house of G	Ezr 10:9	430
unto the LORD G of your fathers	Ezr 10:11	430
until the fierce wrath of our G	Ezr 10:14	430
and prayed before the G of heaven	Neh 1:4	430
O LORD G of heaven	Neh 1:5	430
the great and terrible G	Neh 1:5	410
So I prayed to the G of heaven	Neh 2:4	430
to the good hand of my G upon me	Neh 2:8	430
my G had put in my heart to do at	Neh 2:12	430
of my G which was good upon me	Neh 2:18	430
The G of heaven, he will prosper	Neh 2:20	430
Hear, O our G	Neh 4:4	430
we made our prayer unto our G	Neh 4:9	430
G had brought their counsel to	Neh 4:15	430
our G shall fight for us	Neh 4:20	430
G because of the reproach of the	Neh 5:9	430
So G shake out every man from his	Neh 5:13	430
not I, because of the fear of G	Neh 5:15	430
Think upon me, my G, for good,	Neh 5:19	430
Now therefore, O G, strengthen my	Neh 6:9	
meet together in the house of G	Neh 6:10	430
perceived that G had not sent him	Neh 6:12	430
My G, think thou upon Tobiah and	Neh 6:14	430
this work was wrought of our G	Neh 6:16	430
man, and feared G above many	Neh 7:2	430
my G put into mine heart to	Neh 7:5	430
blessed the LORD, the great G	Neh 8:6	430
book in the law of G distinctly	Neh 8:8	430
day is holy unto the LORD your G	Neh 8:9	430
in the courts of the house of G	Neh 8:16	430
read in the book of the law of G	Neh 8:18	430
G one fourth part of the day	Neh 9:3	430
and worshipped the LORD their G	Neh 9:3	430
loud voice unto the LORD their G	Neh 9:4	430
and bless the LORD your G for ever	Neh 9:5	430
Thou art the LORD the G, who	Neh 9:7	430
but thou art a G ready to pardon,	Neh 9:17	433
This is thy G that brought thee	Neh 9:18	430
thou art a gracious and merciful G	Neh 9:31	410
Now therefore, our G, the great,	Neh 9:32	430
the mighty, and the terrible G	Neh 9:32	410
of the lands unto the law of G	Neh 10:28	430
given by Moses the servant of G	Neh 10:29	430
the service of the house of our G	Neh 10:32	430
the work of the house of our G	Neh 10:33	430
bring it into the house of our G	Neh 10:34	430
upon the altar of the LORD our G	Neh 10:34	430
to bring to the house of our G	Neh 10:36	430
minister in the house of our G	Neh 10:36	430
chambers of the house of our G	Neh 10:37	430
tithes unto the house of our G	Neh 10:38	430
not forsake the house of our G	Neh 10:39	430
was the ruler of the house of G	Neh 11:11	430
business of the house of G	Neh 11:16	430
the business of the house of G	Neh 11:22	430
commandment of David the man of G.	Neh 12:24	430
instruments of David the man of G	Neh 12:36	430
gave thanks in the house of G	Neh 12:40	430
for G had made them rejoice with	Neh 12:43	430
porters kept the ward of their G	Neh 12:45	430
of praise and thanksgiving unto G	Neh 12:46	430
the congregation of G for ever	Neh 13:1	430
howbeit our G turned the curse	Neh 13:2	430
the chamber of the house of our G	Neh 13:4	430
in the courts of the house of G	Neh 13:7	430
the vessels of the house of G	Neh 13:9	430
Why is the house of G forsaken	Neh 13:11	430
Remember me, O my G, concerning	Neh 13:14	430
I have done for the house of my G	Neh 13:14	430
did not our G bring all this evil	Neh 13:18	430
Remember me, O my G, concerning	Neh 13:22	430
hair, and made them swear by G	Neh 13:25	430
him, who was beloved of his G	Neh 13:26	430
G made him king over all Israel	Neh 13:26	430
our G in marrying strange wives	Neh 13:27	430
Remember them, O my G, because	Neh 13:29	430
Remember me, O my G, for good	Neh 13:31	430
and upright, and one that feared G	Job 1:1	430
and cursed G in their hearts	Job 1:5	430
of G came to present themselves	Job 1:6	430
upright man, one that feareth G	Job 1:8	430
said, Doth Job fear G for nought	Job 1:9	430
The fire of G is fallen from	Job 1:16	430
not, nor charged G foolishly	Job 1:22	430
of G came to present themselves	Job 2:1	430
upright man, one that feareth G	Job 2:3	430
curse G, and die	Job 2:9	430
we receive good at the hand of G	Job 2:10	430
let not G regard it from above,	Job 3:4	433
is hid, and whom G hath hedged in	Job 3:23	433
By the blast of G they perish	Job 4:9	433
mortal man be more just than G	Job 4:17	433
I would seek unto G	Job 5:8	410
unto G would I commit my cause	Job 5:8	430
is the man whom G correcteth	Job 5:17	433
the terrors of G do set	Job 6:4	433
that G would grant me the thing	Job 6:8	433
it would please G to destroy me	Job 6:9	433
Doth G pervert judgment	Job 8:3	410
thou wouldest seek unto G betimes	Job 8:5	410
the paths of all that forget G	Job 8:13	410
G will not cast away a perfect	Job 8:20	410
but how should man be just with G	Job 9:2	410
If G will not withdraw his anger,	Job 9:13	433
I will say unto G, Do not condemn	Job 10:2	433
But oh that G would speak	Job 11:5	433
Know therefore that G exacteth of	Job 11:6	433
thou by searching find out G	Job 11:7	433
his neighbour, who calleth upon G	Job 12:4	433
and they that provoke G are secure	Job 12:6	410
into whose hand G bringeth	Job 12:6	433
and I desire to reason with G	Job 13:3	410
Will ye speak wickedly for G	Job 13:7	410
will ye contend for G	Job 13:8	410
and restrainest prayer before G	Job 15:4	410
Hast thou heard the secret of G	Job 15:8	433
consolations of G small with thee	Job 15:11	410
thou turnest thy spirit against G	Job 15:13	410
stretcheth out his hand against G	Job 15:25	410
G hath delivered me to the	Job 16:11	410
mine eye poureth out tears unto G	Job 16:20	433
one might plead for a man with G	Job 16:21	433
place of him that knoweth not G	Job 18:21	410
Know now that G hath overthrown	Job 19:6	433
for the hand of G hath touched me	Job 19:21	433
Why do ye persecute me as G	Job 19:22	410
yet in my flesh shall I see G	Job 19:26	433
G shall cast them out of his	Job 20:15	410
G shall cast the fury of his	Job 20:23	
portion of a wicked man from G	Job 20:29	430
heritage appointed unto him by G	Job 20:29	410
neither is the rod of G upon them	Job 21:9	433
Therefore they say unto G	Job 21:14	410
G distributeth sorrows in his	Job 21:17	
G layeth up his iniquity for his	Job 21:19	433
Shall any teach G knowledge	Job 21:22	410
Can a man be profitable unto G	Job 22:2	410
Is not G in the height of heaven	Job 22:12	433
And thou sayest, How doth G know	Job 22:13	410
Which said unto G, Depart from us	Job 22:17	410
and shalt lift up thy face unto G	Job 22:26	433
For G maketh my heart soft, and	Job 23:16	410
yet G layeth not folly to them	Job 24:12	433
then can man be justified with G	Job 25:4	410
As G liveth, who hath taken away	Job 27:2	410
the spirit of G is in my nostrils	Job 27:3	433
G forbid that I should justify	Job 27:5	
when G taketh away his soul	Job 27:8	433
Will G hear his cry when trouble	Job 27:9	401
will he always call upon G	Job 27:10	433
I will teach you by the hand of G	Job 27:11	410
portion of a wicked man with G	Job 27:13	410
For G shall cast upon him, and not	Job 27:22	
G understandeth the way thereof,	Job 28:23	430
in the days when G preserved me	Job 29:2	433
when the secret of G was upon my	Job 29:4	433
portion of G is there from above	Job 31:2	433
that G may know mine integrity	Job 31:6	433
then shall I do when G riseth up	Job 31:14	410
from G was a terror to me	Job 31:23	410
have denied the G that is above	Job 31:28	410
justified himself rather than G	Job 32:2	430
G thrusteth him down, not man	Job 32:13	410
The spirit of G hath made me	Job 33:4	410
that G is greater than man	Job 33:12	433
For G speaketh once, yea twice,	Job 33:14	410
He shall pray unto G, and he will	Job 33:26	433
worketh G oftentimes with man	Job 33:29	410
G hath taken away my judgment	Job 34:5	410
he should delight himself with G	Job 34:9	430
far be it from G, that he should	Job 34:10	410
surely G will not do wickedly,	Job 34:12	410
should enter into judgment with G	Job 34:23	410
it is meet to be said unto G	Job 34:31	410
multiplieth his words against G	Job 34:37	410
none saith, Where is G my maker	Job 35:10	433
Surely G will not hear vanity,	Job 35:13	410
G is mighty, and despiseth not any	Job 36:5	410
Behold, G exalteth by his power	Job 36:22	410
G is great, and we know him not,	Job 36:26	410
G thundereth marvellously with	Job 37:5	410
By the breath of G frost is given	Job 37:10	410
consider the wondrous works of G	Job 37:14	410
thou know when G disposed them	Job 37:15	433
with G is terrible majesty	Job 37:22	433
all the sons of G shouted for joy	Job 38:7	430
when his young ones cry unto G	Job 38:41	410
Because G hath deprived her of	Job 39:17	433
he that reproveth G, let him	Job 40:2	433
Hast thou an arm like G	Job 40:9	410
He is the chief of the ways of G	Job 40:19	410
There is no help for him in G	Ps 3:2	430
save me, O my G	Ps 3:7	430
I call, O G of my righteousness	Ps 4:1	430
voice of my cry, my King, and my G	Ps 5:2	430
For thou art not a G that hath	Ps 5:4	410
Destroy thou them, O G	Ps 5:10	430
O lord my G, in thee do I put my	Ps 7:1	430
O LORD my G, if I have done this	Ps 7:3	430
the righteous G trieth the hearts	Ps 7:9	430
My defence is of G, which saveth	Ps 7:10	430
G judgeth the righteous	Ps 7:11	430
G is angry with the wicked every	Ps 7:11	410
and all the nations that forget G	Ps 9:17	430
will not seek after G	Ps 10:4	
G is not in all his thoughts	Ps 10:4	430
in his heart, G hath forgotten	Ps 10:11	410
O G, lift up thine hand	Ps 10:12	410
doth the wicked contemn G	Ps 10:13	430
Consider and hear me, O LORD my G	Ps 13:3	430
said in his heart, There is no G	Ps 14:1	430
that did understand, and seek G	Ps 14:2	430
for G is in the generation of the	Ps 14:5	430
Preserve me, O G	Ps 16:1	410
thee, for thou wilt hear me, O G	Ps 17:6	410
my G, my strength, in whom I will	Ps 18:2	410
upon the LORD, and cried unto my G	Ps 18:6	430
not wickedly departed from my G	Ps 18:21	430
the LORD my G will enlighten my	Ps 18:28	430
by my G have I leaped over a wall	Ps 18:29	430
As for G, his way is perfect	Ps 18:30	410
For who is G save the LORD	Ps 18:31	433
or who is a rock save our G	Ps 18:31	430
It is G that girdeth me with	Ps 18:32	410
let the G of my salvation be	Ps 18:46	430
It is G that avengeth me, and	Ps 18:47	410
heavens declare the glory of G	Ps 19:1	410
the name of the G of Jacob defend	Ps 20:1	430
in the name of our G we will set	Ps 20:5	430
the name of the LORD our G	Ps 20:7	430
My G, my G, why hast thou	Ps 22:1	410
O my G, I cry in the daytime, but	Ps 22:2	430
thou art my G from my mother's	Ps 22:10	410
from the G of his salvation	Ps 24:5	430
O my G, I trust in thee	Ps 25:2	430
thou art the G of my salvation	Ps 25:5	430
Redeem Israel, O G, out of all	Ps 25:22	430
forsake me, O G of my salvation	Ps 27:9	430
the G of glory thundereth	Ps 29:3	410
O LORD my G, I cried unto thee,	Ps 30:2	430
O LORD my G, I will give thanks	Ps 30:12	430
redeemed me, O LORD G of truth	Ps 31:5	410
I said, Thou art my G	Ps 31:14	430
is the nation whose G is the LORD	Ps 33:12	430
even unto my cause, my G	Ps 35:23	430
Judge me, O LORD my G, according	Ps 35:24	430
is no fear of G before his eyes	Ps 36:1	430
is thy lovingkindness, O G	Ps 36:7	430
The law of his G is in his heart	Ps 37:31	430
thou wilt hear, O Lord my G	Ps 38:15	430
O my G, be not far from me	Ps 38:21	430
my mouth, even praise unto our G	Ps 40:3	430
Many, O LORD my G, are thy	Ps 40:5	430
I delight to do thy will, O my G	Ps 40:8	430
make no tarrying, O my G	Ps 40:17	430
Blessed be the LORD G of Israel	Ps 41:13	430
panteth my soul after thee, O G	Ps 42:1	430
My soul thirsteth for G	Ps 42:2	430
for the living G	Ps 42:2	410
shall I come and appear before G	Ps 42:2	430
say unto me, Where is thy G	Ps 42:3	430
went with them to the house of G	Ps 42:4	430
hope thou in G	Ps 42:5	430
O my G, my soul is cast down	Ps 42:6	430
my prayer unto the G of my life	Ps 42:8	410
I will say unto G my rock	Ps 42:9	410
say daily unto me, Where is thy G	Ps 42:10	430
hope thou in G	Ps 42:11	430
health of my countenance, and my G	Ps 42:11	430
Judge me, O G, and plead my cause	Ps 43:1	430
For thou art the G of my strength	Ps 43:2	430
will I go unto the altar of G	Ps 43:4	430
of G, unto G my exceeding joy	Ps 43:4	410
will I praise thee, O G my G	Ps 43:4	430
hope in G: for I shall yet praise	Ps 43:5	430
health of my countenance, and my G	Ps 43:5	430
We have heard with our ears, O G	Ps 44:1	430
Thou art my King, O G	Ps 44:4	430
In G we boast all the day long,	Ps 44:8	430
have forgotten the name of our G	Ps 44:20	430
Shall not G search this out	Ps 44:21	430
therefore G hath blessed thee for	Ps 45:2	430
Thy throne, O G, is for ever and	Ps 45:6	430
therefore G, thy G, hath	Ps 45:7	430
G is our refuge and strength, a	Ps 46:1	430
shall make glad the city of G	Ps 46:4	430
G is in the midst of her	Ps 46:5	430
G shall help her, and that right	Ps 46:5	430
the G of Jacob is our refuge	Ps 46:7	430
Be still, and know that I am G	Ps 46:10	430
the G of Jacob is our refuge	Ps 46:11	430
shout unto G with the voice of	Ps 47:1	430
G is gone up with a shout, the	Ps 47:5	430
Sing praises to G, sing praises	Ps 47:6	430
For G is the King of all the	Ps 47:7	430
G reigneth over the heathen	Ps 47:8	430
G sitteth upon the throne of his	Ps 47:8	430
the people of the G of Abraham	Ps 47:9	430
of the earth belong unto G	Ps 47:9	430
be praised in the city of our G	Ps 48:1	430
G is known in her palaces for a	Ps 48:3	430
of hosts, in the city of our G	Ps 48:8	430
G will establish it for ever	Ps 48:8	430
of thy lovingkindness, O G	Ps 48:9	430
According to thy name, O G	Ps 48:10	430
For this G is our G for ever	Ps 48:14	430
nor give to G a ransom for him	Ps 49:7	430
But G will redeem my soul from	Ps 49:15	430
The mighty G, even the LORD, hath	Ps 50:1	410
of beauty, G hath shined	Ps 50:2	430
Our G shall come, and shall not	Ps 50:3	430
for G is judge himself	Ps 50:6	430
I am G, even thy G	Ps 50:7	430
Offer unto G thanksgiving	Ps 50:14	430

Context	Reference	Number
But unto the wicked G saith	Ps 50:16	430
consider this, ye that forget G	Ps 50:22	433
will I shew the salvation of G	Ps 50:23	430
Have mercy upon me, O G,	Ps 51:1	430
Create in me a clean heart, O G	Ps 51:10	430
O G, thou G of my salvation	Ps 51:14	430
The sacrifices of G are a broken	Ps 51:17	430
a broken and a contrite heart, O G	Ps 51:17	430
the goodness of G endureth	Ps 52:1	410
G shall likewise destroy thee for	Ps 52:5	410
man that made not G his strength	Ps 52:7	430
olive tree in the house of G	Ps 52:8	430
trust in the mercy of G for ever	Ps 52:8	430
said in his heart, There is no G	Ps 53:1	430
G looked down from heaven upon	Ps 53:2	430
did understand, that did seek G	Ps 53:2	430
they have not called upon G	Ps 53:4	430
for G hath scattered the bones of	Ps 53:5	430
because G hath despised them	Ps 53:5	430
When G bringeth back the	Ps 53:6	430
Save me, O G, by thy name, and	Ps 54:1	430
Hear my prayer, O G	Ps 54:2	430
they have not set G before them	Ps 54:3	430
Behold, G is mine helper	Ps 54:4	430
Give ear to my prayer, O G	Ps 55:1	430
unto the house of G in company	Ps 55:14	430
As for me, I will call upon G	Ps 55:16	430
G shall hear, and afflict them,	Ps 55:19	410
therefore they fear not G	Ps 55:19	430
But thou, O G, shalt bring them	Ps 55:23	430
Be merciful unto me, O G	Ps 56:1	430
In G I will praise his word	Ps 56:4	430
in G I have put my trust	Ps 56:4	430
anger cast down the people, O G	Ps 56:7	430
for G is for me	Ps 56:9	430
In G will I praise his word	Ps 56:10	430
In G have I put my trust	Ps 56:11	430
Thy vows are upon me, O G	Ps 56:12	430
that I may walk before G in the	Ps 56:13	430
Be merciful unto me, O G, be	Ps 57:1	430
I will cry unto G most high	Ps 57:2	430
unto G that performeth all things	Ps 57:2	410
G shall send forth his mercy and	Ps 57:3	430
Be thou exalted, O G, above the	Ps 57:5	430
My heart is fixed, O G, my heart	Ps 57:7	430
Be thou exalted, O G, above the	Ps 57:11	430
Break their teeth, O G, in their	Ps 58:6	430
verily he is a G that judgeth in	Ps 58:11	430
me from mine enemies, O my G	Ps 59:1	430
O LORD G of hosts, the G of	Ps 59:5	430
for G is my defence	Ps 59:9	430
The G of my mercy shall prevent	Ps 59:10	430
G shall let me see my desire upon	Ps 59:10	430
let them know that G ruleth in	Ps 59:13	430
for G is my defence, and the G	Ps 59:17	430
O G, thou hast cast us off, thou	Ps 60:1	430
G hath spoken in his holiness	Ps 60:6	430
Wilt not thou, O G, which hadst	Ps 60:10	430
and thou, O G, which didst not go	Ps 60:10	430
Through G we shall do valiantly	Ps 60:12	430
Hear my cry, O G	Ps 61:1	430
For thou, O G, hast heard my vows	Ps 61:5	430
He shall abide before G for ever	Ps 61:7	430
Truly my soul waiteth upon G	Ps 62:1	430
My soul, wait thou only upon G	Ps 62:5	430
In G is my salvation and my glory	Ps 62:7	430
strength, and my refuge, is in G	Ps 62:7	430
G is a refuge for us	Ps 62:8	430
G hath spoken once	Ps 62:11	430
that power belongeth unto G	Ps 62:11	430
O g, thou art my G	Ps 63:1	430
O g, thou art my G	Ps 63:1	410
But the king shall rejoice in G	Ps 63:11	430
Hear my voice, O G, in my prayer	Ps 64:1	430
But G shall shoot at them with an	Ps 64:7	430
and shall declare the work of G	Ps 64:9	430
waiteth for thee, O G in Sion	Ps 65:1	430
answer us, O G of our salvation	Ps 65:5	430
enrichest it with the river of G	Ps 65:9	430
Make a joyful noise unto G	Ps 66:1	430
Say unto G, How terrible art thou	Ps 66:3	430
Come and see the works of G	Ps 66:5	430
O bless our G, ye people, and make	Ps 66:8	430
For thou, O G, hast proved us	Ps 66:10	430
Come and hear, all ye that fear G	Ps 66:16	430
But verily G hath heard me	Ps 66:19	430
Blessed be G, which hath not	Ps 66:20	430
G be merciful unto us, and bless	Ps 67:1	430
Let the people praise thee, O G	Ps 67:3	430
Let the people praise thee, O G	Ps 67:5	430
and G, even our own G, shall	Ps 67:6	430
G shall bless us	Ps 67:7	430
Let G arise, let his enemies be	Ps 68:1	430
perish at the presence of G	Ps 68:2	430
let them rejoice before G	Ps 68:3	430
Sing unto G, sing praises to his	Ps 68:4	430
is G in his holy habitation	Ps 68:5	430
G setteth the solitary in	Ps 68:6	430
O G, when thou wentest forth	Ps 68:7	430
also dropped at the presence of G	Ps 68:8	430
presence of G, the G of Israel	Ps 68:8	430
Thou, O G, didst send a plentiful	Ps 68:9	430
thou, O G, hast prepared of thy	Ps 68:10	430
The hill of G is as the hill of	Ps 68:15	430
hill which G desireth to dwell in	Ps 68:16	430
The chariots of G are twenty	Ps 68:17	430
that the LORD G might dwell among	Ps 68:18	430
even the G of our salvation	Ps 68:19	410
is our G is the G of salvation	Ps 68:20	410
unto G the Lord belong the issues	Ps 68:20	3069
But G shall wound the head of his	Ps 68:21	430
They have seen thy goings, O G	Ps 68:24	430
even the goings of my G, my King,	Ps 68:24	410
Bless ye G in the congregations,	Ps 68:26	430
Thy G hath commanded thy strength	Ps 68:28	430
strengthen, O G, that which thou	Ps 68:28	430
soon stretch out her hands unto G	Ps 68:31	430
Sing unto G, ye kingdoms of the	Ps 68:32	430
Ascribe ye strength unto G	Ps 68:34	430
O G, thou art terrible out of thy	Ps 68:35	430
the G of Israel is he that giveth	Ps 68:35	410
Blessed be G	Ps 68:35	430
Save me, O G	Ps 69:1	430
eyes fail while I wait for my G	Ps 69:3	430
O G, thou knowest my foolishness	Ps 69:5	430
O Lord G of hosts, be ashamed for	Ps 69:6	3069
for my sake, O G of Israel	Ps 69:6	430
O G, in the multitude of thy	Ps 69:13	430
let thy salvation, O G, set me up	Ps 69:29	430
praise the name of G with a song	Ps 69:30	430
your heart shall live that seek G	Ps 69:32	430
For G will save Zion, and will	Ps 69:35	430
Make haste, O G, to deliver me	Ps 70:1	430
continually, Let G be magnified	Ps 70:4	430
make haste unto me, O G	Ps 70:5	430
Deliver me, O my G, out of the	Ps 71:4	430
For thou art my hope, O Lord G	Ps 71:5	3069
Saying, G hath forsaken him	Ps 71:11	430
O G, be not far from me	Ps 71:12	430
O my G, make haste for my help	Ps 71:12	430
go in the strength of the Lord G	Ps 71:16	3069
O G, thou hast taught me from my	Ps 71:17	430
when I am old and greyheaded, O G	Ps 71:18	430
Thy righteousness also, O G	Ps 71:19	430
O G, who is like unto thee	Ps 71:19	430
psaltery, even thy truth, O my G	Ps 71:22	430
Give the king thy judgments, O G	Ps 72:1	430
Blessed be the LORD G	Ps 72:18	430
the G of Israel, who only doeth	Ps 72:18	430
Truly G is good to Israel, even	Ps 73:1	430
And they say, How doth G know	Ps 73:11	4010
I went into the sanctuary of G	Ps 73:17	410
but G is the strength of my heart	Ps 73:26	430
is good for me to draw near to G	Ps 73:28	430
I have put my trust in the Lord G	Ps 73:28	3069
O G, why hast thou cast us off	Ps 74:1	430
the synagogues of G in the land	Ps 74:8	410
O G, how long shall the adversary	Ps 74:10	430
For G is my King of old, working	Ps 74:12	430
Arise, O G, plead thine own cause	Ps 74:22	430
Unto thee, O G, do we give thanks	Ps 75:1	430
But G is the judge	Ps 75:7	430
sing praises to the G of Jacob	Ps 75:9	430
In Judah is G known	Ps 76:1	430
O G of Jacob, both the chariot and	Ps 76:6	430
When G arose to judgment, to save	Ps 76:9	430
Vow, and pay unto the LORD your G	Ps 76:11	430
I cried unto G with my voice,	Ps 77:1	430
even unto G with my voice	Ps 77:1	430
I remembered G, and was troubled	Ps 77:3	430
Hath G forgotten to be gracious	Ps 77:9	410
Thy way, O G, is in the sanctuary	Ps 77:13	430
who is so great a G as our G	Ps 77:13	410
who is so great a G as our G	Ps 77:13	430
Thou art the G that doest wonders	Ps 77:14	410
The waters saw thee, O G, the	Ps 77:16	430
they might set their hope in G	Ps 78:7	430
and not forget the works of G	Ps 78:7	410
spirit was not stedfast with G	Ps 78:8	410
They kept not the covenant of G	Ps 78:10	430
they tempted G in their heart by	Ps 78:18	410
Yea, they spake against G	Ps 78:19	430
Can G furnish a table in the	Ps 78:19	410
Because they believed not in G	Ps 78:22	430
The wrath of G came upon them, and	Ps 78:31	430
and enquired early after G	Ps 78:34	410
remembered that G was their rock	Ps 78:35	430
the high G their redeemer	Ps 78:35	410
they turned back and tempted G	Ps 78:41	410
and provoked the most high G	Ps 78:56	430
When G heard this, he was wroth,	Ps 78:59	430
O g, the heathen are come into	Ps 79:1	430
O G of our salvation, for the	Ps 79:9	430
the heathen say, Where is their G	Ps 79:10	430
Turn us again, O G, and cause thy	Ps 80:3	430
O LORD G of hosts, how long wilt	Ps 80:4	430
O G of hosts, and cause thy face	Ps 80:7	430
we beseech thee, O G of hosts	Ps 80:14	430
O LORD G of hosts, cause thy face	Ps 80:19	430
Sing aloud unto G our strength	Ps 81:1	430
joyful noise unto the G of Jacob	Ps 81:1	430
and a law of the G of Jacob	Ps 81:4	430
I am the LORD thy G, which	Ps 81:10	430
G standeth in the congregation of	Ps 82:1	430
Arise, O G, judge the earth	Ps 82:8	430
Keep not thou silence, O G	Ps 83:1	430
thy peace, and be not still, O G	Ps 83:1	410
the houses of G in possession	Ps 83:12	430
O my G, make them like a wheel	Ps 83:13	430
flesh crieth out for the living G	Ps 84:2	410
O LORD of hosts, my King, and my G	Ps 84:3	430
them in Zion appeareth before G	Ps 84:7	430
O LORD G of hosts, hear my prayer	Ps 84:8	430
give ear, O G of Jacob	Ps 84:8	430
O G our shield, and look upon the	Ps 84:9	430
a doorkeeper in the house of my G	Ps 84:10	430
For the LORD G is a sun and shield	Ps 84:11	430
O G of our salvation, and cause	Ps 85:4	430
I will hear what G the LORD will	Ps 85:8	410
O thou my G, save thy servant	Ps 86:2	430
thou art G alone	Ps 86:10	430
I will praise thee, O Lord my G	Ps 86:12	430
O G, the proud are risen against	Ps 86:14	430
art a G full of compassion, and	Ps 86:15	410
are spoken of thee, O city of G	Ps 87:3	430
O lord G of my salvation, I have	Ps 88:1	430
G is greatly to be feared in the	Ps 89:7	410
O LORD G of hosts, who is a	Ps 89:8	430
unto me, Thou art my father, my G	Ps 89:26	410
A Prayer of Moses, the man of G	Ps 90:t	430
to everlasting, thou art G	Ps 90:2	410
of the LORD our G be upon us	Ps 90:17	430
refuge and my fortress: my G	Ps 91:2	430
flourish in the courts of our G	Ps 92:13	430
O LORD G, to whom vengeance	Ps 94:1	410
O G, to whom vengeance belongeth,	Ps 94:1	410
neither shall the G of Jacob	Ps 94:7	430
my G is the rock of my refuge	Ps 94:22	430
the LORD our G shall cut them off	Ps 94:23	430
For the LORD is a great G	Ps 95:3	410
For he is our G	Ps 95:7	430
have seen the salvation of our G	Ps 98:3	430
Exalt ye the LORD our G, and	Ps 99:5	430
answeredst them, O LORD our G	Ps 99:8	430
thou wast a G that forgavest them	Ps 99:8	410
Exalt the LORD our G, and worship	Ps 99:9	430
for the LORD our G is holy	Ps 99:9	430
Know ye that the LORD he is G	Ps 100:3	430
I said, O my G, take me not away	Ps 102:24	410
O LORD my G, thou art very great	Ps 104:1	430
prey, and seek their meat from G	Ps 104:21	410
to my G while I have my being	Ps 104:33	430
He is the LORD our G	Ps 105:7	430
and tempted G in the desert	Ps 106:14	410
They forgat G their saviour,	Ps 106:21	410
Save us, O LORD our G, and gather	Ps 106:47	430
Blessed be the LORD G of Israel	Ps 106:48	430
rebelled against the words of G	Ps 107:11	410
O G, my heart is fixed	Ps 108:1	430
Be thou exalted, O G, above the	Ps 108:5	430
G hath spoken in his holiness	Ps 108:7	430
Wilt not thou, O G, who hast cast	Ps 108:11	430
and wilt not thou, O G, go forth	Ps 108:11	430
Through G we shall do valiantly	Ps 108:13	430
not thy peace, O G of my praise	Ps 109:1	430
O G the Lord, for thy name's sake	Ps 109:21	3069
Help me, O LORD my G	Ps 109:26	430
Who is like unto the LORD our G	Ps 113:5	430
at the presence of the G of Jacob	Ps 114:7	433
heathen say, Where is now their G	Ps 115:2	430
But our G is in the heavens	Ps 115:3	430
yea, our G is merciful	Ps 116:5	430
G is the LORD, which hath shewed	Ps 118:27	410
Thou art my G, and I will praise	Ps 118:28	410
thou art my G, I will exalt thee	Ps 118:28	430
keep the commandments of my G	Ps 119:115	430
LORD our G I will seek thy good	Ps 122:9	430
our eyes wait upon the LORD our G	Ps 123:2	430
vowed unto the mighty G of Jacob	Ps 132:2	
for the mighty G of Jacob	Ps 132:5	
the courts of the house of our G	Ps 135:2	430
O give thanks unto the G of gods	Ps 136:2	430
give thanks unto the G of heaven	Ps 136:26	410
are thy thoughts unto me, O G	Ps 139:17	410
thou wilt slay the wicked, O G	Ps 139:19	433
Search me, O G, and know my heart	Ps 139:23	410
said unto the LORD, Thou art my G	Ps 140:6	410
O G the Lord, the strength of my	Ps 140:7	
eyes are unto thee, O G the Lord	Ps 141:8	3069
for thou art my G	Ps 143:10	430
sing a new song unto thee, O G	Ps 144:9	430
that people, whose G is the LORD	Ps 144:15	430
I will extol thee, my G, O king	Ps 145:1	430
unto my G while I have any being	Ps 146:2	430
hath the G of Jacob for his help	Ps 146:5	410
whose hope is in the LORD his G	Ps 146:5	430
shall reign for ever, even thy G	Ps 146:10	430
good to sing praises unto our G	Ps 147:1	430
praise upon the harp unto our G	Ps 147:7	430
praise thy G, O Zion	Ps 147:12	430
praises of G be in their mouth	Ps 149:6	410
Praise G in his sanctuary	Ps 150:1	410
LORD, and find the knowledge of G	Prov 2:5	430
forgetteth the covenant of her G	Prov 2:17	430
understanding in the sight of G	Prov 3:4	430
but G overthroweth the wicked for	Prov 21:12	
the glory of G to conceal a thing	Prov 25:2	430
The great G that formed all	Prov 26:10	
Every word of G is pure	Prov 30:5	433
and take the name of my G in vain	Prov 30:9	430
this sore travail hath G given to	Eccl 1:13	430
that it was from the hand of G	Eccl 2:24	430
For G giveth to a man that is	Eccl 2:26	
give to him that is good before G	Eccl 2:26	430
which G hath given to the sons of	Eccl 3:10	430
G maketh from the beginning to	Eccl 3:11	430
his labour, it is the gift of G	Eccl 3:13	430
I know that, whatsoever G doeth	Eccl 3:14	430
G doeth it, that men should fear	Eccl 3:14	430
G requireth that which is past	Eccl 3:15	430
G shall judge the righteous and	Eccl 3:17	430
that G might manifest them, and	Eccl 3:18	430
when thou goest to the house of G	Eccl 5:1	430
hasty to utter any thing before G	Eccl 5:2	430
for G is in heaven, and thou upon	Eccl 5:2	430
When thou vowest a vow unto G	Eccl 5:4	430
wherefore should G be angry at	Eccl 5:6	430
but fear thou G	Eccl 5:7	430
of his life, which G giveth him	Eccl 5:18	430
also to whom G hath given riches	Eccl 5:19	430
this is the gift of G	Eccl 5:19	430
because G answereth him in the	Eccl 5:20	430
A man to whom G hath given riches	Eccl 6:2	430
yet G giveth him not power to eat	Eccl 6:2	430
Consider the work of G	Eccl 7:13	430
G also hath set the one over	Eccl 7:14	430
for he that feareth G shall come	Eccl 7:18	430
whoso pleaseth G shall escape	Eccl 7:26	430
that G hath made man upright	Eccl 7:29	430
that in regard of the oath of G	Eccl 8:2	430
be well with them that fear G	Eccl 8:12	430
because he feareth not before G	Eccl 8:13	430

Context	Reference	Number
which G giveth him under the sun	Eccl 8:15	430
Then I beheld all the work of G	Eccl 8:17	430
their works, are in the hand of G	Eccl 9:1	430
for G now accepteth thy works	Eccl 9:7	430
not the works of G who maketh all	Eccl 11:5	430
that for all these things G will	Eccl 11:9	430
shall return unto G who gave it	Eccl 12:7	430
Fear G, and keep his commandments	Eccl 12:13	430
For G shall bring every work into	Eccl 12:14	430
give ear unto the law of our G	Is 1:10	430
to the house of the G of Jacob	Is 2:3	430
saith the Lord G of hosts	Is 3:15	3069
and G that is holy shall be	Is 5:16	410
Thus saith the Lord G, It shall	Is 7:7	3069
Ask thee a sign of the LORD thy G	Is 7:11	430
men, but will ye weary my G also	Is 7:13	430
for G is with us	Is 8:10	410
not a people seek unto their G	Is 8:19	430
and curse their king and their G	Is 8:21	430
Counsellor, The mighty G	Is 9:6	410
of Jacob, unto the mighty G	Is 10:21	410
For the Lord G of hosts shall	Is 10:23	3069
thus saith the Lord G of hosts	Is 10:24	3069
Behold, G is my salvation	Is 12:2	410
be as when G overthrew Sodom	Is 13:19	430
my throne above the stars of G	Is 14:13	410
saith the LORD G of Israel	Is 17:6	430
forgotten the G of thy salvation	Is 17:10	430
but G shall rebuke them, and they	Is 17:13	
the G of Israel, have I declared	Is 21:10	430
for the LORD G of Israel hath	Is 21:17	430
Lord G of hosts in the valley of	Is 22:5	3069
Lord G of hosts call to weeping	Is 22:12	3069
ye die, saith the Lord G of hosts	Is 22:14	3069
Thus saith the Lord G of hosts	Is 22:15	3069
even the name of the LORD G of	Is 24:15	430
O lord, thou art my G	Is 25:1	430
the Lord G will wipe away tears	Is 25:8	3069
in that day, Lo, this is our G	Is 25:9	430
salvation will G appoint for	Is 26:1	
O LORD our G, other lords besides	Is 26:13	430
Therefore thus saith the Lord G	Is 28:16	3069
the Lord G of hosts a consumption	Is 28:22	3069
For his G doth instruct him to	Is 28:26	430
and shall fear the G of Israel	Is 29:23	430
For thus saith the Lord G	Is 30:15	3069
for the LORD is a G of judgment	Is 30:18	430
the Egyptians are men, and not G	Is 31:3	410
LORD, and the excellency of our G	Is 35:2	430
your G will come with vengeance,	Is 35:4	430
even G with a recompence	Is 35:4	430
to me, We trust in the LORD our G	Is 36:7	430
LORD thy G will hear the words of	Is 37:4	430
sent to reproach the living G	Is 37:4	430
which the LORD thy G hath heard	Is 37:4	430
of Judah, saying, Let not thy G	Is 37:10	430
G of Israel, that dwellest	Is 37:16	430
the cherubims, thou art the G	Is 37:16	430
sent to reproach the living G	Is 37:17	430
Now therefore, O LORD our G	Is 37:20	430
Thus saith the LORD G of Israel	Is 37:21	430
in the house of Nisroch his g	Is 37:38	430
the G of David thy father, I have	Is 38:5	430
ye my people, saith your G	Is 40:1	430
in the desert a highway for our G	Is 40:3	430
but the word of our G shall stand	Is 40:8	430
cities of Judah, Behold your G	Is 40:9	430
the Lord G will come with strong	Is 40:10	3069
To whom then will ye liken G	Is 40:18	410
judgment is passed over from my G	Is 40:27	430
not heard, that the everlasting G	Is 40:28	430
for I am thy G	Is 41:10	430
For I the LORD thy G will hold	Is 41:13	430
I the G of Israel will not	Is 41:17	430
Thus saith G the LORD, he that	Is 42:5	410
For I am the LORD thy G, the Holy	Is 43:3	430
before me there was no G formed	Is 43:10	410
saith the LORD, that I am G	Is 43:12	410
and beside me there is no G	Is 44:6	430
Is there a G beside me	Is 44:8	433
yea, there is no G	Is 44:8	6697
by thy name, am the G of Israel	Is 45:3	430
else, there is no G beside me	Is 45:5	430
thee, saying, Surely G is in thee	Is 45:14	410
there is none else, there is no G	Is 45:14	430
Verily thou art a G that hidest	Is 45:15	410
O G of Israel, the Saviour	Is 45:15	430
G himself that formed the earth	Is 45:18	430
there is no G else beside me	Is 45:21	430
a just G and a Saviour	Is 45:21	410
for I am G, and there is none else	Is 45:22	410
for I am G, and there is none else	Is 46:9	410
I am G, and there is none like me,	Is 46:9	430
make mention of the G of Israel	Is 48:1	430
themselves upon the G of Israel	Is 48:2	430
and now the Lord G, and his Spirit,	Is 48:16	3069
I am the LORD thy G which	Is 48:17	430
the LORD, and my work with my G	Is 49:4	430
my G shall be my strength	Is 49:5	430
Thus saith the Lord G, Behold, I	Is 49:22	3069
The Lord G hath given me the	Is 50:4	3069
The Lord G hath opened mine ear,	Is 50:5	3069
For the Lord G will help me	Is 50:7	3069
Behold, the Lord G will help me	Is 50:9	3609
of the LORD, and stay upon his G	Is 50:10	430
But I am the LORD thy G, that	Is 51:15	430
of the LORD, the rebuke of thy G	Is 51:20	430
thy G that pleadeth the cause of	Is 51:22	430
For thus saith the Lord G	Is 52:4	3069
saith unto Zion, Thy G reigneth	Is 52:7	430
shall see the salvation of our G	Is 52:10	430
the G of Israel will be your	Is 52:12	430
esteem him stricken, smitten of G	Is 53:4	430
The G of the whole earth shall he	Is 54:5	430
thou wast refused, saith thy G	Is 54:6	430
thee because of the LORD thy G	Is 55:5	430
and to our G, for he will	Is 55:7	430
The Lord G which gathereth the	Is 56:8	3069
There is no peace, saith my G	Is 57:21	430
not the ordinance of their G	Is 58:2	430
take delight in approaching to G	Is 58:2	430
separated between you and your G	Is 59:2	430
and departing away from our G	Is 59:13	430
unto the name of the LORD thy G	Is 60:9	430
light, and thy G thy glory	Is 60:19	430
Spirit of the Lord G is upon me	Is 61:1	3069
and the day of vengeance of our G	Is 61:2	430
call you the Ministers of our G	Is 61:6	430
my soul shall be joyful in my G	Is 61:10	430
so the Lord G will cause	Is 61:11	3069
royal diadem in the hand of thy G	Is 62:3	430
so shall thy G rejoice over thee	Is 62:5	430
neither hath the eye seen, O G	Is 64:4	430
Therefore thus saith the Lord G	Is 65:13	3069
for the Lord G shall slay thee,	Is 65:15	3069
bless himself in the G of truth	Is 65:16	430
shall swear by the G of truth	Is 65:16	430
saith thy G	Is 66:9	430
Then said I, Ah, Lord G	Jer 1:6	3069
thou hast forsaken the LORD thy G	Jer 2:17	430
thou hast forsaken the LORD thy G	Jer 2:19	430
thee, saith the Lord G of hosts	Jer 2:19	3069
before me, saith the Lord G	Jer 2:22	3069
against the LORD thy G, and hast	Jer 3:13	430
have forgotten the LORD their G	Jer 3:21	430
for thou art the LORD our G	Jer 3:22	430
truly in the LORD our G is the	Jer 3:23	430
sinned against the LORD our G	Jer 3:25	430
the voice of the LORD our G	Jer 3:25	430
Then said I, Ah, Lord G	Jer 4:10	3069
LORD, nor the judgment of their G	Jer 5:4	430
LORD, and the judgment of their G	Jer 5:5	430
thus saith the LORD G of hosts	Jer 5:14	430
our G all these things unto us	Jer 5:19	430
Let us now fear the LORD our G	Jer 5:24	430
the G of Israel, Amend your ways	Jer 7:3	430
Therefore thus saith the Lord G	Jer 7:20	3069
LORD of hosts, the G of Israel	Jer 7:21	430
my voice, and I will be your G	Jer 7:23	430
not the voice of the LORD their G	Jer 7:28	430
for the LORD our G hath put us to	Jer 8:14	430
LORD of hosts, the G of Israel	Jer 9:15	430
the true G, he is the living G	Jer 10:10	430
Thus saith the LORD G of Israel	Jer 11:3	430
be my people, and I will be your G	Jer 11:4	430
Thus saith the LORD G of Israel	Jer 13:12	430
Give glory to the LORD your G	Jer 13:16	430
Then said I, Ah, Lord G	Jer 14:13	3069
art not thou he, O LORD our G	Jer 14:22	430
by thy name, O LORD G of hosts	Jer 15:16	430
LORD of hosts, the G of Israel	Jer 16:9	430
committed against the LORD our G	Jer 16:10	430
LORD of hosts, the G of Israel	Jer 19:3	430
LORD of hosts, the G of Israel	Jer 19:15	430
Thus saith the LORD G of Israel	Jer 21:4	430
the covenant of the LORD their G	Jer 22:9	430
G of Israel against the pastors	Jer 23:2	430
Am I a G at hand, saith the LORD,	Jer 23:23	430
and not a G afar off	Jer 23:23	430
the words of the living G	Jer 23:36	430
of the LORD of hosts our G	Jer 23:36	430
saith the LORD, the G of Israel	Jer 24:5	430
my people, and I will be their G	Jer 24:7	430
the LORD G of Israel unto me	Jer 25:15	430
LORD of hosts, the G of Israel	Jer 25:27	430
obey the voice of the LORD your G	Jer 26:13	430
us in the name of the LORD our G	Jer 26:16	430
LORD of hosts, the G of Israel	Jer 27:4	430
the G of Israel, concerning the	Jer 27:21	430
the G of Israel, saying, I have	Jer 28:2	430
LORD of hosts, the G of Israel	Jer 28:14	430
the G of Israel, unto all that	Jer 29:4	430
LORD of hosts, the G of Israel	Jer 29:8	430
the G of Israel, of Ahab the son	Jer 29:21	430
the G of Israel, saying, Because	Jer 29:25	430
speaketh the LORD G of Israel	Jer 30:2	430
they shall serve the LORD their G	Jer 30:9	430
be my people, and I will be your G	Jer 30:22	430
will I be the G of all the	Jer 31:1	430
go up to Zion unto the LORD our G	Jer 31:6	430
for thou art the LORD my G	Jer 31:18	430
LORD of hosts, the G of Israel	Jer 31:23	430
and will be their G, and they shall	Jer 31:33	430
LORD of hosts, the G of Israel	Jer 32:14	430
LORD of hosts, the G of Israel	Jer 32:15	430
Ah Lord G!	Jer 32:17	3069
the Great, the Mighty G, the LORD	Jer 32:18	410
thou hast said unto me, O Lord G	Jer 32:25	3069
I am the LORD, the G of all flesh	Jer 32:27	430
the G of Israel, concerning this	Jer 32:36	430
my people, and I will be their G	Jer 32:38	430
the G of Israel, concerning the	Jer 33:4	430
saith the LORD, the G of Israel	Jer 34:2	430
saith the LORD, the G of Israel	Jer 34:13	430
the son of Igdaliah, a man of G	Jer 35:4	430
LORD of hosts, the G of Israel	Jer 35:13	430
G of hosts, the G of Israel	Jer 35:17	430
LORD of hosts, the G of Israel	Jer 35:18	430
LORD of hosts, the G of Israel	Jer 35:19	430
now unto the LORD our G for us	Jer 37:3	430
saith the LORD, the G of Israel	Jer 37:7	430
the G of hosts, the G of Israel	Jer 38:17	430
LORD of hosts, the G of Israel	Jer 39:16	430
The LORD thy G hath pronounced	Jer 40:2	430
pray for us unto the LORD thy G	Jer 42:2	430
That the LORD thy G may shew us	Jer 42:3	430
your G according to your words	Jer 42:4	430
LORD thy G shall send thee to us	Jer 42:5	430
obey the voice of the LORD our G	Jer 42:6	430
obey the voice of the LORD our G	Jer 42:6	430
the G of Israel, unto whom ye	Jer 42:9	430
obey the voice of the LORD your G	Jer 42:13	430
LORD of hosts, the G of Israel	Jer 42:15	430
LORD of hosts, the G of Israel	Jer 42:18	430
ye sent me unto the LORD your G	Jer 42:20	430
Pray for us unto the LORD our G	Jer 42:20	430
all that the LORD our G shall say	Jer 42:20	430
the voice of the LORD your G	Jer 42:21	430
all the words of the LORD their G	Jer 43:1	430
LORD their G had sent him to them	Jer 43:1	430
the LORD our G hath not sent thee	Jer 43:2	430
LORD of hosts, the G of Israel	Jer 43:10	430
LORD of hosts, the G of Israel	Jer 44:2	430
the G of hosts, the G of Israel	Jer 44:7	430
LORD of hosts, the G of Israel	Jer 44:11	430
of hosts, the G of Israel, saying	Jer 44:25	430
Egypt, saying, The Lord G liveth	Jer 44:26	3069
the G of Israel, unto thee, O	Jer 45:2	430
is the day of the Lord G of hosts	Jer 46:10	3069
for the Lord G of hosts hath a	Jer 46:10	3069
of hosts, the G of Israel, saith	Jer 46:25	430
LORD of hosts, the G of Israel	Jer 48:1	430
thee, saith the Lord G of hosts	Jer 49:5	3069
go, and seek the LORD their G	Jer 50:4	430
LORD of hosts, the G of Israel	Jer 50:18	430
G of hosts in the land of the	Jer 50:25	3069
the vengeance of the LORD our G	Jer 50:28	430
proud, saith the Lord G of hosts	Jer 50:31	3069
As G overthrew Sodom and Gomorrah	Jer 50:40	430
been forsaken, nor Judah of his G	Jer 51:5	430
Zion the work of the LORD our G	Jer 51:10	430
LORD of hosts, the G of Israel	Jer 51:33	430
for the LORD G of recompences	Jer 51:56	410
our hands unto G in the heavens	Lam 3:41	410
opened, and I saw visions of G	Eze 1:1	430
unto them, Thus saith the Lord G	Eze 2:4	3069
tell them, Thus saith the Lord G	Eze 3:11	3069
unto them, Thus saith the Lord G	Eze 3:27	3069
Then said I, Ah Lord G	Eze 4:14	3069
Thus saith the Lord G	Eze 5:5	3069
Therefore thus saith the Lord G	Eze 5:7	3069
Therefore thus saith the Lord G	Eze 5:8	3069
as I live, saith the Lord G	Eze 5:11	3069
hear the word of the Lord G	Eze 6:3	3069
saith the Lord G to the mountains	Eze 6:3	3069
Thus saith the Lord G	Eze 6:11	3069
thus saith the Lord G unto the	Eze 7:2	3069
Thus saith the Lord G	Eze 7:5	3069
of the Lord G fell there upon me	Eze 8:1	3069
in the visions of G to Jerusalem	Eze 8:3	430
the glory of the G of Israel was	Eze 8:4	430
the glory of the G of Israel was	Eze 9:3	430
and cried, and said, Ah Lord G	Eze 9:8	3069
the Almighty G when he speaketh	Eze 10:5	410
the glory of the G of Israel was	Eze 10:19	430
the G of Israel by the river of	Eze 10:20	430
Therefore thus saith the Lord G	Eze 11:7	3069
sword upon you, saith the Lord G	Eze 11:8	3069
a loud voice, and said, Ah Lord G	Eze 11:13	3069
say, Thus saith the Lord G	Eze 11:16	3069
say, Thus saith the Lord G	Eze 11:17	3069
my people, and I will be their G	Eze 11:20	430
their own heads, saith the Lord G	Eze 11:21	3069
the glory of the G of Israel was	Eze 11:22	430
by the Spirit of G into Chaldea	Eze 11:24	430
unto them, Thus saith the Lord G	Eze 12:10	3069
Thus saith the Lord G of the	Eze 12:19	3069
therefore, Thus saith the Lord G	Eze 12:23	3069
will perform it, saith the Lord G	Eze 12:25	3069
unto them, Thus saith the Lord G	Eze 12:28	3069
shall be done, saith the Lord G	Eze 12:28	3069
Thus saith the Lord G	Eze 13:3	3069
Therefore thus saith the Lord G	Eze 13:8	3069
am against you, saith the Lord G	Eze 13:8	3069
shall know that I am the Lord G	Eze 13:9	3069
Therefore thus saith the Lord G	Eze 13:13	3069
is no peace, saith the Lord G	Eze 13:16	3069
And say, Thus saith the Lord G	Eze 13:18	3069
Wherefore thus saith the Lord G	Eze 13:20	3069
unto them, Thus saith the Lord G	Eze 14:4	3069
of Israel, Thus saith the Lord G	Eze 14:6	3069
be my people, and I may be their G	Eze 14:11	430
saith the Lord G	Eze 14:11	3069
righteousness, saith the Lord G	Eze 14:14	3069
it, as I live, saith the Lord G	Eze 14:16	3069
it, as I live, saith the Lord G	Eze 14:18	3069
it, as I live, saith the Lord G	Eze 14:20	3069
For thus saith the Lord G	Eze 14:21	3069
have done in it, saith the Lord G	Eze 14:23	3069
Therefore thus saith the Lord G	Eze 15:6	3069
a trespass, saith the Lord G	Eze 15:8	3069
saith the Lord G unto Jerusalem	Eze 16:3	3069
with thee, saith the Lord G	Eze 16:8	3069
put upon thee, saith the Lord G	Eze 16:14	3069
and thus it was, saith the Lord G	Eze 16:19	3069
saith the Lord G	Eze 16:23	3069
is thine heart, saith the Lord G	Eze 16:30	3069
Thus saith the Lord G	Eze 16:36	3069
upon thine head, saith the Lord G	Eze 16:43	3069
As I live, saith the Lord G	Eze 16:48	3069
For thus saith the Lord G	Eze 16:59	3069
thou hast done, saith the Lord G	Eze 16:63	3069
And say, Thus saith the Lord G	Eze 17:3	3069
Say thou, Thus saith the Lord G	Eze 17:9	3069
As I live, saith the Lord G	Eze 17:16	3069
Therefore thus saith the Lord G	Eze 17:19	3069
Thus saith the Lord G	Eze 17:22	3069
As I live, saith the Lord G	Eze 18:3	3069
surely live, saith the Lord G	Eze 18:9	3069
saith the Lord G	Eze 18:23	3069
to his ways, saith the Lord G	Eze 18:30	3069
him that dieth, saith the Lord G	Eze 18:32	3069

unto them, Thus saith the Lord G	Eze 20:3	3069
As I live, saith the Lord G	Eze 20:3	3069
unto them, Thus saith the Lord G	Eze 20:5	3069
saying, I am the LORD your G	Eze 20:5	430
I am the LORD your G	Eze 20:7	430
I am the LORD your G	Eze 20:19	430
know that I am the LORD your G	Eze 20:20	430
unto them, Thus saith the Lord G	Eze 20:27	3069
of Israel, Thus saith the Lord G	Eze 20:30	3069
As I live, saith the Lord G	Eze 20:31	3069
As I live, saith the Lord G	Eze 20:33	3069
plead with you, saith the Lord G	Eze 20:36	3069
of Israel, thus saith the Lord G	Eze 20:39	3069
of Israel, saith the Lord G	Eze 20:40	3069
house of Israel, saith the Lord G	Eze 20:44	3069
Thus saith the Lord G	Eze 20:47	3069
Then said I, Ah Lord G	Eze 20:49	3069
brought to pass, saith the Lord G	Eze 21:7	3069
be no more, saith the Lord G	Eze 21:13	3069
Therefore thus saith the Lord G	Eze 21:24	3069
Thus saith the Lord G	Eze 21:26	3069
Thus saith the Lord G concerning	Eze 21:28	3069
say thou, Thus saith the Lord G	Eze 22:3	3069
forgotten me, saith the Lord G	Eze 22:12	3069
Therefore thus saith the Lord G	Eze 22:19	3069
saying, Thus saith the Lord G	Eze 22:28	3069
their heads, saith the Lord G	Eze 22:31	3069
O Aholibah, thus saith the Lord G	Eze 23:22	3069
For thus saith the Lord G	Eze 23:28	3069
Thus saith the Lord G	Eze 23:32	3069
have spoken it, saith the Lord G	Eze 23:34	3069
Therefore thus saith the Lord G	Eze 23:35	3069
For thus saith the Lord G	Eze 23:46	3069
shall know that I am the Lord G	Eze 23:49	3069
unto them, Thus saith the Lord G	Eze 24:3	3069
Wherefore thus saith the Lord G	Eze 24:6	3069
Therefore thus saith the Lord G	Eze 24:9	3069
they judge thee, saith the Lord G	Eze 24:14	3069
of Israel, Thus saith the Lord G	Eze 24:21	3069
shall know that I am the Lord G	Eze 24:24	3069
Hear the word of the Lord G	Eze 25:3	3069
Thus saith the Lord G	Eze 25:3	3069
For thus saith the Lord G	Eze 25:6	3069
Thus saith the Lord G	Eze 25:8	3069
Thus saith the Lord G	Eze 25:12	3069
Therefore thus saith the Lord G	Eze 25:13	3069
my vengeance, saith the Lord G	Eze 25:14	3069
Thus saith the Lord G	Eze 25:15	3069
Therefore thus saith the Lord G	Eze 25:16	3069
Therefore thus saith the Lord G	Eze 26:3	3069
have spoken it, saith the Lord G	Eze 26:5	3069
For thus saith the Lord G	Eze 26:7	3069
have spoken it, saith the Lord G	Eze 26:14	3069
Thus saith the Lord G to Tyrus	Eze 26:15	3069
For thus saith the Lord G	Eze 26:19	3069
be found again, saith the Lord G	Eze 26:21	3069
many isles, Thus saith the Lord G	Eze 27:3	3069
of Tyrus, Thus saith the Lord G	Eze 28:2	3069
up, and thou hast said, I am a G	Eze 28:2	410
I sit in the seat of G	Eze 28:2	430
yet thou art a man, and not G	Eze 28:2	410
set thine heart as the heart of G	Eze 28:2	430
Therefore thus saith the Lord G	Eze 28:6	3069
set thine heart as the heart of G	Eze 28:6	430
him that slayeth thee, I am G	Eze 28:9	430
but thou shalt be a man, and no G	Eze 28:9	410
have spoken it, saith the Lord G	Eze 28:10	3069
unto him, Thus saith the Lord G	Eze 28:12	3069
hast been in Eden the garden of G	Eze 28:13	430
wast upon the holy mountain of G	Eze 28:14	430
profane out of the mountain of G	Eze 28:16	430
And say, Thus saith the Lord G	Eze 28:22	3069
shall know that I am the Lord G	Eze 28:24	3069
Thus saith the Lord G	Eze 28:25	3069
know that I am the LORD their G	Eze 28:26	430
and say, Thus saith the Lord G	Eze 29:3	3069
Therefore thus saith the Lord G	Eze 29:8	3069
Yet thus saith the Lord G	Eze 29:13	3069
shall know that I am the Lord G	Eze 29:16	3069
Therefore thus saith the Lord G	Eze 29:19	3069
wrought for me, saith the Lord G	Eze 29:20	3069
and say, Thus saith the Lord G	Eze 30:2	3069
it by the sword, saith the Lord G	Eze 30:6	3069
Thus saith the Lord G	Eze 30:10	3069
Thus saith the Lord G	Eze 30:13	3069
Therefore thus saith the Lord G	Eze 30:22	3069
garden of G could not hide him	Eze 31:8	430
nor any tree in the garden of G	Eze 31:8	430
that were in the garden of G	Eze 31:9	430
Therefore thus saith the Lord G	Eze 31:10	3069
Thus saith the Lord G	Eze 31:15	430
his multitude, saith the Lord G	Eze 31:18	3069
Thus saith the Lord G	Eze 32:3	3069
upon thy land, saith the Lord G	Eze 32:8	3069
For thus saith the Lord G	Eze 32:11	3069
to run like oil, saith the Lord G	Eze 32:14	3069
her multitude, saith the Lord G	Eze 32:16	3069
by the sword, saith the Lord G	Eze 32:31	3069
his multitude, saith the Lord G	Eze 32:32	3069
them, As I live, saith the Lord G	Eze 33:11	3069
unto them, Thus saith the Lord G	Eze 33:25	3069
unto them, Thus saith the Lord G	Eze 33:27	3069
the Lord G unto the shepherds	Eze 34:2	3069
As I live saith the Lord G	Eze 34:8	3069
Thus saith the Lord G	Eze 34:10	3069
For thus saith the Lord G	Eze 34:11	3069
to lie down, saith the Lord G	Eze 34:15	3069
O my flock, thus saith the Lord G	Eze 34:17	3069
thus saith the Lord G unto them	Eze 34:20	3069
And I the LORD will be their G	Eze 34:24	430
I the LORD their G am with them	Eze 34:30	430
are my people, saith the Lord G	Eze 34:30	3069
pasture, are men, and I am your G	Eze 34:31	430
saith the Lord G	Eze 34:31	3069
unto it, Thus saith the Lord G	Eze 35:3	3069
as I live, saith the Lord G	Eze 35:6	3069
as I live, saith the Lord G	Eze 35:11	3069
Thus saith the Lord G	Eze 35:14	3069
Thus saith the Lord G	Eze 36:2	3069
and say, Thus saith the Lord G	Eze 36:3	3069
hear the word of the Lord G	Eze 36:4	3069
saith the Lord G to the mountains	Eze 36:4	3069
Therefore thus saith the Lord G	Eze 36:5	3069
valleys, Thus saith the Lord G	Eze 36:6	3069
Therefore thus saith the Lord G	Eze 36:7	3069
Thus saith the Lord G	Eze 36:13	3069
any more, saith the Lord G	Eze 36:14	3069
fall any more, saith the Lord G	Eze 36:15	3069
of Israel, Thus saith the Lord G	Eze 36:22	3069
I am the LORD, saith the Lord G	Eze 36:23	3069
be my people, and I will be your G	Eze 36:28	430
sakes do I this, saith the Lord G	Eze 36:32	3069
Thus saith the Lord G	Eze 36:33	3069
Thus saith the Lord G	Eze 36:37	3069
And I answered, O Lord G, thou	Eze 37:3	3069
saith the Lord G unto these bones	Eze 37:5	3069
the wind, Thus saith the Lord G	Eze 37:9	3069
unto them, Thus saith the Lord G	Eze 37:12	3069
unto them, Thus saith the Lord G	Eze 37:19	3069
unto them, Thus saith the Lord G	Eze 37:21	3069
my people, and I will be their G	Eze 37:23	430
yea, I will be their G, and they	Eze 37:27	430
And say, Thus saith the Lord G	Eze 38:3	3069
Thus saith the Lord G	Eze 38:10	3069
unto Gog, Thus saith the Lord G	Eze 38:14	3069
Thus saith the Lord G	Eze 38:17	3069
land of Israel, saith the Lord G	Eze 38:18	3069
my mountains, saith the Lord G	Eze 38:21	3069
and say, Thus saith the Lord G	Eze 39:1	3069
have spoken it, saith the Lord G	Eze 39:5	3069
and it is done, saith the Lord G	Eze 39:8	3069
robbed them, saith the Lord G	Eze 39:10	3069
be glorified, saith the Lord G	Eze 39:13	3069
son of man, thus saith the Lord G	Eze 39:17	3069
all men of war, saith the Lord G	Eze 39:20	3069
am the LORD their G from that day	Eze 39:22	430
Therefore thus saith the Lord G	Eze 39:25	3069
know that I am the LORD their G	Eze 39:28	430
house of Israel, saith the Lord G	Eze 39:29	3069
In the visions of G brought he me	Eze 40:2	430
the glory of the G of Israel came	Eze 43:2	430
Son of man, thus saith the Lord G	Eze 43:18	3069
unto me, saith the Lord G	Eze 43:19	3069
will accept you, saith the Lord G	Eze 43:27	3069
the G of Israel, hath entered in	Eze 44:2	430
of Israel, Thus saith the Lord G	Eze 44:6	3069
Thus saith the Lord G	Eze 44:9	3069
against them, saith the Lord G	Eze 44:12	3069
and the blood, saith the Lord G	Eze 44:15	3069
sin offering, saith the Lord G	Eze 44:27	3069
Thus saith the Lord G	Eze 45:9	3069
from my people, saith the Lord G	Eze 45:9	3069
for them, saith the Lord G	Eze 45:15	3069
Thus saith the Lord G	Eze 45:18	3069
Thus saith the Lord G	Eze 46:1	3069
Thus saith the Lord G	Eze 46:16	3069
Thus saith the Lord G	Eze 47:13	3069
his inheritance, saith the Lord G	Eze 47:23	3069
their portions, saith the Lord G	Eze 48:29	3069
of the vessels of the house of G	Dan 1:2	430
Now G had brought Daniel into	Dan 1:9	430
G gave them knowledge and skill in	Dan 1:17	430
the G of heaven concerning this	Dan 2:18	426
Daniel blessed the G of heaven	Dan 2:19	426
Blessed be the name of G for ever	Dan 2:20	426
O thou G of my fathers, who hast	Dan 2:23	426
But there is a G in heaven that	Dan 2:28	426
for the G of heaven hath given	Dan 2:37	426
the G of heaven set up a kingdom	Dan 2:44	426
the great G hath made known to	Dan 2:45	426
is, that your G is a G of gods	Dan 2:47	426
who is that G that shall deliver	Dan 3:15	426
our G whom we serve is able to	Dan 3:17	426
the fourth is like the Son of G	Dan 3:25	426
ye servants of the most high G	Dan 3:26	426
Blessed be the G of Shadrach	Dan 3:28	426
except their own G	Dan 3:28	426
amiss against the G of Shadrach	Dan 3:29	426
because there is no other G that	Dan 3:29	426
wonders that the high G hath	Dan 4:2	426
house of G which was at Jerusalem	Dan 5:3	426
O thou king, the most high G gave	Dan 5:18	426
G ruled in the kingdom of men	Dan 5:21	426
the G in whose hand thy breath is	Dan 5:23	426
G hath numbered thy kingdom, and	Dan 5:26	426
him concerning the law of his G	Dan 6:5	426
of any G or man for thirty days	Dan 6:7	426
and gave thanks before his G	Dan 6:10	426
making supplication before his G	Dan 6:11	426
any G or man within thirty days	Dan 6:12	426
Daniel, Thy G whom thou servest	Dan 6:16	426
of the living G, is thy G	Dan 6:20	426
My G hath sent his angel, and hath	Dan 6:22	426
him, because he believed in his G	Dan 6:23	426
and fear before the G of Daniel	Dan 6:26	426
for he is the living G, and	Dan 6:26	426
And I set my face unto the Lord G	Dan 9:3	430
And I prayed unto the LORD my G	Dan 9:4	430
O Lord, the great and dreadful G	Dan 9:4	410
To the Lord our G belong mercies	Dan 9:9	430
the voice of the LORD our G	Dan 9:10	430
the law of Moses the servant of G	Dan 9:11	430
our prayer before the LORD our G	Dan 9:13	430
for the LORD our G is righteous	Dan 9:14	430
And now, O Lord our G, that hast	Dan 9:15	430
Now therefore, O our G, hear the	Dan 9:17	430
O my G, incline thine ear, and	Dan 9:18	430
not, for thine own sake, O my G	Dan 9:19	430
G for the holy mountain of my G	Dan 9:20	430
to chasten thyself before thy G	Dan 10:12	430
do know their G shall be strong	Dan 11:32	430
things against the G of gods	Dan 11:36	410
he regard the G of his fathers	Dan 11:37	430
shall he honour the G of forces	Dan 11:38	433
G said unto him, Call her name	Hos 1:6	
save them by the LORD their G	Hos 1:7	430
Then said G, Call his name	Hos 1:9	
people, and I will not be your G	Hos 1:9	
Ye are the sons of the living G	Hos 1:10	410
and they shall say, Thou art my G	Hos 2:23	430
return, and seek the LORD their G	Hos 3:5	430
nor knowledge of G in the land	Hos 4:1	430
hast forgotten the law of thy G	Hos 4:6	430
gone a whoring from under their G	Hos 4:12	430
their doings to turn unto their G	Hos 5:4	430
the knowledge of G more than	Hos 6:6	430
do not return to the LORD their G	Hos 7:10	430
Israel shall cry unto me, My G	Hos 8:2	430
therefore it is not G	Hos 8:6	430
hast gone a whoring from thy G	Hos 9:1	430
watchman of Ephraim was with my G	Hos 9:8	430
and hatred in the house of his G	Hos 9:8	430
My G will cast them away, because	Hos 9:17	430
for I am G, and not man	Hos 11:9	410
but Judah yet ruleth with G	Hos 11:12	430
his strength he had power with G	Hos 12:3	430
Even the LORD G of hosts	Hos 12:5	430
Therefore turn thou to thy G	Hos 12:6	430
and wait on thy G continually	Hos 12:6	430
I that am the LORD thy G from the	Hos 12:9	430
Yet I am the LORD thy G from the	Hos 13:4	430
she hath rebelled against her G	Hos 13:16	430
return unto the LORD thy G	Hos 14:1	430
sackcloth, ye ministers of my G	Joel 1:13	430
from the house of your G	Joel 1:13	430
into the house of the LORD your G	Joel 1:14	430
gladness from the house of our G	Joel 1:16	430
and turn unto the LORD your G	Joel 2:13	430
offering unto the LORD your G	Joel 2:14	430
the people, Where is their G	Joel 2:17	430
and rejoice in the LORD your G	Joel 2:23	430
the name of the LORD your G	Joel 2:26	430
and that I am the LORD your G	Joel 2:27	430
the LORD your G dwelling in Zion	Joel 3:17	430
shall perish, saith the Lord G	Amos 1:8	3069
Surely the Lord G will do nothing	Amos 3:7	3069
the Lord G hath spoken, who can	Amos 3:8	3069
Therefore thus saith the Lord G	Amos 3:11	3069
house of Jacob, saith the Lord G	Amos 3:13	3069
the G of hosts,	Amos 3:13	430
The Lord G hath sworn by his	Amos 4:2	3069
of Israel, saith the Lord G	Amos 4:5	3069
as G overthrew Sodom and Gomorrah,	Amos 4:11	430
unto thee, prepare to meet thy G	Amos 4:12	430
The G of hosts, is his name	Amos 4:13	430
For thus saith the Lord G	Amos 5:3	3069
the G of hosts, shall be with you	Amos 5:14	430
it may be that the LORD G of	Amos 5:15	430
the G of hosts, the Lord, saith	Amos 5:16	430
whose name is The G of hosts	Amos 5:27	430
The Lord G hath sworn by himself,	Amos 6:8	3069
saith the LORD the G of hosts	Amos 6:8	430
saith the LORD the G of hosts	Amos 6:14	430
hath the Lord G shewed unto me	Amos 7:1	3069
the land, then I said, O Lord G	Amos 7:2	3069
hath the Lord G shewed unto me	Amos 7:4	3069
the Lord G called to contend by	Amos 7:4	3069
Then said I, O Lord G, cease, I	Amos 7:5	3069
shall not be, saith the Lord G	Amos 7:6	3069
hath the Lord G shewed unto me	Amos 8:1	3069
in that day, saith the Lord G	Amos 8:3	3069
in that day, saith the Lord G	Amos 8:9	3069
the days come, saith the Lord G	Amos 8:11	3069
the Lord G of hosts is he that	Amos 9:5	3069
the eyes of the Lord G are upon	Amos 9:8	3069
given them, saith the LORD thy G	Amos 9:15	430
saith the Lord G concerning Edom	Obad 1	3069
arise, call upon thy G	Jonah 1:6	430
if so be that G will think upon	Jonah 1:6	
the G of heaven, which hath made	Jonah 1:9	430
his G out of the fish's belly	Jonah 2:1	430
life from corruption, O LORD my G	Jonah 2:6	430
the people of Nineveh believed G	Jonah 3:5	430
sackcloth, and cry mightily unto G	Jonah 3:8	430
Who can tell if G will turn	Jonah 3:9	430
G saw their works, that they	Jonah 3:10	430
G repented of the evil, that he	Jonah 3:10	430
I knew that thou art a gracious G	Jonah 4:2	410
the LORD G prepared a gourd, and	Jonah 4:6	430
But G prepared a worm when the	Jonah 4:7	430
that G prepared a vehement east	Jonah 4:8	430
G said to Jonah, Doest thou well	Jonah 4:9	430
let the Lord G be witness against	Mic 1:2	3069
for there is no answer of G	Mic 3:7	430
and to the house of the G of Jacob	Mic 4:2	430
name of the LORD our G for ever	Mic 4:5	430
of the name of the LORD his G	Mic 5:4	430
and bow myself before the high G	Mic 6:6	430
and to walk humbly with thy G	Mic 6:8	430
wait for the G of my salvation	Mic 7:7	430
my G will hear me	Mic 7:7	430
unto me, Where is the LORD thy G	Mic 7:10	430
shall be afraid of the LORD our G	Mic 7:17	430
Who is a G like unto thee, that	Mic 7:18	410
G is jealous, and the LORD	Nah 1:2	410
not from everlasting, O LORD my G	Hab 1:12	430
and, O mighty G, thou hast	Hab 1:12	6697
G came from Teman, and the Holy	Hab 3:3	433
will joy in the G of my salvation	Hab 3:18	430
The LORD G is my strength, and he	Hab 3:19	136
at the presence of the Lord G	Zeph 1:7	3069
the LORD their G shall visit them	Zeph 2:7	430

the G of Israel, Surely Moab	Zeph 2:9	430
she drew not near to her G	Zeph 3:2	430
The LORD thy G in the midst of	Zeph 3:17	430
the voice of the LORD their G	Hag 1:12	430
as the LORD their G had sent him	Hag 1:12	430
of the LORD of hosts, their G	Hag 1:14	430
obey the voice of the LORD your G	Zec 6:15	430
sent unto the house of G Sherezer	Zec 7:2	1008
my people, and I will be their G	Zec 8:8	430
we have heard that G is with you	Zec 8:23	430
even he, shall be for our G	Zec 9:7	430
the Lord G shall blow the trumpet	Zec 9:14	3069
the LORD their G shall save them	Zec 9:16	430
for I am the LORD their G	Zec 10:6	430
Thus saith the LORD my G	Zec 11:4	430
in the LORD of hosts their G	Zec 12:5	430
the house of David shall be as G	Zec 12:8	430
they shall say, The LORD is my G	Zec 13:9	430
and the LORD my G shall come	Zec 14:5	430
beseech G that he will be	Mal 1:9	410
hath not one G created us	Mal 2:10	410
the G of Israel, saith that he	Mal 2:16	430
or, Where is the G of judgment	Mal 2:17	430
Will a man rob G	Mal 3:8	430
have said, It is vain to serve G	Mal 3:14	430
they that tempt G are even	Mal 3:15	430
between him that serveth G	Mal 3:18	430
being interpreted is, G with us	Mt 1:23	2316
being warned of G in a dream that	Mt 2:12	
being warned of G in a dream	Mt 2:22	
that G is able of these stones to	Mt 3:9	2316
he saw the Spirit of G descending	Mt 3:16	2316
he said, If thou be the Son of G	Mt 4:3	2316
proceedeth out of the mouth of G	Mt 4:4	2316
unto him, If thou be the Son of G	Mt 4:6	2316
shalt not tempt the Lord thy G	Mt 4:7	2316
Thou shalt worship the Lord thy G	Mt 4:10	2316
for they shall see G	Mt 5:8	2316
shall be called the children of G	Mt 5:9	2316
Ye cannot serve G and mammon	Mt 6:24	2316
if G so clothe the grass of the	Mt 6:30	2316
seek ye first the kingdom of G	Mt 6:33	2316
with thee, Jesus, thou Son of G	Mt 8:29	2316
they marvelled, and glorified G	Mt 9:8	2316
he entered into the house of G	Mt 12:4	2316
out devils by the Spirit of G	Mt 12:28	2316
the kingdom of G is come unto you	Mt 12:28	2316
Of a truth thou art the Son of G	Mt 14:33	2316
of G by your tradition	Mt 15:3	2316
For G commanded, saying, Honour	Mt 15:4	2316
of G of none effect by your	Mt 15:6	2316
and they glorified the G of Israel	Mt 15:31	2316
Christ, the Son of the living G	Mt 16:16	2316
not the things that be of G	Mt 16:23	2316
What therefore G hath joined	Mt 19:6	2316
is none good but one, that is, G	Mt 19:17	2316
to enter into the kingdom of G	Mt 19:24	2316
but with G all things are	Mt 19:26	2316
Jesus went into the temple of G	Mt 21:12	2316
into the kingdom of G before you	Mt 21:31	2316
The kingdom of G shall be taken	Mt 21:43	2316
and teachest the way of G in truth	Mt 22:16	2316
unto G the things that are God's	Mt 22:21	2316
scriptures, nor the power of G	Mt 22:29	2316
are as the angels of G in heaven	Mt 22:30	2316
which was spoken unto you by G	Mt 22:31	2316
I am the G of Abraham	Mt 22:32	2316
G of Isaac, and the G of Jacob	Mt 22:32	2316
G is not the G of the dead	Mt 22:32	2316
the Lord thy G with all thy heart	Mt 22:37	2316
sweareth by the throne of G	Mt 23:22	2316
able to destroy the temple of G	Mt 26:61	2316
I adjure thee by the living G	Mt 26:63	2316
thou be the Christ, the Son of G	Mt 26:63	2316
If thou be the Son of G, come	Mt 27:40	2316
He trusted in G	Mt 27:43	2316
for he said, I am the Son of G	Mt 27:43	2316
that is to say, My G, my G	Mt 27:46	2316
Truly this was the Son of G	Mt 27:54	2316
of Jesus Christ, the Son of G	Mk 1:1	2316
the gospel of the kingdom of G	Mk 1:14	2316
and the kingdom of G is at hand	Mk 1:15	2316
who thou art, the Holy One of G	Mk 1:24	2316
who can forgive sins but G only	Mk 2:7	2316
were all amazed, and glorified G	Mk 2:12	2316
of G in the days of Abiathar the	Mk 2:26	2316
saying, Thou art the Son of G	Mk 3:11	2316
whosoever shall do the will of G	Mk 3:35	2316
the mystery of the kingdom of G	Mk 4:11	2316
he said, So is the kingdom of G	Mk 4:26	2316
shall we liken the kingdom of G	Mk 4:30	2316
thou Son of the most high G	Mk 5:7	2316
I adjure thee by G, that thou	Mk 5:7	2316
laying aside the commandment of G	Mk 7:8	2316
ye reject the commandment of G	Mk 7:9	2316
Making the word of G of none	Mk 7:13	2316
not the things that be of G	Mk 8:33	2316
the kingdom of G come with power	Mk 9:1	2316
the kingdom of G with one eye	Mk 9:47	2316
of the creation G made them male	Mk 10:6	2316
What therefore G hath joined	Mk 10:9	2316
for of such is the kingdom of G	Mk 10:14	2316
kingdom of G as a little child	Mk 10:15	2316
is none good but one, that is, G	Mk 10:18	2316
enter into the kingdom of G	Mk 10:23	2316
to enter into the kingdom of G	Mk 10:24	2316
to enter into the kingdom of G	Mk 10:25	2316
it is impossible, but not with G	Mk 10:27	2316
for with G all things are	Mk 10:27	2316
saith unto them, Have faith in G	Mk 11:22	2316
teachest the way of G in truth	Mk 12:14	2316
to G the things that are God's	Mk 12:17	2316
neither the power of G	Mk 12:24	2316
how in the bush G spake unto him	Mk 12:26	2316
I am the G of Abraham	Mk 12:26	2316
G of Isaac, and the G of Jacob	Mk 12:26	2316
He is not the G of the dead	Mk 12:27	2316
but the G of the living	Mk 12:27	2316
The Lord our G is one Lord	Mk 12:29	2316
the Lord thy G with all thy heart	Mk 12:30	2316
for there is one G	Mk 12:32	2316
art not far from the kingdom of G	Mk 12:34	2316
which G created unto this time	Mk 13:19	2316
drink it new in the kingdom of G	Mk 14:25	2316
being interpreted, My G, my G	Mk 15:34	2316
Truly this man was the Son of G	Mk 15:39	2316
also waited for the kingdom of G	Mk 15:43	2316
and sat on the right hand of G	Mk 16:19	2316
they were both righteous before G	Lk 1:6	2316
G in the order of his course	Lk 1:8	2316
shall he turn to the Lord their G	Lk 1:16	2316
that stand in the presence of G	Lk 1:19	2316
from G unto a city of Galilee	Lk 1:26	2316
for thou hast found favour with G	Lk 1:30	2316
the Lord G shall give unto him	Lk 1:32	2316
thee shall be called the Son of G	Lk 1:35	2316
For with G nothing shall be	Lk 1:37	2316
hath rejoiced in G my Saviour	Lk 1:47	2316
loosed, and he spake, and praised G	Lk 1:64	2316
Blessed be the Lord G of Israel	Lk 1:68	2316
Through the tender mercy of our G	Lk 1:78	2316
of the heavenly host praising G	Lk 2:13	2316
Glory to G in the highest, and on	Lk 2:14	2316
praising G for all the things	Lk 2:20	2316
him up in his arms, and blessed G	Lk 2:28	2316
but served G with fastings and	Lk 2:37	
and the grace of G was upon him	Lk 2:40	2316
and stature, and in favour with G	Lk 2:52	2316
the word of G came unto John the	Lk 3:2	2316
shall see the salvation of G	Lk 3:6	2316
That G is able of these stones to	Lk 3:8	2316
of Adam, which was the son of G	Lk 3:38	2316
unto him, If thou be the Son of G	Lk 4:3	2316
alone, but by every word of G	Lk 4:4	2316
Thou shalt worship the Lord thy G	Lk 4:8	2316
unto him, If thou be the Son of G	Lk 4:9	2316
shalt not tempt the Lord thy G	Lk 4:12	2316
the Holy One of G	Lk 4:34	2316
Thou art Christ the Son of G	Lk 4:41	2316
kingdom of G to other cities also	Lk 4:43	2316
upon him to hear the word of G	Lk 5:1	2316
Who can forgive sins, but G alone	Lk 5:21	2316
to his own house, glorifying G	Lk 5:25	2316
all amazed, and they glorified G	Lk 5:26	2316
How he went into the house of G	Lk 6:4	2316
all night in prayer to G	Lk 6:12	2316
for yours is the kingdom of G	Lk 6:20	2316
and they glorified G, saying, That	Lk 7:16	2316
That G hath visited his people	Lk 7:16	2316
kingdom of G is greater than he	Lk 7:28	2316
and the publicans, justified G	Lk 7:29	2316
counsel of G against themselves	Lk 7:30	2316
glad tidings of the kingdom of G	Lk 8:1	2316
the mysteries of the kingdom of G	Lk 8:10	2316
The seed is the word of G	Lk 8:11	2316
these which hear the word of G	Lk 8:21	2316
Jesus, thou Son of G most high	Lk 8:28	2316
things G hath done unto thee	Lk 8:39	2316
them to preach the kingdom of G	Lk 9:2	2316
unto them of the kingdom of G	Lk 9:11	2316
answering said, The Christ of G	Lk 9:20	2316
till they see the kingdom of G	Lk 9:27	2316
amazed at the mighty power of G	Lk 9:43	2316
thou and preach the kingdom of G	Lk 9:60	2316
back, is fit for the kingdom of G	Lk 9:62	2316
The kingdom of G is come nigh	Lk 10:9	2316
that the kingdom of G is come	Lk 10:11	2316
the Lord thy G with all thy heart	Lk 10:27	2316
the finger of G cast out devils	Lk 11:20	2316
the kingdom of G is come upon you	Lk 11:20	2316
are they that hear the word of G	Lk 11:28	2316
over judgment and the love of G	Lk 11:42	2316
also said the wisdom of G	Lk 11:49	2316
one of them is forgotten before G	Lk 12:6	2316
confess before the angels of G	Lk 12:8	2316
be denied before the angels of G	Lk 12:9	2316
But G said unto him, Thou fool,	Lk 12:20	2316
himself, and is not rich toward G	Lk 12:21	2316
and G feedeth them	Lk 12:24	2316
If then G so clothe the grass,	Lk 12:28	2316
rather seek ye the kingdom of G	Lk 12:31	2316
was made straight, and glorified G	Lk 13:13	2316
what is the kingdom of G like	Lk 13:18	2316
shall I liken the kingdom of G	Lk 13:20	2316
the prophets, in the kingdom of G	Lk 13:28	2316
sit down in the kingdom of G	Lk 13:29	2316
eat bread in the kingdom of G	Lk 14:15	2316
the presence of the angels of G	Lk 15:10	2316
Ye cannot serve G and mammon	Lk 16:13	2316
but G knoweth your hearts	Lk 16:15	2316
is abomination in the sight of G	Lk 16:15	2316
time the kingdom of G is preached	Lk 16:16	2316
and with a loud voice glorified G	Lk 17:15	2316
that returned to give glory to G	Lk 17:18	2316
when the kingdom of G should come	Lk 17:20	2316
The kingdom of G cometh not with	Lk 17:20	2316
the kingdom of G is within you	Lk 17:21	2316
city a judge, which feared not G	Lk 18:2	2316
himself, Though I fear not G	Lk 18:4	2316
shall not G avenge his own elect,	Lk 18:7	2316
and prayed thus with himself, G	Lk 18:11	2316
G be merciful to me a sinner	Lk 18:13	2316
for of such is the kingdom of G	Lk 18:16	2316
not receive the kingdom of G as a	Lk 18:17	2316
is good, save one, that is, G	Lk 18:19	2316
enter into the kingdom of G	Lk 18:24	2316
to enter into the kingdom of G	Lk 18:25	2316
with men are possible with G	Lk 18:27	2316
and followed him, glorifying G	Lk 18:43	2316
they saw it, gave praise unto G	Lk 18:43	2316
of G should immediately appear	Lk 19:11	2316
praise G with a loud voice for	Lk 19:37	2316
heard it, they said, G forbid	Lk 20:16	
but teachest the way of G truly	Lk 20:21	2316
unto G the things which be God's	Lk 20:25	2316
and are the children of G, being	Lk 20:36	2316
calleth the Lord the G of Abraham	Lk 20:37	2316
G of Isaac, and the G of Jacob	Lk 20:37	2316
For he is not a G of the dead	Lk 20:38	2316
cast in unto the offerings of G	Lk 21:4	2316
the kingdom of G is nigh at hand	Lk 21:31	2316
be fulfilled in the kingdom of G	Lk 22:16	2316
until the kingdom of G shall come	Lk 22:18	2316
the right hand of the power of G	Lk 22:69	2316
all, Art thou then the Son of G	Lk 22:70	2316
if he be Christ, the chosen of G	Lk 23:35	2316
him, saying, Dost not thou fear G	Lk 23:40	2316
saw what was done, he glorified G	Lk 23:47	2316
waited for the kingdom of G	Lk 23:51	2316
mighty in deed and word before G	Lk 24:19	2316
temple, praising and blessing G	Lk 24:53	2316
was with G, and the Word was G	Jn 1:1	2316
same was in the beginning with G	Jn 1:2	2316
There was a man sent from G	Jn 1:6	2316
he power to become the sons of G	Jn 1:12	2316
nor of the will of man, but of G	Jn 1:13	2316
No man hath seen G at any time	Jn 1:18	2316
and saith, Behold the Lamb of G	Jn 1:29	2316
record that this is the Son of G	Jn 1:34	2316
he saith, Behold the Lamb of G	Jn 1:36	2316
him, Rabbi, thou art the Son of G	Jn 1:49	2316
and the angels of G ascending	Jn 1:51	2316
thou art a teacher come from G	Jn 3:2	2316
thou doest, except G be with him	Jn 3:2	2316
he cannot see the kingdom of G	Jn 3:3	2316
enter into the kingdom of G	Jn 3:5	2316
For G so loved the world, that he	Jn 3:16	2316
For G sent not his Son into the	Jn 3:17	2316
of the only begotten Son of G	Jn 3:18	2316
that they are wrought in G	Jn 3:21	2316
set to his seal that G is true	Jn 3:33	2316
For he whom G hath sent speaketh	Jn 3:34	2316
hath sent speaketh the words of G	Jn 3:34	2316
for G giveth not the Spirit by	Jn 3:34	2316
but the wrath of G abideth on him	Jn 3:36	2316
If thou knewest the gift of G	Jn 4:10	2316
G is a Spirit	Jn 4:24	2316
said also that G was his Father	Jn 5:18	2316
making himself equal with G	Jn 5:18	2316
hear the voice of the Son of G	Jn 5:25	2316
ye have not the love of G in you	Jn 5:42	2316
honour that cometh from G only	Jn 5:44	2316
for him hath G the Father sealed	Jn 6:27	2316
that we might work the works of G	Jn 6:28	2316
unto them, This is the work of G	Jn 6:29	2316
For the bread of G is he which	Jn 6:33	2316
And they shall be all taught of G	Jn 6:45	2316
the Father, save he which is of G	Jn 6:46	2316
Christ, the Son of the living G	Jn 6:69	2316
the doctrine, whether it be of G	Jn 7:17	2316
truth, which I have heard of G	Jn 8:40	2316
we have one Father, even G	Jn 8:41	2316
If G were your Father, ye would	Jn 8:42	2316
I proceeded forth and came from G	Jn 8:42	2316
He that is of G heareth God's	Jn 8:47	2316
them not, because ye are not of G	Jn 8:47	2316
of whom ye say, that he is your G	Jn 8:54	2316
but that the works of G should be	Jn 9:3	2316
Pharisees, This man is not of G	Jn 9:16	2316
said unto him, Give G the praise	Jn 9:24	2316
We know that G spake unto Moses	Jn 9:29	2316
Now we know that G heareth not	Jn 9:31	2316
if any man be a worshipper of G	Jn 9:31	2318
If this man were not of G	Jn 9:33	2316
Dost thou believe on the Son of G	Jn 9:35	2316
being a man, makest thyself G	Jn 10:33	2316
unto whom the word of G came	Jn 10:35	2316
because I said, I am the Son of G	Jn 10:36	2316
death, but for the glory of G	Jn 11:4	2316
that the Son of G might be	Jn 11:4	2316
ask of G, G will give it thee	Jn 11:22	2316
thou art the Christ, the Son of G	Jn 11:27	2316
thou shouldest see the glory of G	Jn 11:40	2316
of G that were scattered abroad	Jn 11:52	2316
of men more than the praise of G	Jn 12:43	2316
was come from G, and went to G	Jn 13:3	2316
and G is glorified in him	Jn 13:31	2316
If G be glorified in him	Jn 13:32	2316
G shall also glorify him in	Jn 13:32	2316
ye believe in G, believe also in	Jn 14:1	2316
think that he doeth G service	Jn 16:2	2316
believed that I came out from G	Jn 16:27	2316
that thou camest forth from G	Jn 16:30	2316
might know thee the only true G	Jn 17:3	2316
he made himself the Son of G	Jn 19:7	2316
and to my G, and your G	Jn 20:17	2316
and said unto him, My Lord and my G	Jn 20:28	2316
Jesus is the Christ, the Son of G	Jn 20:31	2316
by what death he should glorify G	Jn 21:19	2316
pertaining to the kingdom of G	Acts 1:3	2316
tongues the wonderful works of G	Acts 2:11	2316
to pass in the last days, saith G	Acts 2:17	2316
a man approved of G among you by	Acts 2:22	2316
which G did by him in the midst	Acts 2:22	2316
counsel and foreknowledge of G	Acts 2:23	2316
Whom G hath raised up, having	Acts 2:24	2316
knowing that G had sworn with an	Acts 2:30	2316
This Jesus hath G raised up	Acts 2:32	2316
by the right hand of G exalted	Acts 2:33	2316
that G hath made that same Jesus,	Acts 2:36	2316
many as the Lord our G shall call	Acts 2:39	2316
Praising G, and having favour with	Acts 2:47	2316

and leaping, and praising G	Acts 3:8	2316
saw him walking and praising G	Acts 3:9	2316
The G of Abraham, and of Isaac, and	Acts 3:13	2316
the G of our fathers, hath	Acts 3:13	2316
whom G hath raised from the dead	Acts 3:15	2316
which G before had shewed by the	Acts 3:18	2316
which G hath spoken by the mouth	Acts 3:21	2316
your G raise up unto you of your	Acts 3:22	2316
which G made with our fathers	Acts 3:25	2316
Unto you first G, having raised	Acts 3:26	2316
whom G raised from the dead, even	Acts 4:10	2316
it be right in the sight of G to	Acts 4:19	2316
hearken unto you more than unto G	Acts 4:19	2316
for all men glorified G for that	Acts 4:21	2316
their voice to G with one accord	Acts 4:24	2316
and said, Lord, thou art G	Acts 4:24	2316
spake the word of G with boldness	Acts 4:31	2316
not lied unto men, but unto G	Acts 5:4	2316
ought to obey G rather than men	Acts 5:29	2316
The G of our fathers raised up	Acts 5:30	2316
Him hath G exalted with his right	Acts 5:31	2316
whom G hath given to them that	Acts 5:32	2316
But if it be of G, ye cannot	Acts 5:39	2316
be found even to fight against G	Acts 5:39	2314
we should leave the word of G	Acts 6:2	2316
And the word of G increased	Acts 6:7	2316
words against Moses, and against G	Acts 6:11	2316
The G of glory appeared unto our	Acts 7:2	2316
G spake on this wise, That his	Acts 7:6	2316
in bondage will I judge, said G	Acts 7:7	2316
but G was with him,	Acts 7:9	2316
which G had sworn to Abraham, the	Acts 7:17	2316
G by his hand would deliver them	Acts 7:25	2316
I am the G of thy fathers	Acts 7:32	2316
the G of Abraham	Acts 7:32	2316
G of Isaac, and the G of Jacob	Acts 7:32	2316
the same did G send to be a ruler	Acts 7:35	2316
your G raise up unto you of your	Acts 7:37	2316
Then G turned, and gave them up to	Acts 7:42	2316
whom G drave out before the face	Acts 7:45	2316
Who found favour before G	Acts 7:46	2316
a tabernacle for the G of Jacob	Acts 7:46	2316
heaven, and saw the glory of G	Acts 7:55	2316
standing on the right hand of G	Acts 7:55	2316
standing on the right hand of G	Acts 7:56	2316
stoned Stephen, calling upon G	Acts 7:59	
This man is the great power of G	Acts 8:10	2316
concerning the kingdom of G	Acts 8:12	2316
had received the word of G	Acts 8:14	2316
of G may be purchased with money	Acts 8:20	2316
is not right in the sight of G	Acts 8:21	2316
of this thy wickedness, and pray G	Acts 8:22	2316
that Jesus Christ is the Son of G	Acts 8:37	2316
that he is the Son of G	Acts 9:20	2316
one that feared G with all his	Acts 10:2	2316
the people, and prayed to G alway	Acts 10:2	2316
an angel of G coming in to him	Acts 10:3	2316
come up for a memorial before G	Acts 10:4	2316
What G hath cleansed, that call	Acts 10:15	2316
a just man, and one that feareth G	Acts 10:22	2316
was warned from G by an holy	Acts 10:22	
but G hath shewed me that I	Acts 10:28	2316
in remembrance in the sight of G	Acts 10:31	2316
are we all here present before G	Acts 10:33	2316
that are commanded thee of G	Acts 10:33	2316
that G is no respecter of persons	Acts 10:34	2316
The word which G sent unto the	Acts 10:36	
How G anointed Jesus of Nazareth	Acts 10:38	2316
for G was with him	Acts 10:38	2316
Him G raised up the third day, and	Acts 10:40	2316
unto witnesses chosen before of G	Acts 10:41	2316
of G to be the Judge of quick	Acts 10:42	2316
speak with tongues, and magnify G	Acts 10:46	2316
had also received the word of G	Acts 11:1	2316
What G hath cleansed, that call	Acts 11:9	2316
Forasmuch then as G gave them the	Acts 11:17	2316
was I, that I could withstand G	Acts 11:17	2316
held their peace, and glorified G	Acts 11:18	2316
Then hath G also to the Gentiles	Acts 11:18	2316
came, and had seen the grace of G	Acts 11:23	2316
of the church unto G for him	Acts 12:5	2316
because he gave not G the glory	Acts 12:23	2316
But the word of G grew and	Acts 12:24	2316
they preached the word of G in	Acts 13:5	2316
and desired to hear the word of G	Acts 13:7	2316
Men of Israel, and ye that fear G	Acts 13:16	2316
The G of this people of Israel	Acts 13:17	2316
G gave unto them Saul the son of	Acts 13:21	2316
Of this man's seed hath G	Acts 13:23	2316
and whosoever among you feareth G	Acts 13:26	2316
But G raised him from the dead	Acts 13:30	2316
G hath fulfilled the same unto us	Acts 13:33	2316
own generation by the will of G	Acts 13:36	2316
whom G raised again, saw no	Acts 13:37	2316
to continue in the grace of G	Acts 13:43	2316
together to hear the word of G	Acts 13:44	2316
G should first have been spoken	Acts 13:46	2316
these vanities unto the living G	Acts 14:15	2316
enter into the kingdom of G	Acts 14:22	2316
of G for the work which they	Acts 14:26	2316
all that G had done with them	Acts 14:27	2316
things that G had done with them	Acts 15:4	2316
while ago G made choice among us	Acts 15:7	2316
And G, which knoweth the hearts,	Acts 15:8	2316
Now therefore why tempt ye G	Acts 15:10	2316
wonders G had wrought among the	Acts 15:12	2316
Simeon hath declared how G at the	Acts 15:14	2316
Known unto G are all his works	Acts 15:18	2316
the Gentiles are turned to G	Acts 15:19	2316
the brethren unto the grace of G	Acts 15:40	2316
of Thyatira, which worshipped G	Acts 16:14	2316
the servants of the most high G	Acts 16:17	2316
prayed, and sang praises unto G	Acts 16:25	2316
believing in G with all his house	Acts 16:34	2316
G was preached of Paul at Berea	Acts 17:13	2316
inscription, TO THE UNKNOWN G	Acts 17:23	2316
G that made the world and all	Acts 17:24	2316
then as we are the offspring of G	Acts 17:29	2316
of this ignorance G winked at	Acts 17:30	2316
Justus, one that worshipped G	Acts 18:7	2316
teaching the word of G among them	Acts 18:11	2316
to worship G contrary to the law	Acts 18:13	2316
return again unto you, if G will	Acts 18:21	2316
him the way of G more perfectly	Acts 18:26	2316
concerning the kingdom of G	Acts 19:8	2316
G wrought special miracles by the	Acts 19:11	2316
So mightily grew the word of G	Acts 19:20	2962
the Greeks, repentance toward G	Acts 20:21	2316
the gospel of the grace of G	Acts 20:24	2316
gone preaching the kingdom of G	Acts 20:25	2316
unto you all the counsel of G	Acts 20:27	2316
to feed the church of G, which	Acts 20:28	2316
now, brethren, I commend you to G	Acts 20:32	2316
particularly what things G had	Acts 21:19	2316
fathers, and was zealous toward G	Acts 22:3	2316
The G of our fathers hath chosen	Acts 22:14	2316
before G until this day	Acts 23:1	2316
G shall smite thee, thou whited	Acts 23:3	2316
him, let us not fight against G	Acts 23:9	2313
so worship I the G of my fathers	Acts 24:14	2316
And have hope toward G, which they	Acts 24:15	2316
void of offence toward G, and	Acts 24:16	2316
made of G unto our fathers	Acts 26:6	2316
tribes, instantly serving G day	Acts 26:7	
that G should raise the dead	Acts 26:8	2316
and from the power of Satan unto G	Acts 26:18	2316
they should repent and turn to G	Acts 26:20	2316
therefore obtained help of G	Acts 26:22	2316
And Paul said, I would to G	Acts 26:29	2316
by me this night the angel of G	Acts 27:23	2316
G hath given thee all them that	Acts 27:24	2316
for I believe G, that it shall be	Acts 27:25	2316
gave thanks to G in presence of	Acts 27:35	2316
whom when Paul saw, he thanked G	Acts 28:15	2316
and testified the kingdom of G	Acts 28:23	2316
that the salvation of G is sent	Acts 28:28	2316
Preaching the kingdom of G	Acts 28:31	2316
separated unto the gospel of G	Rom 1:1	2316
to be the Son of G with power	Rom 1:4	2316
all that be in Rome, beloved of G	Rom 1:7	2316
to you and peace from G our Father	Rom 1:7	2316
I thank my G through Jesus Christ	Rom 1:8	2316
For G is my witness, whom I serve	Rom 1:9	2316
by the will of G to come unto you	Rom 1:10	2316
for it is the power of G unto	Rom 1:16	2316
of G revealed from faith to faith	Rom 1:17	2316
For the wrath of G is revealed	Rom 1:18	2316
be known of G is manifest in them	Rom 1:19	2316
for G hath shewed it unto them	Rom 1:19	2316
Because that, when they knew G	Rom 1:21	2316
they glorified him not as G	Rom 1:21	2316
G into an image made like to	Rom 1:23	2316
Wherefore G also gave them up to	Rom 1:24	2316
changed the truth of G into a lie	Rom 1:25	2316
For this cause G gave them up	Rom 1:26	2316
to retain G in their knowledge	Rom 1:28	2316
G gave them over to a reprobate	Rom 1:28	2316
Backbiters, haters of G,	Rom 1:30	2319
Who knowing the judgment of G	Rom 1:32	2316
G is according to truth against	Rom 2:2	2316
shalt escape the judgment of G	Rom 2:3	2316
of G leadeth thee to repentance	Rom 2:4	2316
of the righteous judgment of G	Rom 2:5	2316
is no respect of persons with G	Rom 2:11	2316
of the law are just before G	Rom 2:13	2316
In the day when G shall judge the	Rom 2:16	2316
the law, and makest thy boast of G	Rom 2:17	2316
the law dishonourest thou G	Rom 2:23	2316
For the name of G is blasphemed	Rom 2:24	2316
praise is not of men, but of G	Rom 2:29	2316
were committed the oracles of G	Rom 3:2	2316
the faith of G without effect	Rom 3:3	2316
G forbid: yea,	Rom 3:4	
let G be true, but every man a	Rom 3:4	2316
commend the righteousness of G	Rom 3:5	2316
Is G unrighteous who taketh	Rom 3:5	2316
G forbid: for then how	Rom 3:6	
then how shall G judge the world	Rom 3:6	2316
For if the truth of G hath more	Rom 3:7	2316
is none that seeketh after G	Rom 3:11	2316
is no fear of G before their eyes	Rom 3:18	2316
world may become guilty before G	Rom 3:19	2316
But now the righteousness of G	Rom 3:21	2316
Even the righteousness of G which	Rom 3:22	2316
and come short of the glory of G	Rom 3:23	2316
Whom G hath set forth to be a	Rom 3:25	2316
through the forbearance of G	Rom 3:25	2316
Is he the G of the Jews only	Rom 3:29	2316
Seeing it is one G, which shall	Rom 3:30	2316
G forbid: yea, we establish	Rom 3:31	
but not before G	Rom 4:2	2316
Abraham believed G, and it was	Rom 4:3	2316
of the man, unto whom G imputeth	Rom 4:6	2316
him whom he believed, even G	Rom 4:17	2316
the promise of G through unbelief	Rom 4:20	2316
in faith, giving glory to G	Rom 4:20	2316
we have peace with G through our	Rom 5:1	2316
rejoice in hope of the glory of G	Rom 5:2	2316
because the love of G is shed	Rom 5:5	2316
But G commendeth his love toward	Rom 5:8	2316
we were reconciled to G by the	Rom 5:10	2316
but we also joy in G through our	Rom 5:11	2316
be dead, much more the grace of G	Rom 5:15	2316
G forbid. How shall we	Rom 6:2	
that he liveth, he liveth unto G	Rom 6:10	2316
but alive unto G through Jesus	Rom 6:11	2316
but yield yourselves unto G	Rom 6:13	2316
of righteousness unto G	Rom 6:13	2316
but under grace? G forbid	Rom 6:15	
But G be thanked, that ye were	Rom 6:17	2316
from sin, and become servants to G	Rom 6:22	2316
but the gift of G is eternal life	Rom 6:23	2316
should bring forth fruit unto G	Rom 7:4	2316
Is the law sin? G forbid	Rom 7:7	
made death unto me? G forbid	Rom 7:13	
the law of G after the inward man	Rom 7:22	2316
I thank G through Jesus Christ	Rom 7:25	2316
mind I myself serve the law of G	Rom 7:25	2316
G sending his own Son in the	Rom 8:3	2316
carnal mind is enmity against G	Rom 8:7	2316
it is not subject to the law of G	Rom 8:7	2316
are in the flesh cannot please G	Rom 8:8	2316
that the Spirit of G dwell in you	Rom 8:9	2316
as are led by the Spirit of G	Rom 8:14	2316
they are the sons of G	Rom 8:14	2316
that we are the children of G	Rom 8:16	2316
heirs of G, and joint-heirs with	Rom 8:17	2316
manifestation of the sons of G	Rom 8:19	2316
liberty of the children of G	Rom 8:21	2316
saints according to the will of G	Rom 8:27	2316
for good to them that love G	Rom 8:28	2316
If G be for us, who can be	Rom 8:31	2316
It is G that justifieth	Rom 8:33	2316
is even at the right hand of G	Rom 8:34	2316
to separate us from the love of G	Rom 8:39	2316
of the law, and the service of G	Rom 9:4	
is over all, G blessed for ever	Rom 9:5	2316
word of G hath taken none effect	Rom 9:6	2316
these are not the children of G	Rom 9:8	2316
that the purpose of G according	Rom 9:11	2316
Is there unrighteousness with G	Rom 9:14	2316
unrighteousness with G? G forbid	Rom 9:14	
but of G that sheweth mercy	Rom 9:16	2316
art thou that repliest against G	Rom 9:20	2316
What if G, willing to shew his	Rom 9:22	2316
the children of the living G	Rom 9:26	2316
prayer to G for Israel is, that	Rom 10:1	2316
record that they have a zeal of G	Rom 10:2	2316
unto the righteousness of G	Rom 10:3	2316
believe in thine heart that G	Rom 10:9	2316
and hearing by the word of G	Rom 10:17	2316
Hath G cast away his people	Rom 11:1	2316
cast away his people? G forbid	Rom 11:1	
G hath not cast away his people	Rom 11:2	2316
intercession to G against Israel	Rom 11:2	2316
saith the answer of G unto him	Rom 11:4	
G hath given them the spirit of	Rom 11:8	2316
that they should fall? G forbid	Rom 11:11	
For if G spared not the natural	Rom 11:21	2316
the goodness and severity of G	Rom 11:22	2316
for G is able to graff them in	Rom 11:23	2316
gifts and calling of G are without	Rom 11:29	2316
in times past have not believed G	Rom 11:30	2316
For G hath concluded them all in	Rom 11:32	2316
of the wisdom and knowledge of G	Rom 11:33	2316
brethren, by the mercies of G	Rom 12:1	2316
holy, acceptable unto G, which	Rom 12:1	2316
acceptable, and perfect, will of G	Rom 12:2	2316
according as G hath dealt to	Rom 12:3	2316
For there is no power but of G	Rom 13:1	2316
powers that be are ordained of G	Rom 13:1	2316
resisteth the ordinance of G	Rom 13:2	2316
minister of G to thee for good	Rom 13:4	2316
for he is the minister of G	Rom 13:4	2316
for G hath received him	Rom 14:3	2316
for G is able to make him stand	Rom 14:4	2316
the Lord, for he giveth G thanks	Rom 14:6	2316
he eateth not, and giveth G thanks	Rom 14:6	2316
every tongue shall confess to G	Rom 14:11	2316
give account of himself to G	Rom 14:12	2316
For the kingdom of G is not meat	Rom 14:17	2316
serveth Christ is acceptable to G	Rom 14:18	2316
meat destroy not the work of G	Rom 14:20	2316
have it to thyself before G	Rom 14:22	2316
Now the G of patience and	Rom 15:5	2316
one mind and one mouth glorify G	Rom 15:6	2316
received us to the glory of G	Rom 15:7	2316
circumcision for the truth of G	Rom 15:8	2316
might glorify G for his mercy	Rom 15:9	2316
Now the G of hope fill you with	Rom 15:13	2316
grace that is given to me of G	Rom 15:15	2316
ministering the gospel of G	Rom 15:16	2316
those things which pertain to G	Rom 15:17	2316
by the power of the Spirit of G	Rom 15:19	2316
me in your prayers to G for me	Rom 15:30	2316
you with joy by the will of G	Rom 15:32	2316
Now the G of peace be with you	Rom 15:33	2316
the G of peace shall bruise Satan	Rom 16:20	2316
commandment of the everlasting G	Rom 16:26	2316
To G only wise, be glory through	Rom 16:27	2316
Christ through the will of G	1Cor 1:1	2316
Unto the church of G which is at	1Cor 1:2	2316
from G our Father, and from the	1Cor 1:3	2316
I thank my G always on your	1Cor 1:4	2316
for the grace of G which is given	1Cor 1:4	2316
G is faithful, by whom ye were	1Cor 1:9	2316
I thank G that I baptized none of	1Cor 1:14	2316
are saved it is the power of G	1Cor 1:18	2316
hath not G made foolish the	1Cor 1:20	2316
that in the wisdom of G	1Cor 1:21	2316
the world by wisdom knew not G	1Cor 1:21	2316
it pleased G by the foolishness	1Cor 1:21	2316
power of G, and the wisdom of G	1Cor 1:24	2316
of G is wiser than men	1Cor 1:25	2316
the weakness of G is stronger	1Cor 1:25	2316
But G hath chosen the foolish	1Cor 1:27	2316
G hath chosen the weak things of	1Cor 1:27	2316
hath G chosen, yea, and things	1Cor 1:28	2316
who of G is made unto us wisdom,	1Cor 1:30	2316
unto you the testimony of G	1Cor 2:1	2316
of men, but in the power of G	1Cor 2:5	2316
the wisdom of G in a mystery	1Cor 2:7	2316

which G ordained before the world 1Cor 2:7 2316
the things which G hath prepared 1Cor 2:9 2316
But G hath revealed them unto us 1Cor 2:10 2316
things, yea, the deep things of G 1Cor 2:10 2316
so the things of G knoweth no man 1Cor 2:11 2316
but the Spirit of G 1Cor 2:11 2316
but the spirit which is of G 1Cor 2:12 2316
that are freely given to us of G 1Cor 2:12 2316
not the things of the Spirit of G 1Cor 2:14 2316
but G gave the increase 1Cor 3:6 2316
but G that giveth the increase 1Cor 3:7 2316
we are labourers together with G 1Cor 3:9 2316
grace of G which is given unto me 1Cor 3:10 2316
not that ye are the temple of G 1Cor 3:16 2316
the Spirit of G dwelleth in you 1Cor 3:16 2316
If any man defile the temple of G 1Cor 3:17 2316
him shall G destroy 1Cor 3:17 2316
for the temple of G is holy 1Cor 3:17 2316
this world is foolishness with G 1Cor 3:19 2316
and stewards of the mysteries of G 1Cor 4:1 2316
shall every man have praise of G 1Cor 4:5 2316
I would to G ye did reign, that 1Cor 4:8
For I think that G hath set forth 1Cor 4:9 2316
the kingdom of G is not in word 1Cor 4:20 2316
them that are without G judgeth 1Cor 5:13 2316
not inherit the kingdom of G 1Cor 6:9 2316
shall inherit the kingdom of G 1Cor 6:10 2316
Jesus, and by the Spirit of our G 1Cor 6:11 2316
but G shall destroy both it and 1Cor 6:13 2316
G hath both raised up the Lord 1Cor 6:14 2316
members of an harlot? G forbid 1Cor 6:15
is in you, which ye have of G 1Cor 6:19 2316
therefore glorify G in your body 1Cor 6:20 2316
man hath his proper gift of G 1Cor 7:7 2316
but G hath called us to peace 1Cor 7:15 2316
But as G hath distributed to 1Cor 7:17 2316
keeping of the commandments of G 1Cor 7:19 2316
is called, therein abide with G 1Cor 7:24 2316
also that I have the Spirit of G 1Cor 7:40 2316
But if any man love G, the same 1Cor 8:3 2316
there is none other G but one 1Cor 8:4 2316
But to us there is but one G 1Cor 8:6 2316
But meat commendeth us not to G 1Cor 8:8 2316
Doth G take care for oxen 1Cor 9:9 2316
law, (being not without law to G 1Cor 9:21 2316
of them G was not well pleased 1Cor 10:5 2316
But G is faithful, who will not 1Cor 10:13 2316
sacrifice to devils, and not to G 1Cor 10:20 2316
ye do, do all to the glory of G 1Cor 10:31 2316
Gentiles, nor to the church of G 1Cor 10:32 2316
and the head of Christ is G 1Cor 11:3 2316
as he is the image and glory of G 1Cor 11:7 2316
but all things of G 1Cor 11:12 2316
a woman pray unto G uncovered 1Cor 11:13 2316
custom, neither the churches of G 1Cor 11:16 2316
or despise ye the church of G 1Cor 11:22 2316
of G calleth Jesus accursed 1Cor 12:3 2316
but it is the same G which 1Cor 12:6 2316
But now hath G set the members 1Cor 12:18 2316
but G hath tempered the body 1Cor 12:24 2316
G hath set some in the church 1Cor 12:28 2316
speaketh not unto men, but unto G 1Cor 14:2 2316
I thank my G, I speak with 1Cor 14:18 2316
on his face he will worship G 1Cor 14:25 2316
report that G is in you of a 1Cor 14:25 2316
let him speak to himself, and to G 1Cor 14:28 2316
For G is not the author of 1Cor 14:33 2316
came the word of G out from you 1Cor 14:36 2316
I persecuted the church of G 1Cor 15:9 2316
by the grace of G I am what I am 1Cor 15:10 2316
but the grace of G which was with 1Cor 15:10 2316
we are found false witnesses of G 1Cor 15:15 2316
of G that he raised up Christ 1Cor 15:15 2316
delivered up the kingdom to G 1Cor 15:24 2316
him, that G may be all in all 1Cor 15:28 2316
some have not the knowledge of G 1Cor 15:34 2316
But G giveth it a body as it hath 1Cor 15:38 2316
cannot inherit the kingdom of G 1Cor 15:50 2316
But thanks be to G, which giveth 1Cor 15:57 2316
as G hath prospered him, that 1Cor 16:2
of Jesus Christ by the will of G 2Cor 1:1 2316
unto the church of G which is at 2Cor 1:1 2316
to you and peace from G our Father 2Cor 1:2 2316
Blessed be G, even the Father of 2Cor 1:3 2316
mercies, and the G of all comfort 2Cor 1:3 2316
we ourselves are comforted of G 2Cor 1:4 2316
but in G which raiseth the dead 2Cor 1:9 2316
wisdom, but by the grace of G 2Cor 1:12 2316
But as G is true, our word toward 2Cor 1:18 2316
For the Son of G, Jesus Christ 2Cor 1:19 2316
the promises of G in him are yea 2Cor 1:20 2316
Amen, unto the glory of G by us 2Cor 1:20 2316
Christ, and hath anointed us, is G 2Cor 1:21 2316
Moreover I call G for a record 2Cor 1:23 2316
Now thanks be unto G, which 2Cor 2:14 2316
For we are unto G a sweet savour 2Cor 2:15 2316
many, which corrupt the word of G 2Cor 2:17 2316
but as of sincerity, but as of G 2Cor 2:17 2316
in the sight of G speak we in 2Cor 2:17 2316
with the Spirit of the living G 2Cor 3:3 2316
but our sufficiency is of G 2Cor 3:5 2316
the word of G deceitfully 2Cor 4:2 2316
conscience in the sight of G 2Cor 4:2 2316
of Christ, who is the image of G 2Cor 4:4 2316
For G, who commanded the light to 2Cor 4:6 2316
of G in the face of Jesus Christ 2Cor 4:6 2316
of the power may be of G, and not 2Cor 4:7 2316
of many redound to the glory of G 2Cor 4:15 2316
we have a building of G, an 2Cor 5:1 2316
us for the selfsame thing is G 2Cor 5:5 2316
but we are made manifest unto G 2Cor 5:11 2316
be beside ourselves, it is to G 2Cor 5:13 2316
And all things are of G, who hath 2Cor 5:18 2316
that G was in Christ, reconciling 2Cor 5:19 2316
as though G did beseech you by us 2Cor 5:20 2316
stead, be ye reconciled to G 2Cor 5:20 2316
the righteousness of G in him 2Cor 5:21 2316
not the grace of G in vain 2Cor 6:1 2316
ourselves as the ministers of G 2Cor 6:4 2316
word of truth, by the power of G 2Cor 6:7 2316
hath the temple of G with idols 2Cor 6:16 2316
ye are the temple of the living G 2Cor 6:16 2316
as G hath said, I will dwell in 2Cor 6:16 2316
and I will be their G, and they 2Cor 6:16 2316
holiness in the fear of G 2Cor 7:1 2316
Nevertheless G, that comforteth 2Cor 7:6 2316
sight of G might appear unto you 2Cor 7:12 2316
of G bestowed on the churches of 2Cor 8:1 2316
Lord, and unto us by the will of G 2Cor 8:5 2316
But thanks be to G, which put the 2Cor 8:16 2316
for G loveth a cheerful giver 2Cor 9:7 2316
G is able to make all grace 2Cor 9:8 2316
through us thanksgiving to G 2Cor 9:11 2316
also by many thanksgivings unto G 2Cor 9:12 2316
G for your professed subjection 2Cor 9:13 2316
the exceeding grace of G in you 2Cor 9:14 2316
Thanks be unto G for his 2Cor 9:15 2316
but mighty through G to the 2Cor 10:4 2316
itself against the knowledge of G 2Cor 10:5 2316
which G hath distributed to us 2Cor 10:13 2316
Would to G ye could bear with me 2Cor 11:1
to you the gospel of G freely 2Cor 11:7 2316
I love you not? G knoweth 2Cor 11:11 2316
The G and Father of our Lord Jesus 2Cor 11:31 2316
body, I cannot tell: G knoweth 2Cor 12:2 2316
I cannot tell: G knoweth 2Cor 12:3 2316
we speak before G in Christ 2Cor 12:19 2316
my G will humble me among you, and 2Cor 12:21 2316
yet he liveth by the power of G 2Cor 13:4 2316
him by the power of G toward you 2Cor 13:4 2316
Now I pray to G that ye do no 2Cor 13:7 2316
the G of love and peace shall be 2Cor 13:11 2316
Jesus Christ, and the love of G 2Cor 13:14 2316
G the Father, who raised him from Gal 1:1 2316
to you and peace from G the Father Gal 1:3 2316
world, according to the will of G Gal 1:4 2316
For do I now persuade men, or G Gal 1:10 2316
I persecuted the church of G Gal 1:13 2316
But when it pleased G, who Gal 1:15 2316
write unto you, behold, before G Gal 1:20 2316
And they glorified G in me Gal 1:24 2316
G accepteth no man's person Gal 2:6 2316
minister of sin? G forbid Gal 2:17
the law, that I might live unto G Gal 2:19 2316
live by the faith of the Son of G Gal 2:20 2316
I do not frustrate the grace of G Gal 2:21 2316
Even as Abraham believed G Gal 3:6 2316
foreseeing that G would justify Gal 3:8 2316
by the law in the sight of G Gal 3:11 2316
confirmed before of G in Christ Gal 3:17 2316
but G gave it to Abraham by Gal 3:18 2316
a mediator of one, but G is one Gal 3:20 2316
then against the promises of G Gal 3:21 2316
promises of G? G forbid Gal 3:21
of G by faith in Christ Jesus Gal 3:26 2316
G sent forth his Son, made of a Gal 4:4 2316
G hath sent forth the Spirit of Gal 4:6 2316
then an heir of G through Christ Gal 4:7 2316
Howbeit then, when ye knew not G Gal 4:8 2316
now, after that ye have known G Gal 4:9 2316
or rather are known of G Gal 4:9 2316
but received me as an angel of G Gal 4:14 2316
not inherit the kingdom of G Gal 5:21 2316
G is not mocked Gal 6:7 2316
But G forbid that I should glory Gal 6:14
and mercy, and upon the Israel of G Gal 6:16 2316
of Jesus Christ by the will of G Eph 1:1 2316
from G our Father, and from the Eph 1:2 2316
Blessed be the G and Father of our Eph 1:3 2316
That the G of our Lord Jesus Eph 1:17 2316
But G, who is rich in mercy, for Eph 2:4 2316
it is the gift of G Eph 2:8 2316
which G hath before ordained that Eph 2:10 2316
hope, and without G in the world Eph 2:12 112
unto G in one body by the cross Eph 2:16 2316
saints, and of the household of G Eph 2:19 2316
of G through the Spirit Eph 2:22 2316
dispensation of the grace of G Eph 3:2 2316
to the gift of the grace of G Eph 3:7 2316
of the world hath been hid in G Eph 3:9 2316
church the manifold wisdom of G Eph 3:10 2316
filled with all the fulness of G Eph 3:19 2316
One G and Father of all, who is Eph 4:6 2316
of the knowledge of the Son of G Eph 4:13 2316
alienated from the life of G Eph 4:18 2316
which after G is created in Eph 4:24 2316
grieve not the holy Spirit of G Eph 4:30 2316
even as G for Christ's sake hath Eph 4:32 2316
Be ye therefore followers of G Eph 5:1 2316
and a sacrifice to G for a Eph 5:2 2316
in the kingdom of Christ and of G Eph 5:5 2316
wrath of G upon the children of Eph 5:6 2316
always for all things unto G Eph 5:20 2316
one to another in the fear of G Eph 5:21 2316
the will of G from the heart Eph 6:6 2316
Put on the whole armour of G Eph 6:11 2316
unto you the whole armour of G Eph 6:13 2316
Spirit, which is the word of G Eph 6:17 2316
from G the Father and the Lord Eph 6:23 2316
from G our Father, and from the Phil 1:2 2316
I thank my G upon every Phil 1:3 2316
For G is my record, how greatly I Phil 1:8 2316
unto the glory and praise of G Phil 1:11 2316
to you of salvation, and that of G Phil 1:28 2316
Who, being in the form of G Phil 2:6 2316
it not robbery to be equal with G Phil 2:6 2316
Wherefore G also hath highly Phil 2:9 2316
to the glory of G the Father Phil 2:11 2316
For it is G which worketh in you Phil 2:13 2316
and harmless, the sons of G Phil 2:15 2316
but G had mercy on him Phil 2:27 2316
which worship G in the spirit Phil 3:3 2316
which is of G by faith Phil 3:9 2316
high calling of G in Christ Jesus Phil 3:14 2316
G shall reveal even this unto you Phil 3:15 2316
whose G is their belly, and whose Phil 3:19 2316
requests be made known unto G Phil 4:6 2316
And the peace of G, which passeth Phil 4:7 2316
the G of peace shall be with you Phil 4:9 2316
acceptable, wellpleasing to G Phil 4:18 2316
But my G shall supply all your Phil 4:19 2316
Now unto G and our Father be glory Phil 4:20 2316
of Jesus Christ by the will of G Col 1:1 2316
from G our Father and the Lord Col 1:2 2316
We give thanks to G and the Father Col 1:3 2316
and knew the grace of G in truth Col 1:6 2316
increasing in the knowledge of G Col 1:10 2316
is the image of the invisible G Col 1:15 2316
to the dispensation of G which is Col 1:25 2316
for you, to fulfil the word of G Col 1:25 2316
To whom G would make known what Col 1:27 2316
of the mystery of G, and of the Col 2:2 2316
the faith of the operation of G Col 2:12 2316
increaseth with the increase of G Col 2:19 2316
sitteth on the right hand of G Col 3:1 2316
your life is hid with Christ in G Col 3:3 2316
of G cometh on the children of Col 3:6 2316
on therefore, as the elect of G Col 3:12 2316
let the peace of G rule in your Col 3:15 2316
Lord Jesus, giving thanks to G Col 3:17 2316
in singleness of heart, fearing G Col 3:22 2316
that G would open unto us a door Col 4:3 2316
workers unto the kingdom of G Col 4:11 2316
and complete in all the will of G Col 4:12 2316
which is in G the Father and in 1Th 1:1 2316
from G our Father, and the Lord 1Th 1:1 2316
We give thanks to G always for 1Th 1:2 2316
Jesus Christ, in the sight of G 1Th 1:3 2316
beloved, your election of G 1Th 1:4 2316
how ye turned to G from idols to 1Th 1:9 2316
to serve the living and true G 1Th 1:9 2316
we were bold in our G to speak 1Th 2:2 2316
gospel of G with much contention 1Th 2:2 2316
But as we were allowed of G to be 1Th 2:4 2316
not as pleasing men, but G 1Th 2:4 2316
cloke of covetousness; G is witness 1Th 2:5 2316
you, not the gospel of G only 1Th 2:8 2316
preached unto you the gospel of G 1Th 2:9 2316
G also, how holily and justly and 1Th 2:10 2316
That ye would walk worthy of G 1Th 2:12 2316
also thank we G without ceasing 1Th 2:13 2316
word of G which ye heard of us 1Th 2:13 2316
as it is in truth, the word of G 1Th 2:13 2316
followers of the churches of G 1Th 2:14 2316
and they please not G, and are 1Th 2:15 2316
our brother, and minister of G 1Th 3:2 2316
can we render to G again for you 1Th 3:9 2316
joy for your sakes before our G 1Th 3:9 2316
Now G himself and our Father, and 1Th 3:11 2316
unblameable in holiness before G 1Th 3:13 2316
ye ought to walk and to please G 1Th 4:1 2316
For this is the will of G 1Th 4:3 2316
as the Gentiles which know not G 1Th 4:5 2316
For G hath not called us unto 1Th 4:7 2316
despiseth not man, but G 1Th 4:8 2316
taught of G to love one another 1Th 4:9 2312
in Jesus will G bring with him 1Th 4:14 2316
archangel, and with the trump of G 1Th 4:16 2316
For G hath not appointed us to 1Th 5:9 2316
for this is the will of G in 1Th 5:18 2316
the very G of peace sanctify you 1Th 5:23 2316
I pray G your whole spirit and 1Th 5:23
the Thessalonians in G our Father 2Th 1:1 2316
from G our Father and the Lord 2Th 1:2 2316
bound to thank G always for you 2Th 1:3 2316
churches of G for your patience 2Th 1:4 2316
of the righteous judgment of G 2Th 1:5 2316
worthy of the kingdom of G 2Th 1:5 2316
G to recompense tribulation to 2Th 1:6 2316
vengeance on them that know not G 2Th 1:8 2316
that our G would count you worthy 2Th 1:11 2316
according to the grace of our G 2Th 1:12 2316
above all that is called G 2Th 2:4 2316
as G sitteth in the temple of G 2Th 2:4 2316
shewing himself that he is G 2Th 2:4 2316
for this cause G shall send them 2Th 2:11 2316
to give thanks alway to G for you 2Th 2:13 2316
because G hath from the beginning 2Th 2:13 2316
Lord Jesus Christ himself, and G 2Th 2:16 2316
your hearts into the love of G 2Th 3:5 2316
the commandment of G our Saviour 1Ti 1:1 2316
from G our Father and Jesus Christ 1Ti 1:2 2316
glorious gospel of the blessed G 1Ti 1:11 2316
invisible, the only wise G 1Ti 1:17 2316
in the sight of G our Saviour 1Ti 2:3 2316
For there is one G 1Ti 2:5 2316
and one mediator between G 1Ti 2:5 2316
he take care of the church of G 1Ti 3:5 2316
behave thyself in the house of G 1Ti 3:15 2316
is the church of the living G 1Ti 3:15 2316
G was manifest in the flesh 1Ti 3:16 2316
which G hath created to be 1Ti 4:3 2316
For every creature of G is good 1Ti 4:4 2316
it is sanctified by the word of G 1Ti 4:5 2316
because we trust in the living G 1Ti 4:10 2316
is good and acceptable before G 1Ti 5:4 2316
and desolate, trusteth in G 1Ti 5:5 2316
I charge thee before G, and the 1Ti 5:21 2316
of all honour, that the name of G 1Ti 6:1 2316
But thou, O man of G, flee these 1Ti 6:11 2316
thee charge in the sight of G 1Ti 6:13 2316
riches, but in the living G 1Ti 6:17 2316

of Jesus Christ by the will of G	2Ti 1:1	2316
from G the Father and Christ Jesus	2Ti 1:2	2316
I thank G, whom I serve from my	2Ti 1:3	2316
that thou stir up the gift of G	2Ti 1:6	2316
For G hath not given us the	2Ti 1:7	2316
according to the power of G	2Ti 1:8	2316
but the word of G is not bound	2Ti 2:9	2316
to shew thyself approved unto G	2Ti 2:15	2316
the foundation of G standeth sure	2Ti 2:19	2316
if G peradventure will give them	2Ti 2:25	2316
pleasures more than lovers of G	2Ti 3:4	5377
is given by inspiration of G	2Ti 3:16	2315
That the man of G may be perfect	2Ti 3:17	2316
I charge thee therefore before G	2Ti 4:1	2316
I pray G that it may not be laid	2Ti 4:16	
Paul, a servant of G, and an	Titus 1:1	2316
In hope of eternal life, which G	Titus 1:2	2316
the commandment of G our Saviour	Titus 1:3	2316
from G the Father and the Lord	Titus 1:4	2316
be blameless, as the steward of G	Titus 1:7	2316
They profess that they know G	Titus 1:16	2316
that the word of G be not	Titus 2:5	2316
of G our Saviour in all things	Titus 2:10	2316
For the grace of G that bringeth	Titus 2:11	2316
glorious appearing of the great G	Titus 2:13	2316
love of G our Saviour toward man	Titus 3:4	2316
they which have believed in G	Titus 3:8	2316
from G our Father and the Lord	Philem 3	2316
I thank my G, making mention of	Philem 4	2316
G, who at sundry times and in	Heb 1:1	2316
all the angels of G worship him	Heb 1:6	2316
the Son he saith, Thy throne, O G	Heb 1:8	2316
therefore G, even thy G	Heb 1:9	2316
G also bearing them witness, both	Heb 2:4	2316
that he by the grace of G should	Heb 2:9	2316
children which G hath given me	Heb 2:13	2316
priest in things pertaining to G	Heb 2:17	2316
but he that built all things is G	Heb 3:4	2316
in departing from the living G	Heb 3:12	2316
G did rest the seventh day from	Heb 4:4	2316
a rest to the people of G	Heb 4:9	2316
his own works, as G did from his	Heb 4:10	2316
For the word of G is quick	Heb 4:12	2316
the heavens, Jesus the Son of G	Heb 4:14	2316
for men in things pertaining to G	Heb 5:1	2316
but he that is called of G	Heb 5:4	2316
Called of G an high priest after	Heb 5:10	2316
principles of the oracles of G	Heb 5:12	2316
dead works, and of faith toward G	Heb 6:1	2316
And this will we do, if G permit	Heb 6:3	2316
And have tasted the good word of G	Heb 6:5	2316
to themselves the Son of G afresh	Heb 6:6	2316
receiveth blessing from G	Heb 6:7	2316
For G is not unrighteous to	Heb 6:10	2316
For when G made promise to	Heb 6:13	2316
Wherein G, willing more	Heb 6:17	2316
it was impossible for G to lie	Heb 6:18	2316
Salem, priest of the most high G	Heb 7:1	2316
but made like unto the Son of G	Heb 7:3	2316
by the which we draw nigh unto G	Heb 7:19	2316
uttermost that come unto G by him	Heb 7:25	2316
as Moses was admonished of G when	Heb 8:5	5537
and I will be to them a G, and they	Heb 8:10	2316
accomplishing the service of G	Heb 9:6	
offered himself without spot to G	Heb 9:14	2316
dead works to serve the living G	Heb 9:14	2316
which G hath enjoined unto you	Heb 9:20	2316
in the presence of G for us	Heb 9:24	2316
of me,) to do thy will, O G	Heb 10:7	2316
Lo, I come to do thy will, O G	Heb 10:9	2316
sat down on the right hand of G	Heb 10:12	2316
high priest over the house of G	Heb 10:21	2316
trodden under foot the Son of G	Heb 10:29	2316
into the hands of the living G	Heb 10:31	2316
after ye have done the will of G	Heb 10:36	2316
were framed by the word of G	Heb 11:3	2316
By faith Abel offered unto G a	Heb 11:4	2316
G testifying of his gifts	Heb 11:4	2316
because G had translated him	Heb 11:5	2316
this testimony, that he pleased G	Heb 11:5	2316
for he that cometh to G must	Heb 11:6	2316
being warned of G of things not	Heb 11:7	
whose builder and maker is G	Heb 11:10	2316
wherefore G is not ashamed to be	Heb 11:16	2316
not ashamed to be called their G	Heb 11:16	2316
Accounting that G was able to	Heb 11:19	2316
affliction with the people of G	Heb 11:25	2316
G having provided some better	Heb 11:40	2316
the right hand of the throne of G	Heb 12:2	2316
G dealeth with you as with sons	Heb 12:7	2316
any man fail of the grace of G	Heb 12:15	2316
and unto the city of the living G	Heb 12:22	2316
to G the Judge of all, and to the	Heb 12:23	2316
whereby we may serve G acceptably	Heb 12:28	2316
For our G is a consuming fire	Heb 12:29	2316
and adulterers G will judge	Heb 13:4	2316
spoken unto you the word of G	Heb 13:7	2316
of praise to G continually	Heb 13:15	2316
such sacrifices G is well pleased	Heb 13:16	2316
Now the G of peace, that brought	Heb 13:20	2316
James, a servant of G and of the	Jas 1:1	2316
you lack wisdom, let him ask of G	Jas 1:5	2316
he is tempted, I am tempted of G	Jas 1:13	2316
for G cannot be tempted with evil	Jas 1:13	2316
not the righteousness of G	Jas 1:20	2316
religion and undefiled before G	Jas 1:27	2316
Hath not G chosen the poor of	Jas 2:5	2316
believest that there is one G	Jas 2:19	2316
which saith, Abraham believed G	Jas 2:23	2316
and he was called the Friend of G	Jas 2:23	2316
Therewith bless we G, even the	Jas 3:9	2316
made after the similitude of G	Jas 3:9	2316
of the world is enmity with G	Jas 4:4	2316
of the world is the enemy of G	Jas 4:4	2316
G resisteth the proud, but giveth	Jas 4:6	2316
Submit yourselves therefore to G	Jas 4:7	2316
Draw nigh to G, and he will draw	Jas 4:8	2316
the foreknowledge of G the Father	1Pet 1:2	2316
Blessed be the G and Father of our	1Pet 1:3	2316
of G through faith unto salvation	1Pet 1:5	2316
Who by him do believe in G	1Pet 1:21	2316
your faith and hope might be in G	1Pet 1:21	2316
incorruptible, by the word of G	1Pet 1:23	2316
indeed of men, but chosen of G	1Pet 2:4	2316
acceptable to G by Jesus Christ	1Pet 2:5	2316
but are now the people of G	1Pet 2:10	2316
behold, glorify G in the day of	1Pet 2:12	2316
For so is the will of G, that	1Pet 2:15	2316
but as the servants of G	1Pet 2:16	2316
G. Honour the king	1Pet 2:17	2316
conscience toward G endure grief	1Pet 2:19	2316
this is acceptable with G	1Pet 2:20	2316
in the sight of G of great price	1Pet 3:4	2316
holy women also, who trusted in G	1Pet 3:5	2316
the Lord G in your hearts	1Pet 3:15	2316
is better, if the will of G be so	1Pet 3:17	2316
that he might bring us to G	1Pet 3:18	2316
of G waited in the days of Noah	1Pet 3:20	2316
of a good conscience toward G	1Pet 3:21	2316
and is on the right hand of G	1Pet 3:22	2316
of men, but to the will of G	1Pet 4:2	2316
live according to G in the spirit	1Pet 4:6	2316
of the manifold grace of G	1Pet 4:10	2316
let him speak as the oracles of G	1Pet 4:11	2316
as of the ability which G giveth	1Pet 4:11	2316
that G in all things may be	1Pet 4:11	2316
of glory and of G resteth upon you	1Pet 4:14	2316
let him glorify G on this behalf	1Pet 4:16	2316
must begin at the house of G	1Pet 4:17	2316
that obey not the gospel of G	1Pet 4:17	2316
of G commit the keeping of their	1Pet 4:19	2316
Feed the flock of G which is	1Pet 5:2	2316
for G resisteth the proud, and	1Pet 5:5	2316
under the mighty hand of G	1Pet 5:6	2316
But the G of all grace, who hath	1Pet 5:10	2316
true grace of G wherein ye stand	1Pet 5:12	2316
us through the righteousness of G	2Pet 1:1	2316
you through the knowledge of G	2Pet 1:2	2316
received from G the Father honour	2Pet 1:17	2316
but holy men of G spake as they	2Pet 1:21	2316
For if G spared not the angels	2Pet 2:4	2316
that by the word of G the heavens	2Pet 3:5	2316
unto the coming of the day of G	2Pet 3:12	2316
that G is light, and in him is no	1Jn 1:5	2316
verily is the love of G perfected	1Jn 2:5	2316
the word of G abideth in you, and	1Jn 2:14	2316
the will of G abideth for ever	1Jn 2:17	2316
we should be called the sons of G	1Jn 3:1	2316
Beloved, now are we the sons of G	1Jn 3:2	2316
the Son of G was manifested	1Jn 3:8	2316
is born of G doth not commit sin	1Jn 3:9	2316
sin, because he is born of G	1Jn 3:9	2316
the children of G are manifest	1Jn 3:10	2316
not righteousness is not of G	1Jn 3:10	2316
Hereby perceive we the love of G	1Jn 3:16	
how dwelleth the love of G in him	1Jn 3:17	2316
G is greater than our heart, and	1Jn 3:20	2316
then have we confidence toward G	1Jn 3:21	2316
the spirits whether they are of G	1Jn 4:1	2316
Hereby know ye the Spirit of G	1Jn 4:2	2316
is come in the flesh is of G	1Jn 4:2	2316
is come in the flesh is not of G	1Jn 4:3	2316
Ye are of G, little children, and	1Jn 4:4	2316
We are of G	1Jn 4:6	2316
he that knoweth G heareth us	1Jn 4:6	2316
that is not of G heareth not us	1Jn 4:6	2316
for love is of G	1Jn 4:7	2316
is born of G, and knoweth G	1Jn 4:7	2316
He that loveth not knoweth not G	1Jn 4:8	2316
for G is love	1Jn 4:8	2316
the love of G toward us, because	1Jn 4:9	2316
because that G sent his only	1Jn 4:9	2316
is love, not that we loved G	1Jn 4:10	2316
if G so loved us, we ought also	1Jn 4:11	2316
No man hath seen G at any time	1Jn 4:12	2316
G dwelleth in us, and his love is	1Jn 4:12	2316
that Jesus is the Son of G	1Jn 4:15	2316
G dwelleth in him, and he in G	1Jn 4:15	2316
the love that G hath to us	1Jn 4:16	2316
G is love	1Jn 4:16	2316
love dwelleth in G, and G in him	1Jn 4:16	2316
If a man say, I love G, and hateth	1Jn 4:20	2316
how can he love G whom he hath	1Jn 4:20	2316
That he who loveth G love his	1Jn 4:21	2316
Jesus is the Christ is born of G	1Jn 5:1	2316
children of G, when we love G	1Jn 5:2	2316
For this is the love of G	1Jn 5:3	2316
is born of G overcometh the world	1Jn 5:4	2316
that Jesus is the Son of G	1Jn 5:5	2316
men, the witness of G is greater	1Jn 5:9	2316
for this is the witness of G	1Jn 5:9	2316
of G hath the witness in himself	1Jn 5:10	2316
not G hath made him a liar	1Jn 5:10	2316
the record that G gave of his Son	1Jn 5:10	2316
that G hath given to us eternal	1Jn 5:11	2316
not the Son of G hath not life	1Jn 5:12	2316
on the name of the Son of G	1Jn 5:13	2316
on the name of the Son of G	1Jn 5:13	2316
is born of G sinneth not	1Jn 5:18	2316
is begotten of G keepeth himself	1Jn 5:18	2316
And we know that we are of G	1Jn 5:19	2316
we know that the Son of G is come	1Jn 5:20	2316
This is the true G, and eternal	1Jn 5:20	2316
from G the Father, and from the	2Jn 3	2316
doctrine of Christ, hath not G	2Jn 9	2316
house, neither bid him G speed	2Jn 10	
For he that biddeth him G speed	2Jn 11	
He that doeth good is of G	3Jn 11	2316
that doeth evil hath not seen G	3Jn 11	2316
are sanctified by G the Father	Jude 1	2316
of our G into lasciviousness	Jude 4	2316
and denying the only Lord G	Jude 4	2316
Keep yourselves in the love of G	Jude 21	2316
To the only wise G our Saviour	Jude 25	2316
which G gave unto him, to shew	Rev 1:1	2316
Who bare record of the word of G	Rev 1:2	2316
made us kings and priests unto G	Rev 1:6	2316
called Patmos, for the word of G	Rev 1:9	2316
in the midst of the paradise of G	Rev 2:7	2316
These things saith the Son of G	Rev 2:18	2316
that hath the seven Spirits of G	Rev 3:1	2316
found thy works perfect before G	Rev 3:2	2316
a pillar in the temple of my G	Rev 3:12	2316
write upon him the name of my G	Rev 3:12	2316
and the name of the city of my G	Rev 3:12	2316
down out of heaven from my G	Rev 3:12	2316
beginning of the creation of G	Rev 3:14	2316
which are the seven Spirits of G	Rev 4:5	2316
Lord G Almighty, which was, and is	Rev 4:8	2316
G sent forth into all the earth	Rev 5:6	2316
hast redeemed us to G by thy	Rev 5:9	2316
And hast made us unto our G kings	Rev 5:10	2316
that were slain for the word of G	Rev 6:9	2316
having the seal of the living G	Rev 7:2	2316
of our G in their foreheads	Rev 7:3	2316
Salvation to our G which sitteth	Rev 7:10	2316
on their faces, and worshipped G	Rev 7:11	2316
and might, be unto our G for ever	Rev 7:12	2316
are they before the throne of G	Rev 7:15	2316
G shall wipe away all tears from	Rev 7:17	2316
seven angels which stood before G	Rev 8:2	2316
ascended up before G out of the	Rev 8:4	2316
the seal of G in their foreheads	Rev 9:4	2316
golden altar which is before G	Rev 9:13	2316
the mystery of G should be	Rev 10:7	2316
Rise, and measure the temple of G	Rev 11:1	2316
before the G of the earth	Rev 11:4	2316
of life from G entered into them	Rev 11:11	2316
and gave glory to the G of heaven	Rev 11:13	2316
which sat before G on their seats	Rev 11:16	2316
upon their faces, and worshipped G	Rev 11:16	2316
O Lord G Almighty, which art, and	Rev 11:17	2316
the temple of G was opened in	Rev 11:19	2316
and her child was caught up unto G	Rev 12:5	2316
she hath a place prepared of G	Rev 12:6	2316
strength, and the kingdom of our G	Rev 12:10	2316
accused them before our G day	Rev 12:10	2316
which keep the commandments of G	Rev 12:17	2316
his mouth in blasphemy against G	Rev 13:6	2316
men, being the firstfruits unto G	Rev 14:4	2316
fault before the throne of G	Rev 14:5	2316
Saying with a loud voice, Fear G	Rev 14:7	2316
of the wine of the wrath of G	Rev 14:10	2316
that keep the commandments of G	Rev 14:12	2316
great winepress of the wrath of G	Rev 14:19	2316
them is filled up the wrath of G	Rev 15:1	2316
of glass, having the harps of G	Rev 15:2	2316
song of Moses the servant of G	Rev 15:3	2316
are thy works, Lord G Almighty	Rev 15:3	2316
vials full of the wrath of G	Rev 15:7	2316
with smoke from the glory of G	Rev 15:8	2316
of the wrath of G upon the earth	Rev 16:1	2316
Even so, Lord G Almighty, true and	Rev 16:7	2316
heat, and blasphemed the name of G	Rev 16:9	2316
blasphemed the G of heaven	Rev 16:11	2316
of that great day of G Almighty	Rev 16:14	2316
came in remembrance before G	Rev 16:19	2316
men blasphemed G because of the	Rev 16:21	2316
For G hath put in their hearts to	Rev 17:17	2316
the words of G shall be fulfilled	Rev 17:17	2316
G hath remembered her iniquities	Rev 18:5	2316
is the Lord G who judgeth her	Rev 18:8	2316
for G hath avenged you on her	Rev 18:20	2316
and power, unto the Lord our G	Rev 19:1	2316
worshipped G that sat on the	Rev 19:4	2316
the throne, saying, Praise our G	Rev 19:5	2316
for the Lord G omnipotent	Rev 19:6	2316
These are the true sayings of G	Rev 19:9	2316
worship G	Rev 19:10	2316
his name is called The Word of G	Rev 19:13	2316
fierceness and wrath of Almighty G	Rev 19:15	2316
unto the supper of the great G	Rev 19:17	2316
of Jesus, and for the word of G	Rev 20:4	2316
but they shall be priests of G	Rev 20:6	2316
came down from G out of heaven	Rev 20:9	2316
small and great, stand before G	Rev 20:12	2316
coming down from G out of heaven	Rev 21:2	2316
the tabernacle of G is with men	Rev 21:3	2316
G himself shall be with them	Rev 21:3	2316
and be their G	Rev 21:3	2316
G shall wipe away all tears from	Rev 21:4	2316
and I will be his G, and he shall	Rev 21:7	2316
descending out of heaven from G	Rev 21:10	2316
Having the glory of G	Rev 21:11	2316
for the Lord G Almighty and the	Rev 21:22	2316
for the glory of G did lighten it	Rev 21:23	2316
proceeding out of the throne of G	Rev 22:1	2316
but the throne of G and of the	Rev 22:3	2316
for the Lord G giveth them light	Rev 22:5	2316
the Lord G of the holy prophets	Rev 22:6	2316
worship G	Rev 22:9	2316
G shall add unto him the plagues	Rev 22:18	2316
G shall take away his part out of	Rev 22:19	2316

2. Any deity other than God 1.

I have made thee a g to Pharaoh	Ex 7:1	430
He that sacrificeth unto any g	Ex 22:20	430
For thou shalt worship no other g	Ex 34:14	410
there was no strange g with him	Deut 32:12	410
am he, and there is no g with me	Deut 32:39	430
if he be a g, let him plead for	Judg 6:31	430
and made Baal-berith their g	Judg 8:33	430
and went into the house of their g	Judg 9:27	430

hold of the house of the g Berith Judg 9:46 410
thy g giveth thee to possess Judg 11:24 430
sacrifice unto Dagon their g Judg 16:23 430
Our g hath delivered Samson our Judg 16:23 430
saw him, they praised their g Judg 16:24 430
Our g hath delivered into our Judg 16:24 430
sore upon us, and upon Dagon our g 1Sa 5:7 430
Chemosh the g of the Moabites, and 1Kin 11:33 430
Milcom the g of the children of 1Kin 11:33 430
for he is a g 1Kin 18:27 430
the g of Ekron whether I shall 2Kin 1:2 430
of Baal-zebub the g of Ekron 2Kin 1:3 430
of Baal-zebub the g of Ekron 2Kin 1:6 430
of Baal-zebub the g of Ekron 2Kin 1:16 430
in the house of Nisroch his g 2Kin 19:37 430
for no g of any nation or kingdom 2Chr 32:15 433
was come into the house of his g 2Chr 32:21 430
that hasten after another g Ps 16:4
out our hands to a strange g Ps 44:20 410
shall no strange g be in thee Ps 81:9 410
shalt thou worship any strange g Ps 81:9 410
there was no strange g among you Is 43:12
Who hath formed a g, or molten a Is 44:10 410
yea, he maketh a g, and Is 44:15 410
the residue thereof he maketh a g Is 44:17 410
for thou art my g Is 44:17 410
pray unto a g that cannot save Is 45:20 410
and he maketh it a g Is 46:6 410
of Shinar to the house of his g Dan 1:2 430
into the treasure house of his g Dan 1:2 430
might not serve nor worship any g Dan 3:28 426
according to the name of my g Dan 4:8 426
and magnify himself above every g Dan 11:36 410
desire of women, nor regard any g Dan 11:37 433
a g whom his fathers knew not Dan 11:38 433
strong holds with a strange g Dan 11:39 433
and thou shalt know no g but me Hos 13:4 430
condemned in the house of their g Amos 2:8 430
your images, the star of your g Amos 5:26 430
the sin of Samaria, and say, Thy g Amos 8:14 430
and cried every man unto his g Jonah 1:5 430
every one in the name of his g Mic 4:5 430
this his power unto his g Hab 1:11 430
the daughter of a strange g Mal 2:11 410
and the star of your g Remphan Acts 7:43 2316
saying, It is the voice of a g Acts 12:22 2316
minds, and said that he was a g Acts 28:6 2316
In whom the g of this world hath 2Cor 4:4 2316

GODDESS
Ashtoreth the g of the Zidonians 1Kin 11:5 430
Ashtoreth the g of the Zidonians 1Kin 11:33 430
great g Diana should be despised Acts 19:27 2299
a worshipper of the great g Diana Acts 19:35 2299
nor yet blasphemers of your g Acts 19:37 2299

GODHEAD *That which is divine.*
that the G is like unto gold Acts 17:29 2304
made, even his eternal power and G Rom 1:20 2305
all the fulness of the G bodily Col 2:9 2320

GODLINESS
quiet and peaceable life in all g 1Ti 2:2 2150
professing g) with good works 1Ti 2:10 2317
great is the mystery of g 1Ti 3:16 2150
and exercise thyself rather unto g 1Ti 4:7 2150
but g is profitable unto all 1Ti 4:8 2150
doctrine which is according to g 1Ti 6:3 2150
truth, supposing that gain is g 1Ti 6:5 2150
But g with contentment is great 1Ti 6:6 2150
and follow after righteousness, g 1Ti 6:11 2150
Having a form of g, but denying 2Ti 3:5 2150
of the truth which is after g Titus 1:1 2150
that pertain unto life and g 2Pet 1:3 2150
and to patience g 2Pet 1:6 2150
And to g brotherly kindness 2Pet 1:7 2150
be in all holy conversation and g 2Pet 3:11 2150

GODLY
apart him that is g for himself Ps 4:3 2623
for the g man ceaseth Ps 12:1 2623
this shall every one that is g Ps 32:6 2623
That he might seek a g seed Mal 2:15 430
g sincerity, not with fleshly 2Cor 1:12 2316
were made sorry after a g manner 2Cor 7:9
For g sorrow worketh repentance 2Cor 7:10
that ye sorrowed after a g sort 2Cor 7:11
jealous over you with g jealousy 2Cor 11:2 2316
rather than g edifying which is 1Ti 1:4 2316
all that will live g in Christ 2Ti 3:12 2153
live soberly, righteously, and g Titus 2:12 2153
with reverence and g fear Heb 12:28
deliver the g out of temptations 2Pet 2:9 2152
on their journey after a g sort 3Jn 6

GOD'S *Refers to God 1.*
for a pillar, shall be G house Gen 28:22 430
and he said, Am I in G stead Gen 30:2 430
saw them, he said, This is G host Gen 32:2 430
G anger was kindled because he Num 22:22 430
for the judgment is G Deut 1:17 430
the battle is not yours, but G 2Chr 20:15 430
and into an oath, to walk in G law Neh 10:29 430
according to thy wish in G stead Job 33:6 410
My righteousness is more than G Job 35:2 410
I have yet to speak on G behalf Job 36:2 433
for it is G throne Mt 5:34 2316
and unto God the things that are G Mt 22:21 2316
and to God the things that are G Mk 12:17 2316
for the kingdom of G sake Lk 18:29 2316
and unto God the things which be G Lk 20:25 2316
He that is of God heareth G words Jn 8:47 2316
said, Revilest thou G high priest Acts 23:4 2316
thing to the charge of G elect Rom 8:33 2316
being ignorant of G righteousness Rom 10:3 2316
for they are G ministers, Rom 13:6 2316
ye are G husbandry, ye are G 1Cor 3:9 2316
and Christ is G 1Cor 3:23 2316
and in your spirit, which are G 1Cor 6:20 2316
according to the faith of G elect Titus 1:1 2316
as being lords over G heritage 1Pet 5:3 2316

GODS *Refers to God 2.*
be opened, and ye shall be as g Gen 3:5 430
wherefore hast thou stolen my g Gen 31:30 430
whomsoever thou findest thy g Gen 31:32 430
the strange g that are among you Gen 35:2 430
g which were in their hand Gen 35:4 430
against all the g of Egypt I will Ex 12:12 430
unto thee, O LORD, among the g Ex 15:11 410
the LORD is greater than all g Ex 18:11 430
shalt have no other g before me Ex 20:3 430
not make with me g of silver Ex 20:23 430
shall ye make unto you g of gold Ex 20:23 430
Thou shalt not revile the g Ex 22:28 430
no mention of the name of other g Ex 23:13 430
shalt not bow down to their g Ex 23:24 430
with them, nor with their g Ex 23:32 430
for if thou serve their g Ex 23:33 430
and said unto him, Up, make us g Ex 32:1 430
and they said, These be thy g Ex 32:4 430
and said, These be thy g, O Ex 32:8 430
For they said unto me, Make us g Ex 32:23 430
sin, and have made them g of gold Ex 32:31 430
they go a whoring after their g Ex 34:15 430
and do sacrifice unto their g Ex 34:15 430
go a whoring after their g Ex 34:16 430
sons go a whoring after their g Ex 34:16 430
Thou shalt make thee no molten g Ex 34:17 430
nor make to yourselves molten g Lev 19:4 430
unto the sacrifices of their g Num 25:2 430
did eat, and bowed down to their g Num 25:2 430
upon their g also the LORD Num 33:4 430
And there ye shall serve g Deut 4:28 430
shalt have none other g before me Deut 5:7 430
Ye shall not go after other g Deut 6:14 430
of the g of the people which are Deut 6:14 430
me, that they may serve other g Deut 7:4 430
neither shalt thou serve their g Deut 7:16 430
their g shall ye burn with fire Deut 7:25 430
thy God, and walk after other g Deut 8:19 430
For the LORD your God is God of g Deut 10:17 430
ye turn aside, and serve other g Deut 11:16 430
you this day, to go after other g Deut 11:28 430
ye shall possess served their g Deut 12:2 430
down the graven images of their g Deut 12:3 430
thou enquire not after their g Deut 12:30 430
did these nations serve their g Deut 12:30 430
have they done unto their g Deut 12:31 430
have burnt in the fire to their g Deut 12:31 430
saying, Let us go after other g Deut 13:2 430
Let us go and serve other g Deut 13:6 430
of the g of the people which are Deut 13:7 430
Let us go and serve other g Deut 13:13 430
And hath gone and served other g Deut 17:3 430
speak in the name of other g Deut 18:20 430
which they have done unto their g Deut 20:18 430
to go after other g to serve them Deut 28:14 430
and there shalt thou serve other g Deut 28:36 430
and there thou shalt serve other g Deut 28:64 430
serve the g of these nations Deut 29:18 430
For they went and served other g Deut 29:26 430
g whom they knew not, and whom he Deut 29:26 430
be drawn away, and worship other g Deut 30:17 430
go a whoring after the g of the Deut 31:16 430
that they are turned unto other g Deut 31:18 430
then will they turn unto other g Deut 31:20 430
him to jealousy with strange g Deut 32:16
to g whom they knew not Deut 32:17 430
to new g that came newly up, whom Deut 32:17
he shall say, Where are their g Deut 32:37 430
God of g, the LORD God of g Josh 22:22 430
mention of the names of their g Josh 23:7 430
and have gone and served other g Josh 23:16 430
and they served other g Josh 24:2 430
put away the g which your fathers Josh 24:14 430
whether the g which your fathers Josh 24:15 430
or the g of the Amorites, in Josh 24:15 430
the LORD, to serve other g Josh 24:16 430
the LORD, and serve strange g Josh 24:20 430
the strange g which are among you Josh 24:23 430
their g shall be a snare unto you Judg 2:3 430
of Egypt, and followed other g Judg 2:12 430
of the g of the people that were Judg 2:12 430
they went a whoring after other g Judg 2:17 430
following other g to serve them Judg 2:19 430
to their sons, and served their g Judg 3:6 430
They chose new g Judg 5:8 430
fear not the g of the Amorites, Judg 6:10 430
the g of Syria Judg 10:6 430
the g of Zidon Judg 10:6 430
the g of Moab Judg 10:6 430
the g of the children of Ammon Judg 10:6 430
the g of the Philistines, and Judg 10:6 430
forsaken me, and served other g Judg 10:13 430
cry unto the g which ye have Judg 10:14 430
the strange g from among them Judg 10:16 430
the man Micah had an house of g Judg 17:5 430
have taken away my g which I made Judg 18:24 430
unto her people, and unto her g Ruth 1:15 430
out of the hand of these mighty G 1Sa 4:8 430
these are the G that smote the 1Sa 4:8 430
from off you, and from off your g 1Sa 6:5 430
then put away the strange g 1Sa 7:3 430
forsaken me, and served other g 1Sa 8:8 430
Philistine cursed David by his g 1Sa 17:43 430
LORD, saying, Go, serve other g 1Sa 26:19 430
I saw g ascending out of the 1Sa 28:13 430
from the nations and their g 2Sa 7:23 430
you, but go and serve other g 1Kin 9:6 430
and have taken hold upon other g 1Kin 9:9 430
away your heart after their g 1Kin 11:2 430
away his heart after other g 1Kin 11:4 430
and sacrificed unto their g 1Kin 11:8 430
he should not go after other g 1Kin 11:10 430
behold thy g, O Israel, which 1Kin 12:28 430
hast gone and made thee other g 1Kin 14:9 430
And call ye on the name of your g 1Kin 18:24 430
and call on the name of your g 1Kin 18:25 430
saying, So let the g do to me 1Kin 19:2 430
The g do so unto me, and more also 1Kin 20:10 430
Their g are g of the hills 1Kin 20:23 430
Their g are g of the hills 1Kin 20:23 430
nor sacrifice unto other g 2Kin 5:17 430
of Egypt, and had feared other g 2Kin 17:7 430
every nation made g of their own 2Kin 17:29 430
Anammelech, the g of Sepharvaim 2Kin 17:31 430
the LORD, and served their own g 2Kin 17:33 430
saying, Ye shall not fear other g 2Kin 17:35 430
and ye shall not fear other g 2Kin 17:37 430
neither shall ye fear other g 2Kin 17:38 430
Hath any of the g of the nations 2Kin 18:33 430
Where are the g of Hamath 2Kin 18:34 430
where are the g of Sepharvaim 2Kin 18:34 430
among all the g of the countries 2Kin 18:35 430
Have the g of the nations 2Kin 19:12 430
have cast their g into the fire 2Kin 19:18 430
for they were no g, but the work 2Kin 19:18 430
have burned incense unto other g 2Kin 22:17 430
went a whoring after the g of the 1Chr 5:25 430
armour in the house of their g 1Chr 10:10 430
when they had left their g there 1Chr 14:12 430
also is to be feared above all g 1Chr 16:25 430
For all the g of the people are 1Chr 16:26 430
for great is our God above all g 2Chr 2:5 430
you, and shall go and serve other g 2Chr 7:19 430
of Egypt, and laid hold on other g 2Chr 7:22 430
which Jeroboam made you for g 2Chr 13:8 430
be a priest of them that are no g 2Chr 13:9 430
away the altars of the strange g 2Chr 14:3
that he brought the g of the 2Chr 25:14 430
Seir, and set them up to be his g 2Chr 25:14 430
sought after the g of the people 2Chr 25:15 430
they sought after the g of Edom 2Chr 25:20 430
sacrificed unto the g of Damascus 2Chr 28:23 430
Because the g of the kings of 2Chr 28:23 430
to burn incense unto other g 2Chr 28:25 430
were the g of the nations of 2Chr 32:13 430
the g of those nations that my 2Chr 32:14 430
As the g of the nations of other 2Chr 32:17 430
as against the g of the people of 2Chr 32:19 430
And he took away the strange g 2Chr 33:15 430
have burned incense unto other g 2Chr 34:25 430
put them in the house of his g Ezr 1:7 430
he judgeth among the g Ps 82:1 430
I have said, Ye are g Ps 82:6 430
Among the g there is none like Ps 86:8 430
God, and a great King above all g Ps 95:3 430
he is to be feared above all g Ps 96:4 430
For all the g of the nations are Ps 96:5 430
worship him, all ye g Ps 97:7 430
thou art exalted far above all g Ps 97:9 430
and that our Lord is above all g Ps 135:5 430
O give thanks unto the God of g Ps 136:2 430
before the g will I sing praise Ps 138:1 430
all the graven images of her g he Is 21:9 430
Hath any of the g of the nations Is 36:18 430
Where are the g of Hamath Is 36:19 430
where are the g of Sepharvaim Is 36:19 430
among all the g of these lands Is 36:20 430
Have the g of the nations Is 37:12 430
have cast their g into the fire Is 37:19 430
for they were no g, but the work Is 37:19 430
that we may know that ye are g Is 41:23 430
the molten images, Ye are our g Is 42:17 430
have burned incense unto other g Jer 1:16 430
their g, which are yet no g Jer 2:11 430
But where are thy g that thou Jer 2:28 430
number of thy cities are thy g Jer 2:28 430
and sworn by them that are no g Jer 5:7 430
and served strange g in your land Jer 5:19 430
walk after other g to your hurt Jer 7:6 430
after other g whom ye know not Jer 7:9 430
out drink offerings unto other g Jer 7:18 430
The g that have not made the Jer 10:11 426
went after other g to serve them Jer 11:10 430
cry unto the g unto whom they Jer 11:12 430
number of thy cities were thy g Jer 11:13 430
heart, and walk after other g Jer 13:10 430
and have walked after other g Jer 16:11 430
there shall ye serve other g day Jer 16:13 430
Shall a man make g unto himself Jer 16:20 430
and they are no g Jer 16:20 430
burned incense in it unto other g Jer 19:4 430
out drink offerings unto other g Jer 19:13 430
their God, and worshipped other g Jer 22:9 430
not after other g to serve them Jer 25:6 430
out drink offerings unto other g Jer 32:29 430
not after other g to serve them Jer 35:15 430
in the houses of the g of Egypt Jer 43:12 430
the houses of the g of the Jer 43:13 430
burn incense, and to serve other g Jer 44:3 430
to burn no incense unto other g Jer 44:5 430
unto other g in the land of Egypt Jer 44:8 430
had burned incense unto other g Jer 44:15 430
Pharaoh, and Egypt, with their g Jer 46:25 430
him that burneth incense to his g Jer 48:35 430
it before the king, except the g Dan 2:11 426
is, that your God is a God of g Dan 2:47 426
they serve not thy g, nor worship Dan 3:12 426
Abed-nego, do not ye serve my g Dan 3:14 426
that we will not serve thy g Dan 3:18 426
whom is the spirit of the holy g Dan 4:8 426
spirit of the holy g is in thee Dan 4:9 426

spirit of the holy *g* is in thee	Dan 4:18	426
wine, and praised the *g* of gold	Dan 5:4	426
whom is the spirit of the holy *g*	Dan 5:11	426
wisdom, like the wisdom of the *g*	Dan 5:11	426
the spirit of the *g* is in thee	Dan 5:14	426
thou hast praised the *g* of silver	Dan 5:23	426
carry captives into Egypt their *g*	Dan 11:8	430
things against the God of *g*	Dan 11:36	410
of Israel, who look to other *g*	Hos 3:1	430
work of our hands, Ye are our *g*	Hos 14:3	430
out of the house of thy *g* will I	Nah 1:14	430
famish all the *g* of the earth	Zeph 2:11	430
in your law, I said, Ye are *g*	Jn 10:34	*2316*
If he called them *g*, unto whom	Jn 10:35	*2316*
Make us *g* to go before us	Acts 7:40	*2316*
The *g* are come down to us in the	Acts 14:11	*2316*
to be a setter forth of strange *g*	Acts 17:18	*1140*
people, saying that they be no *g*	Acts 19:26	*2316*
though there be that are called *g*	1Cor 8:5	*2316*
or in earth, (as there be *g* many	1Cor 8:5	*2316*
them which by nature are no *g*	Gal 4:8	*2316*

GOD-WARD

Be thou for the people to *G*	Ex 18:19	
trust have we through Christ to *G*	2Cor 3:4	
your faith to *G* is spread abroad	1Th 1:8	

GOEST

as thou *g*, unto Sodom, and	Gen 10:19	935
as thou *g* unto Sephar a mount of	Gen 10:30	935
Egypt, as thou *g* toward Assyria	Gen 25:18	935
thee in all places whither thou *g*	Gen 28:15	3212
and whither *g* thou	Gen 32:17	3212
When thou *g* to return into Egypt,	Ex 4:21	3212
is it not in that thou *g* with us	Ex 33:16	3212
of the land whither thou *g*	Ex 34:12	935
that thou *g* before them, by	Num 14:14	1980
land whither thou *g* to possess it	Deut 7:1	935
whither thou *g* in to possess it,	Deut 11:10	935
land whither thou *g* to possess it	Deut 11:29	935
whither thou *g* to possess them,	Deut 12:29	935
When thou *g* out to battle against	Deut 20:1	3318
When thou *g* forth to war against	Deut 21:10	3318
land whither thou *g* to possess it	Deut 23:20	935
shalt thou be when thou *g* out	Deut 28:6	3318
shalt thou be when thou *g* out	Deut 28:19	3318
whither thou *g* to possess it	Deut 28:21	935
land whither thou *g* to possess it	Deut 28:63	935
land whither thou *g* to possess it	Deut 30:16	935
in the mount whither thou *g* up	Deut 32:50	5927
prosper whithersoever thou *g*	Josh 1:7	3212
is with thee whithersoever thou *g*	Josh 1:9	3212
that thou *g* to take a wife of the	Judg 14:3	1980
the old man said, Whither *g* thou	Judg 19:17	3212
for whither thou *g*, I will go	Ruth 1:16	3212
of the land, as thou *g* to Shur	1Sa 27:8	935
strength, when thou *g* on thy way	1Sa 28:22	3212
Wherefore *g* thou also with us	2Sa 15:19	3212
be, that on the day thou *g* out	1Kin 2:37	3318
a certain, on the day thou *g* out	1Kin 2:42	3318
g not forth with our armies	Ps 44:9	3318
When thou *g*, thy steps shall not	Prov 4:12	3212
When thou *g*, it shall lead thee	Prov 6:22	1980
when thou *g* to the house of God	Eccl 5:1	3212
in the grave, whither thou *g*	Eccl 9:10	1980
prey in all places whither thou *g*	Jer 45:5	3212
Then said I, Whither *g* thou	Zec 2:2	1980
follow thee whithersoever thou *g*	Mt 8:19	
follow thee whithersoever thou *g*	Lk 9:57	*565*
When thou *g* with thine adversary	Lk 12:58	*5217*
and *g* thou thither again	Jn 11:8	*5217*
unto him, Lord, whither *g* thou	Jn 13:36	*5217*
Lord, we know not whither thou *g*	Jn 14:5	*5217*
of you asketh me, Whither *g* thou	Jn 16:5	*5217*

GOETH

that is it which *g* toward the	Gen 2:14	1980
with the present that *g* before me	Gen 32:20	1980
as the cattle that *g* before me	Gen 33:14	
Behold thy father in law *g* up to	Gen 38:13	5927
lo, he *g* out unto the water	Ex 7:15	3318
unto him by that the sun *g* down	Ex 22:26	935
when he *g* in unto the holy place,	Ex 28:29	935
when he *g* in before the LORD	Ex 28:30	935
sound shall be heard when he *g* in	Ex 28:35	935
thing that *g* upon all four	Lev 11:21	1980
whatsoever *g* upon his paws, among	Lev 11:27	1980
Whatsoever *g* upon the belly, and	Lev 11:42	1980
whatsoever *g* upon all four, or	Lev 11:42	1980
Moreover he that *g* into the house	Lev 14:46	935
and of him whose seed *g* from him	Lev 15:32	3318
of the congregation when he *g* in	Lev 16:17	935
that *g* unto the holy things,	Lev 22:3	7126
or a man whose seed *g* from him	Lev 22:4	3318
when it *g* out in the jubile,	Lev 27:21	3318
when a wife *g* aside to another	Num 5:29	7847
that *g* down to the dwelling of Ar	Num 21:15	5186
LORD your God which *g* before you	Deut 1:30	1980
is he which *g* over before thee	Deut 9:3	5674
by the way where the sun *g* down	Deut 11:30	3996
As when a man *g* into the wood	Deut 19:5	935
your God is he that *g* with you	Deut 20:4	1980
When the host *g* forth against	Deut 23:9	3318
pledge again when the sun *g* down	Deut 24:13	935
the way that *g* up to Beth-horon	Josh 10:10	4609
that *g* up to Seir, even unto	Josh 11:17	5927
mount Halak, that *g* up to Seir	Josh 12:7	5927
to the wilderness that *g* up from	Josh 16:1	5927
g out from Beth-el to Luz, and	Josh 16:2	3318
g down westward to the coast of	Josh 16:3	3381
then *g* out to Daberath, and *g*	Josh 19:12	3318
g out to Remmon-methoar to Neah	Josh 19:13	3318
g out to Cabul on the left hand,	Josh 19:27	3318
g out from thence to Hukkok, and	Josh 19:34	3318
sun when he *g* forth in his might	Judg 5:31	3318
of which one *g* up to the house of	Judg 20:31	5927
that *g* up from Beth-el to Shechem	Judg 21:19	5927
if it *g* up by the way of his own	1Sa 6:9	5927
law, and *g* at thy bidding, and is	1Sa 22:14	5493
part is that *g* down to the battle	1Sa 30:24	3381
that when my master *g* into the	2Kin 5:18	935
be ye with the king as he *g* out	2Kin 11:8	3318
of Millo, which *g* down to Silla	2Kin 12:20	3381
he cometh in, and when he *g* out	2Chr 23:7	3318
the walls, and this work *g* fast on	Ezr 5:8	5648
so he that *g* down to the grave	Job 7:9	3381
he *g* by me, and I see him not	Job 9:11	5674
Which *g* in company with the	Job 34:8	732
the sound that *g* out of his mouth	Job 37:2	3318
he *g* on to meet the armed men	Job 39:21	3318
Out of his nostrils *g* smoke	Job 41:20	3318
a flame *g* out of his mouth	Job 41:21	3318
that *g* not out of feigned lips	Ps 17:1	
when he *g* abroad, he telleth it	Ps 41:6	3318
as *g* on still in his trespasses	Ps 68:21	1980
Thy fierce wrath *g* over me	Ps 88:16	5674
A fire *g* before him, and burneth	Ps 97:3	3212
Man *g* forth unto his work and to	Ps 104:23	3318
He that *g* forth and weepeth,	Ps 126:6	3212
His breath *g* forth, he returneth	Ps 146:4	3318
So he that *g* in to his	Prov 6:29	935
He *g* after her straightway	Prov 7:22	1980
as an ox *g* to the slaughter, or	Prov 7:22	925
When it *g* well with the righteous	Prov 11:10	
Pride *g* before destruction, and an	Prov 16:18	
He that *g* about as a talebearer	Prov 20:19	1980
As a thorn *g* up into the hand of	Prov 26:9	5927
no wood is, there the fire *g* out	Prov 26:20	3518
her candle *g* not out by night	Prov 31:18	3518
also ariseth, and the sun *g* down	Eccl 1:5	935
The wind *g* toward the south, and	Eccl 1:6	1980
the spirit of man that *g* upward	Eccl 3:21	5927
that *g* downward to the earth	Eccl 3:21	3381
because man *g* to his long home,	Eccl 12:5	1980
that *g* down sweetly, causing the	Song 7:9	1980
From the time that it *g* forth it	Is 28:19	5674
as when one *g* with a pipe to come	Is 30:29	1980
be that *g* forth out of my mouth	Is 55:11	3318
whosoever *g* therein shall not	Is 59:8	1869
As a beast *g* down into the valley	Is 63:14	3318
every one that *g* out thence shall	Jer 5:6	3318
for the day *g* away, for the	Jer 6:4	6437
but he that *g* out, and falleth to	Jer 21:9	3318
but weep sore for him that *g* away	Jer 22:10	1980
of the LORD *g* forth with fury	Jer 30:23	3318
but he that *g* forth to the	Jer 38:2	3318
g forth out of our own mouth	Jer 44:17	3318
every one that *g* by it shall be	Jer 49:17	5674
every one that *g* by Babylon shall	Jer 50:13	5674
but none *g* to the battle	Eze 7:14	1980
but their heart *g* after their	Eze 33:31	1980
as one *g* up to the entry of the	Eze 40:40	5927
as one *g* into them from the utter	Eze 42:9	935
day that he *g* into the sanctuary	Eze 44:27	935
as one *g* to Hamath, Hazar-enan,	Eze 48:1	935
and as the early dew it *g* away	Hos 6:4	1980
are as the light that *g* forth	Hos 6:5	3318
This is the curse that *g* forth	Zec 5:3	3318
and see what is this that *g* forth	Zec 5:5	3318
This is an ephah that *g* forth	Zec 5:6	3318
and I say to this man, Go, and he *g*	Mt 8:9	*4198*
Then *g* he, and taketh with himself	Mt 12:45	*4198*
he hideth, and for joy thereof *g*	Mt 13:44	*5217*
Not that which *g* into the mouth	Mt 15:11	*1525*
in at the mouth *g* into the belly	Mt 15:17	*5562*
Howbeit this kind *g* not out but	Mt 17:21	*1607*
g into the mountains, and seeketh	Mt 18:12	*4198*
The Son of man *g* as it is written	Mt 26:24	*5217*
he *g* before you into Galilee	Mt 28:7	*4254*
he *g* up into a mountain, and	Mk 3:13	*305*
g out into the draught, purging	Mk 7:19	*1607*
The Son of man indeed *g*, as it is	Mk 14:21	*5217*
he *g* straightway to him, and saith	Mk 14:45	*4334*
Peter that he *g* before you into	Mk 16:7	*4254*
and I say unto one, Go, and he *g*	Lk 7:8	*4198*
Then *g* he, and taketh to him seven	Lk 11:26	*4198*
And truly the Son of man *g*	Lk 22:22	*4198*
whence it cometh, and whither it *g*	Jn 3:8	*5217*
who *g* about to kill thee	Jn 7:20	*2212*
he *g* before them, and the sheep	Jn 10:4	*4198*
She *g* unto the grave to weep	Jn 11:31	*5217*
darkness knoweth not whither he *g*	Jn 12:35	*5217*
the south unto the way that *g*	Acts 8:26	*3597*
But brother *g* to law with brother	1Cor 6:6	
Who *g* a warfare any time at his	1Cor 9:7	
g his way, and straightway	Jas 1:24	*565*
and knoweth not whither he *g*	1Jn 2:11	*5217*
the Lamb whithersoever he *g*	Rev 14:4	*5217*
of the seven, and *g* into perdition	Rev 17:11	*5217*
out of his mouth *g* a sharp sword	Rev 19:15	*1607*

GOG See HAMON-GOG, MAGOG.

1. Son of Shemarah.

G his son, Shimei his son,	1Chr 5:4	1463

2. A prince of Scythia.

of man, set thy face against *G*	Eze 38:2	1463
Behold, I am against thee, O *G*	Eze 38:3	1463
of man, prophesy and say unto *G*	Eze 38:14	1463
shall be sanctified in thee, O *G*	Eze 38:16	1463
to pass at the same time when *G*	Eze 38:18	1463
son of man, prophesy against *G*	Eze 39:1	1463
Behold, I am against thee, O *G*	Eze 39:1	1463
that I will give unto *G* a place	Eze 39:11	1463
and there shall they bury *G*	Eze 39:11	1463
the four quarters of the earth, *G*	Rev 20:8	*1136*

GOIIM See NATIONS.

GOING

g on still toward the south	Gen 12:9	1980
And when the sun was *g* down	Gen 15:12	935
g to carry it down to Egypt	Gen 37:25	1980
until the *g* down of the sun	Ex 17:12	935
enemy's ox or his ass *g* astray	Ex 23:4	8582
six branches *g* out of the sides	Ex 37:18	3318
branches *g* out of the candlestick	Ex 37:19	3318
to the six branches *g* out of it	Ex 37:21	3318
g upon all four, shall be an	Lev 11:20	1980
g over into the land which the	Num 32:7	5674
the *g* forth thereof shall be from	Num 34:4	8444
at the *g* down of the sun, at the	Deut 16:6	935
Rejoice, Zebulun, in thy *g* out	Deut 33:18	3318
sea toward the *g* down of the sun	Josh 1:4	3996
after the ark, the priests *g* on	Josh 6:9	1980
the city, *g* about it once	Josh 6:11	5362
ark of the LORD, the priests *g* on	Josh 6:13	1980
and smote them in the *g* down	Josh 7:5	4174
were in the *g* down to Beth-horon,	Josh 10:11	4174
the time of the *g* down of the sun	Josh 10:27	935
is before the *g* up to Adummim	Josh 15:7	4608
over against the *g* up of Adummim	Josh 18:17	4608
this day I am *g* the way of all	Josh 23:14	1980
was from the *g* up to Akrabbim	Judg 1:36	4608
but I am now *g* to the house of	Judg 19:18	1980
said unto her, Up, and let us be *g*	Judg 19:28	3212
young maidens *g* out to draw water	1Sa 9:11	3318
as they were *g* down to the end of	1Sa 9:27	3381
three men *g* up to God to Beth-el	1Sa 10:3	5927
as the host was *g* forth to the	1Sa 17:20	3318
hast been upright, and thy *g* out	1Sa 29:6	3318
in *g* he turned not to the right	2Sa 2:19	3212
thee, and to know thy *g* out	2Sa 3:25	4161
a *g* in the tops of the mulberry	2Sa 5:24	6807
as she was *g* to fetch it, he	1Kin 17:11	3212
host about the *g* down of the sun	1Kin 22:36	935
as he was *g* up by the way, there	2Kin 2:23	5927
And they did so at the *g* up to Gur	2Kin 9:27	4608
I know thy abode, and thy *g* out	2Kin 19:27	3318
of *g* in the tops of the mulberry	1Chr 14:15	6807
by the causeway of the *g* up	1Chr 26:16	5927
returned from *g* against Jeroboam	2Chr 11:4	3212
time of the sun *g* down he died	2Chr 18:34	935
the *g* up to the armoury at the	Neh 3:19	5927
to the *g* up of the corner	Neh 3:31	5944
between the *g* up of the corner	Neh 3:32	5944
at the *g* up of the wall, above	Neh 12:37	4608
the LORD, and said, From *g* to	Job 1:7	7751
the LORD, and said, From *g* to	Job 2:2	7751
him from *g* down to the pit	Job 33:24	3381
his soul from *g* into the pit	Job 33:28	5674
His *g* forth is from the end of	Ps 19:6	4161
the sun unto the *g* down thereof	Ps 50:1	3996
the sun knoweth his *g* down	Ps 104:19	3996
the *g* down of the same the LORD's	Ps 113:3	3996
The LORD shall preserve thy *g* out	Ps 121:8	3318
be no breaking in, nor *g* out	Ps 144:14	3318
g down to the chambers of death	Prov 7:27	3381
prudent man looketh well to his *g*	Prov 14:15	838
well, yea, four are comely in *g*	Prov 30:29	3212
shall be darkened in his *g* forth	Is 13:10	3318
I know thy abode, and thy *g* out	Is 37:28	3318
For in the *g* up of Luhith	Jer 48:5	4608
for in the *g* down of Horonaim the	Jer 48:5	4174
the children of Judah together, *g*	Jer 50:4	1980
Dan also and Javan *g* to and fro	Eze 27:19	235
the *g* up to it had eight steps	Eze 40:31	4608
the *g* up to it had eight steps	Eze 40:34	4608
the *g* up to it had eight steps	Eze 40:37	4608
with every *g* forth of the	Eze 44:5	4161
after his *g* forth one shall shut	Eze 46:12	3318
he laboured till the *g* down of	Dan 6:14	4606
that from the *g* forth of the	Dan 9:25	4161
his *g* forth is prepared as the	Hos 6:3	4161
and he found a ship *g* to Tarshish	Jonah 1:3	935
g down of the same my name shall	Mal 1:11	3996
g on from thence, he saw other	Mt 4:21	*4260*
Jesus *g* up to Jerusalem took the	Mt 20:17	*305*
Rise, let us be *g*	Mt 26:46	*71*
Now when they were *g*, behold,	Mt 28:11	*4108*
for there were many coming and *g*	Mk 6:31	*5217*
were in the way *g* up to Jerusalem	Mk 10:32	*305*
g to make war against another	Lk 14:31	*4198*
And as he was now *g* down, his	Jn 4:51	*2597*
g through the midst of them, and	Jn 8:59	*1330*
coming in and *g* out at Jerusalem	Acts 9:28	*1607*
These *g* before tarried for us at	Acts 20:5	*4281*
g about to establish their own	Rom 10:3	*2212*
beforehand, *g* before to judgment	1Ti 5:24	*4254*
g before for the weakness	Heb 7:18	*4254*
For ye were as sheep *g* astray	1Pet 2:25	*4105*
g after strange flesh, are set	Jude 7	*565*

GOINGS

Moses wrote their *g* out according	Num 33:2	4161
journeys according to their *g* out	Num 33:2	4161
the *g* out of it shall be at the	Num 34:5	8444
the *g* forth of the border shall	Num 34:8	8444
the *g* out of it shall be at	Num 34:9	8444
the *g* out of it shall be at the	Num 34:12	8444
the *g* out of that coast were at	Josh 15:4	8444
the *g* out thereof were at	Josh 15:7	8444
the *g* out of the border were at	Josh 15:11	8444
the *g* out thereof are at the sea	Josh 16:3	8444
the *g* out thereof were at the sea	Josh 16:8	8444
the *g* out thereof were at the	Josh 18:12	8444
the *g* out thereof were at	Josh 18:14	8444
of man, and he seeth all his *g*	Job 34:21	6806
Hold up my *g* in thy paths, that	Ps 17:5	838
upon a rock, and established my *g*	Ps 40:2	838
They have seen thy *g*, O God	Ps 68:24	1979
even the *g* of my God, my King, in	Ps 68:24	1979

have purposed to overthrow my g Ps 140:4 6471
LORD, and he pondereth all his g Prov 5:21 4570
Man's g are of the LORD Prov 20:24 4703
there is no judgment in their g Is 59:8 4570
all their g out were both Eze 42:11 4161
the g out thereof, and the comings Eze 43:11 4161
these are the g out of the city Eze 48:30 8444
whose g forth have been from of Mic 5:2 4163

GOLAN (*go'-lan*) *A Levitical city in Manasseh.*
G in Bashan, of the Manassites Deut 4:43 1474
G in Bashan out of the tribe of Josh 20:8 1474
gave G in Bashan with her suburbs Josh 21:27 1474
G in Bashan with her suburbs, and 1Chr 6:71 1474

GOLD
land of Havilah, where there is g Gen 2:11 2091
the g of that land is good Gen 2:12 2091
in cattle, in silver, and in g Gen 13:2 2091
hands of ten shekels weight of g Gen 24:22 2091
flocks, and herds, and silver, and g Gen 24:35 2091
jewels of silver, and jewels of g Gen 24:53 2091
put a g chain about his neck Gen 41:42 2091
of thy lord's house silver or g Gen 44:8 2091
jewels of silver, and jewels of g Ex 3:22 2091
jewels of silver, and jewels of g Ex 11:2 2091
jewels of silver, and jewels of g Ex 12:35 2091
shall ye make unto you gods of g Ex 20:23 2091
g, and silver, and brass, Ex 25:3 2091
thou shalt overlay it with pure g Ex 25:11 2091
upon it a crown of g round about Ex 25:11 2091
shalt cast four rings of g for it Ex 25:12 2091
wood, and overlay them with g Ex 25:13 2091
shalt make a mercy seat of pure g Ex 25:17 2091
shalt make two cherubims of g Ex 25:18 2091
thou shalt overlay it with pure g Ex 25:24 2091
thereto a crown of g round about Ex 25:24 2091
shalt make for it four rings of g Ex 25:26 2091
wood, and overlay them with g Ex 25:28 2091
of pure g shalt thou make them Ex 25:29 2091
make a candlestick of pure g Ex 25:31 2091
be one beaten work of pure g Ex 25:36 2091
thereof, shall be of pure g Ex 25:38 2091
talent of pure g shall he make it Ex 25:39 2091
thou shalt make fifty taches of g Ex 26:6 2091
shalt overlay the boards with g Ex 26:29 2091
make their rings of g for places Ex 26:29 2091
shalt overlay the bars with g Ex 26:29 2091
of shittim wood overlaid with g Ex 26:32 2091
their hooks shall be of g Ex 26:32 2091
wood, and overlay them with g Ex 26:37 2091
and their hooks shall be of g Ex 26:37 2091
And they shall take g, and blue, and Ex 28:5 2091
And they shall make the ephod of g Ex 28:6 2091
even of g, of blue, and purple, and Ex 28:8 2091
them to be set in ouches of g Ex 28:11 2091
And thou shalt make ouches of g Ex 28:13 2091
two chains of pure g at the ends Ex 28:14 2091
of g, of blue, and of purple, and Ex 28:15 2091
be set in g in their inclosings Ex 28:20 2091
ends of wreathen work of pure g Ex 28:22 2091
the breastplate two rings of g Ex 28:23 2091
g in the two rings which are on Ex 28:24 2091
And thou shalt make two rings of g Ex 28:26 2091
other rings of g thou shalt make Ex 28:27 2091
bells of g between them round Ex 28:33 2091
thou shalt make a plate of pure g Ex 28:36 2091
thou shalt overlay it with pure g Ex 30:3 2091
unto it a crown of g round about Ex 30:3 2091
wood, and overlay them with g Ex 30:5 2091
cunning works, to work in g Ex 31:4 2091
unto them, Whosoever hath any g Ex 32:24 2091
sin, and have made them gods of g Ex 32:31 2091
g, and silver, and brass, Ex 35:5 2091
and tablets, all jewels of g Ex 35:22 2091
an offering of g unto the LORD Ex 35:22 2091
curious works, to work in g Ex 35:32 2091
And he made fifty taches of g Ex 36:13 2091
And he overlaid the boards with g Ex 36:34 2091
made their rings of g to be Ex 36:34 2091
bars, and overlaid the bars with g Ex 36:34 2091
wood, and overlaid them with g Ex 36:36 2091
their hooks were of g Ex 36:36 2091
chapiters and their fillets with g Ex 36:38 2091
he overlaid it with pure g within Ex 37:2 2091
made a crown of g to it round Ex 37:2 2091
And he cast for it four rings of g Ex 37:3 2091
wood, and overlaid them with g Ex 37:4 2091
he made the mercy seat of pure g Ex 37:6 2091
And he made two cherubims of g Ex 37:7 2091
And he overlaid it with pure g Ex 37:11 2091
a crown of g round about Ex 37:11 2091
made a crown of g for the border Ex 37:12 2091
And he cast for it four rings of g Ex 37:13 2091
wood, and overlaid them with g Ex 37:15 2091
covers to cover withal, of pure g Ex 37:16 2091
he made the candlestick of pure g Ex 37:17 2091
it was one beaten work of pure g Ex 37:22 2091
and his snuffdishes, of pure g Ex 37:23 2091
Of a talent of pure g made he it Ex 37:24 2091
And he overlaid it with pure g Ex 37:26 2091
unto it a crown of g round about Ex 37:26 2091
he made two rings of g for it Ex 37:27 2091
wood, and overlaid them with g Ex 37:28 2091
All the g that was occupied for Ex 38:24 2091
even the g of the offering, was Ex 38:24 2091
And he made the ephod of g Ex 39:2 2091
did beat the g into thin plates Ex 39:3 2091
of g, blue, and purple, and scarlet Ex 39:5 2091
stones inclosed in ouches of g Ex 39:6 2091
of g, blue, and purple, and scarlet Ex 39:8 2091
ouches of g in their inclosings Ex 39:13 2091
ends, of wreathen work of pure g Ex 39:15 2091
And they made two ouches of g Ex 39:16 2091
ouches of g, and two g rings Ex 39:16 2091
put the two wreathen chains of g Ex 39:17 2091
And they made two rings of g Ex 39:19 2091
And they made bells of pure g Ex 39:25 2091
plate of the holy crown of pure g Ex 39:30 2091
thou shalt set the altar of g for Ex 40:5 2091
One spoon of ten shekels of g Num 7:14 2091
One spoon of g of ten shekels, Num 7:20 2091
silver bowls, twelve spoons of g Num 7:84 2091
all the g of the spoons was an Num 7:86 2091
the candlestick was of beaten g Num 8:4 2091
me his house full of silver and g Num 22:18 2091
me his house full of silver and g Num 24:13 2091
Only the g, and the silver, the Num 31:22 2091
man hath gotten, of jewels of g Num 31:50 2091
the priest took the g of them Num 31:51 2091
all the g of the offering that Num 31:52 2091
Eleazar the priest took the g of Num 31:54 2091
the silver or g that is on them Deut 7:25 2091
thy g is multiplied, and all that Deut 8:13 2091
multiply to himself silver and g Deut 17:17 2091
idols, wood and stone, silver and g Deut 29:17 2091
But all the silver, and g, and Josh 6:19 2091
only the silver, and the g Josh 6:24 2091
a wedge of g of fifty shekels Josh 7:21 2091
and the garment, and the wedge of g Josh 7:24 2091
cattle, with silver, and with g Josh 22:8 2091
and seven hundred shekels of g Judg 8:26 2091
and put the jewels of g, which ye 1Sa 6:8 2091
and the coffer with the mice of g 1Sa 6:11 2091
it, wherein the jewels of g were 1Sa 6:15 2091
ornaments of g upon your apparel 2Sa 1:24 2091
David took the shields of g that 2Sa 8:7 2091
of silver, and vessels of g 2Sa 8:10 2091
g that he had dedicated of all 2Sa 8:11 2091
of g with the precious stones 2Sa 12:30 2091
will have no silver nor g of Saul 2Sa 21:4 2091
and he overlaid it with pure g 1Kin 6:20 2091
the house within with pure g 1Kin 6:21 2091
the chains of g before the oracle 1Kin 6:21 2091
and he overlaid it with g 1Kin 6:21 2091
whole house he overlaid with g 1Kin 6:22 2091
by the oracle he overlaid with g 1Kin 6:22 2091
he overlaid the cherubims with g 1Kin 6:28 2091
of the house he overlaid with g 1Kin 6:30 2091
flowers, and overlaid them with g 1Kin 6:32 2091
spread g upon the cherubims, and 1Kin 6:32 2091
covered them with g fitted upon 1Kin 6:35 2091
altar of g, and the table of g 1Kin 7:48 2091
And the candlesticks of pure g 1Kin 7:49 2091
and the lamps, and the tongs of g 1Kin 7:49 2091
spoons, and the censers of pure g 1Kin 7:50 2091
and the hinges of g, both for the 1Kin 7:50 2091
even the silver, and the g 1Kin 7:51 2091
trees and fir trees, and with g 1Kin 9:11 2091
to the king sixscore talents of g 1Kin 9:14 2091
Ophir, and fetched from thence g 1Kin 9:28 2091
that bare spices, and very much g 1Kin 10:2 2091
an hundred and twenty talents of g 1Kin 10:10 2091
Hiram, that brought g from Ophir 1Kin 10:11 2091
Now the weight of g that came to 1Kin 10:14 2091
threescore and six talents of g 1Kin 10:14 2091
two hundred targets of beaten g 1Kin 10:16 2091
shekels of g went to one target 1Kin 10:16 2091
three hundred shields of beaten g 1Kin 10:17 2091
three pound of g went to one 1Kin 10:17 2091
and overlaid it with the best g 1Kin 10:18 2091
drinking vessels were of g 1Kin 10:21 2091
forest of Lebanon were of pure g 1Kin 10:21 2091
the navy of Tharshish, bringing g 1Kin 10:22 2091
of silver, and vessels of g 1Kin 10:25 2091
counsel, and made two calves of g 1Kin 12:28 2091
of g which Solomon had made 1Kin 14:26 2091
house of the LORD, silver, and g 1Kin 15:15 2091
the g that were left in the 1Kin 15:18 2091
thee a present of silver and g 1Kin 15:19 2091
Thy silver and thy g is mine 1Kin 20:3 2091
deliver me thy silver, and thy g 1Kin 20:5 2091
and for my silver, and for my g 1Kin 20:7 2091
of Tharshish to go to Ophir for g 1Kin 22:48 2091
and six thousand pieces of g 2Kin 5:5 2091
and carried thence silver, and g 2Kin 7:8 2091
trumpets, any vessels of g 2Kin 12:13 2091
all the g that was found in the 2Kin 12:18 2091
And he took all the g and silver, 2Kin 14:14 2091
g that was found in the house of 2Kin 16:8 2091
of silver and thirty talents of g 2Kin 18:14 2091
time did Hezekiah cut off the g 2Kin 18:16
things, the silver, and the g 2Kin 20:13 2091
of silver, and a talent of g 2Kin 23:33 2091
the silver and the g to Pharaoh 2Kin 23:35 2091
the g of the people of the land, 2Kin 23:35 2091
of g which Solomon king of Israel 2Kin 24:13 2091
such things as were of g, in g 2Kin 25:15 2091
David took the shields of g that 1Chr 18:7 2091
him all manner of vessels of g 1Chr 18:10 2091
the g that he brought from all 1Chr 18:11 2091
found it to weigh a talent of g 1Chr 20:2 2091
hundred shekels of g by weight 1Chr 21:25 2091
an hundred thousand talents of g 1Chr 22:14 2091
Of the g, the silver, and the 1Chr 22:16 2091
of g by weight for things of g 1Chr 28:14 2091
weight for the candlesticks of g 1Chr 28:15 2091
and for their lamps of g 1Chr 28:15 2091
by weight he gave g for the 1Chr 28:16 2091
Also pure g for the fleshhooks, 1Chr 28:17 2091
gave g by weight for every bason 1Chr 28:17
of incense refined g by weight 1Chr 28:18 2091
g for the pattern of the chariot 1Chr 28:18 2091
g for things to be made of g 1Chr 29:2 2091
of mine own proper good, of g 1Chr 29:3 2091
Even three thousand talents of g 1Chr 29:4 2091
of the g of Ophir, and seven 1Chr 29:4 2091
The g for things of g, and the 1Chr 29:5 2091
of God of g five thousand talents 1Chr 29:7 2091
g at Jerusalem as plenteous as 2Chr 1:15 2091
a man cunning to work in g 2Chr 2:7 2091
man of Tyre, skilful to work in g 2Chr 2:14 2091
he overlaid it within with pure g 2Chr 3:4 2091
which he overlaid with fine g 2Chr 3:5 2091
and the g was g of Parvaim 2Chr 3:6 2091
and the doors thereof, with g 2Chr 3:7 2091
and he overlaid it with fine g 2Chr 3:8 2091
the nails was fifty shekels of g 2Chr 3:9 2091
the upper chambers with g 2Chr 3:9 2091
work, and overlaid them with g 2Chr 3:10 2091
of g according to their form 2Chr 4:7 2091
And he made an hundred basons of g 2Chr 4:8 2091
before the oracle, of pure g 2Chr 4:20 2091
he of g, and that perfect g 2Chr 4:21 2091
spoons, and the censers, of pure g 2Chr 4:22 2091
house of the temple, were of g 2Chr 4:22 2091
and the silver, and the g, and all 2Chr 5:1 2091
hundred and fifty talents of g 2Chr 8:18 2091
g in abundance, and precious 2Chr 9:1 2091
an hundred and twenty talents of g 2Chr 9:9 2091
which brought g from Ophir 2Chr 9:10 2091
Now the weight of g that came to 2Chr 9:13 2091
and threescore and six talents of g 2Chr 9:13 2091
of the country brought g and 2Chr 9:14 2091
two hundred targets of beaten g 2Chr 9:15 2091
of beaten g went to one target 2Chr 9:15 2091
shields made he of beaten g 2Chr 9:16 2091
shekels of g went to one shield 2Chr 9:16 2091
ivory, and overlaid it with pure g 2Chr 9:17 2091
the throne, with a footstool of g 2Chr 9:18 2091
vessels of king Solomon were of g 2Chr 9:20 2091
forest of Lebanon were of pure g 2Chr 9:20 2091
the ships of Tarshish bringing g 2Chr 9:21 2091
of silver, and vessels of g 2Chr 9:24 2091
of g which Solomon had made 2Chr 12:9 2091
the candlestick of g with the 2Chr 13:11 2091
had dedicated, silver, and g 2Chr 15:18 2091
g out of the treasures of the 2Chr 16:2 2091
I have sent thee silver and g 2Chr 16:3 2091
great gifts of silver, and of g 2Chr 21:3 2091
and spoons, and vessels of g 2Chr 24:14 2091
And he took all the g and the 2Chr 25:24 2091
treasuries for silver, and for g 2Chr 32:27 2091
of silver and a talent of g 2Chr 36:3 2091
help him with silver, and with g Ezr 1:4 2091
with vessels of silver, with g Ezr 1:6 2091
thirty chargers of g, a thousand Ezr 1:9 2091
Thirty basons of g, silver basons Ezr 1:10 2091
All the vessels of g and of silver Ezr 1:11 2091
and one thousand drams of g Ezr 2:69 2091
And the vessels also of g and Ezr 5:14 1722
And to carry the silver and g Ezr 7:15 1722
g that thou canst find in all the Ezr 7:16 1722
the rest of the silver and the g Ezr 7:18 1722
unto them the silver, and the g Ezr 8:25 2091
and of g an hundred talents Ezr 8:26 2091
Also twenty basons of g, of a Ezr 8:27 2091
of fine copper, precious as g Ezr 8:27 2091
the g are a freewill offering Ezr 8:28 2091
weight of the silver, and the g Ezr 8:30 2091
day was the silver and the g Ezr 8:33 2091
treasure a thousand drams of g Neh 7:70 2091
work twenty thousand drams of g Neh 7:71 2091
was twenty thousand drams of g Neh 7:72 2091
the beds were of g and silver, Est 1:6 2091
gave them drink in vessels of g Est 1:7 2091
white, and with a great crown of g Est 8:15 2091
Or with princes that had g Job 3:15 2091
Then shalt thou lay up g as dust Job 22:24 1220
the g of Ophir as the stones of Job 22:24 1220
tried me, I shall come forth as g Job 23:10 2091
a place for g where they fine it Job 28:1 2091
and it hath dust of g Job 28:6 2091
It cannot be gotten for g Job 28:15 5458
be valued with the g of Ophir Job 28:16 3800
The g and the crystal cannot equal Job 28:17 2091
shall not be for jewels of fine g Job 28:17 6337
shall it be valued with pure g Job 28:19 3800
If I have made g my hope Job 31:24 2091
or have said to the fine g Job 31:24 3800
no, not g, nor all the forces of Job 36:19 1222
and every one an earring of g Job 42:11 2091
to be desired are they than g Ps 19:10 2091
yea, than much fine g Ps 19:10 6337
a crown of pure g on his head Ps 21:3 6337
did stand the queen in g of Ophir Ps 45:9 3800
her clothing is of wrought g Ps 45:13 2091
and her feathers with yellow g Ps 68:13 2742
shall be given of the g of Sheba Ps 72:15 2091
them forth also with silver and g Ps 105:37 2091
Their idols are silver and g Ps 115:4 2091
unto me than thousands of g Ps 119:72 2091
I love thy commandments above g Ps 119:127 2091
yea, above fine g Ps 119:127 6337
of the heathen are silver and g Ps 135:15 2091
and the gain thereof than fine g Prov 3:14 2742
and knowledge rather than choice g Prov 8:10 2742
My fruit is better than g Prov 8:19 2742
yea, than fine g Prov 8:19 6337
As a jewel of g in a swine's Prov 11:22 2091
better is it to get wisdom than g Prov 16:16 2742
for silver, and the furnace for g Prov 17:3 2091
There is g, and a multitude of Prov 20:15 2091
favour rather than silver and g Prov 22:1 2091
apples of g in pictures of silver Prov 25:11 2091
As an earring of g, and an Prov 25:12 2091
of g, and an ornament of fine g Prov 25:12 3800
for silver, and the furnace for g Prov 27:21 2091
I gathered me also silver and g Eccl 2:8 2091
jewels, thy neck with chains of g Song 1:10
borders of g with studs of silver Song 1:11 2091
silver, the bottom thereof of g Song 3:10 2091
His head is as the most fine g Song 5:11 6337

His hands are as g rings set with Song 5:14 2091
set upon sockets of fine g Song 5:15 6337
land also is full of silver and g Is 2:7 2091
of silver, and his idols of g Is 2:20 2091
a man more precious than fine g Is 13:12 6337
and as for g, they shall not Is 13:17 2091
of thy molten images of g Is 30:22 2091
of silver, and his idols of g Is 31:7 2091
things, the silver, and the g Is 39:2 2091
spreadeth it over with g, and Is 40:19 2091
They lavish g out of the bag, and Is 46:6 2091
they shall bring g and incense Is 60:6 2091
their g with them, unto the name Is 60:9 2091
For brass I will bring g, and for Is 60:17 2091
deckest thee with ornaments of g Jer 4:30 2091
deck it with silver and with g Jer 10:4 2091
g from Uphaz, the work of the Jer 10:9 2091
that which was of g in g Jer 52:19 2091
How is the g become dim Lam 4:1 2091
how is the most fine g changed Lam 4:1 3800
of Zion, comparable to fine g Lam 4:2 6337
and their g shall be removed Eze 7:19 2091
their g shall not be able to Eze 7:19 2091
Thus wast thou decked with g Eze 16:13 2091
taken thy fair jewels of my g Eze 16:17 2091
and with all precious stones, and g Eze 27:22 2091
thee riches, and hast gotten g Eze 28:4 2091
emerald, and the carbuncle, and g Eze 28:13 2091
to carry away silver and g Eze 38:13 2091
This image's head was of fine g Dan 2:32 1722
the brass, the silver, and the g Dan 2:35 1722
Thou art this head of g Dan 2:38 1722
the clay, the silver, and the g Dan 2:45 1722
the king made an image of g Dan 3:1 1722
wine, and praised the gods of g Dan 5:4 1722
have a chain of g about his neck Dan 5:7 1722
have a chain of g about thy neck Dan 5:16 1722
praised the gods of silver, and g Dan 5:23 1722
put a chain of g about his neck Dan 5:29 1722
were girded with fine g of Uphaz Dan 10:5 3800
vessels of silver and of g Dan 11:8 2091
knew not shall he honour with g Dan 11:38 2091
power over the treasures of g Dan 11:43 2091
and multiplied her silver and g Hos 2:8 2091
their g have they made them idols Hos 8:4 2091
ye have taken my silver and my g Joel 3:5 2091
of silver, take the spoil of g Nah 2:9 2091
Behold, it is laid over with g Hab 2:19 2091
g shall be able to deliver them Zeph 1:18 2091
the g is mine, saith the LORD of Hag 2:8 2091
and behold a candlestick all of g Zec 4:2 2091
Then take silver and g, and make Zec 6:11 2091
fine g as the mire of the streets Zec 9:3 2742
and will try them as g is tried Zec 13:9 2091
shall be gathered together, g Zec 14:14 2091
sons of Levi, and purge them as g Mal 3:3 2091
g, and frankincense, and myrrh Mt 2:11 5557
Provide neither g, nor silver, Mt 10:9 5557
swear by the g of the temple Mt 23:16 5557
for whether is greater, the g Mt 23:17 5557
the temple that sanctifieth the g Mt 23:17 5557
said, Silver and g have I none Acts 3:6 5553
that the Godhead is like unto g Acts 17:29 5557
coveted no man's silver, or g Acts 20:33 5553
man build upon this foundation g 1Cor 3:12 5557
not with broided hair, or g 1Ti 2:9 5557
there are not only vessels of g 2Ti 2:20 5552
overlaid round about with g Heb 9:4 5553
your assembly a man with a g ring Jas 2:2 5554
Your g and silver is cankered Jas 5:3 5557
precious than of g that perisheth 1Pet 1:7 5553
things, as silver and g, from your 1Pet 1:18 5553
the hair, and of wearing of g 1Pet 3:3 5553
to buy of me g tried in the fire Rev 3:18 5553
had on their heads crowns of g Rev 4:4 5552
were as it were crowns like g Rev 9:7 5557
not worship devils, and idols of g Rev 9:20 5552
scarlet colour, and decked with g Rev 17:4 5557
The merchandise of g, and silver, Rev 18:12 5557
and scarlet, and decked with g Rev 18:16 5557
and the city was pure g, like unto Rev 21:18 5553
the street of the city was pure g Rev 21:21 5553

GOLDEN

that the man took a g earring of Gen 24:22 2091
thou shalt make a g crown to the Ex 25:25 2091
A g bell and a pomegranate Ex 28:34 2091
a g bell and a pomegranate, upon Ex 28:34 2091
two g rings shalt thou make to it Ex 30:4 2091
them, Break off the g earrings Ex 32:2 2091
g earrings which were in their Ex 32:3 2091
And they made two other g rings Ex 39:20 2091
the g altar, and the anointing oil Ex 39:38 2091
he put the g altar in the tent of Ex 40:26 2091
forefront, did he put the g plate Lev 8:9 2091
upon the g altar they shall Num 4:11 2091
One g spoon of ten shekels, full Num 7:26 2091
One g spoon of ten shekels, full Num 7:32 2091
One g spoon of ten shekels, full Num 7:38 2091
One g spoon of ten shekels, full Num 7:44 2091
One g spoon of ten shekels, full Num 7:50 2091
One g spoon of ten shekels, full Num 7:56 2091
One g spoon of ten shekels, full Num 7:62 2091
One g spoon of ten shekels, full Num 7:68 2091
One g spoon of ten shekels, full Num 7:74 2091
One g spoon of ten shekels, full Num 7:80 2091
The g spoons were twelve, full of Num 7:86 2091
(For they had g earrings, because Judg 8:24 2091
the weight of the g earrings that Judg 8:26 2091
g emerods, and five g mice 1Sa 6:4 2091
these are the g emerods which the 1Sa 6:17 2091
the g mice, according to the 1Sa 6:18 2091
the g calves that were in Beth-el 2Kin 10:29 2091
for the g basons he gave gold by 1Chr 28:17 2091
the g altar also, and the tables 2Chr 4:19 2091
and there are with you g calves 2Chr 13:8 2091
And also let the g and silver Ezr 6:5 1722
king shall hold out the g sceptre Est 4:11 2091
g sceptre that was in his hand Est 5:2 2091
out the g sceptre toward Esther Est 8:4 2091
or the g bowl be broken, or the Eccl 12:6 2091
a man than the g wedge of Ophir Is 13:12 3800
the g city ceased Is 14:4 4062
Babylon hath been a g cup in the Jer 51:7 2091
down and worship the g image that Dan 3:5 1722
worshipped the g image that Dan 3:7 1722
fall down and worship the g image Dan 3:10 1722
nor worship the g image which Dan 3:12 1722
nor worship the g image which I Dan 3:14 1722
nor worship the g image which Dan 3:18 1722
wine, commanded to bring the g Dan 5:2 1722
Then they brought the g vessels Dan 5:3 1722
g pipes empty the g oil out Zec 4:12 2091
Which had the g censer, and the Heb 9:4 *5552*
wherein was the g pot that had Heb 9:4 *5552*
I saw seven g candlesticks Rev 1:12 *5552*
about the paps with a g girdle Rev 1:13 *5552*
hand, and the seven g candlesticks Rev 1:20 *5552*
midst of the seven g candlesticks Rev 2:1 *5552*
g vials full of odours, which are Rev 5:8 *5552*
at the altar, having a g censer Rev 8:3 *5552*
the g altar which was before the Rev 8:3 *5552*
the g altar which is before God Rev 9:13 *5552*
man, having on his head a g crown Rev 14:14 *5552*
breasts girded with g girdles Rev 15:6 *5552*
unto the seven angels seven g Rev 15:7 *5552*
having a g cup in her hand full Rev 17:4 *5552*
had a g reed to measure the city Rev 21:15 *5552*

GOLDSMITH

the g spreadeth it over with gold Is 40:19 6884
So the carpenter encouraged the g Is 41:7 6884
in the balance, and hire a g Is 46:6 6884

GOLDSMITH'S

the g son unto the place of the Neh 3:31 6885

GOLDSMITHS

the son of Harhaiah, of the g Neh 3:8 6884
the sheep gate repaired the g Neh 3:32 6884

GOLGOTHA (*gol'-go-thah*) See CALVARY. *Hill where Jesus was crucified.*

were come unto a place called G Mt 27:33 *1115*
they bring him unto the place G Mk 15:22 *1115*
which is called in the Hebrew G Jn 19:17 *1115*

GOLIATH (*go-li'-ath*) *Philistine warrior killed by David.*

camp of the Philistines, named G 1Sa 17:4 1555
G by name, out of the armies of 1Sa 17:23 1555
The sword of G the Philistine, 1Sa 21:9 1555
him the sword of G the Philistine 1Sa 22:10 1555
slew the brother of G the Gittite 2Sa 21:19 1555
the brother of G the Gittite 1Chr 20:5 1555

GOMER (*go'-mer*)

1. Son of Japheth.

G, and Magog, and Madai, and Javan, Gen 10:2 1586
And the sons of G Gen 10:3 1586
G, and Magog, and Madai, and Javan, 1Chr 1:5 1586
And the sons of G 1Chr 1:6 1586

2. Descendants of Gomer 1.

G, and all his bands Eze 38:6 1586

3. Wife of Hosea.

took G the daughter of Diblaim Hos 1:3 1586

GOMORRAH (*go-mor'-rah*) See GOMORRHA. *City destroyed by God.*

as thou goest, unto Sodom, and G Gen 10:19 6017
the LORD destroyed Sodom and G Gen 13:10 6017
Sodom, and with Birsha king of G Gen 14:2 6017
king of Sodom, and the king of G Gen 14:8 6017
of Sodom and G fled, and fell there Gen 14:10 6017
took all the goods of Sodom and G Gen 14:11 6017
G is great, and because their sin Gen 18:20 6017
upon G brimstone and fire from the Gen 19:24 6017
And he looked toward Sodom and G Gen 19:28 6017
like the overthrow of Sodom, and G Deut 29:23 6017
of Sodom, and of the fields of G Deut 32:32 6017
we should have been like unto G Is 1:9 6017
law of our God, ye people of G Is 1:10 6017
as when God overthrew Sodom and G Is 13:19 6017
and the inhabitants thereof as G Jer 23:14 6017
As in the overthrow of Sodom and G Jer 49:18 6017
As God overthrew Sodom and G Jer 50:40 6017
you, as God overthrew Sodom and G Amos 4:11 6017
and the children of Ammon as G Zeph 2:9 6017
G into ashes condemned them with 2Pet 2:6 *1116*

GOMORRHA (*go-mor'-rah*) See GOMORRAH. *Greek form of Gomorrah.*

G in the day of judgment, than Mt 10:15 *1116*
G in the day of judgment, than Mk 6:11 *1116*
Sodoma, and been made like unto G Rom 9:29 *1116*
Even as Sodom and G, and the cities Jude 7 *1116*

GONE

Jacob was yet scarce g out from Gen 27:30 3318
mother, and was g to Padan-aram Gen 28:7 3212
though thou wouldest needs be g Gen 31:30 1980
our daughter, and we will be g Gen 34:17 1980
of your households, and be g Gen 42:33 3212
when they were g out of the city, Gen 44:4 3318
the prey, my son, thou art g up Gen 49:9 5927
As soon as I am g out of the city Ex 9:29 3318
herds, as ye have said, and be g Ex 12:32 3212
And when the dew that lay was g up Ex 16:14 5927
the children of Israel were g Ex 19:1 3318
Moses, until he was g into the Ex 33:8 935
after whom they have g a whoring Lev 17:7
if thou hast not g aside to Num 5:19 7847
But if thou hast g aside to Num 5:20 7847
when Moses was g into the Num 7:89 935
which we have g to search it Num 13:32 5674
is wrath g out from the LORD Num 16:46 3318
there is a fire g out of Heshbon Num 21:28 3318
When I was g up into the mount to Deut 9:9 5927
are g out from among you, and have Deut 13:13 3318
And hath g and served other gods, Deut 17:3 3212
That which is g out of thy lips Deut 23:23 4161
shall be when ye be g over Jordan Deut 27:4 5674
he seeth that their power is g Deut 32:36 235
pursued after them were g out Josh 2:7 3318
before us, until we were g over Josh 4:23 5674
which he commanded you, and have g Josh 23:16 1980
When he was g out, his servants Judg 3:24 3318
Abinoam was g up to mount Tabor Judg 4:12 5927
is not the LORD g out before thee Judg 4:14 3318
and the priest, and ye are g away Judg 18:24 3212
of Israel were g up to Mizpeh Judg 20:3 5927
of the LORD is g out against me Ruth 1:13 3318
in law is g back unto her people Ruth 1:15 7725
knew not that Jonathan was g 1Sa 14:3 1980
now, and see who is g from us 1Sa 14:17 1980
is g about, and passed on 1Sa 15:12 5437
and g down to Gilgal 1Sa 15:12 3381
have g the way which the LORD 1Sa 15:20 3212
And as soon as the lad was g 1Sa 20:41 935
when the wine was g out of Nabal 1Sa 25:37 3318
in the morning the people had g 2Sa 2:27 5927
Wherefore hast thou g in unto my 2Sa 3:7 935
him away, and he was g in peace 2Sa 3:22 3212
him away, and he is g in peace 2Sa 3:23 3212
sent him away, and he is quite g 2Sa 3:24 3212
ark of the LORD had g six paces 2Sa 6:13 6805
Amnon said unto her, Arise, be g 2Sa 13:15 3212
They be g over the brook of water 2Sa 17:20 5674
them that was not g over Jordan 2Sa 17:22 5674
and the men of Israel were g away 2Sa 23:9 5927
So when they had g through all 2Sa 24:8 7751
For he is g down this day, and 1Kin 1:25 3381
had g from Jerusalem to Gath 1Kin 2:41 1980
Pharaoh king of Egypt had g up 1Kin 9:16 5927
host was g up to bury the slain 1Kin 11:15 5927
And when he was g, a lion met him 1Kin 13:24 3212
for thou hast g and made thee 1Kin 14:9 3212
away dung, till it be all g 1Kin 14:10
pass, as soon as I am g from thee 1Kin 18:12 3212
was busy here and there, he was g 1Kin 20:40 369
whither he is g down to possess 1Kin 21:18 3381
the messenger that was g to call 1Kin 22:13 1980
that bed on which thou art g up 2Kin 1:4 5927
that bed on which thou art g up 2Kin 1:6 5927
that bed on which thou art g up 2Kin 1:16 5927
to pass, when they were g over 2Kin 2:9 5674
And the Syrians had g out by 2Kin 5:2 3318
and g forth, behold, an host 2Kin 6:15 3318
therefore are they g out of the 2Kin 7:12 3318
afore Isaiah was g out into the 2Kin 20:4 3318
by which it had g down in the 2Kin 20:11 3381
for God is g forth before thee to 1Chr 14:15 3318
but have g from tent to tent, and 1Chr 17:5 1961
of their feasting were g about Job 1:5 5362
shall I arise, and the night be g Job 7:4 4059
me on every side, and I am g Job 19:10 3212
Neither have I g back from the Job 23:12 4185
for a little while, but are g Job 24:24 369
up, they are g away from men Job 28:4 5128
They are all g aside, they are Ps 14:3 5493
Their line is g out through all Ps 19:4 3318
iniquities are g over mine head Ps 38:4 5674
mine eyes, it also is g from me Ps 38:10 369
for I had g with the multitude, I Ps 42:4 5674
and thy billows are g over me Ps 42:7 5674
God is g up with a shout, the Ps 47:5 5927
after he had g in to Bath-sheba Ps 51:t 935
Every one of them is g back Ps 53:3 5472
as for me, my feet were almost g Ps 73:2 5186
Is his mercy clean g for ever Ps 77:8 656
thing that is g out of my lips Ps 89:34 4161
wind passeth over it, and it is g Ps 103:16 369
I am g like the shadow when it Ps 109:23 1980
I have g astray like a lost sheep Ps 119:176 8582
the stream had g over our soul Ps 124:4 5674
proud waters had g over our soul Ps 124:5 5674
at home, he is g a long journey Prov 7:19 1980
but when he is g his way, then he Prov 20:14 235
g from the place of the holy, and Eccl 8:10 1980
is past, the rain is over and g Song 2:11 1980
had withdrawn himself, and was g Song 5:6 5674
Whither is thy beloved g, O thou Song 6:1 1980
My beloved is g down into his Song 6:2 3381
anger, they are g away backward Is 1:4 2114
my people are g into captivity Is 5:13
They are g over the passage Is 10:29 5674
He is g up to Bajith, and to Dibon Is 15:2 5927
For the cry is g round about the Is 15:8 5362
out, they are g over the sea Is 16:8 5674
art wholly g up to the housetops Is 22:1 5927
the mirth of the land is g Is 24:11 1540
which is g down in the sun dial Is 38:8 3381
by which degrees it was g down Is 38:8 3381
that he had not g with his feet Is 41:3 935
the word is g out of my mouth in Is 45:23 3318
themselves are g into captivity Is 46:2 1980
my salvation is g forth, and mine Is 51:5 3318
All we like sheep have g astray Is 53:6 8582
to another than me, and art g up Is 57:8 5927
me, that they are g far from me Jer 2:5
I have not g after Baalim Jer 2:23 1980
she is g up upon every high Jer 3:6 1980
he is g forth from his place to Jer 4:7 3318
they are revolted and g Jer 5:23 3212
beast are fled; they are g Jer 9:10 1980
my children are g forth of me Jer 10:20 3318

and the cry of Jerusalem is g up Jer 14:2 5927
the LORD, thou art g backward Jer 15:6 3212
her sun is g down while it was Jer 15:9 935
g forth into all the land Jer 23:15 3318
of the LORD is g forth in fury Jer 23:19 3318
g forth with you into captivity Jer 29:16 3318
army, which are g up from you Jer 34:21 5927
Now while he was not yet g back Jer 40:5 7725
Egypt, whither ye be g to dwell Jer 44:8 935
which are g into the land of Jer 44:14 935
that are g into the land of Egypt Jer 44:28 935
neither hath he g into captivity Jer 48:11 1980
g up out of her cities, and his Jer 48:15 5927
men are g down to the slaughter Jer 48:15 3381
thy plants are g over the sea Jer 48:32 5674
they have g from mountain to hill Jer 50:6 1980
Judah is g into captivity because Lam 1:3
her children are g into captivity Lam 1:5 1980
they are g without strength Lam 1:6 3212
my young men are g into captivity Lam 1:18 1980
the morning is g forth Eze 7:10 3318
Israel was g up from the cherub Eze 9:3 5927
Ye have not g up into the gaps, Eze 13:5 5927
fire is g out of a rod of her Eze 19:14 3318
because thou hast g a whoring Eze 23:30
and whose scum is not g out of it Eze 24:6 3318
earth are g down from his shadow Eze 31:12 3381
they are g down, they lie Eze 32:21 3381
which are g down uncircumcised Eze 32:24 3381
which are g down to hell with Eze 32:27 3381
which are g down with the slain Eze 32:30 3381
are g forth out of his land Eze 36:20 3318
the heathen, whither they be g Eze 37:21 1980
that are g away far from me Eze 44:10
Chaldeans, The thing is g from me Dan 2:5 230
ye see the thing is g from me Dan 2:8 230
which was g forth to slay the Dan 2:14 5312
and when I am g forth, lo, the Dan 10:20 3318
they have g a whoring from under Hos 4:12
For they are g up to Assyria, a Hos 8:9 5927
for thou hast g a whoring from Hos 9:1
they are g because of destruction Hos 9:6 1980
When will the new moon be g Amos 8:5 5674
But Jonah was g down into the Jonah 1:5 3381
for they are g into captivity Mic 1:16
the gate, and are g out by it Mic 2:13 3318
are g away from mine ordinances Mal 3:7 5493
Ye shall not have g over the Mt 10:23 *5055*
unclean spirit is g out of a man Mt 12:43 *1831*
And when they were g over, they Mt 14:34 *1276*
sheep, and one of them be g astray Mt 18:12 *4105*
and seeketh that which is g astray Mt 18:12
for our lamps are g out Mt 25:8 *4570*
when he was g out into the porch, Mt 26:71 *1831*
when he had g a little farther Mk 1:19 *4260*
that virtue had g out of him Mk 5:30 *1831*
the devil is g out of thy Mk 7:29 *1831*
house, she found the devil g out Mk 7:30 *1831*
when he was g forth into the way, Mk 10:17 *1607*
as the angels were g away from Lk 2:15 *565*
the fishermen were g out of them Lk 5:2 *576*
that virtue is g out of me Lk 8:46 *1831*
to pass, when the devil was g out Lk 11:14 *1831*
unclean spirit is g out of a man Lk 11:24 *1831*
That he was g to be guest with a Lk 19:7 *1525*
as though he would have g further Lk 24:28 *4198*
(For his disciples were g away Jn 4:8 *565*
his disciples were g away alone Jn 6:22 *565*
But when his brethren were g up Jn 7:10 *305*
behold, the world is g after him Jn 12:19 *565*
Therefore, when he was g out Jn 13:31 *1831*
when they had g through the isle Acts 13:6 *1330*
when the Jews were g out of the Acts 13:42 *1826*
Now when they had g throughout Acts 16:6 *1330*
the hope of their gains was g Acts 16:19 *1831*
g up, and saluted the church, he Acts 18:22 *305*
when he had g over those parts, Acts 20:2 *1330*
among whom I have g preaching the Acts 20:25 *1330*
Who also hath g about to profane Acts 24:6 *3985*
And when they were g aside Acts 26:31 *402*
when they had g a little further, Acts 27:28 *1339*
They are all g out of the way, Rom 3:12 *1578*
Who is g into heaven, and is on 1Pet 3:22 *4198*
are g astray, following the way 2Pet 2:15 *4105*
prophets are g out into the world 1Jn 4:1 *1831*
for they have g in the way of Jude 11 *4198*

GOOD

God saw the light, that it was g Gen 1:4 2896
and God saw that it was g Gen 1:10 2896
and God saw that it was g Gen 1:12 2896
and God saw that it was g Gen 1:18 2896
and God saw that it was g Gen 1:21 2896
and God saw that it was g Gen 1:25 2896
made, and, behold, it was very g Gen 1:31 2896
to the sight, and g for food Gen 2:9 2896
and the tree of knowledge of g Gen 2:9 2896
And the gold of that land is g Gen 2:12 2896
of the tree of the knowledge of g Gen 2:17 2896
It is not g that the man should Gen 2:18 2896
and ye shall be as gods, knowing g Gen 3:5 2896
saw that the tree was g for food Gen 3:6 2896
is become as one of us, to know g Gen 3:22 2896
shalt be buried in a g old age Gen 15:15 2896
and fetcht a calf tender and g Gen 18:7 2896
ye to them as is g in your eyes Gen 19:8 2896
down over against him a g way off Gen 21:16 7368
send me g speed this day, and shew Gen 24:12
cannot speak unto thee bad or g Gen 24:50 2896
the ghost, and died in a g old age Gen 25:8 2896
have done unto thee nothing but g Gen 26:29 2896
thence two g kids of the goats Gen 27:9 2896
what g shall my life do me Gen 27:46
God hath endued me with a g dowry Gen 30:20 2896
not to Jacob either g or bad Gen 31:24 2896
not to Jacob either g or bad Gen 31:29 2896
saidst, I will surely do thee g Gen 32:12 3190
saw that the interpretation was g Gen 40:16 2896
came up upon one stalk, rank and g Gen 41:5 2896
came up in one stalk, full and g Gen 41:22 2896
ears devoured the seven g ears Gen 41:24 2896
The seven g kine are seven years Gen 41:26 2896
the seven g ears are seven years Gen 41:26 2896
food of those g years that come Gen 41:35 2896
the thing was g in the eyes of Gen 41:37 3190
servant our father is in g health Gen 43:28 7965
have ye rewarded evil for g Gen 44:4 2896
I will give you the g of the land Gen 45:18 2898
for the g of all the land of Gen 45:20 2898
laden with the g things of Egypt Gen 45:23 2898
and wept on his neck a g while Gen 46:29 5750
And he saw that rest was g Gen 49:15 2896
but God meant it unto g, to bring Gen 50:20 2896
up out of that land unto a g land Ex 3:8 2896
thing that thou doest is not g Ex 18:17 2896
owner of the pit shall make it g Ex 21:34 7999
and he shall not make it g Ex 22:11 7999
he shall not make g that which Ex 22:13 7999
it, he shall surely make it g Ex 22:14 7999
with it, he shall not make it g Ex 22:15 7999
his lips to do evil, or to do g Lev 5:4 3190
killeth a beast shall make it g Lev 24:18 7999
g for a bad, or a bad for a g Lev 27:10 2896
value it, whether it be g or bad Lev 27:12 2896
it, whether it be g or bad Lev 27:14 2896
not search whether it be g or bad Lev 27:33 2896
with us, and we will do thee g Num 10:29 2895
hath spoken g concerning Israel Num 10:29 2896
dwell in, whether it be g or bad Num 13:19 2896
And be ye of g courage, and bring Num 13:20
search it, is an exceeding g land Num 14:7 2896
to do either g or bad of mine own Num 24:13 2896
hast spoken is g for us to do Deut 1:14 2896
It is a g land which the LORD our Deut 1:25 2896
evil generation see that g land Deut 1:35 2896
day had no knowledge between g Deut 1:39 2896
take ye g heed unto yourselves Deut 2:4 3966
see the g land that is beyond Deut 3:25 2896
Take ye therefore g heed unto Deut 4:15 3966
should not go in unto that g land Deut 4:21 2896
go over, and possess that g land Deut 4:22 2896
And houses full of all g things Deut 6:11 2898
g in the sight of the LORD Deut 6:18 2896
possess the g land which the LORD Deut 6:18 2896
LORD our God, for our g always Deut 6:24 2896
God bringeth thee into a g land Deut 8:7 2896
g land which he hath given thee Deut 8:10 2896
to do thee g at thy latter end Deut 8:16 3190
this g land to possess it for thy Deut 9:6 2896
I command thee this day for thy g Deut 10:13 2896
g land which the LORD giveth you Deut 11:17 2896
when thou doest that which is g Deut 12:28 2896
thou shalt rejoice in every g Deut 26:11 2896
open unto thee his g treasure Deut 28:12 2896
rejoiced over you to do you g Deut 28:63 3190
and he will do thee g, and multiply Deut 30:5 3190
in the fruit of thy land, for g Deut 30:9 2896
again rejoice over thee for g Deut 30:9 2896
before thee this day life and g Deut 30:15 2896
of a g courage, fear not, nor be Deut 31:6
Be strong and of a g courage Deut 31:7
said, Be strong and of a g courage Deut 31:23
for the g will of him that dwelt Deut 33:16 7522
Be strong and of a g courage Josh 1:6
and then thou shalt have g success Josh 1:8
Be strong and of a g courage Josh 1:9
only be strong and of a g courage Josh 1:18
as it seemeth g and right unto Josh 9:25 2896
be strong and of g courage Josh 10:25
There failed not ought of any g Josh 21:45 2896
Take g heed therefore unto Josh 23:11 3966
g land which the LORD your God Josh 23:13 2896
thing hath failed of all the g Josh 23:14 2896
that as all g things are come Josh 23:15 2896
destroyed you from off this g Josh 23:15 2896
perish quickly from off the g Josh 23:16 2896
after that he hath done you g Josh 24:20 3190
son of Joash died in a g old age Judg 8:32 2896
my g fruit, and go to be promoted Judg 9:11 2896
us whatsoever seemeth g unto thee Judg 10:15 2896
know I that the LORD will do me g Judg 17:13 3190
land, and, behold, it is very g Judg 18:9 2896
when they were a g way from the Judg 18:22 7368
with them what seemeth g unto you Judg 19:24 2896
Ruth her daughter in law, It is g Ruth 2:22 2896
unto her, Do what seemeth thee g 1Sa 1:23 2896
for it is no g report that I hear 1Sa 2:24 2896
let him do what seemeth him g 1Sa 3:18 2896
us all that seemeth g unto you 1Sa 11:10 2896
but I will teach you the g 1Sa 12:23 2896
Do whatsoever seemeth g unto thee 1Sa 14:36 2896
Saul, Do what seemeth g unto thee 1Sa 14:40 2896
and the lambs, and all that was g 1Sa 15:9 2896
Jonathan spake g of David unto 1Sa 19:4 2896
have been to thee-ward very g 1Sa 19:4 2896
if there be g toward David, and I 1Sa 20:12 2896
him as it shall seem g unto thee 1Sa 24:4 3190
for thou hast rewarded me g 1Sa 24:17 2896
wherefore the LORD reward thee g 1Sa 24:19 2896
was a woman of g understanding 1Sa 25:3 2896
for we come in a g day 1Sa 25:8 2896
But the men were very g unto us 1Sa 25:15 2896
and he hath requited me evil for g 1Sa 25:21 2896
g that he hath spoken concerning 1Sa 25:30 2896
This thing is not g that thou 1Sa 26:16 2896
me in the host is g in my sight 1Sa 29:6 2896
know that thou art g in my sight 1Sa 29:9 2896
all that seemed g to Israel 2Sa 3:19 2896
that seemed g to the whole house 2Sa 3:19
to have brought g tidings 2Sa 4:10 1319
a g piece of flesh, and a flagon 2Sa 6:19
Be of g courage, and let us play 2Sa 10:12
LORD do that which seemeth him g 2Sa 10:12 2896
brother Amnon neither g nor bad 2Sa 13:22 2896
is my lord the king to discern g 2Sa 14:17 2896
it had been g for me to have been 2Sa 14:32 2896
unto him, See, thy matters are g 2Sa 15:3 2896
do to me as seemeth g unto him 2Sa 15:26 2896
me g for his cursing this day 2Sa 16:12 2896
hath given is not g at this time 2Sa 17:7 2896
the g counsel of Ahithophel 2Sa 17:14 2896
And the king said, He is a g man 2Sa 18:27 2896
and cometh with g tidings 2Sa 18:27 2896
and to do what he thought g 2Sa 19:18 2896
therefore what is g in thine eyes 2Sa 19:27 2896
and can I discern between g 2Sa 19:35 2896
him what shall seem g unto thee 2Sa 19:37 2896
that which shall seem g unto thee 2Sa 19:38 2896
offer up what seemeth g unto him 2Sa 24:22 2896
man, and bringest g tidings 1Kin 1:42 2896
unto the king, The saying is g 1Kin 2:38 2896
The word that I have heard is g 1Kin 2:42 2896
that I may discern between g 1Kin 3:9 2896
that thou teach them the g way 1Kin 8:36 2896
one word of all his g promise 1Kin 8:56 2896
speak g words to them, then they 1Kin 12:7 2896
in him there is found some g 1Kin 14:13 2896
root up Israel out of this g land 1Kin 14:15 2896
or, if it seem g to thee, I will 1Kin 21:2 2896
doth not prophesy g concerning me 1Kin 22:8 2896
g unto the king with one mouth 1Kin 22:13 2896
of them, and speak that which is g 1Kin 22:13 2896
would prophesy no g concerning me 1Kin 22:18 2896
city, and shall fell every g tree 2Kin 3:19 2896
mar every g piece of land with 2Kin 3:19 2896
on every g piece of land cast 2Kin 3:25 2896
water, and felled all the g trees 2Kin 3:25 2896
this day is a day of g tidings 2Kin 7:9
even of every g thing of Damascus 2Kin 8:9 2898
that which is g in thine eyes 2Kin 10:5 2896
done that which is g in thy sight 2Kin 20:3 2896
G is the word of the LORD which 2Kin 20:19 2896
And he said, Is it not g, if peace 2Kin 20:19
And they found fat pasture and g 1Chr 4:40 2896
of Israel, If it seem g unto you 1Chr 13:2 2895
a g piece of flesh, and a flagon 1Chr 16:3
for he is g 1Chr 16:34 2896
Be of g courage, and let us behave 1Chr 19:13
do that which is g in his sight 1Chr 19:13 2896
do that which is g in his eyes 1Chr 21:23 2896
be strong, and of g courage 1Chr 22:13
that ye may possess this g land 1Chr 28:8 2896
strong and of g courage, and do it 1Chr 28:20
God, I have of mine own proper g 1Chr 29:3
And he died in a g old age 1Chr 29:28 2896
the LORD, saying, For he is g 2Chr 5:13 2896
thou hast taught them the g way 2Chr 6:27 2896
the LORD, saying, For he is g 2Chr 7:3 2896
speak g words to them, they will 2Chr 10:7 2896
And Asa did that which was g 2Chr 14:2 2896
for he never prophesied g unto me 2Chr 18:7 2896
g to the king with one assent 2Chr 18:12 2896
one of theirs, and speak thou g 2Chr 18:12 2896
he would not prophesy g unto me 2Chr 18:17 2896
there are g things found in thee 2Chr 19:3 2896
and the LORD shall be with the g 2Chr 19:11 2896
because he had done g in Israel 2Chr 24:16 2896
The g LORD pardon every one 2Chr 30:18 2896
the g knowledge of the LORD 2Chr 30:22 2896
and wrought that which was g 2Chr 31:20 2896
because he is g, for his mercy Ezr 3:11 2896
if it seem g to the king, let Ezr 5:17 2869
according to the g hand of his Ezr 7:9 2896
whatsoever shall seem g to thee Ezr 7:18 3191
by the g hand of our God upon us Ezr 8:18 2896
upon all them for g that seek him Ezr 8:22 2896
eat the g of the land, and leave Ezr 9:12 2898
be of g courage, and do it Ezr 10:4
according to the g hand of my God Neh 2:8 2896
of my God which was g upon me Neh 2:18 2896
their hands for this g work Neh 2:18 2896
I said, It is not g that ye do Neh 5:9 2896
Think upon me, my God, for g Neh 5:19 2896
reported his g deeds before me Neh 6:19 2896
g statutes and commandments Neh 9:13 2896
Thou gavest also thy g spirit to Neh 9:20 2896
the g thereof, behold, we are Neh 9:36 2898
wipe not out my g deeds that I Neh 13:14 2617
Remember me, O my God, for g Neh 13:31 2896
with them as it seemeth g to thee Est 3:11 2896
If it seem g unto the king, let Est 5:4 2895
who had spoken g for the king Est 7:9 2896
and gladness, a feast and a g day Est 8:17 2896
a g day, and of sending portions Est 9:19 2896
and from mourning into a g day Est 9:22 2896
shall we receive g at the hand of Job 2:10 2896
it, and know thou it for thy g Job 5:27
mine eye shall no more see g Job 7:7 2896
they flee away, they see no g Job 9:25 2896
Is it g unto thee that thou Job 10:3 2896
Is it g that he should search you Job 13:9 2896
speeches wherewith he can do no g Job 15:3 3276
their g is not in their hand Job 21:16 2898
filled their houses with g things Job 22:18 2896
thereby g shall come unto thee Job 22:21 2896
and doeth not g to the widow Job 24:21 3190
When I looked for g, then evil Job 30:26 2896
us know among ourselves what is g Job 34:4 2896
Their young ones are in g liking Job 39:4 2492
that say, Who will shew us any g Ps 4:6 2896
works, there is none that doeth g Ps 14:1 2896
there is none that doeth g Ps 14:3 2896

G and upright is the LORD Ps 25:8 2896
be of g courage, and he shall Ps 27:14
Be of g courage, and he shall Ps 31:24
O taste and see that the LORD is g Ps 34:8 2896
LORD shall not want any g thing Ps 34:10 2896
many days, that he may see g Ps 34:12 2896
Depart from evil, and do g Ps 34:14 2896
They rewarded me evil for g to Ps 35:12 2896
left off to be wise, and to do g Ps 36:3 3190
himself in a way that is not g Ps 36:4 2896
Trust in the LORD, and do g Ps 37:3 2896
The steps of a g man are ordered Ps 37:23
Depart from evil, and do g Ps 37:27 2896
evil for g are mine adversaries Ps 38:20 2896
I follow the thing that g is Ps 38:20 2896
I held my peace, even from g Ps 39:2 2896
My heart is inditing a g matter Ps 45:1 2896
Do g in thy g pleasure unto Ps 51:18 3190
Do g in thy g pleasure unto Ps 51:18
Thou lovest evil more than g Ps 52:3 2896
for it is g before thy saints Ps 52:9 2896
there is none that doeth g Ps 53:1 2896
there is none that doeth g Ps 53:3 2896
for it is g Ps 54:6 2896
for thy lovingkindness is g Ps 69:16 2896
Truly God is g to Israel, even to Ps 73:1 2896
But it is g for me to draw near Ps 73:28 2896
no g thing will he withhold from Ps 84:11 2896
LORD shall give that which is g Ps 85:12 2896
For thou, Lord, art g, and ready Ps 86:5 2896
Shew me a token for g Ps 86:17 2896
It is a g thing to give thanks Ps 92:1 2896
For the LORD is g Ps 100:5 2896
thy mouth with g things Ps 103:5 2896
hand, they are filled with g Ps 104:28 2896
for he is g Ps 106:1 2896
I may see the g of thy chosen Ps 106:5 2896
thanks unto the LORD, for he is g Ps 107:1 2896
they have rewarded me evil for g Ps 109:5 2896
because thy mercy is g, deliver Ps 109:21 2896
a g understanding have all they Ps 111:10 2896
A g man sheweth favour, and Ps 112:5 2896
for he is g Ps 118:1 2896
for he is g Ps 118:29 2896
for thy judgments are g Ps 119:39 2896
Teach me g judgment and knowledge Ps 119:66 2898
Thou art g, and doest g Ps 119:68 2896
Thou art g, and doest g Ps 119:68 2895
It is g for me that I have been Ps 119:71 2896
Be surety for thy servant for g Ps 119:122 2896
LORD our God I will seek thy g Ps 122:9 2896
Do g, O LORD, unto those that be Ps 125:4 2895
O LORD, unto those that be g Ps 125:4 2896
thou shalt see the g of Jerusalem Ps 128:5 2898
Behold, how g and how pleasant it Ps 133:1 2896
for the LORD is g Ps 135:3 2896
for he is g Ps 136:1 2896
thy spirit is g Ps 143:10 2896
The LORD is g to all Ps 145:9 2896
for it is g to sing praises unto Ps 147:1 2896
yea, every g path Prov 2:9 2896
mayest walk in the way of g men Prov 2:20 2896
g understanding in the sight of Prov 3:4 2896
Withhold not g from them to whom Prov 3:27 2896
For I give you g doctrine Prov 4:2 2896
man doeth g to his own soul Prov 11:17 1580
desire of the righteous is only g Prov 11:23 2896
seeketh g procureth favour Prov 11:27 2896
A g man obtaineth favour of the Prov 12:2 2896
with g by the fruit of his mouth Prov 12:14 2896
but a g word maketh it glad Prov 12:25 2896
A man shall eat g by the fruit of Prov 13:2 2896
G understanding giveth favour Prov 13:15 2896
the righteous g shall be repaid Prov 13:21 2896
A g man leaveth an inheritance to Prov 13:22 2896
a g man shall be satisfied from Prov 14:14 2896
The evil bow before the g Prov 14:19 2896
shall be to them that devise g Prov 14:22 2896
beholding the evil and the g Prov 15:3 2896
spoken in due season, how g is it Prov 15:23 2896
a g report maketh the bones fat Prov 15:30 2896
a matter wisely shall find g Prov 16:20 2896
him into the way that is not g Prov 16:29 2896
Whoso rewardeth evil for g Prov 17:13 2896
hath a froward heart findeth no g Prov 17:20 2896
heart doeth g like a medicine Prov 17:22 3190
Also to punish the just is not g Prov 17:26 2896
It is not g to accept the person Prov 18:5 2896
findeth a wife findeth a g thing Prov 18:22 2896
be without knowledge, it is not g Prov 19:2 2896
understanding shall find g Prov 19:8 2896
and with g advice make war Prov 20:18
and a false balance is not g Prov 20:23 2896
A g name is rather to be chosen Prov 22:1
eat thou honey, because it is g Prov 24:13 2896
It is not g to have respect of Prov 24:23 2896
a g blessing shall come upon them Prov 24:25 2896
so is g news from a far country Prov 25:25 2896
It is not g to eat much honey Prov 25:27 2896
shall have g things in possession Prov 28:10 2896
have respect of persons is not g Prov 28:21 2896
She will do him g and not evil all Prov 31:12 2896
that her merchandise is g Prov 31:18 2896
was that g for the sons of men Eccl 2:3 2896
his soul enjoy g in his labour Eccl 2:24 2896
man that is g in his sight wisdom Eccl 2:26 2896
give to him that is g before God Eccl 2:26 2896
I know that there is no g in them Eccl 3:12 2896
rejoice, and to do g in his life Eccl 3:12 2896
enjoy the g of all his labour, it Eccl 3:13 2896
I labour, and bereave my soul of g Eccl 4:8 2896
because they have a g reward for Eccl 4:9 2896
what g is there to the owners Eccl 5:11 3788
it is g and comely for one to eat Eccl 5:18 2896
to enjoy the g of all his labour Eccl 5:18 2896
and his soul be not filled with g Eccl 6:3 2896
twice told, yet hath he seen no g Eccl 6:6 2896
what is g for man in this life Eccl 6:12 2896
A g name is better than precious Eccl 7:1
Wisdom is g with an inheritance Eccl 7:11 2896
It is g that thou shouldest take Eccl 7:18 2896
just man upon earth, that doeth g Eccl 7:20 2896
to the g and to the clean, and to Eccl 9:2 2896
as is the g, so is the sinner Eccl 9:2 2896
but one sinner destroyeth much g Eccl 9:18 2896
they both shall be alike g Eccl 11:6 2896
yea, he gave g heed, and sought Eccl 12:9
secret thing, whether it be g Eccl 12:14 2896
of thy g ointments thy name is as Song 1:3 2896
the tender grape give a g smell Song 2:13
ye shall eat the g of the land Is 1:19 2898
that call evil g, and g evil Is 5:20 2896
refuse the evil, and choose the g Is 7:15 2896
refuse the evil, and choose the g Is 7:16 2896
done that which is g in thy sight Is 38:3 2896
G is the word of the LORD which Is 39:8 2896
O Zion, that bringest g tidings Is 40:9 1319
that bringest g tidings, lift up Is 40:9 1319
to his brother, Be of g courage Is 41:6
yea, do g, or do evil, that we Is 41:23 1390
one that bringeth g tidings Is 41:27 1319
of him that bringeth g tidings Is 52:7 1319
that bringeth g tidings of g Is 52:7 2896
me, and eat ye that which is g Is 55:2 2896
to preach g tidings unto the meek Is 61:1 1319
walketh in a way that was not g Is 65:2 2896
do evil, but to do g they have no Jer 4:22 3190
have withholden g things from you Jer 5:25 2896
the old paths, where is the g way Jer 6:16 2896
looked for peace, but no g came Jer 8:15 2896
also is it in them to do g Jer 10:5 3190
girdle, which is g for nothing Jer 13:10 6743
then may ye also do g, that are Jer 13:23 3190
not for this people for their g Jer 14:11 2896
for peace, and there is no g Jer 14:19 2896
and shall not see when g cometh Jer 17:6 2896
as seemed g to the potter to make Jer 18:4 3474
then I will repent of the g Jer 18:10 2896
make your ways and your doings g Jer 18:11 3190
Shall evil be recompensed for g Jer 18:20 2896
before thee to speak g for them Jer 18:20 2896
this city for evil, and not for g Jer 21:10 2896
One basket had very g figs Jer 24:2 2896
the g figs, very g Jer 24:3 2896
the g figs, very g Jer 24:3 2896
Like these g figs, so will I Jer 24:5 2896
land of the Chaldeans for their g Jer 24:5 2896
set mine eyes upon them for g Jer 24:6 2896
do with me as seemeth g and meet Jer 26:14 2896
perform my g word toward you, in Jer 29:10 2896
neither shall he behold the g Jer 29:32 2896
me for ever, for the g of them Jer 32:39 2896
turn away from them, to do them g Jer 32:40 3190
rejoice over them to do them g Jer 32:41 2895
the g that I have promised them Jer 32:42 2896
all the g that I do unto them Jer 33:9 2896
for the LORD is g Jer 33:11 2896
that I will perform that g thing Jer 33:14 2896
this city for evil, and not for g Jer 39:16 2896
If it seem g unto thee to come Jer 40:4 2896
whither it seemeth g and Jer 40:4 2896
Whether it be g, or whether it be Jer 42:6 2896
over them for evil, and not for g Jer 44:27 2896
The LORD is g unto them that wait Lam 3:25 2896
It is g that a man should both Lam 3:26 2896
It is g for a man that he bear Lam 3:27 2896
High proceedeth not evil and g Lam 3:38 2896
I took them away as I saw g Eze 16:50
It was planted in a g soil by Eze 17:8 2896
which is not g among his people Eze 18:18 2896
also statutes that were not g Eze 20:25 2896
into it, even every g piece Eze 24:4 2896
I will feed them in a g pasture Eze 34:14 2896
there shall they lie in a g fold Eze 34:14 2896
to have eaten up the g pasture Eze 34:18 2896
and your doings that were not g Eze 36:31 2896
I thought it g to shew the signs Dan 4:2 8232
because the shadow thereof is g Hos 4:13 2896
hath cast off the thing that is g Hos 8:3 2896
Seek g, and not evil, that ye may Amos 5:14 2896
Hate the evil, and love the g Amos 5:15 2896
upon them for evil, and not for g Amos 9:4 2896
of Maroth waited carefully for g Mic 1:12 2896
do not my words do g to him that Mic 2:7 3190
Who hate the g, and love the evil Mic 3:2 2896
shewed thee, O man, what is g Mic 6:8 2896
The g man is perished out of the Mic 7:2 2623
The LORD is g, a strong hold in Nah 1:7 2896
of him that bringeth g tidings Nah 1:15 1319
heart, The LORD will not do g Zeph 1:12 3190
that talked with me with g words Zec 1:13 2896
I said unto them, If ye think g Zec 11:12 2896
it with g will at your hand Mal 2:13 7522
is g in the sight of the LORD Mal 2:17 2896
not forth g fruit is hewn down Mt 3:10 *2570*
it is thenceforth g for nothing Mt 5:13 *2480*
that they may see your g works Mt 5:16 *2570*
do g to them that hate you, and Mt 5:44 *2573*
to rise on the evil and on the g Mt 5:45 *18*
know how to give g gifts unto Mt 7:11 *18*
g things to them that ask him Mt 7:11 *18*
Even so every g tree bringeth Mt 7:17 *18*
bringeth forth g fruit Mt 7:17 *2570*
A g tree cannot bring forth evil Mt 7:18 *18*
corrupt tree bring forth g fruit Mt 7:18 *2570*
not forth g fruit is hewn down Mt 7:19 *2570*
there was a g way off from them Mt 8:30 *3112*
Son, be of g cheer Mt 9:2
said, Daughter, be of g comfort Mt 9:22
for so it seemed g in thy sight Mt 11:26 *2107*
the tree g, and his fruit g Mt 12:33 *2570*
ye, being evil, speak g things Mt 12:34 *18*
A g man out of the g treasure Mt 12:35 *18*
the heart bringeth forth g things Mt 12:35 *18*
But other fell into g ground Mt 13:8 *2570*
g ground is he that heareth the Mt 13:23 *2570*
which sowed g seed in his field Mt 13:24 *2570*
not thou sow g seed in thy field Mt 13:27 *2570*
He that soweth the g seed is the Mt 13:37 *2570*
the g seed are the children of Mt 13:38 *2570*
and gathered the g into vessels Mt 13:48 *2570*
unto them, saying, Be of g cheer Mt 14:27
it is g for us to be here Mt 17:4 *2570*
his wife, it is not g to marry Mt 19:10 *4851*
G Master, what g thing shall I Mt 19:16 *18*
unto him, Why callest thou me g Mt 19:17 *18*
there is none g but one, that is, Mt 19:17 *18*
Is thine eye evil, because I am g Mt 20:15 *18*
many as they found, both bad and g Mt 22:10 *18*
said unto him, Well done, thou g Mt 25:21 *18*
lord said unto him, Well done, g Mt 25:23 *18*
she hath wrought a g work upon me Mt 26:10 *18*
it had been g for that man if he Mt 26:24 *18*
Is it lawful to do g on the Mk 3:4 *15*
And other fell on g ground Mk 4:8 *2570*
they which are sown on g ground Mk 4:20 *2570*
and saith unto them, Be of g cheer Mk 6:50
it is g for us to be here Mk 9:5 *2750*
Salt is g Mk 9:50 *2750*
G Master, what shall I do that I Mk 10:17 *18*
unto him, Why callest thou me g Mk 10:18 *18*
there is none g but one, that is, Mk 10:18 *18*
unto him, Be of g comfort, rise Mk 10:49
she hath wrought a g work on me Mk 14:6 *2570*
ye will ye may do them g Mk 14:7 *2095*
g were it for that man if he had Mk 14:21 *2570*
It seemed g to me also, having Lk 1:3
filled the hungry with g things Lk 1:53 *18*
I bring you g tidings of great Lk 2:10 *2097*
on earth peace, g will toward men Lk 2:14 *2107*
not forth g fruit is hewn down Lk 3:9 *2570*
on the sabbath days to do g Lk 6:9 *15*
do g to them which hate you, Lk 6:27 *2573*
do g to them which do g to you Lk 6:33 *15*
But love ye your enemies, and do g Lk 6:35 *15*
g measure, pressed down, and Lk 6:38 *2570*
For a g tree bringeth not forth Lk 6:43 *2570*
corrupt tree bring forth g fruit Lk 6:43 *2570*
A g man out of the g treasure Lk 6:45 *18*
bringeth forth that which is g Lk 6:45 *18*
And other fell on g ground Lk 8:8 *18*
But that on the g ground are they Lk 8:15 *2570*
g heart, having heard the word, Lk 8:15 *18*
her, Daughter, be of g comfort Lk 8:48
it is g for us to be here Lk 9:33 *2570*
for so it seemed g in thy sight Lk 10:21
and Mary hath chosen that g part Lk 10:42 *18*
know how to give g gifts unto Lk 11:13 *18*
for it is your Father's g Lk 12:32
Salt is g Lk 14:34 *2570*
lifetime receivedst thy g things Lk 16:25 *18*
G Master, what shall I do to Lk 18:18 *18*
unto him, Why callest thou me g Lk 18:19 *18*
none is g, save one, that is, God Lk 18:19 *18*
unto him, Well, thou g servant Lk 19:17 *18*
and he was a g man, and a just Lk 23:50 *18*
Can there any g thing come out of Jn 1:46 *18*
beginning doth set forth g wine Jn 2:10 *2570*
hast kept the g wine until now Jn 2:10 *2570*
they that have done g, unto the Jn 5:29 *18*
for some said, He is a g man Jn 7:12 *18*
I am the g shepherd Jn 10:11 *2570*
the g shepherd giveth his life Jn 10:11 *2570*
I am the g shepherd, and know my Jn 10:14 *2570*
Many g works have I shewed you Jn 10:32 *2570*
For a g work we stone thee not Jn 10:33 *2570*
but be of g cheer Jn 16:33
g deed done to the impotent man Acts 4:9 *2108*
this woman was full of g works Acts 9:36 *18*
of g report among all the nation Acts 10:22 *18*
who went about doing g, and Acts 10:38 *2109*
For he was a g man, and full of Acts 11:24 *18*
without witness, in that he did g Acts 14:17 *15*
ye know how that a g while ago Acts 15:7
It seemed g unto us, being Acts 15:25
For it seemed g to the Holy Ghost Acts 15:28
But Paul thought not g to take Acts 15:38 *515*
this tarried there yet a g while Acts 18:18 *2425*
having a g report of all the Jews Acts 22:12
I have lived in all g conscience Acts 23:1 *18*
by him, and said, Be of g cheer Acts 23:11
now I exhort you to be of g cheer Acts 27:22
Wherefore, sirs, be of g cheer Acts 27:25
Then were they all of g cheer Acts 27:36
to every man that worketh g Rom 2:10 *18*
Let us do evil, that g may come Rom 3:8 *18*
there is none that doeth g Rom 3:12 *5544*
yet peradventure for a g man some Rom 5:7 *18*
commandment holy, and just, and g Rom 7:12 *18*
which is g made death unto me Rom 7:13 *18*
death in me by that which is g Rom 7:13 *18*
consent unto the law that it is g Rom 7:16 *2570*
in my flesh,) dwelleth no g thing Rom 7:18 *18*
that which is g I find not Rom 7:18 *2570*
For the g that I would I do not Rom 7:19 *18*
a law, that, when I would do g Rom 7:21 *2570*
for g to them that love God Rom 8:28 *18*
neither having done any g or evil Rom 9:11 *18*
and bring glad tidings of g things Rom 10:15 *18*
to nature into a g olive tree Rom 11:24 *2565*
that ye may prove what is that g Rom 12:2 *18*
cleave to that which is g Rom 12:9 *18*

of evil, but overcome evil with g ... Rom 12:21 18
are not a terror to g works ... Rom 13:3 18
do that which is g, and thou shalt ... Rom 13:3 18
the minister of God to thee for g ... Rom 13:4 18
not then your g be evil spoken of ... Rom 14:16 18
It is g neither to eat flesh, nor ... Rom 14:21 2570
for his g to edification ... Rom 15:2 18
by g words and fair speeches ... Rom 16:18 5542
you wise unto that which is g ... Rom 16:19 18
Your glorying is not g ... 1Cor 5:6 2570
It is g for a man not to touch a ... 1Cor 7:1 2570
It is g for them if they abide ... 1Cor 7:8 2570
is g for the present distress ... 1Cor 7:26 2570
that it is g for a man so to be ... 1Cor 7:26 2570
communications corrupt g manners ... 1Cor 15:33 5543
hath done, whether it be g or bad ... 2Cor 5:10 18
by evil report and g report ... 2Cor 6:8 2162
may abound to every g work ... 2Cor 9:8 18
be of g comfort, be of one mind, ... 2Cor 13:11
But it is g to be zealously ... Gal 4:18 2570
affected always in a g thing ... Gal 4:18 2570
him that teacheth in all g things ... Gal 6:6 18
let us do g unto all men, ... Gal 6:10 18
according to the g pleasure of ... Eph 1:5
according to his g pleasure which ... Eph 1:9
in Christ Jesus unto g works ... Eph 2:10 18
his hands the thing which is g ... Eph 4:28 18
but that which is g to the use of ... Eph 4:29 18
With g will doing service, as to ... Eph 6:7 2133
whatsoever g thing any man doeth ... Eph 6:8 18
that he which hath begun a g work ... Phil 1:6 18
and some also of g will ... Phil 1:15 2107
will and to do of his g pleasure ... Phil 2:13
that I also may be of g comfort ... Phil 2:19
whatsoever things are of g report ... Phil 4:8 2163
being fruitful in every g work ... Col 1:10 18
we thought it g to be left at ... 1Th 3:1 2106
brought us g tidings of your ... 1Th 3:6 2097
that ye have g remembrance of us ... 1Th 3:6 18
but ever follow that which is g ... 1Th 5:15 18
hold fast that which is g ... 1Th 5:21 2570
fulfil all the g pleasure of his ... 2Th 1:11
and g hope through grace, ... 2Th 2:16 18
and stablish you in every g word ... 2Th 2:17 18
of a g conscience, and of faith ... 1Ti 1:5 18
But we know that the law is g ... 1Ti 1:8 2570
by them mightest war a g warfare ... 1Ti 1:18 2570
Holding faith, and a g conscience ... 1Ti 1:19 18
For this is g and acceptable in ... 1Ti 2:3 2570
godliness) with g works ... 1Ti 2:10 18
of a bishop, he desireth a g work ... 1Ti 3:1 2570
sober, of g behaviour, given to ... 1Ti 3:2
Moreover he must have a g report ... 1Ti 3:7 2570
purchase to themselves a g degree ... 1Ti 3:13 2570
For every creature of God is g ... 1Ti 4:4 2570
thou shalt be a g minister of ... 1Ti 4:6 2570
of g doctrine, whereunto thou ... 1Ti 4:6 2570
for that is g and acceptable ... 1Ti 5:4 2570
Well reported of for g works ... 1Ti 5:10 2570
diligently followed every g work ... 1Ti 5:10 18
Likewise also the g works of some ... 1Ti 5:25 2570
Fight the g fight of faith, lay ... 1Ti 6:12 2570
hast professed a g profession ... 1Ti 6:12 2570
Pilate witnessed a g confession ... 1Ti 6:13 2570
That they do g, that they be rich ... 1Ti 6:18 14
that they be rich in g works ... 1Ti 6:18 2570
up in store for themselves a g ... 1Ti 6:19 2570
That g thing which was committed ... 2Ti 1:14 2570
as a g soldier of Jesus Christ ... 2Ti 2:3 2570
and prepared unto every g work ... 2Ti 2:21 18
despisers of those that are g ... 2Ti 3:3 865
furnished unto all g works ... 2Ti 3:17 18
I have fought a g fight, I have ... 2Ti 4:7 2570
of hospitality, a lover of g men ... Titus 1:8 5358
unto every g work reprobate ... Titus 1:16 18
much wine, teachers of g things ... Titus 2:3 2567
chaste, keepers at home, g ... Titus 2:5 18
thyself a pattern of g works ... Titus 2:7 2570
but shewing all g fidelity ... Titus 2:10 18
people, zealous of g works ... Titus 2:14 2570
to be ready to every g work ... Titus 3:1 18
be careful to maintain g works ... Titus 3:8 2570
These things are g and profitable ... Titus 3:8 2570
g works for necessary uses ... Titus 3:14 2570
by the acknowledging of every g ... Philem 6 18
exercised to discern both g ... Heb 5:14 2570
And have tasted the g word of God ... Heb 6:5 2570
high priest of g things to come ... Heb 9:11 18
a shadow of g things to come ... Heb 10:1 18
provoke unto love and to g works ... Heb 10:24 2570
it the elders obtained a g report ... Heb 11:2
him as g as dead, so many as the ... Heb 11:12
having obtained a g report ... Heb 11:39
For it is a g thing that the ... Heb 13:9 2570
But to do g and to communicate ... Heb 13:16 2140
we trust we have a g conscience ... Heb 13:18 2570
in every g work to do his will ... Heb 13:21 18
Every g gift and every perfect ... Jas 1:17 18
him, Sit thou here in a g place ... Jas 2:3 2573
let him shew out of a g ... Jas 3:13 2570
g fruits, without partiality, and ... Jas 3:17 18
to him that knoweth to do g ... Jas 4:17 2570
they may by your g works ... 1Pet 2:12 2570
not only to the g and gentle, but ... 1Pet 2:18 18
see g days, let him refrain his ... 1Pet 3:10 18
Let him eschew evil, and do g ... 1Pet 3:11 18
be followers of that which is g ... 1Pet 3:13 18
Having a g conscience ... 1Pet 3:16 18
your g conversation in Christ ... 1Pet 3:16 18
but the answer of a g conscience ... 1Pet 3:21 18
as g stewards of the manifold ... 1Pet 4:10 2570
But whoso hath this world's g ... 1Jn 3:17 979
is evil, but that which is g ... 3Jn 11 18
He that doeth g is of God ... 3Jn 11 15
Demetrius hath g report of all ... 3Jn 12

GOODLIER
of Israel a g person than he ... 1Sa 9:2 2896

GOODLIEST
your g young men, and your asses, ... 1Sa 8:16 2896
also and thy children, even the g ... 1Kin 20:3 2896

GOODLINESS
all the g thereof is as the ... Is 40:6 2617

GOODLY
Rebekah took g raiment of her ... Gen 27:15 2530
And Joseph was a g person, and well ... Gen 39:6
he giveth g words ... Gen 49:21 8233
she saw him that he was a g child ... Ex 2:2 2896
g bonnets of fine linen, and linen ... Ex 39:28 6287
first day the boughs of g trees ... Lev 23:40 1926
How g are thy tents, O Jacob, and ... Num 24:5 2896
dwelt, and all their g castles ... Num 31:10
that g mountain, and Lebanon ... Deut 3:25 2896
g cities, which thou buildedst ... Deut 6:10 2896
art full, and hast built g houses ... Deut 8:12 2896
the spoils a g Babylonish garment ... Josh 7:21 2896
Saul, a choice young man, and a g ... 1Sa 9:2 2896
countenance, and g to look to ... 1Sa 16:12 2896
And he slew an Egyptian, a g man ... 2Sa 23:21 4758
and he also was a very g man ... 1Kin 1:6 2896
with the g vessels of the house ... 2Chr 36:10 2532
all the g vessels thereof ... 2Chr 36:19 4261
Gavest thou the g wings unto the ... Job 39:13 7443
yea, I have a g heritage ... Ps 16:6 8231
thereof were like the g cedars ... Ps 80:10 410
a g heritage of the hosts of ... Jer 3:19 6643
olive tree, fair, and of g fruit ... Jer 11:16
fruit, that it might be a g vine ... Eze 17:8 155
and bear fruit, and be a g cedar ... Eze 17:23 117
his land they have made g images ... Hos 10:1 2896
your temples my g pleasant things ... Joel 3:5 2896
them as his g horse in the battle ... Zec 10:3 1935
a g price that I was prised at of ... Zec 11:13 145
a merchant man, seeking g pearls ... Mt 13:45 2573
how it was adorned with g stones ... Lk 21:5 2573
in g apparel, and there come in ... Jas 2:2 2986
g are departed from thee, and thou ... Rev 18:14 2986

GOODMAN
For the g is not at home, he is ... Prov 7:19 376
against the g of the house ... Mt 20:11 3611
that if the g of the house had ... Mt 24:43 3611
in, say ye to the g of the house ... Mk 14:14 3611
that if the g of the house had ... Lk 12:39 3611
shall say unto the g of the house ... Lk 22:11 3611

GOODNESS
the g which the LORD had done to ... Ex 18:9 2896
make all my g pass before thee ... Ex 33:19 2898
longsuffering, and abundant in g ... Ex 34:6 2617
that what g the LORD shall do ... Num 10:32 2896
according to all the g which he ... Judg 8:35 2896
promised this g unto thy servant ... 2Sa 7:28 2896
glad of heart for all the g that ... 1Kin 8:66 2896
promised this g unto thy servant ... 1Chr 17:26 2896
and let thy saints rejoice in g ... 2Chr 6:41 2896
merry in heart for the g that the ... 2Chr 7:10 2896
of the acts of Hezekiah, and his g ... 2Chr 32:32 2617
of the acts of Josiah, and his g ... 2Chr 35:26 2617
themselves in thy great g ... Neh 9:25 2898
in thy great g that thou gavest ... Neh 9:35 2898
my g extendeth not to thee ... Ps 16:2 2896
him with the blessings of g ... Ps 21:3 2896
Surely g and mercy shall follow me ... Ps 23:6 2896
I had believed to see the g of ... Ps 27:13 2898
Oh how great is thy g, which thou ... Ps 31:19 2898
is full of the g of the LORD ... Ps 33:5 2617
the g of God endureth continually ... Ps 52:1 2617
satisfied with the g of thy house ... Ps 65:4 2898
Thou crownest the year with thy g ... Ps 65:11 2896
prepared of thy g for the poor ... Ps 68:10 2896
would praise the LORD for his g ... Ps 107:8 2617
and filleth the hungry soul with g ... Ps 107:9 2896
would praise the LORD for his g ... Ps 107:15 2617
would praise the LORD for his g ... Ps 107:21 2617
would praise the LORD for his g ... Ps 107:31 2617
My g, and my fortress ... Ps 144:2 2617
utter the memory of thy great g ... Ps 145:7 2898
will proclaim every one his own g ... Prov 20:6 2617
the great g toward the house of ... Is 63:7 2898
fruit thereof and the g thereof ... Jer 2:7 2898
together to the g of the LORD ... Jer 31:12 2898
shall be satisfied with my g ... Jer 31:14 2898
fear and tremble for all the g ... Jer 33:9 2896
LORD and his g in the latter days ... Hos 3:5 2898
for your g is as a morning cloud, ... Hos 6:4 2617
according to the g of his land ... Hos 10:1 2896
For how great is his g, and how ... Zec 9:17 2898
thou the riches of his g and ... Rom 2:4 5544
not knowing that the g of God ... Rom 2:4 5543
Behold therefore the g and ... Rom 11:22 5544
but toward thee, g ... Rom 11:22 5544
if thou continue in his g ... Rom 11:22 5544
that ye also are full of g ... Rom 15:14 19
longsuffering, gentleness, g ... Gal 5:22 19
fruit of the Spirit is in all g ... Eph 5:9 19
all the good pleasure of his g ... 2Th 1:11 19

GOODNESS'
remember thou me for thy g sake ... Ps 25:7 2898

GOODS
And they took all the g of Sodom ... Gen 14:11 7399
son, who dwelt in Sodom, and his g ... Gen 14:12 7399
And he brought back all the g ... Gen 14:16 7399
again his brother Lot, and his g ... Gen 14:16 7399
persons, and take the g to thyself ... Gen 14:21 7399
for all the g of his master were ... Gen 24:10 2898
all his g which he had gotten, ... Gen 31:18 7399
took their cattle, and their g ... Gen 46:6 7399
his hand unto his neighbour's g ... Ex 22:8 4399
his hand unto his neighbour's g ... Ex 22:11 4399
unto Korah, and all their g ... Num 16:32 7399
all their flocks, and all their g ... Num 31:9 2428
for their cattle, and for their g ... Num 35:3 7399
shall make thee plenteous in g ... Deut 28:11 2896
and thy wives, and all thy g ... 2Chr 21:14 7399
silver, and with gold, and with g ... Ezr 1:4 7399
of silver, with gold, with g ... Ezr 1:6 7399
that of the king's g, even of the ... Ezr 6:8 5232
or to confiscation of g, or to ... Ezr 7:26 5232
and possessed houses full of all g ... Neh 9:25 2898
his hands shall restore their g ... Job 20:10 202
shall no man look for his g ... Job 20:21 2898
his g shall flow away in the day ... Job 20:28
When g increase, they are ... Eccl 5:11 2896
which have gotten cattle and g ... Eze 38:12 7075
and gold, to take away cattle and g ... Eze 38:13 7075
Therefore their g shall become a ... Zeph 1:13 2428
man's house, and spoil his g ... Mt 12:29 4632
make him ruler over all his g ... Mt 24:47 5224
and delivered unto them his g ... Mt 25:14 5224
man's house, and spoil his g ... Mk 3:27 4632
away thy g ask them not again ... Lk 6:30 4674
his palace, his g are in peace ... Lk 11:21 5224
I bestow all my fruits and my g ... Lk 12:18 18
thou hast much g laid up for many ... Lk 12:19 18
portion of g that falleth to me ... Lk 15:12 3776
unto him that he had wasted his g ... Lk 16:1 5224
the half of my g I give to the ... Lk 19:8 5224
And sold their possessions and g ... Acts 2:45 5223
bestow all my g to feed the poor ... 1Cor 13:3 5224
joyfully the spoiling of your g ... Heb 10:34 5224
I am rich, and increased with g ... Rev 3:17 4147

GOPHER
Make thee an ark of g wood ... Gen 6:14 1613

GORE
If an ox g a man or a woman, that ... Ex 21:28 5055

GORED
Whether he have g a son ... Ex 21:31 5055
or have g a daughter, according ... Ex 21:31 5055

GORGEOUS
him, and arrayed him in a g robe ... Lk 23:11 2986

GORGEOUSLY
captains and rulers clothed most g ... Eze 23:12 4358
they which are g apparelled ... Lk 7:25 1741

GOSHEN (*go'-shen*)
1. A district of Egypt.
thou shalt dwell in the land of G ... Gen 45:10 1657
Joseph, to direct his face unto G ... Gen 46:28 1657
and they came into the land of G ... Gen 46:28 1657
to meet Israel his father, to G ... Gen 46:29 1657
ye may dwell in the land of G ... Gen 46:34 1657
behold, they are in the land of G ... Gen 47:1 1657
servants dwell in the land of G ... Gen 47:4 1657
in the land of G let them dwell ... Gen 47:6 1657
of Egypt, in the country of G ... Gen 47:27 1657
herds, they left in the land of G ... Gen 50:8 1657
sever in that day the land of G ... Ex 8:22 1657
Only in the land of G, where the ... Ex 9:26 1657
2. A district in southern Palestine.
Gaza, and all the country of G ... Josh 10:41 1657
country, and all the land of G ... Josh 11:16 1657
3. A town in Judea.
And G, and Holon, and Giloh ... Josh 15:51 1657

GOSPEL
preaching the g of the kingdom, ... Mt 4:23 2098
preaching the g of the kingdom, ... Mt 9:35 2098
poor have the g preached to them ... Mt 11:5 2097
this g of the kingdom shall be ... Mt 24:14 2098
Wheresoever this g shall be ... Mt 26:13 2098
of the g of Jesus Christ, the Son ... Mk 1:1 2098
preaching the g of the kingdom of ... Mk 1:14 2098
repent ye, and believe the g ... Mk 1:15 2098
the g must first be published ... Mk 13:10 2098
Wheresoever this g shall be ... Mk 14:9 2098
preach the g to every creature ... Mk 16:15 2098
me to preach the g to the poor ... Lk 4:18 2097
to the poor the g is preached ... Lk 7:22 2097
the towns, preaching the g ... Lk 9:6 2097
in the temple, and preached the g ... Lk 20:1 2097
preached the g in many villages ... Acts 8:25 2097
And there they preached the g ... Acts 14:7 2097
had preached the g to that city ... Acts 14:21 2097
should hear the word of the g ... Acts 15:7 2098
us for to preach the g unto them ... Acts 16:10 2097
to testify the g of the grace of ... Acts 20:24 2098
separated unto the g of God ... Rom 1:1 2098
my spirit in the g of his Son ... Rom 1:9 2098
I am ready to preach the g to you ... Rom 1:15 2097
am not ashamed of the g of Christ ... Rom 1:16 2098
by Jesus Christ according to my g ... Rom 2:16 2098
them that preach the g of peace ... Rom 10:15 2097
they have not all obeyed the g ... Rom 10:16 2098
As concerning the g, they are ... Rom 11:28 2098
ministering the g of God ... Rom 15:16 2098
fully preached the g of Christ ... Rom 15:19 2098
so have I strived to preach the g ... Rom 15:20 2097
the blessing of the g of Christ ... Rom 15:29 2098
to stablish you according to my g ... Rom 16:25 2098
to baptize, but to preach the g ... 1Cor 1:17 2097
I have begotten you through the g ... 1Cor 4:15 2098
we should hinder the g of Christ ... 1Cor 9:12 2098
the g should live of the g ... 1Cor 9:14 2098
For though I preach the g ... 1Cor 9:16 2097
is unto me, if I preach not the g ... 1Cor 9:16 2097
of the g is committed unto me ... 1Cor 9:17
Verily that, when I preach the g ... 1Cor 9:18 2097
I may make the g of Christ ... 1Cor 9:18 2098

I abuse not my power in the g ... 1Cor 9:18 2098
I declare unto you the g which I ... 1Cor 15:1 2098
to Troas to preach Christ's g ... 2Cor 2:12 2098
But if our g be hid, it is hid to ... 2Cor 4:3 2098
light of the glorious g of Christ ... 2Cor 4:4 2098
brother, whose praise is in the g ... 2Cor 8:18 2098
subjection into the g of Christ ... 2Cor 9:13 2098
also in preaching the g of Christ ... 2Cor 10:14 2098
To preach the g in the regions ... 2Cor 10:16 2097
have not received, or another g ... 2Cor 11:4 2098
to you the g of God freely ... 2Cor 11:7 2098
grace of Christ unto another g ... Gal 1:6 2098
and would pervert the g of Christ ... Gal 1:7 2098
preach any other g unto you than ... Gal 1:8 2097
g unto you than that ye have ... Gal 1:9 2097
that the g which was preached of ... Gal 1:11 2098
that g which I preach among the ... Gal 2:2 2098
that the truth of the g might ... Gal 2:5 2098
when they saw that the g of the ... Gal 2:7 2098
as the g of the circumcision was ... Gal 2:7
according to the truth of the g ... Gal 2:14 2098
before the g unto Abraham ... Gal 3:8 4283
the g unto you at the first ... Gal 4:13 2097
of truth, the g of your salvation ... Eph 1:13 2098
of his promise in Christ by the g ... Eph 3:6 2098
the preparation of the g of peace ... Eph 6:15 2098
make known the mystery of the g ... Eph 6:19 2098
For your fellowship in the g from ... Phil 1:5 2098
defence and comfirmation of the g ... Phil 1:7 2098
unto the furtherance of the g ... Phil 1:12 2098
I am set for the defence of the g ... Phil 1:17 2098
be as it becometh the g of Christ ... Phil 1:27 2098
together for the faith of the g ... Phil 1:27 2098
he hath served with me in the g ... Phil 2:22 2098
which laboured with me in the g ... Phil 4:3 2098
that in the beginning of the g ... Phil 4:15 2098
in the word of the truth of the g ... Col 1:5 2098
moved away from the hope of the g ... Col 1:23 2098
For our g came not unto you in ... 1Th 1:5 2098
the g of God with much contention ... 1Th 2:2 2098
God to be put in trust with the g ... 1Th 2:4 2098
not the g of God only, but also ... 1Th 2:8 2098
we preached unto you the g of God ... 1Th 2:9 2098
fellowlabourer in the g of Christ ... 1Th 3:2 2098
that obey not the g of our Lord ... 2Th 1:8 2098
Whereunto he called you by our g ... 2Th 2:14 2098
the glorious g of the blessed God ... 1Ti 1:11 2098
of the afflictions of the g ... 2Ti 1:8 2098
to light through the g ... 2Ti 1:10 2098
from the dead according to my g ... 2Ti 2:8 2098
unto me in the bonds of the g ... Philem 13 2098
For unto us was the g preached ... Heb 4:2 2097
g unto you with the Holy Ghost ... 1Pet 1:12 2097
by the g is preached unto you ... 1Pet 1:25 2097
For for this cause was the g ... 1Pet 4:6 2097
them that obey not the g of God ... 1Pet 4:17 2098
having the everlasting g to ... Rev 14:6 2098

GOSPEL'S
his life for my sake and the g ... Mk 8:35 2098
or lands, for my sake, and the g ... Mk 10:29 2098
And this I do for the g sake ... 1Cor 9:23 2098

GOT
which he had g in the land of ... Gen 36:6 7408
her hand, and fled, and g him out ... Gen 39:12 3318
with me, and fled, and g him out ... Gen 39:15 3318
For they g not the land in ... Ps 44:3 3423
I g me servants and maidens, and ... Eccl 2:7 7069
So I g a girdle according to the ... Jer 13:2 7069
Take the girdle that thou hast g ... Jer 13:4 7069

GOTTEN
I have g a man from the LORD ... Gen 4:1 7069
souls that they had g in Haran ... Gen 12:5 6213
father's hath he g all this glory ... Gen 31:1 4069
and all his goods which he had g ... Gen 31:18 7408
which he had g in Padan-aram, for ... Gen 31:18 7408
which they had g in the land of ... Gen 46:6 7408
when I have g me honour upon ... Ex 14:18
thing which he hath deceitfully g ... Lev 6:4
the LORD, what every man hath g ... Num 31:50 4672
mine hand hath g me this wealth ... Deut 8:17 6213
if he be g into a city, then ... 2Sa 17:13 622
It cannot be g for gold, neither ... Job 28:15 5414
and because mine hand had g much ... Job 31:25 4672
holy arm, hath g him the victory ... Ps 98:1
Wealth g by vanity shall be ... Prov 13:11
An inheritance may be g hastily ... Prov 20:21
have g more wisdom than all they ... Eccl 1:16 3254
the abundance they have g ... Is 15:7 6213
that he hath g are perished ... Jer 48:36 6213
thou hast g thee riches, and hast ... Eze 28:4 6213
thee riches, and hast g gold ... Eze 28:4 6213
the nations, which have g cattle ... Eze 38:12 6213
hast g thee renown, as at this ... Dan 9:15 6213
that after we were g from them ... Acts 21:1 645
them that had g the victory over ... Rev 15:2

GOURD
And the LORD God prepared a g ... Jonah 4:6 7021
Jonah was exceeding glad of the g ... Jonah 4:6 7021
it smote the g that it withered ... Jonah 4:7 7021
thou well to be angry for the g ... Jonah 4:9 7021
LORD, Thou hast had pity on the g ... Jonah 4:10 7021

GOURDS
thereof wild g his lap full ... 2Kin 4:39 6498

GOVERN
Dost thou now g the kingdom of ... 1Kin 21:7 6213
Shall even he that hateth right g ... Job 34:17 2280
and g the nations upon earth ... Ps 67:4 5148

GOVERNMENT
the g shall be upon his shoulder ... Is 9:6 4951
Of the increase of his g and peace ... Is 9:7 4951
I will commit thy g into his hand ... Is 22:21 4475
lust of uncleanness, and despise g ... 2Pet 2:10 2963

GOVERNMENTS
then gifts of healings, helps, g ... 1Cor 12:28 2941

GOVERNOR
And Joseph was the g over the land ... Gen 42:6 7989
he is g over all the land of ... Gen 45:26 4910
which was the g of his house ... 1Kin 18:3 5921
back unto Amon the g of the city ... 1Kin 22:26 8269
gate of Joshua the g of the city ... 2Kin 23:8 8269
of Babylon had made Gedaliah g ... 2Kin 25:23 6485
unto the LORD to be the chief g ... 1Chr 29:22 5057
to every g in all Israel, the ... 2Chr 1:2 5387
back to Amon the g of the city ... 2Chr 18:25 8269
Azrikam the g of the house, and ... 2Chr 28:7 5057
and Maaseiah the g of the city ... 2Chr 34:8 8269
g on this side the river, and ... Ezr 5:3 6347
g on this side the river, and ... Ezr 5:6 6347
Sheshbazzar, whom he had made g ... Ezr 5:14 6347
Tatnai, g beyond the river ... Ezr 6:6 6347
let the g of the Jews and the ... Ezr 6:7 6347
g on this side the river ... Ezr 6:13 6347
of the g on this side the river ... Neh 3:7 6346
be their g in the land of Judah ... Neh 5:14 6346
have not eaten the bread of the g ... Neh 5:14 6346
required not I the bread of the g ... Neh 5:18 6346
and in the days of Nehemiah the g ... Neh 12:26 6346
he is the g among the nations ... Ps 22:28 4910
who was also chief g in the house ... Jer 20:1 5057
their g shall proceed from the ... Jer 30:21 4910
made g over the cities of Judah ... Jer 40:5 6485
the son of Ahikam g in the land ... Jer 40:7 6485
Babylon had made g over the land ... Jer 41:2 6485
of Babylon made g in the land ... Jer 41:18 6485
g of Judah, and to Joshua the son ... Hag 1:1 6346
g of Judah, and the spirit of ... Hag 1:14 6346
g of Judah, and to Joshua the son ... Hag 2:2 6346
g of Judah, saying, I will shake ... Hag 2:21 6346
and he shall be as a g in Judah ... Zec 9:7 441
offer it now unto thy g ... Mal 1:8 6346
for out of thee shall come a G ... Mt 2:6 2233
him to Pontius Pilate the g ... Mt 27:2 2232
And Jesus stood before the g ... Mt 27:11 2232
the g asked him, saying, Art thou ... Mt 27:11 2232
that the g marvelled greatly ... Mt 27:14 2232
Now at that feast the g was wont ... Mt 27:15 2232
The g answered and said unto them ... Mt 27:21 2232
the g said, Why, what evil hath ... Mt 27:23 2232
Then the soldiers of the g took ... Mt 27:27 2232
made when Cyrenius was g of Syria ... Lk 2:2 2230
Pontius Pilate being g of Judaea ... Lk 3:1 2230
the power and authority of the g ... Lk 20:20 2230
and bear unto the g of the feast ... Jn 2:8 755
the g of the feast called the ... Jn 2:9 755
and he made him g over Egypt ... Acts 7:10 2233
bring him safe unto Felix the g ... Acts 23:24 2232
g Felix sendeth greeting ... Acts 23:26 2232
and delivered the epistle to the g ... Acts 23:33 2232
when the g had read the letter ... Acts 23:34 2232
who informed the g against Paul ... Acts 24:1 2232
after that the g had beckoned ... Acts 24:10 2232
the king rose up, and the g ... Acts 26:30 2232
In Damascus the g under Aretas ... 2Cor 11:32 1481
helm, whithersoever the g listeth ... Jas 3:4 2116

GOVERNOR'S
And if this come to the g ears ... Mt 28:14 2232

GOVERNORS
heart is toward the g of Israel ... Judg 5:9 2710
out of Machir came down g ... Judg 5:14 2710
and of the g of the country ... 1Kin 10:15 6346
for the g of the sanctuary, and ... 1Chr 24:5 8269
g of the house of God, were of ... 1Chr 24:5 8269
g of the country brought gold and ... 2Chr 9:14 6346
the g of the people, and all the ... 2Chr 23:20 4910
to the g on this side the river ... Ezr 8:36 6346
me to the g beyond the river ... Neh 2:7 6346
I came to the g beyond the river ... Neh 2:9 6346
But the former g that had been ... Neh 5:15 6346
to the g that were over every ... Est 3:12 6346
chief of the g over all the wise ... Dan 2:48 5461
together the princes, the g ... Dan 3:2 5461
Then the princes, the g, and ... Dan 3:3 5461
And the princes, g, and captains ... Dan 3:27 5461
presidents of the kingdom, the g ... Dan 6:7 5461
the g of Judah shall say in their ... Zec 12:5 441
In that day will I make the g of ... Zec 12:6 441
And ye shall be brought before g ... Mt 10:18 2232
g until the time appointed of the ... Gal 4:2 3623
Or unto g, as unto them that are ... 1Pet 2:14 2232

GOYIM See NATIONS.

GOZAN *(go'-zan) An Assyrian city.*
and in Habor by the river of G ... 2Kin 17:6 1470
and in Habor by the river of G ... 2Kin 18:11 1470
as G, and Haran, and Rezeph, and the ... 2Kin 19:12 1470
Habor, and Hara, and to the river G ... 1Chr 5:26 1470
my fathers have destroyed, as G ... Is 37:12 1470

GRACE
But Noah found g in the eyes of ... Gen 6:8 2580
servant hath found g in thy sight ... Gen 19:19 2580
that I may find g in thy sight ... Gen 32:5 2580
These are to find g in the sight ... Gen 33:8 2580
now I have found g in thy sight ... Gen 33:10 2580
let me find g in the sight of my ... Gen 33:15 2580
Let me find g in your eyes, and ... Gen 34:11 2580
And Joseph found g in his sight ... Gen 39:4 2580
let us find g in the sight of my ... Gen 47:25 2580
now I have found g in thy sight ... Gen 47:29 2580
now I have found g in your eyes ... Gen 50:4 2580
hast also found g in my sight ... Ex 33:12 2580
if I have found g in thy sight ... Ex 33:13 2580
that I may find g in thy sight ... Ex 33:13 2580
people have found g in thy sight ... Ex 33:16 2580
for thou hast found g in my sight ... Ex 33:17 2580
now I have found g in thy sight ... Ex 34:9 2580
if we have found g in thy sight ... Num 32:5 2580
now I have found g in thy sight ... Judg 6:17 2580
him in whose sight I shall find g ... Ruth 2:2 2580
Why have I found g in thine eyes ... Ruth 2:10 2580
handmaid find g in thy sight ... 1Sa 1:18 2580
that I have found g in thine eyes ... 1Sa 20:3 2580
I have now found g in thine eyes ... 1Sa 27:5 2580
that I have found g in thy sight ... 2Sa 14:22 2580
that I may find g in thy sight ... 2Sa 16:4 2580
now for a little space g hath ... Ezr 9:8 8467
all the women, and she obtained g ... Est 2:17 2580
g is poured into thy lips ... Ps 45:2 2580
the LORD will give g and glory ... Ps 84:11 2580
be an ornament of g unto thy head ... Prov 1:9 2580
unto thy soul, and g to thy neck ... Prov 3:22 2580
but he giveth g unto the lowly ... Prov 3:34 2580
to thine head an ornament of g ... Prov 4:9 2580
for the g of his lips the king ... Prov 22:11 2580
sword found g in the wilderness ... Jer 31:2 2580
crying, G, g unto it ... Zec 4:7 2580
of Jerusalem, the spirit of g ... Zec 12:10 2580
the g of God was upon him ... Lk 2:40 5485
of the Father,) full of g ... Jn 1:14 5485
all we received, and g for g ... Jn 1:16 5485
the law was given by Moses, but g ... Jn 1:17 5485
great g was upon them all ... Acts 4:33 5485
he came, and had seen the g of God ... Acts 11:23 5485
them to continue in the g of God ... Acts 13:43 5485
testimony unto the word of his g ... Acts 14:3 5485
had been recommended to the g of ... Acts 14:26 5485
the g of the Lord Jesus Christ we ... Acts 15:11 5485
by the brethren unto the g of God ... Acts 15:40 5485
much which had believed through g ... Acts 18:27 5485
the gospel of the g of God ... Acts 20:24 5485
to God, and to the word of his g ... Acts 20:32 5485
By whom we have received g ... Rom 1:5 5485
G to you and peace from God our ... Rom 1:7 5485
Being justified freely by his g ... Rom 3:24 5485
is the reward not reckoned of g ... Rom 4:4 5485
of faith, that it might be by g ... Rom 4:16 5485
into this g wherein we stand ... Rom 5:2 5485
g of God, and the gift by g ... Rom 5:15 5485
they which receive abundance of g ... Rom 5:17 5485
abounded, g did much more abound ... Rom 5:20 5485
even so might g reign through ... Rom 5:21 5485
in sin, that g may abound ... Rom 6:1 5485
not under the law, but under g ... Rom 6:14 5485
not under the law, but under g ... Rom 6:15 5485
according to the election of g ... Rom 11:5 5485
And if by g, then is it no more of ... Rom 11:6 5485
otherwise g is no more g ... Rom 11:6 5485
be of works, then is it no more g ... Rom 11:6 5485
through the g given unto me, to ... Rom 12:3 5485
to the g that is given to us ... Rom 12:6 5485
because of the g that is given to ... Rom 15:15 5485
The g of our Lord Jesus Christ be ... Rom 16:20 5485
The g of our Lord Jesus Christ be ... Rom 16:24 5485
G be unto you, and peace, from God ... 1Cor 1:3 5485
for the g of God which is given ... 1Cor 1:4 5485
According to the g of God which ... 1Cor 3:10 5485
For if I by g be a partaker, why ... 1Cor 10:30 5485
But by the g of God I am what I ... 1Cor 15:10 5485
his g which was bestowed upon me ... 1Cor 15:10 5485
but the g of God which was with ... 1Cor 15:10 5485
The g of our Lord Jesus Christ be ... 1Cor 16:23 5485
G be to you and peace from God our ... 2Cor 1:2 5485
wisdom, but by the g of God ... 2Cor 1:12 5485
that the abundant g might through ... 2Cor 4:15 5485
receive not the g of God in vain ... 2Cor 6:1 5485
we do you to wit of the g of God ... 2Cor 8:1 5485
finish in you the same g also ... 2Cor 8:6 5485
see that ye abound in this g also ... 2Cor 8:7 5485
For ye know the g of our Lord ... 2Cor 8:9 5485
to travel with us with this g ... 2Cor 8:19 5485
to make all g abound toward you ... 2Cor 9:8 5485
for the exceeding g of God in you ... 2Cor 9:14 5485
My g is sufficient for thee ... 2Cor 12:9 5485
The g of the Lord Jesus Christ ... 2Cor 13:14 5485
G be to you and peace from God the ... Gal 1:3 5485
him that called you into the g of ... Gal 1:6 5485
womb, and called me by his g ... Gal 1:15 5485
perceived the g that was given ... Gal 2:9 5485
I do not frustrate the g of God ... Gal 2:21 5485
ye are fallen from g ... Gal 5:4 5485
the g of our Lord Jesus Christ be ... Gal 6:18 5485
G be to you, and peace, from God ... Eph 1:2 5485
the praise of the glory of his g ... Eph 1:6 5485
according to the riches of his g ... Eph 1:7 5485
with Christ, (by g ye are saved ... Eph 2:5 5485
his g in his kindness toward us ... Eph 2:7 5485
For by g are ye saved through ... Eph 2:8 5485
of the dispensation of the g of ... Eph 3:2 5485
the g of God given unto me by the ... Eph 3:7 5485
of all saints, is this g given ... Eph 3:8 5485
unto every one of us is given g ... Eph 4:7 5485
may minister g unto the hearers ... Eph 4:29 5485
G be with all them that love our ... Eph 6:24 5485
G be unto you, and peace, from God ... Phil 1:2 5485
ye all are partakers of my g ... Phil 1:7 5485
The g of our Lord Jesus Christ be ... Phil 4:23 5485
G be unto you, and peace, from God ... Col 1:2 5485
knew the g of God in truth ... Col 1:6 5485
singing with g in your hearts to ... Col 3:16 5485
Let your speech be alway with g ... Col 4:6 5485
G be with you ... Col 4:18 5485
G be unto you, and peace, from God ... 1Th 1:1 5485
The g of our Lord Jesus Christ be ... 1Th 5:28 5485
G unto you, and peace, from God ... 2Th 1:2 5485
according to the g of our God ... 2Th 1:12 5485
and good hope through g ... 2Th 2:16 5485

The g of our Lord Jesus Christ be........ 2Th 3:18 5485
G, mercy, and peace, from God our........ 1Ti 1:2 5485
the g of our Lord was exceeding.......... 1Ti 1:14 5485
G be with thee.......... 1Ti 6:21 5485
G, mercy, and peace, from God the........ 2Ti 1:2 5485
according to his own purpose and g........ 2Ti 1:9 5485
be strong in the g that is in.......... 2Ti 2:1 5485
G be with you.......... 2Ti 4:22 5485
G, mercy, and peace, from God the........ Titus 1:4 5485
For the g of God that bringeth.......... Titus 2:11 5485
That being justified by his g.......... Titus 3:7 5485
G be with you all.......... Titus 3:15 5485
G to you, and peace, from God our........ Philem 3 5485
The g of our Lord Jesus Christ be........ Philem 25 5485
that he by the g of God should.......... Heb 2:9 5485
come boldly unto the throne of g.......... Heb 4:16 5485
find g to help in time of need.......... Heb 4:16 5485
done despite unto the Spirit of g.......... Heb 10:29 5485
lest any man fail of the g of God.......... Heb 12:15 5485
cannot be moved, let us have g.......... Heb 12:28 5485
the heart be established with g.......... Heb 13:9 5485
G be with you all.......... Heb 13:25 5485
the g of the fashion of it.......... Jas 1:11 2143
But he giveth more g.......... Jas 4:6 5485
but giveth g unto the humble.......... Jas 4:6 5485
G unto you, and peace, be.......... 1Pet 1:2 5485
who prophesied of the g that.......... 1Pet 1:10 5485
hope to the end for the g that is.......... 1Pet 1:13 5485
heirs together of the g of life.......... 1Pet 3:7 5485
stewards of the manifold g of God........ 1Pet 4:10 5485
proud, and giveth g to the humble........ 1Pet 5:5 5485
But the God of all g, who hath.......... 1Pet 5:10 5485
that this is the true g of God.......... 1Pet 5:12 5485
G and peace be multiplied unto you........ 2Pet 1:2 5485
But grow in g, and in the.......... 2Pet 3:18 5485
G be with you, mercy, and peace,.......... 2Jn 3 5485
turning the g of our God into.......... Jude 4 5485
G be unto you, and peace, from him........ Rev 1:4 5485
The g of our Lord Jesus Christ be........ Rev 22:21 5485

GRACIOUS

God be g unto thee, my son.......... Gen 43:29 2603
for I am g.......... Ex 22:27 2587
be g to whom I will be g.......... Ex 33:19 2603
LORD, The LORD God, merciful and g........ Ex 34:6 2587
upon thee, and be g unto thee.......... Num 6:25 2603
tell whether GOD will be g to me.......... 2Sa 12:22 2603
And the LORD was g unto them.......... 2Kin 13:23 2603
for the LORD your God is g.......... 2Chr 30:9 2587
thou art a God ready to pardon, g........ Neh 9:17 2587
for thou art a g and merciful God........ Neh 9:31 2587
Then he is g unto him, and saith,.......... Job 33:24 2603
Hath God forgotten to be g.......... Ps 77:9 2589
a God full of compassion, and g.......... Ps 86:15 2587
The LORD is merciful and g.......... Ps 103:8 2587
the LORD is g and full of.......... Ps 111:4 2587
he is g, and full of compassion,.......... Ps 112:4 2587
G is the LORD, and righteous.......... Ps 116:5 2587
The LORD is g, and full of.......... Ps 145:8 2587
A g woman retaineth honour.......... Prov 11:16 2580
words of a wise man's mouth are g........ Eccl 10:12 2580
wait, that he may be g unto you.......... Is 30:18 2603
he will be very g unto thee at.......... Is 30:19 2603
O LORD, be g unto us.......... Is 33:2 2603
how g shalt thou be when pangs.......... Jer 22:23 2603
for he is g and merciful, slow to.......... Joel 2:13 2587
be g unto the remnant of Joseph.......... Amos 5:15 2587
for I knew that thou art a g God.......... Jonah 4:2 2587
God that he will be g unto us.......... Mal 1:9 2603
wondered at the g words which.......... Lk 4:22 5485
ye have tasted that the Lord is g.......... 1Pet 2:3 5543

GRACIOUSLY

God hath g given thy servant.......... Gen 33:5 2603
because God hath dealt g with me........ Gen 33:11 2603
and grant me thy law g.......... Ps 119:29 2603
all iniquity, and receive us g.......... Hos 14:2 2896

GRAFT

God is able to g them in again.......... Rom 11:23 1461

GRAFTED

wert g in among them, and with.......... Rom 11:17 1461
broken off, that I might be g in.......... Rom 11:19 1461
still in unbelief, shall be g in.......... Rom 11:23 1461
wert g contrary to nature into a.......... Rom 11:24 1461
be g into their own olive tree.......... Rom 11:24 1461

GRAIN

the least g fall upon the earth.......... Amos 9:9 6872
is like to a g of mustard seed.......... Mt 13:31 2848
have faith as a g of mustard seed........ Mt 17:20 2848
It is like a g of mustard seed,.......... Mk 4:31 2848
It is like a g of mustard seed,.......... Lk 13:19 2848
had faith as a g of mustard seed........ Lk 17:6 2848
body that shall be, but bare g.......... 1Cor 15:37 2848
of wheat, or of some other g.......... 1Cor 15:37

GRANDMOTHER

which dwelt first in thy g Lois.......... 2Ti 1:5 3125

GRANT

shall g a redemption for the land.......... Lev 25:24 5414
The LORD g you that ye may find.......... Ruth 1:9 5414
the God of Israel g thee thy.......... 1Sa 1:17 5414
to Ornan, G me the place of this.......... 1Chr 21:22 5414
thou shalt g it me for the full.......... 1Chr 21:22 5414
them, but I will g them some.......... 2Chr 12:7 5414
according to the g that they had.......... Ezr 3:7 7558
g him mercy in the sight of this.......... Neh 1:11 5414
please the king to g my petition.......... Est 5:8 5414
that God would g me the thing.......... Job 6:8 5414
G thee according to thine own.......... Ps 20:4 5414
O LORD, and g us thy salvation.......... Ps 85:7 5414
and g me thy law graciously.......... Ps 119:29
G not, O LORD, the desires of the.......... Ps 140:8 5414
G that these my two sons may sit,........ Mt 20:21 2036
G unto us that we may sit, one on........ Mk 10:37 1325
That he would g unto us, that we,........ Lk 1:74 1325
g unto thy servants, that with.......... Acts 4:29 1325
and consolation g you to be.......... Rom 15:5 1325
That he would g you, according to........ Eph 3:16 1325
The Lord g unto him that he may........ 2Ti 1:18 1325
I g to sit with me in my throne.......... Rev 3:21 1325

GRANTED

God g him that which he requested........ 1Chr 4:10 935
and knowledge is g unto thee.......... 2Chr 1:12 5414
the king g him all his request,.......... Ezr 7:6 5414
And the king g me, according to.......... Neh 2:8 5414
and it shall be g thee.......... Est 5:6 5414
and it shall be g thee.......... Est 7:2 5414
Wherein the king g the Jews which........ Est 8:11 5414
and it shall be g thee.......... Est 9:12 5414
let it be g to the Jews which are.......... Est 9:13 5414
Thou hast g me life and favour, and........ Job 10:12 6213
of the righteous shall be g.......... Prov 10:24 5414
a murderer to be g unto you.......... Acts 3:14 5483
Gentiles g repentance unto life.......... Acts 11:18 1325
g signs and wonders to be done by........ Acts 14:3 1325
to her was g that she should be.......... Rev 19:8 1325

GRAPE

gather every g of thy vineyard.......... Lev 19:10 6528
drink the pure blood of the g.......... Deut 32:14 6025
off his unripe g as the vine.......... Job 15:33 1154
the tender g give a good smell.......... Song 2:13 5563
whether the tender g appear.......... Song 7:12 5563
the sour g is ripening in the.......... Is 18:5 1155
The fathers have eaten a sour g.......... Jer 31:29 1155
every man that eateth the sour g........ Jer 31:30 1155

GRAPEGATHERER

hand as a g into the baskets.......... Jer 6:9 1219

GRAPEGATHERERS

If g come to thee, would they not........ Jer 49:9 1219
if the g came to thee, would they........ Obad 5 1219

GRAPEGLEANINGS

fruits, as the g of the vintage.......... Mic 7:1 5955

GRAPES

thereof brought forth ripe g.......... Gen 40:10 6025
and I took the g, and pressed them........ Gen 40:11 6025
and his clothes in the blood of g........ Gen 49:11 6025
neither gather the g of thy vine.......... Lev 25:5 6025
nor gather the g in it of thy.......... Lev 25:11
liquor of g, nor eat moist g.......... Num 6:3 6025
was the time of the firstripe g.......... Num 13:20 6025
a branch with one cluster of g.......... Num 13:23 6025
because of the cluster of g which........ Num 13:24
then thou mayest eat g thy fill.......... Deut 23:24 6025
gatherest the g of thy vineyard.......... Deut 24:21
and shalt not gather the g thereof........ Deut 28:30
of the wine, nor gather the g.......... Deut 28:39
their g are g of gall.......... Deut 32:32 6025
the g of Ephraim better than the.......... Judg 8:2
their vineyards, and trode the g.......... Judg 9:27
as also wine, g, and figs, and all........ Neh 13:15 6025
for our vines have tender g.......... Song 2:15 5563
and thy breasts to clusters of g.......... Song 7:7
that it should bring forth g.......... Is 5:2 6025
and it brought forth wild g.......... Is 5:2 891
that it should bring forth g.......... Is 5:4 6025
brought it forth wild g.......... Is 5:4 891
Yet gleaning g shall be left in.......... Is 17:6
as the gleaning g when the.......... Is 24:13
there shall be no g on the vine.......... Jer 8:13 6025
a shout, as they that tread the g........ Jer 25:30
they not leave some gleaning g.......... Jer 49:9
The fathers have eaten sour g.......... Eze 18:2 1154
Israel like g in the wilderness.......... Hos 9:10 6025
the treader of g him that soweth........ Amos 9:13 6025
thee, would they not leave some g........ Obad 5
Do men gather g of thorns.......... Mt 7:16 4718
of a bramble bush gather they g.......... Lk 6:44 4718
for her g are fully ripe.......... Rev 14:18 4718

GRASS

said, Let the earth bring forth g.......... Gen 1:11 1877
And the earth brought forth g.......... Gen 1:12 1877
ox licketh up the g of the field.......... Num 22:4 3418
I will send g in thy fields for.......... Deut 11:15 6212
nor any g groweth therein, like.......... Deut 29:23 6212
and as the showers upon the g.......... Deut 32:2 6212
as the tender g springing out of.......... 2Sa 23:4 1877
we may find g to save the horses........ 1Kin 18:5 2682
they were as the g of the field.......... 2Kin 19:26 6212
as the g on the house tops, and as........ 2Kin 19:26 2682
offspring as the g of the earth.......... Job 5:25 6212
the wild ass bray when he hath g........ Job 6:5 1877
he eateth g as an ox.......... Job 40:15 2682
shall soon be cut down like the g........ Ps 37:2 2682
down like rain upon the mown g.......... Ps 72:6
flourish like g of the earth.......... Ps 72:16 6212
they are like g which groweth up........ Ps 90:5 2682
When the wicked spring as the g........ Ps 92:7 6212
is smitten, and withered like g.......... Ps 102:4 6212
and I am withered like g.......... Ps 102:11 6212
As for man, his days are as g.......... Ps 103:15 2682
He causeth the g to grow for the........ Ps 104:14 2682
similitude of an ox that eateth g........ Ps 106:20 6212
be as the g upon the housetops.......... Ps 129:6 2682
who maketh g to grow upon the.......... Ps 147:8 2682
his favour is as dew upon the g.......... Prov 19:12 6212
the tender g sheweth itself, and.......... Prov 27:25 1877
the g faileth, there is no green.......... Is 15:6 1877
shall be g with reeds and rushes.......... Is 35:7 2682
they were as the g of the field.......... Is 37:27 6212
as the g on the housetops, and as........ Is 37:27 2682
All flesh is g, and all the.......... Is 40:6 2682
The g withereth, the flower.......... Is 40:7 2682
surely the people is g.......... Is 40:7 2682
The g withereth, the flower.......... Is 40:8 2682
shall spring up as among the g.......... Is 44:4 2682
of man which shall be made as g........ Is 51:12 2682
it, because there was no g.......... Jer 14:5 1758
did fail, because there was no g.......... Jer 14:6 6212
are grown fat as the heifer at g.......... Jer 50:11 1877
in the tender g of the field.......... Dan 4:15 1883
the beasts in the g of the earth.......... Dan 4:15 6211
in the tender g of the field.......... Dan 4:23 1883
shall make thee to eat g as oxen.......... Dan 4:25 6211
shall make thee to eat g as oxen.......... Dan 4:32 6211
from men, and did eat g as oxen.......... Dan 4:33 6211
they fed him with g like oxen.......... Dan 5:21 6211
end of eating the g of the land.......... Amos 7:2 6212
LORD, as the showers upon the g.......... Mic 5:7 6212
rain, to every one g in the field.......... Zec 10:1 6212
God so clothe the g of the field.......... Mt 6:30 5528
multitude to sit down on the g.......... Mt 14:19 5528
by companies upon the green g.......... Mk 6:39 5528
If then God so clothe the g.......... Lk 12:28 5528
Now there was much g in the place........ Jn 6:10 5528
of the g he shall pass away.......... Jas 1:10 5528
heat, but it withereth the g.......... Jas 1:11 5528
For all flesh is as g, and all the........ 1Pet 1:24 5528
glory of man as the flower of g.......... 1Pet 1:24 5528
The g withereth, and the flower.......... 1Pet 1:24 5528
up, and all green g was burnt up.......... Rev 8:7 5528
not hurt the g of the earth.......... Rev 9:4 5528

GRASSHOPPER

his kind, and the g after his kind.......... Lev 11:22 2284
Canst thou make him afraid as a g........ Job 39:20 697
the g shall be a burden, and.......... Eccl 12:5 2284

GRASSHOPPERS

and we were in our own sight as g........ Num 13:33 2284
they came as g for multitude.......... Judg 6:5 697
the valley like g for multitude.......... Judg 7:12 697
the inhabitants thereof are as g.......... Is 40:22 2284
because they are more than the g........ Jer 46:23 697
he formed g in the beginning of.......... Amos 7:1 1462
and thy captains as the great g.......... Nah 3:17 1462

GRATE

for it a g of network of brass.......... Ex 27:4 4345
burnt offering, with his brasen g........ Ex 35:16 4345
g of network under the compass.......... Ex 38:4 4345
the four ends of the g of brass.......... Ex 38:5 4345
altar, and the brasen g for it.......... Ex 38:30 4345
his g of brass, his staves, and.......... Ex 39:39 4345

GRAVE

And Jacob set a pillar upon her g........ Gen 35:20 6900
of Rachel's g unto this day.......... Gen 35:20 6900
into the g unto my son mourning.......... Gen 37:35 7585
gray hairs with sorrow to the g.......... Gen 42:38 7585
gray hairs with sorrow to the g.......... Gen 44:29 7585
our father with sorrow to the g.......... Gen 44:31 7585
in my g which I have digged for.......... Gen 50:5 6913
g on them the names of the.......... Ex 28:9 6605
g upon it, like the engravings of.......... Ex 28:36 6605
body, or a bone of a man, or a g........ Num 19:16 6913
or one slain, or one dead, or a g........ Num 19:18 6913
he bringeth down to the g.......... 1Sa 2:6 7585
voice, and wept at the g of Abner........ 2Sa 3:32 6913
be buried by the g of my father.......... 2Sa 19:37 6913
head go down to the g in peace.......... 1Kin 2:6 7585
thou down to the g with blood.......... 1Kin 2:9 7585
he laid his carcase in his own g........ 1Kin 13:30 6913
of Jeroboam shall come to the g........ 1Kin 14:13 6913
be gathered into thy g in peace.......... 2Kin 22:20 6913
that can skill to g with the.......... 2Chr 2:7 6603
also to g any manner of graving,.......... 2Chr 2:14 6605
be gathered to thy g in peace.......... 2Chr 34:28 6913
glad, when they can find the g.......... Job 3:22 6913
shalt come to thy g in a full age........ Job 5:26 6913
to the g shall come up no more.......... Job 7:9 7585
carried from the womb to the g.......... Job 10:19 6913
thou wouldest hide me in the g.......... Job 14:13 7585
If I wait, the g is mine house.......... Job 17:13 7585
and in a moment go down to the g........ Job 21:13 7585
Yet shall he be brought to the g........ Job 21:32 6913
so doth the g those which have.......... Job 24:19 7585
not stretch out his hand to the g........ Job 30:24 1164
his soul draweth near unto the g........ Job 33:22 7845
in the g who shall give thee.......... Ps 6:5 7585
brought up my soul from the g.......... Ps 30:3 7585
and let them be silent in the g.......... Ps 31:17 7585
Like sheep they are laid in the g........ Ps 49:14 7585
in the g from their dwelling.......... Ps 49:14 7585
my soul from the power of the g........ Ps 49:15 7585
my life draweth nigh unto the g........ Ps 88:3 7585
like the slain that lie in the g.......... Ps 88:5 6913
be declared in the g.......... Ps 88:11 6913
his soul from the hand of the g.......... Ps 89:48 7585
us swallow them up alive as the g........ Prov 1:12 7585
The g; and the barren.......... Prov 30:16 7585
knowledge, nor wisdom, in the g.......... Eccl 9:10 7585
jealousy is cruel as the g.......... Song 8:6 7585
Thy pomp is brought down to the g........ Is 14:11 7585
thy g like an abominable branch.......... Is 14:19 6913
I shall go to the gates of the g.......... Is 38:10 7585
For the g cannot praise thee,.......... Is 38:18 7585
he made his g with the wicked, and........ Is 53:9 6913
my mother might have been my g.......... Jer 20:17 6913
down to the g I caused a mourning........ Eze 31:15 7585
her company is round about her g........ Eze 32:23 6900
her multitude round about her g.......... Eze 32:24 6900
them from the power of the g.......... Hos 13:14 7585
O g, I will be thy destruction.......... Hos 13:14 7585
I will make thy g.......... Nah 1:14 6913
lain in the g four days already.......... Jn 11:17 3419
goeth unto the g to weep there.......... Jn 11:31 3419
in himself cometh to the g.......... Jn 11:38 3419
he called Lazarus out of his g.......... Jn 12:17 3419
O g, where is thy victory.......... 1Cor 15:55 86

Likewise must the deacons be g 1Ti 3:8 4586
Even so must their wives be g 1Ti 3:11 4586
That the aged men be sober, g Titus 2:2 4586

GRAVECLOTHES
forth, bound hand and foot with g Jn 11:44 2750

GRAVED
he g cherubims, lions, and palm 1Kin 7:36 6605
and g cherubims on the walls 2Chr 3:7 6605

GRAVEL
his mouth shall be filled with g Prov 20:17 2687
of thy bowels like the g thereof Is 48:19 4579
broken my teeth with g stones Lam 3:16 2687

GRAVEN
not make unto thee any g image Ex 20:4 6459
writing of God, g upon the tables Ex 32:16 2801
inclosed in ouches of gold, g Ex 39:6 6605
of gold, g, as signets are g Ex 39:6 6605
make you no idols nor g image Lev 26:1 6459
yourselves, and make you a g image Deut 4:16 6459
with you, and make you a g image Deut 4:23 6459
yourselves, and make a g image Deut 4:25 6459
shalt not make thee any g image Deut 5:8 6459
burn their g images with fire Deut 7:5 6456
The g images of their gods shall Deut 7:25 6456
down the g images of their gods Deut 12:3 6456
that maketh any g or molten image Deut 27:15 6459
for my son, to make a g image Judg 17:3 6459
who made thereof a g image Judg 17:4 6459
a g image, and a molten image Judg 18:14 6459
in thither, and took the g image Judg 18:17 6459
the g image, and went in the midst Judg 18:20 6459
of Dan set up the g image Judg 18:30 6459
they set them up Micah's g image Judg 18:31 6459
LORD, and served their g images 2Kin 17:41 6456
he set a g image of the grove 2Kin 21:7 6459
g images, before he was humbled 2Chr 33:19 6456
had beaten the g images into 2Chr 34:7 6456
That they were g with an iron pen Job 19:24 2672
to jealousy with their g images Ps 78:58 6456
be all they that serve g images Ps 97:7 6459
whose g images did excel them of Is 10:10 6456
all the g images of her gods he Is 21:9 6456
of thy g images of silver Is 30:22 6456
The workman melteth a g image Is 40:19 6459
workman to prepare a g image Is 40:20 6459
neither my praise to g images Is 42:8 6456
ashamed, that trust in g images Is 42:17 6459
They that make a g image are all Is 44:9 6459
or molten a g image that is Is 44:10 6459
he maketh it a g image, and Is 44:15 6459
he maketh a god, even his g image Is 44:17 6459
set up the wood of their g image Is 45:20 6459
my g image, and my molten image, Is 48:5 6459
I have g thee upon the palms of Is 49:16 2710
me to anger with their g images Jer 8:19 6456
is confounded by the g image Jer 10:14 6459
it is g upon the table of their Jer 17:1 2790
for it is the land of g images Jer 50:38 6456
is confounded by the g image Jer 51:17 6459
upon the g images of Babylon Jer 51:47 6456
do judgment upon her g images Jer 51:52 6456
and burned incense to g images Hos 11:2 6456
all the g images thereof shall be Mic 1:7 6456
Thy g images also will I cut off, Mic 5:13 6456
gods will I cut off the g image Nah 1:14 6459
What profiteth the g image that Hab 2:18 6459
that the maker thereof hath g it Hab 2:18 6458
stone, g by art and man's device Acts 17:29 5480

GRAVE'S
are scattered at the g mouth Ps 141:7 7585

GRAVES
Because there were no g in Egypt Ex 14:11 6913
the powder thereof upon the g of 2Kin 23:6 6913
strowed it upon the g of them 2Chr 34:4 6913
extinct, the g are ready for me Job 17:1 6913
Which remain among the g, and Is 65:4 6913
of Jerusalem, out of their g Jer 8:1 6913
into the g of the common people Jer 26:23 6913
his g are about him Eze 32:22 6913
Whose g are set in the sides of Eze 32:23 6913
her g are round about him Eze 32:25 6913
her g are round about him Eze 32:26 6913
O my people, I will open your g Eze 37:12 6913
you to come up out of your g Eze 37:12 6913
LORD, when I have opened your g Eze 37:13 6913
and brought you up out of your g Eze 37:13 6913
Gog a place there of g in Israel Eze 39:11 6913
And the g were opened Mt 27:52 3419
came out of the g after his Mt 27:53 3419
for ye are as g which appear not, Lk 11:44 3419
are in the g shall hear his voice Jn 5:28 3419
their dead bodies to be put in g Rev 11:9 3418

GRAVETH
that g an habitation for himself Is 22:16 2710

GRAVING
and fashioned it with a g tool Ex 32:4 2747
also to grave any manner of g 2Chr 2:14 6603
I will engrave the g thereof Zec 3:9 6603

GRAVINGS
of it were g with their borders 1Kin 7:31 4734

GRAVITY
children in subjection with all g 1Ti 3:4 4587
doctrine shewing uncorruptness, g Titus 2:7 4587

GRAY
then shall ye bring down my g Gen 42:38 7872
ye shall bring down my g hairs Gen 44:29 7872
servants shall bring down the g Gen 44:31 7872
also with the man of g hairs Deut 32:25 7872
g hairs are here and there upon Hos 7:9 7872

GRAYHEADED
and I am old and g 1Sa 12:2 7867
With us are both the g and very Job 15:10 7867

GREASE
Their heart is as fat as g Ps 119:70 2459

GREAT
And God made two g lights Gen 1:16 1419
And God created g whales, and every Gen 1:21 1419
of man was g in the earth Gen 6:5 7227
fountains of the g deep broken up Gen 7:11 7227
the same is a g city Gen 10:12 1419
And I will make of thee a g nation Gen 12:2 1419
bless thee, and make thy name g Gen 12:2 1431
his house with g plagues because Gen 12:17 1419
for their substance was g Gen 13:6 7227
shield, and thy exceeding g reward Gen 15:1 7235
an horror of g darkness fell upon Gen 15:12 1419
they come out with g substance Gen 15:14 1419
river of Egypt unto the g river Gen 15:18 1419
and I will make him a g nation Gen 17:20 1419
Abraham shall surely become a g Gen 18:18 1419
the cry of Sodom and Gomorrah is g Gen 18:20 7227
with blindness, both small and g Gen 19:11 1419
the cry of them is waxen g before Gen 19:13 1431
on me and on my kingdom a g sin Gen 20:9 1419
Abraham made a g feast the same Gen 21:8 1419
for I will make him a g nation Gen 21:18 1419
and he is become g Gen 24:35 1431
And the man waxed g, and went Gen 26:13 1431
and grew until he became very g Gen 26:13 1431
of herds, and g store of servants Gen 26:14 7227
of his father, he cried with a g Gen 27:34 1419
a g stone was upon the well's Gen 29:2 1419
With g wrestlings have I wrestled Gen 30:8 430
then can I do this g wickedness Gen 39:9 1419
there come seven years of g Gen 41:29 1419
your lives by a g deliverance Gen 45:7 1419
there make of thee a g nation Gen 46:3 1419
a people, and he also shall be g Gen 48:19 1431
and it was a very g company Gen 50:9 3515
and there they mourned with a g Gen 50:10 1419
turn aside, and see this g sight Ex 3:3 1419
out arm, and with g judgments Ex 6:6 1419
the land of Egypt by g judgments Ex 7:4 1419
was very g in the land of Egypt Ex 11:3 1419
there shall be a g cry throughout Ex 11:6 1419
out from Pharaoh in a g anger Ex 11:8 2750
there was a g cry in Egypt Ex 12:30 1419
Israel saw that g work which the Ex 14:31 1419
that every g matter they shall Ex 18:22 1419
upon the g toe of their right Ex 29:20
and I will make of thee a g nation Ex 32:10 1419
of the land of Egypt with g power Ex 32:11 1419
hast brought so g a sin upon them Ex 32:21 1419
people, Ye have sinned a g sin Ex 32:30 1419
this people have sinned a g sin Ex 32:31 1419
upon the g toe of his right foot Lev 8:23
upon the g toes of their right Lev 8:24
and the cormorant, and the g owl Lev 11:17 3244
upon the g toe of his right foot Lev 14:14
upon the g toe of his right foot, Lev 14:17
upon the g toe of his right foot Lev 14:25
upon the g toe of his right foot, Lev 14:28
the people with a very g plague Num 11:33 7227
the cities are walled, and very g Num 13:28 1419
saw in it are men of a g stature Num 13:32
let the power of my LORD be g Num 14:17 1431
of g mercy, forgiving iniquity and Num 14:18 7227
promote thee unto very g honour Num 22:17
people shall rise up as a g lion Num 23:24 3833
down as a lion, and as a g lion Num 24:9 3833
to promote thee unto g honour Num 24:11
had a very g multitude of cattle Num 32:1 6099
even have the g sea for a border Num 34:6 1419
from the g sea ye shall point out Num 34:7 1419
and unto Lebanon, unto the g river Deut 1:7 1419
hear the small as well as the g Deut 1:17 1419
Horeb, we went through all that g Deut 1:19 1419
the cities are g and walled up to Deut 1:28 1419
walking through this g wilderness Deut 2:7 1419
therein in times past, a people g Deut 2:10 1419
A people g, and many, and tall, as Deut 2:21 1419
beside unwalled towns a g many Deut 3:5 3966
Surely this g nation is a wise and Deut 4:6 1419
For what nation is there so g Deut 4:7 1419
And what nation is there so g Deut 4:8 1419
any such thing as this g thing is Deut 4:32 1419
by g terrors, according to all Deut 4:34 1419
earth he shewed thee his g fire Deut 4:36 1419
thick darkness, with a g voice Deut 5:22 1419
for this g fire will consume us Deut 5:25 1419
and to Jacob, to give thee g Deut 6:10 1419
LORD shewed signs and wonders, g Deut 6:22 1419
The g temptations which thine Deut 7:19 1419
Who led thee through that g Deut 8:15 1419
mightier than thyself, cities g Deut 9:1 1419
A people g and tall, the children Deut 9:2 1419
a g God, a mighty, and a terrible Deut 10:17 1419
that hath done for thee these g Deut 10:21 1419
g acts of the LORD which he did Deut 11:7 1419
The little owl, and the g owl Deut 14:16 3244
let me see this g fire any more Deut 18:16 1419
in thy bag divers weights, a g Deut 25:13 1419
thine house divers measures, a g Deut 25:14 1419
few, and became there a nation, g Deut 26:5 1419
with g terribleness, and with Deut 26:8 1419
thou shalt set thee up g stones Deut 27:2 1419
even g plagues, and of long Deut 28:59 1419
The g temptations which thine Deut 29:3 1419
the signs, and those g miracles Deut 29:3 1419
meaneth the heat of this g anger Deut 29:24 1419
in g indignation, and cast them Deut 29:28 1419
in all the g terror which Moses Deut 34:12 1419
Lebanon even unto the g river Josh 1:4 1419
unto the g sea toward the going Josh 1:4 1419
people shall shout with a g shout Josh 6:5 1419
the people shouted with a g shout Josh 6:20 1419
what wilt thou do unto thy g name Josh 7:9 1419
they raised over him a g heap of Josh 7:26 1419
raise thereon a g heap of stones Josh 8:29 1419
of the g sea over against Lebanon Josh 9:1 1419
because Gibeon was a g city Josh 10:2 1419
slew them with a g slaughter at Josh 10:10 1419
that the LORD cast down g stones Josh 10:11 1419
Roll g stones upon the mouth of Josh 10:18 1419
them with a very g slaughter Josh 10:20 1419
laid g stones in the cave's mouth Josh 10:27 1419
them, and chased them unto g Zidon Josh 11:8 7227
there, and that the cities were g Josh 14:12 1419
which Arba was a g man among the Josh 14:15 1419
the west border was to the g sea Josh 15:12 1419
the river of Egypt, and the g sea Josh 15:47 1419
inherit, seeing I am a g people Josh 17:14 7227
them, If thou be a g people Josh 17:15 7227
saying, Thou art a g people Josh 17:17 7227
and hast g power Josh 17:17 1419
and Kanah, even unto g Zidon Josh 19:28 7227
by Jordan, a g altar to see to Josh 22:10 1419
off, even unto the g sea westward Josh 23:4 1419
out from before you g nations Josh 23:9 1419
which did those g signs in our Josh 24:17 1419
the law of God, and took a g stone Josh 24:26 1419
cut off his thumbs and his g toes Judg 1:6
their g toes cut off, gathered Judg 1:7
seen all the g works of the LORD Judg 2:7 1419
there were g thoughts of heart Judg 5:15 1419
there were g searchings of heart Judg 5:16 1419
with a very g slaughter Judg 11:33 1419
my people were at g strife with Judg 12:2 3699
hip and thigh with a g slaughter Judg 15:8 1419
and said, Thou hast given this g Judg 15:18 1419
see wherein his g strength lieth Judg 16:5 1419
wherein thy g strength lieth, and Judg 16:6 1419
me wherein thy g strength lieth Judg 16:15 1419
them together for to offer a g Judg 16:23 1419
that they should make a g flame Judg 20:38 7235
For they had made a g oath Judg 21:5 1419
men was very g before the LORD 1Sa 2:17 1419
all Israel shouted with a g shout 1Sa 4:5 1419
this g shout in the camp of the 1Sa 4:6 1419
and there was a very g slaughter 1Sa 4:10 1419
and there hath been also a g 1Sa 4:17 1419
city with a very g destruction 1Sa 5:9 1419
men of the city, both small and g 1Sa 5:9 1419
then he hath done us this g evil 1Sa 6:9 1419
there, where there was a g stone 1Sa 6:14 1419
were, and put them on the g stone 1Sa 6:15 1419
even unto the g stone of Abel 1Sa 6:18 1419
of the people with a g slaughter 1Sa 6:19 1419
a g thunder on that day upon the 1Sa 7:10 1419
stand and see this g thing 1Sa 12:16 1419
and see that your wickedness is g 1Sa 12:17 7227
his people for his g name's sake 1Sa 12:22 1419
for consider how g things he hath 1Sa 12:24 1431
so it was a very g trembling 1Sa 14:15 430
there was a very g discomfiture 1Sa 14:20 1419
roll a g stone unto me this day 1Sa 14:33 1419
this g salvation in Israel 1Sa 14:45 1419
Hath the LORD as g delight in 1Sa 15:22 1419
will enrich him with g riches 1Sa 17:25 1419
the LORD wrought a g salvation 1Sa 19:5 1419
and slew them with a g slaughter 1Sa 19:8 1419
came to a g well that is in Sechu 1Sa 19:22 1419
will do nothing either g or small 1Sa 20:2 1419
and smote them with a g slaughter 1Sa 23:5 1419
and the man was very g, and he had 1Sa 25:2 1419
a g space being between them 1Sa 26:13 7227
thou shalt both do g things 1Sa 26:25
either g or small, but carried 1Sa 30:2 1419
because of all the g spoil that 1Sa 30:16 1419
to them, neither small nor g 1Sa 30:19 1419
brought in a g spoil with them 2Sa 3:22 7227
a g man fallen this day in Israel 2Sa 3:38 1419
And David went on, and grew g 2Sa 5:10 1419
sight, and have made thee a g name 2Sa 7:9 1419
the g men that are in the earth 2Sa 7:9 1419
house for a g while to come 2Sa 7:19 7350
hast thou done all these g things 2Sa 7:21 1420
Wherefore thou art g, O LORD God 2Sa 7:22 1431
a name, and to do for you g things 2Sa 7:23 1420
by this deed thou hast given g 2Sa 12:14 5006
spoil of the city in g abundance 2Sa 12:30 3966
there was there a g slaughter 2Sa 18:7 1419
under the thick boughs of a g oak 2Sa 18:9 1419
cast him into a g pit in the wood 2Sa 18:17 1419
laid a very g heap of stones upon 2Sa 18:17 1419
me thy servant, I saw a g tumult 2Sa 18:29 1419
for he was a very g man 2Sa 19:32 1419
When they were at the g stone 2Sa 20:8 1419
where was a man of g stature 2Sa 21:20
and thy gentleness hath made me g 2Sa 22:36 7235
LORD wrought a g victory that day 2Sa 23:10 1419
and the LORD wrought a g victory 2Sa 23:12 1419
said unto Gad, I am in a g strait 2Sa 24:14 3966
for his mercies are g 2Sa 24:14 7227
pipes, and rejoiced with g joy 1Kin 1:40 1419
for that was the g high place 1Kin 3:4 1419
servant David my father g mercy 1Kin 3:6 1419
hast kept for him this g kindness 1Kin 3:6 1419
a g people, that cannot be 1Kin 3:8 7227
to judge this thy so g a people 1Kin 3:9 3515
threescore g cities with walls and 1Kin 4:13 1419
a wise son over this g people 1Kin 5:7 7227
and they brought g stones 1Kin 5:17 1419
on the outside toward the g court 1Kin 7:9 1419

Context	Reference	Number
even g stones, stones of ten	1Kin 7:10	1419
the g court round about was with	1Kin 7:12	1419
For they shall hear of thy g name	1Kin 8:42	1419
a g congregation, from the	1Kin 8:65	1419
to Jerusalem with a very g train	1Kin 10:2	3515
gold, and of spices very g store	1Kin 10:10	7235
Ophir g plenty of almug trees	1Kin 10:11	3966
the king made a g throne of ivory	1Kin 10:18	1419
Hadad found g favour in the sight	1Kin 11:19	3966
as g as would contain two	1Kin 18:32	1004
and wind, and there was a g rain	1Kin 18:45	1419
the journey is too g for thee	1Kin 19:7	7227
the LORD passed by, and a g	1Kin 19:11	1419
thou seen all this g multitude	1Kin 20:13	1419
the Syrians with a g slaughter	1Kin 20:21	1419
will I deliver all this g	1Kin 20:28	1419
Fight neither with small nor g	1Kin 22:31	1419
there was g indignation against	2Kin 3:27	1419
to Shunem, where was a g woman	2Kin 4:8	1419
his servant, Set on the g pot	2Kin 4:38	1419
was a g man with his master, and	2Kin 5:1	1419
had bid thee do some g thing	2Kin 5:13	1419
horses, and chariots, and a g host	2Kin 6:14	3515
he prepared g provision for them	2Kin 6:23	1419
there was a g famine in Samaria	2Kin 6:25	1419
even the noise of a g host	2Kin 7:6	1419
all the g things that Elisha hath	2Kin 8:4	1419
that he should do this g thing	2Kin 8:13	1419
were with the g men of the city,	2Kin 10:6	1419
Ahab in Jezreel, and all his g men	2Kin 10:11	1419
for I have a g sacrifice to do to	2Kin 10:19	1419
Upon the g altar burn the morning	2Kin 16:15	1419
LORD, and made them sin a g sin	2Kin 17:21	1419
of the land of Egypt with g power	2Kin 17:36	1419
with a g host against Jerusalem	2Kin 18:17	3515
Hezekiah, Thus saith the g king	2Kin 18:19	1419
Hear the word of the g king	2Kin 18:28	1419
for g is the wrath of the LORD	2Kin 22:13	1419
all the people, both small and g	2Kin 23:2	1419
the fierceness of his g wrath	2Kin 23:26	1419
every g man's house burnt he with	2Kin 25:9	1419
all the people, both small and g	2Kin 25:26	1419
saved them by a g deliverance	1Chr 11:14	
an Egyptian, a man of g stature	1Chr 11:23	
help him, until it was a g host	1Chr 12:22	1419
For g is the LORD, and greatly to	1Chr 16:25	1419
the g men that are in the earth	1Chr 17:8	1419
house for a g while to come	1Chr 17:17	7350
making known all these g things	1Chr 17:19	1420
where was a man of g stature	1Chr 20:6	
said unto Gad, I am in a g strait	1Chr 21:13	3966
for very g are his mercies	1Chr 21:13	7227
abundantly, and hast made g wars	1Chr 22:8	1419
ward, as well the small as the g	1Chr 25:8	1419
lots, as well the small as the g	1Chr 26:13	1419
young and tender, and the work is g	1Chr 29:1	1419
the king also rejoiced with g joy	1Chr 29:9	1419
and in thine hand it is to make g	1Chr 29:12	1431
LORD on that day with g gladness	1Chr 29:22	1419
Thou hast shewed g mercy unto	2Chr 1:8	1419
this thy people, that is so g	2Chr 1:10	1419
And the house which I build is g	2Chr 2:5	1419
for g is our God above all gods	2Chr 2:5	1419
to build shall be wonderful g	2Chr 2:9	1419
the g court, and doors for the	2Chr 4:9	1419
all these vessels in g abundance	2Chr 4:18	3966
far country for thy g name's sake	2Chr 6:32	1419
a very g congregation, from the	2Chr 7:8	1419
Jerusalem, with a very g company	2Chr 9:1	3515
of gold, and of spices g abundance	2Chr 9:9	3966
the king made a g throne of ivory	2Chr 9:17	1419
ye be a g multitude, and there are	2Chr 13:8	7227
slew them with a g slaughter	2Chr 13:17	7227
but g vexations were upon all the	2Chr 15:5	7227
put to death, whether small or g	2Chr 15:13	1419
until his disease was exceeding g	2Chr 16:12	
made a very g burning for him	2Chr 16:14	1419
Jehoshaphat waxed g exceedingly	2Chr 17:12	1432
Fight ye not with small or g	2Chr 18:30	1419
There cometh a g multitude	2Chr 20:2	1419
we have no might against this g	2Chr 20:12	7227
by reason of this g multitude	2Chr 20:15	7227
gave them g gifts of silver	2Chr 21:3	7227
with a g plague will the LORD	2Chr 21:14	1419
thou shalt have g sickness by	2Chr 21:15	7227
a very g host into their hand	2Chr 24:24	7230
(for they left him in g diseases	2Chr 24:25	7227
and they returned home in g anger	2Chr 25:10	2750
shoot arrows and g stones withal	2Chr 26:15	1419
carried away a g multitude of	2Chr 28:5	1419
who smote him with a g slaughter	2Chr 28:5	1419
for our trespass is g, and there	2Chr 28:13	7227
month, a very g congregation	2Chr 30:13	7230
bread seven days with g gladness	2Chr 30:21	1419
a g number of priests sanctified	2Chr 30:24	7230
So there was g joy in Jerusalem	2Chr 30:26	1419
which is left is this g store	2Chr 31:10	
as well to the g as to the small	2Chr 31:15	1419
and raised it up a very g height	2Chr 33:14	
for g is the wrath of the LORD	2Chr 34:21	1419
the Levites, and all the people, g	2Chr 34:30	1419
vessels of the house of God, g	2Chr 36:18	1419
the people shouted with a g shout	Ezr 3:11	1419
rest of the nations whom the g	Ezr 4:10	7229
Judea, to the house of the g God	Ezr 5:8	7229
which is builded with g stones	Ezr 5:8	1560
which a g king of Israel builded	Ezr 5:11	7229
With three rows of g stones	Ezr 6:4	1560
in a g trespass unto this day	Ezr 9:7	1419
for our g trespass, seeing that	Ezr 9:13	1419
a very g congregation of men	Ezr 10:1	7227
of this matter, and for the g rain	Ezr 10:9	
the province are in g affliction	Neh 1:3	1419
thee, O LORD God of heaven, the g	Neh 1:5	1419

Context	Reference	Number
thou hast redeemed by thy g power	Neh 1:10	1419
over against the g tower that	Neh 3:27	1419
took g indignation, and mocked the	Neh 4:1	7235
remember the LORD, which is g	Neh 4:14	1419
rest of the people, The work is g	Neh 4:19	7235
there was a g cry of the people	Neh 5:1	1419
I set a g assembly against them	Neh 5:7	1419
them, saying, I am doing a g work	Neh 6:3	1419
Now the city was large and g	Neh 7:4	1419
Ezra blessed the LORD, the g God	Neh 8:6	1419
send portions, and to make g mirth	Neh 8:12	1419
And there was very g gladness	Neh 8:17	1419
of g kindness, and forsookest them	Neh 9:17	7227
had wrought g provocations	Neh 9:18	1419
themselves in thy g goodness	Neh 9:25	1419
and they wrought g provocations	Neh 9:26	1419
Nevertheless for thy g mercies'	Neh 9:31	7227
Now therefore, our God, the g	Neh 9:32	1419
in thy g goodness that thou	Neh 9:35	7227
pleasure, and we are in g distress	Neh 9:37	1419
the son of one of the g men	Neh 11:14	1419
appointed two g companies of them	Neh 12:31	1419
day they offered g sacrifices	Neh 12:43	1419
had made them rejoice with g joy	Neh 12:43	1419
had prepared for him a g chamber	Neh 13:5	1419
unto you to do all this g evil	Neh 13:27	1419
Shushan the palace, both unto g	Est 1:5	1419
all his empire, (for it is g	Est 1:20	7227
their husbands honour, both to g	Est 1:20	1419
Then the king made a g feast unto	Est 2:18	1419
there was g mourning among the	Est 4:3	1419
with a g crown of gold, and with a	Est 8:15	1419
For Mordecai was g in the king's	Est 9:4	1419
g among the Jews, and accepted of	Est 10:3	1419
she asses, and a very g household	Job 1:3	7227
there came a g wind from the	Job 1:19	1419
saw that his grief was very g	Job 2:13	1431
The small and g are there	Job 3:19	1419
Which doeth g things and	Job 5:9	1419
also that thy seed shall be g	Job 5:25	7227
Which doeth g things past finding	Job 9:10	1419
Is not thy wickedness g	Job 22:5	7227
plead against me with his g power	Job 23:6	7227
By the g force of my disease is	Job 30:18	7227
rejoiced because my wealth was g	Job 31:25	7227
Did I fear a g multitude, or did	Job 31:34	7227
G men are not always wise	Job 32:9	7227
he knoweth it not in g extremity	Job 35:15	3966
then a g ransom cannot deliver	Job 36:18	7227
Behold, God is g, and we know him	Job 36:26	7689
g things doeth he, which we	Job 37:5	1419
to the g rain of his strength	Job 37:6	4306
the number of thy days is g	Job 38:21	7227
him, because his strength is g	Job 39:11	7227
There were they in g fear	Ps 14:5	6343
and thy gentleness hath made me g	Ps 18:35	7235
G deliverance giveth he to his	Ps 18:50	1431
keeping of them there is g reward	Ps 19:11	7227
innocent from the g transgression	Ps 19:13	7227
His glory is g in thy salvation	Ps 21:5	1419
be of thee in the g congregation	Ps 22:25	7227
mine iniquity; for it is g	Ps 25:11	7227
Oh how g is thy goodness, which	Ps 31:19	7227
surely in the floods of g waters	Ps 32:6	7227
he deliver any by his g strength	Ps 33:17	7230
thee thanks in the g congregation	Ps 35:18	7227
is like the g mountains	Ps 36:6	410
thy judgments are a g deep	Ps 36:6	7227
I have seen the wicked in g power	Ps 37:35	
in the g congregation	Ps 40:9	7227
thy truth from the g congregation	Ps 40:10	7227
he is a g King over all the earth	Ps 47:2	1419
G is the LORD, and greatly to be	Ps 48:1	1419
the north, the city of the g King	Ps 48:2	7227
There were they in g fear	Ps 53:5	
thy mercy is g unto the heavens	Ps 57:10	1419
break out the g teeth of the	Ps 58:6	4459
g was the company of those that	Ps 68:11	7227
very high, who hast done g things	Ps 71:19	1419
Thou, which hast shewed me g	Ps 71:20	7229
his name is g in Israel	Ps 76:1	1419
who is so g a God as our God	Ps 77:13	1419
sea, and thy path in the g waters	Ps 77:19	7227
them drink as out of the g depths	Ps 78:15	7227
From following the ewes g with	Ps 78:71	
them tears to drink in g measure	Ps 80:5	7991
For thou art g, and doest wondrous	Ps 86:10	1419
For g is thy mercy toward me	Ps 86:13	1419
O LORD, how g are thy works	Ps 92:5	1431
For the LORD is a g God	Ps 95:3	1419
and a g King above all gods	Ps 95:3	1419
For the LORD is g, and greatly to	Ps 96:4	1419
The LORD is g in Zion	Ps 99:2	1419
Let them praise thy g and terrible	Ps 99:3	1419
so g is his mercy toward them	Ps 103:11	1396
O LORD my God, thou art very g	Ps 104:1	1431
So is this g and wide sea, wherein	Ps 104:25	1419
both small and g beasts	Ps 104:25	1419
which had done g things in Egypt	Ps 106:21	1419
that do business in g waters	Ps 107:23	7227
For thy mercy is g above the	Ps 108:4	1419
The works of the LORD are g	Ps 111:2	1419
fear the LORD, both small and g	Ps 115:13	1419
merciful kindness is g toward us	Ps 117:2	1396
G are thy tender mercies, O LORD	Ps 119:156	7227
word, as one that findeth g spoil	Ps 119:162	7227
G peace have they which love thy	Ps 119:165	7227
LORD hath done g things for them	Ps 126:2	1431
LORD hath done g things for us	Ps 126:3	1431
do I exercise myself in g matters	Ps 131:1	1419
For I know that the LORD is g	Ps 135:5	1419
Who smote g nations, and slew	Ps 135:10	7227
To him who alone doeth g wonders	Ps 136:4	1419
To him that made g lights	Ps 136:7	1419

Context	Reference	Number
To him which smote g kings	Ps 136:17	1419
for g is the glory of the LORD	Ps 138:5	1419
How g is the sum of them	Ps 139:17	6105
me, and deliver me out of g waters	Ps 144:7	7227
G is the LORD, and greatly to be	Ps 145:3	1419
the memory of thy g goodness	Ps 145:7	7227
slow to anger, and of g mercy	Ps 145:8	1419
G is our Lord, and of g power	Ps 147:5	1419
G is our Lord, and of g power	Ps 147:5	7227
himself poor, yet hath g riches	Prov 13:7	7227
to wrath is of g understanding	Prov 14:29	7227
fear of the LORD than g treasure	Prov 15:16	7227
than g revenues without right	Prov 16:8	7230
brother to him that is a g waster	Prov 18:9	1167
him, and bringeth him before g men	Prov 18:16	1419
A man of g wrath shall suffer	Prov 19:19	
rather to be chosen than g riches	Prov 22:1	7227
stand not in the place of g men	Prov 25:6	1419
The g God that formed all things	Prov 26:10	7227
men do rejoice, there is g glory	Prov 28:12	7227
is also a g oppressor	Prov 28:16	7227
saying, Lo, I am come to g estate	Eccl 1:16	1431
my heart had g experience of	Eccl 1:16	7235
I made me g works	Eccl 2:4	1431
also I had g possessions of g	Eccl 2:7	7235
also I had g possessions of g	Eccl 2:7	1241
So I was g, and increased more	Eccl 2:9	1431
This also is vanity and a g evil	Eccl 2:21	7227
the misery of man is g upon him	Eccl 8:6	7227
the sun, and it seemed g unto me	Eccl 9:13	1419
there came a g king against it,	Eccl 9:14	1419
built g bulwarks against it	Eccl 9:14	1419
for yielding pacifieth g offences	Eccl 10:4	1419
Folly is set in g dignity	Eccl 10:6	7227
under his shadow with g delight	Song 2:3	
the g man humbleth himself	Is 2:9	
houses shall be desolate, even g	Is 5:9	1419
there be a g forsaking in the	Is 6:12	7227
said unto me, Take thee a g roll	Is 8:1	1419
in darkness have seen a g light	Is 9:2	1419
for g is the Holy One of Israel	Is 12:6	1419
mountains, like as of a g people	Is 13:4	7227
with all that g multitude	Is 16:14	7227
a g one, and he shall deliver them	Is 19:20	7227
by g waters the seed of Sihor,	Is 23:3	7227
day the LORD with his sore and g	Is 27:1	1419
that the g trumpet shall be blown	Is 27:13	1419
g noise, with storm and tempest,	Is 29:6	1419
in the day of the g slaughter	Is 30:25	7227
as the shadow of a g rock in a	Is 32:2	3515
is the prey of a g spoil divided	Is 33:23	4766
a g slaughter in the land of	Is 34:6	1419
There shall the g owl make her	Is 34:15	7091
unto king Hezekiah with a g army	Is 36:2	3515
Hezekiah, Thus saith the g king	Is 36:4	1419
Hear ye the words of the g king	Is 36:13	1419
for peace I had g bitterness	Is 38:17	
for the g abundance of thine	Is 47:9	3966
the sea, the waters of the g deep	Is 51:10	7227
I divide him a portion with the g	Is 53:12	7227
but with g mercies will I gather	Is 54:7	1419
g shall be the peace of thy	Is 54:13	7227
the g goodness toward the house	Is 63:7	7227
the north, and a g destruction	Jer 4:6	1419
I will get me unto the g men	Jer 5:5	1419
therefore they are become g	Jer 5:27	1431
of the north, and g destruction	Jer 6:1	1419
a g nation shall be raised from	Jer 6:22	1419
thou art g, and thy name is g	Jer 10:6	1419
g, and thy name is g in might	Jer 10:6	1419
a g commotion out of the north	Jer 10:22	1419
with the noise of a g tumult he	Jer 11:16	1419
and the g pride of Jerusalem	Jer 13:9	7227
people is broken with a g breach	Jer 14:17	1419
Both the g and the small shall die	Jer 16:6	1419
all this g evil against us	Jer 16:10	1419
her womb to be always g with me	Jer 20:17	2030
anger, and in fury, and in g wrath	Jer 21:5	1419
they shall die of a g pestilence	Jer 21:6	1419
LORD done thus unto this g city	Jer 22:8	1419
g kings shall serve themselves of	Jer 25:14	1419
a g whirlwind shall be raised up	Jer 25:32	1419
Thus might we procure g evil	Jer 26:19	1419
upon the ground, by my g power	Jer 27:5	1419
g kings shall serve themselves of	Jer 27:7	1419
against g kingdoms, of war, and of	Jer 28:8	1419
for that day is g, so that none	Jer 30:7	1419
a g company shall return thither	Jer 31:8	1419
and the earth by thy g power	Jer 32:17	1419
the G, the Mighty God, the LORD	Jer 32:18	1419
G in counsel, and mighty in work	Jer 32:19	1419
out arm, and with g terror	Jer 32:21	1419
and in my fury, and in g wrath	Jer 32:37	1419
all this g evil upon this people	Jer 32:42	1419
will answer thee, and shew thee g	Jer 33:3	1419
for g is the anger and the fury	Jer 36:7	1419
found him by the g waters that	Jer 41:12	7227
Take g stones in thine hand, and	Jer 43:9	1419
ye this g evil against your souls	Jer 44:7	1419
a g multitude, even all the	Jer 44:15	1419
Behold, I have sworn by my g name	Jer 44:26	1419
seekest thou g things for thyself	Jer 45:5	1419
spoiling and g destruction	Jer 48:3	1419
g nations from the north country	Jer 50:9	1419
in the land, and of g destruction	Jer 50:22	1419
a g nation, and many kings shall	Jer 50:41	1419
g destruction from the land of	Jer 51:54	1419
destroyed out of her the g voice	Jer 51:55	1419
her waves do roar like g waters	Jer 51:55	7227
and all the houses of the g men	Jer 52:13	1419
she that was g among the nations,	Lam 1:1	7227
and because of g servitude	Lam 1:3	7230
for thy breach is g like the sea	Lam 2:13	1419
g is thy faithfulness	Lam 3:23	7227

Context	Reference	Number
a g cloud, and a fire infolding	Eze 1:4	1419
wings, like the noise of g waters	Eze 1:24	7227
behind me a voice of a g rushing	Eze 3:12	1419
them, and a noise of a g rushing	Eze 3:13	1419
even the g abominations that the	Eze 8:6	1419
of Israel and Judah is exceeding g	Eze 9:9	1419
O g hailstones, shall fall	Eze 13:11	417
g hailstones in my fury to	Eze 13:13	417
and thou hast increased and waxen g	Eze 16:7	1431
thy neighbours, g of flesh	Eze 16:26	1432
A g eagle with g wings,	Eze 17:3	1419
he placed it by g waters, and set	Eze 17:5	7227
another g eagle with g wings	Eze 17:7	1419
in a good soil by g waters	Eze 17:8	7227
even without g power or many	Eze 17:9	1419
g company make for him in the war	Eze 17:17	7227
sword of the g men that are slain	Eze 21:14	1419
g lords and renowned, all of them	Eze 23:23	7991
even make the pile for fire g	Eze 24:9	1431
her g scum went not forth out of	Eze 24:12	7227
I will execute g vengeance upon	Eze 25:17	1419
g waters shall cover thee	Eze 26:19	7227
have brought thee into g waters	Eze 27:26	7227
By thy g wisdom and by thy	Eze 28:5	7230
the g dragon that lieth in the	Eze 29:3	1419
serve a g service against Tyrus	Eze 29:18	1419
g pain shall be in Ethiopia, when	Eze 30:4	
g pain shall come upon them, as	Eze 30:9	
Sin shall have g pain, and No	Eze 30:16	2342
The waters made him g, the deep	Eze 31:4	1431
his shadow dwelt all g nations	Eze 31:6	7227
for his root was by g waters	Eze 31:7	7227
and the g waters were stayed	Eze 31:15	7227
thereof from beside the g waters	Eze 32:13	7227
And I will sanctify my g name	Eze 36:23	1419
their feet, an exceeding g army	Eze 37:10	1419
even a g company with bucklers and	Eze 38:4	7227
and goods, to take a g spoil	Eze 38:13	1419
a g company, and a mighty army	Eze 38:15	1419
in that day there shall be a g	Eze 38:19	1419
g hailstones, fire, and brimstone	Eze 38:22	417
even a g sacrifice upon the	Eze 39:17	1419
were a full reed of six g cubits	Eze 41:8	679
be a very g multitude of fish	Eze 47:9	7227
kinds, as the fish of the g sea	Eze 47:10	1419
the north side, from the g sea	Eze 47:15	1419
in Kadesh, the river to the g sea	Eze 47:19	1419
be the g sea from the border	Eze 47:20	1419
and to the river toward the g sea	Eze 48:28	1419
me gifts and rewards and g honour	Dan 2:6	7690
king, sawest, and behold a g image	Dan 2:31	7690
This g image, whose brightness	Dan 2:31	7229
the image became a g mountain	Dan 2:35	7229
the g God hath made known to the	Dan 2:45	7229
Then the king made Daniel a g man	Dan 2:48	7236
and gave him many g gifts	Dan 2:48	7260
How g are his signs	Dan 4:3	7260
and the height thereof was g	Dan 4:10	7690
and said, Is not this g Babylon	Dan 4:30	7227
a g feast to a thousand of his	Dan 5:1	7227
the heaven strove upon the g sea	Dan 7:2	7227
four g beasts came up from the	Dan 7:3	7260
and it had g iron teeth	Dan 7:7	7260
man, and a mouth speaking g things	Dan 7:8	7260
the g words which the horn spake	Dan 7:11	7260
These g beasts, which are four,	Dan 7:17	7260
a mouth that spake very g things	Dan 7:20	7260
he shall speak g words against	Dan 7:25	
to his will, and became g	Dan 8:4	1431
the he goat waxed very g	Dan 8:8	1431
was strong, the g horn was broken	Dan 8:8	1419
horn, which waxed exceeding g	Dan 8:9	1431
And it waxed g, even to the host	Dan 8:10	1431
the g horn that is between his	Dan 8:21	1419
and said, O Lord, the g and	Dan 9:4	1419
us, by bringing upon us a g evil	Dan 9:12	1419
but for thy g mercies	Dan 9:18	7227
I was by the side of the g river	Dan 10:4	1419
but a g quaking fell upon them,	Dan 10:7	1419
left alone, and saw this g vision	Dan 10:8	1419
that shall rule with g dominion	Dan 11:3	7227
dominion shall be a g dominion	Dan 11:5	7227
assemble a multitude of g forces	Dan 11:10	7227
he shall set forth a g multitude	Dan 11:11	7227
after certain years with a g army	Dan 11:13	1419
king of the south with a g army	Dan 11:25	1419
up to battle with a very g	Dan 11:25	1419
into his land with g riches	Dan 11:28	1419
go forth with g fury to destroy	Dan 11:44	1419
the g prince which standeth for	Dan 12:1	1419
land hath committed g whoredom	Hos 1:2	
for g shall be the day of Jezreel	Hos 1:11	1419
to him the g things of my law	Hos 8:12	7239
thine iniquity, and the g hatred	Hos 9:7	7227
you because of your g wickedness	Hos 10:15	7451
in the land of g drought	Hos 13:5	8514
hath the cheek teeth of a g lion	Joel 1:6	3833
a g people and a strong	Joel 2:2	7227
for his camp is very g	Joel 2:11	7227
for the day of the LORD is g	Joel 2:11	1419
of g kindness, and repenteth him	Joel 2:13	7227
up, because he hath done g things	Joel 2:20	1431
for the LORD will do g things	Joel 2:21	1431
my g army which I sent among you	Joel 2:25	1419
the moon into blood, before the g	Joel 2:31	1419
for their wickedness is g	Joel 3:13	7227
behold the g tumults in the midst	Amos 3:9	7227
the g houses shall have an end,	Amos 3:15	7227
from thence go ye to Hamath the g	Amos 6:2	7227
he will smite the g house with	Amos 6:11	1419
fire, and it devoured the g deep	Amos 7:4	7227
the ephah small, and the shekel g	Amos 8:5	1431
Arise, go to Nineveh, that g city	Jonah 1:2	1419
sent out a g wind into the sea	Jonah 1:4	1419
sake this g tempest is upon you	Jonah 1:12	1419
a g fish to swallow up Jonah	Jonah 1:17	1419
go unto Nineveh, that g city	Jonah 3:2	1419
g city of three days' journey	Jonah 3:3	1419
of g kindness, and repentest thee	Jonah 4:2	7227
not I spare Nineveh, that g city	Jonah 4:11	1419
they shall make g noise by reason	Mic 2:12	
for now shall he be g unto the	Mic 5:4	1431
and the g man, he uttereth his	Mic 7:3	1419
g in power, and will not at all	Nah 1:3	1431
slain, and a g number of carcases	Nah 3:3	3514
all her g men were bound in	Nah 3:10	1419
captains as the g grasshoppers	Nah 3:17	1462
through the heap of g waters	Hab 3:15	7227
a g crashing from the hills	Zeph 1:10	1419
The g day of the LORD is near, it	Zeph 1:14	1419
and for Zion with a g jealousy	Zec 1:14	1419
Who art thou, O g mountain	Zec 4:7	1419
therefore came a g wrath from the	Zec 7:12	1419
jealous for Zion with g jealousy	Zec 8:2	1419
I was jealous for her with g fury	Zec 8:2	1419
For how g is his goodness	Zec 9:17	
and how g is his beauty	Zec 9:17	
be a g mourning in Jerusalem	Zec 12:11	1431
and there shall be a very g valley	Zec 14:4	1419
that a g tumult from the LORD	Zec 14:13	7227
and apparel, in g abundance	Zec 14:14	3966
shall be g among the Gentiles	Mal 1:11	1419
name shall be g among the heathen	Mal 1:11	1419
for I am a g King, saith the LORD	Mal 1:14	1419
before the coming of the g	Mal 4:5	1419
rejoiced with exceeding g joy	Mt 2:10	3173
g mourning, Rachel weeping for	Mt 2:18	4183
which sat in darkness saw g light	Mt 4:16	3173
there followed him g multitudes	Mt 4:25	4183
for g is your reward in heaven	Mt 5:12	4183
called g in the kingdom of heaven	Mt 5:19	3173
for it is the city of the g King	Mt 5:35	3173
darkness, how g is that darkness	Mt 6:23	4214
and g was the fall of it	Mt 7:27	3173
g multitudes followed him	Mt 8:1	4183
you, I have not found so g faith	Mt 8:10	5118
Now when Jesus saw g multitudes	Mt 8:18	4183
there arose a g tempest in the	Mt 8:24	3173
and there was a g calm	Mt 8:26	3173
g multitudes followed him, and he	Mt 12:15	4183
g multitudes were gathered	Mt 13:2	4183
he had found one pearl of g price	Mt 13:46	4186
saw a g multitude, and was moved	Mt 14:14	4183
unto her, O woman, g is thy faith	Mt 15:28	3173
g multitudes came unto him,	Mt 15:30	4183
as to fill so g a multitude	Mt 15:33	5118
g multitudes followed him	Mt 19:2	4183
for he had g possessions	Mt 19:22	4183
them, and they that are g exercise	Mt 20:25	3171
but whosoever will be g among you	Mt 20:26	3173
a g multitude followed him	Mt 20:29	4183
a very g multitude spread their	Mt 21:8	4118
which is the g commandment in the	Mt 22:36	3173
is the first and g commandment	Mt 22:38	3173
For then shall be g tribulation	Mt 24:21	3173
prophets, and shall shew g signs	Mt 24:24	3173
of heaven with power and g glory	Mt 24:30	4183
with a g sound of a trumpet	Mt 24:31	3173
with him a g multitude with	Mt 26:47	4183
he rolled a g stone to the door	Mt 27:60	3173
behold, there was a g earthquake	Mt 28:2	3173
the sepulchre with fear and g joy	Mt 28:8	3173
rising up a g while before day,	Mk 1:35	3029
a g multitude from Galilee	Mk 3:7	4183
a g multitude, when they had	Mk 3:8	4183
had heard what g things he did	Mk 3:8	3745
gathered unto him a g multitude	Mk 4:1	4183
herbs, and shooteth out g branches	Mk 4:32	3173
And there arose a g storm of wind	Mk 4:37	3173
ceased, and there was a g calm	Mk 4:39	3173
a g herd of swine feeding	Mk 5:11	3173
tell them how g things the Lord	Mk 5:19	3745
to publish in Decapolis how g	Mk 5:20	3745
astonished with a g astonishment	Mk 5:42	3173
so much the more a g deal they	Mk 7:36	3123
days the multitude being very g	Mk 8:1	3827
he saw a g multitude about them,	Mk 9:14	4183
for he had g possessions	Mk 10:22	4183
their g ones exercise authority	Mk 10:42	3173
but whosoever will be g among you	Mk 10:43	3173
a g number of people, blind	Mk 10:46	2425
but he cried the more a g deal	Mk 10:48	4183
him, Seest thou these g buildings	Mk 13:2	3173
coming in the clouds with g power	Mk 13:26	4183
with him a g multitude with	Mk 14:43	4183
for it was very g	Mk 16:4	3173
For he shall be g in the sight of	Lk 1:15	3173
He shall be g, and shall be called	Lk 1:32	3173
mighty hath done to me g things	Lk 1:49	3167
Lord had shewed g mercy upon her	Lk 1:58	3170
espoused wife, being g with child	Lk 2:5	
I bring you good tidings of g joy	Lk 2:10	3173
she was of a g age, and had lived	Lk 2:36	4183
when g famine was throughout all	Lk 4:25	3173
mother was taken with a g fever	Lk 4:38	3173
they inclosed a g multitude of	Lk 5:6	4183
g multitudes came together to	Lk 5:15	4183
Levi made him a g feast in his	Lk 5:29	3173
and there was a g company of	Lk 5:29	4183
a g multitude of people out of	Lk 6:17	4183
your reward is g in heaven	Lk 6:23	4183
and your reward shall be g	Lk 6:35	4183
and the ruin of that house was g	Lk 6:49	3173
you, I have not found so g faith	Lk 7:9	5118
That a g prophet is risen up	Lk 7:16	3173
for they were taken with g fear	Lk 8:37	3173
shew how g things God hath done	Lk 8:39	3745
throughout the whole city how g	Lk 8:39	3745
you all, the same shall be g	Lk 9:48	3173
unto them, The harvest truly is g	Lk 10:2	4183
they had a g while ago repented,	Lk 10:13	3819
and it grew, and waxed a g tree	Lk 13:19	3173
A certain man made a g supper	Lk 14:16	3173
there went g multitudes with him	Lk 14:25	4183
the other is yet a g way off	Lk 14:32	
But when he was yet a g way off	Lk 15:20	3112
us and you there is a g gulf fixed	Lk 16:26	3173
g earthquakes shall be in divers	Lk 21:11	3173
g signs shall there be from	Lk 21:11	3173
for there shall be g distress in	Lk 21:23	3173
in a cloud with power and g glory	Lk 21:27	4183
his sweat was as it were g drops	Lk 22:44	
him a g company of people	Lk 23:27	4183
returned to Jerusalem with g joy	Lk 24:52	3173
In these lay a g multitude of	Jn 5:3	4183
a g multitude followed him,	Jn 6:2	4183
saw a g company come unto him, he	Jn 6:5	4183
by reason of a g wind that blew	Jn 6:18	3173
that g day of the feast, Jesus	Jn 7:37	3173
the net to land full of g fishes	Jn 21:11	3173
moon into blood, before that g	Acts 2:20	3173
with g power gave the apostles	Acts 4:33	3173
g grace was upon them all	Acts 4:33	3173
g fear came on all them that	Acts 5:5	3173
g fear came upon all the church,	Acts 5:11	3173
a g company of the priests were	Acts 6:7	4183
did g wonders and miracles among	Acts 6:8	3173
Egypt and Chanaan, and g affliction	Acts 7:11	3173
at that time there was a g	Acts 8:1	3173
made g lamentation over him	Acts 8:2	3173
there was g joy in that city	Acts 8:8	3173
out that himself was some g one	Acts 8:9	3173
This man is the g power of God	Acts 8:10	3173
an eunuch of g authority under	Acts 8:27	
For I will shew him how g things	Acts 9:16	3745
as it had been a g sheet knit at	Acts 10:11	3173
descend, as it had been a g sheet	Acts 11:5	3173
a g number believed, and turned	Acts 11:21	4183
g dearth throughout all the world	Acts 11:28	3173
that a g multitude both of the	Acts 14:1	4183
they caused g joy unto all the	Acts 15:3	3173
suddenly there was a g earthquake	Acts 16:26	3173
the devout Greeks a g multitude	Acts 17:4	4183
of the g goddess Diana should be	Acts 19:27	3173
G is Diana of the Ephesians	Acts 19:28	3173
G is Diana of the Ephesians	Acts 19:34	3173
worshipper of the g goddess Diana	Acts 19:35	3173
when there was made a g silence	Acts 21:40	4183
heaven a g light round about me	Acts 22:6	2425
With a g sum obtained I this	Acts 22:28	4183
And there arose a g cry	Acts 23:9	3173
when there arose a g dissension	Acts 23:10	4183
bound ourselves under a g curse	Acts 23:14	
that by thee we enjoy g quietness	Acts 24:2	4183
with g violence took him away out	Acts 24:7	4183
was come, and Bernice, with g pomp	Acts 25:23	4183
witnessing both to small and g	Acts 26:22	3173
after they had looked a g while	Acts 28:6	4183
had g reasoning among themselves	Acts 28:29	4183
That I have g heaviness and	Rom 9:2	3173
having a g desire these many	Rom 15:23	1974
is it a g thing if we shall reap	1Cor 9:11	3173
For a g door and effectual is	1Cor 16:9	3173
delivered us from so g a death	2Cor 1:10	5082
we use g plainness of speech	2Cor 3:12	4183
G is my boldness of speech toward	2Cor 7:4	4183
you, g is my glorying of you	2Cor 7:4	4183
How that in a g trial of	2Cor 8:2	4183
upon the g confidence which I	2Cor 8:22	4183
Therefore it is no g thing if his	2Cor 11:15	3173
for his g love wherewith he loved	Eph 2:4	4183
This is a g mystery	Eph 5:32	3173
what g conflict I have for you	Col 2:1	2245
that he hath a g zeal for you	Col 4:13	4183
to see your face with g desire	1Th 2:17	4183
g boldness in the faith which is	1Ti 3:13	4183
without controversy g is the	1Ti 3:16	3173
with contentment is g gain	1Ti 6:6	3173
But in a g house there are not	2Ti 2:20	3173
glorious appearing of the g God	Titus 2:13	3173
For we have g joy and consolation	Philem 7	4183
if we neglect so g salvation	Heb 2:3	5082
then that we have a g high priest	Heb 4:14	3173
Now consider how g this man was	Heb 7:4	4080
ye endured a g fight of	Heb 10:32	4183
which hath g recompence of reward	Heb 10:35	3173
with so g a cloud of witnesses	Heb 12:1	5118
that g shepherd of the sheep,	Heb 13:20	3173
ships, which though they be so g	Jas 3:4	5082
member, and boasteth g things	Jas 3:5	3166
how g a matter a little fire	Jas 3:5	2245
is in the sight of God of g price	1Pet 3:4	4185
are given unto us exceeding g	2Pet 1:4	3176
For when they speak g swelling	2Pet 2:18	5246
shall pass away with a g noise	2Pet 3:10	
unto the judgment of the g day	Jude 6	3173
mouth speaketh g swelling words	Jude 16	5246
day, and heard behind me a g voice	Rev 1:10	3173
with her into g tribulation	Rev 2:22	3173
was given unto him a g sword	Rev 6:4	3173
and, lo, there was a g earthquake	Rev 6:12	3173
kings of the earth, and the g men	Rev 6:15	3175
For the g day of his wrath is	Rev 6:17	3173
a g multitude, which no man could	Rev 7:9	4183
which came out of g tribulation	Rev 7:14	3173
as it were a g mountain burning	Rev 8:8	3173
there fell a g star from heaven,	Rev 8:10	3173
pit, as the smoke of a g furnace	Rev 9:2	3173
bound in the g river Euphrates	Rev 9:14	3173
lie in the street of the g city	Rev 11:8	3173
g fear fell upon them which saw	Rev 11:11	3173
they heard a g voice from heaven	Rev 11:12	3173

hour was there a g earthquake Rev 11:13 3173
there were g voices in heaven, Rev 11:15 3173
hast taken to thee thy g power Rev 11:17 3173
that fear thy name, small and g Rev 11:18 3173
and an earthquake, and g hail Rev 11:19 3173
appeared a g wonder in heaven Rev 12:1 3173
behold a g red dragon, having Rev 12:3 3173
the g dragon was cast out, that Rev 12:9 3173
down unto you, having g wrath Rev 12:12 3173
were given two wings of a g eagle Rev 12:14 3173
and his seat, and g authority Rev 13:2 3173
him a mouth speaking g things Rev 13:5 3173
And he doeth g wonders, so that he Rev 13:13 3173
he causeth all, both small and g Rev 13:16 3173
and as the voice of a g thunder Rev 14:2 3173
is fallen, is fallen, that g city Rev 14:8 3173
cast it into the g winepress of Rev 14:19 3173
I saw another sign in heaven, g Rev 15:1 3173
the song of the Lamb, saying, G Rev 15:3 3173
I heard a g voice out of the Rev 16:1 3173
And men were scorched with g heat Rev 16:9 3173
vial upon the g river Euphrates Rev 16:12 3173
of that g day of God Almighty Rev 16:14 3173
there came a g voice out of the Rev 16:17 3173
and there was a g earthquake Rev 16:18 3173
so mighty an earthquake, and so g Rev 16:18 3173
the g city was divided into three Rev 16:19 3173
g Babylon came in remembrance Rev 16:19 3173
upon men a g hail out of heaven Rev 16:21 3173
plague thereof was exceeding g Rev 16:21 3173
g whore that sitteth upon many Rev 17:1 3173
BABYLON THE G Rev 17:5 3173
her, I wondered with g admiration Rev 17:6 3173
which thou sawest is that g city Rev 17:18 3173
down from heaven, having g power Rev 18:1 3173
saying, Babylon the g is fallen Rev 18:2 3173
alas that g city Babylon, that Rev 18:10 3173
And saying, Alas, alas that g city Rev 18:16 3173
For in one hour so g riches is Rev 18:17 5118
city is like unto this g city Rev 18:18 3173
saying, Alas, alas that g city Rev 18:19 3173
up a stone like a g millstone Rev 18:21 3173
g city Babylon be thrown down Rev 18:21 3173
were the g men of the earth Rev 18:23 3175
after these things I heard a g Rev 19:1 3173
for he hath judged the g whore Rev 19:2 3173
ye that fear him, both small and g Rev 19:5 3173
were the voice of a g multitude Rev 19:6 4185
unto the supper of the g God Rev 19:17 3173
free and bond, both small and g Rev 19:18 3173
pit and a g chain in his hand Rev 20:1 3173
I saw a g white throne, and him Rev 20:11 3173
And I saw the dead, small and g Rev 20:12 3173
I heard a g voice out of heaven Rev 21:3 3173
me away in the spirit to a g Rev 21:10 3173
and shewed me that g city Rev 21:10 3173
And had a wall g and high, and had Rev 21:12 3173

GREATER

the g light to rule the day, and Gen 1:16 1419
punishment is g than I can bear Gen 4:13 1419
There is none g in this house Gen 39:9 1419
the throne will I be g than thou Gen 41:40 1431
brother shall be g than he Gen 48:19 1431
that the LORD is g than all gods Ex 18:11 1419
and will make of thee a g nation Num 14:12 1419
heart, saying, The people is g Deut 1:28 1419
out nations from before thee g Deut 4:38 1419
and the Jebusites, seven nations g Deut 7:1 7227
to go in to possess nations g Deut 9:1 1419
a nation mightier and g than they Deut 9:14 7227
and ye shall possess g nations Deut 11:23 1419
and because it was g than Ai Josh 10:2 1419
had there not been now a much g 1Sa 14:30 7235
wherewith he hated her was g than 2Sa 13:15 1419
g than the other that thou didst 2Sa 13:16 1419
make his throne g than the throne 1Kin 1:37
make his throne g than thy throne 1Kin 1:47
So David waxed g and g 1Chr 11:9 1980
So David waxed g and g 1Chr 11:9 1419
the g house he cieled with fir 2Chr 3:5 1419
man Mordecai waxed g and g Est 9:4 1419
thee, that God is g than man Job 33:12 7235
g than the punishment of the sin Lam 4:6 1431
and thou shalt see g abominations Eze 8:6 1419
thou shalt see g abominations Eze 8:13 1419
thou shalt see g abominations Eze 8:15 1419
the g settle shall be four cubits Eze 43:14 1419
a multitude g than the former Dan 11:13 7227
or their border g than your Amos 6:2 7227
shall be g than of the former Hag 2:9 1419
risen a g than John the Baptist Mt 11:11 3187
kingdom of heaven is g than he Mt 11:11 3187
place is one g than the temple Mt 12:6 3187
behold, a g than Jonas is here Mt 12:41 4119
behold, a g than Solomon is here Mt 12:42 4119
ye shall receive the g damnation Mt 23:14 4055
for whether is g, the gold, or Mt 23:17 3187
for whether is g, the gift, or Mt 23:19 3187
becometh g than all herbs, and Mk 4:32 3187
other commandment g than these Mk 12:31 3187
these shall receive g damnation Mk 12:40 4055
born of women there is not a g Lk 7:28 3187
the kingdom of God is g than he Lk 7:28 3187
behold, a g than Solomon is here Lk 11:31 4119
behold, a g than Jonas is here Lk 11:32 4119
pull down my barns, and build g Lk 12:18 3187
same shall receive g damnation Lk 20:47 4055
For whether is g, he that sitteth Lk 22:27 3187
thou shalt see g things than Jn 1:50 3187
Art thou g than our father Jacob, Jn 4:12 3187
will shew him g works than these Jn 5:20 3187
But I have g witness than that of Jn 5:36 3187
Art thou g than our father Jn 8:53 3187
which gave them me, is g than all Jn 10:29 3187
servant is not g than his lord Jn 13:16 3187
is sent g than he that sent him Jn 13:16 3187
g works than these shall he do Jn 14:12 3187
for my Father is g than I Jn 14:28 3187
G love hath no man than this, Jn 15:13 3187
servant is not g than his lord Jn 15:20 3187
me unto thee hath the g sin Jn 19:11 3187
to lay upon you no g burden than Acts 15:28 4119
for g is he that prophesieth than 1Cor 14:5 3187
of whom the g part remain unto 1Cor 15:6 4119
because he could swear by no g Heb 6:13 3187
For men verily swear by the g Heb 6:16 3187
of good things to come, by a g Heb 9:11 3187
the reproach of Christ g riches Heb 11:26 3187
shall receive the g condemnation Jas 3:1 3187
angels, which are g in power 2Pet 2:11 3187
God is g than our heart, and 1Jn 3:20 3187
because g is he that is in you, 1Jn 4:4 3187
of men, the witness of God is g 1Jn 5:9 3187
I have no g joy than to hear that 3Jn 4 3186

GREATEST

hundred, and the g over a thousand 1Chr 12:14 1419
for hitherto the g part of them 1Chr 12:29 4768
so that this man was the g of all Job 1:3 1419
g of them every one is given to Jer 6:13 1419
the g is given to covetousness Jer 8:10 1419
least of them unto the g of them Jer 31:34 1419
from the least even unto the g Jer 42:1 1419
from the least even to the g Jer 42:8 1419
from the least even unto the g Jer 44:12 1419
from the g of them even to the Jonah 3:5 1419
it is the g among herbs, and Mt 13:32 3187
Who is the g in the kingdom of Mt 18:1 3187
the same is g in the kingdom of Mt 18:4 3187
But he that is g among you shall Mt 23:11 3187
themselves, who should be the g Mk 9:34 3187
them, which of them should be g Lk 9:46 3187
of them should be accounted the g Lk 22:24 3187
but he that is g among you Lk 22:26 3187
heed, from the least to the g Acts 8:10 3173
but the g of these is charity 1Cor 13:13 3187
know me, from the least to the g Heb 8:11 3173

GREATLY

I will g multiply thy sorrow and Gen 3:16
were increased g upon the earth Gen 7:18 3966
And he pressed upon them g Gen 19:3 3966
the LORD hath blessed my master g Gen 24:35 3966
Then Jacob was g afraid and Gen 32:7 3966
and the whole mount quaked g Ex 19:18 3966
anger of the LORD was kindled g Num 11:10 3966
and the people mourned g Num 14:39 3966
for the LORD shall g bless thee Deut 15:4
neither shall he g multiply to Deut 17:17 3966
That they feared g, because Josh 10:2 3966
and they were g distressed Judg 2:15 3966
Israel was g impoverished because Judg 6:6 3966
and his anger was kindled g 1Sa 11:6 3966
all the men of Israel rejoiced g 1Sa 11:15 3966
all the people g feared the LORD 1Sa 12:18 3966
and he loved him g 1Sa 16:21 3966
they were dismayed, and g afraid 1Sa 17:11 3966
afraid, and his heart g trembled 1Sa 28:5 3966
And David was g distressed 1Sa 30:6 3966
because the men were g ashamed 2Sa 10:5 3966
David's anger was g kindled 2Sa 12:5 3966
I have sinned g in that I have 2Sa 24:10 3966
and his kingdom was established g 1Kin 2:12 3966
of Solomon, that he rejoiced g 1Kin 5:7 3966
(Now Obadiah feared the LORD g 1Kin 18:3 3966
of their fathers increased g 1Chr 4:38 7230
is the LORD, and g to be praised 1Chr 16:25 3966
for the men were g ashamed 1Chr 19:5 3966
said unto God, I have sinned g 1Chr 21:8 3966
anger was g kindled against Judah 2Chr 25:10 3966
humbled himself g before the God 2Chr 33:12 3966
For the thing which I g feared is Job 3:25
thy latter end should g increase Job 8:7 3966
salvation how g shall he rejoice Ps 21:1 3966
therefore my heart g rejoiceth Ps 28:7
I am bowed down g Ps 38:6 3966
the king g desire thy beauty Ps 45:11
he is g exalted Ps 47:9 3966
g to be praised in the city of Ps 48:1 3966
I shall not be g moved Ps 62:2 7227
thou g enrichest it with the Ps 65:9 7227
My lips shall g rejoice when I Ps 71:23
was wroth, and g abhorred Israel Ps 78:59 3966
God is g to be feared in the Ps 89:7 7227
LORD is great, and g to be praised Ps 96:4 3966
And he increased his people g Ps 105:24 3966
so that they are multiplied g Ps 107:38 3966
I will g praise the LORD with my Ps 109:30 3966
LORD, that delighteth g in his Ps 112:1 3966
I was g afflicted Ps 116:10 3966
proud have had me g in derision Ps 119:51 3966
is the LORD, and g to be praised Ps 145:3 3966
of the righteous shall g rejoice Prov 23:24
back, they shall be g ashamed Is 42:17
I will g rejoice in the LORD, my Is 61:10
shall not that land be g polluted Jer 3:1
surely thou hast g deceived this Jer 4:10
we are g confounded, because we Jer 9:19 3966
they shall be g ashamed Jer 20:11 3966
and my sabbaths they g polluted Eze 20:13 3966
hath g offended, and revenged Eze 25:12
was king Belshazzar g troubled Dan 5:9 7690
for thou art g beloved Dan 9:23
a man g beloved, understand the Dan 10:11
O man g beloved, fear not Dan 10:19
thou art g despised Obad 2 3966
is near, it is near, and hasteth g Zeph 1:14 3966
Rejoice g, O daughter of Zion Zec 9:9 3966
that the governor marvelled g Mt 27:14 3029
that were done, they feared g Mt 27:54 4970
And besought him g, saying, My Mk 5:23 4183
and them that wept and wailed g Mk 5:38 4183
were g amazed, and running to him Mk 9:15 1568
ye therefore do g err Mk 12:27 4183
rejoiceth g because of the Jn 3:29 5479
is called Solomon's, g wondering Acts 3:11 1569
multiplied in Jerusalem g Acts 6:7 4970
I g desired him to come unto you 1Cor 16:12 4183
how g I long after you all in the Phil 1:8 1971
But I rejoiced in the Lord g Phil 4:10 3171
desiring g to see us, as we also 1Th 3:6 1971
G desiring to see thee, being 2Ti 1:4 1971
for he hath g withstood our words 2Ti 4:15 3029
Wherein ye g rejoice, though now 1Pet 1:6
I rejoiced g that I found of thy 2Jn 4 3029
For I rejoiced g, when the 3Jn 3 3029

GREATNESS

in the g of thine excellency thou Ex 15:7 7230
by the g of thine arm they shall Ex 15:16 1419
according unto the g of thy mercy Num 14:19 1433
begun to shew thy servant thy g Deut 3:24 1433
hath shewed us his glory and his g Deut 5:24 1433
thou hast redeemed through thy g Deut 9:26 1433
of the LORD your God, his g Deut 11:2 1433
ascribe ye g unto our God Deut 32:3 1433
heart, hast thou done all this g 1Chr 17:19 1420
people, to make thee a name of g 1Chr 17:21 1420
Thine, O LORD, is the g, and the 1Chr 29:11 1420
the one half of the g of thy 2Chr 9:6 4768
the g of the burdens laid upon 2Chr 24:27 7230
according to the g of thy mercy Neh 13:22 7230
declaration of the g of Mordecai Est 10:2 1420
through the g of thy power shall Ps 66:3 7230
Thou shalt increase my g, and Ps 71:21 1420
according to the g of thy power Ps 79:11 1433
and his g is unsearchable Ps 145:3 1420
and I will declare thy g Ps 145:6 1420
him according to his excellent g Ps 150:2 1433
in the g of his folly he shall go Prov 5:23 7230
by names by the g of his might Is 40:26 7230
art wearied in the g of thy way Is 57:10 7230
in the g of his strength Is 63:1 7230
For the g of thine iniquity are Jer 13:22 7230
Whom art thou like in thy g Eze 31:2 1433
Thus was he fair in his g Eze 31:7 1433
in g among the trees of Eden Eze 31:18 1433
for thy g is grown, and reacheth Dan 4:22 7238
the g of the kingdom under the Dan 7:27 7238
what is the exceeding g of his Eph 1:19 3174

GREAVES

he had g of brass upon his legs, 1Sa 17:6 4697

GRECIA See GRECIANS, GREECE. *Latin form of Greece.*

the rough goat is the king of G Dan 8:21 3120
lo, the prince of G shall come Dan 10:20 3120
up all against the realm of G Dan 11:2 3120

GRECIANS See GREEKS.

1. Inhabitants of Greece.

Jerusalem have ye sold unto the G Joel 3:6 3125

2. Hellenistic Jews.

of the G against the Hebrews Acts 6:1 1675
Jesus, and disputed against the G Acts 9:29 1675
come to Antioch, spake unto the G Acts 11:20 1675

GREECE See GRECIA. *Peninsula south of the Balkans.*

O Zion, against thy sons, O G Zec 9:13 3120
much exhortation, he came into G Acts 20:2 1671

GREEDILY

He coveteth g all the day long Prov 21:26 8378
thou hast g gained of thy Eze 22:12
ran g after the error of Balaam Jude 11 1632

GREEDINESS

to work all uncleanness with g Eph 4:19 4124

GREEDY

as a lion that is g of his prey Ps 17:12 3700
of every one that is g of gain Prov 1:19 1214
He that is g of gain troubleth Prov 15:27 1214
they are g dogs which can never Is 56:11
no striker, not g of filthy lucre 1Ti 3:3 866
much wine, not g of filthy lucre 1Ti 3:8 146

GREEK See GREEKS.

1. A native of Greece.

written over him in letters of G Lk 23:38 1673
and it was written in Hebrew, and G Jn 19:20 1676
but his father was a G Acts 16:1 1672
knew all that his father was a G Acts 16:3 1672
the Jew first, and also to the G Rom 1:16 1672
between the Jew and the G Rom 10:12 1672
Titus, who was with me, being a G Gal 2:3 1672
There is neither Jew nor G Gal 3:28 1672
Where there is neither G nor Jew Col 3:11 1672

2. A language.

Who said, Canst thou speak G Acts 21:37 1676
but in the G tongue hath his name Rev 9:11 1673

3. A female.

The woman was a G, a Mk 7:26 1674

GREEKS See GRECIANS. *Plural of Greek 1.*

there were certain G among them Jn 12:20 1672
Jews and also of the G believed Acts 14:1 1672
of the devout G a great multitude Acts 17:4 1672
of honourable women which were G Acts 17:12 1674
and persuaded the Jews and the G Acts 18:4 1672
Then all the G took Sosthenes, Acts 18:17 1672
of the Lord Jesus, both Jews and G Acts 19:10 1672
G also dwelling at Ephesus Acts 19:17 1672
to the Jews, and also to the G Acts 20:21 1672
further brought G also into the Acts 21:28 1672

G

I am debtor both to the G ... Rom 1:14 1672
sign, and the G seek after wisdom ... 1Cor 1:22 1672
and unto the G foolishness ... 1Cor 1:23 1672
which are called, both Jews and G ... 1Cor 1:24 1672

GREEN
have given every g herb for meat ... Gen 1:30 3418
even as the g herb have I given ... Gen 9:3 3418
Jacob took him rods of g poplar ... Gen 30:37 3892
not any g thing in the trees ... Ex 10:15 3418
offering of thy firstfruits g ... Lev 2:14
nor g ears, until the selfsame ... Lev 23:14
the hills, and under every g tree ... Deut 12:2 7488
If they bind me with seven g ... Judg 16:7 3892
brought up to her seven g withs ... Judg 16:8 3892
high hill, and under every g tree ... 1Kin 14:23 7488
the hills, and under every g tree ... 2Kin 16:4 7488
high hill, and under every g tree ... 2Kin 17:10 7488
of the field, and as the g herb ... 2Kin 19:26 3410
the hills, and under every g tree ... 2Chr 28:4 7488
Where were white, g, and blue, ... Est 1:6 3768
He is g before the sun, and his ... Job 8:16 7373
and his branch shall not be g ... Job 15:32 7488
he searcheth after every g thing ... Job 39:8 3387
me to lie down in g pastures ... Ps 23:2 1877
grass, and wither as the g herb ... Ps 37:2 3418
himself like a g bay tree ... Ps 37:35 7488
But I am like a g olive tree in ... Ps 52:8 7488
also our bed is g ... Song 1:16 7488
fig tree putteth forth her g figs ... Song 2:13 6291
faileth, there is no g thing ... Is 15:6 3418
of the field, and as the g herb ... Is 37:27 3419
with idols under every g tree ... Is 57:5 7488
under every g tree thou wanderest ... Jer 2:20 7488
mountain and under every g tree ... Jer 3:6 7488
the strangers under every g tree ... Jer 3:13 7488
A g olive tree, fair, and of ... Jer 11:16 7488
their groves by the g trees upon ... Jer 17:2 7488
cometh, but her leaf shall be g ... Jer 17:8 7488
mountains, and under every g tree ... Eze 6:13 7488
tree, have dried up the g tree ... Eze 17:24 3892
shall devour every g tree in thee ... Eze 20:47 3892
I am like a g fir tree ... Hos 14:8 7488
by companies upon the g grass ... Mk 6:39 5515
they do these things in a g tree ... Lk 23:31 5200
up, and all g grass was burnt up ... Rev 8:7 5515
of the earth, neither any g thing ... Rev 9:4 5515

GREENISH
if the plague be g or reddish in ... Lev 13:49 3422
g or reddish, which in sight are ... Lev 14:37 3422

GREENNESS
Whilst it is yet in his g ... Job 8:12 3

GREET
go to Nabal, and g him in my name ... 1Sa 25:5
G Priscilla and Aquila my helpers ... Rom 16:3 782
Likewise g the church that is in ... Rom 16:5
G Mary, who bestowed much labour ... Rom 16:6 782
G Amplias my beloved in the Lord ... Rom 16:8 782
G them that be of the household ... Rom 16:11 782
All the brethren g you ... 1Cor 16:20 782
G ye one another with an holy ... 1Cor 16:20 782
G one another with an holy kiss ... 2Cor 13:12 782
brethren which are with me g you ... Phil 4:21 782
physician, and Demas, g you ... Col 4:14 782
G all the brethren with an holy ... 1Th 5:26 782
G them that love us in the faith ... Titus 3:15 782
G ye one another with a kiss of ... 1Pet 5:14 782
of thy elect sister g thee ... 2Jn 13 782
G the friends by name ... 3Jn 14 782

GREETETH
Eubulus g thee, and Pudens, and ... 2Ti 4:21 782

GREETING
brethren send g unto the brethren ... Acts 15:23 5463
governor Felix sendeth g ... Acts 23:26 5463
which are scattered abroad, g ... Jas 1:1 5463

GREETINGS
g in the markets, and to be called ... Mt 23:7 783
synagogues, and g in the markets ... Lk 11:43 783
love g in the markets, and the ... Lk 20:46 783

GREW
herb of the field before it g ... Gen 2:5 6779
that which g upon the ground ... Gen 19:25 6780
And the child g, and was weaned ... Gen 21:8 1431
and he g, and dwelt in the ... Gen 21:20 1431
And the boys g ... Gen 25:27 1431
g until he became very great ... Gen 26:13 1432
had possessions therein, and g ... Gen 47:27 6509
the more they multiplied and g ... Ex 1:12 6555
And the child g, and she brought ... Ex 2:10 1431
and his wife's sons g up, and they ... Judg 11:2 1431
and the child g, and the LORD ... Judg 13:24 1431
child Samuel g before the LORD ... 1Sa 2:21 1431
And the child Samuel g on, and was ... 1Sa 2:26 1432
And Samuel g, and the LORD was with ... 1Sa 3:19 1431
g great, and the LORD God of hosts ... 2Sa 5:10
it g up together with him, and ... 2Sa 12:3 1431
And it g, and became a spreading ... Eze 17:6 6779
wither in the furrows where it g ... Eze 17:10 6780
The tree g, and was strong, and the ... Dan 4:11 7236
tree that thou sawest, which g ... Dan 4:20 7236
among thorns, and the thorns g up ... Mk 4:7 305
bettered, but rather g worse ... Mk 5:26 2064
And the child g, and waxed strong ... Lk 1:80 837
And the child g, and waxed strong ... Lk 2:40 837
and it g, and waxed a great tree ... Lk 13:19 837
sworn to Abraham, the people g ... Acts 7:17 837
But the word of God g and ... Acts 12:24 837
So mightily g the word of God and ... Acts 19:20 837

GREY
beauty of old men is the g head ... Prov 20:29 7872

GREYHEADED
Now also when I am old and g ... Ps 71:18 7872

GREYHOUND
A g ... Prov 30:31

GRIEF
Which were a g of mind unto Isaac ... Gen 26:35 4786
and g have I spoken hitherto ... 1Sa 1:16 3708
That this shall be no g unto thee ... 1Sa 25:31 6330
know his own sore and his own g ... 2Chr 6:29 4341
saw that his g was very great ... Job 2:13 3511
O that my g were throughly ... Job 6:2 3708
of my lips should asswage your g ... Job 16:5
I speak, my g is not asswaged ... Job 16:6 3511
Mine eye is consumed because of g ... Ps 6:7 3708
mine eye is consumed with g ... Ps 31:9 3708
For my life is spent with g ... Ps 31:10 3015
they talk to the g of those whom ... Ps 69:26 4341
foolish son is a g to his father ... Prov 17:25 3708
For in much wisdom is much g ... Eccl 1:18 3708
are sorrows, and his travail g ... Eccl 2:23 3708
shall be a heap in the day of g ... Is 17:11 2470
of sorrows, and acquainted with g ... Is 53:3 2483
he hath put him to g ... Is 53:10 2470
before me continually is g ... Jer 6:7 2483
but I said, Truly this is a g ... Jer 10:19 2483
LORD hath added g to my sorrow ... Jer 45:3 3015
But though he cause g, yet will ... Lam 3:32 3013
head, to deliver him from his g ... Jonah 4:6 7451
But if any have caused g, he hath ... 2Cor 2:5 3076
may do it with joy, and not with g ... Heb 13:17 4727
conscience toward God endure g ... 1Pet 2:19 3077

GRIEFS
Surely he hath borne our g ... Is 53:4 2483

GRIEVANCE
iniquity, and cause me to behold g ... Hab 1:3 5999

GRIEVE
thine eyes, and to g thine heart ... 1Sa 2:33 109
from evil, that it may not g me ... 1Chr 4:10 6087
and g him in the desert ... Ps 78:40 6087
nor g the children of men ... Lam 3:33 3013
g not the holy Spirit of God, ... Eph 4:30 3076

GRIEVED
earth, and it g him at his heart ... Gen 6:6 6087
and the men were g, and they were ... Gen 34:7 6087
Now therefore be not g, nor angry ... Gen 45:5 6087
The archers have sorely g him ... Gen 49:23 4843
they were g because of the ... Ex 1:12 6973
thine heart shall not be g when ... Deut 15:10 7489
his soul was g for the misery of ... Judg 10:16 7114
and why is thy heart g ... 1Sa 1:8 7489
And it g Samuel ... 1Sa 15:11 2734
Jonathan know this, lest he be g ... 1Sa 20:3 6087
for he was g for David, because ... 1Sa 20:34 6087
the soul of all the people was g ... 1Sa 30:6 4784
how the king was g for his son ... 2Sa 19:2 6087
it g them exceedingly that there ... Neh 2:10 7489
neither be ye g ... Neh 8:11 6087
And it g me sore ... Neh 13:8 7489
Then was the queen exceedingly g ... Est 4:4 2342
commune with thee, wilt thou be g ... Job 4:2 3811
was not my soul g for the poor ... Job 30:25 5701
Thus my heart was g, and I was ... Ps 73:21 2556
long was I g with this generation ... Ps 95:10 6962
The wicked shall see it, and be g ... Ps 112:10 3707
the transgressors, and was g ... Ps 119:158 6962
am not I g with those that rise ... Ps 139:21 6962
g in spirit, and a wife of youth, ... Is 54:6 6087
therefore thou wast not g ... Is 57:10 2470
them, but they have not g ... Jer 5:3 2342
I Daniel was g in my spirit in ... Dan 7:15 3735
therefore he shall be g, and ... Dan 11:30 3512
but they are not g for the ... Amos 6:6 2470
being g for the hardness of their ... Mk 3:5 4818
at that saying, and went away g ... Mk 10:22 3076
Peter was g because he said unto ... Jn 21:17 3076
Being g that they taught the ... Acts 4:2 1278
But Paul, being g, turned and said ... Acts 16:18 1278
if thy brother be g with thy meat ... Rom 14:15 3076
not that ye should be g, but that ... 2Cor 2:4 3076
caused grief, he hath not g me ... 2Cor 2:5 3076
Wherefore I was g with that ... Heb 3:10 4360
with whom was he g forty years ... Heb 3:17 4360

GRIEVETH
for it g me much for your sakes ... Ruth 1:13 4843
it g him to bring it again to his ... Prov 26:15 3811

GRIEVING
nor any g thorn of all that are ... Eze 28:24 3510

GRIEVOUS
for the famine was g in the land ... Gen 12:10 3515
and because their sin is very g ... Gen 18:20 3513
the thing was very g in Abraham's ... Gen 21:11 7489
Let it not be g in thy sight ... Gen 21:12 7489
for it shall be very g ... Gen 41:31 3515
This is a g mourning to the ... Gen 50:11 3515
there came a g swarm of flies ... Ex 8:24 3515
there shall be a very g murrain ... Ex 9:3 3515
cause it to rain a very g hail ... Ex 9:18 3515
mingled with the hail, very g ... Ex 9:24 3515
very g were they ... Ex 10:14 3515
which cursed me with a g curse in ... 1Kin 2:8 4834
Thy father made our yoke g ... 1Kin 12:4 7185
thou the g service of thy father ... 1Kin 12:4 7186
Thy father made our yoke g ... 2Chr 10:4 7185
ease thou somewhat the g ... 2Chr 10:4 7186
His ways are always g ... Ps 10:5 2342
which speak g things proudly and ... Ps 31:18 6277
but g words stir up anger ... Prov 15:1 6089
Correction is g unto him that ... Prov 15:10 7451
under the sun is g unto me ... Eccl 2:17 7451
his life shall be g unto him ... Is 15:4 3415
A g vision is declared unto me ... Is 21:2 7186
They are all g revolters, walking ... Jer 6:28 5493
my wound is g ... Jer 10:19 2470
great breach, with a very g blow ... Jer 14:17 2470
They shall die of g deaths ... Jer 16:4 8463
forth in fury, even a g whirlwind ... Jer 23:19 2342
is incurable, and thy wound is g ... Jer 30:12 2470
thy wound is g ... Nah 3:19 2470
g to be borne, and lay them on ... Mt 23:4 1418
men with burdens g to be borne ... Lk 11:46 1418
shall g wolves enter in among you ... Acts 20:29 926
g complaints against Paul, which ... Acts 25:7 926
to you, to me indeed is not g ... Phil 3:1 3636
seemeth to be joyous, but g ... Heb 12:11 3077
and his commandments are not g ... 1Jn 5:3 926
g sore upon the men which had the ... Rev 16:2 4190

GRIEVOUSLY
afterward did more g afflict her ... Is 9:1 3513
it shall fall g upon the head of ... Jer 23:19 2342
Jerusalem hath g sinned ... Lam 1:8 2399
for I have g rebelled ... Lam 1:20 4784
against me by trespassing g ... Eze 14:13 4604
sick of the palsy, g tormented ... Mt 8:6 1171
my daughter is g vexed with a ... Mt 15:22 2560

GRIEVOUSNESS
that write g which they have ... Is 10:1 5999
bent bow, and from the g of war ... Is 21:15 3514

GRIND
he did g in the prison house ... Judg 16:21 2912
Then let my wife g unto another ... Job 31:10 2912
and g the faces of the poor ... Is 3:15 2912
Take the millstones, and g meal ... Is 47:2 2912
They took the young men to g ... Lam 5:13 2911
fall, it will g him to powder ... Mt 21:44 3039
fall, it will g him to powder ... Lk 20:18 3039

GRINDERS
the g cease because they are few, ... Eccl 12:3 2912

GRINDING
when the sound of the g is low ... Eccl 12:4 2913
Two women shall be g at the mill ... Mt 24:41 229
Two women shall be g together ... Lk 17:35 229

GRISLED
were ringstraked, speckled, and g ... Gen 31:10 1261
are ringstraked, speckled, and g ... Gen 31:12 1261
and in the fourth chariot g ... Zec 6:3 1261
the g go forth toward the south ... Zec 6:6 1261

GROAN
Men g from out of the city, and ... Job 24:12 5008
all her land the wounded shall g ... Jer 51:52 602
he shall g before him with the ... Eze 30:24 5008
How do the beasts g ... Joel 1:18 584
we ourselves g within ourselves ... Rom 8:23 4727
For in this we g, earnestly ... 2Cor 5:2 4727
that are in this tabernacle do g ... 2Cor 5:4 4727

GROANED
he g in the spirit, and was ... Jn 11:33 1690

GROANETH
we know that the whole creation g ... Rom 8:22 4959

GROANING
And God heard their g, and God ... Ex 2:24 5009
I have also heard the g of the ... Ex 6:5 5009
my stroke is heavier than my g ... Job 23:2 585
I am weary with my g ... Ps 6:6 585
my g is not hid from thee ... Ps 38:9 585
my g my bones cleave to my skin ... Ps 102:5 585
To hear the g of the prisoner ... Ps 102:20 603
Jesus therefore again g in ... Jn 11:38 1690
in Egypt, and I have heard their g ... Acts 7:34 4726

GROANINGS
of their g by reason of them that ... Judg 2:18 5009
the g of a deadly wounded man ... Eze 30:24 5009
us with g which cannot be uttered ... Rom 8:26 4726

GROPE
And thou shalt g at noonday ... Deut 28:29 4959
g in the noonday as in the night ... Job 5:14 4959
They g in the dark without light ... Job 12:25 4959
We g for the wall like the blind, ... Is 59:10 1659
we g as if we had no eyes ... Is 59:10 1659

GROPETH
as the blind g in darkness ... Deut 28:29 4959

GROSS
earth, and g darkness the people ... Is 60:2 6205
of death, and make it g darkness ... Jer 13:16 6205
this people's heart is waxed g ... Mt 13:15 3975
heart of this people is waxed g ... Acts 28:27 3975

GROUND
there was not a man to till the g ... Gen 2:5 127
watered the whole face of the g ... Gen 2:6 127
formed man of the dust of the g ... Gen 2:7 127
out of the g made the LORD God to ... Gen 2:9 127
out of the g the LORD God formed ... Gen 2:19 127
cursed is the g for thy sake ... Gen 3:17 127
till thou return unto the g ... Gen 3:19 127
to till the g from whence he was ... Gen 3:23 127
but Cain was a tiller of the g ... Gen 4:2 127
the g an offering unto the LORD ... Gen 4:3 127
blood crieth unto me from the g ... Gen 4:10 127
When thou tillest the g, it shall ... Gen 4:12 127
because of the g which the LORD ... Gen 5:29 127
which was upon the face of the g ... Gen 7:23 127
abated from off the face of the g ... Gen 8:8 127
behold, the face of the g was dry ... Gen 8:13 127
the g any more for man's sake ... Gen 8:21 127

and bowed himself toward the g .... Gen 18:2 776
with his face toward the g .... Gen 19:1 776
and that which grew upon the g .... Gen 19:25 127
himself to the g seven times .... Gen 33:3 776
wife, that he spilled it on the g .... Gen 38:9 776
down every man his sack to the g .... Gen 44:11 776
and they fell before him on the g .... Gen 44:14 776
whereon thou standest is holy g .... Ex 3:5 127
And he said, Cast it on the g .... Ex 4:3 776
And he cast it on the g, and it .... Ex 4:3 776
also the g whereon they are .... Ex 8:21 127
and the fire ran along upon the g .... Ex 9:23 776
of Israel shall go on dry g .... Ex 14:16
midst of the sea upon the dry g .... Ex 14:22
small as the hoar frost on the g .... Ex 16:14 776
g it to powder, and strawed it .... Ex 32:20 2912
thing that creepeth on the g .... Lev 20:25 127
g it in mills, or beat it in a .... Num 11:8 2912
that the g clave asunder that was .... Num 16:31 127
any thing that creepeth on the g .... Deut 4:18 127
g it very small, even until it .... Deut 9:21 2912
shalt pour it upon the g as water .... Deut 15:23 776
the way in any tree, or on the g .... Deut 22:6 776
thy body, and the fruit of thy g .... Deut 28:4 127
cattle, and in the fruit of thy g .... Deut 28:11 127
foot upon the g for delicateness .... Deut 28:56 776
on dry g in the midst of Jordan .... Josh 3:17
Israelites passed over on dry g .... Josh 3:17
in a parcel of g which Jacob .... Josh 24:32 7704
and fastened it into the g .... Judg 4:21 776
upon all the g let there be dew .... Judg 6:39 776
and there was dew on all the g .... Judg 6:40 776
and fell on their faces to the g .... Judg 13:20 776
destroyed down to the g of the .... Judg 20:21 776
destroyed down to the g of the .... Judg 20:25 776
face, and bowed herself to the g .... Ruth 2:10 776
none of his words fall to the g 1Sa 3:19 776
the g before the ark of the LORD 1Sa 5:4 776
and will set them to ear his g 1Sa 8:12 2758
and there was honey upon the g 1Sa 14:25 7704
and calves, and slew them on the g 1Sa 14:32 776
hair of his head fall to the g 1Sa 14:45 776
son of Jesse liveth upon the g 1Sa 20:31 127
and fell on his face to the g 1Sa 20:41 776
face, and bowed herself to the g 1Sa 25:23 776
stuck in the g at his bolster 1Sa 26:7 776
he stooped with his face to the g 1Sa 28:14 776
should I smite thee to the g 2Sa 2:22 776
line, casting them down to the g 2Sa 8:2 776
she fell on her face to the g 2Sa 14:4 776
and are as water spilt on the g 2Sa 14:14 776
And Joab fell to the g on his face 2Sa 14:22 776
his face to the g before the king 2Sa 14:33 776
him as the dew falleth on the g 2Sa 17:12 127
mouth, and spread g corn thereon 2Sa 17:19 7383
thou not smite him there to the g 2Sa 18:11 776
and shed out his bowels to the g 2Sa 20:10 776
was a piece of g full of lentiles 2Sa 23:11 7704
he stood in the midst of the g 2Sa 23:12 2513
the king on his face upon the g 2Sa 24:20 776
the king with his face to the g 1Kin 1:23 776
in the clay g between Succoth and 1Kin 7:46 127
that they two went over on dry g 2Kin 2:8
themselves to the g before him 2Kin 2:15 776
water is naught, and the g barren 2Kin 2:19 776
feet, and bowed herself to the g 2Kin 4:37 776
and cast him into the plat of g 2Kin 9:26
king of Israel, Smite upon the g 2Kin 13:18 776
was a parcel of g full of barley 1Chr 11:13 7704
to David with his face to the g 1Chr 21:21 776
the g was Ezri the son of Chelub 1Chr 27:26 127
in the clay g between Succoth and 2Chr 4:17 127
faces to the g upon the pavement 2Chr 7:3 776
his head with his face to the g 2Chr 20:18 776
LORD with their faces to the g .... Neh 8:6 776
to bring the firstfruits of our g .... Neh 10:35 127
tithes of our g unto the Levites .... Neh 10:37 127
his head, and fell down upon the g .... Job 1:20 776
with him upon the g seven days .... Job 2:13 776
doth trouble spring out of the g .... Job 5:6 127
and the stock thereof die in the g .... Job 14:8 6083
he poureth out my gall upon the g .... Job 16:13 776
snare is laid for him in the g .... Job 18:10 776
satisfy the desolate and waste g .... Job 38:27
swalloweth the g with fierceness .... Job 39:24 776
place of thy name to the g .... Ps 74:7 776
his crown by casting it to the g .... Ps 89:39 776
and cast his throne down to the g .... Ps 89:44 776
and devoured the fruit of their g .... Ps 105:35 127
and the watersprings into dry g .... Ps 107:33
water, and dry g into watersprings .... Ps 107:35 127
smitten my life down to the g .... Ps 143:3 776
casteth the wicked down to the g .... Ps 147:6 776
desolate shall sit upon the g .... Is 3:26 776
how art thou cut down to the g .... Is 14:12 776
gods he hath broken unto the g .... Is 21:9 776
down, lay low, and bring to the g .... Is 25:12 776
he layeth it low, even to the g .... Is 26:5 776
open and break the clods of his g .... Is 28:24 127
down, and shalt speak out of the g .... Is 29:4 776
a familiar spirit, out of the g .... Is 29:4 776
that thou shalt sow the g withal .... Is 30:23 127
the g shall eat clean provender .... Is 30:24 127
the parched g shall become a pool .... Is 35:7
thirsty, and floods upon the dry g .... Is 44:3
daughter of Babylon, sit on the g .... Is 47:1 776
thou hast laid thy body as the g .... Is 51:23 776
and as a root out of a dry g .... Is 53:2 776
Jerusalem, Break up your fallow g .... Jer 4:3
field, and upon the fruit of the g .... Jer 7:20 127
they are black unto the g .... Jer 14:2 776
Because the g is chapt, for there .... Jer 14:4 127
they shall be dung upon the g .... Jer 25:33 127
and the beast that are upon the g .... Jer 27:5 776
hath brought them down to the g .... Lam 2:2 776
Her gates are sunk into the g .... Lam 2:9 776
daughter of Zion sit upon the g .... Lam 2:10 776
hang down their heads to the g .... Lam 2:10 776
old lie on the g in the streets .... Lam 2:21 776
thy face, that thou see not the g .... Eze 12:6 776
he see not the g with his eyes .... Eze 12:12 776
morter, and bring it down to the g .... Eze 13:14 776
fury, she was cast down to the g .... Eze 19:12 776
wilderness, in a dry and thirsty g .... Eze 19:13 776
she poured it not upon the g .... Eze 24:7 776
garrisons shall go down to the g .... Eze 26:11 776
they shall sit upon the g .... Eze 26:16 776
I will cast thee to the g .... Eze 28:17 776
and every wall shall fall to the g .... Eze 38:20 776
from the g up to the windows, and .... Eze 41:16 776
From the g unto above the door .... Eze 41:20 776
and the middlemost from the g .... Eze 42:6 776
from the bottom upon the g even .... Eze 43:14 776
whole earth, and touched not the g .... Dan 8:5 776
but he cast him down to the g .... Dan 8:7 776
the host and of the stars to the g .... Dan 8:10 776
it cast down the truth to the g .... Dan 8:12 776
sleep on my face toward the g .... Dan 8:18 776
my face, and my face toward the g .... Dan 10:9 776
me, I set my face toward the g .... Dan 10:15 776
with the creeping things of the g .... Hos 2:18 127
break up your fallow g .... Hos 10:12
be cut off, and fall to the g .... Amos 3:14 776
Who shall bring me down to the g .... Obad 3 776
that which the g bringeth forth .... Hag 1:11 127
the g shall give her increase, and .... Zec 8:12 776
not destroy the fruits of your g .... Mal 3:11 127
fall on the g without your Father .... Mt 10:29 *1093*
But other fell into good g .... Mt 13:8 *1093*
g is he that heareth the word .... Mt 13:23 *1093*
multitude to sit down on the g .... Mt 15:35 *1093*
And some fell on stony g, where it .... Mk 4:5
And other fell on good g, and did .... Mk 4:8 *1093*
which are sown on stony g .... Mk 4:16
are they which are sown on good g .... Mk 4:20 *1093*
a man should cast seed into the g .... Mk 4:26 *1093*
the people to sit down on the g .... Mk 8:6 *1093*
and he fell on the g, and wallowed .... Mk 9:20 *1093*
a little, and fell on the g .... Mk 14:35 *1093*
And other fell on good g, and .... Lk 8:8 *1093*
But that on the good g are they .... Lk 8:15 *1093*
The g of a certain rich man .... Lk 12:16 *5561*
why cumbereth it the g .... Lk 13:7 *1093*
him, I have bought a piece of g .... Lk 14:18 *68*
And shall lay thee even with the g .... Lk 19:44 *1474*
of blood falling down to the g .... Lk 22:44 *1093*
near to the parcel of g that .... Jn 4:5 *5564*
and with his finger wrote on the g .... Jn 8:6 *1093*
stooped down, and wrote on the g .... Jn 8:8 *1093*
had thus spoken, he spat on the g .... Jn 9:6 *5476*
a corn of wheat fall into the g .... Jn 12:24 *1093*
went backward, and fell to the g .... Jn 18:6 *5476*
where thou standest is holy g .... Acts 7:33 *1093*
And I fell unto the g, and heard a .... Acts 22:7 *1475*
God, the pillar and g of the truth 1Ti 3:15 *1477*

GROUNDED
where the g staff shall pass .... Is 30:32 4145
ye, being rooted and g in love, ... Eph 3:17 *2311*
If ye continue in the faith g .... Col 1:23 *2311*

GROVE
Abraham planted a g in Beer-sheba .... Gen 21:33 815
a g of any trees near unto the .... Deut 16:21 842
cut down the g that is by it .... Judg 6:25 842
the g which thou shalt cut down .... Judg 6:26 842
the g was cut down that was by it .... Judg 6:28 842
cut down the g that was by it .... Judg 6:30 842
she had made an idol in a g 1Kin 15:13 842
And Ahab made a g 1Kin 16:33 842
remained the g also in Samaria 2Kin 13:6 842
even two calves, and made a g 2Kin 17:16 842
up altars for Baal, and made a g 2Kin 21:3 842
he set a graven image of the g 2Kin 21:7 842
were made for Baal, and for the g 2Kin 23:4 842
he brought out the g from the 2Kin 23:6 842
the women wove hangings for the g 2Kin 23:7 842
small to powder, and burned the g 2Kin 23:15 842
she had made an idol in a g 2Chr 15:16 842

GROVES
their images, and cut down their g .... Ex 34:13 842
their images, and cut down their g .... Deut 7:5 842
and burn their g with fire .... Deut 12:3 842
God, and served Baalim and the g .... Judg 3:7 842
because they have made their g 1Kin 14:15 842
them high places, and images, and g 1Kin 14:23 842
prophets of the g four hundred 1Kin 18:19 842
g in every high hill, and under 2Kin 17:10 842
the images, and cut down the g 2Kin 18:4 842
the images, and cut down the g 2Kin 23:14 842
the images, and cut down the g 2Chr 14:3 842
the high places and g out of Judah 2Chr 17:6 842
taken away the g out of the land 2Chr 19:3 842
God of their fathers, and served g 2Chr 24:18 842
in pieces, and cut down the g 2Chr 31:1 842
up altars for Baalim, and made g 2Chr 33:3 842
he built high places, and set up g 2Chr 33:19 842
from the high places, and the g 2Chr 34:3 842
and the g, and the carved images, ... 2Chr 34:4 842
broken down the altars and the g 2Chr 34:7 842
fingers have made, either the g .... Is 17:8 842
that are beaten in sunder, the g .... Is 27:9 842
their g by the green trees upon .... Jer 17:2 842
I will pluck up thy g out of the .... Mic 5:14 842

GROW
g every tree that is pleasant to .... Gen 2:9 6779
let them g into a multitude in .... Gen 48:16 1711
locks of the hair of his head g .... Num 6:5 1431
to g again after he was shaven .... Judg 16:22 6779
although he make it not to g 2Sa 23:5 6779
such things as g of themselves 2Kin 19:29 5599
why should damage g to the hurt .... Ezr 4:22 7680
Can the rush g up without mire .... Job 8:11 1342
can the flag g without water .... Job 8:11 6779
out of the earth shall others g .... Job 8:19 6779
g out of the dust of the earth .... Job 14:19 5599
Let thistles g instead of wheat, ... Job 31:40 3318
good liking, they g up with corn .... Job 39:4 7235
he shall g like a cedar in .... Ps 92:12 7685
the grass to g for the cattle .... Ps 104:14 6779
grass to g upon the mountains .... Ps 147:8 6779
nor how the bones do g in the .... Eccl 11:5
a Branch shall g out of his roots .... Is 11:1 6509
shalt thou make thy plant to g .... Is 17:11 7735
For he shall g up before him as a .... Is 53:2 5927
they g, yea, they bring forth .... Jer 12:2 3212
righteousness to g up unto David .... Jer 33:15 6779
nor suffer their locks to g long .... Eze 44:20 7971
shall g all trees for meat, whose .... Eze 47:12 5927
he shall g as the lily, and cast .... Hos 14:5 6524
as the corn, and g as the vine .... Hos 14:7 6524
not laboured, neither madest it g .... Jonah 4:10 1431
he shall g up out of his place, ... Zec 6:12 6779
g up as calves of the stall .... Mal 4:2 6335
lilies of the field, how they g .... Mt 6:28 *837*
Let both g together until the .... Mt 13:30 *4886*
unto it, Let no fruit g on thee .... Mt 21:19 *1096*
and g up, he knoweth not how .... Mk 4:27 *3373*
Consider the lilies how they g .... Lk 12:27 *837*
of them whereunto this would g .... Acts 5:24 *1096*
may g up into him in all things, ... Eph 4:15 *837*
the word, that ye may g thereby 1Pet 2:2 *837*
But g in grace, and in the 2Pet 3:18 *837*

GROWETH
which g for you out of the field .... Ex 10:5 6779
freckled spot that g in the skin .... Lev 13:39 6524
That which g of its own accord of .... Lev 25:5 5599
reap that which g of itself in it .... Lev 25:11 5599
beareth, nor any grass g therein .... Deut 29:23 5927
the day g to an end, lodge here, ... Judg 19:9 2583
When the dust g into hardness .... Job 38:38 3332
they are like grass which g up .... Ps 90:5 2498
morning it flourisheth, and g up .... Ps 90:6 2498
which withereth afore it g up .... Ps 129:6 8025
eat this year such as g of itself .... Is 37:30 5599
But when it is sown, it g up .... Mk 4:32 *305*
building fitly framed together g .... Eph 2:21 *837*
that your faith g exceedingly 2Th 1:3 *5232*

GROWN
house, till Shelah my son be g .... Gen 38:11 1431
for she saw that Shelah was g .... Gen 38:14 1431
in those days, when Moses was g .... Ex 2:11 1431
for they were not g up .... Ex 9:32 648
there is black hair g up therein .... Lev 13:37 6779
art waxen fat, thou art g thick .... Deut 32:15
tarry for them till they were g .... Ruth 1:13 1431
at Jericho until your beards be g 2Sa 10:5 6779
young men that were g up with him 1Kin 12:8 1431
the young men that were g up with 1Kin 12:10 1431
And when the child was g, it fell 2Kin 4:18 1431
as corn blasted before it be g up 2Kin 19:26 6965
at Jericho until your beards be g 1Chr 19:5 6779
our trespass is g up unto the .... Ezr 9:6 1431
be as plants g up in their youth .... Ps 144:12 1431
it was all g over with thorns, and .... Prov 24:31 5927
as corn blasted before it be g up .... Is 37:27 6965
because ye are g fat as the .... Jer 50:11 6335
are fashioned, and thine hair is g .... Eze 16:7 6779
It is thou, O king, that art g .... Dan 4:22 7236
for thy greatness is g, and .... Dan 4:22 7236
till his hairs were g like .... Dan 4:33 7236
but when it is g, it is the .... Mt 13:32 *837*

GROWTH
the shooting up of the latter g .... Amos 7:1 3954
it was the latter g after the .... Amos 7:1 3954

GRUDGE
nor bear any g against the .... Lev 19:18 5201
g if they be not satisfied .... Ps 59:15 3885
G not one against another, ... Jas 5:9 *4727*

GRUDGING
one to another without g 1Pet 4:9 *1112*

GRUDGINGLY
not g, or of necessity 2Cor 9:7

GUARD
of Pharaoh's, and captain of the g .... Gen 37:36 2876
of Pharaoh, captain of the g .... Gen 39:1 2876
the house of the captain of the g .... Gen 40:3 2876
the captain of the g charged .... Gen 40:4 2876
servant to the captain of the g .... Gen 41:12 2876
And David set him over his g 2Sa 23:23 4928
the hands of the chief of the g 1Kin 14:27 7323
that the g bare them, and brought 1Kin 14:28 7323
them back into the g chamber 1Kin 14:28 7323
offering, that Jehu said to the g 2Kin 10:25 7323
and the g and the captains cast 2Kin 10:25 7323
with the captains and the g 2Kin 11:4 7323
part at the gate behind the g 2Kin 11:6 7323
the g stood, every man with his 2Kin 11:11 7323
Athaliah heard the noise of the g 2Kin 11:13 7323
and the captains, and the g 2Kin 11:19 7323
gate of the g to the king's house 2Kin 11:19 7323
Nebuzar-adan, captain of the g 2Kin 25:8 2876
were with the captain of the g 2Kin 25:10 2876
the captain of the g carry away 2Kin 25:11 2876
But the captain of the g left of 2Kin 25:12 2876
the captain of the g took away 2Kin 25:15 2876
the captain of the g took Seraiah 2Kin 25:18 2876
captain of the g took these 2Kin 25:20 2876

and David set him over his g ... 1Chr 11:25 4928
the hands of the chief of the g ... 2Chr 12:10 7323
the g came and fetched them, and ... 2Chr 12:11 7323
them again into the g chamber ... 2Chr 12:11 7323
the night they may be a g to us ... Neh 4:22 4929
men of the g which followed me ... Neh 4:23 4929
the g carried away captive into ... Jer 39:9 2876
g left of the poor of the people ... Jer 39:10 2876
Nebuzar-adan the captain of the g ... Jer 39:11 2876
the captain of the g sent ... Jer 39:13 2876
the g had let him go from Ramah ... Jer 40:1 2876
captain of the g took Jeremiah ... Jer 40:2 2876
of the g gave him victuals ... Jer 40:5 2876
g had committed to Gedaliah the ... Jer 41:10 2876
g had left with Gedaliah the son ... Jer 43:6 2876
Nebuzar-adan, captain of the g ... Jer 52:12 2876
were with the captain of the g ... Jer 52:14 2876
g carried away captive certain of ... Jer 52:15 2876
g left certain of the poor of the ... Jer 52:16 2876
took the captain of the g away ... Jer 52:19 2876
the captain of the g took Seraiah ... Jer 52:24 2876
the captain of the g took them ... Jer 52:26 2876
the g carried away captive of the ... Jer 52:30 2876
thee, and be thou a g unto them ... Eze 38:7 4929
the captain of the king's g ... Dan 2:14 2877
prisoners to the captain of the g ... Acts 28:16 *4759*

GUARD'S
in the captain of the g house ... Gen 41:10 2876

GUDGODAH (*gud-go'-dah*) See Hor-hagidgad.
A wilderness encampment of Israel.
From thence they journeyed unto G ... Deut 10:7 1412
from G to Jotbath, a land of ... Deut 10:7 1412

GUEST
That he was gone to be g with a ... Lk 19:7 *2647*

GUESTCHAMBER
The Master saith, Where is the g ... Mk 14:14 *2646*
saith unto thee, Where is the g ... Lk 22:11 *2646*

GUESTS
all the g that were with him ... 1Kin 1:41 7121
all the g that were with Adonijah ... 1Kin 1:49 7121
that her g are in the depths of ... Prov 9:18 7121
a sacrifice, he hath bid his g ... Zeph 1:7 7121
the wedding was furnished with g ... Mt 22:10 *345*
the king came in to see the g ... Mt 22:11 *345*

GUIDE
or canst thou g Arcturus with his ... Job 38:32 5148
The meek will he g in judgment ... Ps 25:9 1869
thy name's sake lead me, and g me ... Ps 31:3 5095
I will g thee with mine eye ... Ps 32:8 3289
he will be our g even unto death ... Ps 48:14 5090
was thou, a man mine equal, my g ... Ps 55:13 441
Thou shalt g me with thy counsel, ... Ps 73:24 5148
he will g his affairs with ... Ps 112:5 3557
forsaketh the g of her youth ... Prov 2:17 441
Which having no g, overseer, or ... Prov 6:7 7101
of the upright shall g them ... Prov 11:3 5148
wise, and g thine heart in the way ... Prov 23:19 833
springs of water shall he g them ... Is 49:10 5095
There is none to g her among all ... Is 51:18 5095
the Lord shall g thee continually ... Is 58:11 5148
thou art the g of my youth ... Jer 3:4 441
put ye not confidence in a g ... Mic 7:5 441
to g our feet into the way of ... Lk 1:79 *2720*
he will g you into all truth ... Jn 16:13 *3594*
which was g to them that took ... Acts 1:16 *3595*
I, except some man should g me ... Acts 8:31 *3594*
thou thyself art a g of the blind ... Rom 2:19 *3595*
g the house, give none occasion ... 1Ti 5:14 *3616*

GUIDED
thou hast g them in thy strength ... Ex 15:13 5095
other, and g them on every side ... 2Chr 32:22 5095
I have g her from my mother's ... Job 31:18 5148
g them in the wilderness like a ... Ps 78:52 5090
g them by the skilfulness of his ... Ps 78:72 5148

GUIDES
Woe unto you, ye blind g, which ... Mt 23:16 *3595*
Ye blind g, which strain at a ... Mt 23:24 *3595*

GUIDING
head, g his hands wittingly ... Gen 48:14

GUILE
his neighbour, to slay him with g ... Ex 21:14 6195
and in whose spirit there is no g ... Ps 32:2 7423
evil, and thy lips from speaking g ... Ps 34:13 4820
g depart not from her streets ... Ps 55:11 4820
Israelite indeed, in whom is no g ... Jn 1:47 *1388*
being crafty, I caught you with g ... 2Cor 12:16 *1388*
nor of uncleanness, nor in g ... 1Th 2:3 *1388*
laying aside all malice, and all g ... 1Pet 2:1 *1388*
neither was g found in his mouth ... 1Pet 2:22 *1388*
and his lips that they speak no g ... 1Pet 3:10 *1388*
And in their mouth was found no g ... Rev 14:5 *1388*

GUILT
but thou shalt put away the g of ... Deut 19:13
So shalt thou put away the g of ... Deut 21:9

GUILTINESS
shouldest have brought g upon us ... Gen 26:10 817

GUILTLESS
g that taketh his name in vain ... Ex 20:7 5352
shall the man be g from iniquity ... Num 5:31 5352
be g before the Lord, and before ... Num 32:22 5355
g that taketh his name in vain ... Deut 5:11 5352
be upon his head, and we will be g ... Josh 2:19 5355
the Lord's anointed, and be g ... 1Sa 26:9 5352
my kingdom are g before the Lord ... 2Sa 3:28 5355
and the king and his throne be g ... 2Sa 14:9 5355
Now therefore hold him not g ... 1Kin 2:9 5352
ye would not have condemned the g ... Mt 12:7 *338*

GUILTY
We are verily g concerning our ... Gen 42:21 816
that will by no means clear the g ... Ex 34:7
should not be done, and are g ... Lev 4:13 816
which should not be done, and is g ... Lev 4:22 816
ought not to be done, and be g ... Lev 4:27 816
he also shall be unclean, and g ... Lev 5:2 816
knoweth of it, then he shall be g ... Lev 5:3 816
he shall be g in one of these ... Lev 5:4 816
when he shall be g in one of ... Lev 5:5 816
he wist it not, yet is he g ... Lev 5:17 816
because he hath sinned, and is g ... Lev 6:4 816
the Lord, and that person be g ... Num 5:6 816
and by no means clearing the g ... Num 14:18
he shall not be g of blood ... Num 35:27
a murderer, which is g of death ... Num 35:31 7563
at this time, that ye should be g ... Judg 21:22 816
and being g, they offered a ram of ... Ezr 10:19 816
he curse thee, and thou be found g ... Prov 30:10 816
Thou art become g in thy blood ... Eze 22:4 816
them, and hold themselves not g ... Zec 11:5 816
the gift that is upon it, he is g ... Mt 23:18 *3784*
and said, He is g of death ... Mt 26:66 *1777*
condemned him to be g of death ... Mk 14:64 *1777*
the world may become g before God ... Rom 3:19 *5267*
shall be g of the body and blood ... 1Cor 11:27 *1777*
in one point, he is g of all ... Jas 2:10 *1777*

GULF
and you there is a great g fixed ... Lk 16:26 *5490*

GUNI (*gu'-ni*) See Gunites.
1. A son of Naphtali.
Jahzeel, and G, and Jezer, and ... Gen 46:24 1476
of G, the family of the Gunites ... Num 26:48 1476
Jahziel, and G, and Jezer, and ... 1Chr 7:13 1476
2. Father of Abdiel.
the son of Abdiel, the son of G ... 1Chr 5:15 1476

GUNITES (*gu'-nites*) *Descendants of Guni 1.*
of Guni, the family of the G ... Num 26:48 1477

GUR (*gur*) See Gur-baal. *A hill near Ibleam.*
they did so at the going up to G ... 2Kin 9:27 1483

GUR-BAAL (*gur-ba'-al*) *Place in western Arabia.*
the Arabians that dwelt in G ... 2Chr 26:7 1485

GUSH
our eyelids g out with waters ... Jer 9:18 5140

GUSHED
till the blood g out upon them ... 1Kin 18:28 8210
the rock, that the waters g out ... Ps 78:20 2100
the rock, and the waters g out ... Ps 105:41 2100
rock also, and the waters g out ... Is 48:21 2100
midst, and all his bowels g out ... Acts 1:18 *1632*

GUTTER
Whosoever getteth up to the g ... 2Sa 5:8 6794

GUTTERS
g in the watering troughs when ... Gen 30:38 7298
the eyes of the cattle in the g ... Gen 30:41 7298

H

HA
saith among the trumpets, H, h ... Job 39:25 1889

HAAHASHTARI (*ha-a-hash'-ta-ri*) *A son of Naarah.*
and Hepher, and Temeni, and H ... 1Chr 4:6 326

HABAIAH (*hab-ah'-yah*) *A family of exiles.*
the children of H, the children ... Ezr 2:61 2252
the children of H, the children ... Neh 7:63 2252

HABAKKUK (*hab'-ak-kuk*) *A prophet of Judah.*
The burden which H the prophet ... Hab 1:1 2265
A prayer of H the prophet upon ... Hab 3:1 2265

HABAZINIAH (*hab-az-in-i'-ah*) *Head of a Rechabite family.*
the son of Jeremiah, the son of H ... Jer 35:3 2262

HABAZZINIAH See Habaziniah.

HABERGEON
it, as it were the hole of an h ... Ex 28:32 8473
of the robe, as the hole of an h ... Ex 39:23 8473
the spear, the dart, nor the h ... Job 41:26 8302

HABERGEONS
and spears, and helmets, and h ... 2Chr 26:14 8302
shields, and the bows, and the h ... Neh 4:16 8302

HABITABLE
Rejoicing in the h part of his ... Prov 8:31 8398

HABITATION
God, and I will prepare him an h ... Ex 15:2 5115
in thy strength unto thy holy h ... Ex 15:13 5116
without the camp shall his h be ... Lev 13:46 4186
even unto his h shall ye seek ... Deut 12:5 7933
Look down from thy holy h ... Deut 26:15 4583
which I have commanded in my h ... 1Sa 2:29 4583
thou shalt see an enemy in my h ... 1Sa 2:32 4583
and shew me both it, and his h ... 2Sa 15:25 5116
have built an house of h for thee ... 2Chr 6:2 2073
faces from the h of the Lord ... 2Chr 29:6 4908
Israel, whose h is in Jerusalem, ... Ezr 7:15 4907
but suddenly I cursed his h ... Job 5:3 5116
and thou shalt visit thy h ... Job 5:24 5116
make the h of thy righteousness ... Job 8:6 5116
shall be scattered upon his h ... Job 18:15 5116
I have loved the h of thy house ... Ps 26:8 4583
From the place of his h he ... Ps 33:14 3427
the widows, is God in his holy h ... Ps 68:5 4583
Let their h be desolate ... Ps 69:25 2918
Be thou my strong h, whereunto I ... Ps 71:3 4583
judgment are the h of thy throne ... Ps 89:14 4349
refuge, even the most High, thy h ... Ps 91:9 4583
judgment are the h of his throne ... Ps 97:2 4349
fowls of the heaven have their h ... Ps 104:12 7931
that they might go to a city of h ... Ps 107:7 4186
they may prepare a city for h ... Ps 107:36 4186
an h for the mighty God of Jacob ... Ps 132:5 4908
he hath desired it for his h ... Ps 132:13 4186
but he blesseth the h of the just ... Prov 3:33 5116
that graveth an h for himself in ... Is 22:16 4908
the h forsaken, and left like a ... Is 27:10 5116
shall dwell in a peaceable h ... Is 32:18 5116
shall see Jerusalem a quiet h ... Is 33:20 5116
and it shall be an h of dragons ... Is 34:13 5116
in the h of dragons, where each ... Is 35:7 5116
behold from the h of thy holiness ... Is 63:15 2073
Thine h is in the midst of deceit ... Jer 9:6 3427
him, and have made his h desolate ... Jer 10:25 5116
utter his voice from his holy h ... Jer 25:30 4583
he shall mightily roar upon his h ... Jer 25:30 5116
O h of justice, and mountain of ... Jer 31:23 5116
shall be an h of shepherds ... Jer 33:12 5116
and dwelt in the h of Chimham ... Jer 41:17 1628
against the h of the strong ... Jer 49:19 5116
the h of justice, even the Lord, ... Jer 50:7 5116
will bring Israel again to his h ... Jer 50:19 5116
Jordan unto the h of the strong ... Jer 50:44 5116
make their h desolate with them ... Jer 50:45 5116
Pathros, into the land of their h ... Eze 29:14 4351
fowls of the heaven had their h ... Dan 4:21 7932
of the rock, whose h is high ... Obad 3 3427
and moon stood still in their h ... Hab 3:11 2073
he is raised up out of his holy h ... Zec 2:13 4583
Let his h be desolate, and let no ... Acts 1:20 *1886*
and the bounds of their h ... Acts 17:26 *2733*
an h of God through the Spirit ... Eph 2:22 *2732*
estate, but left their own h ... Jude 6 *3613*
and is become the h of devils ... Rev 18:2 *2732*

HABITATIONS
according to their h in the land ... Gen 36:43 4186
of cruelty are in their h ... Gen 49:5 4380
in all your h shall ye eat ... Ex 12:20 4186
your h upon the sabbath day ... Ex 35:3 4186
Ye shall bring out of your h two ... Lev 23:17 4186
be come into the land of your h ... Num 15:2 4186
These were their h, and their ... 1Chr 4:33 4186
the h that were found there, and ... 1Chr 4:41 4583
h were, Beth-el and the towns ... 1Chr 7:28 4186
are full of the h of cruelty ... Ps 74:20 4999
their camp, round about their h ... Ps 78:28 4908
forth the curtains of thine h ... Is 54:2 4908
for the h of the wilderness a ... Jer 9:10 4999
or who shall enter into our h ... Jer 21:13 4585
the peaceable h are cut down ... Jer 25:37 4999
make their h desolate with them ... Jer 49:20 5116
swallowed up all the h of Jacob ... Lam 2:2 4999
toward Diblath, in all their h ... Eze 6:14 4186
the h of the shepherds shall ... Amos 1:2 4999
receive you into everlasting h ... Lk 16:9 *4638*

HABOR (*ha'-bor*) *A Mesopotamian district.*
in H by the river of Gozan, and in ... 2Kin 17:6 2249
in H by the river of Gozan, and in ... 2Kin 18:11 2249
and brought them unto Halah, and H ... 1Chr 5:26 2249

HACALIAH See Hachaliah.

HACHALIAH (*hak-a-li'-ah*) *Father of Nehemiah.*
words of Nehemiah the son of H ... Neh 1:1 2446
the Tirshatha, the son of H ... Neh 10:1 2446

HACHILAH (*hak'-i-lah*) *A hill in Judah.*
in the wood, in the hill of H ... 1Sa 23:19 2444
hide himself in the hill of H ... 1Sa 26:1 2444
And Saul pitched in the hill of H ... 1Sa 26:3 2444

HACHMONI (*hak'-mo-ni*) See Hachmonite. *Father of Jehiel.*
Jehiel the son of H was with the ... 1Chr 27:32 2453

HACHMONITE (*hak'-mo-nite*) See Tachmonite. *A descendant of Hachmoni.*
Jashobeam, a H, the chief of the ... 1Chr 11:11 2453

HAD
saw every thing that he h made ... Gen 1:31
ended his work which he h made ... Gen 2:2
from all his work which he h made ... Gen 2:2
because that in it he h rested ... Gen 2:3

for the LORD God *h* not caused it........ Gen 2:5
he put the man whom he *h* formed........ Gen 2:8
the LORD God *h* taken from man......... Gen 2:22
field which the LORD God *h* made......... Gen 3:1
the LORD *h* respect unto Abel and........ Gen 4:4
to his offering he *h* not respect........... Gen 4:5
he *h* begotten Seth were eight............. Gen 5:4
that he *h* made man on the earth......... Gen 6:6
for all flesh *h* corrupted his way.......... Gen 6:12
female, as God *h* commanded Noah....... Gen 7:9
all flesh, as God *h* commanded him...... Gen 7:16
window of the ark which he *h* made...... Gen 8:6
his younger son *h* done unto him.......... Gen 9:24
they *h* brick for stone............................ Gen 11:3 1961
and slime *h* they for morter.................. Gen 11:3 1961
she *h* no child... Gen 11:30
Now the LORD *h* said unto Abram,....... Gen 12:1
as the LORD *h* spoken unto him............ Gen 12:4
substance that they *h* gathered............ Gen 12:5
souls that they *h* gotten in Haran......... Gen 12:5
he *h* sheep, and oxen, and he asses,..... Gen 12:16 1961
and his wife, and all that he *h*.............. Gen 12:20
he, and his wife, and all that he *h*........ Gen 13:1
his tent *h* been at the beginning........... Gen 13:3
which he *h* made there at the.............. Gen 13:4
h flocks, and herds, and tents............. Gen 13:5 1961
And there came one that *h* escaped..... Gen 14:13
she *h* an handmaid, an Egyptian,......... Gen 16:1
after Abram *h* dwelt ten years in......... Gen 16:3
when she saw that she *h* conceived...... Gen 16:4
when she saw that she *h* conceived...... Gen 16:5
day, as God *h* said unto him................. Gen 17:23
and the calf which he *h* dressed........... Gen 18:8
as soon as he *h* left communing............ Gen 18:33
when they *h* brought them forth........... Gen 19:17
But Abimelech *h* not come near her...... Gen 20:4
For the LORD *h* fast closed up all........ Gen 20:18
LORD visited Sarah as he *h* said........... Gen 21:1
did unto Sarah as he *h* spoken.............. Gen 21:1
time of which God *h* spoken to him...... Gen 21:2
days old, as God *h* commanded him...... Gen 21:4
which she *h* born unto Abraham,........... Gen 21:9
servants *h* violently taken away........... Gen 21:25
the place of which God *h* told him....... Gen 22:3
the place which God *h* told him of....... Gen 22:9
which he *h* named in the audience....... Gen 23:16
the LORD *h* blessed Abraham in all....... Gen 24:1
that ruled over all that he *h*................ Gen 24:2
before he *h* done speaking, that,.......... Gen 24:15
neither *h* any man known her.............. Gen 24:16
when she *h* done giving him drink,....... Gen 24:19
to wit whether the LORD *h* made.......... Gen 24:21
as the camels *h* done drinking.............. Gen 24:22
Rebekah *h* a brother, and his name...... Gen 24:29
before I *h* done speaking in mine......... Gen 24:45
which *h* led me in the right way.......... Gen 24:48
For she *h* said unto the servant,.......... Gen 24:65
And the servant *h* said, It is my.......... Gen 24:65
Isaac all things that he *h* done............ Gen 24:66
gave all that he *h* unto Isaac................ Gen 25:5
the concubines, which Abraham *h*......... Gen 25:6
when he *h* been there a long time,....... Gen 26:8
For he *h* possession of flocks, and......... Gen 26:14
which his father's servants *h*............... Gen 26:15
the Philistines *h* stopped them............. Gen 26:15
which they *h* digged in the days........... Gen 26:18
for the Philistines *h* stopped................. Gen 26:18
by which his father *h* called them......... Gen 26:18
the well which they *h* digged................ Gen 26:32
the bread, which she *h* prepared........... Gen 27:17
as soon as Isaac *h* made an end of....... Gen 27:30
he also *h* made savoury meat, and........ Gen 27:31
saw that Isaac *h* blessed Jacob............. Gen 28:6
he *h* Mahalath the daughter of............. Gen 28:9
that he *h* put for his pillows.................. Gen 28:18
And Laban *h* two daughters.................. Gen 29:16
days, for the love he *h* to her............... Gen 29:20
Leah saw that she *h* left bearing.......... Gen 30:9
pass, when Rachel *h* born Joseph.......... Gen 30:25
every one that *h* some white in it......... Gen 30:35
he set the rods which he *h* pilled......... Gen 30:38
h much cattle, and maidservants,......... Gen 30:43 1961
all his goods which he *h* gotten............ Gen 31:18
which he *h* gotten in Padan-aram,........ Gen 31:18
Rachel *h* stolen the images that........... Gen 31:19
So he fled with all that he *h*................. Gen 31:21
Now Jacob *h* pitched his tent in........... Gen 31:25
not that Rachel *h* stolen them............. Gen 31:32
Now Rachel *h* taken the images, and... Gen 31:34
h been with me, surely thou hadst....... Gen 31:42
the brook, and sent over that he *h*...... Gen 32:23
as though I *h* seen the face of.............. Gen 33:10
where he *h* spread his tent, at............. Gen 33:19
Jacob heard that he *h* defiled............... Gen 34:5
because he *h* wrought folly in.............. Gen 34:7
because he *h* defiled Dinah their.......... Gen 34:13
because he *h* delight in Jacob's............ Gen 34:19
because they *h* defiled their................. Gen 34:27
travailed, and she *h* hard labour......... Gen 35:16
which he *h* got in the land of............... Gen 36:6
because she *h* covered her face............ Gen 38:15
that *h* the scarlet thread upon............. Gen 38:30
which *h* brought him down thither....... Gen 39:1
all that he *h* he put into his................. Gen 39:4 3426
to pass from the time that he *h*........... Gen 39:5 3426
his house, and over all that he *h*.......... Gen 39:5 3426
upon all that he *h* in the house............. Gen 39:5 3426
all that he *h* in Joseph's hand.............. Gen 39:6
and he knew not ought he *h*.................. Gen 39:6
when she saw that he *h* left his............ Gen 39:13
his baker *h* offended their lord............ Gen 40:1
I *h* three white baskets on my.............. Gen 40:16
as Joseph *h* interpreted to them.......... Gen 40:22
when they *h* eaten them up, it............. Gen 41:21
be known that they *h* eaten them......... Gen 41:21
in the second chariot which he *h*......... Gen 41:43
come, according as Joseph *h* said......... Gen 41:54
when they *h* eaten up the corn............. Gen 43:2
which they *h* brought out of Egypt...... Gen 43:2
man whether ye *h* yet a brother........... Gen 43:6
For except we *h* lingered...................... Gen 43:10
surely now we *h* returned this.............. Gen 43:10
I *h* your money..................................... Gen 43:23 935
to the word that Joseph *h* spoken......... Gen 44:2
which he *h* said unto them.................... Gen 45:27
which Joseph *h* sent to carry him......... Gen 45:27
his journey with all that he *h*.............. Gen 46:1
which Pharaoh *h* sent to carry him...... Gen 46:5
which they *h* gotten in the land........... Gen 46:6
Rameses, as Pharaoh *h* commanded...... Gen 47:11
for the priests *h* a portion..................... Gen 47:22
they *h* possessions therein, and............. Gen 47:27
I *h* not thought to see thy face............. Gen 48:11
when Jacob *h* made an end of............... Gen 49:33
after he *h* buried his father................... Gen 50:14
when she *h* opened it, she saw the........ Ex 2:6
she *h* compassion on him, and said,...... Ex 2:6
of Midian *h* seven daughters................ Ex 2:16
and God *h* respect unto them............... Ex 2:25
words of the LORD who *h* sent him........ Ex 4:28
signs which he *h* commanded him......... Ex 4:28
the LORD *h* spoken unto Moses.............. Ex 4:30
when they heard that the LORD *h*......... Ex 4:31
that he *h* looked upon their.................. Ex 4:31
taskmasters *h* set over them................. Ex 5:14
did so as the LORD *h* commanded.......... Ex 7:10
as the LORD *h* said................................. Ex 7:13
as the LORD *h* said................................. Ex 7:22
that the LORD *h* smitten the river........ Ex 7:25
he *h* brought against Pharaoh............... Ex 8:12
as the LORD *h* said................................. Ex 8:15
as the LORD *h* said................................. Ex 8:19
as the LORD *h* spoken unto Moses........ Ex 9:12
as the LORD *h* spoken by Moses............ Ex 9:35
the trees which the hail *h* left............... Ex 10:15
Israel *h* light in their dwellings........... Ex 10:23 1961
did as the LORD *h* commanded Moses.. Ex 12:28
neither *h* they prepared for.................. Ex 12:39
when Pharaoh *h* let the people go,....... Ex 13:17
for he *h* straitly sworn the................... Ex 13:19
For it *h* been better for us to................ Ex 14:12
which when he *h* cast into the.............. Ex 15:25
Would to God we *h* died by the............ Ex 16:3
that gathered much *h* nothing over...... Ex 16:18
he that gathered little *h* no lack........... Ex 16:18
Joshua did as Moses *h* said to him........ Ex 17:10
of all that God *h* done for Moses.......... Ex 18:1
that the LORD *h* brought Israel............. Ex 18:1
after he *h* sent her back,...................... Ex 18:2
that the LORD *h* done unto Pharaoh..... Ex 18:8
all the travail that *h* come upon........... Ex 18:8
which the LORD *h* done to Israel.......... Ex 18:9
whom he *h* delivered out of the............ Ex 18:9
in law, and did all that he *h* said......... Ex 18:24
h pitched in the wilderness................... Ex 19:2
Moses, when he *h* made an end of....... Ex 31:18
after he *h* made it a molten calf........... Ex 32:4
took the calf which they *h* made.......... Ex 32:20
(for Aaron *h* made them naked unto..... Ex 32:25
For Moses *h* said, Consecrate............... Ex 32:29
For the LORD *h* said unto Moses,........... Ex 33:5
as the LORD *h* commanded him, and.... Ex 34:4
commandment all that the LORD *h*....... Ex 34:32
till Moses *h* done speaking with........... Ex 34:33
and brought that which they *h* spun.... Ex 35:25
which the LORD *h* commanded to be.... Ex 35:29
to all that the LORD *h* commanded....... Ex 36:1
whose heart the LORD *h* put wisdom.... Ex 36:2
h brought for the work of the.............. Ex 36:3
For the stuff they *h* was....................... Ex 36:7 1961
One board *h* two tenons, equally.......... Ex 36:22
they *h* done it as the LORD *h*............... Ex 39:43
even so *h* they done it.......................... Ex 39:43
as the LORD *h* commanded Moses......... Ex 40:23
as Moses *h* said.................................... Lev 10:5
if I *h* eaten the sin offering to.............. Lev 10:19
unto him, which hath *h* no husband..... Lev 21:3 1961
him that *h* cursed out of the camp....... Lev 24:23
For the LORD *h* spoken unto Moses,...... Num 1:48
of Sinai, and they *h* no children........... Num 3:4 1961
h fully set up the tabernacle................. Num 7:1
h anointed it, and sanctified it,............ Num 7:1
h anointed them, and sanctified........... Num 7:1
which the LORD *h* shewed Moses.......... Num 8:4
as the LORD *h* commanded Moses......... Num 8:22
Ethiopian woman whom he *h* married. Num 12:1
for he *h* married an Ethiopian.............. Num 12:1
If her father *h* but spit in her.............. Num 12:14
h searched unto the children of............ Num 13:32
Would God that we *h* died in the.......... Num 14:2
or would God we *h* died in this............ Num 14:2
because he *h* another spirit with......... Num 14:24 1961
as he *h* made an end of speaking......... Num 16:31
they that were burnt *h* offered............. Num 16:39
Would God that we *h* died when our... Num 20:3
if a serpent *h* bitten any man.............. Num 21:9
who *h* fought against the former......... Num 21:26
Israel *h* done to the Amorites.............. Num 22:2
unless she *h* turned from me,.............. Num 22:33
surely now also I *h* slain thee.............. Num 22:33
And Balak did as Balaam *h* spoken...... Num 23:2
And Balak did as Balaam *h* said.......... Num 23:30
the son of Hepher *h* no sons................ Num 26:33 1961
For the LORD *h* said of them.............. Num 26:65
died in his own sin, and *h* no sons....... Num 27:3 1961
if she *h* at all an husband, when.......... Num 30:6 1961
which the men of war *h* caught........... Num 31:32
of women that *h* not known man by.... Num 31:35
(For the men of war *h* taken spoil........ Num 31:53
the children of Gad *h* a very................. Num 32:1 1961
land which the LORD *h* given them....... Num 32:9
that *h* done evil in the sight of............. Num 32:13
which the LORD *h* smitten among......... Num 33:4
unto all that the LORD *h* given............. Deut 1:3
After he *h* slain Sihon the king............ Deut 1:4
which in that day *h* no knowledge....... Deut 1:39
when ye *h* girded on every man his...... Deut 1:41
when they *h* destroyed them from........ Deut 2:12
he *h* sworn unto your fathers................ Deut 7:8
ye *h* sinned against the LORD your....... Deut 9:16
God, and *h* made you a molten calf...... Deut 9:16
ye *h* turned aside quickly out of........... Deut 9:16
which the LORD *h* commanded you........ Deut 9:16
sin, the calf which ye *h* made................ Deut 9:21 1961
because the LORD *h* said he would........ Deut 9:25 1961
tables in the ark which I *h* made.......... Deut 10:5
Only the LORD *h* a delight in thy........... Deut 10:15
as he *h* thought to have done unto....... Deut 19:19
whom he *h* not given unto them.......... Deut 29:26
when Moses *h* made an end of............. Deut 31:24
except their Rock *h* sold them............. Deut 32:30
and the LORD *h* shut them up............... Deut 32:30
for Moses *h* laid his hands upon.......... Deut 34:9
But she *h* brought them up to the........ Josh 2:6
which she *h* laid in order upon............. Josh 2:6
as soon as we *h* heard these................. Josh 2:11
whom he *h* prepared of the.................. Josh 4:4
heard that the LORD *h* dried up........... Josh 5:1
them they *h* not circumcised............... Josh 5:5
because they *h* not circumcised........... Josh 5:7
when they *h* done circumcising all....... Josh 5:8
h eaten of the old corn of the.............. Josh 5:12
neither *h* the children of Israel............ Josh 5:12 1961
when Joshua *h* spoken unto the............ Josh 6:8
Joshua *h* commanded the people,.......... Josh 6:10
But Joshua *h* said unto the two............ Josh 6:22
men that *h* spied out the country......... Josh 6:22
her brethren, and all that she *h*........... Josh 6:23
household, and all that she *h*................ Josh 6:25
would to God we *h* been content.......... Josh 7:7
and his tent, and all that he *h*.............. Josh 7:24
after they *h* stoned them with.............. Josh 7:25
when they *h* set the people, even......... Josh 8:13
he *h* in his hand toward the city........... Josh 8:18
as he *h* stretched out his hand............. Josh 8:19
they *h* no power to flee this way.......... Josh 8:20
that the ambush *h* taken the city......... Josh 8:21
when Israel *h* made an end of.............. Josh 8:24
until he *h* utterly destroyed all............. Josh 8:26
of the LORD *h* commanded before......... Josh 8:33
what Joshua *h* done unto Jericho......... Josh 9:3
and went and made as if they *h* been.. Josh 9:4
they *h* made a league with them.......... Josh 9:16
h sworn unto them by the LORD God... Josh 9:18
as the princes *h* promised them............ Josh 9:21
h heard how Joshua *h* taken Ai............ Josh 10:1
and *h* utterly destroyed it;.................... Josh 10:1 1961
as he *h* done to Jericho and her.......... Josh 10:1 1961
so he *h* done to Ai and her king........... Josh 10:1 1961
Gibeon *h* made peace with Israel......... Josh 10:1 1961
until the people *h* avenged.................. Josh 10:13
the children of Israel *h* made an.......... Josh 10:20
the cave wherein they *h* been hid........ Josh 10:27
to all that he *h* done to Libnah............ Josh 10:32
people, until he *h* left him none.......... Josh 10:33
to all that he *h* done to Lachish........... Josh 10:35
to all that he *h* done to Eglon............. Josh 10:37
as he *h* done to Hebron, so he did........ Josh 10:39
as he *h* done also to Libnah, and......... Josh 10:39
of Hazor *h* heard those things.............. Josh 11:1
until they *h* destroyed them,................ Josh 11:14
For Moses *h* given the inheritance........ Josh 14:3
And the land *h* rest from war............... Josh 14:15
man of war, therefore he *h* Gilead........ Josh 17:1 1961
h no sons, but daughters..................... Josh 17:3 1961
the daughters of Manasseh *h* an........... Josh 17:6
sons *h* the land of Gilead..................... Josh 17:6 1961
Now Manasseh *h* the land of................ Josh 17:8 1961
Manasseh *h* in Issachar and in............ Josh 17:11 1961
which *h* not yet received their............ Josh 18:2
they *h* in their inheritance.................. Josh 19:2 1961
the children of Simeon *h* their............. Josh 19:9
When they *h* made an end of................ Josh 19:49
h by lot out of the tribe of.................... Josh 21:4 1961
h by lot out of the families of............... Josh 21:5
the children of Gershon *h* by lot........... Josh 21:6
h out of the tribe of Reuben................. Josh 21:7
were of the children of Levi, *h*............... Josh 21:10 1961
even they *h* the cities of their.............. Josh 21:20 1961
any good thing which the LORD *h*......... Josh 21:45
h given possession in Bashan............... Josh 22:7
h given rest unto Israel from all........... Josh 23:1
which *h* known all the works of............. Josh 24:31
that he *h* done for Israel...................... Josh 24:31
Judah *h* fought against Jerusalem........ Judg 1:8
h taken it, and smitten it with.............. Judg 1:8
because they *h* chariots of iron............ Judg 1:19
when Joshua *h* let the people go,......... Judg 2:6
who *h* seen all the great works of......... Judg 2:7
works which he *h* done for Israel.......... Judg 2:10
them for evil, as the LORD *h* said.......... Judg 2:15
as the LORD *h* sworn unto them............ Judg 2:15
as *h* not known all the wars of............... Judg 3:1
the land *h* rest forty years.................... Judg 3:11
because they *h* done evil in the............. Judg 3:12
him a dagger which *h* two edges........... Judg 3:16
when he *h* made an end to offer............ Judg 3:18
which he *h* for himself alone................. Judg 3:20
the land *h* rest fourscore years............. Judg 3:30
for he *h* nine hundred chariots of......... Judg 4:3
h severed himself from the.................... Judg 4:11
when he *h* turned in unto her into........ Judg 4:18

H

until they *h* destroyed Jabin king	Judg 4:24	
off his head, when she *h* pierced	Judg 5:26	
the land *h* rest forty years	Judg 5:31	
And so it was, when Israel *h* sown	Judg 6:3	
did as the LORD *h* said unto him	Judg 6:27	
they *h* but newly set the watch	Judg 7:19	
toward him, when he *h* said that	Judg 8:3	
the men of Succoth *h* answered him	Judg 8:8	
if ye *h* saved them alive, I would	Judg 8:19	
(For they *h* golden earrings,	Judg 8:24	
Gideon *h* threescore and ten sons	Judg 8:30	
for he *h* many wives	Judg 8:30	1961
who *h* delivered them out of the	Judg 8:34	
which he *h* shewed unto Israel	Judg 8:35	
When Abimelech *h* reigned three	Judg 9:22	
he *h* thirty sons that rode on	Judg 10:4	1961
they *h* thirty cities, which are	Judg 10:4	
beside her he *h* neither son nor	Judg 11:34	
to his vow which he *h* vowed	Judg 11:39	
he *h* thirty sons, and thirty	Judg 12:9	1961
he *h* forty sons and thirty nephews	Judg 12:14	1961
h dominion over Israel	Judg 14:4	
kid, and he *h* nothing in his hand	Judg 14:6	
or his mother what he *h* done	Judg 14:6	
he *h* taken the honey out of the	Judg 14:9	
If ye *h* not plowed with my heifer	Judg 14:18	
ye *h* not found out my riddle	Judg 14:18	
whom he *h* used as his friend	Judg 14:20	
when he *h* set the brands on fire,	Judg 15:5	
because he *h* taken his wife, and	Judg 15:6	
when he *h* made an end of speaking	Judg 15:17	
and when he *h* drunk, his spirit	Judg 15:19	
withs which *h* not been dried	Judg 16:8	
that he *h* told her all his heart	Judg 16:18	
when he *h* restored the eleven	Judg 17:3	
I *h* wholly dedicated the silver	Judg 17:3	
the man Micah *h* an house of gods,	Judg 17:5	
h not fallen unto them among the	Judg 18:1	
h no business with any man	Judg 18:7	
the things which Micah *h* made	Judg 18:27	
and the priest which he *h*	Judg 18:27	1961
they *h* no business with any man	Judg 18:28	
father *h* said unto the man	Judg 19:6	
when he *h* lifted up his eyes, he	Judg 19:17	
which they *h* set beside Gibeah	Judg 20:36	
men of Israel *h* sworn in Mizpeh	Judg 21:1	
For they *h* made a great oath	Judg 21:5	
that *h* known no man by lying with	Judg 21:12	
h saved alive of the women of	Judg 21:14	
because that the LORD *h* made a	Judg 21:15	
for she *h* heard in the country of	Ruth 1:6	
of Moab how that the LORD *h*	Ruth 1:6	
And Naomi *h* a kinsman of her	Ruth 2:1	
and beat out that she *h* gleaned	Ruth 2:17	
in law saw what she *h* gleaned	Ruth 2:18	
gave to her that she *h* reserved	Ruth 2:18	
in law with whom she *h* wrought	Ruth 2:19	
And when Boaz *h* eaten	Ruth 3:7	
all that the man *h* done to her	Ruth 3:16	
And he *h* two wives	1Sa 1:2	
and Peninnah *h* children	1Sa 1:2	1961
but Hannah *h* no children	1Sa 1:2	
but the LORD *h* shut up her womb	1Sa 1:5	
the LORD *h* shut up her womb	1Sa 1:6	
up after they *h* eaten in Shiloh	1Sa 1:9	
and after they *h* drunk	1Sa 1:9	
Eli thought she *h* been drunken	1Sa 1:13	
about after Hannah *h* conceived	1Sa 1:20	
when she *h* weaned him, she took	1Sa 1:24	
that the LORD *h* called the child	1Sa 3:8	
he *h* judged Israel forty years	1Sa 4:18	
after they *h* carried it about,	1Sa 5:9	
they *h* emerods in their secret	1Sa 5:9	
when he *h* wrought wonderfully	1Sa 6:6	
of the Philistines *h* seen it	1Sa 6:16	
because they *h* looked into the	1Sa 6:19	
because the LORD *h* smitten many	1Sa 6:19	
cities which the Philistines *h*	1Sa 7:14	
he *h* a son, whose name was Saul,	1Sa 9:2	1961
Now the LORD *h* told Samuel in his	1Sa 9:15	
that when he *h* turned his back to	1Sa 10:9	
And when he *h* made an end of	1Sa 10:13	
when Samuel *h* caused all the	1Sa 10:20	
When he *h* caused the tribe of	1Sa 10:21	
men, whose hearts God *h* touched	1Sa 10:26	
when he *h* reigned two years over	1Sa 13:1	
Saul *h* smitten a garrison of the	1Sa 13:4	
that Israel also was *h* in	1Sa 13:4	
set time that Samuel *h* appointed	1Sa 13:8	
that as soon as he *h* made an end	1Sa 13:10	
Yet they *h* a file for the	1Sa 13:21	
holes where they *h* hid themselves	1Sa 14:11	
And when they *h* numbered, behold,	1Sa 14:17	
all the men of Israel which *h* hid	1Sa 14:22	
for Saul *h* adjured the people,	1Sa 14:24	
for haply the people *h* eaten	1Sa 14:30	
for *h* there not been now a much	1Sa 14:30	
the LORD repented that he *h* made	1Sa 15:35	1961
he *h* an helmet of brass upon his	1Sa 17:5	
he *h* greaves of brass upon his	1Sa 17:6	
and he *h* eight sons	1Sa 17:12	
and went, as Jesse *h* commanded him	1Sa 17:20	
the Philistines *h* put the battle	1Sa 17:21	
for he *h* not proved it	1Sa 17:39	
in a shepherd's bag which he *h*	1Sa 17:40	
when he *h* made an end of speaking	1Sa 18:1	
him all that Saul *h* done to him	1Sa 19:18	
his father *h* done him shame	1Sa 20:34	
the arrow which Jonathan *h* shot	1Sa 20:37	
Saul *h* slain the LORD's priests	1Sa 22:21	
because he *h* cut off Saul's skirt	1Sa 24:5	
have seen how that the LORD *h*	1Sa 24:10	
when David *h* made an end of	1Sa 24:16	
forasmuch as when the LORD *h*	1Sa 24:18	
he *h* three thousand sheep, and a	1Sa 25:2	
Now David *h* said, Surely in vain	1Sa 25:21	1961
surely there *h* not been left unto	1Sa 25:34	
hand that which she *h* brought him	1Sa 25:35	
his wife *h* told him these things,	1Sa 25:37	
But Saul *h* given Michal his	1Sa 25:44	
to the place where Saul *h* pitched	1Sa 26:5	
all Israel *h* lamented him, and	1Sa 28:3	
Saul *h* put away those that *h*	1Sa 28:3	
for he *h* eaten no bread all the	1Sa 28:20	
the woman *h* a fat calf in the	1Sa 28:24	
Amalekites *h* invaded the south	1Sa 30:1	
h taken the women captives, that	1Sa 30:2	
until they *h* no more power to	1Sa 30:4	
and when he *h* eaten, his spirit	1Sa 30:12	
for he *h* eaten no bread, nor	1Sa 30:12	
when he *h* brought him down,	1Sa 30:16	
h taken out of the land of the	1Sa 30:16	
the Amalekites *h* carried away	1Sa 30:18	
thing that they *h* taken to them	1Sa 30:19	
whom they *h* made also to abide at	1Sa 30:21	
the Philistines *h* done to Saul	1Sa 31:11	
David *h* abode two days in Ziklag	2Sa 1:1	
as though he *h* not been anointed	2Sa 1:21	
people *h* gone up every one from	2Sa 2:27	
when he *h* gathered all the people	2Sa 2:30	
of David *h* smitten of Benjamin	2Sa 2:31	
Saul *h* a concubine, whose name	2Sa 3:7	
Abner *h* communication with the	2Sa 3:17	
for he *h* sent him away, and he was	2Sa 3:22	
because he *h* slain their brother	2Sa 3:30	
Saul's son *h* two men that were	2Sa 4:2	1961
h a son that was lame of his feet	2Sa 4:4	
LORD *h* established him king over	2Sa 5:12	
that he *h* exalted his kingdom for	2Sa 5:12	
h anointed David king over Israel	2Sa 5:17	
as the LORD *h* commanded him	2Sa 5:25	
because the LORD *h* made a breach	2Sa 6:8	
ark of the LORD *h* gone six paces	2Sa 6:13	
that David *h* pitched for it	2Sa 6:17	
as soon as David *h* made an end of	2Sa 6:18	
of them shall I be *h* in honour	2Sa 6:22	
Michal the daughter of Saul *h* no	2Sa 6:23	
the LORD *h* given him rest round	2Sa 7:1	
David *h* smitten all the host of	2Sa 8:9	1961
because he *h* fought against	2Sa 8:10	
for Hadadezer *h* wars with Toi	2Sa 8:10	
gold that he *h* dedicated of all	2Sa 8:11	
when they *h* called him unto David	2Sa 9:2	
Now Ziba *h* fifteen sons and twenty	2Sa 9:10	
And Mephibosheth *h* a young son	2Sa 9:12	
when they *h* told David, saying,	2Sa 11:10	
And when David *h* called him	2Sa 11:13	
all that Joab *h* sent him for	2Sa 11:22	
David *h* done displeased the LORD	2Sa 11:27	
The rich man *h* exceeding many	2Sa 12:2	1961
But the poor man *h* nothing	2Sa 12:3	
ewe lamb, which he *h* bought	2Sa 12:3	1961
thing, and because he *h* no pity	2Sa 12:6	
if that *h* been too little, I	2Sa 12:8	
the son of David *h* a fair sister	2Sa 13:1	
But Amnon *h* a friend, whose name	2Sa 13:3	
took the cakes which she *h* made	2Sa 13:10	
when she *h* brought them unto him	2Sa 13:11	
the love wherewith he *h* loved her	2Sa 13:15	
she *h* a garment of divers colours	2Sa 13:18	
because he *h* forced his sister	2Sa 13:22	
that Absalom *h* sheepshearers in	2Sa 13:23	
Now Absalom *h* commanded his	2Sa 13:28	
as Absalom *h* commanded	2Sa 13:29	
as soon as he *h* made an end of	2Sa 13:36	
but be as a woman that *h* a long	2Sa 14:2	
And thy handmaid *h* two sons	2Sa 14:6	
it *h* been good for me to have	2Sa 14:32	
when he *h* called for Absalom, he	2Sa 14:33	
that when any man that *h* a	2Sa 15:2	1961
until all the people *h* done	2Sa 15:24	
h his head covered, and he went	2Sa 15:30	
was as if a man *h* enquired at the	2Sa 16:23	
For the LORD *h* appointed to	2Sa 17:14	
which *h* a well in his court	2Sa 17:18	
And when they *h* sought and could	2Sa 17:20	
Absalom in his lifetime *h* taken	2Sa 18:18	
would God I *h* died for thee, O	2Sa 18:33	
perceive, that if Absalom *h* lived	2Sa 19:6	
all we *h* died this day	2Sa 19:6	
then it *h* pleased thee well	2Sa 19:6	
for Israel *h* fled every man to	2Sa 19:8	
h neither dressed his feet, nor	2Sa 19:24	
he *h* provided the king of	2Sa 19:32	
first *h* in bringing back our king	2Sa 19:43	
whom he *h* left to keep the house,	2Sa 20:3	
set time which he *h* appointed him	2Sa 20:5	
Joab's garment that he *h* put on	2Sa 20:8	
of Israel *h* sworn unto them	2Sa 21:2	
the concubine of Saul, *h* done	2Sa 21:11	
which *h* stolen them from the	2Sa 21:12	
the Philistines *h* hanged them	2Sa 21:12	
h slain Saul in Gilboa	2Sa 21:12	1961
Moreover the Philistines *h* yet	2Sa 21:15	1961
that *h* on every hand six fingers,	2Sa 21:20	
in the day that the LORD *h*	2Sa 22:1	
not again until I *h* consumed them	2Sa 22:38	
of the mighty men whom David *h*	2Sa 23:8	
them, and *h* the name among three	2Sa 23:18	
who *h* done many acts, he slew two	2Sa 23:20	
the Egyptian *h* a spear in his	2Sa 23:21	
h the name among three mighty men	2Sa 23:22	
So when they *h* gone through all	2Sa 24:8	
that he *h* numbered the people	2Sa 24:10	
his father *h* not displeased him	1Kin 1:6	
as they *h* made an end of eating	1Kin 1:41	
for Joab *h* turned after Adonijah,	1Kin 2:28	
h gone from Jerusalem to Gath	1Kin 2:41	
until he *h* made an end of	1Kin 3:1	
that Solomon *h* asked this thing	1Kin 3:10	
but when I *h* considered it in the	1Kin 3:21	
judgment which the king *h* judged	1Kin 3:28	
these were the princes which he *h*	1Kin 4:2	
Solomon *h* twelve officers over	1Kin 4:7	
which *h* Taphath the daughter of	1Kin 4:11	
the son of Iddo *h* Mahanaim	1Kin 4:14	
For he *h* dominion over all the	1Kin 4:24	
he *h* peace on all sides round	1Kin 4:24	1961
Solomon *h* forty thousand stalls	1Kin 4:26	
which *h* heard of his wisdom	1Kin 4:34	
for he *h* heard that they *h*	1Kin 5:1	1961
Solomon *h* threescore and ten	1Kin 5:15	1961
until he *h* finished all the house	1Kin 6:22	1961
his house where he dwelt *h*	1Kin 7:8	
whom he *h* taken to wife, like	1Kin 7:8	1961
pillars *h* pomegranates also above	1Kin 7:20	
they *h* borders, and the borders	1Kin 7:28	
every base *h* four brasen wheels,	1Kin 7:30	
corners thereof *h* undersetters	1Kin 7:30	
all of them *h* one casting	1Kin 7:37	
David his father *h* dedicated	1Kin 7:51	
for the glory of the LORD *h*	1Kin 8:11	
that when Solomon *h* made an end	1Kin 8:54	
LORD *h* done for David his servant	1Kin 8:66	
when Solomon *h* finished the	1Kin 9:1	
as he *h* appeared unto him at	1Kin 9:2	
when Solomon *h* built the two	1Kin 9:10	
(Now Hiram the king of Tyre *h*	1Kin 9:11	
cities which Solomon *h* given him	1Kin 9:12	
Pharaoh king of Egypt *h* gone up	1Kin 9:16	
cities of store that Solomon *h*	1Kin 9:19	1961
which Solomon *h* built for her	1Kin 9:24	
shipmen that *h* knowledge of the	1Kin 9:27	
when the queen of Sheba *h* seen	1Kin 10:4	
and the house that he *h* built	1Kin 10:4	
I came, and mine eyes *h* seen it	1Kin 10:7	
Beside that he *h* of the	1Kin 10:15	
The throne *h* six steps, and the	1Kin 10:19	
For the king *h* at sea a navy of	1Kin 10:22	
which God *h* put in his heart	1Kin 10:24	
he *h* a thousand and four hundred	1Kin 10:26	
Solomon *h* horses brought out of	1Kin 10:28	
he *h* seven hundred wives,	1Kin 11:3	1961
which *h* appeared unto him twice	1Kin 11:9	
h commanded him concerning this	1Kin 11:10	
after he *h* smitten every male in	1Kin 11:15	
until he *h* cut off every male in	1Kin 11:16	
he *h* clad himself with a new	1Kin 11:29	
old men, which they *h* given him	1Kin 12:8	
day, as the king *h* appointed	1Kin 12:12	
unto the calves that he *h* made	1Kin 12:32	
the high places which he *h* made	1Kin 12:32	
h made in Beth-el the fifteenth	1Kin 12:33	
he *h* devised of his own heart	1Kin 12:33	
which *h* cried against the altar	1Kin 13:4	
h given by the word of the LORD	1Kin 13:5	
of God *h* done that day in Beth-el	1Kin 13:11	
the words which he *h* spoken unto	1Kin 13:11	
For his sons *h* seen what way the	1Kin 13:12	
h eaten bread, and after he *h*	1Kin 13:23	
prophet whom he *h* brought back	1Kin 13:23	1961
the lion *h* not eaten the carcase,	1Kin 13:28	
after he *h* buried him, that he	1Kin 13:31	
their sins which they *h* committed	1Kin 14:22	
all that their fathers *h* done	1Kin 14:22	
of gold which Solomon *h* made	1Kin 14:26	
which he *h* done before him	1Kin 15:3	
the idols that his fathers *h* made	1Kin 15:12	
because she *h* made an idol in a	1Kin 15:13	
which his father *h* dedicated	1Kin 15:15	
things which himself *h* dedicated	1Kin 15:15	
he *h* against the cities of Israel	1Kin 15:20	
wherewith Baasha *h* builded	1Kin 15:22	
until he *h* destroyed him,	1Kin 15:29	
as if it *h* been a light thing for	1Kin 16:31	
which he *h* built in Samaria	1Kin 16:32	
because there *h* been no rain in	1Kin 17:7	1961
Jezebel all that Elijah *h* done	1Kin 19:1	
withal how he *h* slain all the	1Kin 19:1	
the Jezreelite *h* a vineyard	1Kin 21:1	1961
the Jezreelite *h* spoken to him	1Kin 21:4	
for he *h* said, I will not give	1Kin 21:4	
did as Jezebel *h* sent unto them	1Kin 21:11	
which she *h* sent unto them	1Kin 21:11	
two captains that *h* rule over his	1Kin 22:31	
to all that his father *h* done	1Kin 22:53	
of the LORD which Elijah *h* spoken	2Kin 1:17	
because he *h* no son	2Kin 1:17	1961
when he also *h* smitten the waters	2Kin 2:14	
of Baal that his father *h* made	2Kin 3:2	
when he *h* called her, she stood	2Kin 4:12	
when he *h* called her, she stood	2Kin 4:15	
that Elisha *h* said unto her	2Kin 4:17	
when he *h* taken him, and brought	2Kin 4:20	
because by him the LORD *h* given	2Kin 5:1	1961
the Syrians *h* gone out by	2Kin 5:2	
h brought away captive out of the	2Kin 5:2	
king of Israel *h* read the letter	2Kin 5:7	
when Elisha the man of God *h*	2Kin 5:8	
king of Israel *h* rent his clothes	2Kin 5:8	
if the prophet *h* bid thee do some	2Kin 5:13	
and when they *h* eaten and drunk, he	2Kin 6:23	
he *h* sackcloth within upon his	2Kin 6:30	
For the LORD *h* made the host of	2Kin 7:6	
which the Syrians *h* cast away in	2Kin 7:15	
he died, as the man of God *h* said	2Kin 7:17	
man of God *h* spoken to the king	2Kin 7:18	
whose son he *h* restored to life,	2Kin 8:1	
he *h* restored a dead body to life	2Kin 8:5	
whose son he *h* restored to life,	2Kin 8:5	
the Syrians *h* given him at Ramah	2Kin 8:29	
(Now Joram *h* kept Ramoth-gilead,	2Kin 9:14	

which the Syrians *h* given him 2Kin 9:15
H Zimri peace, who slew his 2Kin 9:31
Ahab *h* seventy sons in Samaria 2Kin 10:1
Samaria, till he *h* destroyed him, 2Kin 10:17
as soon as he *h* made an end of 2Kin 10:25
For the priest *h* said, Let her 2Kin 11:15
of king Jehoash the priests *h* not 2Kin 12:6
that *h* the oversight of the house 2Kin 12:11
h dedicated, and his own hallowed 2Kin 12:18
king of Syria *h* destroyed them 2Kin 13:7
h made them like the dust by 2Kin 13:7
h compassion on them, and *h* 2Kin 13:23
which he *h* taken out of the hand 2Kin 13:25
which *h* slain the king his father 2Kin 14:5
that his father Amaziah *h* done 2Kin 15:3
the LORD, as his fathers *h* done 2Kin 15:9
all that his father Uzziah *h* done 2Kin 15:34
king Ahaz *h* sent from Damascus 2Kin 16:11
that they *h* built in the house 2Kin 16:18
for he *h* sent messengers to So 2Kin 17:4
as he *h* done year by year 2Kin 17:4
that the children of Israel *h* 2Kin 17:7
which *h* brought them up out of 2Kin 17:7
of Egypt, and *h* feared other gods, 2Kin 17:7
of Israel, which they *h* made 2Kin 17:8
whereof the LORD *h* said unto them 2Kin 17:12
whom the LORD *h* charged them 2Kin 17:15
until he *h* cast them out of his 2Kin 17:20
as he *h* said by all his servants 2Kin 17:23
one of the priests whom they *h* 2Kin 17:28
which the Samaritans *h* made 2Kin 17:29
whom the LORD *h* made a covenant 2Kin 17:35
brasen serpent that Moses *h* made 2Kin 18:4
Hezekiah king of Judah *h* overlaid 2Kin 18:16
when they *h* called to the king, 2Kin 18:18
for he *h* heard that he was 2Kin 19:8
by which it *h* gone down in the 2Kin 20:11
for he *h* heard that Hezekiah *h* 2Kin 20:12
Hezekiah his father *h* destroyed 2Kin 21:3
grove that he *h* made in the house 2Kin 21:7
till he *h* filled Jerusalem from 2Kin 21:16
h conspired against king Amon 2Kin 21:24
when the king *h* heard the words 2Kin 22:11
whom the kings of Judah *h* 2Kin 23:5
the priests *h* burned incense 2Kin 23:8
kings of Judah *h* given to the sun 2Kin 23:11
which the kings of Judah *h* made 2Kin 23:12
the altars which Manasseh *h* made 2Kin 23:12
h builded for Ashtoreth the 2Kin 23:13
h made, both that altar and the 2Kin 23:15
which the kings of Israel *h* made 2Kin 23:19
acts that he *h* done in Beth-el 2Kin 23:19
Manasseh *h* provoked him withal 2Kin 23:26
at Megiddo, when he *h* seen him 2Kin 23:29
to all that his fathers *h* done 2Kin 23:32
to all that his fathers *h* done 2Kin 23:37
for the king of Babylon *h* taken 2Kin 24:7
to all that his father *h* done 2Kin 24:9
which Solomon king of Israel *h* 2Kin 24:13
of the LORD, as the LORD *h* said 2Kin 24:13
to all that Jehoiakim *h* done 2Kin 24:19
until he *h* cast them out from his 2Kin 24:20
the bases which Solomon *h* made 2Kin 25:16
like unto these *h* the second 2Kin 25:17
king of Babylon *h* left, even over 2Kin 25:22
Babylon *h* made Gedaliah governor 2Kin 25:23
who *h* three and twenty cities in 1Chr 2:22 1961
Jerahmeel *h* also another wife, 1Chr 2:26
Now Sheshan *h* no sons, but 1Chr 2:34 1961
Sheshan *h* a servant, an Egyptian, 1Chr 2:34
father of Kirjath-jearim *h* sons 1Chr 2:52
the father of Tekoa *h* two wives 1Chr 4:5 1961
who *h* the dominion in Moab, and 1Chr 4:22
Shimei *h* sixteen sons and six 1Chr 4:27
but his brethren *h* not many 1Chr 4:27
for they of Ham *h* dwelt there of 1Chr 4:40
LORD, after that the ark *h* rest 1Chr 6:31
until Solomon *h* built the house 1Chr 6:32
the servant of God *h* commanded 1Chr 6:49
h cities of their coasts out of 1Chr 6:66 1961
for they *h* many wives and sons 1Chr 7:4
and Zelophehad *h* daughters 1Chr 7:15 1961
after he *h* sent them away 1Chr 8:8
Azel *h* six sons, whose names are 1Chr 8:38
h many sons, and sons' sons, an 1Chr 8:40
their children *h* the oversight of 1Chr 9:23
certain of them *h* the charge of 1Chr 9:28
h the set office over the things 1Chr 9:31
Azel *h* six sons, whose names are 1Chr 9:44
when they *h* stripped him, they 1Chr 10:9
the Philistines *h* done to Saul 1Chr 10:11
of one that *h* a familiar spirit 1Chr 10:13
of the mighty men whom David *h* 1Chr 11:10
of the mighty men whom David *h* 1Chr 11:11
them, and *h* a name among the three 1Chr 11:20 1961
of Kabzeel, who *h* done many acts 1Chr 11:22
h the name among the three 1Chr 11:24
when it *h* overflown all his banks 1Chr 12:15
the greatest part of them *h* kept 1Chr 12:29
Issachar, which were men that *h* 1Chr 12:32
brethren *h* prepared for them 1Chr 12:39
because the LORD *h* made a breach 1Chr 13:11
of Obed-edom, and all that he *h* 1Chr 13:14
David perceived that the LORD *h* 1Chr 14:2
children which he *h* in Jerusalem 1Chr 14:4 1961
when they *h* left their gods there 1Chr 14:12
which he *h* prepared for it 1Chr 15:3
David also *h* upon him an ephod of 1Chr 15:27
tent that David *h* pitched for it 1Chr 16:1
when David *h* made an end of 1Chr 16:2
David *h* smitten all the host of 1Chr 18:9
because he *h* fought against 1Chr 18:10
(for Hadarezer *h* war with Tou 1Chr 18:10 1961
h made themselves odious to David 1Chr 19:6
So when David *h* put the battle in 1Chr 19:17
the LORD *h* answered him in the 1Chr 21:28
Jeush and Beriah *h* not many sons 1Chr 23:11
Eliezer *h* none other sons 1Chr 23:17 1961
died, and *h* no sons, but daughters 1Chr 23:22 1961
their father, and *h* no children 1Chr 24:2 1961
God of Israel *h* commanded him 1Chr 24:19
Mahli came Eleazar, who *h* no sons 1Chr 24:28 1961
And Meshelemiah *h* sons and brethren 1Chr 26:9
of the children of Merari, *h* sons 1Chr 26:10
captains of the host, *h* dedicated 1Chr 26:26
the son of Zeruiah, *h* dedicated 1Chr 26:28
whosoever *h* dedicated any thing, 1Chr 26:28
because the LORD *h* said he would 1Chr 27:23
I *h* in mine heart to build an 1Chr 28:2
h made ready for the building 1Chr 28:2
of all that he *h* by the spirit 1Chr 28:12
upon him such royal majesty as *h* 1Chr 29:25 1961
the LORD *h* made in the wilderness 2Chr 1:3 1961
But the ark of God *h* David 2Chr 1:4
which David *h* prepared for it 2Chr 1:4
for he *h* pitched a tent for it at 2Chr 1:4
h made, he put before the 2Chr 1:5
have *h* that have been before thee 2Chr 1:12 1961
he *h* a thousand and four hundred 2Chr 1:14 1961
Solomon *h* horses brought out of 2Chr 1:16
David his father *h* numbered them 2Chr 2:17
in the place that David *h* 2Chr 3:1
that David his father *h* dedicated 2Chr 5:1
LORD *h* filled the house of God 2Chr 5:14
For Solomon *h* made a brasen 2Chr 6:13
h set it in the midst of the 2Chr 6:13
Now when Solomon *h* made an end of 2Chr 7:1 1961
LORD *h* filled the LORD's house 2Chr 7:2
which David the king *h* made to 2Chr 7:6
h made was not able to receive 2Chr 7:7
that the LORD *h* shewed unto David 2Chr 7:10
wherein Solomon *h* built the house 2Chr 8:1
which Huram *h* restored to Solomon 2Chr 8:2
the store cities that Solomon *h* 2Chr 8:6 1961
the house that he *h* built for her 2Chr 8:11
which he *h* built before the porch 2Chr 8:12
for so *h* David the man of God 2Chr 8:14
servants that *h* knowledge of the 2Chr 8:18
when the queen of Sheba *h* seen 2Chr 9:3
and the house that he *h* built 2Chr 9:3
I came, and mine eyes *h* seen it 2Chr 9:6
which she *h* brought unto the king 2Chr 9:12
that God *h* put in his heart 2Chr 9:23
Solomon *h* four thousand stalls 2Chr 9:25 1961
whither he *h* fled from the 2Chr 10:2
counsel with the old men that *h* 2Chr 10:6 1961
his sons *h* cast them off from 2Chr 11:14
and for the calves which he *h* made 2Chr 11:15
when Rehoboam *h* established the 2Chr 12:1
h strengthened himself, he 2Chr 12:1
because they *h* transgressed 2Chr 12:2
of gold which Solomon *h* made 2Chr 12:9
the city which the LORD *h* chosen 2Chr 12:13
for the land *h* rest, and he *h* no 2Chr 14:6
because the LORD *h* given him rest 2Chr 14:6
Asa *h* an army of men that bare 2Chr 14:8 1961
he *h* taken from mount Ephraim 2Chr 15:8
of the spoil which they *h* brought 2Chr 15:11
for they *h* sworn with all their 2Chr 15:15
because she *h* made an idol in a 2Chr 15:16
that his father *h* dedicated 2Chr 15:18
and that he himself *h* dedicated 2Chr 15:18
which he *h* made for himself in 2Chr 16:14
which Asa his father *h* taken 2Chr 17:2
and he *h* riches and honour in 2Chr 17:5 1961
h the book of the law of the LORD 2Chr 17:9
he *h* much business in the cities 2Chr 17:13 1961
Now Jehoshaphat *h* riches and 2Chr 18:1 1961
for the people that he *h* with him 2Chr 18:2
h made him horns of iron, and said 2Chr 18:10
Now the king of Syria *h* commanded 2Chr 18:30
when he *h* consulted with the 2Chr 20:21
when they *h* made an end of the 2Chr 20:23
for the LORD *h* made them to 2Chr 20:27
when they *h* heard that the LORD 2Chr 20:29
for as yet the people *h* not 2Chr 20:33
he *h* brethren the sons of 2Chr 21:2
for he *h* the daughter of Ahab to 2Chr 21:6 1961
that he *h* made with David 2Chr 21:7
because he *h* forsaken the LORD 2Chr 21:10
the camp *h* slain all the eldest 2Chr 22:1
whom the LORD *h* anointed to cut 2Chr 22:7
and when they *h* slain him, they 2Chr 22:9
So the house of Ahaziah *h* no 2Chr 22:9
Jehoiada the priest *h* commanded 2Chr 23:8
that *h* been king David's, which 2Chr 23:9
whom David *h* distributed in the 2Chr 23:18
after that they *h* slain Athaliah 2Chr 23:21
h broken up the house of God 2Chr 24:7
chest, until they *h* made an end 2Chr 24:10
when they *h* finished it, they 2Chr 24:14
because he *h* done good in Israel, 2Chr 24:16
Jehoiada his father *h* done to him 2Chr 24:22
because they *h* forsaken the LORD 2Chr 24:24
that *h* killed the king his father 2Chr 25:3
who *h* understanding in the 2Chr 26:5
for he *h* much cattle, both in the 2Chr 26:10 1961
Moreover Uzziah *h* an host of 2Chr 26:11
h a censer in his hand to burn 2Chr 26:19
because the LORD *h* smitten him 2Chr 26:20
of the heathen whom the LORD *h* 2Chr 28:3
because they *h* forsaken the LORD 2Chr 28:6
For again the Edomites *h* come 2Chr 28:17
The Philistines also *h* invaded 2Chr 28:18
h taken Beth-shemesh, and Ajalon, 2Chr 28:18
all that David his father *h* done 2Chr 29:2
when they *h* killed the rams, they 2Chr 29:22
when they *h* made an end of 2Chr 29:29
priests *h* sanctified themselves 2Chr 29:34
that God *h* prepared the people 2Chr 29:36
For the king *h* taken counsel, and 2Chr 30:2
because the priests *h* not 2Chr 30:3
neither *h* the people gathered 2Chr 30:3
for they *h* not done it of a long 2Chr 30:5
therefore the Levites *h* the 2Chr 30:17
h not cleansed themselves, yet 2Chr 30:18
until they *h* utterly destroyed 2Chr 31:1
we have *h* enough to eat, and have 2Chr 31:10
Hezekiah *h* exceeding much riches 2Chr 32:27 1961
for God *h* given him substance 2Chr 32:29
whom the LORD *h* cast out before 2Chr 33:2
Hezekiah his father *h* broken down 2Chr 33:3
the LORD, whereof the LORD *h* said 2Chr 33:4
image, the idol which he *h* made 2Chr 33:7
of which God *h* said to David and 2Chr 33:7
whom the LORD *h* destroyed before 2Chr 33:9
all the altars that he *h* built in 2Chr 33:15
which Manasseh his father *h* made 2Chr 33:22
his father *h* humbled himself 2Chr 33:23
h conspired against king Amon 2Chr 33:25
them that *h* sacrificed unto them 2Chr 34:4
when he *h* broken down the altars 2Chr 34:7
h beaten the graven images into 2Chr 34:7
when he *h* purged the land, and the 2Chr 34:8
doors *h* gathered of the hand of 2Chr 34:9
h the oversight of the house of 2Chr 34:10
the kings of Judah *h* destroyed 2Chr 34:11
when the king *h* heard the words 2Chr 34:19
and they that the king *h* appointed 2Chr 34:22
when Josiah *h* prepared the temple 2Chr 35:20
in the second chariot that he *h* 2Chr 35:24
who *h* made him swear by God 2Chr 36:13
which he *h* hallowed in Jerusalem 2Chr 36:14
because he *h* compassion on his 2Chr 36:15
h no compassion upon young man or 2Chr 36:17
them that *h* escaped from the 2Chr 36:20
until the land *h* enjoyed her 2Chr 36:21
them whose spirit God *h* raised Ezr 1:5
which Nebuchadnezzar *h* brought Ezr 1:7
h put them in the house of his Ezr 1:7
of those which *h* been carried Ezr 2:1
the king of Babylon *h* carried Ezr 2:1
to the grant that they *h* of Cyrus Ezr 3:7
that *h* seen the first house, when Ezr 3:12
But after that our fathers *h* Ezr 5:12
whom he *h* made governor Ezr 5:14
that which Darius the king *h* sent Ezr 6:13
and all such as *h* separated Ezr 6:21
for the LORD *h* made them joyful, Ezr 6:22
the LORD God of Israel *h* given Ezr 7:6
For Ezra *h* prepared his heart to Ezr 7:10
the princes *h* appointed for the Ezr 8:20
because we *h* spoken unto the king Ezr 8:22
Israel there present, *h* offered Ezr 8:25
of those that *h* been carried away Ezr 8:35
of those that *h* been carried away Ezr 9:4
Now when Ezra *h* prayed Ezr 10:1
when he *h* confessed, weeping and Ezr 10:1
of them that *h* been carried away Ezr 10:6
of those that *h* been carried away Ezr 10:8
that *h* taken strange wives by the Ezr 10:17
found that *h* taken strange wives Ezr 10:18
All these *h* taken strange wives Ezr 10:44
some of them *h* wives by whom they Ezr 10:44 3426
wives by whom they *h* children Ezr 10:44 7760
the Jews that *h* escaped, which Neh 1:2
Now I *h* not been beforetime sad Neh 2:1
Now the king *h* sent captains of Neh 2:9
my God *h* put in my heart to do at Neh 2:12
neither *h* I as yet told it to the Neh 2:16
words that he *h* spoken unto me Neh 2:18
for the people *h* a mind to work Neh 4:6 1961
God *h* brought their counsel to Neh 4:15
every one *h* his sword girded by Neh 4:18
But the former governors that *h* Neh 5:15
h taken of them bread and wine, Neh 5:15
heard that I *h* builded the wall, Neh 6:1
(though at that time I *h* not set Neh 6:1
perceived that God *h* not sent him Neh 6:12
Tobiah and Sanballat *h* hired him Neh 6:12
his son Johanan *h* taken the Neh 6:18
I *h* set up the doors, and the Neh 7:1
of those that *h* been carried away Neh 7:6
king of Babylon *h* carried away Neh 7:6
they *h* two hundred forty and five Neh 7:67
which the LORD *h* commanded to Neh 8:1
which they *h* made for the purpose Neh 8:4
because they *h* understood the Neh 8:12
the LORD *h* commanded by Moses Neh 8:14
the son of Nun unto that day *h* Neh 8:17
when they *h* made them a molten Neh 9:18
h wrought great provocations Neh 9:18
But after they *h* rest, they did Neh 9:28
so that they *h* the dominion over Neh 9:28
all they that *h* separated Neh 10:28 1961
h the oversight of the outward Neh 11:16
for the singers *h* builded them Neh 12:29
for God *h* made them rejoice with Neh 12:43
when they *h* heard the law, that Neh 13:3
he *h* prepared for him a great Neh 13:5
the Levites *h* not been given them Neh 13:10
that *h* married wives of Ashdod Neh 13:23
for so the king *h* appointed to Est 1:8
Vashti, and what she *h* done Est 2:1
Who *h* been carried away from Est 2:6
with the captivity which *h* been Est 2:6
king of Babylon *h* carried away Est 2:6
for she *h* neither father nor Est 2:7
Esther *h* not shewed her people Est 2:10
for Mordecai *h* charged her that Est 2:10
after that she *h* been twelve Est 2:12
who *h* taken her for his daughter, Est 2:15

Esther *h* not yet shewed her ... Est 2:20
as Mordecai *h* charged her ... Est 2:20
for the king *h* so commanded ... Est 3:2
for he *h* told them that he was a ... Est 3:4
for they *h* shewed him the people ... Est 3:6
Haman *h* commanded unto the king's . Est 3:12
whom he *h* appointed to attend ... Est 4:5
of all that *h* happened unto him ... Est 4:7
h promised to pay to the king's ... Est 4:7
all that Esther *h* commanded him ... Est 4:17
banquet that Esther *h* prepared ... Est 5:5
wherein the king *h* promoted him ... Est 5:11
how he *h* advanced him above the ... Est 5:11
that she *h* prepared but myself ... Est 5:12
that Mordecai *h* told of Bigthana ... Est 6:2
that he *h* prepared for him ... Est 6:4
every thing that *h* befallen him ... Est 6:13
banquet that Esther *h* prepared ... Est 6:14
But if we *h* been sold for bondmen ... Est 7:4
I *h* held my tongue, although the ... Est 7:4
which Haman *h* made for Mordecai, ... Est 7:9
who *h* spoken good for the king, ... Est 7:9
that he *h* prepared for Mordecai ... Est 7:10
for Esther *h* told what he was ... Est 8:1
which he *h* taken from Haman, and ... Est 8:2
his device that he *h* devised ... Est 8:3
The Jews *h* light, and gladness, and ... Est 8:16
his decree came, the Jews *h* joy ... Est 8:17
that the Jews *h* rule over them ... Est 9:1
h rest from their enemies, and ... Est 9:16
undertook to do as they *h* begun ... Est 9:23
as Mordecai *h* written unto them ... Est 9:23
h devised against the Jews to ... Est 9:24
h cast Pur, that is, the lot, to ... Est 9:24
of that which they *h* seen ... Est 9:26
and which *h* come unto them, ... Est 9:26
Esther the queen *h* enjoined them ... Est 9:31
as they *h* decreed for themselves ... Est 9:31
for they *h* made an appointment ... Job 2:11
then *h* I been at rest, ... Job 3:13
Or with princes that *h* gold ... Job 3:15
untimely birth I *h* not been ... Job 3:16
not in safety, neither *h* I rest ... Job 3:26
confounded because they *h* hoped ... Job 6:20
If I *h* called, and he *h* answered ... Job 9:16
that he *h* hearkened unto my voice ... Job 9:16
Oh that I *h* given up the ghost, ... Job 10:18
up the ghost, and no eye *h* seen me ... Job 10:18
have been as though I *h* not been ... Job 10:19
the mighty man, he *h* the earth ... Job 22:8
houses, which they *h* marked for ... Job 24:16
him that *h* none to help him ... Job 29:12
because mine hand *h* gotten much ... Job 31:25
Oh that we *h* of his flesh ... Job 31:31
mine adversary *h* written a book ... Job 31:35
because they *h* found no answer, ... Job 32:3
and yet *h* condemned Job ... Job 32:3
Now Elihu *h* waited till Job *h* ... Job 32:4
h waited till Job *h* spoken ... Job 32:4
When I *h* waited, (for they spake ... Job 32:16
as if it *h* issued out of the womb ... Job 38:8
that after the LORD *h* spoken ... Job 42:7
Job twice as much as he *h* before ... Job 42:10
all they that *h* been of his ... Job 42:11
that the LORD *h* brought upon him ... Job 42:11
for he *h* fourteen thousand sheep, ... Job 42:12 1961
He *h* also seven sons and three ... Job 42:13 1961
I *h* fainted, unless I *h* ... Ps 27:13
he *h* been my friend or brother ... Ps 35:14
for I *h* gone with the multitude, ... Ps 42:4
after he *h* gone in to Bath-sheba ... Ps 51:*t* 1961
Oh that I *h* wings like a dove ... Ps 55:6
my steps *h* well nigh slipped ... Ps 73:2
h lifted up axes upon the thick ... Ps 74:5
his wonders that he *h* shewed them ... Ps 78:11
Though he *h* commanded the clouds ... Ps 78:23
h rained down manna upon them to ... Ps 78:24
h given them of the corn of ... Ps 78:24
How he *h* wrought his signs in ... Ps 78:43
h turned their rivers into blood ... Ps 78:44
which his right hand *h* purchased ... Ps 78:54
my people *h* hearkened unto me ... Ps 81:13
Israel *h* walked in my ways ... Ps 81:13
I *h* rather be a doorkeeper in the ... Ps 84:10
to be *h* in reverence of all them ... Ps 89:7
Unless the LORD *h* been my help ... Ps 94:17
my soul *h* almost dwelt in silence ... Ps 94:17
and Aaron whom he *h* chosen ... Ps 105:26
which *h* done great things in ... Ps 106:21
h not Moses his chosen stood ... Ps 106:23 3884
The proud have *h* me greatly in ... Ps 119:51
This I *h*, because I kept thy ... Ps 119:56 1961
They *h* almost consumed me upon ... Ps 119:87
Unless thy law *h* been my delights ... Ps 119:92
If it *h* not been the LORD who was ... Ps 124:1
If it *h* not been the LORD who was ... Ps 124:2
Then they *h* swallowed us up quick ... Ps 124:3
Then the waters *h* overwhelmed us ... Ps 124:4
the stream *h* gone over our soul ... Ps 124:4
proud waters *h* gone over our soul ... Ps 124:5
While as yet he *h* not made the ... Prov 8:26
nettles *h* covered the face ... Prov 24:31
my heart *h* great experience of ... Eccl 1:16
h servants born in my house ... Eccl 2:7 1961
also I *h* great possessions of ... Eccl 2:7 1961
the works that my hands *h* wrought ... Eccl 2:11
labour that I *h* laboured to do ... Eccl 2:11
which I *h* taken under the sun ... Eccl 2:18
oppressed, and they *h* no comforter ... Eccl 4:1
but they *h* no comforter ... Eccl 4:1
who *h* come and gone from the place .. Eccl 8:10
in the city where they *h* so done ... Eccl 8:10
until I *h* brought him into my ... Song 3:4
but my beloved *h* withdrawn ... Song 5:6

Solomon *h* a vineyard at ... Song 8:11
Except the LORD of hosts *h* left ... Is 1:9
each one *h* six wings ... Is 6:2
which he *h* taken with the tongs ... Is 6:6
neither *h* respect unto him that ... Is 22:11
thee have *h* dominion over us ... Is 26:13
framed it, He *h* no understanding ... Is 29:16
for he *h* heard that he was ... Is 37:8
when he *h* been sick, and was ... Is 38:9
for peace I *h* great bitterness ... Is 38:17
For Isaiah *h* said, Let them take ... Is 38:21
Hezekiah also *h* said, What is the ... Is 38:22
he *h* heard that he *h* been sick ... Is 39:1
that he *h* not gone with his feet ... Is 41:3
then *h* thy peace been as a river, ... Is 48:18
Thy seed also *h* been as the sand, ... Is 48:19
these, where *h* they been ... Is 49:21
for that which *h* not been told ... Is 52:15
that which they *h* not heard shall ... Is 52:15
because he *h* done no violence, ... Is 53:9
and we grope as if we *h* no eyes ... Is 59:10
my favour have I *h* mercy on thee ... Is 60:10
Yet I *h* planted thee a noble vine ... Jer 2:21
I said after she *h* done all these ... Jer 3:7
adultery I *h* put her away ... Jer 3:8
the heavens, and they *h* no light ... Jer 4:23
when I *h* fed them to the full, ... Jer 5:7
when they *h* committed abomination ... Jer 6:15
when they *h* committed abomination ... Jer 8:12
Oh that I *h* in the wilderness a ... Jer 9:2
I knew not that they *h* devised ... Jer 11:19
from the place where I *h* hid it ... Jer 13:7
lands whither he *h* driven them ... Jer 16:15
whither the LORD *h* sent him to ... Jer 19:14
countries whither I *h* driven them ... Jer 23:8
But if they *h* stood in my counsel ... Jer 23:22
h caused my people to hear my ... Jer 23:22
h carried away captive Jeconiah ... Jer 24:1
h brought them to Babylon ... Jer 24:1
One basket *h* very good figs, even ... Jer 24:2
the other basket *h* very naughty ... Jer 24:2
unto whom the LORD *h* sent me ... Jer 25:17
when Jeremiah *h* made an end of ... Jer 26:8
of speaking all that the LORD *h* ... Jer 26:8
he *h* pronounced against them ... Jer 26:19
h broken the yoke from off the ... Jer 28:12
h carried away captive from ... Jer 29:1
king of Judah *h* shut him up ... Jer 32:3
Now when I *h* delivered the ... Jer 32:16
h made a covenant with all the ... Jer 34:8
which *h* entered into the covenant ... Jer 34:10
whom they *h* let go free, to ... Jer 34:11
h done right in my sight, in ... Jer 34:15
ye *h* made a covenant before me in ... Jer 34:15
whom he *h* set at liberty at their ... Jer 34:16
which they *h* made before me ... Jer 34:18
which he *h* spoken unto him, upon ... Jer 36:4
h heard out of the book all the ... Jer 36:11
all the words that he *h* heard ... Jer 36:13
when they *h* heard all the words, ... Jer 36:16
that when Jehudi *h* read three or ... Jer 36:23
Gemariah *h* made intercession to ... Jer 36:25
that the king *h* burned the roll ... Jer 36:27
of Judah *h* burned in the fire ... Jer 36:32
for they *h* not put him into ... Jer 37:4
For though ye *h* smitten the whole ... Jer 37:10
for they *h* made that the prison ... Jer 37:15
Jeremiah *h* remained there many ... Jer 37:16
h spoken unto all the people ... Jer 38:1
heard that they *h* put Jeremiah in ... Jer 38:7
words that the king *h* commanded ... Jer 38:27
and when they *h* taken him, they ... Jer 39:5
which *h* nothing, in the land of ... Jer 39:10
the guard *h* let him go from Ramah ... Jer 40:1
when he *h* taken him being bound ... Jer 40:1
heard that the king of Babylon *h* ... Jer 40:7
h committed unto him men, and ... Jer 40:7
Babylon *h* left a remnant of Judah ... Jer 40:11
that he *h* set over them Gedaliah ... Jer 40:11
whom the king of Babylon *h* made ... Jer 41:2
day after he *h* slain Gedaliah ... Jer 41:4
Now the pit wherein Ishmael *h* ... Jer 41:9
whom he *h* slain because of ... Jer 41:9
was it which Asa the king *h* made ... Jer 41:9
the captain of the guard *h* ... Jer 41:10
the son of Nethaniah *h* done ... Jer 41:11
h carried away captive from ... Jer 41:14
remnant of the people whom he *h* ... Jer 41:16
after that he *h* slain Gedaliah ... Jer 41:16
whom he *h* brought again from ... Jer 41:16
h slain Gedaliah the son of ... Jer 41:18
that when Jeremiah *h* made an end ... Jer 43:1
LORD their God *h* sent him to them ... Jer 43:1
whither they *h* been driven ... Jer 43:5
the captain of the guard *h* left ... Jer 43:6
h burned incense unto other gods ... Jer 44:15
for then *h* we plenty of victuals, ... Jer 44:17 1961
which *h* given him that answer ... Jer 44:20
when he *h* written these words in ... Jer 45:1
to all that Jehoiakim *h* done ... Jer 52:2
till he *h* cast them out from his ... Jer 52:3
which king Solomon *h* made in the ... Jer 52:20
which *h* the charge of the men of ... Jer 52:25 1961
that she *h* in the days of old ... Lam 1:7 1961
she *h* no comforter ... Lam 1:9
hath done that which he *h* devised ... Lam 2:17
he *h* commanded in the days of old ... Lam 2:17
they *h* the likeness of a man ... Eze 1:5
every one *h* four faces ... Eze 1:6
and every one *h* four wings ... Eze 1:6
they *h* the hands of a man under ... Eze 1:8
they four *h* their faces and their ... Eze 1:8
they four *h* the face of a man, and ... Eze 1:10
they four *h* the face of an ox on ... Eze 1:10

they four also *h* the face of an ... Eze 1:10
and they four *h* one likeness ... Eze 1:16
every one *h* two, which covered on ... Eze 1:23
on this side, and every one *h* two ... Eze 1:23
stood, and *h* let down their wings ... Eze 1:25
it *h* brightness round about ... Eze 1:27
h I sent thee to them, they would ... Eze 3:6
when I *h* digged in the wall, ... Eze 8:8
which *h* the writer's inkhorn by ... Eze 9:3
which *h* the inkhorn by his side, ... Eze 9:11
that when he *h* commanded the man ... Eze 10:6
they four *h* one likeness ... Eze 10:10 1961
as if a wheel *h* been in the midst ... Eze 10:10
even the wheels that they four *h* ... Eze 10:12
And every one *h* four faces ... Eze 10:14
Every one *h* four faces apiece, and ... Eze 10:21
that I *h* seen went up from me ... Eze 11:24
things that the LORD *h* shewed me ... Eze 11:25
which I *h* put upon thee, saith ... Eze 16:14
which I *h* given thee, and madest ... Eze 16:17
which *h* divers colours, came unto ... Eze 17:3
he *h* given his hand, and hath done ... Eze 17:18
when she saw that she *h* waited ... Eze 19:5
she *h* strong rods for the ... Eze 19:11 1961
a land that I *h* espied for them ... Eze 20:6
the land which I *h* given them ... Eze 20:15
Because they *h* not executed my ... Eze 20:24
but *h* despised my statutes, and ... Eze 20:24
h polluted my sabbaths, and their ... Eze 20:24
For when I *h* brought them into ... Eze 20:28
for they *h* executed judgment upon ... Eze 23:10
wherein she *h* played the harlot ... Eze 23:19
laughed to scorn and *h* in derision ... Eze 23:32
For when they *h* slain their ... Eze 23:39
yet *h* he no wages, nor his army, ... Eze 29:18 1961
that he *h* served against it ... Eze 29:18
give again that he *h* robbed ... Eze 33:15
that one that *h* escaped out of ... Eze 33:21
h opened my mouth, until he came ... Eze 33:22
Because thou hast *h* a perpetual ... Eze 35:5 1961
time that their iniquity *h* an end ... Eze 35:5
that they *h* shed upon the land ... Eze 36:18
wherewith they *h* polluted it ... Eze 36:18
But I *h* pity for mine holy name, ... Eze 36:21
which the house of Israel *h* ... Eze 36:21
the posts *h* one measure on this ... Eze 40:10
it *h* palm trees, one on this side ... Eze 40:26
the going up to it *h* eight steps ... Eze 40:31
the going up to it *h* eight steps ... Eze 40:34
the going up to it *h* eight steps ... Eze 40:37
but they *h* not hold in the wall ... Eze 41:6 1961
and every cherub *h* two faces ... Eze 41:18
and the sanctuary *h* two doors ... Eze 41:23
the doors *h* two leaves apiece, ... Eze 41:24
but *h* not pillars as the pillars ... Eze 42:6
Now when he *h* made an end of ... Eze 42:15
it *h* a wall round about, five ... Eze 42:20
or a widow that *h* a priest before ... Eze 44:22 1961
for sister that hath *h* no husband ... Eze 44:25 1961
when the man that *h* the line in ... Eze 47:3
Now when I *h* returned, behold, at ... Eze 47:7
such as *h* ability in them to ... Dan 1:4
Now God *h* brought Daniel into ... Dan 1:9
of the eunuchs *h* set over Daniel ... Dan 1:11
Daniel *h* understanding in all ... Dan 1:17
h said he should bring them in ... Dan 1:18
whom the king *h* ordained to ... Dan 2:24
Nebuchadnezzar the king *h* set up ... Dan 3:2
Nebuchadnezzar the king *h* set up ... Dan 3:3
that Nebuchadnezzar *h* set up ... Dan 3:3
Nebuchadnezzar the king *h* set up ... Dan 3:7
whose bodies the fire *h* no power ... Dan 3:27
smell of fire *h* passed on them ... Dan 3:27
of the field *h* shadow under it ... Dan 4:12
of the heaven *h* their habitation ... Dan 4:21
h taken out of the temple which ... Dan 5:2
those men which *h* accused Daniel ... Dan 6:24
the lions *h* the mastery of them, ... Dan 6:24
king of Babylon Daniel *h* a dream ... Dan 7:1 2370
like a lion, and *h* eagle's wings ... Dan 7:4
it *h* three ribs in the mouth of ... Dan 7:5
which *h* upon the back of it four ... Dan 7:6
the beast *h* also four heads ... Dan 7:6
and it *h* great iron teeth ... Dan 7:7
and it *h* ten horns ... Dan 7:7
they *h* their dominion taken away ... Dan 7:12
even of that horn that *h* eyes ... Dan 7:20
the river a ram which *h* two horns ... Dan 8:3
the goat *h* a notable horn between ... Dan 8:5
came to the ram that *h* two horns ... Dan 8:6
which I *h* seen standing before ... Dan 8:6
h seen the vision, and sought for ... Dan 8:15
whom I *h* seen in the vision at ... Dan 9:21
h understanding of the vision ... Dan 10:1
when he *h* spoken this word unto ... Dan 10:11
when he *h* spoken such words unto ... Dan 10:15
when he *h* spoken unto me, I was ... Dan 10:19
Now when she *h* weaned Lo-ruhamah, Hos 1:8
her that *h* not obtained mercy ... Hos 2:23
his strength he *h* power with God ... Hos 12:3
he *h* power over the angel, and ... Hos 12:4
that when they *h* made an end of ... Amos 7:2
have stolen till they *h* enough ... Obad 5
be as though they *h* not been ... Obad 16
the LORD, because he *h* told them ... Jonah 1:10
Now the LORD *h* prepared a great ... Jonah 1:17
that he *h* said that he would do ... Jonah 3:10
Thou hast *h* pity on the gourd, ... Jonah 4:10
that *h* the waters round about it, ... Nah 3:8
he *h* horns coming out of his hand ... Hab 3:4 1961
as the LORD their God *h* sent him ... Hag 1:12
against which thou hast *h* ... Zec 1:12
for they *h* wings like the wings ... Zec 5:9
When they *h* sent unto the house ... Zec 7:2

as though I *h* not cast them off Zec 10:6
I *h* made with all the people Zec 11:10
Yet *h* he the residue of the Mal 2:15
her that *h* been the wife of Urias Mt 1:6
angel of the Lord *h* bidden him Mt 1:24
knew her not till she *h* brought Mt 1:25
the king *h* heard these things Mt 2:3
when he *h* gathered all the chief Mt 2:4
when he *h* privily called the wise Mt 2:7
When they *h* heard the king, they Mt 2:9
and when they *h* opened their Mt 2:11
according to the time which he *h* Mt 2:16
the same John *h* his raiment of Mt 3:4 2192
when he *h* fasted forty days and Mt 4:2
Now when Jesus *h* heard that John Mt 4:12
and those that *h* the palsy Mt 4:24
when Jesus *h* ended these sayings, Mt 7:28
which *h* given such power unto men Mt 9:8
when he *h* called unto him his Mt 10:1
when Jesus *h* made an end of Mt 11:1
Now when John *h* heard in the Mt 11:2
h been done in Tyre and Sidon, Mt 11:21
h been done in Sodom, it would Mt 11:23
But if ye *h* known what this Mt 12:7
a man which *h* his hand withered Mt 12:10 2192
where they *h* not much earth Mt 13:5 2192
because they *h* no deepness of Mt 13:5 2192
and because they *h* no root Mt 13:6 2192
when he *h* found one pearl of Mt 13:46
price, went and sold all that he *h* Mt 13:46 2192
that when Jesus *h* finished these Mt 13:53
For Herod *h* laid hold on John, and Mt 14:3
when the people *h* heard thereof Mt 14:13
they that *h* eaten were about five Mt 14:21
when he *h* sent the multitudes Mt 14:23
of that place *h* knowledge of him Mt 14:35
they *h* forgotten to take bread Mt 16:5
when they *h* lifted up their eyes, Mt 17:8
when he *h* begun to reckon, one Mt 18:24
But forasmuch as he *h* not to pay Mt 18:25 2192
and children, and all that he *h* Mt 18:25 2192
lord, after that he *h* called him Mt 18:32
Shouldest not thou also have *h* Mt 18:33
even as I *h* pity on thee Mt 18:33
that when Jesus *h* finished these Mt 19:1
for he *h* great possessions Mt 19:22
when he *h* agreed with the Mt 20:2
when they *h* received it, they Mt 20:11
So Jesus *h* compassion on them, and Mt 20:34
A certain man *h* two sons Mt 21:28 2192
and ye, when ye *h* seen it, Mt 21:32
Pharisees *h* heard his parables, Mt 21:45
which *h* not on a wedding garment Mt 22:11 1746
When they *h* heard these words, Mt 22:22
when he *h* married a wife, Mt 22:25
for they all *h* her Mt 22:28 2192
But when the Pharisees *h* heard Mt 22:34
he *h* put the Sadducees to silence Mt 22:34
If we *h* been in the days of our Mt 23:30
if the goodman of the house *h* Mt 24:43
Then he that *h* received the five Mt 25:16
likewise he that *h* received two Mt 25:17
But he that *h* received one went Mt 25:18
so he that *h* received five Mt 25:20
He also that *h* received two Mt 25:22
Then he which *h* received the one Mt 25:24
when Jesus *h* finished all these Mt 26:1
they *h* indignation, saying, To Mt 26:8
did as Jesus *h* appointed them Mt 26:19
it *h* been good for that man if he Mt 26:24
that man if he *h* not been born Mt 26:24
when they *h* sung an hymn, they Mt 26:30
they that *h* laid hold on Jesus Mt 26:57
And when they *h* bound him, they Mt 27:2
which *h* betrayeth him, when he Mt 27:3
they *h* then a notable prisoner, Mt 27:16 2192
for envy they *h* delivered him Mt 27:18
when he *h* scourged Jesus, he Mt 27:26
when they *h* platted a crown of Mt 27:29
And after that they *h* mocked him Mt 27:31
when he *h* tasted thereof, he Mt 27:34
when he *h* cried again with a loud Mt 27:50
when Joseph *h* taken the body, he Mt 27:59
which he *h* hewn out in the rock Mt 27:60
h taken counsel, they gave large Mt 28:12
where Jesus *h* appointed them Mt 28:16
when he *h* gone a little farther Mk 1:19
them as one that *h* authority Mk 1:22 2192
the unclean spirit *h* torn him Mk 1:26
And when they *h* found him, they Mk 1:37
And as soon as he *h* spoken Mk 1:42
when they *h* broken it up, they Mk 2:4
what David did, when he *h* need Mk 2:25 2192
man there which *h* a withered hand Mk 3:1 2192
the man which *h* the withered hand Mk 3:3 2192
when he *h* looked round about on Mk 3:5
when they *h* heard what great Mk 3:8
For he *h* healed many Mk 3:10
touch him, as many as *h* plagues Mk 3:10 2192
where it *h* not much earth Mk 4:5 2192
because it *h* no depth of earth Mk 4:5 2192
and because it *h* no root, it Mk 4:6 2192
when they *h* sent away the Mk 4:36
Who *h* his dwelling among the Mk 5:3 2192
Because that he *h* been often Mk 5:4
the chains *h* been plucked asunder Mk 5:4
h the legion, sitting, and clothed Mk 5:15 2192
he that *h* been possessed with the Mk 5:18
hath *h* compassion on thee Mk 5:19
great things Jesus *h* done for him Mk 5:20
which *h* an issue of blood twelve Mk 5:25 1510
h suffered many things of many Mk 5:26
and *h* spent all that she *h* Mk 5:26 3844
When she *h* heard of Jesus, came Mk 5:27

that virtue *h* gone out of him Mk 5:30
to see her that *h* done this thing Mk 5:32
But when he *h* put them all out, Mk 5:40
For Herod himself *h* sent forth Mk 6:17
for he *h* married her Mk 6:17
For John *h* said unto Herod, It is Mk 6:18
Therefore Herodias *h* a quarrel Mk 6:19
h done, and what they *h* taught Mk 6:30
they *h* no leisure so much as to Mk 6:31
when he *h* taken the five loaves Mk 6:41
when he *h* sent them away, he Mk 6:46
they supposed it *h* been a spirit Mk 6:49
when they *h* passed over, they Mk 6:53
when he *h* called all the people Mk 7:14
daughter *h* an unclean spirit Mk 7:25 2192
h an impediment in his speech Mk 7:32
they *h* a few small fishes Mk 8:7 2192
they that *h* eaten were about four Mk 8:9
Now the disciples *h* forgotten to Mk 8:14
neither *h* they in the ship with Mk 8:14 2192
when he *h* spit on his eyes, and Mk 8:23
But when he *h* turned about and Mk 8:33
when he *h* called the people unto Mk 8:34
when they *h* looked round about, Mk 9:8
no man what things they *h* seen Mk 9:9
for by the way they *h* disputed Mk 9:34
when he *h* taken him in his arms, Mk 9:36
for he *h* great possessions Mk 10:22
them even as Jesus *h* commanded Mk 11:6
when he *h* looked round about upon Mk 11:11
for they knew that he *h* spoken Mk 12:12
And the seven *h* her, and left no Mk 12:22 2983
for the seven *h* her to wife Mk 12:23 2192
that he *h* answered them well Mk 12:28
want did cast in all that she *h* Mk 12:44 2192
the Lord *h* shortened those days Mk 13:20
And there were some that *h* Mk 14:4
found as he *h* said unto them Mk 14:16
that man if he *h* never been born Mk 14:21
when he *h* given thanks, he gave Mk 14:23
when they *h* sung an hymn, they Mk 14:26
betrayed him *h* given them a token Mk 14:44
that *h* made insurrection with him Mk 15:7
who *h* committed murder in the Mk 15:7
to do as he *h* ever done unto them Mk 15:8
priests *h* delivered him for envy Mk 15:10
when he *h* scourged him, to be Mk 15:15
when they *h* mocked him, they took Mk 15:20
when they *h* crucified him, they Mk 15:24
whether he *h* been any while dead Mk 15:44
h bought sweet spices, that they Mk 16:1
out of whom he *h* cast seven Mk 16:9
and told them that *h* been with him Mk 16:10
when they *h* heard that he was Mk 16:11
h been seen of her, believed not Mk 16:11
h seen him after he was risen Mk 16:14
after the Lord *h* spoken unto them Mk 16:19
having *h* perfect understanding of Lk 1:3
they *h* no child, because that Lk 1:7 1510
they perceived that he *h* seen a Lk 1:22
h shewed great mercy upon her Lk 1:58
And when they *h* seen it, they made Lk 2:17
all the things that they *h* heard Lk 2:20
before he *h* seen the Lord's Lk 2:26
h lived with an husband seven Lk 2:36
when they *h* performed all things Lk 2:39
when they *h* fulfilled the days, Lk 2:43
all the evils which Herod *h* done Lk 3:19
when the devil *h* ended all the Lk 4:13
where he *h* been brought up Lk 4:16
when he *h* opened the book, he Lk 4:17
which *h* a spirit of an unclean Lk 4:33 2192
when the devil *h* thrown him in Lk 4:35
all they that *h* any sick with Lk 4:40 2192
Now when he *h* left speaking, he Lk 5:4
And when they *h* this done, they Lk 5:6
of the fishes which they *h* taken Lk 5:9
when they *h* brought their ships Lk 5:11
the man which *h* the withered hand Lk 6:8 2192
Now when he *h* ended all his Lk 7:1
servant whole that *h* been sick Lk 7:10
he *h* compassion on her, and said Lk 7:13
which *h* bidden him saw it Lk 7:39
creditor which *h* two debtors Lk 7:41 1510
when they *h* nothing to pay, he Lk 7:42 2192
which *h* been healed of evil Lk 8:2
when he *h* said these things, he Lk 8:8
which *h* devils long time, and ware Lk 8:27 2192
(For he *h* commanded the unclean Lk 8:29
For oftentimes it *h* caught him Lk 8:29
things Jesus *h* done unto him Lk 8:39
For he *h* one only daughter, about Lk 8:42 1510
which *h* spent all her living upon Lk 8:43
for what cause she *h* touched him Lk 8:47
And of some, that Elias *h* appeared Lk 9:8
told him all that they *h* done Lk 9:10
them that *h* need of healing Lk 9:11 2192
of those things which they *h* seen Lk 9:36
mighty works *h* been done in Tyre Lk 10:13
they *h* a great while ago repented Lk 10:13
saw him, he *h* compassion on him, Lk 10:33
she *h* a sister called Mary, which Lk 10:39 1510
he marvelled that he *h* not first Lk 11:38
if the goodman of the house *h* Lk 12:39
whose blood Pilate *h* mingled with Lk 13:1
A certain man *h* a fig tree Lk 13:6 2192
there was a woman which *h* a Lk 13:11 2192
because that Jesus *h* healed on Lk 13:14
when he *h* said these things, all Lk 13:17
man before him which *h* the dropsy Lk 14:2
found the piece which I *h* lost Lk 15:9
he said, A certain man *h* two sons Lk 15:11 2192
when he *h* spent all, there arose Lk 15:14
h compassion, and ran, and fell on Lk 15:20

rich man, which *h* a steward Lk 16:1 2192
him that he *h* wasted his goods Lk 16:1
steward, because he *h* done wisely Lk 16:8
If ye *h* faith as a grain of Lk 17:6 2192
to whom he *h* given the money, Lk 19:15
every man *h* gained by trading Lk 19:15
when he *h* thus spoken, he went Lk 19:28
found even as he *h* said unto them Lk 19:32
the mighty works that they *h* seen Lk 19:37
for they perceived that he *h* Lk 20:19
for seven *h* her to wife Lk 20:33 2192
cast in all the living that she *h* Lk 21:4 2192
found as he *h* said unto them Lk 22:13
when they *h* kindled a fire in the Lk 22:55
how he *h* said unto him, Before Lk 22:61
when they *h* blindfolded him, they Lk 22:64
because he *h* heard many things of Lk 23:8
when he *h* called together the Lk 23:13
into prison, whom they *h* desired Lk 23:25
when Jesus *h* cried with a loud Lk 23:46
(The same *h* not consented to the Lk 23:51
the spices which they *h* prepared Lk 24:1
all these things which *h* happened Lk 24:14
But we trusted that it *h* been he Lk 24:21
that they *h* also seen a vision of Lk 24:23
it even so as the women *h* said Lk 24:24
that they *h* seen a spirit Lk 24:37
when he *h* thus spoken, he shewed Lk 24:40
When the ruler of the feast *h* Jn 2:9
when he *h* made a scourge of small Jn 2:15
that he *h* said this unto them Jn 2:22
and the word which Jesus *h* said Jn 2:22
Pharisees *h* heard that Jesus made Jn 4:1
For thou hast *h* five husbands Jn 4:18 2192
word that Jesus *h* spoken unto him Jn 4:50
whole of whatsoever disease he *h* Jn 5:4 2722
which *h* an infirmity thirty and Jn 5:5 2192
knew that he *h* been now a long Jn 5:6
for Jesus *h* conveyed himself away Jn 5:13
was Jesus, which *h* made him whole Jn 5:15
because he *h* done these things on Jn 5:16
he not only *h* broken the sabbath Jn 5:18
For *h* ye believed Moses, ye would Jn 5:46
when he *h* given thanks, he Jn 6:11
and above unto them that *h* eaten Jn 6:13
when they *h* seen the miracle that Jn 6:14
So when they *h* rowed about five Jn 6:19
that the Lord *h* given thanks Jn 6:23
when they *h* found him on the Jn 6:25
when they *h* heard this, said, Jn 6:60
When he *h* said these words unto Jn 7:9
when they *h* set her in the midst, Jn 8:3
When Jesus *h* lifted up himself, Jn 8:10
if ye *h* known me, ye should have Jn 8:19
When he *h* thus spoken, he spat on Jn 9:6
they which before *h* seen him that Jn 9:8
him how he *h* received his sight Jn 9:15
that he *h* been blind, and received Jn 9:18
of him that *h* received his sight Jn 9:18
for the Jews *h* agreed already, Jn 9:22
heard that they *h* cast him out Jn 9:35
when he *h* found him, he said unto Jn 9:35
When he *h* heard therefore that he Jn 11:6
but they thought that he *h* spoken Jn 11:13
he found that he *h* lain in the Jn 11:17
been here, my brother *h* not died Jn 11:21
And when she *h* so said, she went Jn 11:28
been here, my brother *h* not died Jn 11:32
And when he thus *h* spoken, he Jn 11:43
h seen the things which Jesus did Jn 11:45
them what things Jesus *h* done Jn 11:46
and the Pharisees *h* given a Jn 11:57
Lazarus was which *h* been dead Jn 12:1
h the bag, and bare what was put Jn 12:6 2192
whom he *h* raised from the dead Jn 12:9
when he *h* found a young ass, sat Jn 12:14
that they *h* done these things Jn 12:16
heard that he *h* done this miracle Jn 12:18
But though he *h* done so many Jn 12:37
Jesus knowing that the Father *h* Jn 13:3
So after he *h* washed their feet, Jn 13:12
h taken his garments, and was set Jn 13:12
When Jesus *h* thus said, he was Jn 13:21
when he *h* dipped the sop, he gave Jn 13:26
thought, because Judas *h* the bag Jn 13:29 2192
that Jesus *h* said unto him, Buy Jn 13:29
If ye *h* known me, ye should have Jn 14:7
If I *h* not come and spoken unto Jn 15:22
unto them, they *h* not *h* sin Jn 15:22
unto them, they *h* not *h* sin Jn 15:22 2192
If I *h* not done among them the Jn 15:24
other man did, they *h* not *h* sin Jn 15:24
h with thee before the world was Jn 17:5 2192
When Jesus *h* spoken these words, Jn 18:1
soon then as he *h* said unto them Jn 18:6
who *h* made a fire of coals Jn 18:18
when he *h* thus spoken, one of the Jn 18:22
Now Annas *h* sent him bound unto Jn 18:24
when he *h* said this, he went out Jn 18:38
when they *h* crucified Jesus, took Jn 19:23
therefore *h* received the vinegar Jn 19:30
where the body of Jesus *h* lain Jn 20:12
when she *h* thus said, she turned Jn 20:14
that she *h* seen the Lord Jn 20:18
that he *h* spoken these things Jn 20:18
And when he *h* so said, he shewed Jn 20:20
when he *h* said this, he breathed Jn 20:22
So when they *h* dined, Jesus saith Jn 21:15
when he *h* spoken this, he saith Jn 21:19
h given commandments unto the Acts 1:2
the apostles whom he *h* chosen Acts 1:2
when he *h* spoken these things, Acts 1:9
h obtained part of this ministry Acts 1:17
knowing that God *h* sworn with an Acts 2:30

H

together, and *h* all things common Acts 2:44 *2192*
to all men, as every man *h* need Acts 2:45 *2192*
at that which *h* happened unto him Acts 3:10
we *h* made this man to walk Acts 3:12
which God before *h* shewed by the Acts 3:18
when they *h* set them in the midst Acts 4:7
that they *h* been with Jesus Acts 4:13
But when they *h* commanded them to. Acts 4:15
So when they *h* further threatened Acts 4:21
and elders *h* said unto them Acts 4:23
And when they *h* prayed, the place Acts 4:31
but they *h* all things common Acts 4:32 *1510*
every man according as he *h* need Acts 4:35 *2192*
but when we *h* opened, we found no Acts 5:23
when they *h* brought them, they Acts 5:27
h in reputation among all the Acts 5:34
when they *h* called the apostles, Acts 5:40
and when they *h* prayed, they laid Acts 6:6
saw his face as it *h* been the Acts 6:15
him, when as yet he *h* no child Acts 7:5 *5607*
which God *h* sworn to Abraham, the Acts 7:17
after that he *h* shewed wonders and Acts 7:36
Our fathers *h* the tabernacle of Acts 7:44 *1510*
as he *h* appointed, speaking unto Acts 7:44
to the fashion that he *h* seen Acts 7:44
when he *h* said this, he fell Acts 7:60
And to him they *h* regard Acts 8:11
because that of long time he *h* Acts 8:11
h received the word of God Acts 8:14
And they, when they *h* testified Acts 8:25
who *h* the charge of all her Acts 8:27
h come to Jerusalem for to Acts 8:27
from his eyes as it *h* been scales Acts 9:18
when he *h* received meat, he was Acts 9:19
how he *h* seen the Lord in the way Acts 9:27
that he *h* spoken to him Acts 9:27
how he *h* preached boldly at Acts 9:27
Then *h* the churches rest Acts 9:31 *2192*
which *h* kept his bed eight years, Acts 9:33
whom when they *h* washed, they Acts 9:37
the disciples *h* heard that Peter Acts 9:38
when he *h* called the saints and Acts 9:41
when he *h* declared all these Acts 10:8
as it *h* been a great sheet knit Acts 10:11
which he *h* seen should mean Acts 10:17
h made enquiry for Simon's house Acts 10:17
h called together his kinsmen and Acts 10:24
thine alms are *h* in remembrance Acts 10:31
h also received the word of God Acts 11:1
as it *h* been a great sheet, let Acts 11:5
which when I *h* fastened mine eyes Acts 11:6
he shewed us how he *h* seen an Acts 11:13
h seen the grace of God, was glad Acts 11:23
when he *h* found him, he brought Acts 11:26
when he *h* apprehended him, he put Acts 12:4
when he *h* considered the thing, Acts 12:12
when they *h* opened the door, and Acts 12:16
h brought him out of the prison Acts 12:17
when Herod *h* sought for him, and Acts 12:19
when they *h* fulfilled their Acts 12:25
which *h* been brought up with Acts 13:1
And when they *h* fasted and prayed, Acts 13:3
they *h* also John to their Acts 13:5 *2192*
when they *h* gone through the isle Acts 13:6
when he *h* destroyed seven nations Acts 13:19
when he *h* removed him, he raised Acts 13:22
When John *h* first preached before Acts 13:24
when they *h* fulfilled all that Acts 13:29
after he *h* served his own Acts 13:36
mother's womb, who never *h* walked Acts 14:8
that he *h* faith to be healed Acts 14:9 *2192*
the people saw what Paul *h* done Acts 14:11
that they *h* not done sacrifice Acts 14:18
city, supposing he *h* been dead Acts 14:19
when they *h* preached the gospel Acts 14:21
h taught many, they returned Acts 14:21
when they *h* ordained them elders Acts 14:23
h prayed with fasting, they Acts 14:23
after they *h* passed throughout Acts 14:24
when they *h* preached the word in Acts 14:25
Antioch, from whence they *h* been Acts 14:26
h gathered the church together, Acts 14:27
all that God *h* done with them Acts 14:27
how he *h* opened the door of faith Acts 14:27
Barnabas *h* no small dissension and Acts 15:2
things that God *h* done with them Acts 15:4
when there *h* been much disputing, Acts 15:7
wonders God *h* wrought among the Acts 15:12
after they *h* held their peace, Acts 15:13
and when they *h* gathered the Acts 15:30
Which when they *h* read, they Acts 15:31
after they *h* tarried there a Acts 15:33
Now when they *h* gone throughout Acts 16:6
after he *h* seen the vision, Acts 16:10
gathering that the Lord *h* called Acts 16:10
when they *h* laid many stripes Acts 16:23
that the prisoners *h* been fled Acts 16:27
when he *h* brought them into his Acts 16:34
when they *h* seen the brethren, Acts 16:40
Now when they *h* passed through Acts 17:1
when they *h* taken security of Acts 17:9
when the Jews of Thessalonica *h* Acts 17:13
(because that Claudius *h* Acts 18:2
for he *h* a vow Acts 18:18 *2192*
when he *h* landed at Caesarea, and Acts 18:22
after he *h* spent some time there, Acts 18:23
when Aquila and Priscilla *h* heard Acts 18:26
which *h* believed through grace Acts 18:27
when Paul *h* laid his hands upon Acts 19:6
h evil spirits the name of the Acts 19:13 *2192*
spirit, when he *h* passed through Acts 19:21
when the townclerk *h* appeased the Acts 19:35
when he *h* thus spoken, he Acts 19:41
when he *h* gone over those parts, Acts 20:2
h given them much exhortation, he Acts 20:2
h broken bread, and eaten, and Acts 20:11
for so *h* he appointed, minding Acts 20:13
For Paul *h* determined to sail by Acts 20:16
when he *h* thus spoken, he kneeled Acts 20:36
h launched, we came with a Acts 21:1
Now when we *h* discovered Cyprus, Acts 21:3
when we *h* accomplished those days Acts 21:5
when we *h* taken our leave one of Acts 21:6
when we *h* finished our course Acts 21:7
the same man *h* four daughters, Acts 21:9 *1510*
when he *h* saluted them, he Acts 21:19
particularly what things God *h* Acts 21:19
(For they *h* seen before with him Acts 21:29
Paul *h* brought into the temple Acts 21:29
who he was, and what he *h* done Acts 21:33
when he *h* given him licence, Paul Acts 21:40
Roman, and because he *h* bound him Acts 22:29
And when he *h* so said, there arose Acts 23:7
nor drink till they *h* killed Paul Acts 23:12
which *h* made this conspiracy Acts 23:13
thee what they *h* against him Acts 23:30
the governor *h* read the letter Acts 23:34
after that the governor *h* Acts 24:10
if they *h* ought against me Acts 24:19 *2192*
when he *h* tarried among them more Acts 25:6
when he *h* conferred with the Acts 25:12
when they *h* been there many days, Acts 25:14
But *h* certain questions against Acts 25:19 *2192*
But when Paul *h* appealed to be Acts 25:21
But when I found that he *h* Acts 25:25
that, after examination *h* Acts 25:26 *1096*
when he *h* thus spoken, the king Acts 26:30
if he *h* not appealed unto Caesar Acts 26:32
when we *h* launched from thence, Acts 27:4
when we *h* sailed over the sea of Acts 27:5
when we *h* sailed slowly many days Acts 27:7
supposing that they *h* obtained Acts 27:13
we *h* much work to come by the Acts 27:16
Which when they *h* taken up Acts 27:17
when they *h* gone a little further Acts 27:28
when they *h* let down the boat Acts 27:30
when he *h* thus spoken, he took Acts 27:35
when he *h* broken it, he began to Acts 27:35
when they *h* eaten enough, they Acts 27:38
when they *h* taken up the anchors, Acts 27:40
when Paul *h* gathered a bundle of Acts 28:3
but after they *h* looked a great Acts 28:6
which *h* diseases in the island, Acts 28:9 *2192*
which *h* wintered in the isle, Acts 28:11
when they *h* examined me, would Acts 28:18
not that I *h* ought to accuse my Acts 28:19 *2192*
when they *h* appointed him a day, Acts 28:23
after that Paul *h* spoken one word Acts 28:25
when he *h* said these words, the Acts 28:29
and *h* great reasoning among Acts 28:29 *2192*
(Which he *h* promised afore by his Rom 1:2
of the faith which he *h* yet being Rom 4:11
Abraham, which he *h* being yet Rom 4:12
what he *h* promised, he was able Rom 4:21
even over them that *h* not sinned Rom 5:14
What fruit *h* ye then in those Rom 6:21 *2192*
I *h* not known sin, but by the law Rom 7:7
for I *h* not known lust, except Rom 7:7
known lust, except the law *h* said Rom 7:7
Rebecca also *h* conceived by one Rom 9:10
which he *h* afore prepared unto Rom 9:23
Lord of Sabaoth *h* left us a seed Rom 9:29
we *h* been as Sodoma, and been made. Rom 9:29
I *h* baptized in mine own name 1Cor 1:15
for *h* they known it, they would 1Cor 2:8
wives be as though they *h* none 1Cor 7:29 *2192*
when he *h* given thanks, he brake 1Cor 11:24
he took the cup, when he *h* supped 1Cor 11:25
Yet in the church I *h* rather 1Cor 14:19
But we *h* the sentence of death in 2Cor 1:9 *2192*
we have *h* our conversation in the 2Cor 1:12
I *h* no rest in my spirit, because 2Cor 2:13 *2192*
h no glory in this respect 2Cor 3:10
Macedonia, our flesh *h* no rest 2Cor 7:5 *2192*
his cause that *h* done the wrong 2Cor 7:12
desired Titus, that as he *h* begun 2Cor 8:6
h gathered much *h* nothing over 2Cor 8:15
h gathered little *h* no lack 2Cor 8:15
whereof ye *h* notice before, that 2Cor 9:5
as though we *h* been weak 2Cor 11:21
But they *h* heard only, That he Gal 1:23
I should run, or *h* run, in vain Gal 2:2
for if there *h* been a law given Gal 3:21
if it *h* been possible, ye would Gal 4:15
written, that Abraham *h* two sons Gal 4:22 *2192*
Among whom also we all *h* our Eph 2:3
ye *h* heard that he *h* been sick Phil 2:26
but God *h* mercy on him Phil 2:27
Not as though I *h* already Phil 3:12
of entering in we *h* unto you 1Th 1:9 *2192*
after that we *h* suffered before 1Th 2:2
but *h* pleasure in unrighteousness 2Th 2:12
every city, as I *h* appointed thee Titus 1:5
when he *h* by himself purged our Heb 1:3
him that *h* the power of death Heb 2:14 *2192*
For some, when they *h* heard Heb 3:16
it not with them that *h* sinned Heb 3:17
For if Jesus *h* given them rest, Heb 4:8
when he *h* offered up prayers and Heb 5:7
after he *h* patiently endured, he Heb 6:15
blessed him that *h* the promises Heb 7:6 *2192*
first covenant *h* been faultless Heb 8:7
h also ordinances of divine Heb 9:1 *2192*
Which *h* the golden censer, and the Heb 9:4 *2192*
was the golden pot that *h* manna Heb 9:4 *2192*
For when Moses *h* spoken every Heb 9:19
once purged should have *h* no more Heb 10:2 *2192*
for sin thou hast *h* no pleasure Heb 10:6 *2192*
after he *h* offered one sacrifice Heb 10:12
for after that he *h* said before Heb 10:15
For ye *h* compassion of me in my Heb 10:34
because God *h* translated him Heb 11:5
translation he *h* this testimony Heb 11:5
him faithful who *h* promised Heb 11:11
if they *h* been mindful of that Heb 11:15
they might have *h* opportunity to Heb 11:15 *2192*
he that *h* received the promises Heb 11:17
for he *h* respect unto the Heb 11:26
when she *h* received the spies Heb 11:31
others *h* trial of cruel mockings Heb 11:36 *2983*
Furthermore we have *h* fathers of Heb 12:9 *2192*
when he *h* offered Isaac his son Jas 2:21
by works, when she *h* received the Jas 2:25
h sent them out another way Jas 2:25
which *h* not obtained mercy, but 1Pet 2:10
For it *h* been better for them not 2Pet 2:21
which ye *h* from the beginning 1Jn 2:7 *2192*
for if they *h* been of us, they 1Jn 2:19
but that which we *h* from the 2Jn 5 *2192*
I *h* many things to write, but I 3Jn 13 *2192*
he *h* in his right hand seven Rev 1:16 *2192*
they *h* on their heads crowns of Rev 4:4 *2192*
the third beast *h* a face as a man Rev 4:7 *2192*
the four beasts *h* each of them Rev 4:8 *2192*
stood a Lamb as it *h* been slain Rev 5:6
when he *h* taken the book, the Rev 5:8
and he that sat on him *h* a bow Rev 6:2 *2192*
when he *h* opened the second seal, Rev 6:3
when he *h* opened the third seal, Rev 6:5
he that sat on him *h* a pair of Rev 6:5 *2192*
when he *h* opened the fourth seal, Rev 6:7
when he *h* opened the fifth seal, Rev 6:9
I beheld when he *h* opened the Rev 6:12
when he *h* opened the seventh seal Rev 8:1
the seven angels which *h* the Rev 8:6 *2192*
were in the sea, and *h* life, died Rev 8:9 *2192*
they *h* hair as the hair of women, Rev 9:8 *2192*
they *h* breastplates, as it were Rev 9:9 *2192*
they *h* tails like unto scorpions, Rev 9:10 *2192*
they *h* a king over them, which is Rev 9:11 *2192*
sixth angel which *h* the trumpet Rev 9:14 *2192*
h heads, and with them they do Rev 9:19 *2192*
he *h* in his hand a little book Rev 10:2 *2192*
and when he *h* cried, seven Rev 10:3
thunders *h* uttered their voices Rev 10:4
and as soon as I *h* eaten it Rev 10:10
he *h* two horns like a lamb, and he Rev 13:11 *2192*
of those miracles which he *h* Rev 13:14
which *h* the wound by a sword, and Rev 13:14 *2192*
he *h* power to give life unto the Rev 13:15
or sell, save he that *h* the mark Rev 13:17 *2192*
altar, which *h* power over fire Rev 14:18 *2192*
to him that *h* the sharp sickle Rev 14:18 *2192*
them that *h* gotten the victory Rev 15:2
men which *h* the mark of the beast Rev 16:2 *2192*
angels which *h* the seven vials Rev 17:1 *2192*
h ships in the sea by reason of Rev 18:19 *2192*
he *h* a name written, that no man Rev 19:12 *2192*
which he deceived them that *h* Rev 19:20
which *h* not worshipped the beast, Rev 20:4
neither *h* received his mark upon Rev 20:4
h the seven vials full of the Rev 21:9 *2192*
h a wall great and high, and *h* Rev 21:12 *2192*
of the city *h* twelve foundations Rev 21:14 *2192*
he that talked with me *h* a golden Rev 21:15 *2192*
the city *h* no need of the sun, Rev 21:23 *2192*
And when I *h* heard and seen, I fell Rev 22:8

HADAD (*ha'-dad*) See BEN-HADAD, HADADRIMMON, HADAR.
1. A son of Bedad.
H the son of Bedad, who smote Gen 36:35 1908
H died, and Samlah of Masrekah Gen 36:36 1908
H the son of Bedad, which smote 1Chr 1:46 1908
when *H* was dead, Samlah of 1Chr 1:47 1908
2. A royal Edomite.
unto Solomon, *H* the Edomite 1Kin 11:14 1908
That *H* fled, he and certain 1Kin 11:17 1908
H being yet a little child 1Kin 11:17 1908
H found great favour in the sight 1Kin 11:19 1908
when *H* heard in Egypt that David 1Kin 11:21 1908
H said to Pharaoh, Let me depart, 1Kin 11:21 1908
beside the mischief that *H* did 1Kin 11:25 1908
3. A son of Ishmael.
Mishma, and Dumah, Massa, *H* 1Chr 1:30 1908
4. An early king of Edom.
was dead, *H* reigned in his stead 1Chr 1:50 1908
H died also 1Chr 1:51 1908

HADADEZER (*had-a-de'-zer*) See HADAREZER.
King of Zobah.
David smote also *H*, the son of 2Sa 8:3 1909
came to succour *H* king of Zobah 2Sa 8:5 1909
that were on the servants of *H* 2Sa 8:7 1909
and from Berothai, cities of *H* 2Sa 8:8 1909
had smitten all the host of *H* 2Sa 8:9 1909
because he had fought against *H* 2Sa 8:10 1909
for *H* had wars with Toi 2Sa 8:10 1909
of Amalek, and of the spoil of *H* 2Sa 8:12 1909
from his lord *H* king of Zobah 1Kin 11:23 1909

HADADRIMMON (*ha''-dad-rim'-mom*) *A place in the valley of Megiddo.*
as the mourning of *H* in the Zec 12:11 1910

HADAR (*ha'-dar*) See HADAD.
1. A son of Ishmael.
H, and Tema, Jetur, Naphish, and Gen 25:15 1924
2. An early king of Edom.
died, and *H* reigned in his stead Gen 36:39 1924

HADAREZER (*had-a-re'-zer*) See HADADEZER.
Another name for Hadadezer.
H sent, and brought out the 2Sa 10:16 1928

of the host of *H* went before them........ 2Sa 10:16 1928
to *H* saw that they were smitten........... 2Sa 10:19 1928
David smote *H* king of Zobah unto...... 1Chr 18:3 1928
came to help *H* king of Zobah............. 1Chr 18:5 1928
that were on the servants of *H*............ 1Chr 18:7 1928
and from Chun, cities of *H*.................. 1Chr 18:8 1928
all the host of *H* king of Zobah............ 1Chr 18:9 1928
because he had fought against *H*.......... 1Chr 18:10 1928
(for *H* had war with Tou...................... 1Chr 18:10 1928
of the host of *H* went before them........ 1Chr 19:16 1928
when the servants of *H* saw that.......... 1Chr 19:19 1928

HADASHAH (*had'-a-shah*) *A town in Judah.*
Zenan, and *H*, and Migdal-gad,............. Josh 15:37 2322

HADASSAH (*ha-das'-sah*) See ESTHER. *Another name for Esther.*
And he brought up *H*, that is,................ Est 2:7 1919

HADATTAH (*ha-dat'-tah*) See HAZOR-HADATTAH. *Another name for Hazor.*
And Hazor, *H*, and Kerioth, and............ Josh 15:25 2675

HADES See HELL.

HADID (*ha'-did*) *A city in Benjamin.*
The children of Lod, *H*, and Ono,.......... Ezr 2:33 2307
The children of Lod, *H*, and Ono,.......... Neh 7:37 2307
H, Zeboim, Neballat,.............................. Neh 11:34 2307

HADLAI (*had'-la-i*) *Father of Amasa.*
of Shallum, and Amasa the son of *H*.... 2Chr 28:12 2311

HADORAM (*ha-do'-ram*) See ADORAM.
1. A son of Joktan.
And *H*, and Uzal, and Diklah,................ Gen 10:27 1913
H also, and Uzal, and Diklah,................ 1Chr 1:21 1913
2. A son of Tou.
He sent *H* his son to king David,........... 1Chr 18:10 1913
3. An officer of Rehoboam.
Then king Rehoboam sent *H* that........ 2Chr 10:18 1913

HADRACH (*ha'-drak*) *A district in Syria.*
word of the LORD in the land of *H*........ Zec 9:1 2317

HADST
little which thou *h* before I came.......... Gen 30:30
surely thou *h* sent me away now.......... Gen 31:42
that thou *h* utterly hated her................ Judg 15:2
thee, except thou *h* hasted.................... 1Sa 25:34
God liveth, unless thou *h* spoken.......... 2Sa 2:27
then *h* thou smitten Syria till................ 2Kin 13:19
Syria till thou *h* consumed it................ 2Kin 13:19
with us till thou *h* consumed us............ Ezr 9:14
which thou *h* sworn to give them.......... Neh 9:15
concerning which thou *h* promised......... Neh 9:23
because thou *h* a favour unto them...... Ps 44:3
thou, O God, which *h* cast us off............ Ps 60:10
or ever thou *h* formed the earth............ Ps 90:2
thou *h* removed it far unto all................ Is 26:15
O that thou *h* hearkened to my.............. Is 48:18
thou *h* a whore's forehead, thou............ Jer 3:3
For thou *h* cast me into the deep,.......... Jonah 2:3
Saying, If thou *h* known, even................ Lk 19:42
if thou *h* been here, my brother.............. Jn 11:21
if thou *h* been here, my brother.............. Jn 11:32
as if thou *h* not received it.................... 1Cor 4:7
neither *h* pleasure therein...................... Heb 10:8

HA-ELEPH See ELEPH.

HAFT
the *h* also went in after the.................. Judg 3:22 5325

HAGAB (*ha'-gab*) See HAGABA. *A family of exiles.*
The children of *H*, the children............. Ezr 2:46 2285

HAGABA (*hag'-a-bah*) *Same as Hagab.*
of Lebana, the children of *H*................ Neh 7:48 2286

HAGABAH (*hag'-a-bah*) See HAGABA. *Same as Hagab.*
of Lebanah, the children of *H*............... Ezr 2:45 2286

HAGAR (*ha'-gar*) *Sarah's handmaid.*
an Egyptian, whose name was *H*.............. Gen 16:1 1904
wife took *H* her maid the Egyptian........ Gen 16:3 1904
And he went in unto *H*, and she............ Gen 16:4 1904
And he said, *H*, Sarai's maid,................ Gen 16:8 1904
And *H* bare Abram a son......................... Gen 16:15 1904
his son's name, which *H* bare................ Gen 16:15 1904
when *H* bare Ishmael to Abram.............. Gen 16:16 1904
saw the son of *H* the Egyptian.............. Gen 21:9 1904
of water, and gave it unto *H*.................. Gen 21:14 1904
of God called to *H* out of heaven.......... Gen 21:17 1904
unto her, What aileth thee, *H*................ Gen 21:17 1904
whom *H* the Egyptian, Sarah's.............. Gen 25:12 1904

HAGARENES (*haga-renes'*) See HAGARITES. *A people east of the Jordan.*
of Moab, and the *H*................................. Ps 83:6 1905

HAGARITES (*hag'-a-rites*) *Same as Hagarenes.*
of Saul they made war with the *H*......... 1Chr 5:10 1905
And they made war with the *H*............. 1Chr 5:19 1905
the *H* were delivered into their............. 1Chr 5:20 1905

HAGERITE (*hag'-e-rite*) See HAGARITES, HAGGERI. *Family of David's herdsmen.*
over the flocks was Jaziz the *H*............. 1Chr 27:31 1905

HAGGAI (*hag'-ga-i*) *A prophet.*
H the prophet, and Zechariah the.......... Ezr 5:1 2292
the prophesying of *H* the prophet.......... Ezr 6:14 2292
came the word of the LORD by *H*............ Hag 1:1 2292
word of the LORD by *H* the prophet........ Hag 1:3 2292
and the words of *H* the prophet............. Hag 1:12 2292
Then spake *H* the LORD's messenger...... Hag 1:13 2292
word of the LORD by the prophet *H*........ Hag 2:1 2292
word of the LORD by *H* the prophet........ Hag 2:10 2292
Then said *H*, If one that is..................... Hag 2:13 2292
Then answered *H*, and said, So is.......... Hag 2:14 2292
the LORD came unto *H* in the four.......... Hag 2:20 2292

HAGGEDOLIM See Neh 12:14.

HAGGERI (*hag'-gher-i*) See HAGERITE. *Father of Mibhar.*
of Nathan, Mibhar the son of *H*............. 1Chr 11:38 1905

HAGGI (*hag'-ghi*) See HAGGITES. *A son of Gad.*
Ziphion, and *H*, Shuni, and Ezbon,........ Gen 46:16 2291
of *H*, the family of the Haggites............ Num 26:15 2291

HAGGIAH (*hag-ghi'-ah*) *A descendant of Merari.*
H his son, Asaiah his son......................... 1Chr 6:30 2293

HAGGITES (*hag'-ghites*) See HAGGI. *Descendants of Haggi.*
of Haggi, the family of the *H*................. Num 26:15 2291

HAGGITH (*hag'-ghith*) *A wife of David.*
the fourth, Adonijah the son of *H*......... 2Sa 3:4 2294
the son of *H* exalted himself.................. 1Kin 1:5 2294
Adonijah the son of *H* doth reign.......... 1Kin 1:11 2294
Adonijah the son of *H* came to.............. 1Kin 2:13 2294
the fourth, Adonijah the son of *H*......... 1Chr 3:2 2294

HAGRI See HAGGERI.

HAGRITE See HAGERITE.

HAGRITES See HAGARITES.

HAI (*ha'-i*) See AI. *A form of Ai.*
on the west, and *H* on the east.............. Gen 12:8 5857
beginning, between Beth-el and *H*......... Gen 13:3 5857

HAIL
it to rain a very grievous *h*..................... Ex 9:18 1259
the *h* shall come down upon them,......... Ex 9:19 1259
that there may be *h* in all the................ Ex 9:22 1259
and the LORD sent thunder and *h*........... Ex 9:23 1259
the LORD rained *h* upon the land............ Ex 9:23 1259
h, and fire mingled with the *h*................ Ex 9:24 1259
the *h* smote throughout all the.............. Ex 9:25 1259
the *h* smote every herb of the................ Ex 9:25 1259
of Israel were, was there no *h*............... Ex 9:26 1259
no more mighty thunderings and *h*......... Ex 9:28 1259
neither shall there be any more *h*.......... Ex 9:29 1259
h ceased, and the rain was not.............. Ex 9:33 1259
saw that the rain and the *h*.................... Ex 9:34 1259
remaineth unto you from the *h*.............. Ex 10:5 1259
even all that the *h* hath left.................. Ex 10:12 1259
of the trees which the *h* had left............ Ex 10:15 1259
thou seen the treasures of the *h*............ Job 38:22 1259
h stones and coals of fire...................... Ps 18:12 1259
h stones and coals of fire...................... Ps 18:13 1259
He destroyed their vines with *h*............. Ps 78:47 1259
up their cattle also to the *h*.................. Ps 78:48 1259
He gave them *h* for rain, and................ Ps 105:32 1259
Fire, and *h*; snow, and vapours............. Ps 148:8 1259
one, which as a tempest of *h*................. Is 28:2 1259
the *h* shall sweep away the refuge......... Is 28:17 1259
When it shall *h*, coming down on.......... Is 32:19 1258
with *h* in all the labours of your............ Hag 2:17 1259
he came to Jesus, and said, *H*............... Mt 26:49 5463
him, and mocked him, saying, *H*............ Mt 27:29 5463
Jesus met them, saying, All *h*............... Mt 28:9 5463
And began to salute him, *H*................... Mk 15:18 5463
came in unto her, and said, *H*............... Lk 1:28 5463
And said, *H*, King of the Jews................ Jn 19:3 5463
sounded, and there followed *h*.............. Rev 8:7 5464
and an earthquake, and great *h*............. Rev 11:19 5464
upon men a great *h* out of heaven.......... Rev 16:21 5464
because of the plague of the *h*............... Rev 16:21 5464

HAILSTONES
h than they whom the children of.......... Josh 10:11
with scattering, and tempest, and *h*....... Is 30:30
and ye, O great *h*, shall fall................... Eze 13:11
great *h* in my fury to consume it........... Eze 13:13
and overflowing rain, and great *h*.......... Eze 38:22

HAIR
and fine linen, and goats' *h*.................. Ex 25:4
h to be a covering upon the................... Ex 26:7
and fine linen, and goats' *h*.................. Ex 35:6
and fine linen, and goats' *h*.................. Ex 35:23
them up in wisdom spun goats' *h*........... Ex 35:26
of goats' *h* for the tent over the............ Ex 36:14
when the *h* in the plague is.................. Lev 13:3 8181
the *h* thereof be not turned white.......... Lev 13:4 8181
and it have turned the *h* white............... Lev 13:10 8181
the *h* thereof be turned white............... Lev 13:20 8181
if the *h* in the bright spot be................ Lev 13:25 8181
there be no white *h* in the bright.......... Lev 13:26 8181
and there be in it a yellow thin *h*......... Lev 13:30 8181
and that there is no black *h* in it........... Lev 13:31 8181
and there be in it no yellow *h*.............. Lev 13:32 8181
shall not seek for yellow *h*.................... Lev 13:36 8181
there is black *h* grown up therein......... Lev 13:37 8181
the man whose *h* is fallen off his........... Lev 13:40 4803
he that hath his *h* fallen off................... Lev 13:41 4803
clothes, and shave off all his *h*............. Lev 14:8 8181
shave all his *h* off his head.................... Lev 14:9 8181
even all his *h* he shall shave off............ Lev 14:9 8181
locks of the *h* of his head grow............. Num 6:5 8181
shall take the *h* of the head of............. Num 6:18 8181
after the *h* of his separation is............. Num 6:19
of skins, and all work of goats' *h*.......... Num 31:20
Howbeit the *h* of his head began........... Judg 16:22 8181
sling stones at an *h* breadth.................. Judg 20:16 8185
there shall not one *h* of his head.......... 1Sa 14:45 8185
of goats' *h* for his bolster..................... 1Sa 19:13
of goats' *h* for his bolster..................... 1Sa 19:16
there shall not one *h* of thy son............ 2Sa 14:11 8185
because the *h* was heavy on him,........... 2Sa 14:26
he weighed the *h* of his head at.............. 2Sa 14:26 8181
there shall not an *h* of him fall.............. 1Kin 1:52 8185
and plucked off the *h* of my head........... Ezr 9:3 8181
of them, and plucked off their *h*............. Neh 13:25
the *h* of my flesh stood up...................... Job 4:15 8185
thy *h* is as a flock of goats,................... Song 4:1 8181
thy *h* is as a flock of goats that.............. Song 6:5 8181
the *h* of thine head like purple.............. Song 7:5 1803
and instead of well set *h* baldness......... Is 3:24 4748
the head, and the *h* of the feet.............. Is 7:20 8181
to them that plucked off the *h*.............. Is 50:6
Cut off thine *h*, O Jerusalem, and.......... Jer 7:29 5145
to weigh, and divide the *h*..................... Eze 5:1
thine *h* is grown, whereas thou............. Eze 16:7 8181
nor was an *h* of their head singed......... Dan 3:27 8177
the *h* of his head like the pure.............. Dan 7:9 8177
John had his raiment of camel's *h*......... Mt 3:4 2359
not make one *h* white or black............... Mt 5:36 *2359*
John was clothed with camel's *h*............. Mk 1:6 *2359*
not an *h* of your head perish................. Lk 21:18 *2359*
and wiped his feet with her *h*................ Jn 11:2 *2359*
and wiped his feet with her *h*................ Jn 12:3 *2359*
for there shall not an *h* fall................... Acts 27:34 *2359*
you, that, if a man have long *h*.............. 1Cor 11:14 *2863*
But if a woman have long *h*.................... 1Cor 11:15 *2863*
for her *h* is given her for a.................... 1Cor 11:15 *2864*
not with broided *h*, or gold, or................ 1Ti 2:9 *4117*
adorning of plaiting the *h*...................... 1Pet 3:3 *2359*
became black as sackcloth of *h*.............. Rev 6:12 *5155*
they had *h* as the *h* of women,............... Rev 9:8 *2359*

HAIRS
gray *h* with sorrow to the grave............ Gen 42:38
gray *h* with sorrow to the grave............ Gen 44:29
shall bring down the gray *h* of............... Gen 44:31
there be no white *h* therein................... Lev 13:21 8181
also with the man of gray *h*.................. Deut 32:25
are more than the *h* of mine head......... Ps 40:12 8185
are more than the *h* of mine head......... Ps 69:4 8185
even to hoar *h* will I carry you.............. Is 46:4
till his *h* were grown like........................ Dan 4:33 8177
gray *h* are here and there upon him....... Hos 7:9
But the very *h* of your head are............. Mt 10:30 *2359*
wipe them with the *h* of her head.......... Lk 7:38 *2359*
wiped them with the *h* of her head......... Lk 7:44 *2359*
But even the very *h* of your head........... Lk 12:7 *2359*
his *h* were white like wool, as................ Rev 1:14 *2359*

HAIRY
red, all over like an *h* garment.............. Gen 25:25 8181
Esau my brother is a *h* man.................... Gen 27:11 8163
him not, because his hands were *h*........ Gen 27:23 8163
answered him, He was an *h* man............. 2Kin 1:8 8181
the *h* scalp of such an one as................ Ps 68:21 8181

HAKELDAMA See ACELDAMA.

HAKKATAN (*hak'-ka-tan*) *A family of exiles.*
Johanan the son of *H*, and with him........ Ezr 8:12 6997

HAKKOZ (*hak'-koz*) See KOZ. *A sanctuary servant.*
The seventh to *H*, the eighth to.............. 1Chr 24:10 6976

HAKUPHA (*ha-ku'-fah*) *A family of exiles.*
of Bakbuk, the children of *H*................. Ezr 2:51 2709
of Bakbuk, the children of *H*................. Neh 7:53 2709

HALAH (*ha'-lah*) *An Assyrian district.*
into Assyria, and placed them in *H*........ 2Kin 17:6 2477
unto Assyria, and put them in *H*............ 2Kin 18:11 2477
Manasseh, and brought them unto *H*... 1Chr 5:26 2477

HALAK (*ha'-lak*) *A mountain in southern Canaan.*
Even from the mount *H*, that goeth........ Josh 11:17 2510
of Lebanon even unto the mount *H*...... Josh 12:7 2510

HALE
lest he *h* thee to the judge, and.............. Lk 12:58 *2694*

HALF
earring of *h* a shekel weight.................. Gen 24:22 1235
Moses took *h* of the blood, and put....... Ex 24:6 2677
h of the blood he sprinkled on.............. Ex 24:6 2677
a *h* shall be the length thereof,.............. Ex 25:10 2677
a *h* the breadth thereof........................... Ex 25:10 2677
a cubit and a *h* the height thereof......... Ex 25:10 2677
a *h* shall be the length thereof,.............. Ex 25:17 2677
cubit and a *h* the breadth thereof......... Ex 25:17 2677
a cubit and a *h* the height thereof......... Ex 25:23 2677
the *h* curtain that remaineth,............... Ex 26:12 2677
a *h* shall be the breadth of one............. Ex 26:16 2677
h a shekel after the shekel of................ Ex 30:13 4276
an *h* shekel shall be the........................ Ex 30:13 4276
not give less than *h* a shekel................. Ex 30:15 4276
and of sweet cinnamon *h* so much......... Ex 30:23 4276
of a board one cubit and a *h*.................. Ex 36:21 2677
a *h* was the length of it, and a.............. Ex 37:1 2677
a *h* the breadth of it............................... Ex 37:1 2677
a cubit and a *h* the height of it............. Ex 37:1 2677
a *h* was the length thereof, and............ Ex 37:6 2677
cubit and a *h* the breadth thereof......... Ex 37:6 2677
a cubit and a *h* the height thereof......... Ex 37:10 2677
h a shekel, after the shekel of.............. Ex 38:26 4276
h of it in the morning, and *h*................. Lev 6:20 4276
of whom the flesh is *h* consumed.......... Num 12:12 2677
mingled with *h* an hin of oil................... Num 15:9 2677
a drink offering *h* an hin of wine.......... Num 15:10 2677
h an hin of wine unto a bullock............. Num 28:14 2677
Take it of their *h*, and give it................ Num 31:29 4276
And of the children of Israel's *h*........... Num 31:30 4276
And the *h*, which was the portion.......... Num 31:36 4275
And of the children of Israel's *h*........... Num 31:42 4276
(Now the *h* that pertained unto............ Num 31:43 4275
of the children of Israel's *h*................... Num 31:47 4276
unto the *h* tribe of Manasseh the.......... Num 32:33 2677
nine tribes, and to the *h* tribe.............. Num 34:13 2677
h the tribe of Manasseh have................ Num 34:14 2677
the *h* tribe have received their.............. Num 34:15 2677
h mount Gilead, and the cities.............. Deut 3:12 2677
gave I unto the *h* tribe of...................... Deut 3:13 2677

H

unto the river Arnon *h* the valley ... Deut 3:16 8432
to the *h* tribe of Manasseh ... Deut 29:8 2677
to *h* the tribe of Manasseh, spake ... Josh 1:12 2677
h the tribe of Manasseh, passed ... Josh 4:12 2677
h of them over against mount ... Josh 8:33 2677
h of them over against mount Ebal ... Josh 8:33 2677
from *h* Gilead, even unto the ... Josh 12:2 2677
h Gilead, the border of Sihon ... Josh 12:5 2677
and the *h* tribe of Manasseh ... Josh 12:6 2677
and the *h* tribe of Manasseh, ... Josh 13:7 2677
h the land of the children of ... Josh 13:25 2677
unto the *h* tribe of Manasseh ... Josh 13:29 2677
of the *h* tribe of the children of ... Josh 13:29 2677
h Gilead, and Ashtaroth, and Edrei, ... Josh 13:31 2677
even to the one *h* of the children ... Josh 13:31 2677
nine tribes, and for the *h* tribe ... Josh 14:2 2677
an *h* tribe on the other side ... Josh 14:3 2677
h the tribe of Manasseh, have ... Josh 18:7 2677
out of the *h* tribe of Manasseh, ... Josh 21:5 2677
out of the *h* tribe of Manasseh in ... Josh 21:6 2677
out of the *h* tribe of Manasseh, ... Josh 21:25 4276
out of the other *h* tribe of ... Josh 21:27 2677
and the *h* tribe of Manasseh, ... Josh 22:1 2677
Now to the one *h* of the tribe of ... Josh 22:7 2677
but unto the other *h* thereof gave ... Josh 22:7 2677
the *h* tribe of Manasseh returned, ... Josh 22:9 2677
the *h* tribe of Manasseh built ... Josh 22:10 2677
the *h* tribe of Manasseh have ... Josh 22:11 2677
to the *h* tribe of Manasseh, into ... Josh 22:13 2677
to the *h* tribe of Manasseh, unto ... Josh 22:15 2677
the *h* tribe of Manasseh answered, ... Josh 22:21 2677
as it were an *h* acre of land ... 1Sa 14:14 2677
off the one *h* of their beards ... 2Sa 10:4 2677
neither if *h* of us die, will they ... 2Sa 18:3 2677
also *h* the people of Israel ... 2Sa 19:40 2677
give *h* to the one, and *h* to the ... 1Kin 3:25 2677
work of the base, a cubit and an *h* ... 1Kin 7:31 2677
a wheel was a cubit and *h* a cubit ... 1Kin 7:32 2677
a round compass of *h* a cubit high ... 1Kin 7:35 2677
and, behold, the *h* was not told me ... 1Kin 10:7 2677
thou wilt give me *h* thine house ... 1Kin 13:8 2677
captain of *h* his chariots, ... 1Kin 16:9 4276
h of the people followed Tibni ... 1Kin 16:21 2677
and *h* followed Omri ... 1Kin 16:21 2677
Haroeh, and *h* of the Manahethites ... 1Chr 2:52 2677
h of the Manahethites, the ... 1Chr 2:54 2677
h the tribe of Manasseh, of ... 1Chr 5:18 2677
the children of the *h* tribe of ... 1Chr 5:23 2677
the *h* tribe of Manasseh, and ... 1Chr 5:26 2677
cities given out of the *h* tribe ... 1Chr 6:61 2677
out of the *h* tribe of Manasseh, ... 1Chr 6:61 4276
out of the *h* tribe of Manasseh ... 1Chr 6:70 4276
family of the *h* tribe of Manasseh ... 1Chr 6:71 2677
of the *h* tribe of Manasseh ... 1Chr 12:31 2677
of the *h* tribe of Manasseh, with ... 1Chr 12:37 2677
the *h* tribe of Manasseh, for ... 1Chr 26:32 2677
of the *h* tribe of Manasseh, Joel ... 1Chr 27:20 2677
Of the *h* tribe of Manasseh in ... 1Chr 27:21 2677
the one *h* of the greatness of thy ... 2Chr 9:6 2677
the ruler of the *h* part of ... Neh 3:9 2677
the ruler of the *h* part of ... Neh 3:12 2677
ruler of the *h* part of Beth-zur ... Neh 3:16 2677
the ruler of the *h* part of Keilah ... Neh 3:17 2677
the ruler of the *h* part of Keilah ... Neh 3:18 2677
together unto the *h* thereof ... Neh 4:6 2677
that the *h* of my servants wrought ... Neh 4:16 2677
the other *h* of them held both the ... Neh 4:16 2677
h of them held the spears from ... Neh 4:21 2677
h of the princes of Judah, ... Neh 12:32 2677
the *h* of the people upon the wall ... Neh 12:38 2677
the *h* of the rulers with me ... Neh 12:40 2677
their children spake *h* in the ... Neh 13:24 2677
thee to the *h* of the kingdom ... Est 5:3 2677
even to the *h* of the kingdom it ... Est 5:6 2677
even to the *h* of the kingdom ... Est 7:2 2677
shall not live out *h* their days ... Ps 55:23 2673
Samaria committed *h* of thy sins ... Eze 16:51 2677
an *h* long, and a cubit and an *h* ... Eze 40:42 2677
about it shall be *h* a cubit ... Eze 43:17 2677
be for a time, times, and an *h* ... Dan 12:7 2677
barley, and an *h* homer of barley ... Hos 3:2
h of the city shall go forth into ... Zec 14:2 2677
h of the mountain shall remove ... Zec 14:4 2677
and *h* of it toward the south ... Zec 14:4 2677
h of them toward the former sea, ... Zec 14:8 2677
h of them toward the hinder sea ... Zec 14:8 2677
it thee, unto the *h* of my kingdom ... Mk 6:23 2255
and departed, leaving him *h* dead ... Lk 10:30 2253
the *h* of my goods I give to the ... Lk 19:8 2255
about the space of *h* an hour ... Rev 8:1 2256
dead bodies three days and an *h* ... Rev 11:9 2255
an *h* the Spirit of life from God ... Rev 11:11 2255
h a time, from the face of the ... Rev 12:14 2255

HALHUL (*hal'-hul*) *A city in Judah.*
H, Beth-zur, and Gedor, ... Josh 15:58 2478

HALI (*ha'-li*) *A town in Asher.*
And their border was Helkath, and *H* .. Josh 19:25 2482

HALING
h men and women committed them to Acts 8:3 4951

HALL
took Jesus into the common *h* ... Mt 27:27 4232
soldiers led him away into the *h* ... Mk 15:16 833
a fire in the midst of the *h* ... Lk 22:55 833
Caiaphas unto the *h* of judgment ... Jn 18:28 4232
went not into the judgment *h* ... Jn 18:28 4232
entered into the judgment *h* again ... Jn 18:33 4232
And went again into the judgment *h* ... Jn 19:9 4232
to be kept in Herod's judgment *h* ... Acts 23:35 4232

HALLOHESH (*hal-lo'-hesh*) See HALOHESH. *Father of Shallum.*
H, Pileha, Shobek, ... Neh 10:24 3873

HALLOW
shall *h* in all their holy gifts ... Ex 28:38 6942
thou shalt do unto them to *h* them ... Ex 29:1 6942
that is therein, and shalt *h* it ... Ex 40:9 6942
h it from the uncleanness of the ... Lev 16:19 6942
those things which they *h* unto me ... Lev 22:2 6942
of Israel *h* unto the LORD ... Lev 22:3 6942
I am the LORD which *h* you ... Lev 22:32 6942
ye shall *h* the fiftieth year, and ... Lev 25:10 6942
shall *h* his head that same day ... Num 6:11 6942
The same day did the king *h* the ... 1Kin 8:64 6942
but *h* ye the sabbath day, as I ... Jer 17:22 6942
but *h* the sabbath day, to do no ... Jer 17:24 6942
unto me to *h* the sabbath day ... Jer 17:27 6942
And *h* my sabbaths ... Eze 20:20 6942
and they shall *h* my sabbaths ... Eze 44:24 6942

HALLOWED
blessed the sabbath day, and *h* it ... Ex 20:11 6942
and he shall be *h*, and his garments ... Ex 29:21 6942
she shall touch no *h* thing ... Lev 12:4 6944
profaned the *h* thing of the LORD ... Lev 19:8 6944
but I will be *h* among the ... Lev 22:32 6942
in the land of Egypt I *h* unto me ... Num 3:13 6942
every man's *h* things shall be his ... Num 5:10 6944
for they are *h* ... Num 16:37 6942
the LORD, therefore they are *h* ... Num 16:38 6942
the *h* things of the children of ... Num 18:8 6944
even the *h* part thereof out of it ... Num 18:29 4720
I have brought away the *h* things ... Deut 26:13 6944
mine hand, but there is *h* bread ... 1Sa 21:4 6944
So the priest gave him *h* bread ... 1Sa 21:6 6944
I have *h* this house, which thou ... 1Kin 9:3 6942
house, which I have *h* for my name ... 1Kin 9:7 6942
all the *h* things that Jehoshaphat ... 2Kin 12:18 6944
dedicated, and his own *h* things ... 2Kin 12:18 6944
Moreover Solomon *h* the middle of ... 2Chr 7:7 6942
LORD which he had *h* in Jerusalem ... 2Chr 36:14 6942
art in heaven, *H* be thy name ... Mt 6:9 37
art in heaven, *H* be thy name ... Lk 11:2 37

HALOHESH (*ha-lo'-hesh*) See HALLOHESH. *Same as Hallohesh.*
him repaired Shallum the son of *H* ... Neh 3:12 3873

HALT
How long *h* ye between two ... 1Kin 18:21 6452
For I am ready to *h*, and my sorrow ... Ps 38:17 6761
to enter into life *h* or maimed ... Mt 18:8 5560
for thee to enter *h* into life ... Mk 9:45 5560
the poor, and the maimed, and the *h* ... Lk 14:21 5560
of impotent folk, of blind, *h* ... Jn 5:3 5560

HALTED
upon him, and he *h* upon his thigh ... Gen 32:31 6761
I will make her that *h* a remnant ... Mic 4:7 6761

HALTETH
LORD, will I assemble her that *h* ... Mic 4:6 6761
and I will save her that *h* ... Zeph 3:19 6761

HALTING
All my familiars watched for my *h* ... Jer 20:10 6761

HAM (*ham*)
1. A son of Noah.
and Noah begat Shem, *H*, and Japheth Gen 5:32 2526
And Noah begat three sons, Shem, *H* .. Gen 6:10 2526
day entered Noah, and Shem, and *H* ... Gen 7:13 2526
forth of the ark, were Shem, and *H* ... Gen 9:18 2526
H is the father of Canaan ... Gen 9:18 2526
And *H*, the father of Canaan, saw ... Gen 9:22 2526
of the sons of Noah, Shem, *H* ... Gen 10:1 2526
And the sons of *H* ... Gen 10:6 2526
These are the sons of *H*, after ... Gen 10:20 2526
Karnaim, and the Zuzims in *H* ... Gen 14:5 1990
Noah, Shem, *H*, and Japheth ... 1Chr 1:4 2526
The sons of *H* ... 1Chr 1:8 2526
2. Descendants and land of Ham.
for they of *H* had dwelt there of ... 1Chr 4:40 2526
strength in the tabernacles of *H* ... Ps 78:51 2526
Jacob sojourned in the land of *H* ... Ps 105:23 2526
them, and wonders in the land of *H* ... Ps 105:27 2526
Wondrous works in the land of *H* ... Ps 106:22 2526

HAMAN (*ha'-man*) See HAMAN'S. *Prime minister under King Ahasuerus.*
H the son of Hammedatha the ... Est 3:1 2001
gate, bowed, and reverenced *H* ... Est 3:2 2001
not unto them, that they told *H* ... Est 3:4 2001
when *H* saw that Mordecai bowed ... Est 3:5 2001
then was *H* full of wrath ... Est 3:5 2001
wherefore *H* sought to destroy all ... Est 3:6 2001
before *H* from day to day, and from ... Est 3:7 2001
H said unto king Ahasuerus, There ... Est 3:8 2001
gave it unto *H* the son of ... Est 3:10 2001
And the king said unto *H*, The ... Est 3:11 2001
H had commanded unto the king's ... Est 3:12 2001
the king and *H* sat down to drink ... Est 3:15 2001
that *H* had promised to pay to the ... Est 4:7 2001
H come this day unto the banquet ... Est 5:4 2001
Cause *H* to make haste, that he ... Est 5:5 2001
H came to the banquet that Esther ... Est 5:5 2001
H come to the banquet that I ... Est 5:8 2001
Then went *H* forth that day joyful ... Est 5:9 2001
but when *H* saw Mordecai in the ... Est 5:9 2001
Nevertheless *H* refrained himself ... Est 5:10 2001
H told them of the glory of his ... Est 5:11 2001
H said moreover, Yea, Esther the ... Est 5:12 2001
And the thing pleased *H* ... Est 5:14 2001
Now *H* was come into the outward ... Est 6:4 2001
Behold, *H* standeth in the court ... Est 6:5 2001
So *H* came in ... Est 6:6 2001
Now *H* thought in his heart, To ... Est 6:6 2001
H answered the king, For the man ... Est 6:7 2001
Then the king said to *H*, Make ... Est 6:10 2001
Then took *H* the apparel and the ... Est 6:11 2001
But *H* hasted to his house ... Est 6:12 2001
H told Zeresh his wife and all his ... Est 6:13 2001
hasted to bring *H* unto the ... Est 6:14 2001
H came to banquet with Esther the ... Est 7:1 2001
and enemy is this wicked *H* ... Est 7:6 2001
Then *H* was afraid before the king ... Est 7:6 2001
H stood up to make request for ... Est 7:7 2001
H was fallen upon the bed whereon ... Est 7:8 2001
which *H* had made for Mordecai ... Est 7:9 2001
king, standeth in the house of *H* ... Est 7:9 2001
So they hanged *H* on the gallows ... Est 7:10 2001
Ahasuerus give the house of *H* the ... Est 8:1 2001
ring, which he had taken from *H* ... Est 8:2 2001
set Mordecai over the house of *H* ... Est 8:2 2001
the mischief of *H* the Agagite ... Est 8:3 2001
by *H* the son of Hammedatha the ... Est 8:5 2001
have given Esther the house of *H* ... Est 8:7 2001
The ten sons of *H* the son of ... Est 9:10 2001
the palace, and the ten sons of *H* ... Est 9:12 2001
Because *H* the son of Hammedatha, ... Est 9:24 2001

HAMAN'S (*ha'-mans*)
king's mouth, they covered *H* face ... Est 7:8 2001
let *H* ten sons be hanged upon the ... Est 9:13 2001
and they hanged *H* ten sons ... Est 9:14 2001

HAMATH (*ha'-math*) See HAMATHITE, HAMATH-ZOBAH, HEMATH. *A capital of Syria.*
Zin unto Rehob, as men come to *H* ... Num 13:21 2574
border unto the entrance of *H* ... Num 34:8 2574
Hermon unto the entering into *H* ... Josh 13:5 2574
unto the entering in of *H* ... Judg 3:3 2574
When Toi king of *H* heard that ... 2Sa 8:9 2574
in of *H* unto the river of Egypt ... 1Kin 8:65 2574
of *H* unto the sea of the plain ... 2Kin 14:25 2574
how he recovered Damascus, and *H* ... 2Kin 14:28 2574
Cuthah, and from Ava, and from *H* ... 2Kin 17:24 2574
the men of *H* made Ashima, ... 2Kin 17:30 2574
Where are the gods of *H*, and of ... 2Kin 18:34 2574
Where is the king of *H*, and the ... 2Kin 19:13 2574
bands at Riblah in the land of *H* ... 2Kin 23:33 2574
them at Riblah in the land of *H* ... 2Kin 25:21 2574
Hadarezer king of Zobah unto *H* ... 1Chr 18:3 2574
Now when Tou king of *H* heard how ... 1Chr 18:9 2574
in of *H* unto the river of Egypt ... 2Chr 7:8 2574
store cities, which he built in *H* ... 2Chr 8:4 2574
is not *H* as Arpad ... Is 10:9 2574
Elam, and from Shinar, and from *H* ... Is 11:11 2574
Where are the gods of *H* and Arphad .. Is 36:19 2574
Where is the king of *H*, and the ... Is 37:13 2574
to Riblah in the land of *H* ... Jer 39:5 2574
H is confounded, and Arpad ... Jer 49:23 2574
to Riblah in the land of *H* ... Jer 52:9 2574
death in Riblah in the land of *H* ... Jer 52:27 2574
H, Berothah, Sibraim, which is ... Eze 47:16 2574
of Damascus and the border of *H* ... Eze 47:16 2574
northward, and the border of *H* ... Eze 47:17 2574
till a man come over against *H* ... Eze 47:20 2574
way of Hethlon, as one goeth to *H* ... Eze 48:1 2574
northward, to the coast of *H* ... Eze 48:1 2574
from thence go ye to *H* the great ... Amos 6:2 2579
H also shall border thereby ... Zec 9:2 2574

HAMATHITE
and the Zemarite, and the *H* ... Gen 10:18 2577
and the Zemarite, and the *H* ... 1Chr 1:16 2577

HAMATH-ZOBAH (*ha''-math-zo'-bah*) *Full name of Hamath.*
And Solomon went to *H*, and ... 2Chr 8:3 2578

HAMITES See HAM.

HAMMATH (*ham'-math*) *A city in Naphtali.*
cities are Ziddim, Zer, and *H* ... Josh 19:35 2575

HAMMEDATHA (*ham-med'a-thah*) *Father of Haman.*
Haman the son of *H* the Agagite ... Est 3:1 4099
Haman the son of *H* the Agagite ... Est 3:10 4099
by Haman the son of *H* the Agagite ... Est 8:5 4099
ten sons of Haman the son of *H* ... Est 9:10 4099
Because Haman the son of *H* ... Est 9:24 4099

HAMMELECH (*ham'-me-lek*) *Father of Jerahmeel.*
commanded Jerahmeel the son of *H* ... Jer 36:26 4429
dungeon of Malchiah the son of *H* ... Jer 38:6 4429

HAMMER
took an *h* in her hand, and went ... Judg 4:21 4718
her right hand to the workmen's *h* ... Judg 5:26 1989
with the *h* she smote Sisera, she ... Judg 5:26
so that there was neither *h* nor ... 1Kin 6:7 4717
the *h* him that smote the anvil ... Is 41:7 6360
like a *h* that breaketh the rock ... Jer 23:29 6360
How is the *h* of the whole earth ... Jer 50:23 6360

HAMMERS
thereof at once with axes and *h* ... Ps 74:6 3597
coals, and fashioneth it with *h* ... Is 44:12 4717
fasten it with nails and with *h* ... Jer 10:4 4717

HAMMOLEKETH (*ham-mol'-e-keth*) *Daughter of Machir.*
And his sister *H* bare Ishod ... 1Chr 7:18 4447

HAMMON (*ham'-mon*)
1. A city in Asher.
And Hebron, and Rehob, and *H* ... Josh 19:28 2540
2. A city in Naphtali.
H with her suburbs, and Kirjathaim ... 1Chr 6:76 2540

HAMMOTH-DOR (*ham''-moth-dor'*) *Same as Hammon 2.*
H with her suburbs, and Kartan ... Josh 21:32 2576

HAMMUEL See HAMUEL.

HAMONAH (*ha-mo'-nah*) *Place where Gog is buried.*
the name of the city shall be *H* ... Eze 39:16 1997

HAMON-GOG (*ha''-mon-gog*) *Same as Hamonah.*
shall call it The valley of *H* Eze 39:11 1996
have buried it in the valley of *H* Eze 39:15 1996

HAMOR (*ha'-mor*) See EMMOR, HAMOR'S. *Father of Shechem.*
at the hand of the children of *H* Gen 33:19 2544
Shechem the son of *H* the Hivite Gen 34:2 2544
Shechem spake unto his father *H* Gen 34:4 2544
H the father of Shechem went out Gen 34:6 2544
H communed with them, saying, The .. Gen 34:8 2544
H his father deceitfully, and said Gen 34:13 2544
And their words pleased *H*, and Gen 34:18 2544
And *H* and Shechem his son Gen 34:20 2544
And unto *H* and unto Shechem Gen 34:24 2544
And they slew *H* and Shechem his son Gen 34:26 2544
Jacob bought of the sons of *H* the Josh 24:32 2544
serve the men of *H* the father of Judg 9:28 2544

HAMOR'S (*ha'-mors*)
pleased Hamor, and Shechem *H* son Gen 34:18 2544

HAMRAN See AMRAN.

HAMUEL (*ha-mu'-el*) *Son of Mishma.*
H his son, Zacchur his son, 1Chr 4:26 2536

HAMUL (*ha'-mul*) See HAMULITES. *A son of Pharez.*
sons of Pharez were Hezron and *H* Gen 46:12 2538
of *H*, the family of the Hamulites Num 26:21 2538
Hezron, and *H*. 1Chr 2:5 2538

HAMULITES (*ha'-mu-lites*) *Descendants of Hamul.*
of Hamul, the family of the *H* Num 26:21 2539

HAMUTAL (*ha-mu'-tal*) *Mother of King Jehoahaz.*
And his mother's name was *H* 2Kin 23:31 2537
And his mother's name was *H* 2Kin 24:18 2537
his mother's name was *H* the Jer 52:1 2537

HANAMEAL See HANAMEEL.

HANAMEEL (*ha-nam'-e-el*) *Son of Shallum.*
H the son of Shallum thine uncle Jer 32:7 2601
So *H* mine uncle's son came to me Jer 32:8 2601
the field of *H* my uncle's son Jer 32:9 2601
in the sight of *H* mine uncle's Jer 32:12 2601

HANAMEL See HANAMEEL.

HANAN (*ha'-nan*) See BAAL-HANAN, BEN-HANAN, ELON-BETH-HANAN.
1. A son of Shashak.
And Abdon, and Zichri, and *H* 1Chr 8:23 2605
2. A son of Azel.
and Sheariah, and Obadiah, and *H* 1Chr 8:38 2605
and Sheariah, and Obadiah, and *H* 1Chr 9:44 2605
3. A "mighty man" of David.
H the son of Maachah, and 1Chr 11:43 2605
4. Family of exiles.
of Shalmai, the children of *H* Ezr 2:46 2605
The children of *H*, the children Neh 7:49 2605
5. A priest who assisted Ezra.
Kelita, Azariah, Jozabad, *H* Neh 8:7 2605
6. A Levite who renewed the covenant.
Hodijah, Kelita, Pelaiah, *H* Neh 10:10 2605
next to them was *H* the son of Neh 13:13 2605
7. A chief who renewed the covenant.
Pelatiah, *H*, Anaiah, Neh 10:22 2605
8. Another chief who renewed the covenant.
And Ahijah, *H*, Anan, Neh 10:26 2605
9. Son of Igdaliah.
into the chamber of the sons of *H* Jer 35:4 2605

HANANEAL See HANANEEL.

HANANEEL (*ha-nan'-e-el*) *A tower on Jerusalem's wall.*
it, unto the tower of *H* Neh 3:1 2606
the fish gate, and the tower of *H* Neh 12:39 2606
of *H* unto the gate of the corner Jer 31:38 2606
from the tower of *H* unto the Zec 14:10 2606

HANANEL See HANANEEL.

HANANI (*ha-na'-ni*)
1. A son of Heman.
Shebuel, and Jerimoth, Hananiah, *H* 1Chr 25:4 2607
The eighteenth to *H*, he, his sons 1Chr 25:25 2607
2. A prophet.
at that time *H* the seer came to 2Chr 16:7 2607
3. Father of Jehu.
Jehu the son of *H* against Baasha 1Kin 16:1 2607
of *H* came the word of the LORD 1Kin 16:7 2607
Jehu the son of *H* the seer went 2Chr 19:2 2607
in the book of Jehu the son of *H* 2Chr 20:34 2607
4. Married a foreigner in exile.
of Immer; *H*, and Zebadiah Ezr 10:20 2607
5. Brother of Nehemiah.
That *H*, one of my brethren, came, Neh 1:2 2607
That I gave my brother *H*, and Neh 7:2 2607
6. A priest.
Maai, Nethaneel, and Judah, *H* Neh 12:36 2607

HANANIAH (*han-a-ni'-ah*) See SHADRACH.
1. A son of Heman.
Uzziel, Shebuel, and Jerimoth, *H* 1Chr 25:4 2608
The sixteenth to *H*, he, his sons, 1Chr 25:23 2608
Meraiah; of Jeremiah, *H* Neh 12:12 2608
Hear now, *H*; The LORD hath Jer 28:15 2608
2. A captain of King Uzziah.
the ruler, under the hand of *H* 2Chr 26:11 2608
3. Father of Zedekiah.
Shaphan, and Zedekiah the son of *H* ... Jer 36:12 2608
4. A false prophet.
that *H* the son of Azur the Jer 28:1 2608
H in the presence of the priests Jer 28:5 2608
Then *H* the prophet took the yoke Jer 28:10 2608
H spake in the presence of all Jer 28:11 2608
after that *H* the prophet had Jer 28:12 2608
Go and tell *H*, saying, Thus saith Jer 28:13 2608
Jeremiah unto *H* the prophet Jer 28:15 2608
So *H* the prophet died the same Jer 28:17 2608
5. Grandfather of Irijah.
son of Shelemiah, the son of *H* Jer 37:13 2608
6. Son of Shashak.
And *H*, and Elam, and Antothijah, 1Chr 8:24 2608
7. Hebrew form of Shadrach.
the children of Judah, Daniel, *H* Dan 1:6 2608
and to *H*, of Shadrach Dan 1:7 2608
eunuchs had set over Daniel, *H* Dan 1:11 2608
all was found none like Daniel, *H* Dan 1:19 2608
and made the thing known to *H* Dan 2:17 2608
8. A son of Zerubbabel.
Meshullam, and *H*, and Shelomith 1Chr 3:19 2608
And the sons of *H* 1Chr 3:21 2608
9. Married a foreigner in exile.
Jehohanan, *H*, Zabbai, and Athlai Ezr 10:28 2608
10. A rebuilder of Jerusalem's wall.
repaired *H* the son of one of the Neh 3:8 2608
11. Another rebuilder of Jerusalem's wall.
After him repaired *H* the son of Neh 3:30 2608
12. A palace servant of Nehemiah.
H the ruler of the palace, charge Neh 7:2 2608
13. An Israelite who renewed the covenant.
Hoshea, *H*, Hashub, Neh 10:23 2608
14. A priest.
Elioenai, Zechariah, and *H* Neh 12:41 2608

HAND
and now, lest he put forth his *h* Gen 3:22 3027
thy brother's blood from thy *h* Gen 4:11 3027
then he put forth his *h*, and took Gen 8:9 3027
into your *h* are they delivered Gen 9:2 3027
at the *h* of every beast will I Gen 9:5 3027
I require it, and at the *h* of man Gen 9:5 3027
at the *h* of every man's brother Gen 9:5 3027
if thou wilt take the left *h* Gen 13:9 8041
or if thou depart to the right *h* Gen 13:9 3225
is on the left *h* of Damascus Gen 14:15 8040
thine enemies into thy *h* Gen 14:20 3027
have lift up mine *h* unto the LORD Gen 14:22 3027
Behold, thy maid is in thy *h* Gen 16:6 3027
his *h* will be against every man, Gen 16:12 3027
and every man's *h* against him Gen 16:12 3027
But the men put forth their *h* Gen 19:10 3027
the men laid hold upon his *h* Gen 19:16 3027
upon the *h* of his wife Gen 19:16 3027
upon the *h* of his two daughters Gen 19:16 3027
the lad, and hold him in thine *h* Gen 21:18 3027
ewe lambs shalt thou take of my *h* Gen 21:30 3027
and he took the fire in his *h* Gen 22:6 3027
And Abraham stretched forth his *h* Gen 22:10 3027
Lay not thine *h* upon the lad Gen 22:12 3027
I pray thee, thy *h* under my thigh Gen 24:2 3027
the servant put his *h* under the Gen 24:9 3027
goods of his master were in his *h* Gen 24:10 3027
let down her pitcher upon her *h* Gen 24:18 3027
that I may turn to the right *h* Gen 24:49 3225
his *h* took hold on Esau's heel Gen 25:26 3027
into the *h* of her son Jacob Gen 27:17 3027
mourning for my father are at *h* Gen 27:41 7126
gave them into the *h* of his sons Gen 30:35 3027
the power of my *h* to do you hurt Gen 31:29 3027
of my *h* didst thou require it, Gen 31:39 3027
from the *h* of my brother Gen 32:11 3027
from the *h* of Esau Gen 32:11 3027
h a present for Esau his brother Gen 32:13 3027
them into the *h* of his servants Gen 32:16 3027
then receive my present at my *h* Gen 33:10 3027
at the *h* of the children of Hamor Gen 33:19 3027
gods which were in their *h* Gen 35:4 3027
wilderness, and lay no *h* upon him Gen 37:22 3027
and let not our *h* be upon him Gen 37:27 3027
and thy staff that is in thine *h* Gen 38:18 3027
Judah sent the kid by the *h* of Gen 38:20 3027
his pledge from the woman's *h* Gen 38:20 3027
that the one put out his *h* Gen 38:28 3027
bound upon his *h* a scarlet thread Gen 38:28 3027
to pass, as he drew back his *h* Gen 38:29 3027
had the scarlet thread upon his *h* Gen 38:30 3027
that he did to prosper in his *h* Gen 39:3 3027
all that he had he put into his *h* Gen 39:4 3027
all that he had in Joseph's *h* Gen 39:6 3027
all that he hath to my *h* Gen 39:8 3027
and he left his garment in her *h* Gen 39:12 3027
he had left his garment in her *h* Gen 39:13 3027
prison committed to Joseph's *h* Gen 39:22 3027
to any thing that was under his *h* Gen 39:23 3027
And Pharaoh's cup was in my *h* Gen 40:11 3027
I gave the cup into Pharaoh's *h* Gen 40:11 3709
deliver Pharaoh's cup into his *h* Gen 40:13 3027
he gave the cup into Pharaoh's *h* Gen 40:21 3709
up corn under the *h* of Pharaoh Gen 41:35 3027
took off his ring from his *h* Gen 41:42 3027
h, and put it upon Joseph's *h* Gen 41:42 3027
his *h* or foot in all the land of Gen 41:44 3027
deliver him into my *h*, and I will Gen 42:37 3027
of my *h* shalt thou require him Gen 43:9 3027
And take double money in your *h* Gen 43:12 3027
sacks, carry it again in your *h* Gen 43:12 3027
they took double money in their *h* Gen 43:15 3027
we have brought it again in our *h* Gen 43:21 3027
was in their *h* into the house Gen 43:26 3027
man in whose *h* the cup is found Gen 44:17 3027
shall put his *h* upon thine eyes Gen 46:4 3027
thy *h* under my thigh, and deal Gen 47:29 3027
Ephraim in his right *h* toward Gen 48:13 3225
toward Israel's left *h* Gen 48:13 8040
Manasseh in his left *h* toward Gen 48:13 8040
toward Israel's right *h* Gen 48:13 3225
Israel stretched out his right *h* Gen 48:14 3225
his left *h* upon Manasseh's head, Gen 48:14 8040
right *h* upon the head of Ephraim Gen 48:17 3027
and he held up his father's *h* Gen 48:17 3027
put thy right *h* upon his head Gen 48:18 3225
which I took out of the *h* of the Gen 48:22 3027
thy *h* shall be in the neck of Gen 49:8 3027
us out of the *h* of the shepherds Ex 2:19 3027
out of the *h* of the Egyptians Ex 3:8 3027
let you go, no, not by a mighty *h* Ex 3:19 3027
And I will stretch out my *h* Ex 3:20 3027
unto him, What is that in thine *h* Ex 4:2 3027
unto Moses, Put forth thine *h* Ex 4:4 3027
And he put forth his *h*, and caught Ex 4:4 3027
it, and it became a rod in his *h* Ex 4:4 3709
Put now thine *h* into thy bosom Ex 4:6 3027
he put his *h* into his bosom Ex 4:6 3027
his *h* was leprous as snow Ex 4:6 3027
Put thine *h* into thy bosom again Ex 4:7 3027
he put his *h* into his bosom again Ex 4:7 3027
by the *h* of him whom thou wilt Ex 4:13 3027
shalt take this rod in thine *h* Ex 4:17 3027
took the rod of God in his *h* Ex 4:20 3027
which I have put in thine *h* Ex 4:21 3027
put a sword in their *h* to slay us Ex 5:21 3027
for with a strong *h* shall he let Ex 6:1 3027
with a strong *h* shall he drive Ex 6:1 3027
that I may lay my *h* upon Egypt Ex 7:4 3027
I stretch forth mine *h* upon Egypt Ex 7:5 3027
shalt thou take in thine *h* Ex 7:15 3027
h upon the waters which are in Ex 7:17 3027
stretch out thine *h* upon the Ex 7:19 3027
Stretch forth thine *h* with thy Ex 8:5 3027
Aaron stretched out his *h* over Ex 8:6 3027
stretched out his *h* with his rod Ex 8:17 3027
the *h* of the LORD is upon thy Ex 9:3 3027
For now I will stretch out my *h* Ex 9:15 3027
forth thine *h* toward heaven Ex 9:22 3027
Stretch out thine *h* over the land Ex 10:12 3027
Stretch out thine *h* toward heaven Ex 10:21 3027
forth his *h* toward heaven Ex 10:22 3027
feet, and your staff in your *h* Ex 12:11 3027
for by strength of *h* the LORD Ex 13:3 3027
for a sign unto thee upon thine *h* Ex 13:9 3027
for with a strong *h* hath the LORD Ex 13:9 3027
By strength of *h* the LORD brought Ex 13:14 3027
shall be for a token upon thine *h* Ex 13:16 3027
for by strength of *h* the LORD Ex 13:16 3027
of Israel went out with an high *h* Ex 14:8 3027
stretch out thine *h* over the sea Ex 14:16 3027
stretched out his *h* over the sea Ex 14:21 3027
a wall unto them on their right *h* Ex 14:22 3225
Stretch out thine *h* over the sea Ex 14:26 3027
forth his *h* over the sea, and the Ex 14:27 3027
a wall unto them on their right *h* Ex 14:29 3225
day out of the *h* of the Egyptians Ex 14:30 3027
Thy right *h*, O LORD, is become Ex 15:6 3225
thy right *h*, O LORD, hath dashed Ex 15:6 3225
my sword, my *h* shall destroy them Ex 15:9 3027
Thou stretchedst out thy right *h* Ex 15:12 3225
of Aaron, took a timbrel in her *h* Ex 15:20 3027
the *h* of the LORD in the land of Ex 16:3 3027
the river, take in thine *h* Ex 17:5 3027
with the rod of God in mine *h* Ex 17:9 3027
to pass, when Moses held up his *h* Ex 17:11 3027
and when he let down his *h* Ex 17:11 3027
out of the *h* of the Egyptians Ex 18:9 3027
you out of the *h* of the Egyptians Ex 18:10 3027
and out of the *h* of Pharaoh Ex 18:10 3027
from under the *h* of the Egyptians Ex 18:10 3027
There shall not an *h* touch it Ex 19:13 3027
but God deliver him into his *h* Ex 21:13 3027
him, or if he be found in his *h* Ex 21:16 3027
with a rod, and he die under his *h* Ex 21:20 3027
h for *h*, foot for foot, Ex 21:24 3027
be certainly found in his *h* alive Ex 22:4 3027
his *h* unto his neighbour's goods Ex 22:8 3027
that he hath not put his *h* unto Ex 22:11 3027
put not thine *h* with the wicked Ex 23:1 3027
of the land into your *h* Ex 23:31 3027
of Israel he laid not his *h* Ex 24:11 3027
of an *h* breadth round about Ex 25:25 2948
upon the thumb of their right *h* Ex 29:20 3027
And he received them at their *h* Ex 32:4 3027
great power, and with a mighty *h* Ex 32:11 3027
of the testimony were in his *h* Ex 32:15 3027
thee with my *h* while I pass by Ex 33:22 3709
And I will take away mine *h* Ex 33:23 3709
took in his *h* the two tables of Ex 34:4 3027
tables of testimony in Moses' *h* Ex 34:29 3027
to be made by the *h* of Moses Ex 35:29 3027
gate, on this *h* and that *h* Ex 38:15 3027
by the *h* of Ithamar, son to Aaron Ex 38:21 3027
he shall put his *h* upon the head Lev 1:4 3027
he shall lay his *h* upon the head Lev 3:2 3027
he shall lay his *h* upon the head Lev 3:8 3027
he shall lay his *h* upon the head Lev 3:13 3027
and shall lay his *h* upon the Lev 4:4 3027
he shall lay his *h* upon the head Lev 4:24 3027
he shall lay his *h* upon the head Lev 4:29 3027
he shall lay his *h* upon the head Lev 4:33 3027
and upon the thumb of his right *h* Lev 8:23 3027
LORD commanded by the *h* of Moses ... Lev 8:36 3027
lifted up his *h* toward the people Lev 9:22 3027
unto them by the *h* of Moses Lev 10:11 3027
and upon the thumb of his right *h* Lev 14:14 3027
into the palm of his own left *h* Lev 14:15 8042
in the oil that is in his left *h* Lev 14:16 3709
h shall the priest put upon the Lev 14:17 3709
and upon the thumb of his right *h* Lev 14:17 3027
h he shall pour upon the head of Lev 14:18 3709
and upon the thumb of his right *h* Lev 14:25 3027
into the palm of his own left *h* Lev 14:26 8042
h seven times before the LORD Lev 14:27 3709
h upon the tip of the right ear Lev 14:28 3709

H

and upon the thumb of his right *h* Lev 14:28 3027
h he shall put upon the head of Lev 14:29 3709
whose *h* is not able to get that Lev 14:32 3027
by the *h* of a fit man into the Lev 16:21 3027
Neither from a stranger's *h* shall Lev 22:25 3027
buyest ought of thy neighbour's *h* Lev 25:14 3027
the *h* of him that hath bought it Lev 25:28 3027
delivered into the *h* of the enemy Lev 26:25 3027
in mount Sinai by the *h* of Moses Lev 26:46 3027
h of Ithamar the son of Aaron the Num 4:28 3027
under the *h* of Ithamar the son of Num 4:33 3027
of the LORD by the *h* of Moses Num 4:37 3027
of the LORD by the *h* of Moses Num 4:45 3027
were numbered by the *h* of Moses Num 4:49 3027
the priest shall have in his *h* Num 5:18 3027
offering out of the woman's *h* Num 5:25 3027
beside that that his *h* shall get Num 6:21 3027
under the *h* of Ithamar the son of Num 7:8 3027
of the LORD by the *h* of Moses Num 9:23 3027
of the LORD by the *h* of Moses Num 10:13 3027
kill me, I pray thee, out of *h* Num 11:15 2026
Is the LORD's *h* waxed short Num 11:23 3027
commanded you by the *h* of Moses Num 15:23 3027
said to him by the *h* of Moses Num 16:40 3027
And Moses lifted up his *h*, and with Num 20:11 3027
to the right *h* nor to the left Num 20:17 3225
much people, and with a strong *h* Num 20:20 3027
deliver this people into my *h* Num 21:2 3027
taken all his land out of his *h* Num 21:26 3027
I have delivered him into thy *h* Num 21:34 3027
rewards of divination in their *h* Num 22:7 3027
way, and his sword drawn in his *h* Num 22:23 3027
to the right *h* or to the left Num 22:26 3325
there were a sword in mine *h* Num 22:29 3027
way, and his sword drawn in his *h* Num 22:31 3027
and took a javelin in his *h* Num 25:7 3027
spirit, and lay thine *h* upon him Num 27:18 3027
LORD commanded by the *h* of Moses Num 27:23 3027
and the trumpets to blow in his *h* Num 31:6 3027
their armies under the *h* of Moses Num 33:1 3027
an high *h* in the sight of all the Num 33:3 3027
him with an *h* weapon of wood Num 35:18 3027
Or in enmity smite him with his *h* Num 35:21 3027
of the *h* of the revenger of blood Num 35:25 3027
h of Moses unto the children of Num 36:13 3027
us into the *h* of the Amorites Deut 1:27 3027
thee in all the works of thy *h* Deut 2:7 3027
For indeed the *h* of the LORD was Deut 2:15 3027
into thine *h* Sihon the Amorite Deut 2:24 3027
unto the right *h* nor to the left Deut 2:27 3225
he might deliver him into thy *h* Deut 2:30 3027
people, and his land, into thy *h* Deut 3:2 3027
of the *h* of the two kings of the Deut 3:8 3027
thy greatness, and thy mighty *h* Deut 3:24 3027
and by war, and by a mighty *h* Deut 4:34 3027
out thence through a mighty *h* Deut 5:15 3027
to the right *h* or to the left Deut 5:32 3225
bind them for a sign upon thine *h* Deut 6:8 3027
us out of Egypt with a mighty *h* Deut 6:21 3027
brought you out with a mighty *h* Deut 7:8 3027
from the *h* of Pharaoh king of Deut 7:8 3027
and the wonders, and the mighty *h* Deut 7:19 3027
deliver their kings into thine *h* Deut 7:24 3027
the might of mine *h* hath gotten Deut 8:17 3027
out of Egypt with a mighty *h* Deut 9:26 3027
having the two tables in mine *h* Deut 10:3 3027
God, his greatness, his mighty *h* Deut 11:2 3027
bind them for a sign upon your *h* Deut 11:18 3027
and heave offerings of your *h* Deut 12:6 3027
in all that ye put your *h* unto Deut 12:7 3027
and the heave offering of your *h* Deut 12:11 3027
or heave offering of thine *h* Deut 12:17 3027
thine *h* shall be first upon him Deut 13:9 3027
afterwards the *h* of all the Deut 13:9 3027
of the cursed thing to thine *h* Deut 13:17 3027
and bind up the money in thine *h* Deut 14:25 3027
work of thine *h* which thou doest Deut 14:29 3027
thy brother thine *h* shall release Deut 15:3 3027
nor shut thine *h* from thy poor Deut 15:7 3027
shalt open thine *h* wide unto him Deut 15:8 3027
the year of release, is at *h* Deut 15:9 7126
that thou puttest thine *h* unto Deut 15:10 3027
thine *h* wide unto thy brother Deut 15:11 3027
of a freewill offering of thine *h* Deut 16:10 3027
shall shew thee, to the right *h* Deut 17:11 3225
the commandment, to the right *h* Deut 17:20 3225
his *h* fetcheth a stroke with the Deut 19:5 3027
deliver him into the *h* of the Deut 19:12 3027
h for *h*, foot for foot Deut 19:21 3027
h to in the land whither thou Deut 23:20 3027
pluck the ears with thine *h* Deut 23:25 3027
divorcement, and give it in her *h* Deut 24:1 3027
and giveth it in her *h*, and Deut 24:3 3027
of the *h* of him that smiteth him Deut 25:11 3027
and putteth forth her *h* Deut 25:11 3027
Then thou shalt cut off her *h* Deut 25:12 3709
take the basket out of thine *h* Deut 26:4 3027
out of Egypt with a mighty *h* Deut 26:8 3027
that thou settest thine *h* unto Deut 28:8 3027
to bless all the work of thine *h* Deut 28:12 3027
thee this day, to the right *h* Deut 28:14 3225
settest thine *h* unto for to do Deut 28:20 3027
shall be no might in thine *h* Deut 28:32 3027
in every work of thine *h*, in the Deut 30:9 3027
Our *h* is high, and the LORD hath Deut 32:27 3027
the day of their calamity is at *h* Deut 32:35 7138
any that can deliver out of my *h* Deut 32:39 3027
For I lift up my *h* to heaven Deut 32:40 3027
mine *h* take hold on judgment Deut 32:41 3027
from his right *h* went a fiery law Deut 33:2 3225
all his saints are in thy *h* Deut 33:3 3027
And in all that mighty *h*, and in Deut 34:12 3027
it to the right *h* or to the left Josh 1:7 3225
on our head, if any *h* be upon him Josh 2:19 3027

might know the *h* of the LORD Josh 4:24 3027
him with his sword drawn in his *h* Josh 5:13 3027
I have given into thine *h* Jericho Josh 6:2 3027
us into the *h* of the Amorites Josh 7:7 3027
given into thy *h* the king of Ai Josh 8:1 3027
God will deliver it into your *h* Josh 8:7 3027
spear that is in thy *h* toward Ai Josh 8:18 3027
for I will give it into thine *h* Josh 8:18 3027
he had in his *h* toward the city Josh 8:18 3027
as he had stretched out his *h* Josh 8:19 3027
For Joshua drew not his *h* back Josh 8:26 3027
And now, behold, we are in thine *h* Josh 9:25 3027
the *h* of the children of Israel Josh 9:26 3027
Slack not thy *h* from thy servants Josh 10:6 3027
have delivered them into thine *h* Josh 10:8 3027
hath delivered them into your *h* Josh 10:19 3027
thereof, into the *h* of Israel Josh 10:30 3027
Lachish into the *h* of Israel Josh 10:32 3027
them into the *h* of Israel Josh 11:8 3027
LORD commanded by the *h* of Moses Josh 14:2 3027
right *h* unto the inhabitants of Josh 17:7 3225
goeth out to Cabul on the left *h* Josh 19:27 8040
spake unto you by the *h* of Moses Josh 20:2 3027
deliver the slayer up into his *h* Josh 20:5 3027
not die by the *h* of the avenger Josh 20:9 3027
The LORD commanded by the *h* of Josh 21:2 3027
LORD commanded by the *h* of Moses Josh 21:8 3027
all their enemies into their *h* Josh 21:44 3027
of the LORD by the *h* of Moses Josh 22:9 3027
Israel out of the *h* of the LORD Josh 22:31 3027
to the right *h* or to the left Josh 23:6 3225
and I gave them into your *h* Josh 24:8 3027
so I delivered you out of his *h* Josh 24:10 3027
and I delivered them into your *h* Josh 24:11 3027
delivered the land into his *h* Judg 1:2 3027
and the Perizzites into their *h* Judg 1:4 3027
yet the *h* of the house of Joseph Judg 1:35 3027
the *h* of the LORD was against Judg 2:15 3027
the *h* of those that spoiled them Judg 2:16 3027
delivered them out of the *h* of Judg 2:18 3027
he them into the *h* of Joshua Judg 2:23 3027
their fathers by the *h* of Moses Judg 3:4 3027
he sold them into the *h* of Judg 3:8 3027
king of Mesopotamia into his *h* Judg 3:10 3027
and his *h* prevailed against Judg 3:10 3027
And Ehud put forth his left *h* Judg 3:21 3027
enemies the Moabites into your *h* Judg 3:28 3027
that day under the *h* of Israel Judg 3:30 3027
the *h* of Jabin king of Canaan Judg 4:2 3027
I will deliver him into thine *h* Judg 4:7 3027
sell Sisera into the *h* of a woman Judg 4:9 3027
delivered Sisera into thine *h* Judg 4:14 3027
tent, and took an hammer in her *h* Judg 4:21 3027
the *h* of the children of Israel Judg 4:24 3027
She put her *h* to the nail Judg 5:26 3027
her right *h* to the workmen's Judg 5:26 3225
into the *h* of Midian seven years Judg 6:1 3027
the *h* of Midian prevailed against Judg 6:2 3027
you out of the *h* of the Egyptians Judg 6:9 3027
and out of the *h* of all that Judg 6:9 3027
from the *h* of the Midianites Judg 6:14 3709
of the staff that was in his *h* Judg 6:21 3027
thou wilt save Israel by mine *h* Judg 6:36 3027
thou wilt save Israel by mine *h* Judg 6:37 3027
saying, Mine own *h* hath saved me Judg 7:2 3027
putting their *h* to their mouth, Judg 7:6 3027
the Midianites into thine *h* Judg 7:7 3027
people took victuals in their *h* Judg 7:8 3027
I have delivered it into thine *h* Judg 7:9 3027
for into his *h* hath God delivered Judg 7:14 3027
into your *h* the host of Midian Judg 7:15 3027
he put a trumpet in every man's *h* Judg 7:16 3027
Zebah and Zalmunna now in thine *h* Judg 8:6 3027
Zebah and Zalmunna into mine *h* Judg 8:7 3027
Zebah and Zalmunna now in thine *h* Judg 8:15 3027
delivered us from the *h* of Midian Judg 8:22 3027
you out of the *h* of Midian Judg 9:17 3027
God this people were under my *h* Judg 9:29 3027
and Abimelech took an axe in his *h* Judg 9:48 3027
and I delivered you out of their *h* Judg 10:12 3027
his people into the *h* of Israel Judg 11:21 3027
the LORD delivered them into my *h* Judg 12:3 3027
LORD delivered them into the *h* of Judg 13:1 3027
out of the *h* of the Philistines Judg 13:5 3027
a kid, and he had nothing in his *h* Judg 14:6 3027
into the *h* of the Philistines Judg 15:12 3027
and deliver thee into their *h* Judg 15:13 3027
of an ass, and put forth his *h* Judg 15:15 3027
away the jawbone out of his *h* Judg 15:17 3027
into the *h* of thy servant Judg 15:18 3027
thirst, and fall into the *h* of the Judg 15:18 3027
her, and brought money in their *h* Judg 16:18 3027
Samson our enemy into our *h* Judg 16:23 3027
the lad that held him by the *h* Judg 16:26 3027
up, of the one with his right *h* Judg 16:29
the LORD from my *h* for my son Judg 17:3 3027
lay thine *h* upon thy mouth, and go Judg 18:19 3027
I will deliver them into thine *h* Judg 20:28 3027
the beast, and all that came to *h* Judg 20:48 4672
h of the LORD is gone out against Ruth 1:13 3027
the field of the *h* of Naomi Ruth 4:5 3027
and Mahlon's, of the *h* of Naomi Ruth 4:9 3027
fleshhook of three teeth in his *h* 1Sa 2:13 3027
us out of the *h* of our enemies 1Sa 4:3 3709
out of the *h* of these mighty Gods 1Sa 4:8 3027
But the *h* of the LORD was heavy 1Sa 5:6 3027
for his *h* is sore upon us, and 1Sa 5:7 3027
the *h* of the LORD was against the 1Sa 5:9 3027
the *h* of God was very heavy there 1Sa 5:11 3027
why his *h* is not removed from you 1Sa 6:3 3027
will lighten his *h* from off you 1Sa 6:5 3027
it is not his *h* that smote us 1Sa 6:9 3027
to the right *h* or to the left 1Sa 6:12
out of the *h* of the Philistines 1Sa 7:3 3027

out of the *h* of the Philistines 1Sa 7:8 3027
the *h* of the LORD was against the 1Sa 7:13 3027
I have here at *h* the fourth part 1Sa 9:8 3027
out of the *h* of the Philistines 1Sa 9:16 3027
you out of the *h* of the Egyptians 1Sa 10:18 3027
out of the *h* of all kingdoms, and 1Sa 10:18 3027
or of whose *h* have I received any 1Sa 12:3 3027
thou taken ought of any man's *h* 1Sa 12:4 3027
ye have not found ought in my *h* 1Sa 12:5 3027
he sold them into the *h* of Sisera 1Sa 12:9 3027
into the *h* of the Philistines, and 1Sa 12:9 3027
into the *h* of the king of Moab, 1Sa 12:9 3027
us out of the *h* of our enemies 1Sa 12:10 3027
delivered you out of the *h* of 1Sa 12:11 3027
then shall the *h* of the LORD be 1Sa 12:15 3027
sword nor spear found in the *h* of 1Sa 13:22 3027
hath delivered them into our *h* 1Sa 14:10 3027
them into the *h* of Israel 1Sa 14:12 3027
unto the priest, Withdraw thine *h* 1Sa 14:19 3027
but no man put his *h* to his mouth 1Sa 14:26 3027
end of the rod that was in his *h* 1Sa 14:27 3027
and put his *h* to his mouth 1Sa 14:27 3027
deliver them into the *h* of Israel 1Sa 14:37 3027
end of the rod that was in mine *h* 1Sa 14:43 3027
that he shall play with his *h* 1Sa 16:16 3027
an harp, and played with his *h* 1Sa 16:23 3027
h of the keeper of the carriage 1Sa 17:22 3027
out of the *h* of this Philistine 1Sa 17:37 3027
And he took his staff in his *h* 1Sa 17:40 3027
and his sling was in his *h* 1Sa 17:40 3027
the LORD deliver thee into mine *h* 1Sa 17:46 3027
And David put his *h* in his bag 1Sa 17:49 3027
was no sword in the *h* of David 1Sa 17:50 3027
head of the Philistine in his *h* 1Sa 17:57 3027
and David played with his *h* 1Sa 18:10 3027
there was a javelin in Saul's *h* 1Sa 18:10 3027
said, Let not mine *h* be upon him 1Sa 18:17 3027
but let the *h* of the Philistines 1Sa 18:17 3027
that the *h* of the Philistines may 1Sa 18:21 3027
fall by the *h* of the Philistines 1Sa 18:25 3027
For he did put his life in his *h* 1Sa 19:5 3709
house with his javelin in his *h* 1Sa 19:9 3027
and David played with his *h* 1Sa 19:9 3027
it at the *h* of David's enemies 1Sa 20:16 3027
when the business was in *h* 1Sa 20:19
therefore what is under thine *h* 1Sa 21:3 3027
me five loaves of bread in mine *h* 1Sa 21:3 3027
is no common bread under mine *h* 1Sa 21:4 3027
here under thine *h* spear or sword 1Sa 21:8 3027
Ramah, having his spear in his *h* 1Sa 22:6 3027
because their *h* also is with 1Sa 22:17 3027
king would not put forth their *h* 1Sa 22:17 3027
the Philistines into thine *h* 1Sa 23:4 3027
came down with an ephod in his *h* 1Sa 23:6 3027
hath delivered him into mine *h* 1Sa 23:7 3027
Keilah deliver me up into his *h* 1Sa 23:11 3027
me and my men into the *h* of Saul 1Sa 23:12 3027
God delivered him not into his *h* 1Sa 23:14 3027
and strengthened his *h* in God 1Sa 23:16 3027
for the *h* of Saul my father shall 1Sa 23:17 3027
to deliver him into the king's *h* 1Sa 23:20 3027
deliver thine enemy into thine *h* 1Sa 24:4 3027
stretch forth mine *h* against him 1Sa 24:6 3027
to day into mine *h* in the cave 1Sa 24:10 3027
put forth mine *h* against my lord 1Sa 24:10 3027
see the skirt of thy robe in my *h* 1Sa 24:11 3027
evil nor transgression in mine *h* 1Sa 24:11 3027
but mine *h* shall not be upon thee 1Sa 24:12 3027
but mine *h* shall not be upon thee 1Sa 24:13 3027
and deliver me out of thine *h* 1Sa 24:15 3027
had delivered me into thine *h* 1Sa 24:18 3027
shall be established in thine *h* 1Sa 24:20 3027
to thine *h* unto thy servants 1Sa 25:8 3027
avenging thyself with thine own *h* 1Sa 25:26 3027
avenging myself with mine own *h* 1Sa 25:33 3027
So David received of her *h* that 1Sa 25:35 3027
my reproach from the *h* of Nabal 1Sa 25:39 3027
thine enemy into thine *h* this day 1Sa 26:8 3027
his *h* against the LORD's anointed 1Sa 26:9 3027
h against the LORD's anointed 1Sa 26:11 3027
or what evil is in mine *h* 1Sa 26:18 3027
delivered thee into my *h* to day 1Sa 26:23 3027
h against the LORD's anointed 1Sa 26:23 3027
perish one day by the *h* of Saul 1Sa 27:1 3027
so shall I escape out of his *h* 1Sa 27:1 3027
rent the kingdom out of thine *h* 1Sa 28:17 3027
into the *h* of the Philistines 1Sa 28:19 3027
into the *h* of the Philistines 1Sa 28:19 3027
and I have put my life in my *h* 1Sa 28:21 3709
that came against us into our *h* 1Sa 30:23 3027
afraid to stretch forth thine *h* 2Sa 1:14 3027
he turned not to the right *h* nor 2Sa 2:19
to thy right *h* or to thy left 2Sa 2:21
thee into the *h* of David, that 2Sa 3:8 3027
my *h* shall be with thee, to bring 2Sa 3:12 3027
By the *h* of my servant David I 2Sa 3:18 3027
out of the *h* of the Philistines 2Sa 3:18 3027
out of the *h* of all their enemies 2Sa 3:18 3027
now require his blood of your *h* 2Sa 4:11 3027
thou deliver them into mine *h* 2Sa 5:19 3027
the Philistines into thine *h* 2Sa 5:19 3027
put forth his *h* to the ark of God 2Sa 6:6
out of the *h* of the Philistines 2Sa 8:1 3027
sent to comfort him by the *h* of 2Sa 10:2 3027
into the *h* of Abishai his brother 2Sa 10:10 3027
and sent it by the *h* of Uriah 2Sa 11:14 3027
thee out of the *h* of Saul 2Sa 12:7 3027
he sent by the *h* of Nathan the 2Sa 12:25 3027
I may see it, and eat it at her *h* 2Sa 13:5 3027
my sight, that I may eat at her *h* 2Sa 13:6 3027
that I may eat of thine *h* 2Sa 13:10 3027
laid her *h* on her head, and went 2Sa 13:19 3027
h of the man that would destroy 2Sa 14:16 3709
Is not the *h* of Joab with thee in 2Sa 14:19 3027

none can turn to the right *h* or 2Sa 14:19
him obeisance, he put forth his *h* 2Sa 15:5 3027
mighty men were on his right *h* 2Sa 16:6
into the *h* of Absalom thy son 2Sa 16:8 3027
of the people under the *h* of Joab 2Sa 18:2 3027
a third part under the *h* of 2Sa 18:2 3027
under the *h* of Ittai the Gittite 2Sa 18:2 3027
shekels of silver in mine *h* 2Sa 18:12 3709
mine *h* against the king's son 2Sa 18:12 3027
And he took three darts in his *h* 2Sa 18:14 3027
their *h* against my lord the king 2Sa 18:28 3027
us out of the *h* of our enemies 2Sa 19:9 3709
out of the *h* of the Philistines 2Sa 19:9 3709
with the right *h* to kiss him 2Sa 20:9 3027
to the sword that was in Joab's *h* 2Sa 20:10 3027
lifted up his *h* against the king 2Sa 20:21 3027
that had on every *h* six fingers 2Sa 21:20 3027
Gath, and fell by the *h* of David 2Sa 21:22 3027
and by the *h* of his servants 2Sa 21:22 3027
out of the *h* of all his enemies 2Sa 22:1 3709
enemies, and out of the *h* of Saul 2Sa 22:1 3709
Philistines until his *h* was weary 2Sa 23:10 3027
his *h* clave unto the sword 2Sa 23:10 3027
the Egyptian had a spear in his *h* 2Sa 23:21 3027
the spear out of the Egyptian's *h* 2Sa 23:21 3027
fall now into the *h* of the LORD 2Sa 24:14 3027
let me not fall into the *h* of man 2Sa 24:14 3027
the angel stretched out his *h* 2Sa 24:16 3027
stay now thine *h* 2Sa 24:16 3027
let thine *h*, I pray thee, be 2Sa 24:17 3027
and she sat on his right *h* 1Kin 2:19
king Solomon sent by the *h* of 1Kin 2:25 3027
established in the *h* of Solomon 1Kin 2:46 3027
it was an *h* breadth thick, and the 1Kin 7:26 2947
and hath with his *h* fulfilled it 1Kin 8:15 3027
and hast fulfilled it with thine *h* 1Kin 8:24 3027
great name, and of thy strong *h* 1Kin 8:42 3027
by the *h* of Moses thy servant 1Kin 8:53 3027
by the *h* of Moses his servant 1Kin 8:56 3027
rend it out of the *h* of thy son 1Kin 11:12 3027
lifted up his *h* against the king 1Kin 11:26 3027
lifted up his *h* against the king 1Kin 11:27 3027
kingdom out of the *h* of Solomon 1Kin 11:31 3027
the whole kingdom out of his *h* 1Kin 11:34 3027
the kingdom out of his son's *h* 1Kin 11:35 3027
he put forth his *h* from the altar 1Kin 13:4 3027
And his *h*, which he put forth 1Kin 13:4 3027
that my *h* may be restored me 1Kin 13:6 3027
the king's *h* was restored him 1Kin 13:6 3027
which he spake by the *h* of his 1Kin 14:18 3027
them into the *h* of his servants 1Kin 15:18 3027
also by the *h* of the prophet Jehu 1Kin 16:7 3027
a morsel of bread in thine *h* 1Kin 17:11 3027
thy servant into the *h* of Ahab 1Kin 18:9 3027
out of the sea, like a man's *h* 1Kin 18:44 3709
the *h* of the LORD was on Elijah 1Kin 18:46 3027
they shall put it in their *h* 1Kin 20:6 3027
deliver it into thine *h* this day 1Kin 20:13 3027
this great multitude into thine *h* 1Kin 20:28 3027
thou hast let go out of thy *h* a 1Kin 20:42 3027
out of the *h* of the king of Syria 1Kin 22:3 3027
deliver it into the *h* of the king 1Kin 22:6 3027
deliver it into the king's *h* 1Kin 22:12 3027
deliver it into the *h* of the king 1Kin 22:15 3027
standing by him on his right *h* 1Kin 22:19
of his chariot, Turn thine *h* 1Kin 22:34 3027
deliver them into the *h* of Moab 2Kin 3:10 3027
deliver them into the *h* of Moab 2Kin 3:13 3027
that the *h* of the LORD came upon 2Kin 3:15 3027
the Moabites also into your *h* 2Kin 3:18 3027
and take my staff in thine *h* 2Kin 4:29 3027
strike his *h* over the place, and 2Kin 5:11 3027
there, and he leaneth on my *h* 2Kin 5:18 3027
tower, he took them from their *h* 2Kin 5:24 3027
And he put out his *h*, and took it 2Kin 6:7 3027
Then a lord on whose *h* the king 2Kin 7:2 3027
appointed the lord on whose *h* he 2Kin 7:17 3027
Hazael, Take a present in thine *h* 2Kin 8:8 3027
from under the *h* of Judah 2Kin 8:20 3027
the *h* of Judah unto this day 2Kin 8:22 3027
take this box of oil in thine *h* 2Kin 9:1 3027
of the LORD, at the *h* of Jezebel 2Kin 9:7 3027
If it be, give me thine *h* 2Kin 10:15 3027
And he gave him his *h* 2Kin 10:15 3027
man with his weapons in his *h* 2Kin 11:8 3027
man with his weapons in his *h* 2Kin 11:11 3027
into whose *h* they delivered the 2Kin 12:15 3027
the *h* of Hazael king of Syria 2Kin 13:3 3027
into the *h* of Ben-hadad the son 2Kin 13:3 3027
from under the *h* of the Syrians 2Kin 13:5 3027
Israel, Put thine *h* upon the bow 2Kin 13:16 3027
And he put his *h* upon it 2Kin 13:16 3027
h of Ben-hadad the son of Hazael 2Kin 13:25 3027
h of Jehoahaz his father by war 2Kin 13:25 3027
kingdom was confirmed in his *h* 2Kin 14:5 3027
by the *h* of his servant Jonah 2Kin 14:25 3027
but he saved them by the *h* of 2Kin 14:27 3027
that his *h* might be with him to 2Kin 15:19 3027
to confirm the kingdom in his *h* 2Kin 15:19 3027
save me out of the *h* of the king 2Kin 16:7 3709
out of the *h* of the king of 2Kin 16:7 3709
from under the *h* of Pharaoh king 2Kin 17:7 3027
them into the *h* of spoilers 2Kin 17:20 3027
out of the *h* of all your enemies 2Kin 17:39 3027
a man lean, it will go into his *h* 2Kin 18:21 3709
able to deliver you out of his *h* 2Kin 18:29 3027
into the *h* of the king of Assyria 2Kin 18:30 3027
of the *h* of the king of Assyria 2Kin 18:33 3027
delivered Samaria out of mine *h* 2Kin 18:34 3027
their country out of mine *h* 2Kin 18:35 3027
deliver Jerusalem out of mine *h* 2Kin 18:35 3027
into the *h* of the king of Assyria 2Kin 19:10 3027
letter of the *h* of the messengers 2Kin 19:14 3027
thee, save thou us out of his *h* 2Kin 19:19 3027

this city out of the *h* of the 2Kin 20:6 3709
them into the *h* of their enemies 2Kin 21:14 3027
to the right *h* or to the left 2Kin 22:2
the *h* of the doers of the work 2Kin 22:5 3027
that was delivered into their *h* 2Kin 22:7 3027
the *h* of them that do the work 2Kin 22:9 3027
left *h* at the gate of the city 2Kin 23:8 3027
which were on the right *h* of the 2Kin 23:13
that thine *h* might be with me, and 1Chr 4:10 3027
Hagarites, who fell by their *h* 1Chr 5:10 3027
were delivered into their *h* 1Chr 5:20 3027
Judah and Jerusalem by the *h* of 1Chr 6:15 3027
Asaph, who stood on his right *h* 1Chr 6:39
of Merari stood on the left *h* 1Chr 6:44
in the Egyptian's *h* was a spear 1Chr 11:23 3027
the spear out of the Egyptian's *h* 1Chr 11:23 3027
and could use both the right *h* 1Chr 12:2
put forth his *h* to hold the ark 1Chr 13:9 3027
because he put his *h* to the ark 1Chr 13:10 3027
thou deliver them into mine *h* 1Chr 14:10 3027
I will deliver them into thine *h* 1Chr 14:10 3027
mine *h* like the breaking forth of 1Chr 14:11 3027
the LORD into the *h* of Asaph 1Chr 16:7 3027
out of the *h* of the Philistines 1Chr 18:1 3027
unto the *h* of Abishai his brother 1Chr 19:11 3027
four and twenty, six on each *h* 1Chr 20:6
and they fell by the *h* of David 1Chr 20:8 3027
and by the *h* of his servants 1Chr 20:8 3027
fall now into the *h* of the LORD 1Chr 21:13 3027
let me not fall into the *h* of man 1Chr 21:13 3027
It is enough, stay now thine *h* 1Chr 21:15 3027
having a drawn sword in his *h* 1Chr 21:16 3027
let thine *h*, I pray thee, O LORD 1Chr 21:17 3027
of the land into mine *h* 1Chr 22:18 3027
it was under the *h* of Shelomith 1Chr 26:28 3027
in writing by his *h* upon me 1Chr 28:19 3027
by the *h* of Jehiel the Gershonite 1Chr 29:8 3027
and in thine *h* is power and might 1Chr 29:12 3027
in thine *h* it is to make great 1Chr 29:12 3027
thine holy name cometh of thine *h* 1Chr 29:16 3027
the temple, one on the right *h* 2Chr 3:17
of that on the right *h* Jachin 2Chr 3:17 3027
and put five on the right *h* 2Chr 4:6
the temple, five on the right *h* 2Chr 4:7
and hast fulfilled it with thine *h* 2Chr 6:15 3027
name's sake, and thy mighty *h* 2Chr 6:32 3027
which he spake by the *h* of Ahijah 2Chr 10:15 3027
also left you in the *h* of Shishak 2Chr 12:5 3027
Jerusalem by the *h* of Shishak 2Chr 12:7 3027
in the *h* of the sons of David 2Chr 13:8 3027
God delivered them into their *h* 2Chr 13:16 3027
of Syria escaped out of thine *h* 2Chr 16:7 3027
he delivered them into thine *h* 2Chr 16:8 3027
stablished the kingdom in his *h* 2Chr 17:5 3027
will deliver it into the king's *h* 2Chr 18:5 3027
deliver it into the *h* of the king 2Chr 18:11 3027
shall be delivered into your *h* 2Chr 18:14 3027
of heaven standing on his right *h* 2Chr 18:18
to his chariot man, Turn thine *h* 2Chr 18:33 3027
in thine *h* is there not power and 2Chr 20:6 3027
the *h* of Judah unto this day 2Chr 21:10 3027
Libnah revolt from under his *h* 2Chr 21:10 3027
man with his weapons in his *h* 2Chr 23:7 3027
man having his weapon in his *h* 2Chr 23:10 3027
the *h* of the priests the Levites 2Chr 23:18 3027
office by the *h* of the Levites 2Chr 24:11 3027
a very great host into their *h* 2Chr 24:24 3027
their own people out of thine *h* 2Chr 25:15 3027
them into the *h* of their enemies 2Chr 25:20 3027
by the *h* of Jeiel the scribe 2Chr 26:11 3027
under the *h* of Hananiah, one of 2Chr 26:11 3027
And under their *h* was an army 2Chr 26:13 3027
a censer in his *h* to burn incense 2Chr 26:19 3027
into the *h* of the king of Syria 2Chr 28:5 3027
into the *h* of the king of Israel 2Chr 28:5 3027
hath delivered them into your *h* 2Chr 28:9 3027
of the *h* of the kings of Assyria 2Chr 30:6 3709
Also in Judah the *h* of God was to 2Chr 30:12 3027
received of the *h* of the Levites 2Chr 30:16 3027
overseers under the *h* of Cononiah 2Chr 31:13 3027
of the *h* of the king of Assyria 2Chr 32:11 3709
deliver their lands out of mine *h* 2Chr 32:13 3027
deliver his people out of mine *h* 2Chr 32:14 3027
able to deliver you out of mine *h* 2Chr 32:14 3027
deliver his people out of mine *h* 2Chr 32:15 3027
out of the *h* of my fathers 2Chr 32:15 3027
God deliver you out of mine *h* 2Chr 32:15 3027
their people out of mine *h* 2Chr 32:17 3027
deliver his people out of mine *h* 2Chr 32:17 3027
of Jerusalem from the *h* of 2Chr 32:22 3027
from the *h* of all other, and 2Chr 32:22 3027
the ordinances by the *h* of Moses 2Chr 33:8 3027
declined neither to the right *h* 2Chr 34:2 3225
had gathered of the *h* of Manasseh 2Chr 34:9 3027
they put it in the *h* of the 2Chr 34:10 3027
it into the *h* of the overseers 2Chr 34:17 3027
and to the *h* of the workmen 2Chr 34:17 3027
of the LORD by the *h* of Moses 2Chr 35:6 3027
he gave them all into his *h* 2Chr 36:17 3027
the *h* of Mithredath the treasurer Ezr 1:8 3027
he gave them into the *h* of Ezr 5:12 3028
shall put to their *h* to alter Ezr 6:12 3028
according to the *h* of the LORD Ezr 7:6 3027
to the good *h* of his God upon him Ezr 7:9 3027
of thy God which is in thine *h* Ezr 7:14 3028
of thy God, that is in thine *h* Ezr 7:25 3028
I was strengthened as the *h* of Ezr 7:28 3027
by the good *h* of our God upon us Ezr 8:18 3027
The *h* of our God is upon all them Ezr 8:22 3027
weighed unto their *h* six hundred Ezr 8:26 3027
the *h* of our God was upon us, and Ezr 8:31 3027
us from the *h* of the enemy Ezr 8:31 3709
h of Meremoth the son of Uriah Ezr 8:33 3027
the *h* of the princes and rulers Ezr 9:2 3027

been delivered into the *h* of the Ezr 9:7 3027
great power, and by thy strong *h* Neh 1:10 3027
to the good *h* of my God upon me Neh 2:8 3027
Then I told them of the *h* of my Neh 2:18 3027
and with the other *h* held a weapon Neh 4:17
time with an open letter in his *h* Neh 6:5 3027
and Maaseiah, on his right *h* Neh 8:4 3225
and on his left *h*, Pedaiah, and Neh 8:4 8040
by the *h* of Moses thy servant Neh 9:14 3027
them into the *h* of their enemies Neh 9:27 3027
out of the *h* of their enemies Neh 9:27 3027
them in the *h* of their enemies Neh 9:28 3027
gavest thou them into the *h* of Neh 9:30 3027
was at the king's *h* in all Neh 11:24 3027
h upon the wall toward the dung Neh 12:31 3225
sought to lay *h* on the king Est 2:21 3027
the king took his ring from his *h* Est 3:10 3027
golden sceptre that was in his *h* Est 5:2 3027
who sought to lay *h* on the king Est 6:2 3027
horse be delivered to the *h* of Est 6:9 3027
he laid his *h* upon the Jews Est 8:7 3027
to lay *h* on such as sought their Est 9:2 3027
the spoil laid they not their *h* Est 9:10 3027
on the prey they laid not their *h* Est 9:15 3027
But put forth thine *h* now Job 1:11 3027
himself put not forth thine *h* Job 1:12 3027
But put forth thine *h* now Job 2:5 3027
Satan, Behold, he is in thine *h* Job 2:6 3027
we receive good at the *h* of God Job 2:10 854
and from the *h* of the mighty Job 5:15 3027
that he would let loose his *h* Job 6:9 3027
Or, Deliver me from the enemy's *h* Job 6:23 3027
me from the *h* of the mighty Job 6:23 3027
is given into the *h* of the wicked Job 9:24 3027
that might lay his *h* upon us both Job 9:33 3027
that can deliver out of thine *h* Job 10:7 3027
If iniquity be in thine *h* Job 11:14 3027
into whose *h* God bringeth Job 12:6 3027
not in all these that the *h* of Job 12:9 3027
In whose *h* is the soul of every Job 12:10 3027
teeth, and put my life in mine *h* Job 13:14 3709
Withdraw thine *h* far from me Job 13:21 3709
day of darkness is ready at his *h* Job 15:23 3027
stretcheth out his *h* against God Job 15:25 3027
for the *h* of God hath touched me Job 19:21 3027
every *h* of the wicked shall come Job 20:22 3027
lay your *h* upon your mouth Job 21:5 3027
Lo, their good is not in their *h* Job 21:16 3027
On the left *h*, where he doth work Job 23:9 8040
he hideth himself on the right *h* Job 23:9 3225
his *h* hath formed the crooked Job 26:13 3027
I will teach you by the *h* of God Job 27:11 3027
he would fain flee out of his *h* Job 27:22 3027
putteth forth his *h* upon the rock Job 28:9 3027
laid their *h* on their mouth Job 29:9 3709
my bow was renewed in my *h* Job 29:20 3027
Upon my right *h* rise the youth Job 30:12 3225
with thy strong *h* thou opposest Job 30:21 3027
stretch out his *h* to the grave Job 30:24 3027
up my *h* against the fatherless Job 31:21 3027
because mine *h* had gotten much Job 31:25 3027
or my mouth hath kissed my *h* Job 31:27 3027
neither shall my *h* be heavy upon Job 33:7 405
shall be taken away without *h* Job 34:20 3027
or what receiveth he of thine *h* Job 35:7 3027
He sealeth up the *h* of every man Job 37:7 3027
I will lay mine *h* upon my mouth Job 40:4 3027
thine own right *h* can save thee Job 40:14 3225
Lay thine *h* upon him, remember Job 41:8 3709
O God, lift up thine *h* Ps 10:12 3027
spite, to requite it with thy *h* Ps 10:14 3027
because he is at my right *h* Ps 16:8 3225
at thy right *h* there are Ps 16:11 3225
h them which put their trust in Ps 17:7 3225
From men which are thy *h*, O LORD, Ps 17:14 3027
him from the *h* of all his enemies Ps 18:*t* 3709
and from the *h* of Saul Ps 18:*t* 3027
thy right *h* hath holden me up, and Ps 18:35 3225
saving strength of his right *h* Ps 20:6 3225
Thine *h* shall find out all thine Ps 21:8 3027
thy right *h* shall find out those Ps 21:8 3225
their right *h* is full of bribes Ps 26:10 3225
Into thine *h* I commit my spirit Ps 31:5 3027
me up into the *h* of the enemy Ps 31:8 3027
My times are in thy *h* Ps 31:15 3027
me from the *h* of mine enemies Ps 31:15 3027
night thy *h* was heavy upon me Ps 32:4 3027
let not the *h* of the wicked Ps 36:11 3027
the LORD upholdeth him with his *h* Ps 37:24 3027
LORD will not leave him in his *h* Ps 37:33 3027
in me, and thy *h* presseth me sore Ps 38:2 3027
consumed by the blow of thine *h* Ps 39:10 3027
drive out the heathen with thy *h* Ps 44:2 3027
but thy right *h*, and thine arm, and Ps 44:3 3225
thy right *h* shall teach thee Ps 45:4 3225
upon thy right *h* did stand the Ps 45:9 3225
thy right *h* is full of Ps 48:10 3225
save with thy right *h*, and hear me Ps 60:5 3225
thy right *h* upholdeth me Ps 63:8 3225
out of the *h* of the wicked Ps 71:4 3027
out of the *h* of the unrighteous Ps 71:4 3709
thou hast holden me by my right *h* Ps 73:23 3027
Why withdrawest thou thy *h* Ps 74:11 3027
even thy right *h* Ps 74:11 3225
For in the *h* of the LORD there is Ps 75:8 3027
of the right *h* of the most High Ps 77:10 3225
like a flock by the *h* of Moses Ps 77:20 3027
They remembered not his *h* Ps 78:42 3027
which his right *h* had purchased Ps 78:54 3225
and his glory into the enemy's *h* Ps 78:61 3027
which thy right *h* hath planted Ps 80:15 3225
Let thy *h* be upon the man of thy Ps 80:17 3027
be upon the man of thy right *h* Ps 80:17 3225
turned my *h* against their Ps 81:14 3027

them out of the *h* of the wicked Ps 82:4 3027
and they are cut off from thy *h* Ps 88:5 3027
thy *h*, and high is thy right *h* Ps 89:13 3225
With whom my *h* shall be Ps 89:21 3027
I will set his *h* also in the sea, Ps 89:25 3027
his right *h* in the rivers Ps 89:25 3225
up the right *h* of his adversaries Ps 89:42 3225
his soul from the *h* of the grave Ps 89:48 3027
and ten thousand at thy right *h* Ps 91:7 3225
In his *h* are the deep places of Ps 95:4 3027
pasture, and the sheep of his *h* Ps 95:7 3027
them out of the *h* of the wicked Ps 97:10 3027
his right *h*, and his holy arm, Ps 98:1 3225
thou openest thine *h*, they are Ps 104:28 3027
from the *h* of him that hated them Ps 106:10 3027
them from the *h* of the enemy Ps 106:10 3027
he lifted up his *h* against them Ps 106:26 3027
them into the *h* of the heathen Ps 106:41 3027
into subjection under their *h* Ps 106:42 3027
redeemed from the *h* of the enemy Ps 107:2 3027
save with thy right *h*, and answer Ps 108:6 3225
and let Satan stand at his right *h* Ps 109:6 3225
they may know that this is thy *h* Ps 109:27 3027
stand at the right *h* of the poor Ps 109:31 3225
my Lord, Sit thou at my right *h* Ps 110:1 3225
The LORD at thy right *h* shall Ps 110:5 3225
the right *h* of the LORD doeth Ps 118:15 3225
The right *h* of the LORD is Ps 118:16 3225
the right *h* of the LORD doeth Ps 118:16 3225
My soul is continually in my *h* Ps 119:109 3709
Let thine *h* help me Ps 119:173 3027
is thy shade upon thy right *h* Ps 121:5 3225
look unto the *h* of their masters Ps 123:2 3027
maiden unto the *h* of her mistress Ps 123:2 3027
are in the *h* of a mighty man Ps 127:4 3027
the mower filleth not his *h* Ps 129:7 3709
With a strong *h*, and with a Ps 136:12 3027
let my right *h* forget her cunning Ps 137:5 3225
thine *h* against the wrath of mine Ps 138:7 3027
thy right *h* shall save me Ps 138:7 3225
before, and laid thine *h* upon me Ps 139:5 3709
Even there shall thy *h* lead me Ps 139:10 3027
thy right *h* shall hold me Ps 139:10 3225
I looked on my right *h*, and beheld Ps 142:4 3225
Send thine *h* from above Ps 144:7 3027
from the *h* of strange children Ps 144:7 3027
their right *h* is a right *h* of Ps 144:8 3225
me from the *h* of strange children Ps 144:11 3027
their right *h* is a right *h* of Ps 144:11 3225
Thou openest thine *h*, and Ps 145:16 3027
and a twoedged sword in their *h* Ps 149:6 3027
I have stretched out my *h* Prov 1:24 3027
Length of days is in her right *h* Prov 3:16 3225
and in her left *h* riches and honour Prov 3:16 8040
in the power of thine *h* to do it Prov 3:27 3027
to the right *h* nor to the left Prov 4:27 3227
stricken thy *h* with a stranger Prov 6:1 3709
art come into the *h* of thy friend Prov 6:3 3709
as a roe from the *h* of the hunter Prov 6:5 3027
a bird from the *h* of the fowler Prov 6:5 3027
poor that dealeth with a slack *h* Prov 10:4 3709
but the *h* of the diligent maketh Prov 10:4 3027
Though *h* join in *h*, the wicked Prov 11:21 3027
The *h* of the diligent shall bear Prov 12:24 3027
though *h* join in *h*, he shall Prov 16:5 3027
in the *h* of a fool to get wisdom Prov 17:16 3027
man hideth his *h* in his bosom Prov 19:24 3027
heart is in the *h* of the LORD Prov 21:1 3027
that sendeth a message by the *h* Prov 26:6 3027
goeth up into the *h* of a drunkard Prov 26:9 3027
hideth his *h* in his bosom Prov 26:15 3027
and the ointment of his right *h* Prov 27:16 3225
lay thine *h* upon thy mouth Prov 30:32 3027
stretcheth out her *h* to the poor Prov 31:20 3709
that it was from the *h* of God Eccl 2:24 3027
son, and there is nothing in his *h* Eccl 5:14 3027
which he may carry away in his *h* Eccl 5:15 3027
from this withdraw not thine *h* Eccl 7:18 3027
their works, are in the *h* of God Eccl 9:1 3027
Whatsoever thy *h* findeth to do Eccl 9:10 3027
man's heart is at his right *h* Eccl 10:2 3225
the evening withhold not thine *h* Eccl 11:6 3027
His left *h* is under my head, and Song 2:6 8040
his right *h* doth embrace me Song 2:6 3225
My beloved put in his *h* by the Song 5:4 3027
His left *h* should be under my Song 8:3 8040
his right *h* should embrace me Song 8:3 3225
who hath required this at your *h* Is 1:12 3027
And I will turn my *h* upon thee Is 1:25 3027
and let this ruin be under thy *h* Is 3:6 3027
forth his *h* against them, and hath Is 5:25 3027
but his *h* is stretched out still Is 5:25 3027
me, having a live coal in his *h* Is 6:6 3027
spake thus to me with a strong *h* Is 8:11 3027
but his *h* is stretched out still Is 9:12 3027
but his *h* is stretched out still Is 9:17 3027
And he shall snatch on the right *h* Is 9:20 3225
and he shall eat on the left *h* Is 9:20 8040
but his *h* is stretched out still Is 9:21 3027
but his *h* is stretched out still Is 10:4 3027
the staff in their *h* is mine Is 10:5 3027
As my *h* hath found the kingdoms Is 10:10 3027
strength of my *h* I have done it Is 10:13 3027
my *h* hath found as a nest the Is 10:14 3027
he shall shake his *h* against the Is 10:32 3027
put his *h* on the cockatrice' den Is 11:8 3027
his *h* again the second time to Is 11:11 3027
they shall lay their *h* upon Edom Is 11:14 3027
he shake his *h* over the river Is 11:15 3027
the voice unto them, shake the *h* Is 13:2 3027
for the day of the LORD is at *h* Is 13:6 7138
this is the *h* that is stretched Is 14:26 3027
his *h* is stretched out, and who Is 14:27 3027
over into the *h* of a cruel lord Is 19:4 3027
of the *h* of the LORD of hosts Is 19:16 3027
commit thy government into his *h* Is 22:21 3027
stretched out his *h* over the sea Is 23:11 3027
shall the *h* of the LORD rest Is 25:10 3027
when thy *h* is lifted up, they Is 26:11 3027
cast down to the earth with the *h* Is 28:2 3027
is yet in his *h* he eateth it up Is 28:4 3709
it, when ye turn to the right *h* Is 30:21 3027
the LORD shall stretch out his *h* Is 31:3 3027
his *h* hath divided it unto them Is 34:17 3027
a man lean, it will go into his *h* Is 36:6 3709
into the *h* of the king of Assyria Is 36:15 3027
of the *h* of the king of Assyria Is 36:18 3027
delivered Samaria out of my *h* Is 36:19 3027
delivered their land out of my *h* Is 36:20 3027
deliver Jerusalem out of my *h* Is 36:20 3027
into the *h* of the king of Assyria Is 37:10 3027
from the *h* of the messengers Is 37:14 3027
LORD our God, save us from his *h* Is 37:20 3027
this city out of the *h* of the Is 38:6 3709
LORD's *h* double for all her sins Is 40:2 3027
Lord GOD will come with strong *h* Is 40:10
the waters in the hollow of his *h* Is 40:12
the right *h* of my righteousness Is 41:10 3225
thy God will hold thy right *h* Is 41:13 3225
that the *h* of the LORD hath done Is 41:20 3027
and will hold thine *h*, and will Is 42:6 3027
none that can deliver out of my *h* Is 43:13 3027
with his *h* unto the LORD, and Is 44:5 3027
Is there not a lie in my right *h* Is 44:20 3225
whose right *h* I have holden, to Is 45:1 3225
and given them into thine *h* Is 47:6 3027
Mine *h* also hath laid the Is 48:13 3027
my right *h* hath spanned the Is 48:13 3225
shadow of his *h* hath he hid me Is 49:2 3027
lift up mine *h* to the Gentiles Is 49:22 3027
Is my *h* shortened at all, that it Is 50:2 3027
This shall ye have of mine *h* Is 50:11 3027
thee in the shadow of mine *h* Is 51:16 3027
which hast drunk at the *h* of the Is 51:17 3027
any that taketh her by the *h* of Is 51:18 3027
of thine *h* the cup of trembling Is 51:22 3027
the *h* of them that afflict thee Is 51:23 3027
the LORD shall prosper in his *h* Is 53:10 3027
shalt break forth on the right *h* Is 54:3 3225
keepeth his *h* from doing any evil Is 56:2 3027
hast found the life of thine *h* Is 57:10 3027
the LORD's *h* is not shortened, Is 59:1 3027
of glory in the *h* of the LORD Is 62:3 3027
royal diadem in the *h* of thy God Is 62:3 3709
LORD hath sworn by his right *h* Is 62:8 3225
That led them by the right *h* of Is 63:12 3225
and we all are the work of thy *h* Is 64:8 3027
all those things hath mine *h* made Is 66:2 3027
the *h* of the LORD shall be known Is 66:14 3027
Then the LORD put forth his *h* Jer 1:9 3027
turn back thine *h* as a Jer 6:9 3027
for I will stretch out my *h* upon Jer 6:12 3027
LORD, that thou die not by our *h* Jer 11:21 3027
my soul into the *h* of her enemies Jer 12:7 3709
I stretch out my *h* against thee Jer 15:6 3027
I sat alone because of thy *h* Jer 15:17 3027
thee out of the *h* of the wicked Jer 15:21 3027
thee out of the *h* of the terrible Jer 15:21 3709
I will cause them to know mine *h* Jer 16:21 3027
was marred in the *h* of the potter Jer 18:4 3027
as the clay is in the potter's *h* Jer 18:6 3027
so are ye in mine *h* Jer 18:6 3027
into the *h* of the king of Babylon Jer 20:4 3027
give into the *h* of their enemies Jer 20:5 3027
the poor from the *h* of evildoers Jer 20:13 3027
you with an outstretched *h* Jer 21:5 3027
into the *h* of Nebuchadrezzar king Jer 21:7 3027
into the *h* of their enemies, and Jer 21:7 3027
into the *h* of those that seek Jer 21:7 3027
into the *h* of the king of Babylon Jer 21:10 3027
out of the *h* of the oppressor Jer 21:12 3027
out of the *h* of the oppressor Jer 22:3 3027
were the signet upon my right *h* Jer 22:24 3027
I will give thee into the *h* of Jer 22:25 3027
into the *h* of them whose face Jer 22:25 3027
even into the *h* of Nebuchadrezzar Jer 22:25 3027
into the *h* of the Chaldeans Jer 22:25 3027
Am I a God at *h*, saith the LORD, Jer 23:23 7138
the wine cup of this fury at my *h* Jer 25:15 3027
took I the cup at the LORD's *h* Jer 25:17 3027
take the cup at thine *h* to drink Jer 25:28 3027
As for me, behold, I am in your *h* Jer 26:14 3027
Nevertheless the *h* of Ahikam the Jer 26:24 3027
the *h* of the people to put him to Jer 26:24 3027
by the *h* of the messengers which Jer 27:3 3027
h of Nebuchadnezzar the king of Jer 27:6 3027
I have consumed them by his *h* Jer 27:8 3027
By the *h* of Elasah the son of Jer 29:3 3027
the *h* of Nebuchadrezzar king of Jer 29:21 3027
ransomed him from the *h* of him Jer 31:11 3027
h to bring them out of the land Jer 31:32 3027
into the *h* of the king of Babylon Jer 32:3 3027
out of the *h* of the Chaldeans Jer 32:4 3027
into the *h* of the king of Babylon Jer 32:4 3027
with wonders, and with a strong *h* Jer 32:21 3027
given into the *h* of the Chaldeans Jer 32:24 3027
given into the *h* of the Chaldeans Jer 32:25 3027
city into the *h* of the Chaldeans Jer 32:28 3027
into the *h* of Nebuchadrezzar king Jer 32:28 3027
h of the king of Babylon by the Jer 32:36 3027
given into the *h* of the Chaldeans Jer 32:43 3027
into the *h* of the king of Babylon Jer 34:2 3027
shalt not escape out of his *h* Jer 34:3 3027
be taken, and delivered into his *h* Jer 34:3 3027
them into the *h* of their enemies Jer 34:20 3027
into the *h* of them that seek Jer 34:20 3027
give into the *h* of their enemies Jer 34:21 3027
into the *h* of them that seek Jer 34:21 3027
into the *h* of the king of Jer 34:21 3027
Take in thine *h* the roll wherein Jer 36:14 3027
of Neriah took the roll in his *h* Jer 36:14 3027
into the *h* of the king of Babylon Jer 37:17 3027
h of the king of Babylon's army Jer 38:3 3027
said, Behold, he is in your *h* Jer 38:5 3027
will I give thee into the *h* of Jer 38:16 3027
given into the *h* of the Chaldeans Jer 38:18 3027
shalt not escape out of their *h* Jer 38:18 3027
lest they deliver me into their *h* Jer 38:19 3027
shalt not escape out of their *h* Jer 38:23 3027
by the *h* of the king of Babylon Jer 38:23 3027
the *h* of the men of whom thou art Jer 39:17 3027
chains which were upon thine *h* Jer 40:4 3027
offerings and incense in their *h* Jer 41:5 3027
you, and to deliver you from his *h* Jer 42:11 3027
us into the *h* of the Chaldeans Jer 43:3 3027
Take great stones in thine *h* Jer 43:9 3027
mouths, and fulfilled with your *h* Jer 44:25 3027
Egypt into the *h* of his enemies Jer 44:30 3027
into the *h* of them that seek his Jer 44:30 3027
the *h* of Nebuchadrezzar king of Jer 44:30 3027
the *h* of the people of the north Jer 46:24 3027
I will deliver them into the *h* of Jer 46:26 3027
into the *h* of Nebuchadrezzar king Jer 46:26 3027
into the *h* of his servants Jer 46:26 3027
she hath given her *h* Jer 50:15 3027
been a golden cup in the LORD's *h* Jer 51:7 3027
will stretch out mine *h* upon thee Jer 51:25 3027
fell into the *h* of the enemy Lam 1:7 3027
h upon all her pleasant things Lam 1:10 3027
transgressions is bound by his *h* Lam 1:14 3027
his right *h* from before the enemy Lam 2:3 3225
with his right *h* as an adversary Lam 2:4 3225
he hath given up into the *h* of Lam 2:7 3027
withdrawn his *h* from destroying Lam 2:8 3027
he turneth his *h* against me all Lam 3:3 3027
have given the *h* to the Egyptians Lam 5:6 3027
doth deliver us out of their *h* Lam 5:8 3027
Princes are hanged up by their *h* Lam 5:12 3027
the *h* of the LORD was there upon Eze 1:3 3027
behold, an *h* was sent unto me Eze 2:9 3027
but the *h* of the LORD was strong Eze 3:14 3027
blood will I require at thine *h* Eze 3:18 3027
blood will I require at thine *h* Eze 3:20 3027
the *h* of the LORD was there upon Eze 3:22 3027
Smite with thine *h*, and stamp with Eze 6:11 3709
will I stretch out my *h* upon them Eze 6:14 3027
that the *h* of the Lord GOD fell Eze 8:1 3027
And he put forth the form of an *h* Eze 8:3 3027
every man his censer in his *h* Eze 8:11 3027
his destroying weapon in his *h* Eze 9:1 3027
man a slaughter weapon in his *h* Eze 9:2 3027
fill thine *h* with coals of fire Eze 10:2 2651
one cherub stretched forth his *h* Eze 10:7 3027
of a man's *h* under their wings Eze 10:8 3027
through the wall with mine *h* Eze 12:7 3027
say unto them, The days are at *h* Eze 12:23 7126
mine *h* shall be upon the prophets Eze 13:9 3027
deliver my people out of your *h* Eze 13:21 3027
be no more in your *h* to be hunted Eze 13:21 3027
deliver my people out of your *h* Eze 13:23 3027
I will stretch out my *h* upon him Eze 14:9 3027
will I stretch out mine *h* upon it Eze 14:13 3027
have stretched out my *h* over thee Eze 16:27 3027
will also give thee into their *h* Eze 16:39 3027
that dwell at thy left *h* Eze 16:46 8040
that dwelleth at thy right *h* Eze 16:46 3225
she strengthen the *h* of the poor Eze 16:49 3027
when, lo, he had given his *h* Eze 17:18 3027
withdrawn his *h* from iniquity Eze 18:8 3027
taken off his *h* from the poor Eze 18:17 3027
lifted up mine *h* unto the seed of Eze 20:5 3027
when I lifted up mine *h* unto them Eze 20:5 3027
that I lifted up mine *h* unto them Eze 20:6 3027
Yet also I lifted up my *h* unto Eze 20:15 3027
Nevertheless I withdrew mine *h* Eze 20:22 3027
I lifted up mine *h* unto them also Eze 20:23 3027
up mine *h* to give it to them Eze 20:28 3027
Lord GOD, surely with a mighty *h* Eze 20:33 3027
ye are scattered, with a mighty *h* Eze 20:34 3027
mine *h* to give it to your fathers Eze 20:42 3027
give it into the *h* of the slayer Eze 21:11 3027
or other, either on the right *h* Eze 21:16 3221
At his right *h* was the divination Eze 21:22 3225
ye shall be taken with the *h* Eze 21:24 3079
thee into the *h* of brutish men Eze 21:31 3027
h at thy dishonest gain which Eze 22:13 3079
her into the *h* of her lovers Eze 23:9 3027
into the *h* of the Assyrians, upon Eze 23:9 3027
the *h* of them whom thou hatest Eze 23:28 3027
into the *h* of them from whom thy Eze 23:28 3027
will I give her cup into thine *h* Eze 23:31 3027
will stretch out mine *h* upon thee Eze 25:7 3027
also stretch out mine *h* upon Edom Eze 25:13 3027
Edom by the *h* of my people Israel Eze 25:14 3027
out mine *h* upon the Philistines Eze 25:16 3027
were the merchandise of thine *h* Eze 27:15 3027
in the *h* of him that slayeth thee Eze 28:9 3027
by the *h* of strangers Eze 28:10 3027
they took hold of thee by thy *h* Eze 29:7 3709
of Egypt to cease by the *h* of Eze 30:10 3027
the land into the *h* of the wicked Eze 30:12 3027
is therein, by the *h* of strangers Eze 30:12 3027
the sword to fall out of his *h* Eze 30:22 3027
Babylon, and put my sword in his *h* Eze 30:24 3027
into the *h* of the king of Babylon Eze 30:25 3027
delivered him into the *h* of the Eze 31:11 3027
I require at the watchman's *h* Eze 33:6 3027
blood will I require at thine *h* Eze 33:8 3027
Now the *h* of the LORD was upon me Eze 33:22 3027
will require my flock at their *h* Eze 34:10 3027
delivered them out of the *h* of Eze 34:27 3027
stretch out mine *h* against thee Eze 35:3 3027

I have lifted up mine h, Surely ... Eze 36:7 3027
for they are at h to come ... Eze 36:8 7126
The h of the LORD was upon me, and.. Eze 37:1 3027
they shall become one in thine h ... Eze 37:17 3027
which is in the h of Ephraim ... Eze 37:19 3027
and they shall be one in mine h ... Eze 37:19 3027
be in thine h before their eyes ... Eze 37:20 3027
to turn thine h upon the desolate ... Eze 38:12 3027
smite thy bow out of thy left h ... Eze 39:3 3027
arrows to fall out of thy right h ... Eze 39:3 3027
my h that I have laid upon them ... Eze 39:21 3027
them into the h of their enemies ... Eze 39:23 3027
day the h of the LORD was upon me ... Eze 40:1 3027
with a line of flax in his h ... Eze 40:3 3027
in the man's h a measuring reed ... Eze 40:5 3027
long by the cubit and an h breadth ... Eze 40:5 2948
an h broad, fastened round about ... Eze 40:43 2948
cubit is a cubit and an h breadth ... Eze 43:13 2948
I lifted up mine h against them ... Eze 44:12 3027
as his h shall attain unto ... Eze 46:7 3027
line in his h went forth eastward ... Eze 47:3 3027
the which I lifted up mine h to ... Eze 47:14 3027
king of Judah into his h, with ... Dan 1:2 3027
heaven hath he given into thine h ... Dan 2:38 3028
he will deliver us out of thine h ... Dan 3:17 3028
and none can stay his h, or say ... Dan 4:35 3028
came forth fingers of a man's h ... Dan 5:5 3028
saw the part of the h that wrote ... Dan 5:5 3028
the God in whose h thy breath is ... Dan 5:23 3028
the part of the h sent from him ... Dan 5:24 3028
be given into his h until a time ... Dan 7:25 3028
that could deliver out of his h ... Dan 8:4 3027
deliver the ram out of his h ... Dan 8:7 3027
cause craft to prosper in his h ... Dan 8:25 3027
but he shall be broken without h ... Dan 8:25 3027
the land of Egypt with a mighty h ... Dan 9:15 3027
an h touched me, which set me ... Dan 10:10 3027
shall be given into his h ... Dan 11:11 3027
which by his h shall be consumed ... Dan 11:16 3027
these shall escape out of his h ... Dan 11:41 3027
his h also upon the countries ... Dan 11:42 3027
when he held up his right h ... Dan 12:7 3225
his left h unto heaven, and sware ... Dan 12:7 8040
shall deliver her out of mine h ... Hos 2:10 3027
stretched out his h with scorners ... Hos 7:5 3027
balances of deceit are in his h ... Hos 12:7 3027
for the day of the LORD is at h ... Joel 1:15 7138
LORD cometh, for it is nigh at h ... Joel 2:1
your daughters into the h of the ... Joel 3:8 3027
I will turn mine h against Ekron ... Amos 1:8 3027
leaned his h on the wall, and a ... Amos 5:19 3027
with a plumbline in his h ... Amos 7:7 3027
thence shall mine h take them ... Amos 9:2 3027
discern between their right h ... Jonah 4:11 3235
their right h and their left h ... Jonah 4:11 8040
it is in the power of their h ... Mic 2:1 3027
thee from the h of thine enemies ... Mic 4:10 3709
Thine h shall be lifted up upon ... Mic 5:9 3027
off witchcrafts out of thine h ... Mic 5:12 3027
lay their h upon their mouth ... Mic 7:16 3027
right h shall be turned unto thee ... Hab 2:16 3225
he had horns coming out of his h ... Hab 3:4 3027
stretch out mine h upon Judah ... Zeph 1:4 3027
for the day of the LORD is at h ... Zeph 1:7 7138
out his h against the north ... Zeph 2:13 3027
by her shall hiss, and wag his h ... Zeph 2:15 3027
with a measuring line in his h ... Zec 2:1 3027
I will shake mine h upon them ... Zec 2:9 3027
at his right h to resist him ... Zec 3:1 3225
shall see the plummet in the h of ... Zec 4:10 3027
his staff in his h for very age ... Zec 8:4 3027
every one into his neighbour's h ... Zec 11:6 3027
and into the h of his king ... Zec 11:6 3027
out of their h I will not deliver ... Zec 11:6 3027
round about, on the right h ... Zec 12:6 3225
I will turn mine h upon the ... Zec 13:7 3027
one on the h of his neighbour ... Zec 14:13 3027
his h shall rise up against the ... Zec 14:13 3027
up against the h of his neighbour ... Zec 14:13 3027
I accept an offering at your h ... Mal 1:10 3027
should I accept this of your h ... Mal 1:13 3027
it with good will at your h ... Mal 2:13 3027
for the kingdom of heaven is at h ... Mt 3:2 1448
Whose fan is in his h, and he will ... Mt 3:12 5495
for the kingdom of heaven is at h ... Mt 4:17 1448
And if thy right h offend thee ... Mt 5:30 5495
let not thy left h know what thy ... Mt 6:3
know what thy right h doeth ... Mt 6:3
And Jesus put forth his h, and ... Mt 8:3 5495
And he touched her h, and the fever ... Mt 8:15 5495
lay thy h upon her, and she shall ... Mt 9:18 5495
he went in, and took her by the h ... Mt 9:25 5495
The kingdom of heaven is at h ... Mt 10:7 1448
a man which had his h withered ... Mt 12:10 5495
to the man, Stretch forth thine h ... Mt 12:13 5495
forth his h toward his disciples ... Mt 12:49 5495
Jesus stretched forth his h ... Mt 14:31 5495
Wherefore if thy h or thy foot ... Mt 18:8 5495
may sit, the one on thy right h ... Mt 20:21
but to sit on my right h, and on ... Mt 20:23
king to the servants, Bind him h ... Mt 22:13
my Lord, Sit thou on my right h ... Mt 22:44
set the sheep on his right h ... Mt 25:33
King say unto them on his right h ... Mt 25:34
say also unto them on the left h ... Mt 25:41
The Master saith, My time is at h ... Mt 26:18 1451
dippeth his h with me in the dish ... Mt 26:23 5495
behold, the hour is at h, and the ... Mt 26:45 1448
he is at h that doth betray me ... Mt 26:46 1448
with Jesus stretched out his h ... Mt 26:51 5495
sitting on the right h of power ... Mt 26:64
head, and a reed in his right h ... Mt 27:29
with him, one on the right h ... Mt 27:38
and the kingdom of God is at h ... Mk 1:15 1448
And he came and took her by the h ... Mk 1:31 5495
with compassion, put forth his h ... Mk 1:41 5495
man there which had a withered h ... Mk 3:1 5495
the man which had the withered h ... Mk 3:3 5495
the man, Stretch forth thine h ... Mk 3:5 5495
his h was restored whole as the ... Mk 3:5 5495
And he took the damsel by the h ... Mk 5:41 5495
beseech him to put his h upon him ... Mk 7:32 5495
And he took the blind man by the h ... Mk 8:23 5495
But Jesus took him by the h ... Mk 9:27 5495
if thy h offend thee, cut it off ... Mk 9:43 5495
we may sit, one on thy right h ... Mk 10:37
and the other on thy left h ... Mk 10:37
But to sit on my right h and on my ... Mk 10:40
on my left h is not mine to give ... Mk 10:40
my Lord, Sit thou on my right h ... Mk 12:36
lo, he that betrayeth me is at h ... Mk 14:42 1448
sitting on the right h of power ... Mk 14:62
the one on his right h, and the ... Mk 15:27
and sat on the right h of God ... Mk 16:19
in h to set forth in order a ... Lk 1:1 2021
the h of the Lord was with him ... Lk 1:66 5495
from the h of all that hate us ... Lk 1:71 5495
being delivered out of the h of ... Lk 1:74 5495
Whose fan is in his h, and he will ... Lk 3:17 5495
And he put forth his h, and touched ... Lk 5:13 5495
a man whose right h was withered ... Lk 6:6 5495
the man which had the withered h ... Lk 6:8 5495
unto the man, Stretch forth thy h ... Lk 6:10 5495
his h was restored whole as the ... Lk 6:10 5495
all out, and took her by the h ... Lk 8:54 5495
having put his h to the plough ... Lk 9:62 5495
and put a ring on his h, and shoes ... Lk 15:22 5495
my Lord, Sit thou on my right h ... Lk 20:42
that summer is now nigh at h ... Lk 21:30
the kingdom of God is nigh at h ... Lk 21:31
the h of him that betrayeth me is ... Lk 22:21 5495
the right h of the power of God ... Lk 22:69
malefactors, one on the right h ... Lk 23:33
And the Jews' passover was at h ... Jn 2:13 1451
hath given all things into his h ... Jn 3:35 5495
feast of tabernacles was at h ... Jn 7:2 1451
any man pluck them out of my h ... Jn 10:28 5495
pluck them out of my Father's h ... Jn 10:29 5495
but he escaped out of their h ... Jn 10:39 5495
that was dead came forth, bound h ... Jn 11:44 5495
the Jews' passover was nigh at h ... Jn 11:55
Jesus with the palm of his h ... Jn 18:22
for the sepulchre was nigh at h ... Jn 19:42
thrust my h into his side, I will ... Jn 20:25 5495
and reach hither thy h, and thrust ... Jn 20:27 5495
my face, for he is on my right h ... Acts 2:25
by the right h of God exalted ... Acts 2:33
my Lord, Sit thou on my right h ... Acts 2:34
And he took him by the right h ... Acts 3:7 5495
For to do whatsoever thy h ... Acts 4:28 5495
stretching forth thine h to heal ... Acts 4:30 5495
with his right h to be a Prince ... Acts 5:31
God by his h would deliver them ... Acts 7:25 5495
a deliverer by the h of the angel ... Acts 7:35 5495
Hath not my h made all these ... Acts 7:50 5495
standing on the right h of God ... Acts 7:55
standing on the right h of God ... Acts 7:56
but they led him by the h ... Acts 9:8 5496
in, and putting his h on him ... Acts 9:12 5495
And he gave her his h, and lifted ... Acts 9:41 5495
the h of the Lord was with them ... Acts 11:21 5495
me out of the h of Herod, and from ... Acts 12:11 5495
with the h to hold their peace ... Acts 12:17 5495
the h of the Lord is upon thee, ... Acts 13:11 5495
seeking some to lead him by the h ... Acts 13:11 5497
up, and beckoning with his h said ... Acts 13:16 5495
And Alexander beckoned with the h ... Acts 19:33 5495
Cyprus, we left it on the left h ... Acts 21:3
with the h unto the people ... Acts 21:40 5495
being led by the h of them that ... Acts 22:11 5496
chief captain took him by the h ... Acts 23:19 5495
Then Paul stretched forth the h ... Acts 26:1 5495
of the heat, and fastened on his h ... Acts 28:3 5495
the venomous beast hang on his h ... Acts 28:4 5495
who is even at the right h of God ... Rom 8:34
is far spent, the day is at h ... Rom 13:12 1448
shall say, Because I am not the h ... 1Cor 12:15 5495
And the eye cannot say unto the h ... 1Cor 12:21 5495
of me Paul with mine own h ... 1Cor 16:21 5495
of righteousness on the right h ... 2Cor 6:7
of things made ready to our h ... 2Cor 10:16
by angels in the h of a mediator ... Gal 3:19 5495
written unto you with mine own h ... Gal 6:11 5495
right h in the heavenly places ... Eph 1:20
The Lord is at h ... Phil 4:5 1451
sitteth on the right h of God ... Col 3:1
salutation by the h of me Paul ... Col 4:18 5495
as that the day of Christ is at h ... 2Th 2:2 1764
of Paul with mine own h, which is ... 2Th 3:17 5495
the time of my departure is at h ... 2Ti 4:6 2186
have written it with mine own h ... Philem 19 5495
sat down on the right h of the ... Heb 1:3
at any times, Sit on my right h ... Heb 1:13
who is set on the right h of the ... Heb 8:1
h to lead them out of the land of ... Heb 8:9 5495
sat down on the right h of God ... Heb 10:12
the right h of the throne of God ... Heb 12:2
and is on the right h of God ... 1Pet 3:22
But the end of all things is at h ... 1Pet 4:7 1448
under the mighty h of God ... 1Pet 5:6 5495
for the time is at h ... Rev 1:3 1451
he had in his right h seven stars ... Rev 1:16 5495
And he laid his right h upon me ... Rev 1:17 5495
which thou sawest in my right h ... Rev 1:20
the seven stars in his right h ... Rev 2:1
I saw in the right h of him that ... Rev 5:1
took the book out of the right h ... Rev 5:7
had a pair of balances in his h ... Rev 6:5 5495
before God out of the angel's h ... Rev 8:4 5495
he had in his h a little book ... Rev 10:2 5495
earth lifted up his h to heaven ... Rev 10:5 5495
book which is open in the h of ... Rev 10:8 5495
little book out of the angel's h ... Rev 10:10 5495
receive a mark in their right h ... Rev 13:16 5495
mark in his forehead, or in his h ... Rev 14:9 5495
crown, and in his h a sharp sickle ... Rev 14:14 5495
cup in her h full of abominations ... Rev 17:4 5495
blood of his servants at her h ... Rev 19:2 5495
pit and a great chain in his h ... Rev 20:1 5495
for the time is at h ... Rev 22:10 1451

HANDBREADTH
a border of an h round about ... Ex 37:12 2948
And the thickness of it was an h ... 2Chr 4:5 2947
thou hast made my days as an h ... Ps 39:5 2947

HANDED
him while he is weary and weak h ... 2Sa 17:2 3027

HANDFUL
his h of the flour thereof ... Lev 2:2
the priest shall take his h of it ... Lev 5:12
And he shall take of it his h ... Lev 6:15 7062
offering, and took an h thereof ... Lev 9:17
shall take an h of the offering ... Num 5:26 7061
but an h of meal in a barrel, and ... 1Kin 17:12
There shall be an h of corn in ... Ps 72:16 6451
Better is an h with quietness, ... Eccl 4:6
as the h after the harvestman, and ... Jer 9:22 5995

HANDFULS
the earth brought forth by h ... Gen 41:47 7062
Take to you h of ashes of the ... Ex 9:8
some of the h of purpose for her ... Ruth 2:16 6653
of Samaria shall suffice for h ... 1Kin 20:10 8168
among my people for h of barley ... Eze 13:19 8168

HANDKERCHIEFS
brought unto the sick h or aprons ... Acts 19:12 4676

HANDLE
father of all such as h the harp ... Gen 4:21 8610
they that h the pen of the writer ... Judg 5:14 4900
the battle, that could h shield ... 1Chr 12:8 6186
forth to war, that could h spear ... 2Chr 25:5 270
They have hands, but they h not ... Ps 115:7 4184
they that h the law knew me not ... Jer 2:8 8610
and the Libyans, that h the shield ... Jer 46:9 8610
and the Lydians, that h and bend ... Jer 46:9 8610
And all that h the oar, the ... Eze 27:29 8610
h me, and see ... Lk 24:39 5584
taste not; h not ... Col 2:21 2345

HANDLED
to be furbished, that it may be h ... Eze 21:11
and sent him away shamefully h ... Mk 12:4 821
looked upon, and our hands have h ... 1Jn 1:1 5584

HANDLES
myrrh, upon the h of the lock ... Song 5:5 3709

HANDLETH
He that h a matter wisely shall ... Prov 16:20 5921
him that h the sickle in the time ... Jer 50:16 8610
shall he stand that h the bow ... Amos 2:15 8610

HANDLING
and shields, all of them h swords ... Eze 38:4 8610
nor h the word of God deceitfully ... 2Cor 4:2 1389

HANDMAID
and she had an h, an Egyptian, ... Gen 16:1 8198
Hagar the Egyptian, Sarah's h ... Gen 25:12 8198
Leah Zilpah his maid for an h ... Gen 29:24 8198
Bilhah his h to be her maid ... Gen 29:29 8198
she gave him Bilhah her h to wife ... Gen 30:4 8198
And the sons of Bilhah, Rachel's h ... Gen 35:25 8198
And the sons of Zilpah, Leah's h ... Gen 35:26 8198
ass may rest, and the son of thy h ... Ex 23:12 519
and wine also for me, and for thy h ... Judg 19:19 519
hast spoken friendly unto thine h ... Ruth 2:13 8198
she answered, I am Ruth thine h ... Ruth 3:9 519
therefore thy skirt over thine h ... Ruth 3:9 519
look on the affliction of thine h ... 1Sa 1:11 519
me, and not forget thine h ... 1Sa 1:11 519
give unto thine h a man child ... 1Sa 1:11 519
Count not thine h for a daughter ... 1Sa 1:16 519
Let thine h find grace in thy ... 1Sa 1:18 8198
and let thine h, I pray thee, ... 1Sa 25:24 519
and hear the words of thine h ... 1Sa 25:24 519
but I thine h saw not the young ... 1Sa 25:25 519
thine h hath brought unto my lord ... 1Sa 25:27 8198
forgive the trespass of thine h ... 1Sa 25:28 519
my lord, then remember thine h ... 1Sa 25:31 519
let thine h be a servant to wash ... 1Sa 25:41 519
thine h hath obeyed thy voice, and ... 1Sa 28:21 8198
also unto the voice of thine h ... 1Sa 28:22 8198
thy h had two sons, and they two ... 2Sa 14:6 8198
family is risen against thine h ... 2Sa 14:7 8198
Then the woman said, Let thine h ... 2Sa 14:12 8198
thy h said, I will now speak unto ... 2Sa 14:15 8198
will perform the request of his h ... 2Sa 14:15 519
to deliver his h out of the hand ... 2Sa 14:16 519
Then thine h said, The word of my ... 2Sa 14:17 8198
words in the mouth of thine h ... 2Sa 14:19 8198
him, Hear the words of thine h ... 2Sa 20:17 519
lord, O king, swear unto thine h ... 1Kin 1:13 519
by the LORD thy God unto thine h ... 1Kin 1:17 519
beside me, while thine h slept ... 1Kin 3:20 519
Thine h hath not any thing in the ... 2Kin 4:2 8198
of God, do not lie unto thine h ... 2Kin 4:16 8198
and save the son of thine h ... Ps 86:16 519
servant, and the son of thine h ... Ps 116:16 519
an h that is heir to her mistress ... Prov 30:23 8198
his servant, and every man his h ... Jer 34:16 8198
said, Behold the h of the Lord ... Lk 1:38 1399

HANDMAIDEN

regarded the low estate of his *h*	Lk 1:48	*1399*

HANDMAIDENS

Then the *h* came near, they and	Gen 33:6	8198
I be not like unto one of thine *h*	Ruth 2:13	8198
on my *h* I will pour out in those	Acts 2:18	*1399*

HANDMAIDS

and unto Rachel, and unto the two *h*	Gen 33:1	8198
And he put the *h* and their children	Gen 33:2	8198
the eyes of the *h* of his servants	2Sa 6:20	519
of the LORD for servants and *h*	Is 14:2	8198
and caused the servants and the *h*	Jer 34:11	8198
subjection for servants and for *h*	Jer 34:11	8198
be unto you for servants and for *h*	Jer 34:16	8198
upon the *h* in those days will I	Joel 2:29	8198

HANDS

our work and toil of our *h*	Gen 5:29	3027
and submit thyself under her *h*	Gen 16:9	3027
innocency of my *h* have I done	Gen 20:5	3709
two bracelets for her *h* of ten	Gen 24:22	3027
and bracelets upon his sister's *h*	Gen 24:30	3027
face, and the bracelets upon her *h*	Gen 24:47	3027
the kids of the goats upon his *h*	Gen 27:16	3027
but the *h* are the *h* of Esau	Gen 27:22	3027
him not, because his *h* were hairy	Gen 27:23	3027
as his brother Esau's *h*	Gen 27:23	3027
affliction and the labour of my *h*	Gen 31:42	3709
he delivered him out of their *h*	Gen 37:21	3027
he might rid him out of their *h*	Gen 37:22	3027
bought him of the *h* of the	Gen 39:1	3027
brought down in our *h* to buy food	Gen 43:22	3027
head, guiding his *h* wittingly	Gen 48:14	3027
the arms of his *h* were made	Gen 49:24	3027
the *h* of the mighty God of Jacob	Gen 49:24	3027
spread abroad my *h* unto the LORD	Ex 9:29	3709
spread abroad his *h* unto the LORD	Ex 9:33	3709
which thy *h* have established	Ex 15:17	3027
But Moses' *h* were heavy	Ex 17:12	3027
and Aaron and Hur stayed up his *h*	Ex 17:12	3027
his *h* were steady until the going	Ex 17:12	3027
his sons shall put their *h* upon	Ex 29:10	3027
their *h* upon the head of the ram	Ex 29:15	3027
their *h* upon the head of the ram	Ex 29:19	3027
shalt put all in the *h* of Aaron	Ex 29:24	3709
and in the *h* of his sons	Ex 29:24	3027
shalt receive them of their *h*	Ex 29:25	3027
and his sons shall wash their *h*	Ex 30:19	3027
So they shall wash their *h*	Ex 30:21	3027
he cast the tables out of his *h*	Ex 32:19	3027
hearted did spin with their *h*	Ex 35:25	3027
Aaron and his sons washed their *h*	Ex 40:31	3027
h upon the head of the bullock	Lev 4:15	3027
His own *h* shall bring the	Lev 7:30	3027
his sons laid their *h* upon the	Lev 8:14	3027
his sons laid their *h* upon the	Lev 8:18	3027
his sons laid their *h* upon the	Lev 8:22	3027
upon the thumbs of their right *h*	Lev 8:24	3027
And he put all upon Aaron's *h*	Lev 8:27	3709
and upon his sons' *h*	Lev 8:27	3709
Moses took them from off their *h*	Lev 8:28	3709
and hath not rinsed his *h* in water	Lev 15:11	3027
his *h* full of sweet incense	Lev 16:12	2651
Aaron shall lay both his *h* upon	Lev 16:21	3027
him lay their *h* upon his head	Lev 24:14	3027
the offering of memorial in her *h*	Num 5:18	3709
them upon the *h* of the Nazarite	Num 6:19	3709
put their *h* upon the Levites	Num 8:10	3027
the Levites shall lay their *h*	Num 8:12	3027
and he smote his *h* together	Num 24:10	3709
And he laid his *h* upon him	Num 27:23	3027
the fruit of the land in their *h*	Deut 1:25	3027
God delivered into our *h* Og also	Deut 3:3	3027
serve gods, the work of men's *h*	Deut 4:28	3027
of the covenant were in my two *h*	Deut 9:15	3027
and cast them out of my two *h*	Deut 9:17	3027
that thou puttest thine *h* unto	Deut 12:18	3027
and in all the works of thine *h*	Deut 16:15	3027
The *h* of the witnesses shall be	Deut 17:7	3027
afterward the *h* of all the people	Deut 17:7	3027
hath delivered it into thine *h*	Deut 20:13	3027
shall wash their *h* over the	Deut 21:6	3027
Our *h* have not shed this blood,	Deut 21:7	3027
hath delivered them into thine *h*	Deut 21:10	3027
thee in all the work of thine *h*	Deut 24:19	3027
LORD, the work of the *h* of the	Deut 27:15	3027
anger through the work of your *h*	Deut 31:29	3027
let his *h* be sufficient for him	Deut 33:7	3027
and accept the work of his *h*	Deut 33:11	3027
for Moses had laid his *h* upon him	Deut 34:9	3027
delivered into our *h* all the land	Josh 2:24	3027
he delivered them into the *h* of	Judg 2:14	3027
he sold them into the *h* of their	Judg 2:14	3027
us into the *h* of the Midianites	Judg 6:13	3709
give the Midianites into their *h*	Judg 7:2	3027
afterward shall thine *h* be	Judg 7:11	3027
the pitchers that were in their *h*	Judg 7:19	3027
and held the lamps in their left *h*	Judg 7:20	3027
in their right *h* to blow withal	Judg 7:20	3027
into your *h* the princes of Midian	Judg 8:3	3027
Are the *h* of Zebah and Zalmunna	Judg 8:6	3709
Are the *h* of Zebah and Zalmunna	Judg 8:15	3709
h of all their enemies on every	Judg 8:34	3027
to the deserving of his *h*	Judg 9:16	3027
into the *h* of the Philistines	Judg 10:7	3027
into the *h* of the children of	Judg 10:7	3027
the children of Ammon into mine *h*	Judg 11:30	3027
LORD delivered them into his *h*	Judg 11:32	3027
delivered me not out of their *h*	Judg 12:2	3027
me not, I put my life in my *h*	Judg 12:3	3709
and a meat offering at our *h*	Judg 13:23	3027
And he took thereof in his *h*	Judg 14:9	3709
his bands loosed from off his *h*	Judg 15:14	3027
delivered into our *h* our enemy	Judg 16:24	3027
for God hath given it into your *h*	Judg 18:10	3027
her *h* were upon the threshold	Judg 19:27	3027
both the palms of his *h* were cut	1Sa 5:4	3027
out of the *h* of the Philistines	1Sa 7:14	3027
thou shalt receive of their *h*	1Sa 10:4	3027
of Israel by the *h* of messengers	1Sa 11:7	3027
And Jonathan climbed up upon his *h*	1Sa 14:13	3027
the *h* of them that spoiled them	1Sa 14:48	3027
and he will give you into our *h*	1Sa 17:47	3027
and feigned himself mad in their *h*	1Sa 21:13	3027
me into the *h* of my master	1Sa 30:15	3027
now let your *h* be strengthened	2Sa 2:7	3027
Thy *h* were not bound, nor thy	2Sa 3:34	3027
his *h* were feeble, and all the	2Sa 4:1	3027
slew them, and cut off their *h*	2Sa 4:12	3027
then shall the *h* of all that are	2Sa 16:21	3027
them into the *h* of the Gibeonites	2Sa 21:9	3027
of my *h* hath he recompensed me	2Sa 22:21	3027
He teacheth my *h* to war	2Sa 22:35	3027
they cannot be taken with *h*	2Sa 23:6	3027
spread forth his *h* toward heaven	1Kin 8:22	3027
spread forth his *h* toward this	1Kin 8:38	3027
with his *h* spread up to heaven	1Kin 8:54	3027
committed them unto the *h* of the	1Kin 14:27	3027
to anger with the work of his *h*	1Kin 16:7	3027
poured water on the *h* of Elijah	2Kin 3:11	3027
his eyes, and his *h* upon his *h*	2Kin 4:34	3709
at his *h* that which he brought	2Kin 5:20	3027
And Joram turned his *h*, and fled,	2Kin 9:23	3027
the feet, and the palms of her *h*	2Kin 9:35	3027
I have brought into your *h* escape	2Kin 10:24	3027
and they clapped their *h*, and said,	2Kin 11:12	3709
And they laid *h* on her	2Kin 11:16	3027
into the *h* of them that did the	2Kin 12:11	3027
put his *h* upon the king's *h*	2Kin 13:16	3027
no gods, but the work of men's *h*	2Kin 19:18	3027
with all the works of their *h*	2Kin 22:17	3027
there is no wrong in mine *h*	1Chr 12:17	3709
of Asaph under the *h* of Asaph	1Chr 25:2	3027
under the *h* of their father	1Chr 25:3	3027
All these were under the *h* of	1Chr 25:6	3027
to be made by the *h* of artificers	1Chr 29:5	3027
who hath with his *h* fulfilled	2Chr 6:4	3027
of Israel, and spread forth his *h*	2Chr 6:12	3709
spread forth his *h* toward heaven	2Chr 6:13	3709
spread forth his *h* in this house	2Chr 6:29	3709
by the *h* of his servants ships	2Chr 8:18	3027
committed them to the *h* of the	2Chr 12:10	3027
and let not your *h* be weak	2Chr 15:7	3027
So they laid *h* on her	2Chr 23:15	3027
and they laid their *h* upon them	2Chr 29:23	3027
were the work of the *h* of man	2Chr 32:19	3027
with all the works of their *h*	2Chr 34:25	3027
sprinkled the blood from their *h*	2Chr 35:11	3027
their *h* with vessels of silver	Ezr 1:6	3027
the *h* of the people of Judah	Ezr 4:4	3027
fast on, and prospereth in their *h*	Ezr 5:8	3028
to strengthen their *h* in the work	Ezr 6:22	3027
spread out my *h* unto the LORD my	Ezr 9:5	3709
they gave their *h* that they would	Ezr 10:19	3027
their *h* for this good work	Neh 2:18	3027
one of his *h* wrought in the work	Neh 4:17	3027
Their *h* shall be weakened from	Neh 6:9	3027
therefore, O God, strengthen my *h*	Neh 6:9	3027
Amen, with lifting up their *h*	Neh 8:6	3027
and gavest them into their *h*	Neh 9:24	3027
do so again, I will lay *h* on you	Neh 13:21	3027
scorn to lay *h* on Mordecai alone	Est 3:6	3027
talents of silver to the *h* of	Est 3:9	3027
they laid not their *h* on the prey	Est 9:16	3027
hast blessed the work of his *h*	Job 1:10	3027
thou hast strengthened the weak *h*	Job 4:3	3027
so that their *h* cannot perform	Job 5:12	3027
he woundeth, and his *h* make whole	Job 5:18	3027
and make my *h* never so clean	Job 9:30	3709
despise the work of thine *h*	Job 10:3	3709
Thine *h* have made me and fashioned	Job 10:8	3027
and stretch out thine *h* toward him	Job 11:13	3709
a desire to the work of thine *h*	Job 14:15	3027
me over into the *h* of the wicked	Job 16:11	3027
Not for any injustice in mine *h*	Job 16:17	3709
is he that will strike *h* with me	Job 17:3	3027
hath clean *h* shall be stronger	Job 17:9	3027
his *h* shall restore their goods	Job 20:10	3027
by the pureness of thine *h*	Job 22:30	3709
Men shall clap their *h* at him	Job 27:23	3709
the strength of their *h* profit me	Job 30:2	3027
any blot hath cleaved to mine *h*	Job 31:7	3709
they all are the work of his *h*	Job 34:19	3027
sin, he clappeth his *h* among us	Job 34:37	
if there be iniquity in my *h*	Ps 7:3	3709
dominion over the works of thy *h*	Ps 8:6	3027
snared in the work of his own *h*	Ps 9:16	3709
of my *h* hath he recompensed me	Ps 18:20	3027
cleanness of my *h* in his eyesight	Ps 18:24	3027
He teacheth my *h* to war, so that	Ps 18:34	3027
they pierced my *h* and my feet	Ps 22:16	3027
He that hath clean *h*, and a pure	Ps 24:4	3709
I will wash mine *h* in innocency	Ps 26:6	3709
In whose *h* is mischief, and their	Ps 26:10	3027
when I lift up my *h* toward thy	Ps 28:2	3027
them after the work of their *h*	Ps 28:4	3027
LORD, nor the operation of his *h*	Ps 28:5	3027
out our *h* to a strange god	Ps 44:20	3709
O clap your *h*, all ye people	Ps 47:1	3709
He hath put forth his *h* against	Ps 55:20	3027
violence of your *h* in the earth	Ps 58:2	3027
I will lift up my *h* in thy name	Ps 63:4	3709
soon stretch out her *h* unto God	Ps 68:31	3027
vain, and washed my *h* in innocency	Ps 73:13	3709
men of might have found their *h*	Ps 76:5	3027
them by the skilfulness of his *h*	Ps 78:72	3709
his *h* were delivered from the	Ps 81:6	3709
have stretched out my *h* unto thee	Ps 88:9	3709
thou the work of our *h* upon us	Ps 90:17	3027
the work of our *h* establish thou	Ps 90:17	3027
shall bear thee up in their *h*	Ps 91:12	3709
triumph in the works of thy *h*	Ps 92:4	3027
his *h* formed the dry land	Ps 95:5	3027
Let the floods clap their *h*	Ps 98:8	3709
the heavens are the work of thy *h*	Ps 102:25	3027
The works of his *h* are verity	Ps 111:7	3027
and gold, the work of men's *h*	Ps 115:4	3027
They have *h*, but they handle not	Ps 115:7	3027
My *h* also will I lift up unto thy	Ps 119:48	3709
Thy *h* have made me and fashioned	Ps 119:73	3027
put forth their *h* unto iniquity	Ps 125:3	3027
shalt eat the labour of thine *h*	Ps 128:2	3709
Lift up your *h* in the sanctuary,	Ps 134:2	3027
and gold, the work of men's *h*	Ps 135:15	3027
not the works of thine own *h*	Ps 138:8	3027
O LORD, from the *h* of the wicked	Ps 140:4	3027
the lifting up of my *h* as the	Ps 141:2	3709
I muse on the work of thy *h*	Ps 143:5	3027
I stretch forth my *h* unto thee	Ps 143:6	3027
which teacheth my *h* to war	Ps 144:1	3027
little folding of the *h* to sleep	Prov 6:10	3027
h that shed innocent blood,	Prov 6:17	3027
the recompence of a man's *h* shall	Prov 12:14	3027
plucketh it down with her *h*	Prov 14:1	3027
void of understanding striketh *h*	Prov 17:18	3709
for his *h* refuse to labour	Prov 21:25	3027
thou one of them that strike *h*	Prov 22:26	3709
little folding of the *h* to sleep	Prov 24:33	3027
The spider taketh hold with her *h*	Prov 30:28	3027
and worketh willingly with her *h*	Prov 31:13	3709
with the fruit of her *h* she	Prov 31:16	3709
She layeth her *h* to the spindle	Prov 31:19	3027
and her *h* hold the distaff	Prov 31:19	3709
reacheth forth her *h* to the needy	Prov 31:20	3027
Give her of the fruit of her *h*	Prov 31:31	3027
the works that my *h* had wrought	Eccl 2:11	3027
The fool foldeth his *h* together	Eccl 4:5	3027
than both the *h* full with travail	Eccl 4:6	2651
and destroy the work of thine *h*	Eccl 5:6	3027
snares and nets, and her *h* as bands	Eccl 7:26	3027
through idleness of the *h* the	Eccl 10:18	3027
my *h* dropped with myrrh, and my	Song 5:5	3027
His *h* are as gold rings set with	Song 5:14	3027
the work of the *h* of a cunning	Song 7:1	3027
And when ye spread forth your *h*	Is 1:15	3709
your *h* are full of blood	Is 1:15	3027
worship the work of their own *h*	Is 2:8	3027
of his *h* shall be given him	Is 3:11	3027
consider the operation of his *h*	Is 5:12	3027
Therefore shall all *h* be faint	Is 13:7	3027
to the altars, the work of his *h*	Is 17:8	3027
and Assyria the work of my *h*	Is 19:25	3027
forth his *h* in the midst of them	Is 25:11	3027
spreadeth forth his *h* to swim	Is 25:11	
with the spoils of their *h*	Is 25:11	3027
his children, the work of mine *h*	Is 29:23	3027
which your own *h* have made unto	Is 31:7	3027
that shaketh his *h* from holding	Is 33:15	3709
Strengthen ye the weak *h*, and	Is 35:3	3027
no gods, but the work of men's *h*	Is 37:19	3027
or thy work, He hath no *h*	Is 45:9	3027
the work of my *h* command ye me	Is 45:11	3027
I, even my *h*, have stretched out	Is 45:12	3027
thee upon the palms of my *h*	Is 49:16	3709
of the field shall clap their *h*	Is 55:12	3709
For your *h* are defiled with blood	Is 59:3	3709
the act of violence is in their *h*	Is 59:6	3709
of my planting, the work of my *h*	Is 60:21	3027
I have spread out my *h* all the	Is 65:2	3027
long enjoy the work of their *h*	Is 65:22	3027
the works of their own *h*	Jer 1:16	3027
him, and thine *h* upon thine head	Jer 2:37	3027
herself, that spreadeth her *h*	Jer 4:31	3709
our *h* wax feeble	Jer 6:24	3027
the work of the *h* of the workman	Jer 10:3	3027
and of the *h* of the founder	Jer 10:9	3027
by the *h* of them that seek their	Jer 19:7	3027
weapons of war that are in your *h*	Jer 21:4	3027
also the *h* of evildoers, that	Jer 23:14	3027
to anger with the works of your *h*	Jer 25:6	3027
works of your *h* to your own hurt	Jer 25:7	3027
to the works of their own *h*	Jer 25:14	3027
every man with his *h* on his loins	Jer 30:6	3027
to anger with the work of their *h*	Jer 32:30	3027
the *h* of him that telleth them	Jer 33:13	3027
for thus he weakeneth the *h* of	Jer 38:4	3027
the *h* of all the people, in	Jer 38:4	3027
wrath with the works of your *h*	Jer 44:8	3027
children for feebleness of *h*	Jer 47:3	3027
upon all the *h* shall be cuttings,	Jer 48:37	3027
of them, and his *h* waxed feeble	Jer 50:43	3027
hath delivered me into their *h*	Lam 1:14	3027
Zion spreadeth forth her *h*	Lam 1:17	3027
that pass by clap their *h* at thee	Lam 2:15	3709
lift up thy *h* toward him for the	Lam 2:19	3709
our *h* unto God in the heavens	Lam 3:41	3709
according to the work of their *h*	Lam 3:64	3027
the work of the *h* of the potter	Lam 4:2	3027
a moment, and no *h* stayed on her	Lam 4:6	3027
The *h* of the pitiful women have	Lam 4:10	3027
they had the *h* of a man under	Eze 1:8	3027
All *h* shall be feeble, and all	Eze 7:17	3027
I will give it into the *h* of the	Eze 7:21	3027
the *h* of the people of the land	Eze 7:27	3027
put it into the *h* of him that was	Eze 10:7	2651
body, and their backs, and their *h*	Eze 10:12	3027
the likeness of the *h* of a man	Eze 10:21	3027
you into the *h* of strangers	Eze 11:9	3027
strengthened the *h* of the wicked	Eze 13:22	3027
and I put bracelets upon thy *h*	Eze 16:11	3027
all *h* shall be feeble, and every	Eze 21:7	3027

and smite thine *h* together Eze 21:14 3709
I will also smite mine *h* together Eze 21:17 3709
endure, or can thine *h* be strong Eze 22:14 3027
adultery, and blood is in their *h* Eze 23:37 3027
which put bracelets upon their *h* Eze 23:42 3027
and blood is in their *h* Eze 23:45 3027
Because thou hast clapped thine *h* Eze 25:6 3027
a stone was cut out without *h* Dan 2:34 3028
cut out of the mountain without *h* Dan 2:45 3028
shall deliver you out of my *h* Dan 3:15 3028
knees and upon the palms of my *h* Dan 10:10 3027
say any more to the work of our *h* Hos 14:3 3027
nor have laid *h* on their Obad 13
the violence that is in their *h* Jonah 3:8 3709
more worship the work of thine *h* Mic 5:13 3027
may do evil with both *h* earnestly Mic 7:3 3709
thee shall clap the *h* over thee Nah 3:19 3709
voice, and lifted up his *h* on high Hab 3:10 3027
to Zion, Let not thine *h* be slack Zeph 3:16 3027
and upon all the labour of the *h* Hag 1:11 3709
and so is every work of their *h* Hag 2:14 3027
hail in all the labours of your *h* Hag 2:17 3027
The *h* of Zerubbabel have laid the Zec 4:9 3027
his *h* shall also finish it Zec 4:9 3027
Let your *h* be strong, ye that Zec 8:9 3027
not, but let your *h* be strong Zec 8:13 3027
What are these wounds in thine *h* Zec 13:6 3027
in their *h* they shall bear thee Mt 4:6 *5495*
not their *h* when they eat bread Mt 15:2 *5495*
unwashen *h* defileth not a man Mt 15:20 *5495*
be betrayed into the *h* of men Mt 17:22 *5495*
rather than having two *h* or two Mt 18:8 *5495*
and he laid *h* on him, and took him Mt 18:28 *2902*
that he should put his *h* on them Mt 19:13 *5495*
And he laid his *h* on them, and Mt 19:15 *5495*
when they sought to lay *h* on him Mt 21:46 *2902*
is betrayed into the *h* of sinners Mt 26:45 *5495*
laid *h* on Jesus, and took him Mt 26:50 *5495*
him with the palms of their *h* Mt 26:67
washed his *h* before the multitude Mt 27:24 *5495*
thee, come and lay thy *h* on her Mk 5:23 *5495*
mighty works are wrought by his *h* Mk 6:2 *5495*
laid his *h* upon a few sick folk Mk 6:5 *5495*
that is to say, with unwashen, *h* Mk 7:2 *5495*
except they wash their *h* oft Mk 7:3 *5495*
but eat bread with unwashen *h* Mk 7:5 *5495*
put his *h* upon him, he asked him Mk 8:23 *5495*
he put his *h* again upon his eyes Mk 8:25 *5495*
is delivered into the *h* of men Mk 9:31 *5495*
than having two *h* to go into hell Mk 9:43 *5495*
put his *h* upon them, and blessed Mk 10:16 *5495*
is betrayed into the *h* of sinners Mk 14:41 *5495*
And they laid their *h* on him Mk 14:46 *5495*
this temple that is made with *h* Mk 14:58 *5499*
will build another made without *h* Mk 14:58 *886*
him with the palms of their *h* Mk 14:65
they shall lay *h* on the sick Mk 16:18 *5495*
in their *h* they shall bear thee Lk 4:11 *5495*
he laid his *h* on every one of Lk 4:40 *5495*
did eat, rubbing them in their *h* Lk 6:1 *5495*
be delivered into the *h* of men Lk 9:44 *5495*
And he laid his *h* on her Lk 13:13 *5495*
same hour sought to lay *h* on him Lk 20:19 *5495*
they shall lay their *h* on you Lk 21:12 *5495*
stretched forth no *h* against me Lk 22:53 *5495*
into thy *h* I commend my spirit Lk 23:46 *5495*
into the *h* of sinful men, and be Lk 24:7 *5495*
Behold my *h* and my feet, that it Lk 24:39 *5495*
thus spoken, he shewed them his *h* Lk 24:40 *5495*
to Bethany, and he lifted up his *h* Lk 24:50 *5495*
but no man laid *h* on him, because Jn 7:30 *5495*
but no man laid *h* on him Jn 7:44 *5495*
and no man laid *h* on him Jn 8:20 *4084*
had given all things into his *h* Jn 13:3 *5495*
not my feet only, but also my *h* Jn 13:9 *5495*
and they smote him with their *h* Jn 19:3 *4475*
said, he shewed unto them his *h* Jn 20:20 *5495*
in his *h* the print of the nails Jn 20:25 *5495*
hither thy finger, and behold my *h* Jn 20:27 *5495*
thou shalt stretch forth thy *h* Jn 21:18 *5495*
by wicked *h* have crucified and Acts 2:23 *5495*
And they laid *h* on them, and put Acts 4:3 *5495*
by the *h* of the apostles were Acts 5:12 *5495*
laid their *h* on the apostles, and Acts 5:18 *5495*
prayed, they laid their *h* on them Acts 6:6 *5495*
in the works of their own *h* Acts 7:41 *5495*
not in temples made with *h* Acts 7:48 *5499*
Then laid they their *h* on them Acts 8:17 *5495*
h the Holy Ghost was given Acts 8:18 *5495*
power, that on whomsoever I lay *h* Acts 8:19 *5495*
and putting his *h* on him said Acts 9:17 *5495*
the elders by the *h* of Barnabas Acts 11:30 *5495*
h to vex certain of the church Acts 12:1 *5495*
And his chains fell off from his *h* Acts 12:7 *5495*
prayed, and laid their *h* on them Acts 13:3 *5495*
and wonders to be done by their *h* Acts 14:3 *5495*
not in temples made with *h* Acts 17:24 *5499*
is worshipped with men's *h* Acts 17:25 *5495*
Paul had laid his *h* upon them Acts 19:6 *5495*
special miracles by the *h* of Paul Acts 19:11 *5495*
be no gods, which are made with *h* Acts 19:26 *5495*
that these *h* have ministered unto Acts 20:34 *5495*
Paul's girdle, and bound his own *h* Acts 21:11 *5495*
him into the *h* of the Gentiles Acts 21:11 *5495*
all the people, and laid *h* on him, Acts 21:27 *5495*
took him away out of our *h* Acts 24:7 *5495*
own *h* the tackling of the ship Acts 27:19 *849*
and prayed, and laid his *h* on him Acts 28:8 *5495*
into the *h* of the Romans Acts 28:17 *5495*
forth my *h* unto a disobedient Rom 10:21 *5495*
And labour, working with our own *h* 1Cor 4:12 *5495*
of God, an house not made with *h* 2Cor 5:1 *886*
by the wall, and escaped his *h* 2Cor 11:33 *5495*
the right *h* of fellowship Gal 2:9
in the flesh made by *h* Eph 2:11 *5499*
working with his *h* the thing Eph 4:28 *5495*
the circumcision made without *h* Col 2:11 *886*
and to work with your own *h* 1Th 4:11 *5495*
every where, lifting up holy *h* 1Ti 2:8 *5495*
on of the *h* of the presbytery 1Ti 4:14 *5495*
Lay *h* suddenly on no man, neither 1Ti 5:22 *5495*
in thee by the putting on of my *h* 2Ti 1:6 *5495*
heavens are the works of thine *h* Heb 1:10 *5495*
set him over the works of thy *h* Heb 2:7 *5495*
of baptisms, and of laying on of *h* Heb 6:2 *5495*
tabernacle, not made with *h* Heb 9:11 *5499*
into the holy places made with *h* Heb 9:24 *5499*
fall into the *h* of the living God Heb 10:31 *5495*
lift up the *h* which hang down Heb 12:12 *5495*
Cleanse your *h*, ye sinners Jas 4:8 *5495*
our *h* have handled, of the Word 1Jn 1:1 *5495*
white robes, and palms in their *h* Rev 7:9 *5495*
not of the works of their *h* Rev 9:20 *5495*
their foreheads, or in their *h* Rev 20:4 *5495*

HANDSTAVES
the bows and the arrows, and the *h* Eze 39:9

HANDWRITING
Blotting out the *h* of ordinances Col 2:14 *5498*

HANDYWORK
and the firmament sheweth his *h* Ps 19:1

HANES (*ha'-nees*) See TAHPANES. *A place in Egypt.*
and his ambassadors came to *H* Is 30:4 2609

HANG
thee, and shall *h* thee on a tree Gen 40:19 8518
shall *h* over the backside of the Ex 26:12 5628
it shall *h* over the sides of the Ex 26:13 5628
thou shalt *h* it upon four pillars Ex 26:32 5414
thou shalt *h* up the vail under Ex 26:33 5414
h up the hanging at the court Ex 40:8 5414
h them up before the LORD against Num 25:4 3363
to death, and thou *h* him on a tree Deut 21:22 8518
thy life shall *h* in doubt before Deut 28:66 8511
we will *h* them up unto the LORD 2Sa 21:6 3363
to speak unto the king to *h* Est 6:4 8518
Then the king said, *H* him thereon Est 7:9 8518
whereon there *h* a thousand Song 4:4 8518
they shall *h* upon him all the Is 22:24 8518
the virgins of Jerusalem *h* down Lam 2:10 3381
pin of it to *h* any vessel thereon Eze 15:3 8518
two commandments *h* all the law Mt 22:40 *2910*
the venomous beast *h* on his hand Acts 28:4 *2910*
lift up the hands which *h* down Heb 12:12 *3935*

HANGED
But he *h* the chief baker Gen 40:22 8518
unto mine office, and him he *h* Gen 41:13 8518
(for he that is *h* is accursed of Deut 21:23 8518
the king of Ai he *h* on a tree Josh 8:29 8518
them, and *h* them on five trees Josh 10:26 8518
h them up over the pool in Hebron 2Sa 4:12 8518
h himself, and died, and was buried 2Sa 17:23 2614
Behold, I saw Absalom *h* in an oak 2Sa 18:10 8518
they *h* them in the hill before 2Sa 21:9 3363
where the Philistines had *h* them 2Sa 21:12 8511
the bones of them that were *h* 2Sa 21:13 3363
set up, let him be *h* thereon Ezr 6:11 4223
they were both *h* on a tree Est 2:23 8518
that Mordecai may be *h* thereon Est 5:14 8518
So they *h* Haman on the gallows Est 7:10 8518
him they have *h* upon the gallows, Est 8:7 8518
ten sons be *h* upon the gallows Est 9:13 8518
and they *h* Haman's ten sons Est 9:14 8518
sons should be *h* on the gallows Est 9:25 8518
We *h* our harps upon the willows Ps 137:2 8518
Princes are *h* up by their hand Lam 5:12 8518
they *h* the shield and helmet in Eze 27:10 8518
they *h* their shields upon thy Eze 27:11 8518
a millstone were *h* about his neck Mt 18:6 *2910*
and departed, and went and *h* himself. Mt 27:5 *519*
a millstone were *h* about his neck Mk 9:42 *4029*
a millstone were *h* about his neck Lk 17:2 *4029*
which were *h* railed on him Lk 23:39 *2910*
whom ye slew and *h* on a tree Acts 5:30 *2910*
whom they slew and *h* on a tree Acts 10:39 *2910*

HANGETH
and *h* the earth upon nothing Job 26:7 8518
is every one that *h* on a tree Gal 3:13 *2910*

HANGING
thou shalt make an *h* for the door Ex 26:36 4539
thou shalt make for the *h* five Ex 26:37 4539
shall be an *h* of twenty cubits Ex 27:16 4539
the *h* for the door at the Ex 35:15 4539
the *h* for the door of the court Ex 35:17 4539
he made an *h* for the tabernacle Ex 36:37 4539
the *h* for the gate of the court Ex 38:18 4539
the *h* for the tabernacle door, Ex 39:38 4539
the *h* for the court gate, his Ex 39:40 4539
put the *h* of the door to the Ex 40:5 4539
hang up the *h* at the court gate Ex 40:8 4539
he set up the *h* at the door of Ex 40:28 4539
set up the *h* of the court gate Ex 40:33 4539
the *h* for the door of the Num 3:25 4539
wherewith they minister, and the *h* Num 3:31 4539
the *h* for the door of the Num 4:25 4539
the *h* for the door of the gate of Num 4:26 4539
they were *h* upon the trees until Josh 10:26 8518

HANGINGS
be *h* for the court of fine twined Ex 27:9 7050
be *h* of an hundred cubits long Ex 27:11 7050
side shall be *h* of fifty cubits Ex 27:12 7050
The *h* of one side of the gate Ex 27:14 7050
side shall be *h* fifteen cubits Ex 27:15 7050
The *h* of the court, his pillars, Ex 35:17 7050
the *h* of the court were of fine Ex 38:9 7050
side the *h* were an hundred cubits Ex 38:11
west side were *h* of fifty cubits Ex 38:12 7050
The *h* of the one side of the gate Ex 38:14 7050
hand, were *h* of fifteen cubits Ex 38:15 7050
All the *h* of the court round Ex 38:16 7050
answerable to the *h* of the court Ex 38:18 7050
The *h* of the court, his pillars, Ex 39:40 7050
the *h* of the court, and the Num 3:26 7050
the *h* of the court, and the Num 4:26 7050
the women wove *h* for the grove 2Kin 23:7 1004
were white, green, and blue, *h* Est 1:6

HANIEL (*ha'-ne-el*) See HANNIEL. *A son of Ulla.*
Arah, and *H*, and Rezia 1Chr 7:39 2592

HANNAH (*han'-nah*) *Mother of Samuel.*
the name of the one was *H* 1Sa 1:2 2584
children, but *H* had no children 1Sa 1:2 2584
But unto *H* he gave a worthy 1Sa 1:5 2584
for he loved *H* 1Sa 1:5 2584
Elkanah her husband to her, *H* 1Sa 1:8 2584
So *H* rose up after they had eaten 1Sa 1:9 2584
Now *H*, she spake in her heart 1Sa 1:13 2584
H answered and said, No, my lord, 1Sa 1:15 2584
and Elkanah knew *H* his wife 1Sa 1:19 2584
come about after *H* had conceived 1Sa 1:20 2584
But *H* went not up 1Sa 1:22 2584
H prayed, and said, My heart 1Sa 2:1 2584
And the LORD visited *H*, so that 1Sa 2:21 2584

HANNATHON (*han'-na-thon*) *A city in Zebulun.*
it on the north side to *H* Josh 19:14 2615

HANNIEL (*han'-ne-el*) See HANIEL. *A prince of Manasseh.*
of Manasseh, *H* the son of Ephod Num 34:23 2592

HANOCH (*ha'-nok*) See HANOCHITES, HENOCH.
1. A son of Midian.
Ephah, and Epher, and *H*, and Abidah, Gen 25:4 2585
2. A son of Reuben.
H, and Phallu, and Hezron, and Carmi Gen 46:9 2585
H, and Pallu, Hezron, and Carmi Ex 6:14 2585
H, of whom cometh the family of Num 26:5 2585
the firstborn of Israel were, *H* 1Chr 5:3 2585

HANOCHITES (*ha'-nok-ites*) *Descendants of Hanoch 2.*
whom cometh the family of the *H* Num 26:5 2599

HANUN (*ha'-nun*)
1. A king of Ammon.
H his son reigned in his stead 2Sa 10:1 2586
kindness unto *H* the son of Nahash 2Sa 10:2 2586
of Ammon said unto *H* their lord 2Sa 10:3 2586
Wherefore *H* took David's servants 2Sa 10:4 2586
kindness unto *H* the son of Nahash 1Chr 19:2 2586
of the children of Ammon to *H* 1Chr 19:2 2586
the children of Ammon said to *H* 1Chr 19:3 2586
Wherefore *H* took David's servants 1Chr 19:4 2586
themselves odious to David, *H* 1Chr 19:6 2586
2. A son of Zalaph.
H the sixth son of Zalaph, Neh 3:30 2586
3. A rebuilder of Jerusalem's wall.
The valley gate repaired *H* Neh 3:13 2586

HAP
her *h* was to light on a part of Ruth 2:3 4745

HAPHRAIM (*haf-ra'-im*) *A city in Issachar.*
And *H*, and Shihon, and Anaharath, Josh 19:19 2663

HAPLY
if *h* the people had eaten freely 1Sa 14:30 3863
if *h* he might find any thing Mk 11:13 *686*
Lest *h*, after he hath laid the Lk 14:29 *3379*
lest *h* ye be found even to fight Acts 5:39 *3379*
if *h* they might feel after him, Acts 17:27 *686*
Lest *h* if they of Macedonia come 2Cor 9:4 *3381*

HAPPEN
h to thee for this thing 1Sa 28:10 7136
There shall no evil *h* to the just Prov 12:21 579
forth, and shew us what shall *h* Is 41:22 7136
what things should *h* unto him Mk 10:32 *4819*

HAPPENED
it was a chance that *h* to us 1Sa 6:9 1961
As I *h* by chance upon mount 2Sa 1:6 7136
there *h* to be there a man of 2Sa 20:1 7122
him of all that had *h* unto him Est 4:7 7136
therefore this evil is *h* unto you Jer 44:23 7122
of all these things which had *h* Lk 24:14 *4819*
at that which had *h* unto him Acts 3:10 *4819*
blindness in part is *h* to Israel Rom 11:25 *1096*
Now all these things *h* unto them 1Cor 10:11 *4819*
that the things which *h* unto me Phil 1:12
some strange thing *h* unto you 1Pet 4:12 *4819*
But it is *h* unto them according 2Pet 2:22 *4819*

HAPPENETH
also that one event *h* to them all Eccl 2:14 7136
As it *h* to the fool Eccl 2:15 4745
so it *h* even to me Eccl 2:15 7136
unto whom it *h* according to the Eccl 8:14 5060
to whom it *h* according to the Eccl 8:14 5060
but time and chance *h* to them all Eccl 9:11 7136

HAPPIER
But she is *h* if she so abide, 1Cor 7:40 *3107*

HAPPIZZEZ See APHSES.

HAPPY
H am I, for the daughters will Gen 30:13 837
H art thou, O Israel Deut 33:29 835
H are thy men, *h* are these 1Kin 10:8 835
H are thy men, and *h* are these 2Chr 9:7 835
h is the man whom God correcteth Job 5:17 835
H is the man that hath his quiver Ps 127:5 835

h shalt thou be, and it shall be — Ps 128:2 — 835
h shall he be, that rewardeth — Ps 137:8 — 835
H shall he be, that taketh and — Ps 137:9 — 835
H is that people, that is in such — Ps 144:15 — 835
h is that people, whose God is — Ps 144:15 — 835
H is he that hath the God of — Ps 146:5 — 835
H is the man that findeth wisdom, — Prov 3:13 — 835
h is every one that retaineth her — Prov 3:18 — 835
hath mercy on the poor, *h* is he — Prov 14:21 — 835
trusteth in the LORD, *h* is he — Prov 16:20 — 835
H is the man that feareth alway — Prov 28:14 — 835
he that keepeth the law, *h* is he — Prov 29:18 — 835
wherefore are all they *h* that — Jer 12:1 — 7951
And now we call the proud *h* — Mal 3:15 — 833
things, *h* are ye if ye do them — Jn 13:17 — *3107*
I think myself *h*, king Agrippa, — Acts 26:2 — *3107*
H is he that condemneth not — Rom 14:22 — *3107*
we count them *h* which endure — Jas 5:11 — *3106*
for righteousness' sake, *h* are ye — 1Pet 3:14 — *3107*
for the name of Christ, *h* are ye — 1Pet 4:14 — *3107*

HARA (*ha'-rah*) *An Assyrian province.*
them unto Halah, and Habor, and *H* — 1Chr 5:26 — 2024

HARADAH (*har'-a-dah*) *A Hebrew encampment in the wilderness.*
mount Shapher, and encamped in *H* — Num 33:24 — 2732
And they removed from *H*, and — Num 33:25 — 2732

HARAN (*ha'-ran*) See BETH-HARAN, CHARRAN.
1. A son of Terah.
and begat Abram, Nahor, and *H* — Gen 11:26 — 2309
Terah begat Abram, Nahor, and *H* — Gen 11:27 — 2309
and *H* begat Lot — Gen 11:27 — 2309
H died before his father Terah in — Gen 11:28 — 2309
wife, Milcah, the daughter of *H* — Gen 11:29 — 2309
and Lot the son of *H* his son's son — Gen 11:31 — 2309
2. A Levite.
Shelomith, and Haziel, and *H* — 1Chr 23:9 — 2039
3. A son of Caleb.
Ephah, Caleb's concubine, bare *H* — 1Chr 2:46 — 2771
and *H* begat Gazez — 1Chr 2:46 — 2771
4. A city in northern Mesopotamia.
and they came unto *H*, and dwelt — Gen 11:31 — 2771
and Terah died in *H* — Gen 11:32 — 2771
old when he departed out of *H* — Gen 12:4 — 2771
souls that they had gotten in *H* — Gen 12:5 — 2771
thou to Laban my brother to *H* — Gen 27:43 — 2771
from Beer-sheba, and went toward *H* — Gen 28:10 — 2771
And they said, Of *H* are we — Gen 29:4 — 2771
as Gozan, and *H*, and Rezeph, and the — 2Kin 19:12 — 2771
have destroyed, as Gozan, and *H* — Is 37:12 — 2771
H, and Canneh, and Eden, the — Eze 27:23 — 2771

HARARITE (*har'-a-rite*) *Native of the hill country of Judah.*
was Shammah the son of Agee the *H* — 2Sa 23:11 — 2043
Shammah the *H*, Ahiam the son of — 2Sa 23:33 — 2043
Ahiam the son of Sharar the *H* — 2Sa 23:33 — 2043
Jonathan the son of Shage the *H* — 1Chr 11:34 — 2043
Ahiam the son of Sacar the *H* — 1Chr 11:35 — 2043

HARBONA (*har-bo'-nah*) See HARBONAH. *A servant of King Ahasuerus.*
he commanded Mehuman, Biztha, *H* — Est 1:10 — 2726

HARBONAH (*har-bo'-nah*) See HARBONA. *Same as Harbona.*
And *H*, one of the chamberlains, — Est 7:9 — 2726

HARD
Is any thing too *h* for the LORD — Gen 18:14 — 6381
travailed, and she had *h* labour — Gen 35:16 — 7185
to pass, when she was in *h* labour — Gen 35:17 — 7185
their lives bitter with *h* bondage — Ex 1:14 — 7186
the *h* causes they brought unto — Ex 18:26 — 7186
he take off *h* by the backbone — Lev 3:9 — 5980
the cause that is too *h* for you — Deut 1:17 — 7185
It shall not seem *h* unto thee — Deut 15:18 — 7185
matter too *h* for thee in judgment — Deut 17:8 — 6381
us, and laid upon us *h* bondage — Deut 26:6 — 7186
went *h* unto the door of the tower — Judg 9:52 — 5066
pursued *h* after them unto Gidom, — Judg 20:45
even they also followed *h* after — 1Sa 14:22 — 1692
Philistines followed *h* upon Saul — 1Sa 31:2 — 1692
and horsemen followed *h* after him — 2Sa 1:6 — 1692
sons of Zeruiah be too *h* for me — 2Sa 3:39 — 7186
Amnon thought it *h* for him to do — 2Sa 13:2 — 6381
to prove him with *h* questions — 1Kin 10:1 — 2420
h by the palace of Ahab king of — 1Kin 21:1 — 681
said, Thou hast asked a *h* thing — 2Kin 2:10 — 7185
Philistines followed *h* after Saul — 1Chr 10:2 — 5221
in the midst *h* by their buttocks — 1Chr 19:4
with *h* questions at Jerusalem — 2Chr 9:1 — 2420
as *h* as a piece of the nether — Job 41:24 — 3332
hast shewed thy people *h* things — Ps 60:3 — 7186
My soul followeth *h* after thee — Ps 63:8 — 1692
Thy wrath lieth *h* upon me — Ps 88:7 — 5564
they utter and speak *h* things — Ps 94:4 — 6277
but the way of transgressors is *h* — Prov 13:15 — 386
from the *h* bondage wherein thou — Is 14:3 — 7186
there is nothing too *h* for thee — Jer 32:17 — 6381
is there any thing too *h* for me — Jer 32:27 — 6381
of an *h* language, but to the — Eze 3:5 — 3515
of an *h* language, whose words — Eze 3:6 — 3515
dreams, and shewing of *h* sentences — Dan 5:12 — 280
rowed *h* to bring it to the land — Jonah 1:13
knew thee that thou art an *h* man — Mt 25:24 — *4642*
how *h* is it for them that trust — Mk 10:24 — *1422*
this, said, This is an *h* saying — Jn 6:60 — *4642*
it is *h* for thee to kick against — Acts 9:5 — *4642*
house joined *h* to the synagogue — Acts 18:7 — *4927*
it is *h* for thee to kick against — Acts 26:14 — *4642*
h to be uttered, seeing ye are — Heb 5:11 — *1421*
some things *h* to be understood — 2Pet 3:16 — *1425*
of all their *h* speeches which — Jude 15 — *4642*

HARDEN
but I will *h* his heart, that he — Ex 4:21 — 2388
I will *h* Pharaoh's heart, and — Ex 7:3 — 7185
I will *h* Pharaoh's heart, that he — Ex 14:4 — 2388
I will *h* the hearts of the — Ex 14:17 — 2388
thou shalt not *h* thine heart — Deut 15:7 — 533
was of the LORD to *h* their hearts — Josh 11:20 — 2388
then do ye *h* your hearts, as the — 1Sa 6:6 — 5513
I would *h* myself in sorrow — Job 6:10 — 5539
H not your heart, as in the — Ps 95:8 — 7185
H not your hearts, as in the — Heb 3:8 — *4645*
h not your hearts, as in the — Heb 3:15 — *4645*
hear his voice, *h* not your hearts — Heb 4:7 — *4645*

HARDENED
he *h* Pharaoh's heart, that he — Ex 7:13 — 2388
unto Moses, Pharaoh's heart is *h* — Ex 7:14 — 3515
and Pharaoh's heart was *h*, neither — Ex 7:22 — 2388
he *h* his heart, and hearkened not — Ex 8:15 — 3515
and Pharaoh's heart was *h*, and he — Ex 8:19 — 2388
Pharaoh *h* his heart at this time — Ex 8:32 — 3513
And the heart of Pharaoh was *h* — Ex 9:7 — 3515
the LORD *h* the heart of Pharaoh, — Ex 9:12 — 2388
h his heart, he and his servants — Ex 9:34 — 3513
And the heart of Pharaoh was *h* — Ex 9:35 — 2388
for I have *h* his heart, and the — Ex 10:1 — 3513
But the LORD *h* Pharaoh's heart, — Ex 10:20 — 2388
But the LORD *h* Pharaoh's heart, — Ex 10:27 — 2388
the LORD *h* Pharaoh's heart, so — Ex 11:10 — 2388
the LORD *h* the heart of Pharaoh — Ex 14:8 — 2388
for the LORD thy God *h* his spirit — Deut 2:30 — 7185
and Pharaoh *h* their hearts — 1Sa 6:6 — 3513
but *h* their necks, like to the — 2Kin 17:14 — 7185
h his heart from turning unto the — 2Chr 36:13 — 553
h their necks, and hearkened not — Neh 9:16 — 7185
but *h* their necks, and in their — Neh 9:17 — 7185
h their neck, and would not hear — Neh 9:29 — 7185
who hath *h* himself against him, — Job 9:4 — 7185
She is *h* against her young ones, — Job 39:16 — 7188
h our heart from thy fear — Is 63:17 — 7188
their ear, but *h* their neck — Jer 7:26 — 7185
because they have *h* their necks — Jer 19:15 — 7185
lifted up, and his mind *h* in pride — Dan 5:20 — 8631
for their heart was *h* — Mk 6:52 — *4456*
have ye your heart yet *h* — Mk 8:17 — *4456*
their eyes, and *h* their heart — Jn 12:40 — *4456*
But when divers were *h*, and — Acts 19:9 — *4645*
lest any of you be *h* through the — Heb 3:13 — *4645*

HARDENETH
A wicked man *h* his face — Prov 21:29 — 5810
but he that *h* his heart shall — Prov 28:14 — 7185
being often reproved *h* his neck — Prov 29:1 — 7185
have mercy, and whom he will he *h* — Rom 9:18 — *4645*

HARDER
A brother offended is *h* to be won — Prov 18:19
made their faces *h* than a rock — Jer 5:3 — 2388
As an adamant *h* than flint have I — Eze 3:9 — 2389

HARDHEARTED
house of Israel are impudent and *h* — Eze 3:7

HARDLY
And when Sarai dealt *h* with her — Gen 16:6 — 6031
when Pharaoh would *h* let us go — Ex 13:15 — 7185
through it, *h* bestead and hungry — Is 8:21 — 7185
That a rich man shall *h* enter — Mt 19:23 — *1423*
How *h* shall they that have riches — Mk 10:23 — *1423*
bruising him *h* departeth from him — Lk 9:39 — *3425*
How *h* shall they that have riches — Lk 18:24 — *1423*
h passing it, came unto a place — Acts 27:8 — *3433*

HARDNESS
When the dust groweth into *h* — Job 38:38 — 4165
Moses because of the *h* of your — Mt 19:8 — *4641*
grieved for the *h* of their hearts — Mk 3:5 — *4457*
For the *h* of your heart he wrote — Mk 10:5 — *4641*
h of heart, because they believed — Mk 16:14 — *4641*
But after thy *h* and impenitent — Rom 2:5 — *4643*
Thou therefore endure *h*, as a — 2Ti 2:3 — *2553*

HARE
And the *h*, because he cheweth the — Lev 11:6 — 768
as the camel, and the *h*, and the — Deut 14:7 — 768

HAREPH (*ha'-ref*) *A son of Caleb.*
H the father of Beth-gader — 1Chr 2:51 — 2780

HARETH (*ha'-reth*) *Forest land in Judah.*
and came into the forest of *H* — 1Sa 22:5 — 2802

HARHAIAH (*har-ha-i'-ah*) *Father of Uzziel.*
him repaired Uzziel the son of *H* — Neh 3:8 — 2736

HARHAS (*har'-has*) See HASRAH. *Grandfather of Shallum.*
the son of Tikvah, the son of *H* — 2Kin 22:14 — 2745

HARHUR (*har'-hur*) *A family in exile.*
of Hakupha, the children of *H* — Ezr 2:51 — 2744
of Hakupha, the children of *H* — Neh 7:53 — 2744

HARIM (*ha'-rim*)
1. A priest.
The third to *H*, the fourth to — 1Chr 24:8 — 2766
The children of *H*, a thousand and — Ezr 2:39 — 2766
And of the sons of *H* — Ezr 10:21 — 2766
Malchijah the son of *H*, and Hashub — Neh 3:11 — 2766
The children of *H*, a thousand and — Neh 7:42 — 2766
Of *H*, Adna; of Meraioth — Neh 12:15 — 2766
2. A family in exile.
The children of *H*, three hundred — Ezr 2:32 — 2766
The children of *H*, three hundred — Neh 7:35 — 2766
3. Married a foreigner in exile.
And of the sons of *H* — Ezr 10:31 — 2766
4. An Israelite who renewed the covenant.
H, Meremoth, Obadiah, — Neh 10:5 — 2766
5. A family who renewed the covenant.
Malluch, *H*, Baanah — Neh 10:27 — 2766

HARIPH (*ha'-rif*) See JORAH.
1. A family of exiles.
The children of *H*, an hundred and — Neh 7:24 — 2756
2. A family who renewed the covenant.
H, Anathoth, Nebai, — Neh 10:19 — 2756

HARLOT
deal with our sister as with an *h* — Gen 34:31 — 2181
her, he thought her to be an *h* — Gen 38:15 — 2181
place, saying, Where is the *h* — Gen 38:21 — 6948
There was no *h* in this place — Gen 38:21 — 6948
that there was no *h* in this place — Gen 38:22 — 6948
daughter in law hath played the *h* — Gen 38:24 — 2181
woman, or profane, or an *h* — Lev 21:14 — 2181
only Rahab the *h* shall live — Josh 6:17 — 2181
And Joshua saved Rahab the *h* alive — Josh 6:25 — 2181
valour, and he was the son of an *h* — Judg 11:1 — 2181
Samson to Gaza, and saw there an *h* — Judg 16:1 — 2181
a woman with the attire of an *h* — Prov 7:10 — 2181
is the faithful city become an *h* — Is 1:21 — 2181
years shall Tyre sing as an *h* — Is 23:15 — 2181
thou *h* that hast been forgotten — Is 23:16 — 2181
thou wanderest, playing the *h* — Jer 2:20 — 2181
played the *h* with many lovers — Jer 3:1 — 2181
tree, and there hath played the *h* — Jer 3:6 — 2181
but went and played the *h* also — Jer 3:8 — 2181
playedst the *h* because of thy — Eze 16:15 — 2181
and playedst the *h* thereupon — Eze 16:16 — 2181
thou hast played the *h* with them — Eze 16:28 — 2181
and hast not been as an *h*, in that — Eze 16:31 — 2181
Wherefore, O *h*, hear the word of — Eze 16:35 — 2181
thee to cease from playing the *h* — Eze 16:41 — 2181
played the *h* when she was mine — Eze 23:5 — 2181
played the *h* in the land of Egypt — Eze 23:19 — 2181
unto a woman that playeth the *h* — Eze 23:44 — 2181
their mother hath played the *h* — Hos 2:5 — 2181
thou shalt not play the *h* — Hos 3:3 — 2181
Though thou, Israel, play the *h* — Hos 4:15 — 2181
and have given a boy for an *h* — Joel 3:3 — 2181
wife shall be an *h* in the city — Amos 7:17 — 2181
gathered it of the hire of an *h* — Mic 1:7 — 2181
shall return to the hire of an *h* — Mic 1:7 — 2181
whoredoms of the wellfavoured *h* — Nah 3:4 — 2181
and make them the members of an *h* — 1Cor 6:15 — *4204*
is joined to an *h* is one body — 1Cor 6:16 — *4204*
By faith the *h* Rahab perished not — Heb 11:31 — *4204*
Rahab the *h* justified by works — Jas 2:25 — *4204*

HARLOT'S
went, and came into an *h* house — Josh 2:1 — 2181
the country, Go into the *h* house — Josh 6:22 — 2181

HARLOTS
came there two women, that were *h* — 1Kin 3:16 — 2181
with *h* spendeth his substance — Prov 29:3 — 2181
whores, and they sacrifice with *h* — Hos 4:14 — 6948
the *h* go into the kingdom of God — Mt 21:31 — *4204*
publicans and the *h* believed him — Mt 21:32 — *4204*
hath devoured thy living with *h* — Lk 15:30 — *4204*
THE GREAT, THE MOTHER OF *H* — Rev 17:5 — *4204*

HARLOTS'
by troops in the *h* houses — Jer 5:7 — 2181

HARM
and this pillar unto me, for *h* — Gen 31:52 — 7451
he shall make amends for the *h* — Lev 5:16 — 2398
his enemy, neither sought his *h* — Num 35:23 — 7451
for I will no more do thee *h* — 1Sa 26:21 — 7489
do us more *h* than did Absalom — 2Sa 20:6 — 3415
And there was no *h* in the pot — 2Kin 4:41
anointed, and do my prophets no *h* — 1Chr 16:22 — 7489
anointed, and do my prophets no *h* — Ps 105:15 — 7489
cause, if he have done thee no *h* — Prov 3:30 — 7451
look well to him, and do him no *h* — Jer 39:12 — 7451
voice, saying, Do thyself no *h* — Acts 16:28 — *2556*
Crete, and to have gained this *h* — Acts 27:21 — *5196*
beast into the fire, and felt no *h* — Acts 28:5 — *2556*
saw no *h* come to him, they — Acts 28:6 — *824*
shewed or spake any *h* of thee — Acts 28:21 — *4190*
And who is he that will *h* you — 1Pet 3:13 — *2559*

HAR-MAGEDON See ARMAGEDDON.

HARMLESS
wise as serpents, and *h* as doves — Mt 10:16 — *185*
That ye may be blameless and *h* — Phil 2:15 — *185*
priest became us, who is holy, *h* — Heb 7:26 — *172*

HARNEPHER (*har-ne'-fur*) *A son of Zophah.*
Suah, and *H*, and Shual, and Beri, and — 1Chr 7:36 — 2774

HARNESS
on his *h* boast himself as he that — 1Kin 20:11
between the joints of the *h* — 1Kin 22:34 — 8302
and vessels of gold, and raiment, *h* — 2Chr 9:24 — 5402
between the joints of the *h* — 2Chr 18:33 — 8302
H the horses — Jer 46:4 — 631

HARNESSED
up *h* out of the land of Egypt — Ex 13:18 — 2571

HAROD (*ha'-rod*) See HARODITE. *A spring of water.*
and pitched beside the well of *H* — Judg 7:1 — 5878

HARODITE (*ha-ro'-dite*) See HARORITE. *Family name of two of David's "mighty men."*
Shammah the *H*, Elika the *H* — 2Sa 23:25 — 2733

HAROEH (*ha-ro'-eh*) See REAIAH. *A son of Shobal.*
H, and half of the Manahethites — 1Chr 2:52 — 7204

HARORITE (*ha'-ro-rite*) *Family name of a "mighty man."*
Shammoth the *H*, Helez the — 1Chr 11:27 — 2033

HAROSHETH (*har'-o-sheth*) *A city in Galilee.*
which dwelt in *H* of the Gentiles — Judg 4:2 — 2800
from *H* of the Gentiles unto the — Judg 4:13 — 2800

the host, unto *H* of the Gentiles ... Judg 4:16 2800

HARP
of all such as handle the *h* ... Gen 4:21 3658
songs, with tabret, and with *h* ... Gen 31:27 3658
and a tabret, and a pipe, and a *h* ... 1Sa 10:5 3658
who is a cunning player on an *h* ... 1Sa 16:16 3658
upon Saul, that David took an *h* ... 1Sa 16:23 3658
Jeduthun, who prophesied with a *h* ... 1Chr 25:3 3658
They take the timbrel and *h* ... Job 21:12 3658
My *h* also is turned to mourning, ... Job 30:31 3658
Praise the LORD with *h* ... Ps 33:2 3658
upon the *h* will I praise thee, O ... Ps 43:4 3658
open my dark saying upon the *h* ... Ps 49:4 3658
awake, psaltery and *h* ... Ps 57:8 3658
unto thee will I sing with the *h* ... Ps 71:22 3658
the pleasant *h* with the psaltery ... Ps 81:2 3658
upon the *h* with a solemn sound ... Ps 92:3 3658
Sing unto the LORD with the *h* ... Ps 98:5 3658
with the *h*, and the voice of a ... Ps 98:5 3658
Awake, psaltery and *h* ... Ps 108:2 3658
praise upon the *h* unto our God ... Ps 147:7 3658
unto him with the timbrel and *h* ... Ps 149:3 3658
praise him with the psaltery and *h* ... Ps 150:3 3658
And the *h*, and the viol, the tabret ... Is 5:12 3658
shall sound like an *h* for Moab ... Is 16:11 3658
Take an *h*, go about the city, ... Is 23:16 3658
endeth, the joy of the *h* ceaseth ... Is 24:8 3658
the sound of the cornet, flute, *h* ... Dan 3:5 7030
the sound of the cornet, flute, *h* ... Dan 3:7 7030
the sound of the cornet, flute, *h* ... Dan 3:10 7030
the sound of the cornet, flute, *h* ... Dan 3:15 7030
giving sound, whether pipe or *h* ... 1Cor 14:7 *2788*

HARPED
it be known what is piped or *h* ... 1Cor 14:7 *2789*

HARPERS
I heard the voice of *h* harping ... Rev 14:2 *2790*
And the voice of *h*, and musicians, ... Rev 18:22 *2790*

HARPING
of harpers *h* with their harps ... Rev 14:2 *2789*

HARPS
made of fir wood, even on *h* ... 2Sa 6:5 3658
h also and psalteries for singers ... 1Kin 10:12 3658
might, and with singing, and with *h* ... 1Chr 13:8 3658
of musick, psalteries and *h* ... 1Chr 15:16 3658
with *h* on the Sheminith to excel ... 1Chr 15:21 3658
a noise with psalteries and *h* ... 1Chr 15:28 3658
Jeiel with psalteries and with *h* ... 1Chr 16:5 3658
who should prophesy with *h* ... 1Chr 25:1 3658
with cymbals, psalteries, and *h* ... 1Chr 25:6 3658
having cymbals and psalteries and *h* ... 2Chr 5:12 3658
and to the king's palace, and *h* ... 2Chr 9:11 3658
to Jerusalem with psalteries and *h* ... 2Chr 20:28 3658
with psalteries, and with *h* ... 2Chr 29:25 3658
cymbals, psalteries, and with *h* ... Neh 12:27 3658
We hanged our *h* upon the willows ... Ps 137:2 3658
it shall be with tabrets and *h* ... Is 30:32 3658
the sound of thy *h* shall be no ... Eze 26:13 3658
Lamb, having every one of them *h* ... Rev 5:8 *2788*
of harpers harping with their *h* ... Rev 14:2 *2788*
sea of glass, having the *h* of God ... Rev 15:2 *2788*

HARROW
or will he *h* the valleys after ... Job 39:10 7702

HARROWS
under *h* of iron, and under axes of ... 2Sa 12:31 2757
with *h* of iron, and with axes ... 1Chr 20:3 2757

HARSHA (*har'-shah*) *A family of exiles.*
of Mehida, the children of *H* ... Ezr 2:52 2797
of Mehida, the children of *H* ... Neh 7:54 2797

HART
as of the roebuck, and as of the *h* ... Deut 12:15 354
the *h* is eaten, so thou shalt eat ... Deut 12:22 354
The *h*, and the roebuck, and the ... Deut 14:5 354
as the roebuck, and as the *h* ... Deut 15:22 354
As the *h* panteth after the water ... Ps 42:1 354
is like a roe or a young *h* ... Song 2:9 354
h upon the mountains of Bether ... Song 2:17 354
like to a roe or to a young *h* ... Song 8:14 354
shall the lame man leap as an *h* ... Is 35:6 354

HARTS
and an hundred sheep, beside *h* ... 1Kin 4:23 354
like *h* that find no pasture ... Lam 1:6 354

HARUM (*ha'-rum*) *Father of Aharhel.*
families of Aharhel the son of *H* ... 1Chr 4:8 2037

HARUMAPH (*ha-ru'-maf*) *Father of Jedaiah.*
repaired Jedaiah the son of *H* ... Neh 3:10 2739

HARUPHITE (*ha'-ru-fite*) *A Korhite soldier.*
and Shemariah, and Shephatiah the *H*. 1Chr 12:5 2741

HARUZ (*ha'ruz*) *Father of Meshullemeth.*
the daughter of *H* of Jotbah ... 2Kin 21:19 2743

HARVEST
earth remaineth, seedtime and *h* ... Gen 8:22 7105
went in the days of wheat *h* ... Gen 30:14 7105
shall neither be earing nor *h* ... Gen 45:6 7105
And the feast of *h*, the ... Ex 23:16 7105
time and in *h* thou shalt rest ... Ex 34:21 7105
of the firstfruits of wheat *h* ... Ex 34:22 7105
when ye reap the *h* of your land ... Lev 19:9 7105
gather the gleanings of thy *h* ... Lev 19:9 7105
you, and shall reap the *h* thereof ... Lev 23:10 7105
of your *h* unto the priest ... Lev 23:10 7105
when ye reap the *h* of your land ... Lev 23:22 7105
thou gather any gleaning of thy *h* ... Lev 23:22 7105
of thy *h* thou shalt not reap ... Lev 25:5 7105
cuttest down thine *h* in thy field ... Deut 24:19 7105
all his banks all the time of *h* ... Josh 3:15 7105
after, in the time of wheat *h* ... Judg 15:1 7105
in the beginning of barley *h* ... Ruth 1:22 7105
until they have ended all my *h* ... Ruth 2:21 7105
of barley *h* and of wheat *h* ... Ruth 2:23 7105
their wheat *h* in the valley ... 1Sa 6:13 7105
ear his ground, and to reap his *h* ... 1Sa 8:12 7105
Is it not wheat *h* to day ... 1Sa 12:17 7105
put to death in the days of *h* ... 2Sa 21:9 7105
in the beginning of barley *h* ... 2Sa 21:9 7105
from the beginning of *h* until ... 2Sa 21:10 7105
came to David in the *h* time unto ... 2Sa 23:13 7105
Whose *h* the hungry eateth up, and ... Job 5:5 7105
and gathereth her food in the *h* ... Prov 6:8 7105
but he that sleepeth in *h* is a ... Prov 10:5 7105
therefore shall he beg in *h* ... Prov 20:4 7105
the cold of snow in the time of *h* ... Prov 25:13 7105
snow in summer, and as rain in *h* ... Prov 26:1 7105
thee according to the joy in *h* ... Is 9:3 7105
fruits and for thy *h* is fallen ... Is 16:9 7105
but the *h* shall be a heap in the ... Is 17:11 7105
a cloud of dew in the heat of *h* ... Is 18:4 7105
For afore the *h*, when the bud is ... Is 18:5 7105
the *h* of the river, is her ... Is 23:3 7105
And they shall eat up thine *h* ... Jer 5:17 7105
us the appointed weeks of the *h* ... Jer 5:24 7105
The *h* is past, the summer is ... Jer 8:20 7105
the sickle in the time of *h* ... Jer 50:16 7105
and the time of her *h* shall come ... Jer 51:33 7105
Judah, he hath set an *h* for thee ... Hos 6:11 7105
because the *h* of the field is ... Joel 1:11 7105
in the sickle, for the *h* is ripe ... Joel 3:13 7105
were yet three months to the *h* ... Amos 4:7 7105
The *h* truly is plenteous, but the ... Mt 9:37 *2326*
ye therefore the Lord of the *h* ... Mt 9:38 *2326*
send forth labourers into his *h* ... Mt 9:38 *2326*
both grow together until the *h* ... Mt 13:30 *2326*
in the time of *h* I will say to ... Mt 13:30 *2326*
the *h* is the end of the world ... Mt 13:39 *2326*
the sickle, because the *h* is come ... Mk 4:29 *2326*
The *h* truly is great, but the ... Lk 10:2 *2326*
ye therefore the Lord of the *h* ... Lk 10:2 *2326*
send forth labourers into his *h* ... Lk 10:2 *2326*
yet four months, and then cometh *h* ... Jn 4:35 *2326*
for they are white already to *h* ... Jn 4:35 *2326*
for the *h* of the earth is ripe ... Rev 14:15 *2326*

HARVESTMAN
as when the *h* gathereth the corn ... Is 17:5 7105
and as the handful after the *h* ... Jer 9:22 7114

HASADIAH (*has-a-di'-ah*) *A son of Zerubbabel.*
and Ohel, and Berechiah, and *H* ... 1Chr 3:20 2619

HASENUAH (*has-e-nu'-ah*) See SENUAH. *Father of Hodaviah.*
the son of Hodaviah, the son of *H* ... 1Chr 9:7 5574

HASHABIAH (*hash-a-bi'-ah*)
1. Son of Amaziah.
The son of *H*, the son of Amaziah, ... 1Chr 6:45 2811
2. A Merarite Levite.
the son of Azrikam, the son of *H* ... 1Chr 9:14 2811
3. A son of Jeduthun.
Gedaliah, and Zeri, and Jeshaiah, *H* ... 1Chr 25:3 2811
The twelfth to *H*, he, his sons, ... 1Chr 25:19 2811
4. A descendant of Hebron.
And of the Hebronites, *H* and his ... 1Chr 26:30 2811
5. Son of Kemuel.
the Levites, *H* the son of Kemuel ... 1Chr 27:17 2811
6. A Levite chief.
and Nethaneel, his brethren, and *H* ... 2Chr 35:9 2811
7. A Levite in exile.
And *H*, and with him Jeshaiah of the ... Ezr 8:19 2811
8. A chief priest.
of the priests, Sherebiah, *H* ... Ezr 8:24 2811
9. A rebuilder of Jerusalem's wall.
Next unto him repaired *H*, the ... Neh 3:17 2811
10. A Levite who renewed the covenant.
Micha, Rehob, *H*, ... Neh 10:11 2811
11. Son of Bunni.
the son of Azrikam, the son of *H* ... Neh 11:15 2811
12. Another Levite.
the son of Bani, the son of *H* ... Neh 11:22 2811
13. A priest in Joiakim's time.
Of Hilkiah, *H* ... Neh 12:21 2811
14. A chief Levite.
H, Sherebiah, and Jeshua the son ... Neh 12:24 2811

HASHABNAH (*hash-ab'-nah*) *A clan leader who renewed the covenant.*
Rehum, *H*, Maaseiah, ... Neh 10:25 2812

HASHABNEIAH See HASHABNIAH.

HASHABNIAH (*hash-ab-ni'-ah*)
1. Father of Hattush.
him repaired Hattush the son of *H* ... Neh 3:10 2813
2. A Levite.
Jeshua, and Kadmiel, Bani, *H* ... Neh 9:5 2813

HASHBADANA (*hash-bad'-a-nah*) *A priest.*
and Malchiah, and Hashum, and *H* ... Neh 8:4 2806

HASHBADDANAH See HASHBADANA.

HASHEM (*ha'-shem*) *Father of several "mighty men."*
The sons of *H* the Gizonite, ... 1Chr 11:34 2044

HASHMONAH (*hash-mo'-nah*) *A Hebrew encampment in the wilderness.*
from Mithcah, and pitched in *H* ... Num 33:29 2832
And they departed from *H*, and ... Num 33:30 2832

HASHUB (*ha'-shub*) See HASSHUB.
1. Father of Shemaiah.
Shemaiah the son of *H*, the son of ... Neh 11:15 2815
2. Son of Pahath-moab.
H the son of Pahath-moab, ... Neh 3:11 2815
3. A rebuilder of Jerusalem's wall.
H over against their house ... Neh 3:23 2815
4. A clan leader who renewed the covenant.
Hoshea, Hananiah, *H*, ... Neh 10:23 2815

HASHUBAH (*hash-u'-bah*) *A son of Zerubbabel.*
And *H*, and Ohel, and Berechiah, and .. 1Chr 3:20 2807

HASHUM (*ha'-shum*)
1. A family of exiles.
The children of *H*, two hundred ... Ezr 2:19 2828
Of the sons of *H* ... Ezr 10:33 2828
The children of *H*, three hundred ... Neh 7:22 2828
2. A priest.
and Mishael, and Malchiah, and *H* ... Neh 8:4 2828
3. A clan leader who renewed the covenant.
Hodijah, *H*, Bezai, ... Neh 10:18 2828

HASHUPHA (*hash-u'-fah*) See HASUPHA. *A family of exiles.*
of Ziha, the children of *H* ... Neh 7:46 2817

HASRAH (*has'-rah*) See HARHAS. *Same as Harhas.*
the son of Tikvath, the son of *H* ... 2Chr 34:22 2641

HASSENAAH (*has-se-na'-ah*) See SENAAH. *Father of some rebuilders of Jerusalem's wall.*
fish gate did the sons of *H* build ... Neh 3:3 5574

HASSENUAH See SENUAH.

HASSHUB (*hash'-ub*) See HASHUB. *Father of Shemaiah.*
Shemaiah the son of *H*, the son of ... 1Chr 9:14 2815

HASSPHERETH See SOPHERETH.

HAST
H thou eaten of the tree, whereof ... Gen 3:11
What is this that thou *h* done ... Gen 3:13
serpent, Because thou *h* done this ... Gen 3:14
Because thou *h* hearkened unto the ... Gen 3:17
h eaten of the tree, of which I ... Gen 3:17
And he said, What *h* thou done ... Gen 4:10
thou *h* driven me out this day ... Gen 4:14
is this that thou *h* done unto me ... Gen 12:18
to me thou *h* given no seed ... Gen 15:3
they said, So do, as thou *h* said ... Gen 18:5
unto Lot, *H* thou here any besides ... Gen 19:12
and whatsoever thou *h* in the city ... Gen 19:12
thou *h* magnified thy mercy ... Gen 19:19
which thou *h* shewed unto me in ... Gen 19:19
city, for the which thou *h* spoken ... Gen 19:21
for the woman which thou *h* taken ... Gen 20:3
him, What *h* thou done unto us ... Gen 20:9
that thou *h* brought on me and on ... Gen 20:9
thou *h* done deeds unto me that ... Gen 20:9
that thou *h* done this thing ... Gen 20:10
the land wherein thou *h* sojourned ... Gen 21:23
which thou *h* set by themselves ... Gen 21:29
seeing thou *h* not withheld thy ... Gen 22:12
because thou *h* done this thing ... Gen 22:16
h not withheld thy son, thine ... Gen 22:16
because thou *h* obeyed my voice ... Gen 22:18
let the same be she that thou *h* ... Gen 24:14
h shewed kindness unto my master ... Gen 24:14
What is this thou *h* done unto us ... Gen 26:10
that thou *h* found it so quickly ... Gen 27:20
H thou not reserved a blessing ... Gen 27:36
H thou but one blessing, my ... Gen 27:38
that which thou *h* done to him ... Gen 27:45
What is this thou *h* done unto me ... Gen 29:25
wherefore then *h* thou beguiled me ... Gen 29:25
that thou *h* taken my husband ... Gen 30:15
What *h* thou done, that thou *h* ... Gen 31:26
that thou *h* stolen away unawares ... Gen 31:26
h not suffered me to kiss my sons ... Gen 31:28
thou *h* now done foolishly in so ... Gen 31:28
yet wherefore *h* thou stolen my ... Gen 31:30
that thou *h* so hotly pursued ... Gen 31:36
Whereas thou *h* searched all my ... Gen 31:37
what *h* thou found of all thy ... Gen 31:37
thou *h* changed my wages ten times ... Gen 31:41
which thou *h* shewed unto thy ... Gen 32:10
for as a prince *h* thou power with ... Gen 32:28
God and with men, and *h* prevailed ... Gen 32:28
keep that thou *h* unto thyself ... Gen 33:9
is this dream that thou *h* dreamed ... Gen 37:10
this kid, and thou *h* not found her ... Gen 38:23
she said, How *h* thou broken forth ... Gen 38:29
which thou *h* brought unto us, ... Gen 39:17
and thy herds, and all that thou *h* ... Gen 45:10
thy household, and all that thou *h* ... Gen 45:11
they said, Thou *h* saved our lives ... Gen 47:25
he said, I will do as thou *h* said ... Gen 47:30
When thou *h* brought forth the ... Ex 3:12
nor since thou *h* spoken unto thy ... Ex 4:10
Lord, wherefore *h* thou so evil ... Ex 5:22
why is it that thou *h* sent me ... Ex 5:22
neither *h* thou delivered thy ... Ex 5:23
and all that thou *h* in the field ... Ex 9:19
Thou *h* spoken well, I will see ... Ex 10:29
when thou *h* circumcised him, then ... Ex 12:44
cometh of a beast which thou *h* ... Ex 13:12 1961
h thou taken us away to die in ... Ex 14:11
wherefore *h* thou dealt thus with ... Ex 14:11
of thine excellency thou *h* ... Ex 15:7
Thou in thy mercy *h* led forth the ... Ex 15:13
the people which thou *h* redeemed ... Ex 15:13
thou *h* guided them in thy ... Ex 15:13
pass over, which thou *h* purchased ... Ex 15:16
which thou *h* made for thee to ... Ex 15:17
thou *h* brought us up out of Egypt ... Ex 17:3
tool upon it, thou *h* polluted it ... Ex 20:25
which thou *h* sown in the field ... Ex 23:16

when thou *h* gathered in thy ... Ex 23:16
when thou *h* made an atonement for ... Ex 29:36
which thou *h* brought forth out of ... Ex 32:11
that thou *h* brought so great a ... Ex 32:21
of thy book which thou *h* written ... Ex 32:32
the people which thou *h* brought ... Ex 33:1
thou *h* not let me know whom thou ... Ex 33:12
Yet thou *h* said, I know thee by ... Ex 33:12
thou *h* also found grace in my ... Ex 33:12
thing also that thou *h* spoken ... Ex 33:17
for thou *h* found grace in my ... Ex 33:17
if thou *h* not gone aside to ... Num 5:19
But if thou *h* gone aside to ... Num 5:20
Wherefore *h* thou afflicted thy ... Num 11:11
and thou *h* said, I will give them ... Num 11:21
great, according as thou *h* spoken ... Num 14:17
as thou *h* forgiven this people, ... Num 14:19
h brought us up out of a land ... Num 16:13
Moreover thou *h* not brought us ... Num 16:14
that thou *h* smitten me these ... Num 22:28
the ass, Because thou *h* mocked me ... Num 22:29
upon which thou *h* ridden ever ... Num 22:30
Wherefore *h* thou smitten thine ... Num 22:32
Balaam, What *h* thou done unto me ... Num 23:11
thou *h* blessed them altogether ... Num 23:11
thou *h* altogether blessed them ... Num 24:10
And when thou *h* seen it, thou also ... Num 27:13
The thing which thou *h* spoken is ... Deut 1:14
where thou *h* seen how that the ... Deut 1:31
thou *h* lacked nothing ... Deut 2:7
thou *h* begun to shew thy servant ... Deut 3:24
of the fire, as thou *h* heard ... Deut 4:33
When thou *h* eaten and art full, ... Deut 8:10
Lest when thou *h* eaten and art ... Deut 8:12
h built goodly houses, and dwelt ... Deut 8:12
and all that thou *h* is multiplied ... Deut 8:13
and of whom thou *h* heard say ... Deut 9:2
for thy people which thou *h* ... Deut 9:12
which thou *h* redeemed through thy ... Deut 9:26
which thou *h* brought forth out of ... Deut 9:26
Only thy holy things which thou *h* ... Deut 12:26 1961
gods, which thou *h* not known ... Deut 13:2
gods, which thou *h* not known ... Deut 13:6
after that thou *h* gathered in thy ... Deut 16:13
thou *h* heard of it, and enquired ... Deut 17:4
Israel, whom thou *h* redeemed ... Deut 21:8
thou *h* taken them captive, ... Deut 21:10
h a desire unto her, that thou ... Deut 21:11
her, because thou *h* humbled her ... Deut 21:14
thou *h* found, shalt thou do ... Deut 22:3
of thy seed which thou *h* sown ... Deut 22:9
according as thou *h* vowed unto ... Deut 23:23
which thou *h* promised with thy ... Deut 23:23
h forgot a sheaf in the field, ... Deut 24:19
which thou, O LORD, *h* given me ... Deut 26:10
When thou *h* made an end of ... Deut 26:12
h given it unto the Levite, the ... Deut 26:12
which thou *h* commanded me ... Deut 26:13
to all that thou *h* commanded me ... Deut 26:14
and the land which thou *h* given us ... Deut 26:15
Thou *h* avouched the LORD this day ... Deut 26:17
whereby thou *h* forsaken me ... Deut 28:20
h forgotten God that formed thee ... Deut 32:18
oath which thou *h* made us swear ... Josh 2:17
which thou *h* made us to swear ... Josh 2:20
wherefore *h* thou at all brought ... Josh 7:7
and tell me now what thou *h* done ... Josh 7:19
said, Why *h* thou troubled us ... Josh 7:25
because thou *h* wholly followed ... Josh 14:9
for thou *h* given me a south land ... Josh 15:19
Why *h* thou given me but one lot ... Josh 17:14
a great people, and *h* great power ... Josh 17:17
for thou *h* given me a south land ... Judg 1:15
thou *h* trodden down strength ... Judg 5:21
by mine hand, as thou *h* said ... Judg 6:36
by mine hand, as thou *h* said ... Judg 6:37
Why *h* thou served us thus, that ... Judg 8:1
for thou *h* delivered us from the ... Judg 8:22
the people that thou *h* despised ... Judg 9:38
What *h* thou to do with me, that ... Judg 11:12
thou *h* brought me very low, and ... Judg 11:35
if thou *h* opened thy mouth unto ... Judg 11:36
thou *h* put forth a riddle unto ... Judg 14:16
of my people, and *h* not told it me ... Judg 14:16
is this that thou *h* done unto us ... Judg 15:11
and said, Thou *h* given this great ... Judg 15:18
thou *h* mocked me, and told me lies ... Judg 16:10
Samson, Hitherto thou *h* mocked me ... Judg 16:13
thou *h* mocked me these three ... Judg 16:15
h not told me wherein thy great ... Judg 16:15
and what *h* thou here ... Judg 18:3
all that thou *h* done unto thy ... Ruth 2:11
how thou *h* left thy father and thy ... Ruth 2:11
for that thou *h* comforted me ... Ruth 2:13
for that thou *h* spoken friendly ... Ruth 2:13
Where *h* thou gleaned to day ... Ruth 2:19
for thou *h* shewed more kindness ... Ruth 3:10
the vail that thou *h* upon thee ... Ruth 3:15
petition that thou *h* asked of him ... 1Sa 1:17
for thou *h* born a son ... 1Sa 4:20
Thou *h* not defrauded us, nor ... 1Sa 12:4
neither *h* thou taken ought of any ... 1Sa 12:4
And Samuel said, What *h* thou done ... 1Sa 13:11
to Saul, Thou *h* done foolishly ... 1Sa 13:13
thou *h* not kept the commandment ... 1Sa 13:13
because thou *h* not kept that ... 1Sa 13:14
Tell me what thou *h* done ... 1Sa 14:43
Because thou *h* rejected the word ... 1Sa 15:23
for thou *h* rejected the word of ... 1Sa 15:26
with whom *h* thou left those few ... 1Sa 17:28
of Israel, whom thou *h* defied ... 1Sa 17:45
Why *h* thou deceived me so, and ... 1Sa 19:17
for thou *h* brought thy servant ... 1Sa 20:8
when thou *h* stayed three days, ... 1Sa 20:19

do not I know that thou *h* chosen ... 1Sa 20:30
in that thou *h* given him bread, ... 1Sa 22:13
h enquired of God for him, that ... 1Sa 22:13
for thou *h* rewarded me good, ... 1Sa 24:17
thou *h* shewed this day how that ... 1Sa 24:18
that thou *h* dealt well with me ... 1Sa 24:18
that thou *h* done unto me this day ... 1Sa 24:19
and peace be unto all that thou *h* ... 1Sa 25:6
I have heard that thou *h* shearers ... 1Sa 25:7
either that thou *h* shed blood ... 1Sa 25:31
which *h* kept me this day from ... 1Sa 25:33
wherefore then *h* thou not kept ... 1Sa 26:15
is not good that thou *h* done ... 1Sa 26:16
saying, Why *h* thou deceived me ... 1Sa 28:12
Why *h* thou disquieted me, to ... 1Sa 28:15
place which thou *h* appointed him ... 1Sa 29:4
thou *h* been upright, and thy going ... 1Sa 29:6
what *h* thou found in thy servant ... 1Sa 29:8
very pleasant *h* thou been unto me ... 2Sa 1:26
Wherefore *h* thou gone in unto my ... 2Sa 3:7
king, and said, What *h* thou done ... 2Sa 3:24
is it that thou *h* sent him away ... 2Sa 3:24
which thou *h* spoken of, of them ... 2Sa 6:22
that thou *h* brought me hitherto ... 2Sa 7:18
but thou *h* spoken also of thy ... 2Sa 7:19
h thou done all these great ... 2Sa 7:21
For thou *h* confirmed to thyself ... 2Sa 7:24
the word that thou *h* spoken ... 2Sa 7:25
it for ever, and do as thou *h* said ... 2Sa 7:25
h revealed to thy servant, saying ... 2Sa 7:27
thou *h* promised this goodness ... 2Sa 7:28
for thou, O Lord GOD, *h* spoken it ... 2Sa 7:29
When thou *h* made an end of ... 2Sa 11:19
Wherefore *h* thou despised the ... 2Sa 12:9
thou *h* killed Uriah the Hittite ... 2Sa 12:9
h taken his wife to be thy wife, ... 2Sa 12:9
h slain him with the sword of the ... 2Sa 12:9
because thou *h* despised me ... 2Sa 12:10
h taken the wife of Uriah the ... 2Sa 12:10
because by this deed thou *h* given ... 2Sa 12:14
thing is this that thou *h* done ... 2Sa 12:21
Wherefore then *h* thou thought ... 2Sa 14:13
h thou not there with thee Zadok ... 2Sa 15:35
in whose stead thou *h* reigned ... 2Sa 16:8
say, Wherefore *h* thou done so ... 2Sa 16:10
Go tell the king what thou *h* seen ... 2Sa 18:21
that thou *h* no tidings ready ... 2Sa 18:22
said Thou *h* shamed this day the ... 2Sa 19:5
For thou *h* declared this day, ... 2Sa 19:6
Thou *h* also given me the shield ... 2Sa 22:36
Thou *h* enlarged my steps under me ... 2Sa 22:37
For thou *h* girded me with ... 2Sa 22:40
me *h* thou subdued under me ... 2Sa 22:40
Thou *h* also given me the necks of ... 2Sa 22:41
Thou also *h* delivered me from the ... 2Sa 22:44
thou *h* kept me to be head of the ... 2Sa 22:44
thou also *h* lifted me up on high ... 2Sa 22:49
thou *h* delivered me from the ... 2Sa 22:49
in saying, Why *h* thou done so ... 1Kin 1:6
H thou not heard that Adonijah ... 1Kin 1:11
h thou said, Adonijah shall reign ... 1Kin 1:24
thou *h* not shewed it unto thy ... 1Kin 1:27
thou *h* with thee Shimei the son ... 1Kin 2:8
because thou *h* been afflicted in ... 1Kin 2:26
Why then *h* thou not kept the oath ... 1Kin 2:43
Thou *h* shewed unto thy servant ... 1Kin 3:6
thou *h* kept for him this great ... 1Kin 3:6
that thou *h* given him a son to ... 1Kin 3:6
thou *h* made thy servant king ... 1Kin 3:7
of thy people which thou *h* chosen ... 1Kin 3:8
Because thou *h* asked this thing, ... 1Kin 3:11
h not asked for thyself long life ... 1Kin 3:11
neither *h* asked riches for ... 1Kin 3:11
nor *h* asked the life of thine ... 1Kin 3:11
but *h* asked for thyself ... 1Kin 3:11
thee that which thou *h* not asked ... 1Kin 3:13
Who *h* kept with thy servant David ... 1Kin 8:24
h fulfilled it with thine hand, ... 1Kin 8:24
me as thou *h* walked before me ... 1Kin 8:25
the place of which thou *h* said ... 1Kin 8:29
which thou *h* given to thy people ... 1Kin 8:36
the city which thou *h* chosen ... 1Kin 8:44
the city which thou *h* chosen ... 1Kin 8:48
that thou *h* made before me ... 1Kin 9:3
this house, which thou *h* built ... 1Kin 9:3
are these which thou *h* given me ... 1Kin 9:13
thou *h* not kept my covenant and my ... 1Kin 11:11
But what *h* thou lacked with me, ... 1Kin 11:22
Forasmuch as thou *h* disobeyed the ... 1Kin 13:21
h not kept the commandment which ... 1Kin 13:21
h eaten bread and drunk water in ... 1Kin 13:22
yet thou *h* not been as my servant ... 1Kin 14:8
But *h* done evil above all that ... 1Kin 14:9
for thou *h* gone and made thee ... 1Kin 14:9
h cast me behind thy back ... 1Kin 14:9
thou *h* walked in the way of ... 1Kin 16:2
h made my people Israel to sin, ... 1Kin 16:2
go and do as thou *h* said ... 1Kin 17:13
h thou also brought evil upon the ... 1Kin 17:20
LORD, and thou *h* followed Baalim ... 1Kin 18:18
that thou *h* turned their heart ... 1Kin 18:37
H thou seen all this great ... 1Kin 20:13
like the army that thou *h* lost ... 1Kin 20:25
Because thou *h* not obeyed the ... 1Kin 20:36
thyself *h* decided it ... 1Kin 20:40
Because thou *h* let go out of thy ... 1Kin 20:42
H thou killed, and also taken ... 1Kin 21:19
H thou found me, O mine enemy ... 1Kin 21:20
because thou *h* sold thyself to ... 1Kin 21:20
thou *h* provoked me to anger ... 1Kin 21:22
LORD, Forasmuch as thou *h* sent ... 2Kin 1:16
Thou *h* asked a hard thing ... 2Kin 2:10
tell me, what *h* thou in the house ... 2Kin 4:2 3426
thou *h* been careful for us with ... 2Kin 4:13

Wherefore *h* thou rent thy clothes ... 2Kin 5:8
thou smite those whom thou *h* ... 2Kin 6:22
What *h* thou to do with peace ... 2Kin 9:18
What *h* thou to do with peace ... 2Kin 9:19
Because thou *h* done well in ... 2Kin 10:30
h done unto the house of Ahab ... 2Kin 10:30
Thou *h* indeed smitten Edom, and ... 2Kin 14:10
The nations which thou *h* removed ... 2Kin 17:26
of the words which thou *h* heard ... 2Kin 19:6
thou *h* heard what the kings of ... 2Kin 19:11
thou *h* made heaven and earth ... 2Kin 19:15
That which thou *h* prayed to me ... 2Kin 19:20
Whom *h* thou reproached and ... 2Kin 19:22
against whom *h* thou exalted thy ... 2Kin 19:22
thou *h* reproached the Lord ... 2Kin 19:23
h said, With the multitude of my ... 2Kin 19:23
H thou not heard long ago how I ... 2Kin 19:25
of the LORD which thou *h* spoken ... 2Kin 20:19
thou *h* humbled thyself before the ... 2Kin 22:19
h rent thy clothes, and wept ... 2Kin 22:19
these things that thou *h* done ... 2Kin 23:17
thee whithersoever thou *h* walked ... 1Chr 17:8
that thou *h* brought me hitherto ... 1Chr 17:16
for thou *h* also spoken of thy ... 1Chr 17:17
h regarded me according to the ... 1Chr 17:17
h thou done all this greatness, ... 1Chr 17:19
whom thou *h* redeemed out of Egypt ... 1Chr 17:21
let the thing that thou *h* spoken ... 1Chr 17:23
for ever, and do as thou *h* said ... 1Chr 17:23
h told thy servant that thou wilt ... 1Chr 17:25
h promised this goodness unto thy ... 1Chr 17:26
Thou *h* shed blood abundantly ... 1Chr 22:8
and *h* made great wars ... 1Chr 22:8
because thou *h* shed much blood ... 1Chr 22:8
because thou *h* been a man of war, ... 1Chr 28:3
a man of war, and *h* shed blood ... 1Chr 28:3
until thou *h* finished all the ... 1Chr 28:20
h pleasure in uprightness ... 1Chr 29:17
Thou *h* shewed great mercy unto ... 2Chr 1:8
h made me to reign in his stead ... 2Chr 1:8
for thou *h* made me king over a ... 2Chr 1:9
thou *h* not asked riches, wealth, ... 2Chr 1:11
neither yet *h* asked long life ... 2Chr 1:11
but *h* asked wisdom and knowledge ... 2Chr 1:11
Thou which *h* kept with thy ... 2Chr 6:15
that which thou *h* promised him ... 2Chr 6:15
h fulfilled it with thine hand, ... 2Chr 6:15
that which thou *h* promised him ... 2Chr 6:16
as thou *h* walked before me ... 2Chr 6:16
which thou *h* spoken unto thy ... 2Chr 6:17
upon the place whereof thou *h* ... 2Chr 6:20
when thou *h* taught them the good ... 2Chr 6:27
which thou *h* given unto thy ... 2Chr 6:27
this city which thou *h* chosen ... 2Chr 6:34
the city which thou *h* chosen ... 2Chr 6:38
Because thou *h* relied on the king ... 2Chr 16:7
Herein thou *h* done foolishly ... 2Chr 16:9
in that thou *h* taken away the ... 2Chr 19:3
h prepared thine heart to seek ... 2Chr 19:3
which thou *h* given us to inherit ... 2Chr 20:11
Because thou *h* joined thyself ... 2Chr 20:37
Because thou *h* not walked in the ... 2Chr 21:12
But *h* walked in the way of the ... 2Chr 21:13
h made Judah and the inhabitants ... 2Chr 21:13
also *h* slain thy brethren of thy ... 2Chr 21:13
Why *h* thou not required of the ... 2Chr 24:6
Why *h* thou sought after the gods ... 2Chr 25:15
thee, because thou *h* done this ... 2Chr 25:16
h not hearkened unto my counsel ... 2Chr 25:16
thou *h* smitten the Edomites ... 2Chr 25:19
for thou *h* trespassed ... 2Chr 26:18
the words which thou *h* heard ... 2Chr 34:26
Which thou *h* commanded by thy ... Ezr 9:11
seeing that thou our God *h* ... Ezr 9:13
h given us such deliverance as ... Ezr 9:13
with a loud voice, As thou *h* said ... Ezr 10:12
whom thou *h* redeemed by thy great ... Neh 1:10
thou *h* also appointed prophets to ... Neh 6:7
thou *h* made heaven, the heaven of ... Neh 9:6
seed, and *h* performed thy words ... Neh 9:8
for thou *h* done right, but we ... Neh 9:33
unto the kings whom thou *h* set ... Neh 9:37
and the horse, as thou *h* said ... Est 6:10
fail of all that thou *h* spoken ... Est 6:10
before whom thou *h* begun to fall ... Est 6:13
H thou considered my servant Job, ... Job 1:8
H not thou made an hedge about ... Job 1:10
thou *h* blessed the work of his ... Job 1:10
H thou considered my servant Job, ... Job 2:3
thou *h* instructed many ... Job 4:3
thou *h* strengthened the weak ... Job 4:3
thou *h* strengthened the feeble ... Job 4:4
why *h* thou set me as a mark ... Job 7:20
H thou eyes of flesh ... Job 10:4
that thou *h* made me as the clay ... Job 10:9
H thou not poured me out as milk, ... Job 10:10
Thou *h* clothed me with skin and ... Job 10:11
h fenced me with bones and sinews ... Job 10:11
Thou *h* granted me life and favour, ... Job 10:12
these things *h* thou hid in thine ... Job 10:13
Wherefore then *h* thou brought me ... Job 10:18
For thou *h* said, My doctrine is ... Job 11:4
thou *h* appointed his bounds that ... Job 14:5
H thou heard the secret of God ... Job 15:8
thou *h* made desolate all my ... Job 16:7
thou *h* filled me with wrinkles, ... Job 16:8
For thou *h* hid their heart from ... Job 17:4
For thou *h* taken a pledge from ... Job 22:6
Thou *h* not given water to the ... Job 22:7
thou *h* withholden bread from the ... Job 22:7
Thou *h* sent widows away empty, and ... Job 22:9
H thou marked the old way which ... Job 22:15
How *h* thou helped him that is ... Job 26:2
How *h* thou counseled him that ... Job 26:3

how *h* thou plentifully declared Job 26:3
To whom *h* thou uttered words Job 26:4
Surely thou *h* spoken in mine Job 33:8
If thou *h* any thing to say, Job 33:32 3426
If now thou *h* understanding, hear Job 34:16
But thou *h* fulfilled the judgment Job 36:17
for this *h* thou chosen rather Job 36:21
can say, Thou *h* wrought iniquity Job 36:23
H thou with him spread out the Job 37:18
declare, if thou *h* understanding Job 38:4
H thou commanded the morning Job 38:12
H thou entered into the springs Job 38:16
or *h* thou walked in the search of Job 38:16
or *h* thou seen the doors of the Job 38:17
H thou perceived the breadth of Job 38:18
H thou entered into the treasures Job 38:22
or *h* thou seen the treasures of Job 38:22
h thou clothed his neck with Job 39:19
H thou an arm like God Job 40:9
for thou *h* smitten all mine Ps 3:7
thou *h* broken the teeth of the Ps 3:7
thou *h* enlarged me when I was in Ps 4:1
Thou *h* put gladness in my heart, Ps 4:7
judgment that thou *h* commanded Ps 7:6
who *h* set thy glory above the Ps 8:1
sucklings *h* thou ordained Ps 8:2
the stars, which thou *h* ordained Ps 8:3
For thou *h* made him a little Ps 8:5
h crowned him with glory and Ps 8:5
thou *h* put all things under his Ps 8:6
For thou *h* maintained my right and Ps 9:4
Thou *h* rebuked the heathen Ps 9:5
thou *h* destroyed the wicked Ps 9:5
thou *h* put out their name for Ps 9:5
and thou *h* destroyed cities Ps 9:6
h not forsaken them that seek Ps 9:10
Thou *h* seen it Ps 10:14
h heard the desire of the Ps 10:17
thou *h* said unto the LORD, Thou Ps 16:2
Thou *h* proved mine heart Ps 17:3
thou *h* visited me in the night Ps 17:3
thou *h* tried me, and shalt find Ps 17:3
Thou *h* also given me the shield Ps 18:35
Thou *h* enlarged my steps under me Ps 18:36
For thou *h* girded me with Ps 18:39
thou *h* subdued under me those Ps 18:39
Thou *h* also given me the necks of Ps 18:40
Thou *h* delivered me from the Ps 18:43
thou *h* made me the head of the Ps 18:43
thou *h* delivered me from the Ps 18:48
Thou *h* given him his heart's Ps 21:2
h not withholden the request of Ps 21:2
majesty *h* thou laid upon him Ps 21:5
For thou *h* made him most blessed Ps 21:6
thou *h* made him exceeding glad Ps 21:6
my God, why *h* thou forsaken me Ps 22:1
thou *h* brought me into the dust Ps 22:15
for thou *h* heard me from the Ps 22:21
thou *h* been my help Ps 27:9
for thou *h* lifted me up, and *h* Ps 30:1
unto thee, and thou *h* healed me Ps 30:2
thou *h* brought up my soul from Ps 30:3
thou *h* kept me alive, that I Ps 30:3
by thy favour thou *h* made my Ps 30:7
Thou *h* turned for me my mourning Ps 30:11
thou *h* put off my sackcloth, and Ps 30:11
thou *h* redeemed me, O LORD God of Ps 31:5
for thou *h* considered my trouble Ps 31:7
thou *h* known my soul in Ps 31:7
h not shut me up into the hand of Ps 31:8
thou *h* set my feet in a large Ps 31:8
which thou *h* laid up for them Ps 31:19
which thou *h* wrought for them Ps 31:19
This thou *h* seen, O LORD Ps 35:22
thou *h* made my days as an Ps 39:5
wonderful works which thou *h* done Ps 40:5
mine ears *h* thou opened Ps 40:6
sin offering *h* thou not required Ps 40:6
my rock, Why *h* thou forgotten me Ps 42:9
But thou *h* saved us from our Ps 44:7
h put them to shame that hated us Ps 44:7
But thou *h* cast off, and put us to Ps 44:9
Thou *h* given us like sheep Ps 44:11
h scattered us among the heathen Ps 44:11
Though thou *h* sore broken us in Ps 44:19
What *h* thou to do to declare my Ps 50:16
h been partaker with adulterers Ps 50:18
These things *h* thou done, and I Ps 50:21
which thou *h* broken may rejoice Ps 51:8
for ever, because thou *h* done it Ps 52:9
thou *h* put them to shame, because Ps 53:5
For thou *h* delivered my soul from Ps 56:13
for thou *h* been my defence and Ps 59:16
thou *h* cast us off, thou *h* Ps 60:1
us, thou *h* been displeased Ps 60:1
Thou *h* made the earth to tremble Ps 60:2
thou *h* broken it Ps 60:2
Thou *h* shewed thy people hard Ps 60:3
thou *h* made us to drink the wine Ps 60:3
Thou *h* given a banner to them Ps 60:4
For thou *h* been a shelter for me Ps 61:3
For thou, O God, *h* heard my vows Ps 61:5
thou *h* given me the heritage of Ps 61:5
Because thou *h* been my help Ps 63:7
when thou *h* so provided for it Ps 65:9
For thou, O God, *h* proved us Ps 66:10
thou *h* tried us, as silver is Ps 66:10
Thou *h* caused men to ride over Ps 66:12
h prepared of thy goodness for Ps 68:10
Thou *h* ascended on high Ps 68:18
thou *h* led captivity captive Ps 68:18
thou *h* received gifts for men Ps 68:18
that which thou *h* wrought for us Ps 68:28
Thou *h* known my reproach, and my Ps 69:19
persecute him whom thou *h* smitten Ps 69:26
of those whom thou *h* wounded Ps 69:26
thou *h* given commandment to save Ps 71:3
thou *h* taught me from my youth Ps 71:17
high, who *h* done great things Ps 71:19
which *h* shewed me great and sore Ps 71:20
and my soul, which thou *h* redeemed Ps 71:23
thou *h* holden me by my right hand Ps 73:23
thou *h* destroyed all them that go Ps 73:27
why *h* thou cast us off for ever Ps 74:1
which thou *h* purchased of old Ps 74:2
which thou *h* redeemed Ps 74:2
mount Zion, wherein thou *h* dwelt Ps 74:2
thou *h* prepared the light and the Ps 74:16
Thou *h* set all the borders of the Ps 74:17
thou *h* made summer and winter Ps 74:17
thou *h* declared thy strength Ps 77:14
Thou *h* with thine arm redeemed Ps 77:15
Thou *h* brought a vine out of Ps 80:8
thou *h* cast out the heathen, and Ps 80:8
Why *h* thou then broken down her Ps 80:12
thou *h* been favourable unto thy Ps 85:1
thou *h* brought back the captivity Ps 85:1
Thou *h* forgiven the iniquity of Ps 85:2
thou *h* covered all their sin Ps 85:2
Thou *h* taken away all thy wrath Ps 85:3
thou *h* turned thyself from the Ps 85:3
whom thou *h* made shall come Ps 86:9
thou *h* delivered my soul from the Ps 86:13
h holpen me, and comforted me Ps 86:17
Thou *h* laid me in the lowest pit, Ps 88:6
thou *h* afflicted me with all thy Ps 88:7
Thou *h* put away mine acquaintance Ps 88:8
thou *h* made me an abomination Ps 88:8
friend *h* thou put far from me, and Ps 88:18
Thou *h* broken Rahab in pieces, as Ps 89:10
thou *h* scattered thine enemies Ps 89:10
thereof, thou *h* founded them Ps 89:11
and the south thou *h* created them Ps 89:12
Thou *h* a mighty arm Ps 89:13
But thou *h* cast off and abhorred, Ps 89:38
thou *h* been wroth with thine Ps 89:38
Thou *h* made void the covenant of Ps 89:39
thou *h* profaned his crown by Ps 89:39
Thou *h* broken down all his hedges Ps 89:40
thou *h* brought his strong holds Ps 89:40
Thou *h* set up the right hand of Ps 89:42
thou *h* made all his enemies to Ps 89:42
Thou *h* also turned the edge of Ps 89:43
h not made him to stand in the Ps 89:43
Thou *h* made his glory to cease, Ps 89:44
of his youth *h* thou shortened Ps 89:45
thou *h* covered him with shame Ps 89:45
wherefore *h* thou made all men in Ps 89:47
thou *h* been our dwelling place in Ps 90:1
Thou *h* set our iniquities before Ps 90:8
days wherein thou *h* afflicted us Ps 90:15
Because thou *h* made the LORD, Ps 91:9
h made me glad through thy work Ps 92:4
for thou *h* lifted me up, and cast Ps 102:10
Of old *h* thou laid the foundation Ps 102:25
which thou *h* founded for them Ps 104:8
Thou *h* set a bound that they may Ps 104:9
In wisdom *h* thou made them all Ps 104:24
whom thou *h* made to play therein Ps 104:26
thou, O God, who *h* cast us off Ps 108:11
that thou, LORD, *h* done it Ps 109:27
thou *h* the dew of thy youth Ps 110:3
For thou *h* delivered my soul from Ps 116:8
thou *h* loosed my bonds Ps 116:16
Thou *h* thrust sore at me that I Ps 118:13
for thou *h* heard me, and art Ps 118:21
Thou *h* commanded us to keep thy Ps 119:4
Thou *h* rebuked the proud that are Ps 119:21
upon which thou *h* caused me to Ps 119:49
Thou *h* dealt well with thy Ps 119:65
in faithfulness *h* afflicted me Ps 119:75
thou *h* established the earth, and Ps 119:90
for with them thou *h* quickened me Ps 119:93
Thou through thy commandments *h* Ps 119:98
for thou *h* taught me Ps 119:102
Thou *h* trodden down all them that Ps 119:118
thou *h* commanded are righteous Ps 119:138
that thou *h* founded them for ever Ps 119:152
when thou *h* taught me thy Ps 119:171
thee as thou *h* served us Ps 137:8
for thou *h* magnified thy word Ps 138:2
thou *h* searched me, and known me Ps 139:1
Thou *h* beset me behind and before, Ps 139:5
For thou *h* possessed my reins Ps 139:13
thou *h* covered me in my mother's Ps 139:13
thou *h* covered my head in the day Ps 140:7
when thou *h* it by thee Prov 3:28 3426
if thou *h* stricken thy hand with Prov 6:1
If thou *h* nothing to pay, why Prov 22:27
The morsel which thou *h* eaten Prov 23:8
when thou *h* found it, then there Prov 24:14
H thou found honey Prov 25:16
If thou *h* done foolishly in Prov 30:32
or if thou *h* thought evil, lay Prov 30:32
pay that which thou *h* vowed Eccl 5:4
thyself likewise *h* cursed others Eccl 7:22
thou *h* doves' eyes Song 1:15
thou *h* doves' eyes within thy Song 4:1
Thou *h* ravished my heart, my Song 4:9
thou *h* ravished my heart with one Song 4:9
Therefore thou *h* forsaken thy Is 2:6
Thou *h* clothing, be thou our Is 3:6
Thou *h* multiplied the nation, and Is 9:3
For thou *h* broken the yoke of his Is 9:4
For thou *h* said in thine heart, I Is 14:13
because thou *h* destroyed thy land Is 14:20
Because thou *h* forgotten the God Is 17:10
h not been mindful of the rock of Is 17:10
What *h* thou here Is 22:16
whom *h* thou here, that thou *h* Is 22:16
thou harlot that *h* been forgotten Is 23:16
for thou *h* done wonderful things Is 25:1
For thou *h* made of a city an heap Is 25:2
For thou *h* been a strength to the Is 25:4
for thou also *h* wrought all our Is 26:12
therefore *h* thou visited and Is 26:14
Thou *h* increased the nation, O Is 26:15
thou *h* increased the nation Is 26:15
of the words that thou *h* heard Is 37:6
thou *h* heard what the kings of Is 37:11
thou *h* made heaven and earth Is 37:16
Whereas thou *h* prayed to me Is 37:21
Whom *h* thou reproached and Is 37:23
against whom *h* thou exalted thy Is 37:23
By thy servants *h* thou reproached Is 37:24
h said, By the multitude of my Is 37:24
H thou not heard long ago, how I Is 37:26
but thou *h* in love to my soul Is 38:17
for thou *h* cast all my sins Is 38:17
of the LORD which thou *h* spoken Is 39:8
H thou not known Is 40:28
h thou not heard, that the Is 40:28
thou *h* been honourable, and I have Is 43:4
But thou *h* not called upon me, O Is 43:22
but thou *h* been weary of me, O Is 43:22
Thou *h* not brought me the small Is 43:23
neither *h* thou honoured me with Is 43:23
Thou *h* bought me no sweet cane Is 43:24
neither *h* thou filled me with the Is 43:24
but thou *h* made me to serve with Is 43:24
thou *h* wearied me with thine Is 43:24
though thou *h* not known me Is 45:4
though thou *h* not known me Is 45:5
What *h* thou brought forth Is 45:10
upon the ancient *h* thou very Is 47:6
For thou *h* trusted in thy Is 47:10
thou *h* said, None seeth me Is 47:10
thou *h* said in thine heart, I am, Is 47:10
wherein thou *h* laboured from thy Is 47:12
thee with whom thou *h* laboured Is 47:15
Thou *h* heard, see all this Is 48:6
after thou *h* lost the other, Is 49:20
h feared continually every day Is 51:13
which *h* drunk at the hand of the Is 51:17
thou *h* drunken the dregs of the Is 51:17
thou *h* laid thy body as the Is 51:23
even to them *h* thou poured a Is 57:6
thou *h* offered a meat offering Is 57:6
high mountain *h* thou set thy bed Is 57:7
the posts *h* thou set up thy Is 57:8
for thou *h* discovered thyself to Is 57:8
thou *h* enlarged thy bed, and made Is 57:8
thou *h* found the life of thine Is 57:10
of whom *h* thou been afraid or Is 57:11
or feared, that thou *h* lied Is 57:11
h not remembered me, nor laid it Is 57:11
Whereas thou *h* been forsaken and Is 60:15
for the which thou *h* laboured Is 62:8
why *h* thou made us to err from Is 63:17
for thou *h* hid thy face from us, Is 64:7
h consumed us, because of our Is 64:7
LORD unto me, Thou *h* well seen Jer 1:12
H thou not procured this unto Jer 2:17
in that thou *h* forsaken the LORD Jer 2:17
now what *h* thou to do in the way Jer 2:18
or what *h* thou to do in the way Jer 2:18
that thou *h* forsaken the LORD thy Jer 2:19
the valley, know what thou *h* done Jer 2:23
a stone, Thou *h* brought me forth Jer 2:27
thy gods that thou *h* made thee Jer 2:28
therefore *h* thou also taught the Jer 2:33
but thou *h* played the harlot with Jer 3:1
see where thou *h* not been lien Jer 3:2
In the ways *h* thou sat for them, Jer 3:2
thou *h* polluted the land with thy Jer 3:2
thou *h* spoken and done evil things Jer 3:5
the king, *H* thou seen that which Jer 3:6
that thou *h* transgressed against Jer 3:13
h scattered thy ways to the Jer 3:13
surely thou *h* greatly deceived Jer 4:10
my peace, because thou *h* heard Jer 4:19
thou *h* stricken them, but they Jer 5:3
thou *h* consumed them, but they Jer 5:3
Thou *h* planted them, yea, they Jer 12:2
thou *h* seen me, and tried mine Jer 12:3
If thou *h* run with the footmen, Jer 12:5
Take the girdle that thou *h* got Jer 13:4
for thou *h* taught them to be Jer 13:21
because thou *h* forgotten me Jer 13:25
H thou utterly rejected Judah Jer 14:19
why *h* thou smitten us, and there Jer 14:19
for thou *h* made all these things Jer 14:22
Thou *h* forsaken me, saith the Jer 15:6
that thou *h* borne me a man of Jer 15:10
for thou *h* filled me with Jer 15:17
to whom thou *h* prophesied lies Jer 20:6
thou *h* deceived me, and I was Jer 20:7
stronger than I, and *h* prevailed Jer 20:7
Why *h* thou prophesied in the name Jer 26:9
thy words which thou *h* prophesied Jer 28:6
Thou *h* broken the yokes of wood Jer 28:13
because thou *h* taught rebellion Jer 28:16
Because thou *h* sent letters in Jer 29:25
Now therefore why *h* thou not Jer 29:27
thou *h* no healing medicines Jer 30:13
Thou *h* chastised me, and I was Jer 31:18
thou *h* made the heaven and the Jer 32:17
Which *h* set signs and wonders in Jer 32:20
h made thee a name, as at this Jer 32:20
h brought forth thy people Israel Jer 32:21
h given them this land, which Jer 32:22
therefore thou *h* caused all this Jer 32:23

what thou *h* spoken is come to ... Jer 32:24
thou *h* said unto me, O Lord GOD, ... Jer 32:25
which thou *h* written from my ... Jer 36:6
hand the roll wherein thou *h* read ... Jer 36:14
Thou *h* burned this roll, saying, ... Jer 36:29
Why *h* thou written therein, ... Jer 36:29
what thou *h* said unto the king ... Jer 38:25
because thou *h* put thy trust in ... Jer 39:18
As for the word that thou *h* ... Jer 44:16
For because thou *h* trusted in thy ... Jer 48:7
because thou *h* striven against ... Jer 50:24
thou *h* spoken against this place, ... Jer 51:62
when thou *h* made an end of ... Jer 51:63
they are glad that thou *h* done it ... Lam 1:21
bring the day that thou *h* called ... Lam 1:21
as thou *h* done unto me for all my ... Lam 1:22
consider to whom thou *h* done this ... Lam 2:20
thou *h* slain them in the day of ... Lam 2:21
thou *h* killed, and not pitied ... Lam 2:21
Thou *h* called as in a solemn day ... Lam 2:22
thou *h* removed my soul far off ... Lam 3:17
thou *h* not pardoned ... Lam 3:42
Thou *h* covered with anger, and ... Lam 3:43
h slain, thou *h* not pitied ... Lam 3:43
Thou *h* covered thyself with a ... Lam 3:44
Thou *h* made us as the offscouring ... Lam 3:45
Thou *h* heard my voice ... Lam 3:56
thou *h* pleaded the causes of my ... Lam 3:58
thou *h* redeemed my life ... Lam 3:58
O LORD, thou *h* seen my wrong ... Lam 3:59
Thou *h* seen all their vengeance ... Lam 3:60
Thou *h* heard their reproach, O ... Lam 3:61
But thou *h* utterly rejected us ... Lam 5:22
but thou *h* delivered thy soul ... Eze 3:19
because thou *h* not given him ... Eze 3:20
also thou *h* delivered thy soul ... Eze 3:21
when thou *h* accomplished them, ... Eze 4:6
till thou *h* ended the days of thy ... Eze 4:8
because thou *h* defiled my ... Eze 5:11
h thou seen what the ancients of ... Eze 8:12
H thou seen this, O son of man ... Eze 8:15
H thou seen this, O son of man ... Eze 8:17
have done as thou *h* commanded me ... Eze 9:11
thou *h* increased and waxen great, ... Eze 16:7
Thou *h* also taken thy fair jewels ... Eze 16:17
thou *h* set mine oil and mine ... Eze 16:18
thou *h* even set it before them ... Eze 16:19
Moreover thou *h* taken thy sons and ... Eze 16:20
whom thou *h* borne unto me, and ... Eze 16:20
these *h* thou sacrificed unto them ... Eze 16:20
That thou *h* slain my children, and ... Eze 16:21
and thy whoredoms thou *h* not ... Eze 16:22
That thou *h* also built unto thee ... Eze 16:24
h made thee an high place in ... Eze 16:24
Thou *h* built thy high place at ... Eze 16:25
h made thy beauty to be abhorred, ... Eze 16:25
h opened thy feet to every one ... Eze 16:25
Thou *h* also committed fornication ... Eze 16:26
h increased thy whoredoms, to ... Eze 16:26
Thou *h* played the whore also with ... Eze 16:28
thou *h* played the harlot with ... Eze 16:28
Thou *h* moreover multiplied thy ... Eze 16:29
h not been as an harlot, in that ... Eze 16:31
with whom thou *h* taken pleasure ... Eze 16:37
and all them that thou *h* loved ... Eze 16:37
with all them that thou *h* hated ... Eze 16:37
Because thou *h* not remembered the ... Eze 16:43
but *h* fretted me in all these ... Eze 16:43
Yet *h* thou not walked after their ... Eze 16:47
nor her daughters, as thou *h* done ... Eze 16:48
but thou *h* multiplied thine ... Eze 16:51
h justified thy sisters in all ... Eze 16:51
abominations which thou *h* done ... Eze 16:51
which *h* judged thy sisters, bear ... Eze 16:52
shame for thy sins that thou *h* ... Eze 16:52
in that thou *h* justified thy ... Eze 16:52
in all that thou *h* done, in that ... Eze 16:54
Thou *h* borne thy lewdness and ... Eze 16:58
deal with thee as thou *h* done ... Eze 16:59
which *h* despised the oath in ... Eze 16:59
thee for all that thou *h* done ... Eze 16:63
in thy blood that thou *h* shed ... Eze 22:4
h defiled thyself in thine idols ... Eze 22:4
in thine idols which thou *h* made ... Eze 22:4
thou *h* caused thy days to draw ... Eze 22:4
Thou *h* despised mine holy things, ... Eze 22:8
and *h* profaned my sabbaths ... Eze 22:8
thou *h* taken usury and increase, ... Eze 22:12
thou *h* greedily gained of thy ... Eze 22:12
h forgotten me, saith the Lord ... Eze 22:12
dishonest gain which thou *h* made ... Eze 22:13
because thou *h* gone a whoring ... Eze 23:30
Thou *h* walked in the way of thy ... Eze 23:31
Because thou *h* forgotten me ... Eze 23:35
whereupon thou *h* set mine incense ... Eze 23:41
Because thou *h* clapped thine ... Eze 25:6
O Tyrus, thou *h* said, I am of ... Eze 27:3
is lifted up, and thou *h* said ... Eze 28:2
thou *h* gotten thee riches ... Eze 28:4
h gotten gold and silver into thy ... Eze 28:4
by thy traffick *h* thou increased ... Eze 28:5
Because thou *h* set thine heart as ... Eze 28:6
Thou *h* been in Eden the garden of ... Eze 28:13
thou *h* walked up and down in the ... Eze 28:14
with violence, and thou *h* sinned ... Eze 28:16
thou *h* corrupted thy wisdom by ... Eze 28:17
Thou *h* defiled thy sanctuaries by ... Eze 28:18
Because thou *h* lifted up thyself ... Eze 31:10
countries which thou *h* not known ... Eze 32:9
but thou *h* delivered thy soul ... Eze 33:9
Because thou *h* had a perpetual ... Eze 35:5
h shed the blood of the children ... Eze 35:5
sith thou *h* not hated blood, even ... Eze 35:6
Because thou *h* said, These two ... Eze 35:10
to thine envy which thou *h* used ... Eze 35:11
all thy blasphemies which thou *h* ... Eze 35:12
up men, and *h* bereaved thy nations ... Eze 36:13
h thou gathered thy company to ... Eze 38:13
When thou *h* made an end of ... Eze 43:23
me, Son of man, *h* thou seen this ... Eze 47:6
who *h* given me wisdom and might, ... Dan 2:23
h made known unto me now what we ... Dan 2:23
for thou *h* now made known unto us ... Dan 2:23
h made a decree, that every man ... Dan 3:10
are certain Jews whom thou *h* set ... Dan 3:12
golden image which thou *h* set up ... Dan 3:12
golden image which thou *h* set up ... Dan 3:18
h not humbled thine heart, though ... Dan 5:22
But *h* lifted up thyself against ... Dan 5:23
thou *h* praised the gods of silver ... Dan 5:23
thy ways, *h* thou not glorified ... Dan 5:23
H thou not signed a decree, that ... Dan 6:12
nor the decree that thou *h* signed ... Dan 6:13
whither thou *h* driven them ... Dan 9:7
that *h* brought thy people forth ... Dan 9:15
h gotten thee renown, as at this ... Dan 9:15
for thou *h* strengthened me ... Dan 10:19
because thou *h* rejected knowledge ... Hos 4:6
seeing thou *h* forgotten the law ... Hos 4:6
for thou *h* gone a whoring from ... Hos 9:1
thou *h* loved a reward upon every ... Hos 9:1
thou *h* sinned from the days of ... Hos 10:9
Israel, thou *h* destroyed thyself ... Hos 13:9
for thou *h* fallen by thine ... Hos 14:1
as thou *h* done, it shall be done ... Obad 15
unto him, Why *h* thou done this ... Jonah 1:10
h done as it pleased thee ... Jonah 1:14
yet *h* thou brought up my life ... Jonah 2:6
Thou *h* had pity on the gourd ... Jonah 4:10
for the which thou *h* not laboured ... Jonah 4:10
which thou *h* sworn unto our ... Mic 7:20
Thou *h* multiplied thy merchants ... Nah 3:16
thou *h* ordained them for judgment ... Hab 1:12
thou *h* established them for ... Hab 1:12
Because thou *h* spoiled many ... Hab 2:8
Thou *h* consulted shame to thy ... Hab 2:10
h sinned against thy soul ... Hab 2:10
wherein thou *h* transgressed ... Zeph 3:11
Judah, against which thou *h* had ... Zec 1:12
ye say, Wherein *h* thou loved us ... Mal 1:2
against whom thou *h* dealt ... Mal 2:14
till thou *h* paid the uttermost ... Mt 5:26
when thou *h* shut thy door, pray ... Mt 6:6
as thou *h* believed, so be it done ... Mt 8:13
because thou *h* hid these things ... Mt 11:25
h revealed them unto babes ... Mt 11:25
when thou *h* opened his mouth, ... Mt 17:27
thou *h* gained thy brother ... Mt 18:15
perfect, go and sell that thou *h* ... Mt 19:21 *5224*
thou *h* made them equal unto us, ... Mt 20:12
sucklings thou *h* perfected praise ... Mt 21:16
thou *h* been faithful over a few ... Mt 25:21
thou *h* been faithful over a few ... Mt 25:23
reaping where thou *h* not sown ... Mt 25:24
where thou *h* not strawed ... Mt 25:24
there thou *h* that is thine ... Mt 25:25 *2192*
He said unto him, Thou *h* said ... Mt 26:25
Jesus saith unto him, Thou *h* said ... Mt 26:64
my God, why *h* thou forsaken me ... Mt 27:46
thy way, sell whatsoever thou *h* ... Mk 10:21 *2192*
Master, thou *h* said the truth ... Mk 12:32
my God, why *h* thou forsaken me ... Mk 15:34
wherein thou *h* been instructed ... Lk 1:4
for thou *h* found favour with God ... Lk 1:30
Which thou *h* prepared before the ... Lk 2:31
why *h* thou thus dealt with us ... Lk 2:48
unto him, Thou *h* rightly judged ... Lk 7:43
that thou *h* hid these things from ... Lk 10:21
h revealed them unto babes ... Lk 10:21
unto him, Thou *h* answered right ... Lk 10:28
and the paps which thou *h* sucked ... Lk 11:27
thou *h* much goods laid up for ... Lk 12:19 *2192*
things be, which thou *h* provided ... Lk 12:20
till thou *h* paid the very last ... Lk 12:59
thou *h* taught in our streets ... Lk 13:26
it is done as thou *h* commanded ... Lk 14:22
thou *h* killed for him the fatted ... Lk 15:30
sell all that thou *h*, and ... Lk 18:22 *2192*
because thou *h* been faithful in a ... Lk 19:17
said, Master, thou *h* well said ... Lk 20:39
h not known the things which are ... Lk 24:18
but thou *h* kept the good wine ... Jn 2:10
thou *h* nothing to draw with, and ... Jn 4:11 *2192*
from whence then *h* thou that ... Jn 4:11 *2192*
Thou *h* well said, I have no ... Jn 4:17
For thou *h* had five husbands ... Jn 4:18 *2192*
he whom thou now *h* is not thy ... Jn 4:18 *2192*
thou *h* the words of eternal life ... Jn 6:68 *2192*
answered and said, Thou *h* a devil ... Jn 7:20 *2192*
art a Samaritan, and *h* a devil ... Jn 8:48 *2192*
Now we know that thou *h* a devil ... Jn 8:52 *2192*
years old, and *h* thou seen Abraham ... Jn 8:57
Thou *h* both seen him, and it is he ... Jn 9:37
I thank thee that thou *h* heard me ... Jn 11:41
may believe that thou *h* sent me ... Jn 11:42
thee not, thou *h* no part with me ... Jn 13:8 *2192*
till thou *h* denied me thrice ... Jn 13:38
yet *h* thou not known me, Philip ... Jn 14:9
As thou *h* given him power over ... Jn 17:2
to as many as thou *h* given him ... Jn 17:2
and Jesus Christ, whom thou *h* sent ... Jn 17:3
thou *h* given me are of thee ... Jn 17:7
for them which thou *h* given me ... Jn 17:9
name those whom thou *h* given me ... Jn 17:11
As thou *h* sent me into the world, ... Jn 17:18
may believe that thou *h* sent me ... Jn 17:21
may know that thou *h* sent me ... Jn 17:23
h loved them, as thou *h* loved ... Jn 17:23
they also, whom thou *h* given me ... Jn 17:24
my glory, which thou *h* given me ... Jn 17:24
have known that thou *h* sent me ... Jn 17:25
thou *h* loved me may be in them ... Jn 17:26
what *h* thou done? ... Jn 18:35
tell me where thou *h* laid him ... Jn 20:15
h seen me, thou *h* believed ... Jn 20:29
of these two thou *h* chosen ... Acts 1:24
Thou *h* made known to me the ways ... Acts 2:28
which *h* made heaven, and earth, and ... Acts 4:24
mouth of thy servant David *h* said ... Acts 4:25
child Jesus, whom thou *h* anointed ... Acts 4:27
why *h* thou conceived this thing ... Acts 5:4
thou *h* not lied unto men, but ... Acts 5:4
because thou *h* thought that the ... Acts 8:20
Thou *h* neither part nor lot in ... Acts 8:21 *2076*
thou *h* well done that thou art ... Acts 10:33
unto all men of what thou *h* seen ... Acts 22:15
for as thou *h* testified of me in ... Acts 23:11
What is that thou *h* to tell me ... Acts 23:19 *2192*
thou *h* shewed these things to me ... Acts 23:22
Forasmuch as I know that thou *h* ... Acts 24:10
H thou appealed unto Caesar ... Acts 25:12
of these things which thou *h* seen ... Acts 26:16
which *h* the form of knowledge and ... Rom 2:20 *2192*
it, Why *h* thou made me thus ... Rom 9:20
H thou faith? ... Rom 14:22 *2192*
what *h* thou that thou didst not ... 1Cor 4:7 *2192*
if thou marry, thou *h* not sinned ... 1Cor 7:28
h knowledge sit at meat in the ... 1Cor 8:10 *2192*
which thou *h* received in the Lord ... Col 4:17
whereunto thou *h* attained ... 1Ti 4:6
h professed a good profession ... 1Ti 6:12
which thou *h* heard of me, in ... 2Ti 1:13
the things that thou *h* heard of ... 2Ti 2:2
But thou *h* fully known my ... 2Ti 3:10
the things which thou *h* learned ... 2Ti 3:14
h been assured of, knowing of ... 2Ti 3:14
of whom thou *h* learned them ... 2Ti 3:14
that from a child thou *h* known ... 2Ti 3:15
which thou *h* toward the Lord ... Philem 5 *2192*
Thou *h* loved righteousness, and ... Heb 1:9
in the beginning *h* laid the ... Heb 1:10
Thou *h* put all things in ... Heb 2:8
but a body *h* thou prepared me ... Heb 10:5
for sin thou *h* had no pleasure ... Heb 10:6
Thou *h* faith, and I have works ... Jas 2:18 *2192*
the things which thou *h* seen ... Rev 1:19
thou *h* tried them which say they ... Rev 2:2
and are not, and *h* found them liars ... Rev 2:2
h borne, and *h* patience, and for ... Rev 2:3
h patience, and for my name's sake ... Rev 2:3 *2192*
h laboured, and *h* not fainted ... Rev 2:3
because thou *h* left thy first ... Rev 2:4
But this thou *h*, that thou hatest ... Rev 2:6 *2192*
h not denied my faith, even in ... Rev 2:13
because thou *h* there them that ... Rev 2:14 *2192*
So *h* thou also them that hold the ... Rev 2:15 *2192*
that thou *h* a name that thou ... Rev 3:1 *2192*
therefore how thou *h* received ... Rev 3:3
Thou *h* a few names even in Sardis ... Rev 3:4 *2192*
for thou *h* a little strength, and ... Rev 3:8 *2192*
h kept my word, and *h* not ... Rev 3:8
Because thou *h* kept the word of ... Rev 3:10
hold that fast which thou *h* ... Rev 3:11 *2192*
for thou *h* created all things, and ... Rev 4:11
h redeemed us to God by thy blood ... Rev 5:9
h made us unto our God kings and ... Rev 5:10
because thou *h* taken to thee thy ... Rev 11:17
thy great power, and *h* reigned ... Rev 11:17
be, because thou *h* judged thus ... Rev 16:5
thou *h* given them blood to drink ... Rev 16:6

HASTE

H thee, escape thither ... Gen 19:22 4116
And she made *h*, and let down her ... Gen 24:46 4116
And Joseph made *h* ... Gen 43:30 4116
H ye, and go up to my father, and ... Gen 45:9 4116
and ye shall *h* and bring down my ... Gen 45:13 4116
called for Moses and Aaron in *h* ... Ex 10:16 4116
and ye shall eat it in *h* ... Ex 12:11 2649
send them out of the land in *h* ... Ex 12:33 4116
And Moses made *h*, and bowed his ... Ex 34:8 4116
out of the land of Egypt in *h* ... Deut 16:3 2649
that shall come upon them make *h* ... Deut 32:35 2363
What ye have seen me do, make *h* ... Judg 9:48 4116
And the woman made *h*, and ran, and ... Judg 13:10 4116
make *h* now, for he came to day to ... 1Sa 9:12 4116
after the lad, Make speed, *h* ... 1Sa 20:38 2363
the king's business required *h* ... 1Sa 21:8 5169
David made *h* to get away for fear ... 1Sa 23:26 2648
Saul, saying, *H* thee, and come ... 1Sa 23:27 4116
Then Abigail made *h*, and took two ... 1Sa 25:18 4116
to pass, as she made *h* to flee ... 2Sa 4:4 2648
Syrians had cast away in their *h* ... 2Kin 7:15 2648
for God commanded me to make *h* ... 2Chr 35:21 926
they went up in *h* to Jerusalem ... Ezr 4:23 924
king said, Cause Haman to make *h* ... Est 5:5 4116
the king said to Haman, Make *h* ... Est 6:10 4116
to answer, and for this I make *h* ... Job 20:2 2363
O my strength, *h* thee to help me ... Ps 22:19 2363
For I said in my *h*, I am cut off ... Ps 31:22 2648
Make *h* to help me, O Lord my ... Ps 38:22 2363
O LORD, make *h* to help me ... Ps 40:13 2363
Make *h*, O God, to deliver me ... Ps 70:1
make *h* to help me, O LORD ... Ps 70:1 2363
make *h* unto me, O God ... Ps 70:5 2363
O my God, make *h* for my help ... Ps 71:12 2439
I said in my *h*, All men are liars ... Ps 116:11 2648
I made *h*, and delayed not to keep ... Ps 119:60 2363
make *h* unto me ... Ps 141:1 2363
to evil, and make *h* to shed blood ... Prov 1:16 4116
but he that maketh *h* to be rich ... Prov 28:20 213
Make *h*, my beloved, and be thou ... Song 8:14 1272

that believeth shall not make *h*... Is 28:16 2363
Thy children shall make *h*... Is 49:17 4116
For ye shall not go out with *h*... Is 52:12 2649
they make *h* to shed innocent... Is 59:7 4116
And let them make *h*, and take up a... Jer 9:18 4116
in Daniel before the king in *h*... Dan 2:25 927
was astonied, and rose up in *h*... Dan 3:24 927
went in *h* unto the den of lions... Dan 6:19 927
they shall make *h* to the wall... Nah 2:5 4116
straightway with *h* unto the king... Mk 6:25 *4710*
went into the hill country with *h*... Lk 1:39 *4710*
And they came with *h*, and found... Lk 2:16 *4692*
said unto him, Zacchaeus, make *h*... Lk 19:5 *4692*
And he made *h*, and came down, and... Lk 19:6 *4692*
And saw him saying unto me, Make *h*... Acts 22:18 *4692*

HASTED

and he *h* to dress it... Gen 18:7 4116
and she *h*, and let down her pitcher... Gen 24:18 4116
And she *h*, and emptied her pitcher... Gen 24:20 4116
And the taskmasters *h* them... Ex 5:13 213
and the people *h* and passed over... Josh 4:10 4116
king of Ai saw it, that they *h*... Josh 8:14 4116
into the city, and took it, and *h*... Josh 8:19 4116
h not to go down about a whole... Josh 10:13 213
And the liers in wait *h*, and rushed... Judg 20:37 2363
nigh to meet David, that David *h*... 1Sa 17:48 4116
And when Abigail saw David, she *h*... 1Sa 25:23 4116
hurting thee, except thou hadst *h*... 1Sa 25:34 4116
And Abigail *h*, and arose, and rode... 1Sa 25:42 4116
and she *h*, and killed it, and took... 1Sa 28:24 4116
which was of Bahurim, *h* and came... 2Sa 19:16 4116
And he *h*, and took the ashes away... 1Kin 20:41 4116
Then they *h*, and took every man... 2Kin 9:13 4116
himself *h* also to go out, because... 2Chr 26:20 1765
But Haman *h* to his house mourning... Est 6:12 1765
h to bring Haman unto the banquet... Est 6:14 926
or if my foot hath *h* to deceit... Job 31:5 2363
they were troubled, and *h* away... Ps 48:5 2648
voice of thy thunder they *h* away... Ps 104:7 2648
for he *h*, if it were possible for... Acts 20:16 *4692*

HASTEN

H hither Micaiah the son of Imlah... 1Kin 22:9 4116
year, and see that ye *h* the matter... 2Chr 24:5 4116
that *h* after another god... Ps 16:4 4116
I would *h* my escape from the... Ps 55:8 2363
eat, or who else can *h* hereunto... Eccl 2:25 2363
h his work, that we may see it... Is 5:19 2363
I the LORD will *h* it in his time... Is 60:22 2363
for I will *h* my word to perform... Jer 1:12 8245

HASTENED

Abraham *h* into the tent unto... Gen 18:6 4116
arose, then the angels *h* Lot... Gen 19:15 213
Howbeit the Levites *h* it not... 2Chr 24:5 4116
being *h* by the king's commandment... Est 3:15 1765
mules and camels went out, being *h*... Est 8:14 926
I have not *h* from being a pastor... Jer 17:16 213

HASTENETH

The captive exile *h* that he may... Is 51:14 4116

HASTETH

as the eagle that *h* to the prey... Job 9:26 2907
he drinketh up a river, and *h* not... Job 40:23 2648
as a bird *h* to the snare, and... Prov 7:23 4116
he that *h* with his feet sinneth... Prov 19:2 213
He that *h* to be rich hath an evil... Prov 28:22 926
h to his place where he arose... Eccl 1:5 7602
to come, and his affliction *h* fast... Jer 48:16 4116
fly as the eagle that *h* to eat... Hab 1:8 2363
h greatly, even the voice of the... Zeph 1:14 4116

HASTILY

they brought him *h* out of the... Gen 41:14 7323
without driving them out *h*... Judg 2:23 4118
Then he called *h* unto the young... Judg 9:54 4120
And the man came in *h*, and told Eli... 1Sa 4:14 4116
come from him, and did *h* catch it... 1Kin 20:33 4116
may be gotten *h* at the beginning... Prov 20:21 926
Go not forth *h* to strive, lest... Prov 25:8 4118
they saw Mary, that she rose up *h*... Jn 11:31 *5030*

HASTING

judgment, and *h* righteousness... Is 16:5 4106
h unto the coming of the day of... 2Pet 3:12 *4692*

HASTY

but he that is *h* of spirit... Prov 14:29 7116
every one that is *h* only to want... Prov 21:5 213
thou a man that is *h* in his words... Prov 29:20 213
let not thine heart be *h* to utter... Eccl 5:2 4116
Be not *h* in thy spirit to be... Eccl 7:9 926
Be not *h* to go out of his sight... Eccl 8:3 926
as the *h* fruit before the summer... Is 28:4 1061
is the decree so *h* from the king... Dan 2:15 2685
h nation, which shall march... Hab 1:6 4116

HASUPHA (*has-u'-fah*) *A family of exiles.*
of Ziha, the children of *H*... Ezr 2:43 2817

HATACH (*ha'-tak*) *A servant of King Ahasuerus.*
Then called Esther for *H*, one of... Est 4:5 2047
So *H* went forth to Mordecai unto... Est 4:6 2047
H came and told Esther the words... Est 4:9 2047
Again Esther spake unto *H*... Est 4:10 2047

HATCH

owl make her nest, and lay, and *h*... Is 34:15 1234
They *h* cockatrice' eggs, and weave... Is 59:5 1234

HATCHETH

sitteth on eggs, and *h* them not... Jer 17:11 3205

HATE

the gate of those which *h* them... Gen 24:60 8130
come ye to me, seeing ye *h* me... Gen 26:27 8130
Joseph will peradventure *h* us... Gen 50:15 7852
generation of them that *h* me... Ex 20:5 8130
Thou shalt not *h* thy brother in... Lev 19:17 8130
they that *h* you shall reign over... Lev 26:17 8130
let them that *h* thee flee before... Num 10:35 8130
generation of them that *h* me... Deut 5:9 8130
them that *h* him to their face... Deut 7:10 8130
them upon all them that *h* thee... Deut 7:15 8130
But if any man *h* his neighbour... Deut 19:11 8130
and go in unto her, and *h* her,... Deut 22:13 8130
And if the latter husband *h* her... Deut 24:3 8130
enemies, and on them that *h* thee... Deut 30:7 8130
and will reward them that *h* me... Deut 32:41 8130
him, and of them that *h* him... Deut 33:11 8130
elders of Gilead, Did not ye *h* me... Judg 11:7 8130
him, and said, Thou dost but *h* me... Judg 14:16 8130
I might destroy them that *h* me... 2Sa 22:41 8130
but I *h* him... 1Kin 22:8 8130
but I *h* him... 2Chr 18:7 8130
and love them that *h* the LORD... 2Chr 19:2 8130
They that *h* thee shall be clothed... Job 8:22 8130
which I suffer of them that *h* me... Ps 9:13 8130
I might destroy them that *h* me... Ps 18:40 8130
shall find out those that *h* thee... Ps 21:8 8130
they *h* me with cruel hatred... Ps 25:19 8130
they that *h* the righteous shall... Ps 34:21 8130
the eye that *h* me without a cause... Ps 35:19 8130
they that *h* me wrongfully are... Ps 38:19 8130
All that *h* me whisper together... Ps 41:7 8130
they which *h* us spoil for... Ps 44:10 8130
upon me, and in wrath they *h* me... Ps 55:3 7852
let them also that *h* him flee... Ps 68:1 8130
They that *h* me without a cause... Ps 69:4 8130
be delivered from them that *h* me... Ps 69:14 8130
they that *h* thee have lifted up... Ps 83:2 8130
that they which *h* me may see it... Ps 86:17 8130
face, and plague them that *h* him... Ps 89:23 8130
Ye that love the LORD, *h* evil... Ps 97:10 8130
I *h* the work of them that turn... Ps 101:3 8130
their heart to *h* his people... Ps 105:25 8130
see my desire upon them that *h* me... Ps 118:7 8130
therefore I *h* every false way... Ps 119:104 8130
I *h* vain thoughts... Ps 119:113 8130
and I *h* every false way... Ps 119:128 8130
I *h* and abhor lying... Ps 119:163 8130
and turned back that *h* Zion... Ps 129:5 8130
I *h* them, O LORD, that *h* thee... Ps 139:21 8130
I *h* them with perfect hatred... Ps 139:22 8130
scorning, and fools *h* knowledge... Prov 1:22 8130
These six things doth the LORD *h*... Prov 6:16 8130
The fear of the LORD is to *h* evil... Prov 8:13 8130
way, and the froward mouth, do I *h*... Prov 8:13 8130
all they that *h* me love death... Prov 8:36 8130
not a scorner, lest he *h* thee... Prov 9:8 8130
the brethren of the poor do *h* him... Prov 19:7 8130
he be weary of thee, and so *h* thee... Prov 25:17 8130
The bloodthirsty *h* the upright... Prov 29:10 8130
A time to love, and a time to *h*... Eccl 3:8 8130
I *h* robbery for burnt offering... Is 61:8 8130
this abominable thing that I *h*... Jer 44:4 8130
unto the will of them that *h* thee... Eze 16:27 8130
the dream be to them that *h* thee... Dan 4:19 8131
They *h* him that rebuketh in the... Amos 5:10 8130
H the evil, and love the good, and... Amos 5:15 8130
I *h*, I despise your feast days,... Amos 5:21 8130
of Jacob, and *h* his palaces... Amos 6:8 8130
Who *h* the good, and love the evil... Mic 3:2 8130
for all these are things that I *h*... Zec 8:17 8130
thy neighbour, and *h* thine enemy... Mt 5:43 *3404*
you, do good to them that *h* you... Mt 5:44 *3404*
for either he will *h* the one... Mt 6:24 *3404*
another, and shall *h* one another... Mt 24:10 *3404*
and from the hand of all that *h* us... Lk 1:71 *3404*
are ye, when men shall *h* you... Lk 6:22 *3404*
do good to them which *h* you... Lk 6:27 *3404*
h not his father, and mother, and... Lk 14:26 *3404*
for either he will *h* the one... Lk 16:13 *3404*
The world cannot *h* you... Jn 7:7 *3404*
If the world *h* you, ye know that... Jn 15:18 *3404*
but what I *h*, that do I... Rom 7:15 *3404*
my brethren, if the world *h* you... 1Jn 3:13 *3404*
the Nicolaitanes, which I also *h*... Rev 2:6 *3404*
the Nicolaitanes, which thing I *h*... Rev 2:15 *3404*
beast, these shall *h* the whore... Rev 17:16 *3404*

HATED

Esau *h* Jacob because of the... Gen 27:41 7852
when the LORD saw that Leah was *h*... Gen 29:31 8130
the LORD hath heard that I was *h*... Gen 29:33 8130
than all his brethren, they *h* him... Gen 37:4 8130
and they *h* him yet the more... Gen 37:5 8130
they *h* him yet the more for his... Gen 37:8 8130
him, and shot at him, and *h* him... Gen 49:23 7852
and said, Because the LORD *h* us... Deut 1:27 8135
and *h* him not in times past... Deut 4:42 8130
them, and because he *h* them... Deut 9:28 8135
whom he *h* not in time past... Deut 19:4 8130
inasmuch as he *h* him not in time... Deut 19:6 8130
wives, one beloved, and another *h*... Deut 21:15 8130
both the beloved and the *h*... Deut 21:15 8130
firstborn son be hers that was *h*... Deut 21:15 8146
firstborn before the son of the *h*... Deut 21:16 8130
son of the *h* for the firstborn... Deut 21:17 8130
and *h* him not beforetime... Josh 20:5 8130
that thou hadst utterly *h* her... Judg 15:2 8130
that are *h* of David's soul, he... 2Sa 5:8 8130
Then Amnon *h* her exceedingly... 2Sa 13:15 8130
h her was greater than the love... 2Sa 13:15 8130
for Absalom *h* Amnon, because he... 2Sa 13:22 8130
enemy, and from them that *h* me... 2Sa 22:18 8130
had rule over them that *h* them... Est 9:1 8130
they would unto those that *h* them... Est 9:5 8130
the destruction of him that *h* me... Job 31:29 8130
enemy, and from them which *h* me... Ps 18:17 8130
I have *h* the congregation of... Ps 26:5 8130
I have *h* them that regard lying... Ps 31:6 8130
hast put them to shame that *h* us... Ps 44:7 8130
neither was it he that *h* me that... Ps 55:12 8130
from the hand of him that *h* them... Ps 106:10 8130
they that *h* them ruled over them... Ps 106:41 8130
For that they *h* knowledge... Prov 1:29 8130
How have I *h* instruction, and my... Prov 5:12 8130
and a man of wicked devices is *h*... Prov 14:17 8130
The poor is *h* even of his own... Prov 14:20 8130
Therefore I *h* life... Eccl 2:17 8130
I *h* all my labour which I had... Eccl 2:18 8130
thou hast been forsaken and *h*... Is 60:15 8130
Your brethren that *h* you, that... Is 66:5 8130
therefore have I *h* it... Jer 12:8 8130
with all them that thou hast *h*... Eze 16:37 8130
sith thou hast not *h* blood... Eze 35:6 8130
for there I *h* them... Hos 9:15 8130
I *h* Esau, and laid his mountains... Mal 1:3 8130
ye shall be *h* of all men for my... Mt 10:22 *3404*
ye shall be *h* of all nations for... Mt 24:9 *3404*
ye shall be *h* of all men for my... Mk 13:13 *3404*
But his citizens *h* him, and sent a... Lk 19:14 *3404*
ye shall be *h* of all men for my... Lk 21:17 *3404*
ye know that it *h* me before it... Jn 15:18 *3404*
me before it *h* you... Jn 15:18
seen and *h* both me and my Father... Jn 15:24 *3404*
They *h* me without a cause... Jn 15:25 *3404*
and the world hath *h* them, because... Jn 17:14 *3404*
have I loved, but Esau have I *h*... Rom 9:13 *3404*
no man ever yet *h* his own flesh... Eph 5:29 *3404*
righteousness, and *h* iniquity... Heb 1:9 *3404*

HATEFUL

his iniquity be found to be *h*... Ps 36:2 8130
living in malice and envy, *h*... Titus 3:3 *4767*
a cage of every unclean and *h* bird... Rev 18:2 *3404*

HATEFULLY

And they shall deal with thee *h*... Eze 23:29 8135

HATERS

The *h* of the LORD should have... Ps 81:15 8130
h of God, despiteful, proud,... Rom 1:30 *2319*

HATEST

thine enemies, and *h* thy friends... 2Sa 19:6 8130
thou *h* all workers of iniquity... Ps 5:5 8130
righteousness, and *h* wickedness... Ps 45:7 8130
Seeing thou *h* instruction... Ps 50:17 8130
into the hand of them whom thou *h*... Eze 23:28 8130
that thou *h* the deeds of the... Rev 2:6 *3404*

HATETH

h thee lying under his burden... Ex 23:5 8130
not be slack to him that *h* him... Deut 7:10 8130
to the LORD, which he *h*, have... Deut 12:31 8130
which the LORD thy God *h*... Deut 16:22 8130
this man to wife, and he *h* her... Deut 22:16 8130
teareth me in his wrath, who *h* me... Job 16:9 7852
Shall even he that *h* right govern... Job 34:17 8130
that loveth violence his soul *h*... Ps 11:5 8130
long dwelt with him that *h* peace... Ps 120:6 8130
he that *h* suretiship is sure... Prov 11:15 8130
but he that *h* reproof is brutish... Prov 12:1 8130
A righteous man *h* lying... Prov 13:5 8130
He that spareth his rod *h* his son... Prov 13:24 8130
he that *h* reproof shall die... Prov 15:10 8130
but he that *h* gifts shall live... Prov 15:27 8130
He that *h* dissembleth with his... Prov 26:24 8130
A lying tongue *h* those that are... Prov 26:28 8130
but he that *h* covetousness shall... Prov 28:16 8130
with a thief *h* his own soul... Prov 29:24 8130
your appointed feasts my soul *h*... Is 1:14 8130
saith that he *h* putting away... Mal 2:16 8130
one that doeth evil *h* the light... Jn 3:20 *3404*
but me it *h*, because I testify of... Jn 7:7 *3404*
he that *h* his life in this world... Jn 12:25 *3404*
world, therefore the world *h* you... Jn 15:19 *3404*
He that *h* me *h* my Father... Jn 15:23 *3404*
h his brother, is in darkness... 1Jn 2:9 *3404*
But he that *h* his brother is in... 1Jn 2:11 *3404*
Whosoever *h* his brother is a... 1Jn 3:15 *3404*
h his brother, he is a liar... 1Jn 4:20 *3404*

HATH

the moving creature that *h* life... Gen 1:20
h God said, Ye shall not eat of... Gen 3:1
God *h* said, Ye shall not eat of... Gen 3:3
which *h* opened her mouth to... Gen 4:11
h appointed me another seed... Gen 4:25
ground which the LORD *h* cursed... Gen 5:29
which *h* delivered thine enemies... Gen 14:20
the LORD *h* restrained me from... Gen 16:2
because the LORD *h* heard thy... Gen 16:11
he *h* broken my covenant... Gen 17:14
that which he *h* spoken of him... Gen 18:19
the LORD *h* sent us to destroy it... Gen 19:13
thy servant *h* found grace in thy... Gen 19:19
God *h* made me to laugh, so that... Gen 21:6
all that Sarah *h* said unto thee... Gen 21:12
for God *h* heard the voice of the... Gen 21:17
I wot not who *h* done this thing... Gen 21:26
she *h* also born children unto thy... Gen 22:20
the cave of Machpelah, which he *h*... Gen 23:9
who *h* not left destitute my... Gen 24:27
the LORD *h* blessed my master... Gen 24:35
he *h* given him flocks, and herds,... Gen 24:35
him *h* he given all that he *h*... Gen 24:36
h appointed out for my master's... Gen 24:44
son's wife, as the LORD *h* spoken... Gen 24:51
seeing the LORD *h* prospered my... Gen 24:56
now the LORD *h* made room for us... Gen 26:22
a field which the LORD *h* blessed... Gen 27:27
where is he that *h* taken venison... Gen 27:33
h taken away thy blessing... Gen 27:35
for he *h* supplanted me these two... Gen 27:36
now he *h* taken away my blessing... Gen 27:36

H

Surely the LORD *h* looked upon my Gen 29:32
Because the LORD *h* heard that I Gen 29:33
he *h* therefore given me this son Gen 29:33
who *h* withheld from thee the Gen 30:2
God *h* judged me, and *h* also Gen 30:6
my voice, and *h* given me a son Gen 30:6
God *h* given me my hire, because I Gen 30:18
God *h* endued me with a good dowry Gen 30:20
God *h* taken away my reproach Gen 30:23
LORD *h* blessed me for thy sake Gen 30:27
the LORD *h* blessed thee since my Gen 30:30
Jacob *h* taken away all that was Gen 31:1
h he gotten all this glory Gen 31:1
God of my father *h* been with me Gen 31:5
And your father *h* deceived me Gen 31:7
Thus God *h* taken away the cattle Gen 31:9
for he *h* sold us, and *h* quite Gen 31:15
which God *h* taken from our father Gen 31:16
whatsoever God *h* said unto thee Gen 31:16
God *h* seen mine affliction and the Gen 31:42
he said, The children which God *h* Gen 33:5
because God *h* dealt graciously Gen 33:11
Some evil beast *h* devoured him Gen 37:20
an evil beast *h* devoured him Gen 37:33
in law *h* played the harlot Gen 38:24
She *h* been more righteous than I Gen 38:26
he *h* committed all that he Gen 39:8
all that he *h* to my hand Gen 39:8 3426
neither *h* he kept back any thing Gen 39:9
he *h* brought in an Hebrew unto us Gen 39:14
God *h* shewed Pharaoh what he is Gen 41:25
Forasmuch as God *h* shewed thee Gen 41:39
h made me forget all my toil, and Gen 41:51
For God *h* caused me to be Gen 41:52
is this that God *h* done unto us Gen 42:28
h given you treasure in your Gen 43:23
God *h* found out the iniquity of Gen 44:16
For these two years *h* the famine Gen 45:6
he *h* made me a father to Pharaoh, Gen 45:8
God *h* made me lord of all Egypt Gen 45:9
for their trade *h* been to feed Gen 46:32
Thy servants' trade *h* been about Gen 46:34
my lord also *h* our herds of Gen 47:18 413
whom God *h* given me in this place Gen 48:9
God *h* shewed me also thy seed Gen 48:11
your fathers *h* sent me unto you Ex 3:13
Israel, I AM *h* sent me unto you Ex 3:14
God of Jacob, *h* sent me unto you Ex 3:15
God of the Hebrews *h* met with us Ex 3:18
The LORD *h* not appeared unto thee Ex 4:1
of Jacob, *h* appeared unto thee Ex 4:5
unto him, Who *h* made man's mouth Ex 4:11
God of the Hebrews *h* met with us Ex 5:3
he *h* done evil to this people Ex 5:23
the Hebrews *h* sent me unto thee Ex 7:16
such as *h* not been in Egypt since Ex 9:18
even all that the hail *h* left Ex 10:12
you, according as he *h* promised Ex 12:25
for with a strong hand *h* the LORD Ex 13:9
the wilderness *h* shut them in Ex 14:3
for he *h* triumphed gloriously Ex 15:1
his rider *h* he thrown into the Ex 15:1
his host *h* he cast into the sea Ex 15:4
h dashed in pieces the enemy Ex 15:6
for he *h* triumphed gloriously Ex 15:21
his rider *h* he thrown into the Ex 15:21
ye shall know that the LORD *h* Ex 16:6
for he *h* heard your murmurings Ex 16:9
which the LORD *h* given you to eat Ex 16:15
thing which the LORD *h* commanded Ex 16:16
is that which the LORD *h* said Ex 16:23
for that the LORD *h* given you the Ex 16:29
Because the LORD *h* sworn that the Ex 17:16
who *h* delivered you out of the Ex 18:10
who *h* delivered the people from Ex 18:10
that the LORD *h* spoken we will do Ex 19:8
who *h* betrothed her to himself, Ex 21:8
seeing he *h* dealt deceitfully Ex 21:8
it *h* been testified to his owner, Ex 21:29
he *h* not kept him in Ex 21:29
but that he *h* killed a man or a Ex 21:29
ox *h* used to push in time past Ex 21:36
his owner *h* not kept him in Ex 21:36
that he *h* not put his hand unto Ex 22:11
which the LORD *h* said will we do Ex 24:3
that the LORD *h* said will we do Ex 24:7
which the LORD *h* made with you Ex 24:8
unto them, Whosoever *h* any gold Ex 32:24
Whosoever *h* sinned against me, Ex 32:33
words which the LORD *h* commanded Ex 35:1
all that the LORD *h* commanded Ex 35:10
the LORD *h* called by name Ex 35:30
he *h* filled him with the spirit Ex 35:31
he *h* put in his heart that he may Ex 35:34
Them *h* he filled with wisdom of Ex 35:35
for his sin, which he *h* sinned Lev 4:3
When a ruler *h* sinned, and done Lev 4:22
if his sin, wherein he *h* sinned Lev 4:23
Or if his sin, which he *h* sinned Lev 4:28
for his sin which he *h* sinned Lev 4:28
for his sin that he *h* committed Lev 4:35
whether he *h* seen or known of it Lev 5:1
that he *h* sinned in that thing Lev 5:5
for his sin which he *h* sinned Lev 5:6
which he *h* committed, two Lev 5:7
him for his sin which he *h* sinned Lev 5:10
that he *h* sinned in one of these Lev 5:13
that he *h* done in the holy thing Lev 5:16
he *h* certainly trespassed against Lev 5:19
or *h* deceived his neighbour Lev 6:2
it shall be, because he *h* sinned Lev 6:4
which he *h* deceitfully gotten Lev 6:4
about which he *h* sworn falsely Lev 6:5
he *h* done in trespassing therein Lev 6:7

fire *h* consumed with the burnt Lev 6:10
burnt offering which he *h* offered Lev 7:8
As he *h* done this day Lev 8:34
so the LORD *h* commanded to do, to Lev 8:34
burning which the LORD *h* kindled Lev 10:6
h spoken unto them by the hand of Lev 10:11
as the LORD *h* commanded Lev 10:15
God *h* given it you to bear the Lev 10:17
whatsoever *h* fins and scales in Lev 11:9
Whatsoever *h* no fins nor scales Lev 11:12
or whatsoever *h* more feet among Lev 11:42
that *h* born a male or a female Lev 12:7
him that *h* the plague seven days Lev 13:4
after that he *h* been seen of the Lev 13:7
h the plague from his head even Lev 13:12
him clean that *h* the plague Lev 13:13
him clean that *h* the plague Lev 13:17
h the plague of the scall seven Lev 13:31
that *h* the scall seven days more Lev 13:33
he that *h* his hair fallen off Lev 13:41
shut up it that *h* the plague Lev 13:50
after that he *h* taken away the Lev 14:43
after he *h* scraped the house, and Lev 14:43
the plague *h* not spread in the Lev 14:48
When any man *h* a running issue Lev 15:2 1961
whereon he lieth that *h* the issue Lev 15:4
that *h* the issue shall wash his Lev 15:6
that *h* the issue shall wash his Lev 15:7
if he that *h* the issue spit upon Lev 15:8
that *h* the issue shall be unclean Lev 15:9
he toucheth that *h* the issue Lev 15:11
h not rinsed his hands in water, Lev 15:11
he toucheth which *h* the issue Lev 15:12
when he that *h* an issue is Lev 15:13
is the law of him that *h* an issue Lev 15:32
and of him that *h* an issue Lev 15:33
And when he *h* made an end of Lev 16:20
thing which the LORD *h* commanded Lev 17:2
he *h* shed blood Lev 17:4
because he *h* profaned the Lev 19:8
LORD for his sin which he *h* done Lev 19:22
the sin which he *h* done shall be Lev 19:22
because he *h* given of his seed Lev 20:3
he *h* cursed his father or his Lev 20:9
wife *h* uncovered his father's Lev 20:11
he *h* uncovered his sister's Lev 20:17
he *h* discovered her fountain, and Lev 20:18
she *h* uncovered the fountain of Lev 20:18
he *h* uncovered his uncle's Lev 20:20
he *h* uncovered his brother's Lev 20:21
or woman that *h* a familiar spirit Lev 20:27 1961
unto him, which *h* had no husband Lev 21:3
generations that *h* any blemish Lev 21:17 1961
man he be that *h* a blemish Lev 21:18
or he that *h* a flat nose, or any Lev 21:18
or that *h* a blemish in his eye, Lev 21:20
scabbed, or *h* his stones broken Lev 21:20
No man that *h* a blemish of the Lev 21:21
he *h* a blemish Lev 21:21
the altar, because he *h* a blemish Lev 21:23
is a leper, or *h* a running issue Lev 22:4
whatsoever uncleanness he *h* Lev 22:5
The soul which *h* touched any such Lev 22:6
But whatsoever *h* a blemish Lev 22:20
that *h* any thing superfluous or Lev 22:23
Bring forth him that *h* cursed Lev 24:14
as he *h* done, so shall it be done Lev 24:19
as he *h* caused a blemish in a man Lev 24:20
poor, and *h* sold away some of his Lev 25:25
h bought it until the year of Lev 25:28
LORD a field which he *h* bought Lev 27:22
unto the LORD of all that he *h* Lev 27:28
and every one that *h* an issue Num 5:2
him against whom he *h* trespassed Num 5:7
when he *h* made her to drink the Num 5:27
he *h* defiled the head of his Num 6:9
law of the Nazarite who *h* vowed Num 6:21
for the LORD *h* spoken good Num 10:29
H the LORD indeed spoken only by Num 12:2
h he not spoken also by us Num 12:2
wherefore *h* the LORD brought us Num 14:3
therefore he *h* slain them in the Num 14:16
h followed me fully, him will I Num 14:24
place which the LORD *h* promised Num 14:40
which the LORD *h* spoken unto Num 15:22
Even all that the LORD *h* Num 15:23
Because he *h* despised the word of Num 15:31
h broken his commandment, that Num 15:31
even him whom he *h* chosen will he Num 16:5
Israel *h* separated you from the Num 16:9
he *h* brought thee near to him, and Num 16:10
ye shall know that the LORD *h* Num 16:28
then the LORD *h* not sent me Num 16:29
law which the LORD *h* commanded Num 19:2
which *h* no covering bound upon it Num 19:15
because he *h* defiled the Num 19:20
the water of separation *h* not Num 19:20
all the travel that *h* befallen us Num 20:14
h brought us forth out of Egypt Num 20:16
it *h* consumed Ar of Moab, and the Num 21:28
he *h* given his sons that escaped, Num 21:29
of Moab, *h* sent unto me, saying, Num 22:10
of Moab *h* brought me from Aram Num 23:7
I curse, whom God *h* not cursed Num 23:8
defy, whom the LORD *h* not defied Num 23:8
which the LORD *h* put in my mouth Num 23:12
unto him, What *h* the LORD spoken Num 23:17
h he said, and shall he not do it Num 23:19
and he *h* blessed Num 23:20
He *h* not beheld iniquity in Jacob Num 23:21
neither *h* he seen perverseness in Num 23:21
he *h* as it were the strength of a Num 23:22
and of Israel, What *h* God wrought Num 23:23
Balaam the son of Beor *h* said Num 24:3

man whose eyes are open *h* said Num 24:3
He *h* said, which heard the words Num 24:4
aloes which the LORD *h* planted Num 24:6
he *h* as it were the strength of a Num 24:8
the LORD *h* kept thee back from Num 24:11
Balaam the son of Beor *h* said Num 24:15
man whose eyes are open *h* said Num 24:15
He *h* said, which heard the words Num 24:16
h turned my wrath away from the Num 25:11
his family, because he *h* no son Num 27:4
thing which the LORD *h* commanded Num 30:1
wherewith she *h* bound her soul Num 30:4
every bond wherewith she *h* bound Num 30:4
wherewith she *h* bound her soul Num 30:5
But if her husband *h* utterly made Num 30:12
her husband *h* made them void Num 30:12
void after that he *h* heard them Num 30:15
kill every woman that *h* known man Num 31:17
whosoever *h* killed any person, and Num 31:19
whosoever *h* touched any slain, Num 31:19
the LORD, what every man *h* gotten Num 31:50
land which the LORD *h* given them Num 32:7
until he *h* driven out his enemies Num 32:21
do that which *h* proceeded out of Num 32:24
As the LORD *h* said unto thy Num 32:31
of the sons of Joseph *h* said well Num 36:5
LORD your God *h* multiplied you Deut 1:10
bless you, as he *h* promised you Deut 1:11
the LORD thy God *h* set the land Deut 1:21
of thy fathers *h* said unto thee Deut 1:21
he *h* brought us forth out of the Deut 1:27
the land that he *h* trodden upon Deut 1:36
because he *h* wholly followed the Deut 1:36
For the LORD thy God *h* blessed Deut 2:7
the LORD thy God *h* been with thee Deut 2:7
The LORD your God *h* given you Deut 3:18
God *h* given them beyond Jordan Deut 3:20
God *h* done unto these two kings Deut 3:21
the LORD thy God *h* destroyed them Deut 4:3
who *h* God so nigh unto them, as Deut 4:7
that *h* statutes and judgments so Deut 4:8
which the LORD thy God *h* divided Deut 4:19
But the LORD *h* taken you, and Deut 4:20
the LORD thy God *h* forbidden thee Deut 4:23
whether there *h* been any such Deut 4:32
thing is, or *h* been heard like it Deut 4:32
Or *h* God assayed to go and take Deut 4:34
the LORD thy God *h* commanded thee Deut 5:12
the LORD thy God *h* commanded thee Deut 5:16
the LORD our God *h* shewed us his Deut 5:24
that *h* heard the voice of the Deut 5:26
the LORD your God *h* commanded you Deut 5:32
the LORD your God *h* commanded you Deut 5:33
of thy fathers *h* promised thee Deut 6:3
which he *h* commanded thee Deut 6:17
before thee, as the LORD *h* spoken Deut 6:19
the LORD our God *h* commanded you Deut 6:20
our God, as he *h* commanded us Deut 6:25
h cast out many nations before Deut 7:1
the LORD thy God *h* chosen thee to Deut 7:6
h the LORD brought you out with a Deut 7:8
good land which he *h* given thee Deut 8:10
mine hand *h* gotten me this wealth Deut 8:17
as the LORD *h* said unto thee Deut 9:3
after that the LORD thy God *h* Deut 9:4
h brought me in to possess this Deut 9:4
he *h* brought them out to slay Deut 9:28
Wherefore Levi *h* no part nor Deut 10:9 1961
that *h* done for thee these great Deut 10:21
now the LORD thy God *h* made thee Deut 10:22
how the LORD *h* destroyed them Deut 11:4
tread upon, as he *h* said unto you Deut 11:25
when the LORD thy God *h* brought Deut 11:29
the LORD thy God *h* blessed thee Deut 12:7
forasmuch as he *h* no part nor Deut 12:12
thy God which he *h* given thee Deut 12:15
as he *h* promised thee, and thou Deut 12:20
place which the LORD thy God *h* Deut 12:21
which the LORD *h* given thee Deut 12:21
because he *h* spoken to turn you Deut 13:5
because he *h* sought to thrust Deut 13:10
which the LORD thy God *h* given Deut 13:12
as he *h* sworn unto thy fathers Deut 13:17
the LORD *h* chosen thee to be a Deut 14:2
And whatsoever *h* not fins and Deut 14:10
the LORD thy God *h* blessed thee Deut 14:24
for he *h* no part nor inheritance Deut 14:27
(because he *h* no part nor Deut 14:29
h blessed thee thou shalt give Deut 15:14
for he *h* been worth a double Deut 15:18
the LORD thy God *h* blessed thee Deut 16:10
place which the LORD thy God *h* Deut 16:11
thy God which he *h* given thee Deut 16:17
that *h* wrought wickedness in the Deut 17:2
h gone and served other gods, and Deut 17:3
as the LORD *h* said unto you Deut 17:16
as he *h* said unto them Deut 18:2
For the LORD thy God *h* chosen him Deut 18:5
the LORD thy God *h* not suffered Deut 18:14
word which the LORD *h* not spoken Deut 18:21
thing which the LORD *h* not spoken Deut 18:22
but the prophet *h* spoken it Deut 18:22
thy God *h* cut off the nations Deut 19:1
as he *h* sworn unto thy fathers, Deut 19:8
h testified falsely against his Deut 19:18
is there that *h* built a new house Deut 20:5
and *h* not dedicated it Deut 20:5
is he that *h* planted a vineyard Deut 20:6
and *h* not yet eaten of it Deut 20:6
is there that *h* betrothed a wife Deut 20:7
and *h* not taken her Deut 20:7
when the LORD thy God *h* delivered Deut 20:13
the LORD thy God *h* given thee Deut 20:14
the LORD thy God *h* commanded thee Deut 20:17

it be not known who *h* slain him ... Deut 21:1
which *h* not been wrought with, and ... Deut 21:3
which *h* not drawn in the yoke ... Deut 21:3
for them the LORD thy God *h* ... Deut 21:5
the LORD thy God *h* delivered them ... Deut 21:10
sons to inherit that which he *h* ... Deut 21:16 1961
a double portion of all that he *h* ... Deut 21:17 4672
of thy brother's, which he *h* lost ... Deut 22:3
he *h* given occasions of speech ... Deut 22:17
because he *h* brought up an evil ... Deut 22:19
because she *h* wrought folly in ... Deut 22:21
the man, because he *h* humbled his ... Deut 22:24
because he *h* humbled her, he may ... Deut 22:29
or *h* his privy member cut off, ... Deut 23:1
When a man *h* taken a wife, and ... Deut 24:1
his eyes, because he *h* found some ... Deut 24:1
When a man *h* taken a new wife, he ... Deut 24:5
up his wife which he *h* taken ... Deut 24:5
of him that *h* his shoe loosed ... Deut 25:10
when the LORD thy God *h* given ... Deut 25:19
he *h* brought us into this place, ... Deut 26:9
h given us this land, even a land ... Deut 26:9
LORD thy God *h* given unto thee ... Deut 26:11
This day the LORD thy God *h* ... Deut 26:16
the LORD *h* avouched thee this day ... Deut 26:18
as he *h* promised thee, and that ... Deut 26:18
above all nations which he *h* made ... Deut 26:19
the LORD thy God, as he *h* spoken ... Deut 26:19
of thy fathers *h* promised thee ... Deut 27:3
as he *h* sworn unto thee, if thou ... Deut 28:9
the LORD thy God *h* given thee ... Deut 28:52
the LORD thy God *h* given thee ... Deut 28:53
because he *h* nothing left him in ... Deut 28:55
Yet the LORD *h* not given you an ... Deut 29:4
as he *h* said unto thee ... Deut 29:13
as he *h* sworn unto thy fathers, ... Deut 29:13
which the LORD *h* laid upon it ... Deut 29:22
Wherefore *h* the LORD done thus ... Deut 29:24
the LORD thy God *h* driven thee ... Deut 30:1
the LORD thy God *h* scattered thee ... Deut 30:3
also the LORD *h* said unto me ... Deut 31:2
before thee, as the LORD *h* said ... Deut 31:3
h sworn unto their fathers to ... Deut 31:7
he thy father that *h* bought thee ... Deut 32:6
H he not made thee, and ... Deut 32:6
the LORD *h* not done all this ... Deut 32:27
LORD your God *h* given you rest ... Josh 1:13
and *h* given you this land ... Josh 1:13
as he *h* given you, and they also ... Josh 1:15
the LORD *h* given you the land ... Josh 2:9
when the LORD *h* given us the land ... Josh 2:14
Truly the LORD *h* delivered into ... Josh 2:24
for the LORD *h* given you the city ... Josh 6:16
the woman, and all that she *h* ... Josh 6:22
Israel *h* sinned, and they have ... Josh 7:11
with fire, he and all that he *h* ... Josh 7:15
because he *h* transgressed the ... Josh 7:15
because he *h* wrought folly in ... Josh 7:15
which no man *h* lift up any iron ... Josh 8:31
for it *h* made peace with Joshua ... Josh 10:4
for the LORD your God *h* delivered ... Josh 10:19
the LORD *h* kept me alive, as he ... Josh 14:10
as the LORD *h* blessed me hitherto ... Josh 17:14
God of your fathers *h* given you ... Josh 18:3
now the LORD your God *h* given ... Josh 22:4
For the LORD *h* made Jordan a ... Josh 22:25
God *h* done unto all these nations ... Josh 23:3
God is he that *h* fought for you ... Josh 23:3
LORD your God *h* promised unto you ... Josh 23:5
For the LORD *h* driven out from ... Josh 23:9
no man *h* been able to stand ... Josh 23:9
for you, as he *h* promised you ... Josh 23:10
the LORD your God *h* given you ... Josh 23:13
that not one thing *h* failed of ... Josh 23:14
not one thing *h* failed thereof ... Josh 23:14
the LORD your God *h* given you ... Josh 23:15
land which he *h* given unto you ... Josh 23:16
after that he *h* done you good ... Josh 24:20
for it *h* heard all the words of ... Josh 24:27
I have done, so God *h* requited me ... Judg 1:7
Because that this people *h* ... Judg 2:20
for the LORD *h* delivered your ... Judg 3:28
H not the LORD God of Israel ... Judg 4:6
h delivered Sisera into thine ... Judg 4:14
but now the LORD *h* forsaken us ... Judg 6:13
altar of Baal that thy father *h* ... Judg 6:25
to another, Who *h* done this thing ... Judg 6:29
son of Joash *h* done this thing ... Judg 6:29
because he *h* cast down the altar ... Judg 6:30
because he *h* cut down the grove ... Judg 6:30
because one *h* cast down his altar ... Judg 6:31
because he *h* thrown down his ... Judg 6:32
saying, Mine own hand *h* saved me ... Judg 7:2
for into his hand *h* God delivered ... Judg 7:14
for the LORD *h* delivered into ... Judg 7:15
God *h* delivered into your hands ... Judg 8:3
when the LORD *h* delivered Zebah ... Judg 8:7
So now the LORD God of Israel *h* ... Judg 11:23
h proceeded out of thy mouth ... Judg 11:36
forasmuch as the LORD *h* taken ... Judg 11:36
the man *h* appeared unto me, that ... Judg 13:10
Philistines said, Who *h* done this ... Judg 15:6
to do to him as he *h* done to us ... Judg 15:10
There *h* not come a razor upon ... Judg 16:17
for he *h* shewed me all his heart ... Judg 16:18
Our god *h* delivered Samson our ... Judg 16:23
Our god *h* delivered into our ... Judg 16:24
h hired me, and I am his priest ... Judg 18:4
for God *h* given it into your ... Judg 18:10
and every woman that *h* lain by man ... Judg 21:11
for the Almighty *h* dealt very ... Ruth 1:20
the LORD *h* brought me home again ... Ruth 1:21
seeing the LORD *h* testified ... Ruth 1:21
and the Almighty *h* afflicted me ... Ruth 1:21
h continued even from the morning ... Ruth 2:7
It *h* fully been shewed me, all ... Ruth 2:11
who *h* not left off his kindness ... Ruth 2:20
which *h* not left thee this day ... Ruth 4:14
thee than seven sons, *h* born him ... Ruth 4:15
the LORD *h* given me my petition ... 1Sa 1:27
so that the barren *h* born seven ... 1Sa 2:5
she that *h* many children is waxed ... 1Sa 2:5
he *h* set the world upon them ... 1Sa 2:8
that the LORD *h* said unto thee ... 1Sa 3:17
Wherefore *h* the LORD smitten us ... 1Sa 4:3
for there *h* not been such a thing ... 1Sa 4:7
there *h* been also a great ... 1Sa 4:17
on which there *h* come no yoke ... 1Sa 6:7
then he *h* done us this great evil ... 1Sa 6:9
Hitherto *h* the LORD helped us ... 1Sa 7:12
for unto this time *h* it been kept ... 1Sa 9:24
Is it not because the LORD *h* ... 1Sa 10:1
thy father *h* left the care of the ... 1Sa 10:2
he *h* hid himself among the stuff ... 1Sa 10:22
See ye him whom the LORD *h* chosen ... 1Sa 10:24
for to day the LORD *h* wrought ... 1Sa 11:13
the LORD *h* set a king over you ... 1Sa 12:13
because it *h* pleased the LORD to ... 1Sa 12:22
great things he *h* done for you ... 1Sa 12:24
the LORD *h* sought him a man after ... 1Sa 13:14
the LORD *h* commanded him to be ... 1Sa 13:14
for the LORD *h* delivered them ... 1Sa 14:10
for the LORD *h* delivered them ... 1Sa 14:12
My father *h* troubled the land ... 1Sa 14:29
wherein this sin *h* been this day ... 1Sa 14:38
die, who *h* wrought this great ... 1Sa 14:45
for he *h* wrought with God this ... 1Sa 14:45
h not performed my commandments ... 1Sa 15:11
the LORD *h* said to me this night ... 1Sa 15:16
H the LORD as great delight in ... 1Sa 15:22
he *h* also rejected thee from ... 1Sa 15:23
the LORD *h* rejected thee from ... 1Sa 15:26
The LORD *h* rent the kingdom of ... 1Sa 15:28
h given it to a neighbour of ... 1Sa 15:28
As thy sword *h* made women ... 1Sa 15:33
Neither *h* the LORD chosen this ... 1Sa 16:8
Neither *h* the LORD chosen these ... 1Sa 16:9
The LORD *h* not chosen these ... 1Sa 16:10
for he *h* found favour in my sight ... 1Sa 16:22
seeing he *h* defied the armies of ... 1Sa 17:36
Saul *h* slain his thousands, and ... 1Sa 18:7
the king *h* delight in thee, and ... 1Sa 18:22
because he *h* not sinned against ... 1Sa 19:4
as he *h* been with my father ... 1Sa 20:13
not when the LORD *h* cut off the ... 1Sa 20:15
for the LORD *h* sent thee away ... 1Sa 20:22
Something *h* befallen him, he is ... 1Sa 20:26
for our family *h* a sacrifice in ... 1Sa 20:29
he *h* commanded me to be there ... 1Sa 20:29
what *h* he done? ... 1Sa 20:32
The king *h* commanded me a ... 1Sa 21:2
h said unto me, Let no man know ... 1Sa 21:2
Saul *h* slain his thousands, and ... 1Sa 21:11
that sheweth me that my son *h* ... 1Sa 22:8
h stirred up my servant against ... 1Sa 22:8
God *h* delivered him into mine ... 1Sa 23:7
entering into a town that *h* gates ... 1Sa 23:7
thy servant *h* certainly heard ... 1Sa 23:10
come down, as thy servant *h* heard ... 1Sa 23:11
haunt is, and who *h* seen him there ... 1Sa 23:22
this fellow *h* in the wilderness ... 1Sa 25:21
he *h* requited me evil for good ... 1Sa 25:21
seeing the LORD *h* withholden thee ... 1Sa 25:26
handmaid *h* brought unto my lord ... 1Sa 25:27
evil *h* not been found in thee all ... 1Sa 25:28
that he *h* spoken concerning thee ... 1Sa 25:30
or that my lord *h* avenged himself ... 1Sa 25:31
which *h* kept me back from hurting ... 1Sa 25:34
that *h* pleaded the cause of my ... 1Sa 25:39
h kept his servant from evil ... 1Sa 25:39
for the LORD *h* returned the ... 1Sa 25:39
God *h* delivered thine enemy into ... 1Sa 26:8
He *h* made his people Israel ... 1Sa 27:12
a woman that *h* a familiar spirit ... 1Sa 28:7 1172
there is a woman that *h* a ... 1Sa 28:7 1172
thou knowest what Saul *h* done ... 1Sa 28:9
how he *h* cut off those that have ... 1Sa 28:9
the LORD *h* done to him, as he ... 1Sa 28:17
for the LORD *h* rent the kingdom ... 1Sa 28:17
therefore *h* the LORD done this ... 1Sa 28:18
thine handmaid *h* obeyed thy voice ... 1Sa 28:21
which *h* been with me these days, ... 1Sa 29:3
that which the LORD *h* given us ... 1Sa 30:23
who *h* preserved us, and delivered ... 1Sa 30:23
for thy mouth *h* testified against ... 2Sa 1:16
as the LORD *h* sworn to David, ... 2Sa 3:9
for the LORD *h* spoken of David, ... 2Sa 3:18
he *h* sent him away, and he is gone ... 2Sa 3:23
house of Joab one that *h* an issue ... 2Sa 3:29
the LORD *h* avenged my lord the ... 2Sa 4:8
who *h* redeemed my soul out of all ... 2Sa 4:9
The LORD *h* broken forth upon mine ... 2Sa 5:20
The LORD *h* blessed the house of ... 2Sa 6:12
therefore *h* thy servant found in ... 2Sa 7:27
Jonathan *h* yet a son, which is ... 2Sa 9:3
the king *h* commanded his servant ... 2Sa 9:11
that he *h* sent comforters unto ... 2Sa 10:3
h not David rather sent his ... 2Sa 10:3
the man that *h* done this thing ... 2Sa 12:5
The LORD also *h* put away thy sin ... 2Sa 12:13
H Amnon thy brother been with ... 2Sa 13:20
thy servant *h* sheepshearers ... 2Sa 13:24
Absalom *h* slain all the king's ... 2Sa 13:30
h been determined from the day ... 2Sa 13:32
that my lord the king *h* spoken ... 2Sa 14:19
h thy servant Joab done this ... 2Sa 14:20
in that the king *h* fulfilled the ... 2Sa 14:22
near mine, and he *h* barley there ... 2Sa 14:30
that every man which *h* any suit ... 2Sa 15:4
The LORD *h* returned upon thee all ... 2Sa 16:8
the LORD *h* delivered the kingdom ... 2Sa 16:8
because the LORD *h* said unto him ... 2Sa 16:10
for the LORD *h* bidden him ... 2Sa 16:11
which he *h* left to keep the house ... 2Sa 16:21
Ahithophel *h* spoken after this ... 2Sa 17:6
The counsel that Ahithophel *h* ... 2Sa 17:7
for thus *h* Ahithophel counselled ... 2Sa 17:21
how that the LORD *h* avenged him ... 2Sa 18:19
which *h* delivered up the men that ... 2Sa 18:28
for the LORD *h* avenged thee this ... 2Sa 18:31
he *h* slandered thy servant unto ... 2Sa 19:27
or *h* he given us any gift ... 2Sa 19:42
h lifted up his hand against the ... 2Sa 20:21
of my hands *h* he recompensed me ... 2Sa 22:21
Therefore the LORD *h* recompensed ... 2Sa 22:25
and thy gentleness *h* made me great ... 2Sa 22:36
yet he *h* made with me an ... 2Sa 23:5
he *h* slain oxen and fat cattle and ... 1Kin 1:19
h called all the sons of the king ... 1Kin 1:19
thy servant *h* he not called ... 1Kin 1:19
h slain oxen and fat cattle and ... 1Kin 1:25
h called all the king's sons, and ... 1Kin 1:25
servant Solomon, *h* he not called ... 1Kin 1:26
that *h* redeemed my soul out of ... 1Kin 1:29
As the LORD *h* been with my lord ... 1Kin 1:37
king David *h* made Solomon king ... 1Kin 1:43
the king *h* sent with him Zadok ... 1Kin 1:44
which *h* given one to sit on my ... 1Kin 1:48
he *h* caught hold on the horns of ... 1Kin 1:51
which *h* established me, and set me ... 1Kin 2:24
who *h* made me an house, as he ... 1Kin 2:24
said unto him, Do as he *h* said ... 1Kin 2:31
as my lord the king *h* said ... 1Kin 2:38
But now the LORD my God *h* given ... 1Kin 5:4
which *h* given unto David a wise ... 1Kin 5:7
h with his hand fulfilled it, ... 1Kin 8:15
the LORD *h* performed his word ... 1Kin 8:20
that *h* given rest unto his people ... 1Kin 8:56
there *h* not failed one word of ... 1Kin 8:56
Why *h* the LORD done thus unto ... 1Kin 9:8
therefore *h* the LORD brought upon ... 1Kin 9:9
my father *h* chastised you with ... 1Kin 12:11
the sign which the LORD *h* spoken ... 1Kin 13:3
therefore the LORD *h* delivered ... 1Kin 13:26
which *h* torn him, and slain him, ... 1Kin 13:26
for the LORD *h* spoken it ... 1Kin 14:11
Zimri *h* conspired, and *h* also ... 1Kin 16:16
whither my lord *h* not sent to ... 1Kin 18:10
mouth which *h* not kissed him ... 1Kin 19:18
the LORD *h* put a lying spirit in ... 1Kin 22:23
the LORD *h* spoken evil concerning ... 1Kin 22:23
the LORD *h* not spoken by me ... 1Kin 22:28
Thou man of God, the king *h* said ... 2Kin 1:9
man of God, thus *h* the king said ... 2Kin 1:11
for the LORD *h* sent me to Beth-el ... 2Kin 2:2
for the LORD *h* sent me to Jericho ... 2Kin 2:4
for the LORD *h* sent me to Jordan ... 2Kin 2:6
Spirit of the LORD *h* taken him up ... 2Kin 2:16
The king of Moab *h* rebelled ... 2Kin 3:7
that the LORD *h* called these ... 2Kin 3:10
for the LORD *h* called these three ... 2Kin 3:13
Thine handmaid *h* not any thing in ... 2Kin 4:2
answered, Verily she *h* no child ... 2Kin 4:14
the LORD *h* hid it from me, and ... 2Kin 4:27
and *h* not told me ... 2Kin 4:27
my master *h* spared Naaman this ... 2Kin 5:20
My master *h* sent me, saying, ... 2Kin 5:22
and she *h* hid her son ... 2Kin 6:29
h sent to take away mine head ... 2Kin 6:32
the king of Israel *h* hired ... 2Kin 7:6
for the LORD *h* called for a ... 2Kin 8:1
great things that Elisha *h* done ... 2Kin 8:4
king of Syria *h* sent me to thee ... 2Kin 8:9
howbeit the LORD *h* shewed me that ... 2Kin 8:10
The LORD *h* shewed me that thou ... 2Kin 8:13
for the LORD *h* done that which he ... 2Kin 10:10
thine heart *h* lifted thee up ... 2Kin 14:10
therefore he *h* sent lions among ... 2Kin 17:26
altars Hezekiah *h* taken away ... 2Kin 18:22
h said to Judah and Jerusalem, Ye ... 2Kin 18:22
H my master sent me to thy master ... 2Kin 18:27
h he not sent me to the men which ... 2Kin 18:27
H any of the gods of the nations ... 2Kin 18:33
the king of Assyria his master *h* ... 2Kin 19:4
which the LORD thy God *h* heard ... 2Kin 19:4
which *h* sent him to reproach the ... 2Kin 19:16
the LORD *h* spoken concerning him ... 2Kin 19:21
daughter of Zion *h* despised thee ... 2Kin 19:21
h shaken her head at thee ... 2Kin 19:21
do the thing that he *h* spoken ... 2Kin 20:9
Judah *h* done these abominations ... 2Kin 21:11
h done wickedly above all that ... 2Kin 21:11
h made Judah also to sin with his ... 2Kin 21:11
Hilkiah the priest *h* delivered me ... 2Kin 22:10
which the king of Judah *h* read ... 2Kin 22:16
God *h* broken in upon mine enemies ... 1Chr 14:11
for them *h* the LORD chosen to ... 1Chr 15:2
marvellous works that he *h* done ... 1Chr 16:12
h confirmed the same to Jacob for ... 1Chr 16:17
therefore thy servant *h* found in ... 1Chr 17:25
that he *h* sent comforters unto ... 1Chr 19:3
thy God, as he *h* said of thee ... 1Chr 22:11
h he not given you rest on every ... 1Chr 22:18
for he *h* given the inhabitants of ... 1Chr 22:18
The LORD God of Israel *h* given ... 1Chr 23:25
for he *h* chosen Judah to be the ... 1Chr 28:4
(for the LORD *h* given me many ... 1Chr 28:5
he *h* chosen Solomon my son to ... 1Chr 28:5
for the LORD *h* chosen thee to ... 1Chr 28:10
my son, whom alone God *h* chosen ... 1Chr 29:1
the LORD *h* loved his people ... 2Chr 2:11
he *h* made thee king over them ... 2Chr 2:11

who *h* given to David the king a.......... 2Chr 2:12
wine, which my lord *h* spoken of.......... 2Chr 2:15
The LORD *h* said that he would.......... 2Chr 6:1
who *h* with his hands fulfilled.......... 2Chr 6:4
The LORD therefore *h* performed.......... 2Chr 6:10
his word that he *h* spoken.......... 2Chr 6:10
Why *h* the LORD done thus unto.......... 2Chr 7:21
therefore *h* he brought all this.......... 2Chr 7:22
the ark of the LORD *h* come.......... 2Chr 8:11
h rebelled against his lord.......... 2Chr 13:6
he *h* given us rest on every side.......... 2Chr 14:7
h been without the true God.......... 2Chr 15:3
the LORD *h* put a lying spirit in.......... 2Chr 18:22
the LORD *h* spoken evil against.......... 2Chr 18:22
then *h* not the LORD spoken by me.......... 2Chr 18:27
the LORD *h* broken thy works.......... 2Chr 20:37
as the LORD *h* said of the sons of.......... 2Chr 23:3
the LORD, he *h* also forsaken you.......... 2Chr 24:20
for God *h* power to help, and to.......... 2Chr 25:8 3426
I know that God *h* determined to.......... 2Chr 25:16
he *h* delivered them into your.......... 2Chr 28:9
he *h* delivered them to trouble,.......... 2Chr 29:8
for the LORD *h* chosen you to.......... 2Chr 29:11
which he *h* sanctified for ever.......... 2Chr 30:8
for the LORD *h* blessed his people.......... 2Chr 31:10
H not the same Hezekiah taken.......... 2Chr 32:12
the priest *h* given me a book.......... 2Chr 34:18
All the kingdoms of the earth *h*.......... 2Chr 36:23
he *h* charged me to build him an.......... 2Chr 36:23
The LORD God of heaven *h* given me.......... Ezr 1:2
he *h* charged me to build him an.......... Ezr 1:2
the king of Persia *h* commanded us.......... Ezr 4:3
us *h* been plainly read before me.......... Ezr 4:18
search *h* been made, and it is.......... Ezr 4:19
that this city of old time *h* made.......... Ezr 4:19
Who *h* commanded you to build this.......... Ezr 5:3
until now *h* it been in building.......... Ezr 5:16
the God that *h* caused his name to.......... Ezr 6:12
which *h* put such a thing as this.......... Ezr 7:27
h extended mercy unto me before.......... Ezr 7:28
rulers *h* been chief in this.......... Ezr 9:2
now for a little space grace *h*.......... Ezr 9:8
yet our God *h* not forsaken us in.......... Ezr 9:9
but *h* extended mercy unto us in.......... Ezr 9:9
that *h* come upon us, on our kings.......... Neh 9:32
because she *h* not performed the.......... Est 1:15
Vashti the queen *h* not done wrong.......... Est 1:16
that he may do as Esther *h* said.......... Est 5:5
do to morrow as the king *h* said.......... Est 5:8
dignity *h* been done to Mordecai.......... Est 6:3
about all that he *h* on every side.......... Job 1:10
hand now, and touch all that he *h*.......... Job 1:11
all that he *h* is in thy power.......... Job 1:12
h burned up the sheep, and the.......... Job 1:16
gave, and the LORD *h* taken away.......... Job 1:21
all that a man *h* will he give for.......... Job 2:4
is hid, and whom God *h* hedged in.......... Job 3:23
So the poor *h* hope, and iniquity.......... Job 5:16 1961
the wild ass bray when he *h* grass.......... Job 6:5
The eye of him that *h* seen me.......... Job 7:8
who *h* hardened himself against.......... Job 9:4
against him, and *h* prospered.......... Job 9:4
thy visitation *h* preserved my.......... Job 10:12
hand of the LORD *h* wrought this.......... Job 12:9
he *h* counsel and understanding.......... Job 12:13
mine eye *h* seen all this.......... Job 13:1
seen all this, mine ear *h* heard.......... Job 13:1
But now he *h* made me weary.......... Job 16:7
God *h* delivered me to the ungodly.......... Job 16:11
but he *h* also broken me asunder.......... Job 16:12
he *h* also taken me by my neck, and.......... Job 16:12
He *h* made me also a byword of the.......... Job 17:6
he that *h* clean hands shall be.......... Job 17:9
Know now that God *h* overthrown me Job 19:6
h compassed me with his net.......... Job 19:6
He *h* fenced up my way that I.......... Job 19:8
he *h* set darkness in my paths.......... Job 19:8
He *h* stripped me of my glory, and.......... Job 19:9
He *h* destroyed me on every side,.......... Job 19:10
mine hope *h* he removed like a.......... Job 19:10
He *h* also kindled his wrath.......... Job 19:11
He *h* put my brethren far from me,.......... Job 19:13
for the hand of God *h* touched me.......... Job 19:21
He *h* swallowed down riches, and he.......... Job 20:15
Because he *h* oppressed and *h*.......... Job 20:19
because he *h* violently taken away.......... Job 20:19
For what pleasure *h* he in his.......... Job 21:21
shall repay him what he *h* done.......... Job 21:31
when he *h* tried me, I shall come.......... Job 23:10
My foot *h* held his steps, his way.......... Job 23:11
neither *h* he covered the darkness.......... Job 23:17
thou the arm that *h* no strength.......... Job 26:2
counseled him that *h* no wisdom.......... Job 26:3
him, and destruction *h* no covering.......... Job 26:6
He *h* compassed the waters with.......... Job 26:10
By his spirit he *h* garnished the.......... Job 26:13
his hand *h* formed the crooked.......... Job 26:13
who *h* taken away my judgment.......... Job 27:2
the Almighty, who *h* vexed my soul.......... Job 27:2
the hypocrite, though he *h* gained.......... Job 27:8
and it *h* dust of gold.......... Job 28:6
the vulture's eye *h* not seen.......... Job 28:7
Because he *h* loosed my cord, and.......... Job 30:11
He *h* cast me into the mire, and I.......... Job 30:19
or if my foot *h* hasted to deceit.......... Job 31:5
If my step *h* turned out of the.......... Job 31:7
if any blot *h* cleaved to mine.......... Job 31:7
the fatherless *h* not eaten.......... Job 31:17
my heart *h* been secretly enticed,.......... Job 31:27
or my mouth *h* kissed my hand.......... Job 31:27
Now he *h* not directed his words.......... Job 32:14
belly is as wine which *h* no vent.......... Job 32:19
my tongue *h* spoken in my mouth.......... Job 33:2
The spirit of God *h* made me.......... Job 33:4

of the Almighty *h* given me life.......... Job 33:4
For Job *h* said, I am righteous.......... Job 34:5
God *h* taken away my judgment.......... Job 34:5
For he *h* said, It profiteth a man.......... Job 34:9
Who *h* given him a charge over the.......... Job 34:13
Or who *h* disposed the whole world.......... Job 34:13
Job *h* spoken without knowledge,.......... Job 34:35
he *h* visited in his anger.......... Job 35:15
Who *h* enjoined him his way.......... Job 36:23
Who *h* laid the measures thereof,.......... Job 38:5
or who *h* stretched the line upon.......... Job 38:5
Who *h* divided a watercourse for.......... Job 38:25
H the rain a father.......... Job 38:28 3426
or who *h* begotten the drops of.......... Job 38:28
of heaven, who *h* gendered it.......... Job 38:29
Who *h* put wisdom in the inward.......... Job 38:36
or who *h* given understanding to.......... Job 38:36
Who *h* sent out the wild ass free.......... Job 39:5
or who *h* loosed the bands of the.......... Job 39:5
Because God *h* deprived her of.......... Job 39:17
neither *h* he imparted to her.......... Job 39:17
H thou given the horse strength.......... Job 39:19
Who *h* prevented me, that I should.......... Job 41:11
is right, as my servant Job *h*.......... Job 42:7
The LORD *h* said unto me, Thou art.......... Ps 2:7
But know that the LORD *h* set.......... Ps 4:3
God that *h* pleasure in wickedness.......... Ps 5:4
for the LORD *h* heard the voice of.......... Ps 6:8
The LORD *h* heard my supplication.......... Ps 6:9
he *h* bent his bow, and made it.......... Ps 7:12
He *h* also prepared for him the.......... Ps 7:13
h conceived mischief, and brought.......... Ps 7:14
he *h* prepared his throne for.......... Ps 9:7
He *h* said in his heart, I shall.......... Ps 10:6
He *h* said in his heart, God *h*.......... Ps 10:11
he *h* said in his heart, Thou wilt.......... Ps 10:13
because he *h* dealt bountifully.......... Ps 13:6
The fool *h* said in his heart,.......... Ps 14:1
the LORD, who *h* given me counsel.......... Ps 16:7
of my hands *h* he recompensed me.......... Ps 18:20
Therefore *h* the LORD recompensed.......... Ps 18:24
and thy right hand *h* holden me up.......... Ps 18:35
and thy gentleness *h* made me great.......... Ps 18:35
In them *h* he set a tabernacle for.......... Ps 19:4
For he *h* not despised nor.......... Ps 22:24
neither *h* he hid his face from.......... Ps 22:24
be born, that he *h* done this.......... Ps 22:31
For he *h* founded it upon the seas.......... Ps 24:2
He that *h* clean hands, and a pure.......... Ps 24:4
who *h* not lifted up his soul unto.......... Ps 24:4
because he *h* heard the voice of.......... Ps 28:6
for he *h* shewed me his marvellous.......... Ps 31:21
the people whom he *h* chosen for.......... Ps 33:12
net that he *h* hid catch himself.......... Ps 35:8
said, Aha, aha, our eye *h* seen it.......... Ps 35:21
which *h* pleasure in the.......... Ps 35:27
he *h* left off to be wise, and to.......... Ps 36:3
h is better than the riches of.......... Ps 37:16
he *h* put a new song in my mouth,.......... Ps 40:3
h lifted up his heel against me.......... Ps 41:9
the shame of my face *h* covered me.......... Ps 44:15
therefore God *h* blessed thee for.......... Ps 45:2
h anointed thee with the oil of.......... Ps 45:7
he *h* made in the earth.......... Ps 46:8
h spoken, and called the earth.......... Ps 50:1
of beauty, God *h* shined.......... Ps 50:2
The fool *h* said in his heart,.......... Ps 53:1
for God *h* scattered the bones of.......... Ps 53:5
because God *h* despised them.......... Ps 53:5
For he *h* delivered me out of all.......... Ps 54:7
mine eye *h* seen his desire upon.......... Ps 54:7
me, and horror *h* overwhelmed me.......... Ps 55:5
He *h* delivered my soul in peace.......... Ps 55:18
He *h* put forth his hands against.......... Ps 55:20
he *h* broken his covenant.......... Ps 55:20
God *h* spoken in his holiness.......... Ps 60:6
God *h* spoken once.......... Ps 62:11
uttered, and my mouth *h* spoken.......... Ps 66:14
what he *h* done for my soul.......... Ps 66:16
But verily God *h* heard me.......... Ps 66:19
he *h* attended to the voice of my.......... Ps 66:19
which *h* not turned away my prayer.......... Ps 66:20
Thy congregation *h* dwelt therein.......... Ps 68:10
Thy God *h* commanded thy strength.......... Ps 68:28
shame *h* covered my face.......... Ps 69:7
zeal of thine house *h* eaten me up.......... Ps 69:9
Reproach *h* broken my heart.......... Ps 69:20
an ox or bullock that *h* horns.......... Ps 69:31
Saying, God *h* forsaken him.......... Ps 71:11
also, and him that *h* no helper.......... Ps 72:12
even all that the enemy *h* done.......... Ps 74:3
this, that the enemy *h* reproached.......... Ps 74:18
H God forgotten to be gracious.......... Ps 77:9
h he in anger shut up his tender.......... Ps 77:9
wonderful works that he *h* done.......... Ps 78:4
which he *h* established for ever.......... Ps 78:69
which thy right hand *h* planted.......... Ps 80:15
the sparrow *h* found an house, and.......... Ps 84:3
I am as a man that *h* no strength.......... Ps 88:4
Because he *h* set his love upon me.......... Ps 91:14
because he *h* known my name.......... Ps 91:14
wherewith he *h* girded himself.......... Ps 93:1
for he *h* done marvellous things.......... Ps 98:1
arm, *h* gotten him the victory.......... Ps 98:1
The LORD *h* made known his.......... Ps 98:2
his righteousness *h* he openly.......... Ps 98:2
He *h* remembered his mercy and his.......... Ps 98:3
it is he that *h* made us, and not.......... Ps 100:3
him that *h* an high look and a.......... Ps 101:5
For he *h* looked down from the.......... Ps 102:19
He *h* not dealt with us after our.......... Ps 103:10
the west, so far *h* he removed our.......... Ps 103:12
The LORD *h* prepared his throne in.......... Ps 103:19
of Lebanon, which he *h* planted.......... Ps 104:16

marvellous works that he *h* done.......... Ps 105:5
He *h* remembered his covenant for.......... Ps 105:8
whom he *h* redeemed from the hand.......... Ps 107:2
For he *h* broken the gates of.......... Ps 107:16
God *h* spoken in his holiness.......... Ps 108:7
extortioner catch all that he *h*.......... Ps 109:11
The LORD *h* sworn, and will not.......... Ps 110:4
He *h* made his wonderful works to.......... Ps 111:4
He *h* given meat unto them that.......... Ps 111:5
He *h* shewed his people the power.......... Ps 111:6
he *h* commanded his covenant for.......... Ps 111:9
He *h* dispersed, he *h* given to.......... Ps 112:9
h done whatsoever he *h* pleased.......... Ps 115:3
The LORD *h* been mindful of us.......... Ps 115:12
but the earth *h* he given to the.......... Ps 115:16
because he *h* heard my voice and my.......... Ps 116:1
Because he *h* inclined his ear.......... Ps 116:2
for the LORD *h* dealt bountifully.......... Ps 116:7
The LORD *h* chastened me sore.......... Ps 118:18
but he *h* not given me over unto.......... Ps 118:18
is the day which the LORD *h* made.......... Ps 118:24
the LORD, which *h* shewed us light.......... Ps 118:27
for the longing that it *h* unto.......... Ps 119:20
for thy word *h* quickened me.......... Ps 119:50
Horror *h* taken hold upon me.......... Ps 119:53
My zeal *h* consumed me, because.......... Ps 119:139
My soul *h* kept thy testimonies.......... Ps 119:167
My soul *h* long dwelt with him.......... Ps 120:6
who *h* not given us as a prey to.......... Ps 124:6
The LORD *h* done great things for.......... Ps 126:2
The LORD *h* done great things for.......... Ps 126:3
Happy is the man that *h* his.......... Ps 127:5
he *h* cut asunder the cords of the.......... Ps 129:4
The LORD *h* sworn in truth unto.......... Ps 132:11
For the LORD *h* chosen Zion.......... Ps 132:13
he *h* desired it for his.......... Ps 132:13
For the LORD *h* chosen Jacob unto.......... Ps 135:4
h redeemed us from our enemies.......... Ps 136:24
yet *h* he respect unto the lowly.......... Ps 138:6
For the enemy *h* persecuted my.......... Ps 143:3
he *h* smitten my life down to the.......... Ps 143:3
he *h* made me to dwell in darkness.......... Ps 143:3
Happy is he that *h* the God of.......... Ps 146:5
For he *h* strengthened the bars of.......... Ps 147:13
he *h* blessed thy children within.......... Ps 147:13
He *h* not dealt so with any nation.......... Ps 147:20
He *h* also stablished them for.......... Ps 148:6
he *h* made a decree which shall.......... Ps 148:6
Let every thing that *h* breath.......... Ps 150:6
by wisdom *h* founded the earth.......... Prov 3:19
by understanding *h* he established.......... Prov 3:19
He *h* taken a bag of money with.......... Prov 7:20
For she *h* cast down many wounded.......... Prov 7:26
Wisdom *h* builded her house.......... Prov 9:1
she *h* hewn out her seven pillars.......... Prov 9:1
She *h* killed her beasts.......... Prov 9:2
she *h* mingled her wine.......... Prov 9:2
she *h* also furnished her table.......... Prov 9:2
She *h* sent forth her maidens.......... Prov 9:3
In the lips of him that *h*.......... Prov 10:13
a man of understanding *h* wisdom.......... Prov 10:23
h a servant, is better than he.......... Prov 12:9
sluggard desireth, and *h* nothing.......... Prov 13:4
himself rich, yet *h* nothing.......... Prov 13:7
himself poor, yet *h* great riches.......... Prov 13:7
but the rich *h* many friends.......... Prov 14:20
but he that *h* mercy on the poor,.......... Prov 14:21
honoureth him *h* mercy on the poor.......... Prov 14:31
the righteous *h* hope in his death.......... Prov 14:32
heart of him that *h* understanding.......... Prov 14:33
The heart of him that *h*.......... Prov 15:14
a merry heart *h* a continual feast.......... Prov 15:15
A man *h* joy by the answer of his.......... Prov 15:23
The LORD *h* made all things for.......... Prov 16:4
of life unto him that *h* it.......... Prov 16:22 1167
in the eyes of him that *h* it.......... Prov 17:8 1167
seeing he *h* no heart to it.......... Prov 17:16
He that *h* a froward heart findeth.......... Prov 17:20
he that *h* a perverse tongue.......... Prov 17:20
and the father of a fool *h* no joy.......... Prov 17:21
before him that *h* understanding.......... Prov 17:24
He that *h* knowledge spareth his.......... Prov 17:27
A fool *h* no delight in.......... Prov 18:2
A man that *h* friends must shew.......... Prov 18:24
He that *h* pity upon the poor.......... Prov 19:17
that which he *h* given will he pay.......... Prov 19:17
and he that *h* it shall abide.......... Prov 19:23
reprove one that *h* understanding.......... Prov 19:25
the LORD *h* made even both of them.......... Prov 20:12
He that *h* a bountiful eye shall.......... Prov 22:9
bread of him that *h* an evil eye.......... Prov 23:6
Who *h* woe?.......... Prov 23:29
who *h* sorrow?.......... Prov 23:29
who *h* contentions?.......... Prov 23:29
who *h* babbling?.......... Prov 23:29
who *h* wounds without.......... Prov 23:29
who *h* redness of.......... Prov 23:29
do so to him as he *h* done to me.......... Prov 24:29
thy neighbour *h* put thee to shame.......... Prov 25:8
He that *h* no rule over his own.......... Prov 25:28
but the poor that *h* understanding.......... Prov 28:11
hasteth to be rich *h* an evil eye.......... Prov 28:22
Who *h* ascended up into heaven, or.......... Prov 30:4
who *h* gathered the wind in his.......... Prov 30:4
who *h* bound the waters in a.......... Prov 30:4
who *h* established all the ends of.......... Prov 30:4
The horseleach *h* two daughters.......... Prov 30:15
What profit *h* a man of all his.......... Eccl 1:3
The thing that *h* been, it is that.......... Eccl 1:9
it *h* been already of old time,.......... Eccl 1:10
this sore travail *h* God given to.......... Eccl 1:13
even that which *h* been already.......... Eccl 2:12
yet to a man that *h* not laboured.......... Eccl 2:21
For what *h* man of all his labour,.......... Eccl 2:22 1933

wherein he *h* laboured under the ... Eccl 2:22
What profit *h* he that worketh in ... Eccl 3:9
which God *h* given to the sons of ... Eccl 3:10
He *h* made every thing beautiful ... Eccl 3:11
also he *h* set the world in their ... Eccl 3:11
That which *h* been is now ... Eccl 3:15
which is to be *h* already been ... Eccl 3:15
so that a man *h* no preeminence ... Eccl 3:19
which *h* not yet been ... Eccl 4:3
who *h* not seen the evil work that ... Eccl 4:3
he *h* neither child nor brother ... Eccl 4:8
for he *h* not another to help him ... Eccl 4:10
for he *h* no pleasure in fools ... Eccl 5:4
what profit *h* he that *h* ... Eccl 5:16
he *h* much sorrow and wrath with ... Eccl 5:17
also to whom God *h* given riches ... Eccl 5:19
h given him power to eat thereof, ... Eccl 5:19
A man to whom God *h* given riches ... Eccl 6:2
Moreover he *h* not seen the sun, ... Eccl 6:5
this *h* more rest than the other ... Eccl 6:5
twice told, yet *h* he seen no good ... Eccl 6:6
For what *h* the wise more than the ... Eccl 6:8
what *h* the poor, that knoweth to ... Eccl 6:8
That which *h* been is named ... Eccl 6:10
straight, which he *h* made crooked ... Eccl 7:13
God also *h* set the one over ... Eccl 7:14
that God *h* made man upright ... Eccl 7:29
There is no man that *h* power over ... Eccl 8:8
neither *h* he power in the day of ... Eccl 8:8
because a man *h* no better thing ... Eccl 8:15
which he *h* given thee under the ... Eccl 9:9
that which *h* wings shall tell the ... Eccl 10:20 1167
the king *h* brought me into his ... Song 1:4
because the sun *h* looked upon me ... Song 1:6
every man *h* his sword upon his ... Song 3:8
which *h* a most vehement flame ... Song 8:6
sister, and she *h* no breasts ... Song 8:8
for the LORD *h* spoken, I have ... Is 1:2
who *h* required this at your hand, ... Is 1:12
the mouth of the LORD *h* spoken it ... Is 1:20
and as a garden that *h* no water ... Is 1:30
My wellbeloved *h* a vineyard in a ... Is 5:1
Therefore hell *h* enlarged herself ... Is 5:14
he *h* stretched forth his hand ... Is 5:25
against them, and *h* smitten them ... Is 5:25
said, Lo, this *h* touched thy lips ... Is 6:7
the LORD *h* given me are for signs ... Is 8:18
upon them *h* the light shined ... Is 9:2
and it *h* lighted upon Israel ... Is 9:8
As my hand *h* found the kingdoms ... Is 10:10
that when the Lord *h* performed ... Is 10:12
my hand *h* found as a nest the ... Is 10:14
at Michmash he *h* laid up his ... Is 10:28
for he *h* done excellent things ... Is 12:5
How *h* the oppressor ceased ... Is 14:4
The LORD *h* broken the staff of ... Is 14:5
it *h* raised up from their thrones ... Is 14:9
The LORD of hosts *h* sworn ... Is 14:24
For the LORD of hosts *h* purposed ... Is 14:27
That the LORD *h* founded Zion ... Is 14:32
h spoken concerning Moab since ... Is 16:13
But now the LORD *h* spoken ... Is 16:14
of hosts *h* purposed upon Egypt ... Is 19:12
The LORD *h* mingled a perverse ... Is 19:14
which he *h* determined against it ... Is 19:17
my servant Isaiah *h* walked naked ... Is 20:3
the night of my pleasure *h* he ... Is 21:4
For thus *h* the Lord said unto me, ... Is 21:6
gods he *h* broken unto the ground ... Is 21:9
For thus *h* the Lord said unto me, ... Is 21:16
LORD God of Israel *h* spoken it ... Is 21:17
for the LORD *h* spoken it ... Is 22:25
for the sea *h* spoken, even the ... Is 23:4
Who *h* taken this counsel against ... Is 23:8
The LORD of hosts *h* purposed it ... Is 23:9
the LORD *h* given a commandment ... Is 23:11
for the LORD *h* spoken this word ... Is 24:3
Therefore *h* the curse devoured ... Is 24:6
for the LORD *h* spoken it ... Is 25:8
H he smitten him, as he smote ... Is 27:7
Behold, the Lord *h* a mighty ... Is 28:2
When he *h* made plain the face ... Is 28:25
as of one that *h* a familiar ... Is 29:4
is faint, and his soul *h* appetite ... Is 29:8
For the LORD *h* poured out upon ... Is 29:10
deep sleep, and *h* closed your eyes ... Is 29:10
rulers, the seers *h* he covered ... Is 29:10
which *h* been winnowed with the ... Is 30:24
he *h* made it deep and large ... Is 30:33
For thus *h* the LORD spoken unto ... Is 31:4
he *h* filled Zion with judgment and ... Is 33:5
he *h* broken the covenant, he *h* ... Is 33:8
fearfulness *h* surprised the ... Is 33:14
he *h* utterly destroyed them ... Is 34:2
he *h* delivered them to the ... Is 34:2
for the LORD *h* a sacrifice in ... Is 34:6
for my mouth it *h* commanded ... Is 34:16
and his spirit it *h* gathered them ... Is 34:16
he *h* cast the lot for them, and ... Is 34:17
his hand *h* divided it unto them ... Is 34:17
altars Hezekiah *h* taken away ... Is 36:7
H my master sent me to thy master ... Is 36:12
h he not sent me to the men that ... Is 36:12
H any of the gods of the nations ... Is 36:18
the king of Assyria his master *h* ... Is 37:4
which the LORD thy God *h* heard ... Is 37:4
which *h* sent to reproach the ... Is 37:17
the LORD *h* spoken concerning him ... Is 37:22
h despised thee, and laughed thee ... Is 37:22
h shaken her head at thee ... Is 37:22
do this thing that he *h* spoken ... Is 38:7
He *h* both spoken unto me ... Is 38:15
and himself *h* done it ... Is 38:15
for she *h* received of the LORD'S ... Is 40:2
the mouth of the LORD *h* spoken it ... Is 40:5
Who *h* measured the waters in the ... Is 40:12
Who *h* directed the Spirit of the ... Is 40:13
being his counsellor *h* taught him ... Is 40:13
he *h* no oblation chooseth a tree ... Is 40:20
h it not been told you from the ... Is 40:21
behold who *h* created these things ... Is 40:26
Who *h* wrought and done it, calling ... Is 41:4
the hand of the LORD *h* done this ... Is 41:20
Holy One of Israel *h* created it ... Is 41:20
Who *h* declared from the beginning ... Is 41:26
Therefore he *h* poured upon him ... Is 42:25
it *h* set him on fire round about, ... Is 42:25
Thy first father *h* sinned ... Is 43:27
Who *h* formed a god, or molten a ... Is 44:10
for he *h* shut their eyes, that ... Is 44:18
deceived heart *h* turned him aside ... Is 44:20
for the LORD *h* done it ... Is 44:23
for the LORD *h* redeemed Jacob, and ... Is 44:23
or thy work, He *h* no hands ... Is 45:9
he *h* established it, he created ... Is 45:18
who *h* declared this from ancient ... Is 45:21
who *h* told it from that time ... Is 45:21
knowledge, it *h* perverted thee ... Is 47:10
say, Mine idol *h* done them ... Is 48:5
my molten image, *h* commanded them ... Is 48:5
Mine hand also *h* laid the ... Is 48:13
my right hand *h* spanned the ... Is 48:13
which among them *h* declared these ... Is 48:14
The LORD *h* loved him ... Is 48:14
GOD, and his Spirit, *h* sent me ... Is 48:16
The LORD *h* redeemed his servant ... Is 48:20
The LORD *h* called me from the ... Is 49:1
h he made mention of my name ... Is 49:1
he *h* made my mouth like a sharp ... Is 49:2
shadow of his hand *h* he hid me ... Is 49:2
in his quiver *h* he hid me ... Is 49:2
for he that *h* mercy on them shall ... Is 49:10
for the LORD *h* comforted his ... Is 49:13
The LORD *h* forsaken me ... Is 49:14
and my Lord *h* forgotten me ... Is 49:14
Who *h* begotten me these, seeing I ... Is 49:21
and who *h* brought up these ... Is 49:21
The Lord GOD *h* given me the ... Is 50:4
The Lord GOD *h* opened mine ear, ... Is 50:5
in darkness, and *h* no light ... Is 50:10
Art thou not it that *h* cut Rahab ... Is 51:9
thou not it which *h* dried the sea ... Is 51:10
that *h* made the depths of the sea ... Is 51:10
that *h* stretched forth the ... Is 51:13
the sons whom she *h* brought forth ... Is 51:18
the sons that she *h* brought up ... Is 51:18
for the LORD *h* comforted his ... Is 52:9
people, he *h* redeemed Jerusalem ... Is 52:9
The LORD *h* made bare his holy arm ... Is 52:10
Who *h* believed our report ... Is 53:1
he *h* no form nor comeliness ... Is 53:2
Surely he *h* borne our griefs, and ... Is 53:4
the LORD *h* laid on him the ... Is 53:6
he *h* put him to grief ... Is 53:10
because he *h* poured out his soul ... Is 53:12
For the LORD *h* called thee as a ... Is 54:6
the LORD that *h* mercy on thee ... Is 54:10
the waters, and he that *h* no money ... Is 55:1
for he *h* glorified thee ... Is 55:5
that *h* joined himself to the LORD ... Is 56:3
The LORD *h* utterly separated me ... Is 56:3
the mouth of the LORD *h* spoken it ... Is 58:14
lies, your tongue *h* muttered ... Is 59:3
because he *h* glorified thee ... Is 60:9
because the LORD *h* anointed me to ... Is 61:1
he *h* sent me to bind up the ... Is 61:1
the seed which the LORD *h* blessed ... Is 61:9
for he *h* clothed me with the ... Is 61:10
he *h* covered me with the robe of ... Is 61:10
The LORD *h* sworn by his right ... Is 62:8
the LORD *h* proclaimed unto the ... Is 62:11
that the LORD *h* bestowed on us ... Is 63:7
which he *h* bestowed on them ... Is 63:7
neither *h* the eye seen, O God, ... Is 64:4
what he *h* prepared for him that ... Is 64:4
man that *h* not filled his days ... Is 65:20
all those things *h* mine hand made ... Is 66:2
Who *h* heard such a thing ... Is 66:8
who *h* seen such things ... Is 66:8
H a nation changed their gods, ... Jer 2:11
your own sword *h* devoured your ... Jer 2:30
for the LORD *h* rejected thy ... Jer 2:37
there *h* been no latter rain ... Jer 3:3
which backsliding Israel *h* done ... Jer 3:6
there *h* played the harlot ... Jer 3:6
h not turned unto me with her ... Jer 3:10
unto me, The backsliding Israel *h* ... Jer 3:11
For shame *h* devoured the labour ... Jer 3:24
because she *h* been rebellious ... Jer 4:17
For thus *h* the LORD said, The ... Jer 4:27
But this people *h* a revolting ... Jer 5:23
For thus *h* the LORD of hosts said ... Jer 6:6
anguish *h* taken hold of us, and ... Jer 6:24
because the LORD *h* rejected them ... Jer 6:30
for the LORD *h* rejected and ... Jer 7:29
LORD our God *h* put us to silence ... Jer 8:14
astonishment *h* taken hold on me ... Jer 8:21
the mouth of the LORD *h* spoken ... Jer 9:12
He *h* made the earth by his power, ... Jer 10:12
he *h* established the world by his ... Jer 10:12
h stretched out the heavens by ... Jer 10:12
What *h* my beloved to do in mine ... Jer 11:15
seeing she *h* wrought lewdness ... Jer 11:15
tumult he *h* kindled fire upon it ... Jer 11:16
h pronounced evil against thee, ... Jer 11:17
the LORD *h* given me knowledge of ... Jer 11:18
for the LORD *h* spoken ... Jer 13:15
h thy soul lothed Zion ... Jer 14:19
She that *h* borne seven ... Jer 15:9
she *h* given up the ghost ... Jer 15:9
she *h* been ashamed and confounded ... Jer 15:9
Wherefore *h* the LORD pronounced ... Jer 16:10
heathen, who *h* heard such things ... Jer 18:13
the virgin of Israel *h* done a ... Jer 18:13
Because my people *h* forgotten me ... Jer 18:15
The LORD *h* not called thy name ... Jer 20:3
for he *h* delivered the soul of ... Jer 20:13
Wherefore *h* the LORD done thus ... Jer 22:8
This *h* been thy manner from thy ... Jer 22:21
like a man whom wine *h* overcome ... Jer 23:9
that despise me, The LORD *h* said ... Jer 23:17
For who *h* stood in the counsel of ... Jer 23:18
h perceived and heard his word ... Jer 23:18
who *h* marked his word, and heard ... Jer 23:18
The prophet that *h* a dream ... Jer 23:28
and he that *h* my word, let him ... Jer 23:28
brother, What *h* the LORD answered ... Jer 23:35
and, What *h* the LORD spoken ... Jer 23:35
What *h* the LORD answered thee ... Jer 23:37
and, What *h* the LORD spoken ... Jer 23:37
word of the LORD *h* come unto me ... Jer 25:3
the LORD *h* sent unto you all his ... Jer 25:4
that the LORD *h* given unto you ... Jer 25:5
which Jeremiah *h* prophesied ... Jer 25:13
for the LORD *h* a controversy with ... Jer 25:31
for the LORD *h* spoiled their ... Jer 25:36
He *h* forsaken his covert, as the ... Jer 25:38
for he *h* prophesied against this ... Jer 26:11
that he *h* pronounced against you ... Jer 26:13
for of a truth the LORD *h* sent me ... Jer 26:15
for he *h* spoken to us in the name ... Jer 26:16
as the LORD *h* spoken against the ... Jer 27:13
that the LORD *h* truly sent him ... Jer 28:9
The LORD *h* not sent thee ... Jer 28:15
The LORD *h* raised us up prophets ... Jer 29:15
The LORD *h* made thee priest in ... Jer 29:26
Shemaiah *h* prophesied unto you ... Jer 29:31
because he *h* taught rebellion ... Jer 29:32
The LORD *h* appeared of old unto ... Jer 31:3
For the LORD *h* redeemed Jacob, and ... Jer 31:11
for the LORD *h* created a new ... Jer 31:22
For this city *h* been to me as a ... Jer 32:31
families which the LORD *h* chosen ... Jer 33:24
he *h* even cast them off ... Jer 33:24
which *h* been sold unto thee ... Jer 34:14
when he *h* served thee six years, ... Jer 34:14
in all that he *h* charged us ... Jer 35:8
but this people *h* not hearkened ... Jer 35:16
unto all that he *h* commanded you ... Jer 35:18
anger and the fury that the LORD *h* ... Jer 36:7
the king of Judah *h* burned ... Jer 36:28
word that the LORD *h* shewed me ... Jer 38:21
The LORD thy God *h* pronounced ... Jer 40:2
Now the LORD *h* brought it ... Jer 40:3
and done according as he *h* said ... Jer 40:3
whom the king of Babylon *h* made ... Jer 40:5
h sent Ishmael the son of ... Jer 40:14
my fury *h* been poured forth upon ... Jer 42:18
The LORD *h* said concerning you, O ... Jer 42:19
the which he *h* sent me unto you ... Jer 42:21
the LORD our God *h* not sent thee ... Jer 43:2
for the LORD *h* added grief to my ... Jer 45:3
hosts *h* a sacrifice in the north ... Jer 46:10
thy cry *h* filled the land ... Jer 46:12
for the mighty man *h* stumbled ... Jer 46:12
he *h* passed the time appointed ... Jer 46:17
seeing the LORD *h* given it a ... Jer 47:7
there *h* he appointed it ... Jer 47:7
destroyed, as the LORD *h* spoken ... Jer 48:8
Moab *h* been at ease from his ... Jer 48:11
he *h* settled on his lees, and *h* ... Jer 48:11
neither *h* he gone into captivity ... Jer 48:11
that he *h* gotten are perished ... Jer 48:36
how *h* Moab turned the back with ... Jer 48:39
because he *h* magnified himself ... Jer 48:42
H Israel no sons? ... Jer 49:1
h he no heir? ... Jer 49:1
Thy terribleness *h* deceived thee ... Jer 49:16
that he *h* taken against Edom ... Jer 49:20
that he *h* purposed against the ... Jer 49:20
to flee, and fear *h* seized on her ... Jer 49:24
h taken counsel against you ... Jer 49:30
h conceived a purpose against you ... Jer 49:30
My people *h* been lost sheep ... Jer 50:6
for she *h* sinned against the LORD ... Jer 50:14
she *h* given her hand ... Jer 50:15
as she *h* done, do unto her ... Jer 50:15
king of Assyria *h* devoured him ... Jer 50:17
of Babylon *h* broken his bones ... Jer 50:17
The LORD *h* opened his armoury, and ... Jer 50:25
h brought forth the weapons of ... Jer 50:25
according to all that she *h* done ... Jer 50:29
for she *h* been proud against the ... Jer 50:29
The king of Babylon *h* heard the ... Jer 50:43
that he *h* taken against Babylon ... Jer 50:45
that he *h* purposed against the ... Jer 50:45
For Israel *h* not been forsaken, ... Jer 51:5
Babylon *h* been a golden cup in ... Jer 51:7
The LORD *h* brought forth our ... Jer 51:10
the LORD *h* raised up the spirit ... Jer 51:11
for the LORD *h* both devised ... Jer 51:12
LORD of hosts *h* sworn by himself ... Jer 51:14
He *h* made the earth by his power, ... Jer 51:15
he *h* established the world by his ... Jer 51:15
h stretched out the heaven by his ... Jer 51:15
their might *h* failed ... Jer 51:30
the king of Babylon *h* devoured me ... Jer 51:34
he *h* crushed me, he *h* made me ... Jer 51:34
he *h* swallowed me up like a ... Jer 51:34
he *h* filled his belly with my ... Jer 51:34
my delicates, he *h* cast me out ... Jer 51:34
that which he *h* swallowed up ... Jer 51:44

As Babylon *h* caused the slain of	Jer 51:49	
shame *h* covered our faces	Jer 51:51	
the LORD *h* spoiled Babylon	Jer 51:55	
lovers she *h* none to comfort her	Lam 1:2	
for the LORD *h* afflicted her for	Lam 1:5	
Jerusalem *h* grievously sinned	Lam 1:8	
for the enemy *h* magnified himself	Lam 1:9	
The adversary *h* spread out his	Lam 1:10	
for she *h* seen that the heathen	Lam 1:10	
wherewith the LORD *h* afflicted me	Lam 1:12	
From above *h* he sent fire into my	Lam 1:13	
he *h* spread a net for my feet	Lam 1:13	
he *h* turned me back	Lam 1:13	
he *h* made me desolate and faint	Lam 1:13	
he *h* made my strength to fall,	Lam 1:14	
the Lord *h* delivered me into	Lam 1:14	
The Lord *h* trodden under foot all	Lam 1:15	
he *h* called an assembly against	Lam 1:15	
the Lord *h* trodden the virgin,	Lam 1:15	
the LORD *h* commanded concerning	Lam 1:17	
How *h* the Lord covered the	Lam 2:1	
The Lord *h* swallowed up all the	Lam 2:2	
of Jacob, and *h* not pitied	Lam 2:2	
he *h* thrown down in his wrath the	Lam 2:2	
he *h* brought them down to the	Lam 2:2	
he *h* polluted the kingdom and the	Lam 2:2	
He *h* cut off in his fierce anger	Lam 2:3	
he *h* drawn back his right hand	Lam 2:3	
He *h* bent his bow like an enemy	Lam 2:4	
he *h* swallowed up Israel, he *h*	Lam 2:5	
he *h* destroyed his strong holds,	Lam 2:5	
h increased in the daughter of	Lam 2:5	
he *h* violently taken away his	Lam 2:6	
he *h* destroyed his places of the	Lam 2:6	
the LORD *h* caused the solemn	Lam 2:6	
h despised in the indignation of	Lam 2:6	
The Lord *h* cast off his altar	Lam 2:7	
he *h* abhorred his sanctuary,	Lam 2:7	
he *h* given up into the hand of	Lam 2:7	
The LORD *h* purposed to destroy	Lam 2:8	
he *h* stretched out a line	Lam 2:8	
he *h* not withdrawn his hand from	Lam 2:8	
he *h* destroyed and broken her bars	Lam 2:9	
The LORD *h* done that which he had	Lam 2:17	
he *h* fulfilled his word that he	Lam 2:17	
h thrown down, and *h* not pitied	Lam 2:17	
he *h* caused thine enemy to	Lam 2:17	
he *h* set up the horn of thine	Lam 2:17	
brought up *h* mine enemy consumed	Lam 2:22	
I am the man that *h* seen	Lam 3:1	
He *h* led me, and brought me into	Lam 3:2	
My flesh and my skin *h* he made old	Lam 3:4	
he *h* broken my bones	Lam 3:4	
He *h* builded against me, and	Lam 3:5	
He *h* set me in dark places, as	Lam 3:6	
He *h* hedged me about, that I	Lam 3:7	
he *h* made my chain heavy	Lam 3:7	
He *h* inclosed my ways with hewn	Lam 3:9	
he *h* made my paths crooked	Lam 3:9	
He *h* turned aside my ways, and	Lam 3:11	
he *h* made me desolate	Lam 3:11	
He *h* bent his bow, and set me as a	Lam 3:12	
He *h* caused the arrows of his	Lam 3:13	
He *h* filled me with bitterness,	Lam 3:15	
he *h* made me drunken with	Lam 3:15	
He *h* also broken my teeth with	Lam 3:16	
he *h* covered me with ashes	Lam 3:16	
My soul *h* them still in	Lam 3:20	
because he *h* borne it upon him	Lam 3:28	
The LORD *h* accomplished his fury	Lam 4:11	
he *h* poured out his fierce anger,	Lam 4:11	
h kindled a fire in Zion	Lam 4:11	
it *h* devoured the foundations	Lam 4:11	
anger of the LORD *h* divided them	Lam 4:16	
nation that *h* rebelled against me	Eze 2:3	
there *h* been a prophet among them	Eze 2:5	
his righteousness which he *h* done	Eze 3:20	
my soul *h* not been polluted	Eze 4:14	
she *h* changed my judgments into	Eze 5:6	
which *h* departed from me, and with	Eze 6:9	
the rod *h* blossomed, pride *h*	Eze 7:10	
the LORD *h* forsaken the earth	Eze 8:12	
The LORD *h* forsaken the earth, and	Eze 9:9	
h not the house of Israel, the	Eze 12:9	
and the LORD *h* not sent them	Eze 13:6	
deceived when he *h* spoken a thing	Eze 14:9	
work, when the fire *h* devoured it	Eze 15:5	
GOD, Sodom thy sister *h* not done	Eze 16:48	
Neither *h* Samaria committed half	Eze 16:51	
h taken the king thereof, and the	Eze 17:12	
h taken of the king's seed, and	Eze 17:13	
him, and *h* taken an oath of him	Eze 17:13	
he *h* also taken the mighty of the	Eze 17:13	
h done all these things, he shall	Eze 17:18	
mine oath that he *h* despised	Eze 17:19	
and my covenant that he *h* broken	Eze 17:19	
that he *h* trespassed against me	Eze 17:20	
h not eaten upon the mountains,	Eze 18:6	
neither *h* lifted up his eyes to	Eze 18:6	
neither *h* defiled his neighbour's	Eze 18:6	
wife, neither *h* come near to a	Eze 18:6	
h not oppressed any, but *h*	Eze 18:7	
h spoiled none by violence, *h*	Eze 18:7	
h covered the naked with a	Eze 18:7	
He that *h* not given forth upon	Eze 18:8	
neither *h* taken any increase,	Eze 18:8	
that *h* withdrawn his hand from	Eze 18:8	
h executed true judgment between	Eze 18:8	
H walked in my statutes, and *h*	Eze 18:9	
but even *h* eaten upon the	Eze 18:11	
H oppressed the poor and needy,	Eze 18:12	
h spoiled by violence, *h* not	Eze 18:12	
h lifted up his eyes to the idols	Eze 18:12	
h committed abomination	Eze 18:12	
H given forth upon usury, and *h*	Eze 18:13	
he *h* done all these abominations	Eze 18:13	
his father's sins which he *h* done	Eze 18:14	
That *h* not eaten upon the	Eze 18:15	
neither *h* lifted up his eyes to the	Eze 18:15	
h not defiled his neighbour's	Eze 18:15	
Neither *h* oppressed any, *h* not	Eze 18:16	
neither *h* spoiled by violence,	Eze 18:16	
but *h* given his bread to the	Eze 18:16	
h covered the naked with a	Eze 18:16	
That *h* taken off his hand from	Eze 18:17	
that *h* not received usury nor	Eze 18:17	
h executed my judgments, *h*	Eze 18:17	
When the son *h* done that which is	Eze 18:19	
h kept all my statutes, and *h*	Eze 18:19	
all his sins that he *h* committed	Eze 18:21	
that he *h* committed, they shall	Eze 18:22	
that he *h* done he shall live	Eze 18:22	
he *h* done shall not be mentioned	Eze 18:24	
his trespass that he *h* trespassed	Eze 18:24	
and in his sin that he *h* sinned	Eze 18:24	
that he *h* done shall he die	Eze 18:26	
wickedness that he *h* committed	Eze 18:27	
that he *h* committed, he shall	Eze 18:28	
which *h* devoured her fruit	Eze 19:14	
so that she *h* no strong rod to be	Eze 19:14	
he *h* given it to be furbished,	Eze 21:11	
one *h* committed abomination with	Eze 22:11	
another *h* lewdly defiled his	Eze 22:11	
another in thee *h* humbled his	Eze 22:11	
at thy blood which *h* been in the	Eze 22:13	
GOD, when the LORD *h* not spoken	Eze 22:28	
She *h* wearied herself with lies,	Eze 24:12	
to all that he *h* done shall ye do	Eze 24:24	
Because that Edom *h* dealt against	Eze 25:12	
h greatly offended, and revenged	Eze 25:12	
because that Tyrus *h* said against	Eze 26:2	
the east wind *h* broken thee in	Eze 27:26	
midst of his rivers, which *h* said	Eze 29:3	
because he *h* said, The river is	Eze 29:9	
he *h* shot up his top among the	Eze 31:10	
his iniquity that he *h* committed	Eze 33:13	
None of his sins that he *h*	Eze 33:16	
he *h* done that which is lawful and	Eze 33:16	
of one that *h* a pleasant voice	Eze 33:32	
that a prophet *h* been among them	Eze 33:33	
the enemy *h* said against you	Eze 36:2	
h entered in by it, therefore it	Eze 44:2	
for sister that *h* had no husband	Eze 44:25	
who *h* appointed your meat and your	Dan 1:10	
The secret which the king *h*	Dan 2:27	
of heaven *h* given thee a kingdom	Dan 2:37	
the fowls of the heaven *h* he	Dan 2:38	
h made thee ruler over them all	Dan 2:38	
the great God *h* made known to the	Dan 2:45	
Nebuchadnezzar the king *h* set up	Dan 3:5	
who *h* sent his angel, and	Dan 3:28	
the high God *h* wrought toward me	Dan 4:2	
God *h* numbered thy kingdom, and	Dan 5:26	
My God *h* sent his angel, and *h*	Dan 6:22	
who *h* delivered Daniel from the	Dan 6:27	
he *h* confirmed his words, which	Dan 9:12	
for under the whole heaven *h* not	Dan 9:12	
as *h* been done upon Jerusalem	Dan 9:12	
Therefore *h* the LORD watched upon	Dan 9:14	
And when he *h* taken away the	Dan 11:12	
for the land *h* committed great	Hos 1:2	
For their mother *h* played the	Hos 2:5	
conceived them *h* done shamefully	Hos 2:5	
her fig trees, whereof she *h* said	Hos 2:12	
for the LORD *h* a controversy with	Hos 4:1	
of whoredoms *h* caused them to err	Hos 4:12	
The wind *h* bound her up in her	Hos 4:19	
he *h* withdrawn himself from them	Hos 5:6	
for he *h* torn, and he will heal us	Hos 6:1	
he *h* smitten, and he will bind us	Hos 6:1	
he *h* set an harvest for thee,	Hos 6:11	
after he *h* kneaded the dough	Hos 7:4	
he *h* mixed himself among the	Hos 7:8	
as their congregation *h* heard	Hos 7:12	
Israel *h* cast off the thing that	Hos 8:3	
calf, O Samaria, *h* cast thee off	Hos 8:5	
it *h* no stalk	Hos 8:7	
Ephraim *h* hired lovers	Hos 8:9	
Because Ephraim *h* made many	Hos 8:11	
For Israel *h* forgotten his Maker,	Hos 8:14	
Judah *h* multiplied fenced cities	Hos 8:14	
fruit he *h* increased the altars	Hos 10:1	
The LORD *h* also a controversy	Hos 12:2	
for she *h* rebelled against her	Hos 13:16	
H this been in your days, or even	Joel 1:2	
That which the palmerworm *h* left	Joel 1:4	
that which the locust *h* left *h*	Joel 1:4	
h left *h* the caterpiller eaten	Joel 1:4	
he *h* the cheek teeth of a great	Joel 1:6	
He *h* laid my vine waste, and	Joel 1:7	
he *h* made it clean bare, and cast	Joel 1:7	
for the fire *h* devoured the	Joel 1:19	
the flame *h* burned all the trees	Joel 1:19	
the fire *h* devoured the pastures	Joel 1:20	
there *h* not been ever the like,	Joel 2:2	
because he *h* done great things	Joel 2:20	
for he *h* given you the former	Joel 2:23	
the years that the locust *h* eaten	Joel 2:25	
that *h* dealt wondrously with you	Joel 2:26	
deliverance, as the LORD *h* said	Joel 2:32	
for the LORD *h* spoken it	Joel 3:8	
the LORD *h* spoken against you	Amos 3:1	
in the forest, when he *h* no prey	Amos 3:4	
a city, and the LORD *h* not done it	Amos 3:6	
The lion *h* roared, who will not	Amos 3:8	
the Lord GOD *h* spoken, who can	Amos 3:8	
The Lord GOD *h* sworn by his	Amos 4:2	
The Lord GOD *h* sworn by himself,	Amos 6:8	
Thus *h* the Lord GOD shewed unto	Amos 7:1	
Thus *h* the Lord GOD shewed unto	Amos 7:4	
Amos *h* conspired against thee in	Amos 7:10	
Thus *h* the Lord GOD shewed unto	Amos 8:1	
The LORD *h* sworn by the	Amos 8:7	
h founded his troop in the earth	Amos 9:6	
of thine heart *h* deceived thee	Obad 3	
for the LORD *h* spoken it	Obad 18	
which *h* made the sea and the dry	Jonah 1:9	
he *h* changed the portion of my	Mic 2:4	
how *h* he removed it from me	Mic 2:4	
turning away he *h* divided our	Mic 2:4	
of the LORD of hosts *h* spoken it	Mic 4:4	
he *h* laid siege against us	Mic 5:1	
which travaileth *h* brought forth	Mic 5:3	
for the LORD *h* a controversy with	Mic 6:2	
He *h* shewed thee, O man, what is	Mic 6:8	
ye the rod, and who *h* appointed it	Mic 6:9	
the LORD *h* his way in the	Nah 1:3	
the LORD *h* given a commandment	Nah 1:14	
For the LORD *h* turned away the	Nah 2:2	
for upon whom *h* not thy	Nah 3:19	
the maker thereof *h* graven it	Hab 2:18	
for the LORD *h* prepared a	Zeph 1:7	
a sacrifice, he *h* bid his guests	Zeph 1:7	
The LORD *h* taken away thy	Zeph 3:15	
he *h* cast out thine enemy	Zeph 3:15	
olive tree, *h* not brought forth	Hag 2:19	
The LORD *h* been sore displeased	Zec 1:2	
our doings, so *h* he dealt with us	Zec 1:6	
whom the LORD *h* sent to walk to	Zec 1:10	
After the glory *h* he sent me unto	Zec 2:8	
that the LORD of hosts *h* sent me	Zec 2:9	
LORD of hosts *h* sent me unto thee	Zec 2:11	
even the LORD that *h* chosen	Zec 3:2	
LORD of hosts *h* sent me unto you	Zec 4:9	
For who *h* despised the day of	Zec 4:10	
LORD of hosts *h* sent me unto you	Zec 6:15	
h cried by the former prophets	Zec 7:7	
hosts *h* sent in his spirit by the	Zec 7:12	
for the LORD of hosts *h* visited	Zec 10:3	
h made them as his goodly horse	Zec 10:3	
his vision, when he *h* prophesied	Zec 13:4	
the LORD *h* indignation for ever	Mal 1:4	
this *h* been by your means	Mal 1:9	
which *h* in his flock a male, and	Mal 1:14	
h not one God created us	Mal 2:10	
Judah *h* dealt treacherously, and	Mal 2:11	
for Judah *h* profaned the holiness	Mal 2:11	
h married the daughter of a	Mal 2:11	
Because the LORD *h* been witness	Mal 2:14	
who *h* warned you to flee from the	Mt 3:7	
thy brother *h* ought against thee	Mt 5:23	*2192*
her *h* committed adultery with her	Mt 5:28	
It *h* been said, Whosoever shall	Mt 5:31	
ye have heard that it *h* been said	Mt 5:33	
Ye have heard that it *h* been said	Mt 5:38	
Ye have heard that it *h* been said	Mt 5:43	
but the Son of man *h* not where to	Mt 8:20	*2192*
h power on earth to forgive sins	Mt 9:6	*2192*
thy faith *h* made thee whole	Mt 9:22	
that are born of women there *h*	Mt 11:11	
He that *h* ears to hear, let him	Mt 11:15	*2192*
and they say, He *h* a devil	Mt 11:18	*2192*
Who *h* ears to hear, let him hear	Mt 13:9	*2192*
For whosoever *h*, to him shall be	Mt 13:12	*2192*
but whosoever *h* not, from him	Mt 13:12	*2192*
be taken away even that he *h*	Mt 13:12	*2192*
Yet *h* he not root in himself, but	Mt 13:21	*2192*
from whence then *h* it tares	Mt 13:27	*2192*
unto them, An enemy *h* done this	Mt 13:28	
Who *h* ears to hear, let him hear	Mt 13:43	*2192*
the which when a man *h* found	Mt 13:44	
goeth and selleth all that he *h*	Mt 13:44	*2192*
Whence *h* this man this wisdom, and	Mt 13:54	
Whence then *h* this man all these	Mt 13:56	
my heavenly Father *h* not planted	Mt 15:13	
blood *h* not revealed it unto thee	Mt 16:17	
therefore God *h* joined together	Mt 19:6	
every one that *h* forsaken houses,	Mt 19:29	
him, Because no man *h* hired us	Mt 20:7	
say, The Lord *h* need of them	Mt 21:3	*2192*
whom his lord *h* made ruler over	Mt 24:45	
it unto him which *h* ten talents	Mt 25:28	*2192*
every one that *h* shall be given	Mt 25:29	*2192*
but from him that *h* not shall be	Mt 25:29	*2192*
taken away even that which he *h*	Mt 25:29	*2192*
for she *h* wrought a good work	Mt 26:10	
For in that she *h* poured this	Mt 26:12	
also this, that this woman *h* done	Mt 26:13	
saying, He *h* spoken blasphemy	Mt 26:65	
said, Why, what evil *h* he done	Mt 27:23	
h power on earth to forgive sins	Mk 2:10	*2192*
He *h* Beelzebub, and by the prince	Mk 3:22	*2192*
he cannot stand, but *h* an end	Mk 3:26	*2192*
Holy Ghost *h* never forgiveness	Mk 3:29	*2192*
they said, He *h* an unclean spirit	Mk 3:30	*2192*
He that *h* ears to hear, let him	Mk 4:9	*2192*
For he that *h*, to him shall be	Mk 4:25	*2192*
and he that *h* not, from him shall	Mk 4:25	*2192*
be taken even that which he *h*	Mk 4:25	*2192*
things the Lord *h* done for thee	Mk 5:19	
and *h* had compassion on thee	Mk 5:19	
thy faith *h* made thee whole	Mk 5:34	
From whence *h* this man these	Mk 6:2	
Well *h* Esaias prophesied of you	Mk 7:6	
He *h* done all things well	Mk 7:37	
my son, which *h* a dumb spirit	Mk 9:17	*2192*
ofttimes it *h* cast him into the	Mk 9:22	
therefore God *h* joined together	Mk 10:9	
There is no man that *h* left house	Mk 10:29	
thy faith *h* made thee whole	Mk 10:52	
ye that the Lord *h* need of him	Mk 11:3	*2192*
this poor widow *h* cast more in	Mk 12:43	

elect's sake, whom he *h* chosen	Mk 13:20	
he *h* shortened the days	Mk 13:20	
she *h* wrought a good work on me	Mk 14:6	
She *h* done what she could	Mk 14:8	
this also that she *h* done shall	Mk 14:9	
them, Why, what evil *h* he done	Mk 15:14	
Thus *h* the Lord dealt with me in	Lk 1:25	
she *h* also conceived a son in her	Lk 1:36	
my spirit *h* rejoiced in God my	Lk 1:47	
For he *h* regarded the low estate	Lk 1:48	
For he that is mighty *h* done to	Lk 1:49	
He *h* shewed strength with his arm	Lk 1:51	
he *h* scattered the proud in the	Lk 1:51	
He *h* put down the mighty from	Lk 1:52	
He *h* filled the hungry with good	Lk 1:53	
the rich he *h* sent empty away	Lk 1:53	
He *h* holpen his servant Israel,	Lk 1:54	
for he *h* visited and redeemed his	Lk 1:68	
h raised up an horn of salvation	Lk 1:69	
from on high *h* visited us	Lk 1:78	
which the Lord *h* made known unto	Lk 2:15	
who *h* warned you to flee from the	Lk 3:7	
He that *h* two coats	Lk 3:11	*2192*
let him impart to him that *h* none	Lk 3:11	*2192*
and he that *h* meat, let him do	Lk 3:11	*2192*
because he *h* anointed me to	Lk 4:18	
he *h* sent me to heal the	Lk 4:18	
man *h* power upon earth to forgive	Lk 5:24	*2192*
he *h* built us a synagogue	Lk 7:5	
That God *h* visited his people	Lk 7:16	
John Baptist *h* sent us unto thee,	Lk 7:20	
and ye say, He *h* a devil	Lk 7:33	*2192*
but she *h* washed my feet with	Lk 7:44	
in *h* not ceased to kiss my feet	Lk 7:45	
but this woman *h* anointed my feet	Lk 7:46	
the woman, Thy faith *h* saved thee	Lk 7:50	
He that *h* ears to hear, let him	Lk 8:8	*2192*
when he *h* lighted a candle,	Lk 8:16	
for whosoever *h*, to him shall be	Lk 8:18	*2192*
and whosoever *h* not, from him	Lk 8:18	*2192*
great things God *h* done unto thee	Lk 8:39	
Jesus said, Somebody *h* touched me	Lk 8:46	
thy faith *h* made thee whole	Lk 8:48	
but the Son of man *h* not where to	Lk 9:58	*2192*
sister *h* left me to serve alone	Lk 10:40	
Mary *h* chosen that good part,	Lk 10:42	
when he *h* lighted a candle,	Lk 11:33	*2192*
which after he *h* killed	Lk 12:5	
killed *h* power to cast into hell	Lk 12:5	*2192*
make him ruler over all that he *h*	Lk 12:44	*5224*
of Abraham, whom Satan *h* bound	Lk 13:16	
h shut to the door, and ye begin	Lk 13:25	
after he *h* laid the foundation,	Lk 14:29	
that forsaketh not all that he *h*	Lk 14:33	*5224*
He that *h* ears to hear, let him	Lk 14:35	*2192*
when he *h* found it, he layeth it	Lk 15:5	
And when she *h* found it, she	Lk 15:9	
thy father *h* killed the fatted	Lk 15:27	
because he *h* received him safe and	Lk 15:27	
which *h* devoured thy living with	Lk 15:30	
thy faith *h* made thee whole	Lk 17:19	
There is no man that *h* left house	Lk 18:29	
thy faith *h* saved thee	Lk 18:42	
thy pound *h* gained ten pounds	Lk 19:16	
thy pound *h* gained five pounds	Lk 19:18	
give it to him that *h* ten pounds	Lk 19:24	*2192*
unto him, Lord, he *h* ten pounds	Lk 19:25	*2192*
every one which *h* shall be given	Lk 19:26	*2192*
and from him that *h* not	Lk 19:26	*2192*
even that he *h* shall be taken	Lk 19:26	*2192*
Because the Lord *h* need of him	Lk 19:31	*2192*
they said, The Lord *h* need of him	Lk 19:34	*2192*
image and superscription *h* it	Lk 20:24	*2192*
that this poor widow *h* cast in	Lk 21:3	
but she of her penury *h* cast in	Lk 21:4	
as my Father *h* appointed unto me	Lk 22:29	
Satan *h* desired to have you, that	Lk 22:31	
them, But now, he that *h* a purse	Lk 22:36	*2192*
he that *h* no sword, let him sell	Lk 22:36	*2192*
time, Why, what evil *h* he done	Lk 23:22	
but this man *h* done nothing amiss	Lk 23:41	
indeed, and *h* appeared to Simon	Lk 24:34	
for a spirit *h* not flesh and bones	Lk 24:39	*2192*
No man *h* seen God at any time	Jn 1:18	
of the Father, he *h* declared him	Jn 1:18	
zeal of thine house *h* eaten me up	Jn 2:17	
no man *h* ascended up to heaven,	Jn 3:13	
because he *h* not believed in the	Jn 3:18	
He that *h* the bride is the	Jn 3:29	*2192*
And what he *h* seen and heard, that	Jn 3:32	
He that *h* received his testimony	Jn 3:33	
h set to his seal that God is	Jn 3:33	
For he whom God *h* sent speaketh	Jn 3:34	
h given all things into his hand	Jn 3:35	
on the Son *h* everlasting life	Jn 3:36	*2192*
H any man brought him ought to	Jn 4:33	
that a prophet *h* no honour in his	Jn 4:44	*2192*
but *h* committed all judgment unto	Jn 5:22	
not the Father which *h* sent him	Jn 5:23	
h everlasting life, and shall not	Jn 5:24	*2192*
as the Father *h* life in himself	Jn 5:26	*2192*
so *h* he given to the Son to have	Jn 5:26	
h given him authority to execute	Jn 5:27	
of the Father which *h* sent me	Jn 5:30	
the Father *h* given me to finish	Jn 5:36	
of me, that the Father *h* sent me	Jn 5:36	
which *h* sent me, *h* borne	Jn 5:37	
for whom he *h* sent, him ye	Jn 5:38	
which *h* five barley loaves, and	Jn 6:9	*2192*
for him *h* God the Father sealed	Jn 6:27	
ye believe on him whom he *h* sent	Jn 6:29	
the Father's will which *h* sent me	Jn 6:39	
that of all which he *h* given me I	Jn 6:39	
Father which *h* sent me draw him	Jn 6:44	
Every man therefore that *h* heard	Jn 6:45	
h learned of the Father, cometh	Jn 6:45	
that any man *h* seen the Father	Jn 6:46	
is of God, he *h* seen the Father	Jn 6:46	
on me *h* everlasting life	Jn 6:47	*2192*
drinketh my blood, *h* eternal life	Jn 6:54	*2192*
As the living Father *h* sent me	Jn 6:57	
I am from him, and he *h* sent me	Jn 7:29	
than these which this man *h* done	Jn 7:31	
on me, as the scripture *h* said	Jn 7:38	
H not the scripture said, That	Jn 7:42	
h no man condemned thee	Jn 8:10	
but as my Father *h* taught me	Jn 8:28	
the Father *h* not left me alone	Jn 8:29	
because my word *h* no place in you	Jn 8:37	
a man that *h* told you the truth,	Jn 8:40	
Neither *h* this man sinned, nor	Jn 9:3	
that he *h* opened thine eyes	Jn 9:17	
or who *h* opened his eyes, we know	Jn 9:21	
yet he *h* opened mine eyes	Jn 9:30	
said, He *h* a devil, and is mad	Jn 10:20	*2192*
the words of him that *h* a devil	Jn 10:21	
him, whom the Father *h* sanctified	Jn 10:36	
for he *h* been dead four days	Jn 11:39	
day of my burying *h* she kept this	Jn 12:7	
who *h* believed our report	Jn 12:38	
to whom *h* the arm of the Lord	Jn 12:38	
He *h* blinded their eyes, and	Jn 12:40	
my words, *h* one that judgeth him	Jn 12:48	*2192*
He that eateth bread with me *h*	Jn 13:18	
h seen me *h* seen the Father	Jn 14:9	
He that *h* my commandments, and	Jn 14:21	*2192*
world cometh, and *h* nothing in me	Jn 14:30	*2192*
As the Father *h* loved me, so have	Jn 15:9	
Greater love *h* no man than this,	Jn 15:13	*2192*
sorrow *h* filled your heart	Jn 16:6	
things that the Father *h* are mine	Jn 16:15	*2192*
when she is in travail *h* sorrow	Jn 16:21	*2192*
the world *h* hated them, because	Jn 17:14	
the world *h* not known thee	Jn 17:25	
cup which my Father *h* given me	Jn 18:11	
me unto thee *h* the greater sin	Jn 19:11	*2192*
as my Father *h* sent me, even so	Jn 20:21	
which the Father *h* put in his own	Acts 1:7	
Whom God *h* raised up, having	Acts 2:24	
This Jesus *h* God raised up,	Acts 2:32	
he *h* shed forth this, which ye	Acts 2:33	
that God *h* made that same Jesus,	Acts 2:36	
h glorified his Son Jesus	Acts 3:13	
whom God *h* raised from the dead	Acts 3:15	
his name *h* made this man strong	Acts 3:16	
by him *h* given him this perfect	Acts 3:16	
should suffer, he *h* so fulfilled	Acts 3:18	
which God *h* spoken by the mouth	Acts 3:21	
h been done by them is manifest	Acts 4:16	
why *h* Satan filled thine heart to	Acts 5:3	
Him *h* God exalted with his right	Acts 5:31	
whom God *h* given to them that	Acts 5:32	
H not my hand made all these	Acts 7:50	
h seen in a vision a man named	Acts 9:12	
how much evil he *h* done to thy	Acts 9:13	
here he *h* authority from the	Acts 9:14	*2192*
h sent me, that thou mightest	Acts 9:17	
second time, What God *h* cleansed	Acts 10:15	
but God *h* shewed me that I should	Acts 10:28	
h at any time entered into my	Acts 11:8	
from heaven, What God *h* cleansed	Acts 11:9	
Then *h* God also to the Gentiles	Acts 11:18	
that the Lord *h* sent his angel,	Acts 12:11	
h delivered me out of the hand of	Acts 12:11	
Of this man's seed *h* God	Acts 13:23	
God *h* fulfilled the same unto us	Acts 13:33	
in that he *h* raised up Jesus	Acts 13:33	
For so *h* the Lord commanded us,	Acts 13:47	
Simeon *h* declared how God at the	Acts 15:14	
For Moses of old time *h* in every	Acts 15:21	*2192*
Whom Jason *h* received	Acts 17:7	
h made of one blood all nations	Acts 17:26	
h determined the times before	Acts 17:26	
Because he *h* appointed a day, in	Acts 17:31	
by that man whom he *h* ordained	Acts 17:31	
whereof he *h* given assurance unto	Acts 17:31	
in that he *h* raised him from the	Acts 17:31	
all Asia, this Paul *h* persuaded	Acts 19:26	
Holy Ghost *h* made you overseers	Acts 20:28	
which he *h* purchased with his own	Acts 20:28	
h polluted this holy place	Acts 21:28	
God of our fathers *h* chosen thee	Acts 22:14	
or an angel *h* spoken to him	Acts 23:9	
for he *h* a certain thing to tell	Acts 23:17	*2192*
who *h* something to say unto thee	Acts 23:18	*2192*
Who also *h* gone about to profane	Acts 24:6	*2192*
that he himself *h* appealed to	Acts 25:25	
God *h* given thee all them that	Acts 27:24	
though he *h* escaped the sea, yet	Acts 28:4	
for God *h* shewed it unto them	Rom 1:19	
What advantage then *h* the Jew	Rom 3:1	
For if the truth of God *h* more	Rom 3:7	
Whom God *h* set forth to be a	Rom 3:25	
pertaining to the flesh, *h* found	Rom 4:1	
by works, he *h* whereof to glory	Rom 4:2	*2192*
Christ, *h* abounded unto many	Rom 5:15	
That as sin *h* reigned unto death,	Rom 5:21	
death *h* no more dominion over him	Rom 6:9	
how that the law *h* dominion over	Rom 7:1	
For the woman which *h* an husband	Rom 7:2	*5220*
h made me free from the law of	Rom 8:2	
but by reason of him who *h*	Rom 8:20	
word of God *h* taken none effect	Rom 9:6	
Therefore *h* he mercy on whom he	Rom 9:18	
For who *h* resisted his will	Rom 9:19	
H not the potter power over the	Rom 9:21	*2192*
Even us, whom he *h* called	Rom 9:24	
h not attained to the law of	Rom 9:31	
God *h* raised him from the dead	Rom 10:9	
who *h* believed our report	Rom 10:16	
H God cast away his people	Rom 11:1	
God *h* not cast away his people	Rom 11:2	
Israel *h* not obtained that which	Rom 11:7	
but the election *h* obtained it	Rom 11:7	
God *h* given them the spirit of	Rom 11:8	
For God *h* concluded them all in	Rom 11:32	
For who *h* known the mind of the	Rom 11:34	
or who *h* been his counsellor	Rom 11:34	
Or who *h* first given to him, and	Rom 11:35	
according as God *h* dealt to every	Rom 12:3	
another *h* fulfilled the law	Rom 13:8	
for God *h* received him	Rom 14:3	
which Christ *h* not wrought by me	Rom 15:18	
For it *h* pleased them of	Rom 15:26	
It *h* pleased them verily	Rom 15:27	
business she *h* need of you	Rom 16:2	
for she *h* been a succourer of	Rom 16:2	
For it *h* been declared unto me of	1Cor 1:11	
h not God made foolish the wisdom	1Cor 1:20	
But God *h* chosen the foolish	1Cor 1:27	
God *h* chosen the weak things of	1Cor 1:27	
h God chosen, yea, and things	1Cor 1:28	
Eye *h* not seen, nor ear heard,	1Cor 2:9	
the things which God *h* prepared	1Cor 2:9	
But God *h* revealed them unto us	1Cor 2:10	
For who *h* known the mind of the	1Cor 2:16	
abide which he *h* built thereupon	1Cor 3:14	
For I think that God *h* set forth	1Cor 4:9	
that he that *h* done this deed	1Cor 5:2	
him that *h* so done this deed	1Cor 5:3	
God *h* both raised up the Lord, and	1Cor 6:14	
The wife *h* not power of her own	1Cor 7:4	
h not power of his own body	1Cor 7:4	
But every man *h* his proper gift	1Cor 7:7	*2192*
If any brother *h* a wife that	1Cor 7:12	*2192*
the woman which *h* an husband that	1Cor 7:13	*2192*
but God *h* called us to peace	1Cor 7:15	
But as God *h* distributed to every	1Cor 7:17	
as the Lord *h* called every one,	1Cor 7:17	
as one that *h* obtained mercy of	1Cor 7:25	
a virgin marry, she *h* not sinned	1Cor 7:28	
but *h* power over his own will, and	1Cor 7:37	*2192*
h so decreed in his heart that he	1Cor 7:37	
Even so *h* the Lord ordained that	1Cor 9:14	
There *h* no temptation taken you	1Cor 10:13	
h many members, and all the	1Cor 12:12	*2192*
But now *h* God set the members	1Cor 12:18	
in the body, as it *h* pleased him	1Cor 12:18	
but God *h* tempered the body	1Cor 12:24	
God *h* set some in the church,	1Cor 12:28	
every one of you *h* a psalm	1Cor 14:26	*2192*
h a doctrine, *h* a tongue, *h*	1Cor 14:26	*2192*
a revelation, *h* an interpretation	1Cor 14:26	*2192*
till he *h* put all enemies under	1Cor 15:25	
For he *h* put all things under his	1Cor 15:27	
it a body as it *h* pleased him	1Cor 15:38	
as God *h* prospered him, that	1Cor 16:2	
Christ, and *h* anointed us, is God	2Cor 1:21	
Who *h* also sealed us, and given	2Cor 1:22	
he *h* not grieved me, but in part	2Cor 2:5	
Who also *h* made us able ministers	2Cor 3:6	
In whom the god of this world *h*	2Cor 4:4	
h shined in our hearts, to give	2Cor 4:6	
Now he that *h* wrought us for the	2Cor 5:5	
who also *h* given unto us the	2Cor 5:5	
body, according to that he *h* done	2Cor 5:10	
who *h* reconciled us to himself by	2Cor 5:18	
h given to us the ministry of	2Cor 5:18	
h committed unto us the word of	2Cor 5:19	
For he *h* made him to be sin for	2Cor 5:21	
fellowship *h* righteousness with	2Cor 6:14	
what communion *h* light with	2Cor 6:14	
what concord *h* Christ with Belial	2Cor 6:15	
or what part *h* he that believeth	2Cor 6:15	
what agreement *h* the temple of	2Cor 6:16	
as God *h* said, I will dwell in	2Cor 6:16	
the same epistle *h* made you sorry	2Cor 7:8	
according to that a man *h*	2Cor 8:12	*2192*
and not according to that he *h* not	2Cor 8:12	*2192*
your zeal *h* provoked very many	2Cor 9:2	
is written, He *h* dispersed abroad	2Cor 9:9	
he *h* given to the poor	2Cor 9:9	
which the Lord *h* given us for	2Cor 10:8	
which God *h* distributed to us	2Cor 10:13	
Lord *h* given me to edification	2Cor 13:10	
who *h* bewitched you, that ye	Gal 3:1	
Christ *h* been evidently set forth	Gal 3:1	
Christ *h* redeemed us from the	Gal 3:13	
But the scripture *h* concluded all	Gal 3:22	
God *h* sent forth the Spirit of	Gal 4:6	
for the desolate *h* many more	Gal 4:27	
than she which *h* a husband	Gal 4:27	*2192*
wherewith Christ *h* made us free	Gal 5:1	
who *h* blessed us with all	Eph 1:3	
According as he *h* chosen us in	Eph 1:4	
wherein he *h* made us accepted in	Eph 1:6	
Wherein he *h* abounded toward us	Eph 1:8	
which he *h* purposed in himself	Eph 1:9	
h put all things under his feet,	Eph 1:22	
you *h* he quickened, who were dead	Eph 2:1	
h quickened us together with	Eph 2:5	
h raised us up together, and made	Eph 2:6	
which God *h* before ordained that	Eph 2:10	
who *h* made both one, and *h*	Eph 2:14	
of the world *h* been hid in God	Eph 3:9	
for Christ's sake *h* forgiven you	Eph 4:32	
love, as Christ also *h* loved us	Eph 5:2	
h given himself for us an	Eph 5:2	
h any inheritance in the kingdom	Eph 5:5	*2192*
that he which *h* begun a good work	Phil 1:6	
God also *h* highly exalted him	Phil 2:9	
he *h* served with me in the gospel	Phil 2:22	

h whereof he might trust in the ... Phil 3:4
care of me *h* flourished again ... Phil 4:10
which *h* made us meet to be ... Col 1:12
Who *h* delivered us from the power ... Col 1:13
h translated us into the kingdom ... Col 1:13
works, yet now *h* he reconciled ... Col 1:21
which *h* been hid from ages ... Col 1:26
who *h* raised him from the dead ... Col 2:12
h he quickened together with him, ... Col 2:13
those things which he *h* not seen ... Col 2:18
for the wrong which he *h* done ... Col 3:25
that he *h* a great zeal for you, ... Col 4:13 *2192*
who *h* called you unto his kingdom ... 1Th 2:12
For God *h* not called us unto ... 1Th 4:7
who *h* also given unto us his holy ... 1Th 4:8
For God *h* not appointed us to ... 1Th 5:9
because God *h* from the beginning ... 2Th 2:13
which *h* loved us, and *h* given ... 2Th 2:16
who *h* enabled me, for that he ... 1Ti 1:12
which God *h* created to be ... 1Ti 4:3
he *h* denied the faith, and is ... 1Ti 5:8
Who only *h* immortality, dwelling ... 1Ti 6:16 *2192*
whom no man *h* seen, nor can see ... 1Ti 6:16
For God *h* not given us the spirit ... 2Ti 1:7
Who *h* saved us, and called us with ... 2Ti 1:9
who *h* abolished death, and *h* ... 2Ti 1:10
who *h* chosen him to be a soldier ... 2Ti 2:4
For Demas *h* forsaken me, having ... 2Ti 4:10
for he *h* greatly withstood our ... 2Ti 4:15
But *h* in due times manifested his ... Titus 1:3
faithful word as he *h* been taught ... Titus 1:9
salvation *h* appeared to all men ... Titus 2:11
If he *h* wronged thee, or oweth ... Philem 18
H in these last days spoken unto ... Heb 1:2
whom he *h* appointed heir of all ... Heb 1:2
as he *h* by inheritance obtained a ... Heb 1:4
h anointed thee with the oil of ... Heb 1:9
For unto the angels *h* he not put ... Heb 2:5
the children which God *h* given me ... Heb 2:13
himself *h* suffered being tempted ... Heb 2:18
inasmuch as he who *h* builded the ... Heb 3:3
h more honour than the house ... Heb 3:3 *2192*
he also *h* ceased from his own ... Heb 4:10
h an unchangeable priesthood ... Heb 7:24 *2192*
But now *h* he obtained a more ... Heb 8:6
covenant, he *h* made the first old ... Heb 8:13
which God *h* enjoined unto you ... Heb 9:20
once in the end of the world *h* he ... Heb 9:26
For by one offering he *h* ... Heb 10:14
which he *h* consecrated for us, ... Heb 10:20
who *h* trodden under foot the Son ... Heb 10:29
h counted the blood of the ... Heb 10:29
h done despite unto the Spirit of ... Heb 10:29
For we know him that *h* said ... Heb 10:30
which *h* great recompence of ... Heb 10:35 *2192*
for a city which *h* foundations ... Heb 11:10 *2192*
for he *h* prepared for them a city ... Heb 11:16
but now he *h* promised, saying, ... Heb 12:26
for he *h* said, I will never leave ... Heb 13:5
which the Lord *h* promised to them ... Jas 1:12
Then when lust *h* conceived ... Jas 1:15
H not God chosen the poor of this ... Jas 2:5
heirs of the kingdom which he *h* ... Jas 2:5
mercy, that *h* shewed no mercy ... Jas 2:13
though a man say he *h* faith ... Jas 2:14 *2192*
if it *h* not works, is dead, being ... Jas 2:17 *2192*
tamed, and *h* been tamed of mankind .. Jas 3:7
h long patience for it, until he ... Jas 5:7
h begotten us again unto a lively ... 1Pet 1:3
But as he which *h* called you is ... 1Pet 1:15
forth the praises of him who *h* ... 1Pet 2:9
For Christ also *h* once suffered ... 1Pet 3:18
Forasmuch then as Christ *h* ... 1Pet 4:1
for he that *h* suffered in the ... 1Pet 4:1
in the flesh *h* ceased from sin ... 1Pet 4:1
As every man *h* received the gift, ... 1Pet 4:10
who *h* called us unto his eternal ... 1Pet 5:10
h given unto us all things that ... 2Pet 1:3
of him that *h* called us to glory ... 2Pet 1:3
h forgotten that he was purged ... 2Pet 1:9
our Lord Jesus Christ *h* shewed me ... 2Pet 1:14
given unto him *h* written unto you ... 2Pet 3:15
that darkness *h* blinded his eyes ... 1Jn 2:11
the same *h* not the Father ... 1Jn 2:23 *2192*
the Son *h* the Father also ... 1Jn 2:23 *2192*
the promise that he *h* promised us ... 1Jn 2:25
lie, and even as it *h* taught you ... 1Jn 2:27
the Father *h* bestowed upon us ... 1Jn 3:1
every man that *h* this hope in him ... 1Jn 3:3 *2192*
whosoever sinneth *h* not seen him ... 1Jn 3:6
ye know that no murderer *h* ... 1Jn 3:15 *2192*
But whoso *h* this world's good, and ... 1Jn 3:17 *2192*
by the Spirit which he *h* given us ... 1Jn 3:24
No man *h* seen God at any time ... 1Jn 4:12
because he *h* given us of his ... 1Jn 4:13
the love that God *h* to us ... 1Jn 4:16 *2192*
because fear *h* torment ... 1Jn 4:18 *2192*
not his brother whom he *h* seen ... 1Jn 4:20
he love God whom he *h* not seen ... 1Jn 4:20
which he *h* testified of his Son ... 1Jn 5:9
of God *h* the witness in himself ... 1Jn 5:10 *2192*
not God *h* made him a liar ... 1Jn 5:10
that God *h* given to us eternal ... 1Jn 5:11
He that *h* the Son *h* life ... 1Jn 5:12 *2192*
he that *h* not the Son of God *h* ... 1Jn 5:12 *2192*
h given us an understanding, that ... 1Jn 5:20
the doctrine of Christ, *h* not God ... 2Jn 9 *2192*
he *h* both the Father and the Son ... 2Jn 9 *2192*
he that doeth evil *h* not seen God ... 3Jn 11
Demetrius *h* good report of all ... 3Jn 12
he *h* reserved in everlasting ... Jude 6
h made us kings and priests unto ... Rev 1:6
He that *h* an ear, let him hear ... Rev 2:7 *2192*
He that *h* an ear, let him hear ... Rev 2:11 *2192*
These things saith he which *h* the ... Rev 2:12 *2192*
He that *h* an ear, let him hear ... Rev 2:17 *2192*
who *h* his eyes like unto a flame ... Rev 2:18 *2192*
He that *h* an ear, let him hear ... Rev 2:29 *2192*
that *h* the seven Spirits of God ... Rev 3:1 *2192*
He that *h* an ear, let him hear ... Rev 3:6 *2192*
he that *h* the key of David, he ... Rev 3:7 *2192*
He that *h* an ear, let him hear ... Rev 3:13 *2192*
He that *h* an ear, let him hear ... Rev 3:22 *2192*
h prevailed to open the book, and ... Rev 5:5
Greek tongue *h* his name Apollyon ... Rev 9:11 *2192*
as he *h* declared to his servants ... Rev 10:7
where she *h* a place prepared of ... Rev 12:6 *2192*
that he *h* but a short time ... Rev 12:12 *2192*
Let him that *h* understanding ... Rev 13:18 *2192*
which *h* power over these plagues ... Rev 16:9 *2192*
which *h* the seven heads and ten ... Rev 17:7 *2192*
here is the mind which *h* wisdom ... Rev 17:9 *2192*
For God *h* put in their hearts to ... Rev 17:17
God *h* remembered her iniquities ... Rev 18:5
in the cup which she *h* filled ... Rev 18:6
How much she *h* glorified herself, ... Rev 18:7
for God *h* avenged you on her ... Rev 18:20
for he *h* judged the great whore, ... Rev 19:2
h avenged the blood of his ... Rev 19:2
his wife *h* made herself ready ... Rev 19:7
he *h* on his vesture and on his ... Rev 19:16 *2192*
holy is he that *h* part in the ... Rev 20:6 *2192*
such the second death *h* no power ... Rev 20:6 *2192*

HATHACH See HATACH.

HATHATH (*ha'-thath*) *Son of Othniel.*
sons of Othniel; *H* ... 1Chr 4:13 2867

HATING
God, men of truth, *h* covetousness ... Ex 18:21 8130
envy, hateful, and *h* one another ... Titus 3:3 *3404*
h even the garment spotted by the ... Jude 23 *3404*

HATIPHA (*hat'-if-ah*) *A family of exiles.*
of Neziah, the children of *H* ... Ezr 2:54 2412
of Neziah, the children of *H* ... Neh 7:56 2412

HATITA (*hat'-it-ah*) *A family of exiles.*
of Akkub, the children of *H* ... Ezr 2:42 2410
of Akkub, the children of *H* ... Neh 7:45 2410

HATRED
But if he thrust him of *h* ... Num 35:20 8135
so that the *h* wherewith he hated ... 2Sa 13:15 8135
and they hate me with cruel *h* ... Ps 25:19 8135
me about also with words of *h* ... Ps 109:3 8135
evil for good, and *h* for my love ... Ps 109:5 8135
I hate them with perfect *h* ... Ps 139:22 8135
H stirreth up strifes ... Prov 10:12 8135
He that hideth *h* with lying lips, ... Prov 10:18 8135
than a stalled ox and *h* therewith ... Prov 15:17 8135
Whose *h* is covered by deceit, his ... Prov 26:26 8135
or *h* by all that is before them ... Eccl 9:1 8135
Also their love, and their *h* ... Eccl 9:6 8135
to destroy it for the old *h* ... Eze 25:15 342
thou hast had a perpetual *h* ... Eze 35:5 342
used out of thy *h* against them ... Eze 35:11 8135
of thine iniquity, and the great *h* ... Hos 9:7 4895
h in the house of his God ... Hos 9:8 4895
Idolatry, witchcraft, *h*, variance ... Gal 5:20 *2189*

HATS
coats, their hosen, and their *h* ... Dan 3:21 3737

HATTIL (*hat'-til*) *A family of exiles.*
of Shephatiah, the children of *H* ... Ezr 2:57 2411
of Shephatiah, the children of *H* ... Neh 7:59 2411

HATTUSH (*hat'-tush*)
1. A son of Shemaiah.
H, and Igeal, and Bariah, and ... 1Chr 3:22 2407
the sons of David; *H* ... Ezr 8:2 2407
3. A priest.
Amariah, Malluch, *H*, ... Neh 12:2 2407
4. A rebuilder of Jerusalem's wall.
repaired *H* the son of Hashabniah ... Neh 3:10 2407
5. Renewed the covenant.
H, Shebaniah, Malluch, ... Neh 10:4 2407

HAUGHTILY
neither shall ye go *h* ... Mic 2:3 7317

HAUGHTINESS
the *h* of men shall be bowed down, ... Is 2:11 7312
the *h* of men shall be made low ... Is 2:17 7312
lay low the *h* of the terrible ... Is 13:11 1346
even of his *h*, and his pride, and ... Is 16:6 1346
his pride, and the *h* of his heart ... Jer 48:29 7312

HAUGHTY
but thine eyes are upon the *h* ... 2Sa 22:28 7311
Lord, my heart is not *h*, nor mine ... Ps 131:1 1361
an *h* spirit before a fall ... Prov 16:18 1363
destruction the heart of man is *h* ... Prov 18:12 1361
h scorner is his name, who ... Prov 21:24 3093
the daughters of Zion are *h* ... Is 3:16 1361
down, and the *h* shall be humbled ... Is 10:33 1364
the *h* people of the earth do ... Is 24:4 4791
And they were *h*, and committed ... Eze 16:50 1361
thou shalt no more be *h* because ... Zeph 3:11 1361

HAUNT
and see his place where his *h* is ... 1Sa 23:22 7272
himself and his men were wont to *h* ... 1Sa 30:31 1980
terror to be on all that *h* it ... Eze 26:17 3427

HAURAN (*hau'-ran*) *A province south of Damascus.*
which is by the coast of *H* ... Eze 47:16 2362
east side ye shall measure from *H* ... Eze 47:18 2362

HAVE
let them *h* dominion over the fish ... Gen 1:26
h dominion over the fish of the ... Gen 1:28
I *h* given you every herb bearing ... Gen 1:29
I *h* given every green herb for ... Gen 1:30
I *h* gotten a man from the LORD ... Gen 4:1 1961
in tents, and of such as *h* cattle ... Gen 4:20
for I *h* slain a man to my ... Gen 4:23
I will destroy man whom I *h* ... Gen 6:7
repenteth me that I *h* made them ... Gen 6:7
for thee *h* I seen righteous ... Gen 7:1
I *h* made will I destroy from off ... Gen 7:4
every thing living, as I *h* done ... Gen 8:21
herb *h* I given you all things ... Gen 9:3
which I *h* established between me ... Gen 9:17
one, and they *h* all one language ... Gen 11:6
which they *h* imagined to do ... Gen 11:6
so I might *h* taken her to me to ... Gen 12:19
I *h* lift up mine hand unto the ... Gen 14:22
say, I *h* made Abram rich ... Gen 14:23
that which the young men *h* eaten ... Gen 14:24
Unto thy seed *h* I given this land ... Gen 15:18
I *h* given my maid into thy bosom ... Gen 16:5
H I also here looked after him ... Gen 16:13
of many nations *h* I made thee ... Gen 17:5
And as for Ishmael, I *h* heard thee ... Gen 17:20
I *h* blessed him, and will make him ... Gen 17:20
if now I *h* found favour in thy ... Gen 18:3
lo, Sarah thy wife shall *h* a son ... Gen 18:10
I am waxed old shall I *h* pleasure ... Gen 18:12
of life, and Sarah shall *h* a son ... Gen 18:14
now, and see whether they *h* done ... Gen 18:21
I *h* taken upon me to speak unto ... Gen 18:27
I *h* taken upon me to speak unto ... Gen 18:31
I *h* two daughters which *h* not ... Gen 19:8
I *h* accepted thee concerning this ... Gen 19:21
of my hands *h* I done this ... Gen 20:5
what *h* I offended thee, that thou ... Gen 20:9
I *h* given thy brother a thousand ... Gen 20:16
Who would *h* said unto Abraham, ... Gen 21:7
that Sarah should *h* given ... Gen 21:7
for I *h* born him a son in his old ... Gen 21:7
kindness that I *h* done unto thee ... Gen 21:23
that I *h* digged this well ... Gen 21:30
And said, By myself *h* I sworn ... Gen 22:16
until they *h* done drinking ... Gen 24:19
We *h* both straw and provender ... Gen 24:25
for I *h* prepared the house, and ... Gen 24:31
until I *h* told mine errand ... Gen 24:33
lightly *h* lien with thy wife ... Gen 26:10
and thou shouldest *h* brought ... Gen 26:10
me, and *h* sent me away from you ... Gen 26:27
as we *h* not touched thee ... Gen 26:29
as we *h* done unto thee nothing ... Gen 26:29
h sent thee away in peace ... Gen 26:29 1961
said unto him, We *h* found water ... Gen 26:32
I *h* done according as thou badest ... Gen 27:19
I *h* eaten of all before thou ... Gen 27:33
thou camest, and *h* blessed him ... Gen 27:33
I *h* made him thy lord, and all his ... Gen 27:37
all his brethren *h* I given to him ... Gen 27:37
corn and wine *h* I sustained him ... Gen 27:37
when thou shalt *h* the dominion ... Gen 27:40
until I *h* done that which I *h* ... Gen 28:15
which I *h* set for a pillar, shall ... Gen 28:22
because I *h* born him three sons ... Gen 29:34
that I may also *h* children by her ... Gen 30:3
With great wrestlings *h* I ... Gen 30:8
with my sister, and I *h* prevailed ... Gen 30:8
for surely I *h* hired thee with my ... Gen 30:16
because I *h* given my maiden to my ... Gen 30:18
because I *h* born him six sons ... Gen 30:20
for whom I *h* served thee, and let ... Gen 30:26
my service which I *h* done thee ... Gen 30:26
if I *h* found favour in thine eyes ... Gen 30:27
for I *h* learned by experience ... Gen 30:27
Thou knowest how I *h* served thee ... Gen 30:29
my power I *h* served your father ... Gen 31:6
for I *h* seen all that Laban doeth ... Gen 31:12
that I might *h* sent thee away ... Gen 31:27
twenty years *h* I been with thee ... Gen 31:38
thy she goats *h* not cast their ... Gen 31:38
rams of thy flock *h* I not eaten ... Gen 31:38
Thus *h* I been twenty years in thy ... Gen 31:41
their children which they *h* born ... Gen 31:43
which I *h* cast betwixt me and thee ... Gen 31:51
I *h* sojourned with Laban, and ... Gen 32:4
I *h* oxen, and asses, flocks, and ... Gen 32:5 1961
I *h* sent to tell my lord, that I ... Gen 32:5 1961
for I *h* seen God face to face, and ... Gen 32:30
Esau said, I *h* enough, my brother ... Gen 33:9 3426
if now I *h* found grace in thy ... Gen 33:10
for therefore I *h* seen thy face ... Gen 33:10
with me, and because I *h* enough ... Gen 33:11 3426
Ye *h* troubled me to make me to ... Gen 34:30
thou shalt *h* this son also ... Gen 35:17
you, this dream which I *h* dreamed ... Gen 37:6
thou indeed *h* dominion over us ... Gen 37:8
Behold, I *h* dreamed a dream more ... Gen 37:9
and said, This *h* we found ... Gen 37:32
We *h* dreamed a dream, and there is ... Gen 40:8
here also *h* I done nothing that ... Gen 40:15
I *h* dreamed a dream, and there is ... Gen 41:15
I *h* heard say of thee, that thou ... Gen 41:15
which I *h* spoken unto Pharaoh ... Gen 41:28
I *h* set thee over all the land of ... Gen 41:41
I *h* heard that there is corn in ... Gen 42:2
Me *h* ye bereaved of my children ... Gen 42:36
h ye another brother ... Gen 43:7 3426
we *h* brought it again in our hand ... Gen 43:21
other money *h* we brought down in ... Gen 43:22
Wherefore *h* ye rewarded evil for ... Gen 44:4
ye *h* done evil in so doing ... Gen 44:5
What deed is this that ye *h* done ... Gen 44:15
H ye a father, or a brother ... Gen 44:19 3426
We *h* a father, an old man, and a ... Gen 44:20 3426
Egypt, and of all that ye *h* seen ... Gen 45:13

since I *h* seen thy face, because Gen 46:30
they *h* brought their flocks, and Gen 46:32
their herds, and all that they *h* Gen 46:32
their herds, and all that they *h* Gen 47:1
for thy servants *h* no pasture for Gen 47:4
evil *h* the days of the years of Gen 47:9
h not attained unto the days of Gen 47:9
I *h* bought you this day and your Gen 47:23
Pharaoh should *h* the fifth part Gen 47:26
If now I *h* found grace in thy Gen 47:29
Moreover I *h* given to thee one Gen 48:22
I *h* waited for thy salvation, O Gen 49:18
The archers *h* sorely grieved him, Gen 49:23
The blessings of thy father *h* Gen 49:26
If now I *h* found grace in your Gen 50:4
in my grave which I *h* digged for Gen 50:5
Why *h* ye done this thing, and *h* Ex 1:18
why is it that ye *h* left the man Ex 2:20
I *h* been a stranger in a strange Ex 2:22
I *h* surely seen the affliction of Ex 3:7
h heard their cry by reason of Ex 3:7
I *h* also seen the oppression Ex 3:9
unto thee, that I *h* sent thee Ex 3:12
I *h* surely visited you, and seen Ex 3:16
I *h* said, I will bring you up out Ex 3:17
h not I the LORD Ex 4:11
which I *h* put in thine hand Ex 4:21
Wherefore *h* ye not fulfilled your Ex 5:14
because ye *h* made our savour to Ex 5:21
I *h* also established my covenant Ex 6:4
I *h* also heard the groaning of Ex 6:5
I *h* remembered my covenant Ex 6:5
of Israel *h* not hearkened unto me Ex 6:12
I *h* made thee a god to Pharaoh Ex 7:1
for this cause *h* I raised thee up Ex 9:16
unto them, I *h* sinned this time Ex 9:27
for I *h* hardened his heart, and Ex 10:1
what things I *h* wrought in Egypt, Ex 10:2
signs which I *h* done among them Ex 10:2
nor thy fathers' fathers *h* seen Ex 10:6
I *h* sinned against the LORD your Ex 10:16
for in this selfsame day *h* I Ex 12:17
go, serve the LORD, as ye *h* said Ex 12:31
and your herds, as ye *h* said Ex 12:32
Why *h* we done this, that we *h* Ex 14:5
Egyptians whom ye *h* seen to day Ex 14:13
when I *h* gotten me honour upon Ex 14:18
The depths *h* covered them Ex 15:5
which thy hands *h* established Ex 15:17
which I *h* brought upon the Ex 15:26
for ye *h* brought us forth into Ex 16:3
I *h* heard the murmurings of the Ex 16:12
I *h* fed you in the wilderness Ex 16:32
hath sworn that the LORD will *h* Ex 17:16
I *h* been an alien in a strange Ex 18:3
When they *h* a matter, they come Ex 18:16 1961
Ye *h* seen what I did unto the Ex 19:4
which *h* brought thee out of the Ex 20:2
Thou shalt *h* no other gods before Ex 20:3
Ye *h* seen that I *h* talked with Ex 20:22
If his master *h* given him a wife, Ex 21:4
she *h* born him sons or daughters Ex 21:4
nation he shall *h* no power Ex 21:8
if he *h* betrothed her unto his Ex 21:9
Whether he *h* gored a son, or *h* Ex 21:31
if he *h* nothing, then he shall be Ex 22:3
to see whether he *h* put his hand Ex 22:8
in all things that I *h* said unto Ex 23:13
into the place which I *h* prepared Ex 23:20
and commandments which I *h* written Ex 24:12
if any man *h* any matters to do, Ex 24:14
the curtains shall *h* one measure Ex 26:2
whom I *h* filled with the spirit Ex 28:3
It shall *h* the two shoulderpieces Ex 28:7 1961
it shall *h* a binding of woven Ex 28:32 1961
things which I *h* commanded thee Ex 29:35
I *h* called by name Bezaleel the Ex 31:2
I *h* filled him with the spirit of Ex 31:3
I *h* given with him Aholiab, the Ex 31:6
are wise hearted I *h* put wisdom Ex 31:6
make all that I *h* commanded thee Ex 31:6
according to all that I *h* Ex 31:11
of Egypt, *h* corrupted themselves Ex 32:7
They *h* turned aside quickly out Ex 32:8
they *h* made them a molten calf, Ex 32:8
and *h* worshipped it, and *h* Ex 32:8
which *h* brought thee up out of Ex 32:8
I *h* seen this people, and, behold, Ex 32:9
all this land that I *h* spoken of Ex 32:13
people, Ye *h* sinned a great sin Ex 32:30
this people *h* sinned a great sin, Ex 32:31
and *h* made them gods of gold Ex 32:31
of which I *h* spoken unto thee Ex 32:34
if I *h* found grace in thy sight, Ex 33:13
thy people *h* found grace in thy Ex 33:16
If now I *h* found grace in thy Ex 34:9
such as *h* not been done in all Ex 34:10
I *h* made a covenant with thee Ex 34:27
they *h* done somewhat against any Lev 4:13
which they *h* sinned against it, Lev 4:14
Or *h* found that which was lost, Lev 6:3
I *h* given it unto them for their Lev 6:17
atonement therewith shall *h* it Lev 7:7 1961
even the priest shall *h* to Lev 7:8 1961
shall all the sons of Aaron *h* Lev 7:10 1961
shall *h* the right shoulder for Lev 7:33 1961
the heave shoulder *h* I taken of Lev 7:34
h given them unto Aaron the Lev 7:34
Wherefore *h* ye not eaten the sin Lev 10:17
ye should indeed *h* eaten it in Lev 10:18
this day *h* they offered their sin Lev 10:19
and such things *h* befallen me Lev 10:19
should it *h* been accepted in the Lev 10:19
And all that *h* not fins and scales Lev 11:10

but ye shall *h* their carcases in Lev 11:11
these are they which ye shall *h* Lev 11:13
which *h* legs above their feet, to Lev 11:21
which *h* four feet, shall be an Lev 11:23
If a woman *h* conceived seed, and Lev 12:2
When a man shall *h* in the skin of Lev 13:2 1961
it *h* turned the hair white, and Lev 13:10
if the leprosy *h* covered all his Lev 13:13
burneth *h* a white bright spot Lev 13:24 1961
If a man or woman *h* a plague upon Lev 13:29 1961
If a man also or a woman *h* in the Lev 13:38 1961
if the plague *h* not changed his Lev 13:55
And if a woman *h* an issue, and her Lev 15:19 1961
if a woman *h* an issue of her Lev 15:25 1961
he shall *h* the linen breeches Lev 16:4 1961
h made an atonement for himself, Lev 16:17 1961
after whom they *h* gone a whoring Lev 17:7
I *h* given it to you upon the Lev 17:11
h the men of the land done Lev 18:27
shall *h* planted all manner of Lev 19:23
not them that *h* familiar spirits Lev 19:31
ephah, and a just hin, shall ye *h* Lev 19:36 1961
after such as *h* familiar spirits Lev 20:6
they *h* wrought confusion Lev 20:12
both of them *h* committed an Lev 20:13
But I *h* said unto you, Ye shall Lev 20:24
which *h* separated you from other Lev 20:24
which I *h* separated from you as Lev 20:25
h severed you from other people, Lev 20:26
h no child, and is returned unto Lev 22:13
ye shall *h* an holy convocation Lev 23:7 1961
h brought an offering unto your Lev 23:14
shall ye *h* a sabbath, a memorial Lev 23:24 1961
when ye *h* gathered in the fruit Lev 23:39
Ye shall *h* one manner of law, as Lev 24:22 1961
if the man *h* none to redeem it, Lev 25:26 1961
houses of the villages which *h* no Lev 25:31
thy bondmaids, which thou shalt *h* Lev 25:44 1961
For I will *h* respect unto you, and Lev 26:9
I *h* broken the bands of your yoke Lev 26:13
when I *h* broken the staff of your Lev 26:26
ye shall *h* no power to stand Lev 26:37 1961
that also they *h* walked contrary Lev 26:40
that I also *h* walked contrary Lev 26:41
h brought them into the land of Lev 26:41
or if he *h* sold the field to Lev 27:20
I *h* taken the Levites from among Num 3:12
h the oversight of them that keep Num 3:32
his sons *h* made an end of Num 4:15
their sin which they *h* done Num 5:7
But if the man *h* no kinsman to Num 5:8
the priest shall *h* in his hand Num 5:18 1961
If no man *h* lain with thee, and if Num 5:19
some man *h* lain with thee beside Num 5:20
h done trespass against her Num 5:27
of Israel, *h* I taken them unto me Num 8:16
I *h* taken the Levites for all the Num 8:18
I *h* given the Levites as a gift Num 8:19
ye shall *h* one ordinance, both Num 9:14 1961
wherefore *h* I not found favour in Num 11:11
H I conceived all this people Num 11:12
h I begotten them, that thou Num 11:12
Whence should I *h* flesh to give Num 11:13
if I *h* found favour in thy sight Num 11:15
for ye *h* wept in the ears of the Num 11:18
because that ye *h* despised the Num 11:20
h wept before him, saying, Why Num 11:20
wherein we *h* done foolishly Num 12:11
and wherein we *h* sinned Num 12:11
through which we *h* gone to search Num 13:32
signs which I *h* shewed among them Num 14:11
for they *h* heard that thou LORD Num 14:14
then the nations which *h* heard Num 14:15
I *h* pardoned according to thy Num 14:20
those men which *h* seen my glory Num 14:22
h tempted me now these ten times, Num 14:22
h not hearkened to my voice Num 14:22
I *h* heard the murmurings of the Num 14:27
as ye *h* spoken in mine ears, so Num 14:28
which *h* murmured against me, Num 14:29
know the land which ye *h* despised Num 14:31
I the LORD *h* said, I will surely Num 14:35
for we *h* sinned Num 14:40
And if ye *h* erred, and not observed Num 15:22
Ye shall *h* one law for him that Num 15:29 1961
I *h* not taken one ass from them, Num 16:15
neither *h* I hurt one of them Num 16:15
for I *h* not done them of mine own Num 16:28
these men *h* provoked the LORD Num 16:30
Ye *h* killed the people of the Num 16:41
I *h* taken your brethren the Num 18:6
I *h* given your priest's office Num 18:7
I also *h* given thee the charge of Num 18:8
unto thee *h* I given them by Num 18:8
I *h* given them unto thee, and to Num 18:11
the LORD, them *h* I given thee Num 18:12
h I given thee, and thy sons and Num 18:19
Thou shalt *h* no inheritance in Num 18:20
neither shalt thou *h* any part Num 18:20 1961
I *h* given the children of Levi Num 18:21
of Israel they *h* no inheritance Num 18:23
I *h* given to the Levites to Num 18:24
therefore I *h* said unto them, Num 18:24
they shall *h* no inheritance Num 18:24
I *h* given you from them for your Num 18:26
When ye *h* heaved the best thereof Num 18:30
when ye *h* heaved from it the best Num 18:32
And why *h* ye brought up the Num 20:4
wherefore *h* ye made us to come up Num 20:5
the land which I *h* given them Num 20:12
we *h* dwelt in Egypt a long time Num 20:15
until we *h* passed thy borders Num 20:17
I *h* given unto the children of Num 20:24
Wherefore *h* ye brought us up out Num 21:5

We *h* sinned, for we *h* spoken Num 21:7
We *h* shot at them Num 21:30
we *h* laid them waste even unto Num 21:30
for I *h* delivered him into thy Num 21:34
What *h* I done unto thee, that Num 22:28
the angel of the LORD, I *h* sinned Num 22:34
h I now any power at all to say Num 22:38
I *h* prepared seven altars Num 23:4
I *h* offered upon every altar a Num 23:4
I *h* received commandment to bless Num 23:20
come he that shall *h* dominion Num 24:19
And he shall *h* it, and his seed Num 25:13 1961
wherewith they *h* beguiled you in Num 25:18
h no son, then ye shall cause his Num 27:8
if he *h* no daughter, then ye Num 27:9
if he *h* no brethren, then ye Num 27:10
And if his father *h* no brethren Num 27:11
see the land which I *h* given unto Num 27:12
not as sheep which *h* no shepherd Num 27:17
ye shall *h* an holy convocation Num 28:25 1961
ye shall *h* an holy convocation Num 28:26 1961
ye shall *h* an holy convocation Num 29:1 1961
ye shall *h* on the tenth day of Num 29:7 1961
ye shall *h* an holy covocation Num 29:12 1961
day ye shall *h* a solemn assembly Num 29:35 1961
wherewith they *h* bound their Num 30:9
H ye saved all the women alive Num 31:15
that *h* not known a man by lying Num 31:18
Thy servants *h* taken the sum of Num 31:49
We *h* therefore brought an Num 31:50
cattle, and thy servants *h* cattle Num 32:4
if we *h* found grace in thy sight, Num 32:5
because they *h* not wholly Num 32:11
for they *h* wholly followed the Num 32:12
until we *h* brought them unto Num 32:17
Israel *h* inherited every man his Num 32:18
ye *h* sinned against the LORD Num 32:23
they shall *h* possessions among Num 32:30 270
for I *h* given you the land to Num 33:53
ye shall even *h* the great sea for Num 34:6 1961
h received their inheritance Num 34:14
h received their inheritance Num 34:14
the half tribe *h* received their Num 34:15
cities shall they *h* to dwell in Num 35:3 1961
from them that *h* many ye shall Num 35:8
but from them that *h* few ye shall Num 35:8
six cities shall ye *h* for refuge Num 35:13 1961
or *h* cast upon him any thing Num 35:22
Because he should *h* remained in Num 35:28
Ye *h* dwelt long enough in this Deut 1:6
I *h* set the land before you Deut 1:8
our brethren *h* discouraged our Deut 1:28
moreover we *h* seen the sons of Deut 1:28
We *h* sinned against the LORD, we Deut 1:41
Ye *h* compassed this mountain long Deut 2:3
because I *h* given mount Seir unto Deut 2:5
because I *h* given Ar unto the Deut 2:9
because I *h* given it unto the Deut 2:19
I *h* given into thine hand Sihon Deut 2:24
I *h* begun to give Sihon and his Deut 2:31
(for I know that ye *h* much cattle Deut 3:19
your cities which I *h* given you Deut 3:19
Until the LORD *h* given rest unto Deut 3:20
possession, which I *h* given you Deut 3:20
Thine eyes *h* seen all that the Deut 3:21
Your eyes *h* seen what the LORD Deut 4:3
I *h* taught you statutes and Deut 4:5
things which thine eyes *h* seen Deut 4:9
ye shall *h* remained long in the Deut 4:25
Thou shalt *h* none other gods Deut 5:7 1961
we *h* heard his voice out of the Deut 5:24
we *h* seen this day that God doth Deut 5:24
of the midst of the fire, as we *h* Deut 5:26
I *h* heard the voice of the words Deut 5:28
which they *h* spoken unto thee Deut 5:28
they *h* well said all that they Deut 5:28
well said all that they *h* spoken Deut 5:28
h brought thee into the land Deut 6:10
when thou shalt *h* eaten and be Deut 6:11
thine eye shall *h* no pity upon Deut 7:16
until thou *h* destroyed them Deut 7:24
ye *h* been rebellious against the Deut 9:7
angry with you to *h* destroyed you Deut 9:8
of Egypt *h* corrupted themselves Deut 9:12
they *h* made them a molten image Deut 9:12
I *h* seen this people, and, behold, Deut 9:13
with Aaron to *h* destroyed him Deut 9:20
the land which I *h* given you Deut 9:23
Ye *h* been rebellious against the Deut 9:24
things, which thine eyes *h* seen Deut 10:21
your children which *h* not known Deut 11:2
which *h* not seen the chastisement Deut 11:2
But your eyes *h* seen all the Deut 11:7
other gods, which ye *h* not known Deut 11:28
as I *h* commanded thee, and thou Deut 12:21
h they done unto their gods Deut 12:31
their daughters they *h* burnt in Deut 12:31
h withdrawn the inhabitants of Deut 13:13
other gods, which ye *h* not known Deut 13:13
h compassion upon thee, and Deut 13:17
all that *h* fins and scales shall Deut 14:9
or *h* any ill blemish, thou shalt Deut 15:21
heaven, which I *h* not commanded Deut 17:3
which *h* committed that wicked Deut 17:5
shall *h* no part nor inheritance Deut 18:1
Therefore shall they *h* no Deut 18:2
They shall *h* like portions to eat Deut 18:8
They *h* well spoken that which Deut 18:17
spoken that which they *h* spoken Deut 18:17
which I *h* not commanded him to Deut 18:20
which they of old time *h* set in Deut 19:14
as he had thought to *h* done unto Deut 19:19
when the officers *h* made an end Deut 20:9
which they *h* done unto their gods Deut 20:18

Context	Reference	No.
Our hands *h* not shed this blood,	Deut 21:7	
neither *h* our eyes seen it	Deut 21:7	
thou wouldest *h* her to thy wife	Deut 21:11	
if thou *h* no delight in her, then	Deut 21:14	
If a man *h* two wives, one beloved	Deut 21:15	1961
they *h* born him children, both	Deut 21:15	
If a man *h* a stubborn and	Deut 21:18	1961
when they *h* chastened him, will	Deut 21:18	
if a man *h* committed a sin worthy	Deut 21:22	
Thou shalt *h* a place also without	Deut 23:12	1961
thou shalt *h* a paddle upon thy	Deut 23:13	1961
h no child, the wife of the dead	Deut 25:5	
Thou shalt not *h* in thy bag	Deut 25:13	1961
Thou shalt not *h* in thine house	Deut 25:14	1961
But thou shalt *h* a perfect	Deut 25:15	1961
and just measure shalt thou *h*	Deut 25:15	1961
I *h* brought the firstfruits of	Deut 26:10	
I *h* brought away the hallowed	Deut 26:13	
also *h* given them unto the Levite	Deut 26:13	
I *h* not transgressed thy	Deut 26:13	
neither *h* I forgotten them	Deut 26:13	
I *h* not eaten thereof in my	Deut 26:14	
neither *h* I taken away ought	Deut 26:14	
but I *h* hearkened to the voice of	Deut 26:14	
h done according to all that thou	Deut 26:14	
until he *h* consumed thee from off	Deut 28:21	
thou shalt *h* none to rescue them	Deut 28:31	
thou nor thy fathers *h* known	Deut 28:36	
Thou shalt *h* olive trees	Deut 28:40	1961
until he *h* destroyed thee	Deut 28:48	1961
until he *h* destroyed thee	Deut 28:51	
thou nor thy fathers *h* known	Deut 28:64	
shall the sole of thy foot *h* rest	Deut 28:65	1961
shalt *h* none assurance of thy	Deut 28:66	
Ye *h* seen all that the LORD did	Deut 29:2	
which thine eyes *h* seen, the	Deut 29:3	
I *h* led you forty years in the	Deut 29:5	
Ye *h* not eaten bread	Deut 29:6	
neither *h* ye drunk wine or strong	Deut 29:6	
(For ye know how we *h* dwelt in	Deut 29:16	
ye *h* seen their abominations, and	Deut 29:17	
heart, saying, I shall *h* peace	Deut 29:19	
Because they *h* forsaken the	Deut 29:25	
which I *h* set before thee, and	Deut 30:1	
h compassion upon thee, and will	Deut 30:3	
I *h* set before thee this day life	Deut 30:15	
that I *h* set before you life and	Deut 30:19	
which I *h* commanded you	Deut 31:5	
which *h* not known any thing, may	Deut 31:13	
covenant which I *h* made with them	Deut 31:16	
evils which they shall *h* wrought	Deut 31:18	
For when I shall *h* brought them	Deut 31:20	
and they shall *h* eaten and filled	Deut 31:20	
before I *h* brought them into the	Deut 31:21	
ye *h* been rebellious against the	Deut 31:27	
the way which I *h* commanded you	Deut 31:29	
They *h* corrupted themselves,	Deut 32:5	
They *h* moved me to jealousy with	Deut 32:21	
they *h* provoked me to anger with	Deut 32:21	
to his mother, I *h* not seen him	Deut 33:9	
for they *h* observed thy word, and	Deut 33:9	
I *h* caused thee to see it with	Deut 34:4	
that *h* I given unto you, as I	Josh 1:3	
and then thou shalt *h* good success	Josh 1:8	
H not I commanded thee	Josh 1:9	
Until the LORD *h* given your	Josh 1:15	
they also *h* possessed the land	Josh 1:15	
For we *h* heard how the LORD dried	Josh 2:10	
since I *h* shewed you kindness,	Josh 2:12	
and my sisters, and all that they *h*	Josh 2:13	
for ye *h* not passed this way	Josh 3:4	
This day *h* I rolled away the	Josh 5:9	
I *h* given into thine hand Jericho	Josh 6:2	
they *h* also transgressed my	Josh 7:11	
for they *h* even taken of the	Josh 7:11	
h also stolen, and dissembled also	Josh 7:11	
they *h* put it even among their	Josh 7:11	
Indeed I *h* sinned against the	Josh 7:20	
Israel, and thus and thus *h* I done	Josh 7:20	
I *h* given into thy hand the king	Josh 8:1	
we *h* drawn them from the city	Josh 8:6	
when ye *h* taken the city, that ye	Josh 8:8	
See, I *h* commanded you	Josh 8:8	
for we *h* heard the fame of him,	Josh 9:9	
We *h* sworn unto them by the LORD	Josh 9:19	
Wherefore *h* ye beguiled us,	Josh 9:22	
of you, and *h* done this thing	Josh 9:24	
for I *h* delivered them into thine	Josh 10:8	
and that they might *h* no favour	Josh 11:20	1961
as I *h* commanded thee	Josh 13:6	
the Gadites *h* received their	Josh 13:8	
thy feet *h* trodden shall be thine	Josh 14:9	
of the valley *h* chariots of iron	Josh 17:16	
thou shalt not *h* one lot only	Josh 17:17	1961
though they *h* iron chariots, and	Josh 17:18	
But the Levites *h* no part among	Josh 18:7	
h received their inheritance	Josh 18:7	1961
Ye *h* kept all that Moses the	Josh 22:2	
h obeyed my voice in all that I	Josh 22:2	
Ye *h* not left your brethren these	Josh 22:3	
but *h* kept the charge of the	Josh 22:3	
the half tribe of Manasseh *h*	Josh 22:11	
ye *h* committed against the God of	Josh 22:16	
in that ye *h* builded you an altar	Josh 22:16	
That we *h* built us an altar to	Josh 22:23	
if we *h* not rather done it for	Josh 22:24	
What *h* ye to do with the LORD God	Josh 22:24	
ye *h* no part in the LORD	Josh 22:25	
to come, Ye *h* no part in the LORD	Josh 22:27	
because ye *h* not committed this	Josh 22:31	
now ye *h* delivered the children	Josh 22:31	
ye *h* seen all that the LORD your	Josh 23:3	
I *h* divided unto you by lot these	Josh 23:4	
all the nations that I *h* cut off	Josh 23:4	
as ye *h* done unto this day	Josh 23:8	
until he *h* destroyed you from off	Josh 23:15	
When ye *h* transgressed the	Josh 23:16	
h gone and served other gods, and	Josh 23:16	
h seen what I *h* done in Egypt	Josh 24:7	
I *h* given you a land for which ye	Josh 24:13	
that ye *h* chosen you the LORD	Josh 24:22	
I *h* delivered the land into his	Judg 1:2	
as I *h* done, so God hath requited	Judg 1:7	
h brought you unto the land which	Judg 2:1	
but ye *h* not obeyed my voice	Judg 2:2	
why *h* ye done this	Judg 2:2	
h not hearkened unto my voice	Judg 2:20	
I *h* a secret errand unto thee, O	Judg 3:19	
I *h* a message from God unto thee	Judg 3:20	
h dominion over the nobles among	Judg 5:13	
the LORD made me *h* dominion over	Judg 5:13	
H they not sped?	Judg 5:30	
h they not divided the prey	Judg 5:30	
but ye *h* not obeyed my voice	Judg 6:10	
h not I sent thee	Judg 6:14	
If now I *h* found grace in thy	Judg 6:17	
for because I *h* seen an angel of	Judg 6:22	
for I *h* delivered it into thine	Judg 7:9	
What *h* I done now in comparison	Judg 8:2	
if ye *h* done truly and sincerely,	Judg 9:16	
in that ye *h* made Abimelech king,	Judg 9:16	
if ye *h* dealt well with Jerubbaal	Judg 9:16	
h done unto him according to the	Judg 9:16	
h slain his sons, threescore and	Judg 9:18	
h made Abimelech, the son of his	Judg 9:18	
If ye then *h* dealt truly and	Judg 9:19	
What ye *h* seen me do, make haste,	Judg 9:48	
and do as I *h* done	Judg 9:48	
We *h* sinned against thee	Judg 10:10	
both because we *h* forsaken our	Judg 10:10	
Yet ye *h* forsaken me, and served	Judg 10:13	
unto the gods which ye *h* chosen	Judg 10:14	
said unto the LORD, We *h* sinned	Judg 10:15	
Wherefore I *h* not sinned against	Judg 11:27	
for I *h* opened my mouth unto the	Judg 11:35	
until we shall *h* made ready a kid	Judg 13:15	
surely die, because we *h* seen God	Judg 13:22	
he would not *h* received a burnt	Judg 13:23	
neither would he *h* shewed us all	Judg 13:23	
nor would as at this time *h* told	Judg 13:23	
I *h* seen a woman in Timnath of	Judg 14:2	
rent him as he would *h* rent a kid	Judg 14:6	
h ye called us to take that we	Judg 14:15	
ye called us to take that we *h*	Judg 14:15	
I *h* not told it my father nor my	Judg 14:16	
unto them, Though ye *h* done this	Judg 15:7	
unto me, so *h* I done unto them	Judg 15:11	
an ass *h* I slain a thousand men	Judg 15:16	
for I *h* been a Nazarite unto God	Judg 16:17	
seeing I *h* a Levite to my priest	Judg 17:13	1961
for we *h* seen the land, and,	Judg 18:9	
consider what ye *h* to do	Judg 18:14	
Ye *h* taken away my gods which I	Judg 18:24	
and what *h* I more	Judg 18:24	
night, and thought to *h* slain me	Judg 20:5	
and my concubine *h* they forced	Judg 20:5	
for they *h* committed lewdness and	Judg 20:6	
that they *h* wrought in Israel	Judg 20:10	
seeing we *h* sworn by the LORD	Judg 21:7	
the children of Israel *h* sworn	Judg 21:18	
as ye *h* dealt with the dead, and	Ruth 1:8	
for I am too old to *h* an husband	Ruth 1:12	
I *h* hope, if I should *h* an	Ruth 1:12	
h I not charged the young men	Ruth 2:9	
that which the young men *h* drawn	Ruth 2:9	
Why *h* I found grace in thine eyes	Ruth 2:10	
until they *h* ended all my harvest	Ruth 2:21	
man, until he shall *h* done eating	Ruth 3:3	
until he *h* finished the thing	Ruth 3:18	
that I *h* bought all that was	Ruth 4:9	
h I purchased to be my wife, to	Ruth 4:10	
I *h* drunken neither wine nor	1Sa 1:15	
but *h* poured out my soul before	1Sa 1:15	
grief *h* I spoken hitherto	1Sa 1:16	
Because I *h* asked him of the LORD	1Sa 1:20	
tarry until thou *h* weaned him	1Sa 1:23	
Therefore also I *h* lent him to	1Sa 1:28	
They that were full *h* hired out	1Sa 2:5	
for he will not *h* sodden flesh of	1Sa 2:15	3947
which I *h* commanded in my	1Sa 2:29	
I *h* spoken concerning his house	1Sa 3:12	
For I *h* told him that I will	1Sa 3:13	
therefore I *h* sworn unto the	1Sa 3:14	
Hebrews, as they *h* been to you	1Sa 4:9	
They *h* brought about the ark of	1Sa 5:10	
The Philistines *h* brought again	1Sa 6:21	
We *h* sinned against the LORD	1Sa 7:6	
for they *h* not rejected thee	1Sa 8:7	
but they *h* rejected me, that I	1Sa 8:7	
they *h* done since the day that I	1Sa 8:8	
day, wherewith they *h* forsaken me	1Sa 8:8	
king which ye shall *h* chosen you	1Sa 8:18	
but we will *h* a king over us	1Sa 8:19	1961
what *h* we	1Sa 9:7	
I *h* here at hand the fourth part	1Sa 9:8	4672
for I *h* looked upon my people,	1Sa 9:16	
I said, I *h* invited the people	1Sa 9:24	
ye *h* this day rejected your God,	1Sa 10:19	
ye *h* said unto him, Nay, but set	1Sa 10:19	
the sun be hot, ye shall *h* help	1Sa 11:9	
I *h* hearkened unto your voice in	1Sa 12:1	
me, and *h* made a king over you	1Sa 12:1	
I *h* walked before you from my	1Sa 12:2	
whose ox *h* I taken	1Sa 12:3	
or whose ass *h* I taken	1Sa 12:3	
or whom *h* I defrauded	1Sa 12:3	
whom *h* I oppressed	1Sa 12:3	
or of whose hand *h* I received any	1Sa 12:3	
that ye *h* not found ought in my	1Sa 12:5	
We *h* sinned, because we *h*	1Sa 12:10	
h served Baalim and Ashtaroth	1Sa 12:10	
h chosen, and whom ye *h* desired	1Sa 12:13	
which ye *h* done in the sight of	1Sa 12:17	
for we *h* added unto all our sins	1Sa 12:19	
ye *h* done all this wickedness	1Sa 12:20	
I *h* not made supplication unto	1Sa 13:12	
for now would the LORD *h*	1Sa 13:13	
how mine eyes *h* been enlightened,	1Sa 14:29	
And he said, Ye *h* transgressed	1Sa 14:33	
utterly destroy all that they *h*	1Sa 15:3	
that I *h* set up Saul to be king	1Sa 15:11	
I *h* performed the commandment of	1Sa 15:13	
They *h* brought them from the	1Sa 15:15	
the rest we *h* utterly destroyed	1Sa 15:15	
I *h* obeyed the voice of the LORD,	1Sa 15:20	
h gone the way which the LORD	1Sa 15:20	
h brought Agag the king of Amalek	1Sa 15:20	
and *h* utterly destroyed the	1Sa 15:20	
should *h* been utterly destroyed	1Sa 15:21	
Saul said unto Samuel, I *h* sinned	1Sa 15:24	
for I *h* transgressed the	1Sa 15:24	
Then he said, I *h* sinned	1Sa 15:30	
seeing I *h* rejected him from	1Sa 16:1	
for I *h* provided me a king among	1Sa 16:1	
because I *h* refused him	1Sa 16:7	
I *h* seen a son of Jesse the	1Sa 16:18	
H ye seen this man that is come	1Sa 17:25	
And David said, What *h* I now done	1Sa 17:29	
for I *h* not proved them	1Sa 17:39	
They *h* ascribed unto David ten	1Sa 18:8	
to me they *h* ascribed but	1Sa 18:8	
what can he *h* more but the	1Sa 18:8	
should *h* been given to David	1Sa 18:19	
because his works *h* been to	1Sa 19:4	1961
before Jonathan, What *h* I done	1Sa 20:1	
I *h* found grace in thine eyes	1Sa 20:3	1961
thy servant shall *h* peace	1Sa 20:7	
when I *h* sounded my father about	1Sa 20:12	
I *h* spoken of, behold, the LORD	1Sa 20:23	
if I *h* found favour in thine eyes	1Sa 20:29	
forasmuch as we *h* sworn both of	1Sa 20:42	
thee, and what I *h* commanded thee	1Sa 21:2	
I *h* appointed my servants to such	1Sa 21:2	
if the young men *h* kept	1Sa 21:4	
Of a truth women *h* been kept from	1Sa 21:5	
for I *h* neither brought my sword	1Sa 21:8	
wherefore then *h* ye brought him	1Sa 21:14	
H I need of mad men, that ye *h*	1Sa 21:15	
That all of you *h* conspired	1Sa 22:8	
Why *h* ye conspired against me,	1Sa 22:13	
I *h* occasioned the death of all	1Sa 22:22	
for ye *h* compassion on me	1Sa 23:21	
Philistines *h* invaded the land	1Sa 23:27	
this day thine eyes *h* seen how	1Sa 24:10	
I *h* not sinned against thee	1Sa 24:11	
whereas I *h* rewarded thee evil	1Sa 24:17	
now I *h* heard that thou hast	1Sa 25:7	
my flesh that I *h* killed for my	1Sa 25:11	
Surely in vain *h* I kept all that	1Sa 25:21	
when the LORD shall *h* done to my	1Sa 25:30	
shall *h* appointed thee ruler over	1Sa 25:30	
shall *h* dealt well with my lord	1Sa 25:31	
I *h* hearkened to thy voice	1Sa 25:35	
and *h* accepted thy person	1Sa 25:35	
because ye *h* not kept your master	1Sa 26:16	
for what *h* I done	1Sa 26:18	
If the LORD *h* stirred thee up	1Sa 26:19	
for they *h* driven me out this day	1Sa 26:19	
Then said Saul, I *h* sinned	1Sa 26:21	
I *h* played the fool, and *h*	1Sa 26:21	
If I *h* now found grace in thine	1Sa 27:5	
Whither *h* ye made a road to day	1Sa 27:10	
off those that *h* familiar spirits	1Sa 28:9	
therefore I *h* called thee	1Sa 28:15	
I *h* put my life in my hand, and	1Sa 28:21	
h hearkened unto thy words which	1Sa 28:21	
eat, that thou mayest *h* strength	1Sa 28:22	
I *h* found no fault in him since	1Sa 29:3	
for I *h* not found evil in thee	1Sa 29:6	
unto Achish, But what *h* I done	1Sa 29:8	
in thy servant so long as I *h*	1Sa 29:8	
princes of the Philistines *h* said	1Sa 29:9	
the morning, and *h* light, depart	1Sa 29:10	
of the spoil that we *h* recovered	1Sa 30:22	
h brought them hither unto my	2Sa 1:10	
I *h* slain the LORD's anointed	2Sa 1:16	
that ye *h* shewed this kindness	2Sa 2:5	
even unto Saul, and *h* buried him	2Sa 2:5	
because ye *h* done this thing	2Sa 2:6	
also the house of Judah *h*	2Sa 2:7	
h not delivered thee into the	2Sa 3:8	
though they would *h* fetched wheat	2Sa 4:6	
thinking to *h* brought good	2Sa 4:10	
who thought that I would *h* given	2Sa 4:10	
when wicked men *h* slain a	2Sa 4:11	
Whereas I *h* not dwelt in any	2Sa 7:6	
but *h* walked in a tent and in a	2Sa 7:6	
In all the places wherein I *h*	2Sa 7:7	
h cut off all thine enemies out	2Sa 7:9	
h made thee a great name, like	2Sa 7:9	
h caused thee to rest from all	2Sa 7:11	
all that we *h* heard with our ears	2Sa 7:22	
I *h* given unto thy master's son	2Sa 9:9	
master's son may *h* food to eat	2Sa 9:10	1961
I would moreover *h* given unto	2Sa 12:8	
I *h* sinned against the LORD	2Sa 12:13	
I *h* fought against Rabbah, and	2Sa 12:27	
h taken the city of waters	2Sa 12:27	
Amnon said, *H* out all men from me	2Sa 13:9	3318
h not I commanded you	2Sa 13:28	
h slain all the young men the	2Sa 13:32	
the people *h* made me afraid	2Sa 14:15	

Behold now, I *h* done this thing 2Sa 14:21
that I *h* found grace in thy sight 2Sa 14:22
to *h* sent him to the king 2Sa 14:29
Wherefore *h* thy servants set my 2Sa 14:31
good for me to *h* been there still 2Sa 14:32
which I *h* vowed unto the LORD, in 2Sa 15:7
thus say, I *h* no delight in thee 2Sa 15:26
as I *h* been thy father's servant 2Sa 15:34
they *h* there with them their two 2Sa 15:36
What *h* I to do with you, ye sons 2Sa 16:10
as I *h* served in thy father's 2Sa 16:19
and thus and thus *h* I counselled 2Sa 17:15
I would *h* given thee ten shekels 2Sa 18:11
Otherwise I should *h* wrought 2Sa 18:13
thou thyself wouldest *h* set 2Sa 18:13
I *h* no son to keep my name in 2Sa 18:18
which this day *h* saved thy life 2Sa 19:5
servant doth know that I *h* sinned 2Sa 19:20
What *h* I to do with you, ye sons 2Sa 19:22
What right therefore *h* I yet to 2Sa 19:28 3426
I *h* said, Thou and Ziba divide the 2Sa 19:29
How long *h* I to live, that I 2Sa 19:34
Why *h* our brethren the men of 2Sa 19:41
h brought the king, and his 2Sa 19:41
h we eaten at all of the king's 2Sa 19:42
We *h* ten parts in the king 2Sa 19:43
we *h* also more right in David 2Sa 19:43
We *h* no part in David 2Sa 20:1
neither *h* we inheritance in the 2Sa 20:1
We will *h* no silver nor gold of 2Sa 21:4
sword, thought to *h* slain David 2Sa 21:16
For I *h* kept the ways of the LORD 2Sa 22:22
h not wickedly departed from my 2Sa 22:22
h kept myself from mine iniquity 2Sa 22:24
For by thee I *h* run through a 2Sa 22:30
by my God *h* I leaped over a wall 2Sa 22:30
I *h* pursued mine enemies, and 2Sa 22:38
I *h* consumed them, and wounded 2Sa 22:39
I *h* sinned greatly in that I *h* 2Sa 24:10
for I *h* done very foolishly 2Sa 24:10
h sinned, and I *h* done wickedly 2Sa 24:17
but these sheep, what *h* they done 2Sa 24:17
I *h* appointed him to be ruler 1Kin 1:35
they *h* caused him to ride upon 1Kin 1:44
Nathan the prophet *h* anointed him 1Kin 1:45
This is the noise that ye *h* heard 1Kin 1:45
I *h* somewhat to say unto thee 1Kin 2:14
if Adonijah *h* not spoken this 1Kin 2:23
The word that I *h* heard is good 1Kin 2:42
that I *h* charged thee with 1Kin 2:43
I *h* done according to thy words 1Kin 3:12
I *h* given thee a wise and an 1Kin 3:12
I *h* also given thee that which 1Kin 3:13
I *h* considered the things which 1Kin 5:8
I *h* surely built thee an house to 1Kin 8:13
h built an house for the name of 1Kin 8:20
I *h* set there a place for the ark 1Kin 8:21
less this house that I *h* builded 1Kin 8:27
Yet *h* thou respect unto the 1Kin 8:28
because they *h* sinned against 1Kin 8:33
because they *h* sinned against 1Kin 8:35
this house, which I *h* builded 1Kin 8:43
house that I *h* built for thy name 1Kin 8:44
We *h* sinned, and *h* done 1Kin 8:47
we *h* committed wickedness 1Kin 8:47
the house which I *h* built for thy 1Kin 8:48
people that *h* sinned against thee 1Kin 8:50
they *h* transgressed against thee 1Kin 8:50
that they may *h* compassion on 1Kin 8:50
wherewith I *h* made supplication 1Kin 8:59
I *h* heard thy prayer and thy 1Kin 9:3
I *h* hallowed this house, which 1Kin 9:3
to all that I *h* commanded thee 1Kin 9:4
statutes which I *h* set before you 1Kin 9:6
of the land which I *h* given them 1Kin 9:7
which I *h* hallowed for my name, 1Kin 9:7
h taken hold upon other gods, and 1Kin 9:9
h worshipped them, and served them 1Kin 9:9
which I *h* commanded thee, I will 1Kin 11:11
Jerusalem's sake which I *h* chosen 1Kin 11:13
(But he shall *h* one tribe for my 1Kin 11:32 1961
the city which I *h* chosen out of 1Kin 11:32
Because that they *h* forsaken me 1Kin 11:33
h worshipped Ashtoreth the 1Kin 11:33
h not walked in my ways, to do 1Kin 11:33
that David my servant may *h* a 1Kin 11:36
the city which I *h* chosen me to 1Kin 11:36
who *h* spoken to me, saying, Make 1Kin 12:9
What portion *h* we in David 1Kin 12:16
neither *h* we inheritance in the 1Kin 12:16
because they *h* made their groves, 1Kin 14:15
I *h* sent unto thee a present of 1Kin 15:19
I *h* commanded the ravens to feed 1Kin 17:4
I *h* commanded a widow woman there 1Kin 17:9
I *h* not a cake, but an handful of 1Kin 17:12 3426
What *h* I to do with thee, O thou 1Kin 17:18
What *h* I sinned, that thou 1Kin 18:9
answered, I *h* not troubled Israel 1Kin 18:18
in that ye *h* forsaken the 1Kin 18:18
that I *h* done all these things at 1Kin 18:36
I *h* been very jealous for the 1Kin 19:10
of Israel *h* forsaken thy covenant 1Kin 19:10
I *h* been very jealous for the 1Kin 19:14
of Israel *h* forsaken thy covenant 1Kin 19:14
Yet I *h* left me seven thousand in 1Kin 19:18
knees which *h* not bowed unto Baal 1Kin 19:18
for what *h* I done to thee 1Kin 19:20
I am thine, and all that I *h* 1Kin 20:4
Although I *h* sent unto thee, 1Kin 20:5
LORD, Because the Syrians *h* said 1Kin 20:28
we *h* heard that the kings of the 1Kin 20:31
that I may *h* it for a garden of 1Kin 21:2 1961
And he answered, I *h* found thee 1Kin 21:20
until thou *h* consumed them 1Kin 22:11
as sheep that *h* not a shepherd 1Kin 22:17
the LORD said, These *h* no master 1Kin 22:17
the LORD, I *h* healed these waters 2Kin 2:21
Israel, What *h* I to do with thee 2Kin 3:13
they *h* smitten one another 2Kin 3:23
should *h* reigned in his stead 2Kin 3:27
I *h* therewith sent Naaman my 2Kin 5:6
wouldest thou not *h* done it 2Kin 5:13
you what the Syrians *h* done to us 2Kin 7:12
to *h* the charge of the gate 2Kin 7:17
I *h* anointed thee king over 2Kin 9:3
I *h* an errand to thee, O captain 2Kin 9:5
I *h* anointed thee king over the 2Kin 9:6
I *h* anointed thee king over 2Kin 9:12
Surely I *h* seen yesterday the 2Kin 9:26
They *h* brought the heads of the 2Kin 10:8
for I *h* a great sacrifice to do 2Kin 10:19
If any of the men whom I *h* 2Kin 10:24
H her forth without the ranges 2Kin 11:15 3318
till thou *h* consumed them 2Kin 13:17
Thou shouldest *h* smitten five or 2Kin 13:19
the covenant that I *h* made with 2Kin 17:38
to Lachish, saying, I *h* offended 2Kin 18:14
I *h* counsel and strength for the 2Kin 18:20
h they delivered Samaria out of 2Kin 18:34
that *h* delivered their country 2Kin 18:35
king of Assyria *h* blasphemed me 2Kin 19:6
of Assyria *h* done to all lands 2Kin 19:11
H the gods of the nations 2Kin 19:12
them which my fathers *h* destroyed 2Kin 19:12
the kings of Assyria *h* destroyed 2Kin 19:17
h cast their gods into the fire 2Kin 19:18
therefore they *h* destroyed them 2Kin 19:18
king of Assyria I *h* heard 2Kin 19:20
I *h* digged and drunk strange 2Kin 19:24
with the sole of my feet *h* I 2Kin 19:24
heard long ago how I *h* done it 2Kin 19:25
ancient times that I *h* formed it 2Kin 19:25
now *h* I brought it to pass, that 2Kin 19:25
remember now how I *h* walked 2Kin 20:3
h done that which is good in thy 2Kin 20:3
I *h* heard thy prayer, I *h* seen 2Kin 20:5
sign shalt thou *h* of the LORD 2Kin 20:9
What *h* they seen in thine house 2Kin 20:15
are in mine house *h* they seen 2Kin 20:15
that I *h* not shewed them 2Kin 20:15
that which thy fathers *h* laid up 2Kin 20:17
which I *h* chosen out of all 2Kin 21:7
to all that I *h* commanded them 2Kin 21:8
Because they *h* done that which 2Kin 21:15
h provoked me to anger, since the 2Kin 21:15
the door *h* gathered of the people 2Kin 22:4
that *h* the oversight of the house 2Kin 22:5
I *h* found the book of the law in 2Kin 22:8
Thy servants *h* gathered the money 2Kin 22:9
h delivered it into the hand of 2Kin 22:9
that *h* the oversight of the house 2Kin 22:9
because our fathers *h* not 2Kin 22:13
Because they *h* forsaken me 2Kin 22:17
h burned incense unto other gods, 2Kin 22:17
I also *h* heard thee, saith the 2Kin 22:19
as I *h* removed Israel, and will 2Kin 23:27
city Jerusalem which I *h* chosen 2Kin 23:27
h put their lives in jeopardy 1Chr 11:19
place that I *h* prepared for it 1Chr 15:12
For I *h* not dwelt in an house 1Chr 17:5
but *h* gone from tent to tent, and 1Chr 17:5
Wheresoever I *h* walked with all 1Chr 17:6
Why *h* ye not built me an house of 1Chr 17:6
I *h* been with thee whithersoever 1Chr 17:8
h cut off all thine enemies from 1Chr 17:8
h made thee a name like the name 1Chr 17:8
all that we *h* heard with our ears 1Chr 17:20
I *h* sinned greatly 1Chr 21:8
because I *h* done this thing 1Chr 21:8
for I *h* done very foolishly 1Chr 21:8
even I it is that *h* sinned 1Chr 21:17
for these sheep, what *h* they done 1Chr 21:17
in my trouble I *h* prepared for 1Chr 22:14
timber also and stone *h* I prepared 1Chr 22:14
for I *h* chosen him to be my son, 1Chr 28:6
Now I *h* prepared with all my 1Chr 29:2
because I *h* set my affection to 1Chr 29:3
I *h* of mine own proper good, of 1Chr 29:3 3426
which I *h* given to the house of 1Chr 29:3
above all that I *h* prepared for 1Chr 29:3
of thine own *h* we given thee 1Chr 29:14
all this store that we *h* prepared 1Chr 29:16
I *h* willingly offered all these 1Chr 29:17
now *h* I seen with joy thy people, 1Chr 29:17
for the which I *h* made provision 1Chr 29:19
over whom I *h* made thee king 2Chr 1:11
h had that *h* been before thee 2Chr 1:12
there any after thee *h* the like 2Chr 1:12 1961
now I *h* sent a cunning man, 2Chr 2:13
But I *h* built an house of 2Chr 6:2
But I *h* chosen Jerusalem, that my 2Chr 6:6
h chosen David to be over my 2Chr 6:6
h built the house for the name of 2Chr 6:10
in it *h* I put the ark, wherein is 2Chr 6:11
less this house which I *h* built 2Chr 6:18
H respect therefore to the prayer 2Chr 6:19
because they *h* sinned against 2Chr 6:24
because they *h* sinned against 2Chr 6:26
I *h* built is called by thy name 2Chr 6:33
the house which I *h* built for thy 2Chr 6:34
We *h* sinned, we *h* done amiss, 2Chr 6:37
done amiss, and *h* dealt wickedly 2Chr 6:37
whither they *h* carried them 2Chr 6:38
which I *h* built for thy name 2Chr 6:38
which *h* sinned against thee 2Chr 6:39
I *h* heard thy prayer, and *h* 2Chr 7:12
For now *h* I chosen and sanctified 2Chr 7:16
to all that I *h* commanded thee 2Chr 7:17
according as I *h* covenanted with 2Chr 7:18
which I *h* set before you, and 2Chr 7:19
of my land which I *h* given them 2Chr 7:20
which I *h* sanctified for my name, 2Chr 7:20
which *h* spoken to me, saying, 2Chr 10:9
What portion *h* we in David 2Chr 10:16
we *h* none inheritance in the son 2Chr 10:16
Ye *h* forsaken me, and therefore 2Chr 12:5
therefore *h* I also left you in 2Chr 12:5
They *h* humbled themselves 2Chr 12:7
h strengthened themselves against 2Chr 13:7
H ye not cast out the priests of 2Chr 13:9
h made you priests after the 2Chr 13:9
our God, and we *h* not forsaken him 2Chr 13:10
but ye *h* forsaken him 2Chr 13:11
because we *h* sought the LORD our 2Chr 14:7
we *h* sought him, and he hath given 2Chr 14:7
or with them that *h* no power 2Chr 14:11
I *h* sent thee silver and gold 2Chr 16:3
from henceforth thou shalt *h* wars 2Chr 16:9 3426
as sheep that *h* no shepherd 2Chr 18:16
the LORD said, These *h* no master 2Chr 18:16
h built thee a sanctuary therein 2Chr 20:8
for we *h* no might against this 2Chr 20:12
thou shalt *h* great sickness by 2Chr 21:15
H her forth of the ranges 2Chr 23:14 3318
because ye *h* forsaken the LORD, 2Chr 24:20
I *h* given to the army of Israel 2Chr 25:9
ye *h* slain them in a rage that 2Chr 28:9
which ye *h* taken captive of your 2Chr 28:11
for whereas we *h* offended against 2Chr 28:13
For our fathers *h* trespassed 2Chr 29:6
h forsaken him, and *h* turned 2Chr 29:6
Also they *h* shut up the doors of 2Chr 29:7
h not burned incense nor offered 2Chr 29:7
our fathers *h* fallen by the sword 2Chr 29:9
We *h* cleansed all the house of 2Chr 29:18
h we prepared and sanctified, and, 2Chr 29:19
Now ye *h* consecrated yourselves 2Chr 29:31
we *h* had enough to eat, and *h* 2Chr 31:10
my fathers *h* done unto all the 2Chr 32:13
of the nations of other lands *h* 2Chr 32:17
which I *h* chosen before all the 2Chr 33:7
I *h* appointed for your fathers 2Chr 33:8
to do all that I *h* commanded them 2Chr 33:8
I *h* found the book of the law in 2Chr 34:15
they *h* gathered together the 2Chr 34:17
h delivered it into the hand of 2Chr 34:17
because our fathers *h* not kept 2Chr 34:21
h read before the king of Judah 2Chr 34:24
Because they *h* forsaken me 2Chr 34:25
h burned incense unto other gods, 2Chr 34:25
I *h* even heard thee also, saith 2Chr 34:27
What *h* I to do with thee, thou 2Chr 35:21
the house wherewith I *h* war 2Chr 35:21
said to his servants, *H* me away 2Chr 35:23 5674
Ye *h* nothing to do with us to Ezr 4:3
h set up the walls thereof, and Ezr 4:12
Now because we *h* maintenance from Ezr 4:14
dishonour, therefore *h* we sent Ezr 4:14
that they *h* moved sedition within Ezr 4:15
by this means thou shalt *h* no Ezr 4:16 383
sedition *h* been made therein Ezr 4:19
There *h* been mighty kings also Ezr 4:20 1934
which *h* ruled over all countries Ezr 4:20
And that which they *h* need of Ezr 6:9
Also I *h* made a decree, that Ezr 6:11
I Darius *h* made a decree Ezr 6:12
his counsellors *h* freely offered Ezr 7:15
which thou shalt *h* occasion to Ezr 7:20
h not separated themselves from Ezr 9:1
For they *h* taken of their Ezr 9:2
so that the holy seed *h* mingled Ezr 9:2
h we been in a great trespass Ezr 9:7
and for our iniquities *h* we Ezr 9:7
for we *h* forsaken thy Ezr 9:10
which *h* filled it from one end to Ezr 9:11
We *h* trespassed against our God, Ezr 10:2
h taken strange wives of the Ezr 10:2
Ye *h* transgressed, and *h* taken Ezr 10:10
for we are many that *h* Ezr 10:13
let all them which *h* taken Ezr 10:14
which we *h* sinned against thee Neh 1:6
I and my father's house *h* sinned Neh 1:6
We *h* dealt very corruptly against Neh 1:7
h not kept the commandments, nor Neh 1:7
them unto the place that I *h* Neh 1:9
if thy servant *h* found favour in Neh 2:5
but ye *h* no portion, nor right, Neh 2:20
for they *h* provoked thee to anger Neh 4:5
We *h* mortgaged our lands, Neh 5:3
We *h* borrowed money for the Neh 5:4
for other men *h* our lands Neh 5:5
We after our ability *h* redeemed Neh 5:8
my brethren *h* not eaten the bread Neh 5:14
all that I *h* done for this people Neh 5:19
that they might *h* matter for an Neh 6:13
that would *h* put me in fear Neh 6:14
right, but we *h* done wickedly Neh 9:33
Neither *h* our kings, our princes, Neh 9:34
For they *h* not served thee in Neh 9:35
also they *h* dominion over our Neh 9:37
that the same Levites might *h* the Neh 10:37
I *h* done for the house of my God Neh 13:14
because they *h* defiled the Neh 13:29
which *h* heard of the deed of the Est 1:18
that *h* the charge of the business Est 3:9
but I *h* not been called to come Est 4:11
banquet that I *h* prepared for him Est 5:4
If I *h* found favour in the sight Est 5:8
If I *h* found favour in thy sight, Est 7:3
if I *h* found favour in his sight, Est 8:5
I *h* given Esther the house of Est 8:7
him they *h* hanged upon the Est 8:7

Jews hoped to *h* power over them .... Est 9:1
the queen, The Jews *h* slain .... Est 9:12
what *h* they done in the rest of .... Est 9:12
It may be that my sons *h* sinned .... Job 1:5
they *h* slain the servants with .... Job 1:15
h carried them away, yea, and .... Job 1:17
let it look for light, but *h* none .... Job 3:9
For now should I *h* lain still .... Job 3:13
and been quiet, I should *h* slept .... Job 3:13
Thy words *h* upholden him that was .... Job 4:4
Even as I *h* seen, they that plow .... Job 4:8
I *h* seen the foolish taking root .... Job 5:3
we *h* searched it, so it is .... Job 5:27
Oh that I might *h* my request .... Job 6:8 935
Then should I yet *h* comfort .... Job 6:10 1961
for I *h* not concealed the words .... Job 6:10
My brethren *h* dealt deceitfully .... Job 6:15
to understand wherein I *h* erred .... Job 6:24
I *h* sinned .... Job 7:20
If thy children *h* sinned against .... Job 8:4
he *h* cast them away for their .... Job 8:4
him, saying, I *h* not seen thee .... Job 8:18
Thine hands *h* made me and .... Job 10:8
I should *h* been as though I had .... Job 10:19
I should *h* been carried from the .... Job 10:19
But I *h* understanding as well as .... Job 12:3
Behold now, I *h* ordered my cause .... Job 13:18 1961
thou wilt *h* a desire to the work .... Job 14:15
his flesh upon him shall *h* pain .... Job 14:22
that which I *h* seen I will .... Job 15:17
Which wise men *h* told from their .... Job 15:18
their fathers, and *h* not hid it .... Job 15:18
I *h* heard many such things .... Job 16:2
Shall vain words *h* an end .... Job 16:3
They *h* gaped upon me with their .... Job 16:10
they *h* smitten me upon the cheek .... Job 16:10
they *h* gathered themselves .... Job 16:10
I *h* sewed sackcloth upon my skin, ... Job 16:15
blood, and let my cry *h* no place .... Job 16:18 1961
I *h* made my bed in the darkness .... Job 17:13
I *h* said to corruption, Thou art .... Job 17:14
he shall *h* no name in the street .... Job 18:17
He shall neither *h* son nor nephew .... Job 18:19
These ten times *h* ye reproached .... Job 19:3
And be it indeed that I *h* erred .... Job 19:4
My kinsfolk *h* failed, and my .... Job 19:14
familiar friends *h* forgotten me .... Job 19:14
H pity upon me, *h* pity upon me .... Job 19:21
I *h* heard the check of my .... Job 20:3
they which *h* seen him shall say, ... Job 20:7
and after that I *h* spoken, mock on .... Job 21:3
and what profit should we *h* .... Job 21:15
H ye not asked them that go by .... Job 21:29
of the fatherless *h* been broken .... Job 22:9
way which wicked men *h* trodden .... Job 22:15
thou shalt *h* plenty of silver .... Job 22:25
For then shalt thou *h* thy delight .... Job 22:26
held his steps, his way *h* I kept .... Job 23:11
Neither *h* I gone back from the .... Job 23:12
I *h* esteemed the words of his .... Job 23:12
that they *h* no covering in the .... Job 24:7
the grave those which *h* sinned .... Job 24:19
all ye yourselves *h* seen it .... Job 27:12
lion's whelps *h* not trodden it .... Job 28:8
We *h* heard the fame thereof with .... Job 28:22
younger than I *h* me in derision .... Job 30:1
I would *h* disdained to *h* set .... Job 30:1
they *h* also let loose the bridle .... Job 30:11
my calamity, they *h* no helper .... Job 30:13
affliction *h* taken hold upon me .... Job 30:16
If I *h* walked with vanity, or if .... Job 31:5
If mine heart *h* been deceived by .... Job 31:9
or if I *h* laid wait at my .... Job 31:9
If I *h* withheld the poor from .... Job 31:16
or *h* caused the eyes of the widow .... Job 31:16
Or *h* eaten my morsel myself alone .... Job 31:17
I *h* guided her from my mother's .... Job 31:18
If I *h* seen any perish for want .... Job 31:19
If his loins *h* not blessed me, and .... Job 31:20
If I *h* lifted up my hand against .... Job 31:21
If I *h* made gold my hope, or *h* .... Job 31:24
for I should *h* denied the God .... Job 31:28
(Neither *h* I suffered my mouth to .... Job 31:30
If I *h* eaten the fruits thereof .... Job 31:39
or *h* caused the owners thereof to .... Job 31:39
should say, We *h* found out wisdom .... Job 32:13
now I *h* opened my mouth, my .... Job 33:2
I *h* heard the voice of thy words, ... Job 33:8
I *h* found a ransom .... Job 33:24
I *h* sinned, and perverted that .... Job 33:27
ear unto me, ye that *h* knowledge .... Job 34:2
I *h* borne chastisement, I will .... Job 34:31
if I *h* done iniquity, I will do .... Job 34:32
and, What profit shall I *h* .... Job 35:3
I will shew thee that I *h* yet to .... Job 36:2
that they *h* exceeded .... Job 36:9
Even so would he *h* removed thee .... Job 36:16
H the gates of death been opened .... Job 38:17
Which I *h* reserved against the .... Job 38:23
Whose house I *h* made the .... Job 39:6
Once *h* I spoken .... Job 40:5
therefore *h* I uttered that I .... Job 42:3
I *h* heard of thee by the hearing .... Job 42:5
for ye *h* not spoken of me the .... Job 42:7
in that ye *h* not spoken of me the .... Job 42:8
the Lord shall *h* them in derision .... Ps 2:4
Yet *h* I set my king upon my holy .... Ps 2:6
this day *h* I begotten thee .... Ps 2:7
that *h* set themselves against me .... Ps 3:6
h mercy upon me, and hear my .... Ps 4:1
for they *h* rebelled against thee .... Ps 5:10
H mercy upon me, O LORD .... Ps 6:2
O LORD my God, if I *h* done this .... Ps 7:3
If I *h* rewarded evil unto him .... Ps 7:4

I *h* delivered him that without .... Ps 7:4
Thou madest him to *h* dominion .... Ps 8:6
H mercy upon me, O LORD .... Ps 9:13
the devices that they *h* imagined .... Ps 10:2
Who *h* said, With our tongue will .... Ps 12:4
I *h* prevailed against him .... Ps 13:4
But I *h* trusted in thy mercy .... Ps 13:5
they *h* done abominable works, ... Ps 14:1
H all the workers of iniquity no .... Ps 14:4
Ye *h* shamed the counsel of the .... Ps 14:6
yea, I *h* a goodly heritage .... Ps 16:6 5921
I *h* set the LORD always before me .... Ps 16:8
by the word of thy lips I *h* kept .... Ps 17:4
I *h* called upon thee, for thou .... Ps 17:6
They *h* now compassed us in our .... Ps 17:11
they *h* set their eyes bowing down .... Ps 17:11
which *h* their portion in this .... Ps 17:14
For I *h* kept the ways of the LORD .... Ps 18:21
h not wickedly departed from my .... Ps 18:21
For by thee I *h* run through a .... Ps 18:29
by my God *h* I leaped over a wall .... Ps 18:29
I *h* pursued mine enemies, and .... Ps 18:37
I *h* wounded them that they were .... Ps 18:38
a people whom I *h* not known shall .... Ps 18:43
let them not *h* dominion over me .... Ps 19:13
Many bulls *h* compassed me .... Ps 22:12
bulls of Bashan *h* beset me round .... Ps 22:12
For dogs *h* compassed me .... Ps 22:16
of the wicked *h* inclosed me .... Ps 22:16
for they *h* been ever of old .... Ps 25:6
thee unto me, and *h* mercy upon me .... Ps 25:16
for I *h* walked in mine integrity .... Ps 26:1
I *h* trusted also in the LORD .... Ps 26:1
and I *h* walked in thy truth .... Ps 26:3
I *h* not sat with vain persons, ... Ps 26:4
I *h* hated the congregation of .... Ps 26:5
I *h* loved the habitation of thy .... Ps 26:8
One thing *h* I desired of the LORD .... Ps 27:4
h mercy also upon me, and answer .... Ps 27:7
Hear, O LORD, and *h* mercy upon me .... Ps 30:10
that they *h* laid privily for me .... Ps 31:4
I *h* hated them that regard lying .... Ps 31:6
H mercy upon me, O LORD, for I am .... Ps 31:9
For I *h* heard the slander of many .... Ps 31:13
for I *h* called upon thee .... Ps 31:17
and mine iniquity *h* I not hid .... Ps 32:5
mule, which *h* no understanding .... Ps 32:9
because we *h* trusted in his holy .... Ps 33:21
For without cause *h* they hid for .... Ps 35:7
cause they *h* digged for my soul .... Ps 35:7
hearts, Ah, so would we *h* it .... Ps 35:25
not say, We *h* swallowed him up .... Ps 35:25
The wicked *h* drawn out the sword, ... Ps 37:14
h bent their bow, to cast down .... Ps 37:14
I *h* been young, and now am old .... Ps 37:25
yet *h* I not seen the righteous .... Ps 37:25
I *h* seen the wicked in great .... Ps 37:35
I *h* roared by reason of the .... Ps 38:8
I *h* preached righteousness in the .... Ps 40:9
I *h* not refrained my lips, O LORD .... Ps 40:9
I *h* not hid thy righteousness .... Ps 40:10
I *h* declared thy faithfulness and .... Ps 40:10
I *h* not concealed thy .... Ps 40:10
evils *h* compassed me about .... Ps 40:12
mine iniquities *h* taken hold upon .... Ps 40:12
for I *h* sinned against thee .... Ps 41:4
My tears *h* been my meat day and .... Ps 42:3
We *h* heard with our ears, O God, ... Ps 44:1
our fathers *h* told us .... Ps 44:1
yet *h* we not forgotten thee, ... Ps 44:17
neither *h* we dealt falsely in thy .... Ps 44:17
neither *h* our steps declined from .... Ps 44:18
If we *h* forgotten the name of our .... Ps 44:20
which I *h* made touching the king .... Ps 45:1
whereby they *h* made thee glad .... Ps 45:8
As we *h* heard, so *h* we seen in .... Ps 48:8
We *h* thought of thy .... Ps 48:9
the upright shall *h* dominion over .... Ps 49:14
those that *h* made a covenant with .... Ps 50:5
to *h* been continually before me .... Ps 50:8
H mercy upon me, O God, according .... Ps 51:1
h I sinned, and done this evil in .... Ps 51:4
h done abominable iniquity .... Ps 53:1
H the workers of iniquity no .... Ps 53:4
they *h* not called upon God .... Ps 53:4
they *h* not set God before them .... Ps 54:3
for I *h* seen violence and strife .... Ps 55:9
then I could *h* borne it .... Ps 55:12
then I would *h* hid myself from .... Ps 55:12
Because they *h* no changes .... Ps 55:19
his word, in God I *h* put my trust .... Ps 56:4
In God *h* I put my trust .... Ps 56:11
They *h* prepared a net for my .... Ps 57:6
they *h* digged a pit before me, ... Ps 57:6
thou shalt *h* all the heathen in .... Ps 59:8
twice *h* I heard this .... Ps 62:11
so as I *h* seen thee in the .... Ps 63:2
Which my lips *h* uttered, and my .... Ps 66:14
Though ye *h* lien among the pots, ... Ps 68:13
They *h* seen thy goings, O God .... Ps 68:24
for thy sake I *h* borne reproach .... Ps 69:7
that which should *h* been for .... Ps 69:22
there, and *h* it in possession .... Ps 69:35
By thee *h* I been holden up from .... Ps 71:6
hitherto *h* I declared thy .... Ps 71:17
until I *h* shewed thy strength .... Ps 71:18
He shall *h* dominion also from sea .... Ps 72:8
they *h* more than heart could wish .... Ps 73:7
Verily I *h* cleansed my heart in .... Ps 73:13
all the day long *h* I been plagued .... Ps 73:14
Whom *h* I in heaven but thee .... Ps 73:25
I *h* put my trust in the Lord GOD, ... Ps 73:28
They *h* cast fire into thy .... Ps 74:7
they *h* defiled by casting down .... Ps 74:7

they *h* burned up all the .... Ps 74:8
people *h* blasphemed thy name .... Ps 74:18
H respect unto the covenant .... Ps 74:20
spoiled, they *h* slept their sleep .... Ps 76:5
men of might *h* found their hands .... Ps 76:5
I *h* considered the days of old, ... Ps 77:5
Which we *h* heard and known .... Ps 78:3
and our fathers *h* told us .... Ps 78:3
thy holy temple *h* they defiled .... Ps 79:1
they *h* laid Jerusalem on heaps .... Ps 79:1
h they given to be meat unto the .... Ps 79:2
Their blood *h* they shed like .... Ps 79:3
the heathen that *h* not known thee .... Ps 79:6
upon the kingdoms that *h* not .... Ps 79:6
For they *h* devoured Jacob, and .... Ps 79:7
wherewith they *h* reproached thee, ... Ps 79:12
I should soon *h* subdued their .... Ps 81:14
h submitted themselves unto him .... Ps 81:15
time should *h* endured for ever .... Ps 81:15
He should *h* fed them also with .... Ps 81:16
rock should I *h* satisfied thee .... Ps 81:16
I *h* said, Ye are gods .... Ps 82:6
hate thee *h* lifted up the head .... Ps 83:2
They *h* taken crafty counsel .... Ps 83:3
They *h* said, Come, and let us cut .... Ps 83:4
For they *h* consulted together .... Ps 83:5
they *h* holpen the children of Lot .... Ps 83:8
peace *h* kissed each other .... Ps 85:10
men *h* sought after my soul .... Ps 86:14
h not set thee before them .... Ps 86:14
turn unto me, and *h* mercy upon me .... Ps 86:16
I *h* cried day and night before .... Ps 88:1
I *h* called daily upon thee, I .... Ps 88:9
I *h* stretched out my hands unto .... Ps 88:9
But unto thee *h* I cried, O LORD .... Ps 88:13
thy terrors *h* cut me off .... Ps 88:16
For I *h* said, Mercy shall be .... Ps 89:2
I *h* made a covenant with my .... Ps 89:3
I *h* sworn unto David my servant, ... Ps 89:3
I *h* laid help upon one that is .... Ps 89:19
I *h* exalted one chosen out of the .... Ps 89:19
I *h* found David my servant .... Ps 89:20
with my holy oil *h* I anointed him .... Ps 89:20
Once *h* I sworn by my holiness .... Ps 89:35
thine enemies *h* reproached .... Ps 89:51
wherewith they *h* reproached the .... Ps 89:51
the years wherein we *h* seen evil .... Ps 90:15
The floods *h* lifted up, O LORD, ... Ps 93:3
the floods *h* lifted up their .... Ps 93:3
iniquity *h* fellowship with thee .... Ps 94:20
and they *h* not known my ways .... Ps 95:10
all the ends of the earth *h* seen .... Ps 98:3
For I *h* eaten ashes like bread, ... Ps 102:9
shalt arise, and *h* mercy upon Zion .... Ps 102:13
same, and thy years shall *h* no end .... Ps 102:27
of the heaven *h* their habitation .... Ps 104:12
to my God while I *h* my being .... Ps 104:33
We *h* sinned with our fathers .... Ps 106:6
we *h* committed iniquity, we *h* .... Ps 106:6
they *h* spoken against me with a .... Ps 109:2
they *h* rewarded me evil for good, ... Ps 109:5
all them that *h* pleasure therein .... Ps 111:2
h all they that do his .... Ps 111:10
They *h* mouths, but they speak not .... Ps 115:5
eyes *h* they, but they see not .... Ps 115:5
They *h* ears, but they hear not .... Ps 115:6
noses *h* they, but they smell not .... Ps 115:6
They *h* hands, but they handle not .... Ps 115:7
feet *h* they, but they walk not .... Ps 115:7
I believed, therefore *h* I spoken .... Ps 116:10
we *h* blessed you out of the house .... Ps 118:26
when I *h* respect unto all thy .... Ps 119:6
when I shall *h* learned thy .... Ps 119:7
my whole heart *h* I sought thee .... Ps 119:10
Thy word *h* I hid in mine heart, ... Ps 119:11
With my lips *h* I declared all the .... Ps 119:13
I *h* rejoiced in the way of thy .... Ps 119:14
and *h* respect unto thy ways .... Ps 119:15
for I *h* kept thy testimonies .... Ps 119:22
I *h* declared my ways, and thou .... Ps 119:26
I *h* chosen the way of truth .... Ps 119:30
thy judgments *h* I laid before me .... Ps 119:30
I *h* stuck unto thy testimonies .... Ps 119:31
I *h* longed after thy precepts .... Ps 119:40
So shall I *h* wherewith to answer .... Ps 119:42
for I *h* hoped in thy judgments .... Ps 119:43
thy commandments, which I *h* loved .... Ps 119:47
thy commandments, which I *h* loved .... Ps 119:48
The proud *h* had me greatly in .... Ps 119:51
yet *h* I not declined from thy law .... Ps 119:51
and *h* comforted myself .... Ps 119:52
Thy statutes *h* been my songs in .... Ps 119:54
I *h* remembered thy name, O LORD, ... Ps 119:55
in the night, and *h* kept thy law .... Ps 119:55
I *h* said that I would keep thy .... Ps 119:57
bands of the wicked *h* robbed me .... Ps 119:61
but I *h* not forgotten thy law .... Ps 119:61
for I *h* believed thy commandments .... Ps 119:66
but now *h* I kept thy word .... Ps 119:67
The proud *h* forged a lie against .... Ps 119:69
for me that I *h* been afflicted .... Ps 119:71
Thy hands *h* made me and fashioned .... Ps 119:73
because I *h* hoped in thy word .... Ps 119:74
me, and those that *h* known thy .... Ps 119:79
The proud *h* digged pits for me, ... Ps 119:85
I should then *h* perished in mine .... Ps 119:92
for I *h* sought thy precepts .... Ps 119:94
The wicked *h* waited for me to .... Ps 119:95
I *h* seen an end of all perfection .... Ps 119:96
I *h* more understanding than all .... Ps 119:99
I *h* refrained my feet from every .... Ps 119:101
I *h* not departed from thy .... Ps 119:102
I *h* sworn, and I will perform it, ... Ps 119:106
The wicked *h* laid a snare for me .... Ps 119:110

Thy testimonies *h* I taken as an ... Ps 119:111
I *h* inclined mine heart to ... Ps 119:112
I will *h* respect unto thy ... Ps 119:117
I *h* done judgment and justice ... Ps 119:121
for they *h* made void thy law ... Ps 119:126
any iniquity *h* dominion over me ... Ps 119:133
enemies *h* forgotten thy words ... Ps 119:139
anguish *h* taken hold on me ... Ps 119:143
I *h* known of old that thou hast ... Ps 119:152
Princes *h* persecuted me without a ... Ps 119:161
Great peace *h* they which love thy ... Ps 119:165
I *h* hoped for thy salvation, and ... Ps 119:166
I *h* kept thy precepts and thy ... Ps 119:168
for I *h* chosen thy precepts ... Ps 119:173
I *h* longed for thy salvation, O ... Ps 119:174
I *h* gone astray like a lost sheep ... Ps 119:176
until that he *h* mercy upon us ... Ps 123:2
H mercy upon us, O LORD, *h* ... Ps 123:3
Many a time *h* they afflicted me ... Ps 129:1
Many a time *h* they afflicted me ... Ps 129:2
yet they *h* not prevailed against ... Ps 129:2
of the depths *h* I cried unto thee ... Ps 130:1
Surely I *h* behaved and quieted ... Ps 131:2
for I *h* desired it ... Ps 132:14
I *h* ordained a lamp for mine ... Ps 132:17
They *h* mouths, but they speak not ... Ps 135:16
eyes *h* they, but they see not ... Ps 135:16
They *h* ears, but they hear not ... Ps 135:17
They *h* sharpened their tongues ... Ps 140:3
who *h* purposed to overthrow my ... Ps 140:4
The proud *h* hid a snare for me, ... Ps 140:5
they *h* spread a net by the ... Ps 140:5
they *h* set gins for me ... Ps 140:5
snares which they *h* laid for me ... Ps 141:9
In the way wherein I walked *h* ... Ps 142:3
as those that *h* been long dead ... Ps 143:3
unto my God while I *h* any being ... Ps 146:2
judgments, they *h* not known them ... Ps 147:20
this honour *h* all his saints ... Ps 149:9
let us all *h* one purse ... Prov 1:14 1961
Because I *h* called, and ye refused ... Prov 1:24
I *h* stretched out my hand, and no ... Prov 1:24
But ye *h* set at nought all my ... Prov 1:25
if he *h* done thee no harm ... Prov 3:30
I *h* taught thee in the way of ... Prov 4:11
I *h* led thee in right paths ... Prov 4:11
except they *h* done mischief ... Prov 4:16
How *h* I hated instruction, and my ... Prov 5:12
h not obeyed the voice of my ... Prov 5:13
I *h* peace offerings with me ... Prov 7:14
this day *h* I payed my vows ... Prov 7:14
seek thy face, and I *h* found thee ... Prov 7:15
I *h* decked my bed with coverings ... Prov 7:16
I *h* perfumed my bed with myrrh, ... Prov 7:17
many strong men *h* been slain by ... Prov 7:26
I *h* strength ... Prov 8:14
of the wine which I *h* mingled ... Prov 9:5
wide his lips shall *h* destruction ... Prov 13:3
shall *h* a place of refuge ... Prov 14:26 1961
A wise servant shall *h* rule over ... Prov 17:2
shall *h* part of the inheritance ... Prov 17:2
a servant to *h* rule over princes ... Prov 19:10
he beg in harvest, and *h* nothing ... Prov 20:4
I *h* made my heart clean, I am ... Prov 20:9
I *h* made known to thee this day, ... Prov 22:19
H not I written to thee excellent ... Prov 22:20
landmark, which thy fathers *h* set ... Prov 22:28
a wise child shall *h* joy of him ... Prov 23:24
They *h* stricken me, shalt thou ... Prov 23:35
they *h* beaten me, and I felt it ... Prov 23:35
It is not good to *h* respect of ... Prov 24:23
the prince whom thine eyes *h* seen ... Prov 25:7
thou shalt *h* goats' milk enough ... Prov 27:27
but the upright shall *h* good ... Prov 28:10
and forsaketh them shall *h* mercy ... Prov 28:13
his land shall *h* plenty of bread ... Prov 28:19
persons shall *h* poverty enough ... Prov 28:19
To *h* respect of persons is not ... Prov 28:21
his eyes shall *h* many a curse ... Prov 28:27
shall *h* him become his son at the ... Prov 29:21
h not the understanding of a man ... Prov 30:2
nor *h* the knowledge of the holy ... Prov 30:3 3045
Two things *h* I required of thee ... Prov 30:7
and saith, I *h* done no wickedness ... Prov 30:20
The locusts *h* no king, yet go ... Prov 30:27
that he shall *h* no need of spoil ... Prov 31:11
Many daughters *h* done virtuously, ... Prov 31:29
I *h* seen all the works that are ... Eccl 1:14
h gotten more wisdom than all ... Eccl 1:16
h been before me in Jerusalem ... Eccl 1:16
yet shall he *h* rule over all my ... Eccl 2:19
my labour wherein I *h* laboured ... Eccl 2:19
wherein I *h* shewed myself wise ... Eccl 2:19
I *h* seen the travail, which God ... Eccl 3:10
yea, they *h* all one breath ... Eccl 3:19
because they *h* a good reward for ... Eccl 4:9 3426
lie together, then they *h* heat ... Eccl 4:11
of all that *h* been before them ... Eccl 4:16
evil which I *h* seen under the sun ... Eccl 5:13
Behold that which I *h* seen ... Eccl 5:18
evil which I *h* seen under the sun ... Eccl 6:1
good, and also that he *h* no burial ... Eccl 6:3 1961
giveth life to them that *h* it ... Eccl 7:12 1167
All things *h* I seen in the days ... Eccl 7:15
All this *h* I proved by wisdom ... Eccl 7:23
this *h* I found, saith the ... Eccl 7:27
man among a thousand *h* I found ... Eccl 7:28
among all those *h* I not found ... Eccl 7:28
Lo, this only *h* I found, that God ... Eccl 7:29
but they *h* sought out many ... Eccl 7:29
All this *h* I seen, and applied my ... Eccl 8:9
neither *h* they any more a reward ... Eccl 9:5
neither *h* they any more a portion ... Eccl 9:6
This wisdom *h* I seen also under ... Eccl 9:13
evil which I *h* seen under the sun ... Eccl 10:5
I *h* seen servants upon horses, and ... Eccl 10:7
say, I *h* no pleasure in them ... Eccl 12:1
mine own vineyard *h* I not kept ... Song 1:6
I *h* compared thee, O my love, to ... Song 1:9
for our vines *h* tender grapes ... Song 2:15
I *h* gathered my myrrh with my ... Song 5:1
I *h* eaten my honeycomb with my ... Song 5:1
I *h* drunk my wine with my milk ... Song 5:1
I *h* put off my coat ... Song 5:3
I *h* washed my feet ... Song 5:3
from me, for they *h* overcome me ... Song 6:5
which I *h* laid up for thee, O my ... Song 7:13
We *h* a little sister, and she hath ... Song 8:8
must *h* a thousand, and those that ... Song 8:12
I *h* nourished and brought up ... Is 1:2
they *h* rebelled against me ... Is 1:2
they *h* forsaken the LORD, they ... Is 1:4
they *h* provoked the Holy One of ... Is 1:4
they *h* not been closed, neither ... Is 1:6
we should *h* been as Sodom ... Is 1:9
we should *h* been like unto ... Is 1:9
of the oaks which ye *h* desired ... Is 1:29
for the gardens that ye *h* chosen ... Is 1:29
which their own fingers *h* made ... Is 2:8
for they *h* rewarded evil unto ... Is 3:9
for ye *h* eaten up the vineyard ... Is 3:14
When the Lord shall *h* washed away ... Is 4:4
shall *h* purged the blood of ... Is 4:4
What could *h* been done more to my ... Is 5:4
vineyard, that I *h* not done in it ... Is 5:4
because they *h* no knowledge ... Is 5:13
because they *h* cast away the law ... Is 5:24
for mine eyes *h* seen the King ... Is 6:5
the LORD *h* removed men far away, ... Is 6:12
h taken evil counsel against thee ... Is 7:5
house, days that *h* not come ... Is 7:17
child shall *h* knowledge to cry ... Is 8:4
unto them that *h* familiar spirits ... Is 8:19
in darkness *h* seen a great light ... Is 9:2
Therefore the Lord shall *h* no joy ... Is 9:17
neither shall *h* mercy on their ... Is 9:17
which they *h* prescribed ... Is 10:1
as I *h* done unto Samaria and her ... Is 10:11
strength of my hand I *h* done it ... Is 10:13
I *h* removed the bounds of the ... Is 10:13
h robbed their treasures ... Is 10:13
I *h* put down the inhabitants like ... Is 10:13
h I gathered all the earth ... Is 10:14
they *h* taken up their lodging at ... Is 10:29
I *h* commanded my sanctified ones, ... Is 13:3
I *h* also called my mighty ones ... Is 13:3
they shall *h* no pity on the fruit ... Is 13:18
the LORD will *h* mercy on Jacob ... Is 14:1
saying, Surely as I *h* thought ... Is 14:24
as I *h* purposed, so shall it ... Is 14:24
the abundance they *h* gotten ... Is 15:7
and that which they *h* laid up ... Is 15:7
We *h* heard of the pride of Moab ... Is 16:6
the lords of the heathen *h* broken ... Is 16:8
I *h* made their vintage shouting ... Is 16:10
his eyes shall *h* respect to the ... Is 17:7
that which his fingers *h* made ... Is 17:8
whose land the rivers *h* spoiled ... Is 18:2
whose land the rivers *h* spoiled ... Is 18:7
to them that *h* familiar spirits, ... Is 19:3
they *h* also seduced Egypt, even ... Is 19:13
they *h* caused Egypt to err in ... Is 19:14
sighing thereof *h* I made to cease ... Is 21:2
pangs *h* taken hold upon me, as ... Is 21:3
that which I *h* heard of the LORD ... Is 21:10
of Israel, *h* I declared unto you ... Is 21:10
together, which *h* fled from far ... Is 22:3
Ye *h* seen also the breaches of ... Is 22:9
ye *h* numbered the houses of ... Is 22:10
the houses *h* ye broken down to ... Is 22:10
but ye *h* not looked unto the ... Is 22:11
pass over the sea, *h* replenished ... Is 23:2
there also shalt thou *h* no rest ... Is 23:12
because they *h* transgressed the ... Is 24:5
of the earth *h* we heard songs ... Is 24:16
dealers *h* dealt treacherously ... Is 24:16
the treacherous dealers *h* dealt ... Is 24:16
we *h* waited for him, and he will ... Is 25:9
we *h* waited for him, we will be ... Is 25:9
We *h* a strong city ... Is 26:1
O LORD, *h* we waited for thee ... Is 26:8
With my soul *h* I desired thee in ... Is 26:9
thee *h* had dominion over us ... Is 26:13
in trouble *h* they visited thee ... Is 26:16
so *h* we been in thy sight, O LORD ... Is 26:17
We *h* been with child ... Is 26:18
we *h* been in pain, we *h* as it ... Is 26:18
we *h* not wrought any deliverance ... Is 26:18
neither *h* the inhabitants of the ... Is 26:18
them will not *h* mercy on them ... Is 27:11
But they also *h* erred through ... Is 28:7
the prophet *h* erred through ... Is 28:7
Because ye *h* said, We *h* made a ... Is 28:15
We *h* made a covenant with death, ... Is 28:15
for we *h* made lies our refuge, and ... Is 28:15
and under falsehood *h* we hid ... Is 28:15
for I *h* heard from the Lord GOD ... Is 28:22
but *h* removed their heart far ... Is 29:13
Egypt, and *h* not asked at my mouth ... Is 30:2
therefore *h* I cried concerning ... Is 30:7
that he may *h* mercy upon you ... Is 30:18
Ye shall *h* a song, as in the ... Is 30:29 1961
of Israel *h* deeply revolted ... Is 31:6
which your own hands *h* made unto ... Is 31:7
we *h* waited for thee ... Is 33:2
that are far off, what I *h* done ... Is 33:13
are but vain words) I *h* counsel ... Is 36:5
h they delivered Samaria out of ... Is 36:19
that *h* delivered their land out ... Is 36:20
king of Assyria *h* blasphemed me ... Is 37:6
h done to all lands by destroying ... Is 37:11
H the gods of the nations ... Is 37:12
them which my fathers *h* destroyed ... Is 37:12
the kings of Assyria *h* laid waste ... Is 37:18
h cast their gods into the fire ... Is 37:19
therefore they *h* destroyed them ... Is 37:19
I *h* digged, and drunk water ... Is 37:25
with the sole of my feet *h* I ... Is 37:25
heard long ago, how I *h* done it ... Is 37:26
ancient times, that I *h* formed it ... Is 37:26
now *h* I brought it to pass, that ... Is 37:26
how I *h* walked before thee in ... Is 38:3
h done that which is good in thy ... Is 38:3
I *h* heard thy prayer, I *h* seen ... Is 38:5
I *h* cut off like a weaver my life ... Is 38:12
What *h* they seen in thine house ... Is 39:4
that is in mine house *h* they seen ... Is 39:4
that I *h* not shewed them ... Is 39:4
that which thy fathers *h* laid up ... Is 39:6
H ye not known? ... Is 40:21
h ye not heard? ... Is 40:21
h ye not understood from the ... Is 40:21
to them that *h* no might he ... Is 40:29
my servant, Jacob whom I *h* chosen ... Is 41:8
Thou whom I *h* taken from the ends ... Is 41:9
I *h* chosen thee, and not cast thee ... Is 41:9
I *h* raised up one from the north, ... Is 41:25
I *h* put my spirit upon him ... Is 42:1
till he *h* set judgment in the ... Is 42:4
I the LORD *h* called thee in ... Is 42:6
I *h* long time holden my peace ... Is 42:14
I *h* been still, and refrained ... Is 42:14
in paths that they *h* not known ... Is 42:16
LORD, he against whom we *h* sinned ... Is 42:24
for I *h* redeemed thee, I *h* ... Is 43:1
honourable, and I *h* loved thee ... Is 43:4
for I *h* created him for my glory, ... Is 43:7
I *h* formed him ... Is 43:7
yea, I *h* made him ... Is 43:7
the blind people that *h* eyes ... Is 43:8 3426
and the deaf that *h* ears ... Is 43:8
and my servant whom I *h* chosen ... Is 43:10
I *h* declared, and *h* saved, and I ... Is 43:12
I *h* shewed, when there was no ... Is 43:12
For your sake I *h* sent to Babylon ... Is 43:14
h brought down all their nobles, ... Is 43:14
This people *h* I formed for myself ... Is 43:21
I *h* not caused thee to serve with ... Is 43:23
thy teachers *h* transgressed ... Is 43:27
Therefore I *h* profaned the ... Is 43:28
h given Jacob to the curse, and ... Is 43:28
and Israel, whom I *h* chosen ... Is 44:1
and thou, Jesurun, whom I *h* chosen ... Is 44:2
h not I told thee from that time, ... Is 44:8
from that time, and *h* declared it ... Is 44:8
Aha, I am warm, I *h* seen the fire ... Is 44:16
They *h* not known nor understood ... Is 44:18
I *h* burned part of it in the fire ... Is 44:19
also I *h* baked bread upon the ... Is 44:19
I *h* roasted flesh, and eaten it ... Is 44:19
I *h* formed thee ... Is 44:21
I *h* blotted out, as a thick cloud ... Is 44:22
for I *h* redeemed thee ... Is 44:22
whose right hand I *h* holden ... Is 45:1
I *h* even called thee by thy name ... Is 45:4
I *h* surnamed thee, though thou ... Is 45:4
I the LORD *h* created it ... Is 45:8
I *h* made the earth, and created ... Is 45:12
h stretched out the heavens ... Is 45:12
and all their host *h* I commanded ... Is 45:12
I *h* raised him up in ... Is 45:13
I *h* not spoken in secret, in a ... Is 45:19
they *h* no knowledge that set up ... Is 45:20
h not I the LORD ... Is 45:21
I *h* sworn by myself, the word is ... Is 45:23
in the LORD *h* I righteousness and ... Is 45:24
I *h* made, and I will bear ... Is 46:4
I *h* spoken it, I will also bring ... Is 46:11
I *h* purposed it, I will also do ... Is 46:11
I *h* polluted mine inheritance, and ... Is 47:6
I *h* declared the former things ... Is 48:3
I *h* even from the beginning ... Is 48:5
I *h* shewed thee new things from ... Is 48:6
I *h* refined thee, but not with ... Is 48:10
I *h* chosen thee in the furnace of ... Is 48:10
I, even I, *h* spoken ... Is 48:15
yea, I *h* called him ... Is 48:15
I *h* brought him, and he shall make ... Is 48:15
I *h* not spoken in secret from the ... Is 48:16
his name should not *h* been cut ... Is 48:19
I *h* laboured in vain, I *h* ... Is 49:4
an acceptable time *h* I heard thee ... Is 49:8
day of salvation *h* I helped thee ... Is 49:8
will *h* mercy upon his afflicted ... Is 49:13
that she should not *h* compassion ... Is 49:15
I *h* graven thee upon the palms of ... Is 49:16
The children which thou shalt *h* ... Is 49:20
seeing I *h* lost my children, and ... Is 49:21
divorcement, whom I *h* put away ... Is 50:1
is it to whom I *h* sold you ... Is 50:1
iniquities *h* ye sold yourselves ... Is 50:1
or *h* I no power to deliver ... Is 50:2
therefore *h* I set my face like a ... Is 50:7
in the sparks that ye *h* kindled ... Is 50:11
This shall ye *h* of mine hand ... Is 50:11 1961
I *h* put my words in thy mouth, and ... Is 51:16
I *h* covered thee in the shadow of ... Is 51:16
Thy sons *h* fainted, they lie at ... Is 51:20
I *h* taken out of thine hand the ... Is 51:22
which *h* said to thy soul, Bow ... Is 51:23
Ye *h* sold yourselves for nought ... Is 52:3
what *h* I here, saith the LORD, ... Is 52:5

All we like sheep *h* gone astray.......... Is 53:6
we *h* turned every one to his own .... Is 53:6
a small moment *h* I forsaken thee .... Is 54:7
kindness will I *h* mercy on thee .... Is 54:8
for as I *h* sworn that the waters.......... Is 54:9
so *h* I sworn that I would not be .... Is 54:9
I *h* created the smith that.......... Is 54:16
I *h* created the waster to destroy .... Is 54:16
I *h* given him for a witness to.......... Is 55:4
LORD, and he will *h* mercy upon him ... Is 55:7
dogs which can never *h* enough.......... Is 56:11 3045
h not I held my peace even of old .... Is 57:11
me, and the souls which I *h* made .... Is 57:16
I *h* seen his ways, and will heal.......... Is 57:18
Wherefore *h* we fasted, say they,.......... Is 58:3
wherefore *h* we afflicted our soul.......... Is 58:3
Is it such a fast that I *h* chosen.......... Is 58:5
not this the fast that I *h* chosen.......... Is 58:6
But your iniquities *h* separated.......... Is 59:2
your sins *h* hid his face from you.......... Is 59:2
your lips *h* spoken lies, your.......... Is 59:3
they *h* made them crooked paths.......... Is 59:8
words which I *h* put in thy mouth.......... Is 59:21
but in my favour *h* I had mercy on .... Is 60:10
For your shame ye shall *h* double.......... Is 61:7
I *h* set watchmen upon thy walls,.......... Is 62:6
But they that *h* gathered it shall .... Is 62:9
they that *h* brought it together.......... Is 62:9
I *h* trodden the winepress alone .... Is 63:3
The people of thy holiness *h*.......... Is 63:18
our adversaries *h* trodden down .... Is 63:18
of the world men *h* not heard .... Is 64:4
for we *h* sinned.......... Is 64:5
like the wind, *h* taken us away.......... Is 64:6
I *h* spread out my hands all the.......... Is 65:2
which *h* burned incense upon the.......... Is 65:7
for my people that *h* sought me.......... Is 65:10
made, and all those things *h* been.......... Is 66:2
they *h* chosen their own ways, and .... Is 66:3
that *h* not heard my fame.......... Is 66:19
neither *h* seen my glory.......... Is 66:19
that *h* transgressed against me.......... Is 66:24
I *h* put my words in thy mouth.......... Jer 1:9
I *h* this day set thee over the.......... Jer 1:10
who *h* forsaken me, and *h* burned .... Jer 1:16
I *h* made thee this day a defenced.......... Jer 1:18
What iniquity *h* your fathers.......... Jer 2:5
h walked after vanity, and are.......... Jer 2:5
but my people *h* changed their.......... Jer 2:11
For my people *h* committed two .... Jer 2:13
they *h* forsaken me the fountain .... Jer 2:13
Tahapanes *h* broken the crown of .... Jer 2:16
of old time I *h* broken thy yoke .... Jer 2:20
I *h* not gone after Baalim.......... Jer 2:23
for I *h* loved strangers, and after.......... Jer 2:25
for they *h* turned their back unto.......... Jer 2:27
ye all *h* transgressed against me,.......... Jer 2:29
In vain *h* I smitten your children.......... Jer 2:30
H I been a wilderness unto Israel.......... Jer 2:31
yet my people *h* forgotten me days .... Jer 2:32
I *h* not found it by secret search.......... Jer 2:34
thou sayest, I *h* not sinned .... Jer 2:35
the showers *h* been withholden .... Jer 3:3
ye *h* not obeyed my voice, saith.......... Jer 3:13
I *h* given for an inheritance unto.......... Jer 3:18
so *h* ye dealt treacherously with.......... Jer 3:20
for they *h* perverted their way,.......... Jer 3:21
they *h* forgotten the LORD their.......... Jer 3:21
for we *h* sinned against the LORD.......... Jer 3:25
h not obeyed the voice of the.......... Jer 3:25
saying, Ye shall *h* peace.......... Jer 4:10 1961
thy doings *h* procured these .... Jer 4:18
is foolish, they *h* not known me .... Jer 4:22
they *h* none understanding .... Jer 4:22
to do good they *h* no knowledge.......... Jer 4:22
because I *h* spoken it, I *h*.......... Jer 4:28
For I *h* heard a voice as of a .... Jer 4:31
them, but they *h* not grieved.......... Jer 5:3
but they *h* refused to receive.......... Jer 5:3
they *h* made their faces harder .... Jer 5:3
they *h* refused to return .... Jer 5:3
for they *h* known the way of the.......... Jer 5:5
but these *h* altogether broken the.......... Jer 5:5
thy children *h* forsaken me.......... Jer 5:7
the house of Judah *h* dealt very .... Jer 5:11
They *h* belied the LORD, and said,.......... Jer 5:12
Like as ye *h* forsaken me, and .... Jer 5:19
which *h* eyes, and see not .... Jer 5:21
which *h* ears, and hear not .... Jer 5:21
which *h* placed the sand for the.......... Jer 5:22
Your iniquities *h* turned away .... Jer 5:25
your sins *h* withholden good .... Jer 5:25
and my people love to *h* it so.......... Jer 5:31
I *h* likened the daughter of Zion .... Jer 6:2
they *h* no delight in it.......... Jer 6:10
They *h* healed also the hurt of.......... Jer 6:14
because they *h* not hearkened unto.......... Jer 6:19
they are cruel, and *h* no mercy.......... Jer 6:23
We *h* heard the fame thereof .... Jer 6:24
I *h* set thee for a tower and a .... Jer 6:27
even I *h* seen it, saith the LORD.......... Jer 7:11
because ye *h* done all these works.......... Jer 7:13
fathers, as I *h* done to Shiloh .... Jer 7:14
as I *h* cast out all your brethren.......... Jer 7:15
the ways that I *h* commanded you .... Jer 7:23
day I *h* even sent unto you all my.......... Jer 7:25
of Judah *h* done evil in my sight.......... Jer 7:30
they *h* set their abominations in.......... Jer 7:30
they *h* built the high places of.......... Jer 7:31
host of heaven, whom they *h* loved.......... Jer 8:2
and after whom they *h* walked.......... Jer 8:2
and whom they *h* sought.......... Jer 8:2
and whom they *h* worshipped.......... Jer 8:2
places whither I *h* driven them.......... Jer 8:3
wickedness, saying, What *h* I done.......... Jer 8:6
they *h* rejected the word of the.......... Jer 8:9
For they *h* healed the hurt of the.......... Jer 8:11
the things that I *h* given them.......... Jer 8:13
because we *h* sinned against the .... Jer 8:14
h devoured the land, and all that .... Jer 8:16
Why *h* they provoked me to anger.......... Jer 8:19
they *h* taught their tongue to.......... Jer 9:5
Because they *h* forsaken my law.......... Jer 9:13
h not obeyed my voice, neither.......... Jer 9:13
But *h* walked after the.......... Jer 9:14
they nor their fathers *h* known.......... Jer 9:16
them, till I *h* consumed them .... Jer 9:16
because we *h* forsaken the land,.......... Jer 9:19
our dwellings *h* cast us out.......... Jer 9:19
The gods that *h* not made the.......... Jer 10:11
brutish, and *h* not sought the LORD.......... Jer 10:21
for they *h* eaten up Jacob, and .... Jer 10:25
h made his habitation desolate.......... Jer 10:25
which I *h* sworn unto your fathers.......... Jer 11:5
the house of Judah *h* broken my.......... Jer 11:10
h ye set up altars to that.......... Jer 11:13
which they *h* done against.......... Jer 11:17
for unto thee *h* I revealed my .... Jer 11:20
them, yea, they *h* taken root .... Jer 12:2
they *h* wearied thee, then how .... Jer 12:5
even they *h* dealt treacherously.......... Jer 12:6
they *h* called a multitude after.......... Jer 12:6
I *h* forsaken mine house, I *h*.......... Jer 12:7
I *h* given the dearly beloved of.......... Jer 12:7
therefore *h* I hated it.......... Jer 12:8
Many pastors *h* destroyed my.......... Jer 12:10
they *h* trodden my portion under.......... Jer 12:10
they *h* made my pleasant portion a .... Jer 12:10
They *h* made it desolate, and being .... Jer 12:11
no flesh shall *h* peace.......... Jer 12:12
They *h* sown wheat, but shall reap.......... Jer 12:13
they *h* put themselves to pain,.......... Jer 12:13
I *h* caused my people Israel to.......... Jer 12:14
after that I *h* plucked them out I.......... Jer 12:15
h compassion on them, and will .... Jer 12:15
so *h* I caused to cleave unto me.......... Jer 13:11
nor *h* mercy, but destroy them .... Jer 13:14
I *h* seen thine adulteries, and thy.......... Jer 13:27
their nobles *h* sent their little.......... Jer 14:3
we *h* sinned against thee .... Jer 14:7
Thus *h* they loved to wander.......... Jer 14:10
they *h* not refrained their feet,.......... Jer 14:10
sword, neither shall ye *h* famine.......... Jer 14:13
neither *h* I commanded them,.......... Jer 14:14
they shall *h* none to bury them, ... Jer 14:16
for we *h* sinned against thee .... Jer 14:20
For who shall *h* pity upon thee, O .... Jer 15:5
I *h* brought upon them against the.......... Jer 15:8
I *h* caused him to fall upon it.......... Jer 15:8
I *h* neither lent on usury, nor.......... Jer 15:10
nor men *h* lent to me on usury.......... Jer 15:10
for thy sake I *h* suffered rebuke.......... Jer 15:15
neither shalt thou *h* sons or.......... Jer 16:2
for I *h* taken away my peace from .... Jer 16:5
or what is our sin that we *h*.......... Jer 16:10
your fathers *h* forsaken me.......... Jer 16:11
h walked after other gods, and .... Jer 16:11
h served them, and *h* worshipped.......... Jer 16:11
h forsaken me, and *h* not kept.......... Jer 16:11
ye *h* done worse than your fathers.......... Jer 16:12
because they *h* defiled my land,.......... Jer 16:18
they *h* filled mine inheritance.......... Jer 16:18
our fathers *h* inherited lies.......... Jer 16:19
for ye *h* kindled a fire in mine.......... Jer 17:4
because they *h* forsaken the LORD,.......... Jer 17:13
I *h* not hastened from being a.......... Jer 17:16
neither *h* I desired the woeful .... Jer 17:16
against whom I *h* pronounced .... Jer 18:8
they *h* burned incense to vanity,.......... Jer 18:15
they *h* caused them to stumble in.......... Jer 18:15
for they *h* digged a pit for my.......... Jer 18:20
for they *h* digged a pit to take.......... Jer 18:22
Because they *h* forsaken me.......... Jer 19:4
h estranged this place, and *h*.......... Jer 19:4
they nor their fathers *h* known.......... Jer 19:4
h filled this place with the.......... Jer 19:4
They *h* built also the high places.......... Jer 19:5
h burned incense unto all the.......... Jer 19:13
h poured out drink offerings unto.......... Jer 19:13
that I *h* pronounced against it .... Jer 19:15
because they *h* hardened their.......... Jer 19:15
for unto thee *h* I opened my cause.......... Jer 20:12
my mother might *h* been my grave .... Jer 20:17
neither *h* pity, nor *h* mercy.......... Jer 21:7
For I *h* set my face against this.......... Jer 21:10
Because they *h* forsaken the .... Jer 22:9
whither they *h* led him captive.......... Jer 22:12
Ye *h* scattered my flock, and.......... Jer 23:2
them away, and *h* not visited them .... Jer 23:2
countries whither I *h* driven them .... Jer 23:3
in my house *h* I found their.......... Jer 23:11
I *h* seen folly in the prophets of .... Jer 23:13
I *h* seen also in the prophets of .... Jer 23:14
LORD hath said, Ye shall *h* peace.......... Jer 23:17 1961
not return, until he *h* executed.......... Jer 23:20
till he *h* performed the thoughts.......... Jer 23:20
I *h* not sent these prophets, yet.......... Jer 23:21
I *h* not spoken to them, yet they .... Jer 23:21
then they should *h* turned them.......... Jer 23:22
I *h* heard what the prophets said,.......... Jer 23:25
I *h* dreamed, I *h* dreamed.......... Jer 23:25
as their fathers *h* forgotten my.......... Jer 23:27
for ye *h* perverted the words of.......... Jer 23:36
I *h* sent unto you, saying, Ye .... Jer 23:38
whom I *h* sent out of this place.......... Jer 24:5
I *h* spoken unto you, rising early .... Jer 25:3
but ye *h* not hearkened.......... Jer 25:3
but ye *h* not hearkened, nor.......... Jer 25:4
Yet ye *h* not hearkened unto me,.......... Jer 25:7
Because ye *h* not heard my words,.......... Jer 25:8
which I *h* pronounced against it.......... Jer 25:13
shepherds shall *h* no way to flee .... Jer 25:35
which I *h* set before you,.......... Jer 26:4
them, but ye *h* not hearkened.......... Jer 26:5
as ye *h* heard with your ears.......... Jer 26:11
all the words that ye *h* heard.......... Jer 26:12
I *h* made the earth, the man and.......... Jer 27:5
h given it unto whom it seemed.......... Jer 27:5
now *h* I given all these lands.......... Jer 27:6
the beasts of the field *h* I given .... Jer 27:6
until I *h* consumed them by his.......... Jer 27:8
For I *h* not sent them, saith the .... Jer 27:15
I *h* broken the yoke of the king .... Jer 28:2
prophets that *h* been before me.......... Jer 28:8
I *h* put a yoke of iron upon the .... Jer 28:14
I *h* given him the beasts of the.......... Jer 28:14
whom I *h* caused to be carried.......... Jer 29:4
I *h* caused you to be carried away.......... Jer 29:7
peace thereof shall ye *h* peace .... Jer 29:7
I *h* not sent them, saith the LORD.......... Jer 29:9
the places whither I *h* driven you.......... Jer 29:14
Because ye *h* said, The LORD hath .... Jer 29:15
nations whither I *h* driven them.......... Jer 29:18
Because they *h* not hearkened to.......... Jer 29:19
whom I *h* sent from Jerusalem to.......... Jer 29:20
Because they *h* committed villany .... Jer 29:23
h committed adultery with their.......... Jer 29:23
h spoken lying words in my name,.......... Jer 29:23
which I *h* not commanded them .... Jer 29:23
he shall not *h* a man to dwell.......... Jer 29:32 1961
I *h* spoken unto thee in a book .... Jer 30:2
We *h* heard a voice of trembling,.......... Jer 30:5
whither I *h* scattered thee.......... Jer 30:11
All thy lovers *h* forgotten thee.......... Jer 30:14
for I *h* wounded thee with the.......... Jer 30:14
I *h* done these things unto thee.......... Jer 30:15
h mercy on his dwellingplaces .... Jer 30:18
not return, until he *h* done it.......... Jer 30:24
until he *h* performed the intents.......... Jer 30:24
Yea, I *h* loved thee with an.......... Jer 31:3
lovingkindness *h* I drawn thee.......... Jer 31:3
I *h* surely heard Ephraim.......... Jer 31:18
I will surely *h* mercy upon him,.......... Jer 31:20
For I *h* satiated the weary soul,.......... Jer 31:25
I *h* replenished every sorrowful.......... Jer 31:25
that like as I *h* watched over .... Jer 31:28
The fathers *h* eaten a sour grape,.......... Jer 31:29
Israel for all that they *h* done.......... Jer 31:37
they *h* done nothing of all that.......... Jer 32:23
upon whose roofs they *h* offered .... Jer 32:29
the children of Judah *h* only done .... Jer 32:30
for the children of Israel *h* only.......... Jer 32:30
which they *h* done to provoke me .... Jer 32:32
they *h* turned unto me the back,.......... Jer 32:33
yet they *h* not hearkened to.......... Jer 32:33
whither I *h* driven them in mine.......... Jer 32:37
Like as I *h* brought all this .... Jer 32:42
the good that I *h* promised them.......... Jer 32:42
whom I *h* slain in mine anger and.......... Jer 33:5
I *h* hid my face from this city .... Jer 33:5
whereby they *h* sinned against me.......... Jer 33:8
iniquities, whereby they *h* sinned.......... Jer 33:8
whereby they *h* transgressed.......... Jer 33:8
I *h* promised unto the house of .... Jer 33:14
that he should not *h* a son to.......... Jer 33:21 1961
not what this people *h* spoken .... Jer 33:24
thus they *h* despised my people,.......... Jer 33:24
and if I *h* not appointed the.......... Jer 33:25
to return, and *h* mercy on them .... Jer 33:26
for I *h* pronounced the word,.......... Jer 34:5
Ye *h* not hearkened unto me, in.......... Jer 34:17
that *h* transgressed my covenant .... Jer 34:18
which *h* not performed the words.......... Jer 34:18
nor plant vineyard, nor *h* any .... Jer 35:7
Thus *h* we obeyed the voice of.......... Jer 35:8
neither *h* we vineyard, nor field,.......... Jer 35:9 1961
But we *h* dwelt in tents, and *h*.......... Jer 35:10
I *h* spoken unto you, rising early .... Jer 35:14
I *h* sent also unto you all my .... Jer 35:15
the land which I *h* given to you .... Jer 35:15
but ye *h* not inclined your ear,.......... Jer 35:15
h performed the commandment of.......... Jer 35:16
that I *h* pronounced against them .... Jer 35:17
because I *h* spoken unto them.......... Jer 35:17
but they *h* not heard .... Jer 35:17
I *h* called unto them .... Jer 35:17
but they *h* not answered.......... Jer 35:17
Because ye *h* obeyed the .... Jer 35:18
therein all the words that I *h*.......... Jer 36:2
He shall *h* none to sit upon the .... Jer 36:30 1961
all the evil that I *h* pronounced.......... Jer 36:31
What *h* I offended against thee,.......... Jer 37:18
that ye *h* put me in prison .... Jer 37:18
for he shall *h* his life for a.......... Jer 38:2
these men *h* done evil in all that.......... Jer 38:9
h done to Jeremiah the prophet.......... Jer 38:9
whom they *h* cast into the dungeon.......... Jer 38:9
say, Thy friends *h* set thee on.......... Jer 38:22
and *h* prevailed against thee.......... Jer 38:22
hear that I *h* talked with thee.......... Jer 38:25
because ye *h* sinned against the .... Jer 40:3
h not obeyed his voice, therefore .... Jer 40:3
in your cities that ye *h* taken.......... Jer 40:10
for we *h* treasures in the field, ... Jer 41:8 3426
said unto them, I *h* heard you.......... Jer 42:4
the evil that I *h* done unto you .... Jer 42:10
that he may *h* mercy upon you, and .... Jer 42:12
trumpet, nor *h* hunger of bread.......... Jer 42:14
know certainly that I *h*.......... Jer 42:19
now I *h* this day declared it to.......... Jer 42:21
but ye *h* not obeyed the voice of.......... Jer 42:21
upon these stones that I *h* hid .... Jer 43:10

Ye *h* seen all the evil that I ... Jer 44:2
that I *h* brought upon Jerusalem ... Jer 44:2
they *h* committed to provoke me to ... Jer 44:3
H ye forgotten the wickedness of ... Jer 44:9
which they *h* committed in the ... Jer 44:9
neither *h* they feared, nor walked ... Jer 44:10
that *h* set their faces to go into ... Jer 44:12
as I *h* punished Jerusalem, by the ... Jer 44:13
to the which they *h* a desire to ... Jer 44:14 5375
offerings unto her, as we *h* done ... Jer 44:17
we *h* wanted all things, and *h* ... Jer 44:18
abominations which ye *h* committed ... Jer 44:22
Because ye *h* burned incense, and ... Jer 44:23
because ye *h* sinned against the ... Jer 44:23
h not obeyed the voice of the ... Jer 44:23
your wives *h* both spoken with ... Jer 44:25
perform our vows that we *h* vowed ... Jer 44:25
I *h* sworn by my great name, saith ... Jer 44:26
that which I *h* built will I break ... Jer 45:4
that which I *h* planted I will ... Jer 45:4
Wherefore *h* I seen them dismayed ... Jer 46:5
The nations *h* heard of thy shame, ... Jer 46:12
nations whither I *h* driven thee ... Jer 46:28
in Heshbon they *h* devised evil ... Jer 48:2
her little ones *h* caused a cry to ... Jer 48:4
h heard a cry of destruction ... Jer 48:5
We *h* heard the pride of Moab, (he ... Jer 48:29
I *h* caused wine to fail from the ... Jer 48:33
h they uttered their voice, from ... Jer 48:34
for I *h* broken Moab like a vessel ... Jer 48:38
will destroy till they *h* enough ... Jer 49:9
But I *h* made Esau bare, I *h* ... Jer 49:10
of the cup *h* assuredly drunken ... Jer 49:12
For I *h* sworn by myself, saith ... Jer 49:13
I *h* heard a rumour from the LORD, ... Jer 49:14
for they *h* heard evil tidings ... Jer 49:23
sorrows *h* taken her, as a woman ... Jer 49:24
which *h* neither gates nor bars, ... Jer 49:31
them, till I *h* consumed them ... Jer 49:37
their shepherds *h* caused them to ... Jer 50:6
they *h* turned them away on the ... Jer 50:6
they *h* gone from mountain to hill ... Jer 50:6
they *h* forgotten their ... Jer 50:6
that found them *h* devoured them ... Jer 50:7
because they *h* sinned against the ... Jer 50:7
the lions *h* driven him away ... Jer 50:17
as I *h* punished the king of ... Jer 50:18
to all that I *h* commanded thee ... Jer 50:21
I *h* laid a snare for thee, and ... Jer 50:24
the nations *h* drunken of her wine ... Jer 51:7
We would *h* healed Babylon, but ... Jer 51:9
all their evil that they *h* done ... Jer 51:24
men of Babylon *h* forborn to fight ... Jer 51:30
they *h* remained in their holds ... Jer 51:30
they *h* burned her dwellingplaces ... Jer 51:30
the reeds they *h* burned with fire ... Jer 51:32
Ye that *h* escaped the sword, go ... Jer 51:50
because we *h* heard reproach ... Jer 51:51
all her friends *h* dealt ... Lam 1:2
because they *h* seen her nakedness ... Lam 1:8
they *h* given their pleasant ... Lam 1:11
for I *h* rebelled against his ... Lam 1:18
for I *h* grievously rebelled ... Lam 1:20
They *h* heard that I sigh ... Lam 1:21
all mine enemies *h* heard of my ... Lam 1:21
they *h* made a noise in the house ... Lam 2:7
they *h* cast up dust upon their ... Lam 2:10
they *h* girded themselves with ... Lam 2:10
Thy prophets *h* seen vain and ... Lam 2:14
they *h* not discovered thine ... Lam 2:14
but *h* seen for thee false burdens ... Lam 2:14
All thine enemies *h* opened their ... Lam 2:16
they say, We *h* swallowed her up ... Lam 2:16
we *h* found, we *h* seen it ... Lam 2:16
those that I *h* swaddled and ... Lam 2:22
to my mind, therefore *h* I hope ... Lam 3:21
grief, yet will he *h* compassion ... Lam 3:32
h transgressed and *h* rebelled ... Lam 3:42
All our enemies *h* opened their ... Lam 3:46
They *h* cut off my life in the ... Lam 3:53
women *h* sodden their own children ... Lam 4:10
would not *h* believed that the ... Lam 4:12
the enemy should *h* entered into ... Lam 4:12
that *h* shed the blood of the just ... Lam 4:13
They *h* wandered as blind men in ... Lam 4:14
they *h* polluted themselves with ... Lam 4:14
in our watching we *h* watched for ... Lam 4:17
We *h* drunken our water for money ... Lam 5:4
we labour, and *h* no rest ... Lam 5:5
We *h* given the hand to the ... Lam 5:6
Our fathers *h* sinned, and are not ... Lam 5:7
we *h* borne their iniquities ... Lam 5:7
Servants *h* ruled over us ... Lam 5:8
The elders *h* ceased from the gate ... Lam 5:14
woe unto us, that we *h* sinned ... Lam 5:16
their fathers *h* transgressed ... Eze 2:3
they would *h* hearkened unto thee ... Eze 3:6
I *h* made thy face strong against ... Eze 3:8
than flint *h* I made thy forehead ... Eze 3:9
I *h* made thee a watchman unto the ... Eze 3:17
For I *h* laid upon thee the years ... Eze 4:5
I *h* appointed thee each day for a ... Eze 4:6
from my youth up even till now *h* ... Eze 4:14
I *h* given thee cow's dung for ... Eze 4:15
I *h* set it in the midst of the ... Eze 5:5
for they *h* refused my judgments ... Eze 5:6
they *h* not walked in them ... Eze 5:6
h not walked in my statutes, ... Eze 5:7
neither *h* kept my judgments, ... Eze 5:7
neither *h* done according to the ... Eze 5:7
in thee that which I *h* not done ... Eze 5:9
spare, neither will I *h* any pity ... Eze 5:11
I the LORD *h* spoken it in my zeal ... Eze 5:13
when I *h* accomplished my fury in ... Eze 5:13

I the LORD *h* spoken it ... Eze 5:15
I the LORD *h* spoken it ... Eze 5:17
that ye may *h* some that shall ... Eze 6:8 1961
they *h* committed in all their ... Eze 6:9
that I *h* not said in vain that I ... Eze 6:10
spare thee, neither will I *h* pity ... Eze 7:4
not spare, neither will I *h* pity ... Eze 7:9
They *h* blown the trumpet, even to ... Eze 7:14
therefore *h* I set it far from ... Eze 7:20
for they *h* filled the land with ... Eze 8:17
h returned to provoke me to anger ... Eze 8:17
not spare, neither will I *h* pity ... Eze 8:18
Cause them that *h* charge over the ... Eze 9:1
your eye spare, neither *h* ye pity ... Eze 9:5
not spare, neither will I *h* pity ... Eze 9:10
I *h* done as thou hast commanded ... Eze 9:11
Thus *h* ye said, O house of Israel ... Eze 11:5
Ye *h* multiplied your slain in ... Eze 11:6
ye *h* filled the streets thereof ... Eze 11:6
Your slain whom ye *h* laid in the ... Eze 11:7
Ye *h* feared the sword ... Eze 11:8
for ye *h* not walked in my ... Eze 11:12
but *h* done after the manners of ... Eze 11:12
inhabitants of Jerusalem *h* said ... Eze 11:15
Although I *h* cast them far off ... Eze 11:16
although I *h* scattered them among ... Eze 11:16
where ye *h* been scattered ... Eze 11:17
which *h* eyes to see, and see not ... Eze 12:2
they *h* ears to hear, and hear not ... Eze 12:2
for I *h* set thee for a sign unto ... Eze 12:6
like as I *h* done, so shall it be ... Eze 12:11
that ye *h* in the land of Israel ... Eze 12:22
which I *h* spoken shall be done ... Eze 12:28
own spirit, and *h* seen nothing ... Eze 13:3
Ye *h* not gone up into the gaps, ... Eze 13:5
They *h* seen vanity and lying ... Eze 13:6
they *h* made others to hope that ... Eze 13:6
H ye not seen a vain vision ... Eze 13:7
and *h* ye not spoken a lying ... Eze 13:7
albeit I *h* not spoken ... Eze 13:7
Because ye *h* spoken vanity, and ... Eze 13:8
because they *h* seduced my people ... Eze 13:10
daubing wherewith ye *h* daubed it ... Eze 13:12
h daubed with untempered morter ... Eze 13:14
upon them that *h* daubed it with ... Eze 13:15
Because with lies ye *h* made the ... Eze 13:22
sad, whom I *h* not made sad ... Eze 13:22
these men *h* set up their idols in ... Eze 14:3
I the LORD *h* deceived that ... Eze 14:9
that I *h* brought upon Jerusalem ... Eze 14:22
all that I *h* brought upon it ... Eze 14:22
ye shall know that I *h* not done ... Eze 14:23
cause all that I *h* done in it ... Eze 14:23
which I *h* given to the fire for ... Eze 15:6
because they *h* committed a ... Eze 15:8
to *h* compassion upon thee ... Eze 16:5
I *h* caused thee to multiply as ... Eze 16:7
therefore I *h* stretched out my ... Eze 16:27
h diminished thine ordinary food, ... Eze 16:27
know that I the LORD *h* spoken it ... Eze 17:21
LORD *h* brought down the high tree ... Eze 17:24
h exalted the low tree, *h* ... Eze 17:24
h made the dry tree to flourish ... Eze 17:24
the LORD *h* spoken and *h* done it ... Eze 17:24
The fathers *h* eaten sour grapes, ... Eze 18:2
ye shall not *h* occasion any more ... Eze 18:3
H I any pleasure at all that the ... Eze 18:23
whereby ye *h* transgressed ... Eze 18:31
For I *h* no pleasure in the death ... Eze 18:32
this your fathers *h* blasphemed me ... Eze 20:27
in that they *h* committed a ... Eze 20:27
wherein ye *h* been scattered ... Eze 20:41
wherein ye *h* been defiled ... Eze 20:43
your evils that ye *h* committed ... Eze 20:43
when I *h* wrought with you for my ... Eze 20:44
see that I the LORD *h* kindled it ... Eze 20:48
flesh may know that I the LORD *h* ... Eze 21:5
I *h* set the point of the sword ... Eze 21:15
I the LORD *h* said it ... Eze 21:17
sight, to them that *h* sworn oaths ... Eze 21:23
Because ye *h* made your iniquity ... Eze 21:24
when iniquity shall *h* an end ... Eze 21:25
their iniquity shall *h* an end ... Eze 21:29
for I the LORD *h* spoken it ... Eze 21:32
therefore *h* I made thee a ... Eze 22:4
In thee *h* they set light by ... Eze 22:7
in the midst of thee *h* they dealt ... Eze 22:7
in thee *h* they vexed the ... Eze 22:7
In thee *h* they discovered their ... Eze 22:10
in thee *h* they humbled her that ... Eze 22:10
In thee *h* they taken gifts to ... Eze 22:12
therefore I *h* smitten mine hand ... Eze 22:13
I the LORD *h* spoken it, and will ... Eze 22:14
h poured out my fury upon you ... Eze 22:22
they *h* devoured souls ... Eze 22:25
they *h* taken the treasure and ... Eze 22:25
they *h* made her many widows in ... Eze 22:25
Her priests *h* violated my law, and ... Eze 22:26
h profaned mine holy things ... Eze 22:26
they *h* put no difference between ... Eze 22:26
neither *h* they shewed difference ... Eze 22:26
h hid their eyes from my sabbaths ... Eze 22:26
her prophets *h* daubed them with ... Eze 22:28
of the land *h* used oppression ... Eze 22:29
h vexed the poor and needy ... Eze 22:29
they *h* oppressed the stranger ... Eze 22:29
Therefore *h* I poured out mine ... Eze 22:31
I *h* consumed them with the fire ... Eze 22:31
their own way *h* I recompensed ... Eze 22:31
Wherefore I *h* delivered her into ... Eze 23:9
for I *h* spoken it, saith the Lord ... Eze 23:34
That they *h* committed adultery, ... Eze 23:37
with their idols *h* they committed ... Eze 23:37
h also caused their sons, whom ... Eze 23:37

Moreover this they *h* done unto me ... Eze 23:38
they *h* defiled my sanctuary in ... Eze 23:38
day, and *h* profaned my sabbaths ... Eze 23:38
thus *h* they done in the midst of ... Eze 23:39
that ye *h* sent for men to come ... Eze 23:40
I *h* set her blood upon the top of ... Eze 24:8
because I *h* purged thee, and thou ... Eze 24:13
till I *h* caused my fury to rest ... Eze 24:13
I the LORD *h* spoken it ... Eze 24:14
your daughters whom ye *h* left ... Eze 24:21
And ye shall do as I *h* done ... Eze 24:22
Philistines *h* dealt by revenge ... Eze 25:15
and *h* taken vengeance with a ... Eze 25:15
for I *h* spoken it, saith the Lord ... Eze 26:5
for I the LORD *h* spoken it ... Eze 26:14
thy builders *h* perfected thy ... Eze 27:4
They *h* made all thy ship boards ... Eze 27:5
they *h* taken cedars from Lebanon ... Eze 27:5
of Bashan *h* they made thine oars ... Eze 27:6
h made thy benches of ivory ... Eze 27:6
they *h* made thy beauty perfect ... Eze 27:11
Thy rowers *h* brought thee into ... Eze 27:26
for I *h* spoken it, saith the Lord ... Eze 28:10
and I *h* set thee so ... Eze 28:14
of thy merchandise they *h* filled ... Eze 28:16
when I shall *h* executed judgments ... Eze 28:22
When I shall *h* gathered the house ... Eze 28:25
I *h* given to my servant Jacob ... Eze 28:25
when I *h* executed judgments upon ... Eze 28:26
own, and I *h* made it for myself ... Eze 29:3
I *h* given thee for meat to the ... Eze 29:5
because they *h* been a staff of ... Eze 29:6
The river is mine, and I *h* made it ... Eze 29:9
I *h* given him the land of Egypt ... Eze 29:20
when I *h* set a fire in Egypt, and ... Eze 30:8
I the LORD *h* spoken it ... Eze 30:12
Sin shall *h* great pain, and No ... Eze 30:16
Noph shall *h* distresses daily ... Eze 30:16
I *h* broken the arm of Pharaoh ... Eze 30:21
I *h* made him fair by the ... Eze 31:9
I *h* therefore delivered him into ... Eze 31:11
I *h* driven him out for his ... Eze 31:11
h cut him off, and *h* left him ... Eze 31:12
from his shadow, and *h* left him ... Eze 31:12
yet *h* they borne their shame with ... Eze 32:24
They *h* set her a bed in the midst ... Eze 32:25
yet *h* they borne their shame with ... Eze 32:25
they *h* laid their swords under ... Eze 32:27
For I *h* caused my terror in the ... Eze 32:32
I *h* set thee a watchman unto the ... Eze 33:7
I *h* no pleasure in the death of ... Eze 33:11
when I *h* laid the land most ... Eze 33:29
which they *h* committed ... Eze 33:29
The diseased *h* ye not ... Eze 34:4
neither *h* ye healed that which ... Eze 34:4
neither *h* ye bound up that which ... Eze 34:4
neither *h* ye brought again that ... Eze 34:4
neither *h* ye sought that which ... Eze 34:4
with cruelty *h* ye ruled them ... Eze 34:4
h been scattered in the cloudy ... Eze 34:12
to *h* eaten up the good pasture ... Eze 34:18
to *h* drunk of the deep waters, ... Eze 34:18
which ye *h* trodden with your feet ... Eze 34:19
which ye *h* fouled with your feet ... Eze 34:19
Because ye *h* thrust with side and ... Eze 34:21
till ye *h* scattered them abroad ... Eze 34:21
I the LORD *h* spoken it ... Eze 34:24
when I *h* broken the bands of ... Eze 34:27
among them, when I *h* judged thee ... Eze 35:11
LORD, and that I *h* heard all thy ... Eze 35:12
mouth ye *h* boasted against me ... Eze 35:13
h multiplied your words against ... Eze 35:13
I *h* heard them ... Eze 35:13
Because they *h* made you desolate, ... Eze 36:3
in the fire of my jealousy *h* I ... Eze 36:5
which *h* appointed my land into ... Eze 36:5
I *h* spoken in my jealousy and in ... Eze 36:6
because ye *h* borne the shame of ... Eze 36:6
I *h* lifted up mine hand, Surely ... Eze 36:7
which ye *h* profaned among the ... Eze 36:22
which ye *h* profaned in the midst ... Eze 36:23
In the day that I shall *h* ... Eze 36:33
I the LORD *h* spoken it, and I will ... Eze 36:36
when I *h* opened your graves, O my ... Eze 37:13
know that I the LORD *h* spoken it ... Eze 37:14
wherein they *h* sinned, and will ... Eze 37:23
and they all shall *h* one shepherd ... Eze 37:24 1961
I *h* given unto Jacob my servant ... Eze 37:25
wherein your fathers *h* dwelt ... Eze 37:25
which *h* been always waste ... Eze 38:8
which *h* gotten cattle and goods, ... Eze 38:12
Art thou he of whom I *h* spoken in ... Eze 38:17
the fire of my wrath *h* I spoken ... Eze 38:19
for I *h* spoken it, saith the Lord ... Eze 39:5
is the day whereof I *h* spoken ... Eze 39:8
till the buriers *h* buried it in ... Eze 39:15
which I *h* sacrificed for you ... Eze 39:19
see my judgment that I *h* executed ... Eze 39:21
my hand that I *h* laid upon them ... Eze 39:21
transgressions *h* I done unto them ... Eze 39:24
h mercy upon the whole house of ... Eze 39:25
After that they *h* borne their ... Eze 39:26
they *h* trespassed against me ... Eze 39:26
When I *h* brought them again from ... Eze 39:27
but I *h* gathered them unto their ... Eze 39:28
h left none of them any more ... Eze 39:28
for I *h* poured out my spirit upon ... Eze 39:29
about, that they might *h* hold ... Eze 41:6 1961
they *h* even defiled my holy name ... Eze 43:8
that they *h* committed ... Eze 43:8
wherefore I *h* consumed them in ... Eze 43:8
ashamed of all that they *h* done ... Eze 43:11
In that ye *h* brought into my ... Eze 44:7
they *h* broken my covenant because ... Eze 44:7

H

ye *h* not kept the charge of mine Eze 44:8
but ye *h* set keepers of my charge Eze 44:8
therefore *h* I lifted up mine hand Eze 44:12
which they *h* committed Eze 44:13
They shall *h* linen bonnets upon Eze 44:18 1961
shall *h* linen breeches upon their Eze 44:18 1961
house, *h* for themselves, for a Eze 45:5 1961
Ye shall *h* just balances, and a Eze 45:10 1961
ye shall *h* the passover, a feast Eze 45:21 1961
Joseph shall *h* two portions Eze 47:13
they shall *h* inheritance with you Eze 47:22 5307
which *h* kept my charge, which Eze 48:11
priests the Levites shall *h* five Eze 48:13
side, Benjamin shall *h* a portion Eze 48:23
side, Simeon shall *h* a portion Eze 48:24
I *h* dreamed a dream, and my spirit Dan 2:3
for ye *h* prepared lying and Dan 2:9
I *h* found a man of the captives Dan 2:25
unto me the dream which I *h* seen Dan 2:26
that I *h* more than any living Dan 2:30 383
men, O king, *h* not regarded thee Dan 3:12
the golden image which I *h* set up Dan 3:14
worship the image which I *h* made Dan 3:15
of the fire, and they *h* no hurt Dan 3:25 383
h changed the king's word, and Dan 3:28
visions of my dream that I *h* seen Dan 4:9
I king Nebuchadnezzar *h* seen Dan 4:18
after that thou shalt *h* known Dan 4:26
that I *h* built for the house of Dan 4:30
h a chain of gold about his neck, Dan 5:7
I *h* even heard of thee, that the Dan 5:14
h been brought in before me, that Dan 5:15
I *h* heard of thee, that thou Dan 5:16
h a chain of gold about thy neck, Dan 5:16
they *h* brought the vessels of his Dan 5:23
concubines, *h* drunk wine in them Dan 5:23
and the king should *h* no damage Dan 6:2 1934
h consulted together to establish Dan 6:7
mouths, that they *h* not hurt me Dan 6:22
thee, O king, *h* I done no hurt Dan 6:22
We *h* sinned, and *h* committed Dan 9:5
h done wickedly, and *h* rebelled Dan 9:5
Neither *h* we hearkened unto thy Dan 9:6
they *h* trespassed against thee Dan 9:7
because we *h* sinned against thee Dan 9:8
though we *h* rebelled against him Dan 9:9
Neither *h* we obeyed the voice of Dan 9:10
all Israel *h* transgressed thy law Dan 9:11
because we *h* sinned against him Dan 9:11
h sinned, we *h* done wickedly Dan 9:15
me, and I *h* retained no strength Dan 10:16
strong above him, and *h* dominion Dan 11:5
that which his fathers *h* not done Dan 11:24
h indignation against the holy Dan 11:30
h intelligence with them that Dan 11:30
But he shall *h* power over the Dan 11:43
when he shall *h* accomplished to Dan 12:7
for I will no more *h* mercy upon Hos 1:6
But I will *h* mercy upon the house Hos 1:7
I will not *h* mercy upon her Hos 2:4
rewards that my lovers *h* given me Hos 2:12
I will *h* mercy upon her that had Hos 2:23
they shall eat, and not *h* enough Hos 4:10
because they *h* left off to take Hos 4:10
they *h* gone a whoring from under Hos 4:12
they *h* committed whoredom Hos 4:18
because ye *h* been a snare on Hos 5:1
though I *h* been a rebuker of them Hos 5:2
they *h* not known the LORD Hos 5:4
They *h* dealt treacherously Hos 5:7
for they *h* begotten strange Hos 5:7
among the tribes of Israel *h* I Hos 5:9
Therefore *h* I hewed them by the Hos 6:5
I *h* slain them by the words of my Hos 6:5
But they like men *h* transgressed Hos 6:7
there *h* they dealt treacherously Hos 6:7
I *h* seen an horrible thing in the Hos 6:10
When I would *h* healed Israel, Hos 7:1
own doings *h* beset them about Hos 7:2
h made him sick with bottles of Hos 7:5
For they *h* made ready their heart Hos 7:6
oven, and *h* devoured their judges Hos 7:7
Strangers *h* devoured his strength Hos 7:9
for they *h* fled from me Hos 7:13
because they *h* transgressed Hos 7:13
though I *h* redeemed them Hos 7:13
yet they *h* spoken lies against me Hos 7:13
they *h* not cried unto me with Hos 7:14
Though I *h* bound and strengthened Hos 7:15
because they *h* transgressed my Hos 8:1
They *h* set up kings, but not by Hos 8:4
they *h* made princes, and I knew it Hos 8:4
their gold *h* they made them idols Hos 8:4
For they *h* sown the wind, and they Hos 8:7
though they *h* hired among the Hos 8:10
I *h* written to him the great Hos 8:12
They *h* deeply corrupted Hos 9:9
land they *h* made goodly images Hos 10:1
We *h* no king, because we feared Hos 10:3
They *h* spoken words, swearing Hos 10:4
Ye *h* plowed wickedness, ye *h* Hos 10:13
ye *h* eaten the fruit of lies Hos 10:13
I *h* found me out substance Hos 12:8
I *h* also spoken by the prophets, Hos 12:10
I *h* multiplied visions, and used Hos 12:10
h made them molten images of Hos 13:2
therefore *h* they forgotten me Hos 13:6
What *h* I to do any more with Hos 14:8
I *h* heard him, and observed him Hos 14:8
because they *h* no pasture Joel 1:18
whom they *h* scattered among the Joel 3:2
they *h* cast lots for my people Joel 3:3
h given a boy for an harlot, and Joel 3:3
what *h* ye to do with me, O Tyre, Joel 3:4

Because ye *h* taken my silver and Joel 3:5
h carried into your temples my Joel 3:5
h ye sold unto the Grecians Joel 3:6
the place whither ye *h* sold them Joel 3:7
because they *h* shed innocent Joel 3:19
their blood that I *h* not cleansed Joel 3:21
because they *h* threshed Gilead Amos 1:3
because they *h* ripped up the Amos 1:13
because they *h* despised the law Amos 2:4
h not kept his commandments, and Amos 2:4
the which their fathers *h* walked Amos 2:4
You only *h* I known of all the Amos 3:2
of his den, if he *h* taken nothing Amos 3:4
earth, and *h* taken nothing at all Amos 3:5
the great houses shall *h* an end Amos 3:15
I also *h* given you cleanness of Amos 4:6
yet *h* ye not returned unto me, Amos 4:6
also I *h* withholden the rain from Amos 4:7
yet *h* ye not returned unto me, Amos 4:8
I *h* smitten you with blasting and Amos 4:9
yet *h* ye not returned unto me, Amos 4:9
I *h* sent among you the pestilence Amos 4:10
your young men *h* I slain with the Amos 4:10
and *h* taken away your horses Amos 4:10
I *h* made the stink of your camps Amos 4:10
yet *h* ye not returned unto me, Amos 4:10
I *h* overthrown some of you, as Amos 4:11
yet *h* ye not returned unto me, Amos 4:11
ye *h* built houses of hewn stone, Amos 5:11
ye *h* planted pleasant vineyards, Amos 5:11
shall be with you, as ye *h* spoken Amos 5:14
H ye offered unto me sacrifices Amos 5:25
But ye *h* borne the tabernacle of Amos 5:26
for ye *h* turned judgment into Amos 6:12
H we not taken to us horns by our Amos 6:13
H not I brought up Israel out of Amos 9:7
their land which I *h* given them Amos 9:15
We *h* heard a rumour from the LORD Obad 1
I *h* made thee small among the Obad 2
would they not *h* stolen till Obad 5
All the men of thy confederacy *h* Obad 7
peace with thee *h* deceived thee Obad 7
bread *h* laid a wound under thee Obad 7
But thou shouldest not *h* looked Obad 12
neither shouldest thou *h* rejoiced Obad 12
neither shouldest thou *h* spoken Obad 12
Thou shouldest not *h* entered into Obad 13
thou shouldest not *h* looked on Obad 13
nor *h* laid hands on their Obad 13
thou *h* stood in the crossway Obad 14
neither shouldest thou *h* Obad 14
For as ye *h* drunk upon my holy Obad 16
I will pay that that I *h* vowed Jonah 2:9
Therefore thou shalt *h* none that Mic 2:5 1961
The women of my people *h* ye cast Mic 2:9
from their children *h* ye taken Mic 2:9
they *h* broken up, and *h* passed Mic 2:13
as they *h* behaved themselves ill Mic 3:4
you, that ye shall not *h* a vision Mic 3:6
out, and her that I *h* afflicted Mic 4:6
for pangs *h* taken thee as a woman Mic 4:9
goings forth *h* been from of old Mic 5:2
thou shalt *h* no more soothsayers Mic 5:12 1961
heathen, such as they *h* not heard Mic 5:15
people, what *h* I done unto thee Mic 6:3
and wherein *h* I wearied thee Mic 6:3
inhabitants thereof *h* spoken lies Mic 6:12
for I am as when they *h* gathered Mic 7:1
because I *h* sinned against him, Mic 7:9
he will *h* compassion upon us Mic 7:19
Though I *h* afflicted thee, I will Nah 1:12
the emptiers *h* emptied them out Nah 2:2
that *h* no ruler over them Hab 1:14
I *h* heard thy speech, and was Hab 3:2
those that *h* not sought the LORD, Zeph 1:6
because they *h* sinned against the Zeph 1:17
which *h* wrought his judgment Zeph 2:3
I *h* heard the reproach of Moab, Zeph 2:8
whereby they *h* reproached my Zeph 2:8
This shall they *h* for their pride Zeph 2:10
because they *h* reproached Zeph 2:10
her priests *h* polluted the Zeph 3:4
they *h* done violence to the law Zeph 3:4
I *h* cut off the nations Zeph 3:6
where they *h* been put to shame Zeph 3:19
Ye *h* sown much, and bring in Hag 1:6
ye eat, but ye *h* not enough Hag 1:6
for I *h* chosen thee, saith the Hag 2:23
whom the former prophets *h* cried Zec 1:4
We *h* walked to and fro through the Zec 1:11
thou not *h* mercy on Jerusalem Zec 1:12
the horns which *h* scattered Judah Zec 1:19
the horns which *h* scattered Judah Zec 1:21
for I *h* spread you abroad as the Zec 2:6
I *h* caused thine iniquity to pass Zec 3:4
stone that I *h* laid before Joshua Zec 3:9
I said, I *h* looked, and behold a Zec 4:2
The hands of Zerubbabel *h* laid Zec 4:9
go toward the north country *h* Zec 6:8
as I *h* done these so many years Zec 7:3
So again *h* I thought in these Zec 8:15
for we *h* heard that God is with Zec 8:23
for now *h* I seen with mine eyes Zec 9:8
by the blood of thy covenant I *h* Zec 9:11
When I *h* bent Judah for me, Zec 9:13
For the idols *h* spoken vanity Zec 10:2
and the diviners *h* seen a lie Zec 10:2
and *h* told false dreams Zec 10:2
for I *h* mercy upon them Zec 10:6
for I *h* redeemed them Zec 10:8
increase as they *h* increased Zec 10:8
look upon me whom they *h* pierced Zec 12:10
that *h* fought against Jerusalem Zec 14:12
up, and come not, that *h* no rain Zec 14:18

I *h* loved you, saith the LORD Mal 1:2
Wherein *h* we despised thy name Mal 1:6
Wherein *h* we polluted thee Mal 1:7
I *h* no pleasure in you, saith the Mal 1:10
But ye *h* profaned it, in that ye Mal 1:12
ye *h* snuffed at it, saith the Mal 1:13
I *h* cursed them already, because Mal 2:2
ye shall know that I *h* sent this Mal 2:4
ye *h* caused many to stumble at Mal 2:8
ye *h* corrupted the covenant of Mal 2:8
Therefore *h* I also made you Mal 2:9
according as ye *h* not kept my Mal 2:9
but *h* been partial in the law Mal 2:9
H we not all one father Mal 2:10
this *h* ye done again, covering Mal 2:13
Ye *h* wearied the LORD with your Mal 2:17
ye say, Wherein *h* we wearied him Mal 2:17
ordinances, and *h* not kept them Mal 3:7
Yet ye *h* robbed me Mal 3:8
ye say, Wherein *h* we robbed thee Mal 3:8
for ye *h* robbed me, even this Mal 3:9
Your words *h* been stout against Mal 3:13
What *h* we spoken so much against Mal 3:13
Ye *h* said, It is vain to serve Mal 3:14
it that we *h* kept his ordinance Mal 3:14
that we *h* walked mournfully Mal 3:14
for we *h* seen his star in the Mt 2:2
when ye *h* found him, bring me Mt 2:8
Out of Egypt *h* I called my son Mt 2:15
We *h* Abraham to our father Mt 3:9 *2192*
I *h* need to be baptized of thee, Mt 3:14 *2192*
but if the salt *h* lost his savour Mt 5:13
Ye *h* heard that it was said by Mt 5:21
Ye *h* heard that it was said by Mt 5:27
ye *h* heard that it hath been said Mt 5:33
Ye *h* heard that it hath been said Mt 5:38
coat, let him *h* thy cloke also Mt 5:40
Ye *h* heard that it hath been said Mt 5:43
which love you, what reward *h* ye Mt 5:46 *2192*
otherwise ye *h* no reward of your Mt 6:1 *2192*
that they may *h* glory of men Mt 6:2
say unto you, They *h* their reward Mt 6:2 *568*
say unto you, They *h* their reward Mt 6:5 *568*
knoweth what things ye *h* need of Mt 6:8 *2192*
say unto you, They *h* their reward Mt 6:16 *568*
ye *h* need of all these things Mt 6:32
h we not prophesied in thy name Mt 7:22
in thy name *h* cast out devils Mt 7:22
I *h* not found so great faith, no, Mt 8:10
saith unto him, The foxes *h* holes Mt 8:20 *2192*
and the birds of the air *h* nests Mt 8:20
What *h* we to do with thee, Jesus, Mt 8:29
what that meaneth, I will *h* mercy Mt 9:13
Thou son of David, *h* mercy on us Mt 9:27
freely ye *h* received, freely give Mt 10:8
Ye shall not *h* gone over the Mt 10:23
If they *h* called the master of Mt 10:25
the poor *h* the gospel preached to Mt 11:5
We *h* piped unto you, and ye *h* Mt 11:17
we *h* mourned unto you, and ye *h* Mt 11:17
they would *h* repented long ago in Mt 11:21
which *h* been done in thee, had Mt 11:23
it would *h* remained until this Mt 11:23
H ye not read what David did, Mt 12:3
Or *h* ye not read in the law, how Mt 12:5
what this meaneth, I will *h* mercy Mt 12:7
ye would not *h* condemned the Mt 12:7
among you, that shall *h* one sheep Mt 12:11 *2192*
my servant, whom I *h* chosen Mt 12:18
he shall *h* more abundance Mt 13:12
and their eyes they *h* closed Mt 13:15
righteous men *h* desired to see Mt 13:17
which ye see, and *h* not seen them Mt 13:17
ye hear, and *h* not heard them Mt 13:17
which *h* been kept secret from the Mt 13:35
H ye understood all these things Mt 13:51
is not lawful for thee to *h* her Mt 14:4 *2192*
when he would *h* put him to death, Mt 14:5
We *h* here but five loaves, and two Mt 14:17 *2192*
Thus *h* ye made the commandment of Mt 15:6
H mercy on me, O Lord, thou son Mt 15:22
I *h* compassion on the multitude, Mt 15:32
three days, and *h* nothing to eat Mt 15:32 *2192*
Whence should we *h* so much bread Mt 15:33
unto them, How many loaves *h* ye Mt 15:34 *2192*
It is because we *h* taken no bread Mt 16:7
because ye *h* brought no bread Mt 16:8
but *h* done unto him whatsoever Mt 17:12
Lord, *h* mercy on my son Mt 17:15
If ye *h* faith as a grain of Mt 17:20 *2192*
if a man *h* an hundred sheep, and Mt 18:12 *1099*
h patience with me, and I will pay Mt 18:26
H patience with me, and I will pay Mt 18:29
thou also *h* had compassion on thy Mt 18:33
H ye not read, that he which made Mt 19:4
which *h* made themselves eunuchs Mt 19:12
that I may *h* eternal life Mt 19:16 *2192*
All these things *h* I kept from my Mt 19:20
thou shalt *h* treasure in heaven Mt 19:21 *2192*
we *h* forsaken all, and followed Mt 19:27
what shall we *h* therefore Mt 19:27 *2701*
you, That ye which *h* followed me Mt 19:28
that they should *h* received more Mt 20:10
These last *h* wrought but one hour Mt 20:12
which *h* borne the burden and heat Mt 20:12
H mercy on us, O Lord, thou son Mt 20:30
H mercy on us, O Lord, thou son Mt 20:31
but ye *h* made it a den of thieves Mt 21:13
h ye never read, Out of the mouth Mt 21:16
I say unto you, If ye *h* faith Mt 21:21 *2192*
Behold, I *h* prepared my dinner Mt 22:4
h ye not read that which was Mt 22:31
h omitted the weightier matters Mt 23:23
these ought ye to *h* done, and not Mt 23:23

we would not *h* been partakers	Mt 23:30	
how often would I *h* gathered thy	Mt 23:37	
Behold, I *h* told you before	Mt 24:25	
would come, he would *h* watched	Mt 24:43	
would not *h* suffered his house to	Mt 24:43	
I *h* gained beside them five	Mt 25:20	
I *h* gained two other talents	Mt 25:22	
and gather where I *h* not strawed	Mt 25:26	
Thou oughtest therefore to *h* put	Mt 25:27	
then at my coming I should *h*	Mt 25:27	
be given, and he shall *h* abundance	Mt 25:29	
Inasmuch as ye *h* done it unto one	Mt 25:40	
my brethren, ye *h* done it unto me	Mt 25:40	
might *h* been sold for much	Mt 26:9	
For ye *h* the poor always with you	Mt 26:11	2192
but me ye *h* not always	Mt 26:11	2192
further need *h* we of witnesses	Mt 26:65	2192
now ye *h* heard his blasphemy	Mt 26:65	
I *h* sinned in that I *h*	Mt 27:4	
H thou nothing to do with that	Mt 27:19	
for I *h* suffered many things this	Mt 27:19	
deliver him now, if he will *h* him	Mt 27:43	
said unto them, Ye *h* a watch	Mt 27:65	2192
lo, I *h* told you	Mt 28:7	
whatsoever I *h* commanded you	Mt 28:20	
I indeed *h* baptized you with	Mk 1:8	
what *h* we to do with thee, thou	Mk 1:24	
They that are whole *h* no need of	Mk 2:17	2192
as long as they *h* the bridegroom	Mk 2:19	2192
H ye never read what David did	Mk 2:25	
to *h* power to heal sicknesses, and	Mk 3:15	2192
but when they *h* heard, Satan	Mk 4:15	
when they *h* heard the word	Mk 4:16	
h no root in themselves, and so	Mk 4:17	2192
If any man *h* ears to hear, let	Mk 4:23	2192
how is it that ye *h* no faith	Mk 4:40	2192
What *h* I to do with thee, Jesus	Mk 5:7	
for thee to *h* thy brother's wife	Mk 6:18	2192
him, and would *h* killed him	Mk 6:19	
for they *h* nothing to eat	Mk 6:36	2192
unto them, How many loaves *h* ye	Mk 6:38	2192
sea, and would *h* passed by them	Mk 6:48	
which they *h* received to hold, as	Mk 7:4	
tradition, which ye *h* delivered	Mk 7:13	
If any man *h* ears to hear, let	Mk 7:16	2192
house, and would *h* no man know it	Mk 7:24	
I *h* compassion on the multitude	Mk 8:2	
because they *h* now been with me	Mk 8:2	
three days, and *h* nothing to eat	Mk 8:2	2192
asked them, How many loaves *h* ye	Mk 8:5	2192
It is because we *h* no bread	Mk 8:16	2192
reason ye, because ye *h* no bread	Mk 8:17	2192
h ye your heart yet hardened	Mk 8:17	2192
till they *h* seen the kingdom of	Mk 9:1	
they *h* done unto him whatsoever	Mk 9:13	
I *h* brought unto thee my son	Mk 9:17	
h compassion on us, and help us	Mk 9:22	
but if the salt *h* lost his	Mk 9:50	
H salt in yourselves	Mk 9:50	2192
and *h* peace one with another	Mk 9:50	
all these *h* I observed from my	Mk 10:20	
thou shalt *h* treasure in heaven	Mk 10:21	2192
How hardly shall they that *h*	Mk 10:23	2192
we *h* left all	Mk 10:28	2192
and *h* followed thee	Mk 10:28	
thou son of David, *h* mercy on me	Mk 10:47	
Thou son of David, *h* mercy on me	Mk 10:48	
but ye *h* made it a den of thieves	Mk 11:17	
saith unto them, *H* faith in God	Mk 11:22	2192
he shall *h* whatsoever he saith	Mk 11:23	2071
receive them, and ye shall *h* them	Mk 11:24	2071
if ye *h* ought against any	Mk 11:25	2192
h ye not read this scripture	Mk 12:10	
h ye not read in the book of	Mk 12:26	
than all they which *h* cast into	Mk 12:43	
I *h* foretold you all things	Mk 13:23	
For it might *h* been sold for more	Mk 14:5	
and *h* been given to the poor	Mk 14:5	
For ye *h* the poor with you always	Mk 14:7	2192
but me ye *h* not always	Mk 14:7	2192
Ye *h* heard the blasphemy	Mk 14:64	
Forasmuch as many *h* taken in hand	Lk 1:1	
And thou shalt *h* joy and gladness	Lk 1:14	2071
father, how he would *h* him called	Lk 1:62	
which *h* been since the world	Lk 1:70	
For mine eyes *h* seen thy	Lk 2:30	
supposing him to *h* been in the	Lk 2:44	
I *h* sought thee sorrowing	Lk 2:48	
We *h* Abraham to our father	Lk 3:8	2192
whatsoever we *h* heard done in	Lk 4:23	
what *h* we to do with thee, thou	Lk 4:34	
we *h* toiled all the night	Lk 5:5	
and *h* taken nothing	Lk 5:5	
We *h* seen strange things to day	Lk 5:26	
H ye not read so much as this	Lk 6:3	
for ye *h* received your	Lk 6:24	
which love you, what thank *h* ye	Lk 6:32	2076
do good to you, what thank *h* ye	Lk 6:33	2076
hope to receive, what thank *h* ye	Lk 6:34	2076
I *h* not found so great faith, no	Lk 7:9	
tell John what things ye *h* seen	Lk 7:22	
We *h* piped unto you, and ye *h*	Lk 7:32	
we *h* mourned to you, and ye *h*	Lk 7:32	
would *h* known who and what	Lk 7:39	
I *h* somewhat to say unto thee	Lk 7:40	2192
these *h* no root, which for a	Lk 8:13	2192
they, which, when they *h* heard	Lk 8:14	
even that which he seemeth to *h*	Lk 8:18	2192
What *h* I to do with thee, Jesus	Lk 8:28	
neither *h* two coats apiece	Lk 9:3	2192
And Herod said, John *h* I beheaded	Lk 9:9	
We *h* no more but five loaves and	Lk 9:13	2076
said unto him, Foxes *h* holes	Lk 9:58	2192
and birds of the air *h* nests	Lk 9:58	

which *h* been done in you, they	Lk 10:13	
kings *h* desired to see those	Lk 10:24	
which ye see, and *h* not seen them	Lk 10:24	
ye hear, and *h* not heard them	Lk 10:24	
Which of you shall *h* a friend	Lk 11:5	2192
I *h* nothing to set before him	Lk 11:6	2192
give alms of such things as ye *h*	Lk 11:41	1751
these ought ye to *h* done, and not	Lk 11:42	
for ye *h* taken away the key of	Lk 11:52	
Therefore whatsoever ye *h* spoken	Lk 12:3	
that which ye *h* spoken in the ear	Lk 12:3	
after that *h* no more that they	Lk 12:4	2192
because I *h* no room where to	Lk 12:17	2192
which neither *h* storehouse nor	Lk 12:24	2076
that ye *h* need of these things	Lk 12:30	2192
Sell that ye *h*, and give alms	Lk 12:33	5224
would come, he would *h* watched	Lk 12:39	
not *h* suffered his house to be	Lk 12:39	
to whom men *h* committed much, of	Lk 12:48	
But I *h* a baptism to be baptized	Lk 12:50	2192
We *h* eaten and drunk in thy	Lk 13:26	
how often would I *h* gathered thy	Lk 13:34	
Which of you shall *h* an ass or an	Lk 14:5	
then shalt thou *h* worship in the	Lk 14:10	2071
I *h* bought a piece of ground, and	Lk 14:18	
I pray thee *h* me excused	Lk 14:18	2192
I *h* bought five yoke of oxen, and	Lk 14:19	
I pray thee *h* me excused	Lk 14:19	2192
I *h* married a wife, and therefore	Lk 14:20	
whether he *h* sufficient to finish	Lk 14:28	2192
but if the salt *h* lost his savour	Lk 14:34	
for I *h* found my sheep which was	Lk 15:6	
for I *h* found the piece which I	Lk 15:9	
he would fain *h* filled his belly	Lk 15:16	
of my father's *h* bread enough	Lk 15:17	
I *h* sinned against heaven, and	Lk 15:18	
I *h* sinned against heaven, and in	Lk 15:21	
with me, and all that I *h* is thine	Lk 15:31	1699
If therefore ye *h* not been	Lk 16:11	
if ye *h* not been faithful in that	Lk 16:12	
h mercy on me, and send Lazarus	Lk 16:24	
For I *h* five brethren	Lk 16:28	2192
They *h* Moses and the prophets	Lk 16:29	2192
and serve me, till I *h* eaten	Lk 17:8	
when ye shall *h* done all those	Lk 17:10	
we *h* done that which was our duty	Lk 17:10	
Jesus, Master, *h* mercy on us	Lk 17:13	
All these *h* I kept from my youth	Lk 18:21	
thou shalt *h* treasure in heaven	Lk 18:22	2192
How hardly shall they that *h*	Lk 18:24	2192
we *h* left all, and followed thee	Lk 18:28	
thou son of David, *h* mercy on me	Lk 18:38	
Thou son of David, *h* mercy on me	Lk 18:39	
if I *h* taken any thing from any	Lk 19:8	
We will not *h* this man to reign	Lk 19:14	
h thou authority over ten cities	Lk 19:17	2192
which I *h* kept laid up in a	Lk 19:20	
that at my coming I might *h*	Lk 19:23	
but ye *h* made it a den of thieves	Lk 19:46	
For all these *h* of their	Lk 21:4	
With desire I *h* desired to eat	Lk 22:15	
Ye are they which *h* continued	Lk 22:28	
Satan hath desired to *h* you	Lk 22:31	
But I *h* prayed for thee, that thy	Lk 22:32	
the things concerning me *h* an end	Lk 22:37	2192
for we ourselves *h* heard of his	Lk 22:71	
he hoped to *h* seen some miracle	Lk 23:8	
Ye *h* brought this man unto me, as	Lk 23:14	
h found no fault in this man	Lk 23:14	
I *h* found no cause of death in	Lk 23:22	
these that ye *h* one to another	Lk 24:17	474
to death, and *h* crucified him	Lk 24:20	
he which should *h* redeemed Israel	Lk 24:21	
all that the prophets *h* spoken	Lk 24:25	
Ought not Christ to *h* suffered	Lk 24:26	
as though he would *h* gone further	Lk 24:28	
flesh and bones, as ye see me *h*	Lk 24:39	2192
unto them, *H* ye here any meat	Lk 24:41	2192
of his fulness *h* all we received	Jn 1:16	
We *h* found the Messias, which is	Jn 1:41	
We *h* found him, of whom Moses in	Jn 1:45	
saith unto him, They *h* no wine	Jn 2:3	2192
Woman, what *h* I to do with thee	Jn 2:4	
when men *h* well drunk, then that	Jn 2:10	
know, and testify that we *h* seen	Jn 3:11	
If I *h* told you earthly things	Jn 3:12	
not perish, but *h* eternal life	Jn 3:15	2192
perish, but *h* everlasting life	Jn 3:16	2192
for the Jews *h* no dealings with	Jn 4:9	
thou wouldest *h* asked of him	Jn 4:10	
he would *h* given thee living	Jn 4:10	
answered and said, I *h* no husband	Jn 4:17	2192
hast well said, I *h* no husband	Jn 4:17	2192
I *h* meat to eat that ye know not	Jn 4:32	2192
for we *h* heard him ourselves, and	Jn 4:42	
I *h* no man, when the water is	Jn 5:7	2192
to the Son to *h* life in himself	Jn 5:26	2192
they that *h* done good, unto the	Jn 5:29	
and they that *h* done evil, unto	Jn 5:29	
But I *h* greater witness than that	Jn 5:36	2192
Ye *h* neither heard his voice at	Jn 5:37	
ye *h* not his word abiding in you	Jn 5:38	2192
them ye think ye *h* eternal life	Jn 5:39	2192
come to me, that ye might *h* life	Jn 5:40	2192
that ye *h* not the love of God in	Jn 5:42	2192
Moses, ye would *h* believed me	Jn 5:46	
unto you, That ye also *h* seen me	Jn 6:36	
on him, may *h* everlasting life	Jn 6:40	2192
his blood, ye *h* no life in you	Jn 6:53	2192
H not I chosen you twelve, and one	Jn 6:70	
I *h* done one work, and ye all	Jn 7:21	
because I *h* made a man every whit	Jn 7:23	
And some of them would *h* taken him	Jn 7:44	
them, Why *h* ye not brought him	Jn 7:45	

H any of the rulers or of the	Jn 7:48	
that they might *h* to accuse him	Jn 8:6	2192
but shall *h* the light of life	Jn 8:12	2192
ye should *h* known my Father also	Jn 8:19	
I *h* many things to say and to	Jn 8:26	2192
things which I *h* heard of him	Jn 8:26	
When ye *h* lifted up the Son of	Jn 8:28	
which I *h* seen with my Father	Jn 8:38	
ye do that which ye *h* seen with	Jn 8:38	
the truth, which I *h* heard of God	Jn 8:40	
we *h* one Father, even God	Jn 8:41	2192
Jesus answered, I *h* not a devil	Jn 8:49	2192
Yet ye *h* not known him	Jn 8:55	
I *h* told you already, and ye did	Jn 9:27	
ye were blind, ye should *h* no sin	Jn 9:41	2192
I am come that they might *h* life	Jn 10:10	2192
that they might *h* it more	Jn 10:10	2192
And other sheep I *h*, which are not	Jn 10:16	2192
I *h* power to lay it down	Jn 10:18	2192
I *h* power to take it again	Jn 10:18	2192
This commandment *h* I received of	Jn 10:18	
Many good works *h* I shewed you	Jn 10:32	
And said, Where *h* ye laid him	Jn 11:34	
h caused that even this man	Jn 11:37	
even this man should not *h* died	Jn 11:37	
For the poor always ye *h* with you	Jn 12:8	2192
but me ye *h* not always	Jn 12:8	2192
I *h* both glorified it, and will	Jn 12:28	
We *h* heard out of the law that	Jn 12:34	
Walk while ye *h* the light	Jn 12:35	2192
While ye *h* light, believe in the	Jn 12:36	2192
the word that I *h* spoken, the	Jn 12:48	
For I *h* not spoken of myself	Jn 12:49	
Know ye what I *h* done to you	Jn 13:12	
and Master, *h* washed your feet	Jn 13:14	
For I *h* given you an example	Jn 13:15	
ye should do as I *h* done to you	Jn 13:15	
I know whom I *h* chosen	Jn 13:18	
give a sop, when I *h* dipped it	Jn 13:26	
Buy those things that we *h* need	Jn 13:29	2192
as I *h* loved you, that ye also	Jn 13:34	
if ye *h* love one to another	Jn 13:35	2192
were not so, I would *h* told you	Jn 14:2	
ye should *h* known my Father also	Jn 14:7	
ye know him, and *h* seen him	Jn 14:7	
H I been so long time with you	Jn 14:9	
These things *h* I spoken unto you	Jn 14:25	
whatsoever I *h* said unto you	Jn 14:26	
Ye *h* heard how I said unto you, I	Jn 14:28	
now I *h* told you before it come	Jn 14:29	
word which I *h* spoken unto you	Jn 15:3	
hath loved me, so *h* I loved you	Jn 15:9	
even as I *h* kept my Father's	Jn 15:10	
These things *h* I spoken unto you	Jn 15:11	
one another, as I *h* loved you	Jn 15:12	
but I *h* called you friends	Jn 15:15	
for all things that I *h* heard of	Jn 15:15	
my Father I *h* made known unto you	Jn 15:15	
Ye *h* not chosen me, but I *h*	Jn 15:16	
but I *h* chosen you out of the	Jn 15:19	
If they *h* persecuted me, they	Jn 15:20	
if they *h* kept my saying, they	Jn 15:20	
but now they *h* no cloke for their	Jn 15:22	2192
but now *h* they both seen and hated	Jn 15:24	
because ye *h* been with me from	Jn 15:27	
These things *h* I spoken unto you	Jn 16:1	
because they *h* not known the	Jn 16:3	
But these things *h* I told you	Jn 16:4	
But because I *h* said these things	Jn 16:6	
I *h* yet many things to say unto	Jn 16:12	2192
And ye now therefore *h* sorrow	Jn 16:22	2192
Hitherto *h* ye asked nothing in my	Jn 16:24	
These things *h* I spoken unto you	Jn 16:25	
loveth you, because ye *h* loved me	Jn 16:27	
h believed that I came out from	Jn 16:27	
These things I *h* spoken unto you	Jn 16:33	
that in me ye might *h* peace	Jn 16:33	2192
the world ye shall *h* tribulation	Jn 16:33	2192
I *h* overcome the world	Jn 16:33	
I *h* glorified thee on the earth	Jn 17:4	
I *h* finished the work which thou	Jn 17:4	
I *h* manifested thy name unto the	Jn 17:6	
and they *h* kept thy word	Jn 17:6	
Now they *h* known that all things	Jn 17:7	
For I *h* given unto them the words	Jn 17:8	
they *h* received them, and *h*	Jn 17:8	
they *h* believed that thou didst	Jn 17:8	
that thou gavest me I *h* kept	Jn 17:12	
world, that they might *h* my joy	Jn 17:13	2192
I *h* given them thy word	Jn 17:14	
even so *h* I also sent them into	Jn 17:18	
thou gavest me I *h* given them	Jn 17:22	
but I *h* known thee, and these *h*	Jn 17:25	
I *h* declared unto them thy name	Jn 17:26	
I *h* told you that I am he	Jn 18:8	
thou gavest me *h* I lost none	Jn 18:9	
in secret *h* I said nothing	Jn 18:20	
heard me, what I *h* said unto them	Jn 18:21	
If I *h* spoken evil, bear witness	Jn 18:23	
we would not *h* delivered him up	Jn 18:30	
the chief priests *h* delivered	Jn 18:35	
But ye *h* a custom, that I should	Jn 18:39	2076
We *h* a law, and by our law he	Jn 19:7	2192
that I *h* power to crucify thee	Jn 19:10	2192
and *h* power to release thee	Jn 19:10	2192
Thou couldest *h* no power at all	Jn 19:11	2192
answered, We *h* no king but Caesar	Jn 19:15	2192
What I *h* written I *h* written	Jn 19:22	
They *h* taken away the Lord out of	Jn 20:2	
we know not where they *h* laid him	Jn 20:2	
Because they *h* taken away my Lord	Jn 20:13	
I know not where they *h* laid him	Jn 20:13	
if thou *h* borne him hence, tell	Jn 20:15	
said unto him, We *h* seen the Lord	Jn 20:25	

blessed are they that *h* not seen	Jn 20:29	
and yet *h* believed	Jn 20:29	
ye might *h* life through his name	Jn 20:31	*2192*
them, Children, *h* ye any meat	Jn 21:5	*2192*
of the fish which ye *h* now caught	Jn 21:10	
The former treatise *h* I made	Acts 1:1	
which, saith he, ye *h* heard of me	Acts 1:4	
as ye *h* seen him go into heaven	Acts 1:11	
must needs *h* been fulfilled	Acts 1:16	
Wherefore of these men which *h*	Acts 1:21	
ye *h* taken, and by wicked hands	Acts 2:23	
and by wicked hands *h* crucified	Acts 2:23	
whom ye *h* crucified, both Lord and	Acts 2:36	
said, Silver and gold *h* I none	Acts 3:6	*5225*
but such as I *h* give I thee	Acts 3:6	*2192*
follow after, as many as *h* spoken	Acts 3:24	
h likewise foretold of these days	Acts 3:24	
or by what name, *h* ye done this	Acts 4:7	
speak the things which we *h* seen	Acts 4:20	
How is it that ye *h* agreed	Acts 5:9	
the feet of them which *h* buried	Acts 5:9	
to the prison to *h* them brought	Acts 5:21	
lest they should *h* been stoned	Acts 5:26	
ye *h* filled Jerusalem with your	Acts 5:28	
We *h* heard him speak blasphemous	Acts 6:11	
For we *h* heard him say, that this	Acts 6:14	
h understood how that God by his	Acts 7:25	
would *h* set them at one again,	Acts 7:26	
I *h* seen, I *h* seen the	Acts 7:34	
I *h* heard their groaning, and am	Acts 7:34	
h ye offered to me slain beasts	Acts 7:42	
Which of the prophets *h* not your	Acts 7:52	
they *h* slain them which shewed	Acts 7:52	
of whom ye *h* been now the	Acts 7:52	
Who *h* received the law by the	Acts 7:53	
of angels, and *h* not kept it	Acts 7:53	
which ye *h* spoken come upon me	Acts 8:24	
Lord, what wilt thou *h* me to do	Acts 9:6	
I *h* heard by many of this man,	Acts 9:13	
very hungry, and would *h* eaten	Acts 10:10	
for I *h* never eaten any thing	Acts 10:14	
for I *h* sent them	Acts 10:20	
for what intent ye *h* sent for me	Acts 10:29	
which *h* received the Holy Ghost	Acts 10:47	
when Herod would *h* brought him	Acts 12:6	
work whereunto I *h* called them	Acts 13:2	
if ye *h* any word of exhortation	Acts 13:15	*2076*
I *h* found David the son of Jesse,	Acts 13:22	
day, they *h* fulfilled them in	Acts 13:27	
this day *h* I begotten thee	Acts 13:33	
should first *h* been spoken to you	Acts 13:46	
I *h* set thee to be a light of the	Acts 13:47	
would *h* done sacrifice with the	Acts 14:13	
Forasmuch as we *h* heard, that	Acts 15:24	
from us *h* troubled you with words	Acts 15:24	
Men that *h* hazarded their lives	Acts 15:26	
We *h* sent therefore Judas and	Acts 15:27	
h preached the word of the Lord	Acts 15:36	
Him would Paul *h* to go forth with	Acts 16:3	
If ye *h* judged me to be faithful	Acts 16:15	
would *h* killed himself, supposing	Acts 16:27	
The magistrates *h* sent to let you	Acts 16:36	
them, They *h* beaten us openly	Acts 16:37	
Romans, and *h* cast us into prison	Acts 16:37	
that Christ must needs *h* suffered	Acts 17:3	
These that *h* turned the world	Acts 17:6	
we live, and move, and *h* our being	Acts 17:28	
also of your own poets *h* said	Acts 17:28	
for I *h* much people in this city	Acts 18:10	*2076*
H ye received the Holy Ghost	Acts 19:2	
We *h* not so much as heard whether	Acts 19:2	
After I *h* been there, I must also	Acts 19:21	
by this craft we *h* our wealth	Acts 19:25	*2076*
when Paul would *h* entered in unto	Acts 19:30	
would *h* made his defence unto the	Acts 19:33	
For ye *h* brought hither these men	Acts 19:37	
h a matter against any man, the	Acts 19:38	*2192*
after what manner I *h* been with	Acts 20:18	
but *h* shewed you, and *h* taught	Acts 20:20	
which I *h* received of the Lord	Acts 20:24	
among whom I *h* gone preaching the	Acts 20:25	
For I *h* not shunned to declare	Acts 20:27	
I *h* coveted no man's silver, or	Acts 20:33	
that these hands *h* ministered	Acts 20:34	
I *h* shewed you all things, how	Acts 20:35	
We *h* four men which	Acts 21:23	*1526*
four men which *h* a vow on them	Acts 21:23	*2192*
we *h* written and concluded that	Acts 21:25	
him which should *h* examined him	Acts 22:29	
because he would *h* known the	Acts 22:30	
I *h* lived in all good conscience	Acts 23:1	
fearing lest Paul should *h* been	Acts 23:10	
We *h* bound ourselves under a	Acts 23:14	
eat nothing until we *h* slain Paul	Acts 23:14	
The Jews *h* agreed to desire thee	Acts 23:20	
which *h* bound themselves with an	Acts 23:21	
nor drink till they *h* killed him	Acts 23:21	
should *h* been killed of them	Acts 23:27	
when I would *h* known the cause	Acts 23:28	
but to *h* nothing laid to his	Acts 23:29	*2192*
For we *h* found this man a	Acts 24:5	
would *h* judged according to our	Acts 24:6	
h hope toward God, which they	Acts 24:15	*2192*
to *h* always a conscience void of	Acts 24:16	*2192*
Who ought to *h* been here before	Acts 24:19	
if they *h* found any evil doing in	Acts 24:20	
Paul, and to let him *h* liberty	Acts 24:23	*2192*
when I *h* a convenient season, I	Acts 24:25	*3335*
should *h* been given him of Paul	Acts 24:26	
h I offended any thing at all	Acts 25:8	
to the Jews *h* I done no wrong, as	Acts 25:10	
or *h* committed any thing worthy	Acts 25:11	
desiring to *h* judgment against	Acts 25:15	
h the accusers face to face	Acts 25:16	*2192*
h licence to answer for himself	Acts 25:16	*2983*
of the Jews *h* dealt with me	Acts 25:24	
I *h* determined to send him	Acts 25:25	
Of whom I *h* no certain thing to	Acts 25:26	*2192*
Wherefore I *h* brought him forth	Acts 25:26	
I might *h* somewhat to write	Acts 25:26	*2192*
for I *h* appeared unto thee for	Acts 26:16	
This man might *h* been set at	Acts 26:32	
ye should *h* hearkened unto me, and	Acts 27:21	
not *h* loosed from Crete	Acts 27:21	
to *h* gained this harm and loss	Acts 27:21	
we should *h* fallen upon rocks	Acts 27:29	
would *h* cast anchors out of the	Acts 27:30	
fourteenth day that ye *h* tarried	Acts 27:33	
looked when he should *h* swollen	Acts 28:6	
though I *h* committed nothing	Acts 28:17	
would *h* let me go, because there	Acts 28:18	
therefore *h* I called for you	Acts 28:20	
and their eyes *h* they closed	Acts 28:27	
By whom we *h* received grace and	Rom 1:5	
h a prosperous journey by the	Rom 1:10	
Now I would not *h* you ignorant	Rom 1:13	
that I might *h* some fruit among	Rom 1:13	*2192*
but *h* pleasure in them that do	Rom 1:32	
For as many as *h* sinned without	Rom 2:12	
as many as *h* sinned in the law	Rom 2:12	
which *h* not the law, do by nature	Rom 2:14	*2192*
for we *h* before proved both Jews	Rom 3:9	
their tongues they *h* used deceit	Rom 3:13	
the way of peace *h* they not known	Rom 3:17	
For all *h* sinned, and come short	Rom 3:23	
I *h* made thee a father of many	Rom 4:17	
we *h* peace with God through our	Rom 5:1	*2192*
By whom also we *h* access by faith	Rom 5:2	*2192*
by whom we *h* now received the	Rom 5:11	
all men, for that all *h* sinned	Rom 5:12	
For if we *h* been planted together	Rom 6:5	
sin shall not *h* dominion over you	Rom 6:14	
but ye *h* obeyed from the heart	Rom 6:17	
for as ye *h* yielded your members	Rom 6:19	
ye *h* your fruit unto holiness, and	Rom 6:22	*2192*
Now if any man *h* not the Spirit	Rom 8:9	*2192*
For ye *h* not received the spirit	Rom 8:15	
but ye *h* received the Spirit of	Rom 8:15	
which *h* the firstfruits of the	Rom 8:23	*2192*
That I *h* great heaviness and	Rom 9:2	*2076*
I come, and Sarah shall *h* a son	Rom 9:9	*2071*
Jacob *h* I loved	Rom 9:13	
Esau *h* I hated	Rom 9:13	
h mercy on whom I will *h* mercy	Rom 9:15	
I will *h* compassion on whom I	Rom 9:15	
on whom I will *h* compassion	Rom 9:15	
same purpose *h* I raised thee up	Rom 9:17	
he mercy on whom he will *h* mercy	Rom 9:18	
h attained to righteousness, even	Rom 9:30	
record that they *h* a zeal of God	Rom 10:2	*2192*
h not submitted themselves unto	Rom 10:3	
him in whom they *h* not believed	Rom 10:14	
in him of whom they *h* not heard	Rom 10:14	
But they *h* not all obeyed the	Rom 10:16	
But I say, *H* they not heard	Rom 10:18	
All day long I *h* stretched forth	Rom 10:21	
they *h* killed thy prophets, and	Rom 11:3	
I *h* reserved to myself seven	Rom 11:4	
who *h* not bowed the knee to the	Rom 11:4	
H they stumbled that they should	Rom 11:11	
in times past *h* not believed God	Rom 11:30	
yet *h* now obtained mercy through	Rom 11:30	
Even so *h* these also now not	Rom 11:31	
that he might *h* mercy upon all	Rom 11:32	
For as we *h* many members in one	Rom 12:4	*2192*
all members *h* not the same office	Rom 12:4	*2192*
thou shalt *h* praise of the same	Rom 13:3	*2192*
h it to thyself before God	Rom 14:22	*2192*
of the scriptures might *h* hope	Rom 15:4	*2192*
I *h* written the more boldly unto	Rom 15:15	
I *h* therefore whereof I may glory	Rom 15:17	*2192*
I *h* fully preached the gospel of	Rom 15:19	
so *h* I strived to preach the	Rom 15:20	
they that *h* not heard shall	Rom 15:21	
For which cause also I *h* been	Rom 15:22	
For if the Gentiles *h* been made	Rom 15:27	
When therefore I *h* performed this	Rom 15:28	
h sealed to them this fruit, I	Rom 15:28	
that my service which I *h* for	Rom 15:31	
Who *h* for my life laid down their	Rom 16:4	
the doctrine which ye *h* learned	Rom 16:17	
but yet I would *h* you wise unto	Rom 16:19	
they would not *h* crucified the	1Cor 2:8	
neither *h* entered into the heart	1Cor 2:9	
Now we *h* received, not the spirit	1Cor 2:12	
But we *h* the mind of Christ	1Cor 2:16	*2192*
I *h* fed you with milk, and not	1Cor 3:2	
I *h* planted, Apollos watered	1Cor 3:6	
I *h* laid the foundation, and	1Cor 3:10	
shall every man *h* praise of God	1Cor 4:5	*1096*
I *h* in a figure transferred to	1Cor 4:6	
ye *h* reigned as kings without us	1Cor 4:8	
h no certain dwellingplace place	1Cor 4:11	
For though ye *h* ten thousand	1Cor 4:15	*2192*
yet *h* ye not many fathers	1Cor 4:15	
for in Christ Jesus I *h* begotten	1Cor 4:15	*2192*
For this cause *h* I sent unto you	1Cor 4:17	
that one should *h* his father's	1Cor 5:1	*2192*
h not rather mourned, that he	1Cor 5:2	
h judged already, as though I	1Cor 5:3	
But now I *h* written unto you not	1Cor 5:11	
For what *h* I to do to judge them	1Cor 5:12	
If then ye *h* judgments of things	1Cor 6:4	*2192*
is in you, which ye *h* of God	1Cor 6:19	*2192*
let every man *h* his own wife	1Cor 7:2	*2192*
let every woman *h* her own husband	1Cor 7:2	*2192*
Now concerning virgins I *h* no	1Cor 7:25	*2192*
such shall *h* trouble in the flesh	1Cor 7:28	*2192*
that both they that *h* wives be as	1Cor 7:29	*2192*
But I would *h* you without	1Cor 7:32	
also that I *h* the Spirit of God	1Cor 7:40	*2192*
we know that we all *h* knowledge	1Cor 8:1	*2192*
h I not seen Jesus Christ our	1Cor 9:1	
H we not power to eat and to drink	1Cor 9:4	*2192*
H we not power to lead about a	1Cor 9:5	*2192*
h not we power to forbear working	1Cor 9:6	*2192*
If we *h* sown unto you spiritual	1Cor 9:11	
Nevertheless we *h* not used this	1Cor 9:12	
But I *h* used none of these things	1Cor 9:15	
neither *h* I written these things,	1Cor 9:15	
gospel, I *h* nothing to glory of	1Cor 9:16	*2076*
thing willingly, I *h* a reward	1Cor 9:17	*2192*
yet *h* I made myself servant unto	1Cor 9:19	
when I *h* preached to others, I	1Cor 9:27	
should *h* fellowship with devils	1Cor 10:20	
But I would *h* you know, that the	1Cor 11:3	
to *h* power on her head because of	1Cor 11:10	*2192*
if a man *h* long hair, it is a	1Cor 11:14	
But if a woman *h* long hair	1Cor 11:15	
we *h* no such custom, neither the	1Cor 11:16	*2192*
h ye not houses to eat and to	1Cor 11:22	*2192*
of God, and shame them that *h* not	1Cor 11:22	*2192*
For I *h* received of the Lord that	1Cor 11:23	
I would not *h* you ignorant	1Cor 12:1	
h been all made to drink into one	1Cor 12:13	
the hand, I *h* no need of thee	1Cor 12:21	*2192*
to the feet, I *h* no need of you	1Cor 12:21	*2192*
our uncomely parts *h* more	1Cor 12:23	*2192*
For our comely parts *h* no need	1Cor 12:24	*2192*
but that the members should *h* the	1Cor 12:25	
H all the gifts of healing	1Cor 12:30	*2192*
h not charity, I am become as	1Cor 13:1	*2192*
though I *h* the gift of prophecy,	1Cor 13:2	*2192*
though I *h* all faith, so that I	1Cor 13:2	*2192*
h not charity, I am nothing	1Cor 13:2	*2192*
h not charity, it profiteth me	1Cor 13:3	*2192*
you, which also ye *h* received	1Cor 15:1	
unless ye *h* believed in vain	1Cor 15:2	
because we *h* testified of God	1Cor 15:15	
life only we *h* hope in Christ	1Cor 15:19	*2070*
when he shall *h* delivered up the	1Cor 15:24	
when he shall *h* put down all rule	1Cor 15:24	
I *h* in Christ Jesus our Lord	1Cor 15:31	*2192*
If after the manner of men I *h*	1Cor 15:32	
for some *h* not the knowledge of	1Cor 15:34	*2192*
as we *h* borne the image of the	1Cor 15:49	
shall *h* put on incorruption	1Cor 15:54	
this mortal shall *h* put on	1Cor 15:54	
as I *h* given order to the	1Cor 16:1	
when he shall *h* convenient time	1Cor 16:12	
that they *h* addicted themselves	1Cor 16:15	
on your part they *h* supplied	1Cor 16:17	
For they *h* refreshed my spirit and	1Cor 16:18	
h you ignorant of our trouble	2Cor 1:8	
we *h* had our conversation in the	2Cor 1:12	
As also ye *h* acknowledged us in	2Cor 1:14	
that ye might *h* a second benefit	2Cor 1:15	*2192*
Not for that we *h* dominion over	2Cor 1:24	
I should *h* sorrow from them of	2Cor 2:3	*2192*
I *h* more abundantly unto you	2Cor 2:4	*2192*
But if any *h* caused grief, he	2Cor 2:5	
such trust *h* we through Christ to	2Cor 3:4	*2192*
Seeing then that we *h* such hope	2Cor 3:12	*2192*
seeing we *h* this ministry	2Cor 4:1	*2192*
as we *h* received mercy, we faint	2Cor 4:1	
But *h* renounced the hidden things	2Cor 4:2	
But we *h* this treasure in earthen	2Cor 4:7	*2192*
believed, and therefore *h* I spoken	2Cor 4:13	
we *h* a building of God, an house	2Cor 5:1	*2192*
that ye may *h* somewhat to answer	2Cor 5:12	*2192*
though we *h* known Christ after	2Cor 5:16	
I *h* heard thee in a time accepted	2Cor 6:2	
of salvation *h* I succoured thee	2Cor 6:2	
we *h* wronged no man, we *h*	2Cor 7:2	
no man, we *h* defrauded no man	2Cor 7:2	
for I *h* said before, that ye are	2Cor 7:3	
In all things ye *h* approved	2Cor 7:11	
For if I *h* boasted any thing to	2Cor 7:14	
I rejoice therefore that I *h*	2Cor 7:16	
who *h* begun before, not only to	2Cor 8:10	
also out of that which ye *h*	2Cor 8:11	*2192*
we *h* sent with him the brother,	2Cor 8:18	
we *h* sent with them our brother,	2Cor 8:22	
whom we *h* oftentimes proved	2Cor 8:22	
great confidence which I *h* in you	2Cor 8:22	
Yet *h* I sent the brethren, lest	2Cor 9:3	
for I *h* espoused you to one	2Cor 11:2	
whom we *h* not preached, or if ye	2Cor 11:4	
which ye *h* not received, or	2Cor 11:4	
which ye *h* not accepted, ye might	2Cor 11:4	
but we *h* been throughly made	2Cor 11:6	
H I committed an offence in	2Cor 11:7	
because I *h* preached to you the	2Cor 11:7	
in all things I *h* kept myself	2Cor 11:9	
a day I *h* been in the deep	2Cor 11:25	
ye *h* compelled me	2Cor 12:11	
for I ought to *h* been commended	2Cor 12:11	
many which *h* sinned already	2Cor 12:21	
h not repented of the uncleanness	2Cor 12:21	
which they *h* committed	2Cor 12:21	
to them which heretofore *h* sinned	2Cor 13:2	
that which we *h* preached unto you	Gal 1:8	
unto you than that ye *h* received	Gal 1:9	
For ye *h* heard of my conversation	Gal 1:13	
which we *h* in Christ Jesus	Gal 2:4	*2192*
even we *h* believed in Jesus	Gal 2:16	
H ye suffered so many things in	Gal 3:4	
given which could *h* given life	Gal 3:21	
should *h* been by the law	Gal 3:21	
For as many of you as *h* been	Gal 3:27	
into Christ *h* put on Christ	Gal 3:27	
now, after that ye *h* known God	Gal 4:9	

lest I *h* bestowed upon you labour Gal 4:11
ye *h* not injured me at all Gal 4:12
ye would *h* plucked out your own Gal 4:15
and *h* given them to me Gal 4:15
I *h* confidence in you through the Gal 5:10
ye *h* been called unto liberty Gal 5:13
as I *h* also told you in time past Gal 5:21
And they that are Christ's *h* Gal 5:24
then shall he *h* rejoicing in Gal 6:4 *2192*
As we *h* therefore opportunity, Gal 6:10 *2192*
Ye see how large a letter I *h* Gal 6:11
but desire to *h* you circumcised, Gal 6:13
In whom we *h* redemption through Eph 1:7 *2192*
In whom also we *h* obtained an Eph 1:11
For through him we both *h* access Eph 2:18 *2192*
If ye *h* heard of the dispensation Eph 3:2
In whom we *h* boldness and access Eph 3:12 *2192*
Who being past feeling *h* given Eph 4:19
But ye *h* not so learned Christ Eph 4:20
If so be that ye *h* heard him Eph 4:21
h been taught by him, as the Eph 4:21
that he may *h* to give to him that Eph 4:28 *2192*
And *h* no fellowship with the Eph 5:11
Whom I *h* sent unto you for the Eph 6:22
because I *h* you in my heart Phil 1:7 *2192*
me *h* fallen out rather unto the Phil 1:12
as ye *h* always obeyed, not as in Phil 2:12
that I *h* not run in vain, neither Phil 2:16
For I *h* no man likeminded, who Phil 2:20 *2192*
lest I should *h* sorrow upon Phil 2:27 *2192*
h no confidence in the flesh Phil 3:3
Though I might also *h* confidence Phil 3:4 *2192*
for whom I *h* suffered the loss of Phil 3:8
count not myself to *h* apprehended Phil 3:13
whereto we *h* already attained, Phil 3:16
so as ye *h* us for an ensample Phil 3:17 *2192*
of whom I *h* told you often, and Phil 3:18
which ye *h* both learned, and Phil 4:9
for I *h* learned, in whatsoever Phil 4:11
Notwithstanding ye *h* well done Phil 4:14
But I *h* all, and abound Phil 4:18 *568*
love which ye *h* to all the saints Col 1:4
In whom we *h* redemption through Col 1:14 *2192*
things he might *h* the preeminence Col 1:18
of the gospel, which ye *h* heard Col 1:23
what great conflict I *h* for you Col 2:1 *2192*
for as many as *h* not seen my face Col 2:1
As ye *h* therefore received Christ Col 2:6
as ye *h* been taught, abounding Col 2:7
Which things *h* indeed a shew of Col 2:23 *2192*
seeing that ye *h* put off the old Col 3:9
h put on the new man, which is Col 3:10
if any man *h* a quarrel against Col 3:13 *2192*
that ye also *h* a Master in heaven Col 4:1 *2192*
Whom I *h* sent unto you for the Col 4:8
which *h* been a comfort unto me Col 4:11
when we might *h* been burdensome, 1Th 2:6
willing to *h* imparted unto you 1Th 2:8
for ye also *h* suffered like 1Th 2:14
even as they *h* of the Jews 1Th 2:14
own prophets, and *h* persecuted us 1Th 2:15
we would *h* come unto you, even I 1Th 2:18
means the tempter *h* tempted you 1Th 3:5
that ye *h* good remembrance of us 1Th 3:6 *2192*
that as ye *h* received of us how 1Th 4:1
as we also *h* forewarned you and 1Th 4:6
that ye may *h* lack of nothing 1Th 4:12 *2192*
But I would not *h* you to be 1Th 4:13
even as others which *h* no hope 1Th 4:13 *2192*
ye *h* no need that I write unto 1Th 5:1 *2192*
traditions which ye *h* been taught 2Th 2:15
of the Lord may *h* free course 2Th 3:1
for all men *h* not faith 2Th 3:2
we *h* confidence in the Lord 2Th 3:4
Not because we *h* not power 2Th 3:9 *2192*
h no company with him, that he 2Th 3:14
From which some having swerved *h* 1Ti 1:6
concerning faith *h* made shipwreck 1Ti 1:19
whom I *h* delivered unto Satan, 1Ti 1:20
Who will *h* all men to be saved, 1Ti 2:4
Moreover he must *h* a good report 1Ti 3:7 *2192*
For they that *h* used the office 1Ti 3:13
But if any widow *h* children or 1Ti 5:4 *2192*
if she *h* brought up children 1Ti 5:10
if she *h* lodged strangers 1Ti 5:10
if she *h* washed the saints' feet, 1Ti 5:10
if she *h* relieved the afflicted, 1Ti 5:10
if she *h* diligently followed 1Ti 5:10
for when they *h* begun to wax 1Ti 5:11
because they *h* cast off their 1Ti 5:12
or woman that believeth *h* widows 1Ti 5:16 *2192*
they that *h* believing masters, 1Ti 6:2 *2192*
they *h* erred from the faith, and 1Ti 6:10
Which some professing *h* erred 1Ti 6:21
that without ceasing I *h* 2Ti 1:3 *2192*
for I know whom I *h* believed 2Ti 1:12
h committed unto him against that 2Ti 1:12
Who concerning the truth *h* erred 2Ti 2:18
I *h* fought a good fight, I *h* 2Ti 4:7
my course, I *h* kept the faith 2Ti 4:7
Tychicus *h* I sent to Ephesus 2Ti 4:12
but Trophimus *h* I left at Miletum 2Ti 4:20
of righteousness which we *h* done Titus 3:5
that they which *h* believed in God Titus 3:8
for I *h* determined there to Titus 3:12
For we *h* great joy and consolation Philem 7 *2192*
whom I *h* begotten in my bonds Philem 10
Whom I *h* sent again Philem 12
Whom I would *h* retained with me, Philem 13
that in thy stead he might *h* Philem 13
I Paul *h* written it with mine own Philem 19
let me *h* joy of thee in the Lord Philem 20
this day *h* I begotten thee Heb 1:5
to the things which we *h* heard Heb 2:1

and they *h* not known my ways Heb 3:10
For we which *h* believed do enter Heb 4:3
As I *h* sworn in my wrath, if they Heb 4:3
afterward *h* spoken of another day Heb 4:8
eyes of him with whom we *h* to do Heb 4:13
that we *h* a great high priest Heb 4:14 *2192*
For we *h* not an high priest which Heb 4:15 *2192*
Who can *h* compassion on the Heb 5:2
my Son, to day *h* I begotten thee Heb 5:5
Of whom we *h* many things to say, Heb 5:11
ye *h* need that one teach you Heb 5:12 *2192*
are become such as *h* need of milk Heb 5:12 *2192*
use *h* their senses exercised to Heb 5:14 *2192*
h tasted of the heavenly gift, and Heb 6:4
h tasted the good word of God, and Heb 6:5
which ye *h* shewed toward his name Heb 6:10
in that ye *h* ministered to the Heb 6:10
we might *h* a strong consolation, Heb 6:18 *2192*
who *h* fled for refuge to lay hold Heb 6:18
Which hope we *h* as an anchor of Heb 6:19 *2192*
h a commandment to take tithes of Heb 7:5 *2192*
high priests which *h* infirmity Heb 7:28 *2192*
which we *h* spoken this is the sum Heb 8:1
We *h* such an high priest, who is Heb 8:1 *2192*
this man *h* somewhat also to offer Heb 8:3 *2192*
then should no place *h* been Heb 8:7
For then must he often *h* suffered Heb 9:26
they not *h* ceased to be offered Heb 10:2
h had no more conscience of sins Heb 10:2 *2192*
h received the knowledge of the Heb 10:26
that ye *h* in heaven a better Heb 10:34 *2192*
For ye *h* need of patience, that, Heb 10:36
after ye *h* done the will of God, Heb 10:36
my soul shall *h* no pleasure in Heb 10:38
they might *h* had opportunity to Heb 11:15 *2192*
had opportunity to *h* returned Heb 11:15
Ye *h* not yet resisted unto blood, Heb 12:4
ye *h* forgotten the exhortation Heb 12:5
Furthermore we *h* had fathers of Heb 12:9 *2192*
when he would *h* inherited the Heb 12:17
cannot be moved, let us *h* grace Heb 12:28 *2192*
for thereby some *h* entertained Heb 13:2
content with such things as ye *h* Heb 13:5 *3918*
them which *h* the rule over you Heb 13:7
who *h* spoken unto you the word of Heb 13:7
which *h* not profited them that Heb 13:9
them that *h* been occupied therein Heb 13:9
We *h* an altar, whereof they *h* Heb 13:10 *2192*
For here *h* we no continuing city, Heb 13:14 *2192*
Obey them that *h* the rule over Heb 13:17
for we trust we *h* a good Heb 13:18 *2192*
for I *h* written a letter unto you Heb 13:22
all them that *h* the rule over you Heb 13:24
let patience *h* her perfect work Jas 1:4 *2192*
h not the faith of our Lord Jesus Jas 2:1 *2192*
ye *h* respect to him that weareth Jas 2:3
But ye *h* despised the poor Jas 2:6
But if ye *h* respect to persons, Jas 2:9
For he shall *h* judgment without Jas 2:13
say he hath faith, and *h* not works Jas 2:14 *2192*
Thou hast faith, and I *h* works Jas 2:18
But if ye *h* bitter envying and Jas 3:14 *2192*
Ye lust, and *h* not Jas 4:2 *2192*
ye kill, and desire to *h*, and Jas 4:2 *2192*
ye fight and war, yet ye *h* not Jas 4:2 *2192*
Ye *h* heaped treasure together for Jas 5:3
who *h* reaped down your fields Jas 5:4 *2192*
the cries of them which *h* reaped Jas 5:4
Ye *h* lived in pleasure on the Jas 5:5
ye *h* nourished your hearts, as in Jas 5:5
Ye *h* condemned and killed the just Jas 5:6
who *h* spoken in the name of the Jas 5:10
Ye *h* heard of the patience of Job Jas 5:11
h seen the end of the Lord Jas 5:11
if he *h* committed sins, they Jas 5:15
salvation the prophets *h* enquired 1Pet 1:10
h preached the gospel unto you 1Pet 1:12
Seeing ye *h* purified your souls 1Pet 1:22
If so be ye *h* tasted that the 1Pet 2:3
mercy, but now *h* obtained mercy 1Pet 2:10
us to *h* wrought the will of the 1Pet 4:3
above all things *h* fervent 1Pet 4:8 *2192*
after that ye *h* suffered a while, 1Pet 5:10
I *h* written briefly, exhorting, 1Pet 5:12
to them that *h* obtained like 2Pet 1:1
to *h* these things always in 2Pet 1:15
For we *h* not followed cunningly 2Pet 1:16
We *h* also a more sure word of 2Pet 1:19 *2192*
an heart they *h* exercised with 2Pet 2:14 *2192*
Which *h* forsaken the right way, 2Pet 2:15
For if after they *h* escaped the 2Pet 2:20
h known the way of righteousness 2Pet 2:21
than, after they *h* known it 2Pet 2:21
the beginning, which we *h* heard 1Jn 1:1
which we *h* seen with our eyes, 1Jn 1:1
which we *h* looked upon 1Jn 1:1
and our hands *h* handled 1Jn 1:1
we *h* seen it, and bear witness, and 1Jn 1:2
That which we *h* seen and heard 1Jn 1:3
that ye also may *h* fellowship 1Jn 1:3 *2192*
message which we *h* heard of him 1Jn 1:5
If we say that we *h* fellowship 1Jn 1:6 *2192*
we *h* fellowship one with another, 1Jn 1:7 *2192*
If we say that we *h* no sin 1Jn 1:8 *2192*
If we say that we *h* not sinned 1Jn 1:10
we *h* an advocate with the Father, 1Jn 2:1 *2192*
is the word which ye *h* heard from 1Jn 2:7
because ye *h* known him that is 1Jn 2:13
because ye *h* overcome the wicked 1Jn 2:13
because ye *h* known the Father 1Jn 2:13
I *h* written unto you, fathers, 1Jn 2:14
because ye *h* known him that is 1Jn 2:14
I *h* written unto you, young men, 1Jn 2:14
ye *h* overcome the wicked one 1Jn 2:14

as ye *h* heard that antichrist 1Jn 2:18
no doubt *h* continued with us 1Jn 2:19
But ye *h* an unction from the Holy 1Jn 2:20 *2192*
I *h* not written unto you because 1Jn 2:21
which ye *h* heard from the 1Jn 2:24
If that which ye *h* heard from the 1Jn 2:24
These things *h* I written unto you 1Jn 2:26
But the anointing which ye *h* 1Jn 2:27
we may *h* confidence, and not be 1Jn 2:28 *2192*
We know that we *h* passed from 1Jn 3:14
good, and seeth his brother *h* need 1Jn 3:17 *2192*
then *h* we confidence toward God 1Jn 3:21 *2192*
whereof ye *h* heard that it should 1Jn 4:3
children, and *h* overcome them 1Jn 4:4
we *h* seen and do testify that the 1Jn 4:14
we *h* known and believed the love 1Jn 4:16
that we may *h* boldness in the day 1Jn 4:17 *2192*
And this commandment *h* we 1Jn 4:21 *2192*
These things *h* I written unto you 1Jn 5:13
may know that ye *h* eternal life 1Jn 5:13 *2192*
the confidence that we *h* in him 1Jn 5:14 *2192*
we know that we *h* the petitions 1Jn 5:15 *2192*
all they that *h* known the truth 2Jn 1
as we *h* received a commandment 2Jn 4
as ye *h* heard from the beginning, 2Jn 6
those things which we *h* wrought 2Jn 8
I *h* no greater joy than to hear 3Jn 4 *2192*
Which *h* borne witness of thy 3Jn 6
who loveth to *h* the preeminence 3Jn 9
for they *h* gone in the way of Jude 11
which they *h* ungodly committed Jude 15
sinners *h* spoken against him Jude 15
of some *h* compassion, making a Jude 22
h the keys of hell and of death Rev 1:18 *2192*
Nevertheless I *h* somewhat against Rev 2:4 *2192*
ye shall *h* tribulation ten days Rev 2:10 *2192*
But I *h* a few things against thee Rev 2:14 *2192*
Notwithstanding I *h* a few things Rev 2:20 *2192*
as many as *h* not this doctrine, Rev 2:24
which *h* not known the depths of Rev 2:24 *2192*
But that which ye *h* already hold Rev 2:25 *2192*
for I *h* not found thy works Rev 3:2
h not defiled their garments Rev 3:4
I *h* set before thee an open door, Rev 3:8
and to know that I *h* loved thee Rev 3:9
with goods, and *h* need of nothing Rev 3:17 *2192*
till we *h* sealed the servants of Rev 7:3
h washed their robes, and made Rev 7:14
scorpions of the earth *h* power Rev 9:3 *2192*
but only those men which *h* not Rev 9:4 *2192*
These *h* power to shut heaven, Rev 11:6 *2192*
h power over waters to turn them Rev 11:6 *2192*
when they shall *h* finished their Rev 11:7
h the testimony of Jesus Christ Rev 12:17 *2192*
If any man *h* an ear, let him hear Rev 13:9 *2192*
they *h* no rest day nor night, who Rev 14:11 *2192*
For they *h* shed the blood of Rev 16:6
the earth *h* committed fornication Rev 17:2
the inhabitants of the earth *h* Rev 17:2
which *h* received no kingdom as Rev 17:12
These *h* one mind, and shall give Rev 17:13 *2192*
For all nations *h* drunk of the Rev 18:3
and the kings of the earth *h* Rev 18:3
For her sins *h* reached unto Rev 18:5
who *h* committed fornication and Rev 18:9
of thy brethren that *h* the Rev 19:10 *2192*
shall *h* their part in the lake Rev 21:8
that they may *h* right to the tree Rev 22:14 *2071*
I Jesus *h* sent mine angel to Rev 22:16

HAVEN
shall dwell at the *h* of the sea Gen 49:13 2348
and he shall be for an *h* of ships Gen 49:13 2348
them unto their desired *h* Ps 107:30 4231
because the *h* was not commodious Acts 27:12 *3040*
which is an *h* of Crete, and lieth Acts 27:12 *3040*

HAVENS
place which is called The fair *h* Acts 27:8 *2568*

HAVILAH (*hav'-il-ah*)
1. A son of Cush.
H, and Sabtah, and Raamah, Gen 10:7 2341
Seba, and *H*, and Sabta, and Raamah, 1Chr 1:9 2341
2. A son of Joktan.
And Ophir, and *H*, and Jobab Gen 10:29 2341
And Ophir, and *H*, and Jobab 1Chr 1:23 2341
3. A land west of Ural.
compasseth the whole land of *H* Gen 2:11 2341
4. A district east of Amalek.
And they dwelt from *H* unto Shur Gen 25:18 2341
from *H* until thou comest to Shur 1Sa 15:7 2341

HAVING
h Beth-el on the west, and Hai on Gen 12:8
h his uncleanness upon him, even Lev 7:20
lie with a woman *h* her sickness Lev 20:18
h his uncleanness upon him, that Lev 22:3
or *h* a wen, or scurvy, or scabbed Lev 22:22
a trance, but *h* his eyes open Num 24:4
a trance, but *h* his eyes open Num 24:16
h the two tables in mine hand Deut 10:3
h their thumbs and their great Judg 1:7
h his servant with him, and a Judg 19:3
ye stay for them from *h* husbands Ruth 1:13
h his spear in his hand, and all 1Sa 22:6
h three thousand chosen men of 1Sa 26:2
h put on their robes, in a void 1Kin 22:10
h for their captains Pelatiah, and 1Chr 4:42
h a drawn sword in his hand 1Chr 21:16
h wards one against another, to 1Chr 26:12
h cymbals and psalteries and harps, 2Chr 5:12
h Judah and Benjamin on his side 2Chr 11:12
every man *h* his weapon in his 2Chr 23:10
h rent my garment and my mantle, I Ezr 9:5
h knowledge, and *h* understanding Neh 10:28

H

h the oversight of the chamber of........ Neh 13:4 5414
mourning, and *h* his head covered........ Est 6:12
h sorrow in my heart daily........ Ps 13:2
Which *h* no guide, overseer, or........ Prov 6:7
h separated himself, seeketh and........ Prov 18:1
h a live coal in his hand, which........ Is 6:6
threshing instrument *h* teeth........ Is 41:15 1167
h their beards shaven, and their........ Jer 41:5
h cut themselves, with offerings........ Jer 41:5
h neither bars nor gates,........ Eze 38:11
at the side of the east gate *h*........ Eze 40:44
h charge at the gates of the........ Eze 44:11
The ram which thou sawest *h* two........ Dan 8:20 1167
of Saphir, *h* thy shame naked........ Mic 1:11
he is just, and *h* salvation........ Zec 9:9
he taught them as one *h* authority........ Mt 7:29 *2192*
authority, *h* soldiers under me........ Mt 8:9 *2192*
abroad, as sheep *h* no shepherd........ Mt 9:36 *2192*
h with them those that were lame,........ Mt 15:30 *2192*
rather than *h* two hands or two........ Mt 18:8 *2192*
rather than *h* two eyes to be cast........ Mt 18:9 *2192*
in hither not *h* a wedding garment........ Mt 22:12 *2192*
h no children, his brother shall........ Mt 22:24 *2192*
h no issue, left his wife unto........ Mt 22:25 *2192*
woman *h* an alabaster box of very........ Mt 26:7 *2192*
were as sheep not *h* a shepherd........ Mk 6:34 *2192*
h nothing to eat, Jesus called........ Mk 8:1 *2192*
H eyes, see ye not........ Mk 8:18 *2192*
and *h* ears, hear ye not........ Mk 8:18 *2192*
than *h* two hands to go into hell,........ Mk 9:43 *2192*
than *h* two feet to be cast into........ Mk 9:45 *2192*
than *h* two eyes to be cast into........ Mk 9:47 *2192*
a fig tree afar off *h* leaves........ Mk 11:13 *2192*
H yet therefore one son, his........ Mk 12:6 *2192*
h heard them reasoning together,........ Mk 12:28
there came a woman *h* an alabaster........ Mk 14:3 *2192*
h a linen cloth cast about his........ Mk 14:51
h had perfect understanding of........ Lk 1:3
No man also *h* drunk old wine........ Lk 5:39
h under me soldiers, and I say........ Lk 7:8 *2192*
h heard the word, keep it, and........ Lk 8:15
a woman *h* an issue of blood........ Lk 8:43
h put his hand to the plough, and........ Lk 9:62
h no part dark, the whole shall........ Lk 11:36 *2192*
h an hundred sheep, if he lose........ Lk 15:4 *2192*
Either what woman *h* ten pieces of........ Lk 15:8 *2192*
h a servant plowing or feeding........ Lk 17:7 *2192*
h received the kingdom, then he........ Lk 19:15
h a wife, and he die without........ Lk 20:28 *2192*
h examined him before you, have........ Lk 23:14
h said thus, he gave up the ghost........ Lk 23:46
h seen all the things that he did........ Jn 4:45
tongue Bethesda, *h* five porches........ Jn 5:2 *2192*
this man letters, *h* never learned........ Jn 7:15
h loved his own which were in the........ Jn 13:1
the devil *h* now put into the........ Jn 13:2
He then *h* received the sop went........ Jn 13:30
h received a band of men and........ Jn 18:3
Simon Peter *h* a sword drew it........ Jn 18:10 *2192*
h loosed the pains of death........ Acts 2:24
h received of the Father the........ Acts 2:33
h favour with all the people........ Acts 2:47 *2192*
h raised up his Son Jesus, sent........ Acts 3:26
H land, sold it, and brought the........ Acts 4:37
h made Blastus the king's........ Acts 12:20
h stoned Paul, drew him out of........ Acts 14:19
h received such a charge, thrust........ Acts 16:24
h shorn his head in Cenchrea........ Acts 18:18
Paul *h* passed through the upper........ Acts 19:1
h caught Gaius and Aristarchus,........ Acts 19:29
h a good report of all the Jews........ Acts 22:12
h understood that he was a Roman........ Acts 23:27
h more perfect knowledge of that........ Acts 24:22
h received authority from the........ Acts 26:10
H therefore obtained help of God,........ Acts 26:22
fasting, *h* taken nothing........ Acts 27:33
h not the law, are a law unto........ Rom 2:14 *2192*
neither *h* done any good or evil,........ Rom 9:11
H then gifts differing according........ Rom 12:6 *2192*
But now *h* no more place in these........ Rom 15:23 *2192*
h a great desire these many years........ Rom 15:23 *2192*
h a matter against another, go to........ 1Cor 6:1 *2192*
h no necessity, but hath power........ 1Cor 7:37 *2192*
h his head covered, dishonoureth........ 1Cor 11:4 *2192*
h given more abundant honour to........ 1Cor 12:24
h confidence in you all, that my........ 2Cor 2:3
We *h* the same spirit of faith,........ 2Cor 4:13 *2192*
as *h* nothing, and yet possessing........ 2Cor 6:10 *2192*
H therefore these promises dearly........ 2Cor 7:1 *2192*
always *h* all sufficiency in all........ 2Cor 9:8 *2192*
h in a readiness to revenge all........ 2Cor 10:6 *2192*
but *h* hope, when your faith is........ 2Cor 10:15 *2192*
h begun in the Spirit, are ye now........ Gal 3:3
H predestinated us unto the........ Eph 1:5
H made known unto us the mystery........ Eph 1:9
h no hope, and without God in the........ Eph 2:12 *2192*
H abolished in his flesh the........ Eph 2:15
h slain the enmity thereby........ Eph 2:16
H the understanding darkened,........ Eph 4:18
not *h* spot, or wrinkle, or any........ Eph 5:27 *2192*
evil day, and *h* done all, to stand........ Eph 6:13
h your loins girt about with........ Eph 6:14
truth, and *h* on the breastplate of........ Eph 6:14 *1746*
h a desire to depart, and to be........ Phil 1:23 *2192*
h this confidence, I know that I........ Phil 1:25
H the same conflict which ye saw........ Phil 1:30 *2192*
h the same love, being of one........ Phil 2:2 *2192*
not *h* mine own righteousness,........ Phil 3:9 *2192*
h received of Epaphroditus the........ Phil 4:18
h made peace through the blood of........ Col 1:20
h forgiven you all trespasses........ Col 2:13
h spoiled principalities and........ Col 2:15
bands *h* nourishment ministered,........ Col 2:19
h received the word in much........ 1Th 1:6

From which some *h* swerved have........ 1Ti 1:6
which some *h* put away concerning........ 1Ti 1:19
h his children in subjection with........ 1Ti 3:4 *2192*
h their conscience seared with a........ 1Ti 4:2
h promise of the life that now is........ 1Ti 4:8 *2192*
h been the wife of one man,........ 1Ti 5:9
H damnation, because they have........ 1Ti 5:12 *2192*
h food and raiment let us be........ 1Ti 6:8 *2192*
h this seal, The Lord knoweth........ 2Ti 2:19 *2192*
H a form of godliness, but........ 2Ti 3:5 *2192*
teachers, *h* itching ears........ 2Ti 4:3
h loved this present world, and is........ 2Ti 4:10
h faithful children not accused........ Titus 1:6 *2192*
h no evil thing to say of you........ Titus 2:8 *2192*
H confidence in thy obedience I........ Philem 21
h neither beginning of days, nor........ Heb 7:3 *2192*
h obtained eternal redemption for........ Heb 9:12
For the law *h* a shadow of good........ Heb 10:1 *2192*
H therefore, brethren, boldness........ Heb 10:19 *2192*
h an high priest over the house........ Heb 10:21
h our hearts sprinkled from an........ Heb 10:22
not *h* received the promises........ Heb 11:13
but *h* seen them afar off, and were........ Heb 11:13
h obtained a good report through........ Heb 11:39
God *h* provided some better thing........ Heb 11:40
Whom *h* not seen, ye love........ 1Pet 1:8
H your conversation honest among........ 1Pet 2:12 *2192*
h compassion one of another, love........ 1Pet 3:8
H a good conscience........ 1Pet 3:16 *2192*
h escaped the corruption that is........ 2Pet 1:4
H eyes full of adultery, and that........ 2Pet 2:14 *2192*
H many things to write unto you,........ 2Jn 12 *2192*
h saved the people out of the........ Jude 5
h men's persons in admiration........ Jude 16
sensual, *h* not the Spirit........ Jude 19 *2192*
h seven horns and seven eyes,........ Rev 5:6 *2192*
h every one of them harps, and........ Rev 5:8 *2192*
h the seal of the living God........ Rev 7:2 *2192*
at the altar, *h* a golden censer........ Rev 8:3 *2192*
h breastplates of fire, and of........ Rev 9:17 *2192*
h seven heads and ten horns, and........ Rev 12:3 *2192*
h great wrath, because he knoweth........ Rev 12:12 *2192*
h seven heads and ten horns, and........ Rev 13:1 *2192*
h his Father's name written in........ Rev 14:1 *2192*
h the everlasting gospel to........ Rev 14:6 *2192*
h on his head a golden crown, and........ Rev 14:14 *2192*
heaven, he also *h* a sharp sickle........ Rev 14:17 *2192*
seven angels *h* the seven last........ Rev 15:1 *2192*
sea of glass, *h* the harps of God........ Rev 15:2 *2192*
h the seven plagues, clothed in........ Rev 15:6 *2192*
h their breasts girded with........ Rev 15:6 *2192*
h seven heads and ten horns........ Rev 17:3 *2192*
h a golden cup in her hand full........ Rev 17:4 *2192*
down from heaven, *h* great power........ Rev 18:1 *2192*
h the key of the bottomless pit........ Rev 20:1 *2192*
H the glory of God........ Rev 21:11 *2192*

HAVOCK
he made *h* of the church, entering........ Acts 8:3 *3075*

HAVOTH-JAIR (*ha''-voth-ja'-ir*) See BASHAN-HAVOTH. *Villages in Gilead.*
towns thereof, and called them *H*........ Num 32:41 2334
which are called *H* unto this day........ Judg 10:4 2334

HAWK
And the owl, and the night *h*........ Lev 11:16 8464
cuckow, and the *h* after his kind,........ Lev 11:16 5322
And the owl, and the night *h*........ Deut 14:15 8464
cuckow, and the *h* after his kind,........ Deut 14:15 5322
Doth the *h* fly by thy wisdom, and........ Job 39:26 5322

HAY
The *h* appeareth, and the tender........ Prov 27:25 2682
for the *h* is withered away, the........ Is 15:6 2682
silver, precious stones, wood, *h*........ 1Cor 3:12 *5528*

HAZAEL (*ha'-za-el*) *A king of Syria.*
anoint *H* to be king over Syria........ 1Kin 19:15 2371
the sword of *H* shall Jehu slay........ 1Kin 19:17 2371
And the king said unto *H*, Take a........ 2Kin 8:8 2371
So *H* went to meet him, and took a........ 2Kin 8:9 2371
H said, Why weepeth my lord........ 2Kin 8:12 2371
H said, But what, is thy servant........ 2Kin 8:13 2371
and *H* reigned in his stead........ 2Kin 8:15 2371
H king of Syria in Ramoth-gilead........ 2Kin 8:28 2371
he fought against *H* king of Syria........ 2Kin 8:29 2371
because of *H* king of Syria........ 2Kin 9:14 2371
he fought with *H* king of Syria........ 2Kin 9:15 2371
H smote them in all the coasts of........ 2Kin 10:32 2371
Then *H* king of Syria went up, and........ 2Kin 12:17 2371
H set his face to go up to........ 2Kin 12:17 2371
sent it to *H* king of Syria........ 2Kin 12:18 2371
into the hand of *H* king of Syria........ 2Kin 13:3 2371
hand of Ben-hadad the son of *H*........ 2Kin 13:3 2371
But *H* king of Syria oppressed........ 2Kin 13:22 2371
So *H* king of Syria died........ 2Kin 13:24 2371
Ben-hadad the son of *H* the cities........ 2Kin 13:25 2371
king of Israel to war against *H*........ 2Chr 22:5 2371
he fought with *H* king of Syria........ 2Chr 22:6 2371
send a fire into the house of *H*........ Amos 1:4 2371

HAZAIAH (*ha-za-i'-ah*) *Son of Adaiah.*
the son of Colhozeh, the son of *H*........ Neh 11:5 2382

HAZAR-ADDAR (*ha''-zar-ad'-dar*) See ADDAR. *A place in southern Palestine.*
and shall go on to *H*, and pass on........ Num 34:4 2692

HAZARDED
Men that have *h* their lives for........ Acts 15:26 *3860*

HAZAR-ENAN (*ha''-zar-e'-nan*) *A village in northeastern Palestine.*
goings out of it shall be at *H*........ Num 34:9 2704
east border from *H* to Shepham........ Num 34:10 2704
border from the sea shall be *H*........ Eze 47:17 2703
as one goeth to Hamath, *H*........ Eze 48:1 2704

HAZAR-GADDAH (*ha''-zar-gad'-dah*) *A town in Judah.*
And *H*, and Heshmon, and Beth-palet,. Josh 15:27 2693

HAZAR-HATTICON (*ha''-zar-hat'-ti-con*) *A place in Hauran.*
H, which is by the coast of........ Eze 47:16 2694

HAZARMAVETH (*ha-zar-ma'-veth*) *A son of Joktan.*
begat Almodad, and Sheleph, and *H*..... Gen 10:26 2700
begat Almodad, and Sheleph, and *H*..... 1Chr 1:20 2700

HAZAR-SHUAL (*ha''-zar-shoo'-al*) *A town in Judah.*
And *H*, and Beer-sheba, and........ Josh 15:28 2705
And *H*, and Balah, and Azem,........ Josh 19:3 2705
at Beer-sheba, and Moladah, and *H*........ 1Chr 4:28 2705
And at *H*, and at Beer-sheba, and in..... Neh 11:27 2705

HAZAR-SUSAH (*ha''-zar-soo'-sah*) See HAZAR-SUSIM. *A city in Judah.*
Ziklag, and Beth-marcaboth, and *H*..... Josh 19:5 2701

HAZAR-SUSIM (*ha''-zar-soo'-sim*) See HAZAR-SUSAH. *Same as Hazar-susah.*
And at Beth-marcaboth, and *H*........ 1Chr 4:31 2702

HAZAZON-TAMAR (*haz''-a-zon-ta'-mar*) See HAZEZON-TAMAR. *A name for En-gedi.*
and, behold, they be in *H*, which........ 2Chr 20:2 2688

HAZEL
rods of green poplar, and of the *h*........ Gen 30:37 3869

HAZELELPONI (*haz-el-el-po'-ni*) *Sister of the sons of Etam.*
and the name of their sister was *H*..... 1Chr 4:3 6753

HAZER-HATTICON See HAZAR-HATTICON.

HAZERIM (*haz'-e-rim*) *A district near Gaza.*
And the Avims which dwelt in *H*........ Deut 2:23 2699

HAZEROTH (*haz'-e-roth*) *A Hebrew encampment in the wilderness.*
from Kibroth-hattaavah unto *H*........ Num 11:35 2698
and abode at *H*........ Num 11:35 2698
the people removed from *H*........ Num 12:16 2698
and encamped at *H*........ Num 33:17 2698
And they departed from *H*, and........ Num 33:18 2698
Paran, and Tophel, and Laban, and *H*.. Deut 1:1 2698

HAZEZON-TAMAR (*haz''-e-zon-ta'-mar*) See EN-GEDI, HAZAZON-TAMAR. *Same as Hazazon-tamar.*
the Amorites, that dwelt in *H*........ Gen 14:7 2688

HAZIEL (*ha'-ze-el*) *A Levite.*
Shelomith, and *H*, and Haran, three..... 1Chr 23:9 2381

HAZO (*ha'-zo*) *A son of Nahor.*
And Chesed, and *H*, and Pildash, and... Gen 22:22 2375

HAZOBEBAH See HAZELELPONI.

HAZOR (*ha'-zor*) See BAAL-HAZOR, EN-HAZOR, HEZRON.
1. A fortified city in Naphtali.
when Jabin king of *H* had heard........ Josh 11:1 2674
that time turned back, and took *H*........ Josh 11:10 2674
for *H* beforetime was the head of........ Josh 11:10 2674
and he burnt *H* with fire........ Josh 11:11 2674
burned none of them, save *H* only........ Josh 11:13 2674
the king of *H*, one........ Josh 12:19 2674
And Adamah, and Ramah, and *H*........ Josh 19:36 2674
king of Canaan, that reigned in *H*........ Judg 4:2 2674
peace between Jabin the king of *H*........ Judg 4:17 2674
Sisera, captain of the host of *H*........ 1Sa 12:9 2674
and the wall of Jerusalem, and *H*........ 1Kin 9:15 2674
H, Ramah, Gittaim,........ Neh 11:33 2674
2. A city in Judah.
And Kedesh, and *H*, and Ithnan,........ Josh 15:23 2674
and Janoah, and Kedesh, and *H*........ 2Kin 15:29 2674
3. Another town in Judah.
And *H*, Hadattah, and Kerioth, and..... Josh 15:25 2675
and Kerioth, and Hezron, which is *H*... Josh 15:25 2674
4. Where the Benjamites lived after the Exile.
and concerning the kingdoms of *H*........ Jer 49:28 2674
5. An area in eastern Arabia.
dwell deep, O ye inhabitants of *H*........ Jer 49:30 2674
H shall be a dwelling for dragons........ Jer 49:33 2674

HAZZELELPONI See HAZELELPONI.

HE (*hay*) See PREFACE. *A Hebrew letter.*

HEAD
it shall bruise thy *h*, and thou........ Gen 3:15 7218
And the man bowed down his *h*........ Gen 24:26
And I bowed down my *h*, and........ Gen 24:48
shall Pharaoh lift up thine *h*........ Gen 40:13 7218
I had three white baskets on my *h*........ Gen 40:16 7218
them out of the basket upon my *h*........ Gen 40:17 7218
lift up thy *h* from off thee........ Gen 40:19 7218
he lifted up the *h* of the chief........ Gen 40:20 7218
bowed himself upon the bed's *h*........ Gen 47:31 7218
hand, and laid it upon Ephraim's *h*........ Gen 48:14 7218
his left hand upon Manasseh's *h*........ Gen 48:14 7218
right hand upon the *h* of Ephraim........ Gen 48:17 7218
Ephraim's *h* unto Manasseh's *h*........ Gen 48:17 7218
put thy right hand upon his *h*........ Gen 48:18 7218
they shall be on the *h* of Joseph........ Gen 49:26 7218
on the crown of the *h* of him that........ Gen 49:26 6936
his *h* with his legs, and with the........ Ex 12:9 7218
And the people bowed the *h*........ Ex 12:27
above the *h* of it unto one ring........ Ex 26:24 7218
shalt put the mitre upon his *h*........ Ex 29:6 7218
oil, and pour it upon his *h*........ Ex 29:7 7218
hands upon the *h* of the bullock........ Ex 29:10 7218
their hands upon the *h* of the ram........ Ex 29:15 7218
unto his pieces, and unto his *h*........ Ex 29:17 7218
their hands upon the *h* of the ram........ Ex 29:19 7218

bowed his *h* toward the earth, and ... Ex 34:8
coupled together at the *h* thereof ... Ex 36:29 7218
upon the *h* of the burnt offering ... Lev 1:4 7218
sons, shall lay the parts, the *h* ... Lev 1:8 7218
it into his pieces, with his *h* ... Lev 1:12 7218
the altar, and wring off his *h* ... Lev 1:15 7218
hand upon the *h* of his offering ... Lev 3:2 7218
hand upon the *h* of his offering ... Lev 3:8 7218
lay his hand upon the *h* of it ... Lev 3:13 7218
lay his hand upon the bullock's *h* ... Lev 4:4 7218
and all his flesh, with his *h* ... Lev 4:11 7218
h of the bullock before the LORD ... Lev 4:15 7218
his hand upon the *h* of the goat ... Lev 4:24 7218
upon the *h* of the sin offering ... Lev 4:29 7218
upon the *h* of the sin offering ... Lev 4:33 7218
and wring off his *h* from his neck ... Lev 5:8 7218
And he put the mitre upon his *h* ... Lev 8:9 7218
the anointing oil upon Aaron's *h* ... Lev 8:12 7218
the *h* of the bullock for the sin ... Lev 8:14 7218
their hands upon the *h* of the ram ... Lev 8:18 7218
and Moses burnt the *h*, and the ... Lev 8:20 7218
their hands upon the *h* of the ram ... Lev 8:22 7218
with the pieces thereof, and the *h* ... Lev 9:13 7218
from his *h* even to his foot ... Lev 13:12 7218
a plague upon the *h* or the beard ... Lev 13:29 7218
a leprosy upon the *h* or beard ... Lev 13:30 7218
whose hair is fallen off his *h* ... Lev 13:40 7218
the part of his *h* toward his face ... Lev 13:41 7218
And if there be in the bald *h* ... Lev 13:42
a leprosy sprung up in his bald *h* ... Lev 13:42
be white reddish in his bald *h* ... Lev 13:43
his plague is in his *h* ... Lev 13:44 7218
his *h* bare, and he shall put a ... Lev 13:45 7218
shave all his hair off his *h* ... Lev 14:9 7218
hand he shall pour upon the *h* of ... Lev 14:18 7218
hand he shall put upon the *h* of ... Lev 14:29 7218
hands upon the *h* of the live goat ... Lev 16:21 7218
them upon the *h* of the goat ... Lev 16:21 7218
shalt rise up before the hoary *h* ... Lev 19:32
not make baldness upon their *h* ... Lev 21:5 7218
upon whose *h* the anointing oil ... Lev 21:10 7218
garments, shall not uncover his *h* ... Lev 21:10 7218
him lay their hands upon his *h* ... Lev 24:14 7218
every one *h* of the house of his ... Num 1:4 7218
LORD, and uncover the woman's *h* ... Num 5:18 7218
shall no razor come upon his *h* ... Num 6:5 7218
locks of the hair of his *h* grow ... Num 6:5 7218
of his God is upon his *h* ... Num 6:7 7218
defiled the *h* of his consecration ... Num 6:9 7218
then he shall shave his *h* in the ... Num 6:9 7218
shall hallow his *h* that same day ... Num 6:11 7218
the Nazarite shall shave the *h* of ... Num 6:18 7218
hair of the *h* of his separation ... Num 6:18 7218
for one rod shall be for the *h* of ... Num 17:3 7218
and he bowed down his *h*, and fell ... Num 22:31
he was *h* over a people, and of a ... Num 25:15 7218
the *h* slippeth from the helve, and ... Deut 19:5 1270
and she shall shave her *h*, and pare ... Deut 21:12 7218
And the LORD shall make thee the *h* ... Deut 28:13 7218
that is over thy *h* shall be brass ... Deut 28:23 7218
of thy foot unto the top of thy *h* ... Deut 28:35 6936
he shall be the *h*, and thou shalt ... Deut 28:44 7218
come upon the *h* of Joseph ... Deut 33:16 7218
upon the top of the *h* of him that ... Deut 33:16 6936
the arm with the crown of the *h* ... Deut 33:20 6936
his blood shall be upon his *h* ... Josh 2:19 7218
his blood shall be on our *h* ... Josh 2:19 7218
was the *h* of all those kingdoms ... Josh 11:10 7218
each one was an *h* of the house of ... Josh 22:14 7218
smote Sisera, she smote off his *h* ... Judg 5:26 7218
of a millstone upon Abimelech's *h* ... Judg 9:53 7218
he shall be *h* over all the ... Judg 10:18 7218
be our *h* over all the inhabitants ... Judg 11:8 7218
them before me, shall I be your *h* ... Judg 11:9 7218
Gilead, and the people made him *h* ... Judg 11:11 7218
and no razor shall come on his *h* ... Judg 13:5 7218
seven locks of my *h* with the web ... Judg 16:13 7218
hath not come a razor upon mine *h* ... Judg 16:17 7218
off the seven locks of his *h* ... Judg 16:19 7218
Howbeit the hair of his *h* began ... Judg 16:22 7218
shall no razor come upon his *h* ... 1Sa 1:11 7218
rent, and with earth upon his *h* ... 1Sa 4:12 7218
the *h* of Dagon and both the palms ... 1Sa 5:4 7218
of oil, and poured it upon his *h* ... 1Sa 10:1 7218
hair of his *h* fall to the ground ... 1Sa 14:45 7218
wast thou not made the *h* of the ... 1Sa 15:17 7218
had an helmet of brass upon his *h* ... 1Sa 17:5 7218
his spear's *h* weighed six hundred ... 1Sa 17:7 3852
put an helmet of brass upon his *h* ... 1Sa 17:38 7218
thee, and take thine *h* from thee ... 1Sa 17:46 7218
him, and cut off his *h* therewith ... 1Sa 17:51 7218
And David took the *h* of the ... 1Sa 17:54 7218
him before Saul with the *h* of the ... 1Sa 17:57 7218
of Nabal upon his own *h* ... 1Sa 25:39 7218
thee keeper of mine *h* for ever ... 1Sa 28:2 7218
And they cut off his *h*, and ... 1Sa 31:9 7218
clothes rent, and earth upon his *h* ... 2Sa 1:2 7218
the crown that was upon his *h* ... 2Sa 1:10 7218
unto him, Thy blood be upon thy *h* ... 2Sa 1:16 7218
every one his fellow by the *h* ... 2Sa 2:16 7218
and said, Am I a dog's *h*, which ... 2Sa 3:8 7218
Let it rest on the *h* of Joab ... 2Sa 3:29 7218
and beheaded him, and took his *h* ... 2Sa 4:7 7218
they brought the *h* of Ish-bosheth ... 2Sa 4:8 7218
Behold the *h* of Ish-bosheth the ... 2Sa 4:8 7218
they took the *h* of Ish-bosheth ... 2Sa 4:12 7218
their king's crown from off his *h* ... 2Sa 12:30 7218
and it was set on David's *h* ... 2Sa 12:30 7218
And Tamar put ashes on her *h* ... 2Sa 13:19 7218
on her, and laid her hand on her *h* ... 2Sa 13:19 7218
his *h* there was no blemish in him ... 2Sa 14:25 6936
And when he polled his *h*, (for it ... 2Sa 14:26 7218
he weighed the hair of his *h* at ... 2Sa 14:26 7218
he went up, and had his *h* covered ... 2Sa 15:30 7218
with him covered every man his *h* ... 2Sa 15:30 7218
coat rent, and earth upon his *h* ... 2Sa 15:32 7218
I pray thee, and take off his *h* ... 2Sa 16:9 7218
his *h* caught hold of the oak, and ... 2Sa 18:9 7218
his *h* shall be thrown to thee ... 2Sa 20:21 7218
they cut off the *h* of Sheba the ... 2Sa 20:22 7218
kept me to be *h* of the heathen ... 2Sa 22:44 7218
let not his hoar *h* go down to the ... 1Kin 2:6
but his hoar *h* bring thou down to ... 1Kin 2:9
return his blood upon his own *h* ... 1Kin 2:32 7218
return upon the *h* of Joab ... 1Kin 2:33 7218
upon the *h* of his seed for ever ... 1Kin 2:33 7218
blood shall be upon thine own *h* ... 1Kin 2:37 7218
thy wickedness upon thine own *h* ... 1Kin 2:44 7218
to bring his way upon his *h* ... 1Kin 8:32 7218
and a cruse of water at his *h* ... 1Kin 19:6 4763
away thy master from thy *h* to day ... 2Kin 2:3 7218
away thy master from thy *h* to day ... 2Kin 2:5 7218
said unto him, Go up, thou bald *h* ... 2Kin 2:23
go up, thou bald *h* ... 2Kin 2:23
unto his father, My *h*, my *h* ... 2Kin 4:19 7218
the ax *h* fell into the water ... 2Kin 6:5 1270
until an ass's *h* was sold for ... 2Kin 6:25 7218
if the *h* of Elisha the son of ... 2Kin 6:31 7218
hath sent to take away mine *h* ... 2Kin 6:32 7218
box of oil, and pour it on his *h* ... 2Kin 9:3 7218
and he poured the oil on his *h* ... 2Kin 9:6 7218
painted her face, and tired her *h* ... 2Kin 9:30 7218
hath shaken her *h* at thee ... 2Kin 19:21 7218
began to reign did lift up the *h* ... 2Kin 25:27 7218
had stripped him, they took his *h* ... 1Chr 10:9 7218
fastened his *h* in the temple of ... 1Chr 10:10 1538
of their king from off his *h* ... 1Chr 20:2 7218
and it was set upon David's *h* ... 1Chr 20:2 7218
thou art exalted as *h* above all ... 1Chr 29:11 7218
his way upon his own *h* ... 2Chr 6:23 7218
Jehoshaphat bowed his *h* with his ... 2Chr 20:18
and plucked off the hair of my *h* ... Ezr 9:3 7218
are increased over our *h*, and our ... Ezr 9:6 7218
their reproach upon their own *h* ... Neh 4:4 7218
he set the royal crown upon her *h* ... Est 2:17 7218
royal which is set upon his *h* ... Est 6:8 7218
mourning, and having his *h* covered ... Est 6:12 7218
should return upon his own *h* ... Est 9:25 7218
rent his mantle, and shaved his *h* ... Job 1:20 7218
yet will I not lift up my *h* ... Job 10:15 7218
you, and shake mine *h* at you ... Job 16:4 7218
and taken the crown from my *h* ... Job 19:9 7218
his *h* reach unto the clouds ... Job 20:6 7218
When his candle shined upon my *h* ... Job 29:3 7218
or his *h* with fish spears ... Job 41:7 7218
glory, and the lifter up of mine *h* ... Ps 3:3 7218
shall return upon his own *h* ... Ps 7:16 7218
hast made me the *h* of the heathen ... Ps 18:43 7218
a crown of pure gold on his *h* ... Ps 21:3 7218
out the lip, they shake the *h* ... Ps 22:7 7218
thou anointest my *h* with oil ... Ps 23:5 7218
now shall mine *h* be lifted up ... Ps 27:6 7218
iniquities are gone over mine *h* ... Ps 38:4 7218
are more than the hairs of mine *h* ... Ps 40:12 7218
shaking of the *h* among the people ... Ps 44:14 7218
also is the strength of mine *h* ... Ps 60:7 7218
shall wound the *h* of his enemies ... Ps 68:21 7218
are more than the hairs of mine *h* ... Ps 69:4 7218
hate thee have lifted up the *h* ... Ps 83:2 7218
also is the strength of mine *h* ... Ps 108:8 7218
therefore shall he lift up the *h* ... Ps 110:7 7218
become the *h* stone of the corner ... Ps 118:22 7218
the precious ointment upon the *h* ... Ps 133:2 7218
covered my *h* in the day of battle ... Ps 140:7 7218
As for the *h* of those that ... Ps 140:9 7218
oil, which shall not break my *h* ... Ps 141:5 7218
an ornament of grace unto thy *h* ... Prov 1:9 7218
to thine *h* an ornament of grace ... Prov 4:9 7218
are upon the *h* of the just ... Prov 10:6 7218
upon the *h* of him that selleth it ... Prov 11:26 7218
The hoary *h* is a crown of glory, ... Prov 16:31
beauty of old men is the grey *h* ... Prov 20:29
heap coals of fire upon his *h* ... Prov 25:22 7218
The wise man's eyes are in his *h* ... Eccl 2:14 7218
let thy *h* lack no ointment ... Eccl 9:8 7218
His left hand is under my *h* ... Song 2:6 7218
for my *h* is filled with dew, and ... Song 5:2 7218
His *h* is as the most fine gold, ... Song 5:11 7218
Thine *h* upon thee is like Carmel, ... Song 7:5 7218
the hair of thine *h* like purple ... Song 7:5 7218
left hand should be under my *h* ... Song 8:3 7218
the whole *h* is sick, and the whole ... Is 1:5 7218
the *h* there is no soundness in it ... Is 1:6 7218
of the *h* of the daughters of Zion ... Is 3:17 6936
For the *h* of Syria is Damascus, ... Is 7:8 7218
the *h* of Damascus is Rezin ... Is 7:8 7218
the *h* of Ephraim is Samaria, and ... Is 7:9 7218
the *h* of Samaria is Remaliah's ... Is 7:9 7218
by the king of Assyria, the *h* ... Is 7:20 7218
LORD will cut off from Israel *h* ... Is 9:14 7218
and honourable, he is the *h* ... Is 9:15 7218
for Egypt, which the *h* or tail ... Is 19:15 7218
which are on the *h* of the fat ... Is 28:1 7218
which is on the *h* of the fat ... Is 28:4 7218
hath shaken her *h* at thee ... Is 37:22 7218
joy shall be upon their *h* ... Is 51:11 7218
they lie at the *h* of all the ... Is 51:20 7218
it to bow down his *h* as a bulrush ... Is 58:5 7218
an helmet of salvation upon his *h* ... Is 59:17 7218
have broken the crown of thy *h* ... Jer 2:16 6936
him, and thine hands upon thine *h* ... Jer 2:37 7218
Oh that my *h* were waters, and mine ... Jer 9:1 7218
shall be astonished, and wag his *h* ... Jer 18:16 7218
unto me, and the *h* of Lebanon ... Jer 22:6 7218
upon the *h* of the wicked ... Jer 23:19 7218
pain upon the *h* of the wicked ... Jer 30:23 7218
For every *h* shall be bald, and ... Jer 48:37 7218
the crown of the *h* of the ... Jer 48:45 6936
the *h* of Jehoiachin king of Judah ... Jer 52:31 7218
wag their *h* at the daughter of ... Lam 2:15 7218
Waters flowed over mine *h* ... Lam 3:54 7218
The crown is fallen from our *h* ... Lam 5:16 7218
and cause it to pass upon thine *h* ... Eze 5:1 7218
and took me by a lock of mine *h* ... Eze 8:3 7218
recompense their way upon their *h* ... Eze 9:10 7218
firmament that was above the *h* of ... Eze 10:1 7218
the *h* looked they followed it ... Eze 10:11 7218
make kerchiefs upon the *h* of ... Eze 13:18 7218
and a beautiful crown upon thine *h* ... Eze 16:12 7218
high place at every *h* of the way ... Eze 16:25 7218
place in the *h* of every way ... Eze 16:31 7218
recompense thy way upon thine *h* ... Eze 16:43 7218
will I recompense upon his own *h* ... Eze 17:19 7218
choose it at the *h* of the way to ... Eze 21:19 7218
at the *h* of the two ways, to use ... Eze 21:21 7218
the tire of thine *h* upon thee ... Eze 24:17
every *h* was made bald, and every ... Eze 29:18 7218
his blood shall be upon his own *h* ... Eze 33:4 7218
was a door in the *h* of the way ... Eze 42:12 7218
make me endanger my *h* to the king ... Dan 1:10 7218
the visions of thy *h* upon thy bed ... Dan 2:28 7217
This image's *h* was of fine gold, ... Dan 2:32 7217
Thou art this *h* of gold ... Dan 2:38 7217
nor was an hair of their *h* singed ... Dan 3:27 7217
the visions of my *h* troubled me ... Dan 4:5 7217
the visions of mine *h* in my bed ... Dan 4:10 7217
the visions of my *h* upon my bed ... Dan 4:13 7217
and visions of his *h* upon his bed ... Dan 7:1 7217
the hair of his *h* like the pure ... Dan 7:9 7217
the visions of my *h* troubled me ... Dan 7:15 7217
the ten horns that were in his *h* ... Dan 7:20 7217
and appoint themselves one *h* ... Hos 1:11 7218
your recompence upon your own *h* ... Joel 3:4 7218
your recompence upon your own *h* ... Joel 3:7 7218
of the earth on the *h* of the poor ... Amos 2:7 7218
loins, and baldness upon every *h* ... Amos 8:10 7218
and cut them in the *h*, all of them ... Amos 9:1 7218
shall return upon thine own *h* ... Obad 15 7218
the weeds were wrapped about my *h* ... Jonah 2:5 7218
it might be a shadow over his *h* ... Jonah 4:6 7218
the sun beat upon the *h* of Jonah ... Jonah 4:8 7218
and the LORD on the *h* of them ... Mic 2:13 7218
thou woundedst the *h* out of the ... Hab 3:13 7218
his staves the *h* of his villages ... Hab 3:14 7218
so that no man did lift up his *h* ... Zec 1:21 7218
them set a fair mitre upon his *h* ... Zec 3:5 7218
they set a fair mitre upon his *h* ... Zec 3:5 7218
set them upon the *h* of Joshua the ... Zec 6:11 7218
Neither shalt thou swear by thy *h* ... Mt 5:36 2776
when thou fastest, anoint thine *h* ... Mt 6:17 2776
man hath not where to lay his *h* ... Mt 8:20 2776
hairs of your *h* are all numbered ... Mt 10:30 2776
John Baptist's *h* in a charger ... Mt 14:8 2776
his *h* was brought in a charger, ... Mt 14:11 2776
is become the *h* of the corner ... Mt 21:42 2776
ointment, and poured it on his *h* ... Mt 26:7 2776
of thorns, they put it upon his *h* ... Mt 27:29 2776
the reed, and smote him on the *h* ... Mt 27:30 2776
set up over his *h* his accusation ... Mt 27:37 2776
The *h* of John the Baptist ... Mk 6:24 2776
charger the *h* of John the Baptist ... Mk 6:25 2776
and commanded his *h* to be brought ... Mk 6:27 2776
brought his *h* in a charger, and ... Mk 6:28 2776
stones, and wounded him in the *h* ... Mk 12:4 2775
is become the *h* of the corner ... Mk 12:10 2776
the box, and poured it on his *h* ... Mk 14:3 2776
of thorns, and put it about his *h* ... Mk 15:17 2776
smote him on the *h* with a reed ... Mk 15:19 2776
wipe them with the hairs of her *h* ... Lk 7:38 2776
them with the hairs of her *h* ... Lk 7:44 2776
My *h* with oil thou didst not ... Lk 7:46 2776
man hath not where to lay his *h* ... Lk 9:58 2776
hairs of your *h* are all numbered ... Lk 12:7 2776
is become the *h* of the corner ... Lk 20:17 2776
not an hair of your *h* perish ... Lk 21:18 2776
only, but also my hands and my *h* ... Jn 13:9 2776
of thorns, and put it on his *h* ... Jn 19:2 2776
and he bowed his *h*, and gave up the ... Jn 19:30 2776
the napkin, that was about his *h* ... Jn 20:7 2776
white sitting, the one at the *h* ... Jn 20:12 2776
is become the *h* of the corner ... Acts 4:11 2776
having shorn his *h* in Cenchrea ... Acts 18:18 2776
fall from the *h* of any of you ... Acts 27:34 2776
shalt heap coals of fire on his *h* ... Rom 12:20 2776
that the *h* of every man is Christ ... 1Cor 11:3 2776
the *h* of the woman is the man ... 1Cor 11:3 2776
and the *h* of Christ is God ... 1Cor 11:3 2776
prophesying, having his *h* covered ... 1Cor 11:4 2776
h uncovered dishonoureth her *h* ... 1Cor 11:5 2776
indeed ought not to cover his *h* ... 1Cor 11:7 2776
on her *h* because of the angels ... 1Cor 11:10 2776
nor again the *h* to the feet ... 1Cor 12:21 2776
gave him to be the *h* over all ... Eph 1:22 2776
him in all things, which is the *h* ... Eph 4:15 2776
the husband is the *h* of the wife ... Eph 5:23 2776
as Christ is the *h* of the church ... Eph 5:23 2776
he is the *h* of the body, the ... Col 1:18 2776
in him, which is the *h* of all ... Col 2:10 2776
And not holding the *H*, from which ... Col 2:19 2776
same is made the *h* of the corner ... 1Pet 2:7 2776
His *h* and his hairs were white ... Rev 1:14 2776
and a rainbow was upon his *h* ... Rev 10:1 2776
upon her *h* a crown of twelve ... Rev 12:1 2776
having on his *h* a golden crown, ... Rev 14:14 2776
on his *h* were many crowns ... Rev 19:12 2776

HEADBANDS
ornaments of the legs, and the *h* ... Is 3:20 7196

HEADLONG
of the froward is carried *h* ... Job 5:13
that they might cast him down *h* ... Lk 4:29 2630
and falling *h*, he burst asunder in ... Acts 1:18 4248

HEADS

was parted, and became into four h ..... Gen 2:10 7218
And they bowed down their h ..... Gen 43:28
then they bowed their h and ..... Ex 4:31
These be the h of their fathers' ..... Ex 6:14 7218
these are the h of the fathers of ..... Ex 6:25 7218
made them h over the people, ... Ex 18:25 7218
his sons, Uncover not your h ..... Lev 10:6 7218
not round the corners of your h ..... Lev 19:27 7218
fathers, h of thousands in Israel ..... Num 1:16 7218
h of the house of their fathers, ... Num 7:2 7218
hands upon the h of the bullocks ..... Num 8:12 7218
which are h of the thousands of ..... Num 10:4 7218
... those men were h of the ..... Num 13:3 7218
Take all the h of the people, and ..... Num 25:4 7218
Moses spake unto the h of the ..... Num 30:1 7218
and made them h over you ..... Deut 1:15 7218
even all the h of your tribes, and ..... Deut 5:23 7218
when the h of the people and the ..... Deut 33:5 7218
he came with the h of the people ..... Deut 33:21 7218
Israel, and put dust upon their h ..... Josh 7:6 7218
the h of the fathers of the ..... Josh 14:1 7218
the h of the fathers of the ..... Josh 19:51 7218
Then came near the h of the ..... Josh 21:1 7218
unto the h of the fathers of the ..... Josh 21:1 7218
said unto the h of the thousands ..... Josh 22:21 7218
h of the thousands of Israel ..... Josh 22:30 7218
for their elders, and for their h ..... Josh 23:2 7218
elders of Israel, and for their h ..... Josh 24:1 7218
Midian, and brought the h of Oreb ..... Judg 7:25 7218
they lifted up their h no more ..... Judg 8:28 7218
did God render upon their h ..... Judg 9:57 7218
it not be with the h of these men 1Sa 29:4 7218
all the h of the tribes, the 1Kin 8:1 7218
on our loins, and ropes upon our h 1Kin 20:31 7218
loins, and put ropes on their h 1Kin 20:32 7218
take ye the h of the men your 2Kin 10:6 7218
put their h in baskets, and sent 2Kin 10:7 7218
brought the h of the king's sons 2Kin 10:8 7218
these were the h of the house of 1Chr 5:24 7218
h of the house of their fathers 1Chr 5:24 7218
h of their father's house, to wit 1Chr 7:2 7218
h of the house of their fathers, ... 1Chr 7:7 7218
h of the house of their fathers, ... 1Chr 7:9 7218
by the h of their fathers, mighty 1Chr 7:11 7218
h of their father's house, choice 1Chr 7:40 7218
these are the h of the fathers of 1Chr 8:6 7218
were his sons, h of the fathers 1Chr 8:10 7218
who were h of the fathers of the 1Chr 8:13 7218
These were h of the fathers, by 1Chr 8:28 7218
h of the house of their fathers, ... 1Chr 9:13 7218
Saul to the jeopardy of our h 1Chr 12:19 7218
the h of them were two hundred 1Chr 12:32
fathers, and bowed down their h 1Chr 29:20
put them on the h of the pillars 2Chr 3:16 7218
all the h of the tribes, the 2Chr 5:2 7218
Then certain of the h of the 2Chr 28:12
gladness, and they bowed their h 2Chr 29:30
and they bowed their h, and ..... Neh 8:6
dust upon their h toward heaven ..... Job 2:12 7218
Lift up your h, O ye gates ..... Ps 24:7 7218
Lift up your h, O ye gates ..... Ps 24:9 7218
caused men to ride over our h ..... Ps 66:12 7218
thou brakest the h of the dragons ..... Ps 74:13 7218
Thou brakest the h of leviathan ..... Ps 74:14 7218
upon me they shaked their h ..... Ps 109:25 7218
he shall wound the h over many ..... Ps 110:6 7218
on all their h shall be baldness, ... Is 15:2 7218
and everlasting joy upon their h ..... Is 35:10 7218
and confounded, and covered their h ... Jer 14:3 7218
ashamed, they covered their h ..... Jer 14:4 7218
have cast up dust upon their h ..... Lam 2:10 7218
hang down their h to the ground ..... Lam 2:10 7218
of the firmament upon the h of ..... Eze 1:22 7218
forth over their h above ..... Eze 1:22 7218
firmament that was over their h ..... Eze 1:25 7218
h was the likeness of a throne ..... Eze 1:26 7218
and baldness upon all their h ..... Eze 7:18 7218
their way upon their own h ..... Eze 11:21 7218
have I recompensed upon their h ..... Eze 22:31 7218
in dyed attire upon their h ..... Eze 23:15 7218
and beautiful crowns upon their h ..... Eze 23:42 7218
your tires shall be upon your h ..... Eze 24:23 7218
shall cast up dust upon their h ..... Eze 27:30 7218
laid their swords under their h ..... Eze 32:27 7218
have linen bonnets upon their h ..... Eze 44:18 7218
Neither shall they shave their h ..... Eze 44:20 7218
they shall only poll their h ..... Eze 44:20 7218
the beast had also four h ..... Dan 7:6 7217
O h of Jacob, and ye princes of ..... Mic 3:1 7218
ye h of the house of Jacob, and ..... Mic 3:9 7218
The h thereof judge for reward, ... Mic 3:11 7218
by reviled him, wagging their h ..... Mt 27:39 2776
by railed on him, wagging their h ..... Mk 15:29 2776
then look up, and lift up your h ..... Lk 21:28 2776
Your blood be upon your own h ..... Acts 18:6 2776
them, that they may shave their h ..... Acts 21:24 2776
had on their h crowns of gold ..... Rev 4:4 2776
on their h were as it were crowns ..... Rev 9:7 2776
the h of the horses were as the ..... Rev 9:17 2776
the horses were as the h of lions ..... Rev 9:17 2776
were like unto serpents, and had h ..... Rev 9:19 2776
great red dragon, having seven h ..... Rev 12:3 2776
horns, and seven crowns upon his h ..... Rev 12:3 2776
up out of the sea, having seven h ..... Rev 13:1 2776
upon his h the name of blasphemy ..... Rev 13:1 2776
I saw one of his h as it were ..... Rev 13:3 2776
of blasphemy, having seven h ..... Rev 17:3 2776
her, which hath the seven h ..... Rev 17:7 2776
The seven h are seven mountains, ... Rev 17:9 2776
And they cast dust on their h ..... Rev 18:19 2776

HEADSTONE

the h thereof with shoutings ..... Zec 4:7

HEADY

Traitors, h, highminded, lovers 2Ti 3:4 4312

HEAL

H her now, O God, I beseech thee ..... Num 12:13 7495
I wound, and I h ..... Deut 32:39 7495
behold, I will h thee 2Kin 20:5 7495
the sign that the LORD will h me 2Kin 20:8 7495
their sin, and will h their land 2Chr 7:14 7495
O LORD, h me ..... Ps 6:2 7495
h my soul ..... Ps 41:4 7495
h the breaches thereof ..... Ps 60:2 7495
A time to kill, and a time to h ..... Eccl 3:3 7495
he shall smite and h it ..... Is 19:22 7495
of them, and shall h them ..... Is 19:22 7495
have seen his ways, and will h him ..... Is 57:18 7495
and I will h him ..... Is 57:19 7495
I will h your backslidings ..... Jer 3:22 7495
H me, O LORD, and I shall be ..... Jer 17:14 7495
I will h thee of thy wounds, ... Jer 30:17 7495
who can h thee? ..... Lam 2:13 7495
yet could he not h you, nor cure ..... Hos 5:13 7495
for he hath torn, and he will h us ..... Hos 6:1 7495
I will h their backsliding, I ..... Hos 14:4 7495
nor h that that is broken, nor ..... Zec 11:16 7495
unto him, I will come and h him ..... Mt 8:7 2323
to h all manner of sickness and ..... Mt 10:1 2323
H the sick, cleanse the lepers, ... Mt 10:8 2323
Is it lawful to h on the sabbath ..... Mt 12:10 2323
be converted, and I should h them ..... Mt 13:15 2390
whether he would h him on the ..... Mk 3:2 2323
And to have power to h sicknesses ..... Mk 3:15 2323
sent me to h the brokenhearted ..... Lk 4:18 2390
proverb, Physician, h thyself ..... Lk 4:23 2323
of the Lord was present to h them ..... Lk 5:17 2390
whether he would h on the sabbath ..... Lk 6:7 2323
he would come and h his servant ..... Lk 7:3 1295
kingdom of God, and to h the sick ..... Lk 9:2 2390
h the sick that are therein, and ..... Lk 10:9 2323
Is it lawful to h on the sabbath ..... Lk 14:3 2323
he would come down, and h his son ..... Jn 4:47 2390
be converted, and I should h them ..... Jn 12:40 2390
stretching forth thine hand to h ..... Acts 4:30 2392
be converted, and I should h them ..... Acts 28:27 2392

HEALED

God h Abimelech, and his wife, and ..... Gen 20:17 7495
cause him to be thoroughly h ..... Ex 21:19 7495
skin thereof, was a boil, and is h ..... Lev 13:18 7495
the scall is h, he is clean ..... Lev 13:37 7495
of leprosy be h in the leper ..... Lev 14:3 7495
clean, because the plague is h ..... Lev 14:48 7495
itch, whereof thou canst not be h ..... Deut 28:27 7495
a sore botch that cannot be h ..... Deut 28:35 7495
then ye shall be h, and it shall 1Sa 6:3 7495
the LORD, I have h these waters 2Kin 2:21 7495
the waters were h unto this day 2Kin 2:22 7495
king Joram went back to be h in 2Kin 8:29 7495
king Joram was returned to be h 2Kin 9:15 7495
he returned to be h in Jezreel 2Chr 22:6 7495
to Hezekiah, and h the people 2Chr 30:20 7495
unto thee, and thou hast h me ..... Ps 30:2 7495
h them, and delivered them from ..... Ps 107:20 7495
their heart, and convert, and be h ..... Is 6:10 7495
and with his stripes we are h ..... Is 53:5 7495
They have h also the hurt of the ..... Jer 6:14 7495
For they have h the hurt of the ..... Jer 8:11 7495
incurable, which refuseth to be h ..... Jer 15:18 7495
Heal me, O LORD, and I shall be h ..... Jer 17:14 7495
her pain, if so be she may be h ..... Jer 51:8 7495
h Babylon, but she is not h ..... Jer 51:9 7495
it shall not be bound up to be h ..... Eze 30:21
neither have ye h that which was ..... Eze 34:4 7495
the sea, the waters shall be h ..... Eze 47:8 7495
for they shall be h ..... Eze 47:9 7495
marishes thereof shall not be h ..... Eze 47:11 7495
When I would have h Israel ..... Hos 7:1 7495
but they knew not that I h them ..... Hos 11:3 7495
and he h them ..... Mt 4:24 2323
only, and my servant shall be h ..... Mt 8:8 2390
his servant was h in the selfsame ..... Mt 8:13 2390
his word, and h all that were sick ..... Mt 8:16 2323
followed him, and he h them all ..... Mt 12:15 2323
he h him, insomuch that the blind ..... Mt 12:22 2323
toward them, and he h their sick ..... Mt 14:14 2323
and he h them ..... Mt 15:30 2323
and he h them there ..... Mt 19:2 2323
and he h them ..... Mt 21:14 2323
he h many that were sick of ..... Mk 1:34 2323
For he had h many ..... Mk 3:10 2323
hands on her, that she may be h ..... Mk 5:23 4982
that she was h of that plague ..... Mk 5:29 2390
upon a few sick folk, and h them ..... Mk 6:5 2323
many that were sick, and h them ..... Mk 6:13 2323
on every one of them, and h them ..... Lk 4:40 2323
hear, and to be h by him of their ..... Lk 5:15 2323
to be h of their diseases ..... Lk 6:17 2390
and they were h ..... Lk 6:18 2323
virtue out of him, and h them all ..... Lk 6:19 2390
a word, and my servant shall be h ..... Lk 7:7 2390
which had been h of evil spirits ..... Lk 8:2 2390
was possessed of the devils was h ..... Lk 8:36 4982
neither could be h of any ..... Lk 8:43 2323
him, and how she was h immediately .. Lk 8:47 2390
h them that had need of healing ..... Lk 9:11 2390
h the child, and delivered him ..... Lk 9:42 2390
Jesus had h on the sabbath day ..... Lk 13:14 2323
in them therefore come and be h ..... Lk 13:14 2323
took him, and h him, and let him go ... Lk 14:4 2323
them, when he saw that he was h ..... Lk 17:15 2390
And he touched his ear, and h him ..... Lk 22:51 2390
he that was h wist not who it was ..... Jn 5:13 2390
lame man which was h held Peter ..... Acts 3:11 2390
which was h standing with them ..... Acts 4:14 2323
and they were h every one ..... Acts 5:16 2323
and that were lame, were h ..... Acts 8:7 2323
that he had faith to be h ..... Acts 14:9 4982
laid his hands on him, and h him ..... Acts 28:8 2390
in the island, came, and were h ..... Acts 28:9 2323
but let it rather be h ..... Heb 12:13 2390
one for another, that ye may be h ..... Jas 5:16 2390
by whose stripes ye were h 1Pet 2:24 2390
and his deadly wound was h ..... Rev 13:3 2323
beast, whose deadly wound was h ..... Rev 13:12 2323

HEALER

swear, saying, I will not be an h ..... Is 3:7 2280

HEALETH

for I am the LORD that h thee ..... Ex 15:26 7495
who h all thy diseases ..... Ps 103:3 7495
He h the broken in heart, and ..... Ps 147:3 7495
h the stroke of their wound ..... Is 30:26 7495

HEALING

us, and there is no h for us ..... Jer 14:19 4832
and for the time of h, and behold ..... Jer 14:19 4832
thou hast no h medicines ..... Jer 30:13 8585
There is no h of thy bruise ..... Nah 3:19 3545
arise with h in his wings ..... Mal 4:2 4832
h all manner of sickness and all ..... Mt 4:23 2323
h every sickness and every disease ..... Mt 9:35 2323
the gospel, and h every where ..... Lk 9:6 2323
and healed them that had need of h ..... Lk 9:11 2322
whom this miracle of h was shewed ..... Acts 4:22 2392
h all that were oppressed of the ..... Acts 10:38 2390
the gifts of h by the same Spirit 1Cor 12:9 2386
Have all the gifts of h 1Cor 12:30 2386
were for the h of the nations ..... Rev 22:2 2322

HEALINGS

that miracles, then gifts of h 1Cor 12:28 2386

HEALTH

servant our father is in good h ..... Gen 43:28 7965
Joab said to Amasa, Art thou in h 2Sa 20:9 7965
who is the h of my countenance, ... Ps 42:11 3444
who is the h of my countenance, ... Ps 43:5 3444
thy saving h among all nations ..... Ps 67:2
It shall be h to thy navel, and ..... Prov 3:8 7500
them, and h to all their flesh ..... Prov 4:22 4832
but the tongue of the wise is h ..... Prov 12:18 4832
but a faithful ambassador is h ..... Prov 13:17 4832
to the soul, and h to the bones ..... Prov 16:24 4832
thine h shall spring forth ..... Is 58:8 724
and for a time of h, and behold ..... Jer 8:15 4832
why then is not the h of the ..... Jer 8:22 724
For I will restore h unto thee ..... Jer 30:17 724
Behold, I will bring it h ..... Jer 33:6 724
for this is for your h ..... Acts 27:34 4491
thou mayest prosper and be in h 3Jn 2 5198

HEAP

and they took stones, and made an h .. Gen 31:46 1530
and they did eat there upon the h ..... Gen 31:46 1530
This h is a witness between me and ..... Gen 31:48 1530
said to Jacob, Behold this h ..... Gen 31:51 1530
This h be witness, and this pillar ..... Gen 31:52 1530
will not pass over this h to thee ..... Gen 31:52 1530
thou shalt not pass over this h ..... Gen 31:52 1530
the floods stood upright as an h ..... Ex 15:8 5067
and it shall be an h for ever ..... Deut 13:16 8510
I will h mischiefs upon them ..... Deut 32:23 5595
and they shall stand upon an h ..... Josh 3:13 5067
rose up upon an h very far from ..... Josh 3:16 5067
a great h of stones unto this day ..... Josh 7:26 1530
Ai, and made it an h for ever ..... Josh 8:28 8510
raise thereon a great h of stones ..... Josh 8:29 1530
down at the end of the h of corn ..... Ruth 3:7 6194
laid a very great h of stones 2Sa 18:17 1530
His roots are wrapped about the h ..... Job 8:17 1530
I could h up words against you, ... Job 16:4 2266
Though he h up silver as the dust ..... Job 27:16 6651
hypocrites in heart h up wrath ..... Job 36:13 7760
of the sea together as an h ..... Ps 33:7 5067
made the waters to stand as an h ..... Ps 78:13 5067
For thou shalt h coals of fire ..... Prov 25:22 2846
travail, to gather and to h up ..... Eccl 2:26 3664
thy belly is like an h of wheat ..... Song 7:2 6194
city, and it shall be a ruinous h ..... Is 17:1 4596
shall be a h in the day of grief ..... Is 17:11 5067
For thou hast made of a city an h ..... Is 25:2 1530
shall be builded upon her own h ..... Jer 30:18 8510
and it shall be a desolate h ..... Jer 49:2 8510
H on wood, kindle the fire, ... Eze 24:10 7235
make Samaria as an h of the field ..... Mic 1:6 5856
for they shall h dust, and take it ..... Hab 1:10 6651
through the h of great waters ..... Hab 3:15 2563
came to an h of twenty measures ..... Hag 2:16 6194
shalt h coals of fire on his head ..... Rom 12:20 4987
they h to themselves teachers 2Ti 4:3 2002

HEAPED

h up silver as the dust, and fine ..... Zec 9:3 6651
Ye have h treasure together for ..... Jas 5:3 2343

HEAPETH

he h up riches, and knoweth not ..... Ps 39:6 6651
nations, and h unto him all people ..... Hab 2:5 6908

HEAPS

gathered them together upon h ..... Ex 8:14 2563
h upon h, with the jaw of an ..... Judg 15:16 2565
Lay ye them in two h at the 2Kin 10:8 6632
fenced cities into ruinous h 2Kin 19:25 1530
LORD their God, and laid them by h 2Chr 31:6 6194
to lay the foundation of the h 2Chr 31:7 6194
and the princes came and saw the h 2Chr 31:8 6194
and the Levites concerning the h 2Chr 31:9 6194
revive the stones out of the h of ..... Neh 4:2 6194

which are ready to become *h* Job 15:28 1530
they have laid Jerusalem on *h* Ps 79:1 5856
defenced cities into ruinous *h* Is 37:26 1530
And I will make Jerusalem *h* Jer 9:11 1530
and Jerusalem shall become *h* Jer 26:18 5856
up waymarks, make thee high *h* Jer 31:21 8564
cast her up as *h*, and destroy her Jer 50:26 6194
And Babylon shall become *h* Jer 51:37 1530
their altars are as *h* in the Hos 12:11 1530
and Jerusalem shall become *h* Mic 3:12 5856

HEAR

wives, Adah and Zillah, *H* my voice Gen 4:23 8085
so that all that *h* will laugh Gen 21:6 8085
H us, my lord Gen 23:6 8085
h me, and intreat for me to Ephron Gen 23:8 8085
Nay, my lord, *h* me Gen 23:11 8085
wilt give it, I pray thee, *h* me Gen 23:13 8085
And he said unto them, *H*, I pray Gen 37:6 8085
he besought us, and we would not *h* Gen 42:21 8085
and ye would not *h* Gen 42:22 8085
Gather yourselves together, and *h* Gen 49:2 8085
how then shall Pharaoh *h* me Ex 6:12 8085
hitherto thou wouldest not *h* Ex 7:16 8085
The people shall *h*, and be afraid Ex 15:14 8085
that the people may *h* when I Ex 19:9 8085
Speak thou with us, and we will *h* Ex 20:19 8085
me, I will surely *h* their cry Ex 22:23 8085
he crieth unto me, that I will *h* Ex 22:27 8085
noise of them that sing do I *h* Ex 32:18 8085
h the voice of swearing, and is a Lev 5:1 8085
I will *h* what the LORD will Num 9:8 8085
And he said, *H* now my words Num 12:6 8085
Then the Egyptians shall *h* it Num 14:13 8085
And Moses said unto Korah, *H* Num 16:8 8085
said unto them, *H* now, ye rebels Num 20:10 8085
and said, Rise up, Balak, and *h* Num 23:18 8085
And her father *h* her vow, and her Num 30:4 8085
H the causes between your Deut 1:16 8085
but ye shall *h* the small as well Deut 1:17 8085
bring it unto me, and I will *h* it Deut 1:17 8085
and ye would not *h*, but rebelled Deut 1:43 8085
who shall *h* report of thee, and Deut 2:25 8085
for your sakes, and would not *h* me Deut 3:26 8085
which shall *h* all these statutes, Deut 4:6 8085
and I will make them *h* my words Deut 4:10 8085
stone, which neither see, nor *h* Deut 4:28 8085
Did ever people *h* the voice of Deut 4:33 8085
he made thee to *h* his voice Deut 4:36 8085
all Israel, and said unto them, *H* Deut 5:1 8085
if we *h* the voice of the LORD our Deut 5:25 8085
h all that the LORD our God shall Deut 5:27 8085
and we will *h* it, and do it Deut 5:27 8085
H therefore, O Israel, and observe Deut 6:3 8085
H, O Israel Deut 6:4 8085
H, O Israel Deut 9:1 8085
h all these words which I command Deut 12:28 8085
And all Israel shall *h*, and fear, Deut 13:11 8085
If thou shalt *h* say in one of thy Deut 13:12 8085
And all the people shall *h* Deut 17:13 8085
Let me not *h* again the voice of Deut 18:16 8085
And those which remain shall *h* Deut 19:20 8085
And shall say unto them, *H* Deut 20:3 8085
and all Israel shall *h*, and fear Deut 21:21 8085
and eyes to see, and ears to *h* Deut 29:4 8085
it unto us, that we may *h* it Deut 30:12 8085
it unto us, that we may *h* it Deut 30:13 8085
away, so that thou wilt not *h* Deut 30:17 8085
within thy gates, that they may *h* Deut 31:12 8085
have not known any thing, may *h* Deut 31:13 8085
and *h*, O earth, the words of my Deut 32:1 8085
and he said, *H*, LORD, the voice of Deut 33:7 8085
h the words of the LORD your God Josh 3:9 8085
when ye *h* the sound of the Josh 6:5 8085
of the land shall *h* of it Josh 7:9 8085
H, O ye kings Judg 5:3 8085
to *h* the bleatings of the flocks Judg 5:16 8085
thou shalt *h* what they say Judg 7:11 8085
thy riddle, that we may *h* it Judg 14:13 8085
for I *h* of your evil dealings by 1Sa 2:23 8085
for it is no good report that I *h* 1Sa 2:24 8085
LORD will not *h* you in that day 1Sa 8:18 6030
land, saying, Let the Hebrews *h* 1Sa 13:3 8085
the lowing of the oxen which I *h* 1Sa 15:14 8085
if Saul *h* it, he will kill me 1Sa 16:2 8085
about him, *H* now, ye Benjamites 1Sa 22:7 8085
H now, thou son of Ahitub 1Sa 22:12 8085
h the words of thine handmaid 1Sa 25:24 8085
let my lord the king *h* the words 1Sa 26:19 8085
For the king will *h*, to deliver 2Sa 14:16 8085
man deputed of the king to *h* thee 2Sa 15:3 8085
As soon as ye *h* the sound of the 2Sa 15:10 8085
shalt *h* out of the king's house 2Sa 15:35 8085
unto me every thing that ye can *h* 2Sa 15:36 8085
all Israel shall *h* that thou art 2Sa 16:21 8085
let us *h* likewise what he saith 2Sa 17:5 8085
can I *h* any more the voice of 2Sa 19:35 8085
woman out of the city, *H*, *h* 2Sa 20:16 8085
H the words of thine handmaid 2Sa 20:17 8085
And he answered, I do *h* 2Sa 20:17 8085
he did *h* my voice out of his 2Sa 22:7 8085
as soon as they *h*, they shall be 2Sa 22:45 8085
people to *h* the wisdom of Solomon 1Kin 4:34 8085
h thou in heaven thy dwelling 1Kin 8:30 8085
Then *h* thou in heaven, and do, and 1Kin 8:32 8085
Then *h* thou in heaven, and forgive 1Kin 8:34 8085
Then *h* thou in heaven, and forgive 1Kin 8:36 8085
Then *h* thou in heaven thy 1Kin 8:39 8085
(For they shall *h* of thy great 1Kin 8:42 8085
H thou in heaven thy dwelling 1Kin 8:43 8085
Then *h* thou in heaven their 1Kin 8:45 8085
Then *h* thou their prayer and their 1Kin 8:49 8085
before thee, and that *h* thy wisdom 1Kin 10:8 8085
to *h* his wisdom, which God had 1Kin 10:24 8085

until noon, saying, O Baal, *h* us 1Kin 18:26 6030
H me, O LORD, *h* me, that this 1Kin 18:37 6030
H thou therefore the word of the 1Kin 22:19 8085
H ye the word of the LORD 2Kin 7:1 8085
Syrians to *h* a noise of chariots 2Kin 7:6 8085
But Amaziah would not *h* 2Kin 14:11 8085
Notwithstanding they would not *h* 2Kin 17:14 8085
commanded, and would not *h* them 2Kin 18:12 8085
H the word of the great king, the 2Kin 18:28 8085
h all the words of Rab-shakeh 2Kin 19:4 8085
upon him, and he shall *h* a rumour 2Kin 19:7 8085
LORD, bow down thine ear, and *h* 2Kin 19:16 8085
h the words of Sennacherib, which 2Kin 19:16 8085
Hezekiah, *H* the word of the LORD 2Kin 20:16 8085
when thou shalt *h* a sound of 1Chr 14:15 8085
H me, my brethren, and my people 1Chr 28:2 8085
h thou from thy dwelling place, 2Chr 6:21 8085
Then *h* thou from heaven, and do, 2Chr 6:23 8085
Then *h* thou from the heavens, and 2Chr 6:25 8085
Then *h* thou from heaven, and 2Chr 6:27 8085
Then *h* thou from heaven thy 2Chr 6:30 8085
Then *h* thou from the heavens, 2Chr 6:33 8085
Then *h* thou from the heavens 2Chr 6:35 8085
Then *h* thou from the heavens, 2Chr 6:39 8085
then will I *h* from heaven 2Chr 7:14 8085
before thee, and *h* thy wisdom 2Chr 9:7 8085
to *h* his wisdom, that God had put 2Chr 9:23 8085
H me, thou Jeroboam, and all 2Chr 13:4 8085
H ye me, Asa, and all Judah and 2Chr 15:2 8085
Therefore *h* the word of the LORD 2Chr 18:18 8085
our affliction, then thou wilt *h* 2Chr 20:9 8085
H me, O Judah, and ye inhabitants 2Chr 20:20 8085
But Amaziah would not *h* 2Chr 25:20 8085
Now *h* me therefore, and deliver 2Chr 28:11 8085
H me, ye Levites, sanctify now 2Chr 29:5 8085
that thou mayest *h* the prayer of Neh 1:6 8085
H, O our God Neh 4:4 8085
ye *h* the sound of the trumpet Neh 4:20 8085
women, and all that could *h* with Neh 8:2 8085
their neck, and would not *h* Neh 9:29 8085
they *h* not the voice of the Job 3:18 8085
h it, and know thou it for thy Job 5:27 8085
H now my reasoning, and hearken to Job 13:6 8085
H diligently my speech, and my Job 13:17 8085
I will shew thee, *h* me Job 15:17 8085
H diligently my speech, and let Job 21:2 8085
unto him, and he shall *h* thee Job 22:27 8085
Will God *h* his cry when trouble Job 27:9 8085
unto thee, and thou dost not *h* me Job 30:20 6030
Oh that one would *h* me Job 31:35 8085
h my speeches, and hearken to all Job 33:1 8085
H my words, O ye wise men Job 34:2 8085
thou hast understanding, *h* this Job 34:16 8085
Surely God will not *h* vanity Job 35:13 8085
H attentively the noise of his Job 37:2 8085
H, I beseech thee, and I will Job 42:4 8085
H me when I call, O God of my Ps 4:1 6030
mercy upon me, and *h* my prayer Ps 4:1 8085
the LORD will *h* when I call unto Ps 4:3 8085
voice shalt thou *h* in the morning Ps 5:3 8085
thou wilt cause thine ear to *h* Ps 10:17 7181
Consider and *h* me, O LORD my God Ps 13:3 6030
H the right, O LORD, attend unto Ps 17:1 8085
upon thee, for thou wilt *h* me Ps 17:6 6030
thine ear unto me, and *h* my speech Ps 17:6 8085
As soon as they *h* of me, they Ps 18:44 8085
The LORD *h* thee in the day of Ps 20:1 6030
he will *h* him from his holy Ps 20:6 6030
let the king *h* us when we call Ps 20:9 6030
H, O LORD, when I cry with my Ps 27:7 8085
H the voice of my supplications, Ps 28:2 8085
H, O LORD, and have mercy upon me Ps 30:10 8085
the humble shall *h* thereof Ps 34:2 8085
thou wilt *h*, O Lord my God Ps 38:15 6030
H me, lest otherwise they should Ps 38:16 8085
H my prayer, O LORD, and give ear Ps 39:12 8085
H this, all ye people Ps 49:1 8085
H, O my people, and I will speak Ps 50:7 8085
Make me to *h* joy and gladness Ps 51:8 8085
H my prayer, O God Ps 54:2 8085
Attend unto me, and *h* me Ps 55:2 6030
and he shall *h* my voice Ps 55:17 8085
God shall *h*, and afflict them, Ps 55:19 8085
for who, say they, doth *h* Ps 59:7 8085
save with thy right hand, and *h* me Ps 60:5 6030
H my cry, O God Ps 61:1 8085
H my voice, O God, in my prayer Ps 64:1 8085
Come and *h*, all ye that fear God, Ps 66:16
my heart, the Lord will not *h* me Ps 66:18 8085
the multitude of thy mercy *h* me Ps 69:13 6030
H me, O LORD Ps 69:16 6030
h me speedily Ps 69:17 6030
H, O my people, and I will testify Ps 81:8 8085
O LORD God of hosts, *h* my prayer Ps 84:8 8085
I will *h* what God the LORD will Ps 85:8 8085
Bow down thine ear, O LORD, *h* me Ps 86:1 6030
mine ears shall *h* my desire of Ps 92:11 8085
planted the ear, shall he not *h* Ps 94:9 8085
To day if ye will *h* his voice Ps 95:7 8085
H my prayer, O LORD, and let my Ps 102:1 8085
To *h* the groaning of the prisoner Ps 102:20 8085
They have ears, but they *h* not Ps 115:6 8085
h me, O LORD Ps 119:145 6030
H my voice according unto thy Ps 119:149 8085
Lord, *h* my voice Ps 130:2 8085
They have ears, but they *h* not Ps 135:17 238
when they *h* the words of thy Ps 138:4 8085
h the voice of my supplications, Ps 140:6 238
places, they shall *h* my words Ps 141:6 8085
H my prayer, O LORD, give ear to Ps 143:1 8085
H me speedily, O LORD Ps 143:7 6030
Cause me to *h* thy lovingkindness Ps 143:8 8085
he also will *h* their cry, and will Ps 145:19 8085
A wise man will *h*, and will Prov 1:5 8085

h the instruction of thy father, Prov 1:8 8085
H, ye children, the instruction Prov 4:1 8085
H, O my son, and receive my Prov 4:10 8085
H me now therefore, O ye children Prov 5:7 8085
H; for I will speak Prov 8:6 8085
H instruction, and be wise, and Prov 8:33 8085
H counsel, and receive instruction Prov 19:20 8085
to *h* the instruction that causeth Prov 19:27 8085
h the words of the wise, and apply Prov 22:17 8085
H thou, my son, and be wise, and Prov 23:19 8085
of God, and be more ready to *h* Eccl 5:1 8085
It is better to *h* the rebuke of Eccl 7:5 8085
for a man to *h* the song of fools Eccl 7:5 8085
lest thou *h* thy servant curse Eccl 7:21 8085
Let us *h* the conclusion of the Eccl 12:13 8085
countenance, let me *h* thy voice Song 2:14 8085
cause me to *h* it Song 8:13 8085
H, O heavens, and give ear, O Is 1:2 8085
H the word of the LORD, ye rulers Is 1:10 8085
make many prayers, I will not *h* Is 1:15 8085
H ye indeed, but understand not Is 6:9 8085
h with their ears, and understand Is 6:10 8085
H ye now, O house of David Is 7:13 8085
when he bloweth a trumpet, *h* ye Is 18:3 8085
yet they would not *h* Is 28:12 8085
Wherefore *h* the word of the LORD, Is 28:14 8085
Give ye ear, and *h* my voice Is 28:23 8085
hearken, and *h* my speech Is 28:23 8085
the deaf *h* the words of the book Is 29:18 8085
will not *h* the law of the LORD Is 30:9 8085
when he shall *h* it, he will Is 30:19 8085
thine ears shall *h* a word behind Is 30:21 8085
ears of them that *h* shall hearken Is 32:3 8085
h my voice, ye careless daughters Is 32:9 8085
H, ye that are far off, what I Is 33:13 8085
Come near, ye nations, to *h* Is 34:1 8085
let the earth *h*, and all that is Is 34:1 8085
H ye the words of the great king, Is 36:13 8085
God will *h* the words of Rabshakeh Is 37:4 8085
upon him, and he shall *h* a rumour Is 37:7 8085
Incline thine ear, O LORD, and *h* Is 37:17 8085
h all the words of Sennacherib, Is 37:17 8085
H the word of the LORD of hosts Is 39:5 8085
thirst, I the LORD will *h* them Is 41:17 6030
H, ye deaf Is 42:18 8085
hearken and *h* for the time to come Is 42:23 8085
or let them *h*, and say, It is Is 43:9 8085
Yet now *h*, O Jacob my servant Is 44:1 8085
Therefore *h* now this, thou that Is 47:8 8085
H ye this, O house of Jacob, Is 48:1 8085
All ye, assemble yourselves, and *h* Is 48:14 8085
Come ye near unto me, *h* ye this Is 48:16 8085
mine ear to *h* as the learned Is 50:4 8085
Therefore *h* now this, thou Is 51:21 8085
h, and your soul shall live Is 55:3 8085
his ear heavy, that it cannot *h* Is 59:1 8085
face from you, that he will not *h* Is 59:2 8085
when I spake, ye did not *h* Is 65:12 8085
they are yet speaking, I will *h* Is 65:24 8085
when I spake, they did not *h* Is 66:4 8085
H the word of the LORD, ye that Is 66:5 8085
H ye the word of the LORD, O Jer 2:4 8085
h the sound of the trumpet Jer 4:21 8085
H now this, O foolish people, and Jer 5:21 8085
which have ears, and *h* not Jer 5:21 8085
and give warning, that they may *h* Jer 6:10 8085
Therefore *h*, ye nations, and know, Jer 6:18 8085
H, O earth Jer 6:19 8085
H the word of the LORD, all ye of Jer 7:2 8085
for I will not *h* thee Jer 7:16 8085
neither can men *h* the voice of Jer 9:10 8085
Yet *h* the word of the LORD, O ye Jer 9:20 8085
H ye the word which the LORD Jer 10:1 8085
H ye the words of this covenant, Jer 11:2 8085
H ye the words of this covenant, Jer 11:6 8085
which refused to *h* my words Jer 11:10 8085
for I will not *h* them in the time Jer 11:14 8085
which refuse to *h* my words Jer 13:10 8085
but they would not *h* Jer 13:11 8085
H ye, and give ear Jer 13:15 8085
But if ye will not *h* it, my soul Jer 13:17 8085
they fast, I will not *h* their cry Jer 14:12 8085
H ye the word of the LORD, ye Jer 17:20 8085
neck stiff, that they might not *h* Jer 17:23 8085
I will cause thee to *h* my words Jer 18:2 8085
H ye the word of the LORD, O Jer 19:3 8085
that they might not *h* my words Jer 19:15 8085
let him *h* the cry in the morning, Jer 20:16 8085
H ye the word of the LORD Jer 21:11 8085
H the word of the LORD, O king of Jer 22:2 8085
But if ye will not *h* these words Jer 22:5 8085
but thou saidst, I will not *h* Jer 22:21 8085
earth, *h* the word of the LORD Jer 22:29 8085
caused my people to *h* my words Jer 23:22 8085
nor inclined your ear to *h* Jer 25:4 8085
Nevertheless *h* thou now this word Jer 28:7 8085
the prophet, *H* now, Hananiah Jer 28:15 8085
but ye would not *h*, saith the Jer 29:19 8085
H ye therefore the word of the Jer 29:20 8085
H the word of the LORD, O ye Jer 31:10 8085
which shall *h* all the good that I Jer 33:9 8085
Yet *h* the word of the LORD, O Jer 34:4 8085
h all the evil which I purpose to Jer 36:3 8085
but he would not *h* them Jer 36:25 8085
Therefore *h* now, I pray thee, O Jer 37:20 8085
But if the princes *h* that I have Jer 38:25 8085
nor *h* the sound of the trumpet, Jer 42:14 8085
now therefore *h* the word of the Jer 42:15 8085
H the word of the LORD, all Judah Jer 44:24 8085
Therefore *h* ye the word of the Jer 44:26 8085
Therefore *h* the counsel of the Jer 49:20 8085
Therefore *h* ye the counsel of the Jer 50:45 8085
h, I pray you, all people, and Lam 1:18 8085
And they, whether they will *h* Eze 2:5 8085

Context	Reference	Number
unto them, whether they will *h*	Eze 2:7	8085
of man, *h* what I say unto thee	Eze 2:8	8085
thine heart, and *h* with thine ears	Eze 3:10	8085
whether they will *h*, or whether	Eze 3:11	8085
therefore *h* the word at my mouth,	Eze 3:17	8085
He that heareth, let him *h*	Eze 3:27	8085
h the word of the Lord GOD	Eze 6:3	8085
loud voice, yet will I not *h* them	Eze 8:18	8085
they have ears to *h*, and *h* not	Eze 12:2	8085
H ye the word of the LORD	Eze 13:2	8085
to my people that *h* your lies	Eze 13:19	8085
O harlot, *h* the word of the LORD	Eze 16:35	8085
H now, O house of Israel	Eze 18:25	8085
the south, *H* the word of the LORD	Eze 20:47	8085
to cause thee to *h* it with thine	Eze 24:26	2045
H the word of the Lord GOD	Eze 25:3	8085
thou shalt *h* the word at my mouth	Eze 33:7	8085
h what is the word that cometh	Eze 33:30	8085
they *h* thy words, but they will	Eze 33:31	8085
for they *h* thy words, but they do	Eze 33:32	8085
shepherds, *h* the word of the LORD	Eze 34:7	8085
shepherds, *h* the word of the LORD	Eze 34:9	8085
of Israel, *h* the word of the LORD	Eze 36:1	8085
h the word of the Lord GOD	Eze 36:4	8085
men to *h* in thee the shame of the	Eze 36:15	8085
dry bones, *h* the word of the LORD	Eze 37:4	8085
h with thine ears, and set thine	Eze 40:4	8085
h with thine ears all that I say	Eze 44:5	8085
That at what time ye *h* the sound	Dan 3:5	8086
shall *h* the sound of the cornet	Dan 3:10	8086
time ye *h* the sound of the cornet	Dan 3:15	8086
and stone, which see not, nor *h*	Dan 5:23	8086
h the prayer of thy servant, and	Dan 9:17	8085
O my God, incline thine ear, and *h*	Dan 9:18	8085
O Lord, *h*; O Lord	Dan 9:19	8085
to pass in that day, I will *h*	Hos 2:21	6030
I will *h* the heavens	Hos 2:21	6030
and they shall *h* the earth	Hos 2:21	6030
And the earth shall *h* the corn	Hos 2:22	6030
and they shall *h* Jezreel	Hos 2:22	6030
H the word of the LORD, ye	Hos 4:1	8085
H ye this, O priests	Hos 5:1	8085
H this, ye old men, and give ear,	Joel 1:2	8085
H this word that the LORD hath	Amos 3:1	8085
H ye, and testify in the house of	Amos 3:13	8085
H this word, ye kine of Bashan,	Amos 4:1	8085
H ye this word which I take up	Amos 5:1	8085
for I will not *h* the melody of	Amos 5:23	8085
Now therefore *h* thou the word of	Amos 7:16	8085
H this, O ye that swallow up the	Amos 8:4	8085
H, all ye people	Mic 1:2	8085
And I said, *H*, I pray you, O heads	Mic 3:1	8085
the LORD, but he will not *h* them	Mic 3:4	6030
H this, I pray you, ye heads of	Mic 3:9	8085
H ye now what the LORD saith	Mic 6:1	8085
and let the hills *h* thy voice	Mic 6:1	8085
H ye, O mountains, the LORD's	Mic 6:2	8085
h ye the rod, and who hath	Mic 6:9	8085
my God will *h* me	Mic 7:7	8085
all that *h* the bruit of thee	Nah 3:19	8085
shall I cry, and thou wilt not *h*	Hab 1:2	8085
but they did not *h*, nor hearken	Zec 1:4	8085
H now, O Joshua the high priest,	Zec 3:8	8085
Should ye not *h* the words which	Zec 7:7	
ears, that they should not *h*	Zec 7:11	8085
stone, lest they should *h* the law	Zec 7:12	8085
as he cried, and they would not *h*	Zec 7:13	8085
so they cried, and I would not *h*	Zec 7:13	8085
ye that *h* in these days these	Zec 8:9	8085
LORD their God, and will *h* them	Zec 10:6	6030
call on my name, and I will *h* them	Zec 13:9	6030
If ye will not *h*, and if ye will	Mal 2:2	8085
nor *h* your words, when ye depart	Mt 10:14	191
what ye *h* in the ear, that preach	Mt 10:27	191
again those things which ye do *h*	Mt 11:4	191
are cleansed, and the deaf *h*	Mt 11:5	191
that hath ears to *h*, let him *h*	Mt 11:15	191
neither shall any man *h* his voice	Mt 12:19	191
earth to *h* the wisdom of Solomon	Mt 12:42	191
Who hath ears to *h*, let him *h*	Mt 13:9	191
and hearing they *h* not, neither do	Mt 13:13	191
saith, By hearing ye shall *h*	Mt 13:14	191
h with their ears, and should	Mt 13:15	191
and your ears, for they *h*	Mt 13:16	191
to *h* those things which ye *h*	Mt 13:17	191
H ye therefore the parable of the	Mt 13:18	191
Who hath ears to *h*, let him *h*	Mt 13:43	191
multitude, and said unto them, *H*	Mt 15:10	191
h ye him	Mt 17:5	191
if he shall *h* thee, thou hast	Mt 18:15	191
But if he will not *h* thee	Mt 18:16	191
And if he shall neglect to *h* them	Mt 18:17	3878
but if he neglect to *h* the church	Mt 18:17	3878
H another parable	Mt 21:33	191
And ye shall *h* of wars and rumours	Mt 24:6	191
that hath ears to *h*, let him *h*	Mk 4:9	191
and hearing they may *h*, and not	Mk 4:12	191
such as *h* the word,	Mk 4:18	191
such as *h* the word, and receive it	Mk 4:20	191
man have ears to *h*, let him *h*	Mk 4:23	191
unto them, Take heed what ye *h*	Mk 4:24	191
unto you that *h* shall more be	Mk 4:24	191
them, as they were able to *h* it	Mk 4:33	191
shall not receive you, nor *h* you	Mk 6:11	191
man have ears to *h*, let him *h*	Mk 7:16	191
he maketh both the deaf to *h*	Mk 7:37	191
and having ears, *h* ye not	Mk 8:18	191
h him	Mk 9:7	191
of all the commandments is, *H*	Mk 12:29	191
And when ye shall *h* of wars	Mk 13:7	191
upon him to *h* the word of God	Lk 5:1	191
multitudes came together to *h*	Lk 5:15	191
and Sidon, which came to *h* him	Lk 6:17	191
But I say unto you which *h*	Lk 6:27	191
lepers are cleansed, the deaf *h*	Lk 7:22	191
that hath ears to *h*, let him *h*	Lk 8:8	191
by the way side are they that *h*	Lk 8:12	191
rock are they, which, when they *h*	Lk 8:13	191
Take heed therefore how ye *h*	Lk 8:18	191
are these which *h* the word of God	Lk 8:21	191
is this, of whom I *h* such things	Lk 9:9	191
h him	Lk 9:35	191
to *h* those things which ye *h*,	Lk 10:24	191
are they that *h* the word of God	Lk 11:28	191
earth to *h* the wisdom of Solomon	Lk 11:31	191
that hath ears to *h*, let him *h*	Lk 14:35	191
publicans and sinners for to *h* him	Lk 15:1	191
How is it that I *h* this of thee	Lk 16:2	191
let them *h* them	Lk 16:29	191
If they *h* not Moses and the	Lk 16:31	191
H what the unjust judge saith	Lk 18:6	191
were very attentive to *h* him	Lk 19:48	191
But when ye shall *h* of wars	Lk 21:9	191
him in the temple, for to *h* him	Lk 21:38	191
when the dead shall *h* the voice	Jn 5:25	191
and they that *h* shall live	Jn 5:25	191
in the graves shall *h* his voice	Jn 5:28	191
as I *h*, I judge	Jn 5:30	191
who can *h* it?	Jn 6:60	191
judge any man, before it *h* him	Jn 7:51	191
even because ye cannot *h* my word	Jn 8:43	191
ye therefore *h* them not, because	Jn 8:47	191
told you already, and ye did not *h*	Jn 9:27	191
wherefore would ye *h* it again	Jn 9:27	191
and the sheep *h* his voice	Jn 10:3	191
but the sheep did not *h* them	Jn 10:8	191
bring, and they shall *h* my voice	Jn 10:16	191
why *h* ye him?	Jn 10:20	191
My sheep *h* my voice, and I know	Jn 10:27	191
And if any man *h* my words, and	Jn 12:47	191
the word which ye *h* is not mine	Jn 14:24	191
but whatsoever he shall *h*	Jn 16:13	191
how *h* we every man in our own	Acts 2:8	191
we do *h* them speak in our tongues	Acts 2:11	191
Ye men of Israel, *h* these words	Acts 2:22	191
forth this, which ye now see and *h*	Acts 2:33	191
him shall ye *h* in all things	Acts 3:22	191
which will not *h* that prophet	Acts 3:23	191
him shall ye *h*	Acts 7:37	191
his house, and to *h* words of thee	Acts 10:22	191
God, to *h* all things that are	Acts 10:33	191
desired to *h* the word of God	Acts 13:7	191
together to *h* the word of God	Acts 13:44	191
should *h* the word of the gospel	Acts 15:7	191
to tell, or to *h* some new thing	Acts 17:21	191
We will *h* thee again of this	Acts 17:32	191
Moreover ye see and *h*, that not	Acts 19:26	191
for they will *h* that thou art	Acts 21:22	191
h ye my defence which I make now	Acts 22:1	191
shouldest *h* the voice of his	Acts 22:14	191
I will *h* thee, said he, when	Acts 23:35	1251
h us of thy clemency a few words	Acts 24:4	191
I would also *h* the man myself	Acts 25:22	191
morrow, said he, thou shalt *h* him	Acts 25:22	191
I beseech thee to *h* me patiently	Acts 26:3	191
but also all that *h* me this day	Acts 26:29	191
But we desire to *h* of thee what	Acts 28:22	191
and say, Hearing ye shall *h*	Acts 28:26	191
h with their ears, and understand	Acts 28:27	191
Gentiles, and that they will *h* it	Acts 28:28	191
how shall they *h* without a	Rom 10:14	191
and ears that they should not *h*	Rom 11:8	191
I *h* that there be divisions among	1Cor 11:18	191
for all that will they not *h* me	1Cor 14:21	1522
the law, do ye not *h* the law	Gal 4:21	191
I may *h* of your affairs, that ye	Phil 1:27	191
saw in me, and now *h* to be in me	Phil 1:30	191
For we *h* that there are some	2Th 3:11	191
save thyself, and them that *h* thee	1Ti 4:16	191
and that all the Gentiles might *h*	2Ti 4:17	191
To day if ye will *h* his voice	Heb 3:7	191
To day if ye will *h* his voice	Heb 3:15	191
To day if ye will *h* his voice	Heb 4:7	191
let every man be swift to *h*	Jas 1:19	191
And if we know that he *h* us	1Jn 5:15	191
I have no greater joy than to *h*	3Jn 4	191
they that *h* the words of this	Rev 1:3	191
let him *h* what the Spirit saith	Rev 2:7	191
let him *h* what the Spirit saith	Rev 2:11	191
let him *h* what the Spirit saith	Rev 2:17	191
let him *h* what the Spirit saith	Rev 2:29	191
let him *h* what the Spirit saith	Rev 3:6	191
let him *h* what the Spirit saith	Rev 3:13	191
if any man *h* my voice, and open	Rev 3:20	191
let him *h* what the Spirit saith	Rev 3:22	191
which neither can see, nor *h*	Rev 9:20	191
If any man have an ear, let him *h*	Rev 13:9	191

HEARD

Context	Reference	Number
they *h* the voice of the LORD God	Gen 3:8	8085
I *h* thy voice in the garden, and I	Gen 3:10	8085
when Abram *h* that his brother was	Gen 14:14	8085
the LORD hath *h* thy affliction	Gen 16:11	8085
And as for Ishmael, I have *h* thee	Gen 17:20	8085
Sarah *h* it in the tent door,	Gen 18:10	8085
God *h* the voice of the lad	Gen 21:17	8085
for God hath *h* the voice of the	Gen 21:17	8085
tell me, neither yet *h* I of it	Gen 21:26	8085
when he *h* the words of Rebekah	Gen 24:30	8085
Abraham's servant *h* their words	Gen 24:52	8085
Rebekah *h* when Isaac spake to	Gen 27:5	8085
I *h* thy father speak unto Esau	Gen 27:6	8085
when Esau *h* the words of his	Gen 27:34	8085
when Laban *h* the tidings of Jacob	Gen 29:13	8085
the LORD hath *h* that I was hated	Gen 29:33	8085
me, and hath also *h* my voice	Gen 30:6	8085
he *h* the words of Laban's sons,	Gen 31:1	8085
Jacob *h* that he had defiled Dinah	Gen 34:5	8085
out of the field when they *h* it	Gen 34:7	8085
and Israel *h* it	Gen 35:22	8085
for I *h* them say, Let us go to	Gen 37:17	8085
And Reuben *h* it, and he delivered	Gen 37:21	8085
when he *h* that I lifted up my	Gen 39:15	8085
when his master *h* the words of	Gen 39:19	8085
I have *h* say of thee, that thou	Gen 41:15	8085
I have *h* that there is corn in	Gen 42:2	8085
for they *h* that they should eat	Gen 43:25	8085
and the house of Pharaoh *h*	Gen 45:2	8085
thereof was *h* in Pharaoh's house	Gen 45:16	8085
Now when Pharaoh *h* this thing	Ex 2:15	8085
God *h* their groaning, and God	Ex 2:24	8085
have *h* their cry by reason of	Ex 3:7	8085
when they *h* that the LORD had	Ex 4:31	8085
I have also *h* the groaning of the	Ex 6:5	8085
for he hath *h* your murmurings	Ex 16:9	8085
I have *h* the murmurings of the	Ex 16:12	8085
h of all that God had done for	Ex 18:1	8085
let it be *h* out of thy mouth	Ex 23:13	8085
his sound shall be *h* when he	Ex 28:35	8085
when Joshua *h* the noise of the	Ex 32:17	8085
when the people *h* these evil	Ex 33:4	8085
And when Moses *h* that, he was	Lev 10:20	8085
let all that *h* him lay their	Lev 24:14	8085
then he *h* the voice of one	Num 7:89	8085
and the LORD *h* it	Num 11:1	8085
Then Moses *h* the people weep	Num 11:10	8085
And the LORD *h* it	Num 12:2	8085
for they have *h* that thou LORD	Num 14:14	8085
h the fame of thee will speak	Num 14:15	8085
I have *h* the murmurings of the	Num 14:27	8085
And when Moses *h* it, he fell upon	Num 16:4	8085
he *h* our voice, and sent an angel,	Num 20:16	8085
h tell that Israel came by the	Num 21:1	8085
when Balak *h* that Balaam was come	Num 22:36	8085
which *h* the words of God, which	Num 24:4	8085
which *h* the words of God, and knew	Num 24:16	8085
And her husband *h* it, and held his	Num 30:7	8085
at her in the day that he *h* it	Num 30:7	8085
her on the day that he *h* it	Num 30:8	8085
And her husband *h* it, and held his	Num 30:11	8085
them void on the day he *h* them	Num 30:12	8085
at her in the day that he *h* them	Num 30:14	8085
void after that he hath *h* them	Num 30:15	8085
h of the coming of the children	Num 33:40	8085
the LORD *h* the voice of your	Deut 1:34	8085
ye *h* the voice of the words, but	Deut 4:12	8085
only ye *h* a voice	Deut 4:12	8085
thing is, or hath been *h* like it	Deut 4:32	8085
midst of the fire, as thou hast *h*	Deut 4:33	8085
when ye *h* the voice out of the	Deut 5:23	8085
we have *h* his voice out of the	Deut 5:24	8085
that hath *h* the voice of the	Deut 5:26	8085
the LORD *h* the voice of your	Deut 5:28	8085
I have *h* the voice of the words	Deut 5:28	8085
and of whom thou hast *h* say	Deut 9:2	8085
told thee, and thou hast *h* of it	Deut 17:4	8085
the LORD *h* our voice, and looked	Deut 26:7	8085
For we have *h* how the LORD dried	Josh 2:10	8085
as soon as we had *h* these things	Josh 2:11	8085
h that the LORD had dried up the	Josh 5:1	8085
when the people *h* the sound of	Josh 6:20	8085
and the Jebusite, *h* thereof	Josh 9:1	8085
h what Joshua had done unto	Josh 9:3	8085
for we have *h* the fame of him, and	Josh 9:9	8085
that they *h* that they were their	Josh 9:16	8085
king of Jerusalem had *h* how	Josh 10:1	8085
king of Hazor had *h* those things	Josh 11:1	8085
And the children of Israel *h* say	Josh 22:11	8085
the children of Israel *h* of it	Josh 22:12	8085
h the words that the children of	Josh 22:30	8085
for it hath *h* all the words of	Josh 24:27	8085
when Gideon *h* the telling of the	Judg 7:15	8085
Zebul the ruler of the city *h* the	Judg 9:30	8085
of the tower of Shechem *h* that	Judg 9:46	8085
Let not thy voice be *h* among us	Judg 18:25	8085
h that the children of Israel	Judg 20:3	8085
for she had *h* in the country of	Ruth 1:6	8085
moved, but her voice was not *h*	1Sa 1:13	8085
h all that his sons did unto all	1Sa 2:22	8085
when the Philistines *h* the noise	1Sa 4:6	8085
when Eli *h* the noise of the	1Sa 4:14	8085
when she *h* the tidings that the	1Sa 4:19	8085
when the Philistines *h* that the	1Sa 7:7	8085
when the children of Israel *h* it	1Sa 7:7	8085
and the LORD *h* him	1Sa 7:9	6030
Samuel *h* all the words of the	1Sa 8:21	8085
upon Saul when he *h* those tidings	1Sa 11:6	8085
Geba, and the Philistines *h* of it	1Sa 13:3	8085
all Israel *h* say that Saul had	1Sa 13:4	8085
when they *h* that the Philistines	1Sa 14:22	8085
But Jonathan *h* not when his	1Sa 14:27	8085
all Israel *h* those words of the	1Sa 17:11	8085
and David *h* them	1Sa 17:23	8085
Eliab his eldest brother *h* when	1Sa 17:28	8085
words were *h* which David spake	1Sa 17:31	8085
and all his father's house *h* it	1Sa 22:1	8085
When Saul *h* that David was	1Sa 22:6	8085
thy servant hath certainly *h* that	1Sa 23:10	8085
come down, as thy servant hath *h*	1Sa 23:11	8085
And when Saul *h* that, he pursued	1Sa 23:25	8085
David *h* in the wilderness that	1Sa 25:4	8085
now I have *h* that thou hast	1Sa 25:7	8085
when David *h* that Nabal was dead,	1Sa 25:39	8085
inhabitants of Jabesh-gilead *h* of	1Sa 31:11	8085
And afterward when David *h* it	2Sa 3:28	8085
when Saul's son *h* that Abner was	2Sa 4:1	8085
But when the Philistines *h* that	2Sa 5:17	8085
and David *h* of it, and went down to	2Sa 5:17	8085
all that we have *h* with our ears	2Sa 7:22	8085
When Toi king of Hamath *h* that	2Sa 8:9	8085
And when David *h* of it, he sent	2Sa 10:7	8085
when the wife of Uriah *h* that	2Sa 11:26	8085

king David *h* of all these things	2Sa 13:21	8085
all the people *h* when the king	2Sa 18:5	8085
for the people *h* say that day how	2Sa 19:2	8085
Hast thou not *h* that Adonijah the	1Kin 1:11	8085
h it as they had made an end of	1Kin 1:41	8085
when Joab *h* the sound of the	1Kin 1:41	8085
This is the noise that ye have *h*	1Kin 1:45	8085
The word that I have *h* is good	1Kin 2:42	8085
all Israel *h* of the judgment	1Kin 3:28	8085
which had *h* of his wisdom	1Kin 4:34	8085
for he had *h* that they had	1Kin 5:1	8085
when Hiram *h* the words of Solomon	1Kin 5:7	8085
any tool of iron *h* in the house	1Kin 6:7	8085
I have *h* thy prayer and thy	1Kin 9:3	8085
of Sheba *h* of the fame of Solomon	1Kin 10:1	8085
It was a true report that I *h* in	1Kin 10:6	8085
exceedeth the fame which I *h*	1Kin 10:7	8085
when Hadad *h* in Egypt that David	1Kin 11:21	8085
h of it, (for he was fled from	1Kin 12:2	8085
when all Israel *h* that Jeroboam	1Kin 12:20	8085
when king Jeroboam *h* the saying	1Kin 13:4	8085
him back from the way *h* thereof	1Kin 13:26	8085
when Ahijah *h* the sound of her	1Kin 14:6	8085
to pass, when Baasha *h* thereof	1Kin 15:21	8085
people that were encamped *h* say	1Kin 16:16	8085
the LORD *h* the voice of Elijah	1Kin 17:22	8085
And it was so, when Elijah *h* it	1Kin 19:13	8085
when Ben-hadad *h* this message	1Kin 20:12	8085
we have *h* that the kings of the	1Kin 20:31	8085
when Jezebel *h* that Naboth was	1Kin 21:15	8085
when Ahab *h* that Naboth was dead,	1Kin 21:16	8085
when Ahab *h* those words, that he	1Kin 21:27	8085
when all the Moabites *h* that the	2Kin 3:21	8085
had *h* that the king of Israel had	2Kin 5:8	8085
when the king *h* the words of the	2Kin 6:30	8085
come to Jezreel, Jezebel *h* of it	2Kin 9:30	8085
when Athaliah *h* the noise of the	2Kin 11:13	8085
to pass, when king Hezekiah *h* it	2Kin 19:1	8085
which the LORD thy God hath *h*	2Kin 19:4	8085
of the words which thou hast *h*	2Kin 19:6	8085
for he had *h* that he was departed	2Kin 19:8	8085
when he *h* say of Tirhakah king of	2Kin 19:9	8085
thou hast *h* what the kings of	2Kin 19:11	8085
king of Assyria I have *h*	2Kin 19:20	8085
Hast thou not *h* long ago how I	2Kin 19:25	8085
I have *h* thy prayer, I have seen	2Kin 20:5	8085
for he had *h* that Hezekiah had	2Kin 20:12	8085
when the king had *h* the words of	2Kin 22:11	8085
the words which thou hast *h*	2Kin 22:18	8085
I also have *h* thee, saith the	2Kin 22:19	8085
h that the king of Babylon had	2Kin 25:23	8085
when all Jabesh-gilead *h* all that	1Chr 10:11	8085
when the Philistines *h* that David	1Chr 14:8	8085
And David *h* of it, and went out	1Chr 14:8	8085
all that we have *h* with our ears	1Chr 17:20	8085
Tou king of Hamath *h* how	1Chr 18:9	8085
And when David *h* of it, he sent	1Chr 19:8	8085
one sound to be *h* in praising	2Chr 5:13	8085
I have *h* thy prayer, and have	2Chr 7:12	8085
of Sheba *h* of the fame of Solomon	2Chr 9:1	8085
It was a true report which I *h* in	2Chr 9:5	8085
thou exceedest the fame that I *h*	2Chr 9:6	8085
h it, that Jeroboam returned out	2Chr 10:2	8085
when Asa *h* these words, and the	2Chr 15:8	8085
it came to pass, when Baasha *h* it	2Chr 16:5	8085
when they had *h* that the LORD	2Chr 20:29	8085
Now when Athaliah *h* the noise of	2Chr 23:12	8085
and their voice was *h*, and their	2Chr 30:27	8085
h his supplication, and brought	2Chr 33:13	8085
when the king had *h* the words of	2Chr 34:19	8085
the words which thou hast *h*	2Chr 34:26	8085
I have even *h* thee also, saith	2Chr 34:27	8085
and the noise was *h* afar off	Ezr 3:13	8085
Benjamin *h* that the children of	Ezr 4:1	8085
when I *h* this thing, I rent my	Ezr 9:3	8085
when I *h* these words, that I sat	Neh 1:4	8085
h of it, it grieved them	Neh 2:10	8085
h it, they laughed us to scorn,	Neh 2:19	8085
that when Sanballat *h* that we	Neh 4:1	8085
h that the walls of Jerusalem	Neh 4:7	8085
when our enemies *h* that it was	Neh 4:15	8085
was very angry when I *h* their cry	Neh 5:6	8085
h that I had builded the wall, and	Neh 6:1	8085
when all our enemies *h* thereof	Neh 6:16	8085
when they *h* the words of the law	Neh 8:9	8085
of Jerusalem was *h* even afar off	Neh 12:43	8085
to pass, when they had *h* the law	Neh 13:3	8085
which have *h* of the deed of the	Est 1:18	8085
commandment and his decree was *h*	Est 2:8	8085
Now when Job's three friends *h* of	Job 2:11	8085
silence, and I *h* a voice, saying,	Job 4:16	8085
seen all this, mine ear hath *h*,	Job 13:1	8085
Hast thou *h* the secret of God	Job 15:8	8085
I have *h* many such things	Job 16:2	8085
cry out of wrong, but I am not *h*	Job 19:7	6030
I have *h* the check of my reproach	Job 20:3	8085
how little a portion is *h* of him	Job 26:14	8085
We have *h* the fame thereof with	Job 28:22	8085
When the ear *h* me, then it	Job 29:11	8085
I have *h* the voice of thy words,	Job 33:8	8085
not stay them when his voice is *h*	Job 37:4	8085
I have *h* of thee by the hearing	Job 42:5	8085
he *h* me out of his holy hill	Ps 3:4	6030
for the LORD hath *h* the voice of	Ps 6:8	8085
The LORD hath *h* my supplication	Ps 6:9	8085
thou hast *h* the desire of the	Ps 10:17	8085
he *h* my voice out of his temple,	Ps 18:6	8085
where their voice is not *h*	Ps 19:3	8085
for thou hast *h* me from the horns	Ps 22:21	6030
but when he cried unto him, he *h*	Ps 22:24	8085
because he hath *h* the voice of my	Ps 28:6	8085
For I have *h* the slander of many	Ps 31:13	8085
I sought the LORD, and he *h* me	Ps 34:4	6030
poor man cried, and the LORD *h* him	Ps 34:6	8085
But I, as a deaf man, *h* not	Ps 38:13	8085
he inclined unto me, and *h* my cry	Ps 40:1	8085
We have *h* with our ears, O God,	Ps 44:1	8085
As we have *h*, so have we seen in	Ps 48:8	8085
For thou, O God, hast *h* my vows	Ps 61:5	8085
twice have I *h* this	Ps 62:11	8085
the voice of his praise to be *h*	Ps 66:8	8085
But verily God hath *h* me	Ps 66:19	8085
judgment to be *h* from heaven	Ps 76:8	8085
Which we have *h* and known, and our	Ps 78:3	8085
Therefore the LORD *h* this	Ps 78:21	8085
When God *h* this, he was wroth, and	Ps 78:59	8085
where I *h* a language that I	Ps 81:5	8085
Zion *h*, and was glad	Ps 97:8	8085
affliction, when he *h* their cry	Ps 106:44	8085
LORD, because he hath *h* my voice	Ps 116:1	8085
for thou hast *h* me, and art become	Ps 118:21	6030
I cried unto the LORD, and he *h* me	Ps 120:1	6030
Lo, we *h* of it at Ephratah	Ps 132:6	8085
cry himself, but shall not be *h*	Prov 21:13	6030
despised, and his words are not *h*	Eccl 9:16	8085
The words of wise men are *h* in	Eccl 9:17	8085
of the turtle is *h* in our land	Song 2:12	8085
Also I *h* the voice of the Lord,	Is 6:8	8085
cause it to be *h* unto Laish	Is 10:30	7181
voice shall be *h* even unto Jahaz	Is 15:4	8085
We have *h* of the pride of Moab	Is 16:6	8085
that which I have *h* of the LORD	Is 21:10	8085
part of the earth have we *h* songs	Is 24:16	8085
for I have *h* from the Lord GOD of	Is 28:22	8085
cause his glorious voice to be *h*	Is 30:30	8085
to pass, when king Hezekiah *h* it	Is 37:1	8085
which the LORD thy God hath *h*	Is 37:4	8085
of the words that thou hast *h*	Is 37:6	8085
for he had *h* that he was departed	Is 37:8	8085
he *h* say concerning Tirhakah king	Is 37:9	8085
And when he *h* it, he sent	Is 37:9	8085
thou hast *h* what the kings of	Is 37:11	8085
Hast thou not *h* long ago, how I	Is 37:26	8085
I have *h* thy prayer, I have seen	Is 38:5	8085
for he had *h* that he had been	Is 39:1	8085
have ye not *h*?	Is 40:21	8085
hast thou not *h*, that the	Is 40:28	8085
his voice to be *h* in the street	Is 42:2	8085
Thou hast *h*, see all this	Is 48:6	8085
an acceptable time have I *h* thee	Is 49:8	6030
had not *h* shall they consider	Is 52:15	8085
make your voice to be *h* on high	Is 58:4	8085
shall no more be *h* in thy land	Is 60:18	8085
of the world men have not *h*	Is 64:4	8085
weeping shall be no more *h* in her	Is 65:19	8085
Who hath *h* such a thing	Is 66:8	8085
afar off, that have not *h* my fame	Is 66:19	8085
A voice was *h* upon the high	Jer 3:21	8085
my peace, because thou hast *h*	Jer 4:19	8085
For I have *h* a voice as of a	Jer 4:31	8085
violence and spoil is *h* in her	Jer 6:7	8085
We have *h* the fame thereof	Jer 6:24	8085
early and speaking, but ye *h* not	Jer 7:13	8085
I hearkened and *h*, but they spake	Jer 8:6	8085
of his horses was *h* from Dan	Jer 8:16	8085
voice of wailing is *h* out of Zion	Jer 9:19	8085
heathen, who hath *h* such things	Jer 18:13	8085
Let a cry be *h* from their houses,	Jer 18:22	8085
h that Jeremiah prophesied these	Jer 20:1	8085
For I *h* the defaming of many,	Jer 20:10	8085
and hath perceived and *h* his word	Jer 23:18	8085
who hath marked his word, and *h* it	Jer 23:18	8085
I have *h* what the prophets said,	Jer 23:25	8085
Because ye have not *h* my words	Jer 25:8	8085
of the flock, shall be *h*	Jer 25:36	8085
all the people *h* Jeremiah	Jer 26:7	8085
princes of Judah *h* these things	Jer 26:10	8085
as ye have *h* with your ears	Jer 26:11	8085
city all the words that ye have *h*	Jer 26:12	8085
h his words, the king sought to	Jer 26:21	8085
but when Urijah *h* it, he was	Jer 26:21	8085
We have *h* a voice of trembling,	Jer 30:5	8085
A voice was *h* in Ramah,	Jer 31:15	8085
I have surely *h* Ephraim bemoaning	Jer 31:18	8085
there shall be *h* in this place	Jer 33:10	8085
h that every one should let his	Jer 34:10	8085
unto them, but they have not *h*	Jer 35:17	8085
had *h* out of the book all the	Jer 36:11	8085
them all the words that he had *h*	Jer 36:13	8085
when they had *h* all the words	Jer 36:16	8085
servants that *h* all these words	Jer 36:24	8085
Jerusalem *h* tidings of them	Jer 37:5	8085
h the words that Jeremiah had	Jer 38:1	8085
h that they had put Jeremiah in	Jer 38:7	8085
h that the king of Babylon had	Jer 40:7	8085
h that the king of Babylon had	Jer 40:11	8085
h of all the evil that Ishmael	Jer 41:11	8085
said unto them, I have *h* you	Jer 42:4	8085
The nations have *h* of thy shame	Jer 46:12	8085
ones have caused a cry to be *h*	Jer 48:4	8085
have *h* a cry of destruction	Jer 48:5	8085
We have *h* the pride of Moab, (he	Jer 48:29	8085
be *h* in Rabbah of the Ammonites	Jer 49:2	8085
I have *h* a rumour from the LORD,	Jer 49:14	8085
thereof was *h* in the Red sea	Jer 49:21	8085
for they have *h* evil tidings	Jer 49:23	8085
Babylon hath *h* the report of them	Jer 50:43	8085
the cry is *h* among the nations	Jer 50:46	8085
that shall be *h* in the land	Jer 51:46	8085
because we have *h* reproach	Jer 51:51	8085
They have *h* that I sigh	Lam 1:21	8085
mine enemies have *h* of my trouble	Lam 1:21	8085
Thou hast *h* my voice	Lam 3:56	8085
Thou hast *h* their reproach, O	Lam 3:61	8085
I *h* the noise of their wings,	Eze 1:24	8085
I *h* a voice of one that spake	Eze 1:28	8085
that I *h* him that spake unto me	Eze 2:2	8085
I *h* behind me a voice of a great	Eze 3:12	8085
I *h* also the noise of the wings	Eze 3:13	
was *h* even to the outer court	Eze 10:5	8085
The nations also *h* of him	Eze 19:4	8085
his voice should no more be *h*	Eze 19:9	8085
of thy harps shall be no more *h*	Eze 26:13	8085
their voice to be *h* against thee	Eze 27:30	8085
He *h* the sound of the trumpet, and	Eze 33:5	8085
that I have *h* all thy blasphemies	Eze 35:12	8085
I have *h* them	Eze 35:13	8085
I *h* him speaking unto me out of	Eze 43:6	8085
when all the people *h* the sound	Dan 3:7	8086
I have even *h* of thee, that the	Dan 5:14	8086
I have *h* of thee, that thou canst	Dan 5:16	8086
when he *h* these words, was sore	Dan 6:14	8086
Then I *h* one saint speaking, and	Dan 8:13	8085
I *h* a man's voice between the	Dan 8:16	8085
Yet *h* I the voice of his words	Dan 10:9	8085
when I *h* the voice of his words,	Dan 10:9	8085
before thy God, thy words were *h*	Dan 10:12	8085
I *h* the man clothed in linen,	Dan 12:7	8085
And I *h*, but I understood not	Dan 12:8	8085
as their congregation hath *h*	Hos 7:12	8085
I have *h* him, and observed him	Hos 14:8	6030
We have *h* a rumour from the LORD,	Obad 1	8085
unto the LORD, and he *h* me	Jonah 2:2	6030
heathen, such as they have not *h*	Mic 5:15	8085
thy messengers shall no more be *h*	Nah 2:13	8085
I have *h* thy speech, and was	Hab 3:2	8085
When I *h*, my belly trembled	Hab 3:16	8085
I have *h* the reproach of Moab, and	Zeph 2:8	8085
for we have *h* that God is with	Zec 8:23	8085
h it, and a book of remembrance	Mal 3:16	8085
Herod the king had *h* these things	Mt 2:3	*191*
When they had *h* the king, they	Mt 2:9	*191*
In Rama was there a voice *h*	Mt 2:18	*191*
But when he *h* that Archelaus did	Mt 2:22	*191*
Now when Jesus had *h* that John	Mt 4:12	*191*
Ye have *h* that it was said by	Mt 5:21	*191*
Ye have *h* that it was said by	Mt 5:27	*191*
ye have *h* that it hath been said	Mt 5:33	*191*
Ye have *h* that it hath been said,	Mt 5:38	*191*
Ye have *h* that it hath been said,	Mt 5:43	*191*
be *h* for their much speaking	Mt 6:7	*1522*
When Jesus *h* it, he marvelled, and	Mt 8:10	*191*
But when Jesus *h* that, he said	Mt 9:12	*191*
Now when John had *h* in the prison	Mt 11:2	*191*
But when the Pharisees *h* it	Mt 12:24	*191*
which ye hear, and have not *h* them	Mt 13:17	*191*
tetrarch *h* of the fame of Jesus	Mt 14:1	*191*
When Jesus *h* of it, he departed	Mt 14:13	*191*
and when the people had *h* thereof	Mt 14:13	*191*
after they *h* this saying	Mt 15:12	*191*
And when the disciples *h* it	Mt 17:6	*191*
when the young man *h* that saying	Mt 19:22	*191*
When his disciples *h* it, they	Mt 19:25	*191*
And when the ten *h* it, they were	Mt 20:24	*191*
when they *h* that Jesus passed by,	Mt 20:30	*191*
and Pharisees had *h* his parables	Mt 21:45	*191*
But when the king *h* thereof	Mt 22:7	*191*
When they had *h* these words	Mt 22:22	*191*
And when the multitude *h* this	Mt 22:33	*191*
But when the Pharisees had *h* that	Mt 22:34	*191*
now ye have *h* his blasphemy	Mt 26:65	*191*
stood there, when they *h* that	Mt 27:47	*191*
When Jesus *h* it, he saith unto	Mk 2:17	*191*
when they had *h* what great things	Mk 3:8	*191*
And when his friends *h* of it	Mk 3:21	*191*
but when they have *h*, Satan	Mk 4:15	*191*
who, when they have *h* the word	Mk 4:16	*191*
When she had *h* of Jesus, came in	Mk 5:27	*191*
As soon as Jesus *h* the word that	Mk 5:36	*191*
And king Herod *h* of him	Mk 6:14	*191*
But when Herod *h* thereof, he said	Mk 6:16	*191*
and when he *h* him, he did many	Mk 6:20	*191*
did many things, and *h* him gladly	Mk 6:20	*191*
And when his disciples *h* of it	Mk 6:29	*191*
were sick, where they *h* he was	Mk 6:55	*191*
h of him, and came and fell at his	Mk 7:25	*191*
And when the ten *h* it, they began	Mk 10:41	*191*
when he *h* that it was Jesus of	Mk 10:47	*191*
And his disciples *h* it	Mk 11:14	*191*
the scribes and chief priests *h* it	Mk 11:18	*191*
having *h* them reasoning together,	Mk 12:28	*191*
And the common people *h* him gladly.	Mk 12:37	*191*
And when they *h* it, they were glad	Mk 14:11	*191*
We *h* him say, I will destroy this	Mk 14:58	*191*
Ye have *h* the blasphemy	Mk 14:64	*191*
stood by, when they *h* it said	Mk 15:35	*191*
when they had *h* that he was alive	Mk 16:11	*191*
for thy prayer is *h*	Lk 1:13	*1522*
when Elisabeth *h* the salutation	Lk 1:41	*191*
her cousins *h* how the Lord had	Lk 1:58	*191*
all they that *h* them laid them up	Lk 1:66	*191*
all they that *h* it wondered at	Lk 2:18	*191*
all the things that they had *h*	Lk 2:20	*191*
all that *h* him were astonished at	Lk 2:47	*191*
we have *h* done in Capernaum	Lk 4:23	*191*
when they *h* these things, were	Lk 4:28	*191*
when he *h* of Jesus, he sent unto	Lk 7:3	*191*
When Jesus *h* these things, he	Lk 7:9	*191*
what things ye have seen and *h*	Lk 7:22	*191*
And all the people that *h* him	Lk 7:29	*191*
are they, which, when they have *h*	Lk 8:14	*191*
having *h* the word, keep it, and	Lk 8:15	*191*
But when Jesus *h* it, he answered	Lk 8:50	*191*
Now Herod the tetrarch *h* of all	Lk 9:7	*191*
which ye hear, and have not *h* them	Lk 10:24	*191*
sat at Jesus' feet, and *h* his word	Lk 10:39	*191*
darkness shall be *h* in the light	Lk 12:3	*191*
at meat with him *h* these things	Lk 14:15	*191*
the house, he *h* musick and dancing	Lk 15:25	*191*
were covetous, *h* all these things	Lk 16:14	*191*
Now when Jesus *h* these things	Lk 18:22	*191*
And when he *h* this, he was very	Lk 18:23	*191*

And they that *h* it said, Who then Lk 18:26 *191*
as they *h* these things, he added Lk 19:11 *191*
And when they *h* it, they said, God Lk 20:16 *191*
ourselves have *h* of his own mouth Lk 22:71 *191*
When Pilate *h* of Galilee, he Lk 23:6 *191*
because he had *h* many things of Lk 23:8 *191*
And the two disciples *h* him speak Jn 1:37 *191*
One of the two which *h* John speak Jn 1:40 *191*
And what he hath seen and *h* Jn 3:32 *191*
Pharisees had *h* that Jesus made Jn 4:1 *191*
for we have *h* him ourselves, and Jn 4:42 *191*
When he *h* that Jesus was come out Jn 4:47 *191*
Ye have neither *h* his voice at Jn 5:37 *191*
Every man therefore that hath *h* Jn 6:45 *191*
disciples, when they had *h* this Jn 6:60 *191*
The Pharisees *h* that the people Jn 7:32 *191*
when they *h* this saying, said, Of Jn 7:40 *191*
ground, as though he *h* them not Jn 8:6
And they which *h* it, being Jn 8:9 *191*
things which I have *h* of him Jn 8:26 *191*
the truth, which I have *h* of God Jn 8:40 *191*
the world began was it not *h* that Jn 9:32 *191*
Jesus *h* that they had cast him Jn 9:35 *191*
which were with him *h* these words Jn 9:40 *191*
When Jesus *h* that, he said, This Jn 11:4 *191*
When he had *h* therefore that he Jn 11:6 *191*
as soon as she *h* that Jesus was Jn 11:20 *191*
As soon as she *h* that, she arose Jn 11:29 *191*
I thank thee that thou hast *h* me Jn 11:41 *191*
when they *h* that Jesus was coming Jn 12:12 *191*
for that they *h* that he had done Jn 12:18 *191*
h it, said that it thundered Jn 12:29 *191*
We have *h* out of the law that Jn 12:34 *191*
Ye have *h* how I said unto you, I Jn 14:28 *191*
for all things that I have *h* of Jn 15:15 *191*
ask them which *h* me, what I have Jn 18:21 *191*
Pilate therefore *h* that saying Jn 19:8 *191*
Pilate therefore *h* that saying Jn 19:13 *191*
Peter *h* that it was the Lord Jn 21:7 *191*
which, saith he, ye have *h* of me Acts 1:4 *191*
because that every man *h* them Acts 2:6 *191*
Now when they *h* this, they were Acts 2:37 *191*
of them which *h* the word believed Acts 4:4 *191*
things which we have seen and *h* Acts 4:20 *191*
And when they *h* that, they lifted Acts 4:24 *191*
on all them that *h* these things Acts 5:5 *191*
and upon as many as *h* these things Acts 5:11 *191*
And when they *h* that, they entered Acts 5:21 *191*
the chief priests *h* these things Acts 5:24 *191*
When they *h* that, they were cut Acts 5:33 *191*
We have *h* him speak blasphemous Acts 6:11 *191*
For we have *h* him say, that this Acts 6:14 *191*
But when Jacob *h* that there was Acts 7:12 *191*
I have *h* their groaning, and am Acts 7:34 *191*
When they *h* these things, they Acts 7:54 *191*
which were at Jerusalem *h* that Acts 8:14 *191*
h him read the prophet Esaias, and Acts 8:30 *191*
h a voice saying unto him, Saul Acts 9:4 *191*
I have *h* by many of this man, how Acts 9:13 *191*
But all that *h* him were amazed, Acts 9:21 *191*
the disciples had *h* that Peter Acts 9:38 *191*
said, Cornelius, thy prayer is *h* Acts 10:31 *1522*
fell on all them which *h* the word Acts 10:44 *191*
For they *h* them speak with Acts 10:46 *191*
h that the Gentiles had also Acts 11:1 *191*
I *h* a voice saying unto me, Arise Acts 11:7 *191*
When they *h* these things, they Acts 11:18 *191*
And when the Gentiles *h* this Acts 13:48 *191*
The same *h* Paul speak Acts 14:9 *191*
h of, they rent their clothes, and Acts 14:14 *191*
Forasmuch as we have *h*, that Acts 15:24 *191*
which worshipped God, *h* us Acts 16:14 *191*
and the prisoners *h* them Acts 16:25 *1874*
when they *h* that they were Romans Acts 16:38 *191*
city, when they *h* these things Acts 17:8 *191*
when they *h* of the resurrection Acts 17:32 *191*
when Aquila and Priscilla had *h* Acts 18:26 *191*
We have not so much as *h* whether Acts 19:2 *191*
When they *h* this, they were Acts 19:5 *191*
Asia *h* the word of the Lord Jesus Acts 19:10 *191*
when they *h* these sayings, they Acts 19:28 *191*
when we *h* these things, both we Acts 21:12 *191*
And when they *h* it, they glorified Acts 21:20 *191*
when they *h* that he spake in the Acts 22:2 *191*
h a voice saying unto me, Saul Acts 22:7 *191*
but they *h* not the voice of him Acts 22:9 *191*
men of what thou hast seen and *h* Acts 22:15 *191*
When the centurion *h* that Acts 22:26 *191*
son *h* of their lying in wait Acts 23:16 *191*
when Felix *h* these things, having Acts 24:22 *191*
h him concerning the faith in Acts 24:24 *191*
I *h* a voice speaking unto me, and Acts 26:14 *191*
thence, when the brethren *h* of us Acts 28:15 *191*
in him of whom they have not *h* Rom 10:14 *191*
But I say, Have they not *h* Rom 10:18 *191*
that have not *h* shall understand Rom 15:21 *191*
Eye hath not seen, nor ear *h* 1Cor 2:9 *191*
I have *h* thee in a time accepted, 2Cor 6:2 *1873*
h unspeakable words, which it is 2Cor 12:4 *191*
For ye have *h* of my conversation Gal 1:13 *191*
But they had *h* only, That he Gal 1:23 *191*
after that ye *h* the word of truth Eph 1:13 *191*
after I *h* of your faith in the Eph 1:15 *191*
If ye have *h* of the dispensation Eph 3:2 *191*
If so be that ye have *h* him Eph 4:21 *191*
because that ye had *h* that he had Phil 2:26 *191*
both learned, and received, and *h* Phil 4:9 *191*
Since we *h* of your faith in Col 1:4 *191*
whereof ye *h* before in the word Col 1:5 *4257*
in you, since the day ye *h* of it Col 1:6 *191*
we also, since the day we *h* it Col 1:9 *191*
of the gospel, which ye have *h* Col 1:23 *191*
the word of God which ye *h* of us 1Th 2:13 *189*
words, which thou hast *h* of me 2Ti 1:13 *191*
the things that thou hast *h* of me 2Ti 2:2 *191*
to the things which we have *h* Heb 2:1 *191*
unto us by them that *h* him Heb 2:3 *191*
For some, when they had *h* Heb 3:16 *191*
with faith in them that *h* it Heb 4:2 *191*
death, and was *h* in that he feared Heb 5:7 *1522*
which voice they that *h* intreated Heb 12:19 *191*
Ye have *h* of the patience of Job, Jas 5:11 *191*
voice which came from heaven we *h* 2Pet 1:18 *191*
the beginning, which we have *h* 1Jn 1:1 *191*
h declare we unto you, that ye 1Jn 1:3 *191*
message which we have *h* of him 1Jn 1:5 *191*
ye have *h* from the beginning 1Jn 2:7 *191*
as ye have *h* that antichrist 1Jn 2:18 *191*
in you, which ye have *h* from the 1Jn 2:24 *191*
If that which ye have *h* from the 1Jn 2:24 *191*
that ye *h* from the beginning 1Jn 3:11 *191*
whereof ye have *h* that it should 1Jn 4:3 *191*
as ye have *h* from the beginning, 2Jn 6 *191*
h behind me a great voice, as of Rev 1:10 *191*
how thou hast received and *h* Rev 3:3 *191*
the first voice which I *h* was as Rev 4:1 *191*
I *h* the voice of many angels Rev 5:11 *191*
h I saying, Blessing, and honour, Rev 5:13 *191*
opened one of the seals, and I *h* Rev 6:1 *191*
I *h* the second beast say, Come and Rev 6:3 *191*
I *h* the third beast say, Come and Rev 6:5 *191*
I *h* a voice in the midst of the Rev 6:6 *191*
I *h* the voice of the fourth beast Rev 6:7 *191*
I *h* the number of them which were Rev 7:4 *191*
h an angel flying through the Rev 8:13 *191*
I *h* a voice from the four horns Rev 9:13 *191*
and I *h* the number of them Rev 9:16 *191*
I *h* a voice from heaven saying Rev 10:4 *191*
the voice which I *h* from heaven Rev 10:8 *191*
they *h* a great voice from heaven Rev 11:12 *191*
I *h* a loud voice saying in heaven Rev 12:10 *191*
I *h* a voice from heaven, as the Rev 14:2 *191*
I *h* the voice of harpers harping Rev 14:2 *191*
I *h* a voice from heaven saying Rev 14:13 *191*
I *h* a great voice out of the Rev 16:1 *191*
I *h* the angel of the waters say, Rev 16:5 *191*
I *h* another out of the altar say, Rev 16:7 *191*
I *h* another voice from heaven, Rev 18:4 *191*
shall be *h* no more at all in thee Rev 18:22 *191*
shall be *h* no more at all in thee Rev 18:22 *191*
of the bride shall be *h* no more Rev 18:23 *191*
after these things I *h* a great Rev 19:1 *191*
I *h* as it were the voice of a Rev 19:6 *191*
I *h* a great voice out of heaven Rev 21:3 *191*
John saw these things, and *h* them Rev 22:8 *191*
And when I had *h* and seen, I fell Rev 22:8 *191*

HEARDEST
thou *h* his words out of the midst Deut 4:36 8085
for thou *h* in that day how the Josh 14:12 8085
when thou *h* what I spake against 2Kin 22:19 8085
when thou *h* his words against 2Chr 34:27 8085
h their cry by the Red sea Neh 9:9 8085
thee, thou *h* them from heaven Neh 9:27 8085
thee, thou *h* them from heaven Neh 9:28 8085
nevertheless thou *h* the voice of Ps 31:22 8085
declared my ways, and thou *h* me Ps 119:26 6030
the day when thou *h* them not Is 48:7 8085
Yea, thou *h* not Is 48:8 8085
hell cried I, and thou *h* my voice Jonah 2:2 8085

HEARER
For if any be a *h* of the word Jas 1:23 *202*
he being not a forgetful *h* Jas 1:25 *202*

HEARERS
(For not the *h* of the law are Rom 2:13 *202*
it may minister grace unto the *h* Eph 4:29 *191*
but to the subverting of the *h* 2Ti 2:14 *191*
not *h* only, deceiving your own Jas 1:22 *202*

HEAREST
Ruth, *H* thou not, my daughter Ruth 2:8 8085
Wherefore *h* thou men's words, 1Sa 24:9 8085
when thou *h* the sound of a going 2Sa 5:24 8085
and when thou *h*, forgive 1Kin 8:30 8085
and when thou *h*, forgive 2Chr 6:21 8085
in the daytime, but thou *h* not Ps 22:2 6030
O thou that *h* prayer, unto thee Ps 65:2 8085
unto him, *H* thou what these say Mt 21:16 *191*
H thou not how many things they Mt 27:13 *191*
thou *h* the sound thereof, but Jn 3:8 *191*
And I knew that thou *h* me always Jn 11:42 *191*

HEARETH
for that he *h* your murmurings Ex 16:7 8085
for that the LORD *h* your Ex 16:8 8085
disallow her in the day that he *h* Num 30:5 8085
when he *h* the words of this curse Deut 29:19 8085
for thy servant *h* 1Sa 3:9 8085
for thy servant *h* 1Sa 3:10 8085
every one that *h* it shall tingle 1Sa 3:11 8085
that whosoever *h* it will say 2Sa 17:9 8085
and Judah, that whosoever *h* of it 2Kin 21:12 8085
he *h* the cry of the afflicted Job 34:28 8085
The righteous cry, and the LORD *h* Ps 34:17 8085
Thus I was as a man that *h* not Ps 38:14 8085
For the LORD *h* the poor, and Ps 69:33 8085
Blessed is the man that *h* me Prov 8:34 8085
A wise son *h* his father's Prov 13:1 8085
but a scorner *h* not rebuke Prov 13:1 8085
but the poor *h* not rebuke Prov 13:8 8085
but he *h* the prayer of the Prov 15:29 8085
The ear that *h* the reproof of Prov 15:31 8085
but he that *h* reproof getteth Prov 15:32 8085
answereth a matter before he *h* it Prov 18:13 8085
but the man that *h* speaketh Prov 21:28 8085
Lest he that *h* it put thee to Prov 25:10 8085
he *h* cursing, and bewrayeth it not Prov 29:24 8085
there is none that *h* your words Is 41:26 8085
opening the ears, but he *h* not Is 42:20 8085
this place, the which whosoever *h* Jer 19:3 8085
He that *h*, let him hear Eze 3:27 8085
Then whosoever *h* the sound of the Eze 33:4 8085
Therefore whosoever *h* these Mt 7:24 *191*
every one that *h* these sayings of Mt 7:26 *191*
When any one *h* the word of the Mt 13:19 *191*
the same is he that *h* the word Mt 13:20 *191*
the thorns is he that *h* the word Mt 13:22 *191*
good ground is he that *h* the word Mt 13:23 *191*
h my sayings, and doeth them, I Lk 6:47 *191*
But he that *h*, and doeth not, is Lk 6:49 *191*
He that *h* you *h* me Lk 10:16 *191*
h him, rejoiceth greatly because Jn 3:29 *191*
I say unto you, He that *h* my word Jn 5:24 *191*
He that is of God *h* God's words Jn 8:47 *191*
we know that God *h* not sinners Jn 9:31 *191*
God, and doeth his will, him he *h* Jn 9:31 *191*
that is of the truth *h* my voice Jn 18:37 *191*
me to be, or that he *h* of me 2Cor 12:6 *191*
of the world, and the world *h* them 1Jn 4:5 *191*
he that knoweth God *h* us 1Jn 4:6 *191*
he that is not of God *h* not us 1Jn 4:6 *191*
according to his will, he *h* us 1Jn 5:14 *191*
And let him that *h* say, Come Rev 22:17 *191*
h the words of the prophecy of Rev 22:18 *191*

HEARING
law before all Israel in their *h* Deut 31:11 241
for in our *h* the king charged 2Sa 18:12 241
there was neither voice, nor *h* 2Kin 4:31 7182
Surely thou hast spoken in mine *h* Job 33:8 241
heard of thee by the *h* of the ear Job 42:5 8088
The *h* ear, and the seeing eye, the Prov 20:12 8085
away his ear from *h* the law Prov 28:9 8085
seeing, nor the ear filled with *h* Eccl 1:8 8085
reprove after the *h* of his ears Is 11:3 4926
I was bowed down at the *h* of it Is 21:3 8085
stoppeth his ears from *h* of blood Is 33:15 8085
to the others he said in mine *h* Eze 9:5 241
it was cried unto them in my *h* Eze 10:13 241
but of *h* the words of the LORD Amos 8:11 8085
h they hear not, neither do they Mt 13:13 *191*
By *h* ye shall hear, and shall not Mt 13:14 *189*
and their ears are dull of *h* Mt 13:15 *191*
and *h* they may hear, and not Mk 4:12 *191*
many *h* him were astonished, Mk 6:2 *191*
midst of the doctors, both *h* them Lk 2:46 *191*
h they might not understand Lk 8:10 *191*
h the multitude pass by, he asked Lk 18:36 *191*
Ananias *h* these words fell down, Acts 5:5 *191*
things which Philip spake, *h* Acts 8:6 *191*
h a voice, but seeing no man Acts 9:7 *191*
of the Corinthians *h* believed Acts 18:8 *191*
reserved unto the *h* of Augustus Acts 25:21 *1233*
was entered into the place of *h* Acts 25:23 *201*
H ye shall hear, and shall not Acts 28:26 *189*
and their ears are dull of *h* Acts 28:27 *191*
So then faith cometh by *h* Rom 10:17 *189*
and *h* by the word of God Rom 10:17 *189*
were an eye, where were the *h* 1Cor 12:17 *189*
If the whole were *h*, where were 1Cor 12:17 *189*
of the law, or by the *h* of faith Gal 3:2 *189*
of the law, or by the *h* of faith Gal 3:5 *189*
H of thy love and faith, which Philem 5 *191*
uttered, seeing ye are dull of *h* Heb 5:11 *189*
among them, in seeing and *h* 2Pet 2:8 *189*

HEARKEN
wives of Lamech, *h* unto my speech Gen 4:23 238
said unto thee, *h* unto her voice Gen 21:12 8085
My lord, *h* unto me Gen 23:15 8085
But if ye will not *h* unto us Gen 34:17 8085
h unto Israel your father Gen 49:2 8085
they shall *h* to thy voice Ex 3:18 8085
believe me, nor *h* unto my voice Ex 4:1 8085
neither *h* to the voice of the Ex 4:8 8085
neither *h* unto thy voice, that Ex 4:9 8085
and how shall Pharaoh *h* unto me Ex 6:30 8085
But Pharaoh shall not *h* unto you Ex 7:4 8085
neither did he *h* unto them Ex 7:22 8085
Pharaoh shall not *h* unto you Ex 11:9 8085
If thou wilt diligently *h* to the Ex 15:26 8085
H now unto my voice, I will give Ex 18:19 8085
But if ye will not *h* unto me Lev 26:14 8085
not yet for all this *h* unto me Lev 26:18 8085
unto me, and will not *h* unto me Lev 26:21 8085
will not for all this *h* unto me Lev 26:27 8085
h unto me, thou son of Zippor Num 23:18 238
LORD would not *h* to your voice Deut 1:45 8085
Now therefore *h*, O Israel, unto Deut 4:1 8085
if ye *h* to these judgments, and Deut 7:12 8085
if ye shall *h* diligently unto my Deut 11:13 8085
Thou shalt not *h* unto the words Deut 13:3 8085
consent unto him, nor *h* unto him Deut 13:8 8085
When thou shalt *h* to the voice of Deut 13:18 8085
Only if thou carefully *h* unto the Deut 15:5 8085
will not *h* unto the priest that Deut 17:12 8085
unto him ye shall *h* Deut 18:15 8085
that whosoever will not *h* unto my Deut 18:19 8085
him, will not *h* unto them Deut 21:18 8085
thy God would not *h* unto Balaam Deut 23:5 8085
judgments, and to *h* unto his voice Deut 26:17 8085
Israel, saying, Take heed, and *h* Deut 27:9 8085
if thou shalt *h* diligently unto the Deut 28:1 8085
if thou shalt *h* unto the voice of Deut 28:2 8085
if that thou *h* unto the Deut 28:13 8085
if thou wilt not *h* unto the voice Deut 28:15 8085
If thou shalt *h* unto the voice of Deut 30:10 8085
things, so will we *h* unto thee Josh 1:17 8085
will not *h* unto thy words in all Josh 1:18 8085
But I would not *h* unto Balaam Josh 24:10 8085
would not *h* unto their judges Judg 2:17 8085
to know whether they would *h* unto Judg 3:4 8085
H unto me, ye men of Shechem, Judg 9:7 8085

that God may *h* unto you ... Judg 9:7 8085
king of Edom would not *h* thereto ... Judg 11:17 8085
But the men would not *h* to him ... Judg 19:25 8085
h to the voice of their brethren ... Judg 20:13 8085
H unto the voice of the people in ... 1Sa 8:7 8085
Now therefore *h* unto their voice ... 1Sa 8:9 8085
H unto their voice, and make them ... 1Sa 8:22 8085
now therefore *h* thou unto the ... 1Sa 15:1 8085
to *h* than the fat of rams ... 1Sa 15:22 7181
h thou also unto the voice of ... 1Sa 28:22 8085
For who will *h* unto you in this ... 1Sa 30:24 8085
he would not *h* unto our voice ... 2Sa 12:18 8085
he would not *h* unto her voice ... 2Sa 13:14 8085
But he would not *h* unto her ... 2Sa 13:16 8085
to *h* unto the cry and to the ... 1Kin 8:28 8085
that thou mayest *h* unto the ... 1Kin 8:29 8085
h thou to the supplication of thy ... 1Kin 8:30 8085
to *h* unto them in all that they ... 1Kin 8:52 8085
if thou wilt *h* unto all that I ... 1Kin 11:38 8085
H not unto him, nor consent ... 1Kin 20:8 8085
And he said, *H*, O people, every ... 1Kin 22:28 8085
if ye will *h* unto my voice, take ... 2Kin 10:6 8085
Howbeit they did not *h*, but they ... 2Kin 17:40 8085
H not to Hezekiah ... 2Kin 18:31 8085
h not unto Hezekiah, when he ... 2Kin 18:32 8085
to *h* unto the cry and the prayer ... 2Chr 6:19 8085
to *h* unto the prayer which thy ... 2Chr 6:20 8085
H therefore unto the ... 2Chr 6:21 8085
the king would not *h* unto them ... 2Chr 10:16 8085
And he said, *H*, all ye people ... 2Chr 18:27 8085
he said, *H* ye, all Judah, and ye ... 2Chr 20:15 7181
but they would not *h* ... 2Chr 33:10 7181
Shall we then *h* unto you to do ... Neh 13:27 8085
h to the pleadings of my lips ... Job 13:6 7181
Therefore I said, *H* to me ... Job 32:10 8085
my speeches, and *h* to all my words ... Job 33:1 238
Mark well, O Job, *h* unto me ... Job 33:31 8085
If not, *h* unto me ... Job 33:33 8085
Therefore *h* unto me, ye men of ... Job 34:10 8085
h to the voice of my words ... Job 34:16 238
me, and let a wise man *h* unto me ... Job 34:34 8085
H unto this, O Job ... Job 37:14 238
H unto the voice of my cry, my ... Ps 5:2 7181
Come, ye children, *h* unto me ... Ps 34:11 8085
H, O daughter, and consider, and ... Ps 45:10 8085
Which will not *h* to the voice of ... Ps 58:5 8085
O Israel, if thou wilt *h* unto me ... Ps 81:8 8085
my people would not *h* to my voice ... Ps 81:11 8085
H unto me now therefore, O ye ... Prov 7:24 8085
Now therefore *h* unto me, O ye ... Prov 8:32 8085
H unto thy father that begat thee ... Prov 23:22 8085
If a ruler *h* to lies, all his ... Prov 29:12 7181
the companions *h* to thy voice ... Song 8:13 7181
h, and hear my speech ... Is 28:23 7181
ears of them that hear shall *h* ... Is 32:3 7181
and *h*, ye people ... Is 34:1 7181
H not to Hezekiah ... Is 36:16 8085
who will *h* and hear for the time ... Is 42:23 7181
H unto me, O house of Jacob, and ... Is 46:3 8085
H unto me, ye stouthearted, that ... Is 46:12 8085
H unto me, O Jacob and Israel, my ... Is 48:12 8085
and *h*, ye people, from far ... Is 49:1 7181
H to me, ye that follow after ... Is 51:1 8085
H unto me, my people ... Is 51:4 7181
H unto me, ye that know ... Is 51:7 8085
h diligently unto me, and eat ye ... Is 55:2 8085
uncircumcised, and they cannot *h* ... Jer 6:10 7181
H to the sound of the trumpet ... Jer 6:17 7181
But they said, We will not *h* ... Jer 6:17 7181
but they will not *h* to thee ... Jer 7:27 8085
unto me, I will not *h* unto them ... Jer 11:11 8085
that they may not *h* unto me ... Jer 16:12 8085
pass, if ye diligently *h* unto me ... Jer 17:24 8085
But if ye will not *h* unto me to ... Jer 17:27 8085
h to the voice of them that ... Jer 18:19 8085
H not unto the words of the ... Jer 23:16 8085
If so be they will *h*, and turn ... Jer 26:3 8085
If ye will not *h* to me, to walk ... Jer 26:4 8085
To *h* to the words of my servants ... Jer 26:5 8085
Therefore *h* not ye to your ... Jer 27:9 8085
Therefore *h* not unto the words of ... Jer 27:14 8085
H not to the words of your ... Jer 27:16 8085
H not unto them ... Jer 27:17 8085
neither *h* to your dreams which ye ... Jer 29:8 8085
unto me, and I will *h* unto you ... Jer 29:12 8085
instruction to *h* to my words ... Jer 35:13 8085
did *h* unto the words of the LORD, ... Jer 37:2 8085
counsel, wilt thou not *h* unto me ... Jer 38:15 8085
the LORD, we will not *h* unto thee ... Jer 44:16 8085
of Israel will not *h* unto thee ... Eze 3:7 8085
for they will not *h* unto me ... Eze 3:7 8085
me, and would not *h* unto me ... Eze 20:8 8085
also, if ye will not *h* unto me ... Eze 20:39 8085
O Lord, *h* and do ... Dan 9:19 7181
and *h*, ye house of Israel ... Hos 5:1 7181
because they did not *h* unto him ... Hos 9:17 8085
h, O earth, and all that therein ... Mic 1:2 7181
nor *h* unto me, saith the LORD ... Zec 1:4 7181
But they refused to *h*, and pulled ... Zec 7:11 7181
H; Behold, there went ... Mk 4:3 *191*
H unto me every one of you, and ... Mk 7:14 *191*
known unto you, and *h* to my words ... Acts 2:14 *1801*
to *h* unto you more than unto God ... Acts 4:19 *191*
Men, brethren, and fathers, *h* ... Acts 7:2 *191*
of the gate, a damsel came to *h* ... Acts 12:13 *5219*
Men and brethren, *h* unto me ... Acts 15:13 *191*
H, my beloved brethren, Hath not ... Jas 2:5 *191*

HEARKENED

Because thou hast *h* unto the ... Gen 3:17 8085
Abram *h* to the voice of Sarai ... Gen 16:2 8085
And Abraham *h* unto Ephron ... Gen 23:16 8085
God *h* unto Leah, and she conceived ... Gen 30:17 8085
God *h* to her, and opened her womb ... Gen 30:22 8085
unto Shechem his son *h* all that ... Gen 34:24 8085
that he *h* not unto her, to lie by ... Gen 39:10 8085
but they *h* not unto Moses for ... Ex 6:9 8085
of Israel have not *h* unto me ... Ex 6:12 8085
heart, that he *h* not unto them ... Ex 7:13 8085
his heart, and *h* not unto them ... Ex 8:15 8085
hardened, and he *h* not unto them ... Ex 8:19 8085
of Pharaoh, and he *h* not unto them ... Ex 9:12 8085
they *h* not unto Moses ... Ex 16:20 8085
So Moses *h* to the voice of his ... Ex 18:24 8085
times, and have not *h* to my voice ... Num 14:22 8085
the LORD *h* to the voice of Israel ... Num 21:3 8085
But the LORD *h* unto me at that ... Deut 9:19 8085
him not, nor *h* to his voice ... Deut 9:23 8085
the LORD *h* unto me at that time ... Deut 10:10 8085
h unto observers of times, and ... Deut 18:14 8085
but I have *h* to the voice of the ... Deut 26:14 8085
the children of Israel *h* unto him ... Deut 34:9 8085
According as we *h* unto Moses in ... Josh 1:17 8085
that the LORD *h* unto the voice of ... Josh 10:14 8085
and have not *h* unto my voice ... Judg 2:20 8085
king of the children of Ammon *h* ... Judg 11:28 8085
God *h* to the voice of Manoah ... Judg 13:9 8085
Notwithstanding they *h* not unto ... 1Sa 2:25 8085
I have *h* unto your voice in all ... 1Sa 12:1 8085
Saul *h* unto the voice of Jonathan ... 1Sa 19:6 8085
I have *h* to thy voice, and have ... 1Sa 25:35 8085
have *h* unto thy words which thou ... 1Sa 28:21 8085
and he *h* unto their voice ... 1Sa 28:23 8085
Wherefore the king *h* not unto the ... 1Kin 12:15 8085
saw that the king *h* not unto them ... 1Kin 12:16 8085
They *h* therefore to the word of ... 1Kin 12:24 8085
So Ben-hadad *h* unto king Asa, and ... 1Kin 15:20 8085
he *h* unto their voice, and did so ... 1Kin 20:25 8085
the LORD, and the LORD *h* unto him ... 2Kin 13:4 8085
And the king of Assyria *h* unto him ... 2Kin 16:9 8085
Hezekiah *h* unto them, and shewed ... 2Kin 20:13 8085
But they *h* not ... 2Kin 21:9 8085
not *h* unto the words of this book ... 2Kin 22:13 8085
So the king *h* not unto the people ... 2Chr 10:15 8085
Ben-hadad *h* unto king Asa, and ... 2Chr 16:4 8085
Then the king *h* unto them ... 2Chr 24:17 8085
hast not *h* unto my counsel ... 2Chr 25:16 8085
the LORD *h* to Hezekiah, and healed ... 2Chr 30:20 8085
h not unto the words of Necho ... 2Chr 35:22 8085
h not to thy commandments, ... Neh 9:16 8085
h not unto thy commandments, but ... Neh 9:29 8085
nor *h* unto thy commandments and ... Neh 9:34 7181
he *h* not unto them, that they ... Est 3:4 8085
that he had *h* unto my voice ... Job 9:16 238
Oh that my people had *h* unto me ... Ps 81:13 8085
h not unto the voice of the LORD ... Ps 106:25 8085
he *h* diligently with much heed ... Is 21:7 7181
O that thou hadst *h* to my ... Is 48:18 7181
they have not *h* unto my words ... Jer 6:19 7181
But they *h* not, nor inclined ... Jer 7:24 8085
Yet they *h* not unto me, nor ... Jer 7:26 8085
I *h* and heard, but they spake not ... Jer 8:6 8085
but ye have not *h* ... Jer 25:3 8085
but ye have not *h*, nor inclined ... Jer 25:4 8085
Yet ye have not *h* unto me ... Jer 25:7 8085
sending them, but ye have not *h* ... Jer 26:5 8085
they have not *h* to my words ... Jer 29:19 8085
yet they have not *h* to receive ... Jer 32:33 8085
but your fathers *h* not unto me ... Jer 34:14 8085
Ye have not *h* unto me, in ... Jer 34:17 8085
but ye *h* not unto me ... Jer 35:14 8085
inclined your ear, nor *h* unto me ... Jer 35:15 8085
this people hath not *h* unto me ... Jer 35:16 8085
but they *h* not ... Jer 36:31 8085
But he *h* not to him ... Jer 37:14 8085
But they *h* not, nor inclined ... Jer 44:5 8085
them, they would have *h* unto thee ... Eze 3:6 8085
Neither have we *h* unto thy ... Dan 9:6 8085
and the LORD *h*, and heard it, and a ... Mal 3:16 7181
Sirs, ye should have *h* unto me ... Acts 27:21 *3980*

HEARKENEDST

because thou *h* not unto the voice ... Deut 28:45 8085

HEARKENETH

But whoso *h* unto me shall dwell ... Prov 1:33 8085
but he that *h* unto counsel is ... Prov 12:15 8085

HEARKENING

h unto the voice of his word ... Ps 103:20 8085

HEART

of the thoughts of his *h* was only ... Gen 6:5 3820
earth, and it grieved him at his *h* ... Gen 6:6 3820
and the LORD said in his *h* ... Gen 8:21 3820
of man's *h* is evil from his youth ... Gen 8:21 3820
and laughed, and said in his *h* ... Gen 17:17 3820
in the integrity of my *h* and ... Gen 20:5 3824
this in the integrity of thy *h* ... Gen 20:6 3824
I had done speaking in mine *h* ... Gen 24:45 3820
and Esau said in his *h*, The days ... Gen 27:41 3820
their *h* failed them, and they were ... Gen 42:28 3820
And Jacob's *h* fainted, for he ... Gen 45:26 3820
thee, he will be glad in his *h* ... Ex 4:14 3820
but I will harden his *h*, that he ... Ex 4:21 3820
And I will harden Pharaoh's *h* ... Ex 7:3 3820
And he hardened Pharaoh's *h* ... Ex 7:13 3820
Pharaoh's *h* is hardened, he ... Ex 7:14 3820
Pharaoh's *h* was hardened, neither ... Ex 7:22 3820
did he set his *h* to this also ... Ex 7:23 3820
was respite, he hardened his *h* ... Ex 8:15 3820
Pharaoh's *h* was hardened, and he ... Ex 8:19 3820
hardened his *h* at this time also ... Ex 8:32 3820
the *h* of Pharaoh was hardened, and ... Ex 9:7 3820
LORD hardened the *h* of Pharaoh ... Ex 9:12 3820
send all my plagues upon thine *h* ... Ex 9:14 3820
yet more, and hardened his *h* ... Ex 9:34 3820
the *h* of Pharaoh was hardened, ... Ex 9:35 3820
for I have hardened his *h* ... Ex 10:1 3820
the *h* of his servants, that I ... Ex 10:1 3820
But the LORD hardened Pharaoh's *h* ... Ex 10:20 3820
But the LORD hardened Pharaoh's *h* ... Ex 10:27 3820
and the LORD hardened Pharaoh's *h* ... Ex 11:10 3820
And I will harden Pharaoh's *h* ... Ex 14:4 3820
the *h* of Pharaoh and of his ... Ex 14:5 3824
the LORD hardened the *h* of ... Ex 14:8 3820
congealed in the *h* of the sea ... Ex 15:8 3820
for ye know the *h* of a stranger ... Ex 23:9 5315
his *h* ye shall take my offering ... Ex 25:2 3820
of judgment upon his *h*, when he ... Ex 28:29 3820
and they shall be upon Aaron's *h* ... Ex 28:30 3820
his *h* before the LORD continually ... Ex 28:30 3820
whosoever is of a willing *h* ... Ex 35:5 3820
every one whose *h* stirred him up ... Ex 35:21 3820
all the women whose *h* stirred ... Ex 35:26 3820
whose *h* made them willing to ... Ex 35:29 3820
put in his *h* that he may teach ... Ex 35:34 3820
hath he filled with wisdom of *h* ... Ex 35:35 3820
in whose *h* the LORD had put ... Ex 36:2 3820
even every one whose *h* stirred ... Ex 36:2 3820
not hate thy brother in thine *h* ... Lev 19:17 3824
the eyes, and cause sorrow of *h* ... Lev 26:16 5315
that ye seek not after your own *h* ... Num 15:39 3824
wherefore discourage ye the *h* of ... Num 32:7 3820
they discouraged the *h* of the ... Num 32:9 3820
brethren have discouraged our *h* ... Deut 1:28 3824
made his *h* obstinate, that he ... Deut 2:30 3824
thy *h* all the days of thy life ... Deut 4:9 3824
if thou seek him with all thy *h* ... Deut 4:29 3824
day, and consider it in thine *h* ... Deut 4:39 3824
that there were such an *h* in them ... Deut 5:29 3824
the LORD thy God with all thine *h* ... Deut 6:5 3824
this day, shall be in thine *h* ... Deut 6:6 3824
If thou shalt say in thine *h* ... Deut 7:17 3824
thee, to know what was in thine *h* ... Deut 8:2 3824
shalt also consider in thine *h* ... Deut 8:5 3824
Then thine *h* be lifted up, and ... Deut 8:14 3824
And thou say in thine *h*, My power ... Deut 8:17 3824
Speak not thou in thine *h* ... Deut 9:4 3824
or for the uprightness of thine *h* ... Deut 9:5 3824
the LORD thy God with all thy *h* ... Deut 10:12 3824
therefore the foreskin of your *h* ... Deut 10:16 3824
and to serve him with all your *h* ... Deut 11:13 3824
that your *h* be not deceived, and ... Deut 11:16 3824
lay up these my words in your *h* ... Deut 11:18 3824
the LORD your God with all your *h* ... Deut 13:3 3824
thou shalt not harden thine *h* ... Deut 15:7 3824
be not a thought in thy wicked *h* ... Deut 15:9 3824
thine *h* shall not be grieved when ... Deut 15:10 3824
himself, that his *h* turn not away ... Deut 17:17 3824
That his *h* be not lifted up above ... Deut 17:20 3824
And if thou say in thine *h* ... Deut 18:21 3824
the slayer, while his *h* is hot ... Deut 19:6 3824
h faint as well as his *h* ... Deut 20:8 3824
is poor, and setteth his *h* upon it ... Deut 24:15 5315
keep and do them with all thine *h* ... Deut 26:16 3824
blindness, and astonishment of *h* ... Deut 28:28 3824
joyfulness, and with gladness of *h* ... Deut 28:47 3824
give thee there a trembling *h* ... Deut 28:65 3820
for the fear of thine *h* wherewith ... Deut 28:67 3824
not given you an *h* to perceive ... Deut 29:4 3820
whose *h* turneth away this day ... Deut 29:18 3824
that he bless himself in his *h* ... Deut 29:19 3824
walk in the imagination of mine *h* ... Deut 29:19 3820
and thy children, with all thine *h* ... Deut 30:2 3824
thy God will circumcise thine *h* ... Deut 30:6 3824
the *h* of thy seed, to love the ... Deut 30:6 3824
the LORD thy God with all thine *h* ... Deut 30:6 3824
the LORD thy God with all thine *h* ... Deut 30:10 3824
thee, in thy mouth, and in thy *h* ... Deut 30:14 3824
But if thine *h* turn away, so that ... Deut 30:17 3824
passed over, that their *h* melted ... Josh 5:1 3824
word again as it was in mine *h* ... Josh 14:7 3824
me made the *h* of the people melt ... Josh 14:8 3820
and to serve him with all your *h* ... Josh 22:5 3824
incline your *h* unto the LORD God ... Josh 24:23 3824
My *h* is toward the governors of ... Judg 5:9 3820
there were great thoughts of *h* ... Judg 5:15 3820
there were great searchings of *h* ... Judg 5:16 3820
when thine *h* is not with me ... Judg 16:15 3820
That he told her all his *h* ... Judg 16:17 3820
that he had told her all his *h* ... Judg 16:18 3820
for he hath shewed me all his *h* ... Judg 16:18 3820
And the priest's *h* was glad ... Judg 18:20 3820
Comfort thine *h* with a morsel of ... Judg 19:5 3820
night, and let thine *h* be merry ... Judg 19:6 3820
father said, Comfort thine *h* ... Judg 19:8 3824
that thine *h* may be merry ... Judg 19:9 3824
his *h* was merry, he went to lie ... Ruth 3:7 3820
and why is thy *h* grieved ... 1Sa 1:8 3824
Now Hannah, she spake in her *h* ... 1Sa 1:13 3820
My *h* rejoiceth in the LORD, mine ... 1Sa 2:1 3820
thine eyes, and to grieve thine *h* ... 1Sa 2:33 5315
to that which is in mine *h* ... 1Sa 2:35 3824
for his *h* trembled for the ark of ... 1Sa 4:13 3820
tell thee all that is in thine *h* ... 1Sa 9:19 3824
Samuel, God gave him another *h* ... 1Sa 10:9 3820
serve the LORD with all your *h* ... 1Sa 12:20 3824
him in truth with all your *h* ... 1Sa 12:24 3824
sought him a man after his own *h* ... 1Sa 13:14 3824
him, Do all that is in thine *h* ... 1Sa 14:7 3824
I am with thee according to thy *h* ... 1Sa 14:7 3824
but the LORD looketh on the *h* ... 1Sa 16:7 3824
and the naughtiness of thine *h* ... 1Sa 17:28 3824
Let no man's *h* fail because of ... 1Sa 17:32 3820
laid up these words in his *h* ... 1Sa 21:12 3824
that David's *h* smote him ... 1Sa 24:5 3820
nor offence of *h* unto my lord ... 1Sa 25:31 3820
Nabal's *h* was merry within him ... 1Sa 25:36 3820
that his *h* died within him, and he ... 1Sa 25:37 3820
And David said in his *h*, I shall ... 1Sa 27:1 3820
afraid, and his *h* greatly trembled ... 1Sa 28:5 3820
over all that thine *h* desireth ... 2Sa 3:21 5315
and she despised him in her *h* ... 2Sa 6:16 3820

Go, do all that is in thine *h* 2Sa 7:3 3824
sake, and according to thine own *h* 2Sa 7:21 3820
h to pray this prayer unto thee 2Sa 7:27 3820
when Amnon's *h* is merry with wine 2Sa 13:28 3820
the king take the thing to his *h* 2Sa 13:33 3820
the king's *h* was toward Absalom 2Sa 14:1 3820
whose *h* is as the *h* of a lion 2Sa 17:10 3820
them through the *h* of Absalom 2Sa 18:14 3820
he bowed the *h* of all the men of 2Sa 19:14 3824
Judah, even as the *h* of one man 2Sa 19:14
the king should take it to his *h* 2Sa 19:19 3820
David's *h* smote him after that he 2Sa 24:10 3820
me in truth with all their *h* 1Kin 2:4 3824
which thine *h* is privy to 1Kin 2:44 3824
and in uprightness of *h* with thee 1Kin 3:6 3824
h to judge thy people, that I may 1Kin 3:9 3820
thee a wise and an understanding *h* 1Kin 3:12 3820
exceeding much, and largeness of *h* 1Kin 4:29 3820
it was in the *h* of David my 1Kin 8:17 3824
Whereas it was in thine *h* to 1Kin 8:18 3824
didst well that it was in thine *h* 1Kin 8:18 3824
walk before thee with all their *h* 1Kin 8:23 3820
every man the plague of his own *h* 1Kin 8:38 3824
to his ways, whose *h* thou knowest 1Kin 8:39 3824
return unto thee with all their *h* 1Kin 8:48 3824
Let your *h* therefore be perfect 1Kin 8:61 3824
glad of *h* for all the goodness 1Kin 8:66 3820
mine *h* shall be there perpetually 1Kin 9:3 3820
father walked, in integrity of *h* 1Kin 9:4 3824
with him of all that was in her *h* 1Kin 10:2 3824
which God had put in his *h* 1Kin 10:24 3820
turn away your *h* after their gods 1Kin 11:2 3824
and his wives turned away his *h* 1Kin 11:3 3820
away his *h* after other gods 1Kin 11:4 3824
his *h* was not perfect with the 1Kin 11:4 3824
as was the *h* of David his father 1Kin 11:4 3824
because his *h* was turned from the 1Kin 11:9 3824
And Jeroboam said in his *h* 1Kin 12:26 3820
then shall the *h* of this people 1Kin 12:27 3820
which he had devised of his own *h* 1Kin 12:33 3820
and who followed me with all his *h* 1Kin 14:8 3824
his *h* was not perfect with the 1Kin 15:3 3824
as the *h* of David his father 1Kin 15:3 3824
nevertheless Asa's *h* was perfect 1Kin 15:14 3824
hast turned their *h* back again 1Kin 18:37 3820
bread, and let thine *h* be merry 1Kin 21:7 3820
him, Went not mine *h* with thee 2Kin 5:26 3820
Therefore the *h* of the king of 2Kin 6:11 3820
and the arrow went out at his *h* 2Kin 9:24 3820
and said to him, Is thine *h* right 2Kin 10:15 3824
as my *h* is with thy *h* 2Kin 10:15 3824
to all that was in mine *h* 2Kin 10:30 3824
LORD God of Israel with all his *h* 2Kin 10:31 3824
that cometh into any man's *h* to 2Kin 12:4 3820
thine *h* hath lifted thee up 2Kin 14:10 3820
thee in truth and with a perfect *h* 2Kin 20:3 3820
Because thine *h* was tender 2Kin 22:19 3824
and his statutes with all their *h* 2Kin 23:3 3820
turned to the LORD with all his *h* 2Kin 23:25 3824
mine *h* shall be knit unto you 1Chr 12:17 3824
they were not of double *h* 1Chr 12:33 3820
came with a perfect *h* to Hebron 1Chr 12:38 3824
were of one *h* to make David king 1Chr 12:38 3820
and she despised him in her *h* 1Chr 15:29 3820
let the *h* of them rejoice that 1Chr 16:10 3820
David, Do all that is in thine *h* 1Chr 17:2 3824
sake, and according to thine own *h* 1Chr 17:19 3820
in his *h* to pray before thee 1Chr 17:25
Now set your *h* and your soul to 1Chr 22:19 3824
I had in mine *h* to build an house 1Chr 28:2 3824
and serve him with a perfect *h* 1Chr 28:9 3820
because with perfect *h* they 1Chr 29:9 3820
my God, that thou triest the *h* 1Chr 29:17 3824
in the uprightness of mine *h* I 1Chr 29:17 3824
thoughts of the *h* of thy people 1Chr 29:18 3824
and prepare their *h* unto thee 1Chr 29:18 3824
unto Solomon my son a perfect *h* 1Chr 29:19 3824
Because this was in thine *h* 2Chr 1:11 3824
Now it was in the *h* of David my 2Chr 6:7 3824
Forasmuch as it was in thine *h* to 2Chr 6:8 3824
well in that it was in thine *h* 2Chr 6:8 3824
his ways, whose *h* thou knowest 2Chr 6:30 3824
return to thee with all their *h* 2Chr 6:38 3820
merry in *h* for the goodness that 2Chr 7:10 3820
h to make in the house of the 2Chr 7:11 3820
mine *h* shall be there perpetually 2Chr 7:16 3820
with him of all that was in her *h* 2Chr 9:1 3824
wisdom, that God had put in his *h* 2Chr 9:23 3820
not his *h* to seek the LORD 2Chr 12:14 3820
of their fathers with all their *h* 2Chr 15:12 3824
they had sworn with all their *h* 2Chr 15:15 3824
nevertheless the *h* of Asa was 2Chr 15:17 3824
whose *h* is perfect toward him 2Chr 16:9 3824
his *h* was lifted up in the ways 2Chr 17:6 3820
hast prepared thine *h* to seek God 2Chr 19:3 3824
faithfully, and with a perfect *h* 2Chr 19:9 3824
sought the LORD with all his *h* 2Chr 22:9 3824
LORD, but not with a perfect *h* 2Chr 25:2 3824
thine *h* lifteth thee up to boast 2Chr 25:19 3820
his *h* was lifted up to his 2Chr 26:16 3820
Now it is in mine *h* to make a 2Chr 29:10 3824
were of a free *h* burnt offerings 2Chr 29:31 3820
Levites were more upright in *h* to 2Chr 29:34 3824
of God was to give them one *h* to 2Chr 30:12 3820
That prepareth his *h* to seek God 2Chr 30:19 3824
his God, he did it with all his *h* 2Chr 31:21 3824
for his *h* was lifted up 2Chr 32:25 3820
himself for the pride of his *h* 2Chr 32:26 3820
might know all that was in his *h* 2Chr 32:31 3824
Because thine *h* was tender 2Chr 34:27 3824
and his statutes, with all his *h* 2Chr 34:31 3824
hardened his *h* from turning unto 2Chr 36:13 3824
turned the *h* of the king of Ezr 6:22 3820
For Ezra had prepared his *h* to Ezr 7:10 3824

a thing as this in the king's *h* Ezr 7:27 3820
is nothing else but sorrow of *h* Neh 2:2 3820
put in my *h* to do at Jerusalem Neh 2:12 3820
feignest them out of thine own *h* Neh 6:8 3820
my God put into mine *h* to gather Neh 7:5 3820
foundest his *h* faithful before Neh 9:8 3824
when the *h* of the king was merry Est 1:10 3820
that day joyful and with a glad *h* Est 5:9 3820
Now Haman thought in his *h* Est 6:6 3820
durst presume in his *h* to do so Est 7:5 3820
shouldest set thine *h* upon him Job 7:17 3820
and utter words out of their *h* Job 8:10 3820
He is wise in *h*, and mighty in Job 9:4 3824
things hast thou hid in thine *h* Job 10:13 3824
If thou prepare thine *h*, and Job 11:13 3820
He taketh away the *h* of the chief Job 12:24 3820
Why doth thine *h* carry thee away Job 15:12 3820
hid their *h* from understanding Job 17:4 3820
off, even the thoughts of my *h* Job 17:11 3824
and lay up his words in thine *h* Job 22:22 3824
For God maketh my *h* soft, and the Job 23:16 3820
my *h* shall not reproach me so Job 27:6 3824
the widow's *h* to sing for joy Job 29:13 3820
mine *h* walked after mine eyes, and Job 31:7 3820
If mine *h* have been deceived by a Job 31:9 3820
my *h* hath been secretly enticed, Job 31:27 3820
be of the uprightness of my *h* Job 33:3 3820
If he set his *h* upon man, if he Job 34:14 3820
the hypocrites in *h* heap up wrath Job 36:13 3820
At this also my *h* trembleth Job 37:1 3820
not any that are wise of *h* Job 37:24 3820
hath given understanding to the *h* Job 38:36 7907
His *h* is as firm as a stone Job 41:24 3820
with your own *h* upon your bed Ps 4:4 3824
Thou hast put gladness in my *h* Ps 4:7 3820
which saveth the upright in *h* Ps 7:10 3820
thee, O LORD, with my whole *h* Ps 9:1 3820
He hath said in his *h*, I shall Ps 10:6 3820
He hath said in his *h*, God hath Ps 10:11 3820
he hath said in his *h*, Thou wilt Ps 10:13 3820
thou wilt prepare their *h* Ps 10:17 3820
privily shoot at the upright in *h* Ps 11:2 3820
and with a double *h* do they speak Ps 12:2 3820
soul, having sorrow in my *h* daily Ps 13:2 3824
my *h* shall rejoice in thy Ps 13:5 3820
The fool hath said in his *h* Ps 14:1 3820
and speaketh the truth in his *h* Ps 15:2 3824
Therefore my *h* is glad, and my Ps 16:9 3820
Thou hast proved mine *h* Ps 17:3 3820
LORD are right, rejoicing the *h* Ps 19:8 3820
mouth, and the meditation of my *h* Ps 19:14 3820
thee according to thine own *h* Ps 20:4 3824
my *h* is like wax Ps 22:14 3820
your *h* shall live for ever Ps 22:26 3824
hath clean hands, and a pure *h* Ps 24:4 3824
The troubles of my *h* are enlarged Ps 25:17 3824
try my reins and my *h* Ps 26:2 3820
against me, my *h* shall not fear Ps 27:3 3820
my *h* said unto thee, Thy face, Ps 27:8 3820
and he shall strengthen thine *h* Ps 27:14 3820
my *h* trusted in him, and I am Ps 28:7 3820
therefore my *h* greatly rejoiceth Ps 28:7 3820
and he shall strengthen your *h* Ps 31:24 3824
joy, all ye that are upright in *h* Ps 32:11 3820
of his *h* to all generations Ps 33:11 3820
For our *h* shall rejoice in him, Ps 33:21 3820
unto them that are of a broken *h* Ps 34:18 3820
of the wicked saith within my *h* Ps 36:1 3820
righteousness to the upright in *h* Ps 36:10 3820
give thee the desires of thine *h* Ps 37:4 3820
shall enter into their own *h* Ps 37:15 3820
The law of his God is in his *h* Ps 37:31 3820
of the disquietness of my *h* Ps 38:8 3820
My *h* panteth, my strength faileth Ps 38:10 3820
My *h* was hot within me Ps 39:3 3820
yea, thy law is within my *h* Ps 40:8 4578
hid thy righteousness within my *h* Ps 40:10 3820
therefore my *h* faileth me Ps 40:12 3820
his *h* gathereth iniquity to Ps 41:6 3820
Our *h* is not turned back, neither Ps 44:18 3820
he knoweth the secrets of the *h* Ps 44:21 3820
My *h* is inditing a good matter Ps 45:1 3820
in the *h* of the king's enemies Ps 45:5 3820
the meditation of my *h* shall be Ps 49:3 3820
Create in me a clean *h*, O God Ps 51:10 3820
a broken and a contrite *h*, O God, Ps 51:17 3820
The fool hath said in his *h* Ps 53:1 3820
My *h* is sore pained within me Ps 55:4 3820
than butter, but war was in his *h* Ps 55:21 3820
My *h* is fixed, O God, my *h* is Ps 57:7 3820
Yea, in *h* ye work wickedness Ps 58:2 3820
thee, when my *h* is overwhelmed Ps 61:2 3820
pour out your *h* before him Ps 62:8 3824
set not your *h* upon them Ps 62:10 3820
of every one of them, and the *h* Ps 64:6 3820
all the upright in *h* shall glory Ps 64:10 3820
If I regard iniquity in my *h* Ps 66:18 3820
Reproach hath broken my *h* Ps 69:20 3820
your *h* shall live that seek God Ps 69:32 3824
even to such as are of a clean *h* Ps 73:1 3824
they have more than *h* could wish Ps 73:7 3824
I have cleansed my *h* in vain Ps 73:13 3824
Thus my *h* was grieved, and I was Ps 73:21 3824
My flesh and my *h* faileth Ps 73:26 3824
but God is the strength of my *h* Ps 73:26 3824
I commune with mine own *h* Ps 77:6 3824
that set not their *h* aright Ps 78:8 3820
they tempted God in their *h* by Ps 78:18 3824
For their *h* was not right with Ps 78:37 3820
to the integrity of his *h* Ps 78:72 3824
my *h* and my flesh crieth out for Ps 84:2 3820
in whose *h* are the ways of them Ps 84:5 3824
unite my *h* to fear thy name Ps 86:11 3824
O Lord my God, with all my *h* Ps 86:12 3824

the upright in *h* shall follow it Ps 94:15 3820
Harden not your *h*, as in the Ps 95:8 3824
a people that do err in their *h* Ps 95:10 3824
and gladness for the upright in *h* Ps 97:11 3820
within my house with a perfect *h* Ps 101:2 3824
A froward *h* shall depart from me Ps 101:4 3820
a proud *h* will not I suffer Ps 101:5 3824
My *h* is smitten, and withered like Ps 102:4 3820
that maketh glad the *h* of man Ps 104:15 3824
bread which strengtheneth man's *h* Ps 104:15 3824
let the *h* of them rejoice that Ps 105:3 3820
He turned their *h* to hate his Ps 105:25 3820
brought down their *h* with labour Ps 107:12 3820
O God, my *h* is fixed Ps 108:1 3820
might even slay the broken in *h* Ps 109:16 3824
my *h* is wounded within me Ps 109:22 3820
praise the LORD with my whole *h* Ps 111:1 3824
his *h* is fixed, trusting in the Ps 112:7 3820
His *h* is established, he shall Ps 112:8 3820
and that seek him with the whole *h* Ps 119:2 3820
praise thee with uprightness of *h* Ps 119:7 3824
With my whole *h* have I sought Ps 119:10 3820
Thy word have I hid in mine *h* Ps 119:11 3820
when thou shalt enlarge my *h* Ps 119:32 3820
shall observe it with my whole *h* Ps 119:34 3820
Incline my *h* unto thy testimonies Ps 119:36 3820
thy favour with my whole *h* Ps 119:58 3820
keep thy precepts with my whole *h* Ps 119:69 3820
Their *h* is as fat as grease Ps 119:70 3820
Let my *h* be sound in thy statutes Ps 119:80 3820
they are the rejoicing of my *h* Ps 119:111 3820
I have inclined mine *h* to perform Ps 119:112 3820
I cried with my whole *h* Ps 119:145 3820
but my *h* standeth in awe of thy Ps 119:161 3820
my *h* is not haughty, nor mine Ps 131:1 3820
will praise thee with my whole *h* Ps 138:1 3820
Search me, O God, and know my *h* Ps 139:23 3824
imagine mischiefs in their *h* Ps 140:2 3820
Incline not my *h* to any evil Ps 141:4 3820
my *h* within me is desolate Ps 143:4 3820
He healeth the broken in *h* Ps 147:3 3820
apply thine *h* to understanding Prov 2:2 3820
When wisdom entereth into thine *h* Prov 2:10 3820
but let thine *h* keep my Prov 3:1 3820
them upon the table of thine *h* Prov 3:3 3820
in the LORD with all thine *h* Prov 3:5 3820
Let thine *h* retain my words Prov 4:4 3820
keep them in the midst of thine *h* Prov 4:21 3824
Keep thy *h* with all diligence Prov 4:23 3820
and my *h* despised reproof Prov 5:12 3820
Frowardness is in his *h*, he Prov 6:14 3820
An *h* that deviseth wicked Prov 6:18 3820
them continually upon thine *h* Prov 6:21 3820
not after her beauty in thine *h* Prov 6:25 3824
them upon the table of thine *h* Prov 7:3 3820
of an harlot, and subtil of *h* Prov 7:10 3820
Let not thine *h* decline to her Prov 7:25 3820
be ye of an understanding *h* Prov 8:5 3820
The wise in *h* will receive Prov 10:8 3820
the *h* of the wicked is little Prov 10:20 3820
They that are of a froward *h* are Prov 11:20 3820
shall be servant to the wise of *h* Prov 11:29 3820
of a perverse *h* shall be despised Prov 12:8 3820
Deceit is in the *h* of them that Prov 12:20 3820
but the *h* of fools proclaimeth Prov 12:23 3820
Heaviness in the *h* of man maketh Prov 12:25 3820
Hope deferred maketh the *h* sick Prov 13:12 3820
The *h* knoweth his own bitterness Prov 14:10 3820
in laughter the *h* is sorrowful Prov 14:13 3820
The backslider in *h* shall be Prov 14:14 3820
A sound *h* is the life of the Prov 14:30 3820
Wisdom resteth in the *h* of him Prov 14:33 3820
but the *h* of the foolish doeth Prov 15:7 3820
A merry *h* maketh a cheerful Prov 15:13 3820
of the *h* the spirit is broken Prov 15:13 3820
The *h* of him that hath Prov 15:14 3820
a merry *h* hath a continual feast Prov 15:15 3820
The *h* of the righteous studieth Prov 15:28 3820
light of the eyes rejoiceth the *h* Prov 15:30 3820
The preparations of the *h* in man Prov 16:1 3820
Every one that is proud in *h* is Prov 16:5 3820
A man's *h* deviseth his way Prov 16:9 3820
The wise in *h* shall be called Prov 16:21 3820
The *h* of the wise teacheth his Prov 16:23 3820
wisdom, seeing he hath no *h* to it Prov 17:16 3820
hath a froward *h* findeth no good Prov 17:20 3820
A merry *h* doeth good like a Prov 17:22 3820
but that his *h* may discover Prov 18:2 3820
the *h* of man is haughty Prov 18:12 3820
The *h* of the prudent getteth Prov 18:15 3820
his *h* fretteth against the LORD Prov 19:3 3820
are many devices in a man's *h* Prov 19:21 3820
Counsel in the *h* of man is like Prov 20:5 3820
can say, I have made my *h* clean Prov 20:9 3820
The king's *h* is in the hand of Prov 21:1 3820
An high look, and a proud *h* Prov 21:4 3820
He that loveth pureness of *h* Prov 22:11 3820
is bound in the *h* of a child Prov 22:15 3820
apply thine *h* unto my knowledge Prov 22:17 3820
For as he thinketh in his *h* Prov 23:7 5315
but his *h* is not with thee Prov 23:7 3820
Apply thine *h* unto instruction, Prov 23:12 3820
My son, if thine *h* be wise Prov 23:15 3820
my *h* shall rejoice, even mine Prov 23:15 3820
Let not thine *h* envy sinners Prov 23:17 3820
wise, and guide thine *h* in the way Prov 23:19 3820
My son, give me thine *h*, and let Prov 23:26 3820
thine *h* shall utter perverse Prov 23:33 3820
For their *h* studieth destruction, Prov 24:2 3820
that pondereth the *h* consider it Prov 24:12 3826
let not thine *h* be glad when he Prov 24:17 3820
the *h* of kings is unsearchable Prov 25:3 3820
that singeth songs to an heavy *h* Prov 25:20 3820
a wicked *h* are like a potsherd Prov 26:23 3820

are seven abominations in his *h*	Prov 26:25	3820
Ointment and perfume rejoice the *h*	Prov 27:9	3820
son, be wise, and make my *h* glad	Prov 27:11	3820
to face, so the *h* of man to man	Prov 27:19	3820
his *h* shall fall into mischief	Prov 28:14	3820
of a proud *h* stirreth up strife	Prov 28:25	5315
trusteth in his own *h* is a fool	Prov 28:26	3820
The *h* of her husband doth safely	Prov 31:11	3820
And I gave my *h* to seek and search	Eccl 1:13	3820
I communed with mine own *h*	Eccl 1:16	3820
my *h* had great experience of	Eccl 1:16	3820
I gave my *h* to know wisdom, and to	Eccl 1:17	3820
I said in mine *h*, Go to now, I	Eccl 2:1	3820
I sought in mine *h* to give myself	Eccl 2:3	3820
acquainting mine *h* with wisdom	Eccl 2:3	3820
I withheld not my *h* from any joy	Eccl 2:10	3820
for my *h* rejoiced in all my	Eccl 2:10	3820
Then said I in my *h*, As it	Eccl 2:15	3820
Then I said in my *h*, that this	Eccl 2:15	3820
I went about to cause my *h* to	Eccl 2:20	3820
and of the vexation of his *h*	Eccl 2:22	3820
his *h* taketh not rest in the	Eccl 2:23	3820
he hath set the world in their *h*	Eccl 3:11	3820
I said in mine *h*, God shall judge	Eccl 3:17	3820
I said in mine *h* concerning the	Eccl 3:18	3820
let not thine *h* be hasty to utter	Eccl 5:2	3820
answereth him in the joy of his *h*	Eccl 5:20	3820
the living will lay it to his *h*	Eccl 7:2	3820
countenance the *h* is made better	Eccl 7:3	3820
The *h* of the wise is in the house	Eccl 7:4	3820
but the *h* of fools is in the	Eccl 7:4	3820
and a gift destroyeth the *h*	Eccl 7:7	3820
own *h* knoweth that thou thyself	Eccl 7:22	3820
I applied mine *h* to know, and to	Eccl 7:25	3820
whose *h* is snares and nets, and her	Eccl 7:26	3820
a wise man's *h* discerneth both	Eccl 8:5	3820
applied my *h* unto every work that	Eccl 8:9	3820
therefore the *h* of the sons of	Eccl 8:11	3820
I applied mine *h* to know wisdom	Eccl 8:16	3820
in my *h* even to declare all this	Eccl 9:1	3820
also the *h* of the sons of men is	Eccl 9:3	3820
is in their *h* while they live	Eccl 9:3	3824
and drink thy wine with a merry *h*	Eccl 9:7	3820
A wise man's *h* is at his right	Eccl 10:2	3820
but a fool's *h* at his left	Eccl 10:2	3820
let thy *h* cheer thee in the days	Eccl 11:9	3820
and walk in the ways of thine *h*	Eccl 11:9	3820
remove sorrow from thy *h*, and put	Eccl 11:10	3820
the day of the gladness of his *h*	Song 3:11	3820
Thou hast ravished my *h*, my	Song 4:9	3823
thou hast ravished my *h* with one	Song 4:9	3823
I sleep, but my *h* waketh	Song 5:2	3820
Set me as a seal upon thine *h*	Song 8:6	3820
is sick, and the whole *h* faint	Is 1:5	3824
Make the *h* of this people fat, and	Is 6:10	3820
ears, and understand with their *h*	Is 6:10	3824
his *h* was moved, and the *h* of	Is 7:2	3824
in the pride and stoutness of *h*	Is 9:9	3824
so, neither doth his *h* think so	Is 10:7	3824
but it is in his *h* to destroy	Is 10:7	3824
stout *h* of the king of Assyria	Is 10:12	3824
and every man's *h* shall melt	Is 13:7	3824
For thou hast said in thine *h*	Is 14:13	3824
My *h* shall cry out for Moab	Is 15:5	3820
the *h* of Egypt shall melt in the	Is 19:1	3824
My *h* panted, fearfulness	Is 21:4	3824
have removed their *h* far from me	Is 29:13	3820
and gladness of *h*, as when one	Is 30:29	3824
The *h* also of the rash shall	Is 32:4	3824
his *h* will work iniquity, to	Is 32:6	3820
Thine *h* shall meditate terror	Is 33:18	3820
to them that are of a fearful *h*	Is 35:4	3820
thee in truth and with a perfect *h*	Is 38:3	3820
him, yet he laid it not to *h*	Is 42:25	3820
And none considereth in his *h*	Is 44:19	3820
a deceived *h* hath turned him	Is 44:20	3820
not lay these things to thy *h*	Is 47:7	3820
that sayest in thine *h*, I am, and	Is 47:8	3824
and thou hast said in thine *h*	Is 47:10	3820
Then shalt thou say in thine *h*	Is 49:21	3824
the people in whose *h* is my law	Is 51:7	3820
and no man layeth it to *h*	Is 57:1	3820
me, nor laid it to thy *h*	Is 57:11	3820
to revive the *h* of the contrite	Is 57:15	3820
on frowardly in the way of his *h*	Is 57:17	3820
uttering from the *h* words of	Is 59:13	3820
thine *h* shall fear, and be	Is 60:5	3824
the day of vengeance is in mine *h*	Is 63:4	3820
hardened our *h* from thy fear	Is 63:17	3820
servants shall sing for joy of *h*	Is 65:14	3820
but ye shall cry for sorrow of *h*	Is 65:14	3820
your *h* shall rejoice, and your	Is 66:14	3820
turned unto me with her whole *h*	Jer 3:10	3820
you pastors according to mine *h*	Jer 3:15	3820
the imagination of their evil *h*	Jer 3:17	3820
take away the foreskins of your *h*	Jer 4:4	3824
that the *h* of the king shall	Jer 4:9	3820
perish, and the *h* of the princes	Jer 4:9	3820
wash thine *h* from wickedness	Jer 4:14	3820
because it reacheth unto thine *h*	Jer 4:18	3820
I am pained at my very *h*	Jer 4:19	3820
my *h* maketh a noise in me	Jer 4:19	3820
a revolting and a rebellious *h*	Jer 5:23	3820
Neither say they in their *h*	Jer 5:24	3824
the imagination of their evil *h*	Jer 7:24	3820
not, neither came it into my *h*	Jer 7:31	3820
sorrow, my *h* is faint in me	Jer 8:18	3820
but in *h* he layeth his wait	Jer 9:8	7130
the imagination of their own *h*	Jer 9:14	3820
Israel are uncircumcised in the *h*	Jer 9:26	3820
the imagination of their evil *h*	Jer 11:8	3820
that triest the reins and the *h*	Jer 11:20	3820
me, and tried mine *h* toward thee	Jer 12:3	3820
because no man layeth it to *h*	Jer 12:11	3820

in the imagination of their *h*	Jer 13:10	3820
And if thou say in thine *h*	Jer 13:22	3824
nought, and the deceit of their *h*	Jer 14:14	3820
me the joy and rejoicing of mine *h*	Jer 15:16	3824
the imagination of his evil *h*	Jer 16:12	3820
graven upon the table of their *h*	Jer 17:1	3820
whose *h* departeth from the LORD	Jer 17:5	3820
The *h* is deceitful above all	Jer 17:9	3820
I the LORD search the *h*, I try	Jer 17:10	3820
do the imagination of his evil *h*	Jer 18:12	3820
But his word was in mine *h* as a	Jer 20:9	3820
and seest the reins and the *h*	Jer 20:12	3820
thine *h* are not but for thy	Jer 22:17	3820
Mine *h* within me is broken	Jer 23:9	3820
speak a vision of their own *h*	Jer 23:16	3820
the imagination of his own *h*	Jer 23:17	3820
performed the thoughts of his *h*	Jer 23:20	3820
h of the prophets that prophesy	Jer 23:26	3820
of the deceit of their own *h*	Jer 23:26	3820
I will give them an *h* to know me	Jer 24:7	3820
return unto me with their whole *h*	Jer 24:7	3820
search for me with all your *h*	Jer 29:13	3824
engaged his *h* to approach unto me	Jer 30:21	3820
performed the intents of his *h*	Jer 30:24	3820
set thine *h* toward the highway,	Jer 31:21	3820
And I will give them one *h*	Jer 32:39	3820
land assuredly with my whole *h*	Jer 32:41	3820
and the haughtiness of his *h*	Jer 48:29	3820
mine *h* shall mourn for the men of	Jer 48:31	
Therefore mine *h* shall sound for	Jer 48:36	3820
mine *h* shall sound like pipes for	Jer 48:36	3820
as the *h* of a woman in her pangs	Jer 48:41	3820
thee, and the pride of thine *h*	Jer 49:16	3820
at that day shall the *h* of the	Jer 49:22	3820
as the *h* of a woman in her pangs	Jer 49:22	3820
And lest your *h* faint, and ye fear	Jer 51:46	3824
mine *h* is turned within me	Lam 1:20	3820
sighs are many, and my *h* is faint	Lam 1:22	3820
Their *h* cried unto the Lord, O	Lam 2:18	3820
h like water before the face of	Lam 2:19	3820
Let us lift up our *h* with our	Lam 3:41	3824
Mine eye affecteth mine *h* because	Lam 3:51	5315
Give them sorrow of *h*, thy curse	Lam 3:65	3820
The joy of our *h* is ceased	Lam 5:15	3820
For this our *h* is faint	Lam 5:17	3820
unto thee receive in thine *h*	Eze 3:10	3824
I am broken with their whorish *h*	Eze 6:9	3820
And I will give them one *h*	Eze 11:19	3820
the stony *h* out of their flesh	Eze 11:19	3820
and will give them an *h* of flesh	Eze 11:19	3820
But as for them whose *h* walketh	Eze 11:21	3820
the *h* of their detestable things	Eze 11:21	3820
which prophesy out of their own *h*	Eze 13:17	3820
made the *h* of the righteous sad	Eze 13:22	3820
set up their idols in their *h*	Eze 14:3	3820
setteth up his idols in his *h*	Eze 14:4	3820
house of Israel in their own *h*	Eze 14:5	3820
and setteth up his idols in his *h*	Eze 14:7	3820
How weak is thine *h*, saith the	Eze 16:30	3826
and make you a new *h* and a new	Eze 18:31	3820
for their *h* went after their	Eze 20:16	3820
every *h* shall melt, and all hands	Eze 21:7	3820
gates, that their *h* may faint	Eze 21:15	3820
Can thine *h* endure, or can thine	Eze 22:14	3820
rejoiced in *h* with all thy	Eze 25:6	5315
vengeance with a despiteful *h*	Eze 25:15	5315
for thee with bitterness of *h*	Eze 27:31	5315
Because thine *h* is lifted up	Eze 28:2	3820
set thine *h* as the *h* of God	Eze 28:2	3820
thine *h* is lifted up because of	Eze 28:5	3824
set thine *h* as the *h* of God	Eze 28:6	3824
Thine *h* was lifted up because of	Eze 28:17	3820
his *h* is lifted up in his height	Eze 31:10	3824
but their *h* goeth after their	Eze 33:31	3820
with the joy of all their *h*	Eze 36:5	3824
A new *h* also will I give you, and	Eze 36:26	3820
the stony *h* out of your flesh	Eze 36:26	3820
and I will give you an *h* of flesh	Eze 36:26	3820
set thine *h* upon all that I shall	Eze 40:4	3820
strangers, uncircumcised in *h*	Eze 44:7	3820
No stranger, uncircumcised in *h*	Eze 44:9	3820
in his *h* that he would not defile	Dan 1:8	3820
know the thoughts of thy *h*	Dan 2:30	3825
Let his *h* be changed from man's,	Dan 4:16	3825
let a beast's *h* be given unto him	Dan 4:16	3825
But when his *h* was lifted up, and	Dan 5:20	3825
his *h* was made like the beasts,	Dan 5:21	3825
hast not humbled thine *h*	Dan 5:22	3825
set his *h* on Daniel to deliver	Dan 6:14	1079
a man's *h* was given to it	Dan 7:4	3825
but I kept the matter in my *h*	Dan 7:28	3821
he shall magnify himself in his *h*	Dan 8:25	3824
didst set thine *h* to understand	Dan 10:12	3820
his *h* shall be lifted up	Dan 11:12	3824
his *h* shall be against the holy	Dan 11:28	3824
they set their *h* on their	Hos 4:8	5315
wine and new wine take away the *h*	Hos 4:11	3820
made ready their *h* like an oven	Hos 7:6	3820
is like a silly dove without *h*	Hos 7:11	3820
not cried unto me with their *h*	Hos 7:14	
Their *h* is divided	Hos 10:2	3820
mine *h* is turned within me, my	Hos 11:8	3820
filled, and their *h* was exalted	Hos 13:6	3820
and will rend the caul of their *h*	Hos 13:8	3820
ye even to me with all your *h*	Joel 2:12	3824
And rend your *h*, and not your	Joel 2:13	3824
of thine *h* hath deceived thee	Obad 3	3820
that saith in his *h*, Who shall	Obad 3	3820
the *h* melteth, and the knees smite	Nah 2:10	3820
that say in their *h*, The LORD	Zeph 1:12	3824
carelessly, that said in her *h*	Zeph 2:15	3824
be glad and rejoice with all the *h*	Zeph 3:14	3820
against his brother in your *h*	Zec 7:10	3824
their *h* shall rejoice as through	Zec 10:7	3820

their *h* shall rejoice in the LORD	Zec 10:7	3820
of Judah shall say in their *h*	Zec 12:5	3820
and if ye will not lay it to *h*	Mal 2:2	3820
because ye do not lay it to *h*	Mal 2:2	3820
he shall turn the *h* of the	Mal 4:6	3820
the *h* of the children to their	Mal 4:6	3820
Blessed are the pure in *h*	Mt 5:8	*2588*
with her already in his *h*	Mt 5:28	*2588*
is, there will your *h* be also	Mt 6:21	*2588*
for I am meek and lowly in *h*	Mt 11:29	*2588*
of the *h* the mouth speaketh	Mt 12:34	*2588*
the *h* bringeth forth good things	Mt 12:35	*2588*
nights in the *h* of the earth	Mt 12:40	*2588*
this people's *h* is waxed gross	Mt 13:15	*2588*
and should understand with their *h*	Mt 13:15	*2588*
away that which was sown in his *h*	Mt 13:19	*2588*
but their *h* is far from me	Mt 15:8	*2588*
the mouth come forth from the *h*	Mt 15:18	*2588*
For out of the *h* proceed evil	Mt 15:19	*2588*
the Lord thy God with all thy *h*	Mt 22:37	*2588*
evil servant shall say in his *h*	Mt 24:48	*2588*
for their *h* was hardened	Mk 6:52	*2588*
but their *h* is far from me	Mk 7:6	*2588*
it entereth not into his *h*	Mk 7:19	*2588*
from within, out of the *h* of men	Mk 7:21	*2588*
have ye your *h* yet hardened	Mk 8:17	*2588*
For the hardness of your *h* he	Mk 10:5	*4641*
and shall not doubt in his *h*	Mk 11:23	*2588*
the Lord thy God with all thy *h*	Mk 12:30	*2588*
And to love him with all the *h*	Mk 12:33	*2588*
their unbelief and hardness of *h*	Mk 16:14	*4641*
things, and pondered them in her *h*	Lk 2:19	*2588*
kept all these sayings in her *h*	Lk 2:51	*2588*
h bringeth forth that which is	Lk 6:45	*2588*
h bringeth forth that which is	Lk 6:45	*2588*
of the *h* his mouth speaketh	Lk 6:45	*2588*
which in an honest and good *h*	Lk 8:15	*2588*
perceiving the thought of their *h*	Lk 9:47	*2588*
the Lord thy God with all thy *h*	Lk 10:27	*2588*
is, there will your *h* be also	Lk 12:34	*2588*
and if that servant say in his *h*	Lk 12:45	*2588*
slow of *h* to believe all that the	Lk 24:25	*2588*
Did not our *h* burn within us,	Lk 24:32	*2588*
their eyes, and hardened their *h*	Jn 12:40	*2588*
eyes, nor understand with their *h*	Jn 12:40	*2588*
put into the *h* of Judas Iscariot	Jn 13:2	*2588*
Let not your *h* be troubled	Jn 14:1	*2588*
Let not your *h* be troubled	Jn 14:27	*2588*
you, sorrow hath filled your *h*	Jn 16:6	*2588*
your *h* shall rejoice, and your joy	Jn 16:22	*2588*
Therefore did my *h* rejoice	Acts 2:26	*2588*
they were pricked in their *h*	Acts 2:37	*2588*
with gladness and singleness of *h*	Acts 2:46	*2588*
them that believed were of one *h*	Acts 4:32	*2588*
thine *h* to lie to the Holy Ghost	Acts 5:3	*2588*
conceived this thing in thine *h*	Acts 5:4	*2588*
that, they were cut to the *h*	Acts 5:33	
it came into his *h* to visit his	Acts 7:23	*2588*
stiffnecked and uncircumcised in *h*	Acts 7:51	*2588*
things, they were cut to the *h*	Acts 7:54	*2588*
for thy *h* is not right in the	Acts 8:21	*2588*
of thine *h* may be forgiven thee	Acts 8:22	*2588*
thou believest with all thine *h*	Acts 8:37	*2588*
that with purpose of *h* they would	Acts 11:23	*2588*
of Jesse, a man after mine own *h*	Acts 13:22	*2588*
whose *h* the Lord opened, that she	Acts 16:14	*2588*
ye to weep and to break mine *h*	Acts 21:13	*2588*
For the *h* of this people is waxed	Acts 28:27	*2588*
ears, and understand with their *h*	Acts 28:27	*2588*
and their foolish *h* was darkened	Rom 1:21	*2588*
impenitent *h* treasurest up unto	Rom 2:5	*2588*
and circumcision is that of the *h*	Rom 2:29	*2588*
but ye have obeyed from the *h*	Rom 6:17	*2588*
and continual sorrow in my *h*	Rom 9:2	*2588*
on this wise, Say not in thine *h*	Rom 10:6	*2588*
even in thy mouth, and in thy *h*	Rom 10:8	*2588*
shalt believe in thine *h* that God	Rom 10:9	*2588*
For with the *h* man believeth unto	Rom 10:10	*2588*
have entered into the *h* of man	1Cor 2:9	*2588*
that standeth stedfast in his *h*	1Cor 7:37	*2588*
hath so decreed in his *h* that he	1Cor 7:37	*2588*
secrets of his *h* made manifest	1Cor 14:25	*2588*
anguish of *h* I wrote unto you	2Cor 2:4	*2588*
but in fleshly tables of the *h*	2Cor 3:3	*2588*
is read, the vail is upon their *h*	2Cor 3:15	*2588*
glory in appearance, and not in *h*	2Cor 5:12	*2588*
open unto you, our *h* is enlarged	2Cor 6:11	*2588*
care into the *h* of Titus for you	2Cor 8:16	*2588*
as he purposeth in his *h*, so let	2Cor 9:7	*2588*
of the blindness of their *h*	Eph 4:18	*2588*
melody in your *h* to the Lord	Eph 5:19	*2588*
in singleness of your *h*, as unto	Eph 6:5	*2588*
doing the will of God from the *h*	Eph 6:6	*5590*
all, because I have you in my *h*	Phil 1:7	*2588*
but in singleness of *h*, fearing	Col 3:22	*2588*
short time in presence, not in *h*	1Th 2:17	*2588*
is charity out of a pure *h*	1Ti 1:5	*2588*
call on the Lord out of a pure *h*	2Ti 2:22	*2588*
They do alway err in their *h*	Heb 3:10	*2588*
any of you an evil *h* of unbelief	Heb 3:12	*2588*
the thoughts and intents of the *h*	Heb 4:12	*2588*
true *h* in full assurance of faith	Heb 10:22	*2588*
the *h* be established with grace	Heb 13:9	*2588*
tongue, but deceiveth his own *h*	Jas 1:26	*2588*
another with a pure *h* fervently	1Pet 1:22	*2588*
let it be the hidden man of the *h*	1Pet 3:4	*2588*
an *h* they have exercised with	2Pet 2:14	*2588*
For if our *h* condemn	1Jn 3:20	*2588*
God is greater than our *h*	1Jn 3:20	*2588*
if our *h* condemn us not, then	1Jn 3:21	*2588*
for she saith in her *h*, I sit a	Rev 18:7	*2588*

HEARTED
speak unto all that are wise *h* ... Ex 28:3 3820
that are wise *h* I have put wisdom ... Ex 31:6 3820
every wise *h* among you shall come ... Ex 35:10 3820
women, as many as were willing *h* ... Ex 35:22 3820
wise *h* did spin with their hands ... Ex 35:25 3820
and Aholiab, and every wise *h* man ... Ex 36:1 3820
and Aholiab, and every wise *h* man ... Ex 36:2 3820
every wise *h* man among them that ... Ex 36:8 3820

HEARTH
it, and make cakes upon the *h* ... Gen 18:6
and my bones are burned as an *h* ... Ps 102:3 4168
a sherd to take fire from the *h* ... Is 30:14 3344
fire on the *h* burning before him ... Jer 36:22 254
into the fire that was on the *h* ... Jer 36:23 254
in the fire that was on the *h* ... Jer 36:23 254
like an *h* of fire among the wood ... Zec 12:6 3595

HEARTILY
And whatsoever ye do, do it *h* ... Col 3:23

HEART'S
wicked boasteth of his *h* desire ... Ps 10:3 5315
Thou hast given him his *h* desire ... Ps 21:2 3820
my *h* desire and prayer to God for ... Rom 10:1 *2588*

HEARTS
of bread, and comfort ye your *h* ... Gen 18:5 3820
harden the *h* of the Egyptians ... Ex 14:17 3820
in the *h* of all that are wise ... Ex 31:6 3820
send a faintness into their *h* in ... Lev 26:36 3824
their uncircumcised *h* be humbled ... Lev 26:41 3824
let not your *h* faint, fear not ... Deut 20:3 3824
Set your *h* unto all the words ... Deut 32:46 3824
our *h* did melt, neither did there ... Josh 2:11 3824
wherefore the *h* of the people ... Josh 7:5 3824
was of the LORD to harden their *h* ... Josh 11:20 3820
and ye know in all your *h* and in ... Josh 23:14 3824
their *h* inclined to follow ... Judg 9:3 3820
to pass, when their *h* were merry ... Judg 16:25 3820
as they were making their *h* merry ... Judg 19:22 3820
then do ye harden your *h*, as the ... 1Sa 6:6 3824
and Pharaoh hardened their *h* ... 1Sa 6:6 3820
unto the LORD with all your *h* ... 1Sa 7:3 3824
prepare your *h* unto the LORD, and ... 1Sa 7:3 3824
of men, whose *h* God had touched ... 1Sa 10:26 3820
stole the *h* of the men of Israel ... 2Sa 15:6 3820
The *h* of the men of Israel are ... 2Sa 15:13 3820
knowest the *h* of all the children ... 1Kin 8:39 3824
he may incline our *h* unto him ... 1Kin 8:58 3824
for the LORD searcheth all *h* ... 1Chr 28:9 3824
walk before thee with all their *h* ... 2Chr 6:14 3820
the *h* of the children of men ... 2Chr 6:30 3824
of Israel such as set their *h* to ... 2Chr 11:16 3824
h unto the God of their fathers ... 2Chr 20:33 3824
sinned, and cursed God in their *h* ... Job 1:5 3824
the righteous God trieth the *h* ... Ps 7:9 3826
but mischief is in their *h* ... Ps 28:3 3824
He fashioneth their *h* alike ... Ps 33:15 3820
Let them not say in their *h* ... Ps 35:25 3820
They said in their *h*, Let us ... Ps 74:8 3820
we may apply our *h* unto wisdom ... Ps 90:12 3824
them that are upright in their *h* ... Ps 125:4 3826
then the *h* of the children of men ... Prov 15:11 3826
but the LORD trieth the *h* ... Prov 17:3 3826
but the LORD pondereth the *h* ... Prov 21:2 3826
unto those that be of heavy *h* ... Prov 31:6 5315
and their *h*, that they cannot ... Is 44:18 3826
parts, and write it in their *h* ... Jer 31:33 3820
but I will put my fear in their *h* ... Jer 32:40 3824
For ye dissembled in your *h* ... Jer 42:20 5315
the mighty men's *h* in Moab at ... Jer 48:41 3820
that prophesy out of their own *h* ... Eze 13:2 3820
also vex the *h* of many people ... Eze 32:9 3820
both these kings' *h* shall be to ... Dan 11:27 3824
their *h* that I remember all their ... Hos 7:2 3824
they made their *h* as an adamant ... Zec 7:12 3820
in your *h* against his neighbour ... Zec 8:17 3820
Wherefore think ye evil in your *h* ... Mt 9:4 *2588*
if ye from your *h* forgive not ... Mt 18:35 *2588*
h suffered you to put away your ... Mt 19:8 *4641*
there, and reasoning in their *h* ... Mk 2:6 *2588*
reason ye these things in your *h* ... Mk 2:8 *2588*
for the hardness of their *h* ... Mk 3:5 *2588*
the word that was sown in their *h* ... Mk 4:15 *2588*
to turn the *h* of the fathers to ... Lk 1:17 *2588*
in the imagination of their *h* ... Lk 1:51 *2588*
them laid them up in their *h* ... Lk 1:66 *2588*
of many *h* may be revealed ... Lk 2:35 *2588*
all men mused in their *h* of John ... Lk 3:15 *2588*
them, What reason ye in your *h* ... Lk 5:22 *2588*
away the word out of their *h* ... Lk 8:12 *2588*
but God knoweth your *h* ... Lk 16:15 *2588*
Settle it therefore in your *h* ... Lk 21:14 *2588*
Men's *h* failing them for fear, and ... Lk 21:26 *674*
lest at any time your *h* be ... Lk 21:34 *2588*
why do thoughts arise in your *h* ... Lk 24:38 *2588*
which knowest the *h* of all men ... Acts 1:24 *2589*
in their *h* turned back again into ... Acts 7:39 *2588*
seasons, filling our *h* with food ... Acts 14:17 *2588*
And God, which knoweth the *h* ... Acts 15:8 *2589*
them, purifying their *h* by faith ... Acts 15:9 *2588*
through the lusts of their own *h* ... Rom 1:24 *2588*
of the law written in their *h* ... Rom 2:15 *2588*
our *h* by the Holy Ghost which is ... Rom 5:5 *2588*
he that searcheth the *h* knoweth ... Rom 8:27 *2588*
deceive the *h* of the simple ... Rom 16:18 *2588*
manifest the counsels of the *h* ... 1Cor 4:5 *2588*
earnest of the Spirit in our *h* ... 2Cor 1:22 *2588*
are our epistle written in our *h* ... 2Cor 3:2 *2588*
of darkness, hath shined in our *h* ... 2Cor 4:6 *2588*
that ye are in our *h* to die ... 2Cor 7:3 *2588*
the Spirit of his Son into your *h* ... Gal 4:6 *2588*
may dwell in your *h* by faith ... Eph 3:17 *2588*
and that he might comfort your *h* ... Eph 6:22 *2588*
understanding, shall keep your *h* ... Phil 4:7 *2588*
That their *h* might be comforted ... Col 2:2 *2588*
the peace of God rule in your *h* ... Col 3:15 *2588*
with grace in your *h* to the Lord ... Col 3:16 *2588*
your estate, and comfort your *h* ... Col 4:8 *2588*
men, but God, which trieth our *h* ... 1Th 2:4 *2588*
h unblameable in holiness before ... 1Th 3:13 *2588*
Comfort your *h*, and stablish you ... 2Th 2:17 *2588*
your *h* into the love of God ... 2Th 3:5 *2588*
Harden not your *h*, as in the ... Heb 3:8 *2588*
hear his voice, harden not your *h* ... Heb 3:15 *2588*
hear his voice, harden not your *h* ... Heb 4:7 *2588*
mind, and write them in their *h* ... Heb 8:10 *2588*
I will put my laws into their *h* ... Heb 10:16 *2588*
having our *h* sprinkled from an ... Heb 10:22 *2588*
envying and strife in your *h* ... Jas 3:14 *2588*
and purify your *h*, ye double ... Jas 4:8 *2588*
ye have nourished your *h*, as in a ... Jas 5:5 *2588*
ye also patient; stablish your *h* ... Jas 5:8 *2588*
sanctify the Lord God in your *h* ... 1Pet 3:15 *2588*
and the day star arise in your *h* ... 2Pet 1:19 *2588*
and shall assure our *h* before him ... 1Jn 3:19 *2588*
he which searcheth the reins and *h* ... Rev 2:23 *2588*
put in their *h* to fulfil his will ... Rev 17:17 *2588*

HEARTS'
them up unto their own *h* lust ... Ps 81:12 3820

HEARTY
of a man's friend by *h* counsel ... Prov 27:9 5315

HEAT
seedtime and harvest, and cold and *h* ... Gen 8:22 2527
the tent door in the *h* of the day ... Gen 18:1 2527
what meaneth the *h* of this great ... Deut 29:24 2750
and devoured with burning *h* ... Deut 32:24 7565
Ammonites until the *h* of the day ... 1Sa 11:11 2527
came about the *h* of the day to ... 2Sa 4:5 2527
him with clothes, but he gat no *h* ... 1Kin 1:1 3179
that my lord the king may get *h* ... 1Kin 1:2 2552
h consume the snow waters ... Job 24:19 2527
me, and my bones are burned with *h* ... Job 30:30 2721
is nothing hid from the *h* thereof ... Ps 19:6 2535
lie together, then they have *h* ... Eccl 4:11 2552
shadow in the daytime from the *h* ... Is 4:6 2721
place like a clear *h* upon herbs ... Is 18:4 2527
cloud of dew in the *h* of harvest ... Is 18:4 2527
the storm, a shadow from the *h* ... Is 25:4 2721
as the *h* in a dry place ... Is 25:5 2721
even the *h* with the shadow of a ... Is 25:5 2721
neither shall the *h* nor sun smite ... Is 49:10 8273
and shall not see when *h* cometh ... Jer 17:8 2527
be cast out in the day to the *h* ... Jer 36:30 2721
In their *h* I will make their ... Jer 51:39 2527
bitterness, in the *h* of my spirit ... Eze 3:14 2534
commanded that they should *h* the ... Dan 3:19 228
borne the burden and *h* of the day ... Mt 20:12 *2742*
blow, ye say, There will be *h* ... Lk 12:55 *2742*
there came a viper out of the *h* ... Acts 28:3 *2329*
no sooner risen with a burning *h* ... Jas 1:11 *2742*
shall melt with fervent *h* ... 2Pet 3:10 *2741*
shall melt with fervent *h* ... 2Pet 3:12 *2741*
the sun light on them, nor any *h* ... Rev 7:16 *2738*
And men were scorched with great *h* ... Rev 16:9 *2738*

HEATED
more than it was wont to be *h* ... Dan 3:19 228
as an oven *h* by the baker, who ... Hos 7:4 1197

HEATH
shall be like the *h* in the desert ... Jer 17:6 6176
be like the *h* in the wilderness ... Jer 48:6 6176

HEATHEN
shall be of the *h* that are round ... Lev 25:44 1471
And I will scatter you among the *h* ... Lev 26:33 1471
And ye shall perish among the *h* ... Lev 26:38 1471
of Egypt in the sight of the *h* ... Lev 26:45 1471
be left few in number among the *h* ... Deut 4:27 1471
hast kept me to be head of the *h* ... 2Sa 22:44 1471
unto thee, O LORD, among the *h* ... 2Sa 22:50 1471
to the abominations of the *h* ... 2Kin 16:3 1471
walked in the statutes of the *h* ... 2Kin 17:8 1471
as did the *h* whom the LORD ... 2Kin 17:11 1471
went after the *h* that were round ... 2Kin 17:15 1471
after the abominations of the *h* ... 2Kin 21:2 1471
Declare his glory among the *h* ... 1Chr 16:24 1471
and deliver us from the *h* ... 1Chr 16:35 1471
over all the kingdoms of the *h* ... 2Chr 20:6 1471
the *h* whom the LORD had cast out ... 2Chr 28:3 1471
unto the abominations of the *h* ... 2Chr 33:2 1471
to err, and to do worse than the *h* ... 2Chr 33:9 1471
all the abominations of the *h* ... 2Chr 36:14 1471
filthiness of the *h* of the land ... Ezr 6:21 1471
Jews, which were sold unto the *h* ... Neh 5:8 1471
the reproach of the *h* our enemies ... Neh 5:9 1471
among the *h* that are about us ... Neh 5:17 1471
It is reported among the *h* ... Neh 6:6 1471
all the *h* that were about us saw ... Neh 6:16 1471
Why do the *h* rage, and the people ... Ps 2:1 1471
thee the *h* for thine inheritance ... Ps 2:8 1471
Thou hast rebuked the *h*, thou ... Ps 9:5 1471
The *h* are sunk down in the pit ... Ps 9:15 1471
let the *h* be judged in thy sight ... Ps 9:19 1471
the *h* are perished out of his ... Ps 10:16 1471
hast made me the head of the *h* ... Ps 18:43 1471
unto thee, O LORD, among the *h* ... Ps 18:49 1471
the counsel of the *h* to nought ... Ps 33:10 1471
drive out the *h* with thy hand ... Ps 44:2 1471
and hast scattered us among the *h* ... Ps 44:11 1471
makest us a byword among the *h* ... Ps 44:14 1471
The *h* raged, the kingdoms were ... Ps 46:6 1471
I will be exalted among the *h* ... Ps 46:10 1471
God reigneth over the *h* ... Ps 47:8 1471
Israel, awake to visit all the *h* ... Ps 59:5 1471
shalt have all the *h* in derision ... Ps 59:8 1471
He cast out the *h* also before ... Ps 78:55 1471
the *h* are come into thine ... Ps 79:1 1471
the *h* that have not known thee ... Ps 79:6 1471
Wherefore should the *h* say ... Ps 79:10 1471
let him be known among the *h* in ... Ps 79:10 1471
thou hast cast out the *h*, and ... Ps 80:8 1471
He that chastiseth the *h*, shall ... Ps 94:10 1471
Declare his glory among the *h* ... Ps 96:3 1471
Say among the *h* that the LORD ... Ps 96:10 1471
shewed in the sight of the *h* ... Ps 98:2 1471
So the *h* shall fear the name of ... Ps 102:15 1471
And gave them the lands of the *h* ... Ps 105:44 1471
But were mingled among the *h* ... Ps 106:35 1471
gave them into the hand of the *h* ... Ps 106:41 1471
and gather us from among the *h* ... Ps 106:47 1471
He shall judge among the *h* ... Ps 110:6 1471
give them the heritage of the *h* ... Ps 111:6 1471
Wherefore should the *h* say ... Ps 115:2 1471
then said they among the *h* ... Ps 126:2 1471
The idols of the *h* are silver ... Ps 135:15 1471
To execute vengeance upon the *h* ... Ps 149:7 1471
the lords of the *h* have broken ... Is 16:8 1471
scatter them also among the *h* ... Jer 9:16 1471
LORD, Learn not the way of the *h* ... Jer 10:2 1471
for the *h* are dismayed at them ... Jer 10:2 1471
upon the *h* that know thee not ... Jer 10:25 1471
Ask ye now among the *h*, who hath ... Jer 18:13 1471
an ambassador is sent unto the *h* ... Jer 49:14 1471
will make thee small among the *h* ... Jer 49:15 1471
she dwelleth among the *h*, she ... Lam 1:3 1471
the *h* entered into her sanctuary ... Lam 1:10 1471
wandered, they said among the *h* ... Lam 4:15 1471
shadow we shall live among the *h* ... Lam 4:20 1471
I will bring the worst of the *h* ... Eze 7:24 1471
of the *h* that are round about you ... Eze 11:12 1471
cast them far off among the *h* ... Eze 11:16 1471
among the *h* whither they come ... Eze 12:16 1471
forth among the *h* for thy beauty ... Eze 16:14 1471
not be polluted before the *h* ... Eze 20:9 1471
not be polluted before the *h* ... Eze 20:14 1471
be polluted in the sight of the *h* ... Eze 20:22 1471
I would scatter them among the *h* ... Eze 20:23 1471
that ye say, We will be as the *h* ... Eze 20:32 1471
be sanctified in you before the *h* ... Eze 20:41 1471
I made thee a reproach unto the *h* ... Eze 22:4 1471
I will scatter thee among the *h* ... Eze 22:15 1471
in thyself in the sight of the *h* ... Eze 22:16 1471
hast gone a whoring after the *h* ... Eze 23:30 1471
deliver thee for a spoil to the *h* ... Eze 25:7 1471
of Judah is like unto all the *h* ... Eze 25:8 1471
in them in the sight of the *h* ... Eze 28:25 1471
it shall be the time of the *h* ... Eze 30:3 1471
hand of the mighty one of the *h* ... Eze 31:11 1471
his shadow in the midst of the *h* ... Eze 31:17 1471
shall no more be a prey to the *h* ... Eze 34:28 1471
bear the shame of the *h* any more ... Eze 34:29 1471
unto the residue of the *h* ... Eze 36:3 1471
of the *h* that are round about ... Eze 36:4 1471
against the residue of the *h* ... Eze 36:5 1471
ye have borne the shame of the *h* ... Eze 36:6 1471
Surely the *h* that are about you ... Eze 36:7 1471
thee the shame of the *h* any more ... Eze 36:15 1471
And I scattered them among the *h* ... Eze 36:19 1471
And when they entered unto the *h* ... Eze 36:20 1471
Israel had profaned among the *h* ... Eze 36:21 1471
ye have profaned among the *h* ... Eze 36:22 1471
which was profaned among the *h* ... Eze 36:23 1471
the *h* shall know that I am the ... Eze 36:23 1471
I will take you from among the *h* ... Eze 36:24 1471
reproach of famine among the *h* ... Eze 36:30 1471
Then the *h* that are left round ... Eze 36:36 1471
of Israel from among the *h* ... Eze 37:21 1471
the *h* shall know that I the LORD ... Eze 37:28 1471
that the *h* may know me, when I ... Eze 38:16 1471
the *h* shall know that I am the ... Eze 39:7 1471
I will set my glory among the *h* ... Eze 39:21 1471
all the *h* shall see my judgment ... Eze 39:21 1471
the *h* shall know that the house ... Eze 39:23 1471
be led into captivity among the *h* ... Eze 39:28 1471
that the *h* should rule over them ... Joel 2:17 1471
make you a reproach among the *h* ... Joel 2:19 1471
yourselves, and come, all ye *h* ... Joel 3:11 1471
Let the *h* be wakened, and come up ... Joel 3:12 1471
to judge all the *h* round about ... Joel 3:12 1471
remnant of Edom, and of all the *h* ... Amos 9:12 1471
an ambassador is sent among the *h* ... Obad 1 1471
have made thee small among the *h* ... Obad 2 1471
the LORD is near upon all the *h* ... Obad 15 1471
so shall all the *h* drink ... Obad 16 1471
in anger and fury upon the *h* ... Mic 5:15 1471
Behold ye among the *h*, and regard ... Hab 1:5 1471
thou didst thresh the *h* in anger ... Hab 3:12 1471
even all the isles of the *h* ... Zeph 2:11 1471
strength of the kingdoms of the *h* ... Hag 2:22 1471
with the *h* that are at ease ... Zec 1:15 1471
as ye were a curse among the *h* ... Zec 8:13 1471
he shall speak peace unto the *h* ... Zec 9:10 1471
the wealth of all the *h* round ... Zec 14:14 1471
the LORD will smite the *h* that ... Zec 14:18 1471
name shall be great among the *h* ... Mal 1:11 1471
my name is dreadful among the *h* ... Mal 1:14 1471
not vain repetitions, as the *h* do ... Mt 6:7 *1482*
let him be unto thee as an *h* man ... Mt 18:17 *1482*
hast said, Why did the *h* rage ... Acts 4:25 *1484*
countrymen, in perils by the *h* ... 2Cor 11:26 *1484*
I might preach him among the *h* ... Gal 1:16 *1484*
that we should go unto the *h* ... Gal 2:9 *1484*
would justify the *h* through faith ... Gal 3:8 *1484*

HEAVE
and the shoulder of the *h* offering ... Ex 29:27 8641
for it is an *h* offering ... Ex 29:28 8641
it shall be an *h* offering from ... Ex 29:28 8641
even their *h* offering unto the ... Ex 29:28 8641
for an *h* offering unto the LORD ... Lev 7:14 8641

h offering of the sacrifices of Lev 7:32 8641
the *h* shoulder have I taken of Lev 7:34 8641
h shoulder shall ye eat in a Lev 10:14 8641
The *h* shoulder and the wave breast Lev 10:15 8641
the wave breast and *h* shoulder Num 6:20 8641
ye shall offer up an *h* offering Num 15:19 8641
of your dough for an *h* offering Num 15:20 8641
as ye do the *h* offering of the Num 15:20 8641
threshingfloor, so shall ye *h* it Num 15:20 7311
an *h* offering in your generations Num 15:21 8641
h offerings of all the hallowed Num 18:8 8641
the *h* offering of their gift, Num 18:11 8641
All the *h* offerings of the holy Num 18:19 8641
as an *h* offering unto the LORD Num 18:24 8641
then ye shall offer up an *h* Num 18:26 8641
this your *h* offering shall be Num 18:27 8641
Thus ye also shall offer an *h* Num 18:28 8641
h offering to Aaron the priest Num 18:28 8641
every *h* offering of the LORD Num 18:29 8641
for an *h* offering of the LORD Num 31:29 8641
which was the LORD's *h* offering Num 31:41 8641
h offerings of your hand, and your Deut 12:6 8641
the *h* offering of your hand, and Deut 12:11 8641
or *h* offering of thine hand Deut 12:17 8641

HEAVED

which is waved, and which is *h* up Ex 29:27 7311
When ye have *h* the best thereof Num 18:30 7311
when ye have *h* from it the best Num 18:32 7311

HEAVEN

the beginning God created the *h* Gen 1:1 8064
And God called the firmament *H* Gen 1:8 8064
Let the waters under the *h* be Gen 1:9 8064
the *h* to divide the day from the Gen 1:14 8064
h to give light upon the earth Gen 1:15 8064
h to give light upon the earth Gen 1:17 8064
earth in the open firmament of *h* Gen 1:20 8064
the breath of life, from under *h* Gen 6:17 8064
and the windows of *h* were opened Gen 7:11 8064
that were under the whole *h* Gen 7:19 8064
things, and the fowl of the *h* Gen 7:23 8064
and the windows of *h* were stopped Gen 8:2 8064
the rain from *h* was restrained Gen 8:2 8064
tower, whose top may reach unto *h* Gen 11:4 8064
the most high God, possessor of *h* Gen 14:19 8064
most high God, the possessor of *h* Gen 14:22 8064
and said, Look now toward *h* Gen 15:5 8064
and fire from the LORD out of *h* Gen 19:24 8064
of God called to Hagar out of *h* Gen 21:17 8064
the LORD called unto him out of *h* Gen 22:11 8064
Abraham out of *h* the second time Gen 22:15 8064
thy seed as the stars of the *h* Gen 22:17 8064
swear by the LORD, the God of *h* Gen 24:3 8064
The LORD God of *h*, which took me Gen 24:7 8064
to multiply as the stars of *h* Gen 26:4 8064
God give thee of the dew of *h* Gen 27:28 8064
and of the dew of *h* from above Gen 27:39 8064
and the top of it reached to *h* Gen 28:12 8064
of God, and this is the gate of *h* Gen 28:17 8064
thee with blessings of *h* above Gen 49:25 8064
the *h* in the sight of Pharaoh Ex 9:8 8064
and Moses sprinkled it up toward *h* Ex 9:10 8064
Stretch forth thine hand toward *h* Ex 9:22 8064
stretched forth his rod toward *h* Ex 9:23 8064
Stretch out thine hand toward *h* Ex 10:21 8064
stretched forth his hand toward *h* Ex 10:22 8064
I will rain bread from *h* for you Ex 16:4 8064
of Amalek from under *h* Ex 17:14 8064
of any thing that is in *h* above Ex 20:4 8064
For in six days the LORD made *h* Ex 20:11 8064
I have talked with you from *h* Ex 20:22 8064
the body of *h* in his clearness Ex 24:10 8064
for in six days the LORD made *h* Ex 31:17 8064
your seed as the stars of *h* Ex 32:13 8064
and I will make your *h* as iron Lev 26:19 8064
as the stars of *h* for multitude Deut 1:10 8064
are great and walled up to *h* Deut 1:28 8064
that are under the whole *h* Deut 2:25 8064
God is there in *h* or in earth Deut 3:24 8064
with fire unto the midst of *h* Deut 4:11 8064
thou lift up thine eyes unto *h* Deut 4:19 8064
the stars, even all the host of *h* Deut 4:19 8064
all nations under the whole *h* Deut 4:19 8064
I call *h* and earth to witness Deut 4:26 8064
the one side of *h* unto the other Deut 4:32 8064
Out of *h* he made thee to hear his Deut 4:36 8064
the LORD he is God in *h* above Deut 4:39 8064
of any thing that is in *h* above Deut 5:8 8064
destroy their name from under *h* Deut 7:24 8064
cities great and fenced up to *h* Deut 9:1 8064
blot out their name from under *h* Deut 9:14 8064
Behold, the *h* and the *h* of Deut 10:14 8064
as the stars of *h* for multitude Deut 10:22 8064
drinketh water of the rain of *h* Deut 11:11 8064
against you, and he shut up the *h* Deut 11:17 8064
as the days of *h* upon the earth Deut 11:21 8064
or moon, or any of the host of *h* Deut 17:3 8064
of Amalek from under *h* Deut 25:19 8064
from thy holy habitation, from *h* Deut 26:15 8064
the *h* to give the rain unto thy Deut 28:12 8064
thy *h* that is over thy head shall Deut 28:23 8064
from *h* shall it come down upon Deut 28:24 8064
as the stars of *h* for multitude Deut 28:62 8064
blot out his name from under *h* Deut 29:20 8064
out unto the outmost parts of *h* Deut 30:4 8064
It is not in *h*, that thou Deut 30:12 8064
say, Who shall go up for us to *h* Deut 30:12 8064
I call *h* and earth to record this Deut 30:19 8064
words in their ears, and call *h* Deut 31:28 8064
For I lift up my hand to *h* Deut 32:40 8064
for the precious things of *h* Deut 33:13 8064
who rideth upon the *h* in thy help Deut 33:26 8064
your God, he is God in *h* above Josh 2:11 8064
of the city ascended up to *h* Josh 8:20 8064
from *h* upon them unto Azekah Josh 10:11 8064
sun stood still in the midst of *h* Josh 10:13 8064
They fought from *h* Judg 5:20 8064
up toward *h* from off the altar Judg 13:20 8064
of the city ascended up to *h* Judg 20:40 8064
out of *h* shall he thunder upon 1Sa 2:10 8064
the cry of the city went up to *h* 1Sa 5:12 8064
and he was taken up between the *h* 2Sa 18:9 8064
water dropped upon them out of *h* 2Sa 21:10 8064
the foundations of *h* moved 2Sa 22:8 8064
The LORD thundered from *h* 2Sa 22:14 8064
spread forth his hands toward *h* 1Kin 8:22 8064
in *h* above, or on earth beneath, 1Kin 8:23 8064
behold, the *h* and *h* of 1Kin 8:27 8064
hear thou in *h* thy dwelling place 1Kin 8:30 8064
Then hear thou in *h*, and do, and 1Kin 8:32 8064
Then hear thou in *h*, and forgive 1Kin 8:34 8064
When *h* is shut up, and there is no 1Kin 8:35 8064
Then hear thou in *h*, and forgive 1Kin 8:36 8064
Then hear thou in *h* thy dwelling 1Kin 8:39 8064
Hear thou in *h* thy dwelling place 1Kin 8:43 8064
Then hear thou in *h* their prayer 1Kin 8:45 8064
in *h* thy dwelling place, and 1Kin 8:49 8064
with his hands spread up to *h* 1Kin 8:54 8064
that the *h* was black with clouds 1Kin 18:45 8064
all the host of *h* standing by him 1Kin 22:19 8064
then let fire come down from *h* 2Kin 1:10 8064
And there came down fire from *h* 2Kin 1:10 8064
of God, let fire come down from *h* 2Kin 1:12 8064
the fire of God came down from *h* 2Kin 1:12 8064
there came fire down from *h* 2Kin 1:14 8064
up Elijah into *h* by a whirlwind 2Kin 2:1 8064
went up by a whirlwind into *h* 2Kin 2:11 8064
the LORD would make windows in *h* 2Kin 7:2 8064
the LORD should make windows in *h* 2Kin 7:19 8064
the name of Israel from under *h* 2Kin 14:27 8064
and worshipped all the host of *h* 2Kin 17:16 8064
thou hast made *h* and earth 2Kin 19:15 8064
and worshipped all the host of *h* 2Kin 21:3 8064
altars for all the host of *h* in 2Kin 21:5 8064
grove, and for all the host of *h* 2Kin 23:4 8064
planets, and to all the host of *h* 2Kin 23:5 8064
stand between the earth and the *h* 1Chr 21:16 8064
he answered him from *h* by fire 1Chr 21:26 8064
for all that is in the *h* and in 1Chr 29:11 8064
build him an house, seeing the *h* 2Chr 2:6 8064
h of heavens cannot contain him 2Chr 2:6 8064
LORD God of Israel, that made *h* 2Chr 2:12 8064
spread forth his hands toward *h* 2Chr 6:13 8064
is no God like thee in the *h* 2Chr 6:14 8064
behold, *h* and the *h* of 2Chr 6:18 8064
thy dwelling place, even from *h* 2Chr 6:21 8064
Then hear thou from *h*, and do, and 2Chr 6:23 8064
When the *h* is shut up, and there 2Chr 6:26 8064
Then hear thou from *h*, and forgive 2Chr 6:27 8064
thou from *h* thy dwelling place 2Chr 6:30 8064
the fire came down from *h* 2Chr 7:1 8064
If I shut up *h* that there be no 2Chr 7:13 8064
then will I hear from *h*, and will 2Chr 7:14 8064
all the host of *h* standing on his 2Chr 18:18 8064
fathers, art not thou God in *h* 2Chr 20:6 8064
in a rage that reacheth up unto *h* 2Chr 28:9 8064
holy dwelling place, even unto *h* 2Chr 30:27 8064
son of Amoz, prayed and cried to *h* 2Chr 32:20 8064
and worshipped all the host of *h* 2Chr 33:3 8064
altars for all the host of *h* in 2Chr 33:5 8064
hath the LORD God of *h* given me 2Chr 36:23 8064
The LORD God of *h* hath given me Ezr 1:2 8064
are the servants of the God of *h* Ezr 5:11 8065
provoked the God of *h* unto wrath Ezr 5:12 8065
burnt offerings of the God of *h* Ezr 6:9 8065
sweet savours unto the God of *h* Ezr 6:10 8065
scribe of the law of the God of *h* Ezr 7:12 8065
scribe of the law of the God of *h* Ezr 7:21 8065
is commanded by the God of *h* Ezr 7:23 8065
for the house of the God of *h* Ezr 7:23 8065
and prayed before the God of *h* Neh 1:4 8064
I beseech thee, O LORD God of *h* Neh 1:5 8064
unto the uttermost part of the *h* Neh 1:9 8064
So I prayed to the God of *h* Neh 2:4 8064
and said unto them, The God of *h* Neh 2:20 8064
thou hast made *h*, the *h* of Neh 9:6 8064
the host of *h* worshippeth thee Neh 9:6 8064
and spakest with them from *h* Neh 9:13 8064
bread from *h* for their hunger Neh 9:15 8064
thou as the stars of *h*, and Neh 9:23 8064
thee, thou heardest them from *h* Neh 9:27 8064
thee, thou heardest them from *h* Neh 9:28 8064
The fire of God is fallen from *h* Job 1:16 8064
dust upon their heads toward *h* Job 2:12 8064
It is as high as *h* Job 11:8 8064
now, behold, my witness is in *h* Job 16:19 8064
The *h* shall reveal his iniquity Job 20:27 8064
Is not God in the height of *h* Job 22:12 8064
and he walketh in the circuit of *h* Job 22:14 8064
The pillars of *h* tremble, and are Job 26:11 8064
earth, and seeth under the whole *h* Job 28:24 8064
us wiser than the fowls of *h* Job 35:11 8064
He directeth it under the whole *h* Job 37:3 8064
and the hoary frost of *h*, who hath Job 38:29 8064
Knowest thou the ordinances of *h* Job 38:33 8064
or who can stay the bottles of *h* Job 38:37 8064
is under the whole *h* is mine Job 41:11 8064
temple, the LORD's throne is in *h* Ps 11:4 8064
from *h* upon the children of men Ps 14:2 8064
forth is from the end of the *h* Ps 19:6 8064
he will hear him from his holy *h* Ps 20:6 8064
The LORD looketh from *h* Ps 33:13 8064
God looked down from *h* upon the Ps 53:2 8064
He shall send from *h*, and save me Ps 57:3 8064
Let the *h* and earth praise him, Ps 69:34 8064
Whom have I in *h* but thee Ps 73:25 8064
cause judgment to be heard from *h* Ps 76:8 8064
voice of thy thunder was in the *h* Ps 77:18 1534
above, and opened the doors of *h* Ps 78:23 8064
had given them of the corn of *h* Ps 78:24 8064
an east wind to blow in the *h* Ps 78:26 8064
be meat unto the fowls of the *h* Ps 79:2 8064
look down from *h*, and behold, and Ps 80:14 8064
shall look down from *h* Ps 85:11 8064
For who in the *h* can be compared Ps 89:6 7834
and his throne as the days of *h* Ps 89:29 8064
and as a faithful witness in *h* Ps 89:37 7834
from *h* did the LORD behold the Ps 102:19 8064
For as the *h* is high above the Ps 103:11 8064
of the *h* have their habitation Ps 104:12 8064
them with the bread of *h* Ps 105:40 8064
They mount up to the *h*, they go Ps 107:26 8064
behold the things that are in *h* Ps 113:6 8064
blessed of the LORD which made *h* Ps 115:15 8064
The *h*, even the heavens, are the Ps 115:16 8064
O LORD, thy word is settled in *h* Ps 119:89 8064
from the LORD, which made *h* Ps 121:2 8064
the name of the LORD, who made *h* Ps 124:8 8064
The LORD that made *h* and earth Ps 134:3 8064
LORD pleased, that did he in *h* Ps 135:6 8064
O give thanks unto the God of *h* Ps 136:26 8064
If I ascend up into *h*, thou art Ps 139:8 8064
Which made *h*, and earth, the sea, Ps 146:6 8064
Who covereth the *h* with clouds Ps 147:8 8064
his glory is above the earth and *h* Ps 148:13 8064
fly away as an eagle toward *h* Prov 23:5 8064
The *h* for height, and the earth Prov 25:3 8064
Who hath ascended up into *h* Prov 30:4 8064
all things that are done under *h* Eccl 1:13 8064
the *h* all the days of their life Eccl 2:3 8064
time to every purpose under the *h* Eccl 3:1 8064
for God is in *h*, and thou upon Eccl 5:2 8064
a far country, from the end of *h* Is 13:5 8064
For the stars of *h* and the Is 13:10 8064
How art thou fallen from *h* Is 14:12 8064
thine heart, I will ascend into *h* Is 14:13 8064
all the host of *h* shall be Is 34:4 8064
For my sword shall be bathed in *h* Is 34:5 8064
thou hast made *h* and earth Is 37:16 8064
meted out *h* with the span, and Is 40:12 8064
cometh down, and the snow from *h* Is 55:10 8064
Look down from *h*, and behold from Is 63:15 8064
The *h* is my throne, and the earth Is 66:1 8064
to make cakes to the queen of *h* Jer 7:18 8064
be meat for the fowls of the *h* Jer 7:33 8064
and the moon, and all the host of *h* Jer 8:2 8064
the stork in the *h* knoweth her Jer 8:7 8064
be not dismayed at the signs of *h* Jer 10:2 8064
to tear, and the fowls of the *h* Jer 15:3 8064
shall be meat for the fowls of *h* Jer 16:4 8064
to be meat for the fowls of the *h* Jer 19:7 8064
incense unto all the host of *h* Jer 19:13 8064
Do not I fill *h* and earth Jer 23:24 8064
If *h* above can be measured, and Jer 31:37 8064
behold, thou hast made the *h* Jer 32:17 8064
As the host of *h* cannot be Jer 33:22 8064
not appointed the ordinances of *h* Jer 33:25 8064
for meat unto the fowls of the *h* Jer 34:20 8064
burn incense unto the queen of *h* Jer 44:17 8064
to burn incense to the queen of *h* Jer 44:18 8064
burned incense to the queen of *h* Jer 44:19 8064
to burn incense to the queen of *h* Jer 44:25 8064
winds from the four quarters of *h* Jer 49:36 8064
for her judgment reacheth unto *h* Jer 51:9 8064
out the *h* by his understanding Jer 51:15 8064
Then the *h* and the earth, and all Jer 51:48 8064
Babylon should mount up to *h* Jer 51:53 8064
cast down from *h* unto the earth Lam 2:1 8064
LORD look down, and behold from *h* Lam 3:50 8064
swifter than the eagles of the *h* Lam 4:19 8064
me up between the earth and the *h* Eze 8:3 8064
field and to the fowls of the *h* Eze 29:5 8064
All the fowls of *h* made their Eze 31:6 8064
all the fowls of the *h* remain Eze 31:13 8064
of the *h* to remain upon thee Eze 32:4 8064
put thee out, I will cover the *h* Eze 32:7 8064
All the bright lights of *h* will I Eze 32:8 8064
of the sea, and the fowls of the *h* Eze 38:20 8064
God of *h* concerning this secret Dan 2:18 8065
Then Daniel blessed the God of *h* Dan 2:19 8065
But there is a God in *h* that Dan 2:28 8065
for the God of *h* hath given thee Dan 2:37 8065
the fowls of the *h* hath he given Dan 2:38 8065
the God of *h* set up a kingdom Dan 2:44 8065
the height thereof reached unto *h* Dan 4:11 8065
the fowls of the *h* dwelt in the Dan 4:12 8065
and an holy one came down from *h* Dan 4:13 8065
let it be wet with the dew of *h* Dan 4:15 8065
whose height reached unto the *h* Dan 4:20 8065
of the *h* had their habitation Dan 4:21 8065
is grown, and reacheth unto *h* Dan 4:22 8065
and an holy one coming down from *h* Dan 4:23 8065
let it be wet with the dew of *h* Dan 4:23 8065
shall wet thee with the dew of *h* Dan 4:25 8065
mouth, there fell a voice from *h* Dan 4:31 8065
body was wet with the dew of *h* Dan 4:33 8065
lifted up mine eyes unto *h* Dan 4:34 8065
to his will in the army of *h* Dan 4:35 8065
and extol and honour the King of *h* Dan 4:37 8065
body was wet with the dew of *h* Dan 5:21 8065
up thyself against the Lord of *h* Dan 5:23 8065
he worketh signs and wonders in *h* Dan 6:27 8065
the four winds of the *h* strove Dan 7:2 8065
of man came with the clouds of *h* Dan 7:13 8065
of the kingdom under the whole *h* Dan 7:27 8065
ones toward the four winds of *h* Dan 8:8 8064
great, even to the host of *h* Dan 8:10 8064
for under the whole *h* hath not Dan 9:12 8064
toward the four winds of *h* Dan 11:4 8064
hand and his left hand unto *h* Dan 12:7 8064
the field, and with the fowls of *h* Hos 2:18 8064
the field, and with the fowls of *h* Hos 4:3 8064

them down as the fowls of the *h*	Hos 7:12	8064
though they climb up to *h*	Amos 9:2	8064
buildeth his stories in the *h*	Amos 9:6	8064
and I fear the LORD, the God of *h*	Jonah 1:9	8064
merchants above the stars of *h*	Nah 3:16	8064
I will consume the fowls of the *h*	Zeph 1:3	8064
the host of *h* upon the housetops	Zeph 1:5	8064
Therefore the *h* over you is	Hag 1:10	8064
abroad as the four winds of the *h*	Zec 2:6	8064
ephah between the earth and the *h*	Zec 5:9	8064
not open you the windows of *h*	Mal 3:10	8064
for the kingdom of *h* is at hand	Mt 3:2	3772
And lo a voice from *h*, saying,	Mt 3:17	3772
for the kingdom of *h* is at hand	Mt 4:17	3772
for theirs is the kingdom of *h*	Mt 5:3	3772
for theirs is the kingdom of *h*	Mt 5:10	3772
for great is your reward in *h*	Mt 5:12	3772
glorify your Father which is in *h*	Mt 5:16	3772
For verily I say unto you, Till *h*	Mt 5:18	3772
the least in the kingdom of *h*	Mt 5:19	3772
called great in the kingdom of *h*	Mt 5:19	3772
case enter into the kingdom of *h*	Mt 5:20	3772
Swear not at all; neither by *h*	Mt 5:34	3772
of your Father which is in *h*	Mt 5:45	3772
Father which is in *h* is perfect	Mt 5:48	3772
of your Father which is in *h*	Mt 6:1	3772
Our Father which art in *h*	Mt 6:9	3772
be done in earth, as it is in *h*	Mt 6:10	3772
up for yourselves treasures in *h*	Mt 6:20	3772
h give good things to them that	Mt 7:11	3772
shall enter into the kingdom of *h*	Mt 7:21	3772
will of my Father which is in *h*	Mt 7:21	3772
and Jacob, in the kingdom of *h*	Mt 8:11	3772
The kingdom of *h* is at hand	Mt 10:7	3772
before my Father which is in *h*	Mt 10:32	3772
before my Father which is in *h*	Mt 10:33	3772
kingdom of *h* is greater than he	Mt 11:11	3772
kingdom of *h* suffereth violence	Mt 11:12	3772
which art exalted unto *h*	Mt 11:23	3772
I thank thee, O Father, Lord of *h*	Mt 11:25	3772
will of my Father which is in *h*	Mt 12:50	3772
the mysteries of the kingdom of *h*	Mt 13:11	3772
The kingdom of *h* is likened unto	Mt 13:24	3772
The kingdom of *h* is like to a	Mt 13:31	3772
The kingdom of *h* is like unto	Mt 13:33	3772
the kingdom of *h* is like unto	Mt 13:44	3772
the kingdom of *h* is like unto a	Mt 13:45	3772
the kingdom of *h* is like unto a	Mt 13:47	3772
h is like unto a man that is an	Mt 13:52	3772
two fishes, and looking up to *h*	Mt 14:19	3772
he would shew them a sign from *h*	Mt 16:1	3772
thee, but my Father which is in *h*	Mt 16:17	3772
thee the keys of the kingdom of *h*	Mt 16:19	3772
bind on earth shall be bound in *h*	Mt 16:19	3772
on earth shall be loosed in *h*	Mt 16:19	3772
the greatest in the kingdom of *h*	Mt 18:1	3772
not enter into the kingdom of *h*	Mt 18:3	3772
is greatest in the kingdom of *h*	Mt 18:4	3772
That in *h* their angels do always	Mt 18:10	3772
face of my Father which is in *h*	Mt 18:10	3772
will of your Father which is in *h*	Mt 18:14	3772
bind on earth shall be bound in *h*	Mt 18:18	3772
on earth shall be loosed in *h*	Mt 18:18	3772
them of my Father which is in *h*	Mt 18:19	3772
of *h* likened unto a certain king	Mt 18:23	3772
for of such is the kingdom of *h*	Mt 19:14	3772
and thou shalt have treasure in *h*	Mt 19:21	3772
enter into the kingdom of *h*	Mt 19:23	3772
For the kingdom of *h* is like unto	Mt 20:1	3772
from *h*, or of men	Mt 21:25	3772
saying, If we shall say, From *h*	Mt 21:25	3772
The kingdom of *h* is like unto a	Mt 22:2	3772
but are as the angels of God in *h*	Mt 22:30	3772
one is your Father, which is in *h*	Mt 23:9	3772
up the kingdom of *h* against men	Mt 23:13	3772
And he that shall swear by *h*	Mt 23:22	3772
and the stars shall fall from *h*	Mt 24:29	3772
the sign of the Son of man in *h*	Mt 24:30	3772
in the clouds of *h* with power	Mt 24:30	3772
from one end of *h* to the other	Mt 24:31	3772
H and earth shall pass away, but	Mt 24:35	3772
no man, no, not the angels of *h*	Mt 24:36	3772
Then shall the kingdom of *h* be	Mt 25:1	3772
For the kingdom of *h* is as a man	Mt 25:14	
and coming in the clouds of *h*	Mt 26:64	3772
of the Lord descended from *h*	Mt 28:2	3772
All power is given unto me in *h*	Mt 28:18	3772
And there came a voice from *h*	Mk 1:11	3772
the two fishes, he looked up to *h*	Mk 6:41	3772
And looking up to *h*, he sighed, and	Mk 7:34	3772
him, seeking of him a sign from *h*	Mk 8:11	3772
and thou shalt have treasure in *h*	Mk 10:21	3772
your Father also which is in *h*	Mk 11:25	3772
is in *h* forgive your trespasses	Mk 11:26	3772
baptism of John, was it from *h*	Mk 11:30	3772
saying, If we shall say, From *h*	Mk 11:31	3772
are as the angels which are in *h*	Mk 12:25	3772
And the stars of *h* shall fall	Mk 13:25	3772
that are in *h* shall be shaken	Mk 13:25	3772
earth to the uttermost part of *h*	Mk 13:27	3772
H and earth shall pass away	Mk 13:31	3772
no, not the angels which are in *h*	Mk 13:32	3772
and coming in the clouds of *h*	Mk 14:62	3772
them, he was received up into *h*	Mk 16:19	3772
were gone away from them into *h*	Lk 2:15	3772
and praying, the *h* was opened,	Lk 3:21	3772
upon him, and a voice came from *h*	Lk 3:22	3772
when the *h* was shut up three	Lk 4:25	3772
behold, your reward is great in *h*	Lk 6:23	3772
two fishes, and looking up to *h*	Lk 9:16	3772
command fire to come down from *h*	Lk 9:54	3772
Capernaum, which art exalted to *h*	Lk 10:15	3772
Satan as lightning fall from *h*	Lk 10:18	3772
your names are written in *h*	Lk 10:20	3772
I thank thee, O Father, Lord of *h*	Lk 10:21	3772
say, Our Father which art in *h*	Lk 11:2	3772
Thy will be done, as in *h*	Lk 11:2	3772
him, sought of him a sign from *h*	Lk 11:16	3772
that likewise joy shall be in *h*	Lk 15:7	3772
Father, I have sinned against *h*	Lk 15:18	3772
Father, I have sinned against *h*	Lk 15:21	3772
And it is easier for *h* and earth to	Lk 16:17	3772
out of the one part under *h*	Lk 17:24	3772
unto the other part under *h*	Lk 17:24	3772
rained fire and brimstone from *h*	Lk 17:29	3772
up so much as his eyes unto *h*	Lk 18:13	3772
and thou shalt have treasure in *h*	Lk 18:22	3772
peace in *h*, and glory in the	Lk 19:38	3772
baptism of John, was it from *h*	Lk 20:4	3772
saying, If we shall say, From *h*	Lk 20:5	3772
great signs shall there be from *h*	Lk 21:11	3772
the powers of *h* shall be shaken	Lk 21:26	3772
H and earth shall pass away	Lk 21:33	3772
appeared an angel unto him from *h*	Lk 22:43	3772
from them, and carried up into *h*	Lk 24:51	3772
descending from *h* like a dove	Jn 1:32	3772
Hereafter ye shall see *h* open	Jn 1:51	3772
And no man hath ascended up to *h*	Jn 3:13	3772
but he that came down from *h*	Jn 3:13	3772
even the Son of man which is in *h*	Jn 3:13	3772
except it be given him from *h*	Jn 3:27	3772
that cometh from *h* is above all	Jn 3:31	3772
He gave them bread from *h* to eat	Jn 6:31	3772
gave you not that bread from *h*	Jn 6:32	3772
giveth you the true bread from *h*	Jn 6:32	3772
is he which cometh down from *h*	Jn 6:33	3772
For I came down from *h*, not to do	Jn 6:38	3772
the bread which came down from *h*	Jn 6:41	3772
that he saith, I came down from *h*	Jn 6:42	3772
bread which cometh down from *h*	Jn 6:50	3772
bread which came down from *h*	Jn 6:51	3772
that bread which came down from *h*	Jn 6:58	3772
Then came there a voice from *h*	Jn 12:28	3772
Jesus, and lifted up his eyes to *h*	Jn 17:1	3772
stedfastly toward *h* as he went up	Acts 1:10	3772
why stand ye gazing up into *h*	Acts 1:11	3772
which is taken up from you into *h*	Acts 1:11	3772
as ye have seen him go into *h*	Acts 1:11	3772
there came a sound from *h* as of a	Acts 2:2	3772
men, out of every nation under *h*	Acts 2:5	3772
And I will shew wonders in *h* above	Acts 2:19	3772
Whom the *h* must receive until the	Acts 3:21	3772
name under *h* given among men	Acts 4:12	3772
thou art God, which hast made *h*	Acts 4:24	3772
them up to worship the host of *h*	Acts 7:42	3772
H is my throne, and earth is my	Acts 7:49	3772
looked up stedfastly into *h*	Acts 7:55	3772
round about him a light from *h*	Acts 9:3	3772
saw *h* opened, and a certain vessel	Acts 10:11	3772
was received up again into *h*	Acts 10:16	3772
let down from *h* by four corners	Acts 11:5	3772
voice answered me again from *h*	Acts 11:9	3772
and all were drawn up again into *h*	Acts 11:10	3772
unto the living God, which made *h*	Acts 14:15	3772
did good, and gave us rain from *h*	Acts 14:17	3771
seeing that he is Lord of *h*	Acts 17:24	3772
suddenly there shone from *h* a	Acts 22:6	3772
I saw in the way a light from *h*	Acts 26:13	3771
from *h* against all ungodliness	Rom 1:18	3772
heart, Who shall ascend into *h*	Rom 10:6	3772
whether in *h* or in earth, (as	1Cor 8:5	3772
the second man is the Lord from *h*	1Cor 15:47	3772
with our house which is from *h*	2Cor 5:2	3772
an one caught up to the third *h*	2Cor 12:2	3772
But though we, or an angel from *h*	Gal 1:8	3772
in Christ, both which are in *h*	Eph 1:10	3772
Of whom the whole family in *h*	Eph 3:15	3772
that your Master also is in *h*	Eph 6:9	3772
knee should bow, of things in *h*	Phil 2:10	2032
For our conversation is in *h*	Phil 3:20	3772
which is laid up for you in *h*	Col 1:5	3772
all things created, that are in *h*	Col 1:16	3772
things in earth, or things in *h*	Col 1:20	3772
every creature which is under *h*	Col 1:23	3772
that ye also have a Master in *h*	Col 4:1	3772
And to wait for his Son from *h*	1Th 1:10	3772
shall descend from *h* with a shout	1Th 4:16	3772
from *h* with his mighty angels	2Th 1:7	3772
but into *h* itself, now to appear	Heb 9:24	3772
that ye have in *h* a better	Heb 10:34	3772
firstborn, which are written in *h*	Heb 12:23	3772
from him that speaketh from *h*	Heb 12:25	3772
not the earth only, but also *h*	Heb 12:26	3772
brethren, swear not, neither by *h*	Jas 5:12	3772
the *h* gave rain, and the earth	Jas 5:18	3772
not away, reserved in *h* for you	1Pet 1:4	3772
the Holy Ghost sent down from *h*	1Pet 1:12	3772
Who is gone into *h*, and is on the	1Pet 3:22	3772
voice which came from *h* we heard	2Pet 1:18	3772
are three that bear record in *h*	1Jn 5:7	3772
cometh down out of *h* from my God	Rev 3:12	3772
behold, a door was opened in *h*	Rev 4:1	3772
and, behold, a throne was set in *h*	Rev 4:2	3772
And no man in *h*, nor in earth,	Rev 5:3	3772
And every creature which is in *h*	Rev 5:13	3772
the stars of *h* fell unto the	Rev 6:13	3772
the *h* departed as a scroll when	Rev 6:14	3772
there was silence in *h* about the	Rev 8:1	3772
and there fell a great star from *h*	Rev 8:10	3772
flying through the midst of *h*	Rev 8:13	3321
a star fall from *h* unto the earth	Rev 9:1	3772
mighty angel come down from *h*	Rev 10:1	3772
a voice from *h* saying unto me	Rev 10:4	3772
the earth lifted up his hand to *h*	Rev 10:5	3772
for ever and ever, who created *h*	Rev 10:6	3772
heard from *h* spake unto me again	Rev 10:8	3772
These have power to shut *h*	Rev 11:6	3772
voice from *h* saying unto them	Rev 11:12	3772
they ascended up to *h* in a cloud	Rev 11:12	3772
and gave glory to the God of *h*	Rev 11:13	3772
and there were great voices in *h*	Rev 11:15	3772
the temple of God was opened in *h*	Rev 11:19	3772
appeared a great wonder in *h*	Rev 12:1	3772
appeared another wonder in *h*	Rev 12:3	3772
the third part of the stars of *h*	Rev 12:4	3772
And there was war in *h*	Rev 12:7	3772
their place found any more in *h*	Rev 12:8	3772
I heard a loud voice saying in *h*	Rev 12:10	3772
and them that dwell in *h*	Rev 13:6	3772
h on the earth in the sight of	Rev 13:13	3772
And I heard a voice from *h*	Rev 14:2	3772
angel fly in the midst of *h*	Rev 14:6	3321
and worship him that made *h*	Rev 14:7	3772
a voice from *h* saying unto me	Rev 14:13	3772
out of the temple which is in *h*	Rev 14:17	3772
And I saw another sign in *h*	Rev 15:1	3772
of the testimony in *h* was opened	Rev 15:5	3772
blasphemed the God of *h* because	Rev 16:11	3772
voice out of the temple of *h*	Rev 16:17	3772
upon men a great hail out of *h*	Rev 16:21	3772
another angel come down from *h*	Rev 18:1	3772
And I heard another voice from *h*	Rev 18:4	3772
For her sins have reached unto *h*	Rev 18:5	3772
Rejoice over her, thou *h*, and ye	Rev 18:20	3772
a great voice of much people in *h*	Rev 19:1	3772
I saw *h* opened, and behold a white	Rev 19:11	3772
the armies which were in *h*	Rev 19:14	3772
fowls that fly in the midst of *h*	Rev 19:17	3321
I saw an angel come down from *h*	Rev 20:1	3772
fire came down from God out of *h*	Rev 20:9	3772
face the earth and the *h* fled away	Rev 20:11	3772
And I saw a new *h* and a new earth	Rev 21:1	3772
for the first *h* and the first	Rev 21:1	3772
coming down from God out of *h*	Rev 21:2	3772
a great voice out of *h* saying	Rev 21:3	3772
descending out of *h* from God	Rev 21:10	3772

HEAVENLY

your *h* Father will also forgive	Mt 6:14	3770
yet your *h* Father feedeth them	Mt 6:26	3770
for your *h* Father knoweth that	Mt 6:32	3770
which my *h* Father hath not	Mt 15:13	3770
So likewise shall my *h* Father do	Mt 18:35	2032
of the *h* host praising God	Lk 2:13	3770
how much more shall your *h* Father	Lk 11:13	
if I tell you of *h* things	Jn 3:12	2032
not disobedient unto the *h* vision	Acts 26:19	3770
and as is the *h*, such are they	1Cor 15:48	2032
such are they also that are *h*	1Cor 15:48	2032
also bear the image of the *h*	1Cor 15:49	2032
blessings in *h* places in Christ	Eph 1:3	2032
own right hand in the *h* places	Eph 1:20	2032
in *h* places in Christ Jesus	Eph 2:6	2032
powers in *h* places might be known	Eph 3:10	2032
preserve me unto his *h* kingdom	2Ti 4:18	2032
partakers of the *h* calling	Heb 3:1	2032
and have tasted of the *h* gift	Heb 6:4	2032
the example and shadow of *h* things	Heb 8:5	2032
but the *h* things themselves with	Heb 9:23	2032
a better country, that is, an *h*	Heb 11:16	2032
the *h* Jerusalem, and to an	Heb 12:22	2032

HEAVEN'S

eunuchs for the kingdom of *h* sake	Mt 19:12	3772

HEAVENS

Thus the *h* and the earth were	Gen 2:1	8064
are the generations of the *h*	Gen 2:4	8064
LORD God made the earth and the *h*	Gen 2:4	8064
the heaven of *h* is the LORD's thy	Deut 10:14	8064
Give ear, O ye *h*, and I will speak	Deut 32:1	8064
also his *h* shall drop down dew	Deut 33:28	8064
the *h* dropped, the clouds also	Judg 5:4	8064
He bowed the *h* also, and came down	2Sa 22:10	8064
heaven of *h* cannot contain thee	1Kin 8:27	8064
but the LORD made the *h*	1Chr 16:26	8064
Let the *h* be glad, and let the	1Chr 16:31	8064
Israel like to the stars of the *h*	1Chr 27:23	8064
heaven of *h* cannot contain him	2Chr 2:6	8064
the heaven of *h* cannot contain	2Chr 6:18	8064
Then hear thou from the *h*	2Chr 6:25	8064
Then hear thou from the *h*	2Chr 6:33	8064
hear thou from the *h* their prayer	2Chr 6:35	8064
Then hear thou from the *h*	2Chr 6:39	8064
trespass is grown up unto the *h*	Ezr 9:6	8064
hast made heaven, the heaven of *h*	Neh 9:6	8064
Which alone spreadeth out the *h*	Job 9:8	8064
till the *h* be no more, they shall	Job 14:12	8064
the *h* are not clean in his sight	Job 15:15	8064
his excellency mount up to the *h*	Job 20:6	8064
spirit he hath garnished the *h*	Job 26:13	8064
Look unto the *h*, and see	Job 35:5	8064
that sitteth in the *h* shall laugh	Ps 2:4	8064
hast set thy glory above the *h*	Ps 8:1	8064
When I consider thy *h*, the work	Ps 8:3	8064
He bowed the *h* also, and came down	Ps 18:9	8064
The LORD also thundered in the *h*	Ps 18:13	8064
The *h* declare the glory of God	Ps 19:1	8064
word of the LORD were the *h* made	Ps 33:6	8064
Thy mercy, O LORD, is in the *h*	Ps 36:5	8064
He shall call to the *h* from above	Ps 50:4	8064
And the *h* shall declare his	Ps 50:6	8064
thou exalted, O God, above the *h*	Ps 57:5	8064
For thy mercy is great unto the *h*	Ps 57:10	8064
thou exalted, O God, above the *h*	Ps 57:11	8064
rideth upon the *h* by his name JAH	Ps 68:4	6160
the *h* also dropped at the	Ps 68:8	8064
that rideth upon the *h* of *h*	Ps 68:33	8064
set their mouth against the *h*	Ps 73:9	8064
thou establish in the very *h*	Ps 89:2	8064
the *h* shall praise thy wonders, O	Ps 89:5	8064
The *h* are thine, the earth also	Ps 89:11	8064
but the LORD made the *h*	Ps 96:5	8064

Let the *h* rejoice, and let the ... Ps 96:11 8064
The *h* declare his righteousness, ... Ps 97:6 8064
the *h* are the work of thy hands ... Ps 102:25 8064
hath prepared his throne in the *h* ... Ps 103:19 8064
out the *h* like a curtain ... Ps 104:2 8064
thy mercy is great above the *h* ... Ps 108:4 8064
thou exalted, O God, above the *h* ... Ps 108:5 8064
nations, and his glory above the *h* ... Ps 113:4 8064
But our God is in the *h* ... Ps 115:3 8064
The heaven, even the *h*, are the ... Ps 115:16 8064
O thou that dwellest in the *h* ... Ps 123:1 8064
To him that by wisdom made the *h* ... Ps 136:5 8064
Bow thy *h*, O LORD, and come down ... Ps 144:5 8064
Praise ye the LORD from the *h* ... Ps 148:1 8064
Praise him, ye *h* of *h* ... Ps 148:4 8064
and ye waters that be above the *h* ... Ps 148:4 8064
hath he established the *h* ... Prov 3:19 8064
When he prepared the *h*, I was ... Prov 8:27 8064
Hear, O *h*, and give ear, O earth ... Is 1:2 8064
is darkened in the *h* thereof ... Is 5:30 6183
Therefore I will shake the *h* ... Is 13:13 8064
the *h* shall be rolled together as ... Is 34:4 8064
stretcheth out the *h* as a curtain ... Is 40:22 8064
the LORD, he that created the *h* ... Is 42:5 8064
Sing, O ye *h* ... Is 44:23 8064
that stretcheth forth the *h* alone ... Is 44:24 8064
Drop down, ye *h*, from above, and ... Is 45:8 8064
hands, have stretched out the *h* ... Is 45:12 8064
saith the LORD that created the *h* ... Is 45:18 8064
my right hand hath spanned the *h* ... Is 48:13 8064
Sing, O *h* ... Is 49:13 8064
I clothe the *h* with blackness, and ... Is 50:3 8064
Lift up your eyes to the *h* ... Is 51:6 8064
for the *h* shall vanish away like ... Is 51:6 8064
that hath stretched forth the *h* ... Is 51:13 8064
mine hand, that I may plant the *h* ... Is 51:16 8064
For as the *h* are higher than the ... Is 55:9 8064
Oh that thou wouldest rend the *h* ... Is 64:1 8064
For, behold, I create new *h* ... Is 65:17 8064
For as the new *h* and the new earth ... Is 66:22 8064
Be astonished, O ye *h*, at this, ... Jer 2:12 8064
and the *h*, and they had no light ... Jer 4:23 8064
all the birds of the *h* were fled ... Jer 4:25 8064
mourn, and the *h* above be black ... Jer 4:28 8064
both the fowl of the *h* and the ... Jer 9:10 8064
The gods that have not made the *h* ... Jer 10:11 8065
the earth, and from under these *h* ... Jer 10:11 8065
out the *h* by his discretion ... Jer 10:12 8064
is a multitude of waters in the *h* ... Jer 10:13 8064
or can the *h* give showers ... Jer 14:22 8064
is a multitude of waters in the *h* ... Jer 51:16 8064
with our hands unto God in the *h* ... Lam 3:41 8064
from under the *h* of the LORD ... Lam 3:66 8064
that the *h* were opened, and I saw ... Eze 1:1 8064
have known that the *h* do rule ... Dan 4:26 8065
saith the LORD, I will hear the *h* ... Hos 2:21 8064
the *h* shall tremble ... Joel 2:10 8064
And I will shew wonders in the *h* ... Joel 2:30 8064
and the *h* and the earth shall shake ... Joel 3:16 8064
His glory covered the *h*, and the ... Hab 3:3 8064
while, and I will shake the *h* ... Hag 2:6 8064
Judah, saying, I will shake the *h* ... Hag 2:21 8064
are the four spirits of the *h* ... Zec 6:5 8064
the *h* shall give their dew ... Zec 8:12 8064
which stretcheth forth the *h* ... Zec 12:1 8064
the *h* were opened unto him, and he ... Mt 3:16 *3772*
powers of the *h* shall be shaken ... Mt 24:29 *3772*
of the water, he saw the *h* opened ... Mk 1:10 *3772*
in the *h* that faileth not ... Lk 12:33 *3772*
David is not ascended into the *h* ... Acts 2:34 *3772*
said, Behold, I see the *h* opened ... Acts 7:56 *3772*
made with hands, eternal in the *h* ... 2Cor 5:1 *3772*
that ascended up far above all *h* ... Eph 4:10 *3772*
the *h* are the works of thine ... Heb 1:10 *3772*
priest, that is passed into the *h* ... Heb 4:14 *3772*
and made higher than the *h* ... Heb 7:26 *3772*
throne of the Majesty in the *h* ... Heb 8:1 *3772*
h should be purified with these ... Heb 9:23 *3772*
the word of God the *h* were of old ... 2Pet 3:5 *3772*
But the *h* and the earth, which are ... 2Pet 3:7 *3772*
in the which the *h* shall pass ... 2Pet 3:10 *3772*
wherein the *h* being on fire shall ... 2Pet 3:12 *3772*
to his promise, look for new *h* ... 2Pet 3:13 *3772*
Therefore rejoice, ye *h*, and ye ... Rev 12:12 *3772*

HEAVIER
For now it would be *h* than the ... Job 6:3 3513
my stroke is *h* than my groaning ... Job 23:2 3513
fool's wrath is *h* than them both ... Prov 27:3 3513

HEAVILY
wheels, that they drave them *h* ... Ex 14:25 3517
I bowed down *h*, as one that ... Ps 35:14 6957
hast thou very *h* laid thy yoke ... Is 47:6 3513

HEAVINESS
sacrifice I arose up from my *h* ... Ezr 9:5 8589
complaint, I will leave off my *h* ... Job 9:27 6440
and I am full of *h* ... Ps 69:20 5136
My soul melteth for *h* ... Ps 119:28 8424
son is the *h* of his mother ... Prov 10:1 8424
H in the heart of man maketh it ... Prov 12:25 1674
and the end of that mirth is *h* ... Prov 14:13 8424
Ariel, and there shall be *h* ... Is 29:2 8386
of praise for the spirit of *h* ... Is 61:3 3544
That I have great *h* and continual ... Rom 9:2 *3077*
would not come again to you in *h* ... 2Cor 2:1 *3077*
after you all, and was full of *h* ... Phil 2:26 *85*
to mourning, and your joy to *h* ... Jas 4:9 *2726*
ye are in *h* through manifold ... 1Pet 1:6 *3076*

HEAVY
But Moses' hands were *h* ... Ex 17:12 3515
for this thing is too *h* for thee ... Ex 18:18 3515
alone, because it is too *h* for me ... Num 11:14 3515
for he was an old man, and *h* ... 1Sa 4:18 3513
LORD was *h* upon them of Ashdod ... 1Sa 5:6 3513
the hand of God was very *h* there ... 1Sa 5:11 3513
because the hair was *h* on him ... 2Sa 14:26 3513
his *h* yoke which he put upon us, ... 1Kin 12:4 3515
Thy father made our yoke *h* ... 1Kin 12:10 3513
father did lade you with a *h* yoke ... 1Kin 12:11 3515
My father made your yoke *h* ... 1Kin 12:14 3513
I am sent to thee with *h* tidings ... 1Kin 14:6 7186
of Israel went to his house *h* ... 1Kin 20:43 5620
And Ahab came into his house *h* ... 1Kin 21:4 5620
his *h* yoke that he put upon us, ... 2Chr 10:4 3515
Thy father made our yoke *h* ... 2Chr 10:10 3513
my father put a *h* yoke upon you ... 2Chr 10:11 3515
My father made your yoke *h* ... 2Chr 10:14 3513
bondage was *h* upon this people ... Neh 5:18 3513
shall my hand be *h* upon thee ... Job 33:7 3513
and night thy hand was *h* upon me ... Ps 32:4 3513
as an *h* burden they are too *h* ... Ps 38:4 3515
burden they are too *h* for me ... Ps 38:4 3513
that singeth songs to an *h* heart ... Prov 25:20 7451
A stone is *h*, and the sand weighty ... Prov 27:3 3514
unto those that be of *h* hearts ... Prov 31:6 4751
people fat, and make their ears *h* ... Is 6:10 3513
thereof shall be *h* upon it ... Is 24:20 3513
anger, and the burden thereof is *h* ... Is 30:27 3514
your carriages were *h* loaden ... Is 46:1
wickedness, to undo the *h* burdens ... Is 58:6 4133
neither his ear *h*, that it cannot ... Is 59:1 3513
he hath made my chain *h* ... Lam 3:7 3513
are *h* laden, and I will give you ... Mt 11:28
For they bind *h* burdens and ... Mt 23:4 *926*
began to be sorrowful and very *h* ... Mt 26:37 *85*
for their eyes were *h* ... Mt 26:43 *916*
be sore amazed, and to be very *h* ... Mk 14:33 *85*
again, (for their eyes were *h* ... Mk 14:40 *916*
were with him were *h* with sleep ... Lk 9:32 *916*

HEBER (*he'-bur*) See EBER, HEBER'S, HEBERITES.
1. A son of Beriah.
H, and Malchiel ... Gen 46:17 2268
of *H*, the family of the Heberites ... Num 26:45 2268
H, and Malchiel, who is the father ... 1Chr 7:31 2268
H begat Japhlet, and Shomer, and ... 1Chr 7:32 2268
of Phalec, which was the son of *H* ... Lk 3:35 *1443*
2. Husband of Jael.
Now *H* the Kenite, which was of ... Judg 4:11 2268
of Jael the wife of *H* the Kenite ... Judg 4:17 2268
and the house of *H* the Kenite ... Judg 4:17 2268
Jael the wife of *H* the Kenite be ... Judg 5:24 2268
3. A son of Ezra.
H the father of Socho, and ... 1Chr 4:18 2268
4. A son of Elpaal.
and Meshullam, and Hezeki, and *H* ... 1Chr 8:17 2268
5. A head of a Gadite family.
and Jorai, and Jachan, and Zia, and *H*. 1Chr 5:13 5677
6. A son of Shashak.
And Ishpan, and *H*, and Eliel, ... 1Chr 8:22 5677

HEBERITES (*he'-bur-ites*) *Descendants of Heber.*
of Heber, the family of the *H* ... Num 26:45 2277

HEBER'S (*he'-burs*) *Refers to Heber 2.*
Then Jael *H* wife took a nail of ... Judg 4:21 2268

HEBREW (*he'-broo*) See HEBREWESS, HEBREWS.
1. Descendants of Jacob.
had escaped, and told Abram the *H* ... Gen 14:13 5680
in an *H* unto us to mock us ... Gen 39:14 5680
The *H* servant, which thou hast ... Gen 39:17 5680
there with us a young man, an *H* ... Gen 41:12 5680
of Egypt spake to the *H* midwives ... Ex 1:15 5680
of a midwife to the *H* women ... Ex 1:16 5680
Because the *H* women are not as ... Ex 1:19 5680
to thee a nurse of the *H* women ... Ex 2:7 5680
he spied an Egyptian smiting an *H* ... Ex 2:11 5680
If thou buy an *H* servant, six ... Ex 21:2 5680
an *H* man, or an *H* woman, be ... Deut 15:12 5680
being an *H* or an Hebrewess, go ... Jer 34:9 5680
ye go every man his brother an *H* ... Jer 34:14 5680
And he said unto them, I am an *H* ... Jonah 1:9 5680
of Benjamin, an *H* of the Hebrews ... Phil 3:5 *1446*
2. A language.
letters of Greek, and Latin, and *H* ... Lk 23:38 *1444*
called in the *H* tongue Bethesda ... Jn 5:2 *1447*
called the Pavement, but in the *H* ... Jn 19:13 *1447*
which is called in the *H* Golgotha ... Jn 19:17 *1447*
and it was written in *H*, and Greek, ... Jn 19:20 *1447*
spake unto them in the *H* tongue ... Acts 21:40 *1446*
he spake in the *H* tongue to them ... Acts 22:2 *1446*
me, and saying in the *H* tongue ... Acts 26:14 *1446*
name in the *H* tongue is Abaddon ... Rev 9:11 *1447*
called in the *H* tongue Armageddon ... Rev 16:16 *1447*

HEBREWESS (*he'-broo-ess*)
being an Hebrew or an *H*, go free ... Jer 34:9 5680

HEBREWS (*he'-brooz*) See HEBREWS'.
away out of the land of the *H* ... Gen 40:15 5680
might not eat bread with the *H* ... Gen 43:32 5680
two men of the *H* strove together ... Ex 2:13 5680
God of the *H* hath met with us ... Ex 3:18 5680
The God of the *H* hath met with us ... Ex 5:3 5680
The LORD God of the *H* hath sent ... Ex 7:16 5680
Thus saith the LORD God of the *H* ... Ex 9:1 5680
Thus saith the LORD God of the *H* ... Ex 9:13 5680
Thus saith the LORD God of the *H* ... Ex 10:3 5680
great shout in the camp of the *H* ... 1Sa 4:6 5680
ye be not servants unto the *H* ... 1Sa 4:9 5680
the land, saying, Let the *H* hear ... 1Sa 13:3 5680
some of the *H* went over Jordan to ... 1Sa 13:7 5680
Lest the *H* make them swords or ... 1Sa 13:19 5680
the *H* come forth out of the holes ... 1Sa 14:11 5680
Moreover the *H* that were with the ... 1Sa 14:21 5680
Philistines, What do these *H* here ... 1Sa 29:3 5680
of the Grecians against the *H* ... Acts 6:1 *1445*
Are they *H* ... 2Cor 11:22 *1445*
of Benjamin, an Hebrew of the *H* ... Phil 3:5 *1445*
Written to the *H* from Italy by ... Heb *s*

HEBREWS' (*he'-brooz*)
This is one of the *H* children ... Ex 2:6 5680

HEBRON (*he'-brun*) See HEBRONITES.
1. A city in Asher.
And *H*, and Rehob, and Hammon, and Josh 19:28 2275
2. A city in Judah.
the plain of Mamre, which is in *H* ... Gen 13:18 2275
the same is *H* in the land of ... Gen 23:2 2275
the same is *H* in the land of ... Gen 23:19 2275
the city of Arbah, which is *H* ... Gen 35:27 2275
he sent him out of the vale of *H* ... Gen 37:14 2275
by the south, and came unto *H* ... Num 13:22 2275
(Now *H* was built seven years ... Num 13:22 2275
sent unto Hoham king of *H* ... Josh 10:3 2275
king of Jerusalem, the king of *H* ... Josh 10:5 2275
king of Jerusalem, the king of *H* ... Josh 10:23 2275
and all Israel with him, unto *H* ... Josh 10:36 2275
as he had done to *H*, so he did to ... Josh 10:39 2275
from the mountains, from *H* ... Josh 11:21 2275
the king of *H*, one ... Josh 12:10 2275
of Jephunneh *H* for an inheritance ... Josh 14:13 2275
H therefore became the ... Josh 14:14 2275
And the name of *H* before was ... Josh 14:15 2275
father of Anak, which city is *H* ... Josh 15:13 2275
and Kirjath-arba, which is *H* ... Josh 15:54 2275
and Kirjath-arba, which is *H* ... Josh 20:7 2275
father of Anak, which city is *H* ... Josh 21:11 2275
the priest *H* with her suburbs ... Josh 21:13 2275
the Canaanites that dwelt in *H* ... Judg 1:10 2275
(now the name of *H* before was ... Judg 1:10 2275
they gave *H* unto Caleb, as Moses ... Judg 1:20 2275
top of an hill that is before *H* ... Judg 16:3 2275
And to them which were in *H* ... 1Sa 30:31 2275
And he said, Unto *H* ... 2Sa 2:1 2275
and they dwelt in the cities of *H* ... 2Sa 2:3 2275
in *H* over the house of Judah was ... 2Sa 2:11 2275
they came to *H* at break of day ... 2Sa 2:32 2275
And unto David were sons born in *H* ... 2Sa 3:2 2275
These were born to David in *H* ... 2Sa 3:5 2275
speak in the ears of David in *H* ... 2Sa 3:19 2275
So Abner came to David to *H* ... 2Sa 3:20 2275
but Abner was not with David in *H* ... 2Sa 3:22 2275
And when Abner was returned to *H* ... 2Sa 3:27 2275
And they buried Abner in *H* ... 2Sa 3:32 2275
heard that Abner was dead in *H* ... 2Sa 4:1 2275
of Ish-bosheth unto David to *H* ... 2Sa 4:8 2275
hanged them up over the pool in *H* ... 2Sa 4:12 2275
it in the sepulchre of Abner in *H* ... 2Sa 4:12 2275
tribes of Israel to David unto *H* ... 2Sa 5:1 2275
of Israel came to the king to *H* ... 2Sa 5:3 2275
with them in *H* before the LORD ... 2Sa 5:3 2275
In *H* he reigned over Judah seven ... 2Sa 5:5 2275
after he was come from *H* ... 2Sa 5:13 2275
I have vowed unto the LORD, in *H* ... 2Sa 15:7 2275
So he arose, and went to *H* ... 2Sa 15:9 2275
shall say, Absalom reigneth in *H* ... 2Sa 15:10 2275
seven years reigned he in *H* ... 1Kin 2:11 2275
which were born unto him in *H* ... 1Chr 3:1 2275
Amram, Izhar, and *H*, and Uzziel ... 1Chr 6:2 2275
they gave them *H* in the land of ... 1Chr 6:55 2275
the cities of Judah, namely, *H* ... 1Chr 6:57 2275
themselves to David unto *H* ... 1Chr 11:1 2275
elders of Israel to the king to *H* ... 1Chr 11:3 2275
with them in *H* before the LORD ... 1Chr 11:3 2275
to the war, and came to David to *H* ... 1Chr 12:23 2275
came with a perfect heart to *H* ... 1Chr 12:38 2275
seven years reigned he in *H* ... 1Chr 29:27 2275
And Zorah, and Aijalon, and *H* ... 2Chr 11:10 2275
3. A son of Kohath.
Amram, and Izhar, and *H*, and Uzziel .. Ex 6:18 2275
Amram, and Izehar, *H*, and Uzziel ... Num 3:19 2275
These six were born unto him in *H* ... 1Chr 3:4 2275
were, Amram, and Izhar, and *H* ... 1Chr 6:18 2275
Amram, Izhar, *H*, and Uzziel, four ... 1Chr 23:12 2275
Of the sons of *H* ... 1Chr 23:19 2275
And the sons of *H* ... 1Chr 24:23
4. A son of Mareshah.
sons of Mareshah the father of *H* ... 1Chr 2:42 2275
And the sons of *H* ... 1Chr 2:43 2275
Of the sons of *H* ... 1Chr 15:9 2275

HEBRONITES (*he'-brun-ites*) *Descendants of Hebron 3.*
and the family of the *H*, and the ... Num 3:27 2276
the Libnites, the family of the *H* ... Num 26:58 2276
and the Izharites, the *H*, and the ... 1Chr 26:23 2276
And of the *H*, Hashabiah and his ... 1Chr 26:30 2276
Among the *H* was Jerijah the chief ... 1Chr 26:31 2276
even among the *H*, according to the ... 1Chr 26:31 2276

HEDGE
Hast not thou made an *h* about him ... Job 1:10 7753
slothful man is as an *h* of thorns ... Prov 15:19 4881
and whoso breaketh an *h*, a serpent ... Eccl 10:8 1447
I will take away the *h* thereof ... Is 5:5 4881
neither made up the *h* for the ... Eze 13:5 1447
them, that should make up the *h* ... Eze 22:30 1447
I will *h* up thy way with thorns, ... Hos 2:6 7753
upright is sharper than a thorn *h* ... Mic 7:4 4534
set an *h* about it, and digged a ... Mk 12:1 *5418*

HEDGED
way is hid, and whom God hath *h* in ... Job 3:23 5526
He hath *h* me about, that I cannot ... Lam 3:7 1443
h it round about, and digged a ... Mt 21:33

HEDGES
that dwelt among plants and *h* ... 1Chr 4:23 1448
hast thou then broken down her *h* ... Ps 80:12 1447
Thou hast broken down all his *h* ... Ps 89:40 1448
lament, and run to and fro by the *h* ... Jer 49:3 1448
camp in the *h* in the cold day ... Nah 3:17 1448
Go out into the highways and *h* ... Lk 14:23 *5418*

H

HEED
Take h that thou speak not to Gen 31:24 8104
Take thou h that thou speak not Gen 31:29 8104
take h to thyself, see my face no Ex 10:28 8104
Take h to yourselves, that ye go Ex 19:12 8104
Take h to thyself, lest thou make Ex 34:12 8104
Must I not take h to speak that Num 23:12 8104
take ye good h unto yourselves Deut 2:4 8104
Only take h to thyself, and keep Deut 4:9 8104
therefore good h unto yourselves Deut 4:15 8104
Take h unto yourselves, lest ye Deut 4:23 8104
Take h to yourselves, that your Deut 11:16 8104
Take h to thyself that thou offer Deut 12:13 8104
Take h to thyself that thou Deut 12:19 8104
Take h to thyself that thou be Deut 12:30 8104
Take h in the plague of leprosy, Deut 24:8 8104
unto all Israel, saying, Take h Deut 27:9 5535
But take diligent h to do the Josh 22:5 8104
Take good h therefore unto Josh 23:11 8104
take h to thyself until the 1Sa 19:2 8104
But Amasa took no h to the sword 2Sa 20:10 8104
thy children take h to their way 1Kin 2:4 8104
thy children take h to their way 1Kin 8:25 8104
But Jehu took no h to walk in the 2Kin 10:31 8104
if thou takest h to fulfil the 1Chr 22:13 8104
Take h now 1Chr 28:10 7200
yet so that thy children take h 2Chr 6:16 8104
to the judges, Take h what ye do 2Chr 19:6 7200
take h and do it 2Chr 19:7 8104
so that they will take h to do 2Chr 33:8 8104
Take h now that ye fail not to do Ezr 4:22 2095
Take h, regard not iniquity Job 36:21 8104
I said, I will take h to my ways Ps 39:1 8104
by taking h thereto according to Ps 119:9 8104
doer giveth h to false lips Prov 17:4 7181
Also take no h unto all words Eccl 7:21 3820
yea, he gave good h, and sought Eccl 12:9 238
And say unto him, Take h, and be Is 7:4 8104
hearkened diligently with much h Is 21:7 7182
Take ye h every one of his Jer 9:4 8104
Take h to yourselves, and bear no Jer 17:21 8104
let us not give h to any of his Jer 18:18 7181
Give h to me, O LORD, and hearken Jer 18:19 7181
left off to take h to the LORD Hos 4:10 8104
Therefore take h to your spirit Mal 2:15 8104
therefore take h to your spirit Mal 2:16 8104
Take h that ye do not your alms Mt 6:1 4337
Then Jesus said unto them, Take h Mt 16:6 3708
Take h that ye despise not one of Mt 18:10 3708
Take h that no man deceive you Mt 24:4 991
unto them, Take h what ye hear Mk 4:24 991
he charged them, saying, Take h Mk 8:15 3708
Take h lest any man deceive you Mk 13:5 991
But take h to yourselves Mk 13:9 991
But take ye h Mk 13:23 991
Take ye h, watch and pray Mk 13:33 991
Take h therefore how ye hear Lk 8:18 991
Take h therefore that the light Lk 11:35 4648
And he said unto them, Take h Lk 12:15 3708
Take h to yourselves Lk 17:3 4337
Take h that ye be not deceived Lk 21:8 991
take h to yourselves, lest at any Lk 21:34 4337
he gave h unto them, expecting to Acts 3:5 1907
take h to yourselves what ye Acts 5:35 4337
h unto those things which Philip Acts 8:6 4337
To whom they all gave h, from the Acts 8:10 4337
Take h therefore unto yourselves, Acts 20:28 4337
saying, Take h what thou doest Acts 22:26 3708
take h lest he also spare not Rom 11:21
But let every man take h how he 1Cor 3:10 991
But take h lest by any means this 1Cor 8:9 991
he standeth take h lest he fall 1Cor 10:12 991
take h that ye be not consumed Gal 5:15 991
Take h to the ministry which thou Col 4:17 991
Neither give h to fables and 1Ti 1:4 4337
giving h to seducing spirits, and 1Ti 4:1 4337
Take h unto thyself, and unto the 1Ti 4:16 1907
Not giving h to Jewish fables, and Titus 1:14 4337
h to the things which we have Heb 2:1 4337
Take h, brethren, lest there be Heb 3:12 991
ye do well that ye take h 2Pet 1:19 433

HEEL
head, and thou shalt bruise his h Gen 3:15 6119
and his hand took hold on Esau's h Gen 25:26 6119
The gin shall take him by the h Job 18:9 6119
hath lifted up his h against me Ps 41:9 6119
his brother by the h in the womb Hos 12:3 6117
hath lifted up his h against me Jn 13:18 4418

HEELS
the path, that biteth the horse h Gen 49:17 6119
a print upon the h of my feet Job 13:27 8328
of my h shall compass me about Ps 49:5 6120
discovered, and thy h made bare Jer 13:22 6119

HEGAI (he'-gahee) See HEGE. *Servant of King Ahasuerus.*
the palace, to the custody of H Est 2:8 1896
king's house, to the custody of H Est 2:8 1896
but what H the king's chamberlain Est 2:15 1896

HEGE (he'-ghe) See HEGAI. *Same as Hegai.*
unto the custody of H the king's Est 2:3 1896

HEIFER
Take me an h of three years old, Gen 15:9 5697
bring thee a red h without spot Num 19:2 6510
one shall burn the h in his sight Num 19:5 6510
the midst of the burning of the h Num 19:6 6510
gather up the ashes of the h Num 19:9 6510
of the h shall wash his clothes Num 19:10 6510
burnt h of purification for sin Num 19:17
of that city shall take an h Deut 21:3 5697
down the h unto a rough valley Deut 21:4 5697
h that is beheaded in the valley Deut 21:6 5697
If ye had not plowed with my h Judg 14:18 5697
Take an h with thee, and say, I am 1Sa 16:2 5697
Zoar, an h of three years old Is 15:5 5697
Egypt is like a very fair h Jer 46:20 5697
as an h of three years old Jer 48:34 5697
are grown fat as the h at grass Jer 50:11 5697
slideth back as a backsliding h Hos 4:16 6510
Ephraim is as an h that is taught Hos 10:11 5697
the ashes of an h sprinkling the Heb 9:13 1151

HEIFER'S
shall strike off the h neck there Deut 21:4 5697

HEIGHT
the h of it thirty cubits Gen 6:15 6967
a cubit and a half the h thereof Ex 25:10 6967
a cubit and a half the h thereof Ex 25:23 6967
the h thereof shall be three Ex 27:1 6967
the h five cubits of fine twined Ex 27:18 6967
two cubits shall be the h thereof Ex 30:2 6967
and a cubit and a half the h of it Ex 37:1 6967
a cubit and a half the h thereof Ex 37:10 6967
and two cubits was the h of it Ex 37:25 6967
and three cubits the h thereof Ex 38:1 6967
the h in the breadth was five Ex 38:18 6967
or on the h of his stature 1Sa 16:7 1364
whose h was six cubits and a span 1Sa 17:4 1363
the h thereof thirty cubits 1Kin 6:2 6967
and twenty cubits in the h thereof 1Kin 6:20 6967
The h of the one cherub was ten 1Kin 6:26 6967
the h thereof thirty cubits, upon 1Kin 7:2 6967
the h of the one chapiter was 1Kin 7:16 6967
the h of the other chapiter was 1Kin 7:16 6967
about, and his h was five cubits 1Kin 7:23 6967
and three cubits the h of it 1Kin 7:27 6967
the h of a wheel was a cubit and 1Kin 7:32 6967
come up to the h of the mountains 2Kin 19:23 4791
The h of the one pillar was 2Kin 25:17 6967
the h of the chapiter three 2Kin 25:17 6967
the h was an hundred and twenty 2Chr 3:4 1363
and ten cubits the h thereof 2Chr 4:1 6967
and five cubits the h thereof 2Chr 4:2 6967
and raised it up a very great h 2Chr 33:14 1361
the h thereof threescore cubits, Ezr 6:3 7312
Is not God in the h of heaven Job 22:12 1363
behold the h of the stars, how Job 22:12 7218
down from the h of his sanctuary Ps 102:19 4791
The heaven for h, and the earth Prov 25:3 7312
in the depth, or in the h above Is 7:11 1361
come up to the h of the mountains Is 37:24 4791
enter into the h of his border Is 37:24 4791
come and sing in the h of Zion Jer 31:12 4791
that holdest the h of the hill Jer 49:16 4791
fortify the h of her strength Jer 51:53 4791
the h of one pillar was eighteen Jer 52:21 6967
the h of one chapiter was five Jer 52:22 6967
In the mountain of the h of Eze 17:23 4791
she appeared in her h with the Eze 19:11 1363
the mountain of the h of Israel Eze 20:40 4791
Therefore his h was exalted above Eze 31:5 6967
thou hast lifted up thyself in h Eze 31:10 6967
his heart is lifted up in his h Eze 31:10 1363
exalt themselves for their h Eze 31:14 6967
their trees stand up in their h Eze 31:14 1363
and fill the valleys with thy h Eze 32:5 7419
and the h, one reed Eze 40:5 6967
I saw also the h of the house Eze 41:8 1364
whose h was threescore cubits, and Dan 3:1 7314
earth, and the h thereof was great Dan 4:10 7314
the h thereof reached unto heaven Dan 4:11 7314
whose h reached unto the heaven, Dan 4:20 7314
whose h was like the h of Amos 2:9 1363
was like the h of the cedars Amos 2:9 1363
Nor h, nor depth, nor any other Rom 8:39 5313
and length, and depth, and h Eph 3:18 5311
breadth and the h of it are equal Rev 21:16 5311

HEIGHTS
praise him in the h Ps 148:1 4791
ascend above the h of the clouds Is 14:14 1116

HEINOUS
For this is an h crime Job 31:11 2154

HEIR
one born in my house is mine h Gen 15:3 3423
saying, This shall not be thine h Gen 15:4 3423
thine own bowels shall be thine h Gen 15:4 3423
shall not be h with my son Gen 21:10 3423
and we will destroy the h also 2Sa 14:7 3423
that is h to her mistress Prov 30:23 3423
hath he no h? Jer 49:1 3423
then shall Israel be h unto them Jer 49:2 3423
Yet will I bring an h unto thee Mic 1:15 3423
among themselves, This is the h Mt 21:38 2818
among themselves, This is the h Mk 12:7 2818
themselves, saying, This is the h Lk 20:14 2818
he should be the h of the world Rom 4:13 2818
Now I say, That the h, as long as Gal 4:1 2818
then an h of God through Christ Gal 4:7 2818
of the bondwoman shall not be h Gal 4:30 2816
he hath appointed h of all things Heb 1:2 2818
became h of the righteousness Heb 11:7 2818

HEIRS
be heir unto them that were his h Jer 49:2 3423
if they which are of the law be h Rom 4:14 2818
And if children, then h Rom 8:17 2818
h of God, and joint-heirs with Rom 8:17 2818
h according to the promise Gal 3:29 2818
we should be made h according to Titus 3:7 2818
them who shall be h of salvation Heb 1:14 2816
abundantly to shew unto the h of Heb 6:17 2818
the h with him of the same Heb 11:9 4789
h of the kingdom which he hath Jas 2:5 2818
as being h together of the grace 1Pet 3:7 4789

HELAH (he'-lah) *A wife of Asher.*
father of Tekoa had two wives, H 1Chr 4:5 2458
And the sons of H were, Zereth, and 1Chr 4:7 2458

HELAM (he'-lam) *A place east of the Jordan.*
and they came to H 2Sa 10:16 2431
passed over Jordan, and came to H 2Sa 10:17 2431

HELBAH (hel'-bah) *A town in Asher.*
of Ahlab, nor of Achzib, nor of H Judg 1:31 2462

HELBON (hel'-bon) *A city near Damascus.*
in the wine of H, and white wool Eze 27:18 2463

HELD
man wondering at her h his peace Gen 24:21 2790
Jacob h his peace until they were Gen 34:5 2790
he h up his father's hand, to Gen 48:17 8557
when Moses h up his hand, that Ex 17:11 7311
the loops h one curtain to Ex 36:12 6901
And Aaron h his peace Lev 10:3 1826
h his peace at her in the day Num 30:7 2790
h his peace at her, and disallowed Num 30:11 2790
because he h his peace at her in Num 30:14 2790
h the lamps in their left hands, Judg 7:20 2388
the lad that h him by the hand Judg 16:26 2388
And when she h it, he measured six Ruth 3:15 270
But he h his peace 1Sa 10:27 2790
he h a feast in his house, like 1Sa 25:36
for Joab h back the people 2Sa 18:16 2820
And at that time Solomon h a feast 1Kin 8:65 6213
But the people h their peace 2Kin 18:36 2790
and h three thousand baths 2Chr 4:5 3557
half of them h both the spears Neh 4:16 2388
and with the other hand h a weapon Neh 4:17 2388
half of them h the spears from Neh 4:21 2388
Then h they their peace, and found Neh 5:8 2790
the king h out to Esther the Est 5:2 3447
I had h my tongue, although the Est 7:4 2790
Then the king h out the golden Est 8:4 3447
My foot hath h his steps, his way Job 23:11 270
The nobles h their peace, and Job 29:10 2244
whose mouth must be h in with bit Ps 32:9 1102
I h my peace, even from good Ps 39:2 2814
thy mercy, O LORD, h me up Ps 94:18 5582
I h him, and would not let him go, Song 3:4 270
the king is h in the galleries Song 7:5 631
But they h their peace, and Is 36:21 2790
have not I h my peace even of old Is 57:11 2814
took them captives h them fast Jer 50:33 2388
when he h up his right hand and Dan 12:7 7311
h a council against him, how they Mt 12:14 2983
But Jesus h his peace Mt 26:63 4623
h him by the feet, and worshipped Mt 28:9 2902
But they h their peace Mk 3:4 4623
But they h their peace Mk 9:34 4623
But he h his peace, and answered Mk 14:61 4623
the morning the chief priests h a Mk 15:1 4160
And they h their peace Lk 14:4 2270
at his answer, and h their peace Lk 20:26 4601
the men that h Jesus mocked him, Lk 22:63 4912
lame man which was healed h Peter Acts 3:11 2902
they h their peace, and glorified Acts 11:18 2270
part h with the Jews, and part Acts 14:4 2258
And after they had h their peace Acts 15:13 4601
that being dead wherein we were h Rom 7:6 2722
and for the testimony which they h Rev 6:9 2192

HELDAI (hel'-dahee) See HELED, HELEM.
1. A sanctuary servant.
month was H the Netophathite 1Chr 27:15 2469
2. An honored exile.
them of the captivity, even of H Zec 6:10 2469

HELEB (he'-leb) See HELED. *A "mighty man" of David.*
H the son of Baanah, a 2Sa 23:29 2460

HELECH See HELEK.

HELED (he'-led) See HELEB, HELDAI. *Same as Heleb.*
H the son of Baanah the 1Chr 11:30 2466

HELEK (he'-lek) See HELEKITES. *A son of Gilead.*
of H, the family of the Helekites Num 26:30 2507
Abiezer, and for the children of H Josh 17:2 2507

HELEKITES (he'-lek-ites) *Descendants of Helek.*
of Helek, the family of the H Num 26:30 2516

HELEM (he'-lem)
1. A descendant of Asher.
And the sons of his brother H 1Chr 7:35 2494
2. Same as Heldai.
And the crowns shall be to H Zec 6:14 2494

HELEPH (he'-lef) *A town in Naphtali.*
And their coast was from H Josh 19:33 2501

HELEZ (he'-lez)
1. A "mighty man" of David.
H the Paltite, Ira the son of 2Sa 23:26 2503
the Harorite, H the Pelonite, 1Chr 11:27 2503
seventh month was H the Pelonite 1Chr 27:10 2503
2. A son of Azariah.
And Azariah begat H, and Helez 1Chr 2:39 2503
begat Helez, and H begat Eleasah, 1Chr 2:39 2503

HELI (he'-li) See ELI. *Father of Joseph; ancestor of Jesus.*
of Joseph, which was the son of H Lk 3:23 2242

HELKAI (hel'-kahee) *A priest.*
Adna; of Meraioth, H Neh 12:15 2517

HELKATH (hel'-kath) See HELKATH-HAZZURIM, HUKOK. *A town in Asher.*
And their border was H, and Hali, Josh 19:25 2520
H with her suburbs, and Rehob with Josh 21:31 2520

HELKATH-HAZZURIM (*hel''-kath-haz'zu-rim*) *A plain near the pool of Gibeon.*
wherefore that place was called *H* 2Sa 2:16 2521

HELL
and shall burn unto the lowest *h* Deut 32:22 7585
The sorrows of *h* compassed me 2Sa 22:6 7585
deeper than *h* Job 11:8 7585
H is naked before him, and Job 26:6 7585
The wicked shall be turned into *h* Ps 9:17 7585
thou wilt not leave my soul in *h* Ps 16:10 7585
The sorrows of *h* compassed me Ps 18:5 7585
and let them go down quick into *h* Ps 55:15 7585
my soul from the lowest *h* Ps 86:13 7585
the pains of *h* gat hold upon me Ps 116:3 7585
if I make my bed in *h*, behold, Ps 139:8 7585
her steps take hold on *h* Prov 5:5 7585
Her house is the way to *h* Prov 7:27 7585
her guests are in the depths of *h* Prov 9:18 7585
H and destruction are before the Prov 15:11 7585
that he may depart from *h* beneath Prov 15:24 7585
and shalt deliver his soul from *h* Prov 23:14 7585
H and destruction are never full Prov 27:20 7585
Therefore *h* hath enlarged herself Is 5:14 7585
H from beneath is moved for thee Is 14:9 7585
thou shalt be brought down to *h* Is 14:15 7585
with *h* are we at agreement Is 28:15 7585
agreement with *h* shall not stand Is 28:18 7585
didst debase thyself even unto *h* Is 57:9 7585
when I cast him down to *h* with Eze 31:16 7585
They also went down into *h* with Eze 31:17 7585
of *h* with them that help him Eze 32:21 7585
which are gone down to *h* with Eze 32:27 7585
Though they dig into *h*, thence Amos 9:2 7585
out of the belly of *h* cried I Jonah 2:2 7585
who enlargeth his desire as *h* Hab 2:5 7585
shall be in danger of *h* fire Mt 5:22 *1067*
whole body should be cast into *h* Mt 5:29 *1067*
whole body should be cast into *h* Mt 5:30 *1067*
to destroy both soul and body in *h* Mt 10:28 *1067*
shalt be brought down to *h* Mt 11:23 *86*
the gates of *h* shall not prevail Mt 16:18 *86*
two eyes to be cast into *h* fire Mt 18:9 *1067*
the child of *h* than yourselves Mt 23:15 *1067*
can ye escape the damnation of *h* Mt 23:33 *1067*
having two hands to go into *h* Mk 9:43 *1067*
having two feet to be cast into *h* Mk 9:45 *1067*
two eyes to be cast into *h* fire Mk 9:47 *1067*
heaven, shalt be thrust down to *h* Lk 10:15 *86*
killed hath power to cast into *h* Lk 12:5 *1067*
in *h* he lift up his eyes, being Lk 16:23 *86*
thou wilt not leave my soul in *h* Acts 2:27 *86*
that his soul was not left in *h* Acts 2:31 *86*
and it is set on fire of *h* Jas 3:6 *1067*
sinned, but cast them down to *h* 2Pet 2:4 *5020*
and have the keys of *h* and of death Rev 1:18 *86*
was Death, and *H* followed with him Rev 6:8 *86*
h delivered up the dead which Rev 20:13 *86*
h were cast into the lake of fire Rev 20:14 *86*

HELLENISTS See GRECIANS.

HELM
turned about with a very small *h* Jas 3:4 *4079*

HELMET
he had an *h* of brass upon his 1Sa 17:5 3553
he put an *h* of brass upon his 1Sa 17:38 6959
an *h* of salvation upon his head Is 59:17 3553
and shield and *h* round about Eze 23:24 6959
hanged the shield and *h* in thee Eze 27:10 3553
all of them with shield and *h* Eze 38:5 3553
take the *h* of salvation, and the Eph 6:17 *4030*
and for an *h*, the hope of 1Th 5:8 *4030*

HELMETS
the host shields, and spears, and *h* 2Chr 26:14 3553
and stand forth with your *h* Jer 46:4 3553

HELON (*he'-lon*) *Father of Eliab.*
Eliab the son of *H* Num 1:9 2497
Eliab the son of *H* shall be Num 2:7 2497
the third day Eliab the son of *H* Num 7:24 2497
offering of Eliab the son of *H* Num 7:29 2497
of Zebulun was Eliab the son of *H* Num 10:16 2497

HELP
I will make him an *h* meet for him Gen 2:18 5828
was not found an *h* meet for him Gen 2:20 5828
of thy father, who shall *h* thee Gen 49:25 5826
of my father, said he, was mine *h* Ex 18:4 5828
and wouldest forbear to *h* him Ex 23:5 5800
thou shalt surely *h* with him Ex 23:5 5800
thou shalt surely *h* him to lift Deut 22:4 6965
h you, and be your protection Deut 32:38 5826
be thou an *h* to him from his Deut 33:7 5828
rideth upon the heaven in thy *h* Deut 33:26 5828
by the LORD, the shield of thy *h* Deut 33:29 5828
mighty men of valour, and *h* them Josh 1:14 5826
h me, that we may smite Gibeon Josh 10:4 5826
us quickly, and save us, and *h* us Josh 10:6 5826
of Gezer came up to *h* Lachish Josh 10:33 5826
came not to the *h* of the LORD Judg 5:23 5833
to the *h* of the LORD against the Judg 5:23 5833
the sun be hot, ye shall have *h* 1Sa 11:9 8668
for me, then thou shalt *h* me 2Sa 10:11 3447
thee, then I will come and *h* thee 2Sa 10:11 3467
So the Syrians feared to *h* the 2Sa 10:19 3467
and did obeisance, and said, *H* 2Sa 14:4 3467
cried a woman unto him, saying, *H* 2Kin 6:26 3467
h thee, whence shall I *h* thee 2Kin 6:27 3467
be come peaceably unto me to *h* me 1Chr 12:17 5826
day there came to David to *h* him 1Chr 12:22 5826
came to *h* Hadarezer king of Zobah 1Chr 18:5 5826
for me, then thou shalt *h* me 1Chr 19:12 8668
for thee, then I will *h* thee 1Chr 19:12 3467
neither would the Syrians *h* the 1Chr 19:19 3467
of Israel to *h* Solomon his son 1Chr 22:17 5826
it is nothing with thee to *h* 2Chr 14:11 5826
h us, O LORD our God 2Chr 14:11 5826
Shouldest thou *h* the ungodly 2Chr 19:2 5826
together, to ask *h* of the LORD 2Chr 20:4
then thou wilt hear and *h* 2Chr 20:9 3467
for God hath power to *h*, and to 2Chr 25:8 5826
to *h* the king against the enemy 2Chr 26:13 5826
the kings of Assyria to *h* him 2Chr 28:16 5826
gods of the kings of Syria *h* them 2Chr 28:23 5826
to them, that they may *h* me 2Chr 28:23 5826
brethren the Levites did *h* them 2Chr 29:34 2388
and they did *h* him 2Chr 32:3 5826
us is the LORD our God to *h* us 2Chr 32:8 5826
of his place *h* him with silver Ezr 1:4 5375
horsemen to *h* us against the Ezr 8:22 5826
Is not my *h* in me Job 6:13 5833
neither will he *h* the evil doers Job 8:20 2388
and him that had none to *h* him Job 29:12 5826
when I saw my *h* in the gate Job 31:21 5833
There is no *h* for him in God Ps 3:2 3444
H, LORD; for the godly Ps 12:1 3467
Send thee *h* from the sanctuary, Ps 20:2 5828
for there is none to *h* Ps 22:11 5826
O my strength, haste thee to *h* me Ps 22:19 5833
thou hast been my *h* Ps 27:9 5833
he is our *h* and our shield Ps 33:20 5828
buckler, and stand up for mine *h* Ps 35:2 5833
And the LORD shall *h* them, and Ps 37:40 5826
Make haste to *h* me, O Lord my Ps 38:22 5833
O LORD, make haste to *h* me Ps 40:13 5833
thou art my *h* and my deliverer Ps 40:17 5833
him for the *h* of his countenance Ps 42:5 3444
Arise for our *h*, and redeem us for Ps 44:26 5833
a very present *h* in trouble Ps 46:1 5833
God shall *h* her, and that right Ps 46:5 5826
awake to *h* me, and behold Ps 59:4 7125
Give us *h* from trouble Ps 60:11 5833
for vain is the *h* of man Ps 60:11 8668
Because thou hast been my *h* Ps 63:7 5833
make haste to *h* me, O LORD Ps 70:1 5833
thou art my *h* and my deliverer Ps 70:5 5828
O my God, make haste for my *h* Ps 71:12 5833
H us, O God of our salvation, for Ps 79:9 5826
I have laid *h* upon one that is Ps 89:19 5828
Unless the LORD had been my *h* Ps 94:17 5833
fell down, and there was none to *h* Ps 107:12 5826
Give us *h* from trouble Ps 108:12 5833
for vain is the *h* of man Ps 108:12 8668
H me, O LORD my God Ps 109:26 5826
he is their *h* and their shield Ps 115:9 5828
he is their *h* and their shield Ps 115:10 5828
he is their *h* and their shield Ps 115:11 5828
my part with them that *h* me Ps 118:7 5826
h thou me Ps 119:86 5826
Let thine hand *h* me Ps 119:173 5826
and let thy judgments *h* me Ps 119:175 5826
hills, from whence cometh my *h* Ps 121:1 5828
My *h* cometh from the LORD, which Ps 121:2 5828
Our *h* is in the name of the LORD, Ps 124:8 5828
son of man, in whom there is no *h* Ps 146:3 8668
hath the God of Jacob for his *h* Ps 146:5 5828
he hath not another to *h* him up Eccl 4:10 6965
to whom will ye flee for *h* Is 10:3 5833
whither we flee for *h* to be Is 20:6 5833
nor be an *h* nor profit, but a Is 30:5 5828
For the Egyptians shall *h* in vain Is 30:7 5826
them that go down to Egypt for *h* Is 31:1 5833
against the *h* of them that work Is 31:2 5833
yea, I will *h* thee Is 41:10 5826
I will *h* thee Is 41:13 5826
I will *h* thee, saith the LORD, and Is 41:14 5826
from the womb, which will *h* thee Is 44:2 5826
For the Lord GOD will *h* me Is 50:7 5826
Behold, the Lord GOD will *h* me Is 50:9 5826
I looked, and there was none to *h* Is 63:5 5826
which is come forth to *h* you Jer 37:7 5833
of the enemy, and none did *h* her Lam 1:7 5826
eyes as yet failed for our vain *h* Lam 4:17 5833
all that are about him to *h* him Eze 12:14 5828
of hell with them that *h* him Eze 32:21 5826
the chief princes, came to *h* me Dan 10:13 5826
shall be holpen with a little *h* Dan 11:34 5828
to his end, and none shall *h* him Dan 11:45 5826
but in me is thine *h* Hos 13:9 5828
him, saying, Lord, *h* me Mt 15:25 *997*
have compassion on us, and *h* us Mk 9:22 *997*
h thou mine unbelief Mk 9:24 *997*
that they should come and *h* them Lk 5:7 *4815*
bid her therefore that she *h* me Lk 10:40 *4878*
Come over into Macedonia, and *h* us Acts 16:9 *997*
Crying out, Men of Israel, *h* Acts 21:28 *997*
therefore obtained *h* of God Acts 26:22 *1947*
h those women which laboured with Phil 4:3 *4815*
find grace to *h* in time of need Heb 4:16 *996*

HELPED
h them, and watered their flock Ex 2:17 3467
Hitherto hath the LORD *h* us 1Sa 7:12 5826
and they following Adonijah *h* him 1Kin 1:7 5826
thirty and two kings that *h* him 1Kin 20:16 5826
they were *h* against them, and the 1Chr 5:20 5826
but they *h* them not 1Chr 12:19 5826
they *h* David against the band of 1Chr 12:21 5826
when God *h* the Levites that bare 1Chr 15:26 5826
cried out, and the LORD *h* him 2Chr 18:31 5826
every one *h* to destroy another 2Chr 20:23 5826
God *h* him against the Philistines 2Chr 26:7 5826
for he was marvellously *h* 2Chr 26:15 5826
but he *h* him not 2Chr 28:21 5833
and Shabbethai the Levite *h* them Ezr 10:15 5826
officers of the king, *h* the Jews Est 9:3 5375
How hast thou *h* him that is Job 26:2 5826
heart trusted in him, and I am *h* Ps 28:7 5826
I was brought low, and he *h* me Ps 116:6 3467
but the LORD *h* me Ps 118:13 5826
They *h* every one his neighbour Is 41:6 5826
a day of salvation have I *h* thee Is 49:8 5826
they *h* forward the affliction Zec 1:15 5826
h them much which had believed Acts 18:27 *4820*
And the earth *h* the woman, and the Rev 12:16 *997*

HELPER
any left, nor any *h* for Israel 2Kin 14:26 5826
my calamity, they have no *h* Job 30:13 5826
thou art the *h* of the fatherless Ps 10:14 5826
LORD, be thou my *h* Ps 30:10 5826
Behold, God is mine *h* Ps 54:4 5826
poor also, and him that hath no *h* Ps 72:12 5826
Zidon every *h* that remaineth Jer 47:4 5826
our *h* in Christ, and Stachys my Rom 16:9 *4904*
may boldly say, The Lord is my *h* Heb 13:6 *998*

HELPERS
the mighty men, *h* of the war 1Chr 12:1 5826
unto thee, and peace be to thine *h* 1Chr 12:18 5826
the proud *h* do stoop under him Job 9:13 5826
when all her *h* shall be destroyed Eze 30:8 5826
Put and Lubim were thy *h* Nah 3:9 5833
Aquila my *h* in Christ Jesus Rom 16:3 *4904*
your faith, but are *h* of your joy 2Cor 1:24 *4904*

HELPETH
for thy God *h* thee 1Chr 12:18 5826
hand, both he that *h* shall fall Is 31:3 5826
the Spirit also *h* our infirmities Rom 8:26 *4878*
and to every one that *h* with us 1Cor 16:16 *4903*

HELPING
were the prophets of God *h* them Ezr 5:2 5582
why art thou so far from *h* me Ps 22:1 3467
Ye also *h* together by prayer for 2Cor 1:11 *4943*

HELPS
they had taken up, they used *h* Acts 27:17 *996*
then gifts of healings, *h* 1Cor 12:28 *484*

HELVE
and the head slippeth from the *h* Deut 19:5 6086

HEM
beneath upon the *h* of it thou Ex 28:33 7757
round about the *h* thereof Ex 28:33 7757
upon the *h* of the robe round Ex 28:34 7757
upon the *h* of the robe, round Ex 39:25 7757
round about the *h* of the robe to Ex 39:26 7757
touched the *h* of his garment Mt 9:20 *2899*
only touch the *h* of his garment Mt 14:36 *2899*

HEMAM (*he'-mam*) See HOMAM. *A son of Lotan.*
children of Lotan were Hori and *H* Gen 36:22 1967

HEMAN (*he'-man*)
1. A son of Zerah.
than Ethan the Ezrahite, and *H* 1Kin 4:31 1968
Zimri, and Ethan, and *H*, and Calcol, 1Chr 2:6 1968
Of *H*: the sons of *H* 1Chr 25:4 1968
2. A son of Joel.
H a singer, the son of Joel, the 1Chr 6:33 1968
appointed *H* the son of Joel 1Chr 15:17 1968
So the singers, *H*, Asaph, and 1Chr 15:19 1968
And with them *H* and Jeduthun, and 1Chr 16:41 1968
And with them *H* and Jeduthun with 1Chr 16:42 1968
of the sons of Asaph, and of *H* 1Chr 25:1 1968
All these were the sons of *H* the 1Chr 25:5 1968
God gave to *H* fourteen sons and 1Chr 25:5 1968
order to Asaph, Jeduthun, and *H* 1Chr 25:6 1968
all of them of Asaph, of *H* 2Chr 5:12 1968
And of the sons of *H* 2Chr 29:14 1968
of David, and Asaph, and *H*, and 2Chr 35:15 1968
Maschil of *H* the Ezrahite Ps 88:*t* 1968

HEMATH (*he'-math*) See HAMATH.
1. Same as Hamath.
Egypt even unto the entering of *H* 1Chr 13:5 2574
in of *H* unto the river of the Amos 6:14 2574
2. Father of the Kenites and Rechabites.
are the Kenites that came of *H* 1Chr 2:55 2574

HEMDAN (*hem'-dan*) See AMRAM. *Son of Dishon.*
H, and Eshban, and Ithran, and Gen 36:26 2533

HEMLOCK
as *h* in the furrows of the field Hos 10:4 7219
the fruit of righteousness into *h* Amos 6:12 3939

HEMS
they made upon the *h* of the robe Ex 39:24 7757

HEN (*hen*) *A son of Zephaniah.*
to *H* the son of Zephaniah, for a Zec 6:14 2581
even as a *h* gathereth her Mt 23:37 *3733*
as a *h* doth gather her brood Lk 13:34 *3733*

HENA (*he'-nah*) *A city on the Euphrates.*
are the gods of Sepharvaim, *H* 2Kin 18:34 2012
of the city of Sepharvaim, of *H* 2Kin 19:13 2012
king of the city of Sepharvaim, *H* Is 37:13 2012

HENADAD (*hen'-a-dad*) *A Levite.*
the sons of *H*, with their sons and Ezr 3:9 2582
brethren, Bavai the son of *H* Neh 3:18 2582
Binnui the son of *H* another piece Neh 3:24 2582
Azaniah, Binnui of the sons of *H* Neh 10:9 2582

HENCE
the man said, They are departed *h* Gen 37:17 2088
Pharaoh ye shall not go forth *h* Gen 42:15 2088
ye shall carry up my bones from *h* Gen 50:25 2088
afterwards he will let you go *h* Ex 11:1 2088
thrust you out *h* altogether Ex 11:1 2088
carry up my bones away *h* with you Ex 13:19 2088
unto Moses, Depart, and go up *h* Ex 33:1 2088
go not with me, carry us not up *h* Ex 33:15 2088

get thee down quickly from *h* Deut 9:12 2088
Take you *h* out of the midst of Josh 4:3 2088
Depart not *h*, I pray thee, until Judg 6:18 2088
another field, neither go from *h* Ruth 2:8 2088
Get thee *h*, and turn thee eastward 1Kin 17:3 2088
recover strength, before I go *h* Ps 39:13
shalt say unto it, Get thee *h* Is 30:22 3318
Take from *h* thirty men with thee Jer 38:10 2088
and he said, Get you *h*, walk to and Zec 6:7 3212
saith Jesus unto him, Get thee *h* Mt 4:10 *5217*
Remove *h* to yonder place Mt 17:20 *1782*
of God, cast thyself down from *h* Lk 4:9 *1782*
him, Get thee out, and depart *h* Lk 13:31 *1782*
would pass from *h* to you cannot Lk 16:26 *1782*
sold doves, Take these things *h* Jn 2:16 *1782*
therefore said unto him, Depart *h* Jn 7:3 *1782*
Arise, let us go *h* Jn 14:31 *1782*
but now is my kingdom not from *h* Jn 18:36 *1782*
Sir, if thou have borne him *h* Jn 20:15
the Holy Ghost not many days *h* Acts 1:5
send thee far *h* unto the Gentiles Acts 22:21 *1821*
come they not *h*, even of your Jas 4:1 *1782*

HENCEFORTH
it shall not *h* yield unto thee Gen 4:12 3254
must the children of Israel *h* Num 18:22 5750
Ye shall *h* return no more that Deut 17:16 3254
shall *h* commit no more any such Deut 19:20 3254
I also will not *h* drive out any Judg 2:21 3254
for thy servant will *h* offer 2Kin 5:17 5750
therefore from *h* thou shalt have 2Chr 16:9 6258
his people from *h* even for ever Ps 125:2 6258
Israel hope in the LORD from *h* Ps 131:3 6258
with justice from *h* even for ever Is 9:7 6258
for *h* there shall no more come Is 52:1 6258
seed, saith the LORD, from *h* Is 59:21 3254
thou shalt no more *h* bereave them Eze 36:12
over them in mount Zion from *h* Mic 4:7
unto you, Ye shall not see me *h* Mt 23:39
I will not drink *h* of this fruit Mt 26:29
from *h* all generations shall call Lk 1:48 *3568*
from *h* thou shalt catch men Lk 5:10 *3568*
For from *h* there shall be five in Lk 12:52 *3568*
from *h* ye know him, and have seen Jn 14:7 *737*
H I call you not servants Jn 15:15 *3765*
that they speak *h* to no man in Acts 4:17 *3371*
from *h* I will go unto the Acts 18:6 *3568*
that *h* we should not serve sin Rom 6:6 *3371*
should not *h* live unto themselves 2Cor 5:15 *3371*
Wherefore *h* know we no man after 2Cor 5:16
yet now *h* know we him no more 2Cor 5:16 *2089*
From *h* let no man trouble me Gal 6:17 *3063*
That we *h* be no more children Eph 4:14 *3063*
that ye *h* walk not as other Eph 4:17 *3371*
H there is laid up for me a crown 2Ti 4:8 *3063*
From *h* expecting till his enemies Heb 10:13 *3063*
dead which die in the Lord from *h* Rev 14:13 *534*

HENCEFORWARD
and *h* among your generations Num 15:23 1973
no fruit grow on thee *h* for ever Mt 21:19 *3371*

HENNA See CAMPHIRE.

HENOCH (*he'-nok*) See ENOCH. *Same as Enoch.*
H, Methuselah, Lamech 1Chr 1:3 2585
Ephah, and Epher, and *H*, and Abida 1Chr 1:33 2585

HEPHER (*he'-fer*) See GATH-HEPHER, HEPHERITES.
1. A son of Gilead.
and of *H*, the family of the Num 26:32 2660
the son of *H* had no sons, but Num 26:33 2660
of Zelophehad, the son of *H* Num 27:1 2660
Shechem, and for the children of *H* Josh 17:2 2660
But Zelophehad, the son of *H* Josh 17:3 2660
2. A son of Naarah.
And Naarah bare him Ahuzam, and *H*. 1Chr 4:6 2660
3. A mighty man of David.
H the Mecherathite, Ahijah the 1Chr 11:36 2660
4. A Canaanite city.
the king of *H*, one Josh 12:17 2660
Sochoh, and all the land of *H* 1Kin 4:10 2660

HEPHERITES (*he'-fer-ites*) *Descendants of Hepher 1.*
and of Hepher, the family of the *H* Num 26:32 2662

HEPHZI-BAH (*hef'-zi-bah*)
1. Wife of King Hezekiah.
And his mother's name was *H* 2Kin 21:1 2657
2. A symbolic name for Jerusalem.
but thou shalt be called *H* Is 62:4 2657

HER See PREFACE.

HERALD
Then an *h* cried aloud, To you it Dan 3:4 3744

HERB
the *h* yielding seed, and the fruit Gen 1:11 6212
h yielding seed after his kind Gen 1:12 6212
given you every *h* bearing seed Gen 1:29 6212
have given every green *h* for meat Gen 1:30 6212
every *h* of the field before it Gen 2:5 6212
thou shalt eat the *h* of the field Gen 3:18 6212
even as the green *h* have I given Gen 9:3 6212
upon every *h* of the field Ex 9:22 6212
hail smote every *h* of the field Ex 9:25 6212
eat every *h* of the land, even all Ex 10:12 6212
they did eat every *h* of the land Ex 10:15 6212
the small rain upon the tender *h* Deut 32:2 1877
of the field, and as the green *h* 2Kin 19:26 1877
it withereth before any other *h* Job 8:12 2682
of the tender *h* to spring forth Job 38:27 1877
grass, and wither as the green *h* Ps 37:2 1877
and *h* for the service of man Ps 104:14 6212
of the field, and as the green *h* Is 37:27 1877
bones shall flourish like an *h* Is 66:14 1877

HERBS
or in the *h* of the field, through Ex 10:15 6212
with bitter *h* they shall eat it Ex 12:8
with unleavened bread and bitter *h* Num 9:11
with thy foot, as a garden of *h* Deut 11:10 3419
I may have it for a garden of *h* 1Kin 21:2 3419
out into the field to gather *h* 2Kin 4:39 219
eat up all the *h* in their land Ps 105:35 6212
is a dinner of *h* where love is Prov 15:17 3419
h of the mountains are gathered Prov 27:25 6212
place like a clear heat upon *h* Is 18:4 216
for thy dew is as the dew of *h* Is 26:19 219
and hills, and dry up all their *h* Is 42:15 6212
the *h* of every field wither, for Jer 12:4 6212
grown, it is the greatest among *h* Mt 13:32 *3001*
and becometh greater than all *h* Mk 4:32 *3001*
mint and rue and all manner of *h* Lk 11:42 *3001*
another, who is weak, eateth *h* Rom 14:2 *3001*
bringeth forth *h* meet for them by Heb 6:7 *1008*

HERD
And Abraham ran unto the *h* Gen 18:7 1241
of the cattle, even of the *h* Lev 1:2 1241
be a burnt sacrifice of the *h* Lev 1:3 1241
offering, if he offer it of the *h* Lev 3:1 1241
And concerning the tithe of the *h* Lev 27:32 1241
savour unto the LORD, of the *h* Num 15:3 1241
then thou shalt kill of thy *h* Deut 12:21 1241
males that come of thy *h* and of Deut 15:19 1241
thy God, of the flock and the *h* Deut 16:2 1241
came after the *h* out of the field 1Sa 11:5 1241
of his own flock and of his own *h* 2Sa 12:4 1241
young of the flock and of the *h* Jer 31:12 1241
h nor flock, taste any thing Jonah 3:7 1241
there shall be no *h* in the stalls Hab 3:17 1241
them an *h* of many swine feeding Mt 8:30 *34*
us to go away into the *h* of swine Mt 8:31 *34*
they went into the *h* of swine Mt 8:32 *34*
behold, the whole *h* of swine ran Mt 8:32 *34*
a great *h* of swine feeding Mk 5:11 *34*
the *h* ran violently down a steep Mk 5:13 *34*
there was there an *h* of many Lk 8:32 *34*
the *h* ran violently down a steep Lk 8:33 *34*

HERDMAN
but I was an *h*, and a gatherer of Amos 7:14 951

HERDMEN
between the *h* of Abram's cattle Gen 13:7 7462
cattle and the *h* of Lot's cattle Gen 13:7 7462
and between my *h* and thy *h* Gen 13:8 7462
the *h* of Gerar did strive with Gen 26:20 7462
Gerar did strive with Isaac's *h* Gen 26:20 7462
the chiefest of the *h* that 1Sa 21:7 7462
who was among the *h* of Tekoa Amos 1:1 5349

HERDS
went with Abram, had flocks, and *h* Gen 13:5 1241
and he hath given him flocks, and *h* Gen 24:35 1241
of flocks, and possession of *h* Gen 26:14 1241
was with him, and the flocks, and *h* Gen 32:7 1241
and *h* with young are with me Gen 33:13 1241
children, and thy flocks, and thy *h* Gen 45:10 1241
brought their flocks, and their *h* Gen 46:32 1241
and their flocks, and their *h* Gen 47:1 1241
and for the cattle of the *h* Gen 47:17 1241
my lord also hath our *h* of cattle Gen 47:18 4735
ones, and their flocks, and their *h* Gen 50:8 1241
flocks and with our *h* will we go Ex 10:9 1241
your flocks and your *h* be stayed Ex 10:24 1241
Also take your flocks and your *h* Ex 12:32 1241
and flocks, and *h*, even very much Ex 12:38 1241
nor *h* feed before that mount Ex 34:3 1241
the *h* be slain for them, to Num 11:22 1241
And when thy *h* and thy flocks Deut 8:13 1241
and the firstlings of your *h* Deut 12:6 1241
of thy *h* or of thy flock, nor any Deut 12:17 1241
oil, and the firstlings of thy *h* Deut 14:23 1241
took all the flocks and the *h* 1Sa 30:20 1241
had exceeding many flocks and *h* 2Sa 12:2 1241
over the *h* that fed in Sharon was 1Chr 27:29 1241
over the *h* that were in the 1Chr 27:29 1241
of flocks and *h* in abundance 2Chr 32:29 1241
law, and the firstlings of our *h* Neh 10:36 1241
thy flocks, and look well to thy *h* Prov 27:23 5739
a place for the *h* to lie down in Is 65:10 1241
their flocks and their *h*, their Jer 3:24 1241
eat up thy flocks and thine *h* Jer 5:17 1241
with their *h* to seek the LORD Hos 5:6 1241
the *h* of cattle are perplexed Joel 1:18 5739

HERE
Have I also *h* looked after him Gen 16:13 1988
unto Lot, Hast thou *h* any besides Gen 19:12 6311
and thy two daughters, which are *h* Gen 19:15 4672
Now therefore swear unto me *h* by Gen 21:23 2008
and he said, Behold, *h* I am Gen 22:1
men, Abide ye *h* with the ass Gen 22:5 6311
and he said, *H* am I, my son Gen 22:7 2009
and he said, *H* am I Gen 22:11 2009
I stand *h* by the well of water Gen 24:13
he said unto him, Behold, *h* am I Gen 27:1
and he said, *H* am I Gen 27:18 2009
And I said, *H* am I Gen 31:11 2009
set it *h* before my brethren and Gen 31:37 3541
And he said to him, *H* am I Gen 37:13 2009
h also have I done nothing that Gen 40:15 6311
one of your brethren *h* with me Gen 42:33
And he said, *H* am I Gen 46:2 2009
h is seed for you, and ye shall Gen 47:23
And he said, *H* am I Ex 3:4 2009
the elders, Tarry ye *h* for us Ex 24:14 2088
shall it be known *h* that I Ex 33:16 645
the mountain, saying, Lo, we be *h* Num 14:40
Lodge *h* this night, and I will Num 22:8 6311
you, tarry ye also *h* this night Num 22:19 2088
Build me *h* seven altars, and Num 23:1 2088
and prepare me *h* seven oxen Num 23:1 2088
Stand *h* by thy burnt offering Num 23:15 3541
Build me *h* seven altars, and Num 23:29 2088
prepare me *h* seven bullocks and Num 23:29 2088
go to war, and shall ye sit *h* Num 32:6 6311
build sheepfolds *h* for our cattle Num 32:16 6311
are all of us *h* alive this day Deut 5:3 6311
as for thee, stand thou *h* by me Deut 5:31 6311
the things that we do *h* this day Deut 12:8 6311
But with him that standeth *h* with Deut 29:15 6311
that is not *h* with us this day Deut 29:15 6311
for you *h* before the LORD our God Josh 18:6 6311
that I may *h* cast lots for you Josh 18:8 6311
which are *h* mentioned by name Josh 21:9
thee, and say, Is there any man *h* Judg 4:20 6311
and what hast thou *h* Judg 18:3 6311
day groweth to an end, lodge *h* Judg 19:9 6311
h is my daughter a maiden, and his Judg 19:24
give *h* your advice and counsel Judg 20:7 1988
but abide *h* fast by my maidens Ruth 2:8 3541
turn aside, sit down *h* Ruth 4:1 6311
the city, and said, Sit ye down *h* Ruth 4:2 6311
am the woman that stood by thee *h* 1Sa 1:26 2088
and he answered, *H* am I 1Sa 3:4 2009
he ran unto Eli, and said, *H* am I 1Sa 3:5 2005
and went to Eli, and said, *H* am I 1Sa 3:6 2005
and went to Eli, and said, *H* am I 1Sa 3:8 2005
And he answered, *H* am I 1Sa 3:16 2009
I have *h* at hand the fourth part 1Sa 9:8
and said unto them, Is the seer *h* 1Sa 9:11 2088
Behold, *h* I am 1Sa 12:3
man his sheep, and slay them *h* 1Sa 14:34 2088
Jesse, Are *h* all thy children 1Sa 16:11 8552
is there not *h* under thine hand 1Sa 21:8 6311
it is *h* wrapped in a cloth behind 1Sa 21:9
for there is no other save that *h* 1Sa 21:9 2088
And he answered, *H* I am, my lord 1Sa 22:12 2005
Behold, we be afraid *h* in Judah 1Sa 23:3 6311
What do these Hebrews *h* 1Sa 29:3
And I answered, *H* am I 2Sa 1:7 2009
Tarry *h* to day also, and to morrow 2Sa 11:12 2088
h am I, let him do to me as 2Sa 15:26
unto him, Turn aside, and stand *h* 2Sa 18:30 3541
three days, and be thou *h* present 2Sa 20:4 6311
h be oxen for burnt sacrifice, and 2Sa 24:22
but I will die *h* 1Kin 2:30 6311
thy lord, Behold, Elijah is *h* 1Kin 18:8
thy lord, Behold, Elijah is *h* 1Kin 18:11
thy lord, Behold, Elijah is *h* 1Kin 18:14
said unto him, What doest thou *h* 1Kin 19:9 6311
him, and said, What doest thou *h* 1Kin 19:13 6311
And as thy servant was busy *h* 1Kin 20:40 2008
Is there not *h* a prophet of the 1Kin 22:7 6311
Elijah said unto Elisha, Tarry *h* 2Kin 2:2 6311
said unto him, Elisha, tarry *h* 2Kin 2:4 6311
unto him, Tarry, I pray thee, *h* 2Kin 2:6 6311
Is there not *h* a prophet of the 2Kin 3:11 6311
H is Elisha the son of Shaphat 2Kin 3:11 6311
Why sit we *h* until we die 2Kin 7:3 6311
and if we sit still *h*, we die also 2Kin 7:4 6311
look that there be *h* with you 2Kin 10:23 6311
thy people, which are present *h* 1Chr 29:17 6311
Is there not *h* a prophet of the 2Chr 18:6
h shall thy proud waves be stayed Job 38:11 6311
go, and say unto thee, *H* we are Job 38:35 2009
h will I dwell Ps 132:14 6311
Then said I, *H* am I Is 6:8 2005
h cometh a chariot of men, with a Is 21:9 2088
What hast thou *h* Is 22:16 6311
and whom hast thou *h*, that thou Is 22:16 6311
hast hewed thee out a sepulchre *h* Is 22:16 6311
h a little, and there a little Is 28:10 8033
h a little, and there a little Is 28:13 8033
Now therefore, what have I *h* Is 52:5 6311
cry, and he shall say, *H* I am Is 58:9 2009
the house of Israel committeth *h* Eze 8:6 6311
abominations that they do *h* Eze 8:9 6311
abominations which they commit *h* Eze 8:17 6311
yea, gray hairs are *h* and there Hos 7:9 2236
behold, a greater than Jonas is *h* Mt 12:41 5602
a greater than Solomon is *h* Mt 12:42 5602
Give me *h* John Baptist's head in Mt 14:8 5602
We have *h* but five loaves, and two Mt 14:17 5602
you, There be some standing *h* Mt 16:28 5602
Lord, it is good for us to be *h* Mt 17:4 5602
let us make *h* three tabernacles Mt 17:4 5602
Why stand ye *h* all the day idle Mt 20:6 5602
be left *h* one stone upon another Mt 24:2 5602
you, Lo, *h* is Christ, or there Mt 24:23 5602
unto the disciples, Sit ye *h* Mt 26:36 *848*
tarry ye *h*, and watch with me Mt 26:38 5602
He is not *h* Mt 28:6 5602
and are not his sisters *h* with us Mk 6:3 5602
with bread *h* in the wilderness Mk 8:4 5602
be some of them that stand *h* Mk 9:1 5602
Master, it is good for us to be *h* Mk 9:5 5602
of stones and what buildings are *h* Mk 13:1
shall say to you, Lo, *h* is Christ Mk 13:21 5602
saith to his disciples, Sit ye *h* Mk 14:32 5602
tarry ye *h*, and watch Mk 14:34 5602
he is not *h* Mk 16:6 5602
do also *h* in thy country Lk 4:23 5602
for we are *h* in a desert place Lk 9:12 5602
a truth, there be some standing *h* Lk 9:27 5602
Master, it is good for us to be *h* Lk 9:33 5602
a greater than Solomon is *h* Lk 11:31 5602
behold, a greater than Jonas is *h* Lk 11:32 5602
Neither shall they say, Lo *h* Lk 17:21 5602
And they shall say to you, See *h* Lk 17:23 5602
h is thy pound, which I have kept Lk 19:20
Lord, behold, *h* are two swords Lk 22:38 5602
He is not *h*, but is risen Lk 24:6 5602
unto them, Have ye *h* any meat Lk 24:41 1759

There is a lad *h*, which hath five.......... Jn 6:9 5602
Jesus, Lord, if thou hadst been *h*.......... Jn 11:21 5602
him, Lord, if thou hadst been *h*.......... Jn 11:32 5602
this man stand *h* before you whole.......... Acts 4:10 3936
the eunuch said, See, *h* is water.......... Acts 8:36
And he said, Behold, I am *h*.......... Acts 9:10
h he hath authority from the.......... Acts 9:14 5602
are we all *h* present before God.......... Acts 10:33 3918
for we are all *h*.......... Acts 16:28 1759
ought to have been *h* before thee.......... Acts 24:19 3918
Or else let these same *h* say.......... Acts 24:20
men which are *h* present with us.......... Acts 25:24 4840
me, both at Jerusalem, and also *h*.......... Acts 25:24 1759
you all things which are done *h*.......... Col 4:9 5602
h men that die receive tithes.......... Heb 7:8 5602
For *h* have we no continuing city,.......... Heb 13:14 5602
Sit thou *h* in a good place.......... Jas 2:3 5602
or sit *h* under my footstool.......... Jas 2:3 5602
time of your sojourning *h* in fear.......... 1Pet 1:17
H is the patience and the faith of.......... Rev 13:10 5602
H is wisdom.......... Rev 13:18 5602
H is the patience of the saints.......... Rev 14:12 5602
h are they that keep the.......... Rev 14:12 5602
h is the mind which hath wisdom.......... Rev 17:9 5602

HEREAFTER
the things that are to come *h*.......... Is 41:23 268
h also, if ye will not hearken.......... Eze 20:39 310
bed, what should come to pass *h*.......... Dan 2:29
king what shall come to pass *h*.......... Dan 2:45
H shall ye see the Son of man.......... Mt 26:64
man eat fruit of thee *h* for ever.......... Mk 11:14 3370
H shall the Son of man sit on the.......... Lk 22:69
H ye shall see heaven open, and.......... Jn 1:51 737
but thou shalt know *h*.......... Jn 13:7
H I will not talk much with you.......... Jn 14:30 2089
should *h* believe on him to life.......... 1Ti 1:16 3195
and the things which shall be *h*.......... Rev 1:19
shew thee things which must be *h*.......... Rev 4:1
there come two woes more *h*.......... Rev 9:12

HEREBY
H ye shall be proved.......... Gen 42:15 2063
H shall I know that ye are true.......... Gen 42:33 2063
H ye shall know that the LORD.......... Num 16:28 2063
H ye shall know that the living.......... Josh 3:10 2063
yet am I not *h* justified.......... 1Cor 4:4
h we do know that we know him, if.......... 1Jn 2:3
h know we that we are in him.......... 1Jn 2:5
H perceive we the love of God,.......... 1Jn 3:16
h we know that we are of the.......... 1Jn 3:19
h we know that he abideth in us,.......... 1Jn 3:24
H know ye the Spirit of God.......... 1Jn 4:2
H know we the spirit of truth, and.......... 1Jn 4:6
H know we that we dwell in him,.......... 1Jn 4:13

HEREIN
Only *h* will the men consent unto.......... Gen 34:22 2063
H thou hast done foolishly.......... 2Chr 16:9
h is that saying true, One soweth.......... Jn 4:37
Why *h* is a marvellous thing, that.......... Jn 9:30
H is my Father glorified, that ye.......... Jn 15:8
h do I exercise myself, to have.......... Acts 24:16
And *h* I give my advice.......... 2Cor 8:10
H is love, not that we loved God,.......... 1Jn 4:10
H is our love made perfect, that.......... 1Jn 4:17

HEREOF
the fame *h* went abroad into all.......... Mt 9:26 3778
And by reason *h* he ought, as for.......... Heb 5:3 5026

HERES (*he'-res*) See KIR-HERES, TIMMATH-HERES. *A mountain in Judah.*
would dwell in mount *H* in Aijalon.......... Judg 1:35 2776

HERESH (*he'-resh*) *A Levite.*
And Bakbakkar, *H*, and Galal, and.......... 1Chr 9:15 2792

HERESIES
there must be also *h* among you.......... 1Cor 11:19 139
wrath, strife, seditions, *h*.......... Gal 5:20 139
privily shall bring in damnable *h*.......... 2Pet 2:1 139

HERESY
after the way which they call *h*.......... Acts 24:14 139

HERETH See HARETH.

HERETICK
man that is an *h* after the first.......... Titus 3:10 141

HERETOFORE
I am not eloquent, neither *h*.......... Ex 4:10 8543
people straw to make brick, as *h*.......... Ex 5:7 8543
the bricks, which they did make *h*.......... Ex 5:8 8543
both yesterday and to day, as *h*.......... Ex 5:14 8543
for ye have not passed this way *h*.......... Josh 3:4 8543
a people which thou knewest not *h*.......... Ruth 2:11 8543
hath not been such a thing *h*.......... 1Sa 4:7 865
write to them which *h* have sinned.......... 2Cor 13:2 4258

HEREUNTO
can eat, or who else can hasten *h*.......... Eccl 2:25
For even *h* were ye called.......... 1Pet 2:21

HEREWITH
and yet thou wast not satisfied *h*.......... Eze 16:29 2063
in mine house, and prove me now *h*.......... Mal 3:10 2063

HERITAGE
and I will give it you for an *h*.......... Ex 6:8 4181
the *h* appointed unto him by God.......... Job 20:29 5159
the *h* of oppressors, which they.......... Job 27:13 5159
yea, I have a goodly *h*.......... Ps 16:6 5159
thou hast given me the *h* of those.......... Ps 61:5 3425
O LORD, and afflict thine *h*.......... Ps 94:5 5159
give them the *h* of the heathen.......... Ps 111:6 5159
have I taken as an *h* for ever.......... Ps 119:111 5157
Lo, children are an *h* of the LORD.......... Ps 127:3 5159
And gave their land for an *h*.......... Ps 135:12 5159
an *h* unto Israel his people.......... Ps 135:12 5159
And gave their land for an *h*.......... Ps 136:21 5159
Even an *h* unto Israel his servant.......... Ps 136:22 5159
This is the *h* of the servants of.......... Is 54:17 5159
feed thee with the *h* of Jacob thy.......... Is 58:14 5159
made mine *h* an abomination.......... Jer 2:7 5159
a goodly *h* of the hosts of.......... Jer 3:19 5159
mine house, I have left mine *h*.......... Jer 12:7 5159
Mine *h* is unto me as a lion in.......... Jer 12:8 5159
Mine *h* is unto me as a speckled.......... Jer 12:9 5159
them again, every man to his *h*.......... Jer 12:15 5159
from thine *h* that I gave thee.......... Jer 17:4 5159
O ye destroyers of mine *h*.......... Jer 50:11 5159
and give not thine *h* to reproach.......... Joel 2:17 5159
for my people and for my *h* Israel.......... Joel 3:2 5159
and his house, even a man and his *h*.......... Mic 2:2 5159
thy rod, the flock of thine *h*.......... Mic 7:14 5159
of the remnant of his *h*.......... Mic 7:18 5159
his *h* waste for the dragons of.......... Mal 1:3 5159
as being lords over God's *h*.......... 1Pet 5:3 2819

HERITAGES
cause to inherit the desolate *h*.......... Is 49:8 5159

HERMAS (*her'-mas*) *A Christian acquaintance of Paul.*
Salute Asyncritus, Phlegon, *H*.......... Rom 16:14 2057

HERMES (*her'-mees*) *A Christian acquaintance of Paul.*
Phlegon, Hermas, Patrobas, *H*.......... Rom 16:14 2060

HERMOGENES (*her-mog'-e-nees*) *A false Christian teacher.*
of whom are Phygellus and *H*.......... 2Ti 1:15 2061

HERMON
the river of Arnon unto mount *H*.......... Deut 3:8 2768
(Which *H* the Sidonians call.......... Deut 3:9 2768
even unto mount Sion which is *H*.......... Deut 4:48 2768
to the Hivite under *H* in the land.......... Josh 11:3 2768
valley of Lebanon under mount *H*.......... Josh 11:17 2768
from the river Arnon unto mount *H*.......... Josh 12:1 2768
And reigned in mount *H*, and in.......... Josh 12:5 2768
from Baal-gad under mount *H* unto.......... Josh 13:5 2768
and Maachathites, and all mount *H*.......... Josh 13:11 2768
and Senir, and unto mount *H*.......... 1Chr 5:23 2768
H shall rejoice in thy name.......... Ps 89:12 2768
As the dew of *H*, and as the dew.......... Ps 133:3 2768
from the top of Shenir and *H*.......... Song 4:8 2768

HERMONITES (*her'-mon-ites*) See HERMON. *Inhabitants of Mt. Hermon.*
the land of Jordan, and of the *H*.......... Ps 42:6 2769

HEROD (*her'-od*) See HERODIANS, HEROD'S.
1. Herod the Great.
Judaea in the days of *H* the king.......... Mt 2:1 2264
When *H* the king had heard these.......... Mt 2:3 2264
Then *H*, when he had privily.......... Mt 2:7 2264
that they should not return to *H*.......... Mt 2:12 2264
for *H* will seek the young child.......... Mt 2:13 2264
And was there until the death of *H*.......... Mt 2:15 2264
Then *H*, when he saw that he was.......... Mt 2:16 2264
But when *H* was dead, behold, an.......... Mt 2:19 2264
in the room of his father *H*.......... Mt 2:22 2264
There was in the days of *H*.......... Lk 1:5 2264
No, nor yet *H*: for I sent.......... Lk 23:15 2264
2. Herod Antipas.
At that time *H* the tetrarch heard.......... Mt 14:1 2264
For *H* had laid hold on John, and.......... Mt 14:3 2264
danced before them, and pleased *H*.......... Mt 14:6 2264
And king *H* heard of him.......... Mk 6:14 2264
But when *H* heard thereof, he said.......... Mk 6:16 2264
For *H* himself had sent forth and.......... Mk 6:17 2264
For John had said unto *H*, It is.......... Mk 6:18 2264
For *H* feared John, knowing that.......... Mk 6:20 2264
that *H* on his birthday made a.......... Mk 6:21 2264
came in, and danced, and pleased *H*.......... Mk 6:22 2264
Pharisees, and of the leaven of *H*.......... Mk 8:15 2264
H being tetrarch of Galilee, and.......... Lk 3:1 2264
But *H* the tetrarch, being.......... Lk 3:19 2264
all the evils which *H* had done.......... Lk 3:19 2264
Now *H* the tetrarch heard of all.......... Lk 9:7 2264
H said, John have I beheaded.......... Lk 9:9 2264
for *H* will kill thee.......... Lk 13:31 2264
jurisdiction, he sent him to *H*.......... Lk 23:7 2264
And when *H* saw Jesus, he was.......... Lk 23:8 2264
H with his men of war set him at.......... Lk 23:11 2264
H were made friends together.......... Lk 23:12 2264
whom thou hast anointed, both *H*.......... Acts 4:27 2264
brought up with *H* the tetrarch.......... Acts 13:1 2264
3. Herod Agrippa I.
Now about that time *H* the king.......... Acts 12:1 2264
when *H* would have brought him.......... Acts 12:6 2264
delivered me out of the hand of *H*.......... Acts 12:11 2264
when *H* had sought for him, and.......... Acts 12:19 2264
H was highly displeased with them.......... Acts 12:20 2264
And upon a set day *H*, arrayed in.......... Acts 12:21 2264

HERODIANS (*he-ro'-de-uns*) *Hellenizing Jews.*
him their disciples with the *H*.......... Mt 22:16 2265
counsel with the *H* against him.......... Mk 3:6 2265
of the Pharisees and of the *H*.......... Mk 12:13 2265

HERODIAS (*he-ro'-de-as*) See HERODIAS'. *Granddaughter of Herod I.*
the daughter of *H* danced before.......... Mt 14:6 2266
Therefore *H* had a quarrel against.......... Mk 6:19 2266
daughter of the said *H* came in.......... Mk 6:22 2266
for *H* his brother Philip's wife.......... Lk 3:19 2266

HERODIAS' (*he-ro'-de-as*)
and put him in prison for *H* sake.......... Mt 14:3 2266
and bound him in prison for *H* sake.......... Mk 6:17 2266

HERODION (*he-ro'-de-on*) *A relative of Paul.*
Salute *H* my kinsman.......... Rom 16:11 2267

HEROD'S (*her'-ods*)
1. Refers to Herod 2.
But when *H* birthday was kept, the.......... Mt 14:6 2264
the wife of Chuza *H* steward.......... Lk 8:3 2264
he belonged unto *H* jurisdiction.......... Lk 23:7 2264
2. Refers to Herod 3.
him to be kept in *H* judgment hall.......... Acts 23:35 2264

HERON
the *h* after her kind, and the.......... Lev 11:19 601
the *h* after her kind, and the.......... Deut 14:18 601

HERS
firstborn son be *h* that was hated.......... Deut 21:15
damsels of *h* that went after her.......... 1Sa 25:42
saying, Restore all that was *h*.......... 2Kin 8:6
ones, as though they were not *h*.......... Job 39:16

HERSELF
Therefore Sarah laughed within *h*.......... Gen 18:12
and she, even she *h* said, He is my.......... Gen 20:5
she took a vail, and covered *h*.......... Gen 24:65
her with a vail, and wrapped *h*.......... Gen 38:14
came down to wash *h* at the river.......... Ex 2:5
she shall number to *h* seven days.......... Lev 15:28
if she profane *h* by playing the.......... Lev 21:9
she thrust *h* unto the wall, and.......... Num 22:25
bind *h* by a bond, being in her.......... Num 30:3
yea, she returned answer to *h*.......... Judg 5:29
bowed *h* to the ground, and said.......... Ruth 2:10
husband were dead, she bowed *h*.......... 1Sa 4:19
face, and bowed *h* to the ground,.......... 1Sa 25:23
bowed *h* on her face to the earth,.......... 1Sa 25:41
the roof he saw a woman washing *h*.......... 2Sa 11:2
shall feign *h* to be another woman.......... 1Kin 14:5
bowed *h* to the ground, and took up.......... 2Kin 4:37
time she lifteth up *h* on high.......... Job 39:18
and the swallow a nest for *h*.......... Ps 84:3
She maketh *h* coverings of.......... Prov 31:22
Therefore hell hath enlarged *h*.......... Is 5:14 5315
find for *h* a place of rest.......... Is 34:14
bride adorneth *h* with her jewels.......... Is 61:10
Israel hath justified *h* more than.......... Jer 3:11
of Zion, that bewaileth *h*.......... Jer 4:31
feeble, and turneth *h* to flee.......... Jer 49:24
idols against *h* to defile *h*.......... Eze 22:3
all their idols she defiled *h*.......... Eze 23:7
She hath wearied *h* with lies.......... Eze 24:12
she decked *h* with her earrings and.......... Hos 2:13
Tyrus did build *h* a strong hold.......... Zec 9:3
For she said within *h*, If I may.......... Mt 9:21 1438
earth bringeth forth fruit of *h*.......... Mk 4:28 844
hid *h* five months, saying,.......... Lk 1:24 1438
and could in no wise lift up *h*.......... Lk 13:11
had thus said, she turned *h* back.......... Jn 20:14
She turned *h*, and saith unto him,.......... Jn 20:16
Through faith also Sara *h*.......... Heb 11:11 846
which calleth *h* a prophetess.......... Rev 2:20 1438
How much she hath glorified *h*.......... Rev 18:7 1438
and his wife hath made *h* ready.......... Rev 19:7 1438

HESED (*he'-sed*) See JUSHAB-HESED. *Father of an officer of Solomon.*
The son of *H*, in Aruboth.......... 1Kin 4:10 2618

HESHBON (*hesh'-bon*) *A Levitical city in Reuben and Gad.*
the cities of the Amorites, in *H*.......... Num 21:25 2809
For *H* was the city of Sihon the.......... Num 21:26 2809
in proverbs say, Come into *H*.......... Num 21:27 2809
For there is a fire gone out of *H*.......... Num 21:28 2809
H is perished even unto Dibon, and.......... Num 21:30 2809
of the Amorites, which dwelt at *H*.......... Num 21:34 2809
Dibon, and Jazer, and Nimrah, and *H*.......... Num 32:3 2809
And the children of Reuben built *H*.......... Num 32:37 2809
of the Amorites, which dwelt in *H*.......... Deut 1:4 2809
hand Sihon the Amorite, king of *H*.......... Deut 2:24 2809
king of *H* with words of peace.......... Deut 2:26 2809
But Sihon king of *H* would not let.......... Deut 2:30 2809
of the Amorites, which dwelt at *H*.......... Deut 3:2 2809
as we did unto Sihon king of *H*.......... Deut 3:6 2809
of the Amorites, who dwelt at *H*.......... Deut 4:46 2809
this place, Sihon the king of *H*.......... Deut 29:7 2809
beyond Jordan, to Sihon king of *H*.......... Josh 9:10 2809
of the Amorites, who dwelt in *H*.......... Josh 12:2 2809
the border of Sihon king of *H*.......... Josh 12:5 2809
the Amorites, which reigned in *H*.......... Josh 13:10 2809
H, and all her cities that are in.......... Josh 13:17 2809
the Amorites, which reigned in *H*.......... Josh 13:21 2809
from *H* unto Ramath-mizpeh, and.......... Josh 13:26 2809
of the kingdom of Sihon king of *H*.......... Josh 13:27 2809
H with her suburbs, Jazer with.......... Josh 21:39 2809
of the Amorites, the king of *H*.......... Judg 11:19 2809
While Israel dwelt in *H* and her.......... Judg 11:26 2809
H with her suburbs, and Jazer with.......... 1Chr 6:81 2809
and the land of the king of *H*.......... Neh 9:22 2809
eyes like the fishpools in *H*.......... Song 7:4 2809
And *H* shall cry, and Elealeh.......... Is 15:4 2809
For the fields of *H* languish.......... Is 16:8 2809
water thee with my tears, O *H*.......... Is 16:9 2809
in *H* they have devised evil.......... Jer 48:2 2809
From the cry of *H* even unto.......... Jer 48:34 2809
shadow of *H* because of the force.......... Jer 48:45 2809
a fire shall come forth out of *H*.......... Jer 48:45 2809
Howl, O *H*, for Ai is spoiled.......... Jer 49:3 2809

HESHMON (*hesh'-mon*) See AZMON. *A town in Judah.*
And Hazar-gaddah, and *H*, and.......... Josh 15:27 2829

HESLI See ESLI.

HETH (*heth*) *Son of Canaan.*
begat Sidon his firstborn, and *H*.......... Gen 10:15 2845
dead, and spake unto the sons of *H*.......... Gen 23:3 2845

the children of *H* answered Gen 23:5 2845
land, even to the children of *H* Gen 23:7 2845
dwelt among the children of *H* Gen 23:10 2845
the audience of the children of *H* Gen 23:10 2845
in the audience of the sons of *H* Gen 23:16 2845
the presence of the children of *H* Gen 23:18 2845
a buryingplace by the sons of *H* Gen 23:20 2845
purchased of the sons of *H* Gen 25:10 2845
because of the daughters of *H* Gen 27:46 2845
take a wife of the daughters of *H* Gen 27:46 2845
was from the children of *H* Gen 49:32 2845
begat Zidon his firstborn, and *H* 1Chr 1:13 2845

HETHLON (*heth'-lon*) *A place in northern Palestine.*
from the great sea, the way of *H* Eze 47:15 2855
end to the coast of the way of *H* Eze 48:1 2855

HEW
H thee two tables of stone like Ex 34:1 6458
H thee two tables of stone like Deut 10:1 6458
ye shall *h* down the graven images Deut 12:3 1438
wood with his neighbour to *h* wood Deut 19:5 2404
command thou that they *h* me cedar 1Kin 5:6 3772
h timber like unto the Sidonians 1Kin 5:6 3772
and Hiram's builders did *h* them 1Kin 5:18 6458
he set masons to *h* wrought stones 1Chr 22:2 2672
thousand to *h* in the mountain 2Chr 2:2 2672
H ye down trees, and cast a mount Jer 6:6 3772
H down the tree, and cut off his Dan 4:14 1414
H the tree down, and destroy it Dan 4:23 1414

HEWED
he *h* two tables of stone like Ex 34:4 6458
h two tables of stone like unto Deut 10:3 6458
h them in pieces, and sent them 1Sa 11:7 5408
Samuel *h* Agag in pieces before 1Sa 15:33 8158
h stones, to lay the foundation 1Kin 5:17 1496
court with three rows of *h* stone 1Kin 6:36 1496
to the measures of *h* stones 1Kin 7:9 1496
after the measures of *h* stones 1Kin 7:11 1496
was with three rows of *h* stones 1Kin 7:12 1496
h stone to repair the breaches of 2Kin 12:12 4274
that thou hast *h* thee out a Is 22:16 2672
h them out cisterns, broken Jer 2:13 2672
Therefore have I *h* them by the Hos 6:5 2672

HEWER
from the *h* of thy wood unto the Deut 29:11 2404

HEWERS
but let them be *h* of wood Josh 9:21 2404
h of wood and drawers of water for Josh 9:23 2404
made them that day *h* of wood Josh 9:27 2404
thousand *h* in the mountains 1Kin 5:15 2672
h of stone, and to buy timber and 2Kin 12:12 2672
workmen with thee in abundance, *h* 1Chr 22:15 2672
the *h* that cut timber, twenty 2Chr 2:10 2404
thousand to be *h* in the mountain 2Chr 2:18 2672
her with axes, as *h* of wood Jer 46:22 2404

HEWETH
against him that *h* therewith Is 10:15 2672
as he that *h* him out an sepulchre Is 22:16 2672
He *h* him down cedars, and taketh Is 44:14 3772

HEWN
shalt not build it of *h* stone Ex 20:25 1496
h stone to repair the house 2Kin 22:6 4274
gave they it, to buy *h* stone 2Chr 34:11 4274
she hath *h* out her seven pillars Prov 9:1 2672
but we will build with *h* stones Is 9:10 1496
ones of stature shall be *h* down Is 10:33 1438
Lebanon is ashamed and *h* down Is 33:9 7000
unto the rock whence ye are *h* Is 51:1 2672
inclosed my ways with *h* stone Lam 3:9 1496
the four tables were of *h* stone Eze 40:42 1496
ye have built houses of *h* stone Amos 5:11 1496
not forth good fruit is *h* down Mt 3:10 *1581*
not forth good fruit is *h* down Mt 7:19 *1581*
which he had *h* out in the rock Mt 27:60 *2998*
which was *h* out of a rock Mk 15:46 *2998*
not forth good fruit is *h* down Lk 3:9 *1581*
a sepulchre that was *h* in stone Lk 23:53 *2991*

HEZEKI (*hez'-e-ki*) *A Benjamite.*
And Zebadiah, and Meshullam, and *H*. 1Chr 8:17 2395

HEZEKIAH (*hez-e-ki'-ah*) See EZEKIAS, HIZKIAH.
1. Son of King Ahaz.
H his son reigned in his stead 2Kin 16:20 2396
that *H* the son of Ahaz king of 2Kin 18:1 2396
pass in the fourth year of king *H* 2Kin 18:9 2396
even in the sixth year of *H* 2Kin 18:10 2396
in the fourteenth year of king *H* 2Kin 18:13 2396
H king of Judah sent to the king 2Kin 18:14 2396
H king of Judah three hundred 2Kin 18:14 2396
H gave him all the silver that 2Kin 18:15 2396
At that time did *H* cut off the 2Kin 18:16 2396
from the pillars which *H* king of 2Kin 18:16 2396
king *H* with a great host against 2Kin 18:17 2396
said unto them, Speak ye now to *H* 2Kin 18:19 2396
whose altars *H* hath taken away, 2Kin 18:22 2396
the king, Let not *H* deceive you 2Kin 18:29 2396
Neither let *H* make you trust in 2Kin 18:30 2396
Hearken not to *H* 2Kin 18:31 2396
and hearken not unto *H*, when he 2Kin 18:32 2396
to *H* with their clothes rent, and 2Kin 18:37 2396
to pass, when king *H* heard it 2Kin 19:1 2396
they said unto him, Thus saith *H* 2Kin 19:3 2396
servants of king *H* came to Isaiah 2Kin 19:5 2396
he sent messengers again unto *H* 2Kin 19:9 2396
shall ye speak to *H* king of Judah 2Kin 19:10 2396
H received the letter of the hand 2Kin 19:14 2396
H went up into the house of the 2Kin 19:14 2396
H prayed before the LORD, and said 2Kin 19:15 2396
Isaiah the son of Amoz sent to *H* 2Kin 19:20 2396
those days was *H* sick unto death 2Kin 20:1 2396
And *H* wept sore 2Kin 20:3 2396
tell *H* the captain of my people, 2Kin 20:5 2396
H said unto Isaiah, What shall be 2Kin 20:8 2396
H answered, It is a light thing 2Kin 20:10 2396
sent letters and a present unto *H* 2Kin 20:12 2396
he had heard that *H* had been sick 2Kin 20:12 2396
H hearkened unto them, and shewed 2Kin 20:13 2396
dominion, that *H* shewed them not 2Kin 20:13 2396
Isaiah the prophet unto king *H* 2Kin 20:14 2396
H said, They are come from a far 2Kin 20:14 2396
H answered, All the things that 2Kin 20:15 2396
And Isaiah said unto *H*, Hear the 2Kin 20:16 2396
Then said *H* unto Isaiah, Good is 2Kin 20:19 2396
And the rest of the acts of *H* 2Kin 20:20 2396
And *H* slept with his fathers 2Kin 20:21 2396
which *H* his father had destroyed 2Kin 21:3 2396
H his son, Manasseh his son, 1Chr 3:13 2396
in the days of *H* king of Judah 1Chr 4:41 2396
H his son reigned in his stead 2Chr 28:27 2396
H began to reign when he was five 2Chr 29:1 2396
Then they went in to *H* the king 2Chr 29:18 2396
Then *H* the king rose early, and 2Chr 29:20 2396
H commanded to offer the burnt 2Chr 29:27 2396
Moreover *H* the king and the 2Chr 29:30 2396
Then *H* answered and said, Now ye 2Chr 29:31 2396
H rejoiced, and all the people, 2Chr 29:36 2396
H sent to all Israel and Judah, and 2Chr 30:1 2396
But *H* prayed for them, saying, 2Chr 30:18 2396
And the LORD hearkened to *H* 2Chr 30:20 2396
H spake comfortably unto all the 2Chr 30:22 2396
For *H* king of Judah did give to 2Chr 30:24 2396
H appointed the courses of the 2Chr 31:2 2396
H and the princes came and 2Chr 31:8 2396
Then *H* questioned with the 2Chr 31:9 2396
Then *H* commanded to prepare 2Chr 31:11 2396
at the commandment of *H* the king 2Chr 31:13 2396
thus did *H* throughout all Judah, 2Chr 31:20 2396
when *H* saw that Sennacherib was 2Chr 32:2 2396
upon the words of *H* king of Judah 2Chr 32:8 2396
unto *H* king of Judah, and unto 2Chr 32:9 2396
Doth not *H* persuade you to give 2Chr 32:11 2396
Hath not the same *H* taken away 2Chr 32:12 2396
therefore let not *H* deceive you 2Chr 32:15 2396
God, and against his servant *H* 2Chr 32:16 2396
so shall not the God of *H* deliver 2Chr 32:17 2396
And for this cause *H* the king 2Chr 32:20 2396
Thus the LORD saved *H* and the 2Chr 32:22 2396
presents to *H* king of Judah 2Chr 32:23 2396
In those days *H* was sick to the 2Chr 32:24 2396
But *H* rendered not again 2Chr 32:25 2396
Notwithstanding *H* humbled himself 2Chr 32:26 2396
not upon them in the days of *H* 2Chr 32:26 2396
H had exceeding much riches and 2Chr 32:27 2396
This same *H* also stopped the 2Chr 32:30 2396
H prospered in all his works 2Chr 32:30 2396
Now the rest of the acts of *H* 2Chr 32:32 2396
H slept with his fathers, and they 2Chr 32:33 2396
H his father had broken down 2Chr 33:3 2396
which the men of *H* king of Judah Prov 25:1 2396
of Uzziah, Jotham, Ahaz, and *H* Is 1:1 2396
in the fourteenth year of king *H* Is 36:1 2396
unto king *H* with a great army Is 36:2 2396
said unto them, Say ye now to *H* Is 36:4 2396
whose altars *H* hath taken away, Is 36:7 2396
the king, Let not *H* deceive you Is 36:14 2396
Neither let *H* make you trust in Is 36:15 2396
Hearken not to *H* Is 36:16 2396
Beware lest *H* persuade you, Is 36:18 2396
to *H* with their clothes rent, and Is 36:22 2396
to pass, when king *H* heard it Is 37:1 2396
they said unto him, Thus saith *H* Is 37:3 2396
servants of king *H* came to Isaiah Is 37:5 2396
heard it, he sent messengers to *H* Is 37:9 2396
shall ye speak to *H* king of Judah Is 37:10 2396
H received the letter from the Is 37:14 2396
H went up unto the house of the Is 37:14 2396
H prayed unto the LORD, saying, Is 37:15 2396
the son of Amoz sent unto *H* Is 37:21 2396
those days was *H* sick unto death Is 38:1 2396
Then *H* turned his face toward the Is 38:2 2396
And *H* wept sore Is 38:3 2396
Go, and say to *H*, Thus saith the Is 38:5 2396
The writing of *H* king of Judah Is 38:9 2396
H also had said, What is the sign Is 38:22 2396
sent letters and a present to *H* Is 39:1 2396
H was glad of them, and shewed Is 39:2 2396
dominion, that *H* shewed them not Is 39:2 2396
Isaiah the prophet unto king *H* Is 39:3 2396
H said, They are come from a far Is 39:3 2396
H answered, All that is in mine Is 39:4 2396
Then said Isaiah to *H*, Hear the Is 39:5 2396
Then said *H* to Isaiah, Good is Is 39:8 2396
the son of *H* king of Judah Jer 15:4 2396
in the days of *H* king of Judah Jer 26:18 2396
Did *H* king of Judah and all Judah Jer 26:19 2396
of Uzziah, Jotham, Ahaz, and *H* Hos 1:1 2396
in the days of Jotham, Ahaz, and *H* Mic 1:1 2396
2. A son of Neariah.
Elioenai, and *H*, and Azrikam, three 1Chr 3:23 2396
3. A family of exiles.
The children of Ater of *H* Ezr 2:16 2396
The children of Ater of *H* Neh 7:21 2396

HEZION (*he'-zi-on*) *Grandfather of King Benhadad of Syria.*
the son of Tabrimon, the son of *H* 1Kin 15:18 2383

HEZIR (*he'-zir*)
1. A sanctuary servant.
The seventeenth to *H*, the 1Chr 24:15 2387
2. An Israelite who renewed the covenant.
Magpiash, Meshullam, *H*, Neh 10:20 2387

HEZRAI (*hez'-rahee*) See HEZRO. *A mighty man of David.*
H the Carmelite, Paarai the 2Sa 23:35 2695

HEZRO (*hez'-ro*) See HEZRAI. *Same as Hezrai.*
H the Carmelite, Naarai the son 1Chr 11:37 2695

HEZRON (*hez'-ron*) See HAZOR, HEZRONITES, HEZBON'S.
1. Son of Pharez.
And the sons of Pharez were *H* Gen 46:12 2696
Of *H*, the family of the Num 26:6 2696
of *H*, the family of the Num 26:21 2696
Pharez begat *H*, Ruth 4:18 2696
H begat Ram, and Ram begat Ruth 4:19 2696
of Pharez; *H*, and Hamul 1Chr 2:5 2696
The sons also of *H*, that were 1Chr 2:9 2696
Caleb the son of *H* begat children 1Chr 2:18 2696
afterward *H* went in to the 1Chr 2:21 2696
And after that *H* was dead in 1Chr 2:24 2696
Jerahmeel the firstborn of *H* were 1Chr 2:25 2696
Pharez, *H*, and Carmi, and Hur, and 1Chr 4:1 2696
2. A son of Reuben.
Hanoch, and Phallu, and *H*, and Carmi Gen 46:9 2696
Hanoch, and Pallu, *H*, and Carmi Ex 6:14 2696
Israel were, Hanoch, and Pallu, *H* 1Chr 5:3 2696
3. A town in Judah.
and passed along to *H*, and went up Josh 15:3 2696
Hazor, Hadattah, and Kerioth, and *H* Josh 15:25 2696

HEZRONITES (*hez'-ron-ites*) *Descendants of Hezron 2.*
Of Hezron, the family of the *H* Num 26:6 2697
of Hezron, the family of the *H* Num 26:21 2697

HEZRON'S (*hez'-ronz*) *Refers to Hezron 2.*
then Abiah *H* wife bare him Ashur 1Chr 2:24 2696

HID
his wife *h* themselves from the Gen 3:8 2244
and I *h* myself Gen 3:10 2244
and from thy face shall I be *h* Gen 4:14 5641
Jacob *h* them under the oak which Gen 35:4 2934
child, she *h* him three months Ex 2:2 6845
Egyptian, and *h* him in the sand Ex 2:12 2934
And Moses *h* his face Ex 3:6 5641
the thing be *h* from the eyes of Lev 4:13 5956
withal, and it be *h* from him Lev 5:3 5956
with an oath, and it be *h* from him Lev 5:4 5956
it be *h* from the eyes of her Num 5:13 5956
and of treasures *h* in the sand Deut 33:19 2934
h them, and said thus, There came Josh 2:4 6845
h them with the stalks of flax, Josh 2:6 2934
because she *h* the messengers that Josh 6:17 2244
because she *h* the messengers, Josh 6:25 2244
they are *h* in the earth in the Josh 7:21 2934
it was *h* in his tent, and the Josh 7:22 2934
h themselves in a cave at Josh 10:16 2244
are found *h* in a cave at Makkedah Josh 10:17 2244
the cave wherein they had been *h* Josh 10:27 2244
for he *h* himself Judg 9:5 2244
every whit, and *h* nothing from him 1Sa 3:18 3582
he hath *h* himself among the stuff 1Sa 10:22 2244
holes where they had *h* themselves 1Sa 14:11 2244
had *h* themselves in mount Ephraim 1Sa 14:22 2244
So David *h* himself in the field 1Sa 20:24 5641
he is *h* now in some pit, or in 2Sa 17:9 2244
is no matter *h* from the king 2Sa 18:13 3582
was not any thing *h* from the king 1Kin 10:3 5956
h them by fifty in a cave, and fed 1Kin 18:4 2244
how I *h* an hundred men of the 1Kin 18:13 2244
and the LORD hath *h* it from me 2Kin 4:27 5956
and she hath *h* her son 2Kin 6:29 2244
gold, and raiment, and went and *h* it 2Kin 7:8 2934
thence also, and went and *h* it 2Kin 7:8 2934
and they *h* him, even him and his 2Kin 11:2 5641
he was with her *h* in the house of 2Kin 11:3 2244
four sons with him *h* themselves 1Chr 21:20 2244
there was nothing *h* from Solomon 2Chr 9:2 5956
him, (for he was *h* in Samaria 2Chr 22:9 2244
h him from Athaliah, so that she 2Chr 22:11 5641
he was with them *h* in the house 2Chr 22:12 2244
nor *h* sorrow from mine eyes Job 3:10 5641
for it more than for *h* treasures Job 3:21 4301
given to a man whose way is *h* Job 3:23 5641
Thou shalt be *h* from the scourge Job 5:21 2244
the ice, and wherein the snow is *h* Job 6:16 5956
things hast thou *h* in thine heart Job 10:13 6845
their fathers, and have not *h* it Job 15:18 3582
For thou hast *h* their heart from Job 17:4 6845
shall be *h* in his secret places Job 20:26 2244
the thing that is *h* bringeth he Job 28:11 8587
Seeing it is *h* from the eyes of Job 28:21 5956
young men saw me, and *h* themselves. Job 29:8 2244
The waters are *h* as with a stone, Job 38:30 2244
in the net which they *h* is their Ps 9:15 2934
thou fillest with thy *h* treasure Ps 17:14 6845
there is nothing *h* from the heat Ps 19:6 5641
neither hath he *h* his face from Ps 22:24 5641
and mine iniquity have I not *h* Ps 32:5 3680
they *h* for me their net in a pit Ps 35:7 2934
net that he hath *h* catch himself Ps 35:8 2934
and my groaning is not *h* from thee Ps 38:9 5641
I have not *h* thy righteousness Ps 40:10 3680
I would have *h* myself from him Ps 55:12 5641
and my sins are not *h* from thee Ps 69:5 3582
Thy word have I *h* in mine heart Ps 119:11 6845
My substance was not *h* from thee Ps 139:15 3582
The proud have *h* a snare for me Ps 140:5 2934
for her as for *h* treasures Prov 2:4 4301
falsehood have we *h* ourselves Is 28:15 5641
of their prudent men shall be *h* Is 29:14 5641
My way is *h* from the LORD, and my Is 40:27 5641
they are *h* in prison houses Is 42:22 2244
shadow of his hand hath he *h* me Is 49:2 2244
in his quiver hath he *h* me Is 49:2 5641

I *h* not my face from shame and	Is 50:6	5641
we *h* as it were our faces from	Is 53:3	5641
In a little wrath I *h* my face	Is 54:8	5641
I *h* me, and was wroth, and he went	Is 57:17	5641
your sins have *h* his face from	Is 59:2	5641
for thou hast *h* thy face from us,	Is 64:7	5641
because they are *h* from mine eyes	Is 65:16	5641
h it by Euphrates, as the LORD	Jer 13:5	2934
from the place where I had *h* it	Jer 13:7	2934
they are not *h* from my face	Jer 16:17	5641
their iniquity *h* from mine eyes	Jer 16:17	6845
take me, and *h* snares for my feet	Jer 18:22	2934
I have *h* my face from this city	Jer 33:5	5641
but the LORD *h* them	Jer 36:26	5641
upon these stones that I have *h*	Jer 43:10	2934
have *h* their eyes from my	Eze 22:26	5956
therefore *h* I my face from them,	Eze 39:23	5641
unto them, and *h* my face from them	Eze 39:24	5641
and Israel is not *h* from me	Hos 5:3	3582
his sin is *h*	Hos 13:12	6845
shall be *h* from mine eyes	Hos 13:14	5641
though they be *h* from my sight in	Amos 9:3	5641
thou shalt be *h*, thou also shalt	Nah 3:11	5956
it may be ye shall be *h* in the	Zeph 2:3	5641
is set on an hill cannot be *h*	Mt 5:14	*2928*
and *h*, that shall not be known	Mt 10:26	*2927*
because thou hast *h* these things	Mt 11:25	*613*
h in three measures of meal, till	Mt 13:33	*1470*
like unto treasure *h* in a field	Mt 13:44	*2928*
the earth, and *h* his lord's money	Mt 25:18	*613*
h thy talent in the earth	Mt 25:25	*2928*
For there is nothing *h*, which	Mk 4:22	*2927*
but he could not be *h*	Mk 7:24	*2990*
h herself five months, saying,	Lk 1:24	*4032*
neither any thing *h*, that shall	Lk 8:17	*614*
the woman saw that she was not *h*	Lk 8:47	*2990*
it was *h* from them, that they	Lk 9:45	*3871*
that thou hast *h* these things	Lk 10:21	*613*
neither *h*, that shall not be	Lk 12:2	*2927*
h in three measures of meal, till	Lk 13:21	*1470*
and this saying was *h* from them	Lk 18:34	*2928*
now they are *h* from thine eyes	Lk 19:42	*2928*
but Jesus *h* himself, and went out	Jn 8:59	*2928*
But if our gospel be *h*, it is *h*	2Cor 4:3	*2572*
of the world hath been *h* in God	Eph 3:9	*613*
which hath been *h* from ages	Col 1:26	*613*
In whom are *h* all the treasures	Col 2:3	*614*
your life is *h* with Christ in God	Col 3:3	*2928*
that are otherwise cannot be *h*	1Ti 5:25	*2928*
was *h* three months of his parents	Heb 11:23	*2928*
h themselves in the dens and in	Rev 6:15	*2928*

HIDDAI (*hid'-dahee*) See HURAI. *A mighty man of David.*

H of the brooks of Gaash,	2Sa 23:30	1914

HIDDEKEL (*hid'-de-kel*) *A name for the Tigris River.*

the name of the third river is *H*	Gen 2:14	2313
of the great river, which is *H*	Dan 10:4	2313

HIDDEN

things, and if it be *h* from him	Lev 5:2	5956
this day, it is not *h* from thee	Deut 30:11	6381
Or as an *h* untimely birth I had	Job 3:16	2934
of years is *h* to the oppressor	Job 15:20	6845
times are not *h* from the Almighty	Job 24:1	6845
in the *h* part thou shalt make me	Ps 51:6	5640
and consulted against thy *h* ones	Ps 83:3	6845
when the wicked rise, a man is *h*	Prov 28:12	2664
h riches of secret places, that	Is 45:3	4301
even *h* things, and thou didst not	Is 48:6	5341
how are his *h* things sought up	Obad 6	4710
of these things are *h* from him	Acts 26:26	*2990*
in a mystery, even the *h* wisdom	1Cor 2:7	*613*
to light the *h* things of darkness	1Cor 4:5	*2927*
the *h* things of dishonesty	2Cor 4:2	*2927*
let it be the *h* man of the heart	1Pet 3:4	*2927*
will I give to eat of the *h* manna	Rev 2:17	*2928*

HIDE

Shall I *h* from Abraham that thing	Gen 18:17	3680
We will not *h* it from my lord,	Gen 47:18	3582
when she could not longer *h* him	Ex 2:3	6845
But the bullock, and his *h*	Lev 8:17	5785
the *h* he burnt with fire without	Lev 9:11	5785
ways *h* their eyes from the man	Lev 20:4	5956
h themselves from thee, be	Deut 7:20	5641
go astray, and *h* thyself from them	Deut 22:1	5956
thou mayest not *h* thyself	Deut 22:3	5956
the way, and *h* thyself from them	Deut 22:4	5956
I will *h* my face from them, and	Deut 31:17	5641
I will surely *h* my face in that	Deut 31:18	5641
I will *h* my face from them, I	Deut 32:20	5641
h yourselves there three days,	Josh 2:16	2247
h it not from me	Josh 7:19	3582
to *h* it from the Midianites	Judg 6:11	5127
I pray thee *h* it not from me	1Sa 3:17	3582
if thou *h* any thing from me of	1Sa 3:17	3582
people did *h* themselves in caves	1Sa 13:6	2244
in a secret place, and *h* thyself	1Sa 19:2	2244
my father *h* this thing from me	1Sa 20:2	5641
that I may *h* myself in the field	1Sa 20:5	5641
h thyself when the business was	1Sa 20:19	5641
Doth not David *h* himself with us	1Sa 23:19	5641
Doth not David *h* himself in the	1Sa 26:1	5641
H not from me, I pray thee, the	2Sa 14:18	3582
h thyself by the brook Cherith,	1Kin 17:3	5641
an inner chamber to *h* thyself	1Kin 22:25	2247
camp to *h* themselves in the field	2Kin 7:12	2247
an inner chamber to *h* thyself	2Chr 18:24	2244
then I will not *h* myself from	Job 13:20	5641
thou wouldest *h* me in the grave	Job 14:13	6845
though he *h* it under his tongue	Job 20:12	3582
the earth *h* themselves together	Job 24:4	2244
his purpose, and *h* pride from man	Job 33:17	3680
of iniquity may *h* themselves	Job 34:22	5641
H them in the dust together	Job 40:13	2934
long wilt thou *h* thy face from me	Ps 13:1	5641
h me under the shadow of thy	Ps 17:8	5641
he shall *h* me in his pavilion	Ps 27:5	6845
of his tabernacle shall he *h* me	Ps 27:5	5641
H not thy face far from me	Ps 27:9	5641
thou didst *h* thy face, and I was	Ps 30:7	5641
Thou shalt *h* them in the secret	Ps 31:20	5641
H thy face from my sins, and blot	Ps 51:9	5641
Doth not David *h* himself with us	Ps 54:*t*	5641
and *h* not thyself from my	Ps 55:1	5956
they *h* themselves, they mark my	Ps 56:6	6845
H me from the secret counsel of	Ps 64:2	5641
h not thy face from thy servant	Ps 69:17	5641
We will not *h* them from their	Ps 78:4	3582
wilt thou *h* thyself for ever	Ps 89:46	5641
H not thy face from me in the day	Ps 102:2	5641
h not thy commandments from me	Ps 119:19	5641
h not thy face from me, lest I be	Ps 143:7	5641
I flee unto thee to *h* me	Ps 143:9	3680
h my commandments with thee	Prov 2:1	6845
the wicked rise, men *h* themselves	Prov 28:28	5641
I will *h* mine eyes from you	Is 1:15	5956
h thee in the dust, for fear of	Is 2:10	2934
their sin as Sodom, they *h* it not	Is 3:9	3582
h the outcasts	Is 16:3	5641
h thyself as it were for a little	Is 26:20	2247
to *h* their counsel from the LORD	Is 29:15	5641
that thou *h* not thyself from	Is 58:7	5956
h it there in a hole of the rock	Jer 13:4	2934
which I commanded thee to *h* there	Jer 13:6	2934
Can any *h* himself in secret	Jer 23:24	5641
Go, *h* thee, thou and Jeremiah	Jer 36:19	5641
h nothing from me	Jer 38:14	3582
h it not from us, and we will not	Jer 38:25	3582
h them in the clay in the	Jer 43:9	2934
he shall not be able to *h* himself	Jer 49:10	2247
h not thine ear at my breathing,	Lam 3:56	5956
secret that they can *h* from thee	Eze 28:3	6004
the garden of God could not *h* him	Eze 31:8	6004
Neither will I *h* my face any more	Eze 39:29	5641
so that they fled to *h* themselves	Dan 10:7	2244
though they *h* themselves in the	Amos 9:3	2244
he will even *h* his face from them	Mic 3:4	5641
and did *h* himself from them	Jn 12:36	*2928*
shall *h* a multitude of sins	Jas 5:20	*2572*
h us from the face of him that	Rev 6:16	*2928*

HIDEST

Wherefore *h* thou thy face, and	Job 13:24	5641
why *h* thou thyself in times of	Ps 10:1	5956
Wherefore *h* thou thy face, and	Ps 44:24	5641
why *h* thou thy face from me	Ps 88:14	5641
Thou *h* thy face, they are	Ps 104:29	5641
thou art a God that *h* thyself	Is 45:15	5641

HIDETH

lurking places where he *h* himself	1Sa 23:23	2244
he *h* himself on the right hand,	Job 23:9	5848
when he *h* his face, who then can	Job 34:29	5641
Who is he that *h* counsel without	Job 42:3	5956
he *h* his face	Ps 10:11	5641
the darkness *h* not from thee	Ps 139:12	2821
He that *h* hatred with lying lips,	Prov 10:18	3680
A slothful man *h* his hand in his	Prov 19:24	2934
foreseeth the evil, and *h* himself	Prov 22:3	5641
The slothful *h* his hand in his	Prov 26:15	2934
foreseeth the evil, and *h* himself	Prov 27:12	5641
Whosoever *h* her *h* the wind,	Prov 27:16	6845
but he that *h* his eyes shall have	Prov 28:27	5956
that *h* his face from the house of	Is 8:17	5641
which when a man hath found, he *h*	Mt 13:44	*2928*

HIDING

by *h* mine iniquity in my bosom	Job 31:33	2934
Thou art my *h* place	Ps 32:7	5643
Thou art my *h* place and my shield	Ps 119:114	5643
waters shall overflow the *h* place	Is 28:17	5643
be as an *h* place from the wind	Is 32:2	4224
and there was the *h* of his power	Hab 3:4	2253

HIEL (*hi'-el*) *A Bethelite.*

In his days did *H* the Beth-elite	1Kin 16:34	2419

HIERAPOLIS (*hi-e-rap'-o-lis*) *A city in Phrygia.*

are in Laodicea, and them in *H*	Col 4:13	*2404*

HIGGAION (*hig-gah'-yon*) *A musical notation.*

work of his own hands. *H.*	Ps 9:16	1902

HIGH

and all the *h* hills, that were	Gen 7:19	1364
was the priest of the most *h* God	Gen 14:18	5945
be Abram of the most *h* God	Gen 14:19	5945
And blessed be the most *h* God	Gen 14:20	5945
unto the LORD, the most *h* God	Gen 14:22	5945
And he said, Lo, it is yet *h* day	Gen 29:7	1419
of Israel went out with an *h* hand	Ex 14:8	7311
stretch forth their wings on *h*	Ex 25:20	4605
spread out their wings on *h*	Ex 37:9	4605
to fasten it on *h* upon the mitre	Ex 39:31	4605
he that is the *h* priest among his	Lev 21:10	1419
your *h* ways shall be desolate	Lev 26:22	
And I will destroy your *h* places	Lev 26:30	1116
as it were two cubits *h* upon the	Num 11:31	
we will go by the king's *h* way	Num 20:17	
unto him, We will go by the *h* way	Num 20:19	4546
will go along by the king's *h* way	Num 21:22	
lords of the *h* places of Arnon	Num 21:28	1116
him up into the *h* places of Baal	Num 22:41	1116
And he went to an *h* place	Num 23:3	8205
knew the knowledge of the most *H*	Num 24:16	5945
of Israel went out with an *h* hand	Num 33:3	7311
pluck down all their *h* places	Num 33:52	1116
it unto the death of the *h* priest	Num 35:25	1419
until the death of the *h* priest	Num 35:28	1419
but after the death of the *h*	Num 35:28	1419
I will go along by the *h* way	Deut 2:27	1870
cities were fenced with *h* walls	Deut 3:5	1364
upon the *h* mountains, and upon the	Deut 12:2	7311
to make thee *h* above all nations	Deut 26:19	5945
LORD thy God will set thee on *h*	Deut 28:1	5945
shall get up above thee very *h*	Deut 28:43	4605
in all thy gates, until thy *h*	Deut 28:52	1364
When the Most *H* divided to the	Deut 32:8	5945
ride on the *h* places of the earth	Deut 32:13	1116
they should say, Our hand is *h*	Deut 32:27	7311
shalt tread upon their *h* places	Deut 33:29	1116
until the death of the *h* priest	Josh 20:6	1419
in the *h* places of the field	Judg 5:18	4791
the people to day in the *h* place	1Sa 9:12	1116
he go up to the *h* place to eat	1Sa 9:13	1116
them, for to go up to the *h* place	1Sa 9:14	1116
go up before me unto the *h* place	1Sa 9:19	1116
from the *h* place into the city	1Sa 9:25	1116
from the *h* place with a psaltery	1Sa 10:5	1116
he came to the *h* place	1Sa 10:13	1116
rocks, and in *h* places, and in pits	1Sa 13:6	6877
Israel is slain upon thy *h* places	2Sa 1:19	1116
thou wast slain in thine *h* places	2Sa 1:25	1116
my *h* tower, and my refuge, my	2Sa 22:3	4869
the most *H* uttered his voice	2Sa 22:14	5945
and setteth me upon my *h* places	2Sa 22:34	1116
thou also hast lifted me up on *h*	2Sa 22:49	7311
and the man who was raised up on *h*	2Sa 23:1	5920
the people sacrificed in *h* places	1Kin 3:2	1116
and burnt incense in *h* places	1Kin 3:3	1116
for that was the great *h* place	1Kin 3:4	1116
all the house, five cubits *h*	1Kin 6:10	6967
of olive tree, each ten cubits *h*	1Kin 6:23	6967
of eighteen cubits *h* apiece	1Kin 7:15	6967
a round compass of half a cubit *h*	1Kin 7:35	6967
And at this house, which is *h*	1Kin 9:8	5945
build an *h* place for Chemosh	1Kin 11:7	1116
And he made an house of *h* places	1Kin 12:31	1116
of the *h* places which he had made	1Kin 12:32	1116
he offer the priests of the *h*	1Kin 13:2	1116
against all the houses of the *h*	1Kin 13:32	1116
people priests of the *h* places	1Kin 13:33	1116
of the priests of the *h* places	1Kin 13:33	1116
For they also built them *h* places	1Kin 14:23	1364
and groves, on every *h* hill	1Kin 14:23	1364
But the *h* places were not removed	1Kin 15:14	1116
set Naboth on *h* among the people	1Kin 21:9	7218
set Naboth on *h* among the people	1Kin 21:12	7218
nevertheless the *h* places were	1Kin 22:43	1116
burnt incense yet in the *h* places	1Kin 22:43	1116
But the *h* places were not taken	2Kin 12:3	1116
and burnt incense in the *h* places	2Kin 12:3	1116
the *h* priest came up, and they put	2Kin 12:10	1419
Howbeit the *h* places were not	2Kin 14:4	1116
and burnt incense on the *h* places	2Kin 14:4	1116
Save that the *h* places were not	2Kin 15:4	1116
incense still on the *h* places	2Kin 15:4	1116
Howbeit the *h* places were not	2Kin 15:35	1116
incense still in the *h* places	2Kin 15:35	1116
and burnt incense in the *h* places	2Kin 16:4	1116
they built them *h* places in all	2Kin 17:9	1116
images and groves in every *h* hill	2Kin 17:10	1364
burnt incense in all the *h* places	2Kin 17:11	1116
put them in the houses of the *h*	2Kin 17:29	1116
of them priests of the *h* places	2Kin 17:32	1116
in the houses of the *h* places	2Kin 17:32	1116
He removed the *h* places, and brake	2Kin 18:4	1116
whose *h* places and whose altars	2Kin 18:22	1116
and lifted up thine eyes on *h*	2Kin 19:22	4791
the *h* places which Hezekiah his	2Kin 21:3	1116
Go up to Hilkiah the *h* priest	2Kin 22:4	1419
Hilkiah the *h* priest said unto	2Kin 22:8	1419
commanded Hilkiah the *h* priest	2Kin 23:4	1419
h places in the cities of Judah	2Kin 23:5	1116
defiled the *h* places where the	2Kin 23:8	1116
brake down the *h* places of the	2Kin 23:8	1116
h places came not up to the altar	2Kin 23:9	1116
the *h* places that were before	2Kin 23:13	1116
the *h* place which Jeroboam the	2Kin 23:15	1116
the *h* place he brake down, and	2Kin 23:15	1116
brake down, and burned the *h* place	2Kin 23:15	1116
all the houses also of the *h*	2Kin 23:19	1116
he slew all the priests of the *h*	2Kin 23:20	1116
of great stature, five cubits *h*	1Chr 11:23	
his kingdom was lifted up on *h*	1Chr 14:2	4605
in the *h* place that was at Gibeon	1Chr 16:39	1116
the estate of a man of *h* degree	1Chr 17:17	4608
season in the *h* place at Gibeon	1Chr 21:29	1116
went to the *h* place that was at	2Chr 1:3	1116
the *h* place that was at Gibeon to	2Chr 1:13	1116
of thirty and five cubits *h*	2Chr 3:15	753
cubits broad, and three cubits *h*	2Chr 6:13	6967
And this house, which is *h*	2Chr 7:21	5945
him priests for the *h* places	2Chr 11:15	1116
the *h* places, and brake down the	2Chr 14:3	1116
the cities of Judah the *h* places	2Chr 14:5	1116
But the *h* places were not taken	2Chr 15:17	1116
he took away the *h* places	2Chr 17:6	1116
of Israel with a loud voice on *h*	2Chr 20:19	4605
Howbeit the *h* places were not	2Chr 20:33	1116
Moreover he made *h* places in the	2Chr 21:11	1116
they came through the *h* gate into	2Chr 23:20	5945
the *h* priest's officer came and	2Chr 24:11	7218
He built the *h* gate of the house	2Chr 27:3	5945
and burnt incense in the *h* places	2Chr 28:4	1116
h places to burn incense unto	2Chr 28:25	1116
and threw down the *h* places	2Chr 31:1	1116
Hezekiah taken away his *h* places	2Chr 32:12	1116
For he built again the *h* places	2Chr 33:3	1116
sacrifice still in the *h* places	2Chr 33:17	1116
places wherein he built *h* places	2Chr 33:19	1116
and Jerusalem from the *h* places	2Chr 34:3	1116
images, that were on *h* above them	2Chr 34:4	4605

they came to Hilkiah the *h* priest 2Chr 34:9 1419
Then Eliashib the *h* priest rose Neh 3:1 1419
house of Eliashib the *h* priest Neh 3:20 1419
lieth out from the king's *h* house Neh 3:25 5945
the son of Eliashib the *h* priest Neh 13:28 1419
gallows be made of fifty cubits *h* Est 5:14 1364
also, the gallows fifty cubits *h* Est 7:9 1364
To set up on *h* those that be low Job 5:11 4791
It is as *h* as heaven Job 11:8 1363
in heaven, and my record is on *h* Job 16:19 4791
he judgeth those that are *h* Job 21:22 7311
of the stars, how *h* they are Job 22:12 7311
he maketh peace in his *h* places Job 25:2 4791
of the Almighty from on *h* Job 31:2 4791
the *h* arm shall be broken Job 38:15 7311
time she lifteth up herself on *h* Job 39:18 4791
command, and make her nest on *h* Job 39:27 7311
He beholdeth all *h* things Job 41:34 1364
sakes therefore return thou on *h* Ps 7:7 4791
to the name of the LORD most *h* Ps 7:17 5945
praise to thy name, O thou most *H* Ps 9:2 5945
of my salvation, and my *h* tower Ps 18:2 4869
but wilt bring down *h* looks Ps 18:27 7311
and setteth me upon my *h* places Ps 18:33 1116
the most *H* he shall not be moved Ps 21:7 5945
of the tabernacles of the most *H* Ps 46:4 5945
For the LORD most *h* is terrible Ps 47:2 5945
Both low and *h*, rich and poor, Ps 49:2 376
and pay thy vows unto the most *H* Ps 50:14 5945
fight against me, O thou most *H* Ps 56:2 4791
I will cry unto God most *h* Ps 57:2 5945
men of *h* degree are a lie Ps 62:9 376
an *h* hill as the hill of Bashan Ps 68:15 1386
Why leap ye, ye *h* hills Ps 68:16 1386
Thou hast ascended on *h*, thou Ps 68:18 4791
salvation, O God, set me up on *h* Ps 69:29 7682
also, O God, is very *h*, who hast Ps 71:19 4791
is there knowledge in the most *H* Ps 73:11 5945
Lift not up your horn on *h* Ps 75:5 4791
of the right hand of the most *H* Ps 77:10 5945
the most *H* in the wilderness Ps 78:17 5945
rock, and the *h* God their redeemer Ps 78:35 5945
and provoked the most *h* God Ps 78:56 5945
him to anger with their *h* places Ps 78:58 1116
his sanctuary like *h* palaces Ps 78:69 7311
of you are children of the most *H* Ps 82:6 5945
art the most *h* over all the earth Ps 83:18 5945
thy hand, and *h* is thy right hand Ps 89:13 7311
H shall abide under the shadow of Ps 91:1 5945
is my refuge, even the most *H* Ps 91:9 5945
I will set him on *h*, because he Ps 91:14 7682
praises unto thy name, O most *H* Ps 92:1 5945
LORD, art most *h* for evermore Ps 92:8 4791
The LORD on *h* is mightier than Ps 93:4 4791
art *h* above all the earth Ps 97:9 5945
he is *h* above all the people Ps 99:2 7311
him that hath an *h* look and a Ps 101:5 1362
the heaven is *h* above the earth Ps 103:11 1361
The *h* hills are a refuge for the Ps 104:18 1364
the counsel of the most *H* Ps 107:11 5945
he the poor on *h* from affliction Ps 107:41 7682
The LORD is *h* above all nations, Ps 113:4 7311
LORD our God, who dwelleth on *h* Ps 113:5 1361
or in things too *h* for me Ps 131:1 6381
Though the LORD be *h*, yet hath he Ps 138:6 7311
it is *h*, I cannot attain unto it Ps 139:6 7682
my *h* tower, and my deliverer Ps 144:2 4869
Let the *h* praises of God be in Ps 149:6 7319
him upon the *h* sounding cymbals Ps 150:5 8643
standeth in the top of *h* places Prov 8:2 4791
on a seat in the *h* places of the Prov 9:14 4791
as an *h* wall in his own conceit Prov 18:11 7682
An *h* look, and a proud heart, and Prov 21:4 7312
Wisdom is too *h* for a fool Prov 24:7 7311
be afraid of that which is *h* Eccl 12:5 1364
the cedars of Lebanon, that are *h* Is 2:13 7311
And upon all the *h* mountains Is 2:14 7311
And upon every *h* tower, and upon Is 2:15 1364
the Lord sitting upon a throne, *h* Is 6:1 7311
and the glory of his *h* looks Is 10:12 7312
the *h* ones of stature shall be Is 10:33 7312
up a banner upon the *h* mountain Is 13:2 8192
I will be like the most *H* Is 14:14 5945
to Dibon, the *h* places, to weep Is 15:2 1116
that Moab is weary on the *h* place Is 16:12 1116
heweth him out an sepulchre on *h* Is 22:16 4791
the windows from on *h* are open Is 24:18 4791
of the *h* ones that are on *h* Is 24:21 4791
the fortress of the *h* fort of thy Is 25:12 4869
down them that dwell on *h* Is 26:5 4791
to fall, swelling out in a *h* wall Is 30:13 7682
shall be upon every *h* mountain Is 30:25 1364
and upon every *h* hill Is 30:25 4791
be poured upon us from on *h* Is 32:15 4791
for he dwelleth on *h* Is 33:5 4791
He shall dwell on *h* Is 33:16 4791
whose *h* places and whose altars Is 36:7 1111
and lifted up thine eyes on *h* Is 37:23 4796
get thee up into the *h* mountain Is 40:9 1364
Lift up your eyes on *h*, and behold Is 40:26 4791
I will open rivers in *h* places Is 41:18 8203
pastures shall be in all *h* places Is 49:9 8203
exalted and extolled, and be very *h* Is 52:13 1361
h mountain hast thou set thy bed Is 57:7 5375
For thus saith the *h* and lofty One Is 57:15 7311
I dwell in the *h* and holy place, Is 57:15 4791
make your voice to be heard on *h* Is 58:4 4791
upon the *h* places of the earth Is 58:14 1116
when upon every *h* hill and under Jer 2:20 1364
up thine eyes unto the *h* places Jer 3:2 8205
is gone up upon every *h* mountain Jer 3:6 1364
voice was heard upon the *h* places Jer 3:21 8205
A dry wind of the *h* places in the Jer 4:11 8205
take up a lamentation on *h* places Jer 7:29 8205

have built the *h* places of Tophet Jer 7:31 1116
h places through the wilderness Jer 12:12 8205
asses did stand in the *h* places Jer 14:6 8205
the green trees upon the *h* hills Jer 17:2 1364
thy *h* places for sin, throughout Jer 17:3 1116
A glorious *h* throne from the Jer 17:12 4791
built also the *h* places of Baal Jer 19:5 1116
were in the *h* gate of Benjamin Jer 20:2 5945
The LORD shall roar from on *h* Jer 25:30 4791
house as the *h* places of a forest Jer 26:18 1116
up waymarks, make thee *h* heaps Jer 31:21 8564
they built the *h* places of Baal Jer 32:35 1116
him that offereth in the *h* places Jer 48:35 1116
make thy nest as *h* as the eagle Jer 49:16 1361
her *h* gates shall be burned with Jer 51:58 1364
man before the face of the most *H* Lam 3:35 5945
of the most *H* proceedeth not evil Lam 3:38 5945
they were so *h* that they were Eze 1:18 1362
and I will destroy your *h* places Eze 6:3 1116
the *h* places shall be desolate Eze 6:6 1116
their altars, upon every *h* hill Eze 6:13 7311
deckedst thy *h* places with divers Eze 16:16 1116
hast made thee an *h* place in Eze 16:24 7413
Thou hast built thy *h* place at Eze 16:25 7413
makest thine *h* place in every Eze 16:31 7413
and shall break down thy *h* places Eze 16:39 7413
the highest branch of the *h* cedar Eze 17:22 7311
will plant it upon an *h* mountain Eze 17:22 1364
LORD have brought down the *h* tree Eze 17:24 1364
them, then they saw every *h* hill Eze 20:28 7311
What is the *h* place whereunto ye Eze 20:29 1116
is low, and abase him that is *h* Eze 21:26 1364
shroud, and of an *h* stature Eze 31:3 1362
the deep set him up on *h* with her Eze 31:4 7311
mountains, and upon every *h* hill Eze 34:6 7311
upon the *h* mountains of Israel Eze 34:14 4791
even the ancient *h* places are Eze 36:2 1116
and set me upon a very *h* mountain Eze 40:2 1364
and an half broad, and one cubit *h* Eze 40:42 1363
altar of wood was three cubits *h* Eze 41:22 1364
of their kings in their *h* places Eze 43:7 1116
ye servants of the most *h* God Dan 3:26 5943
wonders that the *h* God hath Dan 4:2 5943
H ruleth in the kingdom of men Dan 4:17 5943
this is the decree of the most *H* Dan 4:24 5943
H ruleth in the kingdom of men Dan 4:25
H ruleth in the kingdom of men Dan 4:32 5943
unto me, and I blessed the most *H* Dan 4:34 5943
O thou king, the most *h* God gave Dan 5:18 5943
till he knew that the most *h* God Dan 5:21 5943
the most *H* shall take the kingdom Dan 7:18 5946
given to the saints of the most *H* Dan 7:22 5946
great words against the most *H* Dan 7:25 5943
wear out the saints of the most *H* Dan 7:25 5946
of the saints of the most *H* Dan 7:27 5946
and the two horns were *h* Dan 8:3 1364
return, but not to the most *H* Hos 7:16 5920
The *h* places also of Aven, the Hos 10:8 1116
they called them to the most *H* Hos 11:7 5920
treadeth upon the *h* places of the Amos 4:13 1116
the *h* places of Isaac shall be Amos 7:9 1116
the rock, whose habitation is *h* Obad 3 4791
tread upon the *h* places of the Mic 1:3 1116
what are the *h* places of Judah Mic 1:5 1116
as the *h* places of the forest Mic 3:12 1116
and bow myself before the *h* God Mic 6:6 4791
that he may set his nest on *h* Hab 2:9 4791
and lifted up his hands on *h* Hab 3:10 7315
me to walk upon mine *h* places Hab 3:19 1116
cities, and against the *h* towers Zeph 1:16 1364
Josedech, the *h* priest, saying, Hag 1:1 1419
the *h* priest, with all the Hag 1:12 1419
the *h* priest, and the spirit of Hag 1:14 1419
the *h* priest, and to the residue Hag 2:2 1419
son of Josedech, the *h* priest Hag 2:4 1419
he shewed me Joshua the *h* priest Zec 3:1 1419
Hear now, O Joshua the *h* priest Zec 3:8 1419
the son of Josedech, the *h* priest Zec 6:11 1419
up into an exceeding *h* mountain Mt 4:8 5308
them up into an *h* mountain apart Mt 17:1 5308
unto the palace of the *h* priest Mt 26:3 749
a servant of the *h* priest's Mt 26:51 749
him away to Caiaphas the *h* priest Mt 26:57 749
off unto the *h* priest's palace Mt 26:58 749
the *h* priest arose, and said unto Mt 26:62 749
the *h* priest answered and said Mt 26:63 749
Then the *h* priest rent his Mt 26:65 749
the days of Abiathar the *h* priest Mk 2:26 749
Jesus, thou Son of the most *h* God Mk 5:7 5310
h captains, and chief estates of Mk 6:21
leadeth them up into an *h* Mk 9:2 5308
smote a servant of the *h* priest Mk 14:47 749
led Jesus away to the *h* priest Mk 14:53 749
into the palace of the *h* priest Mk 14:54 749
the *h* priest stood up in the Mk 14:60 749
Again the *h* priest asked him, and Mk 14:61 749
Then the *h* priest rent his Mk 14:63 749
one of the maids of the *h* priest Mk 14:66 749
from on *h* hath visited us Lk 1:78 5311
and Caiaphas being the *h* priests Lk 3:2 749
taking him up into an *h* mountain Lk 4:5 5308
Jesus, thou Son of God most *h* Lk 8:28 5310
smote the servant of the *h* priest Lk 22:50 749
him into the *h* priest's house Lk 22:54 749
ye be endued with power from on *h* Lk 24:49 5311
being the *h* priest that same year Jn 11:49 749
but being *h* priest that year, he Jn 11:51 749
smote the *h* priest's servant, and Jn 18:10 749
which was the *h* priest that same Jn 18:13 749
was known unto the *h* priest Jn 18:15 749
into the palace of the *h* priest Jn 18:15 749
which was known unto the *h* priest Jn 18:16 749
The *h* priest then asked Jesus of Jn 18:19 749
Answerest thou the *h* priest so Jn 18:22 749

bound unto Caiaphas the *h* priest Jn 18:24 749
of the servants of the *h* priest Jn 18:26 749
for that sabbath day was an *h* day Jn 19:31 3173
And Annas the *h* priest, and Acts 4:6 749
of the kindred of the *h* priest Acts 4:6 749
Then the *h* priest rose up, and all Acts 5:17 749
But the *h* priest came, and they Acts 5:21 749
Now when the *h* priest and the Acts 5:24 2409
and the *h* priest asked them, Acts 5:27 749
Then said the *h* priest, Are these Acts 7:1 749
Howbeit the most *H* dwelleth not Acts 7:48 5310
the Lord, went unto the *h* priest Acts 9:1 749
with an *h* arm brought he them out Acts 13:17 5308
the servants of the most *h* God Acts 16:17 5310
As also the *h* priest doth bear me Acts 22:5 749
the *h* priest Ananias commanded Acts 23:2 749
Revilest thou God's *h* priest Acts 23:4 749
that he was the *h* priest Acts 23:5 749
the *h* priest descended with the Acts 24:1 749
Then the *h* priest and the chief of Acts 25:2 749
Mind not *h* things, but condescend Rom 12:16 5308
that now it is *h* time to awake Rom 13:11
every *h* thing that exalteth 2Cor 10:5 5313
saith, When he ascended up on *h* Eph 4:8 5311
spiritual wickedness in *h* places Eph 6:12 2032
the mark for the prize of the *h* Phil 3:14 507
right hand of the Majesty on *h* Heb 1:3 5308
faithful *h* priest in things Heb 2:17 749
H Priest of our profession, Heb 3:1 749
that we have a great *h* priest Heb 4:14 749
For we have not an *h* priest which Heb 4:15 749
For every *h* priest taken from Heb 5:1 749
himself to be made an *h* priest Heb 5:5 749
Called of God an *h* priest after Heb 5:10 749
made an *h* priest for ever after Heb 6:20 749
Salem, priest of the most *h* God Heb 7:1 5310
For such an *h* priest became us, Heb 7:26 749
not daily, as those *h* priests Heb 7:27 749
For the law maketh men *h* priests Heb 7:28 749
We have such an *h* priest, who is Heb 8:1 749
For every *h* priest is ordained to Heb 8:3 749
h priest alone once every year Heb 9:7 749
But Christ being come an *h* priest Heb 9:11 749
as the *h* priest entereth into the Heb 9:25 749
having an *h* priest over the house Heb 10:21 3173
sanctuary by the *h* priest for sin Heb 13:11 749
h mountain, and shewed me that Rev 21:10 5308
And had a wall great and *h*, and had Rev 21:12 5308

HIGHER

and his king shall be *h* than Agag Num 24:7 7311
upward he was *h* than any of the 1Sa 9:2 1364
he was *h* than any of the people 1Sa 10:23 1361
He built the *h* gate of the house 2Kin 15:35 5945
the wall, and on the *h* places Neh 4:13 6706
the clouds which are *h* than thou Job 35:5 1361
me to the rock that is *h* than I Ps 61:2 7311
h than the kings of the earth Ps 89:27 5945
for he that is *h* than the highest Eccl 5:8 1364
and there be *h* than they Eccl 5:8 1364
the heavens are *h* than the earth Is 55:9 1361
so are my ways *h* than your ways Is 55:9 1361
the scribe, in the *h* court Jer 36:10 5945
came from the way of the *h* gate Eze 9:2 5945
the galleries were *h* than these Eze 42:5 3201
this shall be the *h* place of the Eze 43:13 1354
but one was *h* than the other Dan 8:3 1364
and the *h* came up last Dan 8:3 1364
say unto thee, Friend, go up *h* Lk 14:10 511
soul be subject unto the *h* powers Rom 13:1 5242
and made *h* than the heavens Heb 7:26 5308

HIGHEST

heavens, and the *H* gave his voice Ps 18:13 5945
the *h* himself shall establish her Ps 87:5 5945
nor the *h* part of the dust of the Prov 8:26 7218
upon the *h* places of the city Prov 9:3 4791
is higher than the *h* regardeth Eccl 5:8 1364
took the *h* branch of the cedar Eze 17:3 6788
I will also take of the *h* branch Eze 17:22 6788
chamber to the *h* by the midst Eze 41:7 5945
Hosanna in the *h* Mt 21:9 5310
Hosanna in the *h* Mk 11:10 5310
shall be called the Son of the *H* Lk 1:32 5310
thee, and the power of the *H* shall Lk 1:35 5310
be called the prophet of the *H* Lk 1:76 5310
Glory to God in the *h*, and on Lk 2:14 5310
ye shall be the children of the *H* Lk 6:35 5310
sit not down in the *h* room Lk 14:8 4411
in heaven, and glory in the *h* Lk 19:38 5310
the *h* seats in the synagogues, and Lk 20:46 4410

HIGHLY

Hail, thou that art *h* favoured Lk 1:28
for that which is *h* esteemed Lk 16:15 5308
Herod was *h* displeased with them Acts 12:20 2371
more *h* than he ought to think Rom 12:3 5252
God also hath *h* exalted him Phil 2:9 5251
to esteem them very *h* in love for 1Th 5:13

HIGHMINDED

Be not *h*, but fear Rom 11:20 5309
in this world, that they be not *h* 1Ti 6:17 5309
Traitors, heady, *h*, lovers of 2Ti 3:4 5187

HIGHNESS

by reason of his *h* I could not Job 31:23 7613
even them that rejoice in my *h* Is 13:3 1346

HIGHWAY

on the east side of the *h* that Judg 21:19 4546
Beth-shemesh, and went along the *h* 1Sa 6:12 4546
in blood in the midst of the *h* 2Sa 20:12 4546
Amasa out of the *h* into the field 2Sa 20:12 4546
When he was removed out of the *h* 2Sa 20:13 4546
which is in the *h* of the fuller's 2Kin 18:17 4546
The *h* of the upright is to depart Prov 16:17 4546

in the *h* of the fuller's field Is 7:3 4546
there shall be an *h* for the Is 11:16 4546
be a *h* out of Egypt to Assyria Is 19:23 4546
an *h* shall be there, and a way, and Is 35:8 4547
in the *h* of the fuller's field Is 36:2 4546
in the desert a *h* for our God Is 40:3 4546
set thine heart toward the *h* Jer 31:21 4546
sat by the *h* side begging Mk 10:46 *3598*

HIGHWAYS
the *h* were unoccupied, and the Judg 5:6 734
kill, as at other times, in the *h* Judg 20:31 4546
them from the city unto the *h* Judg 20:32 4546
them in the *h* five thousand men Judg 20:45 4546
The *h* lie waste, the wayfaring Is 33:8 4546
a way, and my *h* shall be exalted Is 49:11 4546
cast up, cast up the *h* Is 62:10 4546
and they shall say in all the *h* Amos 5:16 2351
Go ye therefore into the *h* Mt 22:9
servants went out into the *h* Mt 22:10 *3598*
the servant, Go out into the *h* Lk 14:23 *3598*

HILEN (*hi'-len*) See HOLON. *A Levitical city in Judah.*
H with her suburbs, Debir with 1Chr 6:58 2432

HILKIAH (*hil-ki'-ah*) See HELKAI, HILKIAH'S.
1. Father of Eliakim.
out to them Eliakim the son of *H* 2Kin 18:18 2518
Then said Eliakim the son of *H* 2Kin 18:26 2518
Then came Eliakim the son of *H* 2Kin 18:37 2518
And Shallum begat *H* 1Chr 6:13 2518
and *H* begat Azariah 1Chr 6:13 2518
Of *H*, Hashabiah; of Jedaiah Neh 12:21 2518
my servant Eliakim the son of *H* Is 22:20 2518
Then came Eliakim, the son of *H* Is 36:22 2518
2. A High Priest.
Go up to *H* the high priest, that 2Kin 22:4 2518
H the high priest said unto 2Kin 22:8 2518
H gave the book to Shaphan, and he 2Kin 22:8 2518
H the priest hath delivered me a 2Kin 22:10 2518
the king commanded *H* the priest 2Kin 22:12 2518
So *H* the priest, and Ahikam, and 2Kin 22:14 2518
king commanded *H* the high priest 2Kin 23:4 2518
H the priest found in the house 2Kin 23:24 2518
And Azariah the son of *H*, the son 1Chr 9:11 2518
they came to *H* the high priest 2Chr 34:9 2518
H the priest found a book of the 2Chr 34:14 2518
H answered and said to Shaphan the 2Chr 34:15 2518
H delivered the book to Shaphan 2Chr 34:15 2518
H the priest hath given me a book 2Chr 34:18 2518
And the king commanded *H*, and 2Chr 34:20 2518
And *H*, and they that the king had 2Chr 34:22 2518
H and Zechariah and Jehiel, rulers 2Chr 35:8 2518
the son of Azariah, the son of *H* Ezr 7:1 2518
Shaphan, and Gemariah the son of *H* Jer 29:3 2518
3. A descendant of Merari.
the son of Amaziah, the son of *H* 1Chr 6:45 2518
4. A son of Hosah.
H the second, Tebaliah the third, 1Chr 26:11 2518
5. A priest who assisted Ezra.
Anaiah, and Urijah, and *H* Neh 8:4 2518
Seraiah the son of *H*, the son of Neh 11:11 2518
Sallu, Amok, *H*, Jedaiah Neh 12:7 2518
6. Father of Jeremiah.
words of Jeremiah the son of *H* Jer 1:1 2518

HILKIAH'S (*hil-ki'-ahs*) *Refers to Hilkiah 1.*
H son, which was over the house, Is 36:3 2518

HILL
the *h* with the rod of God in mine Ex 17:9 1389
Hur went up to the top of the *h* Ex 17:10 1389
and builded an altar under the *h* Ex 24:4 2022
presumed to go up unto the *h* top Num 14:44 2022
Canaanites which dwelt in that *h* Num 14:45 2022
ye were ready to go up into the *h* Deut 1:41 2022
went presumptuously up into the *h* Deut 1:43 2022
Israel at the *h* of the foreskins Josh 5:3 1389
the *h* country from Lebanon unto Josh 13:6 2022
was drawn from the top of the *h* Josh 15:9 2022
The *h* is not enough for us Josh 17:16 2022
near the *h* that lieth on the Josh 18:13 2022
from the *h* that lieth before Josh 18:14 2022
in the *h* country of Judah, with Josh 21:11 2022
the north side of the *h* of Gaash Josh 24:30 2022
they buried him in a *h* that Josh 24:33 1389
on the north side of the *h* Gaash Judg 2:9 2022
by the *h* of Moreh, in the valley Judg 7:1 1389
top of an *h* that is before Hebron Judg 16:3 2022
the house of Abinadab in the *h* 1Sa 7:1 1389
as they went up the *h* to the city 1Sa 9:11 4608
thou shalt come to the *h* of God 1Sa 10:5 1389
when they came thither to the *h* 1Sa 10:10 1389
in the *h* of Hachilah, which is on 1Sa 23:19 1389
came down by the covert of the *h* 1Sa 25:20 2022
hide himself in the *h* of Hachilah 1Sa 26:1 1389
Saul pitched in the *h* of Hachilah 1Sa 26:3 1389
stood on the top of an *h* afar off 1Sa 26:13 2022
they were come to the *h* of Ammah 2Sa 2:24 1389
and stood on the top of an *h* 2Sa 2:25 1389
the way of the *h* side behind him 2Sa 13:34 2022
a little past the top of the *h* 2Sa 16:1
them in the *h* before the LORD 2Sa 21:9 2022
in the *h* that is before Jerusalem 1Kin 11:7 2022
and groves, on every high *h* 1Kin 14:23 1389
he bought the *h* Samaria of Shemer 1Kin 16:24 2022
of silver, and built on the *h* 1Kin 16:24 2022
name of Shemer, owner of the *h* 1Kin 16:24 2022
behold, he sat on the top of an *h* 2Kin 1:9 2022
came to the man of God to the *h* 2Kin 4:27 2022
images and groves in every high *h* 2Kin 17:10 1389
my king upon my holy *h* of Zion Ps 2:6 2022
and he heard me out of his holy *h* Ps 3:4 2022
who shall dwell in thy holy *h* Ps 15:1 2022
ascend into the *h* of the LORD Ps 24:3 2022
the Hermonites, from the *h* Mizar Ps 42:6 2022
let them bring me unto thy holy *h* Ps 43:3 2022
h of God is as the *h* of Bashan Ps 68:15 2022
an high *h* as the *h* of Bashan Ps 68:15 2022
this is the *h* which God desireth Ps 68:16 2022
our God, and worship at his holy *h* Ps 99:9 2022
and to the *h* of frankincense Song 4:6 1389
a vineyard in a very fruitful *h* Is 5:1 7161
of Zion, the *h* of Jerusalem Is 10:32 1389
mountain, and as an ensign on an *h* Is 30:17 1389
mountain, and upon every high *h* Is 30:25 1389
mount Zion, and for the *h* thereof Is 31:4 1389
mountain and *h* shall be made low Is 40:4 1389
when upon every high *h* and under Jer 2:20 1389
every mountain, and from every *h* Jer 16:16 1389
over against it upon the *h* Gareb Jer 31:39 1389
that holdest the height of the *h* Jer 49:16 1389
they have gone from mountain to *h* Jer 50:6 1389
their altars, upon every high *h* Eze 6:13 1389
them, then they saw every high *h* Eze 20:28 1389
mountains, and upon every high *h* Eze 34:6 1389
round about my *h* a blessing Eze 34:26 1389
that is set on an *h* cannot be hid Mt 5:14 *3735*
went into the *h* country with Lk 1:39 *3714*
all the *h* country of Judaea Lk 1:65 *3714*
and *h* shall be brought low Lk 3:5 *1015*
h whereon their city was built Lk 4:29 *3735*
they were come down from the *h* Lk 9:37 *3735*
stood in the midst of Mars' *h* Acts 17:22 *697*

HILLEL (*hil'-lel*) *Father of Abdon.*
And after him Abdon the son of *H* Judg 12:13 1985
And Abdon the son of *H* the Judg 12:15 1985

HILL'S
on the *h* side over against him 2Sa 16:13 2022

HILLS
and all the high *h*, that were Gen 7:19 2022
utmost bound of the everlasting *h* Gen 49:26 1389
him, and from the *h* I behold him Num 23:9 1389
thereunto, in the plain, in the *h* Deut 1:7 2022
that spring out of valleys and *h* Deut 8:7 2022
out of whose *h* thou mayest dig Deut 8:9 2042
go to possess it, is a land of *h* Deut 11:11 2022
the high mountains, and upon the *h* Deut 12:2 1389
precious things of the lasting *h* Deut 33:15 1389
on this side Jordan, in the *h* Josh 9:1 2022
smote all the country of the *h* Josh 10:40 2022
Joshua took all that land, the *h* Josh 11:16 2022
him, Their gods are gods of the *h* 1Kin 20:23 2022
said, The LORD is God of the *h* 1Kin 20:28 2022
all Israel scattered upon the *h* 1Kin 22:17 2022
in the high places, and on the *h* 2Kin 16:4 1389
in the high places, and on the *h* 2Chr 28:4 1389
or wast thou made before the *h* Job 15:7 1389
foundations also of the *h* moved Ps 18:7 2022
and the cattle upon a thousand *h* Ps 50:10 2042
the little *h* rejoice on every Ps 65:12 1389
Why leap ye, ye high *h* Ps 68:16 2022
to the people, and the little *h* Ps 72:3 1389
The *h* were covered with the Ps 80:10 2022
the strength of the *h* is his also Ps 95:4 2022
The *h* melted like wax at the Ps 97:5 2022
let the *h* be joyful together Ps 98:8 2022
valleys, which run among the *h* Ps 104:10 2022
He watereth the *h* from his Ps 104:13 2022
The high *h* are a refuge for the Ps 104:18 2022
he toucheth the *h*, and they smoke Ps 104:32 2022
rams, and the little *h* like lambs Ps 114:4 1389
and ye little *h*, like lambs Ps 114:6 1389
will lift up mine eyes unto the *h* Ps 121:1 2022
Mountains, and all *h* Ps 148:9 1389
before the *h* was I brought forth Prov 8:25 1389
mountains, skipping upon the *h* Song 2:8 1389
and shall be exalted above the *h* Is 2:2 1389
upon all the *h* that are lifted up Is 2:14 1389
the *h* did tremble, and their Is 5:25 2022
on all *h* that shall be digged Is 7:25 2022
in scales, and the *h* in a balance Is 40:12 1389
and shalt make the *h* as chaff Is 41:15 1389
I will make waste mountains and *h* Is 42:15 1389
shall depart, and the *h* be removed Is 54:10 1389
the *h* shall break forth before Is 55:12 1389
and blasphemed me upon the *h* Is 65:7 1389
is salvation hoped for from the *h* Jer 3:23 1389
and all the *h* moved lightly Jer 4:24 1389
on the *h* in the fields Jer 13:27 1389
the green trees upon the high *h* Jer 17:2 1389
GOD to the mountains, and to the *h* Eze 6:3 1389
in thy *h*, and in thy valleys, and Eze 35:8 1389
GOD to the mountains, and to the *h* Eze 36:4 1389
unto the mountains, and to the *h* Eze 36:6 1389
and burn incense upon the *h* Hos 4:13 1389
and to the *h*, Fall on us Hos 10:8 1389
the *h* shall flow with milk, and Joel 3:18 1389
wine, and all the *h* shall melt Amos 9:13 1389
it shall be exalted above the *h* Mic 4:1 1389
and let the *h* hear thy voice Mic 6:1 1389
the *h* melt, and the earth is Nah 1:5 1389
the perpetual *h* did bow Hab 3:6 1389
and a great crashing from the *h* Zeph 1:10 1389
and to the *h*, Cover us Lk 23:30 *1015*

HIM See PREFACE.

HIMSELF
he divided *h* against them, he and Gen 14:15
bowed *h* toward the ground, Gen 18:2
he bowed *h* with his face toward Gen 19:1
God will provide *h* a lamb for a Gen 22:8
bowed *h* to the people of the land Gen 23:7
Abraham bowed down *h* before the Gen 23:12
the LORD, bowing *h* to the earth Gen 24:52
as touching thee, doth comfort *h* Gen 27:42
set three days' journey betwixt *h* Gen 30:36
h lodged that night in the Gen 32:21 1931
bowed *h* to the ground seven times Gen 33:3
and he shaved *h*, and changed his Gen 41:14
but made *h* strange unto them, and Gen 42:7
he turned *h* about from them, and Gen 42:24
face, and went out, and refrained *h* Gen 43:31
And they set on for him by *h* Gen 43:32
h before all them that stood by Gen 45:1
while Joseph made *h* known unto Gen 45:1
Goshen, and presented *h* unto him Gen 46:29
Israel bowed *h* upon the bed's Gen 47:31
and Israel strengthened *h*, and sat Gen 48:2
he bowed *h* with his face to the Gen 48:12
And he turned *h*, and went out from Ex 10:6
by *h*, he shall go out by *h* Ex 21:3 1610
master's, and he shall go out by *h* Ex 21:4 1610
who hath betrothed her to *h* Ex 21:8
even the priest shall have to *h* Lev 7:8
the sin offering, which was for *h* Lev 9:8
wash *h* in water, that he may be Lev 14:8
bathe *h* in water, and be unclean Lev 15:5
bathe *h* in water, and be unclean Lev 15:6
bathe *h* in water, and be unclean Lev 15:7
bathe *h* in water, and be unclean Lev 15:8
bathe *h* in water, and be unclean Lev 15:10
bathe *h* in water, and be unclean Lev 15:11
then he shall number to *h* seven Lev 15:13
bathe *h* in water, and be unclean Lev 15:21
bathe *h* in water, and be unclean Lev 15:22
bathe *h* in water, and be unclean Lev 15:27
the sin offering, which is for *h* Lev 16:6
and make an atonement for *h* Lev 16:6
the sin offering, which is for *h* Lev 16:11
and shall make an atonement for *h* Lev 16:11
the sin offering which is for *h* Lev 16:11
and have made an atonement for *h* Lev 16:17
and make an atonement for *h* Lev 16:24
bathe *h* in water, and be unclean Lev 17:15
But he shall not defile *h* Lev 21:4
among his people, to profane *h* Lev 21:4
nor defile *h* for his father, or Lev 21:11
not eat to defile *h* therewith Lev 22:8
it, and *h* be able to redeem it Lev 25:26 3027
sell *h* unto the stranger or Lev 25:47
or if he be able, he may redeem *h* Lev 25:49 3027
shall present *h* before the priest Lev 27:8
He shall separate *h* from wine Num 6:3
he separateth *h* unto the LORD Num 6:5
h unto the LORD he shall come at Num 6:6
He shall not make *h* unclean for Num 6:7
to bring you near to *h* to do the Num 16:9
He shall purify *h* with it on the Num 19:12 1931
if he purify not *h* the third day Num 19:12
that is dead, and purifieth not *h* Num 19:13
the seventh day he shall purify *h* Num 19:19
bathe *h* in water, and shall be Num 19:19
be unclean, and shall not purify *h* Num 19:20
lift up *h* as a young lion Num 23:24
Israel joined *h* unto Baal-peor Num 25:3
had taken spoil, every man for *h* Num 31:53
The revenger of blood *h* shall Num 35:19 1931
children of Israel shall keep *h* Num 36:7
keep *h* to his own inheritance Num 36:9
to be a special people unto *h* Deut 7:6
to be a peculiar people unto *h* Deut 14:2
he shall not multiply horses to *h* Deut 17:16
shall he multiply wives to *h* Deut 17:17
he greatly multiply to *h* silver Deut 17:17
on, he shall wash *h* with water Deut 23:11
thee an holy people unto *h* Deut 28:9
thee to day for a people unto *h* Deut 29:13
that he bless *h* in his heart Deut 29:19
repent *h* for his servants, when Deut 32:36
he provided the first part for *h* Deut 33:21
let the LORD *h* require it Josh 22:23
But he *h* turned again from the Judg 3:19 1931
parlour, which he had for *h* alone Judg 3:20
had severed *h* from the Kenites, Judg 4:11
he be a god, let him plead for *h* Judg 6:31
lappeth, him shalt thou set by *h* Judg 7:5
for he hid *h* Judg 9:5
he bowed *h* with all his might Judg 16:30
the man was afraid, and turned *h* Ruth 3:8
brought up the priest took for *h* 1Sa 2:14
for the LORD revealed *h* to Samuel 1Sa 3:21
your sons, and appoint them for *h* 1Sa 8:11
who *h* saved you out of all your 1Sa 10:19
he hath hid *h* among the stuff 1Sa 10:22 1931
and whithersoever he turned *h* 1Sa 14:47
and presented *h* forty days 1Sa 17:16
Jonathan stripped *h* of the robe 1Sa 18:4
sent him, and behaved *h* wisely 1Sa 18:5
David behaved *h* wisely in all his 1Sa 18:14
saw that he behaved *h* very wisely 1Sa 18:15
that David behaved *h* more wisely 1Sa 18:30
So David hid *h* in the field 1Sa 20:24
ground, and bowed *h* three times 1Sa 20:41
feigned *h* mad in their hands, and 1Sa 21:13
Doth not David hide *h* with us in 1Sa 23:19
lurking places where he hideth *h* 1Sa 23:23
his face to the earth, and bowed *h* 1Sa 24:8
or that my lord hath avenged *h* 1Sa 25:31
Doth not David hide *h* in the hill 1Sa 26:1
And Saul disguised *h*, and put on 1Sa 28:8
face to the ground, and bowed *h* 1Sa 28:14
he reconcile *h* unto his master 1Sa 29:4
encouraged *h* in the LORD his God 1Sa 30:6
to all the places where David *h* 1Sa 30:31
that Abner made *h* strong for the 2Sa 3:6
king David *h* followed the bier 2Sa 3:31
of Israel today, who uncovered *h* 2Sa 6:20
fellows shamelessly uncovereth *h* 2Sa 6:20
went to redeem for a people to *h* 2Sa 7:23
And he bowed *h*, and said, What is 2Sa 9:8

H

how will he then vex *h*, if we 2Sa 12:18
earth, and washed, and anointed *h* 2Sa 12:20
So Amnon lay down, and made *h* sick. 2Sa 13:6
ground on his face, and bowed *h* 2Sa 14:22
bowed *h* on his face to the ground 2Sa 14:33
the king also *h* passed over the 2Sa 15:23
household in order, and hanged *h* 2Sa 17:23
taken and reared up for *h* a pillar 2Sa 18:18
And Cushi bowed *h* unto Joab 2Sa 18:21
bowed *h* before the king on his 2Sa 24:20
the son of Haggith exalted *h* 1Kin 1:5
he bowed *h* before the king with 1Kin 1:23
And the king bowed *h* upon the bed 1Kin 1:47
If he will shew *h* a worthy man 1Kin 1:52
came and bowed *h* to king Solomon 1Kin 1:53
bowed *h* unto her, and sat down on 1Kin 2:19
he had clad *h* with a new garment 1Kin 11:29 1931
the things which *h* had dedicated 1Kin 15:15
drinking *h* drunk in the house of 1Kin 16:9
he stretched *h* upon the child 1Kin 17:21
Elijah went to shew *h* unto Ahab 1Kin 18:2
Ahab went one way by *h*, and 1Kin 18:6
and Obadiah went another way by *h* 1Kin 18:6
he cast *h* down upon the earth, and 1Kin 18:42
But he *h* went a day's journey 1Kin 19:4 1931
he requested for *h* that he might 1Kin 19:4 5315
boast *h* as he that putteth it off 1Kin 20:11
drinking *h* drunk in the pavilions 1Kin 20:16
disguised *h* with ashes upon his 1Kin 20:38
Ahab, which did sell *h* to work 1Kin 21:25
how Ahab humbleth *h* before me 1Kin 21:29
because he humbleth *h* before me 1Kin 21:29
And the king of Israel disguised *h* 1Kin 22:30
he stretched *h* upon the child 2Kin 4:34
went up, and stretched *h* upon him 2Kin 4:35
dipped *h* seven times in Jordan, 2Kin 5:14
warned him of, and saved *h* there 2Kin 6:10
covered *h* with sackcloth, and went 2Kin 19:1
And as Josiah turned *h*, he spied 2Kin 23:16
while he yet kept *h* close because 1Chr 12:1
home to *h* to the city of David 1Chr 13:13
bowed *h* to David with his face to 1Chr 21:21
kingdom, and had strengthened *h* 2Chr 12:1
And when he humbled *h*, the wrath 2Chr 12:12
strengthened *h* in Jerusalem 2Chr 12:13
consecrate *h* with a young bullock 2Chr 13:9 3027
God *h* is with us for our captain, 2Chr 13:12
that he *h* had dedicated, silver, 2Chr 15:18
to shew *h* strong in the behalf of 2Chr 16:9
made for *h* in the city of David 2Chr 16:14
strengthened *h* against Israel 2Chr 17:1
willingly offered *h* unto the LORD 2Chr 17:16
So the king of Israel disguised *h* 2Chr 18:29
the king of Israel stayed *h* up in 2Chr 18:34
set *h* to seek the LORD, and 2Chr 20:3 6440
h with Ahaziah king of Israel 2Chr 20:35
he joined *h* with him to make 2Chr 20:36
of his father, he strengthened *h* 2Chr 21:4
year Jehoiada strengthened *h* 2Chr 23:1
And Amaziah strengthened *h* 2Chr 25:11
bowed down *h* before them, and 2Chr 25:14
for he strengthened *h* exceedingly 2Chr 26:8
h hasted also to go out, because 2Chr 26:20 1931
and thought to win them for *h* 2Chr 32:1
Also he strengthened *h*, and built 2Chr 32:5
(but he *h* laid siege against 2Chr 32:9 1931
Hezekiah humbled *h* for the pride 2Chr 32:26
he made *h* treasuries for silver, 2Chr 32:27
humbled *h* greatly before the God 2Chr 33:12
humbled not *h* before the LORD, as 2Chr 33:23
Manasseh his father had humbled *h* 2Chr 33:23
face from him, but disguised *h* 2Chr 35:22
humbled not *h* before Jeremiah the 2Chr 36:12
casting *h* down before the house Ezr 10:1
h separated from the congregation Ezr 10:8 1931
Nevertheless Haman refrained *h* Est 5:10
only upon *h* put not forth thine Job 1:12
them to present *h* before the LORD Job 2:1
him a potsherd to scrape *h* withal Job 2:8
who can withhold *h* from speaking Job 4:2
who hath hardened *h* against him Job 9:4
strengtheneth *h* against the Job 15:25
stir up *h* against the hypocrite Job 17:8
He teareth *h* in his anger Job 18:4 5315
is wise may be profitable unto *h* Job 22:2
he hideth *h* on the right hand, Job 23:9
Will he delight *h* in the Almighty Job 27:10
he justified *h* rather than God Job 32:2 5315
that he should delight *h* with God Job 34:9
if he gather unto *h* his spirit Job 34:14
When he raiseth up *h*, the mighty Job 41:25
set apart him that is godly for *h* Ps 4:3
He croucheth, and humbleth *h* Ps 10:10
the poor committeth *h* unto thee Ps 10:14
his net that he hath hid catch *h* Ps 35:8
he flattereth *h* in his own eyes Ps 36:2
he setteth *h* in a way that is not Ps 36:4
spreading *h* like a green bay tree Ps 37:35
for God is judge *h* Ps 50:6 1931
strengthened *h* in his wickedness Ps 52:7
Doth not David hide *h* with us Ps 54:t
me that did magnify *h* against me Ps 55:12
submit *h* with pieces of silver Ps 68:30
the highest *h* shall establish her Ps 87:5 1931
wherewith he hath girded *h* Ps 93:1
As he clothed *h* with cursing like Ps 109:18
Who humbleth *h* to behold the Ps 113:6
but upon *h* shall his crown Ps 132:18
the LORD hath chosen Jacob unto *h* Ps 135:4
he will repent *h* concerning his Ps 135:14
shall take the wicked *h*, and he Prov 5:22
a scorner getteth to *h* shame Prov 9:7
a wicked man getteth *h* a blot Prov 9:7
watereth shall be watered also *h* Prov 11:25 1931

better than he that honoureth *h* Prov 12:9
There is that maketh *h* rich Prov 13:7
there is that maketh *h* poor Prov 13:7
man shall be satisfied from *h* Prov 14:14
LORD hath made all things for *h* Prov 16:4 4617
He that laboureth laboureth for *h* Prov 16:26
desire a man, having separated *h* Prov 18:1
hath friends must shew *h* friendly Prov 18:24
of the poor, he also shall cry *h* Prov 21:13 1931
foreseeth the evil, and hideth *h* Prov 22:3
thy cause with thy neighbour *h* Prov 25:9
Whoso boasteth *h* of a false gift Prov 25:14
foreseeth the evil, and hideth *h* Prov 27:12
he shall fall *h* into his own pit Prov 28:10 1931
but a child left to *h* bringeth Prov 29:15
the king *h* is served by the field Eccl 5:9
lips of a fool will swallow up *h* Eccl 10:12
shewing *h* through the lattice Song 2:9
King Solomon made *h* a chariot of Song 3:9
but my beloved had withdrawn *h* Song 5:6
down, and the great man humbleth *h* Is 2:9
made each one for *h* to worship Is 2:20
the child shall behave *h* proudly Is 3:5
Therefore the Lord *h* shall give Is 7:14 1931
Sanctify the LORD of hosts *h* Is 8:13
thereof shall be afraid in *h* Is 19:17
an habitation for *h* in a rock Is 22:16
that a man can stretch *h* on it Is 28:20
than that he can wrap *h* in it Is 28:20
nor abase *h* for the noise of them Is 31:4
covered *h* with sackcloth, and went Is 37:1
spoken unto me, and *h* hath done it Is 38:15 1931
another shall call *h* by the name Is 44:5
surname *h* by the name of Israel Is 44:5
which he strengtheneth for *h* Is 44:14
he will take thereof, and warm *h* Is 44:15
yea, he warmeth *h*, and saith, Aha, Is 44:16
Jacob, and glorified *h* in Israel Is 44:23
God *h* that formed the earth and Is 45:18 1931
that hath joined *h* to the LORD Is 56:3
from evil maketh *h* a prey Is 59:15
decketh *h* with ornaments, and as a Is 61:10
to make *h* an everlasting name Is 63:12
that stirreth up *h* to take hold Is 64:7
That he who blesseth *h* in the Is 65:16
shall bless *h* in the God of truth Is 65:16
that the way of man is not in *h* Jer 10:23
Shall a man make gods unto *h* Jer 16:20
Can any hide *h* in secret places Jer 23:24
maketh *h* a prophet, that thou Jer 29:26
which maketh *h* a prophet to you Jer 29:27
heard Ephraim bemoaning *h* thus Jer 31:18
that none should serve *h* of them Jer 34:9
to separate *h* thence in the midst Jer 37:12
he shall array *h* with the land of Jer 43:12
he magnified *h* against the LORD Jer 48:26
hath magnified *h* against the LORD Jer 48:42
and he shall not be able to hide *h* Jer 49:10
lifteth *h* up in his brigandine Jer 51:3
The LORD of hosts hath sworn by *h* Jer 51:14 5315
for the enemy hath magnified *h* Lam 1:9
h in the iniquity of his life Eze 7:13
which separateth *h* from me Eze 14:7
the king of Babylon set *h* against Eze 24:2
offended, and revenged *h* upon them Eze 25:12
shall the prince prepare for *h* Eze 45:22
h with the portion of the king's Dan 1:8
that he might not defile *h* Dan 1:8
words, was sore displeased with *h* Dan 6:14
he magnified *h* even to the prince Dan 8:11
he shall magnify *h* in his heart Dan 8:25
Messiah be cut off, but not for *h* Dan 9:26
and he shall exalt *h* Dan 11:36
magnify *h* above every god, and Dan 11:36
for he shall magnify *h* above all Dan 11:37
he hath withdrawn *h* from them Hos 5:6
he hath mixed *h* among the people Hos 7:8 1931
to Assyria, a wild ass alone by *h* Hos 8:9
he bringeth forth fruit unto *h* Hos 10:1
trembling, he exalted *h* in Israel Hos 13:1 1931
shall the mighty deliver *h* Amos 2:14 5315
swift of foot shall not deliver *h* Amos 2:15 5315
that rideth the horse deliver *h* Amos 2:15 5315
The Lord GOD hath sworn by *h* Amos 6:8 5315
he fainted, and wished in *h* to die Jonah 4:8
him that ladeth *h* with thick clay Hab 2:6
secret *h* shall reward thee openly Mt 6:4 *846*
H took our infirmities, and bare Mt 8:17 *846*
it, he withdrew *h* from thence Mt 12:15
Satan, he is divided against *h* Mt 12:26 *1438*
taketh with *h* seven other spirits Mt 12:45 *1438*
other spirits more wicked than *h* Mt 12:45 *1438*
Yet hath he not root in *h* Mt 13:21 *1438*
come after me, let him deny *h* Mt 16:24 *1438*
humble *h* as this little child Mt 18:4 *1438*
shall exalt *h* shall be abased Mt 23:12 *1438*
shall humble *h* shall be exalted Mt 23:12 *1438*
that he was condemned, repented *h* Mt 27:3
and departed, and went and hanged *h* Mt 27:5
h he cannot save Mt 27:42 *1438*
who also *h* was Jesus' disciple Mt 27:57 *846*
But Jesus withdrew *h* with his Mk 3:7
for they said, He is beside *h* Mk 3:21
And if Satan rise up against *h* Mk 3:26 *1438*
crying, and cutting *h* with stones Mk 5:5 *1438*
immediately knowing in *h* that Mk 5:30 *1438*
For Herod *h* had sent forth and Mk 6:17 *846*
come after me, let him deny *h* Mk 8:34 *1438*
and to love his neighbour as *h* Mk 12:33 *1438*
For David *h* said by the Holy Mk 12:36 *846*
David therefore *h* calleth him Mk 12:37 *846*
servants, and warmed *h* at the fire Mk 14:54
And when she saw Peter warming *h* Mk 14:67
h he cannot save Mk 15:31 *1438*

Jesus *h* began to be about thirty Lk 3:23 *846*
he withdrew *h* into the wilderness Lk 5:16
when *h* was an hungred, and they Lk 6:3 *846*
him saw it, he spake within *h* Lk 7:39 *1438*
come after me, let him deny *h* Lk 9:23 *1438*
gain the whole world, and lose *h* Lk 9:25 *1438*
and place, whither he *h* would come Lk 10:1 *846*
But he, willing to justify *h* Lk 10:29 *1438*
Satan also be divided against *h* Lk 11:18 *1438*
other spirits more wicked than *h* Lk 11:26 *1438*
And he thought within *h*, saying, Lk 12:17 *1438*
he that layeth up treasure for *h* Lk 12:21 *1438*
unto you, that he shall gird *h* Lk 12:37
lord's will, and prepared not *h* Lk 12:47
exalteth *h* shall be abased Lk 14:11 *1438*
that humbleth *h* shall be exalted Lk 14:11 *1438*
joined *h* to a citizen of that Lk 15:15
And when he came to *h*, he said, Lk 15:17 *1438*
Then the steward said within *h* Lk 16:3 *1438*
but afterward he said within *h* Lk 18:4 *1438*
stood and prayed thus with *h* Lk 18:11 *1438*
that exalteth *h* shall be abased Lk 18:14 *1438*
that humbleth *h* shall be exalted Lk 18:14 *1438*
to receive for *h* a kingdom Lk 19:12 *1438*
David *h* saith in the book of Lk 20:42 *846*
saying that he *h* is Christ a King Lk 23:2 *1438*
who *h* also was at Jerusalem at Lk 23:7 *846*
let him save *h*, if he be Christ, Lk 23:35 *1438*
who also *h* waited for the kingdom Lk 23:51 *846*
wondering in *h* at that which was Lk 24:12 *1438*
Jesus *h* drew near, and went with Lk 24:15 *846*
the things concerning *h* Lk 24:27 *1438*
Jesus *h* stood in the midst of Lk 24:36 *846*
Jesus did not commit *h* unto them Jn 2:24 *1438*
(Though Jesus *h* baptized not Jn 4:2 *846*
us the well, and drank thereof *h* Jn 4:12 *846*
For Jesus *h* testified, that a Jn 4:44 *846*
h believed, and his whole house Jn 4:53 *846*
for Jesus had conveyed *h* away Jn 5:13
Father, making *h* equal with God Jn 5:18 *1438*
you, The Son can do nothing of *h* Jn 5:19 *1438*
him all things that *h* doeth Jn 5:20 *846*
For as the Father hath life in *h* Jn 5:26 *1438*
to the Son to have life in *h* Jn 5:26 *1438*
And the Father *h*, which hath sent Jn 5:37 *846*
for he *h* knew what he would do Jn 6:6 *846*
again into a mountain *h* alone Jn 6:15 *846*
When Jesus knew in *h* that his Jn 6:61 *1438*
he *h* seeketh to be known openly Jn 7:4 *846*
He that speaketh of *h* seeketh his Jn 7:18 *1438*
asking him, he lifted up *h* Jn 8:7
When Jesus had lifted up *h* Jn 8:10
said the Jews, Will he kill *h* Jn 8:22 *1438*
but Jesus hid *h*, and went out of Jn 8:59
he shall speak for *h* Jn 9:21 *848*
groaning in *h* cometh to the grave Jn 11:38 *1438*
And this spake he not of *h* Jn 11:51 *1438*
departed, and did hide *h* from them Jn 12:36
and took a towel, and girded *h* Jn 13:4 *1438*
God shall also glorify him in *h* Jn 13:32 *1438*
for he shall not speak of *h* Jn 16:13 *1438*
For the Father *h* loveth you Jn 16:27 *846*
stood with them, and warmed *h* Jn 18:18
And Simon Peter stood and warmed *h* Jn 18:25
because he made *h* the Son of God Jn 19:7 *1438*
whosoever maketh *h* a king Jn 19:12 *848*
h again to the disciples at the Jn 21:1 *1438*
and on this wise shewed he *h* Jn 21:1
and did cast *h* into the sea Jn 21:7 *1438*
Jesus shewed *h* to his disciples Jn 21:14
To whom also he shewed *h* alive Acts 1:3 *1438*
but he saith *h*, The Lord said Acts 2:34 *846*
rest durst no man join *h* to them Acts 5:13
boasting *h* to be somebody Acts 5:36 *1438*
the next day he shewed *h* unto Acts 7:26
giving out that *h* was some great Acts 8:9 *1448*
Then Simon *h* believed also Acts 8:13 *846*
of *h*, or of some other man Acts 8:34 *1438*
to join *h* to the disciples Acts 9:26
Now while Peter doubted in *h* what Acts 10:17 *1438*
And when Peter was come to *h* Acts 12:11 *1438*
he left not *h* without witness Acts 14:17 *1438*
his sword, and would have killed *h* Acts 16:27 *1438*
but he *h* entered into the Acts 18:19 *846*
but he *h* stayed in Asia for a Acts 19:22 *846*
not adventure *h* into the theatre Acts 19:31 *1438*
appointed, minding *h* to go afoot Acts 20:13 *846*
the next day purifying *h* with Acts 21:26
that he *h* would depart shortly Acts 25:4 *1438*
While he answered for *h*, Neither Acts 25:8
for *h* concerning the crime laid Acts 25:16
that he *h* hath appealed to Acts 25:25 *848*
forth the hand, and answered for *h* Acts 26:1
And as he thus spake for *h* Acts 26:24
go unto his friends to refresh *h* Acts 27:3
by *h* with a soldier that kept him Acts 28:16 *1438*
not to think of *h* more highly Rom 12:3
For none of us liveth to *h* Rom 14:7 *1438*
and no man dieth to *h* Rom 14:7 *1438*
us shall give account of *h* to God Rom 14:12 *1438*
h in that thing which he alloweth Rom 14:22 *1438*
For even Christ pleased not *h* Rom 15:3 *1438*
yet he *h* is judged of no man 1Cor 2:15 *846*
but he *h* shall be saved 1Cor 3:15 *846*
Let no man deceive *h* 1Cor 3:18 *1438*
h uncomely toward his virgin 1Cor 7:36
But let a man examine *h*, and so 1Cor 11:28 *1438*
eateth and drinketh damnation to *h* 1Cor 11:29 *1438*
in an unknown tongue edifieth *h* 1Cor 14:4 *1438*
who shall prepare *h* to the battle 1Cor 14:8
and let him speak to *h*, and to God 1Cor 14:28 *1438*
any man think *h* to be a prophet 1Cor 14:37
then shall the Son also *h* be 1Cor 15:28 *846*
us to *h* by Jesus Christ, and hath 2Cor 5:18 *1438*

reconciling the world unto *h* 2Cor 5:19 *1438*
trust to *h* that he is Christ's 2Cor 10:7 *1438*
let him of *h* think this again, 2Cor 10:7 *1438*
he that commendeth *h* is approved 2Cor 10:18 *1438*
for Satan *h* is transformed into 2Cor 11:14 *846*
man take of you, if a man exalt *h* 2Cor 11:20
Who gave *h* for our sins, that he Gal 1:4 *1438*
come, he withdrew and separated *h* Gal 2:12 *1438*
who loved me, and gave *h* for me Gal 2:20 *1438*
if a man think *h* to be something Gal 6:3
he is nothing, he deceiveth *h* Gal 6:3 *1438*
he have rejoicing in *h* alone Gal 6:4 *1438*
of children by Jesus Christ to *h* Eph 1:5 *848*
which he hath purposed in *h* Eph 1:9 *848*
for to make in *h* of twain one new Eph 2:15 *1438*
Jesus Christ *h* being the chief Eph 2:20 *848*
hath given *h* for us an offering Eph 5:2 *1438*
the church, and gave *h* for it Eph 5:25 *1438*
present it to *h* a glorious church Eph 5:27 *1438*
He that loveth his wife loveth *h* Eph 5:28 *1438*
so love his wife even as *h* Eph 5:33 *1438*
But made *h* of no reputation, and Phil 2:7 *1438*
in fashion as a man, he humbled *h* Phil 2:8 *1438*
even to subdue all things unto *h* Phil 3:21 *1438*
to reconcile all things unto *h* Col 1:20 *848*
Now God *h* and our Father, and our 1Th 3:11 *846*
For the Lord *h* shall descend from 1Th 4:16 *846*
exalteth *h* above all that is 2Th 2:4 *1438*
of God, shewing *h* that he is God 2Th 2:4 *1438*
Now our Lord Jesus Christ *h* 2Th 2:16 *846*
Now the Lord of peace *h* give you 2Th 3:16 *846*
Who gave *h* a ransom for all, to 1Ti 2:6 *1438*
h with the affairs of this life 2Ti 2:4
he cannot deny *h* 2Ti 2:13 *1438*
man therefore purge *h* from these 2Ti 2:21 *1438*
Who gave *h* for us, that he might Titus 2:14 *1438*
purify unto *h* a peculiar people, Titus 2:14 *1438*
and sinneth, being condemned of *h* Titus 3:11 *848*
when he had by *h* purged our sins, Heb 1:3 *1438*
he also *h* likewise took part of Heb 2:14 *846*
For in that he *h* hath suffered Heb 2:18 *846*
for that he *h* also is compassed Heb 5:2 *846*
as for the people, so also for *h* Heb 5:3 *1438*
no man taketh this honour unto *h* Heb 5:4 *1438*
not *h* to be made an high priest Heb 5:5 *1438*
by no greater, he sware by *h* Heb 6:13 *1438*
he did once, when he offered up *h* Heb 7:27 *1438*
blood, which he offered for *h* Heb 9:7 *1438*
offered *h* without spot to God Heb 9:14 *1438*
yet that he should offer *h* often Heb 9:25 *1438*
away sin by the sacrifice of *h* Heb 9:26 *848*
of sinners against *h*, lest ye be Heb 12:3 *848*
For he beholdeth *h*, and goeth his Jas 1:24 *1438*
to keep *h* unspotted from the Jas 1:27 *1438*
but committed *h* to him that 1Pet 2:23
in him ought *h* also so to walk 1Jn 2:6 *846*
hath this hope in him purifieth *h* 1Jn 3:3 *1438*
Son of God hath the witness in *h* 1Jn 5:10 *1438*
that is begotten of God keepeth *h* 1Jn 5:18 *1438*
neither doth he *h* receive the 3Jn 10 *846*
that no man knew, but he *h* Rev 19:12
God *h* shall be with them, and be Rev 21:3 *846*

HIN
fourth part of an *h* of beaten oil Ex 29:40 1969
the fourth part of an *h* of wine Ex 29:40 1969
sanctuary, and of oil olive an *h* Ex 30:24 1969
a just ephah, and a just *h* Lev 19:36 1969
of wine, the fourth part of a *h* Lev 23:13 1969
the fourth part of an *h* of oil Num 15:4 1969
the fourth part of an *h* of wine Num 15:5 1969
the third part of an *h* of oil Num 15:6 1969
the third part of an *h* of wine Num 15:7 1969
mingled with half an *h* of oil Num 15:9 1969
drink offering half an *h* of wine Num 15:10 1969
fourth part of an *h* of beaten oil Num 28:5 1969
part of an *h* for the one lamb Num 28:7 1969
half an *h* of wine unto a bullock Num 28:14 1969
the third part of an *h* unto a ram Num 28:14 1969
a fourth part of an *h* unto a lamb Num 28:14 1969
measure, the sixth part of an *h* Eze 4:11 1969
ram, and an *h* of oil for an ephah Eze 45:24 1969
give, and an *h* of oil to an ephah Eze 46:5 1969
unto, and an *h* of oil to an ephah Eze 46:7 1969
give, and an *h* of oil to an ephah Eze 46:11 1969
and the third part of an *h* of oil Eze 46:14 1969

HIND
Naphtali is a *h* let loose Gen 49:21 355
Let her be as the loving *h* Prov 5:19 365
the *h* also calved in the field, Jer 14:5 365

HINDER
H me not, seeing the LORD hath Gen 24:56 309
h thee from coming unto me Num 22:16 4513
wherefore Abner with the *h* end of 2Sa 2:23 310
all their *h* parts were inward 1Kin 7:25 268
all their *h* parts were inward 2Chr 4:4 268
against Jerusalem, and to *h* it Neh 4:8
he taketh away, who can *h* him Job 9:12 7725
together, then who can *h* him Job 11:10 7725
smote his enemies in the *h* parts Ps 78:66 268
his *h* part toward the utmost sea, Joel 2:20 5490
and half of them toward the *h* sea Zec 14:8 314
he was in the *h* part of the ship, Mk 4:38 *4403*
what doth *h* me to be baptized Acts 8:36 *2967*
but the *h* part was broken with Acts 27:41 *4403*
lest we should *h* the gospel of 1Cor 9:12
who did *h* you that ye should not Gal 5:7 *348*

HINDERED
these men, that they be not *h* Ezr 6:8 989
them that were entering in ye *h* Lk 11:52 *2967*
been much *h* from coming to you Rom 15:22 *1465*
but Satan *h* us 1Th 2:18 *1465*
that your prayers be not *h* 1Pet 3:7 *1581*

HINDERETH
anger, is persecuted, and none *h* Is 14:6 2820

HINDERMOST
after, and Rachel and Joseph *h* Gen 33:2 314
the *h* of the nations shall be a Jer 50:12 319

HINDMOST
They shall go *h* with their Num 2:31 314
the way, and smote the *h* of thee Deut 25:18 2179
enemies, and smite the *h* of them Josh 10:19 2179

HINDS
thou mark when the *h* do calve Job 39:1 355
of the LORD maketh the *h* to calve Ps 29:9 355
by the *h* of the field, that ye Song 2:7 355
by the *h* of the field, that ye Song 3:5 355

HINDS'
He maketh my feet like *h* feet 2Sa 22:34 355
He maketh my feet like *h* feet Ps 18:33 355
he will make my feet like *h* feet Hab 3:19 355

HINGES
the *h* of gold, both for the doors 1Kin 7:50 6596
As the door turneth upon his *h* Prov 26:14 6735

HINNOM (*hin'-nom*) *A valley near Jerusalem.*
of *H* unto the south side of the Josh 15:8 2011
before the valley of *H* westward Josh 15:8 2011
before the valley of the son of *H* Josh 18:16 2011
and descended to the valley of *H* Josh 18:16 2011
the valley of the children of *H* 2Kin 23:10 2011
in the valley of the son of *H* 2Chr 28:3 2011
in the valley of the son of *H* 2Chr 33:6 2011
Beer-sheba unto the valley of *H* Neh 11:30 2011
is in the valley of the son of *H* Jer 7:31 2011
nor the valley of the son of *H* Jer 7:32 2011
unto the valley of the son of *H* Jer 19:2 2011
nor The valley of the son of *H* Jer 19:6 2011
are in the valley of the son of *H* Jer 32:35 2011

HIP
And he smote them *h* and thigh with Judg 15:8 7785

HIRAH (*hi'-rah*) *A friend of Judah.*
Adullamite, whose name was *H* Gen 38:1 2437
his friend *H* the Adullamite Gen 38:12 2437

HIRAM (*hi'-ram*) See HIRAM'S, HURAM.
1. A king of Tyre.
H king of Tyre sent messengers to 2Sa 5:11 2438
H king of Tyre sent his servants 1Kin 5:1 2438
for *H* was ever a lover of David 1Kin 5:1 2438
And Solomon sent to *H*, saying, 1Kin 5:2 2438
when *H* heard the words of Solomon 1Kin 5:7 2438
H sent to Solomon, saying, I have 1Kin 5:8 2438
So *H* gave Solomon cedar trees and 1Kin 5:10 2438
Solomon gave *H* twenty thousand 1Kin 5:11 2438
gave Solomon to *H* year by year 1Kin 5:11 2438
and there was peace between *H* 1Kin 5:12 2438
(Now *H* the king of Tyre had 1Kin 9:11 2438
H twenty cities in the land of 1Kin 9:11 2438
H came out from Tyre to see the 1Kin 9:12 2438
H sent to the king sixscore 1Kin 9:14 2438
H sent in the navy his servants, 1Kin 9:27 2438
And the navy also of *H*, that 1Kin 10:11 2438
of Tharshish with the navy of *H* 1Kin 10:22 2438
Now *H* king of Tyre sent 1Chr 14:1 2438
2. An architect.
sent and fetched *H* out of Tyre 1Kin 7:13 2438
H made the lavers, and the shovels 1Kin 7:40 2438
So *H* made an end of doing all the 1Kin 7:40 2438
which *H* made to king Solomon for 1Kin 7:45 2438

HIRAM'S (*hi'-rams*) *Refers to Hiram 1.*
H builders did hew them, and the 1Kin 5:18 2438

HIRE
Leah said, God hath given me my *h* Gen 30:18 7939
and of such shall be my *h* Gen 30:32 7939
come for my *h* before thy face Gen 30:33 7939
The ringstraked shall be thy *h* Gen 31:8 7939
an hired thing, it came for his *h* Ex 22:15 7939
shalt not bring the *h* of a whore Deut 23:18 868
his day thou shalt give him his *h* Deut 24:15 7939
unto thee will I give *h* for thy 1Kin 5:6 7939
of silver to *h* them chariots 1Chr 19:6 7936
Tyre, and she shall turn to her *h* Is 23:17 868
her *h* shall be holiness to the Is 23:18 868
in the balance, and *h* a goldsmith Is 46:6 7936
harlot, in that thou scornest *h* Eze 16:31 868
also shalt give no *h* any more Eze 16:41 868
gathered it of the *h* of an harlot Mic 1:7 868
return to the *h* of an harlot Mic 1:7 868
the priests thereof teach for *h* Mic 3:11 4242
h for man, nor any *h* for beast Zec 8:10 7939
to *h* labourers into his vineyard Mt 20:1 *3409*
labourers, and give them their *h* Mt 20:8 *3408*
the labourer is worthy of his *h* Lk 10:7 *3408*
the *h* of the labourers who have Jas 5:4 *3408*

HIRED
for surely I have *h* thee with my Gen 30:16 7936
an *h* servant shall not eat Ex 12:45 7916
if it be an *h* thing, it came for Ex 22:15 7916
the wages of him that is *h* shall Lev 19:13 7916
or an *h* servant, shall not eat of Lev 22:10 7916
thy maid, and for thy *h* servant Lev 25:6 7916
But as an *h* servant, and as a Lev 25:40 7916
according to the time of an *h* Lev 25:50 7916
as a yearly *h* servant shall he be Lev 25:53 7916
worth a double *h* servant to thee Deut 15:18 7916
because they *h* against thee Deut 23:4 7936
oppress an *h* servant that is poor Deut 24:14 7916
wherewith Abimelech *h* vain Judg 9:4 7936
Micah with me, and hath *h* me Judg 18:4 7936
have *h* out themselves for bread 1Sa 2:5 7936
h the Syrians of Beth-rehob, and 2Sa 10:6 7936
the king of Israel hath *h* against 2Kin 7:6 7936

So they *h* thirty and two thousand 1Chr 19:7 7936
h masons and carpenters to repair 2Chr 24:12 7936
He *h* also an hundred thousand 2Chr 25:6 7936
h counsellors against them, to Ezr 4:5 7936
for Tobiah and Sanballat had *h* him Neh 6:12 7936
Therefore was he *h*, that I should Neh 6:13 7936
but *h* Balaam against them, that Neh 13:2 7936
Lord shave with a razor that is *h* Is 7:20 7917
Also her *h* men are in the midst Jer 46:21 7916
Ephraim hath *h* lovers Hos 8:9 8566
though they have *h* among the Hos 8:10 8566
him, Because no man hath *h* us Mt 20:7 *3409*
were *h* about the eleventh hour Mt 20:9
in the ship with the *h* servants Mk 1:20 *3411*
How many *h* servants of my Lk 15:17 *3407*
make me as one of thy *h* servants Lk 15:19 *3407*
whole years in his own *h* house Acts 28:30 *3410*

HIRELING
days also like the days of a *h* Job 7:1 7916
as a *h* looketh for the reward of Job 7:2 7916
till he shall accomplish, as an *h* Job 14:6 7916
three years, as the years of an *h* Is 16:14 7916
according to the years of an *h* Is 21:16 7916
that oppress the *h* in his wages Mal 3:5 7916
But he that is an *h*, and not the Jn 10:12 *3411*
h fleeth, because he is an *h* Jn 10:13 *3411*

HIRES
all the *h* thereof shall be burned Mic 1:7 868

HIREST
h them, that they may come unto Eze 16:33 7806

HIS See PREFACE.

HISS
shall be astonished, and shall *h* 1Kin 9:8 8319
shall *h* him out of his place Job 27:23 8319
will *h* unto them from the end of Is 5:26 8319
that the LORD shall *h* for the fly Is 7:18 8319
h because of all the plagues Jer 19:8 8319
shall *h* at all the plagues Jer 49:17 8319
and *h* at all her plagues Jer 50:13 8319
they *h* and wag their head at the Lam 2:15 8319
they *h* and gnash the teeth Lam 2:16 8319
among the people shall *h* at thee Eze 27:36 8319
one that passeth by her shall *h* Zeph 2:15 8319
I will *h* for them, and gather them Zec 10:8 8319

HISSING
trouble, to astonishment, and to *h* 2Chr 29:8 8322
land desolate, and a perpetual *h* Jer 18:16 8292
make this city desolate, and an *h* Jer 19:8 8322
them an astonishment, and an *h* Jer 25:9 8322
desolation, an astonishment, an *h* Jer 25:18 8322
and an astonishment, and an *h* Jer 29:18 8322
dragons, an astonishment, and an *h* Jer 51:37 8322
and the inhabitants thereof an *h* Mic 6:16 8322

HIT
Saul, and the archers *h* him 1Sa 31:3 4672
Saul, and the archers *h* him 1Chr 10:3 4672

HITHER
they shall come *h* again Gen 15:16 2008
your youngest brother come *h* Gen 42:15
yourselves, that ye sold me *h* Gen 45:5
now it was not you that sent me *h* Gen 45:8
haste and bring down my father *h* Gen 45:13
And he said, Draw not nigh *h* Ex 3:5 1988
there came men in *h* to night of Josh 2:2
the children of Israel, Come *h* Josh 3:9 5066
and bring the description *h* to me Josh 18:6
Gazites, saying, Samson is come *h* Judg 16:2
said unto him, Who brought thee *h* Judg 18:3 1988
We will not turn aside *h* into the Judg 19:12
unto her, At mealtime come thou *h* Ruth 2:14 1988
Bring *h* a burnt offering to me, 1Sa 13:9 5066
Ahiah, Bring *h* the ark of God 1Sa 14:18 5066
Bring me *h* every man his ox, and 1Sa 14:34 5066
Let us draw near *h* unto God 1Sa 14:36 1988
And Saul said, Draw ye near *h* 1Sa 14:38 1988
Bring ye *h* to me Agag the king of 1Sa 15:32 5066
will not sit down till he come *h* 1Sa 16:11 6311
he said, Why camest thou down *h* 1Sa 17:28
the priest, Bring *h* the ephod 1Sa 23:9 5066
I pray thee, bring me *h* the ephod 1Sa 30:7 5066
have brought them *h* unto my lord 2Sa 1:10
lame, thou shalt not come in *h* 2Sa 5:6
I sent unto thee, saying, Come *h* 2Sa 14:32
pray you, unto Joab, Come near *h* 2Sa 20:16
Hasten *h* Micaiah the son of Imlah 1Kin 22:9
waters, and they were divided *h* 2Kin 2:8
smitten the waters, they parted *h* 2Kin 2:14
saying, The man of God is come *h* 2Kin 8:7 2008
to David, Thou shalt not come *h* 1Chr 11:5
shall not bring in the captives *h* 2Chr 28:13
of Assur, which brought us up *h* Ezr 4:2
Therefore his people return *h* Ps 73:10 1988
bring *h* the timbrel, the pleasant Ps 81:2
is simple, let him turn in *h* Prov 9:4
is simple, let him turn in *h* Prov 9:16
it be said unto thee, Come up *h* Prov 25:7
But draw near *h*, ye sons of the Is 57:3
them unto thee art thou brought *h* Eze 40:4
high God, come forth, and come *h* Dan 3:26
art thou come *h* to torment us Mt 8:29 *5602*
He said, Bring them *h* to me Mt 14:18 *5602*
bring him *h* to me Mt 17:17 *5602*
how camest thou in *h* not having a Mt 22:12 *5602*
and straightway he will send him *h* Mk 11:3 *5602*
Bring thy son *h* Lk 9:41 *5602*
the city, and bring in *h* the poor Lk 14:21 *5602*
bring *h* the fatted calf, and kill Lk 15:23
I should reign over them, bring *h* Lk 19:27 *5602*
loose him, and bring him *h* Lk 19:30
not, neither come *h* to draw Jn 4:15 *1759*

Go, call thy husband, and come *h* ... Jn 4:16 *1759*
him, Rabbi, when camest thou *h* ... Jn 6:25 *5602*
Reach *h* thy finger, and behold my ... Jn 20:27 *5602*
reach *h* thy hand, and thrust it ... Jn 20:27 *5602*
came *h* for that intent, that he ... Acts 9:21 *5602*
call *h* Simon, whose surname is ... Acts 10:32 *3333*
world upside down are come *h* also ... Acts 17:6 *1759*
For ye have brought *h* these men ... Acts 19:37
Therefore, when they were come *h* ... Acts 25:17 *1759*
which said, Come up *h*, and I will ... Rev 4:1 *5602*
saying unto them, Come up *h* ... Rev 11:12 *5602*
with me, saying unto me, Come *h* ... Rev 17:1 *1204*
and talked with me, saying, Come *h* ... Rev 21:9 *1204*

HITHERTO
behold, *h* thou wouldest not hear ... Ex 7:16
as the LORD hath blessed me *h* ... Josh 17:14
H thou hast mocked me, and told me .. Judg 16:13
and grief have I spoken *h* ... 1Sa 1:16
H hath the LORD helped us ... 1Sa 7:12
that thou hast brought me *h* ... 2Sa 7:18 1988
have been thy father's servant *h* ... 2Sa 15:34 227
Who *h* waited in the king's gate ... 1Chr 9:18
for *h* the greatest part of them ... 1Chr 12:29
that thou hast brought me *h* ... 1Chr 17:16 1988
H shalt thou come, but no further ... Job 38:11
h have I declared thy wondrous ... Ps 71:17 2008
terrible from their beginning *h* ... Is 18:2 1973
terrible from their beginning *h* ... Is 18:7 1973
H is the end of the matter ... Dan 7:28
them, My Father worketh *h* ... Jn 5:17
H have ye asked nothing in my ... Jn 16:24
to come unto you, (but was let *h* ... Rom 1:13
for *h* ye were not able to bear it ... 1Cor 3:2 *3768*

HITTITE (*hit'-tite*) See HITTITES. *A descendant of Heth.*
Ephron the *H* answered Abraham in ... Gen 23:10 2850
of Ephron the son of Zohar the *H* ... Gen 25:9 2850
the daughter of Beeri the *H* ... Gen 26:34 2850
the daughter of Elon the *H* ... Gen 26:34 2850
Adah the daughter of Elon the *H* ... Gen 36:2 2850
is in the field of Ephron the *H* ... Gen 49:29 2850
the *H* for a possession of a ... Gen 49:30 2850
of a buryingplace of Ephron the *H* ... Gen 50:13 2850
Hivite, the Canaanite, and the *H* ... Ex 23:28 2850
Canaanite, the Amorite, and the *H* ... Ex 33:2 2850
and the Canaanite, and the *H* ... Ex 34:11 2850
sea over against Lebanon, the *H* ... Josh 9:1 2850
west, and to the Amorite, and the *H* ... Josh 11:3 2850
David and said to Ahimelech the *H* ... 1Sa 26:6 2850
of Eliam, the wife of Uriah the *H* ... 2Sa 11:3 2850
Joab, saying, Send me Uriah the *H* ... 2Sa 11:6 2850
and Uriah the *H* died also ... 2Sa 11:17 2850
servant Uriah the *H* is dead also ... 2Sa 11:21 2850
servant Uriah the *H* is dead also ... 2Sa 11:24 2850
killed Uriah the *H* with the sword ... 2Sa 12:9 2850
of Uriah the *H* to be thy wife ... 2Sa 12:10 2850
Uriah the *H*: thirty and seven ... 2Sa 23:39 2850
only in the matter of Uriah the *H* ... 1Kin 15:5 2850
Uriah the *H*, Zabad the son of ... 1Chr 11:41 2850
an Amorite, and thy mother an *H* ... Eze 16:3 2850
your mother was an *H*, and your ... Eze 16:45 2850

HITTITES (*hit'-tites*)
And the *H*, and the Perizzites, and ... Gen 15:20 2850
place of the Canaanites, and the *H* ... Ex 3:8 2850
land of the Canaanites, and the *H* ... Ex 3:17 2850
land of the Canaanites, and the *H* ... Ex 13:5 2850
in unto the Amorites, and the *H* ... Ex 23:23 2850
and the *H*, and the Jebusites, and ... Num 13:29 2850
many nations before thee, the *H* ... Deut 7:1 2850
namely, the *H*, and the Amorites ... Deut 20:17 2850
Euphrates, all the land of the *H* ... Josh 1:4 2850
you the Canaanites, and the *H* ... Josh 3:10 2850
the *H*, the Amorites, and the ... Josh 12:8 2850
and the Canaanites, and the *H* ... Josh 24:11 2850
man went into the land of the *H* ... Judg 1:26 2850
dwelt among the Canaanites, *H* ... Judg 3:5 2850
that were left of the Amorites, *H* ... 1Kin 9:20 2850
and so for all the kings of the *H* ... 1Kin 10:29 2850
Edomites, Zidonians, and *H* ... 1Kin 11:1 2850
against us the kings of the *H* ... 2Kin 7:6 2850
horses for all the kings of the *H* ... 2Chr 1:17 2850
people that were left of the *H* ... 2Chr 8:7 2850
even of the Canaanites, the *H* ... Ezr 9:1 2850
the land of the Canaanites, the *H* ... Neh 9:8 2850

HIVITE (*hi'-vite*) *A descendant of Canaan.*
And the *H*, and the Arkite, and the ... Gen 10:17 2340
Shechem the son of Hamor the *H* ... Gen 34:2 2340
Anah the daughter of Zibeon the *H* ... Gen 36:2 2340
thee, which shall drive out the *H* ... Ex 23:28 2340
Hittite, and the Perizzite, the *H* ... Ex 33:2 2340
and the Perizzite, and the *H* ... Ex 34:11 2340
Canaanite, the Perizzite, the *H* ... Josh 9:1 2340
to the *H* under Hermon in the land ... Josh 11:3 2340
And the *H*, and the Arkite, and the ... 1Chr 1:15 2340

HIVITES (*hi'-vites*)
and the Perizzites, and the *H* ... Ex 3:8 2340
and the Perizzites, and the *H* ... Ex 3:17 2340
and the Amorites, and the *H* ... Ex 13:5 2340
and the Canaanites, the *H* ... Ex 23:23 2340
and the Perizzites, and the *H* ... Deut 7:1 2340
and the Perizzites, the *H* ... Deut 20:17 2340
and the Hittites, and the *H* ... Josh 3:10 2340
the men of Israel said unto the *H* ... Josh 9:7 2340
save the *H* the inhabitants of ... Josh 11:19 2340
Canaanites, the Perizzites, the *H* ... Josh 12:8 2340
and the Girgashites, the *H* ... Josh 24:11 2340
the *H* that dwelt in mount Lebanon ... Judg 3:3 2340
and Amorites, and Perizzites, and *H* ... Judg 3:5 2340
and to all the cities of the *H* ... 2Sa 24:7 2340
Amorites, Hittites, Perizzites, *H* ... 1Kin 9:20 2340
and the Perizzites, and the *H* ... 2Chr 8:7 2340

HIZKI See HEZEKI.

HIZKIAH (*hiz-ki'-ah*) See HEZEKIAH, HIZKIJAH. *An ancestor of Zephaniah.*
the son of Amariah, the son of *H* ... Zeph 1:1 2396

HIZKIJAH (*hiz-ki'-jah*) See HIZKIAH. *An Israelite who renewed the covenant.*
Ater, *H*, Azzur, ... Neh 10:17 2396

HO
unto whom he said, *H*, such a one ... Ruth 4:1 1945
H, every one that thirsteth, come ... Is 55:1 1945
H, *h*, come forth, and flee from ... Zec 2:6 1945

HOAR
as small as the *h* frost on the ... Ex 16:14 3713
let not his *h* head go down to the ... 1Kin 2:6 7872
but his *h* head bring thou down to ... 1Kin 2:9 7872
scattereth the *h* frost like ashes ... Ps 147:16 3713
even to *h* hairs will I carry you ... Is 46:4 7872

HOARY
shalt rise up before the *h* head ... Lev 19:32 7872
the *h* frost of heaven, who hath ... Job 38:29 3713
one would think the deep to be *h* ... Job 41:32 7872
The *h* head is a crown of glory ... Prov 16:31 7872

HOBAB (*ho'-bab*) See JETHRO. *Another name for Jethro.*
And Moses said unto *H*, the son of ... Num 10:29 2246
of *H* the father in law of Moses ... Judg 4:11 2246

HOBAH (*ho'-bah*) *Place where Abraham pursued the five kings.*
them, and pursued them unto *H* ... Gen 14:15 2327

HOBAIAH See HABAIAH.

HOD (*hod*) *A son of Zophah.*
Bezer, and *H*, and Shamma, and ... 1Chr 7:37 1963

HODAIAH (*ho-da-i'-ah*) See HODAVIAH. *A royal descendant of Judah.*
And the sons of Elioenai were, *H* ... 1Chr 3:24 1939

HODAVIAH (*ho-da-vi'-ah*) See HODAIAH, HODEVAH.
1. A chief of Manasseh.
and Azriel, and Jeremiah, and *H* ... 1Chr 5:24 1938
2. Son of Hassenuah.
son of Meshullam, the son of *H* ... 1Chr 9:7 1938
3. A family of exiles.
and Kadmiel, of the children of *H* ... Ezr 2:40 1938

HODESH (*ho'-desh*) *Wife of Shaharaim.*
And he begat of *H* his wife ... 1Chr 8:9 2321

HODEVAH (*ho-de'-vah*) See HODAVIAH. *A family of exiles.*
Kadmiel, and of the children of *H* ... Neh 7:43 1937

HODIAH (*ho-di'-ah*) See HODIJAH. *A wife of Mered.*
of his wife *H* the sister of Naham ... 1Chr 4:19 1940

HODIJAH (*ho-di'-jah*) See HODIAH.
1. A Levite.
Jamin, Akkub, Shabbethai, *H* ... Neh 8:7 1940
Bani, Hashabniah, Sherebiah, *H* ... Neh 9:5 1940
And their brethren, Shebaniah, *H* ... Neh 10:10 1940
H, Bani, Beninu ... Neh 10:13 1940
2. A leader of the people.
H, Hashum, Bezai, ... Neh 10:18 1940

HOGLAH (*hog'-lah*) See BETH-HOGLAH. *A daughter of Zelophehad.*
were Mahlah, and Noah, *H*, Milcah ... Num 26:33 2295
Mahlah, Noah, and *H* ... Num 27:1 2295
For Mahlah, Tirzah, and *H*, and ... Num 36:11 2295
his daughters, Mahlah, and Noah, *H* ... Josh 17:3 2295

HOHAM (*ho'-ham*) *An Amorite king.*
sent unto *H* king of Hebron ... Josh 10:3 1944

HOISED
h up the mainsail to the wind, and ... Acts 27:40 *1869*

HOLD
the men laid *h* upon his hand, and ... Gen 19:16 2388
the lad, and *h* him in thine hand ... Gen 21:18 2388
his hand took *h* on Esau's heel ... Gen 25:26 270
that they may *h* a feast unto me ... Ex 5:1
them go, and wilt *h* them still ... Ex 9:2 2388
for we must *h* a feast unto the ... Ex 10:9
for you, and ye shall *h* your peace ... Ex 14:14 2790
sorrow shall take *h* on the ... Ex 15:14 270
trembling shall take *h* upon them ... Ex 15:15 270
for the LORD will not *h* him ... Ex 20:7
loops may take *h* one of another ... Ex 26:5 6901
father shall *h* his peace at her ... Num 30:4 2790
h his peace at her from day to ... Num 30:14 2790
for the LORD will not *h* him ... Deut 5:11
father and his mother lay *h* on him ... Deut 21:19 8610
lay *h* on her, and lie with her, and ... Deut 22:28 8610
and mine hand take *h* on judgment ... Deut 32:41 270
they entered into an *h* of the ... Judg 9:46 6877
Abimelech, and put them to the *h* ... Judg 9:49 6877
set the *h* on fire upon them ... Judg 9:49 6877
Samson took *h* of the two middle ... Judg 16:29 3943
H thy peace, lay thine hand upon ... Judg 18:19 2790
laid *h* on his concubine, and ... Judg 19:29 2388
that thou hast upon thee, and *h* it ... Ruth 3:15 270
he laid *h* upon the skirt of his ... 1Sa 15:27 2388
the while that David was in the *h* ... 1Sa 22:4 4686
unto David, Abide not in the *h* ... 1Sa 22:5 4686
and his men gat them up unto the *h* ... 1Sa 24:22 4686
Then David took *h* on his clothes ... 2Sa 1:11 2388
lay thee *h* on one of the young ... 2Sa 2:21 270
how then should I *h* up my face to ... 2Sa 2:22 5375
good tidings, I took *h* of him ... 2Sa 4:10 270
David took the strong *h* of Zion ... 2Sa 5:7 4686
of it, and went down to the *h* ... 2Sa 5:17 4686
the ark of God, and took *h* of it ... 2Sa 6:6 270
unto him to eat, he took *h* of her ... 2Sa 13:11 2388
but *h* now thy peace, my sister ... 2Sa 13:20 2790
and his head caught *h* of the oak ... 2Sa 18:9 2388
And David was then in an *h* ... 2Sa 23:14 4686
And came to the strong *h* of Tyre ... 2Sa 24:7 4013
caught *h* on the horns of the ... 1Kin 1:50 2388
he hath caught *h* on the horns of ... 1Kin 1:51 270
Now therefore *h* him not guiltless ... 1Kin 2:9
caught *h* on the horns of the ... 1Kin 2:28 2388
have taken *h* upon other gods, and ... 1Kin 9:9 2388
the altar, saying, Lay *h* on him ... 1Kin 13:4 8610
h ye your peace ... 2Kin 2:3 2814
h ye your peace ... 2Kin 2:5 2814
he took *h* of his own clothes, and ... 2Kin 2:12 2388
door, and *h* him fast at the door ... 2Kin 6:32 3905
good tidings, and we *h* our peace ... 2Kin 7:9 2814
And David was then in the *h* ... 1Chr 11:16 4686
h to the wilderness men of might ... 1Chr 12:8 4679
and Judah to the *h* unto David ... 1Chr 12:16 4679
put forth his hand to *h* the ark ... 1Chr 13:9 270
and laid *h* on other gods, and ... 2Chr 7:22 2388
H your peace, for the day is holy ... Neh 8:11 2013
shall *h* out the golden sceptre ... Est 4:11 3447
Teach me, and I will *h* my tongue ... Job 6:24 2790
he shall *h* it fast, but it shall ... Job 8:15 2388
that thou wilt not *h* me innocent ... Job 9:28
thy lies make men *h* their peace ... Job 11:3 2790
ye would altogether *h* your peace ... Job 13:5 2790
H your peace, let me alone, that ... Job 13:13 2790
if I *h* my tongue, I shall give up ... Job 13:19 2790
righteous also shall *h* on his way ... Job 17:9 270
and trembling taketh *h* on my flesh ... Job 21:6 270
My righteousness I *h* fast ... Job 27:6 2388
Terrors take *h* on him as waters ... Job 27:20 5381
affliction have taken *h* upon me ... Job 30:16 270
h thy peace, and I will speak ... Job 33:31 2790
h thy peace, and I shall teach ... Job 33:33 2790
and justice take *h* on thee ... Job 36:17 8551
That it might take *h* of the ends ... Job 38:13 270
him that layeth at him cannot *h* ... Job 41:26 6965
H up my goings in thy paths, that ... Ps 17:5 8551
Take *h* of shield and buckler, and ... Ps 35:2 2388
h not thy peace at my tears ... Ps 39:12 2790
iniquities have taken *h* upon me ... Ps 40:12 5381
Fear took *h* upon them there, and ... Ps 48:6 270
thy wrathful anger take *h* of them ... Ps 69:24 5381
h not thy peace, and be not still ... Ps 83:1 2790
H not thy peace, O God of my ... Ps 109:1 2790
the pains of hell gat *h* upon me ... Ps 116:3 4672
Horror hath taken *h* upon me ... Ps 119:53 270
H thou me up, and I shall be safe ... Ps 119:117 5582
and anguish have taken *h* on me ... Ps 119:143 4672
me, and thy right hand shall *h* me ... Ps 139:10 270
neither take they *h* of the paths ... Prov 2:19 5381
life to them that lay *h* upon her ... Prov 3:18 2388
Take fast *h* of instruction ... Prov 4:13 2388
her steps take *h* on hell ... Prov 5:5 8551
spider taketh *h* with her hands ... Prov 30:28 8610
and her hands *h* the distaff ... Prov 31:19 8551
to lay *h* on folly, till I might ... Eccl 2:3 270
thou shouldest take *h* of this ... Eccl 7:18 270
They all *h* swords, being expert ... Song 3:8 270
I will take *h* of the boughs ... Song 7:8 270
When a man shall take *h* of his ... Is 3:6 8610
women shall take *h* of one man ... Is 4:1 2388
lay *h* of the prey, and shall carry ... Is 5:29 270
and sorrows shall take *h* of them ... Is 13:8 270
pangs have taken *h* upon me ... Is 21:3 270
Or let him take *h* of my strength ... Is 27:5 2388
over to his strong *h* for fear ... Is 31:9 5553
thy God will *h* thy right hand ... Is 41:13 2388
will *h* thine hand, and will keep ... Is 42:6 2388
son of man that layeth *h* on it ... Is 56:2 2388
me, and take *h* of my covenant ... Is 56:4 2388
it, and taketh *h* of my covenant ... Is 56:6 2388
Zion's sake will I not *h* my peace ... Is 62:1 2814
which shall never *h* their peace ... Is 62:6 2814
up himself to take *h* of thee ... Is 64:7 2388
wilt thou *h* thy peace, and afflict ... Is 64:12 2814
cisterns, that can *h* no water ... Jer 2:13 3557
I cannot *h* my peace, because thou ... Jer 4:19 2790
They shall lay *h* on bow and spear ... Jer 6:23 2388
anguish hath taken *h* of us ... Jer 6:24 2388
they *h* fast deceit, they refuse ... Jer 8:5 2388
astonishment hath taken *h* on me ... Jer 8:21 2388
They shall *h* the bow and the lance ... Jer 50:42 2388
anguish took *h* of him, and pangs ... Jer 50:43 2388
When they took *h* of thee by thy ... Eze 29:7 8610
to make it strong to *h* the sword ... Eze 30:21 8610
about, that they might have *h* ... Eze 41:6 270
but they had not *h* in the wall of ... Eze 41:6 270
Then shall he say, *H* thy tongue ... Amos 6:10 2013
the strong *h* of the daughter of ... Mic 4:8 6076
and thou shalt take *h*, but shalt ... Mic 6:14 5253
a strong *h* in the day of trouble ... Nah 1:7 4581
they shall deride every strong *h* ... Hab 1:10 4013
H thy peace at the presence of ... Zeph 1:7
they not take *h* of your fathers ... Zec 1:6 5381
that ten men shall take *h* out of ... Zec 8:23 2388
even shall take *h* of the skirt of ... Zec 8:23 2388
did build herself a strong *h* ... Zec 9:3 4692
Turn you to the strong *h*, ye ... Zec 9:12 1225
them, and *h* themselves not guilty ... Zec 11:5 816
they shall lay *h* every one on the ... Zec 14:13 2388
or else he will *h* to the one ... Mt 6:24 472
day, will he not lay *h* on it ... Mt 12:11 2902
For Herod had laid *h* on John ... Mt 14:3 *2902*
because they should *h* their peace ... Mt 20:31 4623
for all *h* John as a prophet ... Mt 21:26 *2192*
same is he: *h* him fast ... Mt 26:48 *2902*
the temple, and ye laid no *h* on me ... Mt 26:55 *2902*
they that had laid *h* on Jesus led ... Mt 26:57 *2902*
H thy peace, and come out of him ... Mk 1:25 5392

it, they went out to lay *h* on him Mk 3:21 2902
laid *h* upon John, and bound him in Mk 6:17 2902
be, which they have received to *h* Mk 7:4 2902
ye *h* the tradition of men, as the Mk 7:8 2902
him that he should *h* his peace Mk 10:48 4623
And they sought to lay *h* on him Mk 12:12 2902
and the young men laid *h* on him Mk 14:51 2902
H thy peace, and come out of him Lk 4:35 5392
or else he will *h* to the one Lk 16:13 472
him, that he should *h* his peace Lk 18:39 4623
if these should *h* their peace Lk 19:40 4623
they might take *h* of his words Lk 20:20 1949
they could not take *h* of his Lk 20:26 1949
they laid *h* upon one Simon, a Lk 23:26 1949
put them in *h* unto the next day Acts 4:3 5084
with the hand to *h* their peace Acts 12:17 4601
but speak, and *h* not thy peace Acts 18:9 4623
of men, who *h* the truth in Rom 1:18 2722
by, let the first *h* his peace 1Cor 14:30 4601
and *h* such in reputation Phil 2:29 2192
h fast that which is good 1Th 5:21 2722
h the traditions which ye have 2Th 2:15 2902
lay *h* on eternal life, whereunto 1Ti 6:12 1949
they may lay *h* on eternal life 1Ti 6:19 1949
H fast the form of sound words, 2Ti 1:13 2192
if we *h* fast the confidence and Heb 3:6 2722
if we *h* the beginning of our Heb 3:14 2722
let us *h* fast our profession Heb 4:14 2902
lay *h* upon the hope set before us Heb 6:18 2902
Let us *h* fast the profession of Heb 10:23 2722
that *h* the doctrine of Balaam Rev 2:14 2902
them that *h* the doctrine of the Rev 2:15 2902
have already *h* fast till I come Rev 2:25 2902
and heard, and *h* fast, and repent Rev 3:3 5083
h that fast which thou hast, that Rev 3:11 2902
the *h* of every foul spirit, and a Rev 18:2 5438
he laid *h* on the dragon, that old Rev 20:2 2902

HOLDEN
Surely there was not *h* such a 2Kin 23:22 6213
was *h* to the LORD in Jerusalem 2Kin 23:23 6213
be *h* in cords of affliction Job 36:8 3920
and thy right hand hath *h* me up Ps 18:35 5582
have I been *h* up from the womb Ps 71:6 5564
thou hast *h* me by my right hand Ps 73:23 270
he shall be *h* with the cords of Prov 5:22 8551
I have long time *h* my peace Is 42:14 2814
Cyrus, whose right hand I have *h* Is 45:1 2388
But their eyes were *h* that they Lk 24:16 2902
that he should be *h* of it Acts 2:24 2902
Yea, he shall be *h* up Rom 14:4

HOLDEST
h thy peace at this time, then Est 4:14 2790
thy face, and *h* me for thine enemy Job 13:24 2803
Thou *h* mine eyes waking Ps 77:4 270
that *h* the height of the hill Jer 49:16 8610
h thy tongue when the wicked Hab 1:13 2790
thou *h* fast my name, and hast not Rev 2:13 2902

HOLDETH
still he *h* fast his integrity, Job 2:3 2388
He *h* back the face of his throne, Job 26:9 270
Which *h* our soul in life, and Ps 66:9 7760
man of understanding *h* his peace Prov 11:12 2790
when he *h* his peace, is counted Prov 17:28 2790
there is none that *h* with me in Dan 10:21 2388
him that *h* the sceptre from the Amos 1:5 8551
him that *h* the sceptre from Amos 1:8 8551
These things saith he that *h* the Rev 2:1 2902

HOLDING
his hands from *h* of bribes Is 33:15 8551
I am weary with *h* in Jer 6:11 3557
h the tradition of the elders Mk 7:3 2902
H forth the word of life Phil 2:16 1907
not *h* the Head, from which all Col 2:19 2902
H faith, and a good conscience 1Ti 1:19 2192
H the mystery of the faith in a 1Ti 3:9 2192
H fast the faithful word as he Titus 1:9 472
h the four winds of the earth, Rev 7:1 2902

HOLDS
whether in tents, or in strong *h* Num 13:19 4013
mountains, and caves, and strong *h* Judg 6:2 4679
in the wilderness in strong *h* 1Sa 23:14 4679
with us in strong *h* in the wood 1Sa 23:19 4679
and dwelt in strong *h* at En-gedi 1Sa 23:29 4679
their strong *h* wilt thou set on 2Kin 8:12 4013
And he fortified the strong *h* 2Chr 11:11 4694
hast brought his strong *h* to ruin Ps 89:40 4013
to destroy the strong *h* thereof Is 23:11 4581
and he shall destroy thy strong *h* Jer 48:18 4013
the strong *h* are surprised, and Jer 48:41 4679
they have remained in their *h* Jer 51:30 4679
strong *h* of the daughter of Judah Lam 2:2 4013
he hath destroyed his strong *h* Lam 2:5 4013
they brought him into *h*, that his Eze 19:9 4686
his devices against the strong *h* Dan 11:24 4013
most strong *h* with a strange god Dan 11:39 4013
and throw down all thy strong *h* Mic 5:11 4013
All thy strong *h* shall be like Nah 3:12 4013
the siege, fortify thy strong *h* Nah 3:14 4013
to the pulling down of strong *h* 2Cor 10:4

HOLE
shall be an *h* in the top of it Ex 28:32 6310
work round about the *h* of it Ex 28:32 6310
as it were the *h* of an habergeon, Ex 28:32 6310
there was an *h* in the midst of Ex 39:23 6310
as the *h* of an habergeon, with a Ex 39:23 6310
with a band round about the *h* Ex 39:23 6310
bored a *h* in the lid of it, and 2Kin 12:9 2356
in his hand by the *h* of the door Song 5:4 2356
shall play on the *h* of the asp Is 11:8 2356
to the *h* of the pit whence ye are Is 51:1 4718
hide it there in a *h* of the rock Jer 13:4 5357
I looked, behold a *h* in the wall Eze 8:7 2356

HOLE'S
nest in the sides of the *h* mouth Jer 48:28 6354

HOLES
h where they had hid themselves 1Sa 14:11 2356
shall go into the *h* of the rocks Is 2:19 4631
in the *h* of the rocks, and upon Is 7:19 5357
they are all of them snared in *h* Is 42:22 2356
out of the *h* of the rocks Jer 16:16 5357
their *h* like worms of the earth Mic 7:17 4526
and filled his *h* with prey Nah 2:12 2356
wages to put it into a bag with *h* Hag 1:6 5344
shall consume away in their *h* Zec 14:12 2356
saith unto him, The foxes have *h* Mt 8:20 5454
Jesus said unto him, Foxes have *h* Lk 9:58 5454

HOLIER
for I am *h* than thou Is 65:5 6942

HOLIEST
which is called the *H* of all Heb 9:3 39
that the way into the *h* of all Heb 9:8 39
into the *h* by the blood of Jesus Heb 10:19 39

HOLILY
are witnesses, and God also, how *h* 1Th 2:10 3743

HOLINESS
Who is like thee, glorious in *h* Ex 15:11 6944
of a signet, *H* TO THE LORD Ex 28:36 6944
of a signet, *H* TO THE LORD Ex 39:30 6944
the LORD in the beauty of *h* 1Chr 16:29 6944
should praise the beauty of *h* 2Chr 20:21 6944
they sanctified themselves in *h* 2Chr 31:18 6944
the LORD in the beauty of *h* Ps 29:2 6944
at the remembrance of his *h* Ps 30:4 6944
sitteth upon the throne of his *h* Ps 47:8 6944
our God, in the mountain of his *h* Ps 48:1 6944
God hath spoken in his *h* Ps 60:6 6944
Once have I sworn by my *h* that I Ps 89:35 6944
h becometh thine house, O LORD, Ps 93:5 6944
the LORD in the beauty of *h* Ps 96:9 6944
at the remembrance of his *h* Ps 97:12 6944
God hath spoken in his *h* Ps 108:7 6944
in the beauties of *h* from the Ps 110:3 6944
her hire shall be *h* to the LORD Is 23:18 6944
it shall be called The way of *h* Is 35:8 6944
drink it in the courts of my *h* Is 62:9 6944
from the habitation of thy *h* Is 63:15 6944
The people of thy *h* have Is 63:18 6944
Israel was *h* unto the LORD, and Jer 2:3 6944
and because of the words of his *h* Jer 23:9 6944
of justice, and mountain of *h* Jer 31:23 6944
The Lord GOD hath sworn by his *h* Amos 4:2 6944
deliverance, and there shall be *h* Obad 17 6944
of the horses, *H* UNTO THE LORD Zec 14:20 6944
in Judah shall be *h* unto the LORD Zec 14:21 6944
the *h* of the LORD which he loved Mal 2:11 6944
In *h* and righteousness before him, Lk 1:75 3742
or *h* we had made this man to walk Acts 3:12 2150
according to the spirit of *h* Rom 1:4 42
servants to righteousness unto *h* Rom 6:19 38
to God, ye have your fruit unto *h* Rom 6:22 38
perfecting *h* in the fear of God 2Cor 7:1 42
in righteousness and true *h* Eph 4:24 3742
unblameable in *h* before God 1Th 3:13 42
us unto uncleanness, but unto *h* 1Th 4:7 38
and charity and *h* with sobriety 1Ti 2:15 38
be in behaviour as becometh *h* Titus 2:3 2412
we might be partakers of his *h* Heb 12:10 41
Follow peace with all men, and *h* Heb 12:14 38

HOLLOW
he touched the *h* of his thigh Gen 32:25 3709
the *h* of Jacob's thigh was out of Gen 32:25 3709
which is upon the *h* of the thigh Gen 32:32 3709
because he touched the *h* of Gen 32:32 3709
H with boards shalt thou make it Ex 27:8 5014
he made the altar *h* with boards Ex 38:7 5014
walls of the house with *h* strakes Lev 14:37 8258
But God clave an *h* place that was Judg 15:19 4388
the waters in the *h* of his hand Is 40:12 8168
was four fingers: it was *h* Jer 52:21 5014

HOLON (*ho'-lon*) See HILEN.
1. A Levitical city in Judah.
And Goshen, and *H*, and Giloh Josh 15:51 2473
H with her suburbs, and Debir with Josh 21:15 2473
2. A Moabite city.
upon *H*, and upon Jahazah, and upon Jer 48:21 2473

HOLPEN
they have *h* the children of Lot Ps 83:8 2220
because thou, LORD, hast *h* me Ps 86:17 5826
he that is *h* shall fall down, and Is 31:3 5826
they shall be *h* with a little Dan 11:34 5826
He hath *h* his servant Israel, in Lk 1:54 482

HOLY
whereon thou standest is *h* ground Ex 3:5 6944
there shall be an *h* convocation Ex 12:16 6944
shall be an *h* convocation to you Ex 12:16 6944
strength unto thy *h* habitation Ex 15:13 6944
of the *h* sabbath unto the LORD Ex 16:23 6944
of priests, and an *h* nation Ex 19:6 6918
the sabbath day, to keep it *h* Ex 20:8 6942
And ye shall be *h* men unto me Ex 22:31 6944
the *h* place and the most *h* Ex 26:33 6944
the testimony in the most *h* place Ex 26:34 6944
thou shalt make *h* garments for Ex 28:2 6944
they shall make *h* garments for Ex 28:4 6944
when he goeth in unto the *h* place Ex 28:29 6944
unto the *h* place before the LORD Ex 28:35 6944
bear the iniquity of the *h* things Ex 28:38 6944
shall hallow in all their *h* gifts Ex 28:38 6944
altar to minister in the *h* place Ex 28:43 6944
put the *h* crown upon the mitre Ex 29:6 6944
the *h* garments of Aaron shall be Ex 29:29 6944
to minister in the *h* place Ex 29:30 6944
seethe his flesh in the *h* place Ex 29:31 6918
eat thereof, because they are *h* Ex 29:33 6944
not be eaten, because it is *h* Ex 29:34 6944
and it shall be an altar most *h* Ex 29:37 6944
toucheth the altar shall be *h* Ex 29:37 6944
it is most *h* unto the LORD Ex 30:10 6944
make it an oil of *h* ointment Ex 30:25 6944
it shall be an *h* anointing oil Ex 30:25 6944
them, that they may be most *h* Ex 30:29 6944
toucheth them shall be *h* Ex 30:29 6942
This shall be an *h* anointing oil Ex 30:31 6944
it is *h*, and it shall be *h* unto Ex 30:32 6944
tempered together, pure and *h* Ex 30:35 6944
it shall be unto you most *h* Ex 30:36 6944
shall be unto thee *h* for the LORD Ex 30:37 6944
the *h* garments for Aaron the Ex 31:10 6944
and sweet incense for the *h* place Ex 31:11 6944
for it is *h* unto you Ex 31:14 6944
sabbath of rest, *h* to the LORD Ex 31:15 6944
there shall be to you an *h* day Ex 35:2 6944
to do service in the *h* place Ex 35:19 6944
the *h* garments for Aaron the Ex 35:19 6944
service, and for the *h* garments Ex 35:21 6944
he made the *h* anointing oil, and Ex 37:29 6944
in all the work of the *h* place Ex 38:24 6944
to do service in the *h* place Ex 39:1 6944
made the *h* garments for Aaron Ex 39:1 6944
plate of the *h* crown of pure gold Ex 39:30 6944
to do service in the *h* place Ex 39:41 6944
the *h* garments for Aaron the Ex 39:41 6944
and it shall be *h* Ex 40:9 6944
and it shall be an altar most *h* Ex 40:10 6944
put upon Aaron the *h* garments Ex 40:13 6944
it is a thing most *h* of the Lev 2:3 6944
it is a thing most *h* of the Lev 2:10 6944
in the *h* things of the LORD Lev 5:15 6944
that he hath done in the *h* thing Lev 5:16 6944
shall it be eaten in the *h* place Lev 6:16 6918
it is most *h*, as is the sin Lev 6:17 6944
one that toucheth them shall be *h* Lev 6:18 6942
it is most *h* Lev 6:25 6944
in the *h* place shall it be eaten, Lev 6:26 6918
the flesh thereof shall be *h* Lev 6:27 6942
it was sprinkled in the *h* place Lev 6:27 6918
it is most *h* Lev 6:29 6944
reconcile withal in the *h* place Lev 6:30 6944
it is most *h* Lev 7:1 6944
it shall be eaten in the *h* place Lev 7:6 6918
it is most *h* Lev 7:6 6944
put the golden plate, the *h* crown Lev 8:9 6944
ye may put difference between *h* Lev 10:10 6944
for it is most *h* Lev 10:12 6944
And ye shall eat it in the *h* place Lev 10:13 6918
h place, seeing it is most *h* Lev 10:17 6944
not brought in within the *h* place Lev 10:18 6944
have eaten it in the *h* place Lev 10:18 6944
yourselves, and ye shall be *h* Lev 11:44 6918
for I am *h* Lev 11:44 6918
therefore be *h*, for I am *h* Lev 11:45 6918
burnt offering, in the *h* place Lev 14:13 6944
it is most *h* Lev 14:13 6944
h place within the vail before Lev 16:2 6944
shall Aaron come into the *h* place Lev 16:3 6944
He shall put on the *h* linen coat Lev 16:4 6944
these are *h* garments Lev 16:4 6944
make an atonement for the *h* place Lev 16:16 6944
make an atonement in the *h* place Lev 16:17 6944
an end of reconciling the *h* place Lev 16:20 6944
on when he went into the *h* place Lev 16:23 6944
flesh with water in the *h* place Lev 16:24 6918
to make atonement in the *h* place Lev 16:27 6944
clothes, even the *h* garments Lev 16:32 6944
an atonement for the *h* sanctuary Lev 16:33 6944
and say unto them, Ye shall be *h* Lev 19:2 6918
for I the LORD your God am *h* Lev 19:2 6918
be *h* to praise the LORD withal Lev 19:24 6944
and to profane my *h* name Lev 20:3 6944
yourselves therefore, and be ye *h* Lev 20:7 6918
And ye shall be *h* unto me Lev 20:26 6918
for I the LORD am *h*, and have Lev 20:26 6918
They shall be *h* unto their God, Lev 21:6 6918
therefore they shall be *h* Lev 21:6 6944
for he is *h* unto his God Lev 21:7 6918
he shall be *h* unto thee Lev 21:8 6918
LORD, which sanctify you, am *h* Lev 21:8 6918
of the most *h*, and of the *h* Lev 21:22 6944
the *h* things of the children of Lev 22:2 6944
that they profane not my *h* name Lev 22:2 6944
that goeth unto the *h* things Lev 22:3 6944
he shall not eat of the *h* things Lev 22:4 6944
and shall not eat of the *h* things Lev 22:6 6944
afterward eat of the *h* things Lev 22:7 6944
no stranger eat of the *h* thing Lev 22:10 6944
shall not eat of the *h* thing Lev 22:10 6944
of an offering of the *h* things Lev 22:12 6944
eat of the *h* thing unwittingly Lev 22:14 6944
unto the priest with the *h* thing Lev 22:14 6944
the *h* things of the children of Lev 22:15 6944
when they eat their *h* things Lev 22:16 6944
shall ye profane my *h* name Lev 22:32 6944
proclaim to be *h* convocations Lev 23:2 6944
sabbath of rest, an *h* convocation Lev 23:3 6944
even *h* convocations, which ye Lev 23:4 6944
ye shall have an *h* convocation Lev 23:7 6944
seventh day is an *h* convocation Lev 23:8 6944
they shall be *h* to the LORD for Lev 23:20 6944
that it may be an *h* convocation Lev 23:21 6944
of trumpets, an *h* convocation Lev 23:24 6944
it shall be an *h* convocation unto Lev 23:27 6944
day shall be an *h* convocation Lev 23:35 6944
be an *h* convocation unto you Lev 23:36 6944
proclaim to be *h* convocations Lev 23:37 6944

H

they shall eat it in the *h* place	Lev 24:9	6918
for it is most *h* unto him of the	Lev 24:9	6944
it shall be *h* unto you	Lev 25:12	6944
of such unto the LORD shall be *h*	Lev 27:9	6944
the exchange thereof shall be *h*	Lev 27:10	6944
his house to be *h* unto the LORD	Lev 27:14	6944
shall be *h* unto the LORD, as a	Lev 27:21	6944
as a *h* thing unto the LORD	Lev 27:23	6944
thing is most *h* unto the LORD	Lev 27:28	6944
it is *h* unto the LORD	Lev 27:30	6944
tenth shall be *h* unto the LORD	Lev 27:32	6944
and the change thereof shall be *h*	Lev 27:33	6944
about the most *h* things	Num 4:4	6944
they shall not touch any *h* thing	Num 4:15	6944
approach unto the most *h* things	Num 4:19	6944
see when the *h* things are covered	Num 4:20	6944
the *h* things of the children of	Num 5:9	6944
the priest shall take *h* water in	Num 5:17	6918
unto the LORD, he shall be *h*	Num 6:5	6918
separation he is *h* unto the LORD	Num 6:8	6918
this is *h* for the priest, with	Num 6:20	6944
and be *h* unto your God	Num 15:40	6918
seeing all the congregation are *h*	Num 16:3	6918
shew who are his, and who is *h*	Num 16:5	6918
LORD doth choose, he shall be *h*	Num 16:7	6918
be thine of the most *h* things	Num 18:9	6944
unto me, shall be most *h* for thee	Num 18:9	6944
In the most *h* place shalt thou	Num 18:10	6944
it shall be *h* unto thee	Num 18:10	6944
they are *h*	Num 18:17	6944
heave offerings of the *h* things	Num 18:19	6944
the *h* things of the children of	Num 18:32	6944
in the *h* place shalt thou cause	Num 28:7	6944
day shall be an *h* convocation	Num 28:18	6944
ye shall have an *h* convocation	Num 28:25	6944
ye shall have an *h* convocation	Num 28:26	6944
ye shall have an *h* convocation	Num 29:1	6944
seventh month an *h* convocation	Num 29:7	6944
ye shall have an *h* covocation	Num 29:12	6944
with the *h* instruments, and the	Num 31:6	6944
which was anointed with the *h* oil	Num 35:25	6944
For thou art an *h* people unto the	Deut 7:6	6918
Only thy *h* things which thou hast	Deut 12:26	6944
For thou art an *h* people unto the	Deut 14:2	6918
for thou art an *h* people unto the	Deut 14:21	6918
therefore shall thy camp be *h*	Deut 23:14	6918
Look down from thy *h* habitation	Deut 26:15	6944
that thou mayest be an *h* people	Deut 26:19	6918
thee an *h* people unto himself	Deut 28:9	6918
and thy Urim be with thy *h* one	Deut 33:8	2623
place whereon thou standest is *h*	Josh 5:15	6944
for he is an *h* God	Josh 24:19	6918
There is none *h* as the LORD	1Sa 2:2	6918
to stand before this *h* LORD God	1Sa 6:20	6918
vessels of the young men are *h*	1Sa 21:5	6944
oracle, even for the most *h* place	1Kin 6:16	6944
the inner house, the most *h* place	1Kin 7:50	6944
all the *h* vessels that were in	1Kin 8:4	6944
of the house, to the most *h* place	1Kin 8:6	6944
in the *h* place before the oracle	1Kin 8:8	6944
were come out of the *h* place	1Kin 8:10	6944
that this is an *h* man of God	2Kin 4:9	6918
even against the *H* One of Israel	2Kin 19:22	6918
all the work of the place most *h*	1Chr 6:49	6944
Glory ye in his *h* name	1Chr 16:10	6944
we may give thanks to thy *h* name	1Chr 16:35	6944
the *h* vessels of God, into the	1Chr 22:19	6944
should sanctify the most *h* things	1Chr 23:13	6944
in the purifying of all *h* things	1Chr 23:28	6944
and the charge of the *h* place	1Chr 23:32	6944
I have prepared for the *h* house	1Chr 29:3	6944
thine *h* name cometh of thine hand	1Chr 29:16	6944
And he made the most *h* house	2Chr 3:8	6944
in the most *h* house he made two	2Chr 3:10	6944
thereof for the most *h* place	2Chr 4:22	6944
all the *h* vessels that were in	2Chr 5:5	6944
the house, into the most *h* place	2Chr 5:7	6944
were come out of the *h* place	2Chr 5:11	6944
Israel, because the places are *h*	2Chr 8:11	6944
they shall go in, for they are *h*	2Chr 23:6	6944
the filthiness out of the *h* place	2Chr 29:5	6944
h place unto the God of Israel	2Chr 29:7	6944
came up to his *h* dwelling place	2Chr 30:27	6944
the tithe of *h* things which were	2Chr 31:6	6944
of the LORD, and the most *h* things	2Chr 31:14	6944
which were *h* unto the LORD	2Chr 35:3	6918
Put the *h* ark in the house which	2Chr 35:3	6944
stand in the *h* place according to	2Chr 35:5	6944
but the other *h* offerings sod	2Chr 35:13	6944
not eat of the most *h* things	Ezr 2:63	6944
unto them, Ye are *h* unto the LORD	Ezr 8:28	6944
the vessels are *h* also	Ezr 8:28	6944
so that the *h* seed have mingled	Ezr 9:2	6944
to give us a nail in his *h* place	Ezr 9:8	6944
not eat of the most *h* things	Neh 7:65	6944
This day is *h* unto the LORD your	Neh 8:9	6918
for this day is *h* unto our Lord	Neh 8:10	6918
Hold your peace, for the day is *h*	Neh 8:11	6918
known unto them thy *h* sabbath	Neh 9:14	6944
on the sabbath, or on the *h* day	Neh 10:31	6944
set feasts, and for the *h* things	Neh 10:33	6944
to dwell in Jerusalem the *h* city	Neh 11:1	6944
All the Levites in the *h* city	Neh 11:18	6944
they sanctified *h* things unto the	Neh 12:47	6944
concealed the words of the *H* One	Job 6:10	6918
my king upon my *h* hill of Zion	Ps 2:6	6944
and he heard me out of his *h* hill	Ps 3:4	6944
I worship toward thy *h* temple	Ps 5:7	6944
The LORD is in his *h* temple	Ps 11:4	6944
who shall dwell in thy *h* hill	Ps 15:1	6944
thine *H* One to see corruption	Ps 16:10	2623
he will hear him from his *h*	Ps 20:6	6944
But thou art *h*, O thou that	Ps 22:3	6918
or who shall stand in his *h* place	Ps 24:3	6944
up my hands toward thy *h* oracle	Ps 28:2	6944
we have trusted in his *h* name	Ps 33:21	6944
let them bring me unto thy *h* hill	Ps 43:3	6944
the *h* place of the tabernacles of	Ps 46:4	6918
take not thy *h* spirit from me	Ps 51:11	6944
thy house, even of thy *h* temple	Ps 65:4	6918
is God in his *h* habitation	Ps 68:5	6944
them, as in Sinai, in the *h* place	Ps 68:17	6944
art terrible out of thy *h* places	Ps 68:35	4720
the harp, O thou *H* One of Israel	Ps 71:22	6918
limited the *H* One of Israel	Ps 78:41	6918
thy *h* temple have they defiled	Ps 79:1	6944
for I am *h*	Ps 86:2	2623
foundation is in the *h* mountains	Ps 87:1	6944
the *H* One of Israel is our king	Ps 89:18	6918
spakest in vision to thy *h* one	Ps 89:19	2623
with my *h* oil have I anointed him	Ps 89:20	6944
his right hand, and his *h* arm	Ps 98:1	6944
for it is *h*	Ps 99:3	6918
for he is *h*	Ps 99:5	6918
our God, and worship at his *h* hill	Ps 99:9	6944
for the LORD our God is *h*	Ps 99:9	6918
is within me, bless his *h* name	Ps 103:1	6944
Glory ye in his *h* name	Ps 105:3	6944
For he remembered his *h* promise	Ps 105:42	6944
to give thanks unto thy *h* name	Ps 106:47	6944
h and reverend is his name	Ps 111:9	6918
will worship toward thy *h* temple	Ps 138:2	6944
his ways, and *h* in all his works	Ps 145:17	2623
flesh bless his *h* name for ever	Ps 145:21	6944
of the *h* is understanding	Prov 9:10	6918
man who devoureth that which is *h*	Prov 20:25	6944
nor have the knowledge of the *h*	Prov 30:3	6918
and gone from the place of the *h*	Eccl 8:10	6918
they have provoked the *H* One of	Is 1:4	6918
in Jerusalem, shall be called *h*	Is 4:3	6918
God that is *h* shall be sanctified	Is 5:16	6918
let the counsel of the *H* One of	Is 5:19	6918
the word of the *H* One of Israel	Is 5:24	6918
another, and said, *H*, *h*, *h*	Is 6:3	6918
so the *h* seed shall be the	Is 6:13	6944
a fire, and his *H* One for a flame	Is 10:17	6918
the *H* One of Israel, in truth	Is 10:20	6918
nor destroy in all my *h* mountain	Is 11:9	6944
for great is the *H* One of Israel	Is 12:6	6918
respect to the *H* One of Israel	Is 17:7	6918
LORD in the *h* mount at Jerusalem	Is 27:13	6944
rejoice in the *H* One of Israel	Is 29:19	6918
and sanctify the *H* One of Jacob	Is 29:23	6918
cause the *H* One of Israel to	Is 30:11	6918
thus saith the *H* One of Israel	Is 30:12	6918
the Lord GOD, the *H* One of Israel	Is 30:15	6918
night when a *h* solemnity is kept	Is 30:29	6942
look not unto the *H* One of Israel	Is 31:1	6918
even against the *H* One of Israel	Is 37:23	6918
I be equal? saith the *H* One	Is 40:25	6918
thy redeemer, the *H* One of Israel	Is 41:14	6918
glory in the *H* One of Israel	Is 41:16	6918
the *H* One of Israel hath created	Is 41:20	6918
the *H* One of Israel, thy Saviour	Is 43:3	6918
redeemer, the *H* One of Israel	Is 43:14	6918
I am the LORD, your *H* One	Is 43:15	6918
the *H* One of Israel, and his Maker	Is 45:11	6918
is his name, the *H* One of Israel	Is 47:4	6918
call themselves of the *h* city	Is 48:2	6944
thy Redeemer, the *H* One of Israel	Is 48:17	6918
Redeemer of Israel, and his *H* One	Is 49:7	6918
the *H* One of Israel, and he shall	Is 49:7	6918
garments, O Jerusalem, the *h* city	Is 52:1	6944
his *h* arm in the eyes of all the	Is 52:10	6944
thy Redeemer the *H* One of Israel	Is 54:5	6918
God, and for the *H* One of Israel	Is 55:5	6918
will I bring to my *h* mountain	Is 56:7	6944
and shall inherit my *h* mountain	Is 57:13	6944
eternity, whose name is *H*	Is 57:15	6918
h place, with him also that is of	Is 57:15	6918
doing thy pleasure on my *h* day	Is 58:13	6944
the *h* of the LORD, honourable	Is 58:13	6918
to the *H* One of Israel, because	Is 60:9	6918
The Zion of the *H* One of Israel	Is 60:14	6918
The *h* people, The redeemed of the	Is 62:12	6944
rebelled, and vexed his *h* Spirit	Is 63:10	6944
that put his *h* Spirit within him	Is 63:11	6944
Thy *h* cities are a wilderness,	Is 64:10	6944
Our *h* and our beautiful house,	Is 64:11	6944
LORD, that forget my *h* mountain	Is 65:11	6944
nor destroy in all my *h* mountain	Is 65:25	6944
to my *h* mountain Jerusalem, saith	Is 66:20	6944
the *h* flesh is passed from thee	Jer 11:15	6944
his voice from his *h* habitation	Jer 25:30	6944
east, shall be *h* unto the LORD	Jer 31:40	6944
against the *H* One of Israel	Jer 50:29	6918
sin against the *H* One of Israel	Jer 51:5	6918
their *h* places shall be defiled	Eze 7:24	6942
but pollute ye my *h* name no more	Eze 20:39	6944
For in mine *h* mountain, in the	Eze 20:40	6944
oblations, with all your *h* things	Eze 20:40	
drop thy word toward the *h* places	Eze 21:2	4720
Thou hast despised mine *h* things	Eze 22:8	6944
and have profaned mine *h* things	Eze 22:26	6944
put no difference between the *h*	Eze 22:26	6944
wast upon the *h* mountain of God	Eze 28:14	6944
went, they profaned my *h* name	Eze 36:20	6944
But I had pity for mine *h* name	Eze 36:21	6944
but for mine *h* name's sake	Eze 36:22	6944
As the *h* flock, as the flock of	Eze 36:38	6944
So will I make my *h* name known in	Eze 39:7	6944
them pollute my *h* name any more	Eze 39:7	6944
am the LORD, the *H* One in Israel	Eze 39:7	6918
and will be jealous for my *h* name	Eze 39:25	6944
unto me, This is the most *h* place	Eze 41:4	6944
they be *h* chambers, where the	Eze 42:13	6944
LORD shall eat the most *h* things	Eze 42:13	6944
shall they lay the most *h* things	Eze 42:13	6944
for the place is *h*	Eze 42:13	6918
the *h* place into the utter court	Eze 42:14	6944
for they are *h*	Eze 42:14	
my *h* name, shall the house of	Eze 43:7	6944
they have even defiled my *h* name	Eze 43:8	6944
round about shall be most *h*	Eze 43:12	6944
kept the charge of mine *h* things	Eze 44:8	6944
h things, in the most *h* place	Eze 44:13	6944
and lay them in the *h* chambers	Eze 44:19	6944
the difference between the *h*	Eze 44:23	6944
LORD, an *h* portion of the land	Eze 45:1	6944
This shall be *h* in all the	Eze 45:1	6944
the sanctuary and the most *h* place	Eze 45:3	6944
The *h* portion of the land shall	Eze 45:4	6944
an *h* place for the sanctuary	Eze 45:4	4720
the oblation of the *h* portion	Eze 45:6	6944
of the oblation of the *h* portion	Eze 45:7	6944
the oblation of the *h* portion	Eze 45:7	6944
into the *h* chambers of the	Eze 46:19	6944
priests, shall be this *h* oblation	Eze 48:10	6944
h by the border of the Levites	Eze 48:12	6944
for it is *h* unto the LORD	Eze 48:14	6944
against the oblation of the *h*	Eze 48:18	6944
the oblation of the *h* portion	Eze 48:18	6944
ye shall offer the *h* oblation	Eze 48:20	6944
and on the other of the *h* oblation	Eze 48:21	6944
and it shall be the *h* oblation	Eze 48:21	6944
whom is the spirit of the *h* gods	Dan 4:8	6922
spirit of the *h* gods is in thee	Dan 4:9	6922
an *h* one came down from heaven	Dan 4:13	6922
demand by the word of the *h* ones	Dan 4:17	6922
spirit of the *h* gods is in thee	Dan 4:18	6922
an *h* one coming down from heaven,	Dan 4:23	6922
whom is the spirit of the *h* gods	Dan 5:11	6922
the mighty and the *h* people	Dan 8:24	6918
city Jerusalem, thy *h* mountain	Dan 9:16	6944
God for the *h* mountain of my God	Dan 9:20	6944
thy people and upon thy *h* city	Dan 9:24	6944
prophecy, and to anoint the most *H*	Dan 9:24	6944
shall be against the *h* covenant	Dan 11:28	6944
against the *h* covenant	Dan 11:30	6944
them that forsake the *h* covenant	Dan 11:30	6944
seas in the glorious *h* mountain	Dan 11:45	6944
scatter the power of the *h* people	Dan 12:7	6944
the *H* One in the midst of thee	Hos 11:9	6918
sound an alarm in my *h* mountain	Joel 2:1	6944
dwelling in Zion, my *h* mountain	Joel 3:17	6944
then shall Jerusalem be *h*	Joel 3:17	6944
same maid, to profane my *h* name	Amos 2:7	6944
ye have drunk upon my *h* mountain	Obad 16	6944
look again toward thy *h* temple	Jonah 2:4	6944
in unto thee, into thine *h* temple	Jonah 2:7	6944
you, the Lord from his *h* temple	Mic 1:2	6944
O LORD my God, mine *H* One	Hab 1:12	6918
But the LORD is in his *h* temple	Hab 2:20	6944
the *H* One from mount Paran	Hab 3:3	6918
haughty because of my *h* mountain	Zeph 3:11	6944
If one bear *h* flesh in the skirt	Hag 2:12	6944
oil, or any meat, shall it be *h*	Hag 2:12	6942
Judah his portion in the *h* land	Zec 2:12	6944
raised up out of his *h* habitation	Zec 2:13	6944
the LORD of hosts the *h* mountain	Zec 8:3	6944
found with child of the *H* Ghost	Mt 1:18	*40*
in her is of the *H* Ghost	Mt 1:20	*40*
baptize you with the *H* Ghost	Mt 3:11	*40*
taketh him up into the *h* city	Mt 4:5	*40*
not that which is *h* unto the dogs	Mt 7:6	*40*
the *H* Ghost shall not be forgiven	Mt 12:31	
speaketh against the *H* Ghost	Mt 12:32	*40*
the prophet, stand in the *h* place	Mt 24:15	*40*
all the *h* angels with him, then	Mt 25:31	*40*
and went into the *h* city, and	Mt 27:53	*40*
and of the Son, and of the *H* Ghost	Mt 28:19	*40*
baptize you with the *H* Ghost	Mk 1:8	*40*
who thou art, the *H* One of God	Mk 1:24	*40*
shall blaspheme against the *H*	Mk 3:29	*40*
that he was a just man and an *h*	Mk 6:20	*40*
of his Father with the *h* angels	Mk 8:38	*40*
David himself said by the *H* Ghost	Mk 12:36	*40*
ye that speak, but the *H* Ghost	Mk 13:11	*40*
shall be filled with the *H* Ghost	Lk 1:15	*40*
The *H* Ghost shall come upon thee,	Lk 1:35	*40*
therefore also that *h* thing which	Lk 1:35	*40*
was filled with the *H* Ghost	Lk 1:41	*40*
and *h* is his name	Lk 1:49	*40*
was filled with the *H* Ghost	Lk 1:67	*40*
by the mouth of his *h* prophets	Lk 1:70	*40*
and to remember his *h* covenant	Lk 1:72	*40*
shall be called *h* to the Lord	Lk 2:23	*40*
and the *H* Ghost was upon him	Lk 2:25	*40*
revealed unto him by the *H* Ghost	Lk 2:26	*40*
baptize you with the *H* Ghost	Lk 3:16	*40*
the *H* Ghost descended in a bodily	Lk 3:22	*40*
Jesus being full of the *H* Ghost	Lk 4:1	*40*
the *H* One of God	Lk 4:34	*40*
his Father's, and of the *h* angels	Lk 9:26	*40*
the *H* Spirit to them that ask him	Lk 11:13	*40*
that blasphemeth against the *H*	Lk 12:10	*40*
For the *H* Ghost shall teach you	Lk 12:12	*40*
which baptizeth with the *H* Ghost	Jn 1:33	*40*
for the *H* Ghost was not yet given	Jn 7:39	*40*
Comforter, which is the *H* Ghost	Jn 14:26	*40*
H Father, keep through thine own	Jn 17:11	*40*
unto them, Receive ye the *H* Ghost	Jn 20:22	*40*
after that he through the *H* Ghost	Acts 1:2	*40*
the *H* Ghost not many days hence	Acts 1:5	*40*
after that the *H* Ghost is come	Acts 1:8	*40*
which the *H* Ghost by the mouth of	Acts 1:16	*40*
were all filled with the *H* Ghost	Acts 2:4	*40*
thine *H* One to see corruption	Acts 2:27	*3741*
Father the promise of the *H* Ghost	Acts 2:33	*40*
receive the gift of the *H* Ghost	Acts 2:38	*40*
But ye denied the *H* One and the	Acts 3:14	*40*
h prophets since the world began	Acts 3:21	*40*

Peter, filled with the *H* Ghost	Acts 4:8	*40*
a truth against thy *h* child Jesus	Acts 4:27	*40*
by the name of thy *h* child Jesus	Acts 4:30	*40*
were all filled with the *H* Ghost	Acts 4:31	*40*
thine heart to lie to the *H* Ghost	Acts 5:3	*40*
and so is also the *H* Ghost	Acts 5:32	*40*
report, full of the *H* Ghost	Acts 6:3	*40*
full of faith and of the *H* Ghost	Acts 6:5	*40*
words against this *h* place	Acts 6:13	*40*
where thou standest is *h* ground	Acts 7:33	*40*
ye do always resist the *H* Ghost	Acts 7:51	*40*
But he, being full of the *H* Ghost	Acts 7:55	*40*
they might receive the *H* Ghost	Acts 8:15	*40*
and they received the *H* Ghost	Acts 8:17	*40*
hands the *H* Ghost was given	Acts 8:18	*40*
hands, he may receive the *H* Ghost	Acts 8:19	*40*
and be filled with the *H* Ghost	Acts 9:17	*40*
and in the comfort of the *H* Ghost	Acts 9:31	*40*
was warned from God by an *h* angel	Acts 10:22	*40*
of Nazareth with the *H* Ghost	Acts 10:38	*40*
the *H* Ghost fell on all them	Acts 10:44	*40*
out the gift of the *H* Ghost	Acts 10:45	*40*
the *H* Ghost as well as we	Acts 10:47	*40*
the *H* Ghost fell on them, as on	Acts 11:15	*40*
be baptized with the *H* Ghost	Acts 11:16	*40*
good man, and full of the *H* Ghost	Acts 11:24	*40*
the *H* Ghost said, Separate me	Acts 13:2	*40*
being sent forth by the *H* Ghost	Acts 13:4	*40*
Paul,) filled with the *H* Ghost	Acts 13:9	*40*
thine *H* One to see corruption	Acts 13:35	*3741*
with joy, and with the *H* Ghost	Acts 13:52	*40*
witness, giving them the *H* Ghost	Acts 15:8	*40*
For it seemed good to the *H* Ghost	Acts 15:28	*40*
were forbidden of the *H* Ghost to	Acts 16:6	*40*
Have ye received the *H* Ghost	Acts 19:2	*40*
whether there be any *H* Ghost	Acts 19:2	*40*
them, the *H* Ghost came on them	Acts 19:6	*40*
Save that the *H* Ghost witnesseth	Acts 20:23	*40*
over the which the *H* Ghost hath	Acts 20:28	*40*
and said, Thus saith the *H* Ghost	Acts 21:11	*40*
and hath polluted this *h* place	Acts 21:28	*40*
Well spake the *H* Ghost by Esaias	Acts 28:25	*40*
his prophets in the *h* scriptures	Rom 1:2	*40*
abroad in our hearts by the *H*	Rom 5:5	*40*
law is *h*, and the commandment *h*	Rom 7:12	*40*
bearing me witness in the *H* Ghost	Rom 9:1	*40*
be *h*, the lump is also *h*	Rom 11:16	*40*
and if the root be *h*, so are the	Rom 11:16	*40*
your bodies a living sacrifice, *h*	Rom 12:1	*40*
and peace, and joy in the *H* Ghost	Rom 14:17	*40*
through the power of the *H* Ghost	Rom 15:13	*40*
being sanctified by the *H* Ghost	Rom 15:16	*40*
Salute one another with an *h* kiss	Rom 16:16	*40*
but which the *H* Ghost teacheth	1Cor 2:13	*40*
for the temple of God is *h*	1Cor 3:17	*40*
of the *H* Ghost which is in you	1Cor 6:19	*40*
but now are they *h*	1Cor 7:14	*40*
that she may be *h* both in body	1Cor 7:34	*40*
h things live of the things of	1Cor 9:13	*2413*
is the Lord, but by the *H* Ghost	1Cor 12:3	*40*
ye one another with an *h* kiss	1Cor 16:20	*40*
by kindness, by the *H* Ghost	2Cor 6:6	*40*
Greet one another with an *h* kiss	2Cor 13:12	*40*
and the communion of the *H* Ghost	2Cor 13:14	*40*
of the world, that we should be *h*	Eph 1:4	*40*
with that *h* Spirit of promise	Eph 1:13	*40*
unto an *h* temple in the Lord	Eph 2:21	*40*
now revealed unto his *h* apostles	Eph 3:5	*40*
And grieve not the *h* Spirit of God	Eph 4:30	*40*
but that it should be *h* and	Eph 5:27	*40*
through death, to present you *h*	Col 1:22	*40*
therefore, as the elect of God, *h*	Col 3:12	*40*
also in power, and in the *H* Ghost	1Th 1:5	*40*
with joy of the *H* Ghost	1Th 1:6	*40*
also given unto us his *h* Spirit	1Th 4:8	*40*
all the brethren with an *h* kiss	1Th 5:26	*40*
be read unto all the *h* brethren	1Th 5:27	*40*
every where, lifting up *h* hands	1Ti 2:8	*3741*
and called us with an *h* calling	2Ti 1:9	*40*
the *H* Ghost which dwelleth in us	2Ti 1:14	*40*
thou hast known the *h* scriptures	2Ti 3:15	*2413*
lover of good men, sober, just, *h*	Titus 1:8	*3741*
and renewing of the *H* Ghost	Titus 3:5	*40*
miracles, and gifts of the *H* Ghost	Heb 2:4	*40*
h brethren, partakers of the	Heb 3:1	*40*
Wherefore (as the *H* Ghost saith	Heb 3:7	*40*
made partakers of the *H* Ghost	Heb 6:4	*40*
high priest became us, who is *h*	Heb 7:26	*3741*
The *H* Ghost this signifying, that	Heb 9:8	*40*
entered in once into the *h* place	Heb 9:12	*39*
into the *h* places made with hands	Heb 9:24	*39*
high priest entereth into the *h*	Heb 9:25	*39*
Whereof the *H* Ghost also is a	Heb 10:15	*40*
the *H* Ghost sent down from heaven	1Pet 1:12	*40*
as he which hath called you is *h*	1Pet 1:15	*40*
so be ye *h* in all manner of	1Pet 1:15	*40*
Be ye *h*; for I am *h*	1Pet 1:16	*40*
an *h* priesthood, to offer up	1Pet 2:5	*40*
an *h* nation, a peculiar people	1Pet 2:9	*40*
in the old time the *h* women also	1Pet 3:5	*40*
we were with him in the *h* mount	2Pet 1:18	*40*
but *h* men of God spake as they	2Pet 1:21	*40*
as they were moved by the *H* Ghost	2Pet 1:21	*40*
to turn from the *h* commandment	2Pet 2:21	*40*
spoken before by the *h* prophets	2Pet 3:2	*40*
ye to be in all *h* conversation	2Pet 3:11	*40*
ye have an unction from the *H* One	1Jn 2:20	*40*
Father, the Word, and the *H* Ghost	1Jn 5:7	*40*
yourselves on your most *h* faith	Jude 20	*40*
praying in the *H* Ghost	Jude 20	*40*
These things saith he that is *h*	Rev 3:7	*40*
and night, saying, *H*, *h*, *h*	Rev 4:8	*40*
saying, How long, O Lord, *h*	Rev 6:10	*40*
the *h* city shall they tread under	Rev 11:2	*40*
in the presence of the *h* angels	Rev 14:10	*40*
for thou only art *h*	Rev 15:4	*3741*
ye *h* apostles and prophets	Rev 18:20	*40*
h is he that hath part in the	Rev 20:6	*40*
And I John saw the *h* city, new	Rev 21:2	*40*
the *h* Jerusalem, descending out	Rev 21:10	*40*
the Lord God of the *h* prophets	Rev 22:6	*40*
that is *h*, let him be *h* still	Rev 22:11	*37*
of life, and out of the *h* city	Rev 22:19	*40*

HOLYDAY

with a multitude that kept *h*	Ps 42:4	2287
in drink, or in respect of an *h*	Col 2:16	*1859*

HOMAM (*ho'-mam*) See HEMAM. *A son of Lotan.*

of Lotan; Hori, and *H*	1Chr 1:39	1950

HOME

by her, until his lord came *h*	Gen 39:16	1004
of his house, Bring these men *h*	Gen 43:16	1004
And when Joseph came *h*, they	Gen 43:26	1004
field, and shall not be brought *h*	Ex 9:19	1004
mother, whether she be born at *h*	Lev 18:9	1004
shalt bring her *h* to thine house	Deut 21:12	8432
he shall be free at *h* one year	Deut 24:5	1004
father's household, *h* unto thee	Josh 2:18	1004
If ye bring me *h* again to fight	Judg 11:9	7725
your way, that thou mayest go *h*	Judg 19:9	168
hath brought me *h* again empty	Ruth 1:21	7725
And they went unto their own *h*	1Sa 2:20	4725
and bring their calves *h* from them	1Sa 6:7	1004
and shut up their calves at *h*	1Sa 6:10	1004
And Saul also went *h* to Gibeah	1Sa 10:26	1004
no more *h* to his father's house	1Sa 18:2	7725
And Saul went *h*	1Sa 24:22	1004
Then David sent *h* to Tamar	2Sa 13:7	1004
not fetch *h* again his banished	2Sa 14:13	7725
gat him *h* to his house, to his	2Sa 17:23	1004
in Lebanon, and two months at *h*	1Kin 5:14	1004
Come *h* with me, and refresh	1Kin 13:7	1004
Come *h* with me, and eat bread	1Kin 13:15	1004
glory of this, and tarry at *h*	2Kin 14:10	1004
I bring the ark of God *h* to me	1Chr 13:12	
So David brought not the ark *h* to	1Chr 13:13	
him out of Ephraim, to go *h* again	2Chr 25:10	4725
they returned *h* in great anger	2Chr 25:10	4725
abide now at *h*	2Chr 25:19	1004
and when he came *h*, he sent and	Est 5:10	1004
that he will bring *h* thy seed	Job 39:12	7725
tarried at *h* divided the spoil	Ps 68:12	1004
For the goodman is not at *h*	Prov 7:19	1004
will come *h* at the day appointed	Prov 7:20	1004
because man goeth to his long *h*	Eccl 12:5	1004
that he should carry him *h*	Jer 39:14	1004
bereaveth, at *h* there is as death	Lam 1:20	1004
a proud man, neither keepeth at *h*	Hab 2:5	5115
and when ye brought it *h*, I did	Hag 1:9	1004
lieth at *h* sick of the palsy	Mt 8:6	*3614*
Go *h* to thy friends, and tell them	Mk 5:19	*3624*
which are at *h* at my house	Lk 9:61	
And when he cometh *h*, he calleth	Lk 15:6	*3624*
disciple took her unto his own *h*	Jn 19:27	
went away again unto their own *h*	Jn 20:10	*1438*
and they returned *h* again	Acts 21:6	*2398*
any man hunger, let him eat at *h*	1Cor 11:34	*3624*
let them ask their husbands at *h*	1Cor 14:35	*3624*
whilst we are at *h* in the body	2Cor 5:6	*1736*
learn first to shew piety at *h*	1Ti 5:4	*2398*
be discreet, chaste, keepers at *h*	Titus 2:5	*3626*

HOMEBORN

One law shall be to him that is *h*	Ex 12:49	249
is he a *h* slave?	Jer 2:14	1004

HOMER

a *h* of barley seed shall be	Lev 27:16	2563
the seed of an *h* shall yield an	Is 5:10	2563
contain the tenth part of an *h*	Eze 45:11	2563
the ephah the tenth part of an *h*	Eze 45:11	2563
thereof shall be after the *h*	Eze 45:11	2563
part of an ephah of an *h* of wheat	Eze 45:13	2563
of an ephah of an *h* of barley	Eze 45:13	2563
which is an *h* of ten baths	Eze 45:14	2563
for ten baths are an *h*	Eze 45:14	2563
an *h* of barley, and an half *h*	Hos 3:2	2563

HOMERS

gathered least gathered ten *h*	Num 11:32	2563

HONEST

ground are they, which in an *h*	Lk 8:15	*2570*
among you seven men of *h* report	Acts 6:3	
Provide things *h* in the sight of	Rom 12:17	*2570*
Providing for *h* things, not only	2Cor 8:21	*2570*
that ye should do that which is *h*	2Cor 13:7	*2570*
are true, whatsoever things are *h*	Phil 4:8	*4586*
conversation *h* among the Gentiles	1Pet 2:12	*2570*

HONESTLY

Let us walk *h*, as in the day	Rom 13:13	*2156*
That ye may walk *h* toward them	1Th 4:12	*2156*
in all things willing to live *h*	Heb 13:18	*2573*

HONESTY

life in all godliness and *h*	1Ti 2:2	*4587*

HONEY

a little balm, and a little *h*	Gen 43:11	1706
a land flowing with milk and *h*	Ex 3:8	1706
a land flowing with milk and *h*	Ex 3:17	1706
a land flowing with milk and *h*	Ex 13:5	1706
of it was like wafers made with *h*	Ex 16:31	1706
a land flowing with milk and *h*	Ex 33:3	1706
shall burn no leaven, nor any *h*	Lev 2:11	1706
land that floweth with milk and *h*	Lev 20:24	1706
surely it floweth with milk and *h*	Num 13:27	1706
land which floweth with milk and *h*	Num 14:8	1706
land that floweth with milk and *h*	Num 16:13	1706
land that floweth with milk and *h*	Num 16:14	1706
land that floweth with milk and *h*	Deut 6:3	1706
a land of oil olive, and *h*	Deut 8:8	1706
land that floweth with milk and *h*	Deut 11:9	1706
land that floweth with milk and *h*	Deut 26:9	1706
land that floweth with milk and *h*	Deut 26:15	1706
land that floweth with milk and *h*	Deut 27:3	1706
that floweth with milk and *h*	Deut 31:20	1706
him to suck *h* out of the rock	Deut 32:13	1706
land that floweth with milk and *h*	Josh 5:6	1706
h in the carcase of the lion	Judg 14:8	1706
h out of the carcase of the lion	Judg 14:9	1706
went down, What is sweeter than *h*	Judg 14:18	1706
there was *h* upon the ground	1Sa 14:25	1706
the wood, behold, the *h* dropped	1Sa 14:26	1706
I tasted a little of this *h*	1Sa 14:29	1706
I did but taste a little *h* with	1Sa 14:43	1706
And *h*, and butter, and sheep, and	2Sa 17:29	1706
and cracknels, and a cruse of *h*	1Kin 14:3	1706
a land of oil olive and of *h*	2Kin 18:32	1706
of corn, wine, and oil, and *h*	2Chr 31:5	1706
the floods, the brooks of *h*	Job 20:17	1706
sweeter also than *h* and the	Ps 19:10	1706
with *h* out of the rock should I	Ps 81:16	1706
yea, sweeter than *h* to my mouth	Ps 119:103	1706
My son, eat thou *h*, because it is	Prov 24:13	1706
Hast thou found *h*?	Prov 25:16	1706
It is not good to eat much *h*	Prov 25:27	1706
h and milk are under thy tongue	Song 4:11	1706
have eaten my honeycomb with my *h*	Song 5:1	1706
h shall he eat, that he may know	Is 7:15	1706
h shall every one eat that is	Is 7:22	1706
a land flowing with milk and *h*	Jer 11:5	1706
a land flowing with milk and *h*	Jer 32:22	1706
and of barley, and of oil, and of *h*	Jer 41:8	1706
in my mouth as *h* for sweetness	Eze 3:3	1706
thou didst eat fine flour, and *h*	Eze 16:13	1706
thee, fine flour, and oil, and *h*	Eze 16:19	1706
for them, flowing with milk and *h*	Eze 20:6	1706
them, flowing with milk and *h*	Eze 20:15	1706
wheat of Minnith, and Pannag, and *h*	Eze 27:17	1706
and his meat was locusts and wild *h*	Mt 3:4	*3192*
and he did eat locusts and wild *h*	Mk 1:6	*3192*
shall be in thy mouth sweet as *h*	Rev 10:9	*3192*
and it was in my mouth sweet as *h*	Rev 10:10	*3192*

HONEYCOMB

in his hand, and dipped it in an *h*	1Sa 14:27	
sweeter also than honey and the *h*	Ps 19:10	
of a strange woman drop as an *h*	Prov 5:3	5317
Pleasant words are as an *h*	Prov 16:24	
and the *h*, which is sweet to thy	Prov 24:13	5317
The full soul loatheth an *h*	Prov 27:7	5317
lips, O my spouse, drop as the *h*	Song 4:11	5317
I have eaten my *h* with my honey	Song 5:1	3293
of a broiled fish, and of an *h*	Lk 24:42	

HONOUR

unto their assembly, mine *h*	Gen 49:6	3519
and I will get me *h* upon Pharaoh	Ex 14:17	3513
I have gotten me *h* upon Pharaoh	Ex 14:18	3513
H thy father and thy mother	Ex 20:12	3513
nor *h* the person of the mighty	Lev 19:15	1921
h the face of the old man, and	Lev 19:32	1921
promote thee unto very great *h*	Num 22:17	3513
able indeed to promote thee to *h*	Num 22:37	3513
to promote thee unto great *h*	Num 24:11	3513
LORD hath kept thee back from *h*	Num 24:11	3519
put some of thine *h* upon him	Num 27:20	1935
H thy father and thy mother, as	Deut 5:16	3513
in praise, and in name, and in *h*	Deut 26:19	8597
takest shall not be for thine *h*	Judg 4:9	8597
wherewith by me they *h* God	Judg 9:9	3513
come to pass we may do thee *h*	Judg 13:17	3513
for them that *h* me I will *h*	1Sa 2:30	3513
yet *h* me now, I pray thee, before	1Sa 15:30	3513
of, of them shall I be had in *h*	2Sa 6:22	3513
thou that David doth *h* thy father	2Sa 10:3	3513
hast not asked, both riches, and *h*	1Kin 3:13	3519
Glory and *h* are in his presence	1Chr 16:27	1926
to thee for the *h* of thy servant	1Chr 17:18	3519
thou that David doth *h* thy father	1Chr 19:3	3513
h come of thee, and thou reignest	1Chr 29:12	3519
age, full of days, riches, and *h*	1Chr 29:28	3519
not asked riches, wealth, or *h*	2Chr 1:11	3519
give thee riches, and wealth, and *h*	2Chr 1:12	3519
he had riches and *h* in abundance	2Chr 17:5	3519
h in abundance, and joined	2Chr 18:1	3519
be for thine *h* from the LORD God	2Chr 26:18	3519
had exceeding much riches and *h*	2Chr 32:27	3519
Jerusalem did him *h* at his death	2Chr 32:33	3519
the *h* of his excellent majesty	Est 1:4	3366
shall give to their husbands *h*	Est 1:20	3366
And the king said, What *h* and	Est 6:3	3366
man whom the king delighteth to *h*	Est 6:6	3366
to do *h* more than to myself	Est 6:6	3366
man whom the king delighteth to *h*	Est 6:7	3366
whom the king delighteth to *h*	Est 6:9	3366
man whom the king delighteth to *h*	Est 6:9	3366
man whom the king delighteth to *h*	Est 6:11	3366
light, and gladness, and joy, and *h*	Est 8:16	3366
His sons come to *h*, and he knoweth	Job 14:21	3513
earth, and lay mine *h* in the dust	Ps 7:5	3519
hast crowned him with glory and *h*	Ps 8:5	1926
h and majesty hast thou laid upon	Ps 21:5	1935
the place where thine *h* dwelleth	Ps 26:8	3519
man being in *h* abideth not	Ps 49:12	3366
Man that is in *h*, and	Ps 49:20	3366
Sing forth the *h* of his name	Ps 66:2	3519
praise and with thy *h* all the day	Ps 71:8	8597
I will deliver him, and *h* him	Ps 91:15	3515
H and majesty are before him	Ps 96:6	1935
thou art clothed with *h* and	Ps 104:1	1935
his horn shall be exalted with *h*	Ps 112:9	3519
of the glorious *h* of thy majesty	Ps 145:5	1926

H

this *h* have all his saints ... Ps 149:9 1926
H the LORD with thy substance, and ... Prov 3:9 3513
and in her left hand riches and *h* ... Prov 3:16 3519
she shall bring thee to *h* ... Prov 4:8 3513
thou give thine *h* unto others ... Prov 5:9 1935
Riches and *h* are with me ... Prov 8:18 3519
A gracious woman retaineth *h* ... Prov 11:16 3519
of people is the king's *h* ... Prov 14:28 1927
and before *h* is humility ... Prov 15:33 3519
and before *h* is humility ... Prov 18:12 3519
It is an *h* for a man to cease ... Prov 20:3 3519
findeth life, righteousness, and *h* ... Prov 21:21 3519
fear of the LORD are riches, and *h* ... Prov 22:4 3519
but the *h* of kings is to search ... Prov 25:2 3519
so *h* is not seemly for a fool ... Prov 26:1 3519
so is he that giveth *h* to a fool ... Prov 26:8 3519
but *h* shall uphold the humble in ... Prov 29:23 3519
Strength and *h* are her clothing ... Prov 31:25 1926
hath given riches, wealth, and *h* ... Eccl 6:2 3519
is in reputation for wisdom and *h* ... Eccl 10:1 3519
mouth, and with their lips do *h* me ... Is 29:13 3513
The beast of the field shall *h* me ... Is 43:20 3513
and shalt *h* him, not doing thine ... Is 58:13 3513
an *h* before all the nations of ... Jer 33:9 8597
of me gifts and rewards and great *h* ... Dan 2:6 3367
power, and for the *h* of my majesty ... Dan 4:30 3367
the glory of my kingdom, mine *h* ... Dan 4:36 1923
h the King of heaven, all whose ... Dan 4:37 1922
and majesty, and glory, and *h* ... Dan 5:18 1923
not give the *h* of the kingdom ... Dan 11:21 1935
shall he *h* the God of forces ... Dan 11:38 3513
knew not shall he *h* with gold ... Dan 11:38 3513
I be a father, where is mine *h* ... Mal 1:6 3519
them, A prophet is not without *h* ... Mt 13:57 *820*
saying, *H* thy father and mother ... Mt 15:4 *5091*
h not his father or his mother, ... Mt 15:6 *5091*
H thy father and thy mother ... Mt 19:19 *5091*
them, A prophet is not without *h* ... Mk 6:4 *820*
H thy father and thy mother ... Mk 7:10 *5091*
not, *H* thy father and mother ... Mk 10:19 *5091*
H thy father and thy mother ... Lk 18:20 *5091*
hath no *h* in his own country ... Jn 4:44 *5092*
That all men should *h* the Son ... Jn 5:23 *5091*
even as they *h* the Father ... Jn 5:23 *5091*
I receive not *h* from men ... Jn 5:41 *1391*
which receive *h* one of another, ... Jn 5:44 *1391*
seek not the *h* that cometh from ... Jn 5:44 *1391*
but I *h* my Father, and ye do ... Jn 8:49 *5091*
I *h* myself, my *h* is nothing ... Jn 8:54 *1391*
serve me, him will my Father *h* ... Jn 12:26 *5091*
in well doing seek for glory and *h* ... Rom 2:7 *5092*
But glory, *h*, and peace, to every ... Rom 2:10 *5092*
lump to make one vessel unto *h* ... Rom 9:21 *5092*
in *h* preferring one another ... Rom 12:10 *5092*
to whom fear; *h* to whom *h* ... Rom 13:7 *5092*
these we bestow more abundant *h* ... 1Cor 12:23 *5092*
h to that part which lacked ... 1Cor 12:24 *5092*
By *h* and dishonour, by evil report ... 2Cor 6:8 *1391*
H thy father and mother ... Eph 6:2 *5091*
not in any *h* to the satisfying of ... Col 2:23 *5092*
his vessel in sanctification and *h* ... 1Th 4:4 *5092*
the only wise God, be *h* and glory ... 1Ti 1:17 *5092*
H widows that are widows indeed ... 1Ti 5:3 *5091*
be counted worthy of double *h* ... 1Ti 5:17 *5092*
their own masters worthy of all *h* ... 1Ti 6:1 *5092*
to whom be *h* and power everlasting ... 1Ti 6:16 *5092*
and some to *h*, and some to ... 2Ti 2:20 *5092*
he shall be a vessel unto *h* ... 2Ti 2:21 *5092*
crownedst him with glory and *h* ... Heb 2:7 *5092*
of death, crowned with glory and *h* ... Heb 2:9 *5092*
house hath more *h* than the house ... Heb 3:3 *5092*
no man taketh this *h* unto himself ... Heb 5:4 *5092*
might be found unto praise and *h* ... 1Pet 1:7 *5092*
H all men ... 1Pet 2:17 *5091*
H the king ... 1Pet 2:17 *5091*
giving *h* unto the wife, as unto ... 1Pet 3:7 *5092*
he received from God the Father *h* ... 2Pet 1:17 *5092*
when those beasts give glory and *h* ... Rev 4:9 *5092*
O Lord, to receive glory and *h* ... Rev 4:11 *5092*
and wisdom, and strength, and *h* ... Rev 5:12 *5092*
heard I saying, Blessing, and *h* ... Rev 5:13 *5092*
and wisdom, and thanksgiving, and *h* ... Rev 7:12 *5092*
Salvation, and glory, and *h* ... Rev 19:1 *5092*
glad and rejoice, and give *h* to him ... Rev 19:7 *1391*
do bring their glory and *h* into it ... Rev 21:24 *5092*
glory and *h* of the nations into it ... Rev 21:26 *5092*

HONOURABLE

he was more *h* than all the house ... Gen 34:19 3513
more, and more *h* than they ... Num 22:15 3513
a man of God, and he is an *h* man ... 1Sa 9:6 3513
bidding, and is *h* in thine house ... 1Sa 22:14 3513
Was he not most *h* of three ... 2Sa 23:19 3513
He was more *h* than the thirty, ... 2Sa 23:23 3513
a great man with his master, and *h* ... 2Kin 5:1
Jabez was more *h* than his ... 1Chr 4:9 3513
he was more *h* than the two ... 1Chr 11:21 3513
he was *h* among the thirty, but ... 1Chr 11:25 3513
and the *h* man dwelt in it ... Job 22:8
daughters were among thy *h* women ... Ps 45:9 3368
His work is *h* and glorious ... Ps 111:3 1935
captain of fifty, and the *h* man ... Is 3:3
and the base against the *h* ... Is 3:5 3519
their *h* men are famished, and ... Is 5:13 3519
The ancient and *h*, he is the head ... Is 9:15
are the *h* of the earth ... Is 23:8 1935
contempt all the *h* of the earth ... Is 23:9 3513
magnify the law, and make it *h* ... Is 42:21 142
in my sight, thou hast been *h* ... Is 43:4 3513
delight, the holy of the LORD, *h* ... Is 58:13 3513
and they cast lots for her *h* men ... Nah 3:10 3513
an *h* counsellor, which also ... Mk 15:43 *2158*
lest a more *h* man than thou be ... Lk 14:8 *1784*
h women, and the chief men of the ... Acts 13:50 *2158*
also of *h* women which were Greeks ... Acts 17:12 *2158*
ye are *h*, but we are despised ... 1Cor 4:10 *1741*
body, which we think to be less *h* ... 1Cor 12:23 *820*
Marriage is *h* in all, and the bed ... Heb 13:4 *5093*

HONOURED

I will be *h* upon Pharaoh, and upon ... Ex 14:4 3513
that regardeth reproof shall be *h* ... Prov 13:18 3513
waiteth on his master shall be *h* ... Prov 27:18 3513
neither hast thou *h* me with thy ... Is 43:23 3513
all that *h* her despise her, ... Lam 1:8 3513
the faces of elders were not *h* ... Lam 5:12 1921
h him that liveth for ever, whose ... Dan 4:34 1922
Who also *h* us with many honours ... Acts 28:10 *5092*
or one member be *h*, all the ... 1Cor 12:26 *1392*

HONOUREST

h thy sons above me, to make ... 1Sa 2:29 3513

HONOURETH

but he *h* them that fear the LORD ... Ps 15:4 3513
is better than he that *h* himself ... Prov 12:9 3513
but he that *h* him hath mercy on ... Prov 14:31 3513
A son *h* his father, and a servant ... Mal 1:6 3513
mouth, and *h* me with their lips ... Mt 15:8 *5091*
This people *h* me with their lips, ... Mk 7:6 *5091*
He that *h* not the Son *h* not ... Jn 5:23 *5091*
it is my Father that *h* me ... Jn 8:54 *1392*

HONOURS

Who also honoured us with many *h* ... Acts 28:10 *5091*

HOODS

and the fine linen, and the *h* ... Is 3:23 6797

HOOF

shall not an *h* be left behind ... Ex 10:26 6541
Whatsoever parteth the *h*, and is ... Lev 11:3 6541
cud, or of them that divide the *h* ... Lev 11:4 6541
the cud, but divideth not the *h* ... Lev 11:4 6541
the cud, but divideth not the *h* ... Lev 11:5 6541
the cud, but divideth not the *h* ... Lev 11:6 6541
the swine, though he divide the *h* ... Lev 11:7 6541
every beast which divideth the *h* ... Lev 11:26 6541
And every beast that parteth the *h* ... Deut 14:6 6541
of them that divide the cloven *h* ... Deut 14:7 6541
the cud, but divide not the *h* ... Deut 14:7 6541
swine, because it divideth the *h* ... Deut 14:8 6541

HOOFS

or bullock that hath horns and *h* ... Ps 69:31 6536
their horses' *h* shall be counted ... Is 5:28 6541
of the *h* of his strong horses ... Jer 47:3 6541
With the *h* of his horses shall he ... Eze 26:11 6541
nor the *h* of beasts trouble them ... Eze 32:13 6541
iron, and I will make thy *h* brass ... Mic 4:13 6541

HOOK

I will put my *h* in thy nose ... 2Kin 19:28 2397
thou draw out leviathan with an *h* ... Job 41:1 100
Canst thou put an *h* into his nose ... Job 41:2 2443
will I put my *h* in thy nose ... Is 37:29 2397
go thou to the sea, and cast an *h* ... Mt 17:27 *44*

HOOKS

their *h* shall be of gold, upon ... Ex 26:32 2053
gold, and their *h* shall be of gold ... Ex 26:37 2053
the *h* of the pillars and their ... Ex 27:10 2053
the *h* of the pillars and their ... Ex 27:11 2053
their *h* shall be of silver, and ... Ex 27:17 2053
their *h* were of gold ... Ex 36:36 2053
five pillars of it with their *h* ... Ex 36:38 2053
the *h* of the pillars and their ... Ex 38:10 2053
the *h* of the pillars and their ... Ex 38:11 2053
the *h* of the pillars and their ... Ex 38:12 2053
the *h* of the pillars and their ... Ex 38:17 2053
their *h* of silver, and the ... Ex 38:19 2053
shekels he made *h* for the pillars ... Ex 38:28 2053
But I will put *h* in thy jaws ... Eze 29:4 2397
put *h* into thy jaws, and I will ... Eze 38:4 2397
And within were *h*, an hand broad, ... Eze 40:43 8240
that he will take you away with *h* ... Amos 4:2 6793

HOPE

If I should say, I have *h* ... Ruth 1:12 8615
yet now there is *h* in Israel ... Ezr 10:2 4723
thy fear, thy confidence, thy *h* ... Job 4:6 8615
So the poor hath *h*, and iniquity ... Job 5:16 8615
is my strength, that I should *h* ... Job 6:11 3176
shuttle, and are spent without *h* ... Job 7:6 8615
and the hypocrite's *h* shall perish ... Job 8:13 8615
Whose *h* shall be cut off, and ... Job 8:14 3689
be secure, because there is *h* ... Job 11:18 8615
their *h* shall be as the giving up ... Job 11:20 8615
For there is *h* of a tree, if it ... Job 14:7 8615
and thou destroyest the *h* of man ... Job 14:19 8615
And where is now my *h* ... Job 17:15 8615
as for my *h*, who shall see it ... Job 17:15 8615
mine *h* hath he removed like a ... Job 19:10 8615
For what is the *h* of the ... Job 27:8 8615
If I have made gold my *h*, or have ... Job 31:24 3689
Behold, the *h* of him is in vain ... Job 41:9 8431
my flesh also shall rest in *h* ... Ps 16:9 983
thou didst make me *h* when I was ... Ps 22:9 982
heart, all ye that *h* in the LORD ... Ps 31:24 3176
upon them that *h* in his mercy ... Ps 33:18 3176
us, according as we *h* in thee ... Ps 33:22 3176
For in thee, O LORD, do I *h* ... Ps 38:15 3176
my *h* is in thee ... Ps 39:7 8431
h thou in God ... Ps 42:5 3176
h thou in God ... Ps 42:11 3176
h in God ... Ps 43:5 3176
For thou art my *h*, O Lord GOD ... Ps 71:5 8615
But I will *h* continually, and will ... Ps 71:14 3176
they might set their *h* in God ... Ps 78:7 3689
which thou hast caused me to *h* ... Ps 119:49 3176
but I *h* in thy word ... Ps 119:81 3176
I *h* in thy word ... Ps 119:114 3176
and let me not be ashamed of my *h* ... Ps 119:116 7664
doth wait, and in his word do I *h* ... Ps 130:5 3176
Let Israel *h* in the LORD ... Ps 130:7 3176
Let Israel *h* in the LORD from ... Ps 131:3 3176
whose *h* is in the LORD his God ... Ps 146:5 7664
him, in those that *h* in his mercy ... Ps 147:11 3176
The *h* of the righteous shall be ... Prov 10:28 8431
the *h* of unjust men perisheth ... Prov 11:7 8431
H deferred maketh the heart sick, ... Prov 13:12 8431
the righteous hath *h* in his death ... Prov 14:32 2620
Chasten thy son while there is *h* ... Prov 19:18 8615
there is more *h* of a fool than of ... Prov 26:12 8615
there is more *h* of a fool than of ... Prov 29:20 8615
to all the living there is *h* ... Eccl 9:4 986
the pit cannot *h* for thy truth ... Is 38:18 7663
saidst thou not, There is no *h* ... Is 57:10 2976
but thou saidst, There is no *h* ... Jer 2:25 2976
O the *h* of Israel, the saviour ... Jer 14:8 4723
the LORD, and whose *h* the LORD is ... Jer 17:7 4009
the *h* of Israel, all that forsake ... Jer 17:13 4723
thou art my *h* in the day of evil ... Jer 17:17 4268
And they said, There is no *h* ... Jer 18:12 2976
there is *h* in thine end, saith ... Jer 31:17 8615
the LORD, the *h* of their fathers ... Jer 50:7 4723
my *h* is perished from the LORD ... Lam 3:18 8431
to my mind, therefore have I *h* ... Lam 3:21 3176
therefore will I *h* in him ... Lam 3:24 3176
is good that a man should both *h* ... Lam 3:26 2342
if so be there may be *h* ... Lam 3:29 8615
they have made others to *h* that ... Eze 13:6 3176
her *h* was lost, then she took ... Eze 19:5 8615
bones are dried, and our *h* is lost ... Eze 37:11 8615
valley of Achor for a door of *h* ... Hos 2:15 8615
LORD will be the *h* of his people ... Joel 3:16 4268
strong hold, ye prisoners of *h* ... Zec 9:12 8615
to them of whom ye *h* to receive ... Lk 6:34 *1679*
also my flesh shall rest in *h* ... Acts 2:26 *1680*
the *h* of their gains was gone ... Acts 16:19 *1680*
of the *h* and resurrection of the ... Acts 23:6 *1680*
have *h* toward God, which they ... Acts 24:15 *1680*
am judged for the *h* of the ... Acts 26:6 *1680*
God day and night, *h* to come ... Acts 26:7 *1679*
all *h* that we should be saved was ... Acts 27:20 *1680*
because that for the *h* of Israel ... Acts 28:20 *1680*
Who against *h* believed in *h*, ... Rom 4:18 *1680*
Who against *h* believed in *h* ... Rom 4:18 *1680*
rejoice in *h* of the glory of God ... Rom 5:2 *1680*
experience; and experience, *h* ... Rom 5:4 *1680*
And *h* maketh not ashamed ... Rom 5:5 *1680*
who hath subjected the same in *h* ... Rom 8:20 *1680*
For we are saved by *h* ... Rom 8:24 *1680*
but *h* that is seen is not *h* ... Rom 8:24 *1680*
man seeth, why doth he yet *h* for ... Rom 8:24 *1679*
But if we *h* for that we see not, ... Rom 8:25 *1679*
Rejoicing in *h* ... Rom 12:12 *1680*
of the scriptures might have *h* ... Rom 15:4 *1680*
Now the God of *h* fill you with ... Rom 15:13 *1680*
that ye may abound in *h*, through ... Rom 15:13 *1680*
he that ploweth should plow in *h* ... 1Cor 9:10 *1680*
that he that thresheth in *h* ... 1Cor 9:10 *1680*
h should be partaker of his *h* ... 1Cor 9:10 *1680*
And now abideth faith, *h*, charity, ... 1Cor 13:13 *1680*
life only we have *h* in Christ ... 1Cor 15:19 *1679*
our *h* of you is stedfast, knowing ... 2Cor 1:7 *1680*
Seeing then that we have such *h* ... 2Cor 3:12 *1680*
but having *h*, when your faith is ... 2Cor 10:15 *1680*
the *h* of righteousness by faith ... Gal 5:5 *1680*
know what is the *h* of his calling ... Eph 1:18 *1680*
covenants of promise, having no *h* ... Eph 2:12 *1680*
called in one *h* of your calling ... Eph 4:4 *1680*
to my earnest expectation and my *h* ... Phil 1:20 *1680*
Him therefore I *h* to send ... Phil 2:23 *1679*
For the *h* which is laid up for ... Col 1:5 *1680*
away from the *h* of the gospel ... Col 1:23 *1680*
is Christ in you, the *h* of glory ... Col 1:27 *1680*
patience of *h* in our Lord Jesus ... 1Th 1:3 *1680*
For what is our *h*, or joy, or ... 1Th 2:19 *1680*
even as others which have no *h* ... 1Th 4:13 *1680*
for an helmet, the *h* of salvation ... 1Th 5:8 *1680*
and good *h* through grace, ... 2Th 2:16 *1680*
Lord Jesus Christ, which is our *h* ... 1Ti 1:1 *1680*
In *h* of eternal life, which God, ... Titus 1:2 *1680*
Looking for that blessed *h* ... Titus 2:13 *1680*
to the *h* of eternal life ... Titus 3:7 *1680*
of the *h* firm unto the end ... Heb 3:6 *1680*
full assurance of *h* unto the end ... Heb 6:11 *1680*
lay hold upon the *h* set before us ... Heb 6:18 *1680*
Which *h* we have as an anchor of ... Heb 6:19
the bringing in of a better *h* did ... Heb 7:19 *1680*
h by the resurrection of Jesus ... 1Pet 1:3 *1680*
h to the end for the grace that ... 1Pet 1:13 *1679*
your faith and *h* might be in God ... 1Pet 1:21 *1680*
h that is in you with meekness ... 1Pet 3:15 *1680*
this *h* in him purifieth himself ... 1Jn 3:3 *1680*

HOPED

Jews *h* to have power over them ... Est 9:1 7663
confounded because they had *h* ... Job 6:20 982
for I have *h* in thy judgments ... Ps 119:43 3176
because I have *h* in thy word ... Ps 119:74 3176
I *h* in thy word ... Ps 119:147 3176
I have *h* for thy salvation, and ... Ps 119:166 7663
is salvation *h* for from the hills ... Jer 3:23
he *h* to have seen some miracle ... Lk 23:8 *1679*
He *h* also that money should have ... Acts 24:26 *1679*
And this they did, not as we *h* ... 2Cor 8:5 *1679*
is the substance of things *h* for ... Heb 11:1 *1679*

HOPE'S

For which *h* sake, king Agrippa, I ... Acts 26:7 *1679*

HOPETH

h all things, endureth all things ... 1Cor 13:7 *1679*

HOPHNI (*hof'-ni*) *A son of Eli.*

And the two sons of Eli, *H* ... 1Sa 1:3 2652
come upon thy two sons, on *H* ... 1Sa 2:34 2652

and the two sons of Eli, H. 1Sa 4:4 2652
and the two sons of Eli, H. 1Sa 4:11 2652
people, and thy two sons also, H. 1Sa 4:17 2652

HOPING
and lend, h for nothing again Lk 6:35 560
h to come unto thee shortly 1Ti 3:14 1679

HOR (hor) See HOR-HAGIDGAD.
1. A mountain in Moab.
from Kadesh, and came unto mount H Num 20:22 2023
unto Moses and Aaron in mount H Num 20:23 2023
and bring them up unto mount H Num 20:25 2023
mount H in the sight of all the Num 20:27 2023
mount H by the way of the Red sea Num 21:4 2023
Kadesh, and pitched in mount H Num 33:37 2023
the priest went up into mount H Num 33:38 2023
years old when he died in mount H Num 33:39 2023
And they departed from mount H Num 33:41 2023
Aaron thy brother died in mount H Deut 32:50 2023
2. A hill in northern Israel.
shall point out for you mount H Num 34:7 2023
From mount H ye shall point out Num 34:8 2023

HORAM (ho'-ram) *A Canaanite king.*
Then H king of Gezer came up to Josh 10:33 2036

HOREB (ho'-reb) See SINAI. *A mountain range in Sinai.*
to the mountain of God, even to H Ex 3:1 2722
thee there upon the rock in H Ex 17:6 2722
of their ornaments by the mount H Ex 33:6 2722
H by the way of mount Seir unto Deut 1:2 2722
LORD our God spake unto us in H Deut 1:6 2722
And when we departed from H Deut 1:19 2722
before the LORD thy God in H Deut 4:10 2722
in H out of the midst of the fire Deut 4:15 2722
God made a covenant with us in H Deut 5:2 2722
Also in H ye provoked the LORD to Deut 9:8 2722
of the LORD thy God in H in the Deut 18:16 2722
which he made with them in H Deut 29:1 2722
stone, which Moses put there at H 1Kin 8:9 2722
nights unto H the mount of God 1Kin 19:8 2722
which Moses put therein at H 2Chr 5:10 2722
They made a calf in H, and Ps 106:19 2722
unto him in H for all Israel Mal 4:4 2722

HOREM (ho'-rem) *A city in Naphtali.*
And Iron, and Migdal-el, H, and Josh 19:38 2765

HORESH See ZIPH.

HOR-HAGIDGAD (hor-hag-id'-gad) *An encampment of Israel in the wilderness.*
Bene-jaakan, and encamped at H Num 33:32 2735
And they went from H, and pitched Num 33:33 2735

HORI (ho'-ri) See HORITE.
1. Son of Lotan.
And the children of Lotan were H Gen 36:22 2753
are the dukes that came of H Gen 36:30 2753
H, and Homam 1Chr 1:39 2753
2. Father of Shapat.
of Simeon, Shaphat the son of H Num 13:5 2753

HORIMS (ho'-rims) See HORITES. *Inhabitants of Mt. Seir.*
The H also dwelt in Seir Deut 2:12 2752
destroyed the H from before them Deut 2:22 2752

HORITE (ho'-rite) See HORI, HORITES. *An inhabitant of Mt. Seir.*
These are the sons of Seir the H Gen 36:20 2752

HORITES (ho'-rites) See HORIMS. *Same as Horims.*
the H in their mount Seir, unto Gen 14:6 2752
these are the dukes of the H Gen 36:21 2752
are the dukes that came of the H Gen 36:29 2752

HORMAH (hor'-mah) See ZEPHATH. *A Canaanite royal town.*
and discomfited them, even unto H Num 14:45 2767
he called the name of the place H Num 21:3 2767
you in Seir, even unto H Deut 1:44 2767
The king of H, one Josh 12:14 2767
And Eltolad, and Chesil, and H Josh 15:30 2767
And Eltolad, and Bethul, and H Josh 19:4 2767
the name of the city was called H Judg 1:17 2767
And to them which were in H 1Sa 30:30 2767
And at Bethuel, and at H, and at 1Chr 4:30 2767

HORN
to push with his h in time past Ex 21:29
a long blast with the ram's h Josh 6:5 7161
mine h is exalted in the LORD 1Sa 2:1 7161
exalt the h of his anointed 1Sa 2:10 7161
fill thine h with oil, and go, I 1Sa 16:1 7161
Then Samuel took the h of oil 1Sa 16:13 7161
the h of my salvation, my high 2Sa 22:3 7161
Zadok the priest took an h of oil 1Kin 1:39 7161
words of God, to lift up the h 1Chr 25:5 7161
skin, and defiled my h in the dust Job 16:15 7161
the h of my salvation, and my high Ps 18:2 7161
to the wicked, Lift not up the h Ps 75:4 7161
Lift not up your h on high Ps 75:5 7161
thy favour our h shall be exalted Ps 89:17 7161
in my name shall his h be exalted Ps 89:24 7161
But my h shalt thou exalt like Ps 92:10 7161
exalt like the h of an unicorn Ps 92:10
his h shall be exalted with Ps 112:9 7161
will I make the h of David to bud Ps 132:17 7161
also exalteth the h of his people Ps 148:14 7161
The h of Moab is cut off, and his Jer 48:25 7161
fierce anger all the h of Israel Lam 2:3 7161
he hath set up the h of thine Lam 2:17 7161
In that day will I cause the h of Eze 29:21 7161
up among them another little h Dan 7:8 7162
in this h were eyes like the eyes Dan 7:8 7162
the great words which the h spake Dan 7:11 7162
even of that h that had eyes, and Dan 7:20 7162
the same h made war with the Dan 7:21 7162
had a notable h between his eyes Dan 8:5 7161
strong, the great h was broken Dan 8:8 7161
one of them came forth a little h Dan 8:9 7161
the great h that is between his Dan 8:21 7161
for I will make thine h iron Mic 4:13 7161
which lifted up their h over the Zec 1:21 7161
hath raised up an h of salvation Lk 1:69 2768

HORNET
God will send the h among them Deut 7:20 6880
And I sent the h before you Josh 24:12 6880

HORNETS
And I will send h before thee Ex 23:28 6880

HORNS
ram caught in a thicket by his h Gen 22:13 7161
thou shalt make the h of it upon Ex 27:2 7161
his h shall be of the same Ex 27:2 7161
put it upon the h of the altar Ex 29:12 7161
the h thereof shall be of the Ex 30:2 7161
round about, and the h thereof Ex 30:3 7161
make an atonement upon the h of Ex 30:10 7161
the h thereof were of the same Ex 37:25 7161
round about, and the h of it Ex 37:26 7161
he made the h thereof on the four Ex 38:2 7161
the h thereof were of the same Ex 38:2 7161
h of the altar of sweet incense Lev 4:7 7161
h of the altar which is before Lev 4:18 7161
put it upon the h of the altar of Lev 4:25 7161
put it upon the h of the altar of Lev 4:30 7161
put it upon the h of the altar of Lev 4:34 7161
put it upon the h of the altar Lev 8:15 7161
and put it upon the h of the altar Lev 9:9 7161
put it upon the h of the altar Lev 16:18 7161
h are like the h of unicorns Deut 33:17 7161
the ark seven trumpets of rams' h Josh 6:4 3104
h before the ark of the LORD Josh 6:6 3104
rams' h passed on before the LORD Josh 6:8
h before the ark of the LORD went Josh 6:13 3104
caught hold on the h of the altar 1Kin 1:50 7161
caught hold on the h of the altar 1Kin 1:51 7161
caught hold on the h of the altar 1Kin 2:28 7161
of Chenaanah made him h of iron 1Kin 22:11 7161
Chenaanah had made him h of iron 2Chr 18:10 7161
me from the h of the unicorns Ps 22:21 7161
than an ox or bullock that hath h Ps 69:31 7160
All the h of the wicked also will Ps 75:10 7161
but the h of the righteous shall Ps 75:10 7161
even unto the h of the altar Ps 118:27 7161
upon the h of your altars Jer 17:1 7161
thee for a present h of ivory Eze 27:15 7161
all the diseased with your h Eze 34:21 7161
altar and upward shall be four h Eze 43:15 7161
and put it on the four h of it Eze 43:20 7161
and it had ten h Dan 7:7 7162
I considered the h, and, behold, Dan 7:8 7162
first h plucked up by the roots Dan 7:8 7162
of the ten h that were in his Dan 7:20 7162
the ten h out of this kingdom are Dan 7:24 7162
the river a ram which had two h Dan 8:3 7161
and the two h were high Dan 8:3 7161
he came to the ram that had two h Dan 8:6 7161
smote the ram, and brake his two h Dan 8:7 7161
two h are the kings of Media Dan 8:20 7161
the h of the altar shall be cut Amos 3:14 7161
taken to us h by our own strength Amos 6:13 7161
he had h coming out of his hand Hab 3:4 7161
eyes, and saw, and behold four h Zec 1:18 7161
These are the h which have Zec 1:19 7161
These are the h which have Zec 1:21 7161
to cast out the h of the Gentiles Zec 1:21 7161
it had been slain, having seven h Rev 5:6 2768
h of the golden altar which is Rev 9:13 2768
having seven heads and ten h Rev 12:3 2768
sea, having seven heads and ten h Rev 13:1 2768
upon his h ten crowns, and upon Rev 13:1 2768
he had two h like a lamb, and he Rev 13:11 2768
having seven heads and ten h Rev 17:3 2768
hath the seven heads and ten h Rev 17:7 2768
the ten h which thou sawest are Rev 17:12 2768
the ten h which thou sawest upon Rev 17:16 2768

HORONAIM (hor-o-na'-im) See HOLON. *A Moabite city.*
for in the way of H they shall Is 15:5 2773
A voice of crying shall be from H Jer 48:3 2773
for in the going down of H the Jer 48:5 2773
voice, from Zoar even unto H Jer 48:34 2773

HORONITE (ho'-ron-ite) *A native of Horonaim.*
When Sanballat the H, and Tobiah Neh 2:10 2772
But when Sanballat the H, and Neh 2:19 2772
was son in law to Sanballat the H Neh 13:28 2772

HORRIBLE
and brimstone, and an h tempest Ps 11:6 2152
me up also out of an h pit Ps 40:2 7588
h thing is committed in the land Jer 5:30 8186
Israel hath done a very h thing Jer 18:13 8186
prophets of Jerusalem an h thing Jer 23:14 8186
I have seen an h thing in the Hos 6:10 8186

HORRIBLY
be h afraid, be ye very desolate, Jer 2:12 8175
kings shall be h afraid for thee Eze 32:10 8178

HORROR
an h of great darkness fell upon Gen 15:12 367
upon me, and h hath overwhelmed me Ps 55:5 6427
H hath taken hold upon me because Ps 119:53 2152
sackcloth, and h shall cover them Eze 7:18 6427

HORSE
the path, that biteth the h heels Gen 49:17 5483
the h and his rider hath he thrown Ex 15:1 5483
For the h of Pharaoh went in with Ex 15:19 5483
the h and his rider hath he thrown Ex 15:21 5483
an h for an hundred and fifty 1Kin 10:29 5483
escaped on an h with the horsemen 1Kin 20:20 5483
h for h, and chariot for 1Kin 20:25 5483
that thou hast lost, h for h 1Kin 20:25 5483
an h for an hundred and fifty 2Chr 1:17 5483
of the h gate by the king's house 2Chr 23:15 5483
From above the h gate repaired Neh 3:28 5483
the h that the king rideth upon, Est 6:8 5483
h be delivered to the hand of one Est 6:9 5483
and take the apparel and the h Est 6:10 5483
took Haman the apparel and the h Est 6:11 5483
on high, she scorneth the h Job 39:18 5483
Hath thou given the h strength Job 39:19 5483
Be ye not as the h, or as the Ps 32:9 5483
An h is a vain thing for safety Ps 33:17 5483
h are cast into a dead sleep Ps 76:6 5483
not in the strength of the h Ps 147:10 5483
The h is prepared against the day Prov 21:31 5483
A whip for the h, a bridle for Prov 26:3 5483
bringeth forth the chariot and h Is 43:17 5483
as an h in the wilderness, that Is 63:13 5483
as the h rusheth into the battle Jer 8:6 5483
of the h gate toward the east Jer 31:40 5483
thee will I break in pieces the h Jer 51:21 5483
that rideth the h deliver himself Amos 2:15 5483
behold a man riding upon a red h Zec 1:8 5483
the h from Jerusalem, and the Zec 9:10 5483
as his goodly h in the battle Zec 10:3 5483
smite every h with astonishment Zec 12:4 5483
will smite every h of the people Zec 12:4 5483
so shall be the plague of the h Zec 14:15 5483
And I saw, and behold a white h Rev 6:2 2462
went out another h that was red Rev 6:4 2462
And I beheld, and lo a black h Rev 6:5 2462
And I looked, and behold a pale h Rev 6:8 2462
even unto the h bridles, by the Rev 14:20 2462
opened, and behold a white h Rev 19:11 2462
war against him that sat on the h Rev 19:19 2462
sword of him that sat upon the h Rev 19:21 2462

HORSEBACK
there went one on h to meet him 2Kin 9:18
Then he sent out a second on h 2Kin 9:19
bring him on h through the street Est 6:9 7392
brought him on h through the Est 6:11 7392
and sent letters by posts on h Est 8:10 5483

HORSEHOOFS
Then were the h broken by the Judg 5:22

HORSELEACH
The h hath two daughters, crying, Prov 30:15 5936

HORSEMAN
And Joram said, Take an h, and send 2Kin 9:17 7395
The h lifteth up both the bright Nah 3:3 6571

HORSEMEN
up with him both chariots and h Gen 50:9 6571
and chariots of Pharaoh, and his h Ex 14:9 6571
upon his chariots, and upon his h Ex 14:17 6571
upon his chariots, and upon his h Ex 14:18 6571
horses, his chariots, and his h Ex 14:23 6571
their chariots, and upon their h Ex 14:26 6571
and covered the chariots, and the h Ex 14:28 6571
with his h into the sea, and the Ex 15:19 6571
chariots and h unto the Red sea Josh 24:6 6571
for his chariots, and to be his h 1Sa 8:11 6571
chariots, and six thousand h 1Sa 13:5 6571
h followed hard after him 2Sa 1:6 6571
chariots, and seven hundred h 2Sa 8:4 6571
the Syrians, and forty thousand h 2Sa 10:18 6571
and he prepared him chariots and h 1Kin 1:5 6571
chariots, and twelve thousand h 1Kin 4:26 6571
his chariots, and cities for his h 1Kin 9:19 6571
rulers of his chariots, and his h 1Kin 9:22 6571
gathered together chariots and h 1Kin 10:26 6571
chariots, and twelve thousand h 1Kin 10:26 6571
escaped on an horse with the h 1Kin 20:20 6571
of Israel, and the h thereof 2Kin 2:12 6571
people to Jehoahaz but fifty h 2Kin 13:7 6571
of Israel, and the h thereof 2Kin 13:14 6571
on Egypt for chariots and for h 2Kin 18:24 6571
chariots, and seven thousand h 1Chr 18:4 6571
h out of Mesopotamia, and out of 1Chr 19:6 6571
And Solomon gathered chariots and h 2Chr 1:14 6571
chariots, and twelve thousand h 2Chr 1:14 6571
cities, and the cities of the h 2Chr 8:6 6571
and captains of his chariots and h 2Chr 8:9 6571
and chariots, and twelve thousand h 2Chr 9:25 6571
and threescore thousand h 2Chr 12:3 6571
with very many chariots and h 2Chr 16:8 6571
h to help us against the enemy in Ezr 8:22 6571
captains of the army and h with me Neh 2:9 6571
saw a chariot with a couple of h Is 21:7 6571
of men, with a couple of h Is 21:9 6571
quiver with chariots of men and h Is 22:6 6571
the h shall set themselves in Is 22:7 6571
cart, nor bruise it with his h Is 28:28 6571
and in h, because they are very Is 31:1 6571
on Egypt for chariots and for h Is 36:9 6571
shall flee for the noise of the h Jer 4:29 6571
and get up, ye h, and stand forth Jer 46:4 6571
young men, h riding upon horses Eze 23:6 6571
h riding upon horses, all of them Eze 23:12 6571
and with chariots, and with h Eze 26:7 6571
shall shake at the noise of the h Eze 26:10 6571
in thy fairs with horses and h Eze 27:14 6571
and all thine army, horses and h Eze 38:4 6571
with chariots, and with h Dan 11:40 6571
by battle, by horses, nor by h Hos 1:7 6571
and as h, so shall they run Joel 2:4 6571
their h shall spread themselves, Hab 1:8 6571
their h shall come from far Hab 1:8 6571

h threescore and ten, and spearmen Acts 23:23 *2460*
they left the *h* to go with him Acts 23:32 *2460*
the *h* were two hundred thousand Rev 9:16 *2461*

HORSES
gave them bread in exchange for *h* Gen 47:17 5483
which is in the field, upon the *h* Ex 9:3 5483
pursued after them, all the *h* Ex 14:9 5483
of the sea, even all Pharaoh's *h* Ex 14:23 5483
the army of Egypt, unto their *h* Deut 11:4 5483
shall not multiply *h* to himself Deut 17:16 5483
the end that he should multiply *h* Deut 17:16 5483
against thine enemies, and seest *h* Deut 20:1 5483
sea shore in multitude, with *h* Josh 11:4 5483
thou shalt hough their *h*, and burn Josh 11:6 5483
he houghed their *h*, and burnt Josh 11:9 5483
David houghed all the chariot *h* 2Sa 8:4
prepared him chariots and *h* 2Sa 15:1 5483
stalls of *h* for his chariots 1Kin 4:26 5483
Barley also and straw for the *h* 1Kin 4:28 5483
garments, and armour, and spices, *h* 1Kin 10:25 5483
Solomon had *h* brought out of 1Kin 10:28 5483
we may find grass to save the *h* 1Kin 18:5 5483
and two kings with him, and *h* 1Kin 20:1 5483
Israel went out, and smote the *h* 1Kin 20:21 5483
as thy people, my *h* as thy *h* 1Kin 22:4 5483
h of fire, and parted them both 2Kin 2:11 5483
thy people, and my *h* as thy *h* 2Kin 3:7 5483
So Naaman came with his *h* 2Kin 5:9 5483
Therefore sent he thither *h* 2Kin 6:14 5483
compassed the city both with *h* 2Kin 6:15 5483
the mountain was full of *h* 2Kin 6:17 5483
of chariots, and a noise of *h* 2Kin 7:6 5483
and left their tents, and their *h* 2Kin 7:7 5483
but *h* tied, and asses tied, and the 2Kin 7:10 5483
thee, five of the *h* that remain 2Kin 7:13 5483
They took therefore two chariot *h* 2Kin 7:14 5483
on the wall, and on the *h* 2Kin 9:33 5483
there are with you chariots and *h* 2Kin 10:2 5483
the *h* came into the king's house 2Kin 11:16 5483
And they brought him on *h* 2Kin 14:20 5483
will deliver thee two thousand *h* 2Kin 18:23 5483
he took away the *h* that the kings 2Kin 23:11 5483
also houghed all the chariot *h* 1Chr 18:4
Solomon had *h* brought out of 2Chr 1:16 5483
so brought they out *h* for all the 2Chr 1:17 5483
and raiment, harness, and spices, *h* 2Chr 9:24 5483
had four thousand stalls for *h* 2Chr 9:25 5483
unto Solomon *h* out of Egypt 2Chr 9:28 5483
And they brought him upon *h* 2Chr 25:28 5483
Their *h* were seven hundred thirty Ezr 2:66 5483
Their *h*, seven hundred thirty and Neh 7:68 5483
trust in chariots, and some in *h* Ps 20:7
I have seen servants upon *h* Eccl 10:7 5483
to a company of *h* in Pharaoh's Song 1:9 5484
their land is also full of *h* Is 2:7 5483
for we will flee upon *h* Is 30:16 5483
and stay on *h*, and trust in Is 31:1 5483
and their *h* flesh, and not spirit Is 31:3 5483
I will give thee two thousand *h* Is 36:8 5483
LORD out of all nations upon *h* Is 66:20 5483
his *h* are swifter than eagles Jer 4:13 5483
They were as fed *h* in the morning Jer 5:8 5483
and they ride upon *h*, set in array Jer 6:23 5483
of his *h* was heard from Dan Jer 8:16 5483
how canst thou contend with *h* Jer 12:5 5483
David, riding in chariots and on *h* Jer 17:25 5483
David, riding in chariots and on *h* Jer 22:4 5483
Harness the *h* Jer 46:4 5483
Come up, ye *h* Jer 46:9 5483
of the hoofs of his strong *h* Jer 47:3
A sword is upon their *h*, and upon Jer 50:37 5483
sea, and they shall ride upon *h* Jer 50:42 5483
cause the *h* to come up as the Jer 51:27 5483
Egypt, that they might give him *h* Eze 17:15 5483
young men, horsemen riding upon *h* Eze 23:6 5483
horsemen riding upon *h*, all of Eze 23:12 5483
issue is like the issue of *h* Eze 23:20 5483
all of them riding upon *h* Eze 23:23 5483
of kings, from the north, with *h* Eze 26:7 5483
his *h* their dust shall cover thee Eze 26:10 5483
With the hoofs of his *h* shall he Eze 26:11 5483
traded in thy fairs with *h* Eze 27:14 5483
thee forth, and all thine army, *h* Eze 38:4 5483
thee, all of them riding upon *h* Eze 38:15 5483
be filled at my table with *h* Eze 39:20 5483
nor by sword, nor by battle, by *h* Hos 1:7 5483
we will not ride upon *h* Hos 14:3 5483
of them is as the appearance of *h* Joel 2:4 5483
sword, and have taken away your *h* Amos 4:10 5483
Shall *h* run upon the rock Amos 6:12 5483
that I will cut off thy *h* out of Mic 5:10 5483
the wheels, and of the pransing *h* Nah 3:2 5483
Their *h* also are swifter than the Hab 1:8 5483
that thou didst ride upon thine *h* Hab 3:8 5483
walk through the sea with thine *h* Hab 3:15 5483
and the *h* and their riders shall Hag 2:22 5483
and behind him were there red *h* Zec 1:8 5483
In the first chariot were red *h* Zec 6:2 5483
and in the second chariot black *h* Zec 6:2 5483
And in the third chariot white *h* Zec 6:3 5483
fourth chariot grisled and bay *h* Zec 6:3 5483
The black *h* which are therein go Zec 6:6 5483
them, and the riders on *h* shall be Zec 10:5 5483
there be upon the bells of the *h* Zec 14:20 5483
like unto *h* prepared unto battle Rev 9:7 *2462*
of many *h* running to battle Rev 9:9 *2462*
And thus I saw the *h* in the vision Rev 9:17 *2462*
the heads of the *h* were as the Rev 9:17 *2462*
wheat, and beasts, and sheep, and *h* Rev 18:13 *2462*
heaven followed him upon white *h* Rev 19:14 *2462*
of mighty men, and the flesh of *h* Rev 19:18 *2462*

HORSES'
their *h* hoofs shall be counted Is 5:28 5483
we put bits in the *h* mouths Jas 3:3 *2462*

HOSAH (*ho'-sah*)
1. A city in Asher.
and the coast turneth to *H* Josh 19:29 2621
2. A Levite.
of Jeduthun and *H* to be porters 1Chr 16:38 2621
Also *H*, of the children of Merari 1Chr 26:10 2621
brethren of *H* were thirteen 1Chr 26:11 2621
H the lot came forth westward, 1Chr 26:16 2621

HOSANNA
saying, *H* to the son of David Mt 21:9 *5614*
H in the highest Mt 21:9 *5614*
and saying, *H* to the son of David Mt 21:15 *5614*
that followed, cried, saying, *H* Mk 11:9 *5614*
H in the highest Mk 11:10 *5614*
forth to meet him, and cried, *H* Jn 12:13 *5614*

HOSEA (*ho-se'-ah*) See HOSHEA, OSEE, OSHEA.
A prophet.
word of the LORD that came unto *H* Hos 1:1 1954
of the word of the LORD by *H* Hos 1:2 1954
And the LORD said to *H*, Go, take Hos 1:2 1954

HOSEN
bound in their coats, their *h* Dan 3:21 6361

HOSHAIAH (*ho-sha-i'-ah*)
1. Helped dedicate the wall.
And after them went *H*, and half of Neh 12:32 1955
2. Father of Jezaniah.
Kareah, and Jezaniah the son of *H* Jer 42:1 1955
Then spake Azariah the son of *H* Jer 43:2 1955

HOSHAMA (*ho-sha'-mah*) *Father of Jeconiah.*
Pedaiah, and Shenazar, Jecamiah, *H* 1Chr 3:18 1953

HOSHEA (*ho-she'-ah*) See HOSEA.
1. Original name of Joshua.
people, he, and *H* the son of Nun Deut 32:44 1954
2. An Ephramite ruler.
of Ephraim, *H* the son of Azaziah 1Chr 27:20 1954
3. Last king of Israel.
And *H* the son of Elah made a 2Kin 15:30 1954
H the son of Elah to reign in 2Kin 17:1 1954
H became his servant, and gave him 2Kin 17:3 1954
of Assyria found conspiracy in *H* 2Kin 17:4 1954
In the ninth year of *H* the king 2Kin 17:6 1954
of *H* son of Elah king of Israel 2Kin 18:1 1954
of *H* son of Elah king of Israel 2Kin 18:9 1954
ninth year of *H* king of Israel 2Kin 18:10 1954
4. An Israelite who renewed the covenant.
H, Hananiah, Hashub, Neh 10:23 1954

HOSPITALITY
given to *h* Rom 12:13 *5381*
of good behaviour, given to *h* 1Ti 3:2 *5382*
But a lover of *h*, a lover of good Titus 1:8 *5382*
Use *h* one to another without 1Pet 4:9 *5382*

HOST
finished, and all the *h* of them Gen 2:1 6635
of his *h* spake unto Abraham Gen 21:22 6635
the chief captain of his *h* Gen 21:32 6635
them, he said, This is God's *h* Gen 32:2 4264
upon Pharaoh, and upon all his *h* Ex 14:4 2428
upon Pharaoh, and upon all his *h* Ex 14:17 2428
h of the Egyptians through the Ex 14:24 4264
troubled the *h* of the Egyptians, Ex 14:24 4264
all the *h* of Pharaoh that came Ex 14:28 2428
his *h* hath he cast into the sea Ex 15:4 2428
the dew lay round about the *h* Ex 16:13 4264
And his *h*, and those that were Num 2:4 6635
And his *h*, and those that were Num 2:6 6635
And his *h*, and those that were Num 2:8 6635
And his *h*, and those that were Num 2:11 6635
And his *h*, and those that were Num 2:13 6635
And his *h*, and those that were Num 2:15 6635
And his *h*, and those that were Num 2:19 6635
And his *h*, and those that were Num 2:21 6635
And his *h*, and those that were Num 2:23 6635
And his *h*, and those that were Num 2:26 6635
And his *h*, and those that were Num 2:28 6635
And his *h*, and those that were Num 2:30 6635
old, all that enter into the *h* Num 4:3 6635
over his *h* was Nahshon the son of Num 10:14
over the *h* of the tribe of the Num 10:15 6635
over the *h* of the tribe of the Num 10:16 6635
over his *h* was Elizur the son of Num 10:18 6635
over the *h* of the tribe of the Num 10:19 6635
over the *h* of the tribe of Israel Num 10:20 6635
over his *h* was Elishama the son Num 10:22 6635
over the *h* of the tribe of the Num 10:23 6635
over the *h* of the tribe of the Num 10:24 6635
over his *h* was Ahiezer the son of Num 10:25 6635
over the *h* of the tribe of the Num 10:26 6635
over the *h* of the tribe of the Num 10:27 6635
wroth with the officers of the *h* Num 31:14 2428
were over thousands of the *h* Num 31:48 6635
were wasted out from among the *h* Deut 2:14 4264
to destroy them from among the *h* Deut 2:15 4264
stars, even all the *h* of heaven Deut 4:19 6635
moon, or any of the *h* of heaven Deut 17:3 6635
When the *h* goeth forth against Deut 23:9 4264
Pass through the *h*, and command Josh 1:11 4264
the officers went through the *h* Josh 3:2 4264
but as captain of the *h* of the Josh 5:14 6635
of the LORD's *h* said unto Joshua Josh 5:15 6635
even all the *h* that was on the Josh 8:13 4264
to Joshua to the *h* at Shiloh Josh 18:9 4264
the captain of whose *h* was Sisera Judg 4:2 6635
and all his chariots, and all his *h* Judg 4:15 4264
the chariots, and after the *h* Judg 4:16 4264
all the *h* of Sisera fell upon the Judg 4:16 4264
so that the *h* of the Midianites Judg 7:1 4264
the *h* of Midian was beneath him Judg 7:8 4264
Arise, get thee down unto the *h* Judg 7:9 4264
Phurah thy servant down to the *h* Judg 7:10 4264
to go down unto the *h* Judg 7:11 4264
the armed men that were in the *h* Judg 7:11 4264
tumbled into the *h* of Midian Judg 7:13 4264
delivered Midian, and all the *h* Judg 7:14 4264
and returned into the *h* of Israel Judg 7:15 4264
into your hand the *h* of Midian Judg 7:15 4264
and all the *h* ran, and cried, and Judg 7:21 4264
fellow, even throughout all the *h* Judg 7:22 4264
the *h* fled to Beth-shittah in Judg 7:22 4264
Nobah and Jogbehah, and smote the *h* Judg 8:11 4264
for the *h* was secure Judg 8:11 4264
and discomfited all the *h* Judg 8:12 4264
of the *h* in the morning watch 1Sa 11:11 4264
Sisera, captain of the *h* of Hazor 1Sa 12:9 6635
And there was trembling in the *h* 1Sa 14:15 4264
the *h* of the Philistines went on 1Sa 14:19 4264
And he gathered an *h*, and smote the 1Sa 14:48 2428
of the captain of his *h* was Abner 1Sa 14:50 6635
as the *h* was going forth to the 1Sa 17:20 2428
the *h* of the Philistines this day 1Sa 17:46 4264
unto Abner, the captain of the *h* 1Sa 17:55 6635
son of Ner, the captain of his *h* 1Sa 26:5 6635
when Saul saw the *h* of the 1Sa 28:5 4264
h of Israel into the hand of the 1Sa 28:19 4264
me in the *h* is good in my sight 1Sa 29:6 4264
son of Ner, captain of Saul's *h* 2Sa 2:8 6635
all the *h* that was with him were 2Sa 3:23 6635
to smite the *h* of the Philistines 2Sa 5:24 4264
smitten all the *h* of Hadadezer 2Sa 8:9 2428
the son of Zeruiah was over the *h* 2Sa 8:16 6635
all the *h* of the mighty men 2Sa 10:7 6635
Shobach the captain of the *h* of 2Sa 10:16 6635
Shobach the captain of their *h* 2Sa 10:18 6635
captain of the *h* instead of Joab 2Sa 17:25 6635
h before me continually in the 2Sa 19:13 6635
Joab was over all the *h* of Israel 2Sa 20:23 6635
through the *h* of the Philistines 2Sa 23:16 4264
said to Joab the captain of the *h* 2Sa 24:2 2428
and against the captains of the *h* 2Sa 24:4 2428
the captains of the *h* went out 2Sa 24:4 2428
and Joab the captain of the *h* 1Kin 1:19 6635
sons, and the captains of the *h* 1Kin 1:25 6635
Ner, captain of the *h* of Israel 1Kin 2:32 6635
Jether, captain of the *h* of Judah 1Kin 2:32 6635
Jehoiada in his room over the *h* 1Kin 2:35 6635
son of Jehoiada was over the *h* 1Kin 4:4 6635
Joab the captain of the *h* was 1Kin 11:15 6635
the captain of the *h* was dead 1Kin 11:21 6635
made Omri, the captain of the *h* 1Kin 16:16 6635
Syria gathered all his *h* together 1Kin 20:1 2428
all the *h* of heaven standing by 1Kin 22:19
hand, and carry me out of the *h* 1Kin 22:34 4264
a proclamation throughout the *h* 1Kin 22:36 4264
and there was no water for the *h* 2Kin 3:9 4264
king, or to the captain of the *h* 2Kin 4:13 6635
captain of the *h* of the king of 2Kin 5:1 6635
horses, and chariots, and a great *h* 2Kin 6:14 2428
an *h* compassed the city both with 2Kin 6:15 2428
king of Syria gathered all his *h* 2Kin 6:24
us fall unto the *h* of the Syrians 2Kin 7:4 4264
For the LORD had made the *h* of 2Kin 7:6 4264
even the noise of a great *h* 2Kin 7:6 2428
sent after the *h* of the Syrians 2Kin 7:14 4264
captains of the *h* were sitting 2Kin 9:5 2428
hundreds, the officers of the *h* 2Kin 11:15 2428
and worshipped all the *h* of heaven 2Kin 17:16 6635
with a great *h* against Jerusalem 2Kin 18:17 2426
and worshipped all the *h* of heaven 2Kin 21:3 6635
he built altars for all the *h* of 2Kin 21:5 6635
grove, and for all the *h* of heaven 2Kin 23:4 6635
and to all the *h* of heaven 2Kin 23:5 6635
of Babylon came, he, and all his *h* 2Kin 25:1 2428
and the principal scribe of the *h* 2Kin 25:19 6635
being over the *h* of the LORD 1Chr 9:19 4264
the *h* of the Philistines encamped 1Chr 11:15 4264
through the *h* of the Philistines 1Chr 11:18 4264
sons of Gad, captains of the *h* 1Chr 12:14 6635
valour, and were captains in the *h* 1Chr 12:21 6635
a great *h*, like the *h* of God 1Chr 12:22 4264
to smite the *h* of the Philistines 1Chr 14:15 4264
and they smote the *h* of the 1Chr 14:16 4264
the *h* of Hadarezer king of Zobah 1Chr 18:9 2428
the son of Zeruiah was over the *h* 1Chr 18:15 6635
all the *h* of the mighty men 1Chr 19:8 6635
Shophach the captain of the *h* of 1Chr 19:16 6635
Shophach the captain of the *h* 1Chr 19:18 6635
the captains of the *h* separated 1Chr 25:1 6635
and the captains of the *h* 1Chr 26:26 6635
of the *h* for the first month 1Chr 27:3 6635
The third captain of the *h* for 1Chr 27:5 6635
with an *h* of a thousand thousand 2Chr 14:9 2428
before the LORD, and before his *h* 2Chr 14:13 4264
therefore is the *h* of the king of 2Chr 16:7 2428
Ethiopians and the Lubims a huge *h* 2Chr 16:8 2428
all the *h* of heaven standing on 2Chr 18:18 6635
thou mayest carry me out of the *h* 2Chr 18:33 4264
hundreds that were set over the *h* 2Chr 23:14 2428
that the *h* of Syria came up 2Chr 24:23 2428
a very great *h* into their hand 2Chr 24:24 2428
Uzziah had an *h* of fighting men 2Chr 26:11 2428
them throughout all the *h* shields 2Chr 26:14 6635
before the *h* that came to Samaria 2Chr 28:9 6635
and worshipped all the *h* of heaven 2Chr 33:3 6635
he built altars for all the *h* of 2Chr 33:5 6635
of the *h* of the king of Assyria 2Chr 33:11 6635
of heavens, with all their *h* Neh 9:6 6635
the *h* of heaven worshippeth thee Neh 9:6 6635
Though an *h* should encamp against Ps 27:3 4264
all the *h* of them by the breath Ps 33:6 6635
saved by the multitude of an *h* Ps 33:16 2428
Pharaoh and his *h* in the Red sea Ps 136:15 2428

mustereth the *h* of the battle ... Is 13:4 6635
h of the high ones that are on ... Is 24:21 6635
all the *h* of heaven shall be ... Is 34:4 6635
all their *h* shall fall down, as ... Is 34:4 6635
bringeth out their *h* by number ... Is 40:26 6635
all their *h* have I commanded ... Is 45:12 6635
all the *h* of heaven, whom they ... Jer 8:2 6635
incense unto all the *h* of heaven ... Jer 19:13 6635
As the *h* of heaven cannot be ... Jer 33:22 6635
destroy ye utterly all her *h* ... Jer 51:3 6635
and the principal scribe of the *h* ... Jer 52:25 6635
of speech, as the noise of an *h* ... Eze 1:24 4264
great, even to the *h* of heaven ... Dan 8:10 6635
and it cast down some of the *h* ... Dan 8:10 6635
even to the prince of the *h* ... Dan 8:11 6635
an *h* was given him against the ... Dan 8:12 6635
the *h* to be trodden under foot ... Dan 8:13 6635
the captivity of this *h* of the ... Obad 20 2426
them that worship the *h* of heaven ... Zeph 1:5 6635
of the heavenly *h* praising God ... Lk 2:13 *4756*
two pence, and gave them to the *h* ... Lk 10:35 *3830*
up to worship the *h* of heaven ... Acts 7:42 *4756*
Gaius mine *h*, and of the whole ... Rom 16:23 *3581*

HOSTAGES
of the king's house, and *h* ... 2Kin 14:14
the *h* also, and returned to ... 2Chr 25:24

HOSTS
that all the *h* of the LORD went ... Ex 12:41 6635
own standard, throughout their *h* ... Num 1:52 6635
their *h* were six hundred thousand ... Num 2:32 6635
all the camps throughout their *h* ... Num 10:25 6635
and went up, they and all their *h* ... Josh 10:5 4264
they and all their *h* with them ... Josh 11:4 4264
their *h* with them, about fifteen ... Judg 8:10 4264
the *h* of the children of the east ... Judg 8:10 4264
unto the LORD of *h* in Shiloh ... 1Sa 1:3 6635
vowed a vow, and said, O LORD of *h* ... 1Sa 1:11 6635
of the covenant of the LORD of *h* ... 1Sa 4:4 6635
Thus saith the LORD of *h*, I ... 1Sa 15:2 6635
thee in the name of the LORD of *h* ... 1Sa 17:45 6635
and the LORD God of *h* was with him ... 2Sa 5:10 6635
of *h* that dwelleth between the ... 2Sa 6:2 6635
in the name of the LORD of *h* ... 2Sa 6:18 6635
David, Thus saith the LORD of *h* ... 2Sa 7:8 6635
The LORD of *h* is the God over ... 2Sa 7:26 6635
For thou, O LORD of *h*, God of ... 2Sa 7:27 6635
two captains of the *h* of Israel ... 1Kin 2:5 6635
sent the captains of the *h* which ... 1Kin 15:20 2428
said, As the LORD of *h* liveth ... 1Kin 18:15 6635
jealous for the LORD God of *h* ... 1Kin 19:10 6635
jealous for the LORD God of *h* ... 1Kin 19:14 6635
said, As the LORD of *h* liveth ... 2Kin 3:14 6635
of the LORD of *h* shall do this ... 2Kin 19:31
for the LORD of *h* was with him ... 1Chr 11:9 6635
David, Thus saith the LORD of *h* ... 1Chr 17:7 6635
The LORD of *h* is the God of ... 1Chr 17:24 6635
The LORD of *h*, he is the King of ... Ps 24:10 6635
The LORD of *h* is with us ... Ps 46:7 6635
The LORD of *h* is with us ... Ps 46:11 6635
seen in the city of the LORD of *h* ... Ps 48:8 6635
Thou therefore, O LORD God of *h* ... Ps 59:5 6635
wait on thee, O Lord GOD of *h* ... Ps 69:6 6635
O LORD God of *h*, how long wilt ... Ps 80:4 6635
Turn us again, O God of *h* ... Ps 80:7 6635
we beseech thee, O God of *h* ... Ps 80:14 6635
Turn us again, O LORD God of *h* ... Ps 80:19 6635
are thy tabernacles, O LORD of *h* ... Ps 84:1 6635
even thine altars, O LORD of *h* ... Ps 84:3 6635
O LORD God of *h*, hear my prayer ... Ps 84:8 6635
O LORD of *h*, blessed is the man ... Ps 84:12 6635
O LORD God of *h*, who is a strong ... Ps 89:8 6635
Bless ye the LORD, all ye his *h* ... Ps 103:21 6635
thou, O God, go forth with our *h* ... Ps 108:11 6635
praise ye him, all his *h* ... Ps 148:2 6635
Except the LORD of *h* had left ... Is 1:9 6635
saith the Lord, the LORD of *h* ... Is 1:24 6635
For the day of the LORD of *h* ... Is 2:12 6635
behold, the Lord, the LORD of *h* ... Is 3:1 6635
saith the Lord GOD of *h* ... Is 3:15 6635
LORD of *h* is the house of Israel ... Is 5:7 6635
In mine ears said the LORD of *h* ... Is 5:9 6635
But the LORD of *h* shall be ... Is 5:16 6635
away the law of the LORD of *h* ... Is 5:24 6635
holy, holy, is the LORD of *h* ... Is 6:3 6635
have seen the King, the LORD of *h* ... Is 6:5 6635
Sanctify the LORD of *h* himself ... Is 8:13 6635
in Israel from the LORD of *h* ... Is 8:18 6635
the LORD of *h* will perform this ... Is 9:7 6635
do they seek the LORD of *h* ... Is 9:13 6635
LORD of *h* is the land darkened ... Is 9:19 6635
shall the Lord, the Lord of *h* ... Is 10:16 6635
For the Lord GOD of *h* shall make ... Is 10:23 6635
thus saith the Lord GOD of *h* ... Is 10:24 6635
the LORD of *h* shall stir up a ... Is 10:26 6635
Behold, the Lord, the LORD of *h* ... Is 10:33 6635
the LORD of *h* mustereth the host ... Is 13:4 6635
in the wrath of the LORD of *h* ... Is 13:13 6635
against them, saith the LORD of *h* ... Is 14:22 6635
destruction, saith the LORD of *h* ... Is 14:23 6635
The LORD of *h* hath sworn, saying, ... Is 14:24 6635
For the LORD of *h* hath purposed ... Is 14:27 6635
of Israel, saith the LORD of *h* ... Is 17:3 6635
LORD of *h* of a people scattered ... Is 18:7 6635
of the name of the LORD of *h* ... Is 18:7 6635
saith the Lord, the LORD of *h* ... Is 19:4 6635
of *h* hath purposed upon Egypt ... Is 19:12 6635
of the hand of the LORD of *h* ... Is 19:16 6635
of the counsel of the LORD of *h* ... Is 19:17 6635
Canaan, and swear to the LORD of *h* ... Is 19:18 6635
LORD of *h* in the land of Egypt ... Is 19:20 6635
Whom the LORD of *h* shall bless ... Is 19:25 6635
I have heard of the LORD of *h* ... Is 21:10 6635
GOD of *h* in the valley of vision ... Is 22:5 6635
the Lord GOD of *h* call to weeping ... Is 22:12 6635
in mine ears by the LORD of *h* ... Is 22:14 6635
ye die, saith the Lord GOD of *h* ... Is 22:14 6635
Thus saith the Lord GOD of *h* ... Is 22:15 6635
In that day, saith the LORD of *h* ... Is 22:25 6635
The LORD of *h* hath purposed it, ... Is 23:9 6635
when the LORD of *h* shall reign in ... Is 24:23 6635
h make unto all people a feast of ... Is 25:6 6635
LORD of *h* be for a crown of glory ... Is 28:5 6635
the Lord GOD of *h* a consumption ... Is 28:22 6635
cometh forth from the LORD of *h* ... Is 28:29 6635
of the LORD of *h* with thunder ... Is 29:6 6635
so shall the LORD of *h* come down ... Is 31:4 6635
the LORD of *h* defend Jerusalem ... Is 31:5 6635
O LORD of *h*, God of Israel, that ... Is 37:16 6635
of the LORD of *h* shall do this ... Is 37:32 6635
Hear the word of the LORD of *h* ... Is 39:5 6635
and his redeemer the LORD of *h* ... Is 44:6 6635
nor reward, saith the LORD of *h* ... Is 45:13 6635
the LORD of *h* is his name ... Is 47:4 6635
The LORD of *h* is his name ... Is 48:2 6635
The LORD of *h* is his name ... Is 51:15 6635
the LORD of *h* is his name ... Is 54:5 6635
in thee, saith the Lord GOD of *h* ... Jer 2:19 6635
heritage of the *h* of nations ... Jer 3:19 6635
thus saith the LORD God of *h* ... Jer 5:14 6635
For thus hath the LORD of *h* said ... Jer 6:6 6635
Thus saith the LORD of *h*, They ... Jer 6:9 6635
Thus saith the LORD of *h*, the God ... Jer 7:3 6635
Thus saith the LORD of *h*, the God ... Jer 7:21 6635
driven them, saith the LORD of *h* ... Jer 8:3 6635
thus saith the LORD of *h*, Behold, ... Jer 9:7 6635
thus saith the LORD of *h*, the God ... Jer 9:15 6635
Thus saith the LORD of *h*, ... Jer 9:17 6635
The LORD of *h* is his name ... Jer 10:16 6635
For the LORD of *h*, that planted ... Jer 11:17 6635
But, O LORD of *h*, that judgest ... Jer 11:20 6635
thus saith the LORD of *h*, Behold, ... Jer 11:22 6635
by thy name, O LORD God of *h* ... Jer 15:16 6635
For thus saith the LORD of *h* ... Jer 16:9 6635
Thus saith the LORD of *h*, the God ... Jer 19:3 6635
them, Thus saith the LORD of *h* ... Jer 19:11 6635
Thus saith the LORD of *h*, the God ... Jer 19:15 6635
But, O LORD of *h*, that triest the ... Jer 20:12 6635
thus saith the LORD of *h* ... Jer 23:15 6635
Thus saith the LORD of *h*, Hearken ... Jer 23:16 6635
God, of the LORD of *h* our God ... Jer 23:36 6635
thus saith the LORD of *h* ... Jer 25:8 6635
them, Thus saith the LORD of *h* ... Jer 25:27 6635
them, Thus saith the LORD of *h* ... Jer 25:28 6635
of the earth, saith the LORD of *h* ... Jer 25:29 6635
Thus saith the LORD of *h*, Behold, ... Jer 25:32 6635
saying, Thus saith the LORD of *h* ... Jer 26:18 6635
masters, Thus saith the LORD of *h* ... Jer 27:4 6635
intercession to the LORD of *h* ... Jer 27:18 6635
LORD of *h* concerning the pillars ... Jer 27:19 6635
Yea, thus saith the LORD of *h* ... Jer 27:21 6635
Thus speaketh the LORD of *h* ... Jer 28:2 6635
For thus saith the LORD of *h* ... Jer 28:14 6635
Thus saith the LORD of *h*, the God ... Jer 29:4 6635
For thus saith the LORD of *h* ... Jer 29:8 6635
Thus saith the LORD of *h* ... Jer 29:17 6635
Thus saith the LORD of *h*, the God ... Jer 29:21 6635
Thus speaketh the LORD of *h* ... Jer 29:25 6635
in that day, saith the LORD of *h* ... Jer 30:8 6635
Thus saith the LORD of *h*, the God ... Jer 31:23 6635
The LORD of *h* is his name ... Jer 31:35 6635
Thus saith the LORD of *h*, the God ... Jer 32:14 6635
For thus saith the LORD of *h* ... Jer 32:15 6635
the Mighty God, the LORD of *h* ... Jer 32:18 6635
shall say, Praise the LORD of *h* ... Jer 33:11 6635
Thus saith the LORD of *h* ... Jer 33:12 6635
Thus saith the LORD of *h*, the God ... Jer 35:13 6635
thus saith the LORD God of *h* ... Jer 35:17 6635
Thus saith the LORD of *h* ... Jer 35:18 6635
thus saith the LORD of *h*, the God ... Jer 35:19 6635
Thus saith the LORD, the God of *h* ... Jer 38:17 6635
saying, Thus saith the LORD of *h* ... Jer 39:16 6635
Thus saith the LORD of *h*, the God ... Jer 42:15 6635
For thus saith the LORD of *h* ... Jer 42:18 6635
them, Thus saith the LORD of *h* ... Jer 43:10 6635
Thus saith the LORD of *h*, the God ... Jer 44:2 6635
thus saith the LORD, the God of *h* ... Jer 44:7 6635
thus saith the LORD of *h*, the God ... Jer 44:11 6635
Thus saith the LORD of *h*, the God ... Jer 44:25 6635
is the day of the Lord GOD of *h* ... Jer 46:10 6635
for the Lord GOD of *h* hath a ... Jer 46:10 6635
King, whose name is the LORD of *h* ... Jer 46:18 6635
The LORD of *h*, the God of Israel, ... Jer 46:25 6635
Moab thus saith the LORD of *h* ... Jer 48:1 6635
King, whose name is the LORD of *h* ... Jer 48:15 6635
thee, saith the Lord GOD of *h* ... Jer 49:5 6635
Edom, thus saith the LORD of *h* ... Jer 49:7 6635
in that day, saith the LORD of *h* ... Jer 49:26 6635
Thus saith the LORD of *h* ... Jer 49:35 6635
thus saith the LORD of *h*, the God ... Jer 50:18 6635
of *h* in the land of the Chaldeans ... Jer 50:25 6635
proud, saith the Lord GOD of *h* ... Jer 50:31 6635
Thus saith the LORD of *h* ... Jer 50:33 6635
the LORD of *h* is his name ... Jer 50:34 6635
of his God, of the LORD of *h* ... Jer 51:5 6635
The LORD of *h* hath sworn by ... Jer 51:14 6635
the LORD of *h* is his name ... Jer 51:19 6635
For thus saith the LORD of *h* ... Jer 51:33 6635
King, whose name is the LORD of *h* ... Jer 51:57 6635
Thus saith the LORD of *h* ... Jer 51:58 6635
Even the LORD God of *h* ... Hos 12:5 6635
saith the Lord GOD, the God of *h* ... Amos 3:13 6635
the earth, The LORD, The God of *h* ... Amos 4:13 6635
and so the LORD, the God of *h* ... Amos 5:14 6635
of *h* will be gracious unto the ... Amos 5:15 6635
Therefore the LORD, the God of *h* ... Amos 5:16 6635
LORD, whose name is The God of *h* ... Amos 5:27 6635
saith the LORD the God of *h* ... Amos 6:8 6635
saith the LORD the God of *h* ... Amos 6:14 6635
the Lord GOD of *h* is he that ... Amos 9:5 6635
of the LORD of *h* hath spoken it ... Mic 4:4 6635
against thee, saith the LORD of *h* ... Nah 2:13 6635
against thee, saith the LORD of *h* ... Nah 3:5 6635
is it not of the LORD of *h* that ... Hab 2:13 6635
as I live, saith the LORD of *h* ... Zeph 2:9 6635
the people of the LORD of *h* ... Zeph 2:10 6635
Thus speaketh the LORD of *h* ... Hag 1:2 6635
thus saith the LORD of *h* ... Hag 1:5 6635
Thus saith the LORD of *h* ... Hag 1:7 6635
saith the LORD of *h* ... Hag 1:9 6635
in the house of the LORD of *h* ... Hag 1:14 6635
am with you, saith the LORD of *h* ... Hag 2:4 6635
For thus saith the LORD of *h* ... Hag 2:6 6635
with glory, saith the LORD of *h* ... Hag 2:7 6635
gold is mine, saith the LORD of *h* ... Hag 2:8 6635
the former, saith the LORD of *h* ... Hag 2:9 6635
I give peace, saith the LORD of *h* ... Hag 2:9 6635
Thus saith the LORD of *h* ... Hag 2:11 6635
In that day, saith the LORD of *h* ... Hag 2:23 6635
chosen thee, saith the LORD of *h* ... Hag 2:23 6635
them, Thus saith the LORD of *h* ... Zec 1:3 6635
ye unto me, saith the LORD of *h* ... Zec 1:3 6635
unto you, saith the LORD of *h* ... Zec 1:3 6635
saying, Thus saith the LORD of *h* ... Zec 1:4 6635
Like as the LORD of *h* thought to ... Zec 1:6 6635
answered and said, O LORD of *h* ... Zec 1:12 6635
saying, Thus saith the LORD of *h* ... Zec 1:14 6635
built in it, saith the LORD of *h* ... Zec 1:16 6635
saying, Thus saith the LORD of *h* ... Zec 1:17 6635
For thus saith the LORD of *h* ... Zec 2:8 6635
that the LORD of *h* hath sent me ... Zec 2:9 6635
LORD of *h* hath sent me unto thee ... Zec 2:11 6635
Thus saith the LORD of *h* ... Zec 3:7 6635
thereof, saith the LORD of *h* ... Zec 3:9 6635
In that day, saith the LORD of *h* ... Zec 3:10 6635
by my spirit, saith the LORD of *h* ... Zec 4:6 6635
LORD of *h* hath sent me unto you ... Zec 4:9 6635
it forth, saith the LORD of *h* ... Zec 5:4 6635
Thus speaketh the LORD of *h* ... Zec 6:12 6635
LORD of *h* hath sent me unto you ... Zec 6:15 6635
in the house of the LORD of *h* ... Zec 7:3 6635
the word of the LORD of *h* unto me ... Zec 7:4 6635
Thus speaketh the LORD of *h* ... Zec 7:9 6635
the words which the LORD of *h* ... Zec 7:12 6635
a great wrath from the LORD of *h* ... Zec 7:12 6635
not hear, saith the LORD of *h* ... Zec 7:13 6635
word of the LORD of *h* came to me ... Zec 8:1 6635
Thus saith the LORD of *h* ... Zec 8:2 6635
the LORD of *h* the holy mountain ... Zec 8:3 6635
Thus saith the LORD of *h* ... Zec 8:4 6635
Thus saith the LORD of *h* ... Zec 8:6 6635
saith the LORD of *h* ... Zec 8:6 6635
Thus saith the LORD of *h* ... Zec 8:7 6635
Thus saith the LORD of *h* ... Zec 8:9 6635
house of the LORD of *h* was laid ... Zec 8:9 6635
former days, saith the LORD of *h* ... Zec 8:11 6635
For thus saith the LORD of *h* ... Zec 8:14 6635
me to wrath, saith the LORD of *h* ... Zec 8:14 6635
of the LORD of *h* came unto me ... Zec 8:18 6635
Thus saith the LORD of *h* ... Zec 8:19 6635
Thus saith the LORD of *h* ... Zec 8:20 6635
LORD, and to seek the LORD of *h* ... Zec 8:21 6635
seek the LORD of *h* in Jerusalem ... Zec 8:22 6635
Thus saith the LORD of *h* ... Zec 8:23 6635
The LORD of *h* shall defend them ... Zec 9:15 6635
for the LORD of *h* hath visited ... Zec 10:3 6635
in the LORD of *h* their God ... Zec 12:5 6635
in that day, saith the LORD of *h* ... Zec 13:2 6635
is my fellow, saith the LORD of *h* ... Zec 13:7 6635
worship the King, the LORD of *h* ... Zec 14:16 6635
worship the King, the LORD of *h* ... Zec 14:17 6635
be holiness unto the LORD of *h* ... Zec 14:21 6635
in the house of the LORD of *h* ... Zec 14:21 6635
thus saith the LORD of *h*, They ... Mal 1:4 6635
saith the LORD of *h* unto you ... Mal 1:6 6635
saith the LORD of *h* ... Mal 1:8 6635
saith the LORD of *h* ... Mal 1:9 6635
in you, saith the LORD of *h* ... Mal 1:10 6635
the heathen, saith the LORD of *h* ... Mal 1:11 6635
at it, saith the LORD of *h* ... Mal 1:13 6635
a great King, saith the LORD of *h* ... Mal 1:14 6635
unto my name, saith the LORD of *h* ... Mal 2:2 6635
be with Levi, saith the LORD of *h* ... Mal 2:4 6635
is the messenger of the LORD of *h* ... Mal 2:7 6635
of Levi, saith the LORD of *h* ... Mal 2:8 6635
an offering unto the LORD of *h* ... Mal 2:12 6635
his garment, saith the LORD of *h* ... Mal 2:16 6635
shall come, saith the LORD of *h* ... Mal 3:1 6635
fear not me, saith the LORD of *h* ... Mal 3:5 6635
unto you, saith the LORD of *h* ... Mal 3:7 6635
now herewith, saith the LORD of *h* ... Mal 3:10 6635
in the field, saith the LORD of *h* ... Mal 3:11 6635
land, saith the LORD of *h* ... Mal 3:12 6635
mournfully before the LORD of *h* ... Mal 3:14 6635
be mine, saith the LORD of *h* ... Mal 3:17 6635
burn them up, saith the LORD of *h* ... Mal 4:1 6635
do this, saith the LORD of *h* ... Mal 4:3 6635

HOT
and when the sun waxed *h*, it ... Ex 16:21 2552
And my wrath shall wax *h*, and I ... Ex 22:24 2734
my wrath may wax *h* against them ... Ex 32:10 2734
wrath wax *h* against thy people ... Ex 32:11 2734
and Moses' anger waxed *h*, and he ... Ex 32:19 2734
not the anger of my lord wax *h* ... Ex 32:22 2734
skin whereof there is a *h* burning ... Lev 13:24 784
h displeasure, wherewith the LORD ... Deut 9:19 2534
the slayer, while his heart is *h* ... Deut 19:6 3179
This our bread we took *h* for our ... Josh 9:12 2525
of the LORD was *h* against Israel ... Judg 2:14 2734
of the LORD was *h* against Israel ... Judg 2:20 2734
of the LORD was *h* against Israel ... Judg 3:8 2734

H

not thine anger be *h* against me Judg 6:39 2734
of the LORD was *h* against Israel Judg 10:7 2734
morrow, by that time the sun be *h* 1Sa 11:9 2527
to put *h* bread in the day when it 1Sa 21:6 2527
be opened until the sun be *h* Neh 7:3 2527
when it is *h*, they are consumed Job 6:17 2527
chasten me in thy *h* displeasure Ps 6:1 2534
chasten me in thy *h* displeasure Ps 38:1 2534
My heart was *h* within me Ps 39:3 2552
and their flocks to *h* thunderbolts Ps 78:48 7565
Can one go upon *h* coals, and his Prov 6:28
that the brass of it may be *h* Eze 24:11 3179
and the furnace exceeding *h* Dan 3:22 228
They are all *h* as an oven Hos 7:7 2552
conscience seared with a *h* iron 1Ti 4:2 *2743*
that thou art neither cold nor *h* Rev 3:15 *2200*
I would thou wert cold or *h* Rev 3:15 *2200*
lukewarm, and neither cold nor *h* Rev 3:16 *2200*

HOTHAM (*ho'-tham*) See HOTHAN. *A son of Heber.*
begat Japhlet, and Shomer, and *H* 1Chr 7:32 2369

HOTHAN (*ho'-than*) See HOTHAM. *Father of Shama and Jehiel.*
Jehiel the sons of *H* the Aroerite 1Chr 11:44 2369

HOTHIR (*ho'-thir*) *A son of Heman.*
Joshbekashah, Mallothi, *H* 1Chr 25:4 1956
The one and twentieth to *H* 1Chr 25:28 1956

HOTLY
thou hast so *h* pursued after me Gen 31:36 1814

HOTTEST
in the forefront of the *h* battle 2Sa 11:15 2389

HOUGH
thou shalt *h* their horses, and Josh 11:6 6131

HOUGHED
he *h* their horses, and burnt their Josh 11:9 6131
David *h* all the chariot horses, 2Sa 8:4 6131
David also *h* all the chariot 1Chr 18:4 6131

HOUR
worshippeth shall the same *h* be Dan 3:6 8160
ye shall be cast the same *h* into Dan 3:15 8160
was astonied for one *h*, and his Dan 4:19 8160
The same *h* was the thing Dan 4:33 8160
In the same *h* came forth fingers Dan 5:5 8160
was healed in the selfsame *h* Mt 8:13 *5610*
woman was made whole from that *h* Mt 9:22 *5610*
that same *h* what ye shall speak Mt 10:19 *5610*
was made whole from that very *h* Mt 15:28 *5610*
child was cured from that very *h* Mt 17:18 *5610*
And he went out about the third *h* Mt 20:3 *5610*
out about the sixth and ninth *h* Mt 20:5 *5610*
about the eleventh *h* he went out Mt 20:6 *5610*
were hired about the eleventh *h* Mt 20:9 *5610*
These last have wrought but one *h* Mt 20:12 *5610*
h knoweth no man, no, not the Mt 24:36 *5610*
not what *h* your Lord doth come Mt 24:42 *5610*
for in such an *h* as ye think not Mt 24:44 *5610*
in an *h* that he is not aware of, Mt 24:50 *5610*
h wherein the Son of man cometh Mt 25:13 *5610*
could ye not watch with me one *h* Mt 26:40 *5610*
the *h* is at hand, and the Son of Mt 26:45 *5610*
In that same *h* said Jesus to the Mt 26:55 *5610*
Now from the sixth *h* there was Mt 27:45 *5610*
all the land unto the ninth *h* Mt 27:45 *5610*
about the ninth *h* Jesus cried Mt 27:46 *5610*
shall be given you in that *h* Mk 13:11 *5610*
that *h* knoweth no man, no, not Mk 13:32 *5610*
the *h* might pass from him Mk 14:35 *5610*
couldest not thou watch one *h* Mk 14:37 *5610*
it is enough, the *h* is come Mk 14:41 *5610*
And it was the third *h*, and they Mk 15:25 *5610*
And when the sixth *h* was come Mk 15:33 *5610*
the whole land until the ninth *h* Mk 15:33 *5610*
at the ninth *h* Jesus cried with a Mk 15:34 *5610*
in that same *h* he cured many of Lk 7:21 *5610*
In that *h* Jesus rejoiced in Lk 10:21 *5610*
the same *h* what ye ought to say Lk 12:12 *5610*
known what *h* the thief would come Lk 12:39 *5610*
cometh at an *h* when ye think not Lk 12:40 *5610*
at an *h* when he is not aware, and Lk 12:46 *5610*
the scribes the same *h* sought to Lk 20:19 *5610*
And when the *h* was come, he sat Lk 22:14 *5610*
but this is your *h*, and the power Lk 22:53 *5610*
about the space of one *h* after Lk 22:59 *5610*
And it was about the sixth *h* Lk 23:44 *5610*
all the earth until the ninth *h* Lk 23:44 *5610*
And they rose up the same *h* Lk 24:33 *5610*
for it was about the tenth *h* Jn 1:39 *5610*
mine *h* is not yet come Jn 2:4 *5610*
and it was about the sixth *h* Jn 4:6 *5610*
the *h* cometh, when ye shall Jn 4:21 *5610*
But the *h* cometh, and now is, when Jn 4:23 *5610*
them the *h* when he began to amend Jn 4:52 *5610*
the seventh *h* the fever left him Jn 4:52 *5610*
knew that it was at the same *h* Jn 4:53 *5610*
The *h* is coming, and now is, when Jn 5:25 *5610*
for the *h* is coming, in the which Jn 5:28 *5610*
because his *h* was not yet come Jn 7:30 *5610*
for his *h* was not yet come Jn 8:20 *5610*
The *h* is come, that the Son of Jn 12:23 *5610*
Father, save me from this *h* Jn 12:27 *5610*
for this cause came I unto this *h* Jn 12:27 *5610*
when Jesus knew that his *h* was Jn 13:1 *5610*
sorrow, because her *h* is come Jn 16:21 *5610*
the *h* cometh, yea, is now come, Jn 16:32 *5610*
and said, Father, the *h* is come Jn 17:1 *5610*
passover, and about the sixth *h* Jn 19:14 *5610*
from that *h* that disciple took Jn 19:27 *5610*
it is but the third *h* of the day Acts 2:15 *5610*
h of prayer, being the ninth *h* Acts 3:1
evidently about the ninth *h* of Acts 10:3 *5610*
to pray about the sixth *h* Acts 10:9 *5610*
ago I was fasting until this *h* Acts 10:30 *5610*
at the ninth *h* I prayed in my Acts 10:30 *5610*
And he came out the same *h* Acts 16:18 *5610*
took them the same *h* of the night Acts 16:33 *5610*
the same *h* I looked up upon him Acts 22:13 *5610*
at the third *h* of the night Acts 23:23 *5610*
this present *h* we both hunger 1Cor 4:11 *5610*
of the idol unto this *h* eat it as 1Cor 8:7 *734*
why stand we in jeopardy every *h* 1Cor 15:30 *5610*
by subjection, no, not for an *h* Gal 2:5 *5610*
know what *h* I will come upon thee Rev 3:3 *5610*
thee from the *h* of temptation Rev 3:10 *5610*
about the space of half an *h* Rev 8:1 *2256*
which were prepared for an *h* Rev 9:15 *5610*
the same *h* was there a great Rev 11:13 *5610*
for the *h* of his judgment is come Rev 14:7 *5610*
as kings one *h* with the beast Rev 17:12 *5610*
for in one *h* is thy judgment come Rev 18:10 *5610*
For in one *h* so great riches is Rev 18:17 *5610*
for in one *h* is she made desolate Rev 18:19 *5610*

HOURS
Are there not twelve *h* in the day Jn 11:9 *5610*
about the space of three *h* after Acts 5:7 *5610*
the space of two *h* cried out Acts 19:34 *5610*

HOUSE
thou and all thy *h* into the ark Gen 7:1 1004
kindred, and from thy father's *h* Gen 12:1 1004
woman was taken into Pharaoh's *h* Gen 12:15 1004
his *h* with great plagues because Gen 12:17 1004
servants, born in his own *h* Gen 14:14 1004
the steward of my *h* is this Gen 15:2 1004
lo, one born in my *h* is mine heir Gen 15:3 1004
he that is born in the *h* Gen 17:12 1004
He that is born in thy *h*, and he Gen 17:13 1004
and all that were born in his *h* Gen 17:23 1004
male among the men of Abraham's *h* Gen 17:23 1004
men of his *h*, born in the *h* Gen 17:27 1004
I pray you, into your servant's *h* Gen 19:2 1004
unto him, and entered into his *h* Gen 19:3 1004
of Sodom, compassed the *h* round Gen 19:4 1004
and pulled Lot into the *h* to them Gen 19:10 1004
the door of the *h* with blindness Gen 19:11 1004
me to wander from my father's *h* Gen 20:13 1004
the wombs of the *h* of Abimelech Gen 20:18 1004
unto his eldest servant of his *h* Gen 24:2 1004
which took me from my father's *h* Gen 24:7 1004
thy father's *h* for us to lodge in Gen 24:23 1004
the LORD led me to the *h* of my Gen 24:27 1004
of her mother's *h* these things Gen 24:28 1004
for I have prepared the *h* Gen 24:31 1004
And the man came into the *h* Gen 24:32 1004
thou shalt go unto my father's *h* Gen 24:38 1004
my kindred, and of my father's *h* Gen 24:40 1004
which were with her in the *h* Gen 27:15 1004
to the *h* of Bethuel thy mother's Gen 28:2 1004
is none other but the *h* of God Gen 28:17 1004
again to my father's *h* in peace Gen 28:21 1004
for a pillar, shall be God's *h* Gen 28:22 1004
him, and brought him to his *h* Gen 29:13 1004
I provide for mine own *h* also Gen 30:30 1004
for us in our father's *h* Gen 31:14 1004
longedst after thy father's *h* Gen 31:30 1004
have I been twenty years in thy *h* Gen 31:41 1004
to Succoth, and built him an *h* Gen 33:17 1004
than all the *h* of his father Gen 34:19 1004
and took Dinah out of Shechem's *h* Gen 34:26 1004
even all that was in the *h* Gen 34:29 1004
I shall be destroyed, I and my *h* Gen 34:30 1004
and all the persons of his *h* Gen 36:6 1004
Remain a widow at thy father's *h* Gen 38:11 1004
went and dwelt in her father's *h* Gen 38:11 1004
he was in the *h* of his master the Gen 39:2 1004
he made him overseer over his *h* Gen 39:4 1004
he had made him overseer in his *h* Gen 39:5 1004
Egyptian's *h* for Joseph's sake Gen 39:5 1004
was upon all that he had in the *h* Gen 39:5 1004
not what is with me in the *h* Gen 39:8 1004
is none greater in this *h* than I Gen 39:9 1004
into the *h* to do his business Gen 39:11 1004
of the men of the *h* there within Gen 39:11 1004
she called unto the men of her *h* Gen 39:14 1004
he put them in ward in the *h* of Gen 40:3 1004
him in the ward of his lord's *h* Gen 40:7 1004
and bring me out of this *h* Gen 40:14 1004
in the captain of the guard's *h* Gen 41:10 1004
Thou shalt be over my *h*, and Gen 41:40 1004
all my toil, and all my father's *h* Gen 41:51 1004
be bound in the *h* of your prison Gen 42:19 1004
he said to the ruler of his *h* Gen 43:16 1004
brought the men into Joseph's *h* Gen 43:17 1004
they were brought into Joseph's *h* Gen 43:18 1004
near to the steward of Joseph's *h* Gen 43:19 1004
with him at the door of the *h* Gen 43:19 1004
brought the men into Joseph's *h* Gen 43:24 1004
was in their hand into the *h* Gen 43:26 1004
he commanded the steward of his *h* Gen 44:1 1004
of thy lord's *h* silver or gold Gen 44:8 1004
his brethren came to Joseph's *h* Gen 44:14 1004
and the *h* of Pharaoh heard Gen 45:2 1004
to Pharaoh, and lord of all his *h* Gen 45:8 1004
thereof was heard in Pharaoh's *h* Gen 45:16 1004
all the souls of the *h* of Jacob Gen 46:27 1004
brethren, and unto his father's *h* Gen 46:31 1004
My brethren, and my father's *h* Gen 46:31 1004
the money into Pharaoh's *h* Gen 47:14 1004
spake unto the *h* of Pharaoh Gen 50:4 1004
of Pharaoh, the elders of his *h* Gen 50:7 1004
all the *h* of Joseph, and his Gen 50:8 1004
his brethren, and his father's *h* Gen 50:8 1004
in Egypt, he, and his father's *h* Gen 50:22 1004
there went a man of the *h* of Levi Ex 2:1 1004
of her that sojourneth in her *h* Ex 3:22 1004
Pharaoh turned and went into his *h* Ex 7:23 1004
shall go up and come into thine *h* Ex 8:3 1004
into the *h* of thy servants, and Ex 8:3 1004
of flies into the *h* of Pharaoh Ex 8:24 1004
to the *h* of their fathers Ex 12:3 1004
of their fathers, a lamb for an *h* Ex 12:3 1004
his neighbour next unto his *h* Ex 12:4 1004
door of his *h* until the morning Ex 12:22 1004
for there was not a *h* where there Ex 12:30 1004
In one *h* shall it be eaten Ex 12:46 1004
of the flesh abroad out of the *h* Ex 12:46 1004
Egypt, out of the *h* of bondage Ex 13:3 1004
from Egypt, from the *h* of bondage Ex 13:14 1004
the *h* of Israel called the name Ex 16:31 1004
shalt thou say to the *h* of Jacob Ex 19:3 1004
of Egypt, out of the *h* of bondage Ex 20:2 1004
shalt not covet thy neighbour's *h* Ex 20:17 1004
it be stolen out of the man's *h* Ex 22:7 1004
then the master of the *h* shall be Ex 22:8 1004
into the *h* of the LORD thy God Ex 23:19 1004
unto the *h* of the LORD thy God Ex 34:26 1004
the sight of all the *h* of Israel Ex 40:38 1004
brethren, the whole *h* of Israel Lev 10:6 1004
h of the land of your possession Lev 14:34 1004
he that owneth the *h* shall come Lev 14:35 1004
is as it were a plague in the *h* Lev 14:35 1004
command that they empty the *h* Lev 14:36 1004
is in the *h* be not made unclean Lev 14:36 1004
priest shall go in to see the *h* Lev 14:36 1004
of the *h* with hollow strakes Lev 14:37 1004
of the *h* to the door of the *h* Lev 14:38 1004
and shut up the *h* seven days Lev 14:38 1004
be spread in the walls of the *h* Lev 14:39 1004
he shall cause the *h* to be Lev 14:41 1004
morter, and shall plaister the *h* Lev 14:42 1004
come again, and break out in the *h* Lev 14:43 1004
and after he hath scraped the *h* Lev 14:43 1004
if the plague be spread in the *h* Lev 14:44 1004
it is a fretting leprosy in the *h* Lev 14:44 1004
And he shall break down the *h* Lev 14:45 1004
and all the morter of the *h* Lev 14:45 1004
h all the while that it is shut Lev 14:46 1004
he that lieth in the *h* shall wash Lev 14:47 1004
he that eateth in the *h* shall Lev 14:47 1004
plague hath not spread in the *h* Lev 14:48 1004
after the *h* was plaistered Lev 14:48 1004
shall pronounce the *h* clean Lev 14:48 1004
take to cleanse the *h* two birds Lev 14:49 1004
and sprinkle the *h* seven times Lev 14:51 1004
he shall cleanse the *h* with the Lev 14:52 1004
and make an atonement for the *h* Lev 14:53 1004
leprosy of a garment, and of a *h* Lev 14:55 1004
for himself, and for his *h* Lev 16:6 1004
for himself, and for his *h* Lev 16:11 1004
there be of the *h* of Israel Lev 17:3 1004
man there be of the *h* of Israel Lev 17:8 1004
man there be of the *h* of Israel Lev 17:10 1004
it, and he that is born in his *h* Lev 22:11 1004
is returned unto her father's *h* Lev 22:13 1004
he be of the *h* of Israel, or of Lev 22:18 1004
a dwelling *h* in a walled city Lev 25:29 1004
then the *h* that is in the walled Lev 25:30 1004
then the *h* that was sold, and the Lev 25:33 1004
his *h* to be holy unto the LORD Lev 27:14 1004
sanctified it will redeem his *h* Lev 27:15 1004
by the *h* of their fathers, with Num 1:2 1004
one head of the *h* of his fathers Num 1:4 1004
by the *h* of their fathers, Num 1:18 1004
by the *h* of their fathers, Num 1:20 1004
by the *h* of their fathers, those Num 1:22 1004
by the *h* of their fathers, Num 1:24 1004
by the *h* of their fathers, Num 1:26 1004
by the *h* of their fathers, Num 1:28 1004
by the *h* of their fathers, Num 1:30 1004
by the *h* of their fathers, Num 1:32 1004
by the *h* of their fathers, Num 1:34 1004
by the *h* of their fathers, Num 1:36 1004
by the *h* of their fathers, Num 1:38 1004
by the *h* of their fathers, Num 1:40 1004
by the *h* of their fathers, Num 1:42 1004
one was for the *h* of his fathers Num 1:44 1004
by the *h* of their fathers, from Num 1:45 1004
the ensign of their father's *h* Num 2:2 1004
Israel by the *h* of their fathers Num 2:32 1004
to the *h* of their fathers Num 2:34 1004
Levi after the *h* of their fathers Num 3:15 1004
to the *h* of their fathers Num 3:20 1004
the chief of the *h* of the father Num 3:24 1004
the chief of the *h* of the father Num 3:30 1004
the chief of the *h* of the father Num 3:35 1004
by the *h* of their fathers, Num 4:2 1004
by the *h* of their fathers, Num 4:29 1004
after the *h* of their fathers, Num 4:34 1004
by the *h* of their fathers, Num 4:38 1004
by the *h* of their fathers, were Num 4:40 1004
by the *h* of their fathers, Num 4:42 1004
after the *h* of their fathers, Num 4:46 1004
heads of the *h* of their fathers, Num 7:2 1004
so, who is faithful in all mine *h* Num 12:7 1004
to the *h* of their fathers Num 17:2 1004
h of their fathers twelve rods Num 17:2 1004
head of the *h* of their fathers Num 17:3 1004
for the *h* of Levi was budded Num 17:8 1004
thy father's *h* with thee shall Num 18:1 1004
is clean in thy *h* shall eat of it Num 18:11 1004
clean in thine *h* shall eat of it Num 18:13 1004
days, even all the *h* of Israel Num 20:29 1004
give me his *h* full of silver Num 22:18 1004
give me his *h* full of silver Num 24:13 1004
a prince of a chief *h* among the Num 25:14 1004
people, and of a chief *h* in Midian Num 25:15 1004
throughout their fathers' *h* Num 26:2 1004
in her father's *h* in her youth Num 30:3 1004
if she vowed in her husband's *h* Num 30:10 1004

Context	Reference	Number
in her youth in her father's *h*	Num 30:16	1004
to the *h* of their fathers	Num 34:14	1004
to the *h* of their fathers	Num 34:14	1004
of Egypt, from the *h* of bondage	Deut 5:6	1004
thou covet thy neighbour's *h*	Deut 5:21	1004
them when thou sittest in thine *h*	Deut 6:7	1004
them upon the posts of thy *h*	Deut 6:9	1004
of Egypt, from the *h* of bondage	Deut 6:12	1004
you out of the *h* of bondmen	Deut 7:8	1004
bring an abomination into thine *h*	Deut 7:26	1004
of Egypt, from the *h* of bondage	Deut 8:14	1004
them when thou sittest in thine *h*	Deut 11:19	1004
upon the door posts of thine *h*	Deut 11:20	1004
you out of the *h* of bondage	Deut 13:5	1004
of Egypt, from the *h* of bondage	Deut 13:10	1004
because he loveth thee and thine *h*	Deut 15:16	1004
is there that hath built a new *h*	Deut 20:5	1004
let him go and return to his *h*	Deut 20:5	1004
him also go and return unto his *h*	Deut 20:6	1004
let him go and return unto his *h*	Deut 20:7	1004
let him go and return unto his *h*	Deut 20:8	1004
shalt bring her home to thine *h*	Deut 21:12	1004
her, and shall remain in thine *h*	Deut 21:13	1004
shalt bring it unto thine own *h*	Deut 22:2	1004
When thou buildest a new *h*	Deut 22:8	1004
thou bring not blood upon thine *h*	Deut 22:8	1004
to the door of her father's *h*	Deut 22:21	1004
play the whore in her father's *h*	Deut 22:21	1004
into the *h* of the LORD thy God	Deut 23:18	1004
hand, and send her out of his *h*	Deut 24:1	1004
when she is departed out of his *h*	Deut 24:2	1004
hand, and sendeth her out of his *h*	Deut 24:3	1004
go into his *h* to fetch his pledge	Deut 24:10	1004
will not build up his brother's *h*	Deut 25:9	1004
The *h* of him that hath his shoe	Deut 25:10	1004
have in thine *h* divers measures	Deut 25:14	1004
given unto thee, and unto thine *h*	Deut 26:11	1004
the hallowed things out of mine *h*	Deut 26:13	1004
thou shalt build an *h*, and thou	Deut 28:30	1004
went, and came into an harlot's *h*	Josh 2:1	1004
which are entered into thine *h*	Josh 2:3	1004
them up to the roof of the *h*	Josh 2:6	
shew kindness unto my father's *h*	Josh 2:12	1004
for her *h* was upon the town wall,	Josh 2:15	1004
doors of thy *h* into the street	Josh 2:19	1004
shall be with thee in the *h*	Josh 2:19	1004
and all that are with her in the *h*	Josh 6:17	1004
country, Go into the harlot's *h*	Josh 6:22	1004
the treasury of the *h* of the LORD	Josh 6:24	1004
of water for the *h* of my God	Josh 9:23	1004
Joshua spake unto the *h* of Joseph	Josh 17:17	1004
the *h* of Joseph shall abide in	Josh 18:5	1004
his own city, and unto his own *h*	Josh 20:6	1004
had spoken unto the *h* of Israel	Josh 21:45	1004
princes, of each chief *h* a prince	Josh 22:14	1004
the *h* of their fathers among the	Josh 22:14	1004
but as for me and my *h*, we will	Josh 24:15	1004
from the *h* of bondage, and which	Josh 24:17	1004
the *h* of Joseph, they also went	Judg 1:22	1004
the *h* of Joseph sent to descry	Judg 1:23	1004
hand of the *h* of Joseph prevailed	Judg 1:35	1004
the *h* of Heber the Kenite	Judg 4:17	1004
you forth out of the *h* of bondage	Judg 6:8	1004
I am the least in my father's *h*	Judg 6:15	1004
a snare unto Gideon, and to his *h*	Judg 8:27	1004
Joash went and dwelt in his own *h*	Judg 8:29	1004
kindness to the *h* of Jerubbaal	Judg 8:35	1004
of the *h* of his mother's father	Judg 9:1	1004
out of the *h* of Baal-berith	Judg 9:4	1004
unto his father's *h* at Ophrah	Judg 9:5	1004
all the *h* of Millo, and went, and	Judg 9:6	1004
well with Jerubbaal and his *h*	Judg 9:16	1004
up against my father's *h* this day	Judg 9:18	1004
Jerubbaal and with his *h* this day	Judg 9:19	1004
men of Shechem, and the *h* of Millo	Judg 9:20	1004
Shechem, and from the *h* of Millo	Judg 9:20	1004
and went into the *h* of their god	Judg 9:27	1004
hold of the *h* of the god Berith	Judg 9:46	1004
and against the *h* of Ephraim	Judg 10:9	1004
not inherit in our father's *h*	Judg 11:2	1004
and expel me out of my father's *h*	Judg 11:7	1004
of the doors of my *h* to meet me	Judg 11:31	1004
came to Mizpeh unto his *h*	Judg 11:34	1004
we will burn thine *h* upon thee	Judg 12:1	1004
thee and thy father's *h* with fire	Judg 14:15	1004
and he went up to his father's *h*	Judg 14:19	1004
and he did grind in the prison *h*	Judg 16:21	1004
for Samson out of the prison *h*	Judg 16:25	1004
pillars whereupon the *h* standeth	Judg 16:26	1004
Now the *h* was full of men and	Judg 16:27	1004
pillars upon which the *h* stood	Judg 16:29	1004
the *h* fell upon the lords, and	Judg 16:30	1004
all the *h* of his father came down	Judg 16:31	1004
and they were in the *h* of Micah	Judg 17:4	1004
And the man Micah had an *h* of gods	Judg 17:5	1004
mount Ephraim to the *h* of Micah	Judg 17:8	1004
priest, and was in the *h* of Micah	Judg 17:12	1004
to the *h* of Micah, they lodged	Judg 18:2	1004
When they were by the *h* of Micah	Judg 18:3	1004
and came unto the *h* of Micah	Judg 18:13	1004
came to the *h* of the young man	Judg 18:15	1004
Levite, even unto the *h* of Micah	Judg 18:15	1004
And these went into Micah's *h*	Judg 18:18	1004
be a priest unto the *h* of one man	Judg 18:19	1004
a good way from the *h* of Micah	Judg 18:22	1004
Micah's *h* were gathered together	Judg 18:22	1004
he turned and went back unto his *h*	Judg 18:26	1004
that the *h* of God was in Shiloh	Judg 18:31	1004
father's *h* to Beth-lehem-judah	Judg 19:2	1004
brought him into her father's *h*	Judg 19:3	1004
took them into his *h* to lodging	Judg 19:15	1004
am now going to the *h* of the LORD	Judg 19:18	1004
is no man that receiveth me to *h*	Judg 19:18	1004
So he brought him into his *h*	Judg 19:21	1004
beset the *h* round about, and beat	Judg 19:22	1004
and spake to the master of the *h*	Judg 19:22	1004
the man that came into thine *h*	Judg 19:22	1004
And the man, the master of the *h*	Judg 19:23	1004
that this man is come into mine *h*	Judg 19:23	1004
of the man's *h* where her lord was	Judg 19:26	1004
and opened the doors of the *h*	Judg 19:27	1004
fallen down at the door of the *h*	Judg 19:27	1004
And when he was come into his *h*	Judg 19:29	1004
beset the *h* round about upon me	Judg 20:5	1004
will we any of us turn into his *h*	Judg 20:8	1004
arose, and went up to the *h* of God	Judg 20:18	1008
up, and came unto the *h* of God	Judg 20:26	1008
one goeth up to the *h* of God	Judg 20:31	1008
the people came to the *h* of God	Judg 21:2	1008
Go, return each to her mother's *h*	Ruth 1:8	1004
of you in the *h* of her husband	Ruth 1:9	1004
she tarried a little in the *h*	Ruth 2:7	1004
is come into thine *h* like Rachel	Ruth 4:11	1004
two did build the *h* of Israel	Ruth 4:11	1004
thy *h* be like the *h* of Pharez	Ruth 4:12	1004
she went up to the *h* of the LORD	1Sa 1:7	1004
and came to their *h* to Ramah	1Sa 1:19	1004
And the man Elkanah, and all his *h*	1Sa 1:21	1004
brought him unto the *h* of the	1Sa 1:24	1004
And Elkanah went to Ramah to his *h*	1Sa 2:11	1004
appear unto the *h* of thy father	1Sa 2:27	1004
they were in Egypt in Pharaoh's *h*	1Sa 2:27	1004
did I give unto the *h* of thy	1Sa 2:28	1004
saith, I said indeed that thy *h*	1Sa 2:30	1004
the *h* of thy father, should walk	1Sa 2:30	1004
arm, and the arm of thy father's *h*	1Sa 2:31	1004
not be an old man in thine *h*	1Sa 2:31	1004
be an old man in thine *h* for ever	1Sa 2:32	1004
all the increase of thine *h* shall	1Sa 2:33	1004
and I will build him a sure *h*	1Sa 2:35	1004
is left in thine *h* shall come	1Sa 2:36	1004
I have spoken concerning his *h*	1Sa 3:12	1004
told him that I will judge his *h*	1Sa 3:13	1004
I have sworn unto the *h* of Eli	1Sa 3:14	1004
Eli's *h* shall not be purged with	1Sa 3:14	1004
the doors of the *h* of the LORD	1Sa 3:15	1004
brought it into the *h* of Dagon	1Sa 5:2	1004
nor any that come into Dagon's *h*	1Sa 5:5	1004
brought it into the *h* of Abinadab	1Sa 7:1	1004
all the *h* of Israel lamented	1Sa 7:2	1004
spake unto all the *h* of Israel	1Sa 7:3	1004
for there was his *h*	1Sa 7:17	1004
pray thee, where the seer's *h* is	1Sa 9:18	1004
on thee, and on all thy father's *h*	1Sa 9:20	1004
with Saul upon the top of the *h*	1Sa 9:25	
called Saul to the top of the *h*	1Sa 9:26	
people away, every man to his *h*	1Sa 10:25	1004
up to his *h* to Gibeah of Saul	1Sa 15:34	1004
his father's *h* free in Israel	1Sa 17:25	1004
go no more home to his father's *h*	1Sa 18:2	1004
prophesied in the midst of the *h*	1Sa 18:10	1004
as he sat in his *h* with his	1Sa 19:9	1004
sent messengers unto David's *h*	1Sa 19:11	1004
thy kindness from my *h* for ever	1Sa 20:15	1004
a covenant with the *h* of David	1Sa 20:16	1004
shall this fellow come into my *h*	1Sa 21:15	1004
and all his father's *h* heard it	1Sa 22:1	1004
of Ahitub, and all his father's *h*	1Sa 22:11	1004
and is honourable in thine *h*	1Sa 22:14	1004
nor to all the *h* of my father	1Sa 22:15	1004
thou, and all thy father's *h*	1Sa 22:16	1004
all the persons of thy father's *h*	1Sa 22:22	1004
wood, and Jonathan went to his *h*	1Sa 23:18	1004
my name out of my father's *h*	1Sa 24:21	1004
and buried him in his *h* at Ramah	1Sa 25:1	1004
and he was of the *h* of Caleb	1Sa 25:3	1004
to thee, and peace be to thine *h*	1Sa 25:6	1004
certainly make my lord a sure *h*	1Sa 25:28	1004
her, Go up in peace to thine *h*	1Sa 25:35	1004
behold, he held a feast in his *h*	1Sa 25:36	1004
the woman had a fat calf in the *h*	1Sa 28:24	1004
it in the *h* of their idols	1Sa 31:9	1004
his armour in the *h* of Ashtaroth	1Sa 31:10	1004
the LORD, and for the *h* of Israel	2Sa 1:12	1004
David king over the *h* of Judah	2Sa 2:4	1004
also the *h* of Judah have anointed	2Sa 2:7	1004
But the *h* of Judah followed David	2Sa 2:10	1004
the *h* of Judah was seven years	2Sa 2:11	1004
h of Saul and the *h* of David	2Sa 3:1	1004
the *h* of Saul waxed weaker and	2Sa 3:1	1004
was war between the *h* of Saul	2Sa 3:6	1004
the *h* of David, that Abner made	2Sa 3:6	1004
himself strong for the *h* of Saul	2Sa 3:6	1004
day unto the *h* of Saul thy father	2Sa 3:8	1004
the kingdom from the *h* of Saul	2Sa 3:10	1004
good to the whole *h* of Benjamin	2Sa 3:19	1004
of Joab, and on all his father's *h*	2Sa 3:29	1004
let there not fail from the *h* of	2Sa 3:29	1004
the day to the *h* of Ish-bosheth	2Sa 4:5	1004
thither into the midst of the *h*	2Sa 4:6	1004
For when they came into the *h*	2Sa 4:7	1004
person in his own *h* upon his bed	2Sa 4:11	1004
lame shall not come into the *h*	2Sa 5:8	1004
and they built David an *h*	2Sa 5:11	1004
brought it out of the *h* of	2Sa 6:3	1004
they brought it out of the *h* of	2Sa 6:4	1004
all the *h* of Israel played before	2Sa 6:5	1004
the *h* of Obed-edom the Gittite	2Sa 6:10	1004
of the LORD continued in the *h* of	2Sa 6:11	1004
hath blessed the *h* of Obed-edom	2Sa 6:12	1004
up the ark of God from the *h* of	2Sa 6:12	1004
all the *h* of Israel brought up	2Sa 6:15	1004
departed every one to his *h*	2Sa 6:19	1004
thy father, and before all his *h*	2Sa 6:21	1004
pass, when the king sat in his *h*	2Sa 7:1	1004
See now, I dwell in an *h* of cedar	2Sa 7:2	1004
build me an *h* for me to dwell in	2Sa 7:5	1004
h since the time that I brought	2Sa 7:6	1004
Why build ye not me an *h* of cedar	2Sa 7:7	1004
thee that he will make thee an *h*	2Sa 7:11	1004
He shall build an *h* for my name	2Sa 7:13	1004
And thine *h* and thy kingdom shall	2Sa 7:16	1004
and what is my *h*, that thou hast	2Sa 7:18	1004
h for a great while to come	2Sa 7:19	1004
thy servant, and concerning his *h*	2Sa 7:25	1004
let the *h* of thy servant David be	2Sa 7:26	1004
saying, I will build thee an *h*	2Sa 7:27	1004
to bless the *h* of thy servant	2Sa 7:29	1004
with thy blessing let the *h* of	2Sa 7:29	1004
any that is left of the *h* of Saul	2Sa 9:1	1004
there was of the *h* of Saul a	2Sa 9:2	1004
not yet any of the *h* of Saul	2Sa 9:3	1004
Behold, he is in the *h* of Machir	2Sa 9:4	1004
him out of the *h* of Machir	2Sa 9:5	1004
pertained to Saul and to all his *h*	2Sa 9:9	1004
all that dwelt in the *h* of Ziba	2Sa 9:12	1004
upon the roof of the king's *h*	2Sa 11:2	1004
and she returned unto her *h*	2Sa 11:4	1004
said to Uriah, Go down to thy *h*	2Sa 11:8	1004
departed out of the king's *h*	2Sa 11:8	1004
h with all the servants of his	2Sa 11:9	1004
lord, and went not down to his *h*	2Sa 11:9	1004
Uriah went not down unto his *h*	2Sa 11:10	1004
thou not go down unto thine *h*	2Sa 11:10	1004
shall I then go into mine *h*	2Sa 11:11	1004
lord, but went not down to his *h*	2Sa 11:13	1004
sent and fetched her to his *h*	2Sa 11:27	1004
And I gave thee thy master's *h*	2Sa 12:8	1004
and gave thee the *h* of Israel	2Sa 12:8	1004
shall never depart from thine *h*	2Sa 12:10	1004
against thee out of thine own *h*	2Sa 12:11	1004
And Nathan departed unto his *h*	2Sa 12:15	1004
And the elders of his *h* arose	2Sa 12:17	1004
and came into the *h* of the LORD	2Sa 12:20	1004
then he came to his own *h*	2Sa 12:20	1004
Go now to thy brother Amnon's *h*	2Sa 13:7	1004
went to her brother Amnon's *h*	2Sa 13:8	1004
in her brother Absalom's *h*	2Sa 13:20	1004
unto the woman, Go to thine *h*	2Sa 14:8	1004
be on me, and on my father's *h*	2Sa 14:9	1004
said, Let him turn to his own *h*	2Sa 14:24	1004
So Absalom returned to his own *h*	2Sa 14:24	1004
and came to Absalom unto his *h*	2Sa 14:31	1004
were concubines, to keep the *h*	2Sa 15:16	1004
shalt hear out of the king's *h*	2Sa 15:35	1004
Today shall the *h* of Israel	2Sa 16:3	1004
of the family of the *h* of Saul	2Sa 16:5	1004
all the blood of the *h* of Saul	2Sa 16:8	1004
which he hath left to keep the *h*	2Sa 16:21	1004
a tent upon the top of the *h*	2Sa 16:22	1004
and came to a man's *h* in Bahurim	2Sa 17:18	1004
came to the woman to the *h*	2Sa 17:20	1004
arose, and gat him home to his *h*	2Sa 17:23	1004
Joab came into the *h* to the king	2Sa 19:5	1004
to bring the king back to his *h*	2Sa 19:11	1004
come to the king, even to his *h*	2Sa 19:11	1004
Ziba the servant of the *h* of Saul	2Sa 19:17	1004
the first this day of all the *h*	2Sa 19:20	1004
For all of my father's *h* were but	2Sa 19:28	1004
again in peace unto his own *h*	2Sa 19:30	1004
David came to his *h* at Jerusalem	2Sa 20:3	1004
whom he had left to keep the *h*	2Sa 20:3	1004
is for Saul, and for his bloody *h*	2Sa 21:1	1004
nor gold of Saul, nor of his *h*	2Sa 21:4	1004
Although my *h* be not so with God	2Sa 23:5	1004
me, and against my father's *h*	2Sa 24:17	1004
said unto him, Go to thine *h*	1Kin 1:53	1004
father, and who hath made me an *h*	1Kin 2:24	1004
concerning the *h* of Eli in Shiloh	1Kin 2:27	1004
me, and from the *h* of my father	1Kin 2:31	1004
and upon his seed, and upon his *h*	1Kin 2:33	1004
in his own *h* in the wilderness	1Kin 2:34	1004
him, Build thee an *h* in Jerusalem	1Kin 2:36	1004
made an end of building his own *h*	1Kin 3:1	1004
the *h* of the LORD, and the wall of	1Kin 3:1	1004
because there was no *h* built unto	1Kin 3:2	1004
I and this woman dwell in one *h*	1Kin 3:17	1004
of a child with her in the *h*	1Kin 3:17	1004
was no stranger with us in the *h*	1Kin 3:18	1004
save we two in the *h*	1Kin 3:18	1004
my father could not build an *h*	1Kin 5:3	1004
I purpose to build an *h* unto the	1Kin 5:5	1004
he shall build an *h* unto my name	1Kin 5:5	1004
to lay the foundation of the *h*	1Kin 5:17	1004
timber and stones to build the *h*	1Kin 5:18	1004
began to build the *h* of the LORD	1Kin 6:1	1004
the *h* which king Solomon built	1Kin 6:2	1004
porch before the temple of the *h*	1Kin 6:3	1004
according to the breadth of the *h*	1Kin 6:3	1004
the breadth thereof before the *h*	1Kin 6:3	1004
for the *h* he made windows of	1Kin 6:4	1004
against the wall of the *h* he	1Kin 6:5	1004
the walls of the *h* round about	1Kin 6:5	1004
h he made narrowed rests round	1Kin 6:6	1004
be fastened in the walls of the *h*	1Kin 6:6	1004
And the *h*, when it was in building	1Kin 6:7	1004
any tool of iron heard in the *h*	1Kin 6:7	1004
was in the right side of the *h*	1Kin 6:8	1004
So he built the *h*, and finished it	1Kin 6:9	1004
and covered the *h* with beams	1Kin 6:9	1004
built chambers against all the *h*	1Kin 6:10	1004
they rested on the *h* with timber	1Kin 6:10	1004
Concerning this *h* which thou art	1Kin 6:12	1004
So Solomon built the *h*, and	1Kin 6:14	1004
he built the walls of the *h*	1Kin 6:15	1004
of cedar, both the floor of the *h*	1Kin 6:15	1004
floor of the *h* with planks of fir	1Kin 6:15	1004
cubits on the sides of the *h*	1Kin 6:16	1004
And the *h*, that is, the temple	1Kin 6:17	1004
the cedar of the *h* within was	1Kin 6:18	1004
he prepared in the *h* within	1Kin 6:19	1004
the *h* within with pure gold	1Kin 6:21	1004

the whole *h* he overlaid with gold 1Kin 6:22 1004
until he had finished all the *h* 1Kin 6:22 1004
the cherubims within the inner *h* 1Kin 6:27 1004
one another in the midst of the *h* 1Kin 6:27 1004
he carved all the walls of the *h* 1Kin 6:29 1004
the floor of the *h* he overlaid 1Kin 6:30 1004
of the *h* of the LORD laid 1Kin 6:37 1004
was the *h* finished throughout all 1Kin 6:38 1004
building his own *h* thirteen years 1Kin 7:1 1004
and he finished all his *h* 1Kin 7:1 1004
He built also the *h* of the forest 1Kin 7:2 1004
his *h* where he dwelt had another 1Kin 7:8 1004
Solomon made also an *h* for 1Kin 7:8 1004
inner court of the *h* of the LORD 1Kin 7:12 1004
and for the porch of the *h* 1Kin 7:12 1004
bases on the right side of the *h* 1Kin 7:39 1004
and five on the left side of the *h* 1Kin 7:39 1004
sea on the right side of the *h* 1Kin 7:39 1004
Solomon for the *h* of the LORD 1Kin 7:40 1004
Solomon for the *h* of the LORD 1Kin 7:45 1004
pertained unto the *h* of the LORD 1Kin 7:48 1004
both for the doors of the inner *h* 1Kin 7:50 1004
place, and for the doors of the *h* 1Kin 7:50 1004
made for the *h* of the LORD 1Kin 7:51 1004
treasures of the *h* of the LORD 1Kin 7:51 1004
place, into the oracle of the *h* 1Kin 8:6 1004
cloud filled the *h* of the LORD 1Kin 8:10 1004
LORD had filled the *h* of the LORD 1Kin 8:11 1004
built thee an *h* to dwell in 1Kin 8:13 1004
tribes of Israel to build an *h* 1Kin 8:16 1004
of David my father to build an *h* 1Kin 8:17 1004
heart to build an *h* unto my name 1Kin 8:18 1004
thou shalt not build the *h* 1Kin 8:19 1004
he shall build the *h* unto my name 1Kin 8:19 1004
have built an *h* for the name of 1Kin 8:20 1004
how much less this *h* that I have 1Kin 8:27 1004
may be open toward this *h* night 1Kin 8:29 1004
come before thine altar in this *h* 1Kin 8:31 1004
supplication unto thee in this *h* 1Kin 8:33 1004
forth his hands toward this *h* 1Kin 8:38 1004
shall come and pray toward this *h* 1Kin 8:42 1004
and that they may know that this *h* 1Kin 8:43 1004
toward the *h* that I have built 1Kin 8:44 1004
the *h* which I have built for thy 1Kin 8:48 1004
dedicated the *h* of the LORD 1Kin 8:63 1004
that was before the *h* of the LORD 1Kin 8:64 1004
the building of the *h* of the LORD 1Kin 9:1 1004
of the LORD, and the king's *h* 1Kin 9:1 1004
I have hallowed this *h*, which 1Kin 9:3 1004
and this *h*, which I have hallowed 1Kin 9:7 1004
And at this *h*, which is high, 1Kin 9:8 1004
thus unto this land, and to this *h* 1Kin 9:8 1004
the *h* of the LORD, and the king's 1Kin 9:10 1004
of the LORD, and the king's *h* 1Kin 9:10 1004
h of the LORD, and his own *h* 1Kin 9:15 1004
of the city of David unto her *h* 1Kin 9:24 1004
So he finished the *h* 1Kin 9:25 1004
and the *h* that he had built, 1Kin 10:4 1004
he went up unto the *h* of the LORD 1Kin 10:5 1004
pillars for the *h* of the LORD 1Kin 10:12 1004
of the LORD, and for the king's *h* 1Kin 10:12 1004
in the *h* of the forest of Lebanon 1Kin 10:17 1004
all the vessels of the *h* of the 1Kin 10:21 1004
which gave him an *h*, and appointed 1Kin 11:18 1004
Tahpenes weaned in Pharaoh's *h* 1Kin 11:20 1004
all the charge of the *h* of Joseph 1Kin 11:28 1004
with thee, and build thee a sure *h* 1Kin 11:38 1004
now see to thine own *h*, David 1Kin 12:16 1004
the *h* of David unto this day 1Kin 12:19 1004
none that followed the *h* of David 1Kin 12:20 1004
he assembled all the *h* of Judah 1Kin 12:21 1004
to fight against the *h* of Israel 1Kin 12:21 1004
Judah, and unto all the *h* of Judah 1Kin 12:23 1004
return every man to his *h* 1Kin 12:24 1004
kingdom return to the *h* of David 1Kin 12:26 1004
in the *h* of the LORD at Jerusalem 1Kin 12:27 1004
he made an *h* of high places, and 1Kin 12:31 1004
shall be born unto the *h* of David 1Kin 13:2 1004
If thou wilt give me half thine *h* 1Kin 13:8 1004
him back with thee into thine *h* 1Kin 13:18 1004
him, and did eat bread in his *h* 1Kin 13:19 1004
became sin unto the *h* of Jeroboam 1Kin 13:34 1004
and came to the *h* of Ahijah 1Kin 14:4 1004
kingdom away from the *h* of David 1Kin 14:8 1004
bring evil upon the *h* of Jeroboam 1Kin 14:10 1004
the remnant of the *h* of Jeroboam 1Kin 14:10 1004
get thee to thine own *h* 1Kin 14:12 1004
of Israel in the *h* of Jeroboam 1Kin 14:13 1004
off the *h* of Jeroboam that day 1Kin 14:14 1004
treasures of the *h* of the LORD 1Kin 14:26 1004
and the treasures of the king's *h* 1Kin 14:26 1004
kept the door of the king's *h* 1Kin 14:27 1004
king went into the *h* of the LORD 1Kin 14:28 1004
into the *h* of the LORD, silver, 1Kin 15:15 1004
treasures of the *h* of the LORD 1Kin 15:18 1004
and the treasures of the king's *h* 1Kin 15:18 1004
of the *h* of Issachar, conspired 1Kin 15:27 1004
he smote all the *h* of Jeroboam 1Kin 15:29 1004
Baasha, and the posterity of his *h* 1Kin 16:3 1004
thy *h* like the *h* of Jeroboam 1Kin 16:3 1004
against Baasha, and against his *h* 1Kin 16:7 1004
in being like the *h* of Jeroboam 1Kin 16:7 1004
drinking himself drunk in the *h* 1Kin 16:9 1004
Arza steward of his *h* in Tirzah 1Kin 16:9 1004
that he slew all the *h* of Baasha 1Kin 16:11 1004
Zimri destroy all the *h* of Baasha 1Kin 16:12 1004
into the palace of the king's *h* 1Kin 16:18 1004
burnt the king's *h* over him with 1Kin 16:18 1004
altar for Baal in the *h* of Baal 1Kin 16:32 1004
and she, and he, and her *h*, did eat 1Kin 17:15 1004
the woman, the mistress of the *h* 1Kin 17:17 1004
out of the chamber into the *h* 1Kin 17:23 1004
which was the governor of his *h* 1Kin 18:3 1004
but thou, and thy father's *h* 1Kin 18:18 1004
and they shall search thine *h* 1Kin 20:6 1004
heard that the kings of the *h* of 1Kin 20:31 1004
of Israel went to his *h* heavy 1Kin 20:43 1004
because it is near unto my *h* 1Kin 21:2 1004
And Ahab came into his *h* heavy 1Kin 21:4 1004
will make thine *h* like the *h* 1Kin 21:22 1004
h of Jeroboam the son of Nebat 1Kin 21:22 1004
like the *h* of Baasha the son of 1Kin 21:22 1004
will I bring the evil upon his *h* 1Kin 21:29 1004
every man to his *h* in peace 1Kin 22:17 1004
the ivory *h* which he made, and all 1Kin 22:39 1004
tell me, what hast thou in the *h* 2Kin 4:2 1004
hath not any thing in the *h* 2Kin 4:2 1004
when Elisha was come into the *h* 2Kin 4:32 1004
returned, and walked in the *h* to 2Kin 4:35 1004
at the door of the *h* of Elisha 2Kin 5:9 1004
the *h* of Rimmon to worship there 2Kin 5:18 1004
I bow myself in the *h* of Rimmon 2Kin 5:18 1004
down myself in the *h* of Rimmon 2Kin 5:18 1004
hand, and bestowed them in the *h* 2Kin 5:24 1004
But Elisha sat in his *h*, and the 2Kin 6:32 1004
told it to the king's *h* within 2Kin 7:11 1004
to cry unto the king for her *h* 2Kin 8:3 1004
life, cried to the king for her *h* 2Kin 8:5 1004
of Israel, as did the *h* of Ahab 2Kin 8:18 1004
in the way of the *h* of Ahab 2Kin 8:27 1004
of the LORD, as did the *h* of Ahab 2Kin 8:27 1004
the son in law of the *h* of Ahab 2Kin 8:27 1004
And he arose, and went into the *h* 2Kin 9:6 1004
smite the *h* of Ahab thy master 2Kin 9:7 1004
For the whole *h* of Ahab shall 2Kin 9:8 1004
I will make the *h* of Ahab like 2Kin 9:9 1004
h of Jeroboam the son of Nebat 2Kin 9:9 1004
like the *h* of Baasha the son of 2Kin 9:9 1004
fled by the way of the garden *h* 2Kin 9:27 1004
and fight for your master's *h* 2Kin 10:3 1004
And he that was over the *h* 2Kin 10:5 1004
spake concerning the *h* of Ahab 2Kin 10:10 1004
of the *h* of Ahab in Jezreel 2Kin 10:11 1004
was at the shearing *h* in the way 2Kin 10:12 1004
them at the pit of the shearing *h* 2Kin 10:14 1004
And they came into the *h* of Baal 2Kin 10:21 1004
the *h* of Baal was full from one 2Kin 10:21 1004
son of Rechab, into the *h* of Baal 2Kin 10:23 1004
went to the city of the *h* of Baal 2Kin 10:25 1004
the images out of the *h* of Baal 2Kin 10:26 1004
Baal, and brake down the *h* of Baal 2Kin 10:27 1004
made it a draught *h* unto this day 2Kin 10:27
hast done unto the *h* of Ahab 2Kin 10:30 1004
in the *h* of the LORD six years 2Kin 11:3 1004
to him into the *h* of the LORD 2Kin 11:4 1004
oath of them in the *h* of the LORD 2Kin 11:4 1004
of the watch of the king's *h* 2Kin 11:5 1004
shall ye keep the watch of the *h* 2Kin 11:6 1004
the *h* of the LORD about the king 2Kin 11:7 1004
not be slain in the *h* of the LORD 2Kin 11:15 1004
the horses came into the king's *h* 2Kin 11:16 1004
the land went into the *h* of Baal 2Kin 11:18 1004
officers over the *h* of the LORD 2Kin 11:18 1004
the king from the *h* of the LORD 2Kin 11:19 1004
gate of the guard to the king's *h* 2Kin 11:19 1004
the sword beside the king's *h* 2Kin 11:20 1004
is brought into the *h* of the LORD 2Kin 12:4 1004
to bring into the *h* of the LORD 2Kin 12:4 1004
them repair the breaches of the *h* 2Kin 12:5 1004
repaired the breaches of the *h* 2Kin 12:6 1004
ye not the breaches of the *h* 2Kin 12:7 1004
it for the breaches of the *h* 2Kin 12:7 1004
to repair the breaches of the *h* 2Kin 12:8 1004
one cometh into the *h* of the LORD 2Kin 12:9 1004
brought into the *h* of the LORD 2Kin 12:9 1004
was found in the *h* of the LORD 2Kin 12:10 1004
oversight of the *h* of the LORD 2Kin 12:11 1004
wrought upon the *h* of the LORD 2Kin 12:11 1004
the breaches of the *h* of the LORD 2Kin 12:12 1004
laid out for the *h* to repair it 2Kin 12:12 1004
the *h* of the LORD bowls of silver 2Kin 12:13 1004
brought into the *h* of the LORD 2Kin 12:13 1004
therewith the *h* of the LORD 2Kin 12:14 1004
brought into the *h* of the LORD 2Kin 12:16 1004
treasures of the *h* of the LORD 2Kin 12:18 1004
of the LORD, and in the king's *h* 2Kin 12:18 1004
and slew Joash in the *h* of Millo 2Kin 12:20 1004
the sins of the *h* of Jeroboam 2Kin 13:6 1004
were found in the *h* of the LORD 2Kin 14:14 1004
in the treasures of the king's *h* 2Kin 14:14 1004
death, and dwelt in a several *h* 2Kin 15:5 1004
the king's son was over the *h* 2Kin 15:5 1004
in the palace of the king's *h* 2Kin 15:25 1004
higher gate of the *h* of the LORD 2Kin 15:35 1004
was found in the *h* of the LORD 2Kin 16:8 1004
in the treasures of the king's *h* 2Kin 16:8 1004
LORD, from the forefront of the *h* 2Kin 16:14 1004
the *h* of the LORD, and put it on 2Kin 16:14 1004
that they had built in the *h* 2Kin 16:18 1004
turned he from the *h* of the LORD 2Kin 16:18 1004
rent Israel from the *h* of David 2Kin 17:21 1004
was found in the *h* of the LORD 2Kin 18:15 1004
in the treasures of the king's *h* 2Kin 18:15 1004
and went into the *h* of the LORD 2Kin 19:1 1004
went up into the *h* of the LORD 2Kin 19:14 1004
herb, as the grass on the *h* tops 2Kin 19:26
h of Judah shall yet again take 2Kin 19:30 1004
in the *h* of Nisroch his god 2Kin 19:37 1004
the LORD, Set thine *h* in order 2Kin 20:1 1004
go up unto the *h* of the LORD 2Kin 20:5 1004
the *h* of the LORD the third day 2Kin 20:8 1004
shewed them all the *h* of his 2Kin 20:13 1004
all the *h* of his armour, and all 2Kin 20:13 1004
there was nothing in his *h* 2Kin 20:13 1004
What have they seen in thine *h* 2Kin 20:15 1004
that are in mine *h* have they seen 2Kin 20:15 1004
come, that all that is in thine *h* 2Kin 20:17 1004
built altars in the *h* of the LORD 2Kin 21:4 1004
two courts of the *h* of the LORD 2Kin 21:5 1004
grove that he had made in the *h* 2Kin 21:7 1004
and to Solomon his son, In this *h* 2Kin 21:7 1004
and the plummet of the *h* of Ahab 2Kin 21:13 1004
buried in the garden of his own *h* 2Kin 21:18 1004
and slew the king in his own *h* 2Kin 21:23 1004
to the *h* of the LORD, saying, 2Kin 22:3 1004
is brought into the *h* of the LORD 2Kin 22:4 1004
oversight of the *h* of the LORD 2Kin 22:5 1004
which is in the *h* of the LORD 2Kin 22:5 1004
to repair the breaches of the *h* 2Kin 22:5 1004
and hewn stone to repair the *h* 2Kin 22:6 1004
of the law in the *h* of the LORD 2Kin 22:8 1004
the money that was found in the *h* 2Kin 22:9 1004
oversight of the *h* of the LORD 2Kin 22:9 1004
went up into the *h* of the LORD 2Kin 23:2 1004
was found in the *h* of the LORD 2Kin 23:2 1004
the grove from the *h* of the LORD 2Kin 23:6 1004
that were by the *h* of the LORD 2Kin 23:7 1004
entering in of the *h* of the LORD 2Kin 23:11 1004
two courts of the *h* of the LORD 2Kin 23:12 1004
priest found in the *h* of the LORD 2Kin 23:24 1004
the *h* of which I said, My name 2Kin 23:27 1004
treasures of the *h* of the LORD 2Kin 24:13 1004
and the treasures of the king's *h* 2Kin 24:13 1004
And he burnt the *h* of the LORD 2Kin 25:9 1004
of the LORD, and the king's *h* 2Kin 25:9 1004
every great man's *h* burnt he with 2Kin 25:9 1004
that were in the *h* of the LORD 2Kin 25:13 1004
sea that was in the *h* of the LORD 2Kin 25:13 1004
had made for the *h* of the LORD 2Kin 25:16 1004
the *h* of Joab, and half of the 1Chr 2:54 5854
the father of the *h* of Rechab 1Chr 2:55 1004
the families of the *h* of them 1Chr 4:21 1004
fine linen, of the *h* of Ashbea, 1Chr 4:21 1004
the *h* of their fathers increased 1Chr 4:38 1004
of the *h* of their fathers were 1Chr 5:13 1004
chief of the *h* of their fathers 1Chr 5:15 1004
heads of the *h* of their fathers 1Chr 5:24 1004
heads of the *h* of their fathers 1Chr 5:24 1004
of song in the *h* of the LORD 1Chr 6:31 1004
the *h* of the LORD in Jerusalem 1Chr 6:32 1004
of the tabernacle of the *h* of God 1Chr 6:48 1004
heads of their father's *h* 1Chr 7:2 1004
after the *h* of their fathers, 1Chr 7:4 1004
heads of the *h* of their fathers, 1Chr 7:7 1004
heads of the *h* of their fathers, 1Chr 7:9 1004
because it went evil with his *h* 1Chr 7:23 1004
Asher, heads of their father's *h* 1Chr 7:40 1004
fathers in the *h* of their fathers 1Chr 9:9 1004
Ahitub, the ruler of the *h* of God 1Chr 9:11 1004
heads of the *h* of their fathers, 1Chr 9:13 1004
of the service of the *h* of God 1Chr 9:13 1004
of the *h* of his father, the 1Chr 9:19 1004
of the gates of the *h* of the LORD 1Chr 9:23 1004
the *h* of the tabernacle, by wards 1Chr 9:23 1004
and treasuries of the *h* of God 1Chr 9:26 1004
lodged round about the *h* of God 1Chr 9:27 1004
sons, and all his *h* died together 1Chr 10:6 1004
his armour in the *h* of their gods 1Chr 10:10 1004
and of his father's *h* twenty 1Chr 12:28 1004
kept the ward of the *h* of Saul 1Chr 12:29 1004
throughout the *h* of their fathers 1Chr 12:30 1004
new cart out of the *h* of Abinadab 1Chr 13:7 1004
the *h* of Obed-edom the Gittite 1Chr 13:13 1004
Obed-edom in his *h* three months 1Chr 13:14 1004
LORD blessed the *h* of Obed-edom 1Chr 13:14 1004
and carpenters, to build him an *h* 1Chr 14:1 1004
of the *h* of Obed-edom with joy 1Chr 15:25 1004
departed every man to his *h* 1Chr 16:43 1004
and David returned to bless his *h* 1Chr 16:43 1004
to pass, as David sat in his *h* 1Chr 17:1 1004
Lo, I dwell in an *h* of cedars 1Chr 17:1 1004
not build me an *h* to dwell in 1Chr 17:4 1004
For I have not dwelt in an *h* 1Chr 17:5 1004
ye not built me an *h* of cedars 1Chr 17:6 1004
the LORD will build thee an *h* 1Chr 17:10 1004
He shall build me an *h*, and I will 1Chr 17:12 1004
But I will settle him in mine *h* 1Chr 17:14 1004
I, O LORD God, and what is mine *h* 1Chr 17:16 1004
h for a great while to come 1Chr 17:17 1004
concerning his *h* be established 1Chr 17:23 1004
let the *h* of David thy servant be 1Chr 17:24 1004
that thou wilt build him an *h* 1Chr 17:25 1004
to bless the *h* of thy servant 1Chr 17:27 1004
be on me, and on my father's *h* 1Chr 21:17 1004
This is the *h* of the LORD God, and 1Chr 22:1 1004
stones to build the *h* of God 1Chr 22:2 1004
the *h* that is to be builded for 1Chr 22:5 1004
charged him to build an *h* for the 1Chr 22:6 1004
an *h* unto the name of the LORD my 1Chr 22:7 1004
shalt not build an *h* unto my name 1Chr 22:8 1004
He shall build an *h* for my name, 1Chr 22:10 1004
build the *h* of the LORD thy God, 1Chr 22:11 1004
h of the LORD an hundred thousand 1Chr 22:14 1004
into the *h* that is to be built to 1Chr 22:19 1004
the work of the *h* of the LORD 1Chr 23:4 1004
according to their father's *h* 1Chr 23:11 1004
Levi after the *h* of their fathers 1Chr 23:24 1004
the service of the *h* of the LORD 1Chr 23:24 1004
the service of the *h* of the LORD 1Chr 23:28 1004
of the service of the *h* of God 1Chr 23:28 1004
the service of the *h* of the LORD 1Chr 23:32 1004
men of the *h* of their fathers 1Chr 24:4 1004
to the *h* of their fathers 1Chr 24:4 1004
and governors of the *h* of God 1Chr 24:5
to come into the *h* of the LORD 1Chr 24:19 1004
after the *h* of their fathers 1Chr 24:30 1004
for song in the *h* of the LORD 1Chr 25:6 1004
for the service of the *h* of God 1Chr 25:6 1004
throughout the *h* of their father 1Chr 26:6 1004
to minister in the *h* of the LORD 1Chr 26:12 1004
to the *h* of their fathers 1Chr 26:13 1004
and to his sons the *h* of Asuppim 1Chr 26:15 1004

Context	Reference	Number
the treasures of the *h* of God	1Chr 26:20	1004
treasures of the *h* of the LORD	1Chr 26:22	1004
to maintain the *h* of the LORD	1Chr 26:27	1004
an *h* of rest for the ark of the	1Chr 28:2	1004
shalt not build an *h* for my name	1Chr 28:3	1004
h of my father to be king over	1Chr 28:4	1004
h of Judah, the *h* of my father	1Chr 28:4	1004
thy son, he shall build my *h*	1Chr 28:6	1004
to build an *h* for the sanctuary	1Chr 28:10	1004
the courts of the *h* of the LORD	1Chr 28:12	1004
of the treasuries of the *h* of God	1Chr 28:12	1004
the service of the *h* of the LORD	1Chr 28:13	1004
of service in the *h* of the LORD	1Chr 28:13	1004
the service of the *h* of the LORD	1Chr 28:20	1004
all the service of the *h* of God	1Chr 28:21	1004
with all my might for the *h* of my	1Chr 29:2	1004
my affection to the *h* of my God	1Chr 29:3	1004
I have given to the *h* of my God	1Chr 29:3	1004
I have prepared for the holy *h*	1Chr 29:3	1004
gave for the service of the *h* of	1Chr 29:7	1004
the treasure of the *h* of the LORD	1Chr 29:8	1004
h for thine holy name cometh of	1Chr 29:16	1004
an *h* for the name of the LORD	2Chr 2:1	1004
the LORD, and an *h* for his kingdom	2Chr 2:1	1004
build him an *h* to dwell therein	2Chr 2:3	1004
I build an *h* to the name of the	2Chr 2:4	1004
the *h* which I build is great	2Chr 2:5	1004
But who is able to build him an *h*	2Chr 2:6	1004
that I should build him an *h*	2Chr 2:6	1004
for the *h* which I am about to	2Chr 2:9	1004
might build an *h* for the LORD	2Chr 2:12	1004
and an *h* for his kingdom	2Chr 2:12	1004
the *h* of the LORD at Jerusalem in	2Chr 3:1	1004
for the building of the *h* of God	2Chr 3:3	1004
that was in the front of the *h*	2Chr 3:4	
according to the breadth of the *h*	2Chr 3:4	1004
the greater *h* he cieled with fir	2Chr 3:5	1004
he garnished the *h* with precious	2Chr 3:6	1004
He overlaid also the *h*, the beams	2Chr 3:7	1004
And he made the most holy *h*	2Chr 3:8	1004
according to the breadth of the *h*	2Chr 3:8	1004
in the most holy *h* he made two	2Chr 3:10	1004
reaching to the wall of the *h*	2Chr 3:11	1004
reaching to the wall of the *h*	2Chr 3:12	1004
the *h* two pillars of thirty	2Chr 3:15	1004
for king Solomon for the *h* of God	2Chr 4:11	1004
the *h* of the LORD of bright brass	2Chr 4:16	1004
that were for the *h* of God	2Chr 4:19	1004
and the entry of the *h*, the inner	2Chr 4:22	1004
the doors of the *h* of the temple	2Chr 4:22	1004
the *h* of the LORD was finished	2Chr 5:1	1004
the treasures of the *h* of God	2Chr 5:1	1004
his place, to the oracle of the *h*	2Chr 5:7	1004
that then the *h* was filled with a	2Chr 5:13	1004
a cloud, even the *h* of the LORD	2Chr 5:13	1004
the LORD had filled the *h* of God	2Chr 5:14	1004
But I have built an *h* of	2Chr 6:2	1004
tribes of Israel to build an *h* in	2Chr 6:5	1004
of David my father to build an *h*	2Chr 6:7	1004
heart to build an *h* for my name	2Chr 6:8	1004
thou shalt not build the *h*	2Chr 6:9	1004
he shall build the *h* for my name	2Chr 6:9	1004
have built the *h* for the name of	2Chr 6:10	1004
less this *h* which I have built	2Chr 6:18	1004
eyes may be open upon this *h* day	2Chr 6:20	1004
come before thine altar in this *h*	2Chr 6:22	1004
before thee in this *h*	2Chr 6:24	1004
spread forth his hands in this *h*	2Chr 6:29	1004
if they come and pray in this *h*	2Chr 6:32	1004
may know that this *h* which I have	2Chr 6:33	1004
the *h* which I have built for thy	2Chr 6:34	1004
toward the *h* which I have built	2Chr 6:38	1004
glory of the LORD filled the *h*	2Chr 7:1	1004
not enter into the *h* of the LORD	2Chr 7:2	1004
the LORD had filled the LORD's *h*	2Chr 7:2	1004
the glory of the LORD upon the *h*	2Chr 7:3	1004
the people dedicated the *h* of God	2Chr 7:5	1004
that was before the *h* of the LORD	2Chr 7:7	1004
finished the *h* of the LORD	2Chr 7:11	1004
of the LORD, and the king's *h*	2Chr 7:11	1004
to make in the *h* of the LORD	2Chr 7:11	1004
of the LORD, and in his own *h*	2Chr 7:11	1004
to myself for an *h* of sacrifice	2Chr 7:12	1004
I chosen and sanctified this *h*	2Chr 7:16	1004
and this *h*, which I have	2Chr 7:20	1004
And this *h*, which is high, shall	2Chr 7:21	1004
unto this land, and unto this *h*	2Chr 7:21	1004
h of the LORD, and his own *h*	2Chr 8:1	1004
the *h* that he had built for her	2Chr 8:11	1004
in the *h* of David king of Israel	2Chr 8:11	1004
foundation of the *h* of the LORD	2Chr 8:16	1004
So the *h* of the LORD was	2Chr 8:16	1004
and the *h* that he had built,	2Chr 9:3	1004
he went up into the *h* of the LORD	2Chr 9:4	1004
terraces to the *h* of the LORD	2Chr 9:11	1004
in the *h* of the forest of Lebanon	2Chr 9:16	1004
all the vessels of the *h* of the	2Chr 9:20	1004
and now, David, see to thine own *h*	2Chr 10:16	1004
the *h* of David unto this day	2Chr 10:19	1004
he gathered of the *h* of Judah	2Chr 11:1	1004
return every man to his *h*	2Chr 11:4	1004
treasures of the *h* of the LORD	2Chr 12:9	1004
and the treasures of the king's *h*	2Chr 12:9	1004
kept the entrance of the king's *h*	2Chr 12:10	1004
entered into the *h* of the LORD	2Chr 12:11	1004
he brought into the *h* of God the	2Chr 15:18	1004
treasures of the *h* of the LORD	2Chr 16:2	1004
of the LORD and of the king's *h*	2Chr 16:2	1004
seer, and put him in a prison *h*	2Chr 16:10	1004
to the *h* of their fathers	2Chr 17:14	1004
every man to his *h* in peace	2Chr 18:16	1004
to his *h* in peace to Jerusalem	2Chr 19:1	1004
the ruler of the *h* of Judah	2Chr 19:11	1004
in the *h* of the LORD, before the	2Chr 20:5	1004
or famine, we stand before this *h*	2Chr 20:9	1004
(for thy name is in this *h*	2Chr 20:9	1004
trumpets unto the *h* of the LORD	2Chr 20:28	1004
Israel, like as did the *h* of Ahab	2Chr 21:6	1004
would not destroy the *h* of David	2Chr 21:7	1004
to the whoredoms of the *h* of Ahab	2Chr 21:13	1004
thy brethren of thy father's *h*	2Chr 21:13	1004
that was found in the king's *h*	2Chr 21:17	1004
in the ways of the *h* of Ahab	2Chr 22:3	1004
of the LORD like the *h* of Ahab	2Chr 22:4	1004
anointed to cut off the *h* of Ahab	2Chr 22:7	1004
judgment upon the *h* of Ahab	2Chr 22:8	1004
So the *h* of Ahaziah had no power	2Chr 22:9	1004
the seed royal of the *h* of Judah	2Chr 22:10	1004
hid in the *h* of God six years	2Chr 22:12	1004
with the king in the *h* of God	2Chr 23:3	1004
part shall be at the king's *h*	2Chr 23:5	1004
the courts of the *h* of the LORD	2Chr 23:5	1004
none come into the *h* of the LORD	2Chr 23:6	1004
whosoever else cometh into the *h*	2Chr 23:7	1004
which were in the *h* of God	2Chr 23:9	1004
the people into the *h* of the LORD	2Chr 23:12	1004
Slay her not in the *h* of the LORD	2Chr 23:14	1004
of the horse gate by the king's *h*	2Chr 23:15	1004
the people went to the *h* of Baal	2Chr 23:17	1004
appointed the offices of the *h* of	2Chr 23:18	1004
distributed in the *h* of the LORD	2Chr 23:18	1004
at the gates of the *h* of the LORD	2Chr 23:19	1004
the king from the *h* of the LORD	2Chr 23:20	1004
the high gate into the king's *h*	2Chr 23:20	1004
to repair the *h* of the LORD	2Chr 24:4	1004
h of your God from year to year	2Chr 24:5	1004
woman, had broken up the *h* of God	2Chr 24:7	1004
the *h* of the LORD did they bestow	2Chr 24:7	1004
at the gate of the *h* of the LORD	2Chr 24:8	1004
the service of the *h* of the LORD	2Chr 24:12	1004
to repair the *h* of the LORD	2Chr 24:12	1004
brass to mend the *h* of the LORD	2Chr 24:12	1004
they set the *h* of God in his	2Chr 24:13	1004
vessels for the *h* of the LORD	2Chr 24:14	1004
offered burnt offerings in the *h*	2Chr 24:14	1004
both toward God, and toward his *h*	2Chr 24:16	1004
they left the *h* of the LORD God	2Chr 24:18	1004
in the court of the *h* of the LORD	2Chr 24:21	1004
and the repairing of the *h* of God	2Chr 24:27	1004
in the *h* of God with Obed-edom	2Chr 25:24	1004
and the treasures of the king's *h*	2Chr 25:24	1004
the priests in the *h* of the LORD	2Chr 26:19	1004
death, and dwelt in a several *h*	2Chr 26:21	1004
cut off from the *h* of the LORD	2Chr 26:21	1004
his son was over the king's *h*	2Chr 26:21	1004
high gate of the *h* of the LORD	2Chr 27:3	1004
and Azrikam the governor of the *h*	2Chr 28:7	1004
portion out of the *h* of the LORD	2Chr 28:21	1004
out of the *h* of the king, and of	2Chr 28:21	1004
the vessels of the *h* of God	2Chr 28:24	1004
the vessels of the *h* of God	2Chr 28:24	1004
up the doors of the *h* of the LORD	2Chr 28:24	1004
the doors of the *h* of the LORD	2Chr 29:3	1004
sanctify the *h* of the LORD God of	2Chr 29:5	1004
to cleanse the *h* of the LORD	2Chr 29:15	1004
inner part of the *h* of the LORD	2Chr 29:16	1004
the court of the *h* of the LORD	2Chr 29:16	1004
so they sanctified the *h* of the	2Chr 29:17	1004
cleansed all the *h* of the LORD	2Chr 29:18	1004
and went up to the *h* of the LORD	2Chr 29:20	1004
in the *h* of the LORD with cymbals	2Chr 29:25	1004
offerings into the *h* of the LORD	2Chr 29:31	1004
So the service of the *h* of the	2Chr 29:35	1004
to the *h* of the LORD at Jerusalem	2Chr 30:1	1004
offerings into the *h* of the LORD	2Chr 30:15	1004
of the *h* of Zadok answered him	2Chr 31:10	1004
offerings into the *h* of the LORD	2Chr 31:10	1004
chambers in the *h* of the LORD	2Chr 31:11	1004
Azariah the ruler of the *h* of God	2Chr 31:13	1004
entereth into the *h* of the LORD	2Chr 31:16	1004
priests by the *h* of their fathers	2Chr 31:17	1004
in the service of the *h* of God	2Chr 31:21	1004
he was come into the *h* of his god	2Chr 32:21	1004
built altars in the *h* of the LORD	2Chr 33:4	1004
two courts of the *h* of the LORD	2Chr 33:5	1004
he had made, in the *h* of God	2Chr 33:7	1004
and to Solomon his son, In this *h*	2Chr 33:7	1004
the idol out of the *h* of the LORD	2Chr 33:15	1004
in the mount of the *h* of the LORD	2Chr 33:15	1004
and they buried him in his own *h*	2Chr 33:20	1004
him, and slew him in his own *h*	2Chr 33:24	1004
he had purged the land, and the *h*	2Chr 34:8	1004
to repair the *h* of the LORD his	2Chr 34:8	1004
was brought into the *h* of God	2Chr 34:9	1004
oversight of the *h* of the LORD	2Chr 34:10	1004
that wrought in the *h* of the LORD	2Chr 34:10	1004
LORD, to repair and amend the *h*	2Chr 34:10	1004
brought into the *h* of the LORD	2Chr 34:14	1004
of the law in the *h* of the LORD	2Chr 34:15	1004
was found in the *h* of the LORD	2Chr 34:17	1004
went up into the *h* of the LORD	2Chr 34:30	1004
was found in the *h* of the LORD	2Chr 34:30	1004
the service of the *h* of the LORD	2Chr 35:2	1004
Put the holy ark in the *h* which	2Chr 35:3	1004
and Jehiel, rulers of the *h* of God	2Chr 35:8	1004
but against the *h* wherewith I	2Chr 35:21	1004
of the *h* of the LORD to Babylon	2Chr 36:7	1004
vessels of the *h* of the LORD	2Chr 36:10	1004
polluted the *h* of the LORD which	2Chr 36:14	1004
sword in the *h* of their sanctuary	2Chr 36:17	1004
all the vessels of the *h* of God	2Chr 36:18	1004
treasures of the *h* of the LORD	2Chr 36:18	1004
And they burnt the *h* of God	2Chr 36:19	1004
me to build him an *h* in Jerusalem	2Chr 36:23	1004
me to build him an *h* at Jerusalem	Ezr 1:2	1004
build the *h* of the LORD God of	Ezr 1:3	1004
the *h* of God that is in Jerusalem	Ezr 1:4	1004
to go up to build the *h* of the	Ezr 1:5	1004
the vessels of the *h* of the LORD	Ezr 1:7	1004
had put them in the *h* of his gods	Ezr 1:7	1004
of the *h* of Jeshua, nine hundred	Ezr 2:36	1004
could not shew their father's *h*	Ezr 2:59	1004
when they came to the *h* of the	Ezr 2:68	1004
offered freely for the *h* of God	Ezr 2:68	1004
unto the *h* of God at Jerusalem	Ezr 3:8	1004
the work of the *h* of the LORD	Ezr 3:8	1004
the workmen in the *h* of God	Ezr 3:9	1004
of the *h* of the LORD was laid	Ezr 3:11	1004
men, that had seen the first *h*	Ezr 3:12	1004
this *h* was laid before their eyes	Ezr 3:12	1004
us to build an *h* unto our God	Ezr 4:3	1004
Then ceased the work of the *h* of	Ezr 4:24	1005
began to build the *h* of God which	Ezr 5:2	1005
commanded you to build this *h*	Ezr 5:3	1005
to the *h* of the great God, which	Ezr 5:8	1005
Who commanded you to build this *h*	Ezr 5:9	1005
build the *h* that was builded	Ezr 5:11	1005
Chaldean, who destroyed this *h*	Ezr 5:12	1005
a decree to build this *h* of God	Ezr 5:13	1005
of gold and silver of the *h* of God	Ezr 5:14	1005
let the *h* of God be builded in	Ezr 5:15	1005
laid the foundation of the *h* of	Ezr 5:16	1005
made in the king's treasure *h*	Ezr 5:17	1005
build this *h* of God at Jerusalem	Ezr 5:17	1005
was made in the *h* of the rolls	Ezr 6:1	1005
the *h* of God at Jerusalem	Ezr 6:3	1005
Let the *h* be builded, the place	Ezr 6:3	1005
be given out of the king's *h*	Ezr 6:4	1004
and silver vessels of the *h* of God	Ezr 6:5	1005
and place them in the *h* of God	Ezr 6:5	1005
the work of this *h* of God alone	Ezr 6:7	1005
build this *h* of God in his place	Ezr 6:7	1005
for the building of this *h* of God	Ezr 6:8	1005
timber be pulled down from his *h*	Ezr 6:11	1005
let his *h* be made a dunghill for	Ezr 6:11	1005
to destroy this *h* of God which is	Ezr 6:12	1005
this *h* was finished on the third	Ezr 6:15	1005
of this *h* of God with joy	Ezr 6:16	1005
at the dedication of this *h* of	Ezr 6:17	1005
hands in the work of the *h* of God	Ezr 6:22	1004
the *h* of their God which is in	Ezr 7:16	1005
of the *h* of your God which is in	Ezr 7:17	1005
the service of the *h* of thy God	Ezr 7:19	1005
be needful for the *h* of thy God	Ezr 7:20	1005
it out of the king's treasure *h*	Ezr 7:20	1005
for the *h* of the God of heaven	Ezr 7:23	1005
or ministers of this *h* of God	Ezr 7:24	1005
to beautify the *h* of the LORD	Ezr 7:27	1004
us ministers for the *h* of our God	Ezr 8:17	1004
the offering of the *h* of our God	Ezr 8:25	1004
the chambers of the *h* of the LORD	Ezr 8:29	1004
Jerusalem unto the *h* of our God	Ezr 8:30	1004
the *h* of our God by the hand of	Ezr 8:33	1004
the people, and the *h* of God	Ezr 8:36	1004
to set up the *h* of our God	Ezr 9:9	1004
himself down before the *h* of God	Ezr 10:1	1004
rose up from before the *h* of God	Ezr 10:6	1004
sat in the street of the *h* of God	Ezr 10:9	1004
after the *h* of their fathers, and	Ezr 10:16	1004
I and my father's *h* have sinned	Neh 1:6	1004
palace which appertained to the *h*	Neh 2:8	1004
for the *h* that I shall enter into	Neh 2:8	1004
Harumaph, even over against his *h*	Neh 3:10	1004
made, and unto the *h* of the mighty	Neh 3:16	1004
the *h* of Eliashib the high priest	Neh 3:20	1004
from the door of the *h* of	Neh 3:21	1004
to the end of the *h* of Eliashib	Neh 3:21	1004
and Hashub over against their *h*	Neh 3:23	1004
the son of Ananiah by his *h*	Neh 3:23	1004
from the *h* of Azariah unto the	Neh 3:24	1004
lieth out from the king's high *h*	Neh 3:25	1004
every one over against his *h*	Neh 3:28	1004
son of Immer over against his *h*	Neh 3:29	1004
were behind all the *h* of Judah	Neh 4:16	1004
shake out every man from his *h*	Neh 5:13	1004
Afterward I came unto the *h* of	Neh 6:10	1004
us meet together in the *h* of God	Neh 6:10	1004
one to be over against his *h*	Neh 7:3	1004
of the *h* of Jeshua, nine hundred	Neh 7:39	1004
could not shew their father's *h*	Neh 7:61	1004
every one upon the roof of his *h*	Neh 8:16	1004
and in the courts of the *h* of God	Neh 8:16	1004
the service of the *h* of our God	Neh 10:32	1004
all the work of the *h* of our God	Neh 10:33	1004
to bring it into the *h* of our God	Neh 10:34	1004
by year, unto the *h* of the LORD	Neh 10:35	1004
to bring to the *h* of our God	Neh 10:36	1004
that minister in the *h* of our God	Neh 10:36	1004
the chambers of the *h* of our God	Neh 10:37	1004
the tithes unto the *h* of our God	Neh 10:38	1004
the chambers, into the treasure *h*	Neh 10:38	1004
will not forsake the *h* of our God	Neh 10:39	1004
was the ruler of the *h* of God	Neh 11:11	1004
that did the work of the *h* were	Neh 11:12	1004
outward business of the *h* of God	Neh 11:16	1004
over the business of the *h* of God	Neh 11:22	1004
Also from the *h* of Gilgal	Neh 12:29	1004
of the wall, above the *h* of David	Neh 12:37	1004
that gave thanks in the *h* of God	Neh 12:40	1004
the chamber of the *h* of our God	Neh 13:4	1004
in the courts of the *h* of God	Neh 13:7	1004
again the vessels of the *h* of God	Neh 13:9	1004
Why is the *h* of God forsaken	Neh 13:11	1004
I have done for the *h* of my God	Neh 13:14	1004
to all the officers of his *h*	Est 1:8	1004
royal *h* which belonged to king	Est 1:9	1004
man should bear rule in his own *h*	Est 1:22	1004
to the *h* of the women, unto the	Est 2:3	1004
brought also unto the king's *h*	Est 2:8	1004
be given her, out of the king's *h*	Est 2:9	1004
best place of the *h* of the women	Est 2:9	1004
before the court of the women's *h*	Est 2:11	1004

h of the women unto the king's	Est 2:13	1004
of the women unto the king's *h*	Est 2:13	1004
into the second *h* of the women	Est 2:14	1004
his *h* royal in the tenth month	Est 2:16	1004
thou shalt escape in the king's *h*	Est 4:13	1004
thy father's *h* shall be destroyed	Est 4:14	1004
the inner court of the king's *h*	Est 5:1	1004
h, over against the king's *h*	Est 5:1	1004
his royal throne in the royal *h*	Est 5:1	1004
over against the gate of the *h*	Est 5:1	1004
the outward court of the king's *h*	Est 6:4	1004
Haman hasted to his *h* mourning	Est 6:12	1004
the queen also before me in the *h*	Est 7:8	1004
king, standeth in the *h* of Haman	Est 7:9	1004
h of Haman the Jews' enemy unto	Est 8:1	1004
set Mordecai over the *h* of Haman	Est 8:2	1004
have given Esther the *h* of Haman	Est 8:7	1004
was great in the king's *h*	Est 9:4	1004
hedge about him, and about his *h*	Job 1:10	1004
wine in their eldest brother's *h*	Job 1:13	1004
wine in their eldest brother's *h*	Job 1:18	1004
smote the four corners of the *h*	Job 1:19	1004
He shall return no more to his *h*	Job 7:10	1004
He shall lean upon his *h*, but it	Job 8:15	1004
If I wait, the grave is mine *h*	Job 17:13	1004
They that dwell in mine *h*	Job 19:15	1004
away an *h* which he builded not	Job 20:19	1004
increase of his *h* shall depart	Job 20:28	1004
hath he in his *h* after him	Job 21:21	1004
Where is the *h* of the prince	Job 21:28	1004
He buildeth his *h* as a moth	Job 27:18	1004
to the *h* appointed for all living	Job 30:23	1004
know the paths to the *h* thereof	Job 38:20	1004
Whose *h* I have made the	Job 39:6	1004
did eat bread with him in his *h*	Job 42:11	1004
I will come into thy *h* in the	Ps 5:7	1004
I will dwell in the *h* of the LORD	Ps 23:6	1004
loved the habitation of thy *h*	Ps 26:8	1004
that I may dwell in the *h* of the	Ps 27:4	1004
the dedication of the *h* of David	Ps 30:*t*	1004
for an *h* of defence to save me	Ps 31:2	1004
with the fatness of thy *h*	Ps 36:8	1004
I went with them to the *h* of God	Ps 42:4	1004
own people, and thy father's *h*	Ps 45:10	1004
the glory of his *h* is increased	Ps 49:16	1004
will take no bullock out of thy *h*	Ps 50:9	1004
is come to the *h* of Ahimelech	Ps 52:*t*	1004
green olive tree in the *h* of God	Ps 52:8	1004
walked unto the *h* of God in	Ps 55:14	1004
and they watched the *h* to kill him	Ps 59:*t*	1004
with the goodness of thy *h*	Ps 65:4	1004
I will go into thy *h* with burnt	Ps 66:13	1004
zeal of thine *h* hath eaten me up	Ps 69:9	1004
Yea, the sparrow hath found an *h*	Ps 84:3	1004
are they that dwell in thy *h*	Ps 84:4	1004
a doorkeeper in the *h* of my God	Ps 84:10	1004
Those that be planted in the *h* of	Ps 92:13	1004
holiness becometh thine *h*	Ps 93:5	1004
his truth toward the *h* of Israel	Ps 98:3	1004
within my *h* with a perfect heart	Ps 101:2	1004
shall not dwell within my *h*	Ps 101:7	1004
as a sparrow alone upon the *h* top	Ps 102:7	
stork, the fir trees are her *h*	Ps 104:17	1004
He made him lord of his *h*	Ps 105:21	1004
and riches shall be in his *h*	Ps 112:3	1004
maketh the barren woman to keep *h*	Ps 113:9	1004
the *h* of Jacob from a people of	Ps 114:1	1004
O *h* of Aaron, trust in the LORD	Ps 115:10	1004
he will bless the *h* of Israel	Ps 115:12	1004
he will bless the *h* of Aaron	Ps 115:12	1004
In the courts of the LORD's *h*	Ps 116:19	1004
Let the *h* of Aaron now say, that	Ps 118:3	1004
you out of the *h* of the LORD	Ps 118:26	1004
songs in the *h* of my pilgrimage	Ps 119:54	1004
Let us go into the *h* of the LORD	Ps 122:1	1004
the thrones of the *h* of David	Ps 122:5	1004
Because of the *h* of the LORD our	Ps 122:9	1004
Except the LORD build the *h*	Ps 127:1	1004
vine by the sides of thine *h*	Ps 128:3	1004
come into the tabernacle of my *h*	Ps 132:3	1004
night stand in the *h* of the LORD	Ps 134:1	1004
that stand in the *h* of the LORD	Ps 135:2	1004
in the courts of the *h* of our God	Ps 135:2	1004
Bless the LORD, O *h* of Israel	Ps 135:19	1004
bless the LORD, O *h* of Aaron	Ps 135:19	1004
Bless the LORD, O *h* of Levi	Ps 135:20	1004
For her *h* inclineth unto death,	Prov 2:18	1004
LORD is in the *h* of the wicked	Prov 3:33	1004
come not nigh the door of her *h*	Prov 5:8	1004
labours be in the *h* of a stranger	Prov 5:10	1004
give all the substance of his *h*	Prov 6:31	1004
For at the window of my *h* I	Prov 7:6	1004
and he went the way to her *h*	Prov 7:8	1004
her feet abide not in her *h*	Prov 7:11	1004
Her *h* is the way to hell, going	Prov 7:27	1004
Wisdom hath builded her *h*	Prov 9:1	1004
she sitteth at the door of her *h*	Prov 9:14	1004
his own *h* shall inherit the wind	Prov 11:29	1004
but the *h* of the righteous shall	Prov 12:7	1004
Every wise woman buildeth her *h*	Prov 14:1	1004
The *h* of the wicked shall be	Prov 14:11	1004
In the *h* of the righteous is much	Prov 15:6	1004
will destroy the *h* of the proud	Prov 15:25	1004
of gain troubleth his own *h*	Prov 15:27	1004
than an *h* full of sacrifices with	Prov 17:1	1004
evil shall not depart from his *h*	Prov 17:13	1004
H and riches are the inheritance	Prov 19:14	1004
a brawling woman and in a wide *h*	Prov 21:9	1004
considereth the *h* of the wicked	Prov 21:12	1004
Through wisdom is an *h* builded	Prov 24:3	1004
and afterwards build thine *h*	Prov 24:27	1004
thy foot from thy neighbour's *h*	Prov 25:17	1004
a brawling woman and in a wide *h*	Prov 25:24	1004
h in the day of thy calamity	Prov 27:10	1004
and had servants born in my *h*	Eccl 2:7	1004
when thou goest to the *h* of God	Eccl 5:1	1004
better to go to the *h* of mourning	Eccl 7:2	1004
than to go to the *h* of feasting	Eccl 7:2	1004
the wise is in the *h* of mourning	Eccl 7:4	1004
of fools is in the *h* of mirth	Eccl 7:4	1004
the hands the *h* droppeth through	Eccl 10:18	1004
keepers of the *h* shall tremble	Eccl 12:3	1004
The beams of our *h* are cedar	Song 1:17	1004
He brought me to the banqueting *h*	Song 2:4	1004
brought him into my mother's *h*	Song 3:4	1004
and bring thee into my mother's *h*	Song 8:2	1004
the substance of his *h* for love	Song 8:7	1004
h shall be established in the top	Is 2:2	1004
to the *h* of the God of Jacob	Is 2:3	1004
O *h* of Jacob, come ye, and let us	Is 2:5	1004
thy people the *h* of Jacob	Is 2:6	1004
brother of the *h* of his father	Is 3:6	1004
for in my *h* is neither bread nor	Is 3:7	1004
LORD of hosts is the *h* of Israel	Is 5:7	1004
unto them that join *h* to *h*	Is 5:8	1004
the *h* was filled with smoke	Is 6:4	1004
And it was told the *h* of David	Is 7:2	1004
said, Hear ye now, O *h* of David	Is 7:13	1004
people, and upon thy father's *h*	Is 7:17	1004
his face from the *h* of Jacob	Is 8:17	1004
as are escaped of the *h* of Jacob	Is 10:20	1004
shall cleave to the *h* of Jacob	Is 14:1	1004
the *h* of Israel shall possess	Is 14:2	1004
opened not the *h* of his prisoners	Is 14:17	1004
in glory, every one in his own *h*	Is 14:18	1004
the armour of the *h* of the forest	Is 22:8	1004
unto Shebna, which is over the *h*	Is 22:15	1004
be the shame of thy lord's *h*	Is 22:18	1004
Jerusalem, and to the *h* of Judah	Is 22:21	1004
the key of the *h* of David will I	Is 22:22	1004
glorious throne to his father's *h*	Is 22:23	1004
all the glory of his father's *h*	Is 22:24	1004
laid waste, so that there is no *h*	Is 23:1	1004
every *h* is shut up, that no man	Is 24:10	1004
concerning the *h* of Jacob	Is 29:22	1004
against the *h* of the evildoers	Is 31:2	1004
son, which was over the *h*	Is 36:3	1004
and went into the *h* of the LORD	Is 37:1	1004
went up unto the *h* of the LORD	Is 37:14	1004
h of Judah shall again take root	Is 37:31	1004
in the *h* of Nisroch his god	Is 37:38	1004
the LORD, Set thine *h* in order	Is 38:1	1004
of our life in the *h* of the LORD	Is 38:20	1004
shall go up to the *h* of the LORD	Is 38:22	1004
shewed them the *h* of his precious	Is 39:2	1004
all the *h* of his armour, and all	Is 39:2	1004
there was nothing in his *h*	Is 39:2	1004
What have they seen in thine *h*	Is 39:4	1004
that is in mine *h* have they seen	Is 39:4	1004
come, that all that is in thine *h*	Is 39:6	1004
in darkness out of the prison *h*	Is 42:7	1004
that it may remain in the *h*	Is 44:13	1004
O *h* of Jacob, and all the remnant	Is 46:3	1004
the remnant of the *h* of Israel	Is 46:3	1004
O *h* of Jacob, which are called by	Is 48:1	1004
unto them will I give in mine *h*	Is 56:5	1004
them joyful in my *h* of prayer	Is 56:7	1004
for mine *h* shall be called an	Is 56:7	1004
an *h* of prayer for all people	Is 56:7	1004
the *h* of Jacob their sins	Is 58:1	1004
poor that are cast out to thy *h*	Is 58:7	1004
I will glorify the *h* of my glory	Is 60:7	1004
goodness toward the *h* of Israel	Is 63:7	1004
Our holy and our beautiful *h*	Is 64:11	1004
where is the *h* that ye build unto	Is 66:1	1004
vessel into the *h* of the LORD	Is 66:20	1004
O *h* of Jacob, and all the families	Jer 2:4	1004
the families of the *h* of Israel	Jer 2:4	1004
so is the *h* of Israel ashamed	Jer 2:26	1004
In those days the *h* of Judah	Jer 3:18	1004
shall walk with the *h* of Israel	Jer 3:18	1004
O *h* of Israel, saith the LORD	Jer 3:20	1004
h of Israel and the *h* of Judah	Jer 5:11	1004
O *h* of Israel, saith the LORD	Jer 5:15	1004
Declare this in the *h* of Jacob	Jer 5:20	1004
Stand in the gate of the LORD's *h*	Jer 7:2	1004
come and stand before me in this *h*	Jer 7:10	1004
Is this *h*, which is called by my	Jer 7:11	1004
Therefore will I do unto this *h*	Jer 7:14	1004
the *h* which is called by my name	Jer 7:30	1004
and all the *h* of Israel are	Jer 9:26	1004
speaketh unto you, O *h* of Israel	Jer 10:1	1004
h of Israel and the *h* of Judah	Jer 11:10	1004
hath my beloved to do in mine *h*	Jer 11:15	1004
for the evil of the *h* of Israel	Jer 11:17	1004
of the *h* of Judah, which they	Jer 11:17	1004
the *h* of thy father, even they	Jer 12:6	1004
I have forsaken mine *h*, I have	Jer 12:7	1004
pluck out the *h* of Judah from	Jer 12:14	1004
unto me the whole *h* of Israel	Jer 13:11	1004
of Israel and the whole *h* of Judah	Jer 13:11	1004
Enter not into the *h* of mourning	Jer 16:5	1004
also go into the *h* of feasting	Jer 16:8	1004
of praise, unto the *h* of the LORD	Jer 17:26	1004
and go down to the potter's *h*	Jer 18:2	1004
I went down to the potter's *h*	Jer 18:3	1004
O *h* of Israel, cannot I do with	Jer 18:6	1004
ye in mine hand, O *h* of Israel	Jer 18:6	1004
in the court of the LORD's *h*	Jer 19:14	1004
governor in the *h* of the LORD	Jer 20:1	1004
which was by the *h* of the LORD	Jer 20:2	1004
thine *h* shall go into captivity	Jer 20:6	1004
touching the *h* of the king of	Jer 21:11	1004
O *h* of David, thus saith the LORD	Jer 21:12	1004
Go down to the *h* of the king of	Jer 22:1	1004
h kings sitting upon the throne	Jer 22:4	1004
that this *h* shall become a	Jer 22:5	1004
LORD unto the king's *h* of Judah	Jer 22:6	1004
buildeth his *h* by unrighteousness	Jer 22:13	1004
saith, I will build me a wide *h*	Jer 22:14	1004
which led the seed of the *h* of	Jer 23:8	1004
in my *h* have I found their	Jer 23:11	1004
even punish that man and his *h*	Jer 23:34	1004
in the court of the LORD's *h*	Jer 26:2	1004
come to worship in the LORD's *h*	Jer 26:2	1004
will I make this *h* like Shiloh	Jer 26:6	1004
these words in the *h* of the LORD	Jer 26:7	1004
This *h* shall be like Shiloh, and	Jer 26:9	1004
Jeremiah in the *h* of the LORD	Jer 26:9	1004
h unto the *h* of the LORD	Jer 26:10	1004
of the new gate of the LORD's *h*	Jer 26:10	
me to prophesy against this *h*	Jer 26:12	1004
the mountain of the *h* as the high	Jer 26:18	1004
the vessels of the LORD's *h* shall	Jer 27:16	1004
are left in the *h* of the LORD	Jer 27:18	1004
in the *h* of the king of Judah, and	Jer 27:18	1004
that remain in the *h* of the LORD	Jer 27:21	1004
in the *h* of the king of Judah and	Jer 27:21	1004
unto me in the *h* of the LORD	Jer 28:1	1004
all the vessels of the LORD's *h*	Jer 28:3	1004
that stood in the *h* of the LORD	Jer 28:5	1004
again the vessels of the LORD's *h*	Jer 28:6	1004
be officers in the *h* of the LORD	Jer 29:26	1004
that I will sow the *h* of Israel	Jer 31:27	1004
the *h* of Judah with the seed of	Jer 31:27	1004
new covenant with the *h* of Israel	Jer 31:31	1004
and with the *h* of Judah	Jer 31:31	1004
I will make with the *h* of Israel	Jer 31:33	1004
was in the king of Judah's *h*	Jer 32:2	1004
set their abominations in the *h*	Jer 32:34	1004
of praise into the *h* of the LORD	Jer 33:11	1004
promised unto the *h* of Israel	Jer 33:14	1004
of Israel and to the *h* of Judah	Jer 33:14	1004
the throne of the *h* of Israel	Jer 33:17	1004
of Egypt, out of the *h* of bondmen	Jer 34:13	1004
the *h* which is called by my name	Jer 34:15	1004
Go unto the *h* of the Rechabites,	Jer 35:2	1004
bring them into the *h* of the LORD	Jer 35:2	1004
the whole *h* of the Rechabites	Jer 35:3	1004
them into the *h* of the LORD	Jer 35:4	1004
I set before the sons of the *h* of	Jer 35:5	1004
Neither shall ye build *h*, nor sow	Jer 35:7	1004
said unto the *h* of the Rechabites	Jer 35:18	1004
It may be that the *h* of Judah	Jer 36:3	1004
cannot go into the *h* of the LORD	Jer 36:5	1004
the LORD's *h* upon the fasting day	Jer 36:6	1004
words of the LORD in the LORD's *h*	Jer 36:8	1004
of Jeremiah in the *h* of the LORD	Jer 36:10	1004
of the new gate of the LORD's *h*	Jer 36:10	1004
he went down into the king's *h*	Jer 36:12	1004
in the *h* of Jonathan the scribe	Jer 37:15	1004
king asked him secretly in his *h*	Jer 37:17	1004
to the *h* of Jonathan the scribe	Jer 37:20	1004
eunuchs which was in the king's *h*	Jer 38:7	1004
went forth out of the king's *h*	Jer 38:8	1004
went into the *h* of the king under	Jer 38:11	1004
that is in the *h* of the LORD	Jer 38:14	1004
and thou shalt live, and thine *h*	Jer 38:17	1004
h shall be brought forth to the	Jer 38:22	1004
me to return to Jonathan's *h*	Jer 38:26	1004
the Chaldeans burned the king's *h*	Jer 39:8	1004
bring them to the *h* of the LORD	Jer 41:5	1004
entry of Pharaoh's *h* in Tahpanhes	Jer 43:9	1004
as the *h* of Israel was ashamed of	Jer 48:13	1004
the sanctuaries of the LORD's *h*	Jer 51:51	1004
h of the LORD, and the king's *h*	Jer 52:13	1004
that were in the *h* of the LORD	Jer 52:17	1004
sea that was in the *h* of the LORD	Jer 52:17	1004
had made in the *h* of the LORD	Jer 52:20	1004
made a noise in the *h* of the LORD	Lam 2:7	1004
(for they are a rebellious *h*	Eze 2:5	1004
though they be a rebellious *h*	Eze 2:6	
rebellious like that rebellious *h*	Eze 2:8	1004
and go speak unto the *h* of Israel	Eze 3:1	1004
go, get thee unto the *h* of Israel	Eze 3:4	1004
language, but to the *h* of Israel	Eze 3:5	1004
But the *h* of Israel will not	Eze 3:7	1004
for all the *h* of Israel are	Eze 3:7	1004
though they be a rebellious *h*	Eze 3:9	1004
a watchman unto the *h* of Israel	Eze 3:17	1004
Go, shut thyself within thine *h*	Eze 3:24	1004
for they are a rebellious *h*	Eze 3:26	1004
for they are a rebellious *h*	Eze 3:27	1004
be a sign to the *h* of Israel	Eze 4:3	1004
of the *h* of Israel upon it	Eze 4:4	1004
the iniquity of the *h* of Israel	Eze 4:5	1004
of the *h* of Judah forty days	Eze 4:6	1004
forth into all the *h* of Israel	Eze 5:4	1004
abominations of the *h* of Israel	Eze 6:11	1004
of the month, as I sat in mine *h*	Eze 8:1	1004
the *h* of Israel committeth here	Eze 8:6	1004
all the idols of the *h* of Israel	Eze 8:10	1004
the ancients of the *h* of Israel	Eze 8:11	1004
of the *h* of Israel do in the dark	Eze 8:12	1004
h which was toward the north	Eze 8:14	1004
the inner court of the LORD's *h*	Eze 8:16	1004
Is it a light thing to the *h* of	Eze 8:17	1004
he was, to the threshold of the *h*	Eze 9:3	1004
men which were before the *h*	Eze 9:6	1004
he said unto them, Defile the *h*	Eze 9:7	1004
The iniquity of the *h* of Israel	Eze 9:9	1004
stood on the right side of the *h*	Eze 10:3	1004
stood over the threshold of the *h*	Eze 10:4	1004
the *h* was filled with the cloud,	Eze 10:4	1004
from off the threshold of the *h*	Eze 10:18	1004
of the east gate of the LORD's *h*	Eze 10:19	1004
the east gate of the LORD's *h*	Eze 11:1	1004
Thus have ye said, O *h* of Israel	Eze 11:5	1004
all the *h* of Israel wholly, are	Eze 11:15	1004
in the midst of a rebellious *h*	Eze 12:2	1004
for they are a rebellious *h*	Eze 12:2	1004
though they be a rebellious *h*	Eze 12:3	1004

for a sign unto the *h* of Israel	Eze 12:6	1004
h of Israel, the rebellious *h*	Eze 12:9	1004
all the *h* of Israel that are	Eze 12:10	1004
divination within the *h* of Israel	Eze 12:24	1004
for in your days, O rebellious *h*	Eze 12:25	1004
they of the *h* of Israel say, The	Eze 12:27	1004
the *h* of Israel to stand in the	Eze 13:5	1004
in the writing of the *h* of Israel	Eze 13:9	1004
Every man of the *h* of Israel that	Eze 14:4	1004
That I may take the *h* of Israel	Eze 14:5	1004
say unto the *h* of Israel, Thus	Eze 14:6	1004
For every one of the *h* of Israel	Eze 14:7	1004
That the *h* of Israel may go no	Eze 14:11	1004
a parable unto the *h* of Israel	Eze 17:2	1004
Say now to the rebellious *h*	Eze 17:12	1004
to the idols of the *h* of Israel	Eze 18:6	1004
to the idols of the *h* of Israel	Eze 18:15	1004
Hear now, O *h* of Israel	Eze 18:25	1004
Yet saith the *h* of Israel	Eze 18:29	1004
O *h* of Israel, are not my ways	Eze 18:29	1004
you, O *h* of Israel, every one	Eze 18:30	1004
why will ye die, O *h* of Israel	Eze 18:31	1004
unto the seed of the *h* of Jacob	Eze 20:5	1004
But the *h* of Israel rebelled	Eze 20:13	1004
man, speak unto the *h* of Israel	Eze 20:27	1004
say unto the *h* of Israel, Thus	Eze 20:30	1004
enquired of by you, O *h* of Israel	Eze 20:31	1004
O *h* of Israel, thus saith the	Eze 20:39	1004
there shall all the *h* of Israel	Eze 20:40	1004
O ye *h* of Israel, saith the Lord	Eze 20:44	1004
the *h* of Israel is to me become	Eze 22:18	1004
they done in the midst of mine *h*	Eze 23:39	1004
a parable unto the rebellious *h*	Eze 24:3	1004
Speak unto the *h* of Israel	Eze 24:21	1004
and against the *h* of Judah	Eze 25:3	1004
the *h* of Judah is like unto all	Eze 25:8	1004
Edom hath dealt against the *h* of	Eze 25:12	1004
They of the *h* of Togarmah traded	Eze 27:14	1004
brier unto the *h* of Israel	Eze 28:24	1004
When I shall have gathered the *h*	Eze 28:25	1004
staff of reed to the *h* of Israel	Eze 29:6	1004
the confidence of the *h* of Israel	Eze 29:16	1004
of the *h* of Israel to bud forth	Eze 29:21	1004
a watchman unto the *h* of Israel	Eze 33:7	1004
man, speak unto the *h* of Israel	Eze 33:10	1004
why will ye die, O *h* of Israel	Eze 33:11	1004
O ye *h* of Israel, I will judge	Eze 33:20	1004
even the *h* of Israel, are my	Eze 34:30	1004
inheritance of the *h* of Israel	Eze 35:15	1004
all the *h* of Israel, even all of	Eze 36:10	1004
when the *h* of Israel dwelt in	Eze 36:17	1004
which the *h* of Israel had	Eze 36:21	1004
say unto the *h* of Israel, Thus	Eze 36:22	1004
O *h* of Israel, but for mine holy	Eze 36:22	1004
for your own ways, O *h* of Israel	Eze 36:32	1004
be enquired of by the *h* of Israel	Eze 36:37	1004
bones are the whole *h* of Israel	Eze 37:11	1004
for all the *h* of Israel his	Eze 37:16	1004
the *h* of Togarmah of the north	Eze 38:6	1004
seven months shall the *h* of	Eze 39:12	1004
So the *h* of Israel shall know	Eze 39:22	1004
h of Israel went into captivity	Eze 39:23	1004
mercy upon the whole *h* of Israel	Eze 39:25	1004
my spirit upon the *h* of Israel	Eze 39:29	1004
thou seest to the *h* of Israel	Eze 40:4	1004
the outside of the *h* round about	Eze 40:5	1004
keepers of the charge of the *h*	Eze 40:45	1004
the altar that was before the *h*	Eze 40:47	1004
brought me to the porch of the *h*	Eze 40:48	1004
he measured the wall of the *h*	Eze 41:5	1004
round about the *h* on every side	Eze 41:5	1004
the *h* for the side chambers round	Eze 41:6	1004
had not hold in the wall of the *h*	Eze 41:6	1004
for the winding about of the *h*	Eze 41:7	1004
still upward round about the *h*	Eze 41:7	1004
breadth of the *h* was still upward	Eze 41:7	1004
the height of the *h* round about	Eze 41:8	1004
round about the *h* on every side	Eze 41:10	1004
So he measured the *h*, an hundred	Eze 41:13	1004
the breadth of the face of the *h*	Eze 41:14	1004
the door, even unto the inner *h*	Eze 41:17	1004
through all the *h* round about	Eze 41:19	1004
upon the side chambers of the *h*	Eze 41:26	1004
an end of measuring the inner *h*	Eze 42:15	1004
h by the way of the gate whose	Eze 43:4	1004
glory of the LORD filled the *h*	Eze 43:5	1004
him speaking unto me out of the *h*	Eze 43:6	1004
shall the *h* of Israel no more	Eze 43:7	1004
shew the *h* to the *h* of Israel	Eze 43:10	1004
done, shew them the form of the *h*	Eze 43:11	1004
This is the law of the *h*	Eze 43:12	1004
Behold, this is the law of the *h*	Eze 43:12	1004
in the appointed place of the *h*	Eze 43:21	1004
of the north gate before the *h*	Eze 44:4	1004
the LORD filled the *h* of the LORD	Eze 44:4	1004
ordinances of the *h* of the LORD	Eze 44:5	1004
well the entering in of the *h*	Eze 44:5	1004
even to the *h* of Israel, Thus	Eze 44:6	1004
O ye *h* of Israel, let it suffice	Eze 44:6	1004
to pollute it, even my *h*	Eze 44:7	1004
charge at the gates of the *h*	Eze 44:11	1004
h, and ministering to the *h*	Eze 44:11	1004
caused the *h* of Israel to fall	Eze 44:12	1004
keepers of the charge of the *h*	Eze 44:14	1004
of the seed of the *h* of Israel	Eze 44:22	1004
the blessing to rest in thine *h*	Eze 44:30	1004
Levites, the ministers of the *h*	Eze 45:5	1004
be for the whole *h* of Israel	Eze 45:6	1004
h of Israel according to their	Eze 45:8	1004
solemnities of the *h* of Israel	Eze 45:17	1004
for the *h* of Israel	Eze 45:17	1004
and put it upon the posts of the *h*	Eze 45:19	1004
so shall ye reconcile the *h*	Eze 45:20	1004
where the ministers of the *h*	Eze 46:24	1004

me again unto the door of the *h*	Eze 47:1	1004
the threshold of the *h* eastward	Eze 47:1	1004
of the *h* stood toward the east	Eze 47:1	1004
from the right side of the *h*	Eze 47:1	1004
the sanctuary of the *h* shall be	Eze 48:21	1004
of the vessels of the *h* of God	Dan 1:2	1004
of Shinar to the *h* of his god	Dan 1:2	1004
into the treasure *h* of his god	Dan 1:2	1004
Then Daniel went to his *h*	Dan 2:17	1005
was at rest in mine *h*, and	Dan 4:4	1005
that I have built for the *h* of	Dan 4:30	1005
h of God which was at Jerusalem	Dan 5:3	1005
lords, came into the banquet *h*	Dan 5:10	1005
the vessels of his *h* before thee	Dan 5:23	1005
was signed, he went into his *h*	Dan 6:10	1005
of Jezreel upon the *h* of Jehu	Hos 1:4	1004
the kingdom of the *h* of Israel	Hos 1:4	1004
have mercy upon the *h* of Israel	Hos 1:6	1004
have mercy upon the *h* of Judah	Hos 1:7	1004
and hearken, ye *h* of Israel	Hos 5:1	1004
and give ye ear, O *h* of the king	Hos 5:1	1004
to the *h* of Judah as rottenness	Hos 5:12	1004
as a young lion to the *h* of Judah	Hos 5:14	1004
horrible thing in the *h* of Israel	Hos 6:10	1004
eagle against the *h* of the LORD	Hos 8:1	1004
not come into the *h* of the LORD	Hos 9:4	1004
and hatred in the *h* of his God	Hos 9:8	1004
I will drive them out of mine *h*	Hos 9:15	1004
the *h* of Israel with deceit	Hos 11:12	1004
is cut off from the *h* of the LORD	Joel 1:9	1004
withholden from the *h* of your God	Joel 1:13	1004
into the *h* of the LORD your God	Joel 1:14	1004
and gladness from the *h* of our God	Joel 1:16	1004
come forth of the *h* of the LORD	Joel 3:18	1004
send a fire into the *h* of Hazael	Amos 1:4	1004
the sceptre from the *h* of Eden	Amos 1:5	1004
condemned in the *h* of their god	Amos 2:8	1004
ye, and testify in the *h* of Jacob	Amos 3:13	1004
winter *h* with the summer *h*	Amos 3:15	1004
even a lamentation, O *h* of Israel	Amos 5:1	1004
leave ten, to the *h* of Israel	Amos 5:3	1004
the LORD unto the *h* of Israel	Amos 5:4	1004
out like fire in the *h* of Joseph	Amos 5:6	1004
or went into the *h*, and leaned his	Amos 5:19	1004
forty years, O *h* of Israel	Amos 5:25	1004
to whom the *h* of Israel came	Amos 6:1	1004
if there remain ten men in one *h*	Amos 6:9	1004
bring out the bones out of the *h*	Amos 6:10	1004
him that is by the sides of the *h*	Amos 6:10	1004
smite the great *h* with breaches	Amos 6:11	1004
and the little *h* with clefts	Amos 6:11	1004
O *h* of Israel, saith the LORD the	Amos 6:14	1004
I will rise against the *h* of	Amos 7:9	1004
in the midst of the *h* of Israel	Amos 7:10	1004
thy word against the *h* of Isaac	Amos 7:16	1004
utterly destroy the *h* of Jacob	Amos 9:8	1004
I will sift the *h* of Israel among	Amos 9:9	1004
the *h* of Jacob shall possess	Obad 17	1004
the *h* of Jacob shall be a fire,	Obad 18	1004
the *h* of Joseph a flame, and the	Obad 18	1004
the *h* of Esau for stubble, and	Obad 18	1004
be any remaining of the *h* of Esau	Obad 18	1004
for the sins of the *h* of Israel	Mic 1:5	1004
in the *h* of Aphrah roll thyself	Mic 1:10	1035
so they oppress a man and his *h*	Mic 2:2	1004
that art named the *h* of Jacob	Mic 2:7	1004
and ye princes of the *h* of Israel	Mic 3:1	1004
you, ye heads of the *h* of Jacob	Mic 3:9	1004
and princes of the *h* of Israel	Mic 3:9	1004
the mountain of the *h* as the high	Mic 3:12	1004
of the *h* of the LORD shall be	Mic 4:1	1004
to the *h* of the God of Jacob	Mic 4:2	1004
thee out of the *h* of servants	Mic 6:4	1004
wickedness in the *h* of the wicked	Mic 6:10	1004
and all the works of the *h* of Ahab	Mic 6:16	1004
enemies are the men of his own *h*	Mic 7:6	1004
out of the *h* of thy gods will I	Nah 1:14	1004
an evil covetousness to his *h*	Hab 2:9	1004
thy *h* by cutting off many people	Hab 2:10	1004
head out of the *h* of the wicked	Hab 3:13	1004
for the remnant of the *h* of Judah	Zeph 2:7	1004
that the LORD's *h* should be built	Hag 1:2	1004
houses, and this *h* lie waste	Hag 1:4	1004
and bring wood, and build the *h*	Hag 1:8	1004
Because of mine *h* that is waste	Hag 1:9	1004
ye run every man unto his own *h*	Hag 1:9	1004
did work in the *h* of the LORD of	Hag 1:14	1004
saw this *h* in her first glory	Hag 2:3	1004
and I will fill this *h* with glory	Hag 2:7	1004
The glory of this latter *h* shall	Hag 2:9	1004
my *h* shall be built in it, saith	Zec 1:16	1004
then thou shalt also judge my *h*	Zec 3:7	1004
laid the foundation of this *h*	Zec 4:9	1004
enter into the *h* of the thief	Zec 5:4	1004
into the *h* of him that sweareth	Zec 5:4	1004
remain in the midst of his *h*	Zec 5:4	1004
To build it an *h* in the land of	Zec 5:11	1004
go into the *h* of Josiah the son	Zec 6:10	1004
sent unto the *h* of God Sherezer	Zec 7:2	1008
in the *h* of the LORD of hosts	Zec 7:3	1004
h of the LORD of hosts was laid	Zec 8:9	1004
O *h* of Judah, and *h* of Israel	Zec 8:13	1004
Jerusalem and to the *h* of Judah	Zec 8:15	1004
shall be to the *h* of Judah joy	Zec 8:19	1004
about mine *h* because of the army	Zec 9:8	1004
visited his flock the *h* of Judah	Zec 10:3	1004
I will strengthen the *h* of Judah	Zec 10:6	1004
and I will save the *h* of Joseph	Zec 10:6	1004
the potter in the *h* of the LORD	Zec 11:13	1004
mine eyes upon the *h* of Judah	Zec 12:4	1004
that the glory of the *h* of David	Zec 12:7	1004
the *h* of David shall be as God,	Zec 12:8	1004
I will pour upon the *h* of David	Zec 12:10	1004
family of the *h* of David apart	Zec 12:12	1004

family of the *h* of Nathan apart	Zec 12:12	1004
The family of the *h* of Levi apart	Zec 12:13	1004
fountain opened to the *h* of David	Zec 13:1	1004
wounded in the *h* of my friends	Zec 13:6	1004
the pots in the LORD's *h* shall be	Zec 14:20	1004
in the *h* of the LORD of hosts	Zec 14:21	1004
that there may be meat in mine *h*	Mal 3:10	1004
And when they were come into the *h*	Mt 2:11	*3614*
light unto all that are in the *h*	Mt 5:15	*3614*
which built his *h* upon a rock	Mt 7:24	*3614*
winds blew, and beat upon that *h*	Mt 7:25	*3614*
which built his *h* upon the sand	Mt 7:26	*3614*
winds blew, and beat upon that *h*	Mt 7:27	*3614*
Jesus was come into Peter's *h*	Mt 8:14	*3614*
up thy bed, and go unto thine *h*	Mt 9:6	*3624*
And he arose, and departed to his *h*	Mt 9:7	*3624*
as Jesus sat at meat in the *h*	Mt 9:10	*3614*
Jesus came into the ruler's *h*	Mt 9:23	*3614*
And when he was come into the *h*	Mt 9:28	*3614*
the lost sheep of the *h* of Israel	Mt 10:6	*3624*
And when ye come into an *h*	Mt 10:12	*3614*
if the *h* be worthy, let your	Mt 10:13	*3614*
ye depart out of that *h* or city	Mt 10:14	*3614*
the master of the *h* Beelzebub	Mt 10:25	*3617*
How he entered into the *h* of God	Mt 12:4	*3624*
every city or *h* divided against	Mt 12:25	*3614*
one enter into a strong man's *h*	Mt 12:29	*3614*
and then he will spoil his *h*	Mt 12:29	*3614*
I will return into my *h* from	Mt 12:44	*3624*
same day went Jesus out of the *h*	Mt 13:1	*3614*
away, and went into the *h*	Mt 13:36	*3614*
his own country, and in his own *h*	Mt 13:57	*3614*
the lost sheep of the *h* of Israel	Mt 15:24	*3624*
And when he was come into the *h*	Mt 17:25	*3614*
against the goodman of the *h*	Mt 20:11	*3617*
My *h* shall be called the *h* of	Mt 21:13	*3624*
your *h* is left unto you desolate	Mt 23:38	*3624*
to take any thing out of his *h*	Mt 24:17	*3614*
that if the goodman of the *h* had	Mt 24:43	*3617*
suffered his *h* to be broken up	Mt 24:43	*3614*
in the *h* of Simon the leper,	Mt 26:6	*3614*
at thy *h* with my disciples	Mt 26:18	
they entered into the *h* of Simon	Mk 1:29	*3614*
was noised that he was in the *h*	Mk 2:1	*3624*
bed, and go thy way into thine *h*	Mk 2:11	*3624*
as Jesus sat at meat in his *h*	Mk 2:15	*3614*
How he went into the *h* of God in	Mk 2:26	*3624*
and they went into an *h*	Mk 3:19	*3624*
if a *h* be divided against itself,	Mk 3:25	*3614*
that *h* cannot stand	Mk 3:25	*3614*
can enter into a strong man's *h*	Mk 3:27	*3614*
and then he will spoil his *h*	Mk 3:27	*3614*
synagogue's *h* certain which said	Mk 5:35	
he cometh to the *h* of the ruler	Mk 5:38	*3624*
his own kin, and in his own *h*	Mk 6:4	*3614*
place soever ye enter into a *h*	Mk 6:10	*3614*
into the *h* from the people	Mk 7:17	*3624*
and Sidon, and entered into an *h*	Mk 7:24	*3614*
And when she was come to her *h*	Mk 7:30	*3624*
And he sent him away to his *h*	Mk 8:26	*3624*
And when he was come into the *h*	Mk 9:28	*3624*
being in the *h* he asked them,	Mk 9:33	*3614*
in the *h* his disciples asked him	Mk 10:10	*3614*
There is no man that hath left *h*	Mk 10:29	*3614*
My *h* shall be called of all	Mk 11:17	*3624*
of all nations the *h* of prayer	Mk 11:17	*3624*
housetop not go down into the *h*	Mk 13:15	*3614*
to take any thing out of his *h*	Mk 13:15	*3614*
a far journey, who left his *h*	Mk 13:34	*3614*
when the master of the *h* cometh	Mk 13:35	*3614*
in the *h* of Simon the leper	Mk 14:3	*3614*
say ye to the goodman of the *h*	Mk 14:14	*3617*
he departed to his own *h*	Lk 1:23	*3624*
was Joseph, of the *h* of David	Lk 1:27	*3624*
over the *h* of Jacob for ever	Lk 1:33	*3624*
entered into the *h* of Zacharias	Lk 1:40	*3624*
months, and returned to her own *h*	Lk 1:56	*3624*
us in the *h* of his servant David	Lk 1:69	*3624*
(because he was of the *h* and	Lk 2:4	*3624*
and entered into Simon's *h*	Lk 4:38	*3614*
up thy couch, and go into thine *h*	Lk 5:24	*3624*
he lay, and departed to his own *h*	Lk 5:25	*3624*
him a great feast in his own *h*	Lk 5:29	*3614*
How he went into the *h* of God	Lk 6:4	*3624*
He is like a man which built an *h*	Lk 6:48	*3614*
beat vehemently upon that *h*	Lk 6:48	*3614*
built an *h* upon the earth	Lk 6:49	*3614*
and the ruin of that *h* was great	Lk 6:49	*3614*
he was now not far from the *h*	Lk 7:6	*3614*
were sent, returning to the *h*	Lk 7:10	*3624*
And he went into the Pharisee's *h*	Lk 7:36	*3614*
sat at meat in the Pharisee's *h*	Lk 7:37	*3614*
I entered into thine *h*, thou	Lk 7:44	*3614*
clothes, neither abode in any *h*	Lk 8:27	*3614*
Return to thine own *h*, and shew	Lk 8:39	*3624*
him that he would come into his *h*	Lk 8:41	*3624*
the ruler of the synagogue's *h*	Lk 8:49	
And when he came into the *h*	Lk 8:51	*3614*
whatsoever *h* ye enter into, there	Lk 9:4	*3614*
which are at home at my *h*	Lk 9:61	*3624*
And into whatsoever *h* ye enter	Lk 10:5	*3614*
first say, Peace be to this *h*	Lk 10:5	*3624*
And in the same *h* remain, eating	Lk 10:7	*3614*
Go not from *h* to *h*	Lk 10:7	*3614*
Martha received him into her *h*	Lk 10:38	*3624*
h divided against a *h* falleth	Lk 11:17	*3624*
unto my *h* whence I came out	Lk 11:24	*3624*
that if the goodman of the *h* had	Lk 12:39	*3617*
his *h* to be broken through	Lk 12:39	*3624*
shall be five in one *h* divided	Lk 12:52	*3624*
the master of the *h* is risen up	Lk 13:25	*3617*
your *h* is left unto you desolate	Lk 13:35	*3624*
as he went into the *h* of one of	Lk 14:1	*3624*
Then the master of the *h* being	Lk 14:21	*3617*

come in, that my *h* may be filled ... Lk 14:23 3624
light a candle, and sweep the *h* ... Lk 15:8 3614
as he came and drew nigh to the *h* ... Lk 15:25 3614
send him to my father's *h* ... Lk 16:27 3624
housetop, and his stuff in the *h* ... Lk 17:31 3614
this man went down to his *h* ... Lk 18:14 3624
There is no man that hath left *h* ... Lk 18:29 3614
for to day I must abide at thy *h* ... Lk 19:5 3624
day is salvation come to this *h* ... Lk 19:9 3624
My *h* is the *h* of prayer ... Lk 19:46 3624
follow him into the *h* where he ... Lk 22:10 3614
say unto the goodman of the *h* ... Lk 22:11 3614
him into the high priest's *h* ... Lk 22:54 3624
h an *h* of merchandise ... Jn 2:16 3624
zeal of thine *h* hath eaten me up ... Jn 2:17 3624
himself believed, and his whole *h* ... Jn 4:53 3614
And every man went unto his own *h* ... Jn 7:53 3624
abideth not in the *h* for ever ... Jn 8:35 3614
but Mary sat still in the *h* ... Jn 11:20 3624
then which were with her in the *h* ... Jn 11:31 3614
the *h* was filled with the odour ... Jn 12:3 3614
In my Father's *h* are many ... Jn 14:2 3614
it filled all the *h* where they ... Acts 2:2 3624
Therefore let all the *h* of Israel ... Acts 2:36 3624
and breaking bread from *h* to *h* ... Acts 2:46 3624
in the temple, and in every *h* ... Acts 5:42 3624
governor over Egypt and all his *h* ... Acts 7:10 3624
up in his father's *h* three months ... Acts 7:20 3624
O ye *h* of Israel, have ye offered ... Acts 7:42 3624
But Solomon built him an *h* ... Acts 7:47 3624
what *h* will ye build me ... Acts 7:49 3624
the church, entering into every *h* ... Acts 8:3 3624
enquire in the *h* of Judas for one ... Acts 9:11 3614
his way, and entered into the *h* ... Acts 9:17 3614
that feared God with all his *h* ... Acts 10:2 3624
whose *h* is by the sea side ... Acts 10:6 3614
had made enquiry for Simon's *h* ... Acts 10:17 3614
angel to send for thee into his *h* ... Acts 10:22 3624
the ninth hour I prayed in my *h* ... Acts 10:30 3624
he is lodged in the *h* of one ... Acts 10:32 3614
come unto the *h* where I was ... Acts 11:11 3614
and we entered into the man's *h* ... Acts 11:12 3624
how he had seen an angel in his *h* ... Acts 11:13 3624
thou and all thy *h* shall be saved ... Acts 11:14 3624
he came to the *h* of Mary the ... Acts 12:12 3614
to the Lord, come into my *h* ... Acts 16:15 3624
and thou shalt be saved, and thy *h* ... Acts 16:31 3624
and to all that were in his *h* ... Acts 16:32 3614
he had brought them into his *h* ... Acts 16:34 3624
believing in God with all his *h* ... Acts 16:34 3832
and entered into the *h* of Lydia ... Acts 16:40
and assaulted the *h* of Jason ... Acts 17:5 3614
and entered into a certain man's *h* ... Acts 18:7 3614
whose *h* joined hard to the ... Acts 18:7 3614
believed on the Lord with all his *h* ... Acts 18:8 3624
they fled out of that *h* naked ... Acts 19:16 3624
publickly, and from *h* to *h* ... Acts 20:20 3624
we entered into the *h* of Philip ... Acts 21:8 3624
whole years in his own hired *h* ... Acts 28:30
the church that is in their *h* ... Rom 16:5 3624
them which are of the *h* of Chloe ... 1Cor 1:11
(ye know the *h* of Stephanas ... 1Cor 16:15 3614
the church that is in their *h* ... 1Cor 16:19 3624
earthly *h* of this tabernacle were ... 2Cor 5:1 3614
an *h* not made with hands, eternal ... 2Cor 5:1 3614
with our *h* which is from heaven ... 2Cor 5:2 3613
and the church which is in his *h* ... Col 4:15 3624
One that ruleth well his own *h* ... 1Ti 3:4 3624
know not how to rule his own *h* ... 1Ti 3:5 3624
to behave thyself in the *h* of God ... 1Ti 3:15 3624
specially for those of his own *h* ... 1Ti 5:8 3609
wandering about from *h* to *h* ... 1Ti 5:13 3614
marry, bear children, guide the *h* ... 1Ti 5:14 3616
mercy unto the *h* of Onesiphorus ... 2Ti 1:16 3624
But in a great *h* there are not ... 2Ti 2:20 3614
and to the church in thy *h* ... Philem 2 3624
Moses was faithful in all his *h* ... Heb 3:2 3624
h hath more honour than the *h* ... Heb 3:3 3624
For every *h* is builded by some ... Heb 3:4 3624
verily was faithful in all his *h* ... Heb 3:5 3624
Christ as a son over his own *h* ... Heb 3:6 3624
whose *h* are we, if we hold fast ... Heb 3:6 3624
new covenant with the *h* of Israel ... Heb 8:8 3624
of Israel and with the *h* of Judah ... Heb 8:8 3624
that I will make with the *h* of ... Heb 8:10 3624
an high priest over the *h* of God ... Heb 10:21 3624
an ark to the saving of his *h* ... Heb 11:7 3624
are built up a spiritual *h* ... 1Pet 2:5 3624
must begin at the *h* of God ... 1Pet 4:17 3624
receive him not into your *h* ... 2Jn 10 3614

HOUSEHOLD

his *h* after him, and they shall ... Gen 18:19 1004
thou found of all thy *h* stuff ... Gen 31:37 1004
Then Jacob said unto his *h* ... Gen 35:2 1004
lest thou, and thy *h*, and all that ... Gen 45:11 1004
brethren, and all his father's *h* ... Gen 47:12 1004
man and his *h* came with Jacob ... Ex 1:1 1004
if the *h* be too little for the ... Ex 12:4 1004
for himself, and for his *h* ... Lev 16:17 1004
upon Pharaoh, and upon all his *h* ... Deut 6:22 1004
shalt rejoice, thou, and thine *h* ... Deut 14:26 1004
LORD shall choose, thou and thy *h* ... Deut 15:20 1004
brethren, and all thy father's *h* ... Josh 2:18 1004
harlot alive, and her father's *h* ... Josh 6:25 1004
the *h* which the LORD shall take ... Josh 7:14 1004
And he brought his *h* man by man ... Josh 7:18 1004
because he feared his father's *h* ... Judg 6:27 1004
thy life, with the lives of thy *h* ... Judg 18:25 1004
our master, and against all his *h* ... 1Sa 25:17 1004
and his men, every man with his *h* ... 1Sa 27:3 1004
bring up, every man with his *h* ... 2Sa 2:3 1004
blessed Obed-edom, and all his *h* ... 2Sa 6:11 1004
David returned to bless his *h* ... 2Sa 6:20 1004
forth, and all his *h* after him ... 2Sa 15:16 1004
be for the king's *h* to ride on ... 2Sa 16:2 1004
put his *h* in order, and hanged ... 2Sa 17:23 1004
boat to carry over the king's *h* ... 2Sa 19:18 1004
have brought the king, and his *h* ... 2Sa 19:41 1004
And Ahishar was over the *h* ... 1Kin 4:6 1004
victuals for the king and his *h* ... 1Kin 4:7 1004
desire, in giving food for my *h* ... 1Kin 5:9 1004
of wheat for food to his *h* ... 1Kin 5:11 1004
h among the sons of Pharaoh ... 1Kin 11:20 1004
we may go and tell the king's *h* ... 2Kin 7:9 1004
Arise, and go thou and thine *h* ... 2Kin 8:1 1004
and she went with her *h*, and ... 2Kin 8:2 1004
of Hilkiah, which was over the *h* ... 2Kin 18:18 1004
of Hilkiah, which was over the *h* ... 2Kin 18:37 1004
Eliakim, which was over the *h* ... 2Kin 19:2 1004
one principal *h* being taken for ... 1Chr 24:6 1004
the *h* stuff of Tobiah out of the ... Neh 13:8 1004
she asses, and a very great *h* ... Job 1:3 5657
thy food, for the food of thy *h* ... Prov 27:27 1004
night, and giveth meat to her *h* ... Prov 31:15 1004
not afraid of the snow for her *h* ... Prov 31:21 1004
for all her *h* are clothed with ... Prov 31:21 1004
looketh well to the ways of her *h* ... Prov 31:27 1004
of Hilkiah, that was over the *h* ... Is 36:22 1004
sent Eliakim, who was over the *h* ... Is 37:2 1004
shall they call them of his *h* ... Mt 10:25 3615
foes shall be they of his own *h* ... Mt 10:36 3615
lord hath made ruler over his *h* ... Mt 24:45 2322
lord shall make ruler over his *h* ... Lk 12:42 2322
he called two of his *h* servants ... Acts 10:7 3610
when she was baptized, and her *h* ... Acts 16:15 3624
them which are of Aristobulus' *h* ... Rom 16:10
that be of the *h* of Narcissus ... Rom 16:11
baptized also the *h* of Stephanas ... 1Cor 1:16 3624
them who are of the *h* of faith ... Gal 6:10 3609
the saints, and of the *h* of God ... Eph 2:19 3609
they that are of Caesar's *h* ... Phil 4:22 3614
Aquila, and the *h* of Onesiphorus ... 2Ti 4:19 3624

HOUSEHOLDER

So the servants of the *h* came ... Mt 13:27 3617
is like unto a man that is an *h* ... Mt 13:52 3617
is like unto a man that is an *h* ... Mt 20:1 3617
There was a certain *h*, which ... Mt 21:33 3617

HOUSEHOLDS

food for the famine of your *h* ... Gen 42:33 1004
And take your father and your *h* ... Gen 45:18 1004
your food, and for them of your *h* ... Gen 47:24 1004
it in every place, ye and your *h* ... Num 18:31 1004
and swallowed them up, and their *h* ... Deut 11:6 1004
put your hand unto, ye and your *h* ... Deut 12:7 1004
LORD shall take shall come by *h* ... Josh 7:14 1004

HOUSES

corn for the famine of your *h* ... Gen 42:19 1004
feared God, that he made them *h* ... Ex 1:21 1004
be the heads of their fathers' *h* ... Ex 6:14 1004
the frogs from thee and thy *h* ... Ex 8:9 1004
depart from thee, and from thy *h* ... Ex 8:11 1004
and the frogs died out of the *h* ... Ex 8:13 1004
and upon thy people, and into thy *h* ... Ex 8:21 1004
the *h* of the Egyptians shall be ... Ex 8:21 1004
Pharaoh, and into his servants' *h* ... Ex 8:24 1004
and his cattle flee into the *h* ... Ex 9:20 1004
And they shall fill thy *h* ... Ex 10:6 1004
the *h* of all thy servants ... Ex 10:6 1004
the *h* of all the Egyptians ... Ex 10:6 1004
on the upper door post of the *h* ... Ex 12:7 1004
a token upon the *h* where ye are ... Ex 12:13 1004
put away leaven out of your *h* ... Ex 12:15 1004
be no leaven found in your *h* ... Ex 12:19 1004
come in unto your *h* to smite you ... Ex 12:23 1004
who passed over the *h* of the ... Ex 12:27 1004
the Egyptians, and delivered our *h* ... Ex 12:27 1004
But the *h* of the villages which ... Lev 25:31 1004
the *h* of the cities of their ... Lev 25:32 1004
for the *h* of the cities of the ... Lev 25:33 1004
throughout the *h* of their fathers ... Num 4:22 1004
and swallowed them up, and their *h* ... Num 16:32 1004
according to their fathers' *h* ... Num 17:6 1004
We will not return unto our *h* ... Num 32:18 1004
h full of all good things, which ... Deut 6:11 1004
art full, and hast built goodly *h* ... Deut 8:12 1004
in their cities, and in their *h* ... Deut 19:1 1004
for our provision out of our *h* on ... Josh 9:12 1004
that there is in these *h* an ephod ... Judg 18:14 1004
the men that were in the *h* near ... Judg 18:22 1004
when Solomon had built the two *h* ... 1Kin 9:10 1004
against all the *h* of the high ... 1Kin 13:32 1004
house, and the *h* of thy servants ... 1Kin 20:6 1004
put them in the *h* of the high ... 2Kin 17:29 1004
them in the *h* of the high places ... 2Kin 17:32 1004
brake down the *h* of the sodomites ... 2Kin 23:7 1004
all the *h* also of the high places ... 2Kin 23:19 1004
all the *h* of Jerusalem, and every ... 2Kin 25:9 1004
David made him *h* in the city of ... 1Chr 15:1 1004
of the *h* thereof, and of the ... 1Chr 28:11 1004
overlay the walls of the *h* withal ... 1Chr 29:4 1004
to the *h* of their fathers ... 2Chr 25:5 1004
to floor the *h* which the kings of ... 2Chr 34:11 1004
by the *h* of your fathers, after ... 2Chr 35:4 1004
daughters, your wives, and your *h* ... Neh 4:14 1004
our lands, vineyards, and *h* ... Neh 5:3 1004
their oliveyards, and their *h* ... Neh 5:11 1004
and the *h* were not builded ... Neh 7:4
possessed *h* full of all goods ... Neh 9:25 1004
after the *h* of our fathers, at ... Neh 10:34 1004
sons went and feasted in their *h* ... Job 1:4 1004
who filled their *h* with silver ... Job 3:15 1004
in them that dwell in *h* of clay ... Job 4:19 1004
in *h* which no man inhabiteth ... Job 15:28 1004
Their *h* are safe from fear ... Job 21:9 1004
filled their *h* with good things ... Job 22:18 1004
In the dark they dig through *h* ... Job 24:16 1004
that their *h* shall continue for ... Ps 49:11 1004
the *h* of God in possession ... Ps 83:12 4999
we shall fill our *h* with spoil ... Prov 1:13 1004
make they their *h* in the rocks ... Prov 30:26
I builded me *h* ... Eccl 2:4 1004
spoil of the poor is in your *h* ... Is 3:14 1004
Of a truth many *h* shall be ... Is 5:9 1004
the *h* without man, and the land be ... Is 6:11 1004
offence to both the *h* of Israel ... Is 8:14 1004
their *h* shall be spoiled, and ... Is 13:16 1004
their *h* shall be full of doleful ... Is 13:21 1004
shall cry in their desolate *h* ... Is 13:22 490
on the tops of their *h*, and in ... Is 15:3
have numbered the *h* of Jerusalem ... Is 22:10 1004
the *h* have ye broken down to ... Is 22:10 1004
upon all the *h* of joy in the ... Is 32:13 1004
and they are hid in prison *h* ... Is 42:22 1004
And they shall build *h*, and inhabit ... Is 65:21 1004
by troops in the harlots' *h* ... Jer 5:7 1004
so are their *h* full of deceit ... Jer 5:27 1004
their *h* shall be turned unto ... Jer 6:12 1004
out of your *h* on the sabbath day ... Jer 17:22 1004
Let a cry be heard from their *h* ... Jer 18:22 1004
the *h* of Jerusalem ... Jer 19:13 1004
the *h* of the kings of Judah ... Jer 19:13 1004
because of all the *h* upon whose ... Jer 19:13 1004
Build ye *h*, and dwell in them ... Jer 29:5 1004
build ye *h*, and dwell in them ... Jer 29:28 1004
H and fields and vineyards shall be ... Jer 32:15 1004
this city, and burn it with the *h* ... Jer 32:29 1004
concerning the *h* of this city ... Jer 33:4 1004
concerning the *h* of the kings of ... Jer 33:4 1004
Nor to build *h* for us to dwell in ... Jer 35:9 1004
the *h* of the people, with fire ... Jer 39:8 1004
in the *h* of the gods of Egypt ... Jer 43:12 1004
and the *h* of the gods of the ... Jer 43:13 1004
all the *h* of Jerusalem, and all ... Jer 52:13 1004
all the *h* of the great men ... Jer 52:13 1004
to strangers, our *h* to aliens ... Lam 5:2 1004
and they shall possess their *h* ... Eze 7:24 1004
let us build *h* ... Eze 11:3 1004
they shall burn thine *h* with fire ... Eze 16:41 1004
and burn up their *h* with fire ... Eze 23:47 1004
walls, and destroy thy pleasant *h* ... Eze 26:12 1004
safely therein, and shall build *h* ... Eze 28:26 1004
walls and in the doors of the *h* ... Eze 33:30 1004
it shall be a place for their *h* ... Eze 45:4 1004
your *h* shall be made a dunghill ... Dan 2:5 1005
their *h* shall be made a dunghill ... Dan 3:29 1005
and I will place them in their *h* ... Hos 11:11 1004
they shall climb up upon the *h* ... Joel 2:9 1004
the *h* of ivory shall perish, and ... Amos 3:15 1004
the great *h* shall have an end ... Amos 3:15 1004
ye have built *h* of hewn stone ... Amos 5:11 1004
the *h* of Achzib shall be a lie to ... Mic 1:14 1004
and *h*, and take them away ... Mic 2:2 1004
ye cast out from their pleasant *h* ... Mic 2:9 1004
their masters' *h* with violence ... Zeph 1:9 1004
a booty, and their *h* a desolation ... Zeph 1:13 1004
they shall also build *h*, but not ... Zeph 1:13 1004
in the *h* of Ashkelon shall they ... Zeph 2:7 1004
O ye, to dwell in your cieled *h* ... Hag 1:4 1004
the *h* rifled, and the women ... Zec 14:2 1004
soft clothing are in kings' *h* ... Mt 11:8 3624
And every one that hath forsaken *h* ... Mt 19:29 3614
for ye devour widows' *h*, and for a ... Mt 23:14 3614
them away fasting to their own *h* ... Mk 8:3 3624
hundredfold now in this time, *h* ... Mk 10:30 3614
Which devour widows' *h*, and for a ... Mk 12:40 3614
they may receive me into their *h* ... Lk 16:4 3624
Which devour widows' *h*, and for a ... Lk 20:47 3614
of lands or *h* sold them, and ... Acts 4:34 3614
have ye not *h* to eat and to drink ... 1Cor 11:22 3614
children and their own *h* well ... 1Ti 3:12 3624
sort are they which creep into *h* ... 2Ti 3:6 3614
be stopped, who subvert whole *h* ... Titus 1:11 3624

HOUSETOP

to dwell in a corner of the *h* ... Prov 21:9 1406
to dwell in the corner of the *h* ... Prov 25:24 1406
Let him which is on the *h* not ... Mt 24:17 1430
let him that is on the *h* not go ... Mk 13:15 1430
multitude, they went upon the *h* ... Lk 5:19 1430
day, he which shall be upon the *h* ... Lk 17:31 1430
Peter went up upon the *h* to pray ... Acts 10:9 1430

HOUSETOPS

them be as the grass upon the *h* ... Ps 129:6 1406
thou art wholly gone up to the *h* ... Is 22:1 1406
green herb, as the grass on the *h* ... Is 37:27 1406
generally upon all the *h* of Moab ... Jer 48:38 1406
the host of heaven upon the *h* ... Zeph 1:5 1406
ear, that preach ye upon the *h* ... Mt 10:27 1430
shall be proclaimed upon the *h* ... Lk 12:3 1430

HOW

h saidst thou, She is my sister ... Gen 26:9 349
H is it that thou hast found it ... Gen 27:20 4100
and said, *H* dreadful is this place ... Gen 28:17 4100
Thou knowest *h* I have served thee ... Gen 30:29
and *h* thy cattle was with me ... Gen 30:29
said, *H* hast thou broken forth ... Gen 38:29 4100
h then can I do this great ... Gen 39:9 349
h then should we steal out of thy ... Gen 44:8 349
or *h* shall we clear ourselves ... Gen 44:16 4100
For *h* shall I go up to my father ... Gen 44:34 349
said unto Jacob, *H* old art thou ... Gen 47:8 4100
h that our money is spent ... Gen 47:18
H is it that ye are come so soon ... Ex 2:18 4069
h then shall Pharaoh hear me, who ... Ex 6:12
h shall Pharaoh hearken unto me ... Ex 6:30 349
that thou mayest know *h* that the ... Ex 9:29
that ye may know *h* that I am the ... Ex 10:2
H long wilt thou refuse to humble ... Ex 10:3 5704

H long shall this man be a snare Ex 10:7
that ye may know *h* that the LORD Ex 11:7
H long refuse ye to keep my Ex 16:28 5704
h the LORD delivered them Ex 18:8
h I bare you on eagles' wings, and Ex 19:4
understanding to know *h* to work Ex 36:1
knowest *h* we are to encamp in the Num 10:31
H long will this people provoke Num 14:11 5704
h long will it be ere they Num 14:11 5704
H long shall I bear with this Num 14:27 5704
H our fathers went down into Num 20:15
H shall I curse, whom God hath Num 23:8 4100
or *h* shall I defy, whom the LORD Num 23:8 4100
H goodly are thy tents, O Jacob, Num 24:5 4100
H can I myself alone bear your Deut 1:12 349
where thou hast seen *h* that the Deut 1:31
h can I dispossess them Deut 7:17 349
h thou provokedst the LORD thy Deut 9:7 834
h he made the water of the Red Deut 11:4 834
h the LORD hath destroyed them Deut 11:4
h the earth opened her mouth, and Deut 11:6 834
H did these nations serve their Deut 12:30 349
H shall we know the word which Deut 18:21 349
H he met thee by the way, and Deut 25:18 834
(For ye know *h* we have dwelt in Deut 29:16 834
h we came through the nations Deut 29:16 834
h much more after my death Deut 31:27 637
H should one chase a thousand, and Deut 32:30 349
For we have heard *h* the LORD Josh 2:10 834
h shall we make a league with you Josh 9:7 349
h that the LORD thy God commanded Josh 9:24
had heard *h* Joshua had taken Ai Josh 10:1 3588
h the inhabitants of Gibeon had Josh 10:1 3588
that day *h* the Anakims were there Josh 14:12 3588
H long are ye slack to go to Josh 18:3 5704
H shall we order the child Judg 13:12 4100
and *h* shall we do unto him Judg 13:12
H canst thou say, I love thee, Judg 16:15 349
h they dwelt careless, after the Judg 18:7
Tell us, *h* was this wickedness Judg 20:3 349
H shall we do for wives for them Judg 21:7 4100
H shall we do for wives for them Judg 21:16 4100
heard in the country of Moab *h* Ruth 1:6
h thou hast left thy father and Ruth 2:11
until thou know *h* the matter will Ruth 3:18 5704
H long wilt thou be drunken 1Sa 1:14 5704
h they lay with the women that 1Sa 2:22 434
said, *H* shall this man save us 1Sa 10:27 4100
for consider *h* great things he 1Sa 12:24 834
h mine eyes have been enlightened 1Sa 14:29 3588
H much more, if haply the people 1Sa 14:30 637
h he laid wait for him in the way 1Sa 15:2 834
H long wilt thou mourn for Saul, 1Sa 16:1 5704
And Samuel said, *H* can I go 1Sa 16:2 349
look *h* thy brethren fare, and take 1Sa 17:18
h much more then if we come to 1Sa 23:3 637
h that the LORD had delivered 1Sa 24:10 834
thou hast shewed this day *h* that 1Sa 24:18
h he hath cut off those that have 1Sa 28:9
said unto him, *H* went the matter 2Sa 1:4 4100
H knowest thou that Saul and 2Sa 1:5 349
H wast thou not afraid to stretch 2Sa 1:14 349
h are the mighty fallen 2Sa 1:19 349
H are the mighty fallen in the 2Sa 1:25 349
H are the mighty fallen, and the 2Sa 1:27 349
h then should I hold up my face 2Sa 2:22 349
h long shall it be then, ere thou 2Sa 2:26 5704
H much more, when wicked men have 2Sa 4:11 637
H shall the ark of the LORD come 2Sa 6:9
H glorious was the king of Israel 2Sa 6:20 4100
David demanded of him *h* Joab did 2Sa 11:7
h the people did, and *h* the war 2Sa 11:7
h will he then vex himself, if we 2Sa 12:18 349
h much more now may this 2Sa 16:11 637
h that the LORD hath avenged him 2Sa 18:19
h the king was grieved for his 2Sa 19:2
H long have I to live, that I 2Sa 19:34 4100
h many soever they be, an 2Sa 24:3
I know not *h* to go out or come in 1Kin 3:7
Thou knowest *h* that David my 1Kin 5:3
h much less this house that I 1Kin 8:27 637
H do ye advise that I may answer 1Kin 12:6 349
h he warred, and *h* he reigned, 1Kin 14:19 834
h I hid an hundred men of the 1Kin 18:13
H long halt ye between two 1Kin 18:21 5704
withal *h* he had slain all the 1Kin 19:1 834
see *h* this man seeketh mischief 1Kin 20:7 3588
Seest thou *h* Ahab humbleth 1Kin 21:29 3588
H many times shall I adjure thee 1Kin 22:16 5704
h he warred, are they not written 1Kin 22:45 834
see *h* he seeketh a quarrel 2Kin 5:7 3588
h much rather then, when he saith 2Kin 5:13 637
h shall we do? 2Kin 6:15 349
See ye *h* this son of a murderer 2Kin 6:32 3588
as he was telling the king *h* he 2Kin 8:5 834
for remember *h* that, when I and 2Kin 9:25
h then shall we stand 2Kin 10:4 349
h he fought with Amaziah king of 2Kin 14:15 834
h he warred, and *h* he recovered 2Kin 14:28 834
taught them *h* they should fear 2Kin 17:28 349
H then wilt thou turn away the 2Kin 18:24 349
heard long ago *h* I have done it 2Kin 19:25
remember now *h* I have walked 2Kin 20:3 834
h he made a pool, and a conduit, 2Kin 20:20 834
H shall I bring the ark of God 1Chr 13:12 1963
when Tou king of Hamath heard *h* 1Chr 18:9 3588
told David *h* the men were served 1Chr 19:5
h much less this house which I 2Chr 6:18 637
Israel saw *h* the fire came down 2Chr 7:3
H many times shall I adjure thee 2Chr 18:15 5704
h they reward us, to come to cast 2Chr 20:11
h much less shall your God 2Chr 32:15 637
h God was intreated of him, and 2Chr 33:19
salt without prescribing *h* much Ezr 7:22

For *h* long shall thy journey be Neh 2:6 5704
h Jerusalem lieth waste, and the Neh 2:17 834
to know *h* Esther did, and what Est 2:11
h he had advanced him above the Est 5:11 834
For *h* can I endure to see the Est 8:6 346
or *h* can I endure to see the Est 8:6 346
H much less in them that dwell in Job 4:19 637
H forcible are right words Job 6:25 4100
H long wilt thou not depart from Job 7:19 5704
H long wilt thou speak these Job 8:2 5704
h long shall the words of thy Job 8:2
but *h* should man be just with God Job 9:2 4100
H much less shall I answer him, Job 9:14 637
H many are mine iniquities and Job 13:23 4100
H much more abominable and filthy Job 15:16 637
H long will it be ere ye make an Job 18:2 5704
H long will ye vex my soul, and Job 19:2 5704
H oft is the candle of the wicked Job 21:17 4100
h oft cometh their destruction Job 21:17
H then comfort ye me in vain, Job 21:34 349
of the stars, *h* high they are Job 22:12 3588
And thou sayest, *H* doth God know Job 22:13 4100
H then can man be justified with Job 25:4 4100
or *h* can he be clean that is born Job 25:4 4100
H much less man, that is a worm Job 25:6 637
H hast thou helped him that is Job 26:2 4100
h savest thou the arm that hath Job 26:2
H hast thou counseled him that Job 26:3 4100
h hast thou plentifully declared Job 26:3
but *h* little a portion is heard Job 26:14 4100
H much less to him that accepteth Job 34:19 834
H thy garments are warm, when he Job 37:17 834
h are they increased that trouble Ps 3:1 4100
h long will ye turn my glory into Ps 4:2 5704
h long will ye love vanity, and Ps 4:2
but thou, O LORD, *h* long Ps 6:3 5704
h excellent is thy name in all Ps 8:1 4100
h excellent is thy name in all Ps 8:9 4100
h say ye to my soul, Flee as a Ps 11:1 349
H long wilt thou forget me, O Ps 13:1 5704
h long wilt thou hide thy face Ps 13:1 5704
H long shall I take counsel in my Ps 13:2 5704
h long shall mine enemy be Ps 13:2 5704
in thy salvation *h* greatly shall Ps 21:1 4100
Oh *h* great is thy goodness, which Ps 31:19 4100
LORD, *h* long wilt thou look on Ps 35:17 4100
H excellent is thy lovingkindness Ps 36:7 4100
that I may know *h* frail I am Ps 39:4 4100
H thou didst drive out the Ps 44:2
h thou didst afflict the people, Ps 44:2
H long will ye imagine mischief Ps 62:3 5704
H terrible art thou in thy works Ps 66:3 4100
And they say, *H* doth God know Ps 73:11 349
H are they brought into Ps 73:19 349
among us any that knoweth *h* long Ps 74:9 5704
h long shall the adversary Ps 74:10 5704
remember *h* the foolish man Ps 74:22
H oft did they provoke him in the Ps 78:40 4101
H he had wrought his signs in Ps 78:43 834
H long, LORD Ps 79:5 5704
h long wilt thou be angry against Ps 80:4 5704
H long will ye judge unjustly, and Ps 82:2 5704
H amiable are thy tabernacles, O Ps 84:1 4100
H long, LORD Ps 89:46 5704
Remember *h* short my time is Ps 89:47 4100
h I do bear in my bosom the Ps 89:50
Return, O LORD, *h* long Ps 90:13 5704
O LORD, *h* great are thy works Ps 92:5 4100
h long shall the wicked, *h* long Ps 94:3 5704
H long shall they utter and speak Ps 94:4
O LORD, *h* manifold are thy works Ps 104:24 4100
H many are the days of thy Ps 119:84 4100
O *h* love I thy law Ps 119:97 4100
H sweet are thy words unto my Ps 119:103 4100
Consider *h* I love thy precepts Ps 119:159 3588
H he sware unto the LORD, and Ps 132:2 834
h good and *h* pleasant it is for Ps 133:1 4100
H shall we sing the LORD's song Ps 137:4 349
H precious also are thy thoughts Ps 139:17 4100
H great is the sum of them Ps 139:17 4100
H long, ye simple ones, will ye Prov 1:22 5704
H have I hated instruction, and my Prov 5:12 349
H long wilt thou sleep, O Prov 6:9 5704
h much more then the hearts of Prov 15:11 637
in due season, *h* good is it Prov 15:23 4100
H much better is it to get wisdom Prov 16:16 4100
h much more do his friends go far Prov 19:7 637
h can a man then understand his Prov 20:24 4100
h much more, when he bringeth it Prov 21:27 637
O *h* lofty are their eyes Prov 30:13 4100
And *h* dieth the wise man Eccl 2:16 349
but *h* can one be warm alone Eccl 4:11 349
knoweth not *h* to go to the city Eccl 10:15 834
nor *h* the bones do grow in the Eccl 11:5
H fair is thy love, my sister, my Song 4:10 4100
h much better is thy love than Song 4:10 4100
h shall I put it on? Song 5:3 349
h shall I defile them Song 5:3 349
H beautiful are thy feet with Song 7:1 4100
H fair and *h* pleasant art thou, Song 7:6 4100
H is the faithful city become an Is 1:21 349
Then said I, Lord, *h* long Is 6:11 5704
H hath the oppressor ceased Is 14:4 349
H art thou fallen from heaven, O Is 14:12 349
h art thou cut down to the ground Is 14:12 349
h say ye unto Pharaoh, I am the Is 19:11 349
and *h* shall we escape Is 20:6 349
H then wilt thou turn away the Is 36:9 349
heard long ago, *h* I have done it Is 37:26
h I have walked before thee in Is 38:3 834
for *h* should my name be polluted Is 48:11 349
that I should know *h* to speak a Is 50:4
H beautiful upon the mountains Is 52:7 4100
h then art thou turned into the Jer 2:21 349

H canst thou say, I am not Jer 2:23 349
H shall I put thee among the Jer 3:19 349
H long shall thy vain thoughts Jer 4:14 5704
H long shall I see the standard, Jer 4:21 5704
H shall I pardon thee for this Jer 5:7 335
H do ye say, We are wise, and the Jer 8:8 349
for *h* shall I do for the daughter Jer 9:7 349
out of Zion, *H* are we spoiled Jer 9:19 349
H long shall the land mourn, and Jer 12:4 5704
then *h* canst thou contend with Jer 12:5 349
then *h* wilt thou do in the Jer 12:5 349
go aside to ask *h* thou doest Jer 15:5
h gracious shalt thou be when Jer 22:23 4100
H long shall this be in the heart Jer 23:26 5704
H long wilt thou go about, O thou Jer 31:22 5704
H didst thou write all these Jer 36:17 349
h Nebuchadrezzar king of Babylon Jer 46:13
h long wilt thou cut thyself Jer 47:5
h long will it be ere thou be Jer 47:6 5704
H can it be quiet, seeing the Jer 47:7 349
H say ye, We are mighty and strong Jer 48:14 349
H is the strong staff broken, and Jer 48:17 349
howl, saying, *H* is it broken down Jer 48:39 349
h hath Moab turned the back with Jer 48:39 349
H is the city of praise not left, Jer 49:25 349
H is the hammer of the whole Jer 50:23 349
h is Babylon become a desolation Jer 50:23 349
H is Sheshach taken Jer 51:41 349
h is the praise of the whole Jer 51:41
h is Babylon become an Jer 51:41 349
H doth the city sit solitary, Lam 1:1 349
h is she become as a widow Lam 1:1
h is she become tributary Lam 1:1
H hath the Lord covered the Lam 2:1 349
H is the gold become dim Lam 4:1 349
h is the most fine gold changed Lam 4:1
h are they esteemed as earthen Lam 4:2
H much more when I send my four Eze 14:21 637
h much less shall it be meet yet Eze 15:5 637
H weak is thine heart, saith the Eze 16:30 4100
H art thou destroyed, that wast Eze 26:17 349
in them, *h* should we then live Eze 33:10 349
H great are his signs Dan 4:3 4101
and *h* mighty are his wonders Dan 4:3 4101
H long shall be the vision Dan 8:13 5704
For *h* can the servant of this my Dan 10:17 1963
H long shall it be to the end of Dan 12:6 5704
h long will it be ere they attain Hos 8:5 5704
H shall I give thee up, Ephraim Hos 11:8 349
h shall I deliver thee, Israel Hos 11:8
h shall I make thee as Admah Hos 11:8 349
h shall I set thee as Zeboim Hos 11:8
H do the beasts groan Joel 1:18 4100
by night, (*h* art thou cut off Obad 5 349
H are the things of Esau searched Obad 6 349
h are his hidden things sought up Obad 6
h hath he removed it from me Mic 2:4 349
h long shall I cry, and thou wilt Hab 1:2 5704
which is not his! *h* long? Hab 2:6 5704
h is she become a desolation, a Zeph 2:15 349
and *h* do ye see it now Hag 2:3 4100
h long wilt thou not have mercy Zec 1:12 5704
For *h* great is his goodness, and Zec 9:17 4100
and *h* great is his beauty Zec 9:17 4100
h great is that darkness Mt 6:23 *4214*
lilies of the field, *h* they grow Mt 6:28 *4459*
Or *h* wilt thou say to thy brother Mt 7:4 *4459*
know *h* to give good gifts unto Mt 7:11
h much more shall your Father Mt 7:11 *4214*
take no thought *h* or what ye Mt 10:19 *4459*
h much more shall they call them Mt 10:25 *4214*
H he entered into the house of Mt 12:4 *4459*
h that on the sabbath days the Mt 12:5
H much then is a man better than Mt 12:12 *4214*
him, *h* they might destroy him Mt 12:14 *3704*
h shall then his kingdom stand Mt 12:26 *4459*
Or else *h* can one enter into a Mt 12:29 *4459*
h can ye, being evil, speak good Mt 12:34 *4459*
unto them, *H* many loaves have ye Mt 15:34 *4214*
h many baskets ye took up Mt 16:9 *4214*
h many baskets ye took up Mt 16:10 *4214*
H is it that ye do not understand Mt 16:11 *4459*
Then understood they *h* that he Mt 16:12
h that he must go unto Jerusalem, Mt 16:21
h long shall I be with you Mt 17:17 *2193*
h long shall I suffer you Mt 17:17 *4219*
H think ye? Mt 18:12 *5101*
h oft shall my brother sin Mt 18:21 *4212*
H soon is the fig tree withered Mt 21:20 *4459*
h camest thou in hither not Mt 22:12 *4459*
took counsel *h* they might Mt 22:15 *3704*
H then doth David in spirit call Mt 22:43 *4459*
h is he his son? Mt 22:45 *4459*
h can ye escape the damnation of Mt 23:33 *4459*
h often would I have gathered thy Mt 23:37
But *h* then shall the scriptures Mt 26:54 *4459*
Hearest thou not *h* many things Mt 27:13 *4214*
H is it that he eateth and Mk 2:16 *5101*
H he went into the house of God Mk 2:26 *4459*
him, *h* they might destroy him Mk 3:6 *3704*
H can Satan cast out Satan Mk 3:23 *4459*
h then will ye know all parables Mk 4:13 *4459*
and grow up, he knoweth not *h* Mk 4:27 *5613*
h is it that ye have no faith Mk 4:40 *4459*
them *h* it befell to him that was Mk 5:16 *4459*
tell them *h* great things the Lord Mk 5:19 *3745*
began to publish in Decapolis *h* Mk 5:20 *3745*
unto them, *H* many loaves have ye Mk 6:38 *4214*
asked them, *H* many loaves have ye Mk 8:5 *4214*
h many baskets full of fragments Mk 8:19 *4214*
h many baskets full of fragments Mk 8:20 *4214*
H is it that ye do not understand Mk 8:21 *4459*
h it is written of the Son of man Mk 9:12 *4459*
h long shall I be with you Mk 9:19 *2193*

h long shall I suffer you Mk 9:19 2193
H long is it ago since this came Mk 9:21 4214
H hardly shall they that have Mk 10:23 4459
h hard is it for them that trust Mk 10:24 4459
sought *h* they might destroy him Mk 11:18 4459
h in the bush God spake unto him, Mk 12:26 5613
H say the scribes that Christ is Mk 12:35 4459
beheld *h* the people cast money Mk 12:41 4459
the scribes sought *h* they might Mk 14:1 4459
he sought *h* he might conveniently Mk 14:11 4459
behold *h* many things they witness Mk 15:4 4214
H shall this be, seeing I know Lk 1:34 4459
her cousins heard *h* the Lord had Lk 1:58 3754
h he would have him called Lk 1:62 5101
H is it that ye sought me Lk 2:49 5101
H he went into the house of God, Lk 6:4 5613
Either *h* canst thou say to thy Lk 6:42 4459
h that the blind see, the lame Lk 7:22 3754
Take heed therefore *h* ye hear Lk 8:18 4459
shew *h* great things God hath done Lk 8:39 3754
throughout the whole city *h* great Lk 8:39 3754
h she was healed immediately Lk 8:47 5613
h long shall I be with you, and Lk 9:41 2193
h readest thou? Lk 10:26 4459
know *h* to give good gifts unto Lk 11:13
h much more shall your heavenly Lk 11:13 4214
h shall his kingdom stand Lk 11:18 4559
take ye no thought *h* or what Lk 12:11 4559
h much more are ye better than Lk 12:24 4214
Consider the lilies *h* they grow Lk 12:27 4459
h much more will he clothe you, O Lk 12:28 4214
h am I straitened till it be Lk 12:50 4459
but *h* is it that ye do not Lk 12:56 4459
h often would I have gathered thy Lk 13:34 4212
when he marked *h* they chose out Lk 14:7 4459
H many hired servants of my Lk 15:17 4214
H is it that I hear this of thee Lk 16:2 5101
H much owest thou unto my lord Lk 16:5 4214
to another, And *h* much owest thou Lk 16:7 4214
H hardly shall they that have Lk 18:24 4459
that he might know *h* much every Lk 19:15 5101
H say they that Christ is David's Lk 20:41 4459
him Lord, *h* is he then his son Lk 20:44 4459
h it was adorned with goodly Lk 21:5 3754
scribes sought *h* they might kill Lk 22:2 4459
h he might betray him unto them Lk 22:4 4459
h he had said unto him, Before Lk 22:61 5613
sepulchre, and *h* his body was laid Lk 23:55 5613
remember *h* he spake unto you when Lk 24:6 5613
h the chief priests and our rulers Lk 24:20 3704
h he was known of them in Lk 24:35 5613
H can a man be born when he is Jn 3:4 4459
unto him, *H* can these things be Jn 3:9 4459
h shall ye believe, if I tell you Jn 3:12 4459
h the Pharisees had heard that Jn 4:1 3754
H is it that thou, being a Jew, Jn 4:9 4459
H can ye believe, which receive Jn 5:44 4459
h shall ye believe my words Jn 5:47 4459
h is it then that he saith, I Jn 6:42 4459
H can this man give us his flesh Jn 6:52 4459
H knoweth this man letters, Jn 7:15 4459
h sayest thou, Ye shall be made Jn 8:33 4459
him, *H* were thine eyes opened Jn 9:10 4459
him *h* he had received his sight Jn 9:15 4459
H can a man that is a sinner do Jn 9:16 4459
h then doth he now see Jn 9:19 4459
h opened he thine eyes Jn 9:26 4459
H long dost thou make us to doubt Jn 10:24 2193
the Jews, Behold *h* he loved him Jn 11:36 4459
Perceive ye *h* ye prevail nothing Jn 12:19 3754
h sayest thou, The Son of man Jn 12:34 4459
and *h* can we know the way Jn 14:5 4459
h sayest thou then, Shew us the Jn 14:9 4459
h is it that thou wilt manifest Jn 14:22 5101
Ye have heard *h* I said unto you, Jn 14:28 3754
h hear we every man in our own Acts 2:8 4459
finding nothing *h* they might Acts 4:21 4459
H is it that ye have agreed Acts 5:9 5101
h that God by his hand would Acts 7:25
H can I, except some man should Acts 8:31 4459
h much evil he hath done to thy Acts 9:13 3745
For I will shew him *h* great Acts 9:16 3745
declared unto them *h* he had seen Acts 9:27 4459
h he had preached boldly at Acts 9:27 4459
Ye know *h* that it is an unlawful Acts 10:28 5613
H God anointed Jesus of Nazareth Acts 10:38 5613
he shewed us *h* he had seen an Acts 11:13 4459
h that he said, John indeed Acts 11:16 5613
told *h* Peter stood before the Acts 12:14
declared unto them *h* the Lord had Acts 12:17 4459
h that the promise which was made Acts 13:32
h he had opened the door of faith Acts 14:27
ye know *h* that a good while ago Acts 15:7
Simeon hath declared *h* God at the Acts 15:14 2531
of the Lord, and see *h* they do Acts 15:36 4459
man is there that knoweth not *h* Acts 19:35
h I kept back nothing that was Acts 20:20 5613
h that so labouring ye ought to Acts 20:35
h he said, It is more blessed to Acts 20:35 3754
h many thousands of Jews there Acts 21:20 4214
when it was told me *h* that the Acts 23:30
for then *h* shall God judge the Rom 3:6 4459
H was it then reckoned Rom 4:10 4459
H shall we, that are dead to sin, Rom 6:2 4459
h that the law hath dominion Rom 7:1
but *h* to perform that which is Rom 7:18
h shall he not with him also Rom 8:32 4459
H then shall they call on him in Rom 10:14 4459
h shall they believe in him of Rom 10:14 4459
h shall they hear without a Rom 10:14 4459
h shall they preach, except they Rom 10:15 5613
H beautiful are the feet of them Rom 10:15
h he maketh intercession to God Rom 11:2 5613
h much more their fulness Rom 11:12 4214
h much more shall these, which be Rom 11:24 4214
h unsearchable are his judgments, Rom 11:33 5613
h that not many wise men after 1Cor 1:26
take heed *h* he buildeth thereupon 1Cor 3:10 4459
h much more things that pertain 1Cor 6:3 3386
or *h* knowest thou, O man, whether 1Cor 7:16 5101
Lord, *h* he may please the Lord 1Cor 7:32 4459
world, *h* he may please his wife 1Cor 7:33 4459
h she may please her husband 1Cor 7:34 4459
h that all our fathers were under 1Cor 10:1
h shall it be known what is piped 1Cor 14:7 4459
h shall it be known what is 1Cor 14:9 4459
h shall he that occupieth the 1Cor 14:16 4459
H is it then, brethren 1Cor 14:26 5101
h that Christ died for our sins 1Cor 15:3
h say some among you that there 1Cor 15:12 4459
say, *H* are the dead raised up 1Cor 15:35 4459
H shall not the ministration of 2Cor 3:8 4459
h with fear and trembling ye 2Cor 7:15 5613
H that in a great trial of 2Cor 8:2
H that he was caught up into 2Cor 12:4
H that Jesus Christ is in you, 2Cor 13:5
religion, *h* that beyond measure I Gal 1:13
h turn ye again to the weak and Gal 4:9 4459
Ye know *h* through infirmity of Gal 4:13 3754
Ye see *h* large a letter I have Gal 6:11 4080
H that by revelation he made Eph 3:3
h I do, Tychicus, a beloved Eph 6:21 5101
h greatly I long after you all in Phil 1:8 5613
I shall see *h* it will go with me Phil 2:23 4012
I know both *h* to be abased Phil 4:12
and I know *h* to abound Phil 4:12
that ye may know *h* ye ought to Col 4:6 4459
h ye turned to God from idols to 1Th 1:9 4459
h holily and justly and unblameably 1Th 2:10 5613
As ye know *h* we exhorted and 1Th 2:11 5613
received of us *h* ye ought to walk 1Th 4:1 4459
know *h* to possess his vessel in 1Th 4:4
For yourselves know *h* ye ought to 2Th 3:7 4459
know not *h* to rule his own house 1Ti 3:5
h shall he take care of the 1Ti 3:5 4459
that thou mayest know *h* thou 1Ti 3:15 4459
in *h* many things he ministered 2Ti 1:18 3745
but *h* much more unto thee, both Philem 16 4214
albeit I do not say to thee *h* Philem 19 3754
H shall we escape, if we neglect Heb 2:3 4459
Now consider *h* great this man was Heb 7:4 4080
by *h* much also he is the mediator Heb 8:6 3745
H much more shall the blood of Heb 9:14 4214
Of *h* much sorer punishment, Heb 10:29 4214
For ye know *h* that afterward, Heb 12:17 3754
Seest thou *h* faith wrought with Jas 2:22 3754
Ye see then *h* that by works a man Jas 2:24
h great a matter a little fire Jas 3:5 2245
The Lord knoweth *h* to deliver the 2Pet 2:9
h dwelleth the love of God in him 1Jn 3:17 4459
h can he love God whom he hath 1Jn 4:20 4459
h that the Lord, having saved the Jude 5
h that they told you there should Jude 18
h thou canst not bear them which Rev 2:2 3754
therefore *h* thou hast received Rev 3:3 4459
H long, O Lord, holy and true, Rev 6:10 2193
H much she hath glorified herself Rev 18:7 3745

HOWBEIT
H Sisera fled away on his feet to Judg 4:17
H the king of the children of Judg 11:28
H the hair of his head began to Judg 16:22
h the name of the city was Laish Judg 18:29 199
H we may not give them wives of Judg 21:18
h there is a kinsman nearer than Ruth 3:12
h yet protest solemnly unto them, 1Sa 8:9 389
H he refused to turn aside 2Sa 2:23
H, because by this deed thou hast 2Sa 12:14 657
H he would not hearken unto her 2Sa 13:14
h he would not go, but blessed 2Sa 13:25
h he attained not unto the first 2Sa 23:19
h the kingdom is turned about, and 1Kin 2:15
H I believed not the words, until 1Kin 10:7
H I will not rend away all the 1Kin 11:13 7535
h let me go in any wise 1Kin 11:22
H I will not take the whole 1Kin 11:34
h the slingers went about it, and 2Kin 3:25
h the LORD hath shewed me that he 2Kin 8:10
H from the sins of Jeroboam the 2Kin 10:29
H there were not made for the 2Kin 12:13
H the high places were not taken 2Kin 14:4
H the high places were not 2Kin 15:35
H every nation made gods of their 2Kin 17:29
H they did not hearken, but they 2Kin 17:40
H there was no reckoning made 2Kin 22:7
h he attained not to the first 1Chr 11:21
H the LORD God of Israel chose me 1Chr 28:4
H I believed not their words, 2Chr 9:6
h the king of Israel stayed 2Chr 18:34
H the high places were not taken 2Chr 20:33
H the LORD would not destroy the 2Chr 21:7
H they buried him in the city of 2Chr 21:20
H the Levites hastened it not 2Chr 24:5
h he entered not into the temple 2Chr 27:2
H in the business of the 2Chr 32:31 3651
H thou art just in all that is Neh 9:33
h our God turned the curse into a Neh 13:2
H he will not stretch out his Job 30:24
H he meaneth not so, neither doth Is 10:7
H I sent unto you all my servants Jer 44:4
H this kind goeth not out but by Mt 17:21
H Jesus suffered him not, but Mk 5:19
H in vain do they worship me, Mk 7:7
(*H* there came other boats from Jn 6:23 1161
H no man spake openly of him for Jn 7:13 3305
H we know this man whence he is Jn 7:27 235
H Jesus spake of his death Jn 11:13
H when he, the Spirit of truth, Jn 16:13
H many of them which heard the Acts 4:4
H the most High dwelleth not in Acts 7:48 235
H, as the disciples stood round Acts 14:20
H certain men clave unto him, and Acts 17:34
H we must be cast upon a certain Acts 27:26
H they looked when he should have Acts 28:6
H we speak wisdom among them that. 1Cor 2:6
H there is not in every man that 1Cor 8:7 235
h in the spirit he speaketh 1Cor 14:2
h in malice be ye children, but 1Cor 14:20 235
H that was not first which is 1Cor 15:46 235
H whereinsoever any is bold, (I 2Cor 11:21
H then, when ye knew not God, ye Gal 4:8 235
H for this cause I obtained mercy 1Ti 1:16 235
h not all that came out of Egypt Heb 3:16 235

HOWL
H ye; for the day of the LORD Is 13:6 3213
H, O gate Is 14:31 3213
Moab shall *h* over Nebo, and over Is 15:2 3213
their streets, every one shall *h* Is 15:3 3213
h for Moab, every one shall *h* Is 16:7 3213
H, ye ships of Tarshish Is 23:1 3213
h, ye inhabitants of the isle Is 23:6 3213
H, ye ships of Tarshish Is 23:14 3213
rule over them make them to *h* Is 52:5 3213
shall *h* for vexation of spirit Is 65:14 3213
you with sackcloth, lament and *h* Jer 4:8 3213
H, ye shepherds, and cry Jer 25:34 3213
inhabitants of the land shall *h* Jer 47:2 3213
h and cry; tell ye it Jer 48:20 3213
Therefore will I *h* for Moab Jer 48:31 3213
They shall *h*, saying, How is it Jer 48:39 3213
H, O Heshbon, for Ai is spoiled Jer 49:3 3213
h for her; take balm Jer 51:8 3213
Cry and *h*, son of man Eze 21:12 3213
H ye, Woe worth the day Eze 30:2 3213
and *h*, all ye drinkers of wine, Joel 1:5 3213
h, O ye vinedressers, for the Joel 1:11 3213
h, ye ministers of the altar Joel 1:13 3213
Therefore I will wail and *h* Mic 1:8 3213
H, ye inhabitants of Maktesh, for Zeph 1:11 3213
H, fir tree; for the cedar Zec 11:2 3213
h, O ye oaks of Bashan Zec 11:2 3213
h for your miseries that shall Jas 5:1 3649

HOWLED
when they *h* upon their beds Hos 7:14 3213

HOWLING
and in the waste *h* wilderness Deut 32:10 3214
the *h* thereof unto Eglaim, and the Is 15:8 3213
the *h* thereof unto Beer-elim Is 15:8 3213
an *h* of the principal of the Jer 25:36 3213
an *h* from the second, and a great Zeph 1:10 3213
a voice of the *h* of the shepherds Zec 11:3 3213

HOWLINGS
the temple shall be *h* in that day Amos 8:3 3213

HOWSOEVER
h let all thy wants lie upon me Judg 19:20 7535
of Zadok yet again to Joab, But *h* 2Sa 18:22
But *h*, said he, let me run 2Sa 18:23
not be cut off, *h* I punished them Zeph 3:7

HOZAI See SEERS.

HUBBAH See JUHUBBAH.

HUGE
Ethiopians and the Lubims a *h* host 2Chr 16:8 7230

HUKKOK (*huk'-kok*) See HELKATH, HUKOK. *A place in Naphtali.*
and goeth out from thence to *H* Josh 19:34 2712

HUKOK (*hu'-kok*) See HUKKOK. *A city in Asher.*
H with her suburbs, and Rehob with 1Chr 6:75 2712

HUL (*hul*) *A son of Aram.*
Uz, and *H*, and Gether, and Mash Gen 10:23 2343
and Lud, and Aram, and Uz, and *H* 1Chr 1:17 2343

HULDAH (*hul'-dah*) *A prophetess.*
went unto *H* the prophetess, the 2Kin 22:14 2468
went to *H* the prophetess, the 2Chr 34:22 2468

HUMBLE
refuse to *h* thyself before me Ex 10:3 6031
to *h* thee, and to prove thee, to Deut 8:2 6031
knew not, that he might *h* thee Deut 8:16 6031
h ye them, and do with them what Judg 19:24 6031
shall *h* themselves, and pray, and 2Chr 7:14 3665
thou didst *h* thyself before God, 2Chr 34:27 3665
and he shall save the *h* person Job 22:29
forgetteth not the cry of the *h* Ps 9:12 6041
forget not the *h* Ps 10:12 6041
hast heard the desire of the *h* Ps 10:17 6041
the *h* shall hear thereof, and be Ps 34:2 6041
The *h* shall see this, and be glad Ps 69:32 6041
h thyself, and make sure thy Prov 6:3 7511
be of an *h* spirit with the lowly Prov 16:19 8213
shall uphold the *h* in spirit Prov 29:23 8217
that is of a contrite and *h* spirit Is 57:15 8217
to revive the spirit of the *h* Is 57:15 8217
the queen, *H* yourselves, sit down Jer 13:18 8213
Whosoever therefore shall *h* Mt 18:4 5013
he that shall *h* himself shall be Mt 23:12 5013
my God will *h* me among you, and 2Cor 12:21 5013
but giveth grace unto the *h* Jas 4:6 5011
H yourselves in the sight of the Jas 4:10 5013
proud, and giveth grace to the *h* 1Pet 5:5 5011
H yourselves therefore under the 1Pet 5:6 5013

HUMBLED
their uncircumcised hearts be *h* Lev 26:41 3665
he *h* thee, and suffered thee to Deut 8:3 6031
of her, because thou hast *h* her Deut 21:14 6031
because he hath *h* his neighbour's Deut 22:24 6031
because he hath *h* her, he may not Deut 22:29 6031

thou hast *h* thyself before the ... 2Kin 22:19 3665
Israel and the king *h* themselves ... 2Chr 12:6 3665
LORD saw that they *h* themselves ... 2Chr 12:7 3665
saying, They have *h* themselves ... 2Chr 12:7 3665
And when he *h* himself, the wrath ... 2Chr 12:12 3665
and of Zebulun *h* themselves ... 2Chr 30:11 3665
Notwithstanding Hezekiah *h* ... 2Chr 32:26 3665
h himself greatly before the God ... 2Chr 33:12 3665
and graven images, before he was *h* ... 2Chr 33:19 3665
h not himself before the LORD, as ... 2Chr 33:23 3665
Manasseh his father had *h* himself ... 2Chr 33:23 3665
h not himself before Jeremiah the ... 2Chr 36:12 3665
I *h* my soul with fasting ... Ps 35:13 6031
The lofty looks of man shall be *h* ... Is 2:11 8213
and the mighty man shall be *h* ... Is 5:15 8213
the eyes of the lofty shall be *h* ... Is 5:15 8213
down, and the haughty shall be *h* ... Is 10:33 8213
They are not *h* even unto this day ... Jer 44:10 1792
in remembrance, and is *h* in me ... Lam 3:20 7743
in thee have they *h* her that was ... Eze 22:10 6031
another in thee hath *h* his sister ... Eze 22:11 6031
hast not *h* thine heart, though ... Dan 5:22 8214
he *h* himself, and became obedient ... Phil 2:8 *5013*

HUMBLEDST
h thyself before me, and didst ... 2Chr 34:27 3665

HUMBLENESS
kindness, *h* of mind, meekness, ... Col 3:12 *5012*

HUMBLETH
thou how Ahab *h* himself before me ... 1Kin 21:29 3665
because he *h* himself before me, I ... 1Kin 21:29 3665
h himself, that the poor may fall ... Ps 10:10 7817
Who *h* himself to behold the ... Ps 113:6 8213
down, and the great man *h* himself ... Is 2:9 8213
he that *h* himself shall be ... Lk 14:11 *5013*
he that *h* himself shall be ... Lk 18:14 *5013*

HUMBLY
I *h* beseech thee that I may find ... 2Sa 16:4 7812
mercy, and to walk *h* with thy God ... Mic 6:8 6800

HUMILIATION
In his *h* his judgment was taken ... Acts 8:33 *5014*

HUMILITY
and before honour is *h* ... Prov 15:33 6038
and before honour is *h* ... Prov 18:12 6038
By *h* and the fear of the LORD are ... Prov 22:4 6038
the Lord with all *h* of mind ... Acts 20:19 *5012*
of your reward in a voluntary *h* ... Col 2:18 *5012*
of wisdom in will worship, and *h* ... Col 2:23 *5012*
to another, and be clothed with *h* ... 1Pet 5:5 *5012*

HUMTAH (*hum'-tah*) *A city in Judah.*
And *H*, and Kirjath-arba, which is ... Josh 15:54 2457

HUNDRED
And Adam lived an *h* and thirty ... Gen 5:3 3967
begotten Seth were eight *h* years ... Gen 5:4 3967
days that Adam lived were nine *h* ... Gen 5:5 3967
And Seth lived an *h* and five years, ... Gen 5:6 3967
lived after he begat Enos eight *h* ... Gen 5:7 3967
all the days of Seth were nine *h* ... Gen 5:8 3967
after he begat Cainan eight *h* ... Gen 5:10 3967
all the days of Enos were nine *h* ... Gen 5:11 3967
after he begat Mahalaleel eight *h* ... Gen 5:13 3967
the days of Cainan were nine *h* ... Gen 5:14 3967
after he begat Jared eight *h* ... Gen 5:16 3967
of Mahalaleel were eight *h* ninety ... Gen 5:17 3967
And Jared lived an *h* sixty ... Gen 5:18 3967
he begat Enoch eight *h* years ... Gen 5:19 3967
days of Jared were nine *h* sixty ... Gen 5:20 3967
he begat Methuselah three *h* years ... Gen 5:22 3967
days of Enoch were three *h* sixty ... Gen 5:23 3967
And Methuselah lived an *h* eighty ... Gen 5:25 3967
he begat Lamech seven *h* eighty ... Gen 5:26 3967
of Methuselah were nine *h* sixty ... Gen 5:27 3967
And Lamech lived an *h* eighty ... Gen 5:28 3967
after he begat Noah five *h* ninety ... Gen 5:30 3967
of Lamech were seven *h* seventy ... Gen 5:31 3967
And Noah was five *h* years old ... Gen 5:32 3967
yet his days shall be an *h* ... Gen 6:3 3967
the ark shall be three *h* cubits ... Gen 6:15 3967
Noah was six *h* years old when the ... Gen 7:6 3967
prevailed upon the earth an *h* ... Gen 7:24 3967
and after the end of the *h* ... Gen 8:3 3967
lived after the flood three *h* ... Gen 9:28 3967
all the days of Noah were nine *h* ... Gen 9:29 3967
Shem was an *h* years old, and begat ... Gen 11:10 3967
he begat Arphaxad five *h* years ... Gen 11:11 3967
lived after he begat Salah four *h* ... Gen 11:13 3967
lived after he begat Eber four *h* ... Gen 11:15 3967
lived after he begat Peleg four *h* ... Gen 11:17 3967
lived after he begat Reu two *h* ... Gen 11:19 3967
lived after he begat Serug two *h* ... Gen 11:21 3967
after he begat Nahor two *h* years ... Gen 11:23 3967
lived after he begat Terah an *h* ... Gen 11:25 3967
And the days of Terah were two *h* ... Gen 11:32 3967
born in his own house, three *h* ... Gen 14:14 3967
shall afflict them four *h* years ... Gen 15:13 3967
unto him that is an *h* years old ... Gen 17:17 3967
And Abraham was an *h* years old ... Gen 21:5 3967
And Sarah was an *h* and seven and ... Gen 23:1 3967
is worth four *h* shekels of silver ... Gen 23:15 3967
four *h* shekels of silver, current ... Gen 23:16 3967
an *h* threescore and fifteen years ... Gen 25:7 3967
of the life of Ishmael, an *h* ... Gen 25:17 3967
meet thee, and four *h* men with him ... Gen 32:6 3967
Two *h* she goats, and twenty he ... Gen 32:14 3967
two *h* ewes, and twenty rams, ... Gen 32:14 3967
Esau came, and with him four *h* men .. Gen 33:1 3967
father, for an *h* pieces of money ... Gen 33:19 3967
And the days of Isaac were an *h* ... Gen 35:28 3967
he gave three *h* pieces of silver ... Gen 45:22 3967
years of my pilgrimage are an *h* ... Gen 47:9 3967
whole age of Jacob was an *h* forty ... Gen 47:28 3967

and Joseph lived an *h* and ten years ... Gen 50:22 3967
So Joseph died, being an *h* ... Gen 50:26 3967
the life of Levi were an *h* thirty ... Ex 6:16 3967
life of Kohath were an *h* thirty ... Ex 6:18 3967
of the life of Amram were an *h* ... Ex 6:20 3967
about six *h* thousand on foot that ... Ex 12:37 3967
who dwelt in Egypt, was four *h* ... Ex 12:40 3967
to pass at the end of the four *h* ... Ex 12:41 3967
he took six *h* chosen chariots, and ... Ex 14:7 3967
of an *h* cubits long for one side ... Ex 27:9 3967
be hangings of an *h* cubits long ... Ex 27:11 3967
of the court shall be an *h* cubits ... Ex 27:18 3967
of pure myrrh five *h* shekels ... Ex 30:23 3967
cinnamon half so much, even two *h* ... Ex 30:23 3967
and of sweet calamus two *h* ... Ex 30:23 3967
And of cassia five *h* shekels ... Ex 30:24 3967
of fine twined linen, an *h* cubits ... Ex 38:9 3967
the hangings were an *h* cubits ... Ex 38:11 3967
and nine talents, and seven *h* ... Ex 38:24 3967
the congregation was an *h* talents ... Ex 38:25 3967
and a thousand seven *h* and ... Ex 38:25 3967
for six *h* thousand and three ... Ex 38:26 3967
and three thousand and five *h* ... Ex 38:26 3967
of the *h* talents of silver were ... Ex 38:27 3967
h sockets of the *h* talents ... Ex 38:27 3967
of the thousand seven *h* seventy ... Ex 38:28 3967
and two thousand and four *h* shekels .. Ex 38:29 3967
And five of you shall chase an *h* ... Lev 26:8 3967
an *h* of you shall put ten ... Lev 26:8 3967
forty and six thousand and five *h* ... Num 1:21 3967
fifty and nine thousand and three *h* ... Num 1:23 3967
were forty and five thousand six *h* ... Num 1:25 3967
and fourteen thousand and six *h* ... Num 1:27 3967
fifty and four thousand and four *h* ... Num 1:29 3967
fifty and seven thousand and four *h* ... Num 1:31 3967
were forty thousand and five *h* ... Num 1:33 3967
thirty and two thousand and two *h* ... Num 1:35 3967
thirty and five thousand and four *h* ... Num 1:37 3967
and two thousand and seven *h* ... Num 1:39 3967
forty and one thousand and five *h* ... Num 1:41 3967
fifty and three thousand and four *h* ... Num 1:43 3967
were numbered were six *h* thousand ... Num 1:46 3967
and three thousand and five *h* ... Num 1:46 3967
and fourteen thousand and six *h* ... Num 2:4 3967
fifty and four thousand and four *h* ... Num 2:6 3967
fifty and seven thousand and four *h* ... Num 2:8 3967
camp of Judah were an *h* thousand ... Num 2:9 3967
and six thousand and four *h* ... Num 2:9 3967
forty and six thousand and five *h* ... Num 2:11 3967
fifty and nine thousand and three *h* ... Num 2:13 3967
forty and five thousand and six *h* ... Num 2:15 3967
camp of Reuben were an *h* thousand ... Num 2:16 3967
fifty and one thousand and four *h* ... Num 2:16 3967
were forty thousand and five *h* ... Num 2:19 3967
thirty and two thousand and two *h* ... Num 2:21 3967
thirty and five thousand and four *h* ... Num 2:23 3967
of Ephraim were an *h* thousand ... Num 2:24 3967
and eight thousand and an *h* ... Num 2:24 3967
and two thousand and seven *h* ... Num 2:26 3967
forty and one thousand and five *h* ... Num 2:28 3967
fifty and three thousand and four *h* ... Num 2:30 3967
camp of Dan were an *h* thousand ... Num 2:31 3967
fifty and seven thousand and six *h* ... Num 2:31 3967
their hosts were six *h* thousand ... Num 2:32 3967
and three thousand and five *h* ... Num 2:32 3967
were seven thousand and five *h* ... Num 3:22 3967
were eight thousand and six *h* ... Num 3:28 3967
were six thousand and two *h* ... Num 3:34 3967
were twenty and two thousand two *h* . Num 3:43 3967
are to be redeemed of the two *h* ... Num 3:46 3967
a thousand three *h* and threescore ... Num 3:50 3967
were two thousand seven *h* ... Num 4:36 3967
were two thousand and six *h* ... Num 4:40 3967
were three thousand and two *h* ... Num 4:44 3967
were eight thousand and five *h* ... Num 4:48 3967
the weight thereof was an *h* ... Num 7:13 3967
the weight whereof was an *h* ... Num 7:19 3967
the weight whereof was an *h* ... Num 7:25 3967
charger of the weight of an *h* ... Num 7:31 3967
the weight whereof was an *h* ... Num 7:37 3967
charger of the weight of an *h* ... Num 7:43 3967
the weight whereof was an *h* ... Num 7:49 3967
charger of the weight of an *h* ... Num 7:55 3967
the weight whereof was an *h* ... Num 7:61 3967
the weight whereof was an *h* ... Num 7:67 3967
the weight whereof was an *h* ... Num 7:73 3967
the weight whereof was an *h* ... Num 7:79 3967
charger of silver weighing an *h* ... Num 7:85 3967
four *h* shekels, after the shekel ... Num 7:85 3967
the gold of the spoons was an *h* ... Num 7:86 3967
are six *h* thousand footmen ... Num 11:21 3967
of the children of Israel, two *h* ... Num 16:2 3967
LORD every man his censer, two *h* ... Num 16:17 3967
the LORD, and consumed the two *h* ... Num 16:35 3967
were fourteen thousand and seven *h* ... Num 16:49 3967
and three thousand and seven *h* ... Num 26:7 3967
what time the fire devoured two *h* ... Num 26:10 3967
twenty and two thousand and two *h* ... Num 26:14 3967
of them, forty thousand and five *h* ... Num 26:18 3967
and sixteen thousand and five *h* ... Num 26:22 3967
and four thousand and three *h* ... Num 26:25 3967
threescore thousand and five *h* ... Num 26:27 3967
fifty and two thousand and seven *h* ... Num 26:34 3967
thirty and two thousand and five *h* ... Num 26:37 3967
forty and five thousand and six *h* ... Num 26:41 3967
and four thousand and four *h* ... Num 26:43 3967
fifty and three thousand and four *h* ... Num 26:47 3967
forty and five thousand and four *h* ... Num 26:50 3967
six *h* thousand and a thousand ... Num 26:51 3967
and a thousand seven *h* ... Num 26:51 3967
one soul of five *h*, both of the ... Num 31:28 3967
was six *h* thousand and seventy ... Num 31:32 3967
was in number three *h* thousand ... Num 31:36 3967
thirty thousand and five *h* sheep ... Num 31:36 3967

tribute of the sheep was six *h* ... Num 31:37 3967
were thirty thousand and five *h* ... Num 31:39 3967
congregation was three *h* thousand ... Num 31:43 3967
seven thousand and five *h* sheep, ... Num 31:43 3967
thirty thousand asses and five *h* ... Num 31:45 3967
was sixteen thousand seven *h* ... Num 31:52 3967
And Aaron was an *h* and twenty and .. Num 33:39 3967
him in an *h* shekels of silver ... Deut 22:19 3967
And he said unto them, I am an *h* ... Deut 31:2 3967
Moses was an *h* and twenty ... Deut 34:7 3967
two *h* shekels of silver, and a ... Josh 7:21 3967
of the LORD, died, being an *h* ... Josh 24:29 3967
Shechem for an *h* pieces of silver ... Josh 24:32 3967
of the LORD, died, being an *h* ... Judg 2:8 3967
six *h* men with an ox goad ... Judg 3:31 3967
for he had nine *h* chariots of ... Judg 4:3 3967
even nine *h* chariots of iron, and ... Judg 4:13 3967
to their mouth, were three *h* men ... Judg 7:6 3967
By the three *h* men that lapped ... Judg 7:7 3967
and retained those three *h* men ... Judg 7:8 3967
he divided the three *h* men into ... Judg 7:16 3967
the *h* men that were with him, ... Judg 7:19 3967
the three *h* blew the trumpets, and ... Judg 7:22 3967
the three *h* men that were with ... Judg 8:4 3967
for there fell an *h* and twenty ... Judg 8:10 3967
and seven *h* shekels of gold ... Judg 8:26 3967
coasts of Arnon, three *h* years ... Judg 11:26 3967
went and caught three *h* foxes ... Judg 15:4 3967
of us eleven *h* pieces of silver ... Judg 16:5 3967
The eleven *h* shekels of silver ... Judg 17:2 3967
h shekels of silver to his mother ... Judg 17:3 3967
took two *h* shekels of silver ... Judg 17:4 3967
six *h* men appointed with weapons ... Judg 18:11 3967
the six *h* men appointed with ... Judg 18:16 3967
of the gate with the six *h* men ... Judg 18:17 3967
four *h* thousand footmen that drew ... Judg 20:2 3967
we will take ten men of an *h* ... Judg 20:10 3967
an *h* of a thousand, and a thousand ... Judg 20:10 3967
were numbered seven *h* chosen men ... Judg 20:15 3967
seven *h* chosen men lefthanded ... Judg 20:16 3967
were numbered four *h* thousand men .. Judg 20:17 3967
and five thousand and an *h* men ... Judg 20:35 3967
But six *h* men turned and fled to ... Judg 20:47 3967
four *h* young virgins, that had ... Judg 21:12 3967
of Israel were three *h* thousand ... 1Sa 11:8 3967
present with him, about six *h* men ... 1Sa 13:15 3967
with him were about six *h* men ... 1Sa 14:2 3967
two *h* thousand footmen, and ten ... 1Sa 15:4 3967
weighed six *h* shekels of iron ... 1Sa 17:7 3967
but an *h* foreskins of the ... 1Sa 18:25 3967
slew of the Philistines two *h* men ... 1Sa 18:27 3967
were with him about four *h* men ... 1Sa 22:2 3967
his men, which were about six *h* ... 1Sa 23:13 3967
up after David about four *h* men ... 1Sa 25:13 3967
and two *h* abode by the stuff ... 1Sa 25:13 3967
made haste, and took two *h* loaves ... 1Sa 25:18 3967
an *h* clusters of raisins ... 1Sa 25:18 3967
two *h* cakes of figs, and laid them ... 1Sa 25:18 3967
six *h* men that were with him unto ... 1Sa 27:2 3967
the six *h* men that were with him, ... 1Sa 30:9 3967
David pursued, he and four *h* men ... 1Sa 30:10 3967
for two *h* abode behind, which ... 1Sa 30:10 3967
of them, save four *h* young men ... 1Sa 30:17 3967
And David came to the two *h* men ... 1Sa 30:21 3967
of Abner's men, so that three *h* ... 2Sa 2:31 3967
an *h* foreskins of the Philistines ... 2Sa 3:14 3967
seven *h* horsemen, and twenty ... 2Sa 8:4 3967
of them for an *h* chariots ... 2Sa 8:4 3967
seven *h* chariots of the Syrians ... 2Sa 10:18 3967
the hair of his head at two *h* ... 2Sa 14:26 3967
went two *h* men out of Jerusalem ... 2Sa 15:11 3967
six *h* men which came after him ... 2Sa 15:18 3967
upon them two *h* loaves of bread, ... 2Sa 16:1 3967
an *h* bunches of raisins ... 2Sa 16:1 3967
an *h* of summer fruits, and a ... 2Sa 16:1 3967
h shekels of brass in weight ... 2Sa 21:16 3967
lift up his spear against eight *h* ... 2Sa 23:8 3967
up his spear against three *h* ... 2Sa 23:18 3967
there were in Israel eight *h* ... 2Sa 24:9 3967
of Judah were five *h* thousand men ... 2Sa 24:9 3967
an *h* sheep, beside harts, and ... 1Kin 4:23 3967
work, three thousand and three *h* ... 1Kin 5:16 3967
And it came to pass in the four *h* ... 1Kin 6:1 3967
length thereof was an *h* cubits ... 1Kin 7:2 3967
the pomegranates were two *h* in ... 1Kin 7:20 3967
four *h* pomegranates for the two ... 1Kin 7:42 3967
and twenty thousand oxen, and an *h* .. 1Kin 8:63 3967
were over Solomon's work, five *h* ... 1Kin 9:23 3967
fetched from thence gold, four *h* ... 1Kin 9:28 3967
And she gave the king an *h* ... 1Kin 10:10 3967
in one year was six *h* threescore ... 1Kin 10:14 3967
king Solomon made two *h* targets ... 1Kin 10:16 3967
six *h* shekels of gold went to one ... 1Kin 10:16 3967
he made three *h* shields of beaten ... 1Kin 10:17 3967
four *h* chariots, and twelve ... 1Kin 10:26 3967
Egypt for six *h* shekels of silver ... 1Kin 10:29 3967
and an horse for an *h* ... 1Kin 10:29 3967
And he had seven *h* wives, ... 1Kin 11:3 3967
princesses, and three *h* concubines ... 1Kin 11:3 3967
with the tribe of Benjamin, an *h* ... 1Kin 12:21 3967
that Obadiah took an *h* prophets ... 1Kin 18:4 3967
how I hid an *h* men of the LORD's ... 1Kin 18:13 3967
and the prophets of Baal four *h* ... 1Kin 18:19 3967
the prophets of the groves four *h* ... 1Kin 18:19 3967
but Baal's prophets are four *h* ... 1Kin 18:22 3967
the provinces, and they were two *h* ... 1Kin 20:15 3967
an *h* thousand footmen in one day ... 1Kin 20:29 3967
together, about four *h* men ... 1Kin 22:6 3967
of Israel an *h* thousand lambs ... 2Kin 3:4 3967
an *h* thousand rams, with the wool ... 2Kin 3:4 3967
him seven *h* men that drew swords ... 2Kin 3:26 3967
should I set this before an *h* men ... 2Kin 4:43 3967
the corner gate, four *h* cubits ... 2Kin 14:13 3967
Judah three *h* talents of silver ... 2Kin 18:14 3967

of the Assyrians an *h* fourscore ... 2Kin 19:35 3967
tribute of an *h* talents of silver ... 2Kin 23:33 3967
of the sons of Simeon, five *h* men ... 1Chr 4:42 3967
four and forty thousand seven *h* ... 1Chr 5:18 3967
fifty thousand, and of sheep two *h* ... 1Chr 5:21 3967
thousand, and of men an *h* thousand... 1Chr 5:21 3967
two and twenty thousand and six *h* ... 1Chr 7:2 3967
was twenty thousand and two *h* ... 1Chr 7:9 3967
two *h* soldiers, fit to go out for ... 1Chr 7:11 3967
many sons, and sons' sons, an *h* ... 1Chr 8:40 3967
Jeuel, and their brethren, six *h* ... 1Chr 9:6 3967
to their generations, nine *h* ... 1Chr 9:9 3967
fathers, a thousand and seven *h* ... 1Chr 9:13 3967
porters in the gates were two *h* ... 1Chr 9:22 3967
three *h* slain by him at one time ... 1Chr 11:11 3967
up his spear against three *h* ... 1Chr 11:20 3967
one of the least was over an *h* ... 1Chr 12:14 3967
were six thousand and eight *h* ... 1Chr 12:24 3967
the war, seven thousand and one *h* ... 1Chr 12:25 3967
of Levi four thousand and six *h* ... 1Chr 12:26 3967
were three thousand and seven *h* ... 1Chr 12:27 3967
twenty thousand and eight *h* ... 1Chr 12:30 3967
the heads of them were two *h* ... 1Chr 12:32 3967
twenty and eight thousand and six *h*... 1Chr 12:35 3967
of war for the battle, an *h* ... 1Chr 12:37 3967
the chief, and his brethren an *h* ... 1Chr 15:5 3967
the chief, and his brethren two *h* ... 1Chr 15:6 3967
the chief, and his brethren an *h* ... 1Chr 15:7 3967
the chief, and his brethren two *h* ... 1Chr 15:8 3967
the chief, and his brethren an *h* ... 1Chr 15:10 3967
reserved of them an *h* chariots ... 1Chr 18:4 3967
The LORD make his people an *h* ... 1Chr 21:3 3967
an *h* thousand men that drew sword ... 1Chr 21:5 3967
and Judah was four *h* threescore ... 1Chr 21:5 3967
six *h* shekels of gold by weight ... 1Chr 21:25 3967
an *h* thousand talents of gold ... 1Chr 22:14 3967
was two *h* fourscore and eight ... 1Chr 25:7 3967
of valour, a thousand and seven *h* ... 1Chr 26:30 3967
seven *h* chief fathers, whom king ... 1Chr 26:32 3967
one *h* thousand talents of iron ... 1Chr 29:7 3967
four *h* chariots, and twelve ... 2Chr 1:14 3967
for six *h* shekels of silver ... 2Chr 1:17 3967
and an horse for an *h* ... 2Chr 1:17 3967
thousand and six *h* to oversee them ... 2Chr 2:2 3967
and they were found an *h* and fifty ... 2Chr 2:17 3967
and three thousand and six *h* ... 2Chr 2:17 3967
six *h* overseers to set the people ... 2Chr 2:18 3967
cubits, and the height was an *h* ... 2Chr 3:4 3967
gold, amounting to six *h* talents ... 2Chr 3:8 3967
made an *h* pomegranates, and put ... 2Chr 3:16 3967
he made an *h* basons of gold ... 2Chr 4:8 3967
four *h* pomegranates on the two ... 2Chr 4:13 3967
of the altar, and with them an *h* ... 2Chr 5:12 3967
and two thousand oxen, and an *h* ... 2Chr 7:5 3967
Solomon's officers, even two *h* ... 2Chr 8:10 3967
to Ophir, and took thence four *h* ... 2Chr 8:18 3967
And she gave the king an *h* ... 2Chr 9:9 3967
to Solomon in one year was six *h* ... 2Chr 9:13 3967
king Solomon made two *h* targets ... 2Chr 9:15 3967
six *h* shekels of beaten gold went ... 2Chr 9:15 3967
three *h* shields made he of beaten ... 2Chr 9:16 3967
three *h* shekels of gold went to ... 2Chr 9:16 3967
house of Judah and Benjamin an *h* ... 2Chr 11:1 3967
With twelve *h* chariots, and ... 2Chr 12:3 3967
even four *h* thousand chosen men ... 2Chr 13:3 3967
with eight *h* thousand chosen men ... 2Chr 13:3 3967
Israel five *h* thousand chosen men ... 2Chr 13:17 3967
out of Judah three *h* thousand ... 2Chr 14:8 3967
bare shields and drew bows, two *h* ... 2Chr 14:8 3967
thousand, and three *h* chariots ... 2Chr 14:9 3967
they had brought, seven *h* oxen ... 2Chr 15:11 3967
seven thousand and seven *h* rams ... 2Chr 17:11 3967
thousand and seven *h* he goats ... 2Chr 17:11 3967
men of valour three *h* thousand ... 2Chr 17:14 3967
the captain, and with him two *h* ... 2Chr 17:15 3967
with him two *h* thousand mighty ... 2Chr 17:16 3967
with bow and shield two *h* thousand ... 2Chr 17:17 3967
was Jehozabad, and with him an *h* ... 2Chr 17:18 3967
together of prophets four *h* men ... 2Chr 18:5 3967
an *h* and thirty years old was he ... 2Chr 24:15 3967
found them three *h* thousand ... 2Chr 25:5 3967
He hired also an *h* thousand ... 2Chr 25:6 3967
Israel for an *h* talents of silver ... 2Chr 25:6 3967
But what shall we do for the *h* ... 2Chr 25:9 3967
to the corner gate, four *h* cubits ... 2Chr 25:23 3967
valour were two thousand and six *h* ... 2Chr 26:12 3967
three *h* thousand and seven ... 2Chr 26:13 3967
and seven thousand and five *h* ... 2Chr 26:13 3967
same year an *h* talents of silver ... 2Chr 27:5 3967
of Remaliah slew in Judah an *h* ... 2Chr 28:6 3967
of their brethren two *h* thousand ... 2Chr 28:8 3967
an *h* rams, and two *h* lambs ... 2Chr 29:32 3967
an *h* rams, and two *h* lambs ... 2Chr 29:32 3967
things were six *h* oxen and three ... 2Chr 29:33 3967
six *h* small cattle, and three ... 2Chr 35:8 3967
small cattle, and three *h* oxen ... 2Chr 35:8 3967
small cattle, and five *h* oxen ... 2Chr 35:9 3967
land in an *h* talents of silver ... 2Chr 36:3 3967
basons of a second sort four *h* ... Ezr 1:10 3967
were five thousand and four *h* ... Ezr 1:11 3967
Parosh, two thousand an *h* seventy ... Ezr 2:3 3967
three *h* seventy and two ... Ezr 2:4 3967
of Arah, seven *h* seventy and five ... Ezr 2:5 3967
and Joab, two thousand eight *h* ... Ezr 2:6 3967
of Elam, a thousand two *h* fifty ... Ezr 2:7 3967
of Zattu, nine *h* forty and five ... Ezr 2:8 3967
The children of Zaccai, seven *h* ... Ezr 2:9 3967
of Bani, six *h* forty and two ... Ezr 2:10 3967
of Bebai, six *h* twenty and three ... Ezr 2:11 3967
of Azgad, a thousand two *h* twenty ... Ezr 2:12 3967
of Adonikam, six *h* sixty and six ... Ezr 2:13 3967
of Adin, four *h* fifty and four ... Ezr 2:15 3967
of Bezai, three *h* twenty and three ... Ezr 2:17 3967
The children of Jorah, an *h* ... Ezr 2:18 3967

of Hashum, two *h* twenty and three ... Ezr 2:19 3967
Beth-lehem, an *h* twenty and three ... Ezr 2:21 3967
of Anathoth, an *h* twenty and eight ... Ezr 2:23 3967
Chephirah, and Beeroth, seven *h* ... Ezr 2:25 3967
and Gaba, six *h* twenty and one ... Ezr 2:26 3967
of Michmas, an *h* twenty and two ... Ezr 2:27 3967
and Ai, two *h* twenty and three ... Ezr 2:28 3967
of Magbish, an *h* fifty and six ... Ezr 2:30 3967
Elam, a thousand two *h* fifty ... Ezr 2:31 3967
The children of Harim, three *h* ... Ezr 2:32 3967
and Ono, seven *h* twenty and five ... Ezr 2:33 3967
of Jericho, three *h* forty ... Ezr 2:34 3967
Senaah, three thousand and six *h* ... Ezr 2:35 3967
Jeshua, nine *h* seventy and three ... Ezr 2:36 3967
of Pashur, a thousand two *h* forty ... Ezr 2:38 3967
of Asaph, an *h* twenty and eight ... Ezr 2:41 3967
of Shobai, in all an *h* thirty ... Ezr 2:42 3967
servants, were three *h* ninety ... Ezr 2:58 3967
of Nekoda, six *h* fifty and two ... Ezr 2:60 3967
was forty and two thousand three *h* ... Ezr 2:64 3967
seven thousand three *h* thirty ... Ezr 2:65 3967
were among them two *h* singing men .. Ezr 2:65 3967
Their horses were seven *h* thirty ... Ezr 2:66 3967
their mules, two *h* forty and five ... Ezr 2:66 3967
camels, four *h* thirty and five ... Ezr 2:67 3967
their asses, six thousand seven *h* ... Ezr 2:67 3967
and one *h* priests' garments ... Ezr 2:69 3967
this house of God an *h* bullocks ... Ezr 6:17 3969
two *h* rams, four *h* lambs ... Ezr 6:17 3967
Unto an *h* talents of silver, and ... Ezr 7:22 3969
to an *h* measures of wheat, and to ... Ezr 7:22 3969
to an *h* baths of wine ... Ezr 7:22 3969
to an *h* baths of oil, and salt ... Ezr 7:22 3969
by genealogy of the males an *h* ... Ezr 8:3 3967
Zerahiah, and with him two *h* males ... Ezr 8:4 3967
and with him three *h* males ... Ezr 8:5 3967
son of Jehiel, and with him two *h* ... Ezr 8:9 3967
of Josiphiah, and with him an *h* ... Ezr 8:10 3967
son of Hakkatan, and with him an *h* ... Ezr 8:12 3967
the service of the Levites, two *h* ... Ezr 8:20 3967
weighed unto their hand six *h* ... Ezr 8:26 3967
and silver vessels an *h* talents ... Ezr 8:26 3967
and of gold an *h* talents ... Ezr 8:26 3967
there were at my table an *h* ... Neh 5:17 3967
Parosh, two thousand an *h* seventy ... Neh 7:8 3967
three *h* seventy and two ... Neh 7:9 3967
of Arah, six *h* fifty and two ... Neh 7:10 3967
and Joab, two thousand and eight *h* ... Neh 7:11 3967
of Elam, a thousand two *h* fifty ... Neh 7:12 3967
children of Zattu, eight *h* forty ... Neh 7:13 3967
The children of Zaccai, seven *h* ... Neh 7:14 3967
of Binnui, six *h* forty and eight ... Neh 7:15 3967
of Bebai, six *h* twenty and eight ... Neh 7:16 3967
two thousand three *h* twenty ... Neh 7:17 3967
six *h* threescore and seven ... Neh 7:18 3967
of Adin, six *h* fifty and five ... Neh 7:20 3967
Hashum, three *h* twenty and eight ... Neh 7:22 3967
of Bezai, three *h* twenty and four ... Neh 7:23 3967
The children of Hariph, an *h* ... Neh 7:24 3967
Netophah, an *h* fourscore and eight ... Neh 7:26 3967
of Anathoth, an *h* twenty and eight ... Neh 7:27 3967
and Beeroth, seven *h* forty ... Neh 7:29 3967
and Gaba, six *h* twenty and one ... Neh 7:30 3967
The men of Michmas, an *h* and ... Neh 7:31 3967
and Ai, an *h* twenty and three ... Neh 7:32 3967
Elam, a thousand two *h* fifty ... Neh 7:34 3967
The children of Harim, three *h* ... Neh 7:35 3967
of Jericho, three *h* forty ... Neh 7:36 3967
and Ono, seven *h* twenty and one ... Neh 7:37 3967
of Senaah, three thousand nine *h* ... Neh 7:38 3967
Jeshua, nine *h* seventy and three ... Neh 7:39 3967
of Pashur, a thousand two *h* forty ... Neh 7:41 3967
of Asaph, an *h* forty and eight ... Neh 7:44 3967
of Shobai, an *h* thirty and eight ... Neh 7:45 3967
servants, were three *h* ninety ... Neh 7:60 3967
of Nekoda, six *h* forty and two ... Neh 7:62 3967
was forty and two thousand three *h* ... Neh 7:66 3967
seven thousand three *h* thirty ... Neh 7:67 3967
and they had two *h* forty and five ... Neh 7:67 3967
horses, seven *h* thirty and six ... Neh 7:68 3967
their mules, two *h* forty and five ... Neh 7:68 3967
camels, four *h* thirty and five ... Neh 7:69 3967
six thousand seven *h* and twenty ... Neh 7:69 3967
of gold, fifty basons, five *h* ... Neh 7:70 3967
and two *h* pounds of silver ... Neh 7:71 3967
Jerusalem were four *h* threescore ... Neh 11:6 3967
Sallai, nine *h* twenty and eight ... Neh 11:8 3967
of the house were eight *h* twenty ... Neh 11:12 3967
the fathers, two *h* forty and two ... Neh 11:13 3967
of valour, an *h* twenty and eight ... Neh 11:14 3967
holy city were two *h* fourscore ... Neh 11:18 3967
kept the gates, were an *h* seventy ... Neh 11:19 3967
even unto Ethiopia, over an *h* ... Est 1:1 3967
majesty many days, even an *h* ... Est 1:4 3967
an *h* twenty and seven provinces, ... Est 8:9 3967
Jews slew and destroyed five *h* men ... Est 9:6 3967
destroyed five *h* men in Shushan ... Est 9:12 3967
slew three *h* men at Shushan ... Est 9:15 3967
all the Jews, to the *h* twenty ... Est 9:30 3967
five *h* yoke of oxen, and five ... Job 1:3 3967
five *h* she asses, and a very great ... Job 1:3 3967
After this lived Job an *h* ... Job 42:16 3967
man than an *h* stripes into a fool ... Prov 17:10 3967
If a man beget an *h* children ... Eccl 6:3 3967
a sinner do evil an *h* times ... Eccl 8:12 3967
that keep the fruit thereof two *h* ... Song 8:12 3967
in the camp of the Assyrians an *h* ... Is 37:36 3967
child shall die an *h* years old ... Is 65:20 3967
but the sinner being an *h* years ... Is 65:20 3967
the network were an *h* round about ... Jer 52:23 3967
from Jerusalem eight *h* thirty ... Jer 52:29 3967
captive of the Jews seven *h* forty ... Jer 52:30 3967
were four thousand and six *h* ... Jer 52:30 3967
the number of the days, three *h* ... Eze 4:5 3967

shalt lie upon thy side, three *h* ... Eze 4:9 3967
an *h* cubits eastward and northward ... Eze 40:19 3967
from gate to gate an *h* cubits ... Eze 40:23 3967
gate toward the south an *h* cubits ... Eze 40:27 3967
an *h* cubits long, and an *h* ... Eze 40:47 3967
the house, an *h* cubits long ... Eze 41:13 3967
walls thereof, an *h* cubits long ... Eze 41:13 3967
toward the east, an *h* cubits ... Eze 41:14 3967
an *h* cubits, with the inner ... Eze 41:15 3967
Before the length of an *h* cubits ... Eze 42:2 3967
the temple were an *h* cubits ... Eze 42:8 3967
five *h* reeds, with the measuring ... Eze 42:16 520
five *h* reeds, with the measuring ... Eze 42:17 3967
five *h* reeds, with the measuring ... Eze 42:18 3967
measured five *h* reeds with the ... Eze 42:19 3967
five *h* reeds long, and five ... Eze 42:20 3967
long, and five *h* broad, to make a ... Eze 42:20 3967
the sanctuary five *h* in length ... Eze 45:2 3967
with five *h* in breadth, square ... Eze 45:2 3967
out of the flock, out of two *h* ... Eze 45:15 3967
side four thousand and five *h* ... Eze 48:16 3967
side four thousand and five *h* ... Eze 48:16 3967
east side four thousand and five *h* ... Eze 48:16 3967
west side four thousand and five *h* ... Eze 48:16 3967
shall be toward the north two *h* ... Eze 48:17 3967
fifty, and toward the south two *h* ... Eze 48:17 3967
fifty, and toward the east two *h* ... Eze 48:17 3967
fifty, and toward the west two *h* ... Eze 48:17 3967
four thousand and five *h* measures ... Eze 48:30 3967
east side four thousand and five *h* ... Eze 48:32 3967
four thousand and five *h* measures ... Eze 48:33 3967
west side four thousand and five *h* ... Eze 48:34 3967
to set over the kingdom an *h* ... Dan 6:1 3969
Unto two thousand and three *h* days ... Dan 8:14 3967
there shall be a thousand two *h* ... Dan 12:11 3967
and cometh to the thousand three *h* ... Dan 12:12 3967
by a thousand shall leave an *h* ... Amos 5:3 3967
forth by an *h* shall leave ten ... Amos 5:3 3967
if a man have an *h* sheep, and one ... Mt 18:12 *1540*
which owed him an *h* pence ... Mt 18:28 *1540*
and some sixty, and some an *h* ... Mk 4:8 *1540*
some sixty, and some an *h* ... Mk 4:20 *1540*
buy two *h* pennyworth of bread, and ... Mk 6:37 *1250*
sold for more than three *h* pence ... Mk 14:5 *5145*
the one owed five *h* pence ... Lk 7:41 *4001*
man of you, having an *h* sheep ... Lk 15:4 *1540*
And he said, An *h* measures of oil ... Lk 16:6 *1540*
he said, An *h* measures of wheat ... Lk 16:7 *1540*
Two *h* pennyworth of bread is not ... Jn 6:7 *1250*
ointment sold for three *h* pence ... Jn 12:5 *5145*
and aloes, about an *h* pound weight ... Jn 19:39 *1540*
land, but as it were two *h* cubits ... Jn 21:8 *1250*
land full of great fishes, an *h* ... Jn 21:11 *1540*
of names together were about an *h* ... Acts 1:15 *1540*
a number of men, about four *h* ... Acts 5:36 *5071*
and entreat them evil four *h* years ... Acts 7:6 *5071*
judges about the space of four *h* ... Acts 13:20 *5071*
Make ready two *h* soldiers to go ... Acts 23:23 *1250*
and ten, and spearmen two *h* ... Acts 23:23 *1250*
all in the ship two *h* threescore ... Acts 27:37 *1250*
when he was about an *h* years old ... Rom 4:19 *1541*
of above five *h* brethren at once ... 1Cor 15:6 *4001*
Christ, the law, which was four *h* ... Gal 3:17 *5071*
and there were sealed an *h* ... Rev 7:4 *1540*
were two *h* thousand thousand ... Rev 9:16 *3461*
shall prophesy a thousand two *h* ... Rev 11:3 *1250*
feed her there a thousand two *h* ... Rev 12:6 *1250*
and his number is six *h* threescore ... Rev 13:18 *5516*
Sion, and with him an *h* forty ... Rev 14:1 *1540*
could learn that song but the *h* ... Rev 14:3 *1540*
of a thousand and six *h* furlongs ... Rev 14:20 *5516*
measured the wall thereof, an *h* ... Rev 21:17 *1540*

HUNDREDFOLD

and received in the same year an *h* ... Gen 26:12
how many soever they be, an *h* ... 2Sa 24:3
and brought forth fruit, some an *h* ... Mt 13:8 *1540*
and bringeth forth, some an *h* ... Mt 13:23 *1540*
name's sake, shall receive an *h* ... Mt 19:29 *1542*
receive an *h* now in this time ... Mk 10:30 *1542*
and sprang up, and bare fruit an *h* ... Lk 8:8 *1542*

HUNDREDS

of thousands, and rulers of *h* ... Ex 18:21 3967
rulers of thousands, rulers of *h* ... Ex 18:25 3967
thousands, and captains over *h* ... Num 31:14 3967
of thousands, and captains of *h* ... Num 31:48 3967
and of the captains of *h*, was ... Num 31:52 3967
the captains of thousands and of *h* ... Num 31:54 3967
thousands, and captains over *h* ... Deut 1:15 3967
of thousands, and captains of *h* ... 1Sa 22:7 3967
of the Philistines passed on by *h* ... 1Sa 29:2 3967
and captains of *h* over them ... 2Sa 18:1 3967
and all the people came out by *h* ... 2Sa 18:4 3967
sent and fetched the rulers over *h* ... 2Kin 11:4 3967
the captains over the *h* did ... 2Kin 11:9 3967
to the captains over *h* did the ... 2Kin 11:10 3967
commanded the captains of the *h* ... 2Kin 11:15 3967
And he took the rulers over *h* ... 2Kin 11:19 3967
the captains of thousands and *h* ... 1Chr 13:1 3967
the captains over thousands and *h* ... 1Chr 26:26 3967
and captains of thousands and *h* ... 1Chr 27:1 3967
thousands, and captains over the *h* ... 1Chr 28:1 3967
the captains of thousands and of *h* ... 1Chr 29:6 3967
the captains of thousands and of *h* ... 2Chr 1:2 3967
and took the captains of *h* ... 2Chr 23:1 3967
to the captains of *h* spears ... 2Chr 23:9 3967
of *h* that were set over the host ... 2Chr 23:14 3967
And he took the captains of *h* ... 2Chr 23:20 3967
thousands, and captains over *h* ... 2Chr 25:5 3967
And they sat down in ranks, by *h* ... Mk 6:40 *1540*

HUNDREDTH

In the six *h* year of Noah's life, ... Gen 7:11 3967
And it came to pass in the six *h* ... Gen 8:13 3967

also the h part of the money, and ... Neh 5:11 3967

HUNGER
kill this whole assembly with h ... Ex 16:3 7457
thee, and suffered thee to h ... Deut 8:3 7456
shall send against thee, in h ... Deut 28:48 7457
They shall be burnt with h ... Deut 32:24 7457
bread from heaven for their h ... Neh 9:15 7457
young lions do lack, and suffer h ... Ps 34:10 7456
and an idle soul shall suffer h ... Prov 19:15 7456
They shall not h nor thirst ... Is 49:10 7456
he is like to die for h in the ... Jer 38:9 7457
the trumpet, nor have h of bread ... Jer 42:14 7456
that faint for h in the top of ... Lam 2:19 7457
than they that be slain with h ... Lam 4:9 7457
more consumed with h in the land ... Eze 34:29 7457
Blessed are they which do h ... Mt 5:6 3983
Blessed are ye that h now ... Lk 6:21 3983
for ye shall h ... Lk 6:25 3983
and to spare, and I perish with h ... Lk 15:17 3042
that cometh to me shall never h ... Jn 6:35 3983
Therefore if thine enemy h ... Rom 12:20 3983
unto this present hour we both h ... 1Cor 4:11 3983
And if any man h, let him eat at ... 1Cor 11:34 3983
in watchings often, in h ... 2Cor 11:27 3042
to kill with sword, and with h ... Rev 6:8 3042
They shall h no more, neither ... Rev 7:16 3983

HUNGERBITTEN
His strength shall be h, and ... Job 18:12 7457

HUNGERED
he returned into the city, he h ... Mt 21:18 3983
they were ended, he afterward h ... Lk 4:2 3983

HUNGRED
nights, he was afterward an h ... Mt 4:2 3983
and his disciples were an h ... Mt 12:1 3983
what David did, when he was an h ... Mt 12:3 3983
For I was an h, and ye gave me ... Mt 25:35 3983
Lord, when saw we thee an h ... Mt 25:37 3983
For I was an h, and ye gave me no ... Mt 25:42 3983
Lord, when saw we thee an h ... Mt 25:44 3983
when he had need, and was an h ... Mk 2:25 3983
David did, when himself was an h ... Lk 6:3 3983

HUNGRY
and they that were h ceased ... 1Sa 2:5 7456
for they said, The people is h ... 2Sa 17:29 7456
They know that we be h ... 2Kin 7:12 7456
Whose harvest the h eateth up ... Job 5:5 7456
hast withholden bread from the h ... Job 22:7 7456
take away the sheaf from the h ... Job 24:10 7456
If I were h, I would not tell ... Ps 50:12 7456
H and thirsty, their soul fainted ... Ps 107:5 7456
filleth the h soul with goodness ... Ps 107:9 7456
And there he maketh the h to dwell ... Ps 107:36 7456
which giveth food to the h ... Ps 146:7 7456
to satisfy his soul when he is h ... Prov 6:30 7456
If thine enemy be h, give him ... Prov 25:21 7456
but to the h soul every bitter ... Prov 27:7 7456
through it, hardly bestead and h ... Is 8:21 7456
pass, that when they shall be h ... Is 8:21 7456
snatch on the right hand, and be h ... Is 9:20 7456
even be as when an h man dreameth ... Is 29:8 7456
to make empty the soul of the h ... Is 32:6 7456
yea, he is h, and his strength ... Is 44:12 7456
it not to deal thy bread to the h ... Is 58:7 7456
thou draw out thy soul to the h ... Is 58:10 7456
shall eat, but ye shall be h ... Is 65:13 7456
hath given his bread to the h ... Eze 18:7 7456
but hath given his bread to the h ... Eze 18:16 7456
were come from Bethany, he was h ... Mk 11:12 3983
filled the h with good things ... Lk 1:53 3983
And he became very h, and would ... Acts 10:10 4361
and one is h, and another is ... 1Cor 11:21 3983
both to be full and to be h ... Phil 4:12 3983

HUNT
to the field to h for venison ... Gen 27:5 6679
as when one doth h a partridge in ... 1Sa 26:20 7291
Wilt thou h the prey for the lion ... Job 38:39 6679
evil shall h the violent man to ... Ps 140:11 6679
the adulteress will h for the ... Prov 6:26 6679
they shall h them from every ... Jer 16:16 6679
They h our steps, that we cannot ... Lam 4:18 6679
head of every stature to h souls ... Eze 13:18 6679
Will ye h the souls of my people, ... Eze 13:18 6679
wherewith ye there h the souls to ... Eze 13:20 6679
souls that ye h to make them fly ... Eze 13:20 6679
they h every man his brother with ... Mic 7:2 6679

HUNTED
be no more in your hand to be h ... Eze 13:21 4686

HUNTER
He was a mighty h before the LORD ... Gen 10:9 6718
the mighty h before the LORD ... Gen 10:9 6718
and Esau was a cunning h, a man of ... Gen 25:27 6718
as a roe from the hand of the h ... Prov 6:5 6718

HUNTERS
and after will I send for many h ... Jer 16:16 6719

HUNTEST
yet thou h my soul to take it ... 1Sa 24:11 6658
Thou h me as a fierce lion ... Job 10:16 6679

HUNTETH
that sojourn among you, which h ... Lev 17:13 6679

HUNTING
his brother came in from his h ... Gen 27:30 6718
not that which he took in h ... Prov 12:27 6718

HUPHAM (*hu'-fam*) See HUPPIM, HUPHAMITES.
A son of Benjamin.
of H, the family of the ... Num 26:39 2349

HUPHAMITES (*hu'-fam-ites*) *Descendants of Hupham.*
of Hupham, the family of the H ... Num 26:39 2350

HUPPAH (*hup'-pah*) *A priest.*
The thirteenth to H, the ... 1Chr 24:13 2647

HUPPIM (*hup'-pim*) See HUPHAM. *Head of a Benjamite family.*
Ehi, and Rosh, Muppim, and H ... Gen 46:21 2650
Shuppim also, and H, the children ... 1Chr 7:12 2650
took to wife the sister of H ... 1Chr 7:15 2650

HUPPITES See HUPPIM.

HUR (*hur*)
1. Assisted Moses at Rephidim.
H went up to the top of the hill ... Ex 17:10 2354
H stayed up his hands, the one on ... Ex 17:12 2354
behold, Aaron and H are with you ... Ex 24:14 2354
2. A son of Caleb.
the son of Uri, the son of H ... Ex 31:2 2354
the son of Uri, the son of H ... Ex 35:30 2354
the son of Uri, the son of H ... Ex 38:22 2354
him Ephrath, which bare him H ... 1Chr 2:19 2354
H begat Uri, and Uri begat ... 1Chr 2:20 2354
the son of Uri, the son of H ... 2Chr 1:5 2354
3. A Midianite king.
Evi, and Rekem, and Zur, and H ... Num 31:8 2354
Evi, and Rekem, and Zur, and H ... Josh 13:21 2354
4. An officer of Solomon.
The son of H, in mount Ephraim ... 1Kin 4:8 2354
5. Father of Caleb.
the sons of Caleb the son of H ... 1Chr 2:50 2354
These are the sons of H, the ... 1Chr 4:4 2354
6. A descendant of Judah.
Pharez, Hezron, and Carmi, and H ... 1Chr 4:1 2354
7. A rebuilder of Jerusalem's wall.
repaired Rephaiah the son of H ... Neh 3:9 2354

HURAI (*hu'-rahee*) See HIDDAI. *A mighty man of David.*
H of the brooks of Gaash, Abiel ... 1Chr 11:32 2360

HURAM (*hu'-ram*) See HIRAM.
1. Son of Bela.
And Gera, and Shephuphan, and H ... 1Chr 8:5 2361
2. Same as Hiram 1.
Solomon sent to H the king of ... 2Chr 2:3 2361
Then H the king of Tyre answered ... 2Chr 2:11 2438
H said moreover, Blessed be the ... 2Chr 2:12 2361
understanding, of H my father's, ... 2Chr 2:13 2438
That the cities which H had ... 2Chr 8:2 2438
H sent him by the hands of his ... 2Chr 8:18 2438
And the servants also of H ... 2Chr 9:10 2438
Tarshish with the servants of H ... 2Chr 9:21 2438
3. Same as Hiram 2.
H made the pots, and the shovels, ... 2Chr 4:11 2361
H finished the work that he was ... 2Chr 4:11 2361
did H his father make to king ... 2Chr 4:16 2361

HURAM-ABI See HURAM.

HURI (*hu'-ri*) *Father of Abihail.*
children of Abihail the son of H ... 1Chr 5:14 2359

HURL
or h at him by laying of wait, ... Num 35:20 7993

HURLETH
as a storm h him out of his place ... Job 27:21 8175

HURLING
hand and the left in h stones ... 1Chr 12:2

HURT
wounding, and a young man to my h ... Gen 4:23 2250
That thou wilt do us no h ... Gen 26:29 7451
but God suffered him not to h me ... Gen 31:7 7489
the power of my hand to do you h ... Gen 31:29 7451
h a woman with child, so that her ... Ex 21:22 5062
And if one man's ox h another's ... Ex 21:35 5062
and it die, or be h, or driven ... Ex 22:10 7665
of his neighbour, and it be h ... Ex 22:14 7665
neither have I h one of them ... Num 16:15 7489
then he will turn and do you h ... Josh 24:20 7489
there is peace to thee, and no h ... 1Sa 20:21 1697
Behold, David seeketh thy h ... 1Sa 24:9 7451
we h them not, neither was there ... 1Sa 25:7 3637
good unto us, and we were not h ... 1Sa 25:15 3637
rise against thee to do thee h ... 2Sa 18:32 7451
shouldest thou meddle to thy h ... 2Kin 14:10 7451
shouldest thou meddle to thine h ... 2Chr 25:19 7451
damage grow to the h of the kings ... Ezr 4:22 5142
hand on such as sought their h ... Est 9:2 7451
may h a man as thou art ... Job 35:8
He that sweareth to his own h ... Ps 15:4 7489
to confusion that devise my h ... Ps 35:4 7451
together that rejoice at mine h ... Ps 35:26 7451
they that seek my h speak ... Ps 38:12 7451
against me do they devise my h ... Ps 41:7 7451
to confusion, that desire my h ... Ps 70:2 7451
and dishonour that seek my h ... Ps 71:13 7451
unto shame, that seek my h ... Ps 71:24 7451
Whose feet they h with fetters ... Ps 105:18 6031
for the owners thereof to their h ... Eccl 5:13 7451
ruleth over another to his own h ... Eccl 8:9 7451
stones shall be h therewith ... Eccl 10:9 6087
They shall not h nor destroy in ... Is 11:9 7489
lest any h it, I will keep it ... Is 27:3 6485
They shall not h nor destroy in ... Is 65:25 7489
They have healed also the h of ... Jer 6:14 7667
walk after other gods to your h ... Jer 7:6 7451
For they have healed the h of the ... Jer 8:11 7667
For the h of the daughter of my ... Jer 8:21 7667
the daughter of my people am I h ... Jer 8:21 7665
Woe is me for my h ... Jer 10:19 7667
kingdoms of the earth for their h ... Jer 24:9 7451
and I will do you no h ... Jer 25:6 7489
works of your hands to your own h ... Jer 25:7 7451
welfare of this people, but the h ... Jer 38:4 7451
of the fire, and they have no h ... Dan 3:25 2257
mouths, that they have not h me ... Dan 6:22 2255
thee, O king, have I done no h ... Dan 6:22 2248
no manner of h was found upon him ... Dan 6:23 2257
deadly thing, it shall not h them ... Mk 16:18 984
he came out of him, and h him not ... Lk 4:35 984
nothing shall by any means h you ... Lk 10:19 91
man shall set on thee to h thee ... Acts 18:10 2559
that this voyage will be with h ... Acts 27:10 5196
not be h of the second death ... Rev 2:11 91
see thou h not the oil and the ... Rev 6:6 91
whom it was given to h the earth ... Rev 7:2 91
H not the earth, neither the sea, ... Rev 7:3 91
not h the grass of the earth ... Rev 9:4 91
power was to h men five months ... Rev 9:10 91
had heads, and with them they do h ... Rev 9:19 91
And if any man will h them ... Rev 11:5 91
and if any man will h them ... Rev 11:5 91

HURTFUL
h unto kings and provinces, and ... Ezr 4:15 5142
his servant from the h sword ... Ps 144:10 7451
h lusts, which drown men in ... 1Ti 6:9 983

HURTING
hath kept me back from h thee ... 1Sa 25:34 7489

HUSBAND
and gave also unto her h with her ... Gen 3:6 376
and thy desire shall be to thy h ... Gen 3:16 376
gave her to her h Abram to be his ... Gen 16:3 376
now therefore my h will love me ... Gen 29:32 376
time will my h be joined unto me ... Gen 29:34 376
matter that thou hast taken my h ... Gen 30:15 376
I have given my maiden to my h ... Gen 30:18 376
now will my h dwell with me, ... Gen 30:20 376
Surely a bloody h art thou to me ... Ex 4:25 2860
she said, A bloody h thou art ... Ex 4:26 2860
the woman's h will lay upon him ... Ex 21:22 1167
is a bondmaid, betrothed to an h ... Lev 19:20 376
unto him, which hath had no h ... Lev 21:3 376
take a woman put away from her h ... Lev 21:7 376
it be hid from the eyes of her h ... Num 5:13 376
with another instead of thy h ... Num 5:19 376
aside to another instead of thy h ... Num 5:20 376
lain with thee beside thine h ... Num 5:20 376
have done trespass against her h ... Num 5:27 376
aside to another instead of her h ... Num 5:29 376
And if she had at all an h ... Num 30:6 376
her h heard it, and held his peace ... Num 30:7 376
But if her h disallowed her on ... Num 30:8 376
her h heard it, and held his peace ... Num 30:11 376
But if her h hath utterly made ... Num 30:12 376
her h hath made them void ... Num 30:12 376
her h may establish it ... Num 30:13 376
or her h may make it void ... Num 30:13 376
But if her h altogether hold his ... Num 30:14 376
shalt go in unto her, and be her h ... Deut 21:13 1167
with a woman married to an h ... Deut 22:22 1167
a virgin be betrothed unto an h ... Deut 22:23 376
And if the latter h hate her ... Deut 24:3 376
or if the latter h die, which ... Deut 24:3 376
Her former h, which sent her away ... Deut 24:4 1167
her h out of the hand of him that ... Deut 25:11 376
be evil toward the h of her bosom ... Deut 28:56 376
Then the woman came and told her h ... Judg 13:6 376
but Manoah her h was not with her ... Judg 13:9 376
haste, and ran, and shewed her h ... Judg 13:10 376
unto Samson's wife, Entice thy h ... Judg 14:15 376
her h arose, and went after her, ... Judg 19:3 376
the h of the woman that was slain ... Judg 20:4 376
And Elimelech Naomi's h died ... Ruth 1:3 376
was left of her two sons and her h ... Ruth 1:5 376
each of you in the house of her h ... Ruth 1:9 376
for I am too old to have an h ... Ruth 1:12 376
I should have an h also to night ... Ruth 1:12 376
in law since the death of thine h ... Ruth 2:11 376
Then said Elkanah her h to her ... 1Sa 1:8 376
for she said unto her h, I will ... 1Sa 1:22 376
Elkanah her h said unto her, Do ... 1Sa 1:23 376
when she came up with her h to ... 1Sa 2:19 376
her h were dead, she bowed ... 1Sa 4:19 376
of her father in law and her h ... 1Sa 4:21 376
But she told not her h Nabal ... 1Sa 25:19 376
sent, and took her from her h ... 2Sa 3:15 376
her h went with her along weeping ... 2Sa 3:16 376
heard that Uriah her h was dead ... 2Sa 11:26 376
she mourned for her h ... 2Sa 11:26 1167
a widow woman, and mine h is dead ... 2Sa 14:5 376
shall not leave to my h neither ... 2Sa 14:7 376
saying, Thy servant my h is dead ... 2Kin 4:1 376
And she said unto her h, Behold ... 2Kin 4:9 376
hath no child, and her h is old ... 2Kin 4:14 376
And she called unto her h, and said ... 2Kin 4:22 376
is it well with thy h ... 2Kin 4:26 376
woman is a crown to her h ... Prov 12:4 1167
The heart of her h doth safely ... Prov 31:11 1167
Her h is known in the gates, when ... Prov 31:23 1167
her h also, and he praiseth her ... Prov 31:28 1167
For thy Maker is thine h ... Is 54:5 1167
departeth from her h, so have ye ... Jer 3:20 1167
for even the h with the wife ... Jer 6:11 376
although I was an h unto them ... Jer 31:32 1167
taketh strangers instead of her h ... Eze 16:32 376
daughter, that lotheth her h ... Eze 16:45 376
or for sister that hath had no h ... Eze 44:25 376
not my wife, neither am I her h ... Hos 2:2 376
I will go and return to my first h ... Hos 2:7 376
sackcloth for the h of her youth ... Joel 1:8 1167
Jacob begat Joseph the h of Mary ... Mt 1:16 435
Then Joseph her h, being a just ... Mt 1:19 435
if a woman shall put away her h ... Mk 10:12 435
had lived with an h seven years ... Lk 2:36 435
from her h committeth adultery ... Lk 16:18 435

saith unto her, Go, call thy *h* Jn 4:16 *435*
answered and said, I have no *h* Jn 4:17 *435*
Thou hast well said, I have no *h* Jn 4:17 *435*
whom thou now hast is not thy *h* Jn 4:18 *435*
have buried thy *h* are at the door Acts 5:9 *435*
her forth, buried her by her *h* Acts 5:10 *435*
an *h* is bound by the law to her Rom 7:2 *5220*
law to her *h* so long as he liveth Rom 7:2 *435*
but if the *h* be dead, she is Rom 7:2 *435*
is loosed from the law of her *h* Rom 7:2 *435*
So then if, while her *h* liveth Rom 7:3 *435*
but if her *h* be dead, she is free Rom 7:3 *435*
and let every woman have her own *h* 1Cor 7:2 *435*
Let the *h* render unto the wife 1Cor 7:3 *435*
likewise also the wife unto the *h* 1Cor 7:3 *435*
power of her own body, but the *h* 1Cor 7:4 *435*
likewise also the *h* hath not 1Cor 7:4 *435*
not the wife depart from her *h* 1Cor 7:10 *435*
or be reconciled to her *h* 1Cor 7:11 *435*
let not the *h* put away his wife 1Cor 7:11 *435*
hath an *h* that believeth not 1Cor 7:13 *435*
For the unbelieving *h* is 1Cor 7:14 *435*
wife is sanctified by the *h* 1Cor 7:14 *435*
whether thou shalt save thy *h* 1Cor 7:16 *435*
world, how she may please her *h* 1Cor 7:34 *435*
the law as long as her *h* liveth 1Cor 7:39 *435*
but if her *h* be dead, she is at 1Cor 7:39 *435*
for I have espoused you to one *h* 2Cor 11:2 *435*
children than she which hath a *h* Gal 4:27 *435*
For the *h* is the head of the wife Eph 5:23 *435*
wife see that she reverence her *h* Eph 5:33 *435*
the *h* of one wife, vigilant, 1Ti 3:2 *435*
the *h* of one wife, having Titus 1:6 *435*
as a bride adorned for her *h* Rev 21:2 *435*

HUSBANDMAN
And Noah began to be an *h*, and he Gen 9:20
thee will I break in pieces the *h* Jer 51:23 406
they shall call the *h* to mourning Amos 5:16 406
say, I am no prophet, I am an *h* Zec 13:5 5647
true vine, and my Father is the *h* Jn 15:1 *1092*
The *h* that laboureth must be 2Ti 2:6 *1092*
the *h* waiteth for the precious Jas 5:7 *1092*

HUSBANDMEN
the land to be vinedressers and *h* 2Kin 25:12 1461
h also, and vine dressers in the 2Chr 26:10 406
the cities thereof together, *h* Jer 31:24 406
land for vinedressers and for *h* Jer 52:16 3009
Be ye ashamed, O ye *h* Joel 1:11 406
built a tower, and let it out to *h* Mt 21:33 *1092*
he sent his servants to the *h* Mt 21:34 *1092*
the *h* took his servants, and beat Mt 21:35 *1092*
But when the *h* saw the son Mt 21:38 *1092*
what will he do unto those *h* Mt 21:40 *1092*
let out his vineyard unto other *h* Mt 21:41 *1092*
built a tower, and let it out to *h* Mk 12:1 *1092*
season he sent to the *h* a servant Mk 12:2 *1092*
h of the fruit of the vineyard Mk 12:2 *1092*
But those *h* said among themselves Mk 12:7 *1092*
he will come and destroy the *h* Mk 12:9 *1092*
a vineyard, and let it forth to *h* Lk 20:9 *1092*
season he sent a servant to the *h* Lk 20:10 *1092*
but the *h* beat him, and sent him Lk 20:10 *1092*
But when the *h* saw him, they Lk 20:14 *1092*
He shall come and destroy these *h* Lk 20:16 *1092*

HUSBANDRY
for he loved *h* 2Chr 26:10 127
ye are God's *h*, ye are God's 1Cor 3:9 *1091*

HUSBAND'S
And if she vowed in her *h* house Num 30:10 070
her *h* brother shall go in unto Deut 25:5 2993
the duty of an *h* brother unto her Deut 25:5 2992
My *h* brother refuseth to raise up Deut 25:7 2993
perform the duty of my *h* brother Deut 25:7 2992
And Naomi had a kinsman of her *h* Ruth 2:1 376

HUSBANDS
my womb, that they may be your *h* Ruth 1:11 582
ye stay for them from having *h* Ruth 1:13 376
despise their *h* in their eyes Est 1:17 1167
shall give to their *h* honour Est 1:20 1167
sons, and give your daughters to *h* Jer 29:6 582
thy sisters, which lothed their *h* Eze 16:45 582
For thou hast had five *h* Jn 4:18 *435*
let them ask their *h* at home 1Cor 14:35 *435*
submit yourselves unto your own *h* Eph 5:22 *435*
be to their own *h* in every thing Eph 5:24 *435*
H, love your wives, even as Eph 5:25 *435*
submit yourselves unto your own *h* Col 3:18 *435*
H, love your wives, and be not Col 3:19 *435*
the deacons be the *h* of one wife 1Ti 3:12 *435*
to be sober, to love their *h* Titus 2:4 *5362*
good, obedient to their own *h* Titus 2:5 *435*
be in subjection to your own *h* 1Pet 3:1 *435*
in subjection unto their own *h* 1Pet 3:5 *435*
Likewise, ye *h*, dwell with them 1Pet 3:7 *435*

HUSHAH (*hu'-shah*) See HUSHATHITE, SHUAH.
A son of Ezer.
of Gedor, and Ezer the father of *H* 1Chr 4:4 2364

HUSHAI (*hu'-shahee*) *Friend and advisor of David.*
H the Archite came to meet him 2Sa 15:32 2365
So *H* David's friend came into the 2Sa 15:37 2365
when *H* the Archite, David's 2Sa 16:16 2365
that *H* said unto Absalom, God 2Sa 16:16 2365
And Absalom said to *H*, Is this thy 2Sa 16:17 2365
And *H* said unto Absalom, Nay 2Sa 16:18 2365
Call now *H* the Archite also, and 2Sa 17:5 2365
when *H* was come to Absalom, 2Sa 17:6 2365
H said unto Absalom, The counsel 2Sa 17:7 2365
For, said *H*, thou knowest thy 2Sa 17:8 2365
The counsel of *H* the Archite is 2Sa 17:14 2365
Then said *H* unto Zadok and to 2Sa 17:15 2365
Baanah the son of *H* was in Asher 1Kin 4:16 2365
H the Archite was the king's 1Chr 27:33 2365

HUSHAM (*hu'-sham*) *A king of Edom.*
H of the land of Temani reigned Gen 36:34 2367
H died, and Hadad the son of Bedad Gen 36:35 2367
H of the land of the Temanites 1Chr 1:45 2367
when *H* was dead, Hadad the son of 1Chr 1:46 2367

HUSHATHITE (*hu'-shath-ite*) *A descendant of Hushah.*
then Sibbechai the *H* slew Saph 2Sa 21:18 2843
the Anethothite, Mebunnai the *H* 2Sa 23:27 2843
Sibbecai the *H*, Ilai the Ahohite 1Chr 11:29 2843
time Sibbechai the *H* slew Sippai 1Chr 20:4 2843
eighth month was Sibbecai the *H* 1Chr 27:11 2843

HUSHIM (*hu'-shim*) See SHUHAM.
1. A son of Dan.
the sons of Dan; *H* Gen 46:23 2366
2. Son of Aher.
Huppim, the children of Ir, and *H* 1Chr 7:12 2366
3. A wife of Shaharaim.
H and Baara were his wives 1Chr 8:8 2366
of *H* he begat Abitub, and Elpaal 1Chr 8:11 2366

HUSHITES See HUSHIM.

HUSK
from the kernels even to the *h* Num 6:4 2085
ears of corn in the *h* thereof 2Kin 4:42 6861

HUSKS
with the *h* that the swine did eat Lk 15:16 *2769*

HUZ (*huz*) *A son of Nahor.*
H his firstborn, and Buz his Gen 22:21 5780

HUZZAB (*huz'-zab*) *A region in Assyria.*
H shall be led away captive, she Nah 2:7 5324

HYMENAEUS (*hy-men-e'-us*) *A false Christian teacher.*
Of whom is *H* and Alexander 1Ti 1:20 *5211*
of whom is *H* and Philetus 2Ti 2:17 *5211*

HYMN
And when they had sung an *h* Mt 26:30 *5214*
And when they had sung an *h* Mk 14:26

HYMNS
to yourselves in psalms and *h* Eph 5:19 *5215*
one another in psalms and *h* Col 3:16 *5215*

HYPOCRISIES
all malice, and all guile, and *h* 1Pet 2:1 *5272*

HYPOCRISY
will work iniquity, to practise *h* Is 32:6 2612
men, but within ye are full of *h* Mt 23:28 *5272*
But he, knowing their *h*, said Mk 12:15 *5272*
of the Pharisees, which is *h* Lk 12:1 *5272*
Speaking lies in *h* 1Ti 4:2 *5272*
without partiality, and without *h* Jas 3:17 *505*

HYPOCRITE
for an *h* shall not come before Job 13:16 2611
stir up himself against the *h* Job 17:8 2611
the joy of the *h* but for a moment Job 20:5 2611
For what is the hope of the *h* Job 27:8 2611
That the *h* reign not, lest the Job 34:30 2611
An *h* with his mouth destroyeth Prov 11:9 2611
for every one is an *h* and an Is 9:17 2611
Thou *h*, first cast out the beam Mt 7:5 *5273*
Thou *h*, cast out first the beam Lk 6:42 *5273*
answered him, and said, Thou *h* Lk 13:15 *5273*

HYPOCRITE'S
and the *h* hope shall perish Job 8:13 2611

HYPOCRITES
of *h* shall be desolate, and fire Job 15:34 2611
But the *h* in heart heap up wrath Job 36:13 2611
fearfulness hath surprised the *h* Is 33:14
as the *h* do in the synagogues and Mt 6:2 *5273*
thou shalt not be as the *h* are Mt 6:5 *5273*
when ye fast, be not, as the *h* Mt 6:16 *5273*
Ye *h*, well did Esaias prophesy of Mt 15:7 *5273*
O ye *h*, ye can discern the face Mt 16:3 *5273*
and said, Why tempt ye me, ye *h* Mt 22:18 *5273*
unto you, scribes and Pharisees, *h* Mt 23:13 *5273*
unto you, scribes and Pharisees, *h* Mt 23:14 *5273*
unto you, scribes and Pharisees, *h* Mt 23:15 *5273*
unto you, scribes and Pharisees, *h* Mt 23:23 *5273*
unto you, scribes and Pharisees, *h* Mt 23:25 *5273*
unto you, scribes and Pharisees, *h* Mt 23:27 *5273*
unto you, scribes and Pharisees, *h* Mt 23:29 *5273*
him his portion with the *h* Mt 24:51 *5273*
hath Esaias prophesied of you *h* Mk 7:6 *5273*
unto you, scribes and Pharisees, *h* Lk 11:44 *5273*
Ye *h*, ye can discern the face of Lk 12:56 *5273*

HYPOCRITICAL
With *h* mockers in feasts, they Ps 35:16 2611
will send him against an *h* nation Is 10:6 2611

HYSSOP
And ye shall take a bunch of *h* Ex 12:22 231
and cedar wood, and scarlet, and *h* Lev 14:4 231
wood, and the scarlet, and the *h* Lev 14:6 231
and cedar wood, and scarlet, and *h* Lev 14:49 231
take the cedar wood, and the *h* Lev 14:51 231
the cedar wood, and with the *h* Lev 14:52 231
shall take cedar wood, and *h* Num 19:6 231
And a clean person shall take *h* Num 19:18 231
is in Lebanon even unto the *h* 1Kin 4:33 231
Purge me with *h*, and I shall be Ps 51:7 231
with vinegar, and put it upon *h* Jn 19:29 *5301*
with water, and scarlet wool, and *h* Heb 9:19 *5301*

I

I See PREFACE.

IBHAR (*ib'-har*) *A son of David.*
I also, and Elishua, and Nepheg, and 2Sa 5:15 2984
I also, and Elishama, and Eliphelet 1Chr 3:6 2984
And *I*, and Elishua, and Elpalet, 1Chr 14:5 2984

IBLEAM (*ib'-le-am*) *A city in Asher.*
Beth-shean and her towns, and *I* Josh 17:11 2991
towns, nor the inhabitants of *I* Judg 1:27 2991
going up to Gur, which is by *I* 2Kin 9:27 2991

IBNEIAH (*ib-ne-i'-ah*) *A son of Jeroham.*
I the son of Jeroham, and Elah the 1Chr 9:8 2997

IBNIJAH (*ib-ni'-jah*) *A family of exiles.*
the son of Reuel, the son of *I* 1Chr 9:8 2998

IBRI (*ib'-ri*) *A descendant of Levi.*
Beno, and Shoham, and Zaccur, and *I*. 1Chr 24:27 5681

IBSAM See JIBSAM.

IBZAN (*ib'-zan*) *A judge of Israel.*
after him *I* of Beth-lehem judged Judg 12:8 78
Then died *I*, and was buried at Judg 12:10 78

ICE
are blackish by reason of the *i* Job 6:16 7140
Out of whose womb came the *i* Job 38:29 7140
casteth forth his *i* like morsels Ps 147:17 7140

I-CHABOD (*ik'-a-bod*) See I-CHABOD'S. *Son of Phinehas.*
And she named the child *I*, saying, 1Sa 4:21 350

ICHABOD See I-CHABOD.

I-CHABOD'S (*ik'-a-bods*)
I brother, the son of Phinehas, 1Sa 14:3 350

ICONIUM (*i-co'-ne-um*) *A city in Asia Minor.*
feet against them, and came unto *I* Acts 13:51 *2430*
And it came to pass in *I*, that Acts 14:1 *2430*
certain Jews from Antioch and *I* Acts 14:19 *2430*
returned again to Lystra, and to *I* Acts 14:21 *2430*
brethren that were at Lystra and *I* Acts 16:2 *2430*
came unto me at Antioch, at *I* 2Ti 3:11 *2430*

IDALAH (*id'-a-lah*) *A town in Zebulun.*
and Nahallal, and Shimron, and *I* Josh 19:15 3030

IDBASH (*id'-bash*) *A son of Abi-etam.*
Jezreel, and Ishma, and *I* 1Chr 4:3 3031

IDDO (*id'-do*)
1. Father of Ahinadab.
the son of *I* had Mahanaim 1Kin 4:14 5714
2. A descendant of Gershom.
I his son, Zerah his son, 1Chr 6:21 5714
3. A son of Zechariah.
in Gilead, *I* the son of Zechariah 1Chr 27:21 3035
4. A seer.
in the visions of *I* the seer 2Chr 9:29 3260
and of *I* the seer concerning 2Chr 12:15 5714
in the story of the prophet *I* 2Chr 13:22 5714
5. An ancestor of Zechariah.
and Zechariah the son of *I* Ezr 5:1 5714
prophet and Zechariah the son of *I* Ezr 6:14 5714
the son of *I* the prophet, saying, Zec 1:1 5714
the son of *I* the prophet, saying, Zec 1:7 5714
6. A Nethinim chief in exile.
I the chief at the place Casiphia Ezr 8:17 112
them what they should say unto *I* Ezr 8:17 112
7. A priest.
I, Ginnetho, Abijah, Neh 12:4 5714
Of *I*, Zechariah Neh 12:16 5714

IDLE
for they be *i* Ex 5:8 7504
he said, Ye are *i*, ye are *i* Ex 5:17 7504
an *i* soul shall suffer hunger Prov 19:15 7423
That every *i* word that men shall Mt 12:36 *692*
standing *i* in the marketplace Mt 20:3 *692*
out, and found others standing *i* Mt 20:6 *692*
Why stand ye here all the day *i* Mt 20:6 *692*
words seemed to them as *i* tales Lk 24:11 *3026*
And withal they learn to be *i* 1Ti 5:13 *692*
and not only *i*, but tattlers also 1Ti 5:13 *692*

IDLENESS
and eateth not the bread of *i* Prov 31:27 6104
through *i* of the hands the house Eccl 10:18 8220
and abundance of *i* was in her Eze 16:49 8252

IDOL
she had made an *i* in a grove 1Kin 15:13 4656
and Asa destroyed her *i*, and burnt 1Kin 15:13 4656
she had made an *i* in a grove 2Chr 15:16 4656
and Asa cut down her *i*, and stamped 2Chr 15:16 4656
the *i* which he had made, in the 2Chr 33:7 5566
the *i* out of the house of the 2Chr 33:15 5566
Mine *i* hath done them, and my Is 48:5 6090
incense, as if he blessed an *i* Is 66:3 205
man Coniah a despised broken *i* Jer 22:28 6089
Woe to the *i* shepherd that Zec 11:17 457
and offered sacrifice unto the *i* Acts 7:41 *1497*
we know that an *i* is nothing in 1Cor 8:4 *1497*
the *i* unto this hour eat it as a 1Cor 8:7 *1497*
it as a thing offered unto an *i* 1Cor 8:7 *1494*
that the *i* is any thing, or that 1Cor 10:19 *1497*

IDOLATER
fornicator, or covetous, or an *i* 1Cor 5:11 *1496*
nor covetous man, who is an *i* Eph 5:5 *1496*

IDOLATERS
or extortioners, or with *i* 1Cor 5:10 *1496*
neither fornicators, nor *i* 1Cor 6:9 *1496*
Neither be ye *i*, as were some of 1Cor 10:7 *1496*
whoremongers, and sorcerers, and *i* Rev 21:8 *1496*
whoremongers, and murderers, and *i* Rev 22:15 *1496*

IDOLATRIES
banquetings, and abominable *i* 1Pet 4:3 *1495*

IDOLATROUS
And he put down the *i* priests 2Kin 23:5 3649

IDOLATRY
stubbornness is as iniquity and *i* 1Sa 15:23 8655
he saw the city wholly given to *i* Acts 17:16 *2712*
my dearly beloved, flee from *i* 1Cor 10:14 *1495*
I, witchcraft, hatred, variance, Gal 5:20 *1495*
and covetousness, which is *i* Col 3:5 *1495*

IDOL'S
sit at meat in the *i* temple 1Cor 8:10 *1493*

IDOLS
Turn ye not unto *i*, nor make to Lev 19:4 457
make you no *i* nor graven image Lev 26:1 457
upon the carcases of your *i* Lev 26:30 1544
their abominations, and their *i* Deut 29:17 1544
it in the house of their *i* 1Sa 31:9 6091
removed all the *i* that his 1Kin 15:12 1544
very abominably in following *i* 1Kin 21:26 1544
For they served *i*, whereof the 2Kin 17:12 1544
made Judah also to sin with his *i* 2Kin 21:11 1544
served the *i* that his father 2Kin 21:21 1544
wizards, and the images, and the *i* 2Kin 23:24 1544
to carry tidings unto their *i* 1Chr 10:9 6091
all the gods of the people are *i* 1Chr 16:26 457
put away the abominable *i* out of 2Chr 15:8 8251
fathers, and served groves and *i* 2Chr 24:18 6091
cut down all the *i* throughout all 2Chr 34:7 2553
all the gods of the nations are *i* Ps 96:5 457
that boast themselves of *i* Ps 97:7 457
And they served their *i* Ps 106:36 6091
sacrificed unto the *i* of Canaan Ps 106:38 6091
Their *i* are silver and gold, the Ps 115:4 6091
The *i* of the heathen are silver Ps 135:15 6091
Their land also is full of *i* Is 2:8 457
the *i* he shall utterly abolish Is 2:18 457
a man shall cast his *i* of silver Is 2:20 457
his *i* of gold, which they made Is 2:20 457
hath found the kingdoms of the *i* Is 10:10 457
I have done unto Samaria and her *i* Is 10:11 457
so do to Jerusalem and her *i* Is 10:11 6091
the *i* of Egypt shall be moved at Is 19:1 457
and they shall seek to the *i* Is 19:3 457
shall cast away his *i* of silver Is 31:7 457
his *i* of gold, which your own Is 31:7 457
together that are makers of *i* Is 45:16 6736
their *i* were upon the beasts, and Is 46:1 6091
with *i* under every green tree Is 57:5 410
her *i* are confounded, her images Jer 50:2 6091
and they are mad upon their *i* Jer 50:38 367
down your slain men before your *i* Eze 6:4 1544
children of Israel before their *i* Eze 6:5 1544
your *i* may be broken and cease, and Eze 6:6 1544
which go a whoring after their *i* Eze 6:9 1544
their *i* round about their altars Eze 6:13 1544
offer sweet savour to all their *i* Eze 6:13 1544
all the *i* of the house of Israel, Eze 8:10 1544
set up their *i* in their heart Eze 14:3 1544
setteth up his *i* in his heart Eze 14:4 1544
to the multitude of his *i* Eze 14:4 1544
estranged from me through their *i* Eze 14:5 1544
and turn yourselves from your *i* Eze 14:6 1544
and setteth up his *i* in his heart Eze 14:7 1544
lovers, and with all the *i* of thy Eze 16:36 1544
to the *i* of the house of Israel Eze 18:6 1544
hath lifted up his eyes to the *i* Eze 18:12 1544
to the *i* of the house of Israel Eze 18:15 1544
yourselves with the *i* of Egypt Eze 20:7 1544
did they forsake the *i* of Egypt Eze 20:8 1544
their heart went after their *i* Eze 20:16 1544
defile yourselves with their *i* Eze 20:18 1544
eyes were after their fathers' *i* Eze 20:24 1544
yourselves with all your *i* Eze 20:31 1544
Go ye, serve ye every one his *i* Eze 20:39 1544
with your gifts, and with your *i* Eze 20:39 1544
maketh *i* against herself to Eze 22:3 1544
in thine *i* which thou hast made Eze 22:4 1544
with all their *i* she defiled Eze 23:7 1544
thou art polluted with their *i* Eze 23:30 1544
with their *i* have they committed Eze 23:37 1544
slain their children to their *i* Eze 23:39 1544
ye shall bear the sins of your *i* Eze 23:49 1544
I will also destroy the *i* Eze 30:13 1544
lift up your eyes toward your *i* Eze 33:25 1544
for their *i* wherewith they had Eze 36:18 1544
filthiness, and from all your *i* Eze 36:25 1544
themselves any more with their *i* Eze 37:23 1544
astray away from me after their *i* Eze 44:10 1544
unto them before their *i*, and Eze 44:12 1544
Ephraim is joined to *i* Hos 4:17 6091
their gold have they made them *i* Hos 8:4 6091
and *i* according to their own Hos 13:2 6091
What have I to do any more with *i* Hos 14:8 6091
al' the *i* thereof will I lay Mic 1:7 6091
trusteth therein, to make dumb *i* Hab 2:18 457
For the *i* have spoken vanity, and Zec 10:2 8655
names of the *i* out of the land Zec 13:2 6091
they abstain from pollutions of *i* Acts 15:20 *1497*
abstain from meats offered to *i* Acts 15:29 *1494*
from things offered to *i*, and from Acts 21:25 *1494*
thou that abhorrest *i*, dost thou Rom 2:22 *1497*
as touching things offered unto *i* 1Cor 8:1 *1494*
are offered in sacrifice unto *i* 1Cor 8:4 *1494*
things which are offered to *i* 1Cor 8:10 *1494*
in sacrifice to *i* is any thing 1Cor 10:19 *1494*
is offered in sacrifice unto *i* 1Cor 10:28 *1494*
carried away unto these dumb *i* 1Cor 12:2 *1497*
hath the temple of God with *i* 2Cor 6:16 *1497*
to God from *i* to serve the living 1Th 1:9 *1497*
children, keep yourselves from *i* 1Jn 5:21 *1497*
to eat things sacrificed unto *i* Rev 2:14 *1494*
to eat things sacrificed unto *i* Rev 2:20 *1494*
i of gold, and silver, and brass, Rev 9:20 *1497*

IDUMAEA (*i-doo-me'-ah*) See IDUMEA. *Greek form of Edom.*
And from Jerusalem, and from *I* Mk 3:8 *2401*

IDUMEA (*i-doo-me'-ah*) See EDOM, IDUMAEA. *Same as Edom.*
behold, it shall come down upon *I* Is 34:5 123
great slaughter in the land of *I* Is 34:6 123
desolate, O mount Seir, and all *I* Eze 35:15 123
of the heathen, and against all *I* Eze 36:5 123

IEZERITES See JEEZERITES.

IF
I thou doest well, shalt thou not Gen 4:7 518
i thou doest not well, sin lieth Gen 4:7 518
I Cain shall be avenged sevenfold Gen 4:24 3588
to see *i* the waters were abated Gen 8:8
i thou wilt take the left hand, Gen 13:9 518
or *i* thou depart to the right Gen 13:9 518
so that *i* a man can number the Gen 13:16 518
i thou be able to number them Gen 15:5 518
i now I have found favour in thy Gen 18:3 518
and *i* not, I will know Gen 18:21 518
I I find in Sodom fifty righteous Gen 18:26 518
I I find there forty and five, I Gen 18:28 518
not do it, *i* I find thirty there Gen 18:30 518
i thou restore her not, know thou Gen 20:7 518
I it be your mind that I should Gen 23:8
But *i* thou wilt give it, I pray Gen 23:13
i the woman will not be willing Gen 24:8
i they give not thee one, thou Gen 24:41 518
i now thou do prosper my way Gen 24:42 518
now *i* ye will deal kindly and Gen 24:49 518
and *i* not, tell me Gen 24:49 518
I it be so, why am I thus Gen 25:22 518
i Jacob take a wife of the Gen 27:46 518
I God will be with me, and will Gen 28:20 518
i I have found favour in thine Gen 30:27 518
i thou wilt do this thing for me, Gen 30:31 518
I he said thus, The speckled Gen 31:8 518
i he said thus, The ringstraked Gen 31:8 518
I thou shalt afflict my daughters Gen 31:50 518
or *i* thou shalt take other wives Gen 31:50 518
I Esau come to the one company, Gen 32:8 518
i now I have found grace in thy Gen 33:10 518
i men should overdrive them one Gen 33:13 518
I ye will be as we be, that every Gen 34:15 518
But *i* ye will not hearken unto us Gen 34:17 518
people, *i* every male among us be Gen 34:22 518
What profit is it *i* we slay our Gen 37:26 3588
I ye be true men, let one of your Gen 42:19 518
i I bring him not to thee Gen 42:37
i mischief befall him by the way Gen 42:38
I thou wilt send our brother with Gen 43:4 518
But *i* thou wilt not send him, we Gen 43:5 518
i I bring him not unto thee, and Gen 43:9 518
I it must be so now, do this Gen 43:11 518
I I be bereaved of my children, I Gen 43:14 834
for *i* he should leave his father, Gen 44:22
i our youngest brother be with us Gen 44:26 518
i ye take this also from me, and Gen 44:29 518
I I bring him not unto thee, then Gen 44:32 518
i thou knowest any men of Gen 47:6 518
you for your cattle, *i* money fail Gen 47:16 518
I now I have found grace in thy Gen 47:29 518
I now I have found grace in your Gen 50:4 518
i it be a son, then ye shall kill Ex 1:16
but *i* it be a daughter, then she Ex 1:16
i they will not believe thee, Ex 4:8 518
i they will not believe also Ex 4:9 518
i thou refuse to let him go, Ex 4:23
i thou refuse to let them go, Ex 8:2
i thou wilt not let my people go, Ex 8:21 518
For *i* thou refuse to let them go, Ex 9:2 518
i thou refuse to let my people go Ex 10:4 518
i the household be too little for Ex 12:4 518
i thou wilt not redeem it, then Ex 13:13 518
I thou wilt diligently hearken to Ex 15:26 518
I thou shalt do this thing, and Ex 18:23 518
i ye will obey my voice indeed, Ex 19:5 518
i thou wilt make me an altar of Ex 20:25 518
for *i* thou lift up thy tool upon Ex 20:25
I thou buy an Hebrew servant, six Ex 21:2 3588
I he came in by himself, he shall Ex 21:3 518
i he were married, then his wife Ex 21:3 518
I his master have given him a Ex 21:4 518
i the servant shall plainly say, Ex 21:5 518
i a man sell his daughter to be a Ex 21:7 3588
I she please not her master, who Ex 21:8 518
i he have betrothed her unto his Ex 21:9 518
I he take him another wife Ex 21:10 518
i he do not these three unto her, Ex 21:11 518
i a man lie not in wait, but God Ex 21:13 834
But *i* a man come presumptuously Ex 21:14 3588
or *i* he be found in his hand, he Ex 21:16
i men strive together, and one Ex 21:18 3588
I he rise again, and walk abroad Ex 21:19 518
i a man smite his servant, or his Ex 21:20 3588
i he continue a day or two, he Ex 21:21 518
I men strive, and hurt a woman Ex 21:22 518
i any mischief follow, then thou Ex 21:23 518
i a man smite the eye of his Ex 21:26 3588
i he smite out his manservant's Ex 21:27 518
I an ox gore a man or a woman, Ex 21:28 3588
But *i* the ox were wont to push Ex 21:29 518
I there be laid on him a sum of Ex 21:30 518
I the ox shall push a manservant Ex 21:32 518
i a man shall open a pit, or *i* a Ex 21:33 518
i one man's ox hurt another's, Ex 21:35 3588
Or *i* it be known that the ox hath Ex 21:36
I a man shall steal an ox, or a Ex 22:1 3588
I a thief be found breaking up, Ex 22:2 518
I the sun be risen upon him, Ex 22:3 518
i he have nothing, then he shall Ex 22:3 518
I the theft be certainly found in Ex 22:4 518
I a man shall cause a field or Ex 22:5 518
I fire break out, and catch in Ex 22:6 3588
I a man shall deliver unto his Ex 22:7 3588
i the thief be found, let him pay Ex 22:7 518
I the thief be not found, then Ex 22:8 518
I a man deliver unto his Ex 22:10 3588
i it be stolen from him, he shall Ex 22:12 518
I it be torn in pieces, then let Ex 22:13 518
i a man borrow ought of his Ex 22:14 3588
But *i* the owner thereof be with Ex 22:15 518
i it be an hired thing, it came Ex 22:15 518
i a man entice a maid that is not Ex 22:16 3588
I her father utterly refuse to Ex 22:17 518
I thou afflict them in any wise, Ex 22:23 518
I thou lend money to any of my Ex 22:25 518
I thou at all take thy Ex 22:26 518
I thou meet thine enemy's ox or Ex 23:4 3588
I thou see the ass of him that Ex 23:5 3588
But *i* thou shalt indeed obey his Ex 23:22 518
for *i* thou serve their gods, it Ex 23:33
i any man have any matters to do, Ex 24:14
i ought of the flesh of the Ex 29:34 518
i thou wilt forgive their sin Ex 32:32 518
i not, blot me, I pray thee, out Ex 32:32 518
i I have found grace in thy sight Ex 33:13 518
I thy presence go not with me, Ex 33:15 518
I now I have found grace in thy Ex 34:9 518
i thou redeem him not, then shalt Ex 34:20 518
But *i* the cloud were not taken up Ex 40:37 518
I any man of you bring an Lev 1:2 3588
I his offering be a burnt Lev 1:3 518
i his offering be of the flocks, Lev 1:10 518
i the burnt sacrifice for his Lev 1:14 518
i thou bring an oblation of a Lev 2:4 518
i thy oblation be a meat offering Lev 2:5 518
i thy oblation be a meat offering Lev 2:7 518
i thou offer a meat offering of Lev 2:14 518
i his oblation be a sacrifice of Lev 3:1 518
i he offer it of the herd Lev 3:1 518
i his offering for a sacrifice of Lev 3:6 518
I he offer a lamb for his Lev 3:7 518
i his offering be a goat, then he Lev 3:12 518
I a soul shall sin through Lev 4:2 3588
I the priest that is anointed do Lev 4:3 518
i the whole congregation of Lev 4:13 518
Or *i* his sin, wherein he hath Lev 4:23
i any one of the common people Lev 4:27 518
Or *i* his sin, which he hath Lev 4:28 176
i he bring a lamb for a sin Lev 4:32 518
i a soul sin, and hear the voice Lev 5:1 3588
i he do not utter it, then he Lev 5:1 518
Or *i* a soul touch any unclean Lev 5:2 834
and *i* it be hidden from him Lev 5:2
Or *i* he touch the uncleanness of Lev 5:3 3588
Or *i* a soul swear, pronouncing Lev 5:4 3588
i he be not able to bring a lamb, Lev 5:7 518
But *i* he be not able to bring two Lev 5:11 518
I a soul commit a trespass, and Lev 5:15 3588
i a soul sin, and commit any of Lev 5:17 3588
I a soul sin, and commit a Lev 6:2 3588
i it be sodden in a brasen pot, Lev 6:28 518
I he offer it for a thanksgiving, Lev 7:12 518
But *i* the sacrifice of his Lev 7:16 518
i any of the flesh of the Lev 7:18 518
i I had eaten the sin offering to Lev 10:19
i any part of their carcase fall Lev 11:37 3588
But *i* any water be put upon the Lev 11:38 3588
i any beast, of which ye may eat, Lev 11:39 3588
I a woman have conceived seed, and Lev 12:2 3588
But *i* she bear a maid child, then Lev 12:5 518
i she be not able to bring a lamb Lev 12:8 518
I the bright spot be white in the Lev 13:4 518
i the plague in his sight be at a Lev 13:5
i the plague be somewhat dark, and Lev 13:6
But *i* the scab spread much abroad Lev 13:7 518
i the priest see that, behold, Lev 13:8
i the rising be white in the skin Lev 13:10
i a leprosy break out abroad in Lev 13:12 518
i the leprosy have covered all Lev 13:13
Or *i* the raw flesh turn again, and Lev 13:16 3588

I

Phrase	Reference	No.
i the plague be turned into white	Lev 13:17	
And *i*, when the priest seeth it,	Lev 13:20	
But *i* the priest look on it, and,	Lev 13:21	518
i it be not lower than the skin,	Lev 13:21	518
i it spread much abroad in the	Lev 13:22	518
But *i* the bright spot stay in his	Lev 13:23	518
Or *i* there be any flesh, in the	Lev 13:24	3588
i the hair in the bright spot be	Lev 13:25	
But *i* the priest look on it, and,	Lev 13:26	
i it be spread much abroad in the	Lev 13:27	518
i the bright spot stay in his	Lev 13:28	518
I a man or woman have a plague	Lev 13:29	3588
i it be in sight deeper than the	Lev 13:30	3588
i the priest look on the plague	Lev 13:31	3588
i the scall spread not, and there	Lev 13:32	
i the scall be not spread in the	Lev 13:34	
But *i* the scall spread much in	Lev 13:35	3588
i the scall be spread in the skin	Lev 13:36	
But *i* the scall be in his sight	Lev 13:37	518
I a man also or a woman have in	Lev 13:38	
i the bright spots in the skin of	Lev 13:39	
i there be in the bald head, or	Lev 13:42	3588
i the rising of the sore be white	Lev 13:43	
i the plague be greenish or	Lev 13:49	
i the plague be spread in the	Lev 13:51	3588
i the priest shall look, and,	Lev 13:53	518
i the plague have not changed his	Lev 13:55	
i the priest look, and, behold,	Lev 13:56	
i it appear still in the garment,	Lev 13:57	518
i the plague be departed from	Lev 13:58	
i the plague of leprosy be healed	Lev 14:3	
i he be poor, and cannot get so	Lev 14:21	518
i the plague be in the walls of	Lev 14:37	
i the plague be spread in the	Lev 14:39	
i the plague come again, and break	Lev 14:43	518
i the plague be spread in the	Lev 14:44	
i the priest shall come in, and	Lev 14:48	518
i he that hath the issue spit	Lev 15:8	3588
i any man's seed of copulation go	Lev 15:16	3588
i a woman have an issue, and her	Lev 15:19	3588
i it be on her bed, or on any	Lev 15:23	518
i any man lie with her at all, and	Lev 15:24	518
i a woman have an issue of her	Lev 15:25	3588
or *i* it run beyond the time of	Lev 15:25	3588
But *i* she be cleansed of her	Lev 15:28	518
But *i* he wash them not, nor bathe	Lev 17:16	518
which *i* a man do, he shall live	Lev 18:5	
i ye offer a sacrifice of peace	Lev 19:5	3588
i ought remain until the third	Lev 19:6	
i it be eaten at all on the third	Lev 19:7	518
i a stranger sojourn with thee in	Lev 19:33	3588
i the people of the land do any	Lev 20:4	518
i a man lie with his daughter in	Lev 20:12	834
I a man also lie with mankind, as	Lev 20:13	834
i a man take a wife and her mother	Lev 20:14	834
i a man lie with a beast, he	Lev 20:15	834
i a woman approach unto any beast	Lev 20:16	834
i a man shall take his sister,	Lev 20:17	834
i a man shall lie with a woman	Lev 20:18	834
i a man shall lie with his	Lev 20:20	834
i a man shall take his brother's	Lev 20:21	834
i she profane herself by playing	Lev 21:9	3588
die therefore, *i* they profane it	Lev 22:9	3588
But *i* the priest buy any soul	Lev 22:11	3588
I the priest's daughter also be	Lev 22:12	3588
But *i* the priest's daughter be a	Lev 22:13	3588
i a man eat of the holy thing	Lev 22:14	3588
i a man cause a blemish in his	Lev 24:19	3588
i thou sell ought unto thy	Lev 25:14	3588
i ye shall say, What shall we eat	Lev 25:20	3588
I thy brother be waxen poor, and	Lev 25:25	3588
i any of his kin come to redeem	Lev 25:25	
i the man have none to redeem it,	Lev 25:26	3588
But *i* he be not able to restore	Lev 25:28	518
i a man sell a dwelling house in	Lev 25:29	3588
i it be not redeemed within the	Lev 25:30	518
i a man purchase of the Levites,	Lev 25:33	834
i thy brother be waxen poor, and	Lev 25:35	3588
i thy brother that dwelleth by	Lev 25:39	3588
i a sojourner or stranger wax	Lev 25:47	3588
or *i* he be able, he may redeem	Lev 25:49	
I there be yet many years behind,	Lev 25:51	518
i there remain but few years unto	Lev 25:52	518
i he be not redeemed in these	Lev 25:54	518
I ye walk in my statutes, and keep	Lev 26:3	518
But *i* ye will not hearken unto me	Lev 26:14	518
i ye shall despise my statutes,	Lev 26:15	518
or *i* your soul abhor my judgments	Lev 26:15	
i ye will not yet for all this	Lev 26:18	518
i ye walk contrary unto me, and	Lev 26:21	518
i ye will not be reformed by me	Lev 26:23	518
i ye will not for all this	Lev 26:27	518
I they shall confess their	Lev 26:40	
i then their uncircumcised hearts	Lev 26:41	176
i it be a female, then thy	Lev 27:4	518
i it be from five years old even	Lev 27:5	518
i it be from a month old even	Lev 27:6	518
i it be from sixty years old and	Lev 27:7	518
i it be a male, then thy	Lev 27:7	518
But *i* he be poorer than thy	Lev 27:8	518
i it be a beast, whereof men	Lev 27:9	518
i he shall at all change beast	Lev 27:10	518
i it be any unclean beast, of	Lev 27:11	518
But *i* he will at all redeem it,	Lev 27:13	518
i he that sanctified it will	Lev 27:15	518
i a man shall sanctify unto the	Lev 27:16	518
I he sanctify his field from the	Lev 27:17	518
But *i* he sanctify his field after	Lev 27:18	518
i he that sanctified the field	Lev 27:19	518
i he will not redeem the field,	Lev 27:20	518
or *i* he have sold the field to	Lev 27:20	518
i a man sanctify unto the LORD a	Lev 27:22	518
i it be of an unclean beast, then	Lev 27:27	518
or *i* it be not redeemed, then it	Lev 27:27	518
i a man will at all redeem ought	Lev 27:31	518
i he change it at all, then both	Lev 27:33	518
But *i* the man have no kinsman to	Num 5:8	518
I any man's wife go aside, and	Num 5:12	3588
or *i* the spirit of jealousy come	Num 5:14	
I no man have lain with thee, and	Num 5:19	518
i thou hast not gone aside to	Num 5:19	518
But *i* thou hast gone aside to	Num 5:20	3588
i thou be defiled, and some man	Num 5:20	3588
i she be defiled, and have done	Num 5:27	518
i the woman be not defiled, but	Num 5:28	518
i any man die very suddenly by	Num 6:9	3588
I any man of you or of your	Num 9:10	3588
i a stranger shall sojourn among	Num 9:14	3588
i they blow but with one trumpet,	Num 10:4	518
i ye go to war in your land	Num 10:9	3588
i thou go with us, yea, it shall	Num 10:32	3588
i thou deal thus with me, kill me	Num 11:15	518
i I have found favour in thy	Num 11:15	518
I there be a prophet among you, I	Num 12:6	518
I her father had but spit in her	Num 12:14	
I the LORD delight in us, then he	Num 14:8	518
Now *i* thou shalt kill all this	Num 14:15	
i a stranger sojourn with you, or	Num 15:14	3588
i ye have erred, and not observed	Num 15:22	3588
i ought be committed by ignorance	Num 15:24	518
i any soul sin through ignorance,	Num 15:27	518
I these men die the common death	Num 16:29	518
or *i* they be visited after the	Num 16:29	
But *i* the LORD make a new thing,	Num 16:30	518
but *i* he purify not himself the	Num 19:12	
i I and my cattle drink of thy	Num 20:19	518
I thou wilt indeed deliver this	Num 21:2	518
that *i* a serpent had bitten any	Num 21:9	518
I Balak would give me his house	Num 22:18	518
I the men come to call thee, rise	Num 22:20	518
i it displease thee, I will get	Num 22:34	518
I Balak would give me his house	Num 24:13	518
I a man die, and have no son, then	Num 27:8	3588
i he have no daughter, then ye	Num 27:9	518
i he have no brethren, then ye	Num 27:10	518
i his father have no brethren,	Num 27:11	518
I a man vow a vow unto the LORD,	Num 30:2	3588
I a woman also vow a vow unto the	Num 30:3	
But *i* her father disallow her in	Num 30:5	518
i she had at all an husband, when	Num 30:6	518
But *i* her husband disallowed her	Num 30:8	518
i she vowed in her husband's	Num 30:10	518
But *i* her husband hath utterly	Num 30:12	518
But *i* her husband altogether hold	Num 30:14	518
But *i* he shall any ways make them	Num 30:15	518
i we have found grace in thy	Num 32:5	518
For *i* ye turn away from after him	Num 32:15	
I ye will do this thing, *i* ye	Num 32:20	518
But *i* ye will not do so, behold,	Num 32:23	518
I the children of Gad and the	Num 32:29	518
But *i* they will not pass over	Num 32:30	518
But *i* ye will not drive out the	Num 33:55	518
i he smite him with an instrument	Num 35:16	518
i he smite him with throwing a	Num 35:17	518
Or *i* he smite him with an hand	Num 35:18	518
But *i* he thrust him of hatred, or	Num 35:20	518
But *i* he thrust him suddenly	Num 35:22	518
But *i* the slayer shall at any	Num 35:26	518
i they be married to any of the	Num 36:3	
But *i* from thence thou shalt seek	Deut 4:29	
i thou seek him with all thy	Deut 4:29	3588
i thou turn to the LORD thy God,	Deut 4:30	
i we hear the voice of the LORD	Deut 5:25	518
i we observe to do all these	Deut 6:25	3588
i ye hearken to these judgments,	Deut 7:12	6112
I thou shalt say in thine heart,	Deut 7:17	3588
i thou do at all forget the LORD	Deut 8:19	518
i ye shall hearken diligently	Deut 11:13	518
For *i* ye shall diligently keep	Deut 11:22	518
i ye obey the commandments of the	Deut 11:27	834
a curse, *i* ye will not obey the	Deut 11:28	518
I the place which the LORD thy	Deut 12:21	3588
I there arise among you a prophet	Deut 13:1	3588
I thy brother, the son of thy	Deut 13:6	3588
I thou shalt hear say in one of	Deut 13:12	3588
i it be truth, and the thing	Deut 13:14	
i the way be too long for thee,	Deut 14:24	3588
or *i* the place be too far from	Deut 14:24	3588
Only *i* thou carefully hearken	Deut 15:5	518
I there be among you a poor man	Deut 15:7	3588
i thy brother, an Hebrew man, or	Deut 15:12	3588
i he say unto thee, I will not go	Deut 15:16	3588
i there be any blemish therein,	Deut 15:21	3588
as *i* it be lame, or blind, or	Deut 15:21	
I there be found among you,	Deut 17:2	3588
I there arise a matter too hard	Deut 17:8	3588
i a Levite come from any of thy	Deut 18:6	3588
i thou say in thine heart, How	Deut 18:21	3588
i the thing follow not, nor come	Deut 18:22	
i the LORD thy God enlarge thy	Deut 19:8	518
I thou shalt keep all these	Deut 19:9	3588
But *i* any man hate his neighbour,	Deut 19:11	3588
I a false witness rise up against	Deut 19:16	3588
i the witness be a false witness,	Deut 19:18	
i it make thee answer of peace,	Deut 20:11	518
i it will make no peace with thee	Deut 20:12	518
I one be found slain in the land	Deut 21:1	3588
i thou have no delight in her,	Deut 21:14	518
I a man have two wives, one	Deut 21:15	3588
i the firstborn son be hers that	Deut 21:15	
I a man have a stubborn and	Deut 21:18	3588
i a man have committed a sin	Deut 21:22	3588
i thy brother be not nigh unto	Deut 22:2	518
or *i* thou know him not, then thou	Deut 22:2	
I a bird's nest chance to be	Deut 22:6	3588
i any man fall from thence	Deut 22:8	3588
I any man take a wife, and go in	Deut 22:13	3588
But *i* this thing be true, and the	Deut 22:20	518
I a man be found lying with a	Deut 22:22	3588
I a damsel that is a virgin be	Deut 22:23	3588
But *i* a man find a betrothed	Deut 22:25	518
I a man find a damsel that is a	Deut 22:28	3588
I there be among you any man,	Deut 23:10	3588
But *i* thou shalt forbear to vow,	Deut 23:22	3588
i the latter husband hate her, and	Deut 24:3	
or *i* the latter husband die,	Deut 24:3	3588
I a man be found stealing any of	Deut 24:7	3588
i the man be poor, thou shalt not	Deut 24:12	518
I there be a controversy between	Deut 25:1	3588
i the wicked man be worthy to be	Deut 25:2	518
i he should exceed, and beat him	Deut 25:3	
I brethren dwell together, and one	Deut 25:5	3588
i the man like not to take his	Deut 25:7	518
i he stand to it, and say, I like	Deut 25:8	
i thou shalt hearken diligently	Deut 28:1	518
i thou shalt hearken unto the	Deut 28:2	3588
unto thee, *i* thou shalt keep the	Deut 28:9	3588
i that thou hearken unto the	Deut 28:13	3588
i thou wilt not hearken unto the	Deut 28:15	518
I thou wilt not observe to do all	Deut 28:58	518
I any of thine be driven out unto	Deut 30:4	518
I thou shalt hearken unto the	Deut 30:10	3588
i thou turn unto the LORD thy God	Deut 30:10	3588
But *i* thine heart turn away, so	Deut 30:17	
I I whet my glittering sword, and	Deut 32:41	518
i ye utter not this our business	Josh 2:14	518
our head, *i* any hand be upon him	Josh 2:19	518
i thou utter this our business,	Josh 2:20	518
all Israel made as *i* they were	Josh 8:15	
went and made as *i* they had been	Josh 9:4	
i so be the LORD will be with me,	Josh 14:12	194
I thou be a great people, then	Josh 17:15	518
i mount Ephraim be too narrow for	Josh 17:15	3588
i the avenger of blood pursue	Josh 20:5	3588
i the land of your possession be	Josh 22:19	518
i it be in rebellion, or *i* in	Josh 22:22	518
or *i* to offer thereon burnt	Josh 22:23	518
or *i* to offer peace offerings	Josh 22:23	518
i we have not rather done it for	Josh 22:24	518
Else *i* ye do in any wise go back,	Josh 23:12	
i it seem evil unto you to serve	Josh 24:15	518
I ye forsake the LORD, and serve	Josh 24:20	3588
I thou wilt go with me, then I	Judg 4:8	518
but *i* thou wilt not go with me,	Judg 4:8	518
i the LORD be with us, why then	Judg 6:13	
I now I have found grace in thy	Judg 6:17	518
i he be a god, let him plead for	Judg 6:31	518
I thou wilt save Israel by mine	Judg 6:36	518
i the dew be on the fleece only,	Judg 6:37	518
But *i* thou fear to go down, go	Judg 7:10	518
i ye had saved them alive, I	Judg 8:19	3863
I in truth ye anoint me king over	Judg 9:15	518
i not, let fire come out of the	Judg 9:15	518
i ye have done truly and sincerely	Judg 9:16	518
i ye have dealt well with	Judg 9:16	518
I ye then have dealt truly and	Judg 9:19	518
But *i* not, let fire come out from	Judg 9:20	518
the mountains as *i* they were men	Judg 9:36	
I ye bring me home again to fight	Judg 11:9	518
i we do not so according to thy	Judg 11:10	518
I thou shalt without fail deliver	Judg 11:30	518
i thou hast opened thy mouth unto	Judg 11:36	
I he said, Nay	Judg 12:5	
i thou wilt offer a burnt	Judg 13:16	518
I the LORD were pleased to kill	Judg 13:23	3863
i ye can certainly declare it me	Judg 14:12	518
But *i* ye cannot declare it me,	Judg 14:13	518
I ye had not plowed with my	Judg 14:18	3883
I they bind me with seven green	Judg 16:7	518
I they bind me fast with new	Judg 16:11	518
I thou weavest the seven locks of	Judg 16:13	518
i I be shaven, then my strength	Judg 16:17	518
i the daughters of Shiloh come	Judg 21:21	518
I I should say, I have hope, *i* I	Ruth 1:12	3588
i ought but death part thee and me	Ruth 1:17	3588
that *i* he will perform unto thee	Ruth 3:13	518
but *i* he will not do the part of	Ruth 3:13	518
I thou wilt redeem it, redeem it	Ruth 4:4	518
but *i* thou wilt not redeem it,	Ruth 4:4	518
i thou wilt indeed look on the	1Sa 1:11	518
i any man said unto him, Let them	1Sa 2:16	
i not, I will take it by force	1Sa 2:16	518
I one man sin against another,	1Sa 2:25	518
but *i* a man sin against the LORD,	1Sa 2:25	518
i he call thee, that thou shalt	1Sa 3:9	518
i thou hide any thing from me of	1Sa 3:17	518
I ye send away the ark of the God	1Sa 6:3	518
i it goeth up by the way of his	1Sa 6:9	518
but *i* not, then we shall know	1Sa 6:9	518
I ye do return unto the LORD with	1Sa 7:3	518
i we go, what shall we bring the	1Sa 9:7	
i the man should yet come thither	1Sa 10:22	
i there be no man to save us, we	1Sa 11:3	518
I ye will fear the LORD, and serve	1Sa 12:14	518
But *i* ye will not obey the voice	1Sa 12:15	518
But *i* ye shall still do wickedly,	1Sa 12:25	518
I they say thus unto us, Tarry	1Sa 14:9	518
But *i* they say thus, Come up unto	1Sa 14:10	518
i haply the people had eaten	1Sa 14:30	3863
i Saul hear it, he will kill me	1Sa 16:2	
I he be able to fight with me, and	1Sa 17:9	518
but *i* I prevail against him, and	1Sa 17:9	518
I thou save not thy to night, to	1Sa 19:11	518
I thy father at all miss me, then	1Sa 20:6	518
I he say thus, It is well	1Sa 20:7	518
but *i* he be very wroth, then be	1Sa 20:7	518
i there be in me iniquity, slay	1Sa 20:8	518
for *i* I knew certainly that evil	1Sa 20:9	518
or what *i* thy father answer thee	1Sa 20:10	176
i there be good toward David, and	1Sa 20:12	
but *i* it please my father to do	1Sa 20:13	3588
I I expressly say unto the lad,	1Sa 20:21	518

Context	Reference	Strong's
But *i* I say thus unto the young	1Sa 20:22	518
i I have found favour in thine	1Sa 20:29	518
i the young men have kept	1Sa 21:4	518
i thou wilt take that, take it	1Sa 21:9	518
how much more then *i* we come to	1Sa 23:3	3588
i he be in the land, that I will	1Sa 23:23	518
For *i* a man find his enemy, will	1Sa 24:19	3588
i I leave of all that pertain to	1Sa 25:22	518
I the LORD have stirred thee up	1Sa 26:19	518
but *i* they be the children of men	1Sa 26:19	518
I I have now found grace in thine	1Sa 27:5	518
i I taste bread, or ought else,	2Sa 3:35	
I he commit iniquity, I will	2Sa 7:14	834
I the Syrians be too strong for	2Sa 10:11	518
but *i* the children of Ammon be	2Sa 10:11	518
i so be that the king's wrath	2Sa 11:20	518
i that had been too little, I	2Sa 12:8	518
i we tell him that the child is	2Sa 12:18	
I not, I pray thee, let my	2Sa 13:26	3808
i there be any iniquity in me,	2Sa 14:32	518
I the LORD shall bring me again	2Sa 15:8	518
i I shall find favour in the eyes	2Sa 15:25	
But *i* he thus say, I have no	2Sa 15:26	518
I thou passest on with me, then	2Sa 15:33	518
But *i* thou return to the city, and	2Sa 15:34	518
was as *i* a man had enquired at	2Sa 16:23	
thou seekest is as *i* all returned	2Sa 17:3	
i not; speak thou	2Sa 17:6	518
i he be gotten into a city, then	2Sa 17:13	518
for *i* we flee away, they will not	2Sa 18:3	518
neither *i* half of us die, will	2Sa 18:3	518
I he be alone, there is tidings	2Sa 18:25	518
that *i* Absalom had lived, and all	2Sa 19:6	3863
i thou go not forth, there will	2Sa 19:7	3588
i thou be not captain of the host	2Sa 19:13	518
I he will shew himself a worthy	1Kin 1:52	518
but *i* wickedness shall be found	1Kin 1:52	518
I thy children take heed to their	1Kin 2:4	518
i Adonijah have not spoken this	1Kin 2:23	3588
i thou wilt walk in my ways, to	1Kin 3:14	518
i thou wilt walk in my statutes,	1Kin 6:12	518
I any man trespass against his	1Kin 8:31	
i they pray toward this place, and	1Kin 8:35	
I there be in the land famine	1Kin 8:37	3588
i there be pestilence, blasting,	1Kin 8:37	3588
or *i* there be caterpiller	1Kin 8:37	3588
i their enemy besiege them in the	1Kin 8:37	3588
I thy people go out to battle	1Kin 8:44	3588
I they sin against thee, (for	1Kin 8:46	3588
Yet *i* they shall bethink	1Kin 8:47	
i thou wilt walk before me, as	1Kin 9:4	518
But *i* ye shall at all turn from	1Kin 9:6	518
i thou wilt hearken unto all that	1Kin 11:38	518
I thou wilt be a servant unto	1Kin 12:7	518
I this people go up to do	1Kin 12:27	518
I thou wilt give me half thine	1Kin 13:8	518
as *i* it had been a light thing	1Kin 16:31	
i the LORD be God, follow him	1Kin 18:21	518
but *i* Baal, then follow him	1Kin 18:21	518
i I make not thy life as the life	1Kin 19:2	
i the dust of Samaria shall	1Kin 20:10	
i by any means he be missing,	1Kin 20:39	518
i it seem good to thee, I will	1Kin 21:2	518
i it please thee, I will give	1Kin 21:6	518
I thou return at all in peace,	1Kin 22:28	518
I I be a man of God, then let	2Kin 1:10	518
I I be a man of God, let fire	2Kin 1:12	518
i thou see me when I am taken	2Kin 2:10	518
but *i* not, it shall not be so	2Kin 2:10	518
i thou meet any man, salute him	2Kin 4:29	3588
i any salute thee, answer him not	2Kin 4:29	3588
i the prophet had bid thee do	2Kin 5:13	
I the LORD do not help thee,	2Kin 6:27	
i the head of Elisha the son of	2Kin 6:31	518
i the LORD would make windows in	2Kin 7:2	
I we say, We will enter into the	2Kin 7:4	518
i we sit still here, we die also	2Kin 7:4	518
i they save us alive, we shall	2Kin 7:4	518
i they kill us, we shall but die	2Kin 7:4	518
i we tarry till the morning light	2Kin 7:9	
i the LORD should make windows in	2Kin 7:19	
I it be your minds, then let none	2Kin 9:15	518
I ye be mine, and *i* ye will	2Kin 10:6	518
I it be, give me thine hand	2Kin 10:15	
I any of the men whom I have	2Kin 10:24	
on which *i* a man lean, it will go	2Kin 18:21	834
But *i* ye say unto me, We trust in	2Kin 18:22	3588
i thou be able on thy part to set	2Kin 18:23	518
i peace and truth be in my days	2Kin 20:19	518
only *i* they will observe to do	2Kin 21:8	518
I ye be come peaceably unto me to	1Chr 12:17	518
but *i* ye be come to betray me to	1Chr 12:17	518
I it seem good unto you, and that	1Chr 13:2	518
I the Syrians be too strong for	1Chr 19:12	518
but *i* the children of Ammon be	1Chr 19:12	518
i thou takest heed to fulfil the	1Chr 22:13	518
i he be constant to do my	1Chr 28:7	518
i thou seek him, he will be found	1Chr 28:9	518
but *i* thou forsake him, he will	1Chr 28:9	518
I a man sin against his neighbour	2Chr 6:22	518
i thy people Israel be put to the	2Chr 6:24	518
yet *i* they pray toward this place	2Chr 6:26	
I there be dearth in the land	2Chr 6:28	3588
i there be pestilence, *i* there	2Chr 6:28	3588
i their enemies besiege them in	2Chr 6:28	3588
i they come and pray in this house	2Chr 6:32	
i thy people go out to war	2Chr 6:34	3588
I they sin against thee, (for	2Chr 6:36	3588
Yet *i* they bethink themselves in	2Chr 6:37	
I they return to thee with all	2Chr 6:38	
I I shut up heaven that there be	2Chr 7:13	2005
or *i* I command the locusts to	2Chr 7:13	2005
or *i* I send pestilence among my	2Chr 7:13	518
I my people, which are called by	2Chr 7:14	
i thou wilt walk before me, as	2Chr 7:17	518
But *i* ye turn away, and forsake my	2Chr 7:19	518
I thou be kind to this people, and	2Chr 10:7	518
i ye seek him, he will be found	2Chr 15:2	518
but *i* ye forsake him, he will	2Chr 15:2	518
I thou certainly return in peace,	2Chr 18:27	518
I, when evil cometh upon us, as	2Chr 20:9	518
But *i* thou wilt go, do it, be	2Chr 25:8	518
For *i* ye turn again unto the LORD	2Chr 30:9	
from you, *i* ye return unto him	2Chr 30:9	518
i this city be builded, and the	Ezr 4:13	2006
i this city be builded again, and	Ezr 4:16	2006
i it seem good to the king, let	Ezr 5:17	2006
I ye transgress, I will scatter	Neh 1:8	
But *i* ye turn unto me, and keep my	Neh 1:9	
I it please the king, and *i* thy	Neh 2:5	518
I it please the king, let letters	Neh 2:7	
i a fox go up, he shall even	Neh 4:3	518
(which *i* a man do, he shall live	Neh 9:29	
i the people of the land bring	Neh 10:31	
i ye do so again, I will lay	Neh 13:21	518
I it please the king, let there	Est 1:19	518
I it please the king, let it be	Est 3:9	518
For *i* thou altogether holdest thy	Est 4:14	518
and *i* I perish, I perish	Est 4:16	834
I it seem good unto the king, let	Est 5:4	518
I I have found favour in the	Est 5:8	518
i it please the king to grant my	Est 5:8	518
I Mordecai be of the seed of the	Est 6:13	518
I I have found favour in thy	Est 7:3	518
i it please the king, let my life	Est 7:3	518
But *i* we had been sold for	Est 7:4	432
I it please the king, and *i* I	Est 8:5	518
I it please the king, let it be	Est 9:13	518
I we assay to commune with thee,	Job 4:2	
i there be any that will answer	Job 5:1	
it is evident unto you *i* I lie	Job 6:28	518
I thy children have sinned	Job 8:4	518
I thou wouldest seek unto God	Job 8:5	518
I thou wert pure and upright	Job 8:6	518
I he destroy him from his place,	Job 8:18	518
I he will contend with him, he	Job 9:3	518
I God will not withdraw his anger	Job 9:13	
I I had called, and he had	Job 9:16	518
I I speak of strength, lo, he is	Job 9:19	518
i of judgment, who shall set me a	Job 9:19	518
I I justify myself, mine own	Job 9:20	518
i I say, I am perfect, it shall	Job 9:20	
I the scourge slay suddenly, he	Job 9:23	518
i not, where, and who is he	Job 9:24	518
I I say, I will forget my	Job 9:27	518
I I be wicked, why then labour I	Job 9:29	
I I wash myself with snow water,	Job 9:30	518
I I sin, then thou markest me, and	Job 10:14	518
I I be wicked, woe unto me	Job 10:15	518
i I be righteous, yet will I not	Job 10:15	518
I he cut off, and shut up, or	Job 11:10	518
I thou prepare thine heart, and	Job 11:13	518
I iniquity be in thine hand, put	Job 11:14	518
i ye do secretly accept persons	Job 13:10	518
i I hold my tongue, I shall give	Job 13:19	3588
i it be cut down, that it will	Job 14:7	518
I a man die, shall he live again	Job 14:14	518
i your soul were in my soul's	Job 16:4	3863
I I wait, the grave is mine house	Job 17:13	518
I indeed ye will magnify	Job 19:5	518
i it were so, why should not my	Job 21:4	518
we have, *i* we pray unto him	Job 21:15	
I thou return to the Almighty,	Job 22:23	518
i one know them, they are in the	Job 24:17	3588
i it be not so now, who will make	Job 24:25	518
I his children be multiplied, it	Job 27:14	518
I I laughed on them, they	Job 29:24	
I I have walked with vanity, or	Job 31:5	518
or *i* my foot hath hasted to	Job 31:5	
I my step hath turned out of the	Job 31:7	518
i any blot hath cleaved to mine	Job 31:7	
I mine heart have been deceived	Job 31:9	518
or *i* I have laid wait at my	Job 31:9	
I I did despise the cause of my	Job 31:13	518
I I have withheld the poor from	Job 31:16	518
I I have seen any perish for want	Job 31:19	518
I his loins have not blessed me,	Job 31:20	518
i he were not warmed with the	Job 31:20	
I I have lifted up my hand	Job 31:21	518
I I have made gold my hope, or	Job 31:24	518
I I rejoiced because my wealth	Job 31:25	518
I I beheld the sun when it shined	Job 31:26	518
I I rejoiced at the destruction	Job 31:29	518
I the men of my tabernacle said	Job 31:31	518
I I covered my transgressions as	Job 31:33	518
I my land cry against me, or that	Job 31:38	518
I I have eaten the fruits thereof	Job 31:39	518
I thou canst answer me, set thy	Job 33:5	518
I there be a messenger with him,	Job 33:23	518
i any say, I have sinned, and	Job 33:27	
I thou hast any thing to say,	Job 33:32	518
I not, hearken unto me	Job 33:33	518
I he set his heart upon man	Job 34:14	518
i he gather unto himself his	Job 34:14	
I now thou hast understanding,	Job 34:16	518
i I have done iniquity, I will do	Job 34:32	518
i I be cleansed from my sin	Job 35:3	
I thou sinnest, what doest thou	Job 35:6	518
or *i* thy transgressions be	Job 35:6	
I thou be righteous, what givest	Job 35:7	518
i they be bound in fetters, and be	Job 36:8	518
I they obey and serve him, they	Job 36:11	518
But *i* they obey not, they shall	Job 36:12	518
I a man speak, surely he shall be	Job 37:20	518
i thou hast understanding	Job 38:4	
measures thereof, *i* thou knowest	Job 38:5	3588
as *i* it had issued out of the	Job 38:8	
declare *i* thou knowest it all	Job 38:18	518
O LORD my God, *i* I have done this	Ps 7:3	518
i there be iniquity in my hands	Ps 7:3	518
I I have rewarded evil unto him	Ps 7:4	518
I he turn not, he will whet his	Ps 7:12	518
I the foundations be destroyed,	Ps 11:3	3588
to see *i* there were any that did	Ps 14:2	
i thou be silent to me, I become	Ps 28:1	
i I would declare and speak of	Ps 40:5	
i he come to see me, he speaketh	Ps 41:6	518
I we have forgotten the name of	Ps 44:20	518
I I were hungry, I would not tell	Ps 50:12	518
to see *i* there were any that did	Ps 53:2	
grudge *i* they be not satisfied	Ps 59:15	518
i riches increase, set not your	Ps 62:10	
I I regard iniquity in my heart,	Ps 66:18	518
I I say, I will speak thus	Ps 73:15	518
i thou wilt hearken unto me	Ps 81:8	518
I his children forsake my law, and	Ps 89:30	518
I they break my statutes, and keep	Ps 89:31	518
i by reason of strength they be	Ps 90:10	518
To day *i* ye will hear his voice,	Ps 95:7	518
I it had not been the LORD who	Ps 124:1	3884
I it had not been the LORD who	Ps 124:2	3884
I thou, LORD, shouldest mark	Ps 130:3	518
I thy children will keep my	Ps 132:12	518
I I forget thee, O Jerusalem, let	Ps 137:5	518
I I do not remember thee, let my	Ps 137:6	518
i I prefer not Jerusalem above my	Ps 137:6	518
I I ascend up into heaven, thou	Ps 139:8	518
i I make my bed in hell, behold,	Ps 139:8	
I I take the wings of the morning	Ps 139:9	
I I say, Surely the darkness	Ps 139:11	
I I should count them, they are	Ps 139:18	
see *i* there be any wicked way in	Ps 139:24	518
i sinners entice thee, consent	Prov 1:10	518
I they say, Come with us, let us	Prov 1:11	518
i thou wilt receive my words, and	Prov 2:1	518
i thou criest after knowledge, and	Prov 2:3	518
I thou seekest her as silver, and	Prov 2:4	518
i he have done thee no harm	Prov 3:30	518
i thou be surety for thy friend,	Prov 6:1	518
i thou hast stricken thy hand	Prov 6:1	
i he steal to satisfy his soul	Prov 6:30	
But *i* he be found, he shall	Prov 6:31	
I thou be wise, thou shalt be	Prov 9:12	518
but *i* thou scornest, thou alone	Prov 9:12	
i it be found in the way of	Prov 16:31	
for *i* thou deliver him, yet thou	Prov 19:19	518
i thou keep them within thee	Prov 22:18	3588
I thou hast nothing to pay, why	Prov 22:27	518
i thou be a man given to appetite	Prov 23:2	518
for *i* thou beatest him with the	Prov 23:13	
i thine heart be wise, my heart	Prov 23:15	518
I thou faint in the day of	Prov 24:10	
I thou forbear to deliver them	Prov 24:11	
I thou sayest, Behold, we knew it	Prov 24:12	3588
I thine enemy be hungry, give him	Prov 25:21	518
i he be thirsty, give him water	Prov 25:21	518
I a wise man contendeth with a	Prov 29:9	
I a ruler hearken to lies, all	Prov 29:12	
his son's name, *i* thou canst tell	Prov 30:4	
I thou hast done foolishly in	Prov 30:32	518
or *i* thou hast thought evil, lay	Prov 30:32	518
For *i* they fall, the one will	Eccl 4:10	518
i two lie together, then they	Eccl 4:11	
i one prevail against him, two	Eccl 4:12	
I thou seest the oppression of	Eccl 5:8	518
I a man beget an hundred children	Eccl 6:3	518
I the spirit of the ruler rise up	Eccl 10:4	
I the iron be blunt, and he do not	Eccl 10:10	518
I the clouds be full of rain,	Eccl 11:3	518
i the tree fall toward the south,	Eccl 11:3	
But *i* a man live many years, and	Eccl 11:8	
I thou know not, O thou fairest	Song 1:8	518
i ye find my beloved, that ye	Song 5:8	
let us see *i* the vine flourish,	Song 7:12	
i a man would give all the	Song 8:7	518
I she be a wall, we will build	Song 8:9	518
i she be a door, we will inclose	Song 8:9	
I ye be willing and obedient, ye	Is 1:19	518
But *i* ye refuse and rebel, ye	Is 1:20	518
i one look unto the land, behold	Is 5:30	
I ye will not believe, surely ye	Is 7:9	518
i they speak not according to	Is 8:20	518
as *i* the rod should shake itself	Is 10:15	
or as *i* the staff should lift up	Is 10:15	
up itself, as *i* it were no wood	Is 10:15	
i ye will enquire, enquire ye	Is 21:12	518
whereon *i* a man lean, it will go	Is 36:6	
But *i* thou say to me, We trust in	Is 36:7	
i thou be able on thy part to set	Is 36:8	518
shalt not be able to put *i* off	Is 47:11	
i so be thou shalt be able to	Is 47:12	194
i so be thou mayest prevail	Is 47:12	194
as *i* he were ready to destroy	Is 51:13	
I thou take away from the midst	Is 58:9	
i thou draw out thy soul to the	Is 58:10	
I thou turn away thy foot from	Is 58:13	518
we grope as *i* we had no eyes	Is 59:10	
an ox is as *i* he slew a man	Is 66:3	
as *i* he cut off a dog's neck	Is 66:3	
as *i* he offered swine's blood	Is 66:3	
incense, as *i* he blessed an idol	Is 66:3	
see *i* there be such a thing	Jer 2:10	
i they can save thee in the time	Jer 2:28	
I a man put away his wife, and she	Jer 3:1	
I thou wilt return, O Israel,	Jer 4:1	518
i thou wilt put away thine	Jer 4:1	
i ye can find a man, *i* there be	Jer 5:1	518
i there be any that executeth	Jer 5:1	518
For *i* ye throughly amend your	Jer 7:5	518
i ye throughly execute judgment	Jer 7:5	518
I ye oppress not the stranger,	Jer 7:6	
I thou hast run with the footmen,	Jer 12:5	3588

i in the land of peace, wherein ... Jer 12:5
i they will diligently learn the ... Jer 12:16 518
But *i* they will not obey, I will ... Jer 12:17 518
But *i* ye will not hear it, my ... Jer 13:17 518
i thou say in thine heart, ... Jer 13:22 3588
I I go forth into the field, then ... Jer 14:18 518
i I enter into the city, then ... Jer 14:18 518
i they say unto thee, Whither ... Jer 15:2 3588
I thou return, then will I bring ... Jer 15:19 518
i thou take forth the precious ... Jer 15:19 518
i ye diligently hearken unto me, ... Jer 17:24 518
But *i* ye will not hearken unto me ... Jer 17:27 518
I that nation, against whom I ... Jer 18:8
I it do evil in my sight, that it ... Jer 18:10
i so be that the LORD will deal ... Jer 21:2 194
For *i* ye do this thing indeed, ... Jer 22:4 518
But *i* ye will not hear these ... Jer 22:5 518
But *i* they had stood in my ... Jer 23:22
i they refuse to take the cup at ... Jer 25:28
I so be they will hearken, and ... Jer 26:3 194
I ye will not hearken to me, to ... Jer 26:4 518
that *i* ye put me to death, ye ... Jer 26:15 518
But *i* they be prophets, and *i* the ... Jer 27:18 518
I those ordinances depart from ... Jer 31:36 518
I heaven above can be measured, ... Jer 31:37 518
I ye can break my covenant of the ... Jer 33:20 518
I my covenant be not with day and ... Jer 33:25 518
i I have not appointed the ... Jer 33:25
I I declare it unto thee, wilt ... Jer 38:15 518
i I give thee counsel, wilt thou ... Jer 38:15 518
I thou wilt assuredly go forth ... Jer 38:17 518
But *i* thou wilt not go forth to ... Jer 38:18 518
But *i* thou refuse to go forth, ... Jer 38:21
But *i* the princes hear that I ... Jer 38:25 3588
I it seem good unto thee to come ... Jer 40:4 518
but *i* it seem ill unto thee to ... Jer 40:4 518
i we do not even according to all ... Jer 42:5
I ye will still abide in this ... Jer 42:10 518
But *i* ye say, We will not dwell ... Jer 42:13 518
I ye wholly set your faces to ... Jer 42:15 518
I grapegatherers come to thee, ... Jer 49:9 518
i thieves by night, they will ... Jer 49:9 518
i so be she may be healed ... Jer 51:8 194
see *i* there be any sorrow like ... Lam 1:12 518
as *i* it were of a garden ... Lam 2:6
i so be there may be hope ... Lam 3:29 194
Yet *i* thou warn the wicked, and he ... Eze 3:19 3588
Nevertheless *i* thou warn the ... Eze 3:21 3588
as *i* a wheel had been in the ... Eze 10:10 834
i the prophet be deceived when he ... Eze 14:9 3588
I I cause noisome beasts to pass ... Eze 14:15 3863
Or *i* I bring a sword upon that ... Eze 14:17
Or *i* I send a pestilence into ... Eze 14:19
as *i* that were a very little ... Eze 16:47
But *i* a man be just, and do that ... Eze 18:5 3588
I he beget a son that is a robber ... Eze 18:10
i he beget a son, that seeth all ... Eze 18:14
But *i* the wicked will turn from ... Eze 18:21
which *i* a man do, he shall even ... Eze 20:11
which *i* a man do, he shall even ... Eze 20:13
which *i* a man do, he shall even ... Eze 20:21
i ye will not hearken unto me ... Eze 20:39 518
what *i* the sword contemn even the ... Eze 21:13 518
i the people of the land take a ... Eze 33:2
I when he seeth the sword come ... Eze 33:3
i the sword come, and take him ... Eze 33:4
But *i* the watchman see the sword ... Eze 33:6 3588
i the sword come, and take any ... Eze 33:6
i thou dost not speak to warn the ... Eze 33:8
i thou warn the wicked of his way ... Eze 33:9 3588
i he do not turn from his way, he ... Eze 33:9
I our transgressions and our sins ... Eze 33:10 3588
i he trust to his own ... Eze 33:13
i he turn from his sin, and do ... Eze 33:14
I the wicked restore the pledge, ... Eze 33:15
But *i* the wicked turn from his ... Eze 33:19
i they be ashamed of all that ... Eze 43:11 518
I the prince give a gift unto any ... Eze 46:16 3588
But *i* he give a gift of his ... Eze 46:17 3588
i ye will not make known unto me ... Dan 2:5 2006
But *i* ye shew the dream, and the ... Dan 2:6 2006
But *i* ye will not make known unto ... Dan 2:9 2006
Now *i* ye be ready that at what ... Dan 3:15 2006
but *i* ye worship not, ye shall be ... Dan 3:15 2006
I it be so, our God whom we serve ... Dan 3:17 2006
But *i* not, be it known unto thee, ... Dan 3:18
i it may be a lengthening of thy ... Dan 4:27 2006
now *i* thou canst read the writing ... Dan 5:16 2006
i we follow on to know the LORD ... Hos 6:3
i so be it yield, the strangers ... Hos 8:7 194
Who knoweth *i* he will return and ... Joel 2:14
i ye recompense me, swiftly and ... Joel 3:4 518
his den, *i* he have taken nothing ... Amos 3:4 518
As *i* a man did flee from a lion, ... Amos 5:19 834
i there remain ten men in one ... Amos 6:9 518
I thieves came to thee ... Obad 5 518
i robbers by night, (how art thou ... Obad 5 518
i the grapegatherers came to thee ... Obad 5 518
i so be that God will think upon ... Jonah 1:6 194
Who can tell *i* God will turn and ... Jonah 3:9
I a man walking in the spirit and ... Mic 2:11 3863
i he go through, both treadeth ... Mic 5:8 518
i they be shaken, they shall even ... Nah 3:12 518
I one bear holy flesh in the ... Hag 2:12 2005
I one that is unclean by a dead ... Hag 2:13 518
I thou wilt walk in my ways, and ... Zec 3:7 518
i thou wilt keep my charge, then ... Zec 3:7 518
i ye will diligently obey the ... Zec 6:15
I it be marvellous in the eyes of ... Zec 8:6 3588
I ye think good, give me my price ... Zec 11:12 518
and *i* not, forbear ... Zec 11:12 518
i the family of Egypt go not up, ... Zec 14:18
i then I be a father, where is ... Mal 1:6 518
i I be a master, where is my fear ... Mal 1:6 518

And *i* ye offer the blind for ... Mal 1:8 3588
i ye offer the lame and sick, is ... Mal 1:8 3588
I ye will not hear, and *i* ye will ... Mal 2:2 518
i I will not open you the windows ... Mal 3:10
I thou be the Son of God, command ... Mt 4:3 1487
I thou be the Son of God, cast ... Mt 4:6 1487
i thou wilt fall down and worship ... Mt 4:9 1437
but *i* the salt have lost his ... Mt 5:13 1437
Therefore *i* thou bring thy gift ... Mt 5:23
i thy right eye offend thee, ... Mt 5:29 1487
i thy right hand offend thee, cut ... Mt 5:30
i any man will sue thee at the ... Mt 5:40
For *i* ye love them which love you ... Mt 5:46 1437
i ye salute your brethren only, ... Mt 5:47 1437
For *i* ye forgive men their ... Mt 6:14 1437
But *i* ye forgive not men their ... Mt 6:15 1437
i therefore thine eye be single, ... Mt 6:22 1437
But *i* thine eye be evil, thy ... Mt 6:23 1437
I therefore the light that is in ... Mt 6:23 1487
i God so clothe the grass of the ... Mt 6:30 1487
whom *i* his son ask bread, will he ... Mt 7:9 1437
Or *i* he ask a fish, will he give ... Mt 7:10 1437
I ye then, being evil, know how ... Mt 7:11 1487
i thou wilt, thou canst make me ... Mt 8:2 1437
I thou cast us out, suffer us to ... Mt 8:31 1487
I I may but touch his garment, I ... Mt 9:21 1437
i the house be worthy, let your ... Mt 10:13 1437
but *i* it be not worthy, let your ... Mt 10:13 1437
I they have called the master of ... Mt 10:25 1487
i ye will receive it, this is ... Mt 11:14 1487
for *i* the mighty works, which ... Mt 11:21 1487
for *i* the mighty works, which ... Mt 11:23 1487
But *i* ye had known what this ... Mt 12:7 1487
i it fall into a pit on the ... Mt 12:11 1437
i Satan cast out Satan, he is ... Mt 12:26 1487
i I by Beelzebub cast out devils, ... Mt 12:27 1487
But *i* I cast out devils by the ... Mt 12:28 1487
i it be thou, bid me come unto ... Mt 14:28 1487
i the blind lead the blind, both ... Mt 15:14 1437
I any man will come after me, let ... Mt 16:24 1487
i he shall gain the whole world, ... Mt 16:26
i thou wilt, let us make here ... Mt 17:4 1487
I ye have faith as a grain of ... Mt 17:20 1437
Wherefore *i* thy hand or thy foot ... Mt 18:8 1487
i thine eye offend thee, pluck it ... Mt 18:9 1487
i a man have an hundred sheep, and ... Mt 18:12 1437
i so be that he find it, verily I ... Mt 18:13 1437
Moreover *i* thy brother shall ... Mt 18:15 1437
i he shall hear thee, thou hast ... Mt 18:15 1437
But *i* he will not hear thee, then ... Mt 18:16 1437
i he shall neglect to hear them, ... Mt 18:17 1437
but *i* he neglect to hear the ... Mt 18:17 1437
That *i* two of you shall agree on ... Mt 18:19 1437
i ye from your hearts forgive not ... Mt 18:35 1437
I the case of the man be so with ... Mt 19:10 1487
but *i* thou wilt enter into life, ... Mt 19:17 1487
I thou wilt be perfect, go and ... Mt 19:21 1487
i any man say ought unto you, ye ... Mt 21:3 1437
I ye have faith, and doubt not, ye ... Mt 21:21 1437
but also *i* ye shall say unto this ... Mt 21:21 2579
which *i* ye tell me, I in like ... Mt 21:24 1437
I we shall say, From heaven ... Mt 21:25 1437
But *i* we shall say, Of men ... Mt 21:26 1437
I a man die, having no children, ... Mt 22:24 1437
I David then call him Lord ... Mt 22:45 1487
I we had been in the days of our ... Mt 23:30 1487
Then *i* any man shall say unto you ... Mt 24:23 1437
i it were possible, they shall ... Mt 24:24 1487
Wherefore *i* they shall say unto ... Mt 24:26 1437
that *i* the goodman of the house ... Mt 24:43 1487
i that evil servant shall say in ... Mt 24:48 1437
that man *i* he had not been born ... Mt 26:24 1487
i it be possible, let this cup ... Mt 26:39 1487
i this cup may not pass away from ... Mt 26:42 1487
I thou be the Son of God, come ... Mt 27:40 1487
I he be the King of Israel, let ... Mt 27:42 1487
him now, *i* he will have him ... Mt 27:43 1487
i this come to the governor's ... Mt 28:14 1437
I thou wilt, thou canst make me ... Mk 1:40 1437
i a kingdom be divided against ... Mk 3:24 1437
i a house be divided against ... Mk 3:25 1437
i Satan rise up against himself, ... Mk 3:26 1487
I any man have ears to hear, let ... Mk 4:23
as *i* a man should cast seed into ... Mk 4:26 1487
I I may touch but his clothes, I ... Mk 5:28 2579
him that they might touch *i* it ... Mk 6:56 2579
I a man shall say to his father ... Mk 7:11 1437
I any man have ears to hear, let ... Mk 7:16
i I send them away fasting to ... Mk 8:3 1437
him, he asked him *i* he saw ought ... Mk 8:23
i he shall gain the whole world, ... Mk 8:36 1437
but *i* thou canst do any thing, ... Mk 9:22
I thou canst believe, all things ... Mk 9:23 1487
I any man desire to be first, the ... Mk 9:35 1487
i thy hand offend thee, cut it ... Mk 9:43 1437
i thy foot offend thee, cut it ... Mk 9:45 1437
i thine eye offend thee, pluck it ... Mk 9:47 1437
but *i* the salt have lost his ... Mk 9:50 1437
i a woman shall put away her ... Mk 10:12 1437
i any man say unto you, Why do ye ... Mk 11:3 1437
i haply he might find any thing ... Mk 11:13 1487
i ye have ought against any ... Mk 11:25 1487
But *i* ye do not forgive, neither ... Mk 11:26 1487
I we shall say, From heaven ... Mk 11:31 1437
But *i* we shall say, Of men ... Mk 11:32 1437
I a man's brother die, and leave ... Mk 12:19 1437
then *i* any man shall say to you, ... Mk 13:21 1437
i it were possible, even the ... Mk 13:22 1487
that man *i* he had never been born ... Mk 14:21 1487
I I should die with thee, I will ... Mk 14:31 1437
i it were possible, the hour ... Mk 14:35 1487
Pilate marvelled *i* he were ... Mk 15:44 1487
i they drink any deadly thing, it ... Mk 16:18 2579
I thou be the Son of God, command ... Lk 4:3 1487

I thou therefore wilt worship me, ... Lk 4:7 1437
I thou be the Son of God, cast ... Lk 4:9 1487
i thou wilt, thou canst make me ... Lk 5:12 1437
i otherwise, then both the new ... Lk 5:36 1490
For *i* ye love them which love you ... Lk 6:32 1487
i ye do good to them which do ... Lk 6:33 1437
i ye lend to them of whom ye hope ... Lk 6:34 1437
i he were a prophet, would have ... Lk 7:39 1487
I any man will come after me, let ... Lk 9:23 1487
i he gain the whole world, and ... Lk 9:25
i the son of peace be there, your ... Lk 10:6 1437
i not, it shall turn to you again ... Lk 10:6 1490
for *i* the mighty works had been ... Lk 10:13 1487
I a son shall ask bread of any of ... Lk 11:11
or *i* he ask a fish, will he for a ... Lk 11:11
Or *i* he shall ask an egg, will he ... Lk 11:12 1437
I ye then, being evil, know how ... Lk 11:13 1487
I Satan also be divided against ... Lk 11:18 1499
i I by Beelzebub cast out devils, ... Lk 11:19 1487
But *i* I with the finger of God ... Lk 11:20 1487
I thy whole body therefore be ... Lk 11:36 1487
I ye then be not able to do that ... Lk 12:26 1487
I then God so clothe the grass, ... Lk 12:28 1487
i he shall come in the second ... Lk 12:38 1437
that *i* the goodman of the house ... Lk 12:39 1487
i that servant say in his heart, ... Lk 12:45 1437
will I, *i* it be already kindled ... Lk 12:49 1487
And *i* it bear fruit, well ... Lk 13:9 2579
i not, then after that thou shalt ... Lk 13:9 1487
I any man come to me, and hate not ... Lk 14:26
but *i* the salt have lost his ... Lk 14:34 1437
i he lose one of them, doth not ... Lk 15:4
i she lose one piece, doth not ... Lk 15:8 1437
I therefore ye have not been ... Lk 16:11 1487
i ye have not been faithful in ... Lk 16:12 1487
but *i* one went unto them from the ... Lk 16:30 1437
I they hear not Moses and the ... Lk 16:31 1487
I thy brother trespass against ... Lk 17:3 1437
and *i* he repent, forgive him ... Lk 17:3 1437
i he trespass against thee seven ... Lk 17:4 1437
I ye had faith as a grain of ... Lk 17:6 1487
i I have taken any thing from any ... Lk 19:8 1487
i any man ask you, Why do ye ... Lk 19:31 1437
i these should hold their peace, ... Lk 19:40 1437
I thou hadst known, even thou, at ... Lk 19:42 1487
I we shall say, From heaven ... Lk 20:5 1437
But and *i* we say, Of men ... Lk 20:6 1437
I any man's brother die, having a ... Lk 20:28 1437
i thou be willing, remove this ... Lk 22:42 1487
I I tell you, ye will not believe ... Lk 22:67 1437
i I also ask you, ye will not ... Lk 22:68 1437
For *i* they do these things in a ... Lk 23:31 1487
i he be Christ, the chosen of God ... Lk 23:35 1487
I thou be the king of the Jews, ... Lk 23:37 1487
I thou be Christ, save thyself and ... Lk 23:39 1487
i thou be not that Christ, nor ... Jn 1:25 1487
I I have told you earthly things, ... Jn 3:12 1487
i I tell you of heavenly things ... Jn 3:12 1437
I thou knewest the gift of God, ... Jn 4:10 1487
I I bear witness of myself, my ... Jn 5:31 1437
i another shall come in his own ... Jn 5:43 1437
But *i* ye believe not his writings ... Jn 5:47 1487
i any man eat of this bread, he ... Jn 6:51 1437
i ye shall see the Son of man ... Jn 6:62 1437
I thou do these things, shew ... Jn 7:4 1487
I any man will do his will, he ... Jn 7:17 1437
I a man on the sabbath day ... Jn 7:23 1487
I any man thirst, let him come ... Jn 7:37 1437
yet *i* I judge, my judgment is ... Jn 8:16 1437
i ye had known me, ye should have ... Jn 8:19 1487
for *i* ye believe not that I am he ... Jn 8:24 1437
I ye continue in my word, then ... Jn 8:31 1437
I the Son therefore shall make ... Jn 8:36 1437
I ye were Abraham's children, ye ... Jn 8:39 1487
I God were your Father, ye would ... Jn 8:42 1487
i I say the truth, why do ye not ... Jn 8:46 1487
I a man keep my saying, he shall ... Jn 8:51 1437
I a man keep my saying, he shall ... Jn 8:52 1437
I I honour myself, my honour is ... Jn 8:54 1437
i I should say, I know him not, I ... Jn 8:55 1437
that *i* any man did confess that ... Jn 9:22 1437
but *i* any man be a worshipper of ... Jn 9:31 1437
I this man were not of God, he ... Jn 9:33 1487
I ye were blind, ye should have ... Jn 9:41 1487
by me *i* any man enter in, he ... Jn 10:9 1437
I thou be the Christ, tell us ... Jn 10:24 1487
I he called them gods, unto whom ... Jn 10:35 1487
I I do not the works of my Father ... Jn 10:37 1487
But *i* I do, though ye believe not ... Jn 10:38 1487
I any man walk in the day, he ... Jn 11:9 1437
But *i* a man walk in the night, he ... Jn 11:10 1437
i he sleep, he shall do well ... Jn 11:12 1487
i thou hadst been here, my ... Jn 11:21 1487
i thou hadst been here, my ... Jn 11:32 1487
i thou wouldest believe, thou ... Jn 11:40 1437
I we let him thus alone, all men ... Jn 11:48 1437
i any man knew where he were, he ... Jn 11:57 1437
but *i* it die, it bringeth forth ... Jn 12:24 1437
I any man serve me, let him ... Jn 12:26 1437
i any man serve me, him will my ... Jn 12:26 1437
i I be lifted up from the earth, ... Jn 12:32 1437
i any man hear my words, and ... Jn 12:47 1437
I I wash thee not, thou hast no ... Jn 13:8 1437
I I then, your Lord and Master, ... Jn 13:14 1487
I ye know these things ... Jn 13:17 1487
happy are ye *i* ye do them ... Jn 13:17 1437
I God be glorified in him, God ... Jn 13:32 1487
i ye have love one to another ... Jn 13:35 1437
i it were not so, I would have ... Jn 14:2 1490
i I go and prepare a place for you ... Jn 14:3 1437
I ye had known me, ye should have ... Jn 14:7 1487
I ye shall ask any thing in my ... Jn 14:14 1437
I ye love me, keep my ... Jn 14:15 1437
I a man love me, he will keep my ... Jn 14:23 1437

Context	Reference	No.
I ye loved me, ye would rejoice,	Jn 14:28	1487
I a man abide not in me, he is	Jn 15:6	1437
I ye abide in me, and my words	Jn 15:7	1437
I ye keep my commandments, ye	Jn 15:10	1437
i ye do whatsoever I command you	Jn 15:14	1437
I the world hate you, ye know	Jn 15:18	1487
I ye were of the world, the world	Jn 15:19	1487
I they have persecuted me, they	Jn 15:20	1487
i they have kept my saying, they	Jn 15:20	1487
I I had not come and spoken unto	Jn 15:22	1487
I I had not done among them the	Jn 15:24	1487
for *i* I go not away, the	Jn 16:7	1437
but *i* I depart, I will send him	Jn 16:7	1437
i therefore ye seek me, let these	Jn 18:8	1487
I I have spoken evil, bear	Jn 18:23	1487
but *i* well, why smitest thou me	Jn 18:23	1487
I he were not a malefactor, we	Jn 18:30	1487
i my kingdom were of this world,	Jn 18:36	1487
I thou let this man go, thou art	Jn 19:12	1437
i thou have borne him hence, tell	Jn 20:15	1487
I I will that he tarry till I	Jn 21:22	1437
I I will that he tarry till I	Jn 21:23	1437
i they should be written every	Jn 21:25	1437
I we this day be examined of the	Acts 4:9	1487
for *i* this counsel or this work	Acts 5:38	1437
But *i* it be of God, ye cannot	Acts 5:39	1487
i perhaps the thought of thine	Acts 8:22	1487
I thou believest with all thine	Acts 8:37	1487
that *i* he found any of this way,	Acts 9:2	1437
i ye have any word of exhortation	Acts 13:15	1487
from which *i* ye keep yourselves,	Acts 15:29	
I ye have judged me to be	Acts 16:15	1487
i haply they might feel after him	Acts 17:27	1487
I it were a matter of wrong or	Acts 18:14	1487
But *i* it be a question of words	Acts 18:15	1487
return again unto you, *i* God will	Acts 18:21	
Wherefore *i* Demetrius, and the	Acts 19:38	1487
But *i* ye enquire any thing	Acts 19:39	1487
i it were possible for him, to be	Acts 20:16	1487
but *i* a spirit or an angel hath	Acts 23:9	1487
i they had ought against me	Acts 24:19	1487
i they have found any evil doing	Acts 24:20	1487
i there be any wickedness in him	Acts 25:5	1487
For *i* I be an offender, or have	Acts 25:11	1487
but *i* there be none of these	Acts 25:11	1487
i they would testify, that after	Acts 26:5	1437
i he had not appealed unto Caesar	Acts 26:32	1487
i by any means they might attain	Acts 27:12	1513
i it were possible, to thrust in	Acts 27:39	1487
i by any means now at length I	Rom 1:10	1513
profiteth, *i* thou keep the law	Rom 2:25	1437
but *i* thou be a breaker of the	Rom 2:25	1437
Therefore *i* the uncircumcision	Rom 2:26	1437
i it fulfil the law, judge thee,	Rom 2:27	
For what *i* some did not believe	Rom 3:3	1487
But *i* our unrighteousness commend	Rom 3:5	1487
For *i* the truth of God hath more	Rom 3:7	1487
For *i* Abraham were justified by	Rom 4:2	1487
For *i* they which are of the law	Rom 4:14	1487
i we believe on him that raised	Rom 4:24	
For *i*, when we were enemies, we	Rom 5:10	1477
For *i* through the offence of one	Rom 5:15	1477
For *i* by one man's offence death	Rom 5:17	1477
For *i* we have been planted	Rom 6:5	1477
Now *i* we be dead with Christ, we	Rom 6:8	1477
but *i* the husband be dead, she is	Rom 7:2	1437
So then *i*, while her husband	Rom 7:3	1437
but *i* her husband be dead, she is	Rom 7:3	1437
I then I do that which I would	Rom 7:16	1487
Now *i* I do that I would not, it	Rom 7:20	1487
i so be that the Spirit of God	Rom 8:9	1512
Now *i* any man have not the Spirit	Rom 8:9	1487
i Christ be in you, the body is	Rom 8:10	1487
But *i* the Spirit of him that	Rom 8:11	1437
For *i* ye live after the flesh, ye	Rom 8:13	1437
but *i* ye through the Spirit do	Rom 8:13	1437
And *i* children, then heirs	Rom 8:17	1487
i so be that we suffer with him,	Rom 8:17	1512
But *i* we hope for that we see not	Rom 8:25	1487
I God be for us, who can be	Rom 8:31	1487
What *i* God, willing to shew his	Rom 9:22	1487
That *i* thou shalt confess with	Rom 10:9	1437
i by grace, then is it no more of	Rom 11:6	1487
But *i* it be of works, then is it	Rom 11:6	1487
Now *i* the fall of them be the	Rom 11:12	1487
I by any means I may provoke to	Rom 11:14	1513
For *i* the casting away of them be	Rom 11:15	1487
For *i* the firstfruit be holy, the	Rom 11:16	1487
i the root be holy, so are the	Rom 11:16	1487
i some of the branches be broken	Rom 11:17	1487
But *i* thou boast, thou bearest	Rom 11:18	1487
For *i* God spared not the natural	Rom 11:21	1487
i thou continue in his goodness	Rom 11:22	1437
i they abide not still in	Rom 11:23	1437
For *i* thou wert cut out of the	Rom 11:24	1487
I it be possible, as much as	Rom 12:18	1487
Therefore *i* thine enemy hunger,	Rom 12:20	1437
i he thirst, give him drink	Rom 12:20	1437
But *i* thou do that which is evil,	Rom 13:4	1437
i there be any other commandment,	Rom 13:9	1487
But *i* thy brother be grieved with	Rom 14:15	1487
that doubteth is damned *i* he eat	Rom 14:23	1437
i first I be somewhat filled with	Rom 15:24	1437
For *i* the Gentiles have been made	Rom 15:27	1487
Now *i* any man build upon this	1Cor 3:12	1487
I any man's work abide which he	1Cor 3:14	1487
I any man's work shall be burned,	1Cor 3:15	148
I any man defile the temple of	1Cor 3:17	148
I any man among you seemeth to be	1Cor 3:18	148
now *i* thou didst receive it, why	1Cor 4:7	1499
as *i* thou hadst not received it	1Cor 4:7	
i the Lord will, and will know,	1Cor 4:19	1437
i any man that is called a	1Cor 5:11	1437
i the world shall be judged by	1Cor 6:2	1487
I then ye have judgments of	1Cor 6:4	1437
It is good for them *i* they abide	1Cor 7:8	1437
But *i* they cannot contain, let	1Cor 7:9	1487
i she depart, let her remain	1Cor 7:11	1437
I any brother hath a wife that	1Cor 7:12	1487
i he be pleased to dwell with her	1Cor 7:13	
But *i* the unbelieving depart, let	1Cor 7:15	1487
but *i* thou mayest be made free,	1Cor 7:21	1499
i thou marry, thou hast not	1Cor 7:28	1437
i a virgin marry, she hath not	1Cor 7:28	1437
But *i* any man think that he	1Cor 7:36	1487
i she pass the flower of her age,	1Cor 7:36	1437
but *i* her husband be dead, she is	1Cor 7:39	1437
But she is happier *i* she so abide	1Cor 7:40	1437
i any man think that he knoweth	1Cor 8:2	1487
But *i* any man love God, the same	1Cor 8:3	1487
i we eat, are we the better	1Cor 8:8	1437
i we eat not, are we the worse	1Cor 8:8	1437
For *i* any man see thee which hast	1Cor 8:10	1437
i meat make my brother to offend,	1Cor 8:13	1487
I I be not an apostle unto others	1Cor 9:2	1487
I we have sown unto you spiritual	1Cor 9:11	1487
is it a great thing *i* we shall	1Cor 9:11	1487
I others be partakers of this	1Cor 9:12	1487
i I preach not the gospel	1Cor 9:16	1437
For *i* I do this thing willingly,	1Cor 9:17	1487
but *i* against my will, a	1Cor 9:17	1487
I any of them that believe not	1Cor 10:27	1487
But *i* any man say unto you, This	1Cor 10:28	1437
For *i* I by grace be a partaker,	1Cor 10:30	1487
even all one as *i* she were shaven	1Cor 11:5	
For *i* the woman be not covered,	1Cor 11:6	1487
but *i* it be a shame for a woman	1Cor 11:6	1487
i a man have long hair, it is a	1Cor 11:14	1437
But *i* a woman have long hair, it	1Cor 11:15	1437
But *i* any man seem to be	1Cor 11:16	1487
For *i* we would judge ourselves,	1Cor 11:31	1487
i any man hunger, let him eat at	1Cor 11:34	1487
I the foot shall say, Because I	1Cor 12:15	1437
i the ear shall say, Because I am	1Cor 12:16	1437
I the whole body were an eye,	1Cor 12:17	1487
I the whole were hearing, where	1Cor 12:17	1487
i they were all one member, where	1Cor 12:19	1487
i I come unto you speaking with	1Cor 14:6	1437
For *i* the trumpet give an	1Cor 14:8	1437
Therefore *i* I know not the	1Cor 14:11	1437
For *i* I pray in an unknown tongue	1Cor 14:14	1437
I therefore the whole church be	1Cor 14:23	1437
But *i* all prophesy, and there come	1Cor 14:24	1437
I any man speak in an unknown	1Cor 14:27	1535
But *i* there be no interpreter,	1Cor 14:28	1437
I any thing be revealed to	1Cor 14:30	1437
i they will learn any thing, let	1Cor 14:35	1487
I any man think himself to be a	1Cor 14:37	1487
But *i* any man be ignorant, let	1Cor 14:38	1487
i ye keep in memory what I	1Cor 15:2	1487
Now *i* Christ be preached that he	1Cor 15:12	1487
But *i* there be no resurrection of	1Cor 15:13	1487
i Christ be not risen, then is	1Cor 15:14	1487
i so be that the dead rise not	1Cor 15:15	1512
For *i* the dead rise not, then is	1Cor 15:16	1487
i Christ be not raised, your	1Cor 15:17	1487
I in this life only we have hope	1Cor 15:19	1487
i the dead rise not at all	1Cor 15:29	1487
I after the manner of men I have	1Cor 15:32	1487
it me, *i* the dead rise not	1Cor 15:32	1487
i it be meet that I go also, they	1Cor 16:4	1437
while with you, *i* the Lord permit	1Cor 16:7	1437
Now *i* Timotheus come, see that he	1Cor 16:10	1437
I any man love not the Lord Jesus	1Cor 16:22	1487
For *i* I make you sorry, who is he	2Cor 2:2	1487
But *i* any have caused grief, he	2Cor 2:5	1487
for *i* I forgave any thing, to	2Cor 2:10	1487
But *i* the ministration of death,	2Cor 3:7	1487
For *i* the ministration of	2Cor 3:9	1487
For *i* that which is done away was	2Cor 3:11	1487
But *i* our gospel be hid, it is	2Cor 4:3	1499
For we know that *i* our earthly	2Cor 5:1	1437
I so be that being clothed we	2Cor 5:3	1489
that *i* one died for all, then	2Cor 5:14	1487
Therefore *i* any man be in Christ,	2Cor 5:17	1487
For *i* I have boasted any thing to	2Cor 7:14	1487
For *i* there be first a willing	2Cor 8:12	1487
Lest haply *i* they of Macedonia	2Cor 9:4	1437
which think of us as *i* we walked	2Cor 10:2	
I any man trust to himself that	2Cor 10:7	1487
That I may not seem as *i* I would	2Cor 10:9	
For *i* he that cometh preacheth	2Cor 11:4	1487
or *i* ye receive another spirit,	2Cor 11:4	
thing *i* his ministers also be	2Cor 11:15	1499
i otherwise, yet as a fool	2Cor 11:16	1490
i a man bring you into bondage,	2Cor 11:20	1487
i a man devour you, *i* a man take	2Cor 11:20	1487
i a man exalt himself, *i* a man	2Cor 11:20	1487
I I must needs glory, I will	2Cor 11:30	1487
as *i* I were present, the second	2Cor 13:2	1437
i I come again, I will not spare	2Cor 13:2	
I any man preach any other gospel	Gal 1:9	1487
for *i* I yet pleased men, I should	Gal 1:10	1487
I thou, being a Jew, livest after	Gal 2:14	1487
But *i*, while we seek to be	Gal 2:17	1487
For *i* I build again the things	Gal 2:18	1487
for *i* righteousness come by the	Gal 2:21	1487
i it be yet in vain	Gal 3:4	1489
yet *i* it be confirmed, no man	Gal 3:15	
For *i* the inheritance be of the	Gal 3:18	1487
for *i* there had been a law given	Gal 3:21	1487
i ye be Christ's, then are ye	Gal 3:29	1487
i a son, then an heir of God	Gal 4:7	1487
i it had been possible, ye would	Gal 4:15	1487
that *i* ye be circumcised, Christ	Gal 5:2	1437
i I yet preach circumcision, why	Gal 5:11	1487
But *i* ye bite and devour one	Gal 5:15	1487
But *i* ye be led of the Spirit, ye	Gal 5:18	1487
I we live in the Spirit, let us	Gal 5:25	1487
i a man be overtaken in a fault,	Gal 6:1	1437
For *i* a man think himself to be	Gal 6:3	1487
we shall reap, *i* we faint not	Gal 6:9	
I ye have heard of the	Eph 3:2	1489
I so be that ye have heard him,	Eph 4:21	1489
But *i* I live in the flesh, this	Phil 1:22	1487
I there be therefore any	Phil 2:1	1487
i any comfort of love, *i* any	Phil 2:1	1487
Spirit, *i* any bowels and mercies,	Phil 2:1	1487
i I be offered upon the sacrifice	Phil 2:17	1487
I any other man thinketh that he	Phil 3:4	1487
I by any means I might attain	Phil 3:11	1513
i that I may apprehend that for	Phil 3:12	1499
i in any thing ye be otherwise	Phil 3:15	1487
i there be any virtue, and *i*	Phil 4:8	1487
i there be any praise, think on	Phil 4:8	1487
I ye continue in the faith	Col 1:23	1489
Wherefore *i* ye be dead with	Col 2:20	1487
I ye then be risen with Christ,	Col 3:1	1487
i any man have a quarrel against	Col 3:13	1437
i he come unto you, receive him	Col 4:10	1437
i ye stand fast in the Lord	1Th 3:8	1437
For *i* we believe that Jesus died	1Th 4:14	1487
that *i* any would not work,	2Th 3:10	1487
i any man obey not our word by	2Th 3:14	1487
is good, *i* a man use it lawfully	1Ti 1:8	1437
i there be any other thing that	1Ti 1:10	1487
i they continue in faith and	1Ti 2:15	1437
I a man desire the office of a	1Ti 3:1	1487
(For *i* a man know not how to rule	1Ti 3:5	1487
But *i* I tarry long, that thou	1Ti 3:15	1437
be refused, *i* it be received with	1Ti 4:4	
I thou put the brethren in	1Ti 4:6	
But *i* any widow have children or	1Ti 5:4	1487
But *i* any provide not for his own	1Ti 5:8	1487
i she have brought up children,	1Ti 5:10	1487
i she have lodged strangers	1Ti 5:10	1487
i she have washed the saints'	1Ti 5:10	1487
i she have relieved the afflicted	1Ti 5:10	1487
i she have diligently followed	1Ti 5:10	1487
I any man or woman that believeth	1Ti 5:16	1487
I any man teach otherwise, and	1Ti 6:3	1487
i a man also strive for masteries	2Ti 2:5	1437
For *i* we be dead with him, we	2Ti 2:11	1487
I we suffer, we shall also reign	2Ti 2:12	1487
i we deny him, he also will deny	2Ti 2:12	1487
I we believe not, yet he abideth	2Ti 2:13	1487
I a man therefore purge himself	2Ti 2:21	1437
i God peradventure will give them	2Ti 2:25	3379
I any be blameless, the husband	Titus 1:6	1487
I thou count me therefore a	Philem 17	1487
I he hath wronged thee, or oweth	Philem 18	1487
For *i* the word spoken by angels	Heb 2:2	1487
i we neglect so great salvation	Heb 2:3	
i we hold fast the confidence and	Heb 3:6	1437
To day *i* ye will hear his voice,	Heb 3:7	1437
i we hold the beginning of our	Heb 3:14	1437
To day *i* ye will hear his voice,	Heb 3:15	1437
i they shall enter into my rest	Heb 4:3	1487
I they shall enter into my rest	Heb 4:5	1487
To day *i* ye will hear his voice,	Heb 4:7	1437
For *i* Jesus had given them rest,	Heb 4:8	1487
And this will we do, *i* God permit	Heb 6:3	1437
I they shall fall away, to renew	Heb 6:6	
I therefore perfection were by	Heb 7:11	1487
For *i* he were on earth, he should	Heb 8:4	1487
For *i* that first covenant had	Heb 8:7	1487
For *i* the blood of bulls and of	Heb 9:13	1487
For *i* we sin wilfully after that	Heb 10:26	
but *i* any man draw back, my soul	Heb 10:38	1437
i they had been mindful of that	Heb 11:15	1487
I ye endure chastening, God	Heb 12:7	1487
But *i* ye be without chastisement,	Heb 12:8	1487
i so much as a beast touch the	Heb 12:20	
For *i* they escaped not who	Heb 12:25	1487
i we turn away from him that	Heb 12:25	
i he come shortly, I will see you	Heb 13:23	1437
I any of you lack wisdom, let him	Jas 1:5	1487
For *i* any be a hearer of the word	Jas 1:23	1487
I any man among you seem to be	Jas 1:26	1487
For *i* there come unto your	Jas 2:2	1437
I ye fulfil the royal law	Jas 2:8	1487
But *i* ye have respect to persons,	Jas 2:9	1487
Now *i* thou commit no adultery,	Jas 2:11	1487
yet *i* thou kill, thou art become	Jas 2:11	
I a brother or sister be naked,	Jas 2:15	1437
i it hath not works, is dead,	Jas 2:17	1437
I any man offend not in word, the	Jas 3:2	1487
But *i* ye have bitter envying and	Jas 3:14	1487
but *i* thou judge the law, thou	Jas 4:11	1487
I the Lord will, we shall live,	Jas 4:15	1437
i he have committed sins, they	Jas 5:15	
i any of you do err from the	Jas 5:19	1437
i need be, ye are in heaviness	1Pet 1:6	1487
i ye call on the Father, who	1Pet 1:17	1487
I so be ye have tasted that the	1Pet 2:3	1512
i a man for conscience toward God	1Pet 2:19	1487
For what glory is it, *i*, when ye	1Pet 2:20	1487
but *i*, when ye do well, and suffer	1Pet 2:20	1487
i any obey not the word, they	1Pet 3:1	1487
i ye be followers of that which	1Pet 3:13	1437
i ye suffer for righteousness'	1Pet 3:14	
i the will of God be so, that ye	1Pet 3:17	1487
I any man speak, let him speak as	1Pet 4:11	1487
i any man minister, let him do it	1Pet 4:11	1487
I ye be reproached for the name	1Pet 4:14	1487
Yet *i* any man suffer as a	1Pet 4:16	1487
i it first begin at us, what	1Pet 4:17	1487
i the righteous scarcely be saved	1Pet 4:18	1487
For *i* these things be in you, and	2Pet 1:8	
for *i* ye do these things, ye	2Pet 1:10	
For *i* God spared not the angels	2Pet 2:4	1487
For *i* after they have escaped the	2Pet 2:20	1487

I we say that we have fellowship 1Jn 1:6 1437
But *i* we walk in the light, as he 1Jn 1:7 1437
I we say that we have no sin, we 1Jn 1:8 1437
I we confess our sins, he is 1Jn 1:9 1437
I we say that we have not sinned, 1Jn 1:10 1437
i any man sin, we have an 1Jn 2:1 1437
i we keep his commandments 1Jn 2:3 1437
I any man love the world, the 1Jn 2:15 1437
for *i* they had been of us, they 1Jn 2:19 1487
I that which ye have heard from 1Jn 2:24 1437
I ye know that he is righteous, 1Jn 2:29 1437
my brethren, *i* the world hate you 1Jn 3:13 1487
For *i* our heart condemn us, God 1Jn 3:20 1437
i our heart condemn us not, then 1Jn 3:21 1437
i God so loved us, we ought also 1Jn 4:11 1487
I we love one another, God 1Jn 4:12 1437
I a man say, I love God, and 1Jn 4:20 1437
I we receive the witness of men, 1Jn 5:9 1487
i we ask any thing according to 1Jn 5:14 1437
i we know that he hear us, 1Jn 5:15 1437
I any man see his brother sin a 1Jn 5:16 1437
I there come any unto you, and 2Jn 10 1487
whom *i* thou bring forward on 3Jn 6
i I come, I will remember his 3Jn 10 1437
as *i* they burned in a furnace Rev 1:15
I therefore thou shalt not watch, Rev 3:3 1437
i any man hear my voice, and open Rev 3:20 1437
i any man will hurt them, fire Rev 11:5 1487
i any man will hurt them, he must Rev 11:5 1487
I any man have an ear, let him Rev 13:9 1487
I any man worship the beast and Rev 14:9 1487
I any man shall add unto these Rev 22:18 1437
i any man shall take away from Rev 22:19 1437

IGAL (*i'-gal*) See IGEAL.
1. One of the twelve spies.
of Issachar, *I* the son of Joseph Num 13:7 3008
2. A "mighty man" of David.
I the son of Nathan of Zobah, 2Sa 23:36 3008

IGDALIAH (*ig-da-li'-ah*) *Father of Hanan.*
the sons of Hanan, the son of *I* Jer 35:4 3012

IGEAL (*ig'-e-al*) See IGAL. *A royal descendant of Judah.*
Hattush, and *I*, and Bariah, and 1Chr 3:22 3008

IGNOMINY
also contempt, and with *i* reproach Prov 18:3 7036

IGNORANCE
If a soul shall sin through *i* Lev 4:2 7684
of Israel sin through *i*, and the Lev 4:13 7686
done somewhat through *i* against Lev 4:22 7684
the common people sin through *i* Lev 4:27 7684
a trespass, and sin through *i* Lev 5:15 7684
concerning his *i* wherein he erred Lev 5:18 7684
if ought be committed by *i* Num 15:24 7684
for it is *i* Num 15:25 7684
before the LORD, for their *i* Num 15:25 7684
seeing all the people were in *i* Num 15:26 7684
And if any soul sin through *i* Num 15:27 7684
he sinneth by *i* before the LORD Num 15:28 7684
for him that sinneth through *i* Num 15:29 7684
I wot that through *i* ye did it Acts 3:17 52
the times of this *i* God winked at Acts 17:30 52
God through the *i* that is in them Eph 4:18 52
to the former lusts in your *i* 1Pet 1:14 52
to silence the *i* of foolish men 1Pet 2:15 56

IGNORANT
So foolish was I, and *i* Ps 73:22
they are all *i*, they are all dumb Is 56:10
father, though Abraham be *i* of us Is 63:16
and *i* men, they marvelled Acts 4:13 2399
Now I would not have you *i* Rom 1:13 50
For they being *i* of God's Rom 10:3 50
ye should be *i* of this mystery Rom 11:25 50
I would not that ye should be *i* 1Cor 10:1 50
brethren, I would not have you *i* 1Cor 12:1 50
any man be *i*, let him be *i* 1Cor 14:38 50
have you *i* of our trouble which 2Cor 1:8 50
for we are not *i* of his devices 2Cor 2:11 50
But I would not have you to be *i* 1Th 4:13 50
Who can have compassion on the *i* Heb 5:2 50
For this they willingly are *i* of 2Pet 3:5 2990
be not *i* of this one thing, that 2Pet 3:8 2990

IGNORANTLY
for the soul that sinneth *i* Num 15:28 7683
Whoso killeth his neighbour *i* Deut 19:4
Whom therefore ye *i* worship Acts 17:23 50
because I did it *i* in unbelief 1Ti 1:13 50

IIM (*i'-im*) See IJE-ABARIM.
1. A Hebrew encampment in the wilderness.
And they departed from *I*, and Num 33:45 5864
2. A town in Judah.
Baalah, and *I*, and Azem, Josh 15:29 5864

IJE-ABARIM (*i'-je-ab'-a-rim*) See IIM. *Same as Iim 1.*
from Oboth, and pitched at *I* Num 21:11 5863
from Oboth, and pitched in *I* Num 33:44 5863

IJON (*i'-jon*) *A town in Naphtali.*
the cities of Israel, and smote *I* 1Kin 15:20 5859
king of Assyria, and took *I* 2Kin 15:29 5859
and they smote *I*, and Dan, and 2Chr 16:4 5859

IKKESH (*ik'-kesh*) *Father of Ira.*
Ira the son of *I* the Tekoite 2Sa 23:26 6142
Ira the son of *I* the Tekoite 1Chr 11:28 6142
was Ira the son of *I* the Tekoite 1Chr 27:9 6142

ILAI (*i'-lahee*) See ZALMON. *A "mighty man" of David.*
the Hushathite, *I* the Ahohite, 1Chr 11:29 5866

ILL
i favoured and leanfleshed Gen 41:3 7451
the *i* favoured and leanfleshed Gen 41:4 7451
very *i* favoured and leanfleshed, Gen 41:19 7451
the *i* favoured kine did eat up Gen 41:20 7451
but they were still *i* favoured Gen 41:21 7451
i favoured kine that came up Gen 41:27 7451
Wherefore dealt ye so *i* with me Gen 43:6 7489
or blind, or have any *i* blemish Deut 15:21 7451
it shall go *i* with him that is Job 20:26 3415
so that it went *i* with Moses for Ps 106:32 3415
it shall be *i* with him Is 3:11 7451
but if it seem *i* unto thee to Jer 40:4 7489
his *i* savour shall come up, Joel 2:20 6709
themselves *i* in their doings Mic 3:4 7489
Love worketh no *i* to his Rom 13:10 2556

ILLUMINATED
days, in which, after ye were *i* Heb 10:32 5461

ILLYRICUM (*il-lir'-ic-um*) *A Roman Adriatic province.*
Jerusalem, and round about unto *I* Rom 15:19 2437

IMAGE
said, Let us make man in our *i* Gen 1:26 6754
So God created man in his own *i* Gen 1:27 6754
in the *i* of God created he him Gen 1:27 6754
in his own likeness, after his *i* Gen 5:3 6754
for in the *i* of God made he man Gen 9:6 6754
not make unto thee any graven *i* Ex 20:4
make you no idols nor graven *i* Lev 26:1
neither rear you up a standing *i* Lev 26:1 6676
up any *i* of stone in your land Lev 26:1 4906
and make you a graven *i*, the Deut 4:16
with you, and make you a graven *i* Deut 4:23
yourselves, and make a graven *i* Deut 4:25
shalt not make thee any graven *i* Deut 5:8
they have made them a molten *i* Deut 9:12
shalt thou set thee up any *i* Deut 16:22 4676
maketh any graven or molten *i* Deut 27:15
make a graven *i* and a molten *i* Judg 17:3
a graven *i* and a molten *i* Judg 17:4
and a graven *i*, and a molten *i* Judg 18:14
in thither, and took the graven *i* Judg 18:17
and the teraphim, and the molten *i* Judg 18:17
house, and fetched the carved *i* Judg 18:18
and the teraphim, and the molten *i* Judg 18:18
and the teraphim, and the graven *i* Judg 18:20
of Dan set up the graven *i* Judg 18:30
they set them up Micah's graven *i* Judg 18:31
And Michal took an *i*, and laid it 1Sa 19:13 8655
behold, there was an *i* in the bed 1Sa 19:16 8655
for he put away the *i* of Baal 2Kin 3:2 4676
And they brake down the *i* of Baal 2Kin 10:27 4676
he set a graven *i* of the grove 2Kin 21:7
he made two cherubims of *i* work 2Chr 3:10 6816
And he set a carved *i*, the idol 2Chr 33:7
an *i* was before mine eyes, there Job 4:16 8544
thou shalt despise their *i* Ps 73:20 6754
Horeb, and worshipped the molten *i* Ps 106:19
The workman melteth a graven *i* Is 40:19
workman to prepare a graven *i* Is 40:20
a graven *i* are all of them vanity Is 44:9
or molten a graven *i* that is Is 44:10
he maketh it a graven *i*, and Is 44:15
maketh a god, even his graven *i* Is 44:17
set up the wood of their graven *i* Is 45:20
hath done them, and my graven *i* Is 48:5
my graven *i*, and my molten *i* Is 48:5
is confounded by the graven *i* Jer 10:14 6459
for his molten *i* is falsehood Jer 10:14
is confounded by the graven *i* Jer 51:17 6459
for his molten *i* is falsehood Jer 51:17
was the seat of the *i* of jealousy Eze 8:3 5566
this *i* of jealousy in the entry Eze 8:5 5566
king, sawest, and behold a great *i* Dan 2:31 6755
This great *i*, whose brightness Dan 2:31 6755
which smote the *i* upon his feet Dan 2:34 6755
the *i* became a great mountain Dan 2:35 6755
the king made an *i* of gold Dan 3:1 6755
i which Nebuchadnezzar the king Dan 3:2 6755
unto the dedication of the *i* that Dan 3:3 6755
they stood before the *i* that Dan 3:3 6755
worship the golden *i* that Dan 3:5 6755
worshipped the golden *i* that Dan 3:7 6755
fall down and worship the golden *i* Dan 3:10 6755
golden *i* which thou hast set up Dan 3:12 6755
the golden *i* which I have set up Dan 3:14 6755
worship the *i* which I have made Dan 3:15 6755
golden *i* which thou hast set up Dan 3:18 6755
a sacrifice, and without an *i* Hos 3:4 6755
gods will I cut off the graven *i* Nah 1:14
the graven *i* and the molten *i* Nah 1:14
What profiteth the graven *i* that Hab 2:18
the molten *i*, and a teacher of Hab 2:18
saith unto them, Whose is this *i* Mt 22:20 1504
saith unto them, Whose is this *i* Mk 12:16 1504
Whose *i* and superscription hath it Lk 20:24 1504
of the *i* which fell down from Acts 19:35
an *i* made like to corruptible man Rom 1:23 1504
be conformed to the *i* of his Son Rom 8:29 1504
bowed the knee to the *i* of Baal Rom 11:4
head, forasmuch as he is the *i* 1Cor 11:7 1504
we have borne the *i* of the earthy 1Cor 15:49 1504
also bear the *i* of the heavenly 1Cor 15:49
the same *i* from glory to glory 2Cor 3:18 1504
of Christ, who is the *i* of God 2Cor 4:4 1504
Who is the *i* of the invisible God Col 1:15 1504
the *i* of him that created him Col 3:10 1504
the express *i* of his person, and Heb 1:3 5481
not the very *i* of the things, can Heb 10:1 1504
should make an *i* to the beast Rev 13:14 1504
give life unto the *i* of the beast Rev 13:15 1504
that the *i* of the beast should Rev 13:15 1504
i of the beast should be killed Rev 13:15 1504
man worship the beast and his *i* Rev 14:9 1504
who worship the beast and his *i* Rev 14:11 1504
over the beast, and over his *i* Rev 15:2 1504
upon them which worshipped his *i* Rev 16:2 1504
and them that worshipped his *i* Rev 19:20 1504
the beast, neither his *i*, neither Rev 20:4 1504

IMAGERY
man in the chambers of his *i* Eze 8:12 4906

IMAGE'S
This *i* head was of fine gold, his Dan 2:32 6755

IMAGES
Rachel had stolen the *i* that were Gen 31:19 8655
Now Rachel had taken the *i* Gen 31:34 8655
he searched, but found not the *i* Gen 31:35 8655
them, and quite break down their *i* Ex 23:24 4676
their altars, break their *i* Ex 34:13 4676
high places, and cut down your *i* Lev 26:30 2553
and destroy all their molten *i* Num 33:52
altars, and break down their *i* Deut 7:5 4676
and burn their graven *i* with fire Deut 7:5
The graven *i* of their gods shall Deut 7:25
down the graven *i* of their gods Deut 12:3
ye shall make *i* of your emerods 1Sa 6:5 6754
i of your mice that mar the land 1Sa 6:5 6754
of gold and the *i* of their emerods 1Sa 6:11 6754
And there they left their *i* 2Sa 5:21 6091
made thee other gods, and molten *i* 1Kin 14:9
also built them high places, and *i* 1Kin 14:23 4676
they brought forth the *i* out of 2Kin 10:26 4676
his *i* brake they in pieces 2Kin 11:18 6754
And they set them up *i* and groves 2Kin 17:10 4676
their God, and made them molten *i* 2Kin 17:16
LORD, and served their graven *i* 2Kin 17:41
the high places, and brake the *i* 2Kin 18:4 4676
And he brake in pieces the *i* 2Kin 23:14 4676
spirits, and the wizards, and the *i* 2Kin 23:24 8655
high places, and brake down the *i* 2Chr 14:3 4676
of Judah the high places and the *i* 2Chr 14:5
his *i* in pieces, and slew Mattan 2Chr 23:17 6754
and made also molten *i* for Baalim 2Chr 28:2
Judah, and brake the *i* in pieces 2Chr 31:1 4676
and set up groves and graven *i* 2Chr 33:19
i which Manasseh his father had 2Chr 33:22
carved *i*, and the molten *i* 2Chr 34:3
and the *i*, that were on high above 2Chr 34:4 2553
carved *i*, and the molten *i* 2Chr 34:4
beaten the graven *i* into powder 2Chr 34:7 6456
to jealousy with their graven *i* Ps 78:58 6456
be all they that serve graven *i* Ps 97:7
whose graven *i* did excel them of Is 10:10
made, either the groves, or the *i* Is 17:8 2553
all the graven *i* of her gods he Is 21:9
groves and *i* shall not stand up Is 27:9 2553
of thy graven *i* of silver Is 30:22
ornament of thy molten *i* of gold Is 30:22
their molten *i* are wind and Is 41:29
neither my praise to graven *i* Is 42:8
ashamed, that trust in graven *i* Is 42:17
i, that say to the molten *i* Is 42:17
me to anger with their graven *i* Jer 8:19
break also the *i* of Beth-shemesh Jer 43:13 4676
her *i* are broken in pieces Jer 50:2 1544
for it is the land of graven *i* Jer 50:38
upon the graven *i* of Babylon Jer 51:47
do judgment upon her graven *i* Jer 51:52
and your *i* shall be broken Eze 6:4 2553
your *i* may be cut down, and your Eze 6:6 2553
but they made the *i* of their Eze 7:20 6754
and madest to thyself *i* of men Eze 16:17 6754
bright, he consulted with *i* Eze 21:21 8655
the *i* of the Chaldeans pourtrayed Eze 23:14 6754
I will cause their *i* to cease out Eze 30:13 457
his land they have made goodly *i* Hos 10:1 4676
altars, he shall spoil their *i* Hos 10:2 4676
and burned incense to graven *i* Hos 11:2
them molten *i* of their silver Hos 13:2
of your Moloch and Chiun your *i* Amos 5:26 6754
all the graven *i* thereof shall be Mic 1:7
Thy graven *i* also will I cut off Mic 5:13 4676
thy standing *i* out of the midst Mic 5:13

IMAGINATION
that every *i* of the thoughts of Gen 6:5 3336
for the *i* of man's heart is evil Gen 8:21 3336
I walk in the *i* of mine heart Deut 29:19 8307
for I know their *i* which they go Deut 31:21 3336
keep this for ever in the *i* of 1Chr 29:18 3336
after the *i* of their evil heart Jer 3:17 8307
in the *i* of their evil heart, and Jer 7:24 8307
after the *i* of their own heart Jer 9:14 8307
one in the *i* of their evil heart Jer 11:8 8307
walk in the *i* of their heart Jer 13:10 8307
one after the *i* of his evil heart Jer 16:12 8307
one do the *i* of his evil heart Jer 18:12 8307
after the *i* of his own heart Jer 23:17 8307
proud in the *i* of their hearts Lk 1:51 1271

IMAGINATIONS
all the *i* of the thoughts 1Chr 28:9 3336
An heart that deviseth wicked *i* Prov 6:18 4284
and all their *i* against me Lam 3:60 4284
O LORD, and all their *i* against me Lam 3:61 4284
but became vain in their *i* Rom 1:21 1261
Casting down *i*, and every high 2Cor 10:5 3053

IMAGINE
Do ye *i* to reprove words, and the Job 6:26 2803
which ye wrongfully *i* against me Job 21:27 2554
the people *i* a vain thing Ps 2:1 1897
i deceits all the day long Ps 38:12 1897
How long will ye *i* mischief Ps 62:3 2050
Which *i* mischiefs in their heart Ps 140:2 2803
in the heart of them that *i* evil Prov 12:20 2790

yet do they *i* mischief against me ... Hos 7:15 2803
What do ye *i* against the LORD ... Nah 1:9 2803
let none of you *i* evil against ... Zec 7:10 2803
let none of you *i* evil in your ... Zec 8:17 2803
rage, and the people *i* vain things ... Acts 4:25 *3191*

IMAGINED
them, which they have *i* to do ... Gen 11:6 2161
in the devices that they have *i* ... Ps 10:2 2803
they *i* a mischievous device, ... Ps 21:11 2803

IMAGINETH
that *i* evil against the LORD, a ... Nah 1:11 2803

IMLA (*im'-lah*) See IMLAH. *Father of Michaiah.*
the same is Micaiah the son of *I* ... 2Chr 18:7 3229
quickly Micaiah the son of *I* ... 2Chr 18:8 3229

IMLAH (*im'-lah*) See IMLA. *Same as Imla.*
yet one man, Micaiah the son of *I* ... 1Kin 22:8 3229
hither Micaiah the son of *I* ... 1Kin 22:9 3229

IMMANUEL (*im-man'-u-el*) See EMMANUEL. *A Messianic name.*
a son, and shall call his name *I* ... Is 7:14 6005
fill the breadth of thy land, O *I* ... Is 8:8 6005

IMMEDIATELY
they *i* left the ship and their ... Mt 4:22 *2112*
i his leprosy was cleansed ... Mt 8:3 *2112*
i Jesus stretched forth his hand, ... Mt 14:31 *2112*
i their eyes received sight, and ... Mt 20:34 *2112*
I after the tribulation of those ... Mt 24:29 *2112*
And *i* the cock crew ... Mt 26:74 *2112*
i the spirit driveth him into the ... Mk 1:12 *2117*
And *i* his fame spread abroad ... Mk 1:28 *2117*
i the fever left her, and she ... Mk 1:31 *2112*
i the leprosy departed from him, ... Mk 1:42 *2112*
i when Jesus perceived in his ... Mk 2:8 *2112*
i he arose, took up the bed, and ... Mk 2:12 *2112*
i it sprang up, because it had no ... Mk 4:5 *2112*
they have heard, Satan cometh *i* ... Mk 4:15 *2112*
i receive it with gladness ... Mk 4:16 *2112*
word's sake, *i* they are offended ... Mk 4:17 *2112*
i he putteth in the sickle, ... Mk 4:29 *2112*
i there met him out of the tombs ... Mk 5:2 *2112*
i knowing in himself that virtue ... Mk 5:30 *2112*
i the king sent an executioner, ... Mk 6:27 *2112*
i he talked with them, and saith ... Mk 6:50 *2112*
i he received his sight, and ... Mk 10:52 *2112*
And *i*, while he yet spake, cometh ... Mk 14:43 *2112*
And his mouth was opened *i* ... Lk 1:64 *3916*
i she arose and ministered unto ... Lk 4:39 *3916*
i the leprosy departed from him ... Lk 5:13 *2112*
i he rose up before them, and took ... Lk 5:25 *3916*
did beat vehemently, and *i* it fell ... Lk 6:49 *2112*
i her issue of blood stanched ... Lk 8:44 *3916*
him, and how she was healed *i* ... Lk 8:47 *3916*
they may open unto him *i* ... Lk 12:36 *2112*
i she was made straight, and ... Lk 13:13 *3916*
i he received his sight, and ... Lk 18:43 *3916*
kingdom of God should *i* appear ... Lk 19:11 *3916*
peace, the stones would *i* cry out ... Lk 19:40
And *i*, while he yet spake, the ... Lk 22:60 *3916*
i the man was made whole, and took ... Jn 5:9 *2112*
i the ship was at the land ... Jn 6:21 *2112*
received the sop went *i* out ... Jn 13:30 *2112*
and *i* the cock crew ... Jn 18:27 *2112*
forth, and entered into a ship *i* ... Jn 21:3 *2117*
i his feet and ancle bones ... Acts 3:7 *3916*
i there fell from his eyes as it ... Acts 9:18 *2112*
And he arose *i* ... Acts 9:34 *2112*
I therefore I sent to thee ... Acts 10:33 *1824*
i there were three men already ... Acts 11:11 *1824*
i the angel of the Lord smote him ... Acts 12:23 *3916*
i there fell on him a mist and a ... Acts 13:11 *3916*
i we endeavoured to go into ... Acts 16:10 *2112*
i all the doors were opened, and ... Acts 16:26 *3916*
the brethren *i* sent away Paul and ... Acts 17:10 *2112*
then *i* the brethren sent away ... Acts 17:14 *2112*
Who *i* took soldiers and centurions ... Acts 21:32 *1824*
i I conferred not with flesh and ... Gal 1:16 *2112*
And *i* I was in the spirit ... Rev 4:2 *2112*

IMMER (*im'-mur*)
1. Father of Meshillemeth.
son of Meshillemith, the son of *I* ... 1Chr 9:12 564
The children of *I*, a thousand ... Ezr 2:37 564
And of the sons of *I* ... Ezr 10:20 564
The children of *I*, a thousand ... Neh 7:40 564
son of Meshillemoth, the son of *I* ... Neh 11:13 564
2. A sanctuary servant.
to Bilgah, the sixteenth to *I* ... 1Chr 24:14 564
3. An exile.
Tel-harsa, Cherub, Addan, and *I* ... Ezr 2:59 564
Tel-haresha, Cherub, Addon, and *I* ... Neh 7:61 564
4. Father of Zadok.
son of *I* over against his house ... Neh 3:29 564
5. A priest.
Pashur the son of *I* the priest ... Jer 20:1 564

IMMORTAL
Now unto the King eternal, *i* ... 1Ti 1:17 *862*

IMMORTALITY
seek for glory and honour and *i* ... Rom 2:7 *861*
and this mortal must put on *i* ... 1Cor 15:53 *110*
this mortal shall have put on *i* ... 1Cor 15:54 *110*
Who only hath *i*, dwelling in the ... 1Ti 6:16 *110*
i to light through the gospel ... 2Ti 1:10 *861*

IMMUTABILITY
of promise the *i* of his counsel ... Heb 6:17 *276*

IMMUTABLE
That by two *i* things, in which it ... Heb 6:18 *276*

IMNA (*im'-nah*) See IMNAH, JIMNA. *A son of Helem.*
Zophah, and *I*, and Shelesh, and Amal. 1Chr 7:35 3234

IMNAH (*im'-nah*) See IMNA, JIMNAH.
1. Son of Asher.
I, and Isuah, and Ishuai, and Beriah ... 1Chr 7:30 3232
2. Father of Kore.
And Kore the son of *I* the Levite ... 2Chr 31:14 3232

IMPART
let him *i* to him that hath none ... Lk 3:11 *3330*
that I may *i* unto you some ... Rom 1:11 *3330*

IMPARTED
wisdom, neither hath he *i* to her ... Job 39:17 2505
were willing to have *i* unto you ... 1Th 2:8 *3330*

IMPEDIMENT
deaf, and had an *i* in his speech ... Mk 7:32 *3424*

IMPENITENT
i heart treasurest up unto ... Rom 2:5 *279*

IMPERIOUS
the work of an *i* whorish woman ... Eze 16:30 7986

IMPLACABLE
without natural affection, *i* ... Rom 1:31 *786*

IMPLEAD
let them *i* one another ... Acts 19:38 *1458*

IMPORTUNITY
yet because of his *i* he will rise ... Lk 11:8 *335*

IMPOSE
it shall not be lawful to *i* toll ... Ezr 7:24 7412

IMPOSED
i on them until the time of ... Heb 9:10 *1942*

IMPOSSIBLE
and nothing shall be *i* unto you ... Mt 17:20 *101*
unto them, With men this is *i* ... Mt 19:26 *102*
upon them saith, With men it is *i* ... Mk 10:27 *102*
For with God nothing shall be *i* ... Lk 1:37 *101*
It is *i* but that offences will ... Lk 17:1 *418*
The things which are *i* with men ... Lk 18:27 *102*
For it is *i* for those who were ... Heb 6:4 *102*
in which it was *i* for God to lie ... Heb 6:18 *102*
faith it is *i* to please him ... Heb 11:6 *102*

IMPOTENT
lay a great multitude of *i* folk ... Jn 5:3 *770*
The *i* man answered him, Sir, I ... Jn 5:7 *770*
the good deed done to the *i* man ... Acts 4:9 *772*
i in his feet, being a cripple ... Acts 14:8 *102*

IMPOVERISH
they shall *i* thy fenced cities, ... Jer 5:17 7567

IMPOVERISHED
Israel was greatly *i* because of ... Judg 6:6 1809
He that is so *i* that he hath no ... Is 40:20 5533
Whereas Edom saith, We are *i* ... Mal 1:4 7567

IMPRISONED
I said, Lord, they know that I *i* ... Acts 22:19 *5439*

IMPRISONMENT
to confiscation of goods, or to *i* ... Ezr 7:26 613
yea, moreover of bonds and *i* ... Heb 11:36 *5438*

IMPRISONMENTS
In stripes, in *i*, in tumults, in ... 2Cor 6:5 *5438*

IMPUDENT
with an *i* face said unto him, ... Prov 7:13 5810
For they are *i* children and ... Eze 2:4
for all the house of Israel are *i* ... Eze 3:7

IMPUTE
let not the king *i* any thing unto ... 1Sa 22:15 7760
Let not my lord *i* iniquity unto ... 2Sa 19:19 2803
to whom the Lord will not *i* sin ... Rom 4:8 *3049*

IMPUTED
neither shall it be *i* unto him ... Lev 7:18 2803
blood shall be *i* unto that man ... Lev 17:4 2803
might be *i* unto them also ... Rom 4:11 *3049*
therefore it was *i* to him for ... Rom 4:22 *3049*
sake alone, that it was *i* to him ... Rom 4:23 *3049*
us also, to whom it shall be *i* ... Rom 4:24 *3049*
but sin is not *i* when there is no ... Rom 5:13 *1677*
God, and it was *i* unto him for ... Jas 2:23 *3049*

IMPUTETH
unto whom the LORD *i* not iniquity ... Ps 32:2 2803
unto whom God *i* righteousness ... Rom 4:6 *3049*

IMPUTING
i this his power unto his god ... Hab 1:11
not *i* their trespasses unto them ... 2Cor 5:19 *3049*

IMRAH (*im'-rah*) *A chief of Asher.*
and Shual, and Beri, and *I*, ... 1Chr 7:36 3236

IMRI (*im'-ri*)
1. Son of Bani.
the son of Omri, the son of *I* ... 1Chr 9:4 556
2. Father of Zaccur.
them builded Zaccur the son of *I* ... Neh 3:2 556

IN See PREFACE.

INASMUCH
i as he hated him not in time ... Deut 19:6 3588
i as thou followedst not young ... Ruth 3:10 1115
I as ye have done it unto one of ... Mt 25:40
I as ye did it not to one of the ... Mt 25:45
i as I am the apostle of the ... Rom 11:13
i as both in my bonds, and in the ... Phil 1:7
i as he who hath builded the ... Heb 3:3
i as not without an oath he was ... Heb 7:20
i as ye are partakers of Christ's ... 1Pet 4:13 *2526*

INCENSE
for anointing oil, and for sweet *i* ... Ex 25:6 7004
make an altar to burn *i* upon ... Ex 30:1 7004
thereon sweet *i* every morning ... Ex 30:7 7004
lamps, he shall burn *i* upon it ... Ex 30:7
at even, he shall burn *i* upon it ... Ex 30:8 6999
a perpetual *i* before the LORD ... Ex 30:8 7004
shall offer no strange *i* thereon ... Ex 30:9 7004
and his vessels, and the altar of *i* ... Ex 30:27 7004
his furniture, and the altar of *i* ... Ex 31:8 7004
sweet *i* for the holy place ... Ex 31:11 7004
anointing oil, and for the sweet *i* ... Ex 35:8 7004
the *i* altar, and his staves, and ... Ex 35:15 7004
the anointing oil, and the sweet *i* ... Ex 35:15 7004
anointing oil, and for the sweet *i* ... Ex 35:28 7004
he made the *i* altar of shittim ... Ex 37:25 7004
the pure *i* of sweet spices, ... Ex 37:29 7004
the anointing oil, and the sweet *i* ... Ex 39:38 7004
set the altar of gold for the *i* ... Ex 40:5 7004
And he burnt sweet *i* thereon ... Ex 40:27 7004
altar of sweet *i* before the LORD ... Lev 4:7 7004
put *i* thereon, and offered strange ... Lev 10:1 7004
full of sweet *i* beaten small ... Lev 16:12 7004
he shall put the *i* upon the fire ... Lev 16:13 7004
that the cloud of the *i* may cover ... Lev 16:13 7004
oil for the light, and the sweet *i* ... Num 4:16 7004
of ten shekels of gold, full of *i* ... Num 7:14 7004
of gold of ten shekels, full of *i* ... Num 7:20 7004
spoon of ten shekels, full of *i* ... Num 7:26 7004
spoon of ten shekels, full of *i* ... Num 7:32 7004
spoon of ten shekels, full of *i* ... Num 7:38 7004
spoon of ten shekels, full of *i* ... Num 7:44 7004
spoon of ten shekels, full of *i* ... Num 7:50 7004
spoon of ten shekels, full of *i* ... Num 7:56 7004
spoon of ten shekels, full of *i* ... Num 7:62 7004
spoon of ten shekels, full of *i* ... Num 7:68 7004
spoon of ten shekels, full of *i* ... Num 7:74 7004
spoon of ten shekels, full of *i* ... Num 7:80 7004
spoons were twelve, full of *i* ... Num 7:86 7004
put *i* in them before the LORD to ... Num 16:7 7004
put *i* in them, and bring ye before ... Num 16:17 7004
laid *i* thereon, and stood in the ... Num 16:18 7004
and fifty men that offered *i* ... Num 16:35 7004
near to offer *i* before the LORD ... Num 16:40 7004
from off the altar, and put on *i* ... Num 16:46 7004
and he put on *i*, and made an ... Num 16:47 7004
they shall put *i* before thee ... Deut 33:10 7004
offer upon mine altar, to burn *i* ... 1Sa 2:28 7004
and burnt *i* in high places ... 1Kin 3:3 6999
he burnt *i* upon the altar that ... 1Kin 9:25 6999
his strange wives, which burnt *i* ... 1Kin 11:8 6999
upon the altar, and burnt *i* ... 1Kin 12:33 6999
stood by the altar to burn *i* ... 1Kin 13:1 6999
high places that burn *i* upon thee ... 1Kin 13:2 6999
burnt *i* yet in the high places ... 1Kin 22:43 6999
burnt *i* in the high places ... 2Kin 12:3 6999
burnt *i* on the high places ... 2Kin 14:4 6999
burnt *i* still on the high places ... 2Kin 15:4 6999
burned *i* still in the high places ... 2Kin 15:35 6999
burnt *i* in the high places, and on ... 2Kin 16:4 6999
there they burnt *i* in all the ... 2Kin 17:11 6999
of Israel did burn *i* to it ... 2Kin 18:4 6999
have burned *i* unto other gods, ... 2Kin 22:17 6999
burn *i* in the high places in the ... 2Kin 23:5 6999
them also that burned *i* unto Baal ... 2Kin 23:5 6999
where the priests had burned *i* ... 2Kin 23:8 6999
offering, and on the altar of *i* ... 1Chr 6:49 7004
to burn *i* before the LORD, to ... 1Chr 23:13 6999
for the altar of *i* refined gold ... 1Chr 28:18 7004
and to burn before him sweet *i* ... 2Chr 2:4 7004
burnt sacrifices and sweet *i* ... 2Chr 13:11 7004
them, and burned *i* unto them ... 2Chr 25:14 6999
burn *i* upon the altar of *i* ... 2Chr 26:16 6999
to burn *i* unto the LORD, but to ... 2Chr 26:18 6999
that are consecrated to burn *i* ... 2Chr 26:18 6999
a censer in his hand to burn *i* ... 2Chr 26:19 6999
the LORD, from beside the *i* altar ... 2Chr 26:19 7004
Moreover he burnt *i* in the valley ... 2Chr 28:3 6999
burnt *i* in the high places, and on ... 2Chr 28:4 6999
places to burn *i* unto other gods ... 2Chr 28:25 6999
have not burned *i* nor offered ... 2Chr 29:7 7004
minister unto him, and burn *i* ... 2Chr 29:11 6999
the altars for *i* took they away ... 2Chr 30:14 6999
one altar, and burn *i* upon it ... 2Chr 32:12 6999
have burned *i* unto other gods, ... 2Chr 34:25 6999
of fatlings, with the *i* of rams ... Ps 66:15 7004
be set forth before thee as *i* ... Ps 141:2 7004
i is an abomination unto me ... Is 1:13 7004
offering, nor wearied thee with *i* ... Is 43:23 3828
they shall bring gold and *i* ... Is 60:6 3828
burneth *i* upon altars of brick ... Is 65:3 6999
which have burned *i* upon the ... Is 65:7 6999
he that burneth *i*, as if he ... Is 66:3 3828
have burned *i* unto other gods, and ... Jer 1:16 6999
cometh there to me *i* from Sheba ... Jer 6:20 3828
burn *i* unto Baal, and walk after ... Jer 7:9 6999
the gods unto whom they offer *i* ... Jer 11:12 6999
even altars to burn *i* unto Baal ... Jer 11:13 6999
to anger in offering *i* unto Baal ... Jer 11:17 6999
and meat offerings, and *i*, and ... Jer 17:26 3828
me, they have burned *i* to vanity ... Jer 18:15 6999
have burned *i* in it unto other ... Jer 19:4 6999
i unto all the host of heaven ... Jer 19:13 6999
they have offered *i* unto Baal ... Jer 32:29 6999
i in their hand, to bring them to ... Jer 41:5 3828
in that they went to burn *i* ... Jer 44:3 6999
to burn no *i* unto other gods ... Jer 44:5 6999
burning *i* unto other gods in the ... Jer 44:8 6999
had burned *i* unto other gods ... Jer 44:15 6999
to burn *i* unto the queen of ... Jer 44:17 6999
to burn *i* to the queen of heaven ... Jer 44:18 6999
when we burned *i* to the queen of ... Jer 44:19 6999
The *i* that ye burned in the ... Jer 44:21 7002
Because ye have burned *i*, and ... Jer 44:23 6999
to burn *i* to the queen of heaven, ... Jer 44:25 6999
and him that burneth *i* to his gods ... Jer 48:35 6999
and a thick cloud of *i* went up ... Eze 8:11 7004
mine oil and mine *i* before them ... Eze 16:18 7004

I

whereupon thou hast set mine *i* — Eze 23:41 — 7004
wherein she burned *i* to them — Hos 2:13 — 6999
burn *i* upon the hills, under oaks — Hos 4:13 — 6999
burned *i* to graven images — Hos 11:2 — 6999
net, and burn *i* unto their drag — Hab 1:16 — 6999
in every place *i* shall be offered — Mal 1:11 — 6999
his lot was to burn *i* when he — Lk 1:9 — *2370*
praying without at the time of *i* — Lk 1:10 — *2368*
the right side of the altar of *i* — Lk 1:11 — *2368*
there was given unto him much *i* — Rev 8:3 — *2368*
And the smoke of the *i*, which came — Rev 8:4 — *2368*

INCENSED
all they that were *i* against thee — Is 41:11 — 2734
all that are *i* against him shall — Is 45:24 — 2734

INCLINE
i your heart unto the LORD God of — Josh 24:23 — 5186
That he may *i* our hearts unto him — 1Kin 8:58 — 5186
i thine ear unto me, and hear my — Ps 17:6 — 5186
and consider, and *i* thine ear — Ps 45:10 — 5186
I will *i* mine ear to a parable — Ps 49:4 — 5186
i thine ear unto me, and save me — Ps 71:2 — 5186
i your ears to the words of my — Ps 78:1 — 5186
i thine ear unto my cry — Ps 88:2 — 5186
i thine ear unto me — Ps 102:2 — 5186
I my heart unto thy testimonies, — Ps 119:36 — 5186
I not my heart to any evil thing, — Ps 141:4 — 5186
So that thou *i* thine ear unto — Prov 2:2 — 7181
i thine ear unto my sayings — Prov 4:20 — 5186
I thine ear, O LORD, and hear — Is 37:17 — 5186
I your ear, and come unto me — Is 55:3 — 5186
O my God, *i* thine ear, and hear — Dan 9:18 — 5186

INCLINED
and their hearts *i* to follow — Judg 9:3 — 5186
he *i* unto me, and heard my cry — Ps 40:1 — 5186
Because he hath *i* his ear unto me — Ps 116:2 — 5186
I have *i* mine heart to perform — Ps 119:112 — 5186
nor *i* mine ear to them that — Prov 5:13 — 5186
nor *i* their ear, but walked in — Jer 7:24 — 5186
nor *i* their ear, but hardened — Jer 7:26 — 5186
nor *i* their ear, but walked every — Jer 11:8 — 5186
neither *i* their ear, but made — Jer 17:23 — 5186
hearkened, nor *i* your ear to hear — Jer 25:4 — 5186
not unto me, neither *i* their ear — Jer 34:14 — 5186
but ye have not *i* your ear — Jer 35:15 — 5186
nor *i* their ear to turn from — Jer 44:5 — 5186

INCLINETH
For her house *i* unto death — Prov 2:18 — 7743

INCLOSE
we will *i* her with boards of — Song 8:9 — 6696

INCLOSED
onyx stones *i* in ouches of gold — Ex 39:6 — 4142
they were *i* in ouches of gold in — Ex 39:13 — 4142
Thus they *i* the Benjamites round — Judg 20:43 — 3803
They are *i* in their own fat — Ps 17:10 — 5462
assembly of the wicked have *i* me — Ps 22:16 — 5362
A garden *i* is my sister, my — Song 4:12 — 5274
He hath *i* my ways with hewn stone — Lam 3:9 — 1443
they *i* a great multitude of — Lk 5:6 — *4788*

INCLOSINGS
shall be set in gold in their *i* — Ex 28:20 — 4396
in ouches of gold in their *i* — Ex 39:13 — 4396

INCONTINENCY
Satan tempt you not for your *i* — 1Cor 7:5 — *192*

INCONTINENT
trucebreakers, false accusers, *i* — 2Ti 3:3 — *193*

INCORRUPTIBLE
but we an *i* — 1Cor 9:25 — *862*
and the dead shall be raised *i* — 1Cor 15:52 — *862*
To an inheritance *i*, and undefiled — 1Pet 1:4 — *862*
not of corruptible seed, but of *i* — 1Pet 1:23 — *862*

INCORRUPTION
it is raised in *i* — 1Cor 15:42 — *861*
neither doth corruption inherit *i* — 1Cor 15:50 — *861*
this corruptible must put on *i* — 1Cor 15:53 — *861*
corruptible shall have put on *i* — 1Cor 15:54 — *861*

INCREASE
And it shall come to pass in the *i* — Gen 47:24 — 8393
may yield unto you the *i* thereof — Lev 19:25 — 8393
shall all the *i* thereof be meat — Lev 25:7 — 8393
ye shall eat the *i* thereof out of — Lev 25:12 — 8393
thou shalt *i* the price thereof — Lev 25:16 — 7235
not sow, nor gather in our *i* — Lev 25:20 — 8393
Take thou no usury of him, or *i* — Lev 25:36 — 8635
nor lend him thy victuals for *i* — Lev 25:37 — 4768
and the land shall yield her *i* — Lev 26:4 — 2981
your land shall not yield her *i* — Lev 26:20 — 2981
as the *i* of the threshingfloor — Num 18:30 — 8393
as the *i* of the winepress — Num 18:30 — 8393
an *i* of sinful men, to augment — Num 32:14 — 8635
thee, and that ye may *i* mightily — Deut 6:3 — 7235
the *i* of thy kine, and the flocks — Deut 7:13 — 7698
beasts of the field *i* upon thee — Deut 7:22 — 7235
truly tithe all the *i* of thy seed — Deut 14:22 — 8393
tithe of thine *i* the same year — Deut 14:28 — 8393
shall bless thee in all thine *i* — Deut 16:15 — 8393
tithes of thine *i* the third year — Deut 26:12 — 8393
the *i* of thy kine, and the flocks — Deut 28:4 — 7698
the *i* of thy kine, and the flocks — Deut 28:18 — 7698
or the *i* of thy kine, or flocks — Deut 28:51 — 7698
he might eat the *i* of the fields — Deut 32:13 — 8570
consume the earth with her *i* — Deut 32:22 — 2981
and destroyed the *i* of the earth — Judg 6:4 — 2981
I thine army, and come out — Judg 9:29 — 7239
all the *i* of thine house shall — 1Sa 2:33 — 4768
the LORD had said he would *i* — 1Chr 27:23 — 7235
over the *i* of the vineyards for — 1Chr 27:27
of all the *i* of the field — 2Chr 31:5 — 8393
also for the *i* of corn, and wine, — 2Chr 32:28 — 8393
to *i* the trespass of Israel — Ezr 10:10 — 3254
it yieldeth much *i* unto the kings — Neh 9:37 — 8393
thy latter end should greatly *i* — Job 8:7 — 7685
The *i* of his house shall depart, — Job 20:28 — 2981
and would root out all mine *i* — Job 31:12 — 8393
dost not *i* thy wealth by their — Ps 44:12 — 7235
if riches *i*, set not your heart — Ps 62:10 — 5107
Then shall the earth yield her *i* — Ps 67:6 — 2981
Thou shalt *i* my greatness, and — Ps 71:21 — 7235
they *i* in riches — Ps 73:12 — 7685
He gave also their *i* unto the — Ps 78:46 — 2981
and our land shall yield her *i* — Ps 85:12 — 2981
which may yield fruits of *i* — Ps 107:37 — 8393
The LORD shall *i* you more — Ps 115:14 — 3254
man will hear, and will *i* learning — Prov 1:5 — 3254
the firstfruits of all thine *i* — Prov 3:9 — 8393
man, and he will *i* in learning — Prov 9:9 — 3254
that gathereth by labour shall *i* — Prov 13:11 — 7235
but much *i* is by the strength of — Prov 14:4 — 8393
with the *i* of his lips shall he — Prov 18:20 — 8393
the poor to *i* his riches, and he — Prov 22:16 — 7235
when they perish, the righteous *i* — Prov 28:28 — 7235
he that loveth abundance with *i* — Eccl 5:10 — 8393
When goods *i*, they are increased — Eccl 5:11 — 7235
be many things that *i* vanity — Eccl 6:11 — 7235
Of the *i* of his government and — Is 9:7 — 4768
The meek also shall *i* their joy — Is 29:19 — 3254
and bread of the *i* of the earth — Is 30:23 — 8393
didst *i* thy perfumes, and didst — Is 57:9 — 7235
LORD, and the firstfruits of his *i* — Jer 2:3 — 8393
and they shall be fruitful and *i* — Jer 23:3 — 7235
I will *i* the famine upon you, and — Eze 5:16 — 3254
usury, neither hath taken any *i* — Eze 18:8 — 8635
forth upon usury, and hath taken *i* — Eze 18:13 — 8635
hath not received usury nor *i* — Eze 18:17 — 8635
thou hast taken usury and *i* — Eze 22:12 — 8635
and the earth shall yield her *i* — Eze 34:27 — 2981
and they shall *i* and bring fruit — Eze 36:11 — 7235
call for the corn, and will *i* it — Eze 36:29 — 7235
the *i* of the field, that ye shall — Eze 36:30 — 8570
I will *i* them with men like a — Eze 36:37 — 7235
the *i* thereof shall be for food — Eze 48:18 — 8393
shall acknowledge and *i* with glory — Dan 11:39 — 7235
commit whoredom, and shall not *i* — Hos 4:10 — 6555
and the ground shall give her *i* — Zec 8:12 — 2981
they shall *i* as they have — Zec 10:8 — 7235
said unto the Lord, *I* our faith — Lk 17:5 — *4369*
He must *i*, but I must decrease — Jn 3:30 — *837*
but God gave the *i* — 1Cor 3:6 — *837*
but God that giveth the *i* — 1Cor 3:7 — *837*
sown, and *i* the fruits of your — 2Cor 9:10 — *837*
maketh *i* of the body unto the — Eph 4:16 — *838*
increaseth with the *i* of God — Col 2:19 — *838*
And the Lord make you to *i* — 1Th 3:12 — *4121*
you, brethren, that ye *i* more — 1Th 4:10 — *4052*
for they will *i* unto more — 2Ti 2:16 — *4298*

INCREASED
and the waters *i*, and bare up the — Gen 7:17 — 7235
were *i* greatly upon the earth — Gen 7:18 — 7235
it is now *i* unto a multitude — Gen 30:30 — 6555
the man *i* exceedingly, and had — Gen 30:43 — 6555
i abundantly, and multiplied, and — Ex 1:7 — 8317
from before thee, until thou be *i* — Ex 23:30 — 6509
of the Philistines went on and *i* — 1Sa 14:19 — 7227
for the people *i* continually with — 2Sa 15:12 — 7227
And the battle *i* that day — 1Kin 22:35 — 5927
house of their fathers *i* greatly — 1Chr 4:38 — 6555
they *i* from Bashan unto — 1Chr 5:23 — 7235
And the battle *i* that day — 2Chr 18:34 — 5927
iniquities are *i* over our head — Ezr 9:6 — 7235
and his substance is *i* in the land — Job 1:10 — 6555
how are they *i* that trouble me — Ps 3:1 — 7231
that their corn and their wine *i* — Ps 4:7 — 7231
when the glory of his house is *i* — Ps 49:16 — 7235
And he *i* his people greatly — Ps 105:24 — 6509
the years of thy life shall be *i* — Prov 9:11 — 3254
i more than all that were before — Eccl 2:9 — 3254
they are *i* that eat them — Eccl 5:11 — 7231
the nation, and not *i* the joy — Is 9:3 — 1431
Thou hast *i* the nation, O LORD, — Is 26:15 — 3254
thou hast *i* the nation — Is 26:15 — 3254
alone, and blessed him, and *i* him — Is 51:2 — 7235
i in the land, in those days, — Jer 3:16 — 6509
many, and their backslidings are *i* — Jer 5:6 — 6105
Their widows are *i* to me above — Jer 15:8 — 6105
that ye may be *i* there, and not — Jer 29:6 — 7235
because thy sins were *i* — Jer 30:14 — 6105
because thy sins were *i*, I have — Jer 30:15 — 6105
hath *i* in the daughter of Judah — Lam 2:5 — 7235
bud of the field, and thou hast *i* — Eze 16:7 — 7235
hast *i* thy whoredoms, to provoke — Eze 16:26 — 7235
And that she *i* her whoredoms — Eze 23:14 — 3254
traffick hast thou *i* thy riches — Eze 28:5 — 7235
so *i* from the lowest chamber to — Eze 41:7 — 5927
and fro, and knowledge shall be *i* — Dan 12:4 — 7235
As they were *i*, so they sinned — Hos 4:7 — 7230
of his fruit he hath *i* the altars — Hos 10:1 — 7235
fig trees and your olive trees *i* — Amos 4:9 — 7235
shall increase as they have *i* — Zec 10:8 — 7235
yield fruit that sprang up and *i* — Mk 4:8 — *837*
Jesus *i* in wisdom and stature, and — Lk 2:52 — *4298*
And the word of God *i* — Acts 6:7 — *837*
But Saul *i* the more in strength, — Acts 9:22 — *1743*
the faith, and *i* in number daily — Acts 16:5 — *4052*
having hope, when your faith is *i* — 2Cor 10:15 — *837*
i with goods, and have need of — Rev 3:17 — *4147*

INCREASEST
i thine indignation upon me — Job 10:17 — 7235

INCREASETH
For it *i*. Thou huntest me — Job 10:16 — 1342
He *i* the nations, and destroyeth — Job 12:23 — 7679
up against thee *i* continually — Ps 74:23 — 5927
is that scattereth, and yet *i* — Prov 11:24 — 3254
sweetness of the lips *i* learning — Prov 16:21 — 3254
i the transgressors among men — Prov 23:28 — 3254
a man of knowledge *i* strength — Prov 24:5 — 553
unjust gain *i* his substance, he — Prov 28:8 — 7235
are multiplied, transgression *i* — Prov 29:16 — 7235
he that *i* knowledge *i* sorrow — Eccl 1:18 — 3254
that have no might he *i* strength — Is 40:29 — 7235
he daily *i* lies and desolation — Hos 12:1 — 7235
Woe to him that *i* that which is — Hab 2:6 — 7235
i with the increase of God — Col 2:19 — *837*

INCREASING
i in the knowledge of God — Col 1:10 — *837*

INCREDIBLE
it be thought a thing *i* with you — Acts 26:8 — *571*

INCURABLE
in his bowels with an *i* disease — 2Chr 21:18
my wound is *i* without — Job 34:6 — 605
my pain perpetual, and my wound *i* — Jer 15:18 — 605
saith the LORD, Thy bruise is *i* — Jer 30:12 — 605
thy sorrow is *i* for the multitude — Jer 30:15 — 605
For her wound is *i* — Mic 1:9 — 605

INDEBTED
forgive every one that is *i* to us — Lk 11:4 — *3784*

INDEED
thy wife shall bear thee a son *i* — Gen 17:19 — 61
And yet *i* she is my sister — Gen 20:12 — 546
Shalt thou *i* reign over us — Gen 37:8
or shalt thou *i* have dominion — Gen 37:8
thy brethren *i* come to bow down — Gen 37:10
For *i* I was stolen away out of — Gen 40:15
we came *i* down at the first time — Gen 43:20
and whereby *i* he divineth — Gen 44:5
if ye will obey my voice *i* — Ex 19:5
if thou shalt *i* obey his voice — Ex 23:22
ye should *i* have eaten it in the — Lev 10:18
Hath the LORD *i* spoken only by — Num 12:2
If thou wilt *i* deliver this — Num 21:2 — 389
am I not able *i* to promote thee — Num 22:37 — 552
For *i* the hand of the LORD was — Deut 2:15 — 1571
hated, which is *i* the firstborn — Deut 21:16
I I have sinned against the LORD — Josh 7:20 — 546
if thou wilt *i* look on the — 1Sa 1:11
I said *i* that thy house, and the — 1Sa 2:30
I am *i* a widow woman, and mine — 2Sa 14:5 — 61
bring me again *i* to Jerusalem — 2Sa 15:8
But will God *i* dwell on the earth — 1Kin 8:27 — 552
Thou hast *i* smitten Edom, and — 2Kin 14:10
Oh that thou wouldest bless me *i* — 1Chr 4:10
that have sinned and done evil *i* — 1Chr 21:17
be it *i* that I have erred, mine — Job 19:4 — 551
If *i* ye will magnify yourselves — Job 19:5 — 551
Do ye *i* speak righteousness, O — Ps 58:1 — 552
and tell this people, Hear ye *i* — Is 6:9
and see ye *i*, but perceive not — Is 6:9
For if ye do this thing *i* — Jer 22:4
I *i* baptize you with water unto — Mt 3:11 — *3303*
Which *i* is the least of all seeds — Mt 13:32 — *3303*
them, Ye shall drink *i* of my cup — Mt 20:23 — *3303*
which *i* appear beautiful outward, — Mt 23:27 — *3303*
the spirit *i* is willing, but the — Mt 26:41 — *3303*
I *i* have baptized you with water — Mk 1:8 — *3303*
unto you, That Elias is *i* come — Mk 9:13 — *2532*
Ye shall *i* drink of the cup that — Mk 10:39 — *3303*
John, that he was a prophet *i* — Mk 11:32 — *3689*
The Son of man *i* goeth, as it is — Mk 14:21 — *3303*
I *i* baptize you with water — Lk 3:16 — *3303*
for they *i* killed them, and ye — Lk 11:48 — *3303*
And we *i* justly; for we — Lk 23:41 — *0000*
Saying, The Lord is risen *i* — Lk 24:34 — *3689*
of him, Behold an Israelite *i* — Jn 1:47 — *230*
and know that this is *i* the Christ — Jn 4:42 — *230*
For my flesh is meat *i* — Jn 6:55 — *230*
and my blood is drink *i* — Jn 6:55 — *230*
Do the rulers know *i* that this is — Jn 7:26 — *230*
word, then are ye my disciples *i* — Jn 8:31 — *230*
make you free, ye shall be free *i* — Jn 8:36 — *3689*
for that *i* a notable miracle hath — Acts 4:16 — *3303*
John *i* baptized with water — Acts 11:16 — *3303*
that were with me saw *i* the light — Acts 22:9 — *3303*
yourselves to be dead *i* unto sin — Rom 6:11 — *3303*
the law of God, neither *i* can be — Rom 8:7 — *1063*
All things *i* are pure — Rom 14:20 — *3303*
For a man *i* ought not to cover — 1Cor 11:7 — *3303*
For *i* he accepted the exhortation — 2Cor 8:17 — *3303*
and *i* bear with me — 2Cor 11:1 — *235*
Some *i* preach Christ even of envy — Phil 1:15 — *3303*
For *i* he was sick nigh unto death — Phil 2:27 — *2532*
to me *i* is not grievous, but for — Phil 3:1 — *3303*
Which things have *i* a shew of — Col 2:23 — *3303*
i ye do it toward all the — 1Th 4:10 — *1063*
Honour widows that are widows *i* — 1Ti 5:3 — *3689*
Now she that is a widow *i* — 1Ti 5:5 — *3689*
relieve them that are widows *i* — 1Ti 5:16 — *3689*
living stone, disallowed *i* of men — 1Pet 2:4 — *3303*

INDIA (*in'-de-ah*) *Eastern boundary of the Persian Empire.*
reigned from *I* even unto Ethiopia — Est 1:1 — 1912
which are from *I* unto Ethiopia — Est 8:9 — 1912

INDIGNATION
anger, and in wrath, and in great *i* — Deut 29:28 — 7110
there was great *i* against Israel — 2Kin 3:27 — 7110
he was wroth, and took great *i* — Neh 4:1 — 3707
he was full of *i* against Mordecai — Est 5:9 — 2534
me, and increasest thine *i* upon me — Job 10:17 — 3708
Pour out thine *i* upon them — Ps 69:24 — 2195
of his anger, wrath, and *i* — Ps 78:49 — 2195
Because of thine *i* and thy wrath — Ps 102:10 — 2195
the staff in their hand is mine *i* — Is 10:5 — 2195
the *i* shall cease, and mine anger — Is 10:25 — 2195

the LORD, and the weapons of his *i*........ Is 13:5 2195
moment, until the *i* be overpast........ Is 26:20 2195
his lips are full of *i*, and his........ Is 30:27 2195
with the *i* of his anger, and with........ Is 30:30 2197
For the *i* of the LORD is upon all........ Is 34:2 7110
and his *i* toward his enemies........ Is 66:14 2194
shall not be able to abide his *i*........ Jer 10:10 2195
for thou hast filled me with *i*........ Jer 15:17 2195
forth the weapons of his *i*........ Jer 50:25 2195
hath despised in the *i* of his........ Lam 2:6 2195
I will pour out mine *i* upon thee........ Eze 21:31 2195
nor rained upon in the day of *i*........ Eze 22:24 2195
I poured out mine *i* upon them........ Eze 22:31 2195
shall be in the last end of the *i*........ Dan 8:19 2195
have *i* against the holy covenant........ Dan 11:30 2194
till the *i* be accomplished........ Dan 11:36 2195
I will bear the *i* of the LORD........ Mic 7:9 2197
Who can stand before his *i*........ Nah 1:6 2195
didst march through the land in *i*........ Hab 3:12 2195
to pour upon them mine *i*........ Zeph 3:8 2195
thou hast had *i* these threescore........ Zec 1:12 2194
whom the LORD hath *i* for ever........ Mal 1:4 2194
they were moved with *i* against........ Mt 20:24 *23*
his disciples saw it, they had *i*........ Mt 26:8 *23*
some that had *i* within themselves........ Mk 14:4 *23*
of the synagogue answered with *i*........ Lk 13:14 *23*
Sadducees,) and were filled with *i*........ Acts 5:17 *2205*
but obey unrighteousness, *i*........ Rom 2:8 *2372*
of yourselves, yea, what *i*........ 2Cor 7:11 *24*
for of judgment and fiery *i*........ Heb 10:27 *2205*
mixture into the cup of his *i*........ Rev 14:10 *3709*

INDITING
My heart is *i* a good matter........ Ps 45:1 7370

INDUSTRIOUS
the young man that he was *i*........ 1Kin 11:28

INEXCUSABLE
Therefore thou art *i*, O man,........ Rom 2:1 *379*

INFALLIBLE
his passion by many *i* proofs........ Acts 1:3

INFAMOUS
shall mock thee, which art *i*........ Eze 22:5

INFAMY
shame, and thine *i* turn not away........ Prov 25:10 1681
and are an *i* of the people........ Eze 36:3 1681

INFANT
but slay both man and woman, *i*........ 1Sa 15:3 5768
be no more thence an *i* of days........ Is 65:20 5764

INFANTS
as *i* which never saw light........ Job 3:16 5768
their *i* shall be dashed in pieces........ Hos 13:16 5768
And they brought unto him also *i*........ Lk 18:15 *1025*

INFERIOR
I am not *i* to you........ Job 12:3 5307
I am not *i* unto you........ Job 13:2 5307
arise another kingdom *i* to thee........ Dan 2:39 772
ye were *i* to other churches........ 2Cor 12:13 *2274*

INFIDEL
hath he that believeth with an *i*........ 2Cor 6:15 *571*
the faith, and is worse than an *i*........ 1Ti 5:8 *571*

INFINITE
and thine iniquities *i*........ Job 22:5
his understanding is *i*........ Ps 147:5
were her strength, and it was *i*........ Nah 3:9

INFIRMITIES
saying, Himself took our *i*........ Mt 8:17 *769*
and to be healed by him of their *i*........ Lk 5:15 *769*
hour he cured many of their *i*........ Lk 7:21 *3554*
been healed of evil spirits and *i*........ Lk 8:2 *769*
the Spirit also helpeth our *i*........ Rom 8:26 *769*
ought to bear the *i* of the weak........ Rom 15:1 *771*
the things which concern mine *i*........ 2Cor 11:30 *769*
I will not glory, but in mine *i*........ 2Cor 12:5 *769*
will I rather glory in my *i*........ 2Cor 12:9 *769*
Therefore I take pleasure in *i*........ 2Cor 12:10 *769*
stomach's sake and thine often *i*........ 1Ti 5:23 *769*
touched with the feeling of our *i*........ Heb 4:15 *769*

INFIRMITY
for her *i* shall she be unclean........ Lev 12:2 1738
And I said, This is my *i*........ Ps 77:10 2470
of a man will sustain his *i*........ Prov 18:14 4245
had a spirit of *i* eighteen years........ Lk 13:11 *769*
thou art loosed from thine *i*........ Lk 13:12 *769*
was there, which had an *i* thirty........ Jn 5:5 *769*
because of the *i* of your flesh........ Rom 6:19 *769*
Ye know how through *i* of the........ Gal 4:13 *769*
himself also is compassed with *i*........ Heb 5:2 *769*
men high priests which have *i*........ Heb 7:28 *769*

INFLAME
until night, till wine *i* them........ Is 5:11 1814

INFLAMMATION
for it is an *i* of the burning........ Lev 13:28 6867
and with a fever, and with an *i*........ Deut 28:22 1816

INFLICTED
punishment, which was *i* of many........ 2Cor 2:6

INFLUENCES
thou bind the sweet *i* of Pleiades........ Job 38:31 4575

INFOLDING
a great cloud, and a fire *i* itself........ Eze 1:4 3947

INFORM
according to all that they *i* thee........ Deut 17:10 3384

INFORMED
And he *i* me, and talked with me, and. Dan 9:22 995
And they are *i* of thee, that thou........ Acts 21:21 *2727*
they were *i* concerning thee........ Acts 21:24 *2727*
who *i* the governor against Paul........ Acts 24:1 *1718*
of the Jews *i* him against Paul........ Acts 25:2 *1718*
and the elders of the Jews *i* me........ Acts 25:15 *1718*

INGATHERING
and the feast of *i*, which is in........ Ex 23:16 614
the feast of *i* at the year's end........ Ex 34:22 614

INHABIT
the land which ye shall *i*........ Num 35:34 3427
the wicked shall not *i* the earth........ Prov 10:30 7931
the villages that Kedar doth *i*........ Is 42:11 3427
shall build houses, and *i* them........ Is 65:21 3427
shall not build, and another *i*........ Is 65:22 3427
but shall *i* the parched places in........ Jer 17:6 7931
Thou daughter that dost *i* Dibon........ Jer 48:18 3427
they that *i* those wastes of the........ Eze 33:24 3427
build the waste cities, and *i* them........ Amos 9:14 3427
also build houses, but not *i* them........ Zeph 1:13 3427

INHABITANT
The flood breaketh out from the *i*........ Job 28:4 1481
even great and fair, without *i*........ Is 5:9 3427
the cities be wasted without *i*........ Is 6:11 3427
the *i* of Samaria, that say in the........ Is 9:9 3427
Cry out and shout, thou *i* of Zion........ Is 12:6 3427
the *i* of this isle shall say in........ Is 20:6 3427
are upon thee, O *i* of the earth........ Is 24:17 3427
the *i* shall not say, I am sick........ Is 33:24 7934
his cities are burned without *i*........ Jer 2:15 3427
shall be laid waste, without an *i*........ Jer 4:7 3427
of Judah desolate, without an *i*........ Jer 9:11 3427
of the land, O *i* of the fortress........ Jer 10:17 3427
O *i* of the valley, and rock of the........ Jer 21:13 3427
O *i* of Lebanon, that makest thy........ Jer 22:23 3427
shall be desolate without an *i*........ Jer 26:9 3427
without man, and without *i*........ Jer 33:10 3427
Judah a desolation without an *i*........ Jer 34:22 3427
and a curse, without an *i*........ Jer 44:22 3427
be waste and desolate without an *i*........ Jer 46:19 3427
O *i* of Aroer, stand by the way,........ Jer 48:19 3427
O *i* of Moab, saith the LORD........ Jer 48:43 3427
Babylon a desolation without an *i*........ Jer 51:29 3427
Babylon, shall the *i* of Zion say........ Jer 51:35 3427
and an hissing, without an *i*........ Jer 51:37 3427
cut off the *i* from the plain of........ Amos 1:5 3427
I will cut off the *i* from Ashdod........ Amos 1:8 3427
thou *i* of Saphir, having thy........ Mic 1:11 3427
the *i* of Zaanan came not forth in........ Mic 1:11 3427
For the *i* of Maroth waited........ Mic 1:12 3427
O thou *i* of Lachish, bind the........ Mic 1:13 3427
heir unto thee, O *i* of Mareshah........ Mic 1:15 3427
thee, that there shall be no *i*........ Zeph 2:5 3427
is no man, that there is none *i*........ Zeph 3:6 3427

INHABITANTS
all the *i* of the cities, and that........ Gen 19:25 3427
to stink among the *i* of the land........ Gen 34:30 3427
when the *i* of the land, the........ Gen 50:11 3427
take hold on the *i* of Palestina........ Ex 15:14 3427
all the *i* of Canaan shall melt........ Ex 15:15 3427
for I will deliver the *i* of the........ Ex 23:31 3427
thou make a covenant with the *i*........ Ex 34:12 3427
a covenant with the *i* of the land........ Ex 34:15 3427
land itself vomiteth out her *i*........ Lev 18:25 3427
the land unto all the *i* thereof........ Lev 25:10 3427
land that eateth up the *i* thereof........ Num 13:32 3427
tell it to the *i* of this land........ Num 14:14 3427
because of the *i* of the land........ Num 32:17 3427
the *i* of the land from before you........ Num 33:52 3427
dispossess the *i* of the land........ Num 33:53
the *i* of the land from before you........ Num 33:55 3427
withdrawn the *i* of their city........ Deut 13:13 3427
Thou shalt surely smite the *i* of........ Deut 13:15 3427
that all the *i* of the land faint........ Josh 2:9 3427
for even all the *i* of the country........ Josh 2:24 3427
all the *i* of the land shall hear........ Josh 7:9 3427
all the *i* of Ai in the field........ Josh 8:24 3427
utterly destroyed all the *i* of Ai........ Josh 8:26 3427
when the *i* of Gibeon heard what........ Josh 9:3 3427
all the *i* of our country spake to........ Josh 9:11 3427
to destroy all the *i* of the land........ Josh 9:24 3427
how the *i* of Gibeon had made........ Josh 10:1 3427
save the Hivites the *i* of Gibeon........ Josh 11:19 3427
All the *i* of the hill country........ Josh 13:6 3427
went up thence to the *i* of Debir........ Josh 15:15 3427
the Jebusites the *i* of Jerusalem........ Josh 15:63 3427
hand unto the *i* of En-tappuah........ Josh 17:7 3427
the *i* of Dor and her towns........ Josh 17:11 3427
the *i* of En-dor and her towns, and........ Josh 17:11 3427
the *i* of Taanach and her towns, and........ Josh 17:11 3427
the *i* of Megiddo and her towns,........ Josh 17:11 3427
drive out the *i* of those cities........ Josh 17:12
he went against the *i* of Debir........ Judg 1:11 3427
drave out the *i* of the mountain........ Judg 1:19
not drive out the *i* of the valley........ Judg 1:19 3427
drive out the *i* of Beth-shean........ Judg 1:27
and her towns, nor the *i* of Dor........ Judg 1:27 3427
nor the *i* of Ibleam and her towns,........ Judg 1:27 3427
nor the *i* of Megiddo and her towns........ Judg 1:27 3427
Zebulun drive out the *i* of Kitron........ Judg 1:30 3427
nor the *i* of Nahalol........ Judg 1:30 3427
Asher drive out the *i* of Accho........ Judg 1:31 3427
nor the *i* of Zidon, nor of Ahlab,........ Judg 1:31 3427
the Canaanites, the *i* of the land........ Judg 1:32 3427
drive out the *i* of Beth-shemesh........ Judg 1:33 3427
nor the *i* of Beth-anath........ Judg 1:33 3427
the Canaanites, the *i* of the land........ Judg 1:33 3427
the *i* of Beth-shemesh and of........ Judg 1:33 3427
no league with the *i* of this land........ Judg 2:2 3427
The *i* of the villages ceased,........ Judg 5:7
the *i* of his villages in Israel........ Judg 5:11
curse ye bitterly the *i* thereof........ Judg 5:23 3427
be head over all the *i* of Gilead........ Judg 10:18 3427
our head over all the *i* of Gilead........ Judg 11:8 3427
Amorites, the *i* of that country........ Judg 11:21 3427
sword, beside the *i* of Gibeah........ Judg 20:15 3427
of the *i* of Jabesh-gilead there........ Judg 21:9 3427
smite the *i* of Jabesh-gilead with........ Judg 21:10 3427
they found among the *i* of........ Judg 21:12 3427
thee, saying, Buy it before the *i*........ Ruth 4:4 3427
to the *i* of Kirjath-jearim........ 1Sa 6:21 3427
So David saved the *i* of Keilah........ 1Sa 23:5 3427
were of old the *i* of the land........ 1Sa 27:8 3427
when the *i* of Jabesh-gilead heard........ 1Sa 31:11 3427
the Jebusites, the *i* of the land........ 2Sa 5:6 3427
who was of the *i* of Gilead........ 1Kin 17:1 8453
nobles who were the *i* in his city........ 1Kin 21:11 3427
Therefore their *i* were of small........ 2Kin 19:26 3427
this place, and upon the *i* thereof........ 2Kin 22:16 3427
place, and against the *i* thereof........ 2Kin 22:19 3427
all the *i* of Jerusalem with him,........ 2Kin 23:2 3427
of the fathers of the *i* of Geba........ 1Chr 8:6 3427
the fathers of the *i* of Aijalon........ 1Chr 8:13 3427
who drove away the *i* of Gath........ 1Chr 8:13 3427
Now the first *i* that dwelt in........ 1Chr 9:2 3427
Jebusites were, the *i* of the land........ 1Chr 11:4 3427
the *i* of Jebus said to David,........ 1Chr 11:5 3427
for he hath given the *i* of the........ 1Chr 22:18 3427
upon all the *i* of the countries........ 2Chr 15:5 3427
who didst drive out the *i* of this........ 2Chr 20:7 3427
ye *i* of Jerusalem, and thou king........ 2Chr 20:15 3427
the *i* of Jerusalem fell before........ 2Chr 20:18 3427
me, O Judah, and ye *i* of Jerusalem........ 2Chr 20:20 3427
up against the *i* of mount Seir........ 2Chr 20:23 3427
had made an end of the *i* of Seir........ 2Chr 20:23 3427
caused the *i* of Jerusalem to........ 2Chr 21:11 3427
the *i* of Jerusalem to go a........ 2Chr 21:13 3427
the *i* of Jerusalem made Ahaziah........ 2Chr 22:1 3427
the *i* of Jerusalem from the hand........ 2Chr 32:22 3427
the *i* of Jerusalem, so that the........ 2Chr 32:26 3427
the *i* of Jerusalem did him honour........ 2Chr 32:33 3427
the *i* of Jerusalem to err, and to........ 2Chr 33:9 3427
this place, and upon the *i* thereof........ 2Chr 34:24 3427
place, and against the *i* thereof........ 2Chr 34:27 3427
place, and upon the *i* of the same........ 2Chr 34:28 3427
the *i* of Jerusalem, and the........ 2Chr 34:30 3427
the *i* of Jerusalem did according........ 2Chr 34:32 3427
present, and the *i* of Jerusalem........ 2Chr 35:18 3427
accusation against the *i* of Judah........ Ezr 4:6 3427
Hanun, and the *i* of Zanoah........ Neh 3:13 3427
watches of the *i* of Jerusalem........ Neh 7:3 3427
before them the *i* of the land........ Neh 9:24 3427
the waters, and the *i* thereof........ Job 26:5 7934
let all the *i* of the world stand........ Ps 33:8 3427
upon all the *i* of the earth........ Ps 33:14 3427
give ear, all ye *i* of the world........ Ps 49:1 3427
all the *i* thereof are dissolved........ Ps 75:3 3427
Philistines with the *i* of Tyre........ Ps 83:7 3427
O *i* of Jerusalem, and men of Judah........ Is 5:3 3427
for a snare to the *i* of Jerusalem........ Is 8:14 3427
put down the *i* like a valiant man........ Is 10:13 3427
the *i* of Gebim gather themselves........ Is 10:31 3427
All ye *i* of the world, and........ Is 18:3 3427
The *i* of the land of Tema brought........ Is 21:14 3427
be a father to the *i* of Jerusalem........ Is 22:21 3427
Be still, ye *i* of the isle........ Is 23:2 3427
howl, ye *i* of the isle........ Is 23:6 3427
scattereth abroad the *i* thereof........ Is 24:1 3427
is defiled under the *i* thereof........ Is 24:5 3427
therefore the *i* of the earth are........ Is 24:6 3427
the *i* of the world will learn........ Is 26:9 3427
neither have the *i* of the world........ Is 26:18 3427
out of his place to punish the *i*........ Is 26:21 3427
Therefore their *i* were of small........ Is 37:27 3427
no more with the *i* of the world........ Is 38:11 3427
the *i* thereof are as grasshoppers........ Is 40:22 3427
the isles, and the *i* thereof........ Is 42:10 3427
let the *i* of the rock sing, let........ Is 42:11 3427
be too narrow by reason of the *i*........ Is 49:19 3427
forth upon all the *i* of the land........ Jer 1:14 3427
ye men of Judah and *i* of Jerusalem........ Jer 4:4 3427
my hand upon the *i* of the land........ Jer 6:12 3427
the bones of the *i* of Jerusalem........ Jer 8:1 3427
I will sling out the *i* of the........ Jer 10:18 3427
Judah, and to the *i* of Jerusalem........ Jer 11:2 3427
and among the *i* of Jerusalem........ Jer 11:9 3427
i of Jerusalem go, and cry unto........ Jer 11:12 3427
will fill all the *i* of this land........ Jer 13:13 3427
all the *i* of Jerusalem, with........ Jer 13:13 3427
all the *i* of Jerusalem, that........ Jer 17:20 3427
of Judah, and the *i* of Jerusalem........ Jer 17:25 3427
to the *i* of Jerusalem, saying,........ Jer 18:11 3427
kings of Judah, and *i* of Jerusalem........ Jer 19:3 3427
to the *i* thereof, and even make........ Jer 19:12 3427
I will smite the *i* of this city........ Jer 21:6 3427
the *i* thereof as Gomorrah........ Jer 23:14 3427
to all the *i* of Jerusalem, saying........ Jer 25:2 3427
land, and against the *i* thereof........ Jer 25:9 3427
sword upon all the *i* of the earth........ Jer 25:29 3427
against all the *i* of the earth........ Jer 25:30 3427
this city, and upon the *i* thereof........ Jer 26:15 3427
of Judah, and the *i* of Jerusalem........ Jer 32:32 3427
the *i* of Jerusalem, Will ye not........ Jer 35:13 3427
upon all the *i* of Jerusalem all........ Jer 35:17 3427
upon the *i* of Jerusalem, and upon........ Jer 36:31 3427
forth upon the *i* of Jerusalem........ Jer 42:18 3427
destroy the city and the *i* thereof........ Jer 46:8 3427
all the *i* of the land shall howl........ Jer 47:2 3427
back, dwell deep, O *i* of Dedan........ Jer 49:8 3427
purposed against the *i* of Teman........ Jer 49:20 3427
O ye *i* of Hazor, saith the LORD........ Jer 49:30 3427
it, and against the *i* of Pekod........ Jer 50:21 3427
and disquiet the *i* of Babylon........ Jer 50:34 3427
upon the *i* of Babylon, and upon........ Jer 50:35 3427
he spake against the *i* of Babylon........ Jer 51:12 3427
to all the *i* of Chaldea all their........ Jer 51:24 3427
and my blood upon the *i* of Chaldea........ Jer 51:35 3427
all the *i* of the world, would not........ Lam 4:12 3427
whom the *i* of Jerusalem have said........ Eze 11:15 3427

Lord GOD of the *i* of Jerusalem Eze 12:19 3427
so will I give the *i* of Jerusalem Eze 15:6 3427
strong in the sea, she and her *i* Eze 26:17 3427
The *i* of Zidon and Arvad were thy Eze 27:8 3427
All the *i* of the isles shall be Eze 27:35 3427
all the *i* of Egypt shall know Eze 29:6 3427
all the *i* of the earth are Dan 4:35 1753
and among the *i* of the earth Dan 4:35 1753
to the *i* of Jerusalem, and unto Dan 9:7 3427
with the *i* of the land, because Hos 4:1 3427
The *i* of Samaria shall fear Hos 10:5 7934
and give ear, all ye *i* of the land Joel 1:2 3427
all the *i* of the land into the Joel 1:14 3427
let all the *i* of the land tremble Joel 2:1 3427
the *i* thereof have spoken lies, Mic 6:12 3427
and the *i* thereof an hissing Mic 6:16 3427
and upon all the *i* of Jerusalem Zeph 1:4 3427
ye *i* of Maktesh, for all the Zeph 1:11 3427
Woe unto the *i* of the sea coast, Zeph 2:5 3427
people, and the *i* of many cities Zec 8:20 3427
the *i* of one city shall go to Zec 8:21 3427
no more pity the *i* of the land Zec 11:6 3427
The *i* of Jerusalem shall be my Zec 12:5 3427
the glory of the *i* of Jerusalem Zec 12:7 3427
LORD defend the *i* of Jerusalem Zec 12:8 3427
upon the *i* of Jerusalem, the Zec 12:10 3427
to the *i* of Jerusalem for sin and Zec 13:1 3427
the *i* of the earth have been made Rev 17:2 *2730*

INHABITED
Seir the Horite, who *i* the land Gen 36:20 3427
until they came to a land *i* Ex 16:35 3427
iniquities unto a land not *i* Lev 16:22 1509
the Canaanites that *i* Zephath Judg 1:17 3427
the Jebusites that *i* Jerusalem Judg 1:21 3427
eastward he *i* unto the entering 1Chr 5:9 3427
It shall never be *i*, neither Is 13:20 3427
to Jerusalem, Thou shalt be *i* Is 44:26 3427
not in vain, he formed it to be *i* Is 45:18 3427
make the desolate cities to be *i* Is 54:3 3427
make thee desolate, a land not *i* Jer 6:8 3427
in a salt land and not *i* Jer 17:6 3427
and cities which are not *i* Jer 22:6 3427
and afterward it shall be *i* Jer 46:26 7931
of the LORD it shall not be *i* Jer 50:13 3427
and it shall be no more *i* for ever Jer 50:39 3427
that are *i* shall be laid waste Eze 12:20 3427
that wast *i* of seafaring men, the Eze 26:17 3427
like the cities that are not *i* Eze 26:19 3427
to the pit, that thou be not *i* Eze 26:20 3427
neither shall it be *i* forty years Eze 29:11 3427
in all the *i* places of the Eze 34:13 4186
and the cities shall be *i*, and the Eze 36:10 3427
are become fenced, and are *i* Eze 36:35 3427
desolate places that are now *i* Eze 38:12 3427
Jerusalem shall be *i* as towns Zec 2:4 3427
prophets, when Jerusalem was *i* Zec 7:7 3427
when men *i* the south and the plain Zec 7:7 3427
Gaza, and Ashkelon shall not be *i* Zec 9:5 3427
Jerusalem shall be *i* again in her Zec 12:6 3427
i in her place, from Benjamin's Zec 14:10 3427
but Jerusalem shall be safely *i* Zec 14:11 3427

INHABITERS
to the *i* of the earth by reason Rev 8:13 *2730*
Woe to the *i* of the earth and of Rev 12:12 *2730*

INHABITEST
O thou that *i* the praises of Ps 22:3 3427

INHABITETH
and in houses which no man *i* Job 15:28 3427
high and lofty One that *i* eternity Is 57:15 7931

INHABITING
to the people *i* the wilderness Ps 74:14 6728

INHERIT
to give thee this land to *i* it Gen 15:7 3423
shall I know that I shall *i* it Gen 15:8 3423
that thou mayest *i* the land Gen 28:4 3423
thou be increased, and *i* the land Ex 23:30 5157
seed, and they shall *i* it for ever Ex 32:13 5157
Ye shall *i* their land, and I will Lev 20:24 3423
to *i* them for a possession Lev 25:46 3423
I have given to the Levites to *i* Num 18:24 5159
of their fathers they shall *i* Num 26:55 5157
For we will not *i* with them on Num 32:19 5157
tribes of your fathers ye shall *i* Num 33:54 5157
the land which ye shall *i* by lot Num 34:13 5157
for he shall cause Israel to *i* it Deut 1:38 5157
that thou mayest *i* his land Deut 2:31 3423
he shall cause them to *i* the land Deut 3:28 5157
the LORD your God giveth you to *i* Deut 12:10 5157
i the land which the LORD thy God Deut 16:20 3423
the LORD thy God giveth thee to *i* Deut 19:3 5157
which thou shalt *i* in the land Deut 19:14 5157
his sons to *i* that which he hath Deut 21:16 5157
and thou shalt cause them to *i* it Deut 31:7 5157
but one lot and one portion to *i* Josh 17:14 5159
Thou shalt not *i* in our father's Judg 11:2 5157
to make them *i* the throne of 1Sa 2:8 5157
which thou hast given us to *i* 2Chr 20:11 3423
and his seed shall *i* the earth Ps 25:13 3423
the LORD, they shall *i* the earth Ps 37:9 3423
But the meek shall *i* the earth Ps 37:11 3423
blessed of him shall *i* the earth Ps 37:22 3423
The righteous shall *i* the land Ps 37:29 3423
he shall exalt thee to *i* the land Ps 37:34 3423
also of his servants shall *i* it Ps 69:36 5157
for thou shalt *i* all nations Ps 82:8 5157
The wise shall *i* glory Prov 3:35 5157
those that love me to *i* substance Prov 8:21 5157
his own house shall *i* the wind Prov 11:29 5157
The simple *i* folly Prov 14:18 5157
to cause to *i* the desolate Is 49:8 5157
and thy seed shall *i* the Gentiles Is 54:3 3423
land, and shall *i* my holy mountain Is 57:13 3423
they shall *i* the land for ever, Is 60:21 3423
and mine elect shall *i* it, and my Is 65:9 3423
fields to them that shall *i* them Jer 8:10 3423
have caused my people Israel to *i* Jer 12:14 5157
why then doth their king *i* Gad Jer 49:1 3423
whereby ye shall *i* the land Eze 47:13 5157
And ye shall *i* it, one as well as Eze 47:14 3423
the LORD shall *i* Judah his Zec 2:12 5157
for they shall *i* the earth Mt 5:5 *2816*
and shall *i* everlasting life Mt 19:29 *2816*
i the kingdom prepared for you Mt 25:34 *2816*
I do that I may *i* eternal life Mk 10:17 *2816*
what shall I do to *i* eternal life Lk 10:25 *2816*
what shall I do to *i* eternal life Lk 18:18 *2816*
shall not *i* the kingdom of God 1Cor 6:9 *2816*
shall *i* the kingdom of God 1Cor 6:10 *2816*
blood cannot *i* the kingdom of God 1Cor 15:50 *2816*
doth corruption *i* incorruption 1Cor 15:50 *2816*
shall not *i* the kingdom of God Gal 5:21 *2816*
faith and patience *i* the promises Heb 6:12 *2816*
that ye should *i* a blessing 1Pet 3:9 *2816*
overcometh shall *i* all things Rev 21:7 *2816*

INHERITANCE
Is there yet any portion or *i* for Gen 31:14 5159
name of their brethren in their *i* Gen 48:6 5159
them in the mountain of thine *i* Ex 15:17 5159
our sin, and take us for thine *i* Ex 34:9 5157
ye shall take them as an *i* for Lev 25:46 5157
and honey, or given us *i* of fields Num 16:14 5159
shalt have no *i* in their land Num 18:20 5157
thine *i* among the children of Num 18:20 5159
all the tenth in Israel for an *i* Num 18:21 5159
children of Israel they have no *i* Num 18:23 5159
of Israel they shall have no *i* Num 18:24 5159
given you from them for your *i* Num 18:26 5159
an *i* according to the number of Num 26:53 5159
many thou shalt give the more *i* Num 26:54 5159
to few thou shalt give the less *i* Num 26:54 5159
to every one shall his *i* be given Num 26:54 5159
because there was no *i* given them Num 26:62 5159
give them a possession of an *i* Num 27:7 5159
thou shalt cause the *i* of their Num 27:7 5159
then ye shall cause his *i* to pass Num 27:8 5159
give his *i* unto his brethren Num 27:9 5159
then ye shall give his *i* unto his Num 27:10 5159
then ye shall give his *i* unto his Num 27:11 5159
have inherited every man his *i* Num 32:18 5159
because our *i* is fallen to us on Num 32:19 5159
that the possession of our *i* on Num 32:32 5159
lot for an *i* among your families Num 33:54 5157
the more ye shall give the more *i* Num 33:54 5159
fewer ye shall give the less *i* Num 33:54 5159
every man's *i* shall be in the Num 33:54
that shall fall unto you for an *i* Num 34:2 5159
fathers, have received their *i* Num 34:14
of Manasseh have received their *i* Num 34:14 5159
their *i* on this side Jordan near Num 34:15 5159
tribe, to divide the land by *i* Num 34:18 5157
LORD commanded to divide the *i* Num 34:29 5157
give unto the Levites of the *i* of Num 35:2 5159
to his *i* which he inheriteth Num 35:8 5159
an *i* by lot to the children of Num 36:2 5159
by the LORD to give the *i* of Num 36:2 5159
then shall their *i* be taken from Num 36:3 5159
taken from the *i* of our fathers Num 36:3 5159
shall be put to the *i* of the Num 36:3 5159
it be taken from the lot of our *i* Num 36:3 5159
i be put unto the *i* of Num 36:4 5159
so shall their *i* be taken away Num 36:4 5159
be taken away from the *i* of the Num 36:4 5159
So shall not the *i* of the Num 36:7 5159
shall keep himself to the *i* of Num 36:7 5159
that possesseth an *i* in any tribe Num 36:8 5159
every man the *i* of his fathers Num 36:8 5159
Neither shall the *i* remove from Num 36:9 5159
shall keep himself to his own *i* Num 36:9 5159
their *i* remained in the tribe of Num 36:12 5159
to be unto him a people of *i* Deut 4:20 5159
LORD thy God giveth thee for an *i* Deut 4:21 5159
to give thee their land for an *i* Deut 4:38 5159
destroy not thy people and thine *i* Deut 9:26 5159
they are thy people and thine *i* Deut 9:29 5159
no part nor *i* with his brethren Deut 10:9 5159
the LORD is his *i*, according as Deut 10:9 5159
yet come to the rest and to the *i* Deut 12:9 5159
as he hath no part nor *i* with you Deut 12:12 5159
he hath no part nor *i* with thee Deut 14:27 5159
he hath no part nor *i* with thee Deut 14:29 5159
thee for an *i* to possess it Deut 15:4 5159
have no part nor *i* with Israel Deut 18:1 5159
the LORD made by fire, and his *i* Deut 18:1 5159
have no *i* among their brethren Deut 18:2 5159
the LORD is their *i*, as he hath Deut 18:2 5159
LORD thy God giveth thee for an *i* Deut 19:10 5159
of old time have set in thine *i* Deut 19:14 5159
thy God doth give thee for an *i* Deut 20:16 5159
LORD thy God giveth thee for an *i* Deut 21:23 5159
LORD thy God giveth thee for an *i* Deut 24:4 5159
thee for an *i* to possess it Deut 25:19 5159
LORD thy God giveth thee for an *i* Deut 26:1 5159
gave it for an *i* unto the Deut 29:8 5159
divided to the nations their *i* Deut 32:8 5157
Jacob is the lot of his *i* Deut 32:9 5159
even the *i* of the congregation of Deut 33:4 4181
thou divide for an *i* the land Josh 1:6 5157
Joshua gave it for an *i* unto Josh 11:23 5159
lot unto the Israelites for an *i* Josh 13:6 5159
for an *i* unto the nine tribes Josh 13:7 5159
the Gadites have received their *i* Josh 13:8 5159
the tribe of Levi he gave none *i* Josh 13:14 5159
Israel made by fire are their *i* Josh 13:14 5159
i according to their families Josh 13:15
This was the *i* of the children of Josh 13:23 5159
Moses gave *i* unto the tribe of Josh 13:24
This is the *i* of the children of Josh 13:28 5159
Moses gave *i* unto the half tribe Josh 13:29
for *i* in the plains of Moab Josh 13:32 5157
of Levi Moses gave not any *i* Josh 13:33 5159
LORD God of Israel was their *i* Josh 13:33 5159
Israel, distributed for *i* to them Josh 14:1 5157
By lot was their *i*, as the LORD Josh 14:2 5159
had given the *i* of two tribes Josh 14:3 5159
Levites he gave none *i* among them Josh 14:3 5159
have trodden shall be thine *i* Josh 14:9 5159
son of Jephunneh Hebron for an *i* Josh 14:13 5159
Hebron therefore became the *i* of Josh 14:14 5159
This is the *i* of the tribe of the Josh 15:20 5159
Manasseh and Ephraim, took their *i* Josh 16:4 5157
of their *i* on the east side was Josh 16:5 5159
This is the *i* of the tribe of the Josh 16:8 5159
of Ephraim were among the *i* of Josh 16:9 5159
give us an *i* among our brethren Josh 17:4 5159
an *i* among the brethren of their Josh 17:4 5159
Manasseh had an *i* among his sons Josh 17:6 5157
had not yet received their *i* Josh 18:2 5159
it according to the *i* of them Josh 18:4 5159
priesthood of the LORD is their *i* Josh 18:7 5159
have received their *i* beyond Josh 18:7 5159
This was the *i* of the children of Josh 18:20 5159
This is the *i* of the children of Josh 18:28 5159
and their *i* was within the Josh 19:1 5159
the *i* of the children of Judah Josh 19:1 5159
And they had in their *i* Beer-sheba Josh 19:2 5159
This is the *i* of the tribe of the Josh 19:8 5159
the *i* of the children of Simeon Josh 19:9 5159
i within the *i* of them Josh 19:9 5159
border of their *i* was unto Sarid Josh 19:10 5159
This is the *i* of the children of Josh 19:16 5159
This is the *i* of the tribe of the Josh 19:23 5159
This is the *i* of the tribe of the Josh 19:31 5159
This is the *i* of the tribe of the Josh 19:39 5159
And the coast of their *i* was Zorah Josh 19:41 5159
This is the *i* of the tribe of the Josh 19:48 5159
the land for *i* by their coasts Josh 19:49 5157
i to Joshua the son of Nun among Josh 19:49 5159
divided for an *i* by lot in Shiloh Josh 19:51 5157
unto the Levites out of their *i* Josh 21:3 5159
to be an *i* for your tribes, from Josh 23:4 5159
depart, every man unto his *i* Josh 24:28 5159
border of his *i* in Timnath-serah Josh 24:30 5159
it became the *i* of the children Josh 24:32 5159
unto his *i* to possess the land Judg 2:6 5159
border of his *i* in Timnath-heres Judg 2:9 5159
sought them an *i* to dwell in Judg 18:1 5159
for unto that day all their *i* had Judg 18:1 5159
the country of the *i* of Israel Judg 20:6 5159
There must be an *i* for them that Judg 21:17 3425
went and returned unto their *i* Judg 21:23 5159
from thence every man to his *i* Judg 21:24 5159
the name of the dead upon his *i* Ruth 4:5 5159
for myself, lest I mar mine own *i* Ruth 4:6 5159
the name of the dead upon his *i* Ruth 4:10 5159
thee to be captain over his *i* 1Sa 10:1 5159
from abiding in the *i* of the LORD 1Sa 26:19 5159
son together out of the *i* of God 2Sa 14:16 5159
neither have we *i* in the son of 2Sa 20:1 5159
thou swallow up the *i* of the LORD 2Sa 20:19 5159
ye may bless the *i* of the LORD 2Sa 21:3 5159
hast given to thy people for an *i* 1Kin 8:36 5159
they be thy people, and thine *i* 1Kin 8:51 5159
of the earth, to be thine *i* 1Kin 8:53 5159
neither have we *i* in the son of 1Kin 12:16 5159
that I should give the *i* of my 1Kin 21:3 5159
not give thee the *i* of my fathers 1Kin 21:4 5159
forsake the remnant of mine *i* 2Kin 21:14 5159
land of Canaan, the lot of your *i* 1Chr 16:18 5159
leave it for an *i* for your 1Chr 28:8 5157
given unto thy people for an *i* 2Chr 6:27 5159
we have none *i* in the son of 2Chr 10:16 5159
leave it for an *i* to your Ezr 9:12 3423
of Judah, every one in his *i* Neh 11:20 5159
what *i* of the Almighty from on Job 31:2 5159
gave them *i* among their brethren Job 42:15 5159
give thee the heathen for thine *i* Ps 2:8 5159
The LORD is the portion of mine *i* Ps 16:5 2506
Save thy people, and bless thine *i* Ps 28:9 5159
whom he hath chosen for his own *i* Ps 33:12 5159
their *i* shall be for ever Ps 37:18 5159
He shall choose our *i* for us Ps 47:4 5159
thou didst confirm thine *i* Ps 68:9 5159
the rod of thine *i*, which thou Ps 74:2 5159
and divided them an *i* by line Ps 78:55 5159
and was wroth with his *i* Ps 78:62 5159
Jacob his people, and Israel his *i* Ps 78:71 5159
the heathen are come into thine *i* Ps 79:1 5159
neither will he forsake his *i* Ps 94:14 5159
land of Canaan, the lot of your *i* Ps 105:11 5159
that I may glory with thine *i* Ps 106:5 5159
that he abhorred his own *i* Ps 106:40 5159
A good man leaveth an *i* to his Prov 13:22 5157
part of the *i* among the brethren Prov 17:2 5159
and riches are the *i* of fathers Prov 19:14 5159
An *i* may be gotten hastily at the Prov 20:21 5159
Wisdom is good with an *i* Eccl 7:11 5159
of my hands, and Israel mine *i* Is 19:25 5159
my people, I have polluted mine *i* Is 47:6 5159
sake, the tribes of thine *i* Is 63:17 5159
given for an *i* unto your fathers Jer 3:18 5157
and Israel is the rod of his *i* Jer 10:16 5159
that touch the *i* which I have Jer 12:14 5159
they have filled mine *i* with the Jer 16:18 5159
for the right of *i* is thine Jer 32:8 3425
and Israel is the rod of his *i* Jer 51:19 5159
Our *i* is turned to strangers, our Lam 5:2 5159
thou shalt take thine *i* in Eze 22:16 2490
the land is given us for *i* Eze 33:24 4181

at the i of the house of Israel	Eze 35:15	5159
thee, and thou shalt be their i	Eze 36:12	5159
And it shall be unto them for an i	Eze 44:28	5159
I am their i	Eze 44:28	5159
divide by lot the land for i	Eze 45:1	5159
the i thereof shall be his sons'	Eze 46:16	5159
it shall be their possession by i	Eze 46:16	5159
of his i to one of his servants	Eze 46:17	5159
but his i shall be his sons' for	Eze 46:17	5159
of the people's i by oppression	Eze 46:18	5159
sons i out of his own possession	Eze 46:18	5157
land shall fall unto you for i	Eze 47:14	5159
it by lot for an i unto you	Eze 47:22	5159
they shall have i with you among	Eze 47:22	5159
there shall ye give him his i	Eze 47:23	5159
unto the tribes of Israel for i	Eze 48:29	5159
him, and let us seize on his i	Mt 21:38	2817
kill him, and the i shall be ours	Mk 12:7	2817
that he divide the i with me	Lk 12:13	2817
kill him, that the i may be ours	Lk 20:14	2817
And he gave him none i in it	Acts 7:5	2817
to give you an i among all them	Acts 20:32	2817
i among them which are sanctified	Acts 26:18	2819
For if the i be of the law, it is	Gal 3:18	2817
whom also we have obtained an i	Eph 1:11	2820
our i until the redemption of the	Eph 1:14	2817
the glory of his i in the saints	Eph 1:18	2817
hath any i in the kingdom of	Eph 5:5	2817
of the i of the saints in light	Col 1:12	2819
shall receive the reward of the i	Col 3:24	2817
as he hath by i obtained a more	Heb 1:4	2820
receive the promise of eternal i	Heb 9:15	2817
he should after receive for an i	Heb 11:8	2817
To an i incorruptible, and	1Pet 1:4	2817

INHERITANCES

These are the i, which Eleazar	Josh 19:51	5159

INHERITED

have i every man his inheritance	Num 32:18	5157
of Israel i in the land of Canaan	Josh 14:1	5157
they i the labour of the people	Ps 105:44	3423
Surely our fathers have i lies	Jer 16:19	5157
Abraham was one, and he i the land	Eze 33:24	3423
when he would have i the blessing	Heb 12:17	2816

INHERITETH

to his inheritance which he i	Num 35:8	5157

INHERITOR

out of Judah an i of my mountains	Is 65:9	3423

INIQUITIES

confess over him all the i of the	Lev 16:21	5771
their i unto a land not inhabited	Lev 16:22	5771
also in the i of their fathers	Lev 26:39	5771
for a year, shall ye bear your i	Num 14:34	5771
for our i are increased over our	Ezr 9:6	5771
and for our i have we, our kings,	Ezr 9:7	5771
us less than our i deserve	Ezr 9:13	5771
sins, and the i of their fathers	Neh 9:2	5771
How many are mine i and sins	Job 13:23	5771
me to possess the i of my youth	Job 13:26	5771
and thine i infinite	Job 22:5	5771
For mine i are gone over mine	Ps 38:4	5771
mine i have taken hold upon me,	Ps 40:12	5771
my sins, and blot out all mine i	Ps 51:9	5771
They search out i	Ps 64:6	5766
I prevail against me	Ps 65:3	
remember not against us former i	Ps 79:8	5771
Thou hast set our i before thee	Ps 90:8	5771
Who forgiveth all thine i	Ps 103:3	5771
rewarded us according to our i	Ps 103:10	5771
and because of their i, are	Ps 107:17	5771
If thou, LORD, shouldest mark i	Ps 130:3	5771
redeem Israel from all his i	Ps 130:8	5771
His own i shall take the wicked	Prov 5:22	5771
thou hast wearied me with thine i	Is 43:24	5771
Behold, for your i have ye sold	Is 50:1	5771
he was bruised for our i	Is 53:5	5771
for he shall bear their i	Is 53:11	5771
But your i have separated between	Is 59:2	5771
and as for our i, we know them	Is 59:12	5771
and our i, like the wind, have	Is 64:6	5771
consumed us, because of our i	Is 64:7	5771
Your i, and the i of your	Is 65:7	5771
Your i have turned away these	Jer 5:25	5771
to the i of their forefathers	Jer 11:10	5771
though our i testify against us,	Jer 14:7	5771
and I will pardon all their i	Jer 33:8	5771
the i of her priests, that have	Lam 4:13	5771
and we have borne their i	Lam 5:7	5771
but ye shall pine away for your i	Eze 24:23	5771
by the multitude of thine i	Eze 28:18	5771
but their i shall be upon their	Eze 32:27	5771
in your own sight for your i	Eze 36:31	5771
i I will also cause you to dwell	Eze 36:33	5771
they may be ashamed of their i	Eze 43:10	5771
thine i by shewing mercy to the	Dan 4:27	5758
that we might turn from our i	Dan 9:13	5771
for the i of our fathers,	Dan 9:16	5771
I will punish you for all your i	Amos 3:2	5771
he will subdue our i	Mic 7:19	5771
away every one of you from his i	Acts 3:26	4189
are they whose i are forgiven	Rom 4:7	458
their i will I remember no more	Heb 8:12	458
i will I remember no more	Heb 10:17	458
and God hath remembered her i	Rev 18:5	92

INIQUITY

for the i of the Amorites is not	Gen 15:16	5771
be consumed in the i of the city	Gen 19:15	5771
found out the i of thy servants	Gen 44:16	5771
visiting the i of the fathers	Ex 20:5	5771
may bear the i of the holy things	Ex 28:38	5771
that they bear not i, and die	Ex 28:43	5771
mercy for thousands, forgiving i	Ex 34:7	5771
visiting the i of the fathers	Ex 34:7	5771
and pardon our i and our sin, and	Ex 34:9	5771
it, then he shall bear his i	Lev 5:1	5771
is he guilty, and shall bear his i	Lev 5:17	5771
eateth of it shall bear his i	Lev 7:18	5771
to bear the i of the congregation	Lev 10:17	5771
then he shall bear his i	Lev 17:16	5771
I do visit the i thereof upon it	Lev 18:25	5771
that eateth it shall bear his i	Lev 19:8	5771
he shall bear his i	Lev 20:17	5771
they shall bear their i	Lev 20:19	5771
them to bear the i of trespass	Lev 22:16	5771
in their i in your enemies' lands	Lev 26:39	5771
If they shall confess their i	Lev 26:40	5771
the i of their fathers, with	Lev 26:40	5771
of the punishment of their i	Lev 26:41	5771
of the punishment of their i	Lev 26:43	5771
bringing i to remembrance	Num 5:15	5771
shall the man be guiltless from i	Num 5:31	5771
and this woman shall bear her i	Num 5:31	5771
and of great mercy, forgiving i	Num 14:18	5771
visiting the i of the fathers	Num 14:18	5771
the i of this people according	Num 14:19	5771
his i shall be upon him	Num 15:31	5771
shall bear the i of the sanctuary	Num 18:1	5771
bear the i of your priesthood	Num 18:1	5771
and they shall bear their i	Num 18:23	5771
He hath not beheld i in Jacob	Num 23:21	205
then he shall bear her i	Num 30:15	5771
visiting the i of the fathers	Deut 5:9	5771
rise up against a man for any i	Deut 19:15	5771
a God of truth and without i	Deut 32:4	5766
Is the i of Peor too little for	Josh 22:17	5771
man perished not alone in his i	Josh 22:20	5771
ever for the i which he knoweth	1Sa 3:13	5771
that the i of Eli's house shall	1Sa 3:14	5771
and stubbornness is as i and	1Sa 15:23	205
what is mine i?	1Sa 20:1	5771
if there be in me i, slay me	1Sa 20:8	5771
my lord, upon me let this i be	1Sa 25:24	5771
If he commit i, I will chasten	2Sa 7:14	5753
the i be on me, and on my father's	2Sa 14:9	5771
and if there be any i in me	2Sa 14:32	5771
Let not my lord impute i unto me	2Sa 19:19	5771
and have kept myself from mine i	2Sa 22:24	5771
take away the i of thy servant	2Sa 24:10	5771
do away the i of thy servant	1Chr 21:8	5771
for there is no i with the LORD	2Chr 19:7	5766
And cover not their i, and let not	Neh 4:5	5771
as I have seen, they that plow i	Job 4:8	205
hope, and i stoppeth her mouth	Job 5:16	5766
I pray you, let it not be i	Job 6:29	5766
Is there i in my tongue	Job 6:30	5766
and take away mine i	Job 7:21	5771
That thou enquirest after mine i	Job 10:6	5771
wilt not acquit me from mine i	Job 10:14	5771
thee less than thine i deserveth	Job 11:6	5771
If i be in thine hand, put it far	Job 11:14	205
a bag, and thou sewest up mine i	Job 14:17	5771
For thy mouth uttereth thine i	Job 15:5	5771
man, which drinketh i like water	Job 15:16	5766
The heaven shall reveal his i	Job 20:27	5771
layeth up his i for his children	Job 21:19	205
thou shalt put away i far from	Job 22:23	5766
punishment to the workers of i	Job 31:3	205
it is an i to be punished by the	Job 31:11	5771
This also were an i to be	Job 31:28	5771
by hiding mine i in my bosom	Job 31:33	5771
neither is there i in me	Job 33:9	5771
in company with the workers of i	Job 34:8	205
Almighty, that he should commit i	Job 34:10	5766
workers of i may hide themselves	Job 34:22	205
if I have done i, I will do no	Job 34:32	5766
that they return from i	Job 36:10	205
Take heed, regard not i	Job 36:21	205
who can say, Thou hast wrought i	Job 36:23	5766
thou hatest all workers of i	Ps 5:5	205
from me, all ye workers of i	Ps 6:8	205
if there be i in my hands	Ps 7:3	5766
Behold, he travaileth with i	Ps 7:14	205
all the workers of i no knowledge	Ps 14:4	205
him, and I kept myself from mine i	Ps 18:23	5771
sake, O LORD, pardon mine i	Ps 25:11	5771
wicked, and with the workers of i	Ps 28:3	205
faileth because of mine i	Ps 31:10	5771
unto whom the LORD imputeth not i	Ps 32:2	5771
thee, and mine i have I not hid	Ps 32:5	5771
and thou forgavest the i of my sin	Ps 32:5	5771
until his i be found to be	Ps 36:2	5771
The words of his mouth are i	Ps 36:3	205
There are the workers of i fallen	Ps 36:12	205
envious against the workers of i	Ps 37:1	5766
For I will declare mine i	Ps 38:18	5771
rebukes dost correct man for i	Ps 39:11	5771
his heart gathereth i to itself	Ps 41:6	205
when the i of my heels shall	Ps 49:5	5771
Wash me throughly from mine i	Ps 51:2	5771
Behold, I was shapen in i	Ps 51:5	5771
they, and have done abominable i	Ps 53:1	5766
the workers of i no knowledge	Ps 53:4	205
for they cast i upon me, and in	Ps 55:3	205
Shall they escape by i	Ps 56:7	205
Deliver me from the workers of i	Ps 59:2	205
insurrection of the workers of i	Ps 64:2	205
If I regard i in my heart	Ps 66:18	205
Add i unto their i	Ps 69:27	5771
of compassion, forgave their i	Ps 78:38	5771
hast forgiven the i of thy people	Ps 85:2	5771
the rod, and their i with stripes	Ps 89:32	5771
all the workers of i do flourish	Ps 92:7	205
workers of i shall be scattered	Ps 92:9	205
the workers of i boast themselves	Ps 94:4	205
for me against the workers of i	Ps 94:16	205
Shall the throne of i have	Ps 94:20	1942
shall bring upon them their own i	Ps 94:23	205
our fathers, we have committed i	Ps 106:6	5753
and were brought low for their i	Ps 106:43	5771
all i shall stop her mouth	Ps 107:42	5766
Let the i of his fathers be	Ps 109:14	5771
They also do no i	Ps 119:3	5766
let not any i have dominion over	Ps 119:133	205
put forth their hands unto i	Ps 125:3	5766
them forth with the workers of i	Ps 125:5	205
wicked works with men that work i	Ps 141:4	205
and the gins of the workers of i	Ps 141:9	205
shall be to the workers of i	Prov 10:29	205
By mercy and truth i is purged	Prov 16:6	5771
mouth of the wicked devoureth i	Prov 19:28	205
shall be to the workers of i	Prov 21:15	205
He that soweth i shall reap	Prov 22:8	5766
righteousness, that i was there	Eccl 3:16	7562
nation, a people laden with i	Is 1:4	5771
it is i, even the solemn meeting	Is 1:13	205
that draw i with cords of vanity	Is 5:18	5771
thine i is taken away, and thy sin	Is 6:7	5771
evil, and the wicked for their i	Is 13:11	5771
for the i of their fathers	Is 14:21	5771
Surely this i shall not be purged	Is 22:14	5771
of the earth for their i	Is 26:21	5771
shall the i of Jacob be purged	Is 27:9	5771
all that watch for i are cut off	Is 29:20	205
Therefore this i shall be to you	Is 30:13	5771
the help of them that work i	Is 31:2	205
villany, and his heart will work i	Is 32:6	205
therein shall be forgiven their i	Is 33:24	5771
that her i is pardoned	Is 40:2	5771
hath laid on him the i of us all	Is 53:6	5771
For the i of his covetousness was	Is 57:17	5771
blood, and your fingers with i	Is 59:3	5771
mischief, and bring forth i	Is 59:4	205
their works are works of i	Is 59:6	205
their thoughts are thoughts of i	Is 59:7	205
LORD, neither remember i for ever	Is 64:9	5771
What i have your fathers found in	Jer 2:5	5766
yet thine i is marked before me,	Jer 2:22	5771
Only acknowledge thine i, that	Jer 3:13	5771
and weary themselves to commit i	Jer 9:5	5753
thine i are thy skirts discovered	Jer 13:22	5771
he will now remember their i	Jer 14:10	5771
and the i of our fathers	Jer 14:20	5771
or what is our i	Jer 16:10	5771
neither is their i hid from mine	Jer 16:17	5771
first I will recompense their i	Jer 16:18	5771
forgive not their i, neither blot	Jer 18:23	5771
saith the LORD, for their i	Jer 25:12	5771
one, for the multitude of thine i	Jer 30:14	5771
for the multitude of thine i	Jer 30:15	5771
every one shall die for his own i	Jer 31:30	5771
for I will forgive their i	Jer 31:34	5771
recompensest the i of the fathers	Jer 32:18	5771
cleanse them from all their i	Jer 33:8	5771
that I may forgive their i	Jer 36:3	5771
seed and his servants for their i	Jer 36:31	5771
the i of Israel shall be sought	Jer 50:20	5771
be not cut off in her i	Jer 51:6	5771
they have not discovered thine i	Lam 2:14	5771
For the punishment of the i of	Lam 4:6	5771
of thine i is accomplished	Lam 4:22	5771
he will visit thine i, O daughter	Lam 4:22	5771
wicked man shall die in his i	Eze 3:18	5771
wicked way, he shall die in his i	Eze 3:19	5771
his righteousness, and commit i	Eze 3:20	5766
lay the i of the house of Israel	Eze 4:4	5771
upon it thou shalt bear their i	Eze 4:4	5771
upon thee the years of their i	Eze 4:5	5771
bear the i of the house of Israel	Eze 4:5	5771
thou shalt bear the i of the	Eze 4:6	5771
and consume away for their i	Eze 4:17	5771
himself in the i of his life	Eze 7:13	5771
mourning, every one for his i	Eze 7:16	5771
is the stumblingblock of their i	Eze 7:19	5771
The i of the house of Israel and	Eze 9:9	5771
of their i before their face	Eze 14:3	5771
of his i before his face, and	Eze 14:4	5771
of his i before his face, and	Eze 14:7	5771
bear the punishment of their i	Eze 14:10	5771
this was the i of thy sister	Eze 16:49	5771
hath withdrawn his hand from i	Eze 18:8	5766
not die for the i of his father	Eze 18:17	5771
lo, even he shall die in his i	Eze 18:18	5771
the son bear the i of the father	Eze 18:19	5771
not bear the i of the father	Eze 18:20	5771
the father bear the i of the son	Eze 18:20	5771
righteousness, and committeth i	Eze 18:24	5766
righteousness, and committeth i	Eze 18:26	5766
for his i that he hath done shall	Eze 18:26	5766
so i shall not be your ruin	Eze 18:30	5771
he will call to remembrance the i	Eze 21:23	5771
have made your i to be remembered	Eze 21:24	5771
when i shall have an end,	Eze 21:25	5771
when their i shall have an end	Eze 21:29	5771
created, till i was found in thee	Eze 28:15	5766
by the i of thy traffick	Eze 28:18	5766
bringeth their i to remembrance	Eze 29:16	5771
them, he is taken away in his i	Eze 33:6	5771
wicked man shall die in his i	Eze 33:8	5771
his way, he shall die in his i	Eze 33:9	
own righteousness, and commit i	Eze 33:13	5766
but for his i that he hath	Eze 33:13	5766
of life, without committing i	Eze 33:15	5766
righteousness, and committeth i	Eze 33:18	5766
the time that their i had an end	Eze 35:5	5771
went into captivity for their i	Eze 39:23	5771
they shall even bear their i	Eze 44:10	5771
house of Israel to fall into i	Eze 44:12	5771
GOD, and they shall bear their i	Eze 44:12	5771
have sinned, and have committed i	Dan 9:5	5753
and to make reconciliation for i	Dan 9:24	5771

I

they set their heart on their *i* Hos 4:8 5771
Israel and Ephraim fall in their *i* Hos 5:5 5771
is a city of them that work *i* Hos 6:8 205
then the *i* of Ephraim was Hos 7:1 5771
now will he remember their *i* Hos 8:13 5771
mad, for the multitude of thine *i* Hos 9:7 5771
he will remember their *i*, he will Hos 9:9 5771
of *i* did not overtake them Hos 10:9 5932
wickedness, ye have reaped *i* Hos 10:13 5766
find none *i* in me that were sin Hos 12:8 5771
Is there *i* in Gilead Hos 12:11 205
The *i* of Ephraim is bound up Hos 13:12 5771
for thou hast fallen by thine *i* Hos 14:1 5771
say unto him, Take away all *i* Hos 14:2 5771
Woe to them that devise *i* Mic 2:1 205
with blood, and Jerusalem with *i* Mic 3:10 5766
like unto thee, that pardoneth *i* Mic 7:18 5771
Why dost thou shew me *i*, and cause Hab 1:3 205
evil, and canst not look on *i* Hab 1:13 5999
blood, and stablisheth a city by *i* Hab 2:12 5766
he will not do *i* Zeph 3:5 5766
remnant of Israel shall not do *i* Zeph 3:13 5766
caused thine *i* to pass from thee Zec 3:4 5771
I will remove the *i* of that land Zec 3:9 5771
i was not found in his lips Mal 2:6 5766
and did turn many away from *i* Mal 2:6 5771
depart from me, ye that work *i* Mt 7:23 *458*
that offend, and them which do *i* Mt 13:41 *458*
ye are full of hypocrisy and *i* Mt 23:28 *458*
because *i* shall abound, the love Mt 24:12 *458*
from me, all ye workers of *i* Lk 13:27 *93*
a field with the reward of *i* Acts 1:18 *93*
bitterness, and in the bond of *i* Acts 8:23 *93*
uncleanness and to *i* unto *i* Rom 6:19 *458*
Rejoiceth not in *i*, but rejoiceth 1Cor 13:6 *93*
mystery of *i* doth already work 2Th 2:7 *458*
the name of Christ depart from *i* 2Ti 2:19 *93*
he might redeem us from all *i* Titus 2:14 *458*
loved righteousness, and hated *i* Heb 1:9 *458*
tongue is a fire, a world of *i* Jas 3:6 *93*
But was rebuked for his *i* 2Pet 2:16 *3892*

INJURED
ye have not *i* me at all Gal 4:12 *91*

INJURIOUS
blasphemer, and a persecutor, and *i* 1Ti 1:13 *5197*

INJUSTICE
Not for any *i* in mine hands Job 16:17 2555

INK
I wrote them with *i* in the book Jer 36:18 1773
by us, written not with *i* 2Cor 3:3 *3188*
I would not write with paper and *i* 2Jn 12 *3188*
to write, but I will not with *i* 3Jn 13 *3188*

INKHORN
with a writer's *i* by his side Eze 9:2 7083
had the writer's *i* by his side Eze 9:3 7083
which had the *i* by his side Eze 9:11 7083

INN
give his ass provender in the *i* Gen 42:27 4411
to pass, when we came to the *i* Gen 43:21 4411
came to pass by the way in the *i* Ex 4:24 4411
was no room for them in the *i* Lk 2:7 *2646*
own beast, and brought him to an *i* Lk 10:34 *3829*

INNER
the cherubims within the *i* house 1Kin 6:27 6442
he built the *i* court with three 1Kin 6:36 6442
both for the *i* court of the house 1Kin 7:12 6442
both for the doors of the *i* house 1Kin 7:50 6442
into the city, into an *i* chamber 1Kin 20:30 2315
into an *i* chamber to hide thyself 1Kin 22:25 2315
and carry him to an *i* chamber 2Kin 9:2 2315
of the *i* parlours thereof, and of 1Chr 28:11 6442
the *i* doors thereof for the most 2Chr 4:22 6442
into an *i* chamber to hide thyself 2Chr 18:24 2315
the priests went into the *i* part 2Chr 29:16 6441
unto the king into the *i* court Est 4:11 6442
stood in the *i* court of the Est 5:1 6442
to the door of the *i* gate Eze 8:3 6442
he brought me into the *i* court of Eze 8:16 6442
and the cloud filled the *i* court Eze 10:3 6442
of the *i* gate were fifty cubits Eze 40:15 6442
forefront of the *i* court without Eze 40:19 6442
the gate of the *i* court was over Eze 40:23 6442
in the *i* court toward the south Eze 40:27 6442
he brought me to the *i* court by Eze 40:28 6442
into the *i* court toward the east Eze 40:32 6442
without the *i* gate were the Eze 40:44 6442
of the singers in the *i* court Eze 40:44 6442
hundred cubits, with the *i* temple Eze 41:15 6442
the door, even unto the *i* house Eze 41:17 6442
cubits which were for the *i* court Eze 42:3 6442
an end of measuring the *i* house Eze 42:15 6442
and brought me into the *i* court Eze 43:5 6442
in at the gates of the *i* court Eze 44:17 6442
in the gates of the *i* court Eze 44:17 6442
when they enter into the *i* court Eze 44:21 6442
the sanctuary, unto the *i* court Eze 44:27 6442
posts of the gate of the *i* court Eze 45:19 6442
The gate of the *i* court that Eze 46:1 6442
thrust them into the *i* prison Acts 16:24 *2082*
might by his Spirit in the *i* man Eph 3:16 *2080*

INNERMOST
into the *i* parts of the belly Prov 18:8 2315
into the *i* parts of the belly Prov 26:22 2315

INNOCENCY
i of my hands have I done this Gen 20:5 5356
I will wash mine hands in *i* Ps 26:6 5356
in vain, and washed my hands in *i* Ps 73:13 5356
as before him *i* was found in me Dan 6:22 2136
will it be ere they attain to *i* Hos 8:5 5356

INNOCENT
and the *i* and righteous slay thou Ex 23:7 5355
That *i* blood be not shed in thy Deut 19:10 5355
the guilt of *i* blood from Israel Deut 19:13 5355
lay not *i* blood unto thy people Deut 21:8 5355
guilt of *i* blood from among you Deut 21:9 5355
taketh reward to slay an *i* person Deut 27:25 5355
wilt thou sin against *i* blood 1Sa 19:5 5355
thou mayest take away the *i* blood 1Kin 2:31 2600
Manasseh shed *i* blood very much 2Kin 21:16 5355
also for the *i* blood that he shed 2Kin 24:4 5355
he filled Jerusalem with *i* blood 2Kin 24:4 5355
thee, who ever perished, being *i* Job 4:7 5355
will laugh at the trial of the *i* Job 9:23 5355
know that thou wilt not hold me *i* Job 9:28 5352
the *i* shall stir up himself Job 17:8 5355
the *i* laugh them to scorn Job 22:19 5355
shall deliver the island of the *i* Job 22:30 5355
the *i* shall divide the silver Job 27:17 5355
without transgression, I am *i* Job 33:9 2643
places doth he murder the *i* Ps 10:8 5355
nor taketh reward against the *i* Ps 15:5 5355
I shall be *i* from the great Ps 19:13 5352
righteous, and condemn the *i* blood Ps 94:21 5355
shed *i* blood, even the blood of Ps 106:38 5355
privily for the *i* without cause Prov 1:11 5355
and hands that shed *i* blood Prov 6:17 5355
toucheth her shall not be *i* Prov 6:29 5352
haste to be rich shall not be *i* Prov 28:20 5352
they make haste to shed *i* blood Is 59:7 5355
Yet thou sayest, Because I am *i* Jer 2:35 5352
shed not *i* blood in this place, Jer 7:6 5355
neither shed *i* blood in this Jer 22:3 5355
and for to shed *i* blood, and for Jer 22:17 5355
bring *i* blood upon yourselves Jer 26:15 5355
have shed *i* blood in their land Joel 3:19 5355
life, and lay not upon us *i* blood Jonah 1:14 5355
that I have betrayed the *i* blood Mt 27:4 *121*
I am *i* of the blood of this just Mt 27:24 *121*

INNOCENTS
blood of the souls of the poor *i* Jer 2:34 5355
this place with the blood of *i* Jer 19:4 5355

INNUMERABLE
him, as there are *i* before him Job 21:33
For *i* evils have compassed me Ps 40:12
wherein are things creeping *i* Ps 104:25
than the grasshoppers, and are *i* Jer 46:23
together an *i* multitude of people Lk 12:1 *3461*
sand which is by the sea shore *i* Heb 11:12 *382*
to an *i* company of angels, Heb 12:22 *3461*

INORDINATE
corrupt in her *i* love than she Eze 23:11 5691
i affection, evil concupiscence, Col 3:5 *3806*

INQUISITION
the judges shall make diligent *i* Deut 19:18 1875
when *i* was made of the matter, it Est 2:23 1245
When he maketh *i* for blood Ps 9:12 1875

INSCRIPTION
I found an altar with this *i* Acts 17:23 *1924*

INSIDE
covered them on the *i* with wood 1Kin 6:15 1004

INSOMUCH
i that he abhorred his own Ps 106:40
i that he regardeth not the Mal 2:13
i that the ship was covered with Mt 8:24 *5620*
i that the blind and dumb both Mt 12:22 *5620*
i that they were astonished, and Mt 13:54 *5620*
I that the multitude wondered, Mt 15:31 *5620*
i that, if it were possible, they Mt 24:24 *5620*
i that the governor marvelled Mt 27:14 *5620*
i that they questioned among Mk 1:27 *5620*
i that Jesus could no more openly Mk 1:45 *5620*
i that there was no room to Mk 2:2 *5620*
i that they were all amazed, and Mk 2:12 *5620*
i that they pressed upon him for Mk 3:10 *5620*
i that many said, He is dead Mk 9:26 *5620*
i that they trode one upon Lk 12:1 *5620*
i as that field is called in Acts 1:19 *5620*
I that they brought forth the Acts 5:15 *5620*
i that we despaired even of life 2Cor 1:8 *5620*
I that we desired Titus, that as 2Cor 8:6 *1519*
i that Barnabas also was carried Gal 2:13 *5620*

INSPIRATION
the *i* of the Almighty giveth them Job 32:8 5397
scripture is given by *i* of God 2Ti 3:16 *2315*

INSTANT
yea, it shall be at an *i* suddenly Is 29:5 6621
breaking cometh suddenly at an *i* Is 30:13 6621
At what *i* I shall speak Jer 18:7 7281
And at what *i* I shall speak Jer 18:9 7281
she coming in that *i* gave thanks Lk 2:38 *5610*
they were *i* with loud voices, Lk 23:23 *1945*
continuing *i* in prayer Rom 12:12 *4342*
be *i* in season, out of season 2Ti 4:2 *2186*

INSTANTLY
to Jesus, they besought him *i* Lk 7:4 *4705*
i serving God day and night, hope Acts 26:7

INSTEAD
and closed up the flesh *i* thereof Gen 2:21 8478
me another seed *i* of Abel Gen 4:25 8478
let thy servant abide *i* of the Gen 44:33 8478
he shall be to thee *i* of a mouth Ex 4:16
and thou shalt be to him *i* of God Ex 4:16
to gather stubble *i* of straw Ex 5:12
i of all the firstborn that Num 3:12 8478
i of all the firstborn among the Num 3:41 8478
the cattle of the Levites *i* of Num 3:41 8478
Take the Levites *i* of all the Num 3:45 8478
of the Levites *i* of their cattle Num 3:45 8478
with another *i* of thy husband Num 5:19 8478
aside to another *i* of thy husband Num 5:20 8478
aside to another *i* of her husband Num 5:29 8478
i of such as open every womb, Num 8:16 8478
even *i* of the firstborn of all Num 8:16
and thou mayest be to us *i* of eyes Num 10:31 8478
take her, I pray thee, *i* of her Judg 15:2 8478
captain of the host *i* of Joab 2Sa 17:25 8478
servant king *i* of David my father 1Kin 3:7 8478
made him king *i* of his father 2Kin 14:21 8478
i of the children of Israel 2Kin 17:24 8478
as king *i* of David his father 1Chr 29:23 8478
I of which king Rehoboam made 2Chr 12:10 8478
the king be queen *i* of Vashti Est 2:4 8478
and made her queen *i* of Vashti Est 2:17 8478
Let thistles grow *i* of wheat Job 31:40 8478
and cockle *i* of barley Job 31:40 8478
I of thy fathers shall be thy Ps 45:16 8478
that *i* of sweet smell there shall Is 3:24 8478
and *i* of a girdle a rent Is 3:24 8478
i of well set hair baldness Is 3:24 8478
i of a stomacher a girding of Is 3:24 8478
and burning *i* of beauty Is 3:24 8478
I of the the thorn shall come up Is 55:13 8478
i of the brier shall come up the Is 55:13 8478
which reigned *i* of Josiah his Jer 22:11 8478
the son of Josiah reigned *i* of Jer 37:1 8478
taketh strangers *i* of her husband Eze 16:32 8478

INSTRUCT
his voice, that he might *i* thee Deut 4:36 3256
also thy good spirit to *i* them Neh 9:20 7919
with the Almighty *i* him Job 40:2 3250
my reins also *i* me in the night Ps 16:7 3256
I will *i* thee and teach thee in Ps 32:8 7919
my mother's house, who would *i* me Song 8:2 3925
For his God doth *i* him to Is 28:26 3256
among the people shall *i* many Dan 11:33 995
of the Lord, that he may *i* him 1Cor 2:16 *4822*

INSTRUCTED
he *i* him, he kept him as the Deut 32:10 995
wherein Jehoiada the priest *i* him 2Kin 12:2 3384
he *i* about the song, because he 1Chr 15:22 3256
were *i* in the songs of the LORD 1Chr 25:7 3925
i for the building of the house 2Chr 3:3 3245
Behold, thou hast *i* many, and thou Job 4:3 3256
be *i*, ye judges of the earth Ps 2:10 3256
mine ear to them that *i* me Prov 5:13 3925
and when the wise is *i*, he Prov 21:11 7919
i me that I should not walk in Is 8:11 3256
took he counsel, and who *i* him Is 40:14 995
Be thou *i*, O Jerusalem, lest my Jer 6:8 3256
and after that I was *i*, I smote Jer 31:19 3045
i unto the kingdom of heaven is Mt 13:52 *3100*
being before *i* of her mother, Mt 14:8 *4264*
things, wherein thou hast been *i* Lk 1:4 *2727*
This man was *i* in the way of the Acts 18:25 *2727*
excellent, being *i* out of the law Rom 2:18 *2727*
all things I am *i* both to be full Phil 4:12 *3453*

INSTRUCTER
an *i* of every artificer in brass Gen 4:22 3913

INSTRUCTERS
ye have ten thousand *i* in Christ 1Cor 4:15 *3807*

INSTRUCTING
In meekness *i* those that oppose 2Ti 2:25 *3811*

INSTRUCTION
ears of men, and sealeth their *i* Job 33:16 4561
Seeing thou hatest *i*, and castest Ps 50:17 4148
To know wisdom and *i* Prov 1:2 4148
To receive the *i* of wisdom Prov 1:3 4148
but fools despise wisdom and *i* Prov 1:7 4148
hear the *i* of thy father, and Prov 1:8 4148
the *i* of a father, and attend to Prov 4:1 4148
Take fast hold of *i* Prov 4:13 4148
And say, How have I hated *i* Prov 5:12 4148
He shall die without *i* Prov 5:23 4148
reproofs of *i* are the way of life Prov 6:23 4148
Receive my *i*, and not silver Prov 8:10 4148
Hear *i*, and be wise, and refuse it Prov 8:33 4148
Give *i* to a wise man, and he will Prov 9:9
in the way of life that keepeth *i* Prov 10:17 4148
Whoso loveth *i* loveth knowledge Prov 12:1 4148
A wise son heareth his father's *i* Prov 13:1 4148
shall be to him that refuseth *i* Prov 13:18 4148
A fool despiseth his father's *i* Prov 15:5 4148
He that refuseth *i* despiseth his Prov 15:32 4148
of the LORD is the *i* of wisdom Prov 15:33 4148
but the *i* of fools is folly Prov 16:22 4148
Hear counsel, and receive *i* Prov 19:20 4148
to hear the *i* that causeth to err Prov 19:27 4148
Apply thine heart unto *i*, and Prov 23:12 4148
also wisdom, and *i*, and Prov 23:23 4148
I looked upon it, and received *i* Prov 24:32 4148
might not hear, nor receive *i* Jer 17:23 4148
have not hearkened to receive *i* Jer 32:33 4148
Will ye not receive *i* to hearken Jer 35:13 4148
be a reproach and a taunt, an *i* Eze 5:15 4148
wilt fear me, thou wilt receive *i* Zeph 3:7 4148
for *i* in righteousness 2Ti 3:16 *3809*

INSTRUCTOR
An *i* of the foolish, a teacher of Rom 2:20 *3810*

INSTRUMENT
if he smite him with an *i* of iron Num 35:16 3627
psaltery and an *i* of ten strings Ps 33:2
Upon an *i* of ten strings, and upon Ps 92:3
an *i* of ten strings will I sing Ps 144:9
not threshed with a threshing *i* Is 28:27

sharp threshing *i* having teeth ... Is 41:15
bringeth forth an *i* for his work ... Is 54:16 3627
voice, and can play well on an *i* ... Eze 33:32

INSTRUMENTS
i of cruelty are in their ... Gen 49:5 3627
the pattern of all the *i* thereof ... Ex 25:9 3627
they shall keep all the *i* of the ... Num 3:8 3627
shall take all the *i* of ministry ... Num 4:12 3627
all the *i* of their service, and ... Num 4:26 3627
and their cords, with all their *i* ... Num 4:32 3627
by name ye shall reckon the *i* of ... Num 4:32 3627
it, and all the *i* thereof, both ... Num 7:1 3627
to the war, with the holy *i* ... Num 31:6 3627
harvest, and to make his *i* of war ... 1Sa 8:12 3627
and *i* of his chariots ... 1Sa 8:12 3627
with joy, and with *i* of musick ... 1Sa 18:6 7991
all manner of *i* made of fir wood ... 2Sa 6:5
burnt sacrifice, and threshing *i* ... 2Sa 24:22
other *i* of the oxen for wood ... 2Sa 24:22 3627
flesh with the *i* of the oxen ... 1Kin 19:21 3627
all the *i* of the sanctuary, and ... 1Chr 9:29 3627
expert in war, with all *i* of war ... 1Chr 12:33 3627
with all manner of *i* of war for ... 1Chr 12:37 3627
be the singers with *i* of musick ... 1Chr 15:16 3627
a sound, and with musical *i* of God ... 1Chr 16:42 3627
and the threshing *i* for wood ... 1Chr 21:23
the LORD with the *i* which I made ... 1Chr 23:5 3627
for all *i* of all manner of ... 1Chr 28:14 3627
for all *i* of silver by weight ... 1Chr 28:14 3627
for all *i* of every kind of ... 1Chr 28:14 3627
and the fleshhooks, and all their *i* ... 2Chr 4:16 3627
silver, and the gold, and all the *i* ... 2Chr 5:1 3627
i of musick, and praised the LORD, ... 2Chr 5:13 3627
also with *i* of musick of the LORD ... 2Chr 7:6 3627
also the singers with *i* of musick ... 2Chr 23:13 3627
Levites stood with the *i* of David ... 2Chr 29:26 3627
with the *i* ordained by David king ... 2Chr 29:27 3627
singing with loud *i* unto the LORD ... 2Chr 30:21 3627
that could skill of *i* of musick ... 2Chr 34:12 3627
with the musical *i* of David the ... Neh 12:36 3627
prepared for him the *i* of death ... Ps 7:13 3627
the players on *i* followed after ... Ps 68:25
the players on *i* shall be there ... Ps 87:7
praise him with stringed *i* ... Ps 150:4 4482
of the sons of men, as musical *i* ... Eccl 2:8
The *i* also of the churl are evil ... Is 32:7 3627
sing my songs to the stringed *i* ... Is 38:20
whereupon also they laid the *i* ... Eze 40:42 3627
neither were *i* of musick brought ... Dan 6:18 1761
Gilead with threshing *i* of iron ... Amos 1:3
invent to themselves *i* of musick ... Amos 6:5 3627
the chief singer on my stringed *i* ... Hab 3:19
yet the *i* of a foolish shepherd ... Zec 11:15 3627
yield ye your members as *i* of ... Rom 6:13 *3696*
the dead, and your members as *i* of ... Rom 6:13 *3696*

INSURRECTION
time hath made *i* against kings ... Ezr 4:19 5376
from the *i* of the workers of ... Ps 64:2 7285
them that had made *i* with him ... Mk 15:7 *4955*
who had committed murder in the *i* ... Mk 15:7 *4714*
the Jews made *i* with one accord ... Acts 18:12 *2721*

INTEGRITY
in the *i* of my heart and innocency ... Gen 20:5 8537
didst this in the *i* of thy heart ... Gen 20:6 8537
in *i* of heart, and in uprightness, ... 1Kin 9:4 8537
and still he holdeth fast his *i* ... Job 2:3 8538
Dost thou still retain thine *i* ... Job 2:9 8538
I will not remove mine *i* from me ... Job 27:5 8538
balance, that God may know mine *i* ... Job 31:6 8538
according to mine *i* that is in me ... Ps 7:8 8537
Let *i* and uprightness preserve me ... Ps 25:21 8537
for I have walked in mine *i* ... Ps 26:1 8537
as for me, I will walk in mine *i* ... Ps 26:11 8537
me, thou upholdest me in mine *i* ... Ps 41:12 8537
according to the *i* of his heart ... Ps 78:72 8537
The *i* of the upright shall guide ... Prov 11:3 8538
is the poor that walketh in his *i* ... Prov 19:1 8537
The just man walketh in his *i* ... Prov 20:7 8537

INTELLIGENCE
have *i* with them that forsake the ... Dan 11:30 995

INTEND
did not *i* to go up against them ... Josh 22:33 559
ye *i* to add more to our sins and ... 2Chr 28:13 559
i to bring this man's blood upon ... Acts 5:28 *1014*
ye *i* to do as touching these men ... Acts 5:35 *3195*

INTENDED
For they *i* evil against thee ... Ps 21:11 5186

INTENDEST
i thou to kill me, as thou ... Ex 2:14 559

INTENDING
i to build a tower, sitteth not ... Lk 14:28 *2309*
i after Easter to bring him forth ... Acts 12:4 *1011*
Assos, there *i* to take in Paul ... Acts 20:13 *3195*

INTENT
to the *i* that the LORD might ... 2Sa 17:14 5668
to the *i* that he might destroy ... 2Kin 10:19 4616
to the *i* that he might let none ... 2Chr 16:1
for to the *i* that I might shew ... Eze 40:4 4616
to the *i* that the living may know ... Dan 4:17 1701
there, to the *i* ye may believe ... Jn 11:15 *2443*
for what *i* he spake this unto him ... Jn 13:28
and came hither for that *i* ... Acts 9:21
for what *i* ye have sent for me ... Acts 10:29 *3056*
to the *i* we should not lust after ... 1Cor 10:6
To the *i* that now unto the ... Eph 3:10 *2443*

INTENTS
have performed the *i* of his heart ... Jer 30:24 4209
of the thoughts and *i* of the heart ... Heb 4:12 *1771*

INTERCESSION
made *i* for the transgressors ... Is 53:12 6293
for them, neither make *i* to me ... Jer 7:16 6293
let them now make *i* to the LORD ... Jer 27:18 6293
Gemariah had made *i* to the king ... Jer 36:25 6293
i for us with groanings which ... Rom 8:26 *5241*
because he maketh *i* for the ... Rom 8:27 *1793*
of God, who also maketh *i* for us ... Rom 8:34 *1793*
how he maketh *i* to God against ... Rom 11:2 *1793*
he ever liveth to make *i* for them ... Heb 7:25 *1793*

INTERCESSIONS
of all, supplications, prayers, *i* ... 1Ti 2:1 *1783*

INTERCESSOR
and wondered that there was no *i* ... Is 59:16 6293

INTERMEDDLE
stranger doth not *i* with his joy ... Prov 14:10 6148

INTERMEDDLETH
seeketh and *i* with all wisdom ... Prov 18:1 1566

INTERMISSION
and ceaseth not, without any *i* ... Lam 3:49 2014

INTERPRET
that could *i* them unto Pharaoh ... Gen 41:8 6622
according to his dream he did *i* ... Gen 41:12 6622
and there is none that can *i* it ... Gen 41:15 6622
canst understand a dream to *i* it ... Gen 41:15 6622
do all *i*? ... 1Cor 12:30 *1329*
with tongues, except he *i* ... 1Cor 14:5 *1329*
unknown tongue pray that he may *i* ... 1Cor 14:13 *1329*
and let one *i* ... 1Cor 14:27 *1329*

INTERPRETATION
according to the *i* of his dream ... Gen 40:5 6623
unto him, This is the *i* of it ... Gen 40:12 6623
baker saw that the *i* was good ... Gen 40:16 6623
and said, This is the *i* thereof ... Gen 40:18 6623
according to the *i* of his dream ... Gen 41:11 6623
the *i* thereof, that he worshipped ... Judg 7:15 7667
To understand a proverb, and the *i* ... Prov 1:6 4426
and who knoweth the *i* of a thing ... Eccl 8:1 6592
the dream, and we will shew the *i* ... Dan 2:4 6591
me the dream, with the *i* thereof ... Dan 2:5 6591
the *i* thereof, ye shall receive ... Dan 2:6 6591
me the dream, and the *i* thereof ... Dan 2:6 6591
and we will shew the *i* of it ... Dan 2:7 6591
that ye can shew me the *i* thereof ... Dan 2:9 6591
that he would shew the king the *i* ... Dan 2:16 6591
I will shew unto the king the *i* ... Dan 2:24 6591
make known unto the king the *i* ... Dan 2:25 6591
I have seen, and the *i* thereof ... Dan 2:26 6591
make known the *i* to the king ... Dan 2:30 6591
we will tell the *i* thereof before ... Dan 2:36 6591
is certain, and the *i* thereof sure ... Dan 2:45 6591
known unto me the *i* of the dream ... Dan 4:6 6591
make known unto me the *i* thereof ... Dan 4:7 6591
I have seen, and the *i* thereof ... Dan 4:9 6591
declare the *i* thereof, forasmuch ... Dan 4:18 6591
able to make known unto me the *i* ... Dan 4:18 6591
or the *i* thereof, trouble thee ... Dan 4:19 6591
the *i* thereof to thine enemies ... Dan 4:19 6591
This is the *i*, O king, and this is ... Dan 4:24 6591
writing, and shew me the *i* thereof ... Dan 5:7 6591
known to the king the *i* thereof ... Dan 5:8 6591
be called, and he will shew the *i* ... Dan 5:12 6591
make known unto me the *i* thereof ... Dan 5:15 6591
could not shew the *i* of the thing ... Dan 5:15 6591
and make known to me the *i* thereof ... Dan 5:16 6591
king, and make known to him the *i* ... Dan 5:17 6591
This is the *i* of the thing ... Dan 5:26 6591
made me know the *i* of the things ... Dan 7:16 6591
be called Cephas, which is by *i* ... Jn 1:42 *2059*
pool of Siloam, (which is by *i* ... Jn 9:7 *2059*
which by *i* is called Dorcas ... Acts 9:36 *1329*
is his name by *i*) withstood them ... Acts 13:8 *3177*
to another the *i* of tongues ... 1Cor 12:10 *2058*
hath a revelation, hath an *i* ... 1Cor 14:26 *2058*
first being by *i* King of ... Heb 7:2 *2059*
the scripture is of any private *i* ... 2Pet 1:20 *1955*

INTERPRETATIONS
unto them, Do not *i* belong to God ... Gen 40:8 6623
of thee, that thou canst make *i* ... Dan 5:16 6591

INTERPRETED
as Joseph had *i* to them ... Gen 40:22 6622
him, and he *i* to us our dreams ... Gen 41:12 6622
And it came to pass, as he *i* to us ... Gen 41:13 6622
tongue, and *i* in the Syrian tongue ... Ezr 4:7 8638
name Emmanuel, which being *i* is ... Mt 1:23 *3177*
which is, being *i*, Damsel, I say ... Mk 5:41 *3177*
place Golgotha, which is, being *i* ... Mk 15:22 *3177*
which is, being *i*, My God, my God ... Mk 15:34 *3177*
Rabbi, (which is to say, being *i* ... Jn 1:38 *2059*
the Messias, which is, being *i* ... Jn 1:41 *3177*
Barnabas, (which is, being *i* ... Acts 4:36 *3177*

INTERPRETER
a dream, and there is no *i* of it ... Gen 40:8 6622
for he spake unto them by an *i* ... Gen 42:23 3887
be a messenger with him, an *i* ... Job 33:23 3887
But if there be no *i*, let him ... 1Cor 14:28 *1328*

INTERPRETING
i of dreams, and shewing of hard ... Dan 5:12 6591

INTO
breathed *i* his nostrils the ... Gen 2:7
parted, and became *i* four heads ... Gen 2:10
put him *i* the garden of Eden to ... Gen 2:15
and thou shalt come *i* the ark ... Gen 6:18 413
sort shalt thou bring *i* the ark ... Gen 6:19 413
thou and all thy house *i* the ark ... Gen 7:1 413
i the ark, because of the waters ... Gen 7:7 413
in two and two unto Noah *i* the ark ... Gen 7:9 413
of his sons with them, *i* the ark ... Gen 7:13 413
they went in unto Noah *i* the ark ... Gen 7:15 413
she returned unto him *i* the ark ... Gen 8:9 413
pulled her in unto him *i* the ark ... Gen 8:9 413
i your hand are they delivered ... Gen 9:2
to go *i* the land of Canaan ... Gen 11:31 413
forth to go *i* the land of Canaan ... Gen 12:5 413
i the land of Canaan they came ... Gen 12:5 413
Abram went down *i* Egypt to ... Gen 12:10 413
he was come near to enter *i* Egypt ... Gen 12:11 935
that, when Abram was come *i* Egypt ... Gen 12:14
woman was taken *i* Pharaoh's house ... Gen 12:15
had, and Lot with him, *i* the south ... Gen 13:1
thine enemies *i* thy hand ... Gen 14:20
I have given my maid *i* thy bosom ... Gen 16:5
Abraham hastened *i* the tent unto ... Gen 18:6
i your servant's house, and tarry ... Gen 19:2 413
unto him, and entered *i* his house ... Gen 19:3 413
pulled Lot *i* the house to them ... Gen 19:10
the earth when Lot entered *i* Zoar ... Gen 19:23
they returned *i* the land of the ... Gen 21:32 413
get thee *i* the land of Moriah ... Gen 22:2 413
emptied her pitcher *i* the trough ... Gen 24:20 413
And the man came *i* the house ... Gen 24:32
Isaac brought her *i* his mother ... Gen 24:67
him, and said, Go not down *i* Egypt ... Gen 26:2
i the hand of her son Jacob ... Gen 27:17
will bring thee again *i* this land ... Gen 28:15 413
came *i* the land of the people of ... Gen 29:1 413
gave them *i* the hand of his sons ... Gen 30:35
Laban went *i* Jacob's tent, and ... Gen 31:33
i Leah's tent, and *i* the two ... Gen 31:33
i the two maidservants' tents ... Gen 31:33
tent, and entered *i* Rachel's tent ... Gen 31:33
herds, and the camels, *i* two bands ... Gen 32:7
he delivered them *i* the hand of ... Gen 32:16
went *i* the country from the face ... Gen 36:6 413
slay him, and cast him *i* some pit ... Gen 37:20
but cast him *i* this pit that is ... Gen 37:22 413
took him, and cast him *i* a pit ... Gen 37:24
and they brought Joseph *i* Egypt ... Gen 37:28
For I will go down *i* the grave ... Gen 37:35
sold him *i* Egypt unto Potiphar ... Gen 37:36 413
all that he had he put *i* his hand ... Gen 39:4
that Joseph went *i* the house to ... Gen 39:11
put him *i* the prison, a place ... Gen 39:20 413
i the prison, the place where ... Gen 40:3 413
pressed them *i* Pharaoh's cup, and ... Gen 40:11 413
I gave the cup *i* Pharaoh's hand ... Gen 40:11 5921
deliver Pharaoh's cup *i* his hand ... Gen 40:13
they should put me *i* the dungeon ... Gen 40:15
he gave the cup *i* Pharaoh's hand ... Gen 40:21 5921
all countries came *i* Egypt to ... Gen 41:57
all together *i* ward three days ... Gen 42:17 413
every man's money *i* his sack ... Gen 42:25 413
deliver him *i* my hand, and I will ... Gen 42:37 5921
brought the men *i* Joseph's house ... Gen 43:17
were brought *i* Joseph's house ... Gen 43:18
brought the men *i* Joseph's house ... Gen 43:24
was in their hand *i* the house ... Gen 43:26
he entered *i* his chamber, and wept ... Gen 43:30
brother, whom ye sold *i* Egypt ... Gen 45:4
came *i* the land of Canaan unto ... Gen 45:25
fear not to go down *i* Egypt ... Gen 46:3
I will go down with thee *i* Egypt ... Gen 46:4
came *i* Egypt, Jacob, and all his ... Gen 46:6
seed brought he with him *i* Egypt ... Gen 46:7
of Israel, which came *i* Egypt ... Gen 46:8
that came with Jacob *i* Egypt ... Gen 46:26
of Jacob, which came *i* Egypt ... Gen 46:27
they came *i* the land of Goshen ... Gen 46:28
the money *i* Pharaoh's house ... Gen 47:14
before I came unto thee *i* Egypt ... Gen 48:5
let them grow *i* a multitude in ... Gen 48:16
come not thou *i* their secret ... Gen 49:6
he gathered up his feet *i* the bed ... Gen 49:33 413
carried him *i* the land of Canaan ... Gen 50:13
And Joseph returned *i* Egypt ... Gen 50:14
of Israel, which came *i* Egypt ... Ex 1:1
is born ye shall cast *i* the river ... Ex 1:22
days' journey *i* the wilderness ... Ex 3:18
Put now thine hand *i* thy bosom ... Ex 4:6
And he put his hand *i* his bosom ... Ex 4:6
Put thine hand *i* thy bosom again ... Ex 4:7 413
he put his hand *i* his bosom again ... Ex 4:7 413
in Midian, Go, return *i* Egypt ... Ex 4:19
When thou goest to return *i* Egypt ... Ex 4:21
Go *i* the wilderness to meet Moses ... Ex 4:27
three days' journey *i* the desert ... Ex 5:3
went *i* his house, neither did he ... Ex 7:23 413
come *i* thine house, and *i* thy ... Ex 8:3
i the house of thy servants, and ... Ex 8:3
i thine ovens, and *i* thy ... Ex 8:3
upon thy people, and *i* thy houses ... Ex 8:21
of flies *i* the house of Pharaoh ... Ex 8:24
i his servants' houses, and *i* ... Ex 8:24
days' journey *i* the wilderness ... Ex 8:27
and his cattle flee *i* the houses ... Ex 9:20 413
I bring the locusts *i* thy coast ... Ex 10:4
and cast them *i* the Red sea ... Ex 10:19
I go out *i* the midst of Egypt ... Ex 11:4
thee *i* the land of the Canaanites ... Ex 13:5 413
thee *i* the land of the Canaanites ... Ex 13:11 413
the children of Israel went *i* the ... Ex 14:22
that came *i* the sea after them ... Ex 14:28
rider hath he thrown *i* the sea ... Ex 15:1
his host hath he cast *i* the sea ... Ex 15:4
they sank *i* the bottom as a stone ... Ex 15:5
and with his horsemen *i* the sea ... Ex 15:19
rider hath he thrown *i* the sea ... Ex 15:21
they went out *i* the wilderness of ... Ex 15:22 413
when he had cast *i* the waters ... Ex 15:25 413
us forth *i* this wilderness ... Ex 16:3 413
wife unto Moses *i* the wilderness ... Ex 18:5 413
and they came *i* the tent ... Ex 18:7

and he went his way *i* his own land Ex 18:27 413
the same day came they *i* the Ex 19:1
that ye go not up *i* the mount Ex 19:12
but God deliver him *i* his hand Ex 21:13
of thy land thou shalt bring *i* Ex 23:19
to bring thee *i* the place which I Ex 23:20 413
of the land *i* your hand Ex 23:31
Moses, Come up to me *i* the mount Ex 24:12
Moses went up *i* the mount of God Ex 24:13 413
And Moses went up *i* the mount Ex 24:15 413
Moses went *i* the midst of the Ex 24:18
cloud, and gat him up *i* the mount Ex 24:18 413
thou shalt put the staves *i* the Ex 25:14
thou shalt put *i* the ark the Ex 25:16 413
and put the taches *i* the loops Ex 26:11
staves shall be put *i* the rings Ex 27:7
thou shalt put them *i* one basket Ex 29:3 5921
when he cometh *i* the tabernacle Ex 29:30 413
When they go *i* the tabernacle of Ex 30:20 413
then I cast it *i* the fire Ex 32:24
I will come up *i* the midst of Ex 33:5
he was gone *i* the tabernacle Ex 33:8
as Moses entered *i* the tabernacle Ex 33:9
And he turned again *i* the camp Ex 33:11 413
he put the staves *i* the rings by Ex 37:5
he put the staves *i* the rings on Ex 38:7
did beat the gold *i* thin plates Ex 39:3
thin plates, and cut it *i* wires Ex 39:3
and put the testimony *i* the ark Ex 40:20 413
brought the ark *i* the tabernacle Ex 40:21 413
When they went *i* the tent of the Ex 40:32 413
Moses was not able to enter *i* the Ex 40:35 413
offering, and cut it *i* his pieces Lev 1:6
And he shall cut it *i* his pieces Lev 1:12
brought *i* the tabernacle of the Lev 6:30 413
And he cut the ram *i* pieces Lev 8:20
Aaron went *i* the tabernacle of Lev 9:23 413
when ye go *i* the tabernacle of Lev 10:9 413
is done, it must be put *i* water Lev 11:32
nor come *i* the sanctuary, until Lev 12:4 413
if the plague be turned *i* white Lev 13:17
bird loose *i* the open field Lev 14:7 5921
that he shall come *i* the camp Lev 14:8 413
pour it *i* the palm of his own Lev 14:15 5921
priest shall pour of the oil *i* Lev 14:26 5921
When ye be come *i* the land of Lev 14:34 413
priest go *i* it to see the plague Lev 14:36
they shall cast them *i* an unclean Lev 14:40 413
the city *i* an unclean place Lev 14:41 413
of the city *i* an unclean place Lev 14:45 413
Moreover he that goeth *i* the Lev 14:46 413
out of the city *i* the open fields Lev 14:53 413
that he come not at all times *i* Lev 16:2 413
shall Aaron come *i* the holy place Lev 16:3 413
for a scapegoat *i* the wilderness Lev 16:10
of a fit man *i* the wilderness Lev 16:21
Aaron shall come *i* the tabernacle Lev 16:23 413
on when he went *i* the holy place Lev 16:23 413
and afterward come *i* the camp Lev 16:26 413
he shall come *i* the camp Lev 16:28 413
And when ye shall come *i* the land Lev 19:23 413
When ye be come *i* the land which Lev 23:10 413
When ye come *i* the land which I Lev 25:2 413
delivered *i* the hand of the enemy Lev 26:25
will bring the land *i* desolation Lev 26:32
i their hearts in the lands of Lev 26:36
have brought them *i* the land of Lev 26:41
old, all that enter *i* the host Num 4:3
one that entereth *i* the service Num 4:30
one that entereth *i* the service Num 4:35
one that entereth *i* the service Num 4:39
one that entereth *i* the service Num 4:43
shall take, and put it *i* the water Num 5:17 413
the curse shall go *i* thy bowels Num 5:22 413
the curse shall enter *i* her Num 5:24 413
the curse shall enter *i* her Num 5:27
when Moses was gone *i* the Num 7:89 413
And Moses gat him *i* the camp Num 11:30 413
and go up *i* the mountain Num 13:17
better for us to return *i* Egypt Num 14:3
captain, and let us return *i* Egypt Num 14:4
then he will bring us *i* this land Num 14:8 413
i the land which he sware unto Num 14:16 413
him will I bring *i* the land Num 14:24 413
get you *i* the wilderness by the Num 14:25
ye shall not come *i* the land Num 14:30 413
gat them up *i* the top of the Num 14:40 413
When ye be come *i* the land of Num 15:2 413
When ye come *i* the land whither I Num 15:18 413
thou hast not brought us *i* a land Num 16:14
and they go down quick *i* the pit Num 16:30
them, went down alive *i* the pit Num 16:33
and ran *i* the midst of the Num 16:47 413
went *i* the tabernacle of witness Num 17:8 413
cast it *i* the midst of the Num 19:6 413
he shall come *i* the camp, and the Num 19:7 413
all that come *i* the tent, and all Num 19:14 413
i the desert of Zin in the first Num 20:1
of the LORD *i* this wilderness Num 20:4 413
i the land which I have given Num 20:12 413
How our fathers went down *i* Egypt Num 20:15
for he shall not enter *i* the land Num 20:24 413
they went up *i* mount Hor in the Num 20:27 413
deliver this people *i* my hand Num 21:2
we will not turn *i* the fields Num 21:22
the fields, or *i* the vineyards Num 21:22
against Israel *i* the wilderness Num 21:23
Come *i* Heshbon, let the city of Num 21:27
i captivity unto Sihon king of Num 21:29
I have delivered him *i* thy hand Num 21:34
of Balak, Get you *i* your land Num 22:13 413
of the way, and went *i* the field Num 22:23
the ass, to turn her *i* the way Num 22:23
brought him up *i* the high places Num 22:41
he brought him *i* the field of Num 23:14
falling *i* a trance, but having Num 24:4
falling *i* a trance, but having Num 24:16
the man of Israel *i* the tent Num 25:8 413
Get thee up *i* this mount Abarim, Num 27:12 413
ye shall come *i* the camp Num 31:24
And divide the prey *i* two parts Num 31:27 413
brought it *i* the tabernacle of Num 31:54 413
of Israel from going over *i* the Num 32:7 413
that they should not go *i* the Num 32:9 413
the LORD *i* the land of Canaan Num 32:32
midst of the sea *i* the wilderness Num 33:8
Aaron the priest went up *i* mount Num 33:38 413
over Jordan *i* the land of Canaan Num 33:51 413
When ye come *i* the land of Canaan Num 34:2 413
over Jordan *i* the land of Canaan Num 35:10
i the land of his possession Num 35:28 413
they were married *i* the families Num 36:12
i what cities we shall come Deut 1:22
went up *i* the mountain, and came Deut 1:24
to deliver us *i* the hand of the Deut 1:27
went, until ye came *i* this place Deut 1:31 5704
you, and take your journey *i* the Deut 1:40
ye were ready to go up *i* the hill Deut 1:41
went presumptuously up *i* the hill Deut 1:43
took our journey *i* the wilderness Deut 2:1
I have given *i* thine hand Sihon Deut 2:24
i the land which the LORD our God Deut 2:29 413
he might deliver him *i* thy hand Deut 2:30
people, and his land, *i* thy hand Deut 3:2
God delivered *i* our hands Og also Deut 3:3
Get thee up *i* the top of Pisgah, Deut 3:27
fire, and went not up *i* the mount Deut 5:5
Get you *i* your tents again Deut 5:30
i the land which he sware unto Deut 6:10 413
LORD thy God shall bring thee *i* Deut 7:1 413
deliver their kings *i* thine hand Deut 7:24
an abomination *i* thine house Deut 7:26 413
God bringeth thee *i* a good land Deut 8:7 413
When I was gone up *i* the mount to Deut 9:9
I cast the dust thereof *i* the Deut 9:21 413
i the land which he promised them Deut 9:28 413
and come up unto me *i* the mount Deut 10:1
went up *i* the mount, having the Deut 10:3
went down *i* Egypt with threescore Deut 10:22
until ye came *i* this place Deut 11:5 5704
gather all the spoil of it *i* the Deut 13:16 413
and cleaveth the cleft *i* two claws Deut 14:6
Then shalt thou turn it *i* money Deut 14:25
get thee up *i* the place which the Deut 17:8 413
When thou art come *i* the land Deut 18:9 413
i three parts, that every slayer Deut 19:3
As when a man goeth *i* the wood Deut 19:5
fleeth *i* one of these cities Deut 19:11 413
deliver him *i* the hand of the Deut 19:12
hath delivered it *i* thine hands Deut 20:13
hath delivered them *i* thine hands Deut 21:10
cut off, shall not enter *i* the Deut 23:1
A bastard shall not enter *i* the Deut 23:2
i the congregation of the LORD Deut 23:2
or Moabite shall not enter *i* the Deut 23:3
i the congregation of the LORD Deut 23:3
the curse *i* a blessing unto thee Deut 23:5
begotten of them shall enter *i* Deut 23:8
he shall come *i* the camp again Deut 23:11 8432
i the house of the LORD thy God Deut 23:18
When thou comest *i* thy Deut 23:24
When thou comest *i* the standing Deut 23:25
thou shalt not go *i* his house to Deut 24:10 413
father, and he went down *i* Egypt Deut 26:5
he hath brought us *i* this place Deut 26:9 413
shalt be removed *i* all the Deut 28:25
carry much seed out *i* the field Deut 28:38
for they shall go *i* captivity Deut 28:41
thee *i* Egypt again with ships Deut 28:68
That thou shouldest enter *i* Deut 29:12
i his oath, which the LORD thy Deut 29:12
cast them *i* another land, as it Deut 29:28 413
thee *i* the land which thy fathers Deut 30:5 413
i the land which I sware unto Deut 31:20 413
them *i* the land which I sware Deut 31:21 413
i the land which I sware unto Deut 31:23 413
I would scatter them *i* corners Deut 32:26
Get thee up *i* this mountain Deut 32:49 413
came *i* an harlot's house, named Josh 2:1
which are entered *i* thine house Josh 2:3
Behold, when we come *i* the land Josh 2:18
doors of thy house *i* the street Josh 2:19
i our hands all the land Josh 2:24
passeth over before you *i* Jordan Josh 3:11
your God *i* the midst of Jordan Josh 4:5 413
I have given *i* thine hand Jericho Josh 6:2
and they came *i* the camp, and Josh 6:11
city once, and returned *i* the camp Josh 6:14
they shall come *i* the treasury of Josh 6:19
the people went up *i* the city Josh 6:20
Go *i* the harlot's house, and bring Josh 6:22
they put *i* the treasury of the Josh 6:24
to deliver us *i* the hand of the Josh 7:7
I have given *i* thy hand the king Josh 8:1
God will deliver it *i* your hand Josh 8:7
Joshua went that night *i* the Josh 8:13
for I will give it *i* thine hand Josh 8:18
and they entered *i* the city Josh 8:19
have delivered them *i* thine hand Josh 10:8
them not to enter *i* their cities Josh 10:19 413
hath delivered them *i* your hand Josh 10:19
of them entered *i* fenced cities Josh 10:20 413
cast them *i* the cave wherein they Josh 10:27 413
thereof, *i* the hand of Israel Josh 10:30
Lachish *i* the hand of Israel Josh 10:32
them *i* the hand of Israel Josh 11:8
Hermon unto the entering *i* Hamath Josh 13:5
shall divide it *i* seven parts Josh 18:5
describe the land *i* seven parts Josh 18:6
by cities *i* seven parts in a book Josh 18:9
take him *i* the city unto them Josh 20:4
deliver the slayer up *i* his hand Josh 20:5
all their enemies *i* their hand Josh 21:44
i the land of Gilead, Phinehas Josh 22:13 413
and his children went down *i* Egypt Josh 24:4
I brought you *i* the land of the Josh 24:8
and I gave them *i* your hand Josh 24:8
and I delivered them *i* your hand Josh 24:11
delivered the land *i* his hand Judg 1:2
brother, Come up with me *i* my lot Judg 1:3
will go with thee *i* thy lot Judg 1:3
and the Perizzites *i* their hand Judg 1:4
Judah *i* the wilderness of Judah Judg 1:16
thee, the entrance *i* the city Judg 1:24
them the entrance *i* the city Judg 1:25
the man went *i* the land of the Judg 1:26
children of Dan *i* the mountain Judg 1:34
he delivered them *i* the hands of Judg 2:14
he sold them *i* the hands of their Judg 2:14
he them *i* the hand of Joshua Judg 2:23
he sold them *i* the hand of Judg 3:8
king of Mesopotamia *i* his hand Judg 3:10
thigh, and thrust it *i* his belly Judg 3:21
enemies the Moabites *i* your hand Judg 3:28
the LORD sold them *i* the hand of Judg 4:2
I will deliver him *i* thine hand Judg 4:7
sell Sisera *i* the hand of a woman Judg 4:9
delivered Sisera *i* thine hand Judg 4:14
had turned in unto her *i* the tent Judg 4:18
and smote the nail *i* his temples Judg 4:21
and fastened it *i* the ground Judg 4:21
And when he came *i* her tent Judg 4:22
he was sent on foot *i* the valley Judg 5:15
the LORD delivered them *i* the Judg 6:1
they entered *i* the land to Judg 6:5
delivered us *i* the hands of the Judg 6:13
give the Midianites *i* their hands Judg 7:2
the Midianites *i* thine hand Judg 7:7
I have delivered it *i* thine hand Judg 7:9
tumbled *i* the host of Midian Judg 7:13
for *i* his hand hath God delivered Judg 7:14
returned *i* the host of Israel, and Judg 7:15 413
for the LORD hath delivered *i* Judg 7:15
hundred men *i* three companies Judg 7:16
God hath delivered *i* your hands Judg 8:3
Zalmunna *i* mine hand, then I will Judg 8:7
And they went out *i* the fields Judg 9:27
went *i* the house of their god, and Judg 9:27
the people went out *i* the field Judg 9:42
divided them *i* three companies, Judg 9:43
they entered *i* an hold of the Judg 9:46 413
he sold them *i* the hands of the Judg 10:7
i the hands of the children of Judg 10:7
thee, through thy land *i* my place Judg 11:19 5704
all his people *i* the hand of Judg 11:21
children of Ammon *i* mine hands Judg 11:30
LORD delivered them *i* his hands Judg 11:32
the LORD delivered them *i* my hand Judg 12:3
the LORD delivered them *i* the Judg 13:1
go in to my wife *i* the chamber Judg 15:1
he let them go *i* the standing Judg 15:5
that we may deliver thee *i* the Judg 15:12
and deliver thee *i* their hand Judg 15:13
i the hand of thy servant Judg 15:18
thirst, and fall *i* the hand of the Judg 15:18
Samson our enemy *i* our hand Judg 16:23
delivered *i* our hands our enemy Judg 16:24
God hath given it *i* your hands Judg 18:10
these went *i* Micah's house, and Judg 18:18
she brought him *i* her father's Judg 19:3
let us turn in *i* this city of the Judg 19:11 413
hither *i* the city of a stranger Judg 19:12 413
took them *i* his house to lodging Judg 19:15
So he brought him *i* his house Judg 19:21
the man that came *i* thine house Judg 19:22 413
this man is come *i* mine house Judg 19:23 413
And when he was come *i* his house Judg 19:29 413
i twelve pieces, and sent her *i* Judg 19:29
I came *i* Gibeah that belongeth to Judg 20:4
we any of us turn *i* his house Judg 20:8
I will deliver them *i* thine hand Judg 20:28
they came *i* the country of Moab, Ruth 1:2
took it up, and went *i* the city Ruth 2:18
that a woman came *i* the floor Ruth 3:14
and she went *i* the city Ruth 3:15
is come *i* thine house like Rachel Ruth 4:11 413
And he struck it *i* the pan 1Sa 2:14
i one of the priests' offices, 1Sa 2:36 413
the people were come *i* the camp 1Sa 4:3 413
of the LORD came *i* the camp 1Sa 4:5 413
of the LORD was come *i* the camp 1Sa 4:6 413
they said, God is come *i* the camp 1Sa 4:7 413
and they fled every man *i* his tent 1Sa 4:10
And when the man came *i* the city 1Sa 4:13
they brought it *i* the house of 1Sa 5:2
nor any that come *i* Dagon's house 1Sa 5:5
the cart came *i* the field of 1Sa 6:14 413
had looked *i* the ark of the LORD 1Sa 6:19
brought it *i* the house of 1Sa 7:1 413
they came no more *i* the coast of 1Sa 7:13
As soon as ye be come *i* the city 1Sa 9:13
And they went up *i* the city 1Sa 9:14 8432
and when they were come *i* the city 1Sa 9:14
and brought them *i* the parlour 1Sa 9:22
from the high place *i* the city 1Sa 9:25
and shalt be turned *i* another man 1Sa 10:6
they came *i* the midst of the host 1Sa 11:11
When Jacob was come *i* Egypt 1Sa 12:8
he sold them *i* the hand of Sisera 1Sa 12:9
i the hand of the Philistines, and 1Sa 12:9
i the hand of the king of Moab, 1Sa 12:9
hath delivered them *i* our hand 1Sa 14:10

them *i* the hand of Israel 1Sa 14:12
which went up with them *i* the 1Sa 14:21
the people were come *i* the wood 1Sa 14:26 413
deliver them *i* the hand of Israel 1Sa 14:37
ran *i* the army, and came and 1Sa 17:22
the LORD deliver thee *i* mine hand 1Sa 17:46
and he will give you *i* our hands 1Sa 17:47
the stone sunk *i* his forehead 1Sa 17:49
he smote the javelin *i* the wall 1Sa 19:10
i a covenant of the LORD with 1Sa 20:8
and let us go out *i* the field 1Sa 20:11
went out both of them *i* the field 1Sa 20:11
that Jonathan went out *i* the 1Sa 20:35
and Jonathan went *i* the city 1Sa 20:42
shall this fellow come *i* my house 1Sa 21:15 413
get thee *i* the land of Judah 1Sa 22:5
came *i* the forest of Hareth 1Sa 22:5
the Philistines *i* thine hand 1Sa 23:4
hath delivered him *i* mine hand 1Sa 23:7
by entering *i* a town that hath 1Sa 23:7
Keilah deliver me up *i* his hand 1Sa 23:11
my men *i* the hand of Saul 1Sa 23:12
God delivered him not *i* his hand 1Sa 23:14
and went to David *i* the wood 1Sa 23:16
to deliver him *i* the king's hand 1Sa 23:20
wherefore he came down *i* a rock 1Sa 23:25
deliver thine enemy *i* thine hand 1Sa 24:4
to day *i* mine hand in the cave 1Sa 24:10
had delivered me *i* thine hand 1Sa 24:18
came after him *i* the wilderness 1Sa 26:3
thine enemy *i* thine hand this day 1Sa 26:8
or he shall descend *i* battle 1Sa 26:10
delivered thee *i* my hand to day 1Sa 26:23
i the land of the Philistines 1Sa 27:1 413
i the hand of the Philistines 1Sa 28:19
deliver the host of Israel *i* the 1Sa 28:19
to return *i* the land of the 1Sa 29:11 413
nor deliver me *i* the hands of my 1Sa 30:15
that came against us *i* our hand 1Sa 30:23
armour, and sent *i* the land of the 1Sa 31:9
Shall I go up *i* any of the cities 2Sa 2:1
thee *i* the hand of David, that 2Sa 3:8
bound, nor thy feet put *i* fetters 2Sa 3:34
they came thither *i* the midst of 2Sa 4:6 5704
For when they came *i* the house 2Sa 4:7
lame shall not come *i* the house 2Sa 5:8 413
thou deliver them *i* mine hand 2Sa 5:19
the Philistines *i* thine hand 2Sa 5:19
LORD unto him *i* the city of David 2Sa 6:10 5921
i the house of Obed-edom the 2Sa 6:10
i the city of David with gladness 2Sa 6:12
the LORD came *i* the city of David 2Sa 6:16
David's servants came *i* the land 2Sa 10:2
i the hand of Abishai his brother 2Sa 10:10
Abishai, and entered *i* the city 2Sa 10:14
shall I then go *i* mine house 2Sa 11:11 413
and came out unto us *i* the field 2Sa 11:23
and thy master's wives *i* thy bosom 2Sa 12:8
came *i* the house of the LORD, and 2Sa 12:20
Bring the meat *i* the chamber 2Sa 13:10
brought them *i* the chamber to 2Sa 13:10
back the ark of God *i* the city 2Sa 15:25
return *i* the city in peace, and 2Sa 15:27
of Ahithophel *i* foolishness 2Sa 15:31
David's friend came *i* the city 2Sa 15:37
and Absalom came *i* Jerusalem 2Sa 15:37
i the hand of Absalom thy son 2Sa 16:8
if he be gotten *i* a city 2Sa 17:13 413
and we will draw it *i* the river 2Sa 17:13 5704
not be seen to come *i* the city 2Sa 17:17
So the people went out *i* the 2Sa 18:6
cast him *i* a great pit in the 2Sa 18:17 413
i mourning unto all the people 2Sa 19:2
by stealth that day *i* the city 2Sa 19:3
Joab came *i* the house to the king 2Sa 19:5
out of the highway *i* the field 2Sa 20:12
he delivered them *i* the hands of 2Sa 21:9
and my cry did enter *i* his ears 2Sa 22:7
me forth also *i* a large place 2Sa 22:20
were gathered together *i* a troop 2Sa 23:11
let us fall now *i* the hand of the 2Sa 24:14
let me not fall *i* the hand of man 2Sa 24:14
in unto the king *i* the chamber 1Kin 1:15
she came *i* the king's presence 1Kin 1:28
brought her *i* the city of David, 1Kin 3:1 413
stairs *i* the middle chamber 1Kin 6:8 5921
and out of the middle *i* the third 1Kin 6:8 413
i the oracle of the house, to the 1Kin 8:6 413
servants with him, to go *i* Egypt 1Kin 11:17
fled *i* Egypt, unto Shishak king 1Kin 11:40
him back with thee *i* thine house 1Kin 13:18 413
and when thy feet enter *i* the city 1Kin 14:12
when the king went *i* the house of 1Kin 14:28
them back *i* the guard chamber 1Kin 14:28 413
i the house of the LORD, silver, 1Kin 15:15
delivered them *i* the hand of his 1Kin 15:18
that he went *i* the palace of the 1Kin 16:18 413
of Israel divided *i* two parts 1Kin 16:21
bosom, and carried him up *i* a loft 1Kin 17:19 413
child's soul come *i* him again 1Kin 17:21 5921
of the child came *i* him again 1Kin 17:22 5921
out of the chamber *i* the house 1Kin 17:23
Go *i* the land, unto all fountains 1Kin 18:5
thy servant *i* the hand of Ahab 1Kin 18:9
a day's journey *i* the wilderness 1Kin 19:4
to Ahab king of Israel *i* the city 1Kin 20:2
I will deliver it *i* thine hand 1Kin 20:13
this great multitude *i* thine hand 1Kin 20:28
rest fled to Aphek, *i* the city 1Kin 20:30 413
came *i* the city, *i* an inner 1Kin 20:30 413
him to come up *i* the chariot 1Kin 20:33 5921
Thy servant went out *i* the midst 1Kin 20:39
Ahab came *i* his house heavy and 1Kin 21:4 413
deliver it *i* the hand of the king 1Kin 22:6

deliver it *i* the king's hand 1Kin 22:12
deliver it *i* the hand of the king 1Kin 22:15
when thou shalt go *i* an inner 1Kin 22:25
myself, and enter *i* the battle 1Kin 22:30
himself, and went *i* the battle 1Kin 22:30
wound *i* the midst of the chariot 1Kin 22:35 413
up Elijah *i* heaven by a whirlwind 2Kin 2:1
went up by a whirlwind *i* heaven 2Kin 2:11
some mountain, or *i* some valley 2Kin 2:16
to deliver them *i* the hand of 2Kin 3:10
to deliver them *i* the hand of 2Kin 3:13
the Moabites also *i* your hand 2Kin 3:18
shalt pour out *i* all those 2Kin 4:4 5921
he turned *i* the chamber, and lay 2Kin 4:11 413
when Elisha was come *i* the house 2Kin 4:32
one went out *i* the field to 2Kin 4:39 413
shred them *i* the pot of pottage 2Kin 4:39 413
And he cast it *i* the pot 2Kin 4:41 413
that when my master goeth *i* the 2Kin 5:18
the ax head fell *i* the water 2Kin 6:5 413
when they were come *i* Samaria 2Kin 6:20
came no more *i* the land of Israel 2Kin 6:23
we say, We will enter *i* the city 2Kin 7:4
of the camp, they went *i* one tent 2Kin 7:8 413
entered *i* another tent, and 2Kin 7:8 413
them alive, and get *i* the city 2Kin 7:12 413
and the people fled *i* their tents 2Kin 8:21
And he arose, and went *i* the house 2Kin 9:6
cast him *i* the plat of ground, 2Kin 9:26
took him up to him *i* the chariot 2Kin 10:15 413
they came *i* the house of Baal 2Kin 10:21
i the house of Baal, and said unto 2Kin 10:23
have brought *i* your hands escape 2Kin 10:24 5921
brought them to him *i* the house 2Kin 11:4
people *i* the temple of the LORD 2Kin 11:13
horses came *i* the king's house 2Kin 11:16
the land went *i* the house of Baal 2Kin 11:18
brought *i* the house of the LORD 2Kin 12:4
all the money that cometh *i* any 2Kin 12:4 5921
to bring *i* the house of the LORD 2Kin 12:4
cometh *i* the house of the LORD 2Kin 12:9
brought *i* the house of the LORD 2Kin 12:9
i the hands of them that did the 2Kin 12:11 5921
brought *i* the house of the LORD 2Kin 12:13
i whose hand they delivered the 2Kin 12:15 5921
brought *i* the house of the LORD 2Kin 12:16
he delivered them *i* the hand of 2Kin 13:3
i the hand of Ben-hadad the son 2Kin 13:3
they cast the man *i* the sepulchre 2Kin 13:21
and carried Israel away *i* Assyria 2Kin 17:6
delivered them *i* the hand of 2Kin 17:20
a man lean, it will go *i* his hand 2Kin 18:21
city shall not be delivered *i* the 2Kin 18:30
went *i* the house of the LORD 2Kin 19:1
shall not be delivered *i* the hand 2Kin 19:10
Hezekiah went up *i* the house of 2Kin 19:14
have cast their gods *i* the fire 2Kin 19:18
I will enter *i* the lodgings of 2Kin 19:23
i the forest of his Carmel 2Kin 19:23
fenced cities *i* ruinous heaps 2Kin 19:25
thy tumult is come up *i* mine ears 2Kin 19:28
He shall not come *i* this city 2Kin 19:32 413
and shall not come *i* this city 2Kin 19:33 413
they escaped *i* the land of 2Kin 19:37
was gone out *i* the middle court 2Kin 20:4
that I shall go up *i* the house of 2Kin 20:8
day, shall be carried *i* Babylon 2Kin 20:17
and brought water *i* the city 2Kin 20:20
deliver them *i* the hand of their 2Kin 21:14
brought *i* the house of the LORD 2Kin 22:4
let them deliver it *i* the hand of 2Kin 22:5 5921
that was delivered *i* their hand 2Kin 22:7 5921
have delivered it *i* the hand of 2Kin 22:9 5921
be gathered *i* thy grave in peace 2Kin 22:20 413
the king went up *i* the house of 2Kin 23:2
dust of them *i* the brook Kidron 2Kin 23:12 413
those carried he *i* captivity from 2Kin 24:15
were delivered *i* their hand 1Chr 5:20
And Jehozadak went *i* captivity 1Chr 6:15
armour, and sent *i* the land of the 1Chr 10:9
to David, *i* the cave of Adullam 1Chr 11:15 413
i the hold to the wilderness men 1Chr 12:8
but carried it aside *i* the house 1Chr 13:13 413
thou deliver them *i* mine hand 1Chr 14:10
I will deliver them *i* thine hand 1Chr 14:10
of David went out *i* all lands 1Chr 14:17
the LORD *i* the hand of Asaph 1Chr 16:7
i the land of the children of 1Chr 19:2 413
brother, and entered *i* the city 1Chr 19:15
let me fall now *i* the hand of the 1Chr 21:13
let me not fall *i* the hand of man 1Chr 21:13
sword again *i* the sheath thereof 1Chr 21:27 413
of the land *i* mine hand 1Chr 22:18
i the house that is to be built 1Chr 22:19
David divided them *i* courses 1Chr 23:6
to come *i* the house of the LORD 1Chr 24:19
i the most holy place, even under 2Chr 5:7 413
i thy resting place, thou, and the 2Chr 6:41
not enter *i* the house of the LORD 2Chr 7:2 413
the people away *i* their tents 2Chr 7:10
all that came *i* Solomon's heart 2Chr 7:11 5921
went up *i* the house of the LORD 2Chr 9:4
entered *i* the house of the LORD 2Chr 12:11
them again *i* the guard chamber 2Chr 12:11 413
God delivered them *i* their hand 2Chr 13:16
they entered *i* a covenant to seek 2Chr 15:12
he brought *i* the house of God the 2Chr 15:18
he delivered them *i* thine hand 2Chr 16:8
will deliver it *i* the king's hand 2Chr 18:5
deliver it *i* the hand of the king 2Chr 18:11
shall be delivered *i* your hand 2Chr 18:14
go *i* an inner chamber to hide 2Chr 18:24
went forth *i* the wilderness of 2Chr 20:20
And they came up *i* Judah, and brake 2Chr 21:17

came up *i* Judah, and brake *i* it 2Chr 21:17
of Zichri, *i* covenant with him 2Chr 23:1
But let none come *i* the house of 2Chr 23:6
whosoever else cometh *i* the house 2Chr 23:7
people *i* the house of the LORD 2Chr 23:12
the high gate *i* the king's house 2Chr 23:20
cast *i* the chest, until they had 2Chr 24:10
a very great host *i* their hand 2Chr 24:24
them *i* the hand of their enemies 2Chr 25:20
went *i* the temple of the LORD to 2Chr 26:16 413
not *i* the temple of the LORD 2Chr 27:2 413
i the hand of the king of Syria 2Chr 28:5
he was also delivered *i* the hand 2Chr 28:5
hath delivered them *i* your hand 2Chr 28:9
but they brought him not *i* the 2Chr 28:27
them together *i* the east street 2Chr 29:4
the priests went *i* the inner part 2Chr 29:16
i the court of the house of the 2Chr 29:16
it out abroad *i* the brook Kidron 2Chr 29:16
thank offerings *i* the house of 2Chr 29:31
enter *i* his sanctuary, which he 2Chr 30:8
they shall come again *i* this land 2Chr 30:9
cast them *i* the brook Kidron 2Chr 30:14
offerings *i* the house of the LORD 2Chr 30:15
possession, *i* their own cities 2Chr 31:1
offerings *i* the house of the LORD 2Chr 31:10
entereth *i* the house of the LORD 2Chr 31:16
Assyria came, and entered *i* Judah 2Chr 32:1
when he was come *i* the house of 2Chr 32:21
again to Jerusalem *i* his kingdom 2Chr 33:13
beaten the graven images *i* powder 2Chr 34:7
was brought *i* the house of God 2Chr 34:9
brought *i* the house of the LORD 2Chr 34:14
have delivered it *i* the hand of 2Chr 34:17 5921
the king went up *i* the house of 2Chr 34:30
he gave them all *i* his hand 2Chr 36:17
that we went *i* the province of Ezr 5:8
he gave them *i* the hand of Ezr 5:12
carried the people away *i* Babylon Ezr 5:12
brought them *i* the temple of Ezr 5:14
carry them *i* the temple that is Ezr 5:15
been delivered *i* the hand of the Ezr 9:7
went *i* the chamber of Johanan the Ezr 10:6 413
me over till I come *i* Judah Neh 2:7 413
the house that I shall enter *i* Neh 2:8 5921
we bring *i* bondage our sons and Neh 5:5
would go *i* the temple to save his Neh 6:11 413
my God put *i* mine heart to gather Neh 7:5 413
i the street that was before the Neh 8:1 413
thou threwest *i* the deeps Neh 9:11
as a stone *i* the mighty waters Neh 9:11
and didst divide them *i* corners Neh 9:22
and broughtest them *i* the land Neh 9:23 413
and gavest them *i* their hands Neh 9:24
them *i* the hand of their enemies Neh 9:27
therefore gavest thou them *i* the Neh 9:30
nobles, and entered *i* a curse Neh 10:29
i an oath, to walk in God's law, Neh 10:29
to bring it *i* the house of our Neh 10:34
chambers, *i* the treasure house Neh 10:38
to gather *i* them out of the Neh 12:44
i the congregation of God for Neh 13:1
God turned the curse *i* a blessing Neh 13:2
which they brought *i* Jerusalem on Neh 13:15
For he sent letters *i* all the Est 1:22 413
i every province according to the Est 1:22
on the morrow she returned *i* the Est 2:14 413
i his house royal in the tenth Est 2:16 413
to bring it *i* the king's Est 3:9 413
posts *i* all the king's provinces Est 3:13 413
went out *i* the midst of the city, Est 4:1
for none might enter *i* the king's Est 4:2 413
unto the king *i* the inner court Est 4:11 413
Now Haman was come *i* the outward Est 6:4
wrath went *i* the palace garden Est 7:7 413
out of the palace garden *i* the Est 7:8 413
and from mourning *i* a good day Est 9:22
let it not come *i* the number of Job 3:6
The earth is given *i* the hand of Job 9:24
wilt thou bring me *i* dust again Job 10:9 413
i whose hand God bringeth Job 12:6
bringest me *i* judgment with thee Job 14:3
turned me over *i* the hands of the Job 16:11 413
They change the night *i* day Job 17:12
For he is cast *i* a net by his own Job 18:8
be driven from light *i* darkness Job 18:18
he enter with thee *i* judgment Job 22:4
fleeing *i* the wilderness in Job 30:3
He hath cast me *i* the mire Job 30:19
my organ *i* the voice of them that Job 30:31
his soul from going *i* the pit Job 33:28
should enter *i* judgment with God Job 34:23
out of the strait *i* a broad place Job 36:16
Then the beasts go *i* dens Job 37:8 1119
Hast thou entered *i* the springs Job 38:16 5704
Hast thou entered *i* the treasures Job 38:22 413
When the dust groweth *i* hardness Job 38:38
thy seed, and gather it *i* thy barn Job 39:12
he can draw up Jordan *i* his mouth Job 40:23 413
Canst thou put an hook *i* his nose Job 41:2
sorrow is turned *i* joy before him Job 41:22
are turned with him *i* stubble Job 41:28
will ye turn my glory *i* shame Ps 4:2
I will come *i* thy house in the Ps 5:7
is fallen *i* the ditch which he Ps 7:15
The wicked shall be turned *i* hell Ps 9:17
when he draweth him *i* his net Ps 10:9
nor take up their names *i* my lips Ps 16:4 5921
came before him, even *i* his ears Ps 18:6
me forth also *i* a large place Ps 18:19
brought me *i* the dust of death Ps 22:15
Who shall ascend *i* the hill of Ps 24:3
like them that go down *i* the pit Ps 28:1
for me my mourning *i* dancing Ps 30:11

Context	Reference	No.
I thine hand I commit my spirit	Ps 31:5	
hast not shut me up *i* the hand of	Ps 31:8	
is turned *i* the drought of summer	Ps 32:4	
i that very destruction let him	Ps 35:8	
prayer returned *i* mine own bosom	Ps 35:13	5921
shall enter *i* their own heart	Ps 37:15	
i smoke shall they consume away	Ps 37:20	
grace is poured *i* thy lips	Ps 45:2	
they shall enter *i* the king's	Ps 45:15	
be carried *i* the midst of the sea	Ps 46:2	
and let them go down quick *i* hell	Ps 55:15	
shalt bring them down *i* the pit	Ps 55:23	
put thou my tears *i* thy bottle	Ps 56:8	
i the midst whereof they are	Ps 57:6	
will bring me *i* the strong city	Ps 60:9	
who will lead me *i* Edom	Ps 60:9	5704
shall go *i* the lower parts of the	Ps 63:9	
He turned the sea *i* dry land	Ps 66:6	
Thou broughtest us *i* the net	Ps 66:11	
us out *i* a wealthy place	Ps 66:12	
I will go *i* thy house with burnt	Ps 66:13	
I am come *i* deep waters, where	Ps 69:2	
them not come *i* thy righteousness	Ps 69:27	
Until I went *i* the sanctuary of	Ps 73:17	413
castedst them down *i* destruction	Ps 73:18	
How are they brought *i* desolation	Ps 73:19	
have cast fire *i* thy sanctuary	Ps 74:7	
and horse are cast *i* a dead sleep	Ps 76:6	
had turned their rivers *i* blood	Ps 78:44	
his strength *i* captivity, and his	Ps 78:61	
his glory *i* the enemy's hand	Ps 78:61	
are come *i* thine inheritance	Ps 79:1	
i their bosom their reproach	Ps 79:12	413
with them that go down *i* the pit	Ps 88:4	
and mine acquaintance *i* darkness	Ps 88:18	
they should not enter *i* my rest	Ps 95:11	413
an offering, and come *i* his courts	Ps 96:8	
Enter *i* his gates with	Ps 100:4	
and *i* his courts with praise	Ps 100:4	
sendeth the springs *i* the valleys	Ps 104:10	
Israel also came *i* Egypt	Ps 105:23	
He turned their waters *i* blood	Ps 105:29	
but sent leanness *i* their soul	Ps 106:15	
i the similitude of an ox that	Ps 106:20	
he gave them *i* the hand of the	Ps 106:41	
they were brought *i* subjection	Ps 106:42	
He turneth rivers *i* a wilderness	Ps 107:33	
and the watersprings *i* dry ground	Ps 107:33	
A fruitful land *i* barrenness	Ps 107:34	
the wilderness *i* a standing water	Ps 107:35	
dry ground *i* watersprings	Ps 107:35	
will bring me *i* the strong city	Ps 108:10	
who will lead me *i* Edom	Ps 108:10	5704
so let it come *i* his bowels like	Ps 109:18	
water, and like oil *i* his bones	Ps 109:18	
the rock *i* a standing water	Ps 114:8	
the flint *i* a fountain of waters	Ps 114:8	
any that go down *i* silence	Ps 115:17	
I will go *i* them, and I will	Ps 118:19	
i which the righteous shall enter	Ps 118:20	
Let us go *i* the house of the LORD	Ps 122:1	
Surely I will not come *i* the	Ps 132:3	
of my house, nor go up *i* my bed	Ps 132:3	5921
We will go *i* his tabernacles	Ps 132:7	
Arise, O LORD, *i* thy rest	Ps 132:8	
wonders *i* the midst of thee, O	Ps 135:9	
which divided the Red sea *i* parts	Ps 136:13	
If I ascend up *i* heaven, thou art	Ps 139:8	
let them be cast *i* the fire	Ps 140:10	
i deep pits, that they rise not	Ps 140:10	
the wicked fall *i* their own nets	Ps 141:10	
enter not *i* judgment with thy	Ps 143:2	
unto them that go down *i* the pit	Ps 143:7	
lead me *i* the land of uprightness	Ps 143:10	
as those that go down *i* the pit	Prov 1:12	
wisdom entereth *i* thine heart	Prov 2:10	
Enter not *i* the path of the	Prov 4:14	
when thou art come *i* the hand of	Prov 6:3	
messenger falleth *i* mischief	Prov 13:17	
leadeth him *i* the way that is not	Prov 16:29	
The lot is cast *i* the lap	Prov 16:33	
A reproof entereth more *i* a wise	Prov 17:10	
than an hundred stripes *i* a fool	Prov 17:10	
tongue falleth *i* mischief	Prov 17:20	
A fool's lips enter *i* contention	Prov 18:6	
they go down *i* the innermost	Prov 18:8	
the righteous runneth *i* it	Prov 18:10	
casteth *i* a deep sleep	Prov 19:15	
enter not *i* the fields of the	Prov 23:10	
the wicked shall fall *i* mischief	Prov 24:16	
As a thorn goeth up *i* the hand of	Prov 26:9	
they go down *i* the innermost	Prov 26:22	
neither go *i* thy brother's house	Prov 27:10	
shall fall himself *i* his own pit	Prov 28:10	
his heart shall fall *i* mischief	Prov 28:14	
men bring a city *i* a snare	Prov 29:8	
Who hath ascended up *i* heaven	Prov 30:4	
All the rivers run *i* the sea	Eccl 1:7	413
diggeth a pit shall fall *i* it	Eccl 10:8	
God will bring thee *i* judgment	Eccl 11:9	
shall bring every work *i* judgment	Eccl 12:14	
hath brought me *i* his chambers	Song 1:4	
brought him *i* my mother's house	Song 3:4	413
i the chamber of her that	Song 3:4	413
Let my beloved come *i* his garden	Song 4:16	
I am come *i* my garden, my sister,	Song 5:1	
beloved is gone down *i* his garden	Song 6:2	
I went down *i* the garden of nuts	Song 6:11	413
let us go forth *i* the field	Song 7:11	
bring thee *i* my mother's house,	Song 8:2	413
beat their swords *i* plowshares	Is 2:4	
and their spears *i* pruninghooks	Is 2:4	
Enter *i* the rock, and hide thee in	Is 2:10	
they shall go *i* the holes of the	Is 2:19	
i the caves of the earth, for	Is 2:19	
To go *i* the clefts of the rocks,	Is 2:21	
i the tops of the ragged rocks,	Is 2:21	
The LORD will enter *i* judgment	Is 3:14	
my people are gone *i* captivity	Is 5:13	
rejoiceth, shall descend *i* it	Is 5:14	
The Lord sent a word *i* Jacob	Is 9:8	
but we will change them *i* cedars	Is 9:10	
that they may go *i* the gates of	Is 13:2	
and flee every one *i* his own land	Is 13:14	413
they break forth *i* singing	Is 14:7	
heart, I will ascend *i* heaven	Is 14:13	
cloud, and shall come *i* Egypt	Is 19:1	
over *i* the hand of a cruel lord	Is 19:4	
angle *i* the brooks shall lament	Is 19:8	
the Assyrian shall come *i* Egypt	Is 19:23	
and the Egyptian *i* Assyria	Is 19:23	
hath he turned *i* fear unto me	Is 21:4	
like a ball *i* a large country	Is 22:18	413
commit thy government *i* his hand	Is 22:21	
to bring *i* contempt all the	Is 23:9	
of the fear shall fall *i* the pit	Is 24:18	413
enter thou *i* thy chambers, and	Is 26:20	
be turned *i* a fruitful field	Is 29:17	
That walk to go down *i* Egypt	Is 30:2	
i the land of trouble and anguish,	Is 30:6	
be removed *i* a corner any more	Is 30:20	
come *i* the mountain of the LORD	Is 30:29	
thereof shall be turned *i* pitch	Is 34:9	
and the dust thereof *i* brimstone	Is 34:9	
a man lean, it will go *i* his hand	Is 36:6	
city shall not be delivered *i* the	Is 36:15	
went *i* the house of the LORD	Is 37:1	
Jerusalem shall not be given *i*	Is 37:10	
have cast their gods *i* the fire	Is 37:19	
I will enter *i* the height of his	Is 37:24	
defenced cities *i* ruinous heaps	Is 37:26	
tumult, is come up *i* mine ears	Is 37:29	
He shall not come *i* this city	Is 37:33	413
and shall not come *i* this city	Is 37:34	413
they escaped *i* the land of	Is 37:38	
they that go down *i* the pit	Is 38:18	
get thee up *i* the high mountain	Is 40:9	5921
break forth *i* singing, ye	Is 44:23	
themselves are gone *i* captivity	Is 46:2	
silent, and get thee *i* darkness	Is 47:5	
and given them *i* thine hand	Is 47:6	
and break forth *i* singing, O	Is 49:13	
But I will put it *i* the hand of	Is 51:23	
come *i* thee the uncircumcised	Is 52:1	
i Egypt to sojourn there	Is 52:4	
Break forth *i* joy, sing together,	Is 52:9	
break forth *i* singing, and cry	Is 54:1	
break forth before you *i* singing	Is 55:12	
He shall enter *i* peace	Is 57:2	
is crushed breaketh out *i* a viper	Is 59:5	
a beast goeth down *i* the valley	Is 63:14	
even recompense *i* their bosom	Is 65:6	5921
their former work *i* their bosom	Is 65:7	5921
be remembered, nor come *i* mind	Is 65:17	5921
vessel *i* the house of the LORD	Is 66:20	
I brought you *i* a plentiful	Jer 2:7	413
how then art thou turned *i* the	Jer 2:21	
let us go *i* the defenced cities	Jer 4:5	413
they shall go *i* thickets, and	Jer 4:29	
as a grapegatherer *i* the baskets	Jer 6:9	5921
Go not forth *i* the field, nor	Jer 6:25	
not, neither came it *i* my heart	Jer 7:31	5921
as the horse rusheth *i* the battle	Jer 8:6	
let us enter *i* the defenced	Jer 8:14	413
death is come up *i* our windows	Jer 9:21	
is entered *i* our palaces, to cut	Jer 9:21	
Silver spread *i* plates is brought	Jer 10:9	
my soul *i* the hand of her enemies	Jer 12:7	
he turn it *i* the shadow of death,	Jer 13:16	
If I go forth *i* the field	Jer 14:18	
and if I enter *i* the city, then	Jer 14:18	
the priest go about *i* a land that	Jer 14:18	413
i all kingdoms of the earth	Jer 15:4	
i a land which thou knowest not	Jer 15:14	
Enter not *i* the house of mourning	Jer 16:5	
also go *i* the house of feasting	Jer 16:8	
land *i* a land that ye know not	Jer 16:13	5921
I will bring them again *i* their	Jer 16:15	5921
Then shall there enter *i* the	Jer 17:25	
it, neither came it *i* my mind	Jer 19:5	5921
I will give all Judah *i* the hand	Jer 20:4	
carry them captive *i* Babylon	Jer 20:4	
give *i* the hand of their enemies	Jer 20:5	
thine house shall go *i* captivity	Jer 20:6	
I will assemble them *i* the midst	Jer 21:4	413
i the hand of Nebuchadrezzar king	Jer 21:7	
i the hand of their enemies, and	Jer 21:7	
i the hand of those that seek	Jer 21:7	
it shall be given *i* the hand of	Jer 21:10	
who shall enter *i* our habitations	Jer 21:13	
cedars, and cast them *i* the fire	Jer 22:7	5921
thy lovers shall go *i* captivity	Jer 22:22	
I will give thee *i* the hand of	Jer 22:25	
i the hand of them whose face	Jer 22:25	
even *i* the hand of Nebuchadrezzar	Jer 22:25	
i the hand of the Chaldeans	Jer 22:25	
i another country, where ye were	Jer 22:26	5921
are cast *i* a land which they know	Jer 22:28	5921
gone forth *i* all the land	Jer 23:15	
i the land of the Chaldeans for	Jer 24:5	
i all the kingdoms of the earth	Jer 24:9	
afraid, and fled, and went *i* Egypt	Jer 26:21	
the king sent men *i* Egypt	Jer 26:22	
and certain men with him *i* Egypt	Jer 26:22	413
cast his dead body *i* the graves	Jer 26:23	413
i the hand of the people to put	Jer 26:24	
have I given all these lands *i*	Jer 27:6	413
i this place all the vessels of	Jer 28:3	
of Judah, that went *i* Babylon	Jer 28:4	
from Babylon *i* this place	Jer 28:6	413
I will bring you again *i* the	Jer 29:14	413
gone forth with you *i* captivity	Jer 29:16	
I will deliver them *i* the hand of	Jer 29:21	
all faces are turned *i* paleness	Jer 30:6	
one of them, shall go *i* captivity	Jer 30:16	
I will turn their mourning *i* joy	Jer 31:13	
I will give this city *i* the hand	Jer 32:3	
but shall surely be delivered *i*	Jer 32:4	
i the bosom of their children	Jer 32:18	413
the city is given *i* the hand of	Jer 32:24	
for the city is given *i* the hand	Jer 32:25	
I will give this city *i* the hand	Jer 32:28	
i the hand of Nebuchadrezzar king	Jer 32:28	
not, neither came it *i* my mind	Jer 32:35	5921
It shall be delivered *i* the hand	Jer 32:36	
it is given *i* the hand of the	Jer 32:43	
of praise *i* the house of the LORD	Jer 33:11	
I will give this city *i* the hand	Jer 34:2	
be taken, and delivered *i* his hand	Jer 34:3	
which had entered *i* the covenant	Jer 34:10	
brought them *i* subjection for	Jer 34:11	
and brought them *i* subjection	Jer 34:16	
i all the kingdoms of the earth	Jer 34:17	
I will even give them *i* the hand	Jer 34:20	
i the hand of them that seek	Jer 34:20	
his princes will I give *i* the	Jer 34:21	
i the hand of them that seek	Jer 34:21	
i the hand of the king of	Jer 34:21	
bring them *i* the house of the	Jer 35:2	
i one of the chambers, and give	Jer 35:2	413
I brought them *i* the house of the	Jer 35:4	
i the chamber of the sons of	Jer 35:4	413
of Babylon came up *i* the land	Jer 35:11	413
days of Josiah, even *i* this day	Jer 36:2	413
I cannot go *i* the house of the	Jer 36:5	
he went down *i* the king's house	Jer 36:12	
i the scribe's chamber	Jer 36:12	5921
went in to the king *i* the court	Jer 36:20	
cast it *i* the fire that was on	Jer 36:23	413
for they had not put him *i* prison	Jer 37:4	
return to Egypt *i* their own land	Jer 37:7	
to go *i* the land of Benjamin	Jer 37:12	
was entered *i* the dungeon	Jer 37:16	413
i the cabins, and Jeremiah had	Jer 37:16	413
thou shalt be delivered *i* the	Jer 37:17	
i the court of the prison	Jer 37:21	
given *i* the hand of the king of	Jer 38:3	
cast him *i* the dungeon of	Jer 38:6	413
whom they have cast *i* the dungeon	Jer 38:9	413
went *i* the house of the king	Jer 38:11	
let them down by cords *i* the	Jer 38:11	413
Jeremiah the prophet unto him *i*	Jer 38:14	413
neither will I give thee *i* the	Jer 38:16	
given *i* the hand of the Chaldeans	Jer 38:18	
lest they deliver me *i* their hand	Jer 38:19	
i Babylon the remnant of the	Jer 39:9	
thou shalt not be given *i* the	Jer 39:17	
thee to come with me *i* Babylon	Jer 40:4	
thee to come with me *i* Babylon	Jer 40:4	
when they came *i* the midst of the	Jer 41:7	413
cast them *i* the midst of the pit,	Jer 41:7	413
Bethlehem, to go to enter *i* Egypt	Jer 41:17	
but we will go *i* the land of	Jer 42:14	
set your faces to enter *i* Egypt	Jer 42:15	
to go *i* Egypt to sojourn there	Jer 42:17	935
you, when ye shall enter *i* Egypt	Jer 42:18	935
Go ye not *i* Egypt	Jer 42:19	
Go not *i* Egypt to sojourn there	Jer 43:2	
for to deliver us *i* the hand of	Jer 43:3	
carry us away captives *i* Babylon	Jer 43:3	
So they came *i* the land of Egypt	Jer 43:7	
go *i* the land of Egypt to sojourn	Jer 44:12	
which are gone *i* the land of	Jer 44:14	
should return *i* the land of Judah	Jer 44:14	
them, and came it not *i* his mind	Jer 44:21	5921
land of Egypt *i* the land of Judah	Jer 44:28	
that are gone *i* the land of Egypt	Jer 44:28	
Egypt *i* the hand of his enemies	Jer 44:30	
i the hand of them that seek his	Jer 44:30	
I gave Zedekiah king of Judah *i*	Jer 44:30	
Go up *i* Gilead, and take balm, O	Jer 46:11	
furnish thyself to go *i* captivity	Jer 46:19	
she shall be delivered *i* the hand	Jer 46:24	
I will deliver them *i* the hand of	Jer 46:26	
i the hand of Nebuchadrezzar king	Jer 46:26	
i the hand of his servants	Jer 46:26	
put up thyself *i* thy scabbard	Jer 47:6	413
and Chemosh shall go forth *i*	Jer 48:7	
neither hath he gone *i* captivity	Jer 48:11	
the fear shall fall *i* the pit	Jer 48:44	413
their king shall go *i* captivity	Jer 49:3	
I will scatter *i* all winds them	Jer 49:32	
us go every one *i* his own country	Jer 51:9	
and let Jerusalem come *i* your mind	Jer 51:50	5921
for strangers are come *i* the	Jer 51:51	5921
i Babylon in the fourth year of	Jer 51:59	
cast it *i* the midst of Euphrates	Jer 51:63	413
the king of Babylon, *i* Jerusalem,	Jer 52:12	
Judah is gone *i* captivity because	Lam 1:3	1473
her children are gone *i* captivity	Lam 1:5	
when her people fell *i* the hand	Lam 1:7	
heathen entered *i* her sanctuary	Lam 1:10	
not enter *i* thy congregation	Lam 1:10	
hath he sent fire *i* my bones	Lam 1:13	
hath delivered me *i* their hands	Lam 1:14	
my young men are gone *i* captivity	Lam 1:18	
he hath given up *i* the hand of	Lam 2:7	
Her gates are sunk *i* the ground	Lam 2:9	
poured out *i* their mothers' bosom	Lam 2:12	413
led me, and brought me *i* darkness	Lam 3:2	
me *i* darkness, but not *i* light	Lam 3:2	
of his quiver to enter *i* my reins	Lam 3:13	

entered *i* the gates of Jerusalem	Lam 4:12	
more carry thee away *i* captivity	Lam 4:22	
our dance is turned *i* mourning	Lam 5:15	
the spirit entered *i* me when he	Eze 2:2	
go forth *i* the plain, and I will	Eze 3:22	413
arose, and went forth *i* the plain	Eze 3:23	413
Then the spirit entered *i* me	Eze 3:24	
there abominable flesh *i* my mouth	Eze 4:14	
cast them *i* the midst of the fire	Eze 5:4	413
forth *i* all the house of Israel	Eze 5:4	413
i wickedness more than the	Eze 5:6	
will I scatter *i* all the winds	Eze 5:10	
a third part *i* all the winds	Eze 5:12	
is risen up *i* a rod of wickedness	Eze 7:11	
I will give it *i* the hands of the	Eze 7:21	
for the robbers shall enter *i* it	Eze 7:22	
he brought me *i* the inner court	Eze 8:16	413
put it *i* the hands of him that	Eze 10:7	413
the things that come *i* your mind	Eze 11:5	
deliver you *i* the hands of	Eze 11:9	
by the Spirit of God *i* Chaldea	Eze 11:24	
as they that go forth *i* captivity	Eze 12:4	
shall remove and go *i* captivity	Eze 12:11	
Ye have not gone up *i* the gaps	Eze 13:5	
they enter *i* the land of Israel	Eze 13:9	
I send a pestilence *i* that land	Eze 14:19	413
it is cast *i* the fire for fuel	Eze 15:4	
entered *i* a covenant with thee,	Eze 16:8	
and thou didst prosper *i* a kingdom	Eze 16:13	
will also give thee *i* their hand	Eze 16:39	
carried it *i* a land of traffick	Eze 17:4	
sending his ambassadors *i* Egypt	Eze 17:15	
they brought him *i* holds, that	Eze 19:9	
i a land that I had espied for	Eze 20:6	413
brought them *i* the wilderness	Eze 20:10	413
that I would not bring them *i* the	Eze 20:15	413
I had brought them *i* the land	Eze 20:28	413
that which cometh *i* your mind	Eze 20:32	5921
I will bring you *i* the wilderness	Eze 20:35	413
I will bring you *i* the bond of	Eze 20:37	
not enter *i* the land of Israel	Eze 20:38	413
bring you *i* the land of Israel	Eze 20:42	413
i the country for the which I	Eze 20:42	413
to give it *i* the hand of the	Eze 21:11	
which entereth *i* their privy	Eze 21:14	
I cause it to return *i* his sheath	Eze 21:30	
deliver thee *i* the hand of	Eze 21:31	
you *i* the midst of Jerusalem	Eze 22:19	413
i the midst of the furnace, to	Eze 22:20	413
her *i* the hand of her lovers	Eze 23:9	
i the hand of the Assyrians, upon	Eze 23:9	
messengers unto them *i* Chaldea	Eze 23:16	
came to her *i* the bed of love	Eze 23:17	
I will deliver thee *i* the hand of	Eze 23:28	
i the hand of them from whom thy	Eze 23:28	
will I give her cup *i* thine hand	Eze 23:31	
day *i* my sanctuary to profane it	Eze 23:39	413
it on, and also pour water *i* it	Eze 24:3	
Gather the pieces thereof *i* it	Eze 24:4	
Judah, when they went *i* captivity	Eze 25:3	
when he shall enter *i* thy gates	Eze 26:10	
as men enter *i* a city wherein is	Eze 26:10	
with them that descend *i* the pit	Eze 26:20	
have brought thee *i* great waters	Eze 27:26	
shall fall *i* the midst of the	Eze 27:27	
gold and silver *i* thy treasures	Eze 28:4	
For I will send *i* her pestilence	Eze 28:23	
and blood *i* her street	Eze 28:23	
thee thrown *i* the wilderness	Eze 29:5	
to return *i* the land of Pathros	Eze 29:14	
i the land of their habitation	Eze 29:14	5921
sell the land *i* the hand of the	Eze 30:12	
these cities shall go *i* captivity	Eze 30:17	
daughters shall go *i* captivity	Eze 30:18	
when I shall put my sword *i* the	Eze 30:25	
i the hand of the mighty one of	Eze 31:11	
with them that descend *i* the pit	Eze 31:16	
They also went down *i* hell with	Eze 31:17	
i the countries which thou hast	Eze 32:9	5921
with them that go down *i* the pit	Eze 32:18	
are gone down uncircumcised *i* the	Eze 32:24	413
which have appointed my land *i*	Eze 36:5	
and will bring you *i* your own land	Eze 36:24	413
will cause breath to enter *i* you	Eze 37:5	
me, and the breath came *i* them	Eze 37:10	
bring you *i* the land of Israel	Eze 37:12	413
them one to another *i* one stick	Eze 37:17	
bring them *i* their own land	Eze 37:21	413
i two kingdoms any more at all	Eze 37:22	
back, and put hooks *i* thy jaws	Eze 38:4	
latter years thou shalt come *i*	Eze 38:8	413
time shall things come *i* thy mind	Eze 38:10	5921
i captivity for their iniquity	Eze 39:23	
gave them *i* the hand of their	Eze 39:23	
led *i* captivity among the heathen	Eze 39:28	
he me *i* the land of Israel	Eze 40:2	413
brought he me *i* the outward court	Eze 40:17	413
he brought me *i* the inner court	Eze 40:32	413
they entered *i* the wall which was	Eze 41:6	
me forth *i* the utter court	Eze 42:1	413
he brought me *i* the chamber that	Eze 42:1	413
as one goeth *i* them from the	Eze 42:9	
the east, as one entereth *i* them	Eze 42:12	
the holy place *i* the utter court	Eze 42:14	413
the glory of the LORD came *i* the	Eze 43:4	413
brought me *i* the inner court	Eze 43:5	413
brought *i* my sanctuary strangers	Eze 44:7	
shall enter *i* my sanctuary, of	Eze 44:9	413
of Israel to fall *i* iniquity	Eze 44:12	
They shall enter *i* my sanctuary	Eze 44:16	413
they go forth *i* the utter court	Eze 44:19	413
even *i* the utter court to the	Eze 44:19	413
when they enter *i* the inner court	Eze 44:21	413
day that he goeth *i* the sanctuary	Eze 44:27	413
i the holy chambers of the	Eze 46:19	413
them not out *i* the utter court	Eze 46:20	413
me forth *i* the utter court	Eze 46:21	413
go down *i* the desert	Eze 47:8	5921
i the desert, and go *i* the sea	Eze 47:8	
being brought forth *i* the sea	Eze 47:8	
king of Judah *i* his hand, with	Dan 1:2	
which he carried *i* the land of	Dan 1:2	
he brought the vessels *i* the	Dan 1:2	
God had brought Daniel *i* favour	Dan 1:9	
thy thoughts came *i* thy mind upon	Dan 2:29	
heaven hath he given *i* thine hand	Dan 2:38	
shall the same hour be cast *i* the	Dan 3:6	
that he should be cast *i* the	Dan 3:11	
i the midst of a burning fiery	Dan 3:15	
to cast them *i* the burning fiery	Dan 3:20	
were cast *i* the midst of the	Dan 3:21	
fell down bound *i* the midst of	Dan 3:23	
men bound *i* the midst of the fire	Dan 3:24	
lords, came *i* the banquet house	Dan 5:10	
shall be cast *i* the den of lions	Dan 6:7	
was signed, he went *i* his house	Dan 6:10	
shall be cast *i* the den of lions	Dan 6:12	
cast him *i* the den of lions	Dan 6:16	
they cast them *i* the den of lions	Dan 6:24	
they shall be given *i* his hand	Dan 7:25	
was turned in me *i* corruption	Dan 10:8	
shall enter *i* the fortress of the	Dan 11:7	
carry captives *i* Egypt their gods	Dan 11:8	
south shall come *i* his kingdom	Dan 11:9	
and shall return *i* his own land	Dan 11:9	413
shall be given *i* his hand	Dan 11:11	
Then shall he return *i* his land	Dan 11:28	
and he shall enter *i* the countries	Dan 11:40	
enter also *i* the glorious land	Dan 11:41	
bring her *i* the wilderness, and	Hos 2:14	
will I change their glory *i* shame	Hos 4:7	
not come *i* the house of the LORD	Hos 9:4	
not return *i* the land of Egypt	Hos 11:5	413
and I will not enter *i* the city	Hos 11:9	
and oil is carried *i* Egypt	Hos 12:1	
Jacob fled *i* the country of Syria	Hos 12:12	
i the house of the LORD your God	Joel 1:14	
and will drive him *i* a land barren	Joel 2:20	413
sun shall be turned *i* darkness	Joel 2:31	
and the moon *i* blood	Joel 2:31	
will bring them down *i* the valley	Joel 3:2	413
have carried *i* your temples my	Joel 3:5	
your daughters *i* the hand of the	Joel 3:8	
Beat your plowshares *i* swords	Joel 3:10	
and your pruninghooks *i* spears	Joel 3:10	
send a fire *i* the house of Hazael	Amos 1:4	
shall go *i* captivity unto Kir	Amos 1:5	
their king shall go *i* captivity	Amos 1:15	
bones of the king of Edom *i* lime	Amos 2:1	
ye shall cast them *i* the palace	Amos 4:3	
not Beth-el, nor enter *i* Gilgal	Amos 5:5	
shall surely go *i* captivity	Amos 5:5	
the shadow of death *i* the morning	Amos 5:8	
or went *i* the house, and leaned	Amos 5:19	
will I cause you to go *i*	Amos 5:27	
ye have turned judgment *i* gall	Amos 6:12	
fruit of righteousness *i* hemlock	Amos 6:12	
flee thee away *i* the land of	Amos 7:12	413
and Israel shall surely go *i*	Amos 7:17	
will turn your feasts *i* mourning	Amos 8:10	
and all your songs *i* lamentation	Amos 8:10	
Though they dig *i* hell, thence	Amos 9:2	
though they go *i* captivity before	Amos 9:4	
and foreigners entered *i* his gates	Obad 11	
i the gate of my people in the	Obad 13	
fare thereof, and went down *i* it	Jonah 1:3	
sent out a great wind *i* the sea	Jonah 1:4	413
that were in the ship *i* the sea	Jonah 1:5	413
gone down *i* the sides of the ship	Jonah 1:5	413
me up, and cast me forth *i* the sea	Jonah 1:12	413
and cast him forth *i* the sea	Jonah 1:15	413
For thou hadst cast me *i* the deep	Jonah 2:3	
in unto thee, *i* thine holy temple	Jonah 2:7	413
Jonah began to enter *i* the city a	Jonah 3:4	
the stones thereof *i* the valley	Mic 1:6	
for they are gone *i* captivity	Mic 1:16	
that putteth not *i* their mouths	Mic 3:5	5921
beat their swords *i* plowshares	Mic 4:3	
and their spears *i* pruninghooks	Mic 4:3	
them as the sheaves *i* the floor	Mic 4:12	
Assyrian shall come *i* our land	Mic 5:5	
when he cometh *i* our land	Mic 5:6	
sins *i* the depths of the sea	Mic 7:19	
away, she went *i* captivity	Nah 3:10	
they shall even fall *i* the mouth	Nah 3:12	5921
go *i* clay, and tread the morter,	Nah 3:14	
rottenness entered *i* my bones	Hab 3:16	
to put it *i* a bag with holes	Hag 1:6	413
it shall enter *i* the house of the	Zec 5:4	413
i the house of him that sweareth	Zec 5:4	413
he cast it *i* the midst of the	Zec 5:8	413
go forth *i* the north country	Zec 6:6	413
go *i* the house of Josiah the son	Zec 6:10	
I will bring them *i* the land of	Zec 10:10	413
every one *i* his neighbour's hand	Zec 11:6	
and *i* the hand of his king	Zec 11:6	
city shall go forth *i* captivity	Zec 14:2	
all the tithes *i* the storehouse	Mal 3:10	413
away *i* Babylon are fourteen	Mt 1:17	*3350*
from the carrying away *i* Babylon	Mt 1:17	*3350*
when they were come *i* the house	Mt 2:11	*1519*
they departed *i* their own country	Mt 2:12	*1519*
flee *i* Egypt, and be thou there	Mt 2:13	*1519*
by night, and departed *i* Egypt	Mt 2:14	*1519*
and go *i* the land of Israel	Mt 2:20	*1519*
came *i* the land of Israel	Mt 2:21	*1519*
he turned aside *i* the parts of	Mt 2:22	*1519*
is hewn down, and cast *i* the fire	Mt 3:10	*1519*
and gather his wheat *i* the garner	Mt 3:12	*1519*
was Jesus led up of the spirit *i*	Mt 4:1	*1519*
taketh him up *i* the holy city	Mt 4:5	*1519*
the devil taketh him up *i* an	Mt 4:8	*1519*
heard that John was cast *i* prison	Mt 4:12	
he departed *i* Galilee	Mt 4:12	*1519*
brother, casting a net *i* the sea	Mt 4:18	*1519*
he went up *i* a mountain	Mt 5:1	*1519*
enter *i* the kingdom of heaven	Mt 5:20	*1519*
officer, and thou be cast *i* prison	Mt 5:25	*1519*
whole body should be cast *i* hell	Mt 5:29	*1519*
whole body should be cast *i* hell	Mt 5:30	*1519*
enter *i* thy closet, and when thou	Mt 6:6	*1519*
And lead us not *i* temptation	Mt 6:13	*1519*
do they reap, nor gather *i* barns	Mt 6:26	*1519*
and to morrow is cast *i* the oven	Mt 6:30	*1519*
is hewn down, and cast *i* the fire	Mt 7:19	*1519*
shall enter *i* the kingdom of	Mt 7:21	*1519*
Jesus was entered *i* Capernaum	Mt 8:5	*1519*
be cast out *i* outer darkness	Mt 8:12	*1519*
Jesus was come *i* Peter's house	Mt 8:14	*1519*
And when he was entered *i* a ship	Mt 8:23	*1519*
i the country of the Gergesenes	Mt 8:28	*1519*
us to go away *i* the herd of swine	Mt 8:31	*1519*
they went *i* the herd of swine	Mt 8:32	*1519*
down a steep place *i* the sea	Mt 8:32	*1519*
and went their ways *i* the city	Mt 8:33	*1519*
And he entered *i* a ship, and passed	Mt 9:1	*1519*
over, and came *i* his own city	Mt 9:1	*1519*
do men put new wine *i* old bottles	Mt 9:17	*1519*
they put new wine *i* new bottles	Mt 9:17	*1519*
when Jesus came *i* the ruler's	Mt 9:23	*1519*
went abroad *i* all that land	Mt 9:26	*1519*
And when he was come *i* the house	Mt 9:28	*1519*
forth labourers *i* his harvest	Mt 9:38	*1519*
Go not *i* the way of the Gentiles,	Mt 10:5	*1519*
i any city of the Samaritans	Mt 10:5	*1519*
i whatsoever city or town ye	Mt 10:11	*1519*
And when ye come *i* an house	Mt 10:12	*1519*
in this city, flee ye *i* another	Mt 10:23	*1519*
What went ye out *i* the wilderness	Mt 11:7	*1519*
How he entered *i* the house of God	Mt 12:4	*1519*
he went *i* their synagogue	Mt 12:9	*1519*
if it fall *i* a pit on the sabbath	Mt 12:11	*1519*
one enter *i* a strong man's house	Mt 12:29	*1519*
I will return *i* my house from	Mt 12:44	*1519*
him, so that he went *i* a ship	Mt 13:2	*1519*
But other fell *i* good ground	Mt 13:8	*1909*
received the seed *i* stony places	Mt 13:20	*1909*
But he that received seed *i* the	Mt 13:23	*1909*
but gather the wheat *i* my barn	Mt 13:30	*1519*
away, and went *i* the house	Mt 13:36	*1519*
shall cast them *i* a furnace of	Mt 13:42	*1519*
a net, that was cast *i* the sea	Mt 13:47	*1519*
and gathered the good *i* vessels	Mt 13:48	*1519*
shall cast them *i* the furnace of	Mt 13:50	*1519*
he was come *i* his own country	Mt 13:54	*1519*
by ship *i* a desert place apart	Mt 14:13	*1519*
that they may go *i* the villages	Mt 14:15	*1519*
his disciples to get *i* a ship	Mt 14:22	*1519*
he went up *i* a mountain apart to	Mt 14:23	*1519*
And when they were come *i* the ship	Mt 14:32	*1519*
over, they came *i* the land of	Mt 14:34	*1519*
they sent out *i* all that country	Mt 14:35	*1519*
Not that which goeth *i* the mouth	Mt 15:11	*1519*
both shall fall *i* the ditch	Mt 15:14	*1519*
in at the mouth goeth *i* the belly	Mt 15:17	*1519*
and is cast out *i* the draught	Mt 15:17	*1519*
departed *i* the coasts of Tyre and	Mt 15:21	*1519*
went up *i* a mountain, and sat down	Mt 15:29	*1519*
came *i* the coasts of Magdala	Mt 15:39	*1519*
When Jesus came *i* the coasts of	Mt 16:13	*1519*
bringeth them up *i* an high	Mt 17:1	*1519*
i the fire, and oft *i* the water	Mt 17:15	*1519*
be betrayed *i* the hands of men	Mt 17:22	*1519*
And when he was come *i* the house	Mt 17:25	*1519*
ye shall not enter *i* the kingdom	Mt 18:3	*1519*
to enter *i* life halt or maimed	Mt 18:8	*1519*
to be cast *i* everlasting fire	Mt 18:8	*1519*
thee to enter *i* life with one eye	Mt 18:9	*1519*
two eyes to be cast *i* hell fire	Mt 18:9	*1519*
goeth *i* the mountains, and seeketh	Mt 18:12	*1909*
but went and cast him *i* prison	Mt 18:30	*1519*
came *i* the coasts of Judaea	Mt 19:1	*1519*
but if thou wilt enter *i* life	Mt 19:17	*1519*
enter *i* the kingdom of heaven	Mt 19:23	*1519*
man to enter *i* the kingdom of God	Mt 19:24	*1519*
to hire labourers *i* his vineyard	Mt 20:1	*1519*
day, he sent them *i* his vineyard	Mt 20:2	*1519*
Go ye also *i* the vineyard, and	Mt 20:4	*1519*
Go ye also *i* the vineyard	Mt 20:7	*1519*
Go *i* the village over against you	Mt 21:2	*1519*
And when he was come *i* Jerusalem	Mt 21:10	*1519*
Jesus went *i* the temple of God,	Mt 21:12	*1519*
and went out of the city *i* Bethany	Mt 21:17	*1519*
morning as he returned *i* the city	Mt 21:18	*1519*
and be thou cast *i* the sea	Mt 21:21	*1519*
And when he was come *i* the temple	Mt 21:23	*1519*
the harlots go *i* the kingdom of	Mt 21:31	*1519*
and went *i* a far country	Mt 21:33	
Go ye therefore *i* the highways	Mt 22:9	*1909*
servants went out *i* the highways	Mt 22:10	*1519*
cast him *i* outer darkness	Mt 22:13	*1519*
be in Judaea flee *i* the mountains	Mt 24:16	*1909*
day that Noe entered *i* the ark	Mt 24:38	*1519*
a man travelling *i* a far country	Mt 25:14	
enter thou *i* the joy of thy lord	Mt 25:21	*1519*
enter thou *i* the joy of thy lord	Mt 25:23	*1519*
servant *i* outer darkness	Mt 25:30	*1519*
i everlasting fire, prepared for	Mt 25:41	*1519*
these shall go away *i* everlasting	Mt 25:46	*1519*
but the righteous *i* life eternal	Mt 25:46	*1519*
Go *i* the city to such a man, and	Mt 26:18	*1519*
they went out *i* the mount of	Mt 26:30	*1519*

I will go before you *i* Galilee	Mt 26:32	*1519*
that ye enter not *i* temptation	Mt 26:41	*1519*
betrayed *i* the hands of sinners	Mt 26:45	*1519*
up again thy sword *i* his place	Mt 26:52	*1519*
when he was gone out *i* the porch	Mt 26:71	*1519*
for to put them *i* the treasury	Mt 27:6	*1519*
took Jesus *i* the common hall	Mt 27:27	*1519*
went *i* the holy city, and appeared	Mt 27:53	*1519*
he goeth before you *i* Galilee	Mt 28:7	*1519*
brethren that they go *i* Galilee	Mt 28:10	*1519*
some of the watch came *i* the city	Mt 28:11	*1519*
disciples went away *i* Galilee	Mt 28:16	*1519*
i a mountain where Jesus had	Mt 28:16	*1519*
driveth him *i* the wilderness	Mk 1:12	*1519*
in prison, Jesus came *i* Galilee	Mk 1:14	*1519*
brother casting a net *i* the sea	Mk 1:16	*1722*
And they went *i* Capernaum	Mk 1:21	*1519*
day he entered *i* the synagogue	Mk 1:21	*1519*
they entered *i* the house of Simon	Mk 1:29	*1519*
departed *i* a solitary place, and	Mk 1:35	*1519*
Let us go *i* the next towns, that	Mk 1:38	*1519*
no more openly enter *i* the city	Mk 1:45	*1519*
again he entered *i* Capernaum	Mk 2:1	*1519*
bed, and go thy way *i* thine house	Mk 2:11	*1519*
putteth new wine *i* old bottles	Mk 2:22	*1519*
wine must be put *i* new bottles	Mk 2:22	*1519*
How he went *i* the house of God in	Mk 2:26	*1519*
he entered again *i* the synagogue	Mk 3:1	*1519*
And he goeth up *i* a mountain	Mk 3:13	*1519*
and they went *i* an house	Mk 3:19	*1519*
No man can enter *i* a strong man's	Mk 3:27	*1519*
so that he entered *i* a ship	Mk 4:1	*1519*
man should cast seed *i* the ground	Mk 4:26	*1909*
and the waves beat *i* the ship	Mk 4:37	*1519*
i the country of the Gadarenes	Mk 5:1	*1519*
Send us *i* the swine	Mk 5:12	*1519*
that we may enter *i* them	Mk 5:12	*1519*
went out, and entered *i* the swine	Mk 5:13	*1519*
down a steep place *i* the sea	Mk 5:13	*1519*
And when he was come *i* the ship	Mk 5:18	*1519*
thence, and came *i* his own country	Mk 6:1	*1519*
place soever ye enter *i* a house	Mk 6:10	*1519*
yourselves apart *i* a desert place	Mk 6:31	*1519*
they departed *i* a desert place by	Mk 6:32	*1519*
that they may go *i* the country	Mk 6:36	*1519*
i the villages, and buy themselves	Mk 6:36	*1519*
his disciples to get *i* the ship	Mk 6:45	*1519*
he departed *i* a mountain to pray	Mk 6:46	*1519*
he went up unto them *i* the ship	Mk 6:51	*1519*
over, they came *i* the land of	Mk 6:53	*1909*
i villages, or cities, or country	Mk 6:56	*1519*
that entering *i* him can defile	Mk 7:15	*1519*
when he was entered *i* the house	Mk 7:17	*1519*
from without entereth *i* the man	Mk 7:18	*1519*
it entereth not *i* his heart	Mk 7:19	*1519*
but *i* the belly, and goeth out	Mk 7:19	*1519*
goeth out *i* the draught, purging	Mk 7:19	*1519*
went *i* the borders of Tyre and	Mk 7:24	*1519*
entered *i* an house, and would have	Mk 7:24	*1519*
and put his fingers *i* his ears	Mk 7:33	*1519*
straightway he entered *i* a ship	Mk 8:10	*1519*
came *i* the parts of Dalmanutha	Mk 8:10	*1519*
entering *i* the ship again	Mk 8:13	*1519*
saying, Neither go *i* the town	Mk 8:26	*1519*
i the towns of Caesarea Philippi	Mk 8:27	*1519*
leadeth them up *i* an high	Mk 9:2	*1519*
it hath cast him *i* the fire	Mk 9:22	*1519*
i the waters, to destroy him	Mk 9:22	*1519*
of him, and enter no more *i* him	Mk 9:25	*1519*
And when he was come *i* the house	Mk 9:28	*1519*
is delivered *i* the hands of men	Mk 9:31	*1519*
neck, and he were cast *i* the sea	Mk 9:42	*1519*
for thee to enter *i* life maimed	Mk 9:43	*1519*
having two hands to go *i* hell	Mk 9:43	*1519*
i the fire that never shall be	Mk 9:43	*1519*
for thee to enter halt *i* life	Mk 9:45	*1519*
having two feet to be cast *i* hell	Mk 9:45	*1519*
i the fire that never shall be	Mk 9:45	*1519*
it is better for thee to enter *i*	Mk 9:47	*1519*
two eyes to be cast *i* hell fire	Mk 9:47	*1519*
cometh *i* the coasts of Judaea by	Mk 10:1	*1519*
when he was gone forth *i* the way	Mk 10:17	*1519*
riches enter *i* the kingdom of God	Mk 10:23	*1519*
to enter *i* the kingdom of God	Mk 10:24	*1519*
man to enter *i* the kingdom of God	Mk 10:25	*1519*
Go your way *i* the village over	Mk 11:2	*1519*
and as soon as ye be entered *i* it	Mk 11:2	*1519*
i Jerusalem, and *i* the temple	Mk 11:11	*1519*
and Jesus went *i* the temple	Mk 11:15	*1519*
and be thou cast *i* the sea	Mk 11:23	
and went *i* a far country	Mk 12:1	
people cast money *i* the treasury	Mk 12:41	*1519*
which have cast *i* the treasury	Mk 12:43	*1519*
housetop not go down *i* the house	Mk 13:15	*1519*
Go ye *i* the city, and there shall	Mk 14:13	*1519*
came *i* the city, and found as he	Mk 14:16	*1519*
they went out *i* the mount of	Mk 14:26	*1519*
I will go before you *i* Galilee	Mk 14:28	*1519*
pray, lest ye enter *i* temptation	Mk 14:38	*1519*
betrayed *i* the hands of sinners	Mk 14:41	*1519*
even *i* the palace of the high	Mk 14:54	
And he went out *i* the porch	Mk 14:68	*1519*
soldiers led him away *i* the hall	Mk 15:16	*2080*
entering *i* the sepulchre, they	Mk 16:5	*1519*
he goeth before you *i* Galilee	Mk 16:7	*1519*
walked, and went *i* the country	Mk 16:12	*1519*
Go ye *i* all the world, and preach	Mk 16:15	*1519*
them, he was received up *i* heaven	Mk 16:19	*1519*
he went *i* the temple of the Lord	Lk 1:9	*1519*
went *i* the hill country with	Lk 1:39	*1519*
with haste, *i* a city of Juda	Lk 1:39	*1519*
entered *i* the house of Zacharias,	Lk 1:40	*1519*
guide our feet *i* the way of peace	Lk 1:79	*1519*
taxed, every one *i* his own city	Lk 2:3	*1519*
i Judaea, unto the city of David,	Lk 2:4	*1519*
were gone away from them *i* heaven	Lk 2:15	*1519*
came by the Spirit *i* the temple	Lk 2:27	*1519*
the Lord, they returned *i* Galilee	Lk 2:39	*1519*
he came *i* all the country about	Lk 3:3	*1519*
is hewn down, and cast *i* the fire	Lk 3:9	*1519*
gather the wheat *i* his garner	Lk 3:17	*1519*
by the Spirit *i* the wilderness	Lk 4:1	*1519*
taking him up *i* an high mountain,	Lk 4:5	*1519*
the power of the Spirit *i* Galilee	Lk 4:14	*1519*
he went *i* the synagogue on the	Lk 4:16	*1519*
the fame of him went out *i* every	Lk 4:37	*1519*
and entered *i* Simon's house	Lk 4:38	*1519*
departed and went *i* a desert place	Lk 4:42	*1519*
he entered *i* one of the ships,	Lk 5:3	*1519*
unto Simon, Launch out *i* the deep	Lk 5:4	*1519*
withdrew himself *i* the wilderness	Lk 5:16	*1722*
couch *i* the midst before Jesus	Lk 5:19	*1519*
up thy couch, and go *i* thine house	Lk 5:24	*1519*
putteth new wine *i* old bottles	Lk 5:37	*1519*
wine must be put *i* new bottles	Lk 5:38	*1519*
How he went *i* the house of God,	Lk 6:4	*1519*
that he entered *i* the synagogue	Lk 6:6	*1519*
that he went out *i* a mountain to	Lk 6:12	*1519*
over, shall men give *i* your bosom	Lk 6:38	*1519*
they not both fall *i* the ditch	Lk 6:39	*1519*
people, he entered *i* Capernaum	Lk 7:1	*1519*
that he went *i* a city called Nain	Lk 7:11	*1519*
What went ye out *i* the wilderness	Lk 7:24	*1519*
he went *i* the Pharisee's house,	Lk 7:36	*1519*
I entered *i* thine house, thou	Lk 7:44	*1519*
that he went *i* a ship with his	Lk 8:22	*1519*
of the devil *i* the wilderness	Lk 8:29	*1519*
many devils were entered *i* him	Lk 8:30	*1519*
command them to go out *i* the deep	Lk 8:31	*1519*
would suffer them to enter *i* them	Lk 8:32	*1519*
the man, and entered *i* the swine	Lk 8:33	*1519*
down a steep place *i* the lake	Lk 8:33	*1519*
and he went up *i* the ship, and	Lk 8:37	*1519*
that he would come *i* his house	Lk 8:41	*1519*
And when he came *i* the house	Lk 8:51	*1519*
And whatsoever house ye enter *i*	Lk 9:4	*1519*
went aside privately *i* a desert	Lk 9:10	*1519*
that they may go *i* the towns	Lk 9:12	*1519*
went up *i* a mountain to pray	Lk 9:28	*1519*
as they entered *i* the cloud	Lk 9:34	*1519*
sayings sink down *i* your ears	Lk 9:44	*1519*
be delivered *i* the hands of men	Lk 9:44	*1519*
entered *i* a village of the	Lk 9:52	*1519*
two before his face *i* every city	Lk 10:1	*1519*
forth labourers *i* his harvest	Lk 10:2	*1519*
i whatsoever house ye enter,	Lk 10:5	*1519*
i whatsoever city ye enter, and	Lk 10:8	*1519*
But *i* whatsoever city ye enter,	Lk 10:10	*1519*
go your ways out *i* the streets of	Lk 10:10	*1519*
that he entered *i* a certain	Lk 10:38	*1519*
Martha received him *i* her house	Lk 10:38	*1519*
And lead us not *i* temptation	Lk 11:4	*1519*
killed hath power to cast *i* hell	Lk 12:5	*1519*
and to morrow is cast *i* the oven	Lk 12:28	*1519*
and the officer cast thee *i* prison	Lk 12:58	*1519*
a man took, and cast *i* his garden	Lk 13:19	*1519*
as he went *i* the house of one of	Lk 14:1	*1519*
an ass or an ox fallen *i* a pit	Lk 14:5	*1519*
Go out quickly *i* the streets	Lk 14:21	*1519*
Go out *i* the highways and hedges,	Lk 14:23	*1519*
took his journey *i* a far country	Lk 15:13	*1519*
he sent him *i* his fields to feed	Lk 15:15	*1519*
may receive me *i* their houses	Lk 16:4	*1519*
ye fail, they may receive you *i*	Lk 16:9	*1519*
and every man presseth *i* it	Lk 16:16	*1519*
by the angels *i* Abraham's bosom	Lk 16:22	*1519*
lest they also come *i* this place	Lk 16:28	*1519*
his neck, and he cast *i* the sea	Lk 17:2	*1519*
as he entered *i* a certain village	Lk 17:12	*1519*
day that Noe entered *i* the ark	Lk 17:27	*1519*
Two men went up *i* the temple to	Lk 18:10	*1519*
riches enter *i* the kingdom of God	Lk 18:24	*1519*
man to enter *i* the kingdom of God	Lk 18:25	*1519*
climbed up *i* a sycomore tree to	Lk 19:4	*1909*
A certain nobleman went *i* a far	Lk 19:12	*1519*
not thou my money *i* the bank	Lk 19:23	*1909*
Go ye *i* the village over against	Lk 19:30	*1519*
he went *i* the temple, and began to	Lk 19:45	*1519*
went *i* a far country for a long	Lk 20:9	
their gifts *i* the treasury	Lk 21:1	*1519*
i prisons, being brought before	Lk 21:12	
be led away captive *i* all nations	Lk 21:24	*1519*
Then entered Satan *i* Judas	Lk 22:3	*1519*
when ye are entered *i* the city	Lk 22:10	*1519*
follow him *i* the house where he	Lk 22:10	*1519*
both *i* prison, and to death	Lk 22:33	*1519*
that ye enter not *i* temptation	Lk 22:40	*1519*
pray, lest ye enter *i* temptation	Lk 22:46	*1519*
brought him *i* the high priest's	Lk 22:54	*1519*
led him *i* their council, saying,	Lk 22:66	*1519*
and for murder, was cast *i* prison	Lk 23:19	*1519*
and murder was cast *i* prison	Lk 23:25	*1519*
me when thou comest *i* thy kingdom	Lk 23:42	*1722*
i thy hands I commend my spirit	Lk 23:46	*1519*
i the hands of sinful men	Lk 24:7	*1519*
things, and to enter *i* his glory	Lk 24:26	*1519*
from them, and carried up *i* heaven	Lk 24:51	*1519*
every man that cometh *i* the world	Jn 1:9	*1519*
Jesus would go forth *i* Galilee	Jn 1:43	*1519*
second time *i* his mother's womb	Jn 3:4	*1519*
he cannot enter *i* the kingdom of	Jn 3:5	*1519*
For God sent not his Son *i* the	Jn 3:17	*1519*
that light is come *i* the world	Jn 3:19	*1519*
his disciples *i* the land of	Jn 3:22	*1519*
John was not yet cast *i* prison	Jn 3:24	*1519*
hath given all things *i* his hand	Jn 3:35	*1722*
and departed again *i* Galilee	Jn 4:3	*1519*
springing up *i* everlasting life	Jn 4:14	*1519*
and went her way *i* the city	Jn 4:28	*1519*
and ye are entered *i* their labours	Jn 4:38	*1519*
thence, and went *i* Galilee	Jn 4:43	*1519*
Then when he was come *i* Galilee	Jn 4:45	*1519*
came again *i* Cana of Galilee	Jn 4:46	*1519*
was come out of Judaea *i* Galilee	Jn 4:47	*1519*
was come out of Judaea *i* Galilee	Jn 4:54	*1519*
at a certain season *i* the pool	Jn 5:4	*1722*
is troubled, to put me *i* the pool	Jn 5:7	*1519*
and shall not come *i* condemnation	Jn 5:24	*1519*
And Jesus went up *i* a mountain	Jn 6:3	*1519*
that should come *i* the world	Jn 6:14	*1519*
he departed again *i* a mountain	Jn 6:15	*1519*
And entered *i* a ship, and went over	Jn 6:17	*1519*
willingly received him *i* the ship	Jn 6:21	*1519*
not with his disciples *i* the boat	Jn 6:22	*1519*
go *i* Judaea, that thy disciples	Jn 7:3	*1519*
feast Jesus went up *i* the temple	Jn 7:14	*1519*
he came again *i* the temple	Jn 8:2	*1519*
judgment I am come *i* this world	Jn 9:39	*1519*
not by the door *i* the sheepfold	Jn 10:1	*1519*
and sent *i* the world, Thou	Jn 10:36	*1519*
i the place where John at first	Jn 10:40	*1519*
Let us go *i* Judaea again	Jn 11:7	*1519*
which should come *i* the world	Jn 11:27	*1519*
Jesus was not yet come *i* the town	Jn 11:30	*1519*
i a city called Ephraim, and there	Jn 11:54	*1519*
a corn of wheat fall *i* the ground	Jn 12:24	*1519*
I am come a light *i* the world	Jn 12:46	*1519*
the devil having now put *i* the	Jn 13:2	*1519*
had given all things *i* his hands	Jn 13:3	*1519*
that he poureth water *i* a bason	Jn 13:5	*1519*
after the sop Satan entered *i* him	Jn 13:27	*1519*
them, and cast them *i* the fire	Jn 15:6	*1519*
he will guide you *i* all truth	Jn 16:13	*1519*
your sorrow shall be turned *i* joy	Jn 16:20	*1519*
that a man is born *i* the world	Jn 16:21	*1519*
Father, and am come *i* the world	Jn 16:28	*1519*
As thou hast sent me *i* the world	Jn 17:18	*1519*
have I also sent them *i* the world	Jn 17:18	*1519*
i the which he entered, and his	Jn 18:1	*1519*
Put up thy sword *i* the sheath	Jn 18:11	*1519*
went in with Jesus *i* the palace	Jn 18:15	*1519*
went not *i* the judgment hall	Jn 18:28	*1519*
Then Pilate entered *i* the	Jn 18:33	*1519*
for this cause came I *i* the world	Jn 18:37	*1519*
went again *i* the judgment hall,	Jn 19:9	*1519*
i a place called the place of a	Jn 19:17	*1519*
went *i* the sepulchre, and seeth	Jn 20:6	*1519*
down, and looked *i* the sepulchre,	Jn 20:11	*1519*
put my finger *i* the print of the	Jn 20:25	*1519*
and thrust my hand *i* his side	Jn 20:25	*1519*
thy hand, and thrust it *i* my side	Jn 20:27	*1519*
entered *i* a ship immediately	Jn 21:3	*1519*
and did cast himself *i* the sea	Jn 21:7	*1519*
why stand ye gazing up *i* heaven	Acts 1:11	*1519*
is taken up from you *i* heaven	Acts 1:11	*1519*
as ye have seen him go *i* heaven	Acts 1:11	*1519*
they went up *i* an upper room,	Acts 1:13	*1519*
sun shall be turned *i* darkness	Acts 2:20	*1519*
and the moon *i* blood	Acts 2:20	*1519*
is not ascended *i* the heavens	Acts 2:34	*1519*
John went up together *i* the	Acts 3:1	*1519*
of them that entered *i* the temple	Acts 3:2	*1519*
John about to go *i* the temple	Acts 3:3	*1519*
and entered with them *i* the temple	Acts 3:8	*1519*
forth the sick *i* the streets	Acts 5:15	*2596*
they entered *i* the temple early	Acts 5:21	*1519*
come *i* the land which I shall	Acts 7:3	*1519*
dead, he removed him *i* this land	Acts 7:4	*1519*
they should bring them *i* bondage	Acts 7:6	
with envy, sold Joseph *i* Egypt	Acts 7:9	*1519*
So Jacob went down *i* Egypt	Acts 7:15	*1519*
And were carried over *i* Sychem	Acts 7:16	*1519*
it came *i* his heart to visit his	Acts 7:23	*1909*
come, I will send thee *i* Egypt	Acts 7:34	*1519*
hearts turned back again *i* Egypt	Acts 7:39	*1519*
after brought in with Jesus *i* the	Acts 7:45	*1722*
looked up stedfastly *i* heaven	Acts 7:55	*1519*
entering *i* every house, and haling	Acts 8:3	*1531*
they went down both *i* the water	Acts 8:38	*1519*
go *i* the city, and it shall be	Acts 9:6	*1519*
hand, and brought him *i* Damascus	Acts 9:8	*1519*
go *i* the street which is called	Acts 9:11	*1909*
his way, and entered *i* the house	Acts 9:17	*1519*
they brought him *i* the upper	Acts 9:39	*1519*
made ready, he fell *i* a trance,	Acts 10:10	*1909*
was received up again *i* heaven	Acts 10:16	*1519*
to send for thee *i* his house	Acts 10:22	*1519*
after they entered *i* Caesarea	Acts 10:24	*1519*
at any time entered *i* my mouth	Acts 11:8	*1519*
all were drawn up again *i* heaven	Acts 11:10	*1519*
we entered *i* the man's house	Acts 11:12	*1519*
departed, and went *i* another place	Acts 12:17	*1519*
went *i* the synagogue on the	Acts 13:14	*1519*
i the synagogue of the Jews	Acts 14:1	*1519*
he rose up, and came *i* the city	Acts 14:20	*1519*
enter *i* the kingdom of God	Acts 14:22	*1519*
Perga, they went down *i* Attalia	Acts 14:25	*1519*
they assayed to go *i* Bithynia	Acts 16:7	*2596*
saying, Come over *i* Macedonia	Acts 16:9	*1519*
we endeavoured to go *i* Macedonia	Acts 16:10	*1519*
come *i* my house, and abide there	Acts 16:15	*1519*
drew them *i* the marketplace unto	Acts 16:19	*1519*
them, they cast them *i* prison	Acts 16:23	*1519*
thrust them *i* the inner prison,	Acts 16:24	*1519*
he had brought them *i* his house	Acts 16:34	*1519*
Romans, and have cast us *i* prison	Acts 16:37	*1519*
entered *i* the house of Lydia	Acts 16:40	*1519*
who coming thither went *i* the	Acts 17:10	*1519*
entered *i* a certain man's house,	Acts 18:7	*1519*
and sailed thence *i* Syria	Acts 18:18	*1519*
himself entered *i* the synagogue	Acts 18:19	*1519*
he was disposed to pass *i* Achaia	Acts 18:27	*1519*

he went *i* the synagogue, and spake..... Acts 19:8 *1519*
So he sent *i* Macedonia two of.............. Acts 19:22 *1519*
with one accord *i* the theatre.............. Acts 19:29 *1519*
adventure himself *i* the theatre.............. Acts 19:31 *1519*
and departed for to go *i* Macedonia...... Acts 20:1 *1519*
exhortation, he came *i* Greece.............. Acts 20:2 *1519*
as he was about to sail *i* Syria.............. Acts 20:3 *1519*
him *i* Asia Sopater of Berea.................. Acts 20:4 *891*
being fallen *i* a deep sleep.................. Acts 20:9
the first day that I came *i* Asia.............. Acts 20:18 *1519*
the left hand, and sailed *i* Syria.............. Acts 21:3 *1519*
we entered *i* the house of Philip.............. Acts 21:8 *1519*
shall deliver him *i* the hands of.............. Acts 21:11 *1519*
with them entered *i* the temple.............. Acts 21:26 *1519*
brought Greeks also *i* the temple.............. Acts 21:28 *1519*
Paul had brought *i* the temple.............. Acts 21:29 *1519*
him to be carried *i* the castle.............. Acts 21:34 *1519*
Paul was to be led *i* the castle.............. Acts 21:37 *1519*
leddest out *i* the wilderness four.............. Acts 21:38 *1519*
delivering *i* prisons both men and.............. Acts 22:4 *1519*
unto me, Arise, and go *i* Damascus.............. Acts 22:10 *1519*
were with me, I came *i* Damascus.............. Acts 22:11 *1519*
clothes, and threw dust *i* the air.............. Acts 22:23 *1519*
him to be brought *i* the castle.............. Acts 22:24 *1519*
and to bring him *i* the castle.............. Acts 23:10 *1519*
entered *i* the castle, and told.............. Acts 23:16 *1519*
down Paul to morrow *i* the council.............. Acts 23:20 *1519*
brought him forth *i* their council.............. Acts 23:28 *1519*
Porcius Festus came *i* Felix' room.............. Acts 24:27
Festus was come *i* the province.............. Acts 25:1
was entered *i* the place of.............. Acts 25:23 *1519*
that we should sail *i* Italy.............. Acts 27:1 *1519*
entering *i* a ship of Adramyttium,.............. Acts 27:2
of Alexandria sailing *i* Italy.............. Acts 27:6 *1519*
and could not bear up *i* the wind.............. Acts 27:15
they should fall *i* the quicksands.............. Acts 27:17 *1519*
had let down the boat *i* the sea.............. Acts 27:30 *1519*
and cast out the wheat *i* the sea.............. Acts 27:38 *1519*
i the which they were minded, if.............. Acts 27:39 *1519*
falling *i* a place where two seas.............. Acts 27:41 *1519*
cast themselves first *i* the sea.............. Acts 27:43
he shook off the beast *i* the fire.............. Acts 28:5 *1519*
i the hands of the Romans.............. Acts 28:17 *1519*
came many to him *i* his lodging.............. Acts 28:23 *1519*
God *i* an image made like to.............. Rom 1:23 *1722*
changed the truth of God *i* a lie.............. Rom 1:25 *1722*
did change the natural use *i* that.............. Rom 1:26 *1519*
i this grace wherein we stand.............. Rom 5:2 *1519*
one man sin entered *i* the world.............. Rom 5:12 *1519*
so many of us as were baptized *i*.............. Rom 6:3 *1519*
Christ were baptized *i* his death.............. Rom 6:3 *1519*
with him by baptism *i* death.............. Rom 6:4 *1519*
bringing me *i* captivity to the.............. Rom 7:23
i the glorious liberty of the.............. Rom 8:21 *1519*
heart, Who shall ascend *i* heaven.............. Rom 10:6 *1519*
Or, Who shall descend *i* the deep.............. Rom 10:7 *1519*
their sound went *i* all the earth.............. Rom 10:18 *1519*
to nature *i* a good olive tree.............. Rom 11:24 *1519*
be graffed *i* their own olive tree.............. Rom 11:24
I take my journey *i* Spain.............. Rom 15:24 *1519*
fruit, I will come by you *i* Spain.............. Rom 15:28 *1519*
have entered *i* the heart of man.............. 1Cor 2:9 *1909*
who shall bring you *i* remembrance.............. 1Cor 4:17
my body, and bring it *i* subjection.............. 1Cor 9:27
together therefore *i* one place.............. 1Cor 11:20 *1909*
are we all baptized *i* one body.............. 1Cor 12:13 *1519*
all made to drink *i* one Spirit.............. 1Cor 12:13 *1519*
for ye shall speak *i* the air.............. 1Cor 14:9 *1519*
be come together *i* one place.............. 1Cor 14:23 *1909*
And to pass by you *i* Macedonia.............. 2Cor 1:16 *1519*
I went from thence *i* Macedonia.............. 2Cor 2:13 *1519*
are changed *i* the same image from.............. 2Cor 3:18
when we were come *i* Macedonia.............. 2Cor 7:5 *1519*
care *i* the heart of Titus for you.............. 2Cor 8:16 *1722*
subjection *i* the gospel of Christ.............. 2Cor 9:13 *1519*
bringing *i* captivity every.............. 2Cor 10:5
i the apostles of Christ.............. 2Cor 11:13 *1519*
transformed *i* an angel of light.............. 2Cor 11:14 *1519*
if a man bring you *i* bondage.............. 2Cor 11:20
that he was caught up *i* paradise.............. 2Cor 12:4 *1519*
you *i* the grace of Christ unto.............. Gal 1:6 *1722*
but I went *i* Arabia, and returned.............. Gal 1:17 *1519*
Afterwards I came *i* the regions.............. Gal 1:21 *1519*
they might bring us *i* bondage.............. Gal 2:4
i Christ have put on Christ.............. Gal 3:27 *1519*
Spirit of his Son *i* your hearts.............. Gal 4:6 *1519*
i the lower parts of the earth.............. Eph 4:9 *1519*
may grow up *i* him in all things,.............. Eph 4:15 *1519*
hath translated us *i* the kingdom.............. Col 1:13 *1519*
intruding *i* those things which he.............. Col 2:18
your hearts *i* the love of God.............. 2Th 3:5 *1519*
i the patient waiting for Christ.............. 2Th 3:5 *1519*
Ephesus, when I went *i* Macedonia.............. 1Ti 1:3 *1519*
putting me *i* the ministry.............. 1Ti 1:12 *1519*
that Christ Jesus came *i* the.............. 1Ti 1:15 *1519*
lifted up with pride he fall *i*.............. 1Ti 3:6 *1519*
lest he fall *i* reproach and the.............. 1Ti 3:7 *1519*
in the world, received up *i* glory.............. 1Ti 3:16 *1722*
Let not a widow be taken *i* the.............. 1Ti 5:9
we brought nothing *i* this world.............. 1Ti 6:7 *1519*
will be rich fall *i* temptation.............. 1Ti 6:9 *1519*
i many foolish and hurtful lusts,.............. 1Ti 6:9 *1519*
are they which creep *i* houses.............. 2Ti 3:6 *1519*
in the firstbegotten *i* the world.............. Heb 1:6 *1519*
They shall not enter *i* my rest.............. Heb 3:11 *1519*
they should not enter *i* his rest.............. Heb 3:18 *1519*
left us of entering *i* his rest.............. Heb 4:1 *1519*
have believed do enter *i* rest.............. Heb 4:3 *1519*
if they shall enter *i* my rest.............. Heb 4:3 *1519*
If they shall enter *i* my rest.............. Heb 4:5 *1519*
For he that is entered *i* his rest.............. Heb 4:10 *1519*
therefore to enter *i* that rest.............. Heb 4:11 *1519*
that is passed *i* the heavens.............. Heb 4:14
which entereth *i* that within the.............. Heb 6:19 *1519*

I will put my laws *i* their mind.............. Heb 8:10 *1519*
always *i* the first tabernacle.............. Heb 9:6 *1519*
But *i* the second went the high.............. Heb 9:7 *1519*
that the way *i* the holiest of all.............. Heb 9:8
entered in once *i* the holy place.............. Heb 9:12 *1519*
For Christ is not entered *i* the.............. Heb 9:24 *1519*
but *i* heaven itself, now to.............. Heb 9:24 *1519*
as the high priest entereth *i* the.............. Heb 9:25 *1519*
when he cometh *i* the world.............. Heb 10:5 *1519*
I will put my laws *i* their hearts.............. Heb 10:16 *1909*
boldness to enter *i* the holiest.............. Heb 10:19
i the hands of the living God.............. Heb 10:31 *1519*
when he was called to go out *i* a.............. Heb 11:8 *1519*
whose blood is brought *i* the.............. Heb 13:11 *1519*
when ye fall *i* divers temptations.............. Jas 1:2
But whoso looketh *i* the perfect.............. Jas 1:25 *1519*
morrow we will go *i* such a city.............. Jas 4:13 *1519*
which have reaped are entered *i*.............. Jas 5:4 *1519*
lest ye fall *i* condemnation.............. Jas 5:12 *5259*
the angels desire to look *i*.............. 1Pet 1:12 *1519*
darkness *i* his marvellous light.............. 1Pet 2:9 *1519*
Who is gone *i* heaven, and is on.............. 1Pet 3:22 *1519*
i the everlasting kingdom of our.............. 2Pet 1:11 *1519*
delivered them *i* chains of.............. 2Pet 2:4
Gomorrah *i* ashes condemned them.............. 2Pet 2:6
prophets are gone out *i* the world.............. 1Jn 4:1 *1519*
his only begotten Son *i* the world.............. 1Jn 4:9 *1519*
deceivers are entered *i* the world.............. 2Jn 7 *1519*
receive him not *i* your house.............. 2Jn 10 *1519*
grace of our God *i* lasciviousness.............. Jude 4 *1519*
shall cast some of you *i* prison.............. Rev 2:10 *1519*
Behold, I will cast her *i* a bed.............. Rev 2:22 *1519*
with her *i* great tribulation.............. Rev 2:22 *1519*
of God sent forth *i* all the earth.............. Rev 5:6 *1519*
the altar, and cast it *i* the earth.............. Rev 8:5 *1519*
with fire was cast *i* the sea.............. Rev 8:8 *1519*
of life from God entered *i* them.............. Rev 11:11 *1909*
the woman fled *i* the wilderness.............. Rev 12:6 *1519*
he was cast out *i* the earth.............. Rev 12:9 *1519*
she might fly *i* the wilderness.............. Rev 12:14 *1519*
i her place, where she is.............. Rev 12:14 *1519*
He that leadeth *i* captivity shall.............. Rev 13:10
captivity shall go *i* captivity.............. Rev 13:10 *1519*
i the cup of his indignation.............. Rev 14:10 *1722*
thrust in his sickle *i* the earth.............. Rev 14:19 *1519*
cast it *i* the great winepress of.............. Rev 14:19 *1519*
was able to enter *i* the temple.............. Rev 15:8 *1519*
he gathered them together *i* a.............. Rev 16:16 *1519*
poured out his vial *i* the air.............. Rev 16:17 *1519*
city was divided *i* three parts.............. Rev 16:19 *1519*
in the spirit *i* the wilderness.............. Rev 17:3 *1519*
bottomless pit, and go *i* perdition.............. Rev 17:8 *1519*
the seven, and goeth *i* perdition.............. Rev 17:11 *1519*
millstone, and cast it *i* the sea.............. Rev 18:21 *1519*
These both were cast alive *i* a.............. Rev 19:20 *1519*
cast him *i* the bottomless pit, and.............. Rev 20:3 *1519*
them was cast *i* the lake of fire.............. Rev 20:10 *1519*
hell were cast *i* the lake of fire.............. Rev 20:14 *1519*
life was cast *i* the lake of fire.............. Rev 20:15 *1519*
bring their glory and honour *i* it.............. Rev 21:24 *1519*
and honour of the nations *i* it.............. Rev 21:26 *1519*
i it any thing that defileth.............. Rev 21:27 *1519*
in through the gates *i* the city.............. Rev 22:14 *1519*

INTREAT
i for me to Ephron the son of.............. Gen 23:8 6293
I the LORD, that he may take away.............. Ex 8:8 6279
when shall I *i* for thee, and for.............. Ex 8:9 6279
very far away: *i* for me.............. Ex 8:28 6279
I will *i* the LORD that the swarms.............. Ex 8:29 6279
I the LORD (for it is enough).............. Ex 9:28 6279
i the LORD your God, that he may.............. Ex 10:17 6279
I me not to leave thee, or to.............. Ruth 1:16 6293
the LORD, who shall *i* for him.............. 1Sa 2:25 6419
I now the face of the LORD thy.............. 1Kin 13:6 2470
the people shall *i* thy favour.............. Ps 45:12 2470
Many will *i* the favour of the.............. Prov 19:6 2470
Being defamed, we *i*.............. 1Cor 4:13 *3870*
I *i* thee also, true yokefellow,.............. Phil 4:3 *2065*
an elder, but *i* him as a father.............. 1Ti 5:1 *3870*

INTREATED
Isaac *i* the LORD for his wife,.............. Gen 25:21 6279
and the LORD was *i* of him, and.............. Gen 25:21 6279
out from Pharaoh, and *i* the LORD.............. Ex 8:30 6279
out from Pharaoh, and *i* the LORD.............. Ex 10:18 6279
Then Manoah *i* the LORD, and said,.............. Judg 13:8 6279
after that God was *i* for the land.............. 2Sa 21:14 6279
So the LORD was *i* for the land.............. 2Sa 24:25 6279
the battle, and he was *i* of them.............. 1Chr 5:20 6279
and he was *i* of him, and heard his.............. 2Chr 33:13 6279
also, and how God was *i* of him.............. 2Chr 33:19 6279
and he was *i* of us.............. Ezr 8:23 6279
I *i* him with my mouth.............. Job 19:16 2603
though I *i* for the children's.............. Job 19:17 2589
I *i* thy favour with my whole.............. Ps 119:58 2470
LORD, and he shall be *i* of them.............. Is 19:22 6279
came his father out, and *i* him.............. Lk 15:28 *3870*
i that the word should not be.............. Heb 12:19 *3862*
gentle, and easy to be *i*, full of.............. Jas 3:17 *2138*

INTREATIES
The poor useth *i*.............. Prov 18:23 8469

INTREATY
Praying us with much *i* that we.............. 2Cor 8:4 *3874*

INTRUDING
i into those things which he hath.............. Col 2:18 *1687*

INVADE
thou wouldest not let Israel *i*.............. 2Chr 20:10 935
he will *i* them with his troops.............. Hab 3:16 1464

INVADED
the Philistines have *i* the land.............. 1Sa 23:27 6584
i the Geshurites, and the Gezrites.............. 1Sa 27:8 6584
the Amalekites had *i* the south.............. 1Sa 30:1 6584
the bands of the Moabites *i* the.............. 2Kin 13:20 935
The Philistines also had *i* the.............. 2Chr 28:18 6584

INVASION
We made an *i* upon the south of.............. 1Sa 30:14 6584

INVENT
i to themselves instruments of.............. Amos 6:5 2803

INVENTED
i by cunning men, to be on the.............. 2Chr 26:15 2803

INVENTIONS
thou tookest vengeance of their *i*.............. Ps 99:8 5949
him to anger with their *i*.............. Ps 106:29 4611
went a whoring with their own *i*.............. Ps 106:39 4611
and find out knowledge of witty *i*.............. Prov 8:12 4209
but they have sought out many *i*.............. Eccl 7:29 2810

INVENTORS
i of evil things, disobedient to.............. Rom 1:30 *2182*

INVISIBLE
For the *i* things of him from the.............. Rom 1:20 *517*
Who is the image of the *i* God.............. Col 1:15 *517*
that are in earth, visible and *i*.............. Col 1:16 *517*
the King eternal, immortal, *i*.............. 1Ti 1:17 *517*
endured, as seeing him who is *i*.............. Heb 11:27 *517*

INVITED
since I said, I have *i* the people.............. 1Sa 9:24 7121
Absalom *i* all the king's sons.............. 2Sa 13:23 7121
to morrow am I *i* unto her also.............. Est 5:12 7121

INWARD
is in the side of the ephod *i*.............. Ex 28:26 1004
was on the side of the ephod *i*.............. Ex 39:19 1004
it is fret *i*, whether it be bare.............. Lev 13:55
built round about from Millo and *i*.............. 2Sa 5:9 1004
and all their hinder parts were *i*.............. 1Kin 7:25 1004
their feet, and their faces were *i*.............. 2Chr 3:13 1004
and all their hinder parts were *i*.............. 2Chr 4:4 1004
All my *i* friends abhorred me.............. Job 19:19 5475
hath put wisdom in the *i* parts.............. Job 38:36 2910
their *i* part is very wickedness.............. Ps 5:9 7130
Their *i* thought is, that their.............. Ps 49:11 7130
desirest truth in the *i* parts.............. Ps 51:6 2910
both the *i* thought of every one.............. Ps 64:6 7130
searching all the *i* parts of the.............. Prov 20:27 2315
so do stripes the *i* parts of the.............. Prov 20:30 2315
mine *i* parts for Kir-haresh.............. Is 16:11 7130
will put my law in their *i* parts.............. Jer 31:33 7130
and the porch of the gate was *i*.............. Eze 40:9 1004
and windows were round about *i*.............. Eze 40:16 6441
Then went he *i*, and measured the.............. Eze 41:3 6441
a walk of ten cubits breadth *i*.............. Eze 42:4 6442
but your *i* part is full of.............. Lk 11:39 *2081*
in the law of God after the *i* man.............. Rom 7:22 *2080*
yet the *i* man is renewed day by.............. 2Cor 4:16 *2081*
his *i* affection is more abundant.............. 2Cor 7:15 *4698*

INWARDLY
their mouth, but they curse *i*.............. Ps 62:4 7130
but *i* they are ravening wolves.............. Mt 7:15 *2081*
But he is a Jew, which is one *i*.............. Rom 2:29

INWARDS
all the fat that covereth the *i*.............. Ex 29:13 7130
in pieces, and wash the *i* of him.............. Ex 29:17 7130
and the fat that covereth the *i*.............. Ex 29:22 7130
But his *i* and his legs shall he.............. Lev 1:9 7130
But he shall wash the *i* and the.............. Lev 1:13 7130
the fat that covereth the *i*.............. Lev 3:3 7130
and all the fat that is upon the *i*.............. Lev 3:3 7130
and the fat that covereth the *i*.............. Lev 3:9 7130
and all the fat that is upon the *i*.............. Lev 3:9 7130
the fat that covereth the *i*.............. Lev 3:14 7130
and all the fat that is upon the *i*.............. Lev 3:14 7130
the fat that covereth the *i*.............. Lev 4:8 7130
and all the fat that is upon the *i*.............. Lev 4:8 7130
head, and with his legs, and his *i*.............. Lev 4:11 7130
and the fat that covereth the *i*.............. Lev 7:3 7130
all the fat that was upon the *i*.............. Lev 8:16 7130
And he washed the *i* and the legs in.............. Lev 8:21 7130
all the fat that was upon the *i*.............. Lev 8:25 7130
And he did wash the *i* and the legs,.............. Lev 9:14 7130
and that which covereth the *i*.............. Lev 9:19

IOB See JOB.

IPHEDEIAH (*if-e-di'-ah*) *A son of Shashak.*
And *I*, and Penuel, the sons of.............. 1Chr 8:25 3301

IPHTAH See JIPHTAH.

IPHTAH EL See JIPHTHAH-EL.

IR (*ur*) See IR-NAHASH, IR-SHEMESH. *Father of Machir.*
and Huppim, the children of *I*.............. 1Chr 7:12 5893

IRA (*i'-rah*)
1. An officer of David.
I also the Jairite was a chief.............. 2Sa 20:26 5896
2. A mighty man of David.
I the son of Ikkesh the Tekoite,.............. 2Sa 23:26 5896
I an Ithrite, Gareb an Ithrite,.............. 2Sa 23:38 5896
I the son of Ikkesh the Tekoite,.............. 1Chr 11:28 5896
I the Ithrite, Gareb the Ithrite,.............. 1Chr 11:40 5896
I the son of Ikkesh the Tekoite.............. 1Chr 27:9 5896

IRAD (*i'-rad*) *Son of Enoch.*
And unto Enoch was born *I*.............. Gen 4:18 5897
and *I* begat Mehujael.............. Gen 4:18 5897

IRAM (*i'-ram*) *An Edomite leader.*
Duke Magdiel, duke *I*.............. Gen 36:43 5902
Duke Magdiel, duke *I*.............. 1Chr 1:54 5902

IRI (*i'-ri*) *A son of Bela.*
and Uzziel, and Jerimoth, and *I* 1Chr 7:7 5901

IRIJAH (*i-ri'-jah*) *A captain of the guard.*
ward was there, whose name was *I* Jer 37:13 3376
so *I* took Jeremiah, and brought Jer 37:14 3376

IR-NAHASH (*ur-na'-hash*) *A descendant of Chelub.*
and Tehinnah the father of *I* 1Chr 4:12 5904

IRON (*i'-ron*) *A city in Naphtali.*
And *I*, and Migdal-el, Horem, and Josh 19:38 3375
A metal.
of every artificer in brass and *i* Gen 4:22 1270
and I will make your heaven as *i* Lev 26:19 1270
and the silver, the brass, the *i* Num 31:22 1270
smite him with an instrument of *i* Num 35:16 1270
his bedstead was a bedstead of *i* Deut 3:11 1270
you forth out of the *i* furnace Deut 4:20 1270
a land whose stones are *i* Deut 8:9 1270
not lift up any *i* tool upon them Deut 27:5 1270
that is under thee shall be *i* Deut 28:23 1270
put a yoke of *i* upon thy neck Deut 28:48 1270
Thy shoes shall be *i* and brass Deut 33:25 1270
and gold, and vessels of brass and *i* Josh 6:19 1270
and the vessels of brass and of *i* Josh 6:24 1270
which no man hath lift up any *i* Josh 8:31 1270
of the valley have chariots of *i* Josh 17:16 1270
though they have *i* chariots Josh 17:18 1270
gold, and with brass, and with *i* Josh 22:8 1270
because they had chariots of *i* Judg 1:19 1270
he had nine hundred chariots of *i* Judg 4:3 1270
even nine hundred chariots of *i* Judg 4:13 1270
weighed six hundred shekels of *i* 1Sa 17:7 1270
of iron, and under axes of *i* 2Sa 12:31 1270
touch them must be fenced with *i* 2Sa 23:7 1270
any tool of *i* heard in the house 1Kin 6:7 1270
the midst of the furnace of *i* 1Kin 8:51 1270
of Chenaanah made him horns of *i* 1Kin 22:11 1270
and the *i* did swim 2Kin 6:6 1270
with saws, and with harrows of *i* 1Chr 20:3 1270
David prepared *i* in abundance for 1Chr 22:3 1270
and of brass and *i* without weight 1Chr 22:14 1270
silver, and the brass, and the *i* 1Chr 22:16 1270
the *i* for things of iron, and wood 1Chr 29:2 1270
brass, the iron for things of *i* 1Chr 29:2 1270
one hundred thousand talents of *i* 1Chr 29:7 1270
in silver, and in brass, and in *i* 2Chr 2:7 1270
and in silver, in brass, in *i* 2Chr 2:14 1270
Chenaanah had made him horns of *i* 2Chr 18:10 1270
LORD, and also such as wrought *i* 2Chr 24:12 1270
they were graven with an *i* pen Job 19:24 1270
He shall flee from the *i* weapon Job 20:24 1270
I is taken out of the earth, and Job 28:2 1270
his bones are like bars of *i* Job 40:18 1270
He esteemeth *i* as straw, and brass Job 41:27 1270
shalt break them with a rod of *i* Ps 2:9 1270
he was laid in *i* Ps 105:18 1270
being bound in affliction and *i* Ps 107:10 1270
and cut the bars of *i* in sunder Ps 107:16 1270
and their nobles with fetters of *i* Ps 149:8 1270
I sharpeneth iron Prov 27:17 1270
Iron sharpeneth *i* Prov 27:17 1270
If the *i* be blunt, and he do not Eccl 10:10 1270
the thickets of the forest with *i* Is 10:34 1270
and cut in sunder the bars of *i* Is 45:2 1270
and thy neck is an *i* sinew Is 48:4 1270
for *i* I will bring silver, and for Is 60:17 1270
for wood brass, and for stones *i* Is 60:17 1270
an *i* pillar, and brasen walls Jer 1:18 1270
they are brass and *i* Jer 6:28 1270
land of Egypt, from the *i* furnace Jer 11:4 1270
Shall *i* break the northern iron Jer 15:12 1270
Judah is written with a pen of *i* Jer 17:1 1270
shalt make for them yokes of *i* Jer 28:13 1270
I have put a yoke of *i* upon the Jer 28:14 1270
take thou unto thee an *i* pan Eze 4:3 1270
it for a wall of *i* between thee Eze 4:3 1270
all they are brass, and tin, and *i* Eze 22:18 1270
gather silver, and brass, and *i* Eze 22:20 1270
with silver, *i*, tin, and lead, Eze 27:12 1270
bright *i*, cassia, and calamus, Eze 27:19 1270
legs of iron, his feet part of *i* Dan 2:33 6523
upon his feet that were of *i* Dan 2:34 6523
Then was the *i*, the clay, the Dan 2:35 6523
kingdom shall be strong as *i* Dan 2:40 6523
forasmuch as *i* breaketh in pieces Dan 2:40 6523
as *i* that breaketh all these, Dan 2:40 6523
of potters' clay, and part of *i* Dan 2:41 6523
be in it of the strength of the *i* Dan 2:41 6523
sawest the *i* mixed with miry clay Dan 2:41 6523
toes of the feet were part of *i* Dan 2:42 6523
whereas thou sawest *i* mixed with Dan 2:43 6523
even as *i* is not mixed with clay Dan 2:43 6523
and that it brake in pieces the *i* Dan 2:45 6523
the earth, even with a band of *i* Dan 4:15 6523
the earth, even with a band of *i* Dan 4:23 6523
and of silver, of brass, of *i* Dan 5:4 6523
of silver, and gold, of brass, *i* Dan 5:23 6523
and it had great *i* teeth Dan 7:7 6523
dreadful, whose teeth were of *i* Dan 7:19 6523
with threshing instruments of *i* Amos 1:3 1270
for I will make thine horn *i* Mic 4:13 1270
they came unto the *i* gate that Acts 12:10 *4603*
conscience seared with a hot *i* 1Ti 4:2
shall rule them with a rod of *i* Rev 2:27 *4603*
as it were breastplates of *i* Rev 9:9 *4603*
rule all nations with a rod of *i* Rev 12:5 *4603*
precious wood, and of brass, and *i* Rev 18:12 *4604*
shall rule them with a rod of *i* Rev 19:15 *4603*

IRONS
thou fill his skin with barbed *i* Job 41:7 7905

IRPEEL (*ur'-pe-el*) *A city in Benjamin.*
And Rekem, and *I*, and Taralah, Josh 18:27 3416

IR-SHEMESH (*ur-she'-mesh*) *A city in Dan.*
was Zorah, and Eshtaol, and *I* Josh 19:41 5905

IRU (*i'-ru*) *A son of Caleb.*
I, Elah, and Naam 1Chr 4:15 5902

IS See PREFACE.

ISAAC (*i'-za-ak*) See ISAAC'S. *Son of Abraham and Sarah.*
and thou shalt call his name *I* Gen 17:19 3327
covenant will I establish with *I* Gen 17:21 3327
him, whom Sarah bare to him, *I* Gen 21:3 3327
his son *I* being eight days old Gen 21:4 3327
when his son *I* was born unto him Gen 21:5 3327
the same day that *I* was weaned Gen 21:8 3327
be heir with my son, even with *I* Gen 21:10 3327
for in *I* shall thy seed be called Gen 21:12 3327
now thy son, thine only son *I* Gen 22:2 3327
I his son, and clave the wood for Gen 22:3 3327
and laid it upon *I* his son Gen 22:6 3327
I spake unto Abraham his father, Gen 22:7 3327
bound *I* his son, and laid him on Gen 22:9 3327
and take a wife unto my son *I* Gen 24:4 3327
hast appointed for thy servant *I* Gen 24:14 3327
I came from the way of the well Gen 24:62 3327
I went out to meditate in the Gen 24:63 3327
up her eyes, and when she saw *I* Gen 24:64 3327
the servant told *I* all things Gen 24:66 3327
I brought her into his mother Gen 24:67 3327
I was comforted after his Gen 24:67 3327
gave all that he had unto *I* Gen 25:5 3327
and sent them away from *I* his son Gen 25:6 3327
And his sons *I* and Ishmael buried Gen 25:9 3327
that God blessed his son *I* Gen 25:11 3327
I dwelt by the well Lahai-roi Gen 25:11 3327
And these are the generations of *I* Gen 25:19 3327
Abraham begat *I* Gen 25:19 3327
I was forty years old when he Gen 25:20 3327
I intreated the LORD for his wife Gen 25:21 3327
I was threescore years old when Gen 25:26 3327
I loved Esau, because he did eat Gen 25:28 3327
I went unto Abimelech king of the Gen 26:1 3327
And *I* dwelt in Gerar Gen 26:6 3327
I was sporting with Rebekah his Gen 26:8 3327
And Abimelech called *I*, and said, Gen 26:9 3327
I said unto him, Because I said, Gen 26:9 3327
Then *I* sowed in that land, and Gen 26:12 3327
And Abimelech said unto *I*, Go from Gen 26:16 3327
I departed thence, and pitched his Gen 26:17 3327
I digged again the wells of water Gen 26:18 3327
I said unto them, Wherefore come Gen 26:27 3327
I sent them away, and they Gen 26:31 3327
Which were a grief of mind unto *I* Gen 26:35 3327
came to pass, that when *I* was old Gen 27:1 3327
Rebekah heard when *I* spake to Gen 27:5 3327
I said unto his son, How is it Gen 27:20 3327
I said unto Jacob, Come near, I Gen 27:21 3327
Jacob went near unto *I* his father Gen 27:22 3327
his father *I* said unto him, Come Gen 27:26 3327
as soon as *I* had made an end of Gen 27:30 3327
from the presence of *I* his father Gen 27:30 3327
I his father said unto him, Who Gen 27:32 3327
I trembled very exceedingly, and Gen 27:33 3327
I answered and said unto Esau, Gen 27:37 3327
I his father answered and said Gen 27:39 3327
And Rebekah said to *I*, I am weary Gen 27:46 3327
I called Jacob, and blessed him, Gen 28:1 3327
And *I* sent away Jacob Gen 28:5 3327
Esau saw that *I* had blessed Jacob Gen 28:6 3327
Canaan pleased not *I* his father Gen 28:8 3327
thy father, and the God of *I* Gen 28:13 3327
for to go to *I* his father in the Gen 31:18 3327
God of Abraham, and the fear of *I* Gen 31:42 3327
sware by the fear of his father *I* Gen 31:53 3327
Abraham, and God of my father *I* Gen 32:9 3327
land which I gave Abraham and *I* Gen 35:12 3327
Jacob came unto *I* his father unto Gen 35:27 3327
where Abraham and *I* sojourned Gen 35:27 3327
the days of *I* were an hundred and Gen 35:28 3327
I gave up the ghost, and died, and Gen 35:29 3327
unto the God of his father *I* Gen 46:1 3327
I did walk, the God which fed me Gen 48:15 3327
name of my fathers Abraham and *I* Gen 48:16 3327
there they buried *I* and Rebekah Gen 49:31 3327
which he sware to Abraham, to *I* Gen 50:24 3327
his covenant with Abraham, with *I* Ex 2:24 3327
the God of Abraham, the God of *I* Ex 3:6 3327
the God of Abraham, the God of *I* Ex 3:15 3327
fathers, the God of Abraham, of *I* Ex 3:16 3327
the God of Abraham, the God of *I* Ex 4:5 3327
I appeared unto Abraham, unto *I* Ex 6:3 3327
swear to give it to Abraham, to *I* Ex 6:8 3327
Remember Abraham, *I*, and Israel, Ex 32:13 3327
which I sware unto Abraham, to *I* Ex 33:1 3327
Jacob, and also my covenant with *I* Lev 26:42 3327
I sware unto Abraham, unto *I* Num 32:11 3327
unto your fathers, Abraham, *I* Deut 1:8 3327
thy fathers, to Abraham, to *I* Deut 6:10 3327
unto thy fathers, Abraham, *I* Deut 9:5 3327
Remember thy servants, Abraham, *I* Deut 9:27 3327
thy fathers, to Abraham, to *I* Deut 29:13 3327
thy fathers, to Abraham, to *I* Deut 30:20 3327
I sware unto Abraham, unto *I* Deut 34:4 3327
his seed, and gave him *I* Josh 24:3 3327
And I gave unto *I* Jacob and Esau Josh 24:4 3327
and said, LORD God of Abraham, *I* 1Kin 18:36 3327
of his covenant with Abraham, *I* 2Kin 13:23 3327
I, and Ishmael 1Chr 1:28 3327
And Abraham begat *I* 1Chr 1:34 3327
The sons of *I* 1Chr 1:34 3327
Abraham, and of his oath unto *I* 1Chr 16:16 3327
O LORD God of Abraham, *I*, and of 1Chr 29:18 3327
unto the LORD God of Abraham, *I* 2Chr 30:6 3327
with Abraham, and his oath unto *I* Ps 105:9 3446
over the seed of Abraham, *I* Jer 33:26 3446
places of *I* shall be desolate Amos 7:9 3446
thy word against the house of *I* Amos 7:16 3446
Abraham begat *I* Mt 1:2 *2464*
and *I* begat Jacob Mt 1:2 *2464*
shall sit down with Abraham, and *I* Mt 8:11 *2464*
God of Abraham, and the God of *I* Mt 22:32 *2464*
God of Abraham, and the God of *I* Mk 12:26 *2464*
of Jacob, which was the son of *I* Lk 3:34 *2464*
when ye shall see Abraham, and *I* Lk 13:28 *2464*
God of Abraham, and the God of *I* Lk 20:37 *2464*
The God of Abraham, and of *I* Acts 3:13 *2464*
and so Abraham begat *I* Acts 7:8 *2464*
and *I* begat Jacob Acts 7:8 *2464*
God of Abraham, and the God of *I* Acts 7:32 *2464*
In *I* shall thy seed be called Rom 9:7 *2464*
by one, even by our father *I* Rom 9:10 *2464*
as *I* was, are the children of Gal 4:28 *2464*
dwelling in tabernacles with *I* Heb 11:9 *2464*
when he was tried, offered up *I* Heb 11:17 *2464*
That in *I* shall thy seed be Heb 11:18 *2464*
By faith *I* blessed Jacob and Esau Heb 11:20 *2464*
when he had offered *I* his son Jas 2:21 *2464*

ISAAC'S (*i'-za-aks*)
I servants digged in the valley, Gen 26:19 3327
Gerar did strive with *I* herdmen Gen 26:20 3327
there *I* servants digged a well Gen 26:25 3327
that *I* servants came, and told him Gen 26:32 3327

ISAIAH (*i-za'-yah*) See ESAIAS. *A prophet.*
to *I* the prophet the son of Amoz 2Kin 19:2 3470
of king Hezekiah came to *I* 2Kin 19:5 3470
I said unto them, Thus shall ye 2Kin 19:6 3470
Then *I* the son of Amoz sent to 2Kin 19:20 3470
the prophet *I* the son of Amoz 2Kin 20:1 3470
afore *I* was gone out into the 2Kin 20:4 3470
I said, Take a lump of figs 2Kin 20:7 3470
And Hezekiah said unto *I*, What 2Kin 20:8 3470
I said, This sign shalt thou have 2Kin 20:9 3470
I the prophet cried unto the LORD 2Kin 20:11 3470
Then came *I* the prophet unto king 2Kin 20:14 3470
I said unto Hezekiah, Hear the 2Kin 20:16 3470
Then said Hezekiah unto *I* 2Kin 20:19 3470
did *I* the prophet, the son of 2Chr 26:22 3470
the prophet *I* the son of Amoz, 2Chr 32:20 3470
in the vision of *I* the prophet 2Chr 32:32 3470
The vision of *I* the son of Amoz, Is 1:1 3470
The word that *I* the son of Amoz Is 2:1 3470
Then said the LORD unto *I* Is 7:3 3470
which *I* the son of Amoz did see Is 13:1 3470
the LORD by *I* the son of Amoz Is 20:2 3470
as my servant *I* hath walked naked Is 20:3 3470
unto *I* the prophet the son of Is 37:2 3470
of king Hezekiah came to *I* Is 37:5 3470
I said unto them, Thus shall ye Is 37:6 3470
Then *I* the son of Amoz sent unto Is 37:21 3470
I the prophet the son of Amoz Is 38:1 3470
came the word of the LORD to *I* Is 38:4 3470
For *I* had said, Let them take a Is 38:21 3470
Then came *I* the prophet unto king Is 39:3 3470
Then said *I* to Hezekiah, Hear the Is 39:5 3470
Then said Hezekiah to *I*, Good is Is 39:8 3470

ISCAH (*is'-cah*) See SARAH. *A daughter of Haran.*
of Milcah, and the father of *I* Gen 11:29 3252

ISCARIOT (*is-car'-e-ot*) See JUDAS. *Disciple who betrayed Jesus.*
Simon the Canaanite, and Judas *I* Mt 10:4 *2469*
one of the twelve, called Judas *I* Mt 26:14 *2469*
And Judas *I*, which also betrayed Mk 3:19 *2469*
And Judas *I*, one of the twelve, Mk 14:10 *2469*
the brother of James, and Judas *I* Lk 6:16 *2469*
Satan into Judas surnamed *I* Lk 22:3 *2469*
spake of Judas *I* the son of Simon Jn 6:71 *2469*
one of his disciples, Judas *I* Jn 12:4 *2469*
now put into the heart of Judas *I* Jn 13:2 *2469*
the sop, he gave it to Judas *I* Jn 13:26 *2469*
Judas saith unto him, not *I* Jn 14:22 *2469*

ISHBAH (*ish'-bah*) *Father of Eshtemoa.*
and *I* the father of Eshtemoa 1Chr 4:17 3431

ISHBAK (*ish'-bak*) *A son of Abraham.*
and Medan, and Midian, and *I* Gen 25:2 3435
and Medan, and Midian, and *I* 1Chr 1:32 3435

ISHBI-BENOB (*ish''-bi-be'-nob*) *A Philistine giant.*
And *I*, which was of the sons of 2Sa 21:16 3430

ISH-BOSHETH (*ish-bo'-sheth*) See ESH-BAAL. *Son of Saul.*
took *I* the son of Saul, and 2Sa 2:8 378
I Saul's son was forty years old 2Sa 2:10 378
the servants of *I* the son of Saul 2Sa 2:12 378
pertained to *I* the son of Saul 2Sa 2:15 378
I said to Abner, Wherefore hast 2Sa 3:7
very wroth for the words of *I* 2Sa 3:8 378
sent messengers to *I* Saul's son 2Sa 3:14 378
I sent, and took her from her 2Sa 3:15 378
heat of the day to the house of *I* 2Sa 4:5 378
head of *I* unto David to Hebron 2Sa 4:8 378
Behold the head of *I* the son of 2Sa 4:8 378
But they took the head of *I* 2Sa 4:12 378

ISHI (*i'-shi*)
1. A descendant of Pharez.
sons of Appaim; *I* 1Chr 2:31 3469
And the sons of *I* 1Chr 2:31 3469
2. A descendant of Judah.

And the sons of *I* were, Zoheth, and.... 1Chr 4:20 3469
3. A Simeonite.
and Uzziel, the sons of *I*.... 1Chr 4:42 3469
4. A chief of Manasseh.
their fathers, even Epher, and *I*.... 1Chr 5:24 3469
5. A symbolic name for Israel.
LORD, that thou shalt call me *I*.... Hos 2:16 376

ISHIAH (*i-shi'-ah*) See ISHIJAH, ISSHIAH. *A son of Izrahiah.*
Michael, and Obadiah, and Joel, *I*.... 1Chr 7:3 3449

ISHIJAH (*i-shi'-jah*) See ISHIAH, JESIAH. *Married a foreigner in exile.*
Eliezer, *I*, Malchiah, Shemaiah,.... Ezr 10:31 3449

ISHMA (*ish'-mah*) *A descendant of Caleb.*
Jezreel, and *I*, and Idbash.... 1Chr 4:3 3457

ISHMAEL (*ish'-ma-el*) See ISHMAELITE, ISHMAEL'S.
1. Son of Abraham and Hagar.
a son, and shalt call his name *I*.... Gen 16:11 3458
son's name, which Hagar bare, *I*.... Gen 16:15 3458
old, when Hagar bare *I* to Abram.... Gen 16:16 3458
O that *I* might live before thee.... Gen 17:18 3458
And as for *I*, I have heard thee.... Gen 17:20 3458
And Abraham took *I* his son.... Gen 17:23 3458
I his son was thirteen years old,.... Gen 17:25 3458
Abraham circumcised, and *I* his son.... Gen 17:26 3458
I buried him in the cave of.... Gen 25:9 3458
these are the generations of *I*.... Gen 25:12 3458
are the names of the sons of *I*.... Gen 25:13 3458
the firstborn of *I*, Nebajoth.... Gen 25:13 3458
These are the sons of *I*, and these.... Gen 25:16 3458
are the years of the life of *I*.... Gen 25:17 3458
Then went Esau unto *I*, and took.... Gen 28:9 3458
the daughter of *I* Abraham's son.... Gen 28:9 3458
Isaac, and *I*.... 1Chr 1:28 3458
The firstborn of *I*, Nebaioth.... 1Chr 1:29 3458
These are the sons of *I*.... 1Chr 1:31 3458
2. A ruler of Judah.
and Zebadiah the son of *I*, the.... 2Chr 19:11 3458
3. Son of Azel.
are these, Azrikam, Bocheru, and *I*.... 1Chr 8:38 3458
are these, Azrikam, Bocheru, and *I*.... 1Chr 9:44 3458
4. A captain who aided Joash.
I the son of Jehohanan, and.... 2Chr 23:1 3458
5. Married a foreigner in exile.
Elioenai, Maaseiah, *I*, Nethaneel,.... Ezr 10:22 3458
6. The son of Nethaniah.
even *I* the son of Nethaniah, and.... 2Kin 25:23 3458
that *I* the son of Nethaniah, the.... 2Kin 25:25 3458
even *I* the son of Nethaniah, and.... Jer 40:8 3458
I the son of Nethaniah to slay.... Jer 40:14 3458
thee, and I will slay *I* the son of.... Jer 40:15 3458
for thou speakest falsely of *I*.... Jer 40:16 3458
that *I* the son of Nethaniah the.... Jer 41:1 3458
Then arose *I* the son of Nethaniah.... Jer 41:2 3458
I also slew all the Jews that.... Jer 41:3 3458
I the son of Nethaniah went forth.... Jer 41:6 3458
that *I* the son of Nethaniah slew.... Jer 41:7 3458
found among them that said unto *I*.... Jer 41:8 3458
Now the pit wherein *I* had cast.... Jer 41:9 3458
I the son of Nethaniah filled it.... Jer 41:9 3458
Then *I* carried away captive all.... Jer 41:10 3458
I the son of Nethaniah carried.... Jer 41:10 3458
heard of all the evil that *I* the.... Jer 41:11 3458
went to fight with *I* the son of.... Jer 41:12 3458
I saw Johanan the son of Kareah.... Jer 41:13 3458
So all the people that *I* had.... Jer 41:14 3458
But *I* the son of Nethaniah.... Jer 41:15 3458
from *I* the son of Nethaniah.... Jer 41:16 3458
because *I* the son of Nethaniah.... Jer 41:18 3458

ISHMAELITE (*ish'-ma-el-ite*) *Descendants of Ishmael 1.*
the camels also was Obil the *I*.... 1Chr 27:30 3458

ISHMAELITES (*ish'-ma-el-lites*) See ISHMEELITES.
earrings, because they were *I*.... Judg 8:24 3459
The tabernacles of Edom, and the *I*.... Ps 83:6 3459

ISHMAEL'S (*ish'-ma-els*) *Refers to Ishmael 1.*
And Bashemath *I* daughter, sister.... Gen 36:3 3458

ISHMAIAH (*ish-ma-i'-ah*) See ISMAIAH. *A prince of Zebulun.*
Of Zebulun, *I* the son of Obadiah.... 1Chr 27:19 3460

ISHMEELITE (*ish'-me-el-ite*) See ISHMAELITE, ISHMEELITES. *Same as Ishmaelite.*
father of Amasa was Jether the *I*.... 1Chr 2:17 3459

ISHMEELITES (*ish'-me-el-ites*) See ISHMAELITES.
a company of *I* came from Gilead.... Gen 37:25 3459
Come, and let us sell him to the *I*.... Gen 37:27 3459
sold Joseph to the *I* for twenty.... Gen 37:28 3459
bought him of the hands of the *I*.... Gen 39:1 3459

ISHMERAI (*ish'-me-rahee*) *A chief of Benjamin.*
I also, and Jezliah, and Jobab, the.... 1Chr 8:18 3461

ISHOD (*i'-shod*) *A son of Hammoleketh.*
And his sister Hammoleketh bare *I*.... 1Chr 7:18 379

ISHPAH See ISPAH.

ISHPAN (*ish'-pan*) *A son of Shashak.*
And *I*, and Heber, and Eliel,.... 1Chr 8:22 3473

ISH-TOB (*ish'-tob*) *A district of Aram.*
men, and of *I* twelve thousand men.... 2Sa 10:6 382
of Zoba, and of Rehob, and *I*.... 2Sa 10:8 382

ISHUAH (*ish'-u-ah*) See ISUAH. *A son of Asher.*
Jimnah, and *I*, and Isui, and Beriah,.... Gen 46:17 3438

ISHUAI (*ish'-u-i*) *A son of Asher.*
Imnah, and Isuah, and *I*, and Beriah,.... 1Chr 7:30 3440

ISHUI (*ish'-u-i*) See ISHUAI, JESUI. *A son of Saul.*
sons of Saul were Jonathan, and *I*.... 1Sa 14:49 3440

ISLAND
deliver the *i* of the innocent.... Job 22:30 336
with the wild beasts of the *i*.... Is 34:14 338
certain *i* which is called Clauda.... Acts 27:16 *3519*
we must be cast upon a certain *i*.... Acts 27:26 *3520*
knew that the *i* was called Melita.... Acts 28:1 *3520*
of the chief man of the *i*.... Acts 28:7 *3520*
also, which had diseases in the *i*.... Acts 28:9 *3520*
i were moved out of their places.... Rev 6:14 *3520*
every *i* fled away, and the.... Rev 16:20 *3520*

ISLANDS
Hamath, and from the *i* of the sea.... Is 11:11 338
the wild beasts of the *i* shall.... Is 13:22 338
Keep silence before me, O *i*.... Is 41:1 339
and declare his praise in the *i*.... Is 42:12 339
and I will make the rivers *i*.... Is 42:15 339
to the *i* he will repay recompence.... Is 59:18 339
beasts of the *i* shall dwell there.... Jer 50:39 339

ISLE
of this *i* shall say in that day.... Is 20:6 339
Be still, ye inhabitants of the *i*.... Is 23:2 339
howl, ye inhabitants of the *i*.... Is 23:6 339
gone through the *i* unto Paphos.... Acts 13:6 *3520*
which had wintered in the *i*.... Acts 28:11 *3520*
was in the *i* that is called.... Rev 1:9 *3520*

ISLES
By these were the *i* of the.... Gen 10:5 339
land, and upon the *i* of the sea.... Est 10:1 339
of the *i* shall bring presents.... Ps 72:10 339
multitude of *i* be glad thereof.... Ps 97:1 339
God of Israel in the *i* of the sea.... Is 24:15 339
he taketh up the *i* as a very.... Is 40:15 339
The *i* saw it, and feared.... Is 41:5 339
the *i* shall wait for his law.... Is 42:4 339
the *i*, and the inhabitants thereof.... Is 42:10 339
Listen, O *i*, unto me.... Is 49:1 339
the *i* shall wait upon me, and on.... Is 51:5 339
Surely the *i* shall wait for me,.... Is 60:9 339
to the *i* afar off, that have not.... Is 66:19 339
For pass over the *i* of Chittim.... Jer 2:10 339
the kings of the *i* which are.... Jer 25:22 339
and declare it in the *i* afar off.... Jer 31:10 339
Shall not the *i* shake at the.... Eze 26:15 339
Now shall the *i* tremble in the.... Eze 26:18 339
the *i* that are in the sea shall.... Eze 26:18 339
merchant of the people for many *i*.... Eze 27:3 339
brought out of the *i* of Chittim.... Eze 27:6 339
purple from the *i* of Elishah was.... Eze 27:7 339
many *i* were the merchandise of.... Eze 27:15 339
All the inhabitants of the *i*.... Eze 27:35 339
that dwell carelessly in the *i*.... Eze 39:6 339
shall he turn his face unto the *i*.... Dan 11:18 339
even all the *i* of the heathen.... Zeph 2:11 339

ISMACHIAH (*is-ma-ki'-ah*) *A temple servant.*
and Jozabad, and Eliel, and *I*.... 2Chr 31:13 3253

ISMAIAH (*is-ma-i'-ah*) See ISHMAIAH. *A warrior in David's army.*
I the Gibeonite, a mighty man.... 1Chr 12:4 3460

ISPAH (*is'-pah*) *A son of Beriah.*
And Michael, and *I*, and Joha, the.... 1Chr 8:16 3472

ISRAEL (*iz'-ra-el*) See EL-ELOHE-ISRAEL, ISRAELITE, ISRAEL'S, JACOB, JESHURUN.
1. Name given to Jacob.
be called no more Jacob, but *I*.... Gen 32:28 3478
Jacob, but *I* shall be thy name.... Gen 35:10 3478
and he called his name *I*.... Gen 35:10 3478
I journeyed, and spread his tent.... Gen 35:21 3478
when *I* dwelt in that land, that.... Gen 35:22 3478
and *I* heard it.... Gen 35:22 3478
Now *I* loved Joseph more than all.... Gen 37:3 3478
I said unto Joseph, Do not thy.... Gen 37:13 3478
the sons of *I* came to buy corn.... Gen 42:5 3478
I said, Wherefore dealt ye so ill.... Gen 43:6 3478
And Judah said unto *I* his father.... Gen 43:8 3478
their father *I* said unto them, If.... Gen 43:11 3478
And the children of *I* did so.... Gen 45:21 3478
And *I* said, It is enough.... Gen 45:28 3478
I took his journey with all that.... Gen 46:1 3478
God spake unto *I* in the visions.... Gen 46:2 3478
the sons of *I* carried Jacob their.... Gen 46:5 3478
the names of the children of *I*.... Gen 46:8 3478
and went up to meet *I* his father.... Gen 46:29 3478
I said unto Joseph, Now let me.... Gen 46:30 3478
I dwelt in the land of Egypt, in.... Gen 47:27 3478
time drew nigh that *I* must die.... Gen 47:29 3478
I bowed himself upon the bed's.... Gen 47:31 3478
I strengthened himself, and sat.... Gen 48:2 3478
I beheld Joseph's sons, and said,.... Gen 48:8 3478
Now the eyes of *I* were dim for.... Gen 48:10 3478
I said unto Joseph, I had not.... Gen 48:11 3478
I stretched out his right hand,.... Gen 48:14 3478
saying, In thee shall *I* bless.... Gen 48:20 3478
I said unto Joseph, Behold, I die.... Gen 48:21 3478
and hearken unto *I* your father.... Gen 49:2 3478
and the physicians embalmed *I*.... Gen 50:2 3478
the names of the children of *I*.... Ex 1:1 3478
the children of *I* were fruitful.... Ex 1:7 3478
sons of Reuben the firstborn of *I*.... Ex 6:14 3478
Remember Abraham, Isaac, and *I*.... Ex 32:13 3478
Reuben, the eldest son of *I*.... Num 26:5 3478
their father, who was born unto *I*.... Judg 18:29 3478
came, saying, *I* shall be thy name.... 1Kin 18:31 3478
God of Abraham, Isaac, and of *I*.... 1Kin 18:36 3478
of Jacob, whom he named *I*.... 2Kin 17:34 3478
The sons of Isaac; Esau and *I*.... 1Chr 1:34 3478
These are the sons of *I*.... 1Chr 2:1 3478
sons of Reuben the firstborn of *I*.... 1Chr 5:1 3478
the sons of Joseph the son of *I*.... 1Chr 5:1 3478
of Reuben the firstborn of *I* were.... 1Chr 5:3 3478
the son of Levi, the son of *I*.... 1Chr 6:38 3478
children of Joseph the son of *I*.... 1Chr 7:29 3478
be thou, LORD God of *I* our father.... 1Chr 29:10 3478
God of Abraham, Isaac, and of *I*.... 1Chr 29:18 3478
LORD God of Abraham, Isaac, and *I*.... 2Chr 30:6 3478
the son of Levi, the son of *I*.... Ezr 8:18 3478
2. People descended from Jacob.
Therefore the children of *I* eat.... Gen 32:32 3478
I in lying with Jacob's daughter.... Gen 34:7 3478
any king over the children of *I*.... Gen 36:31 3478
in Jacob, and scatter them in *I*.... Gen 49:7 3478
people, as one of the tribes of *I*.... Gen 49:16 3478
is the shepherd, the stone of *I*.... Gen 49:24 3478
these are the twelve tribes of *I*.... Gen 49:28 3478
took an oath of the children of *I*.... Gen 50:25 3478
of the children of *I* are more.... Ex 1:9 3478
because of the children of *I*.... Ex 1:12 3478
of *I* to serve with rigour.... Ex 1:13 3478
the children of *I* sighed by.... Ex 2:23 3478
God looked upon the children of *I*.... Ex 2:25 3478
the children of *I* is come unto me.... Ex 3:9 3478
the children of *I* out of Egypt.... Ex 3:10 3478
the children of *I* out of Egypt.... Ex 3:11 3478
I come unto the children of *I*.... Ex 3:13 3478
thou say unto the children of *I*.... Ex 3:14 3478
thou say unto the children of *I*.... Ex 3:15 3478
gather the elders of *I* together.... Ex 3:16 3478
come, thou and the elders of *I*.... Ex 3:18 3478
I is my son, even my firstborn.... Ex 4:22 3478
the elders of the children of *I*.... Ex 4:29 3478
had visited the children of *I*.... Ex 4:31 3478
Thus saith the LORD God of *I*.... Ex 5:1 3478
should obey his voice to let *I* go.... Ex 5:2 3478
the LORD, neither will I let *I* go.... Ex 5:2 3478
the officers of the children of *I*.... Ex 5:14 3478
of the children of *I* came.... Ex 5:15 3478
I did see that they were in evil.... Ex 5:19 3478
the groaning of the children of *I*.... Ex 6:5 3478
say unto the children of *I*.... Ex 6:6 3478
spake so unto the children of *I*.... Ex 6:9 3478
children of *I* go out of his land.... Ex 6:11 3478
the children of *I* have not.... Ex 6:12 3478
a charge unto the children of *I*.... Ex 6:13 3478
of *I* out of the land of Egypt.... Ex 6:13 3478
of *I* from the land of Egypt.... Ex 6:26 3478
out the children of *I* from Egypt.... Ex 6:27 3478
the children of *I* out of his land.... Ex 7:2 3478
and my people the children of *I*.... Ex 7:4 3478
the children of *I* from among them.... Ex 7:5 3478
sever between the cattle of *I*.... Ex 9:4 3478
all that is the children's of *I*.... Ex 9:4 3478
of the children of *I* died not one.... Ex 9:6 3478
where the children of *I* were.... Ex 9:26 3478
would he let the children of *I* go.... Ex 9:35 3478
not let the children of *I* go.... Ex 10:20 3478
but all the children of *I* had.... Ex 10:23 3478
against any of the children of *I*.... Ex 11:7 3478
between the Egyptians and *I*.... Ex 11:7 3478
children of *I* go out of his land.... Ex 11:10 3478
ye unto all the congregation of *I*.... Ex 12:3 3478
of *I* shall kill it in the evening.... Ex 12:6 3478
that soul shall be cut off from *I*.... Ex 12:15 3478
off from the congregation of *I*.... Ex 12:19 3478
called for all the elders of *I*.... Ex 12:21 3478
of the children of *I* in Egypt.... Ex 12:27 3478
And the children of *I* went away.... Ex 12:28 3478
both ye and the children of *I*.... Ex 12:31 3478
the children of *I* did according.... Ex 12:35 3478
the children of *I* journeyed from.... Ex 12:37 3478
sojourning of the children of *I*.... Ex 12:40 3478
of *I* in their generations.... Ex 12:42 3478
congregation of *I* shall keep it.... Ex 12:47 3478
Thus did all the children of *I*.... Ex 12:50 3478
of *I* out of the land of Egypt by.... Ex 12:51 3478
the womb among the children of *I*.... Ex 13:2 3478
the children of *I* went up.... Ex 13:18 3478
straitly sworn the children of *I*.... Ex 13:19 3478
Speak unto the children of *I*.... Ex 14:2 3478
will say of the children of *I*.... Ex 14:3 3478
that we have let *I* go from.... Ex 14:5 3478
pursued after the children of *I*.... Ex 14:8 3478
the children of *I* went out with.... Ex 14:8 3478
the children of *I* lifted up their.... Ex 14:10 3478
the children of *I* cried out unto.... Ex 14:10 3478
speak unto the children of *I*.... Ex 14:15 3478
the children of *I* shall go on dry.... Ex 14:16 3478
which went before the camp of *I*.... Ex 14:19 3478
of the Egyptians and the camp of *I*.... Ex 14:20 3478
the children of *I* went into the.... Ex 14:22 3478
Let us flee from the face of *I*.... Ex 14:25 3478
But the children of *I* walked upon.... Ex 14:29 3478
Thus the LORD saved *I* that day.... Ex 14:30 3478
I saw the Egyptians dead upon the.... Ex 14:30 3478
I saw that great work which the.... Ex 14:31 3478
the children of *I* this song unto.... Ex 15:1 3478
but the children of *I* went on dry.... Ex 15:19 3478
Moses brought *I* from the Red sea.... Ex 15:22 3478
I came unto the wilderness of Sin.... Ex 16:1 3478
of *I* murmured against Moses.... Ex 16:2 3478
the children of *I* said unto them.... Ex 16:3 3478
said unto all the children of *I*.... Ex 16:6 3478
congregation of the children of *I*.... Ex 16:9 3478
congregation of the children of *I*.... Ex 16:10 3478
murmurings of the children of *I*.... Ex 16:12 3478
And when the children of *I* saw it.... Ex 16:15 3478
And the children of *I* did so.... Ex 16:17 3478
the house of *I* called the name.... Ex 16:31 3478

I

the children of *I* did eat manna ... Ex 16:35 3478
I journeyed from the wilderness ... Ex 17:1 3478
take with thee of the elders of *I* ... Ex 17:5 3478
in the sight of the elders of *I* ... Ex 17:6 3478
the chiding of the children of *I* ... Ex 17:7 3478
and fought with *I* in Rephidim ... Ex 17:8 3478
up his hand, that *I* prevailed ... Ex 17:11 3478
for *I* his people, and that the ... Ex 18:1 3478
LORD had brought *I* out of Egypt ... Ex 18:1 3478
which the LORD had done to *I* ... Ex 18:9 3478
came, and all the elders of *I* ... Ex 18:12 3478
Moses chose able men out of all *I* ... Ex 18:25 3478
when the children of *I* were gone ... Ex 19:1 3478
there *I* camped before the mount ... Ex 19:2 3478
Jacob, and tell the children of *I* ... Ex 19:3 3478
speak unto the children of *I* ... Ex 19:6 3478
shalt say unto the children of *I* ... Ex 20:22 3478
and seventy of the elders of *I* ... Ex 24:1 3478
to the twelve tribes of *I* ... Ex 24:4 3478
young men of the children of *I* ... Ex 24:5 3478
and seventy of the elders of *I* ... Ex 24:9 3478
And they saw the God of *I* ... Ex 24:10 3478
of *I* he laid not his hand ... Ex 24:11 3478
in the eyes of the children of *I* ... Ex 24:17 3478
Speak unto the children of *I* ... Ex 25:2 3478
unto the children of *I* ... Ex 25:22 3478
shalt command the children of *I* ... Ex 27:20 3478
the behalf of the children of *I* ... Ex 27:21 3478
him, from among the children of *I* ... Ex 28:1 3478
the names of the children of *I* ... Ex 28:9 3478
the names of the children of *I* ... Ex 28:11 3478
memorial unto the children of *I* ... Ex 28:12 3478
the names of the children of *I* ... Ex 28:21 3478
the names of the children of *I* in ... Ex 28:29 3478
I upon his heart before the LORD ... Ex 28:30 3478
which the children of *I* shall ... Ex 28:38 3478
for ever from the children of *I* ... Ex 29:28 3478
offering from the children of *I* ... Ex 29:28 3478
will meet with the children of *I* ... Ex 29:43 3478
dwell among the children of *I* ... Ex 29:45 3478
children of *I* after their number ... Ex 30:12 3478
money of the children of *I* ... Ex 30:16 3478
the children of *I* before the LORD ... Ex 30:16 3478
speak unto the children of *I* ... Ex 30:31 3478
thou also unto the children of *I* ... Ex 31:13 3478
of *I* shall keep the sabbath ... Ex 31:16 3478
me and the children of *I* for ever ... Ex 31:17 3478
they said, These be thy gods, O *I* ... Ex 32:4 3478
and said, These be thy gods, O *I* ... Ex 32:8 3478
the children of *I* drink of it ... Ex 32:20 3478
Thus saith the LORD God of *I* ... Ex 32:27 3478
Moses, Say unto the children of *I* ... Ex 33:5 3478
the children of *I* stripped ... Ex 33:6 3478
before the Lord GOD, the God of *I* ... Ex 34:23 3478
a covenant with thee and with *I* ... Ex 34:27 3478
all the children of *I* saw Moses ... Ex 34:30 3478
all the children of *I* came nigh ... Ex 34:32 3478
spake unto the children of *I* that ... Ex 34:34 3478
the children of *I* saw the face of ... Ex 34:35 3478
of the children of *I* together ... Ex 35:1 3478
congregation of the children of *I* ... Ex 35:4 3478
I departed from the presence of ... Ex 35:20 3478
The children of *I* brought a ... Ex 35:29 3478
Moses said unto the children of *I* ... Ex 35:30 3478
which the children of *I* had ... Ex 36:3 3478
the names of the children of *I* ... Ex 39:6 3478
a memorial to the children of *I* ... Ex 39:7 3478
to the names of the children of *I* ... Ex 39:14 3478
the children of *I* did according ... Ex 39:32 3478
children of *I* made all the work ... Ex 39:42 3478
the children of *I* went onward in ... Ex 40:36 3478
the sight of all the house of *I* ... Ex 40:38 3478
Speak unto the children of *I* ... Lev 1:2 3478
Speak unto the children of *I* ... Lev 4:2 3478
of *I* sin through ignorance ... Lev 4:13 3478
Speak unto the children of *I* ... Lev 7:23 3478
Speak unto the children of *I* ... Lev 7:29 3478
of *I* from off the sacrifices of ... Lev 7:34 3478
ever from among the children of *I* ... Lev 7:34 3478
given them of the children of *I* ... Lev 7:36 3478
he commanded the children of *I* to ... Lev 7:38 3478
and his sons, and the elders of *I* ... Lev 9:1 3478
children of *I* thou shalt speak ... Lev 9:3 3478
brethren, the whole house of *I* ... Lev 10:6 3478
ye may teach the children of *I* ... Lev 10:11 3478
offerings of the children of *I* ... Lev 10:14 3478
Speak unto the children of *I* ... Lev 11:2 3478
Speak unto the children of *I* ... Lev 12:2 3478
Speak unto the children of *I* ... Lev 15:2 3478
of *I* from their uncleanness ... Lev 15:31 3478
I two kids of the goats for a sin ... Lev 16:5 3478
uncleanness of the children of *I* ... Lev 16:16 3478
and for all the congregation of *I* ... Lev 16:17 3478
uncleanness of the children of *I* ... Lev 16:19 3478
iniquities of the children of *I* ... Lev 16:21 3478
atonement for the children of *I* ... Lev 16:34 3478
and unto all the children of *I* ... Lev 17:2 3478
soever there be of the house of *I* ... Lev 17:3 3478
of *I* may bring their sacrifices ... Lev 17:5 3478
man there be of the house of *I* ... Lev 17:8 3478
man there be of the house of *I* ... Lev 17:10 3478
I said unto the children of *I* ... Lev 17:12 3478
man there be of the children of *I* ... Lev 17:13 3478
I said unto the children of *I* ... Lev 17:14 3478
Speak unto the children of *I* ... Lev 18:2 3478
congregation of the children of *I* ... Lev 19:2 3478
shalt say to the children of *I* ... Lev 20:2 3478
he be of the children of *I* ... Lev 20:2 3478
the strangers that sojourn in *I* ... Lev 20:2 3478
and unto all the children of *I* ... Lev 21:24 3478
holy things of the children of *I* ... Lev 22:2 3478
of *I* hallow unto the LORD ... Lev 22:3 3478
holy things of the children of *I* ... Lev 22:15 3478
and unto all the children of *I* ... Lev 22:18 3478
he be of the house of *I* ... Lev 22:18 3478
or of the strangers in *I* ... Lev 22:18 3478
hallowed among the children of *I* ... Lev 22:32 3478
Speak unto the children of *I* ... Lev 23:2 3478
Speak unto the children of *I* ... Lev 23:10 3478
Speak unto the children of *I* ... Lev 23:24 3478
Speak unto the children of *I* ... Lev 23:34 3478
children of *I* to dwell in booths ... Lev 23:43 3478
of *I* the feasts of the LORD ... Lev 23:44 3478
Command the children of *I* ... Lev 24:2 3478
of *I* by an everlasting covenant ... Lev 24:8 3478
went out among the children of *I* ... Lev 24:10 3481
a man of *I* strove together in the ... Lev 24:10 3478
speak unto the children of *I* ... Lev 24:15 3478
Moses spake to the children of *I* ... Lev 24:23 3478
the children of *I* did as the LORD ... Lev 24:23 3478
Speak unto the children of *I* ... Lev 25:2 3478
among the children of *I* ... Lev 25:33 3478
your brethren the children of *I* ... Lev 25:46 3478
me the children of *I* are servants ... Lev 25:55 3478
the children of *I* in mount Sinai ... Lev 26:46 3478
Speak unto the children of *I* ... Lev 27:2 3478
the children of *I* in mount Sinai ... Lev 27:34 3478
congregation of the children of *I* ... Num 1:2 3478
are able to go forth to war in *I* ... Num 1:3 3478
fathers, heads of thousands in *I* ... Num 1:16 3478
numbered, and the princes of *I* ... Num 1:44 3478
numbered of the children of *I* ... Num 1:45 3478
were able to go forth to war in *I* ... Num 1:45 3478
of them among the children of *I* ... Num 1:49 3478
the children of *I* shall pitch ... Num 1:52 3478
congregation of the children of *I* ... Num 1:53 3478
the children of *I* did according ... Num 1:54 3478
Every man of the children of *I* ... Num 2:2 3478
numbered of the children of *I* by ... Num 2:32 3478
numbered among the children of *I* ... Num 2:33 3478
the children of *I* did according ... Num 2:34 3478
the charge of the children of *I* ... Num 3:8 3478
unto him out of the children of *I* ... Num 3:9 3478
from among the children of *I* ... Num 3:12 3478
matrix among the children of *I* ... Num 3:12 3478
unto me all the firstborn in *I* ... Num 3:13 3478
the charge of the children of *I* ... Num 3:38 3478
children of *I* from a month old ... Num 3:40 3478
firstborn among the children of *I* ... Num 3:41 3478
the cattle of the children of *I* ... Num 3:41 3478
firstborn among the children of *I* ... Num 3:42 3478
firstborn among the children of *I* ... Num 3:45 3478
firstborn of the children of *I* ... Num 3:46 3478
children of *I* took he the money ... Num 3:50 3478
Aaron and the chief of *I* numbered ... Num 4:46 3478
Command the children of *I* ... Num 5:2 3478
And the children of *I* did so ... Num 5:4 3478
Moses, so did the children of *I* ... Num 5:4 3478
Speak unto the children of *I* ... Num 5:6 3478
holy things of the children of *I* ... Num 5:9 3478
Speak unto the children of *I* ... Num 5:12 3478
Speak unto the children of *I* ... Num 6:2 3478
ye shall bless the children of *I* ... Num 6:23 3478
my name upon the children of *I* ... Num 6:27 3478
That the princes of *I*, heads of ... Num 7:2 3478
was anointed, by the princes of *I* ... Num 7:84 3478
from among the children of *I* ... Num 8:6 3478
of the children of *I* together ... Num 8:9 3478
the children of *I* shall put their ... Num 8:10 3478
an offering of the children of *I* ... Num 8:11 3478
from among the children of *I* ... Num 8:14 3478
me from among the children of *I* ... Num 8:16 3478
of all the children of *I*, have I ... Num 8:16 3478
of the children of *I* are mine ... Num 8:17 3478
firstborn of the children of *I* ... Num 8:18 3478
sons from among the children of *I* ... Num 8:19 3478
of *I* in the tabernacle of the ... Num 8:19 3478
atonement for the children of *I* ... Num 8:19 3478
no plague among the children of *I* ... Num 8:19 3478
when the children of *I* come nigh ... Num 8:19 3478
congregation of the children of *I* ... Num 8:20 3478
did the children of *I* unto them ... Num 8:20 3478
Let the children of *I* also keep ... Num 9:2 3478
spake unto the children of *I* ... Num 9:4 3478
Moses, so did the children of *I* ... Num 9:5 3478
season among the children of *I* ... Num 9:7 3478
Speak unto the children of *I* ... Num 9:10 3478
that the children of *I* journeyed ... Num 9:17 3478
children of *I* pitched their tents ... Num 9:17 3478
LORD the children of *I* journeyed ... Num 9:18 3478
then the children of *I* kept the ... Num 9:19 3478
the children of *I* abode in their ... Num 9:22 3478
are heads of the thousands of *I* ... Num 10:4 3478
the children of *I* took their ... Num 10:12 3478
of *I* according to their armies ... Num 10:28 3478
hath spoken good concerning *I* ... Num 10:29 3478
unto the many thousands of *I* ... Num 10:36 3478
the children of *I* also wept again ... Num 11:4 3478
me seventy men of the elders of *I* ... Num 11:16 3478
the camp, he and the elders of *I* ... Num 11:30 3478
I give unto the children of *I* ... Num 13:2 3478
were heads of the children of *I* ... Num 13:3 3478
of *I* cut down from thence ... Num 13:24 3478
congregation of the children of *I* ... Num 13:26 3478
searched unto the children of *I* ... Num 13:32 3478
all the children of *I* murmured ... Num 14:2 3478
congregation of the children of *I* ... Num 14:5 3478
the company of the children of *I* ... Num 14:7 3478
before all the children of *I* ... Num 14:10 3478
murmurings of the children of *I* ... Num 14:27 3478
unto all the children of *I* ... Num 14:39 3478
Speak unto the children of *I* ... Num 15:2 3478
Speak unto the children of *I* ... Num 15:18 3478
congregation of the children of *I* ... Num 15:25 3478
congregation of the children of *I* ... Num 15:26 3478
is born among the children of *I* ... Num 15:29 3478
while the children of *I* were in ... Num 15:32 3478
Speak unto the children of *I* ... Num 15:38 3478
with certain of the children of *I* ... Num 16:2 3478
that the God of *I* hath separated ... Num 16:9 3478
you from the congregation of *I* ... Num 16:9 3478
and the elders of *I* followed him ... Num 16:25 3478
all *I* that were round about them ... Num 16:34 3478
be a sign unto the children of *I* ... Num 16:38 3478
a memorial unto the children of *I* ... Num 16:40 3478
of *I* murmured against Moses ... Num 16:41 3478
Speak unto the children of *I* ... Num 17:2 3478
murmurings of the children of *I* ... Num 17:5 3478
spake unto the children of *I* ... Num 17:6 3478
LORD unto all the children of *I* ... Num 17:9 3478
the children of *I* spake unto ... Num 17:12 3478
any more upon the children of *I* ... Num 18:5 3478
from among the children of *I* ... Num 18:6 3478
things of the children of *I* ... Num 18:8 3478
offerings of the children of *I* ... Num 18:11 3478
thing devoted in *I* shall be thine ... Num 18:14 3478
children of *I* offer unto the LORD ... Num 18:19 3478
among the children of *I* ... Num 18:20 3478
the tenth in *I* for an inheritance ... Num 18:21 3478
of *I* henceforth come nigh the ... Num 18:22 3478
of *I* they have no inheritance ... Num 18:23 3478
the tithes of the children of *I* ... Num 18:24 3478
Among the children of *I* they ... Num 18:24 3478
I the tithes which I have given ... Num 18:26 3478
ye receive of the children of *I* ... Num 18:28 3478
holy things of the children of *I* ... Num 18:32 3478
Speak unto the children of *I* ... Num 19:2 3478
of *I* for a water of separation ... Num 19:9 3478
shall be unto the children of *I* ... Num 19:10 3478
that soul shall be cut off from *I* ... Num 19:13 3478
Then came the children of *I* ... Num 20:1 3478
in the eyes of the children of *I* ... Num 20:12 3478
of *I* strove with the LORD ... Num 20:13 3478
of Edom, Thus saith thy brother *I* ... Num 20:14 3478
the children of *I* said unto him ... Num 20:19 3478
Thus Edom refused to give *I* ... Num 20:21 3478
wherefore *I* turned away from him ... Num 20:21 3478
And the children of *I*, even the ... Num 20:22 3478
have given unto the children of *I* ... Num 20:24 3478
days, even all the house of *I* ... Num 20:29 3478
heard tell that *I* came by the way ... Num 21:1 3478
then he fought against *I*, and took ... Num 21:1 3478
I vowed a vow unto the LORD, and ... Num 21:2 3478
LORD hearkened to the voice of *I* ... Num 21:3 3478
and much people of *I* died ... Num 21:6 3478
And the children of *I* set forward ... Num 21:10 3478
Then *I* sang this song, Spring up, ... Num 21:17 3478
I sent messengers unto Sihon king ... Num 21:21 3478
Sihon would not suffer *I* to pass ... Num 21:23 3478
went out against *I* into the ... Num 21:23 3478
to Jahaz, and fought against *I* ... Num 21:23 3478
I smote him with the edge of the ... Num 21:24 3478
And *I* took all these cities ... Num 21:25 3478
I dwelt in all the cities of the ... Num 21:25 3478
Thus *I* dwelt in the land of the ... Num 21:31 3478
And the children of *I* set forward ... Num 22:1 3478
that *I* had done to the Amorites ... Num 22:2 3478
because of the children of *I* ... Num 22:3 3478
curse me Jacob, and come, defy *I* ... Num 23:7 3478
number of the fourth part of *I* ... Num 23:10 3478
hath he seen perverseness in *I* ... Num 23:21 3478
is there any divination against *I* ... Num 23:23 3478
it shall be said of Jacob and of *I* ... Num 23:23 3478
it pleased the LORD to bless *I* ... Num 24:1 3478
he saw *I* abiding in his tents ... Num 24:2 3478
O Jacob, and thy tabernacles, O *I* ... Num 24:5 3478
and a Sceptre shall rise out of *I* ... Num 24:17 3478
and *I* shall do valiantly ... Num 24:18 3478
I abode in Shittim, and the people ... Num 25:1 3478
I joined himself unto Baal-peor ... Num 25:3 3478
of the LORD was kindled against *I* ... Num 25:3 3478
LORD may be turned away from *I* ... Num 25:4 3478
Moses said unto the judges of *I* ... Num 25:5 3478
one of the children of *I* came ... Num 25:6 3478
congregation of the children of *I* ... Num 25:6 3478
after the man of *I* into the tent ... Num 25:8 3478
of them through, the man of *I* ... Num 25:8 3478
was stayed from the children of *I* ... Num 25:8 3478
wrath away from the children of *I* ... Num 25:11 3478
the children of *I* in my jealousy ... Num 25:11 3478
atonement for the children of *I* ... Num 25:13 3478
congregation of the children of *I* ... Num 26:2 3478
that are able to go to war in *I* ... Num 26:2 3478
Moses and the children of *I* ... Num 26:4 3478
the numbered of the children of *I* ... Num 26:51 3478
numbered among the children of *I* ... Num 26:62 3478
them among the children of *I* ... Num 26:62 3478
who numbered the children of *I* in ... Num 26:63 3478
of *I* in the wilderness of Sinai ... Num 26:64 3478
speak unto the children of *I* ... Num 27:8 3478
of *I* a statute of judgment ... Num 27:11 3478
have given unto the children of *I* ... Num 27:12 3478
the children of *I* may be obedient ... Num 27:20 3478
and all the children of *I* with him ... Num 27:21 3478
Command the children of *I* ... Num 28:2 3478
Moses told the children of *I* ... Num 29:40 3478
concerning the children of *I* ... Num 30:1 3478
children of *I* of the Midianites ... Num 31:2 3478
throughout all the tribes of *I* ... Num 31:4 3478
out of the thousands of *I* ... Num 31:5 3478
the children of *I* took all the ... Num 31:9 3478
congregation of the children of *I* ... Num 31:12 3478
these caused the children of *I* ... Num 31:16 3478
the children of *I* before the LORD ... Num 31:54 3478
before the congregation of *I* ... Num 32:4 3478
I from going over into the land ... Num 32:7 3478
the heart of the children of *I* ... Num 32:9 3478
anger was kindled against *I* ... Num 32:13 3478
fierce anger of the LORD toward *I* ... Num 32:14 3478
armed before the children of *I* ... Num 32:17 3478
until the children of *I* have ... Num 32:18 3478
before the LORD, and before *I* ... Num 32:22 3478

the tribes of the children of *I* Num 32:28 3478
the journeys of the children of *I* Num 33:1 3478
the passover the children of *I* Num 33:3 3478
the children of *I* removed from Num 33:5 3478
year after the children of *I* were Num 33:38 3478
the coming of the children of *I* Num 33:40 3478
Speak unto the children of *I* Num 33:51 3478
Command the children of *I* Num 34:2 3478
Moses commanded the children of *I* Num 34:13 3478
unto the children of *I* in the Num 34:29 3478
Command the children of *I* Num 35:2 3478
possession of the children of *I* Num 35:8 3478
Speak unto the children of *I* Num 35:10 3478
both for the children of *I* Num 35:15 3478
dwell among the children of *I* Num 35:34 3478
fathers of the children of *I* Num 36:1 3478
by lot to the children of *I* Num 36:2 3478
other tribes of the children of *I* Num 36:3 3478
of the children of *I* shall be Num 36:4 3478
of *I* according to the word of the Num 36:5 3478
of *I* remove from tribe to tribe Num 36:7 3478
of *I* shall keep himself to the Num 36:7 3478
in any tribe of the children of *I* Num 36:8 3478
that the children of *I* may enjoy Num 36:8 3478
I shall keep himself to his own Num 36:9 3478
of Moses unto the children of *I* Num 36:13 3478
all *I* on this side Jordan in the Deut 1:1 3478
spake unto the children of *I* Deut 1:3 3478
he shall cause *I* to inherit it Deut 1:38 3478
as *I* did unto the land of his Deut 2:12 3478
your brethren the children of *I* Deut 3:18 3478
Now therefore hearken, O *I* Deut 4:1 3478
set before the children of *I* Deut 4:44 3478
spake unto the children of *I* Deut 4:45 3478
Moses and the children of *I* smote Deut 4:46 3478
And Moses called all *I* Deut 5:1 3478
and said unto them, Hear, O *I* Deut 5:1 3478
Hear therefore, O *I*, and observe Deut 6:3 3478
Hear, O *I*: The LORD our God Deut 6:4 3478
Hear, O *I*: Thou art to pass Deut 9:1 3478
the children of *I* took their Deut 10:6 3478
And now, *I*, what doth the LORD thy Deut 10:12 3478
possession, in the midst of all *I* Deut 11:6 3478
all *I* shall hear, and fear, and Deut 13:11 3478
such abomination is wrought in *I* Deut 17:4 3478
shalt put away the evil from *I* Deut 17:12 3478
his children, in the midst of *I* Deut 17:20 3478
no part nor inheritance with *I* Deut 18:1 3478
any of thy gates out of all *I* Deut 18:6 3478
guilt of innocent blood from *I* Deut 19:13 3478
And shall say unto them, Hear, O *I* Deut 20:3 3478
O LORD, unto thy people *I* Deut 21:8 3478
all *I* shall hear, and fear Deut 21:21 3478
an evil name upon a virgin of *I* Deut 22:19 3478
she hath wrought folly in *I* Deut 22:21 3478
shalt thou put away evil from *I* Deut 22:22 3478
be no whore of the daughters of *I* Deut 23:17 3478
nor a sodomite of the sons of *I* Deut 23:17 3478
his brethren of the children of *I* Deut 24:7 3478
that his name be not put out of *I* Deut 25:6 3478
up unto his brother a name in *I* Deut 25:7 3478
And his name shall be called in *I* Deut 25:10 3478
heaven, and bless thy people *I* Deut 26:15 3478
elders of *I* commanded the people Deut 27:1 3478
the Levites spake unto all *I* Deut 27:9 3478
Take heed, and hearken, O *I* Deut 27:9 3478
the men of *I* with a loud voice Deut 27:14 3478
children of *I* in the land of Moab Deut 29:1 3478
And Moses called unto all *I* Deut 29:2 3478
officers, with all the men of *I* Deut 29:10 3478
evil out of all the tribes of *I* Deut 29:21 3478
and spake these words unto all *I* Deut 31:1 3478
unto him in the sight of all *I* Deut 31:7 3478
LORD, and unto all the elders of *I* Deut 31:9 3478
When all *I* is come to appear Deut 31:11 3478
law before all *I* in their hearing Deut 31:11 3478
and teach it the children of *I* Deut 31:19 3478
for me against the children of *I* Deut 31:19 3478
and taught it the children of *I* Deut 31:22 3478
of *I* into the land which I sware Deut 31:23 3478
of *I* the words of this song Deut 31:30 3478
the number of the children of *I* Deut 32:8 3478
speaking all these words to all *I* Deut 32:45 3478
children of *I* for a possession Deut 32:49 3478
me among the children of *I* at the Deut 32:51 3478
in the midst of the children of *I* Deut 32:51 3478
which I give the children of *I* Deut 32:52 3478
children of *I* before his death Deut 33:1 3478
the tribes of *I* were gathered Deut 33:5 3478
Jacob thy judgments, and *I* thy law Deut 33:10 3478
the LORD, and his judgments with *I* Deut 33:21 3478
I then shall dwell in safety Deut 33:28 3478
Happy art thou, O *I* Deut 33:29 3478
the children of *I* wept for Moses Deut 34:8 3478
the children of *I* hearkened unto Deut 34:9 3478
since in *I* like unto Moses Deut 34:10 3478
shewed in the sight of all *I* Deut 34:12 3478
them, even to the children of *I* Josh 1:2 3478
of *I* to search out the country Josh 2:2 3478
he and all the children of *I* Josh 3:1 3478
thee in the sight of all *I* Josh 3:7 3478
said unto the children of *I* Josh 3:9 3478
twelve men out of the tribes of *I* Josh 3:12 3478
had prepared of the children of *I* Josh 4:4 3478
the tribes of the children of *I* Josh 4:5 3478
unto the children of *I* for ever Josh 4:7 3478
the children of *I* did so as Josh 4:8 3478
the tribes of the children of *I* Josh 4:8 3478
armed before the children of *I* Josh 4:12 3478
Joshua in the sight of all *I* Josh 4:14 3478
he spake unto the children of *I* Josh 4:21 3478
I came over this Jordan on dry Josh 4:22 3478
from before the children of *I* Josh 5:1 3478
because of the children of *I* Josh 5:1 3478

the children of *I* the second time Josh 5:2 3478
circumcised the children of *I* at Josh 5:3 3478
For the children of *I* walked Josh 5:6 3478
the children of *I* encamped in Josh 5:10 3478
the children of *I* manna any more Josh 5:12 3478
up because of the children of *I* Josh 6:1 3478
and make the camp of *I* a curse Josh 6:18 3478
left them without the camp of *I* Josh 6:23 3478
she dwelleth in *I* even unto this Josh 6:25 3478
But the children of *I* committed a Josh 7:1 3478
kindled against the children of *I* Josh 7:1 3478
eventide, he and the elders of *I* Josh 7:6 3478
when *I* turneth their backs before Josh 7:8 3478
I hath sinned, and they have also Josh 7:11 3478
Therefore the children of *I* could Josh 7:12 3478
for thus saith the LORD God of *I* Josh 7:13 3478
thing in the midst of thee, O *I* Josh 7:13 3478
he hath wrought folly in *I* Josh 7:15 3478
brought *I* by their tribes Josh 7:16 3478
thee, glory to the LORD God of *I* Josh 7:19 3478
sinned against the LORD God of *I* Josh 7:20 3478
and unto all the children of *I* Josh 7:23 3478
all *I* with him, took Achan the Josh 7:24 3478
all *I* stoned him with stones, and Josh 7:25 3478
and went up, he and the elders of *I* Josh 8:10 3478
city went out against *I* to battle Josh 8:14 3478
all *I* made as if they were beaten Josh 8:15 3478
that went not out after *I* Josh 8:17 3478
the city open, and pursued after *I* Josh 8:17 3478
all *I* saw that the ambush had Josh 8:21 3478
so they were in the midst of *I* Josh 8:22 3478
when *I* had made an end of slaying Josh 8:24 3478
the spoil of that city *I* took for Josh 8:27 3478
the LORD God of *I* in mount Ebal Josh 8:30 3478
LORD commanded the children of *I* Josh 8:31 3478
the presence of the children of *I* Josh 8:32 3478
And all *I*, and their elders, and Josh 8:33 3478
they should bless the people of *I* Josh 8:33 3478
before all the congregation of *I* Josh 8:35 3478
to fight with Joshua and with *I* Josh 9:2 3478
said unto him, and to the men of *I* Josh 9:6 3478
the men of *I* said unto the Josh 9:7 3478
And the children of *I* journeyed Josh 9:17 3478
the children of *I* smote them not Josh 9:18 3478
unto them by the LORD God of *I* Josh 9:18 3478
unto them by the LORD God of *I* Josh 9:19 3478
of the hand of the children of *I* Josh 9:26 3478
of Gibeon had made peace with *I* Josh 10:1 3478
Joshua and with the children of *I* Josh 10:4 3478
LORD discomfited them before *I* Josh 10:10 3478
pass, as they fled from before *I* Josh 10:11 3478
children of *I* slew with the sword Josh 10:11 3478
Amorites before the children of *I* Josh 10:12 3478
and he said in the sight of *I* Josh 10:12 3478
for the LORD fought for *I* Josh 10:14 3478
all *I* with him, unto the camp to Josh 10:15 3478
the children of *I* had made an end Josh 10:20 3478
against any of the children of *I* Josh 10:21 3478
called for all the men of *I* Josh 10:24 3478
all *I* with him, unto Libnah, and Josh 10:29 3478
king thereof, into the hand of *I* Josh 10:30 3478
all *I* with him, unto Lachish, and Josh 10:31 3478
Lachish into the hand of *I* Josh 10:32 3478
unto Eglon, and all *I* with him Josh 10:34 3478
all *I* with him, unto Hebron Josh 10:36 3478
and all *I* with him, to Debir Josh 10:38 3478
as the LORD God of *I* commanded Josh 10:40 3478
LORD God of *I* fought for Israel Josh 10:42 3478
LORD God of Israel fought for *I* Josh 10:42 3478
all *I* with him, unto the camp to Josh 10:43 3478
of Merom, to fight against *I* Josh 11:5 3478
them up all slain before *I* Josh 11:6 3478
delivered them into the hand of *I* Josh 11:8 3478
I burned none of them, save Hazor Josh 11:13 3478
the children of *I* took for a prey Josh 11:14 3478
the plain, and the mountain of *I* Josh 11:16 3478
made peace with the children of *I* Josh 11:19 3478
should come against *I* in battle Josh 11:20 3478
and from all the mountains of *I* Josh 11:21 3478
in the land of the children of *I* Josh 11:22 3478
I according to their divisions by Josh 11:23 3478
which the children of *I* smote Josh 12:1 3478
LORD and the children of *I* smite Josh 12:6 3478
the children of *I* smote on this Josh 12:7 3478
I for a possession according to Josh 12:7 3478
out from before the children of *I* Josh 13:6 3478
of *I* expelled not the Geshurites Josh 13:13 3478
God of *I* made by fire are their Josh 13:14 3478
did the children of *I* slay with Josh 13:22 3478
the LORD God of *I* was their Josh 13:33 3478
I inherited in the land of Canaan Josh 14:1 3478
the tribes of the children of *I* Josh 14:1 3478
Moses, so the children of *I* did Josh 14:5 3478
while the children of *I* wandered Josh 14:10 3478
wholly followed the LORD God of *I* Josh 14:14 3478
children of *I* were waxen strong Josh 17:13 3478
of *I* assembled together at Shiloh Josh 18:1 3478
the children of *I* seven tribes Josh 18:2 3478
said unto the children of *I* Josh 18:3 3478
of *I* according to their divisions Josh 18:10 3478
the children of *I* gave an Josh 19:49 3478
the tribes of the children of *I* Josh 19:51 3478
Speak to the children of *I* Josh 20:2 3478
for all the children of *I* Josh 20:9 3478
the tribes of the children of *I* Josh 21:1 3478
the children of *I* gave unto the Josh 21:3 3478
the children of *I* gave by lot Josh 21:8 3478
of the children of *I* were forty Josh 21:41 3478
the LORD gave unto *I* all the land Josh 21:43 3478
had spoken unto the house of *I* Josh 21:45 3478
the children of *I* out of Shiloh Josh 22:9 3478
And the children of *I* heard say Josh 22:11 3478
the passage of the children of *I* Josh 22:11 3478
the children of *I* heard of it Josh 22:12 3478

I gathered themselves together at Josh 22:12 3478
the children of *I* sent unto the Josh 22:13 3478
throughout all the tribes of *I* Josh 22:14 3478
fathers among the thousands of *I* Josh 22:14 3478
committed against the God of *I* Josh 22:16 3478
with the whole congregation of *I* Josh 22:18 3478
fell on all the congregation of *I* Josh 22:20 3478
the heads of the thousands of *I* Josh 22:21 3478
he knoweth, and *I* he shall know Josh 22:22 3478
ye to do with the LORD God of *I* Josh 22:24 3478
of *I* which were with him, heard Josh 22:30 3478
of *I* out of the hand of the LORD Josh 22:31 3478
of Canaan, to the children of *I* Josh 22:32 3478
thing pleased the children of *I* Josh 22:33 3478
and the children of *I* blessed God Josh 22:33 3478
I from all their enemies round Josh 23:1 3478
And Joshua called for all *I* Josh 23:2 3478
all the tribes of *I* to Shechem Josh 24:1 3478
and called for the elders of *I* Josh 24:1 3478
Thus saith the LORD God of *I* Josh 24:2 3478
Moab, arose and warred against *I* Josh 24:9 3478
your heart unto the LORD God of *I* Josh 24:23 3478
I served the LORD all the days of Josh 24:31 3478
the LORD, that he had done for *I* Josh 24:31 3478
which the children of *I* brought Josh 24:32 3478
the children of *I* asked the LORD Judg 1:1 3478
when *I* was strong, that they put Judg 1:28 3478
words unto all the children of *I* Judg 2:4 3478
the children of *I* went every man Judg 2:6 3478
of the LORD, that he did for *I* Judg 2:7 3478
the works which he had done for *I* Judg 2:10 3478
the children of *I* did evil in the Judg 2:11 3478
of the LORD was hot against *I* Judg 2:14 3478
of the LORD was hot against *I* Judg 2:20 3478
That through them I may prove *I* Judg 2:22 3478
the LORD left, to prove *I* by them Judg 3:1 3478
even as many of *I* as had not Judg 3:1
of the children of *I* might know Judg 3:2 3478
And they were to prove *I* by them Judg 3:4 3478
the children of *I* dwelt among the Judg 3:5 3478
the children of *I* did evil in the Judg 3:7 3478
of the LORD was hot against *I* Judg 3:8 3478
and the children of *I* served Judg 3:8 3478
children of *I* cried unto the LORD Judg 3:9 3478
a deliverer to the children of *I* Judg 3:9 3478
came upon him, and he judged *I* Judg 3:10 3478
the children of *I* did evil again Judg 3:12 3478
Eglon the king of Moab against *I* Judg 3:12 3478
and Amalek, and went and smote *I* Judg 3:13 3478
So the children of *I* served Eglon Judg 3:14 3478
children of *I* cried unto the LORD Judg 3:15 3478
by him the children of *I* sent a Judg 3:15 3478
the children of *I* went down with Judg 3:27 3478
that day under the hand of *I* Judg 3:30 3478
and he also delivered *I* Judg 3:31 3478
the children of *I* again did evil Judg 4:1 3478
the children of *I* cried unto the Judg 4:3 3478
oppressed the children of *I* Judg 4:3 3478
she judged *I* at that time Judg 4:4 3478
the children of *I* came up to her Judg 4:5 3478
not the LORD God of *I* commanded Judg 4:6 3478
Canaan before the children of *I* Judg 4:23 3478
of the children of *I* prospered Judg 4:24 3478
ye the LORD for the avenging of *I* Judg 5:2 3478
sing praise to the LORD God of *I* Judg 5:3 3478
from before the LORD God of *I* Judg 5:5 3478
villages ceased, they ceased in *I* Judg 5:7 3478
arose, that I arose a mother in *I* Judg 5:7 3478
seen among forty thousand in *I* Judg 5:8 3478
is toward the governors of *I* Judg 5:9 3478
inhabitants of his villages in *I* Judg 5:11 3478
the children of *I* did evil in the Judg 6:1 3478
of Midian prevailed against *I* Judg 6:2 3478
the Midianites the children of *I* Judg 6:2 3478
when *I* had sown, that the Judg 6:3 3478
Gaza, and left no sustenance for *I* Judg 6:4 3478
I was greatly impoverished Judg 6:6 3478
the children of *I* cried unto the Judg 6:6 3478
when the children of *I* cried unto Judg 6:7 3478
a prophet unto the children of *I* Judg 6:8 3478
Thus saith the LORD God of *I* Judg 6:8 3478
thou shalt save *I* from the hand Judg 6:14 3478
my Lord, wherewith shall I save *I* Judg 6:15 3478
If thou wilt save *I* by mine hand Judg 6:36 3478
thou wilt save *I* by mine hand Judg 6:37 3478
lest *I* vaunt themselves against Judg 7:2 3478
rest of *I* every man unto his tent Judg 7:8 3478
the son of Joash, a man of *I* Judg 7:14 3478
and returned into the host of *I* Judg 7:15 3478
the men of *I* gathered themselves Judg 7:23 3478
Then the men of *I* said unto Judg 8:22 3478
all *I* went thither a whoring Judg 8:27 3478
subdued before the children of *I* Judg 8:28 3478
the children of *I* turned again Judg 8:33 3478
the children of *I* remembered not Judg 8:34 3478
which he had shewed unto *I* Judg 8:35 3478
had reigned three years over *I* Judg 9:22 3478
when the men of *I* saw that Judg 9:55 3478
to defend *I* Tola the son of Puah Judg 10:1 3478
And he judged *I* twenty and three Judg 10:2 3478
a Gileadite, and judged *I* twenty Judg 10:3 3478
the children of *I* did evil again Judg 10:6 3478
of the LORD was hot against *I* Judg 10:7 3478
and oppressed the children of *I* Judg 10:8 3478
all the children of *I* that were Judg 10:8 3478
so that *I* was sore distressed Judg 10:9 3478
the children of *I* cried unto the Judg 10:10 3478
LORD said unto the children of *I* Judg 10:11 3478
the children of *I* said unto the Judg 10:15 3478
was grieved for the misery of *I* Judg 10:16 3478
the children of *I* assembled Judg 10:17 3478
of Ammon made war against *I* Judg 11:4 3478
of Ammon made war against *I* Judg 11:5 3478
Because *I* took away my land, when Judg 11:13 3478

I took not away the land of Moab, Judg 11:15 3478
But when *I* came up from Egypt, and Judg 11:16 3478
Then *I* sent messengers unto the Judg 11:17 3478
and *I* abode in Kadesh Judg 11:17 3478
I sent messengers unto Sihon king Judg 11:19 3478
I said unto him, Let us pass, we Judg 11:19 3478
But Sihon trusted not *I* to pass Judg 11:20 3478
in Jahaz, and fought against *I* Judg 11:20 3478
the LORD God of *I* delivered Sihon Judg 11:21 3478
all his people into the hand of *I* Judg 11:21 3478
so *I* possessed all the land of Judg 11:21 3478
So now the LORD God of *I* hath Judg 11:23 3478
Amorites from before his people *I* Judg 11:23 3478
did he ever strive against *I* Judg 11:25 3478
While *I* dwelt in Heshbon and her Judg 11:26 3478
day between the children of *I* Judg 11:27 3478
subdued before the children of *I* Judg 11:33 3478
And it was a custom in *I*, Judg 11:39 3478
That the daughters of *I* went Judg 11:40 3478
And Jephthah judged *I* six years Judg 12:7 3478
him Ibzan of Beth-lehem judged *I* Judg 12:8 3478
And he judged *I* seven years Judg 12:9 3478
him Elon, a Zebulonite, judged *I* Judg 12:11 3478
and he judged *I* ten years Judg 12:11 3478
Hillel, a Pirathonite, judged *I* Judg 12:13 3478
and he judged *I* eight years Judg 12:14 3478
the children of *I* did evil again Judg 13:1 3478
deliver *I* out of the hand of the Judg 13:5 3478
Philistines had dominion over *I* Judg 14:4 3478
he judged *I* in the days of the Judg 15:20 3478
And he judged *I* twenty years Judg 16:31 3478
those days there was no king in *I* Judg 17:6 3478
those days there was no king in *I* Judg 18:1 3478
unto them among the tribes of *I* Judg 18:1 3478
unto a tribe and a family in *I* Judg 18:19 3478
days, when there was no king in *I* Judg 19:1 3478
that is not of the children of *I* Judg 19:12 3478
sent her into all the coasts of *I* Judg 19:29 3478
of *I* came up out of the land of Judg 19:30 3478
all the children of *I* went out Judg 20:1 3478
even of all the tribes of *I* Judg 20:2 3478
of *I* were gone up to Mizpeh Judg 20:3 3478
Then said the children of *I* Judg 20:3 3478
country of the inheritance of *I* Judg 20:6 3478
committed lewdness and folly in *I* Judg 20:6 3478
Behold, ye are all children of *I* Judg 20:7 3478
throughout all the tribes of *I* Judg 20:10 3478
folly that they have wrought in *I* Judg 20:10 3478
So all the men of *I* were gathered Judg 20:11 3478
the tribes of *I* sent men through Judg 20:12 3478
to death, and put away evil from *I* Judg 20:13 3478
their brethren the children of *I* Judg 20:13 3478
battle against the children of *I* Judg 20:14 3478
And the men of *I*, beside Benjamin, Judg 20:17 3478
And the children of *I* arose Judg 20:18 3478
the children of *I* rose up in the Judg 20:19 3478
the men of *I* went out to battle Judg 20:20 3478
the men of *I* put themselves in Judg 20:20 3478
men of *I* encouraged themselves Judg 20:22 3478
(And the children of *I* went up Judg 20:23 3478
the children of *I* came near Judg 20:24 3478
of *I* again eighteen thousand men Judg 20:25 3478
Then all the children of *I* Judg 20:26 3478
the children of *I* enquired of the Judg 20:27 3478
I set liers in wait round about Judg 20:29 3478
the children of *I* went up against Judg 20:30 3478
the field, about thirty men of *I* Judg 20:31 3478
But the children of *I* said Judg 20:32 3478
all the men of *I* rose up out of Judg 20:33 3478
the liers in wait of *I* came forth Judg 20:33 3478
thousand chosen men out of all *I* Judg 20:34 3478
the LORD smote Benjamin before *I* Judg 20:35 3478
the children of *I* destroyed of Judg 20:35 3478
for the men of *I* gave place to Judg 20:36 3478
sign between the men of *I* Judg 20:38 3478
when the men of *I* retired in the Judg 20:39 3478
kill of the men of *I* about thirty Judg 20:39 3478
And when the men of *I* turned again Judg 20:41 3478
their backs before the men of *I* Judg 20:42 3478
the men of *I* turned again upon Judg 20:48 3478
Now the men of *I* had sworn in Judg 21:1 3478
And said, O LORD God of *I* Judg 21:3 3478
why is this come to pass in *I* Judg 21:3 3478
be to day one tribe lacking in *I* Judg 21:3 3478
And the children of *I* said Judg 21:5 3478
of *I* that came not up with the Judg 21:5 3478
the children of *I* repented them Judg 21:6 3478
one tribe cut off from *I* this day Judg 21:6 3478
I that came not up to Mizpeh to Judg 21:8 3478
made a breach in the tribes of *I* Judg 21:15 3478
a tribe be not destroyed out of *I* Judg 21:17 3478
for the children of *I* have sworn Judg 21:18 3478
the children of *I* departed thence Judg 21:24 3478
those days there was no king in *I* Judg 21:25 3478
given thee of the LORD God of *I* Ruth 2:12 3478
time in *I* concerning redeeming Ruth 4:7 3478
and this was a testimony in *I* Ruth 4:7 3478
two did build the house of *I* Ruth 4:11 3478
that his name may be famous in *I* Ruth 4:14 3478
the God of *I* grant thee thy 1Sa 1:17 3478
all that his sons did unto all *I* 1Sa 2:22 3478
the tribes of *I* to be my priest 1Sa 2:28 3478
made by fire of the children of *I* 1Sa 2:28 3478
all the offerings of *I* my people 1Sa 2:29 3478
Wherefore the LORD God of *I* saith 1Sa 2:30 3478
the wealth which God shall give *I* 1Sa 2:32 3478
Behold, I will do a thing in *I* 1Sa 3:11 3478
all *I* from Dan even to Beer-sheba 1Sa 3:20 3478
the word of Samuel came to all *I* 1Sa 4:1 3478
Now *I* went out against the 1Sa 4:1 3478
put themselves in array against *I* 1Sa 4:2 3478
battle, *I* was smitten before the 1Sa 4:2 3478
the camp, the elders of *I* said 1Sa 4:3 3478
all *I* shouted with a great shout, 1Sa 4:5 3478
I was smitten, and they fled every 1Sa 4:10 3478
for there fell of *I* thirty 1Sa 4:10 3478
I is fled before the Philistines, 1Sa 4:17 3478
And he had judged *I* forty years 1Sa 4:18 3478
The glory is departed from *I* 1Sa 4:21 3478
The glory is departed from *I* 1Sa 4:22 3478
The ark of the God of *I* shall not 1Sa 5:7 3478
do with the ark of the God of *I* 1Sa 5:8 3478
Let the ark of the God of *I* be 1Sa 5:8 3478
ark of the God of *I* about thither 1Sa 5:8 3478
the ark of the God of *I* to us 1Sa 5:10 3478
Send away the ark of the God of *I* 1Sa 5:11 3478
send away the ark of the God of *I* 1Sa 6:3 3478
give glory unto the God of *I* 1Sa 6:5 3478
all the house of *I* lamented after 1Sa 7:2 3478
spake unto all the house of *I* 1Sa 7:3 3478
children of *I* did put away Baalim 1Sa 7:4 3478
said, Gather all *I* to Mizpeh 1Sa 7:5 3478
the children of *I* in Mizpeh 1Sa 7:6 3478
of *I* were gathered together to 1Sa 7:7 3478
the Philistines went up against *I* 1Sa 7:7 3478
when the children of *I* heard it 1Sa 7:7 3478
the children of *I* said to Samuel 1Sa 7:8 3478
Samuel cried unto the LORD for *I* 1Sa 7:9 3478
drew near to battle against *I* 1Sa 7:10 3478
and they were smitten before *I* 1Sa 7:10 3478
the men of *I* went out of Mizpeh, 1Sa 7:11 3478
came no more into the coast of *I* 1Sa 7:13 3478
from *I* were restored to Israel 1Sa 7:14 3478
the coasts thereof did *I* deliver 1Sa 7:14 3478
And there was peace between *I* 1Sa 7:14 3478
Samuel judged *I* all the days of 1Sa 7:15 3478
judged *I* in all those places 1Sa 7:16 3478
and there he judged *I* 1Sa 7:17 3478
he made his sons judges over *I* 1Sa 8:1 3478
Then all the elders of *I* gathered 1Sa 8:4 3478
And Samuel said unto the men of *I* 1Sa 8:22 3478
of *I* a goodlier person than he 1Sa 9:2 3478
(Beforetime in *I*, when a man went 1Sa 9:9 3478
to be captain over my people *I* 1Sa 9:16 3478
And on whom is all the desire of *I* 1Sa 9:20 3478
the smallest of the tribes of *I* 1Sa 9:21 3478
And said unto the children of *I* 1Sa 10:18 3478
Thus saith the LORD God of *I* 1Sa 10:18 3478
I brought up *I* out of Egypt 1Sa 10:18 3478
all the tribes of *I* to come near 1Sa 10:20 3478
lay it for a reproach upon all *I* 1Sa 11:2 3478
unto all the coasts of *I* 1Sa 11:3 3478
of *I* by the hands of messengers 1Sa 11:7 3478
the children of *I* were three 1Sa 11:8 3478
LORD hath wrought salvation in *I* 1Sa 11:13 3478
all the men of *I* rejoiced greatly 1Sa 11:15 3478
And Samuel said unto all *I* 1Sa 12:1 3478
he had reigned two years over *I* 1Sa 13:1 3478
chose him three thousand men of *I* 1Sa 13:2 3478
all *I* heard say that Saul had 1Sa 13:4 3478
and that *I* also was had in 1Sa 13:4 3478
together to fight with *I*, thirty 1Sa 13:5 3478
When the men of *I* saw that they 1Sa 13:6 3478
thy kingdom upon *I* for ever 1Sa 13:13 3478
throughout all the land of *I* 1Sa 13:19 3478
delivered them into the hand of *I* 1Sa 14:12 3478
that time with the children of *I* 1Sa 14:18 3478
Likewise all the men of *I* which 1Sa 14:22 3478
So the LORD saved *I* that day 1Sa 14:23 3478
the men of *I* were distressed that 1Sa 14:24 3478
deliver them into the hand of *I* 1Sa 14:37 3478
the LORD liveth, which saveth *I* 1Sa 14:39 3478
Then said he unto all *I*, Be ye on 1Sa 14:40 3478
Saul said unto the LORD God of *I* 1Sa 14:41 3478
wrought this great salvation in *I* 1Sa 14:45 3478
So Saul took the kingdom over *I* 1Sa 14:47 3478
delivered *I* out of the hands of 1Sa 14:48 3478
be king over his people, over *I* 1Sa 15:1 3478
that which Amalek did to *I* 1Sa 15:2 3478
kindness to all the children of *I* 1Sa 15:6 3478
made the head of the tribes of *I* 1Sa 15:17 3478
LORD anointed thee king over *I* 1Sa 15:17 3478
thee from being king over *I* 1Sa 15:26 3478
kingdom of *I* from thee this day 1Sa 15:28 3478
also the Strength of *I* will not 1Sa 15:29 3478
elders of my people, and before *I* 1Sa 15:30 3478
that he had made Saul king over *I* 1Sa 15:35 3478
rejected him from reigning over *I* 1Sa 16:1 3478
the men of *I* were gathered 1Sa 17:2 3478
I stood on a mountain on the 1Sa 17:3 3478
and cried unto the armies of *I* 1Sa 17:8 3478
I defy the armies of *I* this day 1Sa 17:10 3478
all *I* heard those words of the 1Sa 17:11 3478
and they, and all the men of *I* 1Sa 17:19 3478
For *I* and the Philistines had put 1Sa 17:21 3478
And all the men of *I*, when they 1Sa 17:24 3478
And the men of *I* said, Have ye 1Sa 17:25 3478
surely to defy *I* is he come up 1Sa 17:25 3478
make his father's house free in *I* 1Sa 17:25 3478
taketh away the reproach from *I* 1Sa 17:26 3478
hosts, the God of the armies of *I* 1Sa 17:45 3478
may know that there is a God in *I* 1Sa 17:46 3478
And the men of *I* and of Judah arose 1Sa 17:52 3478
the children of *I* returned from 1Sa 17:53 3478
women came out of all cities of *I* 1Sa 18:6 3478
But all *I* and Judah loved David, 1Sa 18:16 3478
life, or my father's family in *I* 1Sa 18:18 3478
a great salvation for all *I* 1Sa 19:5 3478
said unto David, O LORD God of *I* 1Sa 20:12 3478
Then said David, O LORD God of *I* 1Sa 23:10 3478
O LORD God of *I*, I beseech thee, 1Sa 23:11 3478
and thou shalt be king over *I* 1Sa 23:17 3478
thousand chosen men out of all *I* 1Sa 24:2 3478
whom is the king of *I* come out 1Sa 24:14 3478
that the kingdom of *I* shall be 1Sa 24:20 3478
have appointed thee ruler over *I* 1Sa 25:30 3478
Blessed be the LORD God of *I* 1Sa 25:32 3478
deed, as the LORD God of *I* liveth 1Sa 25:34 3478
thousand chosen men of *I* with him 1Sa 26:2 3478
and who is like to thee in *I* 1Sa 26:15 3478
for the king of *I* is come out to 1Sa 26:20 3478
me any more in any coast of *I* 1Sa 27:1 3478
his people *I* utterly to abhor him 1Sa 27:12 3478
for warfare, to fight with *I* 1Sa 28:1 3478
all *I* had lamented him, and buried 1Sa 28:3 3478
and Saul gathered all *I* together 1Sa 28:4 3478
the LORD will also deliver *I* with 1Sa 28:19 3478
host of *I* into the hand of the 1Sa 28:19 3478
the servant of Saul the king of *I* 1Sa 29:3 3478
an ordinance for *I* unto this day 1Sa 30:25 3478
the Philistines fought against *I* 1Sa 31:1 3478
the men of *I* fled from before the 1Sa 31:1 3478
when the men of *I* that were on 1Sa 31:7 3478
saw that the men of *I* fled 1Sa 31:7 3478
Out of the camp of *I* am I escaped 2Sa 1:3 3478
the LORD, and for the house of *I* 2Sa 1:12 3478
The beauty of *I* is slain upon thy 2Sa 1:19 3478
Ye daughters of *I*, weep over Saul 2Sa 1:24 3478
and over Benjamin, and over all *I* 2Sa 2:9 3478
old when he began to reign over *I* 2Sa 2:10 3478
Abner was beaten, and the men of *I* 2Sa 2:17 3478
still, and pursued after *I* no more 2Sa 2:28 3478
set up the throne of David over *I* 2Sa 3:10 3478
to bring about all *I* unto thee 2Sa 3:12 3478
with the elders of *I*, saying, Ye 2Sa 3:17 3478
people *I* out of the hand of the 2Sa 3:18 3478
Hebron all that seemed good to *I* 2Sa 3:19 3478
will gather all *I* unto my lord 2Sa 3:21 3478
all *I* understood that day that it 2Sa 3:37 3478
a great man fallen this day in *I* 2Sa 3:38 3478
tribes of *I* to David unto Hebron 2Sa 5:1 3478
leddest out and broughtest in *I* 2Sa 5:2 3478
thee, Thou shalt feed my people *I* 2Sa 5:2 3478
and thou shalt be a captain over *I* 2Sa 5:2 3478
So all the elders of *I* came to 2Sa 5:3 3478
they anointed David king over *I* 2Sa 5:3 3478
thirty and three years over all *I* 2Sa 5:5 3478
had established him king over *I* 2Sa 5:12 3478
had anointed David king over *I* 2Sa 5:17 3478
together all the chosen men of *I* 2Sa 6:1 3478
all the house of *I* played before 2Sa 6:5 3478
all the house of *I* brought up the 2Sa 6:15 3478
among the whole multitude of *I* 2Sa 6:19 3478
glorious was the king of *I* today 2Sa 6:20 3478
the people of the LORD, over *I* 2Sa 6:21 3478
up the children of *I* out of Egypt 2Sa 7:6 3478
I spake I a word with any of the 2Sa 7:7 3478
word with any of the tribes of *I* 2Sa 7:7 3478
I commanded to feed my people *I* 2Sa 7:7 3478
be ruler over my people, over *I* 2Sa 7:8 3478
appoint a place for my people *I* 2Sa 7:10 3478
judges to be over my people *I* 2Sa 7:11 3478
is like thy people, even like *I* 2Sa 7:23 3478
I to be a people unto thee for 2Sa 7:24 3478
LORD of hosts is the God over *I* 2Sa 7:26 3478
thou, O LORD of hosts, God of *I* 2Sa 7:27 3478
And David reigned over all *I* 2Sa 8:15 3478
chose of all the choice men of *I* 2Sa 10:9 3478
that they were smitten before *I* 2Sa 10:15 3478
David, he gathered all *I* together 2Sa 10:17 3478
And the Syrians fled before *I* 2Sa 10:18 3478
that they were smitten before *I* 2Sa 10:19 3478
Israel, they made peace with *I* 2Sa 10:19 3478
his servants with him, and all *I* 2Sa 11:1 3478
said unto David, The ark, and *I* 2Sa 11:11 3478
Thus saith the LORD God of *I* 2Sa 12:7 3478
I anointed thee king over *I* 2Sa 12:7 3478
and gave thee the house of *I* 2Sa 12:8 3478
I will do this thing before all *I* 2Sa 12:12 3478
such thing ought to be done in *I* 2Sa 13:12 3478
shalt be as one of the fools in *I* 2Sa 13:13 3478
But in all *I* there was none to be 2Sa 14:25 3478
is of one of the tribes of *I* 2Sa 15:2 3478
all *I* that came to the king for 2Sa 15:6 3478
stole the hearts of the men of *I* 2Sa 15:6 3478
throughout all the tribes of *I* 2Sa 15:10 3478
of the men of *I* are after Absalom 2Sa 15:13 3478
Today shall the house of *I* 2Sa 16:3 3478
and all the people the men of *I* 2Sa 16:15 3478
this people, and all the men of *I* 2Sa 16:18 3478
all *I* shall hear that thou art 2Sa 16:21 3478
concubines in the sight of all *I* 2Sa 16:22 3478
well, and all the elders of *I* 2Sa 17:4 3478
for all *I* knoweth that thy father 2Sa 17:10 3478
Therefore I counsel that all *I* be 2Sa 17:11 3478
then shall all *I* bring ropes to 2Sa 17:13 3478
Absalom and all the men of *I* said 2Sa 17:14 3478
Absalom and the elders of *I* 2Sa 17:15 3478
he and all the men of *I* with him 2Sa 17:24 3478
So *I* and Absalom pitched in the 2Sa 17:26 3478
went out into the field against *I* 2Sa 18:6 3478
Where the people of *I* were slain 2Sa 18:7 3478
returned from pursuing after *I* 2Sa 18:16 3478
all *I* fled every one to his tent 2Sa 18:17 3478
for *I* had fled every man to his 2Sa 19:8 3478
throughout all the tribes of *I* 2Sa 19:9 3478
of all *I* is come to the king 2Sa 19:11 3478
man be put to death this day in *I* 2Sa 19:22 3478
that I am this day king over *I* 2Sa 19:22 3478
and also half the people of *I* 2Sa 19:40 3478
all the men of *I* came to the king 2Sa 19:41 3478
of Judah answered the men of *I* 2Sa 19:42 3478
the men of *I* answered the men of 2Sa 19:43 3478
than the words of the men of *I* 2Sa 19:43 3478
every man to his tents, O *I* 2Sa 20:1 3478
So every man of *I* went up from 2Sa 20:2 3478
all the tribes of *I* unto Abel 2Sa 20:14 3478
are peaceable and faithful in *I* 2Sa 20:19 3478
destroy a city and a mother in *I* 2Sa 20:19 3478
Joab was over all the host of *I* 2Sa 20:23 3478
were not of the children of *I* 2Sa 21:2 3478
the children of *I* had sworn unto 2Sa 21:2 3478

in his zeal to the children of *I* 2Sa 21:2 3478
us shalt thou kill any man in *I* 2Sa 21:4 3478
in any of the coasts of *I* 2Sa 21:5 3478
had yet war again with *I* 2Sa 21:15 3478
thou quench not the light of *I* 2Sa 21:17 3478
And when he defied *I*, Jonathan the 2Sa 21:21 3478
Jacob, and the sweet psalmist of *I* 2Sa 23:1 3478
The God of *I* said, the Rock of 2Sa 23:3 3478
said, the Rock of *I* spake to me 2Sa 23:3 3478
the men of *I* were gone away 2Sa 23:9 3478
of the LORD was kindled against *I* 2Sa 24:1 3478
against them to say, Go, number *I* 2Sa 24:1 3478
now through all the tribes of *I* 2Sa 24:2 3478
king, to number the people of *I* 2Sa 24:4 3478
there were in *I* eight hundred 2Sa 24:9 3478
I from the morning even to the 2Sa 24:15 3478
and the plague was stayed from *I* 2Sa 24:25 3478
throughout all the coasts of *I* 1Kin 1:3 3478
the eyes of all *I* are upon thee 1Kin 1:20 3478
unto thee by the LORD God of *I* 1Kin 1:30 3478
anoint him there king over *I* 1Kin 1:34 3478
appointed him to be ruler over *I* 1Kin 1:35 3478
Blessed be the LORD God of *I* 1Kin 1:48 3478
said he) a man on the throne of *I* 1Kin 2:4 3478
two captains of the hosts of *I* 1Kin 2:5 3478
reigned over *I* were forty years 1Kin 2:11 3478
that all *I* set their faces on me, 1Kin 2:15 3478
of Ner, captain of the host of *I* 1Kin 2:32 3478
all *I* heard of the judgment which 1Kin 3:28 3478
king Solomon was king over all *I* 1Kin 4:1 3478
had twelve officers over all *I* 1Kin 4:7 3478
raised a levy out of all *I* 1Kin 5:13 3478
year after the children of *I* were 1Kin 6:1 3478
year of Solomon's reign over *I* 1Kin 6:1 3478
dwell among the children of *I* 1Kin 6:13 3478
and will not forsake my people *I* 1Kin 6:13 3478
Solomon assembled the elders of *I* 1Kin 8:1 3478
the fathers of the children of *I* 1Kin 8:1 3478
all the men of *I* assembled 1Kin 8:2 3478
And all the elders of *I* came 1Kin 8:3 3478
and all the congregation of *I* 1Kin 8:5 3478
a covenant with the children of *I* 1Kin 8:9 3478
blessed all the congregation of *I* 1Kin 8:14 3478
all the congregation of *I* stood 1Kin 8:14 3478
Blessed be the LORD God of *I* 1Kin 8:15 3478
forth my people *I* out of Egypt 1Kin 8:16 3478
the tribes of *I* to build an house 1Kin 8:16 3478
David to be over my people *I* 1Kin 8:16 3478
for the name of the LORD God of *I* 1Kin 8:17 3478
father, and sit on the throne of *I* 1Kin 8:20 3478
for the name of the LORD God of *I* 1Kin 8:20 3478
of all the congregation of *I* 1Kin 8:22 3478
And he said, LORD God of *I* 1Kin 8:23 3478
Therefore now, LORD God of *I* 1Kin 8:25 3478
sight to sit on the throne of *I* 1Kin 8:25 3478
And now, O God of *I*, let thy word, 1Kin 8:26 3478
thy servant, and of thy people *I* 1Kin 8:30 3478
When thy people *I* be smitten down 1Kin 8:33 3478
forgive the sin of thy people *I* 1Kin 8:34 3478
thy servants, and of thy people *I* 1Kin 8:36 3478
any man, or by all thy people *I* 1Kin 8:38 3478
that is not of thy people *I* 1Kin 8:41 3478
to fear thee, as do thy people *I* 1Kin 8:43 3478
the supplication of thy people *I* 1Kin 8:52 3478
of *I* with a loud voice, saying, 1Kin 8:55 3478
hath given rest unto his people *I* 1Kin 8:56 3478
of his people *I* at all times 1Kin 8:59 3478
all *I* with him, offered sacrifice 1Kin 8:62 3478
all the children of *I* dedicated 1Kin 8:63 3478
feast, and all *I* with him, a great 1Kin 8:65 3478
his servant, and for *I* his people 1Kin 8:66 3478
of thy kingdom upon *I* for ever 1Kin 9:5 3478
thee a man upon the throne of *I* 1Kin 9:5 3478
Then will I cut off *I* out of the 1Kin 9:7 3478
I shall be a proverb and a byword 1Kin 9:7 3478
were not of the children of *I* 1Kin 9:20 3478
whom the children of *I* also were 1Kin 9:21 3478
But of the children of *I* did 1Kin 9:22 3478
to set thee on the throne of *I* 1Kin 10:9 3478
because the LORD loved *I* for ever 1Kin 10:9 3478
LORD said unto the children of *I* 1Kin 11:2 3478
was turned from the LORD God of *I* 1Kin 11:9 3478
did Joab remain there with all *I* 1Kin 11:16 3478
he was an adversary to *I* all the 1Kin 11:25 3478
and he abhorred *I*, and reigned over 1Kin 11:25 3478
thus saith the LORD, the God of *I* 1Kin 11:31 3478
chosen out of all the tribes of *I* 1Kin 11:32 3478
desireth, and shalt be king over *I* 1Kin 11:37 3478
David, and will give *I* unto thee 1Kin 11:38 3478
over all *I* was forty years 1Kin 11:42 3478
for all *I* were come to Shechem to 1Kin 12:1 3478
and all the congregation of *I* came 1Kin 12:3 3478
So when all *I* saw that the king 1Kin 12:16 3478
to your tents, O *I* 1Kin 12:16 3478
So *I* departed unto their tents 1Kin 12:16 3478
But as for the children of *I* 1Kin 12:17 3478
Thus saith the LORD God of *I* 1Kin 14:7 3478
made thee prince over my people *I* 1Kin 14:7 3478
choose out of all the tribes of *I* 1Kin 14:21 3478
cast out before the children of *I* 1Kin 14:24 3478
sin wherewith he made *I* to sin 1Kin 15:34 3478
I to anger than all the kings of 1Kin 16:33 3478
Ahab, As the LORD God of *I* liveth 1Kin 17:1 3478
For thus saith the LORD God of *I* 1Kin 17:14 3478
this day that thou art God in *I* 1Kin 18:36 3478
to anger the LORD God of *I* 1Kin 22:53 3478
my father, the chariot of *I* 2Kin 2:12 3478
him, Thus saith the LORD God of *I* 2Kin 9:6 3478
LORD God of *I* with all his heart 2Kin 10:31 3478
He restored the coast of *I* from 2Kin 14:25 3478
to the word of the LORD God of *I* 2Kin 14:25 3478
of *I* did burn incense to it 2Kin 18:4 3478
He trusted in the LORD God of *I* 2Kin 18:5 3478
LORD, and said, O LORD God of *I* 2Kin 19:15 3478
Thus saith the LORD God of *I* 2Kin 19:20 3478
even against the Holy One of *I* 2Kin 19:22 3478
cast out before the children of *I* 2Kin 21:2 3478
a grove, as did Ahab king of *I* 2Kin 21:3 3478
chosen out of all tribes of *I* 2Kin 21:7 3478
I move any more out of the land 2Kin 21:8 3478
before the children of *I* 2Kin 21:9 3478
thus saith the LORD God of *I* 2Kin 21:12 3478
Thus saith the LORD God of *I* 2Kin 22:15 3478
him, Thus saith the LORD God of *I* 2Kin 22:18 3478
which Solomon the king of *I* had 2Kin 23:13 3478
days of the judges that judged *I* 2Kin 23:22 3478
I had made in the temple of the 2Kin 24:13 3478
reigned over the children of *I* 1Chr 1:43 3478
Achar, the troubler of *I*, who 1Chr 2:7 3478
And Jabez called on the God of *I* 1Chr 4:10 3478
the God of *I* stirred up the 1Chr 5:26 3478
and to make an atonement for *I* 1Chr 6:49 3478
the children of *I* gave to the 1Chr 6:64 3478
So all *I* were reckoned by 1Chr 9:1 3478
the Philistines fought against *I* 1Chr 10:1 3478
the men of *I* fled from before the 1Chr 10:1 3478
when all the men of *I* that were 1Chr 10:7 3478
Then all *I* gathered themselves to 1Chr 11:1 3478
leddest out and broughtest in *I* 1Chr 11:2 3478
thee, Thou shalt feed my people *I* 1Chr 11:2 3478
shalt be ruler over my people *I* 1Chr 11:2 3478
elders of *I* to the king to Hebron 1Chr 11:3 3478
they anointed David king over *I* 1Chr 11:3 3478
all *I* went to Jerusalem, which is 1Chr 11:4 3478
him in his kingdom, and with all *I* 1Chr 11:10 3478
the word of the LORD concerning *I* 1Chr 11:10 3478
times, to know what *I* ought to do 1Chr 12:32 3478
to make David king over all *I* 1Chr 12:38 3478
all the rest also of *I* were of 1Chr 12:38 3478
for there was joy in *I* 1Chr 12:40 3478
unto all the congregation of *I* 1Chr 13:2 3478
are left in all the land of *I* 1Chr 13:2 3478
So David gathered all *I* together 1Chr 13:5 3478
And David went up, and all *I* 1Chr 13:6 3478
all *I* played before God with all 1Chr 13:8 3478
had confirmed him king over *I* 1Chr 14:2 3478
on high, because of his people *I* 1Chr 14:2 3478
was anointed king over all *I* 1Chr 14:8 3478
David gathered all *I* together to 1Chr 15:3 3478
of *I* unto the place that I have 1Chr 15:12 3478
up the ark of the LORD God of *I* 1Chr 15:14 3478
So David, and the elders of *I* 1Chr 15:25 3478
Thus all *I* brought up the ark of 1Chr 15:28 3478
And he dealt to every one of *I* 1Chr 16:3 3478
thank and praise the LORD God of *I* 1Chr 16:4 3478
O ye seed of *I* his servant 1Chr 16:13 3478
to *I* for an everlasting covenant, 1Chr 16:17 3478
be the LORD God of *I* for ever 1Chr 16:36 3478
of the LORD, which he commanded *I* 1Chr 16:40 3478
that I brought up *I* unto this day 1Chr 17:5 3478
I have walked with all *I*, spake I 1Chr 17:6 3478
a word to any of the judges of *I* 1Chr 17:6 3478
be ruler over my people *I* 1Chr 17:7 3478
ordain a place for my people *I* 1Chr 17:9 3478
judges to be over my people *I* 1Chr 17:10 3478
in the earth is like thy people *I* 1Chr 17:21 3478
For thy people *I* didst thou make 1Chr 17:22 3478
God of Israel, even a God to *I* 1Chr 17:24 3478
So David reigned over all *I* 1Chr 18:14 3478
chose out of all the choice of *I* 1Chr 19:10 3478
were put to the worse before *I* 1Chr 19:16 3478
and he gathered all *I*, and passed 1Chr 19:17 3478
But the Syrians fled before *I* 1Chr 19:18 3478
were put to the worse before *I* 1Chr 19:19 3478
But when he defied *I*, Jonathan 1Chr 20:7 3478
And Satan stood up against *I* 1Chr 21:1 3478
and provoked David to number *I* 1Chr 21:1 3478
number *I* from Beer-sheba even to 1Chr 21:2 3478
he be a cause of trespass to *I* 1Chr 21:3 3478
and went throughout all *I* 1Chr 21:4 3478
all they of *I* were a thousand 1Chr 21:5 3478
therefore he smote *I* 1Chr 21:7 3478
throughout all the coasts of *I* 1Chr 21:12 3478
the LORD sent pestilence upon *I* 1Chr 21:14 3478
there fell of *I* seventy thousand 1Chr 21:14 3478
Then David and the elders of *I* 1Chr 21:16
altar of the burnt offering for *I* 1Chr 22:1 3478
that were in the land of *I* 1Chr 22:2 3478
an house for the LORD God of *I* 1Chr 22:6 3478
and quietness unto *I* in his days 1Chr 22:9 3478
of his kingdom over *I* for ever 1Chr 22:10 3478
and give thee charge concerning *I* 1Chr 22:12 3478
charged Moses with concerning *I* 1Chr 22:13 3478
of *I* to help Solomon his son 1Chr 22:17 3478
made Solomon his son king over *I* 1Chr 23:1 3478
together all the princes of *I* 1Chr 23:2 3478
The LORD God of *I* hath given rest 1Chr 23:25 3478
LORD God of *I* had commanded him 1Chr 24:19 3478
for the outward business over *I* 1Chr 26:29 3478
were officers among them of *I* on 1Chr 26:30 3478
children of *I* after their number 1Chr 27:1 3478
Furthermore over the tribes of *I* 1Chr 27:16 3478
the princes of the tribes of *I* 1Chr 27:22 3478
I like to the stars of the 1Chr 27:23 3478
there fell wrath for it against *I* 1Chr 27:24 3478
assembled all the princes of *I* 1Chr 28:1 3478
Howbeit the LORD God of *I* chose 1Chr 28:4 3478
father to be king over *I* for ever 1Chr 28:4 3478
me to make me king over all *I* 1Chr 28:4 3478
of the kingdom of the LORD over *I* 1Chr 28:5 3478
in the sight of all *I* the 1Chr 28:8 3478
and princes of the tribes of *I* 1Chr 29:6 3478
sacrifices in abundance for all *I* 1Chr 29:21 3478
and all *I* obeyed him 1Chr 29:23 3478
exceedingly in the sight of all *I* 1Chr 29:25 3478
been on any king before him in *I* 1Chr 29:25 3478
son of Jesse reigned over all *I* 1Chr 29:26 3478
he reigned over *I* was forty years 1Chr 29:27 3478
that went over him, and over *I* 1Chr 29:30 3478
Then Solomon spake unto all *I* 2Chr 1:2 3478
and to every governor in all *I* 2Chr 1:2 3478
congregation, and reigned over *I* 2Chr 1:13 3478
is an ordinance for ever to *I* 2Chr 2:4 3478
Blessed be the LORD God of *I* 2Chr 2:12 3478
that were in the land of *I* 2Chr 2:17 3478
Solomon assembled the elders of *I* 2Chr 5:2 3478
the fathers of the children of *I* 2Chr 5:2 3478
Wherefore all the men of *I* 2Chr 5:3 3478
And all the elders of *I* came 2Chr 5:4 3478
all the congregation of *I* that 2Chr 5:6 3478
a covenant with the children of *I* 2Chr 5:10 3478
the whole congregation of *I* 2Chr 6:3 3478
all the congregation of *I* stood 2Chr 6:3 3478
Blessed be the LORD God of *I* 2Chr 6:4 3478
tribes of *I* to build an house in 2Chr 6:5 3478
to be a ruler over my people *I* 2Chr 6:5 3478
David to be over my people *I* 2Chr 6:6 3478
for the name of the LORD God of *I* 2Chr 6:7 3478
and am set on the throne of *I* 2Chr 6:10 3478
for the name of the LORD God of *I* 2Chr 6:10 3478
he made with the children of *I* 2Chr 6:11 3478
of all the congregation of *I* 2Chr 6:12 3478
before all the congregation of *I* 2Chr 6:13 3478
And said, O LORD God of *I*, there 2Chr 6:14 3478
Now therefore, O LORD God of *I* 2Chr 6:16 3478
sight to sit upon the throne of *I* 2Chr 6:16 3478
Now then, O LORD God of *I* 2Chr 6:17 3478
thy servant, and of thy people *I* 2Chr 6:21 3478
if thy people *I* be put to the 2Chr 6:24 3478
forgive the sin of thy people *I* 2Chr 6:25 3478
thy servants, and of thy people *I* 2Chr 6:27 3478
any man, or of all thy people *I* 2Chr 6:29 3478
which is not of thy people *I* 2Chr 6:32 3478
fear thee, as doth thy people *I* 2Chr 6:33 3478
when all the children of *I* saw 2Chr 7:3 3478
before them, and all *I* stood 2Chr 7:6 3478
all *I* with him, a very great 2Chr 7:8 3478
and to Solomon, and to *I* his people 2Chr 7:10 3478
fail thee a man to be ruler in *I* 2Chr 7:18 3478
the children of *I* to dwell there 2Chr 8:2 3478
Jebusites, which were not of *I* 2Chr 8:7 3478
the children of *I* consumed not 2Chr 8:8 3478
But of the children of *I* did 2Chr 8:9 3478
in the house of David king of *I* 2Chr 8:11 3478
because thy God loved *I*, to 2Chr 9:8 3478
Jerusalem over all *I* forty years 2Chr 9:30 3478
were all *I* come to make him king 2Chr 10:1 3478
all *I* came and spake to Rehoboam, 2Chr 10:3 3478
when all *I* saw that the king 2Chr 10:16 3478
every man to your tents, O *I* 2Chr 10:16 3478
So all *I* went to their tents 2Chr 10:16 3478
But as for the children of *I* that 2Chr 10:17 3478
to all *I* in Judah and Benjamin, 2Chr 11:3 3478
LORD God of *I* came to Jerusalem 2Chr 11:16 3478
of the LORD, and all *I* with him 2Chr 12:1 3478
Whereupon the princes of *I* 2Chr 12:6 3478
chosen out of all the tribes of *I* 2Chr 12:13 3478
to know that the LORD God of *I* 2Chr 13:5 3478
kingdom over *I* to David for ever 2Chr 13:5 3478
Now for a long season *I* hath been 2Chr 15:3 3478
did turn unto the LORD God of *I* 2Chr 15:4 3478
God of *I* should be put to death 2Chr 15:13 3478
of the chief of the fathers of *I* 2Chr 19:8 3478
of this land before thy people *I* 2Chr 20:7 3478
thou wouldest not let *I* invade 2Chr 20:10 3478
of *I* with a loud voice on high 2Chr 20:19 3478
fought against the enemies of *I* 2Chr 20:29 3478
and the chief of the fathers of *I* 2Chr 23:2 3478
gather of all *I* money to repair 2Chr 24:5 3478
LORD, and of the congregation of *I* 2Chr 24:6 3478
God laid upon *I* in the wilderness 2Chr 24:9 3478
because he had done good in *I* 2Chr 24:16 3478
cast out before the children of *I* 2Chr 28:3 3478
were the ruin of him, and of all *I* 2Chr 28:23 3478
book of the kings of Judah and *I* 2Chr 28:26 3478
the sepulchres of the kings of *I* 2Chr 28:27 3478
the holy place unto the God of *I* 2Chr 29:7 3478
a covenant with the LORD God of *I* 2Chr 29:10 3478
to make an atonement for all *I* 2Chr 29:24 3478
offering should be made for all *I* 2Chr 29:24 3478
ordained by David king of *I* 2Chr 29:27 3478
And Hezekiah sent to all *I* 2Chr 30:1 3478
passover unto the LORD God of *I* 2Chr 30:1 3478
proclamation throughout all *I* 2Chr 30:5 3478
the LORD God of *I* at Jerusalem 2Chr 30:5 3478
king, saying, Ye children of *I* 2Chr 30:6 3478
the son of David king of *I* there 2Chr 30:26 3478
all *I* that were present went out 2Chr 31:1 3478
all the children of *I* returned 2Chr 31:1 3478
the children of *I* brought in 2Chr 31:5 3478
blessed the LORD, and his people *I* 2Chr 31:8 3478
to rail on the LORD God of *I* 2Chr 32:17 3478
cast out before the children of *I* 2Chr 33:2 3478
chosen before all the tribes of *I* 2Chr 33:7 3478
of *I* from out of the land which I 2Chr 33:8 3478
before the children of *I* 2Chr 33:9 3478
Judah to serve the LORD God of *I* 2Chr 33:16 3478
in the name of the LORD God of *I* 2Chr 33:18 3478
in the book of the kings of *I* 2Chr 33:18 3478
throughout all the land of *I* 2Chr 34:7 3478
Thus saith the LORD God of *I* 2Chr 34:23 3478
Thus saith the LORD God of *I* 2Chr 34:26 3478
pertained to the children of *I* 2Chr 34:33 3478
that were present in *I* to serve 2Chr 34:33 3478
the Levites that taught all *I* 2Chr 35:3 3478
son of David king of *I* did build 2Chr 35:3 3478
LORD your God, and his people *I* 2Chr 35:3 3478
to the writing of David king of *I* 2Chr 35:4 3478
the children of *I* that were 2Chr 35:17 3478
in *I* from the days of Samuel the 2Chr 35:18 3478
and made them an ordinance in *I* 2Chr 35:25 3478
turning unto the LORD God of *I* 2Chr 36:13 3478

the house of the LORD God of *I*	Ezr 1:3	3478
of the men of the people of *I*	Ezr 2:2	3478
seed, whether they were of *I*	Ezr 2:59	3478
cities, and all *I* in their cities	Ezr 2:70	3478
the children of *I* were in the	Ezr 3:1	3478
builded the altar of the God of *I*	Ezr 3:2	3478
the ordinance of David king of *I*	Ezr 3:10	3478
mercy endureth for ever toward *I*	Ezr 3:11	3478
the temple unto the LORD God of *I*	Ezr 4:1	3478
of the chief of the fathers of *I*	Ezr 4:3	3478
will build unto the LORD God of *I*	Ezr 4:3	3478
in the name of the God of *I*	Ezr 5:1	3479
which a great king of *I* builded	Ezr 5:11	3479
the commandment of the God of *I*	Ezr 6:14	3479
And the children of *I*, the priests	Ezr 6:16	3479
and for a sin offering for all *I*	Ezr 6:17	3479
to the number of the tribes of *I*	Ezr 6:17	3479
And the children of *I*, which were	Ezr 6:21	3478
land, to seek the LORD God of *I*	Ezr 6:21	3478
of the house of God, the God of *I*	Ezr 6:22	3478
which the LORD God of *I* had given	Ezr 7:6	3478
went up some of the children of *I*	Ezr 7:7	3478
do it, and to teach in *I* statutes	Ezr 7:10	3478
the LORD, and of his statutes to *I*	Ezr 7:11	3478
that all they of the people of *I*	Ezr 7:13	3479
freely offered unto the God of *I*	Ezr 7:15	3479
of *I* chief men to go up with me	Ezr 7:28	3478
all *I* there present, had offered	Ezr 8:25	3478
and chief of the fathers of *I*	Ezr 8:29	3478
burnt offerings unto the God of *I*	Ezr 8:35	3478
twelve bullocks for all *I*	Ezr 8:35	3478
to me, saying, The people of *I*	Ezr 9:1	3478
at the words of the God of *I*	Ezr 9:4	3478
O LORD God of *I*, thou art	Ezr 9:15	3478
of *I* a very great congregation of	Ezr 10:1	3478
hope in *I* concerning this thing	Ezr 10:2	3478
priests, the Levites, and all *I*	Ezr 10:5	3478
to increase the trespass of *I*	Ezr 10:10	3478
Moreover of *I*: of the sons of	Ezr 10:25	3478
the children of *I* thy servants	Neh 1:6	3478
the sins of the children of *I*	Neh 1:6	3478
the welfare of the children of *I*	Neh 2:10	3478
men of the people of *I* was this	Neh 7:7	3478
seed, whether they were of *I*	Neh 7:61	3478
and the Nethinims, and all *I*	Neh 7:73	3478
the children of *I* were in their	Neh 7:73	3478
which the LORD had commanded to *I*	Neh 8:1	3478
that the children of *I* should	Neh 8:14	3478
had not the children of *I* done so	Neh 8:17	3478
of *I* were assembled with fasting	Neh 9:1	3478
And the seed of *I* separated	Neh 9:2	3478
to make an atonement for *I*	Neh 10:33	3478
For the children of *I* and the	Neh 10:39	3478
in their cities, to wit, *I*	Neh 11:3	3478
And the residue of *I*, of the	Neh 11:20	3478
all *I* in the days of Zerubbabel	Neh 12:47	3478
not the children of *I* with bread	Neh 13:2	3478
from *I* all the mixed multitude	Neh 13:3	3478
upon *I* by profaning the sabbath	Neh 13:18	3478
king of *I* sin by these things	Neh 13:26	3478
and God made him king over all *I*	Neh 13:26	3478
of *I* were come out of Zion	Ps 14:7	3478
shall rejoice, and *I* shall be glad	Ps 14:7	3478
that inhabitest the praises of *I*	Ps 22:3	3478
and fear him, all ye the seed of *I*	Ps 22:23	3478
Redeem *I*, O God, out of all his	Ps 25:22	3478
LORD God of *I* from everlasting	Ps 41:13	3478
O *I*, and I will testify against	Ps 50:7	3478
of *I* were come out of Zion	Ps 53:6	3478
shall rejoice, and *I* shall be glad	Ps 53:6	3478
O LORD God of hosts, the God of *I*	Ps 59:5	3478
the presence of God, the God of *I*	Ps 68:8	3478
the Lord, from the fountain of *I*	Ps 68:26	3478
his excellency is over *I*, and his	Ps 68:34	3478
the God of *I* is he that giveth	Ps 68:35	3478
for my sake, O God of *I*	Ps 69:6	3478
the harp, O thou Holy One of *I*	Ps 71:22	3478
be the LORD God, the God of *I*	Ps 72:18	3478
Truly God is good to *I*, even to	Ps 73:1	3478
his name is great in *I*	Ps 76:1	3478
in Jacob, and appointed a law in *I*	Ps 78:5	3478
and anger also came up against *I*	Ps 78:21	3478
and smote down the chosen men of *I*	Ps 78:31	3478
God, and limited the Holy One of *I*	Ps 78:41	3478
made the tribes of *I* to dwell in	Ps 78:55	3478
was wroth, and greatly abhorred *I*	Ps 78:59	3478
his people, and *I* his inheritance	Ps 78:71	3478
Give ear, O Shepherd of *I*	Ps 80:1	3478
For this was a statute for *I*	Ps 81:4	3478
O *I*, if thou wilt hearken unto me	Ps 81:8	3478
and *I* would none of me	Ps 81:11	3478
me, and *I* had walked in my ways	Ps 81:13	3478
that the name of *I* may be no more	Ps 83:4	3478
and the Holy One of *I* is our king	Ps 89:18	3478
his truth toward the house of *I*	Ps 98:3	3478
his acts unto the children of *I*	Ps 103:7	3478
to *I* for an everlasting covenant	Ps 105:10	3478
I also came into Egypt	Ps 105:23	3478
Blessed be the LORD God of *I* from	Ps 106:48	3478
When *I* went out of Egypt, the	Ps 114:1	3478
his sanctuary, and *I* his dominion	Ps 114:2	3478
O *I*, trust thou in the LORD	Ps 115:9	3478
he will bless the house of *I*	Ps 115:12	3478
Let *I* now say, that his mercy	Ps 118:2	3478
he that keepeth *I* shall neither	Ps 121:4	3478
the LORD, unto the testimony of *I*	Ps 122:4	3478
was on our side, now may *I* say	Ps 124:1	3478
but peace shall be upon *I*	Ps 125:5	3478
children, and peace upon *I*	Ps 128:6	3478
me from my youth, may *I* now say	Ps 129:1	3478
Let *I* hope in the LORD	Ps 130:7	3478
he shall redeem *I* from all his	Ps 130:8	3478
Let *I* hope in the LORD from	Ps 131:3	3478
I for his peculiar treasure	Ps 135:4	3478
an heritage unto *I* his people	Ps 135:12	3478
Bless the LORD, O house of *I*	Ps 135:19	3478
brought out *I* from among them	Ps 136:11	3478
made *I* to pass through the midst	Ps 136:14	3478
an heritage unto *I* his servant	Ps 136:22	3478
together the outcasts of *I*	Ps 147:2	3478
statutes and his judgments unto *I*	Ps 147:19	3478
even of the children of *I*	Ps 148:14	3478
Let *I* rejoice in him that made	Ps 149:2	3478
the son of David, king of *I*	Prov 1:1	3478
was king over *I* in Jerusalem	Eccl 1:12	3478
are about it, of the valiant of *I*	Song 3:7	3478
but *I* doth not know, my people	Is 1:3	3478
the Holy One of *I* unto anger	Is 1:4	3478
of hosts, the mighty One of *I*	Is 1:24	3478
for them that are escaped of *I*	Is 4:2	3478
LORD of hosts is the house of *I*	Is 5:7	3478
of the Holy One of *I* draw nigh	Is 5:19	3478
the word of the Holy One of *I*	Is 5:24	3478
offence to both the houses of *I*	Is 8:14	3478
for wonders in *I* from the LORD of	Is 8:18	3478
Jacob, and it hath lighted upon *I*	Is 9:8	3478
shall devour *I* with open mouth	Is 9:12	3478
the LORD will cut off from *I* head	Is 9:14	3478
the light of *I* shall be for a	Is 10:17	3478
that day, that the remnant of *I*	Is 10:20	3478
upon the LORD, the Holy One of *I*	Is 10:20	3478
For though thy people *I* be as the	Is 10:22	3478
shall assemble the outcasts of *I*	Is 11:12	3478
like as it was to *I* in the day	Is 11:16	3478
One of *I* in the midst of thee	Is 12:6	3478
on Jacob, and will yet choose *I*	Is 14:1	3478
the house of *I* shall possess them	Is 14:2	3478
as the glory of the children of *I*	Is 17:3	3478
thereof, saith the LORD God of *I*	Is 17:6	3478
have respect to the Holy One of *I*	Is 17:7	3478
left because of the children of *I*	Is 17:9	3478
In that day shall *I* be the third	Is 19:24	3478
my hands, and *I* mine inheritance	Is 19:25	3478
the LORD of hosts, the God of *I*	Is 21:10	3478
the LORD God of *I* hath spoken it	Is 21:17	3478
God of *I* in the isles of the sea	Is 24:15	3478
I shall blossom and bud, and fill	Is 27:6	3478
one by one, O ye children of *I*	Is 27:12	3478
rejoice in the Holy One of *I*	Is 29:19	3478
Jacob, and shall fear the God of *I*	Is 29:23	3478
cause the Holy One of *I* to cease	Is 30:11	3478
thus saith the Holy One of *I*	Is 30:12	3478
the Lord GOD, the Holy One of *I*	Is 30:15	3478
the LORD, to the mighty One of *I*	Is 30:29	3478
look not unto the Holy One of *I*	Is 31:1	3478
of *I* have deeply revolted	Is 31:6	3478
O LORD of hosts, God of *I*	Is 37:16	3478
Thus saith the LORD God of *I*	Is 37:21	3478
even against the Holy One of *I*	Is 37:23	3478
thou, O Jacob, and speakest, O *I*	Is 40:27	3478
But thou, *I*, art my servant	Is 41:8	3478
thou worm Jacob, and ye men of *I*	Is 41:14	3478
thy redeemer, the Holy One of *I*	Is 41:14	3478
shalt glory in the Holy One of *I*	Is 41:16	3478
I the God of *I* will not forsake	Is 41:17	3478
the Holy One of *I* hath created it	Is 41:20	3478
for a spoil, and *I* to the robbers	Is 42:24	3478
and he that formed thee, O *I*	Is 43:1	3478
LORD thy God, the Holy One of *I*	Is 43:3	3478
your redeemer, the Holy One of *I*	Is 43:14	3478
your Holy One, the creator of *I*	Is 43:15	3478
thou hast been weary of me, O *I*	Is 43:22	3478
to the curse, and *I* to reproaches	Is 43:28	3478
and *I*, whom I have chosen	Is 44:1	3478
surname himself by the name of *I*	Is 44:5	3478
Thus saith the LORD the King of *I*	Is 44:6	3478
Remember these, O Jacob and *I*	Is 44:21	3478
O *I*, thou shalt not be forgotten	Is 44:21	3478
Jacob, and glorified himself in *I*	Is 44:23	3478
thee by thy name, am the God of *I*	Is 45:3	3478
I mine elect, I have even called	Is 45:4	3478
saith the LORD, the Holy One of *I*	Is 45:11	3478
that hidest thyself, O God of *I*	Is 45:15	3478
But *I* shall be saved in the LORD	Is 45:17	3478
all the seed of *I* be justified	Is 45:25	3478
all the remnant of the house of *I*	Is 46:3	3478
salvation in Zion for *I* my glory	Is 46:13	3478
is his name, the Holy One of *I*	Is 47:4	3478
which are called by the name of *I*	Is 48:1	3478
and make mention of the God of *I*	Is 48:1	3478
stay themselves upon the God of *I*	Is 48:2	3478
Hearken unto me, O Jacob and *I*	Is 48:12	3478
thy Redeemer, the Holy One of *I*	Is 48:17	3478
unto me, Thou art my servant, O *I*	Is 49:3	3478
Though *I* be not gathered, yet	Is 49:5	3478
and to restore the preserved of *I*	Is 49:6	3478
saith the LORD, the Redeemer of *I*	Is 49:7	3478
is faithful, and the Holy One of *I*	Is 49:7	3478
the God of *I* will be your	Is 52:12	3478
and thy Redeemer the Holy One of *I*	Is 54:5	3478
thy God, and for the Holy One of *I*	Is 55:5	3478
gathereth the outcasts of *I* saith	Is 56:8	3478
thy God, and to the Holy One of *I*	Is 60:9	3478
The Zion of the Holy One of *I*	Is 60:14	3478
goodness toward the house of *I*	Is 63:7	3478
of us, and *I* acknowledge us not	Is 63:16	3478
as the children of *I* bring an	Is 66:20	3478
I was holiness unto the LORD, and	Jer 2:3	3478
the families of the house of *I*	Jer 2:4	3478
Is *I* a servant?	Jer 2:14	3478
with me, O house of *I*, saith the	Jer 3:20	3478
of the children of *I*	Jer 3:21	3478
our God is the salvation of *I*	Jer 3:23	3478
If thou wilt return, O *I*, saith	Jer 4:1	3478
upon you from far, O house of *I*	Jer 5:15	3478
glean the remnant of *I* as a vine	Jer 6:9	3478
the LORD of hosts, the God of *I*	Jer 7:3	3478
for the wickedness of my people *I*	Jer 7:12	3478
the LORD of hosts, the God of *I*	Jer 7:21	3478
the LORD of hosts, the God of *I*	Jer 9:15	3478
speaketh unto you, O house of *I*	Jer 10:1	3478
I is the rod of his inheritance	Jer 10:16	3478
Thus saith the LORD God of *I*	Jer 11:3	3478
caused my people *I* to inherit	Jer 12:14	3478
unto me the whole house of *I*	Jer 13:11	3478
Thus saith the LORD God of *I*	Jer 13:12	3478
O the hope of *I*, the saviour	Jer 14:8	3478
the LORD of hosts, the God of *I*	Jer 16:9	3478
of *I* out of the land of Egypt	Jer 16:14	3478
of *I* from the land of the north	Jer 16:15	3478
O LORD, the hope of *I*, all that	Jer 17:13	3478
O house of *I*, cannot I do with	Jer 18:6	3478
are ye in mine hand, O house of *I*	Jer 18:6	3478
the virgin of *I* hath done a very	Jer 18:13	3478
the LORD of hosts, the God of *I*	Jer 19:3	3478
the LORD of hosts, the God of *I*	Jer 19:15	3478
Thus saith the LORD God of *I*	Jer 21:4	3478
thus saith the LORD God of *I*	Jer 23:2	3478
of *I* out of the land of Egypt	Jer 23:7	3478
of *I* out of the north country	Jer 23:8	3478
and caused my people *I* to err	Jer 23:13	3478
Thus saith the LORD, the God of *I*	Jer 24:5	3478
saith the LORD God of *I* unto me	Jer 25:15	3478
the LORD of hosts, the God of *I*	Jer 25:27	3478
the LORD of hosts, the God of *I*	Jer 27:4	3478
the LORD of hosts, the God of *I*	Jer 27:21	3478
the LORD of hosts, the God of *I*	Jer 28:2	3478
the LORD of hosts, the God of *I*	Jer 28:14	3478
the LORD of hosts, the God of *I*	Jer 29:4	3478
the LORD of hosts, the God of *I*	Jer 29:8	3478
the LORD of hosts, the God of *I*	Jer 29:21	3478
they have committed villany in *I*	Jer 29:23	3478
the LORD of hosts, the God of *I*	Jer 29:25	3478
Thus speaketh the LORD God of *I*	Jer 30:2	3478
the captivity of my people *I*	Jer 30:3	3478
that the LORD spake concerning *I*	Jer 30:4	3478
neither be dismayed, O *I*	Jer 30:10	3478
the God of all the families of *I*	Jer 31:1	3478
even *I*, when I went to cause him	Jer 31:2	3478
shalt be built, O virgin of *I*	Jer 31:4	3478
save thy people, the remnant of *I*	Jer 31:7	3478
for I am a father to *I*, and	Jer 31:9	3478
that scattered *I* will gather him	Jer 31:10	3478
turn again, O virgin of *I*	Jer 31:21	3478
the LORD of hosts, the God of *I*	Jer 31:23	3478
I will make with the house of *I*	Jer 31:33	3478
then the seed of *I* also shall	Jer 31:36	3478
of *I* for all that they have done	Jer 31:37	3478
the LORD of hosts, the God of *I*	Jer 32:14	3478
the LORD of hosts, the God of *I*	Jer 32:15	3478
even unto this day, and in *I*	Jer 32:20	3478
I out of the land of Egypt with	Jer 32:21	3478
for the children of *I* have only	Jer 32:30	3478
thus saith the LORD, the God of *I*	Jer 32:36	3478
thus saith the LORD, the God of *I*	Jer 33:4	3478
and the captivity of *I* to return	Jer 33:7	3478
have promised unto the house of *I*	Jer 33:14	3478
upon the throne of the house of *I*	Jer 33:17	3478
Thus saith the LORD, the God of *I*	Jer 34:2	3478
Thus saith the LORD, the God of *I*	Jer 34:13	3478
the LORD of hosts, the God of *I*	Jer 35:13	3478
LORD God of hosts, the God of *I*	Jer 35:17	3478
the LORD of hosts, the God of *I*	Jer 35:18	3478
the LORD of hosts, the God of *I*	Jer 35:19	3478
I have spoken unto thee against *I*	Jer 36:2	3478
Thus saith the LORD, the God of *I*	Jer 37:7	3478
the God of hosts, the God of *I*	Jer 38:17	3478
the LORD of hosts, the God of *I*	Jer 39:16	3478
Thus saith the LORD, the God of *I*	Jer 42:9	3478
the LORD of hosts, the God of *I*	Jer 42:15	3478
the LORD of hosts, the God of *I*	Jer 42:18	3478
the LORD of hosts, the God of *I*	Jer 43:10	3478
the LORD of hosts, the God of *I*	Jer 44:2	3478
the God of hosts, the God of *I*	Jer 44:7	3478
the LORD of hosts, the God of *I*	Jer 44:11	3478
the LORD of hosts, the God of *I*	Jer 44:25	3478
Thus saith the LORD, the God of *I*	Jer 45:2	3478
The LORD of hosts, the God of *I*	Jer 46:25	3478
Jacob, and be not dismayed, O *I*	Jer 46:27	3478
the LORD of hosts, the God of *I*	Jer 48:1	3478
For was not *I* a derision unto	Jer 48:27	3478
Hath *I* no sons?	Jer 49:1	3478
then shall *I* be heir unto them	Jer 49:2	3478
the children of *I* shall come	Jer 50:4	3478
I is a scattered sheep	Jer 50:17	3478
the LORD of hosts, the God of *I*	Jer 50:18	3478
I will bring *I* again to his	Jer 50:19	3478
the iniquity of *I* shall be sought	Jer 50:20	3478
LORD, against the Holy One of *I*	Jer 50:29	3478
For *I* hath not been forsaken, nor	Jer 51:5	3478
sin against the Holy One of *I*	Jer 51:5	3478
I is the rod of his inheritance	Jer 51:19	3478
the LORD of hosts, the God of *I*	Jer 51:33	3478
caused the slain of *I* to fall	Jer 51:49	3478
unto the earth the beauty of *I*	Lam 2:1	3478
fierce anger all the horn of *I*	Lam 2:3	3478
he hath swallowed up *I*, he hath	Lam 2:5	3478
I send thee to the children of *I*	Eze 2:3	3478
and go speak unto the house of *I*	Eze 3:1	3478
go, get thee unto the house of *I*	Eze 3:4	3478
language, but to the house of *I*	Eze 3:5	3478
But the house of *I* will not	Eze 3:7	3478
all the house of *I* are impudent	Eze 3:7	3478
a watchman unto the house of *I*	Eze 3:17	3478
shall be a sign to the house of *I*	Eze 4:3	3478
I eat their defiled bread among	Eze 4:13	3478
forth into all the house of *I*	Eze 5:4	3478
face toward the mountains of *I*	Eze 6:2	3478
And say, Ye mountains of *I*	Eze 6:3	3478
children of *I* before their idols	Eze 6:5	3478
abominations of the house of *I*	Eze 6:11	3478
the Lord GOD unto the land of *I*	Eze 7:2	3478

glory of the God of *I* was there	Eze 8:4	3478
the house of *I* committeth here	Eze 8:6	3478
all the idols of the house of *I*	Eze 8:10	3478
of the ancients of the house of *I*	Eze 8:11	3478
of the house of *I* do in the dark	Eze 8:12	3478
the glory of the God of *I* was	Eze 9:3	3478
I in thy pouring out of thy fury	Eze 9:8	3478
the God of *I* was over them above	Eze 10:19	3478
God of *I* by the river of Chebar	Eze 10:20	3478
Thus have ye said, O house of *I*	Eze 11:5	3478
will judge you in the border of *I*	Eze 11:10	3478
will judge you in the border of *I*	Eze 11:11	3478
a full end of the remnant of *I*	Eze 11:13	3478
and all the house of *I* wholly	Eze 11:15	3478
and I will give you the land of *I*	Eze 11:17	3478
the God of *I* was over them above	Eze 11:22	3478
for a sign unto the house of *I*	Eze 12:6	3478
of man, hath not the house of *I*	Eze 12:9	3478
all the house of *I* that are among	Eze 12:10	3478
of Jerusalem, and of the land of *I*	Eze 12:19	3478
that ye have in the land of *I*	Eze 12:22	3478
no more use it as a proverb in *I*	Eze 12:23	3478
divination within the house of *I*	Eze 12:24	3478
they of the house of *I* say	Eze 12:27	3478
the prophets of *I* that prophesy	Eze 13:2	3478
O *I*, thy prophets are like the	Eze 13:4	3478
I to stand in the battle in the	Eze 13:5	3478
in the writing of the house of *I*	Eze 13:9	3478
they enter into the land of *I*	Eze 13:9	3478
the prophets of *I* which prophesy	Eze 13:16	3478
of the elders of *I* unto me	Eze 14:1	3478
Every man of the house of *I* that	Eze 14:4	3478
the house of *I* in their own heart	Eze 14:5	3478
Therefore say unto the house of *I*	Eze 14:6	3478
For every one of the house of *I*	Eze 14:7	3478
the stranger that sojourneth in *I*	Eze 14:7	3478
him from the midst of my people *I*	Eze 14:9	3478
That the house of *I* may go no	Eze 14:11	3478
a parable unto the house of *I*	Eze 17:2	3478
the height of *I* will I plant it	Eze 17:23	3478
proverb concerning the land of *I*	Eze 18:2	3478
any more to use this proverb in *I*	Eze 18:3	3478
to the idols of the house of *I*	Eze 18:6	3478
to the idols of the house of *I*	Eze 18:15	3478
Hear now, O house of *I*	Eze 18:25	3478
Yet saith the house of *I*, The way	Eze 18:29	3478
O house of *I*, are not my ways	Eze 18:29	3478
I will judge you, O house of *I*	Eze 18:30	3478
for why will ye die, O house of *I*	Eze 18:31	3478
lamentation for the princes of *I*	Eze 19:1	3478
be heard upon the mountains of *I*	Eze 19:9	3478
of *I* came to enquire of the LORD	Eze 20:1	3478
man, speak unto the elders of *I*	Eze 20:3	3478
In the day when I chose *I*	Eze 20:5	3478
But the house of *I* rebelled	Eze 20:13	3478
of man, speak unto the house of *I*	Eze 20:27	3478
Wherefore say unto the house of *I*	Eze 20:30	3478
enquired of by you, O house of *I*	Eze 20:31	3478
not enter into the land of *I*	Eze 20:38	3478
As for you, O house of *I*, thus	Eze 20:39	3478
the mountain of the height of *I*	Eze 20:40	3478
there shall all the house of *I*	Eze 20:40	3478
bring you into the land of *I*	Eze 20:42	3478
corrupt doings, O ye house of *I*	Eze 20:44	3478
and prophesy against the land of *I*	Eze 21:2	3478
And say to the land of *I*, Thus	Eze 21:3	3478
be upon all the princes of *I*	Eze 21:12	3478
thou, profane wicked prince of *I*	Eze 21:25	3478
Behold, the princes of *I*, every	Eze 22:6	3478
the house of *I* is to me become	Eze 22:18	3478
Speak unto the house of *I*	Eze 24:21	3478
and against the land of *I*, when it	Eze 25:3	3478
thy despite against the land of *I*	Eze 25:6	3478
Edom by the hand of my people *I*	Eze 25:14	3478
brier unto the house of *I*	Eze 28:24	3478
have gathered the house of *I* from	Eze 28:25	3478
a staff of reed to the house of *I*	Eze 29:6	3478
the confidence of the house of *I*	Eze 29:16	3478
of the house of *I* to bud forth	Eze 29:21	3478
a watchman unto the house of *I*	Eze 33:7	3478
of man, speak unto the house of *I*	Eze 33:10	3478
for why will ye die, O house of *I*	Eze 33:11	3478
O ye house of *I*, I will judge you	Eze 33:20	3478
wastes of the land of *I* speak	Eze 33:24	3478
the mountains of *I* shall be	Eze 33:28	3478
against the shepherds of *I*	Eze 34:2	3478
of *I* that do feed themselves	Eze 34:2	3478
the mountains of *I* by the rivers	Eze 34:13	3478
of *I* shall their fold be	Eze 34:14	3478
they feed upon the mountains of *I*	Eze 34:14	3478
and that they, even the house of *I*	Eze 34:30	3478
of *I* by the force of the sword in	Eze 35:5	3478
spoken against the mountains of *I*	Eze 35:12	3478
the inheritance of the house of *I*	Eze 35:15	3478
prophesy unto the mountains of *I*	Eze 36:1	3478
and say, Ye mountains of *I*	Eze 36:1	3478
Therefore, ye mountains of *I*	Eze 36:4	3478
concerning the land of *I*, and say	Eze 36:6	3478
But ye, O mountains of *I*, ye	Eze 36:8	3478
your fruit to my people of *I*	Eze 36:8	3478
men upon you, all the house of *I*	Eze 36:10	3478
walk upon you, even my people *I*	Eze 36:12	3478
when the house of *I* dwelt in	Eze 36:17	3478
which the house of *I* had profaned	Eze 36:21	3478
Therefore say unto the house of *I*	Eze 36:22	3478
this for your sakes, O house of *I*	Eze 36:22	3478
for your own ways, O house of *I*	Eze 36:32	3478
be enquired of by the house of *I*	Eze 36:37	3478
bones are the whole house of *I*	Eze 37:11	3478
and bring you into the land of *I*	Eze 37:12	3478
all the house of *I* his companions	Eze 37:16	3478
and the tribes of *I* his fellows	Eze 37:19	3478
of *I* from among the heathen	Eze 37:21	3478
the land upon the mountains of *I*	Eze 37:22	3478
that I the LORD do sanctify *I*	Eze 37:28	3478
against the mountains of *I*	Eze 38:8	3478
my people of *I* dwelleth safely	Eze 38:14	3478
come up against my people of *I*	Eze 38:16	3478
by my servants the prophets of *I*	Eze 38:17	3478
shall come against the land of *I*	Eze 38:18	3478
a great shaking in the land of *I*	Eze 38:19	3478
thee upon the mountains of *I*	Eze 39:2	3478
fall upon the mountains of *I*	Eze 39:4	3478
known in the midst of my people *I*	Eze 39:7	3478
I am the LORD, the Holy One in *I*	Eze 39:7	3478
in the cities of *I* shall go forth	Eze 39:9	3478
Gog a place there of graves in *I*	Eze 39:11	3478
the house of *I* be burying of them	Eze 39:12	3478
sacrifice upon the mountains of *I*	Eze 39:17	3478
So the house of *I* shall know that	Eze 39:22	3478
shall know that the house of *I*	Eze 39:23	3478
mercy upon the whole house of *I*	Eze 39:25	3478
out my spirit upon the house of *I*	Eze 39:29	3478
brought he me into the land of *I*	Eze 40:2	3478
that thou seest to the house of *I*	Eze 40:4	3478
the glory of the God of *I* came	Eze 43:2	3478
of the children of *I* for ever	Eze 43:7	3478
the house of *I* no more defile	Eze 43:7	3478
shew the house to the house of *I*	Eze 43:10	3478
because the LORD, the God of *I*	Eze 44:2	3478
even to the house of *I*, Thus	Eze 44:6	3478
O ye house of *I*, let it suffice	Eze 44:6	3478
that is among the children of *I*	Eze 44:9	3478
when *I* went astray, which went	Eze 44:10	3478
caused the house of *I* to fall	Eze 44:12	3478
of the seed of the house of *I*	Eze 44:22	3478
give them no possession in *I*	Eze 44:28	3478
thing in *I* shall be their's	Eze 44:29	3478
shall be for the whole house of *I*	Eze 45:6	3478
land shall be his possession in *I*	Eze 45:8	3478
of *I* according to their tribes	Eze 45:8	3478
it suffice you, O princes of *I*	Eze 45:9	3478
out of the fat pastures of *I*	Eze 45:15	3478
this oblation for the prince in *I*	Eze 45:16	3478
all solemnities of the house of *I*	Eze 45:17	3478
reconciliation for the house of *I*	Eze 45:17	3478
to the twelve tribes of *I*	Eze 47:13	3478
and from the land of *I* by Jordan	Eze 47:18	3478
you according to the tribes of *I*	Eze 47:21	3478
country among the children of *I*	Eze 47:22	3478
with you among the tribes of *I*	Eze 47:22	3478
the children of *I* went astray	Eze 48:11	3478
it out of all the tribes of *I*	Eze 48:19	3478
the tribes of *I* for inheritance	Eze 48:29	3478
the names of the tribes of *I*	Eze 48:31	3478
certain of the children of *I*	Dan 1:3	3478
of Jerusalem, and unto all *I*	Dan 9:7	3478
all *I* have transgressed thy law,	Dan 9:11	3478
my sin and the sin of my people *I*	Dan 9:20	3478
the son of Joash, king of *I*	Hos 1:1	3478
the kingdom of the house of *I*	Hos 1:4	3478
bow of *I* in the valley of Jezreel	Hos 1:5	3478
have mercy upon the house of *I*	Hos 1:6	3478
the number of the children of *I*	Hos 1:10	3478
the children of *I* be gathered	Hos 1:11	3478
the LORD toward the children of *I*	Hos 3:1	3478
For the children of *I* shall abide	Hos 3:4	3478
shall the children of *I* return	Hos 3:5	3478
of the LORD, ye children of *I*	Hos 4:1	3478
Though thou, *I*, play the harlot,	Hos 4:15	3478
For *I* slideth back as a	Hos 4:16	3478
and hearken, ye house of *I*	Hos 5:1	3478
Ephraim, and *I* is not hid from me	Hos 5:3	3478
whoredom, and *I* is defiled	Hos 5:3	3478
the pride of *I* doth testify to	Hos 5:5	3478
therefore shall *I* and Ephraim fall	Hos 5:5	3478
among the tribes of *I* have I made	Hos 5:9	3478
horrible thing in the house of *I*	Hos 6:10	3478
whoredom of Ephraim, *I* is defiled	Hos 6:10	3478
When I would have healed *I*	Hos 7:1	3478
the pride of *I* testifieth to his	Hos 7:10	3478
I shall cry unto me, My God, we	Hos 8:2	3478
I hath cast off the thing that is	Hos 8:3	3478
For from *I* was it also	Hos 8:6	3478
I is swallowed up	Hos 8:8	3478
For *I* hath forgotten his Maker,	Hos 8:14	3478
Rejoice not, O *I*, for joy, as	Hos 9:1	3478
I shall know it	Hos 9:7	3478
I found *I* like grapes in the	Hos 9:10	3478
I is an empty vine, he bringeth	Hos 10:1	3478
I shall be ashamed of his own	Hos 10:6	3478
places also of Aven, the sin of *I*	Hos 10:8	3478
O *I*, thou hast sinned from the	Hos 10:9	3478
the king of *I* utterly be cut off	Hos 10:15	3478
When *I* was a child, then I loved	Hos 11:1	3478
how shall I deliver thee, *I*	Hos 11:8	3478
and the house of *I* with deceit	Hos 11:12	3478
I served for a wife, and for a	Hos 12:12	3478
the LORD brought *I* out of Egypt	Hos 12:13	3478
he exalted himself in *I*	Hos 13:1	3478
O *I*, thou hast destroyed thyself	Hos 13:9	3478
O *I*, return unto the LORD thy God	Hos 14:1	3478
I will be as the dew unto *I*	Hos 14:5	3478
know that I am in the midst of *I*	Joel 2:27	3478
my people and for my heritage *I*	Joel 3:2	3478
the strength of the children of *I*	Joel 3:16	3478
which he saw concerning *I* in the	Amos 1:1	3478
the son of Joash king of *I*	Amos 1:1	3478
For three transgressions of *I*	Amos 2:6	3478
not even thus, O ye children of *I*	Amos 2:11	3478
against you, O children of *I*	Amos 3:1	3478
so shall the children of *I* be	Amos 3:12	3478
visit the transgressions of *I*	Amos 3:14	3478
liketh you, O ye children of *I*	Amos 4:5	3478
thus will I do unto thee, O *I*	Amos 4:12	3478
prepare to meet thy God, O *I*	Amos 4:12	3478
even a lamentation, O house of *I*	Amos 5:1	3478
The virgin of *I* is fallen	Amos 5:2	3478
leave ten, to the house of *I*	Amos 5:3	3478
the LORD unto the house of *I*	Amos 5:4	3478
forty years, O house of *I*	Amos 5:25	3478
to whom the house of *I* came	Amos 6:1	3478
you a nation, O house of *I*	Amos 6:14	3478
in the midst of my people *I*	Amos 7:8	3478
the sanctuaries of *I* shall be	Amos 7:9	3478
sent to Jeroboam king of *I*	Amos 7:10	3478
in the midst of the house of *I*	Amos 7:10	3478
I shall surely be led away	Amos 7:11	3478
me, Go, prophesy unto my people *I*	Amos 7:15	3478
sayest, Prophesy not against *I*	Amos 7:16	3478
I shall surely go into captivity	Amos 7:17	3478
end is come upon my people of *I*	Amos 8:2	3478
unto me, O children of *I*	Amos 9:7	3478
Have not I brought up *I* out of	Amos 9:7	3478
the house of *I* among all nations	Amos 9:9	3478
the captivity of my people of *I*	Amos 9:14	3478
of *I* shall possess that of the	Obad 20	3478
and for the sins of the house of *I*	Mic 1:5	3478
of *I* were found in thee	Mic 1:13	3478
shall be a lie to the kings of *I*	Mic 1:14	3478
come unto Adullam the glory of *I*	Mic 1:15	3478
surely gather the remnant of *I*	Mic 2:12	3478
and ye princes of the house of *I*	Mic 3:1	3478
transgression, and to *I* his sin	Mic 3:8	3478
and princes of the house of *I*	Mic 3:9	3478
of *I* with a rod upon the cheek	Mic 5:1	3478
unto me that is to be ruler in *I*	Mic 5:2	3478
return unto the children of *I*	Mic 5:3	3478
people, and he will plead with *I*	Mic 6:2	3478
of Jacob, as the excellency of *I*	Nah 2:2	3478
the LORD of hosts, the God of *I*	Zeph 2:9	3478
The remnant of *I* shall not do	Zeph 3:13	3478
shout, O *I*	Zeph 3:14	3478
the king of *I*, even the LORD, is	Zeph 3:15	3478
of man, as of all the tribes of *I*	Zec 9:1	3478
of the word of the LORD for *I*	Zec 12:1	3478
word of the LORD to *I* by Malachi	Mal 1:1	3478
be magnified from the border of *I*	Mal 1:5	3478
For the LORD, the God of *I*	Mal 2:16	3478
unto him in Horeb for all *I*	Mal 4:4	3478
that shall rule my people *I*	Mt 2:6	2474
mother, and go into the land of *I*	Mt 2:20	2474
and came into the land of *I*	Mt 2:21	2474
so great faith, no, not in *I*	Mt 8:10	2474
saying, It was never so seen in *I*	Mt 9:33	2474
the lost sheep of the house of *I*	Mt 10:6	2474
have gone over the cities of *I*	Mt 10:23	2474
the lost sheep of the house of *I*	Mt 15:24	2474
and they glorified the God of *I*	Mt 15:31	2474
judging the twelve tribes of *I*	Mt 19:28	2474
of the children of *I* did value	Mt 27:9	2474
If he be the King of *I*, let him	Mt 27:42	2474
the commandments is, Hear, O *I*	Mk 12:29	2474
Let Christ the King of *I* descend	Mk 15:32	2474
many of the children of *I* shall	Lk 1:16	2474
He hath holpen his servant *I*	Lk 1:54	2474
Blessed be the Lord God of *I*	Lk 1:68	2474
the day of his shewing unto *I*	Lk 1:80	2474
waiting for the consolation of *I*	Lk 2:25	2474
and the glory of thy people *I*	Lk 2:32	2474
fall and rising again of many in *I*	Lk 2:34	2474
many widows were in *I* in the days	Lk 4:25	2474
many lepers were in *I* in the time	Lk 4:27	2474
so great faith, no, not in *I*	Lk 7:9	2474
judging the twelve tribes of *I*	Lk 22:30	2474
he which should have redeemed *I*	Lk 24:21	2474
he should be made manifest to *I*	Jn 1:31	2474
thou art the King of *I*	Jn 1:49	2474
unto him, Art thou a master of *I*	Jn 3:10	2474
Blessed is the King of *I* that	Jn 12:13	2474
restore again the kingdom to *I*	Acts 1:6	2474
Ye men of *I*, hear these words	Acts 2:22	2475
all the house of *I* know assuredly	Acts 2:36	2474
unto the people, Ye men of *I*	Acts 3:12	2475
of the people, and elders of *I*	Acts 4:8	2474
all, and to all the people of *I*	Acts 4:10	2474
the Gentiles, and the people of *I*	Acts 4:27	2474
the senate of the children of *I*	Acts 5:21	2474
for to give repentance to *I*	Acts 5:31	2474
And said unto them, Ye men of *I*	Acts 5:35	2475
his brethren the children of *I*	Acts 7:23	2474
which said unto the children of *I*	Acts 7:37	2474
of the prophets, O ye house of *I*	Acts 7:42	2474
and kings, and the children of *I*	Acts 9:15	2474
God sent unto the children of *I*	Acts 10:36	2474
with his hand said, Men of *I*	Acts 13:16	2475
people of *I* chose our fathers	Acts 13:17	2474
promise raised unto *I* a Saviour	Acts 13:23	2474
repentance to all the people of *I*	Acts 13:24	2474
Crying out, Men of *I*, help	Acts 21:28	2475
of *I* I am bound with this chain	Acts 28:20	2474
For they are not all *I*, which are	Rom 9:6	2474
not all Israel, which are of *I*	Rom 9:6	2474
Esaias also crieth concerning *I*	Rom 9:27	2474
of *I* be as the sand of the sea	Rom 9:27	2474
But *I*, which followed after the	Rom 9:31	2474
desire and prayer to God for *I* is	Rom 10:1	2474
But I say, Did not *I* know	Rom 10:19	2474
But to *I* he saith, All day long I	Rom 10:21	2474
intercession to God against *I*	Rom 11:2	2474
I hath not obtained that which he	Rom 11:7	2474
in part is happened to *I*, until	Rom 11:25	2474
And so all *I* shall be saved	Rom 11:26	2474
Behold *I* after the flesh	1Cor 10:18	2474
so that the children of *I* could	2Cor 3:7	2474
that the children of *I* could not	2Cor 3:13	2474
and mercy, and upon the *I* of God	Gal 6:16	2474
aliens from the commonwealth of *I*	Eph 2:12	2474
the eighth day, of the stock of *I*	Phil 3:5	2474
new covenant with the house of *I*	Heb 8:8	2474
the house of *I* after those days	Heb 8:10	2474
departing of the children of *I*	Heb 11:22	2474

before the children of *I*, to eat Rev 2:14 2474
the tribes of the children of *I* Rev 7:4 2474
tribes of the children of *I* Rev 21:12 2474

3. The ten northern tribes.

I were many, as the sand which is 1Kin 4:20 3478
I dwelt safely, every man under 1Kin 4:25 3478
all *I* stoned him with stones, 1Kin 12:18 3478
So *I* rebelled against the house 1Kin 12:19 3478
when all *I* heard that Jeroboam 1Kin 12:20 3478
and made him king over all *I* 1Kin 12:20 3478
to fight against the house of *I* 1Kin 12:21 3478
your brethren the children of *I* 1Kin 12:24 3478
behold thy gods, O *I*, which 1Kin 12:28 3478
a feast unto the children of *I* 1Kin 12:33 3478
him that is shut up and left in *I* 1Kin 14:10 3478
all *I* shall mourn for him, and 1Kin 14:13 3478
God of *I* in the house of Jeroboam 1Kin 14:13 3478
shall raise him up a king over *I* 1Kin 14:14 3478
For the LORD shall smite *I* 1Kin 14:15 3478
he shall root up *I* out of this 1Kin 14:15 3478
he shall give *I* up because of the 1Kin 14:16 3478
who did sin, and who made *I* to sin 1Kin 14:16 3478
all *I* mourned for him, according 1Kin 14:18 3478
the chronicles of the kings of *I* 1Kin 14:19 3478
king of *I* reigned Asa over Judah 1Kin 15:9 3478
Baasha king of *I* all their days 1Kin 15:16 3478
Baasha king of *I* went up against 1Kin 15:17 3478
thy league with Baasha king of *I* 1Kin 15:19 3478
he had against the cities of *I* 1Kin 15:20 3478
I in the second year of Asa king 1Kin 15:25 3478
and reigned over *I* two years 1Kin 15:25 3478
sin wherewith he made *I* to sin 1Kin 15:26 3478
all *I* laid siege to Gibbethon 1Kin 15:27 3478
he sinned, and which he made *I* sin 1Kin 15:30 3478
the LORD God of *I* to anger 1Kin 15:30 3478
the chronicles of the kings of *I* 1Kin 15:31 3478
Baasha king of *I* all their days 1Kin 15:32 3478
to reign over all *I* in Tirzah 1Kin 15:33 3478
made thee prince over my people *I* 1Kin 16:2 3478
and hast made my people *I* to sin 1Kin 16:2 3478
the chronicles of the kings of *I* 1Kin 16:5 3478
Baasha to reign over *I* in Tirzah 1Kin 16:8 3478
and by which they made *I* to sin 1Kin 16:13 3478
of *I* to anger with their vanities 1Kin 16:13 3478
the chronicles of the kings of *I* 1Kin 16:14 3478
wherefore all *I* made Omri 1Kin 16:16 3478
king over *I* that day in the camp 1Kin 16:16 3478
all *I* with him, and they besieged 1Kin 16:17 3478
which he did, to make *I* to sin 1Kin 16:19 3478
the chronicles of the kings of *I* 1Kin 16:20 3478
of *I* divided into two parts 1Kin 16:21 3478
Judah began Omri to reign over *I* 1Kin 16:23 3478
sin wherewith he made *I* to sin 1Kin 16:26 3478
to provoke the LORD God of *I* to 1Kin 16:26 3478
the chronicles of the kings of *I* 1Kin 16:27 3478
the son of Omri to reign over *I* 1Kin 16:29 3478
reigned over *I* in Samaria twenty 1Kin 16:29 3478
kings of *I* that were before him 1Kin 16:33 3478
him, Art thou he that troubleth *I* 1Kin 18:17 3478
answered, I have not troubled *I* 1Kin 18:18 3478
gather to me all *I* unto mount 1Kin 18:19 3478
sent unto all the children of *I* 1Kin 18:20 3478
for the children of *I* have 1Kin 19:10 3478
because the children of *I* have 1Kin 19:14 3478
thou anoint to be king over *I* 1Kin 19:16 3478
have left me seven thousand in *I* 1Kin 19:18 3478
to Ahab king of *I* into the city 1Kin 20:2 3478
And the king of *I* answered 1Kin 20:4 3478
Then the king of *I* called all the 1Kin 20:7 3478
And the king of *I* answered 1Kin 20:11 3478
a prophet unto Ahab king of *I* 1Kin 20:13 3478
even all the children of *I* 1Kin 20:15 3478
and *I* pursued them 1Kin 20:20 3478
And the king of *I* went out 1Kin 20:21 3478
the prophet came to the king of *I* 1Kin 20:22 3478
up to Aphek, to fight against *I* 1Kin 20:26 3478
the children of *I* were numbered 1Kin 20:27 3478
the children of *I* pitched before 1Kin 20:27 3478
God, and spake unto the king of *I* 1Kin 20:28 3478
the children of *I* slew of the 1Kin 20:29 3478
the house of *I* are merciful kings 1Kin 20:31 3478
heads, and go out to the king of *I* 1Kin 20:31 3478
heads, and came to the king of *I* 1Kin 20:32 3478
the king of *I* said unto him, So 1Kin 20:40 3478
the king of *I* discerned him that 1Kin 20:41 3478
the king of *I* went to his house 1Kin 20:43 3478
thou now govern the kingdom of *I* 1Kin 21:7 3478
go down to meet Ahab king of *I* 1Kin 21:18 3478
him that is shut up and left in *I* 1Kin 21:21 3478
me to anger, and made *I* to sin 1Kin 21:22 3478
cast out before the children of *I* 1Kin 21:26 3478
without war between Syria and *I* 1Kin 22:1 3478
Judah came down to the king of *I* 1Kin 22:2 3478
the king of *I* said unto his 1Kin 22:3 3478
Jehoshaphat said to the king of *I* 1Kin 22:4 3478
said unto the king of *I*, Enquire, 1Kin 22:5 3478
Then the king of *I* gathered the 1Kin 22:6 3478
And the king of *I* said unto 1Kin 22:8 3478
Then the king of *I* called an 1Kin 22:9 3478
And the king of *I* and Jehoshaphat 1Kin 22:10 3478
I saw all *I* scattered upon the 1Kin 22:17 3478
And the king of *I* said unto 1Kin 22:18 3478
And the king of *I* said, Take 1Kin 22:26 3478
So the king of *I* and Jehoshaphat 1Kin 22:29 3478
And the king of *I* said unto 1Kin 22:30 3478
the king of *I* disguised himself, 1Kin 22:30 3478
save only with the king of *I* 1Kin 22:31 3478
said, Surely it is the king of *I* 1Kin 22:32 3478
that it was not the king of *I* 1Kin 22:33 3478
smote the king of *I* between the 1Kin 22:34 3478
the chronicles of the kings of *I* 1Kin 22:39 3478
the fourth year of Ahab king of *I* 1Kin 22:41 3478
made peace with the king of *I* 1Kin 22:44 3478
I in Samaria the seventeenth year 1Kin 22:51 3478
and reigned two years over *I* 1Kin 22:51 3478
son of Nebat, who made *I* to sin 1Kin 22:52 3478
against *I* after the death of Ahab 2Kin 1:1 3478
because there is not a God in *I* 2Kin 1:3 3478
because there is not a God in *I* 2Kin 1:6 3478
God in *I* to enquire of his word 2Kin 1:16 3478
the chronicles of the kings of *I* 2Kin 1:18 3478
I in Samaria the eighteenth year 2Kin 3:1 3478
son of Nebat, which made *I* to sin 2Kin 3:3 3478
of *I* an hundred thousand lambs 2Kin 3:4 3478
rebelled against the king of *I* 2Kin 3:5 3478
the same time, and numbered all *I* 2Kin 3:6 3478
So the king of *I* went, and the 2Kin 3:9 3478
And the king of *I* said, Alas 2Kin 3:10 3478
So the king of *I* and Jehoshaphat 2Kin 3:12 3478
And Elisha said unto the king of *I* 2Kin 3:13 3478
the king of *I* said unto him, Nay 2Kin 3:13 3478
when they came to the camp of *I* 2Kin 3:24 3478
was great indignation against *I* 2Kin 3:27 3478
of the land of *I* a little maid 2Kin 5:2 3478
the maid that is of the land of *I* 2Kin 5:4 3478
send a letter unto the king of *I* 2Kin 5:5 3478
the letter to the king of *I* 2Kin 5:6 3478
when the king of *I* had read the 2Kin 5:7 3478
king of *I* had rent his clothes 2Kin 5:8 3478
know that there is a prophet in *I* 2Kin 5:8 3478
better than all the waters of *I* 2Kin 5:12 3478
no God in all the earth, but in *I* 2Kin 5:15 3478
king of Syria warred against *I* 2Kin 6:8 3478
of God sent unto the king of *I* 2Kin 6:9 3478
the king of *I* sent to the place 2Kin 6:10 3478
which of us is for the king of *I* 2Kin 6:11 3478
Elisha, the prophet that is in *I* 2Kin 6:12 3478
telleth the king of *I* the words 2Kin 6:12 3478
the king of *I* said unto Elisha, 2Kin 6:21 3478
came no more into the land of *I* 2Kin 6:23 3478
as the king of *I* was passing by 2Kin 6:26 3478
the king of *I* hath hired against 2Kin 7:6 3478
of *I* that are left in it 2Kin 7:13 3478
wilt do unto the children of *I* 2Kin 8:12 3478
Joram the son of Ahab king of *I* 2Kin 8:16 3478
in the way of the kings of *I* 2Kin 8:18 3478
Joram the son of Ahab king of *I* 2Kin 8:25 3478
the daughter of Omri king of *I* 2Kin 8:26 3478
I have anointed thee king over *I* 2Kin 9:3 3478
people of the LORD, even over *I* 2Kin 9:6 3478
him that is shut up and left in *I* 2Kin 9:8 3478
I have anointed thee king over *I* 2Kin 9:12 3478
kept Ramoth-gilead, he and all *I* 2Kin 9:14 3478
And Joram king of *I* and Ahaziah 2Kin 9:21 3478
And Jehu sent through all *I* 2Kin 10:21 3478
Thus Jehu destroyed Baal out of *I* 2Kin 10:28 3478
son of Nebat, who made *I* to sin 2Kin 10:29 3478
shall sit on the throne of *I* 2Kin 10:30 3478
of Jeroboam, which made *I* to sin 2Kin 10:31 3478
the LORD began to cut *I* short 2Kin 10:32 3478
smote them in all the coasts of *I* 2Kin 10:32 3478
the chronicles of the kings of *I* 2Kin 10:34 3478
over *I* in Samaria was twenty 2Kin 10:36 3478
began to reign over *I* in Samaria 2Kin 13:1 3478
son of Nebat, which made *I* to sin 2Kin 13:2 3478
of the LORD was kindled against *I* 2Kin 13:3 3478
for he saw the oppression of *I* 2Kin 13:4 3478
(And the LORD gave *I* a saviour 2Kin 13:5 3478
the children of *I* dwelt in their 2Kin 13:5 3478
house of Jeroboam, who made *I* sin 2Kin 13:6 3478
the chronicles of the kings of *I* 2Kin 13:8 3478
to reign over *I* in Samaria 2Kin 13:10 3478
the son of Nebat, who made *I* sin 2Kin 13:11 3478
the chronicles of the kings of *I* 2Kin 13:12 3478
in Samaria with the kings of *I* 2Kin 13:13 3478
Joash the king of *I* came down 2Kin 13:14 3478
my father, the chariot of *I* 2Kin 13:14 3478
And he said to the king of *I* 2Kin 13:16 3478
And he said unto the king of *I* 2Kin 13:18 3478
I all the days of Jehoahaz 2Kin 13:22 3478
him, and recovered the cities of *I* 2Kin 13:25 3478
of *I* reigned Amaziah the son of 2Kin 14:1 3478
Jehoahaz son of Jehu, king of *I* 2Kin 14:8 3478
Jehoash the king of *I* sent to 2Kin 14:9 3478
Jehoash king of *I* went up 2Kin 14:11 3478
was put to the worse before *I* 2Kin 14:12 3478
Jehoash king of *I* took Amaziah 2Kin 14:13 3478
the chronicles of the kings of *I* 2Kin 14:15 3478
in Samaria with the kings of *I* 2Kin 14:16 3478
Jehoahaz king of *I* fifteen years 2Kin 14:17 3478
the son of Joash king of *I* began 2Kin 14:23 3478
son of Nebat, who made *I* to sin 2Kin 14:24 3478
the LORD saw the affliction of *I* 2Kin 14:26 3478
any left, nor any helper for *I* 2Kin 14:26 3478
the name of *I* from under heaven 2Kin 14:27 3478
which belonged to Judah, for *I* 2Kin 14:28 3478
the chronicles of the kings of *I* 2Kin 14:28 3478
fathers, even with the kings of *I* 2Kin 14:29 3478
year of Jeroboam king of *I* began 2Kin 15:1 3478
over *I* in Samaria six months 2Kin 15:8 3478
son of Nebat, who made *I* to sin 2Kin 15:9 3478
the chronicles of the kings of *I* 2Kin 15:11 3478
of *I* unto the fourth generation 2Kin 15:12 3478
the chronicles of the kings of *I* 2Kin 15:15 3478
the son of Gadi to reign over *I* 2Kin 15:17 3478
son of Nebat, who made *I* to sin 2Kin 15:18 3478
And Menahem exacted the money of *I* 2Kin 15:20 3478
the chronicles of the kings of *I* 2Kin 15:21 3478
began to reign over *I* in Samaria 2Kin 15:23 3478
son of Nebat, who made *I* to sin 2Kin 15:24 3478
the chronicles of the kings of *I* 2Kin 15:26 3478
began to reign over *I* in Samaria 2Kin 15:27 3478
son of Nebat, who made *I* to sin 2Kin 15:28 3478
of *I* came Tiglath-pileser king of 2Kin 15:29 3478
the chronicles of the kings of *I* 2Kin 15:31 3478
the son of Remaliah king of *I* 2Kin 15:32 3478
in the way of the kings of *I* 2Kin 16:3 3478
out from before the children of *I* 2Kin 16:3 3478
of *I* came up to Jerusalem to war 2Kin 16:5 3478
out of the hand of the king of *I* 2Kin 16:7 3478
in Samaria over *I* nine years 2Kin 17:1 3478
kings of *I* that were before him 2Kin 17:2 3478
carried *I* away into Assyria, and 2Kin 17:6 3478
that the children of *I* had sinned 2Kin 17:7 3478
out from before the children of *I* 2Kin 17:8 3478
and of the kings of *I* 2Kin 17:8 3478
the children of *I* did secretly 2Kin 17:9 3478
Yet the LORD testified against *I* 2Kin 17:13 3478
the LORD was very angry with *I* 2Kin 17:18 3478
the statutes of *I* which they made 2Kin 17:19 3478
LORD rejected all the seed of *I* 2Kin 17:20 3478
For he rent *I* from the house of 2Kin 17:21 3478
Jeroboam drave *I* from following 2Kin 17:21 3478
For the children of *I* walked in 2Kin 17:22 3478
LORD removed *I* out of his sight 2Kin 17:23 3478
So was *I* carried away out of 2Kin 17:23 3478
instead of the children of *I* 2Kin 17:24 3478
of Hoshea son of Elah king of *I* 2Kin 18:1 3478
of Hoshea son of Elah king of *I* 2Kin 18:9 3478
ninth year of Hoshea king of *I* 2Kin 18:10 3478
did carry away *I* unto Assyria 2Kin 18:11 3478
son of Nebat, who made *I* to sin 2Kin 23:15 3478
which the kings of *I* had made to 2Kin 23:19 3478
in all the days of the kings of *I* 2Kin 23:22 3478
of my sight, as I have removed *I* 2Kin 23:27 3478
in the days of Jeroboam king of *I* 1Chr 5:17 3478
in the book of the kings of *I* 1Chr 9:1 3478
the children of *I* stoned him with 2Chr 10:18 3478
I rebelled against the house of 2Chr 10:19 3478
were warriors, to fight against *I* 2Chr 11:1 3478
all *I* resorted to him out of all 2Chr 11:13 3478
of *I* such as set their hearts to 2Chr 11:16 3478
Hear me, thou Jeroboam, and all *I* 2Chr 13:4 3478
O children of *I*, fight ye not 2Chr 13:12 3478
all *I* before Abijah and Judah 2Chr 13:15 3478
the children of *I* fled before 2Chr 13:16 3478
so there fell down slain of *I* 2Chr 13:17 3478
Thus the children of *I* were 2Chr 13:18 3478
fell to him out of *I* in abundance 2Chr 15:9 3478
were not taken away out of *I* 2Chr 15:17 3478
king of *I* came up against Judah 2Chr 16:1 3478
thy league with Baasha king of *I* 2Chr 16:3 3478
armies against the cities of *I* 2Chr 16:4 3478
book of the kings of Judah and *I* 2Chr 16:11 3478
and strengthened himself against *I* 2Chr 17:1 3478
and not after the doings of *I* 2Chr 17:4 3478
And Ahab king of *I* said unto 2Chr 18:3 3478
said unto the king of *I*, Enquire, 2Chr 18:4 3478
Therefore the king of *I* gathered 2Chr 18:5 3478
And the king of *I* said unto 2Chr 18:7 3478
the king of *I* called for one of 2Chr 18:8 3478
And the king of *I* and Jehoshaphat 2Chr 18:9 3478
I did see all *I* scattered upon 2Chr 18:16 3478
the king of *I* said to Jehoshaphat 2Chr 18:17 3478
Who shall entice Ahab king of *I* 2Chr 18:19 3478
Then the king of *I* said, Take ye 2Chr 18:25 3478
So the king of *I* and Jehoshaphat 2Chr 18:28 3478
And the king of *I* said unto 2Chr 18:29 3478
So the king of *I* disguised 2Chr 18:29 3478
save only with the king of *I* 2Chr 18:30 3478
they said, It is the king of *I* 2Chr 18:31 3478
that it was not the king of *I* 2Chr 18:32 3478
smote the king of *I* between the 2Chr 18:33 3478
howbeit the king of *I* stayed 2Chr 18:34 3478
in the book of the kings of *I* 2Chr 20:34 3478
himself with Ahaziah king of *I* 2Chr 20:35 3478
the sons of Jehoshaphat king of *I* 2Chr 21:2 3478
divers also of the princes of *I* 2Chr 21:4 3478
in the way of the kings of *I* 2Chr 21:6 3478
in the way of the kings of *I* 2Chr 21:13 3478
I to war against Hazael king of 2Chr 22:5 3478
of *I* for an hundred talents of 2Chr 25:6 3478
not the army of *I* go with thee 2Chr 25:7 3478
for the LORD is not with *I* 2Chr 25:7 3478
I have given to the army of *I* 2Chr 25:9 3478
the son of Jehu, king of *I* 2Chr 25:17 3478
Joash king of *I* sent to Amaziah 2Chr 25:18 3478
So Joash the king of *I* went up 2Chr 25:21 3478
was put to the worse before *I* 2Chr 25:22 3478
Joash the king of *I* took Amaziah 2Chr 25:23 3478
Jehoahaz king of *I* fifteen years 2Chr 25:25 3478
book of the kings of Judah and *I* 2Chr 25:26 3478
in the book of the kings of *I* 2Chr 27:7 3478
in the ways of the kings of *I* 2Chr 28:2 3478
into the hand of the king of *I* 2Chr 28:5 3478
the children of *I* carried away 2Chr 28:8 3478
there is fierce wrath against *I* 2Chr 28:13 3478
low because of Ahaz king of *I* 2Chr 28:19 3478
and his princes throughout all *I* 2Chr 30:6 3478
the children of *I* that were 2Chr 30:21 3478
congregation that came out of *I* 2Chr 30:25 3478
that came out of the land of *I* 2Chr 30:25 3478
And concerning the children of *I* 2Chr 31:6 3478
book of the kings of Judah and *I* 2Chr 32:32 3478
and of all the remnant of *I* 2Chr 34:9 3478
and for them that are left in *I* 2Chr 34:21 3478
neither did all the kings of *I* 2Chr 35:18 3478
I that were present, and the 2Chr 35:18 3478
in the book of the kings of *I* 2Chr 35:27 3478
in the book of the kings of *I* 2Chr 36:8 3478
the son of Remaliah, king of *I* Is 7:1 3478
so is the house of *I* ashamed Jer 2:26 3478
Have I been a wilderness unto *I* Jer 2:31 3478
which backsliding *I* hath done Jer 3:6 3478
I committed adultery I had put Jer 3:8 3478
The backsliding *I* hath justified Jer 3:11 3478
say, Return, thou backsliding *I* Jer 3:12 3478
shall walk with the house of *I* Jer 3:18 3478
For the house of *I* and the house Jer 5:11 3478
and all the house of *I* are Jer 9:26 3478
the house of *I* and the house of Jer 11:10 3478
for the evil of the house of *I* Jer 11:17 3478

be saved, and I shall dwell safely ... Jer 23:6 3478
that I will sow the house of I ... Jer 31:27 3478
new covenant with the house of I ... Jer 31:31 3478
For the children of I and the ... Jer 32:30 3478
all the evil of the children of I ... Jer 32:32 3478
made for fear of Baasha king of I ... Jer 41:9 3478
as the house of I was ashamed of ... Jer 48:13 3478
The children of I and the children ... Jer 50:33 3478
of the house of I upon it ... Eze 4:4 3478
the iniquity of the house of I ... Eze 4:5 3478
The iniquity of the house of I ... Eze 9:9 3478
Judah, and the land of I, they ... Eze 27:17 3478
the children of I his companions ... Eze 37:16 3478
children of I went astray from me ... Eze 44:15 3478
which have scattered Judah, I ... Zec 1:19 3478
O house of Judah, and house of I ... Zec 8:13 3478
brotherhood between Judah and I ... Zec 11:14 3478
an abomination is committed in I ... Mal 2:11 3478

ISRAELITE (*iz'-ra-el-ite*) See ISRAELITES, ISRAELITISH. *A member of Israel 3.*

the name of the I that was slain ... Num 25:14
son, whose name was Ithra an I ... 2Sa 17:25 3481
saith of him, Behold an I indeed ... Jn 1:47 2475
For I also am an I, of the seed ... Rom 11:1 2475

ISRAELITES (*iz'-ra-el-ites*)

one of the cattle of the I dead ... Ex 9:7 3478
all that are I born shall dwell ... Lev 23:42 3478
all the I passed over on dry ... Josh 3:17 3478
that all the I returned unto Ai, ... Josh 8:24 3478
lot unto the I for an inheritance ... Josh 13:6 3478
dwell among the I until this day ... Josh 13:13 3478
ground of the I that day twenty ... Judg 20:21 3478
unto all the I that came thither ... 1Sa 2:14 3478
But all the I went down to the ... 1Sa 13:20 3478
be with the I that were with Saul ... 1Sa 14:21 3478
all the I were gathered together, ... 1Sa 25:1 3478
the I pitched by a fountain which ... 1Sa 29:1 3478
and all the I were troubled ... 2Sa 4:1 3478
the I rose up and smote the ... 2Kin 3:24 3478
of the I that are consumed ... 2Kin 7:13 3478
in their cities were, the I ... 1Chr 9:2 3478
Who are I ... Rom 9:4 2475
Are they I ... 2Cor 11:22 2475

ISRAELITISH

And the son of an I woman, whose ... Lev 24:10 3482
and this son of the I woman ... Lev 24:10 3482
the I woman's son blasphemed the ... Lev 24:11 3482

ISRAEL'S (*iz'-ra-els*)

1. Refers to Israel 1.
his right hand toward I left hand ... Gen 48:13 3478
his left hand toward I right hand ... Gen 48:13 3478
of Reuben, I eldest son, by their ... Num 1:20 3478
2. Refers to Israel 2.
and to the Egyptians for I sake ... Ex 18:8 3478
And of the children of I half ... Num 31:30 3478
And of the children of I half ... Num 31:42 3478
Even of the children of I half ... Num 31:47 3478
blood unto thy people of I charge ... Deut 21:8 3478
his kingdom for his people I sake ... 2Sa 5:12 3478
3. Refers to Israel 3.
the king of I servants answered ... 2Kin 3:11 3478

ISSACHAR (*is'-sa-kar*)

1. A son of Jacob.
and she called his name I ... Gen 30:18 3485
Simeon, and Levi, and Judah, and I ... Gen 35:23 3485
And the sons of I ... Gen 46:13 3485
I is a strong ass couching down ... Gen 49:14 3485
I, Zebulun, and Benjamin, ... Ex 1:3 3485
Reuben, Simeon, Levi, and Judah, I ... 1Chr 2:1 3485
Now the sons of I were, Tola, and ... 1Chr 7:1 3485
2. Descendants of Issachar 1.
Of I ... Num 1:8 3485
Of the children of I, by their ... Num 1:28 3485
of them, even of the tribe of I ... Num 1:29 3485
unto him shall be the tribe of I ... Num 2:5 3485
be captain of the children of I ... Num 2:5 3485
the son of Zuar, prince of I ... Num 7:18 3485
I was Nethaneel the son of Zuar ... Num 10:15 3485
Of the tribe of I, Igal the son ... Num 13:7 3485
Of the sons of I after their ... Num 26:23 3485
These are the families of I ... Num 26:25 3485
of the tribe of the children of I ... Num 34:26 3485
Simeon, and Levi, and Judah, and I ... Deut 27:12 3485
and, I, in thy tents ... Deut 33:18 3485
on the north, and in I on the east ... Josh 17:10 3485
And Manasseh had in I and in Asher ... Josh 17:11 3485
And the fourth lot came out to I ... Josh 19:17 3485
for the children of I according ... Josh 19:17 3485
of I according to their families ... Josh 19:23 3485
of the families of the tribe of I ... Josh 21:6 3485
And out of the tribe of I, Kishon ... Josh 21:28 3485
the princes of I were with ... Judg 5:15 3485
even I, and also Barak ... Judg 5:15 3485
Puah, the son of Dodo, a man of I ... Judg 10:1 3485
the son of Paruah, in I ... 1Kin 4:17 3485
son of Ahijah, of the house of I ... 1Kin 15:27 3485
families out of the tribe of I ... 1Chr 6:62 3485
And out of the tribe of I ... 1Chr 6:72 3485
of I were valiant men of might ... 1Chr 7:5 3485
And of the children of I, which ... 1Chr 12:32 3485
that were nigh them, even unto I ... 1Chr 12:40 3485
of I, Omri the son of Michael ... 1Chr 27:18 3485
many of Ephraim, and Manasseh, I ... 2Chr 30:18 3485
unto the west side, I a portion ... Eze 48:25 3485
And by the border of I, from the ... Eze 48:26 3485
one gate of Simeon, one gate of I ... Eze 48:33 3485
Of the tribe of I were sealed ... Rev 7:7 2466
3. A porter of the tabernacle.
I the seventh, Peulthai the ... 1Chr 26:5 3485

ISSHIAH (*is-shi'-ah*) See ISAIAH, JESIAH.

1. A descendant of Moses.
sons of Rehabiah, the first was I ... 1Chr 24:21 3449
2. A Levite.
The brother of Michah was I ... 1Chr 24:25 3449
of the sons of I ... 1Chr 24:25

ISSHIJAH See ISHIJAH.

ISSHOD See ISHOD.

ISSUE

And thy i, which thou begettest ... Gen 48:6 4138
cleansed from the i of her blood ... Lev 12:7 4726
hath a running i out of his flesh ... Lev 15:2 2100
because of his i he is unclean ... Lev 15:2 2101
shall be his uncleanness in his i ... Lev 15:3 2101
whether his flesh run with his i ... Lev 15:3 2101
his flesh be stopped from his i ... Lev 15:3 2101
whereon he lieth that hath the i ... Lev 15:4 2100
hath the i shall wash his clothes ... Lev 15:6 2100
hath the i shall wash his clothes ... Lev 15:7 2100
if he that hath the i spit upon ... Lev 15:8 2100
that hath the i shall be unclean ... Lev 15:9 2100
he toucheth that hath the i ... Lev 15:11 2100
that he toucheth which hath the i ... Lev 15:12 2100
when he that hath an i is ... Lev 15:13 2100
an i is cleansed of his i ... Lev 15:13 2101
for him before the LORD for his i ... Lev 15:15 2101
And if a woman have an i ... Lev 15:19 2100
her i in her flesh be blood, she ... Lev 15:19 2101
if a woman have an i of her blood ... Lev 15:25 2100
all the days of the i of her ... Lev 15:25 2101
she lieth all the days of her i ... Lev 15:26 2101
But if she be cleansed of her i ... Lev 15:28 2101
LORD for the i of her uncleanness ... Lev 15:30 2101
is the law of him that hath an i ... Lev 15:32 2100
flowers, and of him that hath an i ... Lev 15:33 2100
is a leper, or hath a running i ... Lev 22:4 2100
and every one that hath an i ... Num 5:2 2100
house of Joab one that hath an i ... 2Sa 3:29 2100
thy sons that shall i from thee ... 2Kin 20:18 3318
house, the offspring and the i ... Is 22:24 6849
thy sons that shall i from thee ... Is 39:7 3318
i is like the i of horses ... Eze 23:20 2231
These waters i out toward the ... Eze 47:8 3318
with an i of blood twelve years ... Mt 9:20 131
a wife, deceased, and, having no i ... Mt 22:25 4690
which had an i of blood twelve ... Mk 5:25 4511
a woman having an i of blood ... Lk 8:43 4511
immediately her i of blood ... Lk 8:44 4511

ISSUED

the other i out of the city ... Josh 8:22 3318
as if it had i out of the womb ... Job 38:8 3318
waters i out from under the ... Eze 47:1 3318
they they i out of the sanctuary ... Eze 47:12 3318
A fiery stream i and came forth ... Dan 7:10 5047
and out of their mouths i fire ... Rev 9:17 1607
which i out of their mouths ... Rev 9:18 1607

ISSUES

the Lord belong the i from death ... Ps 68:20 8444
for out of it are the i of life ... Prov 4:23 8444

ISUAH (*is'-u-ah*) See ISHUAH. *A son of Asher.*

Imnah, and I, and Ishuai, and Beriah ... 1Chr 7:30 3440

ISUI (*is'-u-i*) See ISHUI. *A son of Asher.*

Jimnah, and Ishuah, and I, and ... Gen 46:17 3440

IT See PREFACE.

ITALIAN (*it-al'-yan*)

of the band called the I band ... Acts 10:1 2483

ITALY (*it'-a-lee*) *Homeland of most Roman citizens.*

in Pontus, lately come from I ... Acts 18:2 2482
that we should sail into I ... Acts 27:1 2482
ship of Alexandria sailing into I ... Acts 27:6 2482
They of I salute you ... Heb 13:24 2482
to the Hebrews from I by Timothy ... Heb s

ITCH

and with the scab, and with the i ... Deut 28:27 2775

ITCHING

teachers, having i ears ... 2Ti 4:3 2833

ITHAI (*ith'-a-i*) See ITTAI. *A mighty man of David.*

I the son of Ribai of Gibeah, ... 1Chr 11:31 2833

ITHAMAR (*ith'-a-mar*) *A son of Aaron.*

Nadab, and Abihu, Eleazar, and I ... Ex 6:23 385
Nadab and Abihu, Eleazar and I ... Ex 28:1 385
of the Levites, by the hand of I ... Ex 38:21 385
Aaron, and unto Eleazar and unto I ... Lev 10:6 385
Aaron, and unto Eleazar and unto I ... Lev 10:12 385
and he was angry with Eleazar and I ... Lev 10:16 385
and Abihu, Eleazar, and I ... Num 3:2 385
I ministered in the priest's ... Num 3:4 385
shall be under the hand of I the ... Num 4:28 385
under the hand of I the son of ... Num 4:33 385
under the hand of I the son of ... Num 7:8 385
Nadab, and Abihu, Eleazar, and I ... Num 26:60 385
Nadab, and Abihu, Eleazar, and I ... 1Chr 6:3 385
Nadab, and Abihu, Eleazar, and I ... 1Chr 24:1 385
I executed the priest's office ... 1Chr 24:2 385
and Ahimelech of the sons of I ... 1Chr 24:3 385
of Eleazar than of the sons of I ... 1Chr 24:4 385
eight among the sons of I ... 1Chr 24:4 385
of Eleazar, and of the sons of I ... 1Chr 24:5 385
for Eleazar, and one taken for I ... 1Chr 24:6 385
of the sons of I ... Ezr 8:2 385

ITHIEL (*ith'-e-el*)

1. Son of Jesaiah.
the son of Maaseiah, the son of I ... Neh 11:7 384
2. Person mentioned in Proverbs.
the man spake unto I, even unto ... Prov 30:1 384
spake unto Ithiel, even unto I ... Prov 30:1 384

ITHLAH See JETHLAH.

ITHMAH (*ith'-mah*) *A mighty man of David.*

sons of Elnaam, and I the Moabite, ... 1Chr 11:46 3495

ITHNAN (*ith'-nan*) *A town in Judah.*

And Kedesh, and Hazor, and I ... Josh 15:23 3497

ITHRA (*ith'-rah*) See JETHER. *Father of Amasa.*

whose name was I an Israelite ... 2Sa 17:25 3501

ITHRAN (*ith'-ran*)

1. A son of Dishon.
Hemdan, and Eshban, and I, and ... Gen 36:26 3506
and Eshban, and I, and Cheran ... 1Chr 1:41 3506
2. A son of Zophah.
Shamma, and Shilshah, and I ... 1Chr 7:37 3506

ITHREAM (*ith'-re-am*) *A son of David.*

And the sixth, I, by Eglah David's ... 2Sa 3:5 3507
the sixth, I by Eglah his wife ... 1Chr 3:3 3507

ITHRITE (*ith'-rite*) See ITHRITES. *A descendant of Jether.*

Ira an I, Gareb an I, ... 2Sa 23:38 3505
Ira an I, Gareb an I ... 2Sa 23:38 3505
Ira the I, Gareb the I, ... 1Chr 11:40 3505
Ira the I, Gareb the I ... 1Chr 11:40 3505

ITHRITES (*ith'-rites*)

the I, and the Puhites, and the ... 1Chr 2:53 3505

ITS

That which groweth of i own ... Lev 25:5

ITSELF

his kind, whose seed is in i ... Gen 1:11
fruit, whose seed was in i ... Gen 1:12
fat of the beast that dieth of i ... Lev 7:24
that eateth that which died of i ... Lev 17:15
the land i vomiteth out her ... Lev 18:25
That which dieth of i, or is torn ... Lev 22:8
that which groweth of i in it ... Lev 25:11
eat of any thing that dieth of i ... Deut 14:21
were of the very base i ... 1Kin 7:34
A land of darkness, as darkness i ... Job 10:22
his heart gathereth iniquity to i ... Ps 41:6
even Sinai i was moved at the ... Ps 68:8 2088
but that his heart may discover i ... Prov 18:2
the cup, when it moveth i aright ... Prov 23:31
his right hand, which bewrayeth i ... Prov 27:16
and the tender grass sheweth i ... Prov 27:25
Shall the ax boast i against him ... Is 10:15
or shall the saw magnify i ... Is 10:15
as if the rod should shake i ... Is 10:15
as if the staff should lift up i ... Is 10:15
this year such as groweth of i ... Is 37:30
your soul delight i in fatness ... Is 55:2
neither shall thy moon withdraw i ... Is 60:20
And there shall dwell in Judah i ... Jer 31:24
cloud, and a fire infolding i ... Eze 1:4
eaten of that which dieth of i ... Eze 4:14
base, that it might not lift i up ... Eze 17:14
neither shall it exalt i any more ... Eze 29:15
of any thing that is dead of i ... Eze 44:31
and it raised up i on one side ... Dan 7:5
take thought for the things of i ... Mt 6:34 1438
i is brought to desolation ... Mt 12:25 1438
divided against i shall not stand ... Mt 12:25 1438
if a kingdom be divided against i ... Mk 3:24 1438
if a house be divided against i ... Mk 3:25 1438
i is brought to desolation ... Lk 11:17 1438
the branch cannot bear fruit of i ... Jn 15:4 1438
wrapped together in a place by i ... Jn 20:7 5565
i could not contain the books ... Jn 21:25 846
The Spirit i beareth witness with ... Rom 8:16 846
Because the creature i also shall ... Rom 8:21 846
but the Spirit i maketh ... Rom 8:26 846
there is nothing unclean of i ... Rom 14:14 1438
Doth not even nature i teach you ... 1Cor 11:14 846
charity vaunteth not i, is not ... 1Cor 13:4
Doth not behave i unseemly ... 1Cor 13:5
i against the knowledge of God ... 2Cor 10:5
unto the edifying of i in love ... Eph 4:16 1438
but into heaven i, now to appear ... Heb 9:24 846
of all men, and of the truth i ... 3Jn 12 846

ITTAH-KAZIN (*it''-tah-ka'-zin*) *A city in Zebulun.*

the east to Gittah-hepher, to I ... Josh 19:13 6278

ITTAI (*it'-ta-i*) See ITHAI.

1. A Philistine in David's army.
said the king to I the Gittite ... 2Sa 15:19 863
I answered the king, and said, As ... 2Sa 15:21 863
And David said to I, Go and pass ... 2Sa 15:22 863
I the Gittite passed over, and all ... 2Sa 15:22 863
under the hand of I the Gittite ... 2Sa 18:2 863
commanded Joab and Abishai and I ... 2Sa 18:5 863
king charged thee and Abishai and I ... 2Sa 18:12 863
2. A mighty man of David.
I the son of Ribai out of Gibeah ... 2Sa 23:29 863

ITURAEA (*i-tu-re'-ah*) *A province near Mt. Hermon.*

his brother Philip tetrarch of I ... Lk 3:1 2434

IVAH (*i'-vah*) See AHAVA, AVA. *A Mesopotamian district.*

gods of Sepharvaim, Hena, and I ... 2Kin 18:34 5755
city of Sepharvaim, of Hena, and I ... 2Kin 19:13 5755
city of Sepharvaim, Hena, and I ... Is 37:13 5755

IVORY

the king made a great throne of i ... 1Kin 10:18 8127
bringing gold, and silver, i ... 1Kin 10:22 8143
the i house which he made, and all ... 1Kin 22:39 8127
the king made a great throne of i ... 2Chr 9:17 8127

I

bringing gold, and silver, *i* ... 2Chr 9:21 8143
and cassia, out of the *i* palaces ... Ps 45:8 8127
his belly is as bright *i* overlaid ... Song 5:14 8127
Thy neck is as a tower of *i* ... Song 7:4 8127
have made thy benches of *i* ... Eze 27:6 8127
thee for a present horns of *i* ... Eze 27:15 8127
and the houses of *i* shall perish ... Amos 3:15 8127
That lie upon beds of *i*, and ... Amos 6:4 8127
wood, and all manner vessels of *i* ... Rev 18:12 *1661*

IZEHAR (*iz'-e-har*) See IZEHARITES, IZHAR. *A son of Kohath.*
Amram, and *I*, Hebron, and Uzziel ... Num 3:19 3324

IZEHARITES (*iz'-e-har-ites*) See IZHARITE. *Descendants of Izehar.*
Amramites, and the family of the *I* ... Num 3:27 3325

IZHAR (*iz'-har*) See IZEHAR, IZHARITES. *Same as Izehar.*
Amram, and *I*, and Hebron, and Uzziel Ex 6:18 3324
And the sons of *I* ... Ex 6:21 3324
Now Korah, the son of *I*, the son ... Num 16:1 3324
Amram, *I*, and Hebron, and Uzziel ... 1Chr 6:2 3324
sons of Kohath were, Amram, and *I* ... 1Chr 6:18 3324
The son of *I*, the son of Kohath, ... 1Chr 6:38 3324
Amram, *I*, Hebron, and Uzziel, four ... 1Chr 23:12 3324
Of the sons of *I* ... 1Chr 23:18 3324

IZHARITES (*iz'-har-ites*) See IZEHARITES. *Same as Izeharites.*
Of the *I*; Shelomoth ... 1Chr 24:22 3325
Of the Amramites, and the *I* ... 1Chr 26:23 3325
Of the *I*, Chenaniah and his sons ... 1Chr 26:29 3325

IZLIAH See JEZLIAH.

IZRAHIAH (*iz-ra-hi'-ah*) See JEZRAHIAH. *Grandson of Tola.*
the sons of Uzzi; *I* ... 1Chr 7:3 3156
and the sons of *I* ... 1Chr 7:3 3156

IZRAHITE (*iz'-ra-hite*) See EZRAHITE. *Family name of Shamhuth.*
fifth month was Shamhuth the *I* ... 1Chr 27:8 3155

IZRI (*iz'-ri*) See ZERI. *A sanctuary servant.*
The fourth to *I*, he, his sons, and ... 1Chr 25:11 3342

IZZIAH See JEZIAH.

J

JAAKAN (*ja'-a-kan*) See AKAN, BENE-JAAKAN. *A son of Ezer.*
of the children of *J* to Mosera ... Deut 10:6 3292

JAAKOBAH (*ja-ak'-o-bah*) *A descendant of Simeon.*
And Elioenai, and *J*, and Jeshohaiah, ... 1Chr 4:36 3291

JAALA (*ja'-a-lah*) See JAALAH. *A family of exiles.*
The children of *J*, the children ... Neh 7:58 3279

JAALAH (*ja'-a-lah*) See JAALA. *Same as Jaala.*
The children of *J*, the children ... Ezr 2:56 3279

JAALAM (*ja'-a-lam*) *A son of Esau.*
And Aholibamah bare Jeush, and *J* ... Gen 36:5 3281
and she bare to Esau Jeush, and *J* ... Gen 36:14 3281
duke Jeush, duke *J*, duke Korah ... Gen 36:18 3281
Eliphaz, Reuel, and Jeush, and *J* ... 1Chr 1:35 3281

JAANAI (*ja'-a-nahee*) *A Gadite.*
chief, and Shapham the next, and *J* ... 1Chr 5:12 3285

JAAR See WOOD.

JAARE-OREGIM (*ja''-a-re-or'-eg-im*) See JAIR. *Father of Elhanan.*
where Elhanan the son of *J* ... 2Sa 21:19 3296

JAASAU (*ja-a'-saw*) *Married a foreigner in exile.*
Mattaniah, Mattenai, and *J* ... Ezr 10:37 3299

JAASIEL (*ja-a'-se-el*) *A son of Abner.*
of Benjamin, *J* the son of Abner ... 1Chr 27:21 3300

JAASU See JAASAU.

JAAZANIAH (*ja-az-a-ni'-ah*) See JEZANIAH.
1. A son of a Maachathite.
J the son of a Maachathite, they ... 2Kin 25:23 2970
2. A chief Rechabite.
Then I took *J* the son of Jeremiah ... Jer 35:3 2970
3. Son of Shaphan.
them stood *J* the son of Shaphan ... Eze 8:11 2970
4. Son of Azur.
whom I saw *J* the son of Azur ... Eze 11:1 2970

JAAZER (*ja-a'-zer*) See JAZER. *A city in Gilead.*
And Moses sent to spy out *J* ... Num 21:32 3270
And Atroth, Shophan, and *J*, and ... Num 32:35 3270

JAAZIAH (*ja-a-zi'-ah*) *A descendant of Merari.*
the sons of *J*; Beno ... 1Chr 24:26 3269
The sons of Merari by *J* ... 1Chr 24:27 3269

JA-AZIEL See BEN.

JAAZIEL (*ja-a'-ze-el*) See AZIEL. *A priest.*
degree, Zechariah, Ben, and *J* ... 1Chr 15:18 3268

JABAL (*ja'-bal*) *A son of Adah.*
And Adah bare *J* ... Gen 4:20 2989

JABBOK (*jab'-bok*) *A brook in Bashan.*
sons, and passed over the ford *J* ... Gen 32:22 2999
his land from Arnon unto *J* ... Num 21:24 2999
nor unto any place of the river *J* ... Deut 2:37 2999
the border even unto the river *J* ... Deut 3:16 2999
Gilead, even unto the river *J* ... Josh 12:2 2999
of Egypt, from Arnon even unto *J* ... Judg 11:13 2999
Amorites, from Arnon even unto *J* ... Judg 11:22 2999

JABESH (*ja'-besh*) See JABESH-GILEAD.
1. A city in Gad.
all the men of *J* said unto Nahash ... 1Sa 11:1 3003
And the elders of *J* said unto him ... 1Sa 11:3 3003
him the tidings of the men of *J* ... 1Sa 11:5 3003
came and shewed it to the men of *J* ... 1Sa 11:9 3003
Therefore the men of *J* said ... 1Sa 11:10 3003
wall of Beth-shan, and came to *J* ... 1Sa 31:12 3003
and buried them under a tree at *J* ... 1Sa 31:13 3003
of his sons, and brought them to *J* ... 1Chr 10:12 3003
their bones under the oak in *J* ... 1Chr 10:12 3003
2. Father of Shallum.
Shallum the son of *J* conspired ... 2Kin 15:10 3003
Shallum the son of *J* began to ... 2Kin 15:13 3003
Shallum the son of *J* in Samaria ... 2Kin 15:14 3003

JABESH-GILEAD (*ja''-besh-ghil'-e-ad*) *Same as Jabesh 1.*
the camp from *J* to the assembly ... Judg 21:8
of the inhabitants of *J* there ... Judg 21:9
smite the inhabitants of *J* with ... Judg 21:10
of *J* four hundred young virgins ... Judg 21:12
had saved alive of the women of *J* ... Judg 21:14
came up, and encamped against *J* ... 1Sa 11:1
shall ye say unto the men of *J* ... 1Sa 11:9
of *J* heard of that which the ... 1Sa 31:11
That the men of *J* were they that ... 2Sa 2:4
sent messengers unto the men of *J* ... 2Sa 2:5
his son from the men of *J* ... 2Sa 21:12
when all *J* heard all that the ... 1Chr 10:11

JABEZ (*ja'-bez*)
1. A city in Judah.
of the scribes which dwelt at *J* ... 1Chr 2:55 3258
2. Head of a family of Judah.
J was more honourable than his ... 1Chr 4:9 3258
and his mother called his name *J* ... 1Chr 4:9 3258
J called on the God of Israel, ... 1Chr 4:10 3258

JABIN (*ja'-bin*) See JABIN'S.
1. A king of Hazor.
when *J* king of Hazor had heard ... Josh 11:1 2985
2. Another king of Hazor.
into the hand of *J* king of Canaan ... Judg 4:2 2985
peace between *J* the king of Hazor ... Judg 4:17 2985
So God subdued on that day *J* the ... Judg 4:23 2985
prevailed against *J* the king of ... Judg 4:24 2985
had destroyed *J* king of Canaan ... Judg 4:24 2985
as to Sisera, as to *J*, at the ... Ps 83:9 2985

JABIN'S
Sisera, the captain of *J* army ... Judg 4:7 2985

JABNEEL (*jab'-ne-el*) See JABNEH.
1. A city in Judah.
mount Baalah, and went out unto *J* ... Josh 15:11 2995
2. A city in Naphtali.
Zaanannim, and Adami, Nekeb, and *J*. Josh 19:33 2995

JABNEH (*jab'-neh*) See JABNEEL. *A Philistine city.*
wall of Gath, and the wall of *J* ... 2Chr 26:6 2996

JACAN See JACHAN.

JACHAN (*ja'-kan*) See AKAN. *Head of a Gadite family.*
and Sheba, and Jorai, and *J* ... 1Chr 5:13 3275

JACHIN (*ja'-kin*) See JACHINITES, JARIB.
1. A son of Simeon.
Jemuel, and Jamin, and Ohad, and *J* ... Gen 46:10 3199
Jemuel, and Jamin, and Ohad, and *J* ... Ex 6:15 3199
of *J*, the family of the ... Num 26:12 3199
2. A pillar of Solomon's Temple.
and called the name thereof *J* ... 1Kin 7:21 3199
name of that on the right hand *J* ... 2Chr 3:17 3199
3. A family of exiles.
Jedaiah, and Jehoiarib, and *J* ... 1Chr 9:10 3199
Jedaiah the son of Joiarib, *J* ... Neh 11:10 3199
4. A sanctuary servant.
The one and twentieth to *J* ... 1Chr 24:17 3199

JACHINITES (*ja'-kin-ites*) *Descendants of Jachin 1.*
of Jachin, the family of the *J* ... Num 26:12 3200

JACINTH
breastplates of fire, and of *j* ... Rev 9:17 *5191*
the eleventh, a *j* ... Rev 21:20 *5192*

JACOB (*ja'-cub*) See ISRAEL, JACOB'S, JAMES.
1. Son of Isaac and Rebekah.
and his name was called *J* ... Gen 25:26 3290
J was a plain man, dwelling in ... Gen 25:27 3290
but Rebekah loved *J* ... Gen 25:28 3290
And *J* sod pottage ... Gen 25:29 3290
And Esau said to *J*, Feed me, I ... Gen 25:30 3290
J said, Sell me this day thy ... Gen 25:31 3290
J said, Swear to me this day ... Gen 25:33 3290
and he sold his birthright unto *J* ... Gen 25:33 3290
Then *J* gave Esau bread and pottage ... Gen 25:34 3290
And Rebekah spake unto *J* her son ... Gen 27:6 3290
J said to Rebekah his mother, ... Gen 27:11 3290
put them upon *J* her younger son ... Gen 27:15 3290
into the hand of her son *J* ... Gen 27:17 3290
J said unto his father, I am Esau ... Gen 27:19 3290
And Isaac said unto *J*, Come near, ... Gen 27:21 3290
J went near unto Isaac his father ... Gen 27:22 3290
had made an end of blessing *J* ... Gen 27:30 3290
J was yet scarce gone out from ... Gen 27:30 3290
said, Is not he rightly named *J* ... Gen 27:36 3290
Esau hated *J* because of the ... Gen 27:41 3290
then will I slay my brother *J* ... Gen 27:41 3290
called *J* her younger son, and said ... Gen 27:42 3290
if *J* take a wife of the daughters ... Gen 27:46 3290
And Isaac called *J*, and blessed him ... Gen 28:1 3290
And Isaac sent away *J* ... Gen 28:5 3290
Esau saw that Isaac had blessed *J* ... Gen 28:6 3290
that *J* obeyed his father and his ... Gen 28:7 3290
J went out from Beer-sheba, and ... Gen 28:10 3290
J awaked out of his sleep, and he ... Gen 28:16 3290
J rose up early in the morning, ... Gen 28:18 3290
J vowed a vow, saying, If God ... Gen 28:20 3290
Then *J* went on his journey, and ... Gen 29:1 3290
J said unto them, My brethren, ... Gen 29:4 3290
when *J* saw Rachel the daughter of ... Gen 29:10 3290
that *J* went near, and rolled the ... Gen 29:10 3290
J kissed Rachel, and lifted up his ... Gen 29:11 3290
J told Rachel that he was her ... Gen 29:12 3290
the tidings of *J* his sister's son ... Gen 29:13 3290
And Laban said unto *J*, Because ... Gen 29:15 3290
And *J* loved Rachel ... Gen 29:18 3290
J served seven years for Rachel ... Gen 29:20 3290
J said unto Laban, Give me my ... Gen 29:21 3290
J did so, and fulfilled her week ... Gen 29:28 3290
saw that she bare *J* no children ... Gen 30:1 3290
and said unto *J*, Give me children, ... Gen 30:1 3290
and *J* went in unto her ... Gen 30:4 3290
Bilhah conceived, and bare *J* a son ... Gen 30:5 3290
again, and bare *J* a second son ... Gen 30:7 3290
her maid, and gave her *J* to wife ... Gen 30:9 3290
Zilpah Leah's maid bare *J* a son ... Gen 30:10 3290
Leah's maid bare *J* a second son ... Gen 30:12 3290
J came out of the field in the ... Gen 30:16 3290
and bare *J* the fifth son ... Gen 30:17 3290
again, and bare *J* the sixth son ... Gen 30:19 3290
that *J* said unto Laban, Send me ... Gen 30:25 3290
J said, Thou shalt not give me ... Gen 30:31 3290
journey betwixt himself and *J* ... Gen 30:36 3290
J fed the rest of Laban's flocks ... Gen 30:36 3290
J took him rods of green poplar, ... Gen 30:37 3290
J did separate the lambs, and set ... Gen 30:40 3290
that *J* laid the rods before the ... Gen 30:41 3290
J hath taken away all that was ... Gen 31:1 3290
J beheld the countenance of Laban ... Gen 31:2 3290
And the LORD said unto *J*, Return ... Gen 31:3 3290
J sent and called Rachel and Leah ... Gen 31:4 3290
unto me in a dream, saying, *J* ... Gen 31:11 3290
Then *J* rose up, and set his sons ... Gen 31:17 3290
J stole away unawares to Laban ... Gen 31:20 3290
on the third day that *J* was fled ... Gen 31:22 3290
speak not to *J* either good or bad ... Gen 31:24 3290
Then Laban overtook *J* ... Gen 31:25 3290
Now *J* had pitched his tent in the ... Gen 31:25 3290
And Laban said to *J*, What hast ... Gen 31:26 3290
speak not to *J* either good or bad ... Gen 31:29 3290
J answered and said to Laban, ... Gen 31:31 3290
For *J* knew not that Rachel had ... Gen 31:32 3290
J was wroth, and chode with Laban ... Gen 31:36 3290
J answered and said to Laban, What ... Gen 31:36 3290
And Laban answered and said unto *J* .. Gen 31:43 3290
J took a stone, and set it up for ... Gen 31:45 3290
J said unto his brethren, Gather ... Gen 31:46 3290
but *J* called it Galeed ... Gen 31:47 3290
And Laban said to *J*, Behold this ... Gen 31:51 3290
J sware by the fear of his father ... Gen 31:53 3290
Then *J* offered sacrifice upon the ... Gen 31:54 3290
J went on his way, and the angels ... Gen 32:1 3290
when *J* saw them, he said, This is ... Gen 32:2 3290
J sent messengers before him to ... Gen 32:3 3290
Thy servant *J* saith thus, I have ... Gen 32:4 3290
And the messengers returned to *J* ... Gen 32:6 3290
Then *J* was greatly afraid and ... Gen 32:7 3290
J said, O God of my father ... Gen 32:9 3290
thy servant *J* is behind us ... Gen 32:20 3290
And *J* was left alone ... Gen 32:24 3290
And he said, *J* ... Gen 32:27 3290
name shall be called no more *J* ... Gen 32:28 3290
J asked him, and said, Tell me, I ... Gen 32:29 3290
J called the name of the place ... Gen 32:30 3290
J lifted up his eyes, and looked, ... Gen 33:1 3290
J said, Nay, I pray thee, if now ... Gen 33:10 3290
J journeyed to Succoth, and built ... Gen 33:17 3290
J came to Shalem, a city of ... Gen 33:18 3290
of Leah, which she bare unto *J* ... Gen 34:1 3290
unto Dinah the daughter of *J* ... Gen 34:3 3290
J heard that he had defiled Dinah ... Gen 34:5 3290
J held his peace until they were ... Gen 34:5 3290
out unto *J* to commune with him ... Gen 34:6 3290
the sons of *J* came out of the ... Gen 34:7 3290

the sons of J answered Shechem and... Gen 34:13 3290
sore, that two of the sons of J... Gen 34:25 3290
The sons of J came upon the slain... Gen 34:27 3290
J said to Simeon and Levi, Ye have... Gen 34:30 3290
And God said unto J, Arise, go up... Gen 35:1 3290
Then J said unto his household,... Gen 35:2 3290
they gave unto J all the strange... Gen 35:4 3290
J hid them under the oak which... Gen 35:4 3290
not pursue after the sons of J... Gen 35:5 3290
So J came to Luz, which is in the... Gen 35:6 3290
And God appeared unto J again... Gen 35:9 3290
God said unto him, Thy name is J... Gen 35:10 3290
shall not be called any more J... Gen 35:10 3290
J set up a pillar in the place... Gen 35:14 3290
J called the name of the place... Gen 35:15 3290
J set a pillar upon her grave... Gen 35:20 3290
Now the sons of J were twelve... Gen 35:22 3290
these are the sons of J, which... Gen 35:26 3290
J came unto Isaac his father unto... Gen 35:27 3290
and his sons Esau and J buried him... Gen 35:29 3290
from the face of his brother J... Gen 36:6 3290
J dwelt in the land wherein his... Gen 37:1 3290
These are the generations of J... Gen 37:2 3290
J rent his clothes, and put... Gen 37:34 3290
Now when J saw that there was... Gen 42:1 3290
J said unto his sons, Why do ye... Gen 42:1 3290
J sent not with his brethren... Gen 42:4 3290
they came unto J their father... Gen 42:29 3290
J their father said unto them, Me... Gen 42:36 3290
of Canaan unto J their father... Gen 45:25 3290
the spirit of J their father... Gen 45:27 3290
of the night, and said, J, J... Gen 46:2 3290
J rose up from Beer-sheba... Gen 46:5 3290
of Israel carried J their father... Gen 46:5 3290
of Canaan, and came into Egypt, J... Gen 46:6 3290
Israel, which came into Egypt, J... Gen 46:8 3290
she bare unto J in Padan-aram... Gen 46:15 3290
and these she bare unto J... Gen 46:18 3290
of Rachel, which were born to J... Gen 46:22 3290
and she bare these unto J... Gen 46:25 3290
souls that came with J into Egypt... Gen 46:26 3290
all the souls of the house of J... Gen 46:27 3290
And Joseph brought in J his father... Gen 47:7 3290
and J blessed Pharaoh... Gen 47:7 3290
And Pharaoh said unto J, How old... Gen 47:8 3290
J said unto Pharaoh, The days of... Gen 47:9 3290
J blessed Pharaoh, and went out... Gen 47:10 3290
J lived in the land of Egypt... Gen 47:28 3290
so the whole age of J was an... Gen 47:28 3290
And one told J, and said, Behold,... Gen 48:2 3290
J said unto Joseph, God Almighty... Gen 48:3 3290
J called unto his sons, and said,... Gen 49:1 3290
together, and hear, ye sons of J... Gen 49:2 3290
I will divide them in J, and... Gen 49:7 3290
the hands of the mighty God of J... Gen 49:24 3290
when J had made an end of... Gen 49:33 3290
to Abraham, to Isaac, and to J... Gen 50:24 3290
man and his household came with J... Ex 1:1 3290
the loins of J were seventy souls... Ex 1:5 3290
Abraham, with Isaac, and with J... Ex 2:24 3290
the God of Isaac, and the God of J... Ex 3:6 3290
the God of Isaac, and the God of J... Ex 3:15 3290
God of Abraham, of Isaac, and of J... Ex 3:16 3290
the God of Isaac, and the God of J... Ex 4:5 3290
Abraham, unto Isaac, and unto J... Ex 6:3 3290
it to Abraham, to Isaac, and to J... Ex 6:8 3290
shalt thou say to the house of J... Ex 19:3 3290
unto Abraham, to Isaac, and to J... Ex 33:1 3290
I remember my covenant with J... Lev 26:42 3290
Abraham, unto Isaac, and unto J... Num 32:11 3290
fathers, Abraham, Isaac, and J... Deut 1:8 3290
to Abraham, to Isaac, and to J... Deut 6:10 3290
thy fathers, Abraham, Isaac, and J... Deut 9:5 3290
servants, Abraham, Isaac, and J... Deut 9:27 3290
to Abraham, to Isaac, and to J... Deut 29:13 3290
to Abraham, to Isaac, and to J... Deut 30:20 3290
Abraham, unto Isaac, and unto J... Deut 34:4 3290
And I gave unto Isaac J and Esau... Josh 24:4 3290
but J and his children went down... Josh 24:4 3290
in a parcel of ground which J... Josh 24:32 3290
When J was come into Egypt, and... 1Sa 12:8 3290
with Abraham, Isaac, and J... 2Kin 13:23 3290
yet I loved J,... Mal 1:2 3290
and Isaac begat J... Mt 1:2 *2384*
J begat Judas and his brethren... Mt 1:2 *2384*
down with Abraham, and Isaac, and J. Mt 8:11 *2384*
the God of Isaac, and the God of J... Mt 22:32 *2384*
the God of Isaac, and the God of J... Mk 12:26 *2384*
over the house of J for ever... Lk 1:33 *2384*
Which was the son of J, which was... Lk 3:34 *2384*
shall see Abraham, and Isaac, and J... Lk 13:28 *2384*
the God of Isaac, and the God of J... Lk 20:37 *2384*
that J gave to his son Joseph... Jn 4:5 *2384*
thou greater than our father J... Jn 4:12 *2384*
of Abraham, and of Isaac, and of J... Acts 3:13 *2384*
and Isaac begat J... Acts 7:8 *2384*
J begat the twelve patriarchs... Acts 7:8 *2384*
But when J heard that there was... Acts 7:12 *2384*
and called his father J to him... Acts 7:14 *2384*
So J went down into Egypt, and... Acts 7:15 *2384*
the God of Isaac, and the God of J... Acts 7:32 *2384*
a tabernacle for the God of J... Acts 7:46 *2384*
J have I loved, but Esau have I... Rom 9:13 *2384*
turn away ungodliness from J... Rom 11:26 *2384*
in tabernacles with Isaac and J... Heb 11:9 *2384*
By faith Isaac blessed J and Esau... Heb 11:20 *2384*
By faith J, when he was a dying,... Heb 11:21 *2384*
2. Father of Joseph; ancestor of Jesus.
and Matthan begat J... Mt 1:15 *2384*
J begat Joseph the husband of... Mt 1:16 *2384*
3. Descendants of Jacob.
east, saying, Come, curse me J... Num 23:7 3290
Who can count the dust of J... Num 23:10 3290
He hath not beheld iniquity in J... Num 23:21 3290
there is no enchantment against J... Num 23:23 3290
this time it shall be said of J... Num 23:23 3290
How goodly are thy tents, O J... Num 24:5 3290
there shall come a Star out of J... Num 24:17 3290
Out of J shall come he that shall... Num 24:19 3290
J is the lot of his inheritance... Deut 32:9 3290
of the congregation of J... Deut 33:4 3290
They shall teach J thy judgments... Deut 33:10 3290
the fountain of J shall be upon a... Deut 33:28 3290
the anointed of the God of J... 2Sa 23:1 3290
of the tribes of the sons of J... 1Kin 18:31 3290
LORD commanded the children of J... 2Kin 17:34 3290
his servant, ye children of J... 1Chr 16:13 3290
confirmed the same to J for a law... 1Chr 16:17 3290
J shall rejoice, and Israel shall... Ps 14:7 3290
name of the God of J defend thee... Ps 20:1 3290
all ye the seed of J, glorify him... Ps 22:23 3290
seek him, that seek thy face, O J... Ps 24:6 3290
command deliverances for J... Ps 44:4 3290
the God of J is our refuge... Ps 46:7 3290
the God of J is our refuge... Ps 46:11 3290
the excellency of J whom he loved... Ps 47:4 3290
J shall rejoice, and Israel shall... Ps 53:6 3290
in J unto the ends of the earth... Ps 59:13 3290
will sing praises to the God of J... Ps 75:9 3290
At thy rebuke, O God of J... Ps 76:6 3290
thy people, the sons of J... Ps 77:15 3290
he established a testimony in J... Ps 78:5 3290
so a fire was kindled against J... Ps 78:21 3290
brought him to feed J his people... Ps 78:71 3290
For they have devoured J, and laid... Ps 79:7 3290
a joyful noise unto the God of J... Ps 81:1 3290
Israel, and a law of the God of J... Ps 81:4 3290
give ear, O God of J... Ps 84:8 3290
brought back the captivity of J... Ps 85:1 3290
more than all the dwellings of J... Ps 87:2 3290
shall the God of J regard it... Ps 94:7 3290
judgment and righteousness in J... Ps 99:4 3290
ye children of J his chosen... Ps 105:6 3290
the same unto J for a law... Ps 105:10 3290
J sojourned in the land of Ham... Ps 105:23 3290
the house of J from a people of... Ps 114:1 3290
at the presence of the God of J... Ps 114:7 3290
and vowed unto the mighty God of J... Ps 132:2 3290
for the mighty God of J... Ps 132:5 3290
LORD hath chosen J unto himself... Ps 135:4 3290
hath the God of J for his help... Ps 146:5 3290
He sheweth his word unto J... Ps 147:19 3290
to the house of the God of J... Is 2:3 3290
O house of J, come ye, and let us... Is 2:5 3290
thy people the house of J... Is 2:6 3290
his face from the house of J... Is 8:17 3290
The Lord sent a word into J... Is 9:8 3290
as are escaped of the house of J... Is 10:20 3290
return, even the remnant of J... Is 10:21 3290
For the LORD will have mercy on J... Is 14:1 3290
shall cleave to the house of J... Is 14:1 3290
that the glory of J shall be made... Is 17:4 3290
them that come of J to take root... Is 27:6 3290
shall the iniquity of J be purged... Is 27:9 3290
concerning the house of J... Is 29:22 3290
J shall not now be ashamed,... Is 29:22 3290
and sanctify the Holy One of J... Is 29:23 3290
Why sayest thou, O J, and speakest... Is 40:27 3290
J whom I have chosen, the seed of... Is 41:8 3290
Fear not, thou worm J, and ye men... Is 41:14 3290
reasons, saith the King of J... Is 41:21 3290
Who gave J for a spoil, and Israel... Is 42:24 3290
the LORD that created thee, O J... Is 43:1 3290
thou hast not called upon me, O J... Is 43:22 3290
have given J to the curse, and... Is 43:28 3290
Yet now hear, O J my servant... Is 44:1 3290
Fear not, O J, my servant... Is 44:2 3290
call himself by the name of J... Is 44:5 3290
Remember these, O J and Israel... Is 44:21 3290
for the LORD hath redeemed J... Is 44:23 3290
For J my servant's sake, and... Is 45:4 3290
I said not unto the seed of J... Is 45:19 3290
Hearken unto me, O house of J... Is 46:3 3290
Hear ye this, O house of J... Is 48:1 3290
Hearken unto me, O J and Israel,... Is 48:12 3290
LORD hath redeemed his servant J... Is 48:20 3290
to bring J again to him, Though... Is 49:5 3290
to raise up the tribes of J... Is 49:6 3290
thy Redeemer, the mighty One of J... Is 49:26 3290
and the house of J their sins... Is 58:1 3290
with the heritage of J thy father... Is 58:14 3290
that turn from transgression in J... Is 59:20 3290
thy Redeemer, the mighty One of J... Is 60:16 3290
will bring forth a seed out of J... Is 65:9 3290
word of the LORD, O house of J... Jer 2:4 3290
Declare this in the house of J... Jer 5:20 3290
The portion of J is not like them... Jer 10:16 3290
for they have eaten up J, and... Jer 10:25 3290
fear thou not, O my servant J... Jer 30:10 3290
J shall return, and shall be in... Jer 30:10 3290
Sing with gladness for J, and... Jer 31:7 3290
For the LORD hath redeemed J... Jer 31:11 3290
will I cast away the seed of J... Jer 33:26 3290
the seed of Abraham, Isaac, and J... Jer 33:26 3290
But fear not thou, O my servant J... Jer 46:27 3290
J shall return, and be in rest and... Jer 46:27 3290
O J my servant, saith the LORD... Jer 46:28 3290
The portion of J is not like them... Jer 51:19 3290
LORD hath commanded concerning J... Lam 1:17 3290
up all the habitations of J... Lam 2:2 3290
he burned against J like a... Lam 2:3 3290
unto the seed of the house of J... Eze 20:5 3290
that I have given to my servant J... Eze 28:25 3290
I have given unto J my servant... Eze 37:25 3290
I bring again the captivity of J... Eze 39:25 3290
plow, and J shall break his clods... Hos 10:11 3290
will punish J according to his... Hos 12:2 3290
J fled into the country of Syria,... Hos 12:12 3290
ye, and testify in the house of J... Amos 3:13 3290
I abhor the excellency of J... Amos 6:8 3290
by whom shall J arise... Amos 7:2 3290
by whom shall J arise... Amos 7:5 3290
hath sworn by the excellency of J... Amos 8:7 3290
utterly destroy the house of J... Amos 9:8 3290
brother J shame shall cover thee... Obad 10 3290
the house of J shall possess... Obad 17 3290
the house of J shall be a fire,... Obad 18 3290
transgression of J is all this... Mic 1:5 3290
What is the transgression of J... Mic 1:5 3290
that art named the house of J... Mic 2:7 3290
I will surely assemble, O J... Mic 2:12 3290
Hear, I pray you, O heads of J... Mic 3:1 3290
of might, to declare unto J his... Mic 3:8 3290
you, ye heads of the house of J... Mic 3:9 3290
and to the house of the God of J... Mic 4:2 3290
the remnant of J shall be in the... Mic 5:7 3290
the remnant of J shall be among... Mic 5:8 3290
Thou wilt perform the truth to J... Mic 7:20 3290
turned away the excellency of J... Nah 2:2 3290
out of the tabernacles of J... Mal 2:12 3290
ye sons of J are not consumed... Mal 3:6 3290

JACOB'S (*ja'-cubs*)
1. Refers to Jacob 1.
and said, The voice is J voice... Gen 27:22 3290
Syrian, the brother of Rebekah, J... Gen 28:5 3290
J anger was kindled against... Gen 30:2 3290
were Laban's, and the stronger J... Gen 30:42 3290
And Laban went into J tent... Gen 31:33 3290
shalt say, They be thy servant J... Gen 32:18 3290
the hollow of J thigh was out of... Gen 32:25 3290
he touched the hollow of J thigh... Gen 32:32 3290
Israel in lying with J daughter... Gen 34:7 3290
he had delight in J daughter... Gen 34:19 3290
J firstborn, and Simeon, and Levi,... Gen 35:23 3290
J heart fainted, for he believed... Gen 45:26
Reuben, J firstborn... Gen 46:8 3290
The sons of Rachel J wife... Gen 46:19 3290
besides J sons' wives, all the... Gen 46:26 3290
Was not Esau J brother... Mal 1:2 3290
Now J well was there... Jn 4:6 *2384*
2. Refers to Jacob 3.
it is even the time of J trouble... Jer 30:7 3290
again the captivity of J tents... Jer 30:18 3290

JADA (*ja'-dah*) *A grandson of Jerahmeel.*
sons of Onam were, Shammai, and J... 1Chr 2:28 3047
the sons of J the brother of... 1Chr 2:32 3047

JADAH See JARAH.

JADAI See JADAU.

JADAU (*ja'-daw*) *Married a foreigner in exile.*
Mattithiah, Zabad, Zebina, J... Ezr 10:43 3035

JADDAI See JADAU.

JADDUA (*jad'-du-ah*)
1. A Levite.
Meshezabeel, Zadok, J,... Neh 10:21 3037
2. A priest.
Jonathan, and Jonathan begat J... Neh 12:11 3037
Joiada, and Johanan, and J... Neh 12:22 3037

JADON (*ja'-don*) *A repairer of Jerusalem's wall.*
J the Meronothite, the men of... Neh 3:7 3036

JAEL (*ja'-el*) *The wife of Heber.*
of J the wife of Heber the Kenite... Judg 4:17 3278
J went out to meet Sisera, and... Judg 4:18 3278
Then J Heber's wife took a nail... Judg 4:21 3278
J came out to meet him, and said... Judg 4:22 3278
son of Anath, in the days of J... Judg 5:6 3278
Blessed above women shall J the... Judg 5:24 3278

JAGUR (*ja'-gur*) *A town in Judah.*
were Kabzeel, and Eder, and J... Josh 15:21 3017

JAH (*jah*) See JEHOVAH. *A shortened form of Jehovah.*
upon the heavens by his name J... Ps 68:4 3050

JAHALALEEL See JAHLEEL.

JAHATH (*ja'-hath*)
1. A descendant of Shobal.
Reaiah the son of Shobal begat J... 1Chr 4:2 3189
and J begat Ahumai, and Lahad... 1Chr 4:2 3189
2. A descendant of Gershom.
J his son, Zimmah his son,... 1Chr 6:20 3189
The son of J, the son of Gershom,... 1Chr 6:43 3189
3. Another descendant of Gershom.
And the sons of Shimei were, J... 1Chr 23:10 3189
J was the chief, and Zizah the... 1Chr 23:11 3189
4. A descendant of Kohath.
of the sons of Shelomoth; J... 1Chr 24:22 3189
5. A descendant of Merari.
and the overseers of them were J... 2Chr 34:12 3189

JAHAZ (*ja'-haz*) See JAHAZA, JAHAZAH, JAHZAH.
A Levitical city in Reuben.
and he came to J, and fought... Num 21:23 3096
and all his people, to fight at J... Deut 2:32 3096
people together, and pitched in J... Judg 11:20 3096
voice shall be heard even unto J... Is 15:4 3096
even unto Elealeh, and even unto J... Jer 48:34 3096

JAHAZA (*ja-ha'-zah*) See JAHAZ. *Same as Jahaz.*
And J, and Kedemoth, and Mephaath,. Josh 13:18 3096

JAHAZAH (*ja-ha'-zah*) See JAHAZ. *Same as Jahaz.*
suburbs, and J with her suburbs,... Josh 21:36 3096
upon Holon, and upon J, and upon... Jer 48:21 3096

JAHAZIAH (*ja-ha-zi'-ah*) *Son of Tikvah.*
J the son of Tikvah were employed...... Ezr 10:15 3167

JAHAZIEL (*ja-ha'-ze-el*)
1. A captain in David's army.
and Jeremiah, and J, and........................ 1Chr 12:4 3166
2. A priest.
J the priests with trumpets.................... 1Chr 16:6 3166
3. A son of Hebron.
J the third, and Jekameam the 1Chr 23:19 3166
J the third, Jekameam the fourth.... 1Chr 24:23 3166
4. A Levite.
Then upon J the son of Zechariah,....... 2Chr 20:14 3166
5. A family of exiles.
the son of J, and with him three .... Ezr 8:5 3166

JAHDAI (*jah'-dahee*) *A descendant of Caleb.*
And the sons of J 1Chr 2:47 3056

JAHDIEL (*jah'-de-el*) *Head of a family of Manasseh.*
and Jeremiah, and Hodaviah, and J...... 1Chr 5:24 3164

JAHDO (*jah'-do*) *Son of Buz.*
son of Jeshishai, the son of J.................. 1Chr 5:14 3163

JAHLEEL (*jah'-le-el*) See JAHLEELITES. *A son of Zebulun.*
Sered, and Elon, and J............................. Gen 46:14 3177
of J, the family of the.............................. Num 26:26 3177

JAHLEELITES (*jah'-le-el-ites*) *Descendants of Jahleel.*
of Jahleel, the family of the J................ Num 26:26 3178

JAHMAI (*jah'-mahee*) *A son of Tola.*
and Rephaiah, and Jeriel, and J 1Chr 7:2 3181

JAHZAH (*jah'-zah*) See JAHAZ. *A Levitical city in Reuben.*
suburbs, and J with her suburbs,........... 1Chr 6:78 3096

JAHZEEL (*jah'-ze-el*) See JAHZEELITES, JAHZIEL. *A son of Naphtali.*
J, and Guni, and Jezer, and Shillem...... Gen 46:24 3183
of J, the family of the............................. Num 26:48 3183

JAHZEELITES (*jah'-ze-el-ites*) *Descendants of Jahzeel.*
of Jahzeel, the family of the J................ Num 26:48 3184

JAHZEIAH See JAHAZIAH.

JAHZERAH (*jah'-ze-rah*) See AHAZAI. *The son of Meshullam.*
the son of Adiel, the son of J.................. 1Chr 9:12 3170

JAHZIEL (*jah'-ze-el*) See JAHZEEL. *Same as Jahzeel.*
J, and Guni, and Jezer, and Shallum, ... 1Chr 7:13 3185

JAILER
charging the *j* to keep them .... Acts 16:23 *1200*

JAIR (*ja'-ur*) See HAVOTH-JAIR, JAARE-OREGIM, JAIRITE.
1. A descendant of Judah and Manasseh.
J the son of Manasseh went and........... Num 32:41 2971
J the son of Manasseh took all.............. Deut 3:14 2971
towns of J the son of Manasseh 1Kin 4:13 2971
And Segub begat J, who had three......... 1Chr 2:22 2971
2. A judge.
And after him arose J, a Gileadite........ Judg 10:3 2971
J died, and was buried in Camon .... Judg 10:5 2971
3. A district in Bashan.
of Bashan, and all the towns of J.......... Josh 13:30 2971
and Aram, with the towns of J............... 1Chr 2:23 2971
4. Father of Mordecai.
name was Mordecai, the son of J........... Est 2:5 2971
5. Father of Elhanan.
Elhanan the son of J slew Lahmi 1Chr 20:5 2971

JAIRITE (*ja'-ur-ite*) *A descendant of Jair 1.*
Ira also the J was a chief ruler 2Sa 20:26 2972

JAIRUS (*ja-i'-rus*) *A ruler of a synagogue.*
of the synagogue, J by name................... Mk 5:22 *2383*
behold, there came a man named J........ Lk 8:41 *2383*

JAKAN (*ja'-kan*) See AKAN, JAAKAN. *A son of Ezer.*
Bilhan, and Zavan, and J......................... 1Chr 1:42 3292

JAKEH (*ja'-keh*) *Father of Agur.*
The words of Agur the son of J.............. Prov 30:1 3348

JAKIM (*ja'-kim*)
1. Son of Shimhi.
And J, and Zichri, and Zabdi,................. 1Chr 8:19 3356
2. A sanctuary servant.
to Eliashib, the twelfth to J 1Chr 24:12 3356

JAKIN See JACHINITES.

JAKINITE See JACHINITES.

JALAM See JAALAM.

JALON (*ja'-lon*) *A son of Ezra.*
Jether, and Mered, and Epher, and J.... 1Chr 4:17 3210

JAMBRES (*jam'-brees*) *An opponent of Moses.*
J withstood Moses, so do these.............. 2Ti 3:8 *2387*

JAMES (*james*) See JACOB.
1. Son of Zebedee.
J the son of Zebedee, and John his....... Mt 4:21 *2385*
J the son of Zebedee, and John his....... Mt 10:2 *2385*
six days Jesus taketh Peter, J................ Mt 17:1 *2385*
he saw J the son of Zebedee, and .... Mk 1:19 *2385*
house of Simon and Andrew, with J..... Mk 1:29 *2385*
And J the son of.................................... Mk 3:17 *2385*
and John the brother of J...................... Mk 3:17 *2385*
J, and John the brother of J .... Mk 5:37 *2385*
Jesus taketh with him Peter, and J .... Mk 9:2 *2385*
And J and John, the sons of Zebedee.... Mk 10:35 *2385*
to be much displeased with J .... Mk 10:41 *2385*
against the temple, Peter and J............. Mk 13:3 *2385*
And he taketh with him Peter and J ...... Mk 14:33 *2385*
And so was also J, and John, the .... Lk 5:10 *2385*
Peter,) and Andrew his brother, J .... Lk 6:14 *2385*
no man to go in, save Peter, and J........ Lk 8:51 *2385*
he took Peter and John and J .... Lk 9:28 *2385*
And when his disciples J and John .... Lk 9:54 *2385*
where abode both Peter, and J............... Acts 1:13 *2385*
he killed J the brother of John.............. Acts 12:2 *2385*
2. Son of Alphaeus.
J the son of Alphaeus, and.................... Mt 10:3 *2385*
J the son of Alphaeus, and.................... Mk 3:18 *2385*
J the son of Alphaeus, and Simon......... Lk 6:15 *2385*
J the son of Alphaeus, and Simon......... Acts 1:13 *2385*
3. Brother of Jesus.
and his brethren, J, and Joses, and .... Mt 13:55 *2385*
and Mary the mother of J and Joses.... Mt 27:56 *2385*
the son of Mary, the brother of J........... Mk 6:3 *2385*
and Mary the mother of J the less......... Mk 15:40 *2385*
and Mary the mother of J, and.............. Mk 16:1 *2385*
And Judas the brother of J .... Lk 6:16 *2385*
Joanna, and Mary the mother of J........ Lk 24:10 *2385*
and Judas the brother of J..................... Acts 1:13 *2385*
said, Go shew these things unto J......... Acts 12:17 *2385*
J answered, saying, Men and................ Acts 15:13 *2385*
Paul went in with us unto J .... Acts 21:18 *2385*
After that, he was seen of J.................. 1Cor 15:7 *2385*
save J the Lord's brother...................... Gal 1:19 *2385*
And when J, Cephas, and John, who..... Gal 2:9 *2385*
before that certain came from J .... Gal 2:12 *2385*
J, a servant of God and of the............... Jas 1:1 *2385*
of Jesus Christ, and brother of J.......... Jude 1 *2385*

JAMIN (*ja'-min*) See JAMINITES.
1. A son of Simeon.
Jemuel, and J, and Ohad, and Jachin,.. Gen 46:10 3226
Jemuel, and J, and Ohad, and Jachin,.. Ex 6:15 3226
of J, the family of the Jaminites............ Num 26:12 3226
sons of Simeon were, Nemuel, and J.... 1Chr 4:24 3226
2. A descendant of Hezron.
of Jerahmeel were, Maaz, and J............. 1Chr 2:27 3226
3. A priest.
Jeshua, and Bani, and Sherebiah, J........ Neh 8:7 3226

JAMINITES (*ja'-min-ites*) *Descendants of Jamin.*
of Jamin, the family of the J.................. Num 26:12 3228

JAMLECH (*jam'-lek*) *A royal descendant of Simeon.*
And Meshobab, and J, and Joshah the. 1Chr 4:34 3230

JANAI See JAANAI.

JANGLING
have turned aside unto vain *j*................. 1Ti 1:6 *3150*

JANIM See JANUM.

JANNA (*jan'-nah*) *Father of Melchi; ancestor of Jesus.*
of Melchi, which was the son of J......... Lk 3:24 *2388*

JANNAI See JANNA.

JANNES (*jan'-nees*) *An opponent of Moses.*
Now as J and Jambres withstood........... 2Ti 3:8 *2389*

JANOAH (*ja-no'-ah*) See JANOHAH. *A city in Naphtali.*
Ijon, and Abel-beth-maachah, and J..... 2Kin 15:29 3239

JANOHAH (*ja-no'-hah*) See JANOAH. *A city between Ephraim and Manasseh.*
and passed by it on the east to J........... Josh 16:6 3239
And it went down from J to Ataroth ... Josh 16:7 3239

JANUM (*ja'-num*) *A city in Judah.*
And J, and Beth-tappuah .... Josh 15:53 3241

JAPHETH (*ja'-feth*) *A son of Noah.*
and Noah begat Shem, Ham, and J....... Gen 5:32 3315
begat three sons, Shem, Ham, and J..... Gen 6:10 3315
Noah, and Shem, and Ham, and J......... Gen 7:13 3315
the ark, were Shem, and Ham, and J .... Gen 9:18 3315
J took a garment, and laid it upon......... Gen 9:23 3315
God shall enlarge J, and he shall........... Gen 9:27 3315
the sons of Noah, Shem, Ham, and J.... Gen 10:1 3315
The sons of J; Gomer .... Gen 10:2 3315
Eber, the brother of J the elder.............. Gen 10:21 3315
Noah, Shem, Ham, and J........................ 1Chr 1:4 3315
The sons of J; Gomer............................ 1Chr 1:5 3315

JAPHIA (*ja-fi'-ah*)
1. An Amorite king.
unto J king of Lachish, and unto........... Josh 10:3 3309
2. A town in Zebulun.
out to Daberath, and goeth up to J .... Josh 19:12 3309
3. A son of David.
also, and Elishua, and Nepheg, and J... 2Sa 5:15 3309
And Nogah, and Nepheg, and J.............. 1Chr 3:7 3309
And Nogah, and Nepheg, and J.............. 1Chr 14:6 3309

JAPHLET (*jaf'-let*) See JAPHLETI. *A grandson of Beriah.*
And Heber begat J, and Shomer, and... 1Chr 7:32 3310
And the sons of J..................................... 1Chr 7:33 3310
These are the children of J.................... 1Chr 7:33 3310

JAPHLETI (*jaf'-let-i*) See JAPHLET. *A landmark in Ephraim.*
down westward to the coast of J.......... Josh 16:3 3311

JAPHLETITES See JAPHLETI.

JAPHO (*ja'-fo*) See JOPPA. *A city in Dan.*
Rakkon, with the border before J .... Josh 19:46 3305

JARAH (*ja'-rah*) See JEHOADAH. *A son of Ahaz.*
And Ahaz begat J 1Chr 9:42 3294
J begat Alemeth, and Azmaveth, and... 1Chr 9:42 3294

JAREB (*ja'-reb*) *An Assyrian king.*
the Assyrian, and sent to king J............ Hos 5:13 3377
Assyria for a present to king J.............. Hos 10:6 3377

JARED (*ja'-red*) See JERED.
1. A descendant of Seth.
sixty and five years, and begat J .... Gen 5:15 3382
after he begat J eight hundred............... Gen 5:16 3382
J lived an hundred sixty and two.......... Gen 5:18 3382
J lived after he begat Enoch .... Gen 5:19 3382
all the days of J were nine.................... Gen 5:20 3382
2. Father of Enoch; ancestor of Jesus.
of Enoch, which was the son of J......... Lk 3:37 *2391*

JARESIAH *A descendant of Benjamin.*
And J, and Eliah, and Zichri, the........... 1Chr 8:27 3298

JARHA (*jar'-hah*) *An Egyptian servant.*
an Egyptian, whose name was J............ 1Chr 2:34 3398
daughter to J his servant to wife.......... 1Chr 2:35 3398

JARIB (*ja'-rib*) See JACHIN.
1. A son of Simeon.
Simeon were, Nemuel, and Jamin, J.... 1Chr 4:24 3402
2. A family of exiles.
and for Elnathan, and for J.................. Ezr 8:16 3402
3. Married a foreigner.
Maaseiah, and Eliezer, and J .... Ezr 10:18 3402

JARMUTH (*jar'-muth*) See REMETH.
1. A city in Judah.
Hebron, and unto Piram king of J......... Josh 10:3 3412
the king of Hebron, the king of J.......... Josh 10:5 3412
the king of Hebron, the king of J.......... Josh 10:23 3412
The king of J, one .... Josh 12:11 3412
J, and Adullam, Socoh, and Azekah,.... Josh 15:35 3412
J with her suburbs, En-gannim.............. Josh 21:29 3412
En-rimmon, and at Zareah, and at J..... Neh 11:29 3412

JAROAH (*ja-ro'-ah*) *A descendant of Gad.*
the son of Huri, the son of J.................. 1Chr 5:14 3386

JASHAR See JASHER.

JASHEN (*ja'-shen*) See HASHEM. *Father of several "mighty men" of David.*
the Shaalbonite, of the sons of J........... 2Sa 23:32 3464

JASHER (*ja'-shur*) *A book of songs.*
not this written in the book of J........... Josh 10:13 3477
it is written in the book of J................. 2Sa 1:18 3477

JASHOBEAM (*jash-o'-be-am*)
1. A "mighty man" of David.
J, a Hachmonite, the chief of the.......... 1Chr 11:11 3434
month was J the son of Zabdiel............ 1Chr 27:2 3434
2. Another "mighty man" of David.
and Azareel, and Joezer, and J.............. 1Chr 12:6 3434

JASHUB (*ja'-shub*) See JASHUBI-LEHEM, JOB, JASHUBITES, SHEAR-JASHUB.
1. A son of Issachar.
Of J, the family of the............................ Num 26:24 3437
Issachar were, Tola, and Puah, J.......... 1Chr 7:1 3437
2. Married a foreigner in exile.
Meshullam, Malluch, and Adaiah, J...... Ezr 10:29 3437

JASHUBI-LAHEM See JASHUBI-LEHEM.

JASHUBI-LEHEM (*jash''-u-bi-le'-hem*) *A descendant of Shelah.*
had the dominion in Moab, and J......... 1Chr 4:22 3433

JASHUBITES (*jash'-u-bites*) *Descendants of Jashub.*
Of Jashub, the family of the J............... Num 26:24 3432

JASIEL (*ja'-se-el*) *A "mighty man" of David.*
and Obed, and J the Mesobaite.............. 1Chr 11:47

JASON (*ja'-sun*)
1. A Christian in Thessalonica.
and assaulted the house of J................. Acts 17:5 *2394*
they found them not, they drew J......... Acts 17:6 *2394*
Whom J hath received:.......................... Acts 17:7 *2394*
when they had taken security of J........ Acts 17:9 *2394*
2. A relative of Paul.
my workfellow, and Lucius, and J........ Rom 16:21 *2394*

JASPER
row a beryl, and an onyx, and a *j* .... Ex 28:20 3471
row, a beryl, an onyx, and a *j*............... Ex 39:13 3471
the beryl, the onyx, and the *j*.................. Eze 28:13 3471
sat was to look upon like a *j*................... Rev 4:3 *2393*
precious, even like a *j* stone .... Rev 21:11 *2393*
of the wall of it was of *j* .... Rev 21:18 *2393*
The first foundation was *j* .... Rev 21:19 *2393*

JATHNIEL (*jath'-ne-el*) *A son of Meshelemiah.*
Zebadiah the third, J the fourth,........... 1Chr 26:2 3496

JATTIR (*jat'-tur*) *A Levitical city in Judah.*
And in the mountains, Shamir, and J.... Josh 15:48 3492
J with her suburbs, and Eshtemoa........ Josh 21:14 3492
and to them which were in J.................. 1Sa 30:27 3492
and Libnah with her suburbs, and J...... 1Chr 6:57 3492

JAVAN (*ja'-van*)
1. A son of Japheth.
Gomer, and Magog, and Madai, and J.. Gen 10:2 3120
And the sons of J .... Gen 10:4 3120
Gomer, and Magog, and Madai, and J.. 1Chr 1:5 3120
And the sons of J 1Chr 1:7 3120
2. Descendants of Javan 1.
that draw the bow, to Tubal, and J........ Is 66:19 3120
3. A city in southern Arabia.
J, Tubal, and Meshech, they were.......... Eze 27:13 3120
J going to and fro occupied in thy......... Eze 27:19 3120

JAVELIN
and took a *j* in his hand......................... Num 25:7 7420
there was a *j* in Saul's hand.................. 1Sa 18:10 2595
And Saul cast the *j*................................ 1Sa 18:11 2595
his house with his *j* in his hand............. 1Sa 19:9 2595

David even to the wall with the *j*.......... 1Sa 19:10 2595
he smote the *j* into the wall.................... 1Sa 19:10 2595
Saul cast a *j* at him to smite him.......... 1Sa 20:33 2595

JAW
with the *j* of an ass have I slain........... Judg 15:16 3895
an hollow place that was in the *j*.......... Judg 15:19 3895
or bore his *j* through with a................ Job 41:2 3895
their *j* teeth as knives, to...................... Prov 30:14 4973

JAWBONE
And he found a new *j* of an ass........... Judg 15:15 3895
With the *j* of an ass, heaps upon.......... Judg 15:16 3895
cast away the *j* out of his hand............. Judg 15:17 3895

JAWS
I brake the *j* of the wicked, and........... Job 29:17 4973
and my tongue cleaveth to my *j*........... Ps 22:15 4455
a bridle in the *j* of the people.............. Is 30:28 3895
But I will put hooks in thy *j*................. Eze 29:4 3895
back, and put hooks into thy *j*.............. Eze 38:4 3895
that take off the yoke on their *j*........... Hos 11:4 3895

JAZER *(ja'-zur)* See Jaazer. *A Levitical city in Gad.*
and when they saw the land of J.......... Num 32:1 3270
Ataroth, and Dibon, and J, and............ Num 32:3 3270
And their coast was J, and all the......... Josh 13:25 3270
her suburbs, J with her suburbs............ Josh 21:39 3270
of the river of Gad, and toward J........... 2Sa 24:5 3270
suburbs, and J with her suburbs........... 1Chr 6:81 3270
men of valour at J of Gilead.................. 1Chr 26:31 3270
they are come even unto J..................... Is 16:8 3270
weeping of J the vine of Sibmah........... Is 16:9 3270
for thee with the weeping of J............... Jer 48:32 3270
they reach even to the sea of J.............. Jer 48:32 3270

JAZIZ *(ja'-ziz) Overseer of David's flocks.*
the flocks was J the Hagerite................. 1Chr 27:31 3151

JEALOUS
for I the Lord thy God am a *j* God...... Ex 20:5 7067
whose name is J, is a *j* God.................. Ex 34:14 7065
he be *j* of his wife, and she be.............. Num 5:14 7065
he be *j* of his wife, and she be.............. Num 5:14 7065
he be *j* over his wife, and shall.............. Num 5:30 7065
is a consuming fire, even a *j* God.......... Deut 4:24 7067
for I the Lord thy God am a *j* God..... Deut 5:9 7067
(For the Lord thy God is a *j* God.......... Deut 6:15 7067
he is a *j* God.. Josh 24:19 7072
I have been very *j* for the Lord............ 1Kin 19:10 7065
I have been very *j* for the Lord............ 1Kin 19:14 7065
will be *j* for my holy name................... Eze 39:25 7065
will the Lord be *j* for his land.............. Joel 2:18 7065
God is *j*, and the Lord revengeth.......... Nah 1:2 7072
I am *j* for Jerusalem and for Zion......... Zec 1:14 7065
I was *j* for Zion with great................... Zec 8:2 7065
I was *j* for her with great fury............. Zec 8:2 7065
For I am *j* over you with godly............. 2Cor 11:2 *2206*

JEALOUSIES
This is the law of *j*, when a wife.......... Num 5:29 7068

JEALOUSY
And the spirit of *j* come upon him....... Num 5:14 7068
if the spirit of *j* come upon him........... Num 5:14 7068
for it is an offering of *j*........................ Num 5:15 7068
hands, which is the *j* offering................. Num 5:18 7068
the *j* offering out of the woman's.......... Num 5:25 7068
the spirit of *j* cometh upon him............ Num 5:30 7068
the children of Israel in my *j*................. Num 25:11 7068
his *j* shall smoke against that............... Deut 29:20 7068
him to *j* with strange gods..................... Deut 32:16 7065
They have moved me to *j* with that........ Deut 32:21 7065
I will move them to *j* with those........... Deut 32:21 7065
they provoked him to *j* with their.......... 1Kin 14:22 7065
moved him to *j* with their graven.......... Ps 78:58 7065
shall thy *j* burn like fire........................ Ps 79:5 7068
For *j* is the rage of a man...................... Prov 6:34 7068
j is cruel as the grave............................ Song 8:6 7068
he shall stir up *j* like a man of.............. Is 42:13 7068
of *j*, which provoketh to *j*...................... Eze 8:3 7069
this image of *j* in the entry.................... Eze 8:5 7068
will give thee blood in fury and *j*.......... Eze 16:38 7068
my *j* shall depart from thee, and I......... Eze 16:42 7068
And I will set my *j* against thee........... Eze 23:25 7068
Surely in the fire of my *j* have I............ Eze 36:5 7068
Behold, I have spoken in my *j*................ Eze 36:6 7068
For in my *j* and in the fire of my........... Eze 38:19 7068
be devoured by the fire of his *j*............. Zeph 1:18 7068
be devoured with the fire of my *j*........... Zeph 3:8 7068
and for Zion with a great *j*.................... Zec 1:14 7068
was jealous for Zion with great *j*........... Zec 8:2 7068
I will provoke you to *j* by them............. Rom 10:19
for to provoke them to *j*......................... Rom 11:11
Do we provoke the Lord to *j*................... 1Cor 10:22
am jealous over you with godly *j*........... 2Cor 11:2 *2205*

JEARIM *(je'-a-rim)* See Kirjath-jearim. *A mountain in Judah.*
along unto the side of mount J.............. Josh 15:10 3297

JEATERAI *(je-at'-e-rahee) A descendant of Gershom.*
his son, Zerah his son, J his son........... 1Chr 6:21 2979

JEATHERAI See Jeaterai.

JEBERECHIAH *(je-ber''-e-ki'-ah) Father of Zechariah.*
priest, and Zechariah the son of J.......... Is 8:2 3000

JEBEREKIAH See Jeberechiah.

JEBUS *(je'-bus)* See Jebusi, Jebusite, Jerusalem. *Original name of Jerusalem.*
departed, and came over against J........ Judg 19:10 2982
And when they were by J, the day........ Judg 19:11 2982
went to Jerusalem, which is J.............. 1Chr 11:4 2982
inhabitants of J said to David............... 1Chr 11:5 2982

JEBUSI *(jeb'-u-si)* See Jebusite. *Same as Jebus.*
to the side of J on the south.................. Josh 18:16 2983
And Zelah, Eleph, and J, which is......... Josh 18:28 2983

JEBUSITE *(jeb'-u-site)* See Jebusites. *Descendant of Canaan.*
And the J, and the Amorite, and the.... Gen 10:16 2983
Perizzite, the Hivite, and the J.............. Ex 33:2 2983
and the Hivite, and the J...................... Ex 34:11 2983
Perizzite, the Hivite, and the J.............. Josh 9:1 2983
the J in the mountains, and to the......... Josh 11:3 2983
unto the south side of the J.................. Josh 15:8 2983
threshingplace of Araunah the J........... 2Sa 24:16 2983
threshingfloor of Araunah the J............ 2Sa 24:18 2983
The J also, and the Amorite, and.......... 1Chr 1:14 2983
the threshingfloor of Ornan the J.......... 1Chr 21:15 2983
the threshingfloor of Ornan the J.......... 1Chr 21:18 2983
the threshingfloor of Ornan the J.......... 1Chr 21:28 2983
the threshingfloor of Ornan the J.......... 2Chr 3:1 2983
in Judah, and Ekron as a J.................... Zec 9:7 2983

JEBUSITES *(jeb'-u-sites)*
and the Girgashites, and the J.............. Gen 15:21 2983
and the Hivites, and the J..................... Ex 3:8 2983
and the Hivites, and the J..................... Ex 3:17 2983
and the Hivites, and the J..................... Ex 13:5 2983
Canaanites, the Hivites, and the J......... Ex 23:23 2983
and the Hittites, and the J.................... Num 13:29 2983
and the Hivites, and the J..................... Deut 7:1 2983
Perizzites, the Hivites, and the J.......... Deut 20:17 2983
and the Amorites, and the J.................. Josh 3:10 2983
Perizzites, the Hivites, and the J.......... Josh 12:8 2983
As for the J the inhabitants of............... Josh 15:63 2983
but the J dwell with the children........... Josh 15:63 2983
the Hivites, and the J........................... Josh 24:11 2983
the J that inhabited Jerusalem.............. Judg 1:21 2983
but the J dwell with the children........... Judg 1:21 2983
and Perizzites, and Hivites, and J......... Judg 3:5 2983
turn in into this city of the J................. Judg 19:11 2983
men went to Jerusalem unto the J......... 2Sa 5:6 2983
to the gutter, and smiteth the J............. 2Sa 5:8 2983
Perizzites, Hivites, and J..................... 1Kin 9:20 2983
where the J were, the inhabitants......... 1Chr 11:4 2983
the J first shall be chief........................ 1Chr 11:6 2983
and the Hivites, and the J..................... 2Chr 8:7 2983
Hittites, the Perizzites, the J................ Ezr 9:1 2983
and the Perizzites, and the J................. Neh 9:8 2983

JECAMIAH *(jek-a-mi'-ah)* See Jekamiah. *A son of Jeconiah.*
also, and Pedaiah, and Shenazar, J....... 1Chr 3:18 3359

JECHILIAH See Jecholiah.

JECHOLIAH *(jek-o-li'-ah)* See Jecoliah. *Mother of Uzziah.*
mother's name was J of Jerusalem......... 2Kin 15:2 3203

JECHONIAS *(jek-o-ni'-as)* See Jeconiah. *Greek form of Jeconiah.*
And Josias begat J and his brethren..... Mt 1:11 *2423*
to Babylon, J begat Salathiel................. Mt 1:12 *2423*

JECOLIAH *(jek-o-li'-ah)* See Jecholiah. *Same as Jecholiah.*
name also was J of Jerusalem................ 2Chr 26:3 3203

JECONIAH *(jek-o-ni'-ah)* See Coniah, Jechonias, Jehoiachin. *A king of Judah.*
J his son, Zedekiah his son................... 1Chr 3:16 3204
And the sons of J................................... 1Chr 3:17 3204
carried away with J king of Judah.......... Est 2:6 3204
had carried away captive J the............ Jer 24:1 3204
J the son of Jehoiakim king of.............. Jer 27:20 3204
J the son of Jehoiakim king of.............. Jer 28:4 3204
(After that J the king, and the............. Jer 29:2 3204

JEDAIAH *(jed-a-i'-ah)*
1. A descendant of Simeon.
the son of Allon, the son of J................ 1Chr 4:37 3042
2. A rebuilder of Jerusalem's wall.
repaired J the son of Harumaph............ Neh 3:10 3042
3. A priest in Jerusalem.
J, and Jehoiarib, and Jachin,.............. 1Chr 9:10 3048
to Jehoiarib, the second to J................ 1Chr 24:7 3048
the children of J, of the house.............. Ezr 2:36 3048
the children of J, of the house.............. Neh 7:39 3048
4. A family of exiles.
J the son of Joiarib, Jachin.................. Neh 11:10 3048
Shemaiah, and Joiarib, J,..................... Neh 12:6 3048
Mattenai; of J, Uzzi............................. Neh 12:19 3048
of Heldai, of Tobijah, and of J.............. Zec 6:10 3048
to Helem, and to Tobijah, and to J........ Zec 6:14 3048
5. A priest.
Sallu, Amok, Hilkiah, J......................... Neh 12:7 3048
of J, Nethaneel..................................... Neh 12:21 3048

JEDIAEL *(jed-e-a'-el)*
1. A son of Benjamin.
Bela, and Becher, and J, three.............. 1Chr 7:6 3043
The sons also of J................................. 1Chr 7:10 3043
All these the sons of J, by the............... 1Chr 7:11 3043
2. A "mighty man" of David.
J the son of Shimri, and Joha his.......... 1Chr 11:45 3043
3. A warrior in David's army.
Manasseh, Adnah, and Jozabad, and J. 1Chr 12:20 3043
4. Son of Meshelemiah.
J the second, Zebadiah the third,.......... 1Chr 26:2 3043

JEDIDAH *(je-di'-dah) Mother of King Josiah.*
And his mother's name was J............... 2Kin 22:1 3040

JEDIDIAH *(jed-id-i'-ah) Another name for Solomon.*
and he called his name J, because......... 2Sa 12:25 3041

JEDUTHUN *(jed'-u-thun) A Levite.*
the son of Galal, the son of J................ 1Chr 9:16 3038
Obed-edom also the son of J................ 1Chr 16:38 3038
And with them Heman and J, and the. 1Chr 16:41 3038
J with trumpets and cymbals for........... 1Chr 16:42 3038
the sons of J were porters.................... 1Chr 16:42 3038
of Asaph, and of Heman, and of J.......... 1Chr 25:1 3038
Of J: the sons of J................................ 1Chr 25:3 3038
under the hands of their father J.......... 1Chr 25:3 3038
to the king's order to Asaph, J.............. 1Chr 25:6 3038
of them of Asaph, of Heman, of J.......... 2Chr 5:12 3038
and of the sons of J.............................. 2Chr 29:14 3038
and Heman, and J the king's seer......... 2Chr 35:15 3038
the son of Galal, the son of J................ Neh 11:17 3038
To the chief Musician, even to J........... Ps 39:*t* 3038
To the chief Musician, to J................... Ps 62:*t* 3038
To the chief Musician, to J................... Ps 77:*t* 3038

JEEZER *(je-e'-zur)* See Abiezer, Jeezerites. *A son of Gilead.*
of J, the family of the............................ Num 26:30 372

JEEZERITES *(je-e'-zur-ites) Descendants of Jeezer.*
of Jeezer, the family of the J................. Num 26:30 373

JEGAR-SAHADUTHA
And Laban called it J............................. Gen 31:47 3026

JEHALELEEL *(je-hal-e'-le-el)* See Jehalelel. *A descendant of Judah.*
And the sons of J................................... 1Chr 4:16 3094

JEHALELEL *(je-hal'-e-lel)* See Jehaleleel. *A descendant of Merari.*
of Abdi, and Azariah the son of J.......... 2Chr 29:12 3094

JEHALLELEL See Jehalelel.

JEHDEIAH *(jeh-di'-ah)*
1. A sanctuary servant.
the sons of Shubael; J........................... 1Chr 24:20 3165
2. A herdsman of David.
the asses was J the Meronothite........... 1Chr 27:30 3165

JEHEZEKEL *(je-hez'-e-kel)* See Ezekiel. *A sanctuary servant.*
to Pethahiah, the twentieth to J............ 1Chr 24:16 3168

JEHEZEL See Jehezekel.

JEHIAH *(je-hi'-ah)* See Jehiel. *A priest.*
J were doorkeepers for the ark............. 1Chr 15:24 3174

JEHIEL *(je-hi'-el)* See Jehiah, Jeiel, Jehieli.
1. A Levite.
and Jaaziel, and Shemiramoth, and J... 1Chr 15:18 3171
and Aziel, and Shemiramoth, and J...... 1Chr 15:20 3171
Jeiel, and Shemiramoth, and J.............. 1Chr 16:5 3171
2. A Gershonite.
the chief was J, and Zetham, and......... 1Chr 23:8 3171
by the hand of J the Gershonite........... 1Chr 29:8 3171
3. A friend of David's son.
J the son of Hachmoni was with........... 1Chr 27:32 3171
4. Son of King Jehoshaphat.
of Jehoshaphat, Azariah, and J............. 2Chr 21:2 3171
5. A son of Heman.
sons of Heman; J, and Shimei.............. 2Chr 29:14 3171
6. A Levite in Hezekiah's time.
And J, and Azaziah, and Nahath, and.. 2Chr 31:13 3171
7. A chief priest.
Hilkiah and Zechariah and J................. 2Chr 35:8 3171
8. A family of exiles.
Obadiah the son of J, and with him....... Ezr 8:9 3171
9. The father of Shechaniah.
And Shechaniah the son of J................ Ezr 10:2 3171
10. A son of Harim.
and Elijah, and Shemaiah, and J.......... Ezr 10:21 3171
11. A man of Elam's family who married a foreigner.
Mattaniah, Zechariah, and J.................. Ezr 10:26 3171
12. Father of Gibeon.
dwelt the father of Gibeon, J................ 1Chr 9:35 3273
13. A "mighty man" of David.
J the sons of Hothan the Aroerite......... 1Chr 11:44 3273

JEHIELI *(je-hi'-el-i)* See Jehiel. *A sanctuary servant.*
of Laadan the Gershonite, were J......... 1Chr 26:21 3172
The sons of J; Zetham, and.................... 1Chr 26:22 3172

JEHIELITES See Jehiel.

JEHIZKIAH *(je-hiz-ki'-ah)* See Hezekiah. *A son of Shallum.*
J the son of Shallum, and Amasa.......... 2Chr 28:12 3169

JEHOADAH *(je-ho'-a-dah)* See Jarah. *Son of Ahaz.*
And Ahaz begat J.................................. 1Chr 8:36 3085
J begat Alemeth, and Azmaveth, and... 1Chr 8:36 3085

JEHOADDAH See Jehoadah.

JEHOADDAN *(je-ho-ad'-dan) Mother of King Amaziah.*
mother's name was J of Jerusalem....... 2Kin 14:2 3086
mother's name was J of Jerusalem....... 2Chr 25:1 3086

JEHOADDIN See Jehoaddan.

JEHOAHAZ *(je-ho'-a-haz)* See Ahaziah, Joahaz, Shallum.
1. Son of King Jehu.
J his son reigned in his stead................. 2Kin 10:35 3059
son of Ahaziah king of Judah J.............. 2Kin 13:1 3059
J besought the Lord, and the Lord...... 2Kin 13:4 3059
people to J but fifty horsemen............... 2Kin 13:7 3059
Now the rest of the acts of J................. 2Kin 13:8 3059
And J slept with his fathers................... 2Kin 13:9 3059
Judah began Jehoash the son of J......... 2Kin 13:10 3059
Israel all the days of J.......................... 2Kin 13:22 3059
Jehoash the son of J took again............ 2Kin 13:25 3059
the hand of J his father by war............. 2Kin 13:25 3059
J king of Israel reigned Amaziah........... 2Kin 14:1 3099
the son of J son of Jehu, king of............ 2Kin 14:8 3059
the death of Jehoash son of J............... 2Kin 14:17 3059

J

and sent to Joash, the son of J 2Chr 25:17 3059
of J king of Israel fifteen years 2Chr 25:25 3059
2. Son of King Josiah.
the land took J the son of Josiah 2Kin 23:30 3059
J was twenty and three years old 2Kin 23:31 3059
name to Jehoiakim, and took J away 2Kin 23:34 3059
J was twenty and three years old 2Chr 36:2 3059
Necho took J his brother, and 2Chr 36:4 3059
3. A son of King Jehoram.
was never a son left him, save J 2Chr 21:17 3059
the son of Joash, the son of J 2Chr 25:23 3059

JEHOASH (*je-ho'-ash*) See JOASH.
1. A king of Judah.
Seven years old was J when he 2Kin 11:21 3060
year of Jehu J began to reign 2Kin 12:1 3060
J did that which was right in the 2Kin 12:2 3060
J said to the priests, All the 2Kin 12:4 3060
twentieth year of king J the 2Kin 12:6 3060
Then king J called for Jehoiada 2Kin 12:7 3060
J king of Judah took all the 2Kin 12:18 3060
the son of J the son of Ahaziah, 2Kin 14:13 3060
2. A king of Israel.
J the son of Jehoahaz to reign 2Kin 13:10 3060
J the son of Jehoahaz took again 2Kin 13:25 3060
Then Amaziah sent messengers to J 2Kin 14:8 3060
J the king of Israel sent to 2Kin 14:9 3060
Therefore J king of Israel went 2Kin 14:11 3060
J king of Israel took Amaziah 2Kin 14:13 3060
of the acts of J which he did 2Kin 14:15 3060
J slept with his fathers, and was 2Kin 14:16 3060
J son of Jehoahaz king of Israel 2Kin 14:17 3060

JEHOHANAN (*je-ho'-ha-nan*)
1. A sanctuary servant.
J the sixth, Elioenai the seventh 1Chr 26:3 3076
2. A chief captain.
And next to him was J the captain 2Chr 17:15 3076
3. Father of Ishmael.
Jeroham, and Ishmael the son of J 2Chr 23:1 3076
4. Married a foreigner in exile.
J, Hananiah, Zabbai, and Athlai Ezr 10:28 3076
5. A priest in exile.
Meshullam; of Amariah, J Neh 12:13 3076
6. A priest who dedicated the wall.
and Eleazar, and Uzzi, and J Neh 12:42 3076

JEHOIACHIN (*je-hoy'-a-kin*) See CONIAH, JECONIAH, JECONIAS, JEHOIACHIN'S. *A king of Judah.*
J his son reigned in his stead 2Kin 24:6 3078
J was eighteen years old when he 2Kin 24:8 3078
J the king of Judah went out to 2Kin 24:12 3078
And he carried away J to Babylon 2Kin 24:15 3078
the captivity of J king of Judah 2Kin 25:27 3078
of J king of Judah out of prison 2Kin 25:27 3078
J his son reigned in his stead 2Chr 36:8 3078
J was eight years old when he 2Chr 36:9 3078
the captivity of J king of Judah Jer 52:31 3078
up the head of J king of Judah Jer 52:31 3078

JEHOIACHIN'S (*je-hoy'-a-kins*)
fifth year of king J captivity Eze 1:2 3112

JEHOIADA (*je-hoy'-a-dah*) See BERECHIAS, JOIADA.
1. Father of Benaiah.
Benaiah the son of J was over 2Sa 8:18 3111
Benaiah the son of J was over the 2Sa 20:23 3111
And Benaiah the son of J, the son 2Sa 23:20 3111
things did Benaiah the son of J 2Sa 23:22 3111
priest, and Benaiah the son of J 1Kin 1:8 3111
priest, and Benaiah the son of J 1Kin 1:26 3111
prophet, and Benaiah the son of J 1Kin 1:32 3111
the son of J answered the king 1Kin 1:36 3111
prophet, and Benaiah the son of J 1Kin 1:38 3111
prophet, and Benaiah the son of J 1Kin 1:44 3111
the hand of Benaiah the son of J 1Kin 2:25 3111
Solomon sent Benaiah the son of J 1Kin 2:29 3111
So Benaiah the son of J went up 1Kin 2:34 3111
of J in his room over the host 1Kin 2:35 3111
commanded Benaiah the son of J 1Kin 2:46 3111
the son of J was over the host 1Kin 4:4 3111
Benaiah the son of J, the son of 1Chr 11:22 3111
things did Benaiah the son of J 1Chr 11:24 3111
Benaiah the son of J was over the 1Chr 18:17 3111
month was Benaiah the son of J 1Chr 27:5 3111
2. A high priest.
And the seventh year J sent 2Kin 11:4 3111
that J the priest commanded 2Kin 11:9 3111
sabbath, and came to J the priest 2Kin 11:9 3111
But J the priest commanded the 2Kin 11:15 3111
J made a covenant between the 2Kin 11:17 3111
J the priest instructed him 2Kin 12:2 3111
Jehoash called for J the priest 2Kin 12:7 3111
But J the priest took a chest, and 2Kin 12:9 3111
Jehoram, the wife of J the priest 2Chr 22:11 3111
And in the seventh year J 2Chr 23:1 3111
that J the priest had commanded 2Chr 23:8 3111
for J the priest dismissed not 2Chr 23:8 3111
Moreover J the priest delivered 2Chr 23:9 3111
And J and his sons anointed him, and 2Chr 23:11 3111
Then J the priest brought out the 2Chr 23:14 3111
J made a covenant between him, and 2Chr 23:16 3111
Also J appointed the offices of 2Chr 23:18 3111
LORD all the days of J the priest 2Chr 24:2 3111
And J took for him two wives 2Chr 24:3 3111
the king called for J the chief 2Chr 24:6 3111
J gave it to such as did the work 2Chr 24:12 3111
of the money before the king and J 2Chr 24:14 3111
continually all the days of J 2Chr 24:14 3111
But J waxed old, and was full of 2Chr 24:15 3111
Now after the death of J came the 2Chr 24:17 3111
Zechariah the son of J the priest 2Chr 24:20 3111
not the kindness which J his 2Chr 24:22 3111
blood of the sons of J the priest 2Chr 24:25 3111
3. A captain in David's army.
J was the leader of the Aaronites 1Chr 12:27 3111
4. Son of Benaiah.
was J the son of Benaiah, and 1Chr 27:34 3111
5. A rebuilder of Jerusalem's wall.
gate repaired J the son of Paseah Neh 3:6 3111
6. A pre-exilic priest.
in the stead of J the priest Jer 29:26 3111

JEHOIAKIM (*je-hoy'-a-kim*) See ELIAKIM, JOIAKIM. *A king of Judah.*
father, and turned his name to J 2Kin 23:34 3079
J gave the silver and the gold to 2Kin 23:35 3079
J was twenty and five years old 2Kin 23:36 3079
J became his servant three years 2Kin 24:1 3079
Now the rest of the acts of J 2Kin 24:5 3079
So J slept with his fathers 2Kin 24:6 3079
according to all that J had done 2Kin 24:19 3079
firstborn Johanan, the second J 1Chr 3:15 3079
And the sons of J 1Chr 3:16 3079
and turned his name to J 2Chr 36:4 3079
J was twenty and five years old 2Chr 36:5 3079
Now the rest of the acts of J 2Chr 36:8 3079
It came also in the days of J the Jer 1:3 3079
thus saith the LORD concerning J Jer 22:18 3079
though Coniah the son of J king Jer 22:24 3079
the son of J king of Judah Jer 24:1 3079
of Judah in the fourth year of J Jer 25:1 3079
the beginning of the reign of J Jer 26:1 3079
when J the king, with all his Jer 26:21 3079
J the king sent men into Egypt, Jer 26:22 3079
and brought him unto J the king Jer 26:23 3079
the beginning of the reign of J Jer 27:1 3079
captive Jeconiah the son of J Jer 27:20 3079
the son of J king of Judah Jer 28:4 3079
from the LORD in the days of J Jer 35:1 3079
to pass in the fourth year of J Jer 36:1 3079
to pass in the fifth year of J Jer 36:9 3079
which J the king of Judah hath Jer 36:28 3079
thou shalt say to J king of Judah Jer 36:29 3079
saith the LORD of J king of Judah Jer 36:30 3079
J king of Judah had burned in the Jer 36:32 3079
instead of Coniah the son of J Jer 37:1 3079
in the fourth year of J the son Jer 45:1 3079
smote in the fourth year of J the Jer 46:2 3079
according to all that J had done Jer 52:2 3079
the reign of J king of Judah came Dan 1:1 3079
the Lord gave J king of Judah Dan 1:2 3079

JEHOIARIB (*je-hoy'-a-rib*) See JOIARIB.
1. A priest.
Jedaiah, and J, and Jachin, 1Chr 9:10 3080
2. A sanctuary servant.
Now the first lot came forth to J 1Chr 24:7 3080

JEHONADAB (*je-hon'-a-dab*) See JONADAB. *A son of Rechab.*
he lighted on J the son of Rechab 2Kin 10:15 3082
And J answered, It is 2Kin 10:15 3082
J the son of Rechab, into the 2Kin 10:23 3082

JEHONATHAN (*je-hon'-a-than*) See JONATHAN.
1. A storehouse servant.
castles, was J the son of Uzziah 1Chr 27:25 3083
2. A Levite teacher.
and Asahel, and Shemiramoth, and J 2Chr 17:8 3083
3. A priest.
of Shemaiah, J Neh 12:18 3083

JEHORAM (*je-ho'-ram*) See HADORAM, JORAM.
1. A king of Judah.
J his son reigned in his stead 1Kin 22:50 3088
J the son of Jehoshaphat king of 2Kin 1:17 3088
J the son of Jehoshaphat king of 2Kin 8:16 3088
of J king of Judah begin to reign 2Kin 8:25 3088
Ahaziah the son of J king of 2Kin 8:29 3088
things that Jehoshaphat, and J 2Kin 12:18 3088
J his son reigned in his stead 2Chr 21:1 3088
but the kingdom gave he to J 2Chr 21:3 3088
Now when J was risen up to the 2Chr 21:4 3088
J was thirty and two years old 2Chr 21:5 3088
Then J went forth with his 2Chr 21:9 3088
the LORD stirred up against J the 2Chr 21:16 3088
son of J king of Judah reigned 2Chr 22:1 3088
Azariah the son of J king of 2Chr 22:6 3088
the daughter of king J, the wife 2Chr 22:11 3088
2. A son of Ahab.
J reigned in his stead in the 2Kin 1:17 3088
Now J the son of Ahab began to 2Kin 3:1 3088
king J went out of Samaria the 2Kin 3:6 3088
smote J between his arms, and the 2Kin 9:24 3088
went with J the son of Ahab king 2Chr 22:5 3088
see J the son of Ahab at Jezreel 2Chr 22:6 3088
he went out with J against Jehu 2Chr 22:7 3088
3. A priest.
and with them Elishama and J 2Chr 17:8 3088

JEHOSHABEATH (*je-ho-shab'-e-ath*) See JEHOSHEBA. *A daughter of King Jehoram.*
But J, the daughter of the king, 2Chr 22:11 3090
So J, the daughter of king 2Chr 22:11 3090

JEHOSHAPHAT (*je-hosh'-a-fat*) See JOSAPHAT, JOSHAPHAT.
1. David's recorder.
J the son of Ahilud was recorder 2Sa 8:16 3092
J the son of Ahilud was recorder 2Sa 20:24 3092
J the son of Ahilud, the recorder 1Kin 4:3 3092
J the son of Ahilud, recorder 1Chr 18:15 3092
2. An officer of Solomon.
J the son of Paruah, in Issachar 1Kin 4:17 3092
3. A king of Judah.
J his son reigned in his stead 1Kin 15:24 3092
that J the king of Judah came 1Kin 22:2 3092
And he said unto J, Wilt thou go 1Kin 22:4 3092
J said to the king of Israel, I 1Kin 22:4 3092
J said unto the king of Israel, 1Kin 22:5 3092
J said, Is there not here a 1Kin 22:7 3092
And the king of Israel said unto J 1Kin 22:8 3092
J said, Let not the king say so 1Kin 22:8 3092
J the king of Judah sat each on 1Kin 22:10 3092
And the king of Israel said unto J 1Kin 22:18 3092
J the king of Judah went up to 1Kin 22:29 3092
And the king of Israel said unto J 1Kin 22:30 3092
captains of the chariots saw J 1Kin 22:32 3092
and J cried out 1Kin 22:32 3092
J the son of Asa began to reign 1Kin 22:41 3092
J was thirty and five years old 1Kin 22:42 3092
J made peace with the king of 1Kin 22:44 3092
Now the rest of the acts of J 1Kin 22:45 3092
J made ships of Tharshish to go 1Kin 22:48 3092
Ahaziah the son of Ahab unto J 1Kin 22:49 3092
But J would not 1Kin 22:49 3092
J slept with his fathers, and was 1Kin 22:50 3092
year of J king of Judah, and 1Kin 22:51 3092
the son of J king of Judah 2Kin 1:17 3092
year of J king of Judah, and 2Kin 3:1 3092
sent to J the king of Judah, 2Kin 3:7 3092
But J said, Is there not here a 2Kin 3:11 3092
J said, The word of the LORD is 2Kin 3:12 3092
So the king of Israel and J 2Kin 3:12 3092
presence of J the king of Judah 2Kin 3:14 3092
J being then king of Judah, 2Kin 8:16 3092
Jehoram the son of J king of 2Kin 8:16 3092
all the hallowed things that J 2Kin 12:18 3092
his son, Asa his son, J his son, 1Chr 3:10 3092
J his son reigned in his stead, 2Chr 17:1 3092
And the LORD was with J, because 2Chr 17:3 3092
all Judah brought to J presents 2Chr 17:5 3092
that they made no war against J 2Chr 17:10 3092
Philistines brought J presents 2Chr 17:11 3092
J waxed great exceedingly 2Chr 17:12 3092
Now J had riches and honour in 2Chr 18:1 3092
Israel said unto J king of Judah 2Chr 18:3 3092
J said unto the king of Israel, 2Chr 18:4 3092
But J said, Is there not here a 2Chr 18:6 3092
And the king of Israel said unto J 2Chr 18:7 3092
J said, Let not the king say so 2Chr 18:7 3092
J king of Judah sat either of 2Chr 18:9 3092
And the king of Israel said to J 2Chr 18:17 3092
J the king of Judah went up to 2Chr 18:28 3092
And the king of Israel said unto J 2Chr 18:29 3092
captains of the chariots saw J 2Chr 18:31 3092
but J cried out, and the LORD 2Chr 18:31 3092
J the king of Judah returned to 2Chr 19:1 3092
to meet him, and said to king J 2Chr 19:2 3092
And J dwelt at Jerusalem 2Chr 19:4 3092
did J set of the Levites, and of 2Chr 19:8 3092
came against J to battle 2Chr 20:1 3092
Then there came some that told J 2Chr 20:2 3092
J feared, and set himself to seek 2Chr 20:3 3092
J stood in the congregation of 2Chr 20:5 3092
of Jerusalem, and thou king J 2Chr 20:15 3092
J bowed his head with his face to 2Chr 20:18 3092
J stood and said, Hear me, O Judah 2Chr 20:20 3092
And when J and his people came to 2Chr 20:25 3092
J in the forefront of them, to go 2Chr 20:27 3092
So the realm of J was quiet 2Chr 20:30 3092
And J reigned over Judah 2Chr 20:31 3092
Now the rest of the acts of J 2Chr 20:34 3092
after this did J king of Judah 2Chr 20:35 3092
of Mareshah prophesied against J 2Chr 20:37 3092
Now J slept with his fathers, and 2Chr 21:1 3092
And he had brethren the sons of J 2Chr 21:2 3092
were the sons of J king of Israel 2Chr 21:2 3092
in the ways of J thy father 2Chr 21:12 3092
said they, he is the son of J 2Chr 22:9 3092
4. Father of Jehu.
the son of J the son of Nimshi 2Kin 9:2 3092
So Jehu the son of J the son of 2Kin 9:14 3092
5. A priest.
And Shebaniah, and J, and Nethaneel, 1Chr 15:24 3046
6. A valley near Jerusalem.
them down into the valley of J Joel 3:2 3092
and come up to the valley of J Joel 3:12 3092

JEHOSHEBA (*je-hosh'-e-bah*) See JEHOSHABEATH. *Same as Jehoshabeath.*
But J, the daughter of king Joram 2Kin 11:2 3089

JEHOSHUA (*je-hosh'-u-ah*) See JEHOSHUAH, JOSHUA. *Same as Joshua, son of Nun.*
called Oshea the son of Nun J Num 13:16 3091

JEHOSHUAH (*je-hosh'-u-ah*) *Same as Joshua, son of Nun.*
Non his son, J his son 1Chr 7:27 3091

JEHOVAH (*je-ho'-vah*) See GOD, JAH, JEHOVAH-JIREH, JEHOVAH-NISSI, JEHOVAH-SHALOM, LORD. *A name for God.*
but by my name J was I not known Ex 6:3 3068
that thou, whose name alone is J Ps 83:18 3068
for the LORD J is my strength and Is 12:2 3068
for in the LORD J is everlasting Is 26:4 3068

JEHOVAH-JIREH (*je-ho''-vah-ji'-reh*) *Mt. Moriah.*
called the name of that place J Gen 22:14 3070

JEHOVAH-NISSI (*je-ho''-vah-nis'-si*) *An altar built by Moses.*
altar, and called the name of it J Ex 17:15 3071

JEHOVAH-SHALOM (*je-ho''-vah-sha'-lom*) *An altar built by Gideon.*
unto the LORD, and called it J Judg 6:24 3073

JEHOZABAD (*je-hoz'-a-bad*) See JOZABAD.
1. Son of Shomer.
J the son of Shomer, his servants 2Kin 12:21 3075
J the son of Shimrith a Moabitess 2Chr 24:26 3075
2. A son of Obed-edom.
J the second, Joah the third, and 1Chr 26:4 3075
3. A general of Jehoshaphat.

And next him was J, and with him an. 2Chr 17:18 3075

JEHOZADAK (*je-hoz'-a-dak*) *Great-grandson of Hilkiah.*
begat Seraiah, and Seraiah begat J....... 1Chr 6:14 3087
J went into captivity, when the............ 1Chr 6:15 3087

JEHU (*je-hu*)
1. A son of Hanani.
to J the son of Hanani against.............. 1Kin 16:1 3058
J the son of Hanani came the word...... 1Kin 16:7 3058
against Baasha by J the prophet.......... 1Kin 16:12 3058
J the son of Hanani the seer went........ 2Chr 19:2 3058
the book of J the son of Hanani........... 2Chr 20:34 3058
2. A king of Israel.
J the son of Nimshi shalt thou.............. 1Kin 19:16 3058
the sword of Hazael shall J slay........... 1Kin 19:17 3058
the sword of J shall Elisha slay............ 1Kin 19:17 3058
look out there J the son of..................... 2Kin 9:2 3058
J said, Unto which of all us................... 2Kin 9:5 3058
Then J came forth to the servants........ 2Kin 9:11 3058
with trumpets, saying, J is king............ 2Kin 9:13 3058
So J the son of Jehoshaphat the........... 2Kin 9:14 3058
J said, If it be your minds, then............ 2Kin 9:15 3058
So J rode in a chariot, and went........... 2Kin 9:16 3058
spied the company of J as he came...... 2Kin 9:17 3058
J said, What hast thou to do with......... 2Kin 9:18 3058
J answered, What hast thou to do........ 2Kin 9:19 3058
driving of J the son of Nimshi............... 2Kin 9:20 3058
and they went out against J.................. 2Kin 9:21 3058
it came to pass, when Joram saw J....... 2Kin 9:22 3058
that he said, Is it peace, J..................... 2Kin 9:22 3058
J drew a bow with his full..................... 2Kin 9:24 3058
Then said J to Bidkar his captain......... 2Kin 9:25
J followed after him, and said,.............. 2Kin 9:27 3058
when J was come to Jezreel,.................. 2Kin 9:30 3058
as J entered in at the gate, she............ 2Kin 9:31 3058
J wrote letters, and sent to................... 2Kin 10:1 3058
up of the children, sent to J................... 2Kin 10:5 3058
So J slew all that remained of............... 2Kin 10:11 3058
J met with the brethren of..................... 2Kin 10:13 3058
J gathered all the people...................... 2Kin 10:18 3058
but J shall serve him much................... 2Kin 10:18 3058
But J did it in subtilty, to the............... 2Kin 10:19 3058
J said, Proclaim a solemn...................... 2Kin 10:20 3058
J sent through all Israel....................... 2Kin 10:21 3058
J went, and Jehonadab the son of......... 2Kin 10:23 3058
J appointed fourscore men without...... 2Kin 10:24 3058
that J said to the guard and to............. 2Kin 10:25 3058
Thus J destroyed Baal out of................. 2Kin 10:28 3058
J departed not from after them,............ 2Kin 10:29 3058
And the LORD said unto J, Because...... 2Kin 10:30 3058
But J took no heed to walk in the......... 2Kin 10:31 3058
Now the rest of the acts of J................. 2Kin 10:34 3058
And J slept with his fathers.................. 2Kin 10:35 3058
the time that J reigned over................. 2Kin 10:36 3058
year of J Jehoash began to reign.......... 2Kin 12:1 3058
of Judah Jehoahaz the son of J............. 2Kin 13:1 3058
the son of Jehoahaz son of J................. 2Kin 14:8 3058
of the LORD which he spake unto J....... 2Kin 15:12 3058
against J the son of Nimshi................... 2Chr 22:7 3058
when J was executing judgment............ 2Chr 22:8 3058
in Samaria,) and brought him to J......... 2Chr 22:9 3058
the son of Jehoahaz, the son of J.......... 2Chr 25:17 3058
of Jezreel upon the house of J............... Hos 1:4 3058
3. A son of Obed.
begat Jehu, and J begat Azariah,.......... 1Chr 2:38 3058
4. A son of Josibiah.
J the son of Josibiah, the son of............ 1Chr 4:35 3058
5. A warrior in David's army.
and Berachah, and J the Antothite,...... 1Chr 12:3 3058

JEHUBBAH (*je-hub'-bah*) *A descendant of Shamer.*
Ahi, and Rohgah, J, and Aram.............. 1Chr 7:34 3160

JEHUCAL (*je-hu'-kal*) See JUCAL. *A son of Shelemiah.*
king sent J the son of Shelemiah.......... Jer 37:3 3081

JEHUD (*je'-hud*) *A city in Dan.*
And J, and Bene-berak, and.................. Josh 19:45 3055

JEHUDI (*je-hu'-di*) *Son of Nethaniah.*
sent J the son of Nethaniah.................. Jer 36:14 3065
So the king sent J to fetch the.............. Jer 36:21 3065
J read it in the ears of the king............ Jer 36:21 3065
that when J had read three or.............. Jer 36:23 3065

JEHUDIJAH (*je-hu-di'-jah*) See HODIAH. *A descendant of Judah.*
his wife J bare Jered the father............. 1Chr 4:18 3057

JEHUSH (*je'-hush*) See JEUSH. *A descendant of King Saul.*
J the second, and Eliphelet the.............. 1Chr 8:39 3266

JEIEL (*je-i'-el*) See JEHIEL, JEUEL.
1. A chief Reubenite.
was reckoned, were the chief, J............. 1Chr 5:7 3273
2. A Levite gatekeeper.
and Mikneiah, and Obed-edom, and J.. 1Chr 15:18 3273
and Mikneiah, and Obed-edom, and J.. 1Chr 15:21 3273
and next to him Zechariah, J................ 1Chr 16:5 3273
J with psalteries and with harps........... 1Chr 16:5 3273
3. A Levite of the Asaph family.
the son of Benaiah, the son of J............ 2Chr 20:14 3273
4. A scribe.
by the hand of J the scribe.................. 2Chr 26:11 3273
5. A Levite in Hezekiah's time.
Shimri, and J: and of the sons............... 2Chr 29:13 3273
6. A chief Levite.
his brethren, and Hashabiah and J........ 2Chr 35:9 3273
7. An exile.
names are these, Eliphelet, J................. Ezr 8:13 3273
8. Married a foreigner in exile.
J, Mattithiah, Zabad, Zebina,................. Ezr 10:43 3273

JEKABZEEL (*je-kab'-ze-el*) See KABZEEL. *A city in Judah.*
in the villages thereof, and at J............. Neh 11:25 3343

JEKAMEAM (*je-kam'-e-am*) *Son of Hebron.*
the third, and J the fourth.................... 1Chr 23:19 3360
Jahaziel the third, J the fourth.............. 1Chr 24:23 3360

JEKAMIAH (*jek-a-mi'-ah*) See JECAMIAH. *A descendant of Shallum.*
And Shallum begat J............................. 1Chr 2:41 3359
and J begat Elishama............................ 1Chr 2:41 3359

JEKUTHIEL (*je-ku'-the-el*) *A descendant of Ezra.*
Socho, and J the father of Zanoah........ 1Chr 4:18 3354

JEMIMA (*je-mi'-mah*) *A daughter of Job.*
called the name of the first, J................. Job 42:14 3224

JEMIMAH See JEMIMA.

JEMUEL (*je-mu'-el*) See NEMUEL. *A son of Simeon.*
J, and Jamin, and Ohad, and Jachin,.... Gen 46:10 3223
J, and Jamin, and Ohad, and Jachin,.... Ex 6:15 3223

JEOPARDED
Naphtali were a people that *j*................. Judg 5:18 2778

JEOPARDY
men that went in *j* of their lives........... 2Sa 23:17
that have put their lives in *j*................. 1Chr 11:19
for with the *j* of their lives.................... 1Chr 11:19
master Saul to the *j* of our heads.......... 1Chr 12:19
filled with water, and were in *j*.............. Lk 8:23 *2793*
And why stand we in *j* every hour........ 1Cor 15:30 *2793*

JEPHTHAE (*jef'-thah-e*) See JEPHTHAH. *Same as Jephthah.*
of Barak, and of Samson, and of J........ Heb 11:32 *2422*

JEPHTHAH (*jef'-thah*) See JEPHTHAE, JIPHTHAH-EL. *A judge.*
Now J the Gileadite was a mighty........ Judg 11:1 3316
and Gilead begat J................................. Judg 11:1 3316
grew up, and they thrust out J.............. Judg 11:2 3316
Then J fled from his brethren, and....... Judg 11:3 3316
there were gathered vain men to J....... Judg 11:3 3316
to fetch J out of the land of Tob........... Judg 11:5 3316
And they said unto J, Come, and be..... Judg 11:6 3316
J said unto the elders of Gilead............ Judg 11:7 3316
the elders of Gilead said unto J............ Judg 11:8 3316
J said unto the elders of Gilead,........... Judg 11:9 3316
the elders of Gilead said unto J............ Judg 11:10 3316
Then J went with the elders of.............. Judg 11:11 3316
J uttered all his words before............... Judg 11:11 3316
J sent messengers unto the king........... Judg 11:12 3316
answered unto the messengers of J....... Judg 11:13 3316
J sent messengers again unto the......... Judg 11:14 3316
And said unto him, Thus saith J........... Judg 11:15 3316
the words of J which he sent him.......... Judg 11:28 3316
Spirit of the LORD came upon J............. Judg 11:29 3316
J vowed a vow unto the LORD, and....... Judg 11:30 3316
So J passed over unto the..................... Judg 11:32 3316
J came to Mizpeh unto his house,.......... Judg 11:34 3316
to lament the daughter of J the............ Judg 11:40 3316
and went northward, and said unto J.. Judg 12:1 3316
J said unto them, I and my people........ Judg 12:2 3316
Then J gathered together all the.......... Judg 12:4 3316
J judged Israel six years...................... Judg 12:7 3316
Then died J the Gileadite, and was....... Judg 12:7 3316
sent Jerubbaal, and Bedan, and J......... 1Sa 12:11 3316

JEPHUNNEH (*je-fun'-neh*)
1. Father of Caleb.
of Judah, Caleb the son of J.................. Num 13:6 3312
son of Nun, and Caleb the son of J....... Num 14:6 3312
therein, save Caleb the son of J........... Num 14:30 3312
son of Nun, and Caleb the son of J....... Num 14:38 3312
of them, save Caleb the son of J........... Num 26:65 3312
Caleb the son of J the Kenezite............. Num 32:12 3312
of Judah, Caleb the son of J.................. Num 34:19 3312
Save Caleb the son of J......................... Deut 1:36 3312
Caleb the son of J the Kenezite............. Josh 14:6 3312
of J Hebron for an inheritance.............. Josh 14:13 3312
of J the Kenezite unto this day.............. Josh 14:14 3312
unto Caleb the son of J he gave a.......... Josh 15:13 3312
the son of J for his possession............... Josh 21:12 3312
And the sons of Caleb the son of J........ 1Chr 4:15 3312
they gave to Caleb the son of J............. 1Chr 6:56 3312
2. Head of an Asherite family.
J, and Pispah, and Ara.......................... 1Chr 7:38 3312

JERAH (*je'-rah*) *A son of Joktan.*
and Sheleph, and Hazarmaveth, and J. Gen 10:26 3392
and Sheleph, and Hazarmaveth, and J. 1Chr 1:20 3392

JERAHMEEL (*je-rah'-me-el*) See JERAHMEELITES.
1. A son of Hezron.
J, and Ram, and Chelubai...................... 1Chr 2:9 3396
the sons of J the firstborn of................. 1Chr 2:25 3396
J had also another wife, whose.............. 1Chr 2:26 3396
of Ram the firstborn of J were.............. 1Chr 2:27 3396
These were the sons of J....................... 1Chr 2:33 3396
of Caleb the brother of J were.............. 1Chr 2:42 3396
2. A son of Kish.
the son of Kish was J............................ 1Chr 24:29 3396
3. An officer of Jehoiakim.
commanded J the son of Hammelech... Jer 36:26 3396

JERAHMEELITES (*je-rah'-me-el-ites*) *Descendants of Jerahmeel.*
and against the south of the J.............. 1Sa 27:10 3397
which were in the cities of the J........... 1Sa 30:29 3397

JERED (*je'-red*) See JARED.
1. A descendant of Seth.
Kenan, Mahalaleel, J,............................. 1Chr 1:2 3382
2. A descendant of Ezra.
bare J the father of Gedor..................... 1Chr 4:18 3382

JEREMAI (*jer'-e-mahee*) *Married a foreigner in exile.*
Mattathah, Zabad, Eliphelet, J.............. Ezr 10:33 3413

JEREMIAH (*jer-e-mi'-ah*) See JEREMIAH'S, JEREMIAS, JEREMY.
1. Father of Hamutal.
the daughter of J of Libnah.................. 2Kin 23:31 3414
the daughter of J of Libnah.................. 2Kin 24:18 3414
the daughter of J of Libnah.................. Jer 52:1 3414
2. Head of a Manassite family.
Ishi, and Eliel, and Azriel, and J........... 1Chr 5:24 3414
3. A warrior in David's army.
and J, and Jahaziel, and Johanan, and. 1Chr 12:4 3414
4. A Gadite warrior.
the fourth, J the fifth,............................ 1Chr 12:10 3414
5. Another Gadite warrior.
J the tenth, Machbanai the.................... 1Chr 12:13 3414
6. A prophet.
And J lamented for Josiah..................... 2Chr 35:25 3414
humbled not himself before J the......... 2Chr 36:12 3414
of the LORD by the mouth of J.............. 2Chr 36:21 3414
mouth of J might be accomplished........ 2Chr 36:22 3414
the mouth of J might be fulfilled........... Ezr 1:1 3414
The words of J the son of Hilkiah.......... Jer 1:1 3414
the LORD came unto me, saying, J......... Jer 1:11 3414
word that came to J from the LORD...... Jer 7:1 3414
word that came to J from the LORD...... Jer 11:1 3414
came to J concerning the dearth.......... Jer 14:1 3414
which came to J from the LORD............ Jer 18:1 3414
let us devise devices against J............. Jer 18:18 3414
Then came J from Tophet, whither........ Jer 19:14 3414
heard that J prophesied these............... Jer 20:1 3414
Then Pashur smote J the prophet.......... Jer 20:2 3414
brought forth J out of the stocks.......... Jer 20:3 3414
Then said J unto him, The LORD........... Jer 20:3 3414
which came unto J from the LORD.......... Jer 21:1 3414
Then said J unto them, Thus shall......... Jer 21:3 3414
LORD unto me, What seest thou, J......... Jer 24:3 3414
The word that came to J....................... Jer 25:1 3414
The which J the prophet spake.............. Jer 25:2 3414
which J hath prophesied against........... Jer 25:13 3414
all the people heard J speaking............ Jer 26:7 3414
when J had made an end of.................. Jer 26:8 3414
J in the house of the LORD.................... Jer 26:9 3414
Then spake J unto all the princes......... Jer 26:12 3414
according to all the words of J............. Jer 26:20 3414
the son of Shaphan was with J.............. Jer 26:24 3414
this word unto J from the LORD............ Jer 27:1 3414
Then the prophet J said unto the.......... Jer 28:5 3414
Even the prophet J said, Amen............. Jer 28:6 3414
the prophet J went his way.................. Jer 28:11 3414
the LORD came unto J the prophet........ Jer 28:12 3414
off the neck of the prophet J................ Jer 28:12 3414
Then said the prophet J unto............... Jer 28:15 3414
the words of the letter that J............... Jer 29:1 3414
thou not reproved J of Anathoth.......... Jer 29:27 3414
in the ears of J the prophet................. Jer 29:29 3414
came the word of the LORD unto J........ Jer 29:30 3414
word that came to J from the LORD...... Jer 30:1 3414
The word that came to J from the......... Jer 32:1 3414
J the prophet was shut up in the.......... Jer 32:2 3414
J said, The word of the LORD came........ Jer 32:6 3414
came the word of the LORD unto J........ Jer 32:26 3414
LORD came unto J the second time........ Jer 33:1 3414
the word of the LORD came unto J........ Jer 33:19 3414
the word of the LORD came to J........... Jer 33:23 3414
which came unto J from the LORD.......... Jer 34:1 3414
Then J the prophet spake all................ Jer 34:6 3414
that came unto J from the LORD........... Jer 34:8 3414
the LORD came to J from the LORD........ Jer 34:12 3414
The word which came unto J from......... Jer 35:1 3414
I took Jaazaniah the son of J................ Jer 35:3 3414
came the word of the LORD unto J........ Jer 35:12 3414
J said unto the house of the................ Jer 35:18 3414
word came unto J from the LORD.......... Jer 36:1 3414
Then J called Baruch the son of........... Jer 36:4 3414
of J all the words of the LORD.............. Jer 36:4 3414
J commanded Baruch, saying, I am........ Jer 36:5 3414
that J the prophet commanded him...... Jer 36:8 3414
of J in the house of the LORD............... Jer 36:10 3414
Baruch, Go, hide thee, thou and J........ Jer 36:19 3414
the scribe and J the prophet................ Jer 36:26 3414
the word of the LORD came to J........... Jer 36:27 3414
Baruch wrote at the mouth of J............ Jer 36:27 3414
Then took J another roll, and gave....... Jer 36:32 3414
J all the words of the book which......... Jer 36:32 3414
which he spake by the prophet J........... Jer 37:2 3414
the priest to the prophet J.................. Jer 37:3 3414
Now J came in and went out among..... Jer 37:4 3414
of the LORD unto the prophet J............ Jer 37:6 3414
Then J went forth out of...................... Jer 37:12 3414
he took J the prophet, saying,.............. Jer 37:13 3414
Then said J, It is false........................ Jer 37:14 3414
so Irijah took J, and brought him......... Jer 37:14 3414
the princes were wroth with J.............. Jer 37:15 3414
When J was entered into the................ Jer 37:16 3414
J had remained there many days.......... Jer 37:16 3414
And J said, There is............................ Jer 37:17 3414
Moreover J said unto king.................... Jer 37:18 3414
that they should commit J into............. Jer 37:21 3414
Thus J remained in the court of........... Jer 37:21 3414
heard the words that J had spoken....... Jer 38:1 3414
Then took they J, and cast him............ Jer 38:6 3414
and they let down J with cords............. Jer 38:6 3414
so J sunk in the mire........................... Jer 38:6 3414
they had put J in the dungeon............. Jer 38:7 3414
they have done to J the prophet........... Jer 38:9 3414
take up J the prophet out of the........... Jer 38:10 3414
by cords into the dungeon to J............. Jer 38:11 3414
the Ethiopian said unto J..................... Jer 38:12 3414
And J did so....................................... Jer 38:12 3414
So they drew up J with cords............... Jer 38:13 3414

J

J remained in the court of the Jer 38:13 3414
took J the prophet unto him into Jer 38:14 3414
and the king said unto J, I will Jer 38:14 3414
Then J said unto Zedekiah, If I Jer 38:15 3414
the king sware secretly unto J Jer 38:16 3414
Then said J unto Zedekiah, Thus Jer 38:17 3414
And Zedekiah the king said unto J Jer 38:19 3414
But J said, They shall not Jer 38:20 3414
Then said Zedekiah unto J Jer 38:24 3414
Then came all the princes unto J Jer 38:27 3414
So J abode in the court of the Jer 38:28 3414
J to Nebuzar-adan the captain of Jer 39:11 3414
took J out of the court of the Jer 39:14 3414
the word of the LORD came unto J Jer 39:15 3414
word that came to J from the LORD Jer 40:1 3414
the captain of the guard took J Jer 40:2 3414
Then went J unto Gedaliah the son Jer 40:6 3414
said unto J the prophet, Let, we Jer 42:2 3414
Then J the prophet said unto them Jer 42:4 3414
Then they said to J, The LORD be Jer 42:5 3414
the word of the LORD came unto J Jer 42:7 3414
that when J had made an end of Jer 43:1 3414
all the proud men, saying unto J Jer 43:2 3414
J the prophet, and Baruch the son Jer 43:6 3414
of the LORD unto J in Tahpanhes Jer 43:8 3414
The word that came to J Jer 44:1 3414
of Egypt, in Pathros, answered J Jer 44:15 3414
Then J said unto all the people, Jer 44:20 3414
Moreover J said unto all the Jer 44:24 3414
The word that J the prophet spake Jer 45:1 3414
words in a book at the mouth of J Jer 45:1 3414
came to J the prophet against the Jer 46:1 3414
the LORD spake to J the prophet Jer 46:13 3414
came to J the prophet against the Jer 47:1 3414
word of the LORD that came to J Jer 49:34 3414
of the Chaldeans by J the prophet Jer 50:1 3414
The word which J the prophet Jer 51:59 3414
So J wrote in a book all the evil Jer 51:60 3414
J said to Seraiah, When thou Jer 51:61 3414
Thus far are the words of J Jer 51:64 3414
of the LORD came to J the prophet Dan 9:2 3414
7. A priest.
Seraiah, Azariah, J, Neh 10:2 3414
Seraiah, J, Ezra, Neh 12:1 3414
of J, Hananiah Neh 12:12 3414
and Benjamin, and Shemaiah, and J Neh 12:34 3414

JEREMIAH'S (*jer-e-mi'-ahz*) *Refers to Jeremiah 6.*
yoke from off the prophet J neck Jer 28:10 3414

JEREMIAS (*jer-e-mi'-as*) See JEREMIAH. *Greek form of Jeremiah.*
and others, J, or one of the Mt 16:14 *2408*

JEREMOTH (*jer'-e-moth*) See JERIMOTH.
1. A son of Beriah.
And Ahio, Shashak, and J, 1Chr 8:14 3406
2. A son of Elam.
and Jehiel, and Abdi, and J Ezr 10:26 3406
3. Another who married a foreigner in exile.
Eliashib, Mattaniah, and J Ezr 10:27 3406
4. A son of Mushi.
Mahli, and Eder, and J, three 1Chr 23:23 3406
5. A sanctuary servant.
The fifteenth to J, he, his sons, 1Chr 25:22 3406

JEREMY (*jer'-e-mee*) See JEREMIAH. *Latin form of Jeremiah.*
which was spoken by J the prophet Mt 2:17 *2408*
which was spoken by J the prophet Mt 27:9 *2408*

JERIAH (*je-ri'-ah*) See JERIJAH. *A descendant of Hebron.*
J the first, Amariah the second, 1Chr 23:19 3404
J the first, Amariah the second, 1Chr 24:23 3404

JERIBAI (*jer'-ib-ahee*) *A "mighty man" of David.*
Eliel the Mahavite, and J, and 1Chr 11:46 3403

JERICHO (*jer'-ik-o*) *A city in Benjamin.*
of Moab on this side Jordan by J Num 22:1 3405
plains of Moab by Jordan near J Num 26:3 3405
plains of Moab by Jordan near J Num 26:63 3405
Moab, which are by Jordan near J Num 31:12 3405
plains of Moab by Jordan near J Num 33:48 3405
plains of Moab by Jordan, near J Num 33:50 3405
this side Jordan near J eastward Num 34:15 3405
plains of Moab by Jordan near J Num 35:1 3405
plains of Moab by Jordan near J Num 36:13 3405
of Moab, that is over against J Deut 32:49 3405
of Pisgah, that is over against J Deut 34:1 3405
and the plain of the valley of J Deut 34:3 3405
saying, Go view the land, even J Josh 2:1 3405
And it was told the king of J Josh 2:2 3405
the king of J sent unto Rahab, Josh 2:3 3405
passed over right against J Josh 3:16 3405
unto battle, to the plains of J Josh 4:13 3405
Gilgal, in the east border of J Josh 4:19 3405
month at even in the plains of J Josh 5:10 3405
to pass, when Joshua was by J Josh 5:13 3405
Now J was straitly shut up Josh 6:1 3405
I have given into thine hand J Josh 6:2 3405
which Joshua sent to spy out J Josh 6:25 3405
riseth up and buildeth this city J Josh 6:26 3405
And Joshua sent men from J to Ai Josh 7:2 3405
and her king as thou didst unto J Josh 8:2 3405
heard what Joshua had done unto J Josh 9:3 3405
as he had done to J and her king, Josh 10:1 3405
as he did unto the king of J Josh 10:28 3405
as he did unto the king of J Josh 10:30 3405
The king of J, one Josh 12:9 3405
on the other side Jordan, by J Josh 13:32 3405
of Joseph fell from Jordan by J Josh 16:1 3405
unto the water of J on the east Josh 16:1 3405
from J throughout mount Beth-el Josh 16:1 3405
and to Naarath, and came to J Josh 16:7 3405
the side of J on the north side Josh 18:12 3405
to their families were J, and Josh 18:21 3405
other side Jordan by J eastward Josh 20:8 3405
went over Jordan, and came unto J Josh 24:11 3405
the men of J fought against you, Josh 24:11 3405
Tarry at J until your beards be 2Sa 10:5 3405
did Hiel the Beth-elite build J 1Kin 16:34 3405
for the LORD hath sent me to J 2Kin 2:4 3405
So they came to J 2Kin 2:4 3405
that were at J came to Elisha 2Kin 2:5 3405
which were to view at J saw him 2Kin 2:15 3405
to him, (for he tarried at J 2Kin 2:18 3405
overtook him in the plains of J 2Kin 25:5 3405
And on the other side Jordan by J 1Chr 6:78 3405
Tarry at J until your beards be 1Chr 19:5 3405
upon asses, and brought them to J 2Chr 28:15 3405
The children of J, three hundred Ezr 2:34 3405
unto him builded the men of J Neh 3:2 3405
The children of J, three hundred Neh 7:36 3405
Zedekiah in the plains of J Jer 39:5 3405
Zedekiah in the plains of J Jer 52:8 3405
And as they departed from J Mt 20:29 *2410*
And they came to J Mk 10:46 *2410*
as he went out of J with his Mk 10:46 *2410*
man went down from Jerusalem to J Lk 10:30 *2410*
that as he was come nigh unto J Lk 18:35 *2410*
Jesus entered and passed through J Lk 19:1 *2410*
By faith the walls of J fell down Heb 11:30 *2410*

JERIEL (*je-ri'-el*) *A son of Tola.*
Uzzi, and Rephaiah, and J, and 1Chr 7:2 3400

JERIJAH (*je-ri'-jah*) *Same as Jeriah.*
the Hebronites was J the chief 1Chr 26:31 3404

JERIMOTH (*jer'-im-oth*) See JEREMOTH.
1. A son of Bela.
Ezbon, and Uzzi, and Uzziel, and J 1Chr 7:7 3406
2. A son of Becher.
and Elioenai, and Omri, and J 1Chr 7:8 3406
3. A warrior in David's army.
Eluzai, and J, and Bealiah, and 1Chr 12:5 3406
4. A son of Mushi.
Mahli, and Eder, and J 1Chr 24:30 3406
5. A sanctuary servant.
Mattaniah, Uzziel, Shebuel, and J 1Chr 25:4 3406
6. A Naphtalite ruler.
of Naphtali, J the son of Azriel 1Chr 27:19 3406
7. A son of David.
of J the son of David to wife 2Chr 11:18 3406
8. A Temple servant.
and Nahath, and Asahel, and J 2Chr 31:13 3406

JERIOTH (*je'-re-oth*) *A wife of Caleb.*
of Azubah his wife, and of J 1Chr 2:18 3408

JEROBOAM (*jer-o-bo'-am*) See JEROBOAM'S.
1. A king of Israel.
J the son of Nebat, an Ephrathite 1Kin 11:26 3379
the man J was a mighty man of 1Kin 11:28 3379
time when J went out of Jerusalem 1Kin 11:29 3379
And he said to J, Take thee ten 1Kin 11:31 3379
sought therefore to kill J 1Kin 11:40 3379
J arose, and fled into Egypt, unto 1Kin 11:40 3379
when J the son of Nebat, who was 1Kin 12:2 3379
king Solomon, and J dwelt in Egypt 1Kin 12:2 3379
And J and all the congregation of 1Kin 12:3 3379
So J and all the people came to 1Kin 12:12 3379
Shilonite unto J the son of Nebat 1Kin 12:15 3379
heard that J was come again 1Kin 12:20 3379
Then J built Shechem in mount 1Kin 12:25 3379
J said in his heart, Now shall 1Kin 12:26 3379
J ordained a feast in the eighth 1Kin 12:32 3379
J stood by the altar to burn 1Kin 13:1 3379
when king J heard the saying of 1Kin 13:4 3379
After this thing J returned not 1Kin 13:33 3379
became sin unto the house of J 1Kin 13:34 3379
Abijah the son of J fell sick 1Kin 14:1 3379
J said to his wife, Arise, I pray 1Kin 14:2 3379
be not known to be the wife of J 1Kin 14:2 3379
the wife of J cometh to ask a 1Kin 14:5 3379
he said, Come in, thou wife of J 1Kin 14:6 3379
Go, tell J, Thus saith the LORD 1Kin 14:7 3379
bring evil upon the house of J 1Kin 14:10 3379
will cut off from J him that 1Kin 14:10 3379
the remnant of the house of J 1Kin 14:10 3379
Him that dieth of J in the city 1Kin 14:11 3379
for he only of J shall come to 1Kin 14:13 3379
God of Israel in the house of J 1Kin 14:13 3379
cut off the house of J that day 1Kin 14:14 3379
up because of the sins of J 1Kin 14:16 3379
And the rest of the acts of J 1Kin 14:19 3379
the days which J reigned were two 1Kin 14:20 3379
Rehoboam and J all their days 1Kin 14:30 3379
in the eighteenth year of king J 1Kin 15:1 3379
J all the days of his life 1Kin 15:6 3379
there was war between Abijam and J 1Kin 15:7 3379
in the twentieth year of J king 1Kin 15:9 3379
Nadab the son of J began to reign 1Kin 15:25 3379
that he smote all the house of J 1Kin 15:29 3379
he left not to J any that 1Kin 15:29 3379
of the sins of J which he sinned 1Kin 15:30 3379
LORD, and walked in the way of J 1Kin 15:34 3379
thou hast walked in the way of J 1Kin 16:2 3379
the house of J the son of Nebat 1Kin 16:3 3379
in being like the house of J 1Kin 16:7 3379
LORD, in walking in the way of J 1Kin 16:19 3379
all the way of J the son of Nebat 1Kin 16:26 3379
in the sins of J the son of Nebat 1Kin 16:31 3379
the house of J the son of Nebat 1Kin 21:22 3379
in the way of J the son of Nebat, 1Kin 22:52 3379
the sins of J the son of Nebat 2Kin 3:3 3379
the house of J the son of Nebat 2Kin 9:9 3379
the sins of J the son of Nebat 2Kin 10:29 3379
departed not from the sins of J 2Kin 10:31 3379
the sins of J the son of Nebat 2Kin 13:2 3379
from the sins of the house of J 2Kin 13:6 3379
the sins of J the son of Nebat 2Kin 13:11 3379
the sins of J the son of Nebat 2Kin 14:24 3379
the sins of J the son of Nebat 2Kin 15:9 3379
the sins of J the son of Nebat 2Kin 15:18 3379
the sins of J the son of Nebat 2Kin 15:24 3379
the sins of J the son of Nebat 2Kin 15:28 3379
they made J the son of Nebat king 2Kin 17:21 3379
J drave Israel from following the 2Kin 17:21 3379
in all the sins of J which he did 2Kin 17:22 3379
place which J the son of Nebat 2Kin 23:15 3379
seer against J the son of Nebat 2Chr 9:29 3379
when J the son of Nebat, who was 2Chr 10:2 3379
that J returned out of Egypt 2Chr 10:2 3379
So J and all Israel came and spake 2Chr 10:3 3379
So J and all the people came to 2Chr 10:12 3379
Shilonite to J the son of Nebat 2Chr 10:15 3379
and returned from going against J 2Chr 11:4 3379
for J and his sons had cast them 2Chr 11:14 3379
between Rehoboam and J continually 2Chr 12:15 3379
king J began Abijah to reign over 2Chr 13:1 3379
there was war between Abijah and J 2Chr 13:2 3379
J also set the battle in array 2Chr 13:3 3379
Ephraim, and said, Hear me, thou J 2Chr 13:4 3379
Yet J the son of Nebat, the 2Chr 13:6 3379
which J made you for gods 2Chr 13:8 3379
But J caused an ambushment to 2Chr 13:13 3379
it came to pass, that God smote J 2Chr 13:15 3379
And Abijah pursued after J 2Chr 13:19 3379
Neither did J recover strength 2Chr 13:20 3379
2. Another king of Israel, son of Jehoash.
and J sat upon his throne 2Kin 13:13 3379
J his son reigned in his stead 2Kin 14:16 3379
the son of Joash king of Judah J 2Kin 14:23 3379
by the hand of J the son of Joash 2Kin 14:27 3379
Now the rest of the acts of J 2Kin 14:28 3379
J slept with his fathers, even 2Kin 14:29 3379
seventh year of J king of Israel 2Kin 15:1 3379
of J reign over Israel in Samaria 2Kin 15:8 3379
in the days of J king of Israel 1Chr 5:17 3379
in the days of J the son of Joash Hos 1:1 3379
in the days of J the son of Joash Amos 1:1 3379
the house of J with the sword Amos 7:9 3379
Beth-el sent to J king of Israel Amos 7:10 3379
J shall die by the sword, and Amos 7:11 3379

JEROBOAM'S (*jer-o-bo'-ams*) *Refers to Jeroboam 1.*
J wife did so, and arose, and went 1Kin 14:4 3379
J wife arose, and departed, and 1Kin 14:17 3379

JEROHAM (*je-ro'-ham*)
1. Grandfather of Samuel.
name was Elkanah, the son of J 1Sa 1:1 3395
J his son, Elkanah his son 1Chr 6:27 3395
The son of Elkanah, the son of J 1Chr 6:34 3395
2. Head of a Benjamite family.
Eliah, and Zichri, the sons of J 1Chr 8:27 3395
3. A descendant of Benjamin.
And Ibneiah the son of J, and Elah 1Chr 9:8 3395
4. A family of exiles.
And Adaiah the son of J, the son 1Chr 9:12 3395
and Adaiah the son of J, the son Neh 11:12 3395
5. A warrior in David's army.
Zebadiah, the sons of J of Gedor 1Chr 12:7 3395
6. Father of Azareel.
Of Dan, Azareel the son of J 1Chr 27:22 3395
7. Father of Azariah.
of hundreds, Azariah the son of J 2Chr 23:1 3395

JERUBBAAL (*je-rub'-ba-al*) See GIDEON, JERUBBESHETH. *Another name for Gideon.*
on that day he called him J Judg 6:32 3378
Then J, who is Gideon, and all the Judg 7:1 3378
J the son of Joash went and dwelt Judg 8:29 3378
they kindness to the house of J Judg 8:35 3378
Abimelech the son of J went to Judg 9:1 3378
either that all the sons of J Judg 9:2 3378
slew his brethren the sons of J Judg 9:5 3378
the youngest son of J was left Judg 9:5 3378
and if ye have dealt well with J Judg 9:16 3378
dealt truly and sincerely with J Judg 9:19 3378
and ten sons of J might come Judg 9:24 3378
is not he the son of J Judg 9:28 3378
the curse of Jotham the son of J Judg 9:57 3378
And the LORD sent J, and Bedan, and 1Sa 12:11 3378

JERUBBESHETH (*je-rub'-be-sheth*) See JERUBBAAL. *Another name for Gideon.*
Who smote Abimelech the son of J 2Sa 11:21 3380

JERUEL (*je-ru'-el*) *A wilderness in Judah.*
brook, before the wilderness of J 2Chr 20:16 3385

JERUSALEM (*je-ru'-sa-lem*) See JERUSALEM'S, SALEM. *City where the Temple was located.*
when Adoni-zedek king of J had Josh 10:1 3389
Wherefore Adoni-zedek king of J Josh 10:3 3389
of the Amorites, the king of J Josh 10:5 3389
out of the cave, the king of J Josh 10:23 3389
The king of J, one Josh 12:10 3389
Jebusite; the same is J Josh 15:8 3389
Jebusites the inhabitants of J Josh 15:63 3389
of Judah at J unto this day Josh 15:63 3389
Eleph, and Jebusi, which is J Josh 18:28 3389
And they brought him to J, and Judg 1:7 3389
of Judah had fought against J Judg 1:8 3389
the Jebusites that inhabited J Judg 1:21 3389
of Benjamin in J unto this day Judg 1:21 3389
over against Jebus, which is J Judg 19:10 3389
Philistine, and brought it to J 1Sa 17:54 3389
in J he reigned thirty and three 2Sa 5:5 3389
his men went to J unto the 2Sa 5:6 3389
more concubines and wives out of J 2Sa 5:13 3389
that were born unto him in J 2Sa 5:14 3389
Hadadezer, and brought them to J 2Sa 8:7 3389
So Mephibosheth dwelt in J 2Sa 9:13 3389

Context	Reference	Strong's
children of Ammon, and came to J	2Sa 10:14	3389
But David tarried still at J	2Sa 11:1	3389
So Uriah abode in J that day	2Sa 11:12	3389
and all the people returned unto J	2Sa 12:31	3389
Geshur, and brought Absalom to J	2Sa 14:23	3389
Absalom dwelt two full years in J	2Sa 14:28	3389
shall bring me again indeed to J	2Sa 15:8	3389
went two hundred men out of J	2Sa 15:11	3389
servants that were with him at J	2Sa 15:14	3389
carried the ark of God again to J	2Sa 15:29	3389
the city, and Absalom came into J	2Sa 15:37	3389
the king, Behold, he abideth at J	2Sa 16:3	3389
the men of Israel, came to J	2Sa 16:15	3389
not find them, they returned to J	2Sa 17:20	3389
my lord the king went out of J	2Sa 19:19	3389
he was come to J to meet the king	2Sa 19:25	3389
and I will feed thee with me in J	2Sa 19:33	3389
should go up with the king unto J	2Sa 19:34	3389
their king, from Jordan even to J	2Sa 20:2	3389
And David came to his house at J	2Sa 20:3	3389
and they went out of J, to pursue	2Sa 20:7	3389
Joab returned to J unto the king	2Sa 20:22	3389
they came to J at the end of nine	2Sa 24:8	3389
out his hand upon J to destroy it	2Sa 24:16	3389
and three years reigned he in J	1Kin 2:11	3389
him, Build thee an house in J	1Kin 2:36	3389
And Shimei dwelt in J many days	1Kin 2:38	3389
Shimei had gone from J to Gath	1Kin 2:41	3389
and the wall of J round about	1Kin 3:1	3389
And he came to J, and stood before	1Kin 3:15	3389
of Israel, unto king Solomon in J	1Kin 8:1	3389
house, and Millo, and the wall of J	1Kin 9:15	3389
Solomon desired to build in J	1Kin 9:19	3389
she came to J with a very great	1Kin 10:2	3389
chariots, and with the king at J	1Kin 10:26	3389
made silver to be in J as stones	1Kin 10:27	3389
in the hill that is before J	1Kin 11:7	3389
time when Jeroboam went out of J	1Kin 11:29	3389
have a light alway before me in J	1Kin 11:36	3389
time that Solomon reigned in J	1Kin 11:42	3389
up to his chariot, to flee to J	1Kin 12:18	3389
And when Rehoboam was come to J	1Kin 12:21	3389
in the house of the LORD at J	1Kin 12:27	3389
is too much for you to go up to J	1Kin 12:28	3389
he reigned seventeen years in J	1Kin 14:21	3389
king of Egypt came up against J	1Kin 14:25	3389
Three years reigned he in J	1Kin 15:2	3389
LORD his God give him a lamp in J	1Kin 15:4	3389
son after him, and to establish J	1Kin 15:4	3389
and one years reigned he in J	1Kin 15:10	3389
reigned twenty and five years in J	1Kin 22:42	3389
and he reigned eight years in J	2Kin 8:17	3389
and he reigned one year in J	2Kin 8:26	3389
carried him in a chariot to J	2Kin 9:28	3389
and forty years reigned he in J	2Kin 12:1	3389
Hazael set his face to go up to J	2Kin 12:17	3389
and he went away from J	2Kin 12:18	3389
reigned twenty and nine years in J	2Kin 14:2	3389
mother's name was Jehoaddan of J	2Kin 14:2	3389
at Beth-shemesh, and came to J	2Kin 14:13	3389
brake down the wall of J from the	2Kin 14:13	3389
a conspiracy against him in J	2Kin 14:19	3389
he was buried at J with his	2Kin 14:20	3389
reigned two and fifty years in J	2Kin 15:2	3389
mother's name was Jecholiah of J	2Kin 15:2	3389
and he reigned sixteen years in J	2Kin 15:33	3389
and reigned sixteen years in J	2Kin 16:2	3389
of Israel came up to J to war	2Kin 16:5	3389
reigned twenty and nine years in J	2Kin 18:2	3389
with a great host against J	2Kin 18:17	3389
And they went up and came to J	2Kin 18:17	3389
away, and hath said to Judah and J	2Kin 18:22	3389
worship before this altar in J	2Kin 18:22	3389
should deliver J out of mine hand	2Kin 18:35	3389
J shall not be delivered into the	2Kin 19:10	3389
the daughter of J hath shaken her	2Kin 19:21	3389
For out of J shall go forth a	2Kin 19:31	3389
reigned fifty and five years in J	2Kin 21:1	3389
said, In J will I put my name	2Kin 21:4	3389
his son, In this house, and in J	2Kin 21:7	3389
I am bringing such evil upon J	2Kin 21:12	3389
over J the line of Samaria	2Kin 21:13	3389
I will wipe J as a man wipeth a	2Kin 21:13	3389
till he had filled J from one end	2Kin 21:16	3389
and he reigned two years in J	2Kin 21:19	3389
reigned thirty and one years in J	2Kin 22:1	3389
now she dwelt in J in the college	2Kin 22:14	3389
all the elders of Judah and of J	2Kin 23:1	3389
all the inhabitants of J with him	2Kin 23:2	3389
he burned them without J in the	2Kin 23:4	3389
and in the places round about J	2Kin 23:5	3389
the house of the LORD, without J	2Kin 23:6	3389
up to the altar of the LORD in J	2Kin 23:9	3389
high places that were before J	2Kin 23:13	3389
bones upon them, and returned to J	2Kin 23:20	3389
was holden to the LORD in J	2Kin 23:23	3389
in the land of Judah and in J	2Kin 23:24	3389
this city J which I have chosen	2Kin 23:27	3389
from Megiddo, and brought him to J	2Kin 23:30	3389
and he reigned three months in J	2Kin 23:31	3389
that he might not reign in J	2Kin 23:33	3389
and he reigned eleven years in J	2Kin 23:36	3389
for he filled J with innocent	2Kin 24:4	3389
and he reigned in J three months	2Kin 24:8	3389
the daughter of Elnathan of J	2Kin 24:8	3389
king of Babylon came up against J	2Kin 24:10	3389
And he carried away all J, and all	2Kin 24:14	3389
into captivity from J to Babylon	2Kin 24:15	3389
and he reigned eleven years in J	2Kin 24:18	3389
of the LORD it came to pass in J	2Kin 24:20	3389
he, and all his host, against J	2Kin 25:1	3389
of the king of Babylon, unto J	2Kin 25:8	3389
house, and all the houses of J	2Kin 25:9	3389
down the walls of J round about	2Kin 25:10	3389
in J he reigned thirty and three	1Chr 3:4	3389
And these were born unto him in J	1Chr 3:5	3389
temple that Solomon built in J	1Chr 6:10	3389
J by the hand of Nebuchadnezzar	1Chr 6:15	3389
built the house of the LORD in J	1Chr 6:32	3389
These dwelt in J	1Chr 8:28	3389
dwelt with their brethren in J	1Chr 8:32	3389
in J dwelt of the children of	1Chr 9:3	3389
these dwelt at J	1Chr 9:34	3389
dwelt with their brethren at J	1Chr 9:38	3389
And David and all Israel went to J	1Chr 11:4	3389
And David took more wives at J	1Chr 14:3	3389
of his children which he had in J	1Chr 14:4	3389
gathered all Israel together to J	1Chr 15:3	3389
Hadarezer, and brought them to J	1Chr 18:7	3389
Then Joab came to J	1Chr 19:15	3389
But David tarried at J	1Chr 20:1	3389
and all the people returned to J	1Chr 20:3	3389
all Israel, and came to J	1Chr 21:4	3389
an angel unto J to destroy it	1Chr 21:15	3389
in his hand stretched out over J	1Chr 21:16	3389
that they may dwell in J for ever	1Chr 23:25	3389
with all the valiant men, unto J	1Chr 28:1	3389
and three years reigned he in J	1Chr 29:27	3389
he had pitched a tent for it at J	2Chr 1:4	3389
place that was at Gibeon to J	2Chr 1:13	3389
cities, and with the king at J	2Chr 1:14	3389
gold at J as plenteous as stones	2Chr 1:15	3389
that are with me in Judah and in J	2Chr 2:7	3389
and thou shalt carry it up to J	2Chr 2:16	3389
of the LORD at J in mount Moriah	2Chr 3:1	3389
of the children of Israel, unto J	2Chr 5:2	3389
But I have chosen J, that my name	2Chr 6:6	3389
Solomon desired to build in J	2Chr 8:6	3389
Solomon with hard questions at J	2Chr 9:1	3389
cities, and with the king at J	2Chr 9:25	3389
king made silver in J as stones	2Chr 9:27	3389
Solomon reigned in J over all	2Chr 9:30	3389
up to his chariot, to flee to J	2Chr 10:18	3389
And when Rehoboam was come to J	2Chr 11:1	3389
And Rehoboam dwelt in J, and built	2Chr 11:5	3389
possession, and came to Judah and J	2Chr 11:14	3389
the LORD God of Israel came to J	2Chr 11:16	3389
king of Egypt came up against J	2Chr 12:2	3389
pertained to Judah, and came to J	2Chr 12:4	3389
together to J because of Shishak	2Chr 12:5	3389
out upon J by the hand of Shishak	2Chr 12:7	3389
king of Egypt came up against J	2Chr 12:9	3389
strengthened himself in J	2Chr 12:13	3389
he reigned seventeen years in J	2Chr 12:13	3389
He reigned three years in J	2Chr 13:2	3389
in abundance, and returned to J	2Chr 14:15	3389
together at J in the third month	2Chr 15:10	3389
mighty men of valour, were in J	2Chr 17:13	3389
to his house in peace to J	2Chr 19:1	3389
And Jehoshaphat dwelt at J	2Chr 19:4	3389
Moreover in J did Jehoshaphat set	2Chr 19:8	3389
when they returned to J	2Chr 19:8	3389
in the congregation of Judah and J	2Chr 20:5	3389
all Judah, and ye inhabitants of J	2Chr 20:15	3389
the LORD with you, O Judah and J	2Chr 20:17	3389
the inhabitants of J fell before	2Chr 20:18	3389
O Judah, and ye inhabitants of J	2Chr 20:20	3389
returned, every man of Judah and J	2Chr 20:27	3389
them, to go again to J with joy	2Chr 20:27	3389
they came to J with psalteries and	2Chr 20:28	3389
reigned twenty and five years in J	2Chr 20:31	3389
and he reigned eight years in J	2Chr 21:5	3389
of J to commit fornication	2Chr 21:11	3389
inhabitants of J to go a whoring	2Chr 21:13	3389
and he reigned in J eight years	2Chr 21:20	3389
the inhabitants of J made Ahaziah	2Chr 22:1	3389
and he reigned one year in J	2Chr 22:2	3389
of Israel, and they came to J	2Chr 23:2	3389
and he reigned forty years in J	2Chr 24:1	3389
Judah and out of J the collection	2Chr 24:6	3389
a proclamation through Judah and J	2Chr 24:9	3389
J for this their trespass	2Chr 24:18	3389
and they came to Judah and J	2Chr 24:23	3389
reigned twenty and nine years in J	2Chr 25:1	3389
mother's name was Jehoaddan of J	2Chr 25:1	3389
Beth-shemesh, and brought him to J	2Chr 25:23	3389
brake down the wall of J from the	2Chr 25:23	3389
a conspiracy against him in J	2Chr 25:27	3389
reigned fifty and two years in J	2Chr 26:3	3389
name also was Jecoliah of J	2Chr 26:3	3389
towers in J at the corner gate	2Chr 26:9	3389
And he made in J engines, invented	2Chr 26:15	3389
and he reigned sixteen years in J	2Chr 27:1	3389
and reigned sixteen years in J	2Chr 27:8	3389
and he reigned sixteen years in J	2Chr 28:1	3389
J for bondmen and bondwomen unto	2Chr 28:10	3389
him altars in every corner of J	2Chr 28:24	3389
buried him in the city, even in J	2Chr 28:27	3389
reigned nine and twenty years in J	2Chr 29:1	3389
of the LORD was upon Judah and J	2Chr 29:8	3389
to the house of the LORD at J	2Chr 30:1	3389
and all the congregation in J	2Chr 30:2	3389
gathered themselves together to J	2Chr 30:3	3389
unto the LORD God of Israel at J	2Chr 30:5	3389
humbled themselves, and came to J	2Chr 30:11	3389
there assembled at J much people	2Chr 30:13	3389
away the altars that were in J	2Chr 30:14	3389
at J kept the feast of unleavened	2Chr 30:21	3389
So there was great joy in J	2Chr 30:26	3389
there was not the like in J	2Chr 30:26	3389
the people that dwelt in J to	2Chr 31:4	3389
was purposed to fight against J	2Chr 32:2	3389
of Assyria send his servants to J	2Chr 32:9	3389
and unto all Judah that were at J	2Chr 32:9	3389
that ye abide in the siege in J	2Chr 32:10	3389
altars, and commanded Judah and J	2Chr 32:12	3389
people of J that were on the wall	2Chr 32:18	3389
they spake against the God of J	2Chr 32:19	3389
the inhabitants of J from the	2Chr 32:22	3389
brought gifts unto the LORD to J	2Chr 32:23	3389
upon him, and upon Judah and J	2Chr 32:25	3389
both he and the inhabitants of J	2Chr 32:26	3389
the inhabitants of J did him	2Chr 32:33	3389
reigned fifty and five years in J	2Chr 33:1	3389
In J shall my name be for ever	2Chr 33:4	3389
his son, In this house, and in J	2Chr 33:7	3389
and the inhabitants of J to err	2Chr 33:9	3389
him again to J into his kingdom	2Chr 33:13	3389
of the house of the LORD, and in J	2Chr 33:15	3389
reign, and reigned two years in J	2Chr 33:21	3389
to reign, and he reigned in J one	2Chr 34:1	3389
J from the high places, and the	2Chr 34:3	3389
altars, and cleansed Judah and J	2Chr 34:5	3389
land of Israel, he returned to J	2Chr 34:7	3389
and they returned to J	2Chr 34:9	3389
now she dwelt in J in the college	2Chr 34:22	3389
all the elders of Judah and J	2Chr 34:29	3389
of Judah, and the inhabitants of J	2Chr 34:30	3389
caused all that were present in J	2Chr 34:32	3389
And the inhabitants of J did	2Chr 34:32	3389
a passover unto the LORD in J	2Chr 35:1	3389
present, and the inhabitants of J	2Chr 35:18	3389
and they brought him to J, and he	2Chr 35:24	3389
all Judah and J mourned for Josiah	2Chr 35:24	3389
king in his father's stead in J	2Chr 36:1	3389
and he reigned three months in J	2Chr 36:2	3389
king of Egypt put him down at J	2Chr 36:3	3389
his brother king over Judah and J	2Chr 36:4	3389
and he reigned eleven years in J	2Chr 36:5	3389
three months and ten days in J	2Chr 36:9	3389
his brother king over Judah and J	2Chr 36:10	3389
and reigned eleven years in J	2Chr 36:11	3389
LORD which he had hallowed in J	2Chr 36:14	3389
God, and brake down the wall of J	2Chr 36:19	3389
me to build him an house in J	2Chr 36:23	3389
me to build him an house at J	Ezr 1:2	3389
with him, and let him go up to J	Ezr 1:3	3389
(he is the God,) which is in J	Ezr 1:3	3389
for the house of God that is in J	Ezr 1:4	3389
house of the LORD which is in J	Ezr 1:5	3389
had brought forth out of J	Ezr 1:7	3389
brought up from Babylon unto J	Ezr 1:11	3389
Babylon, and came again unto J	Ezr 2:1	3389
house of the LORD which is at J	Ezr 2:68	3389
together as one man to J	Ezr 3:1	3389
coming unto the house of God at J	Ezr 3:8	3389
come out of the captivity unto J	Ezr 3:8	3389
the inhabitants of Judah and J	Ezr 4:6	3389
scribe wrote a letter against J	Ezr 4:8	3390
from thee to us are come unto J	Ezr 4:12	3390
been mighty kings also over J	Ezr 4:20	3390
up in haste to J unto the Jews	Ezr 4:23	3390
of the house of God which is at J	Ezr 4:24	3390
J in the name of the God of	Ezr 5:1	3390
the house of God which is at J	Ezr 5:2	3390
out of the temple that was in J	Ezr 5:14	3390
them into the temple that is in J	Ezr 5:15	3390
of the house of God which is in J	Ezr 5:16	3390
to build this house of God at J	Ezr 5:17	3390
concerning the house of God at J	Ezr 6:3	3390
out of the temple which is at J	Ezr 6:5	3390
unto the temple which is at J	Ezr 6:5	3390
of the priests which are at J	Ezr 6:9	3390
this house of God which is at J	Ezr 6:12	3390
the service of God, which is at J	Ezr 6:18	3390
porters, and the Nethinims, unto J	Ezr 7:7	3389
he came to J in the fifth month	Ezr 7:8	3389
of the fifth month came he to J	Ezr 7:9	3389
their own freewill to go up to J	Ezr 7:13	3390
to enquire concerning Judah and J	Ezr 7:14	3390
Israel, whose habitation is in J	Ezr 7:15	3390
house of their God which is in J	Ezr 7:16	3390
house of your God which is in J	Ezr 7:17	3390
deliver thou before the God of J	Ezr 7:19	3390
house of the LORD which is in J	Ezr 7:27	3389
of the fathers of Israel, at J	Ezr 8:29	3389
to bring them to J unto the house	Ezr 8:30	3389
of the first month, to go unto J	Ezr 8:31	3389
And we came to J, and abode there	Ezr 8:32	3389
give us a wall in Judah and in J	Ezr 9:9	3389
J unto all the children of the	Ezr 10:7	3389
gather themselves together unto J	Ezr 10:7	3389
together unto J within three days	Ezr 10:9	3389
of the captivity, and concerning J	Neh 1:2	3389
the wall of J also is broken down	Neh 1:3	3389
So I came to J, and was there	Neh 2:11	3389
had put in my heart to do at J	Neh 2:12	3389
port, and viewed the walls of J	Neh 2:13	3389
how J lieth waste, and the gates	Neh 2:17	3389
and let us build up the wall of J	Neh 2:17	3389
nor right, nor memorial, in J	Neh 2:20	3389
they fortified J unto the broad	Neh 3:8	3389
the ruler of the half part of J	Neh 3:9	3389
the ruler of the half part of J	Neh 3:12	3389
that the walls of J were made up	Neh 4:7	3389
to come and to fight against J	Neh 4:8	3389
with his servant lodge within J	Neh 4:22	3389
prophets to preach of thee at J	Neh 6:7	3389
of the palace, charge over J	Neh 7:2	3389
Let not the gates of J be opened	Neh 7:3	3389
watches of the inhabitants of J	Neh 7:3	3389
carried away, and came again to J	Neh 7:6	3389
in all their cities, and in J	Neh 8:15	3389
rulers of the people dwelt at J	Neh 11:1	3389
ten to dwell in J the holy city	Neh 11:1	3389
offered themselves to dwell at J	Neh 11:2	3389
of the province that dwelt in J	Neh 11:3	3389
at J dwelt certain of the	Neh 11:4	3389
at J were four hundred threescore	Neh 11:6	3389
at J was Uzzi the son of Bani	Neh 11:22	3389
the dedication of the wall of J	Neh 12:27	3389
their places, to bring them to J	Neh 12:27	3389

the plain country round about J Neh 12:28 3389
them villages round about J Neh 12:29 3389
so that the joy of J was heard Neh 12:43 3389
in all this time was not I at J Neh 13:6 3389
And I came to J, and understood of Neh 13:7 3389
brought into J on the sabbath day Neh 13:15 3389
the children of Judah, and in J Neh 13:16 3389
that when the gates of J began to Neh 13:19 3389
lodged without J once or twice Neh 13:20 3389
J with the captivity which had Est 2:6 3389
build thou the walls of J Ps 51:18 3389
Because of thy temple at J shall Ps 68:29 3389
they have laid J on heaps Ps 79:1 3389
shed like water round about J Ps 79:3 3389
LORD in Zion, and his praise in J Ps 102:21 3389
house, in the midst of thee, O J Ps 116:19 3389
shall stand within thy gates, O J Ps 122:2 3389
J is builded as a city that is Ps 122:3 3389
Pray for the peace of J Ps 122:6 3389
the mountains are round about J Ps 125:2 3389
of J all the days of thy life Ps 128:5 3389
out of Zion, which dwelleth at J Ps 135:21 3389
If I forget thee, O J, let my Ps 137:5 3389
if I prefer not J above my chief Ps 137:6 3389
children of Edom in the day of J Ps 137:7 3389
The LORD doth build up J Ps 147:2 3389
Praise the LORD, O J Ps 147:12 3389
the son of David, king in J Eccl 1:1 3389
was king over Israel in J Eccl 1:12 3389
that have been before me in J Eccl 1:16 3389
all that were in J before me Eccl 2:7 3389
than all that were before me in J Eccl 2:9 3389
but comely, O ye daughters of J Song 1:5 3389
I charge you, O ye daughters of J Song 2:7 3389
I charge you, O ye daughters of J Song 3:5 3389
with love, for the daughters of J Song 3:10 3389
I charge you, O daughters of J Song 5:8 3389
is my friend, O daughters of J Song 5:16 3389
O my love, as Tirzah, comely as J Song 6:4 3389
I charge you, O daughters of J Song 8:4 3389
J in the days of Uzziah, Jotham, Is 1:1 3389
of Amoz saw concerning Judah and J Is 2:1 3389
and the word of the LORD from J Is 2:3 3389
of hosts, doth take away from J Is 3:1 3389
For J is ruined, and Judah is Is 3:8 3389
Zion, and he that remaineth in J Is 4:3 3389
is written among the living in J Is 4:3 3389
J from the midst thereof by the Is 4:4 3389
And now, O inhabitants of J Is 5:3 3389
went up toward J to war against Is 7:1 3389
a snare to the inhabitants of J Is 8:14 3389
graven images did excel them of J Is 10:10 3389
Samaria and her idols, so do to J Is 10:11 3389
work upon mount Zion and on J Is 10:12 3389
daughter of Zion, the hill of J Is 10:32 3389
ye have numbered the houses of J Is 22:10 3389
a father to the inhabitants of J Is 22:21 3389
reign in mount Zion, and in J Is 24:23 3389
the LORD in the holy mount at J Is 27:13 3389
rule this people which is in J Is 28:14 3389
people shall dwell in Zion at J Is 30:19 3389
will the LORD of hosts defend J Is 31:5 3389
is in Zion, and his furnace in J Is 31:9 3389
shall see J a quiet habitation Is 33:20 3389
sent Rabshakeh from Lachish to J Is 36:2 3389
away, and said to Judah and to J Is 36:7 3389
should deliver J out of my hand Is 36:20 3389
J shall not be given into the Is 37:10 3389
the daughter of J hath shaken her Is 37:22 3389
For out of J shall go forth a Is 37:32 3389
Speak ye comfortably to J Is 40:2 3389
O J, that bringest good tidings, Is 40:9 3389
I will give to J one that Is 41:27 3389
that saith to J, Thou shalt be Is 44:26 3389
even saying to J, Thou shalt be Is 44:28 3389
Awake, awake, stand up, O J Is 51:17 3389
on thy beautiful garments, O J Is 52:1 3389
arise, and sit down, O J Is 52:2 3389
together, ye waste places of J Is 52:9 3389
his people, he hath redeemed J Is 52:9 3389
set watchmen upon thy walls, O J Is 62:6 3389
till he make J a praise in the Is 62:7 3389
is a wilderness, J a desolation Is 64:10 3389
I create J a rejoicing, and her Is 65:18 3389
And I will rejoice in J, and joy in Is 65:19 3389
Rejoice ye with J, and be glad Is 66:10 3389
and ye shall be comforted in J Is 66:13 3389
beasts, to my holy mountain J Is 66:20 3389
unto the carrying away of J Jer 1:3 3389
at the entering of the gates of J Jer 1:15 3389
Go and cry in the ears of J Jer 2:2 3389
call J the throne of the LORD Jer 3:17 3389
it, to the name of the LORD, to J Jer 3:17 3389
the LORD to the men of Judah and J Jer 4:3 3389
men of Judah and inhabitants of J Jer 4:4 3389
ye in Judah, and publish in J Jer 4:5 3389
greatly deceived this people and J Jer 4:10 3389
it be said to this people and to J Jer 4:11 3389
O J, wash thine heart from Jer 4:14 3389
behold, publish against J Jer 4:16 3389
and fro through the streets of J Jer 5:1 3389
to flee out of the midst of J Jer 6:1 3389
trees, and cast a mount against J Jer 6:6 3389
Be thou instructed, O J, lest my Jer 6:8 3389
of Judah and in the streets of J Jer 7:17 3389
Cut off thine hair, O J, and cast Jer 7:29 3389
Judah, and from the streets of J Jer 7:34 3389
the bones of the inhabitants of J Jer 8:1 3389
Why then is this people of J Jer 8:5 3389
And I will make J heaps, and a den Jer 9:11 3389
Judah, and to the inhabitants of J Jer 11:2 3389
of Judah, and in the streets of J Jer 11:6 3389
and among the inhabitants of J Jer 11:9 3389
of Judah and inhabitants of J go Jer 11:12 3389
J have ye set up altars to that Jer 11:13 3389
of Judah, and the great pride of J Jer 13:9 3389
and all the inhabitants of J Jer 13:13 3389
Woe unto thee, O J Jer 13:27 3389
and the cry of J is gone up Jer 14:2 3389
of J because of the famine Jer 14:16 3389
Judah, for that which he did in J Jer 15:4 3389
shall have pity upon thee, O J Jer 15:5 3389
go out, and in all the gates of J Jer 17:19 3389
and all the inhabitants of J Jer 17:20 3389
nor bring it in by the gates of J Jer 17:21 3389
of Judah, and the inhabitants of J Jer 17:25 3389
Judah, and from the places about J Jer 17:26 3389
the gates of J on the sabbath day Jer 17:27 3389
it shall devour the palaces of J Jer 17:27 3389
Judah, and to the inhabitants of J Jer 18:11 3389
of Judah, and inhabitants of J Jer 19:3 3389
of Judah and J in this place Jer 19:7 3389
And the houses of J, and the houses Jer 19:13 3389
cast forth beyond the gates of J Jer 22:19 3389
prophets of J an horrible thing Jer 23:14 3389
for from the prophets of J is Jer 23:15 3389
the carpenters and smiths, from J Jer 24:1 3389
his princes, and the residue of J Jer 24:8 3389
and to all the inhabitants of J Jer 25:2 3389
To wit, J, and the cities of Judah Jer 25:18 3389
J shall become heaps, and the Jer 26:18 3389
to J unto Zedekiah king of Judah Jer 27:3 3389
of the king of Judah, and at J Jer 27:18 3389
king of Judah from J to Babylon Jer 27:20 3389
and all the nobles of Judah and J Jer 27:20 3389
of the king of Judah and of J Jer 27:21 3389
J unto the residue of the elders Jer 29:1 3389
away captive from J to Babylon Jer 29:1 3389
the princes of Judah and J Jer 29:2 3389
the smiths, were departed from J Jer 29:2 3389
carried away from J unto Babylon Jer 29:4 3389
I have sent from J to Babylon Jer 29:20 3389
unto all the people that are at J Jer 29:25 3389
king of Babylon's army besieged J Jer 32:2 3389
of Judah, and the inhabitants of J Jer 32:32 3389
and in the places about J Jer 32:44 3389
of Judah, and in the streets of J Jer 33:10 3389
and in the places about J Jer 33:13 3389
be saved, and J shall dwell safely Jer 33:16 3389
all the people, fought against J Jer 34:1 3389
unto Zedekiah king of Judah in J Jer 34:6 3389
Babylon's army fought against J Jer 34:7 3389
all the people which were at J Jer 34:8 3389
of Judah, and the princes of J Jer 34:19 3389
let us go to J for fear of the Jer 35:11 3389
so we dwell at J Jer 35:11 3389
of Judah and the inhabitants of J Jer 35:13 3389
of J all the evil that I have Jer 35:17 3389
the LORD to all the people in J Jer 36:9 3389
from the cities of Judah unto J Jer 36:9 3389
and upon the inhabitants of J Jer 36:31 3389
besieged J heard tidings of them Jer 37:5 3389
of them, they departed from J Jer 37:5 3389
from J for fear of Pharaoh's army Jer 37:11 3389
J to go into the land of Benjamin Jer 37:12 3389
until the day that J was taken Jer 38:28 3389
and he was there when J was taken Jer 38:28 3389
Babylon and all his army against J Jer 39:1 3389
and brake down the walls of J Jer 39:8 3389
were carried away captive of J Jer 40:1 3389
forth upon the inhabitants of J Jer 42:18 3389
evil that I have brought upon J Jer 44:2 3389
of Judah and in the streets of J Jer 44:6 3389
of Judah, and in the streets of J Jer 44:9 3389
of Egypt, as I have punished J Jer 44:13 3389
of Judah, and in the streets of J Jer 44:17 3389
of Judah, and in the streets of J Jer 44:21 3389
of Chaldea, shall J say Jer 51:35 3389
let J come into your mind Jer 51:50 3389
and he reigned eleven years in J Jer 52:1 3389
of the LORD it came to pass in J Jer 52:3 3389
he and all his army, against J Jer 52:4 3389
the king of Babylon, into J Jer 52:12 3389
and all the houses of J, and all Jer 52:13 3389
all the walls of J round about Jer 52:14 3389
from J eight hundred thirty Jer 52:29 3389
J remembered in the days of her Lam 1:7 3389
J hath grievously sinned Lam 1:8 3389
J is as a menstruous woman among Lam 1:17 3389
the virgins of J hang down their Lam 2:10 3389
I liken to thee, O daughter of J Lam 2:13 3389
their head at the daughter of J Lam 2:15 3389
have entered into the gates of J Lam 4:12 3389
pourtray upon it the city, even J Eze 4:1 3389
thy face toward the siege of J Eze 4:7 3389
break the staff of bread in J Eze 4:16 3389
This is J Eze 5:5 3389
me in the visions of God to J Eze 8:3 3389
the city, through the midst of J Eze 9:4 3389
pouring out of thy fury upon J Eze 9:8 3389
the inhabitants of J have said Eze 11:15 3389
burden concerneth the prince in J Eze 12:10 3389
Lord GOD of the inhabitants of J Eze 12:19 3389
which prophesy concerning J Eze 13:16 3389
my four sore judgments upon J Eze 14:21 3389
evil that I have brought upon J Eze 14:22 3389
will I give the inhabitants of J Eze 15:6 3389
cause J to know her abominations, Eze 16:2 3389
Thus saith the Lord GOD unto J Eze 16:3 3389
the king of Babylon is come to J Eze 17:12 3389
Son of man, set thy face toward J Eze 21:2 3389
to Judah in J the defenced Eze 21:20 3389
hand was the divination for J Eze 21:22 3389
gather you into the midst of J Eze 22:19 3389
Samaria is Aholah, and J Aholibah Eze 23:4 3389
himself against J this same day Eze 24:2 3389
that Tyrus hath said against J Eze 26:2 3389
had escaped out of J came unto me Eze 33:21 3389
as the flock of J in her solemn Eze 36:38 3389
king of Babylon unto J, and Dan 1:1 3389
out of the temple which was in J Dan 5:2 3390
the house of God which was at J Dan 5:3 3390
open in his chamber toward J Dan 6:10 3390
years in the desolations of J Dan 9:2 3389
Judah, and to the inhabitants of J Dan 9:7 3389
done as hath been done upon J Dan 9:12 3389
be turned away from thy city J Dan 9:16 3389
the iniquities of our fathers, J Dan 9:16 3389
to build J unto the Messiah the Dan 9:25 3389
in J shall be deliverance, as the Joel 2:32 3389
again the captivity of Judah and J Joel 3:1 3389
the children of J have ye sold Joel 3:6 3389
Zion, and utter his voice from J Joel 3:16 3389
then shall J be holy, and there Joel 3:17 3389
J from generation to generation Joel 3:20 3389
Zion, and utter his voice from J Amos 1:2 3389
it shall devour the palaces of J Amos 2:5 3389
his gates, and cast lots upon J Obad 11 3389
and the captivity of J, which is Obad 20 3389
he saw concerning Samaria and J Mic 1:1 3389
are they not J? Mic 1:5 3389
the gate of my people, even to J Mic 1:9 3389
from the LORD unto the gate of J Mic 1:12 3389
with blood, and J with iniquity Mic 3:10 3389
J shall become heaps, and the Mic 3:12 3389
and the word of the LORD from J Mic 4:2 3389
shall come to the daughter of J Mic 4:8 3389
and upon all the inhabitants of J Zeph 1:4 3389
that I will search J with candles Zeph 1:12 3389
all the heart, O daughter of J Zeph 3:14 3389
In that day it shall be said to J Zeph 3:16 3389
wilt thou not have mercy on J Zec 1:12 3389
I am jealous for J and for Zion Zec 1:14 3389
I am returned to J with mercies Zec 1:16 3389
shall be stretched forth upon J Zec 1:16 3389
Zion, and shall yet choose J Zec 1:17 3389
scattered Judah, Israel, and J Zec 1:19 3389
And he said unto me, To measure J Zec 2:2 3389
J shall be inhabited as towns Zec 2:4 3389
land, and shall choose J again Zec 2:12 3389
that hath chosen J rebuke thee Zec 3:2 3389
when J was inhabited and in Zec 7:7 3389
and will dwell in the midst of J Zec 8:3 3389
J shall be called a city of truth Zec 8:3 3389
women dwell in the streets of J Zec 8:4 3389
shall dwell in the midst of J Zec 8:8 3389
in these days to do well unto J Zec 8:15 3389
to seek the LORD of hosts in J Zec 8:22 3389
shout, O daughter of J Zec 9:9 3389
from Ephraim, and the horse from J Zec 9:10 3389
I will make J a cup of trembling Zec 12:2 3389
both against Judah and against J Zec 12:2 3389
in that day will I make J a Zec 12:3 3389
The inhabitants of J shall be my Zec 12:5 3389
J shall be inhabited again in her Zec 12:6 3389
again in her own place, even in J Zec 12:6 3389
of J do not magnify themselves Zec 12:7 3389
LORD defend the inhabitants of J Zec 12:8 3389
the nations that come against J Zec 12:9 3389
and upon the inhabitants of J Zec 12:10 3389
there be a great mourning in J Zec 12:11 3389
to the inhabitants of J for sin Zec 13:1 3389
all nations against J to battle Zec 14:2 3389
which is before J on the east Zec 14:4 3389
living waters shall go out from J Zec 14:8 3389
from Geba to Rimmon south of J Zec 14:10 3389
but J shall be safely inhabited Zec 14:11 3389
people that have fought against J Zec 14:12 3389
And Judah also shall fight at J Zec 14:14 3389
J shall even go up from year to Zec 14:16 3389
earth unto J to worship the King Zec 14:17 3389
Yea, every pot in J and in Judah Zec 14:21 3389
is committed in Israel and in J Mal 2:11 3389
J be pleasant unto the LORD, as Mal 3:4 3389
came wise men from the east to J Mt 2:1 *2414*
was troubled, and all J with him Mt 2:3 *2414*
Then went out to him J, and all Mt 3:5 *2414*
and from Decapolis, and from J Mt 4:25 *2414*
neither by J; for it is the city Mt 5:35 *2414*
and Pharisees, which were of J Mt 15:1 *2414*
how that he must go unto J Mt 16:21 *2414*
Jesus going up to J took the Mt 20:17 *2414*
Behold, we go up to J Mt 20:18 *2414*
And when they drew nigh unto J Mt 21:1 *2414*
And when he was come into J Mt 21:10 *2414*
O J, J, thou that killest Mt 23:37 *2419*
the land of Judaea, and they of J Mk 1:5 *2414*
And from J, and from Idumaea, and Mk 3:8 *2414*
which came down from J said Mk 3:22 *2414*
of the scribes, which came from J Mk 7:1 *2414*
were in the way going up to J Mk 10:32 *2414*
Saying, Behold, we go up to J Mk 10:33 *2414*
And when they came nigh to J Mk 11:1 *2419*
And Jesus entered into J, and into Mk 11:11 *2414*
And they come to J Mk 11:15 *2414*
And they come again to J Mk 11:27 *2414*
which came up with him unto J Mk 15:41 *2414*
they brought him to J, to Lk 2:22 *2414*
And, behold, there was a man in J Lk 2:25 *2419*
that looked for redemption in J Lk 2:38 *2419*
Now his parents went to J every Lk 2:41 *2419*
they went up to J after the Lk 2:42 *2414*
child Jesus tarried behind in J Lk 2:43 *2419*
not, they turned back again to J Lk 2:45 *2419*
And he brought him to J, and set Lk 4:9 *2419*
town of Galilee, and Judaea, and J Lk 5:17 *2419*
of people out of all Judaea and J Lk 6:17 *2419*
which he should accomplish at J Lk 9:31 *2419*
set his face to go to J Lk 9:51 *2419*
was as though he would go to J Lk 9:53 *2419*
man went down from J to Jericho Lk 10:30 *2419*
above all men that dwelt in J Lk 13:4 *2419*

teaching, and journeying toward J Lk 13:22 *2419*
be that a prophet perish out of J Lk 13:33 *2419*
O J, J, which killest the Lk 13:34 *2419*
it came to pass, as he went to J Lk 17:11 *2419*
unto them, Behold, we go up to J Lk 18:31 *2414*
parable, because he was nigh to J Lk 19:11 *2419*
he went before, ascending up to J Lk 19:28 *2414*
when ye shall see J compassed Lk 21:20 *2419*
J shall be trodden down of the Lk 21:24 *2419*
also was at J at that time Lk 23:7 *2414*
unto them said, Daughters of J Lk 23:28 *2419*
which was from J about threescore Lk 24:13 *2419*
Art thou only a stranger in J Lk 24:18 *2419*
the same hour, and returned to J Lk 24:33 *2419*
among all nations, beginning at J Lk 24:47 *2419*
but tarry ye in the city of J Lk 24:49 *2419*
returned to J with great joy Lk 24:52 *2419*
and Levites from J to ask him Jn 1:19 *2414*
at hand, and Jesus went up to J Jn 2:13 *2414*
when he was in J at the passover Jn 2:23 *2414*
that in J is the place where men Jn 4:20 *2414*
in this mountain, nor yet at J Jn 4:21 *2414*
that he did at J at the feast Jn 4:45 *2414*
and Jesus went up to J Jn 5:1 *2414*
Now there is at J by the sheep Jn 5:2 *2414*
Then said some of them of J Jn 7:25 *2414*
it was at J the feast of the Jn 10:22 *2414*
Now Bethany was nigh unto J Jn 11:18 *2414*
up to J before the passover Jn 11:55 *2414*
heard that Jesus was coming to J Jn 12:12 *2414*
they should not depart from J Acts 1:4 *2414*
be witnesses unto me both in J Acts 1:8 *2419*
Then returned they unto J from Acts 1:12 *2419*
which is from J a sabbath day's Acts 1:12 *2419*
known unto all the dwellers at J Acts 1:19 *2419*
And there were dwelling at J Jews Acts 2:5 *2419*
Judaea, and all ye that dwell at J Acts 2:14 *2419*
were gathered together at J Acts 4:6 *2419*
to all them that dwell in J Acts 4:16 *2419*
of the cities round about unto J Acts 5:16 *2419*
ye have filled J with your Acts 5:28 *2419*
disciples multiplied in J greatly Acts 6:7 *2419*
against the church which was at J Acts 8:1 *2414*
J heard that Samaria had received Acts 8:14 *2414*
word of the Lord, returned to J Acts 8:25 *2419*
that goeth down from J unto Gaza Acts 8:26 *2419*
had come to J for to worship, Acts 8:27 *2419*
he might bring them bound unto J Acts 9:2 *2419*
he hath done to thy saints at J Acts 9:13 *2419*
which called on this name in J Acts 9:21 *2419*
And when Saul was come to J Acts 9:26 *2419*
them coming in and going out at J Acts 9:28 *2419*
in the land of the Jews, and in J Acts 10:39 *2419*
And when Peter was come up to J Acts 11:2 *2414*
ears of the church which was in J Acts 11:22 *2414*
came prophets from J unto Antioch Acts 11:27 *2414*
Barnabas and Saul returned from J Acts 12:25 *2419*
departing from them returned to J Acts 13:13 *2414*
For they that dwell at J, and Acts 13:27 *2419*
up with him from Galilee to J Acts 13:31 *2419*
should go up to J unto the Acts 15:2 *2419*
And when they were come to J Acts 15:4 *2419*
and elders which were at J Acts 16:4 *2419*
keep this feast that cometh in J Acts 18:21 *2414*
Macedonia and Achaia, to go to J Acts 19:21 *2419*
to be at J the day of Pentecost Acts 20:16 *2414*
I go bound in the spirit unto J Acts 20:22 *2419*
that he should not go up to J Acts 21:4 *2419*
So shall the Jews at J bind the Acts 21:11 *2419*
besought him not to go up to J Acts 21:12 *2419*
but also to die at J for the name Acts 21:13 *2419*
up our carriages, and went up to J Acts 21:15 *2419*
And when we were come to J Acts 21:17 *2414*
that all J was in an uproar Acts 21:31 *2419*
which were there bound unto J Acts 22:5 *2419*
that, when I was come again to J Acts 22:17 *2419*
and get thee quickly out of J Acts 22:18 *2419*
as thou hast testified of me in J Acts 23:11 *2419*
I went up to J for to worship Acts 24:11 *2419*
he ascended from Caesarea to J Acts 25:1 *2414*
that he would send for him to J Acts 25:3 *2419*
down from J stood round about Acts 25:7 *2414*
and said, Wilt thou go up to J Acts 25:9 *2414*
About whom, when I was at J Acts 25:15 *2414*
him whether he would go to J Acts 25:20 *2419*
have dealt with me, both at J Acts 25:24 *2414*
first among mine own nation at J Acts 26:4 *2414*
Which thing I also did in J Acts 26:10 *2414*
unto them of Damascus, and at J Acts 26:20 *2414*
J into the hands of the Romans Acts 28:17 *2414*
so that from J, and round about Rom 15:19 *2419*
But now I go unto J to minister Rom 15:25 *2419*
the poor saints which are at J Rom 15:26 *2419*
my service which I have for J may Rom 15:31 *2419*
to bring your liberality unto J 1Cor 16:3 *2419*
Neither went I up to J to them Gal 1:17 *2414*
years I went up to J to see Peter Gal 1:18 *2414*
went up again to J with Barnabas Gal 2:1 *2414*
and answereth to J which now is Gal 4:25 *2419*
But J which is above is free, Gal 4:26 *2419*
of the living God, the heavenly J Heb 12:22 *2419*
city of my God, which is new J Rev 3:12 *2419*
I John saw the holy city, new J Rev 21:2 *2419*
me that great city, the holy J Rev 21:10 *2419*

JERUSALEM'S (*je-ru'-sa-lems*)
for J sake which I have chosen 1Kin 11:13 3389
for J sake, the city which I have 1Kin 11:32 3389
for J sake I will not rest, until Is 62:1 3389

JERUSHA (*je-ru'-shah*) See JERUSHAH. *Mother of King Jotham of Judah.*
And his mother's name was J 2Kin 15:33 3388

JERUSHAH (*je-ru'-shah*) See JERUSHA. *Same as Jerusha.*
His mother's name also was J 2Chr 27:1 3388

JESAIAH (*jes-a-i'-ah*) See ISAIAH, JESHAIAH.
1. Grandson of Zerubbabel.
Hananiah; Pelatiah, and J 1Chr 3:21 3470
2. A family of exiles.
the son of Ithiel, the son of J Neh 11:7 3470

JESHAIAH (*jesh-a-i'-ah*) See JESAIAH.
1. A sanctuary servant.
Gedaliah, and Zeri, and J, 1Chr 25:3 3740
The eighth to J, he, his sons, and 1Chr 25:15 3740
2. A grandson of Eliezer.
J his son, and Joram his son, and 1Chr 26:25 3740
3. An Elamite exile.
J the son of Athaliah, and with Ezr 8:7 3740
4. A Merarite exile.
with him J of the sons of Merari, Ezr 8:19 3740

JESHANAH (*je-sha'-nah*) *A city near Bethel.*
J with the towns thereof, and 2Chr 13:19 3466

JESHARELAH (*je-shar'-e-lah*) See ASARELAH. *A sanctuary servant.*
The seventh to J, he, his sons, 1Chr 25:14 3480

JESHEBEAB (*je-sheb'-e-ab*) *A sanctuary servant.*
to Huppah, the fourteenth to J 1Chr 24:13 3434

JESHER (*je'-shur*) *A son of Caleb.*
J, and Shobab, and Ardon 1Chr 2:18 3475

JESHIMON (*jesh'-im-on*)
1. A place in the Sinai.
of Pisgah, which looketh toward J Num 21:20 3452
of Peor, that looketh toward J Num 23:28 3452
2. A place in the wilderness of Judah.
which is on the south of J 1Sa 23:19 3452
in the plain on the south of J 1Sa 23:24 3452
of Hachilah, which is before J 1Sa 26:1 3452
of Hachilah, which is before J 1Sa 26:3

JESHISHAI (*jesh'-i-shahee*) *Ancestor of a Gadite family.*
the son of Michael, the son of J 1Chr 5:14 3454

JESHOHAIAH (*je-sho-ha-i'-ah*) *A descendant of Simeon.*
And Elioenai, and Jaakobah, and J 1Chr 4:36 3439

JESHUA (*jesh'-u-ah*) See JESHUAH, JOSHUA.
1. A sanctuary servant.
of Jedaiah, of the house of J Ezr 2:36 3442
of Jedaiah, of the house of J Neh 7:39 3442
2. A Levite in Hezekiah's time.
The ninth to J, the tenth to 1Chr 24:11 3442
him were Eden, and Miniamin, and J 2Chr 31:15 3442
the children of J and Kadmiel, of Ezr 2:40 3442
the children of J, of Kadmiel, and Neh 7:43 3442
3. A priest in exile.
J, Nehemiah, Seraiah, Reelaiah, Ezr 2:2 3442
Then stood up J the son of Ezr 3:2 3442
J the son of Jozadak, and the Ezr 3:8 3442
Then stood J with his sons and his Ezr 3:9 3442
But Zerubbabel, and J, and the rest Ezr 4:3 3442
J the son of Jozadak, and began to Ezr 5:2 3443
of the sons of J the son of Ezr 10:18 3442
Who came with Zerubbabel, J Neh 7:7 3442
the son of Shealtiel, and J Neh 12:1 3442
their brethren in the days of J Neh 12:7 3442
J begat Joiakim, Joiakim also Neh 12:10 3442
the days of Joiakim the son of J Neh 12:26 3442
4. Father of Jozabad.
them was Jozabad the son of J Ezr 8:33 3443
5. A family of exiles.
Pahath-moab, of the children of J Ezr 2:6 3442
Pahath-moab, of the children of J Neh 7:11 3442
6. Father of Ezer.
to him repaired Ezer the son of J Neh 3:19 3442
7. A priest who assisted Ezra.
Also J, and Bani, and Sherebiah, Neh 8:7 3442
the stairs, of the Levites, J, Neh 9:4 3442
Then the Levites, J, and Kadmiel, Neh 9:5 3442
J, Binnui, Kadmiel, Sherebiah, Neh 12:8 3442
J the son of Kadmiel, with their Neh 12:24 3442
8. Same as Joshua, son of Nun.
for since the days of J the son Neh 8:17 3442
9. A Levite who renewed the covenant.
both J the son of Azaniah, Binnui Neh 10:9 3442
10. A city in Benjamin.
And at J, and at Moladah, and at Neh 11:26 3442

JESHURUN (*jesh'-u-run*) *Another name for the people Israel.*
But J waxed fat, and kicked Deut 32:15 3484
And he was king in J, when the Deut 33:5 3484
is none like unto the God of J Deut 33:26 3484

JESIAH (*je-si'-ah*) See ISHIAH.
1. A warrior in David's army.
Elkanah, and J, and Azareel, and 1Chr 12:6 3449
2. A descendant of Uzziel.
Micah the first, and J the second 1Chr 23:20 3449

JESIMIEL (*je-sim'-e-el*) *A descendant of Simeon.*
and Asaiah, and Adiel, and J 1Chr 4:36 3450

JESSE (*jes'-se*) *Father of David.*
he is the father of J, the father Ruth 4:17 3448
begat J, and J begat David Ruth 4:22 3448
send thee to J the Beth-lehemite 1Sa 16:1 3448
call J to the sacrifice, and I 1Sa 16:3 3448
And he sanctified J and his sons, 1Sa 16:5 3448
Then J called Abinadab, and made 1Sa 16:8 3448
Then J made Shammah to pass by 1Sa 16:9 3448
J made seven of his sons to pass 1Sa 16:10 3448
And Samuel said unto J, The LORD 1Sa 16:10 3448
And Samuel said unto J, Are here 1Sa 16:11 3448
And Samuel said unto J, Send and 1Sa 16:11 3448
seen a son of J the Beth-lehemite 1Sa 16:18 3448
Saul sent messengers unto J 1Sa 16:19 3448
J took an ass laden with bread, 1Sa 16:20 3448
And Saul sent to J, saying, Let 1Sa 16:22 3448
whose name was J; and he had 1Sa 17:12 3448
the three eldest sons of J went 1Sa 17:13 3448
J said unto David his son, Take 1Sa 17:17 3448
and went, as J had commanded him 1Sa 17:20 3448
thy servant J the Beth-lehemite 1Sa 17:58 3448
cometh not the son of J to meat 1Sa 20:27 3448
son of J to thine own confusion 1Sa 20:30 3448
son of J liveth upon the ground 1Sa 20:31 3448
will the son of J give every one 1Sa 22:7 3448
made a league with the son of J 1Sa 22:8 3448
I saw the son of J coming to Nob 1Sa 22:9 3448
against me, thou and the son of J 1Sa 22:13 3448
and who is the son of J 1Sa 25:10 3448
we inheritance in the son of J 2Sa 20:1 3448
David the son of J said, and the 2Sa 23:1 3448
we inheritance in the son of J 1Kin 12:16 3448
Boaz begat Obed, and Obed begat J 1Chr 2:12 3448
J begat his firstborn Eliab, and 1Chr 2:13 3448
kingdom unto David the son of J 1Chr 10:14 3448
and on thy side, thou son of J 1Chr 12:18 3448
Thus David the son of J reigned 1Chr 29:26 3448
none inheritance in the son of J 2Chr 10:16 3448
daughter of Eliab the son of J 2Chr 11:18 3448
of David the son of J are ended Ps 72:20 3448
forth a rod out of the stem of J Is 11:1 3448
day there shall be a root of J Is 11:10 3448
and Obed begat J Mt 1:5 *2421*
And J begat David the king Mt 1:6 *2421*
Which was the son of J, which was Lk 3:32 *2421*
I have found David the son of J Acts 13:22 *2421*
saith, There shall be a root of J Rom 15:12 *2421*

JESSHIAH See JESIAH.

JESTING
nor foolish talking, nor j Eph 5:4 *2160*

JESUI (*jes'-u-i*) See ISHUI, JESUITES. *A descendant of Asher.*
of J, the family of the Jesuites Num 26:44 3440

JESUITES (*jes'-u-ites*) *Descendants of Jesui.*
of Jesui, the family of the J Num 26:44 3441

JESURUN (*jes'-u-run*) See JESHURUN. *Same as Jeshurun.*
and thou, J, whom I have chosen Is 44:2 3484

JESUS (*je'-zus*) See BAR-JESUS, CHRIST, JESUS', JOSHUA, JUSTUS.
1. The Christ.
of the generation of J Christ Mt 1:1 *2424*
of Mary, of whom was born J Mt 1:16 *2424*
Now the birth of J Christ was on Mt 1:18 *2424*
and thou shalt call his name J Mt 1:21 *2424*
and he called his name J Mt 1:25 *2424*
Now when J was born in Bethlehem Mt 2:1 *2424*
Then cometh J from Galilee to Mt 3:13 *2424*
J answering said unto him, Suffer Mt 3:15 *2424*
And J, when he was baptized, went Mt 3:16 *2424*
Then was J led up of the spirit Mt 4:1 *2424*
J said unto him, It is written Mt 4:7 *2424*
Then saith J unto him, Get thee Mt 4:10 *2424*
Now when J had heard that John Mt 4:12 *2424*
From that time J began to preach, Mt 4:17 *2424*
And J, walking by the sea of Mt 4:18 *2424*
J went about all Galilee, Mt 4:23 *2424*
when J had ended these sayings, Mt 7:28 *2424*
J put forth his hand, and touched Mt 8:3 *2424*
J saith unto him, See thou tell Mt 8:4 *2424*
when J was entered into Capernaum Mt 8:5 *2424*
J saith unto him, I will come and Mt 8:7 *2424*
When J heard it, he marvelled, and Mt 8:10 *2424*
J said unto the centurion, Go thy Mt 8:13 *2424*
when J was come into Peter's Mt 8:14 *2424*
Now when J saw great multitudes Mt 8:18 *2424*
J saith unto him, The foxes have Mt 8:20 *2424*
But J said unto him, Follow me Mt 8:22 *2424*
What have we to do with thee, J Mt 8:29 *2424*
the whole city came out to meet J Mt 8:34 *2424*
J seeing their faith said unto Mt 9:2 *2424*
J knowing their thoughts said, Mt 9:4 *2424*
as J passed forth from thence, he Mt 9:9 *2424*
as J sat at meat in the house, Mt 9:10 *2424*
But when J heard that, he said Mt 9:12 *2424*
J said unto them, Can the Mt 9:15 *2424*
J arose, and followed him, and so Mt 9:19 *2424*
But J turned him about, and when Mt 9:22 *2424*
when J came into the ruler's Mt 9:23 *2424*
when J departed thence, two blind Mt 9:27 *2424*
J saith unto them, Believe ye Mt 9:28 *2424*
J straitly charged them, saying, Mt 9:30 *2424*
J went about all the cities and Mt 9:35 *2424*
These twelve J sent forth Mt 10:5 *2424*
when J had made an end of Mt 11:1 *2424*
J answered and said unto them, Go Mt 11:4 *2424*
departed, J began to say unto the Mt 11:7 *2424*
At that time J answered and said, Mt 11:25 *2424*
At that time J went on the Mt 12:1 *2424*
But when J knew it, he withdrew Mt 12:15 *2424*
J knew their thoughts, and said Mt 12:25 *2424*
same day went J out of the house Mt 13:1 *2424*
All these things spake J unto the Mt 13:34 *2424*
Then J sent the multitude away, Mt 13:36 *2424*
J saith unto them, Have ye Mt 13:51 *2424*
that when J had finished these Mt 13:53 *2424*
But J said unto them, A prophet Mt 13:57 *2424*
tetrarch heard of the fame of J Mt 14:1 *2424*
and buried it, and went and told J Mt 14:12 *2424*
When J heard of it, he departed Mt 14:13 *2424*
J went forth, and saw a great Mt 14:14 *2424*

J

But J said unto them, They need ... Mt 14:16 2424
straightway J constrained his ... Mt 14:22 2424
of the night J went unto them ... Mt 14:25 2424
But straightway J spake unto them ... Mt 14:27 2424
walked on the water, to go to J ... Mt 14:29 2424
immediately J stretched forth his ... Mt 14:31 2424
Then came to J scribes and ... Mt 15:1 2424
J said, Are ye also yet without ... Mt 15:16 2424
Then J went thence, and departed ... Mt 15:21 2424
Then J answered and said unto her, ... Mt 15:28 2424
J departed from thence, and came ... Mt 15:29 2424
Then J called his disciples unto ... Mt 15:32 2424
J saith unto them, How many ... Mt 15:34 2424
Then J said unto them, Take heed ... Mt 16:6 2424
Which when J perceived, he said ... Mt 16:8 2424
When J came into the coasts of ... Mt 16:13 2424
J answered and said unto him, ... Mt 16:17 2424
no man that he was J the Christ ... Mt 16:20 2424
J to shew unto his disciples ... Mt 16:21 2424
Then said J unto his disciples, ... Mt 16:24 2424
And after six days J taketh Peter ... Mt 17:1 2424
answered Peter, and said unto J ... Mt 17:4 2424
J came and touched them, and said, ... Mt 17:7 2424
they saw no man, save J only ... Mt 17:8 2424
J charged them, saying, Tell the ... Mt 17:9 2424
J answered and said unto them, ... Mt 17:11 2424
Then J answered and said, O ... Mt 17:17 2424
And J rebuked the devil ... Mt 17:18 2424
came the disciples to J apart ... Mt 17:19 2424
J said unto them, Because of your ... Mt 17:20 2424
J said unto them, The Son of man ... Mt 17:22 2424
J prevented him, saying, What ... Mt 17:25 2424
J saith unto him, Then are the ... Mt 17:26 2424
time came the disciples unto J ... Mt 18:1 2424
J called a little child unto him, ... Mt 18:2 2424
J saith unto him, I say not unto ... Mt 18:22 2424
that when J had finished these ... Mt 19:1 2424
But J said, Suffer little ... Mt 19:14 2424
J said, Thou shalt do no murder, ... Mt 19:18 2424
J said unto him, If thou wilt be ... Mt 19:21 2424
Then said J unto his disciples, ... Mt 19:23 2424
But J beheld them, and said unto ... Mt 19:26 2424
J said unto them, Verily I say ... Mt 19:28 2424
J going up to Jerusalem took the ... Mt 20:17 2424
But J answered and said, Ye know ... Mt 20:22 2424
But J called them unto him, and ... Mt 20:25 2424
when they heard that J passed by ... Mt 20:30 2424
J stood still, and called them, and ... Mt 20:32 2424
So J had compassion on them, and ... Mt 20:34 2424
then sent J two disciples, ... Mt 21:1 2424
went, and did as J commanded them, .. Mt 21:6 2424
This is J the prophet of Nazareth ... Mt 21:11 2424
J went into the temple of God, and ... Mt 21:12 2424
And J saith unto them, Yea ... Mt 21:16 2424
J answered and said unto them, ... Mt 21:21 2424
J answered and said unto them, I ... Mt 21:24 2424
And they answered J, and said, We ... Mt 21:27 2424
J saith unto them, Verily I say ... Mt 21:31 2424
J saith unto them, Did ye never ... Mt 21:42 2424
J answered and spake unto them ... Mt 22:1 2424
But J perceived their wickedness, ... Mt 22:18 2424
J answered and said unto them, Ye ... Mt 22:29 2424
J said unto him, Thou shalt love ... Mt 22:37 2424
gathered together, J asked them, ... Mt 22:41 2424
Then spake J to the multitude, and ... Mt 23:1 2424
J went out, and departed from the ... Mt 24:1 2424
J said unto them, See ye not all ... Mt 24:2 2424
J answered and said unto them, ... Mt 24:4 2424
when J had finished all these ... Mt 26:1 2424
they might take J by subtilty ... Mt 26:4 2424
Now when J was in Bethany, in the ... Mt 26:6 2424
When J understood it, he said ... Mt 26:10 2424
bread the disciples came to J ... Mt 26:17 2424
did as J had appointed them ... Mt 26:19 2424
J took bread, and blessed it, and ... Mt 26:26 2424
Then saith J unto them, All ye ... Mt 26:31 2424
J said unto him, Verily I say ... Mt 26:34 2424
Then cometh J with them unto a ... Mt 26:36 2424
And forthwith he came to J ... Mt 26:49 2424
And J said unto him, Friend, ... Mt 26:50 2424
came they, and laid hands on J ... Mt 26:50 2424
with J stretched out his hand ... Mt 26:51 2424
Then said J unto him, Put up ... Mt 26:52 2424
hour said J to the multitudes ... Mt 26:55 2424
they that had laid hold on J led ... Mt 26:57 2424
sought false witness against J ... Mt 26:59 2424
But J held his peace ... Mt 26:63 2424
J saith unto him, Thou hast said ... Mt 26:64 2424
Thou also wast with J of Galilee ... Mt 26:69 2424
was also with J of Nazareth ... Mt 26:71 2424
And Peter remembered the word of J .. Mt 26:75 2424
against J to put him to death ... Mt 27:1 2424
J stood before the governor ... Mt 27:11 2424
J said unto him, Thou sayest ... Mt 27:11 2424
or J which is called Christ ... Mt 27:17 2424
should ask Barabbas, and destroy J ... Mt 27:20 2424
with J which is called Christ ... Mt 27:22 2424
and when he had scourged J ... Mt 27:26 2424
took J into the common hall ... Mt 27:27 2424
THIS IS J THE KING OF THE JEWS .. Mt 27:37 2424
about the ninth hour J cried with ... Mt 27:46 2424
J, when he had cried again with a ... Mt 27:50 2424
that were with him, watching J ... Mt 27:54 2424
which followed J from Galilee ... Mt 27:55 2424
Pilate, and begged the body of J ... Mt 27:58 2424
for I know that ye seek J ... Mt 28:5 2424
J met them, saying, All hail ... Mt 28:9 2424
Then said J unto them, Be not ... Mt 28:10 2424
where J had appointed them ... Mt 28:16 2424
J came and spake unto them, saying ... Mt 28:18 2424
of the gospel of J Christ ... Mk 1:1 2424
that J came from Nazareth of ... Mk 1:9 2424
J came into Galilee, preaching ... Mk 1:14 2424
J said unto them, Come ye after ... Mk 1:17 2424
do with thee, thou J of Nazareth ... Mk 1:24 2424
J rebuked him, saying, Hold thy ... Mk 1:25 2424
And J, moved with compassion, put ... Mk 1:41 2424
insomuch that J could no more ... Mk 1:45 2424
When J saw their faith, he said ... Mk 2:5 2424
immediately when J perceived in ... Mk 2:8 2424
as J sat at meat in his house, ... Mk 2:15 2424
sinners sat also together with J ... Mk 2:15 2424
When J heard it, he saith unto ... Mk 2:17 2424
J said unto them, Can the ... Mk 2:19 2424
But J withdrew himself with his ... Mk 3:7 2424
But when he saw J afar off ... Mk 5:6 2424
What have I to do with thee, J ... Mk 5:7 2424
forthwith J gave them leave ... Mk 5:13 2424
And they come to J, and see him ... Mk 5:15 2424
Howbeit J suffered him not, but ... Mk 5:19 2424
great things J had done for him ... Mk 5:20 2424
when J was passed over again by ... Mk 5:21 2424
And J went with him ... Mk 5:24
When she had heard of J, came in ... Mk 5:27 2424
And J, immediately knowing in ... Mk 5:30 2424
As soon as J heard the word that ... Mk 5:36 2424
But J said unto them, A prophet ... Mk 6:4 2424
themselves together unto J ... Mk 6:30 2424
And J, when he came out, saw much ... Mk 6:34 2424
But J said unto her, Let the ... Mk 7:27 2424
J called his disciples unto him, ... Mk 8:1 2424
when J knew it, he saith unto ... Mk 8:17 2424
J went out, and his disciples, ... Mk 8:27 2424
after six days J taketh with him ... Mk 9:2 2424
and they were talking with J ... Mk 9:4 2424
And Peter answered and said to J ... Mk 9:5 2424
save J only with themselves ... Mk 9:8 2424
J said unto him, If thou canst ... Mk 9:23 2424
When J saw that the people came ... Mk 9:25 2424
But J took him by the hand, and ... Mk 9:27 2424
But J said, Forbid him not ... Mk 9:39 2424
J answered and said unto them, For ... Mk 10:5 2424
But when J saw it, he was much ... Mk 10:14 2424
J said unto him, Why callest thou ... Mk 10:18 2424
Then J beholding him loved him, ... Mk 10:21 2424
J looked round about, and saith ... Mk 10:23 2424
But J answereth again, and saith ... Mk 10:24 2424
J looking upon them saith, With ... Mk 10:27 2424
J answered and said, Verily I say ... Mk 10:29 2424
and J went before them ... Mk 10:32 2424
But J said unto them, Ye know not ... Mk 10:38 2424
J said unto them, Ye shall indeed ... Mk 10:39 2424
But J called them to him, and ... Mk 10:42 2424
heard that it was J of Nazareth ... Mk 10:47 2424
he began to cry out, and say, J ... Mk 10:47 2424
J stood still, and commanded him ... Mk 10:49 2424
his garment, rose, and came to J ... Mk 10:50 2424
J answered and said unto him, What ... Mk 10:51 2424
J said unto him, Go thy way ... Mk 10:52 2424
sight, and followed J in the way ... Mk 10:52 2424
unto them even as J had commanded .. Mk 11:6 2424
And they brought the colt to J ... Mk 11:7 2424
J entered into Jerusalem, and into ... Mk 11:11 2424
J answered and said unto it, No ... Mk 11:14 2424
J went into the temple, and began ... Mk 11:15 2424
J answering saith unto them, Have ... Mk 11:22 2424
J answered and said unto them, I ... Mk 11:29 2424
And they answered and said unto J ... Mk 11:33 2424
J answering saith unto them, ... Mk 11:33 2424
J answering said unto them, ... Mk 12:17 2424
J answering said unto them, Do ye ... Mk 12:24 2424
J answered him, The first of all ... Mk 12:29 2424
when J saw that he answered ... Mk 12:34 2424
J answered and said, while he ... Mk 12:35 2424
J sat over against the treasury, ... Mk 12:41 2424
J answering said unto him, Seest ... Mk 13:2 2424
J answering them began to say, ... Mk 13:5 2424
And J said, Let her alone ... Mk 14:6 2424
J said, Verily I say unto you, ... Mk 14:18 2424
J took bread, and blessed, and ... Mk 14:22 2424
J saith unto them, All ye shall ... Mk 14:27 2424
J saith unto him, Verily I say ... Mk 14:30 2424
J answered and said unto them, Are ... Mk 14:48 2424
they led J away to the high ... Mk 14:53 2424
against J to put him to death ... Mk 14:55 2424
stood up in the midst, and asked J ... Mk 14:60 2424
And J said, I am ... Mk 14:62 2424
thou also wast with J of Nazareth ... Mk 14:67 2424
the word that J said unto him ... Mk 14:72 2424
and the whole council, and bound J ... Mk 15:1 2424
But J yet answered nothing ... Mk 15:5 2424
unto them, and delivered J ... Mk 15:15 2424
at the ninth hour J cried with a ... Mk 15:34 2424
J cried with a loud voice, and ... Mk 15:37 2424
Pilate, and craved the body of J ... Mk 15:43 2424
Ye seek J of Nazareth, which was ... Mk 16:6 2424
Now when J was risen early the ... Mk 16:9
a son, and shalt call his name J ... Lk 1:31 2424
the child, his name was called J ... Lk 2:21 2424
parents brought in the child J ... Lk 2:27 2424
the child J tarried behind in ... Lk 2:43 2424
J increased in wisdom and stature, ... Lk 2:52 2424
that J also being baptized, and ... Lk 3:21 2424
J himself began to be about ... Lk 3:23 2424
J being full of the Holy Ghost ... Lk 4:1 2424
J answered him, saying, It is ... Lk 4:4 2424
J answered and said unto him, Get ... Lk 4:8 2424
J answering said unto him, It is ... Lk 4:12 2424
J returned in the power of the ... Lk 4:14 2424
do with thee, thou J of Nazareth ... Lk 4:34 2424
J rebuked him, saying, Hold thy ... Lk 4:35 2424
J said unto Simon, Fear not ... Lk 5:10 2424
who seeing J fell on his face, and ... Lk 5:12 2424
his couch into the midst before J ... Lk 5:19 2424
But when J perceived their ... Lk 5:22 2424
J answering said unto them, They ... Lk 5:31 2424
J answering them said, Have ye ... Lk 6:3 2424
Then said J unto them, I will ask ... Lk 6:9 2424
another what they might do to J ... Lk 6:11 2424
And when he heard of J, he sent ... Lk 7:3 2424
And when they came to J, they ... Lk 7:4 2424
Then J went with them ... Lk 7:6 2424
When J heard these things, he ... Lk 7:9 2424
of his disciples sent them to J ... Lk 7:19 2424
Then J answering said unto them, ... Lk 7:22 2424
when she knew that J sat at meat ... Lk 7:37
J answering said unto him, Simon, ... Lk 7:40 2424
When he saw J, he cried out, and ... Lk 8:28 2424
What have I to do with thee, J ... Lk 8:28 2424
J asked him, saying, What is thy ... Lk 8:30 2424
and came to J, and found the man, ... Lk 8:35 2424
sitting at the feet of J ... Lk 8:35 2424
but J sent him away, saying, ... Lk 8:38 2424
great things J had done unto him ... Lk 8:39 2424
when J was returned, the people ... Lk 8:40 2424
And J said, Who touched me ... Lk 8:45 2424
J said, Somebody hath touched me ... Lk 8:46 2424
But when J heard it, he answered ... Lk 8:50 2424
from him, Peter said unto J ... Lk 9:33 2424
voice was past, J was found alone ... Lk 9:36 2424
J answering said, O faithless and ... Lk 9:41 2424
J rebuked the unclean spirit, and ... Lk 9:42 2424
one at all things which J did ... Lk 9:43 2424
And J, perceiving the thought of ... Lk 9:47 2424
J said unto him, Forbid him not ... Lk 9:50 2424
J said unto him, Foxes have holes ... Lk 9:58 2424
J said unto him, Let the dead ... Lk 9:60 2424
J said unto him, No man, having ... Lk 9:62 2424
In that hour J rejoiced in spirit ... Lk 10:21 2424
to justify himself, said unto J ... Lk 10:29 2424
J answering said, A certain man ... Lk 10:30 2424
Then said J unto him, Go, and do ... Lk 10:37 2424
J answered and said unto her, ... Lk 10:41 2424
J answering said unto them, ... Lk 13:2 2424
when J saw her, he called her to ... Lk 13:12 2424
because that J had healed on the ... Lk 13:14 2424
J answering spake unto the ... Lk 14:3 2424
up their voices, and said, J ... Lk 17:13 2424
J answering said, Were there not ... Lk 17:17 2424
But J called them unto him, and ... Lk 18:16 2424
J said unto him, Why callest thou ... Lk 18:19 2424
Now when J heard these things, he ... Lk 18:22 2424
when J saw that he was very ... Lk 18:24 2424
that J of Nazareth passeth by ... Lk 18:37 2424
And he cried, saying, J, thou son ... Lk 18:38 2424
J stood, and commanded him to be ... Lk 18:40 2424
J said unto him, Receive thy ... Lk 18:42 2424
J entered and passed through ... Lk 19:1
And he sought to see J who he was ... Lk 19:3 2424
when J came to the place, he ... Lk 19:5 2424
J said unto him, This day is ... Lk 19:9 2424
And they brought him to J ... Lk 19:35 2424
the colt, and they set J thereon ... Lk 19:35 2424
J said unto them, Neither tell I ... Lk 20:8 2424
J answering said unto them, The ... Lk 20:34 2424
and drew near unto J to kiss him ... Lk 22:47 2424
But J said unto him, Judas, ... Lk 22:48 2424
J answered and said, Suffer ye ... Lk 22:51 2424
Then J said unto the chief ... Lk 22:52 2424
And the men that held J mocked him .. Lk 22:63 2424
And when Herod saw J, he was ... Lk 23:8 2424
therefore, willing to release J ... Lk 23:20 2424
but he delivered J to their will ... Lk 23:25 2424
that he might bear it after J ... Lk 23:26 2424
But J turning unto them said, ... Lk 23:28 2424
Then said J, Father, forgive them ... Lk 23:34 2424
And he said unto J, Lord, remember ... Lk 23:42 2424
J said unto him, Verily I say ... Lk 23:43 2424
when J had cried with a loud ... Lk 23:46 2424
Pilate, and begged the body of J ... Lk 23:52 2424
found not the body of the Lord J ... Lk 24:3 2424
J himself drew near, and went with ... Lk 24:15 2424
Concerning J of Nazareth, which ... Lk 24:19 2424
J himself stood in the midst of ... Lk 24:36 2424
grace and truth came by J Christ ... Jn 1:17 2424
day John seeth J coming unto him ... Jn 1:29 2424
And looking upon J as he walked ... Jn 1:36 2424
him speak, and they followed J ... Jn 1:37 2424
Then J turned, and saw them ... Jn 1:38 2424
And he brought him to J ... Jn 1:42 2424
when J beheld him, he said, Thou ... Jn 1:42 2424
The day following J would go ... Jn 1:43 2424
J of Nazareth, the son of Joseph ... Jn 1:45 2424
J saw Nathanael coming to him, and ... Jn 1:47 2424
J answered and said unto him, ... Jn 1:48 2424
J answered and said unto him, ... Jn 1:50 2424
and the mother of J was there ... Jn 2:1 2424
both J was called, and his ... Jn 2:2 2424
the mother of J saith unto him, ... Jn 2:3 2424
J saith unto her, Woman, what ... Jn 2:4 2424
J saith unto them, Fill the ... Jn 2:7 2424
miracles did J in Cana of Galilee ... Jn 2:11 2424
hand, and J went up to Jerusalem, ... Jn 2:13 2424
J answered and said unto them, ... Jn 2:19 2424
and the word which J had said ... Jn 2:22 2424
But J did not commit himself unto ... Jn 2:24 2424
The same came to J by night ... Jn 3:2 2424
J answered and said unto him, ... Jn 3:3 2424
J answered, Verily, verily, I say ... Jn 3:5 2424
J answered and said unto him, Art ... Jn 3:10 2424
After these things came J ... Jn 3:22 2424
Pharisees had heard that J made ... Jn 4:1 2424
(Though J himself baptized not, ... Jn 4:2 2424
J therefore, being wearied with ... Jn 4:6 2424
J saith unto her, Give me to ... Jn 4:7 2424
J answered and said unto her, If ... Jn 4:10 2424
J answered and said unto her, ... Jn 4:13 2424
J saith unto her, Go, call thy ... Jn 4:16 2424
J said unto her, Thou hast well ... Jn 4:17 2424
J saith unto her, Woman, believe ... Jn 4:21 2424
J saith unto her, I that speak ... Jn 4:26 2424
J saith unto them, My meat is to ... Jn 4:34 2424

Context	Reference	Number
For J himself testified, that a	Jn 4:44	2424
So J came again into Cana of	Jn 4:46	2424
When he heard that J was come out	Jn 4:47	2424
Then said J unto him, Except ye	Jn 4:48	2424
J saith unto him, Go thy way	Jn 4:50	2424
word that J had spoken unto him	Jn 4:50	2424
in the which J said unto him, Thy	Jn 4:53	2424
the second miracle that J did	Jn 4:54	2424
and J went up to Jerusalem	Jn 5:1	2424
When J saw him lie, and knew that	Jn 5:6	2424
J saith unto him, Rise, take up	Jn 5:8	2424
for J had conveyed himself away,	Jn 5:13	2424
Afterward J findeth him in the	Jn 5:14	2424
and told the Jews that it was J	Jn 5:15	2424
did the Jews persecute J, and	Jn 5:16	2424
But J answered them, My Father	Jn 5:17	2424
Then answered J and said unto them	Jn 5:19	2424
After these things J went over	Jn 6:1	2424
J went up into a mountain, and	Jn 6:3	2424
When J then lifted up his eyes,	Jn 6:5	2424
J said, Make the men sit down	Jn 6:10	2424
And J took the loaves	Jn 6:11	2424
had seen the miracle that J did	Jn 6:14	2424
When J therefore perceived that	Jn 6:15	2424
dark, and J was not come to them	Jn 6:17	2424
they see J walking on the sea, and	Jn 6:19	2424
and that J went not with his	Jn 6:22	2424
saw that J was not there, neither	Jn 6:24	2424
came to Capernaum, seeking for J	Jn 6:24	2424
J answered them and said, Verily,	Jn 6:26	2424
J answered and said unto them,	Jn 6:29	2424
Then J said unto them, Verily,	Jn 6:32	2424
J said unto them, I am the bread	Jn 6:35	2424
And they said, Is not this J	Jn 6:42	2424
J therefore answered and said unto	Jn 6:43	2424
Then J said unto them, Verily,	Jn 6:53	2424
When J knew in himself that his	Jn 6:61	2424
For J knew from the beginning who	Jn 6:64	2424
Then said J unto the twelve, Will	Jn 6:67	2424
J answered them, Have not I	Jn 6:70	2424
these things J walked in Galilee	Jn 7:1	2424
Then J said unto them, My time is	Jn 7:6	2424
feast J went up into the temple	Jn 7:14	2424
J answered them, and said, My	Jn 7:16	2424
J answered and said unto them, I	Jn 7:21	2424
Then cried J in the temple as he	Jn 7:28	2424
Then said J unto them, Yet a	Jn 7:33	2424
J stood and cried, saying, If any	Jn 7:37	2424
because that J was not yet	Jn 7:39	2424
them, (he that came to J by night	Jn 7:50	846
J went unto the mount of Olives	Jn 8:1	2424
But J stooped down, and with his	Jn 8:6	2424
J was left alone, and the woman	Jn 8:9	2424
When J had lifted up himself, and	Jn 8:10	2424
J said unto her, Neither do I	Jn 8:11	2424
Then spake J again unto them,	Jn 8:12	2424
J answered and said unto them,	Jn 8:14	2424
J answered, Ye neither know me,	Jn 8:19	2424
words spake J in the treasury	Jn 8:20	2424
Then said J again unto them, I go	Jn 8:21	2424
J saith unto them, Even the same	Jn 8:25	2424
Then said J unto them, When ye	Jn 8:28	2424
Then said J to those Jews which	Jn 8:31	2424
J answered them, Verily, verily,	Jn 8:34	2424
J saith unto them, If ye were	Jn 8:39	2424
J said unto them, If God were	Jn 8:42	2424
J answered, I have not a devil	Jn 8:49	2424
J answered, If I honour myself,	Jn 8:54	2424
J said unto them, Verily, verily,	Jn 8:58	2424
but J hid himself, and went out of	Jn 8:59	2424
as J passed by, he saw a man	Jn 9:1	
J answered, Neither hath this man	Jn 9:3	2424
A man that is called J made clay	Jn 9:11	2424
sabbath day when J made the clay	Jn 9:14	2424
J heard that they had cast him	Jn 9:35	2424
J said unto him, Thou hast both	Jn 9:37	2424
J said, For judgment I am come	Jn 9:39	2424
J said unto them, If ye were	Jn 9:41	2424
This parable spake J unto them	Jn 10:6	2424
Then said J unto them again,	Jn 10:7	2424
J walked in the temple in	Jn 10:23	2424
J answered them, I told you, and	Jn 10:25	2424
J answered them, Many good works	Jn 10:32	2424
J answered them, Is it not	Jn 10:34	2424
When J heard that, he said, This	Jn 11:4	2424
Now J loved Martha, and her sister	Jn 11:5	2424
J answered, Are there not twelve	Jn 11:9	2424
Howbeit J spake of his death	Jn 11:13	2424
Then said J unto them plainly,	Jn 11:14	2424
Then when J came, he found that	Jn 11:17	2424
as she heard that J was coming	Jn 11:20	2424
Then said Martha unto J, Lord, if	Jn 11:21	2424
J saith unto her, Thy brother	Jn 11:23	2424
J said unto her, I am the	Jn 11:25	2424
Now J was not yet come into the	Jn 11:30	2424
when Mary was come where J was	Jn 11:32	2424
When J therefore saw her weeping,	Jn 11:33	2424
J wept	Jn 11:35	2424
J therefore again groaning in	Jn 11:38	2424
J said, Take ye away the stone	Jn 11:39	2424
J saith unto her, Said I not unto	Jn 11:40	2424
J lifted up his eyes, and said,	Jn 11:41	2424
J saith unto them, Loose him, and	Jn 11:44	2424
had seen the things which J did	Jn 11:45	2424
told them what things J had done	Jn 11:46	2424
he prophesied that J should die	Jn 11:51	2424
J therefore walked no more openly	Jn 11:54	2424
Then sought they for J, and spake	Jn 11:56	2424
Then J six days before the	Jn 12:1	2424
costly, and anointed the feet of J	Jn 12:3	2424
Then said J, Let her alone	Jn 12:7	2424
Jews went away, and believed on J	Jn 12:11	2424
when they heard that J was coming	Jn 12:12	2424
And J, when he had found a young	Jn 12:14	2424
but when J was glorified, then	Jn 12:16	2424
him, saying, Sir, we would see J	Jn 12:21	2424
and again Andrew and Philip tell J	Jn 12:22	2424
J answered them, saying, The hour	Jn 12:23	2424
J answered and said, This voice	Jn 12:30	2424
Then J said unto them, Yet a	Jn 12:35	2424
These things spake J, and departed	Jn 12:36	2424
J cried and said, He that	Jn 12:44	2424
when J knew that his hour was	Jn 13:1	2424
J knowing that the Father had	Jn 13:3	2424
J answered and said unto him, What	Jn 13:7	2424
J answered him, If I wash thee	Jn 13:8	2424
J saith to him, He that is washed	Jn 13:10	2424
When J had thus said, he was	Jn 13:21	2424
of his disciples, whom J loved	Jn 13:23	2424
J answered, He it is, to whom I	Jn 13:26	2424
Then said J unto him, That thou	Jn 13:27	2424
that J had said unto him, Buy	Jn 13:29	2424
J said, Now is the Son of man	Jn 13:31	2424
J answered him, Whither I go,	Jn 13:36	2424
J answered him, Wilt thou lay	Jn 13:38	2424
J saith unto him, I am the way,	Jn 14:6	2424
J saith unto him, Have I been so	Jn 14:9	2424
J answered and said unto him, If a	Jn 14:23	2424
Now J knew that they were	Jn 16:19	2424
J answered them, Do ye now	Jn 16:31	2424
These words spake J, and lifted up	Jn 17:1	2424
J Christ, whom thou hast sent	Jn 17:3	2424
When J had spoken these words, he	Jn 18:1	2424
for J ofttimes resorted thither	Jn 18:2	2424
J therefore, knowing all things	Jn 18:4	2424
They answered him, J of Nazareth	Jn 18:5	2424
J saith unto them, I am he	Jn 18:5	2424
And they said, J of Nazareth	Jn 18:7	2424
J answered, I have told you that	Jn 18:8	2424
Then said J unto Peter, Put up	Jn 18:11	2424
and officers of the Jews took J	Jn 18:12	2424
And Simon Peter followed J	Jn 18:15	2424
went in with J into the palace of	Jn 18:15	2424
then asked J of his disciples	Jn 18:19	2424
J answered him, I spake openly to	Jn 18:20	2424
J with the palm of his hand	Jn 18:22	2424
J answered him, If I have spoken	Jn 18:23	2424
Then led they J from Caiaphas	Jn 18:28	2424
saying of J might be fulfilled	Jn 18:32	2424
judgment hall again, and called J	Jn 18:33	2424
J answered him, Sayest thou this	Jn 18:34	2424
J answered, My kingdom is not of	Jn 18:36	2424
J answered, Thou sayest that I am	Jn 18:37	2424
Then Pilate therefore took J	Jn 19:1	2424
Then came J forth, wearing the	Jn 19:5	2424
judgment hall, and saith unto J	Jn 19:9	2424
But J gave him no answer	Jn 19:9	2424
J answered, Thou couldest have no	Jn 19:11	2424
that saying, he brought J forth	Jn 19:13	2424
And they took J, and led him away	Jn 19:16	2424
side one, and J in the midst	Jn 19:18	2424
J OF NAZARETH THE	Jn 19:19	2424
for the place where J was	Jn 19:20	2424
when they had crucified J	Jn 19:23	2424
by the cross of J his mother	Jn 19:25	2424
When J therefore saw his mother,	Jn 19:26	2424
J knowing that all things were	Jn 19:28	2424
When J therefore had received the	Jn 19:30	2424
But when they came to J, and saw	Jn 19:33	2424
Arimathaea, being a disciple of J	Jn 19:38	2424
he might take away the body of J	Jn 19:38	2424
therefore, and took the body of J	Jn 19:38	2424
at the first came to J by night	Jn 19:39	2424
Then took they the body of J	Jn 19:40	2424
There laid they J therefore	Jn 19:42	2424
whom J loved, and saith unto them,	Jn 20:2	2424
where the body of J had lain	Jn 20:12	2424
saw J standing, and knew not that	Jn 20:14	2424
and knew not that it was J	Jn 20:14	2424
J saith unto her, Woman, why	Jn 20:15	2424
J saith unto her, Mary	Jn 20:16	2424
J saith unto her, Touch me not	Jn 20:17	2424
for fear of the Jews, came J	Jn 20:19	2424
Then said J to them again, Peace	Jn 20:21	2424
was not with them when J came	Jn 20:24	2424
then came J, the doors being shut	Jn 20:26	2424
J saith unto him, Thomas, because	Jn 20:29	2424
did J in the presence of his	Jn 20:30	2424
believe that J is the Christ	Jn 20:31	2424
After these things J shewed	Jn 21:1	2424
now come, J stood on the shore	Jn 21:4	2424
disciples knew not that it was J	Jn 21:4	2424
Then J saith unto them, Children,	Jn 21:5	2424
whom J loved saith unto Peter	Jn 21:7	2424
J saith unto them, Bring of the	Jn 21:10	2424
J saith unto them, Come and dine	Jn 21:12	2424
J then cometh, and taketh bread,	Jn 21:13	2424
J shewed himself to his disciples	Jn 21:14	2424
J saith to Simon Peter, Simon,	Jn 21:15	2424
J saith unto him, Feed my sheep	Jn 21:17	2424
disciple whom J loved following	Jn 21:20	2424
Peter seeing him saith to J	Jn 21:21	2424
J saith unto him, If I will that	Jn 21:22	2424
yet J said not unto him, He shall	Jn 21:23	2424
many other things which J did	Jn 21:25	2424
of all that J began both to do and	Acts 1:1	2424
this same J, which is taken up	Acts 1:11	2424
women, and Mary the mother of J	Acts 1:14	2424
was guide to them that took J	Acts 1:16	2424
the time that the Lord J went in	Acts 1:21	2424
J of Nazareth, a man approved of	Acts 2:22	2424
This J hath God raised up,	Acts 2:32	2424
that God hath made that same J	Acts 2:36	2424
of J Christ for the remission of	Acts 2:38	2424
In the name of J Christ of	Acts 3:6	2424
fathers, hath glorified his Son J	Acts 3:13	2424
And he shall send J Christ	Acts 3:20	2424
God, having raised up his Son J	Acts 3:26	2424
people, and preached through J the	Acts 4:2	2424
the name of J Christ of Nazareth	Acts 4:10	2424
them, that they had been with J	Acts 4:13	2424
at all nor teach in the name of J	Acts 4:18	2424
a truth against thy holy child J	Acts 4:27	2424
by the name of thy holy child J	Acts 4:30	2424
of the resurrection of the Lord J	Acts 4:33	2424
God of our fathers raised up J	Acts 5:30	2424
should not speak in the name of J	Acts 5:40	2424
not to teach and preach J Christ	Acts 5:42	2424
that this J of Nazareth shall	Acts 6:14	2424
with J into the possession of the	Acts 7:45	2424
J standing on the right hand of	Acts 7:55	2424
upon God, and saying, Lord J	Acts 7:59	2424
of God, and the name of J Christ	Acts 8:12	2424
in the name of the Lord J	Acts 8:16	2424
scripture, and preached unto him J	Acts 8:35	2424
I believe that J Christ is the	Acts 8:37	2424
I am J whom thou persecutest	Acts 9:5	2424
Brother Saul, the Lord, even J	Acts 9:17	2424
at Damascus in the name of J	Acts 9:27	2424
boldly in the name of the Lord J	Acts 9:29	2424
J Christ maketh thee whole	Acts 9:34	2424
preaching peace by J Christ	Acts 10:36	2424
How God anointed J of Nazareth	Acts 10:38	2424
who believed on the Lord J Christ	Acts 11:17	2424
Grecians, preaching the Lord J	Acts 11:20	2424
raised unto Israel a Saviour, J	Acts 13:23	2424
in that he hath raised up J again	Acts 13:33	2424
Lord J Christ we shall be saved	Acts 15:11	2424
for the name of our Lord J Christ	Acts 15:26	2424
of J Christ to come out of her	Acts 16:18	2424
Believe on the Lord J Christ	Acts 16:31	2424
and that this J, whom I preach	Acts 17:3	2424
that there is another king, one J	Acts 17:7	2424
because he preached unto them J	Acts 17:18	2424
to the Jews that J was Christ	Acts 18:5	2424
the scriptures that J was Christ	Acts 18:28	2424
after him, that is, on Christ J	Acts 19:4	2424
in the name of the Lord J	Acts 19:5	2424
Asia heard the word of the Lord J	Acts 19:10	2424
spirits the name of the Lord J	Acts 19:13	2424
We adjure you by J whom Paul	Acts 19:13	2424
and said, J I know, and Paul I know	Acts 19:15	2424
name of the Lord J was magnified	Acts 19:17	2424
and faith toward our Lord J Christ	Acts 20:21	2424
I have received of the Lord J	Acts 20:24	2424
remember the words of the Lord J	Acts 20:35	2424
for the name of the Lord J	Acts 21:13	2424
I am J of Nazareth, whom thou	Acts 22:8	2424
own superstition, and of one J	Acts 25:19	2424
to the name of J of Nazareth	Acts 26:9	2424
I am J whom thou persecutest	Acts 26:15	2424
God, persuading them concerning J	Acts 28:23	2424
which concern the Lord J Christ	Acts 28:31	2424
Paul, a servant of J Christ	Rom 1:1	2424
his Son J Christ our Lord	Rom 1:3	2424
ye also the called of J Christ	Rom 1:6	2424
our Father, and the Lord J Christ	Rom 1:7	2424
God through J Christ for you all	Rom 1:8	2424
judge the secrets of men by J	Rom 2:16	2424
is by faith of J Christ unto all	Rom 3:22	2424
redemption that is in Christ J	Rom 3:24	2424
of him which believeth in J	Rom 3:26	2424
up J our Lord from the dead	Rom 4:24	2424
God through our Lord J Christ	Rom 5:1	2424
in God through our Lord J Christ	Rom 5:11	2424
J Christ, hath abounded unto many	Rom 5:15	2424
reign in life by one, J Christ	Rom 5:17	2424
eternal life by J Christ our Lord	Rom 5:21	2424
of us as were baptized into J	Rom 6:3	2424
God through J Christ our Lord	Rom 6:11	2424
life through J Christ our Lord	Rom 6:23	2424
God through J Christ our Lord	Rom 7:25	2424
to them which are in Christ J	Rom 8:1	2424
the Spirit of life in Christ J	Rom 8:2	2424
up J from the dead dwell in you	Rom 8:11	2424
which is in Christ J our Lord	Rom 8:39	2424
confess with thy mouth the Lord J	Rom 10:9	2424
But put ye on the Lord J Christ	Rom 13:14	2424
and am persuaded by the Lord J	Rom 14:14	2424
another according to Christ J	Rom 15:5	2424
the Father of our Lord J Christ	Rom 15:6	2424
Now I say that J Christ was a	Rom 15:8	2424
of J Christ to the Gentiles	Rom 15:16	2424
whereof I may glory through J	Rom 15:17	2424
for the Lord J Christ's sake, and	Rom 15:30	2424
and Aquila my helpers in Christ J	Rom 16:3	2424
such serve not our Lord J Christ	Rom 16:18	2424
of our Lord J Christ be with you	Rom 16:20	2424
The grace of our Lord J Christ be	Rom 16:24	2424
and the preaching of J Christ	Rom 16:25	2424
glory through J Christ for ever	Rom 16:27	2424
called to be an apostle of J	1Cor 1:1	2424
that are sanctified in Christ J	1Cor 1:2	2424
the name of J Christ our Lord	1Cor 1:2	2424
Father, and from the Lord J Christ	1Cor 1:3	2424
which is given you by J Christ	1Cor 1:4	2424
the coming of our Lord J Christ	1Cor 1:7	2424
in the day of our Lord J Christ	1Cor 1:8	2424
of his Son J Christ our Lord	1Cor 1:9	2424
by the name of our Lord J Christ	1Cor 1:10	2424
But of him are ye in Christ J	1Cor 1:30	2424
save J Christ, and him crucified	1Cor 2:2	2424
that is laid, which is J Christ	1Cor 3:11	2424
for in Christ J I have begotten	1Cor 4:15	2424
In the name of our Lord J Christ	1Cor 5:4	2424
the power of our Lord J Christ	1Cor 5:4	2424
be saved in the day of the Lord J	1Cor 5:5	2424
in the name of the Lord J	1Cor 6:11	2424
and one Lord J Christ, by whom are	1Cor 8:6	2424
have I not seen J Christ our Lord	1Cor 9:1	2424
That the Lord J the same night in	1Cor 11:23	2424
Spirit of God calleth J accursed	1Cor 12:3	2424

no man can say that J is the Lord 1Cor 12:3 2424
which I have in Christ J our Lord 1Cor 15:31 2424
victory through our Lord J Christ 1Cor 15:57 2424
man love not the Lord J Christ 1Cor 16:22 2424
of our Lord J Christ be with you 1Cor 16:23 2424
love be with you all in Christ J 1Cor 16:24 2424
an apostle of J Christ by the 2Cor 1:1 2424
Father, and from the Lord J Christ 2Cor 1:2 2424
the Father of our Lord J Christ 2Cor 1:3 2424
are ours in the day of the Lord J 2Cor 1:14 2424
J Christ, who was preached among 2Cor 1:19 2424
ourselves, but Christ J the Lord 2Cor 4:5 2424
of God in the face of J Christ 2Cor 4:6 2424
the body the dying of the Lord J 2Cor 4:10 2424
that the life also of J might be 2Cor 4:10 2424
that the life also of J might be 2Cor 4:11 2424
he which raised up the Lord J 2Cor 4:14 2424
shall raise up us also by J 2Cor 4:14 2424
us to himself by J Christ 2Cor 5:18 2424
the grace of our Lord J Christ 2Cor 8:9 2424
that cometh preacheth another J 2Cor 11:4 2424
and Father of our Lord J Christ 2Cor 11:31 2424
how that J Christ is in you, ... 2Cor 13:5 2424
The grace of the Lord J Christ 2Cor 13:14 2424
neither by man, but by J Christ .... Gal 1:1 2424
Father, and from our Lord J Christ .... Gal 1:3 2424
but by the revelation of J Christ .... Gal 1:12 2424
liberty which we have in Christ J .... Gal 2:4 2424
law, but by the faith of J Christ .... Gal 2:16 2424
even we have believed in J Christ .... Gal 2:16 2424
before whose eyes J Christ hath .... Gal 3:1 2424
on the Gentiles through J Christ .... Gal 3:14 2424
that the promise by faith of J .... Gal 3:22 2424
of God by faith in Christ J .... Gal 3:26 2424
for ye are all one in Christ J .... Gal 3:28 2424
an angel of God, even as Christ J .... Gal 4:14 2424
For in J Christ neither .... Gal 5:6 2424
in the cross of our Lord J Christ .... Gal 6:14 2424
For in Christ J neither .... Gal 6:15 2424
my body the marks of the Lord J .... Gal 6:17 2424
the grace of our Lord J Christ be .... Gal 6:18 2424
an apostle of J Christ by the .... Eph 1:1 2424
and to the faithful in Christ J .... Eph 1:1 2424
Father, and from the Lord J Christ .... Eph 1:2 2424
and Father of our Lord J Christ .... Eph 1:3 2424
children by J Christ to himself .... Eph 1:5 2424
heard of your faith in the Lord J .... Eph 1:15 2424
That the God of our Lord J Christ .... Eph 1:17 2424
in heavenly places in Christ J .... Eph 2:6 2424
toward us through Christ J .... Eph 2:7 2424
in Christ J unto good works .... Eph 2:10 2424
But now in Christ J ye who .... Eph 2:13 2424
J Christ himself being the chief .... Eph 2:20 2424
the prisoner of J Christ for you .... Eph 3:1 2424
created all things by J Christ .... Eph 3:9 2424
he purposed in Christ J our Lord .... Eph 3:11 2424
the Father of our Lord J Christ .... Eph 3:14 2424
by Christ J throughout all ages .... Eph 3:21 2424
by him, as the truth is in J .... Eph 4:21 2424
in the name of our Lord J Christ .... Eph 5:20 2424
the Father and the Lord J Christ .... Eph 6:23 2424
our Lord J Christ in sincerity .... Eph 6:24 2424
the servants of J Christ .... Phil 1:1 2424
in Christ J which are at Philippi .... Phil 1:1 2424
Father, and from the Lord J Christ .... Phil 1:2 2424
it until the day of J Christ .... Phil 1:6 2424
you all in the bowels of J Christ .... Phil 1:8 2424
which are by J Christ, unto the .... Phil 1:11 2424
supply of the Spirit of J Christ .... Phil 1:19 2424
may be more abundant in J Christ .... Phil 1:26 2424
you, which was also in Christ J .... Phil 2:5 2424
That at the name of J every knee .... Phil 2:10 2424
confess that J Christ is Lord .... Phil 2:11 2424
But I trust in the Lord J to send .... Phil 2:19 2424
the things which are J Christ's .... Phil 2:21 2424
spirit, and rejoice in Christ J .... Phil 3:3 2424
the knowledge of Christ J my Lord .... Phil 3:8 2424
also I am apprehended of Christ J .... Phil 3:12 2424
high calling of God in Christ J .... Phil 3:14 2424
the Saviour, the Lord J Christ .... Phil 3:20 2424
hearts and minds through Christ J .... Phil 4:7 2424
his riches in glory by Christ J .... Phil 4:19 2424
Salute every saint in Christ J .... Phil 4:21 2424
The grace of our Lord J Christ be .... Phil 4:23 2424
an apostle of J Christ by the .... Col 1:1 2424
our Father and the Lord J Christ .... Col 1:2 2424
the Father of our Lord J Christ .... Col 1:3 2424
heard of your faith in Christ J .... Col 1:4 2424
every man perfect in Christ J .... Col 1:28 2424
received Christ J the Lord .... Col 2:6 2424
do all in the name of the Lord J .... Col 3:17 2424
Father and in the Lord J Christ 1Th 1:1 2424
our Father, and the Lord J Christ 1Th 1:1 2424
of hope in our Lord J Christ 1Th 1:3 2424
he raised from the dead, even J 1Th 1:10 2424
which in Judaea are in Christ J 1Th 2:14 2424
Who both killed the Lord J 1Th 2:15 2424
our Lord J Christ at his coming 1Th 2:19 2424
our Father, and our Lord J Christ 1Th 3:11 2424
at the coming of our Lord J 1Th 3:13 2424
and exhort you by the Lord J 1Th 4:1 2424
we gave you by the Lord J 1Th 4:2 2424
For if we believe that J died 1Th 4:14 2424
in J will God bring with him 1Th 4:14 2424
salvation by our Lord J Christ 1Th 5:9 2424
of God in Christ J concerning you 1Th 5:18 2424
the coming of our Lord J Christ 1Th 5:23 2424
of our Lord J Christ be with you 1Th 5:28 2424
our Father and the Lord J Christ 2Th 1:1 2424
our Father and the Lord J Christ 2Th 1:2 2424
when the Lord J shall be revealed 2Th 1:7 2424
the gospel of our Lord J Christ 2Th 1:8 2424
That the name of our Lord J 2Th 1:12 2424
of our God and the Lord J Christ 2Th 1:12 2424
the coming of our Lord J Christ 2Th 2:1 2424
of the glory of our Lord J Christ 2Th 2:14 2424
Now our Lord J Christ himself, and 2Th 2:16 2424
in the name of our Lord J Christ 2Th 3:6 2424
and exhort by our Lord J Christ 2Th 3:12 2424
The grace of our Lord J Christ be 2Th 3:18 2424
an apostle of J Christ by the 1Ti 1:1 2424
Lord J Christ, which is our hope 1Ti 1:1 2424
our Father and J Christ our Lord 1Ti 1:2 2424
And I thank Christ J our Lord 1Ti 1:12 2424
and love which is in Christ J 1Ti 1:14 2424
that Christ J came into the world 1Ti 1:15 2424
that in me first J Christ might 1Ti 1:16 2424
God and men, the man Christ J 1Ti 2:5 2424
in the faith which is in Christ J 1Ti 3:13 2424
be a good minister of J Christ 1Ti 4:6 2424
before God, and the Lord J Christ 1Ti 5:21 2424
the words of our Lord J Christ 1Ti 6:3 2424
all things, and before Christ J 1Ti 6:13 2424
appearing of our Lord J Christ 1Ti 6:14 2424
an apostle of J Christ by the 2Ti 1:1 2424
of life which is in Christ J 2Ti 1:1 2424
the Father and Christ J our Lord 2Ti 1:2 2424
Christ J before the world began 2Ti 1:9 2424
appearing of our Saviour J Christ 2Ti 1:10 2424
and love which is in Christ J 2Ti 1:13 2424
in the grace that is in Christ J 2Ti 2:1 2424
as a good soldier of J Christ 2Ti 2:3 2424
Remember that J Christ of the 2Ti 2:8 2424
is in Christ J with eternal glory 2Ti 2:10 2424
Christ J shall suffer persecution 2Ti 3:12 2424
faith which is in Christ J 2Ti 3:15 2424
before God, and the Lord J Christ 2Ti 4:1 2424
The Lord J Christ be with thy 2Ti 4:22 2424
of God, and an apostle of J Christ .... Titus 1:1 2424
the Lord J Christ our Saviour .... Titus 1:4 2424
great God and our Saviour J Christ .... Titus 2:13 2424
through J Christ our Saviour .... Titus 3:6 2424
Paul, a prisoner of J Christ .... Philem 1 2424
our Father and the Lord J Christ .... Philem 3 2424
which thou hast toward the Lord J .... Philem 5 2424
thing which is in you in Christ J .... Philem 6 2424
now also a prisoner of J Christ .... Philem 9 2424
my fellowprisoner in Christ J .... Philem 23 2424
The grace of our Lord J Christ be .... Philem 25 2424
But we see J, who was made a .... Heb 2:9 2424
of our profession, Christ J .... Heb 3:1 2424
J the Son of God, let us hold .... Heb 4:14 2424
is for us entered, even J .... Heb 6:20 2424
By so much was J made a surety of .... Heb 7:22 2424
the body of J Christ once for all .... Heb 10:10 2424
the holiest by the blood of J .... Heb 10:19 2424
Looking unto J the author .... Heb 12:2 2424
to J the mediator of the new .... Heb 12:24 2424
J Christ the same yesterday, and .... Heb 13:8 2424
Wherefore J also, that he might .... Heb 13:12 2424
again from the dead our Lord J .... Heb 13:20 2424
in his sight, through J Christ .... Heb 13:21 2424
of God and of the Lord J Christ .... Jas 1:1 2424
the faith of our Lord J Christ .... Jas 2:1 2424
Peter, an apostle of J Christ 1Pet 1:1 2424
of the blood of J Christ 1Pet 1:2 2424
and Father of our Lord J Christ 1Pet 1:3 2424
of J Christ from the dead 1Pet 1:3 2424
at the appearing of J Christ 1Pet 1:7 2424
you at the revelation of J Christ 1Pet 1:13 2424
acceptable to God by J Christ 1Pet 2:5 2424
by the resurrection of J Christ 1Pet 3:21 2424
may be glorified through J Christ 1Pet 4:11 2424
his eternal glory by Christ J 1Pet 5:10 2424
with you all that are in Christ J 1Pet 5:14 2424
servant and an apostle of J Christ 2Pet 1:1 2424
of God and our Saviour J Christ 2Pet 1:1 2424
of God, and of J our Lord 2Pet 1:2 2424
knowledge of our Lord J Christ 2Pet 1:8 2424
of our Lord and Saviour J Christ 2Pet 1:11 2424
even as our Lord J Christ hath 2Pet 1:14 2424
and coming of our Lord J Christ 2Pet 1:16 2424
of the Lord and Saviour J Christ 2Pet 2:20 2424
of our Lord and Saviour J Christ 2Pet 3:18 2424
Father, and with his Son J Christ 1Jn 1:3 2424
the blood of J Christ his Son 1Jn 1:7 2424
Father, J Christ the righteous 1Jn 2:1 2424
that denieth that J is the Christ 1Jn 2:22 2424
on the name of his Son J Christ 1Jn 3:23 2424
spirit that confesseth that J 1Jn 4:2 2424
J Christ is come in the flesh is 1Jn 4:3 2424
confess that J is the Son of God 1Jn 4:15 2424
Whosoever believeth that J is the 1Jn 5:1 2424
that J is the Son of God 1Jn 5:5 2424
by water and blood, even J Christ 1Jn 5:6 2424
is true, even in his Son J Christ 1Jn 5:20 2424
Father, and from the Lord J Christ 2Jn 3 2424
who confess not that J Christ is 2Jn 7 2424
Jude, the servant of J Christ .... Jude 1 2424
Father, and preserved in J Christ .... Jude 1 2424
Lord God, and our Lord J Christ .... Jude 4 2424
the apostles of our Lord J Christ .... Jude 17 2424
Lord J Christ unto eternal life .... Jude 21 2424
The Revelation of J Christ .... Rev 1:1 2424
and of the testimony of J Christ .... Rev 1:2 2424
from J Christ, who is the .... Rev 1:5 2424
kingdom and patience of J Christ .... Rev 1:9 2424
and for the testimony of J Christ .... Rev 1:9 2424
and have the testimony of J Christ .... Rev 12:17 2424
of God, and the faith of J .... Rev 14:12 2424
the blood of the martyrs of J .... Rev 17:6 2424
that have the testimony of J .... Rev 19:10 2424
for the testimony of J is the .... Rev 19:10 2424
beheaded for the witness of J .... Rev 20:4 2424
I J have sent mine angel to .... Rev 22:16 2424
Even so, come, Lord J .... Rev 22:20 2424
The grace of our Lord J Christ be .... Rev 22:21 2424

2. Joshua, son of Nun.
For if J had given them rest, ... Heb 4:8 2424
3. Justus, a Roman Christian.
And J, which is called Justus, who .... Col 4:11 2424

JESUS' (*je'-zus*) *Refers to the Christ.*
and cast them down at J feet .... Mt 15:30 2424
who also himself was J disciple .... Mt 27:57 2424
saw it, he fell down at J knees .... Lk 5:8 2424
and he fell down at J feet .... Lk 8:41 2424
Mary, which also sat at J feet .... Lk 10:39 2424
and they came not for J sake only .... Jn 12:9 2424
Now there was leaning on J bosom .... Jn 13:23 2424
He then lying on J breast saith .... Jn 13:25 2424
your servants for J sake 2Cor 4:5 2424
delivered unto death for J sake 2Cor 4:11 2424

JETHER (*je'-thur*) See HOBAB, ITHRA, ITHRITES, JETHRO, RAGUEL.
1. A son of Gideon.
he said unto J his firstborn, Up, ... Judg 8:20 3500
2. Father of Amasa.
Ner, and unto Amasa the son of J 1Kin 2:5 3500
of Israel, and Amasa the son of J 1Kin 2:32 3500
of Amasa was J the Ishmeelite 1Chr 2:17 3500
3. A son of Jerahmeel.
J, and Jonathan 1Chr 2:32 3500
and J died without children 1Chr 2:32 3500
4. A son of Ezra.
And the sons of Ezra were, J 1Chr 4:17 3500
5. A descendant of Asher.
And the sons of J 1Chr 7:38 3500

JETHETH (*je'-theth*) *A prince of Edom.*
duke Timnah, duke Alvah, duke J .... Gen 36:40 3509
duke Timnah, duke Aliah, duke J 1Chr 1:51 3509

JETHLAH (*jeth'-lah*) *A city in Dan.*
And Shaalabbin, and Ajalon, and J .... Josh 19:42 3494

JETHRO (*je'-thro*) See JETHER. *Father-in-law of Moses.*
the flock of J his father in law .... Ex 3:1 3503
returned to J his father in law, ... Ex 4:18 3503
J said to Moses, Go in peace .... Ex 4:18 3503
When J, the priest of Midian, ... Ex 18:1 3503
Then J, Moses' father in law, ... Ex 18:2 3503
And J, Moses' father in law, came .... Ex 18:5 3503
father in law J am come unto thee .... Ex 18:6 3503
J rejoiced for all the goodness .... Ex 18:9 3503
J said, Blessed be the LORD, who .... Ex 18:10 3503
And J, Moses' father in law, took .... Ex 18:12 3503

JETUR (*je'-tur*)
1. A son of Ishmael.
Hadar, and Tema, J, Naphish, and .... Gen 25:15 3195
J, Naphish, and Kedemah 1Chr 1:31 3195
2. Descendants of Jetur.
war with the Hagarites, with J 1Chr 5:19 3195

JEUEL (*je-u'-el*) See JEIEL. *A descendant of Zerah.*
J, and their brethren, six hundred 1Chr 9:6 3262

JEUSH (*je'-ush*) See JEHUSH.
1. A son of Esau.
And Aholibamah bare J, and Jaalam, ... Gen 36:5 3266
and she bare to Esau J, and Jaalam, ... Gen 36:14 3266
duke J, duke Jaalam, duke Korah .... Gen 36:18 3266
Eliphaz, Reuel, and J, and Jaalam, ... 1Chr 1:35 3266
2. Grandson of Jediael.
J, and Benjamin, and Ehud, and 1Chr 7:10 3266
3. A sanctuary servant.
Shimei were, Jahath, Zina, and J 1Chr 23:10 3266
but J and Beriah had not many sons 1Chr 23:11 3266
4. A son of Rehoboam.
J, and Shamariah, and Zaham 2Chr 11:19 3266

JEUZ (*je'-uz*) *Son of Shaharaim.*
And J, and Shachia, and Mirma 1Chr 8:10 3263

JEW (*jew*) See JEWESS, JEWISH, JEWS. *Post-exilic term for the Israelites.*
the palace there was a certain J .... Est 2:5 3064
he had told them that he was a J .... Est 3:4 3064
the J sitting at the king's gate .... Est 5:13 3064
and do even so to Mordecai the J .... Est 6:10 3064
the queen and to Mordecai the J .... Est 8:7 3064
of Abihail, and Mordecai the J .... Est 9:29 3064
according as Mordecai the J .... Est 9:31 3064
For Mordecai the J was next unto .... Est 10:3 3064
them, to wit, of a J his brother .... Jer 34:9 3064
of the skirt of him that is a J .... Zec 8:23 3064
How is it that thou, being a J .... Jn 4:9 2453
Pilate answered, Am I a J .... Jn 18:35 2453
a man that is a J to keep company .... Acts 10:28 2453
sorcerer, a false prophet, a J .... Acts 13:6 2453
And found a certain J named Aquila .... Acts 18:2 2453
a certain J named Apollos, born .... Acts 18:24 2453
were seven sons of one Sceva, a J .... Acts 19:14 2453
when they knew that he was a J .... Acts 19:34 2453
I am a man which am a J of Tarsus .... Acts 21:39 2453
I am verily a man which am a J .... Acts 22:3 2453
to the J first, and also to the .... Rom 1:16 2453
that doeth evil, of the J first .... Rom 2:9 2453
that worketh good, to the J first .... Rom 2:10 2453
Behold, thou art called a J .... Rom 2:17 2453
For he is not a J, which is one .... Rom 2:28 2453
But he is a J, which is one .... Rom 2:29 2453
What advantage then hath the J .... Rom 3:1 2453
is no difference between the J .... Rom 10:12 2453
And unto the Jews I became as a J 1Cor 9:20 2453
them all, If thou, being a J .... Gal 2:14 2453
There is neither J nor Greek .... Gal 3:28 2453
there is neither Greek nor J .... Col 3:11 2453

JEWEL
As a *j* of gold in a swine's snout Prov 11:22 5141
of knowledge are a precious *j* Prov 20:15 3627
I put a *j* on thy forehead, and Eze 16:12 5141

JEWELS
servant brought forth *j* of silver Gen 24:53 3627
j of gold, and raiment, and gave Gen 24:53 3627
j of silver, and *j* of gold, Ex 3:22 3627
j of silver, and *j* of gold Ex 11:2 3627
of the Egyptians *j* of silver Ex 12:35 3627
and *j* of gold, and raiment Ex 12:35 3627
rings, and tablets, all *j* of gold Ex 35:22 3627
gotten, of *j* of gold, chains, and Num 31:50 3627
gold of them, even all wrought *j* Num 31:51 3627
and put the *j* of gold, which ye 1Sa 6:8 3627
wherein the *j* of gold were, and 1Sa 6:15 3627
the dead bodies, and precious *j* 2Chr 20:25 3627
and for all manner of pleasant *j* 2Chr 32:27 3627
shall not be for *j* of fine gold Job 28:17 3627
cheeks are comely with rows of *j* Song 1:10
joints of thy thighs are like *j* Song 7:1 2484
The rings, and nose *j*, Is 3:21 5141
bride adorneth herself with her *j* Is 61:10 3627
also taken thy fair *j* of my gold Eze 16:17 3627
clothes, and shall take thy fair *j* Eze 16:39 3627
clothes, and take away thy fair *j* Eze 23:26 3627
with her earrings and her *j* Hos 2:13 2484
in that day when I make up my *j* Mal 3:17 5459

JEWESS (*jew'-ess*) *A female Jew.*
of a certain woman, which was a *J* Acts 16:1 *2453*
his wife Drusilla, which was a *J* Acts 24:24 *2453*

JEWISH (*jew'-ish*) *Of or relating to the Jews.*
Not giving heed to *J* fables Titus 1:14 *2451*

JEWRY (*jew'-ree*) See JUDEA. *Of or relating to the Jews.*
king my father brought out of *J* Dan 5:13 3061
people, teaching throughout all *J* Lk 23:5 *2449*
for he would not walk in *J* Jn 7:1 *2449*

JEWS (*jews*) See JEWS'.
Syria, and drave the *J* from Elath 2Kin 16:6 3064
Gedaliah, that he died, and the *J* 2Kin 25:25 3064
that the *J* which came up from Ezr 4:12 3062
in haste to Jerusalem unto the *J* Ezr 4:23 3062
unto the *J* that were in Judah Ezr 5:1 3062
God was upon the elders of the *J* Ezr 5:5 3062
let the governor of the *J* Ezr 6:7 3062
the elders of the *J* build this Ezr 6:7 3062
J for the building of this house Ezr 6:8 3062
And the elders of the *J* builded Ezr 6:14 3062
concerning the *J* that had escaped Neh 1:2 3064
had I as yet told it to the *J* Neh 2:16 3064
indignation, and mocked the *J* Neh 4:1 3064
and said, What do these feeble *J* Neh 4:2 3064
that when the *J* which dwelt by Neh 4:12 3064
against their brethren the *J* Neh 5:1 3064
have redeemed our brethren the *J* Neh 5:8 3064
an hundred and fifty of the *J* Neh 5:17 3064
that thou and the *J* think to rebel Neh 6:6 3064
In those days also saw I *J* that Neh 13:23 3064
J that were throughout the whole Est 3:6 3064
and to cause to perish, all *J* Est 3:13 3064
was great mourning among the *J* Est 4:3 3064
the king's treasuries for the *J* Est 4:7 3064
king's house, more than all the *J* Est 4:13 3064
arise to the *J* from another place Est 4:14 3064
gather together all the *J* that Est 4:16 3064
Mordecai be of the seed of the *J* Est 6:13 3064
that he had devised against the *J* Est 8:3 3064
the *J* which are in all the king's Est 8:5 3064
he laid his hand upon the *J* Est 8:7 3064
Write ye also for the *J*, as it Est 8:8 3064
Mordecai commanded unto the *J* Est 8:9 3064
to the *J* according to their Est 8:9 3064
the *J* which were in every city to Est 8:11 3064
that the *J* should be ready Est 8:13 3064
The *J* had light, and gladness, and Est 8:16 3064
the *J* had joy and gladness, a Est 8:17 3064
the people of the land became *J* Est 8:17 3054
the fear of the *J* fell upon them Est 8:17 3064
J hoped to have power over them Est 9:1 3064
that the *J* had rule over them Est 9:1 3064
The *J* gathered themselves Est 9:2 3064
of the king, helped the *J* Est 9:3 3064
Thus the *J* smote all their Est 9:5 3064
in Shushan the palace the *J* slew Est 9:6 3064
of Hammedatha, the enemy of the *J* Est 9:10 3064
The *J* have slain and destroyed Est 9:12 3064
let it be granted to the *J* which Est 9:13 3064
For the *J* that were in Shushan Est 9:15 3064
But the other *J* that were in the Est 9:16 3064
But the *J* that were at Shushan Est 9:18 3064
Therefore the *J* of the villages, Est 9:19 3064
sent letters unto all the *J* that Est 9:20 3064
As the days wherein the *J* rested Est 9:22 3064
the *J* undertook to do as they had Est 9:23 3064
Agagite, the enemy of all the *J* Est 9:24 3064
against the *J* to destroy them Est 9:24 3064
which he devised against the *J* Est 9:25 3064
The *J* ordained, and took upon them Est 9:27 3064
should not fail from among the *J* Est 9:28 3064
sent the letters unto all the *J* Est 9:30 3064
Ahasuerus, and great among the *J* Est 10:3 3064
before all the *J* that sat in the Jer 32:12 3064
I am afraid of the *J* that are Jer 38:19 3064
when all the *J* that were in Moab Jer 40:11 3064
Even all the *J* returned out of Jer 40:12 3064
that all the *J* which are gathered Jer 40:15 3064
slew all the *J* that were with him Jer 41:3 3064
the *J* which dwell in the land of Jer 44:1 3064
the seventh year three thousand *J* Jer 52:28 3064
of the *J* seven hundred forty Jer 52:30 3064
came near, and accused the *J* Dan 3:8 3064
There are certain *J* whom thou Dan 3:12 3064
is he that is born King of the *J* Mt 2:2 *2453*
Art thou the King of the *J* Mt 27:11 *2453*
him, saying, Hail, King of the *J* Mt 27:29 *2453*
THIS IS JESUS THE KING OF THE *J* Mt 27:37 *2453*
among the *J* until this day Mt 28:15 *2453*
For the Pharisees, and all the *J* Mk 7:3 *2453*
him, Art thou the King of the *J* Mk 15:2 *2453*
unto you the King of the *J* Mk 15:9 *2453*
whom ye call the King of the *J* Mk 15:12 *2453*
salute him, Hail, King of the *J* Mk 15:18 *2453*
written over, THE KING OF THE *J* Mk 15:26 *2453*
sent unto him the elders of the *J* Lk 7:3 *2453*
Art thou the King of the *J* Lk 23:3 *2453*
If thou be the king of the *J* Lk 23:37 *2453*
IS THE KING OF THE *J* Lk 23:38 *2453*
of Arimathaea, a city of the *J* Lk 23:51 *2453*
when the *J* sent priests and Jn 1:19 *2453*
manner of the purifying of the *J* Jn 2:6 *2453*
Then answered the *J* and said unto Jn 2:18 *2453*
Then said the *J*, Forty and six Jn 2:20 *2453*
named Nicodemus, a ruler of the *J* Jn 3:1 *2453*
and the *J* about purifying Jn 3:25 *2453*
for the *J* have no dealings with Jn 4:9 *2453*
for salvation is of the *J* Jn 4:22 *2453*
this there was a feast of the *J* Jn 5:1 *2453*
The *J* therefore said unto him Jn 5:10 *2453*
told the *J* that it was Jesus, Jn 5:15 *2453*
did the *J* persecute Jesus Jn 5:16 *2453*
Therefore the *J* sought the more Jn 5:18 *2453*
And the passover, a feast of the *J* Jn 6:4 *2453*
The *J* then murmured at him, Jn 6:41 *2453*
The *J* therefore strove among Jn 6:52 *2453*
because the *J* sought to kill him Jn 7:1 *2453*
Then the *J* sought him at the Jn 7:11 *2453*
openly of him for fear of the *J* Jn 7:13 *2453*
the *J* marvelled, saying, How Jn 7:15 *2453*
Then said the *J* among themselves, Jn 7:35 *2453*
Then said the *J*, Will he kill Jn 8:22 *2453*
to those *J* which believed on him Jn 8:31 *2453*
Then answered the *J*, and said unto Jn 8:48 *2453*
Then said the *J* unto him, Now we Jn 8:52 *2453*
Then said the *J* unto him, Thou Jn 8:57 *2453*
But the *J* did not believe Jn 9:18 *2453*
because they feared the *J* Jn 9:22 *2453*
for the *J* had agreed already, Jn 9:22 *2453*
among the *J* for these sayings Jn 10:19 *2453*
Then came the *J* round about him, Jn 10:24 *2453*
Then the *J* took up stones again Jn 10:31 *2453*
The *J* answered him, saying, For a Jn 10:33 *2453*
the *J* of late sought to stone Jn 11:8 *2453*
many of the *J* came to Martha and Jn 11:19 *2453*
The *J* then which were with her in Jn 11:31 *2453*
the *J* also weeping which came Jn 11:33 *2453*
Then said the *J*, Behold how he Jn 11:36 *2453*
Then many of the *J* which came to Jn 11:45 *2453*
walked no more openly among the *J* Jn 11:54 *2453*
Much people of the *J* therefore Jn 12:9 *2453*
of him many of the *J* went away Jn 12:11 *2453*
and as I said unto the *J*, Whither Jn 13:33 *2453*
and officers of the *J* took Jesus Jn 18:12 *2453*
he, which gave counsel to the *J* Jn 18:14 *2453*
whither the *J* always resort Jn 18:20 *2453*
The *J* therefore said unto him, It Jn 18:31 *2453*
him, Art thou the King of the *J* Jn 18:33 *2453*
should not be delivered to the *J* Jn 18:36 *2453*
he went out again unto the *J* Jn 18:38 *2453*
unto you the King of the *J* Jn 18:39 *2453*
And said, Hail, King of the *J* Jn 19:3 *2453*
The *J* answered him, We have a law Jn 19:7 *2453*
but the *J* cried out, saying, If Jn 19:12 *2453*
and he saith unto the *J*, Behold Jn 19:14 *2453*
KING OF THE *J* Jn 19:19 *2453*
title then read many of the *J* Jn 19:20 *2453*
chief priests of the *J* to Pilate Jn 19:21 *2453*
Write not, The King of the *J* Jn 19:21 *2453*
that he said, I am King of the *J* Jn 19:21 *2453*
The *J* therefore, because it was Jn 19:31 *2453*
but secretly for fear of the *J* Jn 19:38 *2453*
as the manner of the *J* is to bury Jn 19:40 *2453*
were assembled for fear of the *J* Jn 20:19 *2453*
were dwelling at Jerusalem *J* Acts 2:5 *2453*
Cyrene, and strangers of Rome, *J* Acts 2:10 *2453*
confounded the *J* which dwelt at Acts 9:22 *2453*
the *J* took counsel to kill him Acts 9:23 *2453*
among all the nation of the *J* Acts 10:22 *2453*
he did both in the land of the *J* Acts 10:39 *2453*
word to none but unto the *J* only Acts 11:19 *2453*
because he saw it pleased the *J* Acts 12:3 *2453*
of the people of the *J* Acts 12:11 *2453*
of God in the synagogues of the *J* Acts 13:5 *2453*
when the *J* were gone out of the Acts 13:42 *2453*
was broken up, many of the *J* Acts 13:43 *2453*
But when the *J* saw the multitudes Acts 13:45 *2453*
But the *J* stirred up the devout Acts 13:50 *2453*
into the synagogue of the *J* Acts 14:1 *2453*
a great multitude both of the *J* Acts 14:1 *2453*
But the unbelieving *J* stirred up Acts 14:2 *2453*
and part held with the *J*, and part Acts 14:4 *2453*
also of the *J* with their rulers, Acts 14:5 *2453*
thither certain *J* from Antioch Acts 14:19 *2453*
J which were in those quarters Acts 16:3 *2453*
saying, These men, being *J* Acts 16:20 *2453*
where was a synagogue of the *J* Acts 17:1 *2453*
But the *J* which believed not, Acts 17:5 *2453*
went into the synagogue of the *J* Acts 17:10 *2453*
But when the *J* of Thessalonica Acts 17:13 *2453*
he in the synagogue with the *J* Acts 17:17 *2453*
all *J* to depart from Rome Acts 18:2 *2453*
every sabbath, and persuaded the *J* Acts 18:4 *2453*
testified to the *J* that Jesus was Acts 18:5 *2453*
the *J* made insurrection with one Acts 18:12 *2453*
his mouth, Gallio said unto the *J* Acts 18:14 *2453*
wrong or wicked lewdness, O ye *J* Acts 18:14 *2453*
synagogue, and reasoned with the *J* Acts 18:19 *2453*
For he mightily convinced the *J* Acts 18:28 *2453*
word of the Lord Jesus, both *J* Acts 19:10 *2453*
Then certain of the vagabond *J* Acts 19:13 *2453*
And this was known to all the *J* Acts 19:17 *2453*
the *J* putting him forward Acts 19:33 *2453*
when the *J* laid wait for him, as Acts 20:3 *2453*
me by the lying in wait of the *J* Acts 20:19 *2453*
Testifying both to the *J*, and also Acts 20:21 *2453*
So shall the *J* at Jerusalem bind Acts 21:11 *2453*
how many thousands of *J* there are Acts 21:20 *2453*
that thou teachest all the *J* Acts 21:21 *2453*
the *J* which were of Asia, when Acts 21:27 *2453*
of all the *J* which dwelt there Acts 22:12 *2453*
wherefore he was accused of the *J* Acts 22:30 *2453*
certain of the *J* banded together, Acts 23:12 *2453*
The *J* have agreed to desire thee Acts 23:20 *2453*
This man was taken of the *J* Acts 23:27 *2453*
that the *J* laid wait for the man Acts 23:30 *2453*
all the *J* throughout the world Acts 24:5 *2453*
the *J* also assented, saying that Acts 24:9 *2453*
Whereupon certain *J* from Asia Acts 24:18 *2453*
willing to shew the *J* a pleasure Acts 24:27 *2453*
the chief of the *J* informed him Acts 25:2 *2453*
the *J* which came down from Acts 25:7 *2453*
Neither against the law of the *J* Acts 25:8 *2453*
willing to do the *J* a pleasure Acts 25:9 *2453*
to the *J* have I done no wrong, as Acts 25:10 *2453*
the elders of the *J* informed me Acts 25:15 *2453*
of the *J* have dealt with me Acts 25:24 *2453*
whereof I am accused of the *J* Acts 26:2 *2453*
questions which are among the *J* Acts 26:3 *2453*
at Jerusalem, know all the *J* Acts 26:4 *2453*
Agrippa, I am accused of the *J* Acts 26:7 *2453*
For these causes the *J* caught me Acts 26:21 *2453*
the chief of the *J* together Acts 28:17 *2453*
But when the *J* spake against it, Acts 28:19 *2453*
the *J* departed, and had great Acts 28:29 *2453*
for we have before proved both *J* Rom 3:9 *2453*
Is he the God of the *J* only Rom 3:29 *2453*
he hath called, not of the *J* only Rom 9:24 *2453*
For the *J* require a sign, and the 1Cor 1:22 *2453*
unto the *J* a stumblingblock, and 1Cor 1:23 *2453*
them which are called, both *J* 1Cor 1:24 *2453*
unto the *J* I became as a Jew, 1Cor 9:20 *2453*
as a Jew, that I might gain the *J* 1Cor 9:20 *2453*
none offence, neither to the *J* 1Cor 10:32 *2453*
body, whether we be *J* or Gentiles 1Cor 12:13 *2453*
Of the *J* five times received I 2Cor 11:24 *2453*
the other *J* dissembled likewise Gal 2:13 *2453*
of Gentiles, and not as do the *J* Gal 2:14 *2452*
the Gentiles to live as do the *J* Gal 2:14 *2450*
We who are *J* by nature, and not Gal 2:15 *2453*
even as they have of the *J* 1Th 2:14 *2453*
of them which say they are *J* Rev 2:9 *2453*
of Satan, which say they are *J* Rev 3:9 *2453*

JEWS' (*jews*)
talk not with us in the *J* 2Kin 18:26 3066
a loud voice in the *J* language 2Kin 18:28 3066
the *J* speech unto the people of 2Chr 32:18 3066
could not speak in the *J* language Neh 13:24 3066
the Agagite, the *J* enemy Est 3:10 3064
the *J* enemy unto Esther the queen Est 8:1 3064
speak not to us in the *J* language Is 36:11 3064
a loud voice in the *J* language Is 36:13 3064
the *J* passover was at hand, and Jn 2:13 *2453*
Now the *J* feast of tabernacles Jn 7:2 *2453*
the *J* passover was nigh at hand Jn 11:55 *2453*
because of the *J* preparation day Jn 19:42 *2453*
in time past in the *J* religion Gal 1:13 *2454*
profited in the *J* religion above Gal 1:14 *2454*

JEZANIAH (*jez-a-ni'-ah*) See JAAZANIAH. *A Jewish captain.*
J the son of a Maachathite, they Jer 40:8 3153
J the son of Hoshaiah, and all the Jer 42:1 3153

JEZEBEL (*jez'-e-bel*) See JEZEBEL'S. *Wife of King Ahab.*
that he took to wife *J* the 1Kin 16:31 348
when *J* cut off the prophets of 1Kin 18:4 348
told my lord what I did when *J* 1Kin 18:13 348
Ahab told *J* all that Elijah had 1Kin 19:1 348
Then *J* sent a messenger unto 1Kin 19:2 348
But *J* his wife came to him, and 1Kin 21:5 348
J his wife said unto him, Dost 1Kin 21:7 348
did as *J* had sent unto them, and 1Kin 21:11 348
Then they sent to *J*, saying, 1Kin 21:14 348
when *J* heard that Naboth was 1Kin 21:15 348
that *J* said to Ahab, Arise, take 1Kin 21:15 348
of *J* also spake the LORD, saying, 1Kin 21:23 348
The dogs shall eat *J* by the wall 1Kin 21:23 348
whom *J* his wife stirred up 1Kin 21:25 348
of the LORD, at the hand of *J* 2Kin 9:7 348
the dogs shall eat *J* in the 2Kin 9:10 348
as the whoredoms of thy mother *J* 2Kin 9:22 348
come to Jezreel, *J* heard of it 2Kin 9:30 348
shall dogs eat the flesh of *J* 2Kin 9:36 348
the carcase of *J* shall be as dung 2Kin 9:37 348
they shall not say, This is *J* 2Kin 9:37 348
thou sufferest that woman *J* Rev 2:20 *2403*

JEZEBEL'S (*jez'-e-bels*)
hundred, which eat at *J* table 1Kin 18:19 348

JEZER (*je'-zur*) See JEZERITES. *A son of Naphtali.*
Jahzeel, and Guni, and *J*, and Gen 46:24 3337
Of *J*, the family of the Jezerites Num 26:49 3337
Jahziel, and Guni, and *J*, and 1Chr 7:13 3337

JEZERITES (*je'-zur-ites*) *Descendants of Jezer.*
Of Jezer, the family of the J ... Num 26:49 3339

JEZIAH (*je-zi'-ah*) *Married a foreigner in exile.*
Ramiah, and J, and Malchiah, and ... Ezr 10:25 3150

JEZIEL (*je'-ze-el*) *A warrior in David's army.*
and J, and Pelet, the sons of ... 1Chr 12:3 3149

JEZLIAH (*jez-li'-ah*) *A son of Elpaal.*
Ishmerai also, and J, and Jobab, ... 1Chr 8:18 3152

JEZOAR (*je-zo'-ar*) See ZOAR. *A son of Helah.*
sons of Helah were, Zereth, and J ... 1Chr 4:7 3328

JEZRAHIAH (*jez-ra-hi'-ah*) See IZRAHIAH. *A priest.*
sang loud, with J their overseer ... Neh 12:42 3156

JEZREEL (*jez'-re-el*) See JEZREELITE.
1. A city in Judah.
And J, and Jokdeam, and Zanoah, ... Josh 15:56 3157
and pitched in the valley of J ... Judg 6:33 3157
David also took Ahinoam of J ... 1Sa 25:43 3157
by a fountain which is in J ... 1Sa 29:1 3157
And the Philistines went up to J ... 1Sa 29:11 3157
2. A city in Issachar.
And their border was toward J ... Josh 19:18 3157
and over the Ashurites, and over J ... 2Sa 2:9 3157
came of Saul and Jonathan out of J ... 2Sa 4:4 3157
which is by Zartanah beneath J ... 1Kin 4:12 3157
And Ahab rode, and went to J ... 1Kin 18:45 3157
before Ahab to the entrance of J ... 1Kin 18:46 3157
had a vineyard, which was in J ... 1Kin 21:1 3157
eat Jezebel by the wall of J ... 1Kin 21:23 3157
J of the wounds which the Syrians ... 2Kin 8:29 3157
to see Joram the son of Ahab in J ... 2Kin 8:29 3157
eat Jezebel in the portion of J ... 2Kin 9:10 3157
was returned to be healed in J of ... 2Kin 9:15 3157
of the city to go to tell it in J ... 2Kin 9:15 3157
rode in a chariot, and went to J ... 2Kin 9:16 3157
a watchman on the tower in J ... 2Kin 9:17 3157
And when Jehu was come to J ... 2Kin 9:30 3157
In the portion of J shall dogs ... 2Kin 9:36 3157
of the field in the portion of J ... 2Kin 9:37 3157
to Samaria, unto the rulers of J ... 2Kin 10:1 3157
come to me to J by to morrow this ... 2Kin 10:6 3157
in baskets, and sent him them to J ... 2Kin 10:7 3157
of the house of Ahab in J ... 2Kin 10:11 3157
in J because of the wounds which ... 2Chr 22:6 3157
see Jehoram the son of Ahab at J ... 2Chr 22:6 3157
3. A plain.
they who are of the valley of J ... Josh 17:16 3157
bow of Israel in the valley of J ... Hos 1:5 3157
and they shall hear J ... Hos 2:22 3157
4. A descendant of Etam.
J, and Ishma, and Idbash ... 1Chr 4:3 3157
5. Symbolic name for Hosea's eldest son.
said unto him, Call his name J ... Hos 1:4 3157
6. Symbolic name for Hosea's eldest son.
blood of J upon the house of Jehu ... Hos 1:4 3157
for great shall be the day of J ... Hos 1:11 3157

JEZREELITE (*jez'-re-el-ite*) See JEZREELITESS.
An inhabitant of Jezreel.
that Naboth the J had a vineyard ... 1Kin 21:1 3158
Naboth the J had spoken to him ... 1Kin 21:4 3158
Because I spake unto Naboth the J ... 1Kin 21:6 3158
thee the vineyard of Naboth the J ... 1Kin 21:7 3158
of the vineyard of Naboth the J ... 1Kin 21:15 3158
to the vineyard of Naboth the J ... 1Kin 21:16 3158
in the portion of Naboth the J ... 2Kin 9:21 3158
of the field of Naboth the J ... 2Kin 9:25 3158

JEZREELITESS (*jez'-re-el-i-tess*) *A female Jezreelite.*
with his two wives, Ahinoam the J ... 1Sa 27:3 3159
taken captives, Ahinoam the J ... 1Sa 30:5 3159
his two wives also, Ahinoam the J ... 2Sa 2:2 3159
was Amnon, of Ahinoam the J ... 2Sa 3:2 3159
firstborn Amnon, of Ahinoam the J ... 1Chr 3:1 3159

JIBSAM (*jib'-sam*) *A son of Tola.*
and Jeriel, and Jahmai, and J ... 1Chr 7:2 3005

JIDLAPH (*jid'-laf*) *A son of Nahor.*
Chesed, and Hazo, and Pildash, and J .. Gen 22:22 3044

JIMNA (*jim'-nah*) See IMNA, JIMNAH, JIMNITES.
A son of Asher.
of J, the family of the Jimnites ... Num 26:44 3232

JIMNAH (*jim'-nah*) See JIMNA. *Same as Jimna.*
J, and Ishuah, and Isui, and Beriah, ... Gen 46:17 3232

JIMNITES (*jim'-nites*) *Descendants of Jimna.*
of Jimna, the family of the J ... Num 26:44 3232

JIPHTAH (*jif'-tah*) See JEPHTHAH, JIPHTHAH-EL.
A city in Judah.
And J, and Ashnah, and Nezib, ... Josh 15:43 3316

JIPHTHAH-EL (*jif'-thah-el*) *A valley in Zebulun.*
thereof are in the valley of J ... Josh 19:14 3317
to the valley of J toward the ... Josh 19:27 3317

JOAB (*jo'-ab*) See ATAROTH, HOUSE, JOAB'S.
1. Commander of David's army.
the son of Zeruiah, brother to J ... 1Sa 26:6 3097
J the son of Zeruiah, and the ... 2Sa 2:13 3097
And Abner said to J, Let the young ... 2Sa 2:14 3097
And J said, Let them arise ... 2Sa 2:14 3097
three sons of Zeruiah there, J ... 2Sa 2:18 3097
hold up my face to J thy brother ... 2Sa 2:22 3097
J also and Abishai pursued after ... 2Sa 2:24 3097
Then Abner called to J, and said, ... 2Sa 2:26 3097
J said, As God liveth, unless ... 2Sa 2:27 3097
So J blew a trumpet, and all the ... 2Sa 2:28 3097
J returned from following Abner ... 2Sa 2:30 3097
And J and his men went all night, ... 2Sa 2:32 3097
J came from pursuing a troop, and ... 2Sa 3:22 3097
When J and all the host that was ... 2Sa 3:23 3097
with him were come, they told J ... 2Sa 3:23 3097
Then J came to the king, and said, ... 2Sa 3:24 3097
when J was come out from David, ... 2Sa 3:26 3097
J took him aside in the gate to ... 2Sa 3:27 3097
Let it rest on the head of J ... 2Sa 3:29 3097
house of J one that hath an issue ... 2Sa 3:29 3097
So J and Abishai his brother slew ... 2Sa 3:30 3097
And David said to J, and to all the ... 2Sa 3:31 3097
J the son of Zeruiah was over the ... 2Sa 8:16 3097
when David heard of it, he sent J ... 2Sa 10:7 3097
When J saw that the front of the ... 2Sa 10:9 3097
J drew nigh, and the people that ... 2Sa 10:13 3097
So J returned from the children ... 2Sa 10:14 3097
to battle, that David sent J ... 2Sa 11:1 3097
And David sent to J, saying, Send ... 2Sa 11:6 3097
And J sent Uriah to David ... 2Sa 11:6 3097
David demanded of him how J did ... 2Sa 11:7 3097
and my lord J, and the servants of ... 2Sa 11:11 3097
that David wrote a letter to J ... 2Sa 11:14 3097
when J observed the city, that he ... 2Sa 11:16 3097
city went out, and fought with J ... 2Sa 11:17 3097
Then J sent and told David all the ... 2Sa 11:18 3097
David all that J had sent him for ... 2Sa 11:22 3097
Thus shalt thou say unto J ... 2Sa 11:25 3097
J fought against Rabbah of the ... 2Sa 12:26 3097
J sent messengers to David, and ... 2Sa 12:27 3097
Now J the son of Zeruiah ... 2Sa 14:1 3097
J sent to Tekoah, and fetched ... 2Sa 14:2 3097
So J put the words in her mouth ... 2Sa 14:3 3097
Is not the hand of J with thee in ... 2Sa 14:19 3097
for thy servant J, he bade me, and ... 2Sa 14:19 3097
thy servant J done this thing ... 2Sa 14:20 3097
And the king said unto J, Behold ... 2Sa 14:21 3097
J fell to the ground on his face, ... 2Sa 14:22 3097
J said, Today thy servant knoweth ... 2Sa 14:22 3097
So J arose and went to Geshur, and ... 2Sa 14:23 3097
Therefore Absalom sent for J ... 2Sa 14:29 3097
Then J arose, and came to Absalom ... 2Sa 14:31 3097
And Absalom answered J, Behold, I ... 2Sa 14:32 3097
So J came to the king, and told ... 2Sa 14:33 3097
captain of the host instead of J ... 2Sa 17:25 3097
of the people under the hand of J ... 2Sa 18:2 3097
And the king commanded J and ... 2Sa 18:5 3097
a certain man saw it, and told J ... 2Sa 18:10 3097
J said unto the man that told him ... 2Sa 18:11 3097
And the man said unto J, Though I ... 2Sa 18:12 3097
Then said J, I may not tarry thus ... 2Sa 18:14 3097
J blew the trumpet, and the people ... 2Sa 18:16 3097
for J held back the people ... 2Sa 18:16 3097
J said unto him, Thou shalt not ... 2Sa 18:20 3097
Then said J to Cushi, Go tell the ... 2Sa 18:21 3097
And Cushi bowed himself unto J ... 2Sa 18:21 3097
the son of Zadok yet again to J ... 2Sa 18:22 3097
J said, Wherefore wilt thou run, ... 2Sa 18:22 3097
When J sent the king's servant, ... 2Sa 18:29 3097
And it was told J, Behold, the ... 2Sa 19:1 3097
J came into the house to the king ... 2Sa 19:5 3097
me continually in the room of J ... 2Sa 19:13 3097
J said to Amasa, Art thou in ... 2Sa 20:9 3097
J took Amasa, by the beard with ... 2Sa 20:9 3097
So J and Abishai his brother ... 2Sa 20:10 3097
him, and said, He that favoureth J ... 2Sa 20:11 3097
is for David, let him go after J ... 2Sa 20:11 3097
all the people went on after J ... 2Sa 20:13 3097
were with J battered the wall ... 2Sa 20:15 3097
say, I pray you, unto J, Come ... 2Sa 20:16 3097
her, the woman said, Art thou J ... 2Sa 20:17 3097
J answered and said, Far be it ... 2Sa 20:20 3097
And the woman said unto J, Behold, ... 2Sa 20:21 3097
of Bichri, and cast it out to J ... 2Sa 20:22 3097
J returned to Jerusalem unto the ... 2Sa 20:22 3097
Now J was over all the host of ... 2Sa 20:23 3097
And Abishai, the brother of J ... 2Sa 23:18 3097
of J was one of the thirty ... 2Sa 23:24 3097
armourbearer to J the son of ... 2Sa 23:37 3097
For the king said to J the ... 2Sa 24:2 3097
J said unto the king, Now the ... 2Sa 24:3 3097
king's word prevailed against J ... 2Sa 24:4 3097
And J and the captains of the host ... 2Sa 24:4 3097
J gave up the sum of the number ... 2Sa 24:9 3097
he conferred with J the son of ... 1Kin 1:7 3097
J the captain of the host ... 1Kin 1:19 3097
when J heard the sound of the ... 1Kin 1:41 3097
J the son of Zeruiah did to me ... 1Kin 2:5 3097
and for J the son of Zeruiah ... 1Kin 2:22 3097
Then tidings came to J ... 1Kin 2:28 3097
for J had turned after Adonijah, ... 1Kin 2:28 3097
J fled unto the tabernacle of the ... 1Kin 2:28 3097
it was told king Solomon that J ... 1Kin 2:29 3097
word again, saying, Thus said J ... 1Kin 2:30 3097
the innocent blood, which J shed ... 1Kin 2:31 3097
return upon the head of J ... 1Kin 2:33 3097
J the captain of the host was ... 1Kin 11:15 3097
(For six months did J remain ... 1Kin 11:16 3097
that J the captain of the host ... 1Kin 11:21 3097
Abishai, and J, and Asahel, three ... 1Chr 2:16 3097
So J the son of Zeruiah went ... 1Chr 11:6 3097
J repaired the rest of the city ... 1Chr 11:8 3097
And Abishai the brother of J ... 1Chr 11:20 3097
were, Asahel the brother of J ... 1Chr 11:26 3097
of J the son of Zeruiah, ... 1Chr 11:39 3097
J the son of Zeruiah was over the ... 1Chr 18:15 3097
when David heard of it, he sent J ... 1Chr 19:8 3097
Now when J saw that the battle ... 1Chr 19:10 3097
So J and the people that were with ... 1Chr 19:14 3097
Then J came to Jerusalem ... 1Chr 19:15 3097
J led forth the power of the army ... 1Chr 20:1 3097
J smote Rabbah, and destroyed it ... 1Chr 20:1 3097
And David said to J and to the ... 1Chr 21:2 3097
J answered, The LORD make his ... 1Chr 21:3 3097
king's word prevailed against J ... 1Chr 21:4 3097
Wherefore J departed, and went ... 1Chr 21:4 3097
J gave the sum of the number of ... 1Chr 21:5 3097
king's word was abominable to J ... 1Chr 21:6 3097
J the son of Zeruiah, had ... 1Chr 26:28 3097
month was Asahel the brother of J ... 1Chr 27:7 3097
J the son of Zeruiah began to ... 1Chr 27:24 3097
general of the king's army was J ... 1Chr 27:34 3097
when J returned, and smote of Edom .. Ps 60:t 3097
2. A descendant of Caleb.
Ataroth, the house of J, and half ... 1Chr 2:54 5854
3. A grandson of Kenaz.
and Seraiah begat J, the father of ... 1Chr 4:14 3097
4. A family of exiles with Zerubbabel.
of the children of Jeshua and J ... Ezr 2:6 3097
of the children of Jeshua and J ... Neh 7:11 3097
5. A family of exiles with Ezra.
Of the sons of J ... Ezr 8:9 3097

JOAB'S (*jo'-abs*) *Refers to Joab 1.*
J field is near mine, and he hath ... 2Sa 14:30 3097
sister to Zeruiah J mother ... 2Sa 17:25 3097
J brother, and a third part under ... 2Sa 18:2 3097
bare J armour compassed about ... 2Sa 18:15 3097
And there went out after him J men ... 2Sa 20:7 3097
J garment that he had put on was ... 2Sa 20:8 3097
to the sword that was in J hand ... 2Sa 20:10 3097
one of J men stood by him, and ... 2Sa 20:11 3097

JOAH (*jo'-ah*) See ETHAN.
1. A son of Asaph.
J the son of Asaph the recorder ... 2Kin 18:18 3098
son of Hilkiah, and Shebna, and J ... 2Kin 18:26 3098
J the son of Asaph the recorder, ... 2Kin 18:37 3098
house, and Shebna the scribe, and J ... Is 36:3 3098
J unto Rabshakeh, Speak, I pray ... Is 36:11 3098
and Shebna the scribe, and J ... Is 36:22 3098
2. A descendant of Gershom.
J his son, Iddo his son, Zerah ... 1Chr 6:21 3098
J the son of Zimmah ... 2Chr 29:12 3098
and Eden the son of J ... 2Chr 29:12 3098
3. A sanctuary servant.
J the third, and Sacar the fourth, ... 1Chr 26:4 3098
4. A Levite.
J the son of Joahaz the recorder, ... 2Chr 34:8 3098

JOAHAZ (*jo'-a-haz*) See JEHOAHAZ. *Father of Joah.*
and Joah the son of J the recorder ... 2Chr 34:8 3098

JOANAN See JOANNA.

JOANNA (*jo-an'-nah*)
1. A female disciple.
J the wife of Chuza Herod's ... Lk 8:3 *2489*
It was Mary Magdalene, and J ... Lk 24:10 *2489*
2. An ancestor of Jesus.
Which was the son of J, which was ... Lk 3:27 *2489*

JOASH (*jo'-ash*) See JEHOASH.
1. A son of Becher.
Zemira, and J, and Eliezer, and ... 1Chr 7:8 3135
2. A sanctuary servant.
and over the cellars of oil was J ... 1Chr 27:28 3135
3. Father of Gideon.
pertained unto J the Abi-ezrite ... Judg 6:11 3101
Gideon the son of J hath done ... Judg 6:29 3101
the men of the city said unto J ... Judg 6:30 3101
J said unto all that stood ... Judg 6:31 3101
the sword of Gideon the son of J ... Judg 7:14 3101
Gideon the son of J returned from ... Judg 8:13 3101
And Jerubbaal the son of J went ... Judg 8:29 3101
Gideon the son of J died in a ... Judg 8:32 3101
in the sepulchre of J his father ... Judg 8:32 3101
4. A son of King Ahab.
the city, and to J the king's son ... 1Kin 22:26 3101
the city, and to J the king's son ... 2Chr 18:25 3101
5. A son of King Ahaziah.
took J the son of Ahaziah, and ... 2Kin 11:2 3101
And the rest of the acts of J ... 2Kin 12:19 3101
slew J in the house of Millo, ... 2Kin 12:20 3101
twentieth year of J the son of ... 2Kin 13:1 3101
seventh year of J king of Judah ... 2Kin 13:10 3101
the son of J king of Judah ... 2Kin 14:1 3101
to all things as J his father did ... 2Kin 14:3 3101
Amaziah the son of J king of ... 2Kin 14:17 3101
year of Amaziah the son of J king ... 2Kin 14:23 3101
son, Ahaziah his son, J his son, ... 1Chr 3:11 3101
took J the son of Ahaziah, and ... 2Chr 22:11 3101
J was seven years old when he ... 2Chr 24:1 3101
J did that which was right in the ... 2Chr 24:2 3101
that J was minded to repair the ... 2Chr 24:4 3101
Thus J the king remembered not ... 2Chr 24:22 3101
they executed judgment against J ... 2Chr 24:24 3101
king of Judah, the son of J ... 2Chr 25:23 3101
Amaziah the son of J king of ... 2Chr 25:25 3101
6. A king of Israel.
J his son reigned in his stead ... 2Kin 13:9 3101
And the rest of the acts of J ... 2Kin 13:12 3101
And J slept with his fathers ... 2Kin 13:13 3101
J was buried in Samaria with the ... 2Kin 13:13 3101
J the king of Israel came down ... 2Kin 13:14 3101
Three times did J beat him ... 2Kin 13:25 3101
In the second year of J son of ... 2Kin 14:1 3101
of Judah Jeroboam the son of J ... 2Kin 14:23 3101
the hand of Jeroboam the son of J ... 2Kin 14:27 3101
Judah took advice, and sent to J ... 2Chr 25:17 3101
J king of Israel sent to Amaziah ... 2Chr 25:18 3101
So J the king of Israel went up ... 2Chr 25:21 3101
J the king of Israel took Amaziah ... 2Chr 25:23 3101
J son of Jehoahaz king of Israel ... 2Chr 25:25 3101
the days of Jeroboam the son of J ... Hos 1:1 3101
the son of J king of Israel ... Amos 1:1 3101
7. A descendant of Shelah.
and the men of Chozeba, and J ... 1Chr 4:22 3101
8. A captain in David's army.
The chief was Ahiezer, then J ... 1Chr 12:3 3101

JOATHAM (jo'-a-tham) See JOTHAM. *Ancestor of Joseph, husband of Mary.*
And Ozias begat J ... Mt 1:9 2488
and J begat Achaz ... Mt 1:9 2488

JOAZCAR See JOZACHAR.

JOB (jobe) See JASHUB, JOB'S.
1. A descendant of Issachar.
Tola, and Phuvah, and J, and Shimron Gen 46:13 3102
2. A righteous sufferer.
the land of Uz, whose name was J ... Job 1:1 347
were gone about, that J sent ... Job 1:5 347
for J said, It may be that my ... Job 1:5 347
Thus did J continually ... Job 1:5 347
Hast thou considered my servant J ... Job 1:8 347
Doth J fear God for nought ... Job 1:9 347
And there came a messenger unto J ... Job 1:14 347
Then J arose, and rent his mantle, ... Job 1:20 347
In all this J sinned not, nor ... Job 1:22 347
Hast thou considered my servant J ... Job 2:3 347
smote J with sore boils from the ... Job 2:7 347
this did not J sin with his lips ... Job 2:10 347
After this opened J his mouth ... Job 3:1 347
And J spake, and said, ... Job 3:2 347
But J answered and said, ... Job 6:1 347
Then J answered and said, ... Job 9:1 347
And J answered and said, ... Job 12:1 347
Then J answered and said, ... Job 16:1 347
Then J answered and said, ... Job 19:1 347
But J answered and said, ... Job 21:1 347
Then J answered and said, ... Job 23:1 347
But J answered and said, ... Job 26:1 347
Moreover J continued his parable, ... Job 27:1 347
Moreover J continued his parable, ... Job 29:1 347
The words of J are ended ... Job 31:40 347
three men ceased to answer J ... Job 32:1 347
against J was his wrath kindled, ... Job 32:2 347
no answer, and yet had condemned J .. Job 32:3 347
had waited till J had spoken ... Job 32:4 347
was none of you that convinced J ... Job 32:12 347
Wherefore, J, I pray thee, hear ... Job 33:1 347
Mark well, O J, hearken unto me ... Job 33:31 347
For J hath said, I am righteous ... Job 34:5 347
What man is like J, who drinketh ... Job 34:7 347
J hath spoken without knowledge, ... Job 34:35 347
My desire is that J may be tried ... Job 34:36 347
Therefore doth J open his mouth ... Job 35:16 347
Hearken unto this, O J ... Job 37:14 347
answered J out of the whirlwind ... Job 38:1 347
Moreover the LORD answered J ... Job 40:1 347
Then J answered the LORD, and said ... Job 40:3 347
LORD unto J out of the whirlwind ... Job 40:6 347
Then J answered the LORD, and said ... Job 42:1 347
had spoken these words unto J ... Job 42:7 347
is right, as my servant J hath ... Job 42:7 347
seven rams, and go to my servant J ... Job 42:8 347
my servant J shall pray for you ... Job 42:8 347
which is right, like my servant J ... Job 42:8 347
the LORD also accepted J ... Job 42:9 347
LORD turned the captivity of J ... Job 42:10 347
also the LORD gave J twice as ... Job 42:10 347
end of J more than his beginning ... Job 42:12 347
so fair as the daughters of J ... Job 42:15 347
After this lived J an hundred ... Job 42:16 347
So J died, being old and full of ... Job 42:17 347
three men, Noah, Daniel, and J ... Eze 14:14 347
Though Noah, Daniel, and J ... Eze 14:20 347
have heard of the patience of J ... Jas 5:11 2492

JOBAB (jo'-bab)
1. A son of Joktan.
And Ophir, and Havilah, and J ... Gen 10:29 3103
And Ophir, and Havilah, and J ... 1Chr 1:23 3103
2. A king of Edom.
J the son of Zerah of Bozrah ... Gen 36:33 3103
J died, and Husham of the land of ... Gen 36:34 3103
J the son of Zerah of Bozrah ... 1Chr 1:44 3103
when J was dead, Husham of the ... 1Chr 1:45 3103
3. A Canaanite king.
that he sent to J king of Madon ... Josh 11:1 3103
4. A son of Shaharaim.
And he begat of Hodesh his wife, J ... 1Chr 8:9 3103
5. A son of Elpaal.
Ishmerai also, and Jezliah, and J ... 1Chr 8:18 3103

JOB'S (jobes) *Refers to Job 2.*
Now when J three friends heard of ... Job 2:11 347

JOCHEBED (jok'-e-bed) *Wife of Amram.*
Amram took him J his father's ... Ex 6:20 3115
And the name of Amram's wife was J. Num 26:59 3115

JODA See JUDA.

JOED (jo'-ed) *A son of Pedaiah.*
son of Meshullam, the son of J ... Neh 11:7 3133

JOEL (jo'-el)
1. A son of Samuel.
the name of his firstborn was J ... 1Sa 8:2 3100
Heman a singer, the son of J ... 1Chr 6:33 3100
appointed Heman the son of J ... 1Chr 15:17 3100
2. A Simeonite.
And J, and Jehu the son of Josibiah ... 1Chr 4:35 3100
3. Father of Shemaiah.
The sons of J ... 1Chr 5:4 3100
the son of Shema, the son of J ... 1Chr 5:8 3100
4. A chief Gadite.
J the chief, and Shapham the next, ... 1Chr 5:12 3100
5. A Kohathite.
The son of Elkanah, the son of J ... 1Chr 6:36 3100
6. A descendant of Tola.
Michael, and Obadiah, and J ... 1Chr 7:3 3100
7. A "mighty man" of David.
J the brother of Nathan, Mibhar ... 1Chr 11:38 3100
8. A Gershomite.
J the chief, and his brethren an ... 1Chr 15:7 3100
Levites, for Uriel, Asaiah, and J ... 1Chr 15:11 3100
chief was Jehiel, and Zetham, and J ... 1Chr 23:8 3100
9. A treasurer of the Temple.
J his brother, which were over ... 1Chr 26:22 3100
10. A prince of Manasseh.
of Manasseh, J the son of Pedaiah ... 1Chr 27:20 3100
11. A Kohathite who cleansed the Temple.
J the son of Azariah, of the sons ... 2Chr 29:12 3100
12. Married a foreigner in exile.
Zabad, Zebina, Jadau, and J ... Ezr 10:43 3100
13. An overseer of the Benjamites.
J the son of Zichri was their ... Neh 11:9 3100
14. A prophet.
that came to J the son of Pethuel ... Joel 1:1 3100
which was spoken by the prophet J ... Acts 2:16 2493

JOELAH (jo-e'-lah) *A member of David's band.*
And J, and Zebadiah, the sons of ... 1Chr 12:7 3132

JOEZER (jo-e'-zer) *A warrior in David's army.*
and Jesiah, and Azareel, and J ... 1Chr 12:6 3134

JOGBEHAH (jog'-be-hah) *A place in Gad.*
Atroth, Shophan, and Jaazer, and J ... Num 32:35 3011
tents on the east of Nobah and J ... Judg 8:11 3011

JOGLI (jog'-li) *A Danite prince.*
of Dan, Bukki the son of J ... Num 34:22 3020

JOHA (jo'-hah)
1. Son of Beriah.
And Michael, and Ispah, and J ... 1Chr 8:16 3109
2. A "mighty man" of David.
J his brother, the Tizite, ... 1Chr 11:45 3109

JOHANAN (jo-ha'-nan) See JEHOHANAN, JOHN.
1. A son of Kareah.
J the son of Careah, and Seraiah ... 2Kin 25:23 3110
the son of Nethaniah, and J ... Jer 40:8 3110
Moreover J the son of Kareah, and ... Jer 40:13 3110
Then J the son of Kareah spake to ... Jer 40:15 3110
said unto J the son of Kareah ... Jer 40:16 3110
But when J the son of Kareah, and ... Jer 41:11 3110
Ishmael saw J the son of Kareah ... Jer 41:13 3110
went unto J the son of Kareah ... Jer 41:14 3110
escaped from J with eight men ... Jer 41:15 3110
Then took J the son of Kareah, and ... Jer 41:16 3110
J the son of Kareah, and Jezaniah ... Jer 42:1 3110
Then called he J the son of ... Jer 42:8 3110
J the son of Kareah, and all the ... Jer 43:2 3110
So J the son of Kareah, and all ... Jer 43:4 3110
But J the son of Kareah, and all ... Jer 43:5 3110
2. A son of King Josiah.
of Josiah were, the firstborn J ... 1Chr 3:15 3110
3. A son of Elioenai.
and Pelaiah, and Akkub, and J ... 1Chr 3:24 3110
4. A grandson of Ahimaaz.
begat Azariah, and Azariah begat J ... 1Chr 6:9 3110
J begat Azariah, (he it is that ... 1Chr 6:10 3110
5. A warrior in David's army.
and Jeremiah, and Jahaziel, and J ... 1Chr 12:4 3110
6. A Gadite warrior in David's army.
J the eighth, Elzabad the ninth, ... 1Chr 12:12 3110
7. An Ephraimite.
of Ephraim, Azariah the son of J ... 2Chr 28:12 3076
8. An exile with Ezra.
J the son of Hakkatan, and with ... Ezr 8:12 3110
9. A priest in exile with Ezra.
chamber of J the son of Eliashib ... Ezr 10:6 3076
10. A son of Tobiah.
his son J had taken the daughter ... Neh 6:18 3076
11. A priest in exile with Zerubbabel.
days of Eliashib, Joiada, and J ... Neh 12:22 3110
the days of J the son of Eliashib ... Neh 12:23 3110

JOHN (jon) See BAPTIST, JEHOHANAN, JOHN'S, MARK.
1. The Baptizer.
In those days came J the Baptist ... Mt 3:1 2491
the same J had his raiment of ... Mt 3:4 2491
from Galilee to Jordan unto J ... Mt 3:13 2491
But J forbad him, saying, I have ... Mt 3:14 2491
heard that J was cast into prison ... Mt 4:12 2491
came to him the disciples of J ... Mt 9:14 2491
Now when J had heard in the ... Mt 11:2 2491
shew J again those things which ... Mt 11:4 2491
unto the multitudes concerning J ... Mt 11:7 2491
a greater than J the Baptist ... Mt 11:11 2491
from the days of J the Baptist ... Mt 11:12 2491
and the law prophesied until J ... Mt 11:13 2491
For J came neither eating nor ... Mt 11:18 2491
servants, This is J the Baptist ... Mt 14:2 2491
For Herod had laid hold on J ... Mt 14:3 2491
For J said unto him, It is not ... Mt 14:4 2491
Give me here J Baptist's head in ... Mt 14:8 2491
sent, and beheaded J in the prison ... Mt 14:10 2491
say that thou art J the Baptist ... Mt 16:14 2491
spake unto them of J the Baptist ... Mt 17:13 2491
The baptism of J, whence was it ... Mt 21:25 2491
for all hold J as a prophet ... Mt 21:26 2491
For J came unto you in the way of ... Mt 21:32 2491
J did baptize in the wilderness, ... Mk 1:4 2491
J was clothed with camel's hair, ... Mk 1:6 2491
and was baptized of J in Jordan ... Mk 1:9 2491
Now after that J was put in ... Mk 1:14 2491
And the disciples of J and of the ... Mk 2:18 2491
him, Why do the disciples of J ... Mk 2:18 2491
That J the Baptist was risen from ... Mk 6:14 2491
heard thereof, he said, It is J ... Mk 6:16 2491
sent forth and laid hold upon J ... Mk 6:17 2491
For J had said unto Herod, It is ... Mk 6:18 2491
For Herod feared J, knowing that ... Mk 6:20 2491
said, The head of J the Baptist ... Mk 6:24 2491
charger the head of J the Baptist ... Mk 6:25 2491
And they answered, J the Baptist ... Mk 8:28 2491
The baptism of J, was it from ... Mk 11:30 2491
for all men counted J, that he ... Mk 11:32 2491
and thou shalt call his name J ... Lk 1:13 2491
but he shall be called J ... Lk 1:60 2491
and wrote, saying, His name is J ... Lk 1:63 2491
the word of God came unto J the ... Lk 3:2 2491
men mused in their hearts of J ... Lk 3:15 2491
J answered, saying unto them all, ... Lk 3:16 2491
all, that he shut up J in prison ... Lk 3:20 2491
do the disciples of J fast often ... Lk 5:33 2491
the disciples of J shewed him of ... Lk 7:18 2491
J calling unto him two of his ... Lk 7:19 2491
J Baptist hath sent us unto thee, ... Lk 7:20 2491
tell J what things ye have seen ... Lk 7:22 2491
the messengers of J were departed ... Lk 7:24 2491
unto the people concerning J ... Lk 7:24 2491
prophet than J the Baptist ... Lk 7:28 2491
baptized with the baptism of J ... Lk 7:29 2491
For J the Baptist came neither ... Lk 7:33 2491
that J was risen from the dead ... Lk 9:7 2491
And Herod said, J have I beheaded ... Lk 9:9 2491
answering said, J the Baptist ... Lk 9:19 2491
as J also taught his disciples ... Lk 11:1 2491
law and the prophets were until J ... Lk 16:16 2491
The baptism of J, was it from ... Lk 20:4 2491
be persuaded that J was a prophet ... Lk 20:6 2491
sent from God, whose name was J ... Jn 1:6 2491
J bare witness of him, and cried, ... Jn 1:15 2491
And this is the record of J ... Jn 1:19 2491
J answered them, saying, I ... Jn 1:26 2491
Jordan, where J was baptizing ... Jn 1:28 2491
The next day J seeth Jesus coming ... Jn 1:29 2491
J bare record, saying, I saw the ... Jn 1:32 2491
Again the next day after J stood ... Jn 1:35 2491
of the two which heard J speak ... Jn 1:40 2491
J also was baptizing in Aenon ... Jn 3:23 2491
For J was not yet cast into ... Jn 3:24 2491
And they came unto J, and said unto .. Jn 3:26 2491
J answered and said, A man can ... Jn 3:27 2491
and baptized more disciples than J ... Jn 4:1 2491
Ye sent unto J, and he bare ... Jn 5:33 2491
greater witness than that of J ... Jn 5:36 2491
place where J at first baptized ... Jn 10:40 2491
him, and said, J did no miracle ... Jn 10:41 2491
but all things that J spake of ... Jn 10:41 2491
For J truly baptized with water ... Acts 1:5 2491
Beginning from the baptism of J ... Acts 1:22 2491
the baptism which J preached ... Acts 10:37 2491
J indeed baptized with water ... Acts 11:16 2491
When J had first preached before ... Acts 13:24 2491
as J fulfilled his course, he ... Acts 13:25 2491
knowing only the baptism of J ... Acts 18:25 2491
J verily baptized with the ... Acts 19:4 2491
2. Son of Zebedee.
J his brother, in a ship with ... Mt 4:21 2491
son of Zebedee, and J his brother ... Mt 10:2 2491
J his brother, and bringeth them ... Mt 17:1 2491
J his brother, who also were in ... Mk 1:19 2491
Simon and Andrew, with James and J. Mk 1:29 2491
and J the brother of James ... Mk 3:17 2491
James, and J the brother of James ... Mk 5:37 2491
with him Peter, and James, and J ... Mk 9:2 2491
J answered him, saying, Master, ... Mk 9:38 2491
And James and J, the sons of ... Mk 10:35 2491
much displeased with James and J ... Mk 10:41 2491
the temple, Peter and James and J ... Mk 13:3 2491
with him Peter and James and J ... Mk 14:33 2491
And so was also James, and J ... Lk 5:10 2491
and Andrew his brother, James and J .. Lk 6:14 2491
go in, save Peter, and James, and J ... Lk 8:51 2491
these sayings, he took Peter and J ... Lk 9:28 2491
J answered and said, Master, we ... Lk 9:49 2491
J saw this, they said, Lord, wilt ... Lk 9:54 2491
And he sent Peter and J, saying, Go ... Lk 22:8 2491
abode both Peter, and James, and J ... Acts 1:13 2491
J went up together into the ... Acts 3:1 2491
J about to go into the temple ... Acts 3:3 2491
his eyes upon him with J, said, ... Acts 3:4 2491
which was healed held Peter and J ... Acts 3:11 2491
saw the boldness of Peter and J ... Acts 4:13 2491
J answered and said unto them, ... Acts 4:19 2491
they sent unto them Peter and J ... Acts 8:14 2491
the brother of J with the sword ... Acts 12:2 2491
And when James, Cephas, and J ... Gal 2:9 2491
by his angel unto his servant J ... Rev 1:1 2491
J to the seven churches which are ... Rev 1:4 2491
I J, who also am your brother, and ... Rev 1:9 2491
I J saw the holy city, new ... Rev 21:2 2491
I J saw these things, and heard ... Rev 22:8 2491
3. A relative of Annas the priest.
high priest, and Caiaphas, and J ... Acts 4:6 2491
4. Surnamed Mark.
the house of Mary the mother of J ... Acts 12:12 2491
ministry, and took with them J ... Acts 12:25 2491
they had also J to their minister ... Acts 13:5 2491
J departing from them returned to ... Acts 13:13 2491
determined to take with them J ... Acts 15:37 2491

JOHN'S (jonz) *Refers to John 1.*
between some of J disciples ... Jn 3:25 2491
And they said, Unto J baptism ... Acts 19:3 2491

JOIADA (joy'-a-dah) See JEHOIADA. *A priest with Zerubbabel.*
Eliashib, and Eliashib begat J ... Neh 12:10 3111
J begat Jonathan, and Jonathan ... Neh 12:11 3111
in the days of Eliashib, J ... Neh 12:22 3111
And one of the sons of J, the son ... Neh 13:28 3111

JOIAKIM (joy'-a-kim) See JEHOIAKIM. *Another priest with Zerubbabel.*
And Jeshua begat J ... Neh 12:10 3113
J also begat Eliashib ... Neh 12:10 3113
And in the days of J were priests ... Neh 12:12 3113
the days of J the son of Jeshua ... Neh 12:26 3113

JOIARIB (*joy'-a-rib*) See JEHOIARIB.
1. A messenger for Ezra.
also for J, and for Elnathan, men ... Ezr 8:16 3114
2. A descendant of Perez.
the son of Adaiah, the son of J ... Neh 11:5 3114
3. Father of Jedaiah.
Jedaiah the son of J, Jachin ... Neh 11:10 3114
Shemaiah, and J, Jedaiah, ... Neh 12:6 3114
And of J, Mattenai ... Neh 12:19 3114

JOIN
they *j* also unto our enemies, and ... Ex 1:10 3254
j himself with Ahaziah king of ... 2Chr 20:35 2266
j in affinity with the people of ... Ezr 9:14 2859
Though hand *j* in hand, the wicked ... Prov 11:21
though hand *j* in hand, he shall ... Prov 16:5
unto them that *j* house to house ... Is 5:8 5060
him, and *j* his enemies together ... Is 9:11 5526
that *j* themselves to the LORD, to ... Is 56:6 3867
let us *j* ourselves to the LORD in ... Jer 50:5 3867
j them one to another into one ... Eze 37:17 7126
they shall *j* themselves together ... Dan 11:6 2266
durst no man *j* himself to them ... Acts 5:13 2853
j thyself to this chariot ... Acts 8:29 2853
he assayed to *j* himself to the ... Acts 9:26 2853

JOINED
All these were *j* together in the ... Gen 14:3 2266
they *j* battle with them in the ... Gen 14:8 6186
time will my husband be *j* unto me ... Gen 29:34 3867
j at the two edges thereof ... Ex 28:7 2266
and so it shall be *j* together ... Ex 28:7 2266
that they may be *j* unto thee ... Num 18:2 3867
And they shall be *j* unto thee ... Num 18:4 3867
Israel *j* himself unto Baal-peor ... Num 25:3 6775
men that were *j* unto Baal-peor ... Num 25:5 6775
and when they *j* battle, Israel was ... 1Sa 4:2 5208
of the wheels were *j* to the base ... 1Kin 7:32
the seventh day the battle was *j* ... 1Kin 20:29 7126
and *j* affinity with Ahab ... 2Chr 18:1 2859
he *j* himself with him to make ... 2Chr 20:36 2266
Because thou hast *j* thyself with ... 2Chr 20:37 2266
thereof, and *j* the foundations ... Ezr 4:12 2338
all the wall was *j* together unto ... Neh 4:6 7194
upon all such as *j* themselves ... Est 9:27 3867
let it not be *j* unto the days of ... Job 3:6 2302
They are *j* one to another, they ... Job 41:17 1692
of his flesh are *j* together ... Job 41:23 1692
Assur also is *j* with them ... Ps 83:8 3867
They *j* themselves also unto ... Ps 106:28 6775
For to him that is *j* to all the ... Eccl 9:4 977
every one that is *j* unto them ... Is 13:15 5595
strangers shall be *j* with them ... Is 14:1 3867
Thou shalt not be *j* with them in ... Is 14:20 3161
that hath *j* himself to the LORD, ... Is 56:3 3867
Their wings were *j* one to another ... Eze 1:9 2266
every one were *j* one to another ... Eze 1:11 2266
courts *j* of forty cubits long ... Eze 46:22 7000
Ephraim is *j* to idols ... Hos 4:17 2266
many nations shall be *j* to the ... Zec 2:11 3867
therefore God hath *j* together ... Mt 19:6 4801
therefore God hath *j* together ... Mk 10:9 4801
j himself to a citizen of that ... Lk 15:15 2853
about four hundred, *j* themselves ... Acts 5:36 4347
whose house *j* hard to the ... Acts 18:7 4927
but that ye be perfectly *j* ... 1Cor 1:10 2675
is *j* to an harlot is one body ... 1Cor 6:16 2853
But he that is *j* unto the Lord is ... 1Cor 6:17 2853
the whole body fitly *j* together ... Eph 4:16 4883
shall be *j* unto his wife, and they ... Eph 5:31 4347

JOINING
j to the wing of the other cherub ... 2Chr 3:12 1692

JOININGS
doors of the gates, and for the *j* ... 1Chr 22:3 4226

JOINT
of Jacob's thigh was out of *j* ... Gen 32:25 3363
and all my bones are out of *j* ... Ps 22:14 6504
broken tooth, and a foot out of *j* ... Prov 25:19 4154
by that which every *j* supplieth ... Eph 4:16 860

JOINT-HEIRS
heirs of God, and *j* with Christ ... Rom 8:17 4789

JOINTS
between the *j* of the harness ... 1Kin 22:34 1694
between the *j* of the harness ... 2Chr 18:33 1694
the *j* of thy thighs are like ... Song 7:1 2542
so that the *j* of his loins were ... Dan 5:6 7001
from which all the body by *j* ... Col 2:19 860
of soul and spirit, and of the *j* ... Heb 4:12 719

JOKDEAM (*jok'-de-am*) *A city in Judah.*
And Jezreel, and J, and Zanoah, ... Josh 15:56 3347

JOKIM (*jo'-kim*) *A descendant of Shelah.*
And J, and the men of Chozeba, and ... 1Chr 4:22 3137

JOKMEAM (*jok'-me-am*) See JOKNEAM. *A Levitical city in Ephraim.*
J with her suburbs, and Beth-horon ... 1Chr 6:68 3361

JOKNEAM (*jok'-ne-am*) See JOKMEAM, KIBZAIM.
1. A Levitical city in Zebulun.
the king of J of Carmel, one ... Josh 12:22 3362
to the river that is before J ... Josh 19:11 3362
J with her suburbs, and Kartah ... Josh 21:34 3362
2. A Levitical city in Ephraim.
unto the place that is beyond J ... 1Kin 4:12 3362

JOKSHAN (*jok'-shan*) *A son of Abraham.*
And she bare him Zimran, and J ... Gen 25:2 3370
And J begat Sheba, and Dedan ... Gen 25:3 3370
she bare Zimran, and J, and Medan, ... 1Chr 1:32 3370
And the sons of J ... 1Chr 1:32 3370

JOKTAN (*jok'-tan*) *A son of Eber.*
and his brother's name was J ... Gen 10:25 3355
J begat Almodad, and Sheleph, and ... Gen 10:26 3355
all these were the sons of J ... Gen 10:29 3355
and his brother's name was J ... 1Chr 1:19 3355
J begat Almodad, and Sheleph, and ... 1Chr 1:20 3355
All these were the sons of J ... 1Chr 1:23 3355

JOKTHEEL (*jok'-the-el*) See SELAH.
1. A city in Judah.
And Dilean, and Mizpeh, and J ... Josh 15:38 3371
2. Another name for Petra in Edom.
the name of it J unto this day ... 2Kin 14:7 3371

JONA (*jo'-nah*) See BAR-JONA, JONAH, JONAS.
Greek form of Jonah.
said, Thou art Simon the son of J ... Jn 1:42 2495

JONADAB (*jon'-a-dab*) See JEHONADAB.
1. A son of Shimeah.
had a friend, whose name was J ... 2Sa 13:3 3122
and J was a very subtil man ... 2Sa 13:3 3122
J said unto him, Lay thee down on ... 2Sa 13:5 3122
And J, the son of Shimeah David's ... 2Sa 13:32 3122
J said unto the king, Behold, the ... 2Sa 13:35 3122
2. A son of Rechab.
for J the son of Rechab our ... Jer 35:6 3122
have we obeyed the voice of J the ... Jer 35:8 3082
that J our father commanded us ... Jer 35:10 3122
The words of J the son of Rechab, ... Jer 35:14 3082
Because the sons of J the son of ... Jer 35:16 3082
the commandment of J your father ... Jer 35:18 3082
J the son of Rechab shall not ... Jer 35:19 3122

JONAH (*jo'-nah*) See JONA, JONAS. *A prophet.*
by the hand of his servant J ... 2Kin 14:25 3124
came unto J the son of Amittai ... Jonah 1:1 3124
But J rose up to flee unto ... Jonah 1:3 3124
But J was gone down into the ... Jonah 1:5 3124
cast lots, and the lot fell upon J ... Jonah 1:7 3124
So they took up J, and cast him ... Jonah 1:15 3124
a great fish to swallow up J ... Jonah 1:17 3124
J was in the belly of the fish ... Jonah 1:17 3124
Then J prayed unto the LORD his ... Jonah 2:1 3124
it vomited out J upon the dry ... Jonah 2:10 3124
LORD came unto J the second time ... Jonah 3:1 3124
So J arose, and went unto Nineveh, ... Jonah 3:3 3124
J began to enter into the city a ... Jonah 3:4 3124
But it displeased J exceedingly ... Jonah 4:1 3124
So J went out of the city, and sat ... Jonah 4:5 3124
and made it to come up over J ... Jonah 4:6 3124
So J was exceeding glad of the ... Jonah 4:6 3124
the sun beat upon the head of J ... Jonah 4:8 3124
And God said to J, Doest thou well ... Jonah 4:9 3124

JONAM See JONAN.

JONAN (*jo'-nan*) *Ancestor of Joseph, husband of Mary.*
of Joseph, which was the son of J ... Lk 3:30 2494

JONAS (*jo'-nas*) See JONA, JONAH.
1. Same as Jonah.
it, but the sign of the prophet J ... Mt 12:39 2495
For as J was three days and three ... Mt 12:40 2495
repented at the preaching of J ... Mt 12:41 2495
behold, a greater than J is here ... Mt 12:41 2495
it, but the sign of the prophet J ... Mt 16:4 2495
it, but the sign of J the prophet ... Lk 11:29 2495
For as J was a sign unto the ... Lk 11:30 2495
repented at the preaching of J ... Lk 11:32 2495
behold, a greater than J is here ... Lk 11:32 2495
2. Father of Peter.
to Simon Peter, Simon, son of J ... Jn 21:15 2495
the second time, Simon, son of J ... Jn 21:16 2495
the third time, Simon, son of J ... Jn 21:17 2495

JONATHAN (*jon'-a-than*) See JEHONATHAN, JONATHAN'S.
1. A Levite.
and J, the son of Gershom, the son ... Judg 18:30 3129
2. Son of Saul.
a thousand were with J in Gibeah ... 1Sa 13:2 3129
J smote the garrison of the ... 1Sa 13:3 3129
J his son, and the people that ... 1Sa 13:16 3129
people that were with Saul and J ... 1Sa 13:22 3129
with J his son was there found ... 1Sa 13:22 3129
that J the son of Saul said unto ... 1Sa 14:1 3129
people knew not that J was gone ... 1Sa 14:3 3129
by which J sought to go over unto ... 1Sa 14:4 3129
J said to the young man that bare ... 1Sa 14:6 3083
Then said J, Behold, we will pass ... 1Sa 14:8 3083
men of the garrison answered J ... 1Sa 14:12 3129
J said unto his armourbearer, ... 1Sa 14:12 3129
J climbed up upon his hands and ... 1Sa 14:13 3129
and they fell before J ... 1Sa 14:13 3129
And that first slaughter, which J ... 1Sa 14:14 3129
when they had numbered, behold, J ... 1Sa 14:17 3129
that were with Saul and J ... 1Sa 14:21 3129
But J heard not when his father ... 1Sa 14:27 3129
Then said J, My father hath ... 1Sa 14:29 3129
Israel, though it be in J my son ... 1Sa 14:39 3129
J my son will be on the other ... 1Sa 14:40 3129
And Saul and J were taken ... 1Sa 14:41 3129
Cast lots between me and J my son ... 1Sa 14:42 3129
And J was taken ... 1Sa 14:42 3129
Then Saul said to J, Tell me what ... 1Sa 14:43 3129
J told him, and said, I did but ... 1Sa 14:43 3129
for thou shalt surely die, J ... 1Sa 14:44 3129
said unto Saul, Shall J die ... 1Sa 14:45 3129
So the people rescued J, that he ... 1Sa 14:45 3129
Now the sons of Saul were J ... 1Sa 14:49 3129
that the soul of J was knit with ... 1Sa 18:1 3083
J loved him as his own soul ... 1Sa 18:1 3083
Then J and David made a covenant, ... 1Sa 18:3 3083
J stripped himself of the robe ... 1Sa 18:4 3083
And Saul spake to J his son ... 1Sa 19:1 3129
But J Saul's son delighted much ... 1Sa 19:2 3083
J told David, saying, Saul my ... 1Sa 19:2 3083
J spake good of David unto Saul ... 1Sa 19:4 3083
hearkened unto the voice of J ... 1Sa 19:6 3083
J called David, and Jonathan ... 1Sa 19:7 3083
J shewed him all those things ... 1Sa 19:7 3083
J brought David to Saul, and he ... 1Sa 19:7 3083
Ramah, and came and said before J ... 1Sa 20:1 3083
Let not J know this, lest he be ... 1Sa 20:3 3083
Then said J unto David, ... 1Sa 20:4 3083
And David said unto J, Behold, to ... 1Sa 20:5 3083
J said, Far be it from thee ... 1Sa 20:9 3083
Then said David to J, Who shall ... 1Sa 20:10 3083
J said unto David, Come, and let ... 1Sa 20:11 3083
J said unto David, O LORD God of ... 1Sa 20:12 3083
The LORD do so and much more to J ... 1Sa 20:13 3083
So J made a covenant with the ... 1Sa 20:16 3083
J caused David to swear again, ... 1Sa 20:17 3083
Then J said to David, To morrow ... 1Sa 20:18 3083
J arose, and Abner sat by Saul's ... 1Sa 20:25 3083
and Saul said unto J his son ... 1Sa 20:27 3083
J answered Saul, David earnestly ... 1Sa 20:28 3083
anger was kindled against J ... 1Sa 20:30 3083
J answered Saul his father, and ... 1Sa 20:32 3083
whereby J knew that it was ... 1Sa 20:33 3083
So J arose from the table in ... 1Sa 20:34 3083
that J went out into the field at ... 1Sa 20:35 3083
of the arrow which J had shot ... 1Sa 20:37 3083
J cried after the lad, and said, ... 1Sa 20:37 3083
J cried after the lad, Make speed ... 1Sa 20:38 3083
only J and David knew the matter ... 1Sa 20:39 3083
J gave his artillery unto his lad ... 1Sa 20:40 3083
J said to David, Go in peace, ... 1Sa 20:42 3083
and J went into the city ... 1Sa 20:42 3083
J Saul's son arose, and went to ... 1Sa 23:16 3083
the wood, and J went to his house ... 1Sa 23:18 3083
and the Philistines slew J ... 1Sa 31:2 3083
Saul and J his son are dead also ... 2Sa 1:4 3083
that Saul and J his son be dead ... 2Sa 1:5 3083
for J his son, and for the people ... 2Sa 1:12 3083
over Saul and over J his son ... 2Sa 1:17 3083
the bow of J turned not back, and ... 2Sa 1:22 3083
J were lovely and pleasant in ... 2Sa 1:23 3083
O J, thou wast slain in thine ... 2Sa 1:25 3083
distressed for thee, my brother J ... 2Sa 1:26 3083
And J, Saul's son, had a son that ... 2Sa 4:4 3083
J out of Jezreel, and his nurse ... 2Sa 4:4 3083
J hath yet a son, which is lame ... 2Sa 9:3 3083
when Mephibosheth, the son of J ... 2Sa 9:6 3083
kindness for J thy father's sake ... 2Sa 9:7 3083
the son of J the son of Saul, ... 2Sa 21:7 3083
David and J the son of Saul ... 2Sa 21:7 3083
the bones of J his son from the ... 2Sa 21:12 3083
of Saul and the bones of J his son ... 2Sa 21:13 3083
J his son buried they in the ... 2Sa 21:14 3083
Kish begat Saul, and Saul begat J ... 1Chr 8:33 3083
the son of J was Merib-baal ... 1Chr 8:34 3083
and Saul begat J, and Malchi-shua, ... 1Chr 9:39 3083
the son of J was Merib-baal ... 1Chr 9:40 3083
and the Philistines slew J ... 1Chr 10:2 3129
3. A son of Abiathar.
thy son, and J the son of Abiathar ... 2Sa 15:27 3083
Zadok's son, and J Abiathar's son ... 2Sa 15:36 3083
Now J and Ahimaaz stayed by ... 2Sa 17:17 3083
they said, Where is Ahimaaz and J ... 2Sa 17:20 3083
J the son of Abiathar the priest ... 1Kin 1:42 3129
J answered and said to Adonijah, ... 1Kin 1:43 3129
4. A son of Shimea.
J the son of Shimeah the brother ... 2Sa 21:21 3083
J the son of Shimea David's ... 1Chr 20:7 3083
5. A "mighty man" of David.
of the sons of Jashen, J ... 2Sa 23:32 3083
J the son of Shage the Hararite, ... 1Chr 11:34 3129
6. A son of Jada.
Shammai; Jether, and J ... 1Chr 2:32 3129
And the sons of J ... 1Chr 2:33 3129
7. An uncle of David.
Also J David's uncle was a ... 1Chr 27:32 3083
8. A family of exiles.
Ebed the son of J, and with him ... Ezr 8:6 3083
9. Son of Asahel.
Only J the son of Asahel and ... Ezr 10:15 3083
10. A descendant of Jeshua.
And Joiada begat J ... Neh 12:11 3083
and J begat Jaddua ... Neh 12:11 3083
11. A priest descended from Melicu.
Of Melicu, J ... Neh 12:14 3083
12. A priest descended from Shemaiah.
namely, Zechariah the son of J ... Neh 12:35 3083
13. A scribe.
in the house of J the scribe ... Jer 37:15 3083
to the house of J the scribe ... Jer 37:20 3083
14. A son of Kareah.
J the sons of Kareah, and Seraiah ... Jer 40:8 3129

JONATHAN'S (*jon'-a-thans*) *Refers to Jonathan 2.*
J lad gathered up the arrows, and ... 1Sa 20:38 3129
may shew him kindness for J sake ... 2Sa 9:1 3129
not cause me to return to J house ... Jer 38:26 3129

JONATH-ELEM-RECHOKIM (*jo''-nath-e'-lem-re-ko'-kim*) *A musical notation.*
To the chief Musician upon J ... Ps 56:*t* 3128

JOPPA (*jop'-pah*) *A seaport in Dan.*
it to thee in flotes by sea to J ... 2Chr 2:16 3305
from Lebanon to the sea of J ... Ezr 3:7 3305
of the LORD, and went down to J ... Jonah 1:3 3305
Now there was at J a certain ... Acts 9:36 2445
forasmuch as Lydda was nigh to J ... Acts 9:38 2445
And it was known throughout all J ... Acts 9:42 2445
days in J with one Simon a tanner ... Acts 9:43 2445
And now send men to J, and call for ... Acts 10:5 2445
unto them, he sent them to J ... Acts 10:8 2445
brethren from J accompanied him ... Acts 10:23 2445

Send therefore to J, and call ... Acts 10:32 *2445*
I was in the city of J praying ... Acts 11:5 *2445*
and said unto him, Send men to J ... Acts 11:13 *2445*

JORAH (*jo'-rah*) See HARIPH. *A family of exiles.*
The children of J, an hundred and ... Ezr 2:18 3139

JORAI (*jo'-rahee*) *Head of a Gadite family.*
and Meshullam, and Sheba, and J ... 1Chr 5:13 3140

JORAM (*jo'-ram*) See JEHORAM.
1. A son of Toi.
Then Toi sent J his son unto king ... 2Sa 8:10 3141
J brought with him vessels of ... 2Sa 8:10
2. Same as Jehoram.
So J went over to Zair, and all ... 2Kin 8:21 3141
And the rest of the acts of J ... 2Kin 8:23 3141
J slept with his fathers, and was ... 2Kin 8:24 3141
Jehosheba, the daughter of king J ... 2Kin 11:2 3141
J his son, Ahaziah his son, Joash ... 1Chr 3:11 3141
and Josaphat begat J ... Mt 1:8 *2496*
and J begat Ozias ... Mt 1:8 *2496*
3. A son of Ahab.
in the fifth year of J the son of ... 2Kin 8:16 3141
In the twelfth year of J the son ... 2Kin 8:25 3141
he went with J the son of Ahab to ... 2Kin 8:28 3141
and the Syrians wounded J ... 2Kin 8:28 3141
king J went back to be healed in ... 2Kin 8:29 3141
see J the son of Ahab in Jezreel ... 2Kin 8:29 3141
son of Nimshi conspired against J ... 2Kin 9:14 3141
(Now J had kept Ramoth-gilead, he ... 2Kin 9:14 3141
But king J was returned to be ... 2Kin 9:15 3188
for J lay there ... 2Kin 9:16 3141
of Judah was come down to see J ... 2Kin 9:16 3141
J said, Take an horseman, and send ... 2Kin 9:17 3188
And J said, Make ready ... 2Kin 9:21 3188
J king of Israel and Ahaziah king ... 2Kin 9:21 3188
when J saw Jehu, that he said, Is ... 2Kin 9:22 3188
J turned his hands, and fled, and ... 2Kin 9:23 3188
in the eleventh year of J the son ... 2Kin 9:29 3188
and the Syrians smote J ... 2Chr 22:5 3141
Ahaziah was of God by coming to J ... 2Chr 22:7 3141
4. A descendant of Eliezer.
J his son, and Zichri his son, and ... 1Chr 26:25 3141

JORDAN (*jor'-dan*) *A river that runs from the Sea of Galilee to the Dead Sea.*
and beheld all the plain of J ... Gen 13:10 3383
Lot chose him all the plain of J ... Gen 13:11 3383
my staff I passed over this J ... Gen 32:10 3383
of Atad, which is beyond J ... Gen 50:10 3383
Abel-mizraim, which is beyond J ... Gen 50:11 3383
by the sea, and by the coast of J ... Num 13:29 3383
of Moab on this side J by Jericho ... Num 22:1 3383
plains of Moab by J near Jericho ... Num 26:3 3383
plains of Moab by J near Jericho ... Num 26:63 3383
Moab, which are by J near Jericho ... Num 31:12 3383
and bring us not over J ... Num 32:5 3383
with them on yonder side J ... Num 32:19 3383
to us on this side J eastward ... Num 32:19 3383
you armed over J before the LORD ... Num 32:21 3383
Reuben will pass with you over J ... Num 32:29 3383
on this side J may be ours ... Num 32:32 3383
plains of Moab by J near Jericho ... Num 33:48 3383
And they pitched by J, from ... Num 33:49 3383
Moses in the plains of Moab by J ... Num 33:50 3383
over J into the land of Canaan ... Num 33:51 3383
And the border shall go down to J ... Num 34:12 3383
this side J near Jericho eastward ... Num 34:15 3383
plains of Moab by J near Jericho ... Num 35:1 3383
When ye be come over J into the ... Num 35:10 3383
give three cities on this side J ... Num 35:14 3383
plains of Moab by J near Jericho ... Num 36:13 3383
on this side J in the wilderness ... Deut 1:1 3383
On this side J, in the land of ... Deut 1:5 3383
until I shall pass over J into ... Deut 2:29 3383
the land that was on this side J ... Deut 3:8 3383
The plain also, and J, and the ... Deut 3:17 3383
your God hath given them beyond J ... Deut 3:20 3383
the good land that is beyond J ... Deut 3:25 3383
for thou shalt not go over this J ... Deut 3:27 3383
sware that I should not go over J ... Deut 4:21 3383
this land, I must not go over J ... Deut 4:22 3383
ye go over J to possess it ... Deut 4:26 3383
this side J toward the sunrising ... Deut 4:41 3383
On this side J, in the valley ... Deut 4:46 3383
this side J toward the sunrising ... Deut 4:47 3383
the plain on this side J eastward ... Deut 4:49 3383
Thou art to pass over J this day ... Deut 9:1 3383
Are they not on the other side J ... Deut 11:30 3383
For ye shall pass over J to go in ... Deut 11:31 3383
But when ye go over J, and dwell ... Deut 12:10 3383
J unto the land which the LORD ... Deut 27:2 3383
shall be when ye be gone over J ... Deut 27:4 3383
people, when ye are come over J ... Deut 27:12 3383
over J to go to possess it ... Deut 30:18 3383
me, Thou shalt not go over this J ... Deut 31:2 3383
ye go over J to possess it ... Deut 31:13 3383
ye go over J to possess it ... Deut 32:47 3383
therefore arise, go over this J ... Josh 1:2 3383
days ye shall pass over this J ... Josh 1:11 3383
Moses gave you on this side J ... Josh 1:14 3383
this side J toward the sunrising ... Josh 1:15 3383
them the way to J unto the fords ... Josh 2:7 3383
that were on the other side J ... Josh 2:10 3383
from Shittim, and came to J ... Josh 3:1 3383
to the brink of the water of J ... Josh 3:8 3383
J, ye shall stand still in J ... Josh 3:8 3383
passeth over before you into J ... Josh 3:11 3383
shall rest in the waters of J ... Josh 3:13 3383
that the waters of J shall be cut ... Josh 3:13 3383
from their tents, to pass over J ... Josh 3:14 3383
bare the ark were come unto J ... Josh 3:15 3383
(for J overfloweth all his banks ... Josh 3:15 3383
on dry ground in the midst of J ... Josh 3:17 3383
people were passed clean over J ... Josh 3:17 3383
people were clean passed over J ... Josh 4:1 3383
you hence out of the midst of J ... Josh 4:3 3383
LORD your God into the midst of J ... Josh 4:5 3383
That the waters of J were cut off ... Josh 4:7 3383
when it passed over J ... Josh 4:7 3383
the waters of J were cut off ... Josh 4:7 3383
stones out of the midst of J ... Josh 4:8 3383
twelve stones in the midst of J ... Josh 4:9 3383
the ark stood in the midst of J ... Josh 4:10 3383
that they come up out of J ... Josh 4:16 3383
saying, Come ye up out of J ... Josh 4:17 3383
come up out of the midst of J ... Josh 4:18 3383
that the waters of J returned ... Josh 4:18 3383
the people came up out of J on ... Josh 4:19 3383
stones, which they took out of J ... Josh 4:20 3383
came over this J on dry land ... Josh 4:22 3383
the waters of J from before you ... Josh 4:23 3383
were on the side of J westward ... Josh 5:1 3383
of J from before the children of ... Josh 5:1 3383
at all brought this people over J ... Josh 7:7 3383
and dwelt on the other side J ... Josh 7:7 3383
kings which were on this side J ... Josh 9:1 3383
the Amorites, that were beyond J ... Josh 9:10 3383
J toward the rising of the sun ... Josh 12:1 3383
smote on this side J on the west ... Josh 12:7 3383
beyond J eastward, even as Moses ... Josh 13:8 3383
of the children of Reuben was J ... Josh 13:23 3383
of Sihon king of Heshbon, J ... Josh 13:27 3383
on the other side J eastward ... Josh 13:27 3383
of Moab, on the other side J ... Josh 13:32 3383
an half tribe on the other side J ... Josh 14:3 3383
salt sea, even unto the end of J ... Josh 15:5 3383
sea at the uttermost part of J ... Josh 15:5 3383
of Joseph fell from J by Jericho ... Josh 16:1 3383
came to Jericho, and went out at J ... Josh 16:7 3383
which were on the other side J ... Josh 17:5 3383
inheritance beyond J on the east ... Josh 18:7 3383
on the north side was from J ... Josh 18:12 3383
salt sea at the south end of J ... Josh 18:19 3383
J was the border of it on the ... Josh 18:20 3383
of their border were at J ... Josh 19:22 3383
the outgoings thereof were at J ... Josh 19:33 3383
to Judah upon J toward the ... Josh 19:34 3383
on the other side J by Jericho ... Josh 20:8 3383
LORD gave you on the other side J ... Josh 22:4 3383
brethren on this side J westward ... Josh 22:7 3383
they came unto the borders of J ... Josh 22:10 3383
built there an altar by J ... Josh 22:10 3383
of Canaan, in the borders of J ... Josh 22:11 3383
hath made J a border between us ... Josh 22:25 3383
for your tribes, from J, with all ... Josh 23:4 3383
which dwelt on the other side J ... Josh 24:8 3383
And ye went over J, and came unto ... Josh 24:11 3383
took the fords of J toward Moab ... Judg 3:28 3383
Gilead abode beyond J ... Judg 5:17 3383
the waters unto Beth-barah and J ... Judg 7:24 3383
the waters unto Beth-barah and J ... Judg 7:24 3383
to Gideon on the other side J ... Judg 7:25 3383
And Gideon came to J, and passed ... Judg 8:4 3383
J in the land of the Amorites ... Judg 10:8 3383
J to fight also against Judah ... Judg 10:9 3383
Arnon even unto Jabbok, and unto J ... Judg 11:13 3383
from the wilderness even unto J ... Judg 11:22 3383
of J before the Ephraimites ... Judg 12:5 3383
and slew him at the passages of J ... Judg 12:6 3383
went over J to the land of Gad ... 1Sa 13:7 3383
that were on the other side J ... 1Sa 31:7 3383
the plain, and passed over J ... 2Sa 2:29 3383
Israel together, and passed over J ... 2Sa 10:17 3383
with him, and they passed over J ... 2Sa 17:22 3383
of them that was not gone over J ... 2Sa 17:22 3383
And Absalom passed over J, he and ... 2Sa 17:24 3383
the king returned, and came to J ... 2Sa 19:15 3383
king, to conduct the king over J ... 2Sa 19:15 3383
they went over J before the king ... 2Sa 19:17 3383
the king, as he was come over J ... 2Sa 19:18 3383
went over J with the king ... 2Sa 19:31 3383
to conduct him over J ... 2Sa 19:31 3383
a little way over J with the king ... 2Sa 19:36 3383
And all the people went over J ... 2Sa 19:39 3383
all David's men with him, over J ... 2Sa 19:41 3383
king, from J even to Jerusalem ... 2Sa 20:2 3383
And they passed over J, and pitched ... 2Sa 24:5 3383
but he came down to meet me at J ... 1Kin 2:8 3383
In the plain of J did the king ... 1Kin 7:46 3383
brook Cherith, that is before J ... 1Kin 17:3 3383
brook Cherith, that is before J ... 1Kin 17:5 3383
for the LORD hath sent me to J ... 2Kin 2:6 3383
and they two stood by J ... 2Kin 2:7 3383
back, and stood by the bank of J ... 2Kin 2:13 3383
wash in J seven times, and thy ... 2Kin 5:10 3383
dipped himself seven times in J ... 2Kin 5:14 3383
Let us go, we pray thee, unto J ... 2Kin 6:2 3383
And when they came to J, they cut ... 2Kin 6:4 3383
And they went after them unto J ... 2Kin 7:15 3383
From J eastward, all the land of ... 2Kin 10:33 3383
And on the other side J by Jericho ... 1Chr 6:78 3383
on the east side of J ... 1Chr 6:78 3383
went over J in the first month ... 1Chr 12:15 3383
And on the other side of J ... 1Chr 12:37 3383
all Israel, and passed over J ... 1Chr 19:17 3383
them of Israel on this side J ... 1Chr 26:30 3383
In the plain of J did the king ... 2Chr 4:17 3383
he can draw up J into his mouth ... Job 40:23 3383
remember thee from the land of J ... Ps 42:6 3383
J was driven back ... Ps 114:3 3383
thou J, that thou wast driven ... Ps 114:5 3383
by the way of the sea, beyond J ... Is 9:1 3383
wilt thou do in the swelling of J ... Jer 12:5 3383
a lion from the swelling of J ... Jer 49:19 3383
of J unto the habitation of the ... Jer 50:44 3383
and from the land of Israel by J ... Eze 47:18 3383
for the pride of J is spoiled ... Zec 11:3 3383
and all the region round about J ... Mt 3:5 *2446*
And were baptized of him in J ... Mt 3:6 *2446*
Jesus from Galilee to J unto John ... Mt 3:13 *2446*
by the way of the sea, beyond J ... Mt 4:15 *2446*
and from Judaea, and from beyond J ... Mt 4:25 *2446*
the coasts of Judaea beyond J ... Mt 19:1 *2446*
baptized of him in the river of J ... Mk 1:5 *2446*
and was baptized of John in J ... Mk 1:9 *2446*
and from Idumaea, and from beyond J Mk 3:8 *2446*
Judaea by the farther side of J ... Mk 10:1 *2446*
came into all the country about J ... Lk 3:3 *2446*
of the Holy Ghost returned from J ... Lk 4:1 *2446*
were done in Bethabara beyond J ... Jn 1:28 *2446*
he that was with thee beyond J ... Jn 3:26 *2446*
went away again beyond J into the ... Jn 10:40 *2446*

JORIM (*jo'-rim*) *Son of Matthat; ancestor of Jesus.*
Eliezer, which was the son of J ... Lk 3:29 *2497*

JORKEAM See JORKOAM.

JORKOAM (*jor'-ko-am*) *A descendant of Hebron.*
begat Raham, the father of J ... 1Chr 2:44 3421

JOSABAD (*jos'-a-bad*) See JOZABAD. *A warrior in David's army.*
and Johanan, and J the Gederathite, ... 1Chr 12:4 3107

JOSAPHAT (*jos'-a-fat*) See JEHOSHAPHAT. *Son of Asa; ancestor of Jesus.*
And Asa begat J ... Mt 1:8 *2498*
and J begat Joram ... Mt 1:8 *2498*

JOSE (*jo'-ze*) See JOSES. *Son of Eliezer; ancestor of Jesus.*
Which was the son of J, which was ... Lk 3:29 *2499*

JOSECH See JOSEPH.

JOSEDECH (*jos'-e-dek*) See JOZADAK. *Father of Joshua, the priest.*
Judah, and to Joshua the son of J ... Hag 1:1 3087
Shealtiel, and Joshua the son of J ... Hag 1:12 3087
the spirit of Joshua the son of J ... Hag 1:14 3087
Judah, and to Joshua the son of J ... Hag 2:2 3087
and be strong, O Joshua, son of J ... Hag 2:4 3087
the head of Joshua the son of J ... Zec 6:11 3087

JOSEPH (*jo'-zef*) See BARSABAS, JOSEPH'S.
1. Son of Jacob and Rachel.
And she called his name J ... Gen 30:24 3130
to pass, when Rachel had born J ... Gen 30:25 3130
after, and Rachel and J hindermost ... Gen 33:2 3130
and after came J near and Rachel, ... Gen 33:7 3130
sons of Rachel; J, and Benjamin ... Gen 35:24 3130
J, being seventeen years old, was ... Gen 37:2 3130
J brought unto his father their ... Gen 37:2 3130
Now Israel loved J more than all ... Gen 37:3 3130
J dreamed a dream, and he told it ... Gen 37:5 3130
And Israel said unto J, Do not thy ... Gen 37:13 3130
J went after his brethren, and ... Gen 37:17 3130
when J was come unto his brethren ... Gen 37:23 3130
they stript J out of his coat ... Gen 37:23 3130
lifted up J out of the pit, and ... Gen 37:28 3130
sold J to the Ishmeelites for ... Gen 37:28 3130
and they brought J into Egypt ... Gen 37:28 3130
and, behold, J was not in the pit ... Gen 37:29 3130
J is without doubt rent in pieces ... Gen 37:33 3130
J was brought down to Egypt ... Gen 39:1 3130
And the LORD was with J, and he was. Gen 39:2 3130
J found grace in his sight, and he ... Gen 39:4 3130
J was a goodly person, and well ... Gen 39:6 3130
wife cast her eyes upon J ... Gen 39:7 3130
as she spake to J day by day ... Gen 39:10 3130
that J went into the house to do ... Gen 39:11
But the LORD was with J, and ... Gen 39:21 3130
the place where J was bound ... Gen 40:3 3130
of the guard charged J with them ... Gen 40:4 3130
J came in unto them in the ... Gen 40:6 3130
And J said unto them, Do not ... Gen 40:8 3130
chief butler told his dream to J ... Gen 40:9 3130
J said unto him, This is the ... Gen 40:12 3130
was good, he said unto J, I also ... Gen 40:16 3130
J answered and said, This is the ... Gen 40:18 3130
as J had interpreted to them ... Gen 40:22 3130
not the chief butler remember J ... Gen 40:23 3130
Then Pharaoh sent and called J ... Gen 41:14 3130
And Pharaoh said unto J, I have ... Gen 41:15 3130
J answered Pharaoh, saying, It is ... Gen 41:16 3130
And Pharaoh said unto J, In my ... Gen 41:17 3130
J said unto Pharaoh, The dream of ... Gen 41:25 3130
And Pharaoh said unto J, Forasmuch .. Gen 41:39 3130
And Pharaoh said unto J, See, I ... Gen 41:41 3130
And Pharaoh said unto J, I am ... Gen 41:44 3130
J went out over all the land of ... Gen 41:45 3130
J was thirty years old when he ... Gen 41:46 3130
J went out from the presence of ... Gen 41:46 3130
J gathered corn as the sand of ... Gen 41:49 3130
unto J were born two sons before ... Gen 41:50 3130
And J called the name of the ... Gen 41:51 3130
to come, according as J had said ... Gen 41:54 3130
unto all the Egyptians, Go unto J ... Gen 41:55 3130
J opened all the storehouses, and ... Gen 41:56 3130
into Egypt to J for to buy corn ... Gen 41:57 3130
J was the governor over the land, ... Gen 42:6 3130
J saw his brethren, and he knew ... Gen 42:7 3130
J knew his brethren, but they ... Gen 42:8 3130
J remembered the dreams which he ... Gen 42:9 3130
J said unto them, That is it that ... Gen 42:14 3130
J said unto them the third day, ... Gen 42:18 3130
knew not that J understood them ... Gen 42:23 3130
Then J commanded to fill their ... Gen 42:25 3130
J is not, and Simeon is not, and ye ... Gen 42:36 3130
down to Egypt, and stood before J ... Gen 43:15 3130
when J saw Benjamin with them, he ... Gen 43:16 3130
And the man did as J bade ... Gen 43:17 3130
present against J came at noon ... Gen 43:25 3130

J

when *J* came home, they brought Gen 43:26 3130
And *J* made haste Gen 43:30 3130
to the word that *J* had spoken Gen 44:2 3130
J said unto his steward, Up, Gen 44:4 3130
J said unto them, What deed is Gen 44:15 3130
Then *J* could not refrain himself Gen 45:1 3130
while *J* made himself known unto Gen 45:1 3130
J said unto his brethren Gen 45:3 3130
I am *J*; doth my father yet Gen 45:3 3130
J said unto his brethren, Come Gen 45:4 3130
I am *J* your brother, whom ye sold Gen 45:4 3130
unto him, Thus saith thy son *J* Gen 45:9 3130
And Pharaoh said unto *J*, Say unto Gen 45:17 3130
J gave them wagons, according to Gen 45:21 3130
J is yet alive, and he is governor Gen 45:26 3130
they told him all the words of *J* Gen 45:27 3130
which *J* had sent to carry him Gen 45:27 3130
J my son is yet alive Gen 45:28 3130
J shall put his hand upon thine Gen 46:4 3130
Jacob's wife; *J*, and Benjamin Gen 46:19 3130
unto *J* in the land of Egypt were Gen 46:20 3130
And the sons of *J*, which were born Gen 46:27 3130
he sent Judah before him unto *J* Gen 46:28 3130
J made ready his chariot, and went Gen 46:29 3130
And Israel said unto *J*, Now let me Gen 46:30 3130
J said unto his brethren, and unto Gen 46:31 3130
Then *J* came and told Pharaoh, and Gen 47:1 3130
And Pharaoh spake unto *J*, saying, Gen 47:5 3130
J brought in Jacob his father, and Gen 47:7 3130
J placed his father and his Gen 47:11 3130
J nourished his father, and his Gen 47:12 3130
J gathered up all the money that Gen 47:14 3130
and *J* brought the money into Gen 47:14 3130
all the Egyptians came unto *J* Gen 47:15 3130
And *J* said, Give your cattle Gen 47:16 3130
they brought their cattle unto *J* Gen 47:17 3130
J gave them bread in exchange for Gen 47:17 3130
J bought all the land of Egypt Gen 47:20 3130
Then *J* said unto the people, Gen 47:23 3130
J made it a law over the land of Gen 47:26 3130
and he called his son *J*, and said Gen 47:29 3130
these things, that one told *J* Gen 48:1 3130
thy son *J* cometh unto thee Gen 48:2 3130
And Jacob said unto *J*, God Gen 48:3 3130
J said unto his father, They are Gen 48:9 3130
And Israel said unto *J*, I had not Gen 48:11 3130
J brought them out from between Gen 48:12 3130
J took them both, Ephraim in his Gen 48:13 3130
And he blessed *J*, and said, God, Gen 48:15 3130
when *J* saw that his father laid Gen 48:17 3130
J said unto his father, Not so, Gen 48:18 3130
And Israel said unto *J*, Behold, I Gen 48:21 3130
J is a fruitful bough, even a Gen 49:22 3130
they shall be on the head of *J* Gen 49:26 3130
J fell upon his father's face, and Gen 50:1 3130
J commanded his servants the Gen 50:2 3130
J spake unto the house of Pharaoh Gen 50:4 3130
J went up to bury his father Gen 50:7 3130
And all the house of *J*, and his Gen 50:8 3130
J returned into Egypt, he, and his Gen 50:14 3130
J will peradventure hate us, and Gen 50:15 3130
And they sent a messenger unto *J* Gen 50:16 3130
So shall ye say unto *J*, Forgive, Gen 50:17 3130
J wept when they spake unto him Gen 50:17 3130
J said unto them, Fear not Gen 50:19 3130
J dwelt in Egypt, he, and his Gen 50:22 3130
J lived an hundred and ten years Gen 50:22 3130
J saw Ephraim's children of the Gen 50:23 3130
J said unto his brethren, I die Gen 50:24 3130
J took an oath of the children of Gen 50:25 3130
So *J* died, being an hundred and Gen 50:26 3130
for *J* was in Egypt already Ex 1:5 0100
J died, and all his brethren, and Ex 1:6 3130
king over Egypt, which knew not *J* Ex 1:8 3130
took the bones of *J* with him Ex 13:19 3130
families of Manasseh the son of *J* Num 27:1 3130
tribe of Manasseh the son of *J* Num 32:33 3130
The prince of the children of *J* Num 34:23 3130
the sons of Manasseh the son of *J* Num 36:12 3130
Levi, and Judah, and Issachar, and *J* Deut 27:12 3130
the children of *J* were two tribes Josh 14:4 3130
the lot of the children of *J* fell Josh 16:1 3130
So the children of *J*, Manasseh and Josh 16:4 3130
for he was the firstborn of *J* Josh 17:1 3130
the son of *J* by their families Josh 17:2 3130
the children of *J* spake unto Josh 17:14 3130
And the children of *J* said Josh 17:16 3130
And the bones of *J*, which the Josh 24:32 3130
Dan, *J*, and Benjamin, Naphtali, 1Chr 2:2 3130
He sent a man before them, even *J* Ps 105:17 3130
that Jacob gave to his son *J* Jn 4:5 *2501*
with envy, sold *J* into Egypt Acts 7:9 *2501*
at the second time *J* was made Acts 7:13 *2501*
Then sent *J*, and called his father Acts 7:14 *2501*
king arose, which knew not *J* Acts 7:18 *2501*
dying, blessed both the sons of *J* Heb 11:21 *2501*
By faith *J*, when he died, made Heb 11:22 *2501*

2. Descendants of Joseph 1.
Of the children of *J* Num 1:10 3130
Of the children of *J*, namely, of Num 1:32 3130
Of the tribe of *J*, namely, of the Num 13:11 3130
The sons of *J* after their Num 26:28 3130
sons of *J* after their families Num 26:37 3130
of the families of the sons of *J* Num 36:1 3130
of the sons of *J* hath said well Num 36:5 3130
of *J* he said, Blessed of the LORD Deut 33:13 3130
blessing come upon the head of *J* Deut 33:16 3130
Joshua spake unto the house of *J* Josh 17:17 3130
the house of *J* shall abide in Josh 18:5 3130
of Judah and the children of *J* Josh 18:11 3130
inheritance of the children of *J* Josh 24:32 3130
And the house of *J*, they also went Judg 1:22 3130
the house of *J* sent to descry Judg 1:23 3130
hand of the house of *J* prevailed Judg 1:35 3130
this day of all the house of *J* to 2Sa 19:20 3130
all the charge of the house of *J* 1Kin 11:28 3130
the sons of *J* the son of Israel 1Chr 5:1 3130
children of *J* the son of Israel 1Chr 7:29 3130
people, the sons of Jacob and *J* Ps 77:15 3130
he refused the tabernacle of *J* Ps 78:67 3130
thou that leadest *J* like a flock Ps 80:1 3130
he ordained in *J* for a testimony Ps 81:5 3084
stick, and write upon it, For *J* Eze 37:16 3130
I will take the stick of *J* Eze 37:19 3130
J shall have two portions Eze 47:13 3130
and one gate of *J*, one gate of Eze 48:32 3130
out like fire in the house of *J* Amos 5:6 3130
be gracious unto the remnant of *J* Amos 5:15 3130
grieved for the affliction of *J* Amos 6:6 3130
a fire, and the house of *J* a flame Obad 18 3130
and I will save the house of *J* Zec 10:6 3130
Of the tribe of *J* were sealed Rev 7:8 *2501*

3. A spy sent to the Promised Land.
of Issachar, Igal the son of *J* Num 13:7 3130

4. A son of Asaph.
Zaccur, and *J*, and Nethaniah, and 1Chr 25:2 3130
lot came forth for Asaph to *J* 1Chr 25:9 3130

5. Married a foreigner in exile.
Shallum, Amariah, and *J* Ezr 10:42 3130

6. A priest.
Jonathan; of Shebaniah, *J* Neh 12:14 3130

7. Husband of Mary, the mother of Jesus.
Jacob begat *J* the husband of Mary Mt 1:16 *2501*
his mother Mary was espoused to *J* Mt 1:18 *2501*
Then *J* her husband, being a just Mt 1:19 *2501*
unto him in a dream, saying, *J* Mt 1:20 *2501*
Then *J* being raised from sleep Mt 1:24 *2501*
Lord appeareth to *J* in a dream Mt 2:13 *2501*
in a dream to *J* in Egypt, Mt 2:19 *2501*
to a man whose name was *J* Lk 1:27 *2501*
J also went up from Galilee, out Lk 2:4 *2501*
with haste, and found Mary, and *J* Lk 2:16 *2501*
And *J* and his mother marvelled at Lk 2:33 *2501*
and *J* and his mother knew not of it Lk 2:43 *2501*
(as was supposed) the son of *J* Lk 3:23 *2501*
Jesus of Nazareth, the son of *J* Jn 1:45 *2501*
Is not this Jesus, the son of *J* Jn 6:42 *2501*

8. A disciple of Jesus.
a rich man of Arimathaea, named *J* Mt 27:57 *2501*
when *J* had taken the body, he Mt 27:59 *2501*
J of Arimathaea, an honourable Mk 15:43 *2501*
centurion, he gave the body to *J* Mk 15:45 *2501*
behold, there was a man named *J* Lk 23:50 *2501*
after this *J* of Arimathaea, being Jn 19:38 *2501*

9. Son of Mattathias; ancestor of Jesus.
of Janna, which was the son of *J* Lk 3:24 *2501*

10. Son of Juda; ancestor of Jesus.
of Semei, which was the son of *J* Lk 3:26 *2501*

11. Son of Jonan; ancestor of Jesus.
of Juda, which was the son of *J* Lk 3:30 *2501*

12. A nominee for Judas' apostleship.
J called Barsabas, who was Acts 1:23 *2501*

JOSEPH'S (*jo'-zefs*)
1. Refers to Joseph 1.
And they took *J* coat, and killed a Gen 37:31 3130
the Egyptian's house for *J* sake Gen 39:5 3130
he left all that he had in *J* hand Gen 39:6 3130
J master took him, and put him Gen 39:20 3130
of the prison committed to *J* hand Gen 39:22 3130
his hand, and put it upon *J* hand Gen 41:42 3130
And Pharaoh called *J* name Gen 41:45 3130
J ten brethren went down to buy Gen 42:3 3130
J brother, Jacob sent not with Gen 42:4 3130
J brethren came, and bowed down Gen 42:6 3130
man brought the men into *J* house Gen 43:17 3130
they were brought into *J* house Gen 43:18 3130
near to the steward of *J* house Gen 43:19 3130
man brought the men into *J* house Gen 43:24 3130
and his brethren came to *J* house Gen 44:14 3130
saying, *J* brethren are come Gen 45:16 3130
And Israel beheld *J* sons, and said, Gen 48:8 3130
when *J* brethren saw that their Gen 50:15 3130
were brought up upon *J* knees Gen 50:23 3130
but the birthright was *J* 1Chr 5:2 3130
J kindred was made known unto Acts 7:13 *2501*

2. Refers to Joseph 7.
And they said, Is not this *J* son Lk 4:22 *2501*

JOSES (*jo'-zez*) See JOSE.
1. A brother of Jesus.
and his brethren, James, and *J* Mt 13:55 *2500*
Mary, the brother of James, and *J* Mk 6:3 *2500*

2. Same as Barnabas.
and Mary the mother of James and *J* Mt 27:56 *2500*
mother of James the less and of *J* Mk 15:40 *2500*
Mary the mother of *J* beheld where Mk 15:47 *2500*
And *J*, who by the apostles was Acts 4:36 *2500*

JOSHAH (*jo'-shah*) *A descendant of Simeon.*
Jamlech, and *J* the son of Amaziah, 1Chr 4:34 3144

JOSHAPHAT (*josh'-a-fat*) See JEHOSHAPHAT, JOSAPHAT. *A "mighty man" of David.*
of Maachah, and *J* the Mithnite, 1Chr 11:43 3146

JOSHAVIAH (*josh-a-vi'-ah*) *A "mighty man" of David.*
the Mahavite, and Jeribai, and *J* 1Chr 11:46 3145

JOSHBEKASHAH (*josh-bek'-a-shah*) *A sanctuary servant.*
Giddalti, and Romamti-ezer, *J* 1Chr 25:4 3436
The seventeenth to *J*, he, his 1Chr 25:24 3436

JOSHEB-BASSHEBETH See ADINO.

JOSHUA (*josh'-u-ah*) See HOSEA, HOSHEA, JEHOSHUAH, JESHUA, JESHUAH, JESUS, OSEA, OSHEA.
1. Son of Nun.
And Moses said unto *J*, Choose us Ex 17:9 3091
So *J* did as Moses had said to him Ex 17:10 3091
J discomfited Amalek and his Ex 17:13 3091
and rehearse it in the ears of *J* Ex 17:14 3091
Moses rose up, and his minister *J* Ex 24:13 3091
when *J* heard the noise of the Ex 32:17 3091
but his servant *J*, the son of Nun Ex 33:11 3091
J the son of Nun, the servant of Num 11:28 3091
J the son of Nun, and Caleb the Num 14:6 3091
of Jephunneh, and *J* the son of Nun Num 14:30 3091
But *J* the son of Nun, and Caleb Num 14:38 3091
of Jephunneh, and *J* the son of Nun Num 26:65 3091
Take thee *J* the son of Nun, a man Num 27:18 3091
and he took *J*, and set him before Num 27:22 3091
the Kenezite, and *J* the son of Nun Num 32:12 3091
J the son of Nun, and the chief Num 32:28 3091
the priest, and *J* the son of Nun Num 34:17 3091
But *J* the son of Nun, which Deut 1:38 3091
I commanded *J* at that time, Deut 3:21 3091
But charge *J*, and encourage him, Deut 3:28 3091
and *J*, he shall go over before Deut 31:3 3091
And Moses called unto *J*, and said Deut 31:7 3091
call *J*, and present yourselves in Deut 31:14 3091
J went, and presented themselves Deut 31:14 3091
he gave *J* the son of Nun a charge Deut 31:23 3091
J the son of Nun was full of the Deut 34:9 3091
LORD spake unto *J* the son of Nun Josh 1:1 3091
Then *J* commanded the officers of Josh 1:10 3091
the tribe of Manasseh, spake *J* Josh 1:12 3091
And they answered *J*, saying, All Josh 1:16 3091
J the son of Nun sent out of Josh 2:1 3091
came to *J* the son of Nun, and told Josh 2:23 3091
And they said unto *J*, Truly the Josh 2:24 3091
J rose early in the morning Josh 3:1 3091
J said unto the people, Sanctify Josh 3:5 3091
J spake unto the priests, saying, Josh 3:6 3091
And the LORD said unto *J*, This day Josh 3:7 3091
J said unto the children of Josh 3:9 3091
J said, Hereby ye shall know that Josh 3:10 3091
that the LORD spake unto *J* Josh 4:1 3091
Then *J* called the twelve men, Josh 4:4 3091
J said unto them, Pass over Josh 4:5 3091
of Israel did so as *J* commanded Josh 4:8 3091
Jordan, as the LORD spake unto *J* Josh 4:8 3091
J set up twelve stones in the Josh 4:9 3091
that the LORD commanded *J* to Josh 4:10 3091
to all that Moses commanded *J* Josh 4:10 3091
J in the sight of all Israel Josh 4:14 3091
And the LORD spake unto *J*, saying, Josh 4:15 3091
J therefore commanded the priests Josh 4:17 3091
of Jordan, did *J* pitch in Gilgal Josh 4:20 3091
At that time the LORD said unto *J* Josh 5:2 3091
J made him sharp knives, and Josh 5:3 3091
is the cause why *J* did circumcise Josh 5:4 3091
their stead, them *J* circumcised Josh 5:7 3091
And the LORD said unto *J*, This day Josh 5:9 3091
when *J* was by Jericho, that he Josh 5:13 3091
J went unto him, and said unto him Josh 5:13 3091
J fell on his face to the earth, Josh 5:14 3091
of the LORD's host said unto *J* Josh 5:15 3091
And *J* did so Josh 5:15 3091
And the LORD said unto *J*, See, I Josh 6:2 3091
J the son of Nun called the Josh 6:6 3091
when *J* had spoken unto the people Josh 6:8 3091
J had commanded the people, Josh 6:10 3091
J rose early in the morning, and Josh 6:12 3091
J said unto the people, Shout Josh 6:16 3091
But *J* had said unto the two men Josh 6:22 3091
J saved Rahab the harlot alive, Josh 6:25 3091
which *J* sent to spy out Jericho Josh 6:25 3091
J adjured them at that time, Josh 6:26 3091
So the LORD was with *J* Josh 6:27 3091
J sent men from Jericho to Ai, Josh 7:2 3091
And they returned to *J*, and said Josh 7:3 3091
J rent his clothes, and fell to Josh 7:6 3091
J said, Alas, O Lord GOD, Josh 7:7 3091
And the LORD said unto *J*, Get thee Josh 7:10 3091
So *J* rose up early in the morning Josh 7:16 3091
J said unto Achan, My son, give, Josh 7:19 3091
And Achan answered *J*, and said, Josh 7:20 3091
So *J* sent messengers, and they ran Josh 7:22 3091
the tent, and brought them unto *J* Josh 7:23 3091
And *J*, and all Israel with him, Josh 7:24 3091
J said, Why hast thou troubled us Josh 7:25 3091
And the LORD said unto *J*, Fear not Josh 8:1 3091
So *J* arose, and all the people of Josh 8:3 3091
J chose out thirty thousand Josh 8:3 3091
J therefore sent them forth Josh 8:9 3091
but *J* lodged that night among the Josh 8:9 3091
J rose up early in the morning, Josh 8:10 3091
J went that night into the midst Josh 8:13 3091
And *J* and all Israel made as if Josh 8:15 3091
and they pursued after *J*, and were Josh 8:16 3091
And the LORD said unto *J*, Stretch Josh 8:18 3091
J stretched out the spear that he Josh 8:18 3091
And when *J* and all Israel saw that Josh 8:21 3091
took alive, and brought him to *J* Josh 8:23 3091
For *J* drew not his hand back, Josh 8:26 3091
of the LORD which he commanded *J* Josh 8:27 3091
J burnt Ai, and made it an heap Josh 8:28 3091
J commanded that they should take Josh 8:29 3091
Then *J* built an altar unto the Josh 8:30 3091
which *J* read not before all the Josh 8:35 3091
together, to fight with *J* Josh 9:2 3091
of Gibeon heard what *J* had done Josh 9:3 3091
they went to *J* unto the camp at Josh 9:6 3091
And they said unto *J*, We are thy Josh 9:8 3091
J said unto them, Who are ye Josh 9:8 3091
J made peace with them, and made a Josh 9:15 3091
J called for them, and he spake Josh 9:22 3091
And they answered *J*, and said, Josh 9:24 3091
J made them that day hewers of Josh 9:27 3091
had heard how *J* had taken Ai Josh 10:1 3091
for it hath made peace with *J* Josh 10:4 3091
sent unto *J* to the camp to Gilgal Josh 10:6 3091

So J ascended from Gilgal, he, and Josh 10:7 3091
And the LORD said unto J, Fear Josh 10:8 3091
J therefore came unto them Josh 10:9 3091
Then spake J to the LORD in the Josh 10:12 3091
J returned, and all Israel with Josh 10:15 3091
And it was told J, saying, The Josh 10:17 3091
J said, Roll great stones upon Josh 10:18 3091
And it came to pass, when J Josh 10:20 3091
camp to J at Makkedah in peace Josh 10:21 3091
Then said J, Open the mouth of Josh 10:22 3091
brought out those kings unto J Josh 10:24 3091
that J called for all the men of Josh 10:24 3091
J said unto them, Fear not, nor Josh 10:25 3091
afterward J smote them, and slew Josh 10:26 3091
that J commanded, and they took Josh 10:27 3091
that day J took Makkedah, and Josh 10:28 3091
Then J passed from Makkedah, and Josh 10:29 3091
J passed from Libnah, and all Josh 10:31 3091
J smote him and his people, until Josh 10:33 3091
from Lachish J passed unto Eglon, Josh 10:34 3091
J went up from Eglon, and all Josh 10:36 3091
J returned, and all Israel with Josh 10:38 3091
So J smote all the country of the Josh 10:40 3091
J smote them from Kadesh-barnea Josh 10:41 3091
their land did J take at one time Josh 10:42 3091
J returned, and all Israel with Josh 10:43 3091
And the LORD said unto J, Be not Josh 11:6 3091
So J came, and all the people of Josh 11:7 3091
J did unto them as the LORD bade Josh 11:9 3091
J at that time turned back, and Josh 11:10 3091
did J take, and smote them with Josh 11:12 3091
that did J burn Josh 11:13 3091
Moses command J, and so did J Josh 11:15 3091
So J took all that land, the Josh 11:16 3091
J made war a long time with all Josh 11:18 3091
And at that time came J, and cut Josh 11:21 3091
J destroyed them utterly with Josh 11:21 3091
So J took the whole land, Josh 11:23 3091
J gave it for an inheritance unto Josh 11:23 3091
the kings of the country which J Josh 12:7 3091
which J gave unto the tribes of Josh 12:7 3091
Now J was old and stricken in Josh 13:1 3091
J the son of Nun, and the heads of Josh 14:1 3091
of Judah came unto J in Gilgal Josh 14:6 3091
J blessed him, and gave unto Caleb Josh 14:13 3091
the commandment of the LORD to J Josh 15:13 3091
before J the son of Nun, and Josh 17:4 3091
children of Joseph spake unto J Josh 17:14 3091
J answered them, If thou be a Josh 17:15 3091
J spake unto the house of Joseph, Josh 17:17 3091
J said unto the children of Josh 18:3 3091
J charged them that went to Josh 18:8 3091
came again to J to the host at Josh 18:9 3091
J cast lots for them in Shiloh Josh 18:10 3091
there J divided the land unto the Josh 18:10 3091
to J the son of Nun among them Josh 19:49 3091
J the son of Nun, and the heads of Josh 19:51 3091
The LORD also spake unto J Josh 20:1 3091
unto J the son of Nun, and unto Josh 21:1 3091
Then J called the Reubenites, and Josh 22:1 3091
So J blessed them, and sent them Josh 22:6 3091
the other half thereof gave J Josh 22:7 3091
when J sent them away also unto Josh 22:7 3091
that J waxed old and stricken in Josh 23:1 3091
J called for all Israel, and for Josh 23:2 3091
J gathered all the tribes of Josh 24:1 3091
J said unto all the people, Thus Josh 24:2 3091
J said unto the people, Ye cannot Josh 24:19 3091
And the people said unto J Josh 24:21 3091
J said unto the people, Ye are Josh 24:22 3091
And the people said unto J Josh 24:24 3091
So J made a covenant with the Josh 24:25 3091
J wrote these words in the book Josh 24:26 3091
J said unto all the people, Josh 24:27 3091
So J let the people depart, every Josh 24:28 3091
that J the son of Nun, the Josh 24:29 3091
served the LORD all the days of J Josh 24:31 3091
of the elders that overlived J Josh 24:31 3091
the death of J it came to pass Judg 1:1 3091
when J had let the people go, the Judg 2:6 3091
served the LORD all the days of J Judg 2:7 3091
of the elders that outlived J Judg 2:7 3091
J the son of Nun, the servant of Judg 2:8 3091
nations which J left when he died Judg 2:21 3091
he them into the hand of J Judg 2:23 3091
he spake by J the son of Nun 1Kin 16:34 3091
2. A Bethshemite.
the cart came into the field of J 1Sa 6:14 3091
unto this day in the field of J 1Sa 6:18 3091
3. A governor of Jerusalem.
of J the governor of the city 2Kin 23:8 3091
4. A High Priest.
to J the son of Josedech, the Hag 1:1 3091
J the son of Josedech, the high Hag 1:12 3091
the spirit of J the son of Hag 1:14 3091
to J the son of Josedech, the Hag 2:2 3091
and be strong, O J, son of Hag 2:4 3091
he shewed me J the high priest Zec 3:1 3091
Now J was clothed with filthy Zec 3:3 3091
of the LORD protested unto J Zec 3:6 3091
O J the high priest, thou, and thy Zec 3:8 3091
stone that I have laid before J Zec 3:9 3091
the head of J the son of Josedech Zec 6:11 3091

JOSIAH (*jo-si'-ah*) See JOSIAS.
1. A king of Judah.
the house of David, J by name 1Kin 13:2 2977
made J his son king in his stead 2Kin 21:24 2977
J his son reigned in his stead 2Kin 21:26 2977
J was eight years old when he 2Kin 22:1 2977
in the eighteenth year of king J 2Kin 22:3 2977
as J turned himself, he spied the 2Kin 23:16 2977
J took away, and did to them 2Kin 23:19 2977
in the eighteenth year of king J 2Kin 23:23 2977
did J put away, that he might 2Kin 23:24 2977
Now the rest of the acts of J 2Kin 23:28 2977
and king J went against him 2Kin 23:29 2977
land took Jehoahaz the son of J 2Kin 23:30 2977
made Eliakim the son of J king in 2Kin 23:34 2977
king in the room of J his father 2Kin 23:34 2977
Amon his son, J his son 1Chr 3:14 2977
And the sons of J were, the 1Chr 3:15 2977
made J his son king in his stead 2Chr 33:25 2977
J was eight years old when he 2Chr 34:1 2977
J took away all the abominations 2Chr 34:33 2977
Moreover J kept a passover unto 2Chr 35:1 2977
J gave to the people, of the 2Chr 35:7 2977
to the commandment of king J 2Chr 35:16 2977
keep such a passover as J kept 2Chr 35:18 2977
reign of J was this passover kept 2Chr 35:19 2977
when J had prepared the temple, 2Chr 35:20 2977
and J went out against him 2Chr 35:20 2977
Nevertheless J would not turn his 2Chr 35:22 2977
And the archers shot at king J 2Chr 35:23 2977
Judah and Jerusalem mourned for J 2Chr 35:24 2977
And Jeremiah lamented for J 2Chr 35:25 2977
the singing women spake of J in 2Chr 35:25 2977
Now the rest of the acts of J 2Chr 35:26 2977
land took Jehoahaz the son of J 2Chr 36:1 2977
J the son of Amon king of Judah Jer 1:2 2977
the son of J king of Judah Jer 1:3 2977
the son of J king of Judah Jer 1:3 2977
unto me in the days of J the king Jer 3:6 2977
the son of J king of Judah Jer 22:11 2977
reigned instead of J his father Jer 22:11 2977
the son of J king of Judah Jer 22:18 2977
the son of J king of Judah Jer 25:1 2977
From the thirteenth year of J the Jer 25:3 2977
of J king of Judah came this word Jer 26:1 2977
of J king of Judah came this word Jer 27:1 2977
the son of J king of Judah Jer 35:1 2977
the son of J king of Judah Jer 36:1 2977
unto thee, from the days of J Jer 36:2 2977
the son of J king of Judah Jer 36:9 2977
king Zedekiah the son of J Jer 37:1 2977
the son of J king of Judah Jer 45:1 2977
the son of J king of Judah Jer 46:2 2977
in the days of J the son of Amon, Zeph 1:1 2977
2. A son of Zephaniah.
house of J the son of Zephaniah Zec 6:10 2977

JOSIAS (*jo-si'-as*) See JOSIAH. *Son of Amon; ancestor of Jesus.*
and Amon begat J Mt 1:10 2502
J begat Jechonias and his brethren Mt 1:11 2502

JOSIBIAH (*jos-ib-i'-ah*) *A Simeonite.*
And Joel, and Jehu the son of J 1Chr 4:35 3143

JOSIPHIAH (*jos-if-i'-ah*) *A family of exiles.*
the son of J, and with him an Ezr 8:10 3131

JOT
one j or one tittle shall in no Mt 5:18 2503

JOTBAH (*jot'-bah*) *A place near Hebron.*
the daughter of Haruz of J 2Kin 21:19 3192

JOTBATH (*jot'-bath*) See JOTBATHAH. *An encampment during the Exodus.*
and from Gudgodah to J, a land of Deut 10:7 3193

JOTBATHAH (*jot'-ba-thah*) See JOTBATH. *Same as Jotbath.*
Hor-hagidgad, and pitched in J Num 33:33 3193
And they removed from J, and Num 33:34 3193

JOTHAM (*jo'-tham*) See JOATHAM.
1. A son of Gideon.
notwithstanding yet J the Judg 9:5 3147
And when they told it to J Judg 9:7 3147
J ran away, and fled, and went to Judg 9:21 3147
curse of J the son of Jerubbaal Judg 9:57 3147
2. Father of King Ahaz.
J the king's son was over the 2Kin 15:5 3147
J his son reigned in his stead 2Kin 15:7 3147
year of J the son of Uzziah 2Kin 15:30 3147
Remaliah king of Israel began J 2Kin 15:32 3147
Now the rest of the acts of J 2Kin 15:36 3147
J slept with his fathers, and was 2Kin 15:38 3147
of J king of Judah began to reign 2Kin 16:1 3147
son, Azariah his son, J his son, 1Chr 3:12 3147
in the days of J king of Judah 1Chr 5:17 3147
J his son was over the king's 2Chr 26:21 3147
J his son reigned in his stead 2Chr 26:23 3147
J was twenty and five years old 2Chr 27:1 3147
So J became mighty, because he 2Chr 27:6 3147
Now the rest of the acts of J 2Chr 27:7 3147
J slept with his fathers, and they 2Chr 27:9 3147
in the days of Uzziah, J, Ahaz, Is 1:1 3147
in the days of Ahaz the son of J Is 7:1 3147
Beeri, in the days of Uzziah, J, Hos 1:1 3147
the Morasthite in the days of J Mic 1:1 3147
3. A descendant of Caleb.
Regem, and J, and Gesham, and Pelet, 1Chr 2:47 3147

JOURNEY
had made his j prosperous or not Gen 24:21 1870
Then Jacob went on his j, and came Gen 29:1
set three days' j betwixt himself Gen 30:36 1870
pursued after him seven days' j Gen 31:23 1870
And he said, Let us take our j Gen 33:12 5265
Israel took his j with all that Gen 46:1 5265
three days' j into the wilderness Ex 3:18 1870
three days' j into the desert, and Ex 5:3 1870
three days' j into the wilderness Ex 8:27 1870
And they took their j from Succoth Ex 13:20 5265
And they took their j from Elim Ex 16:1 5265
dead body, or be in a j afar off Num 9:10 1870
that is clean, and is not in a j Num 9:13 1870
the south side shall take their j Num 10:6 5265
they first took their j according Num 10:13 5265
mount of the LORD three days' j Num 10:33 1870
before them in the three days' j Num 10:33 1870
as it were a day's j on this side Num 11:31 1870
were a day's j on the other side Num 11:31 1870
went three days' j in the Num 33:8 1870
they took their j out of the Num 33:12 5265
(There are eleven days' j from Deut 1:2
Turn you, and take your j, and go Deut 1:7 5265
take your j into the wilderness Deut 1:40 5265
took our j into the wilderness by Deut 2:1 5265
Rise ye up, take your j, and pass Deut 2:24 5265
children of Israel took their j Deut 10:6 5265
take thy j before the people, Deut 10:11 4550
Take victuals with you for the j Josh 9:11 1870
old by reason of the very long j Josh 9:13 1870
notwithstanding the j that thou Judg 4:9 1870
And the LORD sent thee on a j 1Sa 15:18 1870
Uriah, Camest thou not from thy j 2Sa 11:10 1870
he is pursuing, or he is in a j 1Kin 18:27 1870
a day's j into the wilderness 1Kin 19:4 1870
because the j is too great for 1Kin 19:7 1870
a compass of seven days' j 2Kin 3:9 1870
Then Solomon came from his j to 2Chr 1:13
him,) For how long shall thy j be Neh 2:6 4109
not at home, he is gone a long j Prov 7:19 1870
great city of three days' j Jonah 3:3 4109
to enter into the city a day's j Jonah 3:4 4109
Nor scrip for your j, neither two Mt 10:10 3598
and straightway took his j Mt 25:15 589
should take nothing for their j Mk 6:8 3598
of man is as a man taking a far j Mk 13:34 590
in the company, went a day's j Lk 2:44 3598
them, Take nothing for your j Lk 9:3 3598
of mine in his j is come to me Lk 11:6 3598
took his j into a far country, and Lk 15:13 589
being wearied with his j Jn 4:6 3597
from Jerusalem a sabbath day's j Acts 1:12 3598
morrow, as they went on their j Acts 10:9 3596
to pass, that, as I made my j Acts 22:6 4198
I might have a prosperous j by Rom 1:10 2137
Whensoever I take my j into Spain Rom 15:24 4198
for I trust to see you in my j Rom 15:24 1279
me on my j whithersoever I go 1Cor 16:6
and Apollos on their j diligently Titus 3:13
on their j after a godly sort 3Jn 6

JOURNEYED
as they j from the east, that Gen 11:2 5265
And Abram j, going on still toward Gen 12:9 5265
and Lot j east Gen 13:11 5265
Abraham j from thence toward the Gen 20:1 5265
Jacob j to Succoth, and built him Gen 33:17 5265
And they j: and the terror Gen 35:5 5265
And they j from Beth-el Gen 35:16 5265
And Israel j, and spread his tent Gen 35:21 5265
the children of Israel j from Ex 12:37 5265
of the children of Israel j from Ex 17:1 5265
then they j not till the day that Ex 40:37 5265
that the children of Israel j Num 9:17 5265
the LORD the children of Israel j Num 9:18 5265
the charge of the LORD, and j not Num 9:19 5265
commandment of the LORD they j Num 9:20 5265
up in the morning, then they j Num 9:21 5265
the cloud was taken up, they j Num 9:21 5265
abode in their tents, and j not Num 9:22 5265
but when it was taken up, they j Num 9:22 5265
commandment of the LORD they j Num 9:23 5265
And the people j from Num 11:35 5265
the people j not till Miriam was Num 12:15 5265
j from Kadesh, and came unto mount Num 20:22 5265
they j from mount Hor by the way Num 21:4 5265
they j from Oboth, and pitched at Num 21:11 5265
they j from Rissah, and pitched in Num 33:22 5265
From thence they j unto Gudgodah Deut 10:7 5265
And the children of Israel j Josh 9:17 5265
to the house of Micah, as he j Judg 17:8
But a certain Samaritan, as he j Lk 10:33 3593
And as he j, he came near Damascus Acts 9:3 4198
the men which j with him stood Acts 9:7 4922
about me and them which j with me Acts 26:13 4198

JOURNEYING
and for the j of the camps Num 10:2 4550
We are j unto the place of which Num 10:29 5265
teaching, and j toward Jerusalem Lk 13:22

JOURNEYINGS
Thus were the j of the children Num 10:28 4550
In j often, in perils of waters, 2Cor 11:26 3597

JOURNEYS
he went on his j from the south Gen 13:3 4550
wilderness of Sin, after their j Ex 17:1 4550
Israel went onward in all their j Ex 40:36 4550
of Israel, throughout all their j Ex 40:38 4550
shall blow an alarm for their j Num 10:6 4550
children of Israel took their j Num 10:12 4550
These are the j of the children Num 33:1 4550
goings out according to their j Num 33:2 4550
these are their j according to Num 33:2 4550

JOY
king Saul, with tabrets, with j 1Sa 18:6 8057
pipes, and rejoiced with great j 1Kin 1:40 8057
for there was j in Israel 1Chr 12:40 8057
by lifting up the voice with j 1Chr 15:16 8057
of the house of Obed-edom with j 1Chr 15:25 8057
king also rejoiced with great j 1Chr 29:9 8057
now have I seen with j thy people 1Chr 29:17 8057
to go again to Jerusalem with j 2Chr 20:27 8057
So there was great j in Jerusalem 2Chr 30:26 8057
and many shouted aloud for j Ezr 3:12 8057
the noise of the shout of j from Ezr 3:13 8057
of this house of God with j Ezr 6:16 2305
bread seven days with j Ezr 6:22 8057
for the j of the LORD is your Neh 8:10 2304

made them rejoice with great *j* ..... Neh 12:43 8057
so that the *j* of Jerusalem was ..... Neh 12:43 8057
Jews had light, and gladness, and *j* ..... Est 8:16 8342
his decree came, the Jews had *j* ..... Est 8:17 8057
turned unto them from sorrow to *j* ..... Est 9:22 8057
make them days of feasting and *j* ..... Est 9:22 8057
Behold, this is the *j* of his way ..... Job 8:19 4885
the *j* of the hypocrite but for a ..... Job 20:5 8057
the widow's heart to sing for *j* ..... Job 29:13 7442
and he shall see his face with *j* ..... Job 33:26 8643
all the sons of God shouted for *j* ..... Job 38:7
is turned into *j* before him ..... Job 41:22
let them ever shout for *j* ..... Ps 5:11
in thy presence is fulness of *j* ..... Ps 16:11 8057
The king shall *j* in thy strength, ... Ps 21:1 8055
in his tabernacle sacrifices of *j* ..... Ps 27:6 8643
but *j* cometh in the morning ..... Ps 30:5 7440
and shout for *j*, all ye that are ..... Ps 32:11
Let them shout for *j*, and be glad, ... Ps 35:27
house of God, with the voice of *j* ..... Ps 42:4 7440
of God, unto God my exceeding *j* ..... Ps 43:4 1524
the *j* of the whole earth, is ..... Ps 48:2 4885
Make me to hear *j* and gladness ..... Ps 51:8 8342
unto me the *j* of thy salvation ..... Ps 51:12 8342
they shout for *j*, they also sing ..... Ps 65:13
the nations be glad and sing for *j* ..... Ps 67:4
brought forth his people with *j* ..... Ps 105:43 8342
that sow in tears shall reap in *j* ..... Ps 126:5 7440
and let thy saints shout for *j* ..... Ps 132:9 7442
saints shall shout aloud for *j* ..... Ps 132:16 7442
not Jerusalem above my chief *j* ..... Ps 137:6 8057
to the counsellors of peace is *j* ..... Prov 12:20 8057
doth not intermeddle with his *j* ..... Prov 14:10 8057
Folly is *j* to him that is ..... Prov 15:21 8057
A man hath *j* by the answer of his ..... Prov 15:23 8057
and the father of a fool hath no *j* ..... Prov 17:21 8056
It is *j* to the just to do ..... Prov 21:15 8057
a wise child shall have *j* of him ..... Prov 23:24 8056
withheld not my heart from any *j* ..... Eccl 2:10 8057
sight wisdom, and knowledge, and *j* ..... Eccl 2:26 8057
him in the *j* of his heart ..... Eccl 5:20 8057
Go thy way, eat thy bread with *j* ..... Eccl 9:7 8057
nation, and not increased the *j* ..... Is 9:3 8057
they *j* before thee according to ..... Is 9:3 8055
according to the *j* in harvest ..... Is 9:3 8055
have no *j* in their young men ..... Is 9:17 8055
Therefore with *j* shall ye draw ..... Is 12:3 8342
j out of the plentiful field ..... Is 16:10 1524
And behold *j* and gladness, slaying ..... Is 22:13 8342
the *j* of the harp ceaseth ..... Is 24:8 4885
all *j* is darkened, the mirth of ..... Is 24:11 8057
increase their *j* in the LORD ..... Is 29:19 8057
houses of *j* in the joyous city ..... Is 32:13 4885
a *j* of wild asses, a pasture of ..... Is 32:14 4885
and rejoice even with *j* and ..... Is 35:2 1525
everlasting *j* upon their heads ..... Is 35:10 8057
they shall obtain *j* and gladness, ... Is 35:10 8057
j and gladness shall be found ..... Is 51:3 8342
everlasting *j* shall be upon their ..... Is 51:11 8057
they shall obtain gladness and *j* ..... Is 51:11 8057
Break forth into *j*, sing together ..... Is 52:9
For ye shall go out with *j* ..... Is 55:12 8057
a *j* of many generations ..... Is 60:15 4885
the oil of *j* for mourning, the ..... Is 61:3 8342
everlasting *j* shall be unto them ..... Is 61:7 8057
shall sing for *j* of heart ..... Is 65:14 2898
a rejoicing, and her people a *j* ..... Is 65:18 4885
in Jerusalem, and *j* in my people ..... Is 65:19 7796
but he shall appear to your *j* ..... Is 66:5 8057
rejoice for *j* with her, all ye ..... Is 66:10 4885
and thy word was unto me the *j* ..... Jer 15:16 8342
I will turn their mourning into *j* ..... Jer 31:13 8342
And it shall be to me a name of *j* ..... Jer 33:9 8342
The voice of *j*, and the voice of ..... Jer 33:11 8342
of him, thou skippedst for *j* ..... Jer 48:27
And *j* and gladness is taken from ..... Jer 48:33 8057
praise not left, the city of my *j* ..... Jer 49:25 4885
beauty, The *j* of the whole earth ..... Lam 2:15 4885
The *j* of our heart is ceased ..... Lam 5:15 4885
the *j* of their glory, the desire ..... Eze 24:25 4885
with the *j* of all their heart ..... Eze 36:5 8057
Rejoice not, O Israel, for *j* ..... Hos 9:1 1524
because *j* is withered away from ..... Joel 1:12 8342
cut off before our eyes, yea, *j* ..... Joel 1:16 8057
I will *j* in the God of my ..... Hab 3:18 1523
he will rejoice over thee with *j* ..... Zeph 3:17 8057
he will *j* over thee with singing ..... Zeph 3:17 1523
shall be to the house of Judah *j* ..... Zec 8:19 8342
rejoiced with exceeding great *j* ..... Mt 2:10 5479
word, and anon with *j* receiveth it ..... Mt 13:20 5479
for *j* thereof goeth and selleth ..... Mt 13:44 5479
enter thou into the *j* of thy lord ..... Mt 25:21 5479
enter thou into the *j* of thy lord ..... Mt 25:23 5479
sepulchre with fear and great *j* ..... Mt 28:8 5479
And thou shalt have *j* and gladness ..... Lk 1:14 5479
the babe leaped in my womb for *j* ..... Lk 1:44 20
bring you good tidings of great *j* ..... Lk 2:10 5479
ye in that day, and leap for *j* ..... Lk 6:23
hear, receive the word with *j* ..... Lk 8:13 5479
the seventy returned again with *j* ..... Lk 10:17 5479
that likewise *j* shall be in ..... Lk 15:7 5479
there is *j* in the presence of the ..... Lk 15:10 5479
while they yet believed not for *j* ..... Lk 24:41 5479
to Jerusalem with great *j* ..... Lk 24:52 5479
this my *j* therefore is fulfilled ..... Jn 3:29 5479
that my *j* might remain in you, and ..... Jn 15:11 5479
that your *j* might be full ..... Jn 15:11 5479
sorrow shall be turned into *j* ..... Jn 16:20 5479
for *j* that a man is born into the ..... Jn 16:21 5479
your *j* no man taketh from you ..... Jn 16:22 5479
receive, that your *j* may be full ..... Jn 16:24 5479
have my *j* fulfilled in themselves ..... Jn 17:13 5479
me full of *j* with thy countenance ..... Acts 2:28 2167
And there was great *j* in that city ..... Acts 8:8 5479
the disciples were filled with *j* ..... Acts 13:52 5479
they caused great *j* unto all the ..... Acts 15:3 5479
I might finish my course with *j* ..... Acts 20:24 5479
but we also *j* in God through our ..... Rom 5:11 2744
and peace, and *j* in the Holy Ghost ..... Rom 14:17 5479
God of hope fill you with all *j* ..... Rom 15:13 5479
you with *j* by the will of God ..... Rom 15:32 5479
faith, but are helpers of your *j* 2Cor 1:24 5479
that my *j* is the *j* of you all 2Cor 2:3 5479
that my *j* is the *j* of you all 2Cor 2:3
more joyed we for the *j* of Titus 2Cor 7:13 5479
the abundance of their *j* and their 2Cor 8:2 5479
fruit of the Spirit is love, *j* ..... Gal 5:22 5479
for you all making request with *j* ..... Phil 1:4 5479
your furtherance and *j* of faith ..... Phil 1:25 5479
Fulfil ye my *j*, that ye be ..... Phil 2:2 5479
and service of your faith, I *j* ..... Phil 2:17 5468
For the same cause also do ye *j* ..... Phil 2:18 5468
beloved and longed for, my *j* ..... Phil 4:1 5479
with *j* of the Holy Ghost 1Th 1:6 5479
For what is our hope, or *j* 1Th 2:19 5479
For ye are our glory and *j* 1Th 2:20 5479
for all the *j* wherewith we *j* 1Th 3:9 5479
for all the *j* wherewith we *j* 1Th 3:9 5468
that I may be filled with *j* 2Ti 1:4 5479
For we have great *j* and ..... Philem 7 5485
let me have *j* of thee in the Lord ..... Philem 20 3685
who for the *j* that was set before ..... Heb 12:2 5479
that they may do it with *j* ..... Heb 13:17 5479
count it all *j* when ye fall into ..... Jas 1:2 5479
mourning, and your *j* to heaviness ..... Jas 4:9 5479
ye rejoice with *j* unspeakable 1Pet 1:8 5479
may be glad also with exceeding *j* 1Pet 4:13 21
unto you, that your *j* may be full 1Jn 1:4 5479
to face, that our *j* may be full 2Jn 12 5479
I have no greater *j* than to hear 3Jn 4 5479
of his glory with exceeding *j* ..... Jude 24 20

JOYED

exceedingly the more *j* we for the 2Cor 7:13 5463

JOYFUL

king, and went unto their tents *j* 1Kin 8:66 8056
for the LORD had made them *j* ..... Ezr 6:22 8055
Then went Haman forth that day *j* ..... Est 5:9 8056
let no *j* voice come therein ..... Job 3:7 7445
that love thy name be *j* in thee ..... Ps 5:11 5970
And my soul shall be *j* in the LORD ..... Ps 35:9 1523
shall praise thee with *j* lips ..... Ps 63:5 7445
Make a *j* noise unto God, all ye ..... Ps 66:1
make a *j* noise unto the God of ..... Ps 81:1
the people that know the *j* sound ..... Ps 89:15 8643
let us make a *j* noise to the rock ..... Ps 95:1
make a *j* noise unto him with ..... Ps 95:2
Let the field be *j*, and all that ..... Ps 96:12 5937
Make a *j* noise unto the LORD, all ..... Ps 98:4
make a *j* noise before the LORD ..... Ps 98:6
let the hills be *j* together ..... Ps 98:8 7442
Make a *j* noise unto the LORD, all ..... Ps 100:1
to be a *j* mother of children ..... Ps 113:9 8056
of Zion be *j* in their King ..... Ps 149:2 1523
Let the saints be *j* in glory ..... Ps 149:5 5937
In the day of prosperity be *j* ..... Eccl 7:14 2896
And be *j*, O earth ..... Is 49:13 1523
make them *j* in my house of prayer ..... Is 56:7 8055
my soul shall be *j* in my God ..... Is 61:10 1523
I am exceeding *j* in all our 2Cor 7:4 5479

JOYFULLY

Live *j* with the wife whom thou ..... Eccl 9:9 2416
and came down, and received him *j* ..... Lk 19:6 5463
took *j* the spoiling of your goods ..... Heb 10:34

JOYFULNESS

not the LORD thy God with *j* ..... Deut 28:47 8057
patience and longsuffering with *j* ..... Col 1:11 5479

JOYING

am I with you in the spirit, *j* ..... Col 2:5 5463

JOYOUS

a tumultuous city, a *j* city ..... Is 22:2 5947
Is this your *j* city, whose ..... Is 23:7 5947
the houses of joy in the *j* city ..... Is 32:13 5947
for the present seemeth to be *j* ..... Heb 12:11 5479

JOZABAD

1. Another warrior in David's army.
to him of Manasseh, Adnah, and *J* 1Chr 12:20 3107
and Jediael, and Michael, and *J* 1Chr 12:20 3107
2. A Chief Levite in Josiah's time.
and Asahel, and Jerimoth, and *J* 2Chr 31:13 3107
3. An exile with Ezra.
and Hashabiah and Jeiel and *J* 2Chr 35:9 3107
4. A priest.
with them was *J* the son of Jeshua ..... Ezr 8:33 3107
5. A Levite.
Maaseiah, Ishmael, Nethaneel, *J* ..... Ezr 10:22 3107
6. A priest who helped Ezra.
J, and Shimei, and Kelaiah, (the ..... Ezr 10:23 3107
7. A chief Levite in exile.
Maaseiah, Kelita, Azariah, *J* ..... Neh 8:7 3107
8. A chief Levite in exile.
And Shabbethai and *J*, of the chief ..... Neh 11:16 3107

JOZACHAR (*joz'-a-kar*) See ZABAD. *Son of Shimeath.*
For *J* the son of Shimeath, and 2Kin 12:21 3108

JOZADAK (*joz'-a-dak*) See JEHOZADAK, JOSEDECH. *A priest with Zerubbabel.*
Then stood up Jeshua the son of *J* ..... Ezr 3:2 3136
Shealtiel, and Jeshua the son of *J* ..... Ezr 3:8 3136
Shealtiel, and Jeshua the son of *J* ..... Ezr 5:2 3136
the sons of Jeshua the son of *J* ..... Ezr 10:18 3136
the son of Jeshua, the son of *J* ..... Neh 12:26 3136

JUBAL (*ju'-bal*) *Son of Adah.*
And his brother's name was *J* ..... Gen 4:21 3106

JUBILE

j to sound on the tenth day of ..... Lev 25:9 8643
it shall be a *j* unto you ..... Lev 25:10 3104
A *j* shall that fiftieth year be ..... Lev 25:11 3104
For it is the *j* ..... Lev 25:12 3104
In the year of this *j* ye shall ..... Lev 25:13 3104
the number of years after the *j* ..... Lev 25:15 3104
bought it until the year of *j* ..... Lev 25:28 3104
in the *j* it shall go out, and he ..... Lev 25:28 3104
it shall not go out in the *j* ..... Lev 25:30 3104
and they shall go out in the *j* ..... Lev 25:31 3104
shall go out in the year of *j* ..... Lev 25:33 3104
serve thee unto the year of *j* ..... Lev 25:40 3104
sold to him unto the year of *j* ..... Lev 25:50 3104
but few years unto the year of *j* ..... Lev 25:52 3104
he shall go out in the year of *j* ..... Lev 25:54 3104
his field from the year of *j* ..... Lev 27:17 3104
he sanctify his field after the *j* ..... Lev 27:18 3104
even unto the year of the *j* ..... Lev 27:18 3104
field, when it goeth out in the *j* ..... Lev 27:21 3104
even unto the year of the *j* ..... Lev 27:23 3104
In the year of the *j* the field ..... Lev 27:24 3104
when the *j* of the children of ..... Num 36:4 3104

JUCAL (*ju'-kal*) See JEHUCAL. *An enemy of Jeremiah.*
J the son of Shelemiah, and Pashur ..... Jer 38:1 3116

JUCE

wine of the *j* of my pomegranate ..... Song 8:2 6071

JUDA (*ju'-dah*) See JUDAH.
1. Greek form of Judah, the tribe.
thou Bethlehem, in the land of *J* ..... Mt 2:6 2455
the least among the princes of *J* ..... Mt 2:6 2455
with haste, into a city of *J* ..... Lk 1:39 2448
that our Lord sprang out of *J* ..... Heb 7:14 2455
the Lion of the tribe of *J* ..... Rev 5:5 2455
Of the tribe of *J* were sealed ..... Rev 7:5 2455
2. A brother of Jesus.
of James, and Joses, and of *J* ..... Mk 6:3 2455
3. Son of Jacob; an ancestor of Jesus.
of Phares, which was the son of *J* ..... Lk 3:33 2455

JUDAEA *A Roman province.*
J in the days of Herod the king ..... Mt 2:1 2449
said unto him, In Bethlehem of *J* ..... Mt 2:5 2449
that Archelaus did reign in *J* in ..... Mt 2:22 2499
preaching in the wilderness of *J* ..... Mt 3:1 2449
out to him Jerusalem, and all *J* ..... Mt 3:5 2449
and from Jerusalem, and from *J* ..... Mt 4:25 2449
the coasts of *J* beyond Jordan ..... Mt 19:1 2449
be in *J* flee into the mountains ..... Mt 24:16 2449
out unto him all the land of *J* ..... Mk 1:5 2449
Galilee followed him, and from *J* ..... Mk 3:7 2449
cometh into the coasts of *J* by ..... Mk 10:1 2449
be in *J* flee to the mountains ..... Mk 13:14 2449
the days of Herod, the king of *J* ..... Lk 1:5 2449
all the hill country of *J* ..... Lk 1:65 2449
of the city of Nazareth, into *J* ..... Lk 2:4 2449
Pilate being governor of *J* ..... Lk 3:1 2449
of every town of Galilee, and *J* ..... Lk 5:17 2449
multitude of people out of all *J* ..... Lk 6:17 2449
him went forth throughout all *J* ..... Lk 7:17 2449
are in *J* flee to the mountains ..... Lk 21:21 2449
his disciples into the land of *J* ..... Jn 3:22 2449
He left *J*, and departed again into ..... Jn 4:3 2449
was come out of *J* into Galilee ..... Jn 4:47 2449
he was come out of *J* into Galilee ..... Jn 4:54 2449
him, Depart hence, and go into *J* ..... Jn 7:3 2449
disciples, Let us go into *J* again ..... Jn 11:7 2449
me both in Jerusalem, and in all *J* ..... Acts 1:8 2449
dwellers in Mesopotamia, and in *J* ..... Acts 2:9 2449
and said unto them, Ye men of *J* ..... Acts 2:14 2453
throughout the regions of *J* ..... Acts 8:1 2449
churches rest throughout all *J* ..... Acts 9:31 2449
was published throughout all *J* ..... Acts 10:37 2449
brethren that were in *J* heard ..... Acts 11:1 2449
the brethren which dwelt in *J* ..... Acts 11:29 2449
he went down from *J* to Caesarea ..... Acts 12:19 2449
down from *J* taught the brethren ..... Acts 15:1 2449
down from *J* a certain prophet ..... Acts 21:10 2449
and throughout all the coasts of *J* ..... Acts 26:20 2449
letters out of *J* concerning thee ..... Acts 28:21 2449
them that do not believe in *J* ..... Rom 15:31 2449
to be brought on my way toward *J* 2Cor 1:16 2449
of *J* which were in Christ ..... Gal 1:22 2449
which in *J* are in Christ Jesus 1Th 2:14 2449

JUDAH (*ju'-dah*) See BETHLEHEM-JUDAH, JUDA, JUDAH'S, JUDAS, JUDEA, JUDE.
1. Son of Jacob and Leah.
therefore she called his name *J* ..... Gen 29:35 3063
and Simeon, and Levi, and *J* ..... Gen 35:23 3063
J said unto his brethren, What ..... Gen 37:26 3063
that *J* went down from his ..... Gen 38:1 3063
J saw there a daughter of a ..... Gen 38:2 3063
And *J* took a wife for Er his ..... Gen 38:6 3063
J said unto Onan, Go in unto thy ..... Gen 38:8 3063
Then said *J* to Tamar his daughter ..... Gen 38:11 3063
J was comforted, and went up unto ..... Gen 38:12 3063
When *J* saw her, he thought her to ..... Gen 38:15 3063
J sent the kid by the hand of his ..... Gen 38:20 3063
And he returned to *J*, and said, I ..... Gen 38:22 3063
J said, Let her take it to her, ... Gen 38:23 3063
months after, that it was told *J* ..... Gen 38:24 3063
J said, Bring her forth, and let ..... Gen 38:24 3063
J acknowledged them, and said, She ..... Gen 38:26 3063
J spake unto him, saying, The man ..... Gen 43:3 3063
J said unto Israel his father, ... Gen 43:8 3063
And *J* and his brethren came to ..... Gen 44:14 3063
J said, What shall we say unto my ..... Gen 44:16 3063
Then *J* came near unto him, and ..... Gen 44:18 3063
And the sons of *J* ..... Gen 46:12 3063

he sent J before him unto Joseph, Gen 46:28 3063
J, thou art he whom thy brethren Gen 49:8 3063
J is a lion's whelp Gen 49:9 3063
Reuben, Simeon, Levi, and J Ex 1:2 3063
The sons of J were Er and Onan Num 26:19 3063
of Pharez, whom Tamar bare unto J Ruth 4:12 3063
Reuben, Simeon, Levi, and J 1Chr 2:1 3063
The sons of J; Er, and 1Chr 2:3 3063
And Er, the firstborn of J 1Chr 2:3 3063
All the sons of J were five 1Chr 2:4 3063
prince of the children of J 1Chr 2:10 3063
The sons of J; Pharez 1Chr 4:1 3063
sons of Shelah the son of J were 1Chr 4:21 3063
like to the children of J 1Chr 4:27 3063
For J prevailed above his 1Chr 5:2 3063
children of Pharez the son of J 1Chr 9:4 3063
children of Zerah the son of J Neh 11:24 3063

2. The tribe and its land.

sceptre shall not depart from J Gen 49:10 3063
the son of Hur, of the tribe of J Ex 31:2 3063
the son of Hur, of the tribe of J Ex 35:30 3063
the son of Hur, of the tribe of J Ex 38:22 3063
Of J; Nashon the son Num 1:7 3063
Of the children of J, by their Num 1:26 3063
of them, even of the tribe of J Num 1:27 3063
J pitch throughout their armies Num 2:3 3063
be captain of the children of J Num 2:3 3063
of J were an hundred thousand Num 2:9 3063
of Amminadab, of the tribe of J Num 7:12 3063
of J according to their armies Num 10:14 3063
Of the tribe of J, Caleb the son Num 13:6 3063
the sons of J after their Num 26:20 3063
These are the families of J Num 26:22 3063
Of the tribe of J, Caleb the son Num 34:19 3063
Simeon, and Levi, and J, and Deut 27:12 3063
And this is the blessing of J Deut 33:7 3063
said, Hear, LORD, the voice of J Deut 33:7 3063
and Manasseh, and all the land of J Deut 34:2 3063
son of Zerah, of the tribe of J Josh 7:1 3063
and the tribe of J was taken Josh 7:16 3063
And he brought the family of J Josh 7:17 3063
son of Zerah, of the tribe of J Josh 7:18 3063
and from all the mountains of J Josh 11:21 3063
Then the children of J came unto Josh 14:6 3063
children of J by their families Josh 15:1 3063
J round about according to their Josh 15:12 3063
a part among the children of J Josh 15:13 3063
of J according to their families Josh 15:20 3063
of J toward the coast of Edom Josh 15:21 3063
the children of J could not drive Josh 15:63 3063
of J at Jerusalem unto this day Josh 15:63 3063
J shall abide in their coast on Josh 18:5 3063
forth between the children of J Josh 18:11 3063
a city of the children of J Josh 18:14 3063
inheritance of the children of J Josh 19:1 3063
of J was the inheritance of the Josh 19:9 3063
of J was too much for them Josh 19:9 3063
to J upon Jordan toward the Josh 19:34 3063
is Hebron, in the mountain of J Josh 20:7 3063
had by lot out of the tribe of J Josh 21:4 3063
of the tribe of the children of J Josh 21:9 3063
Hebron, in the hill country of J Josh 21:11 3063
And the LORD said, J shall go up Judg 1:2 3063
J said unto Simeon his brother, Judg 1:3 3063
And J went up Judg 1:4 3063
Now the children of J had fought Judg 1:8 3063
afterward the children of J went Judg 1:9 3063
J went against the Canaanites Judg 1:10 3063
of J into the wilderness of Judah Judg 1:16 3063
of Judah into the wilderness of J Judg 1:16 3063
J went with Simeon his brother, Judg 1:17 3063
Also J took Gaza with the coast Judg 1:18 3063
And the LORD was with J Judg 1:19 3063
Jordan to fight also against J Judg 10:9 3063
went up, and pitched in J, and Judg 15:9 3063
And the men of J said, Why are ye Judg 15:10 3063
Then three thousand men of J went Judg 15:11 3063
of the family of J, who was a Judg 17:7 3063
pitched in Kirjath-jearim, in J Judg 18:12 3063
LORD said, J shall go up first Judg 20:18 3063
way to return unto the land of J Ruth 1:7 3063
the men of J thirty thousand 1Sa 11:8 3063
footmen, and ten thousand men of J 1Sa 15:4 3063
at Shochoh, which belongeth to J 1Sa 17:1 3063
of J arose, and shouted, and 1Sa 17:52 3063
J loved David, because he went 1Sa 18:16 3063
and get thee into the land of J 1Sa 22:5 3063
Behold, we be afraid here in J 1Sa 23:3 3063
throughout all the thousands of J 1Sa 23:23 3063
unto the kings of J unto this day 1Sa 27:6 3063
said, Against the south of J 1Sa 27:10 3063
the coast which belongeth to J 1Sa 30:14 3063
and out of the land of J 1Sa 30:16 3063
of the spoil unto the elders of J 1Sa 30:26 3063
children of J the use of the bow 2Sa 1:18 3063
go up into any of the cities of J 2Sa 2:1 3063
And the men of J came, and there 2Sa 2:4 3063
David king over the house of J 2Sa 2:4 3063
also the house of J have anointed 2Sa 2:7 3063
But the house of J followed David 2Sa 2:10 3063
the house of J was seven years 2Sa 2:11 3063
which against J do shew kindness 2Sa 3:8 3063
of David over Israel and over J 2Sa 3:10 3063
he reigned over J seven years 2Sa 5:5 3063
three years over all Israel and J 2Sa 5:5 3063
were with him from Baale of J 2Sa 6:2 3063
David, The ark, and Israel, and J 2Sa 11:11 3063
thee the house of Israel and of J 2Sa 12:8 3063
Speak unto the elders of J 2Sa 19:11 3063
the heart of all the men of J 2Sa 19:14 3063
J came to Gilgal, to go to meet 2Sa 19:15 3063
the men of J to meet king David 2Sa 19:16 3063
all the people of J conducted the 2Sa 19:40 3063
the men of J stolen thee away 2Sa 19:41 3063
all the men of J answered the men 2Sa 19:42 3063
of Israel answered the men of J 2Sa 19:43 3063
the words of the men of J were 2Sa 19:43 3063
but the men of J clave unto their 2Sa 20:2 3063
me the men of J within three days 2Sa 20:4 3063
went to assemble the men of J 2Sa 20:5 3063
to the children of Israel and J 2Sa 21:2 3063
to say, Go, number Israel and J 2Sa 24:1 3063
they went out to the south of J 2Sa 24:7 3063
the men of J were five hundred 2Sa 24:9 3063
all the men of J the king's 1Kin 1:9 3063
to be ruler over Israel and over J 1Kin 1:35 3063
Jether, captain of the host of J 1Kin 2:32 3063
J and Israel were many, as the 1Kin 4:20 3063
And J and Israel dwelt safely, 1Kin 4:25 3063
gave them Hebron in the land of J 1Chr 6:55 3063
Aaron they gave the cities of J 1Chr 6:57 3063
of the tribe of the children of J 1Chr 6:65 3063
dwelt of the children of J 1Chr 9:3 3063
and J to the hold unto David 1Chr 12:16 3063
The children of J that bare 1Chr 12:24 3063
which belonged to J, to bring up 1Chr 13:6 3063
Of J, Elihu, one of the brethren 1Chr 27:18 3063
he hath chosen J to be the ruler 1Chr 28:4 3063
and of the house of J, the house 1Chr 28:4 3063
cunning men that are with me in J 2Chr 2:7 3063
such seen before in the land of J 2Chr 9:11 3063
house at Jerusalem, which is in J Ezr 1:2 3063
go up to Jerusalem, which is in J Ezr 1:3 3063
up the chief of the fathers of J Ezr 1:5 3063
unto Sheshbazzar, the prince of J Ezr 1:8 3063
the hands of the people of J Ezr 4:4 3063
against the inhabitants of J Ezr 4:6 3063
unto the Jews that were in J Ezr 5:1 3061
to enquire concerning J and Ezr 7:14 3061
and to give us a wall in J Ezr 9:9 3063
made proclamation throughout J Ezr 10:7 3063
Then all the men of J and Benjamin Ezr 10:9 3063
came, he and certain men of J Neh 1:2 3063
that thou wouldest send me unto J Neh 2:5 3063
convey me over till I come into J Neh 2:7 3063
J said, The strength of the Neh 4:10 3063
were behind all the house of J Neh 4:16 3063
their governor in the land of J Neh 5:14 3063
saying, There is a king in J Neh 6:7 3063
in those days the nobles of J Neh 6:17 3063
were many in J sworn unto him Neh 6:18 3063
came again to Jerusalem and to J Neh 7:6 3063
but in the cities of J dwelt Neh 11:3 3063
certain of the children of J Neh 11:4 3063
Of the children of J Neh 11:4 3063
were in all the cities of J Neh 11:20 3063
of J dwelt at Kirjath-arba Neh 11:25 3063
the Levites were divisions in J Neh 11:36 3063
up the princes of J upon the wall Neh 12:31 3063
and half of the princes of J Neh 12:32 3063
for J rejoiced for the priests and Neh 12:44 3063
Then brought all J the tithe of Neh 13:12 3063
In those days saw I in J some Neh 13:15 3063
sabbath unto the children of J Neh 13:16 3063
I contended with the nobles of J Neh 13:17 3063
away with Jeconiah king of J Est 2:6 3063
let the daughters of J be glad Ps 48:11 3063
J is my lawgiver Ps 60:7 3063
he was in the wilderness of J Ps 63:t 3063
their ruler, the princes of J Ps 68:27 3063
and will build the cities of J Ps 69:35 3063
In J is God known Ps 76:1 3063
But chose the tribe of J, the Ps 78:68 3063
the daughters of J rejoiced Ps 97:8 3063
J is my lawgiver Ps 108:8 3063
J was his sanctuary, and Israel Ps 114:2 3063
of Israel and with the house of J Heb 8:8 *2455*

3. The southern kingdom after the revolt of the ten northern tribes.

which dwelt in the cities of J 1Kin 12:17 3063
of David, but the tribe of J only 1Kin 12:20 3063
he assembled all the house of J 1Kin 12:21 3063
the son of Solomon, king of J 1Kin 12:23 3063
Judah, and unto all the house of J 1Kin 12:23 3063
even unto Rehoboam king of J 1Kin 12:27 3063
and go again to Rehoboam king of J 1Kin 12:27 3063
like unto the feast that is in J 1Kin 12:32 3063
of J by the word of the LORD unto 1Kin 13:1 3063
of God went, which came from J 1Kin 13:12 3063
the man of God that camest from J 1Kin 13:14 3063
the man of God that came from J 1Kin 13:21 3063
the son of Solomon reigned in J 1Kin 14:21 3063
J did evil in the sight of the 1Kin 14:22 3063
the chronicles of the kings of J 1Kin 14:29 3063
of Nebat reigned Abijam over J 1Kin 15:1 3063
the chronicles of the kings of J 1Kin 15:7 3063
king of Israel reigned Asa over J 1Kin 15:9 3063
king of Israel went up against J 1Kin 15:17 3063
out or come in to Asa king of J 1Kin 15:17 3063
a proclamation throughout all J 1Kin 15:22 3063
the chronicles of the kings of J 1Kin 15:23 3063
the second year of Asa king of J 1Kin 15:25 3063
Asa king of J did Baasha slay him 1Kin 15:28 3063
the third year of Asa king of J 1Kin 15:33 3063
sixth year of Asa king of J began 1Kin 16:8 3063
and seventh year of Asa king of J 1Kin 16:10 3063
seventh year of Asa king of J did 1Kin 16:15 3063
first year of Asa king of J began 1Kin 16:23 3063
eighth year of Asa king of J 1Kin 16:29 3063
Beer-sheba, which belongeth to J 1Kin 19:3 3063
that Jehoshaphat the king of J 1Kin 22:2 3063
king of J sat each on his throne 1Kin 22:10 3063
Jehoshaphat the king of J went up 1Kin 22:29 3063
son of Asa began to reign over J 1Kin 22:41 3063
the chronicles of the kings of J 1Kin 22:45 3063
year of Jehoshaphat king of J 1Kin 22:51 3063
the son of Jehoshaphat king of J 2Kin 1:17 3063
year of Jehoshaphat king of J 2Kin 3:1 3063
sent to Jehoshaphat the king of J 2Kin 3:7 3063
of Israel went, and the king of J 2Kin 3:9 3063
of Jehoshaphat the king of J 2Kin 3:14 3063
Jehoshaphat being then king of J 2Kin 8:16 3063
king of J began to reign 2Kin 8:16 3063
J for David his servant's sake 2Kin 8:19 3063
revolted from under the hand of J 2Kin 8:20 3063
under the hand of J unto this day 2Kin 8:22 3063
the chronicles of the kings of J 2Kin 8:23 3063
Jehoram king of J begin to reign 2Kin 8:25 3063
the son of Jehoram king of J went 2Kin 8:29 3063
Ahaziah king of J was come down 2Kin 9:16 3063
and Ahaziah king of J went out 2Kin 9:21 3063
Ahaziah the king of J saw this 2Kin 9:27 3063
began Ahaziah to reign over J 2Kin 9:29 3063
the brethren of Ahaziah king of J 2Kin 10:13 3063
Jehoash king of J took all the 2Kin 12:18 3063
Ahaziah, his fathers, kings of J 2Kin 12:18 3063
the chronicles of the kings of J 2Kin 12:19 3063
the son of Ahaziah king of J 2Kin 13:1 3063
of J began Jehoash the son of 2Kin 13:10 3063
fought against Amaziah king of J 2Kin 13:12 3063
the son of Joash king of J 2Kin 14:1 3063
Israel sent to Amaziah king of J 2Kin 14:9 3063
fall, even thou, and J with thee 2Kin 14:10 3063
Amaziah king of J looked one 2Kin 14:11 3063
which belongeth to J 2Kin 14:11 3063
J was put to the worse before 2Kin 14:12 3063
of Israel took Amaziah king of J 2Kin 14:13 3063
he fought with Amaziah king of J 2Kin 14:15 3063
of J lived after the death of 2Kin 14:17 3063
the chronicles of the kings of J 2Kin 14:18 3063
all the people of J took Azariah 2Kin 14:21 3063
built Elath, and restored it to J 2Kin 14:22 3063
the son of Joash king of J 2Kin 14:23 3063
and Hamath, which belonged to J 2Kin 14:28 3063
son of Amaziah king of J to reign 2Kin 15:1 3063
the chronicles of the kings of J 2Kin 15:6 3063
of J did Zachariah the son of 2Kin 15:8 3063
year of Uzziah king of J 2Kin 15:13 3063
year of Azariah king of J began 2Kin 15:17 3063
year of Azariah king of J 2Kin 15:23 3063
year of Azariah king of J Pekah 2Kin 15:27 3063
son of Uzziah king of J to reign 2Kin 15:32 3063
the chronicles of the kings of J 2Kin 15:36 3063
against J Rezin the king of Syria 2Kin 15:37 3063
Jotham king of J began to reign 2Kin 16:1 3063
the chronicles of the kings of J 2Kin 16:19 3063
twelfth year of Ahaz king of J 2Kin 17:1 3063
against Israel, and against J 2Kin 17:13 3063
none left but the tribe of J only 2Kin 17:18 3063
Also J kept not the commandments 2Kin 17:19 3063
of Ahaz king of J began to reign 2Kin 18:1 3063
like him among all the kings of J 2Kin 18:5 3063
all the fenced cities of J 2Kin 18:13 3063
Hezekiah king of J sent to the 2Kin 18:14 3063
J three hundred talents of silver 2Kin 18:14 3063
Hezekiah king of J had overlaid 2Kin 18:16 3063
taken away, and hath said to J 2Kin 18:22 3063
ye speak to Hezekiah king of J 2Kin 19:10 3063
of J shall yet again take root 2Kin 19:30 3063
the chronicles of the kings of J 2Kin 20:20 3063
Because Manasseh king of J hath 2Kin 21:11 3063
hath made J also to sin with his 2Kin 21:11 3063
such evil upon Jerusalem and J 2Kin 21:12 3063
sin wherewith he made J to sin 2Kin 21:16 3063
the chronicles of the kings of J 2Kin 21:17 3063
the chronicles of the kings of J 2Kin 21:25 3063
and for the people, and for all J 2Kin 22:13 3063
which the king of J hath read 2Kin 22:16 3063
But to the king of J which sent 2Kin 22:18 3063
unto him all the elders of J 2Kin 23:1 3063
of the LORD, and all the men of J 2Kin 23:2 3063
whom the kings of J had ordained 2Kin 23:5 3063
high places in the cities of J 2Kin 23:5 3063
priests out of the cities of J 2Kin 23:8 3063
kings of J had given to the sun 2Kin 23:11 3063
which the kings of J had made 2Kin 23:12 3063
the man of God, which came from J 2Kin 23:17 3063
of Israel, nor of the kings of J 2Kin 23:22 3063
that were spied in the land of J 2Kin 23:24 3063
his anger was kindled against J 2Kin 23:26 3063
I will remove J also out of my 2Kin 23:27 3063
the chronicles of the kings of J 2Kin 23:28 3063
sent them against J to destroy it 2Kin 24:2 3063
of the LORD came this upon J 2Kin 24:3 3063
the chronicles of the kings of J 2Kin 24:5 3063
Jehoiachin the king of J went out 2Kin 24:12 3063
it came to pass in Jerusalem and J 2Kin 24:20 3063
So J was carried away out of 2Kin 25:21 3063
that remained in the land of J 2Kin 25:22 3063
captivity of Jehoiachin king of J 2Kin 25:27 3063
king of J out of prison 2Kin 25:27 3063
in the days of Hezekiah king of J 1Chr 4:41 3063
in the days of Jotham king of J 1Chr 5:17 3063
when the LORD carried away J 1Chr 6:15 3063
book of the kings of Israel and J 1Chr 9:1 3063
J was four hundred threescore and 1Chr 21:5 3063
that dwelt in the cities of J 2Chr 10:17 3063
he gathered of the house of J 2Chr 11:1 3063
the son of Solomon, king of J 2Chr 11:3 3063
of Judah, and to all Israel in J 2Chr 11:3 3063
and built cities for defence in J 2Chr 11:5 3063
and Hebron, which are in J 2Chr 11:10 3063
them exceeding strong, having J 2Chr 11:12 3063
and their possession, and came to J 2Chr 11:14 3063
strengthened the kingdom of J 2Chr 11:17 3063
throughout all the countries of J 2Chr 11:23 3063
cities which pertained to J 2Chr 12:4 3063
Rehoboam, and to the princes of J 2Chr 12:5 3063
also in J things went well 2Chr 12:12 3063
began Abijah to reign over J 2Chr 13:1 3063
so they were before J, and the 2Chr 13:13 3063
when J looked back, behold, the 2Chr 13:14 3063

Then the men of J gave a shout 2Chr 13:15 3063
and as the men of J shouted 2Chr 13:15 3063
and all Israel before Abijah and J 2Chr 13:15 3063
children of Israel fled before J 2Chr 13:16 3063
and the children of J prevailed 2Chr 13:18 3063
commanded J to seek the LORD God 2Chr 14:4 3063
the cities of J the high places 2Chr 14:5 3063
And he built fenced cities in J 2Chr 14:6 3063
Therefore he said unto J, Let us 2Chr 14:7 3063
out of J three hundred thousand 2Chr 14:8 3063
before Asa, and before J 2Chr 14:12 3063
him, Hear ye me, Asa, and all J 2Chr 15:2 3063
idols out of all the land of J 2Chr 15:8 3063
And he gathered all J and Benjamin, ... 2Chr 15:9 3063
all J rejoiced at the oath 2Chr 15:15 3063
king of Israel came up against J 2Chr 16:1 3063
out or come in to Asa king of J 2Chr 16:1 3063
Then Asa the king took all J 2Chr 16:6 3063
the seer came to Asa king of J 2Chr 16:7 3063
in the book of the kings of J 2Chr 16:11 3063
in all the fenced cities of J 2Chr 17:2 3063
and set garrisons in the land of J 2Chr 17:2 3063
all J brought to Jehoshaphat 2Chr 17:5 3063
high places and groves out of J 2Chr 17:6 3063
to teach in the cities of J 2Chr 17:7 3063
And they taught in J, and had the 2Chr 17:9 3063
throughout all the cities of J 2Chr 17:9 3063
the lands that were round about J 2Chr 17:10 3063
and he built in J castles, and 2Chr 17:12 3063
much business in the cities of J 2Chr 17:13 3063
Of J, the captains of thousands 2Chr 17:14 3063
fenced cities throughout all J 2Chr 17:19 3063
said unto Jehoshaphat king of J 2Chr 18:3 3063
Jehoshaphat king of J sat either 2Chr 18:9 3063
Jehoshaphat the king of J went up 2Chr 18:28 3063
Jehoshaphat the king of J 2Chr 19:1 3063
all the fenced cities of J 2Chr 19:5 3063
the ruler of the house of J 2Chr 19:11 3063
a fast throughout all J 2Chr 20:3 3063
J gathered themselves together, 2Chr 20:4 3063
of J they came to seek the LORD 2Chr 20:4 3063
stood in the congregation of J 2Chr 20:5 3063
all J stood before the LORD, with 2Chr 20:13 3063
And he said, Hearken ye, all J 2Chr 20:15 3063
of the LORD with you, O J 2Chr 20:17 3063
and all J and the inhabitants of 2Chr 20:18 3063
stood and said, Hear me, O J 2Chr 20:20 3063
Seir, which were come against J 2Chr 20:22 3063
when J came toward the watch 2Chr 20:24 3063
they returned, every man of J 2Chr 20:27 3063
And Jehoshaphat reigned over J 2Chr 20:31 3063
this did Jehoshaphat king of J 2Chr 20:35 3063
things, with fenced cities in J 2Chr 21:3 3063
from under the dominion of J 2Chr 21:8 3063
under the hand of J unto this day 2Chr 21:10 3063
high places in the mountains of J 2Chr 21:11 3063
and compelled J thereto 2Chr 21:11 3063
nor in the ways of Asa king of J 2Chr 21:12 3063
kings of Israel, and hast made J 2Chr 21:13 3063
And they came up into J, and brake 2Chr 21:17 3063
son of Jehoram king of J reigned 2Chr 22:1 3063
the son of Jehoram king of J went 2Chr 22:6 3063
Ahab, and found the princes of J 2Chr 22:8 3063
the seed royal of the house of J 2Chr 22:10 3063
And they went about in J, and 2Chr 23:2 3063
out of all the cities of J 2Chr 23:2 3063
all J did according to all things 2Chr 23:8 3063
them, Go out unto the cities of J 2Chr 24:5 3063
the Levites to bring in out of J 2Chr 24:6 3063
made a proclamation through J 2Chr 24:9 3063
of Jehoiada came the princes of J 2Chr 24:17 3063
and wrath came upon J and Jerusalem 2Chr 24:18 3063
and they came to J and Jerusalem, 2Chr 24:23 3063
Amaziah gathered J together 2Chr 25:5 3063
their fathers, throughout all J 2Chr 25:5 3063
was greatly kindled against J 2Chr 25:10 3063
children of J carry away captive 2Chr 25:12 3063
battle, fell upon the cities of J 2Chr 25:13 3063
Amaziah king of J took advice 2Chr 25:17 3063
Israel sent to Amaziah king of J 2Chr 25:18 3063
fall, even thou, and J with thee 2Chr 25:19 3063
both he and Amaziah king of J 2Chr 25:21 3063
which belongeth to J 2Chr 25:21 3063
J was put to the worse before 2Chr 25:22 3063
of Israel took Amaziah king of J 2Chr 25:23 3063
the son of Joash king of J lived 2Chr 25:25 3063
in the book of the kings of J 2Chr 25:26 3063
with his fathers in the city of J 2Chr 25:28 3063
all the people of J took Uzziah 2Chr 26:1 3063
built Eloth, and restored it to J 2Chr 26:2 3063
cities in the mountains of J 2Chr 27:4 3063
book of the kings of Israel and J 2Chr 27:7 3063
of Remaliah slew in J an hundred 2Chr 28:6 3063
of your fathers was wroth with J 2Chr 28:9 3063
to keep under the children of J 2Chr 28:10 3063
Edomites had come and smitten J 2Chr 28:17 3063
low country, and of the south of J 2Chr 28:18 3063
For the LORD brought J low 2Chr 28:19 3063
for he made J naked, and 2Chr 28:19 3063
in every several city of J he 2Chr 28:25 3063
in the book of the kings of J 2Chr 28:26 3063
the wrath of the LORD was upon J 2Chr 29:8 3063
and for the sanctuary, and for J 2Chr 29:21 3063
Hezekiah sent to all Israel and J 2Chr 30:1 3063
throughout all Israel and J 2Chr 30:6 3063
Also in J the hand of God was to 2Chr 30:12 3063
For Hezekiah king of J did give 2Chr 30:24 3063
And all the congregation of J 2Chr 30:25 3063
of Israel, and that dwelt in J 2Chr 30:25 3063
went out to the cities of J 2Chr 31:1 3063
places and the altars out of all J 2Chr 31:1 3063
the children of Israel and J 2Chr 31:6 3063
that dwelt in the cities of J 2Chr 31:6 3063
did Hezekiah throughout all J 2Chr 31:20 3063
Assyria came, and entered into J 2Chr 32:1 3063
the words of Hezekiah king of J 2Chr 32:8 3063
him,) unto Hezekiah king of J 2Chr 32:9 3063
unto all J that were at Jerusalem 2Chr 32:9 3063
and his altars, and commanded J 2Chr 32:12 3063
and presents to Hezekiah king of J 2Chr 32:23 3063
was wrath upon him, and upon J 2Chr 32:25 3063
and in the book of the kings of J 2Chr 32:32 3063
and all J and the inhabitants of 2Chr 32:33 3063
So Manasseh made J and the 2Chr 33:9 3063
war in all the fenced cities of J 2Chr 33:14 3063
commanded J to serve the LORD God... 2Chr 33:16 3063
twelfth year he began to purge J 2Chr 34:3 3063
upon their altars, and cleansed J 2Chr 34:5 3063
remnant of Israel, and of all J 2Chr 34:9 3063
the kings of J had destroyed 2Chr 34:11 3063
that are left in Israel and in J 2Chr 34:21 3063
have read before the king of J 2Chr 34:24 3063
And as for the king of J, who sent 2Chr 34:26 3063
together all the elders of J 2Chr 34:29 3063
of the LORD, and all the men of J 2Chr 34:30 3063
priests, and the Levites, and all J 2Chr 35:18 3063
I to do with thee, thou king of J 2Chr 35:21 3063
And all J and Jerusalem mourned for .. 2Chr 35:24 3063
book of the kings of Israel and J 2Chr 35:27 3063
Eliakim his brother king over J 2Chr 36:4 3063
book of the kings of Israel and J 2Chr 36:8 3063
Zedekiah his brother king over J 2Chr 36:10 3063
house in Jerusalem, which is in J 2Chr 36:23 3063
and came again unto Jerusalem and J. Ezr 2:1 3063
Now when the adversaries of J Ezr 4:1 3063
of Hezekiah king of J copied out Prov 25:1 3063
Amoz, which he saw concerning J Is 1:1 3063
Ahaz, and Hezekiah, kings of J Is 1:1 3063
the son of Amoz saw concerning J Is 2:1 3063
from J the stay and the staff, the Is 3:1 3063
is ruined, and J is fallen Is 3:8 3063
of Jerusalem, and men of J Is 5:3 3063
the men of J his pleasant plant Is 5:7 3063
the son of Uzziah, king of J Is 7:1 3063
Let us go up against J, and vex it Is 7:6 3063
day that Ephraim departed from J Is 7:17 3063
And he shall pass through J Is 8:8 3063
they together shall be against J Is 9:21 3063
together the dispersed of J from Is 11:12 3063
adversaries of J shall be cut off Is 11:13 3063
Ephraim shall not envy J, and Is 11:13 3063
Judah, and J shall not vex Ephraim Is 11:13 3063
the land of J shall be a terror Is 19:17 3063
he discovered the covering of J Is 22:8 3063
Jerusalem, and to the house of J Is 22:21 3063
song be sung in the land of J Is 26:1 3063
all the defenced cities of J Is 36:1 3063
hath taken away, and said to J Is 36:7 3063
ye speak to Hezekiah king of J Is 37:10 3063
J shall again take root downward Is 37:31 3063
The writing of Hezekiah king of J Is 38:9 3063
say unto the cities of J, Behold Is 40:9 3063
and to the cities of J, Ye shall Is 44:26 3063
come forth out of the waters of J Is 48:1 3063
out of J an inheritor of my Is 65:9 3063
Josiah the son of Amon king of J Jer 1:2 3063
the son of Josiah king of J Jer 1:3 3063
the son of Josiah king of J Jer 1:3 3063
and against all the cities of J Jer 1:15 3063
land, against the kings of J Jer 1:18 3063
of thy cities are thy gods, O J Jer 2:28 3063
her treacherous sister J saw it Jer 3:7 3063
treacherous sister J feared not Jer 3:8 3063
J hath not turned unto me with Jer 3:10 3063
herself more than treacherous J Jer 3:11 3063
In those days the house of J Jer 3:18 3063
saith the LORD to the men of J Jer 4:3 3063
of your heart, ye men of J Jer 4:4 3063
Declare ye in J, and publish in Jer 4:5 3063
voice against the cities of J Jer 4:16 3063
the house of J have dealt very Jer 5:11 3063
of Jacob, and publish it in J Jer 5:20 3063
the word of the LORD, all ye of J Jer 7:2 3063
what they do in the cities of J Jer 7:17 3063
For the children of J have done Jer 7:30 3063
to cease from the cities of J Jer 7:34 3063
out the bones of the kings of J Jer 8:1 3063
make the cities of J desolate Jer 9:11 3063
Egypt, and J, and Edom, and the Jer 9:26 3063
to make the cities of J desolate Jer 10:22 3063
and speak unto the men of J Jer 11:2 3063
these words in the cities of J Jer 11:6 3063
is found among the men of J Jer 11:9 3063
the house of J have broken my Jer 11:10 3063
Then shall the cities of J Jer 11:12 3063
of thy cities were thy gods, O J Jer 11:13 3063
of Israel and of the house of J Jer 11:17 3063
the house of J from among them Jer 12:14 3063
manner will I mar the pride of J Jer 13:9 3063
of Israel and the whole house of J Jer 13:11 3063
J shall be carried away captive Jer 13:19 3063
J mourneth, and the gates thereof Jer 14:2 3063
Hast thou utterly rejected J Jer 14:19 3063
the son of Hezekiah king of J Jer 15:4 3063
The sin of J is written with a Jer 17:1 3063
whereby the kings of J come in Jer 17:19 3063
word of the LORD, ye kings of J Jer 17:20 3063
LORD, ye kings of Judah, and all J Jer 17:20 3063
and their princes, the men of J Jer 17:25 3063
shall come from the cities of J Jer 17:26 3063
go to, speak to the men of J Jer 18:11 3063
word of the LORD, O kings of J Jer 19:3 3063
have known, nor the kings of J Jer 19:4 3063
I will make void the counsel of J Jer 19:7 3063
and the houses of the kings of J Jer 19:13 3063
I will give all J into the hand Jer 20:4 3063
of J will I give into the hand of Jer 20:5 3063
I will deliver Zedekiah king of J Jer 21:7 3063
the house of the king of J Jer 21:11 3063
to the house of the king of J Jer 22:1 3063
the word of the LORD, O king of J Jer 22:2 3063
LORD unto the king's house of J Jer 22:6 3063
the son of Josiah king of J Jer 22:11 3063
the son of Josiah king of J Jer 22:18 3063
the son of Jehoiakim king of J Jer 22:24 3063
of David, and ruling any more in J Jer 22:30 3063
In his days J shall be saved, and Jer 23:6 3063
the son of Jehoiakim king of J Jer 24:1 3063
and the princes of J Jer 24:1 3063
are carried away captive of J Jer 24:5 3063
I give Zedekiah the king of J Jer 24:8 3063
concerning all the people of J in Jer 25:1 3063
the son of Josiah king of J Jer 25:1 3063
spake unto all the people of J Jer 25:2 3063
Josiah the son of Amon king of J Jer 25:3 3063
Jerusalem, and the cities of J Jer 25:18 3063
the son of Josiah king of J came Jer 26:1 3063
and speak unto all the cities of J Jer 26:2 3063
princes of J heard these things Jer 26:10 3063
in the days of Hezekiah king of J Jer 26:18 3063
and spake to all the people of J Jer 26:18 3063
Did Hezekiah king of J and all Jer 26:19 3063
all J put him at all to death Jer 26:19 3063
the son of Josiah king of J came Jer 27:1 3063
Jerusalem unto Zedekiah king of J Jer 27:3 3063
of J according to all these words Jer 27:12 3063
and in the house of the king of J Jer 27:18 3063
of J from Jerusalem to Babylon Jer 27:20 3063
and all the nobles of J Jer 27:20 3063
and in the house of the king of J Jer 27:21 3063
the reign of Zedekiah king of J Jer 28:1 3063
the son of Jehoiakim king of J Jer 28:4 3063
Judah, with all the captives of J Jer 28:4 3063
and the eunuchs, the princes of J Jer 29:2 3063
king of J sent unto Babylon to Jer 29:3 3063
of J which are in Babylon Jer 29:22 3063
of my people Israel and J, saith Jer 30:3 3063
concerning Israel and concerning J Jer 30:4 3063
use this speech in the land of J Jer 31:23 3063
And there shall dwell in J itself Jer 31:24 3063
the house of J with the seed of Jer 31:27 3063
of Israel, and with the house of J Jer 31:31 3063
tenth year of Zedekiah king of J Jer 32:1 3063
king of J had shut him up Jer 32:3 3063
Zedekiah king of J shall not Jer 32:4 3063
the children of J have only done Jer 32:30 3063
of Israel and of the children of J Jer 32:32 3063
their prophets, and the men of J Jer 32:32 3063
abomination, to cause J to sin Jer 32:35 3063
Jerusalem, and in the cities of J Jer 32:44 3063
the houses of the kings of J Jer 33:4 3063
I will cause the captivity of J Jer 33:7 3063
beast, even in the cities of J Jer 33:10 3063
Jerusalem, and in the cities of J Jer 33:13 3063
of Israel and to the house of J Jer 33:14 3063
In those days shall J be saved Jer 33:16 3063
Go and speak to Zedekiah king of J Jer 34:2 3063
of the LORD, O Zedekiah king of J Jer 34:4 3063
Zedekiah king of J in Jerusalem Jer 34:6 3063
the cities of J that were left Jer 34:7 3063
remained of the cities of J Jer 34:7 3063
The princes of J, and the princes Jer 34:19 3063
And Zedekiah king of J and his Jer 34:21 3063
of J a desolation without an Jer 34:22 3063
the son of Josiah king of J Jer 35:1 3063
Go and tell the men of J and the Jer 35:13 3063
Behold, I will bring upon J Jer 35:17 3063
the son of Josiah king of J Jer 36:1 3063
thee against Israel, and against J Jer 36:2 3063
It may be that the house of J Jer 36:3 3063
read them in the ears of all J Jer 36:6 3063
the son of Josiah king of J Jer 36:9 3063
the cities of J unto Jerusalem Jer 36:9 3063
the king of J hath burned Jer 36:28 3063
shalt say to Jehoiakim king of J Jer 36:29 3063
the LORD of Jehoiakim king of J Jer 36:30 3063
Jerusalem, and upon the men of J Jer 36:31 3063
king of J had burned in the fire Jer 36:32 3063
made king in the land of J Jer 37:1 3063
shall ye say to the king of J Jer 37:7 3063
ninth year of Zedekiah king of J Jer 39:1 3063
Zedekiah the king of J saw them Jer 39:4 3063
Babylon slew all the nobles of J Jer 39:6 3063
had nothing, in the land of J Jer 39:10 3063
away captive of Jerusalem and J Jer 40:1 3063
governor over the cities of J Jer 40:5 3063
Babylon had left a remnant of J Jer 40:11 3063
driven, and came to the land of J Jer 40:12 3063
and the remnant in J perish Jer 40:15 3063
word of the LORD, ye remnant of J Jer 42:15 3063
concerning you, O ye remnant of J Jer 42:19 3063
LORD, to dwell in the land of J Jer 43:4 3063
forces, took all the remnant of J Jer 43:5 3063
driven, to dwell in the land of J Jer 43:5 3063
in the sight of the men of J Jer 43:9 3064
and upon all the cities of J Jer 44:2 3063
and was kindled in the cities of J Jer 44:6 3063
child and suckling, out of J Jer 44:7 3063
the wickedness of the kings of J Jer 44:9 3063
have committed in the land of J Jer 44:9 3063
you for evil, and to cut off all J Jer 44:11 3063
And I will take the remnant of J Jer 44:12 3063
So that none of the remnant of J Jer 44:14 3063
should return into the land of J Jer 44:14 3063
our princes, in the cities of J Jer 44:17 3063
that ye burned in the cities of J Jer 44:21 3063
all J that are in the land of Jer 44:24 3063
all J that dwell in the land of Jer 44:26 3063
man of J in all the land of Egypt Jer 44:26 3063
all the men of J that are in the Jer 44:27 3063
land of Egypt into the land of J Jer 44:28 3063
and all the remnant of J Jer 44:28 3063

as I gave Zedekiah king of J into Jer 44:30 3063
the son of Josiah king of J Jer 45:1 3063
the son of Josiah king of J Jer 46:2 3063
the reign of Zedekiah king of J Jer 49:34 3063
and the children of J together Jer 50:4 3063
and the sins of J, and they shall Jer 50:20 3063
the children of J were oppressed Jer 50:33 3063
nor J of his God, of the LORD of Jer 51:5 3063
went with Zedekiah the king of J Jer 51:59 3063
it came to pass in Jerusalem and J Jer 52:3 3063
all the princes of J in Riblah Jer 52:10 3063
Thus J was carried away captive Jer 52:27 3063
captivity of Jehoiachin king of J Jer 52:31 3063
the head of Jehoiachin king of J Jer 52:31 3063
J is gone into captivity because Lam 1:3 3063
the virgin, the daughter of J Lam 1:15 3063
strong holds of the daughter of J Lam 2:2 3063
in the daughter of J mourning Lam 2:5 3063
and the maids in the cities of J Lam 5:11 3063
of the house of J forty days Eze 4:6 3063
and the elders of J sat before me Eze 8:1 3063
house of J that they commit the Eze 8:17 3063
J is exceeding great, and the land Eze 9:9 3063
to J in Jerusalem the defenced Eze 21:20 3063
and against the house of J Eze 25:3 3063
the house of J is like unto all Eze 25:8 3063
house of J by taking vengeance Eze 25:12 3063
J, and the land of Israel, they Eze 27:17 3063
stick, and write upon it, For J Eze 37:16 3063
him, even with the stick of J Eze 37:19 3063
the west side, a portion for J Eze 48:7 3063
And by the border of J, from the Eze 48:8 3063
prince's, between the border of J Eze 48:22 3063
one gate of Reuben, one gate of J Eze 48:31 3063
of J came Nebuchadnezzar king of Dan 1:1 3063
Jehoiakim king of J into his hand Dan 1:2 3063
these were of the children of J Dan 1:6 3063
found a man of the captives of J Dan 2:25 3061
children of the captivity of J Dan 5:13 3061
children of the captivity of J Dan 6:13 3061
to the men of J, and to the Dan 9:7 3063
Ahaz, and Hezekiah, kings of J Hos 1:1 3063
have mercy upon the house of J Hos 1:7 3063
Then shall the children of J Hos 1:11 3063
the harlot, yet let not J offend Hos 4:15 3063
J also shall fall with them Hos 5:5 3063
The princes of J were like them Hos 5:10 3063
to the house of J as rottenness Hos 5:12 3063
J saw his wound, then went Hos 5:13 3063
as a young lion to the house of J Hos 5:14 3063
O J, what shall I do unto thee Hos 6:4 3063
Also, O J, he hath set an harvest Hos 6:11 3063
J hath multiplied fenced cities Hos 8:14 3063
J shall plow, and Jacob shall Hos 10:11 3063
but J yet ruleth with God, and is Hos 11:12 3063
hath also a controversy with J Hos 12:2 3063
bring again the captivity of J Joel 3:1 3063
The children also of J and the Joel 3:6 3063
the hand of the children of J Joel 3:8 3063
all the rivers of J shall flow Joel 3:18 3063
against the children of J Joel 3:19 3063
But J shall dwell for ever, and Joel 3:20 3063
in the days of Uzziah king of J Amos 1:1 3063
For three transgressions of J Amos 2:4 3063
But I will send a fire upon J Amos 2:5 3063
flee thee away into the land of J Amos 7:12 3063
rejoiced over the children of J Obad 12 3063
Ahaz, and Hezekiah, kings of J Mic 1:1 3063
and what are the high places of J Mic 1:5 3063
for it is come unto J Mic 1:9 3063
little among the thousands of J Mic 5:2 3063
O J, keep thy solemn feasts, Nah 1:15 3063
Josiah the son of Amon, king of J Zeph 1:1 3063
also stretch out mine hand upon J Zeph 1:4 3063
for the remnant of the house of J Zeph 2:7 3063
son of Shealtiel, governor of J Hag 1:1 3063
son of Shealtiel, governor of J Hag 1:14 3063
son of Shealtiel, governor of J Hag 2:2 3063
to Zerubbabel, governor of J Hag 2:21 3063
Jerusalem and on the cities of J Zec 1:12 3063
the horns which have scattered J Zec 1:19 3063
the horns which have scattered J Zec 1:21 3063
over the land of J to scatter it Zec 1:21 3063
the LORD shall inherit J his Zec 2:12 3063
among the heathen, O house of J Zec 8:13 3063
Jerusalem and to the house of J Zec 8:15 3063
shall be to the house of J joy Zec 8:19 3063
and he shall be as a governor in J Zec 9:7 3063
When I have bent J for me Zec 9:13 3063
visited his flock the house of J Zec 10:3 3063
I will strengthen the house of J Zec 10:6 3063
break the brotherhood between J Zec 11:14 3063
be in the siege both against J Zec 12:2 3063
mine eyes upon the house of J Zec 12:4 3063
the governors of J shall say in Zec 12:5 3063
of J like an hearth of fire among Zec 12:6 3063
shall save the tents of J first Zec 12:7 3063
not magnify themselves against J Zec 12:7 3063
in the days of Uzziah king of J Zec 14:5 3063
J also shall fight at Jerusalem Zec 14:14 3063
in J shall be holiness unto the Zec 14:21 3063
J hath dealt treacherously, and an Mal 2:11 3063
for J hath profaned the holiness Mal 2:11 3063
Then shall the offering of J Mal 3:4 3063

4. A Levite.
and his sons, the sons of J Ezr 3:9 3063

5. A Levite who married a foreigner.
the same is Kelita,) Pethahiah, J Ezr 10:23 3063

6. An overseer.
J the son of Senuah was second Neh 11:9 3063

7. A Levite with Zerubbabel.
Binnui, Kadmiel, Sherebiah, J Neh 12:8 3063

8. An exile.
J, and Benjamin, and Shemaiah, and Neh 12:34 3063

9. A musician in exile.
Gilalai, Maai, Nethaneel, and J Neh 12:36 3063

JUDAH'S (*ju'-dahs*)
1. Refers to Judah 1.
J firstborn, was wicked in the Gen 38:7 3063
the daughter of Shuah J wife died Gen 38:12 3063
which was in the king of J house Jer 32:2 3063
that are left in the king of J Jer 38:22 3063

JUDAISM See JEWS, PROSELYTES.

JUDAS (*ju'-das*) See BARSABAS, ISCARIOT, JUDAH, JUDE, LEBBAEUS, THADDAEUS.
1. Betrayer of Jesus.
J Iscariot, who also betrayed him Mt 10:4 *2455*
called J Iscariot, went unto the Mt 26:14 *2455*
Then J, which betrayed him, Mt 26:25 *2455*
And while he yet spake, lo, J Mt 26:47 *2455*
Then J, which had betrayeth him, Mt 27:3 *2455*
J Iscariot, which also betrayed Mk 3:19 *2455*
J Iscariot, one of the twelve, Mk 14:10 *2455*
while he yet spake, cometh J Mk 14:43 *2455*
J Iscariot, which also was the Lk 6:16 *2455*
Satan into J surnamed Iscariot Lk 22:3 *2455*
and he that was called J, one of Lk 22:47 *2455*
But Jesus said unto him, J Lk 22:48 *2455*
He spake of J Iscariot the son of Jn 6:71 *2455*
J Iscariot, Simon's son, which Jn 12:4 *2455*
put into the heart of J Iscariot Jn 13:2 *2455*
the sop, he gave it to J Iscariot Jn 13:26 *2455*
because J had the bag, that Jesus Jn 13:29 *2455*
J also, which betrayed him, knew Jn 18:2 *2455*
J then, having received a band of Jn 18:3 *2455*
J also, which betrayed him, stood Jn 18:5 *2455*
David spake before concerning J Acts 1:16 *2455*
from which J by transgression Acts 1:25 *2455*
2. A brother of Jesus.
James, and Joses, and Simon, and J Mt 13:55 *2455*
3. A disciple of Jesus.
J the brother of James, and Judas Lk 6:16 *2455*
J saith unto him, not Iscariot, Jn 14:22 *2455*
and J the brother of James Acts 1:13 *2455*
4. A seditious Galilean.
After this man rose up J of Acts 5:37 *2455*
5. Lodged Paul in Damascus.
house of J for one called Saul Acts 9:11 *2455*
6. Surnamed Barsabas.
J surnamed Barsabas, and Silas, Acts 15:22 *2455*
We have sent therefore J and Silas Acts 15:27 *2455*
And J and Silas, being prophets Acts 15:32 *2455*
7. A Greek form of Joseph.
and Jacob begat J and his brethren Mt 1:2 *2455*
J begat Phares and Zara of Thamar Mt 1:3 *2455*

JUDE (*jood*) See JUDAS. *A brother of Jesus.*
J, the servant of Jesus Christ, Jude 1 *2455*

JUDEA (*ju-de'-ah*) See JEWRY, JUDAH. *Southern portion of Israel.*
we went into the province of J Ezr 5:8 3061

JUDGE
whom they shall serve, will I *j* Gen 15:14 1777
the LORD *j* between me and thee Gen 16:5 8199
Shall not the J of all the earth Gen 18:25 8199
sojourn, and he will needs be a *j* Gen 19:9 8199
that they may *j* betwixt us both Gen 31:37 3198
God of their father, *j* betwixt us Gen 31:53 8199
Dan shall *j* his people, as one of Gen 49:16 1777
made thee a prince and a *j* over us Ex 2:14 8199
The LORD look upon you, and *j* Ex 5:21 8199
that Moses sat to *j* the people Ex 18:13 8199
I *j* between one and another, and I Ex 18:16 8199
let them *j* the people at all Ex 18:22 8199
every small matter they shall *j* Ex 18:22 8199
shalt thou *j* thy neighbour Lev 19:15 8199
shall *j* between the slayer Num 35:24 8199
j righteously between every man Deut 1:16 8199
they shall *j* the people with just Deut 16:18 8199
unto the *j* that shall be in those Deut 17:9 8199
the LORD thy God, or unto the *j* Deut 17:12 8199
that the judges may *j* them Deut 25:1 8199
that the *j* shall cause him to lie Deut 25:2 8199
For the LORD shall *j* his people Deut 32:36 1777
then the LORD was with the *j* Judg 2:18 8199
enemies all the days of the *j* Judg 2:18 8199
came to pass, when the *j* was dead Judg 2:19 8199
the LORD the J be *j* this day Judg 11:27 8199
the LORD shall *j* the ends of the 1Sa 2:10 1777
another, the *j* shall *j* him 1Sa 2:25 430
will *j* his house for ever for the 1Sa 3:13 8199
now make us a king to *j* us like 1Sa 8:5 8199
they said, Give us a king to *j* us 1Sa 8:6 8199
and that our king may *j* us 1Sa 8:20 8199
The LORD *j* between me and thee, and 1Sa 24:12 8199
The LORD therefore be *j* 1Sa 24:15 1784
j between me and thee, and see, and 1Sa 24:15 8199
Oh that I were made *j* in the land 2Sa 15:4 8199
heart to *j* thy people, that I may 1Kin 3:9 8199
for who is able to *j* this thy so 1Kin 3:9 8199
for the throne where he might *j* 1Kin 7:7 8199
j thy servants, condemning the 1Kin 8:32 8199
because he cometh to *j* the earth 1Chr 16:33 8199
for who can *j* this thy people, 2Chr 1:10 8199
that thou mayest *j* my people 2Chr 1:11 8199
j thy servants, by requiting the 2Chr 6:23 8199
for ye *j* not for man, but for the 2Chr 19:6 8199
O our God, wilt thou not *j* them 2Chr 20:12 8199
which may *j* all the people that Ezr 7:25
I would make supplication to my *j* Job 9:15 8199
can he *j* through the dark cloud Job 22:13 8199
I be delivered for ever from my *j* Job 23:7 8199
iniquity to be punished by the *j* Job 31:28 6416
The LORD shall *j* the people Ps 7:8 1777
j me, O LORD, according to my Ps 7:8 8199
And he shall *j* the world in Ps 9:8 8199
To *j* the fatherless and the Ps 10:18 8199
J me, O LORD Ps 26:1 8199
J me, O LORD my God, according to Ps 35:24 8199
J me, O God, and plead my cause Ps 43:1 8199
earth, that he may *j* his people Ps 50:4 1777
for God is *j* himself Ps 50:6 8199
thy name, and *j* me by thy strength Ps 54:1 1777
do ye *j* uprightly, O ye sons of Ps 58:1 8199
for thou shalt *j* the people Ps 67:4 8199
a *j* of the widows, is God in his Ps 68:5 1781
He shall *j* thy people with Ps 72:2 1777
He shall *j* the poor of the people Ps 72:4 8199
congregation I will *j* uprightly Ps 75:2 8199
But God is the *j* Ps 75:7 8199
How long will ye *j* unjustly Ps 82:2 8199
Arise, O God, *j* the earth Ps 82:8 8199
up thyself, thou *j* of the earth Ps 94:2 8199
he shall *j* the people righteously Ps 96:10 1777
for he cometh to *j* the earth Ps 96:13 8199
he shall *j* the world with Ps 96:13 8199
for he cometh to *j* the earth Ps 98:9 8199
shall he *j* the world, and the Ps 98:9 8199
He shall *j* among the heathen, he Ps 110:6 1777
For the LORD will *j* his people Ps 135:14 1777
j righteously, and plead the cause Prov 31:9 8199
God shall *j* the righteous and the Eccl 3:17 8199
j the fatherless, plead for the Is 1:17 8199
they *j* not the fatherless, Is 1:23 8199
he shall *j* among the nations, and Is 2:4 8199
man, and the man of war, the *j* Is 3:2 8199
and standeth to *j* the people Is 3:13 1777
of Jerusalem, and men of Judah, *j* Is 5:3 8199
he shall not *j* after the sight of Is 11:3 8199
righteousness shall he *j* the poor Is 11:4 8199
For the LORD is our *j*, the LORD Is 33:22 8199
and mine arms shall *j* the people Is 51:5 8199
they *j* not the cause, the cause Jer 5:28 1777
right of the needy do they not *j* Jer 5:28 8199
j thou my cause Lam 3:59 8199
will *j* thee according to thy ways Eze 7:3 8199
I will *j* thee according to thy Eze 7:8 8199
to their deserts will I *j* them Eze 7:27 8199
I will *j* you in the border of Eze 11:10 8199
but I will *j* you in the border of Eze 11:11 8199
And I will *j* thee, as women that Eze 16:38 8199
Therefore I will *j* you, O house Eze 18:30 8199
Wilt thou *j* them, son of man, Eze 20:4 8199
son of man, wilt thou *j* them Eze 20:4 8199
I will *j* thee in the place where Eze 21:30 8199
Now, thou son of man, wilt thou *j* Eze 22:2 8199
wilt thou *j* the bloody city Eze 22:2 8199
they shall *j* thee according to Eze 23:24 8199
Son of man, wilt thou *j* Aholah Eze 23:36 8199
they shall *j* them after the Eze 23:45 8199
to thy doings, shall they *j* thee Eze 24:14 8199
I will *j* you every one after his Eze 33:20 8199
I *j* between cattle and cattle, Eze 34:17 8199
will *j* between the fat cattle and Eze 34:20 8199
I will *j* between cattle and cattle Eze 34:22 8199
they shall *j* it according to my Eze 44:24 8199
for there will I sit to *j* all the Joel 3:12 8199
I will cut off the *j* from the Amos 2:3 8199
mount Zion to *j* the mount of Esau Obad 21 8199
The heads thereof *j* for reward Mic 3:11 8199
he shall *j* among many people, and Mic 4:3 8199
they shall smite the *j* of Israel Mic 5:1 8199
the *j* asketh for a reward Mic 7:3 8199
then thou shalt also *j* my house Zec 3:7 1777
adversary deliver thee to the *j* Mt 5:25 *2923*
the *j* deliver thee to the officer Mt 5:25 *2923*
J not, that ye be not judged Mt 7:1 *2919*
For with what judgment ye *j* Mt 7:2 *2919*
J not, and ye shall not be judged Lk 6:37 *2919*
who made me a *j* or a divider over Lk 12:14 *1348*
yourselves *j* ye not what is right Lk 12:57 *2919*
lest he hale thee to the *j* Lk 12:58 *2923*
the *j* deliver thee to the officer Lk 12:58 *2923*
Saying, There was in a city a *j* Lk 18:2 *2923*
Hear what the unjust *j* saith Lk 18:6 *2923*
of thine own mouth will I *j* thee Lk 19:22 *2919*
as I hear, I *j* Jn 5:30 *2919*
J not according to the appearance Jn 7:24 *2919*
but *j* righteous judgment Jn 7:24 *2919*
Doth our law *j* any man, before it Jn 7:51 *2919*
Ye *j* after the flesh Jn 8:15 *2919*
I *j* no man Jn 8:15 *2919*
And yet if I *j*, my judgment is Jn 8:16 *2919*
many things to say and to *j* of you Jn 8:26 *2919*
and believe not, I *j* him not Jn 12:47 *2919*
for I came not to *j* the world Jn 12:47 *2919*
the same shall *j* him in the last Jn 12:48 *2919*
j him according to your law Jn 18:31 *2919*
unto you more than unto God, *j* ye Acts 4:19 *2919*
they shall be in bondage will I *j* Acts 7:7 *2919*
made thee a ruler and a *j* over us Acts 7:27 *1348*
Who made thee a ruler and a *j* Acts 7:35 *1348*
of God to be the J of quick Acts 10:42 *2923*
you, and *j* yourselves unworthy of Acts 13:46 *2919*
in the which he will *j* the world Acts 17:31 *2919*
I will be no *j* of such matters Acts 18:15 *2923*
thou to *j* me after the law Acts 23:3 *2919*
many years a *j* unto this nation Acts 24:10 *2923*
In the day when God shall *j* the Rom 2:16 *2919*
j thee, who by the letter and Rom 2:27 *2919*
then how shall God *j* the world Rom 3:6 *2919*
eateth not *j* him that eateth Rom 14:3 *2919*
But why dost thou *j* thy brother Rom 14:10 *2919*
therefore *j* one another any more Rom 14:13 *2919*
but *j* this rather, that no man Rom 14:13 *2919*
yea, I *j* not mine own self 1Cor 4:3 *350*
Therefore *j* nothing before the 1Cor 4:5 *2919*
For what have I to do to *j* them 1Cor 5:12 *2919*
do not ye *j* them that are within 1Cor 5:12 *2919*

that the saints shall *j* the world 1Cor 6:2 *2919*
are ye unworthy to *j* the smallest 1Cor 6:2 *2922*
ye not that we shall *j* angels 1Cor 6:3 *2919*
set them to *j* who are least 1Cor 6:4
be able to *j* between his brethren 1Cor 6:5 *1252*
j ye what I say 1Cor 10:15 *2919*
J in yourselves 1Cor 11:13 *2919*
For if we would *j* ourselves 1Cor 11:31 *1252*
two or three, and let the other *j* 1Cor 14:29 *1252*
because we thus *j*, that if one 2Cor 5:14 *2919*
no man therefore *j* you in meat Col 2:16 *2919*
Christ, who shall *j* the quick 2Ti 4:1 *2919*
which the Lord, the righteous *j* 2Ti 4:8 *2923*
The Lord shall *j* his people Heb 10:30 *2919*
in heaven, and to God the *J* of all Heb 12:23 *2923*
and adulterers God will *j* Heb 13:4 *2919*
but if thou *j* the law, thou art Jas 4:11 *2919*
not a doer of the law, but a *j* Jas 4:11 *2923*
the *j* standeth before the door Jas 5:9 *2923*
him that is ready to *j* the quick 1Pet 4:5 *2919*
holy and true, dost thou not *j* Rev 6:10 *2919*
and in righteousness he doth *j* Rev 19:11 *2919*

JUDGED

And Rachel said, God hath *j* me Gen 30:6 1777
they *j* the people at all seasons Ex 18:26 8199
small matter they *j* themselves Ex 18:26 8199
he *j* Israel, and went out to war Judg 3:10 8199
she *j* Israel at that time Judg 4:4 8199
he *j* Israel twenty and three years Judg 10:2 8199
j Israel twenty and two years Judg 10:3 8199
Jephthah *j* Israel six years Judg 12:7 8199
him Ibzan of Beth-lehem *j* Israel Judg 12:8 8199
And he *j* Israel seven years Judg 12:9 8199
him Elon, a Zebulonite, *j* Israel Judg 12:11 8199
and he *j* Israel ten years Judg 12:11 8199
Hillel, a Pirathonite, *j* Israel Judg 12:13 8199
and he *j* Israel eight years Judg 12:14 8199
he *j* Israel in the days of the Judg 15:20 8199
And he *j* Israel twenty years Judg 16:31 8199
he had *j* Israel forty years 1Sa 4:18 8199
Samuel *j* the children of Israel 1Sa 7:6 8199
Samuel *j* Israel all the days of 1Sa 7:15 8199
j Israel in all those places 1Sa 7:16 8199
and there he *j* Israel 1Sa 7:17 8199
the judgment which the king had *j* 1Kin 3:28 8199
days of the judges that *j* Israel 2Kin 23:22 8199
let the heathen be *j* in thy sight Ps 9:19 8199
nor condemn him when he is *j* Ps 37:33 8199
When he shall be *j*, let him be Ps 109:7 8199
He *j* the cause of the poor and Jer 22:16 1777
break wedlock and shed blood are *j* Eze 16:38 4941
which hast *j* thy sisters, bear Eze 16:52 6419
the wounded shall be *j* in the Eze 28:23 5307
among them, when I have *j* thee Eze 35:11 8199
to their doings I *j* them Eze 36:19 8199
and against our judges that *j* us Dan 9:12 8199
Judge not, that ye be not *j* Mt 7:1 *2919*
judgment ye judge, ye shall be *j* Mt 7:2 *2919*
Judge not, and ye shall not be *j* Lk 6:37 *2919*
unto him, Thou hast rightly *j* Lk 7:43 *2919*
the prince of this world is *j* Jn 16:11 *2919*
If ye have *j* me to be faithful to Acts 16:15 *2919*
would have *j* according to our law Acts 24:6 *2919*
there be *j* of these things before Acts 25:9 *2919*
seat, where I ought to be *j* Acts 25:10 *2919*
there be *j* of these matters Acts 25:20 *2919*
am *j* for the hope of the promise Acts 26:6 *2919*
in the law shall be *j* by the law Rom 2:12 *2919*
mightest overcome when thou art *j* Rom 3:4 *2919*
why yet am I also *j* as a sinner Rom 3:7 *2919*
yet he himself is *j* of no man 1Cor 2:15 *350*
thing that I should be *j* of you 1Cor 4:3 *350*
have *j* already, as though I were 1Cor 5:3 *2919*
and if the world shall be *j* by you 1Cor 6:2 *2919*
for why is my liberty *j* of 1Cor 10:29 *2919*
ourselves, we should not be *j* 1Cor 11:31 *2919*
But when we are *j*, we are 1Cor 11:32 *2919*
convinced of all, he is *j* of all 1Cor 14:24 *350*
because she *j* him faithful who Heb 11:11 *2233*
shall be *j* by the law of liberty Jas 2:12 *2919*
that they might be *j* according to 1Pet 4:6 *2919*
the dead, that they should be *j* Rev 11:18 *2919*
be, because thou hast *j* thus Rev 16:5 *2919*
for he hath *j* the great whore, Rev 19:2 *2919*
the dead were *j* out of those Rev 20:12 *2919*
they were *j* every man according Rev 20:13 *2919*

JUDGES

master shall bring him unto the *j* Ex 21:6 430
he shall pay as the *j* determine Ex 21:22 6414
house shall be brought unto the *j* Ex 22:8 430
parties shall come before the *j* Ex 22:9 430
whom the *j* shall condemn, he Ex 22:9 430
Moses said unto the *j* of Israel Num 25:5 8199
And I charged your *j* at that time Deut 1:16 8199
J and officers shalt thou make Deut 16:18 8199
LORD, before the priests and the *j* Deut 19:17 8199
the *j* shall make diligent Deut 19:18 8199
thy *j* shall come forth, and they Deut 21:2 8199
that the *j* may judge them Deut 25:1 8199
our enemies themselves being *j* Deut 32:31 6414
elders, and officers, and their *j* Josh 8:33 8199
for their heads, and for their *j* Josh 23:2 8199
for their heads, and for their *j* Josh 24:1 8199
Nevertheless the LORD raised up *j* Judg 2:16 8199
would not hearken unto their *j* Judg 2:17 8199
And when the LORD raised them up *j* Judg 2:18 8199
pass in the days when the *j* ruled Ruth 1:1 8199
he made his sons *j* over Israel 1Sa 8:1 8199
they were *j* in Beer-sheba 1Sa 8:2 8199
j to be over my people Israel 2Sa 7:11 8199
days of the *j* that judged Israel 2Kin 23:22 8199
a word to any of the *j* of Israel 1Chr 17:6 8199
j to be over my people Israel 1Chr 17:10 8199
six thousand were officers and *j* 1Chr 23:4 8199
over Israel, for officers and *j* 1Chr 26:29 8199
and of hundreds, and to the *j* 2Chr 1:2 8199
he set *j* in the land throughout 2Chr 19:5 8199
And said to the *j*, Take heed what 2Chr 19:6 8199
thine hand, set magistrates and *j* Ezr 7:25 1782
the *j* thereof, until the fierce Ezr 10:14 8199
the faces of the *j* thereof Job 9:24 8199
spoiled, and maketh the *j* fools Job 12:17 8199
iniquity to be punished by the *j* Job 31:11 6414
be instructed, ye *j* of the earth Ps 2:10 8199
When their *j* are overthrown in Ps 141:6 8199
princes, and all *j* of the earth Ps 148:11 8199
even all the *j* of the earth Prov 8:16 8199
restore thy *j* as at the first Is 1:26 8199
he maketh the *j* of the earth as Is 40:23 8199
governors, and the captains, the *j* Dan 3:2 148
the governors, and captains, the *j* Dan 3:3 148
against our *j* that judged us, by Dan 9:12 8199
an oven, and have devoured their *j* Hos 7:7 8199
thy *j* of whom thou saidst, Give Hos 13:10 8199
her *j* are evening wolves Zeph 3:3 8199
therefore they shall be your *j* Mt 12:27 *2923*
therefore shall they be your *j* Lk 11:19 *2923*
after that he gave unto them *j* Acts 13:20 *2923*
are become *j* of evil thoughts Jas 2:4 *2923*

JUDGEST

speakest, and be clear when thou *j* Ps 51:4 8199
that *j* righteously, that triest Jer 11:20 8199
O man, whosoever thou art that *j* Rom 2:1 *2919*
for wherein thou *j* another Rom 2:1 *2919*
for thou that *j* doest the same Rom 2:1 *2919*
that *j* them which do such things, Rom 2:3 *2919*
Who art thou that *j* another man's Rom 14:4 *2919*
who art thou that *j* another Jas 4:12 *2919*

JUDGETH

seeing he *j* those that are high Job 21:22 8199
For by them *j* he the people Job 36:31 1777
God *j* the righteous, and God is Ps 7:11 8199
he is a God that *j* in the earth Ps 58:11 8199
he *j* among the gods Ps 82:1 8199
king that faithfully *j* the poor Prov 29:14 8199
For the Father *j* no man, but hath Jn 5:22 *2919*
there is one that seeketh and *j* Jn 8:50 *2919*
not my words, hath one that *j* him Jn 12:48 *2919*
he that is spiritual *j* all things 1Cor 2:15 *350*
but he that *j* me is the Lord 1Cor 4:4 *2919*
But them that are without God *j* 1Cor 5:13 *2919*
j his brother, speaketh evil of Jas 4:11 *2919*
evil of the law, and *j* the law Jas 4:11 *2919*
j according to every man's work 1Pet 1:17 *2919*
himself to him that *j* righteously 1Pet 2:23 *2919*
strong is the Lord God who *j* her Rev 18:8 *2919*

JUDGING

house, *j* the people of the land 2Kin 15:5 8199
house, *j* the people of the land 2Chr 26:21 8199
thou satest in the throne *j* right Ps 9:4 8199
in the tabernacle of David, *j* Is 16:5 8199
j the twelve tribes of Israel Mt 19:28 *2919*
sit on thrones *j* the twelve Lk 22:30 *2919*

JUDGMENT

of the LORD, to do justice and *j* Gen 18:19 4941
gods of Egypt I will execute *j* Ex 12:12 8201
according to this *j* shall it be Ex 21:31 4941
to decline after many to wrest *j* Ex 23:2
the *j* of thy poor in his cause Ex 23:6 4941
of *j* with cunning work Ex 28:15 4941
breastplate of *j* upon his heart Ex 28:29 4941
in the breastplate of *j* the Urim Ex 28:30 4941
Aaron shall bear the *j* of the Ex 28:30 4941
shall do no unrighteousness in *j* Lev 19:15 4941
shall do no unrighteousness in *j* Lev 19:35 4941
children of Israel a statute of *j* Num 27:11 4941
the *j* of Urim before the LORD Num 27:21 4941
before the congregation in *j* Num 35:12 4941
of *j* unto you throughout your Num 35:29 4941
Ye shall not respect persons in *j* Deut 1:17 4941
for the *j* is God's Deut 1:17 4941
execute the *j* of the fatherless Deut 10:18 4941
judge the people with just *j* Deut 16:18 4941
Thou shalt not wrest *j* Deut 16:19 4941
a matter too hard for thee in *j* Deut 17:8 4941
shall shew thee the sentence of *j* Deut 17:9 4941
according to the *j* which they Deut 17:11 4941
not pervert the *j* of the stranger Deut 24:17 4941
between men, and they come unto *j* Deut 25:1 4941
perverteth the *j* of the stranger Deut 27:19 4941
for all his ways are *j* Deut 32:4 4941
and mine hand take hold on *j* Deut 32:41 4941
before the congregation for *j* Josh 20:6 4941
of Israel came up to her for *j* Judg 4:5 4941
on white asses, ye that sit in *j* Judg 5:10 4055
and took bribes, and perverted *j* 1Sa 8:3 4941
and David executed *j* and justice 2Sa 8:15 4941
came to the king for *j*, then 2Sa 15:2 4941
that came to the king for *j* 2Sa 15:6 4941
understanding to discern *j* 1Kin 3:11 4941
all Israel heard of the *j* which 1Kin 3:28 4941
wisdom of God was in him, to do *j* 1Kin 3:28 4941
might judge, even the porch of *j* 1Kin 7:7 4941
made he thee king, to do *j* 1Kin 10:9 4941
said unto him, So shall thy *j* be 1Kin 20:40 4941
and they gave *j* upon him 2Kin 25:6 4941
over all Israel, and executed *j* 1Chr 18:14 4941
he thee king over them, to do *j* 2Chr 9:8 4941
LORD, who is with you in the *j* 2Chr 19:6
for the *j* of the LORD, and for 2Chr 19:8 4941
cometh upon us, as the sword, *j* 2Chr 20:9 8196
j upon the house of Ahab, and 2Chr 22:8 8199
So they executed *j* against Joash 2Chr 24:24 8201
let *j* be executed speedily upon Ezr 7:26 1780
toward all that knew law and *j* Est 1:13 1779
Doth God pervert *j*? Job 8:3 4941
and if of *j*, who shall set me a Job 9:19 4941
and we should come together in *j* Job 9:32 4941
and bringest me into *j* with thee Job 14:3 4941
I cry aloud, but there is no *j* Job 19:7 4941
that ye may know there is a *j* Job 19:29 1779
will he enter with thee into *j* Job 22:4 4941
liveth, who hath taken away my *j* Job 27:2 4941
my *j* was as a robe and a diadem Job 29:14 4941
neither do the aged understand *j* Job 32:9 4941
Let us choose to us *j* Job 34:4 4941
and God hath taken away my *j* Job 34:5 4941
will the Almighty pervert *j* Job 34:12 4941
he should enter into *j* with God Job 34:23 4941
not see him, yet *j* is before him Job 35:14 1779
fulfilled the *j* of the wicked Job 36:17 1779
j and justice take hold on thee Job 36:17 1779
he is excellent in power, and in *j* Job 37:23 4941
Wilt thou also disannul my *j* Job 40:8 4941
ungodly shall not stand in the *j* Ps 1:5 4941
awake for me to the *j* that thou Ps 7:6 4941
he hath prepared his throne for *j* Ps 9:7 4941
he shall minister *j* to the people Ps 9:8 1777
known by the *j* which he executeth Ps 9:16 4941
The meek will he guide in *j* Ps 25:9 4941
He loveth righteousness and *j* Ps 33:5 4941
Stir up thyself, and awake to my *j* Ps 35:23 4941
light, and thy *j* as the noonday Ps 37:6 4941
For the LORD loveth *j*, and Ps 37:28 4941
and his tongue talketh of *j* Ps 37:30 4941
righteousness and thy poor with *j* Ps 72:2 4941
Thou didst cause *j* to be heard Ps 76:8 1779
When God arose to *j*, to save all Ps 76:9 4941
j are the habitation of thy Ps 89:14 4941
But *j* shall return unto Ps 94:15 4941
j are the habitation of his Ps 97:2 4941
The king's strength also loveth *j* Ps 99:4 4941
equity, thou executest *j* and Ps 99:4 4941
I will sing of mercy and *j* Ps 101:1 4941
j for all that are oppressed Ps 103:6 4941
Blessed are they that keep *j* Ps 106:3 4941
stood up Phinehas, and executed *j* Ps 106:30 6419
of his hands are verity and *j* Ps 111:7 4941
Teach me good *j* and knowledge Ps 119:66 2940
when wilt thou execute *j* on them Ps 119:84 4941
I have done *j* and justice Ps 119:121 4941
quicken me according to thy *j* Ps 119:149 4941
For there are set thrones of *j* Ps 122:5 4941
enter not into *j* with thy servant Ps 143:2 4941
Which executeth *j* for the Ps 146:7 4941
execute upon them the *j* written Ps 149:9 4941
of wisdom, justice, and *j*, and Prov 1:3 4941
He keepeth the paths of *j* Prov 2:8 4941
understand righteousness, and *j* Prov 2:9 4941
in the midst of the paths of *j* Prov 8:20 4941
that is destroyed for want of *j* Prov 13:23 4941
his mouth transgresseth not in *j* Prov 16:10 4941
bosom to pervert the ways of *j* Prov 17:23 4941
to overthrow the righteous in *j* Prov 18:5 4941
An ungodly witness scorneth *j* Prov 19:28 4941
j scattereth away all evil with Prov 20:8 1779
j is more acceptable to the LORD Prov 21:3 4941
because they refuse to do *j* Prov 21:7 4941
It is joy to the just to do *j* Prov 21:15 4941
to have respect of persons in *j* Prov 24:23 4941
Evil men understand not *j* Prov 28:5 4941
The king by *j* establisheth the Prov 29:4 4941
but every man's *j* cometh from the Prov 29:26 4941
pervert the *j* of any of the Prov 31:5 1779
saw under the sun the place of *j* Eccl 3:16 4941
poor, and violent perverting of *j* Eccl 5:8 4941
heart discerneth both time and *j* Eccl 8:5 4941
every purpose there is time and *j* Eccl 8:6 4941
things God will bring thee into *j* Eccl 11:9 4941
God shall bring every work into *j* Eccl 12:14 4941
seek *j*, relieve the oppressed, Is 1:17 4941
it was full of *j* Is 1:21 4941
Zion shall be redeemed with *j* Is 1:27 4941
The LORD will enter into *j* with Is 3:14 4941
midst thereof by the spirit of *j* Is 4:4 4941
and he looked for *j*, but behold Is 5:7 4941
of hosts shall be exalted in *j* Is 5:16 4941
it, and to establish it with *j* Is 9:7 4941
To turn aside the needy from *j* Is 10:2 1779
Take counsel, execute *j* Is 16:3 6415
of David, judging, and seeking *j* Is 16:5 4941
j to him that sitteth in *j* Is 28:6 4941
err in vision, they stumble in *j* Is 28:7 6417
J also will I lay to the line, and Is 28:17 4941
for the LORD is a God of *j* Is 30:18 4941
and princes shall rule in *j* Is 32:1 4941
Then *j* shall dwell in the Is 32:16 4941
he hath filled Zion with *j* Is 33:5 4941
upon the people of my curse, to *j* Is 34:5 4941
and taught him in the path of *j* Is 40:14 4941
my *j* is passed over from my God Is 40:27 4941
let us come near together to *j* Is 41:1 4941
bring forth *j* to the Gentiles Is 42:1 4941
he shall bring forth *j* unto truth Is 42:3 4941
till he have set *j* in the earth Is 42:4 4941
yet surely my *j* is with the LORD, Is 49:4 4941
I will make my *j* to rest for a Is 51:4 4941
was taken from prison and from *j* Is 53:8 4941
thee in *j* thou shalt condemn Is 54:17 4941
Thus saith the LORD, Keep ye *j* Is 56:1 4941
there is no *j* in their goings Is 59:8 4941
Therefore is *j* far from us Is 59:9 4941
we look for *j*, but there is none Is 59:11 4941
j is turned away backward, and Is 59:14 4941
him that there was no *j* Is 59:15 4941
For I the LORD love *j*, I hate Is 61:8 4941
The LORD liveth, in truth, in *j* Jer 4:2 4941
if there be any that executeth *j* Jer 5:1 4941
the LORD, nor the *j* of their God Jer 5:4 4941

the LORD, and the j of their God Jer 5:5 4941
throughly execute j between a man Jer 7:5 4941
people know not the j of the LORD Jer 8:7 4941
which exercise lovingkindness, j, Jer 9:24 4941
O LORD, correct me, but with j Jer 10:24 4941
Execute j in the morning, and Jer 21:12 4941
Execute ye j and righteousness, and Jer 22:3 4941
thy father eat and drink, and do j Jer 22:15 4941
and prosper, and shall execute j Jer 23:5 4941
and he shall execute j and Jer 33:15 4941
Hamath, where he gave j upon him Jer 39:5 4941
j is come upon the plain country Jer 48:21 4941
Thus far is the j of Moab Jer 48:47 4941
they whose j was not to drink of Jer 49:12 4941
for her j reacheth unto heaven, Jer 51:9 4941
that I will do j upon the graven Jer 51:47 6485
that I will do j upon her graven Jer 51:52 6485
where he gave j upon him Jer 52:9 4941
hath executed true j between man Eze 18:8 4941
for they had executed j upon her Eze 23:10 8196
I will set j before them, and they Eze 23:24 4941
I will feed them with j Eze 34:16 4941
see my j that I have executed Eze 39:21 4941
controversy they shall stand in j Eze 44:24 8199
violence and spoil, and execute j Eze 45:9 4941
works are truth, and his ways j Dan 4:37 1780
the j was set, and the books were Dan 7:10 1780
j was given to the saints of the Dan 7:22 1780
But the j shall sit, and they Dan 7:26 1780
unto me in righteousness, and in j Hos 2:19 4941
for j is toward you, because ye Hos 5:1 4941
is oppressed and broken in j Hos 5:11 4941
thus j springeth up as hemlock in Hos 10:4 4941
keep mercy and j, and wait on thy Hos 12:6 4941
Ye who turn j to wormwood Amos 5:7 4941
good, and establish j in the gate Amos 5:15 4941
But let j run down as waters, and Amos 5:24 4941
for ye have turned j into gall Amos 6:12 4941
Is it not for you to know j Mic 3:1 4941
the spirit of the LORD, and of j Mic 3:8 4941
the house of Israel, that abhor j Mic 3:9 4941
my cause, and execute j for me Mic 7:9 4941
slacked, and j doth never go forth Hab 1:4 4941
therefore wrong j proceedeth Hab 1:4 4941
their j and their dignity shall Hab 1:7 4941
thou hast ordained them for j Hab 1:12 4941
earth, which have wrought his j Zeph 2:3 4941
doth he bring his j to light Zeph 3:5 4941
of hosts, saying, Execute true j Zec 7:9 4941
execute the j of truth and peace Zec 8:16 4941
or, Where is the God of j Mal 2:17 4941
And I will come near to you to j Mal 3:5 4941
kill shall be in danger of the j Mt 5:21 2920
cause shall be in danger of the j Mt 5:22 2920
For with what j ye judge, ye Mt 7:2 2917
Sodom and Gomorrha in the day of j Mt 10:15 2920
for Tyre and Sidon at the day of j Mt 11:22 2920
the land of Sodom in the day of j Mt 11:24 2920
he shall shew j to the Gentiles Mt 12:18 2920
till he send forth j unto victory Mt 12:20 2920
account thereof in the day of j Mt 12:36 2920
rise in j with this generation Mt 12:41 2920
up in the j with this generation Mt 12:42 2920
weightier matters of the law, j Mt 23:23 2920
he was set down on the j seat Mt 27:19 968
Sodom and Gomorrha in the day of j Mk 6:11 2920
for Tyre and Sidon at the j Lk 10:14 2920
the south shall rise up in the j Lk 11:31 2920
up in the j with this generation Lk 11:32 2920
manner of herbs, and pass over j Lk 11:42 2920
hath committed all j unto the Son Jn 5:22 2920
him authority to execute j also Jn 5:27 2920
and my j is just Jn 5:30 2920
appearance, but judge righteous j Jn 7:24 2920
And yet if I judge, my j is true Jn 8:16 2920
For j I am come into this world, Jn 9:39 2917
Now is the j of this world Jn 12:31 2920
sin, and of righteousness, and of j Jn 16:8 2920
Of j, because the prince of this Jn 16:11 2920
from Caiaphas unto the hall of j Jn 18:28 4232
went not into the j hall, lest Jn 18:28 4232
entered into the j hall again Jn 18:33 4232
And went again into the j hall Jn 19:9 4232
sat down in the j seat in a place Jn 19:13 968
humiliation his j was taken away Acts 8:33 2920
and brought him to the j seat Acts 18:12 968
And he drave them from the j seat Acts 18:16 968
and beat him before the j seat Acts 18:17 968
him to be kept in Herod's j hall Acts 23:35 4232
j to come, Felix trembled, and Acts 24:25 2917
the j seat commanded Paul to be Acts 25:6 968
Paul, I stand at Caesar's j seat Acts 25:10 968
desiring to have j against him Acts 25:15 1349
on the morrow I sat on the j seat Acts 25:17 968
Who knowing the j of God, that Rom 1:32 1345
But we are sure that the j of God Rom 2:2 2917
thou shalt escape the j of God Rom 2:3 2917
of the righteous j of God Rom 2:5 1341
for the j was by one to Rom 5:16 2917
of one j came upon all men to Rom 5:18
stand before the j seat of Christ Rom 14:10 968
in the same mind and in the same j 1Cor 1:10 1106
be judged of you, or of man's j 1Cor 4:3 2250
yet I give my j, as one that hath 1Cor 7:25 1106
if she so abide, after my j 1Cor 7:40 1106
before the j seat of Christ 2Cor 5:10 968
troubleth you shall bear his j Gal 5:10 2917
and more in knowledge and in all j Phil 1:9 144
token of the righteous j of God 2Th 1:5 2920
beforehand, going before to j 1Ti 5:24 2920
of the dead, and of eternal j Heb 6:2 2917
once to die, but after this the j Heb 9:27 2920
certain fearful looking for of j Heb 10:27 2920
and draw you before the j seats Jas 2:6 2922
For he shall have j without mercy Jas 2:13 2920
and mercy rejoiceth against j Jas 2:13 2920
For the time is come that j must 1Pet 4:17 2917
whose j now of a long time 2Pet 2:3 2917
darkness, to be reserved unto j 2Pet 2:4 2920
unto the day of j to be punished 2Pet 2:9 2920
unto fire against the day of j 2Pet 3:7 2920
may have boldness in the day of j 1Jn 4:17 2920
unto the j of the great day Jude 6 2920
To execute j upon all, and to Jude 15 2920
for the hour of his j is come Rev 14:7 2920
I will shew unto thee the j of Rev 17:1 2917
for in one hour is thy j come Rev 18:10 2920
them, and j was given unto them Rev 20:4 2917

JUDGMENTS
out arm, and with great j Ex 6:6 8201
of the land of Egypt by great j Ex 7:4 8201
Now these are the j which thou Ex 21:1 4941
words of the LORD, and all the j Ex 24:3 4941
Ye shall do my j, and keep mine Lev 18:4 4941
keep my statutes, and my j Lev 18:5 4941
keep my statutes and my j, and Lev 18:26 4941
all my statutes, and all my j Lev 19:37 4941
keep all my statutes, and all my j Lev 20:22 4941
do my statutes, and keep my j Lev 25:18 4941
or if your soul abhor my j Lev 26:15 4941
even because they despised my j Lev 26:43 4941
These are the statutes and j Lev 26:46 4941
gods also the LORD executed j Num 33:4 8201
of blood according to these j Num 35:24 4941
are the commandments and the j Num 36:13 4941
unto the statutes and unto the j Deut 4:1 4941
I have taught you statutes and j Deut 4:5 4941
j so righteous as all this law, Deut 4:8 4941
time to teach you statutes and j Deut 4:14 4941
and the statutes, and the j Deut 4:45 4941
j which I speak in your ears this Deut 5:1 4941
and the statutes, and the j Deut 5:31 4941
the statutes, and the j, which Deut 6:1 4941
and the statutes, and the j Deut 6:20 4941
and the statutes, and the j Deut 7:11 4941
to pass, if ye hearken to these j Deut 7:12 4941
his commandments, and his j Deut 8:11 4941
charge, and his statutes, and his j Deut 11:1 4941
j which I set before you this day Deut 11:32 4941
These are the statutes and j Deut 12:1 4941
thee to do these statutes and j Deut 26:16 4941
and his commandments, and his j Deut 26:17 4941
and his statutes and his j, that Deut 30:16 4941
They shall teach Jacob thy j Deut 33:10 4941
of the LORD, and his j with Israel Deut 33:21 4941
For all his j were before me 2Sa 22:23 4941
and his commandments, and his j 1Kin 2:3 4941
in my statutes, and execute my j 1Kin 6:12 4941
and his statutes, and his j 1Kin 8:58 4941
and wilt keep my statutes and my j 1Kin 9:4 4941
and to keep my statutes and my j 1Kin 11:33 4941
wonders, and the j of his mouth 1Chr 16:12 4941
his j are in all the earth 1Chr 16:14 4941
j which the LORD charged Moses 1Chr 22:13 4941
to do my commandments and my j 1Chr 28:7 4941
shalt observe my statutes and my j 2Chr 7:17 4941
law and commandment, statutes and j 2Chr 19:10 4941
to teach in Israel statutes and j Ezr 7:10 4941
nor the statutes, nor the j Neh 1:7 4941
heaven, and gavest them right j Neh 9:13 4941
but sinned against thy j Neh 9:29 4941
of the LORD our Lord, and his j Neh 10:29 4941
thy j are far above out of his Ps 10:5 4941
For all his j were before me, and Ps 18:22 4941
the j of the LORD are true and Ps 19:9 4941
thy j are a great deep Ps 36:6 4941
Judah be glad, because of thy j Ps 48:11 4941
Give the king thy j, O God, and Ps 72:1 4941
my law, and walk not in my j Ps 89:30 4941
Judah rejoiced because of thy j Ps 97:8 4941
wonders, and the j of his mouth Ps 105:5 4941
his j are in all the earth Ps 105:7 4941
have learned thy righteous j Ps 119:7 4941
I declared all the j of thy mouth Ps 119:13 4941
it hath unto thy j at all times Ps 119:20 4941
thy j have I laid before me Ps 119:30 4941
for thy j are good Ps 119:39 4941
for I have hoped in thy j Ps 119:43 4941
I remembered thy j of old Ps 119:52 4941
thee because of thy righteous j Ps 119:62 4941
that thy j are right, and that Ps 119:75 4941
I have not departed from thy j Ps 119:102 4941
that I will keep thy righteous j Ps 119:106 4941
mouth, O LORD, and teach me thy j Ps 119:108 4941
and I am afraid of thy j Ps 119:120 4941
O LORD, and upright are thy j Ps 119:137 4941
quicken me according to thy j Ps 119:156 4941
thy righteous j endureth for ever Ps 119:160 4941
thee because of thy righteous j Ps 119:164 4941
and let thy j help me Ps 119:175 4941
his statutes and his j unto Israel Ps 147:19 4941
and as for his j, they have not Ps 147:20 4941
J are prepared for scorners, and Prov 19:29 8201
Yea, in the way of thy j, O LORD, Is 26:8 4941
for when thy j are in the earth, Is 26:9 4941
I will utter my j against them Jer 1:16 4941
let me talk with thee of thy j Jer 12:1 4941
she hath changed my j into Eze 5:6 4941
for they have refused my j Eze 5:6 4941
statutes, neither have kept my j Eze 5:7 4941
have done according to the j of Eze 5:7 4941
will execute j in the midst of Eze 5:8 4941
and I will execute j in thee Eze 5:10 8201
shall execute j in thee in anger Eze 5:15 8201
and will execute j among you Eze 11:9 8201
statutes, neither executed my j Eze 11:12 4941
my four sore j upon Jerusalem Eze 14:21 8201
execute j upon thee in the sight Eze 16:41 8201
in my statutes, and hath kept my j Eze 18:9 4941
nor increase, hath executed my j Eze 18:17 4941
my statutes, and shewed them my j Eze 20:11 4941
statutes, and they despised my j Eze 20:13 4941
Because they despised my j Eze 20:16 4941
fathers, neither observe their j Eze 20:18 4941
walk in my statutes, and keep my j Eze 20:19 4941
neither kept my j to do them Eze 20:21 4941
they had not executed my j Eze 20:24 4941
j whereby they should not live Eze 20:25 4941
judge thee according to their j Eze 23:24 4941
And I will execute j upon Moab Eze 25:11 8201
I shall have executed j in her Eze 28:22 8201
when I have executed j upon all Eze 28:26 8201
in Zoan, and will execute j in No Eze 30:14 8201
Thus will I execute j in Egypt Eze 30:19 8201
statutes, and ye shall keep my j Eze 36:27 4941
they shall also walk in my j Eze 37:24 4941
shall judge it according to my j Eze 44:24 4941
from thy precepts and from thy j Dan 9:5 4941
thy j are as the light that goeth Hos 6:5 4941
The LORD hath taken away thy j Zeph 3:15 4941
Israel, with the statutes and j Mal 4:4 4941
how unsearchable are his j Rom 11:33 2917
If then ye have j of things 1Cor 6:4 2922
for thy j are made manifest Rev 15:4 1345
true and righteous are thy j Rev 16:7 2920
For true and righteous are his j Rev 19:2 2920

JUDITH (ju'-dith) *A wife of Esau.*
wife J the daughter of Beeri the Gen 26:34 3067

JULIA (ju'-le-ah) *A Christian acquaintance of Paul.*
Salute Philologus, and J, Nereus, Rom 16:15 2456

JULIUS (ju'-le-us) *A Roman centurion.*
other prisoners unto one named J Acts 27:1 2457
J courteously entreated Paul, and Acts 27:3 2457

JUMPING
horses, and of the j chariots Nah 3:2 7540

JUNIA (ju'-ne-ah) *A Christian acquaintance of Paul.*
Salute Andronicus and J, my Rom 16:7 2458

JUNIPER
came and sat down under a j tree 1Kin 19:4 7574
as he lay and slept under a j tree 1Kin 19:5 7574
bushes, and j roots for their meat Job 30:4 7574
of the mighty, with coals of j Ps 120:4 7574

JUPITER (ju'-pit-ur) *Chief god of the Romans.*
And they called Barnabas, J Acts 14:12 2203
Then the priest of J, which was Acts 14:13 2203
the image which fell down from J Acts 19:35 1356

JURISDICTION
that he belonged unto Herod's j Lk 23:7 1849

JUSHAB-HESED (ju''-shab-he'-sed) *A son of Zerubbabel.*
and Berechiah, and Hasadiah, J 1Chr 3:20 3142

JUST
Noah was a j man and perfect in Gen 6:9 6662
J balances, j weights Lev 19:36 6664
a j ephah, and a j hin, shall Lev 19:36 6664
judge the people with j judgment Deut 16:18 6664
is altogether j shalt thou follow Deut 16:20 6664
j weight, a perfect and Deut 25:15 6664
j measure shalt thou have Deut 25:15 6664
of truth and without iniquity, j Deut 32:4 6662
He that ruleth over men must be j 2Sa 23:3 6662
Howbeit thou art j in all that is Neh 9:33 6662
mortal man be more j than God Job 4:17 6663
but how should man be j with God Job 9:2 6663
the j upright man is laughed to Job 12:4 6662
but the j shall put it on, and the Job 27:17 6662
Behold, in this thou art not j Job 33:12 6663
thou condemn him that is most j Job 34:17 6662
but establish the j Ps 7:9 6662
The wicked plotteth against the j Ps 37:12 6662
blesseth the habitation of the j Prov 3:33 6662
But the path of the j is as the Prov 4:18 6662
teach a j man, and he will Prov 9:9 6662
are upon the head of the j Prov 10:6 6662
The memory of the j is blessed Prov 10:7 6662
The tongue of the j is as choice Prov 10:20 6662
The mouth of the j bringeth forth Prov 10:31 6662
but a j weight is his delight Prov 11:1 8003
shall the j be delivered Prov 11:9 6662
but the j shall come out of Prov 12:13 6662
shall no evil happen to the j Prov 12:21 6662
the sinner is laid up for the j Prov 13:22 6662
A j weight and balance are the Prov 16:11 4941
and he that condemneth the j Prov 17:15 6662
Also to punish the j is not good Prov 17:26 6662
first in his own cause seemeth j Prov 18:17 6662
The j man walketh in his Prov 20:7 6662
It is joy to the j to do judgment Prov 21:15 6662
For a j man falleth seven times, Prov 24:16 6662
but the j seek his soul Prov 29:10 3477
man is an abomination to the j Prov 29:27 6662
there is a j man that perisheth Eccl 7:15 6662
there is not a j man upon earth Eccl 7:20 6662
that there be j men, unto whom it Eccl 8:14 6662
The way of the j is uprightness Is 26:7 6662
dost weigh the path of the j Is 26:7 6662
turn aside the j for a thing of Is 29:21 6662
a j God and a Saviour Is 45:21 6662
of the j in the midst of her Lam 4:13 6662
But if a man be j, and do that Eze 18:5 6662
he is j, he shall surely live, Eze 18:9 6662
Ye shall have j balances, and a Eze 45:10 6664
a j ephah, and a j bath Eze 45:10 6664
and the j shall walk in them Hos 14:9 6662

they afflict the *j*, they take a ... Amos 5:12 6662
but the *j* shall live by his faith ... Hab 2:4 6662
The *j* LORD is in the midst ... Zeph 3:5 6662
he is *j*, and having salvation ... Zec 9:9 6662
Joseph her husband, being a *j* man ... Mt 1:19 *1342*
good, and sendeth rain on the *j* ... Mt 5:45 *1342*
sever the wicked from among the *j* ... Mt 13:49 *1342*
nothing to do with that *j* man ... Mt 27:19 *1342*
of the blood of this *j* person ... Mt 27:24 *1342*
John, knowing that he was a *j* man ... Mk 6:20 *1342*
to the wisdom of the *j* ... Lk 1:17 *1342*
and the same man was *j* and devout, ... Lk 2:25 *1342*
at the resurrection of the *j* ... Lk 14:14 *1342*
nine *j* persons, which need no ... Lk 15:7 *1342*
should feign themselves *j* men ... Lk 20:20 *1342*
and he was a good man, and a *j* ... Lk 23:50 *1342*
and my judgment is *j* ... Jn 5:30 *1342*
ye denied the Holy One and the *J* ... Acts 3:14 *1342*
before of the coming of the *J* One ... Acts 7:52 *1342*
a *j* man, and one that feareth God, ... Acts 10:22 *1342*
know his will, and see that *J* One ... Acts 22:14 *1342*
of the dead, both of the *j* ... Acts 24:15 *1342*
The *j* shall live by faith ... Rom 1:17 *1342*
of the law are *j* before God ... Rom 2:13 *1342*
whose damnation is *j* ... Rom 3:8 *1738*
that he might be *j*, and the ... Rom 3:26 *1342*
and the commandment holy, and *j* ... Rom 7:12 *1342*
The *j* shall live by faith ... Gal 3:11 *1342*
honest, whatsoever things are *j* ... Phil 4:8 *1342*
your servants that which is *j* ... Col 4:1 *1342*
a lover of good men, sober, *j* ... Titus 1:8 *1342*
received a *j* recompence of reward ... Heb 2:2 *1738*
Now the *j* shall live by faith ... Heb 10:38 *1342*
the spirits of *j* men made perfect ... Heb 12:23 *1342*
Ye have condemned and killed the *j* ... Jas 5:6 *1342*
the *j* for the unjust, that he ... 1Pet 3:18 *1342*
And delivered *j* Lot, vexed with ... 2Pet 2:7 *1342*
j to forgive us our sins, and to ... 1Jn 1:9 *1342*
j and true are thy ways, thou King ... Rev 15:3 *1342*

JUSTICE
keep the way of the LORD, to do *j* ... Gen 18:19 6666
he executed the *j* of the LORD ... Deut 33:21 6666
judgment and *j* unto all his people ... 2Sa 8:15 6666
come unto me, and I would do him *j* ... 2Sa 15:4 6663
he thee king, to do judgment and *j* ... 1Kin 10:9 6666
and *j* among all his people ... 1Chr 18:14 6666
over them, to do judgment and *j* ... 2Chr 9:8 6666
or doth the Almighty pervert *j* ... Job 8:3 6664
judgment and *j* take hold on thee ... Job 36:17 4941
and in judgment, and in plenty of *j* ... Job 37:23 6666
do *j* to the afflicted and needy ... Ps 82:3 6663
J and judgment are the habitation ... Ps 89:14 6664
I have done judgment and *j* ... Ps 119:121 6664
the instruction of wisdom, *j* ... Prov 1:3 6664
kings reign, and princes decree *j* ... Prov 8:15 6664
To do *j* and judgment is more ... Prov 21:3 6666
j in a province, marvel not at ... Eccl 5:8 6664
with *j* from henceforth even for ... Is 9:7 6666
LORD, Keep ye judgment, and do *j* ... Is 56:1 6666
ask of me the ordinances of *j* ... Is 58:2 6664
None calleth for *j*, nor any ... Is 59:4 6664
us, neither doth *j* overtake us ... Is 59:9 6666
backward, and *j* standeth afar off ... Is 59:14 6666
eat and drink, and do judgment and *j* ... Jer 22:15 6666
judgment and *j* in the earth ... Jer 23:5 6666
bless thee, O habitation of *j* ... Jer 31:23 6664
the LORD, the habitation of *j* ... Jer 50:7 6664
spoil, and execute judgment and *j* ... Eze 45:9 6666

JUSTIFICATION
and was raised again for our *j* ... Rom 4:25 *1347*
gift is of many offences unto *j* ... Rom 5:16 *1345*
came upon all men unto *j* of life ... Rom 5:18 *1347*

JUSTIFIED
and should a man full of talk be *j* ... Job 11:2 6663
I know that I shall be *j* ... Job 13:18 6663
How then can man be *j* with God ... Job 25:4 6663
because he *j* himself rather than ... Job 32:2 6663
mightest be *j* when thou speakest ... Ps 51:4 6663
sight shall no man living be *j* ... Ps 143:2 6663
witnesses, that they may be *j* ... Is 43:9 6663
thou, that thou mayest be *j* ... Is 43:26 6663
shall all the seed of Israel be *j* ... Is 45:25 6663
The backsliding Israel hath *j* ... Jer 3:11 6663
hast *j* thy sisters in all thine ... Eze 16:51 6663
in that thou hast *j* thy sisters ... Eze 16:52 6663
But wisdom is *j* of her children ... Mt 11:19 *1344*
For by thy words thou shalt be *j* ... Mt 12:37 *1344*
j God, being baptized with the ... Lk 7:29 *1344*
But wisdom is *j* of all her ... Lk 7:35 *1344*
his house *j* rather than the other ... Lk 18:14 *1344*
believe are *j* from all things ... Acts 13:39 *1344*
not be *j* by the law of Moses ... Acts 13:39 *1344*
the doers of the law shall be *j* ... Rom 2:13 *1344*
thou mightest be *j* in thy sayings ... Rom 3:4 *1344*
shall no flesh be *j* in his sight ... Rom 3:20 *1344*
Being *j* freely by his grace ... Rom 3:24 *1344*
we conclude that a man is *j* by ... Rom 3:28 *1344*
For if Abraham were *j* by works ... Rom 4:2 *1344*
Therefore being *j* by faith ... Rom 5:1 *1344*
being now *j* by his blood, we ... Rom 5:9 *1344*
and whom he called, them he also *j* ... Rom 8:30 *1344*
and whom he *j*, them he also ... Rom 8:30 *1344*
yet am I not hereby *j* ... 1Cor 4:4 *1344*
but ye are *j* in the name of the ... 1Cor 6:11 *1344*
is not *j* by the works of the law ... Gal 2:16 *1344*
that we might be *j* by the faith ... Gal 2:16 *1344*
of the law shall no flesh be *j* ... Gal 2:16 *1344*
while we seek to be *j* by Christ ... Gal 2:17 *1344*
But that no man is *j* by the law ... Gal 3:11 *1344*
that we might be *j* by faith ... Gal 3:24 *1344*
whosoever of you are *j* by the law ... Gal 5:4 *1344*
j in the Spirit, seen of angels, ... 1Ti 3:16 *1344*
That being *j* by his grace, we ... Titus 3:7 *1344*
not Abraham our father *j* by works ... Jas 2:21 *1344*
then how that by works a man is *j* ... Jas 2:24 *1344*
not Rahab the harlot *j* by works ... Jas 2:25 *1344*

JUSTIFIER
the *j* of him which believeth in ... Rom 3:26 *1344*

JUSTIFIETH
He that *j* the wicked, and he that ... Prov 17:15 6663
He is near that *j* me ... Is 50:8 6663
on him that *j* the ungodly ... Rom 4:5 *1344*
It is God that *j* ... Rom 8:33 *1344*

JUSTIFY
for I will not *j* the wicked ... Ex 23:7 6663
then they shall *j* the righteous ... Deut 25:1 6663
If I *j* myself, mine own mouth ... Job 9:20 6663
God forbid that I should *j* you ... Job 27:5 6663
speak, for I desire to *j* thee ... Job 33:32 6663
Which *j* the wicked for reward, and ... Is 5:23 6663
shall my righteous servant *j* many ... Is 53:11 6663
But he, willing to *j* himself ... Lk 10:29 *1344*
Ye are they which *j* yourselves ... Lk 16:15 *1344*
which shall *j* the circumcision by ... Rom 3:30 *1344*
would *j* the heathen through faith ... Gal 3:8 *1344*

JUSTIFYING
j the righteous, to give him ... 1Kin 8:32 6663
by *j* the righteous, by giving him ... 2Chr 6:23 6663

JUSTLE
they shall *j* one against another ... Nah 2:4 8264

JUSTLY
LORD require of thee, but to do *j* ... Mic 6:8 4941
And we indeed *j*; for we receive ... Lk 23:41 *1346*
and God also, how holily and *j* ... 1Th 2:10 *1346*

JUSTUS (*jus'-tus*) See BARSABAS, JESUS.
1. Surname for Barsabas.
Barsabas, who was surnamed *J* ... Acts 1:23 *2459*
2. A Corinthian Christian.
a certain man's house, named *J* ... Acts 18:7 *2459*
3. A Christian acquaintance of Paul.
And Jesus, which is called *J* ... Col 4:11 *2459*

JUTTAH (*jut'-tah*) *A city in Judah.*
Maon, Carmel, and Ziph, and *J* ... Josh 15:55 3194
and *J* with her suburbs, and ... Josh 21:16 3194

K

KABZEEL (*kab'-ze-el*) See JEKABZEEL. *A city in Judah.*
coast of Edom southward were *K* ... Josh 15:21 6909
the son of a valiant man, of *K* ... 2Sa 23:20 6909
the son of a valiant man of *K* ... 1Chr 11:22 6909

KADESH (*ka'-desh*) See EN-MISHPAT, KADESH-BARNEA, KEDESH. *A place in the wilderness, south of Judah.*
and came to En-mishpat, which is *K* ... Gen 14:7 6946
behold, it is between *K* and Bered ... Gen 16:14 6946
country, and dwelled between *K* ... Gen 20:1 6946
the wilderness of Paran, to *K* ... Num 13:26 6946
and the people abode in *K* ... Num 20:1 6946
from *K* unto the king of Edom ... Num 20:14 6946
and, behold, we are in *K*, a city ... Num 20:16 6946
congregation, journeyed from *K* ... Num 20:22 6946
in *K* in the wilderness of Zin ... Num 27:14 6946
the wilderness of Zin, which is *K* ... Num 33:36 6946
And they removed from *K*, and ... Num 33:37 6946
So ye abode in *K* many days ... Deut 1:46 6946
unto the Red sea, and came to *K* ... Judg 11:16 6946
and Israel abode in *K* ... Judg 11:17 6946
LORD shaketh the wilderness of *K* ... Ps 29:8 6946
even to the waters of strife in *K* ... Eze 47:19 6946
unto the waters of strife in *K* ... Eze 48:28 6946

KADESH-BARNEA (*ka''-desh-bar'-ne-ah*) See KADESH. *Same as Kadesh.*
sent them from *K* to see the land ... Num 32:8 6947
shall be from the south to *K* ... Num 34:4 6947
by the way of mount Seir unto *K* ... Deut 1:2 6947
and we came to *K* ... Deut 1:19 6947
the space in which we came from *K* ... Deut 2:14 6947
when the LORD sent you from *K* ... Deut 9:23 6947
smote them from *K* even unto Gaza ... Josh 10:41 6947
of God concerning me and thee in *K* ... Josh 14:6 6947
me from *K* to espy out the land ... Josh 14:7 6947
up on the south side unto *K* ... Josh 15:3 6947

KADMIEL (*kad'-me-el*)
1. An exile.
the children of Jeshua and *K* ... Ezr 2:40 6934
the children of Jeshua, of *K* ... Neh 7:43 6934
2. A rebuilder of the Temple.
with his sons and his brethren, *K* ... Ezr 3:9 6934
3. A Levite with Nehemiah.
the Levites, Jeshua, and Bani, *K* ... Neh 9:4 6934
Then the Levites, Jeshua, and *K* ... Neh 9:5 6934
Binnui of the sons of Henadad, *K* ... Neh 10:9 6934
Jeshua, Binnui, *K*, Sherebiah, ... Neh 12:8 6934
Sherebiah, and Jeshua the son of *K* ... Neh 12:24 6934

KADMONITES (*kad'-mo-nites*) *A Phoenician tribe.*
and the Kenizzites, and the *K* ... Gen 15:19 6935

KAIN See CAIN.

KAIWAN See CHIUN.

KALLAI (*kal'-la-i*) *A priest.*
Of Sallai, *K*; of Amok ... Neh 12:20 7040

KAMON See CAMON.

KANAH (*ka'-nah*)
1. A brook between Ephraim and Manasseh.
Tappuah westward unto the river *K* ... Josh 16:8 7071
coast descended unto the river *K* ... Josh 17:9 7071
2. A city in Asher.
and Rehob, and Hammon, and *K* ... Josh 19:28 7071

KAREAH (*ka'-re-ah*) See CAREAH. *A captain of the Jews.*
Johanan and Jonathan the sons of *K* ... Jer 40:8 7143
Moreover Johanan the son of *K* ... Jer 40:13 7143
Then Johanan the son of *K* spake ... Jer 40:15 7143
said unto Johanan the son of *K* ... Jer 40:16 7143
But when Johanan the son of *K* ... Jer 41:11 7143
Ishmael saw Johanan the son of *K* ... Jer 41:13 7143
and went unto Johanan the son of *K* ... Jer 41:14 7143
Then took Johanan the son of *K* ... Jer 41:16 7143
forces, and Johanan the son of *K* ... Jer 42:1 7143
called he Johanan the son of *K* ... Jer 42:8 7143
Hoshaiah, and Johanan the son of *K* ... Jer 43:2 7143
So Johanan the son of *K*, and all ... Jer 43:4 7143
But Johanan the son of *K*, and all ... Jer 43:5 7143

KARKA See KARKAA.

KARKAA (*kar'-ka-ah*) *A city in Judah.*
Adar, and fetched a compass to *K* ... Josh 15:3 7173

KARKOR (*kar'-kor*) *A Gadite city.*
Now Zebah and Zalmunna were in *K* ... Judg 8:10 7174

KARNAIM (*kar'-na-im*) See ASHTEROTH. *A city in Og.*
smote the Rephaims in Ashteroth *K* ... Gen 14:5

KARTAH (*kar'-tah*) See KATTATH. *A Levitical city in Zebulun.*
suburbs, and *K* with her suburbs, ... Josh 21:34 7177

KARTAN (*kar'-tan*) See KIRJATHAIM. *A Levitical city in Naphtali.*
suburbs, and *K* with her suburbs ... Josh 21:32 7178

KATTATH (*kat'-tath*) See KARTAH, KITRON. *A city in Zebulun.*
And *K*, and Nahallal, and ... Josh 19:15 7005

KEBAR See CHEBAR.

KEDAR (*ke'-dar*)
1. A son of Ishmael.
and *K*, and Adbeel, and Mibsam, ... Gen 25:13 6938
then *K*, and Adbeel, and Mibsam, ... 1Chr 1:29 6938
2. The tribe.
that I dwell in the tents of *K* ... Ps 120:5 6938
of Jerusalem, as the tents of *K* ... Song 1:5 6938
and all the glory of *K* shall fail ... Is 21:16 6938
mighty men of the children of *K* ... Is 21:17 6938
the villages that *K* doth inhabit ... Is 42:11 6938
All the flocks of *K* shall be ... Is 60:7 6938
and send unto *K*, and consider ... Jer 2:10 6938
Concerning *K*, and concerning the ... Jer 49:28 6938
Arise ye, go up to *K*, and spoil ... Jer 49:28 6938
Arabia, and all the princes of *K* ... Eze 27:21 6938

KEDEMAH (*ked'-e-mah*) *A son of Ishmael.*
and Tema, Jetur, Naphish, and *K* ... Gen 25:15 6929
Jetur, Naphish, and *K* ... 1Chr 1:31 6929

KEDEMOTH (*ked'-e-moth*)
1. A wilderness in Reuben.
out of the wilderness of *K* unto ... Deut 2:26 6932
2. A Levitical city in Reuben.
And Jahaza, and *K*, and Mephaath, ... Josh 13:18 6932
K with her suburbs, and Mephaath ... Josh 21:37 6932
K also with her suburbs, and ... 1Chr 6:79 6932

KEDESH (*ke'-desh*) See KADESH, KEDESH-NAPHTALI, KISHION.
1. A Canaanite city.
The king of *K*, one ... Josh 12:22 6943
And *K*, and Edrei, and En-hazor, ... Josh 19:37 6943
2. A city of refuge in Naphtali.
they appointed *K* in Galilee in ... Josh 20:7 6943
K in Galilee with her suburbs, to ... Josh 21:32 6943
arose, and went with Barak to *K* ... Judg 4:9 6943
called Zebulun and Naphtali to *K* ... Judg 4:10 6943
plain of Zaanaim, which is by *K* ... Judg 4:11 6943
and Janoah, and *K*, and Hazor, and ... 2Kin 15:29 6943
K in Galilee with her suburbs, and ... 1Chr 6:76 6943
3. A Levitical city in Naphtali.

K with her suburbs, Daberath with ... 1Chr 6:72 6943
4. A city in Judah.
And *K*, and Hazor, and Ithnan, ... Josh 15:23 6943

KEDESH-NAPHTALI (*ke''-desh-naf'-ta-li*)
Same as Kedesh 2.
Barak the son of Abinoam out of *K* ... Judg 4:6

KEDOLAOMER See CHEDORLAOMER.

KEEP
of Eden to dress it and to *k* it ... Gen 2:15 8104
to *k* the way of the tree of life ... Gen 3:24 8104
to *k* them alive with thee ... Gen 6:19 8104
come unto thee, to *k* them alive ... Gen 6:20 8104
to *k* seed alive upon the face of ... Gen 7:3
Abraham, Thou shalt *k* my covenant ... Gen 17:9 8104
is my covenant, which ye shall *k* ... Gen 17:10 8104
they shall *k* the way of the LORD, ... Gen 18:19 8104
will *k* thee in all places whither ... Gen 28:15 8104
will *k* me in this way that I go, ... Gen 28:20 8104
I will again feed and *k* thy flock ... Gen 30:31 8104
k that thou hast unto thyself ... Gen 33:9 1961
let them *k* food in the cities ... Gen 41:35 8104
whom the Egyptians *k* in bondage ... Ex 6:5
ye shall *k* it up until the ... Ex 12:6 4931
ye shall *k* it a feast to the LORD ... Ex 12:14 2287
ye shall *k* it a feast by an ... Ex 12:14 2287
that ye shall *k* this service ... Ex 12:25 8104
congregation of Israel shall *k* it ... Ex 12:47 6213
will *k* the passover to the LORD, ... Ex 12:48 6213
and then let him come near and *k* it ... Ex 12:48 6213
that thou shalt *k* this service in ... Ex 13:5 5647
Thou shalt therefore *k* this ... Ex 13:10 8104
k all his statutes, I will put ... Ex 15:26 8104
refuse ye to *k* my commandments ... Ex 16:28 8104
k my covenant, then ye shall be a ... Ex 19:5 8104
love me, and *k* my commandments ... Ex 20:6 8104
the sabbath day, to *k* it holy ... Ex 20:8 6942
his neighbour money or stuff to *k* ... Ex 22:7 8104
or a sheep, or any beast, to *k* ... Ex 22:10 8104
K thee far from a false matter ... Ex 23:7 7368
Three times thou shalt *k* a feast ... Ex 23:14 2287
Thou shalt *k* the feast of ... Ex 23:15 8104
to *k* thee in the way, and to bring ... Ex 23:20 8104
Verily my sabbaths ye shall *k* ... Ex 31:13 8104
Ye shall *k* the sabbath therefore ... Ex 31:14 8104
of Israel shall *k* the sabbath ... Ex 31:16 8104
of unleavened bread shalt thou *k* ... Ex 34:18 8104
that which was delivered him to *k* ... Lev 6:2
that which was delivered him to *k* ... Lev 6:4 6485
k the charge of the LORD, that ye ... Lev 8:35 8104
k mine ordinances, to walk ... Lev 18:4 8104
Ye shall therefore *k* my statutes ... Lev 18:5 8104
Ye shall therefore *k* my statutes ... Lev 18:26 8104
shall ye *k* mine ordinance ... Lev 18:30 8104
and his father, and *k* my sabbaths ... Lev 19:3 8104
Ye shall *k* my statutes ... Lev 19:19 8104
Ye shall *k* my sabbaths, and ... Lev 19:30 8104
ye shall *k* my statutes, and do ... Lev 20:8 8104
shall therefore *k* all my statutes ... Lev 20:22 8104
shall therefore *k* mine ordinance ... Lev 22:9 8104
shall ye *k* my commandments ... Lev 22:31 8104
ye shall *k* a feast unto the LORD ... Lev 23:39 2287
ye shall *k* it a feast unto the ... Lev 23:41 2287
then shall the land *k* a sabbath ... Lev 25:2
k my judgments, and do them ... Lev 25:18 8104
Ye shall *k* my sabbaths, and ... Lev 26:2 8104
k my commandments, and do them ... Lev 26:3 8104
the Levites shall *k* the charge of ... Num 1:53 8104
And they shall *k* his charge ... Num 3:7 8104
they shall *k* all the instruments ... Num 3:8 8104
k the charge of the sanctuary ... Num 3:32 8104
The LORD bless thee, and *k* thee ... Num 6:24 8104
to *k* the charge, and shall do no ... Num 8:26 8104
k the passover at his appointed ... Num 9:2 6213
ye shall *k* it in his appointed ... Num 9:3 6213
ceremonies thereof, shall ye *k* it ... Num 9:3 6213
that they should *k* the passover ... Num 9:4 6213
that they could not *k* the ... Num 9:6 6213
yet he shall *k* the passover unto ... Num 9:10 6213
month at even they shall *k* it ... Num 9:11 6213
of the passover they shall *k* it ... Num 9:12 6213
and forbeareth to *k* the passover ... Num 9:13 6213
will *k* the passover unto the LORD ... Num 9:14 6213
And they shall *k* thy charge ... Num 18:3 8104
k the charge of the tabernacle of ... Num 18:4 8104
ye shall *k* the charge of the ... Num 18:5 8104
thy sons with thee shall *k* your ... Num 18:7 8104
ye shall *k* a feast unto the LORD ... Num 29:12 2287
with him, *k* alive for yourselves ... Num 31:18
which *k* the charge of the ... Num 31:30 8104
k himself to the inheritance of ... Num 36:7 1692
k himself to his own inheritance ... Num 36:9 1692
that ye may *k* the commandments of .. Deut 4:2 8104
K therefore and do them ... Deut 4:6 8104
k thy soul diligently, lest thou ... Deut 4:9 8104
Thou shalt *k* therefore his ... Deut 4:40 8104
day, that ye may learn them, and *k* ... Deut 5:1 8104
and *k* my commandments ... Deut 5:10 8104
K the sabbath day to sanctify it, ... Deut 5:12 8104
thee to *k* the sabbath day ... Deut 5:15 6213
k all my commandments always, ... Deut 5:29 8104
to *k* all his statutes and his ... Deut 6:2 8104
Ye shall diligently *k* the ... Deut 6:17 8104
because he would *k* the oath which ... Deut 7:8 8104
k his commandments to a thousand ... Deut 7:9 8104
therefore *k* the commandments ... Deut 7:11 8104
hearken to these judgments, and *k* ... Deut 7:12 8104
shall *k* unto thee the covenant ... Deut 7:12 8104
thou wouldest *k* his commandments ... Deut 8:2 8104
Therefore thou shalt *k* the ... Deut 8:6 8104
To *k* the commandments of the LORD .. Deut 10:13 8104
k his charge, and his statutes, and ... Deut 11:1 8104
Therefore shall ye *k* all the ... Deut 11:8 8104
For if ye shall diligently *k* all ... Deut 11:22 8104
k his commandments, and obey his ... Deut 13:4 8104
to *k* all his commandments which I ... Deut 13:18 8104
k the passover unto the LORD thy ... Deut 16:1 6213
thou shalt *k* the feast of weeks ... Deut 16:10 6213
Seven days shalt thou *k* a solemn ... Deut 16:15 2287
to *k* all the words of this law and ... Deut 17:19 8104
If thou shalt *k* all these ... Deut 19:9 8104
then *k* thee from every wicked ... Deut 23:9 8104
gone out of thy lips thou shalt *k* ... Deut 23:23 8104
thou shalt therefore *k* and do them ... Deut 26:16 8104
to *k* his statutes, and his ... Deut 26:17 8104
that thou shouldest *k* all his ... Deut 26:18 8104
K all the commandments which I ... Deut 27:1 8104
if thou shalt *k* the commandments ... Deut 28:9 8104
to *k* his commandments and his ... Deut 28:45 8104
K therefore the words of this ... Deut 29:9 8104
to *k* his commandments and his ... Deut 30:10 8104
to *k* his commandments and his ... Deut 30:16 8104
in any wise *k* yourselves from the ... Josh 6:18 8104
and set men by it for to *k* them ... Josh 10:18 8104
to *k* his commandments, and to ... Josh 22:5 8104
ye therefore very courageous to *k* ... Josh 23:6 8104
whether they will *k* the way of ... Judg 2:22 8104
as their fathers did *k* it ... Judg 2:22 8104
who said, *K* silence ... Judg 3:19
Thou shalt *k* fast by my young men ... Ruth 2:21 1692
He will *k* the feet of his saints, ... 1Sa 2:9 8104
his son to *k* the ark of the LORD ... 1Sa 7:1 8104
and with one full line to *k* alive ... 2Sa 8:2
were concubines, to *k* the house ... 2Sa 15:16 8104
which he hath left to *k* the house ... 2Sa 16:21 8104
I have no son to *k* my name in ... 2Sa 18:18
whom he had left to *k* the house ... 2Sa 20:3 8104
k the charge of the LORD thy God, ... 1Kin 2:3 8104
to *k* his statutes, and his ... 1Kin 2:3 8104
my ways, to *k* my statutes and my ... 1Kin 3:14 8104
k all my commandments to walk in ... 1Kin 6:12 8104
k with thy servant David my ... 1Kin 8:25 8104
to *k* his commandments, and his ... 1Kin 8:58 8104
to *k* his commandments, as at this ... 1Kin 8:61 8104
thee, and wilt *k* my statutes and my ... 1Kin 9:4 8104
will not *k* my commandments and my. 1Kin 9:6 8104
to *k* my statutes and my judgments, ... 1Kin 11:33
my sight, to *k* my statutes and my ... 1Kin 11:38 8104
man unto me, and said, *K* this man ... 1Kin 20:39 8104
so shall ye *k* the watch of the ... 2Kin 11:6 8104
even they shall *k* the watch of ... 2Kin 11:7 8104
k my commandments and my ... 2Kin 17:13 8104
to *k* his commandments and his ... 2Kin 23:3 8104
K the passover unto the LORD your ... 2Kin 23:21 6213
that thou wouldest *k* me from evil ... 1Chr 4:10 6213
thousand, which could *k* rank ... 1Chr 12:33 5737
men of war, that could *k* rank ... 1Chr 12:38 5737
that thou mayest *k* the law of the ... 1Chr 22:12 8104
that they should *k* the charge of ... 1Chr 23:32 8104
and in the audience of our God, *k* ... 1Chr 28:8 8104
fathers, *k* this for ever in the ... 1Chr 29:18 8104
to *k* thy commandments, thy ... 1Chr 29:19 8104
k with thy servant David my ... 2Chr 6:16 8104
for we *k* the charge of the LORD ... 2Chr 13:11 8104
no power to *k* still the kingdom ... 2Chr 22:9 6113
shall *k* the watch of the LORD ... 2Chr 23:6 8104
now ye purpose to *k* under the ... 2Chr 28:10 3533
to *k* the passover unto the LORD ... 2Chr 30:1 6213
to *k* the passover in the second ... 2Chr 30:2 6213
they could not *k* it at that time ... 2Chr 30:3 6213
that they should come to *k* the ... 2Chr 30:5 6213
at Jerusalem much people to *k* the ... 2Chr 30:13 6213
counsel to *k* other seven days ... 2Chr 30:23 6213
to *k* his commandments, and his ... 2Chr 34:31 8104
to *k* the passover, and to offer ... 2Chr 35:16 6213
did all the kings of Israel *k* ... 2Chr 35:18 6213
k them, until ye weigh them ... Ezr 8:29 8104
k my commandments, and do them ... Neh 1:9 8104
to *k* the dedication with gladness ... Neh 12:27 6213
k the gates, to sanctify the ... Neh 13:22 8104
neither *k* they the king's laws ... Est 3:8 6213
that they should *k* the fourteenth ... Est 9:21 6213
that they would *k* these two days ... Est 9:27 6213
that thou wouldest *k* me secret ... Job 14:13
but *k* it still within his mouth ... Job 20:13 4513
Thou shalt *k* them, O LORD, thou ... Ps 12:7 8104
K me as the apple of the eye ... Ps 17:8 8104
K back thy servant also from ... Ps 19:13 2820
none can *k* alive his own soul ... Ps 22:29
truth unto such as *k* his covenant ... Ps 25:10 5341
O *k* my soul, and deliver me ... Ps 25:20 8104
thou shalt *k* them secretly in a ... Ps 31:20
to *k* them alive in famine ... Ps 33:19
K thy tongue from evil, and thy ... Ps 34:13 5341
k not silence ... Ps 35:22
k his way, and he shall exalt thee ... Ps 37:34 8104
I will *k* my mouth with a bridle, ... Ps 39:1 8104
will preserve him, and *k* him alive ... Ps 41:2
come, and shall not *k* silence ... Ps 50:3
of God, but *k* his commandments ... Ps 78:7 5341
K not thou silence, O God ... Ps 83:1
My mercy will I *k* for him for ... Ps 89:28 8104
and *k* not my commandments ... Ps 89:31 8104
to *k* thee in all thy ways ... Ps 91:11 8104
neither will he *k* his anger for ... Ps 103:9 5201
To such as *k* his covenant, and to ... Ps 103:18 8104
his statutes, and *k* his laws ... Ps 105:45 5341
Blessed are they that *k* judgment ... Ps 106:3 8104
the barren woman to *k* house ... Ps 113:9
are they that *k* his testimonies ... Ps 119:2 5341
us to *k* thy precepts diligently ... Ps 119:4 8104
were directed to *k* thy statutes ... Ps 119:5 8104
I will *k* thy statutes ... Ps 119:8 8104
that I may live, and *k* thy word ... Ps 119:17 8104
I shall *k* it unto the end ... Ps 119:33 5341
and I shall *k* thy law ... Ps 119:34 5341
So shall I *k* thy law continually ... Ps 119:44 8104
said that I would *k* thy words ... Ps 119:57 8104
delayed not to *k* thy commandments ... Ps 119:60 8104
and of them that *k* thy precepts ... Ps 119:63 8104
but I will *k* thy precepts with my ... Ps 119:69 5341
so shall I *k* the testimony of thy ... Ps 119:88 8104
because I *k* thy precepts ... Ps 119:100 5341
evil way, that I might *k* thy word ... Ps 119:101 8104
that I will *k* thy righteous ... Ps 119:106 8104
for I will *k* the commandments of ... Ps 119:115 5341
therefore doth my soul *k* them ... Ps 119:129 5341
so will I *k* thy precepts ... Ps 119:134 8104
eyes, because they *k* not thy law ... Ps 119:136 8104
I will *k* thy statutes ... Ps 119:145 5341
I shall *k* thy testimonies ... Ps 119:146 8104
except the LORD *k* the city ... Ps 127:1 8104
thy children will *k* my covenant ... Ps 132:12 8104
K me, O LORD, from the hands of ... Ps 140:4 8104
K the door of my lips ... Ps 141:3 5341
K me from the snares which they ... Ps 141:9 8104
thee, understanding shall *k* thee ... Prov 2:11 5341
k the paths of the righteous ... Prov 2:20 8104
let thine heart *k* my commandments ... Prov 3:1 5341
k sound wisdom and discretion ... Prov 3:21 5341
shall *k* thy foot from being taken ... Prov 3:26 8104
k my commandments, and live ... Prov 4:4 8104
love her, and she shall *k* thee ... Prov 4:6 5341
let her not go: *k* her ... Prov 4:13 5341
k them in the midst of thine ... Prov 4:21 8104
K thy heart with all diligence ... Prov 4:23 5341
and that thy lips may *k* knowledge ... Prov 5:2 5341
k thy father's commandment, and ... Prov 6:20 5341
thou sleepest, it shall *k* thee ... Prov 6:22 8104
To *k* thee from the evil woman, ... Prov 6:24 8104
My son, *k* my words, and lay up my ... Prov 7:1 8104
K my commandments, and live ... Prov 7:2 8104
That they may *k* thee from the ... Prov 7:5 8104
blessed are they that *k* my ways ... Prov 8:32 8104
he that doth *k* his soul shall be ... Prov 22:5 8104
thing if thou *k* them within thee ... Prov 22:18 8104
but such as *k* the law contend ... Prov 28:4 8104
a time to *k*, and a time to cast ... Eccl 3:6 8104
a time to *k* silence, and a time to ... Eccl 3:7
K thy foot when thou goest to the ... Eccl 5:1 8104
I counsel thee to *k* the king's ... Eccl 8:2 8104
Fear God, and *k* his commandments ... Eccl 12:13 8104
those that *k* the fruit thereof ... Song 8:12 5201
Thou wilt *k* him in perfect peace, ... Is 26:3 5341
I the LORD do *k* it ... Is 27:3 5341
hurt it, I will *k* it night and day ... Is 27:3 5341
K silence before me, O islands ... Is 41:1
hold thine hand, and will *k* thee ... Is 42:6 5341
and to the south, *K* not back ... Is 43:6 3607
K ye judgment, and do justice ... Is 56:1 8104
the eunuchs that *k* my sabbaths ... Is 56:4 8104
of the LORD, *k* not silence, ... Is 62:6
I will not *k* silence, but will ... Is 65:6
will he *k* it to the end ... Jer 3:5 8104
I will not *k* anger for ever ... Jer 3:12 5201
k him, as a shepherd doth his ... Jer 31:10 8104
I will *k* nothing back from you ... Jer 42:4 4513
sit upon the ground, and *k* silence ... Lam 2:10
k mine ordinances, and do them ... Eze 11:20 8104
k all my statutes, and do that ... Eze 18:21 8104
k my judgments, and do them ... Eze 20:19 8104
ye shall *k* my judgments, and do ... Eze 36:27 8104
that they may *k* the whole form ... Eze 43:11 8104
me, and they shall *k* my charge ... Eze 44:16 8104
and they shall *k* my laws and my ... Eze 44:24 8104
to them that *k* his commandments ... Dan 9:4 8104
k mercy and judgment, and wait on ... Hos 12:6 8104
shall *k* silence in that time ... Amos 5:13
k the doors of thy mouth from her ... Mic 7:5 8104
k thy solemn feasts, perform thy ... Nah 1:15 2287
k the munition, watch the way, ... Nah 2:1 5341
let all the earth *k* silence ... Hab 2:20
ways, and if thou wilt *k* my charge ... Zec 3:7 8104
house, and shalt also *k* my courts ... Zec 3:7 8104
me to *k* cattle from my youth ... Zec 13:5 7069
to *k* the feast of tabernacles ... Zec 14:16 2287
up to *k* the feast of tabernacles ... Zec 14:18 2287
up to *k* the feast of tabernacles ... Zec 14:19 2287
priest's lips should *k* knowledge ... Mal 2:7 2287
into life, *k* the commandments ... Mt 19:17 *5083*
I will *k* the passover at thy ... Mt 26:18 *4160*
that ye may *k* your own tradition ... Mk 7:9 *5083*
charge over thee, to *k* thee ... Lk 4:10 *1314*
k it, and bring forth fruit with ... Lk 8:15 *2722*
hear the word of God, and *k* it ... Lk 11:28 *5442*
and *k* thee in on every side, ... Lk 19:43 *4912*
If a man *k* my saying, he shall ... Jn 8:51 *5083*
If a man *k* my saying, he shall ... Jn 8:52 *5083*
but I know him, and *k* his saying ... Jn 8:55 *5083*
shall *k* it unto life eternal ... Jn 12:25 *5442*
If ye love me, *k* my commandments ... Jn 14:15 *5083*
a man love me, he will *k* my words ... Jn 14:23 *5083*
If ye *k* my commandments, ye shall ... Jn 15:10 *5083*
my saying, they will *k* yours also ... Jn 15:20 *5083*
k through thine own name those ... Jn 17:11 *5083*
shouldest *k* them from the evil ... Jn 17:15 *5083*
to *k* back part of the price of ... Acts 5:3 *3557*
a man that is a Jew to *k* company ... Acts 10:28 *2853*
quaternions of soldiers to *k* him ... Acts 12:4 *5442*
them to *k* the law of Moses ... Acts 15:5 *5083*
must be circumcised, and *k* the law ... Acts 15:24 *5083*
from which if ye *k* yourselves ... Acts 15:29 *1301*
them the decrees for to *k* ... Acts 16:4 *5442*
the jailer to *k* them safely ... Acts 16:23 *5083*
I must by all means *k* this feast ... Acts 18:21 *4160*
save only that they *k* themselves ... Acts 21:25 *5442*
commanded a centurion to *k* Paul ... Acts 24:23 *5083*
profiteth, if thou *k* the law ... Rom 2:25 *4238*
k the righteousness of the law ... Rom 2:26 *5442*
Therefore let us *k* the feast ... 1Cor 5:8 *1858*
written unto you not to *k* company ... 1Cor 5:11 *4874*

heart that he will *k* his virgin ... 1Cor 7:37 *5083*
But I *k* under my body, and bring ... 1Cor 9:27 *5299*
k the ordinances, as I delivered ... 1Cor 11:2 *2722*
let him *k* silence in the church ... 1Cor 14:28 *4601*
Let your women *k* silence in the ... 1Cor 14:34 *4601*
if ye *k* in memory what I preached ... 1Cor 15:2 *2722*
unto you, and so will I *k* myself ... 2Cor 11:9 *5083*
who are circumcised *k* the law ... Gal 6:13 *5442*
Endeavouring to *k* the unity of ... Eph 4:3 *5083*
shall *k* your hearts and minds ... Phil 4:7 *5432*
stablish you, and *k* you from evil ... 2Th 3:3 *5442*
k thyself pure ... 1Ti 5:22 *5083*
That thou *k* this commandment ... 1Ti 6:14 *5083*
k that which is committed to thy ... 1Ti 6:20 *5442*
to *k* that which I have committed ... 2Ti 1:12 *5442*
thee *k* by the Holy Ghost which ... 2Ti 1:14 *5442*
to *k* himself unspotted from the ... Jas 1:27 *5083*
whosoever shall *k* the whole law ... Jas 2:10 *5083*
him, if we *k* his commandments ... 1Jn 2:3 *5083*
because we *k* his commandments, and ... 1Jn 3:22 *5083*
love God, and *k* his commandments ... 1Jn 5:2 *5083*
that we *k* his commandments ... 1Jn 5:3 *5083*
children, *k* yourselves from idols ... 1Jn 5:21 *5442*
K yourselves in the love of God, ... Jude 21 *5083*
is able to *k* you from falling ... Jude 24 *5442*
k those things which are written ... Rev 1:3 *5083*
I also will *k* thee from the hour ... Rev 3:10 *5083*
which *k* the commandments of God, ... Rev 12:17 *5083*
here are they that *k* the ... Rev 14:12 *5083*
of them which *k* the sayings of ... Rev 22:9 *5083*

KEEPER
And Abel was a *k* of sheep, but ... Gen 4:2 7462
Am I my brother's *k* ... Gen 4:9 8104
the sight of the *k* of the prison ... Gen 39:21 8269
the *k* of the prison committed to ... Gen 39:22 8269
The *k* of the prison looked not to ... Gen 39:23 8269
and left the sheep with a *k* ... 1Sa 17:20 8104
the hand of the *k* of the carriage ... 1Sa 17:22 8104
make thee *k* of mine head for ever ... 1Sa 28:2 8104
son of Harhas, *k* of the wardrobe ... 2Kin 22:14 8104
son of Hasrah, *k* of the wardrobe ... 2Chr 34:22 8104
Asaph the *k* of the king's forest ... Neh 2:8 8104
the *k* of the east gate ... Neh 3:29 8104
chamberlain, *k* of the women ... Est 2:3 8104
custody of Hegai, *k* of the women ... Est 2:8 8104
the *k* of the women, appointed ... Est 2:15 8104
and as a booth that the *k* maketh ... Job 27:18 5341
The LORD is thy *k* ... Ps 121:5 8104
made me the *k* of the vineyards ... Song 1:6 5201
son of Shallum, the *k* of the door ... Jer 35:4 8104
the *k* of the prison awaking out ... Acts 16:27 *1200*
the *k* of the prison told this ... Acts 16:36 *1200*

KEEPERS
be *k* of the watch of the king's ... 2Kin 11:5 8104
which the *k* of the door have ... 2Kin 22:4 8104
the *k* of the door, to bring forth ... 2Kin 23:4 8104
and the three *k* of the door ... 2Kin 25:18 8104
k of the gates of the tabernacle ... 1Chr 9:19 8104
of the LORD, were *k* of the entry ... 1Chr 9:19 8104
the *k* of the door, who sought to ... Est 6:2 8104
In the day when the *k* of the ... Eccl 12:3 8104
the *k* of the walls took away my ... Song 5:7 8104
he let out the vineyard unto *k* ... Song 8:11 5201
As *k* of a field, are they against ... Jer 4:17 8104
and the three *k* of the door ... Jer 52:24 8104
the *k* of the charge of the house ... Eze 40:45 8104
the *k* of the charge of the altar ... Eze 40:46 8104
but ye have set *k* of my charge in ... Eze 44:8 8104
But I will make them *k* of the ... Eze 44:14 8104
for fear of him the *k* did shake ... Mt 28:4 *5083*
the *k* standing without before the ... Acts 5:23 *5441*
the *k* before the door kept the ... Acts 12:6 *5441*
found him not, he examined the *k* ... Acts 12:19 *5441*
k at home, good, obedient to ... Titus 2:5 *3626*

KEEPEST
who *k* covenant and mercy with thy ... 1Kin 8:23 8104
which *k* covenant, and shewest ... 2Chr 6:14 8104
who *k* covenant and mercy, let not ... Neh 9:32 8104
walkest orderly, and *k* the law ... Acts 21:24 *5442*

KEEPETH
and he die not, but *k* his bed ... Ex 21:18 5307
which *k* covenant and mercy with ... Deut 7:9 8104
and, behold, he *k* the sheep ... 1Sa 16:11 7462
that *k* covenant and mercy for them ... Neh 1:5 8104
He *k* back his soul from the pit, ... Job 33:18 2820
He *k* all his bones ... Ps 34:20 8104
he that *k* thee will not slumber ... Ps 121:3 8104
he that *k* Israel shall neither ... Ps 121:4 8104
which *k* truth for ever ... Ps 146:6 8104
He *k* the paths of judgment, and ... Prov 2:8 5341
way of life that *k* instruction ... Prov 10:17 8104
He that *k* his mouth *k* his ... Prov 13:3 5341
that *k* his mouth *k* his life ... Prov 13:3 8104
Righteousness *k* him that is ... Prov 13:6 5341
he that *k* his way preserveth his ... Prov 16:17 5341
he that *k* understanding shall ... Prov 19:8 8104
He that *k* the commandment *k* ... Prov 19:16 8104
Whoso *k* his mouth and his tongue ... Prov 21:23 8104
his tongue *k* his soul from ... Prov 21:23 8104
he that *k* thy soul, doth not he ... Prov 24:12 5341
Whoso *k* the fig tree shall eat ... Prov 27:18 5341
Whoso *k* the law is a wise son ... Prov 28:7 5341
but he that *k* company with ... Prov 29:3
but a wise man *k* it in till ... Prov 29:11 7623
but he that *k* the law, happy is ... Prov 29:18 8104
Whoso *k* the commandment shall ... Eccl 8:5 8104
which *k* the truth may enter in ... Is 26:2 8104
that *k* the sabbath from polluting ... Is 56:2 8104
k his hand from doing any evil ... Is 56:2 8104
every one that *k* the sabbath from ... Is 56:6 8104
cursed be he that *k* back his ... Jer 48:10 4513
k silence, because he hath borne ... Lam 3:28
is a proud man, neither *k* at home ... Hab 2:5
a strong man armed *k* his palace ... Lk 11:21 *5442*
law, and yet none of you *k* the law ... Jn 7:19 *4160*
because he *k* not the sabbath day ... Jn 9:16 *5083*
k them, he it is that loveth me ... Jn 14:21 *5083*
loveth me not *k* not my sayings ... Jn 14:24 *5083*
k not his commandments, is a liar ... 1Jn 2:4 *5083*
But whoso *k* his word, in him ... 1Jn 2:5 *5083*
he that *k* his commandments ... 1Jn 3:24 *5083*
that is begotten of God *k* himself ... 1Jn 5:18 *5083*
k my works unto the end, to him ... Rev 2:26 *5083*
k his garments, lest he walk ... Rev 16:15 *5083*
blessed is he that *k* the sayings ... Rev 22:7 *5083*

KEEPING
K mercy for thousands, forgiving ... Ex 34:7 5341
k the charge of the sanctuary ... Num 3:28 8104
k the charge of the sanctuary for ... Num 3:38 8104
in not *k* his commandments, and his ... Deut 8:11 8104
we were with them *k* the sheep ... 1Sa 25:16 7462
were porters *k* the ward at the ... Neh 12:25 8104
in *k* of them there is great ... Ps 19:11 8104
but that by *k* of his covenant it ... Eze 17:14 8104
k the covenant and mercy to them ... Dan 9:4 8104
k watch over their flock by night ... Lk 2:8 *5442*
but the *k* of the commandments of ... 1Cor 7:19 *5084*
k of their souls to him in well ... 1Pet 4:19

KEHELATHAH (*ke-hel'-a-thah*) *An Israelite encampment in the wilderness.*
from Rissah, and pitched in *K* ... Num 33:22 6954
And they went from *K*, and pitched ... Num 33:23 6954

KEILAH (*ki'-lah*)
1. A city in Judah.
And *K*, and Achzib, and Mareshah ... Josh 15:44 7084
the Philistines fight against *K* ... 1Sa 23:1 7084
smite the Philistines, and save *K* ... 1Sa 23:2 7084
to *K* against the armies of the ... 1Sa 23:3 7084
him and said, Arise, go down to *K* ... 1Sa 23:4 7084
So David and his men went to *K* ... 1Sa 23:5 7084
David saved the inhabitants of *K* ... 1Sa 23:5 7084
of Ahimelech fled to David to *K* ... 1Sa 23:6 7084
Saul that David was come to *K* ... 1Sa 23:7 7084
together to war, to go down to *K* ... 1Sa 23:8 7084
that Saul seeketh to come to *K* ... 1Sa 23:10 7084
Will the men of *K* deliver me up ... 1Sa 23:11 7084
Will the men of *K* deliver me ... 1Sa 23:12 7084
arose and departed out of *K* ... 1Sa 23:13 7084
that David was escaped from *K* ... 1Sa 23:13 7084
the ruler of the half part of *K* ... Neh 3:17 7084
the ruler of the half part of *K* ... Neh 3:18 7084
2. A descendant of Caleb.
the father of *K* the Garmite ... 1Chr 4:19 7084

KELAIAH (*kel-ah'-yah*) See KELITA. *Married a foreigner in exile.*
Jozabad, and Shimei, and *K*, (the ... Ezr 10:23 7041

KELAL See CHELAL.

KELITA (*kel'-i-tah*) See KELAIAH.
1. Married a foreigner in exile.
and Kelaiah, (the same is *K* ... Ezr 10:23 7042
2. A priest who assisted Ezra.
Shabbethai, Hodijah, Maaseiah, *K* ... Neh 8:7 7042
3. A Levite who renewed the covenant.
brethren, Shebaniah, Hodijah, *K* ... Neh 10:10 7042

KELUB See CHELUB.

KELUHI See CHELLUH.

KEMUEL (*kem-u'-el*)
1. A son of Nahor.
brother, and *K* the father of Aram, ... Gen 22:21 7055
2. An Ephraimite prince.
of Ephraim, *K* the son of Shiphtan ... Num 34:24 7055
3. Father of Hashabiah.
Levites, Hashabiah the son of *K* ... 1Chr 27:17 7055

KENAANAH See CHENAANAH.

KENAN (*ke'-nan*) See CAINAN. *Son of Enosh.*
K, Mahalaleel, Jered, ... 1Chr 1:2 7018

KENANI See CHENANI.

KENANIAH See CHENANIAH.

KENATH (*ke'-nath*) See NOBAH. *A city in Bashan.*
And Nobah went and took *K*, and the ... Num 32:42 7079
towns of Jair, from them, with *K* ... 1Chr 2:23 7079

KENAZ (*ke'-naz*) See KENEZITE.
1. A son of Eliphaz.
Omar, Zepho, and Gatam, and *K* ... Gen 36:11 7073
duke Omar, duke Zepho, duke *K* ... Gen 36:15 7073
and Omar, Zephi, and Gatam, *K* ... 1Chr 1:36 7073
2. A duke of Edom.
Duke *K*, duke Teman, duke Mibzar, ... Gen 36:42 7073
Duke *K*, duke Teman, duke Mibzar, ... 1Chr 1:53 7073
3. Brother of Caleb.
And Othniel the son of *K*, the ... Josh 15:17 7073
And Othniel the son of *K*, Caleb's ... Judg 1:13 7073
them, even Othniel the son of *K* ... Judg 3:9 7073
And Othniel the son of *K* died ... Judg 3:11 7073
And the sons of *K* ... 1Chr 4:13 7073
4. A grandson of Caleb.
and the sons of Elah, even *K* ... 1Chr 4:15 7073

KENEZITE (*ken'-e-zite*) See KENIZZITES. *Descendants of Jephunneh.*
Caleb the son of Jephunneh the *K* ... Num 32:12 7074
of Jephunneh the *K* said unto him ... Josh 14:6 7074
of Jephunneh the *K* unto this day ... Josh 14:14 7074

KENITE (*ken'-ite*) See KENITES. *A member of a Canaanite tribe.*
the *K* shall be wasted, until ... Num 24:22 7014
And the children of the *K*, Moses' ... Judg 1:16 7017
Now Heber the *K*, which was of the ... Judg 4:11 7014
of Jael the wife of Heber the *K* ... Judg 4:17 7017
Hazor and the house of Heber the *K* ... Judg 4:17 7017
Jael the wife of Heber the *K* be ... Judg 5:24 7017

KENITES (*ken'-ites*) See MIDIANITES.
The *K*, and the Kenizzites, and the ... Gen 15:19 7017
And he looked on the *K*, and took up ... Num 24:21 7017
had severed himself from the *K* ... Judg 4:11 7017
And Saul said unto the *K*, Go, ... 1Sa 15:6 7017
So the *K* departed from among the ... 1Sa 15:6 7017
and against the south of the *K* ... 1Sa 27:10 7017
which were in the cities of the *K* ... 1Sa 30:29 7017
These are the *K* that came of ... 1Chr 2:55 7017

KENIZZITE See KENIZZITES.

KENIZZITES (*ken'-iz-zites*) See KENEZITE. *A Canaanite tribe in Abraham's time.*
The Kenites, and the *K*, and the ... Gen 15:19 7074

KENNIZZITE See KENIZZITES.

KEPHER AMMONI See CHEPHAR-HAAMMONAI.

KEPHIRAH See CHEPHIRAH.

KEPT
k my charge, my commandments, my ... Gen 26:5 8104
father's sheep: for she *k* them ... Gen 29:9 7462
neither hath he *k* back any thing ... Gen 39:9 2820
and ye shall be *k* in prison ... Gen 42:16 631
Now Moses *k* the flock of Jethro ... Ex 3:1 7462
for you to be *k* until the morning ... Ex 16:23 4931
it to be *k* for your generations ... Ex 16:32 4931
to be *k* for your generations ... Ex 16:33 4931
up before the Testimony, to be *k* ... Ex 16:34 4931
owner, and he hath not *k* him in ... Ex 21:29 8104
and his owner hath not *k* him in ... Ex 21:36 8104
be *k* close, and she be defiled, and ... Num 5:13 5641
they *k* the passover on the ... Num 9:5 6213
wherefore are we *k* back, that we ... Num 9:7 1639
Israel *k* the charge of the LORD ... Num 9:19 8104
they *k* the charge of the LORD, at ... Num 9:23 8104
to be *k* for a token against the ... Num 17:10 4931
place, and it shall be *k* for the ... Num 19:9 4931
the LORD hath *k* thee back from ... Num 24:11 4513
which *k* the charge of the ... Num 31:47 8104
he *k* him as the apple of his eye ... Deut 32:10 5341
thy word, and *k* thy covenant ... Deut 33:9 5341
k the passover on the fourteenth ... Josh 5:10 6213
behold, the LORD hath *k* me alive ... Josh 14:10
Ye have *k* all that Moses the ... Josh 22:2 8104
but have *k* the charge of the ... Josh 22:3 8104
So she *k* fast by the maidens of ... Ruth 2:23 1692
it been *k* for thee since I said ... 1Sa 9:24 8104
thou hast not *k* the commandment ... 1Sa 13:13 8104
because thou hast not *k* that ... 1Sa 13:14 8104
Thy servant *k* his father's sheep, ... 1Sa 17:34 7462
if the young men have *k* ... 1Sa 21:4 8104
Of a truth women have been *k* from ... 1Sa 21:5 6113
Surely in vain have I *k* all that ... 1Sa 25:21 8104
which hast *k* me this day from ... 1Sa 25:33 3607
which hath *k* me back from hurting ... 1Sa 25:34 4513
hath *k* his servant from evil ... 1Sa 25:39 2820
hast thou not *k* thy lord the king ... 1Sa 26:15 8104
because ye have not *k* your master ... 1Sa 26:16 8104
the young man that *k* the watch ... 2Sa 13:34
For I have *k* the ways of the LORD ... 2Sa 22:22 8104
have *k* myself from mine iniquity ... 2Sa 22:24 8104
thou hast *k* me to be head of the ... 2Sa 22:44 8104
thou not *k* the oath of the LORD ... 1Kin 2:43 8104
thou hast *k* for him this great ... 1Kin 3:6 8104
Who hast *k* with thy servant David ... 1Kin 8:24 8104
but he *k* not that which the LORD ... 1Kin 11:10 8104
and thou hast not *k* my covenant ... 1Kin 11:11 8104
because he *k* my commandments and ... 1Kin 11:34 8104
hast not *k* the commandment which ... 1Kin 13:21 8104
who *k* my commandments, and who ... 1Kin 14:8 8104
which *k* the door of the king's ... 1Kin 14:27 8104
(Now Joram had *k* Ramoth-gilead ... 2Kin 9:14 8104
the priests that *k* the door put ... 2Kin 12:9 8104
Also Judah *k* not the commandments ... 2Kin 17:19 8104
but *k* his commandments, which the ... 2Kin 18:6 8104
word of the LORD, which he *k* not ... 1Chr 10:13 8104
while he yet *k* himself close ... 1Chr 12:1 6113
k the ward of the house of Saul ... 1Chr 12:29 8104
Thou which hast *k* with thy ... 2Chr 6:15 8104
Solomon *k* the feast seven days ... 2Chr 7:8 6213
for they *k* the dedication of the ... 2Chr 7:9 6213
that *k* the entrance of the king's ... 2Chr 12:10 8104
k the feast of unleavened bread ... 2Chr 30:21 6213
they *k* other seven days with ... 2Chr 30:23 6213
which the Levites that *k* the ... 2Chr 34:9 8104
have not *k* the word of the LORD ... 2Chr 34:21 8104
Moreover Josiah *k* a passover unto ... 2Chr 35:1 6213
k the passover at that time ... 2Chr 35:17 6213
that *k* in Israel from the days of ... 2Chr 35:18 6213
keep such a passover as Josiah *k* ... 2Chr 35:18 6213
of Josiah was this passover *k* ... 2Chr 35:19 6213
as she lay desolate she *k* sabbath ... 2Chr 36:21 7673
They *k* also the feast of ... Ezr 3:4 6213
k the dedication of this house of ... Ezr 6:16 5648
captivity *k* the passover upon the ... Ezr 6:19 6213
k the feast of unleavened bread ... Ezr 6:22 6213
have not *k* the commandments, nor ... Neh 1:7 8104
they *k* the feast seven days ... Neh 8:18 6213
k thy law, nor hearkened unto thy ... Neh 9:34 6213
their brethren that *k* the gates ... Neh 11:19 8104
the porters *k* the ward of their ... Neh 12:45 8104
which *k* the concubines ... Est 2:14 8104
Teresh, of those which *k* the door ... Est 2:21 8104
k throughout every generation, ... Est 9:28 6213
held his steps, his way have I *k* ... Job 23:11 8104
k close from the fowls of the air ... Job 28:21 5641
and *k* silence at my counsel ... Job 29:21
that I *k* silence, and went not out ... Job 31:34

I have *k* me from the paths of the ... Ps 17:4 8104
For I have *k* the ways of the LORD ... Ps 18:21 8104
I *k* myself from mine iniquity ... Ps 18:23 8104
thou hast *k* me alive, that I ... Ps 30:3
When I *k* silence, my bones waxed ... Ps 32:3 2790
with a multitude that *k* holyday ... Ps 42:4 2287
hast thou done, and I *k* silence ... Ps 50:21 2790
They *k* not the covenant of God, ... Ps 78:10 8104
God, and *k* not his testimonies ... Ps 78:56 8104
they *k* his testimonies, and the ... Ps 99:7 8104
for I have *k* thy testimonies ... Ps 119:22 5341
in the night, and have *k* thy law ... Ps 119:55 8104
I had, because I *k* thy precepts ... Ps 119:56 5341
but now have I *k* thy word ... Ps 119:67 8104
because they *k* not thy word ... Ps 119:158 8104
My soul hath *k* thy testimonies ... Ps 119:167 8104
I have *k* thy precepts and thy ... Ps 119:168 8104
eyes desired I *k* not from them ... Eccl 2:10 680
riches *k* for the owners thereof ... Eccl 5:13 8104
mine own vineyard have I not *k* ... Song 1:6 5201
night when a holy solemnity is *k* ... Is 30:29 6942
forsaken me, and have not *k* my law ... Jer 16:11 8104
k all his precepts, and done ... Jer 35:18 8104
neither have *k* my judgments ... Eze 5:7 6213
hath *k* my judgments, to deal ... Eze 18:9 8104
hath *k* all my statutes, and hath ... Eze 18:19 8104
neither *k* my judgments to do them ... Eze 20:21 8104
ye have not *k* the charge of mine ... Eze 44:8 8104
that *k* the charge of my sanctuary ... Eze 44:15 8104
which have *k* my charge, which ... Eze 48:11 8104
and whom he would he *k* alive ... Dan 5:19
but I *k* the matter in my heart ... Dan 7:28 5202
a wife, and for a wife he *k* sheep ... Hos 12:12 8104
and he *k* his wrath for ever ... Amos 1:11 8104
have not *k* his commandments, and ... Amos 2:4 8104
For the statutes of Omri are *k* ... Mic 6:16 8104
as ye have not *k* my ways, but ... Mal 2:9 8104
ordinances, and have not *k* them ... Mal 3:7 8104
it that we have *k* his ordinance ... Mal 3:14 8104
And they that *k* them fled, and went ... Mt 8:33 *1006*
utter things which have been *k* ... Mt 13:35
But when Herod's birthday was *k* ... Mt 14:6 *71*
things have I *k* from my youth up ... Mt 19:20 *5442*
neither was any thing *k* secret ... Mk 4:22 *1096*
And they *k* that saying with ... Mk 9:10 *2902*
But Mary *k* all these things, and ... Lk 2:19 *4933*
but his mother *k* all these ... Lk 2:51 *1301*
he was *k* bound with chains and in ... Lk 8:29 *5442*
they *k* it close, and told no man ... Lk 9:36 *4601*
these have I *k* from my youth up ... Lk 18:21 *5442*
which I have *k* laid up in a ... Lk 19:20 *2192*
but thou hast *k* the good wine ... Jn 2:10 *5083*
day of my burying hath she *k* this ... Jn 12:7 *5083*
even as I have *k* my Father's ... Jn 15:10 *5083*
if they have *k* my saying, they ... Jn 15:20 *5083*
and they have *k* thy word ... Jn 17:6 *5083*
the world, I *k* them in thy name ... Jn 17:12 *5083*
that thou gavest me I have *k* ... Jn 17:12 *5442*
and spake unto her that *k* the door ... Jn 18:16 *2377*
damsel that *k* the door unto Peter ... Jn 18:17 *2377*
k back part of the price, his ... Acts 5:2 *3557*
of angels, and have not *k* it ... Acts 7:53 *5442*
which had *k* his bed eight years, ... Acts 9:33 *2621*
Peter therefore was *k* in prison ... Acts 12:5 *5083*
before the door *k* the prison ... Acts 12:6 *5083*
Then all the multitude *k* silence ... Acts 15:12 *4601*
how I *k* back nothing that was ... Acts 20:20 *5288*
to them, they *k* the more silence ... Acts 22:2 *3930*
k the raiment of them that slew ... Acts 22:20 *5442*
he commanded him to be *k* in ... Acts 23:35 *5442*
that Paul should be *k* at Caesarea ... Acts 25:4 *5083*
I commanded him to be *k* till I ... Acts 25:21 *5083*
k them from their purpose ... Acts 27:43 *2967*
himself with a soldier that *k* him ... Acts 28:16 *5442*
which was *k* secret since the ... Rom 16:25
in all things I have *k* myself ... 2Cor 11:9 *5083*
governor under Aretas the king *k* ... 2Cor 11:32 *5432*
we were *k* under the law, shut up ... Gal 3:23 *5432*
my course, I have *k* the faith ... 2Ti 4:7 *5083*
Through faith he *k* the passover ... Heb 11:28 *4160*
which is of you *k* back by fraud ... Jas 5:4 *650*
Who are *k* by the power of God ... 1Pet 1:5 *5432*
by the same word are *k* in store ... 2Pet 3:7 *2343*
the angels which *k* not their ... Jude 6 *5083*
hast *k* my word, and hast not ... Rev 3:8 *5083*
Because thou hast *k* the word of ... Rev 3:10 *5083*

KERAN See CHERAN.

KERCHIEFS
make *k* upon the head of every ... Eze 13:18 4556
Your *k* also will I tear, and ... Eze 13:21 4556

KEREN-HAPPUCH (*ke''-ren-hap'-puk*) *A daughter of Job.*
and the name of the third, *K* ... Job 42:14 7163

KERETHITE See CHERETHITES.

KERETHITES See CHERETHITES.

KERIOTH (*ke'-re-oth*) See ISCARIOT, KIRIOTH.
1. A city in Judah.
And Hazor, Hadattah, and *K*, and ... Josh 15:25 7152
2. A city in Moab.
And upon *K*, and upon Bozrah, and ... Jer 48:24 7152
K is taken, and the strong holds ... Jer 48:41 7152

KERIOTH HEZRON See KERIOTH.

KERITH See CHERITH.

KERNELS
from the *k* even to the husk ... Num 6:4 2785

KEROS (*ke'-ros*) *A family of exiles.*
The children of *K*, the children ... Ezr 2:44 7026
The children of *K*, the children ... Neh 7:47 7026

KERUB See CHERUB.

KESALON See CHESALON.

KESED See CHESED.

KESIL See CHESIL.

KESULLOTH See CHESULLOTH.

KETTLE
he struck it into the pan, or *k* ... 1Sa 2:14 1731

KETURAH (*ket-u'-rah*) *A wife of Abraham.*
took a wife, and her name was *K* ... Gen 25:1 6989
All these were the children of *K* ... Gen 25:4 6989
Now the sons of *K*, Abraham's ... 1Chr 1:32 6989
All these are the sons of *K* ... 1Chr 1:33 6989

KEY
therefore they took a *k*, and ... Judg 3:25 4668
the *k* of the house of David will ... Is 22:22 4668
taken away the *k* of knowledge ... Lk 11:52 *2807*
true, he that hath the *k* of David ... Rev 3:7 *2807*
to him was given the *k* of the ... Rev 9:1 *2807*
having the *k* of the bottomless ... Rev 20:1 *2807*

KEYS
the *k* of the kingdom of heaven ... Mt 16:19 *2807*
and have the *k* of hell and of death ... Rev 1:18 *2807*

KEZIA (*ke-zi'-ah*) *A daughter of Job.*
and the name of the second, *K* ... Job 42:14 7103

KEZIAH See KEZIA.

KEZIB See CHEZIB.

KEZIZ (*ke'-ziz*) *A valley in Benjamin.*
Beth-hoglah, and the valley of *K* ... Josh 18:21 7104

KIBROTH-HATTAAVAH (*kib''-roth-hat-ta'-a-vah*) *A Hebrew encampment in the wilderness.*
called the name of that place *K* ... Num 11:34 6914
journeyed from *K* unto Hazeroth ... Num 11:35 6914
desert of Sinai, and pitched at *K* ... Num 33:16 6914
And they departed from *K*, and ... Num 33:17 6914
at Taberah, and at Massah, and at *K* ... Deut 9:22 6914

KIBZAIM (*kib-za'-im*) See JOKMEAM. *A Levitical city in Ephraim.*
K with her suburbs, and Beth-horon ... Josh 21:22 6911

KICK
Wherefore *k* ye at my sacrifice and ... 1Sa 2:29 1163
for thee to *k* against the pricks ... Acts 9:5 *2979*
for thee to *k* against the pricks ... Acts 26:14 *2979*

KICKED
But Jeshurun waxed fat, and *k* ... Deut 32:15 1163

KID
killed a *k* of the goats, and ... Gen 37:31 8163
will send thee a *k* from the flock ... Gen 38:17 1423
Judah sent the *k* by the hand of ... Gen 38:20 1423
behold, I sent this *k*, and thou ... Gen 38:23 1423
seethe a *k* in his mother's milk ... Ex 23:19 1423
seethe a *k* in his mother's milk ... Ex 34:26 1423
a *k* of the goats, a male without ... Lev 4:23 8163
a *k* of the goats, a female ... Lev 4:28 8166
a lamb or a *k* of the goats, for a ... Lev 5:6 8166
Take ye a *k* of the goats for a ... Lev 9:3 8163
Then ye shall sacrifice one *k* of ... Lev 23:19 8163
One *k* of the goats for a sin ... Num 7:16 8163
One *k* of the goats for a sin ... Num 7:22 8163
One *k* of the goats for a sin ... Num 7:28 8163
One *k* of the goats for a sin ... Num 7:34 8163
One *k* of the goats for a sin ... Num 7:40 8163
One *k* of the goats for a sin ... Num 7:46 8163
One *k* of the goats for a sin ... Num 7:52 8163
One *k* of the goats for a sin ... Num 7:58 8163
One *k* of the goats for a sin ... Num 7:64 8163
One *k* of the goats for a sin ... Num 7:70 8163
One *k* of the goats for a sin ... Num 7:76 8163
One *k* of the goats for a sin ... Num 7:82 8163
one ram, or for a lamb, or a *k* ... Num 15:11 5795
one *k* of the goats for a sin ... Num 15:24 8163
one *k* of the goats for a sin ... Num 28:15 8163
one *k* of the goats, to make an ... Num 28:30 8163
one *k* of the goats for a sin ... Num 29:5 8163
One *k* of the goats for a sin ... Num 29:11 8163
one *k* of the goats for a sin ... Num 29:16 8163
one *k* of the goats for a sin ... Num 29:19 8163
one *k* of the goats for a sin ... Num 29:25 8163
seethe a *k* in his mother's milk ... Deut 14:21 1423
Gideon went in, and made ready a *k* ... Judg 6:19
have made ready a *k* for thee ... Judg 13:15
So Manoah took a *k* with a meat ... Judg 13:19
him as he would have rent a *k* ... Judg 14:6 1423
Samson visited his wife with a *k* ... Judg 15:1
and a bottle of wine, and a *k* ... 1Sa 16:20
leopard shall lie down with the *k* ... Is 11:6 1423
a *k* of the goats without blemish ... Eze 43:22 8163
a *k* of the goats daily for a sin ... Eze 45:23 8163
and yet thou never gavest me a *k* ... Lk 15:29 *2056*

KIDNEYS
is above the liver, and the two *k* ... Ex 29:13 3629
above the liver, and the two *k* ... Ex 29:22 3629
And the two *k*, and the fat that is ... Lev 3:4 3629
caul above the liver, with the *k* ... Lev 3:4 3629
And the two *k*, and the fat that is ... Lev 3:10 3629
caul above the liver, with the *k* ... Lev 3:10 3629
And the two *k*, and the fat that is ... Lev 3:15 3629
caul above the liver, with the *k* ... Lev 3:15 3629
And the two *k*, and the fat that is ... Lev 4:9 3629
caul above the liver, with the *k* ... Lev 4:9 3629
And the two *k*, and the fat that is ... Lev 7:4 3629
is above the liver, with the *k* ... Lev 7:4 3629
above the liver, and the two *k* ... Lev 8:16 3629
above the liver, and the two *k* ... Lev 8:25 3629
But the fat, and the *k*, and the ... Lev 9:10 3629
covereth the inwards, and the *k* ... Lev 9:19 3629
goats, with the fat of *k* of wheat ... Deut 32:14 3629
with the fat of the *k* of rams ... Is 34:6 3629

KIDON

KIDRON (*kid'-ron*) *A brook near Jerusalem.*
himself passed over the brook *K* ... 2Sa 15:23 6939
out, and passest over the brook *K* ... 1Kin 2:37 6939
idol, and burnt it by the brook *K* ... 1Kin 15:13 6939
Jerusalem in the fields of *K* ... 2Kin 23:4 6939
Jerusalem, unto the brook *K* ... 2Kin 23:6 6939
and burned it at the brook *K* ... 2Kin 23:6 6939
the dust of them into the brook *K* ... 2Kin 23:12 6939
it, and burnt it at the brook *K* ... 2Chr 15:16 6939
it out abroad into the brook *K* ... 2Chr 29:16 6939
and cast them into the brook *K* ... 2Chr 30:14 6939
the fields unto the brook of *K* ... Jer 31:40 6939

KIDS
thence two good *k* of the goats ... Gen 27:9 1423
she put the skins of the *k* of the ... Gen 27:16 1423
of the children of Israel two *k* ... Lev 16:5 8163
the *k* of the goats for sin ... Num 7:87 8163
to Beth-el, one carrying three *k* ... 1Sa 10:3 1423
them like two little flocks of *k* ... 1Kin 20:27 5795
people, of the flock, lambs and *k* ... 2Chr 35:7
feed thy *k* beside the shepherds' ... Song 1:8 1423

KILEAB See CHILEAB.

KILION See CHILION.

KILION'S See CHILION'S.

KILL
lest any finding him should *k* him ... Gen 4:15 5221
and they will *k* me, but they will ... Gen 12:12 2026
the place should *k* me for Rebekah ... Gen 26:7 2026
himself, purposing to *k* thee ... Gen 27:42 2026
and said, Let us not *k* him ... Gen 37:21 5221
it be a son, then ye shall *k* him ... Ex 1:16 4191
intendest thou to *k* me, as thou ... Ex 2:14 2026
LORD met him, and sought to *k* him ... Ex 4:24 4191
Israel shall *k* it in the evening ... Ex 12:6 7819
your families, and *k* the passover ... Ex 12:21 7819
to *k* this whole assembly with ... Ex 16:3 4191
us up out of Egypt, to *k* us ... Ex 17:3 4191
Thou shalt not *k* ... Ex 20:13 7523
or a sheep, and *k* it, or sell it ... Ex 22:1 2873
I will *k* you with the sword ... Ex 22:24 2026
thou shalt *k* the bullock before ... Ex 29:11 7819
Then shalt thou *k* the ram ... Ex 29:20 7819
he shall *k* the bullock before the ... Lev 1:5 7819
he shall *k* it on the side of the ... Lev 1:11 7819
and *k* it at the door of the ... Lev 3:2 7819
k it before the tabernacle of the ... Lev 3:8 7819
k it before the tabernacle of the ... Lev 3:13 7819
k the bullock before the LORD ... Lev 4:4 7819
k it in the place where they *k* ... Lev 4:24 7819
where they *k* the burnt offering ... Lev 4:33 7819
In the place where they *k* the ... Lev 7:2 7819
they *k* the trespass offering ... Lev 7:2 7819
where he shall *k* the sin offering ... Lev 14:13 7819
he shall *k* the burnt offering ... Lev 14:19 7819
he shall *k* the lamb of the ... Lev 14:25 7819
he shall *k* the one of the birds ... Lev 14:50 7819
shall *k* the bullock of the sin ... Lev 16:11 7819
Then shall he *k* the goat of the ... Lev 16:15 7819
seed unto Molech, and *k* him not ... Lev 20:4 4191
thereto, thou shalt *k* the woman ... Lev 20:16 2026
be cow or ewe, ye shall not *k* it ... Lev 22:28 7819
k me, I pray thee, out of hand, ... Num 11:15 2026
Now if thou shalt *k* all this ... Num 14:15 4191
to *k* us in the wilderness, except ... Num 16:13 4191
mine hand, for now would I *k* thee ... Num 22:29 2026
Now therefore *k* every male among ... Num 31:17 2026
k every woman that hath known man ... Num 31:17 2026
revenger of blood *k* the slayer ... Num 35:27 7523
which should *k* his neighbour ... Deut 4:42 7523
Thou shalt not *k* ... Deut 5:17 7523
Notwithstanding thou mayest *k* ... Deut 12:15 2076
then thou shalt *k* of thy herd ... Deut 12:21 2076
But thou shalt surely *k* him ... Deut 13:9 2026
I *k*, and I make alive ... Deut 32:39 4191
If the LORD were pleased to *k* us ... Judg 13:23 4191
but surely we will not *k* thee ... Judg 15:13 4191
when it is day, we shall *k* him ... Judg 16:2 2026
to smite of the people, and *k* ... Judg 20:31 2491
k of the men of Israel about ... Judg 20:39 2491
if Saul hear it, he will *k* me ... 1Sa 16:2 2026
able to fight with me, and to *k* me ... 1Sa 17:9 5221
k him, then shall ye be our ... 1Sa 17:9 5221
that they should *k* David ... 1Sa 19:1 4191
Saul my father seeketh to *k* thee ... 1Sa 19:2 4191
why should I *k* thee ... 1Sa 19:17 4191
and some bade me *k* thee ... 1Sa 24:10 2026
God, that thou wilt neither *k* me ... 1Sa 30:15 4191
then *k* him, fear not ... 2Sa 13:28 4191
his brother, that we may *k* him ... 2Sa 14:7 4191
any iniquity in me, let him *k* me ... 2Sa 14:32 4191
us shalt thou *k* any man in Israel ... 2Sa 21:4 4191
sought therefore to *k* Jeroboam ... 1Kin 11:40 4191
king of Judah, and they shall *k* me ... 1Kin 12:27 2026
clothes, and said, Am I God, to *k* ... 2Kin 5:7 4191
and if they *k* us, we shall but die ... 2Kin 7:4 4191
followeth her *k* with the sword ... 2Kin 11:15 4191
So *k* the passover, and sanctify ... 2Chr 35:6 7819
provinces, to destroy, to *k* ... Est 3:13 2026
they watched the house to *k* him ... Ps 59:*t* 4191
A time to *k*, and a time to heal ... Eccl 3:3 2026
I will *k* thy root with famine, and ... Is 14:30 4191
let them *k* sacrifices ... Is 29:1 5362
the wool, ye *k* them that are fed ... Eze 34:3 2076
of old time, Thou shalt not *k* ... Mt 5:21 *5407*

whosoever shall *k* shall be in Mt 5:21 5407
And fear not them which *k* the body Mt 10:28 *615*
but are not able to *k* the soul Mt 10:28 *615*
And they shall *k* him, and the third Mt 17:23 *615*
come, let us *k* him, and let us Mt 21:38 *615*
and some of them ye shall *k* Mt 23:34 *615*
to be afflicted, and shall *k* you Mt 24:9 *615*
take Jesus by subtilty, and *k* him Mt 26:4 *615*
to save life, or to *k* Mk 3:4 *615*
hands of men, and they shall *k* him Mk 9:31 *615*
Do not commit adultery, Do not *k* Mk 10:19 *5407*
spit upon him, and shall *k* him Mk 10:34 *615*
come, let us *k* him, and the Mk 12:7 *615*
afraid of them that *k* the body Lk 12:4 *615*
for Herod will *k* thee Lk 13:31 *615*
hither the fatted calf, and *k* it Lk 15:23 *2380*
Do not commit adultery, Do not *k* Lk 18:20 *5407*
come, let us *k* him, that the Lk 20:14 *615*
sought how they might *k* him Lk 22:2 *337*
the Jews sought the more to *k* him Jn 5:18 *615*
because the Jews sought to *k* him Jn 7:1 *615*
Why go ye about to *k* me Jn 7:19 *615*
who goeth about to *k* thee Jn 7:20 *615*
not this he, whom they seek to *k* Jn 7:25 *615*
said the Jews, Will he *k* himself Jn 8:22 *615*
but ye seek to *k* me, because my Jn 8:37 *615*
But now ye seek to *k* me, a man Jn 8:40 *615*
not, but for to steal, and to *k* Jn 10:10 *2380*
Wilt thou *k* me, as thou diddest Acts 7:28 *337*
the Jews took counsel to *k* him Acts 9:23 *337*
the gates day and night to *k* him Acts 9:24 *337*
Rise, Peter; *k*, and eat Acts 10:13 *2380*
And as they went about to *k* him Acts 21:31 *615*
he come near, are ready to *k* him Acts 23:15 *337*
laying wait in the way to *k* him Acts 25:3 *337*
the temple, and went about to *k* me Acts 26:21 *1315*
counsel was to *k* the prisoners Acts 27:42 *615*
commit adultery, Thou shalt not *k* Rom 13:9 *5407*
adultery, said also, Do not *k* Jas 2:11 *5407*
commit no adultery, yet if thou *k* Jas 2:11 *5407*
ye *k*, and desire to have, and Jas 4:2 *5407*
I will *k* her children with death Rev 2:23 *615*
and that they should *k* one another Rev 6:4 *4969*
to *k* with sword, and with hunger, Rev 6:8 *615*
given that they should not *k* them Rev 9:5 *615*
and shall overcome them, and *k* them Rev 11:7 *615*

KILLED
k a kid of the goats, and dipped Gen 37:31 7819
that he hath *k* a man or a woman Ex 21:29 4191
shall be *k* before the LORD Lev 4:15 7819
is *k* shall the sin offering be Lev 6:25 7819
sin offering be *k* before the LORD Lev 6:25 7819
And he *k* it; and Moses Lev 8:19 7819
that one of the birds be *k* in an Lev 14:5 7819
that was *k* over the running water Lev 14:6 7819
Ye have *k* the people of the LORD Num 16:41 4191
whosoever hath *k* any person Num 31:19 2026
k thee not, know thou and see that 1Sa 24:11 2026
that I have *k* for my shearers 1Sa 25:11 2873
k it, and took flour, and kneaded 1Sa 28:24 2076
thou hast *k* Uriah the Hittite 2Sa 12:9 5221
and smote the Philistine, and *k* him 2Sa 21:17 4191
and because he *k* him 1Kin 16:7 5221
k him, in the twenty and seventh 1Kin 16:10 4191
Thus saith the LORD, Hast thou *k* 1Kin 21:19 7523
he *k* him, and reigned in his room 2Kin 15:25 4191
k Shophach the captain of the 1Chr 19:18 4191
Ahab *k* sheep and oxen for him in 2Chr 18:2 3076
that had *k* the king his father 2Chr 25:3 5221
So they *k* the bullocks, and the 2Chr 29:22 7819
when they had *k* the rams 2Chr 29:22 7819
they *k* also the lambs, and they 2Chr 29:22 7819
And the priests *k* them, and they 2Chr 29:24 7819
Then they *k* the passover on the 2Chr 30:15 7819
they *k* the passover on the 2Chr 35:1 7819
they *k* the passover, and the 2Chr 35:11 7819
k the passover for all the Ezr 6:20 7819
sake are we *k* all the day long Ps 44:22 2026
She hath *k* her beasts Prov 9:2 2873
thou hast *k*, and not pitied Lam 2:21 2873
chief priests and scribes, and be *k* Mt 16:21 *615*
k another, and stoned another Mt 21:35 *615*
my oxen and my fatlings are *k* Mt 22:4 *2380*
of them which *k* the prophets Mt 23:31 *5407*
against him, and would have *k* him Mk 6:19 *615*
priests, and scribes, and be *k* Mk 8:31 *615*
and after that he is *k*, he shall Mk 9:31 *615*
and him they *k*, and many others Mk 12:5 *615*
k him, and cast him out of the Mk 12:8 *615*
when they *k* the passover, his Mk 14:12 *2380*
prophets, and your fathers *k* them Lk 11:47 *615*
for they indeed *k* them, and ye Lk 11:48 *615*
which after he hath *k* hath power Lk 12:5 *615*
thy father hath *k* the fatted calf Lk 15:27 *2380*
thou hast *k* for him the fatted Lk 15:30 *2380*
him out of the vineyard, and *k* him Lk 20:15 *615*
when the passover must be *k* Lk 22:7 *2380*
k the Prince of life, whom God Acts 3:15 *615*
he *k* James the brother of John Acts 12:2 *337*
sword, and would have *k* himself Acts 16:27 *337*
nor drink till they had *k* Paul Acts 23:12 *615*
nor drink till they have *k* him Acts 23:21 *337*
and should have been *k* of them Acts 23:27 *615*
sake we are *k* all the day long Rom 8:36 *2289*
they have *k* thy prophets, and Rom 11:3 *615*
as chastened, and not *k* 2Cor 6:9 *2289*
Who both *k* the Lord Jesus, and 1Th 2:15 *615*
Ye have condemned and *k* the just Jas 5:6 *5407*
that should be *k* as they were Rev 6:11 *615*
three was the third part of men *k* Rev 9:18 *615*
k by these plagues yet repented Rev 9:20 *615*
them, he must in this manner be *k* Rev 11:5 *615*
sword must be *k* with the sword Rev 13:10 *615*
image of the beast should be *k* Rev 13:15 *615*

KILLEDST
kill me, as thou *k* the Egyptian Ex 2:14 2026
me into thine hand, thou *k* me not 1Sa 24:18 2026

KILLEST
thou that *k* the prophets, and Mt 23:37 *615*
which *k* the prophets, and stonest Lk 13:34 *615*

KILLETH
that *k* an ox, or lamb, or goat, Lev 17:3 7819
or that *k* it out of the camp, Lev 17:3 7819
he that *k* any man shall surely be Lev 24:17 5221
he that *k* a beast shall make it Lev 24:18 5221
And he that *k* a beast, he shall Lev 24:21 5221
and he that *k* a man, he shall be Lev 24:21 5221
which *k* any person at unawares Num 35:11 5221
that every one that *k* any person Num 35:15 5221
Whoso *k* any person, the murderer Num 35:30 5221
Whoso *k* his neighbour ignorantly, Deut 19:4 5221
slayer that *k* any person unawares Josh 20:3 5221
that whosoever *k* any person at Josh 20:9 5221
The LORD *k*, and maketh alive 1Sa 2:6 4191
shall be, that the man who *k* him 1Sa 17:25 5221
to the man that *k* this Philistine 1Sa 17:26 5221
it be done to the man that *k* him 1Sa 17:27 5221
For wrath *k* the foolish man, and Job 5:2 2026
rising with the light *k* the poor Job 24:14 6991
The desire of the slothful *k* him Prov 21:25 4191
He that *k* an ox is as if he slew Is 66:3 7819
that whosoever *k* you will think Jn 16:2 *615*
for the letter *k*, but the spirit 2Cor 3:6 *615*
he that *k* with the sword must be Rev 13:10 *615*

KILLING
him in the *k* of his brethren Judg 9:24 2026
Levites had the charge of the *k* 2Chr 30:17 7821
k sheep, eating flesh, and Is 22:13 7819
By swearing, and lying, and *k* Hos 4:2 7523
beating some, and *k* some Mk 12:5 *615*

KILMAD See CHILMAD.

KIMHAM See CHIMHAM.

KIN
to any that is near of *k* to him Lev 18:6 1320
for he uncovereth his near *k* Lev 20:19 7607
But for his *k*, that is near unto Lev 21:2 7607
if any of his *k* come to redeem it Lev 25:25 7138
or any that is nigh of *k* unto him Lev 25:49 1320
her, The man is near of *k* unto us Ruth 2:20
the king is near of *k* to us 2Sa 19:42
own country, and among his own *k* Mk 6:4 4773

KINAH (*ki'-nah*) *A city in Judah.*
And K, and Dimonah, and Adadah, Josh 15:22 7016

KIND
tree yielding fruit after his *k* Gen 1:11 4327
and herb yielding seed after his *k* Gen 1:12 4327
seed was in itself, after his *k* Gen 1:12 4327
forth abundantly, after their *k* Gen 1:21 4327
and every winged fowl after his *k* Gen 1:21 4327
the living creature after his *k* Gen 1:24 4327
and beast of the earth after his *k* Gen 1:24 4327
his *k*, and cattle after their *k* Gen 1:25 4327
upon the earth after his *k* Gen 1:25 4327
Of fowls after their *k* Gen 6:20 4327
and of cattle after their *k* Gen 6:20 4327
thing of the earth after his *k* Gen 6:20 4327
They, and every beast after his *k* Gen 7:14 4327
and all the cattle after their *k* Gen 7:14 4327
upon the earth after his *k* Gen 7:14 4327
and every fowl after his *k* Gen 7:14 4327
vulture, and the kite after his *k* Lev 11:14 4327
Every raven after his *k* Lev 11:15 4327
cuckow, and the hawk after his *k* Lev 11:16 4327
the stork, the heron after her *k* Lev 11:19 4327
the locust after his *k* Lev 11:22 4327
and the bald locust after his *k* Lev 11:22 4327
and the beetle after his *k* Lev 11:22 4327
and the grasshopper after his *k* Lev 11:22 4327
and the tortoise after his *k* Lev 11:29 4327
cattle gender with a diverse *k* Lev 19:19
kite, and the vulture after his *k* Deut 14:13 4327
And every raven after his *k* Deut 14:14 4327
cuckow, and the hawk after his *k* Deut 14:15 4327
stork, and the heron after her *k* Deut 14:18 4327
instruments of every *k* of service 1Chr 28:14
If thou be *k* to this people, and 2Chr 10:7 2896
sellers of all *k* of ware lodged Neh 13:20
trees in them of all *k* of fruits Eccl 2:5
the multitude of all *k* of riches Eze 27:12
the sea, and gathered of every *k* Mt 13:47 *1085*
Howbeit this *k* goeth not out but Mt 17:21 *1085*
This *k* can come forth by nothing, Mk 9:29 *1085*
for he is *k* unto the unthankful Lk 6:35 *5543*
Charity suffereth long, and is *k* 1Cor 13:4 *5541*
there is one *k* of flesh of men 1Cor 15:39
And be ye *k* one to another, Eph 4:32 *5543*
truth, that we should be a *k* of Jas 1:18 *5100*
For every *k* of beasts, and of Jas 3:7 *5449*

KINDLE
Ye shall *k* no fire throughout Ex 35:3 1197
is a contentious man to *k* strife Prov 26:21 2787
shall *k* in the thickets of the Is 9:18 3341
under his glory he shall *k* a Is 10:16 3344
a stream of brimstone, doth *k* it Is 30:33 1197
shall the flame *k* upon thee Is 43:2 1197
Behold, all ye that *k* a fire Is 50:11 6919
wood, and the fathers *k* the fire Jer 7:18 1197
then will I *k* a fire in the gates Jer 17:27 3341
I will *k* a fire in the forest Jer 21:14 3341
to *k* meat offerings, and to do Jer 33:18 6999
I will *k* a fire in the houses of Jer 43:12 3341
I will *k* a fire in the wall of Jer 49:27 3341
I will *k* a fire in his cities, and Jer 50:32 3341
I will *k* a fire in thee, and it Eze 20:47 3341
k the fire, consume the flesh, and Eze 24:10 1814
But I will *k* a fire in the wall Amos 1:14 3341
stubble, and they shall *k* in them Obad 18 1814
neither do ye *k* fire on mine Mal 1:10 215

KINDLED
anger was *k* against Rachel Gen 30:2 2734
that his wrath was *k* Gen 39:19 2734
of the LORD was *k* against Moses Ex 4:14 2734
he that *k* the fire shall surely Ex 22:6 1197
the burning which the LORD hath *k* Lev 10:6 8313
and his anger was *k* Num 11:1 2734
anger of the LORD was *k* greatly Num 11:10 2734
the LORD was *k* against the people Num 11:33 2734
of the LORD was *k* against them Num 12:9 2734
God's anger was *k* because he went Num 22:22 2734
and Balaam's anger was *k*, and he Num 22:27 2734
anger was *k* against Balaam Num 24:10 2734
of the LORD was *k* against Israel Num 25:3 2734
LORD's anger was *k* the same time Num 32:10 2734
LORD's anger was *k* against Israel Num 32:13
LORD thy God be *k* against thee Deut 6:15 2734
of the LORD be *k* against you Deut 7:4 2734
the LORD's wrath be *k* against you Deut 11:17 2734
the LORD was *k* against this land Deut 29:27 2734
Then my anger shall be *k* against Deut 31:17 2734
For a fire is *k* in mine anger Deut 32:22 6919
the anger of the LORD was *k* Josh 7:1 2734
of the LORD be *k* against you Josh 23:16 2734
the son of Ebed, his anger was *k* Judg 9:30 2734
And his anger was *k*, and he went up Judg 14:19 2734
and his anger was *k* greatly 1Sa 11:6 2734
Eliab's anger was *k* against David 1Sa 17:28 2734
anger was *k* against Jonathan 1Sa 20:30 2734
of the LORD was *k* against Uzzah 2Sa 6:7 2734
was greatly *k* against the man 2Sa 12:5 2734
coals were *k* by it 2Sa 22:9 1197
before him were coals of fire *k* 2Sa 22:13 1197
of the LORD was *k* against Israel 2Sa 24:1 2734
of the LORD was *k* against Israel 2Kin 13:3 2734
of the LORD that is *k* against us 2Kin 22:13 3341
shall be *k* against this place 2Kin 22:17 3341
his anger was *k* against Judah 2Kin 23:26 2734
of the LORD was *k* against Uzza 1Chr 13:10 2734
anger was greatly *k* against Judah 2Chr 25:10 2734
of the LORD was *k* against Amaziah 2Chr 25:15 2734
He hath also *k* his wrath against Job 19:11 2734
Then was *k* the wrath of Elihu the Job 32:2 2734
against Job was his wrath *k* Job 32:2 2734
his three friends was his wrath *k* Job 32:3 2734
three men, then his wrath was *k* Job 32:5 2734
My wrath is *k* against thee, and Job 42:7 2734
when his wrath is *k* but a little Ps 2:12 1197
coals were *k* by it Ps 18:8 1197
so a fire was *k* against Jacob Ps 78:21 5400
a fire was *k* in their company Ps 106:18 1197
of the LORD *k* against his people Ps 106:40 2734
when their wrath was *k* against us Ps 124:3 2734
of the LORD *k* against his people Is 5:25 2734
and in the sparks that ye have *k* Is 50:11 1197
tumult he hath *k* fire upon it Jer 11:16 3341
for a fire is *k* in mine anger Jer 15:14 6919
for ye have *k* a fire in mine Jer 17:4 6919
was *k* in the cities of Judah and Jer 44:6 1197
hath *k* a fire in Zion, and it hath Lam 4:11 3341
see that I the LORD have *k* it Eze 20:48 1197
mine anger is *k* against them Hos 8:5 2734
me, my repentings are *k* together Hos 11:8 3648
Mine anger was *k* against the Zec 10:3 2734
what will I, if it be already *k* Lk 12:49 *381*
when they had *k* a fire in the Lk 22:55 *681*
for they *k* a fire, and received us Acts 28:2 *381*

KINDLETH
His breath *k* coals, and a flame Job 41:21 3857
yea, he *k* it, and baketh bread Is 44:15 5400
great a matter a little fire *k* Jas 3:5 *381*

KINDLY
And now if ye will deal *k* and truly Gen 24:49 2617
and spake *k* unto the damsel Gen 34:3
hand under my thigh, and deal *k* Gen 47:29 2617
them, and spake *k* unto them Gen 50:21
us the land, that we will deal *k* Josh 2:14 2617
the LORD deal *k* with you, as ye Ruth 1:8 2617
shalt deal *k* with thy servant 1Sa 20:8 2617
And he spake *k* to him, and set his 2Kin 25:28 2896
spake *k* unto him, and set his Jer 52:32 2896
Be *k* affectioned one to another Rom 12:10 5387

KINDNESS
This is thy *k* which thou shalt Gen 20:13 2617
but according to the *k* that I Gen 21:23 2617
shew *k* unto my master Abraham Gen 24:12 2617
thou hast shewed *k* unto my master Gen 24:14 2617
be well with thee, and shew *k* Gen 40:14 2617
LORD, since I have shewed you *k* Josh 2:12 2617
shew *k* unto my father's house Josh 2:12 2617
Neither shewed they *k* to the Judg 8:35 2617
not left off his *k* to the living Ruth 2:20 2617
for thou hast shewed more *k* in Ruth 3:10 2617
for ye shewed *k* to all the 1Sa 15:6 2617
I live shew me the *k* of the LORD 1Sa 20:14 2617
off thy *k* from my house for ever 1Sa 20:15 2617
have shewed this *k* unto your lord 2Sa 2:5 2617
And now the LORD shew *k* and truth 2Sa 2:6 2617
and I also will requite you this *k* 2Sa 2:6 2896
which against Judah do shew *k* 2Sa 3:8 2617
shew him *k* for Jonathan's sake 2Sa 9:1 2617
I may shew the *k* of God unto him 2Sa 9:3 2617
for I will surely shew thee *k* for 2Sa 9:7 2617
I will shew *k* unto Hanun the son 2Sa 10:2 2617
as his father shewed *k* unto me 2Sa 10:2 2617
Is this thy *k* to thy friend 2Sa 16:17 2617

But shew *k* unto the sons of 1Kin 2:7 2617
hast kept for him this great *k* 1Kin 3:6 2617
I will shew *k* unto Hanun the son 1Chr 19:2 2617
because his father shewed *k* to me 1Chr 19:2 2617
the king remembered not the *k* 2Chr 24:22 2617
slow to anger, and of great *k* Neh 9:17 2617
him, and she obtained *k* of him Est 2:9 2617
his marvellous *k* in a strong city Ps 31:21 2617
For his merciful *k* is great Ps 117:2 2617
thy merciful *k* be for my comfort, Ps 119:76 2617
it shall be a *k* Ps 141:5 2617
The desire of a man is his *k* Prov 19:22 2617
and in her tongue is the law of *k* Prov 31:26 2617
but with everlasting *k* will I Is 54:8 2617
but my *k* shall not depart from Is 54:10 2617
the *k* of thy youth, the love of Jer 2:2 2617
slow to anger, and of great *k* Joel 2:13 2617
slow to anger, and of great *k* Jonah 4:2 2617
people shewed us no little *k* Acts 28:2 *5363*
knowledge, by longsuffering, by *k* 2Cor 6:6 *5544*
riches of his grace in his *k* Eph 2:7 *5544*
and beloved, bowels of mercies, *k* Col 3:12 *5544*
But after that the *k* and love of Titus 3:4 *5544*
And to godliness brotherly *k* 2Pet 1:7 *5360*
and to brotherly *k* charity 2Pet 1:7 *5360*

KINDRED

out of thy country, and from thy *k* Gen 12:1 4138
go unto my country, and to my *k* Gen 24:4 4138
house, and from the land of my *k* Gen 24:7 4138
my father's house, and to my *k* Gen 24:38 4940
take a wife for my son of my *k* Gen 24:40 4940
my oath, when thou comest to my *k* Gen 24:41 4940
land of thy fathers, and to thy *k* Gen 31:3 4138
and return unto the land of thy *k* Gen 31:13 4138
unto thy country, and to thy *k* Gen 32:9 4138
of our state, and of our *k* Gen 43:7 4138
to mine own land, and to my *k* Num 10:30 4138
and they brought out all her *k* Josh 6:23 4940
who was of the *k* of Elimelech Ruth 2:3 4940
And now is not Boaz of our *k* Ruth 3:2 4130
the *k* of Saul, three thousand 1Chr 12:29 250
not shewed her people nor her *k* Est 2:10 4138
yet shewed her *k* nor her people Est 2:20 4138
to see the destruction of my *k* Est 8:6 4138
the Buzite, of the *k* of Ram Job 32:2 4940
thy brethren, the men of thy *k* Eze 11:15 1353
There is none of thy *k* that is Lk 1:61 *4772*
were of the *k* of the high priest Acts 4:6 *1085*
out of thy country, and from thy *k* Acts 7:3 *4772*
Joseph's *k* was made known unto Acts 7:13 *1085*
father Jacob to him, and all his *k* Acts 7:14 *4772*
same dealt subtilly with our *k* Acts 7:19 *1085*
God by thy blood out of every *k* Rev 5:9 *5443*
earth, and to every nation, and *k* Rev 14:6 *5443*

KINDREDS

ye *k* of the people, give unto the 1Chr 16:28 4940
all the *k* of the nations shall Ps 22:27 4940
O ye *k* of the people, give unto Ps 96:7 4940
all the *k* of the earth be blessed Acts 3:25 *3965*
all *k* of the earth shall wail Rev 1:7 *5443*
number, of all nations, and *k* Rev 7:9 *5443*
And they of the people and *k* Rev 11:9 *5443*
and power was given him over all *k* Rev 13:7 *5443*

KINDS

upon the earth, after their *k* Gen 8:19 4940
divers *k* of spices prepared by 2Chr 16:14 2177
I will appoint over them four *k* Jer 15:3 4940
shall be according to their *k* Eze 47:10 4327
all *k* of musick, ye fall down and Dan 3:5 2177
all *k* of musick, all the people, Dan 3:7 2177
all *k* of musick, shall fall down Dan 3:10 2177
all *k* of musick, ye fall down and Dan 3:15 2177
to another divers *k* of tongues 1Cor 12:10 *1085*
so many *k* of voices in the world, 1Cor 14:10 *1085*

KINE

camels with their colts, forty *k* Gen 32:15 6510
the river seven well favoured *k* Gen 41:2 6510
seven other *k* came up after them Gen 41:3 6510
stood by the other *k* upon the Gen 41:3 6510
leanfleshed *k* did eat up the Gen 41:4 6510
the seven well favoured and fat *k* Gen 41:4 6510
came up out of the river seven *k* Gen 41:18 6510
seven other *k* came up after them, Gen 41:19 6510
the ill favoured *k* did eat up the Gen 41:20 6510
did eat up the first seven fat *k* Gen 41:20 6510
The seven good *k* are seven years Gen 41:26 6510
ill favoured *k* that came up after Gen 41:27 6510
thine oil, the increase of thy *k* Deut 7:13 504
thy cattle, the increase of thy *k* Deut 28:4 504
thy land, the increase of thy *k* Deut 28:18 504
or oil, or the increase of thy *k* Deut 28:51 504
Butter of *k*, and milk of sheep, Deut 32:14 1241
a new cart, and take two milch *k* 1Sa 6:7 6510
tie the *k* to the cart, and bring 1Sa 6:7 6510
and took two milch *k*, and tied them 1Sa 6:10 6510
the *k* took the straight way to 1Sa 6:12 6510
offered the *k* a burnt offering 1Sa 6:14 6510
butter, and sheep, and cheese of *k* 2Sa 17:29 1241
ye *k* of Bashan, that are in the Amos 4:1 6510

KING

the days of Amraphel *k* of Shinar Gen 14:1 4428
Arioch *k* of Ellasar, Chedorlaomer Gen 14:1 4428
Ellasar, Chedorlaomer *k* of Elam Gen 14:1 4428
of Elam, and Tidal *k* of nations Gen 14:1 4428
made war with Bera *k* of Sodom Gen 14:2 4428
and with Birsha *k* of Gomorrah Gen 14:2 4428
Shinab *k* of Admah Gen 14:2 4428
Shemeber *k* of Zeboiim Gen 14:2 4428
the *k* of Bela, which is Zoar Gen 14:2 4428
And there went out the *k* of Sodom Gen 14:8 4428
the *k* of Gomorrah Gen 14:8 4428
the *k* of Admah Gen 14:8 4428
the *k* of Zeboiim Gen 14:8 4428
the *k* of Bela (the same is Zoar Gen 14:8 4428
With Chedorlaomer the *k* of Elam Gen 14:9 4428
and with Tidal *k* of nations Gen 14:9 4428
Amraphel *k* of Shinar, and Arioch Gen 14:9 4428
of Shinar, and Arioch *k* of Ellasar Gen 14:9 4428
the *k* of Sodom went out to meet Gen 14:17 4428
Melchizedek *k* of Salem brought Gen 14:18 4428
the *k* of Sodom said unto Abram, Gen 14:21 4428
And Abram said to the *k* of Sodom Gen 14:22 4428
Abimelech *k* of Gerar sent, and Gen 20:2 4428
Isaac went unto Abimelech *k* of Gen 26:1 4428
time, that Abimelech *k* of the Gen 26:8 4428
before there reigned any *k* over Gen 36:31 4428
that the butler of the *k* of Egypt Gen 40:1 4428
their lord the *k* of Egypt Gen 40:1 4428
and the baker of the *k* of Egypt Gen 40:5 4428
stood before Pharaoh *k* of Egypt Gen 41:46 4428
there arose up a new *k* over Egypt Ex 1:8 4428
the *k* of Egypt spake to the Ex 1:15 4428
did not as the *k* of Egypt Ex 1:17 4428
the *k* of Egypt called for the Ex 1:18 4428
of time, that the *k* of Egypt died Ex 2:23 4428
of Israel, unto the *k* of Egypt Ex 3:18 4428
I am sure that the *k* of Egypt Ex 3:19 4428
the *k* of Egypt said unto them, Ex 5:4 4428
in, speak unto Pharaoh *k* of Egypt Ex 6:11 4428
and unto Pharaoh *k* of Egypt Ex 6:13 4428
which spake to Pharaoh *k* of Egypt Ex 6:27 4428
speak thou unto Pharaoh *k* of Ex 6:29 4428
it was told the *k* of Egypt that Ex 14:5 4428
the heart of Pharaoh *k* of Egypt Ex 14:8 4428
from Kadesh unto the *k* of Edom Num 20:14 4428
when *k* Arad the Canaanite, which Num 21:1 4428
unto Sihon *k* of the Amorites Num 21:21 4428
of Sihon the *k* of the Amorites Num 21:26 4428
against the former *k* of Moab Num 21:26 4428
unto Sihon *k* of the Amorites Num 21:29 4428
Og the *k* of Bashan went out Num 21:33 4428
unto Sihon *k* of the Amorites Num 21:34 4428
Balak the son of Zippor was *k* of Num 22:4 4428
k of Moab, hath sent unto me, Num 22:10 4428
Balak the *k* of Moab hath brought Num 23:7 4428
and the shout of a *k* is among them Num 23:21 4428
his *k* shall be higher than Agag, Num 24:7 4428
of Sihon *k* of the Amorites Num 32:33 4428
and the kingdom of Og *k* of Bashan Num 32:33 4428
k Arad the Canaanite, which dwelt Num 33:40 4428
slain Sihon the *k* of the Amorites Deut 1:4 4428
Og the *k* of Bashan, which dwelt Deut 1:4 4428
k of Heshbon, and his land Deut 2:24 4428
of Kedemoth unto Sihon *k* of Deut 2:26 4428
But Sihon *k* of Heshbon would not Deut 2:30 4428
Og the *k* of Bashan came out Deut 3:1 4428
unto Sihon *k* of the Amorites Deut 3:2 4428
the *k* of Bashan, and all his Deut 3:3 4428
as we did unto Sihon *k* of Heshbon Deut 3:6 4428
For only Og *k* of Bashan remained Deut 3:11 4428
land of Sihon *k* of the Amorites Deut 4:46 4428
and the land of Og *k* of Bashan Deut 4:47 4428
the hand of Pharaoh *k* of Egypt Deut 7:8 4428
Egypt unto Pharaoh *k* of Egypt Deut 11:3 4428
shalt say, I will set a *k* over me Deut 17:14 4428
in any wise set him *k* over thee Deut 17:15 4428
shalt thou set *k* over thee Deut 17:15 4428
thy *k* which thou shalt set over Deut 28:36 4428
Sihon the *k* of Heshbon Deut 29:7 4428
Og the *k* of Bashan, came out Deut 29:7 4428
he was *k* in Jeshurun, when the Deut 33:5 4428
And it was told the *k* of Jericho Josh 2:2 4428
the *k* of Jericho sent unto Rahab, Josh 2:3 4428
the *k* thereof, and the mighty men Josh 6:2 4428
given into thy hand the *k* of Ai Josh 8:1 4428
her *k* as thou didst unto Jericho Josh 8:2 4428
thou didst unto Jericho and her *k* Josh 8:2 4428
when the *k* of Ai saw it, that Josh 8:14 4428
the *k* of Ai they took alive, and Josh 8:23 4428
the *k* of Ai he hanged on a tree Josh 8:29 4428
to Sihon *k* of Heshbon Josh 9:10 4428
to Og *k* of Bashan, which was at Josh 9:10 4428
when Adoni-zedek *k* of Jerusalem Josh 10:1 4428
he had done to Jericho and her *k* Josh 10:1 4428
so he had done to Ai and her *k* Josh 10:1 4428
Wherefore Adoni-zedek *k* of Josh 10:3 4428
sent unto Hoham *k* of Hebron Josh 10:3 4428
and unto Piram *k* of Jarmuth Josh 10:3 4428
and unto Japhia *k* of Lachish Josh 10:3 4428
and unto Debir *k* of Eglon Josh 10:3 4428
the *k* of Jerusalem Josh 10:5 4428
the *k* of Hebron Josh 10:5 4428
the *k* of Jarmuth Josh 10:5 4428
the *k* of Lachish Josh 10:5 4428
the *k* of Eglon, gathered Josh 10:5 4428
the *k* of Jerusalem Josh 10:23 4428
the *k* of Hebron Josh 10:23 4428
the *k* of Jarmuth Josh 10:23 4428
the *k* of Lachish Josh 10:23 4428
and the *k* of Eglon Josh 10:23 4428
and the *k* thereof he utterly Josh 10:28 4428
he did to the *k* of Makkedah as he Josh 10:28 4428
as he did unto the *k* of Jericho Josh 10:28 4428
the *k* thereof, into the hand of Josh 10:30 4428
but did unto the *k* thereof as he Josh 10:30 4428
as he did unto the *k* of Jericho Josh 10:30 4428
Then Horam *k* of Gezer came up to Josh 10:33 4428
the *k* thereof, and all the cities Josh 10:37 4428
the *k* thereof, and all the cities Josh 10:39 4428
did to Debir, and to the *k* thereof Josh 10:39 4428
done also to Libnah, and to her *k* Josh 10:39 4428
when Jabin *k* of Hazor had heard Josh 11:1 4428
that he sent to Jobab *k* of Madon Josh 11:1 4428
to the *k* of Shimron Josh 11:1 4428
and to the *k* of Achshaph Josh 11:1 4428
smote the *k* thereof with the Josh 11:10 4428
Sihon *k* of the Amorites, who Josh 12:2 4428
And the coast of Og *k* of Bashan Josh 12:4 4428
the border of Sihon *k* of Heshbon Josh 12:5 4428
The *k* of Jericho, one Josh 12:9 4428
the *k* of Ai, which is beside Josh 12:9 4428
The *k* of Jerusalem, one Josh 12:10 4428
the *k* of Hebron, one Josh 12:10 4428
The *k* of Jarmuth, one Josh 12:11 4428
the *k* of Lachish, one Josh 12:11 4428
The *k* of Eglon, one Josh 12:12 4428
the *k* of Gezer, one Josh 12:12 4428
The *k* of Debir, one Josh 12:13 4428
the *k* of Geder, one Josh 12:13 4428
The *k* of Hormah, one Josh 12:14 4428
the *k* of Arad, one Josh 12:14 4428
The *k* of Libnah, one Josh 12:15 4428
the *k* of Adullam, one Josh 12:15 4428
The *k* of Makkedah, one Josh 12:16 4428
the *k* of Beth-el, one Josh 12:16 4428
The *k* of Tappuah, one Josh 12:17 4428
the *k* of Hepher, one Josh 12:17 4428
The *k* of Aphek, one Josh 12:18 4428
the *k* of Lasharon, one Josh 12:18 4428
The *k* of Madon, one Josh 12:19 4428
the *k* of Hazor, one Josh 12:19 4428
The *k* of Shimron-meron, one Josh 12:20 4428
the *k* of Achshaph, one Josh 12:20 4428
The *k* of Taanach, one Josh 12:21 4428
the *k* of Megiddo, one Josh 12:21 4428
The *k* of Kedesh, one Josh 12:22 4428
the *k* of Jokneam of Carmel, one Josh 12:22 4428
The *k* of Dor in the coast of Dor, Josh 12:23 4428
the *k* of the nations of Gilgal, Josh 12:23 4428
The *k* of Tirzah, one Josh 12:24 4428
cities of Sihon *k* of the Amorites Josh 13:10 4428
of Sihon *k* of the Amorites Josh 13:21 4428
the kingdom of Sihon *k* of Heshbon Josh 13:27 4428
all the kingdom of Og *k* of Bashan Josh 13:30 4428
k of Moab, arose and warred Josh 24:9 4428
k of Mesopotamia Judg 3:8 4428
k of Mesopotamia into his hand Judg 3:10 4428
the *k* of Moab against Israel Judg 3:12 4428
the *k* of Moab eighteen years Judg 3:14 4428
present unto Eglon the *k* of Moab Judg 3:15 4428
the present unto Eglon *k* of Moab Judg 3:17 4428
a secret errand unto thee, O *k* Judg 3:19 4428
the hand of Jabin *k* of Canaan Judg 4:2 4428
between Jabin the *k* of Hazor Judg 4:17 4428
k of Canaan before the children Judg 4:23 4428
against Jabin the *k* of Canaan Judg 4:24 4428
had destroyed Jabin *k* of Canaan Judg 4:24 4428
one resembled the children of a *k* Judg 8:18 4428
and went, and made Abimelech *k* Judg 9:6 4428
on a time to anoint a *k* over them Judg 9:8 4428
in truth ye anoint me *k* over you Judg 9:15 4428
in that ye have made Abimelech *k* Judg 9:16 4427
k over the men of Shechem, Judg 9:18 4427
the *k* of the children of Ammon Judg 11:12 4428
the *k* of the children of Ammon Judg 11:13 4428
the *k* of the children of Ammon Judg 11:14 4428
messengers unto the *k* of Edom Judg 11:17 4428
but the *k* of Edom would not Judg 11:17 4428
they sent unto the *k* of Moab Judg 11:17 4428
unto Sihon *k* of the Amorites Judg 11:19 4428
of the Amorites, the *k* of Heshbon Judg 11:19 4428
the son of Zippor, *k* of Moab Judg 11:25 4428
Howbeit the *k* of the children of Judg 11:28 4428
days there was no *k* in Israel Judg 17:6 4428
days there was no *k* in Israel Judg 18:1 4428
when there was no *k* in Israel Judg 19:1 4428
days there was no *k* in Israel Judg 21:25 4428
he shall give strength unto his *k* 1Sa 2:10 4428
now make us a *k* to judge us like 1Sa 8:5 4428
said, Give us a *k* to judge us 1Sa 8:6 4428
the *k* that shall reign over them 1Sa 8:9 4428
the people that asked of him a *k* 1Sa 8:10 4428
the *k* that shall reign over you 1Sa 8:11 4428
k which ye shall have chosen you 1Sa 8:18 4428
but we will have a *k* over us 1Sa 8:19 4428
that our *k* may judge us, and go 1Sa 8:20 4428
their voice, and make them a *k* 1Sa 8:22 4428
him, Nay, but set a *k* over us 1Sa 10:19 4428
shouted, and said, God save the *k* 1Sa 10:24 4428
there they made Saul *k* before the 1Sa 11:15 4427
me, and have made a *k* over you 1Sa 12:1 4428
behold, the *k* walketh before you 1Sa 12:2 4428
and into the hand of the *k* of Moab 1Sa 12:9 4428
when ye saw that Nahash the *k* of 1Sa 12:12 4428
but a *k* shall reign over us 1Sa 12:12 4428
when the LORD your God was your *k* 1Sa 12:12 4428
behold the *k* whom ye have chosen 1Sa 12:13 4428
the LORD hath set a *k* over you 1Sa 12:13 4428
also the *k* that reigneth over you 1Sa 12:14 4428
of the LORD, in asking you a *k* 1Sa 12:17 4428
our sins this evil, to ask us a *k* 1Sa 12:19 4428
be consumed, both ye and your *k* 1Sa 12:25 4428
thee to be *k* over his people 1Sa 15:1 4428
he took Agag the *k* of the 1Sa 15:8 4428
that I have set up Saul to be *k* 1Sa 15:11 4428
LORD anointed thee *k* over Israel 1Sa 15:17 4428
have brought Agag the *k* of Amalek 1Sa 15:20 4428
also rejected thee from being *k* 1Sa 15:23 4428
thee from being *k* over Israel 1Sa 15:26 4428
me Agag the *k* of the Amalekites 1Sa 15:32 4428
he had made Saul *k* over Israel 1Sa 15:35 4427
provided me a *k* among his sons 1Sa 16:1 4428
the *k* will enrich him with great 1Sa 17:25 4428
said, As thy soul liveth, O *k* 1Sa 17:55 4428
the *k* said, Enquire thou whose 1Sa 17:56 4428
and dancing, to meet *k* Saul 1Sa 18:6 4428
I should be son in law to the *k* 1Sa 18:18 4428
the *k* hath delight in thee, and 1Sa 18:22 4428
The *k* desireth not any dowry, but 1Sa 18:25 4428

gave them in full tale to the *k*	1Sa 18:27	4428
Let not the *k* sin against his	1Sa 19:4	4428
fail to sit with the *k* at meat	1Sa 20:5	4428
the *k* sat him down to eat meat	1Sa 20:24	4428
the *k* sat upon his seat, as at	1Sa 20:25	4428
The *k* hath commanded me a	1Sa 21:2	4428
and went to Achish the *k* of Gath	1Sa 21:10	4428
not this David the *k* of the land	1Sa 21:11	4428
afraid of Achish the *k* of Gath	1Sa 21:12	4428
and he said unto the *k* of Moab	1Sa 22:3	4428
brought them before the *k* of Moab	1Sa 22:4	4428
Then the *k* sent to call Ahimelech	1Sa 22:11	4428
and they came all of them to the *k*	1Sa 22:11	4428
Then Ahimelech answered the *k*	1Sa 22:14	4428
let not the *k* impute any thing	1Sa 22:15	4428
the *k* said, Thou shalt surely die	1Sa 22:16	4428
the *k* said unto the footmen that	1Sa 22:17	4428
But the servants of the *k* would	1Sa 22:17	4428
the *k* said to Doeg, Turn thou, and	1Sa 22:18	4428
and thou shalt be *k* over Israel	1Sa 23:17	4427
Now therefore, O *k*, come down	1Sa 23:20	4428
after Saul, saying, My lord the *k*	1Sa 24:8	4428
After whom is the *k* of Israel	1Sa 24:14	4428
well that thou shalt surely be *k*	1Sa 24:20	4428
his house, like the feast of a *k*	1Sa 25:36	4428
Who art thou that criest to the *k*	1Sa 26:14	4428
hast thou not kept thy lord the *k*	1Sa 26:15	4428
in to destroy the *k* thy lord	1Sa 26:15	4428
It is my voice, my lord, O *k*	1Sa 26:17	4428
let my lord the *k* hear the words	1Sa 26:19	4428
for the *k* of Israel is come out	1Sa 26:20	4428
the son of Maoch, *k* of Gath	1Sa 27:2	4428
the *k* said unto her, Be not	1Sa 28:13	4428
servant of Saul the *k* of Israel	1Sa 29:3	4428
the enemies of my lord the *k*	1Sa 29:8	4428
David *k* over the house of Judah	2Sa 2:4	4428
have anointed me *k* over them	2Sa 2:7	4428
made him *k* over Gilead, and over	2Sa 2:9	4427
the time that David was *k* in	2Sa 2:11	4428
daughter of Talmai *k* of Geshur	2Sa 3:3	4428
in times past to be *k* over you	2Sa 3:17	4428
all Israel unto my lord the *k*	2Sa 3:21	4428
the son of Ner came to the *k*	2Sa 3:23	4428
Then Joab came to the *k*, and said,	2Sa 3:24	4428
k David himself followed the bier	2Sa 3:31	4428
the *k* lifted up his voice, and	2Sa 3:32	4428
the *k* lamented over Abner, and	2Sa 3:33	4428
as whatsoever the *k* did pleased	2Sa 3:36	4428
k to slay Abner the son of Ner	2Sa 3:37	4428
the *k* said unto his servants,	2Sa 3:38	4428
this day weak, though anointed *k*	2Sa 3:39	4428
David to Hebron, and said to the *k*	2Sa 4:8	4428
my lord the *k* this day of Saul	2Sa 4:8	4428
past, when Saul was *k* over us	2Sa 5:2	4428
of Israel came to the *k* to Hebron	2Sa 5:3	4428
k David made a league with them	2Sa 5:3	4428
they anointed David *k* over Israel	2Sa 5:3	4428
And the *k* and his men went to	2Sa 5:6	4428
Hiram *k* of Tyre sent messengers	2Sa 5:11	4428
had established him *k* over Israel	2Sa 5:12	4428
had anointed David *k* over Israel	2Sa 5:17	4428
And it was told *k* David, saying,	2Sa 6:12	4428
saw *k* David leaping and dancing	2Sa 6:16	4428
was the *k* of Israel today	2Sa 6:20	4428
when the *k* sat in his house, and	2Sa 7:1	4428
That the *k* said unto Nathan the	2Sa 7:2	4428
And Nathan said to the *k*, Go, do	2Sa 7:3	4428
Then went *k* David in, and sat	2Sa 7:18	4428
k of Zobah, as he went to recover	2Sa 8:3	4428
to succour Hadadezer *k* of Zobah	2Sa 8:5	4428
k David took exceeding much brass	2Sa 8:8	4428
When Toi *k* of Hamath heard that	2Sa 8:9	4428
sent Joram his son unto *k* David	2Sa 8:10	4428
Which also *k* David did dedicate	2Sa 8:11	4428
son of Rehob, *k* of Zobah	2Sa 8:12	4428
the *k* said unto him, Art thou	2Sa 9:2	4428
the *k* said, is there not yet any	2Sa 9:3	4428
And Ziba said unto the *k*, Jonathan	2Sa 9:3	4428
the *k* said unto him, Where is he	2Sa 9:4	4428
And Ziba said unto the *k*, Behold,	2Sa 9:4	4428
Then *k* David sent, and fetched him	2Sa 9:5	4428
Then the *k* called to Ziba, Saul's	2Sa 9:9	4428
Then said Ziba unto the *k*	2Sa 9:11	4428
to all that my lord the *k* hath	2Sa 9:11	4428
As for Mephibosheth, said the *k*	2Sa 9:11	4428
that the *k* of the children of	2Sa 10:1	4428
the *k* said, Tarry at Jericho	2Sa 10:5	4428
of *k* Maacah a thousand men, and of	2Sa 10:6	4428
him a mess of meat from the *k*	2Sa 11:8	4428
the matters of the war unto the *k*	2Sa 11:19	4428
I anointed thee *k* over Israel	2Sa 12:7	4428
when the *k* was come to see him,	2Sa 13:6	4428
to see him, Amnon said unto the *k*	2Sa 13:6	4428
I pray thee, speak unto the *k*	2Sa 13:13	4428
But when *k* David heard of all	2Sa 13:21	4428
And Absalom came to the *k*, and said	2Sa 13:24	4428
let the *k*, I beseech thee, and his	2Sa 13:24	4428
the *k* said to Absalom, Nay, my	2Sa 13:25	4428
the *k* said unto him, Why should	2Sa 13:26	4428
Then the *k* arose, and tare his	2Sa 13:31	4428
the *k* take the thing to his heart	2Sa 13:33	4428
And Jonadab said unto the *k*	2Sa 13:35	4428
the *k* also and all his servants	2Sa 13:36	4428
the son of Ammihud, *k* of Geshur	2Sa 13:37	4428
the soul of *k* David longed to go	2Sa 13:39	4428
And come to the *k*, and speak on	2Sa 14:3	4428
woman of Tekoah spake to the *k*	2Sa 14:4	4428
did obeisance, and said, Help, O *k*	2Sa 14:4	4428
the *k* said unto her, What aileth	2Sa 14:5	4428
the *k* said unto the woman, Go to	2Sa 14:8	4428
said unto the *k*, My lord, O *k*	2Sa 14:9	4428
and the *k* and his throne be	2Sa 14:9	4428
the *k* said, Whosoever saith ought	2Sa 14:10	4428
let the *k* remember the LORD thy	2Sa 14:11	4428
speak one word unto my lord the *k*	2Sa 14:12	4428
for the *k* doth speak this thing	2Sa 14:13	4428
in that the *k* doth not fetch home	2Sa 14:13	4428
of this thing unto my lord the *k*	2Sa 14:15	4428
said, I will now speak unto the *k*	2Sa 14:15	4428
it may be that the *k* will perform	2Sa 14:15	4428
For the *k* will hear, to deliver	2Sa 14:16	4428
The word of my lord the *k* shall	2Sa 14:17	4428
is my lord the *k* to discern good	2Sa 14:17	4428
Then the *k* answered and said unto	2Sa 14:18	4428
said, Let my lord the *k* now speak	2Sa 14:18	4428
the *k* said, Is not the hand of	2Sa 14:19	4428
As thy soul liveth, my lord the *k*	2Sa 14:19	4428
that my lord the *k* hath spoken	2Sa 14:19	4428
the *k* said unto Joab, Behold now,	2Sa 14:21	4428
bowed himself, and thanked the *k*	2Sa 14:22	4428
grace in thy sight, my lord, O *k*	2Sa 14:22	4428
in that the *k* hath fulfilled the	2Sa 14:22	4428
the *k* said, Let him turn to his	2Sa 14:24	4428
Joab, to have sent him to the *k*	2Sa 14:29	4428
that I may send thee to the *k*	2Sa 14:32	4428
So Joab came to the *k*, and told	2Sa 14:33	4428
for Absalom, he came to the *k*	2Sa 14:33	4428
face to the ground before the *k*	2Sa 14:33	4428
and the *k* kissed Absalom	2Sa 14:33	4428
came to the *k* for judgment	2Sa 15:2	4428
man deputed of the *k* to hear thee	2Sa 15:3	4428
that came to the *k* for judgment	2Sa 15:6	4428
that Absalom said unto the *k*	2Sa 15:7	4428
the *k* said unto him, Go in peace	2Sa 15:9	4428
king's servants said unto the *k*	2Sa 15:15	4428
my lord the *k* shall appoint	2Sa 15:15	4428
the *k* went forth, and all his	2Sa 15:16	4428
the *k* left ten women, which were	2Sa 15:16	4428
the *k* went forth, and all the	2Sa 15:17	4428
from Gath, passed on before the *k*	2Sa 15:18	4428
Then said the *k* to Ittai the	2Sa 15:19	4428
to thy place, and abide with the *k*	2Sa 15:19	4428
And Ittai answered the *k*, and said,	2Sa 15:21	4428
and as my lord the *k* liveth	2Sa 15:21	4428
what place my lord the *k* shall be	2Sa 15:21	4428
the *k* also himself passed over	2Sa 15:23	4428
the *k* said unto Zadok, Carry back	2Sa 15:25	4428
The *k* said also unto Zadok the	2Sa 15:27	4428
I will be thy servant, O *k*	2Sa 15:34	4428
the *k* said unto Ziba, What	2Sa 16:2	4428
the *k* said, And where is thy	2Sa 16:3	4428
And Ziba said unto the *k*, Behold,	2Sa 16:3	4428
Then said the *k* to Ziba, Behold,	2Sa 16:4	4428
grace in thy sight, my lord, O *k*	2Sa 16:4	4428
when *k* David came to Bahurim,	2Sa 16:5	4428
and at all the servants of *k* David	2Sa 16:6	4428
the son of Zeruiah unto the *k*	2Sa 16:9	4428
this dead dog curse my lord the *k*	2Sa 16:9	4428
the *k* said, What have I to do	2Sa 16:10	4428
And the *k*, and all the people that	2Sa 16:14	4428
God save the *k*, God save the *k*	2Sa 16:16	4428
and I will smite the *k* only	2Sa 17:2	4428
lest the *k* be swallowed up, and	2Sa 17:16	4428
and they went and told *k* David	2Sa 17:17	4428
told *k* David, and said unto David,	2Sa 17:21	4428
the *k* said unto the people, I	2Sa 18:2	4428
the *k* said unto them, What	2Sa 18:4	4428
the *k* stood by the gate side, and	2Sa 18:4	4428
the *k* commanded Joab and Abishai	2Sa 18:5	4428
k gave all the captains charge	2Sa 18:5	4428
in our hearing the *k* charged thee	2Sa 18:12	4428
there is no matter hid from the *k*	2Sa 18:13	4428
me now run, and bear the *k* tidings	2Sa 18:19	4428
Go tell the *k* what thou hast seen	2Sa 18:21	4428
the watchman cried, and told the *k*	2Sa 18:25	4428
the *k* said, If he be alone, there	2Sa 18:25	4428
the *k* said, He also bringeth	2Sa 18:26	4428
the *k* said, He is a good man, and	2Sa 18:27	4428
called, and said unto the *k*	2Sa 18:28	4428
earth upon his face before the *k*	2Sa 18:28	4428
their hand against my lord the *k*	2Sa 18:28	4428
the *k* said, Is the young man	2Sa 18:29	4428
the *k* said unto him, Turn aside,	2Sa 18:30	4428
said, Tidings, my lord the *k*	2Sa 18:31	4428
the *k* said unto Cushi, Is the	2Sa 18:32	4428
The enemies of my lord the *k*	2Sa 18:32	4428
the *k* was much moved, and went up	2Sa 18:33	4428
the *k* weepeth and mourneth for	2Sa 19:1	4428
how the *k* was grieved for his son	2Sa 19:2	4428
But the *k* covered his face, and	2Sa 19:4	4428
the *k* cried with a loud voice, O	2Sa 19:4	4428
Joab came into the house to the *k*	2Sa 19:5	4428
Then the *k* arose, and sat in the	2Sa 19:8	4428
the *k* doth sit in the gate	2Sa 19:8	4428
all the people came before the *k*	2Sa 19:8	4428
The *k* saved us out of the hand of	2Sa 19:9	4428
not a word of bringing the *k* back	2Sa 19:10	4428
k David sent to Zadok and to	2Sa 19:11	4428
to bring the *k* back to his house	2Sa 19:11	4428
of all Israel is come to the *k*	2Sa 19:11	4428
ye the last to bring back the *k*	2Sa 19:12	4428
they sent this word unto the *k*	2Sa 19:14	4428
So the *k* returned, and came to	2Sa 19:15	4428
to Gilgal, to go to meet the *k*	2Sa 19:15	4428
to conduct the *k* over Jordan	2Sa 19:15	4428
the men of Judah to meet *k* David	2Sa 19:16	4428
went over Jordan before the *k*	2Sa 19:17	4428
of Gera fell down before the *k*	2Sa 19:18	4428
And said unto the *k*, Let not my	2Sa 19:19	4428
lord the *k* went out of Jerusalem	2Sa 19:19	4428
that the *k* should take it to his	2Sa 19:19	4428
to go down to meet my lord the *k*	2Sa 19:20	4428
that I am this day *k* over Israel	2Sa 19:22	4428
Therefore the *k* said unto Shimei,	2Sa 19:23	4428
And the *k* sware unto him	2Sa 19:23	4428
of Saul came down to meet the *k*	2Sa 19:24	4428
from the day the *k* departed until	2Sa 19:24	4428
come to Jerusalem to meet the *k*	2Sa 19:25	4428
that the *k* said unto him,	2Sa 19:25	4428
And he answered, My lord, O *k*	2Sa 19:26	4428
may ride thereon, and go to the *k*	2Sa 19:26	4428
thy servant unto my lord the *k*	2Sa 19:27	4428
but my lord the *k* is as an angel	2Sa 19:27	4428
but dead men before my lord the *k*	2Sa 19:28	4428
I yet to cry any more unto the *k*	2Sa 19:28	4428
the *k* said unto him, Why speakest	2Sa 19:29	4428
And Mephibosheth said unto the *k*	2Sa 19:30	4428
forasmuch as my lord the *k* is	2Sa 19:30	4428
and went over Jordan with the *k*	2Sa 19:31	4428
and he had provided the *k* of	2Sa 19:32	4428
the *k* said unto Barzillai, Come	2Sa 19:33	4428
And Barzillai said unto the *k*	2Sa 19:34	4428
go up with the *k* unto Jerusalem	2Sa 19:34	4428
yet a burden unto my lord the *k*	2Sa 19:35	4428
little way over Jordan with the *k*	2Sa 19:36	4428
why should the *k* recompense it me	2Sa 19:36	4428
him go over with my lord the *k*	2Sa 19:37	4428
the *k* answered, Chimham shall go	2Sa 19:38	4428
when the *k* was come over	2Sa 19:39	4428
the *k* kissed Barzillai, and	2Sa 19:39	4428
Then the *k* went on to Gilgal, and	2Sa 19:40	4428
people of Judah conducted the *k*	2Sa 19:40	4428
to the *k*, and said unto the *k*	2Sa 19:41	4428
thee away, and have brought the *k*	2Sa 19:41	4428
Because the *k* is near of kin to	2Sa 19:42	4428
said, We have ten parts in the *k*	2Sa 19:43	4428
first had in bringing back our *k*	2Sa 19:43	4428
men of Judah clave unto their *k*	2Sa 20:2	4428
the *k* took the ten women his	2Sa 20:3	4428
Then said the *k* to Amasa,	2Sa 20:4	4428
lifted up his hand against the *k*	2Sa 20:21	4428
returned to Jerusalem unto the *k*	2Sa 20:22	4428
the *k* called the Gibeonites, and	2Sa 21:2	4428
And they answered the *k*, The man	2Sa 21:5	4428
the *k* said, I will give them	2Sa 21:6	4428
But the *k* spared Mephibosheth,	2Sa 21:7	4428
But the *k* took the two sons of	2Sa 21:8	4428
all that the *k* commanded	2Sa 21:14	4428
the tower of salvation for his *k*	2Sa 22:51	4428
For the *k* said to Joab the	2Sa 24:2	4428
And Joab said unto the *k*, Now the	2Sa 24:3	4428
eyes of my lord the *k* may see it	2Sa 24:3	4428
lord the *k* delight in this thing	2Sa 24:3	4428
out from the presence of the *k*	2Sa 24:4	4428
number of the people unto the *k*	2Sa 24:9	4428
And Araunah looked, and saw the *k*	2Sa 24:20	4428
bowed himself before the *k* on his	2Sa 24:20	4428
my lord the *k* come to his servant	2Sa 24:21	4428
David, Let my lord the *k* take	2Sa 24:22	4428
as a *k*, give unto the *k*	2Sa 24:23	4428
And Araunah said unto the *k*	2Sa 24:23	4428
the *k* said unto Araunah, Nay	2Sa 24:24	4428
Now *k* David was old and stricken	1Kin 1:1	4428
for my lord the *k* a young virgin	1Kin 1:2	4428
and let her stand before the *k*	1Kin 1:2	4428
that my lord the *k* may get heat	1Kin 1:2	4428
and brought her to the *k*	1Kin 1:3	4428
was very fair, and cherished the *k*	1Kin 1:4	4428
but the *k* knew her not	1Kin 1:4	4428
himself, saying, I will be *k*	1Kin 1:5	4427
Go and get thee in unto *k* David	1Kin 1:13	4428
him, Didst not thou, my lord, O *k*	1Kin 1:13	4428
thou yet talkest there with the *k*	1Kin 1:14	4428
in unto the *k* into the chamber	1Kin 1:15	4428
and the *k* was very old	1Kin 1:15	4428
Shunammite ministered unto the *k*	1Kin 1:15	4428
and did obeisance unto the *k*	1Kin 1:16	4428
the *k* said, What wouldest thou	1Kin 1:16	4428
and now, my lord the *k*, thou	1Kin 1:18	4428
hath called all the sons of the *k*	1Kin 1:19	4428
And thou, my lord, O *k*, the eyes	1Kin 1:20	4428
throne of my lord the *k* after him	1Kin 1:20	4428
when my lord the *k* shall sleep	1Kin 1:21	4428
while she yet talked with the *k*	1Kin 1:22	4428
And they told the *k*, saying,	1Kin 1:23	4428
when he was come in before the *k*	1Kin 1:23	4428
the *k* with his face to the ground	1Kin 1:23	4428
And Nathan said, My lord, O *k*	1Kin 1:24	4428
him, and say, God save *k* Adonijah	1Kin 1:25	4428
this thing done by my lord the *k*	1Kin 1:27	4428
throne of my lord the *k* after him	1Kin 1:27	4428
Then *k* David answered and said,	1Kin 1:28	4428
presence, and stood before the *k*	1Kin 1:28	4428
the *k* sware, and said, As the LORD	1Kin 1:29	4428
earth, and did reverence to the *k*	1Kin 1:31	4428
Let my lord *k* David live for ever	1Kin 1:31	4428
k David said, Call me Zadok the	1Kin 1:32	4428
And they came before the *k*	1Kin 1:32	4428
The *k* also said unto them, Take	1Kin 1:33	4428
anoint him there *k* over Israel	1Kin 1:34	4428
and say, God save *k* Solomon	1Kin 1:34	4428
for he shall be *k* in my stead	1Kin 1:35	4427
son of Jehoiada answered the *k*	1Kin 1:36	4428
God of my lord the *k* say so too	1Kin 1:36	4428
LORD hath been with my lord the *k*	1Kin 1:37	4428
the throne of my lord *k* David	1Kin 1:37	4428
to ride upon *k* David's mule	1Kin 1:38	4428
people said, God save *k* Solomon	1Kin 1:39	4428
k David hath made Solomon *k*	1Kin 1:43	4427
the *k* hath sent with him Zadok	1Kin 1:44	4428
have anointed him *k* in Gihon	1Kin 1:45	4428
came to bless our lord *k* David	1Kin 1:47	4428
the *k* bowed himself upon the bed	1Kin 1:47	4428
And also thus said the *k*, Blessed	1Kin 1:48	4428
Adonijah feareth *k* Solomon	1Kin 1:51	4428
Let *k* Solomon swear unto me to	1Kin 1:51	4428
So *k* Solomon sent, and they	1Kin 1:53	4428
and bowed himself to *k* Solomon	1Kin 1:53	4428
I pray thee, unto Solomon the *k*	1Kin 2:17	4428
I will speak for thee unto the *k*	1Kin 2:18	4428
therefore went unto *k* Solomon	1Kin 2:19	4428
the *k* rose up to meet her, and	1Kin 2:19	4428

the *k* said unto her, Ask on, my 1Kin 2:20 4428
k Solomon answered and said unto 1Kin 2:22 4428
Then *k* Solomon sware by the LORD, 1Kin 2:23 4428
k Solomon sent by the hand of 1Kin 2:25 4428
Abiathar the priest said the *k* 1Kin 2:26 4428
it was told *k* Solomon that Joab 1Kin 2:29 4428
said unto him, Thus saith the *k* 1Kin 2:30 4428
Benaiah brought the *k* word again 1Kin 2:30 4428
the *k* said unto him, Do as he 1Kin 2:31 4428
the *k* put Benaiah the son of 1Kin 2:35 4428
Zadok the priest did the *k* put in 1Kin 2:35 4428
the *k* sent and called for Shimei, 1Kin 2:36 4428
And Shimei said unto the *k* 1Kin 2:38 4428
as my lord the *k* hath said 1Kin 2:38 4428
Achish son of Maachah *k* of Gath 1Kin 2:39 4428
the *k* sent and called for Shimei, 1Kin 2:42 4428
The *k* said moreover to Shimei, 1Kin 2:44 4428
k Solomon shall be blessed, and 1Kin 2:45 4428
So the *k* commanded Benaiah the 1Kin 2:46 4428
affinity with Pharaoh *k* of Egypt 1Kin 3:1 4428
the *k* went to Gibeon to sacrifice 1Kin 3:4 4428
k instead of David my father 1Kin 3:7 4427
that were harlots, unto the *k* 1Kin 3:16 4428
Thus they spake before the *k* 1Kin 3:22 4428
Then said the *k*, The one saith, 1Kin 3:23 4428
the *k* said, Bring me a sword 1Kin 3:24 4428
they brought a sword before the *k* 1Kin 3:24 4428
the *k* said, Divide the living 1Kin 3:25 4428
the living child was unto the *k* 1Kin 3:26 4428
Then the *k* answered and said, Give 1Kin 3:27 4428
judgment which the *k* had judged 1Kin 3:28 4428
and they feared the *k* 1Kin 3:28 4428
So *k* Solomon was *k* over all 1Kin 4:1 4428
which provided victuals for the *k* 1Kin 4:7 4428
of Sihon *k* of the Amorites 1Kin 4:19 4428
and of Og *k* of Bashan 1Kin 4:19 4428
provided victual for *k* Solomon 1Kin 4:27 4428
that came unto *k* Solomon's table 1Kin 4:27 4428
Hiram *k* of Tyre sent his servants 1Kin 5:1 4428
him *k* in the room of his father 1Kin 5:1 4428
k Solomon raised a levy out of 1Kin 5:13 4428
the *k* commanded, and they brought 1Kin 5:17 4428
the house which *k* Solomon built 1Kin 6:2 4428
k Solomon sent and fetched Hiram 1Kin 7:13 4428
And he came to *k* Solomon, and 1Kin 7:14 4428
k Solomon for the house of the 1Kin 7:40 4428
which Hiram made to *k* Solomon for 1Kin 7:45 4428
of Jordan did the *k* cast them 1Kin 7:46 4428
k Solomon made for the house of 1Kin 7:51 4428
unto *k* Solomon in Jerusalem, that 1Kin 8:1 4428
assembled themselves unto *k* 1Kin 8:2 4428
And *k* Solomon, and all the 1Kin 8:5 4428
the *k* turned his face about, and 1Kin 8:14 4428
And the *k*, and all Israel with him, 1Kin 8:62 4428
So the *k* and all the children of 1Kin 8:63 4428
The same day did the *k* hallow the 1Kin 8:64 4428
and they blessed the *k*, and went 1Kin 8:66 4428
(Now Hiram the *k* of Tyre had 1Kin 9:11 4428
that then *k* Solomon gave Hiram 1Kin 9:11 4428
Hiram sent to the *k* sixscore 1Kin 9:14 4428
the levy which *k* Solomon raised 1Kin 9:15 4428
For Pharaoh *k* of Egypt had gone 1Kin 9:16 4428
k Solomon made a navy of ships in 1Kin 9:26 4428
and brought it to *k* Solomon 1Kin 9:28 4428
was not any thing hid from the *k* 1Kin 10:3 4428
And she said to the *k*, It was a 1Kin 10:6 4428
ever, therefore made he thee *k* 1Kin 10:9 4428
And she gave the *k* an hundred 1Kin 10:10 4428
queen of Sheba gave to *k* Solomon 1Kin 10:10 4428
the *k* made of the almug trees 1Kin 10:12 4428
k Solomon gave unto the queen of 1Kin 10:13 4428
k Solomon made two hundred 1Kin 10:16 4428
the *k* put them in the house of 1Kin 10:17 4428
Moreover the *k* made a great 1Kin 10:18 4428
all *k* Solomon's drinking vessels 1Kin 10:21 4428
For the *k* had at sea a navy of 1Kin 10:22 4428
So *k* Solomon exceeded all the 1Kin 10:23 4428
and with the *k* at Jerusalem 1Kin 10:26 4428
the *k* made silver to be in 1Kin 10:27 4428
But *k* Solomon loved many strange 1Kin 11:1 4428
to Egypt, unto Pharaoh *k* of Egypt 1Kin 11:18 4428
his lord Hadadezer *k* of Zobah 1Kin 11:23 4428
lifted up his hand against the *k* 1Kin 11:26 4428
lifted up his hand against the *k* 1Kin 11:27 4428
and shalt be *k* over Israel 1Kin 11:37 4428
Egypt, unto Shishak *k* of Egypt 1Kin 11:40 4428
come to Shechem to make him *k* 1Kin 12:1 4427
from the presence of *k* Solomon 1Kin 12:2 4428
k Rehoboam consulted with the old 1Kin 12:6 4428
as the *k* had appointed, saying, 1Kin 12:12 4428
the *k* answered the people roughly 1Kin 12:13 4428
Wherefore the *k* hearkened not 1Kin 12:15 4428
the *k* hearkened not unto them 1Kin 12:16 4428
the people answered the *k* 1Kin 12:16 4428
Then *k* Rehoboam sent Adoram, who 1Kin 12:18 4428
Therefore *k* Rehoboam made speed 1Kin 12:18 4428
made him *k* over all Israel 1Kin 12:20 4427
k of Judah, and unto all the house 1Kin 12:23 4428
even unto Rehoboam *k* of Judah 1Kin 12:27 4428
go again to Rehoboam *k* of Judah 1Kin 12:27 4428
Whereupon the *k* took counsel 1Kin 12:28 4428
when *k* Jeroboam heard the saying 1Kin 13:4 4428
the *k* answered and said unto the 1Kin 13:6 4428
the *k* said unto the man of God, 1Kin 13:7 4428
And the man of God said unto the *k* 1Kin 13:8 4428
which he had spoken unto the *k* 1Kin 13:11 4428
I should be *k* over this people 1Kin 14:2 4428
raise him up a *k* over Israel 1Kin 14:14 4428
in the fifth year of *k* Rehoboam 1Kin 14:25 4428
that Shishak *k* of Egypt came up 1Kin 14:25 4428
k Rehoboam made in their stead 1Kin 14:27 4428
when the *k* went into the house of 1Kin 14:28 4428
of *k* Jeroboam the son of Nebat 1Kin 15:1 4428
k of Israel reigned Asa over 1Kin 15:9 4428

Baasha *k* of Israel all their days 1Kin 15:16 4428
Baasha *k* of Israel went up 1Kin 15:17 4428
out or come in to Asa *k* of Judah 1Kin 15:17 4428
k Asa sent them to Ben-hadad, the 1Kin 15:18 4428
k of Syria, that dwelt at 1Kin 15:18 4428
league with Baasha *k* of Israel 1Kin 15:19 4428
So Ben-hadad hearkened unto *k* Asa 1Kin 15:20 4428
Then *k* Asa made a proclamation 1Kin 15:22 4428
k Asa built with them Geba of 1Kin 15:22 4428
the second year of Asa *k* of Judah 1Kin 15:25 4428
k of Judah did Baasha slay him 1Kin 15:28 4428
Baasha *k* of Israel all their days 1Kin 15:32 4428
In the third year of Asa *k* of 1Kin 15:33 4428
sixth year of Asa *k* of Judah 1Kin 16:8 4428
and seventh year of Asa *k* of Judah 1Kin 16:10 4428
seventh year of Asa *k* of Judah 1Kin 16:15 4428
and hath also slain the *k* 1Kin 16:16 4428
k over Israel that day in the 1Kin 16:16 4427
the son of Ginath, to make him *k* 1Kin 16:21 4427
first year of Asa *k* of Judah 1Kin 16:23 4428
eighth year of Asa *k* of Judah 1Kin 16:29 4428
of Ethbaal *k* of the Zidonians 1Kin 16:31 4428
anoint Hazael to be *k* over Syria 1Kin 19:15 4428
thou anoint to be *k* over Israel 1Kin 19:16 4428
Ben-hadad the *k* of Syria gathered 1Kin 20:1 4428
to Ahab *k* of Israel into the city 1Kin 20:2 4428
the *k* of Israel answered and said, 1Kin 20:4 4428
answered and said, My lord, O *k* 1Kin 20:4 4428
Then the *k* of Israel called all 1Kin 20:7 4428
of Ben-hadad, Tell my lord the *k* 1Kin 20:9 4428
the *k* of Israel answered and said, 1Kin 20:11 4428
a prophet unto Ahab *k* of Israel 1Kin 20:13 4428
Ben-hadad the *k* of Syria escaped 1Kin 20:20 4428
the *k* of Israel went out, and 1Kin 20:21 4428
prophet came to the *k* of Israel 1Kin 20:22 4428
k of Syria will come up against 1Kin 20:22 4428
the servants of the *k* of Syria 1Kin 20:23 4428
and spake unto the *k* of Israel 1Kin 20:28 4428
and go out to the *k* of Israel 1Kin 20:31 4428
heads, and came to the *k* of Israel 1Kin 20:32 4428
and waited for the *k* by the way 1Kin 20:38 4428
as the *k* passed by, he cried unto 1Kin 20:39 4428
passed by, he cried unto the *k* 1Kin 20:39 4428
the *k* of Israel said unto him, So 1Kin 20:40 4428
the *k* of Israel discerned him 1Kin 20:41 4428
the *k* of Israel went to his house 1Kin 20:43 4428
the palace of Ahab *k* of Samaria 1Kin 21:1 4428
Thou didst blaspheme God and the *k* 1Kin 21:10 4428
Naboth did blaspheme God and the *k* 1Kin 21:13 4428
go down to meet Ahab *k* of Israel 1Kin 21:18 4428
that Jehoshaphat the *k* of Judah 1Kin 22:2 4428
came down to the *k* of Israel 1Kin 22:2 4428
the *k* of Israel said unto his 1Kin 22:3 4428
out of the hand of the *k* of Syria 1Kin 22:3 4428
said to the *k* of Israel, I am as 1Kin 22:4 4428
said unto the *k* of Israel 1Kin 22:5 4428
Then the *k* of Israel gathered the 1Kin 22:6 4428
deliver it into the hand of the *k* 1Kin 22:6 4428
the *k* of Israel said unto 1Kin 22:8 4428
said, Let not the *k* say so 1Kin 22:8 4428
Then the *k* of Israel called an 1Kin 22:9 4428
the *k* of Israel and Jehoshaphat 1Kin 22:10 4428
Jehoshaphat the *k* of Judah sat 1Kin 22:10 4428
good unto the *k* with one mouth 1Kin 22:13 4428
So he came to the *k* 1Kin 22:15 4428
the *k* said unto him, Micaiah, 1Kin 22:15 4428
deliver it into the hand of the *k* 1Kin 22:15 4428
the *k* said unto him, How many 1Kin 22:16 4428
the *k* of Israel said unto 1Kin 22:18 4428
the *k* of Israel said, Take 1Kin 22:26 4428
And say, Thus saith the *k*, Put 1Kin 22:27 4428
So the *k* of Israel and Jehoshaphat 1Kin 22:29 4428
Jehoshaphat the *k* of Judah went 1Kin 22:29 4428
the *k* of Israel said unto 1Kin 22:30 4428
the *k* of Israel disguised himself 1Kin 22:30 4428
But the *k* of Syria commanded his 1Kin 22:31 4428
save only with the *k* of Israel 1Kin 22:31 4428
Surely it is the *k* of Israel 1Kin 22:32 4428
that it was not the *k* of Israel 1Kin 22:33 4428
smote the *k* of Israel between the 1Kin 22:34 4428
the *k* was stayed up in his 1Kin 22:35 4428
So the *k* died, and was brought to 1Kin 22:37 4428
and they buried the *k* in Samaria 1Kin 22:37 4428
fourth year of Ahab *k* of Israel 1Kin 22:41 4428
made peace with the *k* of Israel 1Kin 22:44 4428
There was then no *k* in Edom 1Kin 22:47 4428
a deputy was *k* 1Kin 22:47 4428
year of Jehoshaphat *k* of Judah 1Kin 22:51 4428
messengers of the *k* of Samaria 2Kin 1:3 4428
again unto the *k* that sent you 2Kin 1:6 4428
Then the *k* sent unto him a 2Kin 1:9 4428
the *k* hath said, Come down 2Kin 1:9 4428
man of God, thus hath the *k* said 2Kin 1:11 4428
and went down with him unto the *k* 2Kin 1:15 4428
the son of Jehoshaphat *k* of Judah 2Kin 1:17 4428
year of Jehoshaphat *k* of Judah 2Kin 3:1 4428
Mesha *k* of Moab was a sheepmaster 2Kin 3:4 4428
rendered unto the *k* of Israel an 2Kin 3:4 4428
that the *k* of Moab rebelled 2Kin 3:5 4428
rebelled against the *k* of Israel 2Kin 3:5 4428
k Jehoram went out of Samaria the 2Kin 3:6 4428
to Jehoshaphat the *k* of Judah 2Kin 3:7 4428
The *k* of Moab hath rebelled 2Kin 3:7 4428
So the *k* of Israel went 2Kin 3:9 4428
k of Judah, and the *k* of Edom 2Kin 3:9 4428
the *k* of Israel said, Alas 2Kin 3:10 4428
one of the *k* of Israel's servants 2Kin 3:11 4428
So the *k* of Israel and Jehoshaphat 2Kin 3:12 4428
the *k* of Edom went down to him 2Kin 3:12 4428
Elisha said unto the *k* of Israel 2Kin 3:13 4428
the *k* of Israel said unto him, 2Kin 3:13 4428
of Jehoshaphat the *k* of Judah 2Kin 3:14 4428
when the *k* of Moab saw that the 2Kin 3:26 4428
through even unto the *k* of Edom 2Kin 3:26 4428

thou be spoken for to the *k* 2Kin 4:13 4428
of the host of the *k* of Syria 2Kin 5:1 4428
the *k* of Syria said, Go to, go, 2Kin 5:5 4428
a letter unto the *k* of Israel 2Kin 5:5 4428
the letter to the *k* of Israel 2Kin 5:6 4428
when the *k* of Israel had read the 2Kin 5:7 4428
man of God had heard that the *k* 2Kin 5:8 4428
clothes, that he sent to the *k* 2Kin 5:8 4428
Then the *k* of Syria warred 2Kin 6:8 4428
of God sent unto the *k* of Israel 2Kin 6:9 4428
the *k* of Israel sent to the place 2Kin 6:10 4428
Therefore the heart of the *k* of 2Kin 6:11 4428
of us is for the *k* of Israel 2Kin 6:11 4428
servants said, None, my lord, O *k* 2Kin 6:12 4428
telleth the *k* of Israel the words 2Kin 6:12 4428
the *k* of Israel said unto Elisha, 2Kin 6:21 4428
that Ben-hadad *k* of Syria 2Kin 6:24 4428
as the *k* of Israel was passing by 2Kin 6:26 4428
him, saying, Help, my lord, O *k* 2Kin 6:26 4428
the *k* said unto her, What aileth 2Kin 6:28 4428
when the *k* heard the words of the 2Kin 6:30 4428
the *k* sent a man from before him 2Kin 6:32 4428
Then a lord on whose hand the *k* 2Kin 7:2 4428
the *k* of Israel hath hired 2Kin 7:6 4428
the *k* arose in the night, and said 2Kin 7:12 4428
the *k* sent after the host of the 2Kin 7:14 4428
returned, and told the *k* 2Kin 7:15 4428
the *k* appointed the lord on whose 2Kin 7:17 4428
spake when the *k* came down to him 2Kin 7:17 4428
man of God had spoken to the *k* 2Kin 7:18 4428
to cry unto the *k* for her house 2Kin 8:3 4428
the *k* talked with Gehazi the 2Kin 8:4 4428
as he was telling the *k* how he 2Kin 8:5 4428
cried to the *k* for her house and 2Kin 8:5 4428
And Gehazi said, My lord, O *k* 2Kin 8:5 4428
when the *k* asked the woman, she 2Kin 8:6 4428
So the *k* appointed unto her a 2Kin 8:6 4428
Ben-hadad the *k* of Syria was sick 2Kin 8:7 4428
the *k* said unto Hazael, Take a 2Kin 8:8 4428
Thy son Ben-hadad *k* of Syria hath 2Kin 8:9 4428
that thou shalt be *k* over Syria 2Kin 8:13 4428
Joram the son of Ahab *k* of Israel 2Kin 8:16 4428
Jehoshaphat being then *k* of Judah 2Kin 8:16 4428
k of Judah began to reign 2Kin 8:16 4428
and made a *k* over themselves 2Kin 8:20 4428
k of Israel did Ahaziah the son 2Kin 8:25 4428
Jehoram *k* of Judah begin to reign 2Kin 8:25 4428
the daughter of Omri *k* of Israel 2Kin 8:26 4428
k of Syria in Ramoth-gilead 2Kin 8:28 4428
k Joram went back to be healed in 2Kin 8:29 4428
fought against Hazael *k* of Syria 2Kin 8:29 4428
Ahaziah the son of Jehoram *k* of 2Kin 8:29 4428
have anointed thee *k* over Israel 2Kin 9:3 4428
I have anointed thee *k* over the 2Kin 9:6 4428
have anointed thee *k* over Israel 2Kin 9:12 4428
with trumpets, saying, Jehu is *k* 2Kin 9:13 4427
because of Hazael *k* of Syria 2Kin 9:14 4428
But *k* Joram was returned to be 2Kin 9:15 4428
he fought with Hazael *k* of Syria 2Kin 9:15 4428
Ahaziah *k* of Judah was come down 2Kin 9:16 4428
him, and said, Thus saith the *k* 2Kin 9:18 4428
them, and said, Thus saith the *k* 2Kin 9:19 4428
Joram *k* of Israel and Ahaziah *k* 2Kin 9:21 4428
Ahaziah the *k* of Judah saw this 2Kin 9:27 4428
we will not make any *k* 2Kin 10:5 4427
brethren of Ahaziah *k* of Judah 2Kin 10:13 4428
to salute the children of the *k* 2Kin 10:13 4428
the daughter of *k* Joram, sister 2Kin 11:2 4428
the house of the LORD about the *k* 2Kin 11:7 4428
shall compass the *k* round about 2Kin 11:8 4428
be ye with the *k* as he goeth out 2Kin 11:8 4428
the priest give *k* David's spears 2Kin 11:10 4428
in his hand, round about the *k* 2Kin 11:11 4428
and they made him *k*, and anointed 2Kin 11:12 4427
hands, and said, God save the *k* 2Kin 11:12 4428
the *k* stood by a pillar, as the 2Kin 11:14 4428
and the trumpeters by the *k* 2Kin 11:14 4428
between the LORD and the *k* 2Kin 11:17 4428
between the *k* also and the people 2Kin 11:17 4428
they brought down the *k* from the 2Kin 11:19 4428
twentieth year of *k* Jehoash the 2Kin 12:6 4428
Then *k* Jehoash called for 2Kin 12:7 4428
Then Hazael *k* of Syria went up, 2Kin 12:17 4428
Jehoash *k* of Judah took all the 2Kin 12:18 4428
and sent it to Hazael *k* of Syria 2Kin 12:18 4428
of Joash the son of Ahaziah *k* of 2Kin 13:1 4428
the hand of Hazael *k* of Syria 2Kin 13:3 4428
because the *k* of Syria oppressed 2Kin 13:4 4428
for the *k* of Syria had destroyed 2Kin 13:7 4428
seventh year of Joash *k* of Judah 2Kin 13:10 4428
fought against Amaziah *k* of Judah 2Kin 13:12 4428
Joash the *k* of Israel came down 2Kin 13:14 4428
And he said to the *k* of Israel 2Kin 13:16 4428
And he said unto the *k* of Israel 2Kin 13:18 4428
But Hazael *k* of Syria oppressed 2Kin 13:22 4428
So Hazael *k* of Syria died 2Kin 13:24 4428
k of Israel reigned Amaziah the 2Kin 14:1 4428
the son of Joash *k* of Judah 2Kin 14:1 4428
which had slain the *k* his father 2Kin 14:5 4428
k of Israel, saying, Come, let us 2Kin 14:8 4428
Jehoash the *k* of Israel sent to 2Kin 14:9 4428
Israel sent to Amaziah *k* of Judah 2Kin 14:9 4428
Jehoash *k* of Israel went up 2Kin 14:11 4428
Amaziah *k* of Judah looked one 2Kin 14:11 4428
Jehoash *k* of Israel took Amaziah 2Kin 14:13 4428
of Israel took Amaziah *k* of Judah 2Kin 14:13 4428
he fought with Amaziah *k* of Judah 2Kin 14:15 4428
Amaziah the son of Joash *k* of 2Kin 14:17 4428
k of Israel fifteen years 2Kin 14:17 4428
made him *k* instead of his father 2Kin 14:21 4427
after that the *k* slept with his 2Kin 14:22 4428
of Amaziah the son of Joash *k* of 2Kin 14:23 4428
k of Israel began to reign in 2Kin 14:23 4428
seventh year of Jeroboam *k* of 2Kin 15:1 4428

of Amaziah *k* of Judah to reign	2Kin 15:1	4428
And the LORD smote the *k*, so that	2Kin 15:5	4428
eighth year of Azariah *k* of Judah	2Kin 15:8	4428
year of Uzziah *k* of Judah	2Kin 15:13	4428
thirtieth year of Azariah *k* of	2Kin 15:17	4428
Pul the *k* of Assyria came against	2Kin 15:19	4428
to give to the *k* of Assyria	2Kin 15:20	4428
So the *k* of Assyria turned back,	2Kin 15:20	4428
k of Judah Pekahiah the son of	2Kin 15:23	4428
fiftieth year of Azariah *k* of	2Kin 15:27	4428
In the days of Pekah *k* of Israel	2Kin 15:29	4428
came Tiglath-pileser *k* of Assyria	2Kin 15:29	4428
of Pekah the son of Remaliah *k* of	2Kin 15:32	4428
son of Uzziah *k* of Judah to reign	2Kin 15:32	4428
Judah Rezin the *k* of Syria	2Kin 15:37	4428
Jotham *k* of Judah began to reign	2Kin 16:1	4428
Then Rezin *k* of Syria and Pekah	2Kin 16:5	4428
Pekah son of Remaliah *k* of Israel	2Kin 16:5	4428
At that time Rezin *k* of Syria	2Kin 16:6	4428
to Tiglath-pileser *k* of Assyria	2Kin 16:7	4428
out of the hand of the *k* of Syria	2Kin 16:7	4428
of the hand of the *k* of Israel	2Kin 16:7	4428
for a present to the *k* of Assyria	2Kin 16:8	4428
the *k* of Assyria hearkened unto	2Kin 16:9	4428
for the *k* of Assyria went up	2Kin 16:9	4428
k Ahaz went to Damascus to meet	2Kin 16:10	4428
meet Tiglath-pileser *k* of Assyria	2Kin 16:10	4428
k Ahaz sent to Urijah the priest	2Kin 16:10	4428
k Ahaz had sent from Damascus	2Kin 16:11	4428
against *k* Ahaz came from Damascus	2Kin 16:11	4428
when the *k* was come from Damascus	2Kin 16:12	4428
the *k* saw the altar	2Kin 16:12	4428
the *k* approached to the altar, and	2Kin 16:12	4428
k Ahaz commanded Urijah the	2Kin 16:15	4428
to all that *k* Ahaz commanded	2Kin 16:16	4428
k Ahaz cut off the borders of the	2Kin 16:17	4428
of the LORD for the *k* of Assyria	2Kin 16:18	4428
In the twelfth year of Ahaz *k* of	2Kin 17:1	4428
came up Shalmaneser *k* of Assyria	2Kin 17:3	4428
the *k* of Assyria found conspiracy	2Kin 17:4	4428
sent messengers to So *k* of Egypt	2Kin 17:4	4428
no present to the *k* of Assyria	2Kin 17:4	4428
therefore the *k* of Assyria shut	2Kin 17:4	4428
Then the *k* of Assyria came up	2Kin 17:5	4428
the *k* of Assyria took Samaria	2Kin 17:6	4428
the hand of Pharaoh *k* of Egypt	2Kin 17:7	4428
made Jeroboam the son of Nebat *k*	2Kin 17:21	4427
the *k* of Assyria brought men from	2Kin 17:24	4428
they spake to the *k* of Assyria	2Kin 17:26	4428
Then the *k* of Assyria commanded,	2Kin 17:27	4428
of Hoshea son of Elah *k* of Israel	2Kin 18:1	4428
of Ahaz *k* of Judah began to reign	2Kin 18:1	4428
rebelled against the *k* of Assyria	2Kin 18:7	4428
in the fourth year of *k* Hezekiah	2Kin 18:9	4428
of Hoshea son of Elah *k* of Israel	2Kin 18:9	4428
that Shalmaneser *k* of Assyria	2Kin 18:9	4428
ninth year of Hoshea *k* of Israel	2Kin 18:10	4428
the *k* of Assyria did carry away	2Kin 18:11	4428
k Hezekiah did Sennacherib *k*	2Kin 18:13	4428
Hezekiah *k* of Judah sent to the	2Kin 18:14	4428
to the *k* of Assyria to Lachish	2Kin 18:14	4428
the *k* of Assyria appointed unto	2Kin 18:14	4428
k of Judah three hundred talents	2Kin 18:14	4428
Hezekiah *k* of Judah had overlaid	2Kin 18:16	4428
and gave it to the *k* of Assyria	2Kin 18:16	4428
the *k* of Assyria sent Tartan and	2Kin 18:17	4428
to *k* Hezekiah with a great host	2Kin 18:17	4428
And when they had called to the *k*	2Kin 18:18	4428
Hezekiah, Thus saith the great *k*	2Kin 18:19	4428
the *k* of Assyria, What confidence	2Kin 18:19	4428
so is Pharaoh *k* of Egypt unto all	2Kin 18:21	4428
to my lord the *k* of Assyria	2Kin 18:23	4428
the great *k*, the *k* of Assyria	2Kin 18:28	4428
Thus saith the *k*, Let not	2Kin 18:29	4428
into the hand of the *k* of Assyria	2Kin 18:30	4428
for thus saith the *k* of Assyria	2Kin 18:31	4428
of the hand of the *k* of Assyria	2Kin 18:33	4428
when *k* Hezekiah heard it, that he	2Kin 19:1	4428
whom the *k* of Assyria his master	2Kin 19:4	4428
So the servants of *k* Hezekiah	2Kin 19:5	4428
k of Assyria have blasphemed me	2Kin 19:6	4428
found the *k* of Assyria warring	2Kin 19:8	4428
say of Tirhakah *k* of Ethiopia	2Kin 19:9	4428
ye speak to Hezekiah *k* of Judah	2Kin 19:10	4428
into the hand of the *k* of Assyria	2Kin 19:10	4428
Where is the *k* of Hamath	2Kin 19:13	4428
the *k* of Arpad	2Kin 19:13	4428
the *k* of the city of Sepharvaim,	2Kin 19:13	4428
k of Assyria I have heard	2Kin 19:20	4428
LORD concerning the *k* of Assyria	2Kin 19:32	4428
So Sennacherib *k* of Assyria	2Kin 19:36	4428
of the hand of the *k* of Assyria	2Kin 20:6	4428
k of Babylon, sent letters and a	2Kin 20:12	4428
the prophet unto *k* Hezekiah	2Kin 20:14	4428
in the palace of the *k* of Babylon	2Kin 20:18	4428
a grove, as did Ahab *k* of Israel	2Kin 21:3	4428
Because Manasseh *k* of Judah hath	2Kin 21:11	4428
slew the *k* in his own house	2Kin 21:23	4428
that had conspired against *k* Amon	2Kin 21:24	4428
Josiah his son *k* in his stead	2Kin 21:24	4427
the eighteenth year of *k* Josiah	2Kin 22:3	4428
that the *k* sent Shaphan the son	2Kin 22:3	4428
Shaphan the scribe came to the *k*	2Kin 22:9	4428
and brought the *k* word again	2Kin 22:9	4428
Shaphan the scribe shewed the *k*	2Kin 22:10	4428
And Shaphan read it before the *k*	2Kin 22:10	4428
when the *k* had heard the words of	2Kin 22:11	4428
the *k* commanded Hilkiah the	2Kin 22:12	4428
which the *k* of Judah hath read	2Kin 22:16	4428
But to the *k* of Judah which sent	2Kin 22:18	4428
And they brought the *k* word again	2Kin 22:20	4428
the *k* sent, and they gathered unto	2Kin 23:1	4428
the *k* went up into the house of	2Kin 23:2	4428
the *k* stood by a pillar, and made	2Kin 23:3	4428
the *k* commanded Hilkiah the high	2Kin 23:4	4428
did the *k* beat down, and brake	2Kin 23:12	4428
which Solomon the *k* of Israel had	2Kin 23:13	4428
of Ammon, did the *k* defile	2Kin 23:13	4428
the *k* commanded all the people,	2Kin 23:21	4428
the eighteenth year of *k* Josiah	2Kin 23:23	4428
him was there no *k* before him	2Kin 23:25	4428
In his days Pharaoh-nechoh *k* of	2Kin 23:29	4428
the *k* of Assyria to the river	2Kin 23:29	4428
k Josiah went against him	2Kin 23:29	4428
made him *k* in his father's stead	2Kin 23:30	4427
k in the room of Josiah his	2Kin 23:34	4427
k of Babylon came up, and	2Kin 24:1	4428
the *k* of Egypt came not again any	2Kin 24:7	4428
for the *k* of Babylon had taken	2Kin 24:7	4428
that pertained to the *k* of Egypt	2Kin 24:7	4428
k of Babylon came up against	2Kin 24:10	4428
Nebuchadnezzar *k* of Babylon came	2Kin 24:11	4428
Jehoiachin the *k* of Judah went	2Kin 24:12	4428
went out to the *k* of Babylon	2Kin 24:12	4428
the *k* of Babylon took him in the	2Kin 24:12	4428
k of Israel had made in the	2Kin 24:13	4428
even them the *k* of Babylon	2Kin 24:16	4428
the *k* of Babylon made Mattaniah	2Kin 24:17	4428
father's brother *k* in his stead	2Kin 24:17	4427
rebelled against the *k* of Babylon	2Kin 24:20	4428
Nebuchadnezzar *k* of Babylon came	2Kin 25:1	4428
the eleventh year of *k* Zedekiah	2Kin 25:2	4428
the *k* went the way toward the	2Kin 25:4	
the Chaldees pursued after the *k*	2Kin 25:5	4428
So they took the *k*, and brought	2Kin 25:6	4428
up to the *k* of Babylon to Riblah	2Kin 25:6	4428
k Nebuchadnezzar *k* of Babylon	2Kin 25:8	4428
a servant of the *k* of Babylon	2Kin 25:8	4428
fell away to the *k* of Babylon	2Kin 25:11	4428
brought them to the *k* of Babylon	2Kin 25:20	4428
the *k* of Babylon smote them, and	2Kin 25:21	4428
k of Babylon had left, even over	2Kin 25:22	4428
heard that the *k* of Babylon had	2Kin 25:23	4428
land, and serve the *k* of Babylon	2Kin 25:24	4428
of Jehoiachin *k* of Judah, in the	2Kin 25:27	4428
that Evil-merodach *k* of Babylon	2Kin 25:27	4428
k of Judah out of prison	2Kin 25:27	4428
allowance given him of the *k*	2Kin 25:30	4428
k reigned over the children of	1Chr 1:43	4428
daughter of Talmai *k* of Geshur	1Chr 3:2	4428
dwelt with the *k* for his work	1Chr 4:23	4428
the days of Hezekiah *k* of Judah	1Chr 4:41	4428
whom Tilgath-pilneser *k* of	1Chr 5:6	4428
in the days of Jotham *k* of Judah	1Chr 5:17	4428
the days of Jeroboam *k* of Israel	1Chr 5:17	4428
up the spirit of Pul *k* of Assyria	1Chr 5:26	4428
of Tilgath-pilneser *k* of Assyria	1Chr 5:26	4428
time past, even when Saul was *k*	1Chr 11:2	4428
of Israel to the *k* to Hebron	1Chr 11:3	4428
they anointed David *k* over Israel	1Chr 11:3	4428
and with all Israel, to make him *k*	1Chr 11:10	4427
by name, to come and make David *k*	1Chr 12:31	4427
to make David *k* over all Israel	1Chr 12:38	4427
were of one heart to make David *k*	1Chr 12:38	4427
Now Hiram *k* of Tyre sent	1Chr 14:1	4428
had confirmed him *k* over Israel	1Chr 14:2	4428
was anointed *k* over all Israel	1Chr 14:8	4428
at a window saw *k* David dancing	1Chr 15:29	4428
And David the *k* came and sat before	1Chr 17:16	4428
Hadarezer *k* of Zobah unto Hamath	1Chr 18:3	4428
came to help Hadarezer *k* of Zobah	1Chr 18:5	4428
Now when Tou *k* of Hamath heard	1Chr 18:9	4428
the host of Hadarezer *k* of Zobah	1Chr 18:9	4428
sent Hadoram his son to *k* David	1Chr 18:10	4428
Them also *k* David dedicated unto	1Chr 18:11	4428
of David were chief about the *k*	1Chr 18:17	4428
that Nahash the *k* of the children	1Chr 19:1	4428
the *k* said, Tarry at Jericho	1Chr 19:5	4428
the *k* of Maachah and his people	1Chr 19:7	4428
of their *k* from off his head	1Chr 20:2	4428
but, my lord the *k*, are they not	1Chr 21:3	4428
let my lord the *k* do that which	1Chr 21:23	4428
k David said to Ornan, Nay	1Chr 21:24	4428
Solomon his son *k* over Israel	1Chr 23:1	4427
Levites, wrote them before the *k*	1Chr 24:6	4428
in the presence of David the *k*	1Chr 24:31	4428
according to the order of the *k*	1Chr 25:2	4428
things, which David the *k*	1Chr 26:26	4428
LORD, and in the service of the *k*	1Chr 26:30	4428
whom *k* David made rulers over the	1Chr 26:32	4428
to God, and affairs of the *k*	1Chr 26:32	4428
k in any matter of the courses	1Chr 27:1	4428
of the Chronicles of *k* David	1Chr 27:24	4428
the substance which was *k* David's	1Chr 27:31	4428
ministered to the *k* by course	1Chr 28:1	4428
substance and possession of the *k*	1Chr 28:1	4428
Then David the *k* stood up upon	1Chr 28:2	4428
to be *k* over Israel for ever	1Chr 28:4	4428
me to make me *k* over all Israel	1Chr 28:4	4427
Furthermore David the *k* said unto	1Chr 29:1	4428
David the *k* also rejoiced with	1Chr 29:9	4428
and worshipped the LORD, and the *k*	1Chr 29:20	4428
son of David *k* the second time	1Chr 29:22	4427
as *k* instead of David his father	1Chr 29:23	4428
all the sons likewise of *k* David	1Chr 29:24	4428
themselves unto Solomon the *k*	1Chr 29:24	4428
on any *k* before him in Israel	1Chr 29:25	4428
Now the acts of David the *k*	1Chr 29:29	4428
for thou hast made me *k* over a	2Chr 1:9	4427
over whom I have made thee *k*	2Chr 1:11	4427
and with the *k* at Jerusalem	2Chr 1:14	4428
the *k* made silver and gold at	2Chr 1:15	4428
sent to Huram the *k* of Tyre	2Chr 2:3	4428
Then Huram the *k* of Tyre answered	2Chr 2:11	4428
he hath made thee *k* over them	2Chr 2:11	4427
given to David the *k* a wise son	2Chr 2:12	4428
k Solomon for the house of God	2Chr 4:11	4428
to *k* Solomon for the house of the	2Chr 4:16	4428
of Jordan did the *k* cast them	2Chr 4:17	4428
k in the feast which was in the	2Chr 5:3	4428
Also *k* Solomon, and all the	2Chr 5:6	4428
the *k* turned his face, and blessed	2Chr 6:3	4428
Then the *k* and all the people	2Chr 7:4	4428
k Solomon offered a sacrifice of	2Chr 7:5	4428
so the *k* and all the people	2Chr 7:5	4428
which David the *k* had made to	2Chr 7:6	4428
the chief of *k* Solomon's officers	2Chr 8:10	4428
in the house of David *k* of Israel	2Chr 8:11	4428
of the *k* unto the priests	2Chr 8:15	4428
and brought them to *k* Solomon	2Chr 8:18	4428
And she said to the *k*, It was a	2Chr 9:5	4428
to be *k* for the LORD thy God	2Chr 9:8	4428
made he thee *k* over them, to do	2Chr 9:8	4428
And she gave the *k* an hundred	2Chr 9:9	4428
the queen of Sheba gave *k* Solomon	2Chr 9:9	4428
the *k* made of the algum trees	2Chr 9:11	4428
k Solomon gave to the queen of	2Chr 9:12	4428
which she had brought unto the *k*	2Chr 9:12	4428
k Solomon made two hundred	2Chr 9:15	4428
the *k* put them in the house of	2Chr 9:16	4428
Moreover the *k* made a great	2Chr 9:17	4428
vessels of *k* Solomon were of gold	2Chr 9:20	4428
k Solomon passed all the kings of	2Chr 9:22	4428
and with the *k* at Jerusalem	2Chr 9:25	4428
the *k* made silver in Jerusalem as	2Chr 9:27	4428
all Israel come to make him *k*	2Chr 10:1	4427
the presence of Solomon the *k*	2Chr 10:2	4428
k Rehoboam took counsel with the	2Chr 10:6	4428
on the third day, as the *k* bade	2Chr 10:12	4428
the *k* answered them roughly	2Chr 10:13	4428
k Rehoboam forsook the counsel of	2Chr 10:13	4428
So the *k* hearkened not unto the	2Chr 10:15	4428
the *k* would not hearken unto them	2Chr 10:16	4428
the people answered the *k*	2Chr 10:16	4428
Then *k* Rehoboam sent Hadoram that	2Chr 10:18	4428
But *k* Rehoboam made speed to get	2Chr 10:18	4428
k of Judah, and to all Israel in	2Chr 11:3	4428
for he thought to make him *k*	2Chr 11:22	4427
that in the fifth year of *k*	2Chr 12:2	4428
k of Egypt came up against	2Chr 12:2	4428
and the *k* humbled themselves	2Chr 12:6	4428
So Shishak *k* of Egypt came up	2Chr 12:9	4428
Instead of which *k* Rehoboam made	2Chr 12:10	4428
when the *k* entered into the house	2Chr 12:11	4428
So *k* Rehoboam strengthened	2Chr 12:13	4428
Now in the eighteenth year of *k*	2Chr 13:1	4428
Maachah the mother of Asa the *k*	2Chr 15:16	4428
k of Israel came up against Judah	2Chr 16:1	4428
out or come in to Asa *k* of Judah	2Chr 16:1	4428
and sent to Ben-hadad *k* of Syria	2Chr 16:2	4428
league with Baasha *k* of Israel	2Chr 16:3	4428
And Ben-hadad hearkened unto *k* Asa	2Chr 16:4	4428
Then Asa the *k* took all Judah	2Chr 16:6	4428
the seer came to Asa *k* of Judah	2Chr 16:7	4428
hast relied on the *k* of Syria	2Chr 16:7	4428
therefore is the host of the *k* of	2Chr 16:7	4428
These waited on the *k*	2Chr 17:19	4428
beside those whom the *k* put in	2Chr 17:19	4428
Ahab *k* of Israel said unto	2Chr 18:3	4428
said unto Jehoshaphat *k* of Judah	2Chr 18:3	4428
said unto the *k* of Israel	2Chr 18:4	4428
Therefore the *k* of Israel	2Chr 18:5	4428
the *k* of Israel said unto	2Chr 18:7	4428
said, Let not the *k* say so	2Chr 18:7	4428
the *k* of Israel called for one of	2Chr 18:8	4428
the *k* of Israel and Jehoshaphat	2Chr 18:9	4428
Jehoshaphat *k* of Judah sat either	2Chr 18:9	4428
deliver it into the hand of the *k*	2Chr 18:11	4428
good to the *k* with one assent	2Chr 18:12	4428
And when he was come to the *k*	2Chr 18:14	4428
the *k* said unto him, Micaiah,	2Chr 18:14	4428
the *k* said to him, How many times	2Chr 18:15	4428
And the *k* of Israel said to	2Chr 18:17	4428
Who shall entice Ahab *k* of Israel	2Chr 18:19	4428
Then the *k* of Israel said, Take	2Chr 18:25	4428
And say, Thus saith the *k*, Put	2Chr 18:26	4428
So the *k* of Israel and Jehoshaphat	2Chr 18:28	4428
Jehoshaphat the *k* of Judah went	2Chr 18:28	4428
the *k* of Israel said unto	2Chr 18:29	4428
So the *k* of Israel disguised	2Chr 18:29	4428
Now the *k* of Syria had commanded	2Chr 18:30	4428
save only with the *k* of Israel	2Chr 18:30	4428
they said, It is the *k* of Israel	2Chr 18:31	4428
that it was not the *k* of Israel	2Chr 18:32	4428
smote the *k* of Israel between the	2Chr 18:33	4428
howbeit the *k* of Israel stayed	2Chr 18:34	4428
Jehoshaphat the *k* of Judah	2Chr 19:1	4428
said to *k* Jehoshaphat, Shouldest	2Chr 19:2	4428
thou *k* Jehoshaphat, Thus saith	2Chr 20:15	4428
k of Judah join himself with	2Chr 20:35	4428
himself with Ahaziah *k* of Israel	2Chr 20:35	4428
sons of Jehoshaphat *k* of Israel	2Chr 21:2	4428
of Judah, and made themselves a *k*	2Chr 21:8	4428
nor in the ways of Asa *k* of Judah	2Chr 21:12	4428
his youngest son *k* in his stead	2Chr 22:1	4427
son of Jehoram *k* of Judah reigned	2Chr 22:1	4428
with Jehoram the son of Ahab *k* of	2Chr 22:5	4428
k of Syria at Ramoth-gilead	2Chr 22:5	4428
he fought with Hazael *k* of Syria	2Chr 22:6	4428
k of Judah went down to see	2Chr 22:6	4428
the daughter of the *k*, took	2Chr 22:11	4428
the daughter of *k* Jehoram	2Chr 22:11	4428
with the *k* in the house of God	2Chr 23:3	4428
shall compass the *k* round about	2Chr 23:7	4428
ye with the *k* when he cometh in	2Chr 23:7	4428
shields, that had been *k* David's	2Chr 23:9	4428
the temple, by the *k* round about	2Chr 23:10	4428
him the testimony, and made him *k*	2Chr 23:11	4427
him, and said, God save the *k*	2Chr 23:11	4428
people running and praising the *k*	2Chr 23:12	4428
the *k* stood at his pillar at the	2Chr 23:13	4428
princes and the trumpets by the *k*	2Chr 23:13	4428

Context	Reference	No.
all the people, and between the *k*	2Chr 23:16	4428
brought down the *k* from the house	2Chr 23:20	4428
set the *k* upon the throne of the	2Chr 23:20	4428
the *k* called for Jehoiada the	2Chr 24:6	4428
And the *k* and Jehoiada gave it to	2Chr 24:12	4428
rest of the money before the *k*	2Chr 24:14	4428
Judah, and made obeisance to the *k*	2Chr 24:17	4428
Then the *k* hearkened unto them	2Chr 24:17	4428
at the commandment of the *k* in	2Chr 24:21	4428
Thus Joash the *k* remembered not	2Chr 24:22	4428
of them unto the *k* of Damascus	2Chr 24:23	4428
that had killed the *k* his father	2Chr 25:3	4428
a man of God to him, saying, O *k*	2Chr 25:7	4428
that the *k* said unto him, Art	2Chr 25:16	
Then Amaziah *k* of Judah took	2Chr 25:17	4428
k of Israel, saying, Come, let us	2Chr 25:17	4428
Joash *k* of Israel sent to Amaziah	2Chr 25:18	4428
Israel sent to Amaziah *k* of Judah	2Chr 25:18	4428
So Joash the *k* of Israel went up	2Chr 25:21	4428
both he and Amaziah *k* of Judah, at	2Chr 25:21	4428
Joash the *k* of Israel took	2Chr 25:23	4428
of Israel took Amaziah *k* of Judah	2Chr 25:23	4428
Amaziah the son of Joash *k* of	2Chr 25:25	4428
k of Israel fifteen years	2Chr 25:25	4428
made him *k* in the room of his	2Chr 26:1	4427
after that the *k* slept with his	2Chr 26:2	4428
to help the *k* against the enemy	2Chr 26:13	4428
And they withstood Uzziah the *k*	2Chr 26:18	4428
Uzziah the *k* was a leper unto the	2Chr 26:21	4428
also with the *k* of the Ammonites	2Chr 27:5	4428
into the hand of the *k* of Syria	2Chr 28:5	4428
into the hand of the *k* of Israel	2Chr 28:5	4428
and Elkanah that was next to the *k*	2Chr 28:7	4428
At that time did *k* Ahaz send unto	2Chr 28:16	4428
low because of Ahaz *k* of Israel	2Chr 28:19	4428
Tilgath-pilneser *k* of Assyria	2Chr 28:20	4428
and out of the house of the *k*	2Chr 28:21	4428
and gave it unto the *k* of Assyria	2Chr 28:21	4428
this is that *k* Ahaz	2Chr 28:22	4428
to the commandment of the *k*	2Chr 29:15	4428
they went in to Hezekiah the *k*	2Chr 29:18	4428
which *k* Ahaz in his reign did	2Chr 29:19	4428
Then Hezekiah the *k* rose early	2Chr 29:20	4428
for the sin offering before the *k*	2Chr 29:23	4428
for the *k* commanded that the	2Chr 29:24	4428
ordained by David *k* of Israel	2Chr 29:27	4428
made an end of offering, the *k*	2Chr 29:29	4428
Moreover Hezekiah the *k* and the	2Chr 29:30	4428
For the *k* had taken counsel, and	2Chr 30:2	4428
And the thing pleased the *k*	2Chr 30:4	4428
went with the letters from the *k*	2Chr 30:6	4428
to the commandment of the *k*	2Chr 30:6	4428
to do the commandment of the *k*	2Chr 30:12	4428
For Hezekiah *k* of Judah did give	2Chr 30:24	4428
k of Israel there was not the	2Chr 30:26	4428
the commandment of Hezekiah the *k*	2Chr 31:13	4428
Sennacherib *k* of Assyria came, and	2Chr 32:1	4428
nor dismayed for the *k* of Assyria	2Chr 32:7	4428
the words of Hezekiah *k* of Judah	2Chr 32:8	4428
After this did Sennacherib *k* of	2Chr 32:9	4428
him,) unto Hezekiah *k* of Judah	2Chr 32:9	4428
saith Sennacherib *k* of Assyria	2Chr 32:10	4428
of the hand of the *k* of Assyria	2Chr 32:11	4428
And for this cause Hezekiah the *k*	2Chr 32:20	4428
in the camp of the *k* of Assyria	2Chr 32:21	4428
of Sennacherib the *k* of Assyria	2Chr 32:22	4428
presents to Hezekiah *k* of Judah	2Chr 32:23	4428
of the host of the *k* of Assyria	2Chr 33:11	4428
that had conspired against *k* Amon	2Chr 33:25	4428
Josiah his son *k* in his stead	2Chr 33:25	4427
Shaphan carried the book to the *k*	2Chr 34:16	4428
brought the *k* word back again	2Chr 34:16	4428
Shaphan the scribe told the *k*	2Chr 34:18	4428
And Shaphan read it before the *k*	2Chr 34:18	4428
when the *k* had heard the words of	2Chr 34:19	4428
the *k* commanded Hilkiah, and	2Chr 34:20	4428
and they that the *k* had appointed	2Chr 34:22	4428
have read before the *k* of Judah	2Chr 34:24	4428
And as for the *k* of Judah, who	2Chr 34:26	4428
So they brought the *k* word again	2Chr 34:28	4428
Then the *k* sent and gathered	2Chr 34:29	4428
the *k* went up into the house of	2Chr 34:30	4428
the *k* stood in his place, and made	2Chr 34:31	4428
of David *k* of Israel did build	2Chr 35:3	4428
the writing of David *k* of Israel	2Chr 35:4	4428
to the commandment of *k* Josiah	2Chr 35:16	4428
Necho *k* of Egypt came up to fight	2Chr 35:20	4428
to do with thee, thou *k* of Judah	2Chr 35:21	4428
And the archers shot at *k* Josiah	2Chr 35:23	4428
the *k* said to his servants, Have	2Chr 35:23	4428
made him *k* in his father's stead	2Chr 36:1	4427
the *k* of Egypt put him down at	2Chr 36:3	4428
the *k* of Egypt made Eliakim his	2Chr 36:4	4428
Eliakim his brother *k* over Judah	2Chr 36:4	4427
up Nebuchadnezzar *k* of Babylon	2Chr 36:6	4428
k Nebuchadnezzar sent, and brought	2Chr 36:10	4428
Zedekiah his brother *k* over Judah	2Chr 36:10	4427
rebelled against *k* Nebuchadnezzar	2Chr 36:13	4428
upon them the *k* of the Chaldees	2Chr 36:17	4428
LORD, and the treasures of the *k*	2Chr 36:18	4428
first year of Cyrus *k* of Persia	2Chr 36:22	4428
the spirit of Cyrus *k* of Persia	2Chr 36:22	4428
Thus saith Cyrus *k* of Persia	2Chr 36:23	4428
first year of Cyrus *k* of Persia	Ezr 1:1	4428
the spirit of Cyrus *k* of Persia	Ezr 1:1	4428
Thus saith Cyrus *k* of Persia	Ezr 1:2	4428
Also Cyrus the *k* brought forth	Ezr 1:7	4428
Even those did Cyrus *k* of Persia	Ezr 1:8	4428
whom Nebuchadnezzar the *k* of	Ezr 2:1	4428
they had of Cyrus *k* of Persia	Ezr 3:7	4428
ordinance of David *k* of Israel	Ezr 3:10	4428
days of Esar-haddon *k* of Assur	Ezr 4:2	4428
as *k* Cyrus the *k* of Persia	Ezr 4:3	4428
all the days of Cyrus *k* of Persia	Ezr 4:5	4428
the reign of Darius *k* of Persia	Ezr 4:5	4428
unto Artaxerxes *k* of Persia	Ezr 4:7	4428
to Artaxerxes the *k* in this sort	Ezr 4:8	4430
him, even unto Artaxerxes the *k*	Ezr 4:11	4430
Be it known unto the *k*, that the	Ezr 4:12	4430
Be it known now unto the *k*	Ezr 4:13	4430
have we sent and certified the *k*	Ezr 4:14	4430
We certify the *k* that, if this	Ezr 4:16	4430
Then sent the *k* an answer unto	Ezr 4:17	4430
Now when the copy of *k*	Ezr 4:23	4430
the reign of Darius *k* of Persia	Ezr 4:24	4430
the river, sent unto Darius the *k*	Ezr 5:6	4430
Unto Darius the *k*, all peace	Ezr 5:7	4430
Be it known unto the *k*, that we	Ezr 5:8	4430
which a great *k* of Israel builded	Ezr 5:11	4430
Nebuchadnezzar the *k* of Babylon	Ezr 5:12	4430
k of Babylon the same *k* Cyrus	Ezr 5:13	4430
those did Cyrus the *k* take out of	Ezr 5:14	4430
if it seem good to the *k*	Ezr 5:17	4430
k to build this house of God at	Ezr 5:17	4430
let the *k* send his pleasure to us	Ezr 5:17	4430
Then Darius the *k* made a decree	Ezr 6:1	4430
the *k* the same Cyrus the *k*	Ezr 6:3	4430
and pray for the life of the *k*	Ezr 6:10	4430
that which Darius the *k* had sent	Ezr 6:13	4430
Darius, and Artaxerxes *k* of Persia	Ezr 6:14	4430
year of the reign of Darius the *k*	Ezr 6:15	4430
of the *k* of Assyria unto them	Ezr 6:22	4428
reign of Artaxerxes *k* of Persia	Ezr 7:1	4428
the *k* granted him all his request	Ezr 7:6	4428
seventh year of Artaxerxes the *k*	Ezr 7:7	4428
was in the seventh year of the *k*	Ezr 7:8	4428
k Artaxerxes gave unto Ezra the	Ezr 7:11	4428
k of kings, unto Ezra the priest	Ezr 7:12	4430
as thou art sent of the *k*	Ezr 7:14	4430
the silver and gold, which the *k*	Ezr 7:15	4430
And I, even I Artaxerxes the *k*	Ezr 7:21	4430
wrath against the realm of the *k*	Ezr 7:23	4430
of thy God, and the law of the *k*	Ezr 7:26	4430
mercy unto me before the *k*	Ezr 7:28	4428
in the reign of Artaxerxes the *k*	Ezr 8:1	4428
of the *k* a band of soldiers	Ezr 8:22	4428
because we had spoken unto the *k*	Ezr 8:22	4428
the house of our God, which the *k*	Ezr 8:25	4428
year of Artaxerxes the *k*, that	Neh 2:1	4428
the wine, and gave it unto the *k*	Neh 2:1	4428
Wherefore the *k* said unto me	Neh 2:2	4428
the *k*, Let the *k* live for ever	Neh 2:3	4428
Then the *k* said unto me, For what	Neh 2:4	4428
unto the *k*, If it please the *k*	Neh 2:5	4428
the *k* said unto me, (the queen	Neh 2:6	4428
So it pleased the *k* to send me	Neh 2:6	4428
unto the *k*, If it please the *k*	Neh 2:7	4428
the *k* granted me, according to	Neh 2:8	4428
Now the *k* had sent captains of	Neh 2:9	4428
will ye rebel against the *k*	Neh 2:19	4428
year of Artaxerxes the *k*, that is	Neh 5:14	4428
wall, that thou mayest be their *k*	Neh 6:6	4428
saying, There is a *k* in Judah	Neh 6:7	4428
to the *k* according to these words	Neh 6:7	4428
whom Nebuchadnezzar the *k* of	Neh 7:6	4428
and the land of the *k* of Heshbon	Neh 9:22	4428
and the land of Og *k* of Bashan	Neh 9:22	4428
k of Babylon came I unto the *k*	Neh 13:6	4428
days obtained I leave of the *k*	Neh 13:6	4428
Did not Solomon *k* of Israel sin	Neh 13:26	4428
nations was there no *k* like him	Neh 13:26	4428
God made him *k* over all Israel	Neh 13:26	4428
when the *k* Ahasuerus sat on the	Est 1:2	4428
the *k* made a feast unto all the	Est 1:5	4428
according to the state of the *k*	Est 1:7	4428
for so the *k* had appointed to all	Est 1:8	4428
which belonged to *k* Ahasuerus	Est 1:9	4428
of the *k* was merry with wine	Est 1:10	4428
the presence of Ahasuerus the *k*	Est 1:10	4428
before the *k* with the crown royal	Est 1:11	4428
therefore was the *k* very wroth	Est 1:12	4428
Then the *k* said to the wise men	Est 1:13	4428
the commandment of the *k*	Est 1:15	4428
And Memucan answered before the *k*	Est 1:16	4428
hath not done wrong to the *k* only	Est 1:16	4428
the provinces of the *k* Ahasuerus	Est 1:16	4428
The *k* Ahasuerus commanded Vashti	Est 1:17	4428
If it please the *k*, let there go	Est 1:19	4428
come no more before *k* Ahasuerus	Est 1:19	4428
let the *k* give her royal estate	Est 1:19	4428
And the saying pleased the *k*	Est 1:21	4428
the *k* did according to the word	Est 1:21	4428
when the wrath of *k* Ahasuerus was	Est 2:1	4428
young virgins sought for the *k*	Est 2:2	4428
let the *k* appoint officers in all	Est 2:3	4428
the *k* be queen instead of Vashti	Est 2:4	4428
And the thing pleased the *k*	Est 2:4	4428
away with Jeconiah *k* of Judah	Est 2:6	4428
whom Nebuchadnezzar the *k* of	Est 2:6	4428
was come to go in to *k* Ahasuerus	Est 2:12	4428
thus came every maiden unto the *k*	Est 2:13	4428
she came in unto the *k* no more	Est 2:14	4428
except the *k* delighted in her, and	Est 2:14	4428
was come to go in unto the *k*	Est 2:15	4428
So Esther was taken unto *k*	Est 2:16	4428
the *k* loved Esther above all the	Est 2:17	4428
Then the *k* made a great feast	Est 2:18	4428
according to the state of the *k*	Est 2:18	4428
to lay hand on the *k* Ahasuerus	Est 2:21	4428
Esther certified the *k* thereof in	Est 2:22	4428
of the chronicles before the *k*	Est 2:23	4428
After these things did *k*	Est 3:1	4428
for the *k* had so commanded	Est 3:2	4428
the twelfth year of *k* Ahasuerus	Est 3:7	4428
And Haman said unto *k* Ahasuerus	Est 3:8	4428
If it please the *k*, let it be	Est 3:9	4428
the *k* took his ring from his hand	Est 3:10	4428
the *k* said unto Haman, The silver	Est 3:11	4428
in the name of *k* Ahasuerus was it	Est 3:12	4428
And the *k* and Haman sat down to	Est 3:15	4428
that she should go in unto the *k*	Est 4:8	4428
shall come unto the *k* into the	Est 4:11	4428
except such to whom the *k* shall	Est 4:11	4428
in unto the *k* these thirty days	Est 4:11	4428
and so will I go in unto the *k*	Est 4:16	4428
the *k* sat upon his royal throne	Est 5:1	4428
when the *k* saw Esther the queen	Est 5:2	4428
the *k* held out to Esther the	Est 5:2	4428
Then said the *k* unto her, What	Est 5:3	4428
good unto the *k*, let the *k*	Est 5:4	4428
Then the *k* said, Cause Haman to	Est 5:5	4428
So the *k* and Haman came to the	Est 5:5	4428
the *k* said unto Esther at the	Est 5:6	4428
favour in the sight of the *k*	Est 5:8	4428
if it please the *k* to grant my	Est 5:8	4428
to perform my request, let the *k*	Est 5:8	4428
do to morrow as the *k* hath said	Est 5:8	4428
wherein the *k* had promoted him	Est 5:11	4428
the princes and servants of the *k*	Est 5:11	4428
k unto the banquet that she had	Est 5:12	4428
invited unto her also with the *k*	Est 5:12	4428
the *k* that Mordecai may be hanged	Est 5:14	4428
with the *k* unto the banquet	Est 5:14	4428
that night could not the *k* sleep	Est 6:1	4428
and they were read before the *k*	Est 6:1	4428
to lay hand on the *k* Ahasuerus	Est 6:2	4428
the *k* said, What honour and	Est 6:3	4428
the *k* said, Who is in the court	Est 6:4	4428
to speak unto the *k* to hang	Est 6:4	4428
the *k* said, Let him come in	Est 6:5	4428
the *k* said unto him, What shall	Est 6:6	4428
whom the *k* delighteth to honour	Est 6:6	4428
To whom would the *k* delight to do	Est 6:6	4428
And Haman answered the *k*, For the	Est 6:7	4428
whom the *k* delighteth to honour	Est 6:7	4428
brought which the *k* useth to wear	Est 6:8	4428
the horse that the *k* rideth upon	Est 6:8	4428
whom the *k* delighteth to honour	Est 6:9	4428
whom the *k* delighteth to honour	Est 6:9	4428
Then the *k* said to Haman, Make	Est 6:10	4428
whom the *k* delighteth to honour	Est 6:11	4428
So the *k* and Haman came to banquet.	Est 7:1	4428
the *k* said again unto Esther on	Est 7:2	4428
O *k*, and if it please the *k*	Est 7:3	4428
Then the *k* Ahasuerus answered and	Est 7:5	4428
Haman was afraid before the *k*	Est 7:6	4428
the *k* arising from the banquet of	Est 7:7	4428
determined against him by the *k*	Est 7:7	4428
Then the *k* returned out of the	Est 7:8	4428
Then said the *k*, Will he force	Est 7:8	4428
chamberlains, said before the *k*	Est 7:9	4428
who had spoken good for the *k*	Est 7:9	4428
Then the *k* said, Hang him thereon	Est 7:9	4428
On that day did the *k* Ahasuerus	Est 8:1	4428
And Mordecai came before the *k*	Est 8:1	4428
the *k* took off his ring, which he	Est 8:2	4428
spake yet again before the *k*	Est 8:3	4428
Then the *k* held out the golden	Est 8:4	4428
arose, and stood before the *k*	Est 8:4	4428
And said, If it please the *k*	Est 8:5	4428
the thing seem right before the *k*	Est 8:5	4428
Then the *k* Ahasuerus said unto	Est 8:7	4428
he wrote in the *k* Ahasuerus' name	Est 8:10	4428
Wherein the *k* granted the Jews	Est 8:11	4428
all the provinces of *k* Ahasuerus	Est 8:12	4428
of the *k* in royal apparel of blue	Est 8:15	4428
the provinces of the *k* Ahasuerus	Est 9:2	4428
deputies, and officers of the *k*	Est 9:3	4428
palace was brought before the *k*	Est 9:11	4428
the *k* said unto Esther the queen	Est 9:12	4428
said Esther, If it please the *k*	Est 9:13	4428
the *k* commanded it so to be done	Est 9:14	4428
the provinces of the *k* Ahasuerus	Est 9:20	4428
But when Esther came before the *k*	Est 9:25	4428
the *k* Ahasuerus laid a tribute	Est 10:1	4428
whereunto the *k* advanced him	Est 10:2	4428
the Jew was next unto *k* Ahasuerus	Est 10:3	4428
as a *k* ready to the battle	Job 15:24	4428
bring him to the *k* of terrors	Job 18:14	4428
dwelt as a *k* in the army, as one	Job 29:25	4428
Is it fit to say to a *k*, Thou art	Job 34:18	4428
he is a *k* over all the children	Job 41:34	4428
Yet have I set my *k* upon my holy	Ps 2:6	4428
unto the voice of my cry, my *K*	Ps 5:2	4428
The LORD is *K* for ever and ever	Ps 10:16	4428
deliverance giveth he to his *k*	Ps 18:50	4428
let the *k* hear us when we call	Ps 20:9	4428
The *k* shall joy in thy strength	Ps 21:1	4428
For the *k* trusteth in the LORD	Ps 21:7	4428
the *K* of glory shall come in	Ps 24:7	4428
Who is this *K* of glory	Ps 24:8	4428
the *K* of glory shall come in	Ps 24:9	4428
Who is this *K* of glory	Ps 24:10	4428
of hosts, he is the *K* of glory	Ps 24:10	4428
yea, the LORD sitteth *K* for ever	Ps 29:10	4428
There is no *k* saved by the	Ps 33:16	4428
Thou art my *K*, O God	Ps 44:4	4428
which I have made touching the *k*	Ps 45:1	4428
So shall the *k* greatly desire thy	Ps 45:11	4428
the *k* in raiment of needlework	Ps 45:14	4428
he is a great *K* over all the	Ps 47:2	4428
sing praises unto our *K*, sing	Ps 47:6	4428
For God is the *K* of all the earth	Ps 47:7	4428
north, the city of the great *K*	Ps 48:2	4428
But the *k* shall rejoice in God	Ps 63:11	4428
even the goings of my God, my *K*	Ps 68:24	4428
Give the *k* thy judgments, O God	Ps 72:1	4428
For God is my *K* of old, working	Ps 74:12	4428
altars, O LORD of hosts, my *K*	Ps 84:3	4428
the Holy One of Israel is our *k*	Ps 89:18	4428
God, and a great *K* above all gods	Ps 95:3	4428
noise before the LORD, the *K*	Ps 98:6	4428

The *k* sent and loosed him ... Ps 105:20 4428
Sihon *k* of the Amorites ... Ps 135:11 4428
Og *k* of Bashan, and all the ... Ps 135:11 4428
Sihon *k* of the Amorites ... Ps 136:19 4428
And Og the *k* of Bashan ... Ps 136:20 4428
I will extol thee, my God, O *k* ... Ps 145:1 4428
of Zion be joyful in their *K* ... Ps 149:2 4428
the son of David, *k* of Israel ... Prov 1:1 4428
sentence is in the lips of the *k* ... Prov 16:10 4428
The wrath of a *k* is as messengers ... Prov 16:14 4428
The fear of a *k* is as the roaring ... Prov 20:2 4428
A *k* that sitteth in the throne of ... Prov 20:8 4428
A wise *k* scattereth the wicked, ... Prov 20:26 4428
Mercy and truth preserve the *k* ... Prov 20:28 4428
lips the *k* shall be his friend ... Prov 22:11 4428
son, fear thou the LORD and the *k* ... Prov 24:21 4428
of Hezekiah *k* of Judah copied out ... Prov 25:1 4428
away the wicked from before the *k* ... Prov 25:5 4428
thyself in the presence of the *k* ... Prov 25:6 4428
The *k* by judgment establisheth ... Prov 29:4 4428
The *k* that faithfully judgeth the ... Prov 29:14 4428
The locusts have no *k*, yet go ... Prov 30:27 4428
and a *k*, against whom there is no ... Prov 30:31 4428
The words of *k* Lemuel, the ... Prov 31:1 4428
the son of David, *k* in Jerusalem ... Eccl 1:1 4428
I the Preacher was *k* over Israel ... Eccl 1:12 4428
man do that cometh after the *k* ... Eccl 2:12 4428
child than an old and foolish *k* ... Eccl 4:13 4428
the *k* himself is served by the ... Eccl 5:9 4428
Where the word of a *k* is, there ... Eccl 8:4 4428
there came a great *k* against it ... Eccl 9:14 4428
when thy *k* is a child, and thy ... Eccl 10:16 4428
when thy *k* is the son of nobles, ... Eccl 10:17 4428
Curse not the *k*, no not in thy ... Eccl 10:20 4428
the *k* hath brought me into his ... Song 1:4 4428
While the *k* sitteth at his table, ... Song 1:12 4428
K Solomon made himself a chariot ... Song 3:9 4428
behold *k* Solomon with the crown ... Song 3:11 4428
the *k* is held in the galleries ... Song 7:5 4428
In the year that *k* Uzziah died I ... Is 6:1 4428
for mine eyes have seen the *K* ... Is 6:5 4428
k of Judah, that Rezin the *k* ... Is 7:1 4428
Judah, that Rezin the *k* of Syria ... Is 7:1 4428
k of Israel, went up toward ... Is 7:1 4428
set a *k* in the midst of it, even ... Is 7:6 4428
even the *k* of Assyria ... Is 7:17 4428
by the *k* of Assyria, the head, and ... Is 7:20 4428
away before the *k* of Assyria ... Is 8:4 4428
even the *k* of Assyria, and all his ... Is 8:7 4428
fret themselves, and curse their *k* ... Is 8:21 4428
stout heart of the *k* of Assyria ... Is 10:12 4428
proverb against the *k* of Babylon ... Is 14:4 4428
In the year that *k* Ahaz died was ... Is 14:28 4428
a fierce *k* shall rule over them, ... Is 19:4 4428
(when Sargon the *k* of Assyria ... Is 20:1 4428
So shall the *k* of Assyria lead ... Is 20:4 4428
delivered from the *k* of Assyria ... Is 20:6 4428
according to the days of one *k* ... Is 23:15 4428
yea, for the *k* it is prepared ... Is 30:33 4428
a *k* shall reign in righteousness, ... Is 32:1 4428
shall see the *k* in his beauty ... Is 33:17 4428
our lawgiver, the LORD is our *k* ... Is 33:22 4428
the fourteenth year of *k* Hezekiah ... Is 36:1 4428
that Sennacherib *k* of Assyria ... Is 36:1 4428
the *k* of Assyria sent Rabshakeh ... Is 36:2 4428
unto *k* Hezekiah with a great army ... Is 36:2 4428
Hezekiah, Thus saith the great *k* ... Is 36:4 4428
the *k* of Assyria, What confidence ... Is 36:4 4428
so is Pharaoh *k* of Egypt to all ... Is 36:6 4428
to my master the *k* of Assyria ... Is 36:8 4428
the great *k*, the *k* of Assyria ... Is 36:13 4428
Thus saith the *k*, Let not ... Is 36:14 4428
into the hand of the *k* of Assyria ... Is 36:15 4428
for thus saith the *k* of Assyria ... Is 36:16 4428
of the hand of the *k* of Assyria ... Is 36:18 4428
when *k* Hezekiah heard it, that he ... Is 37:1 4428
whom the *k* of Assyria his master ... Is 37:4 4428
So the servants of *k* Hezekiah ... Is 37:5 4428
k of Assyria have blasphemed me ... Is 37:6 4428
found the *k* of Assyria warring ... Is 37:8 4428
concerning Tirhakah *k* of Ethiopia ... Is 37:9 4428
ye speak to Hezekiah *k* of Judah ... Is 37:10 4428
into the hand of the *k* of Assyria ... Is 37:10 4428
Where is the *k* of Hamath ... Is 37:13 4428
the *k* of Arphad ... Is 37:13 4428
the *k* of the city of Sepharvaim, ... Is 37:13 4428
against Sennacherib *k* of Assyria ... Is 37:21 4428
LORD concerning the *k* of Assyria ... Is 37:33 4428
So Sennacherib *k* of Assyria ... Is 37:37 4428
of the hand of the *k* of Assyria ... Is 38:6 4428
writing of Hezekiah *k* of Judah ... Is 38:9 4428
k of Babylon, sent letters and a ... Is 39:1 4428
the prophet unto *k* Hezekiah ... Is 39:3 4428
in the palace of the *k* of Babylon ... Is 39:7 4428
reasons, saith the *K* of Jacob ... Is 41:21 4428
the creator of Israel, your *K* ... Is 43:15 4428
saith the LORD the *K* of Israel ... Is 44:6 4428
wentest to the *k* with ointment ... Is 57:9 4428
Josiah the son of Amon *k* of Judah ... Jer 1:2 4428
the son of Josiah *k* of Judah ... Jer 1:3 4428
the son of Josiah *k* of Judah ... Jer 1:3 4428
me in the days of Josiah the *k* ... Jer 3:6 4428
the heart of the *k* shall perish ... Jer 4:9 4428
is not her *k* in her ... Jer 8:19 4428
not fear thee, O *K* of nations ... Jer 10:7 4428
living God, and an everlasting *k* ... Jer 10:10 4428
Say unto the *k* and to the queen, ... Jer 13:18 4428
the son of Hezekiah *k* of Judah ... Jer 15:4 4428
into the hand of the *k* of Babylon ... Jer 20:4 4428
when *k* Zedekiah sent unto him ... Jer 21:1 4428
for Nebuchadrezzar *k* of Babylon ... Jer 21:2 4428
ye fight against the *k* of Babylon ... Jer 21:4 4428
will deliver Zedekiah *k* of Judah ... Jer 21:7 4428
of Nebuchadrezzar *k* of Babylon ... Jer 21:7 4428

into the hand of the *k* of Babylon ... Jer 21:10 4428
the house of the *k* of Judah ... Jer 21:11 4428
to the house of the *k* of Judah ... Jer 22:1 4428
O *k* of Judah, that sittest upon ... Jer 22:2 4428
the son of Josiah *k* of Judah ... Jer 22:11 4428
the son of Josiah *k* of Judah ... Jer 22:18 4428
Coniah the son of Jehoiakim *k* of ... Jer 22:24 4428
of Nebuchadrezzar *k* of Babylon ... Jer 22:25 4428
a *K* shall reign and prosper, and ... Jer 23:5 4428
after that Nebuchadrezzar *k* of ... Jer 24:1 4428
the son of Jehoiakim *k* of Judah ... Jer 24:1 4428
I give Zedekiah the *k* of Judah ... Jer 24:8 4428
the son of Josiah *k* of Judah ... Jer 25:1 4428
of Nebuchadrezzar *k* of Babylon ... Jer 25:1 4428
Josiah the son of Amon *k* of Judah ... Jer 25:3 4428
Nebuchadrezzar the *k* of Babylon ... Jer 25:9 4428
the *k* of Babylon seventy years ... Jer 25:11 4428
I will punish the *k* of Babylon ... Jer 25:12 4428
Pharaoh *k* of Egypt, and his ... Jer 25:19 4428
the *k* of Sheshach shall drink ... Jer 25:26 4428
k of Judah came this word from ... Jer 26:1 4428
the days of Hezekiah *k* of Judah ... Jer 26:18 4428
Did Hezekiah *k* of Judah and all ... Jer 26:19 4428
And when Jehoiakim the *k*, with all ... Jer 26:21 4428
the *k* sought to put him to death ... Jer 26:21 4428
Jehoiakim the *k* sent men into ... Jer 26:22 4428
brought him unto Jehoiakim the *k* ... Jer 26:23 4428
k of Judah came this word unto ... Jer 27:1 4428
And send them to the *k* of Edom ... Jer 27:3 4428
to the *k* of Moab ... Jer 27:3 4428
to the *k* of the Ammonites ... Jer 27:3 4428
to the *k* of Tyrus ... Jer 27:3 4428
to the *k* of Zidon ... Jer 27:3 4428
unto Zedekiah *k* of Judah ... Jer 27:3 4428
Nebuchadnezzar the *k* of Babylon ... Jer 27:6 4428
Nebuchadnezzar the *k* of Babylon ... Jer 27:8 4428
the yoke of the *k* of Babylon ... Jer 27:8 4428
shall not serve the *k* of Babylon ... Jer 27:9 4428
the yoke of the *k* of Babylon ... Jer 27:11 4428
I spake also to Zedekiah *k* of ... Jer 27:12 4428
the yoke of the *k* of Babylon ... Jer 27:12 4428
will not serve the *k* of Babylon ... Jer 27:13 4428
shall not serve the *k* of Babylon ... Jer 27:14 4428
serve the *k* of Babylon, and live ... Jer 27:17 4428
and in the house of the *k* of Judah ... Jer 27:18 4428
k of Babylon took not, when he ... Jer 27:20 4428
k of Judah from Jerusalem to ... Jer 27:20 4428
and in the house of the *k* of Judah ... Jer 27:21 4428
the reign of Zedekiah *k* of Judah ... Jer 28:1 4428
the yoke of the *k* of Babylon ... Jer 28:2 4428
that Nebuchadnezzar *k* of Babylon ... Jer 28:3 4428
the son of Jehoiakim *k* of Judah ... Jer 28:4 4428
the yoke of the *k* of Babylon ... Jer 28:4 4428
the yoke of Nebuchadnezzar *k* of ... Jer 28:11 4428
serve Nebuchadnezzar *k* of Babylon ... Jer 28:14 4428
(After that Jeconiah the *k* ... Jer 29:2 4428
(whom Zedekiah *k* of Judah sent ... Jer 29:3 4428
k of Babylon) saying, ... Jer 29:3 4428
k that sitteth upon the throne of ... Jer 29:16 4428
of Nebuchadrezzar *k* of Babylon ... Jer 29:21 4428
whom the *k* of Babylon roasted in ... Jer 29:22 4428
LORD their God, and David their *k* ... Jer 30:9 4428
tenth year of Zedekiah *k* of Judah ... Jer 32:1 4428
For then the *k* of Babylon's army ... Jer 32:2 4428
was in the *k* of Judah's house ... Jer 32:2 4428
For Zedekiah *k* of Judah had shut ... Jer 32:3 4428
into the hand of the *k* of Babylon ... Jer 32:3 4428
Zedekiah *k* of Judah shall not ... Jer 32:4 4428
into the hand of the *k* of Babylon ... Jer 32:4 4428
of Nebuchadrezzar *k* of Babylon ... Jer 32:28 4428
of the *k* of Babylon by the sword ... Jer 32:36 4428
when Nebuchadnezzar *k* of Babylon ... Jer 34:1 4428
and speak to Zedekiah *k* of Judah ... Jer 34:2 4428
into the hand of the *k* of Babylon ... Jer 34:2 4428
the eyes of the *k* of Babylon ... Jer 34:3 4428
the LORD, O Zedekiah *k* of Judah ... Jer 34:4 4428
Zedekiah *k* of Judah in Jerusalem ... Jer 34:6 4428
When the *k* of Babylon's army ... Jer 34:7 4428
after that the *k* Zedekiah had ... Jer 34:8 4428
And Zedekiah *k* of Judah and his ... Jer 34:21 4428
hand of the *k* of Babylon's army ... Jer 34:21 4428
the son of Josiah *k* of Judah ... Jer 35:1 4428
when Nebuchadrezzar *k* of Babylon ... Jer 35:11 4428
the son of Josiah *k* of Judah ... Jer 36:1 4428
the son of Josiah *k* of Judah ... Jer 36:9 4428
tell the *k* of all these words ... Jer 36:16 4428
went in to the *k* into the court ... Jer 36:20 4428
the words in the ears of the *k* ... Jer 36:20 4428
So the *k* sent Jehudi to fetch the ... Jer 36:21 4428
read it in the ears of the *k* ... Jer 36:21 4428
princes which stood beside the *k* ... Jer 36:21 4428
Now the *k* sat in the winterhouse ... Jer 36:22 4428
their garments, neither the *k* ... Jer 36:24 4428
had made intercession to the *k* ... Jer 36:25 4428
But the *k* commanded Jerahmeel the ... Jer 36:26 4428
after that the *k* had burned the ... Jer 36:27 4428
which Jehoiakim the *k* of Judah ... Jer 36:28 4428
shalt say to Jehoiakim *k* of Judah ... Jer 36:29 4428
The *k* of Babylon shall certainly ... Jer 36:29 4428
the LORD of Jehoiakim *k* of Judah ... Jer 36:30 4428
of the book which Jehoiakim *k* of ... Jer 36:32 4428
k Zedekiah the son of Josiah ... Jer 37:1 4428
whom Nebuchadrezzar *k* of Babylon ... Jer 37:1 4428
made *k* in the land of Judah ... Jer 37:1 4428
Zedekiah the *k* sent Jehucal the ... Jer 37:3 4428
shall ye say to the *k* of Judah ... Jer 37:7 4428
Then Zedekiah the *k* sent, and took ... Jer 37:17 4428
the *k* asked him secretly in his ... Jer 37:17 4428
into the hand of the *k* of Babylon ... Jer 37:17 4428
Jeremiah said unto *k* Zedekiah ... Jer 37:18 4428
The *k* of Babylon shall not come ... Jer 37:19 4428
now, I pray thee, O my lord the *k* ... Jer 37:20 4428
Then Zedekiah the *k* commanded ... Jer 37:21 4428
hand of the *k* of Babylon's army ... Jer 38:3 4428

the princes said unto the *k* ... Jer 38:4 4428
Then Zedekiah the *k* said, Behold, ... Jer 38:5 4428
for the *k* is not he that can do ... Jer 38:5 4428
the *k* then sitting in the gate of ... Jer 38:7 4428
king's house, and spake to the *k* ... Jer 38:8 4428
My lord the *k*, these men have ... Jer 38:9 4428
Then the *k* commanded Ebed-melech ... Jer 38:10 4428
house of the *k* under the treasury ... Jer 38:11 4428
Then Zedekiah the *k* sent, and took ... Jer 38:14 4428
the *k* said unto Jeremiah, I will ... Jer 38:14 4428
So Zedekiah the *k* sware secretly ... Jer 38:16 4428
unto the *k* of Babylon's princes ... Jer 38:17 4428
to the *k* of Babylon's princes ... Jer 38:18 4428
Zedekiah the *k* said unto Jeremiah ... Jer 38:19 4428
the *k* of Judah's house shall be ... Jer 38:22 4428
to the *k* of Babylon's princes ... Jer 38:22 4428
by the hand of the *k* of Babylon ... Jer 38:23 4428
what thou hast said unto the *k* ... Jer 38:25 4428
also what the *k* said unto thee ... Jer 38:25 4428
my supplication before the *k* ... Jer 38:26 4428
words that the *k* had commanded ... Jer 38:27 4428
ninth year of Zedekiah *k* of Judah ... Jer 39:1 4428
came Nebuchadrezzar *k* of Babylon ... Jer 39:1 4428
of the *k* of Babylon came in ... Jer 39:3 4428
the princes of the *k* of Babylon ... Jer 39:3 4428
Zedekiah the *k* of Judah saw them ... Jer 39:4 4428
him up to Nebuchadnezzar *k* of ... Jer 39:5 4428
Then the *k* of Babylon slew the ... Jer 39:6 4428
also the *k* of Babylon slew all ... Jer 39:6 4428
Now Nebuchadrezzar *k* of Babylon ... Jer 39:11 4428
all the *k* of Babylon's princes ... Jer 39:13 4428
whom the *k* of Babylon hath made ... Jer 40:5 4428
heard that the *k* of Babylon had ... Jer 40:7 4428
serve the *k* of Babylon, and it ... Jer 40:9 4428
heard that the *k* of Babylon had ... Jer 40:11 4428
the *k* of the Ammonites hath sent ... Jer 40:14 4428
royal, and the princes of the *k* ... Jer 41:1 4428
whom the *k* of Babylon had made ... Jer 41:2 4428
was it which Asa the *k* had made ... Jer 41:9 4428
for fear of Baasha *k* of Israel ... Jer 41:9 4428
whom the *k* of Babylon made ... Jer 41:18 4428
Be not afraid of the *k* of Babylon ... Jer 42:11 4428
Nebuchadrezzar the *k* of Babylon ... Jer 43:10 4428
I will give Pharaoh-hophra *k* of ... Jer 44:30 4428
as I gave Zedekiah *k* of Judah ... Jer 44:30 4428
of Nebuchadrezzar *k* of Babylon ... Jer 44:30 4428
the son of Josiah *k* of Judah ... Jer 45:1 4428
army of Pharaoh-necho *k* of Egypt ... Jer 46:2 4428
which Nebuchadrezzar *k* of Babylon ... Jer 46:2 4428
the son of Josiah *k* of Judah ... Jer 46:2 4428
how Nebuchadrezzar *k* of Babylon ... Jer 46:13 4428
Pharaoh *k* of Egypt is but a noise ... Jer 46:17 4428
As I live, saith the *K*, whose ... Jer 46:18 4428
of Nebuchadrezzar *k* of Babylon ... Jer 46:26 4428
to the slaughter, saith the *K* ... Jer 48:15 4428
why then doth their *k* inherit Gad ... Jer 49:1 4428
for their *k* shall go into ... Jer 49:3 4428
which Nebuchadrezzar *k* of Babylon ... Jer 49:28 4428
for Nebuchadrezzar *k* of Babylon ... Jer 49:30 4428
the reign of Zedekiah *k* of Judah ... Jer 49:34 4428
and will destroy from thence the *k* ... Jer 49:38 4428
first the *k* of Assyria hath ... Jer 50:17 4428
last this Nebuchadrezzar *k* of ... Jer 50:17 4428
I will punish the *k* of Babylon ... Jer 50:18 4428
I have punished the *k* of Assyria ... Jer 50:18 4428
The *k* of Babylon hath heard the ... Jer 50:43 4428
to shew the *k* of Babylon that his ... Jer 51:31 4428
Nebuchadrezzar the *k* of Babylon ... Jer 51:34 4428
sleep, and not wake, saith the *K* ... Jer 51:57 4428
k of Judah into Babylon in the ... Jer 51:59 4428
rebelled against the *k* of Babylon ... Jer 52:3 4428
Nebuchadrezzar *k* of Babylon came ... Jer 52:4 4428
the eleventh year of *k* Zedekiah ... Jer 52:5 4428
the Chaldeans pursued after the *k* ... Jer 52:8 4428
Then they took the *k* ... Jer 52:9 4428
carried him up unto the *k* of ... Jer 52:9 4428
the *k* of Babylon slew the sons of ... Jer 52:10 4428
the *k* of Babylon bound him in ... Jer 52:11 4428
of Nebuchadrezzar *k* of Babylon ... Jer 52:12 4428
which served the *k* of Babylon ... Jer 52:12 4428
that fell to the *k* of Babylon ... Jer 52:15 4428
which *k* Solomon had made in the ... Jer 52:20 4428
brought them to the *k* of Babylon ... Jer 52:26 4428
the *k* of Babylon smote them, and ... Jer 52:27 4428
of Jehoiachin *k* of Judah, in the ... Jer 52:31 4428
that Evil-merodach *k* of Babylon ... Jer 52:31 4428
the head of Jehoiachin *k* of Judah ... Jer 52:31 4428
given him of the *k* of Babylon ... Jer 52:34 4428
indignation of his anger the *k* ... Lam 2:6 4428
her *k* and her princes are among ... Lam 2:9 4428
year of *k* Jehoiachin's captivity ... Eze 1:2 4428
The *k* shall mourn, and the prince ... Eze 7:27 4428
the *k* of Babylon is come to ... Eze 17:12 4428
and hath taken the *k* thereof ... Eze 17:12 4428
the *k* dwelleth that made him *k* ... Eze 17:16 4428
the *k* dwelleth that made him *k* ... Eze 17:16 4427
brought him to the *k* of Babylon ... Eze 19:9 4428
of the *k* of Babylon may come ... Eze 21:19 4428
For the *k* of Babylon stood at the ... Eze 21:21 4428
the *k* of Babylon set himself ... Eze 24:2 4428
Tyrus Nebuchadrezzar *k* of Babylon ... Eze 26:7 4428
a *k* of kings, from the north, ... Eze 26:7 4428
a lamentation upon the *k* of Tyrus ... Eze 28:12 4428
face against Pharaoh *k* of Egypt ... Eze 29:2 4428
Pharaoh *k* of Egypt, the great ... Eze 29:3 4428
Nebuchadrezzar *k* of Babylon ... Eze 29:18 4428
unto Nebuchadrezzar *k* of Babylon ... Eze 29:19 4428
of Nebuchadrezzar *k* of Babylon ... Eze 30:10 4428
the arm of Pharaoh *k* of Egypt ... Eze 30:21 4428
I am against Pharaoh *k* of Egypt ... Eze 30:22 4428
the arms of the *k* of Babylon ... Eze 30:24 4428
the arms of the *k* of Babylon ... Eze 30:25 4428
into the hand of the *k* of Babylon ... Eze 30:25 4428
speak unto Pharaoh *k* of Egypt ... Eze 31:2 4428

for Pharaoh *k* of Egypt, and say ... Eze 32:2 4428
The sword of the *k* of Babylon ... Eze 32:11 4428
one *k* shall be *k* to them all ... Eze 37:22 4428
my servant shall be *k* over them ... Eze 37:24 4428
k of Judah came Nebuchadnezzar ... Dan 1:1 4428
k of Babylon unto Jerusalem ... Dan 1:1 4428
k of Judah into his hand, with ... Dan 1:2 4428
the *k* spake unto Ashpenaz the ... Dan 1:3 4428
the *k* appointed them a daily ... Dan 1:5 4428
they might stand before the *k* ... Dan 1:5 4428
unto Daniel, I fear my lord the *k* ... Dan 1:10 4428
make me endanger my head to the *k* ... Dan 1:10 4428
k had said he should bring them ... Dan 1:18 4428
And the *k* communed with them ... Dan 1:19 4428
therefore stood they before the *k* ... Dan 1:19 4428
that the *k* enquired of them, he ... Dan 1:20 4428
unto the first year of *k* Cyrus ... Dan 1:21 4428
Then the *k* commanded to call the ... Dan 2:2 4428
for to shew the *k* his dreams ... Dan 2:2 4428
they came and stood before the *k* ... Dan 2:2 4428
the *k* said unto them, I have ... Dan 2:3 4428
the Chaldeans to the *k* in Syriack ... Dan 2:4 4428
O *k*, live for ever ... Dan 2:4 4430
The *k* answered and said to the ... Dan 2:5 4430
Let the *k* tell his servants the ... Dan 2:7 4430
The *k* answered and said, I know of ... Dan 2:8 4430
Chaldeans answered before the *k* ... Dan 2:10 4430
therefore there is no *k*, lord, ... Dan 2:10 4430
a rare thing that the *k* requireth ... Dan 2:11 4430
that can shew it before the *k* ... Dan 2:11 4430
For this cause the *k* was angry ... Dan 2:12 4430
is the decree so hasty from the *k* ... Dan 2:15 4430
desired of the *k* that he would ... Dan 2:16 4430
shew the *k* the interpretation ... Dan 2:16 4430
whom the *k* had ordained to ... Dan 2:24 4430
bring me in before the *k*, and I ... Dan 2:24 4430
unto the *k* the interpretation ... Dan 2:24 4430
in Daniel before the *k* in haste ... Dan 2:25 4430
unto the *k* the interpretation ... Dan 2:25 4430
The *k* answered and said to Daniel, ... Dan 2:26 4430
answered in the presence of the *k* ... Dan 2:27 4430
The secret which the *k* hath ... Dan 2:27 4430
the soothsayers, shew unto the *k* ... Dan 2:27 4430
secrets, and maketh known to the *k* ... Dan 2:28 4430
As for thee, O *k*, thy thoughts ... Dan 2:29 4430
known the interpretation to the *k* ... Dan 2:30 4430
Thou, O *k*, sawest, and behold a ... Dan 2:31 4430
thereof before the *k* ... Dan 2:36 4430
Thou, O *k*, art a *k* of kings ... Dan 2:37 4430
to the *k* what shall come to pass ... Dan 2:45 4430
Then the *k* Nebuchadnezzar fell ... Dan 2:46 4430
The *k* answered unto Daniel, and ... Dan 2:47 4430
Then the *k* made Daniel a great ... Dan 2:48 4430
Then Daniel requested of the *k* ... Dan 2:49 4430
Daniel sat in the gate of the *k* ... Dan 2:49 4430
Nebuchadnezzar the *k* made an ... Dan 3:1 4430
Then Nebuchadnezzar the *k* sent to ... Dan 3:2 4430
Nebuchadnezzar the *k* had set up ... Dan 3:2 4430
Nebuchadnezzar the *k* had set up ... Dan 3:3 4430
Nebuchadnezzar the *k* hath set up ... Dan 3:5 4430
Nebuchadnezzar the *k* had set up ... Dan 3:7 4430
to the *k* Nebuchadnezzar, O *k* ... Dan 3:9 4430
Thou, O *k*, hast made a decree, ... Dan 3:10 4430
these men, O *k*, have not regarded ... Dan 3:12 4430
brought these men before the *k* ... Dan 3:13 4430
answered and said to the *k* ... Dan 3:16 4430
deliver us out of thine hand, O *k* ... Dan 3:17 4430
not, be it known unto thee, O *k* ... Dan 3:18 4430
Nebuchadnezzar the *k* was astonied ... Dan 3:24 4430
and said unto the *k*, True, O *k* ... Dan 3:24 4430
Then the *k* promoted Shadrach, ... Dan 3:30 4430
Nebuchadnezzar the *k*, unto all ... Dan 4:1 4430
This dream I *k* Nebuchadnezzar ... Dan 4:18 4430
The *k* spake, and said, ... Dan 4:19 4430
It is thou, O *k*, that art grown ... Dan 4:22 4430
whereas the *k* saw a watcher and an ... Dan 4:23 4430
This is the interpretation, O *k* ... Dan 4:24 4430
which is come upon my lord the *k* ... Dan 4:24 4430
Wherefore, O *k*, let my counsel be ... Dan 4:27 4430
came upon the *k* Nebuchadnezzar ... Dan 4:28 4430
The *k* spake, and said, Is not this ... Dan 4:30 4430
O *k* Nebuchadnezzar, to thee it is ... Dan 4:31 4430
extol and honour the *K* of heaven ... Dan 4:37 4430
Belshazzar the *k* made a great ... Dan 5:1 4430
that the *k*, and his princes, his ... Dan 5:2 4430
and the *k*, and his princes, his ... Dan 5:3 4430
the *k* saw the part of the hand ... Dan 5:5 4430
The *k* cried aloud to bring in the ... Dan 5:7 4430
the *k* spake, and said to the wise ... Dan 5:7 4430
nor make known to the *k* the ... Dan 5:8 4430
Then was *k* Belshazzar greatly ... Dan 5:9 4430
by reason of the words of the *k* ... Dan 5:10 4430
and the queen spake and said, O *k* ... Dan 5:10 4430
whom the *k* Nebuchadnezzar thy ... Dan 5:11 4430
Nebuchadnezzar thy father, the *k* ... Dan 5:11 4430
whom the *k* named Belteshazzar ... Dan 5:12 4430
Daniel brought in before the *k* ... Dan 5:13 4430
the *k* spake and said unto Daniel, ... Dan 5:13 4430
whom the *k* my father brought out ... Dan 5:13 4430
answered and said before the *k* ... Dan 5:17 4430
will read the writing unto the *k* ... Dan 5:17 4430
O thou *k*, the most high God gave ... Dan 5:18 4430
the *k* of the Chaldeans slain ... Dan 5:30 4430
the *k* should have no damage ... Dan 6:2 4430
the *k* thought to set him over the ... Dan 6:3 4430
assembled together to the *k* ... Dan 6:6 4430
unto him, *K* Darius, live for ever ... Dan 6:6 4430
thirty days, save of thee, O *k* ... Dan 6:7 4430
Now, O *k*, establish the decree, ... Dan 6:8 4430
Wherefore *k* Darius signed the ... Dan 6:9 4430
spake before the *k* concerning the ... Dan 6:12 4430
thirty days, save of thee, O *k* ... Dan 6:12 4430
The *k* answered and said, The thing ... Dan 6:12 4430
they and said before the *k* ... Dan 6:13 4430
of Judah, regardeth not thee, O *k* ... Dan 6:13 4430
Then the *k*, when he heard these ... Dan 6:14 4430
these men assembled unto the *k* ... Dan 6:15 4430
and said unto the *k*, Know, O *k* ... Dan 6:15 4430
the *k* establisheth may be changed ... Dan 6:15 4430
Then the *k* commanded, and they ... Dan 6:16 4430
Now the *k* spake and said unto ... Dan 6:16 4430
the *k* sealed it with his own ... Dan 6:17 4430
Then the *k* went to his palace, and ... Dan 6:18 4430
Then the *k* arose very early in ... Dan 6:19 4430
the *k* spake and said to Daniel, O ... Dan 6:20 4430
said Daniel unto the *k*, O *k* ... Dan 6:21 4430
and also before thee, O *k*, have I ... Dan 6:22 4430
Then was the *k* exceeding glad for ... Dan 6:23 4430
the *k* commanded, and they brought ... Dan 6:24 4430
Then *k* Darius wrote unto all ... Dan 6:25 4430
k of Babylon Daniel had a dream ... Dan 7:1 4430
of *k* Belshazzar a vision appeared ... Dan 8:1 4428
the rough goat is the *k* of Grecia ... Dan 8:21 4428
between his eyes is the first *k* ... Dan 8:21 4428
a *k* of fierce countenance, and ... Dan 8:23 4428
which was made *k* over the realm ... Dan 9:1 4427
In the third year of Cyrus *k* of ... Dan 10:1 4428
a mighty *k* shall stand up, that ... Dan 11:3 4428
the *k* of the south shall be ... Dan 11:5 4428
to the *k* of the north to make an ... Dan 11:6 4428
fortress of the *k* of the north ... Dan 11:7 4428
years than the *k* of the north ... Dan 11:8 4428
So the *k* of the south shall come ... Dan 11:9 4428
the *k* of the south shall be moved ... Dan 11:11 4428
him, even with the *k* of the north ... Dan 11:11 4428
For the *k* of the north shall ... Dan 11:13 4428
up against the *k* of the south ... Dan 11:14 4428
So the *k* of the north shall come, ... Dan 11:15 4428
his courage against the *k* of the ... Dan 11:25 4428
the *k* of the south shall be ... Dan 11:25 4428
the *k* shall do according to his ... Dan 11:36 4428
the *k* of the south push at him ... Dan 11:40 4428
the *k* of the north shall come ... Dan 11:40 4428
the son of Joash, *k* of Israel ... Hos 1:1 4428
shall abide many days without a *k* ... Hos 3:4 4428
LORD their God, and David their *k* ... Hos 3:5 4428
and give ye ear, O house of the *k* ... Hos 5:1 4428
the Assyrian, and sent to *k* Jareb ... Hos 5:13 4428
They make the *k* glad with their ... Hos 7:3 4428
In the day of our *k* the princes ... Hos 7:5 4428
the burden of the *k* of princes ... Hos 8:10 4428
now they shall say, We have no *k* ... Hos 10:3 4428
what then should a *k* do to us ... Hos 10:3 4428
Assyria for a present to *k* Jareb ... Hos 10:6 4428
her *k* is cut off as the foam upon ... Hos 10:7 4428
in a morning shall the *k* of ... Hos 10:15 4428
but the Assyrian shall be his *k* ... Hos 11:5 4428
I will be thy *k* ... Hos 13:10 4428
of whom thou saidst, Give me a *k* ... Hos 13:10 4428
I gave thee a *k* in mine anger ... Hos 13:11 4428
in the days of Uzziah *k* of Judah ... Amos 1:1 4428
the son of Joash *k* of Israel ... Amos 1:1 4428
their *k* shall go into captivity, ... Amos 1:15 4428
bones of the *k* of Edom into lime ... Amos 2:1 4428
sent to Jeroboam *k* of Israel ... Amos 7:10 4428
word came unto the *k* of Nineveh ... Jonah 3:6 4428
Nineveh by the decree of the *k* ... Jonah 3:7 4428
their *k* shall pass before them, ... Mic 2:13 4428
is there no *k* in thee ... Mic 4:9 4428
what Balak *k* of Moab consulted ... Mic 6:5 4428
shepherds slumber, O *k* of Assyria ... Nah 3:18 4428
the son of Amon, *k* of Judah ... Zeph 1:1 4428
the *k* of Israel, even the LORD, ... Zeph 3:15 4428
the second year of Darius the *k* ... Hag 1:1 4428
the second year of Darius the *k* ... Hag 1:15 4428
in the fourth year of *k* Darius ... Zec 7:1 4428
the *k* shall perish from Gaza, and ... Zec 9:5 4428
behold, thy *K* cometh unto thee ... Zec 9:9 4428
hand, and into the hand of his *k* ... Zec 11:6 4428
in the days of Uzziah *k* of Judah ... Zec 14:5 4428
the LORD shall be *k* over all the ... Zec 14:9 4428
year to year to worship the *K* ... Zec 14:16 4428
unto Jerusalem to worship the *K* ... Zec 14:17 4428
for I am a great *K*, saith the ... Mal 1:14 4428
And Jesse begat David the *k* ... Mt 1:6 *935*
David the *k* begat Solomon of her ... Mt 1:6 *935*
Judaea in the days of Herod the *k* ... Mt 2:1 *935*
is he that is born *K* of the Jews ... Mt 2:2 *935*
When Herod the *k* had heard these ... Mt 2:3 *935*
When they had heard the *k* ... Mt 2:9 *935*
for it is the city of the great *K* ... Mt 5:35 *935*
And the *k* was sorry ... Mt 14:9 *935*
heaven likened unto a certain *k* ... Mt 18:23 *935*
thy *K* cometh unto thee, meek, and ... Mt 21:5 *935*
heaven is like unto a certain *k* ... Mt 22:2 *935*
But when the *k* heard thereof, he ... Mt 22:7 *935*
when the *k* came in to see the ... Mt 22:11 *935*
Then said the *k* to the servants, ... Mt 22:13 *935*
Then shall the *K* say unto them on ... Mt 25:34 *935*
the *K* shall answer and say unto ... Mt 25:40 *935*
Art thou the *K* of the Jews ... Mt 27:11 *935*
him, saying, Hail, *K* of the Jews ... Mt 27:29 *935*
THE *K* OF THE JEWS ... Mt 27:37 *935*
If he be the *K* of Israel, let him ... Mt 27:42 *935*
And *k* Herod heard of him ... Mk 6:14 *935*
the *k* said unto the damsel, Ask ... Mk 6:22 *935*
straightway with haste unto the *k* ... Mk 6:25 *935*
the *k* was exceeding sorry ... Mk 6:26 *935*
immediately the *k* sent an ... Mk 6:27 *935*
him, Art thou the *K* of the Jews ... Mk 15:2 *935*
unto you the *K* of the Jews ... Mk 15:9 *935*
whom ye call the *K* of the Jews ... Mk 15:12 *935*
salute him, Hail, *K* of the Jews ... Mk 15:18 *935*
written over, THE *K* OF THE JEWS ... Mk 15:26 *935*
Let Christ the *K* of Israel ... Mk 15:32 *935*
the *k* of Judaea, a certain priest ... Lk 1:5 *935*
Or what *k*, going to make war ... Lk 14:31 *935*
to make war against another *k* ... Lk 14:31 *935*
Blessed be the *K* that cometh in ... Lk 19:38 *935*
that he himself is Christ a *K* ... Lk 23:2 *935*
Art thou the *K* of the Jews ... Lk 23:3 *935*
If thou be the *k* of the Jews ... Lk 23:37 *935*
THE *K* OF THE JEWS ... Lk 23:38 *935*
thou art the *K* of Israel ... Jn 1:49 *935*
him by force, to make him a *k* ... Jn 6:15 *935*
Blessed is the *K* of Israel that ... Jn 12:13 *935*
thy *K* cometh, sitting on an ass's ... Jn 12:15 *935*
him, Art thou the *K* of the Jews ... Jn 18:33 *935*
said unto him, Art thou a *k* then ... Jn 18:37 *935*
Thou sayest that I am a *k* ... Jn 18:37 *935*
unto you the *K* of the Jews ... Jn 18:39 *935*
And said, Hail, *K* of the Jews ... Jn 19:3 *935*
a *k* speaketh against Caesar ... Jn 19:12 *935*
unto the Jews, Behold your *K* ... Jn 19:14 *935*
unto them, Shall I crucify your *K* ... Jn 19:15 *935*
answered, We have no *k* but Caesar ... Jn 19:15 *935*
THE *K* OF THE JEWS ... Jn 19:19 *935*
Write not, The *K* of the Jews ... Jn 19:21 *935*
that he said, I am *K* of the Jews ... Jn 19:21 *935*
the sight of Pharaoh *k* of Egypt ... Acts 7:10 *935*
Till another *k* arose, which knew ... Acts 7:18 *935*
k stretched forth his hands to ... Acts 12:1 *935*
And afterward they desired a *k* ... Acts 13:21 *935*
up unto them David to be their *k* ... Acts 13:22 *935*
saying that there is another *k* ... Acts 17:7 *935*
And after certain days *k* Agrippa ... Acts 25:13 *935*
declared Paul's cause unto the *k* ... Acts 25:14 *935*
K Agrippa, and all men which are ... Acts 25:24 *935*
thee, O *k* Agrippa, that, after ... Acts 25:26 *935*
k Agrippa, because I shall answer ... Acts 26:2 *935*
k Agrippa, I am accused of the ... Acts 26:7 *935*
At midday, O *k*, I saw in the way ... Acts 26:13 *935*
Whereupon, O *k* Agrippa, I was not ... Acts 26:19 *935*
For the *k* knoweth of these things ... Acts 26:26 *935*
K Agrippa, believest thou the ... Acts 26:27 *935*
the *k* rose up, and the governor, ... Acts 26:30 *935*
the governor under Aretas the *k* ... 2Cor 11:32 *935*
Now unto the *K* eternal, immortal, ... 1Ti 1:17 *935*
the *K* of kings, and Lord of lords ... 1Ti 6:15 *935*
k of Salem, priest of the most ... Heb 7:1 *935*
interpretation *K* of righteousness ... Heb 7:2 *935*
and after that also *K* of Salem ... Heb 7:2 *935*
of Salem, which is, *K* of peace ... Heb 7:2 *935*
not fearing the wrath of the *k* ... Heb 11:27 *935*
whether it be to the *k*, as ... 1Pet 2:13 *935*
Honour the *k* ... 1Pet 2:17 *935*
And they had a *k* over them ... Rev 9:11 *935*
are thy ways, thou *K* of saints ... Rev 15:3 *935*
is Lord of lords, and *K* of kings ... Rev 17:14 *935*
K OF KINGS, AND LORD OF LORDS ... Rev 19:16 *935*

KINGDOM

the beginning of his *k* was Babel ... Gen 10:10 4467
on me and on my *k* a great sin ... Gen 20:9 4467
shall be unto me a *k* of priests ... Ex 19:6 4467
Agag, and his *k* shall be exalted ... Num 24:7 4438
the *k* of Sihon king of the ... Num 32:33 4467
the *k* of Og king of Bashan, the ... Num 32:33 4467
of Argob, the *k* of Og in Bashan ... Deut 3:4 4467
cities of the *k* of Og in Bashan ... Deut 3:10 4467
and all Bashan, being the *k* of Og ... Deut 3:13 4467
sitteth upon the throne of his *k* ... Deut 17:18 4467
he may prolong his days in his *k* ... Deut 17:20 4467
All the *k* of Og in Bashan, which ... Josh 13:12 4468
all the *k* of Sihon king of the ... Josh 13:21 4468
the rest of the *k* of Sihon king ... Josh 13:27 4468
all the *k* of Og king of Bashan, ... Josh 13:30 4468
cities of the *k* of Og in Bashan, ... Josh 13:31 4468
But of the matter of the *k* ... 1Sa 10:16 4410
the people the manner of the *k* ... 1Sa 10:25 4410
to Gilgal, and renew the *k* there ... 1Sa 11:14 4410
thy *k* upon Israel for ever ... 1Sa 13:13 4467
But now thy *k* shall not continue ... 1Sa 13:14 4467
So Saul took the *k* over Israel ... 1Sa 14:47 4410
The LORD hath rent the *k* of ... 1Sa 15:28 4468
what can he have more but the *k* ... 1Sa 18:8 4410
not be established, nor thy *k* ... 1Sa 20:31 4438
that the *k* of Israel shall be ... 1Sa 24:20 4467
hath rent the *k* out of thine hand ... 1Sa 28:17 4467
To translate the *k* from the house ... 2Sa 3:10 4467
my *k* are guiltless before the ... 2Sa 3:28 4467
that he had exalted his *k* for his ... 2Sa 5:12 4467
bowels, and I will establish his *k* ... 2Sa 7:12 4467
the throne of his *k* for ever ... 2Sa 7:13 4467
thy *k* shall be established for ... 2Sa 7:16 4467
restore me the *k* of my father ... 2Sa 16:3 4468
the LORD hath delivered the *k* ... 2Sa 16:8 4410
sitteth on the throne of the *k* ... 1Kin 1:46 4410
his *k* was established greatly ... 1Kin 2:12 4438
Thou knowest that the *k* was mine ... 1Kin 2:15 4410
howbeit the *k* is turned about, and ... 1Kin 2:15 4410
ask for him the *k* also ... 1Kin 2:22 4410
the *k* was established in the hand ... 1Kin 2:46 4467
of thy *k* upon Israel for ever ... 1Kin 9:5 4467
was not the like made in any *k* ... 1Kin 10:20 4467
will surely rend the *k* from thee ... 1Kin 11:11 4467
I will not rend away all the *k* ... 1Kin 11:13 4467
I will rend the *k* out of the hand ... 1Kin 11:31 4467
take the whole *k* out of his hand ... 1Kin 11:34 4467
But I will take the *k* out of his ... 1Kin 11:35 4410
to bring the *k* again to Rehoboam ... 1Kin 12:21 4410
Now shall the *k* return to the ... 1Kin 12:26 4467
rent the *k* away from the house of ... 1Kin 14:8 4467
liveth, there is no nation or *k* ... 1Kin 18:10 4467
he took an oath of the *k* and ... 1Kin 18:10 4467
thou now govern the *k* of Israel ... 1Kin 21:7 4410
as soon as the *k* was confirmed in ... 2Kin 14:5 4467
him to confirm the *k* in his hand ... 2Kin 15:19 4467
turned the *k* unto David the son ... 1Chr 10:14 4410
themselves with him in his *k* ... 1Chr 11:10 4438
to turn the *k* of Saul to him, ... 1Chr 12:23 4438
for his *k* was lifted up on high, ... 1Chr 14:2 4438

Context	Reference	No.
from one *k* to another people	1Chr 16:20	4467
and I will establish his *k*	1Chr 17:11	4438
in mine house and in my *k* for ever	1Chr 17:14	4438
of his *k* over Israel for ever	1Chr 22:10	4438
of the *k* of the LORD over Israel	1Chr 28:5	4438
I will establish his *k* for ever	1Chr 28:7	4438
thine is the *k*, O LORD, and thou	1Chr 29:11	4467
David was strengthened in his *k*	2Chr 1:1	4438
the LORD, and an house for his *k*	2Chr 2:1	4438
the LORD, and an house for his *k*	2Chr 2:12	
I stablish the throne of thy *k*	2Chr 7:18	4438
was not the like made in any *k*	2Chr 9:19	4467
bring the *k* again to Rehoboam	2Chr 11:1	4467
they strengthened the *k* of Judah	2Chr 11:17	4438
Rehoboam had established the *k*	2Chr 12:1	4438
k over Israel to David for ever	2Chr 13:5	4467
now ye think to withstand the *k*	2Chr 13:8	4467
the *k* was quiet before him	2Chr 14:5	4467
LORD stablished the *k* in his hand	2Chr 17:5	4467
but the *k* gave he to Jehoram	2Chr 21:3	4467
risen up to the *k* of his father	2Chr 21:4	4467
had no power to keep still the *k*	2Chr 22:9	4467
the king upon the throne of the *k*	2Chr 23:20	4467
when the *k* was established to him	2Chr 25:3	4467
for a sin offering for the *k*	2Chr 29:21	4467
for no god of any nation or *k* was	2Chr 32:15	4467
him again to Jerusalem into his *k*	2Chr 33:13	4438
the reign of the *k* of Persia	2Chr 36:20	4438
proclamation throughout all his *k*	2Chr 36:22	4438
proclamation throughout all his *k*	Ezr 1:1	4438
have not served thee in their *k*	Neh 9:35	4438
sat on the throne of his *k*	Est 1:2	4438
the riches of his glorious *k*	Est 1:4	4438
and which sat the first in the *k*	Est 1:14	4438
in all the provinces of his *k*	Est 2:3	4438
the whole *k* of Ahasuerus, even	Est 3:6	4438
in all the provinces of thy *k*	Est 3:8	4438
to the *k* for such a time as this	Est 4:14	4438
given thee to the half of the *k*	Est 5:3	4438
of the *k* it shall be performed	Est 5:6	4438
even to the half of the *k*	Est 7:2	4438
provinces of the *k* of Ahasuerus	Est 9:30	4438
For the *k* is the LORD's	Ps 22:28	4410
of thy *k* is a right sceptre	Ps 45:6	4438
and his *k* ruleth over all	Ps 103:19	4438
from one *k* to another people	Ps 105:13	4467
shall speak of the glory of thy *k*	Ps 145:11	4438
and the glorious majesty of his *k*	Ps 145:12	4438
Thy *k* is an everlasting *k*,	Ps 145:13	4438
is born in his *k* becometh poor	Eccl 4:14	4438
throne of David, and upon his *k*	Is 9:7	4467
the *k* from Damascus, and the	Is 17:3	4467
city, and *k* against *k*	Is 19:2	4467
call the nobles thereof to the *k*	Is 34:12	4410
k that will not serve thee shall	Is 60:12	4467
a nation, and concerning a *k*	Jer 18:7	4467
a nation, and concerning a *k*	Jer 18:9	4467
k which will not serve the same	Jer 27:8	4467
he hath polluted the *k* and the	Lam 2:2	4467
and thou didst prosper into a *k*	Eze 16:13	4410
That the *k* might be base, that it	Eze 17:14	4467
and they shall be there a base *k*	Eze 29:14	4467
God of heaven hath given thee a *k*	Dan 2:37	4437
arise another *k* inferior to thee	Dan 2:39	4437
and another third *k* of brass	Dan 2:39	4437
the fourth *k* shall be strong as	Dan 2:40	4437
of iron, the *k* shall be divided	Dan 2:41	4437
so the *k* shall be partly strong,	Dan 2:42	4437
the God of heaven set up a *k*	Dan 2:44	4437
the *k* shall not be left to other	Dan 2:44	4437
his *k* is an everlasting *k*,	Dan 4:3	4437
most High ruleth in the *k* of men	Dan 4:17	4437
as all the wise men of my *k* are	Dan 4:18	4437
most High ruleth in the *k* of men	Dan 4:25	4437
thy *k* shall be sure unto thee,	Dan 4:26	4437
in the palace of the *k* of Babylon	Dan 4:29	4437
of the *k* by the might of my power	Dan 4:30	4437
The *k* is departed from thee	Dan 4:31	4437
most High ruleth in the *k* of men	Dan 4:32	4437
his *k* is from generation to	Dan 4:34	4437
and for the glory of my *k*, mine	Dan 4:36	4437
and I was established in my *k*	Dan 4:36	4437
shall be the third ruler in the *k*	Dan 5:7	4437
There is a man in thy *k*, in whom	Dan 5:11	4437
shalt be the third ruler in the *k*	Dan 5:16	4437
Nebuchadnezzar thy father a *k*	Dan 5:18	4437
high God ruled in the *k* of men	Dan 5:21	4437
God hath numbered thy *k*, and	Dan 5:26	4437
Thy *k* is divided, and given to the	Dan 5:28	4437
be the third ruler in the *k*	Dan 5:29	4437
And Darius the Median took the *k*	Dan 5:31	4437
to set over the *k* an hundred	Dan 6:1	4437
which should be over the whole *k*	Dan 6:1	4437
against Daniel concerning the *k*	Dan 6:4	4437
All the presidents of the *k*	Dan 6:7	4437
dominion of my *k* men tremble	Dan 6:26	4437
his *k* that which shall not be	Dan 6:26	4437
him dominion, and glory, and a *k*	Dan 7:14	4437
his *k* that which shall not be	Dan 7:14	4437
of the most High shall take the *k*	Dan 7:18	4437
and possess the *k* for ever	Dan 7:18	4437
that the saints possessed the *k*	Dan 7:22	4437
shall be the fourth *k* upon earth	Dan 7:23	4437
the ten horns out of this *k* are	Dan 7:24	4437
And the *k* and dominion	Dan 7:27	4437
the greatness of the *k* under the	Dan 7:27	4437
whose *k* is an everlasting *k*	Dan 7:27	4437
And in the latter time of their *k*	Dan 8:23	4438
But the prince of the *k* of Persia	Dan 10:13	4438
his *k* shall be broken, and shall	Dan 11:4	4438
for his *k* shall be plucked up,	Dan 11:4	4438
the south shall come into his *k*	Dan 11:9	4438
with the strength of his whole *k*	Dan 11:17	4438
of taxes in the glory of the *k*	Dan 11:20	4438
not give the honour of the *k*	Dan 11:21	4438
obtain the *k* by flatteries	Dan 11:21	4438
the *k* of the house of Israel	Hos 1:4	4468
Lord GOD are upon the sinful *k*	Amos 9:8	4467
the *k* shall be the LORD's	Obad 21	4410
the *k* shall come to the daughter	Mic 4:8	4467
for the *k* of heaven is at hand	Mt 3:2	932
for the *k* of heaven is at hand	Mt 4:17	932
and preaching the gospel of the *k*	Mt 4:23	932
for theirs is the *k* of heaven	Mt 5:3	932
for theirs is the *k* of heaven	Mt 5:10	932
the least in the *k* of heaven	Mt 5:19	932
called great in the *k* of heaven	Mt 5:19	932
case enter into the *k* of heaven	Mt 5:20	932
Thy *k* come	Mt 6:10	932
For thine is the *k*, and the power,	Mt 6:13	932
But seek ye first the *k* of God	Mt 6:33	932
shall enter into the *k* of heaven	Mt 7:21	932
and Jacob, in the *k* of heaven	Mt 8:11	932
But the children of the *k* shall	Mt 8:12	932
and preaching the gospel of the *k*	Mt 9:35	932
The *k* of heaven is at hand	Mt 10:7	932
he that is least in the *k* of	Mt 11:11	932
k of heaven suffereth violence	Mt 11:12	932
Every *k* divided against itself is	Mt 12:25	932
how shall then his *k* stand	Mt 12:26	932
then the *k* of God is come unto	Mt 12:28	932
the mysteries of the *k* of heaven	Mt 13:11	932
any one heareth the word of the *k*	Mt 13:19	932
The *k* of heaven is likened unto a	Mt 13:24	932
The *k* of heaven is like to a	Mt 13:31	932
The *k* of heaven is like unto	Mt 13:33	932
seed are the children of the *k*	Mt 13:38	932
of his *k* all things that offend	Mt 13:41	932
the sun in the *k* of their Father	Mt 13:43	932
the *k* of heaven is like unto	Mt 13:44	932
the *k* of heaven is like unto a	Mt 13:45	932
the *k* of heaven is like unto a	Mt 13:47	932
k of heaven is like unto a man	Mt 13:52	932
thee the keys of the *k* of heaven	Mt 16:19	932
the Son of man coming in his *k*	Mt 16:28	932
the greatest in the *k* of heaven	Mt 18:1	932
not enter into the *k* of heaven	Mt 18:3	932
is greatest in the *k* of heaven	Mt 18:4	932
Therefore is the *k* of heaven	Mt 18:23	932
for the *k* of heaven's sake	Mt 19:12	932
for of such is the *k* of heaven	Mt 19:14	932
hardly enter into the *k* of heaven	Mt 19:23	932
man to enter into the *k* of God	Mt 19:24	932
For the *k* of heaven is like unto	Mt 20:1	932
the other on the left, in thy *k*	Mt 20:21	932
go into the *k* of God before you	Mt 21:31	932
The *k* of God shall be taken from	Mt 21:43	932
The *k* of heaven is like unto a	Mt 22:2	932
for ye shut up the *k* of heaven	Mt 23:13	932
nation, and *k* against *k*	Mt 24:7	932
this gospel of the *k* shall be	Mt 24:14	932
Then shall the *k* of heaven be	Mt 25:1	932
For the *k* of heaven is as a man	Mt 25:14	932
inherit the *k* prepared for you	Mt 25:34	932
it new with you in my Father's *k*	Mt 26:29	932
the gospel of the *k* of God	Mk 1:14	932
and the *k* of God is at hand	Mk 1:15	932
if a *k* be divided against itself,	Mk 3:24	932
that *k* cannot stand	Mk 3:24	932
know the mystery of the *k* of God	Mk 4:11	932
And he said, So is the *k* of God	Mk 4:26	932
shall we liken the *k* of God	Mk 4:30	932
it thee, unto the half of my *k*	Mk 6:23	932
seen the *k* of God come with power	Mk 9:1	932
into the *k* of God with one eye	Mk 9:47	932
for of such is the *k* of God	Mk 10:14	932
the *k* of God as a little child	Mk 10:15	932
riches enter into the *k* of God	Mk 10:23	932
riches to enter into the *k* of God	Mk 10:24	932
man to enter into the *k* of God	Mk 10:25	932
Blessed be the *k* of our father	Mk 11:10	932
art not far from the *k* of God	Mk 12:34	932
nation, and *k* against *k*	Mk 13:8	932
I drink it new in the *k* of God	Mk 14:25	932
also waited for the *k* of God	Mk 15:43	932
of his *k* there shall be no end	Lk 1:33	932
I must preach the *k* of God to	Lk 4:43	932
for yours is the *k* of God	Lk 6:20	932
the *k* of God is greater than he	Lk 7:28	932
the glad tidings of the *k* of God	Lk 8:1	932
the mysteries of the *k* of God	Lk 8:10	932
sent them to preach the *k* of God	Lk 9:2	932
spake unto them of the *k* of God	Lk 9:11	932
death, till they see the *k* of God	Lk 9:27	932
go thou and preach the *k* of God	Lk 9:60	932
back, is fit for the *k* of God	Lk 9:62	932
The *k* of God is come nigh unto	Lk 10:9	932
that the *k* of God is come nigh	Lk 10:11	932
Thy *k* come	Lk 11:2	932
Every *k* divided against itself is	Lk 11:17	932
himself, how shall his *k* stand	Lk 11:18	932
no doubt the *k* of God is come	Lk 11:20	932
But rather seek ye the *k* of God	Lk 12:31	932
good pleasure to give you the *k*	Lk 12:32	932
Unto what is the *k* of God like	Lk 13:18	932
shall I liken the *k* of God	Lk 13:20	932
all the prophets, in the *k* of God	Lk 13:28	932
and shall sit down in the *k* of God	Lk 13:29	932
shall eat bread in the *k* of God	Lk 14:15	932
time the *k* of God is preached	Lk 16:16	932
when the *k* of God should come, he	Lk 17:20	932
The *k* of God cometh not with	Lk 17:20	932
the *k* of God is within you	Lk 17:21	932
for of such is the *k* of God	Lk 18:16	932
k of God as a little child shall	Lk 18:17	932
riches enter into the *k* of God	Lk 18:24	932
man to enter into the *k* of God	Lk 18:25	932
for the *k* of God's sake,	Lk 18:29	932
the *k* of God should immediately	Lk 19:11	932
to receive for himself a *k*	Lk 19:12	932
returned, having received the *k*	Lk 19:15	932
nation, and *k* against *k*	Lk 21:10	932
know ye that the *k* of God is nigh	Lk 21:31	932
it be fulfilled in the *k* of God	Lk 22:16	932
until the *k* of God shall come	Lk 22:18	932
And I appoint unto you a *k*	Lk 22:29	932
eat and drink at my table in my *k*	Lk 22:30	932
me when thou comest into thy *k*	Lk 23:42	932
himself waited for the *k* of God	Lk 23:51	932
again, he cannot see the *k* of God	Jn 3:3	932
he cannot enter into the *k* of God	Jn 3:5	932
My *k* is not of this world	Jn 18:36	932
if my *k* were of this world, then	Jn 18:36	932
but now is my *k* not from hence	Jn 18:36	932
things pertaining to the *k* of God	Acts 1:3	932
restore again the *k* to Israel	Acts 1:6	932
things concerning the *k* of God	Acts 8:12	932
enter into the *k* of God	Acts 14:22	932
things concerning the *k* of God	Acts 19:8	932
have gone preaching the *k* of God	Acts 20:25	932
and testified the *k* of God	Acts 28:23	932
Preaching the *k* of God, and	Acts 28:31	932
For the *k* of God is not meat and	Rom 14:17	932
For the *k* of God is not in word,	1Cor 4:20	932
shall not inherit the *k* of God	1Cor 6:9	932
shall inherit the *k* of God	1Cor 6:10	932
have delivered up the *k* to God	1Cor 15:24	932
blood cannot inherit the *k* of God	1Cor 15:50	932
shall not inherit the *k* of God	Gal 5:21	932
inheritance in the *k* of Christ	Eph 5:5	932
us into the *k* of his dear Son	Col 1:13	932
fellow workers unto the *k* of God	Col 4:11	932
who hath called you unto his *k*	1Th 2:12	932
be counted worthy of the *k* of God	2Th 1:5	932
dead at his appearing and his *k*	2Ti 4:1	932
preserve me unto his heavenly *k*	2Ti 4:18	932
is the sceptre of thy *k*	Heb 1:8	932
a *k* which cannot be moved	Heb 12:28	932
heirs of the *k* which he hath	Jas 2:5	932
the everlasting *k* of our Lord	2Pet 1:11	932
in tribulation, and in the *k*	Rev 1:9	932
the *k* of our God, and the power of	Rev 12:10	932
his *k* was full of darkness	Rev 16:10	932
which have received no *k* as yet	Rev 17:12	932
give their *k* unto the beast,	Rev 17:17	932

KINGDOMS

Context	Reference	No.
all the *k* whither thou passest	Deut 3:21	4467
into all the *k* of the earth	Deut 28:25	4467
was the head of all those *k*	Josh 11:10	4467
and out of the hand of all *k*	1Sa 10:18	4467
Solomon reigned over all *k* from	1Kin 4:21	4467
of all the *k* of the earth	2Kin 19:15	4467
that all the *k* of the earth may	2Kin 19:19	4467
over all the *k* of the countries	1Chr 29:30	4467
service of the *k* of the countries	2Chr 12:8	4467
k of the lands that were round	2Chr 17:10	4467
over all the *k* of the heathen	2Chr 20:6	4467
on all the *k* of those countries	2Chr 20:29	4467
All the *k* of the earth hath the	2Chr 36:23	4467
given me all the *k* of the earth	Ezr 1:2	4467
Moreover thou gavest them *k*	Neh 9:22	4467
heathen raged, the *k* were moved	Ps 46:6	4467
Sing unto God, ye *k* of the earth	Ps 68:32	4467
upon the *k* that have not called	Ps 79:6	4467
are gathered together, and the *k*	Ps 102:22	4467
of Bashan, and all the *k* of Canaan	Ps 135:11	4467
hath found the *k* of the idols	Is 10:10	4467
a tumultuous noise of the *k* of	Is 13:4	4467
And Babylon, the glory of *k*	Is 13:19	4467
to tremble, that did shake *k*	Is 14:16	4467
hand over the sea, he shook the *k*	Is 23:11	4467
k of the world upon the face of	Is 23:17	4467
of all the *k* of the earth	Is 37:16	4467
that all the *k* of the earth may	Is 37:20	4467
no more be called, The lady of *k*	Is 47:5	4467
over the nations and over the *k*	Jer 1:10	4467
families of the *k* of the north	Jer 1:15	4467
of the nations, and in all their *k*	Jer 10:7	4467
removed into all *k* of the earth	Jer 15:4	4467
the *k* of the earth for their hurt	Jer 24:9	4467
all the *k* of the world, which are	Jer 25:26	4467
countries, and against great *k*	Jer 28:8	4467
removed to all the *k* of the earth	Jer 29:18	4467
all the *k* of the earth of his	Jer 34:1	4467
into all the *k* of the earth	Jer 34:17	4467
and concerning the *k* of Hazor	Jer 49:28	4467
and with thee will I destroy *k*	Jer 51:20	4467
against her the *k* of Ararat	Jer 51:27	4467
It shall be the basest of the *k*	Eze 29:15	4467
into two *k* any more at all	Eze 37:22	4467
in pieces and consume all these *k*	Dan 2:44	4437
which shall be diverse from all *k*	Dan 7:23	4437
four *k* shall stand up out of the	Dan 8:22	4438
be they better than these *k*	Amos 6:2	4467
thy nakedness, and the *k* thy shame	Nah 3:5	4467
that I may assemble the *k*	Zeph 3:8	4467
I will overthrow the throne of *k*	Hag 2:22	4467
strength of the *k* of the heathen	Hag 2:22	4467
him all the *k* of the world	Mt 4:8	932
shewed unto him all the *k* of the	Lk 4:5	932
Who through faith subdued *k*	Heb 11:33	932
The *k* of this world are become	Rev 11:15	932
are become the *k* of our Lord	Rev 11:15	932

KINGLY

Context	Reference	No.
he was deposed from his *k* throne	Dan 5:20	4437

KING'S

Context	Reference	No.
of Shaveh, which is the *k* dale	Gen 14:17	4428
a place where the *k* prisoners	Gen 39:20	4428
we will go by the *k* high way	Num 20:17	4428
will go along by the *k* high way	Num 21:22	4428

now therefore be the *k* son in law 1Sa 18:22 4428
light thing to be a *k* son in law 1Sa 18:23 4428
to be avenged of the *k* enemies 1Sa 18:25 4428
David well to be the *k* son in law 1Sa 18:26 4428
that he might be the *k* son in law 1Sa 18:27 4428
he cometh not unto the *k* table 1Sa 20:29 4428
because the *k* business required 1Sa 21:8 4428
David, which is the *k* son in law 1Sa 22:14 4428
be to deliver him into the *k* hand 1Sa 23:20 4428
And now see where the *k* spear is 1Sa 26:16 4428
and said, Behold the *k* spear 1Sa 26:22 4428
at my table, as one of the *k* sons 2Sa 9:11 4428
eat continually at the *k* table 2Sa 9:13 4428
upon the roof of the *k* house 2Sa 11:2 4428
Uriah departed out of the *k* house 2Sa 11:8 4428
k house with all the servants of 2Sa 11:9 4428
if so be that the *k* wrath arise 2Sa 11:20 4428
some of the *k* servants be dead, 2Sa 11:24 4428
he took their *k* crown from off 2Sa 12:30 4428
Why art thou, being the *k* son 2Sa 13:4 4428
the *k* daughters that were virgins 2Sa 13:18 4428
and Absalom invited all the *k* sons 2Sa 13:23 4428
all the *k* sons go with him 2Sa 13:27 4428
Then all the *k* sons arose 2Sa 13:29 4428
Absalom hath slain all the *k* sons 2Sa 13:30 4428
all the young men the *k* sons 2Sa 13:32 4428
that all the *k* sons are dead 2Sa 13:33 4428
the king, Behold, the *k* sons come 2Sa 13:35 4428
the *k* sons came, and lifted up 2Sa 13:36 4428
the *k* heart was toward Absalom 2Sa 14:1 4428
own house, and saw not the *k* face 2Sa 14:24 4428
shekels after the *k* weight 2Sa 14:26 4428
Jerusalem, and saw not the *k* face 2Sa 14:28 4428
therefore let me see the *k* face 2Sa 14:32 4428
the *k* servants said unto the king 2Sa 15:15 4428
shalt hear out of the *k* house 2Sa 15:35 4428
be for the *k* household to ride on 2Sa 16:2 4428
forth mine hand against the *k* son 2Sa 18:12 4428
a pillar, which is in the *k* dale 2Sa 18:18 4428
because the *k* son is dead 2Sa 18:20 4428
When Joab sent the *k* servant 2Sa 18:29 4428
to carry over the *k* household 2Sa 19:18 4428
we eaten at all of the *k* cost 2Sa 19:42 4428
Notwithstanding the *k* word 2Sa 24:4 4428
all his brethren the *k* sons 1Kin 1:9 4428
the men of Judah the *k* servants 1Kin 1:9 4428
and hath called all the *k* sons 1Kin 1:25 4428
And she came into the *k* presence 1Kin 1:28 4428
him to ride upon the *k* mule 1Kin 1:44 4428
moreover the *k* servants came to 1Kin 1:47 4428
a seat to be set for the *k* mother 1Kin 2:19 4428
officer, and the *k* friend 1Kin 4:5 4428
the *k* house, and all Solomon's 1Kin 9:1 4428
of the LORD, and the *k* house, 1Kin 9:10 4428
of the LORD, and for the *k* house 1Kin 10:12 4428
the *k* merchants received the 1Kin 10:28 4428
he was of the *k* seed in Edom 1Kin 11:14 4428
the *k* hand was restored him again 1Kin 13:6 4428
and the treasures of the *k* house 1Kin 14:26 4428
kept the door of the *k* house 1Kin 14:27 4428
and the treasures of the *k* house 1Kin 15:18 4428
into the palace of the *k* house 1Kin 16:18 4428
burnt the *k* house over him with 1Kin 16:18 4428
shall deliver it into the *k* hand 1Kin 22:12 4428
the city, and to Joash the *k* son 1Kin 22:26 4428
we may go and tell the *k* household 2Kin 7:9 4428
told it to the *k* house within 2Kin 7:11 4428
for she is a *k* daughter 2Kin 9:34 4428
Now the *k* sons, being seventy 2Kin 10:6 4428
them, that they took the *k* sons 2Kin 10:7 4428
brought the heads of the *k* sons 2Kin 10:8 4428
among the *k* sons which were slain 2Kin 11:2 4428
LORD, and shewed them the *k* son 2Kin 11:4 4428
of the watch of the *k* house 2Kin 11:5 4428
And he brought forth the *k* son 2Kin 11:12 4428
the horses came into the *k* house 2Kin 11:16 4428
gate of the guard to the *k* house 2Kin 11:19 4428
with the sword beside the *k* house 2Kin 11:20 4428
in the chest, that the *k* scribe 2Kin 12:10 4428
of the LORD, and in the *k* house 2Kin 12:18 4428
put his hands upon the *k* hands 2Kin 13:16 4428
in the treasures of the *k* house 2Kin 14:14 4428
Jotham the *k* son was over the 2Kin 15:5 4428
in the palace of the *k* house 2Kin 15:25 4428
in the treasures of the *k* house 2Kin 16:8 4428
the *k* burnt sacrifice, and his 2Kin 16:15 4428
the *k* entry without, turned he 2Kin 16:18 4428
in the treasures of the *k* house 2Kin 18:15 4428
for the *k* commandment was, saying 2Kin 18:36 4428
and Asahiah a servant of the *k* 2Kin 22:12 4428
and the treasures of the *k* house 2Kin 24:13 4428
the *k* mother, and the *k* wives 2Kin 24:15 4428
walls, which is by the *k* garden 2Kin 25:4 4428
the *k* house, and all the houses of 2Kin 25:9 4428
them that were in the *k* presence 2Kin 25:19 4428
waited in the *k* gate eastward 1Chr 9:18 4428
Nevertheless the *k* word prevailed 1Chr 21:4 4428
for the *k* word was abominable to 1Chr 21:6 4428
the *k* seer in the words of God 1Chr 25:5 4428
according to the *k* order to Asaph 1Chr 25:6 4428
over the *k* treasures was Azmaveth 1Chr 27:25 4428
of Hachmoni was with the *k* sons 1Chr 27:32 4428
Ahithophel was the *k* counsellor 1Chr 27:33 4428
the Archite was the *k* companion 1Chr 27:33 4428
general of the *k* army was Joab 1Chr 27:34 4428
with the rulers of the *k* work 1Chr 29:6 4428
the *k* merchants received the 2Chr 1:16 4428
house of the LORD, and the *k* house 2Chr 7:11 4428
of the LORD, and to the *k* palace 2Chr 9:11 4428
For the *k* ships went to Tarshish 2Chr 9:21 4428
and the treasures of the *k* house 2Chr 12:9 4428
kept the entrance of the *k* house 2Chr 12:10 4428
of the LORD and of the *k* house 2Chr 16:2 4428
will deliver it into the *k* hand 2Chr 18:5 4428
the city, and to Joash the *k* son 2Chr 18:25 4428
of Judah, for all the *k* matters 2Chr 19:11 4428
that was found in the *k* house 2Chr 21:17 4428
among the *k* sons that were slain 2Chr 22:11 4428
the *k* son shall reign, as the 2Chr 23:3 4428
part shall be at the *k* house 2Chr 23:5 4428
Then they brought out the *k* son 2Chr 23:11 4428
of the horse gate by the *k* house 2Chr 23:15 4428
the high gate into the *k* house 2Chr 23:20 4428
at the *k* commandment they made a 2Chr 24:8 4428
the *k* office by the hand of the 2Chr 24:11 4428
the *k* scribe and the high priest's 2Chr 24:11 4428
Art thou made of the *k* counsel 2Chr 25:16 4428
and the treasures of the *k* house 2Chr 25:24 4428
Hananiah, one of the *k* captains 2Chr 26:11 4428
his son was over the *k* house 2Chr 26:21 4428
Ephraim, slew Maaseiah the *k* son 2Chr 28:7 4428
of David, and of Gad the *k* seer 2Chr 29:25 4428
He appointed also the *k* portion 2Chr 31:3 4428
and Asaiah a servant of the *k* 2Chr 34:20 4428
these were of the *k* substance 2Chr 35:7 4428
according to the *k* commandment 2Chr 35:10 4428
and Heman, and Jeduthun the *k* seer 2Chr 35:15 4428
maintenance from the *k* palace Ezr 4:14 4430
for us to see the *k* dishonour Ezr 4:14 4430
made in the *k* treasure house Ezr 5:17 4430
be given out of the *k* house Ezr 6:4 4430
that of the *k* goods, even of the Ezr 6:8 4430
it out of the *k* treasure house Ezr 7:20 4430
a thing as this in the *k* heart Ezr 7:27 4428
before all the *k* mighty princes Ezr 7:28 4428
they delivered the *k* commissions Ezr 8:36 4428
unto the *k* lieutenants, and to the Ezr 8:36 4428
For I was the *k* cupbearer Neh 1:11 4428
Asaph the keeper of the *k* forest Neh 2:8 4428
river, and gave them the *k* letters Neh 2:9 4428
of the fountain, and to the *k* pool Neh 2:14 4428
as also the *k* words that he had Neh 2:18 4428
pool of Siloah by the *k* garden Neh 3:15 4428
lieth out from the *k* high house Neh 3:25 4428
borrowed money for the *k* tribute Neh 5:4 4428
For it was the *k* commandment Neh 11:23 4428
was at the *k* hand in all matters Neh 11:24 4428
of the garden of the *k* palace Est 1:5 4428
Vashti refused to come at the *k* Est 1:12 4428
(for so was the *k* manner toward Est 1:13 4428
and Media, which saw the *k* face Est 1:14 4428
this day unto all the *k* princes Est 1:18 4428
when the *k* decree which he shall Est 1:20 4428
letters into all the *k* provinces Est 1:22 4428
Then said the *k* servants that Est 2:2 4428
custody of Hege the *k* chamberlain Est 2:3 4428
when the *k* commandment and his Est 2:8 4428
was brought also unto the *k* house Est 2:8 4428
be given her, out of the *k* house Est 2:9 4428
of the women unto the *k* house Est 2:13 4428
the *k* chamberlain, which kept the Est 2:14 4428
but what Hegai the *k* chamberlain Est 2:15 4428
then Mordecai sat in the *k* gate Est 2:19 4428
while Mordecai sat in the *k* gate Est 2:21 4428
two of the *k* chamberlains, Est 2:21 4428
all the *k* servants, that were in Est 3:2 4428
servants, that were in the *k* gate Est 3:2 4428
Then the *k* servants, which were Est 3:3 4428
which were in the *k* gate Est 3:3 4428
thou the *k* commandment Est 3:3 4428
neither keep they the *k* laws Est 3:8 4428
for the *k* profit to suffer them Est 3:8 4428
to bring it into the *k* treasuries Est 3:9 4428
Then were the *k* scribes called on Est 3:12 4428
commanded unto the *k* lieutenants Est 3:12 4428
and sealed with the *k* ring Est 3:12 4428
by posts into all the *k* provinces Est 3:13 4428
hastened by the *k* commandment Est 3:15 4428
And came even before the *k* gate Est 4:2 4428
the *k* gate clothed with sackcloth Est 4:2 4428
whithersoever the *k* commandment Est 4:3 4428
one of the *k* chamberlains, whom Est 4:5 4428
city, which was before the *k* gate Est 4:6 4428
to the *k* treasuries for the Jews Est 4:7 4428
All the *k* servants, and the people Est 4:11 4428
and the people of the *k* provinces Est 4:11 4428
thou shalt escape in the *k* house Est 4:13 4428
in the inner court of the *k* house Est 5:1 4428
over against the *k* house Est 5:1 4428
Haman saw Mordecai in the *k* gate Est 5:9 4428
the Jew sitting at the *k* gate Est 5:13 4428
two of the *k* chamberlains, the Est 6:2 4428
Then said the *k* servants that Est 6:3 4428
the outward court of the *k* house Est 6:4 4428
the *k* servants said unto him, Est 6:5 4428
one of the *k* most noble princes Est 6:9 4428
Jew, that sitteth at the *k* gate Est 6:10 4428
Mordecai came again to the *k* gate Est 6:12 4428
came the *k* chamberlains, and Est 6:14 4428
not countervail the *k* damage Est 7:4 4428
the word went out of the *k* mouth Est 7:8 4428
Then was the *k* wrath pacified Est 7:10 4428
which are in all the *k* provinces Est 8:5 4428
as it liketh you, in the *k* name Est 8:8 4428
and seal it with the *k* ring Est 8:8 4428
which is written in the *k* name Est 8:8 4428
and sealed with the *k* ring Est 8:8 4428
Then were the *k* scribes called at Est 8:9 4428
and sealed it with the *k* ring Est 8:10 4428
pressed on by the *k* commandment Est 8:14 4428
whithersoever the *k* commandment Est 8:17 4428
when the *k* commandment and his Est 9:1 4428
Mordecai was great in the *k* house Est 9:4 4428
in the rest of the *k* provinces Est 9:12 4428
k provinces gathered themselves Est 9:16 4428
in the heart of the *k* enemies Ps 45:5 4428
The *k* daughter is all glorious Ps 45:13 4428
shall enter into the *k* palace Ps 45:15 4428
Thou wilt prolong the *k* life Ps 61:6 4428
thy righteousness unto the *k* son Ps 72:1 4428
The *k* strength also loveth Ps 99:4 4428
of people is the *k* honour Prov 14:28 4428
The *k* favour is toward a wise Prov 14:35 4428
of the *k* countenance is life Prov 16:15 4428
The *k* wrath is as the roaring of Prov 19:12 4428
The *k* heart is in the hand of the Prov 21:1 4428
thee to keep the *k* commandment Eccl 8:2 4428
for the *k* commandment was, saying Is 36:21 4428
LORD unto the *k* house of Judah Jer 22:6 4428
then they came up from the *k* Jer 26:10 4428
he went down into the *k* house Jer 36:12 4428
eunuchs which was in the *k* house Jer 38:7 4428
went forth out of the *k* house Jer 38:8 4428
night, by the way of the *k* garden Jer 39:4 4428
the Chaldeans burned the *k* house Jer 39:8 4428
even the *k* daughters, and all the Jer 41:10 4428
the *k* daughters, and every person Jer 43:6 4428
walls, which was by the *k* garden Jer 52:7 4428
house of the LORD, and the *k* house Jer 52:13 4428
them that were near the *k* person Jer 52:25 4428
And hath taken of the *k* seed Eze 17:13 4410
of Israel, and of the *k* seed Dan 1:3 4410
in them to stand in the *k* palace Dan 1:4 4428
a daily provision of the *k* meat Dan 1:5 4428
with the portion of the *k* meat Dan 1:8 4428
eat of the portion of the *k* meat Dan 1:13 4428
did eat the portion of the *k* meat Dan 1:15 4428
earth that can shew the *k* matter Dan 2:10 4430
Arioch the captain of the *k* guard Dan 2:14 4430
and said to Arioch the *k* captain Dan 2:15 4430
made known unto us the *k* matter Dan 2:23 4430
Therefore because the *k* Dan 3:22 4430
the *k* counsellors, being gathered Dan 3:27 4430
him, and have changed the *k* word Dan 3:28 4430
While the word was in the *k* mouth Dan 4:31 4430
of the wall of the *k* palace Dan 5:5 4430
Then the *k* countenance was Dan 5:6 4430
Then came in all the *k* wise men Dan 5:8 4430
the king concerning the *k* decree Dan 6:12 4430
I rose up, and did the *k* business Dan 8:27 4428
for the *k* daughter of the south Dan 11:6 4428
latter growth after the *k* mowings Amos 7:1 4428
for it is the *k* chapel Amos 7:13 4428
and it is the *k* court Amos 7:13 4467
the *k* children, and all such as Zeph 1:8 4428
Hananeel unto the *k* winepresses Zec 14:10 4428
having made Blastus the *k* Acts 12:20 *935*
was nourished by the *k* country Acts 12:20 *937*
not afraid of the *k* commandment Heb 11:23 *935*

KINGS

the *k* that were with him, and Gen 14:5 4428
four *k* with five Gen 14:9 4428
the *k* of Sodom and Gomorrah fled, Gen 14:10 4428
of the *k* that were with him, at Gen 14:17 4428
thee, and *k* shall come out of thee Gen 17:6 4428
k of people shall be of her Gen 17:16 4428
k shall come out of thy loins Gen 35:11 4428
these are the *k* that reigned in Gen 36:31 4428
And they slew the *k* of Midian Num 31:8 4428
and Hur, and Reba, five *k* of Midian Num 31:8 4428
k of the Amorites the land that Deut 3:8 4428
God hath done unto these two *k* Deut 3:21 4428
two *k* of the Amorites, which were Deut 4:47 4428
deliver their *k* into thine hand Deut 7:24 4428
k of the Amorites, and unto the Deut 31:4 4428
unto the two *k* of the Amorites Josh 2:10 4428
when all the *k* of the Amorites, Josh 5:1 4428
all the *k* of the Canaanites, Josh 5:1 4428
when all the *k* which were on this Josh 9:1 4428
did to the two *k* of the Amorites Josh 9:10 4428
the five *k* of the Amorites Josh 10:5 4428
for all the *k* of the Amorites Josh 10:6 4428
But these five *k* fled, and hid Josh 10:16 4428
The five *k* are found hid in a Josh 10:17 4428
bring out those five *k* unto me Josh 10:22 4428
five *k* unto him out of the cave Josh 10:23 4428
brought out those *k* unto Joshua Josh 10:24 4428
feet upon the necks of these *k* Josh 10:24 4428
and of the springs, and all their *k* Josh 10:40 4428
And all these *k* and their land did Josh 10:42 4428
to the *k* that were on the north Josh 11:2 4428
when all these *k* were met Josh 11:5 4428
those *k*, and all the *k* of them Josh 11:12 4428
and all their *k* he took, and smote Josh 11:17 4428
war a long time with all those *k* Josh 11:18 4428
Now these are the *k* of the land Josh 12:1 4428
these are the *k* of the country Josh 12:7 4428
all the *k* thirty and one Josh 12:24 4428
even the two *k* of the Amorites Josh 24:12 4428
said, Threescore and ten *k* Judg 1:7 4428
Hear, O ye *k* Judg 5:3 4428
The *k* came and fought Judg 5:19 4428
then fought the *k* of Canaan in Judg 5:19 4428
Zebah and Zalmunna, *k* of Midian Judg 8:5 4428
them, and took the two *k* of Midian Judg 8:12 4428
that was on the *k* of Midian Judg 8:26 4428
Edom, and against the *k* of Zobah 1Sa 14:47 4428
unto the *k* of Judah unto this day 1Sa 27:6 4428
when all the *k* that were servants 2Sa 10:19 4428
at the time when *k* go forth to 2Sa 11:1 4428
shall not be any among the *k* like 1Kin 3:13 4428
over all the *k* on this side the 1Kin 4:24 4428
from all *k* of the earth, which 1Kin 4:34 4428
and of all the *k* of Arabia 1Kin 10:15 4428
all the *k* of the earth for riches 1Kin 10:23 4428
so for all the *k* of the Hittites, 1Kin 10:29 4428
for the *k* of Syria, did they 1Kin 10:29 4428
the chronicles of the *k* of Israel 1Kin 14:19 4428
the chronicles of the *k* of Judah 1Kin 14:29 4428
the chronicles of the *k* of Judah 1Kin 15:7 4428
the chronicles of the *k* of Judah 1Kin 15:23 4428

the chronicles of the *k* of Israel 1Kin 15:31 4428
the chronicles of the *k* of Israel 1Kin 16:5 4428
the chronicles of the *k* of Israel 1Kin 16:14 4428
the chronicles of the *k* of Israel 1Kin 16:20 4428
the chronicles of the *k* of Israel 1Kin 16:27 4428
k of Israel that were before him 1Kin 16:33 4428
two *k* with him, and horses, and 1Kin 20:1 4428
the *k* in the pavilions, that he 1Kin 20:12 4428
in the pavilions, he and the *k* 1Kin 20:16 4428
thirty and two *k* that helped him 1Kin 20:16 4428
And do this thing, Take the *k* away 1Kin 20:24 4428
we have heard that the *k* of the 1Kin 20:31 4428
house of Israel are merciful *k* 1Kin 20:31 4428
the chronicles of the *k* of Israel 1Kin 22:39 4428
the chronicles of the *k* of Judah 1Kin 22:45 4428
the chronicles of the *k* of Israel 2Kin 1:18 4428
called these three *k* together 2Kin 3:10 4428
called these three *k* together 2Kin 3:13 4428
k were come up to fight against 2Kin 3:21 4428
the *k* are surely slain, and they 2Kin 3:23 4428
against us the *k* of the Hittites 2Kin 7:6 4428
the *k* of the Egyptians, to come 2Kin 7:6 4428
in the way of the *k* of Israel 2Kin 8:18 4428
the chronicles of the *k* of Judah 2Kin 8:23 4428
two *k* stood not before him 2Kin 10:4 4428
the chronicles of the *k* of Israel 2Kin 10:34 4428
And he sat on the throne of the *k* 2Kin 11:19 4428
k of Judah, had dedicated, and his 2Kin 12:18 4428
the chronicles of the *k* of Judah 2Kin 12:19 4428
the chronicles of the *k* of Israel 2Kin 13:8 4428
the chronicles of the *k* of Israel 2Kin 13:12 4428
in Samaria with the *k* of Israel 2Kin 13:13 4428
the chronicles of the *k* of Israel 2Kin 14:15 4428
in Samaria with the *k* of Israel 2Kin 14:16 4428
the chronicles of the *k* of Judah 2Kin 14:18 4428
the chronicles of the *k* of Israel 2Kin 14:28 4428
even with the *k* of Israel 2Kin 14:29 4428
the chronicles of the *k* of Judah 2Kin 15:6 4428
the chronicles of the *k* of Israel 2Kin 15:11 4428
the chronicles of the *k* of Israel 2Kin 15:15 4428
the chronicles of the *k* of Israel 2Kin 15:21 4428
the chronicles of the *k* of Israel 2Kin 15:26 4428
the chronicles of the *k* of Israel 2Kin 15:31 4428
the chronicles of the *k* of Judah 2Kin 15:36 4428
in the way of the *k* of Israel 2Kin 16:3 4428
the chronicles of the *k* of Judah 2Kin 16:19 4428
but not as the *k* of Israel that 2Kin 17:2 4428
of the *k* of Israel, which they 2Kin 17:8 4428
like him among all the *k* of Judah 2Kin 18:5 4428
thou hast heard what the *k* of 2Kin 19:11 4428
the *k* of Assyria have destroyed 2Kin 19:17 4428
the chronicles of the *k* of Judah 2Kin 20:20 4428
the chronicles of the *k* of Judah 2Kin 21:17 4428
the chronicles of the *k* of Judah 2Kin 21:25 4428
whom the *k* of Judah had ordained 2Kin 23:5 4428
k of Judah had given to the sun 2Kin 23:11 4428
which the *k* of Judah had made, and 2Kin 23:12 4428
which the *k* of Israel had made to 2Kin 23:19 4428
all the days of the *k* of Israel 2Kin 23:22 4428
nor of the *k* of Judah 2Kin 23:22 4428
the chronicles of the *k* of Judah 2Kin 23:28 4428
the chronicles of the *k* of Judah 2Kin 24:5 4428
k that were with him in Babylon 2Kin 25:28 4428
Now these are the *k* that reigned 1Chr 1:43 4428
in the book of the *k* of Israel 1Chr 9:1 4428
he reproved *k* for their sakes, 1Chr 16:21 4428
the *k* that were come were by 1Chr 19:9 4428
the time that *k* go out to battle 1Chr 20:1 4428
such as none of the *k* have had 2Chr 1:12 4428
for all the *k* of the Hittites 2Chr 1:17 4428
for the *k* of Syria, by their 2Chr 1:17 4428
all the *k* of Arabia and governors 2Chr 9:14 4428
all the *k* of the earth in riches 2Chr 9:22 4428
all the *k* of the earth sought the 2Chr 9:23 4428
he reigned over all the *k* from 2Chr 9:26 4428
in the book of the *k* of Judah 2Chr 16:11 4428
in the book of the *k* of Israel 2Chr 20:34 4428
in the way of the *k* of Israel 2Chr 21:6 4428
in the way of the *k* of Israel 2Chr 21:13 4428
not in the sepulchres of the *k* 2Chr 21:20 4428
in the city of David among the *k* 2Chr 24:16 4428
not in the sepulchres of the *k* 2Chr 24:25 4428
in the story of the book of the *k* 2Chr 24:27 4428
in the book of the *k* of Judah 2Chr 25:26 4428
burial which belonged to the *k* 2Chr 26:23 4428
in the book of the *k* of Israel 2Chr 27:7 4428
in the ways of the *k* of Israel 2Chr 28:2 4428
unto the *k* of Assyria to help him 2Chr 28:16 4428
gods of the *k* of Syria help them 2Chr 28:23 4428
in the book of the *k* of Judah 2Chr 28:26 4428
the sepulchres of the *k* of Israel 2Chr 28:27 4428
of the hand of the *k* of Assyria 2Chr 30:6 4428
Why should the *k* of Assyria come, 2Chr 32:4 4428
and in the book of the *k* of Judah 2Chr 32:32 4428
in the book of the *k* of Israel 2Chr 33:18 4428
the *k* of Judah had destroyed 2Chr 34:11 4428
neither did all the *k* of Israel 2Chr 35:18 4428
in the book of the *k* of Israel 2Chr 35:27 4428
in the book of the *k* of Israel 2Chr 36:8 4428
endamage the revenue of the *k* Ezr 4:13 4430
city, and hurtful unto *k* and Ezr 4:15 4430
hath made insurrection against *k* Ezr 4:19 4430
been mighty *k* also over Jerusalem Ezr 4:20 4430
damage grow to the hurt of the *k* Ezr 4:22 4430
name to dwell there destroy all *k* Ezr 6:12 4430
Artaxerxes, king of *k*, unto Ezra Ezr 7:12 4428
for our iniquities have we, our *k* Ezr 9:7 4428
the hand of the *k* of the lands Ezr 9:7 4428
in the sight of the *k* of Persia Ezr 9:9 4428
into their hands, with their *k* Neh 9:24 4428
that hath come upon us, on our *k* Neh 9:32 4428
since the time of the *k* of Neh 9:32 4428
Neither have our *k*, our princes, Neh 9:34 4428
the *k* whom thou hast set over us Neh 9:37 4428
the chronicles of the *k* of Media Est 10:2 4428
With *k* and counsellors of the Job 3:14 4428
He looseth the bond of *k*, and Job 12:18 4428
but with *k* are they on the throne Job 36:7 4428
The *k* of the earth set themselves Ps 2:2 4428
Be wise now therefore, O ye *k* Ps 2:10 4428
the *k* were assembled, they passed Ps 48:4 4428
K of armies did flee apace Ps 68:12 4428
the Almighty scattered *k* in it Ps 68:14 4428
shall *k* bring presents unto thee Ps 68:29 4428
The *k* of Tarshish and of the isles Ps 72:10 4428
the *k* of Sheba and Seba shall Ps 72:10 4428
all *k* shall fall down before him Ps 72:11 4428
is terrible to the *k* of the earth Ps 76:12 4428
higher than the *k* of the earth Ps 89:27 4428
all the *k* of the earth thy glory Ps 102:15 4428
he reproved *k* for their sakes Ps 105:14 4428
in the chambers of their *k* Ps 105:30 4428
through *k* in the day of his wrath Ps 110:5 4428
of thy testimonies also before *k* Ps 119:46 4428
great nations, and slew mighty *k* Ps 135:10 4428
To him which smote great *k* Ps 136:17 4428
And slew famous *k* Ps 136:18 4428
All the *k* of the earth shall Ps 138:4 4428
he that giveth salvation unto *k* Ps 144:10 4428
K of the earth, and all people Ps 148:11 4428
To bind their *k* with chains Ps 149:8 4428
By me *k* reign, and princes decree Prov 8:15 4428
to *k* to commit wickedness Prov 16:12 4428
lips are the delight of *k* Prov 16:13 4428
he shall stand before *k* Prov 22:29 4428
but the honour of *k* is to search Prov 25:2 4428
the heart of *k* is unsearchable Prov 25:3 4428
ways to that which destroyeth *k* Prov 31:3 4428
It is not for *k*, O Lemuel, it is Prov 31:4 4428
it is not for *k* to drink wine Prov 31:4 4428
and the peculiar treasure of *k* Eccl 2:8 4428
Ahaz, and Hezekiah, *k* of Judah Is 1:1 4428
shall be forsaken of both her *k* Is 7:16 4428
Are not my princes altogether *k* Is 10:8 4428
thrones all the *k* of the nations Is 14:9 4428
All the *k* of the nations, even Is 14:18 4428
of the wise, the son of ancient *k* Is 19:11 4428
the *k* of the earth upon the earth Is 24:21 4428
thou hast heard what the *k* of Is 37:11 4428
the *k* of Assyria have laid waste Is 37:18 4428
him, and made him rule over *k* Is 41:2 4428
and I will loose the loins of *k* Is 45:1 4428
K shall see and arise, princes Is 49:7 4428
k shall be thy nursing fathers, Is 49:23 4428
the *k* shall shut their mouths at Is 52:15 4428
k to the brightness of thy rising Is 60:3 4428
their *k* shall minister unto thee Is 60:10 4428
that their *k* may be brought Is 60:11 4428
and shalt suck the breast of *k* Is 60:16 4428
righteousness, and all *k* thy glory Is 62:2 4428
land, against the *k* of Judah Jer 1:18 4428
they, their *k*, their princes, and Jer 2:26 4428
out the bones of the *k* of Judah Jer 8:1 4428
even the *k* that sit upon David's Jer 13:13 4428
whereby the *k* of Judah come in, Jer 17:19 4428
ye *k* of Judah, and all Judah, and Jer 17:20 4428
into the gates of this city *k* Jer 17:25 4428
O *k* of Judah, and inhabitants of Jer 19:3 4428
nor the *k* of Judah, and have Jer 19:4 4428
and the houses of the *k* of Judah Jer 19:13 4428
all the treasures of the *k* of Jer 20:5 4428
k sitting upon the throne of Jer 22:4 4428
great *k* shall serve themselves of Jer 25:14 4428
the *k* thereof, and the princes Jer 25:18 4428
all the *k* of the land of Uz, and Jer 25:20 4428
all the *k* of the land of the Jer 25:20 4428
all the *k* of Tyrus Jer 25:22 4428
all the *k* of Zidon Jer 25:22 4428
the *k* of the isles which are Jer 25:22 4428
all the *k* of Arabia Jer 25:24 4428
all the *k* of the mingled people Jer 25:24 4428
all the *k* of Zimri Jer 25:25 4428
and all the *k* of Elam Jer 25:25 4428
and all the *k* of the Medes Jer 25:25 4428
all the *k* of the north, far and Jer 25:26 4428
great *k* shall serve themselves of Jer 27:7 4428
me to anger, they, their *k* Jer 32:32 4428
the houses of the *k* of Judah Jer 33:4 4428
the former *k* which were before Jer 34:5 4428
the wickedness of the *k* of Judah Jer 44:9 4428
done, we, and our fathers, our *k* Jer 44:17 4428
ye, and your fathers, your *k* Jer 44:21 4428
with their gods, and their *k* Jer 46:25 4428
many *k* shall be raised up from Jer 50:41 4428
the spirit of the *k* of the Medes Jer 51:11 4428
nations with the *k* of the Medes Jer 51:28 4428
k that were with him in Babylon Jer 52:32 4428
The *k* of the earth, and all the Lam 4:12 4428
king of Babylon, a king of *k* Eze 26:7 4428
thou didst enrich the *k* of the Eze 27:33 4428
their *k* shall be sore afraid, Eze 27:35 4428
ground, I will lay thee before *k* Eze 28:17 4428
their *k* shall be horribly afraid Eze 32:10 4428
There is Edom, her *k*, and all her Eze 32:29 4428
defile, neither they, nor their *k* Eze 43:7 4428
of their *k* in their high places Eze 43:7 4428
and the carcases of their *k* Eze 43:9 4428
removeth *k*, and setteth up *k* Dan 2:21 4430
Thou, O king, art a king of *k* Dan 2:37 4430
in the days of these *k* shall the Dan 2:44 4430
is a God of gods, and a LORD of *k* Dan 2:47 4430
which are four, are four *k* Dan 7:17 4430
are ten *k* that shall arise Dan 7:24 4430
first, and he shall subdue three *k* Dan 7:24 4430
two horns are the *k* of Media Dan 8:20 4428
which spake in thy name to our *k* Dan 9:6 4428
confusion of face, to our *k* Dan 9:8 4428
there with the *k* of Persia Dan 10:13 4428
stand up yet three *k* in Persia Dan 11:2 4428
k of Judah, and in the days of Hos 1:1 4428
all their *k* are fallen Hos 7:7 4428
They have set up *k*, but not by me Hos 8:4 4428
k of Judah, which he saw Mic 1:1 4428
shall be a lie to the *k* of Israel Mic 1:14 4428
And they shall scoff at the *k* Hab 1:10 4428
k for my sake, for a testimony Mt 10:18 *935*
of whom do the *k* of the earth Mt 17:25 *935*
k for my sake, for a testimony Mk 13:9 *935*
k have desired to see those Lk 10:24 *935*
prisons, being brought before *k* Lk 21:12 *935*
The *k* of the Gentiles exercise Lk 22:25 *935*
The *k* of the earth stood up, and Acts 4:26 *935*
my name before the Gentiles, and *k* Acts 9:15 *935*
ye have reigned as *k* without us 1Cor 4:8
For *k*, and for all that are in 1Ti 2:2 *935*
and only Potentate, the King of *k* 1Ti 6:15 *936*
from the slaughter of the *k* Heb 7:1 *935*
the prince of the *k* of the earth Rev 1:5 *935*
And hath made us *k* and priests unto Rev 1:6 *935*
And hast made us unto our God *k* Rev 5:10 *935*
the *k* of the earth, and the great Rev 6:15 *935*
and nations, and tongues, and *k* Rev 10:11 *935*
that the way of the *k* of the east Rev 16:12 *935*
go forth unto the *k* of the earth Rev 16:14 *935*
With whom the *k* of the earth have Rev 17:2 *935*
And there are seven *k* Rev 17:10 *935*
horns which thou sawest are ten *k* Rev 17:12 *935*
but receive power as *k* one hour Rev 17:12 *935*
he is Lord of lords, and King of *k* Rev 17:14 *935*
reigneth over the *k* of the earth Rev 17:18 *935*
the *k* of the earth have committed Rev 18:3 *935*
the *k* of the earth, who have Rev 18:9 *935*
thigh a name written, KING OF *K* Rev 19:16 *935*
That ye may eat the flesh of *k* Rev 19:18 *935*
the *k* of the earth, and their Rev 19:19 *935*
the *k* of the earth do bring their Rev 21:24 *935*

KINGS'
K daughters were among thy Ps 45:9 4428
her hands, and is in *k* palaces Prov 30:28 4428
both these *k* hearts shall be to Dan 11:27 4428
soft clothing are in *k* houses Mt 11:8 *935*
live delicately, are in *k* courts Lk 7:25 *933*

KINNERETH See CINNEROTH.

KINSFOLK
My *k* have failed, and my familiar Job 19:14 7138
and they sought him among their *k* Lk 2:44 4773

KINSFOLKS
against a wall, neither of his *k* 1Kin 16:11 1350
and all his great men, and his *k* 2Kin 10:11 3045
by parents, and brethren, and *k* Lk 21:16 4773

KINSMAN
But if the man have no *k* to Num 5:8 1350
his *k* that is next to him of his Num 27:11 7607
Naomi had a *k* of her husband's, a Ruth 2:1 3045
for thou art a near *k* Ruth 3:9 1350
it is true that I am thy near *k* Ruth 3:12 1350
there is a *k* nearer than I Ruth 3:12 1350
perform unto thee the part of a *k* Ruth 3:13 1350
not do the part of a *k* to thee Ruth 3:13 1350
will I do the part of a *k* to thee Ruth 3:13 1350
the *k* of whom Boaz spake came by Ruth 4:1 1350
And he said unto the *k*, Naomi, Ruth 4:3 1350
the *k* said, I cannot redeem it Ruth 4:6 1350
Therefore the *k* said unto Boaz, Ruth 4:8 1350
left thee this day without a *k* Ruth 4:14 1350
being his *k* whose ear Peter cut Jn 18:26 *4773*
Salute Herodion my *k* Rom 16:11 *4773*

KINSMAN'S
let him do the *k* part Ruth 3:13 1350

KINSMEN
of kin unto us, one of our next *k* Ruth 2:20 1350
and my *k* stand afar off Ps 38:11 7138
nor thy brethren, neither thy *k* Lk 14:12 *4773*
and had called together his *k* Acts 10:24 *4773*
my *k* according to the flesh Rom 9:3 *4773*
Salute Andronicus and Junia, my *k* Rom 16:7 *4773*
and Jason, and Sosipater, my *k* Rom 16:21 *4773*

KINSWOMAN
she is thy father's near *k* Lev 18:12 7607
for she is thy mother's near *k* Lev 18:13 7607
and call understanding thy *k* Prov 7:4 4129

KINSWOMEN
for they are her near *k* Lev 18:17 7608

KIOS See CHIOS.

KIR (*kur*) See KIR-HARESH.
1. An Assyrian district on the Kur River.
the people of it captive to *K* 2Kin 16:9 7024
shall go into captivity unto *K* Amos 1:5 7024
Caphtor, and the Syrians from *K* Amos 9:7 7024
2. A Moabite city.
because in the night *K* of Moab is Is 15:1 7024
3. Inhabitants of Kir 1.
and *K* uncovered the shield Is 22:6 7024

KIR-HARASETH (*kur-har'-a-seth*) See KIR-HARESETH. *A Moabite city.*
only in *K* left they the stones 2Kin 3:25 7025

KIR-HARESETH (*kur-har'-e-seth*) See KIR-HARESH. *Same as Kir-haraseth.*
foundations of *K* shall ye mourn Is 16:7 7025

KIR-HARESH (*kur-ha'-resh*) See KIR-HARASETH, KIR-HARESETH, KIR-HERES. *Same as Kir-haraseth.*
Moab, and mine inward parts for *K* Is 16:11 7025

KIR-HERES (kur-he'-res) See KIR-HARESH.
Same as Kir-haraseth.
shall mourn for the men of K... Jer 48:31 7025
sound like pipes for the men of K... Jer 48:36 7025

KIRIATH See KIRJATH.

KIRIATHAIM (kir-e-a-thay'-im) See KIRTAN, KIRJATHAIM.
1. A town east of the Jordan.
in Ham, and the Emims in Shaveh K... Gen 14:5 7741
2. A city in Reuben.
K is confounded and taken... Jer 48:1 7156
upon K, and upon Beth-gamul... Jer 48:23 7156
Beth-jeshimoth, Baal-meon, and K... Eze 25:9 7156

KIRIATH ARBA See KIRJATH-ARBA.

KIRIATH-ARBA See KIRJATH-ARBA.

KIRIATH-ARIM See KIRJATH-ARIM.

KIRIATH-BAAL See KIRJATH-BAAL.

KIRIATH-JEARIM See KIRJATH.

KIRIATH-SANNAH See KIRJATH-SANNAH.

KIRIATH-SEPHER See KIRJATH-SEPHER.

KIRIOTH (kir'-e-oth) See KERIOTH. *A Moabite city.*
it shall devour the palaces of K... Amos 2:2 7152

KIRJATH (kur'-jath) See KIRJATH-ARIM, KIRJATH-BAAL, KIRJATH-JEARIM. *Short form of Kirjath-jearim.*
which is Jerusalem, Gibeath, and K... Josh 18:28 7157

KIRJATHAIM (jur'-jath-a'-im)
1. A city in Reuben.
built Heshbon, and Elealeh, and K... Num 32:37 7156
And K, and Sibmah... Josh 13:19 7156
2. A Levitical city in Naphtali.
suburbs, and K with her suburbs... 1Chr 6:76 7156

KIRJATH-ARBA (kur'-jath-ar'-bah) See HEBRON. *A city in Judah.*
And Sarah died in K... Gen 23:2 7153
the name of Hebron before was K... Josh 14:15 7153
And Humtah, and K, which is Hebron, Josh 15:54 7153
in mount Ephraim, and K... Josh 20:7 7153
the name of Hebron before was K... Judg 1:10 7153
the children of Judah dwelt at K... Neh 11:25 7153

KIRJATH-ARIM (kur'-jath-a'-rim) See KIRJATH-JEARIM. *Same as Kirjath-jearim.*
The children of K, Chephirah, and... Ezr 2:25 7157

KIRJATH-BAAL (kur'-jath-ba'-al) See BAALAH, KIRJATH-JEARIM. *Same as Kirjath-jearim.*
K, which is Kirjath-jearim, and... Josh 15:60 7154
the goings out thereof were at K... Josh 18:14 7154

KIRJATH-HUZOTH (kur'-jath-hu'-zoth) *Residence of Balak, king of Edom.*
with Balak, and they came unto K... Num 22:39 7155

KIRJATH-JEARIM (kur'-jath-je'-a-rim) See KIRJATH, KIRJATH-ARIM, KIRJATH-BAAL.
1. A city in Judah.
and Chephirah, and Beeroth, and K... Josh 9:17 7157
was drawn to Baalah, which is K... Josh 15:9 7157
Kirjath-baal, which is K, and... Josh 15:60 7157
were at Kirjath-baal, which is K... Josh 18:14 7157
quarter was from the end of K... Josh 18:15 7157
And they went up, and pitched in K... Judg 18:12 7157
behold, it is behind K... Judg 18:12 7157
to the inhabitants of K, saying,... 1Sa 6:21 7157
And the men of K came, and brought.. 1Sa 7:1 7157
to pass, while the ark abode in K... 1Sa 7:2 7157
to bring the ark of God from K... 1Chr 13:5 7157
Israel, to Baalah, that is, to K... 1Chr 13:6 7157
K to the place which David had... 2Chr 1:4 7157
The men of K, Chephirah, and... Neh 7:29 7157
Urijah the son of Shemaiah of K... Jer 26:20 7157
2. A descendant of Caleb.
Shobal the father of K,... 1Chr 2:50 7157
Shobal the father of K had sons... 1Chr 2:52 7157
And the families of K... 1Chr 2:53 7157

KIRJATH-SANNAH (kur'-jath-san'-nah) *A city in Judah.*
And Dannah, and K, which is Debir,... Josh 15:49 7158

KIRJATH-SEPHER (kur'-jath-se'-fer) See DEBIR, KIRJATH-SANNAH. *Same as Kirjath-sannah.*
and the name of Debir before was K... Josh 15:15 7158
And Caleb said, He that smiteth K... Josh 15:16 7158
and the name of Debir before was K... Judg 1:11 7158
And Caleb said, He that smiteth K... Judg 1:12 7158

KISH (kish)
1. Father of King Saul.
man of Benjamin, whose name was K. 1Sa 9:1 7027
the asses of K Saul's father were... 1Sa 9:3 7027
K said to Saul his son, Take now... 1Sa 9:3 7027
that is come unto the son of K... 1Sa 10:11 7027
and Saul the son of K was taken... 1Sa 10:21 7027
And K was the father of Saul... 1Sa 14:51 7027
in the sepulchre of K his father... 2Sa 21:14 7027
And Ner begat K... 1Chr 8:33 7027
K begat Saul... 1Chr 8:33 7027
And Ner begat K... 1Chr 9:39 7027
and K begat Saul... 1Chr 9:39 7027
because of Saul the son of K... 1Chr 12:1 7027
the seer, and Saul the son of K... 1Chr 26:28 7027
2. Son of Abi-Gibeon.
firstborn son Abdon, and Zur, and K... 1Chr 8:30 7027
son Abdon, then Zur, and K... 1Chr 9:36 7027
3. A sanctuary servant.
of Mahli; Eleazar, and K... 1Chr 23:21 7027
brethren the sons of K took them... 1Chr 23:22 7027
Concerning K: the son of Kish... 1Chr 24:29 7027
4. A Levite.
K the son of Abdi, and Azariah the... 2Chr 29:12 7027
5. An ancestor of Mordecai.
the son of Shimei, the son of K... Est 2:5 7027

KISHI (kish'-i) See KUSHAIAH. *Father of Ethan.*
Ethan the son of K, the son of... 1Chr 6:44 7029

KISHION (kish'-e-on) See KEDESH, KISHON. *A Levitical city in Issachar.*
And Rabbith, and K, and Abez,... Josh 19:20 7191

KISHON (ki'-shon) See KISHION, KISON.
1. Same as Kishion.
K with her suburbs, Dabareh with... Josh 21:28 7191
the Gentiles unto the river of K... Judg 4:13 7028
The river of K swept them away,... Judg 5:21 7028
that ancient river, the river K... Judg 5:21 7028
brought them down to the brook K... 1Kin 18:40 7028
2. A brook near Mt. Tabor.
draw unto thee to the river K... Judg 4:7 7028

KISLEV See CHISLEU.

KISLON See CHISLON.

KISLOTH TABOR See CHISLOTH-TABOR.

KISON (ki'-son) See KISHON. *Same as Kishon 2.*
as to Jabin, at the brook of K... Ps 83:9 7028

KISS
Come near now, and k me, my son... Gen 27:26 5401
hast not suffered me to k my sons... Gen 31:28 5401
with the right hand to k him... 2Sa 20:9 5401
k my father and my mother, and then. 1Kin 19:20 5401
K the Son, lest he be angry, and... Ps 2:12 5401
Every man shall k his lips that... Prov 24:26 5401
Let him k me with the kisses of... Song 1:2 5401
find thee without, I would k thee... Song 8:1 5401
men that sacrifice k the calves... Hos 13:2 5401
saying, Whomsoever I shall k... Mt 26:48 5368
saying, Whomsoever I shall k... Mk 14:44 5368
Thou gavest me no k... Lk 7:45 5370
in hath not ceased to k my feet... Lk 7:45 2705
and drew near unto Jesus to k him... Lk 22:47 5368
thou the Son of man with a k... Lk 22:48 5370
Salute one another with an holy k... Rom 16:16 5370
ye one another with an holy k... 1Cor 16:20 5370
Greet one another with an holy k... 2Cor 13:12 5370
all the brethren with an holy k... 1Th 5:26 5370
one another with a k of charity... 1Pet 5:14 5370

KISSED
And he came near, and k him... Gen 27:27 5401
Jacob k Rachel, and lifted up his... Gen 29:11 5401
k him, and brought him to his... Gen 29:13 5401
k his sons and his daughters, and... Gen 31:55 5401
and fell on his neck, and k him... Gen 33:4 5401
Moreover he k all his brethren,... Gen 45:15 5401
he k them, and embraced them... Gen 48:10 5401
face, and wept upon him, and k him... Gen 50:1 5401
him in the mount of God, and k him... Ex 4:27 5401
law, and did obeisance, and k him... Ex 18:7 5401
Then she k them... Ruth 1:9 5401
Orpah k her mother in law... Ruth 1:14 5401
k him, and said, Is it not because... 1Sa 10:1 5401
they k one another, and wept one... 1Sa 20:41 5401
and the king k Absalom... 2Sa 14:33 5401
his hand, and took him, and k him... 2Sa 15:5 5401
the king k Barzillai, and blessed... 2Sa 19:39 5401
every mouth which hath not k him... 1Kin 19:18 5401
or my mouth hath k my hand... Job 31:27 5401
and peace have k each other... Ps 85:10 5401
k him, and with an impudent face... Prov 7:13 5401
master; and k him... Mt 26:49 2705
Master, master; and k him... Mk 14:45 2705
k his feet, and anointed them with... Lk 7:38 2705
and fell on his neck, and k him... Lk 15:20 2705
and fell on Paul's neck, and k him,... Acts 20:37 2705

KISSES
but the k of an enemy are... Prov 27:6 5390
kiss me with the k of his mouth... Song 1:2 5390

KITE
vulture, and the k after his kind... Lev 11:14 344
And the glede, and the k, and the... Deut 14:13 344

KITHLISH (kith'-lish) *A city in Judah.*
And Cabbon, and Lahmam, and K... Josh 15:40 3798

KITRON (ki'-tron) See KATTAH. *A city in Zebulun.*
drive out the inhabitants of K... Judg 1:30 7003

KITTIM (kit'-tim) See CHITTIM. *A son of Javan.*
Elishah, and Tarshish, K, and... Gen 10:4 3794
Elishah, and Tarshish, K, and... 1Chr 1:7 3794

KIYYUN See CHIUN.

KNEAD
k it, and make cakes upon the... Gen 18:6 3888
the women k their dough, to make... Jer 7:18 3888

KNEADED
k it, and did bake unleavened... 1Sa 28:24 3888
k it, and made cakes in his sight,... 2Sa 13:8 3888
raising after he hath k the dough... Hos 7:4 3888

KNEADINGTROUGHS
into thine ovens, and into thy k... Ex 8:3 4863
their k being bound up in their... Ex 12:34 4863

KNEE
they cried before him, Bow the k... Gen 41:43
That unto me every k shall bow... Is 45:23 1290
and they bowed the k before him... Mt 27:29
bowed the k to the image of Baal... Rom 11:4 1119
every k shall bow to me, and every... Rom 14:11 1119
name of Jesus every k should bow... Phil 2:10 1119

KNEEL
he made his camels to k down... Gen 24:11 1288
let us k before the LORD our... Ps 95:6 1288

KNEELED
k down upon his knees before all... 2Chr 6:13 1288
he k upon his knees three times a... Dan 6:10 1289
k to him, and asked him, Good... Mk 10:17 1120
cast, and k down, and prayed,... Lk 22:41 1119
he k down, and cried with a loud... Acts 7:60 1119
all forth, and k down, and prayed... Acts 9:40 1119
he k down, and prayed with them... Acts 20:36 1119
we k down on the shore, and prayed... Acts 21:5 1119

KNEELING
from k on his knees with his... 1Kin 8:54 3766
k down to him, and saying,... Mt 17:14 1120
k down to him, and saying unto him... Mk 1:40 1120

KNEES
and she shall bear upon my k... Gen 30:3 1290
them out from between his k... Gen 48:12 1290
were brought up upon Joseph's k... Gen 50:23 1290
LORD shall smite thee in the k... Deut 28:35 1290
boweth down upon his k to drink... Judg 7:5 1290
down upon their k to drink water... Judg 7:6 1290
And she made him sleep upon her k... Judg 16:19 1290
from kneeling on his k with his... 1Kin 8:54 1290
and put his face between his k... 1Kin 18:42 1290
all the k which have not bowed... 1Kin 19:18 1290
fell on his k before Elijah, and... 2Kin 1:13 1290
mother, he sat on her k till noon... 2Kin 4:20 1290
kneeled down upon his k before... 2Chr 6:13 1290
and my mantle, I fell upon my k... Ezr 9:5 1290
Why did the k prevent me... Job 3:12 1290
hast strengthened the feeble k... Job 4:4 1290
My k are weak through fasting... Ps 109:24 1290
hands, and confirm the feeble k... Is 35:3 1290
sides, and be dandled upon her k... Is 66:12 1290
all k shall be weak as water... Eze 7:17 1290
all k shall be weak as water... Eze 21:7 1290
the waters were to the k... Eze 47:4 1290
his k smote one against another... Dan 5:6 755
upon his k three times a day... Dan 6:10 1291
me, which set me upon my k... Dan 10:10 1290
the k smite together, and much... Nah 2:10 1290
bowing their k worshipped him... Mk 15:19 1119
saw it, he fell down at Jesus' k... Lk 5:8 1119
For this cause I bow my k unto... Eph 3:14 1119
which hang down, and the feeble k... Heb 12:12 1119

KNEW
they k that they were naked... Gen 3:7 3045
And Adam k Eve his wife... Gen 4:1 3045
And Cain k his wife... Gen 4:17 3045
And Adam k his wife again... Gen 4:25 3045
so Noah k that the waters were... Gen 8:11 3045
k what his younger son had done... Gen 9:24 3045
and I k it not... Gen 28:16 3045
For Jacob k not that Rachel had... Gen 31:32 3045
And he k it, and said, It is my... Gen 37:33 5234
Onan k that the seed should not... Gen 38:9 3045
(for he k not that she was his... Gen 38:16 3045
And he k her again no more... Gen 38:26 3045
he k not ought he had, save the... Gen 39:6 3045
he k them, but made himself... Gen 42:7 5234
Joseph k his brethren... Gen 42:8 5234
his brethren, but they k not him... Gen 42:8 3045
they k not that Joseph understood... Gen 42:23 3045
over Egypt, which k not Joseph... Ex 1:8 3045
for I k not that thou stoodest in... Num 22:34 3045
k the knowledge of the most High,... Num 24:16 3045
manna, which thy fathers k not... Deut 8:16 3045
LORD from the day that I k you... Deut 9:24 3045
them, gods whom they k not... Deut 29:26 3045
to gods whom they k not, to new... Deut 32:17 3045
brethren, nor k his own children... Deut 33:9 3045
whom the LORD k face to face... Deut 34:10 3045
which k not the LORD, nor yet the... Judg 2:10 3045
such as before k nothing thereof... Judg 3:2 3045
and she k no man... Judg 11:39 3045
For Manoah k not that he was an... Judg 13:16 3045
Then Manoah k that he was an... Judg 13:21 3045
his mother k not that it was of... Judg 14:4 3045
they k the voice of the young man... Judg 18:3 5234
and they k her, and abused her all... Judg 19:25 3045
but they k not that evil was near... Judg 20:34 3045
Elkanah k Hannah his wife... 1Sa 1:19 3045
they k not the LORD... 1Sa 2:12 3045
from Dan even to Beer-sheba k... 1Sa 3:20 3045
when all that k him beforetime... 1Sa 10:11 3045
the people k not that Jonathan... 1Sa 14:3 3045
k that the LORD was with David,... 1Sa 18:28 3045
for if I k certainly that evil... 1Sa 20:9 3045
whereby Jonathan k that it was... 1Sa 20:33 3045
But the lad k not any thing... 1Sa 20:39 3045
Jonathan and David k the matter... 1Sa 20:39 3045
for thy servant k nothing of all... 1Sa 22:15 3045
and because they k when he fled... 1Sa 22:17 3045
I k it that day, when Doeg the... 1Sa 22:22 3045
David k that Saul secretly... 1Sa 23:9 3045
away, and no man saw it, nor k it... 1Sa 26:12 3045
Saul k David's voice, and said, Is... 1Sa 26:17 5234
but David k it not... 2Sa 3:26 3045
where he k that valiant men were... 2Sa 11:16 3045
k ye not that they would shoot... 2Sa 11:20 3045
and they k not any thing... 2Sa 15:11 3045
tumult, but I k not what it was... 2Sa 18:29 3045
a people which I k not shall... 2Sa 22:44 3045
but the king k her not... 1Kin 1:4 3045
he k him, and fell on his face, and... 1Kin 18:7 5234
for they k them not... 2Kin 4:39 3045
Then Manasseh k that the LORD he... 2Chr 33:13 3045
the rulers k not whither I went,... Neh 2:16 3045
which k the times, (for so was... Est 1:13 5234
manner toward all that k law... Est 1:13 5234

k him not, they lifted up their — Job 2:12 — 5234
Oh that I *k* where I might find — Job 23:3 — 3045
the cause which I *k* not I — Job 29:16 — 3045
wonderful for me, which I *k* not — Job 42:3 — 3045
to my charge things that I *k* not — Ps 35:11 — 3045
against me, and I *k* it not — Ps 35:15 — 3045
thou sayest, Behold, we *k* it not — Prov 24:12 — 3045
blind by a way that they *k* not — Is 42:16 — 3045
on fire round about, yet he *k* not — Is 42:25 — 3045
Because I *k* that thou art — Is 48:4 — 1847
shouldest say, Behold, I *k* them — Is 48:7 — 3045
for I *k* that thou wouldest deal — Is 48:8 — 3045
nations that *k* not thee shall run — Is 55:5 — 3045
formed thee in the belly I *k* thee — Jer 1:5 — 3045
they that handle the law *k* me not — Jer 2:8 — 3045
I *k* not that they had devised — Jer 11:19 — 3045
Then I *k* that this was the word — Jer 32:8 — 3045
slain Gedaliah, and no man *k* it — Jer 41:4 — 3045
serve other gods, whom they *k* not — Jer 44:3 — 3045
Then all the men which *k* that — Jer 44:15 — 3045
I *k* that they were the cherubims — Eze 10:20 — 3045
he *k* their desolate palaces, and — Eze 19:7 — 3045
till he *k* that the most high God — Dan 5:21 — 3046
Now when Daniel *k* that the — Dan 6:10 — 3046
a god whom his fathers *k* not — Dan 11:38 — 3045
have made princes, and I *k* it not — Hos 8:4 — 3045
but they *k* not that I healed them — Hos 11:3 — 3045
For the men *k* that he fled from — Jonah 1:10 — 3045
for I *k* that thou art a gracious — Jonah 4:2 — 3045
all the nations whom they *k* not — Zec 7:14 — 3045
me *k* that it was the word of the — Zec 11:11 — 3045
k her not till she had brought — Mt 1:25 — 1097
profess unto them, I never *k* you — Mt 7:23 — 1097
But when Jesus *k* it, he withdrew — Mt 12:15 — 1097
Jesus *k* their thoughts, and said — Mt 12:25 — 1492
they *k* him not, but have done — Mt 17:12 — 1912
k not until the flood came, and — Mt 24:39 — 1097
I *k* thee that thou art an hard — Mt 25:24 — 1097
For he *k* that for envy they had — Mt 27:18 — 1492
to speak, because they *k* him — Mk 1:34 — 1492
saw them departing, and many *k* him — Mk 6:33 — 1921
And when they *k*, they say, Five — Mk 6:38 — 1097
the ship, straightway they *k* him — Mk 6:54 — 1921
And when Jesus *k* it, he saith unto — Mk 8:17 — 1097
for they *k* that he had spoken the — Mk 12:12 — 1097
For he *k* that the chief priests — Mk 15:10 — 1097
when he *k* it of the centurion, he — Mk 15:45 — 1097
Joseph and his mother *k* not of it — Lk 2:43 — 1097
for they *k* that he was Christ — Lk 4:41
But he *k* their thoughts, and said — Lk 6:8 — 1492
when she *k* that Jesus sat at meat — Lk 7:37 — 1921
And the people, when they *k* it — Lk 9:11 — 1097
which *k* his lord's will, and — Lk 12:47 — 1097
But he that *k* not, and did commit — Lk 12:48 — 1097
neither *k* they the things which — Lk 18:34 — 1097
as soon as he *k* that he belonged — Lk 23:7 — 1921
eyes were opened, and they *k* him — Lk 24:31 — 1921
by him, and the world *k* him not — Jn 1:10 — 1097
And I *k* him not — Jn 1:31 — 1492
And I *k* him not — Jn 1:33 — 1492
made wine, and *k* not whence it was — Jn 2:9 — 1492
servants which drew the water *k* — Jn 2:9 — 1492
unto them, because he *k* all men — Jn 2:24 — 1097
for he *k* what was in man — Jn 2:25 — 1097
When therefore the Lord *k* how the — Jn 4:1 — 1097
So the father *k* that it was at — Jn 4:53 — 1097
k that he had been now a long — Jn 5:6 — 1097
for he himself *k* what he would do — Jn 6:6 — 1492
When Jesus *k* in himself that his — Jn 6:61 — 1492
For Jesus *k* from the beginning — Jn 6:64 — 1492
I *k* that thou hearest me always — Jn 11:42 — 1492
if any man *k* where he were, he — Jn 11:57 — 1097
therefore *k* that he was there — Jn 12:9 — 1097
when Jesus *k* that his hour was — Jn 13:1 — 1492
For he *k* who should betray him — Jn 13:11 — 1492
Now no man at the table *k* for — Jn 13:28 — 1097
Now Jesus *k* that they were — Jn 16:19 — 1097
which betrayed him, *k* the place — Jn 18:2 — 1492
For as yet they *k* not the — Jn 20:9 — 1492
and *k* not that it was Jesus — Jn 20:14 — 1492
but the disciples *k* not that it — Jn 21:4 — 1492
they *k* that it was he which sat — Acts 3:10 — 1921
king arose, which *k* not Joseph — Acts 7:18 — 1492
Which when the brethren *k* — Acts 9:30 — 1921
when she *k* Peter's voice, she — Acts 12:14 — 1921
rulers, because they *k* him not — Acts 13:27 — 50
for they *k* all that his father — Acts 16:3 — 1492
the more part *k* not wherefore — Acts 19:32 — 1492
But when they *k* that he was a Jew — Acts 19:34 — 1921
after he *k* that he was a Roman — Acts 22:29 — 1921
Which *k* me from the beginning, if — Acts 26:5 — 4267
it was day, they *k* not the land — Acts 27:39 — 1921
then they *k* that the island was — Acts 28:1 — 1921
Because that, when they *k* God — Rom 1:21 — 1097
God the world by wisdom *k* not God — 1Cor 1:21 — 1097
of the princes of this world *k* — 1Cor 2:8 — 1097
to be sin for us, who *k* no sin — 2Cor 5:21 — 1097
I *k* a man in Christ above — 2Cor 12:2 — 1492
I *k* such a man, (whether in the — 2Cor 12:3 — 1492
Howbeit then, when ye *k* not God — Gal 4:8 — 1492
k the grace of God in truth — Col 1:6 — 1921
For I would that ye *k* what great — Col 2:1 — 1492
us not, because it *k* him not — 1Jn 3:1 — 1097
though ye once *k* this, how that — Jude 5 — 1492
had a name written, that no man *k* — Rev 19:12 — 1492

KNEWEST
thee with manna, which thou *k* not — Deut 8:3 — 3045
which thou *k* not heretofore — Ruth 2:11 — 3045
for thou *k* that they dealt — Neh 9:10 — 3045
within me, then thou *k* my path — Ps 142:3 — 3045
yea, thou *k* not — Is 48:8 — 3045
heart, though thou *k* all this — Dan 5:22 — 3046
thou *k* that I reap where I sowed — Mt 25:26 — 1492
Thou *k* that I was an austere man — Lk 19:22 — 1492
because thou *k* not the time of — Lk 19:44 — 1097
If thou *k* the gift of God, and who — Jn 4:10 — 1492

KNIFE
took the fire in his hand, and a *k* — Gen 22:6 — 3979
took the *k* to slay his son — Gen 22:10 — 3979
come into his house, he took a *k* — Judg 19:29 — 3979
put a *k* to thy throat, if thou be — Prov 23:2 — 7915
son of man, take thee a sharp *k* — Eze 5:1 — 2719
part, and smite about it with a *k* — Eze 5:2 — 2719

KNIT
the city, *k* together as one man — Judg 20:11 — 2270
was *k* with the soul of David — 1Sa 18:1 — 7194
mine heart shall be *k* unto you — 1Chr 12:17 — 3162
great sheet *k* at the four corners — Acts 10:11 — 1210
being *k* together in love, and unto — Col 2:2 — 4822
k together, increaseth with the — Col 2:19 — 4822

KNIVES
unto Joshua, Make thee sharp *k* — Josh 5:2 — 2719
And Joshua made him sharp *k* — Josh 5:3 — 2719
after their manner with *k* — 1Kin 18:28 — 2719
of silver, nine and twenty *k* — Ezr 1:9 — 4252
swords, and their jaw teeth as *k* — Prov 30:14 — 3979

KNOCK
k, and it shall be opened unto you — Mt 7:7 — 2925
k, and it shall be opened unto you — Lk 11:9 — 2925
to *k* at the door, saying, Lord — Lk 13:25 — 2925
Behold, I stand at the door, and *k* — Rev 3:20 — 2925

KNOCKED
as Peter *k* at the door of the — Acts 12:13 — 2925

KNOCKETH
is the voice of my beloved that *k* — Song 5:2 — 1849
to him that *k* it shall be opened — Mt 7:8 — 2925
to him that *k* it shall be opened — Lk 11:10 — 2925
that when he cometh and *k*, they — Lk 12:36 — 2925

KNOCKING
But Peter continued *k* — Acts 12:16 — 2925

KNOP
made like unto almonds, with a *k* — Ex 25:33 — 3730
in the other branch, with a *k* — Ex 25:33 — 3730
there shall be a *k* under two — Ex 25:35 — 3730
a *k* under two branches of the — Ex 25:35 — 3730
a *k* under two branches of the — Ex 25:35 — 3730
of almonds in one branch, a *k* — Ex 37:19 — 3730
almonds in another branch, a *k* — Ex 37:19 — 3730
a *k* under two branches of the — Ex 37:21 — 3730
a *k* under two branches of the — Ex 37:21 — 3730
a *k* under two branches of the — Ex 37:21 — 3730

KNOPS
and his branches, his bowls, his *k* — Ex 25:31 — 3730
like unto almonds, with their *k* — Ex 25:34 — 3730
Their *k* and their branches shall — Ex 25:36 — 3730
and his branch, his bowls, his *k* — Ex 37:17 — 3730
bowls made like almonds, his *k* — Ex 37:20 — 3730
Their *k* and their branches were of — Ex 37:22 — 3730
house within was carved with *k* — 1Kin 6:18 — 6497
about there were *k* compassing it — 1Kin 7:24 — 6497
the *k* were cast in two rows, when — 1Kin 7:24 — 6497

KNOW
For God doth *k* that in the day ye — Gen 3:5 — 3045
as one of us, to *k* good and evil — Gen 3:22 — 3045
And he said, I *k* not — Gen 4:9 — 3045
I *k* that thou art a fair woman to — Gen 12:11 — 3045
whereby shall I *k* that I shall — Gen 15:8 — 3045
K of a surety that thy seed shall — Gen 15:13 — 3045
For I *k* him, that he will command — Gen 18:19 — 3045
and if not, I will *k* — Gen 18:21 — 3045
out unto us, that we may *k* them — Gen 19:5 — 3045
I *k* that thou didst this in the — Gen 20:6 — 3045
k thou that thou shalt surely die — Gen 20:7 — 3045
for now I *k* that thou fearest God — Gen 22:12 — 3045
thereby shall I *k* that thou hast — Gen 24:14 — 3045
I *k* not the day of my death — Gen 27:2 — 3045
K ye Laban the son of Nahor — Gen 29:5 — 3045
And they said, We *k* him — Gen 29:5 — 3045
ye *k* that with all my power I — Gen 31:6 — 3045
k now whether it be thy son's — Gen 37:32 — 5234
Hereby shall I *k* that ye are true — Gen 42:33 — 3045
then shall I *k* that ye are no — Gen 42:34 — 3045
we certainly *k* that he would say — Gen 43:7 — 3045
Ye *k* that my wife bare me two — Gen 44:27 — 3045
I *k* it, my son, I *k* it — Gen 48:19 — 3045
for I *k* their sorrows — Ex 3:7 — 3045
I *k* that he can speak well — Ex 4:14 — 3045
I *k* not the LORD, neither will I — Ex 5:2 — 3045
ye shall *k* that I am the LORD — Ex 6:7 — 3045
shall *k* that I am the LORD — Ex 7:5 — 3045
thou shalt *k* that I am the LORD — Ex 7:17 — 3045
that thou mayest *k* that there is — Ex 8:10 — 3045
to the end thou mayest *k* that I — Ex 8:22 — 3045
that thou mayest *k* that there is — Ex 9:14 — 3045
that thou mayest *k* how that the — Ex 9:29 — 3045
I *k* that ye will not yet fear the — Ex 9:30 — 3045
that ye may *k* how that I am the — Ex 10:2 — 3045
we *k* not with what we must serve — Ex 10:26 — 3045
that ye may *k* how that the LORD — Ex 11:7 — 3045
may *k* that I am the LORD — Ex 14:4 — 3045
shall *k* that I am the LORD — Ex 14:18 — 3045
then ye shall *k* that the LORD — Ex 16:6 — 3045
ye shall *k* that I am the LORD — Ex 16:12 — 3045
Now I *k* that the LORD is greater — Ex 18:11 — 3045
I do make them *k* the statutes of — Ex 18:16 — 3045
for ye *k* the heart of a stranger — Ex 23:9 — 3045
they shall *k* that I am the LORD — Ex 29:46 — 3045
that ye may *k* that I am the LORD — Ex 31:13 — 3045
that I may *k* what to do unto thee — Ex 33:5 — 3045
thou hast not let me *k* whom thou — Ex 33:12 — 3045
I *k* thee by name, and thou hast — Ex 33:12 — 3045
me now thy way, that I may *k* thee — Ex 33:13 — 3045
in my sight, and I *k* thee by name — Ex 33:17 — 3045
understanding to *k* how to work — Ex 36:1 — 3045
That your generations may *k* that — Lev 23:43 — 3045
they shall *k* the land which ye — Num 14:31 — 3045
ye shall *k* my breach of promise — Num 14:34 — 3045
Hereby ye shall *k* that the LORD — Num 16:28 — 3045
that I may *k* what the LORD will — Num 22:19 — 3045
(for I *k* that ye have much cattle — Deut 3:19 — 3045
that thou mightest *k* that the — Deut 4:35 — 3045
K therefore this day, and consider — Deut 4:39 — 3045
K therefore that the LORD thy God — Deut 7:9 — 3045
to *k* what was in thine heart — Deut 8:2 — 3045
not, neither did thy fathers *k* — Deut 8:3 — 3045
that he might make thee *k* that — Deut 8:3 — 3045
And *k* ye this day — Deut 11:2 — 3045
to *k* whether ye love the LORD — Deut 13:3 — 3045
How shall we *k* the word which the — Deut 18:21 — 3045
unto thee, or if thou *k* him not — Deut 22:2 — 3045
that ye might *k* that I am the — Deut 29:6 — 3045
(For ye *k* how we have dwelt in — Deut 29:16 — 3045
for I *k* their imagination which — Deut 31:21 — 3045
For I *k* thy rebellion, and thy — Deut 31:27 — 3045
For I *k* that after my death ye — Deut 31:29 — 3045
I *k* that the LORD hath given you — Josh 2:9 — 3045
that ye may *k* the way by which ye — Josh 3:4 — 3045
all Israel, that they may *k* that — Josh 3:7 — 3045
Hereby ye shall *k* that the living — Josh 3:10 — 3045
Then ye shall let your children *k* — Josh 4:22 — 3045
might *k* the hand of the LORD — Josh 4:24 — 3045
he knoweth, and Israel he shall *k* — Josh 22:22 — 3045
K for a certainty that the LORD — Josh 23:13 — 3045
ye *k* in all your hearts and in all — Josh 23:14 — 3045
of the children of Israel might *k* — Judg 3:2 — 3045
to *k* whether they would hearken — Judg 3:4 — 3045
then shall I *k* that thou wilt — Judg 6:37 — 3045
Now *k* I that the LORD will do me — Judg 17:13 — 3045
that we may *k* whether our way — Judg 18:5 — 3045
Do ye *k* that there is in these — Judg 18:14 — 3045
thine house, that we may *k* him — Judg 19:22 — 3045
k that thou art a virtuous woman — Ruth 3:11 — 3045
up before one could *k* another — Ruth 3:14 — 5234
until thou *k* how the matter will — Ruth 3:18 — 3045
it, then tell me, that I may *k* — Ruth 4:4 — 3045
Now Samuel did not yet *k* the LORD — 1Sa 3:7 — 3045
then we shall *k* that it is not — 1Sa 6:9 — 3045
and *k* and see wherein this sin hath — 1Sa 14:38 — 3045
I *k* thy pride, and the naughtiness — 1Sa 17:28 — 3045
that all the earth may *k* that — 1Sa 17:46 — 3045
all this assembly shall *k* that — 1Sa 17:47 — 3045
he saith, Let not Jonathan *k* this — 1Sa 20:3 — 3045
do not I *k* that thou hast chosen — 1Sa 20:30 — 3045
Let no man *k* any thing of the — 1Sa 21:2 — 3045
till I *k* what God will do for me — 1Sa 22:3 — 3045
Go, I pray you, prepare yet, and *k* — 1Sa 23:22 — 3045
k thou and see that there is — 1Sa 24:11 — 3045
I *k* well that thou shalt surely — 1Sa 24:20 — 3045
whom I *k* not whence they be — 1Sa 25:11 — 3045
Now therefore *k* and consider what — 1Sa 25:17 — 3045
K thou assuredly, that thou shalt — 1Sa 28:1 — 3045
Surely thou shalt *k* what thy — 1Sa 28:2 — 3045
I *k* that thou art good in my — 1Sa 29:9 — 3045
to *k* thy going out and thy coming — 2Sa 3:25 — 3045
in, and to *k* all that thou doest — 2Sa 3:25 — 3045
K ye not that there is a prince — 2Sa 3:38 — 3045
to make thy servant *k* them — 2Sa 7:21 — 3045
to *k* all things that are in the — 2Sa 14:20 — 3045
servant doth *k* that I have sinned — 2Sa 19:20 — 3045
for do not I *k* that I am this day — 2Sa 19:22 — 3045
that I may *k* the number of the — 2Sa 24:2 — 3045
thou shalt *k* for certain that — 1Kin 2:37 — 3045
K for a certain, on the day thou — 1Kin 2:42 — 3045
I *k* not how to go out or come in — 1Kin 3:7 — 3045
which shall *k* every man the — 1Kin 8:38 — 3045
of the earth may *k* thy name — 1Kin 8:43 — 3045
that they may *k* that this house — 1Kin 8:43 — 3045
earth may *k* that the LORD is God — 1Kin 8:60 — 3045
Now by this I *k* that thou art a — 1Kin 17:24 — 3045
shall carry thee whither I *k* not — 1Kin 18:12 — 3045
that this people may *k* that thou — 1Kin 18:37 — 3045
thou shalt *k* that I am the LORD — 1Kin 20:13 — 3045
ye shall *k* that I am the LORD — 1Kin 20:28 — 3045
K ye that Ramoth in Gilead is — 1Kin 22:3 — 3045
And he said, Yea, I *k* it — 2Kin 2:3 — 3045
And he answered, Yea, I *k* it — 2Kin 2:5 — 3045
he shall *k* that there is a — 2Kin 5:8 — 3045
now I *k* that there is no God in — 2Kin 5:15 — 3045
They *k* that we be hungry — 2Kin 7:12 — 3045
Because I *k* the evil that thou — 2Kin 8:12 — 3045
unto them, Ye *k* the man, and his — 2Kin 9:11 — 3045
K now that there shall fall unto — 2Kin 10:10 — 3045
k not the manner of the God of — 2Kin 17:26 — 3045
because they *k* not the manner of — 2Kin 17:26 — 3045
may *k* that thou art the LORD God — 2Kin 19:19 — 3045
But I *k* thy abode, and thy going — 2Kin 19:27 — 3045
to *k* what Israel ought to do — 1Chr 12:32 — 3045
of them to me, that I may *k* it — 1Chr 21:2 — 3045
k thou the God of thy father, and — 1Chr 28:9 — 3045
I *k* also, my God, that thou — 1Chr 29:17 — 3045
for I *k* that thy servants can — 2Chr 2:8 — 3045
every one shall *k* his own sore — 2Chr 6:29 — 3045
of the earth may *k* thy name — 2Chr 6:33 — 3045
may *k* that this house which I — 2Chr 6:33 — 3045
that they may *k* my service — 2Chr 12:8 — 3045
Ought ye not to *k* that the LORD — 2Chr 13:5 — 3045
neither *k* we what to do — 2Chr 20:12 — 3045
I *k* that God hath determined to — 2Chr 25:16 — 3045
K ye not what I and my fathers — 2Chr 32:13 — 3045
that he might *k* all that was in — 2Chr 32:31 — 3045
k that this city is a rebellious — Ezr 4:15 — 3046
all such as *k* the laws of thy God — Ezr 7:25 — 3046
and teach ye them that *k* them not — Ezr 7:25 — 3046
said, They shall not *k*, neither — Neh 4:11 — 3045
to *k* how Esther did, and what — Est 2:11 — 3045
to *k* what it was, and why it was — Est 4:5 — 3045

Context	Reference	Number
of the king's provinces, do *k*	Est 4:11	3045
thou shalt *k* that thy tabernacle	Job 5:24	3045
Thou shalt *k* also that thy seed	Job 5:25	3045
it, and *k* thou it for thy good	Job 5:27	3045
shall his place *k* him any more	Job 7:10	5234
k nothing, because our days upon	Job 8:9	3045
I *k* it is so of a truth	Job 9:2	3045
the mountains, and they *k* not	Job 9:5	3045
yet would I not *k* my soul	Job 9:21	3045
I *k* that thou wilt not hold me	Job 9:28	3045
I *k* that this is with thee	Job 10:13	3045
K therefore that God exacteth of	Job 11:6	3045
what canst thou *k*	Job 11:8	3045
What ye *k*, the same do I *k*	Job 13:2	1847
ye *k*, the same do I *k* also	Job 13:2	3045
I *k* that I shall be justified	Job 13:18	3045
make me to *k* my transgression and	Job 13:23	3045
What knowest thou, that we *k* not	Job 15:9	3045
K now that God hath overthrown me	Job 19:6	3045
For I *k* that my redeemer liveth,	Job 19:25	3045
that ye may *k* there is a judgment	Job 19:29	3045
rewardeth him, and he shall *k* it	Job 21:19	3045
I *k* your thoughts, and the devices	Job 21:27	3045
do ye not *k* their tokens,	Job 21:29	5234
And thou sayest, How doth God *k*	Job 22:13	3045
I would *k* the words which he	Job 23:5	3045
do they that *k* him not see his	Job 24:1	3045
they *k* not the ways thereof, nor	Job 24:13	5234
they *k* not the light	Job 24:16	3045
if one *k* them, they are in the	Job 24:17	5234
For I *k* that thou wilt bring me	Job 30:23	3045
that God may *k* mine integrity	Job 31:6	3045
For I *k* not to give flattering	Job 32:22	3045
let us *k* among ourselves what is	Job 34:4	3045
we *k* him not, neither can the	Job 36:26	3045
that all men may *k* his work	Job 37:7	3045
Dost thou *k* when God disposed	Job 37:15	3045
Dost thou *k* the balancings of the	Job 37:16	3045
the dayspring to *k* his place	Job 38:12	3045
that thou shouldest *k* the paths	Job 38:20	995
I *k* that thou canst do every	Job 42:2	3045
But *k* that the LORD hath set	Ps 4:3	3045
they that *k* thy name will put	Ps 9:10	3045
that the nations may *k* themselves	Ps 9:20	3045
Now *k* I that the LORD saveth his	Ps 20:6	3045
unto them that *k* thee	Ps 36:10	3045
LORD, make me to *k* mine end	Ps 39:4	3045
that I may *k* how frail I am	Ps 39:4	3045
By this I *k* that thou favourest	Ps 41:11	3045
Be still, and *k* that I am God	Ps 46:10	3045
I *k* all the fowls of the	Ps 50:11	3045
thou shalt make me to *k* wisdom	Ps 51:6	3045
enemies turn back: this I *k*	Ps 56:9	3045
let them *k* that God ruleth in	Ps 59:13	3045
for I *k* not the numbers thereof	Ps 71:15	3045
And they say, How doth God *k*	Ps 73:11	3045
When I thought to *k* this, it was	Ps 73:16	3045
generation to come might *k* them	Ps 78:6	3045
They *k* not, neither will they	Ps 82:5	3045
That men may *k* that thou, whose	Ps 83:18	3045
and Babylon to them that *k* me	Ps 87:4	3045
people that *k* the joyful sound	Ps 89:15	3045
man knowledge, shall not he *k*	Ps 94:10	
K ye that the LORD he is God	Ps 100:3	3045
I will not *k* a wicked person	Ps 101:4	3045
place thereof shall *k* it no more	Ps 103:16	5234
That they may *k* that this is thy	Ps 109:27	3045
I *k*, O LORD, that thy judgments	Ps 119:75	3045
that I may *k* thy testimonies	Ps 119:125	3045
For I *k* that the LORD is great,	Ps 135:5	3045
Search me, O God, and *k* my heart	Ps 139:23	3045
try me, and *k* my thoughts	Ps 139:23	3045
I *k* that the LORD will maintain	Ps 140:12	3045
there was no man that would *k* me	Ps 142:4	5234
cause me to *k* the way wherein I	Ps 143:8	3045
To *k* wisdom and instruction	Prov 1:2	3045
attend to *k* understanding	Prov 4:1	3045
they *k* not at what they stumble	Prov 4:19	3045
that thou canst not *k* them	Prov 5:6	3045
righteous *k* what is acceptable	Prov 10:32	3045
That I might make thee *k* the	Prov 22:21	3045
thy soul, doth not he *k* it	Prov 24:12	3045
lest thou *k* not what to do in the	Prov 25:8	
Be thou diligent to *k* the state	Prov 27:23	3045
the wicked regardeth not to *k* it	Prov 29:7	1847
for me, yea, four which I *k* not	Prov 30:18	3045
And I gave my heart to *k* wisdom	Eccl 1:17	3045
and to *k* madness and folly	Eccl 1:17	3045
I *k* that there is no good in them	Eccl 3:12	3045
I *k* that, whatsoever God doeth,	Eccl 3:14	3045
I applied mine heart to *k*	Eccl 7:25	3045
to *k* the wickedness of folly,	Eccl 7:25	3045
yet surely I *k* that it shall be	Eccl 8:12	3045
I applied mine heart to *k* wisdom	Eccl 8:16	3045
though a wise man think to *k* it	Eccl 8:17	3045
For the living *k* that they shall	Eccl 9:5	3045
but the dead *k* not any thing,	Eccl 9:5	3045
but *k* thou, that for all these	Eccl 11:9	3045
If thou *k* not, O thou fairest	Song 1:8	3045
but Israel doth not *k*, my people	Is 1:3	3045
nigh and come, that we may *k* it	Is 5:19	3045
that he may *k* to refuse the evil,	Is 7:15	3045
child shall *k* to refuse the evil	Is 7:16	3045
And all the people shall *k*	Is 9:9	3045
let them *k* what the LORD of hosts	Is 19:12	3045
the Egyptians shall *k* the LORD in	Is 19:21	3045
may *k* that thou art the LORD	Is 37:20	3045
But I *k* thy abode, and thy going	Is 37:28	3045
That they may see, and *k*, and	Is 41:20	3045
them, and *k* the latter end of them	Is 41:22	3045
that we may *k* that ye are gods	Is 41:23	3045
from the beginning, that we may *k*	Is 41:26	3045
that ye may *k* and believe me, and	Is 43:10	3045
shall ye not *k* it	Is 43:19	3045
I *k* not any	Is 44:8	3045
they see not, nor *k*	Is 44:9	3045
places, that thou mayest *k* that I	Is 45:3	3045
That they may *k* from the rising	Is 45:6	3045
neither shall I *k* the loss of	Is 47:8	3045
thou shalt not *k* from whence it	Is 47:11	3045
suddenly, which thou shalt not *k*	Is 47:11	3045
things, and thou didst not *k* them	Is 48:6	3045
thou shalt *k* that I am the LORD	Is 49:23	3045
all flesh shall *k* that I the LORD	Is 49:26	3045
that I should *k* how to speak a	Is 50:4	3045
I *k* that I shall not be ashamed	Is 50:7	3045
ye that *k* righteousness, the	Is 51:7	3045
my people shall *k* my name	Is 52:6	3045
therefore they shall *k* in that	Is 52:6	
me daily, and delight to *k* my ways	Is 58:2	1847
The way of peace they *k* not	Is 59:8	3045
goeth therein shall not *k* peace	Is 59:8	3045
as for our iniquities, we *k* them	Is 59:12	3045
thou shalt *k* that I the LORD am	Is 60:16	3045
For I *k* their works and their	Is 66:18	
k therefore and see that it is an	Jer 2:19	3045
the valley, *k* what thou hast done	Jer 2:23	3045
of Jerusalem, and see now, and *k*	Jer 5:1	3045
for they *k* not the way of the	Jer 5:4	3045
Therefore hear, ye nations, and *k*	Jer 6:18	3045
my people, that thou mayest *k*	Jer 6:27	3045
after other gods whom ye *k* not	Jer 7:9	3045
but my people *k* not the judgment	Jer 8:7	3045
they *k* not me, saith the LORD	Jer 9:3	3045
deceit they refuse to *k* me	Jer 9:6	3045
I *k* that the way of man is not in	Jer 10:23	3045
upon the heathen that *k* thee not	Jer 10:25	3045
me knowledge of it, and I *k* it	Jer 11:18	3045
Do we not certainly *k* that every	Jer 13:12	3045
about into a land that they *k* not	Jer 14:18	3045
k that for thy sake I have	Jer 15:15	3045
land into a land that ye *k* not	Jer 16:13	3045
I will this once cause them to *k*	Jer 16:21	3045
I will cause them to *k* mine hand	Jer 16:21	3045
they shall *k* that my name is The	Jer 16:21	3045
who can *k* it?	Jer 17:9	
was not this to *k* me	Jer 22:16	1847
cast into a land which they *k* not	Jer 22:28	3045
I will give them an heart to *k* me	Jer 24:7	3045
But *k* ye for certain, that if ye	Jer 26:15	3045
For I *k* the thoughts that I think	Jer 29:11	3045
K that thus saith the LORD of the	Jer 29:16	
even I *k*, and am a witness, saith	Jer 29:23	3045
his brother, saying, *K* the LORD	Jer 31:34	3045
for they shall all *k* me, from the	Jer 31:34	3045
and let no man *k* where ye be	Jer 36:19	3045
Let no man *k* of these words, and	Jer 38:24	3045
Dost thou certainly *k* that Baalis	Jer 40:14	3045
Nethaniah, and no man shall *k* it	Jer 40:15	3045
k certainly that I have	Jer 42:19	3045
Now therefore *k* certainly that ye	Jer 42:22	3045
shall *k* whose words shall stand,	Jer 44:28	3045
that ye may *k* that my words shall	Jer 44:29	3045
and all ye that *k* his name	Jer 48:17	3045
I *k* his wrath, saith the LORD	Jer 48:30	3045
yet shall *k* that there hath been	Eze 2:5	3045
they shall *k* that I the LORD have	Eze 5:13	3045
ye shall *k* that I am the LORD	Eze 6:7	3045
they shall *k* that I am the LORD,	Eze 6:10	3045
Then shall ye *k* that I am the	Eze 6:13	3045
they shall *k* that I am the LORD	Eze 6:14	3045
ye shall *k* that I am the LORD	Eze 7:4	3045
ye shall *k* that I am the LORD	Eze 7:9	3045
they shall *k* that I am the LORD	Eze 7:27	3045
for I *k* the things that come into	Eze 11:5	3045
ye shall *k* that I am the LORD	Eze 11:10	3045
ye shall *k* that I am the LORD	Eze 11:12	3045
they shall *k* that I am the LORD,	Eze 12:15	3045
they shall *k* that I am the LORD	Eze 12:16	3045
ye shall *k* that I am the LORD	Eze 12:20	3045
ye shall *k* that I am the Lord GOD	Eze 13:9	3045
ye shall *k* that I am the LORD	Eze 13:14	3045
ye shall *k* that I am the LORD	Eze 13:21	3045
ye shall *k* that I am the LORD	Eze 13:23	3045
ye shall *k* that I am the LORD	Eze 14:8	3045
ye shall *k* that I have not done	Eze 14:23	3045
ye shall *k* that I am the LORD,	Eze 15:7	3045
Jerusalem to *k* her abominations	Eze 16:2	3045
thou shalt *k* that I am the LORD	Eze 16:62	3045
K ye not what these things mean	Eze 17:12	3045
ye shall *k* that I the LORD have	Eze 17:21	3045
k that I the LORD have brought	Eze 17:24	3045
cause them to *k* the abominations	Eze 20:4	3045
that they might *k* that I am the	Eze 20:12	3045
that ye may *k* that I am the LORD	Eze 20:20	3045
they might *k* that I am the LORD	Eze 20:26	3045
ye shall *k* that I am the LORD	Eze 20:38	3045
ye shall *k* that I am the LORD,	Eze 20:42	3045
ye shall *k* that I am the LORD,	Eze 20:44	3045
That all flesh may *k* that I the	Eze 21:5	3045
thou shalt *k* that I am the LORD	Eze 22:16	3045
ye shall *k* that I the LORD have	Eze 22:22	3045
ye shall *k* that I am the Lord GOD	Eze 23:49	3045
ye shall *k* that I am the Lord GOD	Eze 24:24	3045
they shall *k* that I am the LORD	Eze 24:27	3045
ye shall *k* that I am the LORD	Eze 25:5	3045
thou shalt *k* that I am the LORD	Eze 25:7	3045
they shall *k* that I am the LORD	Eze 25:11	3045
they shall *k* my vengeance, saith	Eze 25:14	3045
they shall *k* that I am the LORD,	Eze 25:17	3045
they shall *k* that I am the LORD	Eze 26:6	3045
All they that *k* thee among the	Eze 28:19	3045
they shall *k* that I am the LORD,	Eze 28:22	3045
they shall *k* that I am the LORD	Eze 28:23	3045
they shall *k* that I am the Lord	Eze 28:24	3045
they shall *k* that I am the LORD	Eze 28:26	3045
Egypt shall *k* that I am the LORD	Eze 29:6	3045
they shall *k* that I am the LORD	Eze 29:9	3045
but they shall *k* that I am the	Eze 29:16	3045
they shall *k* that I am the LORD	Eze 29:21	3045
they shall *k* that I am the LORD,	Eze 30:8	3045
they shall *k* that I am the LORD	Eze 30:19	3045
they shall *k* that I am the LORD,	Eze 30:25	3045
they shall *k* that I am the LORD	Eze 30:26	3045
then shall they *k* that I am the	Eze 32:15	3045
Then shall they *k* that I am the	Eze 33:29	3045
then shall they *k* that a prophet	Eze 33:33	3045
shall *k* that I am the LORD, when	Eze 34:27	3045
Thus shall they *k* that I the LORD	Eze 34:30	3045
thou shalt *k* that I am the LORD	Eze 35:4	3045
ye shall *k* that I am the LORD	Eze 35:9	3045
thou shalt *k* that I am the LORD,	Eze 35:12	3045
they shall *k* that I am the LORD	Eze 35:15	3045
ye shall *k* that I am the Lord	Eze 36:11	3045
the heathen shall *k* that I am the	Eze 36:23	3045
shall *k* that I the LORD build the	Eze 36:36	3045
they shall *k* that I am the LORD	Eze 36:38	3045
ye shall *k* that I am the LORD	Eze 37:6	3045
ye shall *k* that I am the LORD,	Eze 37:13	3045
then shall ye *k* that I the LORD	Eze 37:14	3045
the heathen shall *k* that I the	Eze 37:28	3045
safely, shalt thou not *k* it	Eze 38:14	3045
land, that the heathen may *k* me	Eze 38:16	3045
they shall *k* that I am the LORD	Eze 38:23	3045
they shall *k* that I am the LORD	Eze 39:6	3045
the heathen shall *k* that I am the	Eze 39:7	3045
k that I am the LORD their God	Eze 39:22	3045
the heathen shall *k* that the	Eze 39:23	3045
Then shall they *k* that I am the	Eze 39:28	3045
was troubled to *k* the dream	Dan 2:3	3045
I *k* of certainty that ye would	Dan 2:8	3046
I shall *k* that ye can shew me the	Dan 2:9	3046
to them that *k* understanding	Dan 2:21	3046
that thou mightest *k* the thoughts	Dan 2:30	3046
because I *k* that the spirit of	Dan 4:9	3046
k that the most High ruleth in	Dan 4:17	3046
till thou *k* that the most High	Dan 4:25	3046
until thou *k* that the most High	Dan 4:32	3046
which see not, nor hear, nor *k*	Dan 5:23	3046
king, and said unto the king, *K*	Dan 6:15	3046
made me *k* the interpretation of	Dan 7:16	3046
Then I would *k* the truth of the	Dan 7:19	3046
I will make thee *k* what shall be	Dan 8:19	3045
K therefore and understand, that	Dan 9:25	3045
but the people that do *k* their	Dan 11:32	3045
For she did not *k* that I gave her	Hos 2:8	3045
and thou shalt *k* the LORD	Hos 2:20	3045
I *k* Ephraim, and Israel is not hid	Hos 5:3	3045
Then shall we *k*, if we follow on	Hos 6:3	3045
if we follow on to *k* the LORD	Hos 6:3	3045
cry unto me, My God, we *k* thee	Hos 8:2	3045
Israel shall *k* it	Hos 9:7	3045
thou shalt *k* no god but me	Hos 13:4	3045
I did *k* thee in the wilderness,	Hos 13:5	3045
prudent, and he shall *k* them	Hos 14:9	3045
ye shall *k* that I am in the midst	Joel 2:27	3045
So shall ye *k* that I am the LORD	Joel 3:17	3045
For they *k* not to do right, saith	Amos 3:10	3045
For I *k* your manifold	Amos 5:12	3045
that we may *k* for whose cause	Jonah 1:7	3045
for I *k* that for my sake this	Jonah 1:12	3045
Is it not for you to *k* judgment	Mic 3:1	3045
But they *k* not the thoughts of	Mic 4:12	3045
that ye may *k* the righteousness	Mic 6:5	3045
ye shall *k* that the LORD of hosts	Zec 2:9	3045
thou shalt *k* that the LORD of	Zec 2:11	3045
thou shalt *k* that the LORD of	Zec 4:9	3045
ye shall *k* that the LORD of hosts	Zec 6:15	3045
ye shall *k* that I have sent this	Mal 2:4	3045
let not thy left hand *k* what thy	Mt 6:3	*1097*
k how to give good gifts unto	Mt 7:11	*1492*
Ye shall *k* them by their fruits	Mt 7:16	*1921*
by their fruits ye shall *k* them	Mt 7:20	*1921*
But that ye may *k* that the Son of	Mt 9:6	*1492*
saying, See that no man *k* it	Mt 9:30	*1097*
k the mysteries of the kingdom of	Mt 13:11	*1097*
and said, Ye *k* not what ye ask	Mt 20:22	*1492*
Ye *k* that the princes of the	Mt 20:25	*1492*
we *k* that thou art true, and	Mt 22:16	*1492*
leaves, ye *k* that summer is nigh	Mt 24:32	*1097*
k that it is near, even at the	Mt 24:33	*1097*
for ye *k* not what hour your Lord	Mt 24:42	*1492*
But *k* this, that if the goodman	Mt 24:43	*1097*
I say unto you, I *k* you not	Mt 25:12	*1492*
for ye *k* neither the day nor the	Mt 25:13	*1492*
Ye *k* that after two days is the	Mt 26:2	*1492*
saying, I *k* not what thou sayest	Mt 26:70	*1492*
with an oath, I do not *k* the man	Mt 26:72	*1492*
to swear, saying, I *k* not the man	Mt 26:74	*1492*
for I *k* that ye seek Jesus, which	Mt 28:5	*1492*
I *k* thee who thou art, the Holy	Mk 1:24	*1492*
But that ye may *k* that the Son of	Mk 2:10	*1492*
Unto you it is given to *k* the	Mk 4:11	*1097*
unto them, *K* ye not this parable	Mk 4:13	*1492*
how then will ye *k* all parables	Mk 4:13	*1097*
straitly that no man should *k* it	Mk 5:43	*1097*
house, and would have no man *k* it	Mk 7:24	*1097*
not that any man should *k* it	Mk 9:30	*1097*
unto them, Ye *k* not what ye ask	Mk 10:38	*1492*
them, Ye *k* that they which are	Mk 10:42	*1492*
we *k* that thou art true, and	Mk 12:14	*1492*
because ye *k* not the scriptures,	Mk 12:24	*1492*
leaves, ye *k* that summer is near	Mk 13:28	*1097*
k that it is nigh, even at the	Mk 13:29	*1097*
for ye *k* not when the time is	Mk 13:33	*1492*
for ye *k* not when the master of	Mk 13:35	*1492*
I *k* not, neither understand I	Mk 14:68	*1492*
I *k* not this man of whom ye speak	Mk 14:71	*1492*
That thou mightest *k* the	Lk 1:4	*1921*
the angel, Whereby shall I *k* this	Lk 1:18	*1097*
this be, seeing I *k* not a man	Lk 1:34	*1097*
I *k* thee who thou art	Lk 4:34	*1492*

But that ye may *k* that the Son of Lk 5:24 *1492*
Unto you it is given to *k* the Lk 8:10 *1097*
Ye *k* not what manner of spirit ye Lk 9:55 *1492*
k how to give good gifts unto Lk 11:13 *1492*
And this *k*, that if the goodman of Lk 12:39 *1097*
I *k* you not whence ye are Lk 13:25 *1492*
I *k* you not whence ye are Lk 13:27 *1492*
that he might *k* how much every Lk 19:15 *1097*
we *k* that thou sayest and teachest Lk 20:21 *1492*
then *k* that the desolation Lk 21:20 *1097*
k of your own selves that summer Lk 21:30 *1097*
k ye that the kingdom of God is Lk 21:31 *1097*
him, saying, Woman, I *k* him not Lk 22:57 *1492*
Man, I *k* not what thou sayest Lk 22:60 *1492*
for they *k* not what they do Lk 23:34 *1492*
holden that they should not *k* him Lk 24:16 *1921*
one among you, whom ye *k* not Jn 1:26 *1492*
we *k* that thou art a teacher come Jn 3:2 *1492*
unto thee, We speak that we do *k* Jn 3:11 *1492*
Ye worship ye *k* not what Jn 4:22 *1492*
we *k* what we worship Jn 4:22 *1492*
I *k* that Messias cometh, which is Jn 4:25 *1492*
have meat to eat that ye *k* not of Jn 4:32 *1492*
k that this is indeed the Christ, Jn 4:42 *1492*
I *k* that the witness which he Jn 5:32 *1492*
But I *k* you, that ye have not the Jn 5:42 *1097*
whose father and mother we *k* Jn 6:42 *1492*
he shall *k* of the doctrine, Jn 7:17 *1097*
Do the rulers *k* indeed that this Jn 7:26 *1097*
Howbeit we *k* this man whence he Jn 7:27 *1492*
both *k* me, and ye *k* whence I am Jn 7:28 *1492*
sent me is true, whom ye *k* not Jn 7:28 *1492*
But I *k* him Jn 7:29 *1492*
it hear him, and *k* what he doeth Jn 7:51 *1097*
for I *k* whence I came, and whither Jn 8:14 *1492*
Jesus answered, Ye neither *k* me Jn 8:19 *1492*
man, then shall ye *k* that I am he Jn 8:28 *1097*
ye shall *k* the truth, and the Jn 8:32 *1097*
I *k* that ye are Abraham's seed Jn 8:37 *1492*
Now we *k* that thou hast a devil Jn 8:52 *1492*
but I *k* him Jn 8:55 *1492*
I *k* him not, I shall be a liar Jn 8:55 *1492*
but I *k* him, and keep his saying Jn 8:55 *1492*
He said, I *k* not Jn 9:12 *1492*
We *k* that this is our son, and Jn 9:20 *1492*
what means he now seeth, we *k* not Jn 9:21 *1492*
hath opened his eyes, we *k* not Jn 9:21 *1492*
we *k* that this man is a sinner Jn 9:24 *1492*
he be a sinner or no, I *k* not Jn 9:25 *1492*
one thing I *k*, that, whereas I Jn 9:25 *1492*
We *k* that God spake unto Moses Jn 9:29 *1492*
we *k* not from whence he is Jn 9:29 *1492*
that ye *k* not from whence he is, Jn 9:30 *1492*
Now we *k* that God heareth not Jn 9:31 *1492*
for they *k* his voice Jn 10:4 *1492*
for they *k* not the voice of Jn 10:5 *1492*
k my sheep, and am known of mine Jn 10:14 *1097*
me, even so *k* I the Father Jn 10:15 *1097*
I *k* them, and they follow me Jn 10:27 *1097*
that ye may *k*, and believe, that Jn 10:38 *1097*
But I *k*, that even now, Jn 11:22 *1492*
I *k* that he shall rise again in Jn 11:24 *1492*
unto them, Ye *k* nothing at all, Jn 11:49 *1492*
I *k* that his commandment is life Jn 12:50 *1492*
but thou shalt *k* hereafter Jn 13:7 *1097*
K ye what I have done to you Jn 13:12 *1097*
If ye *k* these things, happy are Jn 13:17 *1492*
I *k* whom I have chosen Jn 13:18 *1492*
By this shall all men *k* that ye Jn 13:35 *1097*
I go ye *k*, and the way ye *k* Jn 14:4 *1492*
we *k* not whither thou goest Jn 14:5 *1492*
and how can we *k* the way Jn 14:5 *1492*
and from henceforth ye *k* him Jn 14:7 *1097*
but ye *k* him Jn 14:17 *1492*
At that day ye shall *k* that I am Jn 14:20 *1097*
may *k* that I love the Father Jn 14:31 *1097*
ye *k* that it hated me before it Jn 15:18 *1097*
because they *k* not him that sent Jn 15:21 *1492*
that they might *k* thee the only Jn 17:3 *1097*
that the world may *k* that thou Jn 17:23 *1097*
behold, they *k* what I said Jn 18:21 *1492*
that ye may *k* that I find no Jn 19:4 *1097*
we *k* not where they have laid him Jn 20:2 *1492*
I *k* not where they have laid him Jn 20:13 *1492*
we *k* that his testimony is true Jn 21:24 *1492*
It is not for you to *k* the times Acts 1:7 *1097*
of you, as ye yourselves also *k* Acts 2:22 *1492*
the house of Israel *k* assuredly Acts 2:36 *1097*
this man strong, whom ye see and *k* Acts 3:16 *1492*
Ye *k* how that it is an unlawful Acts 10:28 *1987*
That word, I say, ye *k*, which was Acts 10:37 *1492*
Now I *k* of a surety, that the Acts 12:11 *1492*
ye *k* how that a good while ago Acts 15:7 *1987*
May we *k* what this new doctrine, Acts 17:19 *1097*
we would *k* therefore what these Acts 17:20 *1097*
said, Jesus I *k*, and Paul I *k* Acts 19:15 *1987*
ye *k* that by this craft we have Acts 19:25 *1987*
to him, he said unto them, Ye *k* Acts 20:18 *1987*
I *k* that ye all, among whom I Acts 20:25 *1492*
For I *k* this, that after my Acts 20:29 *1492*
Yea, ye yourselves *k*, that these Acts 20:34 *1097*
all may *k* that those things, Acts 21:24 *1097*
when he could not *k* the certainty Acts 21:34 *1097*
that thou shouldest *k* his will Acts 22:14 *1097*
they *k* that I imprisoned and beat Acts 22:19 *1987*
that he might *k* wherefore they Acts 22:24 *1921*
Forasmuch as I *k* that thou hast Acts 24:10 *1987*
I will *k* the uttermost of your Acts 24:22 *1231*
Especially because I *k* thee to be Acts 26:3
at Jerusalem, *k* all the Jews Acts 26:4 *2467*
I *k* that thou believest Acts 26:27 *1492*
we *k* that every where it is Acts 28:22 *1110*
Now we *k* that what things soever Rom 3:19 *1492*
K ye not, that so many of us as Rom 6:3 *50*
K ye not, that to whom ye yield Rom 6:16 *1492*
K ye not, brethren, (for I speak Rom 7:1 *50*
I speak to them that *k* the law Rom 7:1 *1097*
For we *k* that the law is Rom 7:14 *1492*
For I *k* that in me (that is, in Rom 7:18 *1492*
For we *k* that the whole creation Rom 8:22 *1492*
for we *k* not what we should pray Rom 8:26 *1492*
we *k* that all things work Rom 8:28 *1492*
But I say, Did not Israel *k* Rom 10:19 *1097*
I *k*, and am persuaded by the Lord Rom 14:14 *1492*
I *k* not whether I baptized any 1Cor 1:16 *1492*
not to *k* any thing among you 1Cor 2:2 *1492*
that we might *k* the things that 1Cor 2:12 *1492*
neither can he *k* them, because 1Cor 2:14 *1097*
K ye not that ye are the temple 1Cor 3:16 *1492*
For I *k* nothing by myself 1Cor 4:4 *4892*
if the Lord will, and will *k* 1Cor 4:19 *1097*
K ye not that a little leaven 1Cor 5:6 *1492*
Do ye not *k* that the saints shall 1Cor 6:2 *1492*
K ye not that we shall judge 1Cor 6:3 *1492*
K ye not that the unrighteous 1Cor 6:9 *1492*
K ye not that your bodies are the 1Cor 6:15 *1492*
k ye not that he which is joined 1Cor 6:16 *1492*
k ye not that your body is the 1Cor 6:19 *1492*
we *k* that we all have knowledge 1Cor 8:1 *1492*
nothing yet as he ought to *k* 1Cor 8:2 *1097*
we *k* that an idol is nothing in 1Cor 8:4 *1492*
Do ye not *k* that they which 1Cor 9:13 *1492*
K ye not that they which run in a 1Cor 9:24 *1492*
But I would have you *k*, that the 1Cor 11:3 *1492*
Ye *k* that ye were Gentiles, 1Cor 12:2 *1492*
For we *k* in part, and we prophesy 1Cor 13:9 *1097*
now I *k* in part 1Cor 13:12 *1097*
but then shall I *k* even as also I 1Cor 13:12 *1921*
Therefore if I *k* not the meaning 1Cor 14:11 *1492*
forasmuch as ye *k* that your 1Cor 15:58 *1492*
(ye *k* the house of Stephanas, 1Cor 16:15 *1492*
but that ye might *k* the love 2Cor 2:4 *1097*
that I might *k* the proof of you, 2Cor 2:9 *1097*
For we *k* that if our earthly 2Cor 5:1 *1492*
Wherefore henceforth *k* we no man 2Cor 5:16 *1492*
now henceforth *k* we him no more 2Cor 5:16 *1097*
For ye *k* the grace of our Lord 2Cor 8:9 *1097*
For I *k* the forwardness of your 2Cor 9:2 *1492*
K ye not your own selves, how 2Cor 13:5 *1921*
But I trust that ye shall *k* that 2Cor 13:6 *1097*
K ye therefore that they which Gal 3:7 *1097*
Ye *k* how through infirmity of the Gal 4:13 *1492*
that ye may *k* what is the hope of Eph 1:18 *1492*
to *k* the love of Christ, which Eph 3:19 *1097*
For this ye *k*, that no Eph 5:5 *1097*
But that ye also may *k* my affairs Eph 6:21 *1492*
that ye might *k* our affairs Eph 6:22 *1097*
For I *k* that this shall turn to Phil 1:19 *1492*
I *k* that I shall abide and Phil 1:25 *1492*
good comfort, when I *k* your state Phil 2:19 *1097*
But ye *k* the proof of him, that, Phil 2:22 *1097*
That I may *k* him, and the power of Phil 3:10 *1097*
I *k* both how to be abased Phil 4:12 *1492*
and I *k* how to abound Phil 4:12 *1492*
Now ye Philippians *k* also Phil 4:15 *1492*
that ye may *k* how ye ought to Col 4:6 *1492*
that he might *k* your estate Col 4:8 *1097*
as ye *k* what manner of men we 1Th 1:5 *1492*
k our entrance in unto you, that 1Th 2:1 *1492*
shamefully entreated, as ye *k* 1Th 2:2 *1492*
used we flattering words, as ye *k* 1Th 2:5 *1492*
As ye *k* how we exhorted and 1Th 2:11 *1492*
for yourselves *k* that we are 1Th 3:3 *1492*
even as it came to pass, and ye *k* 1Th 3:4 *1492*
I sent to *k* your faith, lest by 1Th 3:5 *1097*
For ye *k* what commandments we 1Th 4:2 *1492*
k how to possess his vessel in 1Th 4:4 *1492*
as the Gentiles which *k* not God 1Th 4:5 *1492*
For yourselves *k* perfectly that 1Th 5:2 *1492*
to *k* them which labour among you, 1Th 5:12 *1492*
vengeance on them that *k* not God 2Th 1:8 *1492*
now ye *k* what withholdeth that he 2Th 2:6 *1492*
For yourselves *k* how ye ought to 2Th 3:7 *1492*
But we *k* that the law is good, if 1Ti 1:8 *1492*
(For if a man *k* not how to rule 1Ti 3:5 *1492*
that thou mayest *k* how thou 1Ti 3:15 *1492*
them which believe and *k* the truth 1Ti 4:3 *1921*
for I *k* whom I have believed, and 2Ti 1:12 *1492*
This *k* also, that in the last 2Ti 3:1 *1097*
They profess that they *k* God Titus 1:16 *1492*
his brother, saying, *K* the Lord Heb 8:11 *1097*
for all shall *k* me, from the Heb 8:11 *1492*
For we *k* him that hath said, Heb 10:30 *1492*
For ye *k* how that afterward, when Heb 12:17 *2467*
K ye that our brother Timothy is Heb 13:23 *1097*
But wilt thou *k*, O vain man, that Jas 2:20 *1097*
k ye not that the friendship of Jas 4:4 *1492*
Whereas ye *k* not what shall be on Jas 4:14 *1987*
Let him *k*, that he which Jas 5:20 *1097*
Forasmuch as ye *k* that ye were 1Pet 1:18 *1492*
of these things, though ye *k* them 2Pet 1:12 *1492*
seeing ye *k* these things before, 2Pet 3:17 *4267*
hereby we do *k* that we *k* him, 1Jn 2:3 *1097*
hereby we do *k* that we *k* him 1Jn 2:3 *1097*
I *k* him, and keepeth not his 1Jn 2:4 *1097*
hereby *k* we that we are in him 1Jn 2:5 *1097*
whereby we *k* that it is the last 1Jn 2:18 *1097*
the Holy One, and ye *k* all things 1Jn 2:20 *1492*
you because ye *k* not the truth 1Jn 2:21 *1492*
but because ye *k* it 1Jn 2:21 *1492*
If ye *k* that he is righteous 1Jn 2:29 *1492*
ye *k* that every one that doeth 1Jn 2:29 *1097*
but we *k* that, when he shall 1Jn 3:2 *1492*
ye *k* that he was manifested to 1Jn 3:5 *1492*
We *k* that we have passed from 1Jn 3:14 *1492*
ye *k* that no murderer hath 1Jn 3:15 *1492*
hereby we *k* that we are of the 1Jn 3:19 *1097*
hereby we *k* that he abideth in us 1Jn 3:24 *1097*
Hereby *k* ye the Spirit of God 1Jn 4:2 *1097*
Hereby *k* we the spirit of truth, 1Jn 4:6 *1097*
Hereby *k* we that we dwell in him, 1Jn 4:13 *1097*
By this we *k* that we love the 1Jn 5:2 *1097*
that ye may *k* that ye have 1Jn 5:13 *1492*
And if we *k* that he hear us, 1Jn 5:15 *1492*
we *k* that we have the petitions 1Jn 5:15 *1492*
We *k* that whosoever is born of 1Jn 5:18 *1492*
we *k* that we are of God, and the 1Jn 5:19 *1492*
we *k* that the Son of God is come, 1Jn 5:20 *1492*
that we may *k* him that is true, 1Jn 5:20 *1097*
ye *k* that our record is true 3Jn 12 *1492*
of those things which they *k* not Jude 10 *1492*
but what they *k* naturally Jude 10 *1987*
I *k* thy works, and thy labour, and Rev 2:2 *1492*
I *k* thy works, and tribulation, and Rev 2:9 *1492*
I *k* the blasphemy of them which Rev 2:9
I *k* thy works, and where thou Rev 2:13 *1492*
I *k* thy works, and charity, and Rev 2:19 *1492*
all the churches shall *k* that I Rev 2:23 *1097*
I *k* thy works, that thou hast a Rev 3:1 *1492*
thou shalt not *k* what hour I will Rev 3:3 *1097*
I *k* thy works Rev 3:8 *1492*
to *k* that I have loved thee Rev 3:9 *1097*
I *k* thy works, that thou art Rev 3:15 *1492*

KNOWEST

for thou *k* my service which I Gen 30:26 3045
Thou *k* how I have served thee, and Gen 30:29 3045
if thou *k* any men of activity Gen 47:6 3045
k thou not yet that Egypt is Ex 10:7 3045
thou *k* the people, that they are Ex 32:22 3045
forasmuch as thou *k* how we are to Num 10:31 3045
whom thou *k* to be the elders of Num 11:16 3045
Thou *k* all the travel that hath Num 20:14 3045
diseases of Egypt, which thou *k* Deut 7:15 3045
of the Anakims, whom thou *k* Deut 9:2 3045
Only the trees which thou *k* that Deut 20:20 3045
a nation which thou *k* not eat up Deut 28:33 3045
Thou *k* the thing that the LORD Josh 14:6 3045
K thou not that the Philistines Judg 15:11 3045
thou *k* what Saul hath done, how 1Sa 28:9 3045
How *k* thou that Saul and Jonathan 2Sa 1:5 3045
k thou not that it will be 2Sa 2:26 3045
Thou *k* Abner the son of Ner, that 2Sa 3:25 3045
for thou, Lord GOD, *k* thy servant 2Sa 7:20 3045
thou *k* thy father and his men, 2Sa 17:8 3045
my lord the king, thou *k* it not 1Kin 1:18 3045
Moreover thou *k* also what Joab 1Kin 2:5 3045
k what thou oughtest to do unto 1Kin 2:9 3045
Thou *k* that the kingdom was mine, 1Kin 2:15 3045
Thou *k* all the wickedness which 1Kin 2:44 3045
Thou *k* how that David my father 1Kin 5:3 3045
for thou *k* that there is not 1Kin 5:6 3045
to his ways, whose heart thou *k* 1Kin 8:39 3045
k the hearts of all the children 1Kin 8:39 3045
K thou that the LORD will take 2Kin 2:3 3045
K thou that the LORD will take 2Kin 2:5 3045
thou *k* that thy servant did fear 2Kin 4:1 3045
for thou *k* thy servant 1Chr 17:18 3045
all his ways, whose heart thou *k* 2Chr 6:30 3045
(for thou only *k* the hearts of 2Chr 6:30 3045
Thou *k* that I am not wicked Job 10:7 1847
What *k* thou, that we know not Job 15:9 3045
K thou not this of old, since man Job 20:4 3045
therefore speak what thou *k* Job 34:33 3045
the measures thereof, if thou *k* Job 38:5 3045
declare if thou *k* it all Job 38:18 3045
K thou it, because thou wast then Job 38:21 3045
K thou the ordinances of heaven Job 38:33 3045
K thou the time when the wild Job 39:1 3045
or *k* thou the time when they Job 39:2 3045
refrained my lips, O LORD, thou *k* Ps 40:9 3045
O God, thou *k* my foolishness Ps 69:5 3045
Thou *k* my downsitting and mine Ps 139:2 3045
lo, O LORD, thou *k* it altogether Ps 139:4 3045
for thou *k* not what a day may Prov 27:1 3045
for thou *k* not what evil shall be Eccl 11:2 3045
As thou *k* not what is the way of Eccl 11:5 3045
even so thou *k* not the works of Eccl 11:5 3045
for thou *k* not whether shall Eccl 11:6 3045
call a nation that thou *k* not Is 55:5 3045
nation whose language thou *k* not Jer 5:15 3045
But thou, O LORD, *k* me Jer 12:3 3045
into a land which thou *k* not Jer 15:14 3045
O LORD, thou *k* Jer 15:15 3045
in the land which thou *k* not Jer 17:4 3045
thou *k*: that which came Jer 17:16 3045
thou *k* all their counsel against Jer 18:23 3045
mighty things, which thou *k* not Jer 33:3 3045
And I answered, O Lord GOD, thou *k* Eze 37:3 3045
K thou wherefore I come unto thee Dan 10:20 3045
unto me, *K* thou not what these be Zec 4:5 3045
and said, *K* thou not what these be Zec 4:13 3045
K thou that the Pharisees were Mt 15:12 *1492*
Thou *k* the commandments, Do not Mk 10:19 *1492*
Thou *k* the commandments, Do not Lk 18:20 *1492*
shalt thrice deny that thou *k* me Lk 22:34 *1492*
saith unto him, Whence *k* thou me Jn 1:48 *1097*
of Israel, and *k* not these things Jn 3:10 *1097*
him, What I do thou *k* not now Jn 13:7 *1492*
we sure that thou *k* all things Jn 16:30 *1492*
k thou not that I have power to Jn 19:10 *1492*
thou *k* that I love thee Jn 21:15 *1492*
thou *k* that I love thee Jn 21:16 *1492*
unto him, Lord, thou *k* all things Jn 21:17 *1492*
thou *k* that I love thee Jn 21:17 *1097*
which *k* the hearts of all men, Acts 1:24 *2589*
no wrong, as thou very well *k* Acts 25:10 *1921*
k his will, and approvest the Rom 2:18 *1097*
For what *k* thou, O wife, whether 1Cor 7:16 *1492*
or how *k* thou, O man, whether 1Cor 7:16 *1492*
This thou *k*, that all they which 2Ti 1:15 *1492*
me at Ephesus, thou *k* very well 2Ti 1:18 *1097*

k not that thou art wretched, and	Rev 3:17	*1492*
And I said unto him, Sir, thou *k*	Rev 7:14	*1492*

KNOWETH

My lord *k* that the children are	Gen 33:13	3045
when he *k* of it, then he shall be	Lev 5:3	3045
when he *k* of it, then he shall be	Lev 5:4	3045
he *k* thy walking through this	Deut 2:7	3045
but no man *k* of his sepulchre	Deut 34:6	3045
gods, the LORD God of gods, he *k*	Josh 22:22	3045
ever for the iniquity which he *k*	1Sa 3:13	3045
Thy father certainly *k* that I	1Sa 20:3	3045
and that also Saul my father *k*	1Sa 23:17	3045
Today thy servant *k* that I have	2Sa 14:22	3045
for all Israel *k* that thy father	2Sa 17:10	3045
reign, and David our lord *k* it not	1Kin 1:11	3045
who *k* whether thou art come to	Est 4:14	3045
For he *k* vain men	Job 11:11	3045
who *k* not such things as these	Job 12:3	854
Who *k* not in all these that the	Job 12:9	3045
come to honour, and he *k* it not	Job 14:21	3045
he *k* that the day of darkness is	Job 15:23	3045
the place of him that *k* not God	Job 18:21	3045
But he *k* the way that I take	Job 23:10	3045
There is a path which no fowl *k*	Job 28:7	3045
Man *k* not the price thereof	Job 28:13	3045
and he *k* the place thereof	Job 28:23	3045
Therefore he *k* their works	Job 34:25	5234
yet he *k* it not in great	Job 35:15	3045
For the LORD *k* the way of the	Ps 1:6	3045
The LORD *k* the days of the	Ps 37:18	3045
k not who shall gather them	Ps 39:6	3045
for he *k* the secrets of the heart	Ps 44:21	3045
among us any that *k* how long	Ps 74:9	3045
Who *k* the power of thine anger	Ps 90:11	3045
A brutish man *k* not	Ps 92:6	3045
The LORD *k* the thoughts of man,	Ps 94:11	3045
For he *k* our frame	Ps 103:14	3045
the sun *k* his going down	Ps 104:19	3045
but the proud he *k* afar off	Ps 138:6	3045
and that my soul *k* right well	Ps 139:14	3045
k not that it is for his life	Prov 7:23	3045
she is simple, and *k* nothing	Prov 9:13	3045
But he *k* not that the dead are	Prov 9:18	3045
The heart *k* his own bitterness	Prov 14:10	3045
who *k* the ruin of them both	Prov 24:22	3045
who *k* whether he shall be a wise	Eccl 2:19	3045
Who *k* the spirit of man that	Eccl 3:21	3045
that *k* to walk before the living	Eccl 6:8	3045
For who *k* what is good for man in	Eccl 6:12	3045
k that thou thyself likewise hast	Eccl 7:22	3045
who *k* the interpretation of a	Eccl 8:1	3045
For he *k* not that which shall be	Eccl 8:7	3045
no man *k* either love or hatred by	Eccl 9:1	3045
For man also *k* not his time	Eccl 9:12	3045
because he *k* not how to go to the	Eccl 10:15	3045
The ox *k* his owner, and the ass	Is 1:3	3045
and who *k* us?	Is 29:15	3045
the heaven *k* her appointed times	Jer 8:7	3045
k me, that I am the LORD which	Jer 9:24	3045
he *k* what is in the darkness, and	Dan 2:22	3046
his strength, and he *k* it not	Hos 7:9	3045
and there upon him, yet he *k* not	Hos 7:9	3045
Who *k* if he will return and repent	Joel 2:14	3045
he *k* them that trust in him	Nah 1:7	3045
but the unjust *k* no shame	Zeph 3:5	3045
for your Father *k* what things ye	Mt 6:8	*1492*
for your heavenly Father *k* that	Mt 6:32	*1492*
no man *k* the Son, but the Father	Mt 11:27	*1921*
neither *k* any man the Father,	Mt 11:27	*1921*
hour *k* no man, no, not the angels	Mt 24:36	*1492*
spring and grow up, he *k* not how	Mk 4:27	*1492*
of that day and that hour *k* no man	Mk 13:32	*1492*
no man *k* who the Son is, but the	Lk 10:22	*1097*
your Father *k* that ye have need	Lk 12:30	*1492*
but God *k* your hearts	Lk 16:15	*1097*
How *k* this man letters, having	Jn 7:15	*1492*
cometh, no man *k* whence he is	Jn 7:27	*1097*
But this people who *k* not the law	Jn 7:49	*1097*
As the Father *k* me, even so know	Jn 10:15	*1097*
darkness *k* not whither he goeth	Jn 12:35	*1492*
it seeth him not, neither *k* him	Jn 14:17	*1097*
for the servant *k* not what his	Jn 15:15	*1492*
he *k* that he saith true, that ye	Jn 19:35	*1492*
which *k* the hearts, bare them	Acts 15:8	*2589*
what man is there that *k* not how	Acts 19:35	*1097*
For the king *k* of these things,	Acts 26:26	*1987*
he that searcheth the hearts *k*	Rom 8:27	*1492*
For what man *k* the things of a	1Cor 2:11	*1492*
so the things of God *k* no man	1Cor 2:11	*1492*
The Lord *k* the thoughts of the	1Cor 3:20	*1097*
any man think that he *k* any thing	1Cor 8:2	*1492*
he *k* nothing yet as he ought to	1Cor 8:2	*1097*
I love you not? God *k*	2Cor 11:11	*1492*
for evermore, *k* that I lie not	2Cor 11:31	*1492*
I cannot tell: God *k*	2Cor 12:2	*1492*
I cannot tell: God *k*	2Cor 12:3	*1492*
The Lord *k* them that are his	2Ti 2:19	*1097*
to him that *k* to do good, and	Jas 4:17	*1492*
The Lord *k* how to deliver the	2Pet 2:9	*1492*
k not whither he goeth, because	1Jn 2:11	*1492*
therefore the world *k* us not	1Jn 3:1	*1097*
than our heart, and *k* all things	1Jn 3:20	*1097*
he that *k* God heareth us	1Jn 4:6	*1097*
loveth is born of God, and *k* God	1Jn 4:7	*1097*
He that loveth not *k* not God	1Jn 4:8	*1097*
which no man *k* saving he that	Rev 2:17	*1097*
because he *k* that he hath but a	Rev 12:12	*1492*

KNOWING

shall be as gods, *k* good and evil	Gen 3:5	3045
my father David not *k* thereof	1Kin 2:32	3045
Jesus *k* their thoughts said,	Mt 9:4	*1492*
not *k* the scriptures, nor the	Mt 22:29	*1492*
immediately *k* in himself that	Mk 5:30	*1921*
k what was done in her, came and	Mk 5:33	*1492*
k that he was a just man and an	Mk 6:20	*1492*
k their hypocrisy, said unto them	Mk 12:15	*1492*
him to scorn, *k* that she was dead	Lk 8:53	*1492*
not *k* what he said	Lk 9:33	*1492*
k their thoughts, said unto them,	Lk 11:17	*1492*
Jesus *k* that the Father had given	Jn 13:3	*1492*
k all things that should come	Jn 18:4	*1492*
Jesus *k* that all things were now	Jn 19:28	*1492*
k that it was the Lord	Jn 21:12	*1492*
k that God had sworn with an oath	Acts 2:30	*1492*
not *k* what was done, came in	Acts 5:7	*1492*
k only the baptism of John	Acts 18:25	*1987*
not *k* the things that shall	Acts 20:22	*1492*
Who *k* the judgment of God, that	Rom 1:32	*1921*
not *k* that the goodness of God	Rom 2:4	*50*
k that tribulation worketh	Rom 5:3	*1492*
K this, that our old man is	Rom 6:6	*1097*
K that Christ being raised from	Rom 6:9	*1492*
k the time, that now it is high	Rom 13:11	*1492*
And our hope of you is stedfast, *k*	2Cor 1:7	*1492*
K that he which raised up the	2Cor 4:14	*1492*
k that, whilst we are at home in	2Cor 5:6	*1492*
K therefore the terror of the	2Cor 5:11	*1492*
K that a man is not justified by	Gal 2:16	*1492*
K that whatsoever good thing any	Eph 6:8	*1492*
k that your Master also is in	Eph 6:9	*1492*
k that I am set for the defence	Phil 1:17	*1492*
K that of the Lord ye shall	Col 3:24	*1492*
k that ye also have a Master in	Col 4:1	*1492*
K, brethren beloved, your	1Th 1:4	*1492*
K this, that the law is not made	1Ti 1:9	*1492*
k nothing, but doting about	1Ti 6:4	*1987*
k that they do gender strifes	2Ti 2:23	*1492*
k of whom thou hast learned them	2Ti 3:14	*1492*
K that he that is such is	Titus 3:11	*1492*
k that thou wilt also do more	Philem 21	*1492*
k in yourselves that ye have in	Heb 10:34	*1097*
went out, not *k* whither he went	Heb 11:8	*1987*
K this, that the trying of your	Jas 1:3	*1097*
k that we shall receive the	Jas 3:1	*1492*
k that ye are thereunto called,	1Pet 3:9	*1492*
k that the same afflictions are	1Pet 5:9	*1492*
K that shortly I must put off	2Pet 1:14	*1492*
K this first, that no prophecy of	2Pet 1:20	*1097*
K this first, that there shall	2Pet 3:3	*1097*

KNOWLEDGE

garden, and the tree of *k* of good	Gen 2:9	1847
But of the tree of the *k* of good	Gen 2:17	1847
and in understanding, and in *k*	Ex 31:3	1847
wisdom, in understanding, and in *k*	Ex 35:31	1847
he hath sinned, come to his *k*	Lev 4:23	3045
he hath sinned, come to his *k*	Lev 4:28	3045
without the *k* of the congregation	Num 15:24	5869
knew the *k* of the most High,	Num 24:16	1847
in that day had no *k* between good	Deut 1:39	3045
that thou shouldest take *k* of me	Ruth 2:10	5234
be he that did take *k* of thee	Ruth 2:19	5234
for the LORD is a God of *k*	1Sa 2:3	1844
take *k* of all the lurking places	1Sa 23:23	3045
shipmen that had *k* of the sea	1Kin 9:27	3045
Give me now wisdom and *k*, that I	2Chr 1:10	4093
k for thyself, that thou mayest	2Chr 1:11	4093
Wisdom and *k* is granted unto thee	2Chr 1:12	4093
and servants that had *k* of the sea	2Chr 8:18	3045
taught the good *k* of the LORD	2Chr 30:22	7922
daughters, every one having *k*	Neh 10:28	3045
Should a wise man utter vain *k*	Job 15:2	1847
we desire not the *k* of thy ways	Job 21:14	1847
Shall any teach God *k*	Job 21:22	1847
and my lips shall utter *k* clearly	Job 33:3	1847
give ear unto me, ye that have *k*	Job 34:2	3045
Job hath spoken without *k*	Job 34:35	1847
he multiplieth words without *k*	Job 35:16	1847
I will fetch my *k* from afar	Job 36:3	1843
that is perfect in *k* is with thee	Job 36:4	1844
and they shall die without *k*	Job 36:12	1847
of him which is perfect in *k*	Job 37:16	1843
counsel by words without *k*	Job 38:2	1847
he that hideth counsel without *k*	Job 42:3	1847
all the workers of iniquity no *k*	Ps 14:4	3045
and night unto night sheweth *k*	Ps 19:2	1847
Have the workers of iniquity no *k*	Ps 53:4	3045
is there *k* in the most High	Ps 73:11	1844
he that teacheth man *k*, shall not	Ps 94:10	1847
Teach me good judgment and *k*	Ps 119:66	1847
Such *k* is too wonderful for me	Ps 139:6	1847
is man, that thou takest *k* of him	Ps 144:3	3045
to the simple, to the young man *k*	Prov 1:4	1847
of the LORD is the beginning of *k*	Prov 1:7	1847
their scorning, and fools hate *k*	Prov 1:22	1847
For that they hated *k*, and did not	Prov 1:29	1847
Yea, if thou criest after *k*	Prov 2:3	998
of the LORD, and find the *k* of God	Prov 2:5	1847
out of his mouth cometh *k*	Prov 2:6	1847
k is pleasant unto thy soul	Prov 2:10	1847
By his *k* the depths are broken up	Prov 3:20	1847
and that thy lips may keep *k*	Prov 5:2	1847
and right to them that find *k*	Prov 8:9	1847
k rather than choice gold	Prov 8:10	1847
find out *k* of witty inventions	Prov 8:12	1847
and the *k* of the holy is	Prov 9:10	1847
Wise men lay up *k*	Prov 10:14	1847
but through *k* shall the just be	Prov 11:9	1847
Whoso loveth instruction loveth *k*	Prov 12:1	1847
A prudent man concealeth *k*	Prov 12:23	1847
Every prudent man dealeth with *k*	Prov 13:16	1847
but *k* is easy unto him that	Prov 14:6	1847
not in him the lips of *k*	Prov 14:7	1847
the prudent are crowned with *k*	Prov 14:18	1847
tongue of the wise useth *k* aright	Prov 15:2	1847
The lips of the wise disperse *k*	Prov 15:7	1847
that hath understanding seeketh *k*	Prov 15:14	1847
He that hath *k* spareth his words	Prov 17:27	1847
heart of the prudent getteth *k*	Prov 18:15	1847
and the ear of the wise seeketh *k*	Prov 18:15	1847
Also, that the soul be without *k*	Prov 19:2	1847
and he will understand *k*	Prov 19:25	1847
to err from the words of *k*	Prov 19:27	1847
but the lips of *k* are a precious	Prov 20:15	1847
is instructed, he receiveth *k*	Prov 21:11	1847
The eyes of the LORD preserve *k*	Prov 22:12	1847
and apply thine heart unto my *k*	Prov 22:17	1847
excellent things in counsels and *k*	Prov 22:20	1847
and thine ears to the words of *k*	Prov 23:12	1847
by *k* shall the chambers be filled	Prov 24:4	1847
a man of *k* increaseth strength	Prov 24:5	1847
So shall the *k* of wisdom be unto	Prov 24:14	3045
k the state thereof shall be	Prov 28:2	3045
nor have the *k* of the holy	Prov 30:3	1847
great experience of wisdom and *k*	Eccl 1:16	1847
increaseth *k* increaseth sorrow	Eccl 1:18	1847
labour is in wisdom, and in *k*	Eccl 2:21	1847
is good in his sight wisdom, and *k*	Eccl 2:26	1847
but the excellency of *k* is	Eccl 7:12	1847
is no work, nor device, nor *k*	Eccl 9:10	1847
he still taught the people *k*	Eccl 12:9	1847
captivity, because they have no *k*	Is 5:13	1847
the child shall have *k* to cry	Is 8:4	3045
counsel and might, the spirit of *k*	Is 11:2	1847
be full of the *k* of the LORD	Is 11:9	1844
Whom shall he teach *k*	Is 28:9	1844
of the rash shall understand *k*	Is 32:4	1847
k shall be the stability of thy	Is 33:6	1847
path of judgment, and taught him *k*	Is 40:14	1847
his heart, neither is there *k* nor	Is 44:19	1847
and maketh their *k* foolish	Is 44:25	1847
they have no *k* that set up the	Is 45:20	3045
Thy wisdom and thy *k*, it hath	Is 47:10	1847
by his *k* shall my righteous	Is 53:11	1847
our soul, and thou takest no *k*	Is 58:3	3045
which shall feed you with *k*	Jer 3:15	1844
but to do good they have no *k*	Jer 4:22	3045
Every man is brutish in his *k*	Jer 10:14	1847
And the LORD hath given me *k* of it	Jer 11:18	3045
Every man is brutish by his *k*	Jer 51:17	1847
in all wisdom, and cunning in *k*	Dan 1:4	1847
four children, God gave them *k*	Dan 1:17	4093
k to them that know understanding	Dan 2:21	998
as an excellent spirit, and *k*	Dan 5:12	998
and fro, and *k* shall be increased	Dan 12:4	1847
mercy, nor *k* of God in the land	Hos 4:1	1847
are destroyed for lack of *k*	Hos 4:6	1847
because thou hast rejected *k*	Hos 4:6	1847
the *k* of God more than burnt	Hos 6:6	1847
the *k* of the glory of the LORD	Hab 2:14	3045
the priest's lips should keep *k*	Mal 2:7	1847
men of that place had *k* of him	Mt 14:35	*1921*
To give *k* of salvation unto his	Lk 1:77	*1108*
ye have taken away the key of *k*	Lk 11:52	*1108*
and they took *k* of them, that they	Acts 4:13	*1921*
had *k* that the word of God was	Acts 17:13	*1097*
mayest take *k* of all these things	Acts 24:8	*1921*
having more perfect *k* of that way	Acts 24:22	*1492*
not like to retain God in their *k*	Rom 1:28	*1922*
babes, which hast the form of *k*	Rom 2:20	*1108*
for by the law is the *k* of sin	Rom 3:20	*1922*
of God, but not according to *k*	Rom 10:2	*1922*
both of the wisdom and *k* of God	Rom 11:33	*1108*
of goodness, filled with all *k*	Rom 15:14	*1108*
in all utterance, and in all *k*	1Cor 1:5	*1108*
idols, we know that we all have *k*	1Cor 8:1	*1108*
K puffeth up, but charity	1Cor 8:1	*1108*
there is not in every man that *k*	1Cor 8:7	*1108*
hast *k* sit at meat in the idol's	1Cor 8:10	*1108*
through thy *k* shall the weak	1Cor 8:11	*1108*
the word of *k* by the same Spirit	1Cor 12:8	*1108*
all mysteries, and all *k*	1Cor 13:2	*1108*
whether there be *k*, it shall	1Cor 13:8	*1108*
you either by revelation, or by *k*	1Cor 14:6	*1108*
for some have not the *k* of God	1Cor 15:34	*56*
of his *k* by us in every place	2Cor 2:14	*1108*
to give the light of the *k* of the	2Cor 4:6	*1108*
By pureness, by *k*, by	2Cor 6:6	*1108*
in faith, and utterance, and *k*	2Cor 8:7	*1108*
itself against the *k* of God	2Cor 10:5	*1108*
I be rude in speech, yet not in *k*	2Cor 11:6	*1108*
and revelation in the *k* of him	Eph 1:17	*1922*
ye may understand my *k* in the	Eph 3:4	*4907*
love of Christ, which passeth *k*	Eph 3:19	*1108*
of the *k* of the Son of God, unto	Eph 4:13	*1922*
may abound yet more and more in *k*	Phil 1:9	*1922*
of the *k* of Christ Jesus my Lord	Phil 3:8	*1108*
the *k* of his will in all wisdom	Col 1:9	*1922*
and increasing in the *k* of God	Col 1:10	*1922*
all the treasures of wisdom and *k*	Col 2:3	*1108*
which is renewed in *k* after the	Col 3:10	*1922*
to come unto the *k* of the truth	1Ti 2:4	*1922*
to come to the *k* of the truth	2Ti 3:7	*1922*
have received the *k* of the truth	Heb 10:26	*1922*
man and endued with *k* among you	Jas 3:13	*1990*
dwell with them according to *k*	1Pet 3:7	*1108*
unto you through the *k* of God	2Pet 1:2	*1922*
through the *k* of him that hath	2Pet 1:3	*1922*
and to virtue *k*	2Pet 1:5	*1108*
And to *k* temperance	2Pet 1:6	*1108*
in the *k* of our Lord Jesus Christ	2Pet 1:8	*1922*
world through the *k* of the Lord	2Pet 2:20	*1922*
in the *k* of our Lord and Saviour	2Pet 3:18	*1108*

KNOWN

daughters which have not *k* man	Gen 19:8	3045
virgin, neither had any man *k* her	Gen 24:16	3045
it could not be *k* that they had	Gen 41:21	3045
the plenty shall not be *k* in the	Gen 41:31	3045
made himself *k* unto his brethren	Gen 45:1	3045
and said, Surely this thing is *k*	Ex 2:14	3045

name JEHOVAH was I not *k* to them . Ex 6:3 3045
Or if it be *k* that the ox hath Ex 21:36 3045
wherein shall it be *k* here that I Ex 33:16 3045
they have sinned against it, is *k* Lev 4:14 3045
whether he hath seen or *k* of it Lev 5:1 3045
myself *k* unto him in a vision Num 12:6 3045
that hath *k* man by lying with him Num 31:17 3045
that have not *k* a man by lying Num 31:18 3045
had not *k* man by lying with him Num 31:35 3045
k among your tribes, and I will Deut 1:13 3045
of your tribes, wise men, and *k* Deut 1:15 3045
your children which have not *k* Deut 11:2 3045
other gods, which ye have not *k* Deut 11:28 3045
other gods, which thou hast not *k* Deut 13:2 3045
other gods, which thou hast not *k* Deut 13:6 3045
other gods, which ye have not *k* Deut 13:13 3045
it be not *k* who hath slain him Deut 21:1 3045
thou nor thy fathers have *k* Deut 28:36 3045
thou nor thy fathers have *k* Deut 28:64 3045
which have not *k* any thing Deut 31:13 3045
which had *k* all the works of the Josh 24:31 3045
had not *k* all the wars of Canaan Judg 3:1 3045
So his strength was not *k* Judg 16:9 3045
that had *k* no man by lying with Judg 21:12 3045
make not thyself *k* unto the man Ruth 3:3 3045
Let it not be *k* that a woman came Ruth 3:14 3045
it shall be *k* to you why his hand 1Sa 6:3 3045
that thou mayest make *k* unto me 1Sa 28:15 3045
and the thing was not *k* 2Sa 17:19 3045
that thou be not *k* to be the wife 1Kin 14:2 3045
let it be *k* this day that thou 1Kin 18:36 3045
make *k* his deeds among the people 1Chr 16:8 3045
in making *k* all these great 1Chr 17:19 3045
Be it *k* unto the king, that the Ezr 4:12 3046
Be it *k* now unto the king, that, Ezr 4:13 3046
Be it *k* unto the king, that we Ezr 5:8 3046
heard that it was *k* unto us Neh 4:15 3045
madest *k* unto them thy holy Neh 9:14 3045
And the thing was *k* to Mordecai Est 2:22 3045
The LORD is *k* by the judgment Ps 9:16 3045
whom I have not *k* shall serve me Ps 18:43 3045
thou hast *k* my soul in Ps 31:7 3045
God is *k* in her palaces for a Ps 48:3 3045
That thy way may be *k* upon earth Ps 67:2 3045
Thou hast *k* my reproach, and my Ps 69:19 3045
In Judah is God *k* Ps 76:1 3045
and thy footsteps are not *k* Ps 77:19 3045
Which we have heard and *k*, and our Ps 78:3 3045
make them *k* to their children Ps 78:5 3045
the heathen that have not *k* thee Ps 79:6 3045
let him be *k* among the heathen in Ps 79:10 3045
thy wonders be *k* in the dark Ps 88:12 3045
I make *k* thy faithfulness to all Ps 89:1 3045
high, because he hath *k* my name Ps 91:14 3045
heart, and they have not *k* my ways Ps 95:10 3045
LORD hath made *k* his salvation Ps 98:2 3045
He made *k* his ways unto Moses, Ps 103:7 3045
make *k* his deeds among the people Ps 105:1 3045
make his mighty power to be *k* Ps 106:8 3045
those that have *k* thy testimonies Ps 119:79 3045
I have *k* of old that thou hast Ps 119:152 3045
thou hast searched me, and *k* me Ps 139:1 3045
To make *k* to the sons of men his Ps 145:12 3045
judgments, they have not *k* them Ps 147:20 3045
I will make *k* my words unto you Prov 1:23 3045
perverteth his ways shall be *k* Prov 10:9 3045
A fool's wrath is presently *k* Prov 12:16 3045
in the midst of fools is made *k* Prov 14:33 3045
Even a child is *k* by his doings Prov 20:11 5234
I have made *k* to thee this day, Prov 22:19 3045
Her husband is *k* in the gates Prov 31:23 3045
a fool's voice is *k* by multitude Eccl 5:3 3045
not seen the sun, nor *k* any thing Eccl 6:5 3045
and it is *k* that it is man Eccl 6:10 3045
this is *k* in all the earth Is 12:5 3045
And the LORD shall be *k* to Egypt Is 19:21 3045
children shall make *k* thy truth Is 38:19 3045
Have ye not *k*? Is 40:21 3045
Hast thou not *k*? Is 40:28 3045
in paths that they have not *k* Is 42:16 3045
They have not *k* nor understood Is 44:18 3045
thee, though thou hast not *k* me Is 45:4 3045
thee, though thou hast not *k* me Is 45:5 3045
shall be *k* among the Gentiles Is 61:9 3045
to make thy name *k* to thine Is 64:2 3045
shall be *k* toward his servants Is 66:14 3045
is foolish, they have not *k* me Jer 4:22 3045
for they have *k* the way of the Jer 5:5 3045
they nor their fathers have *k* Jer 9:16 3045
they nor their fathers have *k* Jer 19:4 3045
pass, then shall the prophet be *k* Jer 28:9 3045
they are not *k* in the streets Lam 4:8 5234
made myself *k* unto them in the Eze 20:5 3045
sight I made myself *k* unto them Eze 20:9 3045
countries which thou hast not *k* Eze 32:9 3045
I will make myself *k* among them Eze 35:11 3045
the Lord GOD, be it *k* unto you Eze 36:32 3045
I will be *k* in the eyes of many Eze 38:23 3045
name *k* in the midst of my people Eze 39:7 3045
will not make *k* unto me the dream Dan 2:5 3046
will not make *k* unto me the dream Dan 2:9 3046
Arioch made the thing *k* to Daniel Dan 2:15 3046
and made the thing *k* to Hananiah Dan 2:17 3046
hast made *k* unto me now what we Dan 2:23 3046
for thou hast now made *k* unto us Dan 2:23 3046
that will make *k* unto the king Dan 2:25 3046
Art thou able to make *k* unto me Dan 2:26 3046
secrets, and maketh *k* to the king Dan 2:28 3046
that revealeth secrets maketh *k* Dan 2:29 3046
k the interpretation to the king Dan 2:30 3046
the great God hath made *k* to the Dan 2:45 3046
be it *k* unto thee, O king, that Dan 3:18 3046
that they might make *k* unto me Dan 4:6 3046
but they did not make *k* unto me Dan 4:7 3046
make *k* unto me the interpretation Dan 4:18 3046
have *k* that the heavens do rule Dan 4:26 3046
nor make *k* to the king the Dan 5:8 3046
make *k* unto me the interpretation Dan 5:15 3046
make *k* to me the interpretation Dan 5:16 3046
make *k* to him the interpretation Dan 5:17 3046
them, and they have not *k* the LORD Hos 5:4 3045
made *k* that which shall surely be Hos 5:9 3045
You only have I *k* of all the Amos 3:2 3045
place is not *k* where they are Nah 3:17 3045
in the midst of the years make *k* Hab 3:2 3045
day which shall be *k* to the LORD Zec 14:7 3045
and hid, that shall not be *k* Mt 10:26 *1097*
But if ye had *k* what this meaneth Mt 12:7 *1097*
that they should not make him *k* Mt 12:16 *5318*
for the tree is *k* by his fruit Mt 12:33 *1097*
k in what watch the thief would Mt 24:43 *1492*
that they should not make him *k* Mk 3:12 *5318*
the Lord hath made *k* unto us Lk 2:15 *1107*
they made *k* abroad the saying Lk 2:17 *1232*
every tree is *k* by his own fruit Lk 6:44 *1097*
were a prophet, would have *k* who Lk 7:39 *1097*
thing hid, that shall not be *k* Lk 8:17 *1097*
neither hid, that shall not be *k* Lk 12:2 *1097*
k what hour the thief would come Lk 12:39 *1492*
Saying, If thou hadst *k*, even Lk 19:42 *1097*
hast not *k* the things which are Lk 24:18 *1097*
how he was *k* of them in breaking Lk 24:35 *1097*
he himself seeketh to be *k* openly Jn 7:4 *1097*
if ye had *k* me, ye should have Jn 8:19 *1492*
ye should have *k* my Father also Jn 8:19 *1492*
Yet ye have not *k* him Jn 8:55 *1097*
my sheep, and am *k* of mine Jn 10:14 *1097*
If ye had *k* me, ye should have Jn 14:7 *1097*
ye should have *k* my Father also Jn 14:7 *1097*
you, and yet hast thou not *k* me Jn 14:9 *1097*
my Father I have made *k* unto you Jn 15:15 *1107*
they have not *k* the Father Jn 16:3 *1097*
Now they have *k* that all things Jn 17:7 *1097*
have *k* surely that I came out Jn 17:8 *1097*
Father, the world hath not *k* thee Jn 17:25 *1097*
but I have *k* thee, and these have Jn 17:25 *1097*
these have *k* that thou hast sent Jn 17:25 *1097*
that disciple was *k* unto the high Jn 18:15 *1110*
which was *k* unto the high priest, Jn 18:16 *1110*
it was *k* unto all the dwellers at Acts 1:19 *1110*
be this *k* unto you, and hearken to Acts 2:14 *1110*
Thou hast made *k* to me the ways Acts 2:28 *1107*
Be it *k* unto you all, and to all Acts 4:10 *1110*
Joseph was made *k* to his brethren Acts 7:13 *319*
kindred was made *k* unto Pharaoh Acts 7:13 *5318*
their laying await was *k* of Saul Acts 9:24 *1097*
it was *k* throughout all Joppa Acts 9:42 *1110*
Be it *k* unto you therefore, men Acts 13:38 *1110*
K unto God are all his works from Acts 15:18 *1110*
this was *k* to all the Jews and Acts 19:17 *1110*
because he would have *k* the Acts 22:30 *1097*
when I would have *k* the cause Acts 23:28 *1097*
Be it *k* therefore unto you, that Acts 28:28 *1110*
Because that which may be *k* of Rom 1:19 *1110*
the way of peace have they not *k* Rom 3:17 *1097*
Nay, I had not *k* sin, but by the Rom 7:7 *1097*
for I had not *k* lust, except the Rom 7:7 *1492*
his wrath, and to make his power *k* Rom 9:22 *1107*
that he might make *k* the riches Rom 9:23 *1107*
For who hath *k* the mind of the Rom 11:34 *1097*
made *k* to all nations for the Rom 16:26 *1107*
for had they *k* it, they would not 1Cor 2:8 *1097*
For who hath *k* the mind of the 1Cor 2:16 *1097*
love God, the same is *k* of him 1Cor 8:3 *1097*
shall I know even as also I am *k* 1Cor 13:12 *1921*
how shall it be *k* what is piped 1Cor 14:7 *1097*
how shall it be *k* what is spoken 1Cor 14:9 *1097*
epistle written in our hearts, *k* 2Cor 3:2 *1097*
though we have *k* Christ after the 2Cor 5:16 *1097*
As unknown, and yet well *k* 2Cor 6:9 *1921*
But now, after that ye have *k* God Gal 4:9 *1097*
or rather are *k* of God Gal 4:9 *1097*
Having made *k* unto us the mystery Eph 1:9 *1107*
he made *k* unto me the mystery Eph 3:3 *1107*
not made *k* unto the sons of men Eph 3:5 *1107*
be *k* by the church the manifold Eph 3:10 *1107*
to make *k* the mystery of the Eph 6:19 *1107*
shall make *k* to you all things Eph 6:21 *1107*
your moderation be *k* unto all men Phil 4:5 *1097*
your requests be made *k* unto God Phil 4:6 *1107*
To whom God would make *k* what is Col 1:27 *1107*
They shall make *k* unto you all Col 4:9 *1107*
But thou hast fully *k* my doctrine 2Ti 3:10 *3877*
thou hast *k* the holy scriptures 2Ti 3:15 *1492*
me the preaching might be fully *k* 2Ti 4:17 *4135*
and they have not *k* my ways Heb 3:10 *1097*
when we made *k* unto you the power 2Pet 1:16 *1107*
have *k* the way of righteousness 2Pet 2:21 *1921*
than, after they have *k* it 2Pet 2:21 *1921*
because ye have *k* him that is 1Jn 2:13 *1097*
because ye have *k* the Father 1Jn 2:13 *1097*
because ye have *k* him that is 1Jn 2:14 *1097*
hath not seen him, neither *k* him 1Jn 3:6 *1097*
And we have *k* and believed the love 1Jn 4:16 *1097*
all they that have *k* the truth 2Jn 1 *1097*
which have not *k* the depths of Rev 2:24 *1097*

KOA (*ko'-ah*) *An obscure tribe.*
Chaldeans, Pekod, and Shoa, and *K* Eze 23:23 6970

KOHATH (*ko'-hath*) See KOHATHITES. *A son of Levi.*
Gershon, *K*, and Merari Gen 46:11 6955
Gershon, and *K*, and Merari Ex 6:16 6955
And the sons of *K* Ex 6:18 6955
life of *K* were an hundred thirty Ex 6:18 6955
Gershon, and *K*, and Merari Num 3:17 6955
the sons of *K* by their families Num 3:19 6955
of *K* was the family of the Num 3:27 6955
The families of the sons of *K* Num 3:29 6955
of *K* from among the sons of Levi Num 4:2 6955
of *K* in the tabernacle of the Num 4:4 6955
the sons of *K* shall come to bear Num 4:15 6955
of *K* in the tabernacle of the Num 4:15 6955
unto the sons of *K* he gave none Num 7:9 6955
the son of Izhar, the son of *K* Num 16:1 6955
of *K*, the family of the Num 26:57 6955
And *K* begat Amram Num 26:58 6955
the rest of the children of *K* had Josh 21:5 6955
the families of the children of *K* Josh 21:20 6955
remained of the children of *K* Josh 21:20 6955
the children of *K* that remained Josh 21:26 6955
Gershon, *K*, and Merari 1Chr 6:1 6955
And the sons of *K* 1Chr 6:2 6955
Gershom, *K*, and Merari 1Chr 6:16 6955
And the sons of *K* were, Amram, and 1Chr 6:18 6955
The sons of *K* 1Chr 6:22 6955
The son of Izhar, the son of *K* 1Chr 6:38 6955
And unto the sons of *K*, which were 1Chr 6:61 6955
K had cities of their coasts out 1Chr 6:66 6955
of the remnant of the sons of *K* 1Chr 6:70 6955
Of the sons of *K* 1Chr 15:5 6955
sons of Levi, namely, Gershon, *K* 1Chr 23:6 6955
The sons of *K* 1Chr 23:12 6955

KOHATHITES (*ko'-hath-ites*) *Descendants of Kohath.*
these are the families of the *K* Num 3:27 6956
K shall be Elizaphan the son of Num 3:30 6956
of the *K* from among the Levites Num 4:18 6956
of the *K* after their families Num 4:34 6956
numbered of the families of the *K* Num 4:37 6956
the *K* set forward, bearing the Num 10:21 6956
of Kohath, the family of the *K* Num 26:57 6956
out for the families of the *K* Josh 21:4 6956
being of the families of the *K* Josh 21:10 6956
Of the sons of the *K* 1Chr 6:33 6956
Aaron, of the families of the *K* 1Chr 6:54 6956
brethren, of the sons of the *K* 1Chr 9:32 6956
Levites, of the children of the *K* 2Chr 20:19 6956
of Azariah, of the sons of the *K* 2Chr 29:12 6956
Meshullam, of the sons of the *K* 2Chr 34:12 6956

KOLAIAH (*ko-la-i'-ah*)
1. A family of exiles.
the son of Pedaiah, the son of *K* Neh 11:7 6964
2. Father of Ahab.
of Israel, of Ahab the son of *K* Jer 29:21 6964

KORAH (*ko'-rah*) See CORE, KORAHITE, KORE.
1. A son of Esau.
bare Jeush, and Jaalam, and *K* Gen 36:5 7141
to Esau Jeush, and Jaalam, and *K* Gen 36:14 7141
duke Jeush, duke Jaalam, duke *K* Gen 36:18 7141
Reuel, and Jeush, and Jaalam, and *K* 1Chr 1:35 7141
2. A son of Eliphaz.
Duke *K*, duke Gatam, and duke Gen 36:16 7141
3. A conspirator against Moses.
K, and Nepheg, and Zichri Ex 6:21 7141
And the sons of *K* Ex 6:24 7141
Now *K*, the son of Izhar, the son Num 16:1 7141
And he spake unto *K* and unto all Num 16:5 7141
Take you censers, *K*, and all his Num 16:6 7141
And Moses said unto *K*, Hear, I Num 16:8 7141
And Moses said unto *K*, Be thou and Num 16:16 7141
K gathered all the congregation Num 16:19 7141
up from about the tabernacle of *K* Num 16:24 7141
gat up from the tabernacle of *K* Num 16:27 7141
the men that appertained unto *K* Num 16:32 7141
that he be not as *K*, and as his Num 16:40 7141
that died about the matter of *K* Num 16:49 7141
against Aaron in the company of *K* Num 26:9 7141
swallowed them up together with *K* Num 26:10 7141
the children of *K* died not Num 26:11 7141
the LORD in the company of *K* Num 27:3 7141
the son of Ebiasaph, the son of *K* 1Chr 6:37 7141
the son of Ebiasaph, the son of *K* 1Chr 9:19 7141
4. A son of Hebron.
K, and Tappuah, and Rekem 1Chr 2:43 7141
5. A grandson of Kohath.
K his son, Assir his son, 1Chr 6:22 7141
Maschil, for the sons of *K* Ps 42:*t* 7141
chief Musician for the sons of *K* Ps 44:*t* 7141
Shoshannim, for the sons of *K* Ps 45:*t* 7141
chief Musician for the sons of *K* Ps 46:*t* 7141
A Psalm for the sons of *K* Ps 47:*t* 7141
A Song and Psalm for the sons of *K* Ps 48:*t* 7141
A Psalm for the sons of *K* Ps 49:*t* 7141
A Psalm for the sons of *K* Ps 84:*t* 7141
A Psalm for the sons of *K* Ps 85:*t* 7141
A Psalm or Song for the sons of *K* Ps 87:*t* 7141
of *K* to the chief Musician upon Ps 88:*t* 7141

KORAHITE (*ko'-ra-hite*) See KORAHITES, KORE. *A descendant of Korah.*
the firstborn of Shallum the *K* 1Chr 9:31 7145

KORAHITES (*ko'-ra-hites*) See KORATHITES, KORHITES.
of the house of his father, the *K* 1Chr 9:19 7145

KORATHITES (*ko'-ra-thites*) See KORAHITES. *Same as Korahites.*
the Mushites, the family of the *K* Num 26:58 7145

KORAZIN See CHORAZIN.

KORE (*ko'-re*) See KORAH, KORAHITE.
1. Father of Shallum.
And Shallum the son of *K*, the son 1Chr 9:19 6981
was Meshelemiah the son of *K* 1Chr 26:1 6981
the porters among the sons of *K* 1Chr 26:19 7145
2. A Temple servant.
K the son of Imnah the Levite, 2Chr 31:14 6981

KORHITES (*kor'-hites*) See KORAHITES. *Same as Korahites.*
these are the families of the K ... Ex 6:24 7145
and Joezer, and Jashobeam, the K ... 1Chr 12:6 7145
Of the K was Meshelemiah the son ... 1Chr 26:1 7145
and of the children of the K ... 2Chr 20:19 7145

KOUM See CUMI.

KOZ (*coz*) See HAKKOZ.
1. A family of exiles.
of Habaiah, the children of K ... Ezr 2:61 6976
of Habaiah, the children of K ... Neh 7:63 6976
2. Father of two rebuilders of the wall.
the son of Urijah, the son of K ... Neh 3:4 6976
Urijah the son of K another piece ... Neh 3:21 6976

KUSHAIAH (*cu-shah'-yah*) See KISHI. *Father of Ethan.*
brethren, Ethan the son of K ... 1Chr 15:17 6984

L

LAADAH (*la'-a-dah*) *Son of Shelah.*
L the father of Mareshah, and the ... 1Chr 4:21 3935

LAADAN (*la'-a-dan*) See LIBNI.
1. A descendant of Ephraim.
L his son, Ammihud his son, ... 1Chr 7:26 3936
2. A descendant of Gershon.
Of the Gershonites were, L ... 1Chr 23:7 3936
The sons of L ... 1Chr 23:8 3936
the chief of the fathers of L ... 1Chr 23:9 3936
As concerning the sons of L ... 1Chr 26:21 3936
the sons of the Gershonite L ... 1Chr 26:21 3936
even of L the Gershonite, were ... 1Chr 26:21 3936

LABAN (*la'-ban*) See LABAN'S, LIBNAH.
1. Father of Rachel.
had a brother, and his name was L ... Gen 24:29 3837
L ran out unto the man, unto the ... Gen 24:29 3837
Then L and Bethuel answered and ... Gen 24:50 3837
the sister to L the Syrian ... Gen 25:20 3837
flee thou to L my brother to ... Gen 27:43 3837
of L thy mother's brother ... Gen 28:2 3837
and he went to Padan-aram unto L ... Gen 28:5 3837
Know ye L the son of Nahor ... Gen 29:5 3837
of L his mother's brother ... Gen 29:10 3837
the sheep of L his mother's ... Gen 29:10 3837
flock of L his mother's brother ... Gen 29:10 3837
when L heard the tidings of Jacob ... Gen 29:13 3837
he told L all these things ... Gen 29:13 3837
L said to him, Surely thou art my ... Gen 29:14 3837
L said unto Jacob, Because thou ... Gen 29:15 3837
And L had two daughters ... Gen 29:16 3837
L said, It is better that I give ... Gen 29:19 3837
And Jacob said unto L, Give me my ... Gen 29:21 3837
L gathered together all the men ... Gen 29:22 3837
L gave unto his daughter Leah ... Gen 29:24 3837
and he said to L, What is this ... Gen 29:25 3837
L said, It must not be so done in ... Gen 29:26 3837
L gave to Rachel his daughter ... Gen 29:29 3837
Joseph, that Jacob said unto L ... Gen 30:25 3837
L said unto him, I pray thee, if ... Gen 30:27 3837
L said, Behold, I would it might ... Gen 30:34 3837
all the brown in the flock of L ... Gen 30:40 3837
Jacob beheld the countenance of L ... Gen 31:2 3837
seen all that L doeth unto thee ... Gen 31:12 3837
L went to shear his sheep ... Gen 31:19 3837
away unawares to L the Syrian ... Gen 31:20 3837
it was told L on the third day ... Gen 31:22 3837
God came to L the Syrian in a ... Gen 31:24 3837
Then L overtook Jacob ... Gen 31:25 3837
L with his brethren pitched in ... Gen 31:25 3837
L said to Jacob, What hast thou ... Gen 31:26 3837
And Jacob answered and said to L ... Gen 31:31 3837
L went into Jacob's tent, and into ... Gen 31:33 3837
L searched all the tent, but ... Gen 31:34 3837
Jacob was wroth, and chode with L ... Gen 31:36 3837
and Jacob answered and said to L ... Gen 31:36 3837
L answered and said unto Jacob, ... Gen 31:43 3837
L called it Jegar-sahadutha ... Gen 31:47 3837
L said, This heap is a witness ... Gen 31:48 3837
L said to Jacob, Behold this heap ... Gen 31:51 3837
And early in the morning L rose up ... Gen 31:55 3837
L departed, and returned unto his ... Gen 31:55 3837
thus, I have sojourned with L ... Gen 32:4 3837
whom L gave to Leah his daughter, ... Gen 46:18 3837
which L gave unto Rachel his ... Gen 46:25 3837
2. A Hebrew encampment in the wilderness.
between Paran, and Tophel, and L ... Deut 1:1 3837

LABAN'S (*la'-bans*) *Refers to Laban 1.*
and Jacob fed the rest of L flocks ... Gen 30:36 3837
and put them not unto L cattle ... Gen 30:40 3837
so the feebler were L, and the ... Gen 30:42 3837
And he heard the words of L sons ... Gen 31:1 3837

LABOUR
the l of my hands, and rebuked ... Gen 31:42 3018
travailed, and she had hard l ... Gen 35:16 3205
to pass, when she was in hard l ... Gen 35:17 3205
the men, that they may l therein ... Ex 5:9 6213
Six days shalt thou l, and do all ... Ex 20:9 5647
Six days thou shalt l, and do all ... Deut 5:13 5647
on our affliction, and our l ... Deut 26:7 5999
not all the people to l thither ... Josh 7:3 3021
you a land for which ye did not l ... Josh 24:13 3021
be a guard to us, and l on the day ... Neh 4:22 4399
man from his house, and from his l ... Neh 5:13 3018
I be wicked, why then l I in vain ... Job 9:29 3021
or wilt thou leave thy l to him ... Job 39:11 3018
her l is in vain without fear ... Job 39:16 3018
and their l unto the locust ... Ps 78:46 3018
years, yet is their strength l ... Ps 90:10 5999
to his l until the evening ... Ps 104:23 5656
inherited the l of the people ... Ps 105:44 5999
brought down their heart with l ... Ps 107:12 5999
and let the strangers spoil his l ... Ps 109:11 3018
they l in vain that build it ... Ps 127:1 5998
shalt eat the l of thine hands ... Ps 128:2 3018
That our oxen may be strong to l ... Ps 144:14 5445
The l of the righteous tendeth to ... Prov 10:16 6468
gathereth by l shall increase ... Prov 13:11 3027
In all l there is profit ... Prov 14:23 6089
for his hands refuse to l ... Prov 21:25 6213
L not to be rich ... Prov 23:4 3021
profit hath a man of all his l ... Eccl 1:3 5999
All things are full of l ... Eccl 1:8 3023
for my heart rejoiced in all my l ... Eccl 2:10 5999
this was my portion of all my l ... Eccl 2:10 5999
on the l that I had laboured to ... Eccl 2:11 5999
I hated all my l which I had ... Eccl 2:18 5999
all my l wherein I have laboured ... Eccl 2:19 5999
the l which I took under the sun ... Eccl 2:20 5999
is a man whose l is in wisdom ... Eccl 2:21 5999
For what hath man of all his l ... Eccl 2:22 5999
make his soul enjoy good in his l ... Eccl 2:24 5999
and enjoy the good of all his l ... Eccl 3:13 5999
yet is there no end of all his l ... Eccl 4:8 5999
neither saith he, For whom do I l ... Eccl 4:8 6001
have a good reward for their l ... Eccl 4:9 5999
and shall take nothing of his l ... Eccl 5:15 5999
l that he taketh under the sun ... Eccl 5:18 5999
portion, and to rejoice in his l ... Eccl 5:19 5999
All the l of man is for his mouth ... Eccl 6:7 5999
him of his l the days of his life ... Eccl 8:15 5999
though a man l to seek it out ... Eccl 8:17 5998
in thy l which thou takest under ... Eccl 9:9 5999
The l of the foolish wearieth ... Eccl 10:15 5999
l not to comfort me, because of ... Is 22:4 213
The l of Egypt, and merchandise of ... Is 45:14 3018
your l for that which satisfieth ... Is 55:2 3018
They shall not l in vain, nor ... Is 65:23 3021
For shame hath devoured the l of ... Jer 3:24 3018
I forth out of the womb to see l ... Jer 20:18 5999
and the people shall l in vain ... Jer 51:58 3021
we l, and have no rest ... Lam 5:5 3021
and shall take away all thy l ... Eze 23:29 3018
him the land of Egypt for his l ... Eze 29:20 6468
l to bring forth, O daughter of ... Mic 4:10 1518
people shall l in the very fire ... Hab 2:13 3021
the l of the olive shall fail, and ... Hab 3:17 4639
and upon all the l of the hands ... Hag 1:11 3018
Come unto me, all ye that l ... Mt 11:28 2872
that whereon ye bestowed no l ... Jn 4:38 2872
L not for the meat which ... Jn 6:27 2038
Mary, who bestowed much l on us ... Rom 16:6 2872
and Tryphosa, who l in the Lord ... Rom 16:12 2872
own reward according to his own l ... 1Cor 3:8 2873
And l, working with our own hands ... 1Cor 4:12 2872
your l is not in vain in the Lord ... 1Cor 15:58 2873
Wherefore we l, that, whether ... 2Cor 5:9 5389
have bestowed upon you l in vain ... Gal 4:11 2872
but rather let him l, working ... Eph 4:28 2872
flesh, this is the fruit of my l ... Phil 1:22 2041
my brother, and companion in l ... Phil 2:25 4904
Whereunto I also l, striving ... Col 1:29 2872
l of love, and patience of hope in ... 1Th 1:3 2873
For ye remember, brethren, our l ... 1Th 2:9 2873
tempted you, and our l be in vain ... 1Th 3:5 2873
to know them which l among you ... 1Th 5:12 2872
but wrought with l and travail ... 2Th 3:8 2873
For therefore we both l and suffer ... 1Ti 4:10 2872
especially they who l in the word ... 1Ti 5:17 2872
Let us l therefore to enter into ... Heb 4:11 4704
l of love, which ye have shewed ... Heb 6:10 2873
I know thy works, and thy l ... Rev 2:2 2873

LABOURED
So we l in the work ... Neh 4:21 6213
That which he l for shall he ... Job 20:18 3022
on the labour that I had l to do ... Eccl 2:11 5998
all my labour wherein I have l ... Eccl 2:19 5998
yet to a man that hath not l ... Eccl 2:21 5998
wherein he hath l under the sun ... Eccl 2:22 6001
hath he that hath l for the wind ... Eccl 5:16 5998
thou hast l from thy youth ... Is 47:12 3021
unto thee with whom thou hast l ... Is 47:15 3021
I have l in vain, I have spent my ... Is 49:4 3021
wine, for the which thou hast l ... Is 62:8 3021
he l till the going down of the ... Dan 6:14 7712
for the which thou hast not l ... Jonah 4:10 5998
other men l, and ye are entered ... Jn 4:38 2872
Persis, which l much in the Lord ... Rom 16:12 2872
but I l more abundantly than they ... 1Cor 15:10 2872
run in vain, neither l in vain ... Phil 2:16 2872
which l with me in the gospel ... Phil 4:3 4866
and for my name's sake hast l ... Rev 2:3 2872

LABOURER
for the l is worthy of his hire ... Lk 10:7 2040
The l is worthy of his reward ... 1Ti 5:18 2040

LABOURERS
is plenteous, but the l are few ... Mt 9:37 2040
send forth l into his harvest ... Mt 9:38 2040
to hire l into his vineyard ... Mt 20:1 2040
with the l for a penny a day ... Mt 20:2 2040
unto his steward, Call the l ... Mt 20:8 2040
truly is great, but the l are few ... Lk 10:2 2040
send forth l into his harvest ... Lk 10:2 2040
For we are l together with God ... 1Cor 3:9 4904
the hire of the l who have reaped ... Jas 5:4 2040

LABOURETH
He that l l for himself ... Prov 16:26 6001
He that l l for himself ... Prov 16:26 5998
that worketh in that wherein he l ... Eccl 3:9 6001
one that helpeth with us, and l ... 1Cor 16:16 2872
The husbandman that l must be ... 2Ti 2:6 2872

LABOURING
The sleep of a l man is sweet ... Eccl 5:12 5647
how that so l ye ought to support ... Acts 20:35 2872
always l fervently for you in ... Col 4:12 75
for l night and day, because we ... 1Th 2:9 2873

LABOURS
harvest, the firstfruits of thy l ... Ex 23:16 4639
in thy l out of the field ... Ex 23:16 4639
fruit of thy land, and all thy l ... Deut 28:33 3018
thy l be in the house of a ... Prov 5:10 6089
pleasure, and exact all your l ... Is 58:3 6092
this city, and all the l thereof ... Jer 20:5 3018
in all my l they shall find none ... Hos 12:8 3018
hail in all the l of your hands ... Hag 2:17 4639
and ye are entered into their l ... Jn 4:38 2873
imprisonments, in tumults, in l ... 2Cor 6:5 2873
that is, of other men's l ... 2Cor 10:15 2873
in l more abundant, in stripes ... 2Cor 11:23 2873
that they may rest from their l ... Rev 14:13 2873

LACE
of the ephod with a l of blue ... Ex 28:28 6616
And thou shalt put it on a blue l ... Ex 28:37 6616
of the ephod with a l of blue ... Ex 39:21 6616
And they tied unto it a l of blue ... Ex 39:31 6616

LACHISH (*la'-kish*) *An Amorite city.*
Jarmuth, and unto Japhia king of L ... Josh 10:3 3923
king of Jarmuth, the king of L ... Josh 10:5 3923
king of Jarmuth, the king of L ... Josh 10:23 3923
and all Israel with him, unto L ... Josh 10:31 3923
the LORD delivered L into the ... Josh 10:32 3923
king of Gezer came up to help L ... Josh 10:33 3923
from L Joshua passed unto Eglon, ... Josh 10:34 3923
to all that he had done to L ... Josh 10:35 3923
the king of L, one ... Josh 12:11 3923
L, and Bozkath, and Eglon, ... Josh 15:39 3923
and he fled to L ... 2Kin 14:19 3923
but they sent after him to L ... 2Kin 14:19 3923
sent to the king of Assyria to L ... 2Kin 18:14 3923
Rab-shakeh from L to king ... 2Kin 18:17 3923
heard that he was departed from L ... 2Kin 19:8 3923
And Adoraim, and L, and Azekah, ... 2Chr 11:9 3923
and he fled to L ... 2Chr 25:27 3923
but they sent to L after him ... 2Chr 25:27 3923
he himself laid siege against L ... 2Chr 32:9 3923
and in their villages, at L ... Neh 11:30 3923
of Assyria sent Rabshakeh from L ... Is 36:2 3923
heard that he was departed from L ... Is 37:8 3923
Judah that were left, against L ... Jer 34:7 3923
O thou inhabitant of L, bind the ... Mic 1:13 3923

LACK
Peradventure there shall l five ... Gen 18:28 2637
all the city for l of five ... Gen 18:28
he that gathered little had no l ... Ex 16:18 2637
thou shalt not l any thing in it ... Deut 8:9 2637
old lion perisheth for l of prey ... Job 4:11 1097
God, they wander for l of meat ... Job 38:41 1097
The young lions do l, and suffer ... Ps 34:10 7326
giveth unto the poor shall not l ... Prov 28:27 4270
and let thy head l no ointment ... Eccl 9:8 2637
are destroyed for l of knowledge ... Hos 4:6 1097
what l I yet ... Mt 19:20 5302
that had gathered little had no l ... 2Cor 8:15 1641
to supply your l of service ... Phil 2:30 5303
and that ye may have l of nothing ... 1Th 4:12 5332
If any of you l wisdom, let him ... Jas 1:5 3007

LACKED
thou hast l nothing ... Deut 2:7 2637
there l of David's servants ... 2Sa 2:30 6485
by the morning light there l not ... 2Sa 17:22 5737
they l nothing ... 1Kin 4:27 5737
him, But what hast thou l with me ... 1Kin 11:22 2638
so that they l nothing ... Neh 9:21 2637
away, because it l moisture ... Lk 8:6
scrip, and shoes, l ye any thing ... Lk 22:35 5302
was there any among them that l ... Acts 4:34 1729
honour to that part which l ... 1Cor 12:24 5302
careful, but ye l opportunity ... Phil 4:10 170

LACKEST
said unto him, One thing thou l ... Mk 10:21 5302
unto him, Yet l thou one thing ... Lk 18:22 3007

LACKETH
there *l* not one man of us — Num 31:49 — 6485
on the sword, or that *l* bread — 2Sa 3:29 — 2638
with a woman *l* understanding — Prov 6:32 — 2638
honoureth himself, and *l* bread — Prov 12:9 — 2638
But he that *l* these things is — 2Pet 1:9

LACKING
to be *l* from thy meat offering — Lev 2:13 — 7673
superfluous or *l* in his parts — Lev 22:23 — 7038
be to day one tribe *l* in Israel — Judg 21:3 — 6485
And there was nothing *l* to them — 1Sa 30:19 — 5737
dismayed, neither shall they be *l* — Jer 23:4 — 6485
for that which was *l* on your part — 1Cor 16:17 — *5303*
for that which was *l* to me the — 2Cor 11:9 — *5303*
that which is *l* in your faith — 1Th 3:10 — *5303*

LAD
in thy sight because of the *l* — Gen 21:12 — 5288
And God heard the voice of the *l* — Gen 21:17 — 5288
the voice of the *l* where he is — Gen 21:17 — 5288
Arise, lift up the *l*, and hold him — Gen 21:18 — 5288
with water, and gave the *l* drink — Gen 21:19 — 5288
And God was with the *l* — Gen 21:20 — 5288
the *l* will go yonder and worship, — Gen 22:5 — 5288
Lay not thine hand upon the *l* — Gen 22:12 — 5288
the *l* was with the sons of Bilhah — Gen 37:2 — 5288
his father, Send the *l* with me — Gen 43:8 — 5288
The *l* cannot leave his father — Gen 44:22 — 5288
father, and the *l* be not with us — Gen 44:30 — 5288
seeth that the *l* is not with us — Gen 44:31 — 5288
surety for the *l* unto my father — Gen 44:32 — 5288
of the *l* a bondman to my lord — Gen 44:33 — 5288
let the *l* go up with his brethren — Gen 44:33 — 5288
father, and the *l* be not with me — Gen 44:34 — 5288
Samson said unto the *l* that held — Judg 16:26 — 5288
And, behold, I will send a *l* — 1Sa 20:21 — 5288
If I expressly say unto the *l* — 1Sa 20:21 — 5288
David, and a little *l* with him — 1Sa 20:35 — 5288
And he said unto his *l*, Run, find — 1Sa 20:36 — 5288
And as the *l* ran, he shot an arrow — 1Sa 20:36 — 5288
when the *l* was come to the place — 1Sa 20:37 — 5288
shot, Jonathan cried after the *l* — 1Sa 20:37 — 5288
And Jonathan cried after the *l* — 1Sa 20:38 — 5288
Jonathan's *l* gathered up the — 1Sa 20:38 — 5288
But the *l* knew not any thing — 1Sa 20:39 — 5288
gave his artillery unto his *l* — 1Sa 20:40 — 5288
And as soon as the *l* was gone — 1Sa 20:41 — 5288
Nevertheless a *l* saw them — 2Sa 17:18 — 5288
And he said to a *l*, Carry him to — 2Kin 4:19 — 5288
There is a *l* here, which hath — Jn 6:9 — *3808*

LADAN See Laadan.

LADDER
behold a *l* set up on the earth, — Gen 28:12 — 5551

LADE
l your beasts, and go, get you — Gen 45:17 — 2943
did I you with a heavy yoke — 1Kin 12:11 — 6006
for ye *l* men with burdens — Lk 11:46 — *5412*

LADED
they *l* their asses with the corn, — Gen 42:26 — 5375
l every man his ass, and returned — Gen 44:13 — 6006
bare burdens, with those that *l* — Neh 4:17 — 6006
they *l* us with such things as — Acts 28:10 — *2007*

LADEN
ten asses *l* with the good things — Gen 45:23 — 5375
and ten she asses *l* with corn — Gen 45:23 — 5375
And Jesse took an ass *l* with bread — 1Sa 16:20
a people *l* with iniquity, a seed — Is 1:4 — 3515
all ye that labour and are heavy *l* — Mt 11:28 — *5412*
captive silly women *l* with sins — 2Ti 3:6 — *4987*

LADETH
to him that *l* himself with thick — Hab 2:6 — 3515

LADIES
Her wise *l* answered her, yea, she — Judg 5:29 — 8282
Likewise shall the *l* of Persia — Est 1:18 — 8282

LADING
bringing in sheaves, and *l* asses — Neh 13:15 — 6006
and much damage, not only of the *l* — Acts 27:10 — *5414*

LAD'S
life is bound up in the *l* life — Gen 44:30 — 5288

LADS
me from all evil, bless the *l* — Gen 48:16 — 5288

LADY
more be called, The *l* of kingdoms — Is 47:5 — 1404
saidst, I shall be a *l* for ever — Is 47:7 — 1404
The elder unto the elect *l* — 2Jn 1 — *2959*
And now I beseech thee, *l*, not as — 2Jn 5 — *2959*

LAEL (*la'-el*) *A Levite.*
shall be Eliasaph the son of *L* — Num 3:24 — 3815

LAHAD (*la'-had*) *Great-grandson of Shobal.*
and Jahath begat Ahumai, and *L* — 1Chr 4:2 — 3854

LAHAI-ROI (*la-hah'-ee-roy*) See Beer-lahai-roi. *A well in Paran.*
came from the way of the well *L* — Gen 24:62 — 883
and Isaac dwelt by the well *L* — Gen 25:11 — 883

LAHMAM (*lah'-mam*) *A city in Judah.*
And Cabbon, and *L*, and Kithlish, — Josh 15:40 — 3903

LAHMAS See Lahmam.

LAHMI (*lah'-mi*) See Bethlehemite. *A brother of Goliath.*
slew *L* the brother of Goliath the — 1Chr 20:5 — 3902

LAID
l it upon both their shoulders, — Gen 9:23 — 7760
l each piece one against another — Gen 15:10 — 5414
the men *l* hold upon his hand, and — Gen 19:16
and *l* it upon Isaac his son — Gen 22:6 — 7760
l the wood in order, and bound — Gen 22:9
l him on the altar upon the wood — Gen 22:9 — 7760
that Jacob *l* the rods before the — Gen 30:41 — 7760
l by her vail from her, and put on — Gen 38:19 — 5493
she *l* up his garment by her, — Gen 39:16 — 3241
l up the food in the cities — Gen 41:48 — 5414
every city, *l* he up in the same — Gen 41:48 — 5414
l it upon Ephraim's head, who was — Gen 48:14 — 7896
l his right hand upon the head of — Gen 48:17 — 7896
she *l* it in the flags by the — Ex 2:3 — 7760
there more work be *l* upon the men — Ex 5:9 — 3515
they *l* it up till the morning, as — Ex 16:24 — 3241
so Aaron *l* it up before the — Ex 16:34 — 3241
l before their faces all these — Ex 19:7 — 7760
If there be *l* on him a sum of — Ex 21:30 — 7896
his life whatsoever is *l* upon him — Ex 21:30 — 7896
of Israel he *l* not his hand — Ex 24:11 — 7971
his sons *l* their hands upon the — Lev 8:14 — 5564
his sons *l* their hands upon the — Lev 8:18 — 5564
his sons *l* their hands upon the — Lev 8:22 — 5564
l incense thereon, and stood in — Num 16:18 — 7760
Moses *l* up the rods before the — Num 17:7 — 3241
we have *l* them waste even unto — Num 21:30
he *l* his hands upon him, and gave — Num 27:23 — 5564
us, and *l* upon us hard bondage — Deut 26:6 — 5414
which the Lord hath *l* upon it — Deut 29:22 — 2470
Is not this *l* up in store with me — Deut 32:34 — 3647
for Moses had *l* his hands upon — Deut 34:9 — 5564
which she had *l* in order upon the — Josh 2:6
And before they were *l* down — Josh 2:8 — 7901
they lodged, and *l* them down there — Josh 4:8 — 3241
l them out before the Lord — Josh 7:23 — 3332
l great stones in the cave's — Josh 10:27 — 7760
their blood be *l* upon Abimelech — Judg 9:24 — 7760
they *l* wait against Shechem in — Judg 9:34
l wait in the field, and looked, — Judg 9:43
l it on his shoulder, and said — Judg 9:48 — 7760
l wait for him all night in the — Judg 16:2
l hold on his concubine, and — Judg 19:29
uncovered his feet, and *l* her down — Ruth 3:7 — 7901
of barley, and *l* it on her — Ruth 3:15 — 7896
l it in her bosom, and became — Ruth 4:16 — 7896
when Eli was *l* down in his place, — 1Sa 3:2 — 7901
Samuel was *l* down to sleep — 1Sa 3:3 — 7901
they *l* the ark of the Lord upon — 1Sa 6:11 — 7760
book, and *l* it up before the Lord — 1Sa 10:25 — 3241
how he *l* wait for him in the way, — 1Sa 15:2 — 7760
Amalek, and *l* wait in the valley — 1Sa 15:5
he *l* hold upon the skirt of his — 1Sa 15:27
l it in the bed, and put a pillow — 1Sa 19:13 — 7760
David *l* up these words in his — 1Sa 21:12 — 7760
cakes of figs, and *l* them on asses — 1Sa 25:18 — 7760
and he was *l* down — 2Sa 13:8 — 7901
l her hand on her head, and went — 2Sa 13:19 — 7760
l a very great heap of stones — 2Sa 18:17 — 5324
l it in her bosom — 1Kin 3:20 — 7901
l her dead child in my bosom — 1Kin 3:20 — 7901
of the house of the Lord *l* — 1Kin 6:37
an oath be *l* upon him to cause — 1Kin 8:31 — 5375
l it upon the ass, and brought it — 1Kin 13:29 — 3241
he *l* his carcase in his own grave — 1Kin 13:30 — 3241
all Israel *l* siege to Gibbethon — 1Kin 15:27
he *l* the foundation thereof in — 1Kin 16:34
abode, and *l* him upon his own bed — 1Kin 17:19 — 7901
l him on the wood, and said, Fill — 1Kin 18:33 — 7760
eat and drink, and *l* him down again — 1Kin 19:6 — 7901
he *l* him down upon his bed, and — 1Kin 21:4 — 7901
l him on the bed of the man of — 2Kin 4:21 — 7901
l the staff upon the face of the — 2Kin 4:31 — 7760
child was dead, and *l* upon his bed — 2Kin 4:32 — 7901
l them upon two of his servants — 2Kin 5:23 — 5414
the Lord *l* this burden upon him — 2Kin 9:25 — 5375
And they *l* hands on her — 2Kin 11:16 — 7760
they *l* it out to the carpenters — 2Kin 12:11 — 3318
for all that was *l* out for the — 2Kin 12:12 — 3318
l it on the boil, and he recovered — 2Kin 20:7 — 7760
have *l* up in store unto this day — 2Kin 20:17
an oath be *l* upon him to make him — 2Chr 6:22 — 5375
and *l* hold on other gods, and — 2Chr 7:22
l him in the bed which was filled — 2Chr 16:14 — 7901
So they *l* hands on her — 2Chr 23:15 — 7760
l upon Israel in the wilderness — 2Chr 24:9
of the burdens *l* upon him — 2Chr 24:27
they *l* their hands upon them — 2Chr 29:23 — 5564
their God, and *l* them by heaps — 2Chr 31:6 — 5414
(but he himself *l* siege against — 2Chr 32:9
temple of the Lord was not yet *l* — Ezr 3:6
And when the builders *l* the — Ezr 3:10
of the house of the Lord was *l* — Ezr 3:11
house was *l* before their eyes — Ezr 3:12
timber is *l* in the walls, and this — Ezr 5:8 — 7760
l the foundation of the house of — Ezr 5:16 — 3052
treasures were *l* up in Babylon — Ezr 6:1 — 5182
foundations thereof be strongly *l* — Ezr 6:3 — 5446
who also *l* the beams thereof, and — Neh 3:3
they *l* the beams thereof, and set — Neh 3:6
they *l* the meat offerings — Neh 13:5 — 5414
because he *l* his hand upon the — Est 8:7 — 7971
but on the spoil *l* they not their — Est 9:10 — 7971
on the prey they *l* not their hand — Est 9:15 — 7971
but they *l* not their hands on the — Est 9:16 — 7971
the king Ahasuerus *l* a tribute — Est 10:1 — 7760
my calamity *l* in the balances — Job 6:2 — 5375
The snare is *l* for him in the — Job 18:10
l their hand on their mouth — Job 29:9 — 7760
or if I have *l* wait at my — Job 31:9
Where wast thou when I *l* the — Job 38:4
Who hath *l* the measures thereof, — Job 38:5 — 7760
or who *l* the corner stone thereof — Job 38:6 — 3384
I *l* me down and slept — Ps 3:5 — 7901
and majesty hast thou *l* upon him — Ps 21:5 — 7737
that they have *l* privily for me — Ps 31:4 — 2934
which thou hast *l* up for them — Ps 31:19 — 6845
they *l* to my charge things that I — Ps 35:11
sheep they are *l* in the grave — Ps 49:14 — 8371
to be *l* in the balance, they are — Ps 62:9 — 5927
they have *l* Jerusalem on heaps — Ps 79:1 — 7760
l waste his dwelling place — Ps 79:7
Thou hast *l* me in the lowest pit, — Ps 88:6 — 7896
I have *l* help upon one that is — Ps 89:19 — 7737
Of old hast thou *l* the foundation — Ps 102:25
Who *l* the foundations of the — Ps 104:5
he was *l* in iron — Ps 105:18 — 935
thy judgments have I *l* before me — Ps 119:30 — 7737
The wicked have *l* a snare for me — Ps 119:110 — 5414
before, and *l* thine hand upon me — Ps 139:5 — 7896
snares which they have *l* for me — Ps 141:9 — 3369
they privily *l* a snare for me — Ps 142:3 — 2934
the sinner is *l* up for the just — Prov 13:22 — 6845
old, which I have *l* up for thee — Song 7:13 — 6845
he *l* it upon my mouth, and said, — Is 6:7 — 5060
he hath *l* up his carriages — Is 10:28 — 6485
saying, Since thou art *l* down — Is 14:8 — 7901
the night Ar of Moab is *l* waste — Is 15:1
the night Kir of Moab is *l* waste — Is 15:1
and that which they have *l* up — Is 15:7 — 6486
for it is *l* waste, so that there — Is 23:1
for your strength is *l* waste — Is 23:14
shall not be treasured nor *l* up — Is 23:18 — 2630
have *l* waste all the nations — Is 37:18
have *l* up in store until this day — Is 39:6
him, yet he *l* it not to heart — Is 42:25 — 7760
temple, Thy foundation shall be *l* — Is 44:28
hast thou very heavily *l* thy yoke — Is 47:6
Mine hand also hath *l* the — Is 48:13
l the foundations of the earth — Is 51:13
thou hast *l* thy body as the — Is 51:23 — 7760
the Lord hath *l* on him the — Is 53:6 — 6293
me, nor *l* it to thy heart — Is 57:11 — 7760
our pleasant things are *l* waste — Is 64:11
and thy cities shall be *l* waste — Jer 4:7
should this city be *l* waste — Jer 27:17
but they *l* up the roll in the — Jer 36:20 — 6485
I have *l* a snare for thee, and — Jer 50:24
they *l* wait for us in the — Lam 4:19
For I have *l* upon thee the years — Eze 4:5 — 5414
the cities shall be *l* waste — Eze 6:6
that your altars may be *l* waste — Eze 6:6
whom ye have *l* in the midst of it — Eze 11:7 — 7760
are inhabited shall be *l* waste — Eze 12:20
and he *l* waste their cities — Eze 19:7
replenished, now she is *l* waste — Eze 26:2
among the cities that are *l* waste — Eze 29:12
be thou *l* with the uncircumcised — Eze 32:19 — 7901
they have *l* their swords under — Eze 32:27 — 5414
which with their might are *l* by — Eze 32:29 — 5414
he shall be *l* in the midst of the — Eze 32:32 — 7901
when I have *l* the land most — Eze 33:29 — 5414
saying, They are *l* desolate — Eze 35:12
my hand that I have *l* upon them — Eze 39:21 — 7760
whereupon also they *l* the — Eze 40:42 — 3240
l upon the mouth of the den — Dan 6:17 — 7760
their jaws, and I *l* meat unto them — Hos 11:4 — 5186
He hath *l* my vine waste, and — Joel 1:7 — 7760
clods, the garners are *l* desolate — Joel 1:17
l to pledge by every altar — Amos 2:8
of Israel shall be *l* waste — Amos 7:9
bread have *l* a wound under thee — Obad 7 — 7760
nor have *l* hands on their — Obad 13 — 7971
he *l* his robe from him, and — Jonah 3:6 — 5674
he hath *l* siege against us — Mic 5:1 — 7760
thee, and say, Nineveh is *l* waste — Nah 3:7
it is *l* over with gold and silver, — Hab 2:19 — 8610
from before a stone was *l* upon a — Hag 2:15 — 7760
of the Lord's temple was *l* — Hag 2:18
stone that I have *l* before Joshua — Zec 3:9 — 5414
l the foundation of this house — Zec 4:9
for they *l* the pleasant land — Zec 7:14 — 7760
house of the Lord of hosts was *l* — Zec 8:9
l his mountains and his heritage — Mal 1:3 — 7760
now also the ax is *l* unto the — Mt 3:10 — *2749*
house, he saw his wife's mother *l* — Mt 8:14 — *906*
For Herod had *l* hold on John — Mt 14:3
he *l* hands on him, and took him by — Mt 18:28
he *l* his hands on them, and — Mt 19:15 — *2007*
l hands on Jesus, and took him — Mt 26:50 — *1911*
the temple, and ye *l* no hold on me — Mt 26:55
they that had *l* hold on Jesus led — Mt 26:57
l it in his own new tomb, which — Mt 27:60 — *5087*
save that he *l* his hands upon a — Mk 6:5 — *2007*
l hold upon John, and bound him in — Mk 6:17
up his corpse, and *l* it in a tomb — Mk 6:29 — *5087*
they *l* the sick in the streets, — Mk 6:56 — *5087*
and her daughter *l* upon the bed — Mk 7:30 — *906*
they *l* their hands on him, and — Mk 14:46 — *1911*
and the young men *l* hold on him — Mk 14:51
l him in a sepulchre which was — Mk 15:46 — *2698*
of Joses beheld where he was *l* — Mk 15:47 — *5087*
behold the place where they *l* him — Mk 16:6 — *5087*
them *l* them up in their hearts — Lk 1:66 — *5087*
clothes, and *l* him in a manger — Lk 2:7 — *347*
now also the axe is *l* unto the — Lk 3:9 — *2749*
he *l* his hands on every one of — Lk 4:40 — *2007*
l the foundation on a rock — Lk 6:48 — *5087*
much goods *l* up for many years — Lk 12:19 — *2749*
And he *l* his hands on her — Lk 13:13 — *2007*
after he hath *l* the foundation, — Lk 14:29 — *5087*
which was *l* at his gate, full of — Lk 16:20 — *906*
I have kept *l* up in a napkin — Lk 19:20 — *606*
man, taking up that I *l* not down — Lk 19:22 — *5087*
they *l* hold upon one Simon, a — Lk 23:26
and on him they *l* the cross — Lk 23:26 — *2007*
l it in a sepulchre that was hewn — Lk 23:53 — *5087*
wherein never man before was *l* — Lk 23:53 — *2749*
sepulchre, and how his body was *l* — Lk 23:55 — *5087*
the linen clothes *l* by themselves — Lk 24:12 — *2749*
but no man *l* hands on him, — Jn 7:30 — *1911*
but no man *l* hands on him — Jn 7:44 — *1911*

and no man *l* hands on him ... Jn 8:20
And said, Where have ye *l* him ... Jn 11:34 *5087*
the place where the dead was *l* ... Jn 11:41 *2749*
supper, and *l* aside his garments ... Jn 13:4 *5087*
wherein was never man yet *l* ... Jn 19:41 *5087*
There *l* they Jesus therefore ... Jn 19:42 *5087*
we know not where they have *l* him ... Jn 20:2 *5087*
I know not where they have *l* him ... Jn 20:13 *5087*
tell me where thou hast *l* him ... Jn 20:15 *5087*
and fish *l* thereon, and bread ... Jn 21:9 *1945*
whom they *l* daily at the gate of ... Acts 3:2 *5087*
they *l* hands on them, and put them ... Acts 4:3 *1911*
l them down at the apostles' feet ... Acts 4:35 *5087*
l it at the apostles' feet ... Acts 4:37 *5087*
l it at the apostles' feet ... Acts 5:2 *5087*
l them on beds and couches, that ... Acts 5:15 *5087*
l their hands on the apostles, and ... Acts 5:18 *1911*
they *l* their hands on them ... Acts 6:6 *2007*
l in the sepulchre that Abraham ... Acts 7:16 *5087*
the witnesses *l* down their ... Acts 7:58 *659*
Then *l* they their hands on them, ... Acts 8:17 *2007*
they *l* her in an upper chamber ... Acts 9:37 *5087*
l their hands on them, they sent ... Acts 13:3 *2007*
the tree, and *l* him in a sepulchre ... Acts 13:29 *5087*
was *l* unto his fathers, and saw ... Acts 13:36 *4369*
when they had *l* many stripes upon ... Acts 16:23 *2007*
when Paul had *l* his hands upon ... Acts 19:6 *2007*
And when the Jews *l* wait for him ... Acts 20:3 *1096*
the people, and *l* hands on him, ... Acts 21:27 *1911*
but to have nothing *l* to his ... Acts 23:29 *1462*
that the Jews *l* wait for the man ... Acts 23:30 *2071*
l many and grievous complaints ... Acts 25:7 *5342*
the crime *l* against him ... Acts 25:16 *1462*
signify the crimes *l* against him ... Acts 25:27
l them on the fire, there came a ... Acts 28:3 *2007*
l his hands on him, and healed him ... Acts 28:8 *2007*
my life *l* down their own necks ... Rom 16:4 *5294*
I have *l* the foundation, and ... 1Cor 3:10 *5087*
can no man lay than that is *l* ... 1Cor 3:11 *5087*
for necessity is *l* upon me ... 1Cor 9:16 *1945*
which is *l* up for you in heaven ... Col 1:5 *606*
Henceforth there is *l* up for me a ... 2Ti 4:8 *606*
it may not be *l* to their charge ... 2Ti 4:16 *3049*
in the beginning hast *l* the ... Heb 1:10
because he *l* down his life for us ... 1Jn 3:16 *5087*
he *l* his right hand upon me, ... Rev 1:17 *2007*
he *l* hold on the dragon, that old ... Rev 20:2

LAIDST
thou *l* affliction upon our loins ... Ps 66:11 7760

LAIN
woman, If no man have *l* with thee ... Num 5:19 7901
some man have *l* with thee beside ... Num 5:20
and every woman that hath *l* by man ... Judg 21:11
For now should I have *l* still ... Job 3:13 7901
he found that he had *l* in the ... Jn 11:17
where the body of Jesus had *l* ... Jn 20:12 *2749*

LAISH (*la'-ish*) See Dan, Leshem.
1. Same as the city of Dan.
five men departed, and came to *L* ... Judg 18:7 3919
went to spy out the country of *L* ... Judg 18:14 3919
which he had, and came unto *L* ... Judg 18:27 3919
of the city was *L* at the first ... Judg 18:29 3919
cause it to be heard unto *L* ... Is 10:30 3919
2. Father of Phaltiel.
wife, to Phalti the son of *L* ... 1Sa 25:44 3919
even from Phaltiel the son of *L* ... 2Sa 3:15 3919

LAKE
he stood by the *l* of Gennesaret ... Lk 5:1 *3041*
saw two ships standing by the *l* ... Lk 5:2 *3041*
over unto the other side of the *l* ... Lk 8:22 *3041*
down a storm of wind on the *l* ... Lk 8:23 *3041*
down a steep place into the *l* ... Lk 8:33 *3041*
both were cast alive into a *l* of ... Rev 19:20 *3041*
them was cast into the *l* of fire ... Rev 20:10 *3041*
hell were cast into the *l* of fire ... Rev 20:14 *3041*
life was cast into the *l* of fire ... Rev 20:15 *3041*
in the *l* which burneth with fire ... Rev 21:8 *3041*

LAKKUM See Lakum.

LAKUM (*la'-kum*) *A city in Naphtali.*
Adami, Nekeb, and Jabneel, unto *L* ... Josh 19:33 3946

LAMA
saying, Eli, Eli, *l* sabachthani ... Mt 27:46 *2982*
saying, Eloi, Eloi, *l* sabachthani ... Mk 15:34 *2982*

LAMB
but where is the *l* for a burnt ... Gen 22:7 7716
himself a *l* for a burnt offering ... Gen 22:8 7716
shall take to them every man a *l* ... Ex 12:3 7716
their fathers, a *l* for an house ... Ex 12:3 7716
household be too little for the *l* ... Ex 12:4 7716
shall make your count for the *l* ... Ex 12:4 7716
Your *l* shall be without blemish, ... Ex 12:5 7716
take you a *l* according to your ... Ex 12:21 6629
an ass thou shalt redeem with a *l* ... Ex 13:13 7716
The one *l* thou shalt offer in the ... Ex 29:39 3532
the other *l* thou shalt offer at ... Ex 29:39 3532
with the one *l* a tenth deal of ... Ex 29:40 3532
the other *l* thou shalt offer at ... Ex 29:41 3532
an ass thou shalt redeem with a *l* ... Ex 34:20 7716
If he offer a *l* for his offering, ... Lev 3:7 3775
if he bring a *l* for a sin ... Lev 4:32 3532
as the fat of the *l* is taken away ... Lev 4:35 3775
a *l* or a kid of the goats, for a ... Lev 5:6 3776
And if he be not able to bring a *l* ... Lev 5:7 7716
and a calf and a *l*, both of the ... Lev 9:3 3532
she shall bring a *l* of the first ... Lev 12:6 3532
if she be not able to bring a *l* ... Lev 12:8 7716
one ewe *l* of the first year ... Lev 14:10 3535
And the priest shall take one he *l* ... Lev 14:12 3532
he shall slay the *l* in the place ... Lev 14:13 3532
then he shall take one *l* for a ... Lev 14:21 3532
the *l* of the trespass offering ... Lev 14:24 3532
he shall kill the *l* of the ... Lev 14:25 3532
Israel, that killeth an ox, or *l* ... Lev 17:3 3775
Either a bullock or a *l* that hath ... Lev 22:23 7716
he *l* without blemish of the first ... Lev 23:12 3532
shall bring a *l* of the first year ... Num 6:12 3532
one he *l* of the first year ... Num 6:14 3532
one ewe *l* of the first year ... Num 6:14 3535
one *l* of the first year, for a ... Num 7:15 3532
one *l* of the first year, for a ... Num 7:21 3532
one *l* of the first year, for a ... Num 7:27 3532
one *l* of the first year, for a ... Num 7:33 3532
one *l* of the first year, for a ... Num 7:39 3532
one *l* of the first year, for a ... Num 7:45 3532
one *l* of the first year, for a ... Num 7:51 3532
one *l* of the first year, for a ... Num 7:57 3532
one *l* of the first year, for a ... Num 7:63 3532
one *l* of the first year, for a ... Num 7:69 3532
one *l* of the first year, for a ... Num 7:75 3532
one *l* of the first year, for a ... Num 7:81 3532
offering or sacrifice, for one *l* ... Num 15:5 3532
or for one ram, or for a *l* ... Num 15:11 7716
The one *l* shalt thou offer in the ... Num 28:4 3532
the other *l* shalt thou offer at ... Num 28:4 3532
part of an hin for the one *l* ... Num 28:7 3532
the other *l* shalt thou offer at ... Num 28:8 3532
for a meat offering unto one *l* ... Num 28:13 3532
a fourth part of an hin unto a *l* ... Num 28:14 3532
deal shalt thou offer for every *l* ... Num 28:21 3532
A several tenth deal unto one *l* ... Num 28:29 3532
And one tenth deal for one *l* ... Num 29:4 3532
A several tenth deal for one *l* ... Num 29:10 3532
to each *l* of the fourteen lambs ... Num 29:15 3532
And Samuel took a sucking *l* ... 1Sa 7:9 2924
took a *l* out of the flock ... 1Sa 17:34 7716
nothing, save one little ewe *l* ... 2Sa 12:3 3535
but took the poor man's *l* ... 2Sa 12:4 3535
he shall restore the *l* fourfold ... 2Sa 12:6 3535
wolf also shall dwell with the *l* ... Is 11:6 3532
Send ye the *l* to the ruler of the ... Is 16:1 3733
brought as a *l* to the slaughter ... Is 53:7 7716
the *l* shall feed together, and the ... Is 65:25 2924
he that sacrificeth a *l*, as if he ... Is 66:3 7716
But I was like a *l* or an ox that ... Jer 11:19 3532
one *l* out of the flock, out of ... Eze 45:15 7716
of a *l* of the first year without ... Eze 46:13 3532
Thus shall they prepare the *l* ... Eze 46:15 3532
feed them as a *l* in a large place ... Hos 4:16 3532
and saith, Behold the *L* of God ... Jn 1:29 *286*
he saith, Behold the *L* of God ... Jn 1:36 *286*
like a *l* dumb before his shearer, ... Acts 8:32 *286*
as of a *l* without blemish and ... 1Pet 1:19 *286*
stood a *L* as it had been slain, ... Rev 5:6 *721*
elders fell down before the *L* ... Rev 5:8 *721*
Worthy is the *L* that was slain to ... Rev 5:12 *721*
throne, and unto the *L* for ever ... Rev 5:13 *721*
I saw when the *L* opened one of ... Rev 6:1 *721*
and from the wrath of the *L* ... Rev 6:16 *721*
the throne, and before the *L* ... Rev 7:9 *721*
upon the throne, and unto the *L* ... Rev 7:10 *721*
them white in the blood of the *L* ... Rev 7:14 *721*
For the *L* which is in the midst ... Rev 7:17 *721*
him by the blood of the *L* ... Rev 12:11 *721*
in the book of life of the *L* ... Rev 13:8 *721*
and he had two horns like a *l* ... Rev 13:11 *721*
a *L* stood on the mount Sion, and ... Rev 14:1 *721*
the *L* whithersoever he goeth ... Rev 14:4 *721*
firstfruits unto God and to the *L* ... Rev 14:4 *721*
and in the presence of the *L* ... Rev 14:10 *721*
of God, and the song of the *L* ... Rev 15:3 *721*
These shall make war with the *L* ... Rev 17:14 *721*
the *L* shall overcome them ... Rev 17:14 *721*
for the marriage of the *L* is come ... Rev 19:7 *721*
unto the marriage supper of the *L* ... Rev 19:9 *721*
of the twelve apostles of the *L* ... Rev 21:14 *721*
the *L* are the temple of it ... Rev 21:22 *721*
the *L* is the light thereof ... Rev 21:23 *721*
of the throne of God and of the *L* ... Rev 22:1 *721*
of God and of the *L* shall be in it ... Rev 22:3 *721*

LAMB'S
shew thee the bride, the *L* wife ... Rev 21:9 *721*
are written in the *L* book of life ... Rev 21:27 *721*

LAMBS
Abraham set seven ewe *l* of the ... Gen 21:28 3535
ewe *l* which thou hast set by ... Gen 21:29 3535
For these seven ewe *l* shalt thou ... Gen 21:30 3535
And Jacob did separate the *l* ... Gen 30:40 3775
two *l* of the first year day by ... Ex 29:38 3532
take two he *l* without blemish ... Lev 14:10 3532
offer with the bread seven *l* ... Lev 23:18 3532
two *l* of the first year for a ... Lev 23:19 3532
before the Lord, with the two *l* ... Lev 23:20 3532
goats, five *l* of the first year ... Num 7:17 3532
goats, five *l* of the first year ... Num 7:23 3532
goats, five *l* of the first year ... Num 7:29 3532
goats, five *l* of the first year ... Num 7:35 3532
goats, five *l* of the first year ... Num 7:41 3532
goats, five *l* of the first year ... Num 7:47 3532
goats, five *l* of the first year ... Num 7:53 3532
goats, five *l* of the first year ... Num 7:59 3532
goats, five *l* of the first year ... Num 7:65 3532
goats, five *l* of the first year ... Num 7:71 3532
goats, five *l* of the first year ... Num 7:77 3532
goats, five *l* of the first year ... Num 7:83 3532
the *l* of the first year twelve, ... Num 7:87 3532
the *l* of the first year sixty ... Num 7:88 3532
two *l* of the first year without ... Num 28:3 3532
on the sabbath day two *l* of the ... Num 28:9 3532
seven *l* of the first year without ... Num 28:11 3532
seven *l* of the first year ... Num 28:19 3532
lamb, throughout the seven *l* ... Num 28:21 3532
seven *l* of the first year ... Num 28:27 3532
one lamb, throughout the seven *l* ... Num 28:29 3532
seven *l* of the first year without ... Num 29:2 3532
one lamb, throughout the seven *l* ... Num 29:4 3532
seven *l* of the first year ... Num 29:8 3532
one lamb, throughout the seven *l* ... Num 29:10 3532
fourteen *l* of the first year ... Num 29:13 3532
to each lamb of the fourteen *l* ... Num 29:15 3532
fourteen *l* of the first year ... Num 29:17 3532
for the rams, and for the *l* ... Num 29:18 3532
fourteen *l* of the first year ... Num 29:20 3532
for the rams, and for the *l* ... Num 29:21 3532
fourteen *l* of the first year ... Num 29:23 3532
for the rams, and for the *l* ... Num 29:24 3532
fourteen *l* of the first year ... Num 29:26 3532
for the rams, and for the *l* ... Num 29:27 3532
fourteen *l* of the first year ... Num 29:29 3532
for the rams, and for the *l* ... Num 29:30 3532
fourteen *l* of the first year ... Num 29:32 3532
for the rams, and for the *l* ... Num 29:33 3532
seven *l* of the first year without ... Num 29:36 3532
for the ram, and for the *l* ... Num 29:37 3532
and milk of sheep, with fat of *l* ... Deut 32:14 3733
and of the fatlings, and the *l* ... 1Sa 15:9 3733
of Israel an hundred thousand *l* ... 2Kin 3:4 3733
a thousand rams, and a thousand *l* ... 1Chr 29:21 3532
and seven rams, and seven *l* ... 2Chr 29:21 3532
they killed also the *l*, and they ... 2Chr 29:22 3532
an hundred rams, and two hundred *l* ... 2Chr 29:32 3532
to the people, of the flock, *l* ... 2Chr 35:7 3532
young bullocks, and rams, and *l* ... Ezr 6:9 563
two hundred rams, four hundred *l* ... Ezr 6:17 563
with this money bullocks, rams, *l* ... Ezr 7:17 563
and six rams, seventy and seven *l* ... Ezr 8:35 3532
the Lord shall be as the fat of *l* ... Ps 37:20 3733
rams, and the little hills like *l* ... Ps 114:4
and ye little hills, like *l* ... Ps 114:6
The *l* are for thy clothing, and ... Prov 27:26 3532
in the blood of bullocks, or of *l* ... Is 1:11 3532
Then shall the *l* feed after their ... Is 5:17 3532
fatness, and with the blood of *l* ... Is 34:6 3733
shall gather the *l* with his arm ... Is 40:11 2922
them down like *l* to the slaughter ... Jer 51:40 3733
they occupied with thee in *l* ... Eze 27:21 3733
of the earth, of rams, of *l* ... Eze 39:18 3733
shall be six *l* without blemish ... Eze 46:4 3532
the meat offering for the *l* as he ... Eze 46:5 3532
bullock without blemish, and six *l* ... Eze 46:6 3532
for the *l* according as his hand ... Eze 46:7 3532
to the *l* as he is able to give, ... Eze 46:11 3532
eat the *l* out of the flock, and ... Amos 6:4 3733
send you forth as *l* among wolves ... Lk 10:3 *704*
He saith unto him, Feed my *l* ... Jn 21:15 *721*

LAME
a blind man, or a *l*, or he that ... Lev 21:18 6455
blemish therein, as if it be *l* ... Deut 15:21 6455
had a son that was *l* of his feet ... 2Sa 4:4 5223
flee, that he fell, and became *l* ... 2Sa 4:4 6452
thou take away the blind and the *l* ... 2Sa 5:6 6455
smiteth the Jebusites, and the *l* ... 2Sa 5:8 6455
the *l* shall not come into the ... 2Sa 5:8 6455
yet a son, which is *l* on his feet ... 2Sa 9:3 5223
and was *l* on both his feet ... 2Sa 9:13 6455
because thy servant is *l* ... 2Sa 19:26 6455
the blind, and feet was I to the *l* ... Job 29:15 6455
The legs of the *l* are not equal ... Prov 26:7 6455
the *l* take the prey ... Is 33:23 6455
Then shall the *l* man leap as an ... Is 35:6 6455
and with them the blind and the *l* ... Jer 31:8 6455
and if ye offer the *l* and sick, is ... Mal 1:8 6455
that which was torn, and the *l* ... Mal 1:13 6455
the *l* walk, the lepers are ... Mt 11:5 *5560*
with them those that were *l* ... Mt 15:30 *5560*
the *l* to walk, and the blind to ... Mt 15:31 *5560*
the *l* came to him in the temple ... Mt 21:14 *5560*
the *l* walk, the lepers are ... Lk 7:22 *5560*
call the poor, the maimed, the *l* ... Lk 14:13 *5560*
a certain man *l* from his mother's ... Acts 3:2 *5560*
as the *l* man which was healed ... Acts 3:11 *5560*
with palsies, and that were *l* ... Acts 8:7 *5560*
lest that which is *l* be turned ... Heb 12:13 *5560*

LAMECH (*la'-mek*) *A son of Methusaleh.*
and Methusael begat *L* ... Gen 4:18 3929
L took unto him two wives ... Gen 4:19 3929
L said unto his wives, Adah and ... Gen 4:23 3929
ye wives of *L*, hearken unto my ... Gen 4:23 3929
truly *L* seventy and sevenfold ... Gen 4:24 3929
eighty and seven years, and begat *L* ... Gen 5:25 3929
he begat *L* seven hundred eighty ... Gen 5:26 3929
L lived an hundred eighty and two ... Gen 5:28 3929
L lived after he begat Noah five ... Gen 5:30 3929
all the days of *L* were seven ... Gen 5:31 3929
Henoch, Methuselah, *L*, ... 1Chr 1:3 3929
of Noe, which was the son of *L* ... Lk 3:36 *2984*

LAMENT
of Israel went yearly to *l* the ... Judg 11:40 8567
And her gates shall *l* and mourn ... Is 3:26 578
angle into the brooks shall *l* ... Is 19:8 56
They shall *l* for the teats, for ... Is 32:12 5594
this gird you with sackcloth, *l* ... Jer 4:8 5594
neither go to *l* nor bemoan them ... Jer 16:5 5594
neither shall men *l* for them ... Jer 16:6 5594
They shall not *l* for him, saying, ... Jer 22:18 5594
they shall not *l* for him, saying, ... Jer 22:18 5594
and they will *l* thee, saying, Ah ... Jer 34:5 5594
l, and run to and fro by the hedges ... Jer 49:3 5594
made the rampart and the wall to *l* ... Lam 2:8 56
l over thee, saying, What city is ... Eze 27:32 6969
wherewith they shall *l* her ... Eze 32:16 6969
of the nations shall *l* her ... Eze 32:16 6969
they shall *l* for her, even for ... Eze 32:16 6969
L like a virgin girded with ... Joel 1:8 421
Gird yourselves, and *l*, ye priests ... Joel 1:13 5594
l with a doleful lamentation, and ... Mic 2:4 5091

unto you, That ye shall weep and *l*....... Jn 16:20 *2354*
l for her, when they shall see................ Rev 18:9 *2875*

LAMENTABLE
he cried with a *l* voice unto.................. Dan 6:20 6088

LAMENTATION
with a great and very sore *l*.................. Gen 50:10 4553
lamented with this *l* over Saul............... 2Sa 1:17 7015
and their widows made no *l*..................... Ps 78:64 1058
as for an only son, most bitter *l*............ Jer 6:26 4553
take up a *l* on high places...................... Jer 7:29 7015
habitations of the wilderness a *l*.............. Jer 9:10 7015
and every one her neighbour *l*................. Jer 9:20 7015
A voice was heard in Ramah, *l*................. Jer 31:15 5092
There shall be *l* generally upon............... Jer 48:38 4553
daughter of Judah mourning and *l*........... Lam 2:5 592
Moreover take thou up a *l* for the............ Eze 19:1 7015
is a *l*, and shall be for a *l*....................... Eze 19:14 7015
they shall take up a *l* for thee................ Eze 26:17 7015
son of man, take up a *l* for Tyrus............ Eze 27:2 7015
they shall take up a *l* for thee................ Eze 27:32 7015
take up a *l* upon the king of.................... Eze 28:12 7015
take up a *l* for Pharaoh king of................ Eze 32:2 7015
This is the *l* wherewith they.................... Eze 32:16 7015
I take up against you, even a *l*................. Amos 5:1 7015
as are skilful of *l* to wailing..................... Amos 5:16 5092
and all your songs into *l*.......................... Amos 8:10 7015
you, and lament with a doleful *l*............... Mic 2:4 5092
Rama was there a voice heard, *l*............... Mt 2:18 *2355*
burial, and made great *l* over him............ Acts 8:2 *2870*

LAMENTATIONS
of Josiah in their *l* to this day................. 2Chr 35:25 7015
behold, they are written in the *l*............... 2Chr 35:25 7015
and there was written therein *l*................ Eze 2:10 7015

LAMENTED
and the people *l*, because the LORD.......... 1Sa 6:19 56
house of Israel *l* after the LORD................ 1Sa 7:2 5091
l him, and buried him in his house............ 1Sa 25:1 5594
was dead, and all Israel had *l* him............ 1Sa 28:3 5594
David *l* with this lamentation.................... 2Sa 1:17 6969
the king *l* over Abner, and said,................ 2Sa 3:33 6969
And Jeremiah *l* for Josiah......................... 2Chr 35:25 6969
they shall not be *l*...................................... Jer 16:4 5594
they shall not be *l*, neither......................... Jer 25:33 5594
unto you, and ye have not *l*...................... Mt 11:17 *2875*
which also bewailed and *l* him.................. Lk 23:27 *2354*

LAMP
a burning *l* that passed between.............. Gen 15:17 3940
to cause the *l* to burn always.................... Ex 27:20 5216
ere the *l* of God went out in the................. 1Sa 3:3 5216
For thou art my *l*, O LORD.......................... 2Sa 22:29 5216
his God give him a *l* in Jerusalem.............. 1Kin 15:4 5216
to slip with his feet is as a *l*.................... Job 12:5 3940
Thy word is a *l* unto my feet..................... Ps 119:105 5216
ordained a *l* for mine anointed.................. Ps 132:17 5216
For the commandment is a *l*..................... Prov 6:23 5216
but the *l* of the wicked shall be.................. Prov 13:9 5216
his *l* shall be put out in obscure................ Prov 20:20 5216
thereof as a *l* that burneth........................ Is 62:1 3940
heaven, burning as it were a *l*.................... Rev 8:10 *2985*

LAMPS
shalt make the seven *l* thereof.................. Ex 25:37 5216
and they shall light the *l* thereof............... Ex 25:37 5216
when he dresseth the *l*, he shall................. Ex 30:7 5216
when Aaron lighteth the *l* at even.............. Ex 30:8 5216
light, and his furniture, and his *l*............... Ex 35:14 5216
And he made his seven *l*, and his............... Ex 37:23 5216
candlestick, with the *l* thereof.................. Ex 39:37 5216
even with the *l* to be set in......................... Ex 39:37 5216
and light the *l* thereof................................ Ex 40:4 5216
he lighted the *l* before the LORD................ Ex 40:25 5216
the light, to cause the *l* to burn................ Lev 24:2 5216
He shall order the *l* upon the..................... Lev 24:4 5216
of the light, and his *l*, and his..................... Num 4:9 5216
him, When thou lightest the *l*..................... Num 8:2 5216
the seven *l* shall give light over................. Num 8:2 5216
he lighted the *l* thereof over..................... Num 8:3 5216
and *l* within the pitchers............................ Judg 7:16 3940
held the *l* in their left hands,..................... Judg 7:20 3940
with the flowers, and the *l*.......................... 1Kin 7:49 5216
of gold, and for their *l* of gold.................. 1Chr 28:15 5216
candlestick, and for the *l* thereof.............. 1Chr 28:15 5216
and also for the *l* thereof........................... 1Chr 28:15 5216
the candlesticks with their *l*....................... 2Chr 4:20 5216
And the flowers, and the *l*, and the............. 2Chr 4:21 5216
of gold with the *l* thereof.......................... 2Chr 13:11 5216
of the porch, and put out the *l*.................. 2Chr 29:7 5216
Out of his mouth go burning *l*................... Job 41:19 3940
fire, and like the appearance of *l*............... Eze 1:13 3940
and his eyes as *l* of fire............................. Dan 10:6 3940
top of it, and his seven *l* thereon............... Zec 4:2 5216
and seven pipes to the seven *l*.................... Zec 4:2 5216
ten virgins, which took their *l*.................... Mt 25:1 *2985*
that were foolish took their *l*..................... Mt 25:3 *2985*
oil in their vessels with their *l*................... Mt 25:4 *2985*
virgins arose, and trimmed their *l*............. Mt 25:7 *2985*
for our *l* are gone out................................... Mt 25:8 *2985*
there were seven *l* of fire............................ Rev 4:5 *2985*

LANCE
They shall hold the bow and the *l*............. Jer 50:42 3591

LANCETS
their manner with knives and *l*................... 1Kin 18:28 7420

LAND
place, and let the dry *l* appear.................. Gen 1:9
And God called the dry *l* Earth................... Gen 1:10
compasseth the whole *l* of Havilah............ Gen 2:11 776
And the gold of that *l* is good.................... Gen 2:12 776
the whole *l* of Ethiopia............................... Gen 2:13 776
LORD, and dwelt in the *l* of Nod................ Gen 4:16 776
of all that was in the dry *l*........................ Gen 7:22
and Calneh, in the *l* of Shinar.................... Gen 10:10 776
Out of that *l* went forth Asshur,................. Gen 10:11 776
found a plain in the *l* of Shinar.................. Gen 11:2 776
Terah in the *l* of his nativity...................... Gen 11:28 776
to go into the *l* of Canaan.......................... Gen 11:31 776
unto a *l* that I will shew thee..................... Gen 12:1 776
forth to go into the *l* of Canaan.................. Gen 12:5 776
into the *l* of Canaan they came.................. Gen 12:5 776
the *l* unto the place of Sichem.................... Gen 12:6 776
the Canaanite was then in the *l*.................. Gen 12:6 776
Unto thy seed will I give this *l*.................... Gen 12:7 776
And there was a famine in the *l*.................. Gen 12:10 776
the famine was grievous in the *l*................. Gen 12:10 776
the *l* was not able to bear them,................. Gen 13:6 776
Perizzite dwelled then in the *l*.................... Gen 13:7 776
Is not the whole *l* before thee..................... Gen 13:9 776
of the LORD, like the *l* of Egypt.................... Gen 13:10 776
Abram dwelled in the *l* of Canaan................ Gen 13:12 776
For all the *l* which thou seest,..................... Gen 13:15 776
walk through the *l* in the length................. Gen 13:17 776
to give thee this *l* to inherit it.................... Gen 15:7 776
in a *l* that is not theirs............................... Gen 15:13 776
Unto thy seed have I given this *l*................ Gen 15:18 776
ten years in the *l* of Canaan....................... Gen 16:3 776
the *l* wherein thou art a stranger............... Gen 17:8 776
all the *l* of Canaan, for an.......................... Gen 17:8 776
and toward all the *l* of the plain................. Gen 19:28 776
said, Behold, my *l* is before thee................ Gen 20:15 776
him a wife out of the *l* of Egypt.................. Gen 21:21 776
to the *l* wherein thou hast.......................... Gen 21:23 776
into the *l* of the Philistines......................... Gen 21:32 776
in the Philistines' *l* many days.................... Gen 21:34 776
and get thee into the *l* of Moriah............... Gen 22:2 776
same is Hebron in the *l* of Canaan.............. Gen 23:2 776
himself to the people of the *l*..................... Gen 23:7 776
before the people of the *l*........................... Gen 23:12 776
audience of the people of the *l*.................... Gen 23:13 776
the *l* is worth four hundred......................... Gen 23:15 776
same is Hebron in the *l* of Canaan.............. Gen 23:19 776
willing to follow me unto this *l*................... Gen 24:5 776
the *l* from whence thou camest.................. Gen 24:5 776
from the *l* of my kindred, and...................... Gen 24:7 776
Unto thy seed will I give this *l*.................... Gen 24:7 776
Canaanites, in whose *l* I dwell.................... Gen 24:37 776
And there was a famine in the *l*.................. Gen 26:1 776
dwell in the *l* which I shall tell.................... Gen 26:2 776
Sojourn in this *l*, and I will be..................... Gen 26:3 776
Then Isaac sowed in that *l*......................... Gen 26:12 776
and we shall be fruitful in the *l*.................. Gen 26:22 776
are of the daughters of the *l*...................... Gen 27:46 776
the *l* wherein thou art a stranger............... Gen 28:4 776
the *l* whereon thou liest, to thee............... Gen 28:13 776
will bring thee again into this *l*.................. Gen 28:15 127
came into the *l* of the people of.................. Gen 29:1 776
Return unto the *l* of thy fathers.................. Gen 31:3 776
arise, get thee out from this *l*.................... Gen 31:13 776
return unto the *l* of thy kindred................. Gen 31:13 776
his father in the *l* of Canaan...................... Gen 31:18 776
his brother unto the *l* of Seir..................... Gen 32:3 776
which is in the *l* of Canaan......................... Gen 33:18 776
out to see the daughters of the *l*................ Gen 34:1 776
the *l* shall be before you............................ Gen 34:10 776
therefore let them dwell in the *l*................. Gen 34:21 776
for the *l*, behold, it is large......................... Gen 34:21 776
among the inhabitants of the *l*.................... Gen 34:30 776
Luz, which is in the *l* of Canaan.................. Gen 35:6 776
the *l* which I gave Abraham and.................. Gen 35:12 776
seed after thee will I give the *l*.................. Gen 35:12 776
pass, when Israel dwelt in that *l*................ Gen 35:22 776
born unto him in the *l* of Canaan............... Gen 36:5 776
he had got in the *l* of Canaan..................... Gen 36:6 776
the *l* wherein they were strangers.............. Gen 36:7 776
came of Eliphaz in the *l* of Edom................ Gen 36:16 776
came of Reuel in the *l* of Edom................... Gen 36:17 776
the Horite, who inhabited the *l*.................. Gen 36:20 776
children of Seir in the *l* of Edom................ Gen 36:21 776
their dukes in the *l* of Seir........................ Gen 36:30 776
that reigned in the *l* of Edom..................... Gen 36:31 776
Husham of the *l* of Temani reigned............. Gen 36:34 776
in the *l* of their possession........................ Gen 36:43 776
Jacob dwelt in the *l* wherein his.................. Gen 37:1 776
a stranger, in the *l* of Canaan..................... Gen 37:1 776
away out of the *l* of the Hebrews................ Gen 40:15 776
in all the *l* of Egypt for badness.................. Gen 41:19 776
throughout all the *l* of Egypt...................... Gen 41:29 776
be forgotten in the *l* of Egypt.................... Gen 41:30 776
and the famine shall consume the *l*............ Gen 41:30 776
in the *l* by reason of that famine................ Gen 41:31 776
and set him over the *l* of Egypt.................. Gen 41:33 776
him appoint officers over the *l*.................... Gen 41:34 776
take up the fifth part of the *l*..................... Gen 41:34 776
the *l* against the seven years of................. Gen 41:36 776
which shall be in the *l* of Egypt.................. Gen 41:36 776
that the *l* perish not through the............... Gen 41:36 776
set thee over all the *l* of Egypt.................. Gen 41:41 776
him ruler over all the *l* of Egypt................ Gen 41:43 776
or foot in all the *l* of Egypt....................... Gen 41:44 776
went out over all the *l* of Egypt................. Gen 41:45 776
throughout all the *l* of Egypt...................... Gen 41:46 776
which were in the *l* of Egypt...................... Gen 41:48 776
in the *l* of my affliction............................... Gen 41:52 776
that was in the *l* of Egypt.......................... Gen 41:53 776
but in all the *l* of Egypt there.................... Gen 41:54 776
when all the *l* of Egypt was........................ Gen 41:55 776
waxed sore in the *l* of Egypt...................... Gen 41:56 776
the famine was in the *l* of Canaan.............. Gen 42:5 776
was the governor over the *l*........................ Gen 42:6 776
sold to all the people of the *l*.................... Gen 42:6 776
From the *l* of Canaan to buy food............... Gen 42:7 776
nakedness of the *l* ye are come................... Gen 42:9 776
nakedness of the *l* ye are come................... Gen 42:12 776
of one man in the *l* of Canaan.................... Gen 42:13 776
their father unto the *l* of Canaan............... Gen 42:29 776
The man, who is the lord of the *l*................. Gen 42:30 776
our father in the *l* of Canaan...................... Gen 42:32 776
and ye shall traffick in the *l*....................... Gen 42:34 776
And the famine was sore in the *l*................ Gen 43:1 776
fruits in the *l* in your vessels.................... Gen 43:11 776
unto thee out of the *l* of Canaan................ Gen 44:8 776
hath the famine been in the *l*.................... Gen 45:6 776
throughout all the *l* of Egypt...................... Gen 45:8 776
shalt dwell in the *l* of Goshen.................... Gen 45:10 776
go, get you unto the *l* of Canaan................. Gen 45:17 776
you the good of the *l* of Egypt.................... Gen 45:18 776
and ye shall eat the fat of the *l*................... Gen 45:18 776
take you wagons out of the *l* of.................. Gen 45:19 776
of all the *l* of Egypt is yours...................... Gen 45:20 776
came into the *l* of Canaan unto.................. Gen 45:25 776
governor over all the *l* of Egypt.................. Gen 45:26 776
had gotten in the *l* of Canaan.................... Gen 46:6 776
and Onan died in the *l* of Canaan............... Gen 46:12 776
unto Joseph in the *l* of Egypt..................... Gen 46:20 776
and they came into the *l* of Goshen............ Gen 46:28 776
which were in the *l* of Canaan..................... Gen 46:31 776
ye may dwell in the *l* of Goshen.................. Gen 46:34 776
are come out of the *l* of Canaan................. Gen 47:1 776
they are in the *l* of Goshen........................ Gen 47:1 776
to sojourn in the *l* are we come................. Gen 47:4 776
famine is sore in the *l* of Canaan............... Gen 47:4 776
servants dwell in the *l* of Goshen............... Gen 47:4 776
The *l* of Egypt is before thee..................... Gen 47:6 776
the best of the *l* make thy father................ Gen 47:6 776
in the *l* of Goshen let them dwell................ Gen 47:6 776
a possession in the *l* of Egypt.................... Gen 47:11 776
in the best of the *l*..................................... Gen 47:11 776
in the *l* of Rameses, as Pharaoh................ Gen 47:11 776
there was no bread in all the *l*................... Gen 47:13 776
very sore, so that the *l* of Egypt................. Gen 47:13 776
all the *l* of Canaan fainted by.................... Gen 47:13 776
that was found in the *l* of Egypt................. Gen 47:14 776
in the *l* of Canaan, for the corn................. Gen 47:14 776
money failed in the *l* of Egypt.................... Gen 47:15 776
in the *l* of Canaan, all the......................... Gen 47:15 776
thine eyes, both we and our *l*..................... Gen 47:19 127
our *l* for bread, and we and our.................. Gen 47:19 127
our *l* will be servants unto........................ Gen 47:19 127
that the *l* be not desolate.......................... Gen 47:19 127
all the *l* of Egypt for Pharaoh.................... Gen 47:20 127
so the *l* became Pharaoh's......................... Gen 47:20 776
Only the *l* of the priests bought................. Gen 47:22 127
this day and your *l* for Pharaoh................. Gen 47:23 127
for you, and ye shall sow the *l*................... Gen 47:23 127
over the *l* of Egypt unto this day............... Gen 47:26 127
except the *l* of the priests only,................. Gen 47:26 127
And Israel dwelt in the *l* of Egypt.............. Gen 47:27 776
Jacob lived in the *l* of Egypt..................... Gen 47:28 776
unto me at Luz in the *l* of Canaan.............. Gen 48:3 776
will give this *l* to thy seed......................... Gen 48:4 776
were born unto thee in the *l* of.................. Gen 48:5 776
me in the *l* of Canaan in the way............... Gen 48:7 776
again unto the *l* of your fathers.................. Gen 48:21 776
the *l* that it was pleasant........................... Gen 49:15 776
in the *l* of Canaan, which Abraham.............. Gen 49:30 776
digged for me in the *l* of Canaan................ Gen 50:5 776
all the elders of the *l* of Egypt.................. Gen 50:7 776
they left in the *l* of Goshen....................... Gen 50:8 776
And when the inhabitants of the *l*.............. Gen 50:11 776
carried him into the *l* of Canaan................ Gen 50:13 776
bring you out of this *l* unto the.................. Gen 50:24 776
the *l* which he sware to Abraham............... Gen 50:24 776
the *l* was filled with them........................... Ex 1:7 776
and so get them up out of the *l*.................. Ex 1:10 776
and dwelt in the *l* of Midian....................... Ex 2:15 776
been a stranger in a strange *l*.................... Ex 2:22 776
up out of that *l* unto a good *l*.................... Ex 3:8 776
unto a *l* flowing with milk and..................... Ex 3:8 776
unto the *l* of the Canaanites....................... Ex 3:17 776
unto a *l* flowing with milk and..................... Ex 3:17 776
river, and pour it upon the dry *l*................. Ex 4:9
shall become blood upon the dry *l*.............. Ex 4:9
and he returned to the *l* of Egypt............... Ex 4:20 776
the people of the *l* now are many............... Ex 5:5 776
abroad throughout all the *l* of..................... Ex 5:12 776
shall he drive them out of his *l*.................. Ex 6:1 776
to give them the *l* of Canaan..................... Ex 6:4 776
the *l* of their pilgrimage,........................... Ex 6:4 776
And I will bring you in unto the *l*............... Ex 6:8 776
of Israel go out of his *l*............................... Ex 6:11 776
of Israel out of the *l* of Egypt..................... Ex 6:13 776
the *l* of Egypt according to their................. Ex 6:26 776
unto Moses in the *l* of Egypt...................... Ex 6:28 776
children of Israel out of his *l*...................... Ex 7:2 776
and my wonders in the *l* of Egypt............... Ex 7:3 776
out of the *l* of Egypt by great..................... Ex 7:4 776
throughout all the *l* of Egypt...................... Ex 7:19 776
throughout all the *l* of Egypt...................... Ex 7:21 776
to come up upon the *l* of Egypt................... Ex 8:5 776
up, and covered the *l* of Egypt................... Ex 8:6 776
up frogs upon the *l* of Egypt...................... Ex 8:7 776
and the *l* stank.. Ex 8:14 776
rod, and smite the dust of the *l*................. Ex 8:16 776
throughout all the *l* of Egypt...................... Ex 8:16 776
all the dust of the *l* became lice................. Ex 8:17 776
throughout all the *l* of Egypt...................... Ex 8:17 776
sever in that day the *l* of Goshen............... Ex 8:22 776
and into all the *l* of Egypt.......................... Ex 8:24 776
the *l* was corrupted by reason of................ Ex 8:24 776
sacrifice to your God in the *l*..................... Ex 8:25 776
LORD shall do this thing in the *l*................. Ex 9:5 776
small dust in all the *l* of Egypt.................. Ex 9:9 776
throughout all the *l* of Egypt...................... Ex 9:9 776
may be hail in all the *l* of Egypt................ Ex 9:22 776
field, throughout the *l* of Egypt.................. Ex 9:22 776
rained hail upon the *l* of Egypt.................. Ex 9:23 776
the *l* of Egypt since it became a................. Ex 9:24 776
l of Egypt all that was in the...................... Ex 9:25 776
Only in the *l* of Goshen, where.................. Ex 9:26 776
the *l* of Egypt for the locusts..................... Ex 10:12 776

may come up upon the *l* of Egypt	Ex 10:12	776
and eat every herb of the *l*	Ex 10:12	776
forth his rod over the *l* of Egypt	Ex 10:13	776
east wind upon the *l* all that day	Ex 10:13	776
went up over all the *l* of Egypt	Ex 10:14	776
so that the *l* was darkened	Ex 10:15	776
they did eat every herb of the *l*	Ex 10:15	776
field, through all the *l* of Egypt	Ex 10:15	776
be darkness over the *l* of Egypt	Ex 10:21	776
in all the *l* of Egypt three days	Ex 10:22	776
was very great in the *l* of Egypt	Ex 11:3	776
in the *l* of Egypt shall die	Ex 11:5	776
cry throughout all the *l* of Egypt	Ex 11:6	776
be multiplied in the *l* of Egypt	Ex 11:9	776
of Israel go out of his *l*	Ex 11:10	776
Moses and Aaron in the *l* of Egypt	Ex 12:1	776
through the *l* of Egypt this night	Ex 12:12	776
the firstborn in the *l* of Egypt	Ex 12:12	776
you, when I smite the *l* of Egypt	Ex 12:13	776
your armies out of the *l* of Egypt	Ex 12:17	776
be a stranger, or born in the *l*	Ex 12:19	776
when ye be come to the *l* which	Ex 12:25	776
the firstborn in the *l* of Egypt	Ex 12:29	776
send them out of the *l* in haste	Ex 12:33	776
LORD went out from the *l* of Egypt	Ex 12:41	776
them out from the *l* of Egypt	Ex 12:42	776
be as one that is born in the *l*	Ex 12:48	776
of the *l* of Egypt by their armies	Ex 12:51	776
thee into the *l* of the Canaanites	Ex 13:5	776
a *l* flowing with milk and honey,	Ex 13:5	776
thee into the *l* of the Canaanites	Ex 13:11	776
the firstborn in the *l* of Egypt	Ex 13:15	776
way of the *l* of the Philistines	Ex 13:17	776
harnessed out of the *l* of Egypt	Ex 13:18	776
They are entangled in the *l*	Ex 14:3	776
that night, and made the sea dry *l*	Ex 14:21	
dry *l* in the midst of the sea	Ex 14:29	
on dry *l* in the midst of the sea	Ex 15:19	
departing out of the *l* of Egypt	Ex 16:1	776
of the LORD in the *l* of Egypt	Ex 16:3	776
you out from the *l* of Egypt	Ex 16:6	776
you forth from the *l* of Egypt	Ex 16:32	776
until they came to a *l* inhabited	Ex 16:35	776
the borders of the *l* of Canaan	Ex 16:35	776
have been an alien in a strange *l*	Ex 18:3	776
and he went his way into his own *l*	Ex 18:27	776
gone forth out of the *l* of Egypt	Ex 19:1	776
thee out of the *l* of Egypt	Ex 20:2	776
l which the LORD thy God giveth	Ex 20:12	127
were strangers in the *l* of Egypt	Ex 22:21	776
were strangers in the *l* of Egypt	Ex 23:9	776
And six years thou shalt sow thy *l*	Ex 23:10	776
l thou shalt bring into the house	Ex 23:19	127
young, nor be barren, in thy *l*	Ex 23:26	776
lest the *l* become desolate, and	Ex 23:29	776
be increased, and inherit the *l*	Ex 23:30	776
of the *l* into your hand	Ex 23:31	776
They shall not dwell in thy *l*	Ex 23:33	776
them forth out of the *l* of Egypt	Ex 29:46	776
us up out of the *l* of Egypt	Ex 32:1	776
thee up out of the *l* of Egypt	Ex 32:4	776
broughtest out of the *l* of Egypt	Ex 32:7	776
thee up out of the *l* of Egypt	Ex 32:8	776
the *l* of Egypt with great power	Ex 32:11	776
all this *l* that I have spoken of	Ex 32:13	776
us up out of the *l* of Egypt	Ex 32:23	776
brought up out of the *l* of Egypt	Ex 33:1	776
unto the *l* which I sware unto	Ex 33:1	776
Unto a *l* flowing with milk and	Ex 33:3	776
of the *l* whither thou goest	Ex 34:12	776
with the inhabitants of the *l*	Ex 34:15	776
shall any man desire thy *l*	Ex 34:24	776
l thou shalt bring unto the house	Ex 34:26	127
you up out of the *l* of Egypt	Lev 11:45	776
ye be come into the *l* of Canaan	Lev 14:34	776
house of the *l* of your possession	Lev 14:34	776
iniquities unto a *l* not inhabited	Lev 16:22	776
the doings of the *l* of Egypt	Lev 18:3	776
the doings of the *l* of Canaan	Lev 18:3	776
And the *l* is defiled	Lev 18:25	776
the *l* itself vomiteth out her	Lev 18:25	776
have the men of the *l* done	Lev 18:27	776
before you, and the *l* is defiled	Lev 18:27	776
That the *l* spue not you out also,	Lev 18:28	776
ye reap the harvest of your *l*	Lev 19:9	776
And when ye shall come into the *l*	Lev 19:23	776
lest the *l* fall to whoredom, and	Lev 19:29	776
the *l* become full of wickedness	Lev 19:29	776
sojourn with thee in your *l*	Lev 19:33	776
were strangers in the *l* of Egypt	Lev 19:34	776
brought you out of the *l* of Egypt	Lev 19:36	776
the people of the *l* shall stone	Lev 20:2	776
if the people of the *l* do any	Lev 20:4	776
that the *l*, whither I bring you	Lev 20:22	776
you, Ye shall inherit their *l*	Lev 20:24	127
a *l* that floweth with milk and	Lev 20:24	776
any offering thereof in your *l*	Lev 22:24	776
brought you out of the *l* of Egypt	Lev 22:33	776
into the *l* which I give unto you	Lev 23:10	776
ye reap the harvest of your *l*	Lev 23:22	776
gathered in the fruit of the *l*	Lev 23:39	776
them out of the *l* of Egypt	Lev 23:43	776
as he that is born in the *l*	Lev 24:16	249
come into the *l* which I give you	Lev 25:2	776
then shall the *l* keep a sabbath	Lev 25:2	776
be a sabbath of rest unto the *l*	Lev 25:4	776
it is a year of rest unto the *l*	Lev 25:5	776
the sabbath of the *l* shall be	Lev 25:6	776
for the beast that are in thy *l*	Lev 25:7	776
sound throughout all your *l*	Lev 25:9	776
the *l* unto all the inhabitants	Lev 25:10	776
ye shall dwell in the *l* in safety	Lev 25:18	776
the *l* shall yield her fruit, and	Lev 25:19	776
The *l* shall not be sold for ever	Lev 25:23	776
for the *l* is mine	Lev 25:23	776
in all the *l* of your possession	Lev 25:24	776
grant a redemption for the *l*	Lev 25:24	776
you forth out of the *l* of Egypt	Lev 25:38	776
to give you the *l* of Canaan	Lev 25:38	776
forth out of the *l* of Egypt	Lev 25:42	776
you, which they begat in your *l*	Lev 25:45	776
forth out of the *l* of Egypt	Lev 25:55	776
up any image of stone in your *l*	Lev 26:1	776
the *l* shall yield her increase,	Lev 26:4	776
full, and dwell in your *l* safely	Lev 26:5	776
And I will give peace in the *l*	Lev 26:6	776
will rid evil beasts out of the *l*	Lev 26:6	776
shall the sword go through your *l*	Lev 26:6	776
you forth out of the *l* of Egypt	Lev 26:13	776
for your *l* shall not yield her	Lev 26:20	776
trees of the *l* yield their fruits	Lev 26:20	776
will bring the *l* into desolation	Lev 26:32	776
your *l* shall be desolate, and your	Lev 26:33	776
Then shall the *l* enjoy her	Lev 26:34	776
and ye be in your enemies' *l*	Lev 26:34	776
even then shall the *l* rest	Lev 26:34	776
the *l* of your enemies shall eat	Lev 26:38	776
them into the *l* of their enemies	Lev 26:41	776
and I will remember the *l*	Lev 26:42	776
The *l* also shall be left of them,	Lev 26:43	776
they be in the *l* of their enemies	Lev 26:44	776
l of Egypt in the sight of the	Lev 26:45	776
possession of the *l* did belong	Lev 27:24	776
And all the tithe of the *l*	Lev 27:30	776
whether of the seed of the *l*	Lev 27:30	776
were come out of the *l* of Egypt	Num 1:1	776
smote all the firstborn in the *l*	Num 3:13	776
l of Egypt I sanctified them for	Num 8:17	776
were come out of the *l* of Egypt	Num 9:1	776
and for him that was born in the *l*	Num 9:14	776
in your *l* against the enemy that	Num 10:9	776
but I will depart to mine own *l*	Num 10:30	776
unto the *l* which thou swarest	Num 11:12	127
they may search the *l* of Canaan	Num 13:2	776
which Moses sent to spy out the *l*	Num 13:16	776
them to spy out the *l* of Canaan	Num 13:17	776
And see the *l*, what it is	Num 13:18	776
what the *l* is that they dwell in,	Num 13:19	776
And what the *l* is, whether it be	Num 13:20	776
and bring of the fruit of the *l*	Num 13:20	776
up, and searched the *l* from the	Num 13:21	776
of the *l* after forty days	Num 13:25	776
and shewed them the fruit of the *l*	Num 13:26	776
We came unto the *l* whither thou	Num 13:27	776
be strong that dwell in the *l*	Num 13:28	776
dwell in the *l* of the south	Num 13:29	776
up an evil report of the *l* which	Num 13:32	776
children of Israel, saying, The *l*	Num 13:32	776
is a *l* that eateth up the	Num 13:32	776
we had died in the *l* of Egypt	Num 14:2	776
the LORD brought us unto this *l*	Num 14:3	776
were of them that searched the *l*	Num 14:6	776
children of Israel, saying, The *l*	Num 14:7	776
search it, is an exceeding good *l*	Num 14:7	776
then he will bring us into this *l*	Num 14:8	776
a *l* which floweth with milk and	Num 14:8	776
fear ye the people of the *l*	Num 14:9	776
it to the inhabitants of this *l*	Num 14:14	776
the *l* which he sware unto them	Num 14:16	776
the *l* which I sware unto their	Num 14:23	776
into the *l* whereinto he went	Num 14:24	776
ye shall not come into the *l*	Num 14:30	776
they shall know the *l* which ye	Num 14:31	776
days in which ye searched the *l*	Num 14:34	776
which Moses sent to search the *l*	Num 14:36	776
bringing up a slander upon the *l*	Num 14:36	776
up the evil report upon the *l*	Num 14:37	776
the men that went to search the *l*	Num 14:38	776
into the *l* of your habitations	Num 15:2	776
into the *l* whither I bring you	Num 15:18	776
when ye eat of the bread of the *l*	Num 15:19	776
whether he be born in the *l*	Num 15:30	249
brought you out of the *l* of Egypt	Num 15:41	776
out of a *l* that floweth with milk	Num 16:13	776
into a *l* that floweth with milk	Num 16:14	776
whatsoever is first ripe in the *l*	Num 18:13	776
have no inheritance in their *l*	Num 18:20	776
the *l* which I have given them	Num 20:12	776
by the coast of the *l* of Edom	Num 20:23	776
the *l* which I have given unto the	Num 20:24	776
Red sea, to compass the *l* of Edom	Num 21:4	776
Let me pass through thy *l*	Num 21:22	776
possessed his *l* from Arnon unto	Num 21:24	776
taken all his *l* out of his hand,	Num 21:26	776
dwelt in the *l* of the Amorites	Num 21:31	776
hand, and all his people, and his *l*	Num 21:34	776
and they possessed his *l*	Num 21:35	776
which is by the river of the *l* of	Num 22:5	776
I may drive them out of the *l*	Num 22:6	776
of Balak, Get you into your *l*	Num 22:13	776
went forth out of the *l* of Egypt	Num 26:4	776
and Onan died in the *l* of Canaan	Num 26:19	776
Unto these the *l* shall be divided	Num 26:53	776
Notwithstanding the *l* shall be	Num 26:55	776
see the *l* which I have given unto	Num 27:12	776
and when they saw the *l* of Jazer	Num 32:1	776
the *l* of Gilead, that, behold,	Num 32:1	776
is a *l* for cattle, and thy	Num 32:4	776
let this *l* be given unto thy	Num 32:5	776
l which the LORD hath given them	Num 32:7	776
from Kadesh-barnea to see the *l*	Num 32:8	776
valley of Eshcol, and saw the *l*	Num 32:9	776
they should not go into the *l*	Num 32:9	776
shall see the *l* which I sware	Num 32:11	127
of the inhabitants of the *l*	Num 32:17	776
the *l* be subdued before the LORD	Num 32:22	776
this *l* shall be your possession	Num 32:22	776
the *l* shall be subdued before you	Num 32:29	776
the *l* of Gilead for a possession	Num 32:29	776
among you in the *l* of Canaan	Num 32:30	776
the LORD into the *l* of Canaan	Num 32:32	776
of Og king of Bashan, the *l*	Num 32:33	776
the *l* of Egypt with their armies	Num 33:1	776
Hor, in the edge of the *l* of Edom	Num 33:37	776
were come out of the *l* of Egypt	Num 33:38	776
in the south in the *l* of Canaan	Num 33:40	776
over Jordan into the *l* of Canaan	Num 33:51	776
of the *l* from before you, and	Num 33:52	776
the inhabitants of the *l*, and	Num 33:53	776
given you the *l* to possess it	Num 33:53	776
ye shall divide the *l* by lot for	Num 33:54	776
of the *l* from before you	Num 33:55	776
vex you in the *l* wherein ye dwell	Num 33:55	776
When ye come into the *l* of Canaan	Num 34:2	776
(this is the *l* that shall fall	Num 34:2	776
even the *l* of Canaan with the	Num 34:2	776
this shall be your *l* with the	Num 34:12	776
This is the *l* which ye shall	Num 34:13	776
which shall divide the *l* unto you	Num 34:17	776
to divide the *l* by inheritance	Num 34:18	776
of Israel in the *l* of Canaan	Num 34:29	776
over Jordan into the *l* of Canaan	Num 35:10	776
shall ye give in the *l* of Canaan	Num 35:14	776
into the *l* of his possession	Num 35:28	776
come again to dwell in the *l*	Num 35:32	776
not pollute the *l* wherein ye are	Num 35:33	776
for blood it defileth the *l*	Num 35:33	776
the *l* cannot be cleansed of the	Num 35:33	776
the *l* which ye shall inhabit	Num 35:34	776
l for an inheritance by lot to	Num 36:2	776
in the *l* of Moab, began Moses to	Deut 1:5	776
to the *l* of the Canaanites, and	Deut 1:7	776
I have set the *l* before you	Deut 1:8	776
possess the *l* which the LORD	Deut 1:8	776
God hath set the *l* before thee	Deut 1:21	776
and they shall search us out the *l*	Deut 1:22	776
the fruit of the *l* in their hands	Deut 1:25	776
It is a good *l* which the LORD our	Deut 1:25	776
us forth out of the *l* of Egypt	Deut 1:27	776
evil generation see that good *l*	Deut 1:35	776
to him will I give the *l* that he	Deut 1:36	776
I will not give you of their *l*	Deut 2:5	776
thee of their *l* for a possession	Deut 2:9	776
did unto the *l* of his possession	Deut 2:12	776
l of the children of Ammon any	Deut 2:19	776
also was accounted a *l* of giants	Deut 2:20	776
king of Heshbon, and his *l*	Deut 2:24	776
Let me pass through thy *l*	Deut 2:27	776
l which the LORD our God giveth	Deut 2:29	776
give Sihon and his *l* before thee	Deut 2:31	776
that thou mayest inherit his *l*	Deut 2:31	776
Only unto the *l* of the children	Deut 2:37	776
him, and all his people, and his *l*	Deut 3:2	776
l that was on this side Jordan	Deut 3:8	776
And this *l*, which we possessed at	Deut 3:12	776
which was called the *l* of giants	Deut 3:13	776
given you this *l* to possess it	Deut 3:18	776
until they also possess the *l*	Deut 3:20	776
see the good *l* that is beyond	Deut 3:25	776
the *l* which thou shalt see	Deut 3:28	776
possess the *l* which the LORD God	Deut 4:1	776
the *l* whither ye go to possess it	Deut 4:5	776
that ye might do them in the *l*	Deut 4:14	776
should not go in unto that good *l*	Deut 4:21	776
But I must die in this *l*, I must	Deut 4:22	776
go over, and possess that good *l*	Deut 4:22	776
shall have remained long in the *l*	Deut 4:25	776
utterly perish from off the *l*	Deut 4:26	776
thee their *l* for an inheritance	Deut 4:38	776
in the *l* of Sihon king of the	Deut 4:46	776
And they possessed his *l*	Deut 4:47	776
the *l* of Og king of Bashan, two	Deut 4:47	776
thee out of the *l* of Egypt	Deut 5:6	776
wast a servant in the *l* of Egypt	Deut 5:15	776
in the *l* which the LORD thy God	Deut 5:16	127
that they may do them in the *l*	Deut 5:31	776
in the *l* which ye shall possess	Deut 5:33	776
the *l* whither ye go to possess it	Deut 6:1	776
in the *l* that floweth with milk	Deut 6:3	776
have brought thee into the *l*	Deut 6:10	776
thee forth out of the *l* of Egypt	Deut 6:12	776
possess the good *l* which the LORD	Deut 6:18	776
to give us the *l* which he sware	Deut 6:23	776
l whither thou goest to possess	Deut 7:1	776
thy womb, and the fruit of thy *l*	Deut 7:13	127
in the *l* which he sware unto thy	Deut 7:13	127
possess the *l* which the LORD	Deut 8:1	776
God bringeth thee into a good *l*	Deut 8:7	776
a *l* of brooks of water, of	Deut 8:7	776
A *l* of wheat, and barley, and vines	Deut 8:8	776
a *l* of oil olive, and honey	Deut 8:8	776
A *l*, wherein thou shalt eat bread	Deut 8:9	776
a *l* whose stones are iron, and out	Deut 8:9	776
good *l* which he hath given thee	Deut 8:10	776
thee forth out of the *l* of Egypt	Deut 8:14	776
brought me in to possess this *l*	Deut 9:4	776
dost thou go to possess their *l*	Deut 9:5	776
this good *l* to possess it for thy	Deut 9:6	776
depart out of the *l* of Egypt	Deut 9:7	776
possess the *l* which I have given	Deut 9:23	776
Lest the *l* whence thou broughtest	Deut 9:28	776
into the *l* which he promised them	Deut 9:28	776
Jotbath, a *l* of rivers of waters	Deut 10:7	776
they may go in and possess the *l*	Deut 10:11	776
were strangers in the *l* of Egypt	Deut 10:19	776
king of Egypt, and unto all his *l*	Deut 11:3	776
strong, and go in and possess the *l*	Deut 11:8	776
ye may prolong your days in the *l*	Deut 11:9	127
a *l* that floweth with milk and	Deut 11:9	776
For the *l*, whither thou goest in	Deut 11:10	776
it is not as the *l* of Egypt	Deut 11:10	776
But the *l*, whither ye go to	Deut 11:11	776

L

is a *l* of hills and valleys, and	Deut 11:11	776
A *l* which the LORD thy God careth	Deut 11:12	776
rain of your *l* in his due season	Deut 11:14	776
that the *l* yield not her fruit	Deut 11:17	127
good *l* which the LORD giveth you	Deut 11:17	776
in the *l* which the LORD sware	Deut 11:21	127
the *l* that ye shall tread upon	Deut 11:25	776
l whither thou goest to possess	Deut 11:29	776
in the *l* of the Canaanites, which	Deut 11:30	776
l which the LORD your God giveth	Deut 11:31	776
ye shall observe to do in the *l*	Deut 12:1	776
dwell in the *l* which the LORD	Deut 12:10	776
them, and dwellest in their *l*	Deut 12:29	776
brought you out of the *l* of Egypt	Deut 13:5	776
thee out of the *l* of Egypt	Deut 13:10	776
l which the LORD thy God giveth	Deut 15:4	776
l which the LORD thy God giveth	Deut 15:7	776
shall never cease out of the *l*	Deut 15:11	776
poor, and to thy needy, in thy *l*	Deut 15:11	776
wast a bondman in the *l* of Egypt	Deut 15:15	776
out of the *l* of Egypt in haste	Deut 16:3	776
l of Egypt all the days of thy	Deut 16:3	776
inherit the *l* which the LORD thy	Deut 16:20	776
When thou art come unto the *l*	Deut 17:14	776
When thou art come into the *l*	Deut 18:9	776
whose *l* the LORD thy God giveth	Deut 19:1	776
for thee in the midst of thy *l*	Deut 19:2	776
and divide the coasts of thy *l*	Deut 19:3	776
give thee all the *l* which he	Deut 19:8	776
blood be not shed in thy *l*	Deut 19:10	776
l that the LORD thy God giveth	Deut 19:14	776
thee up out of the *l* of Egypt	Deut 20:1	776
If one be found slain in the *l*	Deut 21:1	127
that thy *l* be not defiled, which	Deut 21:23	127
thou wast a stranger in his *l*	Deut 23:7	776
settest thine hand to in the *l*	Deut 23:20	776
thou shalt not cause the *l* to sin	Deut 24:4	776
are in thy *l* within thy gates	Deut 24:14	776
wast a bondman in the *l* of Egypt	Deut 24:22	776
l which the LORD thy God giveth	Deut 25:15	127
in the *l* which the LORD thy God	Deut 25:19	776
l which the LORD thy God giveth	Deut 26:1	776
l that the LORD thy God giveth	Deut 26:2	776
place, and hath given us this *l*	Deut 26:9	776
even a *l* that floweth with milk	Deut 26:9	776
brought the firstfruits of the *l*	Deut 26:10	127
the *l* which thou hast given us,	Deut 26:15	127
a *l* that floweth with milk and	Deut 26:15	776
l which the LORD thy God giveth	Deut 27:2	776
l which the LORD thy God giveth	Deut 27:3	776
a *l* that floweth with milk and	Deut 27:3	776
he shall bless thee in the *l*	Deut 28:8	776
in the *l* which the LORD sware	Deut 28:11	127
the rain unto thy *l* in his season	Deut 28:12	776
thy body, and the fruit of thy *l*	Deut 28:18	127
have consumed thee from off the *l*	Deut 28:21	127
make the rain of thy *l* powder	Deut 28:24	776
The fruit of thy *l*, and all thy	Deut 28:33	127
fruit of thy *l* shall the locust	Deut 28:42	127
thy cattle, and the fruit of thy *l*	Deut 28:51	127
trustedst, throughout all thy *l*	Deut 28:52	776
thy gates throughout all thy *l*	Deut 28:52	776
l whither thou goest to possess	Deut 28:63	127
of Israel in the *l* of Moab	Deut 29:1	776
in the *l* of Egypt unto Pharaoh	Deut 29:2	776
his servants, and unto all his *l*	Deut 29:2	776
And we took their *l*, and gave it	Deut 29:8	776
we have dwelt in the *l* of Egypt	Deut 29:16	776
that shall come from a far *l*	Deut 29:22	776
they see the plagues of that *l*	Deut 29:22	776
that the whole *l* thereof is	Deut 29:23	776
the LORD done thus unto this *l*	Deut 29:24	776
them forth out of the *l* of Egypt	Deut 29:25	776
LORD was kindled against this *l*	Deut 29:27	776
them out of their *l* in anger	Deut 29:28	127
and cast them into another *l*	Deut 29:28	776
the *l* which thy fathers possessed	Deut 30:5	776
cattle, and in the fruit of thy *l*	Deut 30:9	127
l whither thou goest to possess	Deut 30:16	776
not prolong your days upon the *l*	Deut 30:18	127
l which the LORD sware unto thy	Deut 30:20	127
Amorites, and unto the *l* of them	Deut 31:4	776
go with this people unto the *l*	Deut 31:7	776
as long as ye live in the *l*	Deut 31:13	127
gods of the strangers of the *l*	Deut 31:16	776
the *l* which I sware unto their	Deut 31:20	127
them into the *l* which I sware	Deut 31:21	776
the *l* which I sware unto them	Deut 31:23	776
He found him in a desert *l*	Deut 32:10	776
and will be merciful unto his *l*	Deut 32:43	127
shall prolong your days in the *l*	Deut 32:47	127
Nebo, which is in the *l* of Moab	Deut 32:49	776
and behold the *l* of Canaan	Deut 32:49	776
thou shalt see the *l* before thee	Deut 32:52	776
l which I give the children of	Deut 32:52	776
Blessed of the LORD be his *l*	Deut 33:13	776
Jacob shall be upon a *l* of corn	Deut 33:28	776
shewed him all the *l* of Gilead	Deut 34:1	776
the *l* of Ephraim, and Manasseh, and	Deut 34:2	776
all the *l* of Judah, unto the	Deut 34:2	776
This is the *l* which I sware unto	Deut 34:4	776
LORD died there in the *l* of Moab	Deut 34:5	776
him in a valley in the *l* of Moab	Deut 34:6	776
do in the *l* of Egypt to Pharaoh	Deut 34:11	776
all his servants, and to all his *l*	Deut 34:11	776
unto the *l* which I do give to	Josh 1:2	776
all the *l* of the Hittites, and	Josh 1:4	776
divide for an inheritance the *l*	Josh 1:6	776
Jordan, to go in to possess the *l*	Josh 1:11	776
rest, and hath given you this *l*	Josh 1:13	776
shall remain in the *l* which Moses	Josh 1:14	776
they also have possessed the *l*	Josh 1:15	776
unto the *l* of your possession	Josh 1:15	776
secretly, saying, Go view the *l*	Josh 2:1	776
the LORD hath given you the *l*	Josh 2:9	776
of the *l* faint because of you	Josh 2:9	776
when the LORD hath given us the *l*	Josh 2:14	776
Behold, when we come into the *l*	Josh 2:18	776
into our hands all the *l*	Josh 2:24	776
were lifted up unto the dry *l*	Josh 4:18	776
came over this Jordan on dry *l*	Josh 4:22	776
that he would not shew them the *l*	Josh 5:6	776
a *l* that floweth with milk and	Josh 5:6	776
of the *l* on the morrow after the	Josh 5:11	776
eaten of the old corn of the *l*	Josh 5:12	776
of the *l* of Canaan that year	Josh 5:12	776
of the *l* shall hear of it	Josh 7:9	776
his people, and his city, and his *l*	Josh 8:1	776
Moses to give you all the *l*	Josh 9:24	776
of the *l* from before you,	Josh 9:24	776
their *l* did Joshua take at one	Josh 10:42	776
under Hermon in the *l* of Mizpeh	Josh 11:3	776
So Joshua took all that *l*	Josh 11:16	776
all the *l* of Goshen, and the	Josh 11:16	776
the *l* of the children of Israel	Josh 11:22	776
So Joshua took the whole *l*	Josh 11:23	776
And the *l* rested from war	Josh 11:23	776
Now these are the kings of the *l*	Josh 12:1	776
possessed their *l* on the other	Josh 12:1	776
yet very much *l* to be possessed	Josh 13:1	776
This is the *l* that yet remaineth	Josh 13:2	776
all the *l* of the Canaanites, and	Josh 13:4	776
the *l* of the Giblites, and all	Josh 13:5	776
Now therefore divide this *l* for	Josh 13:7	776
half the *l* of the children of	Josh 13:25	776
inherited in the *l* of Canaan	Josh 14:1	776
no part unto the Levites in the *l*	Josh 14:4	776
Israel did, and they divided the *l*	Josh 14:5	776
Kadesh-barnea to espy out the *l*	Josh 14:7	776
Surely the *l* whereon thy feet	Josh 14:9	776
And the *l* had rest from war	Josh 14:15	776
for thou hast given me a south *l*	Josh 15:19	776
Manasseh, beside the *l* of Gilead	Josh 17:5	776
sons had the *l* of Gilead	Josh 17:6	776
Now Manasseh had the *l* of Tappuah	Josh 17:8	776
Canaanites would dwell in that *l*	Josh 17:12	776
there in the *l* of the Perizzites	Josh 17:15	776
Canaanites that dwell in the *l* of	Josh 17:16	776
the *l* was subdued before them	Josh 18:1	776
ye slack to go to possess the *l*	Josh 18:3	776
shall rise, and go through the *l*	Josh 18:4	776
describe the *l* into seven parts	Josh 18:6	776
them that went to describe the *l*	Josh 18:8	776
saying, Go and walk through the *l*	Josh 18:8	776
men went and passed through the *l*	Josh 18:9	776
there Joshua divided the *l* unto	Josh 18:10	776
l for inheritance by their coasts	Josh 19:49	776
them at Shiloh in the *l* of Canaan	Josh 21:2	776
the *l* which he sware to give unto	Josh 21:43	776
unto the *l* of your possession,	Josh 22:4	776
which is in the *l* of Canaan	Josh 22:9	776
to the *l* of their possession,	Josh 22:9	776
that are in the *l* of Canaan	Josh 22:10	776
over against the *l* of Canaan	Josh 22:11	776
into the *l* of Gilead, Phinehas	Josh 22:13	776
unto the *l* of Gilead, and they	Josh 22:15	776
if the *l* of your possession be	Josh 22:19	776
then pass ye over unto the *l* of	Josh 22:19	776
of Gad, out of the *l* of Gilead	Josh 22:32	776
unto the *l* of Canaan, to the	Josh 22:32	776
to destroy the *l* wherein the	Josh 22:33	776
and ye shall possess their *l*	Josh 23:5	776
l which the LORD your God hath	Josh 23:13	127
you from off this good *l* which	Josh 23:15	127
quickly from off the good *l* which	Josh 23:16	776
throughout all the *l* of Canaan	Josh 24:3	776
you into the *l* of the Amorites	Josh 24:8	776
that ye might possess their *l*	Josh 24:8	776
I have given you a *l* for which ye	Josh 24:13	776
the Amorites, in whose *l* ye dwell	Josh 24:15	776
our fathers out of the *l* of Egypt	Josh 24:17	776
the Amorites which dwelt in the *l*	Josh 24:18	776
delivered the *l* into his hand	Judg 1:2	776
for thou hast given me a south *l*	Judg 1:15	776
went into the *l* of the Hittites	Judg 1:26	776
Canaanites would dwell in that *l*	Judg 1:27	776
the inhabitants of the *l*	Judg 1:32	776
the inhabitants of the *l*	Judg 1:33	776
have brought you unto the *l* which	Judg 2:1	776
with the inhabitants of this *l*	Judg 2:2	776
his inheritance to possess the *l*	Judg 2:6	776
them out of the *l* of Egypt	Judg 2:12	776
the *l* had rest forty years	Judg 3:11	776
the *l* had rest fourscore years	Judg 3:30	776
the *l* had rest forty years	Judg 5:31	776
entered into the *l* to destroy it	Judg 6:5	776
before you, and gave you their *l*	Judg 6:9	776
the Amorites, in whose *l* ye dwell	Judg 6:10	776
down by the middle of the *l*	Judg 9:37	776
day, which are in the *l* of Gilead	Judg 10:4	776
Jordan in the *l* of the Amorites	Judg 10:8	776
and dwelt in the *l* of Tob	Judg 11:3	776
Jephthah out of the *l* of Tob	Judg 11:5	776
come against me to fight in my *l*	Judg 11:12	776
Because Israel took away my *l*	Judg 11:13	776
took not away the *l* of Moab	Judg 11:15	776
nor the *l* of the children of	Judg 11:15	776
I pray thee, pass through thy *l*	Judg 11:17	776
and compassed the *l* of Edom	Judg 11:18	776
the *l* of Moab, and came by the	Judg 11:18	776
by the east side of the *l* of Moab	Judg 11:18	776
through thy *l* into my place	Judg 11:19	776
all the *l* of the Amorites	Judg 11:21	776
in Pirathon in the *l* of Ephraim	Judg 12:15	776
and from Eshtaol, to spy out the *l*	Judg 18:2	776
said unto them, Go, search the *l*	Judg 18:2	776
there was no magistrate in the *l*	Judg 18:7	776
for we have seen the *l*, and,	Judg 18:9	776
go, and to enter to possess the *l*	Judg 18:9	776
a people secure, and to a large *l*	Judg 18:10	776
went to spy out the *l* went up	Judg 18:17	776
the day of the captivity of the *l*	Judg 18:30	776
of the *l* of Egypt unto this day	Judg 19:30	776
with the *l* of Gilead, unto the	Judg 20:1	776
which is in the *l* of Canaan	Judg 21:12	776
and go to the *l* of Benjamin	Judg 21:21	776
that there was a famine in the *l*	Ruth 1:1	776
way to return unto the *l* of Judah	Ruth 1:7	776
the *l* of thy nativity, and art	Ruth 2:11	776
of Moab, selleth a parcel of *l*	Ruth 4:3	7704
of your mice that mar the *l*	1Sa 6:5	776
off your gods, and from off your *l*	1Sa 6:5	776
passed through the *l* of Shalisha	1Sa 9:4	776
passed through the *l* of Shalim	1Sa 9:4	776
through the *l* of the Benjamites	1Sa 9:4	776
they were come to the *l* of Zuph	1Sa 9:5	776
a man out of the *l* of Benjamin	1Sa 9:16	776
fathers up out of the *l* of Egypt	1Sa 12:6	776
the trumpet throughout all the *l*	1Sa 13:3	776
went over Jordan to the *l* of Gad	1Sa 13:7	776
to Ophrah, unto the *l* of Shual	1Sa 13:17	776
throughout all the *l* of Israel	1Sa 13:19	776
as it were an half acre of *l*	1Sa 14:14	7704
all they of the *l* came to a wood	1Sa 14:25	776
My father hath troubled the *l*	1Sa 14:29	776
not this David the king of the *l*	1Sa 21:11	776
and get thee into the *l* of Judah	1Sa 22:5	776
come to pass, if he be in the *l*	1Sa 23:23	776
Philistines have invaded the *l*	1Sa 23:27	776
into the *l* of the Philistines	1Sa 27:1	776
of old the inhabitants of the *l*	1Sa 27:8	776
to Shur, even unto the *l* of Egypt	1Sa 27:8	776
And David smote the *l*, and left	1Sa 27:9	776
and the wizards, out of the *l*	1Sa 28:3	776
and the wizards, out of the *l*	1Sa 28:9	776
into the *l* of the Philistines	1Sa 29:11	776
out of the *l* of the Philistines	1Sa 30:16	776
and out of the *l* of Judah	1Sa 30:16	776
armour, and sent into the *l* of the	1Sa 31:9	776
behalf, saying, Whose is the *l*	2Sa 3:12	776
the inhabitants of the *l*	2Sa 5:6	776
things and terrible, for thy *l*	2Sa 7:23	776
thee all the *l* of Saul thy father	2Sa 9:7	7704
shall till the *l* for him	2Sa 9:10	127
the *l* of the children of Ammon	2Sa 10:2	776
that I were made judge in the *l*	2Sa 15:4	776
pitched in the *l* of Gilead	2Sa 17:26	776
is fled out of the *l* for Absalom	2Sa 19:9	776
said, Thou and Ziba divide the *l*	2Sa 19:29	7704
that God was intreated for the *l*	2Sa 21:14	776
to the *l* of Tahtim-hodshi	2Sa 24:6	776
they had gone through all the *l*	2Sa 24:8	776
of famine come unto thee in thy *l*	2Sa 24:13	776
three days' pestilence in thy *l*	2Sa 24:13	776
the LORD was intreated for the *l*	2Sa 24:25	776
Sochoh, and all the *l* of Hepher	1Kin 4:10	776
only officer which was in the *l*	1Kin 4:19	776
unto the *l* of the Philistines	1Kin 4:21	776
were come out of the *l* of Egypt	1Kin 6:1	776
they came out of the *l* of Egypt	1Kin 8:9	776
them out of the *l* of Egypt	1Kin 8:21	776
bring them again unto the *l* which	1Kin 8:34	127
walk, and give rain upon thy *l*	1Kin 8:36	776
If there be in the *l* famine	1Kin 8:37	776
them in the *l* of their cities	1Kin 8:37	776
the *l* which thou gavest unto our	1Kin 8:40	127
captives unto the *l* of the enemy	1Kin 8:46	776
the *l* whither they were carried	1Kin 8:47	776
the *l* of them that carried them	1Kin 8:47	776
in the *l* of their enemies, which	1Kin 8:48	776
and pray unto thee toward their *l*	1Kin 8:48	776
of the *l* which I have given them	1Kin 9:7	127
the LORD done thus unto this *l*	1Kin 9:8	776
fathers out of the *l* of Egypt	1Kin 9:9	776
twenty cities in the *l* of Galilee	1Kin 9:11	776
he called them the *l* of Cabul	1Kin 9:13	776
in the wilderness, in the *l*	1Kin 9:18	776
in all the *l* of his dominion	1Kin 9:19	776
were left after them in the *l*	1Kin 9:21	776
of the Red sea, in the *l* of Edom	1Kin 9:26	776
I heard in mine own *l* of thy acts	1Kin 10:6	776
him victuals, and gave him *l*	1Kin 11:18	776
thee up out of the *l* of Egypt	1Kin 12:28	776
root up Israel out of this good *l*	1Kin 14:15	127
were also sodomites in the *l*	1Kin 14:24	776
away the sodomites out of the *l*	1Kin 15:12	776
with all the *l* of Naphtali	1Kin 15:20	776
there had been no rain in the *l*	1Kin 17:7	776
said unto Obadiah, Go into the *l*	1Kin 18:5	776
So they divided the *l* between	1Kin 18:6	776
called all the elders of the *l*	1Kin 20:7	776
father Asa, he took out of the *l*	1Kin 22:46	776
thence any more death or barren *l*	2Kin 2:21	776
every good piece of *l* with stones	2Kin 3:19	2513
on every good piece of *l* cast	2Kin 3:25	2513
him, and returned to their own *l*	2Kin 3:27	776
and there was a dearth in the *l*	2Kin 4:38	776
of the *l* of Israel a little maid	2Kin 5:2	776
maid that is of the *l* of Israel	2Kin 5:4	776
came no more into the *l* of Israel	2Kin 6:23	776
also come upon the *l* seven years	2Kin 8:1	776
sojourned in the *l* of the	2Kin 8:2	776
out of the *l* of the Philistines	2Kin 8:3	776
king for her house and for her *l*	2Kin 8:3	7704
king for her house and for her *l*	2Kin 8:5	7704
since the day that she left the *l*	2Kin 8:6	776
all the *l* of Gilead, the Gadites,	2Kin 10:33	776
And Athaliah did reign over the *l*	2Kin 11:3	776
all the people of the *l* rejoiced	2Kin 11:14	776
all the people of the *l* went into	2Kin 11:18	776
guard, and all the people of the *l*	2Kin 11:19	776
all the people of the *l* rejoiced	2Kin 11:20	776

of the Moabites invaded the *l* at 2Kin 13:20 776
judging the people of the *l* 2Kin 15:5 776
of Assyria came against the *l* 2Kin 15:19 776
and stayed not there in the *l* 2Kin 15:20 776
all the *l* of Naphtali, and carried 2Kin 15:29 776
of all the people of the *l* 2Kin 16:15 776
came up throughout all the *l* 2Kin 17:5 776
them up out of the *l* of Egypt 2Kin 17:7 776
own *l* to Assyria unto this day 2Kin 17:23 127
the manner of the God of the *l* 2Kin 17:26 776
the manner of the God of the *l* 2Kin 17:26 776
the manner of the God of the *l* 2Kin 17:27 776
the *l* of Egypt with great power 2Kin 17:36 776
said to me, Go up against this *l* 2Kin 18:25 776
away to a *l* like your own *l* 2Kin 18:32 776
a *l* of corn and wine 2Kin 18:32 776
a *l* of bread and vineyards 2Kin 18:32 776
a *l* of oil olive and of honey 2Kin 18:32 776
nations delivered at all his *l* 2Kin 18:33 776
and shall return to his own *l* 2Kin 19:7 776
to fall by the sword in his own *l* 2Kin 19:7 776
escaped into the *l* of Armenia 2Kin 19:37 776
the *l* which I gave their fathers 2Kin 21:8 127
the people of the *l* slew all them 2Kin 21:24 776
the people of the *l* made Josiah 2Kin 21:24 776
that were spied in the *l* of Judah 2Kin 23:24 776
the people of the *l* took Jehoahaz 2Kin 23:30 776
at Riblah in the *l* of Hamath 2Kin 23:33 776
put the *l* to a tribute of an 2Kin 23:33 776
but he taxed the *l* to give the 2Kin 23:35 776
the gold of the people of the *l* 2Kin 23:35 776
not again any more out of his *l* 2Kin 24:7 776
sort of the people of the *l* 2Kin 24:14 776
officers, and the mighty of the *l* 2Kin 24:15 776
no bread for the people of the *l* 2Kin 25:3 776
poor of the *l* to be vinedressers 2Kin 25:12 776
mustered the people of the *l* 2Kin 25:19 776
men of the people of the *l* that 2Kin 25:19 776
them at Riblah in the *l* of Hamath 2Kin 25:21 776
was carried away out of their *l* 2Kin 25:21 127
that remained in the *l* of Judah 2Kin 25:22 776
dwell in the *l*, and serve the king 2Kin 25:24 776
the kings that reigned in the *l* 1Chr 1:43 776
Husham of the *l* of the Temanites 1Chr 1:45 776
twenty cities in the *l* of Gilead 1Chr 2:22 776
the *l* was wide, and quiet, and 1Chr 4:40 776
multiplied in the *l* of Gilead 1Chr 5:9 776
all the east *l* of Gilead 1Chr 5:10
in the *l* of Bashan unto Salchah 1Chr 5:11 776
tribe of Manasseh dwelt in the *l* 1Chr 5:23 776
the gods of the people of the *l* 1Chr 5:25 776
them Hebron in the *l* of Judah 1Chr 6:55 776
that were born in that *l* slew 1Chr 7:21 776
armour, and sent into the *l* of the 1Chr 10:9 776
were, the inhabitants of the *l* 1Chr 11:4 776
are left in all the *l* of Israel 1Chr 13:2 776
thee will I give the *l* of Canaan 1Chr 16:18 776
the *l* of the children of Ammon to 1Chr 19:2 776
to overthrow, and to spy out the *l* 1Chr 19:3 776
even the pestilence, in the *l* 1Chr 21:12 776
that were in the *l* of Israel 1Chr 22:2 776
of the *l* into mine hand 1Chr 22:18 776
the *l* is subdued before the LORD, 1Chr 22:18 776
that ye may possess this good *l* 1Chr 28:8 776
that were in the *l* of Israel 2Chr 2:17 776
forth my people out of the *l* of 2Chr 6:5 776
the *l* which thou gavest to them 2Chr 6:25 127
and send rain upon thy *l*, which 2Chr 6:27 776
If there be dearth in the *l* 2Chr 6:28 776
them in the cities of their *l* 2Chr 6:28 776
the *l* which thou gavest unto our 2Chr 6:31 127
captives unto a *l* far off or near 2Chr 6:36 776
in the *l* whither they are carried 2Chr 6:37 776
thee in the *l* of their captivity 2Chr 6:37 776
soul in the *l* of their captivity 2Chr 6:38 776
captives, and pray toward their *l* 2Chr 6:38 776
the locusts to devour the *l* 2Chr 7:13 776
their sin, and will heal their *l* 2Chr 7:14 776
of my *l* which I have given them 2Chr 7:20 127
the LORD done thus unto this *l* 2Chr 7:21 776
them forth out of the *l* of Egypt 2Chr 7:22 776
all the *l* of his dominion 2Chr 8:6 776
who were left after them in the *l* 2Chr 8:8 776
at the sea side in the *l* of Edom 2Chr 8:17 776
heard in mine own *l* of thine acts 2Chr 9:5 776
seen before in the *l* of Judah 2Chr 9:11 776
turned, and went away to her own *l* 2Chr 9:12 776
unto the *l* of the Philistines 2Chr 9:26 776
In his days the *l* was quiet ten 2Chr 14:1 776
for the *l* had rest, and he had no 2Chr 14:6 776
while the *l* is yet before us 2Chr 14:7 776
idols out of all the *l* of Judah 2Chr 15:8 776
set garrisons in the *l* of Judah 2Chr 17:2 776
away the groves out of the *l* 2Chr 19:3 776
he set judges in the *l* throughout 2Chr 19:5 776
this *l* before thy people Israel 2Chr 20:7 776
they came out of the *l* of Egypt 2Chr 20:10 776
and Athaliah reigned over the *l* 2Chr 22:12 776
all the people of the *l* rejoiced 2Chr 23:13 776
and all the people of the *l* 2Chr 23:20 776
all the people of the *l* rejoiced 2Chr 23:21 776
judging the people of the *l* 2Chr 26:21 776
they shall come again into this *l* 2Chr 30:9 776
that came out of the *l* of Israel 2Chr 30:25 776
ran through the midst of the *l* 2Chr 32:4 776
with shame of face to his own *l* 2Chr 32:21 776
the wonder that was done in the *l* 2Chr 32:31 776
foot of Israel from out of the *l* 2Chr 33:8 127
But the people of the *l* slew all 2Chr 33:25 776
the people of the *l* made Josiah 2Chr 33:25 776
throughout all the *l* of Israel 2Chr 34:7 776
reign, when he had purged the *l* 2Chr 34:8 776
Then the people of the *l* took 2Chr 36:1 776
condemned the *l* in an hundred 2Chr 36:3 776

until the *l* had enjoyed her 2Chr 36:21 776
Then the people of the *l* weakened Ezr 4:4 776
of the heathen of the *l*, to seek Ezr 6:21 776
the prophets, saying, The *l* Ezr 9:11 776
it is an unclean *l* with the Ezr 9:11 776
strong, and eat the good of the *l* Ezr 9:12 776
wives of the people of the *l* Ezr 10:2 776
from the people of the *l*, and from Ezr 10:11 776
for a prey in the *l* of captivity Neh 4:4 776
their governor in the *l* of Judah Neh 5:14 776
wall, neither bought we any *l* Neh 5:16 7704
to give the *l* of the Canaanites Neh 9:8 776
and on all the people of his *l* Neh 9:10 776
the midst of the sea on the dry *l* Neh 9:11
should go in to possess the *l* Neh 9:15 776
so they possessed the *l* of Sihon Neh 9:22 776
the *l* of the king of Heshbon, and Neh 9:22 776
the *l* of Og king of Bashan Neh 9:22 776
and broughtest them into the *l* Neh 9:23 776
went in and possessed the *l* Neh 9:24 776
them the inhabitants of the *l* Neh 9:24 776
kings, and the people of the *l* Neh 9:24 776
took strong cities, and a fat *l* Neh 9:25 127
fat *l* which thou gavest before Neh 9:35 776
for the *l* that thou gavest unto Neh 9:36 776
unto the people of the *l*, nor Neh 10:30 776
if the people of the *l* bring ware Neh 10:31 776
the people of the *l* became Jews Est 8:17 776
laid a tribute upon the *l* Est 10:1 776
There was a man in the *l* of Uz Job 1:1 776
substance is increased in the *l* Job 1:10 776
return, even to the *l* of darkness Job 10:21 776
A *l* of darkness, as darkness Job 10:22 776
it found in the *l* of the living Job 28:13 776
If my *l* cry against me, or that Job 31:38 127
for correction, or for his *l* Job 37:13 776
the barren *l* his dwellings Job 39:6
in all the *l* were no women found Job 42:15 776
heathen are perished out of his *l* Ps 10:16 776
the LORD in the *l* of the living Ps 27:13 776
them that are quiet in the *l* Ps 35:20 776
so shalt thou dwell in the *l* Ps 37:3 776
The righteous shall inherit the *l* Ps 37:29 776
shall exalt thee to inherit the *l* Ps 37:34 776
thee from the *l* of Jordan Ps 42:6 776
For they got not the *l* in Ps 44:3 776
thee out of the *l* of the living Ps 52:5 776
for thee in a dry and thirsty *l* Ps 63:1 776
He turned the sea into dry *l* Ps 66:6 776
the rebellious dwell in a dry *l* Ps 68:6
the synagogues of God in the *l* Ps 74:8 776
in the *l* of Egypt, in the field Ps 78:12 776
deep root, and it filled the *l* Ps 80:9 776
went out through the *l* of Egypt Ps 81:5 776
thee out of the *l* of Egypt Ps 81:10 776
hast been favourable unto thy *l* Ps 85:1 776
that glory may dwell in our *l* Ps 85:9 776
our *l* shall yield her increase Ps 85:12 776
in the *l* of forgetfulness Ps 88:12 776
and his hands formed the dry *l* Ps 95:5
be upon the faithful of the *l* Ps 101:6 776
destroy all the wicked of the *l* Ps 101:8 776
thee will I give the *l* of Canaan Ps 105:11 776
he called for a famine upon the *l* Ps 105:16 776
Jacob sojourned in the *l* of Ham Ps 105:23 776
them, and wonders in the *l* of Ham Ps 105:27 776
Their *l* brought forth frogs in Ps 105:30 776
rain, and flaming fire in their *l* Ps 105:32 776
eat up all the herbs in their *l* Ps 105:35 776
also all the firstborn in their *l* Ps 105:36 776
Wondrous works in the *l* of Ham Ps 106:22 776
Yea, they despised the pleasant *l* Ps 106:24 776
the *l* was polluted with blood Ps 106:38 776
A fruitful *l* into barrenness, for Ps 107:34 776
the LORD in the *l* of the living Ps 116:9 776
gave their *l* for an heritage, an Ps 135:12 776
gave their *l* for an heritage Ps 136:21 776
the LORD's song in a strange *l* Ps 137:4 127
my portion in the *l* of the living Ps 142:5 776
after thee, as a thirsty *l* Ps 143:6 776
lead me into the *l* of uprightness Ps 143:10 776
the upright shall dwell in the *l* Prov 2:21 776
He that tilleth his *l* shall be Prov 12:11 127
For the transgression of a *l* many Prov 28:2 776
He that tilleth his *l* shall have Prov 28:19 127
by judgment establisheth the *l* Prov 29:4 776
sitteth among the elders of the *l* Prov 31:23 776
Woe to thee, O *l*, when thy king Eccl 10:16 776
Blessed art thou, O *l*, when thy Eccl 10:17 776
of the turtle is heard in our *l* Song 2:12 776
your *l*, strangers devour it in Is 1:7 127
ye shall eat the good of the *l* Is 1:19 776
Their *l* also is full of silver and Is 2:7 776
their *l* is also full of horses, Is 2:7 776
Their *l* also is full of idols Is 2:8 776
and if one look unto the *l* Is 5:30 776
the *l* be utterly desolate Is 6:11 127
forsaking in the midst of the *l* Is 6:12 776
the *l* that thou abhorrest shall Is 7:16 127
bee that is in the *l* of Assyria Is 7:18 776
one eat that is left in the *l* Is 7:22 776
because all the *l* shall become Is 7:24 776
shall fill the breadth of thy *l* Is 8:8 776
afflicted the *l* of Zebulun Is 9:1 776
the *l* of Naphtali, and afterward Is 9:1 776
in the *l* of the shadow of death Is 9:2 776
LORD of hosts is the *l* darkened Is 9:19 776
in the midst of all the *l* Is 10:23 776
he came up out of the *l* of Egypt Is 11:16 776
to destroy the whole *l* Is 13:5 776
anger, to lay the *l* desolate Is 13:9 776
and flee every one into his own *l* Is 13:14 776
and set them in their own *l* Is 14:1 127
in the *l* of the LORD for servants Is 14:2 127

because thou hast destroyed thy *l* Is 14:20 776
do not rise, nor possess the *l* Is 14:21 776
I will break the Assyrian in my *l* Is 14:25 776
and upon the remnant of the *l* Is 15:9 127
the *l* from Sela to the wilderness Is 16:1 776
are consumed out of the *l* Is 16:4 776
Woe to the *l* shadowing with wings Is 18:1 776
whose *l* the rivers have spoiled Is 18:2 776
whose *l* the rivers have spoiled, Is 18:7 776
the *l* of Judah shall be a terror Is 19:17 127
day shall five cities in the *l* of Is 19:18 776
in the midst of the *l* of Egypt Is 19:19 776
LORD of hosts in the *l* of Egypt Is 19:20 776
a blessing in the midst of the *l* Is 19:24 776
the desert, from a terrible *l* Is 21:1 776
The inhabitants of the *l* of Tema Is 21:14 776
from the *l* of Chittim it is Is 23:1 776
Pass through thy *l* as a river Is 23:10 776
Behold the *l* of the Chaldeans Is 23:13 776
The *l* shall be utterly emptied, Is 24:3 776
the mirth of the *l* is gone Is 24:11 776
midst of the *l* among the people Is 24:13 776
song be sung in the *l* of Judah Is 26:1 776
in the *l* of uprightness will he Is 26:10 776
to perish in the *l* of Assyria Is 27:13 776
and the outcasts in the *l* of Egypt Is 27:13 776
into the *l* of trouble and anguish, Is 30:6 776
of a great rock in a weary *l* Is 32:2 776
Upon the *l* of my people shall Is 32:13 127
behold the *l* that is very far off Is 33:17 776
slaughter in the *l* of Idumea Is 34:6 776
their *l* shall be soaked with Is 34:7 776
the *l* thereof shall become Is 34:9 776
the thirsty *l* springs of water Is 35:7
LORD against this *l* to destroy it Is 36:10 776
unto me, Go up against this *l* Is 36:10 776
away to a *l* like your own *l* Is 36:17 776
a *l* of corn and wine Is 36:17 776
a *l* of bread and vineyards Is 36:17 776
of the nations delivered his *l* Is 36:18 776
delivered their *l* out of my hand Is 36:20 776
a rumour, and return to his own *l* Is 37:7 776
to fall by the sword in his own *l* Is 37:7 776
escaped into the *l* of Armenia Is 37:38 776
the LORD, in the *l* of the living Is 38:11 776
the dry *l* springs of water Is 41:18 776
and these from the *l* of Sinim Is 49:12 776
the *l* of thy destruction, shall Is 49:19 776
off out of the *l* of the living Is 53:8 776
trust in me shall possess the *l* Is 57:13 776
shall no more be heard in thy *l* Is 60:18 776
they shall inherit the *l* for ever Is 60:21 776
therefore in their *l* they shall Is 61:7 776
neither shall thy *l* any more be Is 62:4 776
Hephzi-bah, and thy *l* Beulah Is 62:4 776
thee, and thy *l* shall be married Is 62:4 776
in Anathoth in the *l* of Benjamin Jer 1:1 776
upon all the inhabitants of the *l* Jer 1:14 776
brasen walls against the whole *l* Jer 1:18 776
and against the people of the *l* Jer 1:18 776
in a *l* that was not sown Jer 2:2 776
us up out of the *l* of Egypt Jer 2:6 776
through a *l* of deserts and of pits Jer 2:6 776
through a *l* of drought, and of the Jer 2:6 776
through a *l* that no man passed Jer 2:6 776
when ye entered, ye defiled my *l* Jer 2:7 776
yelled, and they made his *l* waste Jer 2:15 776
a *l* of darkness Jer 2:31 776
shall not that *l* be greatly Jer 3:1 776
polluted the *l* with thy whoredoms Jer 3:2 776
whoredom, that she defiled the *l* Jer 3:9 776
multiplied and increased in the *l* Jer 3:16 776
shall come together out of the *l* Jer 3:18 776
to the *l* that I have given for an Jer 3:18 776
and give thee a pleasant *l* Jer 3:19 776
say, Blow ye the trumpet in the *l* Jer 4:5 776
his place to make thy *l* desolate Jer 4:7 776
for the whole *l* is spoiled Jer 4:20 776
The whole *l* shall be desolate Jer 4:27 776
and served strange gods in your *l* Jer 5:19 776
in a *l* that is not yours Jer 5:19 776
thing is committed in the *l* Jer 5:30 776
thee desolate, a *l* not inhabited Jer 6:8 776
upon the inhabitants of the *l* Jer 6:12 776
in the *l* that I gave to your Jer 7:7 776
them out of the *l* of Egypt Jer 7:22 776
l of Egypt unto this day I have Jer 7:25 776
for the *l* shall be desolate Jer 7:34 776
the whole *l* trembled at the sound Jer 8:16 776
are come, and have devoured the *l* Jer 8:16 776
it, for what the *l* perisheth Jer 9:12 776
because we have forsaken the *l* Jer 9:19 776
Gather up thy wares out of the *l* Jer 10:17 776
inhabitants of the *l* at this once Jer 10:18 776
them forth out of the *l* of Egypt Jer 11:4 776
to give them a *l* flowing with Jer 11:5 776
them up out of the *l* of Egypt Jer 11:7 776
him off from the *l* of the living Jer 11:19 776
How long shall the *l* mourn Jer 12:4 776
and if in the *l* of peace, wherein Jer 12:5 776
the whole *l* is made desolate, Jer 12:11 776
l even to the other end of the Jer 12:12 776
even to the other end of the *l* Jer 12:12 776
I will pluck them out of their *l* Jer 12:14 127
heritage, and every man to his *l* Jer 12:15 776
all the inhabitants of this *l* Jer 13:13 776
thou be as a stranger in the *l* Jer 14:8 776
and famine shall not be in this *l* Jer 14:15 776
about into a *l* that they know not Jer 14:18 776
with a fan in the gates of the *l* Jer 15:7 776
into a *l* which thou knowest not Jer 15:14 776
fathers that begat them in this *l* Jer 16:3 776
and the small shall die in this *l* Jer 16:6 776
will I cast you out of this *l* Jer 16:13 776

L

into a *l* that ye know not	Jer 16:13	776
of Israel out of the *l* of Egypt	Jer 16:14	776
of Israel from the *l* of the north	Jer 16:15	776
bring them again into their *l*	Jer 16:15	127
because they have defiled my *l*	Jer 16:18	776
in the *l* which thou knowest not	Jer 17:4	776
in the wilderness, in a salt *l*	Jer 17:6	776
from the *l* of Benjamin, and from	Jer 17:26	776
To make their *l* desolate, and a	Jer 18:16	776
and shall see this *l* no more	Jer 22:12	776
But to the *l* whereunto they	Jer 22:27	776
are cast into a *l* which they know	Jer 22:28	776
of Israel out of the *l* of Egypt	Jer 23:7	776
they shall dwell in their own *l*	Jer 23:8	127
For the *l* is full of adulterers	Jer 23:10	776
of swearing the *l* mourneth	Jer 23:10	776
gone forth into all the *l*	Jer 23:15	776
l of the Chaldeans for their good	Jer 24:5	776
I will bring them again to this *l*	Jer 24:6	776
Jerusalem, that remain in this *l*	Jer 24:8	776
them that dwell in the *l* of Egypt	Jer 24:8	776
off the *l* that I gave unto them	Jer 24:10	127
dwell in the *l* that the LORD hath	Jer 25:5	127
and will bring them against this *l*	Jer 25:9	776
And this whole *l* shall be a	Jer 25:11	776
the *l* of the Chaldeans, and will	Jer 25:12	776
I will bring upon that *l* all my	Jer 25:13	776
and all the kings of the *l* of Uz	Jer 25:20	776
kings of the *l* of the Philistines	Jer 25:20	776
for their *l* is desolate because	Jer 25:38	776
up certain of the elders of the *l*	Jer 26:17	776
against this *l* according to all	Jer 26:20	776
until the very time of his *l* come	Jer 27:7	776
to remove you far from your *l*	Jer 27:10	127
I let remain still in their own *l*	Jer 27:11	127
cause them to return to the *l*	Jer 30:3	776
thy seed from the *l* of their	Jer 30:10	776
again from the *l* of the enemy	Jer 31:16	776
use this speech in the *l* of Judah	Jer 31:23	776
bring them out of the *l* of Egypt	Jer 31:32	776
be possessed again in this *l*	Jer 32:15	776
and wonders in the *l* of Egypt	Jer 32:20	776
out of the *l* of Egypt with signs	Jer 32:21	776
And hast given them this *l*	Jer 32:22	776
a *l* flowing with milk and honey	Jer 32:22	776
I will plant them in this *l*	Jer 32:41	776
fields shall be bought in this *l*	Jer 32:43	776
witnesses in the *l* of Benjamin	Jer 32:44	776
to return the captivity of the *l*	Jer 33:11	776
in the *l* of Benjamin, and in the	Jer 33:13	776
and righteousness in the *l*	Jer 33:15	776
them forth out of the *l* of Egypt	Jer 34:13	776
and all the people of the *l*	Jer 34:19	776
in the *l* where ye be strangers	Jer 35:7	127
of Babylon came up into the *l*	Jer 35:11	776
ye shall dwell in the *l* which I	Jer 35:15	127
certainly come and destroy this *l*	Jer 36:29	776
made king in the *l* of Judah	Jer 37:1	776
servants, nor the people of the *l*	Jer 37:2	776
return to Egypt into their own *l*	Jer 37:7	776
to go into the *l* of Benjamin	Jer 37:12	776
against you, nor against this *l*	Jer 37:19	776
to Riblah in the *l* of Hamath	Jer 39:5	776
in the *l* of Judah, and gave them	Jer 39:10	776
behold, all the *l* is before thee	Jer 40:4	776
people that were left in the *l*	Jer 40:6	776
son of Ahikam governor in the *l*	Jer 40:7	776
children, and of the poor of the *l*	Jer 40:7	776
dwell in the *l*, and serve the king	Jer 40:9	776
driven, and came to the *l* of Judah	Jer 40:12	776
had made governor over the *l*	Jer 41:2	776
of Babylon made governor in the *l*	Jer 41:18	776
If ye will still abide in this *l*	Jer 42:10	776
cause you to return to your own *l*	Jer 42:12	127
say, We will not dwell in this *l*	Jer 42:13	776
we will go into the *l* of Egypt	Jer 42:14	776
you there in the *l* of Egypt	Jer 42:16	776
LORD, to dwell in the *l* of Judah	Jer 43:4	776
to dwell in the *l* of Judah	Jer 43:5	776
So they came into the *l* of Egypt	Jer 43:7	776
he shall smite the *l* of Egypt	Jer 43:11	776
array himself with the *l* of Egypt	Jer 43:12	776
that is in the *l* of Egypt	Jer 43:13	776
which dwell in the *l* of Egypt	Jer 44:1	776
unto other gods in the *l* of Egypt	Jer 44:8	776
have committed in the *l* of Judah	Jer 44:9	776
the *l* of Egypt to sojourn there	Jer 44:12	776
and fall in the *l* of Egypt	Jer 44:12	776
them that dwell in the *l* of Egypt	Jer 44:13	776
which are gone into the *l* of	Jer 44:14	776
should return into the *l* of Judah	Jer 44:14	776
that dwelt in the *l* of Egypt	Jer 44:15	776
princes, and the people of the *l*	Jer 44:21	776
therefore is your *l* a desolation	Jer 44:22	776
Judah that are in the *l* of Egypt	Jer 44:24	776
that dwell in the *l* of Egypt	Jer 44:26	776
of Judah in all the *l* of Egypt	Jer 44:26	776
men of Judah that are in the *l* of	Jer 44:27	776
l of Egypt into the *l* of Judah	Jer 44:28	776
that are gone into the *l* of Egypt	Jer 44:28	776
will pluck up, even this whole *l*	Jer 45:4	776
and thy cry hath filled the *l*	Jer 46:12	776
come and smite the *l* of Egypt	Jer 46:13	776
to the *l* of our nativity, from	Jer 46:16	776
thy seed from the *l* of their	Jer 46:27	776
flood, and shall overflow the *l*	Jer 47:2	776
inhabitants of the *l* shall howl	Jer 47:2	776
all the cities of the *l* of Moab	Jer 48:24	776
field, and from the *l* of Moab	Jer 48:33	776
against the *l* of the Chaldeans by	Jer 50:1	776
which shall make her *l* desolate	Jer 50:3	776
out of the *l* of the Chaldeans	Jer 50:8	776
shall be a wilderness, a dry *l*	Jer 50:12	
shall flee every one to his own *l*	Jer 50:16	776
the king of Babylon and his *l*	Jer 50:18	776
Go up against the *l* of Merathaim	Jer 50:21	776
A sound of battle is in the *l*	Jer 50:22	776
hosts in the *l* of the Chaldeans	Jer 50:25	776
and escape out of the *l* of Babylon	Jer 50:28	776
that he may give rest to the *l*	Jer 50:34	776
for it is the *l* of graven images,	Jer 50:38	776
against the *l* of the Chaldeans	Jer 50:45	776
fan her, and shall empty her *l*	Jer 51:2	776
fall in the *l* of the Chaldeans	Jer 51:4	776
though their *l* was filled with	Jer 51:5	776
Set ye up a standard in the *l*	Jer 51:27	776
all the *l* of his dominion	Jer 51:28	776
the *l* shall tremble and sorrow	Jer 51:29	776
to make the *l* of Babylon a	Jer 51:29	776
cities are a desolation, a dry *l*	Jer 51:43	776
a *l* wherein no man dwelleth,	Jer 51:43	776
that shall be heard in the *l*	Jer 51:46	776
a rumour, and violence in the *l*	Jer 51:46	776
her whole *l* shall be confounded,	Jer 51:47	776
through all her *l* the wounded	Jer 51:52	776
from the *l* of the Chaldeans	Jer 51:54	776
no bread for the people of the *l*	Jer 52:6	776
to Riblah in the *l* of Hamath	Jer 52:9	776
poor of the *l* for vinedressers	Jer 52:16	776
who mustered the people of the *l*	Jer 52:25	776
men of the people of the *l*	Jer 52:25	776
in Riblah in the *l* of Hamath	Jer 52:27	776
away captive out of his own *l*	Jer 52:27	127
that dwellest in the *l* of Uz	Lam 4:21	776
in the *l* of the Chaldeans by the	Eze 1:3	776
upon them, and make the *l* desolate	Eze 6:14	776
the Lord GOD unto the *l* of Israel	Eze 7:2	127
upon the four corners of the *l*	Eze 7:2	776
O thou that dwellest in the *l*	Eze 7:7	776
for the *l* is full of bloody	Eze 7:23	776
people of the *l* shall be troubled	Eze 7:27	776
have filled the *l* with violence	Eze 8:17	776
the *l* is full of blood, and the	Eze 9:9	776
unto us is this *l* given in	Eze 11:15	776
I will give you the *l* of Israel	Eze 11:17	127
Babylon to the *l* of the Chaldeans	Eze 12:13	776
And say unto the people of the *l*	Eze 12:19	776
Jerusalem, and of the *l* of Israel	Eze 12:19	127
that her *l* may be desolate from	Eze 12:19	776
waste, and the *l* shall be desolate	Eze 12:20	776
that ye have in the *l* of Israel	Eze 12:22	127
they enter into the *l* of Israel	Eze 13:9	127
when the *l* sinneth against me by	Eze 14:13	776
beasts to pass through the *l*	Eze 14:15	776
but the *l* shall be desolate	Eze 14:16	776
Or if I bring a sword upon that *l*	Eze 14:17	776
and say, Sword, go through the *l*	Eze 14:17	776
I send a pestilence into that *l*	Eze 14:19	776
And I will make the *l* desolate	Eze 15:8	776
nativity is of the *l* of Canaan	Eze 16:3	776
in the *l* of Canaan unto Chaldea	Eze 16:29	776
carried it into a *l* of traffick	Eze 17:4	776
He took also of the seed of the *l*	Eze 17:5	776
also taken the mighty of the *l*	Eze 17:13	776
concerning the *l* of Israel	Eze 18:2	127
with chains unto the *l* of Egypt	Eze 19:4	776
the *l* was desolate, and the	Eze 19:7	776
known unto them in the *l* of Egypt	Eze 20:5	776
to bring them forth of the *l* of	Eze 20:6	776
a *l* that I had espied for them	Eze 20:6	776
in the midst of the *l* of Egypt	Eze 20:8	776
them forth out of the *l* of Egypt	Eze 20:9	776
to go forth out of the *l* of Egypt	Eze 20:10	776
into the *l* which I had given them	Eze 20:15	776
I had brought them into the *l*	Eze 20:28	776
the wilderness of the *l* of Egypt	Eze 20:36	776
not enter into the *l* of Israel	Eze 20:38	127
of Israel, all of them in the *l*	Eze 20:40	776
bring you into the *l* of Israel	Eze 20:42	127
prophesy against the *l* of Israel	Eze 21:2	127
And say to the *l* of Israel	Eze 21:3	127
shall come forth out of one *l*	Eze 21:19	776
created, in the *l* of thy nativity	Eze 21:30	776
shall be in the midst of the *l*	Eze 21:32	776
Thou art the *l* that is not	Eze 22:24	776
The people of the *l* have used	Eze 22:29	776
in the gap before me for the *l*	Eze 22:30	776
Chaldea, the *l* of their nativity	Eze 23:15	776
the harlot in the *l* of Egypt	Eze 23:19	776
brought from the *l* of Egypt	Eze 23:27	776
lewdness to cease out of the *l*	Eze 23:48	776
and against the *l* of Israel	Eze 25:3	127
despite against the *l* of Israel	Eze 25:6	127
set glory in the *l* of the living	Eze 26:20	776
the *l* of Israel, they were thy	Eze 27:17	776
they shall stand upon the *l*	Eze 27:29	776
then shall they dwell in their *l*	Eze 28:25	127
the *l* of gypt shall be desolate	Eze 29:9	776
I will make the *l* of Egypt	Eze 29:10	776
I will make the *l* of Egypt	Eze 29:12	776
to return into the *l* of Pathros	Eze 29:14	776
into the *l* of their habitation	Eze 29:14	776
I will give the *l* of Egypt unto	Eze 29:19	776
I have given him the *l* of Egypt	Eze 29:20	776
the men of the *l* that is in	Eze 30:5	776
shall be brought to destroy the *l*	Eze 30:11	776
fill the *l* with the slain	Eze 30:11	776
sell the *l* into the hand of the	Eze 30:12	776
and I will make the *l* waste	Eze 30:12	776
more a prince of the *l* of Egypt	Eze 30:13	776
will put a fear in the *l* of Egypt	Eze 30:13	776
it out upon the *l* of Egypt	Eze 30:25	776
broken by all the rivers of the *l*	Eze 31:12	776
Then will I leave thee upon the *l*	Eze 32:4	776
blood the *l* wherein thou swimmest	Eze 32:6	776
thee, and set darkness upon thy *l*	Eze 32:8	776
make the *l* of Egypt desolate	Eze 32:15	776
terror in the *l* of the living	Eze 32:23	776
terror in the *l* of the living	Eze 32:24	776
was caused in the *l* of the living	Eze 32:25	776
terror in the *l* of the living	Eze 32:26	776
the mighty in the *l* of the living	Eze 32:27	776
my terror in the *l* of the living	Eze 32:32	776
When I bring the sword upon a *l*	Eze 33:2	776
if the people of the *l* take a man	Eze 33:2	776
seeth the sword come upon the *l*	Eze 33:3	776
wastes of the *l* of Israel speak	Eze 33:24	127
was one, and he inherited the *l*	Eze 33:24	776
the *l* is given us for inheritance	Eze 33:24	776
and shall ye possess the *l*	Eze 33:25	776
and shall ye possess the *l*	Eze 33:26	776
I will lay the *l* most desolate	Eze 33:28	776
when I have laid the *l* most	Eze 33:29	776
and will bring them to their own *l*	Eze 34:13	127
evil beasts to cease out of the *l*	Eze 34:25	776
and they shall be safe in their *l*	Eze 34:27	127
the beast of the *l* devour them	Eze 34:28	776
consumed with hunger in the *l*	Eze 34:29	776
which have appointed my *l* into	Eze 36:5	776
concerning the *l* of Israel	Eze 36:6	127
Thou *l* devourest up men, and hast	Eze 36:13	
of Israel dwelt in their own *l*	Eze 36:17	127
that they had shed upon the *l*	Eze 36:18	776
and are gone forth out of his *l*	Eze 36:20	776
and will bring you into your own *l*	Eze 36:24	127
ye shall dwell in the *l* that I,	Eze 36:28	776
the desolate *l* shall be tilled,	Eze 36:34	776
This *l* that was desolate is	Eze 36:35	776
and bring you into the *l* of Israel	Eze 37:12	127
I shall place you in your own *l*	Eze 37:14	127
and bring them into their own *l*	Eze 37:21	127
make them one nation in the *l*	Eze 37:22	776
they shall dwell in the *l* that I	Eze 37:25	776
the *l* of Magog, the chief prince	Eze 38:2	776
l that is brought back from the	Eze 38:8	776
be like a cloud to cover the *l*	Eze 38:9	776
I will go up to the *l* of unwalled	Eze 38:11	776
that dwell in the midst of the *l*	Eze 38:12	776
Israel, as a cloud to cover the *l*	Eze 38:16	776
and I will bring thee against my *l*	Eze 38:16	776
come against the *l* of Israel	Eze 38:18	127
great shaking in the *l* of Israel	Eze 38:19	127
them, that they may cleanse the *l*	Eze 39:12	776
people of the *l* shall bury them	Eze 39:13	776
passing through the *l* to bury	Eze 39:14	776
that pass through the *l*, when any	Eze 39:15	776
Thus shall they cleanse the *l*	Eze 39:16	776
when they dwelt safely in their *l*	Eze 39:26	127
gathered them unto their own *l*	Eze 39:28	127
he me into the *l* of Israel	Eze 40:2	776
by lot the *l* for inheritance	Eze 45:1	776
LORD, an holy portion of the *l*	Eze 45:1	776
The holy portion of the *l* shall	Eze 45:4	776
In the *l* shall be his possession	Eze 45:8	776
the rest of the *l* shall they give	Eze 45:8	776
All the people of the *l* shall	Eze 45:16	776
for all the people of the *l* a	Eze 45:22	776
Likewise the people of the *l*	Eze 46:3	776
But when the people of the *l*	Eze 46:9	776
whereby ye shall inherit the *l*	Eze 47:13	776
this *l* shall fall unto you for	Eze 47:14	776
of the *l* toward the north side	Eze 47:15	776
from the *l* of Israel by Jordan,	Eze 47:18	776
So shall ye divide this *l* unto	Eze 47:21	776
this oblation of the *l* that is	Eze 48:12	776
alienate the firstfruits of the *l*	Eze 48:14	776
This is the *l* which ye shall	Eze 48:29	776
which he carried into the *l* of	Dan 1:2	776
east, and toward the pleasant *l*	Dan 8:9	
and to all the people of the *l*	Dan 9:6	776
the *l* of Egypt with a mighty hand	Dan 9:15	776
and shall return into his own *l*	Dan 11:9	127
he shall stand in the glorious *l*	Dan 11:16	776
face toward the fort of his own *l*	Dan 11:19	776
into his *l* with great riches	Dan 11:28	776
exploits, and return to his own *l*	Dan 11:28	776
and shall divide the *l* for gain	Dan 11:39	127
enter also into the glorious *l*	Dan 11:41	776
the *l* of Egypt shall not escape	Dan 11:42	776
for the *l* hath committed great	Hos 1:2	776
they shall come up out of the *l*	Hos 1:11	776
and set her like a dry *l*, and slay	Hos 2:3	776
she came up out of the *l* of Egypt	Hos 2:15	776
with the inhabitants of the *l*	Hos 4:1	776
nor knowledge of God in the *l*	Hos 4:1	776
Therefore shall the *l* mourn	Hos 4:3	776
their derision in the *l* of Egypt	Hos 7:16	776
shall not dwell in the LORD's *l*	Hos 9:3	776
to the goodness of his *l* they	Hos 10:1	776
not return into the *l* of Egypt	Hos 11:5	776
as a dove out of the *l* of Assyria	Hos 11:11	776
am the LORD thy God from the *l* of	Hos 12:9	776
LORD thy God from the *l* of Egypt	Hos 13:4	776
in the *l* of great drought	Hos 13:5	776
ear, all ye inhabitants of the *l*	Joel 1:2	776
For a nation is come up upon my *l*	Joel 1:6	776
field is wasted, the *l* mourneth	Joel 1:10	127
all the inhabitants of the *l* into	Joel 1:14	776
the inhabitants of the *l* tremble	Joel 2:1	776
the *l* is as the garden of Eden	Joel 2:3	776
the LORD be jealous for his *l*	Joel 2:18	776
and will drive him into a *l* barren	Joel 2:20	776
Fear not, O *l*	Joel 2:21	127
among the nations, and parted my *l*	Joel 3:2	776
shed innocent blood in their *l*	Joel 3:19	776
you up from the *l* of Egypt	Amos 2:10	776
to possess the *l* of the Amorite	Amos 2:10	776
I brought up from the *l* of Egypt	Amos 3:1	776
in the palaces in the *l* of Egypt	Amos 3:9	776
shall be even round about the *l*	Amos 3:11	776
she is forsaken upon her *l*	Amos 5:2	127
end of eating the grass of the *l*	Amos 7:2	776

the *l* is not able to bear all his ... Amos 7:10 776
away captive out of their own *l* ... Amos 7:11 127
thee away into the *l* of Judah ... Amos 7:12 776
thy *l* shall be divided by line ... Amos 7:17 127
and thou shalt die in a polluted *l* ... Amos 7:17 127
go into captivity forth of his *l* ... Amos 7:17 127
to make the poor of the *l* to fail ... Amos 8:4 776
Shall not the *l* tremble for this, ... Amos 8:8 776
I will send a famine in the *l* ... Amos 8:11 776
hosts is he that toucheth the *l* ... Amos 9:5 776
up Israel out of the *l* of Egypt ... Amos 9:7 776
And I will plant them upon their *l* ... Amos 9:15 127
their *l* which I have given them ... Amos 9:15 127
hath made the sea and the dry *l* ... Jonah 1:9
rowed hard to bring it to the *l* ... Jonah 1:13 3004
vomited out Jonah upon the dry *l* ... Jonah 2:10
Assyrian shall come into our *l* ... Mic 5:5 776
they shall waste the *l* of Assyria ... Mic 5:6 776
the *l* of Nimrod in the entrances ... Mic 5:6 776
when he cometh into our *l* ... Mic 5:6 776
will cut off the cities of thy *l* ... Mic 5:11 776
thee up out of the *l* of Egypt ... Mic 6:4 776
Notwithstanding the *l* shall be ... Mic 7:13 776
l of Egypt will I shew unto him ... Mic 7:15 776
the gates of thy *l* shall be set ... Nah 3:13 776
through the breadth of the *l* ... Hab 1:6 776
and for the violence of the *l* ... Hab 2:8 776
and for the violence of the *l* ... Hab 2:17 776
the curtains of the *l* of Midian ... Hab 3:7 776
through the *l* in indignation ... Hab 3:12 776
consume all things from off the *l* ... Zeph 1:2 127
I will cut off man from off the *l* ... Zeph 1:3 127
but the whole *l* shall be devoured ... Zeph 1:18 776
of all them that dwell in the *l* ... Zeph 1:18 776
the *l* of the Philistines, I will ... Zeph 2:5 776
fame in every *l* where they have ... Zeph 3:19 776
I called for a drought upon the *l* ... Hag 1:11 776
be strong, all ye people of the *l* ... Hag 2:4 776
earth, and the sea, and the dry *l* ... Hag 2:6
over the *l* of Judah to scatter it ... Zec 1:21 776
and flee from the *l* of the north ... Zec 2:6 776
Judah his portion in the holy *l* ... Zec 2:12 127
the iniquity of that *l* in one day ... Zec 3:9 776
it an house in the *l* of Shinar ... Zec 5:11 776
unto all the people of the *l* ... Zec 7:5 776
Thus the *l* was desolate after ... Zec 7:14 776
they laid the pleasant *l* desolate ... Zec 7:14 776
of the LORD in the *l* of Hadrach ... Zec 9:1 776
lifted up as an ensign upon his *l* ... Zec 9:16 127
again also out of the *l* of Egypt ... Zec 10:10 776
bring them into the *l* of Gilead ... Zec 10:10 776
pity the inhabitants of the *l* ... Zec 11:6 776
and they shall smite the *l* ... Zec 11:6 776
will raise up a shepherd in the *l* ... Zec 11:16 776
the *l* shall mourn, every family ... Zec 12:12 776
names of the idols out of the *l* ... Zec 13:2 776
spirit to pass out of the *l* ... Zec 13:2 776
come to pass, that in all the *l* ... Zec 13:8 776
All the *l* shall be turned as a ... Zec 14:10 776
for ye shall be a delightsome *l* ... Mal 3:12 776
in the *l* of Juda, art not the ... Mt 2:6 *1093*
and go into the *l* of Israel ... Mt 2:20 *1093*
and came into the *l* of Israel ... Mt 2:21 *1093*
The *l* of Zabulon ... Mt 4:15 *1093*
the *l* of Nephthalim, by the way ... Mt 4:15 *1093*
went abroad into all that *l* ... Mt 9:26 *1093*
more tolerable for the *l* of Sodom ... Mt 10:15 *1093*
l of Sodom in the day of judgment ... Mt 11:24 *1093*
came into the *l* of Gennesaret ... Mt 14:34 *1093*
l to make one proselyte, and when ... Mt 23:15 *3584*
all the *l* unto the ninth hour ... Mt 27:45 *1093*
out unto him all the *l* of Judaea ... Mk 1:5 *5561*
multitude was by the sea on the *l* ... Mk 4:1 *1093*
of the sea, and he alone on the *l* ... Mk 6:47 *1093*
came into the *l* of Gennesaret ... Mk 6:53 *1093*
the whole *l* until the ninth hour ... Mk 15:33 *1093*
famine was throughout all the *l* ... Lk 4:25 *1093*
thrust out a little from the *l* ... Lk 5:3 *1093*
they had brought their ships to *l* ... Lk 5:11 *1093*
And when he went forth to *l* ... Lk 8:27 *1093*
It is neither fit for the *l* ... Lk 14:35 *1093*
arose a mighty famine in that *l* ... Lk 15:14 *5561*
shall be great distress in the *l* ... Lk 21:23 *1093*
disciples into the *l* of Judaea ... Jn 3:22 *1093*
was at the *l* whither they went ... Jn 6:21 *1093*
(for they were not far from *l* ... Jn 21:8 *1093*
soon then as they were come to *l* ... Jn 21:9 *1093*
drew the net to *l* full of great ... Jn 21:11 *1093*
Having *l*, sold it, and brought the ... Acts 4:37 *68*
back part of the price of the *l* ... Acts 5:3 *5564*
whether ye sold the *l* for so much ... Acts 5:8 *5564*
come into the *l* which I shall ... Acts 7:3 *1093*
he out of the *l* of the Chaldaeans ... Acts 7:4 *1093*
dead, he removed him into this *l* ... Acts 7:4 *1093*
should sojourn in a strange *l* ... Acts 7:6 *1093*
a dearth over all the *l* of Egypt ... Acts 7:11 *1093*
was a stranger in the *l* of Madian ... Acts 7:29 *1093*
and signs in the *l* of Egypt ... Acts 7:36 *1093*
brought us out of the *l* of Egypt ... Acts 7:40 *1093*
he did both in the *l* of the Jews ... Acts 10:39 *5561*
as strangers in the *l* of Egypt ... Acts 13:17 *1093*
seven nations in the *l* of Chanaan ... Acts 13:19 *1093*
he divided their *l* to them by lot ... Acts 13:19 *1093*
it was day, they knew not the *l* ... Acts 27:39 *1093*
first into the sea, and get to *l* ... Acts 27:43 *1093*
that they escaped all safe to *l* ... Acts 27:44 *1093*
lead them out of the *l* of Egypt ... Heb 8:9 *1093*
he sojourned in the *l* of promise ... Heb 11:9 *1093*
through the Red sea as by dry *l* ... Heb 11:29
the people out of the *l* of Egypt ... Jude 5 *1093*

LANDED
And when he had *l* at Caesarea ... Acts 18:22 *2718*
sailed into Syria, and *l* at Tyre ... Acts 21:3 *2609*

LANDING
l at Syracuse, we tarried there ... Acts 28:12 *2609*

LANDMARK
not remove thy neighbour's *l* ... Deut 19:14 1366
that removeth his neighbour's *l* ... Deut 27:17 1366
Remove not the ancient *l*, which ... Prov 22:28 1366
Remove not the old *l* ... Prov 23:10 1366

LANDMARKS
Some remove the *l* ... Job 24:2 1367

LANDS
the Gentiles divided in their *l* ... Gen 10:5 776
after their tongues, in their *l* ... Gen 10:31 776
and the dearth was in all *l* ... Gen 41:54 776
the famine was so sore in all *l* ... Gen 41:57 776
my lord, but our bodies, and our *l* ... Gen 47:18 127
wherefore they sold not their *l* ... Gen 47:22 127
hearts in the *l* of their enemies ... Lev 26:36 776
their iniquity in your enemies' *l* ... Lev 26:39 776
restore those *l* again peaceably ... Judg 11:13
of Assyria have done to all *l* ... 2Kin 19:11 776
destroyed the nations and their *l* ... 2Kin 19:17 776
fame of David went out into all *l* ... 1Chr 14:17 776
out of Egypt, and out of all *l* ... 2Chr 9:28 776
manner of the nations of other *l* ... 2Chr 13:9 776
the *l* that were round about Judah ... 2Chr 17:10 776
unto all the people of other *l* ... 2Chr 32:13 776
gods of the nations of those *l* ... 2Chr 32:13 776
deliver their *l* out of mine hand ... 2Chr 32:13 776
gods of the nations of other *l* ... 2Chr 32:17 776
from the people of the *l*, doing ... Ezr 9:1 776
with the people of those *l* ... Ezr 9:2 776
the hand of the kings of the *l* ... Ezr 9:7 776
filthiness of the people of the *l* ... Ezr 9:11 776
said, We have mortgaged our *l* ... Neh 5:3 7704
tribute, and that upon our *l* ... Neh 5:4 7704
for other men have our *l* and ... Neh 5:5 7704
to them, even this day, their *l* ... Neh 5:11 7704
the hand of the people of the *l* ... Neh 9:30 776
of the *l* unto the law of God ... Neh 10:28 776
they call their *l* after their own ... Ps 49:11 127
a joyful noise unto God, all ye *l* ... Ps 66:1 776
noise unto the LORD, all ye *l* ... Ps 100:1 776
gave them the *l* of the heathen ... Ps 105:44 776
and to scatter them in the *l* ... Ps 106:27 776
And gathered them out of the *l* ... Ps 107:3 776
among all the gods of these *l* ... Is 36:20 776
all *l* by destroying them utterly ... Is 37:11 776
from all the *l* whither he had ... Jer 16:15 776
now have I given all these *l* into ... Jer 27:6 776
which is the glory of all *l* ... Eze 20:6 776
which is the glory of all *l* ... Eze 20:15 776
them out of their enemies' *l* ... Eze 39:27 776
or wife, or children, or *l* ... Mt 19:29 *68*
or wife, or children, or *l* ... Mk 10:29 *68*
and mothers, and children, and *l* ... Mk 10:30 *68*
of *l* or houses sold them, and ... Acts 4:34 *5564*

LANES
l of the city, and bring in hither ... Lk 14:21 *4505*

LANGUAGE
And the whole earth was of one *l* ... Gen 11:1 8193
is one, and they have all one *l* ... Gen 11:6 8193
down, and there confound their *l* ... Gen 11:7 8193
confound the *l* of all the earth ... Gen 11:9 8193
to thy servants in the Syrian *l* ... 2Kin 18:26
talk not with us in the Jews' *l* ... 2Kin 18:26
with a loud voice in the Jews' *l* ... 2Kin 18:28
and could not speak in the Jews' *l* ... Neh 13:24
according to the *l* of each people ... Neh 13:24 3956
and to every people after their *l* ... Est 1:22 3956
to the *l* of every people ... Est 1:22 3956
and to every people after their *l* ... Est 3:12 3956
unto every people after their *l* ... Est 8:9 3956
writing, and according to their *l* ... Est 8:9 3956
There is no speech nor *l*, where ... Ps 19:3 1697
where I heard a *l* that I ... Ps 81:5 8193
Jacob from a people of strange *l* ... Ps 114:1 3937
of Egypt speak the *l* of Canaan ... Is 19:18 8193
unto thy servants in the Syrian *l* ... Is 36:11
and speak not to us in the Jews' *l* ... Is 36:11
with a loud voice in the Jews' *l* ... Is 36:13
a nation whose *l* thou knowest not ... Jer 5:15 3956
a strange speech and of an hard *l* ... Eze 3:5 3956
a strange speech and of an hard *l* ... Eze 3:6 3956
That every people, nation, and *l* ... Dan 3:29 3961
I turn to the people a pure *l* ... Zeph 3:9 8193
man heard them speak in his own *l* ... Acts 2:6 *1258*

LANGUAGES
O people, nations, and *l*, ... Dan 3:4 3961
the people, the nations, and the *l* ... Dan 3:7 3961
unto all people, nations, and *l* ... Dan 4:1 3961
him, all people, nations, and *l* ... Dan 5:19 3961
unto all people, nations, and *l* ... Dan 6:25 3961
that all people, nations, and *l* ... Dan 7:14 3961
hold out of all *l* of the nations ... Zec 8:23 3956

LANGUISH
For the fields of Heshbon *l* ... Is 16:8 535
nets upon the waters shall *l* ... Is 19:8 535
haughty people of the earth do *l* ... Is 24:4 535
mourneth, and the gates thereof *l* ... Jer 14:2 535
one that dwelleth therein shall *l* ... Hos 4:3 535

LANGUISHED
they *l* together ... Lam 2:8 535

LANGUISHETH
and fadeth away, the world *l* ... Is 24:4 535
The new wine mourneth, the vine *l* ... Is 24:7 535
The earth mourneth and *l* ... Is 33:9 535
She that hath borne seven *l* ... Jer 15:9 535
new wine is dried up, the oil *l* ... Joel 1:10 535
is dried up, and the fig tree *l* ... Joel 1:12 535
Bashan *l*, and Carmel ... Nah 1:4 535
and the flower of Lebanon *l* ... Nah 1:4 535

LANGUISHING
strengthen him upon the bed of *l* ... Ps 41:3 1741

LANTERNS
Pharisees, cometh thither with *l* ... Jn 18:3 *5322*

LAODICEA (*la-od-i-se'-ah*) *Chief city of Phrygia.*
I have for you, and for them at *L* ... Col 2:1 *2993*
for you, and them that are in *L* ... Col 4:13 *2993*
the brethren which are in *L* ... Col 4:15 *2993*
likewise read the epistle from *L* ... Col 4:16 *2993*
to Timothy was written from *L* ... 1Ti s
and unto Philadelphia, and unto *L* ... Rev 1:11 *2993*

LAODICEANS (*la-od-i-se'-uns*) *Inhabitants of Laodicea.*
read also in the church of the *L* ... Col 4:16 *2994*
of the church of the *L* write ... Rev 3:14 *2994*

LAP
thereof wild gourds his *l* full ... 2Kin 4:39 899
Also I shook my *l*, and said, So ... Neh 5:13 2684
The lot is cast into the *l* ... Prov 16:33 2436

LAPIDOTH (*lap'-i-doth*) *Husband of Deborah.*
a prophetess, the wife of *L* ... Judg 4:4 3941

LAPPED
And the number of them that *l* ... Judg 7:6 3952
men that *l* will I save you ... Judg 7:7 3952

LAPPETH
Every one that *l* of the water ... Judg 7:5 3952
water with his tongue, as a dog *l* ... Judg 7:5 3952

LAPPIDOTH See LAPIDOTH.

LAPWING
heron after her kind, and the *l* ... Lev 11:19 1744
heron after her kind, and the *l* ... Deut 14:18 1744

LARGE
behold, it is *l* enough for them ... Gen 34:21 7342
that land unto a good land and a *l* ... Ex 3:8 7342
a people secure, and to a *l* land ... Judg 18:10
me forth also into a *l* place ... 2Sa 22:20 4800
people, The work is great and *l* ... Neh 4:19 7342
Now the city was *l* and great ... Neh 7:4
thou gavest them, and in the *l* ... Neh 9:35 7342
me forth also into a *l* place ... Ps 18:19 4800
thou hast set my feet in a *l* room ... Ps 31:8 4800
me, and set me in a *l* place ... Ps 118:5 4800
thee like a ball into a *l* country ... Is 22:18
thy cattle feed in *l* pastures ... Is 30:23 7337
he hath made it deep and *l* ... Is 30:33 7337
l chambers, and cutteth him out ... Jer 22:14 7304
of thy sister's cup deep and *l* ... Eze 23:32 7342
feed them as a lamb in a *l* place ... Hos 4:16 4800
they gave *l* money unto the ... Mt 28:12 *2425*
he will shew you a *l* upper room ... Mk 14:15 *3173*
he shall shew you a *l* upper room ... Lk 22:12 *3173*
Ye see how *l* a letter I have ... Gal 6:11 *4080*
the length is as *l* as the breadth ... Rev 21:16 *5118*

LARGENESS
l of heart, even as the sand that ... 1Kin 4:29 7341

LASCIVIOUSNESS
wickedness, deceit, *l*, an evil ... Mk 7:22 *766*
l which they have committed ... 2Cor 12:21 *766*
fornication, uncleanness, *l* ... Gal 5:19 *766*
have given themselves over unto *l* ... Eph 4:19 *766*
the Gentiles, when we walked in *l* ... 1Pet 4:3 *766*
the grace of our God into *l* ... Jude 4 *766*

LASEA (*la-se'-ah*) *A city on Crete.*
nigh whereunto was the city of *L* ... Acts 27:8 *2996*

LASHA (*la'-shah*) *A place in southern Canaan.*
and Admah, and Zeboim, even unto *L*. Gen 10:19 3962

LASHARON (*lash'-ar-on*) *A Canaanite town.*
the king of *L*, one ... Josh 12:18 8289

LAST
shall befall you in the *l* days ... Gen 49:1 319
but he shall overcome at the *l* ... Gen 49:19 6119
and let my *l* end be like his ... Num 23:10 319
Why are ye the *l* to bring the ... 2Sa 19:11 314
ye the *l* to bring back the king ... 2Sa 19:12 314
Now these be the *l* words of David ... 2Sa 23:1 314
For by the *l* words of David the ... 1Chr 23:27 314
of David the king, first and *l* ... 1Chr 29:29 314
the acts of Solomon, first and *l* ... 2Chr 9:29 314
the acts of Rehoboam, first and *l* ... 2Chr 12:15 314
the acts of Asa, first and *l* ... 2Chr 16:11 314
acts of Jehoshaphat, first and *l* ... 2Chr 20:34 314
the acts of Amaziah, first and *l* ... 2Chr 25:26 314
of the acts of Uzziah, first and *l* ... 2Chr 26:22 314
and of all his ways, first and *l* ... 2Chr 28:26 314
And his deeds, first and *l*, behold, ... 2Chr 35:27 314
of the *l* sons of Adonikam, whose ... Ezr 8:13 314
from the first day unto the *l* day ... Neh 8:18 314
And thou mourn at the *l*, when thy ... Prov 5:11 319
At the *l* it biteth like a serpent ... Prov 23:32 319
shall come to pass in the *l* days ... Is 2:2 319
LORD, the first, and with the *l* ... Is 41:4 314
I am the first, and I am the *l* ... Is 44:6 314
I am the first, I also am the *l* ... Is 48:12 314
said, He shall not see our *l* end ... Jer 12:4 319
l this Nebuchadrezzar king of ... Jer 50:17 314
she remembereth not her *l* end ... Lam 1:9 319
But at the *l* Daniel came in ... Dan 4:8 318
other, and the higher came up *l* ... Dan 8:3 314
in the *l* end of the indignation ... Dan 8:19 319
I will slay the *l* of them with ... Amos 9:1 319
But in the *l* days it shall come ... Mic 4:1 319
the *l* state of that man is worse ... Mt 12:45 *2078*

L

many that are first shall be *l* Mt 19:30 *2078*
and the *l* shall be first Mt 19:30 *2078*
from the *l* unto the first Mt 20:8 *2078*
These *l* have wrought but one hour Mt 20:12 *2078*
I will give unto this *l*, even as Mt 20:14 *2078*
So the *l* shall be first Mt 20:16 *2078*
shall be first, and the first *l* Mt 20:16 *2078*
But *l* of all he sent unto them Mt 21:37 *5305*
l of all the woman died also Mt 22:27 *5305*
At the *l* came two false witnesses Mt 26:60 *5305*
so the *l* error shall be worse Mt 27:64 *2078*
first, the same shall be *l* of all Mk 9:35 *2078*
many that are first shall be *l* Mk 10:31 *2078*
and the *l* first Mk 10:31 *2078*
he sent him also *l* unto them Mk 12:6 *2078*
l of all the woman died also Mk 12:22 *2078*
the *l* state of that man is worse Lk 11:26 *2078*
thou hast paid the very *l* mite Lk 12:59 *2078*
there are *l* which shall be first Lk 13:30 *2078*
there are first which shall be *l* Lk 13:30 *2078*
L of all the woman died also Lk 20:32 5305
raise it up again at the *l* day Jn 6:39 *2078*
I will raise him up at the *l* day Jn 6:40 *2078*
I will raise him up at the *l* day Jn 6:44 *2078*
I will raise him up at the *l* day Jn 6:54 *2078*
In the *l* day, that great day of Jn 7:37 *2078*
at the eldest, even unto the *l* Jn 8:9 *2078*
in the resurrection at the *l* day Jn 11:24 *2078*
same shall judge him in the *l* day Jn 12:48 *2078*
shall come to pass in the *l* days Acts 2:17 *2078*
hath set forth us the apostles *l* 1Cor 4:9 *2078*
l of all he was seen of me also, 1Cor 15:8 *2078*
The *l* enemy that shall be 1Cor 15:26 *2078*
the *l* Adam was made a quickening 1Cor 15:45 *2078*
of an eye, at the *l* trump 1Cor 15:52 *2078*
that now at the *l* your care of me Phil 4:10 *4218*
that in the *l* days perilous times 2Ti 3:1 *2078*
Hath in these *l* days spoken unto Heb 1:2 *2078*
treasure together for the *l* days Jas 5:3 *2078*
to be revealed in the *l* time 1Pet 1:5 *2078*
manifest in these *l* times for you 1Pet 1:20 *2078*
shall come in the *l* days scoffers 2Pet 3:3 *2078*
Little children, it is the *l* time 1Jn 2:18 *2078*
we know that it is the *l* time 1Jn 2:18 *2078*
should be mockers in the *l* time Jude 18 *2078*
and Omega, the first and the *l* Rev 1:11 *2078*
I am the first and the *l* Rev 1:17 *2078*
things saith the first and the *l* Rev 2:8 *2078*
the *l* to be more than the first Rev 2:19 *2078*
angels having the seven *l* plagues Rev 15:1 *2078*
vials full of the seven *l* plagues Rev 21:9 *2078*
and the end, the first and the *l* Rev 22:13 *2078*

LASTED
seven days, while their feast *l* Judg 14:17 1961

LASTING
precious things of the *l* hills Deut 33:15 5769

LATCHET
nor the *l* of their shoes be Is 5:27 8288
the *l* of whose shoes I am not Mk 1:7 *2438*
the *l* of whose shoes I am not Lk 3:16 *2438*
whose shoe's *l* I am not worthy to Jn 1:27 *2438*

LATE
you to rise up early, to sit up *l* Ps 127:2 309
Even of *l* my people is risen up Mic 2:8 865
the Jews of *l* sought to stone Jn 11:8 *3568*

LATELY
l come from Italy, with his wife Acts 18:2 *4373*

LATIN (*lat' in*) *Language spoken by the Romans.*
him in letters of Greek, and *L* Lk 23:38 *4513*
written in Hebrew, and Greek, and *L* Jn 19:20 *4513*

LATTER
believe the voice of the *l* sign Ex 4:8 314
do to thy people in the *l* days Num 24:14 319
but his *l* end shall be that he Num 24:20 319
upon thee, even in the *l* days Deut 4:30 319
to do thee good at thy *l* end Deut 8:16 319
the *l* rain, that thou mayest Deut 11:14 4456
if the *l* husband hate her, and Deut 24:3 314
or if the *l* husband die, which Deut 24:3 314
will befall you in the *l* days Deut 31:29 319
they would consider their *l* end Deut 32:29 319
the *l* end than at the beginning Ruth 3:10 314
will be bitterness in the *l* end 2Sa 2:26 314
yet thy *l* end should greatly Job 8:7 319
stand at the *l* day upon the earth Job 19:25 314
mouth wide as for the *l* rain Job 29:23 4456
So the LORD blessed the *l* end of Job 42:12 319
is as a cloud of the *l* rain Prov 16:15 4456
thou mayest be wise in thy *l* end Prov 19:20 319
them, and know the *l* end of them Is 41:22 319
didst remember the *l* end of it Is 47:7 319
and there hath been no *l* rain Jer 3:3 4456
rain, both the former and the *l* Jer 5:24 4456
in the *l* days ye shall consider Jer 23:20 319
in the *l* days ye shall consider Jer 30:24 319
captivity of Moab in the *l* days Jer 48:47 319
shall come to pass in the *l* days Jer 49:39 319
in the *l* years thou shalt come Eze 38:8 319
it shall be in the *l* days Eze 38:16 319
what shall be in the *l* days Dan 2:28 320
in the *l* time of their kingdom, Dan 8:23 319
befall thy people in the *l* days Dan 10:14 319
not be as the former, or as the *l* Dan 11:29 314
and his goodness in the *l* days Hos 3:5 319
unto us as the rain, as the *l* Hos 6:3 4456
the *l* rain in the first month Joel 2:23 4456
the shooting up of the *l* growth Amos 7:1 3954
it was the *l* growth after the Amos 7:1 3954
The glory of this *l* house shall Hag 2:9 314
rain in the time of the *l* rain Zec 10:1 4456
that in the *l* times some shall 1Ti 4:1 *5305*
he receive the early and *l* rain Jas 5:7 *3797*
the *l* end is worse with them than 2Pet 2:20 *2078*

LATTICE
a window, and cried through the *l* Judg 5:28 822
Ahaziah fell down through a *l* in 2Kin 1:2 7639
shewing himself through the *l* Song 2:9 2762

LAUD
and *l* him, all ye people Rom 15:11 *1867*

LAUGH
Abraham, Wherefore did Sarah *l* Gen 18:13 6711
but thou didst *l* Gen 18:15 6711
Sarah said, God hath made me to *l* Gen 21:6 6712
that all that hear will *l* with me Gen 21:6 6711
and famine thou shalt *l* Job 5:22 7832
he will *l* at the trial of the Job 9:23 3932
the innocent *l* them to scorn Job 22:19 3932
sitteth in the heavens shall *l* Ps 2:4 7832
they that see me *l* me to scorn Ps 22:7 3932
The LORD shall *l* at him Ps 37:13 7832
see, and fear, and shall *l* at him Ps 52:6 7832
But thou, O LORD, shalt *l* at them Ps 59:8 7832
our enemies *l* among themselves Ps 80:6 3932
I also will *l* at your calamity Prov 1:26 7832
foolish man, whether he rage or *l* Prov 29:9 7832
A time to weep, and a time to *l* Eccl 3:4 7832
for ye shall *l* Lk 6:21 *1070*
Woe unto you that *l* now Lk 6:25 *1070*

LAUGHED
Abraham fell upon his face, and *l* Gen 17:17 6711
Therefore Sarah *l* within herself Gen 18:12 6711
Sarah denied, saying, I *l* not Gen 18:15 6711
despised thee, and *l* thee to scorn 2Kin 19:21 3932
but they *l* them to scorn, and 2Chr 30:10 7832
they *l* us to scorn, and despised Neh 2:19 3932
just upright man is *l* to scorn Job 12:4 7832
If I *l* on them, they believed it Job 29:24 7832
despised thee, and *l* thee to scorn Is 37:22 3932
thou shalt be *l* to scorn and had Eze 23:32 6712
And they *l* him to scorn Mt 9:24 *2606*
And they *l* him to scorn Mk 5:40 *2606*
they *l* him to scorn, knowing that Lk 8:53 *2606*

LAUGHETH
he *l* at the shaking of a spear Job 41:29 7832

LAUGHING
Till he fill thy mouth with *l* Job 8:21 7814

LAUGHTER
Then was our mouth filled with *l* Ps 126:2 7814
Even in *l* the heart is sorrowful Prov 14:13 7814
I said of *l*, It is mad Eccl 2:2 7814
Sorrow is better than *l* Eccl 7:3 7814
a pot, so is the *l* of the fool Eccl 7:6 7814
A feast is made for *l*, and wine Eccl 10:19 7814
let your *l* be turned to mourning, Jas 4:9 *1071*

LAUNCH
L out into the deep, and let down Lk 5:4 *1877*

LAUNCHED
And they *l* forth Lk 8:22 *321*
were gotten from them, and had *l* Acts 21:1 *321*
into a ship of Adramyttium, we *l* Acts 27:2 *321*
And when we had *l* from thence Acts 27:4 *321*

LAVER
Thou shalt also make a *l* of brass Ex 30:18 3595
with all his vessels, and the *l* Ex 30:28 3595
with all his furniture, and the *l* Ex 31:9 3595
staves, and all his vessels, the *l* Ex 35:16 3595
And he made the *l* of brass Ex 38:8 3595
staves, and all his vessels, the *l* Ex 39:39 3595
thou shalt set the *l* between the Ex 40:7 3595
And thou shalt anoint the *l* Ex 40:11 3595
he set the *l* between the tent of Ex 40:30 3595
and all his vessels, both the *l* Lev 8:11 3595
under the *l* were undersetters 1Kin 7:30 3595
one *l* contained forty baths 1Kin 7:38 3595
and every *l* was four cubits 1Kin 7:38 3595
every one of the ten bases one *l* 1Kin 7:38 3595
removed the *l* from off them 2Kin 16:17 3595

LAVERS
Then made he ten *l* of brass 1Kin 7:38 3595
And Hiram made the *l*, and the 1Kin 7:40 3595
ten bases, and ten *l* on the bases 1Kin 7:43 3595
He made also ten *l*, and put five 2Chr 4:6 3595
and *l* made he upon the bases 2Chr 4:14 3595

LAVISH
They *l* gold out of the bag, and Is 46:6 2107

LAW
son, and Sarai his daughter in *l* Gen 11:31 3618
son in *l*, and thy sons, and thy Gen 19:12 2859
out, and spake unto his sons in *l* Gen 19:14 2859
that mocked unto his sons in *l* Gen 19:14 2859
Judah to Tamar his daughter in *l* Gen 38:11 3618
Behold thy father in *l* goeth up Gen 38:13 2524
that she was his daughter in *l* Gen 38:16 3618
Tamar thy daughter in *l* hath Gen 38:24 3618
she sent to her father in *l* Gen 38:25 2524
Joseph made it a *l* over the land Gen 47:26 2706
flock of Jethro his father in *l* Ex 3:1 2859
to Jethro his father in *l* Ex 4:18 2859
One *l* shall be to him that is Ex 12:49 8451
that the LORD's *l* may be in thy Ex 13:9 8451
whether they will walk in my *l* Ex 16:4 8451
of Midian, Moses' father in *l* Ex 18:1 2859
Then Jethro, Moses' father in *l* Ex 18:2 2859
And Jethro, Moses' father in *l* Ex 18:5 2859
I thy father in *l* Jethro am come Ex 18:6 2859
went out to meet his father in *l* Ex 18:7 2859
Moses told his father in *l* all Ex 18:8 2859
And Jethro, Moses' father in *l* Ex 18:12 2859
Moses' father in *l* before God Ex 18:12 2859
when Moses' father in *l* saw all Ex 18:14 2859
Moses said unto his father in *l* Ex 18:15 2859
Moses' father in *l* said unto him Ex 18:17 2859
to the voice of his father in *l* Ex 18:24 2859
Moses let his father in *l* depart Ex 18:27 2859
give thee tables of stone, and a *l* Ex 24:12 8451
This is the *l* of the burnt Lev 6:9 8451
this is the *l* of the meat Lev 6:14 8451
This is the *l* of the sin offering Lev 6:25 8451
Likewise this is the *l* of the Lev 7:1 8451
there is one *l* for them Lev 7:7 8451
this is the *l* of the sacrifice of Lev 7:11 8451
This is the *l* of the burnt Lev 7:37 8451
This is the *l* of the beasts, and Lev 11:46 8451
This is the *l* for her that hath Lev 12:7 8451
This is the *l* of the plague of Lev 13:59 8451
This shall be the *l* of the leper Lev 14:2 8451
This is the *l* of him in whom is Lev 14:32 8451
This is the *l* for all manner of Lev 14:54 8451
this is the *l* of leprosy Lev 14:57 8451
This is the *l* of him that hath an Lev 15:32 8451
nakedness of thy daughter in *l* Lev 18:15 3618
a man lie with his daughter in *l* Lev 20:12 3618
Ye shall have one manner of *l* Lev 24:22 4941
This is the *l* of jealousies, when Num 5:29 8451
shall execute upon her all this *l* Num 5:30 8451
this is the *l* of the Nazarite, Num 6:13 8451
This is the *l* of the Nazarite who Num 6:21 8451
do after the *l* of his separation Num 6:21 8451
the Midianite, Moses' father in *l* Num 10:29 2859
One *l* and one manner shall be for Num 15:16 8451
Ye shall have one *l* for him that Num 15:29 8451
This is the ordinance of the *l* Num 19:2 8451
This is the *l*, when a man dieth Num 19:14 8451
This is the ordinance of the *l* Num 31:21 8451
began Moses to declare this *l* Deut 1:5 8451
so righteous as all this *l* Deut 4:8 8451
this is the *l* which Moses set Deut 4:44 8451
to the sentence of the *l* which Deut 17:11 8451
l in a book out of that which is Deut 17:18 8451
to keep all the words of this *l* Deut 17:19 8451
upon them all the words of this *l* Deut 27:3 8451
the words of this *l* very plainly Deut 27:8 8451
that lieth with his mother in *l* Deut 27:23 2859
the words of this *l* to do them Deut 27:26 8451
to do all the words of this *l* Deut 28:58 8451
not written in the book of this *l* Deut 28:61 8451
are written in this book of the *l* Deut 29:21 8451
we may do all the words of this *l* Deut 29:29 8451
are written in this book of the *l* Deut 30:10 8451
And Moses wrote this *l*, and Deut 31:9 8451
thou shalt read this *l* before all Deut 31:11 8451
to do all the words of this *l* Deut 31:12 8451
the words of this *l* in a book Deut 31:24 8451
Take this book of the *l*, and put Deut 31:26 8451
to do, all the words of this *l* Deut 32:46 8451
hand went a fiery *l* for them Deut 33:2 1881
Moses commanded us a *l*, even the Deut 33:4 8451
thy judgments, and Israel thy *l* Deut 33:10 8451
to do according to all the *l* Josh 1:7 8451
This book of the *l* shall not Josh 1:8 8451
in the book of the *l* of Moses Josh 8:31 8451
stones a copy of the *l* of Moses Josh 8:32 8451
he read all the words of the *l* Josh 8:34 8451
is written in the book of the *l* Josh 8:34 8451
to do the commandment and the *l* Josh 22:5 8451
in the book of the *l* of Moses Josh 23:6 8451
words in the book of the *l* of God Josh 24:26 8451
of the Kenite, Moses' father in *l* Judg 1:16 2859
of Hobab the father in *l* of Moses Judg 4:11 2859
the son in *l* of the Timnite, Judg 15:6 2859
And his father in *l*, the damsel's Judg 19:4 2859
father said unto his son in *l* Judg 19:5 2859
depart, his father in *l* urged him Judg 19:7 2859
and his servant, his father in *l* Judg 19:9 2859
she arose with her daughters in *l* Ruth 1:6 3618
her two daughters in *l* with her Ruth 1:7 3618
said unto her two daughters in *l* Ruth 1:8 3618
and Orpah kissed her mother in *l* Ruth 1:14 2545
thy sister in *l* is gone back unto Ruth 1:15 2994
return thou after thy sister in *l* Ruth 1:15 2994
the Moabitess, her daughter in *l* Ruth 1:22 3618
in *l* since the death of thine Ruth 2:11 2545
her mother in *l* saw what she had Ruth 2:18 2545
And her mother in *l* said unto her Ruth 2:19 2545
she shewed her mother in *l* with Ruth 2:19 2545
Naomi said unto her daughter in *l* Ruth 2:20 3618
said unto Ruth her daughter in *l* Ruth 2:22 3618
and dwelt with her mother in *l* Ruth 2:23 2545
her mother in *l* said unto her Ruth 3:1 2545
all that her mother in *l* bade her Ruth 3:6 2545
when she came to her mother in *l* Ruth 3:16 2545
Go not empty unto thy mother in *l* Ruth 3:17 2545
for thy daughter in *l*, which Ruth 4:15 3618
And his daughter in *l*, Phinehas' 1Sa 4:19 3618
taken, and that her father in *l* 1Sa 4:19 2524
and because of her father in *l* 1Sa 4:21 2524
I should be son in *l* to the king 1Sa 18:18 2859
son in *l* in the one of the twain 1Sa 18:21 2860
therefore be the king's son in *l* 1Sa 18:22 2860
thing to be a king's son in *l* 1Sa 18:23 2860
well to be the king's son in *l* 1Sa 18:26 2860
he might be the king's son in *l* 1Sa 18:27 2860
which is the king's son in *l* 1Sa 22:14 2859
it is written in the *l* of Moses 1Kin 2:3 8451
the son in *l* of the house of Ahab 2Kin 8:27 2859
took no heed to walk in the *l* of 2Kin 10:31 8451
in the book of the *l* of Moses 2Kin 14:6 8451
according to all the *l* which I 2Kin 17:13 8451
their ordinances, or after the *l* 2Kin 17:34 8451
and the ordinances, and the *l* 2Kin 17:37 8451

according to all the *l* that my	2Kin 21:8	8451
of the *l* in the house of the LORD	2Kin 22:8	8451
the words of the book of the *l*	2Kin 22:11	8451
l which were written in the book	2Kin 23:24	8451
according to all the *l* of Moses	2Kin 23:25	8451
his daughter in *l* bare him Pharez	1Chr 2:4	3618
the same to Jacob for a *l*	1Chr 16:17	2706
is written in the *l* of the LORD	1Chr 16:40	8451
keep the *l* of the LORD thy God	1Chr 22:12	8451
heed to their way to walk in my *l*	2Chr 6:16	8451
he forsook the *l* of the LORD	2Chr 12:1	8451
of their fathers, and to do the *l*	2Chr 14:4	8451
a teaching priest, and without *l*	2Chr 15:3	8451
had the book of the *l* of the LORD	2Chr 17:9	8451
between blood and blood, between *l*	2Chr 19:10	8451
it is written in the *l* of Moses	2Chr 23:18	8451
in the *l* in the book of Moses	2Chr 25:4	8451
according to the *l* of Moses the	2Chr 30:16	8451
is written in the *l* of the LORD	2Chr 31:3	8451
encouraged in the *l* of the LORD	2Chr 31:4	8451
of the house of God, and in the *l*	2Chr 31:21	8451
them, according to the whole *l*	2Chr 33:8	8451
the *l* of the LORD given by Moses	2Chr 34:14	8451
of the *l* in the house of the LORD	2Chr 34:15	8451
king had heard the words of the *l*	2Chr 34:19	8451
was written in the *l* of the LORD	2Chr 35:26	8451
in the *l* of Moses the man of God	Ezr 3:2	8451
a ready scribe in the *l* of Moses	Ezr 7:6	8451
heart to seek the *l* of the LORD	Ezr 7:10	8451
a scribe of the *l* of the God of	Ezr 7:12	1882
according to the *l* of thy God	Ezr 7:14	1882
the scribe of the *l* of the God of	Ezr 7:21	1882
will not do the *l* of thy God	Ezr 7:26	1882
the *l* of the king, let judgment	Ezr 7:26	1882
let it be done according to the *l*	Ezr 10:3	8451
because he was the son in *l* of	Neh 6:18	2859
bring the book of the *l* of Moses	Neh 8:1	8451
Ezra the priest brought the *l*	Neh 8:2	8451
attentive unto the book of the *l*	Neh 8:3	8451
the people to understand the *l*	Neh 8:7	8451
book in the *l* of God distinctly	Neh 8:8	8451
they heard the words of the *l*	Neh 8:9	8451
to understand the words of the *l*	Neh 8:13	8451
they found written in the *l* which	Neh 8:14	8451
read in the book of the *l* of God	Neh 8:18	8451
read in the book of the *l* of the	Neh 9:3	8451
cast thy *l* behind their backs, and	Neh 9:26	8451
bring them again unto thy *l*	Neh 9:29	8451
nor our fathers, kept thy *l*	Neh 9:34	8451
of the lands unto the *l* of God	Neh 10:28	8451
into an oath, to walk in God's *l*	Neh 10:29	8451
God, as it is written in the *l*	Neh 10:34	8451
cattle, as it is written in the *l*	Neh 10:36	8451
portions of the *l* for the priests	Neh 12:44	8451
pass, when they had heard the *l*	Neh 13:3	8451
was son in *l* to Sanballat the	Neh 13:28	2859
drinking was according to the *l*	Est 1:8	1881
manner toward all that knew *l*	Est 1:13	1881
the queen Vashti according to *l*	Est 1:15	1881
there is one *l* of his to put him	Est 4:11	1881
which is not according to the *l*	Est 4:16	1881
the *l* from his mouth, and lay up	Job 22:22	8451
delight is in the *l* of the LORD	Ps 1:2	8451
in his *l* doth he meditate day and	Ps 1:2	8451
The *l* of the LORD is perfect,	Ps 19:7	8451
The *l* of his God is in his heart	Ps 37:31	8451
yea, thy *l* is within my heart	Ps 40:8	8451
Give ear, O my people, to my *l*	Ps 78:1	8451
Jacob, and appointed a *l* in Israel	Ps 78:5	8451
God, and refused to walk in his *l*	Ps 78:10	8451
and a *l* of the God of Jacob	Ps 81:4	4941
If his children forsake my *l*	Ps 89:30	8451
and teachest him out of thy *l*	Ps 94:12	8451
which frameth mischief by a *l*	Ps 94:20	2706
the same unto Jacob for a *l*	Ps 105:10	2706
who walk in the *l* of the LORD	Ps 119:1	8451
wondrous things out of thy *l*	Ps 119:18	8451
and grant me thy *l* graciously	Ps 119:29	8451
and I shall keep thy *l*	Ps 119:34	8451
So shall I keep thy *l* continually	Ps 119:44	8451
have I not declined from thy *l*	Ps 119:51	8451
of the wicked that forsake thy *l*	Ps 119:53	8451
in the night, and have kept thy *l*	Ps 119:55	8451
but I have not forgotten thy *l*	Ps 119:61	8451
but I delight in thy *l*	Ps 119:70	8451
The *l* of thy mouth is better unto	Ps 119:72	8451
for thy *l* is my delight	Ps 119:77	8451
for me, which are not after thy *l*	Ps 119:85	8451
Unless thy *l* had been my delights	Ps 119:92	8451
O how love I thy *l*	Ps 119:97	8451
yet do I not forget thy *l*	Ps 119:109	8451
but thy *l* do I love	Ps 119:113	8451
for they have made void thy *l*	Ps 119:126	8451
eyes, because they keep not thy *l*	Ps 119:136	8451
and thy *l* is the truth	Ps 119:142	8451
they are far from thy *l*	Ps 119:150	8451
for I do not forget thy *l*	Ps 119:153	8451
but thy *l* do I love	Ps 119:163	8451
peace have they which love thy *l*	Ps 119:165	8451
and thy *l* is my delight	Ps 119:174	8451
forsake not the *l* of thy mother	Prov 1:8	8451
My son, forget not my *l*	Prov 3:1	8451
doctrine, forsake ye not my *l*	Prov 4:2	8451
forsake not the *l* of thy mother	Prov 6:20	8451
and the *l* is light	Prov 6:23	8451
my *l* as the apple of thine eye	Prov 7:2	8451
The *l* of the wise is a fountain	Prov 13:14	8451
forsake the *l* praise the wicked	Prov 28:4	8451
as keep the *l* contend with them	Prov 28:4	8451
Whoso keepeth the *l* is a wise son	Prov 28:7	8451
away his ear from hearing the *l*	Prov 28:9	8451
but he that keepeth the *l*	Prov 29:18	8451
Lest they drink, and forget the *l*	Prov 31:5	2710
her tongue is the *l* of kindness	Prov 31:26	8451
give ear unto the *l* of our God	Is 1:10	8451
out of Zion shall go forth the *l*	Is 2:3	8451
away the *l* of the LORD of hosts	Is 5:24	8451
seal the *l* among my disciples	Is 8:16	8451
To the *l* and to the testimony	Is 8:20	8451
will not hear the *l* of the LORD	Is 30:9	8451
and the isles shall wait for his *l*	Is 42:4	8451
he will magnify the *l*, and make it	Is 42:21	8451
were they obedient unto his *l*	Is 42:24	8451
for a *l* shall proceed from me, and	Is 51:4	8451
the people in whose heart is my *l*	Is 51:7	8451
that handle the *l* knew me not	Jer 2:8	8451
unto my words, nor to my *l*	Jer 6:19	8451
the *l* of the LORD is with us	Jer 8:8	8451
my *l* which I set before them	Jer 9:13	8451
me, and have not kept my *l*	Jer 16:11	8451
for the *l* shall not perish from	Jer 18:18	8451
hearken to me, to walk in my *l*	Jer 26:4	8451
I will put my *l* in their inward	Jer 31:33	8451
was sealed according to the *l*	Jer 32:11	4687
voice, neither walked in thy *l*	Jer 32:23	8451
they feared, nor walked in my *l*	Jer 44:10	8451
of the LORD, nor walked in his *l*	Jer 44:23	8451
the *l* is no more	Lam 2:9	8451
but the *l* shall perish from the	Eze 7:26	8451
lewdly defiled his daughter in *l*	Eze 22:11	3618
Her priests have violated my *l*	Eze 22:26	8451
This is the *l* of the house	Eze 43:12	8451
this is the *l* of the house	Eze 43:12	8451
him concerning the *l* of his God	Dan 6:5	1882
according to the *l* of the Medes	Dan 6:8	1882
according to the *l* of the Medes	Dan 6:12	1882
that the *l* of the Medes and	Dan 6:15	1882
Israel have transgressed thy *l*	Dan 9:11	8451
the *l* of Moses the servant of God	Dan 9:11	8451
it is written in the *l* of Moses	Dan 9:13	8451
hast forgotten the *l* of thy God	Hos 4:6	8451
and trespassed against my *l*	Hos 8:1	8451
to him the great things of my *l*	Hos 8:12	8451
have despised the *l* of the LORD	Amos 2:4	8451
for the *l* shall go forth of Zion,	Mic 4:2	8451
the daughter in *l* against her	Mic 7:6	3618
against her mother in *l*	Mic 7:6	2545
Therefore the *l* is slacked	Hab 1:4	8451
they have done violence to the *l*	Zeph 3:4	8451
now the priests concerning the *l*	Hag 2:11	8451
lest they should hear the *l*	Zec 7:12	8451
The *l* of truth was in his mouth,	Mal 2:6	8451
should seek the *l* at his mouth	Mal 2:7	8451
caused many to stumble at the *l*	Mal 2:8	8451
but have been partial in the *l*	Mal 2:9	8451
Remember ye the *l* of Moses my	Mal 4:4	8451
that I am come to destroy the *l*	Mt 5:17	3551
shall in no wise pass from the *l*	Mt 5:18	3551
if any man will sue thee at the *l*	Mt 5:40	
for this is the *l* and the prophets	Mt 7:12	3551
the daughter in *l* against her	Mt 10:35	3565
against her mother in *l*	Mt 10:35	3994
the *l* prophesied until John	Mt 11:13	3551
Or have ye not read in the *l*	Mt 12:5	3551
is the great commandment in the *l*	Mt 22:36	3551
two commandments hang all the *l*	Mt 22:40	3551
the weightier matters of the *l*	Mt 23:23	3551
the *l* of Moses were accomplished	Lk 2:22	3551
is written in the *l* of the Lord	Lk 2:23	3551
is said in the *l* of the Lord	Lk 2:24	3551
for him after the custom of the *l*	Lk 2:27	3551
according to the *l* of the Lord	Lk 2:39	3551
and doctors of the *l* sitting by	Lk 5:17	3547
him, What is written in the *l*	Lk 10:26	3551
the mother in *l* against her	Lk 12:53	3994
against her daughter in *l*	Lk 12:53	3565
the daughter in *l* against her	Lk 12:53	3565
against her mother in *l*	Lk 12:53	3994
The *l* and the prophets were until	Lk 16:16	3551
than one tittle of the *l* to fail	Lk 16:17	3551
were written in the *l* of Moses	Lk 24:44	3551
For the *l* was given by Moses, but	Jn 1:17	3551
found him, of whom Moses in the *l*	Jn 1:45	3551
Did not Moses give you the *l*	Jn 7:19	3551
and yet none of you keepeth the *l*	Jn 7:19	3551
that the *l* of Moses should not be	Jn 7:23	3551
who knoweth not the *l* are cursed	Jn 7:49	3551
Doth our *l* judge any man, before	Jn 7:51	3551
Now Moses in the *l* commanded us	Jn 8:5	3551
It is also written in your *l*	Jn 8:17	3551
them, Is it not written in your *l*	Jn 10:34	3551
We have heard out of the *l* that	Jn 12:34	3551
that is written in their *l*	Jn 15:25	3551
he was father in *l* to Caiaphas	Jn 18:13	3995
and judge him according to your *l*	Jn 18:31	3551
Jews answered him, We have a *l*	Jn 19:7	3551
by our *l* he ought to die, because	Jn 19:7	3551
named Gamaliel, a doctor of the *l*	Acts 5:34	3547
against this holy place, and the *l*	Acts 6:13	3551
Who have received the *l* by the	Acts 7:53	3551
And after the reading of the *l*	Acts 13:15	3551
be justified by the *l* of Moses	Acts 13:39	3551
them to keep the *l* of Moses	Acts 15:5	3551
be circumcised, and keep the *l*	Acts 15:24	3551
to worship God contrary to the *l*	Acts 18:13	3551
of words and names, and of your *l*	Acts 18:15	3551
the *l* is open, and there are	Acts 19:38	60
and they are all zealous of the *l*	Acts 21:20	3551
walkest orderly, and keepest the *l*	Acts 21:24	3551
against the people, and the *l*	Acts 21:28	3551
manner of the *l* of the fathers	Acts 22:3	3551
a devout man according to the *l*	Acts 22:12	3551
thou to judge me after the *l*	Acts 23:3	3551
to be smitten contrary to the *l*	Acts 23:3	3891
accused of questions of their *l*	Acts 23:29	3551
have judged according to our *l*	Acts 24:6	3551
things which are written in the *l*	Acts 24:14	3551
Neither against the *l* of the Jews	Acts 25:8	3551
Jesus, both out of the *l* of Moses	Acts 28:23	3551
l shall also perish without *l*	Rom 2:12	460
the *l* shall be judged by the *l*	Rom 2:12	3551
of the *l* are just before God	Rom 2:13	3551
doers of the *l* shall be justified	Rom 2:13	3551
Gentiles, which have not the *l*	Rom 2:14	3551
the things contained in the *l*	Rom 2:14	3551
these, having not the *l*	Rom 2:14	3551
the *l*, are a *l* unto themselves	Rom 2:14	3551
of the *l* written in their hearts	Rom 2:15	3551
called a Jew, and restest in the *l*	Rom 2:17	3551
being instructed out of the *l*	Rom 2:18	3551
and of the truth in the *l*	Rom 2:20	3551
that makest thy boast of the *l*	Rom 2:23	3551
through breaking the *l*	Rom 2:23	3551
profiteth, if thou keep the *l*	Rom 2:25	3551
but if thou be a breaker of the *l*	Rom 2:25	3551
keep the righteousness of the *l*	Rom 2:26	3551
is by nature, if it fulfil the *l*	Rom 2:27	3551
dost transgress the *l*	Rom 2:27	3551
what things soever the *l* saith	Rom 3:19	3551
saith to them who are under the *l*	Rom 3:19	3551
of the *l* there shall no flesh be	Rom 3:20	3551
for by the *l* is the knowledge of	Rom 3:20	3551
God without the *l* is manifested	Rom 3:21	3551
being witnessed by the *l*	Rom 3:21	3551
By what *l*?	Rom 3:27	3551
but by the *l* of faith	Rom 3:27	3551
faith without the deeds of the *l*	Rom 3:28	3551
make void the *l* through faith	Rom 3:31	3551
yea, we establish the *l*	Rom 3:31	3551
or to his seed, through the *l*	Rom 4:13	3551
they which are of the *l* be heirs	Rom 4:14	3551
Because the *l* worketh wrath	Rom 4:15	3551
for where no *l* is, there is no	Rom 4:15	3551
to that only which is of the *l*	Rom 4:16	3551
(For until the *l* sin was in the	Rom 5:13	3551
is not imputed when there is no *l*	Rom 5:13	3551
Moreover the *l* entered, that the	Rom 5:20	3551
for ye are not under the *l*	Rom 6:14	3551
because we are not under the *l*	Rom 6:15	3551
I speak to them that know the *l*	Rom 7:1	3551
how that the *l* hath dominion	Rom 7:1	3551
l to her husband so long as he	Rom 7:2	3551
loosed from the *l* of her husband	Rom 7:2	3551
be dead, she is free from that *l*	Rom 7:3	3551
to the *l* by the body of Christ	Rom 7:4	3551
of sins, which were by the *l*	Rom 7:5	3551
now we are delivered from the *l*	Rom 7:6	3551
Is the *l* sin	Rom 7:7	3551
I had not known sin, but by the *l*	Rom 7:7	3551
known lust, except the *l* had said	Rom 7:7	3551
For without the *l* sin was dead	Rom 7:8	3551
I was alive without the *l* once	Rom 7:9	3551
Wherefore the *l* is holy, and the	Rom 7:12	3551
we know that the *l* is spiritual	Rom 7:14	3551
unto the *l* that it is good	Rom 7:16	3551
I find then a *l*, that, when I	Rom 7:21	3551
For I delight in the *l* of God	Rom 7:22	3551
But I see another *l* in my members	Rom 7:23	3551
warring against the *l* of my mind	Rom 7:23	3551
me into captivity to the *l* of sin	Rom 7:23	3551
mind I myself serve the *l* of God	Rom 7:25	3551
but with the flesh the *l* of sin	Rom 7:25	3551
For the *l* of the Spirit of	Rom 8:2	3551
made me free from the *l* of sin	Rom 8:2	3551
For what the *l* could not do	Rom 8:3	3551
of the *l* might be fulfilled in us	Rom 8:4	3551
it is not subject to the *l* of God	Rom 8:7	3551
covenants, and the giving of the *l*	Rom 9:4	3548
after the *l* of righteousness	Rom 9:31	3551
to the *l* of righteousness	Rom 9:31	3551
as it were by the works of the *l*	Rom 9:32	3551
For Christ is the end of the *l*	Rom 10:4	3551
righteousness which is of the *l*	Rom 10:5	3551
another hath fulfilled the *l*	Rom 13:8	3551
love is the fulfilling of the *l*	Rom 13:10	3551
go to *l* before the unjust, and not	1Cor 6:1	2919
brother goeth to *l* with brother	1Cor 6:6	2919
ye go to *l* one with another	1Cor 6:7	2917
The wife is bound by the *l* as	1Cor 7:39	3551
or saith not the *l* the same also	1Cor 9:8	3551
it is written in the *l* of Moses	1Cor 9:9	3551
are under the *l*, as under the *l*	1Cor 9:20	3551
gain them that are under the *l*	1Cor 9:20	3551
are without *l*, as without *l*	1Cor 9:21	459
l, (being not without *l* to God	1Cor 9:21	459
but under the *l* to Christ	1Cor 9:21	1772
gain them that are without *l*	1Cor 9:21	459
In the *l* it is written, With men	1Cor 14:21	3551
obedience, as also saith the *l*	1Cor 14:34	3551
and the strength of sin is the *l*	1Cor 15:56	3551
justified by the works of the *l*	Gal 2:16	3551
and not by the works of the *l*	Gal 2:16	3551
for by the works of the *l* shall	Gal 2:16	3551
For I through the *l* am dead to	Gal 2:19	3551
through the *l* am dead to the *l*	Gal 2:19	3551
if righteousness come by the *l*	Gal 2:21	3551
the Spirit by the works of the *l*	Gal 3:2	3551
doeth he it by the works of the *l*	Gal 3:5	3551
of the *l* are under the curse	Gal 3:10	3551
in the book of the *l* to do them	Gal 3:10	3551
by the *l* in the sight of God	Gal 3:11	3551
And the *l* is not of faith	Gal 3:12	3551
us from the curse of the *l*	Gal 3:13	3551
before of God in Christ, the *l*	Gal 3:17	3551
if the inheritance be of the *l*	Gal 3:18	3551
Wherefore then serveth the *l*	Gal 3:19	3551
Is the *l* then against the	Gal 3:21	3551
for if there had been a *l* given	Gal 3:21	3551
should have been by the *l*	Gal 3:21	3551
came, we were kept under the *l*	Gal 3:23	3551
Wherefore the *l* was our	Gal 3:24	3551
made of a woman, made under the *l*	Gal 4:4	3551

redeem them that were under the *l* Gal 4:5 3551
ye that desire to be under the *l* Gal 4:21 3551
do ye not hear the *l* Gal 4:21 3551
he is a debtor to do the whole *l* Gal 5:3 3551
of you are justified by the *l* Gal 5:4 3551
For all the *l* is fulfilled in one Gal 5:14 3551
Spirit, ye are not under the *l* Gal 5:18 3551
against such there is no *l* Gal 5:23 3551
and so fulfil the *l* of Christ Gal 6:2 3551
who are circumcised keep the *l* Gal 6:13 3551
even the *l* of commandments Eph 2:15 3551
as touching the *l*, a Pharisee Phil 3:5 3551
righteousness which is in the *l* Phil 3:6 3551
righteousness, which is of the *l* Phil 3:9 3551
Desiring to be teachers of the *l* 1Ti 1:7 3547
But we know that the *l* is good 1Ti 1:8 3551
that the *l* is not made for a 1Ti 1:9 3551
and strivings about the *l* Titus 3:9 3544
of the people according to the *l* Heb 7:5 3551
it the people received the *l* Heb 7:11 3549
necessity a change also of the *l* Heb 7:12 3551
not after the *l* of a carnal Heb 7:16 3551
For the *l* made nothing perfect, Heb 7:19 3551
For the *l* maketh men high priests Heb 7:28 3551
the oath, which was since the *l* Heb 7:28 3551
offer gifts according to the *l* Heb 8:4 3551
all the people according to the *l* Heb 9:19 3551
are by the *l* purged with blood Heb 9:22 3551
For the *l* having a shadow of good Heb 10:1 3551
which are offered by the *l* Heb 10:8 3551
He that despised Moses' *l* died Heb 10:28 3551
into the perfect *l* of liberty Jas 1:25 3551
If ye fulfil the royal *l* Jas 2:8 3551
of the *l* as transgressors Jas 2:9 3551
whosoever shall keep the whole *l* Jas 2:10 3551
become a transgressor of the *l* Jas 2:11 3551
be judged by the *l* of liberty Jas 2:12 3551
evil of the *l*, and judgeth the *l* Jas 4:11 3551
but if thou judge the *l* Jas 4:11 3551
thou art not a doer of the *l* Jas 4:11 3551
sin transgresseth also the *l* 1Jn 3:4 3551
sin is the transgression of the *l* 1Jn 3:4 458

LAWFUL
it shall not be *l* to impose toll Ezr 7:24 7990
or the *l* captive delivered Is 49:24 6662
be just, and do that which is *l* Eze 18:5 4941
the son hath done that which is *l* Eze 18:19 4941
statutes, and do that which is *l* Eze 18:21 4941
and doeth that which is *l* Eze 18:27 4941
his sin, and do that which is *l* Eze 33:14 4941
he hath done that which is *l* Eze 33:16 4941
wickedness, and do that which is *l* Eze 33:19 4941
not *l* to do upon the sabbath day Mt 12:2 1832
which was not *l* for him to eat, Mt 12:4 1832
Is it *l* to heal on the sabbath Mt 12:10 1832
Wherefore it is *l* to do well on Mt 12:12 1832
It is not *l* for thee to have her Mt 14:4 1832
Is it *l* for a man to put away his Mt 19:3 1832
Is it not *l* for me to do what I Mt 20:15 1833
Is it *l* to give tribute unto Mt 22:17 1833
It is not *l* for to put them into Mt 27:6 1833
sabbath day that which is not *l* Mk 2:24 1833
which is not *l* to eat but for the Mk 2:26 1833
Is it *l* to do good on the sabbath Mk 3:4 1833
It is not *l* for thee to have thy Mk 6:18 1833
Is it *l* for a man to put away his Mk 10:2 1833
Is it *l* to give tribute to Caesar Mk 12:14 1833
not *l* to do on the sabbath days Lk 6:2 1833
which it is not *l* to eat but for Lk 6:4 1833
Is it *l* on the sabbath days to do Lk 6:9 1833
Is it *l* to heal on the sabbath Lk 14:3 1833
Is it *l* for us to give tribute Lk 20:22 1833
it is not *l* for thee to carry thy Jn 5:10 1833
It is not *l* for us to put any man Jn 18:31 1833
which are not *l* for us to receive Acts 16:21 1833
be determined in a *l* assembly Acts 19:39 1772
Is it *l* for you to scourge a man Acts 22:25 1832
All things are *l* unto me, but all 1Cor 6:12 1832
all things are *l* for me, but I 1Cor 6:12 1832
All things are *l* for me, but all 1Cor 10:23 1832
all things are *l* for me, but all 1Cor 10:23 1832
which it is not *l* for a man to 2Cor 12:4 1832

LAWFULLY
law is good, if a man use it *l* 1Ti 1:8 3545
not crowned, except he strive *l* 2Ti 2:5 3545

LAWGIVER
nor a *l* from between his feet, Gen 49:10 2710
it, by the direction of the *l* Num 21:18 2710
there, in a portion of the *l* Deut 33:21 2710
Judah is my *l* Ps 60:7 2710
Judah is my *l* Ps 108:8 2710
is our judge, the LORD is our *l* Is 33:22 2710
There is one *l*, who is able to Jas 4:12 3550

LAWLESS
a righteous man, but for the *l* 1Ti 1:9 459

LAWS
my statutes, and my *l* Gen 26:5 8451
to keep my commandments and my *l* Ex 16:28 8451
the statutes of God, and his *l* Ex 18:16 8451
shalt teach them ordinances and *l* Ex 18:20 8451
the statutes and judgments and *l* Lev 26:46 8451
all such as know the *l* of thy God Ezr 7:25 1882
them right judgments, and true *l* Neh 9:13 8451
them precepts, statutes, and *l* Neh 9:14 8451
among the *l* of the Persians Est 1:19 1881
their *l* are diverse from all Est 3:8 1881
neither keep they the king's *l* Est 3:8 1881
his statutes, and keep his *l* Ps 105:45 8541
they have transgressed the *l* Is 24:5 8451
thereof, and all the *l* thereof Eze 43:11 8451
of the LORD, and all the *l* thereof Eze 44:5 8451
and they shall keep my *l* and my Eze 44:24 8451
and think to change times and *l* Dan 7:25 1882
LORD our God, to walk in his *l* Dan 9:10 8451
I will put my *l* into their mind, Heb 8:10 3551
I will put my *l* into their hearts Heb 10:16 3551

LAWYER
Then one of them, which was a *l* Mt 22:35 3544
And, behold, a certain *l* stood up Lk 10:25 3544
Bring Zenas the *l* and Apollos on Titus 3:13 3544

LAWYERS
l rejected the counsel of God Lk 7:30 3544
Then answered one of the *l* Lk 11:45 3544
he said, Woe unto you also, ye *l* Lk 11:46 3544
Woe unto you, *l* Lk 11:52 3544
Jesus answering spake unto the *l* Lk 14:3 3544

LAY
But before they *l* down, the men Gen 19:4 7901
went in, and *l* with her father Gen 19:33 7901
he perceived not when she *l* down Gen 19:33 7901
I *l* yesternight with my father Gen 19:34 7901
the younger arose, and *l* with him Gen 19:35 7901
he perceived not when she *l* down Gen 19:35 7901
L not thine hand upon the lad, Gen 22:12 7971
l down in that place to sleep Gen 28:11 7901
And he *l* with her that night Gen 30:16 7901
l with her, and defiled her Gen 34:2 7901
l with Bilhah his father's Gen 35:22 7901
wilderness, and *l* no hand upon him Gen 37:22 7971
l up corn under the hand of Gen 41:35 6651
heretofore, ye shall *l* upon them Ex 5:8 7760
that I may *l* my hand upon Egypt, Ex 7:4 5414
the dew *l* round about the host Ex 16:13 7902
when the dew that *l* was gone up Ex 16:14 7902
there *l* a small round thing Ex 16:14
that which remaineth over *l* up Ex 16:23 3241
l it up before the LORD, to be Ex 16:33 3241
woman's husband will *l* upon him Ex 21:22 7896
shalt thou *l* upon him usury Ex 22:25 7760
l the wood in order upon the fire Lev 1:7
shall *l* the parts, the head, and Lev 1:8
the priest shall *l* them in order Lev 1:12
it, and *l* frankincense thereon Lev 2:15 7760
he shall *l* his hand upon the head Lev 3:2 5564
he shall *l* his hand upon the head Lev 3:8 5564
he shall *l* his hand upon the head Lev 3:13 5564
shall *l* his hand upon the Lev 4:4 5564
of the congregation shall *l* their Lev 4:15 5564
he shall *l* his hand upon the head Lev 4:24 5564
he shall *l* his hand upon the head Lev 4:29 5564
he shall *l* his hand upon the head Lev 4:33 5564
l the burnt offering in order Lev 6:12
Aaron shall *l* both his hands upon Lev 16:21 5564
let all that heard him *l* their Lev 24:14 5564
the Levites shall *l* their hands Num 8:12 5564
l not the sin upon us, wherein we Num 12:11 7896
thou shalt *l* them up in the Num 17:4 3241
l them up without the camp in a Num 19:9 3241
he *l* down as a lion, and as a Num 24:9 7901
spirit, and *l* thine hand upon him Num 27:18 5564
but will *l* them upon all them Deut 7:15 5414
Therefore shall ye *l* up these my Deut 11:18 7760
your God shall *l* the fear of you Deut 11:25 5414
shalt *l* it up within thy gates Deut 14:28 3241
l not innocent blood unto thy Deut 21:8 5414
his mother *l* hold on him, and Deut 21:19
the man that *l* with the woman Deut 22:22 7901
only that *l* with her shall die Deut 22:25 7901
l hold on her, and lie with her, Deut 22:28
Then the man that *l* with her Deut 22:29 7901
he shall *l* the foundation thereof Josh 6:26
l thee an ambush for the city Josh 8:2 7760
all that *l* near Ashdod, with Josh 15:46
her tent, behold, Sisera *l* dead Judg 4:22 5307
feet he bowed, he fell, he *l* down Judg 5:27 7901
l them upon this rock, and pour Judg 6:20 3241
east *l* along in the valley like Judg 7:12 5307
it, that the tent *l* along Judg 7:13 5307
because she *l* sore upon him Judg 14:17
Samson *l* till midnight, and arose Judg 16:3 7901
l thine hand upon thy mouth, and Judg 18:19 7760
uncover his feet, and *l* thee down Ruth 3:4 7901
and, behold, a woman *l* at his feet Ruth 3:8 7901
she *l* at his feet until the Ruth 3:14 7901
how they *l* with the women that 1Sa 2:22 7901
And he went and *l* down 1Sa 3:5 7901
went and *l* down in his place 1Sa 3:9 7901
Samuel *l* until the morning, and 1Sa 3:15 7901
the LORD, and *l* it upon the cart 1Sa 6:8 5414
l it for a reproach upon all 1Sa 11:2 7760
l down naked all that day and all 1Sa 19:24 5307
beheld the place where Saul *l* 1Sa 26:5 7901
Saul *l* in the trench, and the 1Sa 26:5 7901
Saul *l* sleeping within the trench 1Sa 26:7 7901
the people *l* round about him 1Sa 26:7 7901
l thee hold on one of the young 2Sa 2:21
who *l* on a bed at noon 2Sa 4:5 7901
he *l* on his bed in his bedchamber 2Sa 4:7 7901
in unto him, and he *l* with her 2Sa 11:4 7901
l in his bosom, and was unto him 2Sa 12:3 7901
l all night upon the earth 2Sa 12:16 7901
went in unto her, and *l* with her 2Sa 12:24 7901
L thee down on thy bed, and make 2Sa 13:5 7901
So Amnon *l* down, and made himself 2Sa 13:6 7901
she, forced her, and *l* with her 2Sa 13:14 7901
his garments, and *l* on the earth 2Sa 13:31 7901
sustenance while he *l* at Mahanaim 2Sa 19:32 7871
to *l* the foundation of the house 1Kin 5:17
that *l* on forty five pillars, 1Kin 7:3
the altar, saying, *L* hold on him 1Kin 13:4
l my bones beside his bones 1Kin 13:31 3241
l it on wood, and put no fire 1Kin 18:23 7760
l it on wood, and put no fire 1Kin 18:23 7760
And as he *l* and slept under a 1Kin 19:5 7901
l in sackcloth, and went softly 1Kin 21:27 7901
into the chamber, and *l* there 2Kin 4:11 7901
l my staff upon the face of the 2Kin 4:29 7760
l upon the child, and put his 2Kin 4:34 7901
for Joram *l* there 2Kin 9:16 7901
L ye them in two heaps at the 2Kin 10:8 7760
be to *l* waste fenced cities into 2Kin 19:25
to *l* the foundation of the heaps 2Chr 31:7
for as long as she *l* desolate she 2Chr 36:21
of such as *l* in wait by the way Ezr 8:31
so again, I will *l* hands on you Neh 13:21 7971
sought to *l* hand on the king Est 2:21 7971
he thought scorn to *l* hands on Est 3:6 7971
many *l* in sackcloth and ashes Est 4:3 3331
who sought to *l* hand on the king Est 6:2 7971
to *l* hand on such as sought their Est 9:2 7971
that might *l* his hand upon us Job 9:33 7896
L down now, put me in a surety Job 17:3 7760
l your hand upon your mouth Job 21:5 7760
l up his words in thine heart Job 22:22 7760
Then shalt thou *l* up gold as dust Job 22:24 7896
the dew *l* all night upon my Job 29:19 3885
For he will not *l* upon man more Job 34:23 7760
I will *l* mine hand upon my mouth Job 40:4 7760
L thine hand upon him, remember Job 41:8 7760
I will both *l* me down in peace, Ps 4:8 7901
l mine honour in the dust Ps 7:5 7931
after my life *l* snares for me Ps 38:12
they that *l* wait for my soul take Ps 71:10
where she may *l* her young Ps 84:3 7896
l them down in their dens Ps 104:22 7257
let us *l* wait for blood, let us Prov 1:11
they *l* wait for their own blood Prov 1:18
life to them that *l* hold upon her Prov 3:18
l up my commandments with thee Prov 7:1 6845
Wise men *l* up knowledge Prov 10:14 6845
L not wait, O wicked man, against Prov 24:15
l thine hand upon thy mouth Prov 30:32
to *l* hold on folly, till I might Eccl 2:3
the living will *l* it to his heart Eccl 7:2 5414
And I will *l* it waste Is 5:6
that *l* field to field, till there Is 5:8 7126
l hold of the prey, and shall Is 5:29
they shall *l* their hand upon Edom Is 11:14 7971
anger, to *l* the land desolate Is 13:9
will *l* low the haughtiness of the Is 13:11
David will I *l* upon his shoulder Is 22:22 5414
l low, and bring to the ground, Is 25:12
I *l* in Zion for a foundation a Is 28:16
also will I *l* to the line Is 28:17 7760
will *l* siege against thee with a Is 29:3
l a snare for him that reproveth Is 29:21
which the LORD shall *l* upon him Is 30:32 5117
the great owl make her nest, and *l* Is 34:15 4422
of dragons, where each *l*, shall Is 35:7 7258
that thou shouldest be to *l* waste Is 37:26
l it for a plaister upon the boil Is 38:21
so that thou didst not *l* these Is 47:7 7760
l the foundations of the earth, Is 51:16
I will *l* thy stones with fair Is 54:11 7257
l thy foundations with sapphires Is 54:11
they *l* wait, as he that setteth Jer 5:26
I will *l* stumblingblocks before Jer 6:21 5414
They shall *l* hold on bow and spear Jer 6:23
I *l* a stumblingblock before him, Eze 3:20 5414
l it before thee, and pourtray Eze 4:1 5414
l siege against it, and build a Eze 4:2 5414
thou shalt *l* siege against it Eze 4:3
l the iniquity of the house of Eze 4:4 7760
I will *l* bands upon thee, and thou Eze 4:8 5414
I will *l* the dead carcases of the Eze 6:5 5414
she *l* down among lions, she Eze 19:2 7257
for in her youth they *l* with her Eze 23:8 7901
I will *l* my vengeance upon Edom Eze 25:14 5414
when I shall *l* my vengeance upon Eze 25:17 5414
and they shall *l* thy stones Eze 26:12 7760
l away their robes, and put off Eze 26:16 5493
I will *l* thee before kings, that Eze 28:17 5414
I will *l* thy flesh upon the Eze 32:5 5414
For I will *l* the land most Eze 33:28 5414
I will *l* thy cities waste, and Eze 35:4 7760
it, and *l* no famine upon you Eze 36:29 5414
whereas it *l* desolate in the Eze 36:34
I will *l* sinews upon you, and will Eze 37:6 5414
there shall they *l* the most holy Eze 42:13 3241
but there they shall *l* their Eze 42:14 3241
l them in the holy chambers, and Eze 44:19 3241
they *l* themselves down upon Amos 2:8 5186
and he *l*, and was fast asleep Jonah 1:5 7901
l not upon us innocent blood Jonah 1:14 5414
idols thereof will I *l* desolate Mic 1:7 7760
they shall *l* their hand upon Mic 7:16 7760
they shall *l* hold every one on Zec 14:13
and if ye will not *l* it to heart Mal 2:2 7760
because ye do not *l* it to heart Mal 2:2 7760
L not up for yourselves treasures Mt 6:19
But *l* up for yourselves treasures Mt 6:20
man hath not where to *l* his head Mt 8:20 2827
l thy hand upon her, and she shall Mt 9:18 2007
day, will he not *l* hold on it Mt 12:11
they sought to *l* hands on him Mt 21:46
l them on men's shoulders Mt 23:4 2007
see the place where the Lord *l* Mt 28:6 2749
wife's mother *l* sick of a fever Mk 1:30 2621
wherein the sick of the palsy *l* Mk 2:4 2621
they went out to *l* hold on him Mk 3:21
l thy hands on her, that she may Mk 5:23 2007
And they sought to *l* hold on him Mk 12:12
which *l* bound with them that had Mk 15:7
they shall *l* hands on the sick, Mk 16:18 2007
him in, and to *l* him before him Lk 5:18 5087
and took up that whereon he *l* Lk 5:25 2621
years of age, and she *l* a dying Lk 8:42

man hath not where to *l* his head ... Lk 9:58 2827
shall *l* thee even with the ground ... Lk 19:44 1474
hour sought to *l* hands on him ... Lk 20:19 1911
they shall *l* their hands on you, ... Lk 21:12 1911
In these *l* a great multitude of ... Jn 5:3 2621
I *l* down my life for the sheep ... Jn 10:15 5087
because I *l* down my life, that I ... Jn 10:17 5087
but I *l* it down of myself ... Jn 10:18 5087
I have power to *l* it down ... Jn 10:18 5087
was a cave, and a stone *l* upon it ... Jn 11:38 1945
I will *l* down my life for thy ... Jn 13:37 5087
Wilt thou *l* down thy life for my ... Jn 13:38 5087
that a man *l* down his life for ... Jn 15:13 5087
l not this sin to their charge ... Acts 7:60 2476
that on whomsoever I *l* hands ... Acts 8:19 2007
to *l* upon you no greater burden ... Acts 15:28 2007
and no small tempest *l* on us ... Acts 27:20 1945
of Publius *l* sick of a fever ... Acts 28:8 2621
Who shall *l* any thing to the ... Rom 8:33 1458
I *l* in Sion a stumblingstone and ... Rom 9:33 5087
can no man *l* than that is laid ... 1Cor 3:11 5087
one of you *l* by him in store ... 1Cor 16:2 5087
ought not to *l* up for the parents ... 2Cor 12:14 2343
L hands suddenly on no man, ... 1Ti 5:22 2007
l hold on eternal life, whereunto ... 1Ti 6:12 1949
that they may *l* hold on eternal ... 1Ti 6:19 1949
who have fled for refuge to *l* ... Heb 6:18
let us *l* aside every weight, and ... Heb 12:1 659
Wherefore *l* apart all filthiness ... Jas 1:21 659
I *l* in Sion a chief corner stone, ... 1Pet 2:6 5087
we ought to *l* down our lives for ... 1Jn 3:16 5087

LAYEDST
takest up that thou *l* not down ... Lk 19:21 5087

LAYEST
that thou *l* the burden of all ... Num 11:11 7760
wherefore then *l* thou a snare for ... 1Sa 28:9

LAYETH
God *l* up his iniquity for his ... Job 21:19 6845
yet God *l* not folly to them ... Job 24:12 7760
of him that *l* at him cannot hold ... Job 41:26 5381
he *l* up the depth in storehouses ... Ps 33:7 5414
Who *l* the beams of his chambers ... Ps 104:3 7760
He *l* up sound wisdom for the ... Prov 2:7 6845
but a fool *l* open his folly ... Prov 13:16
lips, and *l* up deceit within him ... Prov 26:24 7896
She *l* her hands to the spindle, ... Prov 31:19 7971
the lofty city, he *l* it low ... Is 26:5
he *l* it low, even to the ground ... Is 26:5
the son of man that *l* hold on it ... Is 56:2
and no man *l* it to heart ... Is 57:1 7760
mouth, but in heart he *l* his wait ... Jer 9:8 7760
because no man *l* it to heart ... Jer 12:11 7760
l the foundation of the earth, and ... Zec 12:1
So is he that *l* up treasure for ... Lk 12:21
he *l* it on his shoulders, ... Lk 15:5 2007

LAYING
or hurl at him by *l* of wait ... Num 35:20
him any thing without *l* of wait ... Num 35:22
they commune of *l* snares privily ... Ps 64:5 2934
For *l* aside the commandment of ... Mk 7:8 863
L wait for him, and seeking to ... Lk 11:54 1748
when Simon saw that through *l* on ... Acts 8:18 1936
But their *l* await was known of ... Acts 9:24 1917
l wait in the way to kill him ... Acts 25:3 4160
with the *l* on of the hands of the ... 1Ti 4:14 1936
L up in store for themselves a ... 1Ti 6:19 597
not *l* again the foundation of ... Heb 6:1 2598
and of *l* on of hands, and of ... Heb 6:2 1936
Wherefore *l* aside all malice, and ... 1Pet 2:1 659

LAZARUS (*laz'-a-rus*)
1. Name for a beggar in a parable of Jesus.
was a certain beggar named *L* ... Lk 16:20 2976
afar off, and *L* in his bosom ... Lk 16:23 2976
have mercy on me, and send *L* ... Lk 16:24 2976
things, and likewise *L* evil things ... Lk 16:25 2976
2. Man raised from the dead by Jesus.
a certain man was sick, named *L* ... Jn 11:1 2976
hair, whose brother *L* was sick ... Jn 11:2 2976
loved Martha, and her sister, and *L* ... Jn 11:5 2976
unto them, Our friend *L* sleepeth ... Jn 11:11 2976
unto them plainly, *L* is dead ... Jn 11:14 2976
he cried with a loud voice, *L* ... Jn 11:43 2976
where *L* was which had been dead, ... Jn 12:1 2976
but *L* was one of them that sat at ... Jn 12:2 2976
but that they might see *L* also ... Jn 12:9 2976
they might put *L* also to death ... Jn 12:10 2976
when he called *L* out of his grave ... Jn 12:17 2976

LEAD
I will *l* on softly, according as ... Gen 33:14 5095
of a cloud, to *l* them the way ... Ex 13:21 5148
they sank as *l* in the mighty ... Ex 15:10 5777
l the people unto the place of ... Ex 32:34 5148
them, and which may *l* them out ... Num 27:17 3318
the iron, the tin, and the *l* ... Num 31:22 5777
whither the LORD shall *l* you ... Deut 4:27 5090
of the armies to *l* the people ... Deut 20:9 7218
whither the LORD shall *l* thee ... Deut 28:37 5090
So the LORD alone did *l* him ... Deut 32:12 5148
l thy captivity captive, thou son ... Judg 5:12
that they may *l* them away ... 1Sa 30:22 5090
before them that *l* them captive ... 2Chr 30:9
them by day, to *l* them in the way ... Neh 9:19 5148
pen and *l* in the rock for ever ... Job 19:24 5777
L me, O LORD, in thy ... Ps 5:8 5148
L me in thy truth, and teach me ... Ps 25:5 1869
l me in a plain path, because of ... Ps 27:11 5148
for thy name's sake *l* me, and ... Ps 31:3 5148
let them *l* me ... Ps 43:3 5148
who will *l* me into Edom ... Ps 60:9 5148
l me to the rock that is higher ... Ps 61:2 5148
who will *l* me into Edom ... Ps 108:10 5148

the LORD shall *l* them forth with ... Ps 125:5 3212
Even there shall thy hand *l* me ... Ps 139:10 5148
l me in the way everlasting ... Ps 139:24 5148
l me into the land of uprightness ... Ps 143:10 5148
When thou goest, it shall *l* thee ... Prov 6:22 5148
I *l* in the way of righteousness, ... Prov 8:20 1980
I would *l* thee, and bring thee ... Song 8:2 5090
they which *l* thee cause thee to ... Is 3:12 833
and a little child shall *l* them ... Is 11:6 5090
l away the Egyptians prisoners ... Is 20:4 5090
shall gently *l* those that are ... Is 40:11 5095
I will *l* them in paths that they ... Is 42:16 1869
hath mercy on them shall *l* them ... Is 49:10 5090
I will *l* him also, and restore ... Is 57:18 5148
so didst thou *l* thy people ... Is 63:14 5090
the *l* is consumed of the fire ... Jer 6:29 5777
with supplications will I *l* them ... Jer 31:9 2986
he shall *l* Zedekiah to Babylon, ... Jer 32:5 3212
are brass, and tin, and iron, and *l* ... Eze 22:18 5777
silver, and brass, and iron, and *l* ... Eze 22:20 5777
with silver, iron, tin, and *l* ... Eze 27:12 5777
her maids shall *l* her as with the ... Nah 2:7 5090
there was lifted up a talent of *l* ... Zec 5:7 5777
he cast the weight of *l* upon the ... Zec 5:8 5777
l us not into temptation, but ... Mt 6:13 1533
And if the blind *l* the blind ... Mt 15:14 3594
But when they shall *l* you ... Mk 13:11 71
take him, and *l* him away safely ... Mk 14:44 520
them, Can the blind *l* the blind ... Lk 6:39 3594
And *l* us not into temptation ... Lk 11:4 1533
stall, and *l* him away to watering ... Lk 13:15 520
seeking some to *l* him by the hand ... Acts 13:11 5497
we not power to *l* about a sister ... 1Cor 9:5 4013
that we may *l* a quiet and ... 1Ti 2:2 1236
l captive silly women laden with ... 2Ti 3:6 162
l them out of the land of Egypt ... Heb 8:9 1806
them, and shall *l* them unto living ... Rev 7:17 3594

LEADER
was the *l* of the Aaronites ... 1Chr 12:27 5057
and hundreds, and with every *l* ... 1Chr 13:1 5057
for a witness to the people, a *l* ... Is 55:4 5057

LEADERS
mighty men of valour, and the *l* ... 2Chr 32:21 5057
For the *l* of this people cause ... Is 9:16 833
they be blind *l* of the blind ... Mt 15:14 3595

LEADEST
thou that *l* Joseph like a flock ... Ps 80:1 5090

LEADETH
unto the way that *l* to Ophrah ... 1Sa 13:17
He *l* counsellors away spoiled, and ... Job 12:17 3212
He *l* princes away spoiled, and ... Job 12:19 3212
he *l* me beside the still waters ... Ps 23:2 5095
he *l* me in the paths of ... Ps 23:3 5090
l him into the way that is not ... Prov 16:29 3212
which *l* thee by the way that thou ... Is 48:17 1869
that *l* to destruction, and many ... Mt 7:13 520
which *l* unto life, and few there ... Mt 7:14 520
l them up into an high mountain ... Mk 9:2 399
own sheep by name, and *l* them out ... Jn 10:3 1806
iron gate that *l* unto the city ... Acts 12:10 5342
of God *l* thee to repentance ... Rom 2:4 71
He that *l* into captivity shall go ... Rev 13:10 4863

LEAF
mouth was an olive *l* pluckt off ... Gen 8:11 5929
of a shaken *l* shall chase them ... Lev 26:36 5929
Wilt thou break a *l* driven to ... Job 13:25 5929
his *l* also shall not wither ... Ps 1:3 5929
shall be as an oak whose *l* fadeth ... Is 1:30 5929
as the *l* falleth off from the ... Is 34:4 5929
and we all do fade as a *l* ... Is 64:6 5929
the fig tree, and the *l* shall fade ... Jer 8:13 5929
cometh, but her *l* shall be green ... Jer 17:8 5929
whose *l* shall not fade, neither ... Eze 47:12 5929
the *l* thereof for medicine ... Eze 47:12 5929

LEAGUE
now therefore make ye a *l* with us ... Josh 9:6 1285
and how shall we make a *l* with you ... Josh 9:7 1285
therefore now make ye a *l* with us ... Josh 9:11 1285
made a *l* with them, to let them ... Josh 9:15 1285
after they had made a *l* with them ... Josh 9:16 1285
ye shall make no *l* with the ... Judg 2:2 1285
made a *l* with the son of Jesse ... 1Sa 22:8 3772
saying also, Make thy *l* with me ... 2Sa 3:12 1285
I will make a *l* with thee ... 2Sa 3:13 1285
that they may make a *l* with thee ... 2Sa 3:21 1285
king David made a *l* with them in ... 2Sa 5:3 1285
and they two made a *l* together ... 1Kin 5:12 1285
There is a *l* between me and thee, ... 1Kin 15:19 1285
break thy *l* with Baasha king of ... 1Kin 15:19 1285
There is a *l* between me and thee, ... 2Chr 16:3 1285
break thy *l* with Baasha king of ... 2Chr 16:3 1285
For thou shalt be in *l* with the ... Job 5:23 1285
the men of the land that is in *l* ... Eze 30:5 1285
after the *l* made with him he ... Dan 11:23 2266

LEAH (*le'-ah*) See LEAH'S. *Wife of Jacob.*
the name of the elder was *L* ... Gen 29:16 3812
L was tender eyed ... Gen 29:17 3812
that he took *L* his daughter ... Gen 29:23 3812
Laban gave unto his daughter *L* ... Gen 29:24 3812
in the morning, behold, it was *L* ... Gen 29:25 3812
he loved also Rachel more than *L* ... Gen 29:30 3812
the LORD saw that *L* was hated ... Gen 29:31 3812
L conceived, and bare a son, and ... Gen 29:32 3812
When *L* saw that she had left ... Gen 30:9 3812
And *L* said, A troop cometh ... Gen 30:11 3812
L said, Happy am I, for the ... Gen 30:13 3812
and brought them unto his mother *L* ... Gen 30:14 3812
Then Rachel said to *L*, Give me, I ... Gen 30:14 3812
L went out to meet him, and said, ... Gen 30:16 3812
And God hearkened unto *L*, and she ... Gen 30:17 3812

L said, God hath given me my hire ... Gen 30:18 3812
L conceived again, and bare Jacob ... Gen 30:19 3812
L said, God hath endued me with a ... Gen 30:20 3812
L to the field unto his flock, ... Gen 31:4 3812
L answered and said unto him, Is ... Gen 31:14 3812
And he divided the children unto *L* ... Gen 33:1 3812
and their children foremost, and *L* ... Gen 33:2 3812
L also with her children came ... Gen 33:7 3812
And Dinah the daughter of *L* ... Gen 34:1 3812
The sons of *L*; Reuben ... Gen 35:23 3812
These be the sons of *L*, which she ... Gen 46:15 3812
whom Laban gave to *L* his daughter ... Gen 46:18 3812
and there I buried *L* ... Gen 49:31 3812
thine house like Rachel and like *L* ... Ruth 4:11 3812

LEAH'S (*le'-ahs*)
Zilpah *L* maid bare Jacob a son ... Gen 30:10 3812
Zilpah *L* maid bare Jacob a second ... Gen 30:12 3812
into Jacob's tent, and into *L* tent ... Gen 31:33 3812
Then went he out of *L* tent ... Gen 31:33 3812
And the sons of Zilpah, *L* handmaid ... Gen 35:26 3812

LEAN
And the *l* and the ill favoured kine ... Gen 41:20 7534
land is, whether it be fat or *l* ... Num 13:20 7330
standeth, that I may *l* upon them ... Judg 16:26 8172
the king's son, *l* from day to day ... 2Sa 13:4 1800
upon Egypt, on which if a man *l* ... 2Kin 18:21 5564
He shall *l* upon his house, but it ... Job 8:15 8172
and *l* not unto thine own ... Prov 3:5 8172
fatness of his flesh shall wax *l* ... Is 17:4 7329
whereon if a man *l*, it will go ... Is 36:6 5564
cattle and between the *l* cattle ... Eze 34:20 7330
yet will they *l* upon the LORD ... Mic 3:11 8172

LEANED
behold, Saul *l* upon his spear ... 2Sa 1:6 8172
king *l* answered the man of God ... 2Kin 7:2 8172
the lord on whose hand he *l* to ... 2Kin 7:17 8172
and when they *l* upon thee, thou ... Eze 29:7 8172
l his hand on the wall, and a ... Amos 5:19 5564
which also *l* on his breast at ... Jn 21:20 377

LEANETH
or that *l* on a staff, or that ... 2Sa 3:29 2388
he *l* on my hand, and I bow myself ... 2Kin 5:18 8127

LEANFLESHED
of the river, ill favoured and *l* ... Gen 41:3
l kine did eat up the seven well ... Gen 41:4
poor and very ill favoured and *l* ... Gen 41:19 7534

LEANING
wilderness, *l* upon her beloved ... Song 8:5 7514
Now there was *l* on Jesus' bosom ... Jn 13:23 345
l upon the top of his staff ... Heb 11:21

LEANNESS
my *l* rising up in me beareth ... Job 16:8 3585
but sent *l* into their soul ... Ps 106:15 7332
hosts, send among his fat ones *l* ... Is 10:16 7332
But I said, My *l*, my *l*, ... Is 24:16 7334

LEANNOTH (*le-an'-noth*) *A musical choir.*
chief Musician upon Mahalath *L* ... Ps 88:t 6030

LEAP
all the rams which *l* upon the ... Gen 31:12 5927
to *l* withal upon the earth ... Lev 11:21 5425
he shall *l* from Bashan ... Deut 33:22 2178
lamps, and sparks of fire *l* out ... Job 41:19 4422
Why *l* ye, ye high hills ... Ps 68:16 7520
shall the lame man *l* as an hart ... Is 35:6 1801
tops of mountains shall they *l* ... Joel 2:5 7540
all those that *l* on the threshold ... Zeph 1:9 1801
ye in that day, and *l* for joy ... Lk 6:23 4640

LEAPED
the rams which *l* upon the cattle ... Gen 31:10 5927
by my God have I *l* over a wall ... 2Sa 22:30 1801
they *l* upon the altar which was ... 1Kin 18:26 6452
and by my God have I *l* over a wall ... Ps 18:29 1801
of Mary, the babe *l* in her womb ... Lk 1:41 4640
the babe *l* in my womb for joy ... Lk 1:44 4640
And he *l* and walked ... Acts 14:10 242
the evil spirit was *l* on them ... Acts 19:16 2177

LEAPING
a window, and saw king David *l* ... 2Sa 6:16 6339
he cometh *l* upon the mountains, ... Song 2:8 1801
he *l* up stood, and walked, and ... Acts 3:8 1814
into the temple, walking, and *l* ... Acts 3:8 242

LEARN
that they may *l* to fear me all ... Deut 4:10 3925
ears this day, that ye may *l* them ... Deut 5:1 3925
that thou mayest *l* to fear the ... Deut 14:23 3925
that he may *l* to fear the LORD ... Deut 17:19 3925
thou shalt not *l* to do after the ... Deut 18:9 3925
they may hear, and that they may *l* ... Deut 31:12 3925
l to fear the LORD your God, as ... Deut 31:13 3925
that I might *l* thy statutes ... Ps 119:71 3925
that I may *l* thy commandments ... Ps 119:73 3925
Lest thou *l* his ways, and get a ... Prov 22:25 502
L to do well ... Is 1:17 3925
neither shall they *l* war any more ... Is 2:4 3925
of the world will *l* righteousness ... Is 26:9 3925
yet will he not *l* righteousness ... Is 26:10 3925
that murmured shall *l* doctrine ... Is 29:24 3925
L not the way of the heathen, and ... Jer 10:2 3925
l the ways of my people, to swear ... Jer 12:16 3925
neither shall they *l* war any more ... Mic 4:3 3925
l what that meaneth, I will have ... Mt 9:13 3129
Take my yoke upon you, and *l* of me ... Mt 11:29 3129
Now *l* a parable of the fig tree ... Mt 24:32 3129
Now *l* a parable of the fig tree ... Mk 13:28 3129
that ye might *l* in us not to ... 1Cor 4:6 3129
one by one, that all may *l* ... 1Cor 14:31 3129
And if they will *l* any thing ... 1Cor 14:35 3129
This only would I *l* of you ... Gal 3:2 3129

L

that they may *l* not to blaspheme 1Ti 1:20 *3811*
Let the woman *l* in silence with 1Ti 2:11 *3129*
let them *l* first to shew piety at 1Ti 5:4 *3129*
And withal they *l* to be idle 1Ti 5:13 *3129*
let ours also *l* to maintain good Titus 3:14 *3129*
no man could *l* that song but the Rev 14:3 *3129*

LEARNED
for I have *l* by experience that Gen 30:27 5172
the heathen, and *l* their works Ps 106:35 3925
when I shall have *l* thy righteous Ps 119:7 3925
I neither *l* wisdom, nor have the Prov 30:3 3925
men deliver to one that is *l* Is 29:11
is delivered to him that is not *l* Is 29:12
and he saith, I am not *l* Is 29:12
hath given me the tongue of the *l* Is 50:4 3928
mine ear to hear as the *l* Is 50:4 3928
lion, and it *l* to catch the prey Eze 19:3 3925
l to catch the prey, and devoured Eze 19:6 3925
hath *l* of the Father, cometh unto Jn 6:45 *3129*
this man letters, having never *l* Jn 7:15 *3129*
Moses was *l* in all the wisdom of Acts 7:22 *3811*
to the doctrine which ye have *l* Rom 16:17 *3129*
But ye have not so *l* Christ Eph 4:20 *3129*
things, which ye have both *l* Phil 4:9 *3129*
for I have *l*, in whatsoever state Phil 4:11 *3129*
As ye also *l* of Epaphras our dear Col 1:7 *3129*
in the things which thou hast *l* 2Ti 3:14 *3129*
knowing of whom thou hast *l* them 2Ti 3:14 *3129*
yet *l* he obedience by the things Heb 5:8 *3129*

LEARNING
man will hear, and will increase *l* Prov 1:5 3948
man, and he will increase in *l* Prov 9:9 3948
of the lips increaseth *l* Prov 16:21 3948
mouth, and addeth *l* to his lips Prov 16:23 3948
and whom they might teach the *l* Dan 1:4 5612
them knowledge and skill in all *l* Dan 1:17 5612
much *l* doth make thee mad Acts 26:24 *1121*
aforetime were written for our *l* Rom 15:4 *1319*
Ever *l*, and never able to come to 2Ti 3:7 *3129*

LEASING
ye love vanity, and seek after *l* Ps 4:2 3577
shalt destroy them that speak *l* Ps 5:6 3577

LEAST
with us a few days, at the *l* ten Gen 24:55 176
of the *l* of all the mercies Gen 32:10 6994
he that gathered *l* gathered ten Num 11:32 4591
at the *l* such as before knew Judg 3:2 7535
I am the *l* in my father's house Judg 6:15 6810
my family the *l* of all the 1Sa 9:21 6810
kept themselves at *l* from women 1Sa 21:4 389
of the *l* of my master's servants 2Kin 18:24 6996
one of the *l* was over an hundred, 1Chr 12:14 6996
of the *l* of my master's servants Is 36:9 6996
For from the *l* of them even unto Jer 6:13 6996
for every one from the *l* even Jer 8:10 6996
from the *l* of them unto the Jer 31:34 6996
from the *l* even unto the greatest Jer 42:1 6996
from the *l* even to the greatest Jer 42:8 6996
from the *l* even unto the greatest Jer 44:12 6996
Surely the *l* of the flock shall Jer 49:20 6810
Surely the *l* of the flock shall Jer 50:45 6810
yet shall not the *l* grain fall Amos 9:9
of them even to the *l* of them Jonah 3:5 6996
art not the *l* among the princes Mt 2:6 *1646*
break one of these *l* commandments Mt 5:19 *1646*
he shall be called the *l* in the Mt 5:19 *1646*
notwithstanding he that is *l* in Mt 11:11 *3398*
indeed is the *l* of all seeds Mt 13:32 *3398*
one of the *l* of these my brethren Mt 25:40 *1646*
it not to one of the *l* of these Mt 25:45 *1646*
but he that is *l* in the kingdom Lk 7:28 *3398*
for he that is *l* among you all Lk 9:48 *3398*
able to do that thing which is *l* Lk 12:26 *1646*
is *l* is faithful also in much Lk 16:10 *1646*
in the *l* is unjust also in much Lk 16:10 *1646*
at *l* in this thy day, the things Lk 19:42 *2534*
that at the *l* the shadow of Peter Acts 5:15 *2579*
from the *l* to the greatest, Acts 8:10 *3398*
who are *l* esteemed in the church 1Cor 6:4 *1848*
For I am the *l* of the apostles, 1Cor 15:9 *1646*
am less than the *l* of all saints Eph 3:8 *1647*
from the *l* to the greatest Heb 8:11 *3398*

LEATHER
a girdle of *l* about his loins 2Kin 1:8 5785

LEATHERN
a *l* girdle about his loins Mt 3:4 *1193*

LEAVE
shall a man *l* his father and his Gen 2:24 5800
for I will not *l* thee, until I Gen 28:15 5800
Let me now *l* with thee some of Gen 33:15 3322
l one of your brethren here with Gen 42:33 3241
lord, The lad cannot *l* his father Gen 44:22 5800
for if he should *l* his father Gen 44:22 5800
Let no man *l* of it till the Ex 16:19 3498
what they *l* the beasts of the Ex 23:11 3499
he shall not *l* any of it until Lev 7:15 3241
holy place, and shall *l* them there Lev 16:23 3241
thou shalt *l* them for the poor and Lev 19:10 5800
ye shall *l* none of it until the Lev 22:30 3498
thou shalt *l* them unto the poor, Lev 23:22 5800
They shall *l* none of it unto the Num 9:12 7604
And he said, *L* us not, I pray thee Num 10:31 5800
to give me *l* to go with you Num 22:13 5414
he will yet again *l* them in the Num 32:15 3241
also shall not *l* thee either corn Deut 28:51 7604
of his children which he shall *l* Deut 28:54 3498
l them in the lodging place, Josh 4:3 3241
Should I *l* my fatness, wherewith Judg 9:9 2308
unto them, Should I *l* my wine Judg 9:13 2308
said, Intreat me not to *l* thee Ruth 1:16 5800
l them, that she may glean them, Ruth 2:16 5800
lest my father *l* caring for the 1Sa 9:5 2308
let us not *l* a man of them 1Sa 14:36 7604
David earnestly asked *l* of me 1Sa 20:6
David earnestly asked *l* of me to 1Sa 20:28
if I *l* of all that pertain to him 1Sa 25:22 7604
shall not *l* to my husband neither 2Sa 14:7 7604
let him not *l* us, nor forsake us 1Kin 8:57 5800
soul liveth, I will not *l* thee 2Kin 2:2 5800
soul liveth, I will not *l* thee 2Kin 2:4 5800
soul liveth, I will not *l* thee 2Kin 2:6 5800
soul liveth, I will not *l* thee 2Kin 4:30 5800
shall eat, and shall *l* thereof 2Kin 4:43 3498
Neither did he *l* of the people to 2Kin 13:7 7604
l it for an inheritance for your 1Chr 28:8 5157
to *l* us a remnant to escape, and Ezr 9:8 7604
l it for an inheritance to your Ezr 9:12
pray you, let us *l* off this usury Neh 5:10 5800
the work cease, whilst I *l* it Neh 6:3 7503
that we would *l* the seventh year, Neh 10:31 5203
days obtained I *l* of the king Neh 13:6 7592
I will *l* off my heaviness, and Job 9:27 5800
I will *l* my complaint upon myself Job 10:1 5800
or wilt thou *l* thy labour to him Job 39:11 5800
thou wilt not *l* my soul in hell Ps 16:10 5800
l the rest of their substance to Ps 17:14 3241
l me not, neither forsake me, O Ps 27:9 5203
LORD will not *l* him in his hand Ps 37:33 5800
and *l* their wealth to others Ps 49:10 5800
l me not to mine oppressors Ps 119:121 3241
l not my soul destitute Ps 141:8 6168
Who *l* the paths of uprightness, Prov 2:13 5800
therefore *l* off contention, Prov 17:14 5203
because I should *l* it unto the Eccl 2:18 3241
shall he *l* it for his portion Eccl 2:21 5414
up against thee, *l* not thy place Eccl 10:4 3241
and where will ye *l* your glory Is 10:3 5800
ye shall *l* your name for a curse Is 65:15 3241
that I might *l* my people, and go Jer 9:2 5800
l us not Jer 14:9 3241
shall *l* them in the midst of his Jer 17:11 5800
Will a man *l* the snow of Lebanon Jer 18:14 5800
will not *l* thee altogether Jer 30:11
of Judah, to *l* you none to remain Jer 44:7 3498
yet will I not *l* thee wholly Jer 46:28
l the cities, and dwell in the Jer 48:28 5800
would they not *l* some gleaning Jer 49:9 7604
L thy fatherless children, I will Jer 49:11 5800
Yet will I *l* a remnant, that ye Eze 6:8 3498
But I will *l* a few men of them Eze 12:16 3498
jewels, and *l* thee naked and bare Eze 16:39 3241
I will *l* you there, and melt you Eze 22:20 3241
shall *l* thee naked and bare Eze 23:29 5800
I will *l* thee thrown into the Eze 29:5 5203
Then will I *l* thee upon the land, Eze 32:4 5203
l but the sixth part of thee, and Eze 39:2 8338
Nevertheless *l* the stump of his Dan 4:15 7662
yet *l* the stump of the roots Dan 4:23 7662
whereas they commanded to *l* the Dan 4:26 7662
shall he *l* his blood upon him Hos 12:14 5203
and *l* a blessing behind him Joel 2:14 7604
by a thousand shall *l* an hundred Amos 5:3 7604
forth by an hundred shall *l* ten Amos 5:3 7604
l off righteousness in the earth, Amos 5:7 3241
would they not *l* some grapes Obad 5 7604
I will also *l* in the midst of Zeph 3:12 7604
that it shall *l* them neither root Mal 4:1 5800
L there thy gift before the altar Mt 5:24 *863*
astray, doth he not *l* the ninety Mt 18:12 *863*
this cause shall a man *l* father Mt 19:5 *2641*
not to *l* the other undone Mt 23:23 *863*
And forthwith Jesus gave them *l* Mk 5:13 *2010*
cause shall a man *l* his father Mk 10:7 *2641*
l his wife behind him Mk 12:19 *2641*
l no children, that his brother Mk 12:19 *863*
not to *l* the other undone Lk 11:42 *863*
doth not *l* the ninety and nine in Lk 15:4 *2641*
they shall not *l* in thee one Lk 19:44 *863*
I will not *l* you comfortless Jn 14:18 *863*
Peace I *l* with you, my peace I Jn 14:27 *863*
I *l* the world, and go to the Jn 16:28 *863*
to his own, and shall *l* me alone Jn 16:32 *863*
and Pilate gave him *l* Jn 19:38 *2010*
thou wilt not *l* my soul in hell Acts 2:27 *1459*
that we should *l* the word of God Acts 6:2 *2641*
then took his *l* of the brethren, Acts 18:18 *657*
we had taken our *l* one of another Acts 21:6 *782*
dwell with her, let her not *l* him 1Cor 7:13 *863*
but taking my *l* of them, I went 2Cor 2:13 *657*
cause shall a man *l* his father Eph 5:31 *2641*
he hath said, I will never *l* thee Heb 13:5 *447*
which is without the temple *l* out Rev 11:2 *1544*

LEAVED
open before him the two *l* gates Is 45:1 1817

LEAVEN
put away *l* out of your houses Ex 12:15 7603
be no *l* found in your houses Ex 12:19 7603
neither shall there be *l* seen Ex 13:7 7603
the blood of my sacrifice with *l* Ex 34:25 2557
the LORD, shall be made with *l* Lev 2:11 2557
for ye shall burn no *l*, nor any Lev 2:11 7603
It shall not be baken with *l* Lev 6:17 2557
eat it without *l* beside the altar Lev 10:12 4682
they shall be baken with *l* Lev 23:17 2557
sacrifice of thanksgiving with *l* Amos 4:5 2557
kingdom of heaven is like unto *l* Mt 13:33 *2219*
beware of the *l* of the Pharisees Mt 16:6 *2219*
beware of the *l* of the Pharisees Mt 16:11 *2219*
them not beware of the *l* of bread Mt 16:12 *2219*
beware of the *l* of the Pharisees, Mk 8:15 *2219*
and of the *l* of Herod Mk 8:15 *2219*
ye of the *l* of the Pharisees Lk 12:1 *2219*
It is like *l*, which a woman took Lk 13:21 *2219*
little *l* leaveneth the whole lump 1Cor 5:6 *2219*
Purge out therefore the old *l* 1Cor 5:7 *2219*
us keep the feast, not with old *l* 1Cor 5:8 *2219*
neither with the *l* of malice 1Cor 5:8 *2219*
A little *l* leaveneth the whole Gal 5:9 *2219*

LEAVENED
for whosoever eateth *l* bread from Ex 12:15 2557
whosoever eateth that which is *l* Ex 12:19 2557
Ye shall eat nothing *l* Ex 12:20 2557
took their dough before it was *l* Ex 12:34 2557
out of Egypt, for it was not *l* Ex 12:39 2557
there shall no *l* bread be eaten Ex 13:3 2557
there shall no *l* bread be seen Ex 13:7 2557
of my sacrifice with *l* bread Ex 23:18 2557
l bread with the sacrifice of Lev 7:13 2557
Thou shalt eat no *l* bread with it Deut 16:3 2557
there shall be no *l* bread seen Deut 16:4 7603
kneaded the dough, until it be *l* Hos 7:4 2557
of meal, till the whole was *l* Mt 13:33 *2220*
of meal, till the whole was *l* Lk 13:21 *2220*

LEAVENETH
a little leaven *l* the whole lump 1Cor 5:6 *2220*
A little leaven *l* the whole lump Gal 5:9 *2220*

LEAVES
and they sewed fig *l* together Gen 3:7 2529
the two *l* of the one door were 1Kin 6:34 6763
the two *l* of the other door were 1Kin 6:34 7050
in them, when they cast their *l* Is 6:13
Jehudi had read three or four *l* Jer 36:23 1817
wither in all the *l* of her spring Eze 17:9 2964
two *l* apiece, two turning *l* Eze 41:24 1817
two *l* for the one door Eze 41:24
and two *l* for the other door Eze 41:24 1817
The *l* thereof were fair, and the Dan 4:12 6074
off his branches, shake off his *l* Dan 4:14 6074
Whose *l* were fair, and the fruit Dan 4:21 6074
but *l* only, and said unto it, Let Mt 21:19 *5444*
is yet tender, and putteth forth *l* Mt 24:32 *5444*
a fig tree afar off having *l* Mk 11:13 *5444*
to it, he found nothing but *l* Mk 11:13 *5444*
is yet tender, and putteth forth *l* Mk 13:28 *5444*
the *l* of the tree were for the Rev 22:2 *5444*

LEAVETH
Which *l* her eggs in the earth, and Job 39:14 5800
A good man *l* an inheritance to Prov 13:22
a sweeping rain which *l* no food Prov 28:3
idol shepherd that *l* the flock Zec 11:17 5800
Then the devil *l* him, and, behold, Mt 4:11 *863*
coming, and *l* the sheep, and fleeth Jn 10:12 *863*

LEAVING
l Nazareth, he came and dwelt in Mt 4:13 *2641*
him, and departed, *l* him half dead Lk 10:30 *863*
l the natural use of the woman, Rom 1:27 *863*
Therefore *l* the principles of the Heb 6:1 *863*
l us an example, that ye should 1Pet 2:21 *5277*

LEBANA (*leb'-a-nah*) See LEBANAH. *A family of exiles.*
The children of *L*, the children Neh 7:48 3848

LEBANAH (*leb'-a-nah*) *Same as Lebana.*
The children of *L*, the children Ezr 2:45 3848

LEBANON (*leb'-a-non*) *Chief mountain range in Syria.*
land of the Canaanites, and unto *L* Deut 1:7 3844
that goodly mountain, and *L* Deut 3:25 3844
from the wilderness and *L*, from Deut 11:24 3844
this *L* even unto the great river, Josh 1:4 3844
of the great sea over against *L* Josh 9:1 3844
valley of *L* under mount Hermon Josh 11:17 3844
of *L* even unto the mount Halak Josh 12:7 3844
land of the Giblites, and all *L* Josh 13:5 3844
from *L* unto Misrephoth-maim Josh 13:6 3844
the Hivites that dwelt in mount *L* Judg 3:3 3844
and devour the cedars of *L* Judg 9:15 3844
is in *L* even unto the hyssop that 1Kin 4:33 3844
they hew me cedar trees out of *L* 1Kin 5:6 3844
them down from *L* unto the sea 1Kin 5:9 3844
And he sent them to *L*, ten 1Kin 5:14 3844
a month they were in *L*, and two 1Kin 5:14 3844
also the house of the forest of *L* 1Kin 7:2 3844
to build in Jerusalem, and in *L* 1Kin 9:19 3844
in the house of the forest of *L* 1Kin 10:17 3844
the forest of *L* were of pure gold 1Kin 10:21 3844
The thistle that was in *L* sent to 2Kin 14:9 3844
sent to the cedar that was in *L* 2Kin 14:9 3844
by a wild beast that was in *L* 2Kin 14:9 3844
the mountains, to the sides of *L* 2Kin 19:23 3844
trees, and algum trees, out of *L* 2Chr 2:8 3844
can skill to cut timber in *L* 2Chr 2:8 3844
And we will cut wood out of *L* 2Chr 2:16 3844
to build in Jerusalem, and in *L* 2Chr 8:6 3844
in the house of the forest of *L* 2Chr 9:16 3844
the forest of *L* were of pure gold 2Chr 9:20 3844
The thistle that was in *L* sent to 2Chr 25:18 3844
sent to the cedar that was in *L* 2Chr 25:18 3844
by a wild beast that was in *L* 2Chr 25:18 3844
trees from *L* to the sea of Joppa Ezr 3:7 3844
the LORD breaketh the cedars of *L* Ps 29:5 3844
L and Sirion like a young unicorn Ps 29:6 3844
fruit thereof shall shake like *L* Ps 72:16 3844
he shall grow like a cedar in *L* Ps 92:12 3844
the cedars of *L*, which he hath Ps 104:16 3844
a chariot of the wood of *L* Song 3:9 3844
Come with me from *L*, my spouse, Song 4:8 3844
with me from *L* Song 4:8 3844
garments is like the smell of *L* Song 4:11 3844
living waters, and streams from *L* Song 4:15 3844
his countenance is as *L*, Song 5:15 3844
thy nose is as the tower of *L* Song 7:4 3844
And upon all the cedars of *L* Is 2:13 3844
L shall fall by a mighty one Is 10:34 3844

at thee, and the cedars of L Is 14:8 3844
L shall be turned into a fruitful Is 29:17 3844
L is ashamed and hewn down Is 33:9 3844
the glory of L shall be given Is 35:2 3844
the mountains, to the sides of L Is 37:24 3844
L is not sufficient to burn, nor Is 40:16 3844
The glory of L shall come unto Is 60:13 3844
Will a man leave the snow of L Jer 18:14 3844
Gilead unto me, and the head of L Jer 22:6 3844
Go up to L, and cry Jer 22:20 3844
O inhabitant of L, that makest Jer 22:23 3844
had divers colours, came unto L Eze 17:3 3844
from L to make masts for thee Eze 27:5 3844
a cedar in L with fair branches Eze 31:3 3844
I caused L to mourn for him, and Eze 31:15 3844
of Eden, the choice and best of L Eze 31:16 3844
and cast forth his roots as L Hos 14:5 3844
the olive tree, and his smell as L Hos 14:6 3844
thereof shall be as the wine of L Hos 14:7 3844
and the flower of L languisheth Nah 1:4 3844
violence of L shall cover thee Hab 2:17 3844
them into the land of Gilead and L Zec 10:10 3844
Open thy doors, O L, that the Zec 11:1 3844

LEBAOTH (*leb'-a-oth*) See BETH-LEBAOTH. *A city in Judah.*
And L, and Shilhim, and Ain, and Josh 15:32 3822

LEBBAEUS (*leb-be'-us*) See JUDAS, THADDAEUS. *Same as Thaddaeus.*
James the son of Alphaeus, and L Mt 10:3 *3002*

LEB-KAMAI See MIDST.

LEBONAH (*le-bo'-nah*) *A city in Ephraim.*
to Shechem, and on the south of L Judg 21:19 3829

LECAH (*le'-cah*) *Son of Er.*
of Judah were, Er the father of L 1Chr 4:21 3922

LED
the LORD l me to the house of my Gen 24:27 5148
which had l me in the right way Gen 24:48 5148
he l the flock to the backside of Ex 3:1 5090
that God l them not through the Ex 13:17 5148
But God l the people about, Ex 13:18 5437
Thou in thy mercy hast l forth Ex 15:13 5148
l thee these forty years in the Deut 8:2 3212
Who l thee through that great and Deut 8:15 3212
I have l you forty years in the Deut 29:5 3212
he l him about, he instructed him Deut 32:10 5437
l him throughout all the land of Josh 24:3 3212
which l them away captive, and 1Kin 8:48
But he l them to Samaria 2Kin 6:19 3212
Joab l forth the power of the 1Chr 20:1 5090
l forth his people, and went to 2Chr 25:11 5090
thou hast l captivity captive Ps 68:18
also he l them with a cloud Ps 78:14 5148
he l them on safely, so that they Ps 78:53 5148
so he l them through the depths, Ps 106:9 3212
he l them forth by the right way, Ps 107:7 1869
To him which l his people through Ps 136:16 3212
I have l thee in right paths Prov 4:11 1869
they that are l of them are Is 9:16 833
he l them through the deserts Is 48:21 3212
joy, and be l forth with peace Is 55:12 2986
That l them by the right hand of Is 63:12 3212
That l them through the deep, as Is 63:13 3212
that l us through the wilderness, Jer 2:6 3212
when he l thee by the way Jer 2:17 3212
whither they have l him captive Jer 22:12
which l the seed of the house of Jer 23:8 935
He hath l me, and brought me into Lam 3:2 5090
l them with him to Babylon Eze 17:12 935
which caused them to be l into Eze 39:28
l me about the way without unto Eze 47:2 5437
l you forty years through the Amos 2:10 3212
Israel shall surely be l away Amos 7:11
And Huzzab shall be l away captive Nah 2:7
Then was Jesus l up of the spirit Mt 4:1 *321*
that had laid hold on Jesus l him Mt 26:57 *520*
they l him away, and delivered him Mt 27:2 *520*
l him away to crucify him Mt 27:31 *520*
hand, and l him out of the town Mk 8:23 *1806*
they l Jesus away to the high Mk 14:53 *520*
the soldiers l him away into the Mk 15:16 *520*
him, and l him out to crucify him Mk 15:20 *1806*
was l by the Spirit into the Lk 4:1 *71*
l him unto the brow of the hill Lk 4:29 *71*
shall be l away captive into all Lk 21:24 *163*
l him, and brought him into the Lk 22:54 *71*
l him into their council, saying, Lk 22:66 *321*
them arose, and l him unto Pilate Lk 23:1 *71*
as they l him away, they laid Lk 23:26 *520*
l with him to be put to death Lk 23:32 *71*
he l them out as far as to Lk 24:50 *1806*
l him away to Annas first Jn 18:13 *520*
Then l they Jesus from Caiaphas Jn 18:28 *71*
And they took Jesus, and l him away Jn 19:16 *520*
He was l as a sheep to the Acts 8:32 *71*
but they l him by the hand, and Acts 9:8 *5496*
Paul was to be l into the castle Acts 21:37 *1521*
being l by the hand of them that Acts 22:11 *5496*
For as many as are l by the Rom 8:14 *71*
dumb idols, even as ye were l 1Cor 12:2 *71*
But if ye be l of the Spirit, ye Gal 5:18 *71*
he l captivity captive, and gave Eph 4:8 *162*
l away with divers lusts, 2Ti 3:6 *71*
being l away with the error of 2Pet 3:17 *4879*

LEDDEST
over us, thou wast he that l out 2Sa 5:2 3318
was king, thou wast he that l out 1Chr 11:2 3318
Moreover thou l them in the day Neh 9:12 5148
Thou l thy people like a flock by Ps 77:20 5148
l out into the wilderness four Acts 21:38 *1806*

LEDGES
and the borders were between the l 1Kin 7:28 7948
were between the l were lions 1Kin 7:29 7948
upon the l there was a base above 1Kin 7:29 7948
the top of the base the l thereof 1Kin 7:35 3027
on the plates of the l thereof 1Kin 7:36 3027

LEEKS
and the melons, and the l, and the Num 11:5 2682

LEES
things, a feast of wines on the l Is 25:6 8105
of wines on the l well refined Is 25:6 8105
and he hath settled on his l Jer 48:11 8105
men that are settled on their l Zeph 1:12 8105

LEFT
they l off to build the city Gen 11:8 2308
if thou wilt take the l hand Gen 13:9 8040
hand, then I will go to the l Gen 13:9 8041
which is on the l hand of Gen 14:15 8040
he l off talking with him, and God Gen 17:22 3615
as soon as he had l communing Gen 18:33 3615
who hath not l destitute my Gen 24:27 5800
to the right hand, or to the l Gen 24:49 8040
and l bearing Gen 29:35 5975
Leah saw that she had l bearing Gen 30:9 5975
company which is l shall escape Gen 32:8 7604
And Jacob was l alone Gen 32:24 3498
he l all that he had in Joseph's Gen 39:6 5800
he l his garment in her hand, and Gen 39:12 5800
he had l his garment in her hand Gen 39:13 5800
that he l his garment with me, and Gen 39:15 5800
that he l his garment with me, and Gen 39:18 5800
very much, until he l numbering Gen 41:49 2308
brother is dead, and he is l alone Gen 42:38 7604
the eldest, and l at the youngest Gen 44:12 3615
he alone is l of his mother, and Gen 44:20 3498
there is not ought l in the sight Gen 47:18 7604
right hand toward Israel's l hand Gen 48:13 8040
Manasseh in his l hand toward Gen 48:13 8040
his l hand upon Manasseh's head, Gen 48:14 8040
they l in the land of Goshen Gen 50:8 5800
why is it that ye have l the man Ex 2:20 5800
word of the LORD l his servants Ex 9:21 5800
even all that the hail hath l Ex 10:12 7604
of the trees which the hail had l Ex 10:15 3498
shall not an hoof be l behind Ex 10:26 7604
their right hand, and on their l Ex 14:22 8040
their right hand, and on their l Ex 14:29 8040
but some of them l of it until Ex 16:20 3498
passover be l unto the morning Ex 34:25 3885
that which is l of the meat Lev 2:10 3498
Ithamar, his sons that were l Lev 10:12 3498
sons of Aaron which were l alive Lev 10:16 3498
into the palm of his own l hand Lev 14:15 8042
in the oil that is in his l hand Lev 14:16 8042
into the palm of his own l hand Lev 14:26 8042
his l hand seven times before the Lev 14:27 8042
upon them that are l alive of you Lev 26:36 7604
they that are l of you shall pine Lev 26:39 7604
The land also shall be l of them Lev 26:43 5800
to the right hand nor to the l Num 20:17 8040
until there was none l him alive Num 21:35 7604
to the right hand or to the l Num 22:26 8040
And there was not l a man of them Num 26:65 3498
unto the right hand nor to the l Deut 2:27 8040
every city, we l none to remain Deut 2:34 7604
until none was l to him remaining Deut 3:3 7604
ye shall be l few in number among Deut 4:27 7604
to the right hand or to the l Deut 5:32 8040
among them, until they that are l Deut 7:20 7604
to the right hand, nor to the l Deut 17:11 8040
to the right hand, or to the l Deut 17:20 8040
to the right hand, or to the l Deut 28:14 8040
hath nothing l him in the siege Deut 28:55 7604
ye shall be l few in number, Deut 28:62 7604
and there is none shut up, or l Deut 32:36 5800
it to the right hand or to the l Josh 1:7 8040
l them without the camp of Israel Josh 6:23 3241
was not a man l in Ai or Beth-el Josh 8:17 7604
they l the city open, and pursued Josh 8:17 5800
until he had l him none remaining Josh 10:33 7604
he l none remaining, according to Josh 10:37 7604
he l none remaining Josh 10:39 7604
he l none remaining, but utterly Josh 10:40 7604
until they l them none remaining Josh 11:8 7604
there was not any l to breathe Josh 11:11 3498
neither l they any to breathe Josh 11:14 7604
he l nothing undone of all that Josh 11:15 5493
There was none of the Anakims l Josh 11:22 3498
goeth out to Cabul on the l hand Josh 19:27 8040
Ye have not l your brethren these Josh 22:3 5800
to the right hand or to the l Josh 23:6 8040
which Joshua l when he died Judg 2:21 5800
the LORD l those nations, without Judg 2:23 3241
are the nations which the LORD l Judg 3:1 3241
And Ehud put forth his l hand Judg 3:21 8040
and there was not a man l Judg 4:16 7604
l no sustenance for Israel, Judg 6:4 7604
held the lamps in their l hands Judg 7:20 8040
all that were l of all the hosts Judg 8:10 3498
youngest son of Jerubbaal was l Judg 9:5 3498
hand, and of the other with his l Judg 16:29 8040
and she was l, and her two sons Ruth 1:3 7604
the woman was l of her two sons Ruth 1:5 7604
then she l speaking unto her Ruth 1:18 2308
and how thou hast l thy father Ruth 2:11 5800
did eat, and was sufficed, and l Ruth 2:14 3498
who hath not l off his kindness Ruth 2:20 5800
which hath not l thee this day Ruth 4:14 7673
that every one that is l in thine 1Sa 2:36 3498
the stump of Dagon was l to him 1Sa 5:4 7604
to the right hand or to the l 1Sa 6:12 8040
said, Behold that which is l 1Sa 9:24 7604
thy father hath l the care of the 1Sa 10:2 5203
two of them were not l together 1Sa 11:11 7604
l the sheep with a keeper, and 1Sa 17:20 5203
David l his carriage in the hand 1Sa 17:22 5203
with whom hast thou l those few 1Sa 17:28 5203
surely there had not been l unto 1Sa 25:34 3498
l neither man nor woman alive, and 1Sa 27:9
those that were l behind stayed 1Sa 30:9 3498
and my master l me, because three 1Sa 30:13 5800
nor to the l from following Abner 2Sa 2:19 8040
to thy right hand or to thy l 2Sa 2:21 8040
there they l their images, and 2Sa 5:21 5800
that is l of the house of Saul 2Sa 9:1 3498
and there is not one of them l 2Sa 13:30 3498
shall quench my coal which is l 2Sa 14:7 7604
the l from ought that my lord the 2Sa 14:19 8041
the king l ten women, which were 2Sa 15:16 5800
on his right hand and on his l 2Sa 16:6 8040
which he hath l to keep the house 2Sa 16:21 3240
shall not be l so much as one 2Sa 17:12 3498
whom he had l to keep the house, 2Sa 20:3 3240
and he set up the l pillar 1Kin 7:21 8042
five on the l side of the house 1Kin 7:39 8040
Solomon l all the vessels 1Kin 7:47 3240
the right side, and five on the l 1Kin 7:49 8040
that were l of the Amorites 1Kin 9:20 3498
were l after them in the land 1Kin 9:21 3498
l in Israel, and will take away 1Kin 14:10 5800
the gold that were l in the 1Kin 15:18 3498
that he l off building of Ramah, 1Kin 15:21 2308
he l not to Jeroboam any that 1Kin 15:29 7604
he l him not one that pisseth 1Kin 16:11 7604
that there was no breath l in him 1Kin 17:17 3498
to Judah, and l his servant there 1Kin 19:3 3240
and I, even I only, am l 1Kin 19:10 3498
and I, even I only, am l 1Kin 19:14 3498
Yet I have l me seven thousand in 1Kin 19:18 7604
he l the oxen, and ran after 1Kin 19:20 5800
thousand of the men that were l 1Kin 20:30 3498
that is shut up and l in Israel, 1Kin 21:21 5800
him on his right hand and on his l 1Kin 22:19 8040
only in Kir-haraseth l they the 2Kin 3:25 7604
l thereof, according to the word 2Kin 4:44 3498
l their tents, and their horses, 2Kin 7:7 5800
which are l in the city, (behold, 2Kin 7:13 7604
of Israel that are l in it 2Kin 7:13 7604
since the day that she l the land 2Kin 8:6 5800
that is shut up and l in Israel 2Kin 9:8
until he l him none remaining 2Kin 10:11 7604
neither l he any of them 2Kin 10:14 7604
was not a man l that came not 2Kin 10:21 7604
to the l corner of the temple 2Kin 11:11 8042
was not any shut up, nor any l 2Kin 14:26 5800
they l all the commandments of 2Kin 17:16 5800
there was none l but the tribe of 2Kin 17:18 7604
prayer for the remnant that are l 2Kin 19:4 4672
nothing shall be l, saith the 2Kin 20:17 3498
to the right hand or to the l 2Kin 22:2 8040
which were on a man's l hand at 2Kin 23:8 8040
people that were l in the city 2Kin 25:11 7604
But the captain of the guard l of 2Kin 25:12 7604
king of Babylon had l, even over 2Kin 25:22 7604
of Merari stood on the l hand 1Chr 6:44 8040
which were l of the family of 1Chr 6:61 3498
the l in hurling stones and 1Chr 12:2 8040
that are l in all the land of 1Chr 13:2 7604
when they had l their gods there, 1Chr 14:12 5800
So he l there before the ark of 1Chr 16:37 5800
right hand, and the other on the l 2Chr 3:17 8040
and the name of that on the l Boaz 2Chr 3:17 8042
the right hand, and five on the l 2Chr 4:6 8040
the right hand, and five on the l 2Chr 4:7 8040
the right side, and five on the l 2Chr 4:8 8040
that were l of the Hittites 2Chr 8:7 3498
who were l after them in the land 2Chr 8:8 3498
For the Levites l their suburbs 2Chr 11:14 5800
therefore have I also l you in 2Chr 12:5 5800
that he l off building of Ramah, 2Chr 16:5 2308
on his right hand and on his l 2Chr 18:18 8040
that there was never a son l him 2Chr 21:17 7604
to the l side of the temple 2Chr 23:10 8042
they l the house of the LORD God 2Chr 24:18 5800
(for they l him in great diseases 2Chr 24:25 5800
other ten thousand l alive did 2Chr 25:12
So the armed men l the captives 2Chr 28:14 5800
enough to eat, and have l plenty 2Chr 31:10 3498
that which is l is this great 2Chr 31:10 3498
was done in the land, God l him 2Chr 32:31 5800
to the right hand, nor to the l 2Chr 34:2 8040
and for them that are l in Israel 2Chr 34:21 7604
which were l of the captivity, and Neh 1:2 7604
The remnant that are l of the Neh 1:3 7604
there was no breach l therein Neh 6:1 3498
and on his l hand, Pedaiah, and Neh 8:4 8040
There shall none of his meat be l Job 20:21 8300
him that is l in his tabernacle Job 20:26 8300
On the l hand, where he doth work Job 23:9 8040
they l off speaking Job 32:15 6275
he hath l off to be wise, and to Ps 36:3 2308
there was not one of them l Ps 106:11 3498
in her l hand riches and honour Prov 3:16 8040
to the right hand nor to the l Prov 4:27 8040
but a child l to himself bringeth Prov 29:15 7971
but a fool's heart at his l Eccl 10:2 8040
His l hand is under my head, and Song 2:6 8040
His l hand should be under my Song 8:3 8040
the daughter of Zion is l as a Is 1:8 3498
l unto us a very small remnant Is 1:9 3498
pass, that he that is l in Zion Is 4:3 7604
one eat that is l in the land Is 7:22 3498
and he shall eat on the l hand Is 9:20 8040
as one gathereth eggs that are l Is 10:14 5800
of his people, which shall be l Is 11:11 7604
of his people, which shall be l Is 11:16 7604

L

gleaning grapes shall be *l* in it Is 17:6 7604
which they *l* because of the Is 17:9 5800
They shall be *l* together unto the Is 18:6 5800
earth are burned, and few men *l* Is 24:6 7604
In the city is *l* desolation Is 24:12 7604
forsaken, and *l* like a wilderness Is 27:10 5800
till ye be *l* as a beacon upon the Is 30:17 3498
hand, and when ye turn to the *l* Is 30:21 8041
multitude of the city shall be *l* Is 32:14 5800
prayer for the remnant that is *l* Is 37:4 4672
nothing shall be *l*, saith the Is 39:6 3498
Behold, I was *l* alone Is 49:21 7604
on the right hand and on the *l* Is 54:3 8040
house, I have *l* mine heritage Jer 12:7 5203
such as are *l* in this city from Jer 21:7 7604
are *l* in the house of the LORD Jer 27:18 3498
The people which were *l* of the Jer 31:2 8300
the cities of Judah that were *l* Jer 34:7 3498
all the women that are *l* in the Jer 38:22 7604
So they *l* off speaking with him Jer 38:27 2790
the captain of the guard *l* of the Jer 39:10 7604
people that were *l* in the land Jer 40:6 7604
Babylon had *l* a remnant of Judah Jer 40:11 5414
(for we are *l* but a few of many, Jer 42:2 7604
the captain of the guard had *l* Jer 43:6 3240
But since we *l* off to burn Jer 44:18 2308
How is the city of praise not *l* Jer 49:25 5800
let nothing of her be *l* Jer 50:26 7611
the captain of the guard *l* Jer 52:16 7604
the face of an ox on the *l* side Eze 1:10 8040
Lie thou also upon thy *l* side Eze 4:4 8042
were slaying them, and I was *l* Eze 9:8 7604
therein shall be *l* a remnant that Eze 14:22 3498
that dwell at thy *l* hand Eze 16:46 8040
on the right hand, or on the *l* Eze 21:16 8041
Neither *l* she her whoredoms Eze 23:8 5800
ye have *l* shall fall by the sword Eze 24:21 5800
have cut him off, and have *l* him Eze 31:12 5203
from his shadow, and have *l* him Eze 31:12 5203
Then the heathen that are *l* round Eze 36:36 7604
smite thy bow out of thy *l* hand Eze 39:3 8040
have *l* none of them any more Eze 39:28 3498
that which was *l* was the place of Eze 41:9 3240
were toward the place that was *l* Eze 41:11 3240
was *l* was five cubits round about Eze 41:11 3240
that are *l* in the breadth over Eze 48:15 3498
shall not be *l* to other people Dan 2:44 7662
Therefore I was *l* alone, and saw Dan 10:8 7604
neither is there breath *l* in me Dan 10:17 7604
his *l* hand unto heaven, and sware Dan 12:7 8040
because they have *l* off to take Hos 4:10 5800
that there shall not be a man *l* Hos 9:12
hath *l* hath the locust eaten Joel 1:4 3499
hath *l* hath the cankerworm eaten Joel 1:4 3499
hath *l* hath the caterpiller eaten Joel 1:4 3499
their right hand and their *l* hand Jonah 4:11 8040
Who is *l* among you that saw this Hag 2:3 7604
the other upon the *l* side thereof Zec 4:3 8040
and upon the *l* side thereof Zec 4:11 8040
on the right hand and on the *l* Zec 12:6 8040
but the third shall be *l* therein Zec 13:8 3498
that every one that is *l* of all Zec 14:16 3498
And they straightway *l* their nets Mt 4:20 *863*
And they immediately *l* the ship Mt 4:22 *863*
let not thy *l* hand know what thy Mt 6:3 *710*
her hand, and the fever *l* her Mt 8:15 *863*
that was *l* seven baskets full Mt 15:37 *4052*
And he *l* them, and departed Mt 16:4 *2641*
right hand, and the other on the *l* Mt 20:21 *2176*
sit on my right hand, and on my *l* Mt 20:23 *2176*
he *l* them, and went out of the Mt 21:17 *2641*
and *l* him, and went their way Mt 00:00 *000*
l his wife unto his brother Mt 22:25 *863*
your house is *l* unto you desolate Mt 23:38 *863*
There shall not be *l* here one Mt 24:2 *863*
shall be taken, and the other *l* Mt 24:40 *863*
shall be taken, and the other *l* Mt 24:41 *863*
hand, but the goats on the *l* Mt 25:33 *2176*
say also unto them on the *l* hand Mt 25:41 *2176*
he *l* them, and went away again, and Mt 26:44 *863*
right hand, and another on the *l* Mt 27:38 *2176*
they *l* their father Zebedee in Mk 1:20 *863*
and immediately the fever *l* her Mk 1:31 *863*
meat that was *l* seven baskets Mk 8:8 *4051*
he *l* them, and entering into the Mk 8:13 *863*
say unto him, Lo, we have *l* all Mk 10:28 *863*
There is no man that hath *l* house Mk 10:29 *863*
hand, and the other on thy *l* hand Mk 10:37 *2176*
on my *l* hand is not mine to give Mk 10:40 *2176*
and they *l* him, and went their way Mk 12:12 *863*
took a wife, and dying *l* no seed Mk 12:20 *863*
and died, neither *l* he any seed Mk 12:21 *863*
the seven had her, and *l* no seed Mk 12:22 *863*
there shall not be *l* one stone Mk 13:2 *863*
journey, who *l* his house, and gave Mk 13:34 *863*
he *l* the linen cloth, and fled Mk 14:52 *2641*
right hand, and the other on his *l* Mk 15:27 *2176*
and it *l* her Lk 4:39 *863*
Now when he had *l* speaking Lk 5:4 *3973*
he *l* all, rose up, and followed Lk 5:28 *2641*
sister hath *l* me to serve alone Lk 10:40 *2641*
your house is *l* unto you desolate Lk 13:35 *863*
be taken, and the other shall be *l* Lk 17:34 *863*
shall be taken, and the other *l* Lk 17:35 *863*
shall be taken, and the other *l* Lk 17:36 *863*
Peter said, Lo, we have *l* all Lk 18:28 *863*
There is no man that hath *l* house Lk 18:29 *863*
they *l* no children, and died Lk 20:31 *2641*
not be *l* one stone upon another Lk 21:6 *863*
right hand, and the other on the *l* Lk 23:33 *710*
He *l* Judaea, and departed again Jn 4:3 *863*
The woman then *l* her waterpot Jn 4:28 *863*
the seventh hour the fever *l* him Jn 4:52 *863*
and Jesus was *l* alone, and the Jn 8:9 *2641*
the Father hath not *l* me alone Jn 8:29 *863*
that his soul was not *l* in hell Acts 2:31 *2641*
Nevertheless he *l* not himself Acts 14:17 *863*
came to Ephesus, and *l* them there Acts 18:19 *2641*
we *l* it on the *l* hand, and Acts 21:3 *2641*
Cyprus, we *l* it on the *l* hand Acts 21:3 *2176*
soldiers, they *l* beating of Paul Acts 21:32 *3973*
On the morrow they *l* the horsemen Acts 23:32 *1439*
the Jews a pleasure, *l* Paul bound Acts 24:27 *2641*
a certain man *l* in bonds by Felix Acts 25:14 *2641*
Lord of Sabaoth had *l* us a seed Rom 9:29 *1459*
I am *l* alone, and they seek my Rom 11:3 *5275*
on the right hand and on the *l* 2Cor 6:7 *710*
it good to be *l* at Athens alone 1Th 3:1 *2641*
The cloke that I *l* at Troas with 2Ti 4:13 *620*
have I *l* at Miletum sick 2Ti 4:20 *620*
For this cause *l* I thee in Crete, Titus 1:5 *2641*
he *l* nothing that is not put Heb 2:8 *863*
a promise being *l* us of entering Heb 4:1 *2641*
but *l* their own habitation, he Jude 6 *620*
thou hast *l* thy first love Rev 2:4 *863*
sea, and his *l* foot on the earth, Rev 10:2 *2176*

LEFTEST
therefore *l* thou them in the hand Neh 9:28 5800

LEFTHANDED
son of Gera, a Benjamite, a man *l* Judg 3:15
were seven hundred chosen men *l* Judg 20:16

LEG
thy locks, make bare the *l* Is 47:2 7640

LEGION
he answered, saying, My name is *L* Mk 5:9 *3003*
with the devil, and had the *l* Mk 5:15 *3003*
And he said, *L* Lk 8:30 *3003*

LEGIONS
me more than twelve *l* of angels Mt 26:53 *3003*

LEGS
his head with his *l*, and with the Ex 12:9 3767
wash the inwards of him, and his *l* Ex 29:17 3767
his *l* shall he wash in water Lev 1:9 3767
the inwards and the *l* with water Lev 1:13 3767
with his head, and with his *l* Lev 4:11 3767
the inwards and the *l* in water Lev 8:21 3767
he did wash the inwards and the *l* Lev 9:14 3767
which have *l* above their feet, to Lev 11:21 3767
thee in the knees, and in the *l* Deut 28:35 7785
had greaves of brass upon his *l* 1Sa 17:6 7272
not pleasure in the *l* of a man Ps 147:10 7785
The *l* of the lame are not equal Prov 26:7 7785
His *l* are as pillars of marble, Song 5:15 7785
and the ornaments of the *l* Is 3:20 6807
His *l* of iron, his feet part of Dan 2:33 8243
of the mouth of the lion two *l* Amos 3:12 3767
that their *l* might be broken Jn 19:31 *4628*
brake the *l* of the first, and of Jn 19:32 *4628*
already, they brake not his *l* Jn 19:33 *4628*

LEHAB See LEHABIM.

LEHABIM (*le'-ha-bim*) *A son of Mizraim.*
begat Ludim, and Anamim, and *L* Gen 10:13 3853
begat Ludim, and Anamim, and *L* 1Chr 1:11 3853

LEHABITES See LEHABIM.

LEHI (*le'-hi*) See RAMATH-LEHI. *A district near Jerusalem.*
Judah, and spread themselves in *L* Judg 15:9 3896
And when he came unto *L*, the Judg 15:14 3896
which is in *L* unto this day Judg 15:19 3896

LEISURE
they had no *l* so much as to eat Mk 6:31 *2119*

LEMUEL (*lem'-u-el*) *A king mentioned in Proverbs.*
The words of king *L*, the prophecy Prov 31:1 3927
It is not for kings, O *L*, it is Prov 31:4 3927

LEND
If thou *l* money to any of my Ex 22:25 3867
nor *l* him thy victuals for Lev 25:37 5414
thou shalt *l* unto many nations, Deut 15:6 5670
shalt surely *l* him sufficient for Deut 15:8 5670
Thou shalt not *l* upon usury to Deut 23:19 5391
stranger thou mayest *l* upon usury Deut 23:20 5391
thou shalt not *l* upon usury Deut 23:20 5391
When thou dost *l* thy brother any Deut 24:10 5383
the man to whom thou dost *l* shall Deut 24:11 5383
thou shalt *l* unto many nations, Deut 28:12 3867
He shall *l* to thee, and thou shalt Deut 28:44 3867
and thou shalt not *l* to him Deut 28:44 3867
if ye *l* to them of whom ye hope Lk 6:34 *1155*
for sinners also *l* to sinners Lk 6:34 *1155*
ye your enemies, and do good, and *l* Lk 6:35 *1155*
him, Friend, *l* me three loaves Lk 11:5 *5531*

LENDER
the borrower is servant to the *l* Prov 22:7 3867
as with the *l*, so with the Is 24:2 3867

LENDETH
Every creditor that *l* ought unto Deut 15:2 5383
He is ever merciful, and *l* Ps 37:26 3867
A good man sheweth favour, and *l* Ps 112:5 3867
upon the poor *l* unto the LORD Prov 19:17 3867

LENGTH
The *l* of the ark shall be three Gen 6:15 753
through the land in the *l* of it Gen 13:17 753
and a half shall be the *l* thereof Ex 25:10 753
and a half shall be the *l* thereof Ex 25:17 753
two cubits shall be the *l* thereof Ex 25:23 753
The *l* of one curtain shall be Ex 26:2 753
The *l* of one curtain shall be Ex 26:8 753
the *l* of the curtains of the tent Ex 26:13 753
cubits shall be the *l* of a board Ex 26:16 753
l there shall be hangings of an Ex 27:11 753
The *l* of the court shall be an Ex 27:18 753
a span shall be the *l* thereof Ex 28:16 753
A cubit shall be the *l* thereof Ex 30:2 753
The *l* of one curtain was twenty Ex 36:9 753
The *l* of one curtain was thirty Ex 36:15 753
The *l* of a board was ten cubits, Ex 36:21 753
cubits and a half was the *l* of it Ex 37:1 753
and a half was the *l* thereof Ex 37:6 753
two cubits was the *l* thereof Ex 37:10 753
the *l* of it was a cubit, and the Ex 37:25 753
five cubits was the *l* thereof Ex 38:1 753
and twenty cubits was the *l* Ex 38:18 753
a span was the *l* thereof, and a Ex 39:9 753
nine cubits was the *l* thereof Deut 3:11 753
is thy life, and the *l* of thy days Deut 30:20 753
which had two edges, of a cubit *l* Judg 3:16 753
the *l* thereof was threescore 1Kin 6:2 753
twenty cubits was the *l* thereof 1Kin 6:3 753
forepart was twenty cubits in *l* 1Kin 6:20 753
the *l* thereof was an hundred 1Kin 7:2 753
the *l* thereof was fifty cubits, 1Kin 7:6 753
four cubits was the *l* of one base 1Kin 7:27 753
The *l* by cubits after the first 2Chr 3:3 753
the *l* of it was according to the 2Chr 3:4 753
the *l* whereof was according to 2Chr 3:8 753
twenty cubits the *l* thereof 2Chr 4:1 753
in *l* of days understanding Job 12:12 753
even *l* of days for ever and ever Ps 21:4 753
For *l* of days, and long life, and Prov 3:2 753
L of days is in her right hand Prov 3:16 753
have him become his son at the *l* Prov 29:21 319
in the *l* of his branches Eze 31:7 753
the *l* of the gate, thirteen Eze 40:11 753
the *l* of the gates was the lower Eze 40:18 753
north, he measured the *l* thereof Eze 40:20 753
the *l* thereof was fifty cubits, Eze 40:21 753
the *l* was fifty cubits, and the Eze 40:25 753
the *l* was fifty cubits, and the Eze 40:36 753
The *l* of the porch was twenty Eze 40:49 753
and he measured the *l* thereof Eze 41:2 753
So he measured the *l* thereof Eze 41:4 753
the *l* thereof ninety cubits Eze 41:12 753
he measured the *l* of the building Eze 41:15 753
high, and the *l* thereof two cubits Eze 41:22 753
the *l* thereof, and the walls Eze 41:22 753
Before the *l* of an hundred cubits Eze 42:2 753
the *l* thereof was fifty cubits Eze 42:7 753
For the *l* of the chambers that Eze 42:8 753
the *l* shall be the *l* of five Eze 45:1 753
the sanctuary five hundred in *l* Eze 45:2 753
shalt thou measure the *l* of five Eze 45:3 753
the five and twenty thousand of *l* Eze 45:5 753
the *l* shall be over against one Eze 45:7 753
in *l* as one of the other parts, Eze 48:8 753
of five and twenty thousand in *l* Eze 48:9 753
five and twenty thousand in *l* Eze 48:10 753
five and twenty thousand in *l* Eze 48:10 753
have five and twenty thousand in *l* Eze 48:13 753
all the *l* shall be five and twenty Eze 48:13 753
the residue in *l* over against the Eze 48:18 753
thereof, and what is the *l* thereof Zec 2:2 753
the *l* thereof is twenty cubits, Zec 5:2 753
if by any means now at *l* I might Rom 1:10 *4218*
saints what is the breadth, and *l* Eph 3:18 *3372*
the *l* is as large as the breadth Rev 21:16 *3372*
The *l* and the breadth and the Rev 21:16 *3372*

LENGTHEN
did walk, then I will *l* thy days 1Kin 3:14 748
l thy cords, and strengthen thy Is 54:2 748

LENGTHENED
that thy days may be *l* in the Deut 25:15 748

LENGTHENING
if it may be a *l* of thy Dan 4:27 754

LENT
so that they *l* unto them such Ex 12:36 7592
of any thing that is *l* upon usury Deut 23:19 5391
also I have *l* him to the LORD 1Sa 1:28 7592
liveth he shall be *l* to the LORD 1Sa 1:28 7592
the loan which is *l* to the LORD 1Sa 2:20 7592
I have neither *l* on usury Jer 15:10 5383
nor men have *l* to me on usury Jer 15:10 5383

LENTILES
gave Esau bread and pottage of *l* Gen 25:34 5742
and parched corn, and beans, and *l* 2Sa 17:28 5742
was a piece of ground full of *l* 2Sa 23:11 5742
wheat, and barley, and beans, and *l* Eze 4:9 5742

LEOPARD
the *l* shall lie down with the kid Is 11:6 5246
a *l* shall watch over their cities Jer 5:6 5246
his skin, or the *l* his spots Jer 13:23 5246
I beheld, and lo another, like a *l* Dan 7:6 5245
as a *l* by the way will I observe Hos 13:7 5246
which I saw was like unto a *l* Rev 13:2 *3917*

LEOPARDS
dens, from the mountains of the *l* Song 4:8 5246
also are swifter than the *l* Hab 1:8 5246

LEPER
the *l* in whom the plague is, his Lev 13:45 6879
the *l* in the day of his cleansing Lev 14:2 6879
of leprosy be healed in the *l* Lev 14:3 6879
of the seed of Aaron is a *l* Lev 22:4 6879
they put out of the camp every *l* Num 5:2 6879
hath an issue, or that is a *l* 2Sa 3:29 6879
man in valour, but he was a *l* 2Kin 5:1 6879
over the place, and recover the *l* 2Kin 5:11 6879
his presence a *l* as white as snow 2Kin 5:27 6879
so that he was a *l* unto the day 2Kin 15:5 6879
Uzziah the king was a *l* unto the 2Chr 26:21 6879
in a several house, being a *l* 2Chr 26:21 6879

for they said, He is a *l* 2Chr 26:23 6879
And, behold, there came a *l* Mt 8:2 *3015*
in the house of Simon the *l* Mt 26:6 *3015*
And there came a *l* to him, Mk 1:40 *3015*
in the house of Simon the *l* Mk 14:3 *3015*

LEPERS
And when these *l* came to the 2Kin 7:8 6879
Heal the sick, cleanse the *l* Mt 10:8 *3015*
the *l* are cleansed, and the deaf Mt 11:5 *3015*
many *l* were in Israel in the time Lk 4:27 *3015*
the *l* are cleansed, the deaf hear Lk 7:22 *3015*
there met him ten men that were *l* Lk 17:12 *3015*

LEPROSY
of his flesh like the plague of *l* Lev 13:2 6883
of his flesh, it is a plague of *l* Lev 13:3 6883
it is a *l* Lev 13:8 6883
When the plague of *l* is in a man Lev 13:9 6883
It is an old *l* in the skin of his Lev 13:11 6883
if a *l* break out abroad in the Lev 13:12 6883
the *l* cover all the skin of him Lev 13:12 6883
if the *l* have covered all his Lev 13:13 6883
it is a *l* Lev 13:15 6883
it is a plague of *l* broken out of Lev 13:20 6883
it is a *l* broken out of the Lev 13:25 6883
it is the plague of *l* Lev 13:25 6883
it is the plague of *l* Lev 13:27 6883
even a *l* upon the head or beard Lev 13:30 6883
it is a *l* sprung up in his bald Lev 13:42 6883
as the *l* appeareth in the skin of Lev 13:43 6883
also that the plague of *l* is in Lev 13:47 6883
it is a plague of *l*, and shall be Lev 13:49 6883
the plague is a fretting *l* Lev 13:51 6883
for it is a fretting *l* Lev 13:52 6883
of *l* in a garment of woollen or Lev 13:59 6883
if the plague of *l* be healed in Lev 14:3 6883
cleansed from the *l* seven times Lev 14:7 6883
of him in whom is the plague of *l* Lev 14:32 6883
I put the plague of *l* in a house Lev 14:34 6883
it is a fretting *l* in the house Lev 14:44 6883
law for all manner of plague of *l* Lev 14:54 6883
for the *l* of a garment, and of a Lev 14:55 6883
this is the law of *l* Lev 14:57 6883
Take heed in the plague of *l* Deut 24:8 6883
for he would recover him of his *l* 2Kin 5:3 6883
thou mayest recover him of his *l* 2Kin 5:6 6883
unto me to recover a man of his *l* 2Kin 5:7 6883
The *l* therefore of Naaman shall 2Kin 5:27 6883
the *l* even rose up in his 2Chr 26:19 6883
And immediately his *l* was cleansed Mt 8:3 *3014*
immediately the *l* departed from Mk 1:42 *3014*
city, behold a man full of *l* Lk 5:12 *3014*
immediately the *l* departed from Lk 5:13 *3014*

LEPROUS
behold, his hand was *l* as snow Ex 4:6 6879
He is a *l* man, he is unclean Lev 13:44 6879
and, behold, Miriam became *l* Num 12:10 6879
Miriam, and, behold, she was *l* Num 12:10 6879
there were four *l* men at the 2Kin 7:3 6879
he was *l* in his forehead, and they 2Chr 26:20 6879

LESHEM *(le'-shem)* See LAISH. *Same as Laish.*
of Dan went up to fight against *L* Josh 19:47 3959
it, and dwelt therein, and called *L* Josh 19:47 3959

LESS
and gathered, some more, some *l* Ex 16:17 4591
not give *l* than half a shekel Ex 30:15 4591
the LORD my God, to do *l* or more Num 22:18 6996
thou shalt give the *l* inheritance Num 26:54 4591
ye shall give the *l* inheritance Num 33:54 4591
nothing of all this, *l* or more 1Sa 22:15 6996
l or more, until the morning 1Sa 25:36 6996
how much *l* this house that I have 1Kin 8:27
how much *l* this house which I 2Chr 6:18
how much *l* shall your God deliver 2Chr 32:15
us *l* than our iniquities deserve Ezr 9:13 4295
How much *l* in them that dwell in Job 4:19
How much *l* shall I answer him, and Job 9:14
that God exacteth of thee *l* than Job 11:6
How much *l* man, that is a worm Job 25:6
How much *l* to him that accepteth Job 34:19
much *l* do lying lips a prince Prov 17:7
much *l* for a servant to have rule Prov 19:10
are counted to him *l* than nothing Is 40:17 657
how much *l* shall it be meet yet Eze 15:5
is *l* than all the seeds that be Mk 4:31 *3398*
and Mary the mother of James the *l* Mk 15:40 *3398*
which we think to be *l* honourable 1Cor 12:23 *820*
I love you, the *l* I be loved 2Cor 12:15 *2276*
who am *l* than the least of all Eph 3:8 *1647*
and that I may be the *l* sorrowful Phil 2:28 *253*
the *l* is blessed of the better Heb 7:7 *1640*

LESSER
the *l* light to rule the night Gen 1:16 6996
and for the treading of *l* cattle Is 7:25 7716
from the *l* settle even to the Eze 43:14 6996

LEST
shall ye touch it, *l* ye die Gen 3:3 6435
l he put forth his hand, and take Gen 3:22 6435
l any finding him should kill him Gen 4:15 1115
l we be scattered abroad upon the Gen 11:4 6435
l thou shouldest say, I have made Gen 14:23 3808
l thou be consumed in the Gen 19:15 6435
the mountain, *l* thou be consumed Gen 19:17 6435
l some evil take me, and I die Gen 19:19 6435
l, said he, the men of the place Gen 26:7 6435
Because I said, *L* I die for her Gen 26:9 6435
l he will come and smite me, and Gen 32:11 6435
l that he should give seed to his Gen 38:9 1115
L peradventure he die also, as Gen 38:11 6435
take it to her, *l* we be shamed Gen 38:23 6435
L peradventure mischief befall Gen 42:4 6435
l peradventure I see the evil Gen 44:34 6435
l thou, and thy household, and all Gen 45:11 6435
l they multiply, and it come to Ex 1:10 6435
l he fall upon us with pestilence Ex 5:3 6435
L peradventure the people repent Ex 13:17 6435
l they break through unto the Ex 19:21 6435
l the LORD break forth upon them Ex 19:22 6435
l he break forth upon them Ex 19:24 6435
not God speak with us, *l* we die Ex 20:19 6435
l the land become desolate, and Ex 23:29 6435
l they make thee sin against me Ex 23:33 6435
l I consume thee in the way Ex 33:3 6435
l thou make a covenant with the Ex 34:12 6435
l it be for a snare in the midst Ex 34:12 6435
L thou make a covenant with the Ex 34:15 6435
l ye die, and *l* wrath come upon Lev 10:6 3808
l wrath come upon all the people Lev 10:6
of the congregation, *l* ye die Lev 10:7 6435
of the congregation, *l* ye die Lev 10:9 3808
l the land fall to whoredom, and Lev 19:29 3808
l they bear sin for it, and die Lev 22:9 3808
touch any holy thing, *l* they die Num 4:15
things are covered, *l* they die Num 4:20
l ye be consumed in all their Num 16:26 6435
L the earth swallow us up also Num 16:34 6435
l they bear sin, and die Num 18:22
the children of Israel, *l* ye die Num 18:32 3808
l I come out against thee with Num 20:18 6435
l ye be smitten before your Deut 1:42 3808
l thou forget the things which Deut 4:9 6435
l they depart from thy heart all Deut 4:9 6435
L ye corrupt yourselves, and make Deut 4:16 6435
l thou lift up thine eyes unto Deut 4:19 6435
l ye forget the covenant of the Deut 4:23 6435
Then beware *l* thou forget the Deut 6:12 6435
l the anger of the LORD thy God Deut 6:15 6435
l the beasts of the field Deut 7:22 6435
thee, *l* thou be snared therein Deut 7:25 6435
l thou be a cursed thing like it Deut 7:26
L when thou hast eaten and art Deut 8:12 6435
L the land whence thou broughtest Deut 9:28 6435
l ye perish quickly from off the Deut 11:17
L the avenger of the blood pursue Deut 19:6 6435
l he die in the battle, and Deut 20:5 6435
l he die in the battle, and Deut 20:6 6435
l he die in the battle, and Deut 20:7 6435
l his brethren's heart faint as Deut 20:8 6435
l the fruit of thy seed which Deut 22:9 6435
l he cry against thee unto the Deut 24:15 3808
l, if he should exceed, and beat Deut 25:3 6435
L there should be among you man, Deut 29:18 6435
l there should be among you a Deut 29:18 6435
l their adversaries should behave Deut 32:27 6435
l they should say, Our hand is Deut 32:27 6435
mountain, *l* the pursuers meet you Josh 2:16 6435
l ye make yourselves accursed Josh 6:18 6435
l wrath be upon us, because of Josh 9:20 3808
unto you, *l* ye deny your God Josh 24:27 6435
l Israel vaunt themselves against Judg 7:2 6435
l we burn thee and thy father's Judg 14:15 6435
l angry fellows run upon thee, and Judg 18:25 6435
l I mar mine own inheritance Ruth 4:6 6435
l my father leave caring for the 1Sa 9:5 6435
L the Hebrews make them swords or 1Sa 13:19 6435
l I destroy you with them 1Sa 15:6 6435
know this, *l* he be grieved 1Sa 20:3 6435
L they should tell on us, saying, 1Sa 27:11 6435
battle, *l* in the battle he be an 1Sa 29:4 3808
l these uncircumcised come and 1Sa 31:4 6435
l the daughters of the 2Sa 1:20 6435
rejoice, *l* the daughters of the 2Sa 1:20 6435
l I take the city, and it be 2Sa 12:28 6435
l we be chargeable unto thee 2Sa 13:25 3808
any more, *l* they destroy my son 2Sa 14:11
l he overtake us suddenly, and 2Sa 15:14 6435
l the king be swallowed up, and 2Sa 17:16 6435
l he get him fenced cities, and 2Sa 20:6 6435
l peradventure the Spirit of the 2Kin 2:16 6435
l these uncircumcised come and 1Chr 10:4 6435
L ye should say, We have found Job 32:13 6435
not, *l* the people be ensnared Job 34:30
beware *l* he take thee away with Job 36:18 6435
l I deal with you after your Job 42:8 1115
l he be angry, and ye perish from Ps 2:12 6435
L he tear my soul like a lion, Ps 7:2 6435
l I sleep the sleep of death Ps 13:3 6435
L mine enemy say, I have Ps 13:4 6435
l, if thou be silent to me, I Ps 28:1 6435
l they come near unto thee Ps 32:9 1077
l otherwise they should rejoice Ps 38:16 6435
l I tear you in pieces, and there Ps 50:22 6435
Slay them not, *l* my people forget Ps 59:11 6435
l thou dash thy foot against a Ps 91:12 6435
wrath, *l* he should destroy them Ps 106:23
l the righteous put forth their Ps 125:3
l they exalt themselves Ps 140:8
l I be like unto them that go Ps 143:7
L thou shouldest ponder the path Prov 5:6 6435
L thou give thine honour unto Prov 5:9 6435
L strangers be filled with thy Prov 5:10 6435
not a scorner, *l* he hate thee Prov 9:8 6435
not sleep, *l* thou come to poverty Prov 20:13 6435
L thou learn his ways, and get a Prov 22:25 6435
L the LORD see it, and it Prov 24:18 6435
l thou know not what to do in the Prov 25:8 6435
L he that heareth it put thee to Prov 25:10 6435
l thou be filled therewith, and Prov 25:16 6435
l he be weary of thee, and so hate Prov 25:17 6435
l thou also be like unto him Prov 26:4 6435
l he be wise in his own conceit Prov 26:5 6435
l he reprove thee, and thou be Prov 30:6 6435
L I be full, and deny thee, and say Prov 30:9 6435
or *l* I be poor, and steal, and take Prov 30:9 6435
l he curse thee, and thou be found Prov 30:10 6435
L they drink, and forget the law, Prov 31:5 6435
l thou hear thy servant curse Eccl 7:21
l they see with their eyes, and Is 6:10 6435
l any hurt it, I will keep it Is 27:3 6435
l your bands be made strong Is 28:22 6435
Beware *l* Hezekiah persuade you, Is 36:18 6435
l thou shouldest say, Mine idol Is 48:5 6435
l thou shouldest say, Behold, I Is 48:7 6435
l I confound thee before them Jer 1:17 6435
l my fury come forth like fire, Jer 4:4 6435
l my soul depart from thee Jer 6:8 6435
l I make thee desolate, a land Jer 6:8 6435
l thou bring me to nothing Jer 10:24 6435
l my fury go out like fire, and Jer 21:12 6435
the scribe, *l* I die there Jer 37:20 3808
l they deliver me into their hand Jer 38:19 6435
l your heart faint, and ye fear Jer 51:46 6435
L I strip her naked, and set her Hos 2:3 6435
l he break out like fire in the Amos 5:6 6435
l they should hear the law, and Zec 7:12
l I come and smite the earth with Mal 4:6 6435
l at any time thou dash thy foot Mt 4:6 *3379*
l at any time the adversary Mt 5:25 *3379*
l they trample them under their Mt 7:6 *3379*
l at any time they should see Mt 13:15 *3379*
l while ye gather up the tares, Mt 13:29 *3379*
fasting, *l* they faint in the way Mt 15:32 *3379*
l we should offend them, go thou Mt 17:27
l there be not enough for us and Mt 25:9 *3379*
l there be an uproar among the Mt 26:5
l his disciples come by night, and Mt 27:64 *3379*
l they should throng him Mk 3:9
l at any time they should be Mk 4:12 *3379*
Take heed *l* any man deceive you Mk 13:5 *3361*
L coming suddenly he find you Mk 13:36 *3361*
l there be an uproar of the Mk 14:2 *3379*
l ye enter into temptation Mk 14:38
l at any time thou dash thy foot Lk 4:11 *3379*
l they should believe and be saved Lk 8:12
l he hale thee to the judge, and Lk 12:58 *3379*
l a more honourable man than thou Lk 14:8 *3379*
l they also bid thee again, and a Lk 14:12 *3379*
L haply, after he hath laid the Lk 14:29
l they also come into this place Lk 16:28
l by her continual coming she Lk 18:5
l at any time your hearts be Lk 21:34 *3379*
l ye enter into temptation Lk 22:46
l his deeds should be reproved Jn 3:20
l a worse thing come unto thee Jn 5:14
light, *l* darkness come upon you Jn 12:35
l they should be put out of the Jn 12:42
hall, *l* they should be defiled Jn 18:28
l they should have been stoned Acts 5:26
l haply ye be found even to fight Acts 5:39 *3379*
l that come upon you, which is Acts 13:40 *3361*
fearing *l* Paul should have been Acts 23:10 *3361*
fearing *l* they should fall into Acts 27:17 *3361*
Then fearing *l* we should have Acts 27:29 *3381*
l any of them should swim out, and Acts 27:42 *3361*
l they should see with their eyes Acts 28:27 *3379*
take heed *l* he also spare not Rom 11:21 *3381*
l ye should be wise in your own Rom 11:25
l I should build upon another Rom 15:20
L any should say that I had 1Cor 1:15
l the cross of Christ should be 1Cor 1:17
But take heed *l* by any means this 1Cor 8:9 *3381*
l I make my brother to offend 1Cor 8:13
l we should hinder the gospel of 1Cor 9:12
l that by any means, when I have 1Cor 9:27 *3381*
he standeth take heed *l* he fall 1Cor 10:12 *3361*
And I wrote this same unto you, *l* 2Cor 2:3
l perhaps such a one should be 2Cor 2:7 *3381*
L Satan should get an advantage 2Cor 2:11
l the light of the glorious 2Cor 4:4
l our boasting of you should be 2Cor 9:3
L haply if they of Macedonia come 2Cor 9:4 *3381*
l by any means, as the serpent 2Cor 11:3 *3381*
l any man should think of me 2Cor 12:6 *3361*
l I should be exalted above 2Cor 12:7
l I should be exalted above 2Cor 12:7
For I fear, *l*, when I come, I 2Cor 12:20 *3381*
l there be debates, envyings, 2Cor 12:20 *3381*
And *l*, when I come again, my God 2Cor 12:21 *3361*
l being present I should use 2Cor 13:10
l by any means I should run, or Gal 2:2 *3381*
l I have bestowed upon you labour Gal 4:11 *3381*
thyself, *l* thou also be tempted Gal 6:1 *3361*
only *l* they should suffer Gal 6:12
of works, *l* any man should boast Eph 2:9
l I should have sorrow upon Phil 2:27
l any man should beguile you with Col 2:4
Beware *l* any man spoil you Col 2:8 *3361*
to anger, *l* they be discouraged Col 3:21
l by some means the tempter have 1Th 3:5 *3381*
l being lifted up with pride he 1Ti 3:6
l he fall into reproach and the 1Ti 3:7
l at any time we should let them Heb 2:1 *3379*
l there be in any of you an evil Heb 3:12 *3379*
l any of you be hardened through Heb 3:13
Let us therefore fear, *l*, a Heb 4:1 *3379*
l any man fall after the same Heb 4:11
l he that destroyed the firstborn Heb 11:28
l ye be wearied and faint in your Heb 12:3
l that which is lame be turned Heb 12:13
Looking diligently *l* any man fail Heb 12:15 *3361*
l any root of bitterness Heb 12:15 *3361*
L there be any fornicator, or Heb 12:16
brethren, *l* ye be condemned Jas 5:9
l ye fall into condemnation Jas 5:12
beware *l* ye also, being led away 2Pet 3:17
l he walk naked, and they see his Rev 16:15

LET

And God said, *L* there be light	Gen 1:3	
L there be a firmament in the	Gen 1:6	
l it divide the waters from the	Gen 1:6	
L the waters under the heaven be	Gen 1:9	
place, and *l* the dry land appear	Gen 1:9	
L the earth bring forth grass,	Gen 1:11	
said, *L* there be lights in the	Gen 1:14	
l them be for signs, and for	Gen 1:14	
l them be for lights in the	Gen 1:15	
said, *L* the waters bring forth	Gen 1:20	
l fowl multiply in the earth	Gen 1:22	
L the earth bring forth the	Gen 1:24	
L us make man in our image, after	Gen 1:26	
l them have dominion over the	Gen 1:26	
l us make brick, and burn them	Gen 11:3	
l us build us a city and a tower,	Gen 11:4	
l us make us a name, lest we be	Gen 11:4	
l us go down, and there confound	Gen 11:7	
L there be no strife, I pray thee	Gen 13:8	
l them take their portion	Gen 14:24	
L a little water, I pray you, be	Gen 18:4	
Oh *l* not the LORD be angry, and I	Gen 18:30	
Oh *l* not the Lord be angry, and I	Gen 18:32	
l me, I pray you, bring them out	Gen 19:8	
l me escape thither, (is it not a	Gen 19:20	
l us make our father drink wine,	Gen 19:32	
l us make him drink wine this	Gen 19:34	
L it not be grievous in thy sight	Gen 21:12	
L me not see the death of the	Gen 21:16	
l it come to pass, that the	Gen 24:14	
L down thy pitcher, I pray thee,	Gen 24:14	5186
l the same be she that thou hast	Gen 24:14	
L me, I pray thee, drink a little	Gen 24:17	
l down her pitcher upon her hand,	Gen 24:18	3381
l the same be the woman whom the	Gen 24:44	
unto her, *L* me drink, I pray thee	Gen 24:45	
l down her pitcher from her	Gen 24:46	3381
l her be thy master's son's wife,	Gen 24:51	
L the damsel abide with us a few	Gen 24:55	
l thy seed possess the gate of	Gen 24:60	
L there be now an oath betwixt us	Gen 26:28	
l us make a covenant with thee	Gen 26:28	
L people serve thee, and nations	Gen 27:29	
l thy mother's sons bow down to	Gen 27:29	
L my father arise, and eat of his	Gen 27:31	
I have served thee, and *l* me go	Gen 30:26	
findest thy gods, *l* him not live	Gen 31:32	
L it not displease my lord that I	Gen 31:35	
l us make a covenant, I and thou	Gen 31:44	
l it be for a witness between me	Gen 31:44	
L me go, for the day breaketh	Gen 32:26	
And he said, I will not *l* thee go	Gen 32:26	
L us take our journey, and *l* us	Gen 33:12	
L my lord, I pray thee, pass over	Gen 33:14	
l me now leave with thee some of	Gen 33:15	
l me find grace in the sight of	Gen 33:15	
L me find grace in your eyes, and	Gen 34:11	
therefore *l* them dwell in the	Gen 34:21	
l us take their daughters to us	Gen 34:21	
l us give them our daughters	Gen 34:21	
only *l* us consent unto them, and	Gen 34:23	
l us arise, and go up to Beth-el	Gen 35:3	
heard them say, *L* us go to Dothan	Gen 37:17	
l us slay him, and cast him into	Gen 37:20	
and said, *L* us not kill him	Gen 37:21	
l us sell him to the Ishmeelites,	Gen 37:27	
l not our hand be upon him	Gen 37:27	
pray thee, *l* me come in unto thee	Gen 38:16	
L her take it to her, lest we be	Gen 38:23	
her forth, and *l* her be burnt	Gen 38:24	
Now therefore *l* Pharaoh look out	Gen 41:33	
L Pharaoh do this, and *l* him	Gen 41:34	
l them gather all the food of	Gen 41:35	
l them keep food in the cities	Gen 41:35	
l him fetch your brother, and ye	Gen 42:16	
l one of your brethren be bound	Gen 42:19	
then *l* me bear the blame for ever	Gen 43:9	
both *l* him die, and we also will	Gen 44:9	
Now also *l* it be according unto	Gen 44:10	
l thy servant, I pray thee, speak	Gen 44:18	
l not thine anger burn against	Gen 44:18	
l thy servant abide instead of	Gen 44:33	
l the lad go up with his brethren	Gen 44:33	
Now *l* me die, since I have seen	Gen 46:30	
l thy servants dwell in the land	Gen 47:4	
the land of Goshen *l* them dwell	Gen 47:6	
l us find grace in the sight of	Gen 47:25	
l my name be named on them, and	Gen 48:16	
l them grow into a multitude in	Gen 48:16	
Naphtali is a hind *l* loose	Gen 49:21	
Now therefore *l* me go up, I pray	Gen 50:5	
l us deal wisely with them	Ex 1:10	
now *l* us go, we beseech thee,	Ex 3:18	
king of Egypt will not *l* you go	Ex 3:19	5414
and after that he will *l* you go	Ex 3:20	
L me go, I pray thee, and return	Ex 4:18	
that he shall not *l* the people go	Ex 4:21	
L my son go, that he may serve me	Ex 4:23	
and if thou refuse to *l* him go	Ex 4:23	
So he *l* him go	Ex 4:26	
L my people go, that they may	Ex 5:1	
obey his voice to *l* Israel go	Ex 5:2	
LORD, neither will I *l* Israel go	Ex 5:2	
l us go, we pray thee, three	Ex 5:3	
l the people from their works	Ex 5:4	6544
l them go and gather straw for	Ex 5:7	
L us go and sacrifice to our God	Ex 5:8	
L there more work be laid upon	Ex 5:9	
l them not regard vain words	Ex 5:9	
L us go and do sacrifice to the	Ex 5:17	
a strong hand shall he *l* them go	Ex 6:1	
that he *l* the children of Israel	Ex 6:11	
he refuseth to *l* the people go	Ex 7:14	
L my people go, that they may	Ex 7:16	
L my people go, that they may	Ex 8:1	
And if thou refuse to *l* them go	Ex 8:2	
I will *l* the people go, that they	Ex 8:8	
L my people go, that they may	Ex 8:20	
if thou wilt not *l* my people go	Ex 8:21	
And Pharaoh said, I will *l* you go	Ex 8:28	
but *l* not Pharaoh deal	Ex 8:29	
neither would he *l* the people go	Ex 8:32	
L my people go, that they may	Ex 9:1	
For if thou refuse to *l* them go	Ex 9:2	
he did not *l* the people go	Ex 9:7	
l Moses sprinkle it toward the	Ex 9:8	
L my people go, that they may	Ex 9:13	
that thou wilt not *l* them go	Ex 9:17	
and I will *l* you go, and ye shall	Ex 9:28	
neither would he *l* the children	Ex 9:35	
l my people go, that they may	Ex 10:3	
if thou refuse to *l* my people go	Ex 10:4	
l the men go, that they may serve	Ex 10:7	
L the LORD be so with you, as I	Ex 10:10	
so with you, as I will *l* you go	Ex 10:10	
so that he would not *l* the	Ex 10:20	
only *l* your flocks and your herds	Ex 10:24	
l your little ones also go with	Ex 10:24	
heart, and he would not *l* them go	Ex 10:27	
afterwards he will *l* you go hence	Ex 11:1	
when he shall *l* you go, he shall	Ex 11:1	
l every man borrow of his	Ex 11:2	
so that he would not *l* the	Ex 11:10	
l him and his neighbour next unto	Ex 12:4	
ye shall *l* nothing of it remain	Ex 12:10	
l all his males be circumcised,	Ex 12:48	
then *l* him come near and keep it	Ex 12:48	
when Pharaoh would hardly *l* us go	Ex 13:15	
when Pharaoh had *l* the people go	Ex 13:17	
that we have *l* Israel go from	Ex 14:5	
L us alone, that we may serve the	Ex 14:12	
L us flee from the face of Israel	Ex 14:25	
L no man leave of it till the	Ex 16:19	
l no man go out of his place on	Ex 16:29	
when he *l* down his hand, Amalek	Ex 17:11	5117
l them judge the people at all	Ex 18:22	
Moses *l* his father in law depart	Ex 18:27	
l them wash their clothes,	Ex 19:10	
l the priests also, which come	Ex 19:22	
but *l* not the priests and the	Ex 19:24	
but *l* not God speak with us, lest	Ex 20:19	
then shall he *l* her be redeemed	Ex 21:8	
he shall *l* him go free for his	Ex 21:26	
he shall *l* him go free for his	Ex 21:27	
thief be found, *l* him pay double	Ex 22:7	
then *l* him bring it for witness,	Ex 22:13	
seventh year thou shalt *l* it rest	Ex 23:11	
neither *l* it be heard out of thy	Ex 23:13	
to do, *l* him come unto them	Ex 24:14	
l them make me a sanctuary	Ex 25:8	
Now therefore *l* me alone, that my	Ex 32:10	
L not the anger of my lord wax	Ex 32:22	
any gold, *l* them break it off	Ex 32:24	
l him come unto me	Ex 32:26	
thou hast not *l* me know whom thou	Ex 33:12	
neither *l* any man be seen	Ex 34:3	
neither *l* the flocks nor herds	Ex 34:3	
l my Lord, I pray thee, go among	Ex 34:9	
l him bring it, an offering of	Ex 35:5	
L neither man nor woman make any	Ex 36:6	
l him offer a male without	Lev 1:3	
then *l* him bring for his sin,	Lev 4:3	
but *l* your brethren, the whole	Lev 10:6	
shall *l* the living bird loose	Lev 14:7	
But he shall *l* go the living bird	Lev 14:53	
to *l* him go for a scapegoat into	Lev 16:10	
he shall *l* go the goat in the	Lev 16:22	
he that *l* go the goat for the	Lev 16:26	
thou shalt not *l* any of thy seed	Lev 18:21	
Thou shalt not *l* thy cattle	Lev 19:19	
l him not approach to offer the	Lev 21:17	
l all that heard him lay their	Lev 24:14	
l all the congregation stone him	Lev 24:14	
Then *l* him count the years of the	Lev 25:27	
l the trespass be recompensed	Num 5:8	
shall *l* the locks of the hair of	Num 6:5	
l them shave all their flesh, and	Num 8:7	
l them wash their clothes, and so	Num 8:7	
Then *l* them take a young bullock	Num 8:8	
L the children of Israel also	Num 9:2	
l thine enemies be scattered	Num 10:35	
l them that hate thee flee before	Num 10:35	
l me not see my wretchedness	Num 11:15	
l them fall by the camp, as it	Num 11:31	
L her not be as one dead, of whom	Num 12:12	
l her be shut out from the camp	Num 12:14	
after that *l* her be received in	Num 12:14	
L us go up at once, and possess it	Num 13:30	
L us make a captain, and *l* us	Num 14:4	
l the power of my LORD be great,	Num 14:17	
l them make them broad plates for	Num 16:38	
L us pass, I pray thee, through	Num 20:17	
L me pass through thy land	Num 21:22	
l the city of Sihon be built and	Num 21:27	
L nothing, I pray thee, hinder	Num 22:16	
L me die the death of the	Num 23:10	
l my last end be like his	Num 23:10	
L the LORD, the God of the	Num 27:16	
l them go against the Midianites,	Num 31:3	
l this land be given unto thy	Num 32:5	
that those which ye *l* remain of	Num 33:55	
L them marry to whom they think	Num 36:6	
L me pass through thy land	Deut 2:27	
would not *l* us pass by him	Deut 2:30	
l me go over, and see the good	Deut 3:25	
said unto me, *L* it suffice thee	Deut 3:26	
L me alone, that I may destroy	Deut 9:14	
L us go after other gods, which	Deut 13:2	
not known, and *l* us serve them	Deut 13:2	
L us go and serve other gods,	Deut 13:6	
L us go and serve other gods,	Deut 13:13	
shalt *l* him go free from thee	Deut 15:12	
thou shalt not *l* him go away	Deut 15:13	
L me not hear again the voice of	Deut 18:16	
neither *l* me see this great fire	Deut 18:16	
l not your hearts faint, fear not	Deut 20:3	
l him go and return to his house,	Deut 20:5	
l him also go and return unto his	Deut 20:6	
l him go and return unto his house	Deut 20:7	
l him go and return unto his house	Deut 20:8	
then thou shalt *l* her go whither	Deut 21:14	
shalt in any wise *l* the dam go	Deut 22:7	
then *l* him write her a bill of	Deut 24:1	
then *l* his brother's wife go up	Deut 25:7	
L them rise up and help you, and be	Deut 32:38	
L Reuben live, and not die	Deut 33:6	
and *l* not his men be few	Deut 33:6	
l his hands be sufficient for him	Deut 33:7	
L thy Thummim and thy Urim with	Deut 33:8	
l the blessing come upon the head	Deut 33:16	
L Asher be blessed with children	Deut 33:24	
l him be acceptable to his	Deut 33:24	
l him dip his foot in oil	Deut 33:24	
Then she *l* them down by a cord	Josh 2:15	3381
which thou didst *l* us down by	Josh 2:18	3381
Then ye shall *l* your children	Josh 4:22	
l seven priests bear seven	Josh 6:6	
l him that is armed pass on	Josh 6:7	
L not all the people go up	Josh 7:3	
but *l* about two or three thousand	Josh 7:3	
so that they *l* none of them	Josh 8:22	
league with them, to *l* them live	Josh 9:15	
we will even *l* them live, lest	Josh 9:20	
said unto them, *L* them live	Josh 9:21	
but *l* them be hewers of wood and	Josh 9:21	
he *l* none remain	Josh 10:28	
he *l* none remain in it	Josh 10:30	
l the LORD himself require it	Josh 22:23	
L us now prepare to build us an	Josh 22:26	
So Joshua *l* the people depart,	Josh 24:28	
but they *l* go the man and all his	Judg 1:25	
when Joshua had *l* the people go	Judg 2:6	
So *l* all thine enemies perish, O	Judg 5:31	
but *l* them that love him be as	Judg 5:31	
l him be put to death whilst it	Judg 6:31	
l him plead for himself, because	Judg 6:31	
L Baal plead against him, because	Judg 6:32	
L not thine anger be hot against	Judg 6:39	
l me prove, I pray thee, but this	Judg 6:39	
l it now be dry only upon the	Judg 6:39	
all the ground *l* there be dew	Judg 6:39	
l him return and depart early from	Judg 7:3	
l all the other people go every	Judg 7:7	
l fire come out of the bramble,	Judg 9:15	
l him also rejoice in you	Judg 9:19	
l fire come out from Abimelech,	Judg 9:20	
l fire come out from the men of	Judg 9:20	
l them deliver you in the time of	Judg 10:14	
L me, I pray thee, pass through	Judg 11:17	
L us pass, we pray thee, through	Judg 11:19	
L this thing be done for me	Judg 11:37	
l me alone two months, that I may	Judg 11:37	
were escaped said, *L* me go over	Judg 12:5	
l the man of God which thou didst	Judg 13:8	
Now *l* thy words come to pass	Judg 13:12	
said unto the woman *l* her beware	Judg 13:13	
neither *l* her drink wine or	Judg 13:14	
I commanded her *l* her observe	Judg 13:14	
l us detain thee, until we shall	Judg 13:15	
he *l* them go into the standing	Judg 15:5	
L me die with the Philistines	Judg 16:30	
L not thy voice be heard among us	Judg 18:25	
night, and *l* thine heart be merry	Judg 19:6	
l us turn in into this city of	Judg 19:11	
l us draw near to one of these	Judg 19:13	
howsoever *l* all thy wants lie	Judg 19:20	
began to spring, they *l* her go	Judg 19:25	
unto her, Up, and *l* us be going	Judg 19:28	
L us flee, and draw them from the	Judg 20:32	
L me now go to the field, and	Ruth 2:2	
l me glean and gather after the	Ruth 2:7	
L thine eyes be on the field that	Ruth 2:9	
L me find favour in thy sight, my	Ruth 2:13	
L her glean even among the	Ruth 2:15	
l fall also some of the handfuls	Ruth 2:16	
l him do the kinsman's part	Ruth 3:13	
L it not be known that a woman	Ruth 3:14	
l thy house be like the house of	Ruth 4:12	
L thine handmaid find grace in	1Sa 1:18	
l not arrogancy come out of your	1Sa 2:3	
L them not fail to burn the fat	1Sa 2:16	
l him do what seemeth him good	1Sa 3:18	
did *l* none of his words fall to	1Sa 3:19	
L us fetch the ark of the	1Sa 4:3	
L the ark of the God of Israel be	1Sa 5:8	
l it go again to his own place,	1Sa 5:11	
did they not *l* the people go, and	1Sa 6:6	
with him, Come, and *l* us return	1Sa 9:5	
now *l* us go thither	1Sa 9:6	
Come, and *l* us go to the seer	1Sa 9:9	
come, *l* us go	1Sa 9:10	
and to morrow I will *l* thee go	1Sa 9:19	
l it be, when these signs are	1Sa 10:7	
l us go to Gilgal, and renew the	1Sa 11:14	
land, saying, *L* the Hebrews hear	1Sa 13:3	
l us go over to the Philistines'	1Sa 14:1	
l us go over unto the garrison of	1Sa 14:6	
Saul said, *L* us go down after the	1Sa 14:36	
l us not leave a man of them	1Sa 14:36	
L us draw near hither unto God	1Sa 14:36	
L our lord now command thy	1Sa 16:16	

L David, I pray thee, stand 1Sa 16:22
for you, and *l* him come down to me 1Sa 17:8
L no man's heart fail because of 1Sa 17:32
would *l* him go no more home to 1Sa 18:2
L not mine hand be upon him 1Sa 18:17
but *l* the hand of the Philistines 1Sa 18:17
L not the king sin against his 1Sa 19:4
So Michal *l* David down through a 1Sa 19:12 3381
Saul, He said unto me, *L* me go 1Sa 19:17
L not Jonathan know this, lest he 1Sa 20:3
but *l* me go, that I may hide 1Sa 20:5
l us go out into the field 1Sa 20:11
L the LORD even require it at the 1Sa 20:16
And he said, *L* me go, I pray thee 1Sa 20:29
l me get away, I pray thee, and 1Sa 20:29
L no man know any thing of the 1Sa 21:2
l his spittle fall down upon his 1Sa 21:13
L my father and my mother, I pray 1Sa 22:3
l not the king impute any thing 1Sa 22:15
will he *l* him go well away 1Sa 24:19
Wherefore *l* the young men find 1Sa 25:8
upon me *l* this iniquity be 1Sa 25:24
l thine handmaid, I pray thee, 1Sa 25:24
L not my lord, I pray thee, 1Sa 25:25
now *l* thine enemies, and they that 1Sa 25:26
l it even be given unto the young 1Sa 25:27
l thine handmaid be a servant to 1Sa 25:41
now therefore *l* me smite him 1Sa 26:8
and the cruse of water, and *l* us go 1Sa 26:11
l my lord the king hear the words 1Sa 26:19
me, *l* him accept an offering 1Sa 26:19
l not my blood fall to the earth 1Sa 26:20
l one of the young men come over 1Sa 26:22
so *l* my life be much set by in 1Sa 26:24
l him deliver me out of all 1Sa 26:24
l them give me a place in some 1Sa 27:5
l me set a morsel of bread before 1Sa 28:22
l him not go down with us to 1Sa 29:4
l there be no dew 2Sa 1:21
neither *l* there be rain, upon you 2Sa 1:21
Therefore now *l* your hands be 2Sa 2:7
L the young men now arise, and 2Sa 2:14
And Joab said, *L* them arise 2Sa 2:14
L it rest on the head of Joab, and 2Sa 3:29
l there not fail from the house 2Sa 3:29
l it be, when thou hearest the 2Sa 5:24
l thy name be magnified for ever, 2Sa 7:26
l the house of thy servant David 2Sa 7:26
Therefore now *l* it please thee to 2Sa 7:29
with thy blessing *l* the house of 2Sa 7:29
l us play the men for our people, 2Sa 10:12
and to morrow I will *l* thee depart 2Sa 11:12
L not this thing displease thee, 2Sa 11:25
l my sister Tamar come, and give 2Sa 13:5
l Tamar my sister come, and make 2Sa 13:6
l the king, I beseech thee, and 2Sa 13:24 3381
l us not all now go, lest we be 2Sa 13:25
l my brother Amnon go with us 2Sa 13:26
pressed him, that he *l* Amnon 2Sa 13:27
L not my lord suppose that they 2Sa 13:32
Now therefore *l* not my lord the 2Sa 13:33
l the king remember the LORD thy 2Sa 14:11
L thine handmaid, I pray thee, 2Sa 14:12
L my lord the king now speak 2Sa 14:18
L him turn to his own house 2Sa 14:24
and *l* him not see my face 2Sa 14:24
now therefore *l* me see the king's 2Sa 14:32
any iniquity in me, *l* him kill me 2Sa 14:32
l me go and pay my vow, which I 2Sa 15:7
at Jerusalem, Arise, and *l* us flee 2Sa 15:14
l him do to me as seemeth good 2Sa 15:26
l me go over, I pray thee, and 2Sa 16:9
so *l* him curse, because the LORD 2Sa 16:10
l him alone, and *l* him curse 2Sa 16:11 3240
L me now choose out twelve 2Sa 17:1
l us hear likewise what he saith 2Sa 17:5
L me now run, and bear the king 2Sa 18:19
l me, I pray thee, also run after 2Sa 18:22
But howsoever, said he, *l* me run 2Sa 18:23
L not my lord impute iniquity 2Sa 19:19
l him take all, forasmuch as my 2Sa 19:30
L thy servant, I pray thee, turn 2Sa 19:37
l him go over with my lord the 2Sa 19:37
is for David, *l* him go after Joab 2Sa 20:11
L seven men of his sons be 2Sa 21:6
l us fall now into the hand of 2Sa 24:14
l me not fall into the hand of 2Sa 24:14
l thine hand, I pray thee, be 2Sa 24:17
L my lord the king take and offer 2Sa 24:22
L there be sought for my lord the 1Kin 1:2
l her stand before the king, and 1Kin 1:2
l her cherish him, and *l* her lie 1Kin 1:2
l her lie in thy bosom, that my 1Kin 1:2
l me, I pray thee, give thee 1Kin 1:12
L my lord king David live for 1Kin 1:31
l Zadok the priest and Nathan the 1Kin 1:34
L king Solomon swear unto me to 1Kin 1:51
l not his hoar head go down to 1Kin 2:6
l them be of those that eat at 1Kin 2:7
L Abishag the Shunammite be given 1Kin 2:21
L it be neither mine nor thine, 1Kin 3:26
l thy word, I pray thee, be 1Kin 8:26
l him not leave us, nor forsake 1Kin 8:57
l these my words, wherewith I 1Kin 8:59
L your heart therefore be perfect 1Kin 8:61
L me depart, that I may go to 1Kin 11:21
howbeit *l* me go in any wise 1Kin 11:22
l this child's soul come into him 1Kin 17:21
L them therefore give us two 1Kin 18:23
l them choose one bullock for 1Kin 18:23
answereth by fire, *l* him be God 1Kin 18:24
l it be known this day that thou 1Kin 18:36
l not one of them escape 1Kin 18:40
So *l* the gods do to me, and more 1Kin 19:2

L me, I pray thee, kiss my father 1Kin 19:20
L not him that girdeth on his 1Kin 20:11
but *l* us fight against them in 1Kin 20:23
l us, I pray thee, put sackcloth 1Kin 20:31
saith, I pray thee, *l* me live 1Kin 20:32
Because thou hast *l* go out of thy 1Kin 20:42
bread, and *l* thine heart be merry 1Kin 21:7
said, *L* not the king say so 1Kin 22:8
l thy word, I pray thee, be like 1Kin 22:13
l them return every man to his 1Kin 22:17
L my servants go with thy 1Kin 22:49
then *l* fire come down from heaven 2Kin 1:10
l fire come down from heaven, and 2Kin 1:12
l my life, and the life of these 2Kin 1:13
therefore *l* my life now be 2Kin 1:14
l a double portion of thy spirit 2Kin 2:9
l them go, we pray thee, and seek 2Kin 2:16
L us make a little chamber, I 2Kin 4:10
l us set for him there a bed, and 2Kin 4:10
the man of God said, *L* her alone 2Kin 4:27
l him come now to me, and he shall 2Kin 5:8
he *l* the men go, and they departed 2Kin 5:24
L us go, we pray thee, unto 2Kin 6:2
l us make us a place there, where 2Kin 6:2
now *l* us fall unto the host of the 2Kin 7:4
L some take, I pray thee, five of 2Kin 7:13
and *l* us send and see 2Kin 7:13
then *l* none go forth nor escape 2Kin 9:15
them, and *l* him say, Is it peace 2Kin 9:17
l none be wanting 2Kin 10:19
l none come forth 2Kin 10:25
within the ranges, *l* him be slain 2Kin 11:8
L her not be slain in the house 2Kin 11:15
L the priests take it to them, 2Kin 12:5
l them repair the breaches of the 2Kin 12:5
and when the man was *l* down 2Kin 13:21 3212
l us look one another in the face 2Kin 14:8
l them go and dwell there 2Kin 17:27
l him teach them the manner of 2Kin 17:27
L not Hezekiah deceive you 2Kin 18:29
Neither *l* Hezekiah make you trust 2Kin 18:30
L not thy God in whom thou 2Kin 19:10
but *l* the shadow return backward 2Kin 20:10
l them deliver it into the hand 2Kin 22:5
l them give it to the doers of 2Kin 22:5
And he said, *L* him alone 2Kin 23:18 3240
l no man move his bones 2Kin 23:18 3240
So they *l* his bones alone, with 2Kin 23:18
l us send abroad unto our 1Chr 13:2
l us bring again the ark of our 1Chr 13:3
l the heart of them rejoice that 1Chr 16:10
L the heavens be glad, and *l* the 1Chr 16:31
l men say among the nations, The 1Chr 16:31
L the sea roar, and the fulness 1Chr 16:32
l the fields rejoice, and all that 1Chr 16:32
l the thing that thou hast spoken 1Chr 17:23
L it even be established, that 1Chr 17:24
l the house of David thy servant 1Chr 17:24
Now therefore *l* it please thee to 1Chr 17:27
l us behave ourselves valiantly 1Chr 19:13
l the LORD do that which is good 1Chr 19:13
l me fall now into the hand of 1Chr 21:13
but *l* me not fall into the hand 1Chr 21:13
l thine hand, I pray thee, O LORD 1Chr 21:17
l my lord the king do that which 1Chr 21:23
l thy promise unto David my 2Chr 1:9
l him send unto his servants 2Chr 2:15
l thy word be verified, which 2Chr 6:17
Now, my God, *l*, I beseech thee, 2Chr 6:40
l thine ears be attent unto the 2Chr 6:40
l thy priests, O LORD God, be 2Chr 6:41
l thy saints rejoice in goodness 2Chr 6:41
L us build these cities, and make 2Chr 14:7
l not man prevail against thee 2Chr 14:11
and *l* not your hands be weak 2Chr 15:7
to the intent that he might *l* 2Chr 16:1 5414
of Ramah, and *l* his work cease 2Chr 16:5
said, *L* not the king say so 2Chr 18:7
l thy word therefore, I pray thee 2Chr 18:12
l them return therefore every man 2Chr 18:16
Wherefore now *l* the fear of the 2Chr 19:7
thou wouldest not *l* Israel invade 2Chr 20:10
But *l* none come into the house of 2Chr 23:6
l him be slain with the sword 2Chr 23:14
l not the army of Israel go with 2Chr 25:7
l us see one another in the face 2Chr 25:17
Now therefore *l* not Hezekiah 2Chr 32:15
God be with him, and *l* him go up 2Chr 36:23
l him go up to Jerusalem, which Ezr 1:3
l the men of his place help him Ezr 1:4
unto them, *L* us build with you Ezr 4:2
l the house of God be builded in Ezr 5:15
l there be search made in the Ezr 5:17
l the king send his pleasure to Ezr 5:17
L the house be builded, the place Ezr 6:3
l the foundations thereof be Ezr 6:3
l the expences be given out of Ezr 6:4
also *l* the golden and silver Ezr 6:5
L the work of this house of God Ezr 6:7
l the governor of the Jews and the Ezr 6:7
l it be given them day by day Ezr 6:9
l timber be pulled down from his Ezr 6:11
set up, *l* him be hanged thereon Ezr 6:11
l his house be made a dunghill Ezr 6:11
l it be done with speed Ezr 6:12
l it be diligently done for the Ezr 7:23
l judgment be executed speedily Ezr 7:26
Now therefore *l* us make a Ezr 10:3
l it be done according to the law Ezr 10:3
L now our rulers of all the Ezr 10:14
l all them which have taken Ezr 10:14
L thine ear now be attentive, and Neh 1:6
l now thine ear be attentive to Neh 1:11
king, *L* the king live for ever Neh 2:3

l letters be given me to the Neh 2:7
l us build up the wall of Neh 2:17
they said, *L* us rise up and build Neh 2:18
l not their sin be blotted out Neh 4:5
L every one with his servant Neh 4:22
l us leave off this usury Neh 5:10
l us meet together in some one of Neh 6:2
l us take counsel together Neh 6:7
L us meet together in the house Neh 6:10
l us shut the doors of the temple Neh 6:10
L not the gates of Jerusalem be Neh 7:3
l them shut the doors, and bar Neh 7:3
l not all the trouble seem little Neh 9:32
l there go a royal commandment Est 1:19
l it be written among the laws of Est 1:19
l the king give her royal estate Est 1:19
L there be fair young virgins Est 2:2
l the king appoint officers in Est 2:3
l their things for purification Est 2:3
l the maiden which pleaseth the Est 2:4
l it be written that they may be Est 3:9
l the king and Haman come this day Est 5:4
l the king and Haman come to the Est 5:8
Esther the queen did *l* no man Est 5:12
L a gallows be made of fifty Est 5:14
And the king said, *L* him come in Est 6:5
L the royal apparel be brought Est 6:8
l this apparel and horse be Est 6:9
l nothing fail of all that thou Est 6:10
l my life be given me at my Est 7:3
l it be written to reverse the Est 8:5
l it be granted to the Jews which Est 9:13
l Haman's ten sons be hanged upon Est 9:13
L the day perish wherein I was Job 3:3
L that day be darkness Job 3:4
l not God regard it from above, Job 3:4
neither *l* the light shine upon it Job 3:4
L darkness and the shadow of death Job 3:5
l a cloud dwell upon it Job 3:5
l the blackness of the day Job 3:5
night, *l* darkness seize upon it Job 3:6
l it not be joined unto the days Job 3:6
l it not come into the number of Job 3:6
Lo, *l* that night be solitary Job 3:7
l no joyful voice come therein Job 3:7
L them curse it that curse the Job 3:8
L the stars of the twilight Job 3:9
l it look for light, but have Job 3:9
neither *l* it see the dawning of Job 3:9
that he would *l* loose his hand, Job 6:9
l him not spare Job 6:10
I pray you, *l* it not be iniquity Job 6:29
l me alone Job 7:16
nor *l* me alone till I swallow Job 7:19
L him take his rod away from me, Job 9:34
l not his fear terrify me Job 9:34
l me alone, that I may take Job 10:20
l not wickedness dwell in thy Job 11:14
Hold your peace, *l* me alone, Job 13:13
and *l* come on me what will Job 13:13
l not thy dread make me afraid Job 13:21
or *l* me speak, and answer thou me Job 13:22
L not him that is deceived trust Job 15:31
blood, and *l* my cry have no place Job 16:18
l this be your consolations Job 21:2
I hold fast, and will not *l* it go Job 27:6
L mine enemy be as the wicked, and Job 27:7
they have also *l* loose the bridle Job 30:11
L me be weighed in an even Job 31:6
Then *l* me sow, and *l* another eat Job 31:8
l my offspring be rooted out Job 31:8
Then *l* my wife grind unto another Job 31:10
l others bow down upon her Job 31:10
Then *l* mine arm fall from my Job 31:22
L thistles grow instead of wheat, Job 31:40
L me not, I pray you, accept any Job 32:21
neither *l* me give flattering Job 32:21
L us choose to us judgment Job 34:4
l us know among ourselves what is Job 34:4
L men of understanding tell me, Job 34:34
l a wise man hearken unto me Job 34:34
reproveth God, *l* him answer it Job 40:2
L us break their bands asunder, Ps 2:3
l them fall by their own counsels Ps 5:10
But *l* all those that put their Ps 5:11
l them ever shout for joy, Ps 5:11
l them also that love thy name be Ps 5:11
L all mine enemies be ashamed and Ps 6:10
l them return and be ashamed Ps 6:10
L the enemy persecute my soul, and Ps 7:5
l him tread down my life upon the Ps 7:5
Oh *l* the wickedness of the wicked Ps 7:9
l not man prevail Ps 9:19
l the heathen be judged in thy Ps 9:19
l them be taken in the devices Ps 10:2
L my sentence come forth from thy Ps 17:2
l thine eyes behold the things Ps 17:2
l the God of my salvation be Ps 18:46
l them not have dominion over me Ps 19:13
L the words of my mouth, and the Ps 19:14
l the king hear us when we call Ps 20:9
l him deliver him, seeing he Ps 22:8
l me not be ashamed, *l* not mine Ps 25:2
l none that wait on thee be Ps 25:3
l them be ashamed which Ps 25:3
l me not be ashamed Ps 25:20
L integrity and uprightness Ps 25:21
l me never be ashamed Ps 31:1
L me not be ashamed, O LORD Ps 31:17
l the wicked be ashamed Ps 31:17
l them be silent in the grave Ps 31:17
L the lying lips be put to Ps 31:18
L all the earth fear the LORD Ps 33:8
l all the inhabitants of the Ps 33:8

L thy mercy, O LORD, be upon us, Ps 33:22
l us exalt his name together Ps 34:3
L them be confounded and put to Ps 35:4
l them be turned back and brought Ps 35:4
L them be as chaff before the Ps 35:5
l the angel of the LORD chase Ps 35:5
L their way be dark and slippery Ps 35:6
l the angel of the LORD persecute Ps 35:6
L destruction come upon him at Ps 35:8
l his net that he hath hid catch Ps 35:8
that very destruction *l* him fall Ps 35:8
L not them that are mine enemies Ps 35:19
neither *l* them wink with the eye Ps 35:19
l them not rejoice over me Ps 35:24
L them not say in their hearts, Ps 35:25
l them not say, We have swallowed Ps 35:25
L them be ashamed and brought to Ps 35:26
l them be clothed with shame and Ps 35:26
L them shout for joy, and be glad, Ps 35:27
l them say continually Ps 35:27
L the LORD be magnified, which Ps 35:27
L not the foot of pride come Ps 36:11
l not the hand of the wicked Ps 36:11
l thy lovingkindness and thy truth Ps 40:11
L them be ashamed and confounded Ps 40:14
l them be driven backward and put Ps 40:14
L them be desolate for a reward Ps 40:15
L all those that seek thee Ps 40:16
l such as love thy salvation say Ps 40:16
l them lead me Ps 43:3
l them bring me unto thy holy Ps 43:3
L mount Zion rejoice Ps 48:11
l the daughters of Judah be glad, Ps 48:11
L death seize upon them Ps 55:15
l them go down quick into hell Ps 55:15
l thy glory be above all the Ps 57:5
l thy glory be above all the Ps 57:11
L them melt away as waters which Ps 58:7
l them be as cut in pieces Ps 58:7
l every one of them pass away Ps 58:8
God shall *l* me see my desire upon Ps 59:10
the words of their lips *l* them Ps 59:12
l them know that God ruleth in Ps 59:13
And at evening *l* them return Ps 59:14
l them make a noise like a dog, Ps 59:14
L them wander up and down for meat Ps 59:15
l not the rebellious exalt Ps 66:7
L the people praise thee, O God Ps 67:3
l all the people praise thee Ps 67:3
O *l* the nations be glad and sing Ps 67:4
L the people praise thee, O God Ps 67:5
l all the people praise thee Ps 67:5
L God arise, *l* his enemies be Ps 68:1
l his enemies be scattered Ps 68:1
l them also that hate him flee Ps 68:1
so *l* the wicked perish at the Ps 68:2
But *l* the righteous be glad Ps 68:3
l them rejoice before God Ps 68:3
l them exceedingly rejoice Ps 68:3
L not them that wait on thee, O Ps 69:6
l not those that seek thee be Ps 69:6
out of the mire, and *l* me not sink Ps 69:14
l me be delivered from them that Ps 69:14
L not the waterflood overflow me, Ps 69:15
neither *l* the deep swallow me up, Ps 69:15
l not the pit shut her mouth upon Ps 69:15
L their table become a snare Ps 69:22
their welfare, *l* it become a trap Ps 69:22
L their eyes be darkened, that Ps 69:23
l thy wrathful anger take hold of Ps 69:24
L their habitation be desolate Ps 69:25
l none dwell in their tents Ps 69:25
and *l* them not come into thy Ps 69:27
L them be blotted out of the book Ps 69:28
l thy salvation, O God, set me up Ps 69:29
L the heaven and earth praise him, Ps 69:34
L them be ashamed and confounded Ps 70:2
l them be turned backward, and put Ps 70:2
L them be turned back for a Ps 70:3
L all those that seek thee Ps 70:4
l such as love thy salvation say Ps 70:4
continually, *L* God be magnified Ps 70:4
l me never be put to confusion Ps 71:1 3381
L my mouth be filled with thy Ps 71:8
L them be confounded and consumed Ps 71:13
l them be covered with reproach Ps 71:13
l the whole earth be filled with Ps 72:19
L us destroy them together Ps 74:8
O *l* not the oppressed return Ps 74:21
l the poor and needy praise thy Ps 74:21
l all that be round about him Ps 76:11
he *l* it fall in the midst of Ps 78:28
l thy tender mercies speedily Ps 79:8
l him be known among the heathen Ps 79:10
L the sighing of the prisoner Ps 79:11
L thy hand be upon the man of thy Ps 80:17
l us cut them off from being a Ps 83:4
L us take to ourselves the houses Ps 83:12
L them be confounded and troubled Ps 83:17
l them be put to shame, and perish Ps 83:17
but *l* them not turn again to Ps 85:8
L my prayer come before thee Ps 88:2
l it repent thee concerning thy Ps 90:13
L thy work appear unto thy Ps 90:16
l the beauty of the LORD our God Ps 90:17
O come, *l* us sing unto the LORD Ps 95:1
l us make a joyful noise to the Ps 95:1
L us come before his presence Ps 95:2
O come, *l* us worship and bow down Ps 95:6
l us kneel before the LORD our Ps 95:6
L the heavens rejoice Ps 96:11
and *l* the earth be glad Ps 96:11
l the sea roar, and the fulness Ps 96:11
L the field be joyful, and all Ps 96:12
l the earth rejoice Ps 97:1
l the multitude of isles be glad Ps 97:1
L the sea roar, and the fulness Ps 98:7
L the floods clap their hands Ps 98:8
l the hills be joyful together Ps 98:8
l the people tremble Ps 99:1
l the earth be moved Ps 99:1
L them praise thy great and Ps 99:3
LORD, and *l* my cry come unto thee Ps 102:1
L the sinners be consumed out of Ps 104:35
earth, and *l* the wicked be no more Ps 104:35
l the heart of them rejoice that Ps 105:3
of the people, and *l* him go free Ps 105:20
l all the people say, Amen Ps 106:48
L the redeemed of the LORD say so Ps 107:2
l them sacrifice the sacrifices Ps 107:22
L them exalt him also in the Ps 107:32
l Satan stand at his right hand Ps 109:6
be judged, *l* him be condemned Ps 109:7
and *l* his prayer become sin Ps 109:7
L his days be few Ps 109:8
l another take his office Ps 109:8
L his children be fatherless, and Ps 109:9
L his children be continually Ps 109:10
l them seek their bread also out Ps 109:10
L the extortioner catch all that Ps 109:11
l the strangers spoil his labour Ps 109:11
L there be none to extend mercy Ps 109:12
neither *l* there be any to favour Ps 109:12
L his posterity be cut off Ps 109:13
l their name be blotted out Ps 109:13
L the iniquity of his fathers be Ps 109:14
l not the sin of his mother be Ps 109:14
L them be before the LORD Ps 109:15
cursing, so *l* it come unto him Ps 109:17
blessing, so *l* it be far from him Ps 109:17
so *l* it come into his bowels like Ps 109:18
L it be unto him as the garment Ps 109:19
L this be the reward of mine Ps 109:20
L them curse, but bless thou Ps 109:28
they arise, *l* them be ashamed Ps 109:28
but *l* thy servant rejoice Ps 109:28
L mine adversaries be clothed Ps 109:29
l them cover themselves with Ps 109:29
L Israel now say, that his mercy Ps 118:2
L the house of Aaron now say, Ps 118:3
L them now that fear the LORD say Ps 118:4
O *l* me not wander from thy Ps 119:10
L thy mercies come also unto me, Ps 119:41
L, I pray thee, thy merciful Ps 119:76
L thy tender mercies come unto me Ps 119:77
L the proud be ashamed Ps 119:78
L those that fear thee turn unto Ps 119:79
L my heart be sound in thy Ps 119:80
l me not be ashamed of my hope Ps 119:116
l not the proud oppress me Ps 119:122
l not any iniquity have dominion Ps 119:133
L my cry come near before thee, O Ps 119:169
L my supplication come before Ps 119:170
L thine hand help me Ps 119:173
L my soul live, and it shall Ps 119:175
and *l* thy judgments help me Ps 119:175
L us go into the house of the Ps 122:1
L them all be confounded and Ps 129:5
L them be as the grass upon the Ps 129:6
l thine ears be attentive to the Ps 130:2
L Israel hope in the LORD Ps 130:7
L Israel hope in the LORD from Ps 131:3
L thy priests be clothed with Ps 132:9
l thy saints shout for joy Ps 132:9
l my right hand forget her Ps 137:5
l my tongue cleave to the roof of Ps 137:6
l the mischief of their own lips Ps 140:9
L burning coals fall upon them Ps 140:10
l them be cast into the fire Ps 140:10
L not an evil speaker be Ps 140:11
L my prayer be set forth before Ps 141:2
l me not eat of their dainties Ps 141:4
L the righteous smite me Ps 141:5
and *l* him reprove me Ps 141:5
L the wicked fall into their own Ps 141:10
l all flesh bless his holy name Ps 145:21
L them praise the name of the Ps 148:5
L them praise the name of the Ps 148:13
L Israel rejoice in him that made Ps 149:2
l the children of Zion be joyful Ps 149:2
L them praise his name in the Ps 149:3
l them sing praises unto him with Ps 149:3
L the saints be joyful in glory Ps 149:5
l them sing aloud upon their beds Ps 149:5
L the high praises of God be in Ps 149:6
L every thing that hath breath Ps 150:6
l us lay wait for blood Prov 1:11
l us lurk privily for the Prov 1:11
L us swallow them up alive as the Prov 1:12
l us all have one purse Prov 1:14
but *l* thine heart keep my Prov 3:1
L not mercy and truth forsake thee Prov 3:3
l not them depart from thine eyes Prov 3:21
L thine heart retain my words Prov 4:4
l her not go Prov 4:13
L them not depart from thine eyes Prov 4:21
L thine eyes look right on, and Prov 4:25
l thine eyelids look straight Prov 4:25
l all thy ways be established Prov 4:26
L thy fountains be dispersed Prov 5:16
L them be only thine own, and not Prov 5:17
L thy fountain be blessed Prov 5:18
L her be as the loving hind and Prov 5:19
l her breasts satisfy thee at all Prov 5:19
neither *l* her take thee with her Prov 6:25
l us take our fill of love until Prov 7:18
l us solace ourselves with loves Prov 7:18
L not thine heart decline to her Prov 7:25
is simple, *l* him turn in hither Prov 9:4
is simple, *l* him turn in hither Prov 9:16
L a bear robbed of her whelps Prov 17:12
l not thy soul spare for his Prov 19:18
L not thine heart envy sinners Prov 23:17
l thine eyes observe my ways Prov 23:26
l not thine heart be glad when he Prov 24:17
L another man praise thee, and not Prov 27:2
l no man stay him Prov 28:17
L him drink, and forget his Prov 31:7
l her own works praise her in the Prov 31:31
l not thine heart be hasty to Eccl 5:2
therefore *l* thy words be few Eccl 5:2
L thy garments be always white Eccl 9:8
l thy head lack no ointment Eccl 9:8
yet *l* him remember the days of Eccl 11:8
l thy heart cheer thee in the Eccl 11:9
L us hear the conclusion of the Eccl 12:13
L him kiss me with the kisses of Song 1:2
l me see thy countenance, *l* me Song 2:14
I held him, and would not *l* him go Song 3:4
L my beloved come into his garden Song 4:16
l us go forth into the field Song 7:11
l us lodge in the villages Song 7:11
L us get up early to the Song 7:12
l us see if the vine flourish, Song 7:12
he *l* out the vineyard unto Song 8:11 5414
l us reason together, saith the Is 1:18
l us go up to the mountain of the Is 2:3
l us walk in the light of the Is 2:5
l this ruin be under thy hand Is 3:6
only *l* us be called by thy name, Is 4:1
L him make speed, and hasten his Is 5:19
l the counsel of the Holy One of Is 5:19
L us go up against Judah, and vex Is 7:6
l us make a breach therein for us Is 7:6
l him be your fear, and *l* him be Is 8:13
L mine outcasts dwell with thee, Is 16:4
l them tell thee now, and *l* them Is 19:12
l him declare what he seeth Is 21:6
l us eat and drink Is 22:13
L favour be shewed to the wicked, Is 26:10
Or *l* him take hold of my strength Is 27:5
l them kill sacrifices Is 29:1
l the earth hear, and all that is Is 34:1
L not Hezekiah deceive you Is 36:14
Neither *l* Hezekiah make you trust Is 36:15
L not thy God, in whom thou Is 37:10
L them take a lump of figs, and Is 38:21
l the people renew their strength Is 41:1
l them come near Is 41:1
then *l* them speak Is 41:1
l us come near together to Is 41:1
L them bring them forth, and shew Is 41:22
l them shew the former things, Is 41:22
L the wilderness and the cities Is 42:11
l the inhabitants of the rock Is 42:11
l them shout from the top of the Is 42:11
L them give glory unto the LORD, Is 42:12
L all the nations be gathered Is 43:9
and *l* the people be assembled Is 43:9
l them bring forth their Is 43:9
or *l* them hear, and say, It is Is 43:9
I will work, and who shall *l* it Is 43:13 7725
l us plead together Is 43:26
shall come, *l* them shew unto them Is 44:7
l them all be gathered together, Is 44:11
l them stand up Is 44:11
above, and *l* the skies pour down Is 45:8
l the earth open Is 45:8
l them bring forth salvation, and Is 45:8
l righteousness spring up Is 45:8
L the potsherd strive with the Is 45:9
he shall *l* go my captives, not Is 45:13
l them take counsel together Is 45:21
L now the astrologers, the Is 47:13
l us stand together Is 50:8
l him come near to me Is 50:8
l him trust in the name of the Is 50:10
l them stretch forth the curtains Is 54:2
l your soul delight itself in Is 55:2
L the wicked forsake his way, and Is 55:7
l him return unto the LORD, and he Is 55:7
Neither *l* the son of the stranger Is 56:3
neither *l* the eunuch say, Behold, Is 56:3
l thy companies deliver thee Is 57:13
to *l* the oppressed go free, and Is 58:6
said, *L* the LORD be glorified Is 66:5
l them arise, if they can save Jer 2:28
l us go into the defenced cities Jer 4:5
L us now fear the LORD our God, Jer 5:24
arise, and *l* us go up at noon Jer 6:4
l us go by night, and *l* us Jer 6:5
l us enter into the defenced Jer 8:14
cities, and *l* us be silent there Jer 8:14
l them make haste, and take up a Jer 9:18
l your ear receive the word of Jer 9:20
L not the wise man glory in his Jer 9:23
neither *l* the mighty man glory in Jer 9:23
l not the rich man glory in his Jer 9:23
But *l* him that glorieth glory in Jer 9:24
L us destroy the tree with the Jer 11:19
l us cut him off from the land of Jer 11:19
l me see thy vengeance on them Jer 11:20
yet *l* me talk with thee of thy Jer 12:1
L mine eyes run down with tears Jer 14:17
night and day, and *l* them not cease Jer 14:17
of my sight, and *l* them go forth Jer 15:1
l them return unto thee Jer 15:19
l it come now Jer 17:15
L them be confounded that Jer 17:18
but *l* not me be confounded Jer 17:18
l them be dismayed, but *l* not Jer 17:18
l us devise devices against Jer 18:18

l us smite him with the tongue,	Jer 18:18	
l us not give heed to any of his	Jer 18:18	
l their wives be bereaved of	Jer 18:21	
l their men be put to death	Jer 18:21	
l their young men be slain by the	Jer 18:21	
L a cry be heard from their	Jer 18:22	
but *l* them be overthrown before	Jer 18:23	
l me see thy vengeance on them	Jer 20:12	
l not the day wherein my mother	Jer 20:14	
l that man be as the cities which	Jer 20:16	
l him hear the cry in the morning	Jer 20:16	
hath a dream, *l* him tell a dream	Jer 23:28	
l him speak my word faithfully	Jer 23:28	
those will I *l* remain still in	Jer 27:11	
l them now make intercession to	Jer 27:18	
L not your prophets and your	Jer 29:8	
l us go up to Zion unto the LORD	Jer 31:6	
every man should *l* his manservant	Jer 34:9	
every one should *l* his manservant	Jer 34:10	
then they obeyed, and *l* them go	Jer 34:10	
whom they had *l* go free, to	Jer 34:11	
At the end of seven years *l* ye go	Jer 34:14	
thou shalt *l* him go free from	Jer 34:14	
l us go to Jerusalem for fear of	Jer 35:11	
l no man know where ye be	Jer 36:19	
l my supplication, I pray thee,	Jer 37:20	
l this man be put to death	Jer 38:4	
they *l* down Jeremiah with cords	Jer 38:6	7971
l them down by cords into the	Jer 38:11	7971
L no man know of these words, and	Jer 38:24	
the guard had *l* him go from Ramah	Jer 40:1	
victuals and a reward, and *l* him go	Jer 40:5	
L me go, I pray thee, and I will	Jer 40:15	
said unto Jeremiah the prophet, *L*	Jer 42:2	
L not the swift flee away, nor	Jer 46:6	
l the mighty men come forth	Jer 46:9	
l us go again to our own people,	Jer 46:16	
l us cut it off from being a	Jer 48:2	
and *l* thy widows trust in me	Jer 49:11	
l us join ourselves to the LORD	Jer 50:5	
l nothing of her be left	Jer 50:26	
l them go down to the slaughter	Jer 50:27	
l none thereof escape	Jer 50:29	
they refused to *l* them go	Jer 50:33	
bendeth *l* the archer bend his bow	Jer 51:3	
l us go every one into his own	Jer 51:9	
l us declare in Zion the work of	Jer 51:10	
l Jerusalem come into your mind	Jer 51:50	
L all their wickedness come	Lam 1:22	
l tears run down like a river day	Lam 2:18	
l not the apple of thine eye	Lam 2:18	
L us search and try our ways, and	Lam 3:40	
L us lift up our heart with our	Lam 3:41	
stood, they *l* down their wings	Eze 1:24	7503
stood, and had *l* down their wings	Eze 1:25	7503
He that heareth, *l* him hear	Eze 3:27	
he that forbeareth, *l* him forbear	Eze 3:27	
l not the buyer rejoice, nor the	Eze 7:12	
l not your eye spare, neither	Eze 9:5	
l us build houses	Eze 11:3	
will *l* the souls go, even the	Eze 13:20	
l the sword be doubled the third	Eze 21:14	
l them seethe the bones of it	Eze 24:5	
l no lot fall upon it	Eze 24:6	
it well, and *l* the bones be burned	Eze 24:10	
I will not *l* them pollute my holy	Eze 39:7	
Now *l* them put away their	Eze 43:9	
l them measure the pattern	Eze 43:10	
l it suffice you of all your	Eze 44:6	
L it suffice you, O princes of	Eze 45:9	
l them give us pulse to eat, and	Dan 1:12	
Then *l* our countenances be looked	Dan 1:13	
L the king tell his servants the	Dan 2:7	
l the beasts get away from under	Dan 4:14	
l it be wet with the dew of	Dan 4:15	
l his portion be with the beasts	Dan 4:15	
L his heart be changed from man's	Dan 4:16	
l a beast's heart be given unto	Dan 4:16	
l seven times pass over him	Dan 4:16	
l not the dream, or the	Dan 4:19	
l it be wet with the dew of	Dan 4:23	
l his portion be with the beasts	Dan 4:23	
l my counsel be acceptable unto	Dan 4:27	
l not thy thoughts trouble thee,	Dan 5:10	
nor *l* thy countenance be changed	Dan 5:10	
now *l* Daniel be called, and he	Dan 5:12	
L thy gifts be to thyself, and	Dan 5:17	
l thine anger and thy fury be	Dan 9:16	
and said, *L* my lord speak	Dan 10:19	
l her therefore put away her	Hos 2:2	
Yet *l* no man strive, nor reprove	Hos 4:4	
harlot, yet *l* not Judah offend	Hos 4:15	
l him alone	Hos 4:17	
l us return unto the LORD	Hos 6:1	
L the men that sacrifice kiss the	Hos 13:2	
l your children tell their	Joel 1:3	
l all the inhabitants of the land	Joel 2:1	
l the bridegroom go forth of his	Joel 2:16	
L the priests, the ministers of	Joel 2:17	
l them say, Spare thy people, O	Joel 2:17	
l all the men of war draw near	Joel 3:9	
l them come up	Joel 3:9	
l the weak say, I am strong	Joel 3:10	
L the heathen be wakened, and come	Joel 3:12	
masters, Bring, and *l* us drink	Amos 4:1	
But *l* judgment run down as waters	Amos 5:24	
l us rise up against her in	Obad 1	
l us cast lots, that we may know	Jonah 1:7	
l us not perish for this man's	Jonah 1:14	
L neither man nor beast, herd nor	Jonah 3:7	
l them not feed, nor drink water	Jonah 3:7	
But *l* man and beast be covered	Jonah 3:8	
l them turn every one from his	Jonah 3:8	
l the Lord GOD be witness against	Mic 1:2	
l us go up to the mountain of the	Mic 4:2	
L her be defiled, and *l* our eye	Mic 4:11	
l the hills hear thy voice	Mic 6:1	
l them feed in Bashan and Gilead,	Mic 7:14	
l thy foreskin be uncovered	Hab 2:16	
l all the earth keep silence	Hab 2:20	
L not thine hands be slack	Zeph 3:16	
L them set a fair mitre upon his	Zec 3:5	
l none of you imagine evil	Zec 7:10	
L your hands be strong, ye that	Zec 8:9	
but *l* your hands be strong	Zec 8:13	
l none of you imagine evil in	Zec 8:17	
L us go speedily to pray before	Zec 8:21	
that that dieth, *l* it die	Zec 11:9	
is to be cut off, *l* it be cut off	Zec 11:9	
l the rest eat every one the	Zec 11:9	
l none deal treacherously against	Mal 2:15	
L your light so shine before men,	Mt 5:16	
l him give her a writing of	Mt 5:31	
But *l* your communication be, Yea,	Mt 5:37	
l him have thy cloke also	Mt 5:40	
l not thy left hand know what thy	Mt 6:3	
L me pull out the mote out of	Mt 7:4	863
l the dead bury their dead	Mt 8:22	863
l your peace come upon it	Mt 10:13	
l your peace return to you	Mt 10:13	
hath ears to hear, *l* him hear	Mt 11:15	
Who hath ears to hear, *l* him hear	Mt 13:9	
L both grow together until the	Mt 13:30	863
Who hath ears to hear, *l* him hear	Mt 13:43	
or mother, *l* him die the death	Mt 15:4	
L them alone	Mt 15:14	863
l him deny himself, and take up	Mt 16:24	
l us make here three tabernacles	Mt 17:4	
l him be unto thee as an heathen	Mt 18:17	
together, *l* not man put asunder	Mt 19:6	
to receive it, *l* him receive it	Mt 19:12	
among you, *l* him be your minister	Mt 20:26	
among you, *l* him be your servant	Mt 20:27	
unto it, *L* no fruit grow on thee	Mt 21:19	
l it out to husbandmen, and went	Mt 21:33	1554
l us kill him, and *l* us seize on	Mt 21:38	
will *l* out his vineyard unto	Mt 21:41	1554
(whoso readeth, *l* him understand	Mt 24:15	
Then *l* them which be in Judaea	Mt 24:16	
L him which is on the housetop	Mt 24:17	
Neither *l* him which is in the	Mt 24:18	
possible, *l* this cup pass from me	Mt 26:39	
Rise, *l* us be going	Mt 26:46	
say unto him, *L* him be crucified	Mt 27:22	
more, saying, *L* him be crucified	Mt 27:23	
l him now come down from the	Mt 27:42	
l him deliver him now, if he will	Mt 27:43	
L be, *l* us see whether Elias	Mt 27:49	863
l us see whether Elias will come	Mt 27:49	
Saying, *L* us alone	Mk 1:24	1439
L us go into the next towns, that	Mk 1:38	
they *l* down the bed wherein the	Mk 2:4	5465
hath ears to hear, *l* him hear	Mk 4:9	
man have ears to hear, *l* him hear	Mk 4:23	
L us pass over unto the other	Mk 4:35	
or mother, *l* him die the death	Mk 7:10	
man have ears to hear, *l* him hear	Mk 7:16	
L the children first be filled	Mk 7:27	863
l him deny himself, and take up	Mk 8:34	
l us make three tabernacles	Mk 9:5	
together, *l* not man put asunder	Mk 10:9	
and they *l* them go	Mk 11:6	863
l it out to husbandmen, and went	Mk 12:1	1554
l us kill him, and the inheritance	Mk 12:7	
(*l* him that readeth understand,)	Mk 13:14	
then *l* them that be in Judaea	Mk 13:14	
l him that is on the housetop not	Mk 13:15	
l him that is in the field not	Mk 13:16	
And Jesus said, *L* her alone	Mk 14:6	863
Rise up, *l* us go	Mk 14:42	
L Christ the King of Israel	Mk 15:32	
him to drink, saying, *L* alone	Mk 15:36	863
l us see whether Elias will come	Mk 15:36	
L us now go even unto Bethlehem,	Lk 2:15	
l him impart to him that hath	Lk 3:11	
that hath meat, *l* him do likewise	Lk 3:11	
Saying, *L* us alone	Lk 4:34	1439
l down your nets for a draught	Lk 5:4	5465
at thy word I will *l* down the net	Lk 5:5	5465
l him down through the tiling	Lk 5:19	2524
l me pull out the mote that is in	Lk 6:42	863
hath ears to hear, *l* him hear	Lk 8:8	
L us go over unto the other side	Lk 8:22	
l him deny himself, and take up	Lk 9:23	
l us make three tabernacles	Lk 9:33	
L these sayings sink down into	Lk 9:44	
L the dead bury their dead	Lk 9:60	863
but *l* me first go bid them	Lk 9:61	2010
L your loins be girded about, and	Lk 12:35	
l it alone this year also, till I	Lk 13:8	863
him, and healed him, and *l* him go	Lk 14:4	
hath ears to hear, *l* him hear	Lk 14:35	
and *l* us eat, and be merry	Lk 15:23	
l them hear them	Lk 16:29	
l him not come down to take it	Lk 17:31	
l him likewise not return back	Lk 17:31	
l it forth to husbandmen, and went	Lk 20:9	1554
come, *l* us kill him, that the	Lk 20:14	
Then *l* them which are in Judaea	Lk 21:21	
l them which are in the midst of	Lk 21:21	
l not them that are in the	Lk 21:21	
you, *l* him be as the younger	Lk 22:26	
l him take it, and likewise his	Lk 22:36	
l him sell his garment, and buy	Lk 22:36	
will not answer me, nor *l* me go	Lk 22:68	630
chastise him, and *l* him go	Lk 23:22	
l him save himself, if he be	Lk 23:35	
l him come unto me, and drink	Jn 7:37	
l him first cast a stone at her	Jn 8:7	
L us go into Judaea again	Jn 11:7	
nevertheless *l* us go unto him	Jn 11:15	
L us also go, that we may die	Jn 11:16	
unto them, Loose him, and *l* him go	Jn 11:44	863
If we *l* him thus alone, all men	Jn 11:48	863
Then said Jesus, *L* her alone	Jn 12:7	863
any man serve me, *l* him follow me	Jn 12:26	
L not your heart be troubled	Jn 14:1	
L not your heart be troubled,	Jn 14:27	
neither *l* it be afraid	Jn 14:27	
Arise, *l* us go hence	Jn 14:31	
ye seek me, *l* these go their way	Jn 18:8	863
If thou *l* this man go, thou art	Jn 19:12	630
L us not rend it, but cast lots	Jn 19:24	
L his habitation be desolate	Acts 1:20	
and *l* no man dwell therein	Acts 1:20	
and his bishoprick *l* another take	Acts 1:20	
l me freely speak unto you of the	Acts 2:29	1832
Therefore *l* all the house of	Acts 2:36	
he was determined to *l* him go	Acts 3:13	630
l us straitly threaten them, that	Acts 4:17	
they *l* them go, finding nothing	Acts 4:21	
And being *l* go, they went to their	Acts 4:23	
from these men, and *l* them alone	Acts 5:38	1439
the name of Jesus, and *l* them go	Acts 5:40	630
l him down by the wall in a	Acts 9:25	
corners, and *l* down to the earth	Acts 10:11	
l down from heaven by four	Acts 11:5	
they were *l* go in peace from the	Acts 15:33	630
L us go again and visit our	Acts 15:36	
serjeants, saying, *L* those men go	Acts 16:35	630
magistrates have sent to *l* you go	Acts 16:36	630
but *l* them come themselves and	Acts 16:37	
and of the other, they *l* them go	Acts 17:9	630
l them implead one another	Acts 19:38	
l us not fight against God	Acts 23:9	
then *l* the young man depart	Acts 23:22	630
Or else *l* these same here say, if	Acts 24:20	
to *l* him have liberty, and that he	Acts 24:23	
L them therefore, said he, which	Acts 25:5	
up into the wind, we *l* her drive	Acts 27:15	1929
when they had *l* down the boat	Acts 27:30	5465
of the boat, and *l* her fall off	Acts 27:32	1439
examined me, would have *l* me go	Acts 28:18	630
unto you, (but was *l* hitherto	Rom 1:13	2967
l God be true, but every man a	Rom 3:4	
L us do evil, that good may come	Rom 3:8	
L not sin therefore reign in your	Rom 6:12	
L their table be made a snare, and	Rom 11:9	
L their eyes be darkened, that	Rom 11:10	
l us prophesy according to the	Rom 12:6	
l us wait on our ministering	Rom 12:7	
l him do it with simplicity	Rom 12:8	
L love be without dissimulation	Rom 12:9	
L every soul be subject unto the	Rom 13:1	
l us therefore cast off the works	Rom 13:12	
l us put on the armour of light	Rom 13:12	
L us walk honestly, as in the day	Rom 13:13	
L not him that eateth despise him	Rom 14:3	
l not him which eateth not judge	Rom 14:3	
L every man be fully persuaded in	Rom 14:5	
L us not therefore judge one	Rom 14:13	
L not then your good be evil	Rom 14:16	
L us therefore follow after the	Rom 14:19	
L every one of us please his	Rom 15:2	
glorieth, *l* him glory in the Lord	1Cor 1:31	
But *l* every man take heed how he	1Cor 3:10	
L no man deceive himself	1Cor 3:18	
l him become a fool, that he may	1Cor 3:18	
Therefore *l* no man glory in men	1Cor 3:21	
L a man so account of us, as of	1Cor 4:1	
Therefore *l* us keep the feast,	1Cor 5:8	
l every man have his own wife, and	1Cor 7:2	
l every woman have her own	1Cor 7:2	
L the husband render unto the	1Cor 7:3	
they cannot contain, *l* them marry	1Cor 7:9	
L not the wife depart from her	1Cor 7:10	
l her remain unmarried, or be	1Cor 7:11	
l not the husband put away his	1Cor 7:11	
with him, *l* him not put her away	1Cor 7:12	
with her, *l* her not leave him	1Cor 7:13	
unbelieving depart, *l* him depart	1Cor 7:15	
called every one, so *l* him walk	1Cor 7:17	
l him not become uncircumcised	1Cor 7:18	
l him not be circumcised	1Cor 7:18	
L every man abide in the same	1Cor 7:20	
l every man, wherein he is called	1Cor 7:24	
l him do what he will, he sinneth	1Cor 7:36	
l them marry	1Cor 7:36	
Neither *l* us commit fornication,	1Cor 10:8	
Neither *l* us tempt Christ, as	1Cor 10:9	
Wherefore *l* him that thinketh he	1Cor 10:12	
L no man seek his own, but every	1Cor 10:24	
not covered, *l* her also be shorn	1Cor 11:6	
shorn or shaven, *l* her be covered	1Cor 11:6	
But *l* a man examine himself, and	1Cor 11:28	
so *l* him eat of that bread, and	1Cor 11:28	
any man hunger, *l* him eat at home	1Cor 11:34	
Wherefore *l* him that speaketh in	1Cor 14:13	
L all things be done unto	1Cor 14:26	
l it be by two, or at the most by	1Cor 14:27	
and *l* one interpret	1Cor 14:27	
l him keep silence in the church	1Cor 14:28	
l him speak to himself, and to God	1Cor 14:28	
L the prophets speak two or three	1Cor 14:29	
or three, and *l* the other judge	1Cor 14:29	
l the first hold his peace	1Cor 14:30	
L your women keep silence in the	1Cor 14:34	
l them ask their husbands at home	1Cor 14:35	
l him acknowledge that the things	1Cor 14:37	
be ignorant, *l* him be ignorant	1Cor 14:38	
L all things be done decently and	1Cor 14:40	
l us eat and drink	1Cor 15:32	

l every one of you lay by him in 1Cor 16:2
L no man therefore despise him 1Cor 16:11
L all your things be done with 1Cor 16:14
l him be Anathema Maranatha 1Cor 16:22
l us cleanse ourselves from all 2Cor 7:1
in his heart, so l him give 2Cor 9:7
l him of himself think this again 2Cor 10:7
L such an one think this, that, 2Cor 10:11
glorieth, l him glory in the Lord 2Cor 10:17
again, L no man think me a fool 2Cor 11:16
a basket was I l down by the wall 2Cor 11:33 *5465*
unto you, l him be accursed Gal 1:8
have received, l him be accursed Gal 1:9
l us also walk in the Spirit Gal 5:25
L us not be desirous of vain Gal 5:26
But l every man prove his own Gal 6:4
L him that is taught in the word Gal 6:6
l us not be weary in well doing Gal 6:9
l us do good unto all men, Gal 6:10
From henceforth l no man trouble Gal 6:17
l not the sun go down upon your Eph 4:26
L him that stole steal no more Eph 4:28
but rather l him labour, working Eph 4:28
L no corrupt communication Eph 4:29
L all bitterness, and wrath, and Eph 4:31
l it not be once named among you, Eph 5:3
L no man deceive you with vain Eph 5:6
so l the wives be to their own Eph 5:24
Nevertheless l every one of you Eph 5:33
Only l your conversation be as it Phil 1:27
L nothing be done through strife Phil 2:3
but in lowliness of mind l each Phil 2:3
L this mind be in you, which was Phil 2:5
L us therefore, as many as be Phil 3:15
l us walk by the same rule Phil 3:16
l us mind the same thing Phil 3:16
L your moderation be known unto Phil 4:5
l your requests be made known Phil 4:6
L no man therefore judge you in Col 2:16
L no man beguile you of your Col 2:18
l the peace of God rule in your Col 3:15
L the word of Christ dwell in you Col 3:16
L your speech be alway with grace Col 4:6
Therefore l us not sleep, as do 1Th 5:6
but l us watch and be sober 1Th 5:6
But l us, who are of the day, be 1Th 5:8
L no man deceive you by any means 2Th 2:3
only he who now letteth will l 2Th 2:7 *2722*
L the woman learn in silence with 1Ti 2:11
l these also first be proved 1Ti 3:10
then l them use the office of a 1Ti 3:10
L the deacons be the husbands of 1Ti 3:12
L no man despise thy youth 1Ti 4:12
l them learn first to shew piety 1Ti 5:4
L not a widow be taken into the 1Ti 5:9
l them relieve them 1Ti 5:16
l not the church be charged 1Ti 5:16
L the elders that rule well be 1Ti 5:17
L as many servants as are under 1Ti 6:1
l them not despise them, because 1Ti 6:2
raiment l us be therewith content 1Ti 6:8
L every one that nameth the name 2Ti 2:19
L no man despise thee Titus 2:15
l ours also learn to maintain Titus 3:14
l me have joy of thee in the Lord Philem 20
l all the angels of God worship Heb 1:6
at any time we should l them slip Heb 2:1
L us therefore fear, lest, a Heb 4:1
L us labour therefore to enter Heb 4:11
l us hold fast our profession Heb 4:14
L us therefore come boldly unto Heb 4:16
l us go on unto perfection Heb 6:1
L us draw near with a true heart Heb 10:22
L us hold fast the profession of Heb 10:23
l us consider one another to Heb 10:24
l us lay aside every weight, and Heb 12:1
l us run with patience the race Heb 12:1
but l it rather be healed Heb 12:13
l us have grace, whereby we may Heb 12:28
L brotherly love continue Heb 13:1
L your conversation be without Heb 13:5
L us go forth therefore unto him Heb 13:13
By him therefore l us offer the Heb 13:15
But l patience have her perfect Jas 1:4
l him ask of God, that giveth to Jas 1:5
But l him ask in faith, nothing Jas 1:6
For l not that man think that he Jas 1:7
L the brother of low degree Jas 1:9
L no man say when he is tempted, Jas 1:13
l every man be swift to hear, Jas 1:19
l him shew out of a good Jas 3:13
l your laughter be turned to Jas 4:9
but l your yea be yea Jas 5:12
l him pray Jas 5:13
l him sing psalms Jas 5:13
l him call for the elders of the Jas 5:14
l them pray over him, anointing Jas 5:14
L him know, that he which Jas 5:20
Whose adorning l it not be that 1Pet 3:3
But l it be the hidden man of the 1Pet 3:4
l him refrain his tongue from 1Pet 3:10
L him eschew evil, and do good 1Pet 3:11
l him seek peace, and ensue it 1Pet 3:11
l him speak as the oracles of God 1Pet 4:11
l him do it as of the ability 1Pet 4:11
But l none of you suffer as a 1Pet 4:15
a Christian, l him not be ashamed 1Pet 4:16
but l him glorify God on this 1Pet 4:16
Wherefore l them that suffer 1Pet 4:19
L that therefore abide in you, 1Jn 2:24
children, l no man deceive you 1Jn 3:7
l us not love in word, neither in 1Jn 3:18
Beloved, l us love one another 1Jn 4:7
l him hear what the Spirit saith Rev 2:7
l him hear what the Spirit saith Rev 2:11
l him hear what the Spirit saith Rev 2:17
l him hear what the Spirit saith Rev 2:29
l him hear what the Spirit saith Rev 3:6
l him hear what the Spirit saith Rev 3:13
l him hear what the Spirit saith Rev 3:22
any man have an ear, l him hear Rev 13:9
L him that hath understanding Rev 13:18
L us be glad and rejoice, and give Rev 19:7
is unjust, l him be unjust still Rev 22:11
is filthy, l him be filthy still Rev 22:11
l him be righteous still Rev 22:11
that is holy, l him be holy still Rev 22:11
l him that heareth say, Come Rev 22:17
l him that is athirst come Rev 22:17
l him take the water of life Rev 22:17

LETHEK See HOMER.

LETTER
that David wrote a l to Joab 2Sa 11:14 5612
And he wrote in the l, saying, Set 2Sa 11:15 5612
I will send a l unto the king of 2Kin 5:5 5612
he brought the l to the king of 2Kin 5:6 5612
Now when this l is come unto thee 2Kin 5:6 5612
the king of Israel had read the l 2Kin 5:7 5612
as soon as this l cometh to you 2Kin 10:2 5612
Then he wrote a l the second time 2Kin 10:6 5612
when the l came to them, that 2Kin 10:7 5612
Hezekiah received the l of the 2Kin 19:14 5612
the writing of the l was written Ezr 4:7 5406
Shimshai the scribe wrote a l Ezr 4:8 104
of the l that they sent unto him Ezr 4:11 104
The l which ye sent unto us hath Ezr 4:18 5407
l was read before Rehum, and Ezr 4:23 5407
by l concerning this matter Ezr 5:5 5407
The copy of the l that Tatnai Ezr 5:6 104
They sent a l unto him, wherein Ezr 5:7 6600
Now this is the copy of the l Ezr 7:11 5406
a l unto Asaph the keeper of the Neh 2:8 107
time with an open l in his hand Neh 6:5 107
for all the words of this l Est 9:26 107
to confirm this second l of Purim Est 9:29 107
Hezekiah received the l from the Is 37:14 5612
l that Jeremiah the prophet sent Jer 29:1 5612
l in the ears of Jeremiah the Jer 29:29 5612
he wrote a l after this manner Acts 23:25 *1992*
when the governor had read the l Acts 23:34
the law, judge thee, who by the l Rom 2:27 *1121*
in the spirit, and not in the l Rom 2:29 *1121*
and not in the oldness of the l Rom 7:6 *1121*
not of the l, but of the spirit 2Cor 3:6 *1121*
for the l killeth, but the spirit 2Cor 3:6 *1121*
though I made you sorry with a l 2Cor 7:8 *1992*
Ye see how large a l I have Gal 6:11 *1121*
nor by l as from us, as that the 2Th 2:2 *1992*
for I have written a l unto you Heb 13:22 *1989*

LETTERS
So she wrote l in Ahab's name, and 1Kin 21:8 5612
sent the l unto the elders and to 1Kin 21:8 5612
And she wrote in the l, saying, 1Kin 21:9 5612
as it was written in the l which 1Kin 21:11 5612
And Jehu wrote l, and sent to 2Kin 10:1 5612
Baladan, king of Babylon, sent l 2Kin 20:12 5612
wrote l also to Ephraim and 2Chr 30:1 107
went with the l from the king 2Chr 30:6 107
He wrote also l to rail on the 2Chr 32:17 5612
king, let l be given me to the Neh 2:7 107
river, and gave them the king's l Neh 2:9 107
of Judah sent many l unto Tobiah Neh 6:17 107
the l of Tobiah came unto them Neh 6:17
Tobiah sent l to put me in fear Neh 6:19 107
For he sent l into all the king's Est 1:22 5612
the l were sent by posts into all Est 3:13 5612
the l devised by Haman the son of Est 8:5 5612
sent l by posts on horseback, and Est 8:10 5612
sent l unto all the Jews that Est 9:20 5612
he commanded by l that his wicked Est 9:25 5612
he sent the l unto all the Jews, Est 9:30 5612
Baladan, king of Babylon, sent l Is 39:1 5612
Because thou hast sent l in thy Jer 29:25 5612
written over him in l of Greek Lk 23:38 *1121*
saying, How knoweth this man l Jn 7:15 *1121*
desired of him l to Damascus to Acts 9:2 *1992*
they wrote l by them after this Acts 15:23
I received l unto the brethren Acts 22:5 *1992*
We neither received l out of Acts 28:21 *1121*
ye shall approve by your l 1Cor 16:3 *1992*
or l of commendation from you 2Cor 3:1
as if I would terrify you by l 2Cor 10:9 *1992*
For his l, say they, are weighty 2Cor 10:10 *1992*
in word by l when we are absent 2Cor 10:11 *1992*

LETTEST
l such words go out of thy mouth Job 15:13
with a cord which thou l down Job 41:1 8257
now l thou thy servant depart in Lk 2:29 *630*

LETTETH
hands escape, he that l him go 2Kin 10:24
strife is as when one l out water Prov 17:14 6362
only he who now l will let 2Th 2:7 *2722*

LETTING
deceitfully any more in not l the Ex 8:29

LETUSHIM (*le-tu'-shim*) *A son of Dedan.*
sons of Dedan were Asshurim, and L Gen 25:3 3912

LETUSHITES See LETUSHIM.

LEUMMIM (*le-um'-mim*) *A son of Dedan.*
were Asshurim, and Letushim, and L Gen 25:3 3817

LEVI (*le'-vi*) See LEVITE, LEVITICAL, MATTHEW.
1. A son of Jacob.
therefore was his name called L Gen 29:34 3878
of the sons of Jacob, Simeon and L Gen 34:25 3878
And Jacob said to Simeon and L Gen 34:30 3878
firstborn, and Simeon, and L Gen 35:23 3878
Simeon and L are brethren Gen 49:5 3878
Reuben, Simeon, L, and Judah, Ex 1:2 3878
are the names of the sons of L Ex 6:16 3878
life of L were an hundred thirty Ex 6:16 3878
were the sons of L by their names Num 3:17 3878
the son of Kohath, the son of L Num 16:1 3878
was Jochebed, the daughter of L Num 26:59 3878
her mother bare to L in Egypt Num 26:59 3878
the son of Kohath, the son of L 1Chr 6:38 3878
the son of Gershom, the son of L 1Chr 6:43 3878
the son of Merari, the son of L 1Chr 6:47 3878
the sons of Mahli, the son of L Ezr 8:18 3878
2. The tribe.
And the sons of L Gen 46:11 3878
went a man of the house of L Ex 2:1 3878
and took to wife a daughter of L Ex 2:1 3878
these are the families of L Ex 6:19 3878
all the sons of L gathered Ex 32:26 3878
the children of L did according Ex 32:28 3878
shalt not number the tribe of L Num 1:49 3878
Bring the tribe of L near Num 3:6 3878
Number the children of L after Num 3:15 3878
Kohath from among the sons of L Num 4:2 3878
too much upon you, ye sons of L Num 16:7 3878
Hear, I pray you, ye sons of L Num 16:8 3878
brethren the sons of L with thee Num 16:10 3878
Aaron's name upon the rod of L Num 17:3 3878
for the house of L was budded Num 17:8 3878
brethren also of the tribe of L Num 18:2 3878
I have given the children of L Num 18:21 3878
the LORD separated the tribe of L Deut 10:8 3878
Wherefore L hath no part nor Deut 10:9 3878
Levites, and all the tribe of L Deut 18:1 3878
the sons of L shall come near Deut 21:5 3878
Simeon, and L, and Judah, and Deut 27:12 3878
it unto the priests the sons of L Deut 31:9 3878
of L he said, Let thy Thummim and Deut 33:8 3878
Only unto the tribe of L he gave Josh 13:14 3878
But unto the tribe of L Moses Josh 13:33 3878
who were of the children of L Josh 21:10 3878
which were not of the sons of L 1Kin 12:31 3878
Reuben, Simeon, L, and Judah, 1Chr 2:1 3878
The sons of L; Gershon 1Chr 6:1 3878
The sons of L; Gershom 1Chr 6:16 3878
companies of the children of L 1Chr 9:18 3878
the children of L four thousand 1Chr 12:26 3878
But L and Benjamin counted he not 1Chr 21:6 3878
into courses among the sons of L 1Chr 23:6 3878
sons were named of the tribe of L 1Chr 23:14 3878
These were the sons of L after 1Chr 23:24 3878
rest of the sons of L were these 1Chr 24:20 3878
found there none of the sons of L Ezr 8:15 3878
the children of L shall bring the Neh 10:39 3878
The sons of L, the chief of the Neh 12:23 3878
Bless the LORD, O house of L Ps 135:20 3878
sons of Zadok among the sons of L Eze 40:46 3878
one gate of Judah, one gate of L Eze 48:31 3878
family of the house of L apart Zec 12:13 3878
that my covenant might be with L Mal 2:4 3878
have corrupted the covenant of L Mal 2:8 3878
and he shall purify the sons of L Mal 3:3 3878
they that are of the sons of L Heb 7:5 *3017*
L also, who receiveth tithes, Heb 7:9 *3017*
Of the tribe of L were sealed Rev 7:7 *3017*
3. Same as Matthew the apostle.
he saw L the son of Alphaeus Mk 2:14 *3018*
forth, and saw a publican, named L Lk 5:27 *3018*
L made him a great feast in his Lk 5:29 *3018*
4. Father of Matthat; ancestor of Jesus.
Matthat, which was the son of L Lk 3:24 *3017*
5. Father of another Matthat; ancestor of Jesus.
Matthat, which was the son of L Lk 3:29 *3017*

LEVIATHAN
thou draw out l with an hook Job 41:1 3882
brakest the heads of l in pieces Ps 74:14 3882
there is that l, whom thou hast Ps 104:26 3882
punish l the piercing serpent Is 27:1 3882
even l that crooked serpent Is 27:1 3882

LEVITE (*le'-vite*) See LEVITES, LEVITICAL. *A descendant of Levi.*
Is not Aaron the L thy brother Ex 4:14 3881
the L that is within your gates Deut 12:12 3881
the L that is within thy gates Deut 12:18 3881
that thou forsake not the L as Deut 12:19 3881
the L that is within thy gates Deut 14:27 3881
And the L, (because he hath no Deut 14:29 3881
the L that is within thy gates, Deut 16:11 3881
and thy maidservant, and the L Deut 16:14 3881
if a L come from any of thy gates Deut 18:6 3881
unto thine house, thou, and the L Deut 26:11 3881
and hast given it unto the L Deut 26:12 3881
also have given them unto the L Deut 26:13 3881
the family of Judah, who was a L Judg 17:7 3881
I am a L of Beth-lehem-judah, and Judg 17:9 3881
So the L went in Judg 17:10 3881
the L was content to dwell with Judg 17:11 3881
And Micah consecrated the L Judg 17:12 3881
seeing I have a L to my priest Judg 17:13 3881
the voice of the young man the L Judg 18:3 3881
the house of the young man the L Judg 18:15 3881
that there was a certain L Judg 19:1 3881
And the L, the husband of the Judg 20:4 3881
a L of the sons of Asaph, came 2Chr 20:14 3881
which Cononiah the L was ruler 2Chr 31:12 3881
And Kore the son of Imnah the L 2Chr 31:14 3881
and Shabbethai the L helped them Ezr 10:15 3881
And likewise a L, when he was at Lk 10:32 *3019*
The son of consolation,) a L Acts 4:36 *3019*

LEVITES
the *L* according to their families Ex 6:25 3881
Moses, for the service of the *L* Ex 38:21 3881
the cities of the *L*, and the Lev 25:32 3881
may the *L* redeem at any time Lev 25:32 3881
And if a man purchase of the *L* Lev 25:33 3881
L are their possession among the Lev 25:33 3881
But the *L* after the tribe of Num 1:47 3881
the *L* over the tabernacle of Num 1:50 3881
forward, the *L* shall take it down Num 1:51 3881
be pitched, the *L* shall set it up Num 1:51 3881
But the *L* shall pitch round about Num 1:53 3881
the *L* shall keep the charge of Num 1:53 3881
of the *L* in the midst of the camp Num 2:17 3881
But the *L* were not numbered among Num 2:33 3881
thou shalt give the *L* unto Aaron Num 3:9 3881
I have taken the *L* from among the Num 3:12 3881
therefore the *L* shall be mine Num 3:12 3881
These are the families of the *L* Num 3:20 3881
be chief over the chief of the *L* Num 3:32 3881
All that were numbered of the *L* Num 3:39 3881
thou shalt take the *L* for me (I Num 3:41 3881
the cattle of the *L* instead of Num 3:41 3881
Take the *L* instead of all the Num 3:45 3881
the cattle of the *L* instead of Num 3:45 3881
and the *L* shall be mine Num 3:45 3881
Israel, which are more than the *L* Num 3:46 3881
them that were redeemed by the *L* Num 3:49 3881
the Kohathites from among the *L* Num 4:18 3881
those that were numbered of the *L* Num 4:46 3881
thou shalt give them unto the *L* Num 7:5 3881
the oxen, and gave them unto the *L* Num 7:6 3881
Take the *L* from among the Num 8:6 3881
thou shalt bring the *L* before the Num 8:9 3881
shalt bring the *L* before the LORD Num 8:10 3881
shall put their hands upon the *L* Num 8:10 3881
Aaron shall offer the *L* before Num 8:11 3881
the *L* shall lay their hands upon Num 8:12 3881
to make an atonement for the *L* Num 8:12 3881
thou shalt set the *L* before Aaron Num 8:13 3881
the *L* from among the children of Num 8:14 3881
and the *L* shall be mine Num 8:14 3881
after that shall the *L* go in to Num 8:15 3881
I have taken the *L* for all the Num 8:18 3881
I have given the *L* as a gift to Num 8:19 3881
did to the *L* according unto all Num 8:20 3881
commanded Moses concerning the *L* Num 8:20 3881
the *L* were purified, and they Num 8:21 3881
after that went the *L* in to do Num 8:22 3881
commanded Moses concerning the *L* Num 8:22 3881
is it that belongeth unto the *L* Num 8:24 3881
unto the *L* touching their charge Num 8:26 3881
the *L* from among the children of Num 18:6 3881
But the *L* shall do the service of Num 18:23 3881
I have given to the *L* to inherit Num 18:24 3881
Thus speak unto the *L*, and say Num 18:26 3881
unto the *L* as the increase of the Num 18:30 3881
of the *L* after their families Num 26:57 3881
These are the families of the *L* Num 26:58 3881
beasts, and give them unto the *L* Num 31:30 3881
of beast, and gave them unto the *L* Num 31:47 3881
that they give unto the *L* of the Num 35:2 3881
ye shall give also unto the *L* Num 35:2 3881
which ye shall give unto the *L* Num 35:4 3881
which ye shall give unto the *L* Num 35:6 3881
give to the *L* shall be forty Num 35:7 3881
give of his cities unto the *L* Num 35:8 3881
shalt come unto the priests the *L* Deut 17:9 3881
which is before the priests the *L* Deut 17:18 3881
The priests the *L*, and all the Deut 18:1 3881
God, as all his brethren the *L* do Deut 18:7 3881
the priests the *L* shall teach you Deut 24:8 3881
the priests the *L* spake unto all Deut 27:9 3881
the *L* shall speak, and say unto Deut 27:14 3881
That Moses commanded the *L* Deut 31:25 3881
and the priests the *L* bearing it Josh 3:3 3881
side before the priests the *L* Josh 8:33 3881
but unto the *L* he gave none Josh 14:3 3881
no part unto the *L* in the land Josh 14:4 3881
But the *L* have no part among you Josh 18:7 3881
of the *L* unto Eleazar the priest Josh 21:1 3881
of Israel gave unto the *L* out of Josh 21:3 3881
the priest, which were of the *L* Josh 21:4 3881
of Israel gave by lot unto the *L* Josh 21:8 3881
the *L* which remained of the Josh 21:20 3881
Gershon, of the families of the *L* Josh 21:27 3881
of Merari, the rest of the *L* Josh 21:34 3881
of the families of the *L*, were by Josh 21:40 3881
All the cities of the *L* within Josh 21:41 3881
the *L* took down the ark of the 1Sa 6:15 3881
all the *L* were with him, bearing 2Sa 15:24 3881
did the priests and the *L* bring up 1Kin 8:4 3881
the *L* according to their fathers 1Chr 6:19 3881
Their brethren also the *L* were 1Chr 6:48 3881
children of Israel gave to the *L* 1Chr 6:64 3881
the Israelites, the priests, *L* 1Chr 9:2 3881
And of the *L* 1Chr 9:14 3881
For these *L*, the four chief 1Chr 9:26 3881
And Mattithiah, one of the *L* 1Chr 9:31 3881
chief of the fathers of the *L* 1Chr 9:33 3881
These chief fathers of the *L* were 1Chr 9:34 3881
L which are in their cities and 1Chr 13:2 3881
to carry the ark of God but the *L* 1Chr 15:2 3881
the children of Aaron, and the *L* 1Chr 15:4 3881
the priests, and for the *L* 1Chr 15:11 3881
the chief of the fathers of the *L* 1Chr 15:12 3881
the *L* sanctified themselves to 1Chr 15:14 3881
the children of the *L* bare the 1Chr 15:15 3881
L to appoint their brethren to be 1Chr 15:16 3881
So the *L* appointed Heman the son 1Chr 15:17 3881
And Chenaniah, chief of the *L* 1Chr 15:22 3881
when God helped the *L* that bare 1Chr 15:26 3881
all the *L* that bare the ark, and 1Chr 15:27 3881
he appointed certain of the *L* to 1Chr 16:4 3881
Israel, with the priests and the *L* 1Chr 23:2 3881
Now the *L* were numbered from the 1Chr 23:3 3881
And also unto the *L* 1Chr 23:26 3881
by the last words of David the *L* 1Chr 23:27 3881
the scribe, one of the *L*, wrote 1Chr 24:6 3878
the fathers of the priests and *L* 1Chr 24:6 3881
of the *L* after the house of their 1Chr 24:30 3881
the fathers of the priests and *L* 1Chr 24:31 3881
Eastward were six *L*, northward 1Chr 26:17 3881
And of the *L*, Ahijah was over the 1Chr 26:20 3881
Of the *L*, Hashabiah the son of 1Chr 27:17 3881
courses of the priests and the *L* 1Chr 28:13 3881
courses of the priests and the *L* 1Chr 28:21 3881
and the *L* took up the ark 2Chr 5:4 3881
did the priests and the *L* bring up 2Chr 5:5 3881
Also the *L* which were the singers 2Chr 5:12 3881
the *L* also with instruments of 2Chr 7:6 3881
the *L* to their charges, to praise 2Chr 8:14 3881
L concerning any matter, or 2Chr 8:15 3881
the *L* that were in all Israel 2Chr 11:13 3881
For the *L* left their suburbs and 2Chr 11:14 3881
LORD, the sons of Aaron, and the *L* 2Chr 13:9 3881
the *L* wait upon their business 2Chr 13:10 3881
And with them he sent *L*, even 2Chr 17:8 3881
and Tobijah, and Tob-adonijah, *L* 2Chr 17:8 3881
did Jehoshaphat set of the *L* 2Chr 19:8 3881
also the *L* shall be officers 2Chr 19:11 3881
And the *L*, of the children of the 2Chr 20:19 3881
gathered the *L* out of all the 2Chr 23:2 3881
of the priests and of the *L* 2Chr 23:4 3881
and they that minister of the *L* 2Chr 23:6 3881
the *L* shall compass the king 2Chr 23:7 3881
So the *L* and all Judah did 2Chr 23:8 3881
by the hand of the priests the *L* 2Chr 23:18 3881
together the priests and the *L* 2Chr 24:5 3881
Howbeit the *L* hastened it not 2Chr 24:5 3881
of the *L* to bring in out of Judah 2Chr 24:6 3881
office by the hand of the *L* 2Chr 24:11 3881
brought in the priests and the *L* 2Chr 29:4 3881
And said unto them, Hear me, ye *L* 2Chr 29:5 3881
Then the *L* arose, Mahath the son 2Chr 29:12 3881
the *L* took it, to carry it out 2Chr 29:16 3881
he set the *L* in the house of the 2Chr 29:25 3881
the *L* stood with the instruments 2Chr 29:26 3881
the princes commanded the *L* to 2Chr 29:30 3881
brethren the *L* did help them 2Chr 29:34 3881
for the *L* were more upright in 2Chr 29:34 3881
the *L* were ashamed, and sanctified 2Chr 30:15 3881
received of the hand of the *L* 2Chr 30:16 3881
therefore the *L* had the charge of 2Chr 30:17 3881
and the *L* and the priests praised 2Chr 30:21 3881
L that taught the good knowledge 2Chr 30:22 3881
Judah, with the priests and the *L* 2Chr 30:25 3881
Then the priests the *L* arose 2Chr 30:27 3881
the *L* after their courses, every 2Chr 31:2 3881
L for burnt offerings and for 2Chr 31:2 3881
portion of the priests and the *L* 2Chr 31:4 3881
the *L* concerning the heaps 2Chr 31:9 3881
the *L* from twenty years old and 2Chr 31:17 3881
by genealogies among the *L* 2Chr 31:19 3881
which the *L* that kept the doors 2Chr 34:9 3881
were Jahath and Obadiah, the *L* 2Chr 34:12 3881
and other of the *L*, all that could 2Chr 34:12 3881
of the *L* there were scribes, and 2Chr 34:13 3881
and the priests, and the *L* 2Chr 34:30 3881
said unto the *L* that taught all 2Chr 35:3 3881
division of the families of the *L* 2Chr 35:5 3881
to the priests, and to the *L* 2Chr 35:8 3881
Jeiel and Jozabad, chief of the *L* 2Chr 35:9 3881
gave unto the *L* for passover 2Chr 35:9 3881
the *L* in their courses, according 2Chr 35:10 3881
their hands, and the *L* flayed them 2Chr 35:11 3881
therefore the *L* prepared for 2Chr 35:14 3881
brethren the *L* prepared for them 2Chr 35:15 3881
kept, and the priests, and the *L* 2Chr 35:18 3881
and the priests, and the *L* Ezr 1:5 3881
The *L*: the children Ezr 2:40 3881
So the priests, and the *L*, and some Ezr 2:70 3881
brethren the priests and the *L* Ezr 3:8 3881
and appointed the *L*, from twenty Ezr 3:8 3881
sons and their brethren the *L* Ezr 3:9 3881
the *L* the sons of Asaph with Ezr 3:10 3881
But many of the priests and *L* Ezr 3:12 3881
of Israel, the priests, and the *L* Ezr 6:16 3879
the *L* in their courses, for the Ezr 6:18 3879
the *L* were purified together, all Ezr 6:20 3881
and of the priests, and the *L* Ezr 7:7 3881
of Israel, and of his priests and *L* Ezr 7:13 3879
touching any of the priests and *L* Ezr 7:24 3879
for the service of the *L*, two Ezr 8:20 3881
the chief of the priests and the *L* Ezr 8:29 3881
the *L* the weight of the silver Ezr 8:30 3881
and Noadiah the son of Binnui, *L* Ezr 8:33 3881
Israel, and the priests, and the *L* Ezr 9:1 3881
and made the chief priests, the *L* Ezr 10:5 3881
Also of the *L* Ezr 10:23 3881
After him repaired the *L*, Rehum Neh 3:17 3881
singers and the *L* were appointed Neh 7:1 3881
The *L*: the children Neh 7:43 3881
So the priests, and the *L*, and the Neh 7:73 3881
Jozabad, Hanan, Pelaiah, and the *L* Neh 8:7 3881
the *L* that taught the people Neh 8:9 3881
So the *L* stilled all the people Neh 8:11 3881
the people, the priests, and the *L* Neh 8:13 3881
up upon the stairs, of the *L* Neh 9:4 3881
Then the *L*, Jeshua, and Kadmiel Neh 9:5 3881
and our princes, *L*, and priests Neh 9:38 3881
And the *L*: both Jeshua Neh 10:9 3881
of the people, the priests, the *L* Neh 10:28 3881
the lots among the priests, the *L* Neh 10:34 3881
tithes of our ground unto the *L* Neh 10:37 3881
that the same *L* might have the Neh 10:37 3881
son of Aaron shall be with the *L* Neh 10:38 3881
when the *L* take tithes Neh 10:38 3881
the *L* shall bring up the tithe of Neh 10:38 3881
Israel, the priests, and the *L* Neh 11:3 3881
Also of the *L* Neh 11:15 3881
and Jozabad, of the chief of the *L* Neh 11:16 3881
All the *L* in the holy city were Neh 11:18 3881
Israel, of the priests, and the *L* Neh 11:20 3881
The overseer also of the *L* at Neh 11:22 3881
of the *L* were divisions in Judah Neh 11:36 3881
and the *L* that went up with Neh 12:1 3881
Moreover the *L*: Jeshua Neh 12:8 3881
The *L* in the days of Eliashib Neh 12:22 3881
And the chief of the *L* Neh 12:24 3881
the *L* out of all their places Neh 12:27 3881
the *L* purified themselves, and Neh 12:30 3881
of the law for the priests and *L* Neh 12:44 3881
priests and for the *L* that waited Neh 12:44 3881
sanctified holy things unto the *L* Neh 12:47 3881
the *L* sanctified them unto the Neh 12:47 3881
commanded to be given to the *L* Neh 13:5 3881
of the *L* had not been given them Neh 13:10 3881
for the *L* and the singers, that Neh 13:10 3881
and Zadok the scribe, and of the *L* Neh 13:13 3881
I commanded the *L* that they Neh 13:22 3881
of the priesthood, and of the *L* Neh 13:29 3881
the wards of the priests and the *L* Neh 13:30 3881
take of them for priests and for *L* Is 66:21 3881
L want a man before me to offer Jer 33:18 3881
with the *L* the priests, my Jer 33:21 3881
the *L* that minister unto me Jer 33:22 3881
L that be of the seed of Zadok Eze 43:19 3881
the *L* that are gone away far from Eze 44:10 3881
But the priests the *L*, the sons Eze 44:15 3881
of breadth, shall also the *L* Eze 45:5 3881
went astray, as the *L* went astray Eze 48:11 3881
most holy by the border of the *L* Eze 48:12 3881
the priests the *L* shall have five Eze 48:13 3881
from the possession of the *L* Eze 48:22 3881
L from Jerusalem to ask him, Who Jn 1:19 *3019*

LEVITICAL (*le-vit'-i-cal*) *Belonging to the Levites.*
were by the *L* priesthood, (for Heb 7:11 *3020*

LEVY
l a tribute unto the LORD of the Num 31:28 7311
raised a *l* of all Israel 1Kin 5:13 4522
the *l* was thirty thousand men 1Kin 5:13 4522
and Adoniram was over the *l* 1Kin 5:14 4522
the *l* which king Solomon raised 1Kin 9:15 4522
upon those did Solomon *l* a 1Kin 9:21 5927

LEWD
which are ashamed of thy *l* way Eze 16:27 2154
and unto Aholibah, the *l* women Eze 23:44 2154
took unto them certain *l* fellows Acts 17:5 *4190*

LEWDLY
another hath *l* defiled his Eze 22:11 2154

LEWDNESS
for they have committed *l* Judg 20:6 2154
she hath wrought *l* with many Jer 11:15 4209
the *l* of thy whoredom, and thine Jer 13:27 2154
thou shalt not commit this *l* Eze 16:43 2154
Thou hast borne thy *l* and thine Eze 16:58 2154
the midst of thee they commit *l* Eze 22:9 2154
to remembrance the *l* of thy youth Eze 23:21 2154
I make thy *l* to cease from thee Eze 23:27 2154
shall be discovered, both thy *l* Eze 23:29 2154
therefore bear thou also thy *l* Eze 23:35 2154
Thus will I cause *l* to cease out Eze 23:48 2154
be taught not to do after your *l* Eze 23:48 2154
shall recompense your *l* upon you Eze 23:49 2154
In thy filthiness is *l* Eze 24:13 2154
now will I discover her *l* in the Hos 2:10 5040
for they commit *l* Hos 6:9 2154
a matter of wrong or wicked *l* Acts 18:14 *4467*

LIAR
not so now, who will make me a *l* Job 24:25 3576
a *l* giveth ear to a naughty Prov 17:4 8267
and a poor man is better than a *l* Prov 19:22 3576
thee, and thou be found a *l* Prov 30:6 3576
thou be altogether unto me as a *l* Jer 15:18 391
for he is a *l*, and the father of Jn 8:44 *5583*
I shall be a *l* like unto you Jn 8:55 *5583*
God be true, but every man a *l* Rom 3:4 *5583*
have not sinned, we make him a *l* 1Jn 1:10 *5583*
not his commandments, is a *l* 1Jn 2:4 *5583*
Who is a *l* but he that denieth 1Jn 2:22 *5583*
and hateth his brother, he is a *l* 1Jn 4:20 *5583*
not God hath made him a *l* 1Jn 5:10 *5583*

LIARS
shall be found *l* unto thee Deut 33:29 3584
I said in my haste, All men are *l* Ps 116:11 3576
frustrateth the tokens of the *l* Is 44:25 907
A sword is upon the *l* Jer 50:36 907
mankind, for menstealers, for *l* 1Ti 1:10 *5583*
said, The Cretians are alway *l* Titus 1:12 *5583*
and are not, and hast found them *l* Rev 2:2 *5571*
sorcerers, and idolaters, and all *l* Rev 21:8 *5571*

LIBERAL
The *l* soul shall be made fat Prov 11:25 1293
person shall be no more called *l* Is 32:5 5081
But the *l* deviseth *l* things Is 32:8 5081
by *l* things shall he stand Is 32:8 5081
for your *l* distribution unto them 2Cor 9:13 *572*

LIBERALITY
to bring your *l* unto Jerusalem 1Cor 16:3 *5485*
unto the riches of their *l* 2Cor 8:2 *572*

LIBERALLY
furnish him *l* out of thy flock Deut 15:14 6059
of God, that giveth to all men *l* Jas 1:5 *574*

L

LIBERTINES (*lib'-ur-tins*) *Former Jewish slaves.*
is called the synagogue of the *L* Acts 6:9 *3032*

LIBERTY
proclaim *l* throughout all the Lev 25:10 1865
And I will walk at *l* Ps 119:45 7342
to proclaim *l* to the captives, and Is 61:1 1865
to proclaim *l* unto them Jer 34:8 1865
in proclaiming *l* every man to his Jer 34:15 1865
he had set at *l* at their pleasure Jer 34:16 2670
unto me, in proclaiming *l* Jer 34:17 1865
behold, I proclaim a *l* for you Jer 34:17 1865
it shall be his to the year of *l* Eze 46:17 1865
to set at *l* them that are bruised Lk 4:18 *859*
keep Paul, and to let him have *l* Acts 24:23 *425*
This man might have been set at *l* Acts 26:32 *630*
gave him *l* to go unto his friends Acts 27:3 *2010*
glorious *l* of the children of God Rom 8:21 *1657*
she is at *l* to be married to whom 1Cor 7:39 *1658*
means this *l* of yours become a 1Cor 8:9 *1849*
for why is my *l* judged of another 1Cor 10:29 *1657*
Spirit of the Lord is, there is *l* 2Cor 3:17 *1657*
l which we have in Christ Jesus Gal 2:4 *1657*
Stand fast therefore in the *l* Gal 5:1 *1657*
ye have been called unto *l* Gal 5:13 *1657*
only use not *l* for an occasion to Gal 5:13 *1657*
our brother Timothy is set at *l* Heb 13:23 *630*
looketh into the perfect law of *l* Jas 1:25 *1657*
shall be judged by the law of *l* Jas 2:12 *1657*
not using your *l* for a cloke of 1Pet 2:16 *1657*
While they promise them *l* 2Pet 2:19 *1657*

LIBNAH (*lib'-nah*) See LABAN.
1. A Hebrew encampment in the wilderness.
Rimmon-parez, and pitched in *L* Num 33:20 3841
And they removed from *L*, and Num 33:21 3841
2. A Levitical city in Judah.
and all Israel with him, unto *L* Josh 10:29 3841
unto Libnah, and fought against *L* Josh 10:29 3841
And Joshua passed from *L*, and all Josh 10:31 3841
to all that he had done to *L* Josh 10:32 3841
as he had done also to *L*, and to Josh 10:39 3841
The king of *L*, one Josh 12:15 3841
L, and Ether, and Ashan, Josh 15:42 3841
and *L* with her suburbs, Josh 21:13 3841
Then *L* revolted at the same time 2Kin 8:22 3841
king of Assyria warring against *L* 2Kin 19:8 3841
the daughter of Jeremiah of *L* 2Kin 23:31 3841
the daughter of Jeremiah of *L* 2Kin 24:18 3841
L with her suburbs, and Jattir, and 1Chr 6:57 3841
The same time also did *L* revolt 2Chr 21:10 3841
king of Assyria warring against *L* Is 37:8 3841
the daughter of Jeremiah of *L* Jer 52:1 3841

LIBNI (*lib'-ni*) See LAADAN, LIBNITES.
1. Son of Gershon.
L, and Shimi, according to their Ex 6:17 3845
their families; *L*, and Shimei Num 3:18 3845
of Gershom; *L*, and Shimei 1Chr 6:17 3845
L his son, Jahath his son, Zimmah 1Chr 6:20 3845
2. Grandson of Merari.
L his son, Shimei his son, Uzza 1Chr 6:29 3845

LIBNITES (*lib'-nites*) *Descendants of Libni 1.*
Gershon was the family of the *L* Num 3:21 3864
the family of the *L*, the family Num 26:58 3864

LIBYA (*lib'-e-ah*) See LIBYANS. *A land in north Africa.*
Ethiopia, and *L*, and Lydia, and all Eze 30:5 6316
Persia, Ethiopia, and *L* with them Eze 38:5 6316
and in the parts of *L* about Cyrene Acts 2:10 *3033*

LIBYANS (*lib'-e-uns*) See LEHABIM. *Inhabitants of Libya.*
the Ethiopians and the *L*, that Jer 46:9 6316
and the *L* and the Ethiopians shall Dan 11:43 3864

LICE
that it may become *l* throughout Ex 8:16 3654
the earth, and it became *l* in man Ex 8:17 3654
l throughout all the land of Ex 8:17 3654
enchantments to bring forth *l* Ex 8:18 3654
so there were *l* upon man, and upon Ex 8:18 3654
flies, and *l* in all their coasts Ps 105:31 3654

LICENCE
And when he had given him *l* Acts 21:40 *2010*
have *l* to answer for himself Acts 25:16 *5117*

LICK
Now shall this company *l* up all Num 22:4 3897
of Naboth shall dogs *l* thy blood 1Kin 21:19 3952
and his enemies shall *l* the dust Ps 72:9 3897
l up the dust of thy feet Is 49:23 3897
They shall *l* the dust like a Mic 7:17 3897

LICKED
l up the water that was in the 1Kin 18:38 3897
In the place where dogs *l* the 1Kin 21:19 3952
and the dogs *l* up his blood 1Kin 22:38 3952
the dogs came and *l* his sores Lk 16:21 *621*

LICKETH
as the ox *l* up the grass of the Num 22:4 3897

LID
and bored a hole in the *l* of it 2Kin 12:9 1817

LIE
we will *l* with him, that we may Gen 19:32 7901
l with him, that we may preserve Gen 19:34 7901
Therefore he shall *l* with thee to Gen 30:15 7901
and she said, *L* with me Gen 39:7 7901
to *l* by her, or to be with her Gen 39:10 7901
by his garment, saying, *L* with me Gen 39:12 7901
he came in unto me to *l* with me Gen 39:14 7901
But I will *l* with my fathers, and Gen 47:30 7901
if a man *l* not in wait, but God Ex 21:13 6658
l with her, he shall surely endow Ex 22:16 7901
thou shalt let it rest and *l* still Ex 23:11 5203
l unto his neighbour in that Lev 6:2 3584
shall *l* with seed of copulation Lev 15:18 7901
if any man *l* with her at all, and Lev 15:24 7901
Moreover thou shalt not *l* Lev 18:20 7903
Thou shalt not *l* with mankind Lev 18:22 7901
Neither shalt thou *l* with any Lev 18:23 7903
before a beast to *l* down thereto Lev 18:23 7250
falsely, neither *l* one to another Lev 19:11 8266
if a man *l* with his daughter in Lev 20:12 7901
If a man also *l* with mankind Lev 20:13 7901
if a man *l* with a beast, he shall Lev 20:15 7903
l down thereto, thou shalt kill Lev 20:16 7250
if a man shall *l* with a woman Lev 20:18 7901
if a man shall *l* with his uncle's Lev 20:20 7901
in the land, and ye shall *l* down Lev 26:6 7901
a man *l* with her carnally, and it Num 5:13 7901
then the camps that *l* on the east Num 10:5 2583
then the camps that *l* on the Num 10:6 2583
is not a man, that he should *l* Num 23:19 3576
he shall not *l* down until he eat Num 23:24 7901
l in wait for him, and rise up Deut 19:11 693
her in the city, and *l* with her Deut 22:23 7901
the man force her, and *l* with her Deut 22:25 7901
l with her, and they be found Deut 22:28 7901
judge shall cause him to *l* down Deut 25:2 5307
and another man shall *l* with her Deut 28:30 7693
in this book shall *l* upon him Deut 29:20 7257
ye shall *l* in wait against the Josh 8:4 693
and they went to *l* in ambush Josh 8:9
set them to *l* in ambush between Josh 8:12
thee, and *l* in wait in the field Judg 9:32
let all thy wants *l* upon me Judg 19:20
l in wait in the vineyards Judg 21:20
mark the place where he shall *l* Ruth 3:4 7901
he went to *l* down at the end of Ruth 3:7 7901
l down until the morning Ruth 3:13 7901
l down again 1Sa 3:5 7901
l down again 1Sa 3:6 7901
Eli said unto Samuel, Go, *l* down 1Sa 3:9 7901
of Israel will not *l* nor repent 1Sa 15:29 8266
to *l* in wait, as at this day 1Sa 22:8 8266
to *l* in wait, as at this day 1Sa 22:13 8266
and to drink, and to *l* with my wife 2Sa 11:11 7901
at even he went out to *l* on his 2Sa 11:13 7901
he shall *l* with thy wives in the 2Sa 12:11 7901
Come *l* with me, my sister 2Sa 13:11 7901
let her *l* in thy bosom, that my 1Kin 1:2 7901
do not *l* unto thine handmaid 2Kin 4:16 3576
for it is evident unto you if I *l* Job 6:28 3576
When I *l* down, I say, When shall Job 7:4 7901
Also thou shalt *l* down, and none Job 11:19 7257
which shall *l* down with him in Job 20:11 7901
They shall *l* down alike in the Job 21:26 7901
The rich man shall *l* down Job 27:19 7901
Should I *l* against my right Job 34:6 3576
abide in the covert to *l* in wait Job 38:40
He maketh me to *l* down in green Ps 23:2 7257
I *l* even among them that are set Ps 57:4 7901
they *l* in wait for my soul Ps 59:3
and men of high degree are a *l* Ps 62:9 3576
the slain that *l* in the grave Ps 88:5 7901
that I will not *l* unto David Ps 89:35 3576
proud have forged a *l* against me Ps 119:69 3576
yea, thou shalt *l* down, and thy Prov 3:24 7901
wicked are to *l* in wait for blood Prov 12:6
A faithful witness will not *l* Prov 14:5 3576
if two *l* together, then they have Eccl 4:11 7901
he shall *l* all night betwixt my Song 1:13 3885
leopard shall *l* down with the kid Is 11:6 7257
young ones shall *l* down together Is 11:7 7257
of the desert shall *l* there Is 13:21 7257
l in glory, every one in his own Is 14:18 7901
the needy shall *l* down in safety Is 14:30 7257
be for flocks, which shall *l* down Is 17:2 7257
feed, and there shall he *l* down Is 27:10 7257
The highways *l* waste, the Is 33:8
to generation it shall *l* waste Is 34:10
they shall *l* down together, they Is 43:17 7901
Is there not a *l* in my right hand Is 44:20 3576
ye shall *l* down in sorrow Is 50:11 7901
they *l* at the head of all the Is 51:20 7901
people, children that will not *l* Is 63:8 8266
place for the herds to *l* down in Is 65:10 7258
We *l* down in our shame, and our Jer 3:25 7901
For they prophesy a *l* unto you Jer 27:10 8267
for they prophesy a *l* unto you Jer 27:14 8267
yet they prophesy a *l* in my name Jer 27:15 8267
for they prophesy a *l* unto you Jer 27:16 8267
this people to trust in a *l* Jer 28:15 8267
which prophesy a *l* unto you in my Jer 29:21 8267
and he caused you to trust in a *l* Jer 29:31 8267
causing their flocks to *l* down Jer 33:12 7257
the old *l* on the ground in the Lam 2:21 7901
L thou also upon thy left side, Eze 4:4 7901
of the days that thou shalt *l* Eze 4:4 7901
l again on thy right side, and Eze 4:6 7901
that thou shalt *l* upon thy side Eze 4:9 7901
whiles they divine a *l* unto thee Eze 21:29 3576
thou shalt *l* in the midst of the Eze 31:18 7901
they *l* uncircumcised, slain by Eze 32:21 7901
they shall not *l* with the mighty Eze 32:27 7901
shalt *l* with them that are slain Eze 32:28 7901
they shall *l* with the Eze 32:29 7901
they *l* uncircumcised with them Eze 32:30 7901
there shall they *l* in a good fold Eze 34:14 7257
and I will cause them to *l* down Eze 34:15 7257
will make them to *l* down safely Hos 2:18 7901
an oven, whiles they *l* in wait Hos 7:6
l all night in sackcloth, ye Joel 1:13 3885
That *l* upon beds of ivory, and Amos 6:4 7901
be a *l* to the kings of Israel Mic 1:14 391
in the spirit and falsehood do *l* Mic 2:11 3576
they all *l* in wait for blood Mic 7:2
the end it shall speak, and not *l* Hab 2:3 3576
shall they *l* down in the evening Zeph 2:7 7257
flocks shall *l* down in the midst Zeph 2:14 7257
a place for beasts to *l* down in Zeph 2:15 4769
l down, and none shall make them Zeph 3:13 7257
houses, and this house *l* waste Hag 1:4
and the diviners have seen a *l* Zec 10:2 8267
When Jesus saw him *l*, and knew Jn 5:6 *2621*
When he speaketh a *l*, he speaketh Jn 8:44 *5579*
and seeth the linen clothes *l* Jn 20:6 *2749*
heart to *l* to the Holy Ghost Acts 5:3 *5574*
for there *l* in wait for him of Acts 23:21
changed the truth of God into a *l* Rom 1:25 *5579*
through my *l* unto his glory Rom 3:7 *3582*
I *l* not, my conscience also Rom 9:1 *5574*
evermore, knoweth that I *l* not 2Cor 11:31 *5574*
you, behold, before God, I *l* not Gal 1:20 *5574*
whereby they *l* in wait to deceive Eph 4:14 *3180*
L not one to another, seeing that Col 3:9 *5574*
that they should believe a *l* 2Th 2:11 *5579*
the truth in Christ, and *l* not 1Ti 2:7 *5574*
life, which God, that cannot *l* Titus 1:2 *893*
it was impossible for God to *l* Heb 6:18 *5574*
not, and *l* not against the truth Jas 3:14 *5574*
him, and walk in darkness, we *l* 1Jn 1:6 *5574*
that no *l* is of the truth 1Jn 2:21 *5579*
things, and is truth, and is no *l* 1Jn 2:27 *5579*
are Jews, and are not, but do *l* Rev 3:9 *5574*
their dead bodies shall *l* in the Rev 11:8 *5574*
abomination, or maketh a *l* Rev 21:27 *5579*
and whosoever loveth and maketh a *l* Rev 22:15 *5579*

LIED
But he *l* unto him 1Kin 13:18 3584
they *l* unto him with their Ps 78:36 3576
or feared, that thou hast *l* Is 57:11 3576
thou hast not *l* unto men, but Acts 5:4 *5574*

LIEN
lightly have *l* with thy wife Gen 26:10 7901
Though ye have *l* among the pots Ps 68:13 7901
where thou hast not been *l* with Jer 3:2 7693

LIERS
their *l* in wait on the west of Josh 8:13
l in ambush against him behind Josh 8:14
the men of Shechem set *l* in wait Judg 9:25
there were *l* in wait abiding in Judg 16:12
Israel set *l* in wait round about Judg 20:29
the *l* in wait of Israel came Judg 20:33
the *l* in wait which they had set Judg 20:36
the *l* in wait hasted, and rushed Judg 20:37
the *l* in wait drew themselves Judg 20:37
the *l* in wait, that they should Judg 20:38

LIES
thou hast mocked me, and told me *l* Judg 16:10 3576
thou hast mocked me, and told me *l* Judg 16:13 3576
Should thy *l* make men hold their Job 11:3 907
But ye are forgers of *l*, ye are Job 13:4 8267
nor such as turn aside to *l* Ps 40:4 3576
soon as they be born, speaking *l* Ps 58:3 3576
they delight in *l* Ps 62:4 3576
that speak *l* shall be stopped Ps 63:11 8267
he that telleth *l* shall not tarry Ps 101:7 8267
A false witness that speaketh *l* Prov 6:19 3576
but a false witness will utter *l* Prov 14:5 3576
a deceitful witness speaketh *l* Prov 14:25 3576
that speaketh *l* shall not escape Prov 19:5 3576
he that speaketh *l* shall perish Prov 19:9 3576
If a ruler hearken to *l*, all his Prov 29:12
Remove far from me vanity and *l* Prov 30:8
and the prophet that teacheth *l* Is 9:15 8267
but his *l* shall not be so Is 16:6 907
for we have made *l* our refuge Is 28:15 3576
shall sweep away the refuge of *l* Is 28:17 3576
your lips have spoken *l*, your Is 59:3 8267
they trust in vanity, and speak *l* Is 59:4 7723
tongues like their bow for *l* Jer 9:3 8267
taught their tongue to speak *l* Jer 9:5 8267
prophets prophesy *l* in my name Jer 14:14 8267
our fathers have inherited *l* Jer 16:19 8267
to whom thou hast prophesied *l* Jer 20:6 8267
commit adultery, and walk in *l* Jer 23:14 8267
said, that prophesy *l* in my name Jer 23:25 8267
of the prophets that prophesy *l* Jer 23:26 8267
cause my people to err by their *l* Jer 23:32 8267
his *l* shall not so effect it Jer 48:30 907
ye have spoken vanity, and seen *l* Eze 13:8 3576
that see vanity, and that divine *l* Eze 13:9 3576
to my people that hear your *l* Eze 13:19 3576
Because with *l* ye have made the Eze 13:22 3576
divining *l* unto them, saying, Eze 22:28 3576
She hath wearied herself with *l* Eze 24:12 8383
they shall speak *l* at one table Dan 11:27 3576
and the princes with their *l* Hos 7:3 3585
yet they have spoken *l* against me Hos 7:13 3576
ye have eaten the fruit of *l* Hos 10:13 3585
compasseth me about with *l* Hos 11:12 3585
he daily increaseth *l* and Hos 12:1 3576
their *l* caused them to err, after Amos 2:4 3576
inhabitants thereof have spoken *l* Mic 6:12 8267
it is all full of *l* and robbery Nah 3:1 3585
molten image, and a teacher of *l* Hab 2:18 8267
not do iniquity, nor speak *l* Zeph 3:13 3576
for thou speakest *l* in the name Zec 13:3 8267
Speaking *l* in hypocrisy 1Ti 4:2 *5573*

LIEST
the land whereon thou *l*, to thee Gen 28:13 7901
by the way, and when thou *l* down Deut 6:7 7901
by the way, when thou *l* down Deut 11:19 7901
wherefore *l* thou thus upon thy Josh 7:10 5307
When thou *l* down, thou shalt not Prov 3:24 7901

LIETH

doest not well, sin *l* at the door Gen 4:7 7257
of the deep that *l* under, Gen 49:25 7257
Whosoever *l* with a beast shall Ex 22:19 7901
l concerning it, and sweareth Lev 6:3 3584
he that *l* in the house shall wash Lev 14:47 7901
whereon he *l* that hath the issue, Lev 15:4 7901
every thing that she *l* upon in Lev 15:20 7901
bed whereon he *l* shall be unclean Lev 15:24 7901
Every bed whereon she *l* all the Lev 15:26 7901
of him that *l* with her that is Lev 15:33 7901
whosoever *l* carnally with a woman Lev 19:20 7901
the man that *l* with his father's Lev 20:11 7901
as he *l* with a woman, both of Lev 20:13 4904
as long as it *l* desolate Lev 26:34
As long as it *l* desolate it shall Lev 26:35
while she *l* desolate without them Lev 26:43
l upon the border of Moab Num 21:15 8172
Cursed be he that *l* with his Deut 27:20 7901
Cursed be he that *l* with any Deut 27:21 7901
be he that *l* with his sister Deut 27:22 7901
Cursed be he that *l* with his Deut 27:23 7901
l before the valley of Hinnom Josh 15:8
Michmethah, that *l* before Shechem Josh 17:7
near the hill that *l* on the south Josh 18:13
from the hill that *l* before Josh 18:14
l before the valley of the son of Josh 18:16
which *l* in the south of Arad Judg 1:16
see wherein his great strength *l* Judg 16:5
wherein thy great strength *l* Judg 16:6
me wherein thy great strength *l* Judg 16:15
the valley that *l* by Beth-rehob Judg 18:28
And it shall be, when he *l* down Ruth 3:4 7901
that *l* before Giah by the way of 2Sa 2:24
l in the midst of the river of 2Sa 24:5
l waste, and the gates thereof are Neh 2:3
we are in, how Jerusalem *l* waste Neh 2:17
the tower which *l* out from the Neh 3:25 3318
the east, and the tower that *l* out Neh 3:26 3318
the great tower that *l* out Neh 3:27 3318
So man *l* down, and riseth not Job 14:12 7901
He *l* under the shady trees, in Job 40:21 7901
He *l* in wait secretly as a lion Ps 10:9
he *l* in wait to catch the poor Ps 10:9
now that he *l* he shall rise up no Ps 41:8 7901
Thy wrath *l* hard upon me, and thou Ps 88:7 5564
l in wait at every corner Prov 7:12
She also *l* in wait as for a prey, Prov 23:28
thou shalt be as he that *l* down Prov 23:34 7901
or as he that *l* upon the top of a Prov 23:34 7901
which *l* toward the north, and Eze 9:2
the great dragon that *l* in the Eze 29:3 6437
from her that *l* in thy bosom Mic 7:5 7901
my servant *l* at home sick of the Mt 8:6 *906*
My little daughter *l* at the point Mk 5:23 *2192*
the region that *l* round about Acts 14:6
l toward the south west and north Acts 27:12 *991*
be possible, as much as *l* in you Rom 12:18
the whole world *l* in wickedness 1Jn 5:19 *2749*
the city *l* foursquare, and the Rev 21:16 *2749*

LIEUTENANTS

commissions unto the king's *l* Ezr 8:36 323
had commanded unto the king's *l* Est 3:12 323
unto the Jews, and to the *l* Est 8:9 323
rulers of the provinces, and the *l* Est 9:3 323

LIFE

the moving creature that hath *l* Gen 1:20 2416
the earth, wherein there is *l* Gen 1:30 2416
into his nostrils the breath of *l* Gen 2:7 2416
the tree of *l* also in the midst Gen 2:9 2416
thou eat all the days of thy *l* Gen 3:14 2416
eat of it all the days of thy *l* Gen 3:17 2416
and take also of the tree of *l* Gen 3:22 2416
to keep the way of the tree of *l* Gen 3:24 2416
flesh, wherein is the breath of *l* Gen 6:17 2416
six hundredth year of Noah's *l* Gen 7:11 2416
flesh, wherein is the breath of *l* Gen 7:15 2416
nostrils was the breath of *l* Gen 7:22 2416
But flesh with the *l* thereof Gen 9:4 5315
will I require the *l* of man Gen 9:5 5315
thee according to the time of *l* Gen 18:10 2416
thee, according to the time of *l* Gen 18:14 2416
that he said, Escape for thy *l* Gen 19:17 5315
shewed unto me in saving my *l* Gen 19:19 5315
were the years of the *l* of Sarah Gen 23:1 2416
of Abraham's *l* which he lived Gen 25:7 2416
are the years of the *l* of Ishmael Gen 25:17 2416
I am weary of my *l* because of the Gen 27:46 2416
land, what good shall my *l* do me Gen 27:46 2416
to face, and my *l* is preserved Gen 32:30 5315
By the *l* of Pharaoh ye shall not Gen 42:15 2416
or else by the *l* of Pharaoh Gen 42:16 2416
seeing that his *l* is bound up in Gen 44:30 5315
is bound up in the lad's *l* Gen 44:30
send me before you to preserve *l* Gen 45:5
days of the years of my *l* been Gen 47:9 2416
l of my fathers in the days of Gen 47:9 2416
me all my *l* long unto this day Gen 48:15
men are dead which sought thy *l* Ex 4:19 5315
the years of the *l* of Levi were Ex 6:16 2416
the years of the *l* of Kohath were Ex 6:18 2416
the years of the *l* of Amram were Ex 6:20 2416
then thou shalt give *l* for *l* Ex 21:23 5315
give for the ransom of his *l* Ex 21:30 5315
For the *l* of the flesh is in the Lev 17:11 5315
For it is the *l* of all flesh Lev 17:14 5315
blood of it is for the *l* thereof Lev 17:14 5315
for the *l* of all flesh is the Lev 17:14 5315
beside the other in her *l* time Lev 18:18 2416
for the *l* of a murderer, which is Num 35:31 5315
thy heart all the days of thy *l* Deut 4:9 2416
son's son, all the days of thy *l* Deut 6:2 2416
for the blood is the *l* Deut 12:23 5315
not eat the *l* with the flesh Deut 12:23 5315
of Egypt all the days of thy *l* Deut 16:3 2416
therein all the days of his *l* Deut 17:19 2416
but *l* shall go for *l*, eye for Deut 19:21 5315
l) to employ them in the siege Deut 20:19
for he taketh a man's *l* to pledge Deut 24:6 5315
thy *l* shall hang in doubt before Deut 28:66 2416
have none assurance of thy *l* Deut 28:66 2416
I have set before thee this day *l* Deut 30:15 2416
you, that I have set before you *l* Deut 30:19 2416
therefore choose *l*, that both Deut 30:19 2416
for he is thy *l*, and the length of Deut 30:20 2416
because it is your *l* Deut 32:47 2416
before thee all the days of thy *l* Josh 1:5 2416
Our *l* for yours, if ye utter not Josh 2:14 5315
Moses, all the days of his *l* Josh 4:14 2416
for you, and adventured his *l* far Judg 9:17 5315
I put my *l* in my hands, and passed Judg 12:3 5315
than they which he slew in his *l* Judg 16:30 2416
run upon thee, and thou lose thy *l* Judg 18:25 5315
be unto thee a restorer of thy *l* Ruth 4:15 5315
the LORD all the days of his *l* 1Sa 1:11 2416
Israel all the days of his *l* 1Sa 7:15 2416
and what is my *l*, or my father's 1Sa 18:18 2416
For he did put his *l* in his hand 1Sa 19:5 5315
thy father, that he seeketh my *l* 1Sa 20:1 5315
seeketh my *l* seeketh thy *l* 1Sa 22:23 5315
Saul was come out to seek his *l* 1Sa 23:15 5315
bundle of *l* with the LORD thy God 1Sa 25:29 2416
as thy *l* was much set by this day 1Sa 26:24 5315
so let my *l* be much set by in the 1Sa 26:24 5315
then layest thou a snare for my *l* 1Sa 28:9 5315
and I have put my *l* in my hand 1Sa 28:21 5315
because my *l* is yet whole in me 2Sa 1:9 5315
thine enemy, which sought thy *l* 2Sa 4:8 5315
for the *l* of his brother whom he 2Sa 14:7 5315
shall be, whether in death or *l* 2Sa 15:21 2416
forth of my bowels, seeketh my *l* 2Sa 16:11 5315
falsehood against mine own *l* 2Sa 18:13 5315
which this day have saved thy *l* 2Sa 19:5 5315
that thou mayest save thine own *l* 1Kin 1:12 5315
and the *l* of thy son Solomon 1Kin 1:12 5315
this word against his own *l* 1Kin 2:23 5315
hast not asked for thyself long *l* 1Kin 3:11 3117
hast asked the *l* of thine enemies 1Kin 3:11 5315
Solomon all the days of his *l* 1Kin 4:21 2416
his *l* for David my servant's sake 1Kin 11:34 2416
him all the days of his *l* 1Kin 15:5 2416
and Jeroboam all the days of his *l* 1Kin 15:6 2416
if I make not thy *l* as the *l* 1Kin 19:2 5315
that, he arose, and went for his *l* 1Kin 19:3 5315
now, O LORD, take away my *l* 1Kin 19:4 5315
and they seek my *l*, to take it 1Kin 19:10 5315
and they seek my *l*, to take it 1Kin 19:14 5315
peradventure he will save thy *l* 1Kin 20:31 5315
then shall thy *l* be for his *l*, 1Kin 20:39 5315
thy *l* shall go for his *l* 1Kin 20:42 5315
man of God, I pray thee, let my *l* 2Kin 1:13 5315
the *l* of these fifty thy servants 2Kin 1:13
therefore let my *l* now be 2Kin 1:14 5315
according to the time of *l* 2Kin 4:16 2416
her, according to the time of *l* 2Kin 4:17 2416
as it was, and fled for their *l* 2Kin 7:7 5315
whose son he had restored to *l* 2Kin 8:1 2421
he had restored a dead body to *l* 2Kin 8:5 2421
whose son he had restored to *l* 2Kin 8:5 2421
son, whom Elisha restored to *l* 2Kin 8:5 2421
his *l* shall be for the *l* of 2Kin 10:24 2421
l shall be for the *l* of him 2Kin 10:24 5315
before him all the days of his *l* 2Kin 25:29 2416
every day, all the days of his *l* 2Kin 25:30 2416
nor the *l* of thine enemies, 2Chr 1:11 5315
neither yet hast asked long *l* 2Chr 1:11 3117
and pray for the *l* of the king Ezr 6:10 2417
go into the temple to save his *l* Neh 6:11 2425
let my *l* be given me at my Est 7:3 5315
for his *l* to Esther the queen Est 7:7 5315
together, and to stand for their *l* Est 8:11 5315
a man hath will he give for his *l* Job 2:4 5315
but save his *l* Job 2:6 5315
l unto the bitter in soul Job 3:20 2416
end, that I should prolong my *l* Job 6:11 5315
O remember that my *l* is wind Job 7:7 2416
and death rather than my *l* Job 7:15 6106
I would despise my *l* Job 9:21 2416
My soul is weary of my *l* Job 10:1 2416
Thou hast granted me *l* and favour, Job 10:12 2416
teeth, and put my *l* in mine hand Job 13:14 5315
riseth up, and no man is sure of *l* Job 24:22 2416
owners thereof to lose their *l* Job 31:39 5315
of the Almighty hath given me *l* Job 33:4 2421
his *l* from perishing by the sword Job 33:18 2416
So that his *l* abhorreth bread, and Job 33:20 2416
grave, and his *l* to the destroyers Job 33:22 2416
his *l* shall see the light Job 33:28 2416
not the *l* of the wicked Job 36:6 2421
their *l* is among the unclean Job 36:14 2416
tread down my *l* upon the earth Ps 7:5 2416
Thou wilt shew me the path of *l* Ps 16:11 2416
have their portion in this *l* Ps 17:14 2416
He asked *l* of thee, and thou Ps 21:4 2416
follow me all the days of my *l* Ps 23:6 2416
sinners, nor my *l* with bloody men Ps 26:9 2416
the LORD is the strength of my *l* Ps 27:1 2416
of the LORD all the days of my *l* Ps 27:4 2416
in his favour is *l* Ps 30:5 2416
For my *l* is spent with grief, and Ps 31:10 2416
they devised to take away my *l* Ps 31:13 5315
What man is he that desireth *l* Ps 34:12 2416
with thee is the fountain of *l* Ps 36:9 2416
seek after my *l* lay snares for me Ps 38:12 5315
and my prayer unto the God of my *l* Ps 42:8 2416
Thou wilt prolong the king's *l* Ps 61:6 2416
lovingkindness is better than *l* Ps 63:3 2416
preserve my *l* from fear of the Ps 64:1 2416
Which holdeth our soul in *l* Ps 66:9 2416
but gave their *l* over to the Ps 78:50 2416
my *l* draweth nigh unto the grave Ps 88:3 2416
With long *l* will I satisfy him, Ps 91:16 3117
redeemeth thy *l* from destruction Ps 103:4 2416
Jerusalem all the days of thy *l* Ps 128:5 2416
the blessing, even *l* for evermore Ps 133:3 2416
smitten my *l* down to the ground Ps 143:3 2416
away the *l* of the owners thereof Prov 1:19 5315
take they hold of the paths of *l* Prov 2:19 2416
For length of days, and long *l* Prov 3:2 2416
She is a tree of *l* to them that Prov 3:18 2416
So shall they be *l* unto thy soul Prov 3:22 2416
the years of thy *l* shall be many Prov 4:10 2416
for she is thy *l* Prov 4:13 2416
For they are *l* unto those that Prov 4:22 2416
for out of it are the issues of *l* Prov 4:23 2416
shouldest ponder the path of *l* Prov 5:6 2416
of instruction are the way of *l* Prov 6:23 2416
will hunt for the precious *l* Prov 6:26 5315
knoweth not that it is for his *l* Prov 7:23 5315
For whoso findeth me findeth *l* Prov 8:35 2416
the years of thy *l* shall be Prov 9:11 2416
of a righteous man is a well of *l* Prov 10:11 2416
of the righteous tendeth to *l* Prov 10:16 2416
He is in the way of *l* that Prov 10:17 2416
As righteousness tendeth to *l* Prov 11:19 2416
of the righteous is a tree of *l* Prov 11:30 2416
man regardeth the *l* of his beast Prov 12:10 5315
In the way of righteousness is *l* Prov 12:28 2416
keepeth his mouth keepeth his *l* Prov 13:3 5315
of a man's *l* are his riches Prov 13:8 5315
desire cometh, it is a tree of *l* Prov 13:12 2416
of the wise is a fountain of *l* Prov 13:14 2416
of the LORD is a fountain of *l* Prov 14:27 2416
sound heart is the *l* of the flesh Prov 14:30 2416
A wholesome tongue is a tree of *l* Prov 15:4 2416
The way of *l* is above to the wise Prov 15:24 2416
of *l* abideth among the wise Prov 15:31 2416
of the king's countenance is *l* Prov 16:15 2416
is a wellspring of *l* unto him Prov 16:22 2416
l are in the power of the tongue Prov 18:21 2416
The fear of the LORD tendeth to *l* Prov 19:23 2416
righteousness and mercy findeth *l* Prov 21:21 2416
LORD are riches, and honour, and *l* Prov 22:4 2416
and not evil all the days of her *l* Prov 31:12 2416
heaven all the days of their *l* Eccl 2:3 2416
Therefore I hated *l* Eccl 2:17 2416
rejoice, and to do good in his *l* Eccl 3:12 2416
the sun all the days of his *l* Eccl 5:18 2416
much remember the days of his *l* Eccl 5:20 2416
what is good for man in this *l* Eccl 6:12 2416
all the days of his vain *l* which Eccl 6:12 2416
that wisdom giveth *l* to them that Eccl 7:12 2421
his *l* in his wickedness Eccl 7:15
of his labour the days of his *l* Eccl 8:15 2416
the days of the *l* of thy vanity Eccl 9:9 2416
for that is thy portion in this *l* Eccl 9:9 2416
his *l* shall be grievous unto him Is 15:4 5315
I have cut off like a weaver my *l* Is 38:12 2416
things is the *l* of my spirit Is 38:16 2416
of our *l* in the house of the LORD Is 38:20 2416
men for thee, and people for thy *l* Is 43:4 5315
hast found the *l* of thine hand Is 57:10 2416
thee, they will seek thy *l* Jer 4:30 5315
shall be chosen rather than *l* by Jer 8:3 2416
men of Anathoth, that seek thy *l* Jer 11:21 5315
hand of those that seek their *l* Jer 21:7 5315
I set before you the way of *l* Jer 21:8 2416
his *l* shall be unto him for a Jer 21:9 5315
the hand of them that seek thy *l* Jer 22:25 5315
hand of them that seek their *l* Jer 34:20 5315
hand of them that seek their *l* Jer 34:21 5315
he shall have his *l* for a prey Jer 38:2 5315
hand of these men that seek thy *l* Jer 38:16 5315
but thy *l* shall be for a prey Jer 39:18 5315
the hand of them that seek his *l* Jer 44:30 5315
his enemy, and that sought his *l* Jer 44:30 5315
but thy *l* will I give unto thee Jer 45:5 5315
and before them that seek their *l* Jer 49:37 5315
before him all the days of his *l* Jer 52:33 2416
his death, all the days of his *l* Jer 52:34 2416
for the *l* of thy young children Lam 2:19 5315
have cut off my *l* in the dungeon Lam 3:53 2416
thou hast redeemed my *l* Lam 3:58
his wicked way, to save his *l* Eze 3:18 2421
himself in the iniquity of his *l* Eze 7:13 2416
wicked way, by promising him *l* Eze 13:22 2421
moment, every man for his own *l* Eze 32:10 5315
robbed, walk in the statutes of *l* Eze 33:15 2416
awake, some to everlasting *l* Dan 12:2 2416
us not perish for this man's *l* Jonah 1:14 5315
brought up my *l* from corruption Jonah 2:6 2416
I beseech thee, my *l* from me Jonah 4:3 5315
My covenant was with him of *l* Mal 2:5 2416
which sought the young child's *l* Mt 2:20 *5590*
you, Take no thought for your *l* Mt 6:25 *5590*
Is not the *l* more than meat, and Mt 6:25 *5590*
is the way, which leadeth unto *l* Mt 7:14 *2222*
that findeth his *l* shall lose it Mt 10:39 *5590*
he that loseth his *l* for my sake Mt 10:39 *5590*
will save his *l* shall lose it Mt 16:25 *5590*
whosoever will lose his *l* for my Mt 16:25 *5590*
to enter into *l* halt or maimed Mt 18:8 *2222*
thee to enter into *l* with one eye Mt 18:9 *2222*
I do, that I may have eternal *l* Mt 19:16 *2222*
but if thou wilt enter into *l* Mt 19:17 *2222*
and shall inherit everlasting *l* Mt 19:29 *2222*
to give his *l* a ransom for many Mt 20:28 *5590*
but the righteous into *l* eternal Mt 25:46 *2222*
to save *l*, or to kill Mk 3:4 *5590*
will save his *l* shall lose it Mk 8:35 *5590*
shall lose his *l* for my sake Mk 8:35 *5590*

for thee to enter into *l* maimed	Mk 9:43	2222
for thee to enter halt into *l*	Mk 9:45	2222
I do that I may inherit eternal *l*	Mk 10:17	2222
and in the world to come eternal *l*	Mk 10:30	2222
to give his *l* a ransom for many	Mk 10:45	5590
before him, all the days of our *l*	Lk 1:75	2222
to save *l*, or to destroy it	Lk 6:9	5590
and riches and pleasures of this *l*	Lk 8:14	979
will save his *l* shall lose it	Lk 9:24	5590
will lose his *l* for my sake	Lk 9:24	5590
shall I do to inherit eternal *l*	Lk 10:25	2222
for a man's *l* consisteth not in	Lk 12:15	2222
you, Take no thought for your *l*	Lk 12:22	5590
The *l* is more than meat, and the	Lk 12:23	5590
sisters, yea, and his own *l* also	Lk 14:26	5590
seek to save his *l* shall lose it	Lk 17:33	5590
lose his *l* shall preserve it	Lk 17:33	5590
shall I do to inherit eternal *l*	Lk 18:18	2222
the world to come *l* everlasting	Lk 18:30	2222
drunkenness, and cares of this *l*	Lk 21:34	982
In him was *l*	Jn 1:4	2222
the *l* was the light of men	Jn 1:4	2222
not perish, but have eternal *l*	Jn 3:15	2222
perish, but have everlasting *l*	Jn 3:16	2222
on the Son hath everlasting *l*	Jn 3:36	2222
not the Son shall not see *l*	Jn 3:36	2222
springing up into everlasting *l*	Jn 4:14	2222
and gathereth fruit unto *l* eternal	Jn 4:36	2222
that sent me, hath everlasting *l*	Jn 5:24	2222
but is passed from death unto *l*	Jn 5:24	2222
as the Father hath *l* in himself	Jn 5:26	2222
to the Son to have *l* in himself	Jn 5:26	2222
good, unto the resurrection of *l*	Jn 5:29	2222
them ye think ye have eternal *l*	Jn 5:39	2222
come to me, that ye might have *l*	Jn 5:40	2222
which endureth unto everlasting *l*	Jn 6:27	2222
and giveth *l* unto the world	Jn 6:33	2222
unto them, I am the bread of *l*	Jn 6:35	2222
on him, may have everlasting *l*	Jn 6:40	2222
on me hath everlasting *l*	Jn 6:47	2222
I am that bread of *l*	Jn 6:48	2222
will give for the *l* of the world	Jn 6:51	2222
his blood, ye have no *l* in you	Jn 6:53	2222
drinketh my blood, hath eternal *l*	Jn 6:54	2222
they are spirit, and they are *l*	Jn 6:63	2222
thou hast the words of eternal *l*	Jn 6:68	2222
but shall have the light of *l*	Jn 8:12	2222
I am come that they might have *l*	Jn 10:10	2222
giveth his *l* for the sheep	Jn 10:11	5590
and I lay down my *l* for the sheep	Jn 10:15	5590
love me, because I lay down my *l*	Jn 10:17	5590
And I give unto them eternal *l*	Jn 10:28	2222
I am the resurrection, and the *l*	Jn 11:25	2222
that loveth his *l* shall lose it	Jn 12:25	5590
he that hateth his *l* in this	Jn 12:25	5590
shall keep it unto *l* eternal	Jn 12:25	2222
his commandment is *l* everlasting	Jn 12:50	2222
I will lay down my *l* for thy sake	Jn 13:37	5590
thou lay down thy *l* for my sake	Jn 13:38	5590
I am the way, the truth, and the *l*	Jn 14:6	2222
lay down his *l* for his friends	Jn 15:13	5590
that he should give eternal *l* to	Jn 17:2	2222
And this is *l* eternal, that they	Jn 17:3	2222
ye might have *l* through his name	Jn 20:31	2222
made known to me the ways of *l*	Acts 2:28	2222
And killed the Prince of *l*	Acts 3:15	2222
people all the words of this *l*	Acts 5:20	2222
for his *l* is taken from the earth	Acts 8:33	2222
granted repentance unto *l*	Acts 11:18	2222
unworthy of everlasting *l*	Acts 13:46	2222
ordained to eternal *l* believed	Acts 13:48	2222
thing, seeing he giveth to all *l*	Acts 17:25	2222
for his *l* is in him	Acts 20:10	5590
count I my *l* dear unto myself	Acts 20:24	5590
My manner of *l* from my youth,	Acts 26:4	981
no loss of any man's *l* among you	Acts 27:22	5590
honour and immortality, eternal *l*	Rom 2:7	2222
we shall be saved by his *l*	Rom 5:10	2222
shall reign in *l* by one, Jesus	Rom 5:17	2222
all men unto justification of *l*	Rom 5:18	2222
l by Jesus Christ our Lord	Rom 5:21	2222
also should walk in newness of *l*	Rom 6:4	2222
and the end everlasting *l*	Rom 6:22	2222
l through Jesus Christ our Lord	Rom 6:23	2222
which was ordained to *l*, I found	Rom 7:10	2222
of *l* in Christ Jesus hath made me	Rom 8:2	2222
but to be spiritually minded is *l*	Rom 8:6	2222
but the Spirit is *l* because of	Rom 8:10	2222
that neither death, nor *l*	Rom 8:38	2222
am left alone, and they seek my *l*	Rom 11:3	5590
of them be, but *l* from the dead	Rom 11:15	2222
Who have for my *l* laid down their	Rom 16:4	5590
or Cephas, or the world, or *l*	1Cor 3:22	2222
things that pertain to this *l*	1Cor 6:3	982
of things pertaining to this *l*	1Cor 6:4	982
things without *l* giving sound	1Cor 14:7	895
If in this *l* only we have hope in	1Cor 15:19	2222
that we despaired even of *l*	2Cor 1:8	2198
other the savour of *l* unto *l*	2Cor 2:16	2222
killeth, but the spirit giveth *l*	2Cor 3:6	2227
that the *l* also of Jesus might be	2Cor 4:10	2222
that the *l* also of Jesus might be	2Cor 4:11	2222
death worketh in us, but *l* in you	2Cor 4:12	2222
might be swallowed up of *l*	2Cor 5:4	2222
the *l* which I now live in the	Gal 2:20	
given which could have given *l*	Gal 3:21	2227
of the Spirit reap *l* everlasting	Gal 6:8	2222
being alienated from the *l* of God	Eph 4:18	2222
in my body, whether it be by *l*	Phil 1:20	2222
Holding forth the word of *l*	Phil 2:16	2222
unto death, not regarding his *l*	Phil 2:30	5590
whose names are in the book of *l*	Phil 4:3	2222
your *l* is hid with Christ in God	Col 3:3	2222
When Christ, who is our *l*	Col 3:4	2222
believe on him to *l* everlasting	1Ti 1:16	2222
peaceable *l* in all godliness and	1Ti 2:2	979
promise of the *l* that now is	1Ti 4:8	2222
of faith, lay hold on eternal *l*	1Ti 6:12	2222
they may lay hold on eternal *l*	1Ti 6:19	2222
of *l* which is in Christ Jesus	2Ti 1:1	2222
death, and hath brought *l* and	2Ti 1:10	2222
with the affairs of this *l*	2Ti 2:4	979
known my doctrine, manner of *l*	2Ti 3:10	72
In hope of eternal *l*, which God,	Titus 1:2	2222
to the hope of eternal *l*	Titus 3:7	2222
beginning of days, nor end of *l*	Heb 7:3	2222
after the power of an endless *l*	Heb 7:16	2222
their dead raised to *l* again	Heb 11:35	
he shall receive the crown of *l*	Jas 1:12	2222
For what is your *l*	Jas 4:14	2222
heirs together of the grace of *l*	1Pet 3:7	2222
For he that will love *l*, and see	1Pet 3:10	2222
For the time past of our *l* may	1Pet 4:3	979
us all things that pertain unto *l*	2Pet 1:3	2222
have handled, of the Word of *l*	1Jn 1:1	2222
(For the *l* was manifested, and we	1Jn 1:2	2222
and shew unto you that eternal *l*	1Jn 1:2	2222
of the eyes, and the pride of *l*	1Jn 2:16	979
hath promised us, even eternal *l*	1Jn 2:25	2222
we have passed from death unto *l*	1Jn 3:14	2222
hath eternal *l* abiding in him	1Jn 3:15	2222
because he laid down his *l* for us	1Jn 3:16	5590
God hath given to us eternal *l*	1Jn 5:11	2222
and this *l* is in his Son	1Jn 5:11	2222
He that hath the Son hath *l*	1Jn 5:12	2222
not the Son of God hath not *l*	1Jn 5:12	2222
may know that ye have eternal *l*	1Jn 5:13	2222
he shall give him *l* for them that	1Jn 5:16	2222
is the true God, and eternal *l*	1Jn 5:20	2222
Lord Jesus Christ unto eternal *l*	Jude 21	2222
I give to eat of the tree of *l*	Rev 2:7	2222
and I will give thee a crown of *l*	Rev 2:10	2222
out his name out of the book of *l*	Rev 3:5	2222
which were in the sea, and had *l*	Rev 8:9	5590
an half the Spirit of *l* from God	Rev 11:11	2222
of *l* of the Lamb slain from the	Rev 13:8	2222
he had power to give *l* unto the	Rev 13:15	4151
of *l* from the foundation of the	Rev 17:8	2222
opened, which is the book of *l*	Rev 20:12	2222
found written in the book of *l*	Rev 20:15	2222
fountain of the water of *l* freely	Rev 21:6	2222
written in the Lamb's book of *l*	Rev 21:27	2222
me a pure river of water of *l*	Rev 22:1	2222
river, was there the tree of *l*	Rev 22:2	2222
may have right to the tree of *l*	Rev 22:14	2222
him take the water of *l* freely	Rev 22:17	2222
his part out of the book of *l*	Rev 22:19	2222

LIFETIME

Now Absalom in his *l* had taken	2Sa 18:18	2416
remember that thou in thy *l*	Lk 16:25	2222
all their *l* subject to bondage	Heb 2:15	2198

LIFT

it was *l* up above the earth	Gen 7:17	7311
L up now thine eyes, and look from	Gen 13:14	5375
I have *l* up mine hand unto the	Gen 14:22	7311
he *l* up his eyes and looked, and,	Gen 18:2	5375
him, and *l* up her voice, and wept	Gen 21:16	5375
l up the lad, and hold him in	Gen 21:18	5375
L up now thine eyes, and see, all	Gen 31:12	5375
shall Pharaoh *l* up thine head	Gen 40:13	5375
l up thy head from off thee	Gen 40:19	5375
without thee shall no man *l* up	Gen 41:44	7311
But *l* thou up thy rod, and stretch	Ex 14:16	7311
for if thou *l* up thy tool upon it	Ex 20:25	5130
The LORD *l* up his countenance	Num 6:26	5375
wherefore then *l* ye up yourselves	Num 16:3	5375
l up himself as a young lion	Num 23:24	5375
l up thine eyes westward, and	Deut 3:27	5375
lest thou *l* up thine eyes unto	Deut 4:19	5375
help him to *l* them up again	Deut 22:4	6965
thou shalt not *l* up any iron tool	Deut 27:5	5130
For I *l* up my hand to heaven, and	Deut 32:40	5375
which no man hath *l* up any iron	Josh 8:31	5130
he *l* up his spear against eight	2Sa 23:8	
wherefore *l* up thy prayer for the	2Kin 19:4	5375
l up the head of Jehoiachin king	2Kin 25:27	5375
words of God, to *l* up the horn	1Chr 25:5	7311
blush to *l* up my face to thee, my	Ezr 9:6	7311
yet will I not *l* up my head	Job 10:15	5375
For then shalt thou *l* up thy face	Job 11:15	5375
shalt *l* up thy face unto God	Job 22:26	5375
Canst thou *l* up thy voice to the	Job 38:34	7311
l thou up the light of thy	Ps 4:6	5375
l up thyself because of the rage	Ps 7:6	5375
O God, *l* up thine hand	Ps 10:12	5375
L up your heads, O ye gates	Ps 24:7	5375
L up your heads, O ye gates	Ps 24:9	5375
even *l* them up, ye everlasting	Ps 24:9	5375
thee, O LORD, do I *l* up my soul	Ps 25:1	5375
when I *l* up my hands toward thy	Ps 28:2	5375
them also, and *l* them up for ever	Ps 28:9	5375
I will *l* up my hands in thy name	Ps 63:4	5375
L up thy feet unto the perpetual	Ps 74:3	7311
to the wicked, *L* not up the horn	Ps 75:4	7311
L not up your horn on high	Ps 75:5	7311
thee, O Lord, do I *l* up my soul	Ps 86:4	5375
the floods *l* up their waves	Ps 93:3	5375
L up thyself, thou judge of the	Ps 94:2	5375
therefore shall he *l* up the head	Ps 110:7	7311
My hands also will I *l* up unto	Ps 119:48	5375
I will *l* up mine eyes unto the	Ps 121:1	5375
Unto thee *l* I up mine eyes, O	Ps 123:1	5375
L up your hands in the sanctuary,	Ps 134:2	5375
for I *l* up my soul unto thee	Ps 143:8	5375
the one will *l* up his fellow	Eccl 4:10	6965
nation shall not *l* up sword	Is 2:4	5375
he will *l* up an ensign to the	Is 5:26	5375
itself against them that *l* it up	Is 10:15	7311
if the staff should *l* up itself	Is 10:15	7311
shall *l* up his staff against thee	Is 10:24	5375
so shall he *l* it up after the	Is 10:26	5375
L up thy voice, O daughter of	Is 10:30	6670
L ye up a banner upon the high	Is 13:2	5375
They shall *l* up their voice, they	Is 24:14	5375
now will I *l* up myself	Is 33:10	5375
wherefore *l* up thy prayer for the	Is 37:4	5375
l up thy voice with strength	Is 40:9	7311
l it up, be not afraid	Is 40:9	7311
L up your eyes on high, and behold	Is 40:26	5375
He shall not cry, nor *l* up	Is 42:2	5375
cities thereof *l* up their voice	Is 42:11	5375
L up thine eyes round about, and	Is 49:18	5375
I will *l* up mine hand to the	Is 49:22	5375
L up your eyes to the heavens, and	Is 51:6	5375
Thy watchmen shall *l* up the voice	Is 52:8	5375
l up thy voice like a trumpet, and	Is 58:1	7311
shall *l* up a standard against him	Is 59:19	5127
L up thine eyes round about, and	Is 60:4	5375
l up a standard for the people	Is 62:10	7311
L up thine eyes unto the high	Jer 3:2	5375
neither *l* up cry nor prayer for	Jer 7:16	5375
neither *l* up a cry or prayer for	Jer 11:14	5375
L up your eyes, and behold them	Jer 13:20	5375
l up thy voice in Bashan, and cry	Jer 22:20	5414
they shall *l* up a shout against	Jer 51:14	6030
l up thy hands toward him for the	Lam 2:19	5375
Let us *l* up our heart with our	Lam 3:41	5375
l up thine eyes now the way	Eze 8:5	5375
the cherubims *l* up their wings	Eze 11:22	5375
that it might not *l* itself up	Eze 17:14	5375
to *l* up the voice with shouting,	Eze 21:22	7311
so that thou shalt not *l* up thine	Eze 23:27	5375
l up the buckler against thee	Eze 26:8	6965
l up your eyes toward your idols,	Eze 33:25	5375
nation shall not *l* up a sword	Mic 4:3	5375
so that no man did *l* up his head	Zec 1:21	5375
L up now thine eyes, and see what	Zec 5:5	5375
not lay hold on it, and *l* it out	Mt 12:11	1458
and could in no wise *l* up herself	Lk 13:11	352
in hell he *l* up his eyes, being	Lk 16:23	1869
would not *l* up so much as his	Lk 18:13	1869
then look up, and *l* up your heads	Lk 21:28	1869
L up your eyes, and look on the	Jn 4:35	1869
Wherefore *l* up the hands which	Heb 12:12	461
of the Lord, and he shall *l* you up	Jas 4:10	5312

LIFTED

Lot *l* up his eyes, and beheld all	Gen 13:10	5375
third day Abraham *l* up his eyes	Gen 22:4	5375
Abraham *l* up his eyes, and looked,	Gen 22:13	5375
he *l* up his eyes, and saw, and,	Gen 24:63	5375
Rebekah *l* up her eyes, and when	Gen 24:64	5375
Esau *l* up his voice, and wept	Gen 27:38	5375
and *l* up his voice, and wept	Gen 29:11	5375
that I *l* up mine eyes, and saw in	Gen 31:10	5375
Jacob *l* up his eyes, and looked,	Gen 33:1	5375
he *l* up his eyes, and saw the	Gen 33:5	5375
they *l* up their eyes and looked,	Gen 37:25	5375
l up Joseph out of the pit, and	Gen 37:28	5927
he heard that I *l* up my voice	Gen 39:15	7311
as I *l* up my voice and cried, that	Gen 39:18	7311
he *l* up the head of the chief	Gen 40:20	5375
he *l* up his eyes, and saw his	Gen 43:29	5375
he *l* up the rod, and smote the	Ex 7:20	7311
of Israel *l* up their eyes	Ex 14:10	5375
Aaron *l* up his hand toward the	Lev 9:22	5375
the congregation *l* up their voice	Num 14:1	5375
Moses *l* up his hand, and with his	Num 20:11	7311
Balaam *l* up his eyes, and he saw	Num 24:2	5375
Then thine heart be *l* up, and thou	Deut 8:14	7311
be not *l* up above his brethren	Deut 17:20	7311
feet were *l* up unto the dry land	Josh 4:18	5423
that he *l* up his eyes and looked,	Josh 5:13	5375
that the people *l* up their voice	Judg 2:4	5375
so that they *l* up their heads no	Judg 8:28	5375
l up his voice, and cried, and said	Judg 9:7	5375
And when he had *l* up his eyes	Judg 19:17	5375
l up their voices, and wept sore	Judg 21:2	5375
they *l* up their voice, and wept	Ruth 1:9	5375
they *l* up their voice, and wept	Ruth 1:14	5375
they *l* up their eyes, and saw the	1Sa 6:13	5375
all the people *l* up their voices,	1Sa 11:4	5375
Saul *l* up his voice, and wept	1Sa 24:16	5375
were with him *l* up their voice	1Sa 30:4	5375
the king *l* up his voice, and wept	2Sa 3:32	5375
that kept the watch *l* up his eyes	2Sa 13:34	5375
came, and *l* up their voice and wept	2Sa 13:36	5375
l up his eyes, and looked, and	2Sa 18:24	5375
l up their hand against my lord	2Sa 18:28	5375
hath *l* up his hand against the	2Sa 20:21	5375
thou also hast *l* me up on high	2Sa 22:49	7311
he *l* up his spear against three	2Sa 23:18	5782
even he *l* up his hand against the	1Kin 11:26	7311
this was the cause that he *l* up	1Kin 11:27	7311
he *l* up his face to the window,	2Kin 9:32	5375
and thine heart hath *l* thee up	2Kin 14:10	5375
voice, and *l* up thine eyes on high	2Kin 19:22	5375
he *l* up his spear against three	1Chr 11:11	5782
for his kingdom was *l* up on high	1Chr 14:2	5375
David *l* up his eyes, and saw the	1Chr 21:16	5375
when they *l* up their voice with	2Chr 5:13	7311
his heart was *l* up in the ways of	2Chr 17:6	1361
his heart was *l* up to his	2Chr 26:16	1361
for his heart was *l* up	2Chr 32:25	1361
when they *l* up their eyes afar	Job 2:12	5375
they *l* up their voice, and wept	Job 2:12	5375
If I have *l* up my hand against	Job 31:21	5130
or *l* up myself when evil found	Job 31:29	5782
who hath not *l* up his soul unto	Ps 24:4	5375
and be ye *l* up, ye everlasting	Ps 24:7	5375
now shall mine head be *l* up above	Ps 27:6	7311

for thou hast *l* me up, and hast	Ps 30:1	1802
hath *l* up his heel against me	Ps 41:9	1431
l axes upon the thick trees	Ps 74:5	935
that hate thee have *l* up the head	Ps 83:2	5375
The floods have *l* up, O LORD, the	Ps 93:3	5375
the floods have *l* up their voice	Ps 93:3	5375
for thou hast *l* me up, and cast me	Ps 102:10	5375
Therefore he *l* up his hand	Ps 106:26	5375
and their eyelids are *l* up	Prov 30:13	5375
and upon every one that is *l* up	Is 2:12	5375
l up, and upon all the oaks of	Is 2:13	5375
upon all the hills that are *l* up	Is 2:14	5375
l up, and his train filled the	Is 6:1	5375
LORD, when thy hand is *l* up	Is 26:11	5375
voice, and *l* up thine eyes on high	Is 37:23	5375
is *l* up even to the skies	Jer 51:9	5375
l up the head of Jehoiachin king	Jer 52:31	5375
were *l* up from the earth, the	Eze 1:19	5375
the earth, the wheels were *l* up	Eze 1:19	5375
the wheels were *l* up over against	Eze 1:20	5375
when those were *l* up from the	Eze 1:21	5375
the wheels were *l* up over against	Eze 1:21	5375
So the spirit *l* me up, and took me	Eze 3:14	5375
the spirit *l* me up between the	Eze 8:3	5375
So I *l* up mine eyes the way	Eze 8:5	5375
And the cherubims were *l* up	Eze 10:15	7426
when the cherubims *l* up their	Eze 10:16	5375
and when they were *l* up	Eze 10:17	7311
these *l* up themselves also	Eze 10:17	7426
the cherubims *l* up their wings,	Eze 10:19	5375
Moreover the spirit *l* me up	Eze 11:1	5375
neither hath *l* up his eyes to the	Eze 18:6	5375
hath *l* up his eyes to the idols,	Eze 18:12	5375
neither hath *l* up his eyes to the	Eze 18:15	5375
l up mine hand unto the seed of	Eze 20:5	5375
when I *l* up mine hand unto them,	Eze 20:5	5375
In the day that I *l* up mine hand	Eze 20:6	5375
Yet also I *l* up my hand unto them	Eze 20:15	5375
I *l* up mine hand unto them also	Eze 20:23	5375
for the which I *l* up mine hand to	Eze 20:28	5375
the country for the which I *l* up	Eze 20:42	5375
Because thine heart is *l* up	Eze 28:2	1361
thine heart is *l* up because of	Eze 28:5	1361
Thine heart was *l* up because of	Eze 28:17	1361
Because thou hast *l* up thyself in	Eze 31:10	1361
his heart is *l* up in his height	Eze 31:10	7311
I have *l* up mine hand, Surely the	Eze 36:7	5375
therefore have I *l* up mine hand	Eze 44:12	5375
concerning the which I *l* up mine	Eze 47:14	5375
l up mine eyes unto heaven	Dan 4:34	5191
But when his heart was *l* up	Dan 5:20	7313
But hast *l* up thyself against the	Dan 5:23	7313
it was *l* up from the earth, and	Dan 7:4	5191
Then I *l* up mine eyes, and saw, and	Dan 8:3	5375
Then I *l* up mine eyes, and looked,	Dan 10:5	5375
his heart shall be *l* up	Dan 11:12	7311
Thine hand shall be *l* up upon	Mic 5:9	7311
his soul which is *l* up is not	Hab 2:4	6075
voice, and *l* up his hands on high	Hab 3:10	5375
Then I *l* up mine eyes, and saw, and	Zec 1:18	5375
which *l* up their horn over the	Zec 1:21	5375
I *l* up mine eyes again, and looked	Zec 2:1	5375
l up mine eyes, and looked, and	Zec 5:1	5375
there was *l* up a talent of lead	Zec 5:7	
Then I *l* up mine eyes, and looked,	Zec 5:9	5375
they *l* up the ephah between the	Zec 5:9	5375
l up mine eyes, and looked, and,	Zec 6:1	5375
l up as an ensign upon his land	Zec 9:16	5264
and it shall be *l* up, and inhabited	Zec 14:10	7213
And when they had *l* up their eyes	Mt 17:8	*1869*
took her by the hand, and *l* her up	Mk 1:31	*1453*
took him by the hand, and *l* him up	Mk 9:27	*1453*
he *l* up his eyes on his disciples	Lk 6:20	*1869*
of the company *l* up her voice	Lk 11:27	*1869*
they *l* up their voices, and said,	Lk 17:13	*142*
he *l* up his hands, and blessed	Lk 24:50	*1869*
as Moses *l* up the serpent in the	Jn 3:14	*5312*
so must the Son of man be *l* up	Jn 3:14	*5312*
When Jesus then *l* up his eyes	Jn 6:5	*1869*
he *l* up himself, and said unto	Jn 8:7	*352*
When Jesus had *l* up himself	Jn 8:10	*352*
When ye have *l* up the Son of man,	Jn 8:28	*5312*
Jesus *l* up his eyes, and said,	Jn 11:41	*142*
if I be *l* up from the earth, will	Jn 12:32	*5312*
thou, The Son of man must be *l* up	Jn 12:34	*5312*
me hath *l* up his heel against me	Jn 13:18	*1869*
l up his eyes to heaven, and said,	Jn 17:1	*1869*
l up his voice, and said unto them	Acts 2:14	*1869*
by the right hand, and *l* him up	Acts 3:7	*1453*
they *l* up their voice to God with	Acts 4:24	*142*
l her up, and when he had called	Acts 9:41	*450*
they *l* up their voices, saying in	Acts 14:11	*1869*
then *l* up their voices, and said,	Acts 22:22	*1869*
lest being *l* up with pride he	1Ti 3:6	*5188*
upon the earth *l* up his hand to	Rev 10:5	*142*

LIFTER

glory, and the *l* up of mine head	Ps 3:3	7311

LIFTEST

Thou *l* me up to the wind	Job 30:22	5375
thou that *l* me up from the gates	Ps 9:13	7311
thou *l* me up above those that	Ps 18:48	7311
l up thy voice for understanding	Prov 2:3	5414

LIFTETH

he bringeth low, and *l* up	1Sa 2:7	7311
l up the beggar from the dunghill	1Sa 2:8	7311
thine heart *l* thee up to boast	2Chr 25:19	5375
What time she *l* up herself on	Job 39:18	4754
which *l* up the waves thereof	Ps 107:25	7311
l the needy out of the dunghill	Ps 113:7	7311
The LORD *l* up the meek	Ps 147:6	5749
when he *l* up an ensign on the	Is 18:3	5375
against him that *l* himself up in	Jer 51:3	5927
The horseman *l* up both the bright	Nah 3:3	5927

LIFTING

for *l* up his spear against three	1Chr 11:20	5782
by *l* up the voice with joy	1Chr 15:16	7311
Amen, Amen, with *l* up their hands	Neh 8:6	4607
thou shalt say, There is *l* up	Job 22:29	1466
the *l* up of my hands as the	Ps 141:2	4864
done foolishly in *l* up thyself	Prov 30:32	5375
mount up like the *l* up of smoke	Is 9:18	1348
at the *l* up of thyself the	Is 33:3	7427
l up holy hands, without wrath and	1Ti 2:8	*1869*

LIGHT

And God said, Let there be *l*	Gen 1:3	216
and there was *l*	Gen 1:3	216
And God saw the *l*, that it was	Gen 1:4	216
God divided the *l* from the	Gen 1:4	216
And God called the *l* Day, and the	Gen 1:5	216
heaven to give *l* upon the earth	Gen 1:15	216
the greater *l* to rule the day, and	Gen 1:16	3974
the lesser *l* to rule the night	Gen 1:16	3974
heaven to give *l* upon the earth	Gen 1:17	216
to divide the *l* from the darkness	Gen 1:18	216
As soon as the morning was *l*	Gen 44:3	216
Israel had *l* in their dwellings	Ex 10:23	216
a pillar of fire, to give them *l*	Ex 13:21	216
but it gave *l* by night to these	Ex 14:20	216
Oil for the *l*, spices for	Ex 25:6	3974
they shall *l* the lamps thereof,	Ex 25:37	5927
they may give *l* over against it	Ex 25:37	216
pure oil olive beaten for the *l*	Ex 27:20	3974
And oil for the *l*, and spices for	Ex 35:8	3974
The candlestick also for the *l*	Ex 35:14	3974
his lamps, with the oil for the *l*	Ex 35:14	3974
And spice, and oil for the *l*	Ex 35:28	3974
vessels thereof, and the oil for *l*	Ex 39:37	3974
and *l* the lamps thereof	Ex 40:4	5927
pure oil olive beaten for the *l*	Lev 24:2	3974
and cover the candlestick of the *l*	Num 4:9	3974
pertaineth the oil for the *l*	Num 4:16	3974
the seven lamps shall give *l* over	Num 8:2	216
and our soul loatheth this *l* bread	Num 21:5	7052
Cursed be he that setteth *l* by	Deut 27:16	7034
l persons, which followed him	Judg 9:4	6348
where her lord was, till it was *l*	Judg 19:26	216
her hap was to *l* on a part of the	Ruth 2:3	7136
and spoil them until the morning *l*	1Sa 14:36	216
Seemeth it to you a *l* thing to be	1Sa 18:23	7043
l any that pisseth against the	1Sa 25:22	216
l any that pisseth against the	1Sa 25:34	216
less or more, until the morning *l*	1Sa 25:36	216
early in the morning, and have *l*	1Sa 29:10	216
Asahel was as *l* of foot as a wild	2Sa 2:18	7031
we will *l* upon him as the dew	2Sa 17:12	5117
by the morning *l* there lacked not	2Sa 17:22	216
thou quench not the *l* of Israel	2Sa 21:17	5216
shall be as the *l* of the morning	2Sa 23:4	216
l was against *l* in three	1Kin 7:4	4237
l was against *l* in three	1Kin 7:5	4237
was against *l* in three ranks	1Kin 7:5	216
David my servant may have a *l*	1Kin 11:36	5216
as if it had been a *l* thing for	1Kin 16:31	7043
this is but a *l* thing in the	2Kin 3:18	7043
if we tarry till the morning *l*	2Kin 7:9	216
him to give him alway a *l*	2Kin 8:19	5216
It is a *l* thing for the shadow to	2Kin 20:10	7043
as he promised to give a *l* to him	2Chr 21:7	5216
to give them *l* in the way wherein	Neh 9:12	216
of fire by night, to shew them *l*	Neh 9:19	216
The Jews had *l*, and gladness, and	Est 8:16	219
neither let the *l* shine upon it	Job 3:4	5105
let it look for *l*, but have none	Job 3:9	216
as infants which never saw *l*	Job 3:16	216
Wherefore is *l* given to him that	Job 3:20	216
Why is *l* given to a man whose way	Job 3:23	
where the *l* is as darkness	Job 10:22	3313
bringeth out to *l* the shadow of	Job 12:22	216
They grope in the dark without *l*	Job 12:25	216
the *l* is short because of	Job 17:12	216
the *l* of the wicked shall be put	Job 18:5	216
The *l* shall be dark in his	Job 18:6	216
be driven from *l* into darkness	Job 18:18	216
the *l* shall shine upon thy ways	Job 22:28	216
of those that rebel against the *l*	Job 24:13	216
with the *l* killeth the poor	Job 24:14	216
they know not the *l*	Job 24:16	216
and upon whom doth not his *l* arise	Job 25:3	216
is hid bringeth he forth to *l*	Job 28:11	216
when by his *l* I walked through	Job 29:3	216
the *l* of my countenance they cast	Job 29:24	216
and when I waited for *l*, there	Job 30:26	216
pit, and his life shall see the *l*	Job 33:28	216
with the *l* of the living	Job 33:30	216
he spreadeth his *l* upon it	Job 36:30	216
With clouds he covereth the *l*	Job 36:32	216
caused the *l* of his cloud to	Job 37:15	216
bright *l* which is in the clouds	Job 37:21	216
the wicked their *l* is withholden	Job 38:15	216
Where is the way where *l* dwelleth	Job 38:19	216
By what way is the *l* parted	Job 38:24	216
By his neesings a *l* doth shine	Job 41:18	216
lift thou up the *l* of thy	Ps 4:6	216
For thou wilt *l* my candle	Ps 18:28	215
The LORD is my *l* and my salvation	Ps 27:1	216
in thy *l* shall we see *l*	Ps 36:9	216
in thy *l* shall we see *l*	Ps 36:9	216
forth thy righteousness as the *l*	Ps 37:6	216
as for the *l* of mine eyes, it	Ps 38:10	216
O send out thy *l* and thy truth	Ps 43:3	216
the *l* of thy countenance, because	Ps 44:3	216
they shall never see *l*	Ps 49:19	216
before God in the *l* of the living	Ps 56:13	216
thou hast prepared the *l* and the	Ps 74:16	3974
and all the night with a *l* of fire	Ps 78:14	216
in the *l* of thy countenance	Ps 89:15	216
sins in the *l* of thy countenance	Ps 90:8	3974
L is sown for the righteous, and	Ps 97:11	216
thyself with *l* as with a garment	Ps 104:2	216
and fire to give *l* in the night	Ps 105:39	216
there ariseth *l* in the darkness	Ps 112:4	216
the LORD, which hath shewed us *l*	Ps 118:27	216
unto my feet, and a *l* unto my path	Ps 119:105	216
entrance of thy words giveth *l*	Ps 119:130	216
the night shall be *l* about me	Ps 139:11	216
the *l* are both alike to thee	Ps 139:12	219
praise him, all ye stars of *l*	Ps 148:3	216
of the just is as the shining *l*	Prov 4:18	216
and the law is *l*	Prov 6:23	216
The *l* of the righteous rejoiceth	Prov 13:9	216
The *l* of the eyes rejoiceth the	Prov 15:30	3974
In the *l* of the king's	Prov 16:15	216
as far as *l* excelleth darkness	Eccl 2:13	216
Truly the *l* is sweet, and a	Eccl 11:7	216
While the sun, or the *l*, or the	Eccl 12:2	216
let us walk in the *l* of the LORD	Is 2:5	216
for *l*, and *l* for darkness	Is 5:20	216
the *l* is darkened in the heavens	Is 5:30	216
is because there is no *l* in them	Is 8:20	7837
in darkness have seen a great *l*	Is 9:2	216
upon them hath the *l* shined	Is 9:2	216
the *l* of Israel shall be for a	Is 10:17	216
thereof shall not give their *l*	Is 13:10	216
shall not cause her *l* to shine	Is 13:10	216
Moreover the *l* of the moon shall	Is 30:26	216
moon shall be as the *l* of the sun	Is 30:26	216
the *l* of the sun shall be	Is 30:26	216
as the *l* of seven days, in the	Is 30:26	216
people, for a *l* of the Gentiles	Is 42:6	216
will make darkness *l* before them	Is 42:16	216
I form the *l*, and create darkness	Is 45:7	216
It is a *l* thing that thou	Is 49:6	7043
give thee for a *l* to the Gentiles	Is 49:6	216
walketh in darkness, and hath no *l*	Is 50:10	5051
walk in the *l* of your fire, and in	Is 50:11	217
to rest for a *l* of the people	Is 51:4	216
Then shall thy *l* break forth as	Is 58:8	216
then shall thy *l* rise in	Is 58:10	216
we wait for *l*, but behold	Is 59:9	216
for thy *l* is come, and the glory	Is 60:1	216
the Gentiles shall come to thy *l*	Is 60:3	216
sun shall be no more thy *l* by day	Is 60:19	216
shall the moon give *l* unto thee	Is 60:19	216
be unto thee an everlasting *l*	Is 60:19	216
LORD shall be thine everlasting *l*	Is 60:20	216
and the heavens, and they had no *l*	Jer 4:23	216
and, while ye look for *l*, he turn	Jer 13:16	216
and the *l* of the candle	Jer 25:10	216
giveth the sun for a *l* by day	Jer 31:35	216
and of the stars for a *l* by night	Jer 31:35	216
me into darkness, but not into *l*	Lam 3:2	216
Is it a *l* thing to the house of	Eze 8:17	7043
In thee have they set *l* by father	Eze 22:7	7043
and the moon shall not give her *l*	Eze 32:7	216
and the *l* dwelleth with him	Dan 2:22	5094
and in the days of thy father *l*	Dan 5:11	5094
of the gods is in thee, and that *l*	Dan 5:14	5094
are as the *l* that goeth forth	Hos 6:5	216
of the LORD is darkness, and not *l*	Amos 5:18	216
of the LORD be darkness, and not *l*	Amos 5:20	216
when the morning is *l*, they	Mic 2:1	216
the LORD shall be a *l* unto me	Mic 7:8	216
he will bring me forth to the *l*	Mic 7:9	216
And his brightness was as the *l*	Hab 3:4	216
at the *l* of thine arrows they	Hab 3:11	216
Her prophets are *l* and treacherous	Zeph 3:4	6348
doth he bring his judgment to *l*	Zeph 3:5	216
that the *l* shall not be clear,	Zec 14:6	216
at evening time it shall be *l*	Zec 14:7	216
which sat in darkness saw great *l*	Mt 4:16	*5457*
and shadow of death *l* is sprung up	Mt 4:16	*5457*
Ye are the *l* of the world	Mt 5:14	*5457*
Neither do men *l* a candle	Mt 5:15	*2545*
it giveth *l* unto all that are in	Mt 5:15	*2989*
Let your *l* so shine before men,	Mt 5:16	*5457*
The *l* of the body is the eye	Mt 6:22	*5460*
thy whole body shall be full of *l*	Mt 6:22	*3088*
If therefore the *l* that is in	Mt 6:23	*5457*
in darkness, that speak ye in *l*	Mt 10:27	*5457*
yoke is easy, and my burden is *l*	Mt 11:30	*1645*
and his raiment was white as the *l*	Mt 17:2	*5457*
But they made *l* of it, and went	Mt 22:5	*272*
and the moon shall not give her *l*	Mt 24:29	*5338*
and the moon shall not give her *l*	Mk 13:24	*5338*
To give *l* to them that sit in	Lk 1:79	*2014*
A *l* to lighten the Gentiles, and	Lk 2:32	*5457*
they which enter in may see the *l*	Lk 8:16	*5457*
they which come in may see the *l*	Lk 11:33	*5338*
The *l* of the body is the eye	Lk 11:34	*3088*
thy whole body also is full of *l*	Lk 11:34	*5460*
the *l* which is in thee be not	Lk 11:35	*5457*
whole body therefore be full of *l*	Lk 11:36	*5460*
the whole shall be full of *l*	Lk 11:36	*5460*
of a candle doth give thee *l*	Lk 11:36	*5461*
darkness shall be heard in the *l*	Lk 12:3	*5457*
one piece, doth not *l* a candle	Lk 15:8	*681*
wiser than the children of *l*	Lk 16:8	*5457*
and the life was the *l* of men	Jn 1:4	*5457*
the *l* shineth in darkness	Jn 1:5	*5457*
witness, to bear witness of the *L*	Jn 1:7	*5457*
He was not that *L*, but was sent	Jn 1:8	*5457*
sent to bear witness of that *L*	Jn 1:8	*5457*
That was the true *L*, which	Jn 1:9	*5457*
that *l* is come into the world, and	Jn 3:19	*5457*
men loved darkness rather than *l*	Jn 3:19	*5457*
one that doeth evil hateth the *l*	Jn 3:20	*5457*
neither cometh to the *l*	Jn 3:20	*5457*
that doeth truth cometh to the *l*	Jn 3:21	*5457*
He was a burning and a shining *l*	Jn 5:35	*3088*

L

for a season to rejoice in his *l* Jn 5:35 *5457*
saying, I am the *l* of the world Jn 8:12 *5457*
but shall have the *l* of life Jn 8:12 *5457*
world, I am the *l* of the world Jn 9:5 *5457*
he seeth the *l* of this world Jn 11:9 *5457*
because there is no *l* in him Jn 11:10 *5457*
a little while is the *l* with you Jn 12:35 *5457*
Walk while ye have the *l*, lest Jn 12:35 *5457*
ye have *l*, believe in the *l* Jn 12:36 *5457*
that ye may be the children of *l* Jn 12:36 *5457*
I am come a *l* into the world, Jn 12:46 *5457*
round about him a *l* from heaven Acts 9:3 *5457*
him, and a *l* shined in the prison Acts 12:7 *5457*
thee to be a *l* of the Gentiles Acts 13:47 *5457*
Then he called for a *l*, and sprang Acts 16:29 *5457*
heaven a great *l* round about me Acts 22:6 *5457*
were with me saw indeed the *l* Acts 22:9 *5457*
not see for the glory of that *l* Acts 22:11 *5457*
I saw in the way a *l* from heaven Acts 26:13 *5457*
to turn them from darkness to *l* Acts 26:18 *5457*
should shew *l* unto the people, and Acts 26:23 *5457*
a *l* of them which are in darkness Rom 2:19 *5457*
and let us put on the armour of *l* Rom 13:12 *5457*
who both will bring to *l* the 1Cor 4:5 *5461*
lest the *l* of the glorious gospel 2Cor 4:4 *5462*
who commanded the *l* to shine out 2Cor 4:6 *5457*
to give the *l* of the knowledge of 2Cor 4:6 *5462*
For our *l* affliction, which is 2Cor 4:17 *1645*
communion hath *l* with darkness 2Cor 6:14 *5457*
is transformed into an angel of *l* 2Cor 11:14 *5457*
but now are ye *l* in the Lord Eph 5:8 *5457*
walk as children of *l* Eph 5:8 *5457*
are made manifest by the *l* Eph 5:13 *5457*
doth make manifest is *l* Eph 5:13 *5457*
dead, and Christ shall give thee *l* Eph 5:14 *2017*
inheritance of the saints in *l* Col 1:12 *5457*
Ye are all the children of *l* 1Th 5:5 *5457*
dwelling in the *l* which no man 1Ti 6:16 *5457*
immortality to *l* through the 2Ti 1:10 *5461*
of darkness into his marvellous *l* 1Pet 2:9 *5457*
as unto a *l* that shineth in a 2Pet 1:19 *3088*
declare unto you, that God is *l* 1Jn 1:5 *5457*
in the *l*, as he is in the *l* 1Jn 1:7 *5457*
past, and the true *l* now shineth 1Jn 2:8 *5457*
He that saith he is in the *l* 1Jn 2:9 *5457*
his brother abideth in the *l* 1Jn 2:10 *5457*
neither shall the sun *l* on them Rev 7:16 *4098*
the *l* of a candle shall shine no Rev 18:23 *5457*
her *l* was like unto a stone most Rev 21:11 *5458*
it, and the Lamb is the *l* thereof Rev 21:23 *3088*
saved shall walk in the *l* of it Rev 21:24 *5457*
no candle, neither *l* of the sun Rev 22:5 *5457*
for the Lord God giveth them *l* Rev 22:5 *5461*

LIGHTED
saw Isaac, she *l* off the camel Gen 24:64 5307
he *l* upon a certain place, and Gen 28:11 6293
he *l* the lamps before the LORD Ex 40:25 5927
he *l* the lamps thereof over Num 8:3 5927
and she *l* off her ass Josh 15:18 6795
and she *l* from off her ass Judg 1:14 6795
so that Sisera *l* down off his Judg 4:15 3381
l off the ass, and fell before 1Sa 25:23 3381
he *l* down from the chariot to 2Kin 5:21 5307
he *l* on Jehonadab the son of 2Kin 10:15 4672
Jacob, and it hath *l* upon Israel Is 9:8 5307
No man, when he hath *l* a candle Lk 8:16 *681*
No man, when he hath *l* a candle Lk 11:33 *681*

LIGHTEN
peradventure he will *l* his hand 1Sa 6:5 7043
and the LORD will *l* my darkness 2Sa 22:29 5050
that our God may *l* our eyes Ezr 9:8 215
l mine eyes, lest I sleep the Ps 13:3 215
into the sea, to *l* it of them Jonah 1:5 7043
A light to *l* the Gentiles, and the Lk 2:32 *602*
for the glory of God did *l* it Rev 21:23 *5461*

LIGHTENED
They looked unto him, and were *l* Ps 34:5 5102
the lightnings *l* the world Ps 77:18 215
the next day they *l* the ship Acts 27:18 *4160*
they *l* the ship, and cast out the Acts 27:38 *2893*
the earth was *l* with his glory Rev 18:1 *5461*

LIGHTENETH
the LORD *l* both their eyes Prov 29:13 215
that *l* out of the one part under Lk 17:24 *797*

LIGHTER
yoke which he put upon us, *l* 1Kin 12:4 7043
thy father did put upon us *l* 1Kin 12:9 7043
heavy, but make thou it *l* unto us 1Kin 12:10 7043
make thou it somewhat *l* for us 2Chr 10:10 7043
they are altogether *l* than vanity Ps 62:9

LIGHTEST
unto him, When thou *l* the lamps Num 8:2 5927

LIGHTETH
when Aaron *l* the lamps at even, Ex 30:8 5927
l upon his neighbour, that he die Deut 19:5 4672
which *l* every man that cometh Jn 1:9 *5461*

LIGHTING
shall shew the *l* down of his arm, Is 30:30 5183
like a dove, and *l* upon him Mt 3:16 *2064*

LIGHTLY
might *l* have lien with thy wife Gen 26:10 4592
l esteemed the Rock of his Deut 32:15 5034
despise me shall be *l* esteemed 1Sa 2:30 7043
I am a poor man, and *l* esteemed 1Sa 18:23 7034
when at the first he *l* afflicted Is 9:1 7043
and all the hills moved *l* Jer 4:24 7043
that can *l* speak evil of me Mk 9:39 *5035*

LIGHTNESS
through the *l* of her whoredom Jer 3:9 6963
err by their lies, and by their *l* Jer 23:32 6350
was thus minded, did I use *l* 2Cor 1:17 *1644*

LIGHTNING
l, and discomfited them 2Sa 22:15 1300
a way for the *l* of the thunder Job 28:26 2385
his *l* unto the ends of the earth Job 37:3 216
or a way for the *l* of thunder Job 38:25 2385
Cast forth *l*, and scatter them Ps 144:6 1300
and out of the fire went forth *l* Eze 1:13 1300
as the appearance of a flash of *l* Eze 1:14 965
his face as the appearance of *l* Dan 10:6 1300
his arrow shall go forth as the *l* Zec 9:14 1300
For as the *l* cometh out of the Mt 24:27 *796*
His countenance was like *l* Mt 28:3 *796*
Satan as *l* fall from heaven Lk 10:18 *796*
For as the *l*, that lighteneth out Lk 17:24 *796*

LIGHTNINGS
that there were thunders and *l* Ex 19:16 1300
saw the thunderings, and the *l* Ex 20:18 3940
Canst thou send *l*, that they may Job 38:35 1300
and he shot out *l*, and discomfited Ps 18:14 1300
the *l* lightened the world Ps 77:18 1300
His *l* enlightened the world Ps 97:4 1300
he maketh *l* for the rain Ps 135:7 1300
he maketh *l* with rain, and Jer 10:13 1300
he maketh *l* with rain, and Jer 51:16 1300
they shall run like the *l* Nah 2:4 1300
And out of the throne proceeded *l* Rev 4:5 *796*
were voices, and thunderings, and *l* Rev 8:5 *796*
and there were *l*, and voices, and Rev 11:19 *796*
were voices, and thunders, and *l* Rev 16:18 *796*

LIGHTS
Let there be *l* in the firmament Gen 1:14 3974
And let them be for *l* in the Gen 1:15 3974
And God made two great *l* Gen 1:16 3974
house he made windows of narrow *l* 1Kin 6:4 8261
To him that made great *l* Ps 136:7 216
All the bright *l* of heaven will I Eze 32:8 3974
girded about, and your *l* burning Lk 12:35 *3088*
there were many *l* in the upper Acts 20:8 *2985*
whom ye shine as *l* in the world Phil 2:15 *5458*
cometh down from the Father of *l* Jas 1:17 *5457*

LIGN
as the trees of *l* aloes which the Num 24:6

LIGURE
And the third row a *l*, an agate, Ex 28:19 3958
And the third row, a *l*, an agate, Ex 39:12 3958

LIKE
l the land of Egypt, as thou Gen 13:10
all over *l* an hairy garment Gen 25:25
they also did in *l* manner with Ex 7:11 3651
is none *l* unto the LORD our God Ex 8:10 3644
is none *l* me in all the earth Ex 9:14 3644
such as there was none *l* it in Ex 9:24 3644
such as there was none *l* it Ex 11:6 3644
nor shall be *l* it any more Ex 11:6 3644
Who is *l* unto thee, O LORD, among Ex 15:11 3644
Who is *l* thee, glorious in Ex 15:11 3644
it was *l* coriander seed, white Ex 16:31
the taste of it was *l* wafers made Ex 16:31
In *l* manner thou shalt deal with Ex 23:11 3651
l devouring fire on the top of Ex 24:17
Three bowls made *l* unto almonds Ex 25:33
three bowls made *l* almonds in the Ex 25:33
be four bowls made *l* unto almonds Ex 25:34
l the engravings of a signet, Ex 28:11
l the engravings of a signet Ex 28:21
l the engravings of a signet, Ex 28:36
shall ye make any other *l* it Ex 30:32 3644
Whosoever compoundeth any *l* it Ex 30:33 3644
of each shall there be a *l* weight Ex 30:34
Whosoever shall make *l* unto that Ex 30:38 3644
tables of stone *l* unto the first Ex 34:1
tables of stone *l* unto the first Ex 34:4
three bowls made *l* almonds in Ex 37:19
were four bowls made *l* almonds Ex 37:20
work, *l* the work of the ephod Ex 39:8
l the engravings of a signet, Ex 39:14
l to the engravings of a signet, Ex 39:30
his flesh *l* the plague of leprosy Lev 13:2
and let my last end be *l* his Num 23:10 3644
thing is, or hath been heard *l* it Deut 4:32 3644
lest thou be a cursed thing *l* it Deut 7:26 3644
tables of stone *l* unto the first Deut 10:1
tables of stone *l* unto the first Deut 10:3
l as all the nations that are Deut 17:14
They shall have *l* portions to eat Deut 18:8
thee, of thy brethren, *l* unto me Deut 18:15 3644
l unto thee, and will put my words Deut 18:18 3644
In *l* manner shalt thou do with Deut 22:3 3651
if the man *l* not to take his Deut 25:7 2654
it, and say, I *l* not to take her Deut 25:8 2654
l the overthrow of Sodom, and Deut 29:23
His glory is *l* the firstling of Deut 33:17
his horns are *l* the horns of Deut 33:17
There is none *l* unto the God of Deut 33:26
who is *l* unto thee, O people Deut 33:29 3644
since in Israel *l* unto Moses Deut 34:10
there was no day *l* that before it Josh 10:14
l grasshoppers for multitude Judg 7:12
in *l* manner they sent unto the Judg 11:17 1571
his countenance was *l* the Judg 13:6
them from off his arms *l* a thread Judg 16:12
weak, and be *l* any other man Judg 16:17
though I be not *l* unto one of Ruth 2:13
is come into thine house *l* Rachel Ruth 4:11
l Leah, which two did build the Ruth 4:11
let thy house be *l* the house of Ruth 4:12
is there any rock *l* our God 1Sa 2:2
strong, and quit yourselves *l* men 1Sa 4:9
quit yourselves *l* men, and fight 1Sa 4:9
to judge us *l* all the nations 1Sa 8:5
we also may be *l* all the nations 1Sa 8:20
that there is none *l* him among 1Sa 10:24 3644
his spear was *l* a weaver's beam 1Sa 17:7
before Samuel in *l* manner 1Sa 19:24 1571
David said, There is none *l* that 1Sa 21:9
his house, *l* the feast of a king 1Sa 25:36
who is *l* to thee in Israel 1Sa 26:15 3644
l unto the name of the great men 2Sa 7:9
for there is none *l* thee, neither 2Sa 7:22 3644
in the earth is *l* thy people 2Sa 7:23
even *l* Israel, whom God went to 2Sa 7:23
l the running of Ahimaaz the son 2Sa 18:27
whose spear was *l* a weaver's beam 2Sa 21:19
He maketh my feet *l* hinds' feet 2Sa 22:34 7737
there was none *l* thee before thee 1Kin 3:12 3644
thee shall any arise *l* unto thee 1Kin 3:12 3644
kings *l* unto thee all thy days 1Kin 3:13 3644
hew timber *l* unto the Sidonians 1Kin 5:6
porch, which was of the *l* work 1Kin 7:8
taken to wife, *l* unto this porch 1Kin 7:8
was wrought *l* the brim of a cup 1Kin 7:26
the work of the wheels was *l* the 1Kin 7:33
of Israel, there is no God *l* thee 1Kin 8:23 3644
there was not the *l* made in any 1Kin 10:20 3651
l unto the feast that is in Judah 1Kin 12:32
will make thy house *l* the house 1Kin 16:3
in being *l* the house of Jeroboam 1Kin 16:7
out of the sea, *l* a man's hand 1Kin 18:44
l the army that thou hast lost, 1Kin 20:25
them *l* two little flocks of kids 1Kin 20:27
will make thine house *l* the house 1Kin 21:22
l the house of Baasha the son of 1Kin 21:22
But there was none *l* unto Ahab 1Kin 21:25
be *l* the word of one of them, and 1Kin 22:13
but not *l* his father, and *l* his 2Kin 3:2
l his father, and *l* his mother 2Kin 3:2
his flesh came again *l* unto the 2Kin 5:14
l the house of Jeroboam the son 2Kin 9:9
l the house of Baasha the son of 2Kin 9:9
the driving is *l* the driving of 2Kin 9:20
had made them *l* the dust by 2Kin 13:7
yet not *l* David his father 2Kin 14:3
LORD his God, *l* David his father 2Kin 16:2
l to the neck of their fathers, 2Kin 17:14
that they should not do *l* them 2Kin 17:15
none *l* him among all the kings of 2Kin 18:5 3644
away to a land *l* your own land 2Kin 18:32
l unto him was there no king 2Kin 23:25 3644
after him arose there any *l* him 2Kin 23:25 3644
l unto these had the second 2Kin 25:17
l to the children of Judah 1Chr 4:27
was a spear *l* a weaver's beam 1Chr 11:23
whose faces were *l* the faces of 1Chr 12:8
a great host, *l* the host of God 1Chr 12:22
l the breaking forth of waters 1Chr 14:11
have made thee a name *l* the name 1Chr 17:8
O LORD, there is none *l* thee 1Chr 17:20 3644
the earth is *l* thy people Israel 1Chr 17:21
spear staff was *l* a weaver's beam 1Chr 20:5
l to the stars of the heavens 1Chr 27:23
people *l* the dust of the earth in 2Chr 1:9
there any after thee have the *l* 2Chr 1:12 3651
the brim of it *l* the work of the 2Chr 4:5 3651
there is no God *l* thee in the 2Chr 6:14 3644
There was not the *l* made in any 2Chr 9:19 3651
be *l* one of theirs, and speak thou 2Chr 18:12
l as did the house of Ahab 2Chr 21:6
l to the whoredoms of the house 2Chr 21:13
l the burning of his fathers 2Chr 21:19
of the LORD *l* the house of Ahab 2Chr 22:4
of the LORD, *l* David his father 2Chr 28:1
be not ye *l* your fathers 2Chr 30:7
l your brethren, which trespassed 2Chr 30:7
there was not the *l* in Jerusalem 2Chr 30:26
l unto the abominations of the 2Chr 33:2
there was no passover *l* to that 2Chr 35:18 3644
his servant unto me in *l* manner Neh 6:5 2088
nations was there no king *l* him Neh 13:26 3644
l as when she was brought up with Est 2:20
there is none *l* him in the earth Job 1:8 3644
there is none *l* him in the earth Job 2:3 3644
are poured out *l* the waters Job 3:24
l as a shock of corn cometh in in Job 5:26
are not his days also *l* the days Job 7:1
of thy mouth be *l* a strong wind Job 8:2
as milk, and curdled me *l* cheese Job 10:10
man be born *l* a wild ass's colt Job 11:12
them to stagger *l* a drunken man Job 12:25
remembrances are *l* unto ashes Job 13:12 4911
He cometh forth *l* a flower Job 14:2
and bring forth boughs *l* a plant Job 14:9 3644
which drinketh iniquity *l* water Job 15:16
he runneth upon me *l* a giant Job 16:14
hope hath he removed *l* a tree Job 19:10
perish for ever *l* his own dung Job 20:7
forth their little ones *l* a flock Job 21:11
the mire, and I am become *l* dust Job 30:19 4911
is ready to burst *l* new bottles Job 32:19
What man is *l* Job Job 34:7
who drinketh up scorning *l* water Job 34:7
who teacheth *l* him Job 36:22 3644
Gird up now thy loins *l* a man Job 38:3 3644
Gird up thy loins now *l* a man Job 40:7
Hast thou an arm *l* God Job 40:9
thou thunder with a voice *l* him Job 40:9 3644
He moveth his tail *l* a cedar Job 40:17 3644
his bones are *l* bars of iron Job 40:18
his eyes are *l* the eyelids of the Job 41:18
maketh the deep to boil *l* a pot Job 41:31
the sea *l* a pot of ointment Job 41:31
Upon earth there is not his *l* Job 41:33 4915

which is right, *l* my servant Job	Job 42:8	
he shall be *l* a tree planted by	Ps 1:3	
but are *l* the chaff which the	Ps 1:4	
in pieces *l* a potter's vessel	Ps 2:9	
Lest he tear my soul *l* a lion	Ps 7:2	
L as a lion that is greedy of his	Ps 17:12	1825
He maketh my feet *l* hinds' feet	Ps 18:33	
I am poured out *l* water, and all	Ps 22:14	
my heart is *l* wax	Ps 22:14	
strength is dried up *l* a potsherd	Ps 22:15	
I become *l* them that go down into	Ps 28:1	5973
maketh them also to skip *l* a calf	Ps 29:6	3644
and Sirion *l* a young unicorn	Ps 29:6	3644
I am *l* a broken vessel	Ps 31:12	3644
who is *l* unto thee, which	Ps 35:10	
is *l* the great mountains	Ps 36:6	
soon be cut down *l* the grass	Ps 37:2	
himself *l* a green bay tree	Ps 37:35	
beauty to consume away *l* a moth	Ps 39:11	
Thou hast given us *l* sheep	Ps 44:11	
he is *l* the beasts that perish	Ps 49:12	4911
L sheep they are laid in the	Ps 49:14	
is *l* the beasts that perish	Ps 49:20	4711
l a sharp rasor, working	Ps 52:2	
But I am *l* a green olive tree in	Ps 52:8	
Oh that I had wings *l* a dove	Ps 55:6	
Their poison is *l* the poison of a	Ps 58:4	1823
they are *l* the deaf adder that	Ps 58:4	3644
l the untimely birth of a woman	Ps 58:8	
they make a noise *l* a dog	Ps 59:6	
and let them make a noise *l* a dog	Ps 59:14	
Who whet their tongue *l* a sword	Ps 64:3	
O God, who is *l* unto thee	Ps 71:19	3644
He shall come down *l* rain upon	Ps 72:6	
thereof shall shake *l* Lebanon	Ps 72:16	
flourish *l* grass of the earth	Ps 72:16	
are they plagued *l* other men	Ps 73:5	5973
Thou leddest thy people *l* a flock	Ps 77:20	
waters to run down *l* rivers	Ps 78:16	
feathered fowls *l* as the sand of	Ps 78:27	
own people to go forth *l* sheep	Ps 78:52	
them in the wilderness *l* a flock	Ps 78:52	
unfaithfully *l* their fathers	Ps 78:57	
turned aside *l* a deceitful bow	Ps 78:57	
l a mighty man that shouteth by	Ps 78:65	
his sanctuary *l* high palaces	Ps 78:69	
l the earth which he hath	Ps 78:69	
Their blood have they shed *l*	Ps 79:3	
shall thy jealousy burn *l* fire	Ps 79:5	
that leadest Joseph *l* a flock	Ps 80:1	
thereof were *l* the goodly cedars	Ps 80:10	
But ye shall die *l* men	Ps 82:7	
fall *l* one of the princes	Ps 82:7	
their nobles *l* Oreb, and *l* Zeeb	Ps 83:11	
O my God, make them *l* a wheel	Ps 83:13	
gods there is none *l* unto thee	Ps 86:8	
there any works *l* unto thy works	Ps 86:8	
l the slain that lie in the grave	Ps 88:5	3644
came round about me daily *l* water	Ps 88:17	
who is a strong LORD *l* unto thee	Ps 89:8	3644
shall thy wrath burn *l* fire	Ps 89:46	
they are *l* grass which groweth up	Ps 90:5	
exalt *l* the horn of an unicorn	Ps 92:10	
shall flourish *l* the palm tree	Ps 92:12	
he shall grow *l* a cedar in	Ps 92:12	
The hills melted *l* wax at the	Ps 97:5	
For my days are consumed *l* smoke	Ps 102:3	
is smitten, and withered *l* grass	Ps 102:4	
I am *l* a pelican of the	Ps 102:6	1819
I am *l* an owl of the desert	Ps 102:6	
For I have eaten ashes *l* bread	Ps 102:9	
My days are *l* a shadow that	Ps 102:11	
and I am withered *l* grass	Ps 102:11	
of them shall wax old *l* a garment	Ps 102:26	1819
youth is renewed *l* the eagle's	Ps 103:5	
L as a father pitieth his	Ps 103:13	
out the heavens *l* a curtain	Ps 104:2	
ran in the dry places *l* a river	Ps 105:41	
stagger *l* a drunken man, and are	Ps 107:27	
and maketh him families *l* a flock	Ps 107:41	
cursing *l* as with his garment	Ps 109:18	
it come into his bowels *l* water	Ps 109:18	
water, and *l* oil into his bones	Ps 109:18	
I am gone *l* the shadow when it	Ps 109:23	
Who is *l* unto the LORD our God,	Ps 113:5	
The mountains skipped *l* rams	Ps 114:4	
and the little hills *l* lambs	Ps 114:4	
mountains, that ye skipped *l* rams	Ps 114:6	
and ye little hills, *l* lambs	Ps 114:6	
that make them are *l* unto them	Ps 115:8	3644
They compassed me about *l* bees	Ps 118:12	
For I am become *l* a bottle in the	Ps 119:83	
the wicked of the earth *l* dross	Ps 119:119	
I have gone astray *l* a lost sheep	Ps 119:176	
we were *l* them that dream	Ps 126:1	
thy children *l* olive plants round	Ps 128:3	
It is *l* the precious ointment	Ps 133:2	
that make them are *l* unto them	Ps 135:18	3644
their tongues *l* a serpent	Ps 140:3	3644
lest I be *l* unto them that go	Ps 143:7	4911
Man is *l* to vanity	Ps 144:4	1819
He giveth snow *l* wool	Ps 147:16	
scattereth the hoar frost *l* ashes	Ps 147:16	
casteth forth his ice *l* morsels	Ps 147:17	
There is that speaketh *l* the	Prov 12:18	
heart doeth good *l* a medicine	Prov 17:22	
are *l* the bars of a castle	Prov 18:19	
the heart of man is *l* deep water	Prov 20:5	
At the last it biteth *l* a serpent	Prov 23:32	
and stingeth *l* an adder	Prov 23:32	
A word fitly spoken is *l* apples	Prov 25:11	
of a false gift is *l* clouds	Prov 25:14	
of trouble is *l* a broken tooth	Prov 25:19	
is *l* a city that is broken down	Prov 25:28	
lest thou also be *l* unto him	Prov 26:4	7737
is *l* one that taketh a dog by the	Prov 26:17	
a wicked heart are *l* a potsherd	Prov 26:23	
l a sweeping rain which leaveth	Prov 28:3	
She is *l* the merchants' ships	Prov 31:14	
My beloved is *l* a roe or a young	Song 2:9	1819
be thou *l* a roe or a young hart	Song 2:17	1819
the wilderness *l* pillars of smoke	Song 3:6	
Thy teeth are *l* a flock of sheep	Song 4:2	
Thy lips are *l* a thread of	Song 4:3	
thy temples are *l* a piece of a	Song 4:3	
Thy neck is *l* the tower of David	Song 4:4	
Thy two breasts are *l* two young	Song 4:5	
is *l* the smell of Lebanon	Song 4:11	
his lips *l* lilies, dropping sweet	Song 5:13	
my soul made me *l* the chariots of	Song 6:12	
joints of thy thighs are *l* jewels	Song 7:1	3644
Thy navel is *l* a round goblet,	Song 7:2	
thy belly is *l* an heap of wheat	Song 7:2	
Thy two breasts are *l* two young	Song 7:3	
thine eyes *l* the fishpools in	Song 7:4	
Thine head upon thee is *l* Carmel	Song 7:5	
the hair of thine head *l* purple	Song 7:5	
thy stature is *l* to a palm tree	Song 7:7	1819
and the smell of thy nose *l* apples	Song 7:8	
the roof of thy mouth *l* the best	Song 7:9	
am a wall, and my breasts *l* towers	Song 8:10	
be thou *l* to a roe or to a young	Song 8:14	1819
should have been *l* unto Gomorrah	Is 1:9	1819
though they be red *l* crimson	Is 1:18	1819
are soothsayers *l* the Philistines	Is 2:6	
and their round tires *l* the moon	Is 3:18	
hoofs shall be counted *l* flint	Is 5:28	
and their wheels *l* a whirlwind	Is 5:28	
Their roaring shall be *l* a lion	Is 5:29	
they shall roar *l* young lions	Is 5:29	
them *l* the roaring of the sea	Is 5:30	
they shall mount up *l* the lifting	Is 9:18	
to tread them down *l* the mire of	Is 10:6	
the inhabitants *l* a valiant man	Is 10:13	
a burning *l* the burning of a fire	Is 10:16	
the lion shall eat straw *l* the ox	Is 11:7	
l as it was to Israel in the day	Is 11:16	
mountains, *l* as of a great people	Is 13:4	1823
art thou become *l* unto us	Is 14:10	4911
I will be *l* the most High	Is 14:14	1819
thy grave *l* an abominable branch	Is 14:19	
shall sound *l* an harp for Moab	Is 16:11	
which make a noise *l* the noise of	Is 17:12	
that make a rushing *l* the rushing	Is 17:12	
The nations shall rush *l* the	Is 17:13	
l a rolling thing before the	Is 17:13	
place *l* a clear heat upon herbs	Is 18:4	
l a cloud of dew in the heat of	Is 18:4	
day shall Egypt be *l* unto women	Is 19:16	
L as my servant Isaiah hath	Is 20:3	
toss thee *l* a ball into a large	Is 22:18	
fro *l* a drunkard, and shall be	Is 24:20	
and shall be removed *l* a cottage	Is 24:20	
L as a woman with child, that	Is 26:17	3644
forsaken, and left *l* a wilderness	Is 27:10	
strangers shall be *l* small dust	Is 29:5	
l a stream of brimstone, doth	Is 30:33	
L as the lion and the young lion	Is 31:4	
gathered *l* the gathering of the	Is 33:4	
Sharon is *l* a wilderness	Is 33:9	
away to a land *l* your own land	Is 36:17	
I have cut off *l* a weaver my life	Is 38:12	
L a crane or a swallow, so did I	Is 38:14	
shall feed his flock *l* a shepherd	Is 40:11	
stir up jealousy *l* a man of war	Is 42:13	
now will I cry *l* a travailing	Is 42:14	
and compare me, that we may be *l*	Is 46:5	1819
I am God, and there is none *l* me	Is 46:9	3644
thy bowels *l* the gravel thereof	Is 48:19	
made my mouth *l* a sharp sword	Is 49:2	
have I set my face *l* a flint	Is 50:7	
will make her wilderness *l* Eden	Is 51:3	
her desert *l* the garden of the	Is 51:3	
heavens shall vanish away *l* smoke	Is 51:6	
earth shall wax old *l* a garment	Is 51:6	
therein shall die in *l* manner	Is 51:6	3644
shall eat them up *l* a garment	Is 51:8	
and the worm shall eat them *l* wool	Is 51:8	
All we *l* sheep have gone astray	Is 53:6	
the wicked are *l* the troubled sea	Is 57:20	
lift up thy voice *l* a trumpet	Is 58:1	
thou shalt be *l* a watered garden,	Is 58:11	
l a spring of water, whose waters	Is 58:11	
We grope for the wall *l* the blind	Is 59:10	
l bears, and mourn sore *l* doves	Is 59:11	
the enemy shall come in *l* a flood	Is 59:19	
thy garments *l* him that treadeth	Is 63:2	
l the wind, have taken us away	Is 64:6	
shall eat straw *l* the bullock	Is 65:25	
extend peace to her *l* a river	Is 66:12	
the Gentiles *l* a flowing stream	Is 66:12	
bones shall flourish *l* an herb	Is 66:14	
with his chariots *l* a whirlwind	Is 66:15	
prophets, *l* a destroying lion	Jer 2:30	
lest my fury come forth *l* fire	Jer 4:4	
L as ye have forsaken me, and	Jer 5:19	
their voice roareth *l* the sea	Jer 6:23	
tongues *l* their bow for lies	Jer 9:3	
and is burned up *l* a wilderness	Jer 9:12	
as there is none *l* unto thee	Jer 10:6	3644
there is none *l* unto thee	Jer 10:7	3644
portion of Jacob is not *l* them	Jer 10:16	
But I was *l* a lamb or an ox that	Jer 11:19	
pull them out *l* sheep for the	Jer 12:3	
snuffed up the wind *l* dragons	Jer 14:6	
For he shall be *l* the heath in	Jer 17:6	
lest my fury go out *l* fire	Jer 21:12	
I am *l* a drunken man	Jer 23:9	
l a man whom wine hath overcome,	Jer 23:9	
Is not my word *l* as a fire	Jer 23:29	3541
l a hammer that breaketh the rock	Jer 23:29	
even *l* the figs that are first	Jer 24:2	
L these good figs, so will I	Jer 24:5	
ye shall fall *l* a pleasant vessel	Jer 25:34	
will I make this house *l* Shiloh	Jer 26:6	
This house shall be *l* Shiloh	Jer 26:9	
Zion shall be plowed *l* a field	Jer 26:18	
and will make them *l* vile figs	Jer 29:17	
The LORD make thee *l* Zedekiah	Jer 29:22	
l Ahab, whom the king of Babylon	Jer 29:22	
is great, so that none is *l* it	Jer 30:7	3644
that *l* as I have watched over	Jer 31:28	
L as I have brought all this	Jer 32:42	
besides unto them many *l* words	Jer 36:32	1922
he is *l* to die for hunger in the	Jer 38:9	
Egypt riseth up *l* a flood	Jer 46:8	
his waters are moved *l* the rivers	Jer 46:8	
Egypt is *l* a very fair heifer,	Jer 46:20	
midst of her *l* fatted bullocks	Jer 46:21	
thereof shall go *l* a serpent	Jer 46:22	
be *l* the heath in the wilderness	Jer 48:6	2421
be *l* the dove that maketh her	Jer 48:28	
shall sound for Moab *l* pipes	Jer 48:36	
mine heart shall sound *l* pipes	Jer 48:36	
for I have broken Moab *l* a vessel	Jer 48:38	
he shall come up *l* a lion from	Jer 49:19	
for who is *l* me	Jer 49:19	3644
their voice shall roar *l* the sea	Jer 50:42	
l a man to the battle, against	Jer 50:42	
he shall come up *l* a lion from	Jer 50:44	
for who is *l* me	Jer 50:44	3644
portion of Jacob is not *l* them	Jer 51:19	
of Babylon is *l* a threshingfloor	Jer 51:33	
hath swallowed me up *l* a dragon	Jer 51:34	
They shall roar together *l* lions	Jer 51:38	
down *l* lambs to the slaughter	Jer 51:40	
l rams with he goats	Jer 51:40	
her waves do roar *l* great waters	Jer 51:55	
pomegranates were *l* unto these	Jer 52:22	
her princes are become *l* harts	Lam 1:6	
be any sorrow *l* unto my sorrow	Lam 1:12	
and they shall be *l* unto me	Lam 1:21	3644
against Jacob *l* a flaming fire	Lam 2:3	
He hath bent his bow *l* an enemy	Lam 2:4	
he poured out his fury *l* fire	Lam 2:4	
for thy breach is great *l* the sea	Lam 2:13	
let tears run down *l* a river day	Lam 2:18	
l water before the face of the	Lam 2:19	
me sore, *l* a bird, without cause	Lam 3:52	
l the ostriches in the wilderness	Lam 4:3	
withered, it is become *l* a stick	Lam 4:8	3644
Our skin was black *l* an oven	Lam 5:10	
was *l* the sole of a calf's foot	Eze 1:7	
they sparkled *l* the colour of	Eze 1:7	
their appearance was *l* burning	Eze 1:13	
l the appearance of lamps	Eze 1:13	
their work was *l* unto the colour	Eze 1:16	
l the noise of great waters, as	Eze 1:24	
l that rebellious house	Eze 2:8	
I will not do any more the *l*	Eze 5:9	3644
mountains *l* doves of the valleys	Eze 7:16	
l as I have done, so shall it be	Eze 12:11	
thy prophets are *l* the foxes in	Eze 13:4	
the *l* things shall not come,	Eze 16:16	
that doeth the *l* to any one of	Eze 18:10	251
considereth, and doeth not such *l*	Eze 18:14	
Thy mother is *l* a vine in thy	Eze 19:10	
L as I pleaded with your fathers	Eze 20:36	
l a roaring lion ravening the	Eze 22:25	
are *l* wolves ravening the prey	Eze 22:27	
l as my mind was alienated from	Eze 23:18	
whose issue is *l* the issue of	Eze 23:20	
Judah is *l* unto all the heathen	Eze 25:8	
make her *l* the top of a rock	Eze 26:4	
I will make thee *l* the top of a	Eze 26:14	
l the cities that are not	Eze 26:19	
saying, What city is *l* Tyrus	Eze 27:32	
l the destroyed in the midst of	Eze 27:32	
Whom art thou *l* in thy greatness	Eze 31:2	1819
fir trees were not *l* his boughs	Eze 31:8	1819
trees were not *l* his branches	Eze 31:8	1819
God was *l* unto him in his beauty	Eze 31:8	1819
To whom art thou thus *l* in glory	Eze 31:18	1819
Thou art *l* a young lion of the	Eze 32:2	
cause their rivers to run *l* oil	Eze 32:14	
is become *l* the garden of Eden	Eze 36:35	
increase them with men *l* a flock	Eze 36:37	
come *l* a storm, thou shalt be	Eze 38:9	
thou shalt be *l* a cloud to cover	Eze 38:9	
whose appearance was *l* the	Eze 40:3	
round about, *l* those windows	Eze 40:25	
l as were made upon the walls	Eze 41:25	
the way before them was *l* the	Eze 42:11	
his voice was *l* a noise of many	Eze 43:2	
the visions were *l* the vision	Eze 43:3	
shall he do the *l* in the feast of	Eze 45:25	
them all was found none *l* Daniel	Dan 1:19	
became *l* the chaff of the summer	Dan 2:35	
of the fourth is *l* the Son of God	Dan 3:25	1821
were grown *l* eagles' feathers	Dan 4:33	
and his nails *l* birds' claws	Dan 4:33	
l the wisdom of the gods, was	Dan 5:11	
his heart was made *l* the beasts	Dan 5:21	5974
they fed him with grass *l* oxen	Dan 5:21	
The first was *l* a lion, and had	Dan 7:4	
l to a bear, and it raised up	Dan 7:5	1821
l a leopard, which had upon the	Dan 7:6	
horn were eyes *l* the eyes of man	Dan 7:8	
hair of his head *l* the pure wool	Dan 7:9	
his throne was *l* the fiery flame,	Dan 7:9	
one *l* the Son of man came with	Dan 7:13	
His body also was *l* the beryl	Dan 10:6	

his feet *l* in colour to polished ... Dan 10:6
the voice of his words *l* the ... Dan 10:6
one *l* the similitude of the sons ... Dan 10:16
touched me one *l* the appearance ... Dan 10:18
come against him *l* a whirlwind ... Dan 11:40
set her *l* a dry land, and slay her ... Hos 2:3
shall be, *l* people, *l* priest ... Hos 4:9
The princes of Judah were *l* them ... Hos 5:10
out my wrath upon them *l* water ... Hos 5:10
But they *l* men have transgressed ... Hos 6:7
made ready their heart *l* an oven ... Hos 7:6
Ephraim also is *l* a silly dove ... Hos 7:11
they are *l* a deceitful bow ... Hos 7:16
I found Israel *l* grapes in the ... Hos 9:10
glory shall fly away *l* a bird ... Hos 9:11
he shall roar *l* a lion ... Hos 11:10
there will I devour them *l* a lion ... Hos 13:8
I am *l* a green fir tree ... Hos 14:8
Lament *l* a virgin girded with ... Joel 1:8
there hath not been ever the *l* ... Joel 2:2 3644
L the noise of chariots on the ... Joel 2:5
l the noise of a flame of fire ... Joel 2:5
They shall run *l* mighty men ... Joel 2:7
shall climb the wall *l* men of war ... Joel 2:7
enter in at the windows *l* a thief ... Joel 2:9
whose height was *l* the height of ... Amos 2:9
lest he break out *l* fire in the ... Amos 5:6
instruments of musick, *l* David ... Amos 6:5
it shall rise up wholly *l* a flood ... Amos 9:5
l as corn is sifted in a sieve, ... Amos 9:9
that the ship was *l* to be broken ... Jonah 1:4 2803
will make a wailing *l* the dragons ... Mic 1:8
of Zion, *l* a woman in travail ... Mic 4:10
shall lick the dust *l* a serpent ... Mic 7:17
their holes *l* worms of the earth ... Mic 7:17
Who is a God *l* unto thee, that ... Mic 7:18 3644
his fury is poured out *l* fire ... Nah 1:6
they shall seem *l* torches ... Nah 2:4
they shall run *l* the lightnings ... Nah 2:4
is of old *l* a pool of water ... Nah 2:8
be *l* fig trees with the firstripe ... Nah 3:12
eat thee up *l* the cankerworm ... Nah 3:15
will make my feet *l* hinds' feet ... Hab 3:19
that they shall walk *l* blind men ... Zeph 1:17
desolation, and dry *l* a wilderness ... Zeph 2:13
L as the LORD of hosts thought to ... Zec 1:6
for they had wings *l* the wings of ... Zec 5:9
and they shall be filled *l* bowls ... Zec 9:15
Ephraim shall be *l* a mighty man ... Zec 10:7
l an hearth of fire among the ... Zec 12:6
l a torch of fire in a sheaf ... Zec 12:6
l as ye fled from before the ... Zec 14:5
be *l* the bowls before the altar ... Zec 14:20
for he is *l* a refiner's fire ... Mal 3:2
and *l* fullers' sope ... Mal 3:2
Spirit of God descending *l* a dove ... Mt 3:16 *5616*
Be not ye therefore *l* unto them ... Mt 6:8 *3666*
was not arrayed *l* one of these ... Mt 6:29 *5613*
It is *l* unto children sitting in ... Mt 11:16 *3664*
restored whole, *l* as the other ... Mt 12:13 *5613*
The kingdom of heaven is *l* to a ... Mt 13:31 *3664*
of heaven is *l* unto leaven ... Mt 13:33 *3664*
the kingdom of heaven is *l* unto ... Mt 13:44 *3664*
heaven is *l* unto a merchant man ... Mt 13:45 *3664*
kingdom of heaven is *l* unto a net ... Mt 13:47 *3664*
heaven is *l* unto a man that is an ... Mt 13:52 *3664*
heaven is *l* unto a man that is an ... Mt 20:1 *3664*
I in *l* wise will tell you by what ... Mt 21:24 *2504*
heaven is *l* unto a certain king ... Mt 22:2 *3666*
And the second is *l* unto it ... Mt 22:39 *3664*
for ye are *l* unto whited ... Mt 23:27 *3945*
His countenance was *l* lightning ... Mt 28:3 *5613*
the Spirit *l* a dove descending ... Mk 1:10 *5616*
It is *l* a grain of mustard seed, ... Mk 4:31 *5613*
and many other such *l* things ye do ... Mk 7:8 *3946*
and many such *l* things do ye ... Mk 7:13 *3946*
And the second is *l*, namely this ... Mk 12:31 *3664*
So ye in *l* manner, when ye shall ... Mk 13:29 *2532*
a bodily shape *l* a dove upon him ... Lk 3:22 *5616*
for in the *l* manner did their ... Lk 6:23 *5024*
I will shew you to whom he is *l* ... Lk 6:47 *3664*
He is *l* a man which built an ... Lk 6:48 *3664*
is *l* a man that without a ... Lk 6:49 *3664*
and to what are they *l* ... Lk 7:31 *3664*
They are *l* unto children sitting ... Lk 7:32 *3664*
was not arrayed *l* one of these ... Lk 12:27 *5613*
ye yourselves *l* unto men that ... Lk 12:36 *3664*
Unto what is the kingdom of God *l* ... Lk 13:18 *3664*
It is *l* a grain of mustard seed, ... Lk 13:19 *3664*
It is *l* leaven, which a woman ... Lk 13:21 *3664*
in *l* manner the seven also ... Lk 20:31 *5615*
descending from heaven *l* a dove ... Jn 1:32 *5616*
Never man spake *l* this man ... Jn 7:46 *3779*
not, I shall be a liar *l* unto you ... Jn 8:55 *3664*
others said, He is *l* him ... Jn 9:9 *3664*
shall so come in *l* manner as ye ... Acts 1:11 *3779*
them cloven tongues *l* as of fire ... Acts 2:3 *5616*
you of your brethren, *l* unto me ... Acts 3:22 *3945*
you of your brethren, *l* unto me ... Acts 7:37 *5613*
l a lamb dumb before his shearer, ... Acts 8:32 *5613*
them the *l* gift as he did unto us ... Acts 11:17 *2470*
are men of *l* passions with you ... Acts 14:15 *3663*
that the Godhead is *l* unto gold ... Acts 17:29 *3664*
with the workmen of *l* occupation ... Acts 19:25 *5108*
image made *l* to corruptible man ... Rom 1:23 *3667*
even as they did not *l* to retain ... Rom 1:28 *1381*
that *l* as Christ was raised up ... Rom 6:4 *5618*
been made *l* unto Gomorrha ... Rom 9:29 *3666*
fast in the faith, quit you *l* men ... 1Cor 16:13 *407*
revellings, and such *l* ... Gal 5:21 *3664*
l unto his glorious body, ... Phil 3:21 *4832*
for ye also have suffered *l* ... 1Th 2:14 *5024*
In *l* manner also, that women ... 1Ti 2:9 *5615*
to be made *l* unto his brethren ... Heb 2:17 *3666*
in all points tempted *l* as we are ... Heb 4:15 *3665*
but made *l* unto the Son of God ... Heb 7:3 *871*
For he that wavereth is *l* a wave ... Jas 1:6 *1503*
he is *l* unto a man beholding his ... Jas 1:23 *1503*
subject to *l* passions as we are ... Jas 5:17 *3663*
The *l* figure whereunto even ... 1Pet 3:21 *499*
to them that have obtained *l* ... 2Pet 1:1 *2472*
shall appear, we shall be *l* him ... 1Jn 3:2 *3664*
the cities about them in *l* manner ... Jude 7 *3664*
one *l* unto the Son of man ... Rev 1:13 *3664*
and his hairs were white *l* wool ... Rev 1:14 *5616*
his feet *l* unto fine brass, as if ... Rev 1:15 *3664*
who hath his eyes *l* unto a flame ... Rev 2:18 *5613*
and his feet are *l* fine brass ... Rev 2:18 *3664*
sat was to look upon *l* a jasper ... Rev 4:3 *3664*
in sight *l* unto an emerald ... Rev 4:3 *3664*
was a sea of glass *l* unto crystal ... Rev 4:6 *3664*
And the first beast was *l* a lion ... Rev 4:7 *3664*
and the second beast *l* a calf ... Rev 4:7 *3664*
fourth beast was *l* a flying eagle ... Rev 4:7 *3664*
were *l* unto horses prepared unto ... Rev 9:7 *3664*
were as it were crowns *l* gold ... Rev 9:7 *3664*
they had tails *l* unto scorpions ... Rev 9:10 *3664*
their tails were *l* unto serpents ... Rev 9:19 *3664*
was given me a reed *l* unto a rod ... Rev 11:1 *3664*
which I saw was *l* unto a leopard ... Rev 13:2 *3664*
saying, Who is *l* unto the beast ... Rev 13:4 *3664*
and he had two horns *l* a lamb ... Rev 13:11 *3664*
one sat *l* unto the Son of man ... Rev 14:14 *3664*
I saw three unclean spirits *l* ... Rev 16:13 *3664*
What city is *l* unto this great ... Rev 18:18 *3664*
up a stone *l* a great millstone ... Rev 18:21 *5613*
her light was *l* unto a stone most ... Rev 21:11 *3664*
even *l* a jasper stone, clear as ... Rev 21:11 *5613*
was pure gold, *l* unto clear glass ... Rev 21:18 *3664*

LIKED
he *l* me to make me king over all ... 1Chr 28:4 7521

LIKEMINDED
consolation grant you to be *l* one ... Rom 15:5
Fulfil ye my joy, that ye be *l* ... Phil 2:2
For I have no man *l*, who will ... Phil 2:20 *2473*

LIKEN
To whom then will ye *l* God ... Is 40:18 1819
To whom then will ye *l* me ... Is 40:25 1819
To whom will ye *l* me, and make me ... Is 46:5 1819
what thing shall I *l* to thee ... Lam 2:13 1819
I will *l* him unto a wise man, ... Mt 7:24 *3666*
shall I *l* this generation ... Mt 11:16 *3666*
shall we *l* the kingdom of God ... Mk 4:30 *3666*
Whereunto then shall I *l* the men ... Lk 7:31 *3666*
Whereunto shall I *l* the kingdom ... Lk 13:20 *3666*

LIKENED
the mighty can be *l* unto the LORD ... Ps 89:6 1819
I have *l* the daughter of Zion to ... Jer 6:2 1819
shall be *l* unto a foolish man, ... Mt 7:26 *3666*
The kingdom of heaven is *l* unto a ... Mt 13:24 *3666*
of heaven *l* unto a certain king ... Mt 18:23 *3666*
of heaven be *l* unto ten virgins ... Mt 25:1 *3666*

LIKENESS
man in our image, after our *l* ... Gen 1:26 1823
in the *l* of God made he him ... Gen 5:1 1823
and begat a son in his own *l* ... Gen 5:3 1823
or any *l* of any thing that is in ... Ex 20:4 8544
figure, the *l* of male or female, ... Deut 4:16 8403
The *l* of any beast that is on the ... Deut 4:17 8403
the *l* of any winged fowl that ... Deut 4:17 8403
The *l* of any thing that creepeth ... Deut 4:18 8403
the *l* of any fish that is in the ... Deut 4:18 8403
or the *l* of any thing, which the ... Deut 4:23 8544
or the *l* of any thing, and shall ... Deut 4:25 8544
or any *l* of any thing that is in ... Deut 5:8 8544
when I awake, with thy *l* ... Ps 17:15 8544
or what *l* will ye compare unto ... Is 40:18 1823
the *l* of four living creatures ... Eze 1:5 1823
they had the *l* of a man ... Eze 1:5 1823
As for the *l* of their faces, they ... Eze 1:10 1823
As for the *l* of the living ... Eze 1:13 1823
and they four had one *l* ... Eze 1:16 1823
the *l* of the firmament upon the ... Eze 1:22 1823
their heads was the *l* of a throne ... Eze 1:26 1823
upon the *l* of the throne was the ... Eze 1:26 1823
the *l* as the appearance of a man ... Eze 1:26 1823
of the *l* of the glory of the LORD ... Eze 1:28 1823
lo a *l* as the appearance of fire ... Eze 8:2 1823
appearance of the *l* of a throne ... Eze 10:1 1823
appearances, they four had one *l* ... Eze 10:10 1823
the *l* of the hands of a man was ... Eze 10:21 1823
the *l* of their faces was the same ... Eze 10:22 1823
come down to us in the *l* of men ... Acts 14:11 *3666*
together in the *l* of his death ... Rom 6:5 *3667*
also in the *l* of his resurrection ... Rom 6:5
own Son in the *l* of sinful flesh ... Rom 8:3 *3667*
and was made in the *l* of men ... Phil 2:7 *3667*

LIKETH
of thy gates, where it *l* him best ... Deut 23:16 2896
ye also for the Jews, as it *l* you ... Est 8:8 2896
for this *l* you, O ye children of ... Amos 4:5 157

LIKEWISE
L shalt thou do with thine oxen, ... Ex 22:30 3651
and *l* shalt thou make in the ... Ex 26:4 3651
l for the north side in length ... Ex 27:11 3651
l he made in the uttermost side ... Ex 36:11 3651
L this is the law of the trespass ... Lev 7:1 2063
L when the LORD sent you from ... Deut 9:23
even so will I do *l* ... Deut 12:30 3651
thy maidservant thou shalt do *l* ... Deut 15:17 3651
thou hast found, shalt thou do *l* ... Deut 22:3 3651
I *l* will go with thee into thy ... Judg 1:3 3651
l every one that boweth down upon ... Judg 7:5
unto them, Look on me, and do *l* ... Judg 7:17 3651
to Penuel, and spake unto them *l* ... Judg 8:8 2063
all the people *l* cut down every ... Judg 9:49 1571
L all the men of Israel which had ... 1Sa 14:22 1571
messengers, and they prophesied *l* ... 1Sa 19:21 1571
he fell *l* upon his sword, and died ... 1Sa 31:5 1571
l all the men that were with him ... 2Sa 1:11 1571
let us hear *l* what he saith ... 2Sa 17:5 1571
l did he for all his strange ... 1Kin 11:8 3651
he fell *l* on the sword, and died ... 1Chr 10:5 1571
L from Tibhath, and from Chun, ... 1Chr 18:8
they *l* fled before Abishai his ... 1Chr 19:15 1571
and praise the LORD, and *l* at even ... 1Chr 23:30 3651
These *l* cast lots over against ... 1Chr 24:31 1571
in his course *l* were twenty ... 1Chr 27:4
l silver for the tables of silver ... 1Chr 28:16
l silver by weight for every ... 1Chr 28:17
all the sons *l* of king David, ... 1Chr 29:24 1571
the other wing was *l* five cubits ... 2Chr 3:11
l, when they had killed the rams, ... 2Chr 29:22
L at the same time said I unto ... Neh 4:22 1571
I *l*, and my brethren, and my ... Neh 5:10 1571
L shall the ladies of Persia and ... Est 1:18
I also and my maidens will fast *l* ... Est 4:16 3651
the furrows *l* thereof complain ... Job 31:38 3162
l to the small rain, and to the ... Job 37:6
l the fool and the brutish person ... Ps 49:10
God shall *l* destroy thee for ever ... Ps 52:5 1571
thou thyself *l* hast cursed others ... Eccl 7:22 1571
The oxen *l* and the young asses ... Is 30:24
L when all the Jews that were in ... Jer 40:11 1571
L, thou son of man, set thy face ... Eze 13:17
round about, and *l* to the arches ... Eze 40:16 3651
L the people of the land shall ... Eze 46:3
l many, yet thus shall they be ... Nah 1:12 3651
L shall also the Son of man ... Mt 17:12 *3779*
So *l* shall my heavenly Father do ... Mt 18:35 *2532*
the sixth and ninth hour, and did *l* ... Mt 20:5 *5615*
they *l* received every man a penny ... Mt 20:10 *2532*
he came to the second, and said *l* ... Mt 21:30 *5615*
and they did unto them *l* ... Mt 21:36 *5615*
L the second also, and the third, ... Mt 22:26 *3668*
So *l* ye, when ye shall see all ... Mt 24:33 *2532*
l he that had received two, he ... Mt 25:17 *5615*
L also said all the disciples ... Mt 26:35 *3668*
L also the chief priests mocking ... Mt 27:41 *3668*
these are they *l* which are sown ... Mk 4:16 *3668*
and the third *l* ... Mk 12:21 *5615*
L also said they all ... Mk 14:31 *5615*
L also the chief priests mocking ... Mk 15:31 *3668*
gave thanks *l* unto the Lord ... Lk 2:38 *437*
he that hath meat, let him do *l* ... Lk 3:11 *3668*
the soldiers *l* demanded of him, ... Lk 3:14 *2532*
l the disciples of the Pharisees ... Lk 5:33 *3668*
do to you, do ye also to them *l* ... Lk 6:31 *3668*
l a Levite, when he was at the ... Lk 10:32 *3668*
Jesus unto him, Go, and do thou *l* ... Lk 10:37 *3668*
ye repent, ye shall all *l* perish ... Lk 13:3 *5615*
ye repent, ye shall all *l* perish ... Lk 13:5 *3668*
So *l*, whosoever he be of you that ... Lk 14:33 *3779*
that *l* joy shall be in heaven ... Lk 15:7 *3779*
L, I say unto you, there is joy ... Lk 15:10 *3779*
things, and *l* Lazarus evil things ... Lk 16:25 *3668*
So *l* ye, when ye shall have done ... Lk 17:10 *2532*
L also as it was in the days of ... Lk 17:28 *3668*
let him *l* not return back ... Lk 17:31 *3668*
And he said *l* to him, Be thou also ... Lk 19:19 *2532*
So *l* ye, when ye see these things ... Lk 21:31 *2532*
L also the cup after supper, ... Lk 22:20 *5615*
let him take it, and *l* his scrip ... Lk 22:36 *3668*
doeth, these also doeth the Son *l* ... Jn 5:19 *3668*
l of the fishes as much as they ... Jn 6:11 *3668*
bread, and giveth them, and fish *l* ... Jn 21:13 *3668*
have *l* foretold of these days ... Acts 3:24 *2532*
l also the men, leaving the ... Rom 1:27 *3668*
L reckon ye also yourselves to be ... Rom 6:11 *3779*
L the Spirit also helpeth our ... Rom 8:26 *5615*
L greet the church that is in ... Rom 16:5 *2532*
l also the wife unto the husband ... 1Cor 7:3 *3668*
l also the husband hath not power ... 1Cor 7:4 *3668*
l also he that is called, being ... 1Cor 7:22 *3668*
So *l* ye, except ye utter by the ... 1Cor 14:9 *2532*
other Jews dissembled *l* with him ... Gal 2:13 *3668*
that ye *l* read the epistle from ... Col 4:16 *3668*
L must the deacons be grave, not ... 1Ti 3:8 *5615*
L also the good works of some are ... 1Ti 5:25 *5615*
The aged women *l*, that they be in ... Titus 2:3 *5615*
Young men *l* exhort to be sober ... Titus 2:6 *5615*
he also himself *l* took part of ... Heb 2:14 *3898*
L also was not Rahab the harlot ... Jas 2:25 *3668*
L, ye wives, be in subjection to ... 1Pet 3:1 *3668*
L, ye husbands, dwell with them ... 1Pet 3:7 *36*
arm yourselves *l* with the same ... 1Pet 4:1 *2532*
L, ye younger, submit yourselves ... 1Pet 5:5 *3668*
L also these filthy dreamers ... Jude 8 *3668*
third part of it, and the night *l* ... Rev 8:12 *3668*

LIKHI (*lik'-hi*) *Son of Shemidah.*
were, Ahian, and Shechem, and *L* ... 1Chr 7:19 3949

LIKING
Their young ones are in good *l* ... Job 39:4 2492
l than the children which are of ... Dan 1:10

LILIES
brim of a cup, with flowers of *l* ... 1Kin 7:26 7799
brim of a cup, with flowers of *l* ... 2Chr 4:5 7799
he feedeth among the *l* ... Song 2:16 7799
are twins, which feed among the *l* ... Song 4:5 7799
his lips like *l*, dropping sweet ... Song 5:13 7799
in the gardens, and to gather *l* ... Song 6:2 7799
he feedeth among the *l* ... Song 6:3 7799
an heap of wheat set about with *l* ... Song 7:2 7799
Consider the *l* of the field ... Mt 6:28 *2918*
Consider the *l* how they grow ... Lk 12:27 *2918*

LILY
were of *l* work in the porch ... 1Kin 7:19 7799
the top of the pillars was *l* work ... 1Kin 7:22 7799
Sharon, and the *l* of the valleys ... Song 2:1 7799
As the *l* among thorns, so is my ... Song 2:2 7799
he shall grow as the *l*, and cast ... Hos 14:5 7799

LIME
shall be as the burnings of *l* ... Is 33:12 7875
bones of the king of Edom into *l* ... Amos 2:1 7875

LIMIT
l thereof round about shall be ... Eze 43:12 1366

LIMITED
God, and *l* the Holy One of Israel ... Ps 78:41 8428

LIMITETH
he *l* a certain day, saying in ... Heb 4:7 *3724*

LINE
thou shalt bind this *l* of scarlet ... Josh 2:18 8615
bound the scarlet *l* in the window ... Josh 2:21 8515
Moab, and measured them with a *l* ... 2Sa 8:2 2256
and with one full *l* to keep alive ... 2Sa 8:2 2256
a *l* of twelve cubits did compass ... 1Kin 7:15 2339
a *l* of thirty cubits did compass ... 1Kin 7:23 6957
over Jerusalem the *l* of Samaria ... 2Kin 21:13 6957
a *l* of thirty cubits did compass ... 2Chr 4:2 6957
who hath stretched the *l* upon it ... Job 38:5 6957
Their *l* is gone out through all ... Ps 19:4 6957
divided them an inheritance by *l* ... Ps 78:55 2256
l upon *l*, *l* upon *l* ... Is 28:10 6957
l upon *l*, *l* upon *l* ... Is 28:13 6957
Judgment also will I lay to the *l* ... Is 28:17 6957
out upon it the *l* of confusion ... Is 34:11 6957
hath divided it unto them by *l* ... Is 34:17 6957
he marketh it out with a *l* ... Is 44:13 8279
the measuring *l* shall yet go ... Jer 31:39 6957
he hath stretched out a *l* ... Lam 2:8 6957
with a *l* of flax in his hand, and ... Eze 40:3 6616
when the man that had the *l* in ... Eze 47:3 6957
and thy land shall be divided by *l* ... Amos 7:17 2256
a *l* shall be stretched forth upon ... Zec 1:16 6957
with a measuring *l* in his hand ... Zec 2:1 2256
l of things made ready to our ... 2Cor 10:16 *2583*

LINEAGE
he was of the house and *l* of David ... Lk 2:4 *3965*

LINEN
arrayed him in vestures of fine *l* ... Gen 41:42 8336
and purple, and scarlet, and fine *l* ... Ex 25:4 8336
ten curtains of fine twined *l* ... Ex 26:1 8336
fine twined *l* of cunning work ... Ex 26:31 8336
and scarlet, and fine twined *l* ... Ex 26:36 8336
for the court of fine twined *l* of ... Ex 27:9 8336
and scarlet, and fine twined *l* ... Ex 27:16 8336
five cubits of fine twined *l* ... Ex 27:18 8336
and purple, and scarlet, and fine *l* ... Ex 28:5 8336
of scarlet, and fine twined *l* ... Ex 28:6 8336
and scarlet, and fine twined *l* ... Ex 28:8 8336
of scarlet, and of fine twined *l* ... Ex 28:15 8336
embroider the coat of fine *l* ... Ex 28:39 8336
shalt make the mitre of fine *l* ... Ex 28:39 8336
thou shalt make them *l* breeches ... Ex 28:42 906
and purple, and scarlet, and fine *l* ... Ex 35:6 8336
and purple, and scarlet, and fine *l* ... Ex 35:23 8336
and of scarlet, and of fine *l* ... Ex 35:25 8336
purple, in scarlet, and in fine *l* ... Ex 35:35 8336
ten curtains of fine twined *l* ... Ex 36:8 8336
and scarlet, and fine twined *l* ... Ex 36:35 8336
and scarlet, and fine twined *l* ... Ex 36:37 8336
the court were of fine twined *l* ... Ex 38:9 8336
round about were of fine twined *l* ... Ex 38:16 8336
and scarlet, and fine twined *l* ... Ex 38:18 8336
purple, and in scarlet, and fine *l* ... Ex 38:23 8336
and scarlet, and fine twined *l* ... Ex 39:2 8336
in the scarlet, and in the fine *l* ... Ex 39:3 8336
and scarlet, and fine twined *l* ... Ex 39:5 8336
and scarlet, and fine twined *l* ... Ex 39:8 8336
purple, and scarlet, and twined *l* ... Ex 39:24
of fine *l* of woven work for Aaron ... Ex 39:27 8336
And a mitre of fine *l* ... Ex 39:28 8336
and goodly bonnets of fine *l* ... Ex 39:28 8336
l breeches of fine twined *l*, ... Ex 39:28 906
l breeches of fine twined *l* ... Ex 39:28 8336
And a girdle of fine twined *l* ... Ex 39:29 8336
priest shall put on his *l* garment ... Lev 6:10 906
his *l* breeches shall he put upon ... Lev 6:10 906
a woollen garment, or a *l* garment ... Lev 13:47 6593
of *l*, or of woollen ... Lev 13:48 6593
warp or woof, in woollen or in *l* ... Lev 13:52 6593
in a garment of woollen or *l* ... Lev 13:59 6593
He shall put on the holy *l* coat ... Lev 16:4 906
he shall have the *l* breeches upon ... Lev 16:4 906
shall be girded with a *l* girdle ... Lev 16:4 906
with the *l* mitre shall he be ... Lev 16:4 906
and shall put off the *l* garments ... Lev 16:23 906
and shall put on the *l* clothes ... Lev 16:32 906
shall a garment mingled of *l* ... Lev 19:19 8162
as of woollen and *l* together ... Deut 22:11 6593
a child, girded with a *l* ephod ... 1Sa 2:18 906
persons that did wear a *l* ephod ... 1Sa 22:18 906
David was girded with a *l* ephod ... 2Sa 6:14 906
brought out of Egypt, and *l* yarn ... 1Kin 10:28 4723
received the *l* yarn at a price ... 1Kin 10:28 4723
house of them that wrought fine *l* ... 1Chr 4:21 948
was clothed with a robe of fine *l* ... 1Chr 15:27 948
also had upon him an ephod of *l* ... 1Chr 15:27 906
brought out of Egypt, and *l* yarn ... 2Chr 1:16 4723
received the *l* yarn at a price ... 2Chr 1:16 4723
in purple, in blue, and in fine *l* ... 2Chr 2:14 948
and purple, and crimson, and fine *l* ... 2Chr 3:14 948
being arrayed in white *l* ... 2Chr 5:12 948
fastened with cords of fine *l* ... Est 1:6 948
gold, and with a garment of fine *l* ... Est 8:15 948
works, with fine *l* of Egypt ... Prov 7:16 948
She maketh fine *l*, and selleth it ... Prov 31:24 5466
The glasses, and the fine *l* ... Is 3:23 5466
me, Go and get thee a *l* girdle ... Jer 13:1 6593
man among them was clothed with *l* ... Eze 9:2 906
called to the man clothed with *l* ... Eze 9:3 906
behold, the man clothed with *l* ... Eze 9:11 906
spake unto the man clothed with *l* ... Eze 10:2 906
commanded the man clothed with *l* ... Eze 10:6 906
of him that was clothed with *l* ... Eze 10:7 906
I girded thee about with fine *l* ... Eze 16:10 8336
and thy raiment was of fine *l* ... Eze 16:13 8336
Fine *l* with broidered work from ... Eze 27:7 8336
and broidered work, and fine *l* ... Eze 27:16 948
shall be clothed with *l* garments ... Eze 44:17 6593
They shall have *l* bonnets upon ... Eze 44:18 6593
shall have *l* breeches upon their ... Eze 44:18 6593
behold a certain man clothed in *l* ... Dan 10:5 906
one said to the man clothed in *l* ... Dan 12:6 906
And I heard the man clothed in *l* ... Dan 12:7 906
he wrapped it in a clean *l* cloth ... Mt 27:59 *4616*
having a *l* cloth cast about his ... Mk 14:51 *4616*
And he left the *l* cloth, and fled ... Mk 14:52 *4616*
And he bought fine *l*, and took him ... Mk 15:46 *4616*
him down, and wrapped him in the *l* ... Mk 15:46 *4616*
was clothed in purple and fine *l* ... Lk 16:19 *1040*
took it down, and wrapped it in *l* ... Lk 23:53 *4616*
he beheld the *l* clothes laid by ... Lk 24:12 *3608*
wound it in *l* clothes with the ... Jn 19:40 *3608*
in, saw the *l* clothes lying ... Jn 20:5 *3608*
and seeth the *l* clothes lie, ... Jn 20:6 *3608*
not lying with the *l* clothes ... Jn 20:7 *3608*
clothed in pure and white *l* ... Rev 15:6 *3043*
stones, and of pearls, and fine *l* ... Rev 18:12 *1040*
city, that was clothed in fine *l* ... Rev 18:16 *1039*
she should be arrayed in fine *l* ... Rev 19:8 *1039*
for the fine *l* is the ... Rev 19:8 *1039*
white horses, clothed in fine *l* ... Rev 19:14 *1039*

LINES
even with two *l* measured he to ... 2Sa 8:2 2256
The *l* are fallen unto me in ... Ps 16:6 2256

LINGERED
And while he *l*, the men laid hold ... Gen 19:16 4102
For except we had *l*, surely now ... Gen 43:10 4102

LINGERETH
judgment now of a long time *l* not ... 2Pet 2:3 *691*

LINTEL
is in the bason, and strike the *l* ... Ex 12:22 4947
he seeth the blood upon the *l* ... Ex 12:23 4947
the *l* and side posts were a fifth ... 1Kin 6:31 352
Smite the *l* of the door, that the ... Amos 9:1 3730

LINTELS
shall lodge in the upper *l* of it ... Zeph 2:14 3730

LINUS *(li'-nus) A Christian at Rome.*
greeteth thee, and Pudens, and *L* ... 2Ti 4:21 *3044*

LION
stooped down, he couched as a *l* ... Gen 49:9 738
and as an old *l* ... Gen 49:9 3833
people shall rise up as a great *l* ... Num 23:24 3833
and lift up himself as a young *l* ... Num 23:24 738
He couched, he lay down as a *l* ... Num 24:9 738
and as a great *l* ... Num 24:9 3833
he dwelleth as a *l*, and teareth ... Deut 33:20 3833
a young *l* roared against him ... Judg 14:5 738
aside to see the carcase of the *l* ... Judg 14:8 738
and honey in the carcase of the *l* ... Judg 14:8 738
honey out of the carcase of the *l* ... Judg 14:9 738
And what is stronger than a *l* ... Judg 14:18 738
father's sheep, and there came a *l* ... 1Sa 17:34 738
Thy servant slew both the *l* ... 1Sa 17:36 738
me out of the paw of the *l* ... 1Sa 17:37 738
heart is as the heart of a *l* ... 2Sa 17:10 738
slew a *l* in the midst of a pit in ... 2Sa 23:20 738
a *l* met him by the way, and slew ... 1Kin 13:24 738
the *l* also stood by the carcase ... 1Kin 13:24 738
the *l* standing by the carcase ... 1Kin 13:25 738
hath delivered him unto the *l* ... 1Kin 13:26 738
the *l* standing by the carcase ... 1Kin 13:28 738
the *l* had not eaten the carcase, ... 1Kin 13:28 738
from me, a *l* shall slay thee ... 1Kin 20:36 738
a *l* found him, and slew him ... 1Kin 20:36 738
slew a *l* in a pit in a snowy day ... 1Chr 11:22 738
The roaring of the *l* ... Job 4:10 738
and the voice of the fierce *l* ... Job 4:10 7826
The old *l* perisheth for lack of ... Job 4:11 3918
Thou huntest me as a fierce *l* ... Job 10:16 7826
it, nor the fierce *l* passed by it ... Job 28:8 7826
Wilt thou hunt the prey for the *l* ... Job 38:39 3833
Lest he tear my soul like a *l* ... Ps 7:2 738
wait secretly as a *l* in his den ... Ps 10:9 738
Like as a *l* that is greedy of his ... Ps 17:12 738
as it were a young *l* lurking in ... Ps 17:12 3715
as a ravening and a roaring *l* ... Ps 22:13 738
Thou shalt tread upon the *l* ... Ps 91:13 7826
the young *l* and the dragon shalt ... Ps 91:13 3715
wrath is as the roaring of a *l* ... Prov 19:12 3715
a king is as the roaring of a *l* ... Prov 20:2 3715
man saith, There is a *l* without ... Prov 22:13 738
saith, There is a *l* in the way ... Prov 26:13 738
a *l* is in the streets ... Prov 26:13 738
but the righteous are bold as a *l* ... Prov 28:1 3715
As a roaring *l*, and a ranging bear ... Prov 28:15 739
A *l* which is strongest among ... Prov 30:30 3918
dog is better than a dead *l* ... Eccl 9:4 738
Their roaring shall be like a *l* ... Is 5:29 3833
and the calf and the young *l* ... Is 11:6 3715
the *l* shall eat straw like the ox ... Is 11:7 738
And he cried, A *l* ... Is 21:8 738
whence come the young and old *l* ... Is 30:6 3918
spoken unto me, Like as the *l* ... Is 31:4 738
the young *l* roaring on his prey, ... Is 31:4 3715
No *l* shall be there, nor any ... Is 35:9 738
till morning, that, as a *l* ... Is 38:13 738
the *l* shall eat straw like the ... Is 65:25 738
prophets, like a destroying *l* ... Jer 2:30 738
The *l* is come up from his thicket ... Jer 4:7 738
Wherefore a *l* out of the forest ... Jer 5:6 738
is unto me as a *l* in the forest ... Jer 12:8 738
forsaken his covert, as the *l* ... Jer 25:38 3715
he shall come up like a *l* from ... Jer 49:19 738
he shall come up like a *l* from ... Jer 50:44 738
wait, and as a *l* in secret places ... Lam 3:10 738
face of a man, and the face of a *l* ... Eze 1:10 738
man, and the third the face of a *l* ... Eze 10:14 738
it became a young *l*, and it ... Eze 19:3 3715
her whelps, and made him a young *l* ... Eze 19:5 3715
the lions, he became a young *l* ... Eze 19:6 3715
like a roaring *l* ravening the ... Eze 22:25 738
art like a young *l* of the nations ... Eze 32:2 3715
the face of a young *l* toward the ... Eze 41:19 3715
The first was like a *l*, and had ... Dan 7:4 738
For I will be unto Ephraim as a *l* ... Hos 5:14 7826
as a young *l* to the house of ... Hos 5:14 3715
he shall roar like a *l* ... Hos 11:10 738
I will be unto them as a *l* ... Hos 13:7 7826
there will I devour them like a *l* ... Hos 13:8 3833
whose teeth are the teeth of a *l* ... Joel 1:6 738
hath the cheek teeth of a great *l* ... Joel 1:6 3833
Will a *l* roar in the forest, when ... Amos 3:4 738
will a young *l* cry out of his den ... Amos 3:4 3715
The *l* hath roared, who will not ... Amos 3:8 738
of the mouth of the *l* two legs ... Amos 3:12 738
As if a man did flee from a *l* ... Amos 5:19 738
the midst of many people as a *l* ... Mic 5:8 738
as a young *l* among the flocks of ... Mic 5:8 3715
of the young lions, where the *l* ... Nah 2:11 739
even the old *l* ... Nah 2:11 3833
The *l* did tear in pieces enough ... Nah 2:12 738
out of the mouth of the *l* ... 2Ti 4:17 *3023*
the devil, as a roaring *l* ... 1Pet 5:8 *3023*
And the first beast was like a *l* ... Rev 4:7 *3023*
the *L* of the tribe of Juda, the ... Rev 5:5 *3023*
a loud voice, as when a *l* roareth ... Rev 10:3 *3023*
and his mouth as the mouth of a *l* ... Rev 13:2 *3023*

LIONESS
A *l*: she lay down ... Eze 19:2 3833

LIONESSES
whelps, and strangled for his *l* ... Nah 2:12 3833

LIONLIKE
acts, he slew two *l* men of Moab ... 2Sa 23:20 739
he slew two *l* men of Moab ... 1Chr 11:22 739

LION'S
Judah is a *l* whelp ... Gen 49:9 738
of Dan he said, Dan is a *l* whelp ... Deut 33:22 738
the stout *l* whelps are scattered ... Job 4:11 3833
The *l* whelps have not trodden it, ... Job 28:8 7830
Save me from the *l* mouth ... Ps 22:21 738
the *l* whelp, and none made them ... Nah 2:11 738

LIONS
eagles, they were stronger than *l* ... 2Sa 1:23 738
were between the ledges were *l* ... 1Kin 7:29 738
and beneath the *l* and oxen were ... 1Kin 7:29 738
thereof, he graved cherubims, *l* ... 1Kin 7:36 738
two *l* stood beside the stays ... 1Kin 10:19 738
twelve *l* stood there on the one ... 1Kin 10:20 738
the LORD sent *l* among them ... 2Kin 17:25 738
he hath sent *l* among them ... 2Kin 17:26 738
faces were like the faces of *l* ... 1Chr 12:8 738
two *l* standing by the stays ... 2Chr 9:18 738
twelve *l* stood there on the one ... 2Chr 9:19 738
lion, and the teeth of the young *l* ... Job 4:10 3715
fill the appetite of the young *l* ... Job 38:39 3715
The young *l* do lack, and suffer ... Ps 34:10 3715
my darling from the *l* ... Ps 35:17 3715
My soul is among *l* ... Ps 57:4 3833
the great teeth of the young *l* ... Ps 58:6 3715
The young *l* roar after their prey ... Ps 104:21 3715
they shall roar like young *l* ... Is 5:29 3715
l upon him that escapeth of Moab, ... Is 15:9 738
The young *l* roared upon him, and ... Jer 2:15 3715
the *l* have driven him away ... Jer 50:17 738
They shall roar together like *l* ... Jer 51:38 3715
she lay down among *l*, she ... Eze 19:2 738
her whelps among young *l* ... Eze 19:2 3715
went up and down among the *l* ... Eze 19:6 738
with all the young *l* thereof ... Eze 38:13 3715
shall be cast into the den of *l* ... Dan 6:7 744
shall be cast into the den of *l* ... Dan 6:12 744
and cast him into the den of *l* ... Dan 6:16 744
went in haste unto the den of *l* ... Dan 6:19 744
able to deliver thee from the *l* ... Dan 6:20 744
they cast them into the den of *l* ... Dan 6:24 744
the *l* had the mastery of them, and ... Dan 6:24 744
Daniel from the power of the *l* ... Dan 6:27 744
Where is the dwelling of the *l* ... Nah 2:11 738
the feeding place of the young *l* ... Nah 2:11 3715
sword shall devour thy young *l* ... Nah 2:13 3715
princes within her are roaring *l* ... Zeph 3:3 738
a voice of the roaring of young *l* ... Zec 11:3 3715
promises, stopped the mouths of *l* ... Heb 11:33 *3023*
teeth were as the teeth of *l* ... Rev 9:8 *3023*
the horses were as the heads of *l* ... Rev 9:17 *3023*

LIONS'
Shenir and Hermon, from the *l* dens ... Song 4:8 738
they shall yell as *l* whelps ... Jer 51:38 738
angel, and hath shut the *l* mouths ... Dan 6:22 744

LIP
put a covering upon his upper *l* ... Lev 13:45 8222
they shoot out the *l*, they shake ... Ps 22:7 8193
The *l* of truth shall be ... Prov 12:19 8193

LIPS
me, who am of uncircumcised l Ex 6:12 8193
Behold, I am of uncircumcised l Ex 6:30 8193
pronouncing with his l to do evil Lev 5:4 8193
or uttered ought out of her l Num 30:6 8193
that which she uttered with her l Num 30:8 8193
out of her l concerning her vows Num 30:12 8193
gone out of thy l thou shalt keep Deut 23:23 8193
only her l moved, but her voice 1Sa 1:13 8193
thy nose, and my bridle in thy l 2Kin 19:28 8193
this did not Job sin with his l Job 2:10 8193
laughing, and thy l with rejoicing Job 8:21 8193
speak, and open his l against thee Job 11:5 8193
hearken to the pleadings of my l Job 13:6 8193
thine own l testify against thee Job 15:6 8193
the moving of my l should asswage Job 16:5 8193
from the commandment of his l Job 23:12 8193
My l shall not speak wickedness, Job 27:4 8193
I will open my l and answer Job 32:20 8193
my l shall utter knowledge Job 33:3 8193
with flattering l and with a Ps 12:2 8193
shall cut off all flattering l Ps 12:3 8193
our l are our own Ps 12:4 8193
nor take up their names into my l Ps 16:4 8193
that goeth not out of feigned l Ps 17:1 8193
by the word of thy l I have kept Ps 17:4 8193
withholden the request of his l Ps 21:2 8193
Let the lying l be put to silence Ps 31:18 8193
thy l from speaking guile Ps 34:13 8193
lo, I have not refrained my l Ps 40:9 8193
grace is poured into thy l Ps 45:2 8193
O Lord, open thou my l Ps 51:15 8193
swords are in their l Ps 59:7 8193
the words of their l let them Ps 59:12 8193
than life, my l shall praise thee Ps 63:3 8193
shall praise thee with joyful l Ps 63:5 8193
Which my l have uttered, and my Ps 66:14 8193
My l shall greatly rejoice when I Ps 71:23 8193
thing that is gone out of my l Ps 89:34 8193
he spake unadvisedly with his l Ps 106:33 8193
With my l have I declared all the Ps 119:13 8193
My l shall utter praise, when Ps 119:171 8193
my soul, O LORD, from lying l Ps 120:2 8193
adders' poison is under their l Ps 140:3 8193
of their own l cover them Ps 140:9 8193
Keep the door of my l Ps 141:3 8193
perverse l put far from thee Prov 4:24 8193
that thy l may keep knowledge Prov 5:2 8193
For the l of a strange woman drop Prov 5:3 8193
of her l she forced him Prov 7:21 8193
the opening of my l shall be Prov 8:6 8193
is an abomination to my l Prov 8:7 8193
In the l of him that hath Prov 10:13 8193
that hideth hatred with lying l Prov 10:18 8193
he that refraineth his l is wise Prov 10:19 8193
The l of the righteous feed many Prov 10:21 8193
The l of the righteous know what Prov 10:32 8193
by the transgression of his l Prov 12:13 8193
Lying l are abomination to the Prov 12:22 8193
wide his l shall have destruction Prov 13:3 8193
but the l of the wise shall Prov 14:3 8193
not in him the l of knowledge Prov 14:7 8193
but the talk of the l tendeth Prov 14:23 8193
The l of the wise disperse Prov 15:7 8193
sentence is in the l of the king Prov 16:10 8193
Righteous l are the delight of Prov 16:13 8193
of the l increaseth learning Prov 16:21 8193
and addeth learning to his l Prov 16:23 8193
in his l there is as a burning Prov 16:27 8193
moving his l he bringeth evil to Prov 16:30 8193
doer giveth heed to false l Prov 17:4 8193
much less do lying l a prince Prov 17:7 8193
his l is esteemed a man of Prov 17:28 8193
A fool's l enter into contention, Prov 18:6 8193
his l are the snare of his soul Prov 18:7 8193
of his l shall he be filled Prov 18:20 8193
than he that is perverse in his l Prov 19:1 8193
but the l of knowledge are a Prov 20:15 8193
him that flattereth with his l Prov 20:19 8193
for the grace of his l the king Prov 22:11 8193
shall withal be fitted in thy l Prov 22:18 8193
when thy l speak right things Prov 23:16 8193
and their l talk of mischief Prov 24:2 8193
Every man shall kiss his l that Prov 24:26 8193
and deceive not with thy l Prov 24:28 8193
Burning l and a wicked heart are Prov 26:23 8193
hateth dissembleth with his l Prov 26:24 8193
a stranger, and not thine own l Prov 27:2 8193
but the l of a fool will swallow Eccl 10:12 8193
Thy l are like a thread of Song 4:3 8193
Thy l, O my spouse, drop as the Song 4:11 8193
his l like lilies, dropping sweet Song 5:13 8193
causing the l of those that are Song 7:9 8193
because I am a man of unclean l Is 6:5 8193
midst of a people of unclean l Is 6:5 8193
said, Lo, this hath touched thy l Is 6:7 8193
with the breath of his l shall he Is 11:4 8193
For with stammering l and another Is 28:11 8193
with their l do honour me, but Is 29:13 8193
his l are full of indignation, and Is 30:27 8193
thy nose, and my bridle in thy l Is 37:29 8193
I create the fruit of the l Is 57:19 8193
your l have spoken lies, your Is 59:3 8193
out of my l was right before thee Jer 17:16 8193
The l of those that rose up Lam 3:62 8193
upon thy feet, and cover not thy l Eze 24:17 8222
ye shall not cover your l Eze 24:22 8222
are taken up in the l of talkers Eze 36:3 8193
of the sons of men touched my l Dan 10:16 8193
we render the calves of our l Hos 14:2 8193
yea, they shall all cover their l Mic 3:7 8222
my l quivered at the voice Hab 3:16 8193
iniquity was not found in his l Mal 2:6 8193
For the priest's l should keep Mal 2:7 8193
and honoureth me with their l Mt 15:8 *5491*
people honoureth me with their l Mk 7:6 *5491*
poison of asps is under their l Rom 3:13 *5491*
other l will I speak unto this 1Cor 14:21 *5491*
the fruit of our l giving thanks Heb 13:15 *5491*
his l that they speak no guile 1Pet 3:10 *5491*

LIQUOR
shall he drink any l of grapes Num 6:3 4952
round goblet, which wanteth not l Song 7:2 4197

LIQUORS
of thy ripe fruits, and of thy l Ex 22:29 1831

LISTED
done unto him whatsoever they l Mt 17:12 *2309*
done unto him whatsoever they l Mk 9:13 *2309*

LISTEN
L, O isles, unto me Is 49:1 8085

LISTETH
The wind bloweth where it l Jn 3:8 *2309*
whithersoever the governor l Jas 3:4

LITTERS
horses, and in chariots, and in l Is 66:20 6632

LITTLE
Let a l water, I pray you, be Gen 18:4 4592
to flee unto, and it is a l one Gen 19:20 4705
thither, (is it not a l one Gen 19:20 4705
drink a l water of thy pitcher Gen 24:17 4592
a l water of thy pitcher to drink Gen 24:43 4592
For it was l which thou hadst Gen 30:30 4592
their wealth, and all their l ones Gen 34:29 2945
there was but a l way to come to Gen 35:16 3530
them, Go again, buy us a l food Gen 43:2 4592
we, and thou, and also our l ones Gen 43:8 2945
a l balm, and a l honey, Gen 43:11 4592
a child of his old age, a l one Gen 44:20 6966
Go again, and buy us a l food Gen 44:25 4592
the land of Egypt for your l ones Gen 45:19 2945
their father, and their l ones Gen 46:5 2945
and for food for your l ones Gen 47:24 2945
but a l way to come unto Ephrath Gen 48:7 3530
only their l ones, and their Gen 50:8 2945
will nourish you, and your l ones Gen 50:21 2945
I will let you go, and your l ones Ex 10:10 2945
let your l ones also go with you Ex 10:24 2945
household be too l for the lamb Ex 12:4 4591
and he that gathered l had no lack Ex 16:18 4591
By l and l I will drive them Ex 23:30 4592
And the l owl, and the cormorant, Lev 11:17 3563
But your l ones, which ye said Num 14:31 2945
their sons, and their l children Num 16:27 2945
Midian captives, and their l ones Num 31:9 2945
kill every male among the l ones Num 31:17 2945
cattle, and cities for our l ones Num 32:16 2945
our l ones shall dwell in the Num 32:17 2945
Build you cities for your l ones Num 32:24 2945
Our l ones, our wives, our flocks Num 32:26 2945
Moreover your l ones, which ye Deut 1:39 2945
the l ones, of every city, we Deut 2:34 2945
But your wives, and your l ones Deut 3:19 2945
before thee by l and l Deut 7:22 4592
The l owl, and the great owl, and Deut 14:16 3563
the l ones, and the cattle, and all Deut 20:14 2945
field, and shalt gather but l in Deut 28:38 4592
Your l ones, your wives, and thy Deut 29:11 2945
Your wives, your l ones, and your Josh 1:14 2945
the l ones, and the strangers that Josh 8:35 2945
of Dan went out too l for them Josh 19:47
the iniquity of Peor too l for us Josh 22:17 4592
I pray thee, a l water to drink Judg 4:19 4592
and departed, and put the l ones Judg 18:21 2945
that she tarried a l in the house Ruth 2:7 4592
his mother made him a l coat 1Sa 2:19 6996
I tasted a l of this honey 1Sa 14:29 4592
I did but taste a l honey with 1Sa 14:43 4592
When thou wast l in thine own 1Sa 15:17 6996
with David, and a l lad with him 1Sa 20:35 6996
had nothing, save one l ewe lamb 2Sa 12:3 6996
and if that had been too l 2Sa 12:8 4592
all the l ones that were with him 2Sa 15:22 2945
when David was a l past the top 2Sa 16:1 4592
Thy servant will go a l way over 2Sa 19:36 4592
and I am but a l child 1Kin 3:7 6996
was before the LORD was too l to 1Kin 8:64 6996
Hadad being yet a l child 1Kin 11:17 6996
My l finger shall be thicker than 1Kin 12:10 6996
a l water in a vessel, that I may 1Kin 17:10 4592
a barrel, and a l oil in a cruse 1Kin 17:12 4592
make me thereof a l cake first 1Kin 17:13 6996
there ariseth a l cloud out of 1Kin 18:44 6996
them like two l flocks of kids 1Kin 20:27 2835
there came forth l children out 2Kin 2:23 6996
Let us make a l chamber, I pray 2Kin 4:10 6996
of the land of Israel a l maid 2Kin 5:2 6996
like unto the flesh of a l child 2Kin 5:14 6995
So he departed from him a l way 2Kin 5:19 3530
unto them, Ahab served Baal a l 2Kin 10:18 4592
My l finger shall be thicker than 2Chr 10:10 6996
the LORD, with their l ones 2Chr 20:13 2945
the genealogy of all their l ones 2Chr 31:18 2945
way for us, and for our l ones Ezr 8:21 2945
now for a l space grace hath been Ezr 9:8 4592
give us a l reviving in our Ezr 9:8 4592
the trouble seem l before thee Neh 9:32 4591
l children and women, in one day, Est 3:13 2945
would assault them, both l ones Est 8:11 2945
and mine ear received a l thereof Job 4:12 8102
that I may take comfort a l Job 10:20 4592
forth their l ones like a flock Job 21:11 5759
They are exalted for a l while Job 24:24 4592
but how l a portion is heard of Job 26:14 8102
Suffer me a l, and I will shew Job 36:2 2191
when his wrath is kindled but a l Ps 2:12 4592
him a l lower than the angels Ps 8:5 4592
For yet a l while, and the wicked Ps 37:10 4592
A l that a righteous man hath is Ps 37:16 4592
the l hills rejoice on every side Ps 65:12
There is l Benjamin with their Ps 68:27 6810
the l hills, by righteousness Ps 72:3
rams, and the l hills like lambs Ps 114:4
and ye l hills, like lambs Ps 114:6
dasheth thy l ones against the Ps 137:9 5768
Yet a l sleep, a l slumber, Prov 6:10 4592
a l folding of the hands to sleep Prov 6:10 4592
heart of the wicked is l worth Prov 10:20 4592
Better is l with the fear of the Prov 15:16 4592
Better is a l with righteousness Prov 16:8 4592
Yet a l sleep, a l slumber, Prov 24:33 4592
a l folding of the hands to sleep Prov 24:33 4592
things which are l upon the earth Prov 30:24 6996
sweet, whether he eat l or much Eccl 5:12 4592
There was a l city, and few men Eccl 9:14 6996
so doth a l folly him that is in Eccl 10:1 4592
the l foxes, that spoil the vines Song 2:15 6996
It was but a l that I passed from Song 3:4 4592
We have a l sister, and she hath Song 8:8 6996
For yet a very l while, and the Is 10:25 4592
a l child shall lead them Is 11:6 6995
thyself as it were for a l moment Is 26:20 4592
here a l, and there a l Is 28:10 2191
here a l, and there a l Is 28:13 2191
Is it not yet a very l while Is 29:17 4592
up the isles as a very l thing Is 40:15 1851
In a l wrath I hid my face from Is 54:8 8241
A l one shall become a thousand, Is 60:22 6996
have possessed it but a l while Is 63:18 4705
sent their l ones to the waters Jer 14:3 6810
her l ones have caused a cry to Jer 48:4 6810
yet a l while, and the time of her Jer 51:33 4592
maids, and l children, and women Eze 9:6 2945
as a l sanctuary in the countries Eze 11:16 4592
as if that were a very l thing Eze 16:47 4592
sent out her l rivers unto all Eze 31:4 8585
every l chamber was one reed long Eze 40:7
between the l chambers were five Eze 40:7
the l chambers of the gate Eze 40:10
The space also before the l Eze 40:12
the l chambers were six cubits on Eze 40:12
the gate from the roof of one l Eze 40:13
narrow windows to the l chambers Eze 40:16
the l chambers thereof were three Eze 40:21
the l chambers thereof, and the Eze 40:29
the l chambers thereof, and the Eze 40:33
The l chambers thereof, the posts Eze 40:36
came up among them another l horn Dan 7:8 2192
one of them came forth a l horn Dan 8:9 4704
shall be holpen with a l help Dan 11:34 4592
for yet a l while, and I will Hos 1:4 4592
they shall sorrow a l for the Hos 8:10 4592
and the l house with clefts Amos 6:11 6996
though thou be l among the Mic 5:2 6810
Ye have sown much, and bring in l Hag 1:6 4592
for much, and, lo, it came to l Hag 1:9 4592
Yet once, it is a l while Hag 2:6 4592
for I was but a l displeased Zec 1:15 4592
turn mine hand upon the l ones Zec 13:7 6819
more clothe you, O ye of l faith Mt 6:30 *3640*
are ye fearful, O ye of l faith Mt 8:26 *3640*
l ones a cup of cold water only Mt 10:42 *3398*
said unto him, O thou of l faith Mt 14:31 *3640*
said, Seven, and a few l fishes Mt 15:34 *2485*
said unto them, O ye of l faith Mt 16:8 *3640*
Jesus called a l child unto him Mt 18:2 *3813*
and become as l children, ye Mt 18:3 *3813*
humble himself as this l child Mt 18:4 *3813*
whoso shall receive one such l Mt 18:5 *3813*
these l ones which believe in me Mt 18:6 *3398*
despise not one of these l ones Mt 18:10 *3398*
that one of these l ones should Mt 18:14 *3398*
there brought unto him l children Mt 19:13 *3813*
Suffer l children, and forbid them Mt 19:14 *3813*
And he went a l farther, and fell Mt 26:39 *3397*
he had gone a l farther thence Mk 1:19 *3641*
were also with him other l ships Mk 4:36 *4142*
My l daughter lieth at the point Mk 5:23 *2365*
these l ones that believe in me Mk 9:42 *3398*
Suffer the l children to come Mk 10:14 *3813*
the kingdom of God as a l child Mk 10:15 *3813*
And he went forward a l, and fell Mk 14:35 *3397*
a l after, they that stood by Mk 14:70 *3397*
thrust out a l from the land Lk 5:3 *3641*
but to whom l is forgiven Lk 7:47 *3641*
is forgiven, the same loveth l Lk 7:47 *3641*
he clothe you, O ye of l faith Lk 12:28 *3640*
Fear not, l flock Lk 12:32 *3398*
should offend one of these l ones Lk 17:2 *3398*
Suffer l children to come unto me Lk 18:16 *3813*
a l child shall in no wise enter Lk 18:17 *3813*
because he was l of stature Lk 19:3 *3398*
hast been faithful in a very l Lk 19:17 *1646*
after a l while another saw him, Lk 22:58 *1024*
every one of them may take a l Jn 6:7 *1024*
Yet a l while am I with you, and Jn 7:33 *3398*
Yet a l while is the light with Jn 12:35 *3398*
L children, yet a l while I Jn 13:33 *5040*
Yet a l while, and the world seeth Jn 14:19 *3397*
A l while, and ye shall not see me Jn 16:16 *3397*
a l while, and ye shall see me, Jn 16:16 *3397*
A l while, and ye shall not see me Jn 16:17 *3397*
a l while, and ye shall see me Jn 16:17 *3397*
is this that he saith, A l while Jn 16:18 *3397*
A l while, and ye shall not see me Jn 16:19 *3397*
a l while, and ye shall see me Jn 16:19 *3397*
other disciples came in a l ship Jn 21:8 *4142*
put the apostles forth a l space Acts 5:34 *1024*
alive, and were not a l comforted Acts 20:12 *3357*

and when they had gone a *l* further Acts 27:28 1024
people shewed us no *l* kindness Acts 28:2 5177
Know ye not that a *l* leaven 1Cor 5:6 3398
that had gathered *l* had no lack 2Cor 8:15 3641
bear with me a *l* in my folly 2Cor 11:1 3397
me, that I may boast myself a *l* 2Cor 11:16 3397
My *l* children, of whom I travail Gal 4:19 5040
A *l* leaven leaveneth the whole Gal 5:9 3398
For bodily exercise profiteth *l* 1Ti 4:8 3641
water, but use a *l* wine for thy 1Ti 5:23 3641
Thou madest him a *l* lower than Heb 2:7 1024
who was made a *l* lower than the Heb 2:9 1024
For yet a *l* while, and he that Heb 10:37 3397
Even so the tongue is a *l* member Jas 3:5 3398
great a matter a *l* fire kindleth Jas 3:5 3641
that appeareth for a *l* time Jas 4:14 3641
My *l* children, these things write 1Jn 2:1 5040
l children, because your sins are 1Jn 2:12 5040
l children, because ye have known 1Jn 2:13 3813
L children, it is the last time 1Jn 2:18 3813
And now, *l* children, abide in him 1Jn 2:28 5040
L children, let no man deceive 1Jn 3:7 5040
My *l* children, let us not love in 1Jn 3:18 5040
l children, and have overcome them 1Jn 4:4 5040
L children, keep yourselves from 1Jn 5:21 5040
for thou hast a *l* strength Rev 3:8 3398
should rest yet for a *l* season Rev 6:11 3398
he had in his hand a *l* book open Rev 10:2 974
take the *l* book which is open in Rev 10:8 974
said unto him, Give me the *l* book Rev 10:9 974
I took the *l* book out of the Rev 10:10 974
that he must be loosed a *l* season Rev 20:3 3398

LIVE

of life, and eat, and *l* for ever Gen 3:22 2425
my soul shall *l* because of thee Gen 12:13 2421
that Ishmael might *l* before thee Gen 17:18 2421
and my soul shall *l* Gen 19:20 2421
pray for thee, and thou shalt *l* Gen 20:7 2421
And by thy sword shalt thou *l* Gen 27:40 2421
findest thy gods, let him not *l* Gen 31:32 2421
that we may *l*, and not die Gen 42:2 2421
them the third day, This do, and *l* Gen 42:18 2421
that we may *l*, and not die, both Gen 43:8 2421
doth my father yet *l* Gen 45:3 2416
and give us seed, that we may *l* Gen 47:19 2421
be a daughter, then she shall *l* Ex 1:16 2425
be beast or man, it shall not *l* Ex 19:13 2421
then they shall sell the *l* ox Ex 21:35 2416
shalt not suffer a witch to *l* Ex 22:18 2421
there shall no man see me, and *l* Ex 33:20 2425
altar, he shall bring the *l* goat Lev 16:20 2416
hands upon the head of the *l* goat Lev 16:21 2416
if a man do, he shall *l* in them Lev 18:5 2425
that he may *l* with thee Lev 25:35 2416
that thy brother may *l* with thee Lev 25:36 2416
do unto them, that they may *l* Num 4:19 2421
But as truly as I *l*, all the Num 14:21 2416
Say unto them, As truly as I *l* Num 14:28 2416
when he looketh upon it, shall *l* Num 21:8 2425
who shall *l* when God doeth this Num 24:23 2421
for to do them, that ye may *l* Deut 4:1 2421
that they shall *l* upon the earth Deut 4:10 2416
fire, as thou hast heard, and *l* Deut 4:33 2421
one of these cities he might *l* Deut 4:42 2425
hath commanded you, that ye may *l* Deut 5:33 2421
ye observe to do, that ye may *l* Deut 8:1 2421
that man doth not *l* by bread only Deut 8:3 2421
the mouth of the LORD doth man *l* Deut 8:3 2421
the days that ye *l* upon the earth Deut 12:1 2416
thou follow, that thou mayest *l* Deut 16:20 2421
shall flee thither, that he may *l* Deut 19:4 2425
unto one of those cities, and *l* Deut 19:5 2425
all thy soul, that thou mayest *l* Deut 30:6 2416
his judgments, that thou mayest *l* Deut 30:16 2421
that both thou and thy seed may *l* Deut 30:19 2421
as long as ye *l* in the land Deut 31:13 2416
to heaven, and say, I *l* for ever Deut 32:40 2416
Let Reuben *l*, and not die Deut 33:6 2421
only Rahab the harlot shall *l* Josh 6:17 2421
a league with them, to let them *l* Josh 9:15 2421
we will even let them *l*, lest Josh 9:20 2421
said unto them, Let them *l* Josh 9:21 2421
I *l* shew me the kindness of the 1Sa 20:14 2416
not *l* after that he was fallen 2Sa 1:10 2421
to me, that the child may *l* 2Sa 12:22 2416
the king, How long have I to *l* 2Sa 19:34 2416
Let my lord king David *l* for ever 1Kin 1:31 2421
thee all the days that they *l* in 1Kin 8:40 2416
saith, I pray thee, let me *l* 1Kin 20:32 2421
l thou and thy children of the 2Kin 4:7 2421
if they save us alive, we shall *l* 2Kin 7:4 2421
shall be wanting, he shall not *l* 2Kin 10:19 2421
olive and of honey, that ye may *l* 2Kin 18:32 2421
for thou shalt die, and not *l* 2Kin 20:1 2421
so long as they *l* in the land 2Chr 6:31 2416
the king, Let the king *l* for ever Neh 2:3 2421
for them, that we may eat, and *l* Neh 5:2 2421
if a man do, he shall *l* in them Neh 9:29 2421
the golden sceptre, that he may *l* Est 4:11 2421
I would not *l* alway Job 7:16 2421
If a man die, shall he *l* again Job 14:14 2421
Wherefore do the wicked *l* Job 21:7 2421
not reproach me so long as I *l* Job 27:6 3117
your heart shall *l* for ever Ps 22:26 2421
That he should still *l* for ever Ps 49:9 2421
shall not *l* out half their days Ps 55:23
Thus will I bless thee while I *l* Ps 63:4 2416
your heart shall *l* that seek God Ps 69:32 2421
And he shall *l*, and to him shall be Ps 72:15 2421
sing unto the LORD as long as I *l* Ps 104:33 2416
I call upon him as long as I *l* Ps 116:2 3117
I shall not die, but *l*, and Ps 118:17 2421
with thy servant, that I may *l* Ps 119:17 2421
come unto me, that I may *l* Ps 119:77 2421
unto thy word, that I may *l* Ps 119:116 2421
me understanding, and I shall *l* Ps 119:144 2421
Let my soul *l*, and it shall praise Ps 119:175 2421
While I *l* will I praise the LORD Ps 146:2 2416
keep my commandments, and *l* Prov 4:4 2421
Keep my commandments, and *l* Prov 7:2 2421
Forsake the foolish, and *l* Prov 9:6 2421
but he that hateth gifts shall *l* Prov 15:27 2421
l many years, so that the days of Eccl 6:3 2421
though he *l* a thousand years Eccl 6:6 2421
is in their heart while they *l* Eccl 9:3 2416
L joyfully with the wife whom Eccl 9:9 2416
But if a man *l* many years Eccl 11:8 2421
having a *l* coal in his hand, Is 6:6 7531
They are dead, they shall not *l* Is 26:14 2421
Thy dead men shall *l*, together Is 26:19 2421
for thou shalt die, and not *l* Is 38:1 2421
O Lord, by these things men *l* Is 38:16 2421
thou recover me, and make me to *l* Is 38:16 2421
As I *l*, saith the LORD, thou Is 49:18 2416
hear, and your soul shall *l* Is 55:3 2421
that besiege you, he shall *l* Jer 21:9 2421
As I *l*, saith the LORD, though Jer 22:24 2416
and serve him and his people, and *l* Jer 27:12 2421
serve the king of Babylon, and *l* Jer 27:17 2421
that ye may *l* many days in the Jer 35:7 2421
forth to the Chaldeans shall *l* Jer 38:2 2421
his life for a prey, and shall *l* Jer 38:2 2425
princes, then thy soul shall *l* Jer 38:17 2421
and thou shalt *l*, and thine house Jer 38:17 2421
unto thee, and thy soul shall *l* Jer 38:20 2421
As I *l*, saith the King, whose Jer 46:18 2416
we shall *l* among the heathen Lam 4:20 2421
doth not sin, he shall surely *l* Eze 3:21 2421
Wherefore, as I *l*, saith the Lord Eze 5:11 2416
the souls alive that should not *l* Eze 13:19 2421
three men were in it, as I *l* Eze 14:16 2416
three men were in it, as I *l* Eze 14:18 2416
and Job, were in it, as I *l* Eze 14:20 2416
when thou wast in thy blood, *L* Eze 16:6 2421
when thou wast in thy blood, *L* Eze 16:6 2421
As I *l*, saith the Lord GOD, Sodom Eze 16:48 2416
As I *l*, saith the Lord GOD, Eze 17:16 2416
As I *l*, surely mine oath that he Eze 17:19 2416
As I *l*, saith the Lord GOD, ye Eze 18:3 2416
he is just, he shall surely *l* Eze 18:9 2421
shall he then *l* Eze 18:13 2425
he shall not *l* Eze 18:13 2421
of his father, he shall surely *l* Eze 18:17 2421
hath done them, he shall surely *l* Eze 18:19 2421
and right, he shall surely *l* Eze 18:21 2421
that he hath done he shall *l* Eze 18:22 2421
should return from his ways, and *l* Eze 18:23 2421
the wicked man doeth, shall he *l* Eze 18:24 2425
hath committed, he shall surely *l* Eze 18:28 2421
turn yourselves, and *l* ye Eze 18:32 2421
As I *l*, saith the Lord GOD, I Eze 20:3 2416
a man do, he shall even *l* in them Eze 20:11 2425
a man do, he shall even *l* in them Eze 20:13 2425
a man do, he shall even *l* in them Eze 20:21 2425
whereby they should not *l* Eze 20:25 2421
As I *l*, saith the Lord GOD, I Eze 20:31 2416
As I *l*, saith the Lord GOD, Eze 20:33
in them, how should we then *l* Eze 33:10 2421
Say unto them, As I *l*, saith the Eze 33:11 2416
the wicked turn from his way and *l* Eze 33:11 2421
to *l* for his righteousness in the Eze 33:12 2421
righteous, that he shall surely *l* Eze 33:13 2421
he shall surely *l*, he shall not Eze 33:15 2421
he shall surely *l* Eze 33:16 2421
and right, he shall *l* thereby Eze 33:19 2421
As I *l*, surely they that are in Eze 33:27 2416
As I *l* saith the Lord GOD, surely Eze 34:8 2416
Therefore, as I *l*, saith the Lord Eze 35:6 2416
Therefore, as I *l*, saith the Lord Eze 35:11 2416
me, Son of man, can these bones *l* Eze 37:3 2421
to enter into you, and ye shall *l* Eze 37:5 2421
put breath in you, and ye shall *l* Eze 37:6 2421
upon these slain, that they may *l* Eze 37:9 2421
my spirit in you, and ye shall *l* Eze 37:14 2421
the rivers shall come, shall *l* Eze 47:9 2421
every thing shall *l* whither the Eze 47:9 2425
in Syriack, O king, *l* for ever Dan 2:4 2418
O king, *l* for ever Dan 3:9 2418
spake and said, O king, *l* for ever Dan 5:10 2414
unto him, King Darius, *l* for ever Dan 6:6 2414
unto the king, O king, *l* for ever Dan 6:21 2414
us up, and we shall *l* in his sight Hos 6:2 2421
Israel, Seek ye me, and ye shall *l* Amos 5:4 2421
Seek the LORD, and ye shall *l* Amos 5:6 2421
good, and not evil, that ye may *l* Amos 5:14 2421
is better for me to die than to *l* Jonah 4:3 2416
is better for me to die than to *l* Jonah 4:8 2416
but the just shall *l* by his faith Hab 2:4 2421
Therefore as I *l*, saith the LORD Zeph 2:9 2416
the prophets, do they *l* for ever Zec 1:5 2421
they shall *l* with their children, Zec 10:9 2421
say unto him, Thou shalt not *l* Zec 13:3 2421
Man shall not *l* by bread alone Mt 4:4 2198
thy hand upon her, and she shall *l* Mt 9:18 2198
and she shall *l* Mk 5:23 2198
man shall not *l* by bread alone Lk 4:4 2198
l delicately, are in kings' Lk 7:25 5225
this do, and thou shalt *l* Lk 10:28 2198
for all *l* unto him Lk 20:38 2198
and they that hear shall *l* Jn 5:25 2198
this bread, he shall *l* for ever Jn 6:51 2198
sent me, and I *l* by the Father Jn 6:57 2198
eateth me, even he shall *l* by me Jn 6:57 2198
of this bread shall *l* for ever Jn 6:58 2198
he were dead, yet shall he *l* Jn 11:25 2198
because I *l*, ye shall *l* also Jn 14:19 2198
to the end they might not *l* Acts 7:19 2225
For in him we *l*, and move, and have Acts 17:28 2198
it is not fit that he should *l* Acts 22:22 2198
that he ought not to *l* any longer Acts 25:24 2198
yet vengeance suffereth not to *l* Acts 28:4 2198
The just shall *l* by faith Rom 1:17 2198
dead to sin, *l* any longer therein Rom 6:2 2198
that we shall also *l* with him Rom 6:8 4800
the flesh, to *l* after the flesh Rom 8:12 2198
For if ye *l* after the flesh, ye Rom 8:13 2198
the deeds of the body, ye shall *l* Rom 8:13 2198
those things shall *l* by them Rom 10:5 2198
in you, *l* peaceably with all men Rom 12:18 1514
we *l*, we *l* unto the Lord Rom 14:8 2198
whether we *l* therefore, or die, Rom 14:8 2198
For it is written, As I *l* Rom 14:11 2198
minister about holy things *l* of 1Cor 9:13 2068
the gospel should *l* of the gospel 1Cor 9:14 2198
For we which *l* are alway 2Cor 4:11 2198
that they which *l* should not 2Cor 5:15 2198
not henceforth *l* unto themselves 2Cor 5:15 2198
as dying, and, behold, we *l* 2Cor 6:9 2198
our hearts to die and *l* with you 2Cor 7:3 4800
but we shall *l* with him by the 2Cor 13:4 2198
be of one mind, *l* in peace 2Cor 13:11 1514
the Gentiles to *l* as do the Jews Gal 2:14 2198
the law, that I might *l* unto God Gal 2:19 2198
nevertheless I *l* Gal 2:20 2198
the life which I now *l* in the Gal 2:20 2198
l by the faith of the Son of God Gal 2:20 2198
for, The just shall *l* by faith Gal 3:11 2198
that doeth them shall *l* in them Gal 3:12 2198
If we *l* in the Spirit, let us Gal 5:25 2198
thou mayest *l* long on the earth Eph 6:3
For to me to *l* is Christ, and to Phil 1:21 2198
But if I *l* in the flesh, this is Phil 1:22 2198
For now we *l*, if ye stand fast in 1Th 3:8 2198
we should *l* together with him 1Th 5:10 2198
him, we shall also *l* with him 2Ti 2:11 4800
all that will *l* godly in Christ 2Ti 3:12 2198
lusts, we should *l* soberly Titus 2:12 2198
Now the just shall *l* by faith Heb 10:38 2198
unto the Father of spirits, and *l* Heb 12:9 2198
all things willing to *l* honestly Heb 13:18 390
say, If the Lord will, we shall *l* Jas 4:15 2198
should *l* unto righteousness 1Pet 2:24 2198
That he no longer should *l* the 1Pet 4:2 980
but *l* according to God in the 1Pet 4:6 2198
those that after should *l* ungodly 2Pet 2:6
escaped from them who *l* in error 2Pet 2:18 390
that we might *l* through him 1Jn 4:9 2198
the wound by a sword, and did *l* Rev 13:14 2198

LIVED

Adam *l* an hundred and thirty years Gen 5:3 2421
that Adam *l* were nine hundred Gen 5:5 2425
Seth *l* an hundred and five years, Gen 5:6 2421
Seth *l* after he begat Enos eight Gen 5:7 2421
Enos *l* ninety years, and begat Gen 5:9 2421
Enos *l* after he begat Cainan Gen 5:10 2421
Cainan *l* seventy years, and begat Gen 5:12 2421
And Cainan *l* after he begat Gen 5:13 2421
And Mahalaleel *l* sixty and five Gen 5:15 2421
Mahalaleel *l* after he begat Jared Gen 5:16 2421
Jared *l* an hundred sixty and two Gen 5:18 2421
Jared *l* after he begat Enoch Gen 5:19 2421
And Enoch *l* sixty and five years, Gen 5:21 2421
Methuselah *l* an hundred eighty and Gen 5:25 2421
Methuselah *l* after he begat Gen 5:26 2421
Lamech *l* an hundred eighty and two Gen 5:28 2421
Lamech *l* after he begat Noah five Gen 5:30 2421
Noah *l* after the flood three Gen 9:28 2421
Shem *l* after he begat Arphaxad Gen 11:11 2421
And Arphaxad *l* five and thirty Gen 11:12 2425
Arphaxad *l* after he begat Salah Gen 11:13 2421
Salah *l* thirty years, and begat Gen 11:14 2425
Salah *l* after he begat Eber four Gen 11:15 2421
And Eber *l* four and thirty years, Gen 11:16 2421
Eber *l* after he begat Peleg four Gen 11:17 2421
Peleg *l* thirty years, and begat Gen 11:18 2421
Peleg *l* after he begat Reu two Gen 11:19 2421
And Reu *l* two and thirty years, and Gen 11:20 2421
Reu *l* after he begat Serug two Gen 11:21 2421
Serug *l* thirty years, and begat Gen 11:22 2421
Serug *l* after he begat Nahor two Gen 11:23 2421
And Nahor *l* nine and twenty years, Gen 11:24 2421
Nahor *l* after he begat Terah an Gen 11:25 2421
Terah *l* seventy years, and begat Gen 11:26 2421
Isaac his son, while he yet *l* Gen 25:6 2416
of Abraham's life which he *l* Gen 25:7 2425
Jacob *l* in the land of Egypt Gen 47:28 2421
Joseph *l* an hundred and ten years Gen 50:22 2421
went to search the land, *l* still Num 14:38 2421
beheld the serpent of brass, he *l* Num 21:9 2425
of the fire, as we have, and *l* Deut 5:26 2421
I perceive, that if Absalom had *l* 2Sa 19:6 2416
Solomon his father while he yet *l* 1Kin 12:6 2416
l after the death of Jehoash son 2Kin 14:17 2421
Solomon his father while he yet *l* 2Chr 10:6 2416
the son of Joash king of Judah *l* 2Chr 25:25 2421
After this *l* Job an hundred and Job 42:16 2421
Though while he *l* he blessed his Ps 49:18 2416
breath came into them, and they *l* Eze 37:10 2421
had *l* with an husband seven years Lk 2:36 2198
I have *l* in all good conscience Acts 23:1 4176
of our religion I *l* a Pharisee Acts 26:5 2198
some time, when ye *l* in them Col 3:7 2198
Ye have *l* in pleasure on the Jas 5:5 5171
l deliciously, so much torment and Rev 18:7
l deliciously with her, shall Rev 18:9
and they *l* and reigned with Christ Rev 20:4 2198
But the rest of the dead *l* not Rev 20:5 326

LIVELY

for they are *l*, and are delivered Ex 1:19 2422
But mine enemies are *l*, and they Ps 38:19 2416

L

who received the *l* oracles to	Acts 7:38	*2198*
a *l* hope by the resurrection of	1Pet 1:3	*2198*
as *l* stones, are built up a	1Pet 2:5	*2198*

LIVER

and the caul that is above the *l*	Ex 29:13	3516
inwards, and the caul above the *l*	Ex 29:22	3516
flanks, and the caul above the *l*	Lev 3:4	3516
flanks, and the caul above the *l*	Lev 3:10	3516
flanks, and the caul above the *l*	Lev 3:15	3516
flanks, and the caul above the *l*	Lev 4:9	3516
and the caul that is above the *l*	Lev 7:4	3516
inwards, and the caul above the *l*	Lev 8:16	3516
inwards, and the caul above the *l*	Lev 8:25	3516
the caul above the *l* of the sin	Lev 9:10	3516
kidneys, and the caul above the *l*	Lev 9:19	3516
Till a dart strike through his *l*	Prov 7:23	3516
my *l* is poured upon the earth,	Lam 2:11	3516
with images, he looked in the *l*	Eze 21:21	3516

LIVES

blood of your *l* will I require	Gen 9:5	5315
to save your *l* by a great	Gen 45:7	2421
they said, Thou hast saved our *l*	Gen 47:25	2421
they made their *l* bitter with	Ex 1:14	2416
have, and deliver our *l* from death	Josh 2:13	5315
afraid of our *l* because of you	Josh 9:24	5315
l unto the death in the high	Judg 5:18	5315
with the *l* of thy household	Judg 18:25	5315
lovely and pleasant in their *l*	2Sa 1:23	2416
the *l* of thy sons and of thy	2Sa 19:5	5315
the *l* of thy wives	2Sa 19:5	5315
and the *l* of thy concubines	2Sa 19:5	5315
that went in jeopardy of their *l*	2Sa 23:17	5315
that have put their *l* in jeopardy	1Chr 11:19	5315
of their *l* they brought it	1Chr 11:19	5315
together, and stood for their *l*	Est 9:16	5315
they lurk privily for their own *l*	Prov 1:18	5315
hands of them that seek their *l*	Jer 19:7	5315
and they that seek their *l*	Jer 19:9	5315
hand of those that seek their *l*	Jer 46:26	5315
Flee, save your *l*, and be like the	Jer 48:6	5315
our *l* because of the sword of the	Lam 5:9	5315
yet their *l* were prolonged for a	Dan 7:12	2417
is not come to destroy men's *l*	Lk 9:56	*5590*
Men that have hazarded their *l*	Acts 15:26	*5590*
lading and ship, but also of our *l*	Acts 27:10	*5590*
lay down our *l* for the brethren	1Jn 3:16	*5590*
loved not their *l* unto the death	Rev 12:11	*5590*

LIVEST

as long as thou *l* upon the earth	Deut 12:19	3117
as thou *l*, and as thy soul liveth,	2Sa 11:11	2416
l after the manner of Gentiles,	Gal 2:14	*2198*
that thou hast a name that thou *l*	Rev 3:1	*2198*

LIVETH

that *l* shall be meat for you	Gen 9:3	2416
God doth talk with man, and he *l*	Deut 5:24	2425
as the LORD *l*, if ye had saved	Judg 8:19	2416
a kinsman to thee, as the LORD *l*	Ruth 3:13	2416
said, Oh my lord, as thy soul *l*	1Sa 1:26	2416
as long as he *l* he shall be lent	1Sa 1:28	3117
For, as the LORD *l*, which saveth	1Sa 14:39	2416
as the LORD *l*, there shall not	1Sa 14:45	2416
And Abner said, As thy soul *l*	1Sa 17:55	2416
and Saul sware, As the LORD *l*	1Sa 19:6	2416
the LORD *l*, and as thy soul *l*	1Sa 20:3	2416
as the LORD *l*	1Sa 20:21	2416
son of Jesse *l* upon the ground	1Sa 20:31	2425
say to him that *l* in prosperity	1Sa 25:6	2416
the LORD *l*, and as thy soul *l*	1Sa 25:26	2416
deed, as the LORD God of Israel *l*	1Sa 25:34	2416
said furthermore, As the LORD *l*	1Sa 26:10	2416
As the LORD *l*, ye are worthy to	1Sa 26:16	2416
the LORD, saying, As the LORD *l*	1Sa 28:10	2416
unto him, Surely, as the LORD *l*	1Sa 29:6	2416
And Joab said, As God *l*, unless	2Sa 2:27	2416
and said unto them, As the LORD *l*	2Sa 4:9	2416
as thou livest, and as thy soul *l*	2Sa 11:11	2416
he said to Nathan, As the LORD *l*	2Sa 12:5	2416
And he said, As the LORD *l*	2Sa 14:11	2416
answered and said, As thy soul *l*	2Sa 14:19	2416
the king, and said, As the LORD *l*	2Sa 15:21	2416
and as my lord the king *l*	2Sa 15:21	2416
The LORD *l*	2Sa 22:47	2416
sware, and said, As the LORD *l*	1Kin 1:29	2416
Now therefore, as the LORD *l*	1Kin 2:24	2416
one saith, This is my son that *l*	1Kin 3:23	2416
Ahab, As the LORD God of Israel *l*	1Kin 17:1	2416
she said, As the LORD thy God *l*	1Kin 17:12	2416
and Elijah said, See, thy son *l*	1Kin 17:23	2416
As the LORD thy God *l*, there is	1Kin 18:10	2416
said, As the LORD of hosts *l*	1Kin 18:15	2416
And Micaiah said, As the LORD *l*	1Kin 22:14	2416
the LORD *l*, and as thy soul *l*	2Kin 2:2	2416
the LORD *l*, and as thy soul *l*	2Kin 2:4	2416
the LORD *l*, and as thy soul *l*	2Kin 2:6	2416
said, As the LORD of hosts *l*	2Kin 3:14	2416
the LORD *l*, and as thy soul *l*	2Kin 4:30	2416
But he said, As the LORD *l*	2Kin 5:16	2416
but, as the LORD *l*, I will run	2Kin 5:20	2416
And Micaiah said, As the LORD *l*	2Chr 18:13	2416
For I know that my redeemer *l*	Job 19:25	2416
As God *l*, who hath taken away my	Job 27:2	2416
The LORD *l*	Ps 18:46	2416
What man is he that *l*, and shall	Ps 89:48	2421
And thou shalt swear, The LORD *l*	Jer 4:2	2416
And though they say, The LORD *l*	Jer 5:2	2416
to swear by my name, The LORD *l*	Jer 12:16	2416
shall no more be said, The LORD *l*	Jer 16:14	2416
But, The LORD *l*, that brought up	Jer 16:15	2416
shall no more say, The LORD *l*	Jer 23:7	2416
But, The LORD *l*, which brought up	Jer 23:8	2416
Jeremiah, saying, As the LORD *l*	Jer 38:16	2416
of Egypt, saying, The Lord GOD *l*	Jer 44:26	2416
to pass, that every thing that *l*	Eze 47:9	2416
and honoured him that *l* for ever	Dan 4:34	2416
sware by him that *l* for ever that	Dan 12:7	2416
Beth-aven, nor swear, The LORD *l*	Hos 4:15	2416
and say, Thy god, O Dan, *l*	Amos 8:14	2416
and, The manner of Beer-sheba *l*	Amos 8:14	2416
thy son *l*	Jn 4:50	*2198*
and told him, saying, Thy son *l*	Jn 4:51	*2198*
Jesus said unto him, Thy son *l*	Jn 4:53	*2198*
And whosoever *l* and believeth in me	Jn 11:26	*2198*
in that he *l*, he *l* unto God	Rom 6:10	*2198*
over a man as long as he *l*	Rom 7:1	*2198*
to her husband so long as he *l*	Rom 7:2	*2198*
So then if, while her husband *l*	Rom 7:3	*2198*
For none of us *l* to himself	Rom 14:7	*2198*
the law as long as her husband *l*	1Cor 7:39	*2198*
yet he *l* by the power of God	2Cor 13:4	*2198*
yet not I, but Christ *l* in me	Gal 2:20	*2198*
But she that *l* in pleasure is	1Ti 5:6	*2198*
in pleasure is dead while she *l*	1Ti 5:6	*2198*
of whom it is witnessed that he *l*	Heb 7:8	*2198*
by him, seeing he ever *l* to make	Heb 7:25	*2198*
at all while the testator *l*	Heb 9:17	*2198*
by the word of God, which *l*	1Pet 1:23	*2198*
I am he that *l*, and was dead	Rev 1:18	*2198*
throne, who *l* for ever and ever,	Rev 4:9	*2198*
and worship him that *l* for ever	Rev 4:10	*2198*
and worshipped him that *l* for ever	Rev 5:14	*2198*
And sware by him that *l* for ever	Rev 10:6	*2198*
of God, who *l* for ever and ever	Rev 15:7	*2198*

LIVING

every *l* creature that moveth,	Gen 1:21	2416
the *l* creature after his kind	Gen 1:24	2416
over every *l* thing that moveth	Gen 1:28	2416
and man became a *l* soul	Gen 2:7	2416
Adam called every *l* creature	Gen 2:19	2416
she was the mother of all *l*	Gen 3:20	2416
of every *l* thing of all flesh,	Gen 6:19	2416
every *l* substance that I have	Gen 7:4	
every *l* substance was destroyed	Gen 7:23	
remembered Noah, and every *l* thing	Gen 8:1	2416
every *l* thing that is with thee	Gen 8:17	2416
smite any more every thing *l*	Gen 8:21	2416
with every *l* creature that is	Gen 9:10	2416
every *l* creature that is with you	Gen 9:12	2416
every *l* creature of all flesh	Gen 9:15	2416
every *l* creature of all flesh	Gen 9:16	2416
of any *l* thing which is in the	Lev 11:10	2416
of every *l* creature that moveth	Lev 11:46	2416
As for the *l* bird, he shall take	Lev 14:6	2416
the *l* bird in the blood of the	Lev 14:6	2416
shall let the *l* bird loose into	Lev 14:7	2416
the *l* bird, and dip them in the	Lev 14:51	2416
running water, and with the *l* bird	Lev 14:52	2416
But he shall let go the *l* bird	Lev 14:53	2416
or by any manner of *l* thing that	Lev 20:25	2416
stood between the dead and the *l*	Num 16:48	2416
hath heard the voice of the *l* God	Deut 5:26	2416
know that the *l* God is among you	Josh 3:10	2416
left off his kindness to the *l*	Ruth 2:20	2416
defy the armies of the *l* God	1Sa 17:26	2416
defied the armies of the *l* God	1Sa 17:36	2416
of their death, *l* in widowhood	2Sa 20:3	2424
but the *l* is my son, and the dead	1Kin 3:22	2416
is thy son, and the *l* is my son	1Kin 3:22	2416
is the dead, and my son is the *l*	1Kin 3:23	2416
Divide the *l* child in two, and	1Kin 3:25	2416
the *l* child was unto the king	1Kin 3:26	2416
O my lord, give her the *l* child	1Kin 3:26	2416
and said, Give her the *l* child	1Kin 3:27	2416
hath sent to reproach the *l* God	2Kin 19:4	2416
sent him to reproach the *l* God	2Kin 19:16	2416
hand is the soul of every *l* thing	Job 12:10	2416
is it found in the land of the *l*	Job 28:13	2416
it is hid from the eyes of all *l*	Job 28:21	2416
to the house appointed for all *l*	Job 30:23	2416
with the light of the *l*	Job 33:30	2416
of the LORD in the land of the *l*	Ps 27:13	2416
thirsteth for God, for the *l* God	Ps 42:2	2416
thee out of the land of the *l*	Ps 52:5	2416
before God in the light of the *l*	Ps 56:13	2416
away as with a whirlwind, both *l*	Ps 58:9	2416
blotted out of the book of the *l*	Ps 69:28	2416
my flesh crieth out for the *l* God	Ps 84:2	2416
the LORD in the land of the *l*	Ps 116:9	2416
my portion in the land of the *l*	Ps 142:5	2416
sight shall no man *l* be justified	Ps 143:2	2416
the desire of every *l* thing	Ps 145:16	2416
than the *l* which are yet alive	Eccl 4:2	2416
I considered all the *l* which walk	Eccl 4:15	2416
that knoweth to walk before the *l*	Eccl 6:8	2416
the *l* will lay it to his heart	Eccl 7:2	2416
joined to all the *l* there is hope	Eccl 9:4	2416
for a *l* dog is better than a dead	Eccl 9:4	2416
For the *l* know that they shall	Eccl 9:5	2416
of gardens, a well of *l* waters	Song 4:15	2416
written among the *l* in Jerusalem	Is 4:3	2416
for the *l* to the dead	Is 8:19	2416
hath sent to reproach the *l* God	Is 37:4	2416
hath sent to reproach the *l* God	Is 37:17	2416
the LORD, in the land of the *l*	Is 38:11	2416
The *l*, the *l*, he shall	Is 38:19	2416
cut off out of the land of the *l*	Is 53:8	2416
me the fountain of *l* waters	Jer 2:13	2416
is the true God, he is the *l* God	Jer 10:10	2416
him off from the land of the *l*	Jer 11:19	2416
LORD, the fountain of *l* waters	Jer 17:13	2416
perverted the words of the *l* God	Jer 23:36	2416
Wherefore doth a *l* man complain	Lam 3:39	2416
the likeness of four *l* creatures	Eze 1:5	2416
the likeness of the *l* creatures	Eze 1:13	2416
up and down among the *l* creatures	Eze 1:13	2416
the *l* creatures ran and returned	Eze 1:14	2416
Now as I beheld the *l* creatures	Eze 1:15	2416
upon the earth by the *l* creatures	Eze 1:15	2416
when the *l* creatures went, the	Eze 1:19	2416
when the *l* creatures were lifted	Eze 1:19	2416
for the spirit of the *l* creature	Eze 1:20	2416
for the spirit of the *l* creature	Eze 1:21	2416
l creature was as the colour of	Eze 1:22	2416
the *l* creatures that touched one	Eze 3:13	2416
This is the *l* creature that I saw	Eze 10:15	2416
of the *l* creature was in them	Eze 10:17	2416
This is the *l* creature that I saw	Eze 10:20	2416
set glory in the land of the *l*	Eze 26:20	2416
terror in the land of the *l*	Eze 32:23	2416
their terror in the land of the *l*	Eze 32:24	2416
was caused in the land of the *l*	Eze 32:25	2416
their terror in the land of the *l*	Eze 32:26	2416
the mighty in the land of the *l*	Eze 32:27	2416
my terror in the land of the *l*	Eze 32:32	2416
that I have more than any *l*	Dan 2:30	2417
to the intent that the *l* may know	Dan 4:17	2417
O Daniel, servant of the *l* God	Dan 6:20	2417
for he is the *l* God, and stedfast	Dan 6:26	2417
Ye are the sons of the *l* God	Hos 1:10	2416
that *l* waters shall go out from	Zec 14:8	2416
the Christ, the Son of the *l* God	Mt 16:16	*2198*
the God of the dead, but of the *l*	Mt 22:32	*2198*
him, I adjure thee by the *l* God	Mt 26:63	*2198*
of the dead, but the God of the *l*	Mk 12:27	*2198*
all that she had, even all her *l*	Mk 12:44	*979*
spent all her *l* upon physicians	Lk 8:43	*979*
And he divided unto them his *l*	Lk 15:12	*979*
his substance with riotous *l*	Lk 15:13	*2198*
hath devoured thy *l* with harlots	Lk 15:30	*979*
a God of the dead, but of the *l*	Lk 20:38	*2198*
cast in all the *l* that she had	Lk 21:4	*979*
Why seek ye the *l* among the dead	Lk 24:5	*2198*
he would have given thee *l* water	Jn 4:10	*2198*
then hast thou that *l* water	Jn 4:11	*2198*
I am the *l* bread which came down	Jn 6:51	*2198*
As the *l* Father hath sent me, and	Jn 6:57	*2198*
that Christ, the Son of the *l* God	Jn 6:69	*2198*
shall flow rivers of *l* water	Jn 7:38	*2198*
these vanities unto the *l* God	Acts 14:15	*2198*
called the children of the *l* God	Rom 9:26	*2198*
present your bodies a *l* sacrifice	Rom 12:1	*2198*
be Lord both of the dead and *l*	Rom 14:9	*2198*
first man Adam was made a *l* soul	1Cor 15:45	*2198*
but with the Spirit of the *l* God	2Cor 3:3	*2198*
ye are the temple of the *l* God	2Cor 6:16	*2198*
as though *l* in the world, are ye	Col 2:20	*2198*
to God from idols to serve the *l*	1Th 1:9	*2198*
which is the church of the *l* God	1Ti 3:15	*2198*
because we trust in the *l* God	1Ti 4:10	*2198*
riches, but in the *l* God, who	1Ti 6:17	*2198*
l in malice and envy, hateful, and	Titus 3:3	*1236*
in departing from the *l* God	Heb 3:12	*2198*
dead works to serve the *l* God	Heb 9:14	*2198*
l way, which he hath consecrated	Heb 10:20	*2198*
fall into the hands of the *l* God	Heb 10:31	*2198*
and unto the city of the *l* God	Heb 12:22	*2198*
To whom coming, as unto a *l* stone	1Pet 2:4	*2198*
having the seal of the *l* God	Rev 7:2	*2198*
them unto *l* fountains of waters	Rev 7:17	*2198*
every *l* soul died in the sea	Rev 16:3	*2198*

LIZARD

and the chameleon, and the *l*	Lev 11:30	3911

LO

and, *l*, in her mouth was an olive	Gen 8:11	2009
and, *l*, one born in my house is	Gen 15:3	2009
and, *l*, an horror of great	Gen 15:12	2009
lift up his eyes and looked, and, *l*	Gen 18:2	2009
and, *l*, Sarah thy wife shall have	Gen 18:10	2009
of the plain, and beheld, and, *l*	Gen 19:28	2009
behold a well in the field, and, *l*	Gen 29:2	2009
And he said, *L*, it is yet high day	Gen 29:7	2005
sheaves in the field, and, *l*	Gen 37:7	2009
and, *l*, it is even in my sack	Gen 42:28	2009
l, here is seed for you, and ye	Gen 47:23	1883
and, *l*, God hath shewed me also	Gen 48:11	2009
father made me swear, saying, *L*	Gen 50:5	2009
l, he goeth out unto the water	Ex 7:15	2009
l, he cometh forth to the water	Ex 8:20	2009
l, shall we sacrifice the	Ex 8:26	2005
And the LORD said unto Moses, *L*	Ex 19:9	2009
top of the mountain, saying, *L*	Num 14:40	2009
And Balaam said unto Balak, *L*	Num 22:38	2009
And he returned unto him and, *l*	Num 23:6	2009
l, the people shall dwell alone,	Num 23:9	2005
but, *l*, the LORD hath kept thee	Num 24:11	2009
And, *l*, he hath given occasions of	Deut 22:17	2009
and now, *l*, I am this day	Josh 14:10	2009
Behold, I dreamed a dream, and, *l*	Judg 7:13	2009
For, *l*, thou shalt conceive, and	Judg 13:5	2009
And when he came, *l*, Eli sat upon	1Sa 4:13	2009
and, *l*, thy father hath left the	1Sa 10:2	2009
rod that was in mine hand, and, *l*	1Sa 14:43	2114
said Achish unto his servants, *L*	1Sa 21:14	2009
and, *l*, the chariots and horsemen	2Sa 1:6	2009
l Zadok also, and all the Levites	2Sa 15:24	2009
that smote the people, and said, *L*	2Sa 24:17	2009
And, *l*, while she yet talked with	1Kin 1:22	2009
for, *l*, he hath caught hold on	1Kin 1:51	2009
l, I have given thee a wise and an	1Kin 3:12	2009
and they said one to another, *L*	2Kin 7:6	2009
and, *l*, all the way was full of	2Kin 7:15	2009
said to Nathan the prophet, *L*	1Chr 17:1	2009
l, I give thee the oxen also for	1Chr 21:23	7200
the acts of Asa, first and last, *l*	2Chr 16:11	2009
Thou sayest, *L*, thou hast smitten	2Chr 25:19	2009
and all his wars, and his ways, *l*	2Chr 27:7	2005
For, *l*, our fathers have fallen	2Chr 29:9	2009
and, *l*, we bring into bondage our	Neh 5:5	2009
And, *l*, I perceived that God had	Neh 6:12	2009

L, let that night be solitary ... Job 3:7 2009
L this, we have searched it, so ... Job 5:27 2009
L, he goeth by me, and I see him ... Job 9:11 2005
If I speak of strength, *l* ... Job 9:19 2009
L, mine eye hath seen all this, ... Job 13:1 2005
L, their good is not in their ... Job 21:16 2005
L, these are parts of his ways ... Job 26:14 2005
L, all these things worketh God ... Job 33:29 2005
L now, his strength is in his ... Job 40:16 2009
For, *l*, the wicked bend their bow ... Ps 11:2 2009
Yet he passed away, and, *l* ... Ps 37:36 2009
Then said I, *L*, I come ... Ps 40:7 2009
l, I have not refrained my lips, ... Ps 40:9 2009
For, *l*, the kings were assembled, ... Ps 48:4 2009
L, this is the man that made not ... Ps 52:7 2009
L, then would I wander far off, ... Ps 55:7 2009
For, *l*, they lie in wait for my ... Ps 59:3 2009
l, he doth send out his voice, and ... Ps 68:33 2005
For, *l*, they that are far from ... Ps 73:27 2005
For, *l*, thine enemies make a ... Ps 83:2 2009
l, thine enemies, O LORD, for, *l* ... Ps 92:9 2009
L, children are an heritage of ... Ps 127:3 2009
L, we heard of it at Ephratah ... Ps 132:6 2009
not a word in my tongue, but, *l* ... Ps 139:4 2005
And, *l*, it was all grown over with ... Prov 24:31 2009
with mine own heart, saying, *L* ... Eccl 1:16 2009
L, this only have I found, that ... Eccl 7:29 7200
For, *l*, the winter is past, the ... Song 2:11 2009
laid it upon my mouth, and said, *L* ... Is 6:7 2009
it shall be said in that day, *L* ... Is 25:9 2009
L, thou trustest in the staff of ... Is 36:6 2009
and, *l*, these from the north and ... Is 49:12 2009
l, they all shall wax old as a ... Is 50:9 2005
For, *l*, I will call all the ... Jer 1:15 2009
I beheld the earth, and, *l* ... Jer 4:23 2009
I beheld the mountains, and, *l* ... Jer 4:24 2009
I beheld, and, *l*, there was no man ... Jer 4:25 2009
I beheld, and, *l*, the fruitful ... Jer 4:26 2009
L, I will bring a nation upon you ... Jer 5:15 2009
L, certainly in vain made he it ... Jer 8:8 2009
l, they have rejected the word of ... Jer 8:9 2009
For, *l*, I begin to bring evil on ... Jer 25:29 2009
For, *l*, the days come, saith the ... Jer 30:3 2009
for, *l*, I will save thee from ... Jer 30:10 2009
and, *l*, all the princes sat there, ... Jer 36:12 2009
For, *l*, I will make thee small ... Jer 49:15 2009
For, *l*, I will raise and cause to ... Jer 50:9 2009
and, *l*, a roll of a book was ... Eze 2:9 2009
Then he said unto me, *L*, I have ... Eze 4:15 7200
l a likeness as the appearance of ... Eze 8:2 2009
and, *l*, they put the branch to ... Eze 8:17 2009
and one built up a wall, and, *l* ... Eze 13:10 2009
L, when the wall is fallen, shall ... Eze 13:12 2009
by breaking the covenant, when, *l* ... Eze 17:18 2009
Now, *l*, if he beget a son, that ... Eze 18:14 2009
is not good among his people, *l* ... Eze 18:18 2009
and, *l*, thus have they done in the ... Eze 23:39 2009
and, *l*, they came ... Eze 23:40 2009
for, *l*, it cometh ... Eze 30:9 2009
and, *l*, it shall not be bound up ... Eze 30:21 2009
And, *l*, thou art unto them as a ... Eze 33:32 2009
And when this cometh to pass, (*l* ... Eze 33:33 2009
and, *l*, they were very dry ... Eze 37:2 2009
And when I beheld, *l*, the sinews ... Eze 37:8 2009
me into the outward court, and, *l* ... Eze 40:17 2009
and, *l*, before the temple were an ... Eze 42:8 2009
He answered and said, *L*, I see ... Dan 3:25 1888
l another, like a leopard, which ... Dan 7:6 718
but, *l*, Michael, one of the chief ... Dan 10:13 2009
and when I am gone forth, *l* ... Dan 10:20 2009
For, *l*, they are gone because of ... Hos 9:6 2009
sworn by his holiness, that, *l* ... Amos 4:2 2009
For, *l*, he that formeth the ... Amos 4:13 2009
and, *l*, it was the latter growth ... Amos 7:1 2009
For, *l*, I will command, and I will ... Amos 9:9 2009
For, *l*, I raise up the Chaldeans, ... Hab 1:6 2009
Ye looked for much, and, *l* ... Hag 1:9 2009
for, *l*, I come, and I will dwell ... Zec 2:10
but, *l*, I will deliver the men ... Zec 11:6
For, *l*, I will raise up a ... Zec 11:16
and, *l*, the star, which they saw ... Mt 2:9 *2400*
and, *l*, the heavens were opened ... Mt 3:16 *2400*
l a voice from heaven, saying, ... Mt 3:17 *2400*
if any man shall say unto you, *L* ... Mt 24:23 *2400*
l, there thou hast that is thine ... Mt 25:25 *2395*
And while he yet spake, *l*, Judas, ... Mt 26:47 *2400*
l, I have told you ... Mt 28:7 *2400*
and, *l*, I am with you alway, even ... Mt 28:20 *2400*
Peter began to say unto him, *L* ... Mk 10:28 *2400*
if any man shall say to you, *L* ... Mk 13:21 *2400*
or, *l*, he is there ... Mk 13:21 *2400*
l, he that betrayeth me is at ... Mk 14:42 *2400*
For, *l*, as soon as the voice of ... Lk 1:44 *2400*
And, *l*, the angel of the Lord came ... Lk 2:9 *2400*
And, *l*, a spirit taketh him, and he ... Lk 9:39 *2400*
Abraham, whom Satan hath bound, *l* ... Lk 13:16 *2400*
answering said to his father, *L* ... Lk 15:29 *2400*
Neither shall they say, *L* here ... Lk 17:21 *2400*
or, *l* there ... Lk 17:21 *2400*
Then Peter said, *L*, we have left ... Lk 18:28 *2400*
and, *l*, nothing worthy of death is ... Lk 23:15 *2400*
But, *l*, he speaketh boldly, and ... Jn 7:26 *2396*
His disciples said unto him, *L* ... Jn 16:29 *2396*
unworthy of everlasting life, *l* ... Acts 13:46 *2400*
and, *l*, God hath given thee all ... Acts 27:24 *2400*
Then said I, *L*, I come (in the ... Heb 10:7 *2400*
Then said he, *L*, I come to do thy ... Heb 10:9 *2400*
And I beheld, and, *l*, in the midst ... Rev 5:6 *2400*
And I beheld, and *l* a black horse ... Rev 6:5 *2400*
had opened the sixth seal, and, *l* ... Rev 6:12 *2400*
After this I beheld, and, *l* ... Rev 7:9 *2400*
And I looked, and, *l*, a Lamb stood ... Rev 14:1 *2400*

LOADEN
your carriages were heavy *l* ... Is 46:1 6006

LOADETH
who daily *l* us with benefits, ... Ps 68:19 6006

LOAF
one *l* of bread, and one cake of ... Ex 29:23 3603
woman, to every one a *l* of bread ... 1Chr 16:3 3603
ship with them more than one *l* ... Mk 8:14 *740*

LO-AMMI (*lo-am'-mi*) *Symbolic name meaning 'Not My People.'*
Then said God, Call his name *L* ... Hos 1:9 3818

LOAN
the *l* which is lent to the LORD ... 1Sa 2:20 7596

LOATHE
I *l* it ... Job 7:16 3988

LOATHETH
our soul *l* this light bread ... Num 21:5 6973
The full soul *l* an honeycomb ... Prov 27:7 947

LOATHSOME
nostrils, and it be *l* unto you ... Num 11:20 2214
my skin is broken, and become *l* ... Job 7:5 3988
loins are filled with a *l* disease ... Ps 38:7 7033
but a wicked man is *l*, and cometh ... Prov 13:5 887

LOAVES
two wave *l* of two tenth deals ... Lev 23:17 3899
l of bread unto the people that ... Judg 8:5 3603
another carrying three *l* of bread ... 1Sa 10:3 3603
thee, and give thee two *l* of bread ... 1Sa 10:4
this parched corn, and these ten *l* ... 1Sa 17:17 3899
give me five *l* of bread in mine ... 1Sa 21:3
made haste, and took two hundred *l* ... 1Sa 25:18 3899
upon them two hundred *l* of bread ... 2Sa 16:1
And take with thee ten *l*, and ... 1Kin 14:3 3899
twenty *l* of barley, and full ears ... 2Kin 4:42 3899
unto him, We have here but five *l* ... Mt 14:17 *740*
on the grass, and took the five *l* ... Mt 14:19 *740*
gave the *l* to his disciples, and ... Mt 14:19 *740*
unto them, How many *l* have ye ... Mt 15:34 *740*
And he took the seven *l* and the ... Mt 15:36 *740*
the five *l* of the five thousand ... Mt 16:9 *740*
Neither the seven *l* of the four ... Mt 16:10 *740*
unto them, How many *l* have ye ... Mk 6:38 *740*
And when he had taken the five *l* ... Mk 6:41 *740*
and blessed, and brake the *l* ... Mk 6:41 *740*
they that did eat of the *l* were ... Mk 6:44 *740*
not the miracle of the *l* ... Mk 6:52 *740*
he asked them, How many *l* have ye ... Mk 8:5 *740*
and he took the seven *l*, and gave ... Mk 8:6 *740*
the five *l* among five thousand ... Mk 8:19 *740*
said, We have no more but five *l* ... Lk 9:13 *740*
Then he took the five *l* and the ... Lk 9:16 *740*
unto him, Friend, lend me three *l* ... Lk 11:5 *740*
here, which hath five barley *l* ... Jn 6:9 *740*
And Jesus took the *l* ... Jn 6:11 *740*
fragments of the five barley *l* ... Jn 6:13 *740*
but because ye did eat of the *l* ... Jn 6:26 *740*

LOCK
myrrh, upon the handles of the *l* ... Song 5:5 4514
and took me by a *l* of mine head ... Eze 8:3 6734

LOCKED
the parlour upon him, and *l* them ... Judg 3:23 5274
the doors of the parlour were *l* ... Judg 3:24 5274

LOCKS
shall let the *l* of the hair of ... Num 6:5 6545
seven *l* of my head with the web ... Judg 16:13 4253
shave off the seven *l* of his head ... Judg 16:19 4253
the *l* thereof, and the bars ... Neh 3:3 4514
the *l* thereof, and the bars ... Neh 3:6 4514
the *l* thereof, and the bars ... Neh 3:13 4514
the *l* thereof, and the bars ... Neh 3:14 4514
the *l* thereof, and the bars ... Neh 3:15 4514
hast doves' eyes within thy *l* ... Song 4:1 6777
of a pomegranate within thy *l* ... Song 4:3 6777
my *l* with the drops of the night ... Song 5:2 6977
his *l* are bushy, and black as a ... Song 5:11 6977
are thy temples within thy *l* ... Song 6:7 6777
uncover thy *l*, make bare the leg, ... Is 47:2 6777
nor suffer their *l* to grow long ... Eze 44:20 6545

LOCUST
there remained not one *l* in all ... Ex 10:19 697
the *l* after his kind, and the bald ... Lev 11:22 697
the bald *l* after his kind, and the ... Lev 11:22 5556
for the *l* shall consume it ... Deut 28:38 697
of thy land shall the *l* consume ... Deut 28:42 6767
pestilence, blasting, mildew, *l* ... 1Kin 8:37 697
and their labour unto the *l* ... Ps 78:46 697
I am tossed up and down as the *l* ... Ps 109:23 697
hath left hath the *l* eaten ... Joel 1:4 697
that which the *l* hath left hath ... Joel 1:4 697
the years that the *l* hath eaten ... Joel 2:25 697

LOCUSTS
will I bring the *l* into thy coast ... Ex 10:4 697
over the land of Egypt for the *l* ... Ex 10:12 697
the east wind brought the *l* ... Ex 10:13 697
the *l* went up over all the land ... Ex 10:14 697
them there were no such *l* as they ... Ex 10:14 697
west wind, which took away the *l* ... Ex 10:19 697
there be blasting, or mildew, *l* ... 2Chr 6:28 697
command the *l* to devour the land ... 2Chr 7:13 2284
the *l* came, and caterpillers, and ... Ps 105:34 697
The *l* have no king, yet go they ... Prov 30:27 697
fro of *l* shall he run upon them ... Is 33:4 1357
make thyself many as the *l* ... Nah 3:15 697
Thy crowned are as the *l*, and thy ... Nah 3:17 697
and his meat was *l* and wild honey ... Mt 3:4 *200*
and he did eat *l* and wild honey ... Mk 1:6 *200*
out of the smoke *l* upon the earth ... Rev 9:3 *200*
the shapes of the *l* were like ... Rev 9:7 *200*

LOD *A city in Benjamin.*
and Shamed, who built Ono, and *L* ... 1Chr 8:12 3850
The children of *L*, Hadid, and Ono, ... Ezr 2:33 3850
The children of *L*, Hadid, and Ono, ... Neh 7:37 3850
L, and Ono, the valley of ... Neh 11:35 3850

LO-DEBAR (*lo-de'-bar*) *A city in Manasseh.*
Machir, the son of Ammiel, in *L* ... 2Sa 9:4 3810
Machir, the son of Ammiel, from *L* ... 2Sa 9:5 3810
and Machir the son of Ammiel of *L* ... 2Sa 17:27 3810

LODGE
thy father's house for us to *l* in ... Gen 24:23 3885
provender enough, and room to *l* in ... Gen 24:25 3885
L here this night, and I will ... Num 22:8 3885
where ye shall *l* this night ... Josh 4:3 3885
l here, that thine heart may be ... Judg 19:9 3885
city of the Jebusites, and *l* in it ... Judg 19:11 3885
of these places to *l* all night ... Judg 19:13 3885
to go in and to *l* in Gibeah ... Judg 19:15 3885
only *l* not in the street ... Judg 19:20 3885
Benjamin, I and my concubine, to *l* ... Judg 20:4 3885
and where thou lodgest, I will *l* ... Ruth 1:16 3885
will not *l* with the people ... 2Sa 17:8 3885
L not this night in the plains of ... 2Sa 17:16 3885
his servant *l* within Jerusalem ... Neh 4:22 3885
them, Why *l* ye about the wall ... Neh 13:21 3885
the naked to *l* without clothing ... Job 24:7 3885
stranger did not *l* in the street ... Job 31:32 3885
let us *l* in the villages ... Song 7:11 3885
as a *l* in a garden of cucumbers, ... Is 1:8 4412
the forest in Arabia shall ye *l* ... Is 21:13 3885
l in the monuments, which eat ... Is 65:4 3885
thy vain thoughts *l* within thee ... Jer 4:14 3885
the bittern shall *l* in the upper ... Zeph 2:14 3885
l in the branches thereof ... Mt 13:32 *2681*
air may *l* under the shadow of it ... Mk 4:32 *2681*
and country round about, and *l* ... Lk 9:12 *2647*
disciple, with whom we should *l* ... Acts 21:16 *3579*

LODGED
he *l* there that same night ... Gen 32:13 3885
himself *l* that night in the ... Gen 32:21 3885
house, named Rahab, and *l* there ... Josh 2:1 7901
l there before they passed over ... Josh 3:1 3885
them unto the place where they *l* ... Josh 4:8 4411
into the camp, and *l* in the camp ... Josh 6:11 3885
but Joshua *l* that night among the ... Josh 8:9 3885
the house of Micah, they *l* there ... Judg 18:2 3885
they did eat and drink, and *l* there ... Judg 19:4 3885
therefore he *l* there again ... Judg 19:7 3885
thither unto a cave, and *l* there ... 1Kin 19:9 3885
they *l* round about the house of ... 1Chr 9:27 3885
sellers of all kind of ware *l* ... Neh 13:20 3885
righteousness *l* in it ... Is 1:21 3885
and he *l* there ... Mt 21:17 *835*
the fowls of the air *l* in the ... Lk 13:19 *2681*
was surnamed Peter, were *l* there ... Acts 10:18 *3579*
Then called he them in, and *l* them ... Acts 10:23 *3579*
he is *l* in the house of one Simon ... Acts 10:32 *3579*
l us three days courteously ... Acts 28:7 *3579*
children, if she have *l* strangers ... 1Ti 5:10 *3580*

LODGEST
and where thou *l*, I will lodge ... Ruth 1:16 3885

LODGETH
He *l* with one Simon a tanner, ... Acts 10:6 *3579*

LODGING
you, and leave them in the *l* place ... Josh 4:3 4411
took them into his house to *l* ... Judg 19:15 3885
have taken up their *l* at Geba ... Is 10:29 4411
a *l* place of wayfaring men ... Jer 9:2 4411
there came many to him into his *l* ... Acts 28:23 *3578*
But withal prepare me also a *l* ... Philem 22 *3578*

LODGINGS
enter into the *l* of his borders ... 2Kin 19:23 4411

LOFT
bosom, and carried him up into a *l* ... 1Kin 17:19 5944
and fell down from the third *l* ... Acts 20:9

LOFTILY
they speak *l* ... Ps 73:8 4791

LOFTINESS
the *l* of man shall be bowed down, ... Is 2:17 1365
(he is exceeding proud) his *l* ... Jer 48:29 1363

LOFTY
is not haughty, nor mine eyes *l* ... Ps 131:1 7311
O how *l* are their eyes ... Prov 30:13 7311
The *l* looks of man shall be ... Is 2:11 1365
upon every one that is proud and *l* ... Is 2:12 7311
the eyes of the *l* shall be ... Is 5:15 1364
the *l* city, he layeth it low ... Is 26:5 7682
Upon a *l* and high mountain hast ... Is 57:7 1364
l One that inhabiteth eternity, ... Is 57:15 5375

LOG
mingled with oil, and one *l* of oil ... Lev 14:10 3849
the *l* of oil, and wave them for a ... Lev 14:12 3849
shall take some of the *l* of oil ... Lev 14:15 3849
a meat offering, and a *l* of oil ... Lev 14:21 3849
the *l* of oil, and the priest shall ... Lev 14:24 3849

LOINS
and kings shall come out of thy *l* ... Gen 35:11 2504
and put sackcloth upon his *l* ... Gen 37:34 4975
Egypt, which came out of his *l* ... Gen 46:26 3409
the *l* of Jacob were seventy souls ... Ex 1:5 3409
with your *l* girded, your shoes on ... Ex 12:11 4975
from the *l* even unto the thighs ... Ex 28:42 4975
smite through the *l* of them that ... Deut 33:11 4975
upon his *l* in the sheath thereof ... 2Sa 20:8 4975
his girdle that was about his *l* ... 1Kin 2:5 4975
shall come forth out of thy *l* ... 1Kin 8:19 2504

be thicker than my father's *l* 1Kin 12:10 4975
and he girded up his *l*, and ran 1Kin 18:46 4975
pray thee, put sackcloth on our *l* 1Kin 20:31 4975
they girded sackcloth on their *l* 1Kin 20:32 4975
a girdle of leather about his *l* 2Kin 1:8 4975
he said to Gehazi, Gird up thy *l* 2Kin 4:29 4975
and said unto him, Gird up thy *l* 2Kin 9:1 4975
shall come forth out of thy *l* 2Chr 6:9 2504
be thicker than my father's *l* 2Chr 10:10 4975
and girdeth their *l* with a girdle Job 12:18 4975
If his *l* have not blessed me, and Job 31:20 2504
Gird up now thy *l* like a man Job 38:3 2504
Gird up thy *l* now like a man Job 40:7 2504
Lo now, his strength is in his *l* Job 40:16 4975
For my *l* are filled with a Ps 38:7 3689
thou laidst affliction upon our *l* Ps 66:11 4975
make their *l* continually to shake Ps 69:23 4975
She girdeth her *l* with strength Prov 31:17 4975
the girdle of their *l* be loosed Is 5:27 2504
shall be the girdle of his *l* Is 11:5 4975
the sackcloth from off thy *l* Is 20:2 4975
are my *l* filled with pain Is 21:3 4975
and gird sackcloth upon your *l* Is 32:11 2504
and I will loose the *l* of kings Is 45:1 4975
Thou therefore gird up thy *l* Jer 1:17 4975
girdle, and put it upon thy *l* Jer 13:1 4975
of the LORD, and put it on my *l* Jer 13:2 4975
hast got, which is upon thy *l* Jer 13:4 4975
girdle cleaveth to the *l* of a man Jer 13:11 4975
every man with his hands on his *l* Jer 30:6 2504
cuttings, and upon the *l* sackcloth Jer 48:37 4975
appearance of his *l* even upward Eze 1:27 4975
appearance of his *l* even downward Eze 1:27 4975
appearance of his *l* even downward Eze 8:2 4975
from his *l* even upward, as the Eze 8:2 4975
man, with the breaking of thy *l* Eze 21:6 4975
Girded with girdles upon their *l* Eze 23:15 4975
all their *l* to be at a stand Eze 29:7 4975
have linen breeches upon their *l* Eze 44:18 4975
the waters were to the *l* Eze 47:4 4975
the joints of his *l* were loosed Dan 5:6 2788
whose *l* were girded with fine Dan 10:5 4975
bring up sackcloth upon all *l* Amos 8:10 4975
watch the way, make thy *l* strong Nah 2:1 4975
and much pain is in all *l* Nah 2:10 4975
and a leathern girdle about his *l* Mt 3:4 *3751*
a girdle of a skin about his *l* Mk 1:6 *3751*
Let your *l* be girded about, and Lk 12:35 *3751*
him, that of the fruit of his *l* Acts 2:30 *3751*
having your *l* girt about with Eph 6:14 *3751*
they come out of the *l* of Abraham Heb 7:5 *3751*
he was yet in the *l* of his father Heb 7:10 *3751*
gird up the *l* of your mind 1Pet 1:13 *3751*

LOIS (*lo'-is*) *Grandmother of Timothy.*
dwelt first in thy grandmother *L* 2Ti 1:5 *3090*

LONG
when he had been there a *l* time Gen 26:8 748
me all my life *l* unto this day Gen 48:15 5750
How *l* wilt thou refuse to humble Ex 10:3 4970
How *l* shall this man be a snare Ex 10:7 5704
How *l* refuse ye to keep my Ex 16:28 5704
when the trumpet soundeth *l* Ex 19:13 4900
voice of the trumpet sounded *l* Ex 19:19
that thy days may be *l* upon the Ex 20:12 748
of shittim wood, five cubits *l* Ex 27:1 753
an hundred cubits *l* for one side Ex 27:9 753
hangings of an hundred cubits *l* Ex 27:11 753
as *l* as she is put apart for her Lev 18:19
as *l* as it lieth desolate, and ye Lev 26:34 3117
As *l* as it lieth desolate it Lev 26:35 3117
as *l* as the cloud abode upon the Num 9:18 3117
when the cloud tarried *l* upon the Num 9:19
How *l* will this people provoke me Num 14:11 5704
how *l* will it be ere they believe Num 14:11 5704
How *l* shall I bear with this evil Num 14:27 5704
we have dwelt in Egypt a *l* time Num 20:15 7227
Ye have dwelt *l* enough in this Deut 1:6 7227
compassed this mountain *l* enough Deut 2:3 7227
shall have remained *l* in the land Deut 4:25
l as thou livest upon the earth Deut 12:19 3117
And if the way be too *l* for thee Deut 14:24 7235
him, because the way is *l* Deut 19:6 7235
shalt besiege a city a *l* time Deut 20:19 7227
longing for them all the day *l* Deut 28:32
of *l* continuance, and sore Deut 28:59
sicknesses, and of *l* continuance Deut 28:59
as *l* as ye live in the land Deut 31:13 3117
shall cover him all the day *l* Deut 33:12
that when they make a *l* blast Josh 6:5 4900
by reason of the very *l* journey Josh 9:13 7230
Joshua made war a *l* time with all Josh 11:18 7227
How *l* are ye slack to go to Josh 18:3 5704
it came to pass a *l* time after Josh 23:1 7227
in the wilderness a *l* season Josh 24:7 7227
Why is his chariot so *l* in coming Judg 5:28 954
How *l* wilt thou be drunken 1Sa 1:14 3117
as *l* as he liveth he shall be 1Sa 1:28 3117
that the time was *l* 1Sa 7:2 7235
How *l* wilt thou mourn for Saul 1Sa 16:1 5704
For as *l* as the son of Jesse 1Sa 20:31 3117
as *l* as we were conversant with 1Sa 25:15 3117
thou found in thy servant so *l* as 1Sa 29:8 3117
how *l* shall it be then, ere thou 2Sa 2:26 5704
Now there was *l* war between the 2Sa 3:1 752
had a *l* time mourned for the dead 2Sa 14:2 7227
How *l* have I to live, that I 2Sa 19:34 3117
hast not asked for thyself *l* life 1Kin 3:11 7221
before it, was forty cubits *l* 1Kin 6:17
How *l* halt ye between two 1Kin 18:21 5704
so *l* as the whoredoms of thy 2Kin 9:22 5704
Hast thou not heard *l* ago how I 2Kin 19:25 7350
neither yet hast asked *l* life 2Chr 1:11 7227
cherubims were twenty cubits *l* 2Chr 3:11 753
brasen scaffold, of five cubits *l* 2Chr 6:13 753
so *l* as they live in the land 2Chr 6:31 3117
Now for a *l* season Israel hath 2Chr 15:3 7227
as *l* as he sought the LORD, God 2Chr 26:5 3117
a *l* time in such sort as it was 2Chr 30:5 7230
for as *l* as she lay desolate she 2Chr 36:21 3117
For how *l* shall thy journey be Neh 2:6 5704
so *l* as I see Mordecai the Jew Est 5:13 6256
Which *l* for death, but it cometh Job 3:21 2442
grant me the thing that I *l* for Job 6:8 8615
How *l* wilt thou not depart from Job 7:19 4101
How *l* wilt thou speak these Job 8:2 5704
how *l* shall the words of thy Job 8:2
How *l* will it be ere ye make an Job 18:2 5704
How *l* will ye vex my soul, and Job 19:2 5704
not reproach me so *l* as I live Job 27:6 3117
how *l* will ye turn my glory into Ps 4:2 5704
how *l* will ye love vanity, and Ps 4:2
but thou, O LORD, how *l* Ps 6:3 5704
How *l* wilt thou forget me, O LORD Ps 13:1 5704
how *l* wilt thou hide thy face Ps 13:1 5704
How *l* shall I take counsel in my Ps 13:2 5704
how *l* shall mine enemy be exalted Ps 13:2 5704
through my roaring all the day *l* Ps 32:3
LORD, how *l* wilt thou look on Ps 35:17 5704
and of thy praise all the day *l* Ps 35:28
I go mourning all the day *l* Ps 38:6
and imagine deceits all the day *l* Ps 38:12
In God we boast all the day *l* Ps 44:8
sake are we killed all the day *l* Ps 44:22
How *l* will ye imagine mischief Ps 62:3 5704
thy righteousness all the day *l* Ps 71:24
shall fear thee as *l* as the sun Ps 72:5 5973
peace so *l* as the moon endureth Ps 72:7 5704
be continued as *l* as the sun Ps 72:17 6440
For all the day *l* have I been Ps 73:14
among us any that knoweth how *l* Ps 74:9 5704
how *l* shall the adversary Ps 74:10 5704
How *l*, LORD Ps 79:5 5704
how *l* wilt thou be angry against Ps 80:4 5704
How *l* will ye judge unjustly, and Ps 82:2 5704
How *l*, LORD? Ps 89:46 5704
Return, O LORD, how *l* Ps 90:13 5704
With *l* life will I satisfy him, Ps 91:16 753
how *l* shall the wicked Ps 94:3 5704
how *l* shall the wicked triumph Ps 94:3 5704
How *l* shall they utter and speak Ps 94:4 5704
Forty years *l* was I grieved with Ps 95:10
sing unto the LORD as *l* as I live Ps 104:33 5704
I call upon him as *l* as I live Ps 116:2 3117
My soul hath *l* dwelt with him Ps 120:6 7227
they made *l* their furrows Ps 129:3 748
as those that have been *l* dead Ps 143:3 5769
How *l*, ye simple ones, will ye Prov 1:22 5704
l life, and peace, shall they add Prov 3:2 753
How *l* wilt thou sleep, O sluggard Prov 6:9 5704
at home, he is gone a *l* journey Prov 7:19 7350
coveteth greedily all the day *l* Prov 21:26
fear of the LORD all the day *l* Prov 23:17
They that tarry *l* at the wine Prov 23:30
By *l* forbearing is a prince Prov 25:15 753
because man goeth to his *l* home Eccl 12:5 5769
Then said I, Lord, how *l* Is 6:11 5704
unto him that fashioned it *l* ago Is 22:11 7350
Hast thou not heard *l* ago Is 37:26 5704
I have *l* time holden my peace Is 42:14 5769
mine elect shall *l* enjoy the work Is 65:22
How *l* shall thy vain thoughts Jer 4:14 5704
How *l* shall I see the standard Jer 4:21 5704
How *l* shall the land mourn, and Jer 12:4 5704
How *l* shall this be in the heart Jer 23:26 5704
saying, This captivity is *l* Jer 29:28 752
How *l* wilt thou go about, O thou Jer 31:22 5704
how *l* wilt thou cut thyself Jer 47:5 5704
how *l* will it be ere thou be Jer 47:6 5704
fruit, and children of a span *l* Lam 2:20
for ever, and forsake us so *l* time Lam 5:20 753
his branches became *l* because of Eze 31:5 748
reed of six cubits *l* by the cubit Eze 40:5
little chamber was one reed *l* Eze 40:7 753
it was fifty cubits *l*, and five and Eze 40:29 753
were five and twenty cubits *l* Eze 40:30 753
it was fifty cubits *l*, and five and Eze 40:33 753
offering, of a cubit and an half *l* Eze 40:42 753
the court, an hundred cubits *l* Eze 40:47 753
the house, an hundred cubits *l* Eze 41:13 753
thereof, an hundred cubits *l* Eze 41:13 753
as *l* as they, and as broad as they Eze 42:11 753
round about, five hundred reeds *l* Eze 42:20 753
altar shall be twelve cubits *l* Eze 43:16 753
settle shall be fourteen cubits *l* Eze 43:17 753
nor suffer their locks to grow *l* Eze 44:20
and five and twenty thousand *l* Eze 45:6 753
courts joined of forty cubits *l* Eze 46:22 753
How *l* shall be the vision Dan 8:13 5704
but the time appointed was *l* Dan 10:1 1419
How *l* shall it be to the end of Dan 12:6 5704
how *l* will it be ere they attain Hos 8:5 5704
for he should not stay *l* in the Hos 13:13
how *l* shall I cry, and thou wilt Hab 1:2 5704
which is not his! how *l*? Hab 2:6 5704
how *l* wilt thou not have mercy on Zec 1:12 5704
as *l* as the bridegroom is with Mt 9:15 *1909*
have repented *l* ago in sackcloth Mt 11:21 *3819*
how *l* shall I be with you Mt 17:17 *2193*
how *l* shall I suffer you Mt 17:17 *2193*
and for a pretence make *l* prayer Mt 23:14 *3117*
After a *l* time the lord of those Mt 25:19 *4183*
as *l* as they have the bridegroom Mk 2:19 *5550*
how *l* shall I be with you Mk 9:19 *2193*
how *l* shall I suffer you Mk 9:19 *2193*
How *l* is it ago since this came Mk 9:21 *4214*
which love to go in *l* clothing Mk 12:38
and for a pretence make *l* prayers Mk 12:40 *3117*
clothed in a *l* white garment Mk 16:5
he tarried so *l* in the temple Lk 1:21
man, which had devils *l* time Lk 8:27 *2425*
how *l* shall I be with you, and Lk 9:41 *2193*
him, though he bear *l* with them Lk 18:7 *3114*
into a far country for a *l* time Lk 20:9 *2425*
which desire to walk in *l* robes Lk 20:46
and for a shew make *l* prayers Lk 20:47 *3117*
desirous to see him of a *l* season Lk 23:8 *2425*
been now a *l* time in that case Jn 5:6 *4183*
As *l* as I am in the world, I am Jn 9:5 *3752*
How *l* dost thou make us to doubt Jn 10:24 *2193*
Have I been so *l* time with you Jn 14:9 *5118*
because that of *l* time he had Acts 8:11 *2425*
L time therefore abode they Acts 14:3 *2425*
there they abode *l* time with the Acts 14:28
and as Paul was *l* preaching Acts 20:9
and eaten, and talked a *l* while Acts 20:11 *2425*
But not *l* after there arose Acts 27:14 *4183*
But after *l* abstinence Paul stood Acts 27:21 *4183*
For I *l* to see you, that I may Rom 1:11 *1971*
over a man as *l* as he liveth Rom 7:1 *5550*
to her husband so *l* as he liveth Rom 7:2
sake we are killed all the day *l* Rom 8:36
All day *l* I have stretched forth Rom 10:21
law as *l* as her husband liveth 1Cor 7:39 *5550*
you, that, if a man have *l* hair 1Cor 11:14 *2863*
But if a woman have *l* hair 1Cor 11:15 *2863*
Charity suffereth *l*, and is kind 1Cor 13:4 *3114*
which *l* after you for the 2Cor 9:14 *1971*
as *l* as he is a child, differeth Gal 4:1 *5550*
thou mayest live *l* on the earth Eph 6:3 *2118*
how greatly I *l* after you all in Phil 1:8 *1971*
But if I tarry *l*, that thou 1Ti 3:15
David, To day, after so *l* a time Heb 4:7 *5118*
hath *l* patience for it, until he Jas 5:7 *3114*
as *l* as ye do well, and are not 1Pet 3:6
as *l* as I am in this tabernacle, 2Pet 1:13
now of a *l* time lingereth not 2Pet 2:3
with a loud voice, saying, How *l* Rev 6:10 *2193*

LONGED
the soul of king David *l* to go 2Sa 13:39 3615
And David *l*, and said, Oh that one 2Sa 23:15 183
And David *l*, and said, Oh that one 1Chr 11:17 183
I have *l* after thy precepts Ps 119:40 8373
for I *l* for thy commandments Ps 119:131 2968
I have *l* for thy salvation, O Ps 119:174 8373
For he *l* after you all, and was Phil 2:26 *1971*
l for, my joy and crown, so stand Phil 4:1 *1973*

LONGEDST
because thou sore *l* after thy Gen 31:30 3700

LONGER
And when she could not *l* hide him Ex 2:3 5750
let you go, and ye shall stay no *l* Ex 9:28 3254
any *l* stand before their enemies Judg 2:14 5750
but he tarried *l* than the set 2Sa 20:5
should I wait for the LORD any *l* 2Kin 6:33 5750
thereof is *l* than the earth Job 11:9 752
So that the LORD could no *l* bear Jer 44:22 5750
for thou mayest be no *l* steward Lk 16:2 *2089*
him to tarry *l* time with them Acts 18:20 *4119*
that he ought not to live any *l* Acts 25:24 *3370*
dead to sin, live any *l* therein Rom 6:2 *2089*
we are no *l* under a schoolmaster Gal 3:25 *2089*
when we could no *l* forbear 1Th 3:1 *3370*
cause, when I could no *l* forbear 1Th 3:5 *3370*
Drink no *l* water, but use a 1Ti 5:23 *3370*
That he no *l* should live the rest 1Pet 4:2 *3370*
that there should be time no *l* Rev 10:6 *2089*

LONGETH
son Shechem *l* for your daughter Gen 34:8 2836
because thy soul *l* to eat flesh Deut 12:20 183
my flesh *l* for thee in a dry and Ps 63:1 3642
My soul *l*, yea, even fainteth for Ps 84:2 3700

LONGING
fail with *l* for them all the day Deut 28:32
For he satisfieth the *l* soul Ps 107:9 8264
My soul breaketh for the *l* that Ps 119:20 8375

LONGSUFFERING
LORD God, merciful and gracious, *l* Ex 34:6
The LORD is *l*, and of great mercy, Num 14:18
of compassion, and gracious, *l* Ps 86:15
take me not away in thy *l* Jer 15:15
his goodness and forbearance and *l* Rom 2:4 *3115*
endured with much *l* the vessels Rom 9:22 *3115*
By pureness, by knowledge, by *l* 2Cor 6:6 *3115*
the Spirit is love, joy, peace, *l* Gal 5:22 *3115*
all lowliness and meekness, with *l* Eph 4:2 *3115*
all patience and *l* with joyfulness Col 1:11 *3115*
humbleness of mind, meekness, *l* Col 3:12 *3115*
Christ might shew forth all *l* 1Ti 1:16 *3115*
manner of life, purpose, faith, *l* 2Ti 3:10 *3115*
rebuke, exhort with all *l* 2Ti 4:2 *3115*
when once the *l* of God waited in 1Pet 3:20 *3115*
but is *l* to us-ward, not willing 2Pet 3:9 *3114*
account that the *l* of our Lord is 2Pet 3:15 *3115*

LONGWINGED
A great eagle with great wings, *l* Eze 17:3

LOOK
I will *l* upon it, that I may Gen 9:16 7200
thou art a fair woman to *l* upon Gen 12:11 4758
l from the place where thou art Gen 13:14 7200
L now toward heaven, and tell the Gen 15:5 5027
l not behind thee, neither stay Gen 19:17 5027
damsel was very fair to *l* upon Gen 24:16 4758
because she was fair to *l* upon Gen 26:7 4758
Wherefore *l* ye so sadly to day Gen 40:7 6440
let Pharaoh *l* out a man discreet Gen 41:33 7200
Why do ye *l* one upon another Gen 42:1 7200
for he was afraid to *l* upon God Ex 3:6 5027

unto them, The LORD l upon you Ex 5:21 7200
l to it Ex 10:10 7200
faces shall l one to another Ex 25:20
l that thou make them after their Ex 25:40 7200
Moses did l upon all the work, and Ex 39:43 7200
the priest shall l on the plague Lev 13:3 7200
and the priest shall l on him Lev 13:3 7200
the priest shall l on him the Lev 13:5 7200
the priest shall l on him again Lev 13:6 7200
But if the priest l on it Lev 13:21 7200
Then the priest shall l upon it Lev 13:25 7200
But if the priest l on it Lev 13:26 7200
the priest shall l upon him the Lev 13:27 7200
if the priest l on the plague of Lev 13:31 7200
the priest shall l on the plague Lev 13:32 7200
the priest shall l on the scall Lev 13:34 7200
Then the priest shall l on him Lev 13:36 7200
Then the priest shall l Lev 13:39 7200
Then the priest shall l upon it Lev 13:43 7200
priest shall l upon the plague Lev 13:50 7200
he shall l on the plague on the Lev 13:51 7200
And if the priest shall l, and, Lev 13:53 7200
the priest shall l on the plague Lev 13:55 7200
And if the priest l, and, behold, Lev 13:56 7200
and the priest shall l, and, behold Lev 14:3 7200
he shall l on the plague, and, Lev 14:37 7200
again the seventh day, and shall l Lev 14:39 7200
Then the priest shall come and l Lev 14:44 7200
l upon it, and, behold, the plague Lev 14:48 7200
a fringe, that ye may l upon it Num 15:39 7200
l not unto the stubbornness of Deut 9:27 6437
L down from thy holy habitation, Deut 26:15 8259
people, and thine eyes shall l Deut 28:32 7200
them, L on me, and do likewise Judg 7:17 7200
if thou wilt indeed l on the 1Sa 1:11 7200
L not on his countenance, or on 1Sa 16:7 5027
countenance, and goodly to l to 1Sa 16:12 7210
l how thy brethren fare, and take 1Sa 17:18 6485
that thou shouldest l upon such a 2Sa 9:8 6437
was very beautiful to l upon 2Sa 11:2 4758
LORD will l on mine affliction 2Sa 16:12 7200
Go up now, l toward the sea 1Kin 18:43 5027
Judah, I would not l toward thee 2Kin 3:14 5027
l, when the messenger cometh, 2Kin 6:32 7200
l out there Jehu the son of 2Kin 9:2 7200
L even out the best and meetest of 2Kin 10:3 7200
l that there be here with you 2Kin 10:23 7200
let us l one another in the face 2Kin 14:8 7200
the God of our fathers l thereon 1Chr 12:17 7200
died, he said, The LORD l upon it 2Chr 24:22 7200
for she was fair to l on Est 1:11 4758
let it l for light, but have none Job 3:9 6960
therefore be content, l upon me Job 6:28 6437
shall no man l for his goods Job 20:21 2342
L unto the heavens, and see Job 35:5 5027
L on every one that is proud, and Job 40:12 7200
my prayer unto thee, and will l up Ps 5:3 6822
they l and stare upon me Ps 22:17 5027
L upon mine affliction and my pain Ps 25:18 7200
LORD, how long wilt thou l on Ps 35:17 7200
me, so that I am not able to l up Ps 40:12 7200
l down from heaven, and behold, and Ps 80:14 5027
l upon the face of thine anointed Ps 84:9 5027
shall l down from heaven Ps 85:11 8259
him that hath an high l and a Ps 101:5 5869
L thou upon me, and be merciful Ps 119:132 6437
as the eyes of servants l unto Ps 123:2
Let thine eyes l right on Prov 4:25 5027
let thine eyelids l straight Prov 4:25
A proud l, a lying tongue, and Prov 6:17 5869
An high l, and a proud heart, and Prov 21:4 5869
L not thou upon the wine when it Prov 23:31 7200
flocks, and l well to thy herds Prov 27:23 7896
those that l out of the windows Eccl 12:3 7200
L not upon me, because I am black Song 1:6 7200
l from the top of Amana, from the Song 4:8 7789
return, that we may l upon thee Song 6:13 2372
if one l unto the land, behold Is 5:30 5027
of Jacob, and I will l for him Is 8:17 6960
king and their God, and l upward Is 8:21 6437
they shall l unto the earth Is 8:22 5027
thee shall narrowly l upon thee Is 14:16 7688
day shall a man l to his Maker Is 17:7 8159
he shall not l to the altars, the Is 17:8 8159
Therefore said I, L away from me Is 22:4 8159
thou didst l in that day to the Is 22:8 5027
but they l not unto the Holy One Is 31:1 8159
L upon Zion, the city of our Is 33:20 2372
and l, ye blind, that ye may see Is 42:18 5027
L unto me, and be ye saved, all Is 45:22 6437
l unto the rock whence ye are Is 51:1 5027
L unto Abraham your father, and Is 51:2 5027
and l upon the earth beneath Is 51:6 5027
they all l to their own way, Is 56:11 6437
we l for judgment, but there is Is 59:11 6960
L down from heaven, and behold Is 63:15 5027
but to this man will I l, even to Is 66:2 5027
l upon the carcases of the men Is 66:24 7200
while ye l for light, he turn it Jer 13:16 6960
l well to him, and do him no harm Jer 39:12 7760
and I will l well unto thee Jer 40:4 7760
and are fled apace, and l not back Jer 46:5 6437
the fathers shall not l back to Jer 47:3 6437
Till the LORD l down, and behold Lam 3:50 8259
all of them princes to l to Eze 23:15 4758
when they shall l after them Eze 29:16 6437
stairs shall l toward the east Eze 43:17 6437
whose l was more stout than his Dan 7:20 2376
who l to other gods, and love Hos 3:1 6437
yet I will l again toward thy Jonah 2:4 5027
and let our eye l upon Zion Mic 4:11 2372
Therefore I will l unto the LORD Mic 7:7 6822
but none shall l back Nah 2:8 6437
that all they that l upon thee Nah 3:7 7200
evil, and canst not l on iniquity Hab 1:13 5027
that thou mayest l on their Hab 2:15 5027
they shall l upon me whom they Zec 12:10 5027
come, or do we l for another Mt 11:3 4328
upon his eyes, and made him l up Mk 8:25 308
or l we for another Lk 7:19 4328
or l we for another Lk 7:20 4328
I beseech thee, l upon my son Lk 9:38 1914
begin to come to pass, then l up Lk 21:28 352
up your eyes, and l on the fields Jn 4:35 2300
Search, and l Jn 7:52 1492
They shall l on him whom they Jn 19:37 3700
upon him with John, said, L on us Acts 3:4 991
or why l ye so earnestly on us, Acts 3:12 816
l ye out among you seven men of Acts 6:3 1980
names, and of your law, l ye to it Acts 18:15 3700
for I l for him with the brethren 1Cor 16:11 1551
l to the end of that which is 2Cor 3:13 816
While we l not at the things 2Cor 4:18 4648
Do ye l on things after the 2Cor 10:7 991
L not every man on his own things Phil 2:4 4648
whence also we l for the Saviour Phil 3:20 553
unto them that l for him shall he Heb 9:28 553
the angels desire to l into 1Pet 1:12 3879
l for new heavens and a new earth, 2Pet 3:13 4328
seeing that ye l for such things, 2Pet 3:14 4328
L to yourselves, that we lose not 2Jn 8 991
sat was to l upon like a jasper Rev 4:3 3706
the book, neither to l thereon Rev 5:3 991
the book, neither to l thereon Rev 5:4 991

LOOKED

God l upon the earth, and, behold, Gen 6:12 7200
the covering of the ark, and l Gen 8:13 7200
Have I also here l after him that Gen 16:13 7200
And he lift up his eyes and l Gen 18:2 7200
up from thence, and l toward Sodom Gen 18:16 8259
But his wife l back from behind Gen 19:26 5027
he l toward Sodom and Gen 19:28 8259
Abraham lifted up his eyes, and l Gen 22:13 7200
the Philistines l out at a window Gen 26:8 8259
And he l, and behold a well in the Gen 29:2 7200
LORD hath l upon my affliction Gen 29:32 7200
And Jacob lifted up his eyes, and l Gen 33:1 7200
and they lifted up their eyes and l Gen 37:25 7200
The keeper of the prison l not to Gen 39:23 7200
l upon them, and, behold, they Gen 40:6 7200
brethren, and l on their burdens Ex 2:11 7200
he l this way and that way, and Ex 2:12 6437
God l upon the children of Israel Ex 2:25 7200
and he l, and, behold, the bush Ex 3:2 7200
and that he had l upon their Ex 4:31 7200
in the morning watch the LORD l Ex 14:24 8259
that they l toward the wilderness Ex 16:10 6437
l after Moses, until he was gone Ex 33:8 5027
Aaron l upon Miriam, and, behold, Num 12:10 6437
that they l toward the tabernacle Num 16:42 6437
and they l, and took every man his Num 17:9 7200
when he l on Amalek, he took up Num 24:20 7200
he l on the Kenites, and took up Num 24:21 7200
And I l, and, behold, ye had sinned Deut 9:16 7200
l on our affliction, and our Deut 26:7 7200
that he lifted up his eyes and l Josh 5:13 7200
when the men of Ai l behind them Josh 8:20 6437
of Sisera l out at a window Judg 5:28 8259
And the LORD l upon him, and said, Judg 6:14 6437
and laid wait in the field, and l Judg 9:43 7200
and Manoah and his wife l on Judg 13:19 7200
And Manoah and his wife l on it Judg 13:20 7200
the Benjamites l behind them Judg 20:40 6437
because they had l into the ark 1Sa 6:19 7200
for I have l upon my people, 1Sa 9:16 7200
of Saul in Gibeah of Benjamin l 1Sa 14:16 7200
that he l on Eliab, and said, 1Sa 16:6 7200
And when the Philistine l about 1Sa 17:42 5027
when Saul l behind him, David 1Sa 24:8 5027
when he l behind him, he saw me, 2Sa 1:7 6437
Then Abner l behind him, and said, 2Sa 2:20 6437
daughter l through a window 2Sa 6:16 8259
watch lifted up his eyes, and l 2Sa 13:34 7200
wall, and lifted up his eyes, and l 2Sa 18:24 7200
They l, but there was none to 2Sa 22:42 8159
And Araunah l, and saw the king and 2Sa 24:20 8259
And he went up, and l, and said, 1Kin 18:43 5027
And he l, and, behold, there was a 1Kin 19:6 5027
l on them, and cursed them in the 2Kin 2:24 7200
by upon the wall, and the people l 2Kin 6:30 7200
her head, and l out at a window 2Kin 9:30 8259
there l out to him two or three 2Kin 9:32 8259
And when she l, behold, the king 2Kin 11:14 7200
Amaziah king of Judah l one 2Kin 14:11 7200
as David came to Ornan, Ornan l 1Chr 21:21 5027
And when Judah l back, behold, the 2Chr 13:14 6437
they l unto the multitude, and, 2Chr 20:24 6437
And she l, and, behold, the king 2Chr 23:13 7200
l upon him, and, behold, he was 2Chr 26:20 6437
And I l, and rose up, and said unto Neh 4:14 7200
sight of all them that l upon her Est 2:15 7200
The troops of Tema l, the Job 6:19 5027
When I l for good, then evil came Job 30:26 6960
The LORD l down from heaven upon Ps 14:2 8559
They l unto him, and were Ps 34:5 5027
God l down from heaven upon the Ps 53:2 8259
I l for some to take pity, but Ps 69:20 6960
For he hath l down from the Ps 102:19 8259
when they l upon me they shaked Ps 109:25 7200
I l on my right hand, and beheld, Ps 142:4 5027
my house I l through my casement Prov 7:6 8259
I l upon it, and received Prov 24:32 7200
Then I l on all the works that my Eccl 2:11 6437
because the sun hath l upon me Song 1:6 7805
he l that it should bring forth Is 5:2 6960
when I l that it should bring Is 5:4 6960
he l for judgment, but behold Is 5:7 6970
but ye have not l unto the maker Is 22:11 5027
And I l, and there was none to help Is 63:5 5027
things which we l not for Is 64:3 6960
We l for peace, but no good came Jer 8:15 6960
we l for peace, and there is no Jer 14:19 6960
this is the day that we l for Lam 2:16 6960
And I l, and, behold, a whirlwind Eze 1:4 7200
And when I l, behold, an hand was Eze 2:9 7200
and when I l, behold a hole in the Eze 8:7 7200
Then I l, and, behold, in the Eze 10:1 7200
And when I l, behold the four Eze 10:9 7200
the head l they followed it Eze 10:11 6437
l upon thee, behold, thy time was Eze 16:8 7200
with images, he l in the liver Eze 21:21 7200
court that l toward the north Eze 40:20 6440
and I l, and, behold, the glory of Eze 44:4 7200
priests, which l toward the north Eze 46:19 6437
be l upon before thee, and the Dan 1:13 7200
Then I lifted up mine eyes, and l Dan 10:5 7200
Then I Daniel l, and, behold, Dan 12:5 7200
But thou shouldest not have l on Obad 12 7200
thou shouldest not have l on Obad 13 7200
Ye l for much, and, lo, it came to Hag 1:9 6437
I lifted up mine eyes again, and l Zec 2:1 7200
And I said, I have l, and behold a Zec 4:2 7200
and lifted up mine eyes, and l Zec 5:1 7200
Then lifted I up mine eyes, and l Zec 5:9 7200
and lifted up mine eyes, and l Zec 6:1 7200
when he had l round about on them Mk 3:5 4017
he l round about on them which Mk 3:34 4017
he l round about to see her that Mk 5:32 4017
he l up to heaven, and blessed, and Mk 6:41 308
And he l up, and said, I see men as Mk 8:24 308
l on his disciples, he rebuked Mk 8:33 1492
when they had l round about Mk 9:8 4017
Jesus l round about, and saith Mk 10:23 4017
when he had l round about upon Mk 11:11 4017
she l upon him, and said, And thou Mk 14:67 1689
And when they l, they saw that the Mk 16:4 308
me in the days wherein he l on me Lk 1:25 1869
l for redemption in Jerusalem Lk 2:38 4327
l on him, and passed by on the Lk 10:32 1492
Jesus came to the place, he l up Lk 19:5 308
And he l up, and saw the rich men Lk 21:1 308
the fire, and earnestly l upon him Lk 22:56 816
the Lord turned, and l upon Peter Lk 22:61 1689
the disciples l one on another Jn 13:22 991
down, and l into the sepulchre, Jn 20:11
while they l stedfastly toward Acts 1:10 816
l up stedfastly into heaven, and Acts 7:55 816
And when he l on him, he was Acts 10:4 816
And the same hour I l up upon him Acts 22:13 308
Howbeit they l when he should Acts 28:6 4328
after they had l a great while Acts 28:6 4328
For he l for a city which hath Heb 11:10 1551
our eyes, which we have l upon 1Jn 1:1 2300
After this I l, and, behold, a Rev 4:1 1492
And I l, and behold a pale horse Rev 6:8 1492
And I l, and, lo, a Lamb stood on Rev 14:1 1492
And I l, and behold a white cloud, Rev 14:14 1492
And after that I l, and, behold, Rev 15:5 1492

LOOKEST

l narrowly unto all my paths Job 13:27 8104
wherefore l thou upon them that Hab 1:13 5027

LOOKETH

foot, wheresoever the priest l Lev 13:12
that is bitten, when he l upon it Num 21:8 7200
Pisgah, which l toward Jeshimon Num 21:20 8259
of Peor, that l toward Jeshimon Num 23:28 8259
from the bay that l southward Josh 15:2 6437
to the way of the border that l 1Sa 13:18 8259
for man l on the outward 1Sa 16:7 7200
but the LORD l on the heart 1Sa 16:7 7200
as a hireling l for the reward of Job 7:2 6960
For he l to the ends of the earth Job 28:24 5027
He l upon men, and if any say, I Job 33:27 7789
The LORD l from heaven Ps 33:13 5027
the place of his habitation he l Ps 33:14 7688
He l on the earth, and it Ps 104:32 5027
prudent man l well to his going Prov 14:15 995
She l well to the ways of her Prov 31:27 6822
he l forth at the windows, Song 2:9 7688
Who is she that l forth as the Song 6:10 8259
Lebanon which l toward Damascus Song 7:4 6822
when he that l upon it seeth Is 28:4 7200
gate, that l toward the north Eze 8:3 6437
LORD's house, which l eastward Eze 11:1 6437
the gate which l toward the east Eze 40:6 6440
the gate that l toward the east Eze 40:22 6440
the gate that l toward the east Eze 43:1 6437
sanctuary which l toward the east Eze 44:1 6437
gate of the inner court that l Eze 46:1 6437
the gate that l toward the east Eze 46:12 6437
gate by the way that l eastward Eze 47:2 6437
That whosoever l on a woman to Mt 5:28 991
in a day when he l not for him Mt 24:50 4328
in a day when he l not for him Lk 12:46 4328
But whoso l into the perfect law Jas 1:25 3879

LOOKING

l toward Gilgal, that is before Josh 15:7 6437
three l toward the north, and 1Kin 7:25 6437
three l toward the west 1Kin 7:25 6437
three l toward the south 1Kin 7:25 6437
and three l toward the east 1Kin 7:25 6437
Michal the daughter of Saul l out 1Chr 15:29 8259
three l toward the north, and 2Chr 4:4 6437
three l toward the west 2Chr 4:4 6437
three l toward the south 2Chr 4:4 6437
and three l toward the east 2Chr 4:4 6437
is strong, and as a molten l glass Job 37:18 7209
mine eyes fail with l upward Is 38:14
l up to heaven, he blessed, and Mt 14:19 308

L

l up to heaven, he sighed, and Mk 7:34 *308*
Jesus *l* upon them saith, With men Mk 10:27 *1689*
were also women *l* on afar off Mk 15:40 *2334*
l round about upon them all, he Lk 6:10 *4017*
l up to heaven, he blessed them, Lk 9:16 *308*
l back, is fit for the kingdom of Lk 9:62 *991*
for *l* after those things which Lk 21:26 *4329*
l upon Jesus as he walked, he Jn 1:36 *1689*
l in, saw the linen clothes lying Jn 20:5 *1689*
l stedfastly on him, saw his face Acts 6:15 *816*
l for a promise from thee Acts 23:21 *4327*
L for that blessed hope, and the Titus 2:13 *4327*
certain fearful *l* for of judgment Heb 10:27 *1561*
L unto Jesus the author and Heb 12:2 *872*
L diligently lest any man fail of Heb 12:15 *1983*
L for and hasting unto the coming 2Pet 3:12 *4328*
l for the mercy of our Lord Jesus Jude 21 *4327*

LOOKINGGLASSES
of the *l* of the women assembling, Ex 38:8 4759

LOOKS
but wilt bring down high *l* Ps 18:27 5869
The lofty *l* of man shall be Is 2:11 5869
and the glory of his high *l* Is 10:12 5869
words, nor be dismayed at their *l* Eze 2:6 6400
neither be dismayed at their *l* Eze 3:9 6400

LOOPS
thou shalt make *l* of blue upon Ex 26:4 3924
Fifty *l* shalt thou make in the Ex 26:5 3924
fifty *l* shalt thou make in the Ex 26:5 3924
that the *l* may take hold one of Ex 26:5 3924
thou shalt make fifty *l* on the Ex 26:10 3924
fifty *l* in the edge of the Ex 26:10 3924
and put the taches into the *l* Ex 26:11 3924
he made *l* of blue on the edge of Ex 36:11 3924
Fifty *l* made he in one curtain, Ex 36:12 3924
fifty *l* made he in the edge of Ex 36:12 3924
the *l* held one curtain to another Ex 36:12 3924
And he made fifty *l* upon the Ex 36:17 3924
fifty *l* made he upon the edge of Ex 36:17 3924

LOOSE
Naphtali is a hind let *l* Gen 49:21 7971
living bird *l* into the open field Lev 14:7 7971
l his shoe from off his foot, and Deut 25:9 2502
L thy shoe from off thy foot Josh 5:15 5394
that he would let *l* his hand Job 6:9 5425
they have also let *l* the bridle Job 30:11 7971
Pleiades, or *l* the bands of Orion Job 38:31 6605
to *l* those that are appointed to Ps 102:20 6605
l the sackcloth from off thy Is 20:2 6605
I will *l* the loins of kings, to Is 45:1 6605
l thyself from the bands of thy Is 52:2 6605
to *l* the bands of wickedness, to Is 58:6 6605
I *l* thee this day from the chains Jer 40:4 6605
and said, Lo, I see four men *l* Dan 3:25 8271
whatsoever thou shalt *l* on earth Mt 16:19 *3089*
whatsoever ye shall *l* on earth Mt 18:18 *3089*
l them, and bring them unto me Mt 21:2 *3089*
l him, and bring him Mk 11:2 *3089*
and they *l* him Mk 11:4 *3089*
l his ox or his ass from the Lk 13:15 *3089*
l him, and bring him hither Lk 19:30 *3089*
any man ask you, Why do ye *l* him Lk 19:31 *3089*
said unto them, Why *l* ye the colt Lk 19:33 *3089*
unto them, *L* him, and let him go Jn 11:44 *3089*
of his feet I am not worthy to *l* Acts 13:25 *3089*
him of Paul, that he might *l* him Acts 24:26 *3089*
book, and to *l* the seals thereof Rev 5:2 *3089*
to *l* the seven seals thereof Rev 5:5 *3089*
L the four angels which are bound Rev 9:14 *3089*

LOOSED
be not *l* from the ephod Ex 28:28 2118
might not be *l* from the ephod Ex 39:21 2118
house of him that hath his shoe *l* Deut 25:10 2502
his bands *l* from off his hands Judg 15:14 4549
Because he hath *l* my cord Job 30:11 6605
or who hath *l* the bands of the Job 39:5 6605
The king sent and *l* him Ps 105:20 5425
thou hast *l* my bonds Ps 116:16 6605
Or ever the silver cord be *l* Eccl 12:6 7368
the girdle of their loins be *l* Is 5:27 6605
Thy tacklings are *l* Is 33:23 5203
exile hasteneth that he may be *l* Is 51:14 6605
the joints of his loins were *l* Dan 5:6 8271
on earth shall be *l* in heaven Mt 16:19 *3089*
on earth shall be *l* in heaven Mt 18:18 *3089*
l him, and forgave him the debt Mt 18:27 *630*
and the string of his tongue was *l* Mk 7:35 *3089*
immediately, and his tongue *l* Lk 1:64
thou art *l* from thine infirmity Lk 13:12 *630*
be *l* from this bond on the Lk 13:16 *3089*
having *l* the pains of death Acts 2:24 *3089*
Paul and his company *l* from Paphos Acts 13:13 *321*
and every one's bands were *l* Acts 16:26 *447*
he *l* him from his bands, and Acts 22:30 *3089*
not have *l* from Crete, and to have Acts 27:21 *321*
l the rudder bands, and hoised up Acts 27:40 *447*
she is *l* from the law of her Rom 7:2 *2673*
seek not to be *l* 1Cor 7:27 *3089*
Art thou *l* from a wife 1Cor 7:27 *3080*
And the four angels were *l* Rev 9:15 *3089*
that he must be *l* a little season Rev 20:3 *3089*
Satan shall be *l* out of his Rev 20:7 *3089*

LOOSETH
He *l* the bond of kings, and Job 12:18 6605
The LORD *l* the prisoners Ps 146:7 5425

LOOSING
unto them, What do ye, *l* the colt Mk 11:5 *3089*
And as they were *l* the colt Lk 19:33 *3089*
Therefore *l* from Troas, we came Acts 16:11 *321*
l thence, they sailed close by Acts 27:13 *142*

LOP
shall *l* the bough with terror Is 10:33 5586

LORD
1. God.
day that the *L* God made the earth Gen 2:4 3068
for the *L* God had not caused it Gen 2:5 3068
the *L* God formed man of the dust Gen 2:7 3068
the *L* God planted a garden Gen 2:8 3068
out of the ground made the *L* God Gen 2:9 3068
the *L* God took the man, and put Gen 2:15 3068
the *L* God commanded the man, Gen 2:16 3068
the *L* God said, It is not good Gen 2:18 3068
out of the ground the *L* God Gen 2:19 3068
the *L* God caused a deep sleep to Gen 2:21 3068
which the *L* God had taken from Gen 2:22 3068
field which the *L* God had made Gen 3:1 3068
they heard the voice of the *L* God Gen 3:8 3068
from the presence of the *L* God Gen 3:8 3068
the *L* God called unto Adam, and Gen 3:9 3068
the *L* God said unto the woman, Gen 3:13 3068
the *L* God said unto the serpent, Gen 3:14 3068
to his wife did the *L* God make Gen 3:21 3068
the *L* God said, Behold, the man Gen 3:22 3068
Therefore the *L* God sent him Gen 3:23 3068
I have gotten a man from the *L* Gen 4:1 3068
the ground an offering unto the *L* Gen 4:3 3068
the *L* had respect unto Abel and to Gen 4:4 3068
the *L* said unto Cain, Why art Gen 4:6 3068
the *L* said unto Cain, Where is Gen 4:9 3068
And Cain said unto the *L*, My Gen 4:13 3068
the *L* said unto him, Therefore Gen 4:15 3068
the *L* set a mark upon Cain, lest Gen 4:15 3068
out from the presence of the *L* Gen 4:16 3068
to call upon the name of the *L* Gen 4:26 3068
ground which the *L* hath cursed Gen 5:29 3068
the *L* said, My spirit shall not Gen 6:3 3068
it repented the *L* that he had Gen 6:6 3068
the *L* said, I will destroy man Gen 6:7 3068
found grace in the eyes of the *L* Gen 6:8 3068
the *L* said unto Noah, Come thou Gen 7:1 3068
unto all that the *L* commanded him Gen 7:5 3068
and the *L* shut him in Gen 7:16 3068
Noah builded an altar unto the *L* Gen 8:20 3068
the *L* smelled a sweet savour Gen 8:21 3068
the *L* said in his heart, I will Gen 8:21 3068
Blessed be the *L* God of Shem Gen 9:26 3068
was a mighty hunter before the *L* Gen 10:9 3068
the mighty hunter before the *L* Gen 10:9 3068
the *L* came down to see the city Gen 11:5 3068
the *L* said, Behold, the people is Gen 11:6 3068
So the *L* scattered them abroad Gen 11:8 3068
because the *L* did there confound Gen 11:9 3068
from thence did the *L* scatter Gen 11:9 3068
Now the *L* had said unto Abram, Gen 12:1 3068
as the *L* had spoken unto him Gen 12:4 3068
the *L* appeared unto Abram, and Gen 12:7 3068
builded he an altar unto the *L* Gen 12:7 3068
he builded an altar unto the *L* Gen 12:8 3068
and called upon the name of the *L* Gen 12:8 3068
the *L* plagued Pharaoh and his Gen 12:17 3068
Abram called on the name of the *L* Gen 13:4 3068
before the *L* destroyed Sodom and Gen 13:10 3068
even as the garden of the *L* Gen 13:10 3068
sinners before the *L* exceedingly Gen 13:13 3068
the *L* said unto Abram, after that Gen 13:14 3068
built there an altar unto the *L* Gen 13:18 3068
have lift up mine hand unto the *L* Gen 14:22 3068
the *L* came unto Abram in a vision Gen 15:1 3068
L GOD, what wilt thou give me, Gen 15:2 136
the word of the *L* came unto him Gen 15:4 3068
And he believed in the *L* Gen 15:6 3068
I am the *L* that brought thee out Gen 15:7 3068
L GOD, whereby shall I know that Gen 15:8 136
the *L* hath restrained me from Gen 16:2 3068
the *L* judge between me and thee Gen 16:5 3068
the angel of the *L* found her by a Gen 16:7 3068
the angel of the *L* said unto her Gen 16:9 3068
the angel of the *L* said unto her Gen 16:10 3068
the angel of the *L* said unto her Gen 16:11 3068
because the *L* hath heard thy Gen 16:11 3068
name of the *L* that spake unto her Gen 16:13 3068
the *L* appeared to Abram, and said Gen 17:1 3068
the *L* appeared unto him in the Gen 18:1 3068
And said, My *L*, if now I have Gen 18:3 136
And the *L* said unto Abraham, Gen 18:13 3068
Is any thing too hard for the *L* Gen 18:14 3068
the *L* said, Shall I hide from Gen 18:17 3068
they shall keep the way of the *L* Gen 18:19 3068
that the *L* may bring upon Abraham Gen 18:19 3068
the *L* said, Because the cry of Gen 18:20 3068
Abraham stood yet before the *L* Gen 18:22 3068
the *L* said, If I find in Sodom Gen 18:26 3068
taken upon me to speak unto the *L* Gen 18:27 136
him, Oh let not the *L* be angry Gen 18:30 136
taken upon me to speak unto the *L* Gen 18:31 136
said, Oh let not the *L* be angry Gen 18:32 136
the *L* went his way, as soon as he Gen 18:33 3068
great before the face of the *L* Gen 19:13 3068
the *L* hath sent us to destroy it Gen 19:13 3068
for the *L* will destroy this city Gen 19:14 3068
the *L* being merciful unto him Gen 19:16 3068
Then the *L* rained upon Sodom and Gen 19:24 3068
and fire from the *L* out of heaven Gen 19:24 3068
place where he stood before the *L* Gen 19:27 3068
and he said, *L*, wilt thou slay Gen 20:4 136
For the *L* had fast closed up all Gen 20:18 3068
the *L* visited Sarah as he had Gen 21:1 3068
the *L* did unto Sarah as he had Gen 21:1 3068
called there on the name of the *L* Gen 21:33 3068
the angel of the *L* called unto Gen 22:11 3068
mount of the *L* it shall be seen Gen 22:14 3068
the angel of the *L* called unto Gen 22:15 3068
myself have I sworn, saith the *L* Gen 22:16 3068
the *L* had blessed Abraham in all Gen 24:1 3068
I will make thee swear by the *L* Gen 24:3 3068
The *L* God of heaven, which took Gen 24:7 3068
O *L* God of my master Abraham, I Gen 24:12 3068
to wit whether the *L* had made his Gen 24:21 3068
his head, and worshipped the *L* Gen 24:26 3068
Blessed be the *L* God of my master Gen 24:27 3068
the *L* led me to the house of my Gen 24:27 3068
Come in, thou blessed of the *L* Gen 24:31 3068
the *L* hath blessed my master Gen 24:35 3068
And he said unto me, The *L* Gen 24:40 3068
O *L* God of my master Abraham, if Gen 24:42 3068
the *L* hath appointed out for my Gen 24:44 3068
down my head, and worshipped the *L* Gen 24:48 3068
blessed the *L* God of my master Gen 24:48 3068
The thing proceedeth from the *L* Gen 24:50 3068
son's wife, as the *L* hath spoken Gen 24:51 3068
their words, he worshipped the *L* Gen 24:52 3068
seeing the *L* hath prospered my Gen 24:56 3068
intreated the *L* for his wife Gen 25:21 3068
the *L* was intreated of him, and Gen 25:21 3068
And she went to enquire of the *L* Gen 25:22 3068
the *L* said unto her, Two nations Gen 25:23 3068
the *L* appeared unto him, and said, Gen 26:2 3068
and the *L* blessed him Gen 26:12 3068
For now the *L* hath made room for Gen 26:22 3068
the *L* appeared unto him the same Gen 26:24 3068
and called upon the name of the *L* Gen 26:25 3068
that the *L* was with thee Gen 26:28 3068
thou art now the blessed of the *L* Gen 26:29 3068
thee before the *L* before my death Gen 27:7 3068
Because the *L* thy God brought it Gen 27:20 3068
a field which the *L* hath blessed Gen 27:27 3068
the *L* stood above it, and said Gen 28:13 3068
I am the *L* God of Abraham thy Gen 28:13 3068
Surely the *L* is in this place Gen 28:16 3068
then shall the *L* be my God Gen 28:21 3068
when the *L* saw that Leah was Gen 29:31 3068
Surely the *L* hath looked upon my Gen 29:32 3068
Because the *L* hath heard that I Gen 29:33 3068
she said, Now will I praise the *L* Gen 29:35 3068
The *L* shall add to me another son Gen 30:24 3068
L hath blessed me for thy sake Gen 30:27 3068
the *L* hath blessed thee since my Gen 30:30 3068
the *L* said unto Jacob, Return Gen 31:3 3068
The *L* watch between me and thee, Gen 31:49 3068
the *L* which saidst unto me, Gen 32:9 3068
was wicked in the sight of the *L* Gen 38:7 3068
and the *L* slew him Gen 38:7 3068
which he did displeased the *L* Gen 38:10 3068
the *L* was with Joseph, and he was Gen 39:2 3068
saw that the *L* was with him Gen 39:3 3068
that the *L* made all that he did Gen 39:3 3068
that the *L* blessed the Egyptian's Gen 39:5 3068
the blessing of the *L* was upon Gen 39:5 3068
But the *L* was with Joseph, and Gen 39:21 3068
because the *L* was with him, and Gen 39:23 3068
he did, the *L* made it to prosper Gen 39:23 3068
waited for thy salvation, O *L* Gen 49:18 3068
the angel of the *L* appeared unto Ex 3:2 3068
when the *L* saw that he turned Ex 3:4 3068
the *L* said, I have surely seen Ex 3:7 3068
The *L* God of your fathers, the Ex 3:15 3068
The *L* God of your fathers, the Ex 3:16 3068
The *L* God of the Hebrews hath met Ex 3:18 3068
we may sacrifice to the *L* our God Ex 3:18 3068
The *L* hath not appeared unto thee Ex 4:1 3068
the *L* said unto him, What is that Ex 4:2 3068
the *L* said unto Moses, Put forth Ex 4:4 3068
that the *L* God of their fathers Ex 4:5 3068
the *L* said furthermore unto him, Ex 4:6 3068
And Moses said unto the *L* Ex 4:10 136
O my *L*, I am not eloquent Ex 4:10 3068
the *L* said unto him, Who hath Ex 4:11 3068
have not I the *L* Ex 4:11 3068
And he said, O my *L*, send, I pray Ex 4:13 136
the anger of the *L* was kindled Ex 4:14 3068
the *L* said unto Moses in Midian, Ex 4:19 3068
the *L* said unto Moses, When thou Ex 4:21 3068
unto Pharaoh, Thus saith the *L* Ex 4:22 3068
in the inn, that the *L* met him Ex 4:24 3068
the *L* said to Aaron, Go into the Ex 4:27 3068
words of the *L* who had sent him Ex 4:28 3068
which the *L* had spoken unto Moses Ex 4:30 3068
when they heard that the *L* had Ex 4:31 3068
Thus saith the *L* God of Israel Ex 5:1 3068
And Pharaoh said, Who is the *L* Ex 5:2 3068
I know not the *L*, neither will I Ex 5:2 3068
and sacrifice unto the *L* our God Ex 5:3 3068
us go and do sacrifice to the *L* Ex 5:17 3068
The *L* look upon you, and judge Ex 5:21 3068
And Moses returned unto the *L* Ex 5:22 136
and said, *L*, wherefore hast Ex 5:22 3068
Then the *L* said unto Moses, Now Ex 6:1 3068
and said unto him, I am the *L* Ex 6:2 3068
children of Israel, I am the *L* Ex 6:6 3068
know that I am the *L* your God Ex 6:7 3068
I am the *L* Ex 6:8 3068
the *L* spake unto Moses, saying, Ex 6:10 3068
And Moses spake before the *L* Ex 6:12 3068
the *L* spake unto Moses and unto Ex 6:13 3068
and Moses, to whom the *L* said Ex 6:26 3068
to pass on the day when the *L* Ex 6:28 3068
That the *L* spake unto Moses, Ex 6:29 3068
unto Moses, saying, I am the *L* Ex 6:29 3068
And Moses said before the *L* Ex 6:30 3068
the *L* said unto Moses, See, I Ex 7:1 3068
shall know that I am the *L* Ex 7:5 3068
Aaron did as the *L* commanded them Ex 7:6 3068
the *L* spake unto Moses and unto Ex 7:8 3068
did so as the *L* had commanded Ex 7:10 3068
as the *L* had said Ex 7:13 3068
the *L* said unto Moses, Pharaoh's Ex 7:14 3068
The *L* God of the Hebrews hath Ex 7:16 3068

Thus saith the *L*, In this thou	Ex 7:17	3068
thou shalt know that I am the *L*	Ex 7:17	3068
the *L* spake unto Moses, Say unto	Ex 7:19	3068
Aaron did so, as the *L* commanded	Ex 7:20	3068
as the *L* had said	Ex 7:22	3068
after that the *L* had smitten the	Ex 7:25	3068
the *L* spake unto Moses, Go unto	Ex 8:1	3068
and say unto him, Thus saith the *L*	Ex 8:1	3068
the *L* spake unto Moses, Say unto	Ex 8:5	3068
and Aaron, and said, Intreat the *L*	Ex 8:8	3068
they may do sacrifice unto the *L*	Ex 8:8	3068
is none like unto the *L* our God	Ex 8:10	3068
Moses cried unto the *L* because of	Ex 8:12	3068
the *L* did according to the word	Ex 8:13	3068
as the *L* had said	Ex 8:15	3068
the *L* said unto Moses, Say unto	Ex 8:16	3068
as the *L* had said	Ex 8:19	3068
the *L* said unto Moses, Rise up	Ex 8:20	3068
and say unto him, Thus saith the *L*	Ex 8:20	3068
the *L* in the midst of the earth	Ex 8:22	3068
And the *L* did so	Ex 8:24	3068
of the Egyptians to the *L* our God	Ex 8:26	3068
and sacrifice to the *L* our God	Ex 8:27	3068
the *L* your God in the wilderness	Ex 8:28	3068
I will intreat the *L* that the	Ex 8:29	3068
people go to sacrifice to the *L*	Ex 8:29	3068
from Pharaoh, and intreated the *L*	Ex 8:30	3068
the *L* did according to the word	Ex 8:31	3068
Then the *L* said unto Moses, Go in	Ex 9:1	3068
Thus saith the *L* God of the	Ex 9:1	3068
the hand of the *L* is upon thy	Ex 9:3	3068
the *L* shall sever between the	Ex 9:4	3068
the *L* appointed a set time,	Ex 9:5	3068
To morrow the *L* shall do this	Ex 9:5	3068
the *L* did that thing on the	Ex 9:6	3068
the *L* said unto Moses and unto	Ex 9:8	3068
the *L* hardened the heart of	Ex 9:12	3068
as the *L* had spoken unto Moses	Ex 9:12	3068
the *L* said unto Moses, Rise up	Ex 9:13	3068
Thus saith the *L* God of the	Ex 9:13	3068
L among the servants of Pharaoh	Ex 9:20	3068
word of the *L* left his servants	Ex 9:21	3068
the *L* said unto Moses, Stretch	Ex 9:22	3068
the *L* sent thunder and hail, and	Ex 9:23	3068
the *L* rained hail upon the land	Ex 9:23	3068
the *L* is righteous, and I and my	Ex 9:27	3068
Intreat the *L* (for it is enough)	Ex 9:28	3068
spread abroad my hands unto the *L*	Ex 9:29	3068
ye will not yet fear the *L* God	Ex 9:30	3068
abroad his hands unto the *L*	Ex 9:33	3068
as the *L* had spoken by Moses	Ex 9:35	3068
the *L* said unto Moses, Go in unto	Ex 10:1	3068
ye may know how that I am the *L*	Ex 10:2	3068
Thus saith the *L* God of the	Ex 10:3	3068
they may serve the *L* their God	Ex 10:7	3068
them, Go, serve the *L* your God	Ex 10:8	3068
we must hold a feast unto the *L*	Ex 10:9	3068
Let the *L* be so with you, as I	Ex 10:10	3068
ye that are men, and serve the *L*	Ex 10:11	3068
the *L* said unto Moses, Stretch	Ex 10:12	3068
the *L* brought an east wind upon	Ex 10:13	3068
sinned against the *L* your God	Ex 10:16	3068
once, and intreat the *L* your God	Ex 10:17	3068
from Pharaoh, and intreated the *L*	Ex 10:18	3068
the *L* turned a mighty strong west	Ex 10:19	3068
But the *L* hardened Pharaoh's	Ex 10:20	3068
the *L* said unto Moses, Stretch	Ex 10:21	3068
and said, Go ye, serve the *L*	Ex 10:24	3068
may sacrifice unto the *L* our God	Ex 10:25	3068
we take to serve the *L* our God	Ex 10:26	3068
not with what we must serve the *L*	Ex 10:26	3068
But the *L* hardened Pharaoh's	Ex 10:27	3068
the *L* said unto Moses, Yet will I	Ex 11:1	3068
the *L* gave the people favour in	Ex 11:3	3068
And Moses said, Thus saith the *L*	Ex 11:4	3068
L doth put a difference between	Ex 11:7	3068
the *L* said unto Moses, Pharaoh	Ex 11:9	3068
the *L* hardened Pharaoh's heart,	Ex 11:10	3068
the *L* spake unto Moses and Aaron	Ex 12:1	3068
I am the *L*	Ex 12:12	3068
the *L* throughout your generations	Ex 12:14	3068
For the *L* will pass through to	Ex 12:23	3068
the *L* will pass over the door, and	Ex 12:23	3068
land which the *L* will give you	Ex 12:25	3068
did as the *L* had commanded Moses	Ex 12:28	3068
that at midnight the *L* smote all	Ex 12:29	3068
and go, serve the *L*, as ye have	Ex 12:31	3068
the *L* gave the people favour in	Ex 12:36	3068
that all the hosts of the *L* went	Ex 12:41	3068
to be much observed unto the *L*	Ex 12:42	3068
the *L* to be observed of all the	Ex 12:42	3068
the *L* said unto Moses and Aaron,	Ex 12:43	3068
will keep the passover to the *L*	Ex 12:48	3068
L commanded Moses and	Ex 12:50	3068
that the *L* did bring the children	Ex 12:51	3068
the *L* spake unto Moses, saying,	Ex 13:1	3068
for by strength of hand the *L*	Ex 13:3	3068
it shall be when the *L* shall	Ex 13:5	3068
day shall be a feast to the *L*	Ex 13:6	3068
L did unto me when I came forth	Ex 13:8	3068
the *L* brought thee out of Egypt	Ex 13:9	3068
it shall be when the *L* shall	Ex 13:11	3068
the *L* all that openeth the matrix	Ex 13:12	3068
By strength of hand the *L* brought	Ex 13:14	3068
that the *L* slew all the firstborn	Ex 13:15	3068
the *L* all that openeth the matrix	Ex 13:15	3068
for by strength of hand the *L*	Ex 13:16	3068
the *L* went before them by day in	Ex 13:21	3068
the *L* spake unto Moses, saying,	Ex 14:1	3068
may know that I am the *L*	Ex 14:4	3068
the *L* hardened the heart of	Ex 14:8	3068
of Israel cried out unto the *L*	Ex 14:10	3068
and see the salvation of the *L*	Ex 14:13	3068
The *L* shall fight for you, and ye	Ex 14:14	3068
the *L* said unto Moses, Wherefore	Ex 14:15	3068
shall know that I am the *L*	Ex 14:18	3068
the *L* caused the sea to go back	Ex 14:21	3068
the *L* looked unto the host of the	Ex 14:24	3068
for the *L* fighteth for them	Ex 14:25	3068
the *L* said unto Moses, Stretch	Ex 14:26	3068
the *L* overthrew the Egyptians in	Ex 14:27	3068
Thus the *L* saved Israel that day	Ex 14:30	3068
the *L* did upon the Egyptians	Ex 14:31	3068
and the people feared the *L*	Ex 14:31	3068
and believed the *L*	Ex 14:31	3068
of Israel this song unto the *L*	Ex 15:1	3068
saying, I will sing unto the *L*	Ex 15:1	3068
The *L* is my strength and song, and	Ex 15:2	3068
The *L* is a man of war	Ex 15:3	3068
the *L* is his name	Ex 15:3	3068
Thy right hand, O *L*, is become	Ex 15:6	3068
thy right hand, O *L*, hath dashed	Ex 15:6	3068
Who is like unto thee, O *L*	Ex 15:11	3068
till thy people pass over, O *L*	Ex 15:16	3068
inheritance, in the place, O *L*	Ex 15:17	3068
dwell in, in the Sanctuary, O *L*	Ex 15:17	3068
The *L* shall reign for ever and	Ex 15:18	3068
the *L* brought again the waters of	Ex 15:19	3068
answered them, Sing ye to the *L*	Ex 15:21	3068
And he cried unto the *L*	Ex 15:25	3068
the *L* shewed him a tree, which	Ex 15:25	3068
to the voice of the *L* thy God	Ex 15:26	3068
for I am the *L* that healeth thee	Ex 15:26	3068
of the *L* in the land of Egypt	Ex 16:3	3068
Then said the *L* unto Moses	Ex 16:4	3068
then ye shall know that the *L*	Ex 16:6	3068
ye shall see the glory of the *L*	Ex 16:7	3068
your murmurings against the *L*	Ex 16:7	3068
when the *L* shall give you in the	Ex 16:8	3068
for that the *L* heareth your	Ex 16:8	3068
not against us, but against the *L*	Ex 16:8	3068
of Israel, Come near before the *L*	Ex 16:9	3068
the glory of the *L* appeared in	Ex 16:10	3068
the *L* spake unto Moses, saying,	Ex 16:11	3068
know that I am the *L* your God	Ex 16:12	3068
which the *L* hath given you to eat	Ex 16:15	3068
thing which the *L* hath commanded	Ex 16:16	3068
is that which the *L* hath said	Ex 16:23	3068
of the holy sabbath unto the *L*	Ex 16:23	3068
to day is a sabbath unto the *L*	Ex 16:25	3068
the *L* said unto Moses, How long	Ex 16:28	3068
for that the *L* hath given you the	Ex 16:29	3068
the thing which the *L* commandeth	Ex 16:32	3068
and lay it up before the *L*	Ex 16:33	3068
As the *L* commanded Moses, so	Ex 16:34	3068
to the commandment of the *L*	Ex 17:1	3068
wherefore do ye tempt the *L*	Ex 17:2	3068
And Moses cried unto the *L*	Ex 17:4	3068
the *L* said unto Moses, Go on	Ex 17:5	3068
and because they tempted the *L*	Ex 17:7	3068
Is the *L* among us, or not	Ex 17:7	3068
the *L* said unto Moses, Write this	Ex 17:14	3068
the *L* hath sworn that the *L*	Ex 17:16	3068
that the *L* had brought Israel out	Ex 18:1	3068
that the *L* had done unto Pharaoh	Ex 18:8	3068
way, and how the *L* delivered them	Ex 18:8	3068
which the *L* had done to Israel	Ex 18:9	3068
And Jethro said, Blessed be the *L*	Ex 18:10	3068
Now I know that the *L* is greater	Ex 18:11	3068
the *L* called unto him out of the	Ex 19:3	3068
words which the *L* commanded him	Ex 19:7	3068
All that the *L* hath spoken we	Ex 19:8	3068
words of the people unto the *L*	Ex 19:8	3068
the *L* said unto Moses, Lo, I come	Ex 19:9	3068
words of the people unto the *L*	Ex 19:9	3068
the *L* said unto Moses, Go unto	Ex 19:10	3068
for the third day the *L* will come	Ex 19:11	3068
because the *L* descended upon it	Ex 19:18	3068
the *L* came down upon mount Sinai,	Ex 19:20	3068
the *L* called Moses up to the top	Ex 19:20	3068
the *L* said unto Moses, Go down,	Ex 19:21	3068
break through unto the *L* to gaze	Ex 19:21	3068
also, which come near to the *L*	Ex 19:22	3068
lest the *L* break forth upon them	Ex 19:22	3068
And Moses said unto the *L*, The	Ex 19:23	3068
the *L* said unto him, Away, get	Ex 19:24	3068
through to come up unto the *L*	Ex 19:24	3068
I am the *L* thy God, which have	Ex 20:2	3068
for I the *L* thy God am a jealous	Ex 20:5	3068
the name of the *L* thy God in vain	Ex 20:7	3068
for the *L* will not hold him	Ex 20:7	3068
is the sabbath of the *L* thy God	Ex 20:10	3068
For in six days the *L* made heaven	Ex 20:11	3068
wherefore the *L* blessed the	Ex 20:11	3068
which the *L* thy God giveth thee	Ex 20:12	3068
the *L* said unto Moses, Thus thou	Ex 20:22	3068
of the *L* be between them both	Ex 22:11	3068
any god, save unto the *L* only	Ex 22:20	3068
shall appear before the *L* God	Ex 23:17	3068
into the house of the *L* thy God	Ex 23:19	3068
And ye shall serve the *L* your God	Ex 23:25	3068
unto Moses, Come up unto the *L*	Ex 24:1	3068
Moses alone shall come near the *L*	Ex 24:2	3068
the people all the words of the *L*	Ex 24:3	3068
which the *L* hath said will we do	Ex 24:3	3068
wrote all the words of the *L*	Ex 24:4	3068
offerings of oxen unto the *L*	Ex 24:5	3068
All that the *L* hath said will we	Ex 24:7	3068
which the *L* hath made with you	Ex 24:8	3068
the *L* said unto Moses, Come up to	Ex 24:12	3068
the glory of the *L* abode upon	Ex 24:16	3068
the sight of the glory of the *L*	Ex 24:17	3068
the *L* spake unto Moses, saying,	Ex 25:1	3068
evening to morning before the *L*	Ex 27:21	3068
bear their names before the *L*	Ex 28:12	3068
memorial before the *L* continually	Ex 28:29	3068
when he goeth in before the *L*	Ex 28:30	3068
heart before the *L* continually	Ex 28:30	3068
unto the holy place before the *L*	Ex 28:35	3068
of a signet, HOLINESS TO THE *L*	Ex 28:36	3068
they may be accepted before the *L*	Ex 28:38	3068
kill the bullock before the *L*	Ex 29:11	3068
it is a burnt offering unto the *L*	Ex 29:18	3068
offering made by fire unto the *L*	Ex 29:18	3068
bread that is before the *L*	Ex 29:23	3068
for a wave offering before the *L*	Ex 29:24	3068
for a sweet savour before the *L*	Ex 29:25	3068
offering made by fire unto the *L*	Ex 29:25	3068
for a wave offering before the *L*	Ex 29:26	3068
their heave offering unto the *L*	Ex 29:28	3068
offering made by fire unto the *L*	Ex 29:41	3068
of the congregation before the *L*	Ex 29:42	3068
know that I am the *L* their God	Ex 29:46	3068
I am the *L* their God	Ex 29:46	3068
the *L* throughout your generations	Ex 30:8	3068
it is most holy unto the *L*	Ex 30:10	3068
the *L* spake unto Moses, saying,	Ex 30:11	3068
a ransom for his soul unto the *L*	Ex 30:12	3068
shall be the offering of the *L*	Ex 30:13	3068
shall give an offering unto the *L*	Ex 30:14	3068
they give an offering unto the *L*	Ex 30:15	3068
children of Israel before the *L*	Ex 30:16	3068
the *L* spake unto Moses, saying,	Ex 30:17	3068
offering made by fire unto the *L*	Ex 30:20	3068
Moreover the *L* spake unto Moses,	Ex 30:22	3068
the *L* said unto Moses, Take unto	Ex 30:34	3068
shall be unto thee holy for the *L*	Ex 30:37	3068
the *L* spake unto Moses, saying,	Ex 31:1	3068
the *L* spake unto Moses, saying,	Ex 31:12	3068
I am the *L* that doth sanctify you	Ex 31:13	3068
sabbath of rest, holy to the *L*	Ex 31:15	3068
for in six days the *L* made heaven	Ex 31:17	3068
To morrow is a feast to the *L*	Ex 32:5	3068
the *L* said unto Moses, Go, get	Ex 32:7	3068
the *L* said unto Moses, I have	Ex 32:9	3068
the *L* his God, and said, *L*	Ex 32:11	3068
the *L* repented of the evil which	Ex 32:14	3068
Thus saith the *L* God of Israel	Ex 32:27	3068
yourselves to day to the *L*	Ex 32:29	3068
and now I will go up unto the *L*	Ex 32:30	3068
And Moses returned unto the *L*	Ex 32:31	3068
the *L* said unto Moses, Whosoever	Ex 32:33	3068
the *L* plagued the people, because	Ex 32:35	3068
the *L* said unto Moses, Depart, and	Ex 33:1	3068
For the *L* had said unto Moses,	Ex 33:5	3068
L went out unto the tabernacle of	Ex 33:7	3068
and the *L* talked with Moses	Ex 33:9	
the *L* spake unto Moses face to	Ex 33:11	3068
And Moses said unto the *L*, See,	Ex 33:12	3068
the *L* said unto Moses, I will do	Ex 33:17	3068
the name of the *L* before thee	Ex 33:19	3068
the *L* said, Behold, there is a	Ex 33:21	3068
the *L* said unto Moses, Hew thee	Ex 34:1	3068
as the *L* had commanded him, and	Ex 34:4	3068
the *L* descended in the cloud, and	Ex 34:5	3068
and proclaimed the name of the *L*	Ex 34:5	3068
the *L* passed by before him, and	Ex 34:6	3068
proclaimed, The *L*, The *L* God	Ex 34:6	3068
in thy sight, O *L*, let my *L*	Ex 34:9	136
art shall see the work of the *L*	Ex 34:10	3068
for the *L*, whose name is Jealous,	Ex 34:14	3068
children appear before the *L* God	Ex 34:23	3068
the *L* thy God thrice in the year	Ex 34:24	3068
unto the house of the *L* thy God	Ex 34:26	3068
the *L* said unto Moses, Write thou	Ex 34:27	3068
was there with the *L* forty days	Ex 34:28	3068
in commandment all that the *L* had	Ex 34:32	3068
in before the *L* to speak with him	Ex 34:34	3068
words which the *L* hath commanded	Ex 35:1	3068
day, a sabbath of rest to the *L*	Ex 35:2	3068
the thing which the *L* commanded	Ex 35:4	3068
among you an offering unto the *L*	Ex 35:5	3068
bring it, an offering of the *L*	Ex 35:5	3068
all that the *L* hath commanded	Ex 35:10	3068
an offering of gold unto the *L*	Ex 35:22	3068
a willing offering unto the *L*	Ex 35:29	3068
which the *L* had commanded to be	Ex 35:29	3068
the *L* hath called by name	Ex 35:30	3068
man, in whom the *L* put wisdom	Ex 36:1	3068
to all that the *L* had commanded	Ex 36:1	3068
whose heart the *L* had put wisdom	Ex 36:2	3068
which the *L* commanded to make	Ex 36:5	3068
all that the *L* commanded Moses	Ex 38:22	3068
as the *L* commanded Moses	Ex 39:1	3068
as the *L* commanded Moses	Ex 39:5	3068
as the *L* commanded Moses	Ex 39:7	3068
as the *L* commanded Moses	Ex 39:21	3068
as the *L* commanded Moses	Ex 39:26	3068
as the *L* commanded Moses	Ex 39:29	3068
of a signet, HOLINESS TO THE *L*	Ex 39:30	3068
as the *L* commanded Moses	Ex 39:31	3068
to all that the *L* commanded Moses	Ex 39:32	3068
to all that the *L* commanded Moses	Ex 39:42	3068
done it as the *L* had commanded	Ex 39:43	3068
the *L* spake unto Moses, saying,	Ex 40:1	3068
to all that the *L* commanded him	Ex 40:16	3068
as the *L* commanded Moses	Ex 40:19	3068
as the *L* commanded Moses	Ex 40:21	3068
in order upon it before the *L*	Ex 40:23	3068
as the *L* had commanded Moses	Ex 40:23	3068
he lighted the lamps before the *L*	Ex 40:25	3068
as the *L* commanded Moses	Ex 40:25	3068
as the *L* commanded Moses	Ex 40:27	3068
as the *L* commanded Moses	Ex 40:29	3068
as the *L* commanded Moses	Ex 40:32	3068
the glory of the *L* filled the	Ex 40:34	3068
the glory of the *L* filled the	Ex 40:35	3068
For the cloud of the *L* was upon	Ex 40:38	3068
the *L* called unto Moses, and spake	Lev 1:1	3068
you bring an offering unto the *L*	Lev 1:2	3068
of the congregation before the *L*	Lev 1:3	3068
kill the bullock before the *L*	Lev 1:5	3068

of a sweet savour unto the *L*	Lev 1:9	3068
the altar northward before the *L*	Lev 1:11	3068
of a sweet savour unto the *L*	Lev 1:13	3068
his offering to the *L* be of fowls	Lev 1:14	3068
of a sweet savour unto the *L*	Lev 1:17	3068
offer a meat offering unto the *L*	Lev 2:1	3068
of a sweet savour unto the *L*	Lev 2:2	3068
offerings of the *L* made by fire	Lev 2:3	3068
made of these things unto the *L*	Lev 2:8	3068
of a sweet savour unto the *L*	Lev 2:9	3068
offerings of the *L* made by fire	Lev 2:10	3068
which ye shall bring unto the *L*	Lev 2:11	3068
offering of the *L* made by fire	Lev 2:11	3068
ye shall offer them unto the *L*	Lev 2:12	3068
of thy firstfruits unto the *L*	Lev 2:14	3068
offering made by fire unto the *L*	Lev 2:16	3068
it without blemish before the *L*	Lev 3:1	3068
offering made by fire unto the *L*	Lev 3:3	3068
of a sweet savour unto the *L*	Lev 3:5	3068
unto the *L* be of the flock	Lev 3:6	3068
shall he offer it before the *L*	Lev 3:7	3068
offering made by fire unto the *L*	Lev 3:9	3068
offering made by fire unto the *L*	Lev 3:11	3068
he shall offer it before the *L*	Lev 3:12	3068
offering made by fire unto the *L*	Lev 3:14	3068
the *L* spake unto Moses, saying,	Lev 4:1	3068
L concerning things which ought	Lev 4:2	3068
unto the *L* for a sin offering	Lev 4:3	3068
of the congregation before the *L*	Lev 4:4	3068
and kill the bullock before the *L*	Lev 4:4	3068
blood seven times before the *L*	Lev 4:6	3068
of sweet incense before the *L*	Lev 4:7	3068
L concerning things which should	Lev 4:13	3068
head of the bullock before the *L*	Lev 4:15	3068
shall be killed before the *L*	Lev 4:15	3068
it seven times before the *L*	Lev 4:17	3068
the altar which is before the *L*	Lev 4:18	3068
any of the commandments of the *L*	Lev 4:22	3068
the burnt offering before the *L*	Lev 4:24	3068
L concerning things which ought	Lev 4:27	3068
for a sweet savour unto the *L*	Lev 4:31	3068
offerings made by fire unto the *L*	Lev 4:35	3068
the *L* for his sin which he hath	Lev 5:6	3068
or two young pigeons, unto the *L*	Lev 5:7	3068
offerings made by fire unto the *L*	Lev 5:12	3068
the *L* spake unto Moses, saying,	Lev 5:14	3068
in the holy things of the *L*	Lev 5:15	3068
L a ram without blemish out of	Lev 5:15	3068
done by the commandments of the *L*	Lev 5:17	3068
trespassed against the *L*	Lev 5:19	3068
the *L* spake unto Moses, saying,	Lev 6:1	3068
commit a trespass against the *L*	Lev 6:2	3068
his trespass offering unto the *L*	Lev 6:6	3068
an atonement for him before the *L*	Lev 6:7	3068
the *L* spake unto Moses, saying,	Lev 6:8	3068
Aaron shall offer it before the *L*	Lev 6:14	3068
the memorial of it, unto the *L*	Lev 6:15	3068
offerings of the *L* made by fire	Lev 6:18	3068
the *L* spake unto Moses, saying,	Lev 6:19	3068
L in the day when he is anointed	Lev 6:20	3068
for a sweet savour unto the *L*	Lev 6:21	3068
is a statute for ever unto the *L*	Lev 6:22	3068
the *L* spake unto Moses, saying,	Lev 6:24	3068
offering be killed before the *L*	Lev 6:25	3068
offering made by fire unto the *L*	Lev 7:5	3068
which he shall offer unto the *L*	Lev 7:11	3068
for an heave offering unto the *L*	Lev 7:14	3068
that pertain unto the *L*, having	Lev 7:20	3068
which pertain unto the *L*	Lev 7:21	3068
the *L* spake unto Moses, saying,	Lev 7:22	3068
offering made by fire unto the *L*	Lev 7:25	3068
the *L* spake unto Moses, saying,	Lev 7:28	3068
L shall bring his oblation unto	Lev 7:29	3068
bring his oblation unto the *L* of	Lev 7:29	3068
offerings of the *L* made by fire	Lev 7:30	3068
for a wave offering before the *L*	Lev 7:30	3068
offerings of the *L* made by fire	Lev 7:35	3068
unto the *L* in the priest's office	Lev 7:35	3068
Which the *L* commanded to be given	Lev 7:36	3068
Which the *L* commanded Moses in	Lev 7:38	3068
offer their oblations unto the *L*	Lev 7:38	3068
the *L* spake unto Moses, saying,	Lev 8:1	3068
Moses did as the *L* commanded him	Lev 8:4	3068
which the *L* commanded to be done	Lev 8:5	3068
as the *L* commanded Moses	Lev 8:9	3068
as the *L* commanded Moses	Lev 8:13	3068
as the *L* commanded Moses	Lev 8:17	3068
offering made by fire unto the *L*	Lev 8:21	3068
as the *L* commanded Moses	Lev 8:21	3068
bread, that was before the *L*	Lev 8:26	3068
for a wave offering before the *L*	Lev 8:27	3068
offering made by fire unto the *L*	Lev 8:28	3068
for a wave offering before the *L*	Lev 8:29	3068
as the *L* commanded Moses	Lev 8:29	3068
so the *L* hath commanded to do, to	Lev 8:34	3068
days, and keep the charge of the *L*	Lev 8:35	3068
sons did all things which the *L*	Lev 8:36	3068
and offer them before the *L*	Lev 9:2	3068
to sacrifice before the *L*	Lev 9:4	3068
for to day the *L* will appear unto	Lev 9:4	3068
drew near and stood before the *L*	Lev 9:5	3068
the *L* commanded that ye should do	Lev 9:6	3068
the glory of the *L* shall appear	Lev 9:6	3068
as the *L* commanded	Lev 9:7	3068
as the *L* commanded Moses	Lev 9:10	3068
for a wave offering before the *L*	Lev 9:21	3068
the glory of the *L* appeared unto	Lev 9:23	3068
came a fire out from before the *L*	Lev 9:24	3068
offered strange fire before the *L*	Lev 10:1	3068
And there went out fire from the *L*	Lev 10:2	3068
them, and they died before the *L*	Lev 10:2	3068
This is it that the *L* spake	Lev 10:3	3068
burning which the *L* hath kindled	Lev 10:6	3068
oil of the *L* is upon you	Lev 10:7	3068
the *L* spake unto Aaron, saying,	Lev 10:8	3068
all the statutes which the *L* hath	Lev 10:11	3068
offerings of the *L* made by fire	Lev 10:12	3068
sacrifices of the *L* made by fire	Lev 10:13	3068
for a wave offering before the *L*	Lev 10:15	3068
as the *L* hath commanded	Lev 10:15	3068
atonement for them before the *L*	Lev 10:17	3068
their burnt offering before the *L*	Lev 10:19	3068
accepted in the sight of the *L*	Lev 10:19	3068
the *L* spake unto Moses and to	Lev 11:1	3068
For I am the *L* your God	Lev 11:44	3068
For I am the *L* that bringeth you	Lev 11:45	3068
the *L* spake unto Moses, saying,	Lev 12:1	3068
Who shall offer it before the *L*	Lev 12:7	3068
the *L* spake unto Moses and Aaron,	Lev 13:1	3068
the *L* spake unto Moses, saying,	Lev 14:1	3068
and those things, before the *L*	Lev 14:11	3068
for a wave offering before the *L*	Lev 14:12	3068
finger seven times before the *L*	Lev 14:16	3068
an atonement for him before the *L*	Lev 14:18	3068
of the congregation, before the *L*	Lev 14:23	3068
for a wave offering before the *L*	Lev 14:24	3068
hand seven times before the *L*	Lev 14:27	3068
an atonement for him before the *L*	Lev 14:29	3068
is to be cleansed before the *L*	Lev 14:31	3068
the *L* spake unto Moses and unto	Lev 14:33	3068
the *L* spake unto Moses and to	Lev 15:1	3068
come before the *L* unto the door	Lev 15:14	3068
him before the *L* for his issue	Lev 15:15	3068
before the *L* for the issue of her	Lev 15:30	3068
the *L* spake unto Moses after the	Lev 16:1	3068
when they offered before the *L*	Lev 16:1	3068
the *L* said unto Moses, Speak unto	Lev 16:2	3068
present them before the *L* at the	Lev 16:7	3068
one lot for the *L*, and the other	Lev 16:8	3068
be presented alive before the *L*	Lev 16:10	3068
from off the altar before the *L*	Lev 16:12	3068
upon the fire before the *L*	Lev 16:13	3068
the altar that is before the *L*	Lev 16:18	3068
from all your sins before the *L*	Lev 16:30	3068
he did as the *L* commanded Moses	Lev 16:34	3068
the *L* spake unto Moses, saying,	Lev 17:1	3068
thing which the *L* hath commanded	Lev 17:2	3068
L before the tabernacle of the	Lev 17:4	3068
before the tabernacle of the *L*	Lev 17:4	3068
they may bring them unto the *L*	Lev 17:5	3068
for peace offerings unto the *L*	Lev 17:5	3068
L at the door of the tabernacle	Lev 17:6	3068
fat for a sweet savour unto the *L*	Lev 17:6	3068
to offer it unto the *L*	Lev 17:9	3068
the *L* spake unto Moses, saying,	Lev 18:1	3068
unto them, I am the *L* your God	Lev 18:2	3068
I am the *L* your God	Lev 18:4	3068
I am the *L*	Lev 18:5	3068
I am the *L*	Lev 18:6	3068
I am the *L*	Lev 18:21	3068
I am the *L* your God	Lev 18:30	3068
the *L* spake unto Moses, saying,	Lev 19:1	3068
for I the *L* your God am holy	Lev 19:2	3068
I am the *L* your God	Lev 19:3	3068
I am the *L* your God	Lev 19:4	3068
of peace offerings unto the *L*	Lev 19:5	3068
the hallowed thing of the *L*	Lev 19:8	3068
I am the *L* your God	Lev 19:10	3068
I am the *L*	Lev 19:12	3068
I am the *L*	Lev 19:14	3068
I am the *L*	Lev 19:16	3068
I am the *L*	Lev 19:18	3068
his trespass offering unto the *L*	Lev 19:21	3068
trespass offering before the *L*	Lev 19:22	3068
be holy to praise the *L* withal	Lev 19:24	3068
I am the *L* your God	Lev 19:25	3068
I am the *L*	Lev 19:28	3068
I am the *L*	Lev 19:30	3068
I am the *L* your God	Lev 19:31	3068
I am the *L*	Lev 19:32	3068
I am the *L* your God	Lev 19:34	3068
I am the *L* your God, which	Lev 19:36	3068
I am the *L*	Lev 19:37	3068
the *L* spake unto Moses, saying,	Lev 20:1	3068
for I am the *L* your God	Lev 20:7	3068
I am the *L* which sanctify you	Lev 20:8	3068
I am the *L* your God, which have	Lev 20:24	3068
for I the *L* am holy, and have	Lev 20:26	3068
the *L* said unto Moses, Speak unto	Lev 21:1	3068
offerings of the *L* made by fire	Lev 21:6	3068
for I the *L*, which sanctify you,	Lev 21:8	3068
I am the *L*	Lev 21:12	3068
for I the *L* do sanctify him	Lev 21:15	3068
the *L* spake unto Moses, saying,	Lev 21:16	3068
offerings of the *L* made by fire	Lev 21:21	3068
for I the *L* do sanctify them	Lev 21:23	3068
the *L* spake unto Moses, saying,	Lev 22:1	3068
I am the *L*	Lev 22:2	3068
of Israel hallow unto the *L*	Lev 22:3	3068
I am the *L*	Lev 22:3	3068
I am the *L*	Lev 22:8	3068
I the *L* do sanctify them	Lev 22:9	3068
which they offer unto the *L*	Lev 22:15	3068
for I the *L* do sanctify them	Lev 22:16	3068
the *L* spake unto Moses, saying,	Lev 22:17	3068
unto the *L* for a burnt offering	Lev 22:18	3068
unto the *L* to accomplish his vow	Lev 22:21	3068
shall not offer these unto the *L*	Lev 22:22	3068
of them upon the altar unto the *L*	Lev 22:22	3068
unto the *L* that which is bruised	Lev 22:24	3068
the *L* spake unto Moses, saying,	Lev 22:26	3068
offering made by fire unto the *L*	Lev 22:27	3068
of thanksgiving unto the *L*	Lev 22:29	3068
I am the *L*	Lev 22:30	3068
I am the *L*	Lev 22:31	3068
I am the *L* which hallow you,	Lev 22:32	3068
I am the *L*	Lev 22:33	3068
the *L* spake unto Moses, saying,	Lev 23:1	3068
Concerning the feasts of the *L*	Lev 23:2	3068
of the *L* in all your dwellings	Lev 23:3	3068
These are the feasts of the *L*	Lev 23:4	3068
of unleavened bread unto the *L*	Lev 23:6	3068
by fire unto the *L* seven days	Lev 23:8	3068
the *L* spake unto Moses, saying,	Lev 23:9	3068
shall wave the sheaf before the *L*	Lev 23:11	3068
for a burnt offering unto the *L*	Lev 23:12	3068
unto the *L* for a sweet savour	Lev 23:13	3068
a new meat offering unto the *L*	Lev 23:16	3068
are the firstfruits unto the *L*	Lev 23:17	3068
for a burnt offering unto the *L*	Lev 23:18	3068
fire, of sweet savour unto the *L*	Lev 23:18	3068
for a wave offering before the *L*	Lev 23:20	3068
be holy to the *L* for the priest	Lev 23:20	3068
I am the *L* your God	Lev 23:22	3068
the *L* spake unto Moses, saying,	Lev 23:23	3068
offering made by fire unto the *L*	Lev 23:25	3068
the *L* spake unto Moses, saying,	Lev 23:26	3068
offering made by fire unto the *L*	Lev 23:27	3068
for you before the *L* your God	Lev 23:28	3068
the *L* spake unto Moses, saying,	Lev 23:33	3068
for seven days unto the *L*	Lev 23:34	3068
offering made by fire unto the *L*	Lev 23:36	3068
offering made by fire unto the *L*	Lev 23:36	3068
These are the feasts of the *L*	Lev 23:37	3068
offering made by fire unto the *L*	Lev 23:37	3068
Beside the sabbaths of the *L*	Lev 23:38	3068
which ye give unto the *L*	Lev 23:38	3068
a feast unto the *L* seven days	Lev 23:39	3068
before the *L* your God seven days	Lev 23:40	3068
unto the *L* seven days in the year	Lev 23:41	3068
I am the *L* your God	Lev 23:43	3068
of Israel the feasts of the *L*	Lev 23:44	3068
the *L* spake unto Moses, saying,	Lev 24:1	3068
morning before the *L* continually	Lev 24:3	3068
before the *L* continually	Lev 24:4	3068
upon the pure table before the *L*	Lev 24:6	3068
offering made by fire unto the *L*	Lev 24:7	3068
in order before the *L* continually	Lev 24:8	3068
the *L* made by fire by a perpetual	Lev 24:9	3068
son blasphemed the name of the *L*	Lev 24:11	
of the *L* might be shewed them	Lev 24:12	3068
the *L* spake unto Moses, saying,	Lev 24:13	3068
blasphemeth the name of the *L*	Lev 24:16	3068
he blasphemeth the name of the *L*	Lev 24:16	3068
for I am the *L* your God	Lev 24:22	3068
did as the *L* commanded Moses	Lev 24:23	3068
the *L* spake unto Moses in mount	Lev 25:1	3068
land keep a sabbath unto the *L*	Lev 25:2	3068
the land, a sabbath for the *L*	Lev 25:4	3068
for I am the *L* your God	Lev 25:17	3068
I am the *L* your God, which	Lev 25:38	3068
I am the *L* your God	Lev 25:55	3068
for I am the *L* your God	Lev 26:1	3068
I am the *L*	Lev 26:2	3068
I am the *L* your God, which	Lev 26:13	3068
for I am the *L* their God	Lev 26:44	3068
I am the *L*	Lev 26:45	3068
which the *L* made between him and	Lev 26:46	3068
the *L* spake unto Moses, saying,	Lev 27:1	3068
be for the *L* by thy estimation	Lev 27:2	3068
men bring an offering unto the *L*	Lev 27:9	3068
of such unto the *L* shall be holy	Lev 27:9	3068
not offer a sacrifice unto the *L*	Lev 27:11	3068
his house to be holy unto the *L*	Lev 27:14	3068
the *L* some part of a field of his	Lev 27:16	3068
jubile, shall be holy unto the *L*	Lev 27:21	3068
if a man sanctify unto the *L* a	Lev 27:22	3068
day, as a holy thing unto the *L*	Lev 27:23	3068
unto the *L* of all that he hath	Lev 27:28	3068
thing is most holy unto the *L*	Lev 27:28	3068
it is holy unto the *L*	Lev 27:30	3068
tenth shall be holy unto the *L*	Lev 27:32	3068
which the *L* commanded Moses for	Lev 27:34	3068
the *L* spake unto Moses in the	Num 1:1	3068
As the *L* commanded Moses, so he	Num 1:19	3068
For the *L* had spoken unto Moses,	Num 1:48	3068
to all that the *L* commanded Moses	Num 1:54	3068
the *L* spake unto Moses and unto	Num 2:1	3068
as the *L* commanded Moses	Num 2:33	3068
to all that the *L* commanded Moses	Num 2:34	3068
Moses in the day that the *L* spake	Num 3:1	3068
Nadab and Abihu died before the *L*	Num 3:4	3068
offered strange fire before the *L*	Num 3:4	3068
the *L* spake unto Moses, saying,	Num 3:5	3068
the *L* spake unto Moses, saying,	Num 3:11	3068
I am the *L*	Num 3:13	3068
the *L* spake unto Moses in the	Num 3:14	3068
according to the word of the *L*	Num 3:16	3068
at the commandment of the *L*	Num 3:39	3068
the *L* said unto Moses, Number all	Num 3:40	3068
the Levites for me (I am the *L*)	Num 3:41	3068
as the *L* commanded him, all the	Num 3:42	3068
the *L* spake unto Moses, saying,	Num 3:44	3068
I am the *L*	Num 3:45	3068
according to the word of the *L*	Num 3:51	3068
as the *L* commanded Moses	Num 3:51	3068
the *L* spake unto Moses and unto	Num 4:1	3068
the *L* spake unto Moses and unto	Num 4:17	3068
the *L* spake unto Moses, saying,	Num 4:21	3068
of the *L* by the hand of Moses	Num 4:37	3068
to the commandment of the *L*	Num 4:41	3068
of the *L* by the hand of Moses	Num 4:45	3068
to the commandment of the *L* they	Num 4:49	3068
of him, as the *L* commanded Moses	Num 4:49	3068
the *L* spake unto Moses, saying,	Num 5:1	3068
as the *L* spake unto Moses, so did	Num 5:4	3068
the *L* spake unto Moses, saying,	Num 5:5	3068
to do a trespass against the *L*	Num 5:6	3068
be recompensed unto the *L*	Num 5:8	3068
the *L* spake unto Moses, saying,	Num 5:11	3068
her near, and set her before the *L*	Num 5:16	3068
shall set the woman before the *L*	Num 5:18	3068

The *L* make thee a curse and an .... Num 5:21 3068
when the *L* doth make thy thigh to ..... Num 5:21 3068
wave the offering before the *L*.............. Num 5:25 3068
shall set the woman before the *L*.......... Num 5:30 3068
the *L* spake unto Moses, saying,............ Num 6:1 3068
to separate themselves unto the *L* .... Num 6:2 3068
he separateth himself unto the *L*............ Num 6:5 3068
L he shall come at no dead body.......... Num 6:6 3068
separation he is holy unto the *L*............ Num 6:8 3068
the *L* the days of his separation .... Num 6:12 3068
offer his offering unto the *L* .... Num 6:14 3068
shall bring them before the *L*............... Num 6:16 3068
of peace offerings unto the *L* .... Num 6:17 3068
for a wave offering before the *L*............ Num 6:20 3068
unto the *L* for his separation.................. Num 6:21 3068
the *L* spake unto Moses, saying,............ Num 6:22 3068
The *L* bless thee, and keep thee .... Num 6:24 3068
The *L* make his face shine upon.............. Num 6:25 3068
The *L* lift up his countenance .... Num 6:26 3068
their offering before the *L*................... Num 7:3 3068
the *L* spake unto Moses, saying,............ Num 7:4 3068
the *L* said unto Moses, They shall.......... Num 7:11 3068
the *L* spake unto Moses, saying,............ Num 8:1 3068
as the *L* commanded Moses.................... Num 8:3 3068
which the *L* had shewed Moses............... Num 8:4 3068
the *L* spake unto Moses, saying,............ Num 8:5 3068
bring the Levites before the *L*.............. Num 8:10 3068
offer the Levites before the *L*............... Num 8:11 3068
may execute the service of the *L* .... Num 8:11 3068
for a burnt offering, unto the *L* .... Num 8:12 3068
them for an offering unto the *L*............. Num 8:13 3068
according unto all that the *L*................ Num 8:20 3068
them as an offering before the *L* .... Num 8:21 3068
as the *L* had commanded Moses.............. Num 8:22 3068
the *L* spake unto Moses, saying,............ Num 8:23 3068
the *L* spake unto Moses in the............... Num 9:1 3068
to all that the *L* commanded Moses ..... Num 9:5 3068
not offer an offering of the *L* in............ Num 9:7 3068
I will hear what the *L* will .... Num 9:8 3068
the *L* spake unto Moses, saying,............ Num 9:9 3068
keep the passover unto the *L*................. Num 9:10 3068
of the *L* in his appointed season........... Num 9:13 3068
will keep the passover unto the *L*......... Num 9:14 3068
of the *L* the children of Israel .... Num 9:18 3068
commandment of the *L* they pitched ... Num 9:18 3068
Israel kept the charge of the *L* .... Num 9:19 3068
the *L* they abode in their tents .... Num 9:20 3068
of the *L* they journeyed......................... Num 9:20 3068
of the *L* they rested in the tents........... Num 9:23 3068
of the *L* they journeyed......................... Num 9:23 3068
they kept the charge of the *L* .... Num 9:23 3068
of the *L* by the hand of Moses.............. Num 9:23 3068
the *L* spake unto Moses, saying,............ Num 10:1 3068
remembered before the *L* your God...... Num 10:9 3068
I am the *L* your God............................ Num 10:10 3068
of the *L* by the hand of Moses.............. Num 10:13 3068
the place of which the *L* said .... Num 10:29 3068
for the *L* hath spoken good .... Num 10:29 3068
goodness the *L* shall do unto us .... Num 10:32 3068
of the *L* three days' journey .... Num 10:33 3068
L went before them in the three............ Num 10:33 3068
the cloud of the *L* was upon them........ Num 10:34 3068
that Moses said, Rise up, *L* .... Num 10:35 3068
it rested, he said, Return, O *L*.............. Num 10:36 3068
complained, it displeased the *L*............. Num 11:1 3068
and the *L* heard it .... Num 11:1 3068
the fire of the *L* burnt among .... Num 11:1 3068
and when Moses prayed unto the *L* ..... Num 11:2 3068
fire of the *L* burnt among them............. Num 11:3 3068
the anger of the *L* was kindled............. Num 11:10 3068
And Moses said unto the *L*,................... Num 11:11 3068
the *L* said unto Moses, Gather.............. Num 11:16 3068
ye have wept in the ears of the *L* .... Num 11:18 3068
therefore the *L* will give you .... Num 11:18 3068
despised the *L* which is among you..... Num 11:20 3068
the *L* said unto Moses, Is the................ Num 11:23 3068
the people the words of the *L* .... Num 11:24 3068
the *L* came down in a cloud, and.......... Num 11:25 3068
that the *L* would put his spirit .... Num 11:29 3068
went forth a wind from the *L* .... Num 11:31 3068
the wrath of the *L* was kindled............. Num 11:33 3068
the *L* smote the people with a.............. Num 11:33 3068
Hath the *L* indeed spoken only by .... Num 12:2 3068
And the *L* heard it................................ Num 12:2 3068
the *L* spake suddenly unto Moses, ... Num 12:4 3068
the *L* came down in the pillar of .... Num 12:5 3068
I the *L* will make myself known............ Num 12:6 3068
of the *L* shall he behold .... Num 12:8 3068
the anger of the *L* was kindled............. Num 12:9 3068
And Moses cried unto the *L* .... Num 12:13 3068
the *L* said unto Moses, If her .... Num 12:14 3068
the *L* spake unto Moses, saying,............ Num 13:1 3068
L sent them from the wilderness........... Num 13:3 3068
wherefore hath the *L* brought us .... Num 14:3 3068
If the *L* delight in us, then he............... Num 14:8 3068
Only rebel not ye against the *L* .... Num 14:9 3068
from them, and the *L* is with us .... Num 14:9 3068
the glory of the *L* appeared in.............. Num 14:10 3068
the *L* said unto Moses, How long.......... Num 14:11 3068
And Moses said unto the *L*, Then .... Num 14:13 3068
that thou *L* art among this people .... Num 14:14 3068
that thou *L* art seen face to face.......... Num 14:14 3068
Because the *L* was not able to .... Num 14:16 3068
let the power of my *L* be great .... Num 14:17 136
The *L* is longsuffering, and of.............. Num 14:18 3068
the *L* said, I have pardoned .... Num 14:20 3068
be filled with the glory of the *L*........... Num 14:21 3068
the *L* spake unto Moses and unto.......... Num 14:26 3068
As truly as I live, saith the *L*............... Num 14:28 3068
I the *L* have said, I will surely .... Num 14:35 3068
died by the plague before the *L*........... Num 14:37 3068
place which the *L* hath promised .... Num 14:40 3068
the commandment of the *L* .... Num 14:41 3068
for the *L* is not among you.................. Num 14:42 3068
ye are turned away from the *L*.............. Num 14:43 3068
therefore the *L* will not be with............ Num 14:43 3068
the ark of the covenant of the *L*........... Num 14:44 3068
the *L* spake unto Moses, saying,............ Num 15:1 3068
an offering by fire unto the *L*.............. Num 15:3 3068
to make a sweet savour unto the *L*...... Num 15:3 3068
the *L* bring a meat offering of a .... Num 15:4 3068
for a sweet savour unto the *L*.............. Num 15:7 3068
or peace offerings unto the *L* .... Num 15:8 3068
of a sweet savour unto the *L*................ Num 15:10 3068
of a sweet savour unto the *L*................ Num 15:13 3068
of a sweet savour unto the *L*................ Num 15:14 3068
the stranger be before the *L*................ Num 15:15 3068
the *L* spake unto Moses, saying,............ Num 15:17 3068
up an heave offering unto the *L*........... Num 15:19 3068
the *L* an heave offering in your............ Num 15:21 3068
which the *L* hath spoken unto............... Num 15:22 3068
Even all that the *L* hath .... Num 15:23 3068
day that the *L* commanded Moses .... Num 15:23 3068
for a sweet savour unto the *L*.............. Num 15:24 3068
sacrifice made by fire unto the *L*.......... Num 15:25 3068
their sin offering before the *L* .... Num 15:25 3068
sinneth by ignorance before the *L* .... Num 15:28 3068
the same reproacheth the *L* .... Num 15:30 3068
hath despised the word of the *L*........... Num 15:31 3068
the *L* said unto Moses, The man .... Num 15:35 3068
as the *L* commanded Moses................... Num 15:36 3068
the *L* spake unto Moses, saying,............ Num 15:37 3068
all the commandments of the *L*............. Num 15:39 3068
I am the *L* your God, which .... Num 15:41 3068
I am the *L* your God............................ Num 15:41 3068
of them, and the *L* is among them........ Num 16:3 3068
above the congregation of the *L*........... Num 16:3 3068
Even to morrow the *L* will shew .... Num 16:5 3068
in them before the *L* to morrow............ Num 16:7 3068
the man whom the *L* doth choose .... Num 16:7 3068
of the tabernacle of the *L*................... Num 16:9 3068
gathered together against the *L* .... Num 16:11 3068
very wroth, and said unto the *L*............ Num 16:15 3068
and all thy company before the *L*.......... Num 16:16 3068
bring ye before the *L* every man .... Num 16:17 3068
the glory of the *L* appeared unto.......... Num 16:19 3068
the *L* spake unto Moses and unto .... Num 16:20 3068
the *L* spake unto Moses, saying,............ Num 16:23 3068
L hath sent me to do all these .... Num 16:28 3068
then the *L* hath not sent me................. Num 16:29 3068
But if the *L* make a new thing, and...... Num 16:30 3068
these men have provoked the *L* .... Num 16:30 3068
there came out a fire from the *L* .... Num 16:35 3068
the *L* spake unto Moses, saying,............ Num 16:36 3068
they offered them before the *L* .... Num 16:38 3068
to offer incense before the *L*............... Num 16:40 3068
as the *L* said to him by the hand.......... Num 16:40 3068
have killed the people of the *L*............ Num 16:41 3068
and the glory of the *L* appeared .... Num 16:42 3068
the *L* spake unto Moses, saying,............ Num 16:44 3068
is wrath gone out from the *L*................ Num 16:46 3068
the *L* spake unto Moses, saying,............ Num 17:1 3068
laid up the rods before the *L* in .... Num 17:7 3068
all the rods from before the *L* .... Num 17:9 3068
the *L* said unto Moses, Bring................ Num 17:10 3068
as the *L* commanded him, so did he ..... Num 17:11 3068
the tabernacle of the *L* shall die .... Num 17:13 3068
the *L* said unto Aaron, Thou and.......... Num 18:1 3068
are given as a gift for the *L*................ Num 18:6 3068
the *L* spake unto Aaron, Behold, I .... Num 18:8 3068
which they shall offer unto the *L*.......... Num 18:12 3068
which they shall bring unto the *L*.......... Num 18:13 3068
which they bring unto the *L*.................. Num 18:15 3068
for a sweet savour unto the *L*............... Num 18:17 3068
of Israel offer unto the *L*..................... Num 18:19 3068
for ever before the *L* unto thee............ Num 18:19 3068
the *L* spake unto Aaron, Thou .... Num 18:20 3068
as an heave offering unto the *L*............ Num 18:24 3068
the *L* spake unto Moses, saying,............ Num 18:25 3068
an heave offering of it for the *L* .... Num 18:26 3068
unto the *L* of all your tithes .... Num 18:28 3068
every heave offering of the *L* .... Num 18:29 3068
the *L* spake unto Moses and unto.......... Num 19:1 3068
law which the *L* hath commanded.......... Num 19:2 3068
defileth the tabernacle of the *L*........... Num 19:13 3068
defiled the sanctuary of the *L*............. Num 19:20 3068
our brethren died before the *L*............. Num 20:3 3068
of the *L* into this wilderness .... Num 20:4 3068
the glory of the *L* appeared unto.......... Num 20:6 3068
the *L* spake unto Moses, saying,............ Num 20:7 3068
took the rod from before the *L*.............. Num 20:9 3068
the *L* spake unto Moses and Aaron, ... Num 20:12 3068
of Israel strove with the *L* .... Num 20:13 3068
And when we cried unto the *L* .... Num 20:16 3068
the *L* spake unto Moses and Aaron ..... Num 20:23 3068
And Moses did as the *L* commanded..... Num 20:27 3068
And Israel vowed a vow unto the *L* ...... Num 21:2 3068
the *L* hearkened to the voice of............ Num 21:3 3068
the *L* sent fiery serpents among .... Num 21:6 3068
for we have spoken against the *L* .... Num 21:7 3068
pray unto the *L*, that he take............... Num 21:7 3068
the *L* said unto Moses, Make thee .... Num 21:8 3068
in the book of the wars of the *L*........... Num 21:14 3068
whereof the *L* spake unto Moses............ Num 21:16 3068
the *L* said unto Moses, Fear him.......... Num 21:34 3068
as the *L* shall speak unto me............... Num 22:8 3068
for the *L* refuseth to give me .... Num 22:13 3068
beyond the word of the *L* my God......... Num 22:18 3068
what the *L* will say unto me more......... Num 22:19 3068
the angel of the *L* stood in the............. Num 22:22 3068
of the *L* standing in the way .... Num 22:23 3068
But the angel of the *L* stood in a .... Num 22:24 3068
the ass saw the angel of the *L* .... Num 22:25 3068
the angel of the *L* went further .... Num 22:26 3068
the ass saw the angel of the *L* .... Num 22:27 3068
the *L* opened the mouth of the ass .... Num 22:28 3068
Then the *L* opened the eyes of.............. Num 22:31 3068
of the *L* standing in the way .... Num 22:31 3068
the angel of the *L* said unto him .... Num 22:32 3068
said unto the angel of the *L* .... Num 22:34 3068
angel of the *L* said unto Balaam............ Num 22:35 3068
peradventure the *L* will come to........... Num 23:3 3068
the *L* put a word in Balaam's................. Num 23:5 3068
whom the *L* hath not defied .... Num 23:8 3068
which the *L* hath put in my mouth ...... Num 23:12 3068
while I meet the *L* yonder..................... Num 23:15
the *L* met Balaam, and put a word .... Num 23:16 3068
unto him, What hath the *L* spoken........ Num 23:17 3068
the *L* his God is with him, and the .... Num 23:21 3068
saying, All that the *L* speaketh............. Num 23:26 3068
it pleased the *L* to bless Israel............. Num 24:1 3068
aloes which the *L* hath planted............. Num 24:6 3068
the *L* hath kept thee back from............. Num 24:11 3068
beyond the commandment of the *L*........ Num 24:13 3068
but what the *L* saith, that will I .... Num 24:13 3068
the anger of the *L* was kindled............. Num 25:3 3068
the *L* said unto Moses, Take all .... Num 25:4 3068
up before the *L* against the sun............ Num 25:4 3068
that the fierce anger of the *L*.............. Num 25:4 3068
the *L* spake unto Moses, saying,............ Num 25:10 3068
the *L* spake unto Moses, saying,............ Num 25:16 3068
that the *L* spake unto Moses and........... Num 26:1 3068
as the *L* commanded Moses and the .... Num 26:4 3068
when they strove against the *L* .... Num 26:9 3068
the *L* spake unto Moses, saying,............ Num 26:52 3068
offered strange fire before the *L*.......... Num 26:61 3068
For the *L* had said of them, They.......... Num 26:65 3068
the *L* in the company of Korah .... Num 27:3 3068
brought their cause before the *L*.......... Num 27:5 3068
the *L* spake unto Moses, saying,............ Num 27:6 3068
as the *L* commanded Moses.................... Num 27:11 3068
the *L* said unto Moses, Get thee........... Num 27:12 3068
And Moses spake unto the *L*.................. Num 27:15 3068
Let the *L*, the God of the spirits .... Num 27:16 3068
that the congregation of the *L* be .... Num 27:17 3068
the *L* said unto Moses, Take thee .... Num 27:18 3068
the judgment of Urim before the *L*........ Num 27:21 3068
Moses did as the *L* commanded him...... Num 27:22 3068
as the *L* commanded by the hand of.... Num 27:23 3068
the *L* spake unto Moses, saying,............ Num 28:1 3068
which ye shall offer unto the *L*............ Num 28:3 3068
sacrifice made by fire unto the *L*......... Num 28:6 3068
unto the *L* for a drink offering.............. Num 28:7 3068
of a sweet savour unto the *L*................ Num 28:8 3068
offer a burnt offering unto the *L* .... Num 28:11 3068
sacrifice made by fire unto the *L*......... Num 28:13 3068
unto the *L* shall be offered................... Num 28:15 3068
month is the passover of the *L* .... Num 28:16 3068
for a burnt offering unto the *L* .... Num 28:19 3068
of a sweet savour unto the *L*................ Num 28:24 3068
a new meat offering unto the *L*............ Num 28:26 3068
for a sweet savour unto the *L*.............. Num 28:27 3068
for a sweet savour unto the *L*.............. Num 29:2 3068
sacrifice made by fire unto the *L*......... Num 29:6 3068
unto the *L* for a sweet savour.............. Num 29:8 3068
a feast unto the *L* seven days.............. Num 29:12 3068
of a sweet savour unto the *L*................ Num 29:13 3068
of a sweet savour unto the *L*................ Num 29:36 3068
do unto the *L* in your set feasts........... Num 29:39 3068
to all that the *L* commanded Moses ..... Num 29:40 3068
thing which the *L* hath commanded..... Num 30:1 3068
If a man vow a vow unto the *L*............. Num 30:2 3068
a woman also vow a vow unto the *L* ... Num 30:3 3068
the *L* shall forgive her, because .... Num 30:5 3068
and the *L* shall forgive her................... Num 30:8 3068
and the *L* shall forgive her................... Num 30:12 3068
which the *L* commanded Moses, ... Num 30:16 3068
the *L* spake unto Moses, saying,............ Num 31:1 3068
and avenge the *L* of Midian................... Num 31:3 3068
as the *L* commanded Moses.................... Num 31:7 3068
the *L* in the matter of Peor.................. Num 31:16 3068
among the congregation of the *L*........... Num 31:16 3068
law which the *L* commanded Moses..... Num 31:21 3068
the *L* spake unto Moses, saying,............ Num 31:25 3068
levy a tribute unto the *L* of the .... Num 31:28 3068
for an heave offering of the *L* .... Num 31:29 3068
charge of the tabernacle of the *L*......... Num 31:30 3068
did as the *L* commanded Moses............. Num 31:31 3068
priest, as the *L* commanded Moses .... Num 31:41 3068
charge of the tabernacle of the *L* .... Num 31:47 3068
as the *L* commanded Moses.................... Num 31:47 3068
brought an oblation for the *L*............... Num 31:50 3068
for our souls before the *L*.................... Num 31:50 3068
that they offered up to the *L*............... Num 31:52 3068
children of Israel before the *L*............. Num 31:54 3068
Even the country which the *L* .... Num 32:4 3068
land which the *L* hath given them........ Num 32:7 3068
land which the *L* had given them .... Num 32:9 3068
they have wholly followed the *L*............ Num 32:12 3068
done evil in the sight of the *L*............. Num 32:13 3068
anger of the *L* toward Israel................... Num 32:14 3068
will go armed before the *L* to war......... Num 32:20 3068
armed over Jordan before the *L* .... Num 32:21 3068
the land be subdued before the *L* .... Num 32:22 3068
and be guiltless before the *L*................ Num 32:22 3068
be your possession before the *L*............ Num 32:22 3068
ye have sinned against the *L*................ Num 32:23 3068
for war, before the *L* to battle.............. Num 32:27 3068
to battle, as my *l* saith......................... Num 32:27 113
man armed to battle, before the *L* .... Num 32:29 3068
As the *L* hath said unto thy.................. Num 32:31 3068
the *L* into the land of Canaan................ Num 32:32 3068
by the commandment of the *L*............... Num 33:2 3068
which the *L* had smitten among............. Num 33:4 3068
also the *L* executed judgments .... Num 33:4 3068
Hor at the commandment of the *L*........ Num 33:38 3068
the *L* spake unto Moses in the.............. Num 33:50 3068
the *L* spake unto Moses, saying,............ Num 34:1 3068
which the *L* commanded to give .... Num 34:13 3068
the *L* spake unto Moses, saying,............ Num 34:16 3068
the *L* commanded to divide the............. Num 34:29 3068
the *L* spake unto Moses in the............... Num 35:1 3068

the *L* spake unto Moses, saying,	Num 35:9	3068
for I the *L* dwell among the	Num 35:34	3068
The *L* commanded my l to give	Num 36:2	3068
was commanded by the *L* to give	Num 36:2	3068
according to the word of the *L*	Num 36:5	3068
the *L* doth command concerning the	Num 36:6	3068
Even as the *L* commanded Moses, so	Num 36:10	3068
which the *L* commanded by the hand	Num 36:13	3068
according unto all that the *L* had	Deut 1:3	3068
The *L* our God spake unto us in	Deut 1:6	3068
the *L* sware unto your fathers	Deut 1:8	3068
The *L* your God hath multiplied	Deut 1:10	3068
(The *L* God of your fathers make	Deut 1:11	3068
as the *L* our God commanded us	Deut 1:19	3068
which the *L* our God doth give	Deut 1:20	3068
the *L* thy God hath set the land	Deut 1:21	3068
as the *L* God of thy fathers hath	Deut 1:21	3068
which the *L* our God doth give us	Deut 1:25	3068
the commandment of the *L* your God	Deut 1:26	3068
and said, Because the *L* hated us	Deut 1:27	3068
The *L* your God which goeth before	Deut 1:30	3068
how that the *L* thy God bare thee	Deut 1:31	3068
ye did not believe the *L* your God	Deut 1:32	3068
the *L* heard the voice of your	Deut 1:34	3068
he hath wholly followed the *L*	Deut 1:36	3068
Also the *L* was angry with me for	Deut 1:37	3068
me, We have sinned against the *L*	Deut 1:41	3068
that the *L* our God commanded us	Deut 1:41	3068
the *L* said unto me, Say unto them	Deut 1:42	3068
against the commandment of the *L*	Deut 1:43	3068
ye returned and wept before the *L*	Deut 1:45	3068
but the *L* would not hearken to	Deut 1:45	3068
Red sea, as the *L* spake unto me	Deut 2:1	3068
the *L* spake unto me, saying,	Deut 2:2	3068
For the *L* thy God hath blessed	Deut 2:7	3068
these forty years the *L* thy God	Deut 2:7	3068
the *L* said unto me, Distress not	Deut 2:9	3068
which the *L* gave unto them	Deut 2:12	3068
host, as the *L* sware unto them	Deut 2:14	3068
hand of the *L* was against them	Deut 2:15	3068
That the *L* spake unto me, saying,	Deut 2:17	3068
but the *L* destroyed them before	Deut 2:21	3068
which the *L* our God giveth us	Deut 2:29	3068
for the *L* thy God hardened his	Deut 2:30	3068
the *L* said unto me, Behold, I	Deut 2:31	3068
the *L* our God delivered him	Deut 2:33	3068
the *L* our God delivered all unto	Deut 2:36	3068
the *L* our God forbad us	Deut 2:37	3068
the *L* said unto me, Fear him not	Deut 3:2	3068
So the *L* our God delivered into	Deut 3:3	3068
The *L* your God hath given you	Deut 3:18	3068
Until the *L* have given rest unto	Deut 3:20	3068
L your God hath given them beyond	Deut 3:20	3068
eyes have seen all that the *L*	Deut 3:21	3068
so shall the *L* do unto all the	Deut 3:21	3068
for the *L* your God he shall fight	Deut 3:22	3068
And I besought the *L* at that time	Deut 3:23	3068
O *L* God, thou hast begun to shew	Deut 3:24	136
But the *L* was wroth with me for	Deut 3:26	3068
the *L* said unto me, Let it	Deut 3:26	3068
possess the land which the *L* God	Deut 4:1	3068
L your God which I command you	Deut 4:2	3068
the *L* did because of Baal-peor	Deut 4:3	3068
the *L* thy God hath destroyed them	Deut 4:3	3068
L your God are alive every one of	Deut 4:4	3068
even as the *L* my God commanded me	Deut 4:5	3068
as the *L* our God is in all things	Deut 4:7	3068
before the *L* thy God in Horeb	Deut 4:10	3068
when the *L* said unto me, Gather	Deut 4:10	3068
the *L* spake unto you out of the	Deut 4:12	3068
the *L* commanded me at that time	Deut 4:14	3068
L spake unto you in Horeb out of	Deut 4:15	3068
which the *L* thy God hath divided	Deut 4:19	3068
But the *L* hath taken you, and	Deut 4:20	3068
Furthermore the *L* was angry with	Deut 4:21	3068
which the *L* thy God giveth thee	Deut 4:21	3068
the covenant of the *L* your God	Deut 4:23	3068
thing, which the *L* thy God hath	Deut 4:23	3068
For the *L* thy God is a consuming	Deut 4:24	3068
in the sight of the *L* thy God	Deut 4:25	3068
the *L* shall scatter you among the	Deut 4:27	3068
whither the *L* shall lead you	Deut 4:27	3068
thou shalt seek the *L* thy God	Deut 4:29	3068
if thou turn to the *L* thy God	Deut 4:30	3068
(For the *L* thy God is a merciful	Deut 4:31	3068
according to all that the *L* your	Deut 4:34	3068
know that the *L* he is God	Deut 4:35	3068
that the *L* he is God in heaven	Deut 4:39	3068
which the *L* thy God giveth thee,	Deut 4:40	3068
The *L* our God made a covenant	Deut 5:2	3068
The *L* made not this covenant with	Deut 5:3	3068
The *L* talked with you face to	Deut 5:4	3068
(I stood between the *L* and you at	Deut 5:5	3068
to shew you the word of the *L*	Deut 5:5	3068
I am the *L* thy God, which brought	Deut 5:6	3068
for I the *L* thy God am a jealous	Deut 5:9	3068
the name of the *L* thy God in vain	Deut 5:11	3068
for the *L* will not hold him	Deut 5:11	3068
as the *L* thy God hath commanded	Deut 5:12	3068
is the sabbath of the *L* thy God	Deut 5:14	3068
that the *L* thy God brought thee	Deut 5:15	3068
therefore the *L* thy God commanded	Deut 5:15	3068
as the *L* thy God hath commanded	Deut 5:16	3068
which the *L* thy God giveth thee	Deut 5:16	3068
These words the *L* spake unto all	Deut 5:22	3068
the *L* our God hath shewed us his	Deut 5:24	3068
voice of the *L* our God any more	Deut 5:25	3068
all that the *L* our God shall say	Deut 5:27	3068
L our God shall speak unto thee	Deut 5:27	3068
the *L* heard the voice of your	Deut 5:28	3068
the *L* said unto me, I have heard	Deut 5:28	3068
the *L* your God hath commanded you	Deut 5:32	3068
the *L* your God hath commanded you	Deut 5:33	3068
which the *L* your God commanded to	Deut 6:1	3068
thou mightest fear the *L* thy God	Deut 6:2	3068
as the *L* God of thy fathers hath	Deut 6:3	3068
The *L* our God is one *L*	Deut 6:4	3068
thou shalt love the *L* thy God	Deut 6:5	3068
when the *L* thy God shall have	Deut 6:10	3068
beware lest thou forget the *L*	Deut 6:12	3068
Thou shalt fear the *L* thy God	Deut 6:13	3068
(For the *L* thy God is a jealous	Deut 6:15	3068
you) lest the anger of the *L* thy	Deut 6:15	3068
Ye shall not tempt the *L* your God	Deut 6:16	3068
commandments of the *L* your God	Deut 6:17	3068
and good in the sight of the *L*	Deut 6:18	3068
the *L* sware unto thy fathers	Deut 6:18	3068
before thee, as the *L* hath spoken	Deut 6:19	3068
which the *L* our God hath	Deut 6:20	3068
the *L* brought us out of Egypt	Deut 6:21	3068
the *L* shewed signs and wonders,	Deut 6:22	3068
the *L* commanded us to do all	Deut 6:24	3068
statutes, to fear the *L* our God	Deut 6:24	3068
commandments before the *L* our God	Deut 6:25	3068
When the *L* thy God shall bring	Deut 7:1	3068
when the *L* thy God shall deliver	Deut 7:2	3068
of the *L* be kindled against you	Deut 7:4	3068
an holy people unto the *L* thy God	Deut 7:6	3068
the *L* thy God hath chosen thee to	Deut 7:6	3068
The *L* did not set his love upon	Deut 7:7	3068
But because the *L* loved you	Deut 7:8	3068
hath the *L* brought you out with a	Deut 7:8	3068
Know therefore that the *L* thy God	Deut 7:9	3068
that the *L* thy God shall keep	Deut 7:12	3068
the *L* will take away from thee	Deut 7:15	3068
all the people which the *L* thy	Deut 7:16	3068
the *L* thy God did unto Pharaoh	Deut 7:18	3068
whereby the *L* thy God brought	Deut 7:19	3068
so shall the *L* thy God do unto	Deut 7:19	3068
Moreover the *L* thy God will send	Deut 7:20	3068
for the *L* thy God is among you, a	Deut 7:21	3068
the *L* thy God will put out those	Deut 7:22	3068
But the *L* thy God shall deliver	Deut 7:23	3068
an abomination to the *L* thy God	Deut 7:25	3068
the *L* sware unto your fathers	Deut 8:1	3068
L thy God led thee these forty	Deut 8:2	3068
the mouth of the *L* doth man live	Deut 8:3	3068
so the *L* thy God chasteneth thee	Deut 8:5	3068
the commandments of the *L* thy God	Deut 8:6	3068
For the *L* thy God bringeth thee	Deut 8:7	3068
then thou shalt bless the *L* thy	Deut 8:10	3068
thou forget not the *L* thy God	Deut 8:11	3068
up, and thou forget the *L* thy God	Deut 8:14	3068
thou shalt remember the *L* thy God	Deut 8:18	3068
do at all forget the *L* thy God	Deut 8:19	3068
As the nations which the *L*	Deut 8:20	3068
unto the voice of the *L* your God	Deut 8:20	3068
that the *L* thy God is he which	Deut 9:3	3068
as the *L* hath said unto thee	Deut 9:3	3068
after that the *L* thy God hath	Deut 9:4	3068
For my righteousness the *L* hath	Deut 9:4	3068
L doth drive them out from before	Deut 9:4	3068
the *L* thy God doth drive them out	Deut 9:5	3068
the *L* sware unto thy fathers	Deut 9:5	3068
that the *L* thy God giveth thee	Deut 9:6	3068
the *L* thy God to wrath in the	Deut 9:7	3068
been rebellious against the *L*	Deut 9:7	3068
Horeb ye provoked the *L* to wrath	Deut 9:8	3068
so that the *L* was angry with you	Deut 9:8	3068
which the *L* made with you	Deut 9:9	3068
the *L* delivered unto me two	Deut 9:10	3068
which the *L* spake with you in the	Deut 9:10	3068
that the *L* gave me the two tables	Deut 9:11	3068
the *L* said unto me, Arise, get	Deut 9:12	3068
Furthermore the *L* spake unto me	Deut 9:13	3068
had sinned against the *L* your God	Deut 9:16	3068
way which the *L* had commanded you	Deut 9:16	3068
And I fell down before the *L*	Deut 9:18	3068
wickedly in the sight of the *L*	Deut 9:18	3068
wherewith the *L* was wroth against	Deut 9:19	3068
But the *L* hearkened unto me at	Deut 9:19	3068
the *L* was very angry with Aaron	Deut 9:20	3068
ye provoked the *L* to wrath	Deut 9:22	3068
Likewise when the *L* sent you from	Deut 9:23	3068
the commandment of the *L* your God	Deut 9:23	3068
been rebellious against the *L*	Deut 9:24	3068
fell down before the *L* forty days	Deut 9:25	3068
because the *L* had said he would	Deut 9:25	3068
I prayed therefore unto the *L*	Deut 9:26	3068
O *L* God, destroy not thy people	Deut 9:26	136
Because the *L* was not able to	Deut 9:28	3068
At that time the *L* said unto me	Deut 10:1	3068
which the *L* spake unto you in the	Deut 10:4	3068
and the *L* gave them unto me	Deut 10:4	3068
they be, as the *L* commanded me	Deut 10:5	3068
At that time the *L* separated the	Deut 10:8	3068
the ark of the covenant of the *L*	Deut 10:8	3068
to stand before the *L* to minister	Deut 10:8	3068
the *L* is his inheritance,	Deut 10:9	3068
according as the *L* thy God	Deut 10:9	3068
the *L* hearkened unto me at that	Deut 10:10	3068
the *L* would not destroy thee	Deut 10:10	3068
the *L* said unto me, Arise, take	Deut 10:11	3068
what doth the *L* thy God require	Deut 10:12	3068
thee, but to fear the *L* thy God	Deut 10:12	3068
to serve the *L* thy God with all	Deut 10:12	3068
To keep the commandments of the *L*	Deut 10:13	3068
Only the *L* had a delight in thy	Deut 10:15	3068
For the *L* your God is God of gods	Deut 10:17	3068
L of lords, a great God, a mighty	Deut 10:17	113
Thou shalt fear the *L* thy God	Deut 10:20	3068
now the *L* thy God hath made thee	Deut 10:22	3068
thou shalt love the *L* thy God	Deut 11:1	3068
chastisement of the *L* your God	Deut 11:2	3068
how the *L* hath destroyed them	Deut 11:4	3068
great acts of the *L* which he did	Deut 11:7	3068
which the *L* sware unto your	Deut 11:9	3068
A land which the *L* thy God careth	Deut 11:12	3068
the eyes of the *L* thy God are	Deut 11:12	3068
this day, to love the *L* your God	Deut 11:13	3068
good land which the *L* giveth you	Deut 11:17	3068
in the land which the *L* sware	Deut 11:21	3068
do them, to love the *L* your God	Deut 11:22	3068
Then will the *L* drive out all	Deut 11:23	3068
for the *L* your God shall lay the	Deut 11:25	3068
commandments of the *L* your God	Deut 11:27	3068
commandments of the *L* your God	Deut 11:28	3068
when the *L* thy God hath brought	Deut 11:29	3068
which the *L* your God giveth you	Deut 11:31	3068
which the *L* God of thy fathers	Deut 12:1	3068
not do so unto the *L* your God	Deut 12:4	3068
L your God shall choose out of	Deut 12:5	3068
shall eat before the *L* your God	Deut 12:7	3068
wherein the *L* thy God hath	Deut 12:7	3068
which the *L* your God giveth you	Deut 12:9	3068
dwell in the land which the *L*	Deut 12:10	3068
shall be a place which the *L* your	Deut 12:11	3068
vows which ye vow unto the *L*	Deut 12:11	3068
rejoice before the *L* your God	Deut 12:12	3068
the *L* shall choose in one of thy	Deut 12:14	3068
to the blessing of the *L* thy God	Deut 12:15	3068
thou must eat them before the *L*	Deut 12:18	3068
which the *L* thy God shall choose	Deut 12:18	3068
the *L* thy God in all that thou	Deut 12:18	3068
When the *L* thy God shall enlarge	Deut 12:20	3068
If the place which the *L* thy God	Deut 12:21	3068
which the *L* hath given thee, as I	Deut 12:21	3068
is right in the sight of the *L*	Deut 12:25	3068
place which the *L* shall choose	Deut 12:26	3068
upon the altar of the *L* thy God	Deut 12:27	3068
upon the altar of the *L* thy God	Deut 12:27	3068
in the sight of the *L* thy God	Deut 12:28	3068
When the *L* thy God shall cut off	Deut 12:29	3068
not do so unto the *L* thy God	Deut 12:31	3068
for every abomination to the *L*	Deut 12:31	3068
for the *L* your God proveth you,	Deut 13:3	3068
to know whether ye love the *L*	Deut 13:3	3068
shall walk after the *L* your God	Deut 13:4	3068
turn you away from the *L* your God	Deut 13:5	3068
thee out of the way which the *L*	Deut 13:5	3068
thee away from the *L* thy God	Deut 13:10	3068
which the *L* thy God hath given	Deut 13:12	3068
every whit, for the *L* thy God	Deut 13:16	3068
that the *L* may turn from the	Deut 13:17	3068
to the voice of the *L* thy God	Deut 13:18	3068
in the eyes of the *L* thy God	Deut 13:18	3068
the children of the *L* your God	Deut 14:1	3068
an holy people unto the *L* thy God	Deut 14:2	3068
the *L* hath chosen thee to be a	Deut 14:2	3068
an holy people unto the *L* thy God	Deut 14:21	3068
shalt eat before the *L* thy God	Deut 14:23	3068
to fear the *L* thy God always	Deut 14:23	3068
which the *L* thy God shall choose	Deut 14:24	3068
when the *L* thy God hath blessed	Deut 14:24	3068
which the *L* thy God shall choose	Deut 14:25	3068
eat there before the *L* thy God	Deut 14:26	3068
that the *L* thy God may bless thee	Deut 14:29	3068
for the *L* shall greatly bless	Deut 15:4	3068
the *L* thy God giveth thee for an	Deut 15:4	3068
unto the voice of the *L* thy God	Deut 15:5	3068
For the *L* thy God blesseth thee,	Deut 15:6	3068
which the *L* thy God giveth thee	Deut 15:7	3068
and he cry unto the *L* against thee	Deut 15:9	3068
L thy God shall bless thee in all	Deut 15:10	3068
of that wherewith the *L* thy God	Deut 15:14	3068
the *L* thy God redeemed thee	Deut 15:15	3068
the *L* thy God shall bless thee in	Deut 15:18	3068
shalt sanctify unto the *L* thy God	Deut 15:19	3068
the *L* thy God year by year in the	Deut 15:20	3068
place which the *L* shall choose	Deut 15:20	3068
sacrifice it unto the *L* thy God	Deut 15:21	3068
the passover unto the *L* thy God	Deut 16:1	3068
for in the month of Abib the *L*	Deut 16:1	3068
the passover unto the *L* thy God	Deut 16:2	3068
in the place which the *L* shall	Deut 16:2	3068
which the *L* thy God giveth thee	Deut 16:5	3068
But at the place which the *L* thy	Deut 16:6	3068
which the *L* thy God shall choose	Deut 16:7	3068
solemn assembly to the *L* thy God	Deut 16:8	3068
the *L* thy God with a tribute of a	Deut 16:10	3068
shalt give unto the *L* thy God	Deut 16:10	
according as the *L* thy God hath	Deut 16:10	3068
rejoice before the *L* thy God	Deut 16:11	3068
in the place which the *L* thy God	Deut 16:11	3068
keep a solemn feast unto the *L*	Deut 16:15	3068
place which the *L* shall choose	Deut 16:15	3068
because the *L* thy God shall bless	Deut 16:15	3068
L thy God in the place which he	Deut 16:16	3068
not appear before the *L* empty	Deut 16:16	3068
to the blessing of the *L* thy God	Deut 16:17	3068
which the *L* thy God giveth thee,	Deut 16:18	3068
which the *L* thy God giveth thee	Deut 16:20	3068
unto the altar of the *L* thy God	Deut 16:21	3068
which the *L* thy God hateth	Deut 16:22	3068
unto the *L* thy God any bullock	Deut 17:1	3068
an abomination unto the *L* thy God	Deut 17:1	3068
which the *L* thy God giveth thee	Deut 17:2	3068
in the sight of the *L* thy God	Deut 17:2	3068
which the *L* thy God shall choose	Deut 17:8	3068
L shall choose shall shew thee	Deut 17:10	3068
there before the *L* thy God	Deut 17:12	3068
which the *L* thy God giveth thee	Deut 17:14	3068
whom the *L* thy God shall choose	Deut 17:15	3068
forasmuch as the *L* hath said unto	Deut 17:16	3068
may learn to fear the *L* his God	Deut 17:19	3068
offerings of the *L* made by fire	Deut 18:1	3068
the *L* is their inheritance, as he	Deut 18:2	3068
For the *L* thy God hath chosen him	Deut 18:5	3068
to minister in the name of the *L*	Deut 18:5	3068
place which the *L* shall choose	Deut 18:6	3068
in the name of the *L* his God	Deut 18:7	3068
which stand there before the *L*	Deut 18:7	3068

which the *L* thy God giveth thee	Deut 18:9	3068
are an abomination unto the *L*	Deut 18:12	3068
of these abominations the *L* thy	Deut 18:12	3068
be perfect with the *L* thy God	Deut 18:13	3068
the *L* thy God hath not suffered	Deut 18:14	3068
The *L* thy God will raise up unto	Deut 18:15	3068
L thy God in Horeb in the day of	Deut 18:16	3068
again the voice of the *L* my God	Deut 18:16	3068
the *L* said unto me, They have	Deut 18:17	3068
word which the *L* hath not spoken	Deut 18:21	3068
speaketh in the name of the *L*	Deut 18:22	3068
thing which the *L* hath not spoken	Deut 18:22	3068
When the *L* thy God hath cut off	Deut 19:1	3068
whose land the *L* thy God giveth	Deut 19:1	3068
which the *L* thy God giveth thee	Deut 19:2	3068
which the *L* thy God giveth thee	Deut 19:3	3068
if the *L* thy God enlarge thy	Deut 19:8	3068
this day, to love the *L* thy God	Deut 19:9	3068
which the *L* thy God giveth thee	Deut 19:10	3068
inherit in the land that the *L*	Deut 19:14	3068
is, shall stand before the *L*	Deut 19:17	3068
for the *L* thy God is with thee,	Deut 20:1	3068
For the *L* your God is he that	Deut 20:4	3068
when the *L* thy God hath delivered	Deut 20:13	3068
which the *L* thy God hath given	Deut 20:14	3068
which the *L* thy God doth give	Deut 20:16	3068
as the *L* thy God hath commanded	Deut 20:17	3068
ye sin against the *L* your God	Deut 20:18	3068
slain in the land which the *L* thy	Deut 21:1	3068
for them the *L* thy God hath	Deut 21:5	3068
and to bless in the name of the *L*	Deut 21:5	3068
Be merciful, O *L*, unto thy people	Deut 21:8	3068
is right in the sight of the *L*	Deut 21:9	3068
the *L* thy God hath delivered them	Deut 21:10	3068
which the *L* thy God giveth thee	Deut 21:23	3068
abomination unto the *L* thy God	Deut 22:5	3068
into the congregation of the *L*	Deut 23:1	3068
into the congregation of the *L*	Deut 23:2	3068
into the congregation of the *L*	Deut 23:2	3068
into the congregation of the *L*	Deut 23:3	3068
congregation of the *L* for ever	Deut 23:3	3068
Nevertheless the *L* thy God would	Deut 23:5	3068
but the *L* thy God turned the	Deut 23:5	3068
because the *L* thy God loved thee	Deut 23:5	3068
the *L* in their third generation	Deut 23:8	3068
For the *L* thy God walketh in the	Deut 23:14	3068
of the *L* thy God for any vow	Deut 23:18	3068
abomination unto the *L* thy God	Deut 23:18	3068
that the *L* thy God may bless thee	Deut 23:20	3068
vow a vow unto the *L* thy God	Deut 23:21	3068
for the *L* thy God will surely	Deut 23:21	3068
hast vowed unto the *L* thy God	Deut 23:23	3068
that is abomination before the *L*	Deut 24:4	3068
which the *L* thy God giveth thee	Deut 24:4	3068
Remember what the *L* thy God did	Deut 24:9	3068
unto thee before the *L* thy God	Deut 24:13	3068
he cry against thee unto the *L*	Deut 24:15	3068
the *L* thy God redeemed thee	Deut 24:18	3068
that the *L* thy God may bless thee	Deut 24:19	3068
which the *L* thy God giveth thee	Deut 25:15	3068
an abomination unto the *L* thy God	Deut 25:16	3068
when the *L* thy God hath given	Deut 25:19	3068
in the land which the *L* thy God	Deut 25:19	3068
the *L* thy God giveth thee for an	Deut 26:1	3068
that the *L* thy God giveth thee	Deut 26:2	3068
go unto the place which the *L* thy	Deut 26:2	3068
this day unto the *L* thy God	Deut 26:3	3068
L sware unto our fathers for to	Deut 26:3	3068
before the altar of the *L* thy God	Deut 26:4	3068
speak and say before the *L* thy God	Deut 26:5	3068
unto the *L* God of our fathers	Deut 26:7	3068
the *L* heard our voice, and looked	Deut 26:7	3068
the *L* brought us forth out of	Deut 26:8	3068
of the land, which thou, O *L*	Deut 26:10	3068
shalt set it before the *L* thy God	Deut 26:10	3068
and worship before the *L* thy God	Deut 26:10	3068
L thy God hath given unto thee	Deut 26:11	3068
shalt say before the *L* thy God	Deut 26:13	3068
to the voice of the *L* my God	Deut 26:14	3068
This day the *L* thy God hath	Deut 26:16	3068
the *L* this day to be thy God	Deut 26:17	3068
the *L* hath avouched thee this day	Deut 26:18	3068
an holy people unto the *L* thy God	Deut 26:19	3068
which the *L* thy God giveth thee	Deut 27:2	3068
which the *L* thy God giveth thee	Deut 27:3	3068
as the *L* God of thy fathers hath	Deut 27:3	3068
build an altar unto the *L* thy God	Deut 27:5	3068
of the *L* thy God of whole stones	Deut 27:6	3068
thereon unto the *L* thy God	Deut 27:6	3068
and rejoice before the *L* thy God	Deut 27:7	3068
the people of the *L* thy God	Deut 27:9	3068
obey the voice of the *L* thy God	Deut 27:10	3068
image, an abomination unto the *L*	Deut 27:15	3068
unto the voice of the *L* thy God	Deut 28:1	3068
that the *L* thy God will set thee	Deut 28:1	3068
unto the voice of the *L* thy God	Deut 28:2	3068
The *L* shall cause thine enemies	Deut 28:7	3068
The *L* shall command the blessing	Deut 28:8	3068
which the *L* thy God giveth thee	Deut 28:8	3068
The *L* shall establish thee an	Deut 28:9	3068
the commandments of the *L* thy God	Deut 28:9	3068
art called by the name of the *L*	Deut 28:10	3068
the *L* shall make thee plenteous	Deut 28:11	3068
in the land which the *L* sware	Deut 28:11	3068
The *L* shall open unto thee his	Deut 28:12	3068
the *L* shall make thee the head,	Deut 28:13	3068
the commandments of the *L* thy God	Deut 28:13	3068
unto the voice of the *L* thy God	Deut 28:15	3068
The *L* shall send upon thee	Deut 28:20	3068
The *L* shall make the pestilence	Deut 28:21	3068
The *L* shall smite thee with a	Deut 28:22	3068
The *L* shall make the rain of thy	Deut 28:24	3068
The *L* shall cause thee to be	Deut 28:25	3068
The *L* will smite thee with the	Deut 28:27	3068
The *L* shall smite thee with	Deut 28:28	3068
The *L* shall smite thee in the	Deut 28:35	3068
The *L* shall bring thee, and thy	Deut 28:36	3068
whither the *L* shall lead thee	Deut 28:37	3068
unto the voice of the *L* thy God	Deut 28:45	3068
not the *L* thy God with joyfulness	Deut 28:47	3068
the *L* shall send against thee	Deut 28:48	3068
The *L* shall bring a nation	Deut 28:49	3068
which the *L* thy God hath given	Deut 28:52	3068
which the *L* thy God hath given	Deut 28:53	3068
and fearful name, THE *L* THY GOD	Deut 28:58	3068
Then the *L* will make thy plagues	Deut 28:59	3068
them will the *L* bring upon thee,	Deut 28:61	3068
obey the voice of the *L* thy God	Deut 28:62	3068
that as the *L* rejoiced over you	Deut 28:63	3068
so the *L* will rejoice over you to	Deut 28:63	3068
the *L* shall scatter thee among	Deut 28:64	3068
but the *L* shall give thee there a	Deut 28:65	3068
the *L* shall bring thee into Egypt	Deut 28:68	3068
which the *L* commanded Moses to	Deut 29:1	3068
Ye have seen all that the *L* did	Deut 29:2	3068
Yet the *L* hath not given you an	Deut 29:4	3068
know that I am the *L* your God	Deut 29:6	3068
all of you before the *L* your God	Deut 29:10	3068
into covenant with the *L* thy God	Deut 29:12	3068
which the *L* thy God maketh with	Deut 29:12	3068
us this day before the *L* our God	Deut 29:15	3068
away this day from the *L* our God	Deut 29:18	3068
The *L* will not spare him	Deut 29:20	3068
but then the anger of the *L*	Deut 29:20	3068
the *L* shall blot out his name	Deut 29:20	3068
the *L* shall separate him unto	Deut 29:21	3068
which the *L* hath laid upon it	Deut 29:22	3068
which the *L* overthrew in his	Deut 29:23	3068
Wherefore hath the *L* done thus	Deut 29:24	3068
of the *L* God of their fathers	Deut 29:25	3068
the anger of the *L* was kindled	Deut 29:27	3068
the *L* rooted them out of their	Deut 29:28	3068
things belong unto the *L* our God	Deut 29:29	3068
whither the *L* thy God hath driven	Deut 30:1	3068
shalt return unto the *L* thy God	Deut 30:2	3068
That then the *L* thy God will turn	Deut 30:3	3068
whither the *L* thy God hath	Deut 30:3	3068
will the *L* thy God gather thee	Deut 30:4	3068
the *L* thy God will bring thee	Deut 30:5	3068
the *L* thy God will circumcise	Deut 30:6	3068
to love the *L* thy God with all	Deut 30:6	3068
the *L* thy God will put all these	Deut 30:7	3068
return and obey the voice of the *L*	Deut 30:8	3068
the *L* thy God will make thee	Deut 30:9	3068
for the *L* will again rejoice over	Deut 30:9	3068
unto the voice of the *L* thy God	Deut 30:10	3068
if thou turn unto the *L* thy God	Deut 30:10	3068
this day to love the *L* thy God	Deut 30:16	3068
the *L* thy God shall bless thee in	Deut 30:16	3068
thou mayest love the *L* thy God	Deut 30:20	3068
the *L* sware unto thy fathers	Deut 30:20	3068
also the *L* hath said unto me,	Deut 31:2	3068
The *L* thy God, he will go over	Deut 31:3	3068
before thee, as the *L* hath said	Deut 31:3	3068
the *L* shall do unto them as he	Deut 31:4	3068
the *L* shall give them up before	Deut 31:5	3068
for the *L* thy God, he it is that	Deut 31:6	3068
L hath sworn unto their fathers	Deut 31:7	3068
And the *L*, he it is that doth go	Deut 31:8	3068
the ark of the covenant of the *L*	Deut 31:9	3068
is come to appear before the *L*	Deut 31:11	3068
may learn, and fear the *L* your God	Deut 31:12	3068
and learn to fear the *L* your God	Deut 31:13	3068
the *L* said unto Moses, Behold,	Deut 31:14	3068
the *L* appeared in the tabernacle	Deut 31:15	3068
the *L* said unto Moses, Behold,	Deut 31:16	3068
the ark of the covenant of the *L*	Deut 31:25	3068
of the covenant of the *L* your God	Deut 31:26	3068
been rebellious against the *L*	Deut 31:27	3068
do evil in the sight of the *L*	Deut 31:29	3068
I will publish the name of the *L*	Deut 32:3	3068
Do ye thus requite the *L*, O	Deut 32:6	3068
So the *L* alone did lead him, and	Deut 32:12	3068
And when the *L* saw it, he abhorred	Deut 32:19	3068
the *L* hath not done all this	Deut 32:27	3068
them, and the *L* had shut them up	Deut 32:30	3068
For the *L* shall judge his people,	Deut 32:36	3068
the *L* spake unto Moses that	Deut 32:48	3068
The *L* came from Sinai, and rose up	Deut 33:2	3068
and he said, Hear, *L*, the voice of	Deut 33:7	3068
Bless, *L*, his substance, and	Deut 33:11	3068
The beloved of the *L* shall dwell	Deut 33:12	3068
the *L* shall cover him all the day	Deut 33:12	
Blessed of the *L* be his land	Deut 33:13	3068
he executed the justice of the *L*	Deut 33:21	3068
full with the blessing of the *L*	Deut 33:23	3068
thee, O people saved by the *L*	Deut 33:29	3068
the *L* shewed him all the land of	Deut 34:1	3068
the *L* said unto him, This is the	Deut 34:4	3068
So Moses the servant of the *L*	Deut 34:5	3068
according to the word of the *L*	Deut 34:5	3068
did as the *L* commanded Moses	Deut 34:9	3068
whom the *L* knew face to face,	Deut 34:10	3068
which the *L* sent him to do in the	Deut 34:11	3068
servant of the *L* it came to pass	Josh 1:1	3068
that the *L* spake unto Joshua the	Josh 1:1	3068
for the *L* thy God is with thee	Josh 1:9	3068
which the *L* your God giveth you	Josh 1:11	3068
servant of the *L* commanded you	Josh 1:13	3068
The *L* your God hath given you	Josh 1:13	3068
Until the *L* have given your	Josh 1:15	3068
which the *L* your God giveth them	Josh 1:15	3068
only the *L* thy God be with thee,	Josh 1:17	3068
I know that the *L* hath given you	Josh 2:9	3068
For we have heard how the *L* dried	Josh 2:10	3068
for the *L* your God, he is God in	Josh 2:11	3068
pray you, swear unto me by the *L*	Josh 2:12	3068
when the *L* hath given us the land	Josh 2:14	3068
Truly the *L* hath delivered into	Josh 2:24	3068
of the covenant of the *L* your God	Josh 3:3	3068
for to morrow the *L* will do	Josh 3:5	3068
the *L* said unto Joshua, This day	Josh 3:7	3068
hear the words of the *L* your God	Josh 3:9	3068
L of all the earth passeth over	Josh 3:11	113
that bear the ark of the *L*	Josh 3:13	3068
the *L* of all the earth, shall	Josh 3:13	113
the ark of the covenant of the *L*	Josh 3:17	3068
that the *L* spake unto Joshua,	Josh 4:1	3068
the *L* your God into the midst of	Josh 4:5	3068
the ark of the covenant of the *L*	Josh 4:7	3068
as the *L* spake unto Joshua,	Josh 4:8	3068
thing was finished that the *L*	Josh 4:10	3068
that the ark of the *L* passed over	Josh 4:11	3068
over before the *L* unto battle	Josh 4:13	3068
On that day the *L* magnified	Josh 4:14	3068
the *L* spake unto Joshua, saying,	Josh 4:15	3068
L were come up out of the midst	Josh 4:18	3068
For the *L* your God dried up the	Josh 4:23	3068
as the *L* your God did to the Red	Josh 4:23	3068
might know the hand of the *L*	Josh 4:24	3068
fear the *L* your God for ever	Josh 4:24	3068
heard that the *L* had dried up the	Josh 5:1	3068
that time the *L* said unto Joshua	Josh 5:2	3068
obeyed not the voice of the *L*	Josh 5:6	3068
unto whom the *L* sware that he	Josh 5:6	3068
which the *L* sware unto their	Josh 5:6	3068
the *L* said unto Joshua, This day	Josh 5:9	3068
the host of the *L* am I now come	Josh 5:14	113
What saith my *l* unto his servant	Josh 5:14	3068
the *L* said unto Joshua, See, I	Josh 6:2	3068
horns before the ark of the *L*	Josh 6:6	3068
pass on before the ark of the *L*	Josh 6:7	3068
horns passed on before the *L*	Josh 6:8	3068
covenant of the *L* followed them	Josh 6:8	3068
So the ark of the *L* compassed the	Josh 6:11	3068
priests took up the ark of the *L*	Josh 6:12	3068
ark of the *L* went on continually	Josh 6:13	3068
came after the ark of the *L*	Josh 6:13	3068
for the *L* hath given you the city	Josh 6:16	3068
and all that are therein, to the *L*	Josh 6:17	3068
iron, are consecrated unto the *L*	Josh 6:19	3068
come into the treasury of the *L*	Josh 6:19	3068
treasury of the house of the *L*	Josh 6:24	3068
Cursed be the man before the *L*	Josh 6:26	3068
So the *L* was with Joshua	Josh 6:27	3068
the anger of the *L* was kindled	Josh 7:1	3068
ark of the *L* until the eventide	Josh 7:6	3068
O *L* GOD, wherefore hast thou at	Josh 7:7	136
O *L*, what shall I say, when	Josh 7:8	136
the *L* said unto Joshua, Get thee	Josh 7:10	3068
thus saith the *L* God of Israel	Josh 7:13	3068
that the tribe which the *L* taketh	Josh 7:14	3068
the family which the *L* shall take	Josh 7:14	3068
the household which the *L* shall	Josh 7:14	3068
the covenant of the *L*, and because	Josh 7:15	3068
glory to the *L* God of Israel, and	Josh 7:19	3068
against the *L* God of Israel	Josh 7:20	3068
and laid them out before the *L*	Josh 7:23	3068
the *L* shall trouble thee this day	Josh 7:25	3068
So the *L* turned from the	Josh 7:26	3068
the *L* said unto Joshua, Fear not,	Josh 8:1	3068
for the *L* your God will deliver	Josh 8:7	3068
commandment of the *L* shall ye do	Josh 8:8	3068
the *L* said unto Joshua, Stretch	Josh 8:18	3068
the *L* which he commanded Joshua	Josh 8:27	3068
the *L* God of Israel in mount Ebal	Josh 8:30	3068
the *L* commanded the children of	Josh 8:31	3068
burnt offerings unto the *L*	Josh 8:31	3068
the ark of the covenant of the *L*	Josh 8:33	3068
of the *L* had commanded before	Josh 8:33	3068
of the name of the *L* thy God	Josh 9:9	3068
not counsel at the mouth of the *L*	Josh 9:14	3068
unto them by the *L* God of Israel	Josh 9:18	3068
unto them by the *L* God of Israel	Josh 9:19	3068
how that the *L* thy God commanded	Josh 9:24	3068
and for the altar of the *L*	Josh 9:27	3068
the *L* said unto Joshua, Fear them	Josh 10:8	3068
the *L* discomfited them before	Josh 10:10	3068
that the *L* cast down great stones	Josh 10:11	3068
to the *L* in the day when the *L*	Josh 10:12	3068
that the *L* hearkened unto the	Josh 10:14	3068
for the *L* fought for Israel	Josh 10:14	3068
for the *L* your God hath delivered	Josh 10:19	3068
for thus shall the *L* do to all	Josh 10:25	3068
the *L* delivered it also, and the	Josh 10:30	3068
the *L* delivered Lachish into the	Josh 10:32	3068
as the *L* God of Israel commanded	Josh 10:40	3068
because the *L* God of Israel	Josh 10:42	3068
the *L* said unto Joshua, Be not	Josh 11:6	3068
the *L* delivered them into the	Josh 11:8	3068
did unto them as the *L* bade him	Josh 11:9	3068
the servant of the *L* commanded	Josh 11:12	3068
As the *L* commanded Moses his	Josh 11:15	3068
of all that the *L* commanded Moses	Josh 11:15	3068
For it was of the *L* to harden	Josh 11:20	3068
them, as the *L* commanded Moses	Josh 11:20	3068
to all that the *L* said unto Moses	Josh 11:23	3068
did Moses the servant of the *L*	Josh 12:6	3068
Moses the servant of the *L* gave	Josh 12:6	3068
the *L* said unto him, Thou art old	Josh 13:1	3068
the servant of the *L* gave them	Josh 13:8	3068
the sacrifices of the *L* God of	Josh 13:14	3068
the *L* God of Israel was their	Josh 13:33	3068
as the *L* commanded by the hand of	Josh 14:2	3068
As the *L* commanded Moses, so the	Josh 14:5	3068
L said unto Moses the man of God	Josh 14:6	3068
L sent me from Kadesh-barnea to	Josh 14:7	3068
I wholly followed the *L* my God	Josh 14:8	3068
hast wholly followed the *L* my God	Josh 14:9	3068
the *L* hath kept me alive, as he	Josh 14:10	3068
even since the *L* spake this word	Josh 14:10	3068
whereof the *L* spake in that day	Josh 14:12	3068

if so be the *L* will be with me,	Josh 14:12	3068
to drive them out, as the *L* said	Josh 14:12	3068
followed the *L* God of Israel	Josh 14:14	3068
commandment of the *L* to Joshua	Josh 15:13	3068
The *L* commanded Moses to give us	Josh 17:4	3068
to the commandment of the *L* he	Josh 17:4	3068
forasmuch as the *L* hath blessed	Josh 17:14	3068
which the *L* God of your fathers	Josh 18:3	3068
for you here before the *L* our God	Josh 18:6	3068
of the *L* is their inheritance	Josh 18:7	3068
the servant of the *L* gave them	Josh 18:7	3068
for you before the *L* in Shiloh	Josh 18:8	3068
for them in Shiloh before the *L*	Josh 18:10	3068
According to the word of the *L*	Josh 19:50	3068
by lot in Shiloh before the *L*	Josh 19:51	3068
The *L* also spake unto Joshua,	Josh 20:1	3068
The *L* commanded by the hand of	Josh 21:2	3068
at the commandment of the *L*	Josh 21:3	3068
as the *L* commanded by the hand of	Josh 21:8	3068
the *L* gave unto Israel all the	Josh 21:43	3068
the *L* gave them rest round about,	Josh 21:44	3068
the *L* delivered all their enemies	Josh 21:44	3068
of any good thing which the *L* had	Josh 21:45	3068
servant of the *L* commanded you	Josh 22:2	3068
the commandment of the *L* your God	Josh 22:3	3068
now the *L* your God hath given	Josh 22:4	3068
the *L* gave you on the other side	Josh 22:4	3068
the servant of the *L* charged you	Josh 22:5	3068
you, to love the *L* your God	Josh 22:5	3068
of the *L* by the hand of Moses	Josh 22:9	3068
the whole congregation of the *L*	Josh 22:16	3068
this day from following the *L*	Josh 22:16	3068
rebel this day against the *L*	Josh 22:16	3068
in the congregation of the *L*	Josh 22:17	3068
this day from following the *L*	Josh 22:18	3068
ye rebel to day against the *L*	Josh 22:18	3068
land of the possession of the *L*	Josh 22:19	3068
but rebel not against the *L*	Josh 22:19	3068
beside the altar of the *L* our God	Josh 22:19	3068
The *L* God of gods, the *L* God	Josh 22:22	3068
if in transgression against the *L*	Josh 22:22	3068
to turn from following the *L*	Josh 22:23	3068
let the *L* himself require it	Josh 22:23	3068
ye to do with the *L* God of Israel	Josh 22:24	3068
For the *L* hath made Jordan a	Josh 22:25	3068
ye have no part in the *L*	Josh 22:25	3068
children cease from fearing the *L*	Josh 22:25	3068
the *L* before him with our burnt	Josh 22:27	3068
to come, Ye have no part in the *L*	Josh 22:27	3068
the pattern of the altar of the *L*	Josh 22:28	3068
we should rebel against the *L*	Josh 22:29	3068
this day from following the *L*	Josh 22:29	3068
beside the altar of the *L* our God	Josh 22:29	3068
perceive that the *L* is among us	Josh 22:31	3068
this trespass against the *L*	Josh 22:31	3068
Israel out of the hand of the *L*	Josh 22:31	3068
between us that the *L* is God	Josh 22:34	3068
L had given rest unto Israel from	Josh 23:1	3068
ye have seen all that the *L* your	Josh 23:3	3068
for the *L* your God is he that	Josh 23:3	3068
the *L* your God, he shall expel	Josh 23:5	3068
as the *L* your God hath promised	Josh 23:5	3068
But cleave unto the *L* your God	Josh 23:8	3068
For the *L* hath driven out from	Josh 23:9	3068
for the *L* your God, he it is that	Josh 23:10	3068
that ye love the *L* your God	Josh 23:11	3068
Know for a certainty that the *L*	Josh 23:13	3068
the *L* your God hath given you	Josh 23:13	3068
L your God spake concerning you	Josh 23:14	3068
which the *L* your God promised you	Josh 23:15	3068
so shall the *L* bring upon you all	Josh 23:15	3068
the *L* your God hath given you	Josh 23:15	3068
the covenant of the *L* your God	Josh 23:16	3068
of the *L* be kindled against you	Josh 23:16	3068
Thus saith the *L* God of Israel	Josh 24:2	3068
And when they cried unto the *L*	Josh 24:7	3068
Now therefore fear the *L*, and	Josh 24:14	3068
and serve ye the *L*	Josh 24:14	3068
seem evil unto you to serve the *L*	Josh 24:15	3068
and my house, we will serve the *L*	Josh 24:15	3068
that we should forsake the *L*	Josh 24:16	3068
For the *L* our God, he it is that	Josh 24:17	3068
the *L* drave out from before us	Josh 24:18	3068
will we also serve the *L*	Josh 24:18	3068
the people, Ye cannot serve the *L*	Josh 24:19	3068
If ye forsake the *L*, and serve	Josh 24:20	3068
but we will serve the *L*	Josh 24:21	3068
that ye have chosen you the *L*	Josh 24:22	3068
heart unto the *L* God of Israel	Josh 24:23	3068
The *L* our God will we serve, and	Josh 24:24	3068
was by the sanctuary of the *L*	Josh 24:26	3068
of the *L* which he spake unto us	Josh 24:27	3068
son of Nun, the servant of the *L*	Josh 24:29	3068
Israel served the *L* all the days	Josh 24:31	3068
had known all the works of the *L*	Josh 24:31	3068
children of Israel asked the *L*	Judg 1:1	3068
the *L* said, Judah shall go up	Judg 1:2	3068
the *L* delivered the Canaanites and	Judg 1:4	3068
And the *L* was with Judah	Judg 1:19	3068
and the *L* was with them	Judg 1:22	3068
an angel of the *L* came up from	Judg 2:1	3068
when the angel of the *L* spake	Judg 2:4	3068
they sacrificed there unto the *L*	Judg 2:5	3068
the people served the *L* all the	Judg 2:7	3068
seen all the great works of the *L*	Judg 2:7	3068
son of Nun, the servant of the *L*	Judg 2:8	3068
after them, which knew not the *L*	Judg 2:10	3068
did evil in the sight of the *L*	Judg 2:11	3068
they forsook the *L* God of their	Judg 2:12	3068
them, and provoked the *L* to anger	Judg 2:12	3068
And they forsook the *L*, and served	Judg 2:13	3068
the anger of the *L* was hot	Judg 2:14	3068
the hand of the *L* was against	Judg 2:15	3068
as the *L* had said, and as the *L*	Judg 2:15	3068
the *L* raised up judges, which	Judg 2:16	3068
obeying the commandments of the *L*	Judg 2:17	3068
when the *L* raised them up judges,	Judg 2:18	3068
then the *L* was with the judge, and	Judg 2:18	3068
for it repented the *L* because of	Judg 2:18	3068
the anger of the *L* was hot	Judg 2:20	3068
the way of the *L* to walk therein	Judg 2:22	3068
Therefore the *L* left those	Judg 2:23	3068
are the nations which the *L* left	Judg 3:1	3068
unto the commandments of the *L*	Judg 3:4	3068
did evil in the sight of the *L*	Judg 3:7	3068
and forgat the *L* their God	Judg 3:7	3068
of the *L* was hot against Israel	Judg 3:8	3068
of Israel cried unto the *L*	Judg 3:9	3068
the *L* raised up a deliverer to	Judg 3:9	3068
the spirit of the *L* came upon him	Judg 3:10	3068
and the *L* delivered	Judg 3:10	3068
evil again in the sight of the *L*	Judg 3:12	3068
the *L* strengthened Eglon the king	Judg 3:12	3068
done evil in the sight of the *L*	Judg 3:12	3068
of Israel cried unto the *L*	Judg 3:15	3068
the *L* raised them up a deliverer,	Judg 3:15	3068
for the *L* hath delivered your	Judg 3:28	3068
did evil in the sight of the *L*	Judg 4:1	3068
the *L* sold them into the hand of	Judg 4:2	3068
of Israel cried unto the *L*	Judg 4:3	3068
Hath not the *L* God of Israel	Judg 4:6	3068
for the *L* shall sell Sisera into	Judg 4:9	3068
the *L* hath delivered Sisera into	Judg 4:14	3068
is not the *L* gone out before thee	Judg 4:14	3068
the *L* discomfited Sisera, and all	Judg 4:15	3068
Praise ye the *L* for the avenging	Judg 5:2	3068
I, even I, will sing unto the *L*	Judg 5:3	3068
praise to the *L* God of Israel	Judg 5:3	3068
L, when thou wentest out of Seir,	Judg 5:4	3068
melted from before the *L*, even	Judg 5:5	3068
from before the *L* God of Israel	Judg 5:5	3068
Bless ye the *L*	Judg 5:9	3068
the righteous acts of the *L*	Judg 5:11	3068
of the *L* go down to the gates	Judg 5:11	3068
the *L* made me have dominion over	Judg 5:13	3068
ye Meroz, said the angel of the *L*	Judg 5:23	3068
came not to the help of the *L*	Judg 5:23	3068
help of the *L* against the mighty	Judg 5:23	3068
let all thine enemies perish, O *L*	Judg 5:31	3068
did evil in the sight of the *L*	Judg 6:1	3068
the *L* delivered them into the	Judg 6:1	3068
of Israel cried unto the *L*	Judg 6:6	3068
of Israel cried unto the *L*	Judg 6:7	3068
That the *L* sent a prophet unto	Judg 6:8	3068
Thus saith the *L* God of Israel	Judg 6:8	3068
unto you, I am the *L* your God	Judg 6:10	3068
And there came an angel of the *L*	Judg 6:11	3068
the angel of the *L* appeared unto	Judg 6:12	3068
The *L* is with thee, thou mighty	Judg 6:12	3068
if the *L* be with us, why then is	Judg 6:13	3068
Did not the *L* bring us up from	Judg 6:13	3068
but now the *L* hath forsaken us,	Judg 6:13	3068
the *L* looked upon him, and said,	Judg 6:14	3068
And he said unto him, Oh my *L*	Judg 6:15	136
the *L* said unto him, Surely I	Judg 6:16	3068
Then the angel of the *L* put forth	Judg 6:21	3068
Then the angel of the *L* departed	Judg 6:21	3068
that he was an angel of the *L*	Judg 6:22	3068
Gideon said, Alas, O *L* GOD	Judg 6:22	136
an angel of the *L* face to face	Judg 6:22	3068
the *L* said unto him, Peace be	Judg 6:23	3068
built an altar there unto the *L*	Judg 6:24	3068
that the *L* said unto him, Take	Judg 6:25	3068
build an altar unto the *L* thy God	Judg 6:26	3068
did as the *L* had said unto him	Judg 6:27	3068
Spirit of the *L* came upon Gideon	Judg 6:34	3068
the *L* said unto Gideon, The	Judg 7:2	3068
the *L* said unto Gideon, The	Judg 7:4	3068
the *L* said unto Gideon, Every one	Judg 7:5	3068
the *L* said unto Gideon, By the	Judg 7:7	3068
that the *L* said unto him, Arise,	Judg 7:9	3068
for the *L* hath delivered into	Judg 7:15	3068
camp, and say, The sword of the *L*	Judg 7:18	3068
and they cried, The sword of the *L*	Judg 7:20	3068
the *L* set every man's sword	Judg 7:22	3068
Therefore when the *L* hath	Judg 8:7	3068
as the *L* liveth, if ye had saved	Judg 8:19	3068
the *L* shall rule over you	Judg 8:23	3068
remembered not the *L* their God	Judg 8:34	3068
evil again in the sight of the *L*	Judg 10:6	3068
the Philistines, and forsook the *L*	Judg 10:6	3068
the anger of the *L* was hot	Judg 10:7	3068
of Israel cried unto the *L*	Judg 10:10	3068
the *L* said unto the children of	Judg 10:11	3068
of Israel said unto the *L*	Judg 10:15	3068
from among them, and served the *L*	Judg 10:16	3068
the *L* deliver them before me,	Judg 11:9	3068
The *L* be witness between us, if	Judg 11:10	3068
his words before the *L* in Mizpeh	Judg 11:11	3068
the *L* God of Israel delivered	Judg 11:21	3068
So now the *L* God of Israel hath	Judg 11:23	3068
So whomsoever the *L* our God shall	Judg 11:24	3068
the *L* the Judge be judge this day	Judg 11:27	3068
of the *L* came upon Jephthah	Judg 11:29	3068
Jephthah vowed a vow unto the *L*	Judg 11:30	3068
the *L* delivered them into his	Judg 11:32	3068
I have opened my mouth unto the *L*	Judg 11:35	3068
hast opened thy mouth unto the *L*	Judg 11:36	3068
forasmuch as the *L* hath taken	Judg 11:36	3068
the *L* delivered them into my hand	Judg 12:3	3068
evil again in the sight of the *L*	Judg 13:1	3068
the *L* delivered them into the	Judg 13:1	3068
the angel of the *L* appeared unto	Judg 13:3	3068
the *L*, and said, O my *L*	Judg 13:8	3068
angel of the *L* said unto Manoah	Judg 13:13	3068
said unto the angel of the *L*	Judg 13:15	3068
angel of the *L* said unto Manoah	Judg 13:16	3068
thou must offer it unto the *L*	Judg 13:16	3068
not that he was an angel of the *L*	Judg 13:16	3068
said unto the angel of the *L*	Judg 13:17	3068
the angel of the *L* said unto him	Judg 13:18	3068
offered it upon a rock unto the *L*	Judg 13:19	3068
that the angel of the *L* ascended	Judg 13:20	3068
But the angel of the *L* did no	Judg 13:21	3068
that he was an angel of the *L*	Judg 13:21	3068
If the *L* were pleased to kill us,	Judg 13:23	3068
child grew, and the *L* blessed him	Judg 13:24	3068
the Spirit of the *L* began to move	Judg 13:25	3068
knew not that it was of the *L*	Judg 14:4	3068
the Spirit of the *L* came mightily	Judg 14:6	3068
the Spirit of the *L* came upon him	Judg 14:19	3068
the Spirit of the *L* came mightily	Judg 15:14	3068
sore athirst, and called on the *L*	Judg 15:18	3068
he wist not that the *L* was	Judg 16:20	3068
And Samson called unto the *L*	Judg 16:28	3068
O *L* GOD, remember me, I pray thee	Judg 16:28	136
said, Blessed be thou of the *L*	Judg 17:2	3068
the *L* from my hand for my son	Judg 17:3	3068
know I that the *L* will do me good	Judg 17:13	3068
before the *L* is your way wherein	Judg 18:6	3068
now going to the house of the *L*	Judg 19:18	3068
the man's house where her *l* was	Judg 19:26	113
her *l* rose up in the morning, and	Judg 19:27	113
of Gilead, unto the *L* in Mizpeh	Judg 20:1	3068
the *L* said, Judah shall go up	Judg 20:18	3068
and wept before the *L* until even	Judg 20:23	3068
and asked counsel of the *L*	Judg 20:23	3068
the *L* said, Go up against him	Judg 20:23	3068
wept, and sat there before the *L*	Judg 20:26	3068
and peace offerings before the *L*	Judg 20:26	3068
of Israel enquired of the *L*	Judg 20:27	3068
And the *L* said, Go up	Judg 20:28	3068
the *L* smote Benjamin before	Judg 20:35	3068
O *L* God of Israel, why is this	Judg 21:3	3068
with the congregation unto the *L*	Judg 21:5	3068
came not up to the *L* to Mizpeh	Judg 21:5	3068
seeing we have sworn by the *L*	Judg 21:7	3068
came not up to Mizpeh to the *L*	Judg 21:8	3068
because that the *L* had made a	Judg 21:15	3068
there is a feast of the *L* in	Judg 21:19	3068
the *L* had visited his people in	Ruth 1:6	3068
the *L* deal kindly with you, as ye	Ruth 1:8	3068
The *L* grant you that ye may find	Ruth 1:9	3068
of the *L* is gone out against me	Ruth 1:13	113
the *L* do so to me, and more also,	Ruth 1:17	3068
the *L* hath brought me home again	Ruth 1:21	3068
seeing the *L* hath testified	Ruth 1:21	3068
the reapers, The *L* be with you	Ruth 2:4	3068
answered him, The *L* bless thee	Ruth 2:4	3068
The *L* recompense thy work, and a	Ruth 2:12	3068
given thee of the *L* God of Israel	Ruth 2:12	3068
in law, Blessed be he of the *L*	Ruth 2:20	3068
he said, Blessed be thou of the *L*	Ruth 3:10	3068
kinsman to thee, as the *L* liveth	Ruth 3:13	3068
The *L* make the woman that is come	Ruth 4:11	3068
of the seed which the *L* shall	Ruth 4:12	3068
the *L* gave her conception, and she	Ruth 4:13	3068
said unto Naomi, Blessed be the *L*	Ruth 4:14	3068
unto the *L* of hosts in Shiloh	1Sa 1:3	3068
and Phinehas, the priests of the *L*	1Sa 1:3	3068
but the *L* had shut up her womb	1Sa 1:5	3068
because the *L* had shut up her	1Sa 1:6	3068
she went up to the house of the *L*	1Sa 1:7	3068
by a post of the temple of the *L*	1Sa 1:9	3068
of soul, and prayed unto the *L*	1Sa 1:10	3068
O *L* of hosts, if thou wilt indeed	1Sa 1:11	3068
the *L* all the days of his life	1Sa 1:11	3068
continued praying before the *L*	1Sa 1:12	3068
Hannah answered and said, No, my *l*	1Sa 1:15	113
poured out my soul before the *L*	1Sa 1:15	3068
early, and worshipped before the *L*	1Sa 1:19	3068
and the *L* remembered her	1Sa 1:19	3068
Because I have asked him of the *L*	1Sa 1:20	3068
unto the *L* the yearly sacrifice	1Sa 1:21	3068
that he may appear before the *L*	1Sa 1:22	3068
only the *L* establish his word	1Sa 1:23	3068
unto the house of the *L* in Shiloh	1Sa 1:24	3068
And she said, Oh my *l*, as thy soul	1Sa 1:26	113
by thee here, praying unto the *L*	1Sa 1:26	113
the *L* hath given me my petition	1Sa 1:27	3068
also I have lent him to the *L*	1Sa 1:28	3068
liveth he shall be lent to the *L*	1Sa 1:28	3068
And he worshipped the *L* there	1Sa 1:28	3068
said, My heart rejoiceth in the *L*	1Sa 2:1	3068
mine horn is exalted in the *L*	1Sa 2:1	3068
There is none holy as the *L*	1Sa 2:2	3068
for the *L* is a God of knowledge,	1Sa 2:3	3068
The *L* killeth, and maketh alive	1Sa 2:6	3068
The *L* maketh poor, and maketh rich	1Sa 2:7	3068
The adversaries of the *L* shall be	1Sa 2:10	3068
the *L* shall judge the ends of the	1Sa 2:10	3068
unto the *L* before Eli the priest	1Sa 2:11	3068
they knew not the *L*	1Sa 2:12	3068
men was very great before the *L*	1Sa 2:17	3068
abhorred the offering of the *L*	1Sa 2:17	3068
Samuel ministered before the *L*	1Sa 2:18	3068
The *L* give thee seed of this	1Sa 2:20	3068
the loan which is lent to the *L*	1Sa 2:20	3068
the *L* visited Hannah, so that she	1Sa 2:21	3068
child Samuel grew before the *L*	1Sa 2:21	3068
but if a man sin against the *L*	1Sa 2:25	3068
because the *L* would slay them	1Sa 2:25	3068
and was in favour both with the *L*	1Sa 2:26	3068
said unto him, Thus saith the *L*	1Sa 2:27	3068
Wherefore the *L* God of Israel	1Sa 2:30	3068
but now the *L* saith, Be it far	1Sa 2:30	3068
ministered unto the *L* before Eli	1Sa 3:1	3068
the word of the *L* was precious in	1Sa 3:1	3068
went out in the temple of the *L*	1Sa 3:3	3068
That the *L* called Samuel	1Sa 3:4	3068
the *L* called yet again, Samuel	1Sa 3:6	3068
Now Samuel did not yet know the *L*	1Sa 3:7	3068

of the *L* yet revealed unto him	1Sa 3:7	3068
the *L* called Samuel again the	1Sa 3:8	3068
that the *L* had called the child	1Sa 3:8	3068
that thou shalt say, Speak, *L*	1Sa 3:9	3068
the *L* came, and stood, and called	1Sa 3:10	3068
the *L* said to Samuel, Behold, I	1Sa 3:11	3068
the doors of the house of the *L*	1Sa 3:15	3068
that the *L* hath said unto thee	1Sa 3:17	
And he said, It is the *L*	1Sa 3:18	3068
the *L* was with him, and did let	1Sa 3:19	3068
to be a prophet of the *L*	1Sa 3:20	3068
the *L* appeared again in Shiloh	1Sa 3:21	3068
for the *L* revealed himself to	1Sa 3:21	3068
in Shiloh by the word of the *L*	1Sa 3:21	3068
Wherefore hath the *L* smitten us	1Sa 4:3	3068
of the *L* out of Shiloh unto us	1Sa 4:3	3068
of the covenant of the *L* of hosts	1Sa 4:4	3068
of the *L* came into the camp	1Sa 4:5	3068
of the *L* was come into the camp	1Sa 4:6	3068
the earth before the ark of the *L*	1Sa 5:3	3068
ground before the ark of the *L*	1Sa 5:4	3068
But the hand of the *L* was heavy	1Sa 5:6	3068
the hand of the *L* was against the	1Sa 5:9	3068
the ark of the *L* was in the	1Sa 6:1	3068
shall we do to the ark of the *L*	1Sa 6:2	3068
And take the ark of the *L*, and lay	1Sa 6:8	3068
the ark of the *L* upon the cart	1Sa 6:11	3068
kine a burnt offering unto the *L*	1Sa 6:14	3068
took down the ark of the *L*	1Sa 6:15	3068
the same day unto the *L*	1Sa 6:15	3068
a trespass offering unto the *L*	1Sa 6:17	3068
they set down the ark of the *L*	1Sa 6:18	3068
had looked into the ark of the *L*	1Sa 6:19	3068
because the *L* had smitten many of	1Sa 6:19	3068
to stand before this holy *L* God	1Sa 6:20	3068
brought again the ark of the *L*	1Sa 6:21	3068
and brought up the ark of the *L*	1Sa 7:1	3068
his son to keep the ark of the *L*	1Sa 7:1	3068
of Israel lamented after the *L*	1Sa 7:2	3068
unto the *L* with all your hearts	1Sa 7:3	3068
and prepare your hearts unto the *L*	1Sa 7:3	3068
Ashtaroth, and served the *L* only	1Sa 7:4	3068
and I will pray for you unto the *L*	1Sa 7:5	3068
and poured it out before the *L*	1Sa 7:6	3068
We have sinned against the *L*	1Sa 7:6	3068
to cry unto the *L* our God for us	1Sa 7:8	3068
burnt offering wholly unto the *L*	1Sa 7:9	3068
cried unto the *L* for Israel	1Sa 7:9	3068
and the *L* heard him	1Sa 7:9	3068
but the *L* thundered with a great	1Sa 7:10	3068
Hitherto hath the *L* helped us	1Sa 7:12	3068
the hand of the *L* was against the	1Sa 7:13	3068
he built an altar unto the *L*	1Sa 7:17	3068
And Samuel prayed unto the *L*	1Sa 8:6	3068
the *L* said unto Samuel, Hearken	1Sa 8:7	3068
told all the words of the *L* unto	1Sa 8:10	3068
the *L* will not hear you in that	1Sa 8:18	3068
them in the ears of the *L*	1Sa 8:21	3068
the *L* said to Samuel, Hearken	1Sa 8:22	3068
Now the *L* had told Samuel in his	1Sa 9:15	3068
the *L* said unto him, Behold the	1Sa 9:17	3068
Is it not because the *L* hath	1Sa 10:1	3068
the Spirit of the *L* will come	1Sa 10:6	3068
together unto the *L* to Mizpeh	1Sa 10:17	3068
Thus saith the *L* God of Israel	1Sa 10:18	3068
before the *L* by your tribes	1Sa 10:19	3068
they enquired of the *L* further	1Sa 10:22	3068
the *L* answered, Behold, he hath	1Sa 10:22	3068
See ye him whom the *L* hath chosen	1Sa 10:24	3068
book, and laid it up before the *L*	1Sa 10:25	3068
the fear of the *L* fell on the	1Sa 11:7	3068
for to day the *L* hath wrought	1Sa 11:13	3068
Saul king before the *L* in Gilgal	1Sa 11:15	3068
of peace offerings before the *L*	1Sa 11:15	3068
witness against me before the *L*	1Sa 12:3	3068
The *L* is witness against you, and	1Sa 12:5	3068
It is the *L* that advanced Moses	1Sa 12:6	3068
L of all the righteous acts of	1Sa 12:7	3068
all the righteous acts of the *L*	1Sa 12:7	3068
and your fathers cried unto the *L*	1Sa 12:8	3068
then the *L* sent Moses and Aaron,	1Sa 12:8	3068
when they forgat the *L* their God	1Sa 12:9	3068
And they cried unto the *L*, and said	1Sa 12:10	3068
because we have forsaken the *L*	1Sa 12:10	3068
the *L* sent Jerubbaal, and Bedan,	1Sa 12:11	3068
when the *L* your God was your king	1Sa 12:12	3068
the *L* hath set a king over you	1Sa 12:13	3068
If ye will fear the *L*, and serve	1Sa 12:14	3068
of the *L* then shall both ye	1Sa 12:14	3068
continue following the *L* your God	1Sa 12:14	3068
will not obey the voice of the *L*	1Sa 12:15	3068
against the commandment of the *L*	1Sa 12:15	3068
the hand of the *L* be against you	1Sa 12:15	3068
which the *L* will do before your	1Sa 12:16	3068
I will call unto the *L*, and he	1Sa 12:17	3068
have done in the sight of the *L*	1Sa 12:17	3068
So Samuel called unto the *L*	1Sa 12:18	3068
the *L* sent thunder and rain that	1Sa 12:18	3068
the people greatly feared the *L*	1Sa 12:18	3068
thy servants unto the *L* thy God	1Sa 12:19	3068
not aside from following the *L*	1Sa 12:20	3068
but serve the *L* with all your	1Sa 12:20	3068
For the *L* will not forsake his	1Sa 12:22	3068
the *L* to make you his people	1Sa 12:22	3068
the *L* in ceasing to pray for you	1Sa 12:23	3068
Only fear the *L*, and serve him in	1Sa 12:24	3068
not made supplication unto the *L*	1Sa 13:12	3068
the commandment of the *L* thy God	1Sa 13:13	3068
for now would the *L* have	1Sa 13:13	3068
the *L* hath sought him a man after	1Sa 13:14	3068
the *L* hath commanded him to be	1Sa 13:14	3068
that which the *L* commanded thee	1Sa 13:14	3068
be that the *L* will work for us	1Sa 14:6	3068
the *L* to save by many or by few	1Sa 14:6	3068
for the *L* hath delivered them	1Sa 14:10	3068
for the *L* hath delivered them	1Sa 14:12	3068
So the *L* saved Israel that day	1Sa 14:23	3068
the people sin against the *L*	1Sa 14:33	3068
sin not against the *L* in eating	1Sa 14:34	3068
And Saul built an altar unto the *L*	1Sa 14:35	3068
altar that he built unto the *L*	1Sa 14:35	3068
For, as the *L* liveth, which	1Sa 14:39	3068
said unto the *L* God of Israel	1Sa 14:41	3068
as the *L* liveth, there shall not	1Sa 14:45	3068
The *L* sent me to anoint thee to	1Sa 15:1	3068
the voice of the words of the *L*	1Sa 15:1	3068
Thus saith the *L* of hosts	1Sa 15:2	3068
the word of the *L* unto Samuel	1Sa 15:10	3068
and he cried unto the *L* all night	1Sa 15:11	3068
him, Blessed be thou of the *L*	1Sa 15:13	3068
the commandment of the *L*	1Sa 15:13	3068
to sacrifice unto the *L* thy God	1Sa 15:15	3068
I will tell thee what the *L* hath	1Sa 15:16	3068
the *L* anointed thee king over	1Sa 15:17	3068
the *L* sent thee on a journey, and	1Sa 15:18	3068
thou not obey the voice of the *L*	1Sa 15:19	3068
didst evil in the sight of the *L*	1Sa 15:19	3068
I have obeyed the voice of the *L*	1Sa 15:20	3068
gone the way which the *L* sent me	1Sa 15:20	3068
unto the *L* thy God in Gilgal	1Sa 15:21	3068
Hath the *L* as great delight in	1Sa 15:22	3068
as in obeying the voice of the *L*	1Sa 15:22	3068
hast rejected the word of the *L*	1Sa 15:23	3068
the commandment of the *L*, and thy	1Sa 15:24	3068
with me, that I may worship the *L*	1Sa 15:25	3068
hast rejected the word of the *L*	1Sa 15:26	3068
the *L* hath rejected thee from	1Sa 15:26	3068
The *L* hath rent the kingdom of	1Sa 15:28	3068
that I may worship the *L* thy God	1Sa 15:30	3068
and Saul worshipped the *L*	1Sa 15:31	3068
in pieces before the *L* in Gilgal	1Sa 15:33	3068
the *L* repented that he had made	1Sa 15:35	3068
the *L* said unto Samuel, How long	1Sa 16:1	3068
the *L* said, Take an heifer with	1Sa 16:2	3068
I am come to sacrifice to the *L*	1Sa 16:2	3068
Samuel did that which the *L* spake	1Sa 16:4	3068
I am come to sacrifice unto the *L*	1Sa 16:5	3068
But the *L* said unto Samuel, Look	1Sa 16:7	3068
for the *L* seeth not as man seeth	1Sa 16:7	3068
but the *L* looketh on the heart	1Sa 16:7	3068
Neither hath the *L* chosen this	1Sa 16:8	3068
Neither hath the *L* chosen this	1Sa 16:9	3068
The *L* hath not chosen these	1Sa 16:10	3068
the *L* said, Arise, anoint him	1Sa 16:12	3068
the Spirit of the *L* came upon	1Sa 16:13	3068
of the *L* departed from Saul	1Sa 16:14	3068
spirit from the *L* troubled him	1Sa 16:14	3068
person, and the *L* is with him	1Sa 16:18	3068
The *L* that delivered me out of	1Sa 17:37	3068
David, Go, and the *L* be with thee	1Sa 17:37	3068
in the name of the *L* of hosts	1Sa 17:45	3068
This day will the *L* deliver thee	1Sa 17:46	3068
that the *L* saveth not with sword	1Sa 17:47	3068
because the *L* was with him, and	1Sa 18:12	3068
and the *L* was with him	1Sa 18:14	3068
knew that the *L* was with David,	1Sa 18:28	3068
the *L* wrought a great salvation	1Sa 19:5	3068
and Saul sware, As the *L* liveth	1Sa 19:6	3068
spirit from the *L* was upon Saul	1Sa 19:9	3068
but truly as the *L* liveth	1Sa 20:3	3068
a covenant of the *L* with thee	1Sa 20:8	3068
O *L* God of Israel, when I have	1Sa 20:12	3068
The *L* do so and much more to	1Sa 20:13	3068
the *L* be with thee, as he hath	1Sa 20:13	3068
shew me the kindness of the *L*	1Sa 20:14	3068
not when the *L* hath cut off the	1Sa 20:15	3068
Let the *L* even require it at the	1Sa 20:16	3068
as the *L* liveth	1Sa 20:21	3068
for the *L* hath sent thee away	1Sa 20:22	3068
the *L* be between thee and me for	1Sa 20:23	3068
both of us in the name of the *L*	1Sa 20:42	3068
The *L* be between me and thee, and	1Sa 20:42	3068
that was taken from before the *L*	1Sa 21:6	3068
that day, detained before the *L*	1Sa 21:7	3068
And he enquired of the *L* for him	1Sa 22:10	3068
and slay the priests of the *L*	1Sa 22:17	3068
to fall upon the priests of the *L*	1Sa 22:17	3068
Therefore David enquired of the *L*	1Sa 23:2	3068
the *L* said unto David, Go, and	1Sa 23:2	3068
David enquired of the *L* yet again	1Sa 23:4	3068
the *L* answered him and said, Arise	1Sa 23:4	3068
O *L* God of Israel, thy servant	1Sa 23:10	3068
O *L* God of Israel, I beseech thee	1Sa 23:11	3068
the *L* said, He will come down	1Sa 23:11	3068
the *L* said, They will deliver	1Sa 23:12	3068
two made a covenant before the *L*	1Sa 23:18	3068
Saul said, Blessed be ye of the *L*	1Sa 23:21	3068
day of which the *L* said unto thee	1Sa 24:4	3068
The *L* forbid that I should do	1Sa 24:6	3068
he is the anointed of the *L*	1Sa 24:6	3068
eyes have seen how that the *L* had	1Sa 24:10	3068
The *L* judge between me and thee,	1Sa 24:12	3068
and the *L* avenge me of thee	1Sa 24:12	3068
The *L* therefore be judge, and	1Sa 24:15	3068
forasmuch as when the *L* had	1Sa 24:18	3068
wherefore the *L* reward thee good	1Sa 24:19	3068
now therefore unto me by the *L*	1Sa 24:21	3068
as the *L* liveth	1Sa 25:26	3068
seeing the *L* hath withholden thee	1Sa 25:26	3068
for the *L* will certainly make my	1Sa 25:28	3068
fighteth the battles of the *L*	1Sa 25:28	3068
bundle of life with the *L* thy God	1Sa 25:29	3068
when the *L* shall have done to my	1Sa 25:30	3068
but when the *L* shall have dealt	1Sa 25:31	3068
Blessed be the *L* God of Israel	1Sa 25:32	3068
as the *L* God of Israel liveth,	1Sa 25:34	3068
that the *L* smote Nabal, that he	1Sa 25:38	3068
dead, he said, Blessed be the *L*	1Sa 25:39	3068
for the *L* hath returned the	1Sa 25:39	3068
said furthermore, As the *L* liveth	1Sa 26:10	3068
the *L* shall smite him	1Sa 26:10	3068
The *L* forbid that I should	1Sa 26:11	3068
from the *L* was fallen upon them	1Sa 26:12	113
As the *L* liveth, ye are worthy to	1Sa 26:16	3068
If the *L* have stirred thee up	1Sa 26:19	3068
men, cursed be they before the *L*	1Sa 26:19	3068
in the inheritance of the *L*	1Sa 26:19	3068
earth before the face of the *L*	1Sa 26:20	3068
The *L* render to every man his	1Sa 26:23	3068
for the *L* delivered thee into my	1Sa 26:23	3068
much set by in the eyes of the *L*	1Sa 26:24	3068
And when Saul enquired of the *L*	1Sa 28:6	3068
the *L* answered him not, neither	1Sa 28:6	3068
the *L*, saying, As the *L* liveth	1Sa 28:10	3068
seeing the *L* is departed from	1Sa 28:16	3068
the *L* hath done to him, as he	1Sa 28:17	3068
for the *L* hath rent the kingdom	1Sa 28:17	3068
obeyedst not the voice of the *L*	1Sa 28:18	3068
therefore hath the *L* done this	1Sa 28:18	3068
Moreover the *L* will also deliver	1Sa 28:19	3068
the *L* also shall deliver the host	1Sa 28:19	3068
unto him, Surely, as the *L* liveth	1Sa 29:6	3068
himself in the *L* his God	1Sa 30:6	3068
And David enquired at the *L*	1Sa 30:8	3068
that which the *L* hath given us	1Sa 30:23	3068
the spoil of the enemies of the *L*	1Sa 30:26	3068
son, and for the people of the *L*	2Sa 1:12	3068
that David enquired of the *L*	2Sa 2:1	3068
the *L* said unto him, Go up	2Sa 2:1	3068
unto them, Blessed be ye of the *L*	2Sa 2:5	3068
now the *L* shew kindness and truth	2Sa 2:6	3068
as the *L* hath sworn to David,	2Sa 3:9	3068
for the *L* hath spoken of David,	2Sa 3:18	3068
are guiltless before the *L* for	2Sa 3:28	3068
the *L* shall reward the doer of	2Sa 3:39	3068
the *L* hath avenged my	2Sa 4:8	3068
said unto them, As the *L* liveth	2Sa 4:9	3068
the *L* said to thee, Thou shalt	2Sa 5:2	3068
with them in Hebron before the *L*	2Sa 5:3	3068
the *L* God of hosts was with him	2Sa 5:10	3068
David perceived that the *L* had	2Sa 5:12	3068
And David enquired of the *L*	2Sa 5:19	3068
the *L* said unto David, Go up	2Sa 5:19	3068
The *L* hath broken forth upon mine	2Sa 5:20	3068
And when David enquired of the *L*	2Sa 5:23	3068
shall the *L* go out before thee	2Sa 5:24	3068
as the *L* had commanded him	2Sa 5:25	3068
is called by the name of the *L* of	2Sa 6:2	3068
of Israel played before the *L* on	2Sa 6:5	3068
the anger of the *L* was kindled	2Sa 6:7	3068
because the *L* had made a breach	2Sa 6:8	3068
was afraid of the *L* that day	2Sa 6:9	3068
shall the ark of the *L* come to me	2Sa 6:9	3068
L unto him into the city of David	2Sa 6:10	3068
the ark of the *L* continued in the	2Sa 6:11	3068
the *L* blessed Obed-edom, and all	2Sa 6:11	3068
The *L* hath blessed the house of	2Sa 6:12	3068
ark of the *L* had gone six paces	2Sa 6:13	3068
before the *L* with all his might	2Sa 6:14	3068
up the ark of the *L* with shouting	2Sa 6:15	3068
as the ark of the *L* came into the	2Sa 6:16	3068
leaping and dancing before the *L*	2Sa 6:16	3068
they brought in the ark of the *L*	2Sa 6:17	3068
and peace offerings before the *L*	2Sa 6:17	3068
in the name of the *L* of hosts	2Sa 6:18	3068
unto Michal, It was before the *L*	2Sa 6:21	3068
me ruler over the people of the *L*	2Sa 6:21	3068
will I play before the *L*	2Sa 6:21	3068
the *L* had given him rest round	2Sa 7:1	3068
for the *L* is with thee	2Sa 7:3	3068
word of the *L* came unto Nathan	2Sa 7:4	3068
servant David, Thus saith the *L*	2Sa 7:5	3068
David, Thus saith the *L* of hosts	2Sa 7:8	3068
Also the *L* telleth thee that he	2Sa 7:11	3068
David in, and sat before the *L*	2Sa 7:18	3068
and he said, Who am I, O *L* GOD	2Sa 7:18	136
small thing in thy sight, O *L* GOD	2Sa 7:19	136
this the manner of man, O *L* GOD	2Sa 7:19	136
L GOD, knowest thy servant	2Sa 7:20	136
Wherefore thou art great, O *L* God	2Sa 7:22	3068
and thou, *L*, art become their God	2Sa 7:24	3068
O *L* God, the word that thou hast	2Sa 7:25	3068
The *L* of hosts is the God over	2Sa 7:26	3068
O *L* of hosts, God of Israel, hast	2Sa 7:27	3068
O *L* GOD, thou art that God, and	2Sa 7:28	136
for thou, O *L* GOD, hast spoken it	2Sa 7:29	136
And the *L* preserved David	2Sa 8:6	3068
David did dedicate unto the *L*	2Sa 8:11	3068
And the *L* preserved David	2Sa 8:14	3068
the *L* do that which seemeth him	2Sa 10:12	3068
David had done displeased the *L*	2Sa 11:27	3068
the *L* sent Nathan unto David	2Sa 12:1	3068
said to Nathan, As the *L* liveth	2Sa 12:5	3068
Thus saith the *L* God of Israel	2Sa 12:7	3068
despised the commandment of the *L*	2Sa 12:9	3068
Thus saith the *L*, Behold, I will	2Sa 12:11	3068
I have sinned against the *L*	2Sa 12:13	3068
The *L* also hath put away thy sin	2Sa 12:13	3068
the enemies of the *L* to blaspheme	2Sa 12:14	3068
the *L* struck the child that	2Sa 12:15	3068
and came into the house of the *L*	2Sa 12:20	3068
and the *L* loved him	2Sa 12:24	3068
name Jedidiah, because of the *L*	2Sa 12:25	3068
the king remember the *L* thy God	2Sa 14:11	3068
And he said, As the *L* liveth	2Sa 14:11	3068
therefore the *L* thy God will be	2Sa 14:17	3068
which I have vowed unto the *L*	2Sa 15:7	3068
If the *L* shall bring me again	2Sa 15:8	3068
then I will serve the *L*	2Sa 15:8	3068
king, and said, As the *L* liveth	2Sa 15:21	3068
find favour in the eyes of the *L*	2Sa 15:25	3068
And David said, O *L*, I pray thee,	2Sa 15:31	3068

The *L* hath returned upon thee all 2Sa 16:8 3068
the *L* hath delivered the kingdom 2Sa 16:8 3068
because the *L* hath said unto him, 2Sa 16:10 3068
for the *L* hath bidden him 2Sa 16:11 3068
It may be that the *L* will look on 2Sa 16:12 3068
that the *L* will requite me good 2Sa 16:12 3068
but whom the *L*, and this people, 2Sa 16:18 3068
For the *L* had appointed to defeat 2Sa 17:14 3068
to the intent that the *L* might 2Sa 17:14 3068
how that the *L* hath avenged him 2Sa 18:19 3068
and said, Blessed be the *L* thy God 2Sa 18:28 3068
for the *L* hath avenged thee this 2Sa 18:31 3068
for I swear by the *L*, if thou go 2Sa 19:7 3068
up the inheritance of the *L* 2Sa 20:19 3068
and David enquired of the *L* 2Sa 21:1 3068
the *L* answered, It is for Saul, 2Sa 21:1 3068
bless the inheritance of the *L* 2Sa 21:3 3068
up unto the *L* in Gibeah of Saul 2Sa 21:6 3068
of Saul, whom the *L* did choose 2Sa 21:6 3068
them in the hill before the *L* 2Sa 21:9 3068
David spake unto the *L* the words 2Sa 22:1 3068
in the day that the *L* had 2Sa 22:1 3068
The *L* is my rock, and my fortress, 2Sa 22:2 3068
I will call on the *L*, who is 2Sa 22:4 3068
my distress I called upon the *L* 2Sa 22:7 3068
The *L* thundered from heaven, and 2Sa 22:14 3068
at the rebuking of the *L* 2Sa 22:16 3068
but the *L* was my stay 2Sa 22:19 3068
The *L* rewarded me according to my 2Sa 22:21 3068
For I have kept the ways of the *L* 2Sa 22:22 3068
Therefore the *L* hath recompensed 2Sa 22:25 3068
For thou art my lamp, O *L* 2Sa 22:29 3068
the *L* will lighten my darkness 2Sa 22:29 3068
the word of the *L* is tried 2Sa 22:31 3068
For who is God, save the *L* 2Sa 22:32 3068
even unto the *L*, but he answered 2Sa 22:42 3068
The *L* liveth 2Sa 22:47 3068
I will give thanks unto thee, O *L* 2Sa 22:50 3068
The Spirit of the *L* spake by me 2Sa 23:2 3068
the *L* wrought a great victory 2Sa 23:10 3068
the *L* wrought a great victory 2Sa 23:12 3068
but poured it out unto the *L* 2Sa 23:16 3068
he said, Be it far from me, O *L* 2Sa 23:17 3068
again the anger of the *L* was 2Sa 24:1 3068
Now the *L* thy God add unto the 2Sa 24:3 3068
And David said unto the *L*, I have 2Sa 24:10 3068
and now, I beseech thee, O *L* 2Sa 24:10 3068
the word of the *L* came unto the 2Sa 24:11 3068
say unto David, Thus saith the *L* 2Sa 24:12 3068
fall now into the hand of the *L* 2Sa 24:14 3068
So the *L* sent a pestilence upon 2Sa 24:15 3068
the *L* repented him of the evil, 2Sa 24:16 3068
the angel of the *L* was by the 2Sa 24:16 3068
David spake unto the *L* when he 2Sa 24:17 3068
rear an altar unto the *L* in the 2Sa 24:18 3068
Gad, went up as the *L* commanded 2Sa 24:19 3068
to build an altar unto the *L* 2Sa 24:21 3068
The *L* thy God accept thee 2Sa 24:23 3068
L my God of that which doth cost 2Sa 24:24 3068
built there an altar unto the *L* 2Sa 24:25 3068
So the *L* was intreated for the 2Sa 24:25 3068
thou swarest by the *L* thy God 1Kin 1:17 3068
sware, and said, As the *L* liveth 1Kin 1:29 3068
unto thee by the *L* God of Israel 1Kin 1:30 3068
the *L* God of my 1Kin 1:36 3068
As the *L* hath been with my 1Kin 1:37 3068
Blessed be the *L* God of Israel 1Kin 1:48 3068
keep the charge of the *L* thy God 1Kin 2:3 3068
That the *L* may continue his word 1Kin 2:4 3068
and I sware to him by the *L* 1Kin 2:8 3068
for it was his from the *L* 1Kin 2:15 3068
Then king Solomon sware by the *L* 1Kin 2:23 3068
Now therefore, as the *L* liveth 1Kin 2:24 3068
the *L* GOD before David my father 1Kin 2:26 136
from being priest unto the *L* 1Kin 2:27 3068
he might fulfil the word of the *L* 1Kin 2:27 3068
fled unto the tabernacle of the *L* 1Kin 2:28 3068
fled unto the tabernacle of the *L* 1Kin 2:29 3068
came to the tabernacle of the *L* 1Kin 2:30 3068
the *L* shall return his blood upon 1Kin 2:32 3068
be peace for ever from the *L* 1Kin 2:33 3068
I not make thee to swear by the *L* 1Kin 2:42 3068
thou not kept the oath of the *L* 1Kin 2:43 3068
therefore the *L* shall return thy 1Kin 2:44 3068
established before the *L* for ever 1Kin 2:45 3068
own house, and the house of the *L* 1Kin 3:1 3068
built unto the name of the *L* 1Kin 3:2 3068
And Solomon loved the *L*, walking 1Kin 3:3 3068
In Gibeon the *L* appeared to 1Kin 3:5 3068
O *L* my God, thou hast made thy 1Kin 3:7 3068
And the speech pleased the *L* 1Kin 3:10 136
the ark of the covenant of the *L* 1Kin 3:15 3068
an house unto the name of the *L* 1Kin 5:3 3068
until the *L* put them under the 1Kin 5:3 3068
But now the *L* my God hath given 1Kin 5:4 3068
unto the name of the *L* my God 1Kin 5:5 3068
as the *L* spake unto David my 1Kin 5:5 3068
said, Blessed be the *L* this day 1Kin 5:7 3068
the *L* gave Solomon wisdom, as he 1Kin 5:12 3068
began to build the house of the *L* 1Kin 6:1 3068
king Solomon built for the *L* 1Kin 6:2 3068
the word of the *L* came to Solomon 1Kin 6:11 3068
the ark of the covenant of the *L* 1Kin 6:19 3068
of the house of the *L* laid 1Kin 6:37 3068
inner court of the house of the *L* 1Kin 7:12 3068
Solomon for the house of the *L* 1Kin 7:40 3068
Solomon for the house of the *L* 1Kin 7:45 3068
pertained unto the house of the *L* 1Kin 7:48 3068
made for the house of the *L* 1Kin 7:51 3068
treasures of the house of the *L* 1Kin 7:51 3068
of the *L* out of the city of David 1Kin 8:1 3068
they brought up the ark of the *L* 1Kin 8:4 3068
covenant of the *L* unto his place 1Kin 8:6 3068
when the *L* made a covenant with 1Kin 8:9 3068

cloud filled the house of the *L* 1Kin 8:10 3068
for the glory of the *L* had filled 1Kin 8:11 3068
had filled the house of the *L* 1Kin 8:11 3068
The *L* said that he would dwell in 1Kin 8:12 3068
Blessed be the *L* God of Israel 1Kin 8:15 3068
the name of the *L* God of Israel 1Kin 8:17 3068
the *L* said unto David my father, 1Kin 8:18 3068
the *L* hath performed his word 1Kin 8:20 3068
as the *L* promised, and have built 1Kin 8:20 3068
the name of the *L* God of Israel 1Kin 8:20 3068
wherein is the covenant of the *L* 1Kin 8:21 3068
the *L* in the presence of all the 1Kin 8:22 3068
L God of Israel, there is no God 1Kin 8:23 3068
L God of Israel, keep with thy 1Kin 8:25 3068
O *L* my God, to hearken unto the 1Kin 8:28 3068
shall pray unto the *L* toward the 1Kin 8:44 3068
our fathers out of Egypt, O *L* GOD 1Kin 8:53 136
prayer and supplication unto the *L* 1Kin 8:54 3068
from before the altar of the *L* 1Kin 8:54 3068
Blessed be the *L*, that hath given 1Kin 8:56 3068
The *L* our God be with us, as he 1Kin 8:57 3068
made supplication before the *L* 1Kin 8:59 3068
be nigh unto the *L* our God day 1Kin 8:59 3068
earth may know that the *L* is God 1Kin 8:60 3068
be perfect with the *L* our God 1Kin 8:61 3068
offered sacrifice before the *L* 1Kin 8:62 3068
which he offered unto the *L* 1Kin 8:63 3068
dedicated the house of the *L* 1Kin 8:63 3068
was before the house of the *L* 1Kin 8:64 3068
altar that was before the *L* was 1Kin 8:64 3068
of Egypt, before the *L* our God 1Kin 8:65 3068
for all the goodness that the *L* 1Kin 8:66 3068
building of the house of the *L* 1Kin 9:1 3068
That the *L* appeared to Solomon 1Kin 9:2 3068
the *L* said unto him, I have heard 1Kin 9:3 3068
Why hath the *L* done thus unto 1Kin 9:8 3068
they forsook the *L* their God 1Kin 9:9 3068
therefore hath the *L* brought upon 1Kin 9:9 3068
two houses, the house of the *L* 1Kin 9:10 3068
for to build the house of the *L* 1Kin 9:15 3068
altar which he built unto the *L* 1Kin 9:25 3068
the altar that was before the *L* 1Kin 9:25 3068
concerning the name of the *L* 1Kin 10:1 3068
went up unto the house of the *L* 1Kin 10:5 3068
Blessed be the *L* thy God, which 1Kin 10:9 3068
because the *L* loved Israel for 1Kin 10:9 3068
pillars for the house of the *L* 1Kin 10:12 3068
the *L* said unto the children of 1Kin 11:2 3068
not perfect with the *L* his God 1Kin 11:4 3068
did evil in the sight of the *L* 1Kin 11:6 3068
and went not fully after the *L* 1Kin 11:6 3068
the *L* was angry with Solomon, 1Kin 11:9 3068
turned from the *L* God of Israel 1Kin 11:9 3068
not that which the *L* commanded 1Kin 11:10 3068
Wherefore the *L* said unto Solomon 1Kin 11:11 3068
the *L* stirred up an adversary 1Kin 11:14 3068
for thus saith the *L*, the God of 1Kin 11:31 3068
for the cause was from the *L* 1Kin 12:15 3068
which the *L* spake by Ahijah the 1Kin 12:15 3068
Thus saith the *L*, Ye shall not go 1Kin 12:24 3068
therefore to the word of the *L* 1Kin 12:24 3068
according to the word of the *L* 1Kin 12:24 3068
the house of the *L* at Jerusalem 1Kin 12:27 3068
by the word of the *L* unto Beth-el 1Kin 13:1 3068
the altar in the word of the *L* 1Kin 13:2 3068
O altar, altar, thus saith the *L* 1Kin 13:2 3068
the sign which the *L* hath spoken 1Kin 13:3 3068
had given by the word of the *L* 1Kin 13:5 3068
now the face of the *L* thy God 1Kin 13:6 3068
And the man of God besought the *L* 1Kin 13:6 3068
charged me by the word of the *L* 1Kin 13:9 3068
said to me by the word of the *L* 1Kin 13:17 3068
unto me by the word of the *L* 1Kin 13:18 3068
that the word of the *L* came unto 1Kin 13:20 3068
Judah, saying, Thus saith the *L* 1Kin 13:21 3068
hast disobeyed the mouth of the *L* 1Kin 13:21 3068
the *L* thy God commanded thee 1Kin 13:21 3068
the which the *L* did say to thee 1Kin 13:22
unto the word of the *L* 1Kin 13:26 3068
therefore the *L* hath delivered 1Kin 13:26 3068
according to the word of the *L* 1Kin 13:26 3068
he cried by the word of the *L* 1Kin 13:32 3068
the *L* said unto Ahijah, Behold, 1Kin 14:5 3068
Thus saith the *L* God of Israel 1Kin 14:7 3068
for the *L* hath spoken it 1Kin 14:11 3068
some good thing toward the *L* God 1Kin 14:13 3068
Moreover the *L* shall raise him up 1Kin 14:14 3068
For the *L* shall smite Israel, as 1Kin 14:15 3068
groves, provoking the *L* to anger 1Kin 14:15 3068
according to the word of the *L* 1Kin 14:18 3068
the city which the *L* did choose 1Kin 14:21 3068
did evil in the sight of the *L* 1Kin 14:22 3068
of the nations which the *L* cast 1Kin 14:24 3068
treasures of the house of the *L* 1Kin 14:26 3068
king went into the house of the *L* 1Kin 14:28 3068
not perfect with the *L* his God 1Kin 15:3 3068
for David's sake did the *L* his 1Kin 15:4 3068
was right in the eyes of the *L* 1Kin 15:5 3068
was right in the eyes of the *L* 1Kin 15:11 3068
perfect with the *L* all his days 1Kin 15:14 3068
into the house of the *L*, silver, 1Kin 15:15 3068
treasures of the house of the *L* 1Kin 15:18 3068
he did evil in the sight of the *L* 1Kin 15:26 3068
unto the saying of the *L*, which 1Kin 15:29 3068
the *L* God of Israel to anger 1Kin 15:30 3068
he did evil in the sight of the *L* 1Kin 15:34 3068
Then the word of the *L* came to 1Kin 16:1 3068
the word of the *L* against Baasha 1Kin 16:7 3068
that he did in the sight of the *L* 1Kin 16:7 3068
according to the word of the *L* 1Kin 16:12 3068
in provoking the *L* God of Israel 1Kin 16:13 3068
doing evil in the sight of the *L* 1Kin 16:19 3068
wrought evil in the eyes of the *L* 1Kin 16:25 3068
to provoke the *L* God of Israel to 1Kin 16:26 3068

did evil in the sight of the *L* 1Kin 16:30 3068
Ahab did more to provoke the *L* 1Kin 16:33 3068
according to the word of the *L* 1Kin 16:34 3068
As the *L* God of Israel liveth, 1Kin 17:1 3068
the word of the *L* came unto him 1Kin 17:2 3068
according unto the word of the *L* 1Kin 17:5 3068
the word of the *L* came unto him 1Kin 17:8 3068
As the *L* thy God liveth, I have 1Kin 17:12 3068
thus saith the *L* God of Israel 1Kin 17:14 3068
until the day that the *L* sendeth 1Kin 17:14 3068
according to the word of the *L* 1Kin 17:16 3068
And he cried unto the *L*, and said, 1Kin 17:20 3068
O *L* my God, hast thou also 1Kin 17:20 3068
three times, and cried unto the *L* 1Kin 17:21 3068
O *L* my God, I pray thee, let this 1Kin 17:21 3068
the *L* heard the voice of Elijah 1Kin 17:22 3068
that the word of the *L* in thy 1Kin 17:24 3068
that the word of the *L* came to 1Kin 18:1 3068
(Now Obadiah feared the *L* greatly 1Kin 18:3 3068
cut off the prophets of the *L* 1Kin 18:4 3068
As the *L* thy God liveth, there is 1Kin 18:10 3068
that the Spirit of the *L* shall 1Kin 18:12 3068
servant fear the *L* from my youth 1Kin 18:12 3068
slew the prophets of the *L* 1Kin 18:13 3068
As the *L* of hosts liveth, before 1Kin 18:15 3068
the commandments of the *L* 1Kin 18:18 3068
if the *L* be God, follow him 1Kin 18:21 3068
I only, remain a prophet of the *L* 1Kin 18:22 3068
I will call on the name of the *L* 1Kin 18:24 3068
of the *L* that was broken down 1Kin 18:30 3068
unto whom the word of the *L* came 1Kin 18:31 3068
an altar in the name of the *L* 1Kin 18:32 3068
L God of Abraham, Isaac, and of 1Kin 18:36 3068
Hear me, O *L*, hear me, that this 1Kin 18:37 3068
may know that thou art the *L* God 1Kin 18:37 3068
Then the fire of the *L* fell 1Kin 18:38 3068
and they said, The *L*, he is the 1Kin 18:39 3068
the *L*, he is the God 1Kin 18:39 3068
the hand of the *L* was on Elijah 1Kin 18:46 3068
now, O *L*, take away my life 1Kin 19:4 3068
the angel of the *L* came again the 1Kin 19:7 3068
the word of the *L* came to him 1Kin 19:9 3068
jealous for the *L* God of hosts 1Kin 19:10 3068
stand upon the mount before the *L* 1Kin 19:11 3068
the *L* passed by, and a great and 1Kin 19:11 3068
in pieces the rocks before the *L* 1Kin 19:11 3068
but the *L* was not in the wind 1Kin 19:11 3068
but the *L* was not in the 1Kin 19:11 3068
but the *L* was not in the fire 1Kin 19:12 3068
jealous for the *L* God of hosts 1Kin 19:14 3068
the *L* said unto him, Go, return 1Kin 19:15 3068
Israel, saying, Thus saith the *L* 1Kin 20:13 3068
thou shalt know that I am the *L* 1Kin 20:13 3068
And he said, Thus saith the *L* 1Kin 20:14 3068
Israel, and said, Thus saith the *L* 1Kin 20:28 3068
The *L* is God of the hills, but he 1Kin 20:28 3068
and ye shall know that I am the *L* 1Kin 20:28 3068
neighbour in the word of the *L* 1Kin 20:35 3068
not obeyed the voice of the *L* 1Kin 20:36 3068
said unto him, Thus saith the *L* 1Kin 20:42 3068
The *L* forbid it me, that I should 1Kin 21:3 3068
the word of the *L* came to Elijah 1Kin 21:17 3068
him, saying, Thus saith the *L* 1Kin 21:19 3068
him, saying, Thus saith the *L* 1Kin 21:19 3068
work evil in the sight of the *L* 1Kin 21:20 3068
And of Jezebel also spake the *L* 1Kin 21:23 3068
wickedness in the sight of the *L* 1Kin 21:25 3068
whom the *L* cast out before the 1Kin 21:26 3068
the word of the *L* came to Elijah 1Kin 21:28 3068
thee, at the word of the *L* to day 1Kin 22:5 3068
for the *L* shall deliver it into 1Kin 22:6 136
here a prophet of the *L* besides 1Kin 22:7 3068
by whom we may enquire of the *L* 1Kin 22:8 3068
and he said, Thus saith the *L* 1Kin 22:11 3068
for the *L* shall deliver it into 1Kin 22:12 3068
And Micaiah said, As the *L* liveth 1Kin 22:14 3068
what the *L* saith unto me, that 1Kin 22:14 3068
for the *L* shall deliver it into 1Kin 22:15 3068
is true in the name of the *L* 1Kin 22:16 3068
the *L* said, These have no master 1Kin 22:17 3068
thou therefore the word of the *L* 1Kin 22:19 3068
I saw the *L* sitting on his throne 1Kin 22:19 3068
the *L* said, Who shall persuade 1Kin 22:20 3068
a spirit, and stood before the *L* 1Kin 22:21 3068
the *L* said unto him, Wherewith 1Kin 22:22 3068
the *L* hath put a lying spirit in 1Kin 22:23 3068
the *L* hath spoken evil concerning 1Kin 22:23 3068
the *L* from me to speak unto thee 1Kin 22:24 3068
the *L* hath not spoken by me 1Kin 22:28 3068
the word of the *L* which he spake 1Kin 22:38 3068
was right in the eyes of the *L* 1Kin 22:43 3068
he did evil in the sight of the *L* 1Kin 22:52 3068
to anger the *L* God of Israel 1Kin 22:53 3068
But the angel of the *L* said to 2Kin 1:3 3068
Now therefore thus saith the *L* 2Kin 1:4 3068
and say unto him, Thus saith the *L* 2Kin 1:6 3068
angel of the *L* said unto Elijah 2Kin 1:15 3068
said unto him, Thus saith the *L* 2Kin 1:16 3068
of the *L* which Elijah had spoken 2Kin 1:17 3068
when the *L* would take up Elijah 2Kin 2:1 3068
for the *L* hath sent me to Beth-el 2Kin 2:2 3068
said unto him, As the *L* liveth 2Kin 2:2 3068
Knowest thou that the *L* will take 2Kin 2:3 3068
for the *L* hath sent me to Jericho 2Kin 2:4 3068
And he said, As the *L* liveth 2Kin 2:4 3068
Knowest thou that the *L* will take 2Kin 2:5 3068
for the *L* hath sent me to Jordan 2Kin 2:6 3068
And he said, As the *L* liveth 2Kin 2:6 3068
Where is the *L* God of Elijah 2Kin 2:14 3068
Spirit of the *L* hath taken him up 2Kin 2:16 3068
there, and said, Thus saith the *L* 2Kin 2:21 3068
cursed them in the name of the *L* 2Kin 2:24 3068
evil in the sight of the *L* 2Kin 3:2 3068
that the *L* hath called these 2Kin 3:10 3068

Context	Reference	Strong's
there not here a prophet of the L	2Kin 3:11	3068
we may enquire of the L by him	2Kin 3:11	3068
The word of the L is with him	2Kin 3:12	3068
for the L hath called these three	2Kin 3:13	3068
As the L of hosts liveth, before	2Kin 3:14	3068
the hand of the L came upon him	2Kin 3:15	3068
And he said, Thus saith the L	2Kin 3:16	3068
For thus saith the L, Ye shall	2Kin 3:17	3068
light thing in the sight of the L	2Kin 3:18	3068
that thy servant did fear the L	2Kin 4:1	3068
the L hath hid it from me, and	2Kin 4:27	3068
the child said, As the L liveth	2Kin 4:30	3068
them twain, and prayed unto the L	2Kin 4:33	3068
for thus saith the L, They shall	2Kin 4:43	3068
according to the word of the L	2Kin 4:44	3068
because by him the L had given	2Kin 5:1	3068
call on the name of the L his God	2Kin 5:11	3068
But he said, As the L liveth	2Kin 5:16	3068
unto other gods, but unto the L	2Kin 5:17	3068
In this thing the L pardon thy	2Kin 5:18	3068
the L pardon thy servant in this	2Kin 5:18	3068
but, as the L liveth, I will run	2Kin 5:20	3068
And Elisha prayed, and said, L	2Kin 6:17	3068
the L opened the eyes of the	2Kin 6:17	3068
to him, Elisha prayed unto the L	2Kin 6:18	3068
into Samaria, that Elisha said, L	2Kin 6:20	3068
the L opened their eyes, and they	2Kin 6:20	3068
If the L do not help thee, whence	2Kin 6:27	3068
Behold, this evil is of the L	2Kin 6:33	3068
I wait for the L any longer	2Kin 6:33	3068
said, Hear ye the word of the L	2Kin 7:1	3068
Thus saith the L, To morrow about	2Kin 7:1	3068
if the L would make windows in	2Kin 7:2	3068
For the L had made the host of	2Kin 7:6	136
according to the word of the L	2Kin 7:16	3068
if the L should make windows in	2Kin 7:19	3068
for the L hath called for a	2Kin 8:1	3068
God, and enquire of the L by him	2Kin 8:8	3068
howbeit the L hath shewed me that	2Kin 8:10	3068
The L hath shewed me that thou	2Kin 8:13	3068
he did evil in the sight of the L	2Kin 8:18	3068
Yet the L would not destroy Judah	2Kin 8:19	3068
and did evil in the sight of the L	2Kin 8:27	3068
head, and say, Thus saith the L	2Kin 9:3	3068
Thus saith the L God of Israel	2Kin 9:6	3068
king over the people of the L	2Kin 9:6	3068
of all the servants of the L	2Kin 9:7	3068
to me, saying, Thus saith the L	2Kin 9:12	3068
the L laid this burden upon him	2Kin 9:25	3068
blood of his sons, saith the L	2Kin 9:26	3068
thee in this plat, saith the L	2Kin 9:26	3068
according to the word of the L	2Kin 9:26	3068
said, This is the word of the L	2Kin 9:36	3068
nothing of the word of the L	2Kin 10:10	3068
which the L spake concerning the	2Kin 10:10	3068
for the L hath done that which he	2Kin 10:10	3068
with me, and see my zeal for the L	2Kin 10:16	3068
according to the saying of the L	2Kin 10:17	3068
you none of the servants of the L	2Kin 10:23	3068
the L said unto Jehu, Because	2Kin 10:30	3068
the L God of Israel with all his	2Kin 10:31	3068
In those days the L began to cut	2Kin 10:32	3068
in the house of the L six years	2Kin 11:3	3068
to him into the house of the L	2Kin 11:4	3068
of them in the house of the L	2Kin 11:4	3068
the house of the L about the king	2Kin 11:7	3068
that were in the temple of the L	2Kin 11:10	3068
people into the temple of the L	2Kin 11:13	3068
be slain in the house of the L	2Kin 11:15	3068
made a covenant between the L	2Kin 11:17	3068
officers over the house of the L	2Kin 11:18	3068
the king from the house of the L	2Kin 11:19	3068
L all his days wherein Jehoiada	2Kin 12:2	3068
brought into the house of the L	2Kin 12:4	3068
to bring into the house of the L	2Kin 12:4	3068
cometh into the house of the L	2Kin 12:9	3068
brought into the house of the L	2Kin 12:9	3068
was found in the house of the L	2Kin 12:10	3068
oversight of the house of the L	2Kin 12:11	3068
wrought upon the house of the L	2Kin 12:11	3068
breaches of the house of the L	2Kin 12:12	3068
house of the L bowls of silver	2Kin 12:13	3068
brought into the house of the L	2Kin 12:13	3068
therewith the house of the L	2Kin 12:14	3068
brought into the house of the L	2Kin 12:16	3068
treasures of the house of the L	2Kin 12:18	3068
was evil in the sight of the L	2Kin 13:2	3068
the anger of the L was kindled	2Kin 13:3	3068
And Jehoahaz besought the L	2Kin 13:4	3068
and the L hearkened unto him	2Kin 13:4	3068
the L gave Israel a saviour, so	2Kin 13:5	3068
was evil in the sight of the L	2Kin 13:11	3068
the L was gracious unto them, and	2Kin 13:23	3068
was right in the sight of the L	2Kin 14:3	3068
of Moses, wherein the L commanded	2Kin 14:6	3068
were found in the house of the L	2Kin 14:14	3068
was evil in the sight of the L	2Kin 14:24	3068
the word of the L God of Israel	2Kin 14:25	3068
For the L saw the affliction of	2Kin 14:26	3068
the L said not that he would blot	2Kin 14:27	3068
was right in the sight of the L	2Kin 15:3	3068
the L smote the king, so that he	2Kin 15:5	3068
was evil in the sight of the L	2Kin 15:9	3068
of the L which he spake unto Jehu	2Kin 15:12	3068
was evil in the sight of the L	2Kin 15:18	3068
was evil in the sight of the L	2Kin 15:24	3068
was evil in the sight of the L	2Kin 15:28	3068
was right in the sight of the L	2Kin 15:34	3068
higher gate of the house of the L	2Kin 15:35	3068
In those days the L began to send	2Kin 15:37	3068
in the sight of the L his God	2Kin 16:2	3068
whom the L cast out from before	2Kin 16:3	3068
was found in the house of the L	2Kin 16:8	3068
altar, which was before the L	2Kin 16:14	3068
the altar and the house of the L	2Kin 16:14	3068
of the L for the king of Assyria	2Kin 16:18	3068
was evil in the sight of the L	2Kin 17:2	3068
sinned against the L their God	2Kin 17:7	3068
whom the L cast out from before	2Kin 17:8	3068
not right against the L their God	2Kin 17:9	3068
the L carried away before them	2Kin 17:11	3068
things to provoke the L to anger	2Kin 17:11	3068
whereof the L had said unto them,	2Kin 17:12	3068
Yet the L testified against	2Kin 17:13	3068
not believe in the L their God	2Kin 17:14	3068
whom the L had charged them	2Kin 17:15	3068
commandments of the L their God	2Kin 17:16	3068
to do evil in the sight of the L	2Kin 17:17	3068
Therefore the L was very angry	2Kin 17:18	3068
commandments of the L their God	2Kin 17:19	3068
the L rejected all the seed of	2Kin 17:20	3068
drave Israel from following the L	2Kin 17:21	3068
Until the L removed Israel out of	2Kin 17:23	3068
there, that they feared not the L	2Kin 17:25	3068
therefore the L sent lions among	2Kin 17:25	3068
them how they should fear the L	2Kin 17:28	3068
So they feared the L, and made	2Kin 17:32	3068
They feared the L, and served	2Kin 17:33	3068
they fear not the L, neither do	2Kin 17:34	3068
commandment which the L	2Kin 17:34	3068
With whom the L had made a	2Kin 17:35	3068
But the L, who brought you up out	2Kin 17:36	3068
But the L your God ye shall fear	2Kin 17:39	3068
So these nations feared the L	2Kin 17:41	3068
was right in the sight of the L	2Kin 18:3	3068
He trusted in the L God of Israel	2Kin 18:5	3068
For he clave to the L, and	2Kin 18:6	3068
which the L commanded Moses	2Kin 18:6	3068
And the L was with him	2Kin 18:7	3068
not the voice of the L their God	2Kin 18:12	3068
the servant of the L commanded	2Kin 18:12	3068
was found in the house of the L	2Kin 18:15	3068
the doors of the temple of the L	2Kin 18:16	3068
me, We trust in the L our God	2Kin 18:22	3068
Am I now come up without the L	2Kin 18:25	3068
The L said to me, Go up against	2Kin 18:25	3068
Hezekiah make you trust in the L	2Kin 18:30	3068
The L will surely deliver us, and	2Kin 18:30	3068
saying, The L will deliver us	2Kin 18:32	3068
that the L should deliver	2Kin 18:35	3068
and went into the house of the L	2Kin 19:1	3068
It may be the L thy God will hear	2Kin 19:4	3068
which the L thy God hath heard	2Kin 19:4	3068
to your master, Thus saith the L	2Kin 19:6	3068
went up into the house of the L	2Kin 19:14	3068
and spread it before the L	2Kin 19:14	3068
And Hezekiah prayed before the L	2Kin 19:15	3068
O L God of Israel, which dwellest	2Kin 19:15	3068
L, bow down thine ear, and hear	2Kin 19:16	3068
open, L, thine eyes, and see	2Kin 19:16	3068
Of a truth, L, the kings of	2Kin 19:17	3068
O L our God, I beseech thee, save	2Kin 19:19	3068
may know that thou art the L God	2Kin 19:19	3068
Thus saith the L God of Israel	2Kin 19:20	3068
This is the word that the L hath	2Kin 19:21	3068
thou hast reproached the L	2Kin 19:23	3068
the zeal of the L of hosts shall	2Kin 19:31	3068
Therefore thus saith the L	2Kin 19:32	3068
come into this city, saith the L	2Kin 19:33	3068
that the angel of the L went out	2Kin 19:35	3068
said unto him, Thus saith the L	2Kin 20:1	3068
to the wall, and prayed unto the L	2Kin 20:2	3068
I beseech thee, O L, remember now	2Kin 20:3	3068
the word of the L came to him	2Kin 20:4	3068
of my people, Thus saith the L	2Kin 20:5	3068
go up unto the house of the L	2Kin 20:5	3068
the sign that the L will heal me	2Kin 20:8	3068
the house of the L the third day	2Kin 20:8	3068
sign shalt thou have of the L	2Kin 20:9	3068
that the L will do the thing that	2Kin 20:9	3068
the prophet cried unto the L	2Kin 20:11	3068
Hezekiah, Hear the word of the L	2Kin 20:16	3068
shall be left, saith the L	2Kin 20:17	3068
of the L which thou hast spoken	2Kin 20:19	3068
was evil in the sight of the L	2Kin 21:2	3068
whom the L cast out before the	2Kin 21:2	3068
of the L, of which the L said	2Kin 21:4	3068
two courts of the house of the L	2Kin 21:5	3068
wickedness in the sight of the L	2Kin 21:6	3068
of which the L said to David, and	2Kin 21:7	3068
L destroyed before the children	2Kin 21:9	3068
the L spake by his servants the	2Kin 21:10	3068
thus saith the L God of Israel	2Kin 21:12	3068
was evil in the sight of the L	2Kin 21:16	3068
was evil in the sight of the L	2Kin 21:20	3068
he forsook the L God of his	2Kin 21:22	3068
and walked not in the way of the L	2Kin 21:22	3068
was right in the sight of the L	2Kin 22:2	3068
the scribe, to the house of the L	2Kin 22:3	3068
brought into the house of the L	2Kin 22:4	3068
oversight of the house of the L	2Kin 22:5	3068
which is in the house of the L	2Kin 22:5	3068
of the law in the house of the L	2Kin 22:8	3068
oversight of the house of the L	2Kin 22:9	3068
Go ye, enquire of the L for me	2Kin 22:13	3068
the L that is kindled against us	2Kin 22:13	3068
Thus saith the L God of Israel	2Kin 22:15	3068
Thus saith the L, Behold, I will	2Kin 22:16	3068
sent you to enquire of the L	2Kin 22:18	3068
Thus saith the L God of Israel	2Kin 22:18	3068
hast humbled thyself before the L	2Kin 22:19	3068
also have heard thee, saith the L	2Kin 22:19	3068
went up into the house of the L	2Kin 23:2	3068
was found in the house of the L	2Kin 23:2	3068
and made a covenant before the L	2Kin 23:3	3068
to walk after the L	2Kin 23:3	3068
L all the vessels that were made	2Kin 23:4	3068
the grove from the house of the L	2Kin 23:6	3068
that were by the house of the L	2Kin 23:7	3068
the altar of the L in Jerusalem	2Kin 23:9	3068
entering in of the house of the L	2Kin 23:11	3068
two courts of the house of the L	2Kin 23:12	3068
according to the word of the L	2Kin 23:16	3068
made to provoke the L to anger	2Kin 23:19	
the passover unto the L your God	2Kin 23:21	3068
was holden to the L in Jerusalem	2Kin 23:23	3068
found in the house of the L	2Kin 23:24	3068
to the L with all his heart	2Kin 23:25	3068
Notwithstanding the L turned not	2Kin 23:26	3068
the L said, I will remove Judah	2Kin 23:27	3068
was evil in the sight of the L	2Kin 23:32	3068
was evil in the sight of the L	2Kin 23:37	3068
the L sent against him bands of	2Kin 24:2	3068
according to the word of the L	2Kin 24:2	3068
of the L came this upon Judah	2Kin 24:3	3068
which the L would not pardon	2Kin 24:4	3068
was evil in the sight of the L	2Kin 24:9	3068
treasures of the house of the L	2Kin 24:13	3068
had made in the temple of the L	2Kin 24:13	3068
as the L had said	2Kin 24:13	3068
was evil in the sight of the L	2Kin 24:19	3068
L it came to pass in Jerusalem	2Kin 24:20	3068
And he burnt the house of the L	2Kin 25:9	3068
that were in the house of the L	2Kin 25:13	3068
that was in the house of the L	2Kin 25:13	3068
had made for the house of the L	2Kin 25:16	3068
was evil in the sight of the L	1Chr 2:3	3068
when the L carried away Judah and	1Chr 6:15	3068
of song in the house of the L	1Chr 6:31	3068
the house of the L in Jerusalem	1Chr 6:32	3068
being over the host of the L	1Chr 9:19	3068
time past, and the L was with him	1Chr 9:20	3068
the gates of the house of the L	1Chr 9:23	3068
which he committed against the L	1Chr 10:13	3068
even against the word of the L	1Chr 10:13	3068
And enquired not of the L	1Chr 10:14	3068
the L thy God said unto thee,	1Chr 11:2	3068
with them in Hebron before the L	1Chr 11:3	3068
to the word of the L by Samuel	1Chr 11:3	3068
for the L of hosts was with him	1Chr 11:9	3068
word of the L concerning Israel	1Chr 11:10	3068
the L saved them by a great	1Chr 11:14	3068
of it, but poured it out to the L	1Chr 11:18	3068
according to the word of the L	1Chr 12:23	3068
and that it be of the L our God	1Chr 13:2	3068
up thence the ark of God the L	1Chr 13:6	3068
the anger of the L was kindled	1Chr 13:10	3068
because the L had made a breach	1Chr 13:11	3068
the L blessed the house of	1Chr 13:14	3068
David perceived that the L had	1Chr 14:2	3068
the L said unto him, Go up	1Chr 14:10	3068
the L brought the fear of him	1Chr 14:17	3068
for them hath the L chosen to	1Chr 15:2	3068
the ark of the L unto his place	1Chr 15:3	3068
L God of Israel unto the place	1Chr 15:12	3068
the L our God made a breach upon	1Chr 15:13	3068
up the ark of the L God of Israel	1Chr 15:14	3068
according to the word of the L	1Chr 15:15	3068
L out of the house of Obed-edom	1Chr 15:25	3068
the ark of the covenant of the L	1Chr 15:26	3068
covenant of the L with shouting	1Chr 15:28	3068
the L came to the city of David	1Chr 15:29	3068
the people in the name of the L	1Chr 16:2	3068
minister before the ark of the L	1Chr 16:4	3068
praise the L God of Israel	1Chr 16:4	3068
the L into the hand of Asaph	1Chr 16:7	3068
Give thanks unto the L, call upon	1Chr 16:8	3068
of them rejoice that seek the L	1Chr 16:10	3068
Seek the L and his strength, seek	1Chr 16:11	3068
He is the L our God	1Chr 16:14	3068
Sing unto the L, all the earth	1Chr 16:23	3068
For great is the L, and greatly to	1Chr 16:25	3068
but the L made the heavens	1Chr 16:26	3068
Give unto the L, ye kindreds of	1Chr 16:28	3068
the people, give unto the L glory	1Chr 16:28	3068
Give unto the L the glory due	1Chr 16:29	3068
worship the L in the beauty of	1Chr 16:29	3068
among the nations, The L reigneth	1Chr 16:31	3068
sing out at the presence of the L	1Chr 16:33	3068
O give thanks unto the L	1Chr 16:34	3068
Blessed be the L God of Israel	1Chr 16:36	3068
said, Amen, and praised the L	1Chr 16:36	3068
of the covenant of the L Asaph	1Chr 16:37	3068
before the tabernacle of the L in	1Chr 16:39	3068
the L upon the altar of the burnt	1Chr 16:40	3068
is written in the law of the L	1Chr 16:40	3068
by name, to give thanks to the L	1Chr 16:41	3068
of the L remaineth under curtains	1Chr 17:1	3068
my servant, Thus saith the L	1Chr 17:4	3068
David, Thus saith the L of hosts	1Chr 17:7	3068
I tell thee that the L will build	1Chr 17:10	3068
the king came and sat before the L	1Chr 17:16	3068
O L God, and what is mine house,	1Chr 17:16	3068
of a man of high degree, O L God	1Chr 17:17	3068
O L, for thy servant's sake, and	1Chr 17:19	3068
O L, there is none like thee,	1Chr 17:20	3068
and thou, L, becamest their God	1Chr 17:22	3068
Therefore now, L, let the thing	1Chr 17:23	3068
The L of hosts is the God of	1Chr 17:24	3068
And now, L, thou art God, and hast	1Chr 17:26	3068
for thou blessest, O L, and it	1Chr 17:27	3068
Thus the L preserved David	1Chr 18:6	3068
king David dedicated unto the L	1Chr 18:11	3068
Thus the L preserved David	1Chr 18:13	3068
let the L do that which is good	1Chr 19:13	3068
The L make his people an hundred	1Chr 21:3	3068
the L spake unto Gad, David's	1Chr 21:9	3068
David, saying, Thus saith the L	1Chr 21:10	3068
said unto him, Thus saith the L	1Chr 21:11	3068
three days the sword of the L	1Chr 21:12	3068
the angel of the L destroying	1Chr 21:12	3068
fall now into the hand of the L	1Chr 21:13	3068

So the *L* sent pestilence upon 1Chr 21:14 3068
the *L* beheld, and he repented him 1Chr 21:15 3068
the angel of the *L* stood by the 1Chr 21:15 3068
saw the angel of the *L* stand 1Chr 21:16 3068
O *L* my God, be on me, and on my 1Chr 21:17 3068
Then the angel of the *L* commanded 1Chr 21:18 3068
set up an altar unto the *L* in the 1Chr 21:18 3068
he spake in the name of the *L* 1Chr 21:19 3068
build an altar therein unto the *L* 1Chr 21:22 3068
that which is thine for the *L* 1Chr 21:24 3068
built there an altar unto the *L* 1Chr 21:26 3068
offerings, and called upon the *L* 1Chr 21:26 3068
the *L* commanded the angel 1Chr 21:27 3068
the *L* had answered him in the 1Chr 21:28 3068
For the tabernacle of the *L* 1Chr 21:29 3068
the sword of the angel of the *L* 1Chr 21:30 3068
This is the house of the *L* God 1Chr 22:1 3068
L must be exceeding magnifical 1Chr 22:5 3068
an house for the *L* God of Israel 1Chr 22:6 3068
unto the name of the *L* my God 1Chr 22:7 3068
But the word of the *L* came to me 1Chr 22:8 3068
Now, my son, the *L* be with thee 1Chr 22:11 3068
build the house of the *L* thy God 1Chr 22:11 3068
Only the *L* give thee wisdom and 1Chr 22:12 3068
keep the law of the *L* thy God 1Chr 22:12 3068
judgments which the *L* charged 1Chr 22:13 3068
prepared for the house of the *L* 1Chr 22:14 3068
be doing, and the *L* be with thee 1Chr 22:16 3068
Is not the *L* your God with you 1Chr 22:18 3068
the land is subdued before the *L* 1Chr 22:18 3068
your soul to seek the *L* your God 1Chr 22:19 3068
ye the sanctuary of the *L* God 1Chr 22:19 3068
the ark of the covenant of the *L* 1Chr 22:19 3068
to be built to the name of the *L* 1Chr 22:19 3068
the work of the house of the *L* 1Chr 23:4 3068
four thousand praised the *L* with 1Chr 23:5 3068
to burn incense before the *L* 1Chr 23:13 3068
the service of the house of the *L* 1Chr 23:24 3068
The *L* God of Israel hath given 1Chr 23:25 3068
the service of the house of the *L* 1Chr 23:28 3068
morning to thank and praise the *L* 1Chr 23:30 3068
unto the *L* in the sabbaths 1Chr 23:31 3068
them, continually before the *L* 1Chr 23:31 3068
the service of the house of the *L* 1Chr 23:32 3068
to come into the house of the *L* 1Chr 24:19 3068
as the *L* God of Israel had 1Chr 24:19 3068
to give thanks and to praise the *L* 1Chr 25:3 3068
for song in the house of the *L* 1Chr 25:6 3068
instructed in the songs of the *L* 1Chr 25:7 3068
to minister in the house of the *L* 1Chr 26:12 3068
treasures of the house of the *L* 1Chr 26:22 3068
to maintain the house of the *L* 1Chr 26:27 3068
in all the business of the *L* 1Chr 26:30 3068
because the *L* had said he would 1Chr 27:23 3068
the ark of the covenant of the *L* 1Chr 28:2 3068
Howbeit the *L* God of Israel chose 1Chr 28:4 3068
(for the *L* hath given me many 1Chr 28:5 3068
the kingdom of the *L* over Israel 1Chr 28:5 3068
Israel the congregation of the *L* 1Chr 28:8 3068
commandments of the *L* your God 1Chr 28:8 3068
for the *L* searcheth all hearts, 1Chr 28:9 3068
for the *L* hath chosen thee to 1Chr 28:10 3068
the courts of the house of the *L* 1Chr 28:12 3068
the service of the house of the *L* 1Chr 28:13 3068
of service in the house of the *L* 1Chr 28:13 3068
the ark of the covenant of the *L* 1Chr 28:18 3068
the *L* made me understand in 1Chr 28:19 3068
for the *L* God, even my God, will 1Chr 28:20 3068
the service of the house of the *L* 1Chr 28:20 3068
is not for man, but for the *L* God 1Chr 29:1 3068
his service this day unto the *L* 1Chr 29:5 3068
treasure of the house of the *L* 1Chr 29:8 3068
they offered willingly to the *L* 1Chr 29:9 3068
the *L* before all the congregation 1Chr 29:10 3068
L God of Israel our father, for 1Chr 29:10 3068
Thine, O *L*, is the greatness, and 1Chr 29:11 3068
thine is the kingdom, O *L* 1Chr 29:11 3068
O *L* our God, all this store that 1Chr 29:16 3068
O *L* God of Abraham, Isaac, and of 1Chr 29:18 3068
Now bless the *L* your God 1Chr 29:20 3068
the *L* God of their fathers 1Chr 29:20 3068
their heads, and worshipped the *L* 1Chr 29:20 3068
sacrificed sacrifices unto the *L* 1Chr 29:21 3068
burnt offerings unto the *L* 1Chr 29:21 3068
drink before the *L* on that day 1Chr 29:22 3068
anointed him unto the *L* to be the 1Chr 29:22 3068
sat on the throne of the *L* as 1Chr 29:23 3068
And the *L* magnified Solomon 1Chr 29:25 3068
the *L* his God was with him, and 2Chr 1:1 3068
the *L* had made in the wilderness 2Chr 1:3 3068
before the tabernacle of the *L* 2Chr 1:5 3068
to the brasen altar before the *L* 2Chr 1:6 3068
O *L* God, let thy promise unto 2Chr 1:9 3068
an house for the name of the *L* 2Chr 2:1 3068
house to the name of the *L* my God 2Chr 2:4 3068
solemn feasts of the *L* our God 2Chr 2:4 3068
Because the *L* hath loved his 2Chr 2:11 3068
Blessed be the *L* God of Israel 2Chr 2:12 3068
might build an house for the *L* 2Chr 2:12 3068
L at Jerusalem in mount Moriah 2Chr 3:1 3068
where the *L* appeared unto David 2Chr 3:1
house of the *L* of bright brass 2Chr 4:16 3068
the house of the *L* was finished 2Chr 5:1 3068
of the *L* out of the city of David 2Chr 5:2 3068
covenant of the *L* unto his place 2Chr 5:7 3068
when the *L* made a covenant with 2Chr 5:10 3068
in praising and thanking the *L* 2Chr 5:13 3068
of musick, and praised the *L* 2Chr 5:13 3068
a cloud, even the house of the *L* 2Chr 5:13 3068
for the glory of the *L* had filled 2Chr 5:14 3068
The *L* hath said that he would 2Chr 6:1 3068
Blessed be the *L* God of Israel 2Chr 6:4 3068
the name of the *L* God of Israel 2Chr 6:7 3068
But the *L* said to David my father 2Chr 6:8 3068
The *L* therefore hath performed 2Chr 6:10 3068
as the *L* promised, and have built 2Chr 6:10 3068
the name of the *L* God of Israel 2Chr 6:10 3068
wherein is the covenant of the *L* 2Chr 6:11 3068
the *L* in the presence of all the 2Chr 6:12 3068
O *L* God of Israel, there is no 2Chr 6:14 3068
O *L* God of Israel, keep with thy 2Chr 6:16 3068
O *L* God of Israel, let thy word 2Chr 6:17 3068
O *L* my God, to hearken unto the 2Chr 6:19 3068
O *L* God, into thy resting place, 2Chr 6:41 3068
priests, O *L* God, be clothed with 2Chr 6:41 3068
O *L* God, turn not away the face 2Chr 6:42 3068
glory of the *L* filled the house 2Chr 7:1 3068
not enter into the house of the *L* 2Chr 7:2 3068
because the glory of the *L* had 2Chr 7:2 3068
the glory of the *L* upon the house 2Chr 7:3 3068
and worshipped, and praised the *L* 2Chr 7:3 3068
offered sacrifices before the *L* 2Chr 7:4 3068
instruments of musick of the *L* 2Chr 7:6 3068
the king had made to praise the *L* 2Chr 7:6 3068
was before the house of the *L* 2Chr 7:7 3068
that the *L* had shewed unto David 2Chr 7:10 3068
finished the house of the *L* 2Chr 7:11 3068
to make in the house of the *L* 2Chr 7:11 3068
the *L* appeared to Solomon by 2Chr 7:12 3068
Why hath the *L* done thus unto 2Chr 7:21 3068
the *L* God of their fathers 2Chr 7:22 3068
had built the house of the *L* 2Chr 8:1 3068
the ark of the *L* hath come 2Chr 8:11 3068
the *L* on the altar of the *L* 2Chr 8:12 3068
foundation of the house of the *L* 2Chr 8:16 3068
the house of the *L* was perfected 2Chr 8:16 3068
went up into the house of the *L* 2Chr 9:4 3068
Blessed be the *L* thy God, which 2Chr 9:8 3068
to be king for the *L* thy God 2Chr 9:8 3068
terraces to the house of the *L* 2Chr 9:11 3068
that the *L* might perform his word 2Chr 10:15 3068
But the word of the *L* came to 2Chr 11:2 3068
Thus saith the *L*, Ye shall not go 2Chr 11:4 3068
And they obeyed the words of the *L* 2Chr 11:4 3068
the priest's office unto the *L* 2Chr 11:14 3068
L God of Israel came to Jerusalem 2Chr 11:16 3068
unto the *L* God of their fathers 2Chr 11:16 3068
he forsook the law of the *L* 2Chr 12:1 3068
had transgressed against the *L* 2Chr 12:2 3068
said unto them, Thus saith the *L* 2Chr 12:5 3068
and they said, The *L* is righteous 2Chr 12:6 3068
when the *L* saw that they humbled 2Chr 12:7 3068
the word of the *L* came to 2Chr 12:7 3068
treasures of the house of the *L* 2Chr 12:9 3068
entered into the house of the *L* 2Chr 12:11 3068
wrath of the *L* turned from him 2Chr 12:12 3068
the city which the *L* had chosen 2Chr 12:13 3068
not his heart to seek the *L* 2Chr 12:14 3068
Ought ye not to know that the *L* 2Chr 13:5 3068
the *L* in the hand of the sons of 2Chr 13:8 3068
not cast out the priests of the *L* 2Chr 13:9 3068
the *L* is our God, and we have not 2Chr 13:10 3068
which minister unto the *L* 2Chr 13:10 3068
burn unto the *L* every morning 2Chr 13:11 3068
keep the charge of the *L* our God 2Chr 13:11 3068
against the *L* God of your fathers 2Chr 13:12 3068
and they cried unto the *L*, and the 2Chr 13:14 3068
upon the *L* God of their fathers 2Chr 13:18 3068
the *L* struck him, and he died 2Chr 13:20 3068
in the eyes of the *L* his God 2Chr 14:2 3068
seek the *L* God of their fathers 2Chr 14:4 3068
because the *L* had given him rest 2Chr 14:6 3068
we have sought the *L* our God 2Chr 14:7 3068
unto the *L* his God, and said, *L* 2Chr 14:11 3068
help us, O *L* our God 2Chr 14:11 3068
O *L*, thou art our God 2Chr 14:11 3068
So the *L* smote the Ethiopians 2Chr 14:12 3068
they were destroyed before the *L* 2Chr 14:13 3068
the fear of the *L* came upon them 2Chr 14:14 3068
The *L* is with you, while ye be 2Chr 15:2 3068
did turn unto the *L* God of Israel 2Chr 15:4 3068
and renewed the altar of the *L* 2Chr 15:8 3068
was before the porch of the *L* 2Chr 15:8 3068
that the *L* his God was with him 2Chr 15:9 3068
offered unto the *L* the same time 2Chr 15:11 3068
into a covenant to seek the *L* God 2Chr 15:12 3068
whosoever would not seek the *L* 2Chr 15:13 3068
unto the *L* with a loud voice 2Chr 15:14 3068
the *L* gave them rest round about 2Chr 15:15 3068
treasures of the house of the *L* 2Chr 16:2 3068
and not relied on the *L* thy God 2Chr 16:7 3068
because thou didst rely on the *L* 2Chr 16:8 3068
For the eyes of the *L* run to 2Chr 16:9 3068
disease he sought not to the *L* 2Chr 16:12 3068
the *L* was with Jehoshaphat, 2Chr 17:3 3068
sought to the *L* God of his father 2Chr 17:4 3068
Therefore the *L* stablished the 2Chr 17:5 3068
lifted up in the ways of the *L* 2Chr 17:6 3068
of the law of the *L* with them 2Chr 17:9 3068
the fear of the *L* fell upon all 2Chr 17:10 3068
offered himself unto the *L* 2Chr 17:16 3068
thee, at the word of the *L* to day 2Chr 18:4 3068
here a prophet of the *L* besides 2Chr 18:6 3068
by whom we may enquire of the *L* 2Chr 18:7 3068
iron, and said, Thus saith the *L* 2Chr 18:10 3068
for the *L* shall deliver it into 2Chr 18:11 3068
And Micaiah said, As the *L* liveth 2Chr 18:13 3068
truth to me in the name of the *L* 2Chr 18:15 3068
the *L* said, These have no master 2Chr 18:16 3068
Therefore hear the word of the *L* 2Chr 18:18 3068
I saw the *L* sitting upon his 2Chr 18:18 3068
the *L* said, Who shall entice Ahab 2Chr 18:19 3068
a spirit, and stood before the *L* 2Chr 18:20 3068
the *L* said unto him, Wherewith 2Chr 18:20 3068
the *L* said, Thou shalt entice him 2Chr 18:21
the *L* hath put a lying spirit in 2Chr 18:22 3068
the *L* hath spoken evil against 2Chr 18:22 3068
the *L* from me to speak unto thee 2Chr 18:23 3068
then hath not the *L* spoken by me 2Chr 18:27 3068
cried out, and the *L* helped him 2Chr 18:31 3068
and love them that hate the *L* 2Chr 19:2 3068
wrath upon thee from before the *L* 2Chr 19:2 3068
unto the *L* God of their fathers 2Chr 19:4 3068
judge not for man, but for the *L* 2Chr 19:6 3068
let the fear of the *L* be upon you 2Chr 19:7 3068
is no iniquity with the *L* our God 2Chr 19:7 3068
Israel, for the judgment of the *L* 2Chr 19:8 3068
shall ye do in the fear of the *L* 2Chr 19:9 3068
they trespass not against the *L* 2Chr 19:10 3068
over you in all matters of the *L* 2Chr 19:11 3068
the *L* shall be with the good 2Chr 19:11 3068
and set himself to seek the *L* 2Chr 20:3 3068
together, to ask help of the *L* 2Chr 20:4 3068
of Judah they came to seek the *L* 2Chr 20:4 3068
Jerusalem, in the house of the *L* 2Chr 20:5 3068
O *L* God of our fathers, art not 2Chr 20:6 3068
And all Judah stood before the *L* 2Chr 20:13 3068
of the *L* in the midst of the 2Chr 20:14 3068
Thus saith the *L* unto you 2Chr 20:15 3068
the salvation of the *L* with you 2Chr 20:17 3068
for the *L* will be with you 2Chr 20:17 3068
the *L*, worshipping the *L* 2Chr 20:18 3068
stood up to praise the *L* God of 2Chr 20:19 3068
Believe in the *L* your God 2Chr 20:20 3068
he appointed singers unto the *L* 2Chr 20:21 3068
the army, and to say, Praise the *L* 2Chr 20:21 3068
the *L* set ambushments against the 2Chr 20:22 3068
for there they blessed the *L* 2Chr 20:26 3068
for the *L* had made them to 2Chr 20:27 3068
trumpets unto the house of the *L* 2Chr 20:28 3068
when they had heard that the *L* 2Chr 20:29 3068
was right in the sight of the *L* 2Chr 20:32 3068
the *L* hath broken thy works 2Chr 20:37 3068
was evil in the eyes of the *L* 2Chr 21:6 3068
Howbeit the *L* would not destroy 2Chr 21:7 3068
forsaken the *L* God of his fathers 2Chr 21:10 3068
Thus saith the *L* God of David thy 2Chr 21:12 3068
will the *L* smite thy people 2Chr 21:14 3068
Moreover the *L* stirred up against 2Chr 21:16 3068
after all this the *L* smote him in 2Chr 21:18 3068
of the *L* like the house of Ahab 2Chr 22:4 3068
whom the *L* had anointed to cut 2Chr 22:7 3068
who sought the *L* with all his 2Chr 22:9 3068
as the *L* hath said of the sons of 2Chr 23:3 3068
the courts of the house of the *L* 2Chr 23:5 3068
none come into the house of the *L* 2Chr 23:6 3068
shall keep the watch of the *L* 2Chr 23:6 3068
people into the house of the *L* 2Chr 23:12 3068
her not in the house of the *L* 2Chr 23:14 3068
L by the hand of the priests the 2Chr 23:18 3068
distributed in the house of the *L* 2Chr 23:18 3068
the burnt offerings of the *L* 2Chr 23:18 3068
the gates of the house of the *L* 2Chr 23:19 3068
the king from the house of the *L* 2Chr 23:20 3068
L all the days of Jehoiada the 2Chr 24:2 3068
to repair the house of the *L* 2Chr 24:4 3068
of Moses the servant of the *L* 2Chr 24:6 3068
things of the house of the *L* did 2Chr 24:7 3068
at the gate of the house of the *L* 2Chr 24:8 3068
to bring in to the *L* the 2Chr 24:9 3068
the service of the house of the *L* 2Chr 24:12 3068
to repair the house of the *L* 2Chr 24:12 3068
brass to mend the house of the *L* 2Chr 24:12 3068
vessels for the house of the *L* 2Chr 24:14 3068
the *L* continually all the days of 2Chr 24:14 3068
of the *L* God of their fathers 2Chr 24:18 3068
to bring them again unto the *L* 2Chr 24:19 3068
ye the commandments of the *L* 2Chr 24:20 3068
because ye have forsaken the *L* 2Chr 24:20 3068
the court of the house of the *L* 2Chr 24:21 3068
The *L* look upon it, and require it 2Chr 24:22 3068
the *L* delivered a very great host 2Chr 24:24 3068
the *L* God of their fathers 2Chr 24:24 3068
was right in the sight of the *L* 2Chr 25:2 3068
of Moses, where the *L* commanded 2Chr 25:4 3068
for the *L* is not with Israel, to 2Chr 25:7 3068
The *L* is able to give thee much 2Chr 25:9 3068
Wherefore the anger of the *L* was 2Chr 25:15 3068
turn away from following the *L* 2Chr 25:27 3068
was right in the sight of the *L* 2Chr 26:4 3068
and as long as he sought the *L* 2Chr 26:5 3068
against the *L* his God 2Chr 26:16 3068
went into the temple of the *L* to 2Chr 26:16 3068
him fourscore priests of the *L* 2Chr 26:17 3068
to burn incense unto the *L* 2Chr 26:18 3068
for thine honour from the *L* God 2Chr 26:18 3068
the priests in the house of the *L* 2Chr 26:19 3068
because the *L* had smitten him 2Chr 26:20 3068
cut off from the house of the *L* 2Chr 26:21 3068
was right in the sight of the *L* 2Chr 27:2 3068
not into the temple of the *L* 2Chr 27:2 3068
high gate of the house of the *L* 2Chr 27:3 3068
his ways before the *L* his God 2Chr 27:6 3068
was right in the sight of the *L* 2Chr 28:1 3068
the *L* had cast out before the 2Chr 28:3 3068
Wherefore the *L* his God delivered 2Chr 28:5 3068
the *L* God of their fathers 2Chr 28:6 3068
But a prophet of the *L* was there 2Chr 28:9 3068
because the *L* God of your fathers 2Chr 28:9 3068
you, sins against the *L* your God 2Chr 28:10 3068
fierce wrath of the *L* is upon you 2Chr 28:11 3068
offended against the *L* already 2Chr 28:13 3068
For the *L* brought Judah low 2Chr 28:19 3068
transgressed sore against the *L* 2Chr 28:19 3068
portion out of the house of the *L* 2Chr 28:21 3068
trespass yet more against the *L* 2Chr 28:22 3068
the doors of the house of the *L* 2Chr 28:24 3068
to anger the *L* God of his fathers 2Chr 28:25 3068
was right in the sight of the *L* 2Chr 29:2 3068
the doors of the house of the *L* 2Chr 29:3 3068
of the *L* God of your fathers 2Chr 29:5 3068
evil in the eyes of the *L* our God 2Chr 29:6 3068

from the habitation of the *L*	2Chr 29:6	3068
the wrath of the *L* was upon Judah	2Chr 29:8	3068
covenant with the *L* God of Israel	2Chr 29:10	3068
for the *L* hath chosen you to	2Chr 29:11	3068
the king, by the words of the *L*	2Chr 29:15	3068
to cleanse the house of the *L*	2Chr 29:15	3068
inner part of the house of the *L*	2Chr 29:16	3068
L into the court of the house of	2Chr 29:16	3068
the court of the house of the *L*	2Chr 29:16	3068
came they to the porch of the *L*	2Chr 29:17	3068
the house of the *L* in eight days	2Chr 29:17	3068
cleansed all the house of the *L*	2Chr 29:18	3068
are before the altar of the *L*	2Chr 29:19	3068
and went up to the house of the *L*	2Chr 29:20	3068
offer them on the altar of the *L*	2Chr 29:21	3068
the house of the *L* with cymbals	2Chr 29:25	3068
of the *L* by his prophets	2Chr 29:25	3068
the song of the *L* began also with	2Chr 29:27	3068
the *L* with the words of David	2Chr 29:30	3068
consecrated yourselves unto the *L*	2Chr 29:31	3068
offerings into the house of the *L*	2Chr 29:31	3068
for a burnt offering to the *L*	2Chr 29:32	3068
house of the *L* was set in order	2Chr 29:35	3068
the house of the *L* at Jerusalem	2Chr 30:1	3068
passover unto the *L* God of Israel	2Chr 30:1	3068
the *L* God of Israel at Jerusalem	2Chr 30:5	3068
again unto the *L* God of Abraham	2Chr 30:6	3068
the *L* God of their fathers	2Chr 30:7	3068
but yield yourselves unto the *L*	2Chr 30:8	3068
and serve the *L* your God, that the	2Chr 30:8	3068
For if ye turn again unto the *L*	2Chr 30:9	3068
for the *L* your God is gracious and	2Chr 30:9	3068
the princes, by the word of the *L*	2Chr 30:12	3068
offerings into the house of the *L*	2Chr 30:15	3068
to sanctify them unto the *L*	2Chr 30:17	3068
The good *L* pardon every one	2Chr 30:18	3068
the *L* God of his fathers, though	2Chr 30:19	3068
the *L* hearkened to Hezekiah, and	2Chr 30:20	3068
priests praised the *L* day by day	2Chr 30:21	3068
with loud instruments unto the *L*	2Chr 30:21	3068
the good knowledge of the *L*	2Chr 30:22	3068
to the *L* God of their fathers	2Chr 30:22	3068
the gates of the tents of the *L*	2Chr 31:2	3068
it is written in the law of the *L*	2Chr 31:3	3068
be encouraged in the law of the *L*	2Chr 31:4	3068
consecrated unto the *L* their God	2Chr 31:6	3068
saw the heaps, they blessed the *L*	2Chr 31:8	3068
offerings into the house of the *L*	2Chr 31:10	3068
for the *L* hath blessed his people	2Chr 31:10	3068
chambers in the house of the *L*	2Chr 31:11	3068
distribute the oblations of the *L*	2Chr 31:14	3068
entereth into the house of the *L*	2Chr 31:16	3068
and truth before the *L* his God	2Chr 31:20	3068
us is the *L* our God to help us	2Chr 32:8	3068
The *L* our God shall deliver us	2Chr 32:11	3068
spake yet more against the *L* God	2Chr 32:16	3068
to rail on the *L* God of Israel	2Chr 32:17	3068
the *L* sent an angel, which cut	2Chr 32:21	3068
Thus the *L* saved Hezekiah and the	2Chr 32:22	3068
gifts unto the *L* to Jerusalem	2Chr 32:23	3068
the death, and prayed unto the *L*	2Chr 32:24	3068
so that the wrath of the *L* came	2Chr 32:26	3068
was evil in the sight of the *L*	2Chr 33:2	3068
whom the *L* had cast out before	2Chr 33:2	3068
altars in the house of the *L*	2Chr 33:4	3068
whereof the *L* had said	2Chr 33:4	3068
two courts of the house of the *L*	2Chr 33:5	3068
much evil in the sight of the *L*	2Chr 33:6	3068
whom the *L* had destroyed before	2Chr 33:9	3068
the *L* spake to Manasseh, and to	2Chr 33:10	3068
Wherefore the *L* brought upon them	2Chr 33:11	3068
he besought the *L* his God	2Chr 33:12	3068
knew that the *L* he was God	2Chr 33:13	3068
idol out of the house of the *L*	2Chr 33:15	3068
the mount of the house of the *L*	2Chr 33:15	3068
And he repaired the altar of the *L*	2Chr 33:16	3068
to serve the *L* God of Israel	2Chr 33:16	3068
yet unto the *L* their God only	2Chr 33:17	3068
the name of the *L* God of Israel	2Chr 33:18	3068
was evil in the sight of the *L*	2Chr 33:22	3068
humbled not himself before the *L*	2Chr 33:23	3068
was right in the sight of the *L*	2Chr 34:2	3068
repair the house of the *L* his God	2Chr 34:8	3068
oversight of the house of the *L*	2Chr 34:10	3068
wrought in the house of the *L*	2Chr 34:10	3068
brought into the house of the *L*	2Chr 34:14	3068
the law of the *L* given by Moses	2Chr 34:14	3068
of the law in the house of the *L*	2Chr 34:15	3068
was found in the house of the *L*	2Chr 34:17	3068
Go, enquire of the *L* for me	2Chr 34:21	3068
the *L* that is poured out upon us	2Chr 34:21	3068
have not kept the word of the *L*	2Chr 34:21	3068
Thus saith the *L* God of Israel	2Chr 34:23	3068
Thus saith the *L*, Behold, I will	2Chr 34:24	3068
who sent you to enquire of the *L*	2Chr 34:26	3068
Thus saith the *L* God of Israel	2Chr 34:26	3068
even heard thee also, saith the *L*	2Chr 34:27	3068
went up into the house of the *L*	2Chr 34:30	3068
was found in the house of the *L*	2Chr 34:30	3068
and made a covenant before the *L*	2Chr 34:31	3068
to walk after the *L*	2Chr 34:31	3068
even to serve the *L* their God	2Chr 34:33	3068
departed not from following the *L*	2Chr 34:33	3068
passover unto the *L* in Jerusalem	2Chr 35:1	3068
the service of the house of the *L*	2Chr 35:2	3068
which were holy unto the *L*	2Chr 35:3	3068
serve now the *L* your God, and his	2Chr 35:3	3068
of the *L* by the hand of Moses	2Chr 35:6	3068
the people, to offer unto the *L*	2Chr 35:12	3068
the *L* was prepared the same day	2Chr 35:16	3068
offerings upon the altar of the *L*	2Chr 35:16	3068
was written in the law of the *L*	2Chr 35:26	3068
in the sight of the *L* his God	2Chr 36:5	3068
of the house of the *L* to Babylon	2Chr 36:7	3068
was evil in the sight of the *L*	2Chr 36:9	3068
vessels of the house of the *L*	2Chr 36:10	3068
in the sight of the *L* his God	2Chr 36:12	3068
speaking from the mouth of the *L*	2Chr 36:12	3068
turning unto the *L* God of Israel	2Chr 36:13	3068
of the *L* which he had hallowed in	2Chr 36:14	3068
the *L* God of their fathers sent	2Chr 36:15	3068
until the wrath of the *L* arose	2Chr 36:16	3068
treasures of the house of the *L*	2Chr 36:18	3068
of the *L* by the mouth of Jeremiah	2Chr 36:21	3068
that the word of the *L* spoken by	2Chr 36:22	3068
the *L* stirred up the spirit of	2Chr 36:22	3068
hath the *L* God of heaven given me	2Chr 36:23	3068
The *L* his God be with him, and let	2Chr 36:23	3068
that the word of the *L* by the	Ezr 1:1	3068
the *L* stirred up the spirit of	Ezr 1:1	3068
The *L* God of heaven hath given me	Ezr 1:2	3068
the house of the *L* God of Israel	Ezr 1:3	3068
of the *L* which is in Jerusalem	Ezr 1:5	3068
the vessels of the house of the *L*	Ezr 1:7	3068
of the *L* which is at Jerusalem	Ezr 2:68	3068
offerings thereon unto the *L*	Ezr 3:3	3068
of the *L* that were consecrated	Ezr 3:5	3068
a freewill offering unto the *L*	Ezr 3:5	3068
offer burnt offerings unto the *L*	Ezr 3:6	3068
temple of the *L* was not yet laid	Ezr 3:6	3068
the work of the house of the *L*	Ezr 3:8	3068
foundation of the temple of the *L*	Ezr 3:10	3068
with cymbals, to praise the *L*	Ezr 3:10	3068
and giving thanks unto the *L*	Ezr 3:11	3068
shout, when they praised the *L*	Ezr 3:11	3068
of the house of the *L* was laid	Ezr 3:11	3068
temple unto the *L* God of Israel	Ezr 4:1	3068
build unto the *L* God of Israel	Ezr 4:3	3068
to seek the *L* God of Israel, did	Ezr 6:21	3068
for the *L* had made them joyful,	Ezr 6:22	3068
which the *L* God of Israel had	Ezr 7:6	3068
hand of the *L* his God upon him	Ezr 7:6	3068
heart to seek the law of the *L*	Ezr 7:10	3068
of the commandments of the *L*	Ezr 7:11	3068
Blessed be the *L* God of our	Ezr 7:27	3068
of the *L* which is in Jerusalem	Ezr 7:27	3068
hand of the *L* my God was upon me	Ezr 7:28	3068
unto them, Ye are holy unto the *L*	Ezr 8:28	3068
unto the *L* God of your fathers	Ezr 8:28	3068
chambers of the house of the *L*	Ezr 8:29	3068
was a burnt offering unto the *L*	Ezr 8:35	3068
out my hands unto the *L* my God	Ezr 9:5	3068
been shewed from the *L* our God	Ezr 9:8	3068
O *L* God of Israel, thou art	Ezr 9:15	3068
unto the *L* God of your fathers	Ezr 10:11	3068
O *L* God of heaven, the great and	Neh 1:5	3068
O *L*, I beseech thee, let now	Neh 1:11	136
remember the *L*, which is great and	Neh 4:14	136
said, Amen, and praised the *L*	Neh 5:13	3068
which the *L* had commanded to	Neh 8:1	3068
And Ezra blessed the *L*, the great	Neh 8:6	3068
worshipped the *L* with their faces	Neh 8:6	3068
day is holy unto the *L* your God	Neh 8:9	3068
for this day is holy unto our *L*	Neh 8:10	113
the joy of the *L* is your strength	Neh 8:10	3068
the *L* had commanded by Moses	Neh 8:14	3068
L their God one fourth part of	Neh 9:3	3068
and worshipped the *L* their God	Neh 9:3	3068
a loud voice unto the *L* their God	Neh 9:4	3068
bless the *L* your God for ever and	Neh 9:5	3068
Thou, even thou, art *L* alone	Neh 9:6	3068
Thou art the *L* the God, who didst	Neh 9:7	3068
commandments of the *L* our *L*	Neh 10:29	3068
commandments of the *L* our *L*	Neh 10:29	113
upon the altar of the *L* our God	Neh 10:34	3068
by year, unto the house of the *L*	Neh 10:35	3068
present themselves before the *L*	Job 1:6	3068
the *L* said unto Satan, Whence	Job 1:7	3068
Then Satan answered the *L*	Job 1:7	3068
the *L* said unto Satan, Hast thou	Job 1:8	3068
Then Satan answered the *L*	Job 1:9	3068
the *L* said unto Satan, Behold,	Job 1:12	3068
forth from the presence of the *L*	Job 1:12	3068
the *L* gave, and the *L* hath	Job 1:21	3068
blessed be the name of the *L*	Job 1:21	3068
present themselves before the *L*	Job 2:1	3068
to present himself before the *L*	Job 2:1	3068
the *L* said unto Satan, From	Job 2:2	3068
And Satan answered the *L*, and said,	Job 2:2	3068
the *L* said unto Satan, Hast thou	Job 2:3	3068
And Satan answered the *L*, and said,	Job 2:4	3068
the *L* said unto Satan, Behold, he	Job 2:6	3068
forth from the presence of the *L*	Job 2:7	3068
hand of the *L* hath wrought this	Job 12:9	3068
said, Behold, the fear of the *L*	Job 28:28	136
Then the *L* answered Job out of	Job 38:1	3068
Moreover the *L* answered Job	Job 40:1	3068
Then Job answered the *L*, and said,	Job 40:3	3068
Then answered the *L* unto Job out	Job 40:6	3068
Then Job answered the *L*, and said,	Job 42:1	3068
that after the *L* had spoken these	Job 42:7	3068
the *L* said to Eliphaz the	Job 42:7	3068
according as the *L* commanded them	Job 42:9	3068
the *L* also accepted Job	Job 42:9	3068
the *L* turned the captivity of Job	Job 42:10	3068
also the *L* gave Job twice as much	Job 42:10	3068
that the *L* had brought upon him	Job 42:11	3068
So the *L* blessed the latter end	Job 42:12	3068
delight is in the law of the *L*	Ps 1:2	3068
For the *L* knoweth the way of the	Ps 1:6	3068
counsel together, against the *L*	Ps 2:2	3068
the *L* shall have them in derision	Ps 2:4	136
The *L* hath said unto me, Thou art	Ps 2:7	3068
Serve the *L* with fear, and rejoice	Ps 2:11	3068
L, how are they increased that	Ps 3:1	3068
But thou, O *L*, art a shield for	Ps 3:3	3068
I cried unto the *L* with my voice	Ps 3:4	3068
for the *L* sustained me	Ps 3:5	3068
Arise, O *L*	Ps 3:7	3068
Salvation belongeth unto the *L*	Ps 3:8	3068
But know that the *L* hath set	Ps 4:3	3068
the *L* will hear when I call unto	Ps 4:3	3068
and put your trust in the *L*	Ps 4:5	3068
L, lift thou up the light of thy	Ps 4:6	3068
for thou, *L*, only makest me dwell	Ps 4:8	3068
Give ear to my words, O *L*	Ps 5:1	3068
thou hear in the morning, O *L*	Ps 5:3	3068
the *L* will abhor the bloody and	Ps 5:6	3068
Lead me, O *L*, in thy	Ps 5:8	3068
For thou, *L*, wilt bless the	Ps 5:12	3068
O *l*, rebuke me not in thine anger	Ps 6:1	3068
Have mercy upon me, O *L*	Ps 6:2	3068
O *L*, heal me	Ps 6:2	3068
but thou, O *L*, how long	Ps 6:3	3068
Return, O *L*, deliver my soul	Ps 6:4	3068
for the *L* hath heard the voice of	Ps 6:8	3068
The *L* hath heard my supplication	Ps 6:9	3068
the *L* will receive my prayer	Ps 6:9	3068
David, which he sang unto the *L*	Ps 7:*t*	3068
O *l* my God, in thee do I put my	Ps 7:1	3068
O *L* my God, if I have done this	Ps 7:3	3068
Arise, O *L*, in thine anger, lift	Ps 7:6	3068
The *L* shall judge the people	Ps 7:8	3068
judge me, O *L*, according to my	Ps 7:8	3068
I will praise the *L* according to	Ps 7:17	3068
to the name of the *L* most high	Ps 7:17	3068
O *l* our *L*, how excellent is	Ps 8:1	3068
O *l* our *L*, how excellent is	Ps 8:1	113
O *L* our *L*, how excellent is	Ps 8:9	3068
O *L* our *L*, how excellent is	Ps 8:9	113
I will praise thee, O *L*, with my	Ps 9:1	3068
But the *L* shall endure for ever	Ps 9:7	3068
The *L* also will be a refuge for	Ps 9:9	3068
for thou, *L*, hast not forsaken	Ps 9:10	3068
Sing praises to the *L*, which	Ps 9:11	3068
Have mercy upon me, O *L*	Ps 9:13	3068
The *L* is known by the judgment	Ps 9:16	3068
Arise, O *L*	Ps 9:19	3068
Put them in fear, O *L*	Ps 9:20	3068
Why standest thou afar off, O *L*	Ps 10:1	3068
covetous, whom the *L* abhorreth	Ps 10:3	3068
Arise, O *L*	Ps 10:12	3068
The *L* is King for ever and ever	Ps 10:16	3068
L, thou hast heard the desire of	Ps 10:17	3068
In the *L* put I my trust	Ps 11:1	3068
The *L* is in his holy temple, the	Ps 11:4	3068
The *L* trieth the righteous	Ps 11:5	3068
For the righteous *L* loveth	Ps 11:7	3068
Help, *L*; for the	Ps 12:1	3068
The *L* shall cut off all	Ps 12:3	3068
now will I arise, saith the *L*	Ps 12:5	3068
The words of the *L* are pure words	Ps 12:6	3068
Thou shalt keep them, O *L*	Ps 12:7	3068
How long wilt thou forget me, O *L*	Ps 13:1	3068
Consider and hear me, O *L* my God	Ps 13:3	3068
I will sing unto the *L*, because	Ps 13:6	3068
The *L* looked down from heaven	Ps 14:2	3068
eat bread, and call not upon the *L*	Ps 14:4	3068
because the *L* is his refuge	Ps 14:6	3068
when the *L* bringeth back the	Ps 14:7	3068
L, who shall abide in thy	Ps 15:1	3068
he honoureth them that fear the *L*	Ps 15:4	3068
soul, thou hast said unto the *L*	Ps 16:2	3068
Thou art my *L*	Ps 16:2	136
The *L* is the portion of mine	Ps 16:5	3068
I will bless the *L*, who hath	Ps 16:7	3068
I have set the *L* always before me	Ps 16:8	3068
Hear the right, O *L*, attend unto	Ps 17:1	3068
Arise, O *L*, disappoint him, cast	Ps 17:13	3068
From men which are thy hand, O *L*	Ps 17:14	3068
of David, the servant of the *L*	Ps 18:*t*	3068
who spake unto the *L* the words of	Ps 18:*t*	3068
this song in the day that the *L*	Ps 18:*t*	3068
I will love thee, O *L*, my	Ps 18:1	3068
The *L* is my rock, and my fortress,	Ps 18:2	3068
I will call upon the *L*, who is	Ps 18:3	3068
my distress I called upon the *L*	Ps 18:6	3068
The *L* also thundered in the	Ps 18:13	3068
discovered at thy rebuke, O *L*	Ps 18:15	3068
but the *L* was my stay	Ps 18:18	3068
The *L* rewarded me according to my	Ps 18:20	3068
For I have kept the ways of the *L*	Ps 18:21	3068
Therefore hath the *L* recompensed	Ps 18:24	3068
the *L* my God will enlighten my	Ps 18:28	3068
the word of the *L* is tried	Ps 18:30	3068
For who is God save the *L*	Ps 18:31	3068
even unto the *L*, but he answered	Ps 18:41	3068
The *L* liveth	Ps 18:46	3068
will I give thanks unto thee, O *L*	Ps 18:49	3068
The law of the *L* is perfect	Ps 19:7	3068
the testimony of the *L* is sure	Ps 19:7	3068
The statutes of the *L* are right	Ps 19:8	3068
the commandment of the *L* is pure	Ps 19:8	3068
The fear of the *L* is clean	Ps 19:9	3068
the judgments of the *L* are true	Ps 19:9	3068
be acceptable in thy sight, O *L*	Ps 19:14	3068
The *L* hear thee in the day of	Ps 20:1	3068
the *L* fulfil all thy petitions	Ps 20:5	3068
I that the *L* saveth his anointed	Ps 20:6	3068
the name of the *L* our God	Ps 20:7	3068
Save, *L*	Ps 20:9	3068
shall joy in thy strength, O *L*	Ps 21:1	3068
For the king trusteth in the *L*	Ps 21:7	3068
the *L* shall swallow them up in	Ps 21:9	3068
Be thou exalted, *L*, in thine own	Ps 21:13	3068
He trusted on the *L* that he would	Ps 22:8	3068
But be not thou far from me, O *L*	Ps 22:19	3068
Ye that fear the *L*, praise him	Ps 22:23	3068
shall praise the *L* that seek him	Ps 22:26	3068
shall remember and turn unto the *L*	Ps 22:27	3068
to the *L* for a generation	Ps 22:30	136
The *L* is my shepherd	Ps 23:1	3068

in the house of the *L* for ever Ps 23:6 3068
ascend into the hill of the *L* Ps 24:3 3068
receive the blessing from the *L* Ps 24:5 3068
The *L* strong and mighty, the *L* Ps 24:8 3068
The *L* of hosts, he is the King of Ps 24:10 3068
Unto thee, O *L*, do I lift up my Ps 25:1 3068
Shew me thy ways, O *L* Ps 25:4 3068
Remember, O *L*, thy tender mercies Ps 25:6 3068
me for thy goodness' sake, O *L* Ps 25:7 3068
Good and upright is the *L* Ps 25:8 3068
All the paths of the *L* are mercy Ps 25:10 3068
For thy name's sake, O *L*, pardon Ps 25:11 3068
What man is he that feareth the *L* Ps 25:12 3068
The secret of the *L* is with them Ps 25:14 3068
Mine eyes are ever toward the *L* Ps 25:15 3068
Judge me, O *L* Ps 26:1 3068
I have trusted also in the *L* Ps 26:1 3068
Examine me, O *L*, and prove me Ps 26:2 3068
will I compass thine altar, O *L* Ps 26:6 3068
L, I have loved the habitation of Ps 26:8 3068
congregations will I bless the *L* Ps 26:12 3068
The *L* is my light and my salvation Ps 27:1 3068
the *L* is the strength of my life Ps 27:1 3068
One thing have I desired of the *L* Ps 27:4 3068
of the *L* all the days of my life Ps 27:4 3068
to behold the beauty of the *L* Ps 27:4 3068
I will sing praises unto the *L* Ps 27:6 3068
Hear, O *L*, when I cry with my Ps 27:7 3068
heart said unto thee, Thy face, *L* Ps 27:8 3068
then the *L* will take me up Ps 27:10 3068
Teach me thy way, O *L*, and lead me Ps 27:11 3068
the *L* in the land of the living Ps 27:13 3068
Wait on the *L* Ps 27:14 3068
wait, I say, on the *L* Ps 27:14 3068
Unto thee will I cry, O *L* my rock Ps 28:1 3068
regard not the works of the *L* Ps 28:5 3068
Blessed be the *L*, because he hath Ps 28:6 3068
The *L* is my strength and my shield Ps 28:7 3068
The *L* is their strength, and he is Ps 28:8 3068
Give unto the *L*, O ye mighty, Ps 29:1 3068
give unto the *L* glory Ps 29:1 3068
Give unto the *L* the glory due Ps 29:2 3068
worship the *L* in the beauty of Ps 29:2 3068
The voice of the *L* is upon the Ps 29:3 3068
the *L* is upon many waters Ps 29:3 3068
The voice of the *L* is powerful Ps 29:4 3068
the voice of the *L* is full of Ps 29:4 3068
The voice of the *L* breaketh the Ps 29:5 3068
the *L* breaketh the cedars of Ps 29:5 3068
The voice of the *L* divideth the Ps 29:7 3068
The voice of the *L* shaketh the Ps 29:8 3068
the *L* shaketh the wilderness of Ps 29:8 3068
The voice of the *L* maketh the Ps 29:9 3068
The *L* sitteth upon the flood Ps 29:10 3068
the *L* sitteth King for ever Ps 29:10 3068
The *L* will give strength unto his Ps 29:11 3068
the *L* will bless his people with Ps 29:11 3068
I will extol thee, O *L* Ps 30:1 3068
O *L* my God, I cried unto thee, and Ps 30:2 3068
O *L*, thou hast brought up my soul Ps 30:3 3068
Sing unto the *L*, O ye saints of Ps 30:4 3068
L, by thy favour thou hast made Ps 30:7 3068
I cried to thee, O *L* Ps 30:8 3068
unto the *L* I made supplication Ps 30:8 136
Hear, O *L*, and have mercy upon me Ps 30:10 3068
L, be thou my helper Ps 30:10 3068
O *L* my God, I will give thanks Ps 30:12 3068
IN thee, O *L*, do I put my trust Ps 31:1 3068
redeemed me, O *L* God of truth Ps 31:5 3068
but I trust in the *L* Ps 31:6 3068
Have mercy upon me, O *L*, for I am Ps 31:9 3068
But I trusted in thee, O *L* Ps 31:14 3068
Let me not be ashamed, O *L* Ps 31:17 3068
Blessed be the *L* Ps 31:21 3068
O love the *L*, all ye his saints Ps 31:23 3068
for the *L* preserveth the faithful Ps 31:23 3068
heart, all ye that hope in the *L* Ps 31:24 3068
whom the *L* imputeth not iniquity Ps 32:2 3068
my transgressions unto the *L* Ps 32:5 3068
but he that trusteth in the *L* Ps 32:10 3068
Be glad in the *L*, and rejoice, ye Ps 32:11 3068
Rejoice in the *L*, O ye righteous Ps 33:1 3068
Praise the *L* with harp Ps 33:2 3068
For the word of the *L* is right Ps 33:4 3068
is full of the goodness of the *L* Ps 33:5 3068
By the word of the *L* were the Ps 33:6 3068
Let all the earth fear the *L* Ps 33:8 3068
The *L* bringeth the counsel of the Ps 33:10 3068
of the *L* standeth for ever Ps 33:11 3068
is the nation whose God is the *L* Ps 33:12 3068
The *L* looketh from heaven Ps 33:13 3068
the eye of the *L* is upon them Ps 33:18 3068
Our soul waiteth for the *L* Ps 33:20 3068
Let thy mercy, O *L*, be upon us, Ps 33:22 3068
I will bless the *L* at all times Ps 34:1 3068
shall make her boast in the *L* Ps 34:2 3068
O magnify the *L* with me, and let Ps 34:3 3068
I sought the *L*, and he heard me, Ps 34:4 3068
the *L* heard him, and saved him out Ps 34:6 3068
The angel of the *L* encampeth Ps 34:7 3068
O taste and see that the *L* is good Ps 34:8 3068
O fear the *L*, ye his saints Ps 34:9 3068
but they that seek the *L* shall Ps 34:10 3068
will teach you the fear of the *L* Ps 34:11 3068
The eyes of the *L* are upon the Ps 34:15 3068
The face of the *L* is against them Ps 34:16 3068
the *L* heareth, and delivereth them Ps 34:17 3068
The *L* is nigh unto them that are Ps 34:18 3068
but the *L* delivereth him out of Ps 34:19 3068
The *L* redeemeth the soul of his Ps 34:22 3068
Plead my cause, O *L*, with them Ps 35:1 3068
let the angel of the *L* chase them Ps 35:5 3068
the angel of the *L* persecute them Ps 35:6 3068
my soul shall be joyful in the *L* Ps 35:9 3068
All my bones shall say, *L* Ps 35:10 3068
L, how long wilt thou look on Ps 35:17 136
This thou hast seen, O *L* Ps 35:22 3068
O *L*, be not far from me Ps 35:22 136
unto my cause, my God and my *L* Ps 35:23 136
O *L* my God, according to thy Ps 35:24 3068
Let the *L* be magnified, which Ps 35:27 3068
of David, the servant of the *L* Ps 36:t 3068
Thy mercy, O *L*, is in the heavens Ps 36:5 3068
O *L*, thou preservest man and beast Ps 36:6 3068
Trust in the *L*, and do good Ps 37:3 3068
Delight thyself also in the *L* Ps 37:4 3068
Commit thy way unto the *L* Ps 37:5 3068
Rest in the *L*, and wait patiently Ps 37:7 3068
but those that wait upon the *L* Ps 37:9 3068
The *L* shall laugh at him Ps 37:13 136
but the *L* upholdeth the righteous Ps 37:17 3068
The *L* knoweth the days of the Ps 37:18 3068
the enemies of the *L* shall be as Ps 37:20 3068
a good man are ordered by the *L* Ps 37:23 3068
for the *L* upholdeth him with his Ps 37:24 3068
For the *L* loveth judgment, and Ps 37:28 3068
The *L* will not leave him in his Ps 37:33 3068
Wait on the *L*, and keep his way, Ps 37:34 3068
of the righteous is of the *L* Ps 37:39 3068
the *L* shall help them, and deliver Ps 37:40 3068
O *L*, rebuke me not in thy wrath Ps 38:1 3068
L, all my desire is before thee Ps 38:9 136
For in thee, O *L*, do I hope Ps 38:15 3068
thou wilt hear, O *L* my God Ps 38:15 136
Forsake me not, O *L* Ps 38:21 3068
to help me, O *L* my salvation Ps 38:22 136
L, make me to know mine end, and Ps 39:4 3068
And now, *L*, what wait I for Ps 39:7 136
Hear my prayer, O *L*, and give ear Ps 39:12 3068
I waited patiently for the *L* Ps 40:1 3068
and fear, and shall trust in the *L* Ps 40:3 3068
man that maketh the *L* his trust Ps 40:4 3068
O *L* my God, are thy wonderful Ps 40:5 3068
I have not refrained my lips, O *L* Ps 40:9 3068
thy tender mercies from me, O *L* Ps 40:11 3068
Be pleased, O *L*, to deliver me Ps 40:13 3068
O *L*, make haste to help me Ps 40:13 3068
continually, The *L* be magnified Ps 40:16 3068
yet the *L* thinketh upon me Ps 40:17 136
the *L* will deliver him in time of Ps 41:1 3068
The *L* will preserve him, and keep Ps 41:2 3068
The *L* will strengthen him upon Ps 41:3 3068
I said, *L*, be merciful unto me Ps 41:4 3068
But thou, O *L*, be merciful unto Ps 41:10 3068
Blessed be the *L* God of Israel Ps 41:13 3068
Yet the *L* will command his Ps 42:8 3068
Awake, why sleepest thou, O *L* Ps 44:23 136
for he is thy *L* Ps 45:11 113
The *L* of hosts is with us Ps 46:7 3068
Come, behold the works of the *L* Ps 46:8 3068
The *L* of hosts is with us Ps 46:11 3068
For the *L* most high is terrible Ps 47:2 3068
the *L* with the sound of a trumpet Ps 47:5 3068
Great is the *L*, and greatly to be Ps 48:1 3068
in the city of the *L* of hosts Ps 48:8 3068
The mighty God, even the *L* Ps 50:1 3068
O *L*, open thou my lips Ps 51:15 136
the *L* is with them that uphold my Ps 54:4 136
I will praise thy name, O *L* Ps 54:6 3068
Destroy, O *L*, and divide their Ps 55:9 136
and the *L* shall save me Ps 55:16 3068
Cast thy burden upon the *L* Ps 55:22 3068
in the *L* will I praise his word Ps 56:10 3068
I will praise thee, O *L*, among Ps 57:9 136
teeth of the young lions, O *L* Ps 58:6 3068
nor for my sin, O *L* Ps 59:3 3068
O *L* God of hosts, the God of Ps 59:5 3068
But thou, O *L*, shalt laugh at Ps 59:8 3068
bring them down, O *L* our shield Ps 59:11 136
Also unto thee, O *L*, belongeth Ps 62:12 136
righteous shall be glad in the *L* Ps 64:10 3068
my heart, the *L* will not hear me Ps 66:18 136
The *L* gave the word Ps 68:11 136
the *L* will dwell in it for ever Ps 68:16 3068
the *L* is among them, as in Sinai, Ps 68:17 136
that the *L* God might dwell among Ps 68:18 136
Blessed be the *L*, who daily Ps 68:19 136
unto GOD the *L* belong the issues Ps 68:20 136
The *L* said, I will bring again Ps 68:22 136
in the congregations, even the *L* Ps 68:26 136
O sing praises unto the *L* Ps 68:32 136
O *L* GOD of hosts, be ashamed for Ps 69:6 136
me, my prayer is unto thee, O *L* Ps 69:13 3068
Hear me, O *L* Ps 69:16 3068
This also shall please the *L* Ps 69:31 3068
For the *L* heareth the poor, and Ps 69:33 3068
make haste to help me, O *L* Ps 70:1 3068
O *L*, make no tarrying Ps 70:5 3068
In thee, O *L*, do I put my trust Ps 71:1 3068
For thou art my hope, O *L* GOD Ps 71:5 136
go in the strength of the *L* GOD Ps 71:16 136
Blessed be the *L* God, the God of Ps 72:18 3068
so, O *L*, when thou awakest, thou Ps 73:20 136
I have put my trust in the *L* GOD Ps 73:28 136
the enemy hath reproached, O *L* Ps 74:18 3068
the hand of the *L* there is a cup Ps 75:8 3068
Vow, and pay unto the *L* your God Ps 76:11 3068
day of my trouble I sought the *L* Ps 77:2 136
Will the *L* cast off for ever Ps 77:7 136
will remember the works of the *L* Ps 77:11 3050
to come the praises of the *L* Ps 78:4 3068
Therefore the *L* heard this Ps 78:21 3068
Then the *L* awaked as one out of Ps 78:65 136
How long, *L*? Ps 79:5 3068
they have reproached thee, O *L* Ps 79:12 136
O *L* God of hosts, how long wilt Ps 80:4 3068
O *L* God of hosts, cause thy face Ps 80:19 3068
I am the *L* thy God, which brought Ps 81:10 3068
The haters of the *L* should have Ps 81:15 3068
that they may seek thy name, O *L* Ps 83:16 3068
are thy tabernacles, O *L* of hosts Ps 84:1 3068
fainteth for the courts of the *L* Ps 84:2 3068
O *L* of hosts, my King, and my God Ps 84:3 3068
O *L* God of hosts, hear my prayer Ps 84:8 3068
For the *L* God is a sun and shield Ps 84:11 3068
the *L* will give grace and glory Ps 84:11 3068
O *L* of hosts, blessed is the man Ps 84:12 3068
L, thou hast been favourable unto Ps 85:1 3068
Shew us thy mercy, O *L*, and grant Ps 85:7 3068
hear what God the *L* will speak Ps 85:8 3068
the *L* shall give that which is Ps 85:12 3068
Bow down thine ear, O *L*, hear me Ps 86:1 3068
Be merciful unto me, O *L* Ps 86:3 136
for unto thee, O *L*, do I lift up Ps 86:4 136
For thou, *L*, art good, and ready Ps 86:5 136
Give ear, O *L*, unto my prayer Ps 86:6 3068
there is none like unto thee, O *L* Ps 86:8 136
come and worship before thee, O *L* Ps 86:9 136
Teach me thy way, O *L* Ps 86:11 3068
O *L* my God, with all my heart Ps 86:12 136
But thou, O *L*, art a God full of Ps 86:15 136
because thou, *L*, hast holpen me, Ps 86:17 3068
The *L* loveth the gates of Zion Ps 87:2 3068
The *L* shall count, when he Ps 87:6 3068
O *l* God of my salvation, I have Ps 88:1 3068
L, I have called daily upon thee, Ps 88:9 3068
But unto thee have I cried, O *L* Ps 88:13 3068
L, why castest thou off my soul Ps 88:14 3068
of the mercies of the *L* for ever Ps 89:1 3068
shall praise thy wonders, O *L* Ps 89:5 3068
heaven can be compared unto the *L* Ps 89:6 3068
mighty can be likened unto the *L* Ps 89:6 3068
O *L* God of hosts, who is a strong Ps 89:8 3068
who is a strong *L* like unto thee Ps 89:8 3050
they shall walk, O *L*, in the Ps 89:15 3068
For the *L* is our defence Ps 89:18 3068
How long, *L*? Ps 89:46 3068
L, where are thy former Ps 89:49 136
Remember, *L*, the reproach of thy Ps 89:50 136
enemies have reproached, O *L* Ps 89:51 3068
Blessed be the *L* for evermore Ps 89:52 3068
L, thou hast been our dwelling Ps 90:1 136
Return, O *L*, how long Ps 90:13 3068
of the *L* our God be upon us Ps 90:17 136
I will say of the *L*, He is my Ps 91:2 3068
Because thou hast made the *L* Ps 91:9 3068
thing to give thanks unto the *L* Ps 92:1 3068
For thou, *L*, hast made me glad Ps 92:4 3068
O *L*, how great are thy works Ps 92:5 3068
But thou, *L*, art most high for Ps 92:8 3068
For, lo, thine enemies, O *L* Ps 92:9 3068
be planted in the house of the *L* Ps 92:13 3068
To shew that the *L* is upright Ps 92:15 3068
The *L* reigneth, he is clothed Ps 93:1 3068
the *L* is clothed with strength, Ps 93:1 3068
The floods have lifted up, O *L* Ps 93:3 3068
The *L* on high is mightier than Ps 93:4 3068
becometh thine house, O *L* Ps 93:5 3068
O *L* God, to whom vengeance Ps 94:1 3068
L, how long shall the wicked, how Ps 94:3 3068
break in pieces thy people, O *L* Ps 94:5 3068
The *L* shall not see, neither Ps 94:7 3050
The *L* knoweth the thoughts of man Ps 94:11 3068
the man whom thou chastenest, O *L* Ps 94:12 3050
For the *L* will not cast off his Ps 94:14 3068
Unless the *L* had been my help, my Ps 94:17 3068
thy mercy, O *L*, held me up Ps 94:18 3068
But the *L* is my defence Ps 94:22 3068
the *L* our God shall cut them off Ps 94:23 3068
O come, let us sing unto the *L* Ps 95:1 3068
For the *L* is a great God, and a Ps 95:3 3068
us kneel before the *L* our maker Ps 95:6 3068
O sing unto the *L* a new song Ps 96:1 3068
sing unto the *L*, all the earth Ps 96:1 3068
Sing unto the *L*, bless his name Ps 96:2 3068
For the *L* is great, and greatly to Ps 96:4 3068
but the *L* made the heavens Ps 96:5 3068
Give unto the *L*, O ye kindreds of Ps 96:7 3068
the people, give unto the *L* glory Ps 96:7 3068
Give unto the *L* the glory due Ps 96:8 3068
O worship the *L* in the beauty of Ps 96:9 3068
the heathen that the *L* reigneth Ps 96:10 3068
Before the *L*: for he cometh Ps 96:13 3068
The *L* reigneth Ps 97:1 3068
like wax at the presence of the *L* Ps 97:5 113
of the *L* of the whole earth Ps 97:5 3068
because of thy judgments, O *L* Ps 97:8 3068
For thou, *L*, art high above all Ps 97:9 3068
Ye that love the *L*, hate evil Ps 97:10 3068
Rejoice in the *L*, ye righteous Ps 97:12 3068
O sing unto the *L* a new song Ps 98:1 3068
The *L* hath made known his Ps 98:2 3068
Make a joyful noise unto the *L* Ps 98:4 3068
Sing unto the *L* with the harp Ps 98:5 3068
make a joyful noise before the *L* Ps 98:6 3068
Before the *L*; for he cometh Ps 98:9 3068
The *L* reigneth Ps 99:1 3068
The *L* is great in Zion Ps 99:2 3068
Exalt ye the *L* our God, and Ps 99:5 3068
they called upon the *L*, and he Ps 99:6 3068
Thou answeredst them, O *L* our God Ps 99:8 3068
Exalt the *L* our God, and worship Ps 99:9 3068
for the *L* our God is holy Ps 99:9 3068
Make a joyful noise unto the *L* Ps 100:1 3068
Serve the *L* with gladness Ps 100:2 3068
Know ye that the *L* he is God Ps 100:3 3068
For the *L* is good Ps 100:5 3068
unto thee, O *L*, will I sing Ps 101:1 3068
doers from the city of the *L* Ps 101:8 3068
out his complaint before the *L* Ps 102:t 3068
Hear my prayer, O *L*, and let my Ps 102:1 3068
But thou, O *L*, shalt endure for Ps 102:12 3068

shall fear the name of the *L*	Ps 102:15	3068
When the *L* shall build up Zion,	Ps 102:16	3068
be created shall praise the *L*	Ps 102:18	3050
heaven did the *L* behold the earth	Ps 102:19	3068
declare the name of the *L* in Zion	Ps 102:21	3068
and the kingdoms, to serve the *L*	Ps 102:22	3068
Bless the *L*, O my soul	Ps 103:1	3068
Bless the *L*, O my soul, and forget	Ps 103:2	3068
The *L* executeth righteousness and	Ps 103:6	3068
The *L* is merciful and gracious,	Ps 103:8	3068
so the *L* pitieth them that fear	Ps 103:13	3068
But the mercy of the *L* is from	Ps 103:17	3068
The *L* hath prepared his throne in	Ps 103:19	3068
Bless the *L*, ye his angels, that	Ps 103:20	3068
Bless ye the *L*, all ye his hosts	Ps 103:21	3068
Bless the *L*, all his works in all	Ps 103:22	3068
bless the *L*, O my soul	Ps 103:22	3068
Bless the *L*, O my soul	Ps 104:1	3068
O *L* my God, thou art very great	Ps 104:1	3068
trees of the *L* are full of sap	Ps 104:16	3068
O *L*, how manifold are thy works	Ps 104:24	3068
The glory of the *L* shall endure	Ps 104:31	3068
the *L* shall rejoice in his works	Ps 104:31	3068
sing unto the *L* as long as I live	Ps 104:33	3068
I will be glad in the *L*	Ps 104:34	3068
Bless thou the *L*, O my soul	Ps 104:35	3050
Praise ye the *L*	Ps 104:35	3050
O give thanks unto the *L*	Ps 105:1	3050
of them rejoice that seek the *L*	Ps 105:3	3050
Seek the *L*, and his strength	Ps 105:4	3050
He is the *L* our God	Ps 105:7	3050
the word of the *L* tried him	Ps 105:19	3050
Praise ye the *L*	Ps 105:45	3050
Praise ye the *L*	Ps 106:1	3050
O give thanks unto the *L*	Ps 106:1	3068
utter the mighty acts of the *L*	Ps 106:2	3068
Remember me, O *L*, with the favour	Ps 106:4	3068
camp, and Aaron the saint of the *L*	Ps 106:16	3068
not unto the voice of the *L*	Ps 106:25	3068
whom the *L* commanded them	Ps 106:34	3068
the *L* kindled against his people	Ps 106:40	3068
O *L* our God, and gather us from	Ps 106:47	3068
Blessed be the *L* God of Israel	Ps 106:48	3068
Praise ye the *L*	Ps 106:48	3050
O give thanks unto the *L*, for he	Ps 107:1	3068
Let the redeemed of the *L* say so	Ps 107:2	3068
cried unto the *L* in their trouble	Ps 107:6	3068
praise the *L* for his goodness	Ps 107:8	3068
cried unto the *L* in their trouble	Ps 107:13	3068
praise the *L* for his goodness	Ps 107:15	3068
cry unto the *L* in their trouble	Ps 107:19	3068
praise the *L* for his goodness	Ps 107:21	3068
These see the works of the *L*	Ps 107:24	3068
cry unto the *L* in their trouble	Ps 107:28	3068
praise the *L* for his goodness	Ps 107:31	3068
the lovingkindness of the *L*	Ps 107:43	3068
I will praise thee, O *L*, among	Ps 108:3	3068
fathers be remembered with the *L*	Ps 109:14	3068
them be before the *L* continually	Ps 109:15	3068
of mine adversaries from the *L*	Ps 109:20	3068
But do thou for me, O GOD the *L*	Ps 109:21	136
Help me, O *L* my God	Ps 109:26	3068
that thou, *L*, hast done it	Ps 109:27	3068
praise the *L* with my mouth	Ps 109:30	3068
The *L* said unto my	Ps 110:1	3068
said unto my *L*, Sit thou	Ps 110:1	113
The *L* shall send the rod of thy	Ps 110:2	3068
The *L* hath sworn, and will not	Ps 110:4	3068
The *L* at thy right hand shall	Ps 110:5	136
Praise ye the *L*	Ps 111:1	3050
I will praise the *L* with my whole	Ps 111:1	3068
The works of the *L* are great	Ps 111:2	3068
the *L* is gracious and full of	Ps 111:4	3068
The fear of the *L* is the	Ps 111:10	3068
Praise ye the *L*	Ps 112:1	3050
is the man that feareth the *L*	Ps 112:1	3068
heart is fixed, trusting in the *L*	Ps 112:7	3068
Praise ye the *L*	Ps 113:1	3050
Praise, O ye servants of the *L*	Ps 113:1	3068
praise the name of the *L*	Ps 113:1	3068
of the *L* from this time forth	Ps 113:2	3068
The *L* is high above all nations,	Ps 113:4	3068
Who is like unto the *L* our God	Ps 113:5	3068
Praise ye the *L*	Ps 113:9	3050
earth, at the presence of the *L*	Ps 114:7	113
Not unto us, O *L*, not unto us,	Ps 115:1	3068
O Israel, trust thou in the *L*	Ps 115:9	3068
O house of Aaron, trust in the *L*	Ps 115:10	3068
fear the *L*, trust in the *L*	Ps 115:11	3068
The *L* hath been mindful of us	Ps 115:12	3068
will bless them that fear the *L*	Ps 115:13	3068
The *L* shall increase you more and	Ps 115:14	3068
of the *L* which made heaven	Ps 115:15	3068
The dead praise not the *L*	Ps 115:17	3050
bless the *L* from this time forth	Ps 115:18	3050
Praise the *L*	Ps 115:18	3050
I love the *L*, because he hath	Ps 116:1	3068
called I upon the name of the *L*	Ps 116:4	3068
O *L*, I beseech thee, deliver my	Ps 116:4	3068
Gracious is the *L*, and righteous	Ps 116:5	3068
The *L* preserveth the simple	Ps 116:6	3068
for the *L* hath dealt bountifully	Ps 116:7	3068
I will walk before the *L* in the	Ps 116:9	3068
What shall I render unto the *L*	Ps 116:12	3068
and call upon the name of the *L*	Ps 116:13	3068
I will pay my vows unto the *L* now	Ps 116:14	3068
the *L* is the death of his saints	Ps 116:15	3068
O *L*, truly I am thy servant	Ps 116:16	3068
will call upon the name of the *L*	Ps 116:17	3068
I will pay my vows unto the *L* now	Ps 116:18	3068
Praise ye the *L*	Ps 116:19	3068
O praise the *L*, all ye nations	Ps 117:1	3068
the truth of the *L* endureth for	Ps 117:2	3068
Praise ye the *L*	Ps 117:2	3050
O give thanks unto the *L*	Ps 118:1	3068
Let them now that fear the *L* say	Ps 118:4	3068
I called upon the *L* in distress	Ps 118:5	3050
the *L* answered me, and set me in a	Ps 118:5	3050
The *L* is on my side	Ps 118:6	3068
The *L* taketh my part with them	Ps 118:7	3068
It is better to trust in the *L*	Ps 118:8	3068
the *L* than to put confidence in	Ps 118:9	3068
name of the *L* will I destroy them	Ps 118:10	3068
name of the *L* I will destroy them	Ps 118:11	3068
name of the *L* I will destroy them	Ps 118:12	3068
but the *L* helped me	Ps 118:13	3068
The *L* is my strength and song, and	Ps 118:14	3050
hand of the *L* doeth valiantly	Ps 118:15	3068
right hand of the *L* is exalted	Ps 118:16	3068
hand of the *L* doeth valiantly	Ps 118:16	3068
and declare the works of the *L*	Ps 118:17	3050
The *L* hath chastened me sore	Ps 118:18	3050
into them, and I will praise the *L*	Ps 118:19	3050
This gate of the *L*, into which	Ps 118:20	3068
is the day which the *L* hath made	Ps 118:24	3068
Save now, I beseech thee, O *L*	Ps 118:25	3068
O *L*, I beseech thee, send now	Ps 118:25	3068
that cometh in the name of the *L*	Ps 118:26	3068
you out of the house of the *L*	Ps 118:26	3068
God is the *L*, which hath shewed	Ps 118:27	3068
O give thanks unto the *L*	Ps 118:29	3068
way, who walk in the law of the *L*	Ps 119:1	3068
Blessed art thou, O *L*	Ps 119:12	3068
O *L*, put me not to shame	Ps 119:31	3068
Teach me, O *L*, the way of thy	Ps 119:33	3068
mercies come also unto me, O *L*	Ps 119:41	3068
thy judgments of old, O *L*	Ps 119:52	3068
I have remembered thy name, O *L*	Ps 119:55	3068
Thou art my portion, O *L*	Ps 119:57	3068
The earth, O *L*, is full of thy	Ps 119:64	3068
dealt well with thy servant, O *L*	Ps 119:65	3068
I know, O *L*, that thy judgments	Ps 119:75	3068
For ever, O *L*, thy word is	Ps 119:89	3068
quicken me, O *L*, according unto	Ps 119:107	3068
offerings of my mouth, O *L*	Ps 119:108	3068
It is time for thee, *L*, to work	Ps 119:126	3068
Righteous art thou, O *L*, and	Ps 119:137	3068
hear me, O *L*	Ps 119:145	3068
O *L*, quicken me according to thy	Ps 119:149	3068
Thou art near, O *L*	Ps 119:151	3068
Great are thy tender mercies, O *L*	Ps 119:156	3068
quicken me, O *L*, according to thy	Ps 119:159	3068
L, I have hoped for thy salvation	Ps 119:166	3068
my cry come near before thee, O *L*	Ps 119:169	3068
longed for thy salvation, O *L*	Ps 119:174	3068
In my distress I cried unto the *L*	Ps 120:1	3068
Deliver my soul, O *L*, from lying	Ps 120:2	3068
My help cometh from the *L*	Ps 121:2	3068
The *L* is thy keeper	Ps 121:5	3068
the *L* is thy shade upon thy right	Ps 121:5	3068
The *L* shall preserve thee from	Ps 121:7	3068
The *L* shall preserve thy going	Ps 121:8	3068
Let us go into the house of the *L*	Ps 122:1	3068
tribes go up, the tribes of the *L*	Ps 122:4	3050
thanks unto the name of the *L*	Ps 122:4	3068
Because of the house of the *L* our	Ps 122:9	3068
our eyes wait upon the *L* our God	Ps 123:2	3068
Have mercy upon us, O *L*, have	Ps 123:3	3068
been the *L* who was on our side	Ps 124:1	3068
been the *L* who was on our side	Ps 124:2	3068
Blessed be the *L*, who hath not	Ps 124:6	3068
Our help is in the name of the *L*	Ps 124:8	3068
in the *L* shall be as mount Zion	Ps 125:1	3068
so the *L* is round about his	Ps 125:2	3068
Do good, O *L*, unto those that be	Ps 125:4	3068
the *L* shall lead them forth with	Ps 125:5	3068
When the *L* turned again the	Ps 126:1	3068
The *L* hath done great things for	Ps 126:2	3068
The *L* hath done great things for	Ps 126:3	3068
Turn again our captivity, O *L*	Ps 126:4	3068
Except the *L* build the house,	Ps 127:1	3068
except the *L* keep the city, the	Ps 127:1	3068
children are an heritage of the *L*	Ps 127:3	3068
is every one that feareth the *L*	Ps 128:1	3068
man be blessed that feareth the *L*	Ps 128:4	3068
The *L* shall bless thee out of	Ps 128:5	3068
The *L* is righteous	Ps 129:4	3068
The blessing of the *L* be upon you	Ps 129:8	3068
we bless you in the name of the *L*	Ps 129:8	3068
have I cried unto thee, O *L*	Ps 130:1	3068
L, hear my voice	Ps 130:2	136
If thou, *L*, shouldest mark	Ps 130:3	3050
shouldest mark iniquities, O *L*	Ps 130:3	136
I wait for the *L*, my soul doth	Ps 130:5	3068
My soul waiteth for the *L* more	Ps 130:6	136
Let Israel hope in the *L*	Ps 130:7	3068
for with the *L* there is mercy, and	Ps 130:7	3068
L, my heart is not haughty, nor	Ps 131:1	3068
hope in the *L* from henceforth	Ps 131:3	3068
L, remember David, and all his	Ps 132:1	3068
How he sware unto the *L*, and vowed	Ps 132:2	3068
I find out a place for the *L*	Ps 132:5	3068
Arise, O *L*, into thy rest	Ps 132:8	3068
The *L* hath sworn in truth unto	Ps 132:11	3068
For the *L* hath chosen Zion	Ps 132:13	3068
for there the *L* commanded the	Ps 133:3	3068
Behold, bless ye the *L*	Ps 134:1	3068
all ye servants of the *L*	Ps 134:1	3068
night stand in the house of the *L*	Ps 134:1	3068
in the sanctuary, and bless the *L*	Ps 134:2	3068
The *L* that made heaven and earth	Ps 134:3	3068
Praise ye the *L*	Ps 135:1	3050
Praise ye the name of the *L*	Ps 135:1	3068
him, O ye servants of the *L*	Ps 135:1	3068
that stand in the house of the *L*	Ps 135:2	3068
Praise the *L*	Ps 135:3	3050
for the *L* is good	Ps 135:3	3068
For the *L* hath chosen Jacob unto	Ps 135:4	3050
For I know that the *L* is great	Ps 135:5	3068
that our *L* is above all gods	Ps 135:5	113
Whatsoever the *L* pleased, that	Ps 135:6	3068
Thy name, O *L*, endureth for ever	Ps 135:13	3068
and thy memorial, O *L*, throughout	Ps 135:13	3068
For the *L* will judge his people,	Ps 135:14	3068
Bless the *L*, O house of Israel	Ps 135:19	3068
bless the *L*, O house of Aaron	Ps 135:19	3068
Bless the *L*, O house of Levi	Ps 135:20	3068
that fear the *L*, bless the *L*	Ps 135:20	3068
Blessed be the *L* out of Zion	Ps 135:21	3068
Praise ye the *L*	Ps 135:21	3050
O Give thanks unto the *L*	Ps 136:1	3068
O give thanks to the *L* of lords	Ps 136:3	113
Remember, O *L*, the children of	Ps 137:7	3068
the earth shall praise thee, O *L*	Ps 138:4	3068
shall sing in the ways of the *L*	Ps 138:5	3068
for great is the glory of the *L*	Ps 138:5	3068
Though the *L* be high, yet hath he	Ps 138:6	3068
The *L* will perfect that which	Ps 138:8	3068
thy mercy, O *L*, endureth for ever	Ps 138:8	3068
O *L*, thou hast searched me, and	Ps 139:1	3068
a word in my tongue, but, lo, O *L*	Ps 139:4	3068
Do not I hate them, O *L*, that	Ps 139:21	3068
Deliver me, O *L*, from the evil	Ps 140:1	3068
Keep me, O *L*, from the hands of	Ps 140:4	3068
I said unto the *L*, Thou art my	Ps 140:6	3068
voice of my supplications, O *L*	Ps 140:6	3068
O God the *L*, the strength of my	Ps 140:7	136
Grant not, O *L*, the desires of	Ps 140:8	3068
I know that the *L* will maintain	Ps 140:12	3068
L, I cry unto thee	Ps 141:1	3068
Set a watch, O *L*, before my mouth	Ps 141:3	3068
eyes are unto thee, O GOD the *L*	Ps 141:8	136
I cried unto the *L* with my voice	Ps 142:1	3068
with my voice unto the *L* did I	Ps 142:1	3068
I cried unto thee, O *L*	Ps 142:5	3068
Hear my prayer, O *L*, give ear to	Ps 143:1	3068
Hear me speedily, O *L*	Ps 143:7	3068
Deliver me, O *L*, from mine	Ps 143:9	3068
Quicken me, O *L*, for thy name's	Ps 143:11	3068
Blessed be the *L* my strength	Ps 144:1	3068
L, what is man, that thou takest	Ps 144:3	3068
Bow thy heavens, O *L*, and come	Ps 144:5	3068
that people, whose God is the *L*	Ps 144:15	3068
Great is the *L*, and greatly to be	Ps 145:3	3068
The *L* is gracious, and full of	Ps 145:8	3068
The *L* is good to all	Ps 145:9	3068
thy works shall praise thee, O *L*	Ps 145:10	3068
The *L* upholdeth all that fall, and	Ps 145:14	3068
The *L* is righteous in all his	Ps 145:17	3068
The *L* is nigh unto all them that	Ps 145:18	3068
The *L* preserveth all them that	Ps 145:20	3068
shall speak the praise of the *L*	Ps 145:21	3068
Praise ye the *L*	Ps 146:1	3050
Praise the *L*, O my soul	Ps 146:1	3068
While I live will I praise the *L*	Ps 146:2	3068
whose hope is in the *L* his God	Ps 146:5	3068
The *L* looseth the prisoners	Ps 146:7	3068
The *L* openeth the eyes of the	Ps 146:8	3068
the *L* raiseth them that are bowed	Ps 146:8	3068
the *L* loveth the righteous	Ps 146:8	3068
The *L* preserveth the strangers	Ps 146:9	3068
The *L* shall reign for ever, even	Ps 146:10	3068
Praise ye the *L*	Ps 146:10	3050
Praise ye the *L*	Ps 147:1	3050
The *L* doth build up Jerusalem	Ps 147:2	3068
Great is our *L*, and of great power	Ps 147:5	113
The *L* lifteth up the meek	Ps 147:6	3068
Sing unto the *L* with thanksgiving	Ps 147:7	3068
The *L* taketh pleasure in them	Ps 147:11	3068
Praise the *L*, O Jerusalem	Ps 147:12	3068
Praise ye the *L*	Ps 147:20	3050
Praise ye the *L*	Ps 148:1	3050
Praise ye the *L* from the heavens	Ps 148:1	3068
Let them praise the name of the *L*	Ps 148:5	3068
Praise the *L* from the earth, ye	Ps 148:7	3068
Let them praise the name of the *L*	Ps 148:13	3068
Praise ye the *L*	Ps 148:14	3050
Praise ye the *L*	Ps 149:1	3050
Sing unto the *L* a new song	Ps 149:1	3068
For the *L* taketh pleasure in his	Ps 149:4	3068
Praise ye the *L*	Ps 149:9	3050
Praise ye the *L*	Ps 150:1	3050
that hath breath praise the *L*	Ps 150:6	3050
Praise ye the *L*	Ps 150:6	3050
The fear of the *L* is the	Prov 1:7	3068
did not choose the fear of the *L*	Prov 1:29	3068
thou understand the fear of the *L*	Prov 2:5	3068
For the *L* giveth wisdom	Prov 2:6	3068
Trust in the *L* with all thine	Prov 3:5	3068
fear the *L*, and depart from evil	Prov 3:7	3068
Honour the *L* with thy substance,	Prov 3:9	3068
not the chastening of the *L*	Prov 3:11	3068
For whom the *L* loveth he	Prov 3:12	3068
The *L* by wisdom hath founded the	Prov 3:19	3068
For the *L* shall be thy confidence	Prov 3:26	3068
froward is abomination to the *L*	Prov 3:32	3068
The curse of the *L* is in the	Prov 3:33	3068
man are before the eyes of the *L*	Prov 5:21	3068
These six things doth the *L* hate	Prov 6:16	3068
The fear of the *L* is to hate evil	Prov 8:13	3068
The *L* possessed me in the	Prov 8:22	3068
and shall obtain favour of the *L*	Prov 8:35	3068
The fear of the *L* is the	Prov 9:10	3068
The *L* will not suffer the soul of	Prov 10:3	3068
The blessing of the *L*, it maketh	Prov 10:22	3068
The fear of the *L* prolongeth days	Prov 10:27	3068
The way of the *L* is strength to	Prov 10:29	3068
balance is abomination to the *L*	Prov 11:1	3068
heart are abomination to the *L*	Prov 11:20	3068
man obtaineth favour of the *L*	Prov 12:2	3068
lips are abomination to the *L*	Prov 12:22	3068
in his uprightness feareth the *L*	Prov 14:2	3068

In the fear of the *L* is strong	Prov 14:26	3068
The fear of the *L* is a fountain	Prov 14:27	3068
The eyes of the *L* are in every	Prov 15:3	3068
wicked is an abomination to the *L*	Prov 15:8	3068
is an abomination unto the *L*	Prov 15:9	3068
and destruction are before the *L*	Prov 15:11	3068
fear of the *L* than great treasure	Prov 15:16	3068
The *L* will destroy the house of	Prov 15:25	3068
are an abomination to the *L*	Prov 15:26	3068
The *L* is far from the wicked	Prov 15:29	3068
The fear of the *L* is the	Prov 15:33	3068
of the tongue, is from the *L*	Prov 16:1	3068
but the *L* weigheth the spirits	Prov 16:2	3068
Commit thy works unto the *L*	Prov 16:3	3068
The *L* hath made all things for	Prov 16:4	3068
heart is an abomination to the *L*	Prov 16:5	3068
by the fear of the *L* men depart	Prov 16:6	3068
When a man's ways please the *L*	Prov 16:7	3068
but the *L* directeth his steps	Prov 16:9	3068
and whoso trusteth in the *L*	Prov 16:20	3068
disposing thereof is of the *L*	Prov 16:33	3068
but the *L* trieth the hearts	Prov 17:3	3068
both are abomination to the *L*	Prov 17:15	3068
The name of the *L* is a strong	Prov 18:10	3068
and obtaineth favour of the *L*	Prov 18:22	3068
his heart fretteth against the *L*	Prov 19:3	3068
and a prudent wife is from the *L*	Prov 19:14	3068
upon the poor lendeth unto the *L*	Prov 19:17	3068
nevertheless the counsel of the *L*	Prov 19:21	3068
The fear of the *L* tendeth to life	Prov 19:23	3068
are alike abomination to the *L*	Prov 20:10	3068
the *L* hath made even both of them	Prov 20:12	3068
but wait on the *L*, and he shall	Prov 20:22	3068
are an abomination unto the *L*	Prov 20:23	3068
Man's goings are of the *L*	Prov 20:24	3068
of man is the candle of the *L*	Prov 20:27	3068
heart is in the hand of the *L*	Prov 21:1	3068
but the *L* pondereth the hearts	Prov 21:2	3068
to the *L* than sacrifice	Prov 21:3	3068
nor counsel against the *L*	Prov 21:30	3068
but safety is of the *L*	Prov 21:31	3068
the *L* is the maker of them all	Prov 22:2	3068
and the fear of the *L* are riches	Prov 22:4	3068
The eyes of the *L* preserve	Prov 22:12	3068
of the *L* shall fall therein	Prov 22:14	3068
That thy trust may be in the *L*	Prov 22:19	3068
For the *L* will plead their cause,	Prov 22:23	3068
fear of the *L* all the day long	Prov 23:17	3068
Lest the *L* see it, and it	Prov 24:18	3068
My son, fear thou the *L* and the	Prov 24:21	3068
head, and the *L* shall reward thee	Prov 25:22	3068
seek the *L* understand all things	Prov 28:5	3068
trust in the *L* shall be made fat	Prov 28:25	3068
the *L* lighteneth both their eyes	Prov 29:13	3068
his trust in the *L* shall be safe	Prov 29:25	3068
man's judgment cometh from the *L*	Prov 29:26	3068
deny thee, and say, Who is the *L*	Prov 30:9	3068
but a woman that feareth the *L*	Prov 31:30	3068
for the *L* hath spoken, I have	Is 1:2	3068
they have forsaken the *L*, they	Is 1:4	3068
Except the *L* of hosts had left	Is 1:9	3068
Hear the word of the *L*, ye rulers	Is 1:10	3068
saith the *L*	Is 1:11	3068
us reason together, saith the *L*	Is 1:18	3068
the mouth of the *L* hath spoken it	Is 1:20	3068
Therefore saith the *L*, the *L*	Is 1:24	113
the *L* of hosts, the mighty One of	Is 1:24	3068
forsake the *L* shall be consumed	Is 1:28	3068
us go up to the mountain of the *L*	Is 2:3	3068
the word of the *L* from Jerusalem	Is 2:3	3068
let us walk in the light of the *L*	Is 2:5	3068
In the dust, for fear of the *L*	Is 2:10	3068
the *L* alone shall be exalted in	Is 2:11	3068
For the day of the *L* of hosts	Is 2:12	3068
the *L* alone shall be exalted in	Is 2:17	3068
of the earth, for fear of the *L*	Is 2:19	3068
ragged rocks, for fear of the *L*	Is 2:21	3068
For, behold, the *L*, the *L* of	Is 3:1	113
the *L* of hosts, doth take away	Is 3:1	3068
and their doings are against the *L*	Is 3:8	3068
The *L* standeth up to plead, and	Is 3:13	3068
The *L* will enter into judgment	Is 3:14	3068
saith the *L* GOD of hosts	Is 3:15	136
Moreover the *L* saith, Because the	Is 3:16	3068
Therefore the *L* will smite with a	Is 3:17	136
the *L* will discover their secret	Is 3:17	3068
In that day the *L* will take away	Is 3:18	136
the branch of the *L* be beautiful	Is 4:2	3068
When the *L* shall have washed away	Is 4:4	136
the *L* will create upon every	Is 4:5	3068
For the vineyard of the *L* of	Is 5:7	3068
In mine ears said the *L* of hosts	Is 5:9	3068
they regard not the work of the *L*	Is 5:12	3068
But the *L* of hosts shall be	Is 5:16	3068
away the law of the *L* of hosts	Is 5:24	3068
the *L* kindled against his people	Is 5:25	3068
also the *L* sitting upon a throne	Is 6:1	136
holy, holy, is the *L* of hosts	Is 6:3	3068
seen the King, the *L* of hosts	Is 6:5	3068
Also I heard the voice of the *L*	Is 6:8	136
Then said I, *L*, how long	Is 6:11	136
the *L* have removed men far away,	Is 6:12	3068
Then said the *L* unto Isaiah	Is 7:3	3068
Thus saith the *L* GOD, It shall	Is 7:7	136
Moreover the *L* spake again unto	Is 7:10	3068
Ask thee a sign of the *L* thy God	Is 7:11	3068
ask, neither will I tempt the *L*	Is 7:12	3068
Therefore the *L* himself shall	Is 7:14	136
The *L* shall bring upon thee, and	Is 7:17	3068
that the *L* shall hiss for the fly	Is 7:18	3068
In the same day shall the *L* shave	Is 7:20	136
Moreover the *L* said unto me	Is 8:1	3068
Then said the *L* to me, Call his	Is 8:3	3068
The *L* spake also unto me again,	Is 8:5	3068
the *L* bringeth up upon them the	Is 8:7	136
For the *L* spake thus to me with a	Is 8:11	3068
Sanctify the *L* of hosts himself	Is 8:13	3068
And I will wait upon the *L*	Is 8:17	3068
the children whom the *L* hath	Is 8:18	3068
in Israel from the *L* of hosts	Is 8:18	3068
The zeal of the *L* of hosts will	Is 9:7	3068
The *L* sent a word into Jacob, and	Is 9:8	3068
Therefore the *L* shall set up the	Is 9:11	3068
do they seek the *L* of hosts	Is 9:13	3068
Therefore the *L* will cut off from	Is 9:14	3068
Therefore the *L* shall have no joy	Is 9:17	136
Through the wrath of the *L* of	Is 9:19	3068
that when the *L* hath performed	Is 10:12	136
Therefore shall the *L*	Is 10:16	113
the *L* of hosts, send among his	Is 10:16	136
but shall stay upon the *L*	Is 10:20	3068
For the *L* GOD of hosts shall make	Is 10:23	136
thus saith the *L* GOD of hosts	Is 10:24	136
the *L* of hosts shall stir up a	Is 10:26	3068
Behold, the *L*	Is 10:33	113
the *L* of hosts, shall lop the	Is 10:33	3068
the spirit of the *L* shall rest	Is 11:2	3068
knowledge and of the fear of the *L*	Is 11:2	3068
in the fear of the *L*	Is 11:3	3068
be full of the knowledge of the *L*	Is 11:9	3068
that the *L* shall set his hand	Is 11:11	136
the *L* shall utterly destroy the	Is 11:15	3068
in that day thou shalt say, O *L*	Is 12:1	3068
for the *L* JEHOVAH is my strength	Is 12:2	3050
day shall ye say, Praise the *L*	Is 12:4	3068
Sing unto the *L*	Is 12:5	3068
the *L* of hosts mustereth the host	Is 13:4	3068
the end of heaven, even the *L*	Is 13:5	3068
for the day of the *L* is at hand	Is 13:6	3068
Behold, the day of the *L* cometh	Is 13:9	3068
in the wrath of the *L* of hosts	Is 13:13	3068
For the *L* will have mercy on	Is 14:1	3068
in the land of the *L* for servants	Is 14:2	3068
to pass in the day that the *L*	Is 14:3	3068
The *L* hath broken the staff of	Is 14:5	3068
them, saith the *L* of hosts	Is 14:22	3068
and son, and nephew, saith the *L*	Is 14:22	3068
destruction, saith the *L* of hosts	Is 14:23	3068
The *L* of hosts hath sworn, saying	Is 14:24	3068
For the *L* of hosts hath purposed,	Is 14:27	3068
That the *L* hath founded Zion, and	Is 14:32	3068
This is the word that the *L* hath	Is 16:13	3068
But now the *L* hath spoken	Is 16:14	3068
of Israel, saith the *L* of hosts	Is 17:3	3068
saith the *L* God of Israel	Is 17:6	3068
For so the *L* said unto me, I will	Is 18:4	3068
L of hosts of a people scattered	Is 18:7	3068
of the name of the *L* of hosts	Is 18:7	3068
the *L* rideth upon a swift cloud,	Is 19:1	3068
shall rule over them, saith the *L*	Is 19:4	113
the *L* of hosts	Is 19:4	3068
let them know what the *L* of hosts	Is 19:12	3068
The *L* hath mingled a perverse	Is 19:14	3068
of the hand of the *L* of hosts	Is 19:16	3068
of the counsel of the *L* of hosts	Is 19:17	3068
and swear to the *L* of hosts	Is 19:18	3068
the *L* in the midst of the land of	Is 19:19	3068
at the border thereof to the *L*	Is 19:19	3068
for a witness unto the *L* of hosts	Is 19:20	3068
the *L* because of the oppressors	Is 19:20	3068
the *L* shall be known to Egypt, and	Is 19:21	3068
shall know the *L* in that day	Is 19:21	3068
they shall vow a vow unto the *L*	Is 19:21	3068
And the *L* shall smite Egypt	Is 19:22	3068
they shall return even to the *L*	Is 19:22	3068
Whom the *L* of hosts shall bless,	Is 19:25	3068
the *L* by Isaiah the son of Amoz	Is 20:2	3068
the *L* said, Like as my servant	Is 20:3	3068
For thus hath the *L* said unto me	Is 21:6	136
I have heard of the *L* of hosts	Is 21:10	3068
For thus hath the *L* said unto me	Is 21:16	136
for the *L* God of Israel hath	Is 21:17	3068
of perplexity by the *L* GOD of	Is 22:5	136
in that day did the *L* GOD of	Is 22:12	136
in mine ears by the *L* of hosts	Is 22:14	3068
ye die, saith the *L* GOD of hosts	Is 22:14	136
Thus saith the *L* GOD of hosts	Is 22:15	136
the *L* will carry thee away with a	Is 22:17	3068
In that day, saith the *L* of hosts	Is 22:25	3068
for the *L* hath spoken it	Is 22:25	3068
The *L* of hosts hath purposed it,	Is 23:9	3068
the *L* hath given a commandment	Is 23:11	3068
that the *L* will visit Tyre, and	Is 23:17	3068
hire shall be holiness to the *L*	Is 23:18	3068
for them that dwell before the *L*	Is 23:18	3068
the *L* maketh the earth empty, and	Is 24:1	3068
for the *L* hath spoken this word	Is 24:3	3068
sing for the majesty of the *L*	Is 24:14	3068
glorify ye the *L* in the fires	Is 24:15	3068
even the name of the *L* God of	Is 24:15	3068
that the *L* shall punish the host	Is 24:21	3068
when the *L* of hosts shall reign	Is 24:23	3068
O *l*, thou art my God	Is 25:1	3068
in this mountain shall the *L* of	Is 25:6	3068
the *L* GOD will wipe away tears	Is 25:8	136
for the *L* hath spoken it	Is 25:8	3068
this is the *L*	Is 25:9	3068
shall the hand of the *L* rest	Is 25:10	3068
Trust ye in the *L* for ever	Is 26:4	3068
for in the *L* JEHOVAH is	Is 26:4	3050
in the way of thy judgments, O *L*	Is 26:8	3068
not behold the majesty of the *L*	Is 26:10	3068
L, when thy hand is lifted up,	Is 26:11	3068
L, thou wilt ordain peace for us	Is 26:12	3068
O *L* our God, other lords besides	Is 26:13	3068
hast increased the nation, O *L*	Is 26:15	3068
L, in trouble have they visited	Is 26:16	3068
so have we been in thy sight, O *L*	Is 26:17	3068
the *L* cometh out of his place to	Is 26:21	3068
In that day the *L* with his sore	Is 27:1	3068
I the *L* do keep it	Is 27:3	3068
that the *L* shall beat off from	Is 27:12	3068
shall worship the *L* in the holy	Is 27:13	3068
the *L* hath a mighty and strong one	Is 28:2	136
In that day shall the *L* of hosts	Is 28:5	3068
But the word of the *L* was unto	Is 28:13	3068
Wherefore hear the word of the *L*	Is 28:14	3068
Therefore thus saith the *L* GOD	Is 28:16	136
For the *L* shall rise up as in	Is 28:21	3068
for I have heard from the *L* GOD	Is 28:22	136
cometh forth from the *L* of hosts	Is 28:29	3068
of the *L* of hosts with thunder	Is 29:6	3068
For the *L* hath poured out upon	Is 29:10	3068
Wherefore the *L* said, Forasmuch	Is 29:13	136
to hide their counsel from the *L*	Is 29:15	3068
shall increase their joy in the *L*	Is 29:19	3068
Therefore thus saith the *L*	Is 29:22	3068
rebellious children, saith the *L*	Is 30:1	3068
will not hear the law of the *L*	Is 30:9	3068
For thus saith the *L* GOD, the	Is 30:15	136
And therefore will the *L* wait	Is 30:18	3068
for the *L* is a God of judgment	Is 30:18	3068
though the *L* give you the bread	Is 30:20	136
in the day that the *L* bindeth up	Is 30:26	3068
the name of the *L* cometh from far	Is 30:27	3068
come into the mountain of the *L*	Is 30:29	3068
the *L* shall cause his glorious	Is 30:30	3068
L shall the Assyrian be beaten	Is 30:31	3068
which the *L* shall lay upon him,	Is 30:32	3068
the breath of the *L*, like a	Is 30:33	3068
One of Israel, neither seek the *L*	Is 31:1	3068
When the *L* shall stretch out his	Is 31:3	3068
thus hath the *L* spoken unto me	Is 31:4	3068
so shall the *L* of hosts come down	Is 31:4	3068
so will the *L* of hosts defend	Is 31:5	3068
afraid of the ensign, saith the *L*	Is 31:9	3068
and to utter error against the *L*	Is 32:6	3068
O *L*, be gracious unto us	Is 33:2	3068
The *L* is exalted	Is 33:5	3068
the fear of the *L* is his treasure	Is 33:6	3068
Now will I rise, saith the *L*	Is 33:10	3068
But there the glorious *L* will be	Is 33:21	3068
For the *L* is our judge	Is 33:22	3068
the *L* is our lawgiver	Is 33:22	3068
the *L* is our king	Is 33:22	3068
of the *L* is upon all nations	Is 34:2	3068
The sword of the *L* is filled with	Is 34:6	3068
for the *L* hath a sacrifice in	Is 34:6	3068
Seek ye out of the book of the *L*	Is 34:16	3068
they shall see the glory of the *L*	Is 35:2	3068
ransomed of the *L* shall return	Is 35:10	3068
to me, We trust in the *L* our God	Is 36:7	3068
am I now come up without the *L*	Is 36:10	3068
the *L* said unto me, Go up against	Is 36:10	3068
Hezekiah make you trust in the *L*	Is 36:15	3068
The *L* will surely deliver us	Is 36:15	3068
saying, The *L* will deliver us	Is 36:18	3068
that the *L* should deliver	Is 36:20	3068
and went into the house of the *L*	Is 37:1	3068
It may be the *L* thy God will hear	Is 37:4	3068
which the *L* thy God hath heard	Is 37:4	3068
your master, Thus saith the *L*	Is 37:6	3068
went up unto the house of the *L*	Is 37:14	3068
and spread it before the *L*	Is 37:14	3068
And Hezekiah prayed unto the *L*	Is 37:15	3068
O *L* of hosts, God of Israel, that	Is 37:16	3068
Incline thine ear, O *L*, and hear	Is 37:17	3068
open thine eyes, O *L*, and see	Is 37:17	3068
Of a truth, *L*, the kings of	Is 37:18	3068
O *L* our God, save us from his	Is 37:20	3068
may know that thou art the *L*	Is 37:20	3068
Thus saith the *L* God of Israel	Is 37:21	3068
the *L* hath spoken concerning him	Is 37:22	3068
hast thou reproached the *L*	Is 37:24	136
the zeal of the *L* of hosts shall	Is 37:32	3068
Therefore thus saith the *L*	Is 37:33	3068
come into this city, saith the *L*	Is 37:34	3068
the angel of the *L* went forth	Is 37:36	3068
said unto him, Thus saith the *L*	Is 38:1	3068
the wall, and prayed unto the *L*	Is 38:2	3068
And said, Remember now, O *L*	Is 38:3	3068
came the word of the *L* to Isaiah	Is 38:4	3068
say to Hezekiah, Thus saith the *L*	Is 38:5	3068
be a sign unto thee from the *L*	Is 38:7	3068
that the *L* will do this thing	Is 38:7	3068
not see the *L*, even the *L*	Is 38:11	3050
O *L*, I am oppressed	Is 38:14	3068
O *L*, by these things men live, and	Is 38:16	136
The *L* was ready to save me	Is 38:20	3068
of our life in the house of the *L*	Is 38:20	3068
shall go up to the house of the *L*	Is 38:22	3068
Hear the word of the *L* of hosts	Is 39:5	3068
shall be left, saith the *L*	Is 39:6	3068
of the *L* which thou hast spoken	Is 39:8	3068
Prepare ye the way of the *L*	Is 40:3	3068
the glory of the *L* shall be	Is 40:5	3068
the mouth of the *L* hath spoken it	Is 40:5	3068
spirit of the *L* bloweth upon it	Is 40:7	3068
the *L* GOD will come with strong	Is 40:10	136
hath directed the Spirit of the *L*	Is 40:13	3068
Israel, My way is hid from the *L*	Is 40:27	3068
that the everlasting God, the *L*	Is 40:28	3068
the *L* shall renew their strength	Is 40:31	3068
I the *L*, the first, and with the	Is 41:4	3068
For I the *L* thy God will hold thy	Is 41:13	3068
I will help thee, saith the *L*	Is 41:14	3068
and thou shalt rejoice in the *L*	Is 41:16	3068
I the *L* will hear them, I the God	Is 41:17	3068
the hand of the *L* hath done this	Is 41:20	3068
Produce your cause, saith the *L*	Is 41:21	3068
Thus saith God the *L*, he that	Is 42:5	3068
I the *L* have called thee in	Is 42:6	3068

I am the *L* Is 42:8 3068
Sing unto the *L* a new song Is 42:10 3068
Let them give glory unto the *L* Is 42:12 3068
The *L* shall go forth as a mighty Is 42:13 3068
The *L* is well pleased for his Is 42:21 3068
did not the *L*, he against whom we Is 42:24 3068
saith the *L* that created thee Is 43:1 3068
For I am the *L* thy God, the Holy Is 43:3 3068
Ye are my witnesses, saith the *L* Is 43:10 3068
I, even I, am the *L* Is 43:11 3068
ye are my witnesses, saith the *L* Is 43:12 3068
Thus saith the *L*, your redeemer, Is 43:14 3068
I am the *L*, your Holy One, the Is 43:15 3068
Thus saith the *L*, which maketh a Is 43:16 3068
Thus saith the *L* that made thee Is 44:2 3068
with his hand unto the *L*, and Is 44:5 3068
Thus saith the *L* the King of Is 44:6 3068
and his redeemer the *L* of hosts Is 44:6 3068
for the *L* hath done it Is 44:23 3068
for the *L* hath redeemed Jacob, and Is 44:23 3068
Thus saith the *L*, thy redeemer, Is 44:24 3068
I am the *L* that maketh all things Is 44:24 3068
Thus saith the *L* to his anointed, Is 45:1 3068
thou mayest know that I, the *L* Is 45:3 3068
I am the *L*, and there is none else Is 45:5 3068
I am the *L*, and there is none else Is 45:6 3068
I the *L* do all these things Is 45:7 3068
I the *L* have created it Is 45:8 3068
Thus saith the *L*, the Holy One of Is 45:11 3068
nor reward, saith the *L* of hosts Is 45:13 3068
Thus saith the *L*, The labour of Is 45:14 3068
Israel shall be saved in the *L* Is 45:17 3068
For thus saith the *L* that created Is 45:18 3068
I am the *L* Is 45:18 3068
I the *L* speak righteousness, I Is 45:19 3068
have not I the *L* Is 45:21 3068
in the *L* have I righteousness and Is 45:24 3068
In the *L* shall all the seed of Is 45:25 3068
the *L* of hosts is his name, the Is 47:4 3068
which swear by the name of the *L* Is 48:1 3068
The *L* of hosts is his name Is 48:2 3068
The *L* hath loved him Is 48:14 3068
and now the *L* GOD, and his Spirit, Is 48:16 136
Thus saith the *L*, thy Redeemer, Is 48:17 3068
I am the *L* thy God which teacheth Is 48:17 3068
The *L* hath redeemed his servant Is 48:20 3068
There is no peace, saith the *L* Is 48:22 3068
The *L* hath called me from the Is 49:1 3068
surely my judgment is with the *L* Is 49:4 3068
saith the *L* that formed me from Is 49:5 3068
be glorious in the eyes of the *L* Is 49:5 3068
Thus saith the *L*, the Redeemer of Is 49:7 3068
because of the *L* that is faithful Is 49:7 3068
Thus saith the *L*, In an Is 49:8 3068
for the *L* hath comforted his Is 49:13 3068
The *L* hath forsaken me Is 49:14 3068
and my *L* hath forgotten me Is 49:14 136
As I live, saith the *L*, thou Is 49:18 3068
Thus saith the *L* GOD, Behold, I Is 49:22 136
thou shalt know that I am the *L* Is 49:23 3068
But thus saith the *L*, Even the Is 49:25 3068
know that I the *L* am thy Saviour Is 49:26 3068
Thus saith the *L*, Where is the Is 50:1 3068
The *L* GOD hath given me the Is 50:4 136
The *L* GOD hath opened mine ear, Is 50:5 136
For the *L* GOD will help me Is 50:7 136
Behold, the *L* GOD will help me Is 50:9 136
is among you that feareth the *L* Is 50:10 3068
him trust in the name of the *L* Is 50:10 3068
righteousness, ye that seek the *L* Is 51:1 3068
For the *L* shall comfort Zion Is 51:3 3068
desert like the garden of the *L* Is 51:3 3068
put on strength, O arm of the *L* Is 51:9 3068
redeemed of the *L* shall return Is 51:11 3068
And forgettest the *L* thy maker Is 51:13 3068
But I am the *L* thy God, that Is 51:15 3068
The *L* of hosts is his name Is 51:15 3068
hand of the *L* the cup of his fury Is 51:17 3068
are full of the fury of the *L* Is 51:20 3068
Thus saith thy *L* Is 51:22 113
the *L*, and thy God Is 51:22 3068
For thus saith the *L*, Ye have Is 52:3 3068
For thus saith the *L* GOD, My Is 52:4 136
what have I here, saith the *L* Is 52:5 3068
make them to howl, saith the *L* Is 52:5 3068
when the *L* shall bring again Zion Is 52:8 3068
for the *L* hath comforted his Is 52:9 3068
The *L* hath made bare his holy arm Is 52:10 3068
that bear the vessels of the *L* Is 52:11 3068
for the *L* will go before you Is 52:12 3068
whom is the arm of the *L* revealed Is 53:1 3068
the *L* hath laid on him the Is 53:6 3068
it pleased the *L* to bruise him Is 53:10 3068
the pleasure of the *L* shall Is 53:10 3068
of the married wife, saith the *L* Is 54:1 3068
the *L* of hosts is his name Is 54:5 3068
For the *L* hath called thee as a Is 54:6 3068
on thee, saith the *L* thy Redeemer Is 54:8 3068
saith the *L* that hath mercy on Is 54:10 3068
children shall be taught of the *L* Is 54:13 3068
heritage of the servants of the *L* Is 54:17 3068
is of me, saith the *L* Is 54:17 3068
thee because of the *L* thy God Is 55:5 3068
Seek ye the *L* while he may be Is 55:6 3068
and let him return unto the *L* Is 55:7 3068
your ways my ways, saith the *L* Is 55:8 3068
it shall be to the *L* for a name Is 55:13 3068
Thus saith the *L*, Keep ye Is 56:1 3068
that hath joined himself to the *L* Is 56:3 3068
The *L* hath utterly separated me Is 56:3 3068
For thus saith the *L* unto the Is 56:4 3068
that join themselves to the *L* Is 56:6 3068
him, and to love the name of the *L* Is 56:6 3068
The *L* GOD which gathereth the Is 56:8 136
to him that is near, saith the *L* Is 57:19 3068
and an acceptable day to the *L* Is 58:5 3068
the glory of the *L* shall be thy Is 58:8 3068
thou call, and the *L* shall answer Is 58:9 3068
And the *L* shall guide thee Is 58:11 3068
a delight, the holy of the *L* Is 58:13 3068
thou delight thyself in the *L* Is 58:14 3068
the mouth of the *L* hath spoken it Is 58:14 3068
and lying against the *L*, and Is 59:13 3068
the *L* saw it, and it displeased Is 59:15 3068
the name of the *L* from the west Is 59:19 3068
the Spirit of the *L* shall lift up Is 59:19 3068
in Jacob, saith the *L* Is 59:20 3068
covenant with them, saith the *L* Is 59:21 3068
of thy seed's seed, saith the *L* Is 59:21 3068
the glory of the *L* is risen upon Is 60:1 3068
but the *L* shall arise upon thee, Is 60:2 3068
shew forth the praises of the *L* Is 60:6 3068
unto the name of the *L* thy God Is 60:9 3068
call thee, The city of the *L* Is 60:14 3068
know that I the *L* am thy Saviour Is 60:16 3068
but the *L* shall be unto thee an Is 60:19 3068
for the *L* shall be thine Is 60:20 3068
I the *L* will hasten it in his Is 60:22 3068
Spirit of the *L* GOD is upon me Is 61:1 136
because the *L* hath anointed me to Is 61:1 3068
the acceptable year of the *L* Is 61:2 3068
the planting of the *L*, that he Is 61:3 3068
be named the Priests of the *L* Is 61:6 3068
For I the *L* love judgment, I hate Is 61:8 3068
the seed which the *L* hath blessed Is 61:9 3068
I will greatly rejoice in the *L* Is 61:10 3068
so the *L* GOD will cause Is 61:11 136
the mouth of the *L* shall name Is 62:2 3068
of glory in the hand of the *L* Is 62:3 3068
for the *L* delighteth in thee, and Is 62:4 3068
ye that make mention of the *L* Is 62:6 3068
The *L* hath sworn by his right Is 62:8 3068
it shall eat it, and praise the *L* Is 62:9 3068
the *L* hath proclaimed unto the Is 62:11 3068
people, The redeemed of the *L* Is 62:12 3068
the lovingkindnesses of the *L* Is 63:7 3068
and the praises of the *L* Is 63:7 3068
that the *L* hath bestowed on us Is 63:7 3068
the Spirit of the *L* caused him to Is 63:14 3068
thou, O *L*, art our father, our Is 63:16 3068
O *L*, why hast thou made us to err Is 63:17 3068
But now, O *L*, thou art our father Is 64:8 3068
Be not wroth very sore, O *L* Is 64:9 3068
thyself for these things, O *L* Is 64:12 3068
fathers together, saith the *L* Is 65:7 3068
Thus saith the *L*, As the new wine Is 65:8 3068
ye are they that forsake the *L* Is 65:11 3068
Therefore thus saith the *L* GOD Is 65:13 136
for the *L* GOD shall slay thee, and Is 65:15 136
the seed of the blessed of the *L* Is 65:23 3068
all my holy mountain, saith the *L* Is 65:25 3068
Thus saith the *L*, The heaven is Is 66:1 3068
things have been, saith the *L* Is 66:2 3068
Hear the word of the *L*, ye that Is 66:5 3068
said, Let the *L* be glorified Is 66:5 3068
a voice of the *L* that rendereth Is 66:6 3068
saith the *L* Is 66:9 3068
For thus saith the *L*, Behold, I Is 66:12 3068
the hand of the *L* shall be known Is 66:14 3068
the *L* will come with fire, and Is 66:15 3068
will the *L* plead with all flesh Is 66:16 3068
the slain of the *L* shall be many Is 66:16 3068
be consumed together, saith the *L* Is 66:17 3068
for an offering unto the *L* out of Is 66:20 3068
mountain Jerusalem, saith the *L* Is 66:20 3068
vessel into the house of the *L* Is 66:20 3068
and for Levites, saith the *L* Is 66:21 3068
remain before me, saith the *L* Is 66:22 3068
to worship before me, saith the *L* Is 66:23 3068
To whom the word of the *L* came in Jer 1:2 3068
the word of the *L* came unto me Jer 1:4 3068
Then said I, Ah, *L* GOD Jer 1:6 136
But the *L* said unto me, Say not, Jer 1:7 3068
thee to deliver thee, saith the *L* Jer 1:8 3068
Then the *L* put forth his hand, and Jer 1:9 3068
the *L* said unto me, Behold, I Jer 1:9 3068
the word of the *L* came unto me Jer 1:11 3068
Then said the *L* unto me, Thou Jer 1:12 3068
the word of the *L* came unto me Jer 1:13 3068
Then the *L* said unto me, Out of Jer 1:14 3068
of the north, saith the *L* Jer 1:15 3068
for I am with thee, saith the *L* Jer 1:19 3068
the word of the *L* came to me Jer 2:1 3068
saying, Thus saith the *L* Jer 2:2 3068
Israel was holiness unto the *L* Jer 2:3 3068
shall come upon them, saith the *L* Jer 2:3 3068
Hear ye the word of the *L* Jer 2:4 3068
Thus saith the *L*, What iniquity Jer 2:5 3068
Where is the *L* that brought us up Jer 2:6 3068
priests said not, Where is the *L* Jer 2:8 3068
yet plead with you, saith the *L* Jer 2:9 3068
be ye very desolate, saith the *L* Jer 2:12 3068
thou hast forsaken the *L* thy God Jer 2:17 3068
thou hast forsaken the *L* thy God Jer 2:19 3068
in thee, saith the *L* GOD of hosts Jer 2:19 136
marked before me, saith the *L* GOD Jer 2:22 136
against me, saith the *L* Jer 2:29 3068
see ye the word of the *L* Jer 2:31 3068
for the *L* hath rejected thy Jer 2:37 3068
return again to me, saith the *L* Jer 3:1 3068
The *L* said also unto me in the Jer 3:6 3068
heart, but feignedly, saith the *L* Jer 3:10 3068
And the *L* said unto me, The Jer 3:11 3068
backsliding Israel, saith the *L* Jer 3:12 3068
for I am merciful, saith the *L* Jer 3:12 3068
against the *L* thy God, and hast Jer 3:13 3068
not obeyed my voice, saith the *L* Jer 3:13 3068
backsliding children, saith the *L* Jer 3:14 3068
land, in those days, saith the *L* Jer 3:16 3068
The ark of the covenant of the *L* Jer 3:16 3068
Jerusalem the throne of the *L* Jer 3:17 3068
unto it, to the name of the *L* Jer 3:17 3068
O house of Israel, saith the *L* Jer 3:20 3068
have forgotten the *L* their God Jer 3:21 3068
for thou art the *L* our God Jer 3:22 3068
truly in the *L* our God is the Jer 3:23 3068
have sinned against the *L* our God Jer 3:25 3068
obeyed the voice of the *L* our God Jer 3:25 3068
return, O Israel, saith the *L* Jer 4:1 3068
The *L* liveth, in truth, in Jer 4:2 3068
For thus saith the *L* to the men Jer 4:3 3068
Circumcise yourselves to the *L* Jer 4:4 3068
the *L* is not turned back from us Jer 4:8 3068
to pass at that day, saith the *L* Jer 4:9 3068
Then said I, Ah, *L* GOD Jer 4:10 136
against me, saith the *L* Jer 4:17 3068
down at the presence of the *L* Jer 4:26 3068
For thus hath the *L* said, The Jer 4:27 3068
And though they say, The *L* liveth Jer 5:2 3068
O *L*, are not thine eyes upon the Jer 5:3 3068
they know not the way of the *L* Jer 5:4 3068
they have known the way of the *L* Jer 5:5 3068
for these things? saith the *L* Jer 5:9 3068
against me, saith the *L* Jer 5:11 3068
They have belied the *L*, and said, Jer 5:12 3068
thus saith the *L* God of hosts Jer 5:14 3068
O house of Israel, saith the *L* Jer 5:15 3068
in those days, saith the *L* Jer 5:18 3068
Wherefore doeth the *L* our God all Jer 5:19 3068
Fear ye not me? saith the *L* Jer 5:22 3068
Let us now fear the *L* our God Jer 5:24 3068
these things? saith the *L* Jer 5:29 3068
For thus hath the *L* of hosts said Jer 6:6 3068
Thus saith the *L* of hosts Jer 6:9 3068
the word of the *L* is unto them a Jer 6:10 3068
I am full of the fury of the *L* Jer 6:11 3068
of the land, saith the *L* Jer 6:12 3068
shall be cast down, saith the *L* Jer 6:15 3068
Thus saith the *L*, Stand ye in the Jer 6:16 3068
Therefore thus saith the *L* Jer 6:21 3068
Thus saith the *L*, Behold, a Jer 6:22 3068
because the *L* hath rejected them Jer 6:30 3068
that came to Jeremiah from the *L* Jer 7:1 3068
and say, Hear the word of the *L* Jer 7:2 3068
at these gates to worship the *L* Jer 7:2 3068
Thus saith the *L* of hosts Jer 7:3 3068
saying, The temple of the *L* Jer 7:4 3068
of the *L*, The temple of the *L* Jer 7:4 3068
even I have seen it, saith the *L* Jer 7:11 3068
done all these works, saith the *L* Jer 7:13 3068
to anger? saith the *L* Jer 7:19 3068
Therefore thus saith the *L* GOD Jer 7:20 136
Thus saith the *L* of hosts Jer 7:21 3068
not the voice of the *L* their God Jer 7:28 3068
for the *L* hath rejected and Jer 7:29 3068
evil in my sight, saith the *L* Jer 7:30 3068
the days come, saith the *L* Jer 7:32 3068
At that time, saith the *L* Jer 8:1 3068
driven them, saith the *L* of hosts Jer 8:3 3068
say unto them, Thus saith the *L* Jer 8:4 3068
know not the judgment of the *L* Jer 8:7 3068
and the law of the *L* is with us Jer 8:8 3068
have rejected the word of the *L* Jer 8:9 3068
shall be cast down, saith the *L* Jer 8:12 3068
surely consume them, saith the *L* Jer 8:13 3068
for the *L* our God hath put us to Jer 8:14 3068
we have sinned against the *L* Jer 8:14 3068
they shall bite you, saith the *L* Jer 8:17 3068
Is not the *L* in Zion Jer 8:19 3068
and they know not me, saith the *L* Jer 9:3 3068
refuse to know me, saith the *L* Jer 9:6 3068
thus saith the *L* of hosts Jer 9:7 3068
these things? saith the *L* Jer 9:9 3068
the mouth of the *L* hath spoken Jer 9:12 3068
the *L* saith, Because they have Jer 9:13 3068
thus saith the *L* of hosts Jer 9:15 3068
Thus saith the *L* of hosts Jer 9:17 3068
Yet hear the word of the *L* Jer 9:20 3068
Speak, Thus saith the *L*, Even the Jer 9:22 3068
Thus saith the *L*, Let not the Jer 9:23 3068
that I am the *L* which exercise Jer 9:24 3068
things I delight, saith the *L* Jer 9:24 3068
the days come, saith the *L* Jer 9:25 3068
which the *L* speaketh unto you Jer 10:1 3068
Thus saith the *L*, Learn not the Jer 10:2 3068
there is none like unto thee, O *L* Jer 10:6 3068
But the *L* is the true God, he is Jer 10:10 3068
The *L* of hosts is his name Jer 10:16 3068
For thus saith the *L*, Behold, I Jer 10:18 3068
brutish, and have not sought the *L* Jer 10:21 3068
O *L*, I know that the way of man Jer 10:23 3068
O *L*, correct me, but with Jer 10:24 3068
that came to Jeremiah from the *L* Jer 11:1 3068
Thus saith the *L* God of Israel Jer 11:3 3068
I, and said, So be it, O *L* Jer 11:5 3068
Then the *L* said unto me, Proclaim Jer 11:6 3068
the *L* said unto me, A conspiracy Jer 11:9 3068
Therefore thus saith the *L* Jer 11:11 3068
The *L* called thy name, A green Jer 11:16 3068
For the *L* of hosts, that planted Jer 11:17 3068
the *L* hath given me knowledge of Jer 11:18 3068
O *L* of hosts, that judgest Jer 11:20 3068
the *L* of the men of Anathoth Jer 11:21 3068
Prophesy not in the name of the *L* Jer 11:21 3068
thus saith the *L* of hosts Jer 11:22 3068
Righteous art thou, O *L*, when I Jer 12:1 3068
But thou, O *L*, knowest me Jer 12:3 3068
for the sword of the *L* shall Jer 12:12 3068
of the fierce anger of the *L* Jer 12:13 3068
Thus saith the *L* against all mine Jer 12:14 3068
to swear by my name, The *L* liveth Jer 12:16 3068
destroy that nation, saith the *L* Jer 12:17 3068

Thus saith the *L* unto me, Go and	Jer 13:1	3068
according to the word of the *L*	Jer 13:2	3068
the word of the *L* came unto me	Jer 13:3	3068
Euphrates, as the *L* commanded me	Jer 13:5	3068
that the *L* said unto me, Arise,	Jer 13:6	3068
the word of the *L* came unto me	Jer 13:8	3068
Thus saith the *L*, After this	Jer 13:9	3068
whole house of Judah, saith the *L*	Jer 13:11	3068
Thus saith the *L* God of Israel	Jer 13:12	3068
say unto them, Thus saith the *L*	Jer 13:13	3068
and the sons together, saith the *L*	Jer 13:14	3068
for the *L* hath spoken	Jer 13:15	3068
Give glory to the *L* your God	Jer 13:16	3068
thy measures from me, saith the *L*	Jer 13:25	3068
The word of the *L* that came to	Jer 14:1	3068
O *L*, though our iniquities	Jer 14:7	3068
yet thou, O *L*, art in the midst	Jer 14:9	3068
Thus saith the *L* unto this people	Jer 14:10	3068
therefore the *L* doth not accept	Jer 14:10	3068
Then said the *L* unto me, Pray not	Jer 14:11	3068
Then said I, Ah, *L* God	Jer 14:13	136
Then the *L* said unto me, The	Jer 14:14	3068
Therefore thus saith the *L*	Jer 14:15	3068
We acknowledge, O *L*, our	Jer 14:20	3068
art not thou he, O *L* our God	Jer 14:22	3068
Then said the *L* unto me, Though	Jer 15:1	3068
shalt tell them, Thus saith the *L*	Jer 15:2	3068
over them four kinds, saith the *L*	Jer 15:3	3068
hast forsaken me, saith the *L*	Jer 15:6	3068
before their enemies, saith the *L*	Jer 15:9	3068
The *L* said, Verily it shall be	Jer 15:11	3068
O *L*, thou knowest	Jer 15:15	3068
by thy name, O *L* God of hosts	Jer 15:16	3068
Therefore thus saith the *L*	Jer 15:19	3068
and to deliver thee, saith the *L*	Jer 15:20	3068
The word of the *L* came also unto	Jer 16:1	3068
For thus saith the *L* concerning	Jer 16:3	3068
For thus saith the *L*, Enter not	Jer 16:5	3068
from this people, saith the *L*	Jer 16:5	3068
For thus saith the *L* of hosts	Jer 16:9	3068
Wherefore hath the *L* pronounced	Jer 16:10	3068
committed against the *L* our God	Jer 16:10	3068
have forsaken me, saith the *L*	Jer 16:11	3068
the days come, saith the *L*	Jer 16:14	3068
The *L* liveth, that brought up the	Jer 16:14	3068
The *L* liveth, that brought up the	Jer 16:15	3068
for many fishers, saith the *L*	Jer 16:16	3068
O *L*, my strength, and my fortress,	Jer 16:19	3068
shall know that my name is The *L*	Jer 16:21	3068
Thus saith the *L*	Jer 17:5	3068
whose heart departeth from the *L*	Jer 17:5	3068
is the man that trusteth in the *L*	Jer 17:7	3068
and whose hope the *L* is	Jer 17:7	3068
I the *L* search the heart, I try	Jer 17:10	3068
O *L*, the hope of Israel, all that	Jer 17:13	3068
because they have forsaken the *L*	Jer 17:13	3068
Heal me, O *L*, and I shall be	Jer 17:14	3068
me, Where is the word of the *L*	Jer 17:15	3068
Thus said the *L* unto me	Jer 17:19	3068
them, Hear ye the word of the *L*	Jer 17:20	3068
Thus saith the *L*	Jer 17:21	3068
hearken unto me, saith the *L*	Jer 17:24	3068
praise, unto the house of the *L*	Jer 17:26	3068
which came to Jeremiah from the *L*	Jer 18:1	3068
Then the word of the *L* came to me	Jer 18:5	3068
this potter? saith the *L*	Jer 18:6	3068
saying, Thus saith the *L*	Jer 18:11	3068
Therefore thus saith the *L*	Jer 18:13	3068
Give heed to me, O *L*, and hearken	Jer 18:19	3068
Yet, *L*, thou knowest all their	Jer 18:23	3068
Thus saith the *L*, Go and get a	Jer 19:1	3068
And say, Hear ye the word of the *L*	Jer 19:3	3068
Thus saith the *L* of hosts	Jer 19:3	3068
the days come, saith the *L*	Jer 19:6	3068
them, Thus saith the *L* of hosts	Jer 19:11	3068
I do unto this place, saith the *L*	Jer 19:12	3068
whither the *L* had sent him to	Jer 19:14	3068
Thus saith the *L* of hosts	Jer 19:15	3068
governor in the house of the *L*	Jer 20:1	3068
which was by the house of the *L*	Jer 20:2	3068
The *L* hath not called thy name	Jer 20:3	3068
For thus saith the *L*, Behold, I	Jer 20:4	3068
O *L*, thou hast deceived me, and I	Jer 20:7	3068
because the word of the *L* was	Jer 20:8	3068
But the *L* is with me as a mighty	Jer 20:11	3068
O *L* of hosts, that triest the	Jer 20:12	3068
unto the *L*, praise ye the *L*	Jer 20:13	3068
the cities which the *L* overthrew	Jer 20:16	3068
came unto Jeremiah from the *L*	Jer 21:1	3068
I pray thee, of the *L* for us	Jer 21:2	3068
if so be that the *L* will deal	Jer 21:2	3068
Thus saith the *L* God of Israel	Jer 21:4	3068
And afterward, saith the *L*	Jer 21:7	3068
thou shalt say, Thus saith the *L*	Jer 21:8	3068
and not for good, saith the *L*	Jer 21:10	3068
say, Hear ye the word of the *L*	Jer 21:11	3068
house of David, thus saith the *L*	Jer 21:12	3068
and rock of the plain, saith the *L*	Jer 21:13	3068
fruit of your doings, saith the *L*	Jer 21:14	3068
Thus saith the *L*	Jer 22:1	3068
And say, Hear the word of the *L*	Jer 22:2	3068
Thus saith the *L*	Jer 22:3	3068
I swear by myself, saith the *L*	Jer 22:5	3068
For thus saith the *L* unto the	Jer 22:6	3068
Wherefore hath the *L* done thus	Jer 22:8	3068
the covenant of the *L* their God	Jer 22:9	3068
For thus saith the *L* touching	Jer 22:11	3068
know me? saith the *L*	Jer 22:16	3068
Therefore thus saith the *L*	Jer 22:18	3068
As I live, saith the *L*, though	Jer 22:24	3068
earth, hear the word of the *L*	Jer 22:29	3068
Thus saith the *L*, Write ye this	Jer 22:30	3068
my pasture! saith the *L*	Jer 23:1	3068
Therefore thus saith the *L* God of	Jer 23:2	3068
evil of your doings, saith the *L*	Jer 23:2	3068
they be lacking, saith the *L*	Jer 23:4	3068
the days come, saith the *L*	Jer 23:5	3068
called, THE *L* OUR RIGHTEOUSNESS	Jer 23:6	3068
the days come, saith the *L*	Jer 23:7	3068
The *L* liveth, which brought up	Jer 23:7	3068
The *L* liveth, which brought up and	Jer 23:8	3068
hath overcome, because of the *L*	Jer 23:9	3068
their wickedness, saith the *L*	Jer 23:11	3068
of their visitation, saith the *L*	Jer 23:12	3068
the *L* of hosts concerning the	Jer 23:15	3068
Thus saith the *L* of hosts	Jer 23:16	3068
and not out of the mouth of the *L*	Jer 23:16	3068
The *L* hath said, Ye shall have	Jer 23:17	3068
stood in the counsel of the *L*	Jer 23:18	3068
a whirlwind of the *L* is gone	Jer 23:19	3068
anger of the *L* shall not return	Jer 23:20	3068
Am I a God at hand, saith the *L*	Jer 23:23	3068
see him? saith the *L*	Jer 23:24	3068
and earth? saith the *L*	Jer 23:24	3068
the wheat? saith the *L*	Jer 23:28	3068
a fire? saith the *L*	Jer 23:29	3068
against the prophets, saith the *L*	Jer 23:30	3068
against the prophets, saith the *L*	Jer 23:31	3068
false dreams, saith the *L*	Jer 23:32	3068
this people at all, saith the *L*	Jer 23:32	3068
What is the burden of the *L*	Jer 23:33	3068
even forsake you, saith the *L*	Jer 23:33	3068
shall say, The burden of the *L*	Jer 23:34	3068
brother, What hath the *L* answered	Jer 23:35	3068
and, What hath the *L* spoken	Jer 23:35	3068
the burden of the *L* shall ye	Jer 23:36	3068
of the *L* of hosts our God	Jer 23:36	3068
What hath the *L* answered thee	Jer 23:37	3068
and, What hath the *L* spoken	Jer 23:37	3068
since ye say, The burden of the *L*	Jer 23:38	3068
therefore thus saith the *L*	Jer 23:38	3068
this word, The burden of the *L*	Jer 23:38	3068
not say, The burden of the *L*	Jer 23:38	3068
The *L* shewed me, and, behold, two	Jer 24:1	3068
set before the temple of the *L*	Jer 24:1	3068
Then said the *L* unto me, What	Jer 24:3	3068
the word of the *L* came unto me	Jer 24:4	3068
Thus saith the *L*, the God of	Jer 24:5	3068
heart to know me, that I am the *L*	Jer 24:7	3068
surely thus saith the *L*, So will	Jer 24:8	3068
the word of the *L* hath come unto	Jer 25:3	3068
the *L* hath sent unto you all his	Jer 25:4	3068
that the *L* hath given unto you	Jer 25:5	3068
hearkened unto me, saith the *L*	Jer 25:7	3068
thus saith the *L* of hosts	Jer 25:8	3068
of the north, saith the *L*	Jer 25:9	3068
and that nation, saith the *L*	Jer 25:12	3068
For thus saith the *L* God of	Jer 25:15	3068
unto whom the *L* had sent me	Jer 25:17	3068
them, Thus saith the *L* of hosts	Jer 25:27	3068
them, Thus saith the *L* of hosts	Jer 25:28	3068
the earth, saith the *L* of hosts	Jer 25:29	3068
The *L* shall roar from on high, and	Jer 25:30	3068
for the *L* hath a controversy with	Jer 25:31	3068
wicked to the sword, saith the *L*	Jer 25:31	3068
Thus saith the *L* of hosts	Jer 25:32	3068
the slain of the *L* shall be at	Jer 25:33	3068
for the *L* hath spoiled their	Jer 25:36	3068
of the fierce anger of the *L*	Jer 25:37	3068
Judah came this word from the *L*	Jer 26:1	3068
Thus saith the *L*	Jer 26:2	3068
say unto them, Thus saith the *L*	Jer 26:4	3068
these words in the house of the *L*	Jer 26:7	3068
L had commanded him to speak unto	Jer 26:8	3068
prophesied in the name of the *L*	Jer 26:9	3068
Jeremiah in the house of the *L*	Jer 26:9	3068
house unto the house of the *L*	Jer 26:10	3068
The *L* sent me to prophesy against	Jer 26:12	3068
obey the voice of the *L* your God	Jer 26:13	3068
the *L* will repent him of the evil	Jer 26:13	3068
for of a truth the *L* hath sent me	Jer 26:15	3068
us in the name of the *L* our God	Jer 26:16	3068
saying, Thus saith the *L* of hosts	Jer 26:18	3068
did he not fear the *L*, and	Jer 26:19	3068
fear the *L*, and besought the *L*	Jer 26:19	3068
prophesied in the name of the *L*	Jer 26:20	3068
word unto Jeremiah from the *L*	Jer 27:1	3068
Thus saith the *L* to me	Jer 27:2	3068
Thus saith the *L* of hosts	Jer 27:4	3068
nation will I punish, saith the *L*	Jer 27:8	3068
in their own land, saith the *L*	Jer 27:11	3068
as the *L* hath spoken against the	Jer 27:13	3068
I have not sent them, saith the *L*	Jer 27:15	3068
people, saying, Thus saith the *L*	Jer 27:16	3068
if the word of the *L* be with them	Jer 27:18	3068
intercession to the *L* of hosts	Jer 27:18	3068
are left in the house of the *L*	Jer 27:18	3068
For thus saith the *L* of hosts	Jer 27:19	3068
Yea, thus saith the *L* of hosts	Jer 27:21	3068
that remain in the house of the *L*	Jer 27:21	3068
that I visit them, saith the *L*	Jer 27:22	3068
unto me in the house of the *L*	Jer 28:1	3068
Thus speaketh the *L* of hosts	Jer 28:2	3068
went into Babylon, saith the *L*	Jer 28:4	3068
that stood in the house of the *L*	Jer 28:5	3068
the *L* do so	Jer 28:6	3068
the *L* perform thy words which	Jer 28:6	3068
that the *L* hath truly sent him	Jer 28:9	3068
people, saying, Thus saith the *L*	Jer 28:11	3068
Then the word of the *L* came unto	Jer 28:12	3068
saying, Thus saith the *L*	Jer 28:13	3068
For thus saith the *L* of hosts	Jer 28:14	3068
The *L* hath not sent thee	Jer 28:15	3068
Therefore thus saith the *L*	Jer 28:16	3068
taught rebellion against the *L*	Jer 28:16	3068
Thus saith the *L* of hosts	Jer 29:4	3068
and pray unto the *L* for it	Jer 29:7	3068
For thus saith the *L* of hosts	Jer 29:8	3068
I have not sent them, saith the *L*	Jer 29:9	3068
For thus saith the *L*, That after	Jer 29:10	3068
I think toward you, saith the *L*	Jer 29:11	3068
will be found of you, saith the *L*	Jer 29:14	3068
I have driven you, saith the *L*	Jer 29:14	3068
The *L* hath raised us up prophets	Jer 29:15	3068
Know that thus saith the *L* of the	Jer 29:16	3068
Thus saith the *L* of hosts	Jer 29:17	3068
to my words, saith the *L*, which I	Jer 29:19	3068
ye would not hear, saith the *L*	Jer 29:19	3068
ye therefore the word of the *L*	Jer 29:20	3068
Thus saith the *L* of hosts	Jer 29:21	3068
The *L* make thee like Zedekiah and	Jer 29:22	3068
and am a witness, saith the *L*	Jer 29:23	3068
Thus speaketh the *L* of hosts	Jer 29:25	3068
The *L* hath made thee priest in	Jer 29:26	3068
be officers in the house of the *L*	Jer 29:26	3068
the word of the *L* unto Jeremiah	Jer 29:30	3068
Thus saith the *L* concerning	Jer 29:31	3068
Therefore thus saith the *L*	Jer 29:32	3068
do for my people, saith the *L*	Jer 29:32	3068
taught rebellion against the *L*	Jer 29:32	3068
that came to Jeremiah from the *L*	Jer 30:1	3068
Thus speaketh the *L* God of Israel	Jer 30:2	3068
lo, the days come, saith the *L*	Jer 30:3	3068
Israel and Judah, saith the *L*	Jer 30:3	3068
the *L* spake concerning Israel	Jer 30:4	3068
For thus saith the *L*	Jer 30:5	3068
in that day, saith the *L* of hosts	Jer 30:8	3068
they shall serve the *L* their God	Jer 30:9	3068
O my servant Jacob, saith the *L*	Jer 30:10	3068
For I am with thee, saith the *L*	Jer 30:11	3068
For thus saith the *L*, Thy bruise	Jer 30:12	3068
thee of thy wounds, saith the *L*	Jer 30:17	3068
Thus saith the *L*	Jer 30:18	3068
unto me? saith the *L*	Jer 30:21	3068
the whirlwind of the *L* goeth	Jer 30:23	3068
anger of the *L* shall not return	Jer 30:24	3068
At the same time, saith the *L*	Jer 31:1	3068
Thus saith the *L*, The people	Jer 31:2	3068
The *L* hath appeared of old unto	Jer 31:3	3068
go up to Zion unto the *L* our God	Jer 31:6	3068
For thus saith the *L*	Jer 31:7	3068
ye, praise ye, and say, O *L*	Jer 31:7	3068
Hear the word of the *L*, O ye	Jer 31:10	3068
For the *L* hath redeemed Jacob, and	Jer 31:11	3068
together to the goodness of the *L*	Jer 31:12	3068
with my goodness, saith the *L*	Jer 31:14	3068
Thus saith the *L*	Jer 31:15	3068
Thus saith the *L*	Jer 31:16	3068
shall be rewarded, saith the *L*	Jer 31:16	3068
is hope in thine end, saith the *L*	Jer 31:17	3068
for thou art the *L* my God	Jer 31:18	3068
have mercy upon him, saith the *L*	Jer 31:20	3068
for the *L* hath created a new	Jer 31:22	3068
Thus saith the *L* of hosts	Jer 31:23	3068
The *L* bless thee, O habitation of	Jer 31:23	3068
the days come, saith the *L*	Jer 31:27	3068
build, and to plant, saith the *L*	Jer 31:28	3068
the days come, saith the *L*	Jer 31:31	3068
an husband unto them, saith the *L*	Jer 31:32	3068
After those days, saith the *L*	Jer 31:33	3068
his brother, saying, Know the *L*	Jer 31:34	3068
the greatest of them, saith the *L*	Jer 31:34	3068
Thus saith the *L*, which giveth	Jer 31:35	3068
The *L* of hosts is his name	Jer 31:35	3068
from before me, saith the *L*	Jer 31:36	3068
Thus saith the *L*	Jer 31:37	3068
that they have done, saith the *L*	Jer 31:37	3068
the days come, saith the *L*	Jer 31:38	3068
the city shall be built to the *L*	Jer 31:38	3068
east, shall be holy unto the *L*	Jer 31:40	3068
L in the tenth year of Zedekiah	Jer 32:1	3068
and say, Thus saith the *L*	Jer 32:3	3068
be until I visit him, saith the *L*	Jer 32:5	3068
The word of the *L* came unto me	Jer 32:6	3068
according to the word of the *L*	Jer 32:8	3068
that this was the word of the *L*	Jer 32:8	3068
Thus saith the *L* of hosts	Jer 32:14	3068
For thus saith the *L* of hosts	Jer 32:15	3068
of Neriah, I prayed unto the *L*	Jer 32:16	3068
Ah *L* God	Jer 32:17	136
the *L* of hosts, is his name,	Jer 32:18	3068
O *L* God, Buy thee the field for	Jer 32:25	136
the word of the *L* unto Jeremiah	Jer 32:26	3068
Behold, I am the *L*, the God of	Jer 32:27	3068
Therefore thus saith the *L*	Jer 32:28	3068
work of their hands, saith the *L*	Jer 32:30	3068
And now therefore thus saith the *L*	Jer 32:36	3068
For thus saith the *L*	Jer 32:42	3068
captivity to return, saith the *L*	Jer 32:44	3068
Moreover the word of the *L* came	Jer 33:1	3068
Thus saith the *L* the maker	Jer 33:2	3068
thereof, the *L* that formed it, to	Jer 33:2	3068
the *L* is his name	Jer 33:2	3068
For thus saith the *L*, the God of	Jer 33:4	3068
Thus saith the *L*	Jer 33:10	3068
shall say, Praise the *L* of hosts	Jer 33:11	3068
for the *L* is good	Jer 33:11	3068
of praise into the house of the *L*	Jer 33:11	3068
as at the first, saith the *L*	Jer 33:11	3068
Thus saith the *L* of hosts	Jer 33:12	3068
that telleth them, saith the *L*	Jer 33:13	3068
the days come, saith the *L*	Jer 33:14	3068
called, The *L* our righteousness	Jer 33:16	3068
For thus saith the *L*	Jer 33:17	3068
the word of the *L* came unto	Jer 33:19	3068
Thus saith the *L*	Jer 33:20	3068
word of the *L* came to Jeremiah	Jer 33:23	3068
families which the *L* hath chosen	Jer 33:24	3068
Thus saith the *L*	Jer 33:25	3068
came unto Jeremiah from the *L*	Jer 34:1	3068
Thus saith the *L*, the God of	Jer 34:2	3068
and tell him, Thus saith the *L*	Jer 34:2	3068

Yet hear the word of the *L*	Jer 34:4	3068
Thus saith the *L* of thee, Thou	Jer 34:4	3068
pronounced the word, saith the *L*	Jer 34:5	3068
came unto Jeremiah from the *L*	Jer 34:8	3068
Therefore the word of the *L* came	Jer 34:12	3068
came to Jeremiah from the *L*	Jer 34:12	3068
Thus saith the *L*, the God of	Jer 34:13	3068
Therefore thus saith the *L*	Jer 34:17	3068
a liberty for you, saith the *L*	Jer 34:17	3068
I will command, saith the *L*	Jer 34:22	3068
came unto Jeremiah from the *L* in	Jer 35:1	3068
them into the house of the *L*	Jer 35:2	3068
them into the house of the *L*	Jer 35:4	3068
the word of the *L* unto Jeremiah	Jer 35:12	3068
Thus saith the *L* of hosts	Jer 35:13	3068
my words? saith the *L*	Jer 35:13	3068
thus saith the *L* God of hosts	Jer 35:17	3068
Thus saith the *L* of hosts	Jer 35:18	3068
thus saith the *L* of hosts	Jer 35:19	3068
came unto Jeremiah from the *L*	Jer 36:1	3068
Jeremiah all the words of the *L*	Jer 36:4	3068
cannot go into the house of the *L*	Jer 36:5	3068
the words of the *L* in the ears of	Jer 36:6	3068
their supplication before the *L*	Jer 36:7	3068
anger and the fury that the *L* hath	Jer 36:7	3068
of the *L* in the LORD's house	Jer 36:8	3068
proclaimed a fast before the *L* to	Jer 36:9	3068
of Jeremiah in the house of the *L*	Jer 36:10	3068
the book all the words of the *L*	Jer 36:11	3068
but the *L* hid them	Jer 36:26	3068
word of the *L* came to Jeremiah	Jer 36:27	3068
king of Judah, Thus saith the *L*	Jer 36:29	3068
Therefore thus saith the *L* of	Jer 36:30	3068
hearken unto the words of the *L*	Jer 37:2	3068
now unto the *L* our God for us	Jer 37:3	3068
the *L* unto the prophet Jeremiah	Jer 37:6	3068
Thus saith the *L*, the God of	Jer 37:7	3068
Thus saith the *L*	Jer 37:9	3068
Is there any word from the *L*	Jer 37:17	3068
Thus saith the *L*, He that	Jer 38:2	3068
Thus saith the *L*, This city shall	Jer 38:3	3068
that is in the house of the *L*	Jer 38:14	3068
Jeremiah, saying, As the *L* liveth	Jer 38:16	3068
unto Zedekiah, Thus saith the *L*	Jer 38:17	3068
beseech thee, the voice of the *L*	Jer 38:20	3068
word that the *L* hath shewed me	Jer 38:21	3068
word of the *L* came unto Jeremiah	Jer 39:15	3068
saying, Thus saith the *L* of hosts	Jer 39:16	3068
thee in that day, saith the *L*	Jer 39:17	3068
put thy trust in me, saith the *L*	Jer 39:18	3068
that came to Jeremiah from the *L*	Jer 40:1	3068
The *L* thy God hath pronounced	Jer 40:2	3068
Now the *L* hath brought it, and	Jer 40:3	3068
ye have sinned against the *L*	Jer 40:3	3068
bring them to the house of the *L*	Jer 41:5	3068
and pray for us unto the *L* thy God	Jer 42:2	3068
That the *L* thy God may shew us	Jer 42:3	3068
I will pray unto the *L* your God	Jer 42:4	3068
thing the *L* shall answer you	Jer 42:4	3068
The *L* be a true and faithful	Jer 42:5	3068
L thy God shall send thee to us	Jer 42:5	3068
obey the voice of the *L* our God	Jer 42:6	3068
obey the voice of the *L* our God	Jer 42:6	3068
word of the *L* came unto Jeremiah	Jer 42:7	3068
said unto them, Thus saith the *L*	Jer 42:9	3068
be not afraid of him, saith the *L*	Jer 42:11	3068
obey the voice of the *L* your God	Jer 42:13	3068
therefore hear the word of the *L*	Jer 42:15	3068
Thus saith the *L* of hosts	Jer 42:15	3068
For thus saith the *L* of hosts	Jer 42:18	3068
The *L* hath said concerning you, O	Jer 42:19	3068
ye sent me unto the *L* your God	Jer 42:20	3068
Pray for us unto the *L* our God	Jer 42:20	3068
all that the *L* our God shall say	Jer 42:20	3068
the voice of the *L* your God	Jer 42:21	3068
all the words of the *L* their God	Jer 43:1	3068
for which the *L* their God had	Jer 43:1	3068
the *L* our God hath not sent thee	Jer 43:2	3068
obeyed not the voice of the *L*	Jer 43:4	3068
obeyed not the voice of the *L*	Jer 43:7	3068
Then came the word of the *L* unto	Jer 43:8	3068
them, Thus saith the *L* of hosts	Jer 43:10	3068
Thus saith the *L* of hosts	Jer 44:2	3068
Therefore now thus saith the *L*	Jer 44:7	3068
thus saith the *L* of hosts	Jer 44:11	3068
unto us in the name of the *L*	Jer 44:16	3068
did not the *L* remember them, and	Jer 44:21	3068
So that the *L* could no longer	Jer 44:22	3068
ye have sinned against the *L*	Jer 44:23	3068
not obeyed the voice of the *L*	Jer 44:23	3068
the women, Hear the word of the *L*	Jer 44:24	3068
Thus saith the *L* of hosts	Jer 44:25	3068
hear ye the word of the *L*	Jer 44:26	3068
by my great name, saith the *L*	Jer 44:26	3068
Egypt, saying, The *L* GOD liveth	Jer 44:26	136
be a sign unto you, saith the *L*	Jer 44:29	3068
Thus saith the *L*	Jer 44:30	3068
Thus saith the *L*, the God of	Jer 45:2	3068
for the *L* hath added grief to my	Jer 45:3	3068
say unto him, The *L* saith thus	Jer 45:4	3068
evil upon all flesh, saith the *L*	Jer 45:5	3068
The word of the *L* which came to	Jer 46:1	3068
fear was round about, saith the *L*	Jer 46:5	3068
is the day of the *L* GOD of hosts	Jer 46:10	136
for the *L* GOD of hosts hath a	Jer 46:10	136
The word that the *L* spake to	Jer 46:13	3068
because the *L* did drive them	Jer 46:15	3068
whose name is the *L* of hosts	Jer 46:18	3068
cut down her forest, saith the *L*	Jer 46:23	3068
The *L* of hosts, the God of Israel	Jer 46:25	3068
in the days of old, saith the *L*	Jer 46:26	3068
O Jacob my servant, saith the *L*	Jer 46:28	3068
The word of the *L* that came to	Jer 47:1	3068
Thus saith the *L*	Jer 47:2	3068
for the *L* will spoil the	Jer 47:4	3068
O thou sword of the *L*, how long	Jer 47:6	3068
seeing the *L* hath given it a	Jer 47:7	3068
Moab thus saith the *L* of hosts	Jer 48:1	3068
destroyed, as the *L* hath spoken	Jer 48:8	3068
the work of the *L* deceitfully	Jer 48:10	3068
the days come, saith the *L*	Jer 48:12	3068
whose name is the *L* of hosts	Jer 48:15	3068
and his arm is broken, saith the *L*	Jer 48:25	3068
magnified himself against the *L*	Jer 48:26	3068
I know his wrath, saith the *L*	Jer 48:30	3068
to cease in Moab, saith the *L*	Jer 48:35	3068
is no pleasure, saith the *L*	Jer 48:38	3068
For thus saith the *L*	Jer 48:40	3068
magnified himself against the *L*	Jer 48:42	3068
O inhabitant of Moab, saith the *L*	Jer 48:43	3068
of their visitation, saith the *L*	Jer 48:44	3068
in the latter days, saith the *L*	Jer 48:47	3068
The Ammonites, thus saith the *L*	Jer 49:1	3068
the days come, saith the *L*	Jer 49:2	3068
that were his heirs, saith the *L*	Jer 49:2	3068
saith the *L* GOD of hosts, from	Jer 49:5	136
children of Ammon, saith the *L*	Jer 49:6	3068
Edom, thus saith the *L* of hosts	Jer 49:7	3068
For thus saith the *L*	Jer 49:12	3068
have sworn by myself, saith the *L*	Jer 49:13	3068
I have heard a rumour from the *L*	Jer 49:14	3068
down from thence, saith the *L*	Jer 49:16	3068
cities thereof, saith the *L*	Jer 49:18	3068
hear the counsel of the *L*	Jer 49:20	3068
in that day, saith the *L* of hosts	Jer 49:26	3068
shall smite, thus saith the *L*	Jer 49:28	3068
inhabitants of Hazor, saith the *L*	Jer 49:30	3068
without care, saith the *L*	Jer 49:31	3068
all sides thereof, saith the *L*	Jer 49:32	3068
The word of the *L* that came to	Jer 49:34	3068
Thus saith the *L* of hosts	Jer 49:35	3068
even my fierce anger, saith the *L*	Jer 49:37	3068
king and the princes, saith the *L*	Jer 49:38	3068
captivity of Elam, saith the *L*	Jer 49:39	3068
The word that the *L* spake against	Jer 50:1	3068
and in that time, saith the *L*	Jer 50:4	3068
shall go, and seek the *L* their God	Jer 50:4	3068
L in a perpetual covenant that	Jer 50:5	3068
they have sinned against the *L*	Jer 50:7	3068
habitation of justice, even the *L*	Jer 50:7	3068
shall be satisfied, saith the *L*	Jer 50:10	3068
the *L* it shall not be inhabited	Jer 50:13	3068
for she hath sinned against the *L*	Jer 50:14	3068
for it is the vengeance of the *L*	Jer 50:15	3068
thus saith the *L* of hosts	Jer 50:18	3068
and in that time, saith the *L*	Jer 50:20	3068
destroy after them, saith the *L*	Jer 50:21	3068
thou hast striven against the *L*	Jer 50:24	3068
The *L* hath opened his armoury, and	Jer 50:25	3068
for this is the work of the *L* GOD	Jer 50:25	136
the vengeance of the *L* our God	Jer 50:28	3068
she hath been proud against the *L*	Jer 50:29	3068
cut off in that day, saith the *L*	Jer 50:30	3068
proud, saith the *L* GOD of hosts	Jer 50:31	136
Thus saith the *L* of hosts	Jer 50:33	3068
the *L* of hosts is his name	Jer 50:34	3068
upon the Chaldeans, saith the *L*	Jer 50:35	3068
cities thereof, saith the *L*	Jer 50:40	3068
hear ye the counsel of the *L*	Jer 50:45	3068
Thus saith the *L*	Jer 51:1	3068
of his God, of the *L* of hosts	Jer 51:5	3068
The *L* hath brought forth our	Jer 51:10	3068
in Zion the work of the *L* our God	Jer 51:10	3068
the *L* hath raised up the spirit	Jer 51:11	3068
it is the vengeance of the *L*	Jer 51:11	3068
for the *L* hath both devised and	Jer 51:12	3068
The *L* of hosts hath sworn by	Jer 51:14	3068
the *L* of hosts is his name	Jer 51:19	3068
Zion in your sight, saith the *L*	Jer 51:24	3068
destroying mountain, saith the *L*	Jer 51:25	3068
be desolate for ever, saith the *L*	Jer 51:26	3068
for every purpose of the *L* shall	Jer 51:29	3068
For thus saith the *L* of hosts	Jer 51:33	3068
Therefore thus saith the *L*	Jer 51:36	3068
sleep, and not wake, saith the *L*	Jer 51:39	3068
from the fierce anger of the *L*	Jer 51:45	3068
her from the north, saith the *L*	Jer 51:48	3068
remember the *L* afar off, and let	Jer 51:50	3068
the days come, saith the *L*	Jer 51:52	3068
come unto her, saith the *L*	Jer 51:53	3068
Because the *L* hath spoiled	Jer 51:55	3068
for the *L* God of recompences	Jer 51:56	3068
whose name is the *L* of hosts	Jer 51:57	3068
Thus saith the *L* of hosts	Jer 51:58	3068
Then shalt thou say, O *L*, thou	Jer 51:62	3068
was evil in the eyes of the *L*	Jer 52:2	3068
L it came to pass in Jerusalem	Jer 52:3	3068
And burned the house of the *L*	Jer 52:13	3068
that were in the house of the *L*	Jer 52:17	3068
that was in the house of the *L*	Jer 52:17	3068
had made in the house of the *L*	Jer 52:20	3068
for the *L* hath afflicted her for	Lam 1:5	3068
O *L*, behold my affliction	Lam 1:9	3068
see, O *L*, and consider	Lam 1:11	3068
wherewith the *L* hath afflicted me	Lam 1:12	3068
the *L* hath delivered me into	Lam 1:14	136
The *L* hath trodden under foot all	Lam 1:15	136
the *L* hath trodden the virgin	Lam 1:15	136
the *L* hath commanded concerning	Lam 1:17	3068
The *L* is righteous	Lam 1:18	3068
Behold, O *L*	Lam 1:20	3068
How hath the *L* covered the	Lam 2:1	136
The *L* hath swallowed up all the	Lam 2:2	136
The *L* was as an enemy	Lam 2:5	136
the *L* hath caused the solemn	Lam 2:6	3068
The *L* hath cast off his altar, he	Lam 2:7	136
a noise in the house of the *L*	Lam 2:7	3068
The *L* hath purposed to destroy	Lam 2:8	3068
also find no vision from the *L*	Lam 2:9	3068
The *L* hath done that which he had	Lam 2:17	3068
Their heart cried unto the *L*	Lam 2:18	136
water before the face of the *L*	Lam 2:19	136
Behold, O *L*, and consider to whom	Lam 2:20	3068
slain in the sanctuary of the *L*	Lam 2:20	136
and my hope is perished from the *L*	Lam 3:18	3068
The *L* is my portion, saith my	Lam 3:24	3068
The *L* is good unto them that wait	Lam 3:25	3068
wait for the salvation of the *L*	Lam 3:26	3068
For the *L* will not cast off for	Lam 3:31	136
in his cause, the *L* approveth not	Lam 3:36	136
when the *L* commandeth it not	Lam 3:37	136
our ways, and turn again to the *L*	Lam 3:40	3068
Till the *L* look down, and behold	Lam 3:50	3068
I called upon thy name, O *L*	Lam 3:55	3068
O *L*, thou hast pleaded the causes	Lam 3:58	136
O *L*, thou hast seen my wrong	Lam 3:59	3068
hast heard their reproach, O *L*	Lam 3:61	3068
unto them a recompence, O *L*	Lam 3:64	3068
from under the heavens of the *L*	Lam 3:66	3068
The *L* hath accomplished his fury	Lam 4:11	3068
The anger of the *L* hath divided	Lam 4:16	3068
nostrils, the anointed of the *L*	Lam 4:20	3068
Remember, O *L*, what is come upon	Lam 5:1	3068
Thou, O *L*, remainest for ever	Lam 5:19	3068
Turn thou us unto thee, O *L*	Lam 5:21	3068
The word of the *L* came expressly	Eze 1:3	3068
the hand of the *L* was there upon	Eze 1:3	3068
likeness of the glory of the *L*	Eze 1:28	3068
unto them, Thus saith the *L* GOD	Eze 2:4	136
tell them, Thus saith the *L* GOD	Eze 3:11	136
the glory of the *L* from his place	Eze 3:12	3068
hand of the *L* was strong upon me	Eze 3:14	3068
the word of the *L* came unto me	Eze 3:16	3068
the hand of the *L* was there upon	Eze 3:22	3068
the glory of the *L* stood there	Eze 3:23	3068
unto them, Thus saith the *L* GOD	Eze 3:27	136
the *L* said, Even thus shall the	Eze 4:13	3068
Then said I, Ah *L* GOD	Eze 4:14	136
Thus saith the *L* GOD	Eze 5:5	136
Therefore thus saith the *L* GOD	Eze 5:7	136
Therefore thus saith the *L* GOD	Eze 5:8	136
as I live, saith the *L* GOD	Eze 5:11	136
I the *L* have spoken it in my zeal	Eze 5:13	3068
I the *L* have spoken it	Eze 5:15	3068
I the *L* have spoken it	Eze 5:17	3068
And the word of the *L* came unto me	Eze 6:1	3068
hear the word of the *L* GOD	Eze 6:3	136
Thus saith the *L* GOD to the	Eze 6:3	136
and ye shall know that I am the *L*	Eze 6:7	3068
they shall know that I am the *L*	Eze 6:10	3068
Thus saith the *L* GOD	Eze 6:11	136
shall ye know that I am the *L*	Eze 6:13	3068
they shall know that I am the *L*	Eze 6:14	3068
the word of the *L* came unto me	Eze 7:1	3068
thus saith the *L* GOD unto the	Eze 7:2	136
and ye shall know that I am the *L*	Eze 7:4	3068
Thus saith the *L* GOD	Eze 7:5	136
know that I am the *L* that smiteth	Eze 7:9	3068
in the day of the wrath of the *L*	Eze 7:19	3068
they shall know that I am the *L*	Eze 7:27	3068
that the hand of the *L* GOD fell	Eze 8:1	136
for they say, The *L* seeth us not	Eze 8:12	3068
the *L* hath forsaken the earth	Eze 8:12	3068
the door of the temple of the *L*	Eze 8:16	3068
backs toward the temple of the *L*	Eze 8:16	3068
the *L* said unto him, Go through	Eze 9:4	3068
face, and cried, and said, Ah *L* GOD	Eze 9:8	136
The *L* hath forsaken the earth	Eze 9:9	3068
and the *L* seeth not	Eze 9:9	3068
Then the glory of the *L* went up	Eze 10:4	3068
Then the glory of the *L* departed	Eze 10:18	3068
the Spirit of the *L* fell upon me	Eze 11:5	3068
Thus saith the *L*	Eze 11:5	3068
Therefore thus saith the *L* GOD	Eze 11:7	136
a sword upon you, saith the *L* GOD	Eze 11:8	136
and ye shall know that I am the *L*	Eze 11:10	3068
And ye shall know that I am the *L*	Eze 11:12	3068
a loud voice, and said, Ah *L* GOD	Eze 11:13	136
the word of the *L* came unto me	Eze 11:14	3068
have said, Get you far from the *L*	Eze 11:15	3068
say, Thus saith the *L* GOD	Eze 11:16	136
say, Thus saith the *L* GOD	Eze 11:17	136
their own heads, saith the *L* GOD	Eze 11:21	136
the glory of the *L* went up from	Eze 11:23	3068
things that the *L* had shewed me	Eze 11:25	3068
The word of the *L* also came unto	Eze 12:1	3068
came the word of the *L* unto me	Eze 12:8	3068
unto them, Thus saith the *L* GOD	Eze 12:10	136
they shall know that I am the *L*	Eze 12:15	3068
they shall know that I am the *L*	Eze 12:16	3068
the word of the *L* came to me	Eze 12:17	3068
Thus saith the *L* GOD of the	Eze 12:19	136
and ye shall know that I am the *L*	Eze 12:20	3068
And the word of the *L* came unto me	Eze 12:21	3068
therefore, Thus saith the *L* GOD	Eze 12:23	136
For I am the *L*	Eze 12:25	3068
will perform it, saith the *L* GOD	Eze 12:25	136
the word of the *L* came to me	Eze 12:26	3068
unto them, Thus saith the *L* GOD	Eze 12:28	136
shall be done, saith the *L* GOD	Eze 12:28	136
And the word of the *L* came unto me	Eze 13:1	3068
hearts, Hear ye the word of the *L*	Eze 13:2	3068
Thus saith the *L* GOD	Eze 13:3	136
in the battle in the day of the *L*	Eze 13:5	3068
divination, saying, The *L* saith	Eze 13:6	3068
and the *L* hath not sent them	Eze 13:6	3068
whereas ye say, The *L* saith it	Eze 13:7	3068
Therefore thus saith the *L* GOD	Eze 13:8	136
I am against you, saith the *L* GOD	Eze 13:8	136
ye shall know that I am the *L* GOD	Eze 13:9	136
Therefore thus saith the *L* GOD	Eze 13:13	136
and ye shall know that I am the *L*	Eze 13:14	3068

is no peace, saith the *L* GOD	Eze 13:16	136
And say, Thus saith the *L* GOD	Eze 13:18	136
Wherefore thus saith the *L* GOD	Eze 13:20	136
and ye shall know that I am the *L*	Eze 13:21	3068
and ye shall know that I am the *L*	Eze 13:23	3068
And the word of the *L* came unto me	Eze 14:2	3068
unto them, Thus saith the *L* GOD	Eze 14:4	136
I the *L* will answer him that	Eze 14:4	3068
of Israel, Thus saith the *L* GOD	Eze 14:6	136
I the *L* will answer him by myself	Eze 14:7	3068
and ye shall know that I am the *L*	Eze 14:8	3068
I the *L* have deceived that	Eze 14:9	3068
may be their God, saith the *L* GOD	Eze 14:11	136
The word of the *L* came again to	Eze 14:12	3068
righteousness, saith the *L* GOD	Eze 14:14	136
in it, as I live, saith the *L* GOD	Eze 14:16	136
in it, as I live, saith the *L* GOD	Eze 14:18	136
in it, as I live, saith the *L* GOD	Eze 14:20	136
For thus saith the *L* GOD	Eze 14:21	136
have done in it, saith the *L* GOD	Eze 14:23	136
And the word of the *L* came unto me	Eze 15:1	3068
Therefore thus saith the *L* GOD	Eze 15:6	136
and ye shall know that I am the *L*	Eze 15:7	3068
a trespass, saith the *L* GOD	Eze 15:8	136
the word of the *L* came unto me	Eze 16:1	3068
Thus saith the *L* GOD unto	Eze 16:3	136
with thee, saith the *L* GOD	Eze 16:8	136
put upon thee, saith the *L* GOD	Eze 16:14	136
and thus it was, saith the *L* GOD	Eze 16:19	136
saith the *L* GOD	Eze 16:23	136
is thine heart, saith the *L* GOD	Eze 16:30	136
O harlot, hear the word of the *L*	Eze 16:35	3068
Thus saith the *L* GOD	Eze 16:36	136
upon thine head, saith the *L* GOD	Eze 16:43	136
As I live, saith the *L* GOD	Eze 16:48	136
thine abominations, saith the *L*	Eze 16:58	3068
For thus saith the *L* GOD	Eze 16:59	136
thou shalt know that I am the *L*	Eze 16:62	3068
thou hast done, saith the *L* GOD	Eze 16:63	136
And the word of the *L* came unto me	Eze 17:1	3068
And say, Thus saith the *L* GOD	Eze 17:3	136
Say thou, Thus saith the *L* GOD	Eze 17:9	136
the word of the *L* came unto me	Eze 17:11	3068
As I live, saith the *L* GOD	Eze 17:16	136
Therefore thus saith the *L* GOD	Eze 17:19	136
know that I the *L* have spoken it	Eze 17:21	3068
Thus saith the *L* GOD	Eze 17:22	136
L have brought down the high tree	Eze 17:24	3068
I the *L* have spoken and have done	Eze 17:24	3068
The word of the *L* came unto me	Eze 18:1	3068
As I live, saith the *L* GOD	Eze 18:3	136
surely live, saith the *L* GOD	Eze 18:9	136
saith the *L* GOD	Eze 18:23	136
The way of the *L* is not equal	Eze 18:25	136
The way of the *L* is not equal	Eze 18:29	136
to his ways, saith the *L* GOD	Eze 18:30	136
him that dieth, saith the *L* GOD	Eze 18:32	136
Israel came to enquire of the *L*	Eze 20:1	3068
came the word of the *L* unto me	Eze 20:2	3068
unto them, Thus saith the *L* GOD	Eze 20:3	136
As I live, saith the *L* GOD	Eze 20:3	136
unto them, Thus saith the *L* GOD	Eze 20:5	136
them, saying, I am the *L* your God	Eze 20:5	3068
I am the *L* your God	Eze 20:7	3068
I am the *L* that sanctify them	Eze 20:12	3068
I am the *L* your God	Eze 20:19	3068
may know that I am the *L* your God	Eze 20:20	3068
they might know that I am the *L*	Eze 20:26	3068
unto them, Thus saith the *L* GOD	Eze 20:27	136
of Israel, Thus saith the *L* GOD	Eze 20:30	136
As I live, saith the *L* GOD	Eze 20:31	136
As I live, saith the *L* GOD	Eze 20:33	136
I plead with you, saith the *L* GOD	Eze 20:36	136
and ye shall know that I am the *L*	Eze 20:38	3068
of Israel, thus saith the *L* GOD	Eze 20:39	136
height of Israel, saith the *L* GOD	Eze 20:40	136
And ye shall know that I am the *L*	Eze 20:42	3068
And ye shall know that I am the *L*	Eze 20:44	3068
house of Israel, saith the *L* GOD	Eze 20:44	136
the word of the *L* came unto me	Eze 20:45	3068
the south, Hear the word of the *L*	Eze 20:47	3068
Thus saith the *L* GOD	Eze 20:47	136
see that I the *L* have kindled it	Eze 20:48	3068
Then said I, Ah *L* GOD	Eze 20:49	136
And the word of the *L* came unto me	Eze 21:1	3068
land of Israel, Thus saith the *L*	Eze 21:3	3068
L have drawn forth my sword out	Eze 21:5	3068
brought to pass, saith the *L* GOD	Eze 21:7	136
the word of the *L* came unto me	Eze 21:8	3068
and say, Thus saith the *L*	Eze 21:9	3068
shall be no more, saith the *L* GOD	Eze 21:13	136
I the *L* have said it	Eze 21:17	3068
The word of the *L* came unto me	Eze 21:18	3068
Therefore thus saith the *L* GOD	Eze 21:24	136
Thus saith the *L* GOD	Eze 21:26	136
Thus saith the *L* GOD concerning	Eze 21:28	136
for I the *L* have spoken it	Eze 21:32	3068
the word of the *L* came unto me	Eze 22:1	3068
say thou, Thus saith the *L* GOD	Eze 22:3	136
forgotten me, saith the *L* GOD	Eze 22:12	136
I the *L* have spoken it, and will	Eze 22:14	3068
thou shalt know that I am the *L*	Eze 22:16	3068
And the word of the *L* came unto me	Eze 22:17	3068
Therefore thus saith the *L* GOD	Eze 22:19	136
ye shall know that I the *L* have	Eze 22:22	3068
And the word of the *L* came unto me	Eze 22:23	3068
saying, Thus saith the *L* GOD	Eze 22:28	136
when the *L* hath not spoken	Eze 22:28	3068
upon their heads, saith the *L* GOD	Eze 22:31	136
The word of the *L* came again unto	Eze 23:1	3068
O Aholibah, thus saith the *L* GOD	Eze 23:22	136
For thus saith the *L* GOD	Eze 23:28	136
Thus saith the *L* GOD	Eze 23:32	136
I have spoken it, saith the *L* GOD	Eze 23:34	136
Therefore thus saith the *L* GOD	Eze 23:35	136
The *L* said moreover unto me	Eze 23:36	3068
For thus saith the *L* GOD	Eze 23:46	136
ye shall know that I am the *L* GOD	Eze 23:49	136
the word of the *L* came unto me	Eze 24:1	3068
unto them, Thus saith the *L* GOD	Eze 24:3	136
Wherefore thus saith the *L* GOD	Eze 24:6	136
Therefore thus saith the *L* GOD	Eze 24:9	136
I the *L* have spoken it	Eze 24:14	3068
they judge thee, saith the *L* GOD	Eze 24:14	136
the word of the *L* came unto me	Eze 24:15	3068
The word of the *L* came unto me	Eze 24:20	3068
of Israel, Thus saith the *L* GOD	Eze 24:21	136
ye shall know that I am the *L* GOD	Eze 24:24	136
they shall know that I am the *L*	Eze 24:27	3068
The word of the *L* came again unto	Eze 25:1	3068
Hear the word of the *L* GOD	Eze 25:3	136
Thus saith the *L* GOD	Eze 25:3	136
and ye shall know that I am the *L*	Eze 25:5	3068
For thus saith the *L* GOD	Eze 25:6	136
thou shalt know that I am the *L*	Eze 25:7	3068
Thus saith the *L* GOD	Eze 25:8	136
they shall know that I am the *L*	Eze 25:11	3068
Thus saith the *L* GOD	Eze 25:12	136
Therefore thus saith the *L* GOD	Eze 25:13	136
my vengeance, saith the *L* GOD	Eze 25:14	136
Thus saith the *L* GOD	Eze 25:15	136
Therefore thus saith the *L* GOD	Eze 25:16	136
they shall know that I am the *L*	Eze 25:17	3068
the word of the *L* came unto me	Eze 26:1	3068
Therefore thus saith the *L* GOD	Eze 26:3	136
I have spoken it, saith the *L* GOD	Eze 26:5	136
they shall know that I am the *L*	Eze 26:6	3068
For thus saith the *L* GOD	Eze 26:7	136
for I the *L* have spoken it	Eze 26:14	3068
have spoken it, saith the *L* GOD	Eze 26:14	136
Thus saith the *L* GOD to Tyrus	Eze 26:15	136
For thus saith the *L* GOD	Eze 26:19	136
be found again, saith the *L* GOD	Eze 26:21	136
The word of the *L* came again unto	Eze 27:1	3068
many isles, Thus saith the *L* GOD	Eze 27:3	136
The word of the *L* came again unto	Eze 28:1	3068
of Tyrus, Thus saith the *L* GOD	Eze 28:2	136
Therefore thus saith the *L* GOD	Eze 28:6	136
I have spoken it, saith the *L* GOD	Eze 28:10	136
the word of the *L* came unto me	Eze 28:11	3068
unto him, Thus saith the *L* GOD	Eze 28:12	136
the word of the *L* came unto me	Eze 28:20	3068
And say, Thus saith the *L* GOD	Eze 28:22	136
they shall know that I am the *L*	Eze 28:22	3068
they shall know that I am the *L*	Eze 28:23	3068
shall know that I am the *L* GOD	Eze 28:24	136
Thus saith the *L* GOD	Eze 28:25	136
know that I am the *L* their God	Eze 28:26	3068
the word of the *L* came unto me	Eze 29:1	3068
and say, Thus saith the *L* GOD	Eze 29:3	136
Egypt shall know that I am the *L*	Eze 29:6	3068
Therefore thus saith the *L* GOD	Eze 29:8	136
they shall know that I am the *L*	Eze 29:9	3068
Yet thus saith the *L* GOD	Eze 29:13	136
shall know that I am the *L* GOD	Eze 29:16	136
the word of the *L* came unto me	Eze 29:17	3068
Therefore thus saith the *L* GOD	Eze 29:19	136
wrought for me, saith the *L* GOD	Eze 29:20	136
they shall know that I am the *L*	Eze 29:21	3068
The word of the *L* came again unto	Eze 30:1	3068
and say, Thus saith the *L* GOD	Eze 30:2	136
even the day of the *L* is near	Eze 30:3	3068
Thus saith the *L*	Eze 30:6	3068
it by the sword, saith the *L* GOD	Eze 30:6	136
they shall know that I am the *L*	Eze 30:8	3068
Thus saith the *L* GOD	Eze 30:10	136
I the *L* have spoken it	Eze 30:12	3068
Thus saith the *L* GOD	Eze 30:13	136
they shall know that I am the *L*	Eze 30:19	3068
the word of the *L* came unto me	Eze 30:20	3068
Therefore thus saith the *L* GOD	Eze 30:22	136
they shall know that I am the *L*	Eze 30:25	3068
they shall know that I am the *L*	Eze 30:26	3068
the word of the *L* came unto me	Eze 31:1	3068
Therefore thus saith the *L* GOD	Eze 31:10	136
Thus saith the *L* GOD	Eze 31:15	136
his multitude, saith the *L* GOD	Eze 31:18	136
the word of the *L* came unto me	Eze 32:1	3068
Thus saith the *L* GOD	Eze 32:3	136
upon thy land, saith the *L* GOD	Eze 32:8	136
For thus saith the *L* GOD	Eze 32:11	136
to run like oil, saith the *L* GOD	Eze 32:14	136
shall they know that I am the *L*	Eze 32:15	3068
her multitude, saith the *L* GOD	Eze 32:16	136
the word of the *L* came unto me	Eze 32:17	3068
by the sword, saith the *L* GOD	Eze 32:31	136
his multitude, saith the *L* GOD	Eze 32:32	136
the word of the *L* came unto me	Eze 33:1	3068
them, As I live, saith the *L* GOD	Eze 33:11	136
The way of the *L* is not equal	Eze 33:17	136
The way of the *L* is not equal	Eze 33:20	136
Now the hand of the *L* was upon me	Eze 33:22	3068
the word of the *L* came unto me	Eze 33:23	3068
unto them, Thus saith the *L* GOD	Eze 33:25	136
unto them, Thus saith the *L* GOD	Eze 33:27	136
shall they know that I am the *L*	Eze 33:29	3068
word that cometh forth from the *L*	Eze 33:30	3068
And the word of the *L* came unto me	Eze 34:1	3068
Thus saith the *L* GOD unto the	Eze 34:2	136
shepherds, hear the word of the *L*	Eze 34:7	3068
As I live saith the *L* GOD	Eze 34:8	136
shepherds, hear the word of the *L*	Eze 34:9	3068
Thus saith the *L* GOD	Eze 34:10	136
For thus saith the *L* GOD	Eze 34:11	136
them to lie down, saith the *L* GOD	Eze 34:15	136
O my flock, thus saith the *L* GOD	Eze 34:17	136
thus saith the *L* GOD unto them	Eze 34:20	136
I the *L* will be their God, and my	Eze 34:24	3068
I the *L* have spoken it	Eze 34:24	3068
and shall know that I am the *L*	Eze 34:27	3068
I the *L* their God am with them	Eze 34:30	3068
are my people, saith the *L* GOD	Eze 34:30	136
and I am your God, saith the *L* GOD	Eze 34:31	136
the word of the *L* came unto me	Eze 35:1	3068
say unto it, Thus saith the *L* GOD	Eze 35:3	136
thou shalt know that I am the *L*	Eze 35:4	3068
as I live, saith the *L* GOD	Eze 35:6	136
and ye shall know that I am the *L*	Eze 35:9	3068
whereas the *L* was there	Eze 35:10	3068
as I live, saith the *L* GOD	Eze 35:11	136
thou shalt know that I am the *L*	Eze 35:12	3068
Thus saith the *L* GOD	Eze 35:14	136
they shall know that I am the *L*	Eze 35:15	3068
of Israel, hear the word of the *L*	Eze 36:1	3068
Thus saith the *L* GOD	Eze 36:2	136
and say, Thus saith the *L* GOD	Eze 36:3	136
hear the word of the *L* GOD	Eze 36:4	136
Thus saith the *L* GOD to the	Eze 36:4	136
Therefore thus saith the *L* GOD	Eze 36:5	136
the valleys, Thus saith the *L* GOD	Eze 36:6	136
Therefore thus saith the *L* GOD	Eze 36:7	136
and ye shall know that I am the *L*	Eze 36:11	3068
Thus saith the *L* GOD	Eze 36:13	136
nations any more, saith the *L* GOD	Eze 36:14	136
to fall any more, saith the *L* GOD	Eze 36:15	136
the word of the *L* came unto me	Eze 36:16	3068
These are the people of the *L*	Eze 36:20	3068
of Israel, Thus saith the *L* GOD	Eze 36:22	136
shall know that I am the *L*	Eze 36:23	3068
saith the *L* GOD	Eze 36:23	136
sakes do I this, saith the *L* GOD	Eze 36:32	136
Thus saith the *L* GOD	Eze 36:33	136
I the *L* build the ruined places	Eze 36:36	3068
I the *L* have spoken it, and I will	Eze 36:36	3068
Thus saith the *L* GOD	Eze 36:37	136
they shall know that I am the *L*	Eze 36:38	3068
The hand of the *L* was upon me	Eze 37:1	3068
me out in the spirit of the *L*	Eze 37:1	3068
I answered, O *L* GOD, thou knowest	Eze 37:3	136
dry bones, hear the word of the *L*	Eze 37:4	3068
Thus saith the *L* GOD unto these	Eze 37:5	136
and ye shall know that I am the *L*	Eze 37:6	3068
to the wind, Thus saith the *L* GOD	Eze 37:9	136
unto them, Thus saith the *L* GOD	Eze 37:12	136
And ye shall know that I am the *L*	Eze 37:13	3068
know that I the *L* have spoken it	Eze 37:14	3068
and performed it, saith the *L*	Eze 37:14	3068
The word of the *L* came again unto	Eze 37:15	3068
unto them, Thus saith the *L* GOD	Eze 37:19	136
unto them, Thus saith the *L* GOD	Eze 37:21	136
that I the *L* do sanctify Israel	Eze 37:28	3068
And the word of the *L* came unto me	Eze 38:1	3068
And say, Thus saith the *L* GOD	Eze 38:3	136
Thus saith the *L* GOD	Eze 38:10	136
unto Gog, Thus saith the *L* GOD	Eze 38:14	136
Thus saith the *L* GOD	Eze 38:17	136
land of Israel, saith the *L* GOD	Eze 38:18	136
all my mountains, saith the *L* GOD	Eze 38:21	136
they shall know that I am the *L*	Eze 38:23	3068
Gog, and say, Thus saith the *L* GOD	Eze 39:1	136
I have spoken it, saith the *L* GOD	Eze 39:5	136
they shall know that I am the *L*	Eze 39:6	3068
shall know that I am the *L*	Eze 39:7	3068
and it is done, saith the *L* GOD	Eze 39:8	136
that robbed them, saith the *L* GOD	Eze 39:10	136
be glorified, saith the *L* GOD	Eze 39:13	136
son of man, thus saith the *L* GOD	Eze 39:17	136
all men of war, saith the *L* GOD	Eze 39:20	136
am the *L* their God from that day	Eze 39:22	3068
Therefore thus saith the *L* GOD	Eze 39:25	136
know that I am the *L* their God	Eze 39:28	3068
house of Israel, saith the *L* GOD	Eze 39:29	136
day the hand of the *L* was upon me	Eze 40:1	3068
to the *L* to minister unto him	Eze 40:46	3068
is the table that is before the *L*	Eze 41:22	3068
L shall eat the most holy things	Eze 42:13	3068
the glory of the *L* came into the	Eze 43:4	3068
glory of the *L* filled the house	Eze 43:5	3068
Son of man, thus saith the *L* GOD	Eze 43:18	136
minister unto me, saith the *L* GOD	Eze 43:19	136
shalt offer them before the *L*	Eze 43:24	3068
for a burnt offering unto the *L*	Eze 43:24	3068
will accept you, saith the *L* GOD	Eze 43:27	136
Then said the *L* unto me	Eze 44:2	3068
because the *L*, the God of Israel,	Eze 44:2	3068
in it to eat bread before the *L*	Eze 44:3	3068
L filled the house of the *L*	Eze 44:4	3068
the *L* said unto me, Son of man,	Eze 44:5	3068
ordinances of the house of the *L*	Eze 44:5	3068
of Israel, Thus saith the *L* GOD	Eze 44:6	136
Thus saith the *L* GOD	Eze 44:9	136
against them, saith the *L* GOD	Eze 44:12	136
fat and the blood, saith the *L* GOD	Eze 44:15	136
his sin offering, saith the *L* GOD	Eze 44:27	136
offer an oblation unto the *L*	Eze 45:1	3068
come near to minister unto the *L*	Eze 45:4	3068
Thus saith the *L* GOD	Eze 45:9	136
from my people, saith the *L* GOD	Eze 45:9	136
for them, saith the *L* GOD	Eze 45:15	136
Thus saith the *L* GOD	Eze 45:18	136
prepare a burnt offering to the *L*	Eze 45:23	3068
Thus saith the *L* GOD	Eze 46:1	136
gate before the *L* in the sabbaths	Eze 46:3	3068
L in the sabbath day shall be six	Eze 46:4	3068
before the *L* in the solemn feasts	Eze 46:9	3068
offerings voluntarily unto the *L*	Eze 46:12	3068
a burnt offering unto the *L* of a	Eze 46:13	3068
a perpetual ordinance unto the *L*	Eze 46:14	3068
Thus saith the *L* GOD	Eze 46:16	136
Thus saith the *L* GOD	Eze 47:13	136
his inheritance, saith the *L* GOD	Eze 47:23	136
offer unto the *L* shall be of five	Eze 48:9	3068

the sanctuary of the L shall be	Eze 48:10	3068
for it is holy unto the L	Eze 48:14	3068
their portions, saith the L GOD	Eze 48:29	136
that day shall be, The L is there	Eze 48:35	3068
the L gave Jehoiakim king of	Dan 1:2	136
a L of kings, and a revealer of	Dan 2:47	4756
thyself against the L of heaven	Dan 5:23	4756
whereof the word of the L came to	Dan 9:2	3068
And I set my face unto the L God	Dan 9:3	136
And I prayed unto the L my God	Dan 9:4	3068
made my confession, and said, O L	Dan 9:4	136
O L, righteousness belongeth unto	Dan 9:7	136
O L, to us belongeth confusion of	Dan 9:8	136
To the L our God belong mercies	Dan 9:9	136
obeyed the voice of the L our God	Dan 9:10	3068
our prayer before the L our God	Dan 9:13	3068
Therefore hath the L watched upon	Dan 9:14	3068
for the L our God is righteous in	Dan 9:14	3068
O L our God, that hast brought	Dan 9:15	136
O L, according to all thy	Dan 9:16	136
O L, hear	Dan 9:19	136
O L, forgive	Dan 9:19	136
O L, hearken and do	Dan 9:19	136
my supplication before the L my	Dan 9:20	3068
then said I, O my L, what shall	Dan 12:8	113
The word of the L that came unto	Hos 1:1	3068
of the word of the L by Hosea	Hos 1:2	3068
the L said to Hosea, Go, take	Hos 1:2	3068
whoredom, departing from the L	Hos 1:2	3068
the L said unto him, Call his	Hos 1:4	3068
will save them by the L their God	Hos 1:7	3068
lovers, and forgat me, saith the L	Hos 2:13	3068
shall be at that day, saith the L	Hos 2:16	3068
and thou shalt know the L	Hos 2:20	3068
day, I will hear, saith the L	Hos 2:21	3068
Then said the L unto me, Go yet,	Hos 3:1	3068
according to the love of the L	Hos 3:1	3068
seek the L their God, and David	Hos 3:5	3068
and shall fear the L and his	Hos 3:5	3068
Hear the word of the L, ye	Hos 4:1	3068
for the L hath a controversy with	Hos 4:1	3068
left off to take heed to the L	Hos 4:10	3068
nor swear, The L liveth	Hos 4:15	3068
now the L will feed them as a	Hos 4:16	3068
and they have not known the L	Hos 5:4	3068
and with their herds to seek the L	Hos 5:6	3068
dealt treacherously against the L	Hos 5:7	3068
Come, and let us return unto the L	Hos 6:1	3068
if we follow on to know the L	Hos 6:3	3068
do not return to the L their God	Hos 7:10	3068
eagle against the house of the L	Hos 8:1	3068
but the L accepteth them not	Hos 8:13	3068
not offer wine offerings to the L	Hos 9:4	3068
not come into the house of the L	Hos 9:4	3068
in the day of the feast of the L	Hos 9:5	3068
Give them, O L	Hos 9:14	3068
king, because we feared not the L	Hos 10:3	3068
for it is time to seek the L	Hos 10:12	3068
They shall walk after the L	Hos 11:10	3068
them in their houses, saith the L	Hos 11:11	3068
The L hath also a controversy	Hos 12:2	3068
Even the L God of hosts	Hos 12:5	3068
the L is his memorial	Hos 12:5	3068
I that am the L thy God from the	Hos 12:9	3068
by a prophet the L brought Israel	Hos 12:13	3068
shall his L return unto him	Hos 12:14	113
Yet I am the L thy God from the	Hos 13:4	3068
the wind of the L shall come up	Hos 13:15	3068
Israel, return unto the L thy God	Hos 14:1	3068
with you words, and turn to the L	Hos 14:2	3068
for the ways of the L are right	Hos 14:9	3068
The word of the L that came to	Joel 1:1	3068
cut off from the house of the L	Joel 1:9	3068
into the house of the L your God	Joel 1:14	3068
and cry unto the L	Joel 1:14	3068
for the day of the L is at hand	Joel 1:15	3068
O L, to thee will I cry	Joel 1:19	3068
for the day of the L cometh	Joel 2:1	3068
the L shall utter his voice	Joel 2:11	3068
for the day of the L is great	Joel 2:11	3068
Therefore also now, saith the L	Joel 2:12	3068
and turn unto the L your God	Joel 2:13	3068
offering unto the L your God	Joel 2:14	3068
priests, the ministers of the L	Joel 2:17	3068
them say, Spare thy people, O L	Joel 2:17	3068
Then will the L be jealous for	Joel 2:18	3068
the L will answer and say unto his	Joel 2:19	3068
for the L will do great things	Joel 2:21	3068
and rejoice in the L your God	Joel 2:23	3068
praise the name of the L your God	Joel 2:26	3068
and that I am the L your God	Joel 2:27	3068
and the terrible day of the L come	Joel 2:31	3068
name of the L shall be delivered	Joel 2:32	3068
as the L hath said, and in the	Joel 2:32	3068
the remnant whom the L shall call	Joel 2:32	3068
for the L hath spoken it	Joel 3:8	3068
thy mighty ones to come down, O L	Joel 3:11	3068
for the day of the L is near in	Joel 3:14	3068
The L also shall roar out of Zion	Joel 3:16	3068
but the L will be the hope of his	Joel 3:16	3068
the L your God dwelling in Zion	Joel 3:17	3068
come forth of the house of the L	Joel 3:18	3068
for the L dwelleth in Zion	Joel 3:21	3068
The L will roar from Zion, and	Amos 1:2	3068
Thus saith the L	Amos 1:3	3068
captivity unto Kir, saith the L	Amos 1:5	3068
Thus saith the L	Amos 1:6	3068
shall perish, saith the L GOD	Amos 1:8	136
Thus saith the L	Amos 1:9	3068
Thus saith the L	Amos 1:11	3068
Thus saith the L	Amos 1:13	3068
his princes together, saith the L	Amos 1:15	3068
Thus saith the L	Amos 2:1	3068
thereof with him, saith the L	Amos 2:3	3068
Thus saith the L	Amos 2:4	3068
have despised the law of the L	Amos 2:4	3068
Thus saith the L	Amos 2:6	3068
saith the L	Amos 2:11	3068
naked in that day, saith the L	Amos 2:16	3068
the L hath spoken against you	Amos 3:1	3068
a city, and the L hath not done it	Amos 3:6	3068
Surely the L GOD will do nothing,	Amos 3:7	136
the L GOD hath spoken, who can	Amos 3:8	136
know not to do right, saith the L	Amos 3:10	3068
Therefore thus saith the L GOD	Amos 3:11	136
Thus saith the L	Amos 3:12	3068
house of Jacob, saith the L GOD	Amos 3:13	136
shall have an end, saith the L	Amos 3:15	3068
The L GOD hath sworn by his	Amos 4:2	136
them into the palace, saith the L	Amos 4:3	3068
of Israel, saith the L GOD	Amos 4:5	136
not returned unto me, saith the L	Amos 4:6	3068
not returned unto me, saith the L	Amos 4:8	3068
not returned unto me, saith the L	Amos 4:9	3068
not returned unto me, saith the L	Amos 4:10	3068
not returned unto me, saith the L	Amos 4:11	3068
high places of the earth, The L	Amos 4:13	3068
For thus saith the L GOD	Amos 5:3	136
For thus saith the L unto the	Amos 5:4	3068
Seek the L, and ye shall live	Amos 5:6	3068
The L is his name	Amos 5:8	3068
and so the L, the God of hosts,	Amos 5:14	3068
it may be that the L God of hosts	Amos 5:15	3068
Therefore the L, the God of hosts	Amos 5:16	3068
the God of hosts, the L	Amos 5:16	136
pass through thee, saith the L	Amos 5:17	3068
you that desire the day of the L	Amos 5:18	3068
the day of the L is darkness	Amos 5:18	3068
not the day of the L be darkness	Amos 5:20	3068
beyond Damascus, saith the L	Amos 5:27	3068
The L GOD hath sworn by himself,	Amos 6:8	136
saith the L the God of hosts, I	Amos 6:8	3068
make mention of the name of the L	Amos 6:10	3068
the L commandeth, and he will	Amos 6:11	3068
saith the L the God of hosts	Amos 6:14	3068
Thus hath the L GOD shewed unto	Amos 7:1	136
O L GOD, forgive, I beseech thee	Amos 7:2	136
The L repented for this	Amos 7:3	3068
It shall not be, saith the L	Amos 7:3	3068
Thus hath the L GOD shewed unto	Amos 7:4	136
the L GOD called to contend by	Amos 7:4	136
O L GOD, cease, I beseech thee	Amos 7:5	136
The L repented for this	Amos 7:6	3068
shall not be, saith the L GOD	Amos 7:6	136
the L stood upon a wall made by a	Amos 7:7	136
the L said unto me, Amos, what	Amos 7:8	3068
Then said the L, Behold, I will	Amos 7:8	136
the L took me as I followed the	Amos 7:15	3068
the L said unto me, Go, prophesy	Amos 7:15	3068
hear thou the word of the L	Amos 7:16	3068
Therefore thus saith the L	Amos 7:17	3068
Thus hath the L GOD shewed unto	Amos 8:1	136
Then said the L unto me, The end	Amos 8:2	3068
in that day, saith the L GOD	Amos 8:3	136
The L hath sworn by the	Amos 8:7	3068
pass in that day, saith the L GOD	Amos 8:9	136
the days come, saith the L GOD	Amos 8:11	136
but of hearing the words of the L	Amos 8:11	3068
and fro to seek the word of the L	Amos 8:12	3068
I saw the L standing upon the	Amos 9:1	136
the L GOD of hosts is he that	Amos 9:5	136
The L is his name	Amos 9:6	3068
of Israel? saith the L	Amos 9:7	3068
the eyes of the L GOD are upon	Amos 9:8	136
the house of Jacob, saith the L	Amos 9:8	3068
saith the L that doeth this	Amos 9:12	3068
the days come, saith the L	Amos 9:13	3068
given them, saith the L thy God	Amos 9:15	3068
Thus saith the L GOD concerning	Obad 1	136
We have heard a rumour from the L	Obad 1	3068
I bring thee down, saith the L	Obad 4	3068
I not in that day, saith the L	Obad 8	3068
For the day of the L is near upon	Obad 15	3068
for the L hath spoken it	Obad 18	3068
Now the word of the L came unto	Jonah 1:1	3068
from the presence of the L	Jonah 1:3	3068
from the presence of the L	Jonah 1:3	3068
But the L sent out a great wind	Jonah 1:4	3068
and I fear the L, the God of	Jonah 1:9	3068
fled from the presence of the L	Jonah 1:10	3068
Wherefore they cried unto the L	Jonah 1:14	3068
and said, We beseech thee, O L	Jonah 1:14	3068
for thou, O L, hast done as it	Jonah 1:14	3068
the men feared the L exceedingly	Jonah 1:16	3068
and offered a sacrifice unto the L	Jonah 1:16	3068
Now the L had prepared a great	Jonah 1:17	3068
Then Jonah prayed unto the L his	Jonah 2:1	3068
of mine affliction unto the L	Jonah 2:2	3068
life from corruption, O L my God	Jonah 2:6	3068
within me I remembered the L	Jonah 2:7	3068
Salvation is of the L	Jonah 2:9	3068
the L spake unto the fish, and it	Jonah 2:10	3068
the word of the L came unto Jonah	Jonah 3:1	3068
according to the word of the L	Jonah 3:3	3068
And he prayed unto the L	Jonah 4:2	3068
and said, I pray thee, O L	Jonah 4:2	3068
Therefore now, O L, take, I	Jonah 4:3	3068
Then said the L, Doest thou well	Jonah 4:4	3068
the L God prepared a gourd, and	Jonah 4:6	3068
Then said the L, Thou hast had	Jonah 4:10	3068
The word of the L that came to	Mic 1:1	3068
let the L GOD be witness against	Mic 1:2	136
the L from his holy temple	Mic 1:2	136
the L cometh forth out of his	Mic 1:3	3068
the L unto the gate of Jerusalem	Mic 1:12	3068
Therefore thus saith the L	Mic 2:3	3068
lot in the congregation of the L	Mic 2:5	3068
is the spirit of the L straitened	Mic 2:7	3068
the L on the head of them	Mic 2:13	3068
Then shall they cry unto the L	Mic 3:4	3068
Thus saith the L concerning the	Mic 3:5	3068
of power by the spirit of the L	Mic 3:8	3068
yet will they lean upon the L	Mic 3:11	3068
and say, Is not the L among us	Mic 3:11	3068
mountain of the house of the L	Mic 4:1	3068
us go up to the mountain of the L	Mic 4:2	3068
the word of the L from Jerusalem	Mic 4:2	3068
for the mouth of the L of hosts	Mic 4:4	3068
name of the L our God for ever	Mic 4:5	3068
In that day, saith the L, will I	Mic 4:6	3068
the L shall reign over them in	Mic 4:7	3068
there the L shall redeem thee	Mic 4:10	3068
know not the thoughts of the L	Mic 4:12	3068
consecrate their gain unto the L	Mic 4:13	3068
unto the L of the whole earth	Mic 4:13	113
and feed in the strength of the L	Mic 5:4	3068
of the name of the L his God	Mic 5:4	3068
many people as a dew from the L	Mic 5:7	3068
to pass in that day, saith the L	Mic 5:10	3068
Hear ye now what the L saith	Mic 6:1	3068
for the L hath a controversy with	Mic 6:2	3068
know the righteousness of the L	Mic 6:5	3068
shall I come before the L	Mic 6:6	3068
Will the L be pleased with	Mic 6:7	3068
what doth the L require of thee,	Mic 6:8	3068
Therefore I will look unto the L	Mic 7:7	3068
the L shall be a light unto me	Mic 7:8	3068
bear the indignation of the L	Mic 7:9	3068
unto me, Where is the L thy God	Mic 7:10	3068
shall be afraid of the L our God	Mic 7:17	3068
is jealous, and the L revengeth	Nah 1:2	3068
the L revengeth, and is furious	Nah 1:2	3068
the L will take vengeance on his	Nah 1:2	3068
The L is slow to anger, and great	Nah 1:3	3068
the L hath his way in the	Nah 1:3	3068
The L is good, a strong hold in	Nah 1:7	3068
What do ye imagine against the L	Nah 1:9	3068
that imagineth evil against the L	Nah 1:11	3068
Thus saith the L	Nah 1:12	3068
the L hath given a commandment	Nah 1:14	3068
For the L hath turned away the	Nah 2:2	3068
thee, saith the L of hosts	Nah 2:13	3068
thee, saith the L of hosts	Nah 3:5	3068
O L, how long shall I cry, and	Hab 1:2	3068
O L my God, mine Holy One	Hab 1:12	3068
O L, thou hast ordained them for	Hab 1:12	3068
the L answered me, and said, Write	Hab 2:2	3068
is it not of the L of hosts that	Hab 2:13	3068
knowledge of the glory of the L	Hab 2:14	3068
But the L is in his holy temple	Hab 2:20	3068
O L, I have heard thy speech, and	Hab 3:2	3068
O L, revive thy work in the midst	Hab 3:2	3068
Was the L displeased against the	Hab 3:8	3068
Yet I will rejoice in the L	Hab 3:18	3068
The L God is my strength, and he	Hab 3:19	3068
The word of the L which came unto	Zeph 1:1	3068
from off the land, saith the L	Zeph 1:2	3068
from off the land, saith the L	Zeph 1:3	3068
worship and that swear by the L	Zeph 1:5	3068
that are turned back from the L	Zeph 1:6	3068
those that have not sought the L	Zeph 1:6	3068
at the presence of the L GOD	Zeph 1:7	136
for the day of the L is at hand	Zeph 1:7	3068
for the L hath prepared a	Zeph 1:7	3068
to pass in that day, saith the L	Zeph 1:10	3068
The L will not do good, neither	Zeph 1:12	3068
The great day of the L is near	Zeph 1:14	3068
the voice of the day of the L	Zeph 1:14	3068
they have sinned against the L	Zeph 1:17	3068
anger of the L come upon you	Zeph 2:2	3068
Seek ye the L, all ye meek of the	Zeph 2:3	3068
the word of the L is against you	Zeph 2:5	3068
for the L their God shall visit	Zeph 2:7	3068
as I live, saith the L of hosts	Zeph 2:9	3068
the people of the L of hosts	Zeph 2:10	3068
The L will be terrible unto them	Zeph 2:11	3068
she trusted not in the L	Zeph 3:2	3068
The just L is in the midst	Zeph 3:5	3068
wait ye upon me, saith the L	Zeph 3:8	3068
all call upon the name of the L	Zeph 3:9	3068
shall trust in the name of the L	Zeph 3:12	3068
The L hath taken away thy	Zeph 3:15	3068
the king of Israel, even the L	Zeph 3:15	3068
The L thy God in the midst of	Zeph 3:17	3068
before your eyes, saith the L	Zeph 3:20	3068
came the word of the L by Haggai	Hag 1:1	3068
Thus speaketh the L of hosts	Hag 1:2	3068
of the L by Haggai the prophet	Hag 1:3	3068
thus saith the L of hosts	Hag 1:5	3068
Thus saith the L of hosts	Hag 1:7	3068
I will be glorified, saith the L	Hag 1:8	3068
saith the L of hosts	Hag 1:9	3068
the voice of the L their God	Hag 1:12	3068
as the L their God had sent him,	Hag 1:12	3068
the people did fear before the L	Hag 1:12	3068
I am with you, saith the L	Hag 1:13	3068
the L stirred up the spirit of	Hag 1:14	3068
in the house of the L of hosts	Hag 1:14	3068
came the word of the L by the	Hag 2:1	3068
strong, O Zerubbabel, saith the L	Hag 2:4	3068
people of the land, saith the L	Hag 2:4	3068
am with you, saith the L of hosts	Hag 2:4	3068
For thus saith the L of hosts	Hag 2:6	3068
with glory, saith the L of hosts	Hag 2:7	3068
is mine, saith the L of hosts	Hag 2:8	3068
the former, saith the L of hosts	Hag 2:9	3068
give peace, saith the L of hosts	Hag 2:9	3068
came the word of the L by Haggai	Hag 2:10	3068
Thus saith the L of hosts	Hag 2:11	3068
nation before me, saith the L	Hag 2:14	3068
a stone in the temple of the L	Hag 2:15	3068
ye turned not to me, saith the L	Hag 2:17	3068

Context	Reference	Strong's
again the word of the L came unto	Hag 2:20	3068
In that day, saith the L of hosts	Hag 2:23	3068
the son of Shealtiel, saith the L	Hag 2:23	3068
chosen thee, saith the L of hosts	Hag 2:23	3068
the word of the L unto Zechariah	Zec 1:1	3068
The L hath been sore displeased	Zec 1:2	3068
them, Thus saith the L of hosts	Zec 1:3	3068
ye unto me, saith the L of hosts	Zec 1:3	3068
unto you, saith the L of hosts	Zec 1:3	3068
saying, Thus saith the L of hosts	Zec 1:4	3068
nor hearken unto me, saith the L	Zec 1:4	3068
Like as the L of hosts thought to	Zec 1:6	3068
the word of the L unto Zechariah	Zec 1:7	3068
Then said I, O my l, what are	Zec 1:9	113
whom the L hath sent to walk to	Zec 1:10	3068
the L that stood among the myrtle	Zec 1:11	3068
Then the angel of the L answered	Zec 1:12	3068
O L of hosts, how long wilt thou	Zec 1:12	3068
the L answered the angel that	Zec 1:13	3068
saying, Thus saith the L of hosts	Zec 1:14	3068
Therefore thus saith the L	Zec 1:16	3068
built in it, saith the L of hosts	Zec 1:16	3068
saying, Thus saith the L of hosts	Zec 1:17	3068
the L shall yet comfort Zion, and	Zec 1:17	3068
the L shewed me four carpenters	Zec 1:20	3068
For I, saith the L, will be unto	Zec 2:5	3068
land of the north, saith the L	Zec 2:6	3068
winds of the heaven, saith the L	Zec 2:6	3068
For thus saith the L of hosts	Zec 2:8	3068
that the L of hosts hath sent me	Zec 2:9	3068
in the midst of thee, saith the L	Zec 2:10	3068
be joined to the L in that day	Zec 2:11	3068
thou shalt know that the L of	Zec 2:11	3068
the L shall inherit Judah his	Zec 2:12	3068
silent, O all flesh, before the L	Zec 2:13	3068
before the angel of the L	Zec 3:1	3068
the L said unto Satan	Zec 3:2	3068
The L rebuke thee, O Satan	Zec 3:2	3068
even the L that hath chosen	Zec 3:2	3068
And the angel of the L stood by	Zec 3:5	3068
the angel of the L protested unto	Zec 3:6	3068
Thus saith the L of hosts	Zec 3:7	3068
thereof, saith the L of hosts	Zec 3:9	3068
In that day, saith the L of hosts	Zec 3:10	3068
the word of the L unto Zerubbabel	Zec 4:6	3068
my spirit, saith the L of hosts	Zec 4:6	3068
the word of the L came unto me	Zec 4:8	3068
thou shalt know that the L of	Zec 4:9	3068
they are the eyes of the L	Zec 4:10	3068
that stand by the L of the whole	Zec 4:14	113
it forth, saith the L of hosts	Zec 5:4	3068
before the L of all the earth	Zec 6:5	113
And the word of the L came unto me	Zec 6:9	3068
Thus speaketh the L of hosts	Zec 6:12	3068
shall build the temple of the L	Zec 6:12	3068
shall build the temple of the L	Zec 6:13	3068
a memorial in the temple of the L	Zec 6:14	3068
and build in the temple of the L	Zec 6:15	3068
ye shall know that the L of hosts	Zec 6:15	3068
obey the voice of the L your God	Zec 6:15	3068
that the word of the L came unto	Zec 7:1	3068
their men, to pray before the L	Zec 7:2	3068
in the house of the L of hosts	Zec 7:3	3068
word of the L of hosts unto me	Zec 7:4	3068
the L hath cried by the former	Zec 7:7	3068
the word of the L came unto	Zec 7:8	3068
Thus speaketh the L of hosts	Zec 7:9	3068
the words which the L of hosts	Zec 7:12	3068
a great wrath from the L of hosts	Zec 7:12	3068
not hear, saith the L of hosts	Zec 7:13	3068
word of the L of hosts came to me	Zec 8:1	3068
Thus saith the L of hosts	Zec 8:2	3068
Thus saith the L	Zec 8:3	3068
the mountain of the L of hosts	Zec 8:3	3068
Thus saith the L of hosts	Zec 8:4	3068
Thus saith the L of hosts	Zec 8:6	3068
saith the L of hosts	Zec 8:6	3068
Thus saith the L of hosts	Zec 8:7	3068
Thus saith the L of hosts	Zec 8:9	3068
house of the L of hosts was laid	Zec 8:9	3068
former days, saith the L of hosts	Zec 8:11	3068
For thus saith the L of hosts	Zec 8:14	3068
me to wrath, saith the L of hosts	Zec 8:14	3068
things that I hate, saith the L	Zec 8:17	3068
the word of the L of hosts came	Zec 8:18	3068
Thus saith the L of hosts	Zec 8:19	3068
Thus saith the L of hosts	Zec 8:20	3068
go speedily to pray before the L	Zec 8:21	3068
and to seek the L of hosts	Zec 8:21	3068
seek the L of hosts in Jerusalem	Zec 8:22	3068
and to pray before the L	Zec 8:22	3068
Thus saith the L of hosts	Zec 8:23	3068
of the L in the land of Hadrach	Zec 9:1	3068
of Israel, shall be toward the L	Zec 9:1	3068
the L will cast her out, and he	Zec 9:4	136
the L shall be seen over them, and	Zec 9:14	3068
the L God shall blow the trumpet,	Zec 9:14	136
The L of hosts shall defend them	Zec 9:15	3068
the L their God shall save them	Zec 9:16	3068
Ask ye of the L rain in the time	Zec 10:1	3068
so the L shall make bright clouds	Zec 10:1	3068
for the L of hosts hath visited	Zec 10:3	3068
because the L is with them, and	Zec 10:5	3068
for I am the L their God, and will	Zec 10:6	3068
heart shall rejoice in the L	Zec 10:7	3068
I will strengthen them in the L	Zec 10:12	3068
and down in his name, saith the L	Zec 10:12	3068
Thus saith the L my God	Zec 11:4	3068
sell them say, Blessed be the L	Zec 11:5	3068
of the land, saith the L	Zec 11:6	3068
that it was the word of the L	Zec 11:11	3068
the L said unto me, Cast it unto	Zec 11:13	3068
the potter in the house of the L	Zec 11:13	3068
the L said unto me, Take unto	Zec 11:15	3068
of the word of the L for Israel	Zec 12:1	3068
for Israel, saith the L	Zec 12:1	3068
In that day, saith the L, I will	Zec 12:4	3068
in the L of hosts their God	Zec 12:5	3068
The L also shall save the tents	Zec 12:7	3068
In that day shall the L defend	Zec 12:8	3068
as the angel of the L before them	Zec 12:8	3068
in that day, saith the L of hosts	Zec 13:2	3068
lies in the name of the L	Zec 13:3	3068
my fellow, saith the L of hosts	Zec 13:7	3068
that in all the land, saith the L	Zec 13:8	3068
they shall say, The L is my God	Zec 13:9	3068
Behold, the day of the L cometh	Zec 14:1	3068
Then shall the L go forth	Zec 14:3	3068
the L my God shall come, and all	Zec 14:5	3068
day which shall be known to the L	Zec 14:7	3068
the L shall be king over all the	Zec 14:9	3068
in that day shall there be one L	Zec 14:9	3068
be the plague wherewith the L	Zec 14:12	3068
from the L shall be among them	Zec 14:13	3068
the L of hosts, and to keep the	Zec 14:16	3068
the L of hosts, even upon them	Zec 14:17	3068
wherewith the L will smite the	Zec 14:18	3068
the horses, HOLINESS UNTO THE L	Zec 14:20	3068
be holiness unto the L of hosts	Zec 14:21	3068
in the house of the L of hosts	Zec 14:21	3068
of the L to Israel by Malachi	Mal 1:1	3068
I have loved you, saith the L	Mal 1:2	3068
Jacob's brother? saith the L	Mal 1:2	3068
thus saith the L of hosts	Mal 1:4	3068
the L hath indignation for ever	Mal 1:4	3068
The L will be magnified from the	Mal 1:5	3068
saith the L of hosts unto you, O	Mal 1:6	3068
table of the L is contemptible	Mal 1:7	3068
saith the L of hosts	Mal 1:8	3068
saith the L of hosts	Mal 1:9	3068
in you, saith the L of hosts	Mal 1:10	3068
the heathen, saith the L of hosts	Mal 1:11	3068
The table of the L is polluted	Mal 1:12	3068
at it, saith the L of hosts	Mal 1:13	3068
your hand? saith the L	Mal 1:13	3068
unto the L a corrupt thing	Mal 1:14	136
great King, saith the L of hosts	Mal 1:14	3068
my name, saith the L of hosts	Mal 2:2	3068
with Levi, saith the L of hosts	Mal 2:4	3068
the messenger of the L of hosts	Mal 2:7	3068
of Levi, saith the L of hosts	Mal 2:8	3068
holiness of the L which he loved	Mal 2:11	3068
The L will cut off the man that	Mal 2:12	3068
an offering unto the L of hosts	Mal 2:12	3068
the altar of the L with tears	Mal 2:13	3068
Because the L hath been witness	Mal 2:14	3068
For the L, the God of Israel,	Mal 2:16	3068
his garment, saith the L of hosts	Mal 2:16	3068
wearied the L with your words	Mal 2:17	3068
is good in the sight of the L	Mal 2:17	3068
and the L, whom ye seek, shall	Mal 3:1	113
shall come, saith the L of hosts	Mal 3:1	3068
L an offering in righteousness	Mal 3:3	3068
Jerusalem be pleasant unto the L	Mal 3:4	3068
fear not me, saith the L of hosts	Mal 3:5	3068
For I am the L, I change not	Mal 3:6	3068
unto you, saith the L of hosts	Mal 3:7	3068
herewith, saith the L of hosts	Mal 3:10	3068
the field, saith the L of hosts	Mal 3:11	3068
land, saith the L of hosts	Mal 3:12	3068
stout against me, saith the L	Mal 3:13	3068
mournfully before the L of hosts	Mal 3:14	3068
Then they that feared the L spake	Mal 3:16	3068
the L hearkened, and heard it, and	Mal 3:16	3068
him for them that feared the L	Mal 3:16	3068
be mine, saith the L of hosts	Mal 3:17	3068
them up, saith the L of hosts	Mal 4:1	3068
do this, saith the L of hosts	Mal 4:3	3068
great and dreadful day of the L	Mal 4:5	3068
the angel of the L appeared unto	Mt 1:20	2962
spoken of the L by the prophet	Mt 1:22	2962
the angel of the L had bidden him	Mt 1:24	2962
the angel of the L appeareth to	Mt 2:13	2962
spoken of the L by the prophet	Mt 2:15	2962
an angel of the L appeareth in a	Mt 2:19	2962
Prepare ye the way of the L	Mt 3:3	2962
shalt not tempt the L thy God	Mt 4:7	2962
Thou shalt worship the L thy God	Mt 4:10	2962
perform unto the L thine oaths	Mt 5:33	2962
one that saith unto me, L, L	Mt 7:21	2962
say to me in that day, L, L	Mt 7:22	2962
and worshipped him, saying, L	Mt 8:2	2962
And saying, L, my servant lieth at	Mt 8:6	2962
The centurion answered and said, L	Mt 8:8	2962
of his disciples said unto him, L	Mt 8:21	2962
to him, and awoke him, saying, L	Mt 8:25	2962
They said unto him, Yea, L	Mt 9:28	2962
ye therefore the L of the harvest	Mt 9:38	2962
L of heaven and earth, because	Mt 11:25	2962
For the Son of man is L even of	Mt 12:8	2962
They say unto him, Yea, L	Mt 13:51	2962
And Peter answered him and said, L	Mt 14:28	2962
to sink, he cried, saying, L	Mt 14:30	2962
saying, Have mercy on me, O L	Mt 15:22	2962
she and worshipped him, saying, L	Mt 15:25	2962
And she said, Truth, L	Mt 15:27	2962
saying, Be it far from thee, L	Mt 16:22	2962
Peter, and said unto Jesus, L	Mt 17:4	2962
L, have mercy on my son	Mt 17:15	2962
came Peter to him, and said, L	Mt 18:21	2962
and worshipped him, saying, L	Mt 18:26	2962
saying, Have mercy on us, O L	Mt 20:30	2962
saying, Have mercy on us, O L	Mt 20:31	2962
They say unto him, L, that our	Mt 20:33	2962
say, The L hath need of them	Mt 21:3	2962
that cometh in the name of the L	Mt 21:9	2962
When the l therefore of the	Mt 21:40	2962
Thou shalt love the L thy God	Mt 22:37	2962
doth David in spirit call him L	Mt 22:43	2962
The L said unto my L, Sit thou	Mt 22:44	2962
If David then call him L	Mt 22:45	2962
that cometh in the name of the L	Mt 23:39	2962
not what hour your L doth come	Mt 24:42	2962
other virgins, saying, L, L	Mt 25:11	2962
righteous answer him, saying, L	Mt 25:37	2962
they also answer him, saying, L	Mt 25:44	2962
one of them to say unto him, L	Mt 26:22	2962
field, as the L appointed me	Mt 27:10	2962
for the angel of the L descended	Mt 28:2	2962
see the place where the L lay	Mt 28:6	2962
Prepare ye the way of the L	Mk 1:3	2962
of man is L also of the sabbath	Mk 2:28	2962
things the L hath done for thee	Mk 5:19	2962
answered and said unto him, Yes, L	Mk 7:28	2962
cried out, and said with tears, L	Mk 9:24	2962
The blind man said unto him, L	Mk 10:51	4462
say ye that the L hath need of	Mk 11:3	2962
that cometh in the name of the L	Mk 11:9	2962
that cometh in the name of the L	Mk 11:10	2962
The L our God is one L	Mk 12:29	2962
thou shalt love the L thy God	Mk 12:30	2962
The L said to my L, Sit thou	Mk 12:36	2962
therefore himself calleth him L	Mk 12:37	2962
except that the L had shortened	Mk 13:20	2962
So then after the L had spoken	Mk 16:19	2962
the L working with them, and	Mk 16:20	2962
and ordinances of the L blameless	Lk 1:6	2962
he went into the temple of the L	Lk 1:9	2962
unto him an angel of the L	Lk 1:11	2962
be great in the sight of the L	Lk 1:15	2962
shall he turn to the L their God	Lk 1:16	2962
ready a people prepared for the L	Lk 1:17	2962
Thus hath the L dealt with me in	Lk 1:25	2962
favoured, the L is with thee	Lk 1:28	2962
the L God shall give unto him the	Lk 1:32	2962
Behold the handmaid of the L	Lk 1:38	2962
mother of my L should come to me	Lk 1:43	2962
which were told her from the L	Lk 1:45	2962
said, My soul doth magnify the L	Lk 1:46	2962
her cousins heard how the L had	Lk 1:58	2962
And the hand of the L was with him	Lk 1:66	2962
Blessed be the L God of Israel	Lk 1:68	2962
face of the L to prepare his ways	Lk 1:76	2962
the angel of the L came upon them	Lk 2:9	2962
the glory of the L shone round	Lk 2:9	2962
a Saviour, which is Christ the L	Lk 2:11	2962
which the L hath made known unto	Lk 2:15	2962
to present him to the L	Lk 2:22	2962
it is written in the law of the L	Lk 2:23	2962
shall be called holy to the L	Lk 2:23	2962
which is said in the law of the L	Lk 2:24	2962
L, now lettest thou thy servant	Lk 2:29	1203
gave thanks likewise unto the L	Lk 2:38	2962
according to the law of the L	Lk 2:39	2962
Prepare ye the way of the L	Lk 3:4	2962
Thou shalt worship the L thy God	Lk 4:8	2962
shalt not tempt the L thy God	Lk 4:12	2962
The Spirit of the L is upon me	Lk 4:18	2962
the acceptable year of the L	Lk 4:19	2962
for I am a sinful man, O L	Lk 5:8	2962
face, and besought him, saying, L	Lk 5:12	2962
the power of the L was present to	Lk 5:17	2962
of man is L also of the sabbath	Lk 6:5	2962
And why call ye me, L, L	Lk 6:46	2962
to him, saying unto him, L	Lk 7:6	2962
And when the L saw her, he had	Lk 7:13	2962
the L said, Whereunto then shall	Lk 7:31	2962
and John saw this, they said, L	Lk 9:54	2962
a certain man said unto him, L	Lk 9:57	2962
But he said, L, suffer me first	Lk 9:59	2962
And another also said, L, I will	Lk 9:61	2962
After these things the L	Lk 10:1	2962
ye therefore the L of the harvest	Lk 10:2	2962
again with joy, saying, L	Lk 10:17	2962
L of heaven and earth, that thou	Lk 10:21	2962
Thou shalt love the L thy God	Lk 10:27	2962
and came to him, and said, L	Lk 10:40	2962
of his disciples said unto him, L	Lk 11:1	2962
the L said unto him, Now do ye	Lk 11:39	2962
Then Peter said unto him, L	Lk 12:41	2962
the L said, Who then is that	Lk 12:42	2962
And he answering said unto him, L	Lk 13:8	2962
The L then answered him, and said,	Lk 13:15	2962
Then said one unto him, L	Lk 13:23	2962
at the door, saying, L, L	Lk 13:25	2962
that cometh in the name of the L	Lk 13:35	2962
And the apostles said unto the L	Lk 17:5	2962
the L said, If ye had faith as a	Lk 17:6	2962
and said unto him, Where, L	Lk 17:37	2962
the L said, Hear what the unjust	Lk 18:6	2962
And he said, L, that I may receive	Lk 18:41	2962
stood, and said unto the L	Lk 19:8	2962
Behold, L, the half of my goods I	Lk 19:8	2962
Then came the first, saying, L	Lk 19:16	2962
And the second came, saying, L	Lk 19:18	2962
And another came, saying, L	Lk 19:20	2962
(And they said unto him, L	Lk 19:25	2962
Because the L hath need of him	Lk 19:31	2962
they said, The L hath need of him	Lk 19:34	2962
that cometh in the name of the L	Lk 19:38	2962
calleth the L the God of Abraham	Lk 20:37	2962
The L said unto my L, Sit thou	Lk 20:42	2962
David therefore calleth him L	Lk 20:44	2962
the L said, Simon, Simon, behold,	Lk 22:31	2962
And he said unto him, L, I am	Lk 22:33	2962
And they said, L, behold, here are	Lk 22:38	2962
follow, they said unto him, L	Lk 22:49	2962
the L turned, and looked upon	Lk 22:61	2962
remembered the word of the L	Lk 22:61	2962
And he said unto Jesus, L,	Lk 23:42	2962
found not the body of the L Jesus	Lk 24:3	2962
The L is risen indeed, and hath	Lk 24:34	2962

Make straight the way of the *L*	Jn 1:23	2962
When therefore the *L* knew how the	Jn 4:1	2962
after that the *L* had given thanks	Jn 6:23	2962
Then said they unto him, *L*	Jn 6:34	2962
Then Simon Peter answered him, *L*	Jn 6:68	2962
She said, No man, *L*	Jn 8:11	2962
He answered and said, Who is he, *L*	Jn 9:36	2962
And he said, *L*, I believe	Jn 9:38	2962
anointed the *L* with ointment	Jn 11:2	2962
sisters sent unto him, saying, *L*	Jn 11:3	2962
Then said his disciples, *L*	Jn 11:12	2962
Then said Martha unto Jesus, *L*	Jn 11:21	2962
She saith unto him, Yea, *L*	Jn 11:27	2962
at his feet, saying unto him, *L*	Jn 11:32	2962
They said unto him, *L*, come and	Jn 11:34	2962
that was dead, saith unto him, *L*	Jn 11:39	2962
that cometh in the name of the *L*	Jn 12:13	2962
be fulfilled, which he spake, *L*	Jn 12:38	2962
the arm of the *L* been revealed	Jn 12:38	2962
and Peter saith unto him, *L*	Jn 13:6	2962
Simon Peter saith unto him, *L*	Jn 13:9	2962
Ye call me Master and *L*	Jn 13:13	2962
If I then, your *L* and Master, have	Jn 13:14	2962
Jesus' breast saith unto him, *L*	Jn 13:25	2962
Simon Peter said unto him, *L*	Jn 13:36	2962
Peter said unto him, *L*, why	Jn 13:37	2962
Thomas saith unto him, *L*, we know	Jn 14:5	2962
Philip saith unto him, *L*, shew us	Jn 14:8	2962
saith unto him, not Iscariot, *L*	Jn 14:22	2962
away the *L* out of the sepulchre	Jn 20:2	2962
Because they have taken away my *L*	Jn 20:13	2962
disciples that she had seen the *L*	Jn 20:18	2962
glad, when they saw the *L*	Jn 20:20	2962
said unto him, We have seen the *L*	Jn 20:25	2962
answered and said unto him, My *L*	Jn 20:28	2962
saith unto Peter, It is the *L*	Jn 21:7	2962
Peter heard that it was the *L*	Jn 21:7	2962
knowing that it was the *L*	Jn 21:12	2962
He saith unto him, Yea, *L*	Jn 21:15	2962
He saith unto him, Yea, *L*	Jn 21:16	2962
And he said unto him, *L*, thou	Jn 21:17	2962
his breast at supper, and said, *L*	Jn 21:20	2962
seeing him saith to Jesus, *L*	Jn 21:21	2962
they asked of him, saying, *L*	Acts 1:6	2962
the time that the *L* Jesus went in	Acts 1:21	2962
And they prayed, and said, Thou, *L*	Acts 1:24	2962
and notable day of the *L* come	Acts 2:20	2962
the name of the *L* shall be saved	Acts 2:21	2962
I foresaw the *L* always before my	Acts 2:25	2962
The *L* said unto my *L*, Sit thou	Acts 2:34	2962
whom ye have crucified, both *L*	Acts 2:36	2962
many as the *L* our God shall call	Acts 2:39	2962
the *L* added to the church daily	Acts 2:47	2962
come from the presence of the *L*	Acts 3:19	2962
A prophet shall the *L* your God	Acts 3:22	2962
God with one accord, and said, *L*	Acts 4:24	1203
gathered together against the *L*	Acts 4:26	2962
And now, *L*, behold their	Acts 4:29	2962
the resurrection of the *L* Jesus	Acts 4:33	2962
to tempt the Spirit of the *L*	Acts 5:9	2962
were the more added to the *L*	Acts 5:14	2962
But the angel of the *L* by night	Acts 5:19	2962
L in a flame of fire in a bush	Acts 7:30	2962
the voice of the *L* came unto him	Acts 7:31	2962
Then said the *L* to him, Put off	Acts 7:33	2962
A prophet shall the *L* your God	Acts 7:37	2962
build me? saith the *L*	Acts 7:49	2962
L Jesus, receive my spirit	Acts 7:59	2962
and cried with a loud voice, *L*	Acts 7:60	2962
in the name of the *L* Jesus	Acts 8:16	2962
and said, Pray ye to the *L* for me	Acts 8:24	2962
and preached the word of the *L*	Acts 8:25	2962
the angel of the *L* spake unto	Acts 8:26	2962
the Spirit of the *L* caught away	Acts 8:39	2962
against the disciples of the *L*	Acts 9:1	2962
And he said, Who art thou, *L*	Acts 9:5	2962
the *L* said, I am Jesus whom thou	Acts 9:5	2962
trembling and astonished said, *L*	Acts 9:6	2962
the *L* said unto him, Arise, and go	Acts 9:6	2962
and to him said the *L* in a vision	Acts 9:10	2962
And he said, Behold, I am here, *L*	Acts 9:10	2962
the *L* said unto him, Arise, and go	Acts 9:11	2962
Then Ananias answered, *L*, I have	Acts 9:13	2962
But the *L* said unto him, Go thy	Acts 9:15	2962
on him said, Brother Saul, the *L*	Acts 9:17	2962
how he had seen the *L* in the way	Acts 9:27	2962
boldly in the name of the *L* Jesus	Acts 9:29	2962
and walking in the fear of the *L*	Acts 9:31	2962
Saron saw him, and turned to the *L*	Acts 9:35	2962
and many believed in the *L*	Acts 9:42	2962
afraid, and said, What is it, *L*	Acts 10:4	2962
But Peter said, Not so, *L*	Acts 10:14	2962
(he is *L* of all	Acts 10:36	2962
be baptized in the name of the *L*	Acts 10:48	2962
But I said, Not so, *L*	Acts 11:8	2962
remembered I the word of the *L*	Acts 11:16	2962
believed on the *L* Jesus Christ	Acts 11:17	2962
Grecians, preaching the *L* Jesus	Acts 11:20	2962
the hand of the *L* was with them	Acts 11:21	2962
believed, and turned unto the *L*	Acts 11:21	2962
they would cleave unto the *L*	Acts 11:23	2962
much people was added unto the *L*	Acts 11:24	2962
the angel of the *L* came upon him	Acts 12:7	2962
that the *L* hath sent his angel,	Acts 12:11	2962
the *L* had brought him out of the	Acts 12:17	2962
the angel of the *L* smote him	Acts 12:23	2962
As they ministered to the *L*	Acts 13:2	2962
pervert the right ways of the *L*	Acts 13:10	2962
the hand of the *L* is upon thee	Acts 13:11	2962
at the doctrine of the *L*	Acts 13:12	2962
For so hath the *L* commanded us	Acts 13:47	2962
and glorified the word of the *L*	Acts 13:48	2962
the word of the *L* was published	Acts 13:49	2962
they speaking boldly in the *L*	Acts 14:3	2962
they commended them to the *L*	Acts 14:23	2962
that through the grace of the *L*	Acts 15:11	2962
of men might seek after the *L*	Acts 15:17	2962
my name is called, saith the *L*	Acts 15:17	2962
the name of our *L* Jesus Christ	Acts 15:26	2962
and preaching the word of the *L*	Acts 15:35	2962
have preached the word of the *L*	Acts 15:36	2962
assuredly gathering that the *L*	Acts 16:10	2962
whose heart the *L* opened, that	Acts 16:14	2962
judged me to be faithful to the *L*	Acts 16:15	2962
Believe on the *L* Jesus Christ	Acts 16:31	2962
spake unto him the word of the *L*	Acts 16:32	2962
seeing that he is *L* of heaven	Acts 17:24	2962
That they should seek the *L*	Acts 17:27	2962
believed on the *L* with all his	Acts 18:8	2962
Then spake the *L* to Paul in the	Acts 18:9	2962
instructed in the way of the *L*	Acts 18:25	2962
diligently the things of the *L*	Acts 18:25	2962
in the name of the *L* Jesus	Acts 19:5	2962
heard the word of the *L* Jesus	Acts 19:10	2962
spirits the name of the *L* Jesus	Acts 19:13	2962
the name of the *L* Jesus was	Acts 19:17	2962
Serving the *L* with all humility	Acts 20:19	2962
faith toward our *L* Jesus Christ	Acts 20:21	2962
I have received of the *L* Jesus	Acts 20:24	2962
remember the words of the *L* Jesus	Acts 20:35	2962
for the name of the *L* Jesus	Acts 21:13	2962
saying, The will of the *L* be done	Acts 21:14	2962
heard it, they glorified the *L*	Acts 21:20	2962
And I answered, Who art thou, *L*	Acts 22:8	2962
And I said, What shall I do, *L*	Acts 22:10	2962
the *L* said unto me, Arise, and go	Acts 22:10	2962
calling on the name of the *L*	Acts 22:16	2962
And I said, *L*, they know that I	Acts 22:19	2962
following the *L* stood by him	Acts 23:11	2962
And I said, Who art thou, *L*	Acts 26:15	2962
which concern the *L* Jesus Christ	Acts 28:31	2962
his Son Jesus Christ our *L*	Rom 1:3	2962
our Father, and the *L* Jesus Christ	Rom 1:7	2962
to whom the *L* will not impute sin	Rom 4:8	2962
up Jesus our *L* from the dead	Rom 4:24	2962
God through our *L* Jesus Christ	Rom 5:1	2962
in God through our *L* Jesus Christ	Rom 5:11	2962
life by Jesus Christ our *L*	Rom 5:21	2962
God through Jesus Christ our *L*	Rom 6:11	2962
life through Jesus Christ our *L*	Rom 6:23	2962
God through Jesus Christ our *L*	Rom 7:25	2962
which is in Christ Jesus our *L*	Rom 8:39	2962
will the *L* make upon the earth	Rom 9:28	2962
Except the *L* of Sabaoth had left	Rom 9:29	2962
with thy mouth the *L* Jesus	Rom 10:9	2962
for the same *L* over all is rich	Rom 10:12	2962
the name of the *L* shall be saved	Rom 10:13	2962
For Esaias saith, *L*, who hath	Rom 10:16	2962
L, they have killed thy prophets,	Rom 11:3	2962
who hath known the mind of the *L*	Rom 11:34	2962
fervent in spirit; serving the *L*	Rom 12:11	2962
I will repay, saith the *L*	Rom 12:19	2962
But put ye on the *L* Jesus Christ	Rom 13:14	2962
the day, regardeth it unto the *L*	Rom 14:6	2962
to the *L* he doth not regard it	Rom 14:6	2962
He that eateth, eateth to the *L*	Rom 14:6	2962
to the *L* he eateth not, and giveth	Rom 14:6	2962
we live, we live unto the *L*	Rom 14:8	2962
whether we die, we die unto the *L*	Rom 14:8	2962
he might be *L* both of the dead	Rom 14:9	2961
written, As I live, saith the *L*	Rom 14:11	2962
and am persuaded by the *L* Jesus	Rom 14:14	2962
the Father of our *L* Jesus Christ	Rom 15:6	2962
And again, Praise the *L*, all ye	Rom 15:11	2962
for the *L* Jesus Christ's sake, and	Rom 15:30	2962
That ye receive her in the *L*	Rom 16:2	2962
Greet Amplias my beloved in the *L*	Rom 16:8	2962
of Narcissus, which are in the *L*	Rom 16:11	2962
and Tryphosa, who labour in the *L*	Rom 16:12	2962
which laboured much in the *L*	Rom 16:12	2962
Salute Rufus chosen in the *L*	Rom 16:13	2962
such serve not our *L* Jesus Christ	Rom 16:18	2962
The grace of our *L* Jesus Christ	Rom 16:20	2962
this epistle, salute you in the *L*	Rom 16:22	2962
The grace of our *L* Jesus Christ	Rom 16:24	2962
the name of Jesus Christ our *L*	1Cor 1:2	2962
and from the *L* Jesus Christ	1Cor 1:3	2962
the coming of our *L* Jesus Christ	1Cor 1:7	2962
in the day of our *L* Jesus Christ	1Cor 1:8	2962
of his Son Jesus Christ our *L*	1Cor 1:9	2962
by the name of our *L* Jesus Christ	1Cor 1:10	2962
glorieth, let him glory in the *L*	1Cor 1:31	2962
not have crucified the *L* of glory	1Cor 2:8	2962
who hath known the mind of the *L*	1Cor 2:16	2962
even as the *L* gave to every man	1Cor 3:5	2962
The *L* knoweth the thoughts of the	1Cor 3:20	2962
but he that judgeth me is the *L*	1Cor 4:4	2962
before the time, until the *L* come	1Cor 4:5	2962
beloved son, and faithful in the *L*	1Cor 4:17	2962
to you shortly, if the *L* will	1Cor 4:19	2962
In the name of our *L* Jesus Christ	1Cor 5:4	2962
the power of our *L* Jesus Christ	1Cor 5:4	2962
saved in the day of the *L* Jesus	1Cor 5:5	2962
in the name of the *L* Jesus	1Cor 6:11	2962
for fornication, but for the *L*	1Cor 6:13	2962
and the *L* for the body	1Cor 6:13	2962
And God hath both raised up the *L*	1Cor 6:14	2962
joined unto the *L* is one spirit	1Cor 6:17	2962
I command, yet not I, but the *L*	1Cor 7:10	2962
to the rest speak I, not the *L*	1Cor 7:12	2962
as the *L* hath called every one,	1Cor 7:17	2962
For he that is called in the *L*	1Cor 7:22	2962
I have no commandment of the *L*	1Cor 7:25	2962
mercy of the *L* to be faithful	1Cor 7:25	2962
the things that belong to the *L*	1Cor 7:32	2962
how he may please the *L*	1Cor 7:32	2962
careth for the things of the *L*	1Cor 7:34	2962
upon the *L* without distraction	1Cor 7:35	2962
whom she will; only in the *L*	1Cor 7:39	2962
one *L* Jesus Christ, by whom are	1Cor 8:6	2962
I not seen Jesus Christ our *L*	1Cor 9:1	2962
are not ye my work in the *L*	1Cor 9:1	2962
mine apostleship are ye in the *L*	1Cor 9:2	2962
and as the brethren of the *L*	1Cor 9:5	2962
Even so hath the *L* ordained that	1Cor 9:14	2962
Ye cannot drink the cup of the *L*	1Cor 10:21	2962
Do we provoke the *L* to jealousy	1Cor 10:22	2962
woman without the man, in the *L*	1Cor 11:11	2962
For I have received of the *L* that	1Cor 11:23	2962
That the *L* Jesus the same night	1Cor 11:23	2962
bread, and drink this cup of the *L*	1Cor 11:27	2962
of the body and blood of the *L*	1Cor 11:27	2962
judged, we are chastened of the *L*	1Cor 11:32	2962
man can say that Jesus is the *L*	1Cor 12:3	2962
administrations, but the same *L*	1Cor 12:5	2962
they not hear me, saith the *L*	1Cor 14:21	2962
you are the commandments of the *L*	1Cor 14:37	2962
I have in Christ Jesus our *L*	1Cor 15:31	2962
second man is the *L* from heaven	1Cor 15:47	2962
through our *L* Jesus Christ	1Cor 15:57	2962
abounding in the work of the *L*	1Cor 15:58	2962
labour is not in vain in the *L*	1Cor 15:58	2962
a while with you, if the *L* permit	1Cor 16:7	2962
for he worketh the work of the *L*	1Cor 16:10	2962
salute you much in the *L*, with	1Cor 16:19	2962
man love not the *L* Jesus Christ	1Cor 16:22	2962
The grace of our *L* Jesus Christ	1Cor 16:23	2962
and from the *L* Jesus Christ	2Cor 1:2	2962
the Father of our *L* Jesus Christ	2Cor 1:3	2962
ours in the day of the *L* Jesus	2Cor 1:14	2962
door was opened unto me of the *L*	2Cor 2:12	2962
when it shall turn to the *L*	2Cor 3:16	2962
Now the *L* is that Spirit	2Cor 3:17	2962
and where the Spirit of the *L* is	2Cor 3:17	2962
as in a glass the glory of the *L*	2Cor 3:18	2962
even as by the Spirit of the *L*	2Cor 3:18	2962
ourselves, but Christ Jesus the *L*	2Cor 4:5	2962
the body the dying of the *L* Jesus	2Cor 4:10	2962
that he which raised up the *L*	2Cor 4:14	2962
body, we are absent from the *L*	2Cor 5:6	2962
body, and to be present with the *L*	2Cor 5:8	2962
therefore the terror of the *L*	2Cor 5:11	2962
and be ye separate, saith the *L*	2Cor 6:17	2962
daughters, saith the *L* Almighty	2Cor 6:18	2962
gave their own selves to the *L*	2Cor 8:5	2962
the grace of our *L* Jesus Christ	2Cor 8:9	2962
by us to the glory of the same *L*	2Cor 8:19	2962
not only in the sight of the *L*	2Cor 8:21	2962
which the *L* hath given us for	2Cor 10:8	2962
glorieth, let him glory in the *L*	2Cor 10:17	2962
but whom the *L* commendeth	2Cor 10:18	2962
speak, I speak it not after the *L*	2Cor 11:17	2962
and Father of our *L* Jesus Christ	2Cor 11:31	2962
visions and revelations of the *L*	2Cor 12:1	2962
thing I besought the *L* thrice	2Cor 12:8	2962
to the power which the *L* hath	2Cor 13:10	2962
The grace of the *L* Jesus Christ	2Cor 13:14	2962
and from our *L* Jesus Christ,	Gal 1:3	2962
confidence in you through the *L*	Gal 5:10	2962
the cross of our *L* Jesus Christ	Gal 6:14	2962
my body the marks of the *L* Jesus	Gal 6:17	2962
the grace of our *L* Jesus Christ	Gal 6:18	2962
and from the *L* Jesus Christ	Eph 1:2	2962
and Father of our *L* Jesus Christ	Eph 1:3	2962
of your faith in the *L* Jesus	Eph 1:15	2962
the God of our *L* Jesus Christ	Eph 1:17	2962
unto an holy temple in the *L*	Eph 2:21	2962
he purposed in Christ Jesus our *L*	Eph 3:11	2962
the Father of our *L* Jesus Christ	Eph 3:14	2962
therefore, the prisoner of the *L*	Eph 4:1	2962
One *L*, one faith, one baptism,	Eph 4:5	2962
therefore, and testify in the *L*	Eph 4:17	2962
but now are ye light in the *L*	Eph 5:8	2962
what is acceptable unto the *L*	Eph 5:10	2962
what the will of the *L* is	Eph 5:17	2962
melody in your heart to the *L*	Eph 5:19	2962
in the name of our *L* Jesus Christ	Eph 5:20	2962
your own husbands, as unto the *L*	Eph 5:22	2962
it, even as the *L* the church	Eph 5:29	2962
obey your parents in the *L*	Eph 6:1	2962
nurture and admonition of the *L*	Eph 6:4	2962
will doing service, as to the *L*	Eph 6:7	2962
same shall he receive of the *L*	Eph 6:8	2962
my brethren, be strong in the *L*	Eph 6:10	2962
and faithful minister in the *L*	Eph 6:21	2962
the Father and the *L* Jesus Christ	Eph 6:23	2962
our *L* Jesus Christ in sincerity	Eph 6:24	2962
and from the *L* Jesus Christ	Phil 1:2	2962
And many of the brethren in the *L*	Phil 1:14	2962
confess that Jesus Christ is *L*	Phil 2:11	2962
But I trust in the *L* Jesus to	Phil 2:19	2962
But I trust in the *L* that I also	Phil 2:24	2962
in the *L* with all gladness	Phil 2:29	2962
my brethren, rejoice in the *L*	Phil 3:1	2962
knowledge of Christ Jesus my *L*	Phil 3:8	2962
the Saviour, the *L* Jesus Christ	Phil 3:20	2962
and crown, so stand fast in the *L*	Phil 4:1	2962
they be of the same mind in the *L*	Phil 4:2	2962
Rejoice in the *L* alway	Phil 4:4	2962
The *L* is at hand	Phil 4:5	2962
But I rejoiced in the *L* greatly	Phil 4:10	2962
The grace of our *L* Jesus Christ	Phil 4:23	2962
our Father and the *L* Jesus Christ	Col 1:2	2962
the Father of our *L* Jesus Christ	Col 1:3	2962
worthy of the *L* unto all pleasing	Col 1:10	2962
received Christ Jesus the *L*	Col 2:6	2962
grace in your hearts to the *L*	Col 3:16	2962
do all in the name of the *L* Jesus	Col 3:17	2962
husbands, as it is fit in the *L*	Col 3:18	2962
this is well pleasing unto the *L*	Col 3:20	2962
do, do it heartily, as to the *L*	Col 3:23	2962
Knowing that of the *L* ye shall	Col 3:24	2962

for ye serve the *L* Christ Col 3:24 2962
and fellowservant in the *L* Col 4:7 2962
which thou hast received in the *L* Col 4:17 2962
Father and in the *L* Jesus Christ 1Th 1:1 2962
our Father, and the *L* Jesus Christ 1Th 1:1 2962
of hope in our *L* Jesus Christ 1Th 1:3 2962
followers of us, and of the *L* 1Th 1:6 2962
of the *L* not only in Macedonia 1Th 1:8 2962
Who both killed the *L* Jesus 1Th 2:15 2962
our *L* Jesus Christ at his coming 1Th 2:19 2962
live, if ye stand fast in the *L* 1Th 3:8 2962
our *L* Jesus Christ, direct our 1Th 3:11 2962
the *L* make you to increase and 1Th 3:12 2962
at the coming of our *L* Jesus 1Th 3:13 2962
and exhort you by the *L* Jesus 1Th 4:1 2962
we gave you by the *L* Jesus 1Th 4:2 2962
because that the *L* is the avenger 1Th 4:6 2962
say unto you by the word of the *L* 1Th 4:15 2962
L shall not prevent them which 1Th 4:15 2962
For the *L* himself shall descend 1Th 4:16 2962
clouds, to meet the *L* in the air 1Th 4:17 2962
and so shall we ever be with the *L* 1Th 4:17 2962
the *L* so cometh as a thief in the 1Th 5:2 2962
salvation by our *L* Jesus Christ 1Th 5:9 2962
you, and are over you in the *L* 1Th 5:12 2962
the coming of our *L* Jesus Christ 1Th 5:23 2962
I charge you by the *L* that this 1Th 5:27 2962
The grace of our *L* Jesus Christ 1Th 5:28 2962
our Father and the *L* Jesus Christ 2Th 1:1 2962
our Father and the *L* Jesus Christ 2Th 1:2 2962
when the *L* Jesus shall be 2Th 1:7 2962
the gospel of our *L* Jesus Christ 2Th 1:8 2962
from the presence of the *L* 2Th 1:9 2962
That the name of our *L* Jesus 2Th 1:12 2962
of our God and the *L* Jesus Christ 2Th 1:12 2962
the coming of our *L* Jesus Christ 2Th 2:1 2962
whom the *L* shall consume with the 2Th 2:8 2962
you, brethren beloved of the *L* 2Th 2:13 2962
the glory of our *L* Jesus Christ 2Th 2:14 2962
Now our *L* Jesus Christ himself, 2Th 2:16 2962
of the *L* may have free course 2Th 3:1 2962
But the *L* is faithful, who shall 2Th 3:3 2962
confidence in the *L* touching you 2Th 3:4 2962
the *L* direct your hearts into the 2Th 3:5 2962
in the name of our *L* Jesus Christ 2Th 3:6 2962
and exhort by our *L* Jesus Christ 2Th 3:12 2962
Now the *L* of peace himself give 2Th 3:16 2962
The *L* be with you all 2Th 3:16 2962
The grace of our *L* Jesus Christ 2Th 3:18 2962
L Jesus Christ, which is our hope 1Ti 1:1 2962
our Father and Jesus Christ our *L* 1Ti 1:2 2962
And I thank Christ Jesus our *L* 1Ti 1:12 2962
the grace of our *L* was exceeding 1Ti 1:14 2962
the *L* Jesus Christ, and the elect 1Ti 5:21 2962
the words of our *L* Jesus Christ 1Ti 6:3 2962
appearing of our *L* Jesus Christ 1Ti 6:14 2962
the King of kings, and *L* of lords 1Ti 6:15 2962
the Father and Christ Jesus our *L* 2Ti 1:2 2962
ashamed of the testimony of our *L* 2Ti 1:8 2962
The *L* give mercy unto the house 2Ti 1:16 2962
The *L* grant unto him that he may 2Ti 1:18 2962
find mercy of the *L* in that day 2Ti 1:18 2962
the *L* give thee understanding in 2Ti 2:7 2962
charging them before the *L* that 2Ti 2:14 2962
The *L* knoweth them that are his 2Ti 2:19 2962
call on the *L* out of a pure heart 2Ti 2:22 2962
servant of the *L* must not strive 2Ti 2:24 2962
of them all the *L* delivered me 2Ti 3:11 2962
the *L* Jesus Christ, who shall 2Ti 4:1 2962
of righteousness, which the *L* 2Ti 4:8 2962
the *L* reward him according to his 2Ti 4:14 2962
the *L* stood with me, and 2Ti 4:17 2962
the *L* shall deliver me from every 2Ti 4:18 2962
The *L* Jesus Christ be with thy 2Ti 4:22 2962
the *L* Jesus Christ our Saviour Titus 1:4 2962
our Father and the *L* Jesus Christ Philem 3 2962
thou hast toward the *L* Jesus Philem 5 2962
both in the flesh, and in the *L* Philem 16 2962
let me have joy of thee in the *L* Philem 20 2962
refresh my bowels in the *L* Philem 20 2962
The grace of our *L* Jesus Christ Philem 25 2962
And, Thou, *L*, in the beginning Heb 1:10 2962
first began to be spoken by the *L* Heb 2:3 2962
that our *L* sprang out of Juda Heb 7:14 2962
The *L* sware and will not repent, Heb 7:21 2962
tabernacle, which the *L* pitched Heb 8:2 2962
the days come, saith the *L* Heb 8:8 2962
I regarded them not, saith the *L* Heb 8:9 2962
after those days, saith the *L* Heb 8:10 2962
his brother, saying, Know the *L* Heb 8:11 2962
after those days, saith the *L* Heb 10:16 2962
I will recompense, saith the *L* Heb 10:30 2962
The *L* shall judge his people Heb 10:30 2962
not thou the chastening of the *L* Heb 12:5 2962
For whom the *L* loveth he Heb 12:6 2962
which no man shall see the *L* Heb 12:14 2962
The *L* is my helper, and I will not Heb 13:6 2962
again from the dead our *L* Jesus Heb 13:20 2962
of the *L* Jesus Christ, to the Jas 1:1 2962
shall receive any thing of the *L* Jas 1:7 2962
which the *L* hath promised to them Jas 1:12 2962
the faith of our *L* Jesus Christ Jas 2:1 2962
the *L* of glory, with respect of Jas 2:1
yourselves in the sight of the *L* Jas 4:10 2962
ye ought to say, If the *L* will Jas 4:15 2962
into the ears of the *L* of Sabaoth Jas 5:4 2962
unto the coming of the *L* Jas 5:7 2962
the coming of the *L* draweth nigh Jas 5:8 2962
have spoken in the name of the *L* Jas 5:10 2962
and have seen the end of the *L* Jas 5:11 2962
that the *L* is very pitiful, and of Jas 5:11 2962
him with oil in the name of the *L* Jas 5:14 2962
sick, and the *L* shall raise him up Jas 5:15 2962
and Father of our *L* Jesus Christ 1Pet 1:3 2962

word of the *L* endureth for ever 1Pet 1:25 2962
tasted that the *L* is gracious 1Pet 2:3 2962
For the eyes of the *L* are over 1Pet 3:12 2962
but the face of the *L* is against 1Pet 3:12 2962
But sanctify the *L* God in your 1Pet 3:15 2962
of God, and of Jesus our *L* 2Pet 1:2 2962
knowledge of our *L* Jesus Christ 2Pet 1:8 2962
the everlasting kingdom of our *L* 2Pet 1:11 2962
even as our *L* Jesus Christ hath 2Pet 1:14 2962
and coming of our *L* Jesus Christ 2Pet 1:16 2962
denying the *L* that bought them 2Pet 2:1 1203
The *L* knoweth how to deliver the 2Pet 2:9 2962
against them before the *L* 2Pet 2:11 2962
through the knowledge of the *L* 2Pet 2:20 2962
of us the apostles of the *L* 2Pet 3:2 2962
is with the *L* as a thousand years 2Pet 3:8 2962
The *L* is not slack concerning his 2Pet 3:9 2962
But the day of the *L* will come as 2Pet 3:10 2962
of our *L* is salvation 2Pet 3:15 2962
and in the knowledge of our *L* 2Pet 3:18 2962
from the *L* Jesus Christ, the Son 2Jn 3 2962
and denying the only *L* God Jude 4 2962
and our *L* Jesus Christ Jude 4 2962
ye once knew this, how that the *L* Jude 5 2962
but said, The *L* rebuke thee Jude 9 2962
the *L* cometh with ten thousands Jude 14 2962
apostles of our *L* Jesus Christ Jude 17 2962
looking for the mercy of our *L* Jude 21 2962
and the ending, saith the *L* Rev 1:8 2962
L God Almighty, which was, and is, Rev 4:8 2962
Thou art worthy, O *L*, to receive Rev 4:11 2962
loud voice, saying, How long, O *L* Rev 6:10 1203
where also our *L* was crucified Rev 11:8 2962
are become the kingdoms of our *L* Rev 11:15 2962
O *L* God Almighty, which art, and Rev 11:17 2962
die in the *L* from henceforth Rev 14:13 2962
are thy works, *L* God Almighty Rev 15:3 2962
Who shall not fear thee, O *L* Rev 15:4 2962
say, Thou art righteous, O *L* Rev 16:5 2962
L God Almighty, true and righteous Rev 16:7 2962
for he is *L* of lords, and King of Rev 17:14 2962
for strong is the *L* God who Rev 18:8 2962
and power, unto the *L* our God Rev 19:1 2962
for the *L* God omnipotent reigneth Rev 19:6 2962
KING OF KINGS, AND *L* OF LORDS. Rev 19:16 2962
for the *L* God Almighty and the Rev 21:22 2962
for the *L* God giveth them light Rev 22:5 2962
the *L* God of the holy prophets Rev 22:6 2962
Even so, come, *L* Jesus Rev 22:20 2962
The grace of our *L* Jesus Christ Rev 22:21 2962

2. A human title of honor.

In the same day the *L* made a Gen 15:18 3068
pleasure, my *l* being old also Gen 18:12 113
said unto them, Oh, not so, my *L* Gen 19:18 113
Hear us, my *l* Gen 23:6 113
Nay, my *l*, hear me Gen 23:11 113
My *l*, hearken unto me Gen 23:15 113
And she said, Drink, my *l* Gen 24:18 113
be *l* over thy brethren, and let Gen 27:29 1376
Behold, I have made him thy *l* Gen 27:37 1376
Let it not displease my *l* that I Gen 31:35 113
shall ye speak unto my *l* Esau Gen 32:4 113
and I have sent to tell my *l* Gen 32:5 113
is a present sent unto my *l* Esau Gen 32:18 113
find grace in the sight of my *l* Gen 33:8 113
My *l* knoweth that the children Gen 33:13 113
Let my *l*, I pray thee, pass over Gen 33:14 113
until I come unto my *l* unto Seir Gen 33:14 113
find grace in the sight of my *l* Gen 33:15 113
by her, until his *l* came home Gen 39:16 113
their *l* the king of Egypt Gen 40:1 113
And they said unto him, Nay, my *l* Gen 42:10 113
who is the *l* of the land, spake Gen 42:30 113
the *l* of the country, said unto Gen 42:33 113
this it in which my *l* drinketh Gen 44:5 113
Wherefore saith my *l* these words Gen 44:7 113
said, What shall we say unto my *l* Gen 44:16 113
near unto him, and said, Oh my *l* Gen 44:18 113
My *l* asked his servants, saying, Gen 44:19 113
And we said unto my *l*, We have a Gen 44:20 113
And we said unto my *l*, The lad Gen 44:22 113
we told him the words of my *l* Gen 44:24 113
of the lad a bondman to my *l* Gen 44:33 113
l of all his house, and a ruler Gen 45:8 113
God hath made me *l* of all Egypt Gen 45:9 113
We will not hide it from my *l* Gen 47:18 113
my *l* also hath our herds of Gen 47:18 113
ought left in the sight of my *l* Gen 47:18 113
find grace in the sight of my *l* Gen 47:25 113
Let not the anger of my *l* wax hot Ex 32:22 113
and said, My *l* Moses, forbid them Num 11:28 113
Aaron said unto Moses, Alas, my *l* Num 12:11 113
will do as my *l* commandeth Num 32:25 113
their *l* was fallen down dead on Judg 3:25 113
and said unto him, Turn in, my *l* Judg 4:18 3068
And Gideon said unto him, Oh my *L* Judg 6:13 113
me find favour in thy sight, my *l* Ruth 2:13 3068
my lord, as thy soul liveth, my *l* 1Sa 1:26 113
Let our *l* now command thy 1Sa 16:16 113
And he answered, Here I am, my *l* 1Sa 22:12 113
after Saul, saying, My *l* the king 1Sa 24:8 113
put forth mine hand against my *l* 1Sa 24:10 113
his feet, and said, Upon me, my *l* 1Sa 25:24 113
Let not my *l*, I pray thee, regard 1Sa 25:25 113
saw not the young men of my *l* 1Sa 25:25 113
and they that seek evil to my *l* 1Sa 25:26 113
handmaid hath brought unto my *l* 1Sa 25:27 113
the young men that follow my *l* 1Sa 25:27 113
certainly make my *l* a sure house 1Sa 25:28 113
because my *l* fighteth the battles 1Sa 25:28 113
but the soul of my *l* shall be 1Sa 25:29 113
l according to all the good that 1Sa 25:30 113
nor offence of heart unto my *l* 1Sa 25:31 136
or that my *l* hath avenged himself 1Sa 25:31 136

shall have dealt well with my *l* 1Sa 25:31 113
the feet of the servants of my *l* 1Sa 25:41 113
hast thou not kept thy *l* the king 1Sa 26:15 113
in to destroy the king thy *l* 1Sa 26:15 3068
David said, It is my voice, my *l* 1Sa 26:17 113
Wherefore doth my *l* thus pursue 1Sa 26:18 113
let my *l* the king hear the words 1Sa 26:19 113
the enemies of my *l* the king 1Sa 29:8 113
brought them hither unto my *l* 2Sa 1:10 113
shewed this kindness unto your *l* 2Sa 2:5 113
all Israel unto my *l* the king 2Sa 3:21 113
According to all that my *l* the 2Sa 9:11 113
of Ammon said unto Hanun their *l* 2Sa 10:3 113
with all the servants of his *l* 2Sa 11:9 113
my *l* Joab, and the servants of my 2Sa 11:11 113
Joab, and the servants of my *l* 2Sa 11:11 113
bed with the servants of his *l* 2Sa 11:13 113
Let not my *l* suppose that they 2Sa 13:32 113
Now therefore let not my *l* the 2Sa 13:33 113
Tekoah said unto the king, My *l* 2Sa 14:9 113
speak one word unto my *l* the king 2Sa 14:12 113
of this thing unto my *l* the king 2Sa 14:15 113
The word of my *l* the king shall 2Sa 14:17 113
so is my *l* the king to discern 2Sa 14:17 113
Let my *l* the king now speak 2Sa 14:18 113
my *l* the king, none can turn to 2Sa 14:19 113
that my *l* the king hath spoken 2Sa 14:19 113
my *l* is wise, according to the 2Sa 14:20 113
found grace in thy sight, my *l* 2Sa 14:22 113
my *l* the king shall appoint 2Sa 15:15 113
as my *l* the king liveth, surely 2Sa 15:21 113
what place my *l* the king shall be 2Sa 15:21 113
may find grace in thy sight, my *l* 2Sa 16:4 113
this dead dog curse my *l* the king 2Sa 16:9 113
their hand against my *l* the king 2Sa 18:28 113
said, Tidings, my *l* the king 2Sa 18:31 113
The enemies of my *l* the king 2Sa 18:32 113
Let not my *l* impute iniquity unto 2Sa 19:19 113
l the king went out of Jerusalem 2Sa 19:19 113
to go down to meet my *l* the king 2Sa 19:20 113
And he answered, My *l*, O king, my 2Sa 19:26 113
thy servant unto my *l* the king 2Sa 19:27 113
but my *l* the king is as an angel 2Sa 19:27 113
but dead men before my *l* the king 2Sa 19:28 113
forasmuch as my *l* the king is 2Sa 19:30 113
yet a burden unto my *l* the king 2Sa 19:35 113
him go over with my *l* the king 2Sa 19:37 3068
eyes of my *l* the king may see it 2Sa 24:3 113
but why doth my *l* the king 2Sa 24:3 113
Wherefore is my *l* the king come 2Sa 24:21 113
Let my *l* the king take and offer 2Sa 24:22 113
for my *l* the king a young virgin 1Kin 1:2 113
that my *l* the king may get heat 1Kin 1:2 113
David our *l* knoweth it not 1Kin 1:11 113
unto him, Didst not thou, my *l* 1Kin 1:13 113
And she said unto him, My *l* 1Kin 1:17 113
my *l* the king, thou knowest it 1Kin 1:18 113
And thou, my *l*, O king, the eyes 1Kin 1:20 113
throne of my *l* the king after him 1Kin 1:20 113
when my *l* the king shall sleep 1Kin 1:21 113
And Nathan said, My *l*, O king, 1Kin 1:24 113
this thing done by my *l* the king 1Kin 1:27 113
throne of my *l* the king after him 1Kin 1:27 113
Let my *l* king David live for ever 1Kin 1:31 113
with you the servants of your *l* 1Kin 1:33 113
the throne of my *l* king David 1Kin 1:37 113
Verily our *l* king David hath made 1Kin 1:43 113
came to bless our *l* king David 1Kin 1:47 113
as my *l* the king hath said, so 1Kin 2:38 113
And the one woman said, O my *l* 1Kin 3:17 113
upon her son, and she said, O my *l* 1Kin 3:26 113
which fled from his *l* Hadadezer 1Kin 11:23 113
people turn again unto their *l* 1Kin 12:27 3068
said, Art thou that my *l* Elijah 1Kin 18:7 113
go, tell thy *l*, Behold, Elijah is 1Kin 18:8 113
whither my *l* hath not sent to 1Kin 18:10 113
now thou sayest, Go, tell thy *l* 1Kin 18:11 3068
Was it not told my *l* what I did 1Kin 18:13 113
now thou sayest, Go, tell thy *l* 1Kin 18:14 113
of Israel answered and said, My *l* 1Kin 20:4 113
Tell my *l* the king, All that thou 1Kin 20:9 113
city is pleasant, as my *l* seeth 2Kin 2:19 113
And she said, Nay, my *l*, thou man 2Kin 4:16 113
said, Did I desire a son of my *l* 2Kin 4:28 113
Would God my *l* were with the 2Kin 5:3 113
And one went in, and told his *l* 2Kin 5:4 113
of his servants said, None, my *l* 2Kin 6:12 113
unto him, saying, Help, my *l* 2Kin 6:26 113
Then a *l* on whose hand the king 2Kin 7:2 7991
the king appointed the *l* on whose 2Kin 7:17 7991
that *l* answered the man of God, 2Kin 7:19 7991
And Gehazi said, My *l*, O king, 2Kin 8:5 113
And Hazael said, Why weepeth my *l* 2Kin 8:12 113
forth to the servants of his *l* 2Kin 9:11 113
give pledges to my *l* the king of 2Kin 18:23 113
my *l* the king, are they not all 1Chr 21:3 113
why then doth my *l* require this 1Chr 21:3 113
let my *l* the king do that which 1Chr 21:23 113
men of my *l* David thy father 2Chr 2:14 113
which my *l* hath spoken of, let 2Chr 2:15 113
and hath rebelled against his *l* 2Chr 13:6 113
according to the counsel of my *l* Ezr 10:3 136
necks to the work of their *L* Neh 3:5 113
who is *l* over us Ps 12:4 113
He made him *l* of his house, and Ps 105:21 3050
over into the hand of a cruel *l* Is 19:4 113
My *l*, I stand continually upon Is 21:8 136
not lament for him, saying, Ah *l* Jer 22:18 113
will lament thee, saying, Ah *l* Jer 34:5 113
now, I pray thee, O my *l* the king Jer 37:20 113
My *l* the king, these men have Jer 38:9 113
unto Daniel, I fear my *l* the king Dan 1:10 113
therefore there is no king, *l* Dan 2:10 7229
answered and said, My *l*, the dream Dan 4:19 4756

which is come upon my *l* the king Dan 4:24 4756
him that stood before me, O my *l* Dan 10:16 113
this my *l* talk with this my lord Dan 10:17 113
and said, Let my *l* speak Dan 10:19 113
me, saying, What are these, my *l* Zec 4:4 113
And I said, No, my *l* Zec 4:5 113
And I said, No, my *l* Zec 4:13 113
with me, What are these, my *l* Zec 6:4 113
nor the servant above his *l* Mt 10:24 *2962*
master, and the servant as his *l* Mt 10:25 *2962*
his *l* commanded him to be sold, Mt 18:25 *2962*
Then the *l* of that servant was Mt 18:27 *2962*
told unto their *l* all that was Mt 18:31 *2962*
Then his *l*, after that he had Mt 18:32 *2962*
his *l* was wroth, and delivered him Mt 18:34 *2962*
the *l* of the vineyard saith unto Mt 20:8 *2962*
whom his *l* hath made ruler over Mt 24:45 *2962*
whom his *l* when he cometh shall Mt 24:46 *2962*
heart, My *l* delayeth his coming Mt 24:48 *2962*
The *l* of that servant shall come Mt 24:50 *2962*
After a long time the *l* of those Mt 25:19 *2962*
other five talents, saying, *L* Mt 25:20 *2962*
His *l* said unto him, Well done, Mt 25:21 *2962*
enter thou into the joy of thy *l* Mt 25:21 *2962*
two talents came and said, *L* Mt 25:22 *2962*
His *l* said unto him, Well done, Mt 25:23 *2962*
enter thou into the joy of thy *l* Mt 25:23 *2962*
the one talent came and said, *L* Mt 25:24 *2962*
His *l* answered and said unto him, Mt 25:26 *2962*
the *l* of the vineyard do Mk 12:9 *2962*
unto men that wait for their *l* Lk 12:36 *2962*
whom the *l* when he cometh shall Lk 12:37 *2962*
whom his *l* shall make ruler over Lk 12:42 *2962*
whom his *l* when he cometh shall Lk 12:43 *2962*
heart, My *l* delayeth his coming Lk 12:45 *2962*
The *l* of that servant will come Lk 12:46 *2962*
shewed his *l* these things Lk 14:21 *2962*
And the servant said, *L*, it is Lk 14:22 *2962*
the *l* said unto the servant, Go Lk 14:23 *2962*
for my *l* taketh away from me the Lk 16:3 *2962*
How much owest thou unto my *l* Lk 16:5 *2962*
the *l* commended the unjust Lk 16:8 *2962*
Then said the *l* of the vineyard, Lk 20:13 *2962*
What therefore shall the *l* of the Lk 20:15 *2962*
servant is not greater than his *l* Jn 13:16 *2962*
knoweth not what his *l* doeth Jn 15:15 *2962*
servant is not greater than his *l* Jn 15:20 *2962*
certain thing to write unto my *l* Acts 25:26 *2962*
a servant, though he be *l* of all Gal 4:1 *2962*
obeyed Abraham, calling him *l* 1Pet 3:6 *2962*

LORDLY
brought forth butter in a *l* dish Judg 5:25 117

LORD'S
1. Refers to Lord 1.
know how that the earth is the *L* Ex 9:29 3068
it is the *L* passover Ex 12:11 3068
the sacrifice of the *L* passover Ex 12:27 3068
that the *L* law may be in thy Ex 13:9 3068
the males shall be the *L* Ex 13:12 3068
and said, Who is on the *L* side Ex 32:26 3068
they brought the *L* offering to Ex 35:21 3068
and brass brought the *L* offering Ex 35:24 3068
all the fat is the *L* Lev 3:16 3068
goat upon which the *L* lot fell Lev 16:9 3068
month at even is the *L* passover Lev 23:5 3068
which should be the *L* firstling Lev 27:26 3068
it is the *L* Lev 27:26 3068
the fruit of the tree, is the *L* Lev 27:30 3068
Is the *L* hand waxed short Num 11:23 3068
all the *L* people were prophets Num 11:29 3068
ye shall give thereof the *L* heave Num 18:28 3068
the *L* tribute of the sheep was Num 31:37 3068
of which the *L* tribute was Num 31:38 3068
of which the *L* tribute was Num 31:39 3068
of which the *L* tribute was thirty Num 31:40 3068
which was the *L* heave offering, Num 31:41 3068
the *L* anger was kindled the same Num 32:10 3068
the *L* anger was kindled against Num 32:13 3068
of heavens is the *L* thy God Deut 10:14 3068
then the *L* wrath be kindled Deut 11:17 3068
it is called the *L* release Deut 15:2 3068
For the *L* portion is his people Deut 32:9 3068
which Moses the *L* servant gave Josh 1:15 3068
the captain of the *L* host said Josh 5:15 3068
wherein the *L* tabernacle dwelleth Josh 22:19 3068
of Ammon, shall surely be the *L* Judg 11:31 3068
pillars of the earth are the *L* 1Sa 2:8 3068
ye make the *L* people to 1Sa 2:24 3068
the *L* priest in Shiloh, wearing 1Sa 14:3 3068
Surely the *L* anointed is before 1Sa 16:6 3068
for the battle is the *L*, and he 1Sa 17:47 3068
for me, and fight the *L* battles 1Sa 18:17 3068
that Saul had slain the *L* priests 1Sa 22:21 3068
the *L* anointed, to stretch forth 1Sa 24:6 3068
for he is the *L* anointed 1Sa 24:10 3068
his hand against the *L* anointed 1Sa 26:9 3068
mine hand against the *L* anointed 1Sa 26:11 3068
kept your master, the *L* anointed 1Sa 26:16 3068
mine hand against the *L* anointed 1Sa 26:23 3068
hand to destroy the *L* anointed 2Sa 1:14 3068
I have slain the *L* anointed 2Sa 1:16 3068
because he cursed the *L* anointed 2Sa 19:21 3068
because of the *L* oath that was 2Sa 21:7 3068
the *L* prophets by fifty in a cave 1Kin 18:13 3068
that they should be the *L* people 2Kin 11:17 3068
The arrow of the *L* deliverance 2Kin 13:17 3068
the LORD had filled the *L* house 2Chr 7:2 3068
that they should be the *L* people 2Chr 23:16 3068
the *L* throne is in heaven Ps 11:4 3068
For the kingdom is the *L* Ps 22:28 3068
The earth is the *L*, and the Ps 24:1 3068
same the *L* name is to be praised Ps 113:3 3068
even the heavens, are the *L* Ps 115:16 3068
In the courts of the *L* house Ps 116:19 3068
This is the *L* doing Ps 118:23 3068
How shall we sing the *L* song in a Ps 137:4 3068
just weight and balance are the *L* Prov 16:11 3068
that the mountain of the *L* house Is 2:2 3068
it is the day of the *L* vengeance Is 34:8 3068
L hand double for all her sins Is 40:2 3068
and blind as the *L* servant Is 42:19 3068
One shall say, I am the *L* Is 44:5 3068
the *L* hand is not shortened, that Is 59:1 3068
for they are not the *L* Jer 5:10 3068
Stand in the gate of the *L* house Jer 7:2 3068
because the *L* flock is carried Jer 13:17 3068
stood in the court of the *L* house Jer 19:14 3068
Then took I the cup at the *L* hand Jer 25:17 3068
Stand in the court of the *L* house Jer 26:2 3068
come to worship in the *L* house Jer 26:2 3068
of the new gate of the *L* house Jer 26:10 3068
the vessels of the *L* house shall Jer 27:16 3068
all the vessels of the *L* house Jer 28:3 3068
again the vessels of the *L* house Jer 28:6 3068
the *L* house upon the fasting day Jer 36:6 3068
words of the LORD in the *L* house Jer 36:8 3068
of the new gate of the *L* house Jer 36:10 3068
is the time of the *L* vengeance Jer 51:6 3068
been a golden cup in the *L* hand Jer 51:7 3068
the sanctuaries of the *L* house Jer 51:51 3068
so that in the day of the *L* anger Lam 2:22 3068
It is of the *L* mercies that we Lam 3:22 3068
the *L* house which was toward the Eze 8:14 3068
the inner court of the *L* house Eze 8:16 3068
of the brightness of the *L* glory Eze 10:4 3068
of the east gate of the *L* house Eze 10:19 3068
unto the east gate of the *L* house Eze 11:1 3068
that is desolate, for the *L* sake Dan 9:17 136
shall not dwell in the *L* land Hos 9:3 3068
priests, the *L* ministers, mourn Joel 1:9 3068
and the kingdom shall be the *L* Obad 21 3068
the *L* controversy, and ye strong Mic 6:2 3068
The *L* voice crieth unto the city, Mic 6:9 3068
the cup of the *L* right hand shall Hab 2:16 3068
in the day of the *L* sacrifice Zeph 1:8 3068
them in the day of the *L* wrath Zeph 1:18 3068
day of the *L* anger come upon you Zeph 2:2 3068
be hid in the day of the *L* anger Zeph 2:3 3068
the time that the *L* house should Hag 1:2 3068
Then spake Haggai the *L* messenger Hag 1:13 3068
in the *L* message unto the people Hag 1:13 3068
of the *L* temple was laid, Hag 2:18 3068
the pots in the *L* house shall be Zec 14:20 3068
this is the *L* doing, and it is Mt 21:42 *2962*
This was the *L* doing, and it is Mk 12:11 *2962*
before he had seen the *L* Christ Lk 2:26 *2962*
therefore, or die, we are the *L* Rom 14:8 *2962*
being a servant, is the *L* freeman 1Cor 7:22 *2962*
be partakers of the *L* table 1Cor 10:21 *2962*
For the earth is the *L*, and the 1Cor 10:26 *2962*
for the earth is the *L*, and the 1Cor 10:28 *2962*
this is not to eat the *L* supper 1Cor 11:20 *2960*
ye do shew the *L* death till he 1Cor 11:26 *2962*
not discerning the *L* body 1Cor 11:29 *2962*
I none, save James the *L* brother Gal 1:19 *2962*
ordinance of man for the *L* sake 1Pet 2:13 *2962*
I was in the Spirit on the *L* day Rev 1:10 *2960*
2. Refers to Lord 2.
him in the ward of his *l* house Gen 40:7 113
out of thy *l* house silver or gold Gen 44:8 113
and we also will be my *l* bondmen Gen 44:9 113
behold, we are my *l* servants Gen 44:16 113
thee, speak a word in my *l* ears Gen 44:18 113
take thou thy *l* servants, and 2Sa 20:6 113
are they not all my *l* servants 1Chr 21:3 113
shall be the shame of thy *l* house Is 22:18 113
in the earth, and hid his *l* money Mt 25:18 *2962*
servant, which knew his *l* will Lk 12:47 *2962*
one of his *l* debtors unto him Lk 16:5 *2962*

LORDS
And he said, Behold now, my *l* Gen 19:2 113
the *l* of the high places of Arnon Num 21:28 1167
God is God of gods, and Lord of *l* Deut 10:17 113
five *l* of the Philistines Josh 13:3 5633
five *l* of the Philistines, and all Judg 3:3 5633
the *l* of the Philistines came up Judg 16:5 5633
Then the *l* of the Philistines Judg 16:8 5633
sent and called for the *l* of the Judg 16:18 5633
Then the *l* of the Philistines Judg 16:18 5633
Then the *l* of the Philistines Judg 16:23 5633
all the *l* of the Philistines were Judg 16:27 5633
and the house fell upon the *l* Judg 16:30 5633
gathered all the *l* of the 1Sa 5:8 5633
all the *l* of the Philistines 1Sa 5:11 5633
of the *l* of the Philistines 1Sa 6:4 5633
was on you all, and on your *l* 1Sa 6:4 5633
the *l* of the Philistines went 1Sa 6:12 5633
And when the five *l* of the 1Sa 6:16 5633
belonging to the five *l*, both of 1Sa 6:18 5633
the *l* of the Philistines went up 1Sa 7:7 5633
the *l* of the Philistines passed 1Sa 29:2 5633
the *l* favour thee not 1Sa 29:6 5633
not the *l* of the Philistines 1Sa 29:7 5633
for the *l* of the Philistines upon 1Chr 12:19 5633
and his counsellors, and his *l* Ezr 8:25 8269
O give thanks to the Lord of *l* Ps 136:3 113
the *l* of the heathen have broken Is 16:8 1167
other *l* besides thee have had Is 26:13 113
wherefore say my people, We are *l* Jer 2:31 7300
men, captains and rulers, great *l* Eze 23:23 7991
and my *l* sought unto me Dan 4:36 7261
feast to a thousand of his *l* Dan 5:1 7261
in him, and his *l* were astonied Dan 5:9 7261
of the words of the king and his *l* Dan 5:10 7261
before thee, and thou, and thy *l* Dan 5:23 7261
and with the signet of his *l* Dan 6:17 7261
birthday made a supper to his *l* Mk 6:21 *3175*
there be gods many, and *l* many,) 1Cor 8:5 *2962*
the King of kings, and Lord of *l* 1Ti 6:15 *2961*
Neither as being *l* over God's 1Pet 5:3 *2634*
for he is Lord of *l*, and King of Rev 17:14 *2962*
KING OF KINGS, AND LORD OF L Rev 19:16 *2962*

LORDSHIP
the Gentiles exercise *l* over them Mk 10:42 *2634*
the Gentiles exercise *l* over them Lk 22:25 *2961*

LO-RUHAMAH (*lo-ru-ha'-mah*) *Symbolic name meaning 'Not pitied.'*
said unto him, Call her name *L* Hos 1:6 3819
Now when she had weaned *L* Hos 1:8 3819

LOSE
thou *l* thy life, with the lives Judg 18:25 622
that we *l* not all the beasts 1Kin 18:5 3772
owners thereof to *l* their life Job 31:39 5307
vomit up, and *l* thy sweet words Prov 23:8 7843
A time to get, and a time to *l* Eccl 3:6 6
that findeth his life shall *l* it Mt 10:39 *622*
he shall in no wise *l* his reward Mt 10:42 *622*
will save his life shall *l* it Mt 16:25 *622*
whosoever will *l* his life for my Mt 16:25 *622*
whole world, and *l* his own soul Mt 16:26 *2210*
will save his life shall *l* it Mk 8:35 *622*
but whosoever shall *l* his life Mk 8:35 *622*
whole world, and *l* his own soul Mk 8:36 *2210*
you, he shall not *l* his reward Mk 9:41 *622*
will save his life shall *l* it Lk 9:24 *622*
but whosoever will *l* his life for Lk 9:24 *622*
l himself, or be cast away Lk 9:25 *622*
if he *l* one of them, doth not Lk 15:4 *622*
if she *l* one piece, doth not Lk 15:8 *622*
seek to save his life shall *l* it Lk 17:33 *622*
whosoever shall *l* his life shall Lk 17:33 *622*
hath given me I should *l* nothing Jn 6:39 *622*
that loveth his life shall *l* it Jn 12:25 *622*
that we *l* not those things which 2Jn 8 *622*

LOSETH
he that *l* his life for my sake Mt 10:39 *622*

LOSS
I bare the *l* of it Gen 31:39 2398
shall pay for the *l* of his time Ex 21:19 7674
shall I know the *l* of children Is 47:8 7921
the *l* of children, and widowhood Is 47:9 7921
and to have gained this harm and *l* Acts 27:21 *2209*
for there shall be no *l* of any Acts 27:22 *580*
be burned, he shall suffer *l* 1Cor 3:15 *2210*
me, those I counted *l* for Christ Phil 3:7 *2209*
I count all things but *l* for the Phil 3:8 *2209*
have suffered the *l* of all things Phil 3:8 *2210*

LOST
or for any manner of *l* thing Ex 22:9 9
Or have found that which was *l* Lev 6:3 9
or the *l* thing which he found, Lev 6:4 9
days that were before shall be *l* Num 6:12 5307
and with all *l* things of thy Deut 22:3 9
of thy brother's, which he hath *l* Deut 22:3 6
of Kish Saul's father were *l* 1Sa 9:3 6
asses that were *l* three days ago 1Sa 9:20 6
like the army that thou hast *l* 1Kin 20:25 5307
I have gone astray like a *l* sheep Ps 119:176 6
have, after thou hast *l* the other Is 49:20 7923
seeing I have *l* my children Is 49:21 7908
My people hath been *l* sheep Jer 50:6 6
she had waited, and her hope was *l* Eze 19:5 6
have ye sought that which was *l* Eze 34:4 6
I will seek that which was *l* Eze 34:16 6
bones are dried, and our hope is *l* Eze 37:11 6
but if the salt have *l* his savour Mt 5:13 *3471*
But go rather to the *l* sheep of Mt 10:6 *622*
I am not sent but unto the *l* Mt 15:24 *622*
is come to save that which was *l* Mt 18:11 *622*
if the salt have *l* his saltness Mk 9:50
but if the salt have *l* his savour Lk 14:34 *3471*
and go after that which is *l* Lk 15:4 *622*
I have found my sheep which was *l* Lk 15:6 *622*
found the piece which I had *l* Lk 15:9 *622*
he was *l*, and is found Lk 15:24 *622*
and was *l*, and is found Lk 15:32 *622*
seek and to save that which was *l* Lk 19:10 *622*
that remain, that nothing be *l* Jn 6:12 *622*
I have kept, and none of them is *l* Jn 17:12 *622*
thou gavest me have I *l* none Jn 18:9 *622*
hid, it is hid to them that are *l* 2Cor 4:3 *622*

LOT (*lot*) See LOT'S. *Abraham's nephew.*
and Haran begat *L* Gen 11:27 3876
L the son of Haran his son's son, Gen 11:31 3876
and *L* went with him Gen 12:4 3876
L his brother's son, and all their Gen 12:5 3876
L with him, into the south Gen 13:1 3876
L also, which went with Abram, Gen 13:5 3876
And Abram said unto *L*, Let there Gen 13:8 3876
L lifted up his eyes, and beheld Gen 13:10 3876
Then *L* chose him all the plain of Gen 13:11 3876
and *L* journeyed east Gen 13:11 3876
L dwelled in the cities of the Gen 13:12 3876
after that *L* was separated from Gen 13:14 3876
And they took *L*, Abram's brother's Gen 14:12 3876
also brought again his brother *L* Gen 14:16 3876
L sat in the gate of Sodom Gen 19:1 3876
L seeing them rose up to meet Gen 19:1 3876
And they called unto *L*, and said Gen 19:5 3876
L went out at the door unto them, Gen 19:6 3876
pressed sore upon the man, even *L* Gen 19:9 3876
pulled *L* into the house to them, Gen 19:10 3876
And the men said unto *L*, Hast thou Gen 19:12 3876
L went out, and spake unto his Gen 19:14 3876
arose, then the angels hastened *L* Gen 19:15 3876

L said unto them, Oh, not so, my Gen 19:18 3876
earth when L entered into Zoar Gen 19:23 3876
sent L out of the midst of the Gen 19:29 3876
the cities in the which L dwelt Gen 19:29 3876
L went up out of Zoar, and dwelt Gen 19:30 3876
of L with child by their father Gen 19:36 3876
children of L for a possession Deut 2:9 3876
children of L for a possession Deut 2:19 3876
have holpen the children of L Ps 83:8 3876
also as it was in the days of L Lk 17:28 3091
But the same day that L went out Lk 17:29 3091
And delivered just L, vexed with 2Pet 2:7 3091

A die.
one l for the LORD, and the other l Lev 16:8 1486
goat upon which the LORD's l fell Lev 16:9 1486
on which the l fell to be the Lev 16:10 1486
the land shall be divided by l Num 26:55 1486
According to the l shall the Num 26:56 1486
ye shall divide the land by l for Num 33:54 1486
in the place where his l falleth Num 33:54 1486
land which ye shall inherit by l Num 34:13 1486
by l to the children of Israel Num 36:2 1486
from the l of our inheritance Num 36:3 1486
Jacob is the l of his inheritance Deut 32:9 2256
only divide thou it by l unto the Josh 13:6
By l was their inheritance, as Josh 14:2 1486
This then was the l of the tribe Josh 15:1 1486
the l of the children of Joseph Josh 16:1 1486
There was also a l for the tribe Josh 17:1 1486
There was also a l for the rest Josh 17:2
Why hast thou given me but one l Josh 17:14 1486
thou shalt not have one l only Josh 17:17 1486
the l of the tribe of the Josh 18:11 1486
the coast of their l came forth Josh 18:11 1486
the second l came forth to Simeon Josh 19:1 1486
the third l came up for the Josh 19:10 1486
the fourth l came out to Issachar Josh 19:17 1486
the fifth l came out for the Josh 19:24 1486
The sixth l came out to the Josh 19:32 1486
the seventh l came out for the Josh 19:40 1486
by l in Shiloh before the LORD Josh 19:51 1486
the l came out for the families Josh 21:4 1486
had by l out of the tribe of Josh 21:4 1486
by l out of the families of the Josh 21:5 1486
by l out of the families of the Josh 21:6 1486
l unto the Levites these cities Josh 21:8 1486
for theirs was the first l Josh 21:10 1486
l out of the tribe of Ephraim Josh 21:20 1486
were by their l twelve cities Josh 21:40 1486
by l these nations that remain Josh 23:4
Come up with me into my l Judg 1:3 1486
will go with thee into thy l Judg 1:3 1486
we will go up by l against it Judg 20:9 1486
God of Israel, Give a perfect l 1Sa 14:41
for theirs was the l 1Chr 6:54 1486
the half tribe of Manasseh, by l 1Chr 6:61 1486
sons of Merari were given by l 1Chr 6:63 1486
they gave by l out of the tribe 1Chr 6:65 1486
the l of your inheritance 1Chr 16:18 2256
Thus were they divided by l 1Chr 24:5 1486
Now the first l came forth to 1Chr 24:7 1486
Now the first l came forth for 1Chr 25:9 1486
the l eastward fell to Shelemiah 1Chr 26:14 1486
and his l came out northward 1Chr 26:14 1486
Hosah the l came forth westward, 1Chr 26:16
they cast Pur, that is, the l Est 3:7 1486
and had cast Pur, that is, the l Est 9:24 1486
thou maintainest my l Ps 16:5 1486
the l of your inheritance Ps 105:11 2256
rest upon the l of the righteous Ps 125:3 1486
Cast in thy l among us Prov 1:14 1486
The l is cast into the lap Prov 16:33 1486
The l causeth contentions to Prov 18:18 1486
the l of them that rob us Is 17:14 1486
And he hath cast the l for them Is 34:17 1486
they, they are thy l Is 57:6 1486
This is thy l, the portion of thy Jer 13:25 1486
let no l fall upon it Eze 24:6 1486
when ye shall divide by l the Eze 45:1
that ye shall divide it by l for Eze 47:22
l unto the tribes of Israel for Eze 48:29
stand in thy l at the end of the Dan 12:13 1486
lots, and the l fell upon Jonah Jonah 1:7 1486
none that shall cast a cord by l Mic 2:5 1486
his l was to burn incense when he Lk 1:9 2975
and the l fell upon Matthias Acts 1:26 2819
neither part nor l in this matter Acts 8:21 2819
divided their land to them by l Acts 13:19 2624

LOTAN (*lo'-tan*) See LOTAN's. *Son of Seir.*
L, and Shobal, and Zibeon, and Anah, Gen 36:20 3877
And the children of L were Hori Gen 36:22 3877
duke L, duke Shobal, duke Zibeon, Gen 36:29 3877
L, and Shobal, and Zibeon, and Anah, 1Chr 1:38 3877
And the sons of L 1Chr 1:39 3877

LOTAN'S (*lo'-tans*)
and L sister was Timna Gen 36:22 3877
and Timna was L sister 1Chr 1:39 3877

LOTHE
the Egyptians shall l to drink of Ex 7:18 3811
they shall l themselves for the Eze 6:9 6962
ye shall l yourselves in your own Eze 20:43 6962
shall l yourselves in your own Eze 36:31 6962

LOTHED
hath thy soul l Zion Jer 14:19 1602
which l their husbands and their Eze 16:45 1602
and my soul l them, and their soul Zec 11:8 7114

LOTHETH
that l her husband and her Eze 16:45 1602

LOTHING
to the l of thy person, in the Eze 16:5 1604

LOT'S (*lots*)
cattle and the herdmen of L cattle Gen 13:7 3876
Remember L wife Lk 17:32

LOTS
Aaron shall cast l upon the two Lev 16:8 1486
that I may cast l for you here Josh 18:6 1486
that I may here cast l for you Josh 18:8 1486
Joshua cast l for them in Shiloh Josh 18:10 1486
Cast l between me and Jonathan my 1Sa 14:42
These likewise cast l over 1Chr 24:31 1486
And they cast l, ward against ward 1Chr 25:8 1486
And they cast l, as well the small 1Chr 26:13 1486
a wise counsellor, they cast l 1Chr 26:14 1486
we cast the l among the priests, Neh 10:34 1486
rest of the people also cast l Neh 11:1 1486
them, and cast l upon my vesture Ps 22:18 1486
And they have cast l for my people Joel 3:3 1486
cast l upon Jerusalem, even thou Obad 11 1486
fellow, Come, and let us cast l Jonah 1:7 1486
So they cast l, and the lot fell Jonah 1:7 1486
they cast l for her honourable Nah 3:10 1486
and parted his garments, casting l Mt 27:35 2819
upon my vesture did they cast l Mt 27:35 2819
casting l upon them, what every Mk 15:24 2819
parted his raiment, and cast l Lk 23:34 2819
us not rend it, but cast l for it Jn 19:24 2819
and for my vesture they did cast l Jn 19:24 2975
And they gave forth their l Acts 1:26 2819

LOUD
me, and I cried with a l voice Gen 39:14 1419
voice of the trumpet exceeding l Ex 19:16 2389
the men of Israel with a l voice Deut 27:14 7311
Samuel, she cried with a l voice 1Sa 28:12 1419
the country wept with a l voice 2Sa 15:23 1419
and the king cried with a l voice 2Sa 19:4 1419
of Israel with a l voice, saying, 1Kin 8:55 1419
cried with a l voice in the Jews' 2Kin 18:28 1419
unto the LORD with a l voice 2Chr 15:14 1419
of Israel with a l voice on high 2Chr 20:19 1419
singing with l instruments unto 2Chr 30:21 5797
Then they cried with a l voice in 2Chr 32:18 1419
their eyes, wept with a l voice Ezr 3:12 1419
the people shouted with a l shout Ezr 3:13 1419
answered and said with a l voice Ezr 10:12 1419
cried with a l voice unto the Neh 9:4 1419
And the singers sang l, with Neh 12:42 8085
of the city, and cried with a l Est 4:1 1419
play skilfully with a l noise Ps 33:3
make a l noise, and rejoice, and Ps 98:4
Praise him upon the l cymbals Ps 150:5 8085
(She is l and stubborn Prov 7:11 1993
his friend with a l voice Prov 27:14 1419
cried with a l voice in the Jews' Is 36:13 1419
cry in mine ears with a l voice Eze 8:18 1419
also in mine ears with a l voice Eze 9:1 1419
my face, and cried with a l voice Eze 11:13 1419
hour Jesus cried with a l voice Mt 27:46 3173
he had cried again with a l voice Mt 27:50 3173
torn him, and cried with a l voice Mk 1:26 3173
And cried with a l voice, and said, Mk 5:7 3173
hour Jesus cried with a l voice Mk 15:34 3173
And Jesus cried with a l voice Mk 15:37 3173
And she spake out with a l voice Lk 1:42 3173
and cried out with a l voice Lk 4:33 3173
with a l voice said, What have I Lk 8:28 3173
with a l voice glorified God, Lk 17:15 3173
praise God with a l voice for all Lk 19:37 3173
they were instant with l voices Lk 23:23 3173
Jesus had cried with a l voice Lk 23:46 3173
spoken, he cried with a l voice Jn 11:43 3173
they cried out with a l voice Acts 7:57 3173
down, and cried with a l voice Acts 7:60 3173
spirits, crying with l voice Acts 8:7 3173
Said with a l voice, Stand Acts 14:10 3173
But Paul cried with a l voice Acts 16:28 3173
Festus said with a l voice Acts 26:24 3173
angel proclaiming with a l voice Rev 5:2 3173
Saying with a l voice, Worthy is Rev 5:12 3173
And they cried with a l voice Rev 6:10 3173
he cried with a l voice to the Rev 7:2 3173
And cried with a l voice, saying, Rev 7:10 3173
of heaven, saying with a l voice Rev 8:13 3173
And cried with a l voice, as when Rev 10:3 3173
I heard a l voice saying in Rev 12:10 3173
Saying with a l voice, Fear God, Rev 14:7 3173
them, saying with a l voice Rev 14:9 3173
crying with a l voice to him that Rev 14:15 3173
cried with a l cry to him that Rev 14:18 3173
and he cried with a l voice Rev 19:17 3173

LOUDER
long, and waxed l and l Ex 19:19 3966

LOVE
make me savoury meat, such as I l Gen 27:4 157
few days, for the l he had to her Gen 29:20 160
therefore my husband will l me Gen 29:32 157
unto thousands of them that l me Ex 20:6 157
I l my master, my wife, and my Ex 21:5 157
but thou shalt l thy neighbour as Lev 19:18 157
thou shalt l him as thyself Lev 19:34 157
unto thousands of them that l me Deut 5:10 157
thou shalt l the LORD thy God Deut 6:5 157
LORD did not set his l upon you Deut 7:7 2836
and mercy with them that l him Deut 7:9 157
And he will l thee, and bless thee, Deut 7:13 157
to l him, and to serve the LORD Deut 10:12 157
delight in thy fathers to l them Deut 10:15 157
L ye therefore the stranger Deut 10:19 157
thou shalt l the LORD thy God Deut 11:1 157
to l the LORD your God, and to Deut 11:13 157
to l the LORD your God, to walk Deut 11:22 157
to know whether ye l the LORD Deut 13:3 157
to l the LORD thy God, and to walk Deut 19:9 157
to l the LORD thy God with all Deut 30:6 157
this day to l the LORD thy God Deut 30:16 157
thou mayest l the LORD thy God Deut 30:20 157
to l the LORD your God, and to Josh 22:5 157
that ye l the LORD your God Josh 23:11 157
but let them that l him be as the Judg 5:31 157
I l thee, when thine heart is not Judg 16:15 157
thee, and all his servants l thee 1Sa 18:22 157
thy l to me was wonderful, 2Sa 1:26 160
passing the l of women 2Sa 1:26 160
I l Tamar, my brother Absalom's 2Sa 13:4 157
the l wherewith he had loved her 2Sa 13:15 160
Solomon clave unto these in l 1Kin 11:2 160
l them that hate the LORD 2Chr 19:2 157
and mercy for them that l him Neh 1:5 157
how long will ye l vanity Ps 4:2 157
let them also that l thy name be Ps 5:11 157
I will l thee, O LORD, my Ps 18:1 7355
O l the LORD, all ye his saints Ps 31:23 157
let such as l thy salvation say Ps 40:16 157
they that l his name shall dwell Ps 69:36 157
let such as l thy salvation say Ps 70:4 157
Because he hath set his l upon me Ps 91:14 2836
Ye that l the LORD, hate evil Ps 97:10 157
For my l they are my adversaries Ps 109:4 160
evil for good, and hatred for my l Ps 109:5 160
I l the LORD, because he hath Ps 116:1 157
O how l I thy law Ps 119:97 157
but thy law do I l Ps 119:113 157
therefore I l thy testimonies Ps 119:119 157
Therefore I l thy commandments Ps 119:127 157
to do unto those that l thy name Ps 119:132 157
Consider how I l thy precepts Ps 119:159 157
but thy law do I l Ps 119:163 157
peace have they which l thy law Ps 119:165 157
and I l them exceedingly Ps 119:167 157
they shall prosper that l thee Ps 122:6 157
preserveth all them that l him Ps 145:20 157
simple ones, will ye l simplicity Prov 1:22 157
l her, and she shall keep thee Prov 4:6 157
thou ravished always with her l Prov 5:19 160
our fill of l until the morning Prov 7:18 1730
I l them that l me Prov 8:17 157
that l me to inherit substance Prov 8:21 157
all they that hate me l death Prov 8:36 157
a wise man, and he will l thee Prov 9:8 157
but l covereth all sins Prov 10:12 160
is a dinner of herbs where l is Prov 15:17 160
they l him that speaketh right Prov 16:13 157
a transgression seeketh l Prov 17:9 160
they that l it shall eat the Prov 18:21 157
L not sleep, lest thou come to Prov 20:13 157
rebuke is better than secret l Prov 27:5 160
A time to l, and a time to hate Eccl 3:8 157
no man knoweth either l or hatred Eccl 9:1 160
Also their l, and their hatred, and Eccl 9:6 160
for thy l is better than wine Song 1:2 1730
therefore do the virgins l thee Song 1:3 157
remember thy l more than wine Song 1:4 1730
the upright l thee Song 1:4 157
I have compared thee, O my l Song 1:9 7474
Behold, thou art fair, my l Song 1:15 7474
so is my l among the daughters Song 2:2 7474
and his banner over me was l Song 2:4 160
for I am sick of l Song 2:5 160
ye stir not up, nor awake my l Song 2:7 160
and said unto me, Rise up, my l Song 2:10 7474
Arise, my l, my fair one, and come Song 2:13 7474
ye stir not up, nor awake my l Song 3:5 160
midst thereof being paved with l Song 3:10 160
Behold, thou art fair, my l Song 4:1 7474
Thou art all fair, my l Song 4:7 7474
How fair is thy l, my sister, my Song 4:10 1730
much better is thy l than wine Song 4:10 1730
Open to me, my sister, my l Song 5:2 7474
ye tell him, that I am sick of l Song 5:8 160
Thou art beautiful, O my l Song 6:4 7474
and how pleasant art thou, O l Song 7:6 160
ye stir not up, nor awake my l Song 8:4 160
for l is strong as death Song 8:6 160
Many waters cannot quench l Song 8:7 160
the substance of his house for l Song 8:7 160
but thou hast in l to my soul Is 38:17 2836
to l the name of the LORD, to be Is 56:6 157
For I the LORD l judgment Is 61:8 157
in his l and in his pity he Is 63:9 160
glad with her, all ye that l her Is 66:10 157
the l of thine espousals, when Jer 2:2 160
trimmest thou thy way to seek l Jer 2:33 160
my people l to have it so Jer 5:31 157
loved thee with an everlasting l Jer 31:3 160
thy time was the time of l Eze 16:8 1730
in her inordinate l than she Eze 23:11 5691
came to her into the bed of l Eze 23:17 1730
with their mouth they shew much l Eze 33:31 5690
tender l with the prince of the Dan 1:9
and mercy to them that l him Dan 9:4 157
l a woman beloved of her friend, Hos 3:1 157
according to the l of the LORD Hos 3:1 160
other gods, and l flagons of wine Hos 3:1 157
her rulers with shame do l Hos 4:18 157
mine house, I will l them no more Hos 9:15 160
cords of a man, with bands of l Hos 11:4 160
backsliding, I will l them freely Hos 14:4 157
l the good, and establish judgment Amos 5:15 157
Who hate the good, and l the evil Mic 3:2 157
to l mercy, and to walk humbly Mic 6:8 160
he will rest in his l, he will Zeph 3:17 160
and l no false oath Zec 8:17 157

therefore *l* the truth and peace — Zec 8:19 — 157
Thou shalt *l* thy neighbour, and — Mt 5:43 — 25
L your enemies, bless them that — Mt 5:44 — 25
For if ye *l* them which *l* you, — Mt 5:46 — 25
for they *l* to pray standing in — Mt 6:5 — 5368
will hate the one, and *l* the other — Mt 6:24 — 25
Thou shalt *l* thy neighbour as — Mt 19:19 — 25
Thou shalt *l* the Lord thy God — Mt 22:37 — 25
Thou shalt *l* thy neighbour as — Mt 22:39 — 25
l the uppermost rooms at feasts, — Mt 23:6 — 5368
the *l* of many shall wax cold — Mt 24:12 — 26
thou shalt *l* the Lord thy God — Mk 12:30 — 25
Thou shalt *l* thy neighbour as — Mk 12:31 — 25
to *l* him with all the heart, and — Mk 12:33 — 25
to *l* his neighbour as himself, is — Mk 12:33 — 25
which *l* to go in long clothing, — Mk 12:38 — 2309
l salutations in the marketplaces — Mk 12:38
L your enemies, do good to them — Lk 6:27 — 25
For if ye *l* them which *l* you — Lk 6:32 — 25
also *l* those that *l* them — Lk 6:32 — 25
But *l* ye your enemies, and do good — Lk 6:35 — 25
which of them will *l* him most — Lk 7:42 — 25
Thou shalt *l* the Lord thy God — Lk 10:27 — 25
over judgment and the *l* of God — Lk 11:42 — 26
for ye *l* the uppermost seats in — Lk 11:43 — 25
will hate the one, and *l* the other — Lk 16:13 — 25
l greetings in the markets, and — Lk 20:46 — 5368
ye have not the *l* of God in you — Jn 5:42 — 26
were your Father, ye would *l* me — Jn 8:42 — 25
Therefore doth my Father *l* me — Jn 10:17 — 25
unto you, That ye *l* one another — Jn 13:34 — 25
you, that ye also *l* one another — Jn 13:34 — 25
if ye have *l* one to another — Jn 13:35 — 26
If ye *l* me, keep my commandments — Jn 14:15 — 25
of my Father, and I will *l* him — Jn 14:21 — 25
and said unto him, If a man *l* me — Jn 14:23 — 25
and my Father will *l* him, and we — Jn 14:23 — 25
may know that I *l* the Father — Jn 14:31 — 25
continue ye in my *l* — Jn 15:9 — 26
ye shall abide in my *l* — Jn 15:10 — 26
commandments, and abide in his *l* — Jn 15:10 — 26
That ye *l* one another, as I have — Jn 15:12 — 25
Greater *l* hath no man than this, — Jn 15:13 — 26
you, that ye *l* one another — Jn 15:17 — 25
world, the world would *l* his own — Jn 15:19 — 5368
that the *l* wherewith thou hast — Jn 17:26 — 26
thou knowest that I *l* thee — Jn 21:15 — 5368
thou knowest that I *l* thee — Jn 21:16 — 5368
thou knowest that I *l* thee — Jn 21:17 — 5368
because the *l* of God is shed — Rom 5:5 — 26
God commendeth his *l* toward us — Rom 5:8 — 26
for good to them that *l* God — Rom 8:28 — 25
separate us from the *l* of Christ — Rom 8:35 — 26
to separate us from the *l* of God — Rom 8:39 — 26
Let *l* be without dissimulation — Rom 12:9 — 26
one to another with brotherly *l* — Rom 12:10 — 5360
any thing, but to *l* one another — Rom 13:8 — 25
Thou shalt *l* thy neighbour as — Rom 13:9 — 25
L worketh no ill to his neighbour — Rom 13:10 — 26
therefore *l* is the fulfilling of — Rom 13:10 — 26
for the *l* of the Spirit, that ye — Rom 15:30 — 26
hath prepared for them that *l* him — 1Cor 2:9 — 25
come unto you with a rod, or in *l* — 1Cor 4:21 — 26
But if any man *l* God, the same is — 1Cor 8:3 — 25
If any man *l* not the Lord Jesus — 1Cor 16:22 — 5368
My *l* be with you all in Christ — 1Cor 16:24 — 26
but that ye might know the *l* — 2Cor 2:4 — 26
would confirm your *l* toward him — 2Cor 2:8 — 26
For the *l* of Christ constraineth — 2Cor 5:14 — 26
the Holy Ghost, by *l* unfeigned, — 2Cor 6:6 — 26
all diligence, and in your *l* to us — 2Cor 8:7 — 26
to prove the sincerity of your *l* — 2Cor 8:8 — 26
the churches, the proof of your *l* — 2Cor 8:24 — 26
because I *l* you not — 2Cor 11:11 — 25
the more abundantly I *l* you — 2Cor 12:15 — 25
and the God of *l* and peace shall be — 2Cor 13:11 — 26
the *l* of God, and the communion of — 2Cor 13:14 — 26
but faith which worketh by *l* — Gal 5:6 — 26
but by *l* serve one another — Gal 5:13 — 26
Thou shalt *l* thy neighbour as — Gal 5:14 — 25
But the fruit of the Spirit is *l* — Gal 5:22 — 26
and without blame before him in *l* — Eph 1:4 — 26
Jesus, and *l* unto all the saints, — Eph 1:15 — 26
for his great *l* wherewith he — Eph 2:4 — 26
ye, being rooted and grounded in *l* — Eph 3:17 — 26
And to know the *l* of Christ — Eph 3:19 — 26
forbearing one another in *l* — Eph 4:2 — 26
But speaking the truth in *l* — Eph 4:15 — 26
unto the edifying of itself in *l* — Eph 4:16 — 26
And walk in *l*, as Christ also hath — Eph 5:2 — 26
l your wives, even as Christ also — Eph 5:25 — 25
So ought men to *l* their wives as — Eph 5:28 — 25
so *l* his wife even as himself — Eph 5:33 — 25
l with faith, from God the Father — Eph 6:23 — 26
that *l* our Lord Jesus Christ in — Eph 6:24 — 25
that your *l* may abound yet more — Phil 1:9 — 26
But the other of *l*, knowing that — Phil 1:17 — 26
in Christ, if any comfort of *l* — Phil 2:1 — 26
be likeminded, having the same *l* — Phil 2:2 — 26
of the *l* which ye have to all the — Col 1:4 — 26
unto us your *l* in the Spirit — Col 1:8 — 26
being knit together in *l* — Col 2:2 — 26
l your wives, and be not bitter — Col 3:19 — 25
work of faith, and labour of *l* — 1Th 1:3 — 26
abound in *l* one toward another, — 1Th 3:12 — 26
But as touching brotherly *l* ye — 1Th 4:9 — 5360
taught of God to *l* one another — 1Th 4:9 — 25
on the breastplate of faith and *l* — 1Th 5:8 — 26
highly in *l* for their work's sake — 1Th 5:13 — 26
received not the *l* of the truth — 2Th 2:10 — 26
your hearts into the *l* of God — 2Th 3:5 — 26
l which is in Christ Jesus — 1Ti 1:14 — 26
For the *l* of money is the root of — 1Ti 6:10 — 5365
godliness, faith, *l*, patience, — 1Ti 6:11 — 26
but of power, and of *l*, and of a — 2Ti 1:7 — 26
l which is in Christ Jesus — 2Ti 1:13 — 26
them also that *l* his appearing — 2Ti 4:8 — 25
be sober, to *l* their husbands — Titus 2:4 — 5362
to *l* their children — Titus 2:4 — 5388
l of God our Saviour toward man — Titus 3:4 — 5363
Greet them that *l* us in the faith — Titus 3:15 — 5368
Hearing of thy *l* and faith, which — Philem 5 — 26
great joy and consolation in thy *l* — Philem 7 — 26
forget your work and labour of *l* — Heb 6:10 — 26
one another to provoke unto *l* — Heb 10:24 — 26
Let brotherly *l* continue — Heb 13:1 — 5360
hath promised to them that *l* him — Jas 1:12 — 25
hath promised to them that *l* him — Jas 2:5 — 25
Thou shalt *l* thy neighbour as — Jas 2:8 — 25
Whom having not seen, ye *l* — 1Pet 1:8 — 25
unto unfeigned *l* of the brethren — 1Pet 1:22 — 5360
see that ye *l* one another with a — 1Pet 1:22 — 25
L the brotherhood — 1Pet 2:17 — 25
l as brethren, be pitiful, be — 1Pet 3:8 — 5361
For he that will *l* life, and see — 1Pet 3:10 — 25
verily is the *l* of God perfected — 1Jn 2:5 — 26
L not the world, neither the — 1Jn 2:15 — 25
If any man *l* the world — 1Jn 2:15 — 25
the *l* of the Father is not in him — 1Jn 2:15 — 26
what manner of *l* the Father hath — 1Jn 3:1 — 26
that we should *l* one another — 1Jn 3:11 — 25
because we *l* the brethren — 1Jn 3:14 — 25
Hereby perceive we the *l* of God — 1Jn 3:16 — 26
how dwelleth the *l* of God in him — 1Jn 3:17 — 26
children, let us not *l* in word — 1Jn 3:18 — 25
l one another, as he gave us — 1Jn 3:23 — 25
Beloved, let us *l* one another — 1Jn 4:7 — 25
for *l* is of God — 1Jn 4:7 — 26
for God is *l* — 1Jn 4:8 — 26
manifested the *l* of God toward us — 1Jn 4:9 — 26
Herein is *l*, not that we loved — 1Jn 4:10 — 26
we ought also to *l* one another — 1Jn 4:11 — 25
If we *l* one another, God dwelleth — 1Jn 4:12 — 25
us, and his *l* is perfected in us — 1Jn 4:12 — 26
believed the *l* that God hath to — 1Jn 4:16 — 26
God is *l* — 1Jn 4:16 — 26
dwelleth in *l* dwelleth in God — 1Jn 4:16 — 26
Herein is our *l* made perfect — 1Jn 4:17 — 26
There is no fear in *l* — 1Jn 4:18 — 26
but perfect *l* casteth out fear — 1Jn 4:18 — 26
feareth is not made perfect in *l* — 1Jn 4:18 — 26
We *l* him, because he first loved — 1Jn 4:19 — 25
I *l* God, and hateth his brother, — 1Jn 4:20 — 25
how can he *l* God whom he hath not — 1Jn 4:20 — 25
who loveth God *l* his brother also — 1Jn 4:21 — 25
that we *l* the children of God — 1Jn 5:2 — 25
children of God, when we *l* God — 1Jn 5:2 — 25
For this is the *l* of God, that we — 1Jn 5:3 — 26
children, whom I *l* in the truth — 2Jn 1 — 25
Son of the Father, in truth and *l* — 2Jn 3 — 26
beginning, that we *l* one another — 2Jn 5 — 25
And this is *l*, that we walk after — 2Jn 6 — 26
Gaius, whom I *l* in the truth — 3Jn 1 — 25
Mercy unto you, and peace, and *l* — Jude 2 — 26
Keep yourselves in the *l* of God — Jude 21 — 26
thou hast left thy first *l* — Rev 2:4 — 26
As many as I *l*, I rebuke and — Rev 3:19 — 5368

LOVED

his wife; and he *l* her — Gen 24:67 — 157
And Isaac *l* Esau, because he did — Gen 25:28 — 157
but Rebekah *l* Jacob — Gen 25:28 — 157
meat, such as his father *l* — Gen 27:14 — 157
And Jacob *l* Rachel — Gen 29:18 — 157
he *l* also Rachel more than Leah, — Gen 29:30 — 157
he *l* the damsel, and spake kindly — Gen 34:3 — 157
Now Israel *l* Joseph more than all — Gen 37:3 — 157
l him more than all his brethren — Gen 37:4 — 157
because he *l* thy fathers, — Deut 4:37 — 157
But because the LORD *l* you — Deut 7:8 — 160
because the LORD thy God *l* thee — Deut 23:5 — 157
Yea, he *l* the people — Deut 33:3 — 2245
that he *l* a woman in the valley — Judg 16:4 — 157
for he *l* Hannah — 1Sa 1:5 — 157
and he *l* him greatly — 1Sa 16:21 — 157
Jonathan *l* him as his own soul — 1Sa 18:1 — 157
because he *l* him as his own soul — 1Sa 18:3 — 160
But all Israel and Judah *l* David — 1Sa 18:16 — 157
And Michal Saul's daughter *l* David — 1Sa 18:20 — 157
that Michal Saul's daughter *l* him — 1Sa 18:28 — 157
to swear again, because he *l* him — 1Sa 20:17 — 160
for he *l* him as he — 1Sa 20:17 — 157
him as he *l* his own soul — 1Sa 20:17 — 160
and the LORD *l* him — 2Sa 12:24 — 157
and Amnon the son of David *l* her — 2Sa 13:1 — 157
the love wherewith he had *l* her — 2Sa 13:15 — 157
Solomon *l* the LORD, walking in — 1Kin 3:3 — 157
the LORD *l* Israel for ever — 1Kin 10:9 — 160
But king Solomon *l* many strange — 1Kin 11:1 — 157
the LORD hath *l* his people — 2Chr 2:11 — 160
because thy God *l* Israel, to — 2Chr 9:8 — 160
Rehoboam *l* Maachah the daughter — 2Chr 11:21 — 157
for he *l* husbandry — 2Chr 26:10 — 157
the king *l* Esther above all the — Est 2:17 — 157
they whom I *l* are turned against — Job 19:19 — 157
I have *l* the habitation of thy — Ps 26:8 — 157
the excellency of Jacob whom he *l* — Ps 47:4 — 157
Judah, the mount Zion which he *l* — Ps 78:68 — 157
As he *l* cursing, so let it come — Ps 109:17 — 157
thy commandments, which I have *l* — Ps 119:47 — 157
thy commandments, which I have *l* — Ps 119:48 — 157
been honourable, and I have *l* thee — Is 43:4 — 157
The LORD hath *l* him — Is 48:14 — 157
for I have *l* strangers, and after — Jer 2:25 — 157
host of heaven, whom they have *l* — Jer 8:2 — 157
Thus have they *l* to wander — Jer 14:10 — 157
I have *l* thee with an everlasting — Jer 31:3 — 157
and all them that thou hast *l* — Eze 16:37 — 157
thou hast *l* a reward upon every — Hos 9:1 — 157
were according as they *l* — Hos 9:10 — 157
Israel was a child, then I *l* him — Hos 11:1 — 157
I have *l* you, saith the LORD — Mal 1:2 — 157
ye say, Wherein hast thou *l* us — Mal 1:2 — 157
yet I *l* Jacob, — Mal 1:2 — 157
holiness of the LORD which he *l* — Mal 2:11 — 157
Then Jesus beholding him *l* him — Mk 10:21 — 25
for she *l* much — Lk 7:47 — 25
For God so *l* the world, that he — Jn 3:16 — 25
men *l* darkness rather than light, — Jn 3:19 — 25
Now Jesus *l* Martha, and her sister — Jn 11:5 — 25
the Jews, Behold how he *l* him — Jn 11:36 — 5368
For they *l* the praise of men more — Jn 12:43 — 25
having *l* his own which were in — Jn 13:1 — 25
the world, he *l* them unto the end — Jn 13:1 — 25
of his disciples, whom Jesus *l* — Jn 13:23 — 25
as I have *l* you, that ye also — Jn 13:34 — 25
loveth me shall be *l* of my Father — Jn 14:21 — 25
If ye *l* me, ye would rejoice, — Jn 14:28 — 25
hath *l* me, so have I *l* you — Jn 15:9 — 25
love one another, as I have *l* you — Jn 15:12 — 25
loveth you, because ye have *l* me — Jn 16:27 — 5368
thou hast sent me, and hast *l* them — Jn 17:23 — 25
as thou hast *l* me — Jn 17:23 — 25
thou hast *l* me may be in them — Jn 17:26 — 25
disciple standing by, whom he *l* — Jn 19:26 — 25
the other disciple, whom Jesus *l* — Jn 20:2 — 5368
whom Jesus *l* saith unto Peter — Jn 21:7 — 25
disciple whom Jesus *l* following — Jn 21:20 — 25
conquerors through him that *l* us — Rom 8:37 — 25
As it is written Jacob have I *l* — Rom 9:13 — 25
I love you, the less I be *l* — 2Cor 12:15 — 25
faith of the Son of God, who *l* me — Gal 2:20 — 25
his great love wherewith he *l* us — Eph 2:4 — 25
in love, as Christ also hath *l* us — Eph 5:2 — 26
even as Christ also *l* the church — Eph 5:25 — 25
even our Father, which hath *l* us — 2Th 2:16 — 25
having *l* this present world, and — 2Ti 4:10 — 25
Thou hast *l* righteousness, and — Heb 1:9 — 25
son of Bosor, who *l* the wages of — 2Pet 2:15 — 25
Herein is love, not that we *l* God — 1Jn 4:10 — 25
but that he *l* us — 1Jn 4:10 — 25
Beloved, if God so *l* us, we ought — 1Jn 4:11 — 25
love him, because he first *l* us — 1Jn 4:19 — 25
Unto him that *l* us, and washed us — Rev 1:5 — 25
and to know that I have *l* thee — Rev 3:9 — 25
they *l* not their lives unto the — Rev 12:11 — 25

LOVEDST

thou *l* their bed where thou — Is 57:8 — 157
for thou *l* me before the — Jn 17:24 — 25

LOVELY

Saul and Jonathan were *l* and — 2Sa 1:23 — 157
yea, he is altogether *l* — Song 5:16 — 4261
a very *l* song of one that hath a — Eze 33:32 — 5690
are pure, whatsoever things are *l* — Phil 4:8 — 4375

LOVER

for Hiram was ever a *l* of David — 1Kin 5:1 — 157
L and friend hast thou put far — Ps 88:18 — 157
But a *l* of hospitality — Titus 1:8 — 5382
a *l* of good men, sober, just, — Titus 1:8 — 5358

LOVERS

My *l* and my friends stand aloof — Ps 38:11 — 157
played the harlot with many *l* — Jer 3:1 — 7453
thy *l* will despise thee, they — Jer 4:30 — 5689
for all thy *l* are destroyed — Jer 22:20 — 157
thy *l* shall go into captivity — Jer 22:22 — 157
All thy *l* have forgotten thee — Jer 30:14 — 157
among all her *l* she hath none to — Lam 1:2 — 157
I called for my *l*, but they — Lam 1:19 — 157
givest thy gifts to all thy *l* — Eze 16:33 — 157
through thy whoredoms with thy *l* — Eze 16:36 — 157
therefore I will gather all thy *l* — Eze 16:37 — 157
and she doted on her *l*, on the — Eze 23:5 — 157
her into the hand of her *l* — Eze 23:9 — 157
will raise up thy *l* against thee — Eze 23:22 — 157
she said, I will go after my *l* — Hos 2:5 — 157
And she shall follow after her *l* — Hos 2:7 — 157
lewdness in the sight of her *l* — Hos 2:10 — 157
rewards that my *l* have given me — Hos 2:12 — 157
jewels, and she went after her *l* — Hos 2:13 — 157
Ephraim hath hired *l* — Hos 8:9 — 158
For men shall be *l* of their own — 2Ti 3:2 — 5367
l of pleasures more than — 2Ti 3:4 — 5369
of pleasures more than *l* of God — 2Ti 3:4 — 5377

LOVE'S

Yet for *l* sake I rather beseech — Philem 9 — 26

LOVES

of Korah, A Maschil, A Song of *l* — Ps 45:*t* — 3039
let us solace ourselves with *l* — Prov 7:18 — 159
there will I give thee my *l* — Song 7:12 — 1730

LOVEST

thine only son Isaac, whom thou *l* — Gen 22:2 — 157
dost but hate me, and *l* me not — Judg 14:16 — 157
In that thou *l* thine enemies, and — 2Sa 19:6 — 157
Thou *l* righteousness, and hatest — Ps 45:7 — 157
Thou *l* evil more than good — Ps 52:3 — 157
Thou *l* all devouring words, O — Ps 52:4 — 157
with the wife whom thou *l* all the — Eccl 9:9 — 157
behold, he whom thou *l* is sick — Jn 11:3 — 5368
l thou me more than these — Jn 21:15 — 25
Simon, son of Jonas, *l* thou me — Jn 21:16 — 25
Simon, son of Jonas, *l* thou me — Jn 21:17 — 5368
him the third time, *L* thou me — Jn 21:17 — 5368

LOVETH

meat for thy father, such as he *l* — Gen 27:9 — 157
his mother, and his father *l* him — Gen 44:20 — 157
l the stranger, in giving him — Deut 10:18 — 157
because he *l* thee and thine house, — Deut 15:16 — 157
thy daughter in law, which *l* thee — Ruth 4:15 — 157

him that *l* violence his soul Ps 11:5 157
righteous LORD *l* righteousness Ps 11:7 157
He *l* righteousness and judgment Ps 33:5 157
l many days, that he may see good Ps 34:12 157
For the LORD *l* judgment, and Ps 37:28 157
The LORD *l* the gates of Zion more Ps 87:2 157
king's strength also *l* judgment Ps 99:4 157
therefore thy servant *l* it Ps 119:140 157
the LORD *l* the righteous Ps 146:8 157
For whom the LORD *l* he correcteth Prov 3:12 157
l instruction *l* knowledge Prov 12:1 157
but he that *l* him chasteneth him Prov 13:24 157
but he *l* him that followeth after Prov 15:9 157
A scorner *l* not one that Prov 15:12 157
A friend *l* at all times, and a Prov 17:17 157
He *l* transgression that Prov 17:19 157
transgression that *l* strife Prov 17:19 157
getteth wisdom *l* his own soul Prov 19:8 157
He that *l* pleasure shall be a Prov 21:17 157
he that *l* wine and oil shall not Prov 21:17 157
He that *l* pureness of heart, for Prov 22:11 157
Whoso *l* wisdom rejoiceth his Prov 29:3 157
He that *l* silver shall not be Eccl 5:10 157
nor he that *l* abundance with Eccl 5:10 157
Tell me, O thou whom my soul *l* Song 1:7 157
bed I sought him whom my soul *l* Song 3:1 157
I will seek him whom my soul *l* Song 3:2 157
I said, Saw ye him whom my soul *l* Song 3:3 157
but I found him whom my soul *l* Song 3:4 157
every one *l* gifts, and followeth Is 1:23 157
and *l* to tread out the corn Hos 10:11 157
he *l* to oppress Hos 12:7 157
He that *l* father or mother more Mt 10:37 *5368*
he that *l* son or daughter more Mt 10:37 *5368*
For he *l* our nation, and he hath Lk 7:5 *25*
is forgiven, the same *l* little Lk 7:47 *25*
The Father *l* the Son, and hath Jn 3:35 *25*
For the Father *l* the Son, and Jn 5:20 *5368*
He that *l* his life shall lose it Jn 12:25 *5368*
keepeth them, he it is that *l* me Jn 14:21 *25*
he that *l* me shall be loved of my Jn 14:21 *25*
He that *l* me not keepeth not my Jn 14:24 *25*
For the Father himself *l* you Jn 16:27 *5368*
for he that *l* another hath Rom 13:8 *25*
for God *l* a cheerful giver 2Cor 9:7 *25*
He that *l* his wife *l* himself Eph 5:28 *25*
For whom the Lord *l* he chasteneth Heb 12:6 *25*
He that *l* his brother abideth in 1Jn 2:10 *25*
neither he that *l* not his brother 1Jn 3:10 *25*
He that *l* not his brother abideth 1Jn 3:14 *25*
every one that *l* is born of God 1Jn 4:7 *25*
He that *l* not knoweth not God 1Jn 4:8 *25*
for he that *l* not his brother 1Jn 4:20 *25*
That he who *l* God love his 1Jn 4:21 *25*
every one that *l* him that begat 1Jn 5:1 *25*
l him also that is begotten of 1Jn 5:1 *25*
who *l* to have the preeminence 3Jn 9 *5383*
and idolaters, and whosoever *l* Rev 22:15 *5368*

LOVING
Let her be as the *l* hind and Prov 5:19 158
l favour rather than silver and Prov 22:1 2896
lying down, *l* to slumber Is 56:10 157

LOVINGKINDNESS
Shew thy marvellous *l*, O thou Ps 17:7 2617
For thy *l* is before mine eyes Ps 26:3 2617
How excellent is thy *l*, O God Ps 36:7 2617
O continue thy *l* unto them that Ps 36:10 2617
I have not concealed thy *l* Ps 40:10 2617
let thy *l* and thy truth Ps 40:11 2617
will command his *l* in the daytime Ps 42:8 2617
We have thought of thy *l*, O God, Ps 48:9 2617
me, O God, according to thy *l* Ps 51:1 2617
Because thy *l* is better than life Ps 63:3 2617
for thy *l* is good Ps 69:16 2617
Shall thy *l* be declared in the Ps 88:11 2617
Nevertheless my *l* will I not Ps 89:33 2617
shew forth thy *l* in the morning Ps 92:2 2617
who crowneth thee with *l* and Ps 103:4 2617
understand the *l* of the LORD Ps 107:43 2617
Quicken me after thy *l* Ps 119:88 2617
my voice according unto thy *l* Ps 119:149 2617
me, O LORD, according to thy *l* Ps 119:159 2617
and praise thy name for thy *l* Ps 138:2 2617
me to hear thy *l* in the morning Ps 143:8 2617
I am the LORD which exercise *l* Jer 9:24 2617
people, saith the LORD, even *l* Jer 16:5 2617
therefore with *l* have I drawn Jer 31:3 2617
Thou shewest *l* unto thousands, and Jer 32:18 2617
and in judgment, and in *l*, and in Hos 2:19 2617

LOVINGKINDNESSES
LORD, thy tender mercies and thy *l* Ps 25:6 2617
Lord, where are thy former *l* Ps 89:49 2617
I will mention the *l* of the LORD Is 63:7 2617
to the multitude of his *l* Is 63:7 2617

LOW
and thou shalt come down very *l* Deut 28:43 4295
thou hast brought me very *l* Judg 11:35 3766
he bringeth *l*, and lifteth up 1Sa 2:7 8213
the *l* plains was Baal-hanan the 1Chr 27:28 8219
are in the *l* plains in abundance 2Chr 9:27 8219
cattle, both in the *l* country 2Chr 26:10 8219
the cities of the *l* country 2Chr 28:18 8219
For the LORD brought Judah *l* 2Chr 28:19 3665
To set up on high those that be *l* Job 5:11 8217
and they are brought *l*, but he Job 14:21 6819
while, but are gone and brought *l* Job 24:24 4355
one that is proud, and bring him *l* Job 40:12 3665
Both *l* and high, rich and poor, Ps 49:2 120
Surely men of *l* degree are vanity Ps 62:9
for we are brought very *l* Ps 79:8 1809
were brought *l* for their iniquity Ps 106:43 4355
brought *l* through oppression, Ps 107:39 7817
I was brought *l*, and he helped me Ps 116:6 1809
Who remembered us in our *l* estate Ps 136:23 8213
for I am brought very *l* Ps 142:6 1809
A man's pride shall bring him *l* Prov 29:23 8213
and the rich sit in *l* place Eccl 10:6 8216
the sound of the grinding is *l* Eccl 12:4 8217
of musick shall be brought *l* Eccl 12:4 7817
and he shall be brought *l* Is 2:12 8213
of men shall be made *l* Is 2:17 8213
will lay *l* the haughtiness of the Is 13:11 8213
terrible ones shall be brought *l* Is 25:5 6030
walls shall he bring down, lay *l* Is 25:12 8213
the lofty city, he layeth it *l* Is 26:5 8213
he layeth it *l*, even to the Is 26:5 8213
speech shall be *l* out of the dust Is 29:4 7817
city shall be *l* in a *l* place Is 32:19 8213
city shall be *l* in a *l* place Is 32:19 8219
mountain and hill shall be made *l* Is 40:4 8213
O LORD, out of the *l* dungeon Lam 3:55 8482
a spreading vine of *l* stature Eze 17:6 8217
tree, have exalted the *l* tree Eze 17:24 8217
exalt him that is *l*, and abase him Eze 21:26 8217
thee in the *l* parts of the earth Eze 26:20 8482
the *l* estate of his handmaiden Lk 1:48 *5014*
and exalted them of *l* degree Lk 1:52 *5011*
and hill shall be brought *l* Lk 3:5 *5013*
but condescend to men of *l* estate Rom 12:16 *5011*
Let the brother of *l* degree Jas 1:9 *5011*
the rich, in that he is made *l* Jas 1:10 *5014*

LOWER
with *l*, second, and third stories Gen 6:16 8482
it be in sight *l* than the skin Lev 13:20 8217
if it be not *l* than the skin, but Lev 13:21 8217
it be no *l* than the other skin, Lev 13:26 8217
in sight are *l* than the wall Lev 14:37 8217
I in the *l* places behind the wall Neh 4:13 8482
him a little *l* than the angels Ps 8:5 2637
shall go into the *l* parts of the Ps 63:9 8482
l in the presence of the prince Prov 25:7 8213
together the waters of the *l* pool Is 22:9 8481
shout, ye *l* parts of the earth Is 44:23 8482
of the gates was the *l* pavement Eze 40:18 8481
from the forefront of the *l* gate Eze 40:19 8481
higher than these, than the *l* Eze 42:5 8481
the *l* settle shall be two cubits Eze 43:14 8481
into the *l* parts of the earth Eph 4:9 *2737*
him a little *l* than the angels Heb 2:7 *1642*
who was made a little *l* than the Heb 2:9 *1642*

LOWEST
and shall burn unto the *l* hell Deut 32:22 8482
priests of the *l* of the people 1Kin 12:31 7098
but made again of the *l* of the 1Kin 13:33 7098
the *l* of them priests of the high 2Kin 17:32 7098
delivered my soul from the *l* hell Ps 86:13 8482
Thou hast laid me in the *l* pit Ps 88:6 8482
in the *l* parts of the earth Ps 139:15 8482
so increased from the *l* chamber Eze 41:7 8481
was straitened more than the *l* Eze 42:6 8481
with shame to take the *l* room Lk 14:9 *2078*
go and sit down in the *l* room Lk 14:10 *2078*

LOWETH
or *l* the ox over his fodder Job 6:5 1600

LOWING
l as they went, and turned not 1Sa 6:12 1600
the *l* of the oxen which I hear 1Sa 15:14 6963

LOWLINESS
With all *l* and meekness, with Eph 4:2 *5012*
but in *l* of mind let each esteem Phil 2:3 *5012*

LOWLY
yet hath he respect unto the *l* Ps 138:6 8217
but he giveth grace unto the *l* Prov 3:34 6041
but with the *l* is wisdom Prov 11:2 6800
be of an humble spirit with the *l* Prov 16:19 6041
l, and riding upon an ass, and upon Zec 9:9 6041
for I am meek and *l* in heart Mt 11:29 *5011*

LOWRING
for the sky is red and *l* Mt 16:3 *4768*

LUBIM (*lu'-bim*) See LUBIMS. *An African race.*
the *L*, the Sukkiims, and the 2Chr 12:3 3864
Put and *L* were thy helpers Nah 3:9 3864

LUBIMS (*lu'-bims*) See LEHABIM, LUBIM. *Same as Lubim.*
the *L* a huge host, with very many 2Chr 16:8 3864

LUCAS (*lu'-cas*) See LUKE. *Same as Luke.*
city of Macedonia, by Titus and *L* 2Cor s *3065*
Marcus, Aristarchus, Demas, *L* Philem 24 *3065*

LUCIFER (*lu'-sif-ur*) *Title applied to king of Babylon.*
art thou fallen from heaven, O *L* Is 14:12 1966

LUCIUS (*lu'-she-us*)
1. A Christian from Cyrene.
L of Cyrene, and Manaen, which had Acts 13:1 *3066*
2. A relative of Paul.
Timotheus my workfellow, and *L* Rom 16:21 *3066*

LUCRE
ways, but turned aside after *l* 1Sa 8:3 1215
striker, not greedy of filthy *l* 1Ti 3:3 *866*
much wine, not greedy of filthy *l* 1Ti 3:8 *146*
no striker, not given to filthy *l* Titus 1:7 *146*
not for filthy *l*, but of a ready 1Pet 5:2 *147*

LUCRE'S
they ought not, for filthy *l* sake Titus 1:11 *2771*

LUD (*lud*) See LUDIM, LYDIA.
1. Son of Shem.
and Asshur, and Arphaxad, and *L* Gen 10:22 3865
and Asshur, and Arphaxad, and *L* 1Chr 1:17 3865
2. Descendants of Lud 1.
nations, to Tarshish, Pul, and *L* Is 66:19 3865
They of Persia and of *L* and of Phut Eze 27:10 3865

LUDIM (*lu'-dim*) See LUD. *Son of Mizraim.*
And Mizraim begat *L* Gen 10:13 3866
And Mizraim begat *L* 1Chr 1:11 3866

LUHITH (*lu'-hith*) *A Moabite city.*
for by the mounting up of *L* with Is 15:5 3872
For in the going up of *L* Jer 48:5 3872

LUKE (*luke*) See LUCAS. *A companion of Paul.*
L, the beloved physician, and Col 4:14 *3065*
Only *L* is with me 2Ti 4:11 *3065*

LUKEWARM
So then because thou art *l* Rev 3:16 *5513*

LUMP
And Isaiah said, Take a *l* of figs 2Kin 20:7 1690
said, Let them take a *l* of figs Is 38:21 1690
of the same *l* to make one vessel Rom 9:21 *5445*
be holy, the *l* is also holy Rom 11:16 *5445*
leaven leaveneth the whole *l* 1Cor 5:6 *5445*
leaven, that ye may be a new *l* 1Cor 5:7 *5445*
leaven leaveneth the whole *l* Gal 5:9 *5445*

LUNATICK
devils, and those which were *l* Mt 4:24 *4583*
for he is *l*, and sore vexed Mt 17:15 *4583*

LURK
let us *l* privily for the innocent Prov 1:11 6845
they *l* privily for their own Prov 1:18 6845

LURKING
take knowledge of all the *l* 1Sa 23:23 4224
He sitteth in the *l* places of the Ps 10:8 3993
a young lion *l* in secret places Ps 17:12 3427

LUST
my *l* shall be satisfied upon them Ex 15:9 5315
heart by asking meat for their *l* Ps 78:18 5315
were not estranged from their *l* Ps 78:30 8378
them up unto their own hearts' *l* Ps 81:12 8307
L not after her beauty in thine Prov 6:25 2530
to *l* after her hath committed Mt 5:28 *1937*
burned in their *l* one toward Rom 1:27 *3715*
for I had not known *l*, except the Rom 7:7 *1939*
we should not *l* after evil things 1Cor 10:6
not fulfil the *l* of the flesh Gal 5:16 *1939*
Not in the *l* of concupiscence, 1Th 4:5 *3806*
he is drawn away of his own *l* Jas 1:14 *1939*
Then when *l* hath conceived, it Jas 1:15 *1939*
Ye *l*, and have not Jas 4:2 *1937*
that is in the world through *l* 2Pet 1:4 *1939*
the flesh in the *l* of uncleanness 2Pet 2:10 *1939*
the *l* of the flesh 1Jn 2:16 *1939*
the *l* of the eyes, and the pride 1Jn 2:16 *1939*
passeth away, and the *l* thereof 1Jn 2:17 *1939*

LUSTED
they buried the people that *l* Num 11:34 183
But *l* exceedingly in the Ps 106:14 183
after evil things, as they also *l* 1Cor 10:6 *1937*
the fruits that thy soul *l* after Rev 18:14 *1937*

LUSTETH
whatsoever thy soul *l* after Deut 12:15 183
whatsoever thy soul *l* after Deut 12:20 183
gates whatsoever thy soul *l* after Deut 12:21 183
for whatsoever thy soul *l* after Deut 14:26 183
For the flesh *l* against the Gal 5:17 *1937*
that dwelleth in us *l* to envy Jas 4:5 *1971*

LUSTING
that was among them fell a *l* Num 11:4 8378

LUSTS
the *l* of other things entering in Mk 4:19 *1939*
the *l* of your father ye will do Jn 8:44 *1939*
through the *l* of their own hearts Rom 1:24 *1939*
should obey it in the *l* thereof Rom 6:12 *1939*
flesh, to fulfil the *l* thereof Rom 13:14 *1939*
flesh with the affections and *l* Gal 5:24 *1939*
times past in the *l* of our flesh Eph 2:3 *1939*
according to the deceitful *l* Eph 4:22 *1939*
and into many foolish and hurtful *l* 1Ti 6:9 *1939*
Flee also youthful *l* 2Ti 2:22 *1939*
with sins, led away with divers *l* 2Ti 3:6 *1939*
but after their own *l* shall they 2Ti 4:3 *1939*
denying ungodliness and worldly *l* Titus 2:12 *1939*
deceived, serving divers *l* Titus 3:3 *1939*
even of your *l* that war in your Jas 4:1 *2237*
ye may consume it upon your *l* Jas 4:3 *2237*
to the former *l* in your ignorance 1Pet 1:14 *1939*
pilgrims, abstain from fleshly *l* 1Pet 2:11 *1939*
time in the flesh to the *l* of men 1Pet 4:2 *1939*
we walked in lasciviousness, *l* 1Pet 4:3 *1939*
allure through the *l* of the flesh 2Pet 2:18 *1939*
walking after their own *l* 2Pet 3:3 *1939*
walking after their own *l* Jude 16 *1939*
walk after their own ungodly *l* Jude 18 *1939*

LUSTY
about ten thousand men, all *l* Judg 3:29 8082

LUZ (*luz*) See BETH-EL.
1. A Canaanite city.
city was called *L* at the first Gen 28:19 3870
So Jacob came to *L*, which is in Gen 35:6 3870
me at *L* in the land of Canaan Gen 48:3 3870
And goeth out from Beth-el to *L* Josh 16:2 3870
toward *L*, to the side of *L* Josh 18:13 3870
the name of the city before was *L* Judg 1:23 3870
2. A Hittite city.
and called the name thereof *L* Judg 1:26 3870

LYCAONIA *(li-ca-o'-ne-ah) A Roman province in Asia Minor.*
unto Lystra and Derbe, cities of *L* ... Acts 14:6 *3071*
voices, saying in the speech of *L* ... Acts 14:11 *3071*

LYCAONIAN See LYCAONIA.

LYCIA *(lish'-e-ah) A Roman province in Asia Minor.*
we came to Myra, a city of *L* ... Acts 27:5 *3073*

LYDDA *(lid'-dah)* See LOD. *A city in Judea.*
to the saints which dwelt at *L* ... Acts 9:32 *3069*
And all that dwelt at *L* and Saron ... Acts 9:35 *3069*
forasmuch as *L* was nigh to Joppa, ... Acts 9:38 *3069*

LYDIA *(lid'-e-ah)* See LUDIM, LYDIANS.
1. A people in North Africa.
Ethiopia, and Libya, and *L*, and all ... Eze 30:5 3865
2. A Christian woman.
And a certain woman named *L* ... Acts 16:14 *3070*
and entered into the house of *L* ... Acts 16:40 *3070*

LYDIANS *(lid'-e-uns) Same as Lydia 1.*
and the *L*, that handle and bend the ... Jer 46:9 3866

LYING
three flocks of sheep *l* by it ... Gen 29:2 7257
Israel in *l* with Jacob's daughter ... Gen 34:7 7901
hateth thee *l* under his burden ... Ex 23:5 7257
that hath known man by *l* with him ... Num 31:17 4904
not known a man by *l* with him ... Num 31:18 4904
had not known man by *l* with him ... Num 31:35 4904
l in the field, and it be not ... Deut 21:1 5307
If a man be found *l* with a woman ... Deut 22:22 7901
were with him, from *l* in wait ... Judg 9:35
Now there were men *l* in wait ... Judg 16:9
known no man by *l* with any male ... Judg 21:12 4904
I will be a *l* spirit in the mouth ... 1Kin 22:22 8267
the LORD hath put a *l* spirit in ... 1Kin 22:23 8267
be a *l* spirit in the mouth of all ... 2Chr 18:21 8267
the LORD hath put a *l* spirit in ... 2Chr 18:22 8267
hated them that regard *l* vanities ... Ps 31:6 7723
Let the *l* lips be put to silence ... Ps 31:18 8267
and *l* rather than to speak ... Ps 52:3 8267
for cursing and *l* which they speak ... Ps 59:12 3585
spoken against me with a *l* tongue ... Ps 109:2 8267
Remove from me the way of *l* ... Ps 119:29 8267
I hate and abhor *l* ... Ps 119:163 8267
my soul, O LORD, from *l* lips ... Ps 120:2 8267
my *l* down, and art acquainted with ... Ps 139:3 7252
a *l* tongue, and hands that shed ... Prov 6:17 8267
He that hideth hatred with *l* lips ... Prov 10:18 8267
but a *l* tongue is but for a ... Prov 12:19 8267
L lips are abomination to the ... Prov 12:22 8267
A righteous man hateth *l* ... Prov 13:5
much less do *l* lips a prince ... Prov 17:7 8267
a *l* tongue is a vanity tossed to ... Prov 21:6 8267
A *l* tongue hateth those that are ... Prov 26:28 8267
l children, children that will ... Is 30:9 3586
to destroy the poor with *l* words ... Is 32:7 8267
l down, loving to slumber ... Is 56:10 7901
l against the LORD, and departing ... Is 59:13 3584
Trust ye not in *l* words, saying, ... Jer 7:4 8267
Behold, ye trust in *l* words ... Jer 7:8 8267
have spoken *l* words in my name, ... Jer 29:23 8267
was unto me as a bear *l* in wait ... Lam 3:10
l divination, saying, The LORD ... Eze 13:6 3577
have ye not spoken a *l* divination ... Eze 13:7 3577
by your *l* to my people that hear ... Eze 13:19 3576
for ye have prepared *l* and corrupt ... Dan 2:9 3538
By swearing, and *l*, and killing, and ... Hos 4:2 3584
They that observe *l* vanities ... Jonah 2:8 7723
man sick of the palsy, *l* on a bed ... Mt 9:2 *906*
in where the damsel was *l* ... Mk 5:40 *345*
swaddling clothes, *l* in a manger ... Lk 2:12 *2749*
Joseph, and the babe *l* in a manger ... Lk 2:16 *2749*
He then *l* on Jesus' breast saith ... Jn 13:25 *1968*
in, saw the linen clothes *l* ... Jn 20:5 *2749*
not *l* with the linen clothes, but ... Jn 20:7 *2749*
me by the *l* in wait of the Jews ... Acts 20:19
son heard of their *l* in wait ... Acts 23:16
Wherefore putting away *l*, speak ... Eph 4:25 *5579*
all power and signs and *l* wonders, ... 2Th 2:9 *5579*

LYSANIAS *(li-sa'-ne-as) Governor of Abilene.*
L the tetrarch of Abilene, ... Lk 3:1 *3078*

LYSIAS *(lis'-e-as) A Roman commander.*
Claudius *L* unto the most ... Acts 23:26 *3079*
the chief captain *L* came upon us ... Acts 24:7 *3079*
When *L* the chief captain shall ... Acts 24:22 *3079*

LYSTRA *(lis'-trah) A city in Lycaonia.*
were ware of it, and fled unto *L* ... Acts 14:6 *3082*
And there sat a certain man at *L* ... Acts 14:8 *3082*
many, they returned again to *L* ... Acts 14:21 *3082*
Then came he to Derbe and *L* ... Acts 16:1 *3082*
of by the brethren that were at *L* ... Acts 16:2 *3082*
me at Antioch, at Iconium, at *L* ... 2Ti 3:11 *3082*

M

MAACAH *(ma'-a-kah)* See MAACHAH.
1. A wife of David.
Absalom the son of *M* the daughter ... 2Sa 3:3 4601
2. A king of Maacah 3.
of king *M* a thousand men, and of ... 2Sa 10:6 4601
3. A district of Syria.
and of Rehob, and Ish-tob, and *M* ... 2Sa 10:8 4601

MAACATH See MAACHATHITES.

MAACATHITE See MAACHATHITE.

MAACHAH *(ma'-a-kah)* See BETH-MAACHAH, MAACAH, MAACHATHITE, SYRIA-MAACHAH.
1. A son of Nahor.
Gaham, and Thahash, and *M* ... Gen 22:24 4601
2. Father of Achish.
unto Achish son of *M* king of Gath ... 1Kin 2:39 4601
3. Wife of King Rehoboam.
And his mother's name was *M* ... 1Kin 15:2 4601
And his mother's name was *M* ... 1Kin 15:10 4601
after her he took *M* the daughter ... 2Chr 11:20 4601
Rehoboam loved *M* the daughter of ... 2Chr 11:21 4601
Abijah the son of *M* the chief ... 2Chr 11:22 4601
4. Mother of King Asa.
also *M* his mother, even her he ... 1Kin 15:13 4601
also concerning *M* the mother of ... 2Chr 15:16 4601
5. Concubine of Caleb.
M, Caleb's concubine, bare Sheber ... 1Chr 2:48 4601
6. A wife of David.
Absalom the son of *M* the daughter ... 1Chr 3:2 4601
7. A wife of Machir.
whose sister's name was *M* ... 1Chr 7:15 4601
M the wife of Machir bare a son, ... 1Chr 7:16 4601
8. Wife of Jehiel.
whose wife's name was *M* ... 1Chr 8:29 4601
Jehiel, whose wife's name was *M* ... 1Chr 9:35 4601
9. Father of Hanan.
Hanan the son of *M*, and Joshaphat ... 1Chr 11:43 4601
10. A district of Syria.
chariots, and the king of *M* ... 1Chr 19:7 4601
11. Father of Shephatiah.
Shephatiah the son of *M* ... 1Chr 27:16 4601

MAACHATHI *(ma-ak'-a-thi)* See MAACHATHITE. *Inhabitants of Maachah 10.*
unto the coasts of Geshuri and *M* ... Deut 3:14 4602

MAACHATHITE *(ma-ak'-a-thite)* See MAACHATHI, MAACHATHITES. *Same as Maachathi.*
son of Ahasbai, the son of the *M* ... 2Sa 23:34 4602
and Jaazaniah the son of a *M* ... 2Kin 25:23 4602
the Garmite, and Eshtemoa the *M* ... 1Chr 4:19 4602
and Jezaniah the son of a *M* ... Jer 40:8 4602

MAACHATHITES
border of the Geshurites and the *M* ... Josh 12:5 4602
the border of the Geshurites and *M* ... Josh 13:11 4602
not the Geshurites, nor the *M* ... Josh 13:13 4602
the *M* dwell among the Israelites ... Josh 13:13 4602

MAADAI *(ma'-a-dahee) Married a foreigner in exile.*
M, Amram, and Uel, ... Ezr 10:34 4572

MAADIAH *(ma-a-di'-ah)* See MOADIAH. *A priest with Zerubbabel.*
Miamin, *M*, Bilgah, ... Neh 12:5 4573

MAAI *(ma'-ahee) A priest.*
and Azarael, Milalai, Gilalai, *M* ... Neh 12:36 4597

MAALEH-ACRABBIM *(ma'-a-leh-ac-rab'-bim)* See AKRABBIM. *A pass on Judah's southern border.*
went out to the south side to *M* ... Josh 15:3 4610

MAARATH *(ma'-a-rath) A city in Judah.*
And *M*, and Beth-anoth, and Eltekon ... Josh 15:59 4638

MAAREH-GEBA See GIBEAH.

MAASAI See MAASIAI.

MAASEIAH *(ma-a-si'-ah)*
1. A priest who relocated the Ark.
and Unni, Eliab, and Benaiah, and *M* ... 1Chr 15:18 4641
Jehiel, and Unni, and Eliab, and *M* ... 1Chr 15:20 4641
2. Son of Adaiah.
Obed, and *M* the son of Adaiah, and ... 2Chr 23:1 4641
3. An officer of King Uzziah.
M the ruler, under the hand of ... 2Chr 26:11 4641
4. A son of King Ahaz.
slew *M* the king's son, and Azrikam ... 2Chr 28:7 4641
5. A governor of Jerusalem.
M the governor of the city, and ... 2Chr 34:8 4641
6. A priest who married a foreigner.
M, and Eliezer, and Jarib, and ... Ezr 10:18 4641
7. A priest of the Harim family.
M, and Elijah, and Shemaiah, and ... Ezr 10:21 4641
8. A priest of the Pashur family.
Elioenai, *M*, Ishmael, Nethaneel, ... Ezr 10:22 4641
9. A priest of the Pahath-moab family.
Adna, and Chelal, Benaiah, *M* ... Ezr 10:30 4641
10. Father of Azariah.
M the son of Ananiah by his house ... Neh 3:23 4641
11. A priest with Ezra.
and Urijah, and Hilkiah, and *M* ... Neh 8:4 4641
12. Another priest with Ezra.
Akkub, Shabbethai, Hodijah, *M* ... Neh 8:7 4641
13. An Israelite who renewed the covenant.
Rehum, Hashabnah, *M*, ... Neh 10:25 4641
14. A family of exiles.
M the son of Baruch, the son of ... Neh 11:5 4641
15. A descendant of Benjamin.
the son of Kolaiah, the son of *M* ... Neh 11:7 4641
16. A priest who dedicated the wall.
Eliakim, *M*, Miniamin, Michaiah, ... Neh 12:41 4641
17. Another priest who dedicated the wall.
And *M*, and Shemaiah, and ... Neh 12:42 4641
18. Father of Zephaniah.
Zephaniah the son of *M* the priest ... Jer 21:1 4641
Zephaniah the son of *M* the priest ... Jer 29:25 4641
Zephaniah the son of *M* the priest ... Jer 37:3 4641
19. Father of Zedekiah.
and of Zedekiah the son of *M* ... Jer 29:21 4641
20. A Temple officer.
chamber of *M* the son of Shallum ... Jer 35:4 4641
21. Grandfather of Baruch.
the son of Neriah, the son of *M* ... Jer 32:12 4271
the son of Neriah, the son of *M* ... Jer 51:59 4271

MAASIAI *(ma-a'-see-ahee) A family of exiles.*
M the son of Adiel, the son of ... 1Chr 9:12 4640

MAATH *(ma'-ath) Father of Nagge; ancestor of Jesus.*
Which was the son of *M*, which was ... Lk 3:26 *3092*

MAAZ *(ma'-az) A son of Ram.*
firstborn of Jerahmeel were, *M* ... 1Chr 2:27 4619

MAAZIAH *(ma-a-zi'-ah)*
1. A sanctuary servant.
the four and twentieth to *M* ... 1Chr 24:18 4590
2. A priest who renewed the covenant.
M, Bilgai, Shemaiah ... Neh 10:8 4590

MACBENNAH See MACHBENAH.

MACEDONIA *(mas-e-do'-nee-ah)* See MACEDONIAN. *A Roman province north of Greece.*
There stood a man of *M*, and prayed ... Acts 16:9 *3110*
him, saying, Come over into *M* ... Acts 16:9 *3109*
we endeavoured to go into *M* ... Acts 16:10 *3109*
the chief city of that part of *M* ... Acts 16:12 *3109*
and Timotheus were come from *M* ... Acts 18:5 *3109*
when he had passed through *M* ... Acts 19:21 *3109*
So he sent into *M* two of them ... Acts 19:22 *3109*
Gaius and Aristarchus, men of *M* ... Acts 19:29 *3110*
and departed for to go into *M* ... Acts 20:1 *3109*
he purposed to return through *M* ... Acts 20:3 *3109*
For it hath pleased them of *M* ... Rom 15:26 *3109*
you, when I shall pass through *M* ... 1Cor 16:5 *3109*
for I do pass through *M* ... 1Cor 16:5 *3109*
And to pass by you into *M* ... 2Cor 1:16 *3109*
to come again out of *M* unto you ... 2Cor 1:16 *3109*
them, I went from thence into *M* ... 2Cor 2:13 *3109*
For, when we were come into *M* ... 2Cor 7:5 *3109*
God bestowed on the churches of *M* ... 2Cor 8:1 *3109*
which I boast of you to them of *M* ... 2Cor 9:2 *3110*
haply if they of *M* come with me ... 2Cor 9:4 *3110*
which came from *M* supplied ... 2Cor 11:9 *3109*
from Philippi, a city of *M* ... 2Cor *s* *3109*
gospel, when I departed from *M* ... Phil 4:15 *3109*
to all that believe in *M* and ... 1Th 1:7 *3109*
word of the Lord not only in *M* ... 1Th 1:8 *3109*
the brethren which are in all *M* ... 1Th 4:10 *3109*
at Ephesus, when I went into *M* ... 1Ti 1:3 *3109*
the Cretians, from Nicopolis of *M* ... Titus *s* *3109*

MACEDONIAN *(mas-e-do'-nee-an) An inhabitant of Macedonia.*
a *M* of Thessalonica, being with ... Acts 27:2 *3110*

MACHBANAI *(mak'-ba-nahee) A warrior in David's army.*
the tenth, *M* the eleventh ... 1Chr 12:13 4344

MACHBANNAI See MACEBANAI.

MACHBENA See MACHBENAH.

MACHBENAH *(mak'-be-nah) A descendant of Caleb.*
Madmannah, Sheva the father of *M* ... 1Chr 2:49 4343

MACHI *(ma'-ki) Father of Geuel.*
tribe of Gad, Geuel the son of *M* ... Num 13:15 4352

MACHIR *(ma'-kur)* See MACHIRITE.
1. Son of Manasseh.
the children also of *M* the son of ... Gen 50:23 4353
of *M*, the family of the ... Num 26:29 4353
and *M* begat Gilead ... Num 26:29 4353
the son of Gilead, the son of *M* ... Num 27:1 4353
the children of *M* the son of ... Num 32:39 4353
Gilead unto *M* the son of Manasseh ... Num 32:40 4353
children of Gilead, the son of *M* ... Num 36:1 4353
And I gave Gilead unto *M* ... Deut 3:15 4353
children of *M* the son of Manasseh ... Josh 13:31 4353
children of *M* by their families ... Josh 13:31 4353
for *M* the firstborn of Manasseh, ... Josh 17:1 4353
the son of Gilead, the son of *M* ... Josh 17:3 4353
out of *M* came down governors, and ... Judg 5:14 4353
of *M* the father of Gilead ... 1Chr 2:21 4353
sons of *M* the father of Gilead ... 1Chr 2:23 4353
bare *M* the father of Gilead ... 1Chr 7:14 4353
M took to wife the sister of ... 1Chr 7:15 4353

Maachah the wife of *M* bare a son 1Chr 7:16 4353
the sons of Gilead, the son of *M*........... 1Chr 7:17 4353
2. Son of Ammiel.
Behold, he is in the house of *M*............ 2Sa 9:4 4353
fetched him out of the house of *M*.......... 2Sa 9:5 4353
M the son of Ammiel of Lo-debar,........ 2Sa 17:27 4353

MACHIRITES (*ma'-kur-ites*) *Descendants of Machir 1.*
of Machir, the family of the *M*.............. Num 26:29 4354

MACHNADEBAI (*mak-nad'-e-bahee*) *Married a foreigner in exile.*
M, Shashai, Sharai,.................................. Ezr 10:40 4367

MACHPELAH (*mak-pe'-lah*) *Burial place of Abraham.*
That he may give me the cave of *M*...... Gen 23:9 4375
field of Ephron, which was in *M*.......... Gen 23:17 4375
of the field of *M* before Mamre............. Gen 23:19 4375
buried him in the cave of *M*.................. Gen 25:9 4375
cave that is in the field of *M*............... Gen 49:30 4375
him in the cave of the field of *M*........... Gen 50:13 4375

MAD
So that thou shalt be *m* for the............. Deut 28:34 7696
feigned himself *m* in their hands........... 1Sa 21:13 1984
servants, Lo, ye see the man is *m*......... 1Sa 21:14 7696
Have I need of *m* men, that ye.............. 1Sa 21:15 7696
to play the *m* man in my presence......... 1Sa 21:15 7696
came this *m* fellow to thee..................... 2Kin 9:11 7696
they that are *m* against me are.............. Ps 102:8 1984
As a *m* man who casteth firebrands..... Prov 26:18 3856
I said of laughter, It is *m*...................... Eccl 2:2 1984
oppression maketh a wise man *m*........... Eccl 7:7 1984
the liars, and maketh diviners *m*........... Is 44:25 1984
shall drink, and be moved, and be *m*..... Jer 25:16 1984
the LORD, for every man that is *m*......... Jer 29:26 7696
they are *m* upon their idols.................. Jer 50:38 1984
therefore the nations are *m*................... Jer 51:7 1984
is a fool, the spiritual man is *m*............ Hos 9:7 7696
said, He hath a devil, and is *m*.............. Jn 10:20 *3105*
And they said unto her, Thou art *m*..... Acts 12:15 *3105*
being exceedingly *m* against them........ Acts 26:11 *1693*
much learning doth make thee *m*......... Acts 26:24
But he said, I am not *m*, most.............. Acts 26:25 *3105*
will they not say that ye are *m*............. 1Cor 14:23 *3105*

MADAI (*ma'-dahee*) See MEDE, MEDIA. *Son of Japheth.*
Gomer, and Magog, and *M*..................... Gen 10:2 4074
Gomer, and Magog, and *M*..................... 1Chr 1:5 4074

MADE
God *m* the firmament, and divided .... Gen 1:7 6213
And God *m* two great lights.................. Gen 1:16 6213
he *m* the stars also.................................. Gen 1:16
God *m* the beast of the earth................ Gen 1:25 6213
God saw every thing that he had *m*...... Gen 1:31 6213
God ended his work which he had *m*.... Gen 2:2 6213
from all his work which he had *m*......... Gen 2:2 6213
his work which God created and *m*....... Gen 2:3 6213
day that the LORD God *m* the earth...... Gen 2:4 6213
out of the ground *m* the LORD God ...... Gen 2:9
m he a woman, and brought her unto. Gen 2:22 1129
field which the LORD God had *m*........... Gen 3:1 6213
together, and *m* themselves aprons ...... Gen 3:7 6213
in the likeness of God *m* he him........... Gen 5:1 6213
that he had *m* man on the earth........... Gen 6:6 6213
repenteth me that I have *m* them.......... Gen 6:7 6213
m will I destroy from off the .... Gen 7:4 6213
God *m* a wind to pass over the............. Gen 8:1
window of the ark which he had *m*....... Gen 8:6 6213
for in the image of God *m* he man......... Gen 9:6 6213
which he had *m* there at the first.......... Gen 13:4 6213
That these *m* war with Bera king.......... Gen 14:2 6213
say, I have *m* Abram rich....................... Gen 14:23 6213
the LORD *m* a covenant with Abram..... Gen 15:18 3772
of many nations have I *m* thee............... Gen 17:5 5414
he *m* them a feast, and did bake .... Gen 19:3 6213
they *m* their father drink wine.............. Gen 19:33
they *m* their father drink wine.............. Gen 19:35
God hath *m* me to laugh, so that.......... Gen 21:6
Abraham *m* a great feast the same...... Gen 21:8 6213
and both of them *m* a covenant............. Gen 21:27 3772
Thus they *m* a covenant at.................... Gen 21:32 3772
borders round about, were *m* sure .... Gen 23:17
were *m* sure unto Abraham for a......... Gen 23:20
he *m* his camels to kneel down............. Gen 24:11
to wit whether the LORD had *m* his...... Gen 24:21 6743
And my master *m* me swear, saying,.... Gen 24:37
she *m* haste, and let down her.............. Gen 24:46
she *m* the camels drink also .... Gen 24:46
now the LORD hath *m* room for us........ Gen 26:22
he *m* them a feast, and they did.......... Gen 26:30 6213
his mother *m* savoury meat, such......... Gen 27:14 6213
as soon as Isaac had *m* an end of......... Gen 27:30
he also had *m* savoury meat, and......... Gen 27:31 6213
I have *m* him thy lord, and all his......... Gen 27:37 7760
men of the place, and *m* a feast............ Gen 29:22 6213
m the white appear which was in .... Gen 30:37
and they took stones, and *m* an heap .. Gen 31:46 6213
house, and *m* booths for his cattle........ Gen 33:17 6213
he *m* him a coat of many colours......... Gen 37:3 6213
about, and *m* obeisance to my sheaf.... Gen 37:7
eleven stars *m* obeisance to me............ Gen 37:9
that the LORD *m* all that he did............ Gen 39:3
he *m* him overseer over his house,........ Gen 39:4
had *m* him overseer in his house.......... Gen 39:5
he did, the LORD *m* it to prosper........... Gen 39:23
that he *m* a feast unto all his................. Gen 40:20 6213
he *m* him to ride in the second............. Gen 41:43
he *m* him ruler over all the land........... Gen 41:43 5414
hath *m* me forget all my toil, and .... Gen 41:51
but *m* himself strange unto them,......... Gen 42:7
they *m* ready the present against.......... Gen 43:25
down their heads, and *m* obeisance...... Gen 43:28

And Joseph *m* haste................................ Gen 43:30
while Joseph *m* himself known unto.... Gen 45:1
he hath *m* me a father to Pharaoh,....... Gen 45:8 7760
God hath *m* me lord of all Egypt.......... Gen 45:9 7760
Joseph *m* ready his chariot, and........... Gen 46:29
Joseph *m* it a law over the land............ Gen 47:26 7760
were *m* strong by the hands of the...... Gen 49:24
when Jacob had *m* an end of .... Gen 49:33
My father *m* me swear, saying, Lo,...... Gen 50:5
according as he *m* thee swear.............. Gen 50:6
he *m* a mourning for his father............. Gen 50:10 6213
the Egyptians *m* the children of .... Ex 1:13
they *m* their lives bitter with................. Ex 1:14
wherein they *m* them serve .... Ex 1:14
feared God, that he *m* them houses...... Ex 1:21 6213
Who *m* thee a prince and a judge.......... Ex 2:14 7760
unto him, Who hath *m* man's mouth... Ex 4:11 7760
because ye have *m* our savour to.......... Ex 5:21
I have *m* thee a god to Pharaoh .... Ex 7:1 5414
of Pharaoh *m* his servants..................... Ex 9:20
he *m* ready his chariot, and took........... Ex 14:6
m the sea dry land, and the waters....... Ex 14:21 7760
which thou hast *m* for thee to .... Ex 15:17 6466
waters, the waters were *m* sweet.......... Ex 15:25
there he *m* for them a statute and........ Ex 15:25 7760
it was like wafers *m* with honey............ Ex 16:31
m them heads over the people,............. Ex 18:25 5414
For in six days the LORD *m* heaven ...... Ex 20:11 6213
which the LORD hath *m* with you .... Ex 24:8 3772
work shall the candlestick be *m*........... Ex 25:31 6213
Three bowls *m* like unto almonds,......... Ex 25:33
three bowls *m* like almonds in the........ Ex 25:33
be four bowls *m* like unto almonds....... Ex 25:34
with cherubims shall it be *m*................. Ex 26:31 6213
an offering *m* by fire unto the............... Ex 29:18
it is an offering *m* by fire unto............. Ex 29:25
wherewith the atonement was *m*........... Ex 29:33
when thou hast *m* an atonement for..... Ex 29:36
an offering *m* by fire unto the............... Ex 29:41
to burn offering *m* by fire unto .... Ex 30:20
for in six days the LORD *m* heaven .... Ex 31:17 6213
when he had *m* an end of communing ... Ex 31:18
after he had *m* it a molten calf............. Ex 32:4 6213
Aaron *m* proclamation, and said, To..... Ex 32:5
they have *m* them a molten calf,........... Ex 32:8 6213
he took the calf which they had *m*......... Ex 32:20 6213
m the children of Israel drink of .... Ex 32:20
(for Aaron had *m* them naked unto...... Ex 32:25
sin, and have *m* them gods of gold .... Ex 32:31 6213
they *m* the calf, which Aaron *m*............ Ex 32:35 6213
And Moses *m* haste, and bowed his...... Ex 34:8
I have *m* a covenant with thee............. Ex 34:27 3772
one whom his spirit *m* willing.............. Ex 35:21
whose heart *m* them willing to.............. Ex 35:29
to be *m* by the hand of Moses............... Ex 35:29 6213
man from his work which they *m*........... Ex 36:4 6213
the work of the tabernacle *m* ten.......... Ex 36:8 6213
of cunning work *m* he them.................. Ex 36:8 6213
he *m* loops of blue on the edge of......... Ex 36:11 6213
likewise he *m* in the uttermost .... Ex 36:11 6213
Fifty loops *m* he in one curtain,............ Ex 36:12 6213
fifty loops *m* he in the edge of.............. Ex 36:12 6213
he *m* fifty taches of gold, and................ Ex 36:13 6213
he *m* curtains of goats' hair for .... Ex 36:14 6213
eleven curtains he *m* them.................... Ex 36:14 6213
he *m* fifty loops upon the...................... Ex 36:17 6213
fifty loops *m* he upon the edge of .... Ex 36:17 6213
he *m* fifty taches of brass to .... Ex 36:18 6213
he *m* a covering for the tent of............. Ex 36:19 6213
he *m* boards for the tabernacle of......... Ex 36:20 6213
he *m* boards for the tabernacle .... Ex 36:23 6213
he *m* under the twenty boards.............. Ex 36:24 6213
north corner, he *m* twenty boards, ... Ex 36:25 6213
westward he *m* six boards..................... Ex 36:27 6213
two boards *m* he for the corners .... Ex 36:28 6213
he *m* bars of shittim wood .... Ex 36:31 6213
he *m* the middle bar to shoot .... Ex 36:33 6213
m their rings of gold to be .... Ex 36:34 6213
he *m* a vail of blue, and purple, ... Ex 36:35 6213
with cherubims *m* he it of cunning........ Ex 36:35 6213
he *m* thereunto four pillars of .... Ex 36:36 6213
And he *m* an hanging for the................ Ex 36:37 6213
Bezaleel *m* the ark of shittim .... Ex 37:1 6213
m a crown of gold to it round................ Ex 37:2 6213
he *m* staves of shittim wood, and.......... Ex 37:4 6213
he *m* the mercy seat of pure gold .... Ex 37:6 6213
he *m* two cherubims of gold,................. Ex 37:7 6213
beaten out of one piece *m* he them ...... Ex 37:7 6213
out of the mercy seat *m* he the .... Ex 37:8 6213
he *m* the table of shittim wood............. Ex 37:10 6213
m thereunto a crown of gold round........ Ex 37:11 6213
Also he *m* thereunto a border of........... Ex 37:12 6213
m a crown of gold for the border .... Ex 37:12 6213
he *m* the staves of shittim wood, ... Ex 37:15 6213
he *m* the vessels which were upon .... Ex 37:16 6213
he *m* the candlestick of pure gold......... Ex 37:17 6213
of beaten work *m* he the .... Ex 37:17 6213
Three bowls *m* after the fashion............ Ex 37:19
three bowls *m* like almonds in .... Ex 37:19
were four bowls *m* like almonds............ Ex 37:20
he *m* his seven lamps, and his.............. Ex 37:23 6213
Of a talent of pure gold *m* he it............. Ex 37:24 6213
he *m* the incense altar of shittim.......... Ex 37:25 6213
also he *m* unto it a crown of gold.......... Ex 37:26 6213
he *m* two rings of gold for it .... Ex 37:27 6213
he *m* the staves of shittim wood, ... Ex 37:28 6213
he *m* the holy anointing oil, and............ Ex 37:29 6213
he *m* the altar of burnt offering............. Ex 38:1 6213
he *m* the horns thereof on the.............. Ex 38:2 6213
he *m* all the vessels of the altar............ Ex 38:3 6213
the vessels thereof *m* he of brass .... Ex 38:3 6213
he *m* for the altar a brasen grate .... Ex 38:4 6213
he *m* the staves of shittim wood, ... Ex 38:6 6213
he *m* the altar hollow with boards........ Ex 38:7 6213

he *m* the laver of brass, and the............ Ex 38:8 6213
And he *m* the court .... Ex 38:9 6213
m all that the LORD commanded............ Ex 38:22 6213
five shekels he *m* hooks for the............ Ex 38:28 6213
therewith he *m* the sockets to the........ Ex 38:30 6213
they *m* cloths of service, to do............. Ex 39:1 6213
m the holy garments for Aaron .... Ex 39:1 6213
he *m* the ephod of gold, blue, and......... Ex 39:2 6213
They *m* shoulderpieces for it, to .... Ex 39:4 6213
he *m* the breastplate of cunning........... Ex 39:8 6213
they *m* the breastplate double.............. Ex 39:9 6213
they *m* upon the breastplate................. Ex 39:15 6213
they *m* two ouches of gold, and two..... Ex 39:16 6213
they *m* two rings of gold, and put........ Ex 39:19 6213
they *m* two other golden rings, and..... Ex 39:20 6213
he *m* the robe of the ephod of.............. Ex 39:22 6213
they *m* upon the hems of the robe........ Ex 39:24 6213
they *m* bells of pure gold, and put....... Ex 39:25 6213
they *m* coats of fine linen of................ Ex 39:27 6213
they *m* the plate of the holy................ Ex 39:30 6213
children of Israel *m* all the work .... Ex 39:42 6213
sacrifice, an offering *m* by fire.............. Lev 1:9
sacrifice, an offering *m* by fire.............. Lev 1:13
sacrifice, an offering *m* by fire.............. Lev 1:17
to be an offering *m* by fire .... Lev 2:2
offerings of the LORD *m* by fire .... Lev 2:3
it shall be *m* of fine flour with............... Lev 2:7 6213
m of these things unto the LORD........... Lev 2:8 6213
it is an offering *m* by fire...................... Lev 2:9
offerings of the LORD *m* by fire............... Lev 2:10
the LORD, shall be *m* with leaven .... Lev 2:11 6213
offering of the LORD *m* by fire................ Lev 2:11
it is an offering *m* by fire unto............... Lev 2:16
offering *m* by fire unto the LORD........... Lev 3:3
it is an offering *m* by fire...................... Lev 3:5
offering *m* by fire unto the LORD........... Lev 3:9
offering *m* by fire unto the LORD........... Lev 3:11
even an offering *m* by fire unto .... Lev 3:14
m by fire for a sweet savour.................. Lev 3:16
offerings *m* by fire unto the LORD.......... Lev 4:35
offerings *m* by fire unto the LORD.......... Lev 5:12
portion of my offerings *m* by fire .... Lev 6:17
offerings of the LORD *m* by fire............... Lev 6:18
In a pan it shall be *m* with oil................ Lev 6:21 6213
offering *m* by fire unto the LORD........... Lev 7:5
offering *m* by fire unto the LORD........... Lev 7:25
offerings of the LORD *m* by fire............... Lev 7:30
offerings of the LORD *m* by fire............... Lev 7:35
an offering *m* by fire unto the............... Lev 8:21
it is an offering *m* by fire unto .... Lev 8:28
offerings of the LORD *m* by fire............... Lev 10:12
sacrifices of the LORD *m* by fire .... Lev 10:13
offerings *m* by fire of the fat................. Lev 10:15
a skin, or in any thing *m* of skin .... Lev 13:48 4399
or in any work that is *m* of skin............. Lev 13:51 6213
the man that is to be *m* clean .... Lev 14:11
is in the house be not *m* unclean .... Lev 14:36
have *m* an atonement for himself, ... Lev 16:17
And when he hath *m* an end of............. Lev 16:20
offerings of the LORD *m* by fire............... Lev 21:6
offerings of the LORD *m* by fire............... Lev 21:21
whereby he may be *m* unclean .... Lev 22:5
offering *m* by fire unto the LORD........... Lev 22:27
m by fire unto the LORD seven............... Lev 23:8
an offering *m* by fire unto the............... Lev 23:13
even an offering *m* by fire..................... Lev 23:18
offering *m* by fire unto the LORD........... Lev 23:25
offer an offering *m* by fire unto .... Lev 23:27
offering *m* by fire unto the LORD........... Lev 23:36
offering *m* by fire unto the LORD........... Lev 23:36
to offer an offering *m* by fire .... Lev 23:37
generations may know that I *m* the..... Lev 23:43
even an offering *m* by fire unto .... Lev 24:7
of the offerings of the LORD *m* by .... Lev 24:9
of your yoke, and *m* you go upright...... Lev 26:13
which the LORD *m* between him............. Lev 26:46 5414
his sons have *m* an end of..................... Num 4:15
and all that is *m* for them .... Num 4:26 6213
an atonement shall be *m* for him .... Num 5:8
when he hath *m* her to drink the........... Num 5:27
that is *m* of the vine tree...................... Num 6:4 6213
Moses, so he *m* the candlestick............. Num 8:4 6213
Aaron *m* an atonement for them to....... Num 8:21
it in pans, and *m* cakes of it .... Num 11:8 6213
m all the congregation to murmur........ Num 14:36
wine, for an offering *m* by fire.............. Num 15:10
in offering an offering *m* by fire............ Num 15:13
will offer an offering *m* by fire .... Num 15:14
a sacrifice *m* by fire unto the .... Num 15:25
as he had *m* an end of speaking .... Num 16:31
they were *m* broad plates for a............. Num 16:39
m an atonement for the people............. Num 16:47
fat for an offering *m* by fire.................. Num 18:17
wherefore have ye *m* us to come up .... Num 20:5
Moses *m* a serpent of brass, and.......... Num 21:9 6213
m an atonement for the children........... Num 25:13
bread for my sacrifices *m* by fire .... Num 28:2
This is the offering *m* by fire................. Num 28:3
a sacrifice *m* by fire unto the .... Num 28:6
offer it, a sacrifice *m* by fire................. Num 28:8
a sacrifice *m* by fire unto the .... Num 28:13
m by fire for a burnt offering .... Num 28:19
meat of the sacrifice *m* by fire .... Num 28:24
a sacrifice *m* by fire unto the .... Num 29:6
offering, a sacrifice *m* by fire............... Num 29:13
offering, a sacrifice *m* by fire............... Num 29:36
m them void on the day he heard .... Num 30:12
her husband hath *m* them void............. Num 30:12
and all that is *m* of skins..................... Num 31:20 3627
hair, and all things *m* of wood .... Num 31:20
and he *m* them wander in the............... Num 32:13
m them heads over you, captains.......... Deut 1:15 5414
m his heart obstinate, that he .... Deut 2:30
your God, which he *m* with you............. Deut 4:23

Out of heaven he *m* thee to hear ... Deut 4:36
The LORD our God *m* a covenant ... Deut 5:2 3772
The LORD *m* not this covenant with ... Deut 5:3 3772
which the LORD *m* with you ... Deut 9:9 3772
they have *m* them a molten image ... Deut 9:12 6213
God, and had *m* you a molten calf ... Deut 9:16 6213
your sin, the calf which ye had *m* ... Deut 9:21 6213
I *m* an ark of shittim wood, and ... Deut 10:3 6213
tables in the ark which I had *m* ... Deut 10:5 6213
now the LORD thy God hath *m* thee ... Deut 10:22 7760
how he *m* the water of the Red sea ... Deut 11:4
offerings of the LORD *m* by fire ... Deut 18:1
when the officers have *m* an end ... Deut 20:9
When thou hast *m* an end of ... Deut 26:12
above all nations which he hath *m* ... Deut 26:19 6213
which he *m* with them in Horeb ... Deut 29:1 3772
which he *m* with them when he ... Deut 29:25 3772
covenant which I have *m* with them ... Deut 31:16 3772
when Moses had *m* an end of ... Deut 31:24
Hath he not *m* thee, and ... Deut 32:6 6213
He *m* him ride on the high places ... Deut 32:13
he *m* him to suck honey out of the ... Deut 32:13
then he forsook God which *m* him ... Deut 32:15 6213
Moses *m* an end of speaking all ... Deut 32:45
oath which thou hast *m* us swear ... Josh 2:17
which thou hast *m* us to swear ... Josh 2:20
Joshua *m* him sharp knives, and ... Josh 5:3 6213
all Israel *m* as if they were ... Josh 8:15
when Israel had *m* an end of ... Josh 8:24
m it an heap for ever, even a ... Josh 8:28 7760
m as if they had been ambassadors ... Josh 9:4
Joshua *m* peace with them ... Josh 9:15 6213
m a league with them, to let them ... Josh 9:15 6213
they had *m* a league with them ... Josh 9:16 3772
Joshua *m* them that day hewers of ... Josh 9:27 5414
of Gibeon had *m* peace with Israel ... Josh 10:1
for it hath *m* peace with Joshua ... Josh 10:4
Gibeon, and *m* war against it ... Josh 10:5
the children of Israel had *m* an ... Josh 10:20
Joshua *m* war a long time with all ... Josh 11:18 6213
There was not a city that *m* peace ... Josh 11:19
of the LORD God of Israel *m* by ... Josh 13:14
me *m* the heart of the people melt ... Josh 14:8
When they had *m* an end of ... Josh 19:49
So they *m* an end of dividing the ... Josh 19:51
For the LORD hath *m* Jordan a ... Josh 22:25 5414
of the LORD, which our fathers *m* ... Josh 22:28 6213
So Joshua *m* a covenant with the ... Josh 24:25 3772
I *m* you to go up out of Egypt, and ... Judg 2:1
But Ehud *m* him a dagger which had ... Judg 3:16 6213
when he had *m* an end to offer the ... Judg 3:18
Then he *m* him that remaineth have ... Judg 5:13
the LORD *m* me have dominion over ... Judg 5:13
the children of Israel *m* them the ... Judg 6:2 6213
m ready a kid, and unleavened ... Judg 6:19 6213
Gideon *m* an ephod thereof, and put ... Judg 8:27 6213
and *m* Baal-berith their god ... Judg 8:33 7760
m Abimelech king, by the plain of ... Judg 9:6
in that ye have *m* Abimelech king ... Judg 9:16
have *m* Abimelech, the son of his ... Judg 9:18
m merry, and went into the house ... Judg 9:27 6213
of Ammon *m* war against Israel ... Judg 11:4
of Ammon *m* war against Israel ... Judg 11:5
Gilead, and the people *m* him head ... Judg 11:11 7760
And the woman *m* haste, and ran, and ... Judg 13:10
until we shall have *m* ready a kid ... Judg 13:15 6213
and Samson *m* there a feast ... Judg 14:10 6213
when he had *m* an end of speaking, ... Judg 15:17
she *m* him sleep upon her knees ... Judg 16:19
and he *m* them sport ... Judg 16:25
that beheld while Samson *m* sport ... Judg 16:27
who *m* thereof a graven image and a ... Judg 17:4 6213
m an ephod, and teraphim, and ... Judg 17:5 6213
have taken away my gods which I *m* ... Judg 18:24 6213
took the things which Micah had *m* ... Judg 18:27 6213
Micah's graven image, which he *m* ... Judg 18:31 6213
For they had *m* a great oath ... Judg 21:5
had *m* a breach in the tribes of ... Judg 21:15 6213
his mother *m* him a little coat ... 1Sa 2:19 6213
m by fire of the children of ... 1Sa 2:28
his sons *m* themselves vile ... 1Sa 3:13
when he *m* mention of the ark of ... 1Sa 4:18
that he *m* his sons judges over ... 1Sa 8:1 7760
m them sit in the chiefest place ... 1Sa 9:22 5414
And when he had *m* an end of ... 1Sa 10:13
there they *m* Saul king before the ... 1Sa 11:15
me, and have *m* a king over you ... 1Sa 12:1
m them dwell in this place ... 1Sa 12:8
that as soon as he had *m* an end ... 1Sa 13:10
I have not *m* supplication unto ... 1Sa 13:12
Jonathan and his armourbearer *m* ... 1Sa 14:14 5221
wast thou not *m* the head of the ... 1Sa 15:17
thy sword hath *m* women childless ... 1Sa 15:33
he had *m* Saul king over Israel ... 1Sa 15:35
and *m* him pass before Samuel ... 1Sa 16:8
Then Jesse *m* Shammah to pass by ... 1Sa 16:9
Jesse *m* seven of his sons to pass ... 1Sa 16:10
when he had *m* an end of speaking ... 1Sa 18:1
David *m* a covenant, because he ... 1Sa 18:3 3772
m him his captain over a thousand ... 1Sa 18:13 7760
So Jonathan *m* a covenant with the ... 1Sa 20:16 3772
sheweth me that my son hath *m* a ... 1Sa 22:8 3772
they two *m* a covenant before the ... 1Sa 23:18 3772
David *m* haste to get away for ... 1Sa 23:26
when David had *m* an end of ... 1Sa 24:16
Then Abigail *m* haste, and took two ... 1Sa 25:18
Whither have ye *m* a road to day ... 1Sa 27:10
He hath *m* his people Israel ... 1Sa 27:12
and they *m* him drink water ... 1Sa 30:11
We *m* an invasion upon the south ... 1Sa 30:14
whom they had *m* also to abide at ... 1Sa 30:21
that he *m* it a statute and an ... 1Sa 30:25 7760
m him king over Gilead, and over ... 2Sa 2:9
that Abner *m* himself strong for ... 2Sa 3:6
And David *m* Abner and the men that ... 2Sa 3:20 6213
as she *m* haste to flee, that he ... 2Sa 4:4
king David *m* a league with them ... 2Sa 5:3 3772
of instruments *m* of fir wood ... 2Sa 6:5
LORD had *m* a breach upon Uzzah ... 2Sa 6:8 6555
as soon as David had *m* an end of ... 2Sa 6:18
have *m* thee a great name, like ... 2Sa 7:9 6213
they *m* peace with Israel, and ... 2Sa 10:19
and he *m* him drunk ... 2Sa 11:13
When thou hast *m* an end of ... 2Sa 11:19
m them pass through the brickkiln ... 2Sa 12:31
Amnon lay down, and *m* himself sick ... 2Sa 13:6
m cakes in his sight, and did bake ... 2Sa 13:8 3835
took the cakes which she had *m* ... 2Sa 13:10 6213
as soon as he had *m* an end of ... 2Sa 13:36
the people have *m* me afraid ... 2Sa 14:15
Oh that I were *m* judge in the ... 2Sa 15:4 7760
Absalom *m* Amasa captain of the ... 2Sa 17:25 7760
floods of ungodly men *m* me afraid ... 2Sa 22:5 1204
he *m* darkness pavilions round ... 2Sa 22:12 7896
and thy gentleness hath *m* me great ... 2Sa 22:36
yet he hath *m* with me an ... 2Sa 23:5 7760
it as they had *m* an end of eating ... 1Kin 1:41
king David hath *m* Solomon king ... 1Kin 1:43
who hath *m* me an house, as he ... 1Kin 2:24 6213
Solomon *m* affinity with Pharaoh ... 1Kin 3:1
until he had *m* an end of building ... 1Kin 3:1
thou hast *m* thy servant king ... 1Kin 3:7
m a feast to all his servants ... 1Kin 3:15 6213
his month in a year *m* provision ... 1Kin 4:7
they two *m* a league together ... 1Kin 5:12 3772
for the house he *m* windows of ... 1Kin 6:4 6213
he *m* chambers round about ... 1Kin 6:5 6213
he *m* narrowed rests round about ... 1Kin 6:6 5414
was built of stone *m* ready before ... 1Kin 6:7
he *m* a partition by the chains of ... 1Kin 6:21
within the oracle he *m* two ... 1Kin 6:23 6213
oracle he *m* doors of olive tree ... 1Kin 6:31 6213
So also *m* he for the door of the ... 1Kin 6:33 6213
And he *m* a porch of pillars ... 1Kin 7:6 6213
Then he *m* a porch for the throne ... 1Kin 7:7 6213
Solomon *m* also an house for ... 1Kin 7:8 6213
he *m* two chapiters of molten ... 1Kin 7:16 6213
he *m* the pillars, and two rows ... 1Kin 7:18 6213
he *m* a molten sea, ten cubits ... 1Kin 7:23 6213
And he *m* ten bases of brass ... 1Kin 7:27 6213
certain additions *m* of thin work ... 1Kin 7:29 6213
this manner he *m* the ten bases ... 1Kin 7:37 6213
Then *m* he ten lavers of brass ... 1Kin 7:38 6213
Hiram *m* the lavers, and the ... 1Kin 7:40 6213
So Hiram *m* an end of doing all ... 1Kin 7:40 6213
m king Solomon for the house of ... 1Kin 7:40 6213
which Hiram *m* to king Solomon for ... 1Kin 7:45 6213
Solomon *m* all the vessels that ... 1Kin 7:48 6213
m for the house of the LORD ... 1Kin 7:51 6213
when the LORD *m* a covenant with ... 1Kin 8:9 3772
which he *m* with our fathers, when ... 1Kin 8:21 3772
soever be *m* by any man, or by all ... 1Kin 8:38
that when Solomon had *m* an end of ... 1Kin 8:54
wherewith I have *m* supplication ... 1Kin 8:59
that thou hast *m* before me ... 1Kin 9:3
king Solomon *m* a navy of ships in ... 1Kin 9:26 6213
therefore *m* he thee king, to do ... 1Kin 10:9 7760
the king *m* of the almug trees ... 1Kin 10:12 6213
king Solomon *m* two hundred ... 1Kin 10:16 6213
he *m* three hundred shields of ... 1Kin 10:17
Moreover the king *m* a great ... 1Kin 10:18 6213
was not the like *m* in any kingdom ... 1Kin 10:20 6213
the king *m* silver to be in ... 1Kin 10:27 5414
cedars *m* he to be as the sycomore ... 1Kin 10:27 5414
he *m* him ruler over all the ... 1Kin 11:28
Thy father *m* our yoke grievous ... 1Kin 12:4
Thy father *m* our yoke heavy, but ... 1Kin 12:10
My father *m* your yoke heavy, and I ... 1Kin 12:14
Therefore king Rehoboam *m* speed ... 1Kin 12:18
m him king over all Israel ... 1Kin 12:20
m two calves of gold, and said ... 1Kin 12:28 6213
he *m* an house of high places, and ... 1Kin 12:31 6213
m priests of the lowest of the ... 1Kin 12:31 6213
unto the calves that he had *m* ... 1Kin 12:32 6213
of the high places which he had *m* ... 1Kin 12:32 6213
upon the altar which he had *m* in ... 1Kin 12:33 6213
but *m* again of the lowest of the ... 1Kin 13:33 6213
m thee prince over my people ... 1Kin 14:7 5414
m thee other gods, and molten ... 1Kin 14:9 6213
because they have *m* their groves ... 1Kin 14:15 6213
did sin, and who *m* Israel to sin ... 1Kin 14:16
of gold which Solomon had *m* ... 1Kin 14:26 6213
king Rehoboam *m* in their stead ... 1Kin 14:27 6213
the idols that his fathers had *m* ... 1Kin 15:12 6213
because she had *m* an idol in a ... 1Kin 15:13 6213
Then king Asa *m* a proclamation ... 1Kin 15:22 6213
sin wherewith he *m* Israel to sin ... 1Kin 15:26
which he *m* Israel sin, by his ... 1Kin 15:30
sin wherewith he *m* Israel to sin ... 1Kin 15:34
m thee prince over my people ... 1Kin 16:2 5414
hast *m* my people Israel to sin, ... 1Kin 16:2
and by which they *m* Israel to sin ... 1Kin 16:13
wherefore all Israel *m* Omri ... 1Kin 16:16
sin wherewith he *m* Israel to sin ... 1Kin 16:26
And Ahab *m* a grove ... 1Kin 16:33 6213
leaped upon the altar which was *m* ... 1Kin 18:26 6213
he *m* a trench about the altar, as ... 1Kin 18:32 6213
as my father *m* in Samaria ... 1Kin 20:34 7760
So he *m* a covenant with him, and ... 1Kin 20:34 3772
me to anger, and *m* Israel to sin ... 1Kin 21:22
of Chenaanah *m* him horns of iron ... 1Kin 22:11 6213
and the ivory house which he *m* ... 1Kin 22:39 1129
Jehoshaphat *m* peace with the king ... 1Kin 22:44
Jehoshaphat *m* ships of Tharshish ... 1Kin 22:48 6235
son of Nebat, who *m* Israel to sin ... 1Kin 22:52
of Baal that his father had *m* ... 2Kin 3:2 6213
of Nebat, which *m* Israel to sin ... 2Kin 3:3
For the LORD had *m* the host of ... 2Kin 7:6
and *m* a king over themselves ... 2Kin 8:20
And his chariot was *m* ready ... 2Kin 9:21
So they *m* him ride in his chariot ... 2Kin 10:16
as soon as he had *m* an end of ... 2Kin 10:25
m it a draught house unto this ... 2Kin 10:27 7760
who *m* Israel to sin, Jehu ... 2Kin 10:29
Jeroboam, which *m* Israel to sin ... 2Kin 10:31
m a covenant with them, and took ... 2Kin 11:4 3772
they *m* him king, and anointed him ... 2Kin 11:12
Jehoiada *m* a covenant between the ... 2Kin 11:17 3772
Howbeit there were not *m* for the ... 2Kin 12:13 6213
m a conspiracy, and slew Joash in ... 2Kin 12:20
of Nebat, which *m* Israel to sin ... 2Kin 13:2
who *m* Israel sin, but walked ... 2Kin 13:6
had *m* them like the dust by ... 2Kin 13:7 7760
son of Nebat, who *m* Israel sin ... 2Kin 13:11
Now they *m* a conspiracy against ... 2Kin 14:19
m him king instead of his father ... 2Kin 14:21
son of Nebat, who *m* Israel to sin ... 2Kin 14:24
son of Nebat, who *m* Israel to sin ... 2Kin 15:9
and his conspiracy which he *m* ... 2Kin 15:15 7194
son of Nebat, who *m* Israel to sin ... 2Kin 15:18
son of Nebat, who *m* Israel to sin ... 2Kin 15:24
son of Nebat, who *m* Israel to sin ... 2Kin 15:28
Hoshea the son of Elah *m* a ... 2Kin 15:30
m his son to pass through the ... 2Kin 16:3
so Urijah the priest *m* it against ... 2Kin 16:11 6213
kings of Israel, which they had *m* ... 2Kin 17:8 6213
that he *m* with their fathers ... 2Kin 17:15 3772
m them molten images, even two ... 2Kin 17:16 6213
m a grove, and worshipped all the ... 2Kin 17:16 6213
statutes of Israel which they *m* ... 2Kin 17:19 6213
they *m* Jeroboam the son of Nebat ... 2Kin 17:21
LORD, and *m* them sin a great sin ... 2Kin 17:21
every nation *m* gods of their own ... 2Kin 17:29 6213
places which the Samaritans had *m* ... 2Kin 17:29 6213
men of Babylon *m* Succoth-benoth ... 2Kin 17:30 6213
and the men of Cuth *m* Nergal ... 2Kin 17:30 6213
and the men of Hamath *m* Ashima ... 2Kin 17:30 6213
And the Avites *m* Nibhaz and Tartak, ... 2Kin 17:31 6213
m unto themselves of the lowest ... 2Kin 17:32 6213
whom the LORD had *m* a covenant ... 2Kin 17:35 3772
the covenant that I have *m* with ... 2Kin 17:38 3772
brasen serpent that Moses had *m* ... 2Kin 18:4 6213
thou hast *m* heaven and earth ... 2Kin 19:15 6213
all his might, and how he *m* a pool ... 2Kin 20:20 6213
m a grove, as did Ahab king of ... 2Kin 21:3 6213
he *m* his son pass through the ... 2Kin 21:6
grove that he had *m* in the house ... 2Kin 21:7 6213
hath *m* Judah also to sin with his ... 2Kin 21:11
sin wherewith he *m* Judah to sin ... 2Kin 21:16
the people of the land *m* Josiah ... 2Kin 21:24
Howbeit there was no reckoning *m* ... 2Kin 22:7
m a covenant before the LORD, to ... 2Kin 23:3 3772
the vessels that were *m* for Baal ... 2Kin 23:4
which the kings of Judah had *m* ... 2Kin 23:12 6213
the altars which Manasseh had *m* ... 2Kin 23:12 6213
who *m* Israel to sin ... 2Kin 23:15
had *m*, both that altar ... 2Kin 23:15 6213
m to provoke the LORD to anger ... 2Kin 23:19 6213
m him king in his father's stead ... 2Kin 23:30
Pharaoh-nechoh *m* Eliakim the son ... 2Kin 23:34
had *m* in the temple of the LORD ... 2Kin 24:13 6213
the king of Babylon *m* Mattaniah ... 2Kin 24:17
had *m* for the house of the LORD ... 2Kin 25:16 6213
even over them he *m* Gedaliah the ... 2Kin 25:22
Babylon had *m* Gedaliah governor ... 2Kin 25:23
they *m* war with the Hagarites ... 1Chr 5:10 6213
they *m* war with the Hagarites, ... 1Chr 5:19 6213
m the ointment of the spices ... 1Chr 9:30 7543
things that were *m* in the pans ... 1Chr 9:31 4639
David *m* a covenant with them in ... 1Chr 11:3 3772
m them captains of the band ... 1Chr 12:18 5414
the LORD had *m* a breach upon Uzza ... 1Chr 13:11
David *m* him houses in the city of ... 1Chr 15:1 6213
LORD our God *m* a breach upon us ... 1Chr 15:13
when David had *m* an end of ... 1Chr 16:2
but Asaph *m* a sound with cymbals ... 1Chr 16:5
covenant which he *m* with Abraham ... 1Chr 16:16 3772
but the LORD *m* the heavens ... 1Chr 16:26 6213
have *m* thee a name like the name ... 1Chr 17:8 6213
Solomon *m* the brasen sea, and the ... 1Chr 18:8 6213
had *m* themselves odious to David ... 1Chr 19:6
they *m* peace with David, and ... 1Chr 19:19
which Moses *m* in the wilderness, ... 1Chr 21:29 6213
abundantly, and hast *m* great wars ... 1Chr 22:8 6213
he *m* Solomon his son king over ... 1Chr 23:1
with the instruments which I *m* ... 1Chr 23:5 6213
yet his father *m* him the chief ... 1Chr 26:10 7760
whom king David *m* rulers over the ... 1Chr 26:32
had *m* ready for the building ... 1Chr 28:2 6213
the LORD *m* me understand in ... 1Chr 28:19
gold for things to be *m* of gold ... 1Chr 29:2
be *m* by the hands of artificers ... 1Chr 29:5
for the which I have *m* provision ... 1Chr 29:19
they *m* Solomon the son of David ... 1Chr 29:22
the LORD had *m* in the wilderness ... 2Chr 1:3 6213
son of Uri, the son of Hur, had *m* ... 2Chr 1:5 6213
hast *m* me to reign in his stead ... 2Chr 1:8
for thou hast *m* me king over a ... 2Chr 1:9
over whom I have *m* thee king ... 2Chr 1:11
And the king *m* silver and gold at ... 2Chr 1:15 5414
cedar trees *m* he as the sycomore ... 2Chr 1:15 5414
he hath *m* thee king over them ... 2Chr 2:11 5414
that *m* heaven and earth, who hath ... 2Chr 2:12 6213
he *m* the most holy house, the ... 2Chr 3:8 6213
in the most holy house he *m* two ... 2Chr 3:10 6213
he *m* the vail of blue, and purple, ... 2Chr 3:14 6213
Also he *m* before the house two ... 2Chr 3:15 6213
he *m* chains, as in the oracle, and ... 2Chr 3:16 6213
m an hundred pomegranates, and put ... 2Chr 3:16 6213
Moreover he *m* an altar of brass, ... 2Chr 4:1 6213
Also he *m* a molten sea of ten ... 2Chr 4:2 6213
He *m* also ten lavers, and put five ... 2Chr 4:6 6213

he *m* ten candlesticks of gold 2Chr 4:7 6213
He *m* also ten tables, and placed 2Chr 4:8 6213
he *m* an hundred basons of gold 2Chr 4:8 6213
Furthermore he *m* the court of the 2Chr 4:9 6213
Huram *m* the pots, and the shovels, 2Chr 4:11 6213
He *m* also bases, and lavers *m* 2Chr 4:14 6213
Thus Solomon *m* all these vessels 2Chr 4:18 6213
Solomon *m* all the vessels that 2Chr 4:19 6213
m he of gold, and that perfect 2Chr 4:21
m for the house of the LORD was 2Chr 5:1 6213
when the LORD *m* a covenant with 2Chr 5:10 3772
that he *m* with the children of 2Chr 6:11 3772
For Solomon had *m* a brasen 2Chr 6:13 6213
soever shall be *m* of any man 2Chr 6:29
prayer that is *m* in this place 2Chr 6:40
Solomon had *m* an end of praying 2Chr 7:1
the king had *m* to praise the LORD 2Chr 7:6 6213
had *m* was not able to receive the 2Chr 7:7 6213
day they *m* a solemn assembly 2Chr 7:9 6213
prayer that is *m* in this place 2Chr 7:15
therefore *m* he thee king over 2Chr 9:8 5414
the king *m* of the algum trees 2Chr 9:11 6213
king Solomon *m* two hundred 2Chr 9:15 6213
shields *m* he of beaten gold 2Chr 9:16
Moreover the king *m* a great 2Chr 9:17 6213
was not the like *m* in any kingdom 2Chr 9:19 6213
the king *m* silver in Jerusalem as 2Chr 9:27 5414
cedar trees *m* he as the sycomore 2Chr 9:27 5414
Thy father *m* our yoke grievous 2Chr 10:4
Thy father *m* our yoke heavy, but 2Chr 10:10
My father *m* your yoke heavy, but 2Chr 10:14
But king Rehoboam *m* speed to get 2Chr 10:18
m them exceeding strong, having 2Chr 11:12
and for the calves which he had *m* 2Chr 11:15 6213
m Rehoboam the son of Solomon 2Chr 11:17
Rehoboam *m* Abijah the son of 2Chr 11:22
of gold which Solomon had *m* 2Chr 12:9 6213
king Rehoboam *m* shields of brass 2Chr 12:10 6213
which Jeroboam *m* you for gods 2Chr 13:8 6213
have *m* you priests after the 2Chr 13:9 6213
because she had *m* an idol in a 2Chr 15:16 6213
which he had *m* for himself in the 2Chr 16:14 3738
they *m* a very great burning for 2Chr 16:14
so that they *m* no war against 2Chr 17:10
Chenaanah had *m* him horns of iron 2Chr 18:10 6213
when they had *m* an end of the 2Chr 20:23
for the LORD had *m* them to 2Chr 20:27
they *m* the ships in Ezion-gaber 2Chr 20:36 6213
covenant that he had *m* with David 2Chr 21:7 3772
of Judah, and *m* themselves a king 2Chr 21:8
Moreover he *m* high places in the 2Chr 21:11 6213
hast *m* Judah and the inhabitants 2Chr 21:13
his people *m* no burning for him, 2Chr 21:19 6213
the inhabitants of Jerusalem *m* 2Chr 22:1
all the congregation *m* a covenant 2Chr 23:3 3772
him the testimony, and *m* him king 2Chr 23:11
Jehoiada *m* a covenant between him 2Chr 23:16 3772
king's commandment they *m* a chest 2Chr 24:8 6213
they *m* a proclamation through 2Chr 24:9 5414
chest, until they had *m* an end 2Chr 24:10
whereof were *m* vessels for the 2Chr 24:14 6213
Judah, and *m* obeisance to the king 2Chr 24:17
m them captains over thousands, 2Chr 25:5
Art thou *m* of the king's counsel 2Chr 25:16 5414
m a conspiracy against him in 2Chr 25:27
m him king in the room of his 2Chr 26:1
the LORD, God *m* him to prosper 2Chr 26:5
that *m* war with mighty power, to 2Chr 26:13 6213
he *m* in Jerusalem engines, 2Chr 26:15 6213
m also molten images for Baalim 2Chr 28:2 6213
for he *m* Judah naked, and 2Chr 28:19
he *m* him altars in every corner 2Chr 28:24 6213
he *m* high places to burn incense 2Chr 28:25 6213
of the first month they *m* an end 2Chr 29:17
they *m* reconciliation with their 2Chr 29:24
should be *m* for all Israel 2Chr 29:24
when they had *m* an end of 2Chr 29:29
m darts and shields in abundance 2Chr 32:5 6213
he *m* himself treasuries for 2Chr 32:27 6213
m groves, and worshipped all the 2Chr 33:3 6213
image, the idol which he had *m* 2Chr 33:7 6213
So Manasseh *m* Judah and the 2Chr 33:9
which Manasseh his father had *m* 2Chr 33:22 6213
the people of the land *m* Josiah 2Chr 33:25
m dust of them, and strowed it 2Chr 34:4
m a covenant before the LORD, to 2Chr 34:31 3772
m all that were present in Israel 2Chr 34:33
afterward they *m* ready for 2Chr 35:14
m them an ordinance in Israel 2Chr 35:25 5414
m him king in his father's stead 2Chr 36:1
the king of Egypt *m* Eliakim his 2Chr 36:4
m Zedekiah his brother king over 2Chr 36:10
who had *m* him swear by God 2Chr 36:13
Persia, that he *m* a proclamation 2Chr 36:22
Persia, that he *m* a proclamation Ezr 1:1
That search may be *m* in the book Ezr 4:15
commanded, and search hath been *m* Ezr 4:19
hath *m* insurrection against kings Ezr 4:19
and sedition have been *m* therein Ezr 4:19 5648
m them to cease by force and power Ezr 4:23
of Babylon the same king Cyrus *m* Ezr 5:13 7761
whom he had *m* governor Ezr 5:14 7761
let there be search *m* in the Ezr 5:17
that a decree was *m* of Cyrus the Ezr 5:17 7761
Then Darius the king *m* a decree Ezr 6:1 7761
search was *m* in the house of the Ezr 6:1
king the same Cyrus the king *m* a Ezr 6:3 7761
Also I have *m* a decree, that Ezr 6:11 7761
let his house be *m* a dunghill for Ezr 6:11 5648
I Darius have *m* a decree Ezr 6:12 7761
for the LORD had *m* them joyful Ezr 6:22
m the chief priests, the Levites, Ezr 10:5
they *m* proclamation throughout Ezr 10:7
they *m* an end with all the men Ezr 10:17

David, and to the pool that was *m* Neh 3:16 6213
the walls of Jerusalem were *m* up Neh 4:7
Nevertheless we *m* our prayer unto Neh 4:9
For they all *m* us afraid, saying, Neh 6:9
which they had *m* for the purpose Neh 8:4 6213
m themselves booths, every one Neh 8:16 6213
out of the captivity *m* booths Neh 8:17 6213
thou hast *m* heaven, the heaven of Neh 9:6 6213
when they had *m* them a molten Neh 9:18 6213
Also we *m* ordinances for us, to Neh 10:32 5975
for God had *m* them rejoice with Neh 12:43
And I *m* treasurers over the Neh 13:13
m them swear by God, saying, Ye Neh 13:25
God *m* him king over all Israel Neh 13:26 5414
he *m* a feast unto all his princes Est 1:3 6213
the king *m* a feast unto all the Est 1:5 6213
Also Vashti the queen *m* a feast Est 1:9 6213
m her queen instead of Vashti Est 2:17
Then the king *m* a great feast Est 2:18 6213
he *m* a release to the provinces, Est 2:18 6213
inquisition was *m* of the matter Est 2:23
Let a gallows be *m* of fifty Est 5:14 6213
and he caused the gallows to be *m* Est 5:14 6213
which Haman had *m* for Mordecai Est 7:9 6213
m it a day of feasting and Est 9:17 6213
m it a day of feasting and Est 9:18 6213
m the fourteenth day of the month Est 9:19 6213
Hast not thou *m* an hedge about Job 1:10
The Chaldeans *m* out three bands, Job 1:17 7760
for they had *m* an appointment Job 2:11
which *m* all my bones to shake Job 4:14
So am I *m* to possess months of Job 7:3
Thine hands have *m* me and Job 10:8 6087
that thou hast *m* me as the clay Job 10:9 6213
or wast thou *m* before the hills Job 15:7 2342
But now he hath *m* me weary Job 16:7
thou hast *m* desolate all my Job 16:7
He hath *m* me also a byword of the Job 17:6 3322
I have *m* my bed in the darkness Job 17:13 7502
No mention shall be *m* of coral Job 28:18
When he *m* a decree for the rain, Job 28:26 6213
I *m* a covenant with mine eyes Job 31:1 3772
Did not he that *m* me in the womb Job 31:15 6213
If I have *m* gold my hope, or have Job 31:24 7760
The spirit of God hath *m* me Job 33:4 6213
When I *m* the cloud the garment Job 38:9 7760
house I have *m* the wilderness Job 39:6 7760
now behemoth, which I *m* with thee Job 40:15 6213
he that *m* him can make his sword Job 40:19 6213
his like, who is *m* without fear Job 41:33 6213
hath bent his bow, and *m* it ready Ps 7:12
He *m* a pit, and digged it, and is Ps 7:15 3738
fallen into the ditch which he *m* Ps 7:15 6466
For thou hast *m* him a little Ps 8:5
sunk down in the pit that they *m* Ps 9:15 6213
floods of ungodly men *m* me afraid Ps 18:4
He *m* darkness his secret place Ps 18:11 7896
and thy gentleness hath *m* me great Ps 18:35
thou hast *m* me the head of the Ps 18:43 7760
For thou hast *m* him most blessed Ps 21:6 7896
thou hast *m* him exceeding glad Ps 21:6
hast not *m* my foes to rejoice Ps 30:1
by thy favour thou hast *m* my Ps 30:7
and unto the LORD I *m* supplication Ps 30:8
of the LORD were the heavens *m* Ps 33:6 6213
thou hast *m* my days as an Ps 39:5 5414
which I have *m* touching the king Ps 45:1 4639
whereby they have *m* thee glad Ps 45:8
he hath *m* in the earth Ps 46:8 7760
thou afraid when one is *m* rich Ps 49:16
those that have *m* a covenant with Ps 50:5 3772
man that *m* not God his strength Ps 52:7 7760
Thou hast *m* the earth to tremble Ps 60:2
thou hast *m* us to drink the wine Ps 60:3
I *m* sackcloth also my garment Ps 69:11 5414
shall be *m* for him continually Ps 72:15
thou hast *m* summer and winter Ps 74:17 3335
my spirit *m* diligent search Ps 77:6
he *m* the waters to stand as an Ps 78:13
He *m* a way to his anger Ps 78:50
But *m* his own people to go forth Ps 78:52
m the tribes of Israel to dwell Ps 78:55
their widows *m* no lamentation Ps 78:64
whom thou hast *m* shall come Ps 86:9 6213
thou hast *m* me an abomination Ps 88:8 7896
I have *m* a covenant with my Ps 89:3 3772
Thou hast *m* void the covenant of Ps 89:39
thou hast *m* all his enemies to Ps 89:42
hast not *m* him to stand in the Ps 89:43
Thou hast *m* his glory to cease, Ps 89:44
hast thou *m* all men in vain Ps 89:47
Because thou hast *m* the LORD Ps 91:9 7760
hast *m* me glad through thy work Ps 92:4
The sea is his, and he *m* it Ps 95:5 6213
but the LORD *m* the heavens Ps 96:5 6213
The LORD hath *m* known his Ps 98:2
it is he that hath *m* us, and not Ps 100:3 6213
He *m* known his ways unto Moses, Ps 103:7
In wisdom hast thou *m* them all Ps 104:24 6213
whom thou hast *m* to play therein Ps 104:26 3335
Which covenant he *m* with Abraham Ps 105:9 3772
He *m* him lord of his house, and Ps 105:21 7760
m them stronger than their Ps 105:24
He sent darkness, and *m* it dark Ps 105:28
They *m* a calf in Horeb, and Ps 106:19 6213
He *m* them also to be pitied of Ps 106:46 5414
He hath *m* his wonderful works to Ps 111:4 6213
of the LORD which *m* heaven Ps 115:15 6213
is the day which the LORD hath *m* Ps 118:24 6213
I *m* haste, and delayed not to keep Ps 119:60
Thy hands have *m* me and fashioned Ps 119:73 6213
hast *m* me wiser than mine enemies Ps 119:98
for they have *m* void thy law Ps 119:126
the LORD, which *m* heaven and earth Ps 121:2 6213

the LORD, who *m* heaven and earth Ps 124:8 6213
they *m* long their furrows Ps 129:3
The LORD that *m* heaven and earth Ps 134:3 6213
him that by wisdom *m* the heavens Ps 136:5 6213
To him that *m* great lights Ps 136:7 6213
m Israel to pass through the Ps 136:14
I am fearfully and wonderfully *m* Ps 139:14
from thee, when I was *m* in secret Ps 139:15 6213
he hath *m* me to dwell in darkness Ps 143:3
Which *m* heaven, and earth, the sea Ps 146:6 6213
he hath *m* a decree which shall Ps 148:6 5414
Israel rejoice in him that *m* him Ps 149:2 6213
as yet he had not *m* the earth Prov 8:26 6213
The liberal soul shall be *m* fat Prov 11:25
of the diligent shall be *m* fat Prov 13:4
in the midst of fools is *m* known Prov 14:33
way of the righteous is *m* plain Prov 15:19
The LORD hath *m* all things for Prov 16:4 6466
I have *m* my heart clean, I am Prov 20:9
the LORD hath *m* even both of them Prov 20:12 6213
is punished, the simple is *m* wise Prov 21:11
I have *m* known to thee this day, Prov 22:19
trust in the LORD shall be *m* fat Prov 28:25
is crooked cannot be *m* straight Eccl 1:15
I *m* me great works Eccl 2:4
I *m* me gardens and orchards, and I Eccl 2:5 6213
I *m* me pools of water, to water Eccl 2:6 6213
He hath *m* every thing beautiful Eccl 3:11 6213
countenance the heart is *m* better Eccl 7:3
straight, which he hath *m* crooked Eccl 7:13
that God hath *m* man upright Eccl 7:29 6213
A feast is *m* for laughter, and Eccl 10:19 6213
they *m* me the keeper of the Song 1:6 7760
King Solomon *m* himself a chariot Song 3:9 6213
He *m* the pillars thereof of Song 3:10 6213
my soul *m* me like the chariots of Song 6:12 7760
which their own fingers have *m* Is 2:8 6213
haughtiness of men shall be *m* low Is 2:17
which they *m* each one for himself Is 2:20
also *m* a winepress therein Is 5:2 2672
wherein thou wast *m* to serve Is 14:3
man that *m* the earth to tremble Is 14:16
That *m* the world as a wilderness, Is 14:17 7760
I have *m* their vintage shouting Is 16:10
glory of Jacob shall be *m* thin Is 17:4
that which his fingers have *m* Is 17:8 6213
sighing thereof have I *m* to cease Is 21:2
Ye *m* also a ditch between the two Is 22:11 6213
For thou hast *m* of a city an heap Is 25:2 7760
m all their memory to perish Is 26:14
therefore he that *m* them will not Is 27:11 6213
We have *m* a covenant with death, Is 28:15 3772
for we have *m* lies our refuge, and Is 28:15 7760
lest your bands be *m* strong Is 28:22
When he hath *m* plain the face Is 28:25
of him that *m* it, He *m* me not Is 29:16 6213
he hath *m* it deep and large Is 30:33
hands have *m* unto you for a sin Is 31:7 6213
it is *m* fat with fatness, and with Is 34:6
their dust *m* fat with fatness Is 34:7
thou hast *m* heaven and earth Is 37:16 6213
mountain and hill shall be *m* low Is 40:4
the crooked shall be *m* straight Is 40:4
him, and *m* him rule over kings Is 41:2
yea, I have *m* him Is 43:7 6213
but thou hast *m* me to serve with Is 43:24
Thus saith the LORD that *m* thee Is 44:2 6213
I have *m* the earth, and created Is 45:12 6213
that formed the earth and *m* it Is 45:18 6213
I have *m*, and I will bear Is 46:4 6213
hath he *m* mention of my name Is 49:1
he hath *m* my mouth like a sharp Is 49:2 7760
hid me, and *m* me a polished shaft Is 49:2 7760
they that *m* thee waste shall go Is 49:17
that hath *m* the depths of the sea Is 51:10 7760
of man which shall be *m* as grass Is 51:12 5414
The LORD hath *m* bare his holy arm Is 52:10
he *m* his grave with the wicked, Is 53:9 5414
many, and *m* intercession for the Is 53:12
m thee a covenant with them Is 57:8 3772
me, and the souls which I have *m* Is 57:16 6213
they have *m* them crooked paths Is 59:8
why hast thou *m* us to err from Is 63:17
all those things hath mine hand *m* Is 66:2 6213
Shall the earth be *m* to bring Is 66:8
I have *m* thee this day a defenced Jer 1:18 5414
m mine heritage an abomination Jer 2:7 7760
yelled, and they *m* his land waste Jer 2:15 7896
thy gods that thou hast *m* thee Jer 2:28 6213
they have *m* their faces harder Jer 5:3
Lo, certainly in vain *m* he it Jer 8:8 6213
gods that have not *m* the heavens Jer 10:11 5648
He hath *m* the earth by his power, Jer 10:12 6213
have *m* his habitation desolate Jer 10:25
which I *m* with their fathers Jer 11:10 3772
they have *m* my pleasant portion a Jer 12:10 5414
They have *m* it desolate, and being Jer 12:11 7760
the whole land is *m* desolate Jer 12:11
discovered, and thy heels *m* bare Jer 13:22
wilt thou not be *m* clean Jer 13:27
for thou hast *m* all these things Jer 14:22 6213
but *m* their neck stiff, that they Jer 17:23
the vessel that he *m* of clay was Jer 18:4 6213
so he *m* it again another vessel, Jer 18:4 6213
that cannot be *m* whole again Jer 19:11 7495
the LORD was *m* a reproach unto me Jer 20:8 1961
m all the nations to drink, unto Jer 25:17
when Jeremiah had *m* an end of Jer 26:8
I have *m* the earth, the man and Jer 27:5 6213
The LORD hath *m* thee priest in Jer 29:26 5414
to the covenant that I *m* with Jer 31:32 3772
thou hast *m* the heaven and the Jer 32:17 6213
hast *m* thee a name, as at this Jer 32:20 6213
that the king Zedekiah had *m* a Jer 34:8 3772

I *m* a covenant with your fathers Jer 34:13 3772
ye had *m* a covenant before me in Jer 34:15 3772
which they had *m* before me Jer 34:18 3772
Gemariah had *m* intercession to Jer 36:25
m king in the land of Judah Jer 37:1
for they had *m* that the prison Jer 37:15 6213
that *m* us this soul, I will not Jer 38:16 6213
m governor over the cities of Jer 40:5
had *m* Gedaliah the son of Ahikam Jer 40:7
had *m* governor over the land Jer 41:2
had *m* for fear of Baasha king of Jer 41:9 6213
of Babylon *m* governor in the land Jer 41:18
that when Jeremiah had *m* an end Jer 43:1
and *m* drunk with their blood Jer 46:10
He *m* many to fall, yea, one fell Jer 46:16
But I have *m* Esau bare, I have Jer 49:10
that *m* all the earth drunken Jer 51:7
He hath *m* the earth by his power, Jer 51:15 6213
he hath *m* me an empty vessel, he Jer 51:34 3322
when thou hast *m* an end of Jer 51:63
which king Solomon had *m* in the Jer 52:20 6213
he hath *m* me desolate and faint Lam 1:13 5414
he hath *m* my strength to fall, Lam 1:14
they have *m* a noise in the house Lam 2:7 5414
therefore he *m* the rampart Lam 2:8
My flesh and my skin hath he *m* old Lam 3:4
he hath *m* my chain heavy Lam 3:7
he hath *m* my paths crooked Lam 3:9
he hath *m* me desolate Lam 3:11 7760
he hath *m* me drunken with Lam 3:15
Thou hast *m* us as the offscouring Lam 3:45 7760
I have *m* thy face strong against Eze 3:8 5414
than flint have I *m* thy forehead Eze 3:9 5414
I have *m* thee a watchman unto the Eze 3:17 5414
m desolate, and your idols may be Eze 6:6
but they *m* the images of their Eze 7:20 6213
neither *m* up the hedge for the Eze 13:5 1443
they have *m* others to hope that Eze 13:6
Because with lies ye have *m* the Eze 13:22
sad, whom I have not *m* sad Eze 13:22
hast *m* thee an high place in Eze 16:24 6213
hast *m* thy beauty to be abhorred, Eze 16:25
m a covenant with him, and hath Eze 17:13 3772
the king dwelleth that *m* him king Eze 17:16
have *m* the dry tree to flourish Eze 17:24
her whelps, and *m* him a young lion Eze 19:5 7760
m myself known unto them in the Eze 20:5
in whose sight I *m* myself known Eze 20:9
there also they *m* their sweet Eze 20:28 7760
it is *m* bright, it is wrapped up Eze 21:15
he *m* his arrows bright, he Eze 21:21
Because ye have *m* your iniquity Eze 21:24
in thine idols which thou hast *m* Eze 22:4 6213
therefore have I *m* thee a Eze 22:4 5414
dishonest gain which thou hast *m* Eze 22:13 6213
they have *m* her many widows in Eze 22:25
into a city wherein is *m* a breach Eze 26:10
is *m* in the midst of thee Eze 26:15
They have *m* all thy ship boards Eze 27:5 1129
of Bashan have they *m* thine oars Eze 27:6 6213
have *m* thy benches of ivory Eze 27:6 6213
they have *m* thy beauty perfect Eze 27:11 6213
m of cedar, among thy merchandise Eze 27:24
m very glorious in the midst of Eze 27:25
own, and I have *m* it for myself Eze 29:3 6213
The river is mine, and I have *m* it Eze 29:9 6213
every head was *m* bald, and every Eze 29:18
The waters *m* him great, the deep Eze 31:4
All the fowls of heaven *m* their Eze 31:6
I have *m* him fair by the Eze 31:9
I *m* the nations to shake at the Eze 31:16
Because they have *m* you desolate Eze 36:3
their land, and none *m* them afraid Eze 39:26
He *m* also posts of threescore Eze 40:14 6213
a pavement *m* for the court round Eze 40:17 6213
it was *m* with cherubims and palm Eze 41:18 6213
it was *m* through all the house Eze 41:19 6213
were cherubims and palm trees *m* Eze 41:20 6213
And there were *m* on them, on the Eze 41:25 6213
like as were *m* upon the walls Eze 41:25 6213
Now when he had *m* an end of Eze 42:15
When thou hast *m* an end of Eze 43:23
it was *m* with boiling places Eze 46:23 6213
your houses shall be *m* a dunghill Dan 2:5 7761
Then Arioch *m* the thing known to Dan 2:15
m the thing known to Hananiah, Dan 2:17
hast *m* known unto me now what we Dan 2:23
for thou hast now *m* known unto us Dan 2:23
hath *m* thee ruler over them all Dan 2:38
the great God hath *m* known to the Dan 2:45
Then the king *m* Daniel a great Dan 2:48 7236
m him ruler over the whole Dan 2:48
the king *m* an image of gold Dan 3:1 5648
hast *m* a decree, that every man Dan 3:10 7761
worship the image which I have *m* Dan 3:15 5648
houses shall be *m* a dunghill Dan 3:29 7739
I saw a dream which *m* me afraid Dan 4:5
Therefore *m* I a decree to bring Dan 4:6 7761
Belshazzar the king *m* a great Dan 5:1 5648
m master of the magicians, Dan 5:11
his heart was *m* like the beasts, Dan 5:21 7737
m a proclamation concerning him, Dan 5:29
m stand upon the feet as a man, Dan 7:4
m me know the interpretation of Dan 7:16
the same horn *m* war with the Dan 7:21 5648
which was *m* king over the realm Dan 9:1
m my confession, and said, O Lord, Dan 9:4
yet *m* we not our prayer before Dan 9:13
after the league *m* with him he Dan 11:23
be purified, and *m* white, and tried Dan 12:10
the tribes of Israel have I *m* Hos 5:9
of our king the princes have *m* Hos 7:5
For they have *m* ready their heart Hos 7:6
they have *m* princes, and I knew it Hos 8:4

their gold have they *m* them idols Hos 8:4 6213
the workman *m* it Hos 8:6 6213
Ephraim hath *m* many altars to sin Hos 8:11
land they have *m* goodly images Hos 10:1
wept, and *m* supplication unto him Hos 12:4
have *m* them molten images of Hos 13:2 6213
he hath *m* it clean bare, and cast Joel 1:7
the branches thereof are *m* white Joel 1:7
flocks of sheep are *m* desolate Joel 1:18
I have *m* the stink of your camps Amos 4:10
god, which ye *m* to yourselves Amos 5:26 6213
that when they had *m* an end of Amos 7:2
upon a wall *m* by a plumbline Amos 7:7
I have *m* thee small among the Obad 2 5414
of heaven, which hath *m* the sea Jonah 1:9 6213
unto the LORD, and *m* vows Jonah 1:16
there *m* him a booth, and sat under Jonah 4:5 6213
m it to come up over Jonah, that Jonah 4:6
shield of his mighty men is *m* red Nah 2:3
whelp, and none *m* them afraid Nah 2:11
which *m* them afraid, because of Hab 2:17
Thy bow was *m* quite naked Hab 3:9
I *m* their streets waste, that Zeph 3:6
they *m* their hearts as an adamant Zec 7:12 7760
m thee as the sword of a mighty Zec 9:13 7760
hath *m* them as his goodly horse Zec 10:3 7760
which I had *m* with all the people Zec 11:10 3772
have I also *m* you contemptible Mal 2:9 5414
that these stones be *m* bread Mt 4:3 *1096*
garment, and the rent is *m* worse Mt 9:16 *1096*
thy faith hath *m* thee whole Mt 9:22 *4982*
the woman was *m* whole from that Mt 9:22 *4982*
when Jesus had *m* an end of Mt 11:1 *5055*
as touched were *m* perfectly whole Mt 14:36 *1295*
Thus have ye *m* the commandment of Mt 15:6 *208*
her daughter was *m* whole from Mt 15:28 *2390*
that he had, and payment to be *m* Mt 18:25 *591*
that he which *m* them at the Mt 19:4 *4160*
them at the beginning *m* them male Mt 19:4 *4160*
which were *m* eunuchs of men Mt 19:12 *2134*
which have *m* themselves eunuchs Mt 19:12 *2134*
thou hast *m* them equal unto us, Mt 20:12 *4160*
but ye have *m* it a den of thieves Mt 21:13 *4160*
which *m* a marriage for his son, Mt 22:2 *4160*
But they *m* light of it, and went Mt 22:5 *272*
one proselyte, and when he is *m* Mt 23:15 *1096*
whom his lord hath *m* ruler over Mt 24:45 *2525*
And at midnight there was a cry *m* Mt 25:6 *1096*
m them other five talents Mt 25:16 *4160*
they *m* ready the passover Mt 26:19 *2090*
but that rather a tumult was *m* Mt 27:24 *1096*
be *m* sure until the third day Mt 27:64 *805*
m the sepulchre sure, sealing the Mt 27:66 *805*
the old, and the rent is *m* worse Mk 2:21 *1096*
them, The sabbath was *m* for man Mk 2:27 *1096*
thy faith hath *m* thee whole Mk 5:34 *4982*
birthday *m* a supper to his lords Mk 6:21 *4160*
many as touched him were *m* whole Mk 6:56 *4982*
upon his eyes, and *m* him look up Mk 8:25 *4160*
of the creation God *m* them male Mk 10:6 *4160*
thy faith hath *m* thee whole Mk 10:52 *4982*
but ye have *m* it a den of thieves Mk 11:17 *4160*
was this waste of the ointment *m* Mk 14:4 *1096*
they *m* ready the passover Mk 14:16 *2090*
this temple that is *m* with hands Mk 14:58 *5499*
build another *m* without hands Mk 14:58 *886*
that had *m* insurrection with him Mk 15:7 *4955*
they *m* signs to his father, how Lk 1:62 *1770*
this taxing was first *m* when Lk 2:2 *1096*
the Lord hath *m* known unto us Lk 2:15 *1107*
they *m* known abroad the saying Lk 2:17 *1232*
the crooked shall be *m* straight Lk 3:5 *1519*
the rough ways shall be *m* smooth Lk 3:5 *1519*
this stone that it be *m* bread Lk 4:3 *1096*
Levi *m* him a great feast in his Lk 5:29 *4160*
that shall not be *m* manifest Lk 8:17 *1096*
thy faith hath *m* thee whole Lk 8:48 4982
only, and she shall be *m* whole Lk 8:50 *4982*
did so, and *m* them all sit down Lk 9:15 *347*
did not he that *m* that which is Lk 11:40 *4160*
who *m* me a judge or a divider Lk 12:14 *2525*
and immediately she was *m* straight Lk 13:13 *461*
again, and a recompence be *m* thee Lk 14:12 *1096*
A certain man *m* a great supper, Lk 14:16 *4160*
thy faith hath *m* thee whole Lk 17:19 *4982*
he *m* haste, and came down, and Lk 19:6 *4692*
but ye have *m* it a den of thieves Lk 19:46 *4160*
they *m* ready the passover Lk 22:13 *2090*
Herod were *m* friends together Lk 23:12 *1096*
a certain sedition *m* in the city Lk 23:19 *1096*
of our company *m* us astonished Lk 24:22 *1839*
he *m* as though he would have gone Lk 24:28 *4364*
All things were *m* by him Jn 1:3 *1096*
was not any thing *m* that was *m* Jn 1:3 *1096*
world, and the world was *m* by him Jn 1:10 *1096*
And the Word was *m* flesh, and dwelt Jn 1:14 *1096*
he should be *m* manifest to Israel Jn 1:31 *5319*
tasted the water that was *m* wine Jn 2:9 *1096*
when he had *m* a scourge of small Jn 2:15 *4160*
that his deeds may be *m* manifest Jn 3:21 *5319*
Pharisees had heard that Jesus *m* Jn 4:1 *4160*
where he *m* the water wine Jn 4:46 *4160*
of the water stepped in was *m* Jn 5:4 *1096*
unto him, Wilt thou be *m* whole Jn 5:6 *1096*
immediately the man was *m* whole Jn 5:9 *1096*
He that *m* me whole, the same said Jn 5:11 *4160*
him, Behold, thou art *m* whole Jn 5:14 *1096*
was Jesus, which had *m* him whole Jn 5:15 *4160*
because I have *m* a man every whit Jn 7:23 *4160*
sayest thou, Ye shall be *m* free Jn 8:33 *1096*
God should be *m* manifest in him Jn 9:3
m clay of the spittle, and he Jn 9:6 *4160*
A man that is called Jesus *m* clay Jn 9:11 *4160*
sabbath day when Jesus *m* the clay Jn 9:14 *4160*

they which see might be *m* blind Jn 9:39 *1096*
There they *m* him a supper Jn 12:2 *4160*
my Father I have *m* known unto you Jn 15:15 *1107*
that they may be *m* perfect in one Jn 17:23 *5048*
who had *m* a fire of coals Jn 18:18 *4160*
because he *m* himself the Son of Jn 19:7 *4160*
m four parts, to every soldier a Jn 19:23 *4160*
The former treatise have I *m* Acts 1:1 *4160*
Thou hast *m* known to me the ways Acts 2:28 *1107*
that God hath *m* that same Jesus, Acts 2:36 *4160*
we had *m* this man to walk Acts 3:12 *4160*
his name hath *m* this man strong Acts 3:16 *4732*
which God *m* with our fathers Acts 3:25 *1303*
man, by what means he is *m* whole Acts 4:9 *4982*
thou art God, which hast *m* heaven Acts 4:24 *4160*
distribution was *m* unto every man Acts 4:35 *1239*
he *m* him governor over Egypt and Acts 7:10 *2525*
was *m* known to his brethren Acts 7:13 *319*
kindred was *m* known unto Pharaoh Acts 7:13 *1096*
Who *m* thee a ruler and a judge Acts 7:27 *2525*
Who *m* thee a ruler and a judge Acts 7:35 *2525*
they *m* a calf in those days, and Acts 7:41 *3447*
which ye *m* to worship them Acts 7:43 *4160*
not in temples *m* with hands Acts 7:48 *5499*
not my hand *m* all these things Acts 7:50 *4160*
m great lamentation over him Acts 8:2 *4160*
he *m* havock of the church, Acts 8:3 *1096*
coats and garments which Dorcas *m* Acts 9:39 *4160*
but while they *m* ready, he fell Acts 10:10 *3903*
had *m* enquiry for Simon's house Acts 10:17 *1239*
but prayer was *m* without ceasing Acts 12:5 *1096*
having *m* Blastus the king's Acts 12:20 *3982*
throne, and *m* an oration unto them Acts 12:21 *1215*
which was *m* unto the fathers Acts 13:32 *1096*
m their minds evil affected Acts 14:2 *2559*
an assault *m* both of the Gentiles Acts 14:5 *1096*
which *m* heaven, and earth, and the Acts 14:15 *4160*
while ago God *m* choice among us Acts 15:7 *1586*
where prayer was wont to be *m* Acts 16:13 *1511*
m their feet fast in the stocks Acts 16:24 *805*
God that *m* the world and all Acts 17:24 *4160*
not in temples *m* with hands Acts 17:24 *5499*
hath *m* of one blood all nations Acts 17:26 *4160*
the Jews *m* insurrection with one Acts 18:12 *2721*
which *m* silver shrines for Diana, Acts 19:24 *4160*
no gods, which are *m* with hands Acts 19:26 *1096*
would have *m* his defence unto the Acts 19:33 *626*
Holy Ghost hath *m* you overseers Acts 20:28 *5087*
when there was *m* a great silence, Acts 21:40 *1096*
as I *m* my journey, and was come Acts 22:6 *4198*
forty which had *m* this conspiracy Acts 23:13 *4160*
promise *m* of God unto our fathers Acts 26:6 *1096*
to the wind, and *m* toward shore Acts 27:40 *2722*
which was *m* of the seed of David Rom 1:3 *1096*
by the things that are *m*, even Rom 1:20 *4161*
image *m* like to corruptible man Rom 1:23
circumcision is *m* uncircumcision Rom 2:25 *1096*
the law be heirs, faith is *m* void Rom 4:14 *2758*
the promise *m* of none effect Rom 4:14 *2673*
I have *m* thee a father of many Rom 4:17 *5087*
disobedience many were *m* sinners Rom 5:19 *2525*
of one shall many be *m* righteous Rom 5:19 *2525*
Being then *m* free from sin, ye Rom 6:18 *1659*
But now being *m* free from sin Rom 6:22 *1659*
which is good *m* death unto me Rom 7:13 *1096*
m me free from the law of sin Rom 8:2 *1659*
creature was *m* subject to vanity Rom 8:20 *5293*
it, Why hast thou *m* me thus Rom 9:20 *4160*
been *m* like unto Gomorrha Rom 9:29 *3666*
confession is *m* unto salvation Rom 10:10 *3670*
I was *m* manifest unto them that Rom 10:20 *1096*
Let their table be *m* a snare Rom 11:9 *1096*
or is offended, or is *m* weak Rom 14:21 *770*
the promises *m* unto the fathers Rom 15:8
m partakers of their spiritual Rom 15:27 *2841*
But now is *m* manifest, and by the Rom 16:26 *5319*
m known to all nations for the Rom 16:26 *1107*
Christ should be *m* of none effect 1Cor 1:17 *2758*
hath not God *m* foolish the wisdom 1Cor 1:20 *3471*
who of God is *m* unto us wisdom, 1Cor 1:30 *1096*
man's work shall be *m* manifest 1Cor 3:13 *1096*
for we are *m* a spectacle unto the 1Cor 4:9 *1096*
we are *m* as the filth of the 1Cor 4:13 *1096*
but if thou mayest be *m* free 1Cor 7:21 *1096*
yet have I *m* myself servant unto 1Cor 9:19 *1402*
I am *m* all things to all men, 1Cor 9:22 *1096*
may be *m* manifest among you 1Cor 11:19 *1096*
have been all *m* to drink into one 1Cor 12:13 *4222*
secrets of his heart *m* manifest 1Cor 14:25 *1096*
so in Christ shall all be *m* alive 1Cor 15:22 *2227*
man Adam was *m* a living soul 1Cor 15:45 *1096*
the last Adam was *m* a quickening 1Cor 15:45
the same which is *m* sorry by me 2Cor 2:2 *3076*
Who also hath *m* us able ministers 2Cor 3:6 *2427*
For even that which was *m* 2Cor 3:10 *1392*
might be *m* manifest in our body 2Cor 4:10 *5319*
be *m* manifest in our mortal flesh 2Cor 4:11 *5319*
of God, an house not *m* with hands 2Cor 5:1 *886*
but we are *m* manifest unto God 2Cor 5:11 *5319*
I trust also are *m* manifest in 2Cor 5:11 *5319*
For he hath *m* him to be sin for 2Cor 5:21 *4160*
that we might be *m* the 2Cor 5:21 *1096*
For though I *m* you sorry with a 2Cor 7:8 *3076*
the same epistle hath *m* you sorry 2Cor 7:8 *3076*
rejoice, not that ye were *m* sorry 2Cor 7:9 *3076*
for ye were *m* sorry after a godly 2Cor 7:9 *3076*
which I *m* before Titus, is found 2Cor 7:14
of things *m* ready to our hand 2Cor 10:16 *2092*
m manifest among you in all 2Cor 11:6 *5319*
for my strength is *m* perfect in 2Cor 12:9 *5048*
are ye now *m* perfect by the flesh Gal 3:3 *2005*
the law, being *m* a curse for us Gal 3:13 *1096*
and his seed were the promises *m* Gal 3:16 *4483*
come to whom the promise was *m* Gal 3:19 *1861*

m of a woman, *m* under the law, ... Gal 4:4 *1096*
wherewith Christ hath *m* us free... Gal 5:1 *1659*
wherein he hath *m* us accepted in... Eph 1:6 *5487*
Having *m* known unto us the ... Eph 1:9 *1107*
m us sit together in heavenly... Eph 2:6 *4776*
in the flesh *m* by hands... Eph 2:11 *5499*
are *m* nigh by the blood of Christ... Eph 2:13 *1096*
is our peace, who hath *m* both one ... Eph 2:14 *4160*
he *m* known unto me the mystery... Eph 3:3 *1107*
not *m* known unto the sons of men ... Eph 3:5 *1107*
Whereof I was *m* a minister... Eph 3:7 *1096*
are *m* manifest by the light... Eph 5:13 *5319*
But *m* himself of no reputation,... Phil 2:7 *1096*
was *m* in the likeness of men... Phil 2:7 *1096*
being *m* conformable unto his... Phil 3:10 *4832*
your requests be *m* known unto God... Phil 4:6 *1107*
which hath *m* us meet to be... Col 1:12 *2427*
having *m* peace through the blood... Col 1:20 *1517*
whereof I Paul am *m* a minister... Col 1:23 *1096*
Whereof I am *m* a minister... Col 1:25 *1096*
but now is *m* manifest to his... Col 1:26 *5319*
the circumcision *m* without hands... Col 2:11 *1096*
he *m* a shew of them openly, ... Col 2:15 *1165*
law is not *m* for a righteous man... 1Ti 1:9 *2749*
concerning faith have *m* shipwreck... 1Ti 1:19 *3489*
of thanks, be *m* for all men... 1Ti 2:1 *4160*
But is now *m* manifest by the... 2Ti 1:10 *5319*
we should be *m* heirs according to ... Titus 3:7 *1096*
by whom also he *m* the worlds... Heb 1:2 *4160*
Being *m* so much better than the... Heb 1:4 *1096*
who was *m* a little lower than the... Heb 2:9 *1642*
to be *m* like unto his brethren... Heb 2:17 *3666*
For we are *m* partakers of Christ,... Heb 3:14 *1096*
himself to be *m* an high priest... Heb 5:5 *1096*
being *m* perfect, he became the... Heb 5:9 *5048*
were *m* partakers of the Holy... Heb 6:4 *1096*
For when God *m* promise to Abraham Heb 6:13 *1861*
m an high priest for ever after... Heb 6:20 *1096*
but *m* like unto the Son of God... Heb 7:3 *871*
there is *m* of necessity a change... Heb 7:12 *1096*
Who is *m*, not after the law of a ... Heb 7:16 *1096*
For the law *m* nothing perfect,... Heb 7:19 *5048*
without an oath he was *m* priest... Heb 7:20
priests were *m* without an oath... Heb 7:21 *1096*
By so much was Jesus *m* a surety... Heb 7:22 *1096*
m higher than the heavens... Heb 7:26 *1096*
that I *m* with their fathers... Heb 8:9 *4160*
covenant, he hath *m* the first old... Heb 8:13 *3822*
For there was a tabernacle *m*... Heb 9:2 *2680*
of all was not yet *m* manifest... Heb 9:8 *5319*
not *m* with hands, that is to say,... Heb 9:11 *5499*
into the holy places *m* with hands... Heb 9:24 *5499*
again *m* of sins every year... Heb 10:3
his enemies be *m* his footstool... Heb 10:13 5087
whilst ye were *m* a gazingstock... Heb 10:33 *2301*
not *m* of things which do appear... Heb 11:3 *1096*
m mention of the departing of the... Heb 11:22 *3421*
out of weakness were *m* strong... Heb 11:34 *1743*
us should not be *m* perfect... Heb 11:40 *5048*
the spirits of just men *m* perfect... Heb 12:23 *5048*
shaken, as of things that are *m*... Heb 12:27 *4160*
But the rich, in that he is *m* low... Jas 1:10 *5014*
and by works was faith *m* perfect... Jas 2:22 *5048*
which are *m* after the similitude... Jas 3:9 *1096*
the same is *m* the head of the... 1Pet 2:7 *1096*
powers being *m* subject unto him... 1Pet 3:22 *5293*
when we *m* known unto you the... 2Pet 1:16 *1107*
m to be taken and destroyed, speak... 2Pet 2:12 *1080*
that they might be *m* manifest... 1Jn 2:19 *5319*
Herein is our love *m* perfect... 1Jn 4:17 *5048*
feareth is not *m* perfect in love... 1Jn 4:18 5048
not God hath *m* him a liar... 1Jn 5:10 *4160*
hath *m* us kings and priests unto... Rev 1:6 *4160*
hast *m* us unto our God kings and... Rev 5:10 *4160*
m them white in the blood of the... Rev 7:14 *3021*
because they were *m* bitter... Rev 8:11 *4087*
and worship him that *m* heaven... Rev 14:7 *4160*
because she *m* all nations drink... Rev 14:8 *4222*
for thy judgments are *m* manifest... Rev 15:4 *5319*
of the earth have been *m* drunk... Rev 17:2 *3182*
which were *m* rich by her, shall... Rev 18:15 *4147*
wherein were *m* rich all that had... Rev 18:19 *4147*
for in one hour is she *m* desolate... Rev 18:19 *2049*
and his wife hath *m* herself ready... Rev 19:7 *2090*

MADEST
m a covenant with him to give the... Neh 9:8 3772
m known unto them thy holy... Neh 9:14 3045
Thou *m* him to have dominion over... Ps 8:6
that thou *m* strong for thyself... Ps 80:15
whom thou *m* strong for thyself... Ps 80:17
m to thyself images of men, and... Eze 16:17 6213
m all their loins to be at a... Eze 29:7
not laboured, neither *m* it grow... Jonah 4:10
before these days *m* an uproar... Acts 21:38 *387*
Thou *m* him a little lower than... Heb 2:7 *1642*

MADIAN (*ma'-de-an*) See MIDIAN. *Same as Midian 2.*
was a stranger in the land of *M*... Acts 7:29 *3099*

MADMANNAH (*mad-man'-nah*)
1. A city in Judah.
And Ziklag, and *M*, and Sansannah,... Josh 15:31 4089
2. Grandson of Caleb.
bare also Shaaph the father of *M*... 1Chr 2:49 4089

MADMEN (*mad'-men*) See MADMENAH. *A Moabite city.*
Also thou shalt be cut down, O *M*... Jer 48:2 4086

MADMENAH (*mad-me'-nah*) See MADMEN. *A city in Benjamin.*
M is removed... Is 10:31 4088

MADNESS
The LORD shall smite thee with *m*... Deut 28:28 7697
to know wisdom, and to know *m*... Eccl 1:17 1947
myself to behold wisdom, and *m*... Eccl 2:12 1947
folly, even of foolishness and *m*... Eccl 7:25 1947
m is in their heart while they... Eccl 9:3 1947
end of his talk is mischievous *m*... Eccl 10:13 1948
astonishment, and his rider with *m*... Zec 12:4 7697
And they were filled with *m*... Lk 6:11 *454*
voice forbad the *m* of the prophet... 2Pet 2:16 *3913*

MADON (*ma'-don*) *A Canaanite city.*
that he sent to Jobab king of *M*... Josh 11:1 4068
The king of *M*, one... Josh 12:19 4068

MAGADAN See MAGDALA.

MAGBISH (*mag'-bish*) *A family of exiles.*
The children of *M*, an hundred... Ezr 2:30 4019

MAGDALA (*mag'-da-lah*) See MAGDALENE. *A city in Galilee.*
and came into the coasts of *M*... Mt 15:39 *3093*

MAGDALENE (*mag'-da-leen*) *A woman acquaintance of Jesus.*
Among which was Mary *M*, and Mary. Mt 27:56 *3094*
And there was Mary *M*, and the other. Mt 27:61 *3094*
day of the week, came Mary *M*... Mt 28:1 *3094*
among whom was Mary *M*, and Mary. Mk 15:40 *3094*
And Mary *M* and Mary the mother of.. Mk 15:47 *3094*
when the sabbath was past, Mary *M*... Mk 16:1 *3094*
week, he appeared first to Mary *M*... Mk 16:9 *3094*
and infirmities, Mary called *M*... Lk 8:2 *3094*
It was Mary *M*, and Joanna, and Mary Lk 24:10 *3094*
the wife of Cleophas, and Mary *M*... Jn 19:25 *3094*
of the week cometh Mary *M* early... Jn 20:1 *3094*
Mary *M* came and told the disciples... Jn 20:18 *3094*

MAGDIEL (*mag'-de-el*) *A duke of Edom.*
Duke *M*, duke Iram... Gen 36:43 4025
Duke *M*, duke Iram... 1Chr 1:54 4025

MAGICIAN
that asked such things at any *m*... Dan 2:10 2749

MAGICIANS
and called for all the *m* of Egypt... Gen 41:8 2748
and I told this unto the *m*... Gen 41:24 2748
now the *m* of Egypt, they also did... Ex 7:11 2748
the *m* of Egypt did so with their... Ex 7:22 2748
And the *m* did so with their... Ex 8:7 2748
And the *m* did so with their... Ex 8:18 2748
Then the *m* said unto Pharaoh,... Ex 8:19 2748
the *m* could not stand before... Ex 9:11 2748
for the boil was upon the *m*... Ex 9:11 2748
ten times better than all the *m*... Dan 1:20 2748
the king commanded to call the *m*... Dan 2:2 2748
wise men, the astrologers, the *m*... Dan 2:27 2749
Then came in the *m*, the... Dan 4:7 2749
O Belteshazzar, master of the *m*... Dan 4:9 2749
thy father, made master of the *m*... Dan 5:11 2749

MAGISTRATE
and there was no *m* in the land... Judg 18:7
with thine adversary to the *m*... Lk 12:58 *758*

MAGISTRATES
God, that is in thine hand, set *m*... Ezr 7:25 8200
unto the synagogues, and unto *m*... Lk 12:11 *746*
And brought them to the *m*, saying,... Acts 16:20 *4755*
the *m* rent off their clothes, and... Acts 16:22 *4755*
the *m* sent the serjeants, saying,... Acts 16:35 *4755*
The *m* have sent to let you go... Acts 16:36 *4755*
told these words unto the *m*... Acts 16:38 *4755*
and powers, to obey *m*, to be ready... Titus 3:1 *3980*

MAGNIFICAL
for the LORD must be exceeding *m*... 1Chr 22:5 1431

MAGNIFICENCE
her *m* should be destroyed, whom... Acts 19:27 *3168*

MAGNIFIED
sight, and thou hast *m* thy mercy... Gen 19:19 1431
On that day the LORD *m* Joshua in... Josh 4:14 1431
And let thy name be *m* for ever... 2Sa 7:26 1431
that thy name may be *m* for ever... 1Chr 17:24 1431
the LORD *m* Solomon exceedingly in... 1Chr 29:25 1431
with him, and *m* him exceedingly... 2Chr 1:1 1431
so that he was *m* in the sight of... 2Chr 32:23 5375
continually, Let the LORD be *m*... Ps 35:27 1431
say continually, The LORD be *m*... Ps 40:16 1431
say continually, Let God be *m*... Ps 70:4 1431
for thou hast *m* thy word above... Ps 138:2 1431
for he *m* himself against the LORD... Jer 48:26 1431
because he hath *m* himself against... Jer 48:42 1431
for the enemy hath *m* himself... Lam 1:9 1431
he *m* himself even to the prince... Dan 8:11 1431
m themselves against their border... Zeph 2:8 1431
m themselves against the people... Zeph 2:10 1431
The LORD will be *m* from the... Mal 1:5 1431
but the people *m* them... Acts 5:13 *3170*
the name of the Lord Jesus was *m*... Acts 19:17 *3170*
also Christ shall be *m* in my body... Phil 1:20 *3170*

MAGNIFY
This day will I begin to *m* thee... Josh 3:7 1431
is man, that thou shouldest *m* him... Job 7:17 1431
If indeed ye will *m* yourselves... Job 19:5 1431
Remember that thou *m* his work... Job 36:24 7679
O *m* the LORD with me, and let us... Ps 34:3 1431
dishonour that *m* themselves... Ps 35:26 1431
they *m* themselves against me... Ps 38:16 1431
me that did *m* himself against me... Ps 55:12 1431
will *m* him with thanksgiving... Ps 69:30 1431
or shall the saw *m* itself against... Is 10:15 1431
he will *m* the law, and make it... Is 42:21 1431
Thus will I *m* myself, and sanctify... Eze 38:23 1431
he shall *m* himself in his heart,... Dan 8:25 1431
m himself above every god, and... Dan 11:36 1431
for he shall *m* himself above all... Dan 11:37 1431
do not *m* themselves against Judah... Zec 12:7 1431
said, My soul doth *m* the Lord... Lk 1:46 *3170*
them speak with tongues, and *m* God.. Acts 10:46 *3170*
of the Gentiles, I *m* mine office... Rom 11:13 *1392*

MAGOG (*ma'-gog*)
1. A son of Japheth.
Gomer, and *M*, and Madai, and Javan,. Gen 10:2 4031
Gomer, and *M*, and Madai, and Javan,. 1Chr 1:5 4031
2. Descendants of Magog.
face against Gog, the land of *M*... Eze 38:2 4031
And I will send a fire on *M*... Eze 39:6 4031
quarters of the earth, Gog and *M*... Rev 20:8 *3098*

MAGOR-MISSABIB (*ma''-gor-mis'-sa-bib*) *A symbolic name of Pashur.*
not called thy name Pashur, but *M*... Jer 20:3 4036

MAGPIASH (*mag'-pe-ash*) *A chief Israelite who renewed the covenant.*
M, Meshullam, Hezir,... Neh 10:20 4047

MAHALAH (*ma'-ha-lah*) See MAHLAH. *Great-grandson of Manasseh.*
bare Ishod, and Abiezer, and *M*... 1Chr 7:18 4244

MAHALALEEL (*ma-hal'-a-le-el*) See MALELEEL.
1. Son of Cainan.
lived seventy years, and begat *M*... Gen 5:12 4111
after he begat *M* eight hundred... Gen 5:13 4111
M lived sixty and five years, and... Gen 5:15 4111
M lived after he begat Jared... Gen 5:16 4111
all the days of *M* were eight... Gen 5:17 4111
Kenan, *M*, Jered,... 1Chr 1:2 4111
2. A family of exiles.
son of Shephatiah, the son of *M*... Neh 11:4 4111

MAHALALEL See MAHALALEEL.

MAHALATH (*ma'-ha-lath*) See BASHEMATH.
1. A daughter of Ishmael.
he had *M* the daughter of Ishmael... Gen 28:9 4258
2. A granddaughter of David.
Rehoboam took him *M* the daughter... 2Chr 11:18 4258
3. A musical choir.
To the chief Musician upon *M*... Ps 53:t 4257
chief Musician upon *M* Leannoth... Ps 88:t 4257

MAHALI (*ma'-ha-li*) See MAHLI. *Same as Lahli 1.*
sons of Merari; *M* and Mushi... Ex 6:19 4249

MAHANAIM (*ma-ha-na'-im*) *A town east of the Jordan.*
called the name of that place *M*... Gen 32:2 4266
from *M* unto the border of Debir... Josh 13:26 4266
And their coast was from *M*... Josh 13:30 4266
and *M* with her suburbs,... Josh 21:38 4266
of Saul, and brought him over to *M*... 2Sa 2:8 4266
Saul, went out from *M* to Gibeon... 2Sa 2:12 4266
all Bithron, and they came to *M*... 2Sa 2:29 4266
Then David came to *M*... 2Sa 17:24 4266
to pass, when David was come to *M*... 2Sa 17:27 4266
of sustenance while he lay at *M*... 2Sa 19:32 4266
curse in the day when I went to *M*... 1Kin 2:8 4266
Ahinadab the son of Iddo had *M*... 1Kin 4:14 4266
suburbs, and *M* with her suburbs,... 1Chr 6:80 4266

MAHANEH-DAN (*ma'-ha-neh-dan*) *A place in Judah.*
called that place *M* unto this day... Judg 18:12 4265

MAHARAI (*ma'-ha-rahee*) *A warrior of David.*
the Ahohite, *M* the Netophathite,... 2Sa 23:28 4121
M the Netophathite, Heled the son... 1Chr 11:30 4121
month was *M* the Netophathite... 1Chr 27:13 4121

MAHATH (*ma'-hath*)
1. A descendant of Kohath.
the son of Elkanah, the son of *M*... 1Chr 6:35 4287
M the son of Amasai, and Joel the... 2Chr 29:12 4287
2. A Temple servant.
and Eliel, and Ismachiah, and *M*... 2Chr 31:13 4287

MAHAVITE (*ma'-ha-vite*) *Family name of Eliel.*
Eliel the *M*, and Jeribai, and... 1Chr 11:46 4233

MAHAZIOTH (*ma-ha'-ze-oth*) *A sanctuary servant.*
Mallothi, Hothir, and *M*... 1Chr 25:4 4238
The three and twentieth to *M*... 1Chr 25:30 4238

MAHER-SHALAL-HASH-BAZ (*ma''-her-sha''-lal-hash'-baz*) *A son of Isaiah.*
it with a man's pen concerning *M*... Is 8:1 4122
the LORD to me, Call his name *M*... Is 8:3 4122

MAHLAH (*mah'-lah*) *A daughter of Zelophehad.*
daughters of Zelophehad were *M*... Num 26:33 4244
M, Noah, and Hoglah, and Milcah, and Num 27:1 4244
For *M*, Tirzah, and Hoglah, and... Num 36:11 4244
are the names of his daughters, *M*... Josh 17:3 4244

MAHLI (*mah'-li*) See MAHALI, MAHLITES.
1. Son of Merari.
their families; *M*, and Mushi... Num 3:20 4249
of Merari; *M*, and Mushi... 1Chr 6:19 4249
M, Libni his son, Shimei his son,... 1Chr 6:29 4249
M, and Mushi. The sons of *M*... 1Chr 23:21 4249
The sons of Merari were *M*... 1Chr 24:26 4249
Of *M* came Eleazar, who had no... 1Chr 24:28 4249
understanding, of the sons of *M*... Ezr 8:18 4249
2. Son of Mushi.
The son of *M*, the son of Mushi,... 1Chr 6:47 4249
M, and Eder, and Jeremoth, three... 1Chr 23:23 4249
M, and Eder, and Jerimoth... 1Chr 24:30 4249

MAHLITES (*mah'-lites*) *Descendants of Mahli 1.*
Of Merari was the family of the *M*... Num 3:33 4250
Hebronites, the family of the *M*... Num 26:58 4250

MAHLON (*mah'-lon*) See Mahlon's. *A son of Naomi.*
and the name of his two sons *M* Ruth 1:2 4248
And *M* and Chilion died also both of Ruth 1:5 4248
Ruth the Moabitess, the wife of *M* Ruth 4:10 4248

MAHLON'S (*mah'-lons*)
and all that was Chilion's and *M* Ruth 4:9 4248

MAHOL (*ma'-hol*) *Father of some wise men.*
Chalcol, and Darda, the sons of *M* 1Kin 4:31 4235

MAHSEIAH See Maseiah.

MAID
I pray thee, go in unto my *m* Gen 16:2 8198
took Hagar her *m* the Egyptian Gen 16:3 8198
I have given my *m* into thy bosom Gen 16:5 8198
Behold, thy *m* is in thy hand Gen 16:6 8198
And he said, Hagar, Sarai's *m* Gen 16:8 8198
Leah Zilpah his *m* for an handmaid Gen 29:24 8198
Bilhah his handmaid to be her *m* Gen 29:29 8198
And she said, Behold my *m* Bilhah Gen 30:3 519
Bilhah Rachel's *m* conceived again Gen 30:7 8198
bearing, she took Zilpah her *m* Gen 30:9 8198
Zilpah Leah's *m* bare Jacob a son Gen 30:10 8198
Zilpah Leah's *m* bare Jacob a Gen 30:12 8198
flags, she sent her *m* to fetch it Ex 2:5 519
the *m* went and called the child's Ex 2:8 5959
a man smite his servant, or his *m* Ex 21:20 519
his servant, or the eye of his *m* Ex 21:26 519
if a man entice a *m* that is not Ex 22:16 1330
But if she bear a *m* child Lev 12:5 5347
and for thy servant, and for thy *m* Lev 25:6 519
came to her, I found her not a *m* Deut 22:14 1331
I found not thy daughter a *m* Deut 22:17 1331
of the land of Israel a little *m* 2Kin 5:2 5291
thus said the *m* that is of the 2Kin 5:4 5291
the *m* was fair and beautiful Est 2:7 5291
why then should I think upon a *m* Job 31:1 1330
and the way of a man with a *m* Prov 30:19 5959
as with the *m*, so with her Is 24:2 8198
Can a *m* forget her ornaments, or Jer 2:32 1330
in pieces the young man and the *m* Jer 51:22 1330
father will go in unto the same *m* Amos 2:7 5291
for the *m* is not dead, but Mt 9:24 *2877*
her by the hand, and the *m* arose Mt 9:25 *2877*
into the porch, another *m* saw him Mt 26:71
a *m* saw him again, and began to Mk 14:69 *3814*
by the hand, and called, saying, *M* Lk 8:54 *3816*
But a certain *m* beheld him as he Lk 22:56 *3814*

MAIDEN
I have given my *m* to my husband Gen 30:18 8198
Behold, here is my daughter a *m* Judg 19:24 1330
no compassion upon young man or *m* 2Chr 36:17 1330
let the *m* which pleaseth the king Est 2:4 5291
the *m* pleased him, and she Est 2:9 5291
thus came every *m* unto the king Est 2:13 5291
as the eyes of a *m* unto the hand Ps 123:2 8198
the father and the mother of the *m* Lk 8:51 *3816*

MAIDENS
her *m* walked along by the river's Ex 2:5 5291
but abide here fast by my *m* Ruth 2:8 5291
that thou go out with his *m* Ruth 2:22 5291
So she kept fast by the *m* of Boaz Ruth 2:23 5291
kindred, with whose *m* thou wast Ruth 3:2 5291
they found young *m* going out to 1Sa 9:11 5291
when many *m* were gathered Est 2:8 5291
as belonged to her, and seven *m* Est 2:9 5291
I also and my *m* will fast likewise Est 4:16 5291
or wilt thou bind him for thy *m* Job 41:5 5291
their *m* were not given to Ps 78:63 1330
Both young men, and *m* Ps 148:12 1330
She hath sent forth her *m* Prov 9:3 5291
and for the maintenance for thy *m* Prov 27:27 5291
household, and a portion to her *m* Prov 31:15 5291
I got me servants and *m*, and had Eccl 2:7 8198
but they shall take *m* of the seed Eze 44:22 1330
to beat the menservants and *m* Lk 12:45 *3814*

MAID'S
Now when every *m* turn was come to. Est 2:12 5291

MAIDS
Beside their servants and their *m* Ezr 2:65 519
her *m* unto the best place of the Est 2:9 5291
So Esther's *m* and her chamberlains Est 4:4 5291
that dwell in mine house, and my *m* Job 19:15 519
the *m* in the cities of Judah Lam 5:11 1330
Slay utterly old and young, both *m* Eze 9:6 1330
her *m* shall lead her as with the Nah 2:7 519
men cheerful, and new wine the *m* Zec 9:17 1330
one of the *m* of the high priest Mk 14:66 *3814*

MAIDSERVANT
of the *m* that is behind the mill Ex 11:5 8198
thy manservant, nor thy *m* Ex 20:10 519
nor his manservant, nor his *m* Ex 20:17 519
a man sell his daughter to be a *m* Ex 21:7 519
ox shall push a manservant or a *m* Ex 21:32 519
nor thy manservant, nor thy *m* Deut 5:14 519
thy *m* may rest as well as thou Deut 5:14 519
or his manservant, or his *m* Deut 5:21 519
and thy manservant, and thy *m* Deut 12:18 519
also unto thy *m* thou shalt do Deut 15:17 519
and thy manservant, and thy *m* Deut 16:11 519
and thy manservant, and thy *m* Deut 16:14 519
made Abimelech, the son of his *m* Judg 9:18 519
cause of my manservant or of my *m* Job 31:13 519
manservant, and every man his *m* Jer 34:9 8198
manservant, and every one his *m* Jer 34:10 8198

MAIDSERVANT'S
tooth, or his *m* tooth Ex 21:27 519

MAIDSERVANTS
and he asses, and menservants, and *m* Gen 12:16 8198
Abimelech, and his wife, and his *m* Gen 20:17 519
and gold, and menservants, and *m* Gen 24:35 8198
and had much cattle, and *m* Gen 30:43 8198
and your menservants, and your *m* Deut 12:12 519
take your menservants, and your *m* 1Sa 8:16 8198
of the *m* which thou hast spoken 2Sa 6:22 519
and oxen, and menservants, and *m* 2Kin 5:26 8198
their manservants and their *m* Neh 7:67 519

MAIDSERVANTS'
tent, and into the two *m* tents Gen 31:33 519

MAIL
and he was armed with a coat of *m* 1Sa 17:5 7193
he armed him with a coat of *m* 1Sa 17:38 7193

MAIMED
Blind, or broken, or *m*, or having Lev 22:22 2782
that were lame, blind, dumb, *m* Mt 15:30 *2948*
the *m* to be whole, the lame to Mt 15:31 *2948*
thee to enter into life halt or *m* Mt 18:8 *2948*
for thee to enter into life *m* Mk 9:43 *2948*
a feast, call the poor, the *m* Lk 14:13 *376*
in hither the poor, and the *m* Lk 14:21 *376*

MAINSAIL
and hoised up the *m* to the wind Acts 27:40 *736*

MAINTAIN
supplication, and *m* their cause 1Kin 8:45 6213
dwelling place, and *m* their cause, 1Kin 8:49 6213
that he *m* the cause of his 1Kin 8:59 6213
to *m* the house of the Lord 1Chr 26:27 2388
supplication, and *m* their cause 2Chr 6:35 6213
m their cause, and forgive thy 2Chr 6:39 6213
but I will *m* mine own ways before Job 13:15 3198
I know that the Lord will *m* the Ps 140:12 6213
might be careful to *m* good works Titus 3:8 *4291*
let ours also learn to *m* good Titus 3:14 *4291*

MAINTAINED
For thou hast *m* my right and my Ps 9:4 6213

MAINTAINEST
thou *m* my lot Ps 16:5 8551

MAINTENANCE
Now because we have *m* from the Ezr 4:14 4415
for the *m* for thy maidens Prov 27:27 2416

MAJESTY
glory, and the victory, and the *m* 1Chr 29:11 1935
m as had not been on any king 1Chr 29:25 1935
of his excellent *m* many days Est 1:4 1420
with God is terrible *m* Job 37:22 1935
Deck thyself now with *m* and Job 40:10 1347
m hast thou laid upon him Ps 21:5 1926
voice of the Lord is full of *m* Ps 29:4 1926
mighty, with thy glory and thy *m* Ps 45:3 1926
in thy *m* ride prosperously Ps 45:4 1926
reigneth, he is clothed with *m* Ps 93:1 1348
Honour and *m* are before him Ps 96:6 1926
thou art clothed with honour and *m* Ps 104:1 1926
of the glorious honour of thy *m* Ps 145:5 1935
the glorious *m* of his kingdom Ps 145:12 1926
Lord, and for the glory of his *m* Is 2:10 1347
Lord, and for the glory of his *m* Is 2:19 1347
Lord, and for the glory of his *m* Is 2:21 1347
shall sing for the *m* of the Lord Is 24:14 1347
will not behold the *m* of the Lord Is 26:10 1348
of his ornament, he set it in *m* Eze 7:20 1347
power, and for the honour of my *m* Dan 4:30 1923
excellent *m* was added unto me Dan 4:36 7238
thy father a kingdom and *m* Dan 5:18 7238
for the *m* that he gave him, all Dan 5:19 7238
in the *m* of the name of the Lord Mic 5:4 1347
the right hand of the *M* on high Heb 1:3 *3172*
throne of the *M* in the heavens Heb 8:1 *3172*
but were eyewitnesses of his *m* 2Pet 1:16 *3168*
God our Saviour, be glory and *m* Jude 25 *3172*

MAKAZ (*ma'-kaz*) *A town in Judah.*
The son of Dekar, in *M*, and in 1Kin 4:9 4739

MAKE
Let us *m* man in our image, after Gen 1:26 6213
I will *m* him an help meet for him Gen 2:18 6213
tree to be desired to *m* one wise Gen 3:6
did the Lord God *m* coats of skins Gen 3:21 6213
M thee an ark of gopher wood Gen 6:14 6213
rooms shalt thou *m* in the ark Gen 6:14 6213
fashion which thou shalt *m* it of Gen 6:15 6213
A window shalt thou *m* to the ark Gen 6:16 6213
and third stories shalt thou *m* it Gen 6:16 6213
the covenant which I *m* between me Gen 9:12 5414
to another, Go to, let us *m* brick Gen 11:3
let us *m* us a name, lest we be Gen 11:4 6213
I will *m* of thee a great nation, Gen 12:2 6213
bless thee, and *m* thy name great Gen 12:2
I will *m* thy seed as the dust of Gen 13:16 7760
I will *m* my covenant between me Gen 17:2 5414
I will *m* thee exceeding fruitful, Gen 17:6
I will *m* nations of thee, and Gen 17:6 5414
will *m* him fruitful, and will Gen 17:20
I will *m* him a great nation Gen 17:20 5414
M ready quickly three measures of Gen 18:6
it, and *m* cakes upon the hearth Gen 18:6 6213
let us *m* our father drink wine, Gen 19:32
let us *m* him drink wine this Gen 19:34
the bondwoman will I *m* a nation Gen 21:13 7760
for I will *m* him a great nation Gen 21:18 7760
I will *m* thee swear by the Lord, Gen 24:3
I will *m* thy seed to multiply as Gen 26:4
let us *m* a covenant with thee Gen 26:28 3772
m me savoury meat, such as I love Gen 27:4 6213
m me savoury meat, that I may eat Gen 27:7 6213
I will *m* them savoury meat for Gen 27:9 6213
m thee fruitful, and multiply thee Gen 28:3
let us *m* a covenant, I and thou Gen 31:44 3772
m thy seed as the sand of the sea Gen 32:12 7760
m ye marriages with us, and give Gen 34:9
me to *m* me to stink among the Gen 34:30
m there an altar unto God, that Gen 35:1 6213
I will *m* there an altar unto God, Gen 35:3 6213
m mention of me unto Pharaoh, and Gen 40:14
men home, and slay, and *m* ready Gen 43:16
for I will there *m* of thee a Gen 46:3 6213
the best of the land *m* thy father Gen 47:6
then *m* them rulers over my cattle Gen 47:6 7760
I will *m* thee fruitful, and Gen 48:4
I will *m* of thee a multitude of Gen 48:4 5414
God *m* thee as Ephraim and as Gen 48:20 6213
ye *m* them rest from their burdens Ex 5:5
give the people straw to *m* brick Ex 5:7
which they did *m* heretofore Ex 5:8 6213
and they say to us, *M* brick Ex 5:16 6213
shall *m* your count for the lamb Ex 12:4
I do *m* them know the statutes of Ex 18:16 5414
Thou shalt not *m* unto thee any Ex 20:4 6213
Ye shall not *m* with me gods of Ex 20:23 6213
neither shall ye *m* unto you gods Ex 20:23 6213
of earth thou shalt *m* unto me Ex 20:24 6213
if thou wilt *m* me an altar of Ex 20:25 6213
owner of the pit shall *m* it good Ex 21:34
for he should *m* full restitution Ex 22:3
vineyard, shall he *m* restitution Ex 22:5
fire shall surely *m* restitution Ex 22:6
and he shall not *m* it good Ex 22:11
he shall *m* restitution unto the Ex 22:12
he shall not *m* good that which Ex 22:13
it, he shall surely *m* it good Ex 22:14
with it, he shall not *m* it good Ex 22:15
m no mention of the name of other Ex 23:13
I will *m* all thine enemies turn Ex 23:27 5414
Thou shalt *m* no covenant with Ex 23:32 3772
lest they *m* thee sin against me Ex 23:33
let them *m* me a sanctuary Ex 25:8 6213
thereof, even so shall ye *m* it Ex 25:9 6213
they shall *m* an ark of shittim Ex 25:10 6213
shalt *m* upon it a crown of gold Ex 25:11 6213
thou shalt *m* staves of shittim Ex 25:13 6213
thou shalt *m* a mercy seat of pure Ex 25:17 6213
thou shalt *m* two cherubims of Ex 25:18 6213
of beaten work shalt thou *m* them Ex 25:18 6213
m one cherub on the one end, and Ex 25:19 6213
m the cherubims on the two ends Ex 25:19 6213
Thou shalt also *m* a table of Ex 25:23 6213
m thereto a crown of gold round Ex 25:24 6213
thou shalt *m* unto it a border of Ex 25:25 6213
thou shalt *m* a golden crown to Ex 25:25 6213
thou shalt *m* for it four rings of Ex 25:26 6213
thou shalt *m* the staves of Ex 25:28 6213
thou shalt *m* the dishes thereof, Ex 25:29 6213
of pure gold shalt thou *m* them Ex 25:29 6213
thou shalt *m* a candlestick of Ex 25:31 6213
thou shalt *m* the seven lamps Ex 25:37 6213
talent of pure gold shall he *m* it Ex 25:39 6213
look that thou *m* them after their Ex 25:40 6213
Moreover thou shalt *m* the Ex 26:1 6213
of cunning work shalt thou *m* them Ex 26:1 6213
thou shalt *m* loops of blue upon Ex 26:4 6213
likewise shalt thou *m* in the Ex 26:4 6213
shalt thou *m* in the one curtain Ex 26:5 6213
fifty loops shalt thou *m* in the Ex 26:5 6213
thou shalt *m* fifty taches of gold Ex 26:6 6213
thou shalt *m* curtains of goats' Ex 26:7 6213
eleven curtains shalt thou *m* Ex 26:7 6213
thou shalt *m* fifty loops on the Ex 26:10 6213
thou shalt *m* fifty taches of Ex 26:11 6213
thou shalt *m* a covering for the Ex 26:14 6213
thou shalt *m* boards for the Ex 26:15 6213
thus shalt thou *m* for all the Ex 26:17 6213
thou shalt *m* the boards for the Ex 26:18 6213
thou shalt *m* forty sockets of Ex 26:19 6213
westward thou shalt *m* six boards Ex 26:22 6213
two boards shalt thou *m* for the Ex 26:23 6213
thou shalt *m* bars of shittim wood Ex 26:26 6213
m their rings of gold for places Ex 26:29 6213
thou shalt *m* a vail of blue, and Ex 26:31 6213
thou shalt *m* an hanging for the Ex 26:36 6213
thou shalt *m* for the hanging five Ex 26:37 6213
thou shalt *m* an altar of shittim Ex 27:1 6213
thou shalt *m* the horns of it upon Ex 27:2 6213
thou shalt *m* his pans to receive Ex 27:3 6213
thereof thou shalt *m* of brass Ex 27:3 6213
thou shalt *m* for it a grate of Ex 27:4 6213
upon the net shalt thou *m* four Ex 27:4 6213
thou shalt *m* staves for the altar Ex 27:6 6213
with boards shalt thou *m* it Ex 27:8 6213
in the mount, so shall they *m* it Ex 27:8 6213
thou shalt *m* the court of the Ex 27:9 6213
thou shalt *m* holy garments for Ex 28:2 6213
that they may *m* Aaron's garments Ex 28:3 6213
the garments which they shall *m* Ex 28:4 6213
they shall *m* holy garments for Ex 28:4 6213
they shall *m* the ephod of gold, Ex 28:6 6213
thou shalt *m* them to be set in Ex 28:11 6213
thou shalt *m* ouches of gold Ex 28:13 6213
wreathen work shalt thou *m* them Ex 28:14 6213
thou shalt *m* the breastplate of Ex 28:15 6213
work of the ephod thou shalt *m* it Ex 28:15 6213
twined linen, shalt thou *m* it Ex 28:15 6213
thou shalt *m* upon the breastplate Ex 28:22 6213
thou shalt *m* upon the breastplate Ex 28:23 6213
thou shalt *m* two rings of gold, Ex 28:26 6213
other rings of gold thou shalt *m* Ex 28:27 6213
thou shalt *m* the robe of the Ex 28:31 6213
thou shalt *m* pomegranates of blue Ex 28:33 6213
thou shalt *m* a plate of pure gold Ex 28:36 6213

M

thou shalt *m* the mitre of fine Ex 28:39 6213
thou shalt *m* the girdle of Ex 28:39 6213
Aaron's sons thou shalt *m* coats Ex 28:40 6213
thou shalt *m* for them girdles, and Ex 28:40 6213
and bonnets shalt thou *m* for them Ex 28:40 6213
thou shalt *m* them linen breeches Ex 28:42 6213
wheaten flour shalt thou *m* them Ex 29:2 6213
Seven days thou shalt *m* an Ex 29:37
thou shalt *m* an altar to burn Ex 30:1 6213
of shittim wood shalt thou *m* it Ex 30:1 6213
thou shalt *m* unto it a crown of Ex 30:3 6213
m to it under the crown of it Ex 30:4 6213
two sides of it shalt thou *m* it Ex 30:4 6213
thou shalt *m* the staves of Ex 30:5 6213
Aaron shall *m* an atonement upon Ex 30:10
once in the year shall he *m* Ex 30:10
to *m* an atonement for your souls Ex 30:15
to *m* an atonement for your souls Ex 30:16
Thou shalt also *m* a laver of Ex 30:18 6213
thou shalt *m* it an oil of holy Ex 30:25 6213
neither shall ye *m* any other like Ex 30:32 6213
thou shalt *m* it a perfume, a Ex 30:35 6213
the perfume which thou shalt *m* Ex 30:37 6213
ye shall not *m* to yourselves Ex 30:37 6213
Whosoever shall *m* like unto that Ex 30:38 6213
that they may *m* all that I have Ex 31:6 6213
m us gods, which shall go before Ex 32:1 6213
I will *m* of thee a great nation Ex 32:10 6213
M us gods, which shall go before Ex 32:23 6213
peradventure I shall *m* an Ex 32:30
I will *m* all my goodness pass Ex 33:19
he said, Behold, I *m* a covenant Ex 34:10 3772
lest thou *m* a covenant with the Ex 34:12 3772
Lest thou *m* a covenant with the Ex 34:15 3772
m thy sons go a whoring after Ex 34:16
Thou shalt *m* thee no molten gods Ex 34:17 6213
come, and *m* all that the LORD hath Ex 35:10 6213
to *m* any manner of cunning work Ex 35:33 6213
of the sanctuary, to *m* it withal Ex 36:3 6213
which the LORD commanded to *m* Ex 36:5 6213
Let neither man nor woman *m* any Ex 36:6 6213
for all the work to *m* it, and too Ex 36:7 6213
thus did he *m* for all the boards Ex 36:22 6213
for him to *m* atonement for him Lev 1:4
the priest shall *m* an atonement Lev 4:20
the priest shall *m* an atonement Lev 4:26
the priest shall *m* an atonement Lev 4:31
the priest shall *m* an atonement Lev 4:35
the priest shall *m* an atonement Lev 5:6
the priest shall *m* an atonement Lev 5:10
the priest shall *m* an atonement Lev 5:13
he shall *m* amends for the harm Lev 5:16
the priest shall *m* an atonement Lev 5:16
the priest shall *m* an atonement Lev 5:18
the priest shall *m* an atonement Lev 6:7
to *m* reconciliation upon it Lev 8:15
to *m* an atonement for you Lev 8:34
m an atonement for thyself, and Lev 9:7
and *m* an atonement for them Lev 9:7
to *m* atonement for them before Lev 10:17
Ye shall not *m* yourselves Lev 11:43
neither shall ye *m* yourselves Lev 11:43
To *m* a difference between the Lev 11:47
LORD, and *m* an atonement for her Lev 12:7
the priest shall *m* an atonement Lev 12:8
the priest shall *m* an atonement Lev 14:18
m an atonement for him that is to Lev 14:19
the priest shall *m* an atonement Lev 14:20
to *m* an atonement for him, and one Lev 14:21
to *m* an atonement for him before Lev 14:29
the priest shall *m* an atonement Lev 14:31
m an atonement for the house Lev 14:53
the priest shall *m* an atonement Lev 15:15
the priest shall *m* an atonement Lev 15:30
m an atonement for himself, and Lev 16:6
to *m* an atonement with him, and to Lev 16:10
shall *m* an atonement for himself, Lev 16:11
he shall *m* an atonement for the Lev 16:16
when he goeth in to *m* an Lev 16:17
LORD, and *m* an atonement for it Lev 16:18
m an atonement for himself, and Lev 16:24
to *m* atonement in the holy place Lev 16:27
the priest *m* an atonement for you Lev 16:30
shall *m* the atonement, and shall Lev 16:32
he shall *m* an atonement for the Lev 16:33
he shall *m* an atonement for the Lev 16:33
he shall *m* an atonement for the Lev 16:33
to *m* an atonement for the Lev 16:34
to *m* an atonement for your souls Lev 17:11
nor *m* to yourselves molten gods Lev 19:4 6213
the priest shall *m* an atonement Lev 19:22
Ye shall not *m* any cuttings in Lev 19:28 5414
ye shall not *m* your souls Lev 20:25
They shall not *m* baldness upon Lev 21:5
nor *m* any cuttings in their flesh Lev 21:5
nor *m* an offering by fire of them Lev 22:22 5414
neither shall ye *m* any offering Lev 22:24 6213
thou shalt not *m* clean riddance Lev 23:22
to *m* an atonement for you before Lev 23:28
killeth a beast shall *m* it good Lev 24:18
ye *m* the trumpet sound throughout Lev 25:9
Ye shall *m* you no idols nor Lev 26:1 6213
down, and none shall *m* you afraid Lev 26:6
m you fruitful, and multiply you, Lev 26:9
I will *m* your heaven as iron, and Lev 26:19 5414
cattle, and *m* you few in number Lev 26:22
I will *m* your cities waste, and Lev 26:31 5414
When a man shall *m* a singular vow Lev 27:2
The LORD *m* thee a curse and an Num 5:21 5414
the LORD doth *m* thy thigh to rot Num 5:21 5414
to *m* thy belly to swell, and thy Num 5:22
He shall not *m* himself unclean Num 6:7
m an atonement for him, for that Num 6:11
The LORD *m* his face shine upon Num 6:25
clothes, and so *m* themselves clean Num 8:7
to *m* an atonement for the Levites Num 8:12
to *m* an atonement for the Num 8:19
M thee two trumpets of silver Num 10:2 6213
a whole piece shalt thou *m* them Num 10:2 6213
I the LORD will *m* myself known Num 12:6
Let us *m* a captain, and let us Num 14:4 5414
will *m* of thee a greater nation Num 14:12 6213
I sware to *m* you dwell therein Num 14:30
will *m* an offering by fire unto Num 15:3 6213
to *m* a sweet savour unto the LORD Num 15:3 6213
the priest shall *m* an atonement Num 15:25
the priest shall *m* an atonement Num 15:28
to *m* an atonement for him Num 15:28
bid them that they *m* them fringes Num 15:38 6213
except thou *m* thyself altogether Num 16:13
But if the LORD *m* a new thing Num 16:30 1254
let them *m* them broad plates for Num 16:38
and *m* an atonement for them Num 16:46
I will *m* to cease from me the Num 17:5
M thee a fiery serpent, and set it Num 21:8 6213
to *m* an atonement for you Num 28:22
to *m* an atonement for you Num 28:30
to *m* an atonement for you Num 29:5
then he shall *m* her vow which she Num 30:8
it, or her husband may *m* it void Num 30:13
But if he shall any ways *m* them Num 30:15
ye shall *m* it go through the fire Num 31:23 5674
ye shall *m* go through the water Num 31:23 5674
to *m* an atonement for our souls Num 31:50
m you a thousand times so many Deut 1:11
I will *m* them rulers over you Deut 1:13 7760
I will *m* them hear my words, that Deut 4:10
m you a graven image, the Deut 4:16 6213
m you a graven image, or the Deut 4:23 6213
m a graven image, or the likeness Deut 4:25 6213
Thou shalt not *m* thee any graven Deut 5:8 6213
thou shalt *m* no covenant with Deut 7:2 3772
Neither shalt thou *m* marriages Deut 7:3
that he might *m* thee know that Deut 8:3
I will *m* of thee a nation Deut 9:14 6213
mount, and *m* thee an ark of wood Deut 10:1 6213
m search, and ask diligently Deut 13:14
nor *m* any baldness between your Deut 14:1 7760
years thou shalt *m* a release Deut 15:1 6213
officers shalt thou *m* thee in all Deut 16:18 5414
thy God, which thou shalt *m* thee Deut 16:21 6213
the judges shall *m* diligent Deut 19:18
that they shall *m* captains of the Deut 20:9
if it *m* thee answer of peace, and Deut 20:11
if it will *m* no peace with thee, Deut 20:12
but will *m* war against thee, then Deut 20:12 6213
thou shalt not *m* merchandise of Deut 21:14 6014
that he may not *m* the son of the Deut 21:16
then thou shalt *m* a battlement Deut 22:8 6213
Thou shalt *m* thee fringes upon Deut 22:12 6213
to *m* thee high above all nations Deut 26:19 6213
the LORD shall *m* thee plenteous Deut 28:11
And the LORD shall *m* thee the head Deut 28:13 5414
The LORD shall *m* the pestilence Deut 28:21
The LORD shall *m* the rain of thy Deut 28:24 5414
Then the LORD will *m* thy plagues Deut 28:59 6381
the LORD commanded Moses to *m* Deut 29:1 3772
you only do I *m* this covenant Deut 29:14 3772
the LORD thy God will *m* thee Deut 30:9
I would *m* the remembrance of them Deut 32:26
that shall come upon them *m* haste Deut 32:35
I kill, and I *m* alive Deut 32:39
I will *m* mine arrows drunk with Deut 32:42
thou shalt *m* thy way prosperous Josh 1:8
Joshua, *M* thee sharp knives, and Josh 5:2 6213
that when they *m* a long blast Josh 6:5
nor *m* any noise with your voice, Josh 6:10
lest ye *m* yourselves accursed, Josh 6:18
m the camp of Israel a curse, and Josh 6:18 7760
m not all the people to labour Josh 7:3
Israel, and *m* confession unto him Josh 7:19 5414
now therefore *m* ye a league with Josh 9:6 3772
how shall we *m* a league with you Josh 9:7 3772
therefore now *m* ye a league with Josh 9:11 3772
so shall your children *m* our Josh 22:25
neither *m* mention of the names of Josh 23:7
shall *m* marriages with them, and Josh 23:12
ye shall *m* no league with the Judg 2:2 3772
m haste, and do as I have done Judg 9:48
Samson, that he may *m* us sport Judg 16:25
to *m* a graven image and a molten Judg 17:3 6213
that they should *m* a great flame Judg 20:38
but *m* not thyself known unto the Ruth 3:3
The LORD *m* the woman that is come Ruth 4:11 5414
for to *m* her fret, because the 1Sa 1:6
to *m* them inherit the throne of 1Sa 2:8
ye *m* the LORD's people to 1Sa 2:24
to *m* yourselves fat with the 1Sa 2:29
I begin, I will also *m* an end 1Sa 3:12
Wherefore ye shall *m* images of 1Sa 6:5 6213
Now therefore *m* a new cart 1Sa 6:7 6213
now *m* us a king to judge us like 1Sa 8:5 7760
to *m* his instruments of war, and 1Sa 8:12 6213
their voice, and *m* them a king 1Sa 8:22
m haste now, for he came to day 1Sa 9:12
M a covenant with us, and we will 1Sa 11:1 3772
will I *m* a covenant with you 1Sa 11:2 3772
the LORD to *m* you his people 1Sa 12:22 6213
Lest the Hebrews *m* them swords or 1Sa 13:19 6213
m his father's house free in 1Sa 17:25 6213
But Saul thought to *m* David fall 1Sa 18:25
the lad, *M* speed, haste, stay not 1Sa 20:38
m you all captains of thousands, 1Sa 22:7 7760
certainly *m* my lord a sure house 1Sa 25:28 6213
Therefore will I *m* thee keeper of 1Sa 28:2 7760
the Philistines *m* war against me 1Sa 28:15
that thou mayest *m* known unto me 1Sa 28:15
M this fellow return, that he may 1Sa 29:4
M thy league with me, and, behold, 2Sa 3:12 3772
I will *m* a league with thee 2Sa 3:13 3772
that they may *m* a league with 2Sa 3:21 3772
thee that he will *m* thee an house 2Sa 7:11 6213
to *m* thy servant know them 2Sa 7:21
to *m* him a name, and to do for you 2Sa 7:23 7760
m thy battle more strong against 2Sa 11:25
on thy bed, and *m* thyself sick 2Sa 13:5
m me a couple of cakes in my 2Sa 13:6 3823
m speed to depart, lest he 2Sa 15:14
should I this day *m* thee go up 2Sa 15:20
weak handed, and will *m* him afraid 2Sa 17:2
wherewith shall I *m* the atonement 2Sa 21:3
although he *m* it not to grow 2Sa 23:5
m his throne greater than the 1Kin 1:37
God *m* the name of Solomon better 1Kin 1:47
m his throne greater than thy 1Kin 1:47
Did I not *m* thee to swear by the 1Kin 2:42
servant shall *m* toward this place 1Kin 8:29
m supplication unto thee in this 1Kin 8:33
m supplication unto thee in the 1Kin 8:47
Israel did Solomon *m* no bondmen 1Kin 9:22 5414
but I will *m* him prince all the 1Kin 11:34
come to Shechem to *m* him king 1Kin 12:1
now therefore *m* thou the grievous 1Kin 12:4
M the yoke which thy father did 1Kin 12:9
but *m* thou it lighter unto us 1Kin 12:10
will *m* thy house like the house 1Kin 16:3 5414
which he did, to *m* Israel to sin 1Kin 16:19
the son of Ginath, to *m* him king 1Kin 16:21
but *m* me thereof a little cake 1Kin 17:13 6213
after *m* for thee and for thy son 1Kin 17:13 6213
if I *m* not thy life as the life 1Kin 19:2 7760
thou shalt *m* streets for thee in 1Kin 20:34 7760
will *m* thine house like the house 1Kin 21:22 5414
M this valley full of ditches 2Kin 3:16 6213
Let us *m* a little chamber, I pray 2Kin 4:10 6213
to *m* alive, that this man doth 2Kin 5:7
let us *m* us a place there, where 2Kin 6:2 6213
LORD would *m* windows in heaven 2Kin 7:2 6213
LORD should *m* windows in heaven 2Kin 7:19 6213
m him arise up from among his 2Kin 9:2
I will *m* the house of Ahab like 2Kin 9:9 5414
And Joram said, *M* ready 2Kin 9:21
we will not *m* any king 2Kin 10:5
Neither let Hezekiah *m* you trust 2Kin 18:30
M an agreement with me by a 2Kin 18:31 6213
Neither will I *m* the feet of 2Kin 21:8
that no man might *m* his son or 2Kin 23:10
to *m* an atonement for Israel, 1Chr 6:49
to *m* him king, according to the 1Chr 11:10
by name, to come and *m* David king 1Chr 12:31
to *m* David king over all Israel 1Chr 12:38
were of one heart to *m* David king 1Chr 12:38
m known his deeds among the 1Chr 16:8
for those that should *m* a sound 1Chr 16:42
to *m* thee a name of greatness and 1Chr 17:21 7760
thou *m* thine own people for ever 1Chr 17:22 5414
The LORD *m* his people an hundred 1Chr 21:3
now *m* preparation for it 1Chr 22:5
me to *m* me king over all Israel 1Chr 28:4
and in thine hand it is to *m* great 1Chr 29:12
the work that he was to *m* for 2Chr 4:11 6213
did Huram his father *m* to king 2Chr 4:16 6213
to *m* one sound to be heard in 2Chr 5:13
which they shall *m* toward this 2Chr 6:21
be laid upon him to *m* him swear 2Chr 6:22
m supplication before thee in 2Chr 6:24
to *m* in the house of the LORD 2Chr 7:11 6213
will *m* it to be a proverb and a 2Chr 7:20 5414
them did Solomon *m* to pay tribute 2Chr 8:8
m no servants for his work 2Chr 8:9 5414
all Israel come to *m* him king 2Chr 10:1
but *m* thou it somewhat lighter 2Chr 10:10
for he thought to *m* him king 2Chr 11:22
m about them walls, and towers, 2Chr 14:7
him to *m* ships to go to Tarshish 2Chr 20:36 6213
God shall *m* thee fall before the 2Chr 25:8
Now it is in mine heart to *m* a 2Chr 29:10 3772
to *m* an atonement for all Israel 2Chr 29:24
to *m* proclamation throughout all 2Chr 30:5
for God commanded me to *m* haste 2Chr 35:21
this house, and to *m* up this wall Ezr 5:3 3635
of the men that *m* this building Ezr 5:4 1124
house, and to *m* up these walls Ezr 5:9 3635
Moreover I *m* a decree what ye Ezr 6:8 7761
I *m* a decree, that all they of Ezr 7:13 7761
king, do *m* a decree to all the Ezr 7:21 7761
Now therefore let us *m* a covenant Ezr 10:3 3772
Now therefore *m* confession unto Ezr 10:11 5414
me, For what dost thou *m* request Neh 2:4
to *m* beams for the gates of the Neh 2:8
will they *m* an end in a day Neh 4:2
to *m* great mirth, because they Neh 8:12 6213
to *m* booths, as it is written Neh 8:15 6213
of all this we *m* a sure covenant Neh 9:38 3772
to *m* an atonement for Israel Neh 10:33
king's decree which he shall *m* Est 1:20 6213
to *m* supplication unto him, and to Est 4:8
to *m* request before him for her Est 4:8
king said, Cause Haman to *m* haste Est 5:5
M haste, and take the apparel and Est 6:10
Haman stood up to *m* request for Est 7:7
that they should *m* them days of Est 9:22 6213
he woundeth, and his hands *m* whole Job 5:18
m thy supplication to the Job 8:5
thee, and *m* the habitation of thy Job 8:6
but I would *m* supplication to my Job 9:15
m my hands never so clean Job 9:30
Should thy lies *m* men hold their Job 11:3
shall no man *m* thee ashamed Job 11:3
down, and none shall *m* thee afraid Job 11:19
many shall *m* suit unto thee Job 11:19
not his excellency *m* you afraid Job 13:11

and let not thy dread *m* me afraid	Job 13:21	
m me to know my transgression and	Job 13:23	
and anguish shall *m* him afraid	Job 15:24	
it be ere ye *m* an end of words	Job 18:2	7760
Terrors shall *m* him afraid on	Job 18:11	
ye *m* yourselves strange to me	Job 19:3	
to answer, and for this I *m* haste	Job 20:2	
Thou shalt *m* thy prayer unto him,	Job 22:27	
Which *m* oil within their walls,	Job 24:11	
who will *m* me a liar	Job 24:25	7760
m my speech nothing worth	Job 24:25	7760
To *m* the weight for the winds	Job 28:25	6213
he that made me in the womb *m* him	Job 31:15	6213
my terror shall not *m* thee afraid	Job 33:7	
quietness, who then can *m* trouble	Job 34:29	
they *m* the oppressed to cry	Job 35:9	
Canst thou *m* him afraid as a	Job 39:20	
command, and *m* her nest on high	Job 39:27	
he that made him can *m* his sword	Job 40:19	
Will he *m* many supplications unto	Job 41:3	
Will he *m* a covenant with thee	Job 41:4	3772
the companions *m* a banquet of him	Job 41:6	
The arrow cannot *m* him flee	Job 41:28	
m thy way straight before my face	Ps 5:8	
all the night *m* I my bed to swim	Ps 6:6	
they *m* ready their arrow upon the	Ps 11:2	
Thou shalt *m* them as a fiery oven	Ps 21:9	7896
shalt thou *m* them turn their back	Ps 21:12	
when thou shalt *m* ready thine	Ps 21:12	
thou didst *m* me hope when I was	Ps 22:9	
M thy face to shine upon thy	Ps 31:16	
My soul shall *m* her boast in the	Ps 34:2	
thou shalt *m* them drink of the	Ps 36:8	
M haste to help me, O Lord my	Ps 38:22	
m me to know mine end, and the	Ps 39:4	
m me not the reproach of the	Ps 39:8	7760
O LORD, *m* haste to help me	Ps 40:13	
m no tarrying, O my God	Ps 40:17	
thou wilt *m* all his bed in his	Ps 41:3	2015
whom thou mayest *m* princes in all	Ps 45:16	
I will *m* thy name to be	Ps 45:17	
shall *m* glad the city of God	Ps 46:4	
thou shalt *m* me to know wisdom	Ps 51:6	
M me to hear joy and gladness	Ps 51:8	
in my complaint, and *m* a noise	Ps 55:2	
of thy wings will I *m* my refuge	Ps 57:1	
they *m* a noise like a dog, and go	Ps 59:6	
let them *m* a noise like a dog, and	Ps 59:14	
So they shall *m* their own tongue	Ps 64:8	
M a joyful noise unto God, all ye	Ps 66:1	
m his praise glorious	Ps 66:2	7760
m the voice of his praise to be	Ps 66:8	
m their loins continually to	Ps 69:23	
M haste, O God, to deliver me	Ps 70:1	
m haste to help me, O LORD	Ps 70:1	
m haste unto me, O God	Ps 70:5	
O LORD, *m* no tarrying	Ps 70:5	
O my God, *m* haste for my help	Ps 71:12	
I will *m* mention of thy	Ps 71:16	
that they should *m* them known to	Ps 78:5	
m a joyful noise unto the God of	Ps 81:1	
For, lo, thine enemies *m* a tumult	Ps 83:2	
M their nobles like Oreb, and like	Ps 83:11	7896
O my God, *m* them like a wheel	Ps 83:13	7896
m them afraid with thy storm	Ps 83:15	
the valley of Baca *m* it a well	Ps 84:6	6213
I will *m* mention of Rahab and	Ps 87:4	
with my mouth will I *m* known thy	Ps 89:1	
Also I will *m* him my firstborn,	Ps 89:27	5414
also will I *m* to endure for ever	Ps 89:29	7760
M us glad according to the days	Ps 90:15	
let us *m* a joyful noise to the	Ps 95:1	
m a joyful noise unto him with	Ps 95:2	
M a joyful noise unto the LORD,	Ps 98:4	
m a loud noise, and rejoice, and	Ps 98:4	
sound of cornet *m* a joyful noise	Ps 98:6	
M a joyful noise unto the LORD,	Ps 100:1	
oil to *m* his face to shine, and	Ps 104:15	
Where the birds *m* their nests	Ps 104:17	
m known his deeds among the	Ps 105:1	
that he might *m* his mighty power	Ps 106:8	
until I *m* thine enemies thy	Ps 110:1	7896
They that *m* them are like unto	Ps 115:8	6213
M me to understand the way of thy	Ps 119:27	
M me to go in the path of thy	Ps 119:35	
M thy face to shine upon thy	Ps 119:135	
There will I *m* the horn of David	Ps 132:17	6213
They that *m* them are like unto	Ps 135:18	6213
if I *m* my bed in hell, behold,	Ps 139:8	3331
m haste unto me	Ps 141:1	
the LORD did I *m* my supplication	Ps 142:1	
To *m* known to the sons of men his	Ps 145:12	
to evil, and *m* haste to shed blood	Prov 1:16	
I will *m* known my words unto you	Prov 1:23	
thyself, and *m* sure thy friend	Prov 6:3	
Fools *m* a mock at sin	Prov 14:9	
and with good advice *m* war	Prov 20:18	6213
holy, and after vows to *m* enquiry	Prov 20:25	
That I might *m* thee know the	Prov 22:21	
M no friendship with an angry man	Prov 22:24	
certainly *m* themselves wings	Prov 23:5	6213
wise counsel thou shalt *m* thy war	Prov 24:6	
m it fit for thyself in the field	Prov 24:27	
m my heart glad, that I may	Prov 27:11	
yet *m* they their houses in the	Prov 30:26	7760
that he should *m* his soul enjoy	Eccl 2:24	
for who can *m* that straight,	Eccl 7:13	
neither *m* thyself over wise	Eccl 7:16	
We will *m* thee borders of gold	Song 1:11	6213
M haste, my beloved, and be thou	Song 8:14	
when ye *m* many prayers, I will	Is 1:15	
Wash you, *m* you clean	Is 1:16	
m me not a ruler of the people	Is 3:7	7760
That say, Let him *m* speed	Is 5:19	
M the heart of this people fat,	Is 6:10	
m their ears heavy, and shut their	Is 6:10	
let us *m* a breach therein for us,	Is 7:6	
of hosts shall *m* a consumption	Is 10:23	6213
And shall *m* him of quick	Is 11:3	
streams, and *m* men go over dryshod	Is 11:15	
m mention that his name is	Is 12:4	
I will *m* a man more precious than	Is 13:12	
the shepherds *m* their fold there	Is 13:20	
I will also *m* it a possession for	Is 14:23	7760
m thy shadow as the night in the	Is 16:3	7896
down, and none shall *m* them afraid	Is 17:2	
shalt thou *m* thy plant to grow	Is 17:11	
shalt thou *m* thy seed to flourish	Is 17:11	
which *m* a noise like the noise of	Is 17:12	
that *m* a rushing like the rushing	Is 17:12	
thereof, all that *m* sluices	Is 19:10	6213
m sweet melody, sing many songs,	Is 23:16	
shall the LORD of hosts *m* unto	Is 25:6	6213
will we *m* mention of thy name	Is 26:13	
that he may *m* peace with me	Is 27:5	6213
and he shall *m* peace with me	Is 27:5	6213
whom shall he *m* to understand	Is 28:9	
that believeth shall not *m* haste	Is 28:16	
That *m* a man an offender for a	Is 29:21	
to *m* empty the soul of the hungry	Is 32:6	
m you bare, and gird sackcloth	Is 32:11	
when thou shalt *m* an end to deal	Is 33:1	
shall the great owl *m* her nest	Is 34:15	
Neither let Hezekiah *m* you trust	Is 36:15	
M an agreement with me by a	Is 36:16	6213
is come forth to *m* war with thee	Is 37:9	
to night wilt thou *m* an end of me	Is 38:12	
to night wilt thou *m* an end of me	Is 38:13	
thou recover me, and *m* me to live	Is 38:16	
children shall *m* known thy truth	Is 38:19	
m straight in the desert a	Is 40:3	
I will *m* thee a new sharp	Is 41:15	7760
shalt *m* the hills as chaff	Is 41:15	7760
I will *m* the wilderness a pool of	Is 41:18	7760
I will *m* waste mountains and hills	Is 42:15	7760
I will *m* the rivers islands, and I	Is 42:15	7760
I will *m* darkness light before	Is 42:16	7760
the law, and *m* it honourable	Is 42:21	
I will even *m* a way in the	Is 43:19	7760
They that *m* a graven image are	Is 44:9	3335
shall I *m* the residue thereof an	Is 44:19	6213
m the crooked places straight	Is 45:2	
I *m* peace, and create evil	Is 45:7	6213
they shall *m* supplication unto	Is 45:14	
m me equal, and compare me, that	Is 46:5	
m bare the leg, uncover the thigh	Is 47:2	
m mention of the God of Israel,	Is 48:1	
he shall *m* his way prosperous	Is 48:15	
I will *m* all my mountains a way,	Is 49:11	7760
Thy children shall *m* haste	Is 49:17	
I *m* the rivers a wilderness	Is 50:2	7760
I *m* sackcloth their covering	Is 50:3	7760
he will *m* her wilderness like	Is 51:3	7760
I will *m* my judgment to rest for	Is 51:4	
rule over them *m* them to howl	Is 52:5	
when thou shalt *m* his soul an	Is 53:10	7760
m the desolate cities to be	Is 54:3	
I will *m* thy windows of agates,	Is 54:12	7760
I will *m* an everlasting covenant	Is 55:3	3772
m them joyful in my house of	Is 56:7	
against whom *m* ye a wide mouth,	Is 57:4	
to *m* your voice to be heard on	Is 58:4	
in drought, and *m* fat thy bones	Is 58:11	
they *m* haste to shed innocent	Is 59:7	
I will *m* the place of my feet	Is 60:13	7760
thee, I will *m* thee an eternal	Is 60:15	7760
I will also *m* thy officers peace,	Is 60:17	7760
I will *m* an everlasting covenant	Is 61:8	3772
ye that *m* mention of the LORD,	Is 62:6	
till he *m* Jerusalem a praise in	Is 62:7	7760
m them drunk in my fury, and I	Is 63:6	
to *m* himself an everlasting name	Is 63:12	6213
to *m* thyself a glorious name	Is 63:14	6213
to *m* thy name known to thine	Is 64:2	
and the new earth, which I will *m*	Is 66:22	6213
his place to *m* thy land desolate	Jer 4:7	7760
M ye mention to the nations	Jer 4:16	
yet will I not *m* a full end	Jer 4:27	6213
in vain shalt thou *m* thyself fair	Jer 4:30	
but *m* not a full end	Jer 5:10	6213
I will *m* my words in thy mouth	Jer 5:14	5414
I will not *m* a full end with you	Jer 5:18	6213
lest I *m* thee desolate, a land	Jer 6:8	7760
m thee mourning, as for an only	Jer 6:26	6213
neither *m* intercession to me	Jer 7:16	
to *m* cakes to the queen of heaven	Jer 7:18	6213
I will *m* Jerusalem heaps, and a	Jer 9:11	5414
I will *m* the cities of Judah	Jer 9:11	5414
And let them *m* haste, and take up a	Jer 9:18	
to *m* the cities of Judah desolate	Jer 10:22	7760
of death, and *m* it gross darkness	Jer 13:16	7896
I will *m* thee to pass with thine	Jer 15:14	
I will *m* thee unto this people a	Jer 15:20	5414
nor *m* themselves bald for them	Jer 16:6	
Shall a man *m* gods unto himself,	Jer 16:20	6213
seemed good to the potter to *m* it	Jer 18:4	6213
m your ways and your doings good	Jer 18:11	
To *m* their land desolate, and a	Jer 18:16	7760
I will *m* void the counsel of	Jer 19:7	
I will *m* this city desolate, and	Jer 19:8	7760
even *m* this city as Tophet	Jer 19:12	5414
I will *m* thee a terror to thyself	Jer 20:4	5414
I will not *m* mention of him, nor	Jer 20:9	
surely I will *m* thee a wilderness	Jer 22:6	7896
m them drink the water of gall	Jer 23:15	
they *m* you vain	Jer 23:16	
m them an astonishment, and an	Jer 25:9	7760
will *m* it perpetual desolations	Jer 25:12	7760
to *m* them a desolation, an	Jer 25:18	5414
Then will I *m* this house like	Jer 26:6	5414
will *m* this city a curse to all	Jer 26:6	5414
M thee bonds and yokes, and put	Jer 27:2	6213
let them now *m* intercession to	Jer 27:18	
but thou shalt *m* for them yokes	Jer 28:13	6213
will *m* them like vile figs, that	Jer 29:17	5414
The LORD *m* thee like Zedekiah and	Jer 29:22	7760
quiet, and none shall *m* him afraid	Jer 30:10	
though I *m* a full end of all	Jer 30:11	6213
yet will I not *m* a full end of	Jer 30:11	6213
and the voice of them that *m* merry	Jer 30:19	
the dances of them that *m* merry	Jer 31:4	
m them rejoice from their sorrow	Jer 31:13	
up waymarks, *m* thee high heaps	Jer 31:21	7760
that I will *m* a new covenant with	Jer 31:31	3772
I will *m* with the house of Israel	Jer 31:33	3772
I will *m* an everlasting covenant	Jer 32:40	3772
I will *m* you to be removed into	Jer 34:17	5414
I will *m* the cities of Judah a	Jer 34:22	5414
did we *m* her cakes to worship her	Jer 44:19	6213
ease, and none shall *m* him afraid	Jer 46:27	
for I will *m* a full end of all	Jer 46:28	6213
but I will not *m* a full end of	Jer 46:28	6213
M ye him drunken	Jer 48:26	
I will *m* thee small among the	Jer 49:15	5414
though thou shouldest *m* thy nest	Jer 49:16	
but I will suddenly *m* him run	Jer 49:19	
surely he shall *m* their	Jer 49:20	
which shall *m* her land desolate,	Jer 50:3	7896
but I will *m* them suddenly run	Jer 50:44	
surely he shall *m* their	Jer 50:45	
M bright the arrows	Jer 51:11	
m the watch strong, set up the	Jer 51:12	
will *m* thee a burnt mountain	Jer 51:25	5414
to *m* the land of Babylon a	Jer 51:29	7760
up her sea, and *m* her springs dry	Jer 51:36	
their heat I will *m* their feasts	Jer 51:39	7896
I will *m* them drunken, that they	Jer 51:39	
I will *m* drunk her princes, and	Jer 51:57	
drunken, and shalt *m* thyself naked	Lam 4:21	
I will *m* thy tongue cleave to the	Eze 3:26	
m thee bread thereof, according	Eze 4:9	6213
Moreover I will *m* thee waste	Eze 5:14	5414
m the land desolate, yea, more	Eze 6:14	5414
the trumpet, even to *m* all ready	Eze 7:14	
M a chain: for the land	Eze 7:23	6213
I will also *m* the pomp of the	Eze 7:24	
wilt thou *m* a full end of the	Eze 11:13	6213
I will *m* this proverb to cease,	Eze 12:23	
m kerchiefs upon the head of	Eze 13:18	6213
hunt the souls to *m* them fly	Eze 13:20	
souls that ye hunt to *m* them fly	Eze 13:20	
will *m* him a sign and a proverb,	Eze 14:8	8074
I will *m* the land desolate,	Eze 15:8	5414
So will I *m* my fury toward thee	Eze 16:42	
great company *m* for him in the	Eze 17:17	6213
m you a new heart and a new spirit	Eze 18:31	6213
neither did I *m* an end of them in	Eze 20:17	6213
that I might *m* them desolate, to	Eze 20:26	
when ye *m* your sons to pass	Eze 20:31	
sharpened to *m* a sore slaughter	Eze 21:10	
should we then *m* mirth	Eze 21:10	
that should *m* up the hedge, and	Eze 22:30	1443
Thus will I *m* thy lewdness to	Eze 23:27	
m it boil well, and let them	Eze 24:5	
I will even *m* the pile for fire	Eze 24:9	
m no mourning for the dead, bind	Eze 24:17	6213
m their dwellings in thee	Eze 25:4	5414
I will *m* Rabbah a stable for	Eze 25:5	5414
I will *m* it desolate from Teman	Eze 25:13	5414
m her like the top of a rock	Eze 26:4	5414
he shall *m* a fort against thee,	Eze 26:8	5414
they shall *m* a spoil of thy	Eze 26:12	5414
m a prey of thy merchandise	Eze 26:12	
I will *m* thee like the top of a	Eze 26:14	
When I shall *m* thee a desolate	Eze 26:19	5414
I will *m* thee a terror, and thou	Eze 26:21	5414
from Lebanon to *m* masts for thee	Eze 27:5	6213
they shall *m* themselves utterly	Eze 27:31	
I will *m* the land of Egypt	Eze 29:10	5414
I will *m* the land of Egypt	Eze 29:12	5414
go forth from me in ships to *m*	Eze 30:9	
I will also *m* the multitude of	Eze 30:10	
I will *m* the rivers dry, and sell	Eze 30:12	
I will *m* the land waste, and all	Eze 30:12	
I will *m* Pathros desolate, and	Eze 30:14	
to *m* it strong to hold the sword	Eze 30:21	
and *m* the stars thereof dark	Eze 32:7	
of heaven will I *m* dark over thee	Eze 32:8	
I will *m* many people amazed at	Eze 32:10	
Then will I *m* their waters deep,	Eze 32:14	
When I shall *m* the land of Egypt	Eze 32:15	5414
I will *m* with them a covenant of	Eze 34:25	3772
And I will *m* them and the places	Eze 34:26	5414
and none shall *m* them afraid	Eze 34:28	
I will *m* thee most desolate	Eze 35:3	5414
Thus will I *m* mount Seir most	Eze 35:7	5414
I will *m* thee perpetual	Eze 35:9	5414
I will *m* myself known among them,	Eze 35:11	6213
rejoiceth, I will *m* thee desolate	Eze 35:14	6213
m them one stick, and they shall	Eze 37:19	6213
I will *m* them one nation in the	Eze 37:22	6213
Moreover I will *m* a covenant of	Eze 37:26	3772
So will I *m* my holy name known in	Eze 39:7	
to *m* a separation between the	Eze 42:20	
in the day when they shall *m* it	Eze 43:18	6213
the priests shall *m* your burnt	Eze 43:27	6213
But I will *m* them keepers of the	Eze 44:14	
to *m* reconciliation for them,	Eze 45:15	
to *m* reconciliation for the house	Eze 45:17	
then shall ye *m* me endanger my	Dan 1:10	
if ye will not *m* known unto me	Dan 2:5	
But if ye will not *m* known unto	Dan 2:9	

that will *m* known unto the king........ Dan 2:25
Art thou able to *m* known unto me....... Dan 2:26
but for their sakes that shall *m*.............. Dan 2:30
Therefore I *m* a decree, That.................. Dan 3:29 7761
that they might *m* known unto me...... Dan 4:6
but they did not *m* known unto me........ Dan 4:7
not able to *m* known unto me the........ Dan 4:18
they shall *m* thee to eat grass as.......... Dan 4:25
they shall *m* thee to eat grass as.......... Dan 4:32
nor *m* known to the king the.................. Dan 5:8
writing, and *m* known unto me the...... Dan 5:15
that thou canst *m* interpretations......... Dan 5:16
m known to me the interpretation......... Dan 5:16
m known to him the interpretation...... Dan 5:17
and to *m* a firm decree, that.................. Dan 6:7
I *m* a decree, That in every.................... Dan 6:26 7761
m this man to understand the................ Dan 8:16
I will *m* thee know what shall be......... Dan 8:19
to *m* an end of sins.............................. Dan 9:24
to *m* reconciliation for iniquity,........... Dan 9:24
he shall *m* it desolate, even.................. Dan 9:27
Now I am come to *m* thee...................... Dan 10:14
of the north to *m* an agreement............. Dan 11:6 6213
to *m* them white, even to the time....... Dan 11:35
and utterly to *m* away many................. Dan 11:44
m her as a wilderness, and set her....... Hos 2:3 7760
m a wall, that she shall not find.......... Hos 2:6 1443
I will *m* them a forest, and the............. Hos 2:12 7760
in that day will I *m* a covenant............. Hos 2:18 3772
will *m* them to lie down safely.............. Hos 2:18
are profound to *m* slaughter................... Hos 5:2
They *m* the king glad with their............. Hos 7:3
I will *m* Ephraim to ride........................ Hos 10:11
how shall I *m* thee as Admah................. Hos 11:8 5414
they do *m* a covenant with the............... Hos 12:1 3772
m thee to dwell in tabernacles............... Hos 12:9
I will no more *m* you a reproach........... Joel 2:19 5414
for we may not *m* mention of the......... Amos 6:10
even to *m* the poor of the land to......... Amos 8:4
I will *m* it as the mourning of an......... Amos 8:10 7760
they shall also *m* gardens..................... Amos 9:14 6213
Therefore I will *m* Samaria as an......... Mic 1:6 7760
I will *m* a wailing like the................... Mic 1:8 6213
M thee bald, and poll thee for thy........ Mic 1:16
they shall *m* great noise by................... Mic 2:12
the prophets that *m* my people err....... Mic 3:5
and none shall *m* them afraid.............. Mic 4:4
I will *m* her that halted a.................... Mic 4:7 7760
for I will *m* thine horn iron.................. Mic 4:13 7760
and I will *m* thy hoofs brass................ Mic 4:13 7760
Therefore also will I *m* thee sick.......... Mic 6:13
that I should *m* thee a desolation........ Mic 6:16 5414
will *m* an utter end of the place........... Nah 1:8 6213
he will *m* an utter end......................... Nah 1:9 6213
I will *m* thy grave.............................. Nah 1:14 7760
m thy loins strong, fortify thy............. Nah 2:1
they shall *m* haste to the wall.............. Nah 2:5
m thee vile, and will set thee as.......... Nah 3:6
morter, *m* strong the brickkiln............... Nah 3:14
m thyself many as the cankerworm,...... Nah 3:15
m thyself many as the locusts............... Nah 3:15
m it plain upon tables, that he.............. Hab 2:2
trusteth therein, to *m* dumb idols......... Hab 2:18 6213
in the midst of the years *m* known....... Hab 3:2
he will *m* my feet like hinds'................ Hab 3:19 7760
he will *m* me to walk upon mine........... Hab 3:19
for he shall *m* even a speedy.............. Zeph 1:18 6213
will *m* Nineveh a desolation, and......... Zeph 2:13 7760
down, and none shall *m* them afraid..... Zeph 3:13
for I will *m* you a name and a............. Zeph 3:20 5414
LORD, and will *m* thee as a signet......... Hag 2:23 7760
m crowns, and set them upon the.......... Zec 6:11 6213
m a noise as through wine.................. Zec 9:15
corn shall *m* the young men................. Zec 9:17
so the LORD shall *m* bright clouds......... Zec 10:1 6213
I will *m* Jerusalem a cup of.................. Zec 12:2 7760
in that day will I *m* Jerusalem a........... Zec 12:3 7760
In that day will I *m* the...................... Zec 12:6 7760
And did not he *m* one........................ Mal 2:15 6213
in that day when I *m* up my jewels........ Mal 3:17 6213
not willing to *m* her a publick.............. Mt 1:19 *3856*
of the Lord, *m* his paths straight.......... Mt 3:3 *4160*
I will *m* you fishers of men................. Mt 4:19 *4160*
because thou canst not *m* one hair........ Mt 5:36 *4160*
thou wilt, thou canst *m* me clean........... Mt 8:2 *2511*
that they should not *m* him known...... Mt 12:16 *4160*
Either *m* the tree good, and his............ Mt 12:33 *4160*
or else *m* the tree corrupt, and............ Mt 12:33 *4160*
let us *m* here three tabernacles............ Mt 17:4 *4160*
till I *m* thine enemies thy.................... Mt 22:44 *5087*
they *m* broad their phylacteries,........... Mt 23:5 *4115*
and for a pretence *m* long prayer.......... Mt 23:14 *4336*
land to *m* one proselyte, and when....... Mt 23:15 *4160*
ye *m* him twofold more the child........... Mt 23:15 *4160*
for ye *m* clean the outside of the......... Mt 23:25 *2511*
That he shall *m* him ruler over............. Mt 24:47 *2525*
I will *m* thee ruler over many.............. Mt 25:21 *2525*
I will *m* thee ruler over many.............. Mt 25:23 *2525*
your way, *m* it as sure as ye can.......... Mt 27:65 *805*
of the Lord, *m* his paths straight.......... Mk 1:3 *4160*
I will *m* you to become fishers of......... Mk 1:17 *4160*
thou wilt, thou canst *m* me clean.......... Mk 1:40 *2511*
that they should not *m* him known...... Mk 3:12 *4160*
Why *m* ye this ado, and weep................ Mk 5:39 *2350*
he commanded them to *m* all sit........... Mk 6:39 *347*
let us *m* three tabernacles.................. Mk 9:5 *4160*
till I *m* thine enemies thy.................... Mk 12:36 *5087*
and for a pretence *m* long prayers........ Mk 12:40 *4336*
in two mites, which *m* a farthing......... Mk 12:42 *1510*
there *m* ready for us............................. Mk 14:15 *2090*
to *m* ready a people prepared for.......... Lk 1:17 *2090*
of the Lord, *m* his paths straight.......... Lk 3:4 *4160*
thou wilt, thou canst *m* me clean.......... Lk 5:12 *2511*
m prayers, and likewise the................. Lk 5:33 *4160*
Can ye *m* the children of the............... Lk 5:34 *4160*
M them sit down by fifties in a............. Lk 9:14 *2625*
let us *m* three tabernacles.................. Lk 9:33 *4160*
Samaritans, to *m* ready for him............ Lk 9:52 *2090*
Now do ye Pharisees *m* clean the......... Lk 11:39 *2511*
m that which is within also.................. Lk 11:40 *4160*
m them to sit down to meat, and.......... Lk 12:37 *347*
whom his lord shall *m* ruler over.......... Lk 12:42 *2525*
that he will *m* him ruler over all........... Lk 12:44 *2525*
one consent began to *m* excuse............ Lk 14:18 *3868*
going to *m* war against another............ Lk 14:31 *4820*
m me as one of thy hired servants......... Lk 15:19 *4160*
that I might *m* merry with my............... Lk 15:29 *2165*
was meet that we should *m* merry......... Lk 15:32 *2165*
M to yourselves friends of the............. Lk 16:9 *4160*
M ready wherewith I may sup, and......... Lk 17:8 *2090*
Zacchaeus, *m* haste, and come down.... Lk 19:5 *4692*
Till I *m* thine enemies thy................... Lk 20:43 *5087*
for a shew *m* long prayers.................... Lk 20:47 *4336*
there *m* ready....................................... Lk 22:12 *2090*
M straight the way of the Lord,............. Jn 1:23 *2116*
m not my Father's house an house........ Jn 2:16 *4160*
And Jesus said, *M* the men sit down..... Jn 6:10 *4160*
to *m* him a king, he departed............... Jn 6:15 *4160*
and the truth shall *m* you free.............. Jn 8:32 *1659*
Son therefore shall *m* you free.............. Jn 8:36 *1659*
How long dost thou *m* us to doubt........ Jn 10:24 *142*
unto him, and *m* our abode with him..... Jn 14:23 *4160*
thou shalt *m* me full of joy with............ Acts 2:28 *4137*
Until I *m* thy foes thy footstool............. Acts 2:35 *5087*
M us gods to go before us.................... Acts 7:40 *4160*
that he should *m* it according to........... Acts 7:44 *4160*
arise, and *m* thy bed........................... Acts 9:34 *4766*
my defence which I *m* now unto you..... Acts 22:1
M haste, and get thee quickly out......... Acts 22:18 *4692*
M ready two hundred soldiers to.......... Acts 23:23 *2090*
to *m* thee a minister and a witness....... Acts 26:16 *4400*
much learning doth *m* thee mad........... Acts 26:24 *4062*
that without ceasing I *m* mention.......... Rom 1:9 *4160*
shall their unbelief *m* the faith.............. Rom 3:3 *2673*
Do we then *m* void the law through....... Rom 3:31 *2673*
of the same lump to *m* one vessel........ Rom 9:21 *4160*
to *m* his power known, endured............ Rom 9:22 *1107*
that he might *m* known the riches........ Rom 9:23 *1107*
will the Lord *m* upon the earth............. Rom 9:28 *4160*
m not provision for the flesh, to............. Rom 13:14 *4160*
for God is able to *m* him stand............ Rom 14:4 *2476*
the things which *m* for peace................ Rom 14:19 *3753*
to *m* the Gentiles obedient, by............. Rom 15:18 *1519*
and Achaia to *m* a certain.................... Rom 15:26 *4160*
will *m* manifest the counsels of............. 1Cor 4:5 *5319*
m them the members of an harlot......... 1Cor 6:15 *4160*
if meat *m* my brother to offend, I.......... 1Cor 8:13 *4624*
lest I *m* my brother to offend............... 1Cor 8:13 *4624*
any man should *m* my glorying void..... 1Cor 9:15 *2758*
I may *m* the gospel of Christ............... 1Cor 9:18 *5087*
temptation also *m* a way to escape....... 1Cor 10:13 *4160*
For if I *m* you sorry, who is he............ 2Cor 2:2 *3076*
m up beforehand your bounty,.............. 2Cor 9:5 *4294*
God is able to *m* all grace abound........ 2Cor 9:8 *4052*
For we dare not *m* ourselves of............ 2Cor 10:12
Did I *m* a gain of you by any of............ 2Cor 12:17 *4122*
Did Titus *m* a gain of you.................... 2Cor 12:18 *4122*
I *m* myself a transgressor..................... Gal 2:18 *4921*
that it should *m* the promise of............. Gal 3:17 *2673*
As many as desire to *m* a fair.............. Gal 6:12 *2146*
for to *m* in himself of twain one............ Eph 2:15 *2936*
to *m* all men see what is the................ Eph 3:9 *5461*
doth *m* manifest is light....................... Eph 5:13 *4160*
to *m* known the mystery of the............... Eph 6:19 *1107*
shall *m* known to you all things............ Eph 6:21 *1107*
To whom God would *m* known............... Col 1:27 *1107*
That I may *m* it manifest, as I.............. Col 4:4 *5319*
They shall *m* known unto you all.......... Col 4:9 *1107*
the Lord *m* you to increase and............ 1Th 3:12 *4121*
but to *m* ourselves an ensample............ 2Th 3:9 *1325*
which are able to *m* thee wise............. 2Ti 3:15 *4679*
m full proof of thy ministry.................. 2Ti 4:5 *4135*
until I *m* thine enemies thy.................. Heb 1:13 *5087*
to *m* the captain of their....................... Heb 2:10 *5055*
to *m* reconciliation for the sins.............. Heb 2:17 *2433*
liveth to *m* intercession for them.......... Heb 7:25 *1793*
he was about to *m* the tabernacle.......... Heb 8:5 *2005*
that thou *m* all things according........... Heb 8:5 *4160*
when I will *m* a new covenant with....... Heb 8:8 *4931*
is the covenant that I will *m*................. Heb 8:10 *1303*
that could not *m* him that did the......... Heb 9:9 *5055*
year by year continually *m* the.............. Heb 10:1 *5055*
will *m* with them after those days......... Heb 10:16 *1303*
m straight paths for your feet,.............. Heb 12:13 *4160*
M you perfect in every good work.......... Heb 13:21 *2675*
in peace of them that *m* peace.............. Jas 3:18 *4160*
a while, *m* you perfect, stablish,........... 1Pet 5:10 *2675*
they *m* you that ye shall neither............ 2Pet 1:8 *2525*
give diligence to *m* your calling........... 2Pet 1:10 *4160*
words *m* merchandise of you................. 2Pet 2:3 *1710*
we *m* him a liar, and his word is............ 1Jn 1:10 *4160*
I will *m* them of the synagogue of......... Rev 3:9 *1325*
I will *m* them to come and worship........ Rev 3:9 *4160*
Him that overcometh will I *m* a.............. Rev 3:12 *4160*
it shall *m* thy belly bitter, but.............. Rev 10:9 *4087*
pit shall *m* war against them................. Rev 11:7 *4160*
m merry, and shall send gifts one......... Rev 11:10 *2165*
went to *m* war with the remnant of...... Rev 12:17 *4160*
who is able to *m* war with him.............. Rev 13:4 *4170*
unto him to *m* war with the saints......... Rev 13:7 *4160*
that they should *m* an image to............ Rev 13:14 *4160*
These shall *m* war with the Lamb,........ Rev 17:14 *4170*
shall *m* her desolate and naked, and.... Rev 17:16 *4160*
he doth judge and *m* war...................... Rev 19:11 *4170*
gathered together to *m* war................. Rev 19:19 *4160*
said, Behold, I *m* all things new........... Rev 21:5 *4160*

MAKER

a man be more pure than his *m*.............. Job 4:17 6213
in so doing my *m* would soon take........ Job 32:22 6213
But none saith, Where is God my *m*.... Job 35:10 6213
ascribe righteousness to my *M*............ Job 36:3 6466
us kneel before the LORD our *m*........... Ps 95:6 6213
the poor reproacheth his *M*.................. Prov 14:31 6213
the poor reproacheth his *M*.................. Prov 17:5 6213
the LORD is the *m* of them all.............. Prov 22:2 6213
the *m* of it as a spark, and they........... Is 1:31 6467
day shall a man look to his *M*.............. Is 17:7 6213
not looked unto the *m* thereof.............. Is 22:11 6213
unto him that striveth with his *M*......... Is 45:9 3335
the Holy One of Israel, and his *M*........ Is 45:11 3335
And forgettest the LORD thy *m*.............. Is 51:13 6213
For thy *M* is thine husband.................. Is 54:5 6213
Thus saith the LORD the *m* thereof....... Jer 33:2 6213
For Israel hath forgotten his *M*............ Hos 8:14 6213
that the *m* thereof hath graven it......... Hab 2:18 3335
that the *m* of his work trusteth............ Hab 2:18 3335
whose builder and *m* is God................ Heb 11:10 *1217*

MAKERS

together that are *m* of idols................... Is 45:16 2796

MAKEST

what *m* thou in this place..................... Judg 18:3 6213
m me to possess the iniquities of........... Job 13:26
that thou *m* thy ways perfect................. Job 22:3
only *m* me dwell in safety.................... Ps 4:8
thou *m* his beauty to consume away.... Ps 39:11
Thou *m* us to turn back from the.......... Ps 44:10
Thou *m* us a reproach to our.............. Ps 44:13 6213
Thou *m* us a byword among the........... Ps 44:14 6213
thou *m* the outgoings of the.................. Ps 65:8
thou *m* it soft with showers.................. Ps 65:10
Thou *m* us a strife unto our................. Ps 80:6 7760
Thou *m* darkness, and it is night.......... Ps 104:20 7896
that thou *m* account of him................. Ps 144:3
where thou *m* thy flock to rest at......... Song 1:7
that fashioneth it, What *m* thou........... Is 45:9 6213
that *m* thy nest in the cedars,............... Jer 22:23
but thou *m* this people to trust............. Jer 28:15
m thine high place in every................. Eze 16:31 6213
m men as the fishes of the sea,............. Hab 1:14 6213
m him drunken also, that thou............ Hab 2:15
When thou *m* a dinner or a supper,....... Lk 14:12 *4160*
But when thou *m* a feast, call the......... Lk 14:13 *4160*
whom *m* thou thyself............................ Jn 8:53 *4160*
thou, being a man, *m* thyself God......... Jn 10:33 *4160*
the law, and *m* thy boast of God,.......... Rom 2:17 *2744*
Thou that *m* thy boast of the law,.......... Rom 2:23 *2744*

MAKETH

or who *m* the dumb, or deaf, or............ Ex 4:11 7760
the priest that *m* atonement................. Lev 7:7
the priest that *m* him clean shall........... Lev 14:11
for it is the blood that *m* an................. Lev 17:11
m his son or his daughter to pass......... Deut 18:10
the city that *m* war with thee.............. Deut 20:20 6213
when he *m* his sons to inherit............... Deut 21:16
m merchandise of him, or selleth........... Deut 24:7
Cursed be the man that *m* any.............. Deut 27:15 6213
Cursed be he that *m* the blind to.......... Deut 27:18
LORD thy God *m* with thee this day...... Deut 29:12 3772
The LORD killeth, and *m* alive............... 1Sa 2:6
The LORD *m* poor, and *m* rich............... 1Sa 2:7
and he *m* my way perfect...................... 2Sa 22:33
He *m* my feet like hinds' feet............... 2Sa 22:34 7737
For he *m* sore, and bindeth up............. Job 5:18
Which *m* Arcturus, Orion, and.............. Job 9:9 6213
spoiled, and *m* the judges fools............ Job 12:17
he *m* them to stagger like a................. Job 12:25
m collops of fat on his flanks.............. Job 15:27 6213
For God *m* my heart soft, and the........ Job 23:16
he *m* peace in his high places............... Job 25:2 6213
and as a booth that the keeper *m*......... Job 27:18 6213
m us wiser than the fowls of............... Job 35:11
For he *m* small the drops of water......... Job 36:27
He *m* the deep to boil like a pot........... Job 41:31
he *m* the sea like a pot of..................... Job 41:31 7760
He *m* a path to shine after him............. Job 41:32
When he *m* inquisition for blood,.......... Ps 9:12
strength, and *m* my way perfect............ Ps 18:32 5414
He *m* my feet like hinds' feet, and........ Ps 18:33 7737
He *m* me to lie down in green.............. Ps 23:2
He *m* them also to skip like a.............. Ps 29:6
of the LORD *m* the hinds to calve.......... Ps 29:9
he *m* the devices of the people of......... Ps 33:10
man that *m* the LORD his trust.............. Ps 40:4 7760
He *m* wars to cease unto the end.......... Ps 46:9
who *m* the clouds his chariot............... Ps 104:3 7706
Who *m* his angels spirits...................... Ps 104:4 6213
wine that *m* glad the heart of man....... Ps 104:15
He *m* the storm a calm, so that............ Ps 107:29
there he *m* the hungry to dwell,............ Ps 107:36
m him families like a flock.................. Ps 107:41 7760
He *m* the barren woman to keep.......... Ps 113:9
he *m* lightnings for the rain.................. Ps 135:7 6213
who *m* grass to grow upon the............. Ps 147:8
He *m* peace in thy borders, and........... Ps 147:14 7760
A wise son *m* a glad father.................. Prov 10:1
the hand of the diligent *m* rich............. Prov 10:4
it *m* rich, and he addeth no sorrow....... Prov 10:22
but she that *m* ashamed is as............... Prov 12:4
in the heart of man *m* it stoop............. Prov 12:25
but a good word *m* it glad.................... Prov 12:25
There is that *m* himself rich................. Prov 13:7
there is that *m* himself poor................ Prov 13:7
Hope deferred *m* the heart sick,........... Prov 13:12
A merry heart *m* a cheerful.................. Prov 15:13
A wise son *m* a glad father.................. Prov 15:20
and a good report *m* the bones fat........ Prov 15:30
he *m* even his enemies to be at............. Prov 16:7
A man's gift *m* room for him................ Prov 18:16

Wealth *m* many friends ... Prov 19:4
but he that *m* haste to be rich ... Prov 28:20
She *m* herself coverings of ... Prov 31:22 6213
She *m* fine linen, and selleth it ... Prov 31:24 6213
m from the beginning to the end ... Eccl 3:11 6213
oppression *m* a wise man mad ... Eccl 7:7
a man's wisdom *m* his face to ... Eccl 8:1
for laughter, and wine *m* merry ... Eccl 10:19
not the works of God who *m* all ... Eccl 11:5 6213
every one that *m* mention thereof ... Is 19:17
the LORD *m* the earth empty, and ... Is 24:1
m it waste, and turneth it upside ... Is 24:1
when he *m* all the stones of the ... Is 27:9 7760
he *m* the judges of the earth as ... Is 40:23 6213
which *m* a way in the sea, and a ... Is 43:16 5414
m it after the figure of a man, ... Is 44:13 6213
he *m* a god, and worshippeth it ... Is 44:15 6466
he *m* it a graven image, and ... Is 44:15 6213
And the residue thereof he *m* a god ... Is 44:17 6213
I am the LORD that *m* all things ... Is 44:24 6213
of the liars, and *m* diviners mad ... Is 44:25
m their knowledge foolish ... Is 44:25
and he *m* it a god ... Is 46:6 6213
m it bring forth and bud, that it ... Is 55:10
from evil *m* himself a prey ... Is 59:15
my heart *m* a noise in me ... Jer 4:19
he *m* lightnings with rain, and ... Jer 10:13 6213
m flesh his arm, and whose heart ... Jer 17:5
king of Babylon *m* war against us ... Jer 21:2
m himself a prophet, that thou ... Jer 29:26
which *m* himself a prophet to you ... Jer 29:27
be like the dove that *m* her nest ... Jer 48:28
he *m* lightnings with rain, and ... Jer 51:16 6213
m idols against herself to defile ... Eze 22:3 6213
secrets, and *m* known to the king ... Dan 2:28
he that revealeth secrets *m* known ... Dan 2:29
but *m* his petition three times a ... Dan 6:13
the abomination that *m* desolate ... Dan 11:31
that *m* desolate set up, there ... Dan 12:11
that *m* the morning darkness, and ... Amos 4:13 6213
Seek him that *m* the seven stars ... Amos 5:8 6213
m the day dark with night ... Amos 5:8
m it dry, and drieth up all the ... Nah 1:4
for he *m* his sun to rise on the ... Mt 5:45 *393*
he *m* both the deaf to hear, and ... Mk 7:37 *4160*
then both the new *m* a rent ... Lk 5:36 *4977*
whosoever *m* himself a king ... Jn 19:12 *4160*
Aeneas, Jesus Christ *m* thee whole ... Acts 9:34 *2390*
And hope *m* not ashamed ... Rom 5:5 *2617*
but the Spirit itself *m* ... Rom 8:26 *5241*
because he *m* intercession for the ... Rom 8:27 *1793*
who also *m* intercession for us ... Rom 8:34 *1793*
how he *m* intercession to God ... Rom 11:2 *1793*
For who *m* thee to differ from ... 1Cor 4:7 *1252*
who is he then that *m* me glad ... 2Cor 2:2 *2165*
m manifest the savour of his ... 2Cor 2:14 *5319*
they were, it *m* no matter to me ... Gal 2:6 *1308*
m increase of the body unto the ... Eph 4:16 *4160*
Who *m* his angels spirits, and his ... Heb 1:7 *4160*
For the law *m* men high priests ... Heb 7:28 *2525*
m the Son, who is consecrated for ... Heb 7:28
so that he *m* fire come down from ... Rev 13:13 *4160*
worketh abomination, or *m* a lie ... Rev 21:27
and whosoever loveth and *m* a lie ... Rev 22:15 *4160*

MAKHELOTH (*mak'-he-loth*) *An Israelite encampment in the wilderness.*
from Haradah, and pitched in *M* ... Num 33:25 4721
And they removed from *M*, and ... Num 33:26 4721

MAKI See MACHI.

MAKING
task in *m* brick both yesterday ... Ex 5:14
in *m* war against it to take it, ... Deut 20:19
Now as they were *m* their hearts ... Judg 19:22
eating and drinking, and *m* merry ... 1Kin 4:20
m a noise with psalteries and ... 1Chr 15:28
in *m* known all these great things ... 1Chr 17:19
m confession to the LORD God of ... 2Chr 30:22
LORD is sure, *m* wise the simple ... Ps 19:7
of *m* many books there is no end ... Eccl 12:12 6213
m a tinkling with their feet ... Is 3:16
m him very glad ... Jer 20:15
multitude of the wares of thy *m* ... Eze 27:16 4639
multitude of the wares of thy *m* ... Eze 27:18 4639
m supplication before his God ... Dan 6:11
swearing falsely in *m* a covenant ... Hos 10:4 3772
m the ephah small, and the shekel ... Amos 8:5
in *m* thee desolate because of thy ... Mic 6:13
minstrels and the people *m* a noise ... Mt 9:23 *2350*
M the word of God of none effect ... Mk 7:13 *208*
Father, *m* himself equal with God ... Jn 5:18 *4160*
M request, if by any means now at ... Rom 1:10 *1189*
as poor, yet *m* many rich ... 2Cor 6:10 *4148*
m mention of you in my prayers ... Eph 1:16 *4160*
of twain one new man, so *m* peace ... Eph 2:15 *4160*
m melody in your heart to the ... Eph 5:19 *5567*
for you all *m* request with joy ... Phil 1:4 *4160*
m mention of you in our prayers ... 1Th 1:2 *4160*
m mention of thee always in my ... Philem 4 *4160*
m them an ensample unto those ... 2Pet 2:6 *4160*
have compassion, *m* a difference ... Jude 22 *1252*

MAKIR See MACHIR.

MAKIRITE See MACHIRITES.

MAKKEDAH (*mak'-ke-dah*) *A city in Judah.*
smote them to Azekah, and unto *M* ... Josh 10:10 4719
and hid themselves in a cave at *M* ... Josh 10:16 4719
are found hid in a cave at *M* ... Josh 10:17 4719
the camp to Joshua at *M* in peace ... Josh 10:21 4719
And that day Joshua took *M* ... Josh 10:28 4719
he did to the king of *M* as he did ... Josh 10:28 4719
Then Joshua passed from *M* ... Josh 10:29 4719
The king of *M*, one ... Josh 12:16 4719
Beth-dagon, and Naamah, and *M* ... Josh 15:41 4719

MAKTESH (*mak'-tesh*) *A district near Jerusalem.*
Howl, ye inhabitants of *M* ... Zeph 1:11 4389

MALACHI (*mal'-a-ki*) *A prophet.*
word of the LORD to Israel by *M* ... Mal 1:1 4401

MALCAM See MALCHAM.

MALCHAM (*mal'-kam*) See MILCOM.
1. Son of Shaharaim.
Jobab, and Zibia, and Mesha, and *M* ... 1Chr 8:9 4445
2. An Ammonite idol.
by the LORD, and that swear by *M* ... Zeph 1:5 4445

MALCHIAH (*mal-ki'-ah*) See MALCHIJAH, MELCHIAH.
1. Father of Baaseiah.
the son of Baaseiah, the son of *M* ... 1Chr 6:40 4441
2. A descendant of Parosh.
Ramiah, and Jeziah, and *M*, and ... Ezr 10:25 4441
the son of Pashur, the son of *M* ... Neh 11:12 4441
3. Another descendant of Parosh.
Eliezer, Ishijah, *M*, Shemaiah, ... Ezr 10:31 4441
4. A repairer of Jerusalem's wall.
gate repaired *M* the son of Rechab ... Neh 3:14 4441
5. Another repairer of Jerusalem's wall.
After him repaired *M* the ... Neh 3:31 4441
6. A priest who aided Ezra.
hand, Pedaiah, and Mishael, and *M* ... Neh 8:4 4441
7. A priest who dedicated the wall.
Shelemiah, and Pashur the son of *M* ... Jer 38:1 4441
dungeon of *M* the son of Hammelech ... Jer 38:6 4441

MALCHIEL (*mal'-ke-el*) See MALCHIELITES. *A son of Beriah.*
Heber, and *M* ... Gen 46:17 4439
of *M*, the family of the ... Num 26:45 4439
Heber, and *M*, who is the father of ... 1Chr 7:31 4439

MALCHIELITES (*mal'-ke-el-ites*) *Descendants of Malchiel.*
of Malchiel, the family of the *M* ... Num 26:45 4440

MALCHIJAH (*mal-ki'-jah*) See MALCHIAH.
1. A family of exiles.
the son of Pashur, the son of *M* ... 1Chr 9:12 4441
2. A sanctuary servant.
The fifth to *M*, the sixth to ... 1Chr 24:9 4441
3. Married a foreigner in exile.
and Miamin, and Eleazar, and *M* ... Ezr 10:25 4441
4. A rebuilder of Jerusalem's wall.
M the son of Harim, and Hashub the ... Neh 3:11 4441
5. A priest who dedicated the wall.
Pashur, Amariah, *M*, ... Neh 10:3 4441
and Uzzi, and Jehohanan, and *M* ... Neh 12:42 4441

MALCHIRAM (*mal'-ki-ram*) *A descendant of King Jehoiakim.*
M also, and Pedaiah, and Shenazar, ... 1Chr 3:18 4443

MALCHI-SHUA (*mal''-ki-shu'-ah*) See MELCHISHUA. *A son of King Saul.*
and Saul begat Jonathan, and *M* ... 1Chr 8:33 4444
and Saul begat Jonathan, and *M* ... 1Chr 9:39 4444
slew Jonathan, and Abinadab, and *M* ... 1Chr 10:2 4444

MALCHUS (*mal'-kus*) *A servant wounded by Simon Peter.*
The servant's name was *M* ... Jn 18:10 *3124*

MALE
m and female created he them ... Gen 1:27 2145
M and female created he them ... Gen 5:2 2145
they shall be *m* and female ... Gen 6:19 2145
take to thee by sevens, the *m* ... Gen 7:2 376
that are not clean by two, the *m* ... Gen 7:2 376
also of the air by sevens, the *m* ... Gen 7:3 2145
two unto Noah into the ark, the *m* ... Gen 7:9 2145
And they that went in, went in *m* ... Gen 7:16 2145
money, every *m* among the men of ... Gen 17:23 2145
as we be, that every *m* of you be ... Gen 34:15 2145
people, if every *m* among us be ... Gen 34:22 2145
every *m* was circumcised, all that ... Gen 34:24 2145
blemish, a *m* of the first year ... Ex 12:5 2145
whether ox or sheep, that is *m* ... Ex 34:19 2142
let him offer a *m* without blemish ... Lev 1:3 2145
bring it a *m* without blemish ... Lev 1:10 2145
whether it be a *m* or female ... Lev 3:1 2145
m or female, he shall offer it ... Lev 3:6 2145
of the goats, a *m* without blemish ... Lev 4:23 2145
Every *m* among the priests shall ... Lev 7:6 2145
that hath born a *m* or a female ... Lev 12:7 2145
your own will a *m* without blemish ... Lev 22:19 2145
thy estimation shall be of the *m* ... Lev 27:3 2145
shall be of the *m* twenty shekels ... Lev 27:5 2145
of the *m* five shekels of silver ... Lev 27:6 2145
if it be a *m*, then thy estimation ... Lev 27:7 2145
names, every *m* by their polls ... Num 1:2 2145
every *m* from twenty years old and ... Num 1:20 2145
every *m* from twenty years old and ... Num 1:22 2145
every *m* from a month old and ... Num 3:15 2145
Both *m* and female shall ye put out ... Num 5:3 2145
every *m* shall eat it ... Num 18:10 2145
every *m* among the little ones ... Num 31:17 2145
the likeness of *m* or female ... Deut 4:16 2145
there shall not be *m* or female ... Deut 7:14
thou shalt smite every *m* thereof ... Deut 20:13 2138
these were the *m* children of ... Josh 17:2 2145
Ye shall utterly destroy every *m* ... Judg 21:11 2145
known no man by lying with any *m* ... Judg 21:12 2145
he had smitten every *m* in Edom ... 1Kin 11:15 2145
he had cut off every *m* in Edom ... 1Kin 11:16 2145
which hath in his flock a *m* ... Mal 1:14 2145
them at the beginning made them *m* ... Mt 19:4 *730*
of the creation God made them *m* ... Mk 10:6 *730*
Every *m* that openeth the womb ... Lk 2:23 *730*
there is neither *m* nor female ... Gal 3:28 *730*

MALEFACTOR
said unto him, If he were not a *m* ... Jn 18:30 *2555*

MALEFACTORS
And there were also two others, *m* ... Lk 23:32 *2557*
they crucified him, and the *m* ... Lk 23:33 *2557*
one of the *m* which were hanged ... Lk 23:39 *2557*

MALELEEL (*mal'-e-le-el*) See MAHALALEEL. *Son of Cainan; ancestor of Jesus.*
of Jared, which was the son of *M* ... Lk 3:37 *3121*

MALES
city boldly, and slew all the *m* ... Gen 34:25 2145
let all his *m* be circumcised, and ... Ex 12:48 2145
the *m* shall be the LORD's ... Ex 13:12 2145
that openeth the matrix, being *m* ... Ex 13:15 2145
m shall appear before the Lord ... Ex 23:17 2138
All the *m* among the children of ... Lev 6:18 2145
All the *m* among the priests shall ... Lev 6:29 2145
to the number of all the *m* ... Num 3:22 2145
In the number of all the *m* ... Num 3:28 2145
to the number of all the *m* ... Num 3:34 2145
all the *m* from a month old and ... Num 3:39 2145
m of the children of Israel from ... Num 3:40 2145
all the firstborn *m* by the number ... Num 3:43 2145
all *m* from a month old and upward ... Num 26:62 2145
and they slew all the *m* ... Num 31:7 2145
All the firstling *m* that come of ... Deut 15:19 2145
times in a year shall all thy *m* ... Deut 16:16 2138
came out of Egypt, that were *m* ... Josh 5:4 2145
Beside their genealogy of *m* ... 2Chr 31:16 2145
to all the *m* among the priests ... 2Chr 31:19 2145
by genealogy of the *m* an hundred ... Ezr 8:3 2145
and with him two hundred *m* ... Ezr 8:4 2145
and with him three hundred *m* ... Ezr 8:5 2145
of Jonathan, and with him fifty *m* ... Ezr 8:6 2145
Athaliah, and with him seventy *m* ... Ezr 8:7 2145
Michael, and with him fourscore *m* ... Ezr 8:8 2145
him two hundred and eighteen *m* ... Ezr 8:9 2145
him an hundred and threescore *m* ... Ezr 8:10 2145
and with him twenty and eight *m* ... Ezr 8:11 2145
and with him an hundred and ten *m* ... Ezr 8:12 2145
and with them threescore *m* ... Ezr 8:13 2145
and with them seventy *m* ... Ezr 8:14 2145

MALICE
neither with the leaven of *m* ... 1Cor 5:8 *2549*
howbeit in *m* be ye children, but ... 1Cor 14:20 *2549*
be put away from you, with all *m* ... Eph 4:31 *2549*
anger, wrath, *m*, blasphemy, ... Col 3:8 *2549*
lusts and pleasures, living in *m* ... Titus 3:3 *2549*
Wherefore laying aside all *m* ... 1Pet 2:1 *2549*

MALICIOUS
prating against us with *m* words ... 3Jn 10 *4190*

MALICIOUSNESS
wickedness, covetousness, *m* ... Rom 1:29 *2549*
your liberty for a cloke of *m* ... 1Pet 2:16 *2549*

MALIGNITY
envy, murder, debate, deceit, *m* ... Rom 1:29 *2550*

MALLOTHI (*mal'-lo-thi*) *A son of Heman.*
and Romamti-ezer, Joshbekashah, *M* ... 1Chr 25:4 4413
The nineteenth to *M*, he, his sons ... 1Chr 25:26 4413

MALLOWS
Who cut up *m* by the bushes, and ... Job 30:4 4408

MALLUCH (*mal'-luk*) See MELICU.
1. Ancestor of Ethan.
the son of Abdi, the son of *M* ... 1Chr 6:44 4409
2. A son of Bani.
Meshullam, *M*, and Adaiah, Jashub, ... Ezr 10:29 4409
3. A descendant of Harim.
Benjamin, *M*, and Shemariah ... Ezr 10:32 4409
4. A priest who renewed the covenant.
Hattush, Shebaniah, *M*, ... Neh 10:4 4409
Amariah, *M*, Hattush, ... Neh 12:2 4409
5. A clan leader who renewed the covenant.
M, Harim, Baanah ... Neh 10:27 4409

MALLUCHI See MELICU.

MALTA See MELITA.

MAMMON
Ye cannot serve God and *m* ... Mt 6:24 *3126*
of the *m* of unrighteousness ... Lk 16:9 *3126*
faithful in the unrighteous *m* ... Lk 16:11 *3126*
Ye cannot serve God and *m* ... Lk 16:13 *3126*

MAMRE (*mam'-re*)
1. A place near Hebron.
came and dwelt in the plain of *M* ... Gen 13:18 4471
unto him in the plains of *M* ... Gen 18:1 4471
in Machpelah, which was before *M* ... Gen 23:17 4471
the field of Machpelah before *M* ... Gen 23:19 4471
the Hittite, which is before *M* ... Gen 25:9 4471
came unto Isaac his father unto *M* ... Gen 35:27 4471
of Machpelah, which is before *M* ... Gen 49:30 4471
of Ephron the Hittite, before *M* ... Gen 50:13 4471
2. An Amorite ally of Abraham.
in the plain of *M* the Amorite ... Gen 14:13 4471
went with me, Aner, Eshcol, and *M* ... Gen 14:24 4471

MAN
Let us make *m* in our image, after ... Gen 1:26 120
So God created *m* in his own image ... Gen 1:27 120
there was not a *m* to till the ... Gen 2:5 120
the LORD God formed *m* of the dust ... Gen 2:7 120
and *m* became a living soul ... Gen 2:7 120
there he put the *m* whom he had ... Gen 2:8 120
And the LORD God took the *m* ... Gen 2:15 120
And the LORD God commanded the *m* ... Gen 2:16 120
good that the *m* should be alone ... Gen 2:18 120
the LORD God had taken from *m* ... Gen 2:22 120
woman, and brought her unto the *m* ... Gen 2:22 120
because she was taken out of *M* ... Gen 2:23 376

shall a *m* leave his father	Gen 2:24	376
And they were both naked, the *m*	Gen 2:25	120
the *m* said, The woman whom thou	Gen 3:12	120
the *m* is become as one of us, to	Gen 3:22	120
So he drove out the *m*	Gen 3:24	120
I have gotten a *m* from the LORD	Gen 4:1	376
I have slain a *m* to my wounding	Gen 4:23	376
and a young *m* to my hurt	Gen 4:23	
In the day that God created *m*	Gen 5:1	120
shall not always strive with *m*	Gen 6:3	120
of *m* was great in the earth	Gen 6:5	120
that he had made *m* on the earth	Gen 6:6	120
I will destroy *m* whom I have	Gen 6:7	120
both *m*, and beast, and the creeping	Gen 6:7	120
Noah was a just *m* and perfect in	Gen 6:9	376
upon the earth, and every *m*	Gen 7:21	120
the face of the ground, both *m*	Gen 7:23	120
I require it, and at the hand of *m*	Gen 9:5	120
will I require the life of *m*	Gen 9:5	120
by *m* shall his blood be shed	Gen 9:6	120
for in the image of God made he *m*	Gen 9:6	120
so that if a *m* can number the	Gen 13:16	376
And he will be a wild *m*	Gen 16:12	120
his hand will be against every *m*	Gen 16:12	
Every *m* child among you shall be	Gen 17:10	2145
every *m* child in your generations	Gen 17:12	2145
the uncircumcised *m* child whose	Gen 17:14	2145
good, and gave it unto a young *m*	Gen 18:7	
daughters which have not known *m*	Gen 19:8	376
And they pressed sore upon the *m*	Gen 19:9	376
there is not a *m* in the earth to	Gen 19:31	376
Behold, thou art but a dead *m*	Gen 20:3	376
therefore restore the *m* his wife	Gen 20:7	376
neither had any *m* known her	Gen 24:16	376
the *m* wondering at her held his	Gen 24:21	376
that the *m* took a golden earring	Gen 24:22	376
the *m* bowed down his head, and	Gen 24:26	376
and Laban ran out unto the *m*	Gen 24:29	376
saying, Thus spake the *m* unto me	Gen 24:30	376
that he came unto the *m*	Gen 24:30	376
the *m* came into the house	Gen 24:32	376
her, Wilt thou go with this *m*	Gen 24:58	376
the camels, and followed the *m*	Gen 24:61	376
What *m* is this that walketh in	Gen 24:65	376
died in a good old age, an old *m*	Gen 25:8	
cunning hunter, a *m* of the field	Gen 25:27	376
and Jacob was a plain *m*, dwelling	Gen 25:27	376
He that toucheth this *m* or his	Gen 26:11	376
the *m* waxed great, and went	Gen 26:13	376
Esau my brother is a hairy *m*	Gen 27:11	376
and I am a smooth *m*	Gen 27:11	376
I should give her to another *m*	Gen 29:19	376
the *m* increased exceedingly, and	Gen 30:43	376
my daughters, no *m* is with us	Gen 31:50	376
there wrestled a *m* with him until	Gen 32:24	376
the young *m* deferred not to do	Gen 34:19	
brethren, took each *m* his sword	Gen 34:25	376
And a certain *m* found him, and,	Gen 37:15	376
the *m* asked him, saying, What	Gen 37:15	376
the *m* said, They are departed	Gen 37:17	376
father in law, saying, By the *m*	Gen 38:25	376
Joseph, and he was a prosperous *m*	Gen 39:2	376
each *m* his dream in one night,	Gen 40:5	376
each *m* according to the	Gen 40:5	376
we dreamed each *m* according to	Gen 41:11	376
there was there with us a young *m*	Gen 41:12	376
to each *m* according to his dream	Gen 41:12	376
let Pharaoh look out a *m* discreet	Gen 41:33	376
a *m* in whom the Spirit of God is	Gen 41:38	376
without thee shall no *m* lift up	Gen 41:44	376
the sons of one *m* in the land of	Gen 42:13	376
The *m*, who is the lord of the	Gen 42:30	376
And the *m*, the lord of the country	Gen 42:33	376
The *m* did solemnly protest unto	Gen 43:3	376
for the *m* said unto us, Ye shall	Gen 43:5	376
as to tell the *m* whether ye had	Gen 43:6	376
The *m* asked us straitly of our	Gen 43:7	376
and carry down the *m* a present	Gen 43:11	376
and arise, go again unto the *m*	Gen 43:13	376
give you mercy before the *m*	Gen 43:14	376
And the *m* did as Joseph bade	Gen 43:17	376
the *m* brought the men into	Gen 43:17	376
the *m* brought the men into	Gen 43:24	376
the old *m* of whom ye spake	Gen 43:27	
every *m* his sack to the ground	Gen 44:11	376
and opened every *m* his sack	Gen 44:11	376
clothes, and laded every *m* his ass	Gen 44:13	376
wot ye not that such a *m* as I can	Gen 44:15	376
but the *m* in whose hand the cup	Gen 44:17	376
lord, We have a father, an old *m*	Gen 44:20	376
Cause every *m* to go out from me	Gen 45:1	376
And there stood no *m* with him	Gen 45:1	376
he gave each *m* changes of raiment	Gen 45:22	376
Egyptians sold every *m* his field	Gen 47:20	376
for in their anger they slew a *m*	Gen 49:6	376
every *m* and his household came	Ex 1:1	376
there went a *m* of the house of	Ex 2:1	376
when he saw that there was no *m*	Ex 2:12	376
why is it that ye have left the *m*	Ex 2:20	376
was content to dwell with the *m*	Ex 2:21	376
they cast down every *m* his rod	Ex 7:12	376
the earth, and it became lice in *m*	Ex 8:17	120
so there were lice upon *m*	Ex 8:18	120
breaking forth with blains upon *m*	Ex 9:9	120
breaking forth with blains upon *m*	Ex 9:10	120
for upon every *m* and beast which	Ex 9:19	120
in all the land of Egypt, upon *m*	Ex 9:22	120
all that was in the field, both *m*	Ex 9:25	120
shall this *m* be a snare unto us	Ex 10:7	
let every *m* borrow of his	Ex 11:2	376
Moreover the *m* Moses was very	Ex 11:3	376
his tongue, against *m* or beast	Ex 11:7	376
shall take to them every *m* a lamb	Ex 12:3	376
every *m* according to his eating	Ex 12:4	376
in the land of Egypt, both *m*	Ex 12:12	120
save that which every *m* must eat	Ex 12:16	5315
the children of Israel, both of *m*	Ex 13:2	120
all the firstborn of *m* among thy	Ex 13:13	120
of Egypt, both the firstborn of *m*	Ex 13:15	120
The LORD is a *m* of war	Ex 15:3	376
Gather of it every *m* according to	Ex 16:16	376
his eating, an omer for every *m*	Ex 16:16	1538
take ye every *m* for them which	Ex 16:16	376
they gathered every *m* according	Ex 16:18	376
Let no *m* leave of it till the	Ex 16:19	376
every *m* according to his eating	Ex 16:21	376
much bread, two omers for one *m*	Ex 16:22	
abide ye every *m* in his place	Ex 16:29	376
let no *m* go out of his place on	Ex 16:29	376
whether it be beast or *m*, it	Ex 19:13	376
if a *m* sell his daughter to be a	Ex 21:7	376
He that smiteth a *m*, so that he	Ex 21:12	376
if a *m* lie not in wait, but God	Ex 21:13	
But if a *m* come presumptuously	Ex 21:14	376
And he that stealeth a *m*, and	Ex 21:16	376
if a *m* smite his servant, or his	Ex 21:20	376
if a *m* smite the eye of his	Ex 21:26	376
If an ox gore a *m* or a woman	Ex 21:28	376
he hath killed a *m* or a woman	Ex 21:29	376
if a *m* shall open a pit	Ex 21:33	376
or if a *m* shall dig a pit, and not	Ex 21:33	376
If a *m* shall steal an ox, or a	Ex 22:1	376
If a *m* shall cause a field or	Ex 22:5	376
If a *m* shall deliver unto his	Ex 22:7	376
If a *m* deliver unto his neighbour	Ex 22:10	376
or driven away, no *m* seeing it	Ex 22:10	
if a *m* borrow ought of his	Ex 22:14	376
if a *m* entice a maid that is not	Ex 22:16	376
countenance a poor *m* in his cause	Ex 23:3	
if any *m* have any matters to do,	Ex 24:14	1167
of every *m* that giveth it	Ex 25:2	376
then shall they give every *m* a	Ex 30:12	376
the *m* that brought us up out of	Ex 32:1	376
the *m* that brought us up out of	Ex 32:23	376
Put every *m* his sword by his side	Ex 32:27	376
slay every *m* his brother, and	Ex 32:27	376
every *m* his companion	Ex 32:27	376
and every *m* his neighbour	Ex 32:27	376
even every *m* upon his son, and	Ex 32:29	376
no *m* did put on him his ornaments	Ex 33:4	376
stood every *m* at his tent door,	Ex 33:8	376
every *m* in his tent door	Ex 33:10	376
as a *m* speaketh unto his friend	Ex 33:11	376
Joshua, the son of Nun, a young *m*	Ex 33:11	
for there shall no *m* see me	Ex 33:20	120
no *m* shall come up with thee,	Ex 34:3	376
neither let any *m* be seen	Ex 34:3	376
shall any *m* desire thy land	Ex 34:24	376
every *m* that offered offered an	Ex 35:22	376
And every *m*, with whom was found	Ex 35:23	376
and every *m*, with whom was found	Ex 35:24	376
offering unto the LORD, every *m*	Ex 35:29	376
Aholiab, and every wise hearted *m*	Ex 36:1	376
Aholiab, and every wise hearted *m*	Ex 36:2	376
came every *m* from his work which	Ex 36:4	376
Let neither *m* nor woman make any	Ex 36:6	376
every wise hearted *m* among them	Ex 36:8	
A bekah for every *m*, that is,	Ex 38:26	1538
If any *m* of you bring an offering	Lev 1:2	120
if he touch the uncleanness of *m*	Lev 5:3	120
that a *m* shall be defiled withal	Lev 5:3	
whatsoever it be that a *m* shall	Lev 5:4	120
any of all these that a *m* doeth	Lev 6:3	120
thing, as the uncleanness of *m*	Lev 7:21	120
conceived seed, and born a *m* child	Lev 12:2	2145
When a *m* shall have in the skin	Lev 13:2	120
the plague of leprosy is in a *m*	Lev 13:9	120
If a *m* or woman have a plague	Lev 13:29	376
If a *m* also or a woman have in	Lev 13:38	376
the *m* whose hair is fallen off	Lev 13:40	376
He is a leprous *m*, he is unclean	Lev 13:44	376
the *m* that is to be made clean	Lev 14:11	376
When any *m* hath a running issue	Lev 15:2	376
whom *m* shall lie with seed of	Lev 15:18	376
if any *m* lie with her at all, and	Lev 15:24	376
him that hath an issue, of the *m*	Lev 15:33	2145
there shall be no *m* in the	Lev 16:17	120
of a fit *m* into the wilderness	Lev 16:21	376
What *m* soever there be of the	Lev 17:3	376
shall be imputed unto that *m*	Lev 17:4	376
that *m* shall be cut off from	Lev 17:4	376
Whatsoever *m* there be of the	Lev 17:8	376
even that *m* shall be cut off from	Lev 17:9	376
whatsoever *m* there be of the	Lev 17:10	376
whatsoever *m* there be of the	Lev 17:13	376
which if a *m* do, he shall live in	Lev 18:5	120
Ye shall fear every *m* his mother	Lev 19:3	376
and honour the face of the old *m*	Lev 19:32	
I will set my face against that *m*	Lev 20:3	376
ways hide their eyes from the *m*	Lev 20:4	376
I will set my face against that *m*	Lev 20:5	376
the *m* that committeth adultery	Lev 20:10	376
the *m* that lieth with his	Lev 20:11	376
if a *m* lie with his daughter in	Lev 20:12	376
If a *m* also lie with mankind, as	Lev 20:13	376
if a *m* take a wife and her mother,	Lev 20:14	376
if a *m* lie with a beast, he shall	Lev 20:15	376
if a *m* shall take his sister, his	Lev 20:17	376
if a *m* shall lie with a woman	Lev 20:18	376
if a *m* shall lie with his uncle's	Lev 20:20	376
if a *m* shall take his brother's	Lev 20:21	376
A *m* also or woman that hath a	Lev 20:27	376
being a chief *m* among his people,	Lev 21:4	1167
For whatsoever *m* he be that hath	Lev 21:18	376
a blind *m*, or a lame, or he that	Lev 21:18	376
Or a *m* that is brokenfooted, or	Lev 21:19	376
No *m* that hath a blemish of the	Lev 21:21	376
What *m* soever of the seed of	Lev 22:4	376
or a *m* whose seed goeth from him	Lev 22:4	376
or a *m* of whom he may take	Lev 22:5	120
if a *m* eat of the holy thing	Lev 22:14	376
a *m* of Israel strove together in	Lev 24:10	376
he that killeth any *m* shall	Lev 24:17	
if a *m* cause a blemish in his	Lev 24:19	376
he hath caused a blemish in a *m*	Lev 24:20	120
and he that killeth a *m*, he shall	Lev 24:21	120
every *m* unto his possession	Lev 25:10	376
return every *m* unto his family	Lev 25:10	376
every *m* unto his possession	Lev 25:13	376
if the *m* have none to redeem it,	Lev 25:26	376
unto the *m* to whom he sold it	Lev 25:27	376
if a *m* sell a dwelling house in a	Lev 25:29	376
if a *m* purchase of the Levites,	Lev 25:33	
When a *m* shall make a singular	Lev 27:2	376
all that any *m* giveth of such	Lev 27:9	
when a *m* shall sanctify his house	Lev 27:14	376
if a *m* shall sanctify unto the	Lev 27:16	376
have sold the field to another *m*	Lev 27:20	376
if a *m* sanctify unto the LORD a	Lev 27:22	
firstling, no *m* shall sanctify it	Lev 27:26	376
that a *m* shall devote unto the	Lev 27:28	376
of all that he hath, both of *m*	Lev 27:28	120
if a *m* will at all redeem ought	Lev 27:31	376
there shall be a *m* of every tribe	Num 1:4	376
every *m* by his own camp, and every	Num 1:52	376
every *m* by his own standard,	Num 1:52	376
Every *m* of the children of Israel	Num 2:2	376
every *m* in his place by their	Num 2:17	376
the firstborn in Israel, both *m*	Num 3:13	120
When a *m* or woman shall commit	Num 5:6	376
But if the *m* have no kinsman to	Num 5:8	376
whatsoever any *m* giveth the	Num 5:10	376
a *m* lie with her carnally, and it	Num 5:13	376
Then shall the *m* bring his wife	Num 5:15	376
If no *m* have lain with thee, and	Num 5:19	376
some *m* have lain with thee beside	Num 5:20	376
Then shall the *m* be guiltless	Num 5:31	376
When either *m* or woman shall	Num 6:2	376
if any *m* die very suddenly by him	Num 6:9	
to every *m* according to his	Num 7:5	376
of Israel are mine, both *m*	Num 8:17	120
defiled by the dead body of a *m*	Num 9:6	120
defiled by the dead body of a *m*	Num 9:7	120
If any *m* of you or of your	Num 9:10	376
But the *m* that is clean, and is	Num 9:13	376
that *m* shall bear his sin	Num 9:13	376
every *m* in the door of his tent	Num 11:10	376
And there ran a young *m*, and told	Num 11:27	
(Now the *m* Moses was very meek,	Num 12:3	376
their fathers shall ye send a *m*	Num 13:2	376
kill all this people as one *m*	Num 14:15	376
they found a *m* that gathered	Num 15:32	376
The *m* shall be surely put to	Num 15:35	376
it shall be that the *m* whom the	Num 16:7	376
And take every *m* his censer	Num 16:17	376
the LORD every *m* his censer	Num 16:17	376
And they took every *m* his censer	Num 16:18	376
of all flesh, shall one *m* sin	Num 16:22	376
looked, and took every *m* his rod	Num 17:9	376
of *m* shalt thou surely redeem	Num 18:15	120
a *m* that is clean shall gather up	Num 19:9	376
any *m* shall be unclean seven days	Num 19:11	120
dead body of any *m* that is dead	Num 19:13	120
the law, when a *m* dieth in a tent	Num 19:14	120
or a dead body, or a bone of a *m*	Num 19:16	120
But the *m* that shall be unclean,	Num 19:20	376
if a serpent had bitten any *m*	Num 21:9	376
God is not a *m*, that he should	Num 23:19	376
neither the son of *m*, that he	Num 23:19	120
the *m* whose eyes are open hath	Num 24:3	1397
the *m* whose eyes are open hath	Num 24:15	1397
he went after the *m* of Israel	Num 25:8	376
the *m* of Israel, and the woman	Num 25:8	376
was not a *m* of them whom Moses	Num 26:64	376
And there was not left a *m* of them	Num 26:65	376
of Israel, saying, If a *m* die	Num 27:8	376
set a *m* over the congregation,	Num 27:16	376
a *m* in whom is the spirit, and lay	Num 27:18	376
If a *m* vow a vow unto the LORD,	Num 30:2	376
Moses, between a *m*	Num 30:16	376
hath known *m* by lying with him	Num 31:17	
not known a *m* by lying with him	Num 31:18	2145
prey that was taken, both of *m*	Num 31:26	120
had not known *m* by lying with him	Num 31:35	2145
one portion of fifty, both of *m*	Num 31:47	120
and there lacketh not one *m* of us	Num 31:49	376
what every *m* hath gotten, of	Num 31:50	376
taken spoil, every *m* for himself	Num 31:53	376
inherited every *m* his inheritance	Num 32:18	376
every *m* armed for war, before the	Num 32:27	
every *m* armed to battle, before	Num 32:29	
any stone, wherewith a *m* may die	Num 35:23	
of Israel may enjoy every *m* the	Num 36:8	376
judge righteously between every *m*	Deut 1:16	376
not be afraid of the face of *m*	Deut 1:17	376
as a *m* doth bear his son, in all	Deut 1:31	376
on every *m* his weapons of war	Deut 1:41	376
of it, after the cubit of a *m*	Deut 3:11	376
every *m* unto his possession	Deut 3:20	376
that God created *m* upon the earth	Deut 4:32	120
day that God doth talk with *m*	Deut 5:24	120
there shall no *m* be able to stand	Deut 7:24	375
m doth not live by bread only	Deut 8:3	120
the mouth of the LORD doth *m* live	Deut 8:3	120
as a *m* chasteneth his son, so the	Deut 8:5	376
There shall no *m* be able to stand	Deut 11:25	376
every *m* whatsoever is right in	Deut 12:8	376
If there be among you a poor *m* of	Deut 15:7	
And if thy brother, an Hebrew *m*	Deut 15:12	
Every *m* shall give as he is able,	Deut 16:17	376
m or woman, that hath wrought	Deut 17:2	376
bring forth that *m* or that woman	Deut 17:5	376

even that *m* or that woman, and Deut 17:5 376
the *m* that will do presumptuously Deut 17:12 376
the judge, even that *m* shall die Deut 17:12 376
As when a *m* goeth into the wood Deut 19:5
But if any *m* hate his neighbour, Deut 19:11 376
up against a *m* for any iniquity Deut 19:15 376
any *m* to testify against him that Deut 19:16 376
What *m* is there that hath built a Deut 20:5 376
battle, and another *m* dedicate it Deut 20:5 376
what *m* is he that hath planted a Deut 20:6 376
battle, and another *m* eat of it Deut 20:6 376
what *m* is there that hath Deut 20:7 376
the battle, and another *m* take her Deut 20:7 376
What *m* is there that is fearful Deut 20:8 376
which is next unto the slain *m* Deut 21:3 376
that are next unto the slain *m* Deut 21:6
If a *m* have two wives, one Deut 21:15 376
If a *m* have a stubborn and Deut 21:18 376
if a *m* have committed a sin Deut 21:22 376
that which pertaineth unto a *m* Deut 22:5 1397
neither shall a *m* put on a Deut 22:5 1397
if any *m* fall from thence Deut 22:8
If any *m* take a wife, and go in Deut 22:13 376
my daughter unto this *m* to wife Deut 22:16 376
of that city shall take that *m* Deut 22:18 376
If a *m* be found lying with a Deut 22:22 376
both the *m* that lay with the Deut 22:22 376
a *m* find her in the city, and lie Deut 22:23 376
and the *m*, because he hath humbled Deut 22:24 376
But if a *m* find a betrothed Deut 22:25 376
the *m* force her, and lie with her Deut 22:25 376
then the *m* only that lay with her Deut 22:25 376
for as when a *m* riseth against Deut 22:26 376
If a *m* find a damsel that is a Deut 22:28 376
Then the *m* that lay with her Deut 22:29 376
A *m* shall not take his father's Deut 22:30 376
If there be among you any *m* Deut 23:10 376
When a *m* hath taken a wife, and Deut 24:1 376
When a *m* hath taken a new wife, Deut 24:5 376
No *m* shall take the nether or the Deut 24:6
If a *m* be found stealing any of Deut 24:7 376
the *m* to whom thou dost lend Deut 24:11 376
if the *m* be poor, thou shalt not Deut 24:12 376
every *m* shall be put to death for Deut 24:16 376
if the wicked *m* be worthy to be Deut 25:2
if the *m* like not to take his Deut 25:7 376
that *m* that will not build up his Deut 25:9 376
Cursed be the *m* that maketh any Deut 27:15 376
no *m* shall fray them away Deut 28:26
evermore, and no *m* shall save thee Deut 28:29
another *m* shall lie with her Deut 28:30 376
So that the *m* that is tender Deut 28:54 376
bondwomen, and no *m* shall buy you Deut 28:68
Lest there should be among you *m* Deut 29:18 376
shall smoke against that *m* Deut 29:20 376
shall destroy both the young *m* Deut 32:25
also with the *m* of gray hairs Deut 32:25 376
wherewith Moses the *m* of God Deut 33:1 376
but no *m* knoweth of his sepulchre Deut 34:6 376
There shall not any *m* be able to Josh 1:5 376
remain any more courage in any *m* Josh 2:11 376
of Israel, out of every tribe a *m* Josh 3:12 376
people, out of every tribe a *m* Josh 4:2 376
of Israel, out of every tribe a *m* Josh 4:4 376
take you up every *m* of you a Josh 4:5 376
there stood a *m* over against him Josh 5:13 376
up every *m* straight before him Josh 6:5 376
every *m* straight before him, and Josh 6:20 376
all that was in the city, both *m* Josh 6:21 376
Cursed be the *m* before the LORD, Josh 6:26 376
shall take shall come *m* by *m* Josh 7:14 1397
family of the Zarhites *m* by *m* Josh 7:17 1397
he brought his household *m* by *m* Josh 7:18 1397
there was not a *m* left in Ai or Josh 8:17 376
over which no *m* hath lift up any Josh 8:31
there shall not a *m* of them stand Josh 10:8 376
hearkened unto the voice of a *m* Josh 10:14 376
but every *m* they smote with the Josh 11:14 120
Moses the *m* of God concerning me Josh 14:6 376
was a great *m* among the Anakims Josh 14:15 120
because he was a *m* of war Josh 17:1 376
there stood not a *m* of all their Josh 21:44 376
that *m* perished not alone in his Josh 22:20 376
no *m* hath been able to stand Josh 23:9 376
One *m* of you shall chase a Josh 23:10 376
every *m* unto his inheritance Josh 24:28 376
the spies saw a *m* come forth out Judg 1:24 376
but they let go the *m* and all his Judg 1:25 376
the *m* went into the land of the Judg 1:26 376
children of Israel went every *m* Judg 2:6 376
Gera, a Benjamite, a *m* lefthanded Judg 3:15 376
and Eglon was a very fat *m* Judg 3:17 376
and suffered not a *m* to pass over Judg 3:28 376
and there escaped not a *m* Judg 3:29 376
and there was not a *m* left Judg 4:16
when any *m* doth come and enquire Judg 4:20 376
thee, and say, Is there any *m* here Judg 4:20 376
shew thee the *m* whom thou seekest Judg 4:22 376
to every *m* a damsel or two Judg 5:30 1397
thee, thou mighty *m* of valour Judg 6:12
smite the Midianites as one *m* Judg 6:16 376
people go every *m* unto his place Judg 7:7 376
of Israel every *m* unto his tent Judg 7:8 376
there was a *m* that told a dream Judg 7:13 376
the son of Joash, a *m* of Israel Judg 7:14 376
they stood every *m* in his place Judg 7:21 376
caught a young *m* of the men of Judg 8:14
for as the *m* is, so is his Judg 8:21 376
every *m* the earrings of his prey Judg 8:24 376
did cast therein every *m* the Judg 8:25 376
by me they honour God and *m* Judg 9:9 376
my wine, which cheereth God and *m* Judg 9:13 376
cut down every *m* his bough Judg 9:49 376
unto the young *m* his armourbearer Judg 9:54
his young *m* thrust him through, Judg 9:54
departed every *m* unto his place Judg 9:55 376
the son of Dodo, a *m* of Issachar Judg 10:1 376
What *m* is he that will begin to Judg 10:18 376
was a mighty *m* of valour, and he Judg 11:1
and she knew no *m* Judg 11:39 376
And there was a certain *m* of Zorah Judg 13:2 376
A *m* of God came unto me, and his Judg 13:6 376
let the *m* of God which thou didst Judg 13:8 376
the *m* hath appeared unto me, that Judg 13:10 376
after his wife, and came to the *m* Judg 13:11 376
Art thou the *m* that spakest unto Judg 13:11 376
I be weak, and be as another *m* Judg 16:7 120
I be weak, and be as another *m* Judg 16:11 120
weak, and be like any other *m* Judg 16:17 120
and she called for a *m*, and she Judg 16:19 376
there was a *m* of mount Ephraim, Judg 17:1 376
the *m* Micah had an house of gods, Judg 17:5 376
but every *m* did that which was Judg 17:6 376
there was a young *m* out of Judg 17:7
the *m* departed out of the city Judg 17:8 376
was content to dwell with the *m* Judg 17:11 376
the young *m* was unto him as one Judg 17:11
the young *m* became his priest, and Judg 17:12
voice of the young *m* the Levite Judg 18:3
and had no business with any *m* Judg 18:7 120
house of the young *m* the Levite Judg 18:15
a priest unto the house of one *m* Judg 18:19 376
they had no business with any *m* Judg 18:28 120
father had said unto the *m* Judg 19:6 376
when the *m* rose up to depart, his Judg 19:7 376
when the *m* rose up to depart, he, Judg 19:9 376
But the *m* would not tarry that Judg 19:10 376
for there was no *m* that took them Judg 19:15 376
there came an old *m* from his work Judg 19:16 376
he saw a wayfaring *m* in the Judg 19:17 376
and the old *m* said, Whither goest Judg 19:17 376
there is no *m* that receiveth me Judg 19:18 376
for the young *m* which is with thy Judg 19:19
And the old *m* said, Peace be with Judg 19:20 376
master of the house, the old *m* Judg 19:22 376
Bring forth the *m* that came into Judg 19:22 376
And the *m*, the master of the house Judg 19:23 376
seeing that this *m* is come into Judg 19:23 376
but unto this *m* do not so vile a Judg 19:24 376
so the *m* took his concubine, and Judg 19:25 376
Then the *m* took her up upon an Judg 19:28 376
the *m* rose up, and gat him unto Judg 19:28 376
was gathered together as one *m* Judg 20:1 376
And all the people arose as one *m* Judg 20:8 376
the city, knit together as one *m* Judg 20:11 376
every woman that hath lain by *m* Judg 21:11 2145
that had known no *m* by lying with Judg 21:12 376
catch you every *m* his wife of the Judg 21:21 376
not to each *m* his wife in the war Judg 21:22 376
every *m* to his tribe and to his Judg 21:24 376
thence every *m* to his inheritance Judg 21:24 376
every *m* did that which was right Judg 21:25 376
a certain *m* of Beth-lehem-judah Ruth 1:1 376
the name of the *m* was Elimelech Ruth 1:2 376
a mighty *m* of wealth, of the Ruth 2:1 376
The *m* is near of kin unto us, one Ruth 2:20 376
make not thyself known unto the *m* Ruth 3:3 376
that the *m* was afraid, and turned Ruth 3:8 376
all that the *m* had done to her Ruth 3:16 376
for the *m* will not be in rest, Ruth 3:18 376
a *m* plucked off his shoe, and gave Ruth 4:7 376
a certain *m* of Ramathaim-zophim 1Sa 1:1 376
this *m* went up out of his city 1Sa 1:3 376
unto thine handmaid a *m* child 1Sa 1:11 582
the *m* Elkanah, and all his house, 1Sa 1:21 376
by strength shall no *m* prevail 1Sa 2:9 376
when any *m* offered sacrifice, the 1Sa 2:13 376
said to the *m* that sacrificed, 1Sa 2:15 376
if any *m* said unto him, Let them 1Sa 2:16 376
If one *m* sin against another, the 1Sa 2:25 376
but if a *m* sin against the LORD, 1Sa 2:25 376
there came a *m* of God unto Eli, 1Sa 2:27 376
not be an old *m* in thine house 1Sa 2:31
an old *m* in thine house for ever 1Sa 2:32
the *m* of thine, whom I shall not 1Sa 2:33 376
they fled every *m* into his tent 1Sa 4:10 376
there ran a *m* of Benjamin out of 1Sa 4:12 376
when the *m* came into the city, and 1Sa 4:13 376
the *m* came in hastily, and told 1Sa 4:14 376
the *m* said unto Eli, I am he that 1Sa 4:16 376
for he was an old *m*, and heavy 1Sa 4:18 376
Go ye every *m* unto his city 1Sa 8:22 376
Now there was a *m* of Benjamin 1Sa 9:1 376
a Benjamite, a mighty *m* of power 1Sa 9:1 376
name was Saul, a choice young *m* 1Sa 9:2
there is in this city a *m* of God 1Sa 9:6 376
and he is an honourable *m* 1Sa 9:6 376
we go, what shall we bring the *m* 1Sa 9:7 376
present to bring to the *m* of God 1Sa 9:7 376
that will I give to the *m* of God 1Sa 9:8 376
when a *m* went to enquire of God, 1Sa 9:9 376
the city where the *m* of God was 1Sa 9:10 376
a *m* out of the land of Benjamin 1Sa 9:16 376
Behold the *m* whom I spake to thee 1Sa 9:17 376
and shalt be turned into another *m* 1Sa 10:6 376
if the *m* should yet come thither 1Sa 10:22 376
people away, every *m* to his house 1Sa 10:25 376
said, How shall this *m* save us 1Sa 10:27
then, if there be no *m* to save us 1Sa 11:3
There shall not a *m* be put to 1Sa 11:13 376
he sent every *m* to his tent 1Sa 13:2 376
him a *m* after his own heart 1Sa 13:14 376
to sharpen every *m* his share 1Sa 13:20 376
the young *m* that bare his armour 1Sa 14:1
the young *m* that bare his armour 1Sa 14:6
Cursed be the *m* that eateth any 1Sa 14:24 376
but no *m* put his hand to his 1Sa 14:26
Cursed be the *m* that eateth any 1Sa 14:28 376
Bring me hither every *m* his ox 1Sa 14:34 376
every *m* his sheep, and slay them 1Sa 14:34 376
m his ox with him that night 1Sa 14:34 376
and let us not leave a *m* of them 1Sa 14:36 376
But there was not a *m* among all 1Sa 14:39
and when Saul saw any strong *m* 1Sa 14:52 376
or any valiant *m* 1Sa 14:52 1121
but slay both *m* and woman, infant 1Sa 15:3 376
for he is not a *m*, that he should 1Sa 15:29 120
for the LORD seeth not as *m* seeth 1Sa 16:7 120
for *m* looketh on the outward 1Sa 16:7 120
are before thee, to seek out a *m* 1Sa 16:16 376
Provide me now a *m* that can play 1Sa 16:17 376
in playing, and a mighty valiant *m* 1Sa 16:18
a *m* of war, and prudent in matters 1Sa 16:18 376
choose you a *m* for you, and let 1Sa 17:8 376
give me a *m*, that we may fight 1Sa 17:10 376
the *m* went among men for an old 1Sa 17:12 376
for an old *m* in the days of Saul 1Sa 17:12
of Israel, when they saw the *m* 1Sa 17:24 376
ye seen this *m* that is come up 1Sa 17:25 376
that the *m* who killeth him, the 1Sa 17:25 376
What shall be done to the *m* that 1Sa 17:26 376
be done to the *m* that killeth him 1Sa 17:27 376
he a *m* of war from his youth 1Sa 17:33 376
the *m* that bare the shield went 1Sa 17:41 376
Whose son art thou, thou young *m* 1Sa 17:58
in law, seeing that I am a poor *m* 1Sa 18:23 376
if I say thus unto the young *m* 1Sa 20:22 5958
art thou alone, and no *m* with thee 1Sa 21:1 376
Let no *m* know any thing of the 1Sa 21:2 376
Now a certain *m* of the servants 1Sa 21:7 376
servants, Lo, ye see the *m* is mad 1Sa 21:14 376
to play the mad *m* in my presence 1Sa 21:15
For if a *m* find his enemy, will 1Sa 24:19 376
And there was a *m* in Maon, whose 1Sa 25:2 376
the *m* was very great, and he had 1Sa 25:2 376
Now the name of the *m* was Nabal 1Sa 25:3 376
but the *m* was churlish and evil in 1Sa 25:3 376
away every *m* from his master 1Sa 25:10 376
men, Gird ye on every *m* his sword 1Sa 25:13 376
they girded on every *m* his sword 1Sa 25:13 376
that a *m* cannot speak to him 1Sa 25:17
thee, regard this *m* of Belial 1Sa 25:25 376
Yet a *m* is risen to pursue thee, 1Sa 25:29 120
no *m* saw it, nor knew it, neither 1Sa 26:12
Abner, Art not thou a valiant *m* 1Sa 26:15 376
to every *m* his righteousness 1Sa 26:23 376
every *m* with his household, even 1Sa 27:3 376
left neither *m* nor woman alive, 1Sa 27:9 376
saved neither *m* nor woman alive 1Sa 27:11 376
And she said, An old *m* cometh up 1Sa 28:14 376
every *m* for his sons and for his 1Sa 30:6 376
he said, I am a young *m* of Egypt 1Sa 30:13
and there escaped not a *m* of them 1Sa 30:17 376
save to every *m* his wife 1Sa 30:22 376
a *m* came out of the camp from 2Sa 1:2 376
unto the young *m* that told him 2Sa 1:5
the young *m* that told him said, 2Sa 1:6
unto the young *m* that told him 2Sa 1:13
every *m* with his household 2Sa 2:3 376
as a *m* falleth before wicked men, 2Sa 3:34 1121
a great *m* fallen this day in 2Sa 3:38
And is this the manner of *m* 2Sa 7:19 120
The rich *m* had exceeding many 2Sa 12:2
But the poor *m* had nothing 2Sa 12:3
came a traveller unto the rich *m* 2Sa 12:4 376
m that was come unto him 2Sa 12:4
dressed it for the *m* that was 2Sa 12:4 376
was greatly kindled against the *m* 2Sa 12:5 376
the *m* that hath done this thing 2Sa 12:5 376
said to David, Thou art the *m* 2Sa 12:7 376
and Jonadab was a very subtil *m* 2Sa 13:3 376
And they went out every *m* from him 2Sa 13:9 376
every *m* gat him up upon his mule, 2Sa 13:29 376
the young *m* that kept the watch 2Sa 13:34
of the *m* that would destroy me 2Sa 14:16 376
bring the young *m* Absalom again 2Sa 14:21
that when any *m* that had a 2Sa 15:2 376
but there is no *m* deputed of the 2Sa 15:3
that every *m* which hath any suit 2Sa 15:4 376
that when any *m* came nigh to him 2Sa 15:5 376
with him covered every *m* his head 2Sa 15:30 376
thence came out a *m* of the family 2Sa 16:5 376
bloody *m*, and thou *m* of Belial 2Sa 16:7 376
because thou art a bloody *m* 2Sa 16:8 376
was as if a *m* had enquired at the 2Sa 16:23 376
the *m* whom thou seekest is as if 2Sa 17:3 376
and thy father is a *m* of war 2Sa 17:8 376
that thy father is a mighty *m* 2Sa 17:10
for my sake with the young *m* 2Sa 18:5
And a certain *m* saw it, and told 2Sa 18:10 376
said unto the *m* that told him 2Sa 18:11 376
the *m* said unto Joab, Though I 2Sa 18:12 376
none touch the young *m* Absalom 2Sa 18:12
and behold a *m* running alone 2Sa 18:24 376
watchman saw another *m* running 2Sa 18:26 376
Behold another *m* running alone 2Sa 18:26 376
And the king said, He is a good *m* 2Sa 18:27 376
said, Is the young *m* Absalom safe 2Sa 18:29
Is the young *m* Absalom safe 2Sa 18:32
thee hurt, be as that young *m* is 2Sa 18:32
had fled every *m* to his tent 2Sa 19:8 376
Judah, even as the heart of one *m* 2Sa 19:14 376
shall there any *m* be put to death 2Sa 19:22 376
Now Barzillai was a very aged *m* 2Sa 19:32
for he was a very great *m* 2Sa 19:32 376
to be there a *m* of Belial 2Sa 20:1 376
every *m* to his tents, O Israel 2Sa 20:1 376
So every *m* of Israel went up from 2Sa 20:2 376
when the *m* saw that all the 2Sa 20:12 376
but a *m* of mount Ephraim, Sheba 2Sa 20:21 376
the city, every *m* to his tent 2Sa 20:22 376
shalt thou kill any *m* in Israel 2Sa 21:4 376

The *m* that consumed us, and that 2Sa 21:5 376
where was a *m* of great stature, 2Sa 21:20 376
with the upright *m* thou wilt shew 2Sa 22:26
delivered me from the violent *m* 2Sa 22:49 376
the *m* who was raised up on high, 2Sa 23:1 1397
But the *m* that shall touch them 2Sa 23:7 376
Jehoiada, the son of a valiant *m* 2Sa 23:20 376
he slew an Egyptian, a goodly *m* 2Sa 23:21 376
me not fall into the hand of *m* 2Sa 24:14 120
and he also was a very goodly *m* 1Kin 1:6
for thou art a valiant *m*, and 1Kin 1:42 376
rose up, and went every *m* his way 1Kin 1:49 376
he will shew himself a worthy *m* 1Kin 1:52 1121
therefore, and shew thyself a *m* 1Kin 2:2 376
he) a *m* on the throne of Israel 1Kin 2:4 376
for thou art a wise *m*, and knowest 1Kin 2:9 376
each *m* his month in a year made 1Kin 4:7
every *m* under his vine and under 1Kin 4:25 376
table, every *m* in his month 1Kin 4:27 376
every *m* according to his charge 1Kin 4:28 376
and his father was a *m* of Tyre 1Kin 7:14 376
a *m* in my sight to sit on the 1Kin 8:25 376
If any *m* trespass against his 1Kin 8:31 376
soever be made by any *m*, or by 1Kin 8:38 120
which shall know every *m* the 1Kin 8:38 376
give to every *m* according to his 1Kin 8:39 376
there is no *m* that sinneth not 1Kin 8:46 120
a *m* upon the throne of Israel 1Kin 9:5 376
they brought every *m* his present 1Kin 10:25 376
the *m* Jeroboam was a mighty 1Kin 11:28 376
Jeroboam was a mighty *m* of valour 1Kin 11:28
young *m* that he was industrious 1Kin 11:28
came unto Shemaiah the *m* of God 1Kin 12:22 376
return every *m* to his house 1Kin 12:24 376
there came a *m* of God out of 1Kin 13:1 376
heard the saying of the *m* of God 1Kin 13:4 376
m of God had given by the word of 1Kin 13:5 376
and said unto the *m* of God 1Kin 13:6 376
the *m* of God besought the LORD, 1Kin 13:6 376
the king said unto the *m* of God 1Kin 13:7 376
the *m* of God said unto the king, 1Kin 13:8 376
the *m* of God had done that day in 1Kin 13:11 376
seen what way the *m* of God went 1Kin 13:12 376
And went after the *m* of God 1Kin 13:14 376
Art thou the *m* of God that camest 1Kin 13:14 376
he cried unto the *m* of God that 1Kin 13:21 376
he said, It is the *m* of God 1Kin 13:26 376
up the carcase of the *m* of God 1Kin 13:29 376
wherein the *m* of God is buried 1Kin 13:31 376
as a *m* taketh away dung, till it 1Kin 14:10
to do with thee, O thou *m* of God 1Kin 17:18 376
I know that thou art a *m* of God 1Kin 17:24 376
see how this *m* seeketh mischief 1Kin 20:7
And they slew every one his *m* 1Kin 20:20 376
every *m* out of his place, and put 1Kin 20:24 376
And there came a *m* of God, and 1Kin 20:28 376
a certain *m* of the sons of the 1Kin 20:35 376
the *m* refused to smite him 1Kin 20:35 376
Then he found another *m*, and said, 1Kin 20:37 376
the *m* smote him, so that in 1Kin 20:37 376
a *m* turned aside, and brought a 1Kin 20:39 376
m unto me, and said, Keep this *m* 1Kin 20:39 376
a *m* whom I appointed to utter 1Kin 20:42 376
Jehoshaphat, There is yet one *m* 1Kin 22:8 376
every *m* to his house in peace 1Kin 22:17 376
a certain *m* drew a bow at a 1Kin 22:34 376
Every *m* to his city 1Kin 22:36 376
every *m* to his own country 1Kin 22:36 376
There came a *m* up to meet us, and 2Kin 1:6 376
What manner of *m* was he which 2Kin 1:7 376
answered him, He was an hairy *m* 2Kin 1:8 376
Thou *m* of God, the king hath said 2Kin 1:9 376
of fifty, If I be a *m* of God 2Kin 1:10 376
O *m* of God, thus hath the king 2Kin 1:11 376
unto them, If I be a *m* of God 2Kin 1:12 376
O *m* of God, I pray thee, let my 2Kin 1:13 376
of land cast every *m* his stone 2Kin 3:25 376
she came and told the *m* of God 2Kin 4:7 376
that this is an holy *m* of God 2Kin 4:9 376
thou *m* of God, do not lie unto 2Kin 4:16 376
him on the bed of the *m* of God 2Kin 4:21 376
that I may run to the *m* of God 2Kin 4:22 376
came unto the *m* of God to mount 2Kin 4:25 376
when the *m* of God saw her afar 2Kin 4:25 376
came to the *m* of God to the hill 2Kin 4:27 376
the *m* of God said, Let her alone 2Kin 4:27 376
if thou meet any *m*, salute him 2Kin 4:29 376
out, and said, O thou *m* of God 2Kin 4:40 376
there came a *m* from Baal-shalisha 2Kin 4:42 376
brought the *m* of God bread of the 2Kin 4:42 376
was a great *m* with his master, and 2Kin 5:1 376
he was also a mighty *m* in valour 2Kin 5:1 376
that this *m* doth send unto me to 2Kin 5:7
me to recover a *m* of his leprosy 2Kin 5:7 376
when Elisha the *m* of God had 2Kin 5:8 376
to the saying of the *m* of God 2Kin 5:14 376
And he returned to the *m* of God 2Kin 5:15 376
servant of Elisha the *m* of God 2Kin 5:20 376
when the *m* turned again from his 2Kin 5:26 376
and take thence every *m* a beam 2Kin 6:2 376
the *m* of God said, Where fell it 2Kin 6:6 376
the *m* of God sent unto the king 2Kin 6:9 376
place which the *m* of God told him 2Kin 6:10 376
of the *m* of God was risen early 2Kin 6:15 376
opened the eyes of the young *m* 2Kin 6:17
bring you to the *m* whom ye seek 2Kin 6:19 376
the king sent a *m* from before him 2Kin 6:32 376
king leaned answered the *m* of God 2Kin 7:2 376
behold, there was no *m* there 2Kin 7:5 376
and, behold, there was no *m* there 2Kin 7:10 376
neither voice of *m* 2Kin 7:10 120
as the *m* of God had said, who 2Kin 7:17 376
it came to pass as the *m* of God 2Kin 7:18 376
that lord answered the *m* of God 2Kin 7:19 376
after the saying of the *m* of God 2Kin 8:2 376
the servant of the *m* of God 2Kin 8:4 376
The *m* of God is come hither 2Kin 8:7 376
hand, and go, meet the *m* of God 2Kin 8:8 376
and the *m* of God wept 2Kin 8:11 376
So the young *m*, even the young 2Kin 9:4
even the young *m* the prophet 2Kin 9:4 376
he said unto them, Ye know the *m* 2Kin 9:11 376
took every *m* his garment, and put 2Kin 9:13 376
was not a *m* left that came not 2Kin 10:21 376
every *m* with his weapons in his 2Kin 11:8 376
they took every *m* his men that 2Kin 11:9 376
every *m* with his weapons in his 2Kin 11:11 376
the money that every *m* is set at 2Kin 12:4 5315
every *m* of his acquaintance 2Kin 12:5 376
the *m* of God was wroth with him, 2Kin 13:19 376
to pass, as they were burying a *m* 2Kin 13:21 376
and they cast the *m* into the 2Kin 13:21 376
when the *m* was let down, and 2Kin 13:21 376
but every *m* shall be put to death 2Kin 14:6 376
they fled every *m* to their tents 2Kin 14:12 376
of each *m* fifty shekels of silver 2Kin 15:20 376
upon Egypt, on which if a *m* lean 2Kin 18:21 376
eat ye every *m* of his own vine 2Kin 18:31 376
Jerusalem as a *m* wipeth a dish 2Kin 21:13
Tell the *m* that sent you to me, 2Kin 22:15 376
that no *m* might make his son or 2Kin 23:10 376
which the *m* of God proclaimed 2Kin 23:16 376
is the sepulchre of the *m* of God 2Kin 23:17 376
let no *m* move his bones 2Kin 23:18 376
the son of a valiant *m* of Kabzeel 1Chr 11:22 376
a *m* of great stature, five cubits 1Chr 11:23 376
a mighty *m* among the thirty, and 1Chr 12:4
a young *m* mighty of valour, and of 1Chr 12:28
to every one of Israel, both *m* 1Chr 16:3 376
He suffered no *m* to do them wrong 1Chr 16:21 376
departed every *m* to his house 1Chr 16:43 376
the estate of a *m* of high degree 1Chr 17:17 120
where was a *m* of great stature, 1Chr 20:6 376
me not fall into the hand of *m* 1Chr 21:13 120
to thee, who shall be a *m* of rest 1Chr 22:9 376
m by *m*, was thirty and eight 1Chr 23:3 376
number by their polls, *m* by *m* 1Chr 23:3 1397
Now concerning Moses the *m* of God 1Chr 23:14 376
uncle was a counsellor, a wise *m* 1Chr 27:32 376
because thou hast been a *m* of war 1Chr 28:3 376
every willing skilful *m*, for any 1Chr 28:21
for the palace is not for *m* 1Chr 29:1 120
a *m* cunning to work in gold 2Chr 2:7 376
And now I have sent a cunning *m* 2Chr 2:13 376
and his father was a *m* of Tyre 2Chr 2:14 376
neither chose I any *m* to be a 2Chr 6:5 376
a *m* in my sight to sit upon the 2Chr 6:16 376
If a *m* sin against his neighbour, 2Chr 6:22 376
soever shall be made of any *m* 2Chr 6:29 120
render unto every *m* according 2Chr 6:30 120
(for there is no *m* which sinneth 2Chr 6:36 120
thee a *m* to be ruler in Israel 2Chr 7:18 376
had David the *m* of God commanded 2Chr 8:14 376
they brought every *m* his present 2Chr 9:24 376
every *m* to your tents, O Israel, 2Chr 10:16 376
came to Shemaiah the *m* of God 2Chr 11:2 376
return every *m* to his house 2Chr 11:4 376
let not *m* prevail against thee 2Chr 14:11 582
or great, whether *m* or woman 2Chr 15:13 376
Eliada a mighty *m* of valour 2Chr 17:17
Jehoshaphat, There is yet one *m* 2Chr 18:7 376
every *m* to his house in peace 2Chr 18:16 376
a certain *m* drew a bow at a 2Chr 18:33
he said to his chariot *m*, Turn 2Chr 18:33 376
for ye judge not for *m*, but for 2Chr 19:6 120
every *m* of Judah and Jerusalem, and 2Chr 20:27 376
every *m* with his weapons in his 2Chr 23:7 376
took every *m* his men that were to 2Chr 23:8 376
every *m* having his weapon in his 2Chr 23:10 376
but every *m* shall die for his own 2Chr 25:4 376
But there came a *m* of God to him 2Chr 25:7 376
And Amaziah said to the *m* of God 2Chr 25:9 376
the *m* of God answered, The LORD 2Chr 25:9 376
and they fled every *m* to his tent 2Chr 25:22 376
a mighty *m* of Ephraim, slew 2Chr 28:7
to the law of Moses the *m* of God 2Chr 30:16 376
every *m* to his possession, into 2Chr 31:1 376
every *m* according to his service, 2Chr 31:2 376
were the work of the hands of *m* 2Chr 32:19 120
Tell ye the *m* that sent you to me 2Chr 34:23 376
upon young *m* or maiden, old *m* 2Chr 36:17
together as one *m* to Jerusalem Ezr 3:1 376
in the law of Moses the *m* of God Ezr 3:2 376
brought us a *m* of understanding Ezr 8:18 376
him mercy in the sight of this *m* Neh 1:11 376
that there was come a *m* to seek Neh 2:10 120
neither told I any *m* what my God Neh 2:12 120
shake out every *m* from his house Neh 5:13 376
I said, Should such a *m* as I flee Neh 6:11 376
for he was a faithful *m*, and Neh 7:2 376
themselves together as one *m* into Neh 8:1 376
thy judgments, (which if a *m* do Neh 9:29 120
commandment of David the *m* of God. Neh 12:24 376
instruments of David the *m* of God Neh 12:36 376
that every *m* should bear rule in Est 1:22 376
whether *m* or woman, shall come Est 4:11 376
Esther the queen did let no *m* Est 5:12
the *m* whom the king delighteth to Est 6:6 376
the king, For the *m* whom the king Est 6:7 376
that they may array the *m* withal Est 6:9 376
the *m* whom the king delighteth to Est 6:9 376
the *m* whom the king delighteth to Est 6:11 376
the king's ring, may no *m* reverse Est 8:8
no *m* could withstand them Est 9:2 376
for this *m* Mordecai waxed greater Est 9:4 376
There was a *m* in the land of Uz, Job 1:1 376
that *m* was perfect and upright, and Job 1:1 376
so that this *m* was the greatest Job 1:3 376
earth, a perfect and an upright *m* Job 1:8 376
earth, a perfect and an upright *m* Job 2:3 376
all that a *m* hath will he give Job 2:4 376
There is a *m* child conceived Job 3:3 1397
given to a *m* whose way is hid Job 3:23 1397
Shall mortal *m* be more just than Job 4:17 582
shall a *m* be more pure than his Job 4:17 1396
For wrath killeth the foolish *m* Job 5:2
Yet *m* is born unto trouble, as Job 5:7 120
Behold, happy is the *m* whom God Job 5:17 582
an appointed time to *m* upon earth Job 7:1 582
What is *m*, that thou shouldest Job 7:17 582
will not cast away a perfect *m* Job 8:20
but how should *m* be just with God Job 9:2 582
For he is not a *m*, as I am, that Job 9:32 376
or seest thou as *m* seeth Job 10:4 582
Are thy days as the days of *m* Job 10:5 582
should a *m* full of talk be Job 11:2 376
shall no *m* make thee ashamed Job 11:3
For vain *m* would be wise, though Job 11:12 376
though *m* be born like a wild Job 11:12 120
the just upright *m* is laughed to Job 12:4
he shutteth up a *m*, and there can Job 12:14 376
them to stagger like a drunken *m* Job 12:25
or as one *m* mocketh another, do Job 13:9 582
M that is born of a woman is of Job 14:1 120
But *m* dieth, and wasteth away Job 14:10 1397
m giveth up the ghost, and where Job 14:10 120
So *m* lieth down, and riseth not Job 14:12 376
If a *m* die, shall he live again Job 14:14 1397
and thou destroyest the hope of *m* Job 14:19 582
Should a wise *m* utter vain Job 15:2
thou the first *m* that was born Job 15:7 120
What is *m*, that he should be Job 15:14 582
more abominable and filthy is *m* Job 15:16 376
The wicked *m* travaileth with pain Job 15:20
in houses which no *m* inhabiteth Job 15:28
one might plead for a *m* with God Job 16:21 1397
as a *m* pleadeth for his neighbour Job 16:21 120
cannot find one wise *m* among you Job 17:10
since *m* was placed upon earth, Job 20:4 120
shall no *m* look for his goods Job 20:21
portion of a wicked *m* from God Job 20:29 120
As for me, is my complaint to *m* Job 21:4 120
every *m* shall draw after him, as Job 21:33 120
Can a *m* be profitable unto God, Job 22:2 1397
But as for the mighty *m*, he had Job 22:8 376
and the honourable *m* dwelt in it Job 22:8
up, and no *m* is sure of life Job 24:22
How then can *m* be justified with Job 25:4 582
How much less *m*, that is a worm Job 25:6 582
and the son of *m*, which is a worm Job 25:6 120
portion of a wicked *m* with God Job 27:13 120
The rich *m* shall lie down, but he Job 27:19
M knoweth not the price thereof Job 28:13 582
unto *m* he said, Behold, the fear Job 28:28 120
But there is a spirit in *m* Job 32:8 582
God thrusteth him down, not *m* Job 32:13 376
me give flattering titles unto *m* Job 32:21 120
thee, that God is greater than *m* Job 33:12 582
twice, yet *m* perceiveth it not Job 33:14
may withdraw *m* from his purpose Job 33:17 120
his purpose, and hide pride from *m* Job 33:17 1397
to shew unto *m* his uprightness Job 33:23 120
render unto *m* his righteousness Job 33:26 582
worketh God oftentimes with *m* Job 33:29 1397
What *m* is like Job, who drinketh Job 34:7 1397
It profiteth a *m* nothing that he Job 34:9 1397
For the work of a *m* shall he Job 34:11 120
cause every *m* to find according Job 34:11 376
If he set his heart upon *m* Job 34:14
m shall turn again unto dust Job 34:15 120
his eyes are upon the ways of *m* Job 34:21 376
not lay upon *m* more than right Job 34:23 376
a nation, or against a *m* only Job 34:29 120
let a wise *m* hearken unto me Job 34:34 1397
may hurt a *m* as thou art Job 35:8 376
may profit the son of *m* Job 35:8 120
Every *m* may see it Job 36:25 120
m may behold it afar off Job 36:25 582
drop and distil upon *m* abundantly Job 36:28 120
He sealeth up the hand of every *m* Job 37:7 120
If a *m* speak, surely he shall be Job 37:20 376
Gird up now thy loins like a *m* Job 38:3 1397
rain on the earth, where no *m* is Job 38:26 376
wilderness, wherein there is no *m* Job 38:26 120
Gird up thy loins now like a *m* Job 40:7 1397
every *m* also gave him a piece of Job 42:11 376
Blessed is the *m* that walketh not Ps 1:1 376
abhor the bloody and deceitful *m* Ps 5:6 376
What is *m*, that thou art mindful Ps 8:4 582
and the son of *m*, that thou Ps 8:4 120
let not *m* prevail Ps 9:19 582
arm of the wicked and the evil *m* Ps 10:15
that the *m* of the earth may no Ps 10:18 582
for the godly *m* ceaseth Ps 12:1 376
with an upright *m* thou wilt shew Ps 18:25 1397
delivered me from the violent *m* Ps 18:48 376
as a strong *m* to run a race Ps 19:5
But I am a worm, and no *m* Ps 22:6 376
What *m* is he that feareth the Ps 25:12 376
forgotten as a dead *m* out of mind Ps 31:12
thy presence from the pride of *m* Ps 31:20 376
Blessed is the *m* unto whom the Ps 32:2 120
a mighty *m* is not delivered by Ps 33:16
This poor *m* cried, and the LORD Ps 34:6
blessed is the *m* that trusteth in Ps 34:8 1397
What *m* is he that desireth life, Ps 34:12 376
O LORD, thou preservest *m* Ps 36:6 120
because of the *m* who bringeth Ps 37:7 376
A little that a righteous *m* hath Ps 37:16
The steps of a good *m* are ordered Ps 37:23 1397
Mark the perfect *m*, and behold the Ps 37:37
for the end of that *m* is peace Ps 37:37 376

But I, as a deaf *m*, heard not Ps 38:13
I was as a dumb *m* that openeth Ps 38:13
Thus I was as a *m* that heareth Ps 38:14 376
verily every *m* at his best state Ps 39:5 120
Surely every *m* walketh in a vain Ps 39:6 376
dost correct *m* for iniquity Ps 39:11 376
surely every *m* is vanity Ps 39:11 120
Blessed is that *m* that maketh the Ps 40:4 1397
me from the deceitful and unjust *m* Ps 43:1 376
Nevertheless *m* being in honour Ps 49:12 120
M that is in honour, and Ps 49:20 120
thyself in mischief, O mighty *m* Ps 52:1
this is the *m* that made not God Ps 52:7 1397
a *m* mine equal, my guide, and mine Ps 55:13 582
for *m* would swallow me up Ps 56:1 582
be afraid what *m* can do unto me Ps 56:11 120
So that a *m* shall say, Verily Ps 58:11 120
for vain is the help of *m* Ps 60:11 120
ye imagine mischief against a *m* Ps 62:3 376
to every *m* according to his work Ps 62:12 376
Blessed is the *m* whom thou Ps 65:4
of the unrighteous and cruel *m* Ps 71:4
A *m* was famous according as he Ps 74:5
foolish *m* reproacheth thee daily Ps 74:22
the wrath of *m* shall praise thee Ps 76:10 120
M did eat angels' food Ps 78:25 376
like a mighty *m* that shouteth by Ps 78:65
be upon the *m* of thy right hand Ps 80:17 376
upon the son of *m* whom thou Ps 80:17 120
Blessed is the *m* whose strength Ps 84:5 120
blessed is the *m* that trusteth in Ps 84:12 120
this *m* was born there Ps 87:4
This and that *m* was born in her Ps 87:5 376
that this *m* was born there Ps 87:6
I am as a *m* that hath no strength Ps 88:4 1397
What *m* is he that liveth, and Ps 89:48 1397
A Prayer of Moses, the *m* of God Ps 90:*t* 376
Thou turnest *m* to destruction Ps 90:3 582
A brutish *m* knoweth not Ps 92:6 376
he that teacheth *m* knowledge Ps 94:10 120
LORD knoweth the thoughts of *m* Ps 94:11 120
Blessed is the *m* whom thou Ps 94:12 1397
As for *m*, his days are as grass Ps 103:15 582
and herb for the service of *m* Ps 104:14 120
that maketh glad the heart of *m* Ps 104:15 582
M goeth forth unto his work and to Ps 104:23 120
He suffered no *m* to do them wrong Ps 105:14 120
He sent a *m* before them, even Ps 105:17 376
fro, and stagger like a drunken *m* Ps 107:27
for vain is the help of *m* Ps 108:12 120
Set thou a wicked *m* over him Ps 109:6
persecuted the poor and needy *m* Ps 109:16 376
Blessed is the *m* that feareth the Ps 112:1 376
A good *m* sheweth favour, and Ps 112:5 376
what can *m* do unto me Ps 118:6 120
LORD than to put confidence in *m* Ps 118:8 120
shall a young *m* cleanse his way Ps 119:9
me from the oppression of *m* Ps 119:134 120
are in the hand of a mighty *m* Ps 127:4
Happy is the *m* that hath his Ps 127:5 1397
that thus shall the *m* be blessed Ps 128:4 1397
the firstborn of Egypt, both of *m* Ps 135:8 120
me, O LORD, from the evil *m* Ps 140:1 120
preserve me from the violent *m* Ps 140:1 376
preserve me from the violent *m* Ps 140:4 376
the violent *m* to overthrow him Ps 140:11 376
but there was no *m* that would Ps 142:4
no *m* cared for my soul Ps 142:4
shall no *m* living be justified Ps 143:2
LORD, what is *m*, that thou takest Ps 144:3 120
or the son of *m*, that thou makest Ps 144:3 582
M is like to vanity Ps 144:4 120
in princes, nor in the son of *m* Ps 146:3 120
not pleasure in the legs of a *m* Ps 147:10 376
simple, to the young *m* knowledge Prov 1:4
A wise *m* will hear, and will Prov 1:5
a *m* of understanding shall attain Prov 1:5
out my hand, and no *m* regarded Prov 1:24
thee from the way of the evil *m* Prov 2:12
from the *m* that speaketh froward Prov 2:12 376
in the sight of God and *m* Prov 3:4 120
Happy is the *m* that findeth Prov 3:13 120
the *m* that getteth understanding Prov 3:13 120
Strive not with a *m* without cause Prov 3:30 120
For the ways of *m* are before the Prov 5:21 376
and thy want as an armed *m* Prov 6:11 376
A naughty person, a wicked *m* Prov 6:12 376
by means of a whorish woman a *m* Prov 6:26
Can a *m* take fire in his bosom, Prov 6:27 376
For jealousy is the rage of a *m* Prov 6:34 1397
a young *m* void of understanding, Prov 7:7
and my voice is to the sons of *m* Prov 8:4 120
Blessed is the *m* that heareth me, Prov 8:34 120
a wicked *m* getteth himself a blot Prov 9:7
rebuke a wise *m*, and he will love Prov 9:8
Give instruction to a wise *m* Prov 9:9
teach a just *m*, and he will Prov 9:9
a righteous *m* is a well of life Prov 10:11
but a *m* of understanding hath Prov 10:23 376
When a wicked *m* dieth, his Prov 11:7 120
but a *m* of understanding holdeth Prov 11:12 376
The merciful *m* doeth good to his Prov 11:17 376
A good *m* obtaineth favour of the Prov 12:2
but a *m* of wicked devices will he Prov 12:2 376
A *m* shall not be established by Prov 12:3 120
A *m* shall be commended according Prov 12:8 376
A righteous *m* regardeth the life Prov 12:10
A *m* shall be satisfied with good Prov 12:14 376
but a prudent *m* covereth shame Prov 12:16
A prudent *m* concealeth knowledge Prov 12:23 120
in the heart of *m* maketh it stoop Prov 12:25 376
The slothful *m* roasteth not that Prov 12:27
of a diligent *m* is precious Prov 12:27 120
A *m* shall eat good by the fruit Prov 13:2 376
A righteous *m* hateth lying Prov 13:5
but a wicked *m* is loathsome Prov 13:5
Every prudent *m* dealeth with Prov 13:16
A good *m* leaveth an inheritance Prov 13:22
from the presence of a foolish *m* Prov 14:7 376
way which seemeth right unto a *m* Prov 14:12 376
a good *m* shall be satisfied from Prov 14:14 376
but the prudent *m* looketh well to Prov 14:15
A wise *m* feareth, and departeth Prov 14:16
a *m* of wicked devices is hated Prov 14:17 376
A wrathful *m* stirreth up strife Prov 15:18 376
The way of the slothful *m* is as Prov 15:19
but a foolish *m* despiseth his Prov 15:20 120
but a *m* of understanding walketh Prov 15:21 376
A *m* hath joy by the answer of his Prov 15:23 376
preparations of the heart in *m* Prov 16:1 120
All the ways of a *m* are clean in Prov 16:2 376
but a wise *m* will pacify it Prov 16:14 376
a way that seemeth right unto a *m* Prov 16:25 376
An ungodly *m* diggeth up evil Prov 16:27 376
A froward *m* soweth strife Prov 16:28 376
A violent *m* enticeth his Prov 16:29 376
entereth more into a wise *m* than Prov 17:10
An evil *m* seeketh only rebellion Prov 17:11
robbed of her whelps meet a *m* Prov 17:12 376
A *m* void of understanding Prov 17:18 120
A wicked *m* taketh a gift out of Prov 17:23
a *m* of understanding is of an Prov 17:27 376
is esteemed a *m* of understanding Prov 17:28
Through desire a *m*, having Prov 18:1
the heart of *m* is haughty Prov 18:12 376
The spirit of a *m* will sustain Prov 18:14 376
A *m* that hath friends must shew Prov 18:24 376
of *m* perverteth his way Prov 19:3 120
every *m* is a friend to him that Prov 19:6
of a *m* deferreth his anger Prov 19:11 120
A *m* of great wrath shall suffer Prov 19:19
The desire of a *m* is his kindness Prov 19:22 120
a poor *m* is better than a liar Prov 19:22
A slothful *m* hideth his hand in Prov 19:24
for a *m* to cease from strife Prov 20:3 376
the heart of *m* is like deep water Prov 20:5 376
but a *m* of understanding will Prov 20:5 376
but a faithful *m* who can find Prov 20:6 376
The just *m* walketh in his Prov 20:7
Bread of deceit is sweet to a *m* Prov 20:17 376
how can a *m* then understand his Prov 20:24 120
It is a snare to the *m* who Prov 20:25 120
The spirit of *m* is the candle of Prov 20:27 120
Every way of a *m* is right in his Prov 21:2 376
The way of *m* is froward and Prov 21:8 376
The righteous *m* wisely Prov 21:12
The *m* that wandereth out of the Prov 21:16 120
loveth pleasure shall be a poor *m* Prov 21:17 376
but a foolish *m* spendeth it up Prov 21:20 120
A wise *m* scaleth the city of the Prov 21:22
but the *m* that heareth speaketh Prov 21:28 376
A wicked *m* hardeneth his face Prov 21:29 376
A prudent *m* foreseeth the evil, Prov 22:3
The slothful *m* saith, There is a Prov 22:13
no friendship with an angry *m* Prov 22:24 1167
with a furious *m* thou shalt not Prov 22:24 376
Seest thou a *m* diligent in his Prov 22:29 376
if thou be a *m* given to appetite Prov 23:2 1167
shall clothe a *m* with rags Prov 23:21
A wise *m* is strong Prov 24:5 1397
a *m* of knowledge increaseth Prov 24:5 376
to every *m* according to his works Prov 24:12 120
Lay not wait, O wicked *m*, against Prov 24:15 376
For a just *m* falleth seven times, Prov 24:16
shall be no reward to the evil *m* Prov 24:20
Every *m* shall kiss his lips that Prov 24:26
I will render to the *m* according Prov 24:29 376
of the *m* void of understanding Prov 24:30 120
and thy want as an armed *m* Prov 24:34 376
A *m* that beareth false witness Prov 25:18 376
Confidence in an unfaithful *m* in Prov 25:19
A righteous *m* falling down before Prov 25:26
Seest thou a *m* wise in his own Prov 26:12 376
The slothful *m* saith, There is a Prov 26:13
As a mad *m* who casteth firebrands Prov 26:18
So is the *m* that deceiveth his Prov 26:19 376
a contentious *m* to kindle strife Prov 26:21 376
Let another *m* praise thee Prov 27:2
so is a *m* that wandereth from his Prov 27:8 376
A prudent *m* foreseeth the evil, Prov 27:12
so a *m* sharpeneth the countenance Prov 27:17 376
to face, so the heart of *m* to *m* Prov 27:19 120
so the eyes of *m* are never Prov 27:20 120
so is a *m* to his praise Prov 27:21 376
wicked flee when no *m* pursueth Prov 28:1
but by a *m* of understanding and Prov 28:2 120
A poor *m* that oppresseth the poor Prov 28:3 1397
The rich *m* is wise in his own Prov 28:11 376
the wicked rise, a *m* is hidden Prov 28:12 120
Happy is the *m* that feareth alway Prov 28:14 120
A *m* that doeth violence to the Prov 28:17 120
let no *m* stay him Prov 28:17 376
A faithful *m* shall abound with Prov 28:20 376
of bread that *m* will transgress Prov 28:21 1397
He that rebuketh a *m* afterwards Prov 28:23 120
A *m* that flattereth his neighbour Prov 29:5 1397
of an evil *m* there is a snare Prov 29:6 376
m contendeth with a foolish *m* Prov 29:9 376
but a wise *m* keepeth it in till Prov 29:11
and the deceitful *m* meet together Prov 29:13 376
Seest thou a *m* that is hasty in Prov 29:20 376
An angry *m* stirreth up strife Prov 29:22 376
and a furious *m* aboundeth in Prov 29:22 1167
The fear of *m* bringeth a snare Prov 29:25 120
An unjust *m* is an abomination to Prov 29:27 376
the *m* spake unto Ithiel, even Prov 30:1 1397
I am more brutish than any *m* Prov 30:2 376
have not the understanding of a *m* Prov 30:2 120
and the way of a *m* with a maid Prov 30:19 1397
What profit hath a *m* of all his Eccl 1:3 120
m cannot utter it Eccl 1:8 376
of *m* to be exercised therewith Eccl 1:13 120
for what can the *m* do that cometh Eccl 2:12 120
And how dieth the wise *m* Eccl 2:16
unto the *m* that shall be after me Eccl 2:18 120
he shall be a wise *m* or a fool Eccl 2:19
For there is a *m* whose labour is Eccl 2:21 120
yet to a *m* that hath not laboured Eccl 2:21 120
For what hath *m* of all his labour Eccl 2:22 120
There is nothing better for a *m* Eccl 2:24 120
For God giveth to a *m* that is Eccl 2:26 120
so that no *m* can find out the Eccl 3:11 120
but for a *m* to rejoice, and to do Eccl 3:12
And also that every *m* should eat Eccl 3:13 120
so that a *m* hath no preeminence Eccl 3:19 120
the spirit of *m* that goeth upward Eccl 3:21
than that a *m* should rejoice in Eccl 3:22 120
that for this a *m* is envied of Eccl 4:4 376
sleep of a labouring *m* is sweet Eccl 5:12
Every *m* also to whom God hath Eccl 5:19 120
A *m* to whom God hath given riches Eccl 6:2 376
If a *m* beget an hundred children, Eccl 6:3 376
the labour of *m* is for his mouth Eccl 6:7 120
and it is known that it is *m* Eccl 6:10 120
vanity, what is *m* the better Eccl 6:11 120
what is good for *m* in this life Eccl 6:12 120
for who can tell a *m* what shall Eccl 6:12 120
than for a *m* to hear the song of Eccl 7:5 376
oppression maketh a wise *m* mad Eccl 7:7
to the end that *m* should find Eccl 7:14 120
there is a just *m* that perisheth Eccl 7:15
and there is a wicked *m* that Eccl 7:15
there is not a just *m* upon earth Eccl 7:20 120
one *m* among a thousand have I Eccl 7:28 120
that God hath made *m* upright Eccl 7:29 120
Who is as the wise *m* Eccl 8:1 376
the misery of *m* is great upon him Eccl 8:6 120
There is no *m* that hath power Eccl 8:8 120
there is a time wherein one *m* Eccl 8:9 120
because a *m* hath no better thing Eccl 8:15 120
that a *m* cannot find out the work Eccl 8:17 120
because though a *m* labour to seek Eccl 8:17 120
though a wise *m* think to know it, Eccl 8:17
no *m* knoweth either love or Eccl 9:1 120
For *m* also knoweth not his time Eccl 9:12 120
was found in it a poor wise *m* Eccl 9:15 376
m remembered that same poor *m* Eccl 9:15 376
a *m* cannot tell what shall be Eccl 10:14 120
But if a *m* live many years, and Eccl 11:8 120
Rejoice, O young *m*, in thy youth Eccl 11:9
because *m* goeth to his long home, Eccl 12:5 120
for this is the whole duty of *m* Eccl 12:13 120
every *m* hath his sword upon his Song 3:8 376
if a *m* would give all the Song 8:7 376
the mean *m* boweth down, and the Is 2:9 1201
the great *m* humbleth himself Is 2:9 376
lofty looks of *m* shall be humbled Is 2:11 120
the loftiness of *m* shall be bowed Is 2:17 120
In that day a *m* shall cast his Is 2:20 120
Cease ye from *m*, whose breath is Is 2:22 120
The mighty *m*, and the Is 3:2
the *m* of war, the judge, and the Is 3:2 376
of fifty, and the honourable *m* Is 3:3
When a *m* shall take hold of his Is 3:6 376
women shall take hold of one *m* Is 4:1 376
the mean *m* shall be brought down, Is 5:15 120
the mighty *m* shall be humbled, and Is 5:15 376
because I am a *m* of unclean lips, Is 6:5 376
and the houses without *m*, and the Is 6:11 120
that a *m* shall nourish a young Is 7:21 376
no *m* shall spare his brother Is 9:19 376
they shall eat every *m* the flesh Is 9:20 376
the inhabitants like a valiant *m* Is 10:13
I will make a *m* more precious Is 13:12 582
even a *m* than the golden wedge of Is 13:12 120
and as a sheep that no *m* taketh up Is 13:14
they shall every *m* turn to his Is 13:14 376
Is this the *m* that made the earth Is 14:16 376
day shall a *m* look to his Maker Is 17:7 120
as a drunken *m* staggereth in his Is 19:14
is shut up, that no *m* may come in Is 24:10 935
a *m* can stretch himself on it Is 28:20 376
be as when an hungry *m* dreameth Is 29:8
or as when a thirsty *m* dreameth Is 29:8
That make a *m* an offender for a Is 29:21 120
For in that day every *m* shall Is 31:7 376
with the sword, not of a mighty *m* Is 31:8 376
and the sword, not of a mean *m* Is 31:8 120
a *m* shall be as an hiding place Is 32:2 376
waste, the wayfaring *m* ceaseth Is 33:8
the cities, he regardeth no *m* Is 33:8 582
shall the lame *m* leap as an hart Is 35:6
whereon if a *m* lean, it will go Is 36:6 376
I shall behold *m* no more with the Is 38:11 120
up the righteous *m* from the east Is 41:2
For I beheld, and there was no *m* Is 41:28 376
LORD shall go forth as a mighty *m* Is 42:13 376
stir up jealousy like a *m* of war Is 42:13 376
maketh it after the figure of a *m* Is 44:13 376
according to the beauty of a *m* Is 44:13 120
Then shall it be for a *m* to burn Is 44:15 120
the earth, and created *m* upon it Is 45:12 120
the *m* that executeth my counsel Is 46:11 376
and I will not meet thee as a *m* Is 47:3 120
Holy One, to him whom *m* despiseth Is 49:7 5315
when I came, was there no *m* Is 50:2 376
be afraid of a *m* that shall die Is 51:12 582
of the son of *m* which shall be Is 51:12 120
was so marred more than any *m* Is 52:14 376
a *m* of sorrows, and acquainted Is 53:3 376
and the unrighteous *m* his thoughts Is 55:7 376
Blessed is the *m* that doeth this, Is 56:2 582

the son of *m* that layeth hold on Is 56:2 120
and no *m* layeth it to heart Is 57:1 376
a day for a *m* to afflict his soul Is 58:5 120
And he saw that there was no *m* Is 59:16 376
so that no *m* went through thee, I Is 60:15
For as a young *m* marrieth a Is 62:5
nor an old *m* that hath not filled Is 65:20
but to this *m* will I look Is 66:2
an ox is as if he slew a *m* Is 66:3 376
she was delivered of a *m* child Is 66:7 2145
a land that no *m* passed through Jer 2:6 376
and where no *m* dwelt Jer 2:6 120
If a *m* put away his wife, and she Jer 3:1 376
I beheld, and, lo, there was no *m* Jer 4:25 120
and not a *m* dwell therein Jer 4:29 376
thereof, if ye can find a *m* Jer 5:1 376
execute judgment between a *m* Jer 7:5 376
out upon this place, upon *m* Jer 7:20 120
no *m* repented him of his Jer 8:6 376
Who is the wise *m*, that may Jer 9:12 376
Let not the wise *m* glory in his Jer 9:23
the mighty *m* glory in his might Jer 9:23
let not the rich *m* glory in his Jer 9:23
Every *m* is brutish in his Jer 10:14 120
the way of *m* is not in himself Jer 10:23 120
it is not in *m* that walketh to Jer 10:23
Cursed be the *m* that obeyeth not Jer 11:3 376
because no *m* layeth it to heart Jer 12:11 376
every *m* to his heritage Jer 12:15 376
and every *m* to his land Jer 12:15 376
cleaveth to the loins of a *m* Jer 13:11 376
as a wayfaring *m* that turneth Jer 14:8
shouldest thou be as a *m* astonied Jer 14:9 376
as a mighty *m* that cannot save Jer 14:9 376
thou hast borne me a *m* of strife Jer 15:10 376
a *m* of contention to the whole Jer 15:10 376
Shall a *m* make gods unto himself, Jer 16:20 120
Cursed be the *m* that trusteth in Jer 17:5 1397
that trusteth in *m* Jer 17:5 120
Blessed is the *m* that trusteth in Jer 17:7 1397
even to give every *m* according to Jer 17:10 376
Will a *m* leave the snow of Jer 18:14
Cursed be the *m* who brought Jer 20:15 376
A *m* child is born unto thee Jer 20:15 2145
let that *m* be as the cities which Jer 20:16 376
inhabitants of this city, both *m* Jer 21:6 120
say every *m* to his neighbour Jer 22:8 376
Is this *m* Coniah a despised Jer 22:28 376
LORD, Write ye this *m* childless Jer 22:30 376
a *m* that shall not prosper in his Jer 22:30 1397
for no *m* of his seed shall Jer 22:30 376
I am like a drunken *m*, and like a Jer 23:9 376
like a *m* whom wine hath overcome, Jer 23:9 1397
tell every *m* to his neighbour Jer 23:27 376
LORD, I will even punish that *m* Jer 23:34 376
turn every *m* from his evil way, Jer 26:3 376
saying, This *m* is worthy to die Jer 26:11 376
This *m* is not worthy to die Jer 26:16 376
And there was also a *m* that Jer 26:20 376
I have made the earth, the *m* Jer 27:5 120
for every *m* that is mad, and Jer 29:26 376
he shall not have a *m* to dwell Jer 29:32 376
see whether a *m* doth travail with Jer 30:6 2145
wherefore do I see every *m* with Jer 30:6 1397
is Zion, whom no *m* seeketh after Jer 30:17
earth, A woman shall compass a *m* Jer 31:22 1397
house of Judah with the seed of *m* Jer 31:27 120
every *m* that eateth the sour Jer 31:30 120
no more every *m* his neighbour Jer 31:34 376
every *m* his brother, saying, Know Jer 31:34 376
It is desolate without *m* or beast Jer 32:43 120
say shall be desolate without *m* Jer 33:10 120
that are desolate, without *m* Jer 33:10 120
which is desolate without *m* Jer 33:12 120
David shall never want a *m* to sit Jer 33:17 376
want a *m* before me to offer burnt Jer 33:18 376
That every *m* should let his Jer 34:9 376
every *m* his maidservant, being an Jer 34:9 376
go every *m* his brother an Hebrew Jer 34:14 376
liberty every *m* to his neighbour Jer 34:15 376
and caused every *m* his servant Jer 34:16 376
every *m* his handmaid, whom he had Jer 34:16 376
and every *m* to his neighbour Jer 34:17 376
a *m* of God, which was by the Jer 35:4 376
ye now every *m* from his evil way Jer 35:15 376
a *m* to stand before me for ever Jer 35:19 376
return every *m* from his evil way Jer 36:3 376
let no *m* know where ye be Jer 36:19 376
cause to cease from thence *m* Jer 36:29 120
they rise up every *m* in his tent Jer 37:10 376
let this *m* be put to death Jer 38:4 376
for this *m* seeketh not the Jer 38:4 376
Let no *m* know of these words, and Jer 38:24 376
Nethaniah, and no *m* shall know it Jer 40:15 376
slain Gedaliah, and no *m* knew it, Jer 41:4 376
and no *m* dwelleth therein, Jer 44:2
your souls, to cut off from you *m* Jer 44:7 376
any *m* of Judah in all the land of Jer 44:26 376
away, nor the mighty *m* escape Jer 46:6
for the mighty *m* hath stumbled Jer 46:12
be driven out every *m* right forth Jer 49:5 376
no *m* shall abide there, neither Jer 49:18 376
shall a son of *m* dwell in it Jer 49:18 120
and who is a chosen *m*, that I may Jer 49:19
there shall no *m* abide there Jer 49:33 376
nor any son of *m* dwell in it Jer 49:33 120
remove, they shall depart, both *m* Jer 50:3 120
shall be as of a mighty expert *m* Jer 50:9
so shall no *m* abide there Jer 50:40 376
shall any son of *m* dwell therein Jer 50:40 120
like a *m* to the battle, against Jer 50:42 376
and who is a chosen *m*, that I may Jer 50:44
and deliver every *m* his soul Jer 51:6 376
Every *m* is brutish by his Jer 51:17 120

also will I break in pieces *m* Jer 51:22 376
I break in pieces the young *m* Jer 51:22
a land wherein no *m* dwelleth Jer 51:43 376
doth any son of *m* pass thereby Jer 51:43 120
deliver ye every *m* his soul from Jer 51:45 376
neither *m* nor beast, but that it Jer 51:62 120
I am the *m* that hath seen Lam 3:1 1397
is good that a *m* should both hope Lam 3:26
It is good for a *m* that he bear Lam 3:27 1397
a *m* before the face of the most Lam 3:35 1397
To subvert a *m* in his cause Lam 3:36 120
doth a living *m* complain Lam 3:39 120
a *m* for the punishment of his Lam 3:39 1397
no *m* breaketh it unto them Lam 4:4
they had the likeness of a *m* Eze 1:5 120
they had the hands of a *m* under Eze 1:8 120
they four had the face of a *m* Eze 1:10 120
appearance of a *m* above upon it Eze 1:26 120
And he said unto me, Son of *m* Eze 2:1 120
And he said unto me, Son of *m* Eze 2:3 120
And thou, son of *m*, be not afraid Eze 2:6 120
But thou, son of *m*, hear what I Eze 2:8 120
he said unto me, Son of *m* Eze 3:1 120
And he said unto me, Son of *m* Eze 3:3 120
And he said unto me, Son of *m* Eze 3:4 120
he said unto me, Son of *m* Eze 3:10 120
Son of *m*, I have made thee a Eze 3:17 120
the same wicked *m* shall die in Eze 3:18
When a righteous *m* doth turn from Eze 3:20
if thou warn the righteous *m* Eze 3:21
But thou, O son of *m*, behold, Eze 3:25 120
Thou also, son of *m*, take thee a Eze 4:1 120
it with dung that cometh out of *m* Eze 4:12 120
he said unto me, Son of *m* Eze 4:16 120
And thou, son of *m*, take thee a Eze 5:1 120
Son of *m*, set thy face toward the Eze 6:2 120
Also, thou son of *m*, thus saith Eze 7:2 120
Then said he unto me, Son of *m* Eze 8:5 120
furthermore unto me, Son of *m* Eze 8:6 120
Then said he unto me, Son of *m* Eze 8:8 120
with every *m* his censer in his Eze 8:11 376
Then said he unto me, Son of *m* Eze 8:12 120
every *m* in the chambers of his Eze 8:12 376
Hast thou seen this, O son of *m* Eze 8:15 120
Hast thou seen this, O son of *m* Eze 8:17 120
even every *m* with his destroying Eze 9:1 376
every *m* a slaughter weapon in his Eze 9:2 376
one *m* among them was clothed with Eze 9:2 376
he called to the *m* clothed with Eze 9:3 376
near any *m* upon whom is the mark Eze 9:6 376
the *m* clothed with linen, which Eze 9:11 376
he spake unto the *m* clothed with Eze 10:2 376
of the house, when the *m* went in Eze 10:3 376
the *m* clothed with linen, saying, Eze 10:6 376
second face was the face of a *m* Eze 10:14 120
of a *m* was under their wings Eze 10:21 120
Then said he unto me, Son of *m* Eze 11:2 120
them, prophesy, O son of *m* Eze 11:4 120
Son of *m*, thy brethren, even thy Eze 11:15 120
Son of *m*, thou dwellest in the Eze 12:2 120
Therefore, thou son of *m*, prepare Eze 12:3 120
Son of *m*, hath not the house of Eze 12:9 120
Son of *m*, eat thy bread with Eze 12:18 120
Son of *m*, what is that proverb Eze 12:22 120
Son of *m*, behold, they of the Eze 12:27 120
Son of *m*, prophesy against the Eze 13:2 120
Likewise, thou son of *m*, set thy Eze 13:17 120
Son of *m*, these men have set up Eze 14:3 120
Every *m* of the house of Israel Eze 14:4 376
I will set my face against that *m* Eze 14:8 376
Son of *m*, when the land sinneth Eze 14:13 120
famine upon it, and will cut off *m* Eze 14:13 120
that no *m* may pass through Eze 14:15
so that I cut off *m* and beast from Eze 14:17 120
it in blood, to cut off from it *m* Eze 14:19 120
pestilence, to cut off from it *m* Eze 14:21 120
Son of *m*, What is the vine tree Eze 15:2 120
Son of *m*, cause Jerusalem to know Eze 16:2 120
Son of *m*, put forth a riddle, and Eze 17:2 120
But if a *m* be just, and do that Eze 18:5 376
true judgment between *m* and *m* Eze 18:8 376
that the wicked *m* doeth, shall he Eze 18:24
When a righteous *m* turneth away Eze 18:26
when the wicked *m* turneth away Eze 18:27
Son of *m*, speak unto the elders Eze 20:3 120
Wilt thou judge them, son of *m* Eze 20:4 120
them, Cast ye away every *m* the Eze 20:7 376
they did not every *m* cast away Eze 20:8 376
my judgments, which if a *m* do Eze 20:11 120
my judgments, which if a *m* do Eze 20:13 120
to do them, which if a *m* do Eze 20:21 120
Therefore, son of *m*, speak unto Eze 20:27 120
Son of *m*, set thy face toward the Eze 20:46 120
Son of *m*, set thy face toward Eze 21:2 120
Sigh therefore, thou son of *m* Eze 21:6 120
Son of *m*, prophesy, and say, Thus Eze 21:9 120
Cry and howl, son of *m* Eze 21:12 120
Thou therefore, son of *m*, Eze 21:14 120
Also, thou son of *m*, appoint thee Eze 21:19 120
And thou, son of *m*, prophesy and Eze 21:28 120
Now, thou son of *m*, wilt thou Eze 22:2 120
Son of *m*, the house of Israel is Eze 22:18 120
Son of *m*, say unto her, Thou art Eze 22:24 120
And I sought for a *m* among them Eze 22:30 376
Son of *m*, there were two women, Eze 23:2 120
Son of *m*, wilt thou judge Aholah Eze 23:36 120
Son of *m*, write thee the name of Eze 24:2 120
Son of *m*, behold, I take away Eze 24:16 120
Also, thou son of *m*, shall it not Eze 24:25 120
Son of *m*, set thy face against Eze 25:2 120
hand upon Edom, and will cut off *m* Eze 25:13 120
Son of *m*, because that Tyrus hath Eze 26:2 120
Now, thou son of *m*, take up a Eze 27:2 120
Son of *m*, say unto the prince of Eze 28:2 120

yet thou art a *m*, and not God, Eze 28:2 120
but thou shalt be a *m*, and no God, Eze 28:9 120
Son of *m*, take up a lamentation Eze 28:12 120
Son of *m*, set thy face against Eze 28:21 120
Son of *m*, set thy face against Eze 29:2 120
a sword upon thee, and cut off *m* Eze 29:8 120
No foot of *m* shall pass through Eze 29:11 120
Son of *m*, Nebuchadrezzar king of Eze 29:18 120
Son of *m*, prophesy and say, Thus Eze 30:2 120
Son of *m*, I have broken the arm Eze 30:21 120
groanings of a deadly wounded *m* Eze 30:24
Son of *m*, speak unto Pharaoh king Eze 31:2 120
Son of *m*, take up a lamentation Eze 32:2 120
every *m* for his own life, in the Eze 32:10 376
foot of *m* trouble them any more Eze 32:13 120
Son of *m*, wail for the multitude Eze 32:18 120
Son of *m*, speak to the children Eze 33:2 120
the land take a *m* of their coasts Eze 33:2 376
So thou, O son of *m*, I have set Eze 33:7 120
I say unto the wicked, O wicked *m* Eze 33:8
that wicked *m* shall die in his Eze 33:8
Therefore, O thou son of *m* Eze 33:10 120
Therefore, thou son of *m*, say Eze 33:12 120
Son of *m*, they that inhabit those Eze 33:24 120
Also, thou son of *m*, the children Eze 33:30 120
Son of *m*, prophesy against the Eze 34:2 120
Son of *m*, set thy face against Eze 35:2 120
Also, thou son of *m*, prophesy Eze 36:1 120
And I will multiply upon you *m* Eze 36:11 120
Son of *m*, when the house of Eze 36:17 120
And he said unto me, Son of *m* Eze 37:3 120
unto the wind, prophesy, son of *m* Eze 37:9 120
Then he said unto me, Son of *m* Eze 37:11 120
Moreover, thou son of *m*, take Eze 37:16 120
Son of *m*, set thy face against Eze 38:2 120
Therefore, son of *m*, prophesy and Eze 38:14 120
Therefore, thou son of *m*, Eze 39:1 120
And, thou son of *m*, thus saith the Eze 39:17 120
and, behold, there was a *m* Eze 40:3 376
And the *m* said unto me Eze 40:4 376
said unto me, Son of *m* Eze 40:4 120
So that the face of a *m* was Eze 41:19 120
and the *m* stood by me Eze 43:6 376
And he said unto me, Son of *m* Eze 43:7 120
Thou son of *m*, shew the house to Eze 43:10 120
And he said unto me, Son of *m* Eze 43:18 120
no *m* shall enter in by it Eze 44:2 376
the LORD said unto me, Son of *m* Eze 44:5 120
every *m* from his possession Eze 46:18 376
when the *m* that had the line in Eze 47:3 376
And he said unto me, Son of *m* Eze 47:6 120
till a *m* come over against Hamath Eze 47:20
There is not a *m* upon the earth Dan 2:10 606
I have found a *m* of the captives Dan 2:25 1400
the king made Daniel a great *m* Dan 2:48
that every *m* that shall hear the Dan 3:10 606
There is a *m* in thy kingdom, in Dan 5:11 1400
of any God or *m* for thirty days Dan 6:7 606
that every *m* that shall ask a Dan 6:12 606
any God or *m* within thirty days Dan 6:12 606
made stand upon the feet as a *m* Dan 7:4 606
horn were eyes like the eyes of *m* Dan 7:8 606
one like the Son of *m* came with Dan 7:13 606
me as the appearance of a *m* Dan 8:15 1397
make this *m* to understand the Dan 8:16
unto me, Understand, O son of *m* Dan 8:17 120
in prayer, even the *m* Gabriel Dan 9:21 376
a certain *m* clothed in linen Dan 10:5 376
a *m* greatly beloved, understand Dan 10:11 376
me one like the appearance of a *m* Dan 10:18 120
O *m* greatly beloved, fear not Dan 10:19 376
one said to the *m* clothed in Dan 12:6 376
I heard the *m* clothed in linen, Dan 12:7 376
thou shalt not be for another *m* Hos 3:3 376
Yet let no *m* strive, nor reprove Hos 4:4 376
as troops of robbers wait for a *m* Hos 6:9 376
is a fool, the spiritual *m* is mad Hos 9:7 376
that there shall not be a *m* left Hos 9:12 120
I drew them with cords of a *m* Hos 11:4 120
for I am God, and not *m* Hos 11:9 376
and a *m* and his father will go in Amos 2:7 376
declareth unto *m* what is his Amos 4:13 120
As if a *m* did flee from a lion, Amos 5:19 376
cried every *m* unto his god, and Jonah 1:5
saying, Let neither *m* nor beast Jonah 3:7 120
But let *m* and beast be covered Jonah 3:8 120
so they oppress a *m* and his house, Mic 2:2 1397
and his house, even a *m* Mic 2:2 376
If a *m* walking in the spirit and Mic 2:11 376
shall sit every *m* under his vine Mic 4:4 376
this *m* shall be the peace, when Mic 5:5
grass, that tarrieth not for *m* Mic 5:7 376
He hath shewed thee, O *m*, what is Mic 6:8 120
the *m* of wisdom shall see thy Mic 6:9
The good *m* is perished out of the Mic 7:2
they hunt every *m* his brother Mic 7:2 376
and the great *m*, he uttereth his Mic 7:3
mountains, and no *m* gathereth them Nah 3:18
when the wicked devoureth the *m* Hab 1:13
by wine, he is a proud *m*, neither Hab 2:5 1397
I will consume *m* and beast Zeph 1:3 120
I will cut off *m* from off the Zeph 1:3 120
the mighty *m* shall cry there Zeph 1:14
destroyed, so that there is no *m* Zeph 3:6 376
ye run every *m* unto his own house Hag 1:9 376
behold a *m* riding upon a red Zec 1:8 376
the *m* that stood among the myrtle Zec 1:10 376
so that no *m* did lift up his head Zec 1:21 376
behold a *m* with a measuring line Zec 2:1 376
him, Run, speak to this young *m* Zec 2:4
shall ye call every *m* his Zec 3:10
as a *m* that is wakened out of his Zec 4:1 376
Behold the *m* whose name is The Zec 6:12 376
every *m* to his brother Zec 7:9 376

that no *m* passed through nor	Zec 7:14	
every *m* with his staff in his	Zec 8:4	376
days there was no hire for *m*	Zec 8:10	120
Speak ye every *m* the truth to his	Zec 8:16	376
when the eyes of *m*, as of all the	Zec 9:1	120
thee as the sword of a mighty *m*	Zec 9:13	
Ephraim shall be like a mighty *m*	Zec 10:7	
the spirit of *m* within him	Zec 12:1	120
for *m* taught me to keep cattle	Zec 13:5	120
against the *m* that is my fellow,	Zec 13:7	1397
every *m* against his brother	Mal 2:10	376
cut off the *m* that doeth this	Mal 2:12	376
Will a *m* rob God	Mal 3:8	120
as a *m* spareth his own son that	Mal 3:17	376
her husband, being a just *m*	Mt 1:19	
M shall not live by bread alone,	Mt 4:4	444
if any *m* will sue thee at the law	Mt 5:40	
No *m* can serve two masters	Mt 6:24	3762
Or what *m* is there of you, whom	Mt 7:9	444
I will liken him unto a wise *m*	Mt 7:24	435
shall be likened unto a foolish *m*	Mt 7:26	435
unto him, See thou tell no *m*	Mt 8:4	3367
For I am a *m* under authority,	Mt 8:9	444
and I say to this *m*, Go, and he	Mt 8:9	
but the Son of *m* hath not where	Mt 8:20	444
saying, What manner of *m* is this	Mt 8:27	
so that no *m* might pass by that	Mt 8:28	5100
to him a *m* sick of the palsy	Mt 9:2	
themselves, This *m* blasphemeth	Mt 9:3	
ye may know that the Son of *m*	Mt 9:6	444
forth from thence, he saw a *m*	Mt 9:9	444
No *m* putteth a piece of new cloth	Mt 9:16	3762
saying, See that no *m* know it	Mt 9:30	3367
a dumb *m* possessed with a devil	Mt 9:32	444
Israel, till the Son of *m* be come	Mt 10:23	444
For I am come to set a *m* at	Mt 10:35	444
he that receiveth a righteous *m*	Mt 10:41	
in the name of a righteous *m*	Mt 10:41	
A *m* clothed in soft raiment	Mt 11:8	444
The Son of *m* came eating and	Mt 11:19	444
Behold a *m* gluttonous, and a	Mt 11:19	444
no *m* knoweth the Son, but the	Mt 11:27	3762
neither knoweth any *m* the Father	Mt 11:27	
For the Son of *m* is Lord even of	Mt 12:8	444
there was a *m* which had his hand	Mt 12:10	444
What *m* shall there be among you,	Mt 12:11	444
How much then is a *m* better than	Mt 12:12	444
Then saith he to the *m*, Stretch	Mt 12:13	444
neither shall any *m* hear his	Mt 12:19	
except he first bind the strong *m*	Mt 12:29	
a word against the Son of *m*	Mt 12:32	444
A good *m* out of the good treasure	Mt 12:35	444
an evil *m* out of the evil	Mt 12:35	444
shall the Son of *m* be three days	Mt 12:40	444
unclean spirit is gone out of a *m*	Mt 12:43	444
the last state of that *m* is worse	Mt 12:45	444
of heaven is likened unto a *m*	Mt 13:24	444
of mustard seed, which a *m* took	Mt 13:31	444
the good seed is the Son of *m*	Mt 13:37	444
The Son of *m* shall send forth his	Mt 13:41	444
the which when a *m* hath found	Mt 13:44	444
heaven is like unto a merchant *m*	Mt 13:45	444
unto a *m* that is an householder	Mt 13:52	444
Whence hath this *m* this wisdom	Mt 13:54	
then hath this *m* all these things	Mt 13:56	
goeth into the mouth defileth a *m*	Mt 15:11	444
of the mouth, this defileth a *m*	Mt 15:11	444
and they defile the *m*	Mt 15:18	444
are the things which defile a *m*	Mt 15:20	444
unwashen hands defileth not a *m*	Mt 15:20	444
do men say that I the Son of *m* am	Mt 16:13	444
that they should tell no *m* that	Mt 16:20	3367
If any *m* will come after me, let	Mt 16:24	
For what is a *m* profited, if he	Mt 16:26	444
or what shall a *m* give in	Mt 16:26	444
For the Son of *m* shall come in	Mt 16:27	444
every *m* according to his works	Mt 16:27	
Son of *m* coming in his kingdom	Mt 16:28	444
up their eyes, they saw no *m*	Mt 17:8	3762
saying, Tell the vision to no *m*	Mt 17:9	3367
until the Son of *m* be risen again	Mt 17:9	444
also the Son of *m* suffer of them	Mt 17:12	444
there came to him a certain *m*	Mt 17:14	444
The Son of *m* shall be betrayed	Mt 17:22	444
but woe to that *m* by whom the	Mt 18:7	444
For the Son of *m* is come to save	Mt 18:11	444
if a *m* have an hundred sheep, and	Mt 18:12	444
him be unto thee as an heathen *m*	Mt 18:17	
Is it lawful for a *m* to put away	Mt 19:3	444
this cause shall a *m* leave father	Mt 19:5	444
together, let not *m* put asunder	Mt 19:6	444
If the case of the *m* be so with	Mt 19:10	444
The young *m* saith unto him, All	Mt 19:20	3495
the young *m* heard that saying	Mt 19:22	3495
That a rich *m* shall hardly enter	Mt 19:23	
than for a rich *m* to enter into	Mt 19:24	
regeneration when the Son of *m*	Mt 19:28	444
unto a *m* that is an householder	Mt 20:1	444
Because no *m* hath hired us	Mt 20:7	3762
they received every *m* a penny	Mt 20:9	
likewise received every *m* a penny	Mt 20:10	
the Son of *m* shall be betrayed	Mt 20:18	444
Even as the Son of *m* came not to	Mt 20:28	444
if any *m* say ought unto you, ye	Mt 21:3	
A certain *m* had two sons	Mt 21:28	444
he saw there a *m* which had not on	Mt 22:11	444
neither carest thou for any *m*	Mt 22:16	3762
Master, Moses said, If a *m* die	Mt 22:24	5100
no *m* was able to answer him a	Mt 22:46	3762
neither durst any *m* from that day	Mt 22:46	
call no *m* your father upon the	Mt 23:9	
Take heed that no *m* deceive you	Mt 24:4	5100
Then if any *m* shall say unto you,	Mt 24:23	
the coming of the Son of *m* be	Mt 24:27	444
sign of the Son of *m* in heaven	Mt 24:30	444
they shall see the Son of *m*	Mt 24:30	444
of that day and hour knoweth no *m*	Mt 24:36	3762
the coming of the Son of *m* be	Mt 24:37	444
the coming of the Son of *m* be	Mt 24:39	444
ye think not the Son of *m* cometh	Mt 24:44	444
hour wherein the Son of *m* cometh	Mt 25:13	444
a *m* travelling into a far country	Mt 25:14	444
to every *m* according to his	Mt 25:15	
knew thee that thou art an hard *m*	Mt 25:24	444
When the Son of *m* shall come in	Mt 25:31	444
the Son of *m* is betrayed to be	Mt 26:2	444
Go into the city to such a *m*	Mt 26:18	
The Son of *m* goeth as it is	Mt 26:24	444
but woe unto that *m* by whom the	Mt 26:24	444
by whom the Son of *m* is betrayed	Mt 26:24	444
that *m* if he had not been born	Mt 26:24	444
the Son of *m* is betrayed into the	Mt 26:45	444
shall ye see the Son of *m* sitting	Mt 26:64	444
with an oath, I do not know the *m*	Mt 26:72	444
swear, saying, I know not the *m*	Mt 26:74	444
nothing to do with that just *m*	Mt 27:19	
out, they found a *m* of Cyrene	Mt 27:32	444
said, This *m* calleth for Elias	Mt 27:47	
there came a rich *m* of Arimathaea	Mt 27:57	444
a *m* with an unclean spirit	Mk 1:23	444
See thou say nothing to any *m*	Mk 1:44	3367
Why doth this *m* thus speak	Mk 2:7	
ye may know that the Son of *m*	Mk 2:10	444
No *m* also seweth a piece of new	Mk 2:21	3762
no *m* putteth new wine into old	Mk 2:22	3762
them, The sabbath was made for *m*	Mk 2:27	444
and not *m* for the sabbath	Mk 2:27	444
Therefore the Son of *m* is Lord	Mk 2:28	444
there was a *m* there which had a	Mk 3:1	444
he saith unto the *m* which had the	Mk 3:3	444
their hearts, he saith unto the *m*	Mk 3:5	444
No *m* can enter into a strong	Mk 3:27	3762
he will first bind the strong *m*	Mk 3:27	2478
If any *m* have ears to hear, let	Mk 4:23	
as if a *m* should cast seed into	Mk 4:26	444
another, What manner of *m* is this	Mk 4:41	
tombs a *m* with an unclean spirit	Mk 5:2	444
no *m* could bind him, no, not with	Mk 5:3	3762
neither could any *m* tame him	Mk 5:4	
said unto him, Come out of the *m*	Mk 5:8	444
And he suffered no *m* to follow him	Mk 5:37	3762
straitly that no *m* should know it	Mk 5:43	3367
whence hath this *m* these things	Mk 6:2	
knowing that he was a just *m*	Mk 6:20	435
If a *m* shall say to his father or	Mk 7:11	444
There is nothing from without a *m*	Mk 7:15	444
those are they that defile the *m*	Mk 7:15	444
If any *m* have ears to hear, let	Mk 7:16	
from without entereth into the *m*	Mk 7:18	444
of the *m*, that defileth the *m*	Mk 7:20	444
come from within, and defile the *m*	Mk 7:23	444
house, and would have no *m* know it	Mk 7:24	3762
them that they should tell no *m*	Mk 7:36	3367
From whence can a *m* satisfy these	Mk 8:4	5100
and they bring a blind *m* unto him	Mk 8:22	
he took the blind *m* by the hand	Mk 8:23	
restored, and saw every *m* clearly	Mk 8:25	
that they should tell no *m* of him	Mk 8:30	3367
that the Son of *m* must suffer	Mk 8:31	444
For what shall it profit a *m*	Mk 8:36	444
Or what shall a *m* give in	Mk 8:37	444
shall the Son of *m* be ashamed	Mk 8:38	444
about, they saw no *m* any more	Mk 9:8	3762
no *m* what things they had seen	Mk 9:9	3367
till the Son of *m* were risen from	Mk 9:9	444
how it is written of the Son of *m*	Mk 9:12	444
not that any *m* should know it	Mk 9:30	
The Son of *m* is delivered into	Mk 9:31	444
If any *m* desire to be first, the	Mk 9:35	
for there is no *m* which shall do	Mk 9:39	3762
Is it lawful for a *m* to put away	Mk 10:2	435
cause shall a *m* leave his father	Mk 10:7	444
together, let not *m* put asunder	Mk 10:9	444
than for a rich *m* to enter into	Mk 10:25	
There is no *m* that hath left	Mk 10:29	3762
the Son of *m* shall be delivered	Mk 10:33	444
For even the Son of *m* came not to	Mk 10:45	444
And they call the blind *m*, saying	Mk 10:49	
The blind *m* said unto him, Lord,	Mk 10:51	
a colt tied, whereon never *m* sat	Mk 11:2	444
if any *m* say unto you, Why do ye	Mk 11:3	
No *m* eat fruit of thee hereafter	Mk 11:14	3367
would not suffer that any *m*	Mk 11:16	
A certain *m* planted a vineyard,	Mk 12:1	444
thou art true, and carest for no *m*	Mk 12:14	444
no *m* after that durst ask him any	Mk 12:34	3762
Take heed lest any *m* deceive you	Mk 13:5	
then if any *m* shall say to you,	Mk 13:21	
then shall they see the Son of *m*	Mk 13:26	444
day and that hour knoweth no *m*	Mk 13:32	3762
For the Son of *m* is as a	Mk 13:34	
is as a *m* taking a far journey	Mk 13:34	444
servants, and to every *m* his work	Mk 13:34	
there shall meet you a *m* bearing	Mk 14:13	444
The Son of *m* indeed goeth, as it	Mk 14:21	444
but woe to that *m* by whom the Son	Mk 14:21	444
by whom the Son of *m* is betrayed	Mk 14:21	444
good were it for that *m* if he had	Mk 14:21	444
the Son of *m* is betrayed into the	Mk 14:41	444
followed him a certain young *m*	Mk 14:51	3495
ye shall see the Son of *m* sitting	Mk 14:62	444
I know not this *m* of whom ye	Mk 14:71	444
them, what every *m* should take	Mk 15:24	
Truly this *m* was the Son of God	Mk 15:39	444
they saw a young *m* sitting on the	Mk 16:5	3495
to any *m* for they were afraid	Mk 16:8	3762
for I am an old *m*, and my wife	Lk 1:18	
to a *m* whose name was Joseph	Lk 1:27	435
this be, seeing I know not a *m*	Lk 1:34	435
there was a *m* in Jerusalem, whose	Lk 2:25	444
and the same *m* was just and devout,	Lk 2:25	444
and in favour with God and *m*	Lk 2:52	444
unto them, Do violence to no *m*	Lk 3:14	3367
That *m* shall not live by bread	Lk 4:4	444
And in the synagogue there was a *m*	Lk 4:33	444
for I am a sinful *m*, O Lord	Lk 5:8	435
behold a *m* full of leprosy	Lk 5:12	435
And he charged him to tell no *m*	Lk 5:14	3367
men brought in a bed a *m* which	Lk 5:18	444
their faith, he said unto him, *M*	Lk 5:20	444
Son of *m* hath power upon earth to	Lk 5:24	444
No *m* putteth a piece of a new	Lk 5:36	3762
no *m* putteth new wine into old	Lk 5:37	3762
No *m* also having drunk old wine	Lk 5:39	3762
That the Son of *m* is Lord also of	Lk 6:5	444
there was a *m* whose right hand	Lk 6:6	444
said to the *m* which had the	Lk 6:8	444
upon them all, he said unto the *m*	Lk 6:10	444
Give to every *m* that asketh of	Lk 6:30	
A good *m* out of the good treasure	Lk 6:45	444
an evil *m* out of the evil	Lk 6:45	444
He is like a *m* which built an	Lk 6:48	444
is like a *m* that without a	Lk 6:49	444
For I also am a *m* set under	Lk 7:8	444
there was a dead *m* carried out	Lk 7:12	
And he said, Young *m*, I say unto	Lk 7:14	3495
A *m* clothed in soft raiment	Lk 7:25	444
The Son of *m* is come eating and	Lk 7:34	444
and ye say, Behold a gluttonous *m*	Lk 7:34	444
within himself, saying, This *m*	Lk 7:39	
No *m*, when he hath lighted a	Lk 8:16	3762
another, What manner of *m* is this	Lk 8:25	
him out of the city a certain *m*	Lk 8:27	435
spirit to come out of the *m*	Lk 8:29	444
Then went the devils out of the *m*	Lk 8:33	444
and came to Jesus, and found the *m*	Lk 8:35	444
Now the *m* out of whom the devils	Lk 8:38	435
there came a *m* named Jairus	Lk 8:41	435
house, he suffered no *m* to go in	Lk 8:51	3762
should tell no *m* what was done	Lk 8:56	3367
them to tell no *m* that thing	Lk 9:21	3367
The Son of *m* must suffer many	Lk 9:22	444
If any *m* will come after me, let	Lk 9:23	
For what is a *m* advantaged	Lk 9:25	444
him shall the Son of *m* be ashamed	Lk 9:26	444
told no *m* in those days any of	Lk 9:36	3762
a *m* of the company cried out,	Lk 9:38	435
for the Son of *m* shall be	Lk 9:44	444
For the Son of *m* is not come to	Lk 9:56	444
a certain *m* said unto him, Lord,	Lk 9:57	
but the Son of *m* hath not where	Lk 9:58	444
And Jesus said unto him, No *m*	Lk 9:62	3762
and salute no *m* by the way	Lk 10:4	3367
no *m* knoweth who the Son is, but	Lk 10:22	3762
A certain *m* went down from	Lk 10:30	444
When a strong *m* armed keepeth his	Lk 11:21	
unclean spirit is gone out of a *m*	Lk 11:24	444
the last state of that *m* is worse	Lk 11:26	444
Son of *m* be to this generation	Lk 11:30	444
No *m*, when he hath lighted a	Lk 11:33	3762
him shall the Son of *m* also	Lk 12:8	444
speak a word against the Son of *m*	Lk 12:10	444
And he said unto him, *M*, who made	Lk 12:14	444
rich *m* brought forth plentifully	Lk 12:16	444
for the Son of *m* cometh at an	Lk 12:40	444
A certain *m* had a fig tree	Lk 13:6	
of mustard seed, which a *m* took	Lk 13:19	444
there was a certain *m* before him	Lk 14:2	444
art bidden of any *m* to a wedding	Lk 14:8	
lest a more honourable *m* than	Lk 14:8	
and say to thee, Give this *m* place	Lk 14:9	
A certain *m* made a great supper,	Lk 14:16	444
If any *m* come to me, and hate not	Lk 14:26	
This *m* began to build, and was not	Lk 14:30	444
This *m* receiveth sinners, and	Lk 15:2	
What *m* of you, having an hundred	Lk 15:4	444
he said, A certain *m* had two sons	Lk 15:11	444
and no *m* gave unto him	Lk 15:16	3762
There was a certain rich *m*	Lk 16:1	444
and every *m* presseth into it	Lk 16:16	
There was a certain rich *m*	Lk 16:19	444
the rich *m* also died, and was	Lk 16:22	
one of the days of the Son of *m*	Lk 17:22	444
also the Son of *m* be in his day	Lk 17:24	444
also in the days of the Son of *m*	Lk 17:26	444
day when the Son of *m* is revealed	Lk 17:30	444
not God, neither regarded *m*	Lk 18:2	444
I fear not God, nor regard *m*	Lk 18:4	444
when the Son of *m* cometh, shall	Lk 18:8	444
this *m* went down to his house	Lk 18:14	
than for a rich *m* to enter into	Lk 18:25	
There is no *m* that hath left	Lk 18:29	3762
Son of *m* shall be accomplished	Lk 18:31	444
a certain blind *m* sat by the way	Lk 18:35	
there was a *m* named Zacchaeus,	Lk 19:2	435
guest with a *m* that is a sinner	Lk 19:7	435
from any *m* by false accusation	Lk 19:8	
For the Son of *m* is come to seek	Lk 19:10	444
not have this *m* to reign over us	Lk 19:14	
every *m* had gained by trading	Lk 19:15	
because thou art an austere *m*	Lk 19:21	444
knewest that I was an austere *m*	Lk 19:22	444
tied, whereon yet never *m* sat	Lk 19:30	444
if any *m* ask you, Why do ye loose	Lk 19:31	
A certain *m* planted a vineyard,	Lk 20:9	444
of *m* coming in a cloud with power	Lk 21:27	444
and to stand before the Son of *m*	Lk 21:36	444
city, there shall a *m* meet you	Lk 22:10	444
And truly the Son of *m* goeth	Lk 22:22	444
but woe unto that *m* by whom he is	Lk 22:22	444
thou the Son of *m* with a kiss	Lk 22:48	444
and said, This *m* was also with him	Lk 22:56	

And Peter said, *M*, I am not	Lk 22:58	444
And Peter said, *M*, I know not what	Lk 22:60	444
Hereafter shall the Son of *m* sit	Lk 22:69	444
people, I find no fault in this *m*	Lk 23:4	444
whether the *m* were a Galilaean	Lk 23:6	444
Ye have brought this *m* unto me	Lk 23:14	444
have found no fault in this *m*	Lk 23:14	444
at once, saying, Away with this *m*	Lk 23:18	
but this *m* hath done nothing	Lk 23:41	
Certainly this was a righteous *m*	Lk 23:47	444
there was a *m* named Joseph, a	Lk 23:50	435
and he was a good *m*, and a just	Lk 23:50	435
This *m* went unto Pilate, and	Lk 23:52	
wherein never *m* before was laid	Lk 23:53	3762
The Son of *m* must be delivered	Lk 24:7	444
There was a *m* sent from God,	Jn 1:6	444
which lighteth every *m* that	Jn 1:9	444
the flesh, nor of the will of *m*	Jn 1:13	435
No *m* hath seen God at any time	Jn 1:18	3762
After me cometh a *m* which is	Jn 1:30	435
and descending upon the Son of *m*	Jn 1:51	444
Every *m* at the beginning doth set	Jn 2:10	444
not that any should testify of *m*	Jn 2:25	444
for he knew what was in *m*	Jn 2:25	444
There was a *m* of the Pharisees,	Jn 3:1	444
for no *m* can do these miracles	Jn 3:2	3762
Except a *m* be born again, he	Jn 3:3	5100
How can a *m* be born when he is	Jn 3:4	444
Except a *m* be born of water and of	Jn 3:5	5100
no *m* hath ascended up to heaven,	Jn 3:13	3762
even the Son of *m* which is in	Jn 3:13	444
so must the Son of *m* be lifted up	Jn 3:14	444
A *m* can receive nothing, except	Jn 3:27	444
no *m* receiveth his testimony	Jn 3:32	3762
yet no *m* said, What seekest thou	Jn 4:27	3762
Come, see a *m*, which told me all	Jn 4:29	444
Hath any *m* brought him ought to	Jn 4:33	
the *m* believed the word that	Jn 4:50	444
And a certain *m* was there, which	Jn 5:5	444
The impotent *m* answered him	Jn 5:7	
answered him, Sir, I have no *m*	Jn 5:7	444
immediately the *m* was made whole	Jn 5:9	444
What *m* is that which said unto	Jn 5:12	444
The *m* departed, and told the Jews	Jn 5:15	444
For the Father judgeth no *m*	Jn 5:22	3762
also, because he is the Son of *m*	Jn 5:27	444
I receive not testimony from *m*	Jn 5:34	444
which the Son of *m* shall give	Jn 6:27	444
No *m* can come to me, except the	Jn 6:44	3762
Every *m* therefore that hath heard	Jn 6:45	
Not that any *m* hath seen the	Jn 6:46	
that a *m* may eat thereof, and not	Jn 6:50	5100
if any *m* eat of this bread, he	Jn 6:51	
How can this *m* give us his flesh	Jn 6:52	
ye eat the flesh of the Son of *m*	Jn 6:53	444
if ye shall see the Son of *m*	Jn 6:62	444
that no *m* can come unto me,	Jn 6:65	3762
For there is no *m* that doeth any	Jn 7:4	3762
for some said, He is a good *m*	Jn 7:12	
Howbeit no *m* spake openly of him	Jn 7:13	3762
How knoweth this *m* letters	Jn 7:15	
If any *m* will do his will, he	Jn 7:17	
on the sabbath day circumcise a *m*	Jn 7:22	444
If a *m* on the sabbath day receive	Jn 7:23	444
because I have made a *m* every	Jn 7:23	444
we know this *m* whence he is	Jn 7:27	
no *m* knoweth whence he is	Jn 7:27	3762
but no *m* laid hands on him,	Jn 7:30	3762
than these which this *m* hath done	Jn 7:31	
and cried, saying, If any *m* thirst	Jn 7:37	
but no *m* laid hands on him	Jn 7:44	3762
Never *m* spake like this *m*	Jn 7:46	444
Doth our law judge any *m*, before	Jn 7:51	444
every *m* went unto his own house	Jn 7:53	
hath no *m* condemned thee	Jn 8:10	3762
She said, No *m*, Lord	Jn 8:11	3762
I judge no *m*	Jn 8:15	3762
and no *m* laid hands on him	Jn 8:20	3762
ye have lifted up the Son of *m*	Jn 8:28	444
and were never in bondage to any *m*	Jn 8:33	
a *m* that hath told you the truth,	Jn 8:40	444
If a *m* keep my saying, he shall	Jn 8:51	5100
If a *m* keep my saying, he shall	Jn 8:52	5100
he saw a *m* which was blind from	Jn 9:1	444
Master, who did sin, this *m*	Jn 9:2	
Neither hath this *m* sinned	Jn 9:3	
night cometh, when no *m* can work	Jn 9:4	3762
eyes of the blind *m* with the clay	Jn 9:6	
A *m* that is called Jesus made	Jn 9:11	444
This *m* is not of God, because he	Jn 9:16	444
How can a *m* that is a sinner do	Jn 9:16	444
They say unto the blind *m* again	Jn 9:17	
that if any *m* did confess that he	Jn 9:22	
called they the *m* that was blind	Jn 9:24	444
we know that this *m* is a sinner	Jn 9:24	444
The *m* answered and said unto them,	Jn 9:30	444
but if any *m* be a worshipper of	Jn 9:31	
m opened the eyes of one that was	Jn 9:32	
If this *m* were not of God, he	Jn 9:33	
by me if any *m* enter in, he shall	Jn 10:9	
No *m* taketh it from me, but I lay	Jn 10:18	3762
neither shall any *m* pluck them	Jn 10:28	
no *m* is able to pluck them out of	Jn 10:29	3762
and because that thou, being a *m*	Jn 10:33	444
John spake of this *m* were true	Jn 10:41	
Now a certain *m* was sick, named	Jn 11:1	
If any *m* walk in the day, he	Jn 11:9	
But if a *m* walk in the night, he	Jn 11:10	5100
of them said, Could not this *m*	Jn 11:37	
even this *m* should not have died	Jn 11:37	
for this *m* doeth many miracles	Jn 11:47	444
that one *m* should die for the	Jn 11:50	444
if any *m* knew where he were, he	Jn 11:57	
that the Son of *m* should be	Jn 12:23	444
If any *m* serve me, let him follow	Jn 12:26	
if any *m* serve me, him will my	Jn 12:26	
The Son of *m* must be lifted up	Jn 12:34	444
who is this Son of *m*	Jn 12:34	444
if any *m* hear my words, and	Jn 12:47	
Now no *m* at the table knew for	Jn 13:28	3762
Now is the Son of *m* glorified	Jn 13:31	444
no *m* cometh unto the Father, but	Jn 14:6	3762
If a *m* love me, he will keep my	Jn 14:23	5100
If a *m* abide not in me, he is	Jn 15:6	5100
Greater love hath no *m* than this	Jn 15:13	3762
that a *m* lay down his life for	Jn 15:13	5100
the works which none other *m* did	Jn 15:24	
for joy that a *m* is born into the	Jn 16:21	444
your joy no *m* taketh from you	Jn 16:22	3762
not that any *m* should ask thee	Jn 16:30	
every *m* to his own, and shall	Jn 16:32	
one *m* should die for the people	Jn 18:14	444
bring ye against this *m*	Jn 18:29	444
for us to put any *m* to death	Jn 18:31	3762
all again, saying, Not this *m*	Jn 18:40	444
saith unto them, Behold the *m*	Jn 19:5	444
saying, If thou let this *m* go	Jn 19:12	444
wherein was never *m* yet laid	Jn 19:41	3762
Lord, and what shall this *m* do	Jn 21:21	
Now this *m* purchased a field with	Acts 1:18	
and let no *m* dwell therein	Acts 1:20	
because that every *m* heard them	Acts 2:6	1520
hear we every *m* in our own tongue	Acts 2:8	1520
a *m* approved of God among you by	Acts 2:22	435
to all men, as every *m* had need	Acts 2:45	
a certain *m* lame from his	Acts 3:2	435
as the lame *m* which was healed	Acts 3:11	
we had made this *m* to walk	Acts 3:12	
his name hath made this *m* strong	Acts 3:16	
good deed done to the impotent *m*	Acts 4:9	444
even by him doth this *m* stand	Acts 4:10	
beholding the *m* which was healed	Acts 4:14	444
henceforth to no *m* in this name	Acts 4:17	444
For the *m* was above forty years	Acts 4:22	444
was made unto every *m* according	Acts 4:35	
But a certain *m* named Ananias	Acts 5:1	435
durst no *m* join himself to them	Acts 5:13	3762
had opened, we found no *m* within	Acts 5:23	3762
After this *m* rose up Judas of	Acts 5:37	
a *m* full of faith and of the Holy	Acts 6:5	435
This *m* ceaseth not to speak	Acts 6:13	444
the Son of *m* standing on the	Acts 7:56	444
But there was a certain *m*	Acts 8:9	435
This *m* is the great power of God	Acts 8:10	
a *m* of Ethiopia, an eunuch of	Acts 8:27	435
except some *m* should guide me	Acts 8:31	
of himself, or of some other *m*	Acts 8:34	
hearing a voice, but seeing no *m*	Acts 9:7	3367
his eyes were opened, he saw no *m*	Acts 9:8	3762
a *m* named Ananias coming in	Acts 9:12	435
I have heard by many of this *m*	Acts 9:13	435
he found a certain *m* named Aeneas	Acts 9:33	444
There was a certain *m* in Caesarea	Acts 10:1	435
A devout *m*, and one that feared	Acts 10:2	
Cornelius the centurion, a just *m*	Acts 10:22	435
I myself also am a *m*	Acts 10:26	444
a *m* that is a Jew to keep company	Acts 10:28	435
not call any *m* common or unclean	Acts 10:28	444
a *m* stood before me in bright	Acts 10:30	435
Can any *m* forbid water, that	Acts 10:47	5100
For he was a good *m*, and full of	Acts 11:24	435
every *m* according to his ability,	Acts 11:29	1538
the voice of a god, and not of a *m*	Acts 12:22	444
Sergius Paulus, a prudent *m*	Acts 13:7	435
a *m* of the tribe of Benjamin, by	Acts 13:21	435
a *m* after mine own heart, which	Acts 13:22	435
that through this *m* is preached	Acts 13:38	
though a *m* declare it unto you	Acts 13:41	5100
there sat a certain *m* at Lystra	Acts 14:8	435
There stood a *m* of Macedonia	Acts 16:9	435
by that *m* whom he hath ordained	Acts 17:31	435
no *m* shall set on thee to hurt	Acts 18:10	3762
born at Alexandria, an eloquent *m*	Acts 18:24	435
This *m* was instructed in the way	Acts 18:25	
the *m* in whom the evil spirit was	Acts 19:16	444
For a certain *m* named Demetrius,	Acts 19:24	
what *m* is there that knoweth not	Acts 19:35	444
him, have a matter against any *m*	Acts 19:38	
a certain young *m* named Eutychus	Acts 20:9	3494
And they brought the young *m* alive	Acts 20:12	
the same *m* had four daughters,	Acts 21:9	
the *m* that owneth this girdle	Acts 21:11	435
This is the *m*, that teacheth all	Acts 21:28	444
I am a *m* which am a Jew of Tarsus	Acts 21:39	444
I am verily a *m* which am a Jew,	Acts 22:3	435
a devout *m* according to the law,	Acts 22:12	435
to scourge a *m* that is a Roman	Acts 22:25	444
for this *m* is a Roman	Acts 22:26	444
saying, We find no evil in this *m*	Acts 23:9	444
Bring this young *m* unto the chief	Acts 23:17	3494
to bring this young *m* unto thee	Acts 23:18	3494
then let the young *m* depart	Acts 23:22	3494
See thou tell no *m* that thou hast	Acts 23:22	3367
This *m* was taken of the Jews, and	Acts 23:27	435
that the Jews laid wait for the *m*	Acts 23:30	435
found this *m* a pestilent fellow	Acts 24:5	435
the temple disputing with any *m*	Acts 24:12	
go down with me, and accuse this *m*	Acts 25:5	435
no *m* may deliver me unto them	Acts 25:11	3762
There is a certain *m* left in	Acts 25:14	435
Romans to deliver any *m* to die	Acts 25:16	444
commanded the *m* to be brought	Acts 25:17	435
I would also hear the *m* myself	Acts 25:22	444
present with us, ye see this *m*	Acts 25:24	
This *m* doeth nothing worthy of	Acts 26:31	444
This *m* might have been set at	Acts 26:32	444
No doubt this *m* is a murderer	Acts 28:4	444
of the chief *m* of the island	Acts 28:7	
confidence, no *m* forbidding him	Acts 28:31	
image made like to corruptible *m*	Rom 1:23	444
thou art inexcusable, O *m*	Rom 2:1	444
And thinkest thou this, O *m*	Rom 2:3	444
to every *m* according to his deeds	Rom 2:6	
every soul of *m* that doeth evil	Rom 2:9	444
to every *m* that worketh good, to	Rom 2:10	3956
preachest a *m* should not steal	Rom 2:21	
Thou that sayest a *m* should not	Rom 2:22	
God be true, but every *m* a liar	Rom 3:4	444
(I speak as a *m*)	Rom 3:5	444
Therefore we conclude that a *m* is	Rom 3:28	444
the blessedness of the *m*, unto	Rom 4:6	444
Blessed is the *m* to whom the Lord	Rom 4:8	435
for a righteous *m* will one die	Rom 5:7	
m some would even dare to die	Rom 5:7	
as by one *m* sin entered into the	Rom 5:12	444
gift by grace, which is by one *m*	Rom 5:15	
that our old *m* is crucified with	Rom 6:6	444
over a *m* as long as he liveth	Rom 7:1	444
she be married to another *m*	Rom 7:3	435
she be married to another *m*	Rom 7:3	435
the law of God after the inward *m*	Rom 7:22	444
O wretched *m* that I am	Rom 7:24	444
Now if any *m* have not the Spirit	Rom 8:9	
for what a *m* seeth, why doth he	Rom 8:24	5100
Nay but, O *m*, who art thou that	Rom 9:20	444
That the *m* which doeth those	Rom 10:5	444
For with the heart *m* believeth	Rom 10:10	
to every *m* that is among you, not	Rom 12:3	
to every *m* the measure of faith	Rom 12:3	
Recompense to no *m* evil for evil	Rom 12:17	3367
Owe no *m* any thing, but to love	Rom 13:8	3367
One *m* esteemeth one day above	Rom 14:5	
Let every *m* be fully persuaded in	Rom 14:5	
himself, and no *m* dieth to himself	Rom 14:7	3762
that no *m* put a stumblingblock or	Rom 14:13	
that *m* who eateth with offence	Rom 14:20	444
have entered into the heart of *m*	1Cor 2:9	444
For what *m* knoweth the things of	1Cor 2:11	444
knoweth the things of a *m*	1Cor 2:11	444
the spirit of *m* which is in him	1Cor 2:11	444
so the things of God knoweth no *m*	1Cor 2:11	3762
But the natural *m* receiveth not	1Cor 2:14	444
yet he himself is judged of no *m*	1Cor 2:15	3762
even as the Lord gave to every *m*	1Cor 3:5	
every *m* shall receive his own	1Cor 3:8	
But let every *m* take heed how he	1Cor 3:10	
can no *m* lay than that is laid	1Cor 3:11	3762
Now if any *m* build upon this	1Cor 3:12	
If any *m* defile the temple of God	1Cor 3:17	
Let no *m* deceive himself	1Cor 3:18	3367
If any *m* among you seemeth to be	1Cor 3:18	
Therefore let no *m* glory in men	1Cor 3:21	3367
Let a *m* so account of us, as of	1Cor 4:1	444
that a *m* be found faithful	1Cor 4:2	5100
then shall every *m* have praise of	1Cor 4:5	
if any *m* that is called a brother	1Cor 5:11	
there is not a wise *m* among you	1Cor 6:5	
Every sin that a *m* doeth is	1Cor 6:18	444
It is good for a *m* not to touch a	1Cor 7:1	444
let every *m* have his own wife, and	1Cor 7:2	
But every *m* hath his proper gift	1Cor 7:7	
or how knowest thou, O *m*, whether	1Cor 7:16	435
God hath distributed to every *m*	1Cor 7:17	
Is any *m* called being circumcised	1Cor 7:18	
Let every *m* abide in the same	1Cor 7:20	
Brethren, let every *m*, wherein he	1Cor 7:24	
that it is good for a *m* so to be	1Cor 7:26	444
But if any *m* think that he	1Cor 7:36	
If any *m* think that he knoweth	1Cor 8:2	
But if any *m* love God, the same	1Cor 8:3	
is not in every *m* that knowledge	1Cor 8:7	3956
For if any *m* see thee which hast	1Cor 8:10	
Say I these things as a *m*	1Cor 9:8	444
than that any *m* should make my	1Cor 9:15	
every *m* that striveth for the	1Cor 9:25	
you but such as is common to *m*	1Cor 10:13	442
Let no *m* seek his own	1Cor 10:24	3367
but every *m* another's wealth	1Cor 10:24	
But if any *m* say unto you, This	1Cor 10:28	
the head of every *m* is Christ	1Cor 11:3	435
and the head of the woman is the *m*	1Cor 11:3	435
Every *m* praying or prophesying,	1Cor 11:4	435
For a *m* indeed ought not to cover	1Cor 11:7	435
the woman is the glory of the *m*	1Cor 11:7	435
For the *m* is not of the woman	1Cor 11:8	435
but the woman of the *m*	1Cor 11:8	435
Neither was the *m* created for the	1Cor 11:9	435
but the woman for the *m*	1Cor 11:9	435
is the *m* without the woman	1Cor 11:11	435
neither the woman without the *m*	1Cor 11:11	435
For as the woman is of the *m*	1Cor 11:12	435
even so is the *m* also by the	1Cor 11:12	435
if a *m* have long hair, it is a	1Cor 11:14	435
But if any *m* seem to be	1Cor 11:16	
But let a *m* examine himself, and	1Cor 11:28	444
And if any *m* hunger, let him eat	1Cor 11:34	
that no *m* speaking by the Spirit	1Cor 12:3	3762
that no *m* can say that Jesus is	1Cor 12:3	3762
given to every *m* to profit withal	1Cor 12:7	1538
dividing to every *m* severally as	1Cor 12:11	1538
but when I became a *m*, I put away	1Cor 13:11	435
for no *m* understandeth him	1Cor 14:2	3762
If any *m* speak in an unknown	1Cor 14:27	
If any *m* think himself to be a	1Cor 14:37	
But if any *m* be ignorant, let him	1Cor 14:38	
For since by *m* came death	1Cor 15:21	444
by *m* came also the resurrection	1Cor 15:21	444
But every *m* in his own order	1Cor 15:23	
But some *m* will say, How are the	1Cor 15:35	
The first *m* Adam was made a	1Cor 15:45	444
The first *m* is of the earth,	1Cor 15:47	444
the second *m* is the Lord from	1Cor 15:47	444

Let no *m* therefore despise him ... 1Cor 16:11 *5100*
If any *m* love not the Lord Jesus ... 1Cor 16:22
to such a *m* is this punishment ... 2Cor 2:6
but though our outward *m* perish ... 2Cor 4:16 *444*
yet the inward *m* is renewed day ... 2Cor 4:16
know we no *m* after the flesh ... 2Cor 5:16 *3762*
Therefore if any *m* be in Christ ... 2Cor 5:17
we have wronged no *m* ... 2Cor 7:2 *3762*
we have corrupted no *m* ... 2Cor 7:2 *3762*
we have defrauded no *m* ... 2Cor 7:2 *3762*
according to that a *m* hath ... 2Cor 8:12 *5100*
that no *m* should blame us in this ... 2Cor 8:20 *5100*
Every *m* according as he purposeth ... 2Cor 9:7
If any *m* trust to himself that he ... 2Cor 10:7
wanted, I was chargeable to no *m* ... 2Cor 11:9 *3762*
no *m* shall stop me of this ... 2Cor 11:10
again, Let no *m* think me a fool ... 2Cor 11:16 *5100*
if a *m* bring you into bondage ... 2Cor 11:20 *5100*
if a *m* devour you ... 2Cor 11:20 *5100*
if a *m* take of you ... 2Cor 11:20 *5100*
if a *m* exalt himself ... 2Cor 11:20 *5100*
if a *m* smite you on the face ... 2Cor 11:20 *5100*
I knew a *m* in Christ above ... 2Cor 12:2 *444*
And I knew such a *m*, (whether in ... 2Cor 12:3 *444*
it is not lawful for a *m* to utter ... 2Cor 12:4 *444*
lest any *m* should think of me ... 2Cor 12:6
(not of men, neither by *m* ... Gal 1:1 *444*
If any *m* preach any other gospel ... Gal 1:9
was preached of me is not after *m* ... Gal 1:11 *444*
For I neither received it of *m* ... Gal 1:12 *444*
Knowing that a *m* is not justified ... Gal 2:16 *444*
But that no *m* is justified by the ... Gal 3:11 *3762*
The *m* that doeth them shall live ... Gal 3:12 *444*
no *m* disannulleth, or addeth ... Gal 3:15 *3762*
to every *m* that is circumcised ... Gal 5:3 *444*
if a *m* be overtaken in a fault, ... Gal 6:1 *444*
For if a *m* think himself to be ... Gal 6:3 *5100*
But let every *m* prove his own ... Gal 6:4
For every *m* shall bear his own ... Gal 6:5
for whatsoever a *m* soweth ... Gal 6:7 *444*
henceforth let no *m* trouble me ... Gal 6:17 *3367*
of works, lest any *m* should boast ... Eph 2:9
in himself of twain one new *m* ... Eph 2:15 *444*
by his Spirit in the inner *m* ... Eph 3:16 *444*
the Son of God, unto a perfect *m* ... Eph 4:13 *435*
the former conversation the old *m* ... Eph 4:22 *444*
And that ye put on the new *m* ... Eph 4:24 *444*
speak every *m* truth with his ... Eph 4:25
unclean person, nor covetous *m* ... Eph 5:5 *444*
Let no *m* deceive you with vain ... Eph 5:6 *3367*
For no *m* ever yet hated his own ... Eph 5:29 *3762*
cause shall a *m* leave his father ... Eph 5:31 *444*
whatsoever good thing any *m* doeth ... Eph 6:8
Look not every *m* on his own ... Phil 2:4
but every *m* also on the things of ... Phil 2:4
And being found in fashion as a *m* ... Phil 2:8 *444*
For I have no *m* likeminded ... Phil 2:20 *3762*
If any other *m* thinketh that he ... Phil 3:4
Whom we preach, warning every *m* ... Col 1:28 *444*
and teaching every *m* in all wisdom ... Col 1:28 *444*
every *m* perfect in Christ Jesus ... Col 1:28 *444*
lest any *m* should beguile you ... Col 2:4
Beware lest any *m* spoil you ... Col 2:8
Let no *m* therefore judge you in ... Col 2:16 *5100*
Let no *m* beguile you of your ... Col 2:18 *3367*
put off the old *m* with his deeds ... Col 3:9 *444*
And have put on the new *m*, which ... Col 3:10
if any *m* have a quarrel against ... Col 3:13
how ye ought to answer every *m* ... Col 4:6 *1520*
That no *m* should be moved by ... 1Th 3:3 *3367*
That no *m* go beyond and defraud ... 1Th 4:6
that despiseth, despiseth not *m* ... 1Th 4:8 *444*
render evil for evil unto any *m* ... 1Th 5:15
Let no *m* deceive you by any means ... 2Th 2:3 *5100*
that *m* of sin be revealed, the ... 2Th 2:3 *444*
if any *m* obey not our word by ... 2Th 3:14
word by this epistle, note that *m* ... 2Th 3:14
is good, if a *m* use it lawfully ... 1Ti 1:8 *5100*
law is not made for a righteous *m* ... 1Ti 1:9
God and men, the *m* Christ Jesus ... 1Ti 2:5 *444*
nor to usurp authority over the *m* ... 1Ti 2:12 *435*
If a *m* desire the office of a ... 1Ti 3:1 *5100*
(For if a *m* know not how to rule ... 1Ti 3:5 *5100*
Let no *m* despise thy youth ... 1Ti 4:12 *3367*
having been the wife of one *m* ... 1Ti 5:9 *435*
If any *m* or woman that believeth ... 1Ti 5:16
Lay hands suddenly on no *m* ... 1Ti 5:22 *3367*
If any *m* teach otherwise, and ... 1Ti 6:3
O *m* of God, flee these things ... 1Ti 6:11 *444*
which no *m* can approach unto ... 1Ti 6:16
whom no *m* hath seen, nor can see ... 1Ti 6:16 *444*
No *m* that warreth entangleth ... 2Ti 2:4 *3762*
if a *m* also strive for masteries, ... 2Ti 2:5 *5100*
If a *m* therefore purge himself ... 2Ti 2:21 *5100*
That the *m* of God may be perfect, ... 2Ti 3:17 *444*
first answer no *m* stood with me ... 2Ti 4:16 *3762*
Let no *m* despise thee ... Titus 2:15 *3367*
To speak evil of no *m*, to be no ... Titus 3:2 *3367*
God our Saviour toward *m* appeared ... Titus 3:4
A *m* that is an heretick after the ... Titus 3:10 *444*
testified, saying, What is *m* ... Heb 2:6 *444*
or the son of *m*, that thou ... Heb 2:6 *444*
should taste death for every *m* ... Heb 2:9
For this *m* was counted worthy of ... Heb 3:3
every house is builded by some *m* ... Heb 3:4
lest any *m* fall after the same ... Heb 4:11
no *m* taketh this honour unto ... Heb 5:4 *5100*
Now consider how great this *m* was ... Heb 7:4
of which no *m* gave attendance at ... Heb 7:13 *3762*
But this *m*, because he continueth ... Heb 7:24
which the Lord pitched, and not *m* ... Heb 8:2 *444*
m have somewhat also to offer ... Heb 8:3
not teach every *m* his neighbour ... Heb 8:11
every *m* his brother, saying, Know ... Heb 8:11
But this *m*, after he had offered ... Heb 10:12
but if any *m* draw back, my soul ... Heb 10:38
without which no *m* shall see the ... Heb 12:14 *3762*
any *m* fail of the grace of God ... Heb 12:15
not fear what *m* shall do unto me ... Heb 13:6 *444*
For let not that *m* think that he ... Jas 1:7 *444*
A double minded *m* is unstable in ... Jas 1:8 *435*
the rich *m* fade away in his ways ... Jas 1:11
Blessed is the *m* that endureth ... Jas 1:12 *435*
Let no *m* say when he is tempted, ... Jas 1:13 *3367*
evil, neither tempteth he any *m* ... Jas 1:13 *3762*
But every *m* is tempted, when he ... Jas 1:14
let every *m* be swift to hear, ... Jas 1:19 *444*
For the wrath of *m* worketh not ... Jas 1:20 *435*
he is like unto a *m* beholding his ... Jas 1:23 *435*
what manner of *m* he was ... Jas 1:24
this *m* shall be blessed in his ... Jas 1:25
If any *m* among you seem to be ... Jas 1:26
assembly a *m* with a gold ring ... Jas 2:2 *435*
in also a poor *m* in vile raiment ... Jas 2:2
though a *m* say he hath faith, and ... Jas 2:14 *5100*
a *m* may say, Thou hast faith, and ... Jas 2:18 *5100*
But wilt thou know, O vain *m* ... Jas 2:20 *444*
that by works a *m* is justified ... Jas 2:24 *444*
If any *m* offend not in word ... Jas 3:2
the same is a perfect *m* ... Jas 3:2 *435*
But the tongue can no *m* tame ... Jas 3:8 *444*
Who is a wise *m* and endued with ... Jas 3:13
of a righteous *m* availeth much ... Jas 5:16
Elias was a *m* subject to like ... Jas 5:17 *444*
all the glory of *m* as the flower ... 1Pet 1:24 *444*
of *m* for the Lord's sake ... 1Pet 2:13 *442*
if a *m* for conscience toward God ... 1Pet 2:19 *5100*
it be the hidden *m* of the heart ... 1Pet 3:4 *444*
to give an answer to every *m* that ... 1Pet 3:15
As every *m* hath received the gift ... 1Pet 4:10
If any *m* speak, let him speak as ... 1Pet 4:11
if any *m* minister, let him do it ... 1Pet 4:11
Yet if any *m* suffer as a ... 1Pet 4:16
not in old time by the will of *m* ... 2Pet 1:21 *444*
righteous *m* dwelling among them ... 2Pet 2:8
for of whom a *m* is overcome ... 2Pet 2:19 *5100*
And if any *m* sin, we have an ... 1Jn 2:1
If any *m* love the world, the love ... 1Jn 2:15
ye need not that any *m* teach you ... 1Jn 2:27
every *m* that hath this hope in ... 1Jn 3:3
children, let no *m* deceive you ... 1Jn 3:7 *3367*
No *m* hath seen God at any time ... 1Jn 4:12 *3762*
If a *m* say, I love God, and hateth ... 1Jn 4:20
If any *m* see his brother sin a ... 1Jn 5:16
one like unto the Son of *m* ... Rev 1:13 *444*
which no *m* knoweth saving he that ... Rev 2:17 *3762*
he that openeth, and no *m* shutteth ... Rev 3:7 *3762*
and shutteth, and no *m* openeth ... Rev 3:7 *3762*
an open door, and no *m* can shut it ... Rev 3:8 *3762*
hast, that no *m* take thy crown ... Rev 3:11 *3367*
if any *m* hear my voice, and open ... Rev 3:20
the third beast had a face as a *m* ... Rev 4:7 *444*
no *m* in heaven, nor in earth, ... Rev 5:3 *3762*
because no *m* was found worthy to ... Rev 5:4 *3762*
and every bondman, and every free *m*. Rev 6:15
which no *m* could number, of all ... Rev 7:9 *3762*
a scorpion, when he striketh a *m* ... Rev 9:5 *444*
if any *m* will hurt them, fire ... Rev 11:5
if any *m* will hurt them, he must ... Rev 11:5
And she brought forth a *m* child ... Rev 12:5 *730*
which brought forth the *m* child ... Rev 12:13 *730*
If any *m* have an ear, let him ... Rev 13:9
that no *m* might buy or sell, save ... Rev 13:17 *5100*
for it is the number of a *m* ... Rev 13:18 *444*
no *m* could learn that song but ... Rev 14:3 *3762*
If any *m* worship the beast and his ... Rev 14:9
one sat like unto the Son of *m* ... Rev 14:14 *444*
no *m* was able to enter into the ... Rev 15:8 *3762*
became as the blood of a dead *m* ... Rev 16:3
for no *m* buyeth their merchandise ... Rev 18:11 *3762*
a name written, that no *m* knew ... Rev 19:12 *3762*
and they were judged every *m* ... Rev 20:13
according to the measure of a *m* ... Rev 21:17 *444*
to give every *m* according as his ... Rev 22:12
For I testify unto every *m* that ... Rev 22:18 *3956*
If any *m* shall add unto these ... Rev 22:18
if any *m* shall take away from the ... Rev 22:19

MANAEN (*man'-a-en*) *A Christian teacher at Antioch.*
Niger, and Lucius of Cyrene, and *M* ... Acts 13:1 *3127*

MANAHATH (*man'-a-hath*)
1. A son of Shobal.
Alvan, and *M*, and Ebal, Shepho, and ... Gen 36:23 4506
Alian, and *M*, and Ebal, Shephi, and ... 1Chr 1:40 4506
2. A city in Benjamin.
Geba, and they removed them to *M* ... 1Chr 8:6 4506

MANAHETHITES (*man'-a-heth-ites*) *Descendants of Shobal.*
Haroeh, and half of the *M* ... 1Chr 2:52 2679
house of Joab, and half of the *M* ... 1Chr 2:54 2680

MANASSEH (*ma-nas'-seh*) See MANASSEH'S, MANASSES, MANASSITES.
1. A son of Joseph.
the name of the firstborn *M* ... Gen 41:51 4519
in the land of Egypt were born *M* ... Gen 46:20 4519
he took with him his two sons, *M* ... Gen 48:1 4519
two sons, Ephraim and *M* ... Gen 48:5 4519
M in his left hand toward ... Gen 48:13 4519
for *M* was the firstborn ... Gen 48:14 4519
God make thee as Ephraim and as *M* ... Gen 48:20 4519
and he set Ephraim before *M* ... Gen 48:20 4519
also of Machir the son of *M* were ... Gen 50:23 4519
after their families were *M* ... Num 26:28 4519
Of the sons of *M* ... Num 26:29 4519
the son of Machir, the son of *M* ... Num 27:1 4519
families of *M* the son of Joseph ... Num 27:1 4519
the son of *M* went to Gilead ... Num 32:39 4519
Gilead unto Machir the son of *M* ... Num 32:40 4519
And Jair the son of *M* went ... Num 32:41 4519
the son of Machir, the son of *M* ... Num 36:1 4519
Jair the son of *M* took all the ... Deut 3:14 4519
children of Machir the son of *M* ... Josh 13:31 4519
for Machir the firstborn of *M* ... Josh 17:1 4519
of *M* the son of Joseph by their ... Josh 17:2 4519
the son of Machir, the son of *M* ... Josh 17:3 4519
the towns of Jair the son of *M* ... 1Kin 4:13 4519
The sons of *M* ... 1Chr 7:14 4519
the son of Machir, the son of *M* ... 1Chr 7:17 4519
2. Descendants and land of Manasseh 1.
of *M*; Gamaliel the son ... Num 1:10 4519
Of the children of *M*, by their ... Num 1:34 4519
of them, even of the tribe of *M* ... Num 1:35 4519
And by him shall be the tribe of *M* ... Num 2:20 4519
of *M* shall be Gamaliel the son of ... Num 2:20 4519
prince of the children of *M* ... Num 7:54 4519
of *M* was Gamaliel the son of ... Num 10:23 4519
Joseph, namely, of the tribe of *M* ... Num 13:11 4519
These are the families of *M* ... Num 26:34 4519
the tribe of *M* the son of Joseph ... Num 32:33 4519
half the tribe of *M* have received ... Num 34:14 4519
the tribe of the children of *M* ... Num 34:23 4519
the sons of *M* the son of Joseph ... Num 36:12 4519
gave I unto the half tribe of *M* ... Deut 3:13 4519
and to the half tribe of *M* ... Deut 29:8 4520
and they are the thousands of *M* ... Deut 33:17 4519
and the land of Ephraim, and *M* ... Deut 34:2 4519
and to half the tribe of *M* ... Josh 1:12 4519
of Gad, and half the tribe of *M* ... Josh 4:12 4519
Gadites, and the half tribe of *M* ... Josh 12:6 4519
tribes, and the half tribe of *M* ... Josh 13:7 4519
unto the half tribe of *M* ... Josh 13:29 4519
children of *M* by their families ... Josh 13:29 4519
of Joseph were two tribes, *M* ... Josh 14:4 4519
So the children of Joseph, *M* ... Josh 16:4 4519
inheritance of the children of *M* ... Josh 16:9 4519
was also a lot for the tribe of *M* ... Josh 17:1 4519
children of *M* by their families ... Josh 17:2 4519
And there fell ten portions to *M* ... Josh 17:5 4519
Because the daughters of *M* had an ... Josh 17:6 4519
the coast of *M* was from Asher to ... Josh 17:7 4519
Now *M* had the land of Tappuah ... Josh 17:8 4519
of *M* belonged to the children of ... Josh 17:8 4519
Ephraim are among the cities of *M* ... Josh 17:9 4519
the coast of *M* also was on the ... Josh 17:9 4519
M had in Issachar and in Asher ... Josh 17:11 4519
Yet the children of *M* could not ... Josh 17:12 4519
Joseph, even to Ephraim and to *M* ... Josh 17:17 4519
and Reuben, and half the tribe of *M* ... Josh 18:7 4519
in Bashan out of the tribe of *M* ... Josh 20:8 4519
and out of the half tribe of *M* ... Josh 21:5 4519
of the half tribe of *M* in Bashan ... Josh 21:6 4519
And out of the half tribe of *M* ... Josh 21:25 4519
M they gave Golan in Bashan with ... Josh 21:27 4519
Gadites, and the half tribe of *M* ... Josh 22:1 4519
M Moses had given possession in ... Josh 22:7 4519
and the half tribe of *M* returned ... Josh 22:9 4519
the half tribe of *M* built there ... Josh 22:10 4519
the half tribe of *M* have built an ... Josh 22:11 4519
of Gad, and to the half tribe of *M* ... Josh 22:13 4519
of Gad, and to the half tribe of *M* ... Josh 22:15 4519
and the half tribe of *M* answered ... Josh 22:21 4519
of Gad and the children of *M* spake ... Josh 22:30 4519
of Gad, and to the children of *M* ... Josh 22:31 4519
Neither did *M* drive out the ... Judg 1:27 4519
behold, my family is poor in *M* ... Judg 6:15 4519
sent messengers throughout all *M* ... Judg 6:35 4519
and out of Asher, and out of all *M* ... Judg 7:23 4519
and he passed over Gilead, and *M* ... Judg 11:29 4519
Gadites, and half the tribe of *M* ... 1Chr 5:18 4519
half tribe of *M* dwelt in the land ... 1Chr 5:23 4519
Gadites, and the half tribe of *M* ... 1Chr 5:26 4519
out of the half tribe of *M* ... 1Chr 6:61 4519
out of the tribe of *M* in Bashan ... 1Chr 6:62 4519
And out of the half tribe of *M* ... 1Chr 6:70 4519
the family of the half tribe of *M* ... 1Chr 6:71 4519
the borders of the children of *M* ... 1Chr 7:29 4519
of the children of Ephraim, and *M* ... 1Chr 9:3 4519
And there fell some of *M* to David ... 1Chr 12:19 4519
to Ziklag, there fell to him of *M* ... 1Chr 12:20 4519
of the thousands that were of *M* ... 1Chr 12:20 4519
half tribe of *M* eighteen thousand ... 1Chr 12:31 4519
and of the half tribe of *M* ... 1Chr 12:37 4519
Gadites, and the half tribe of *M* ... 1Chr 26:32 4520
of the half tribe of *M*, Joel the ... 1Chr 27:20 4519
Of the half tribe of *M* in Gilead ... 1Chr 27:21 4519
with them out of Ephraim and *M* ... 2Chr 15:9 4519
letters also to Ephraim and *M* ... 2Chr 30:1 4519
of Ephraim and *M* even unto Zebulun. 2Chr 30:10 4519
Nevertheless divers of Asher and *M* ... 2Chr 30:11 4519
even many of Ephraim, and *M* ... 2Chr 30:18 4519
and Benjamin, in Ephraim also and *M*. 2Chr 31:1 4519
And so did he in the cities of *M* ... 2Chr 34:6 4519
had gathered of the hand of *M* ... 2Chr 34:9 4519
Gilead is mine, and *M* is mine ... Ps 60:7 4519
M stir up thy strength, and come ... Ps 80:2 4519
M is mine ... Ps 108:8 4519
M, Ephraim; and Ephraim ... Is 9:21 4519
and Ephraim, *M* ... Is 9:21 4519
the west side, a portion for *M* ... Eze 48:4 4519
And by the border of *M*, from the ... Eze 48:5 4519
3. Grandfather of Jonathan.
the son of Gershom, the son of *M* ... Judg 18:30 4519
4. Son of King Hezekiah.
M his son reigned in his stead ... 2Kin 20:21 4519
M was twelve years old when he ... 2Kin 21:1 4519
M seduced them to do more evil ... 2Kin 21:9 4519
Because *M* king of Judah hath done ... 2Kin 21:11 4519
Moreover *M* shed innocent blood ... 2Kin 21:16 4519
Now the rest of the acts of *M* ... 2Kin 21:17 4519
M slept with his fathers, and was ... 2Kin 21:18 4519

M

of the LORD, as his father *M* did 2Kin 21:20 4519
the altars which *M* had made in 2Kin 23:12 4519
that *M* had provoked him withal 2Kin 23:26 4519
of his sight, for the sins of *M* 2Kin 24:3 4519
son, Hezekiah his son, *M* his son, 1Chr 3:13 4519
M his son reigned in his stead 2Chr 32:33 4519
M was twelve years old when he 2Chr 33:1 4519
So *M* made Judah and the 2Chr 33:9 4519
And the LORD spake to *M*, and to his 2Chr 33:10 4519
which took *M* among the thorns, and 2Chr 33:11 4519
Then *M* knew that the LORD he was 2Chr 33:13 4519
Now the rest of the acts of *M* 2Chr 33:18 4519
So *M* slept with his fathers, and 2Chr 33:20 4519
of the LORD, as did *M* his father 2Chr 33:22 4519
which *M* his father had made 2Chr 33:22 4519
as *M* his father had humbled 2Chr 33:23 4519
because of *M* the son of Hezekiah Jer 15:4 4519
5. Married a foreigner in exile.
Bezaleel, and Binnui, and *M* Ezr 10:30 4519
6. A descendant of Hashum.
Zabad, Eliphelet, Jeremai, *M* Ezr 10:33 4519

MANASSEH'S (*ma-nas'-sez*)
1. Refers to Manasseh 1.
and his left hand upon *M* head Gen 48:14 4519
from Ephraim's head unto *M* head Gen 48:17 4519
the rest of *M* sons had the land Josh 17:6 4519
2. Refers to Manasseh 2.
Ephraim's, and northward it was *M* Josh 17:10 4519

MANASSES (*ma-nas'-seez*) See MANASSEH.
1. Greek form of Manasseh; ancestor of Jesus.
And Ezekias begat *M* Mt 1:10 *3128*
and *M* begat Amon Mt 1:10 *3128*
2. Greek form of Manasseh 2.
Of the tribe of *M* were sealed Rev 7:6 *3128*

MANASSITES (*ma-nas'-sites*) *Same as Manasseh 2.*
and Golan in Bashan, of the *M* Deut 4:43 4520
the Ephraimites, and among the *M* Judg 12:4 4519
and the Reubenites, and the *M* 2Kin 10:33 4520

MANDRAKES
found *m* in the field, and brought Gen 30:14 1736
me, I pray thee, of thy son's *m* Gen 30:14 1736
thou take away my son's *m* also Gen 30:15 1736
thee to night for thy son's *m* Gen 30:15 1736
I have hired thee with my son's *m* Gen 30:16 1736
The *m* give a smell, and at our Song 7:13 1736

MANEH
fifteen shekels, shall be your *m* Eze 45:12 4488

MANGER
clothes, and laid him in a *m* Lk 2:7 *5336*
swaddling clothes, lying in a *m* Lk 2:12 *5336*
Joseph, and the babe lying in a *m* Lk 2:16 *5336*

MANIFEST
of men, that God might *m* them Eccl 3:18 1305
secret, that shall not be made *m* Lk 8:17 *5318*
he should be made *m* to Israel Jn 1:31 *5319*
that his deeds may be made *m* Jn 3:21 *5319*
of God should be made *m* in him Jn 9:3 *5319*
love him, and will *m* myself to him Jn 14:21 *1718*
that thou wilt *m* thyself unto us Jn 14:22 *1718*
is *m* to all them that dwell in Acts 4:16 *5319*
may be known of God is *m* in them Rom 1:19 *5319*
I was made *m* unto them that asked Rom 10:20 *1717*
But now is made *m*, and by the Rom 16:26 *5319*
Every man's work shall be made *m* 1Cor 3:13 *5318*
will make *m* the counsels of the 1Cor 4:5 *5319*
approved may be made *m* among you 1Cor 11:19 *5318*
the secrets of his heart made *m* 1Cor 14:25 *5318*
it is *m* that he is excepted, 1Cor 15:27 *1212*
maketh *m* the savour of his 2Cor 2:14 *5319*
Jesus might be made *m* in our body 2Cor 4:10 *5319*
be made *m* in our mortal flesh 2Cor 4:11 *5319*
but we are made *m* unto God 2Cor 5:11 *5319*
are made *m* in your consciences 2Cor 5:11 *5319*
made *m* among you in all things 2Cor 11:6 *5319*
Now the works of the flesh are *m* Gal 5:19 *5318*
reproved are made *m* by the light Eph 5:13 *5319*
whatsoever doth make *m* is light Eph 5:13 *5319*
in Christ are *m* in all the palace Phil 1:13 *5318*
but now is made *m* to his saints Col 1:26 *5319*
That I may make it *m*, as I ought Col 4:4 *5319*
Which is a *m* token of the 2Th 1:5
God was *m* in the flesh, justified 1Ti 3:16 *5319*
works of some are *m* beforehand 1Ti 5:25 *4271*
But is now made *m* by the 2Ti 1:10 *5319*
folly shall be *m* unto all men 2Ti 3:9 *1552*
that is not *m* in his sight Heb 4:13 *852*
holiest of all was not yet made *m* Heb 9:8 *5319*
but was *m* in these last times for 1Pet 1:20 *5319*
that they might be made *m* that 1Jn 2:19 *5319*
In this the children of God are *m* 1Jn 3:10 *5318*
for thy judgments are made *m* Rev 15:4 *5319*

MANIFESTATION
for the *m* of the sons of God Rom 8:19 *602*
But the *m* of the Spirit is given 1Cor 12:7 *5321*
but by *m* of the truth commending 2Cor 4:2 *5321*

MANIFESTED
nothing hid, which shall not be *m* Mk 4:22 *5319*
of Galilee, and *m* forth his glory Jn 2:11 *5319*
I have *m* thy name unto the men Jn 17:6 *5319*
of God without the law is *m* Rom 3:21 *5319*
But hath in due times *m* his word Titus 1:3 *5319*
(For the life was *m*, and we have 1Jn 1:2 *5319*
with the Father, and was *m* unto us 1Jn 1:2 *5319*
ye know that he was *m* to take 1Jn 3:5 *5319*
this purpose the Son of God was *m* 1Jn 3:8 *5319*
In this was *m* the love of God 1Jn 4:9 *5319*

MANIFESTLY
Forasmuch as ye are *m* declared to 2Cor 3:3 *5319*

MANIFOLD
Yet thou in thy *m* mercies Neh 9:19 7227
according to thy *m* mercies thou Neh 9:27 7227
O LORD, how *m* are thy works Ps 104:24 7231
For I know your *m* transgressions Amos 5:12 7227
Who shall not receive *m* more in Lk 18:30 *4179*
by the church the *m* wisdom of God Eph 3:10 *4182*
heaviness through *m* temptations 1Pet 1:6 *4164*
stewards of the *m* grace of God 1Pet 4:10 *4164*

MANKIND
Thou shalt not lie with *m* Lev 18:22 2145
If a man also lie with *m*, as he Lev 20:13 2145
thing, and the breath of all *m* Job 12:10
nor abusers of themselves with *m* 1Cor 6:9 *733*
that defile themselves with *m* 1Ti 1:10 *733*
is tamed, and hath been tamed of *m* Jas 3:7

MANNA
they said one to another, It is *m* Ex 16:15 4478
Israel called the name thereof *M* Ex 16:31 4478
and put an omer full of *m* therein Ex 16:33 4478
of Israel did eat *m* forty years Ex 16:35 4478
they did eat *m*, until they came Ex 16:35 4478
is nothing at all, beside this *m* Num 11:6 4478
the *m* was as coriander seed, and Num 11:7 4478
in the night, the *m* fell upon it Num 11:9 4478
to hunger, and fed thee with *m* Deut 8:3 4478
fed thee in the wilderness with *m* Deut 8:16 4478
the *m* ceased on the morrow after Josh 5:12 4478
the children of Israel *m* any more Josh 5:12 4478
not thy *m* from their mouth Neh 9:20 4478
had rained down *m* upon them to Ps 78:24 4478
fathers did eat *m* in the desert Jn 6:31 *3131*
did eat *m* in the wilderness Jn 6:49 *3131*
not as your fathers did eat *m* Jn 6:58 *3131*
was the golden pot that had *m* Heb 9:4 *3131*
I give to eat of the hidden *m* Rev 2:17 *3131*

MANNER
with Sarah after the *m* of women Gen 18:11 734
far from thee to do after this *m* Gen 18:25 1697
us after the *m* of all the earth Gen 19:31 1870
womb, and two *m* of people shall be Gen 25:23
On this *m* shall ye speak unto Gen 32:19 1697
After this *m* did thy servant to Gen 39:19 1697
after the former *m* when thou wast Gen 40:13 4941
basket there was of all *m* of Gen 40:17
his father he sent after this *m* Gen 45:23
in all *m* of service in the field Ex 1:14
they also did in like *m* with Ex 7:11 3651
no *m* of work shall be done in Ex 12:16
with her after the *m* of daughters Ex 21:9 4941
For all *m* of trespass, whether it Ex 22:9 1697
or for any *m* of lost thing, which Ex 22:9
In like *m* thou shalt deal with Ex 23:11 3651
and in all *m* of workmanship, Ex 31:3
to work in all *m* of workmanship Ex 31:5
to bring for all *m* of work Ex 35:29
and in all *m* of workmanship Ex 35:31
to make any *m* of cunning work Ex 35:33
of heart, to work all *m* of work Ex 35:35 3605
to know how to work all *m* of work Ex 36:1
offering, according to the *m* Lev 5:10 4941
saying, Ye shall eat no *m* of fat Lev 7:23
ye shall eat no *m* of blood Lev 7:26
it be that eateth any *m* of blood Lev 7:27
and offered it according to the *m* Lev 9:16 4941
among all *m* of beasts that go on Lev 11:27
ye defile yourselves with any *m* Lev 11:44
for all *m* of plague of leprosy Lev 14:54
you, that eateth any *m* of blood Lev 17:10
eat the blood of no *m* of flesh Lev 17:14
planted all *m* of trees for food Lev 19:23
or by any *m* of living thing that Lev 20:25
Ye shall do no *m* of work Lev 23:31
Ye shall have one *m* of law Lev 24:22 4941
neither she be taken with the *m* Num 5:13
and according to the *m* thereof Num 9:14 4941
do these things after this *m* Num 15:13 3541
one *m* shall be for you, and for Num 15:16 4941
offering, according to the *m* Num 15:24 4941
ye shall do no *m* of servile work Num 28:18
After this *m* ye shall offer daily Num 28:24
offerings, according unto their *m* Num 29:6 4941
to their number, after the *m* Num 29:18 4941
to their number, after the *m* Num 29:21 4941
to their number, after the *m* Num 29:24 4941
to their number, after the *m* Num 29:27 4941
to their number, after the *m* Num 29:30 4941
to their number, after the *m* Num 29:33 4941
to their number, after the *m* Num 29:37 4941
of all *m* of beasts, and give them Num 31:30
for ye saw no *m* of similitude on Deut 4:15
this is the *m* of the release Deut 15:2 1697
In like *m* shalt thou do with his Deut 22:3 3651
he that lieth with any *m* of beast Deut 27:21
city after the same *m* seven times Josh 6:15 4941
What *m* of men were they whom ye Judg 8:18
in like *m* they sent unto the king Judg 11:17
after the *m* of the Zidonians, Judg 18:7 4941
Now this was the *m* in former time Ruth 4:7
shew them the *m* of the king that 1Sa 8:9 4941
This will be the *m* of the king 1Sa 8:11 4941
the people the *m* of the kingdom 1Sa 10:25 4941
people answered him after this *m* 1Sa 17:27 1697
and spake after the same *m* 1Sa 17:30 1697
him again after the former *m* 1Sa 17:30 1697
saying, On this *m* spake David 1Sa 18:24 1697
before Samuel in like *m*, and lay 1Sa 19:24 1571
and the bread is in a *m* common 1Sa 21:5 1870
so will be his *m* all the while he 1Sa 27:11 3541
played before the LORD on all *m* 2Sa 6:5
And is this the *m* of man, O Lord 2Sa 7:19 8452
king, and speak on this *m* unto him 2Sa 14:3 1697
on this *m* did Absalom to all 2Sa 15:6 1697
hath spoken after this *m* 2Sa 17:6 1697
work of the bases was on this *m* 1Kin 7:28
After this *m* he made the ten 1Kin 7:37
after their *m* with knives 1Kin 18:28 4941
And one said on this *m* 1Kin 22:20 3541
and another said on that *m* 1Kin 22:20 3541
What *m* of man was he which came 2Kin 1:7 4941
stood by a pillar, as the *m* was 2Kin 11:14 4941
know not the *m* of the God of the 2Kin 17:26 4941
not the *m* of the God of the land 2Kin 17:26 4941
them the *m* of the God of the land 2Kin 17:27 4941
after the *m* of the nations whom 2Kin 17:33 4941
but they did after their former *m* 2Kin 17:40 4941
m of service of the tabernacle of 1Chr 6:48
with all *m* of instruments of war 1Chr 12:37
with him all *m* of vessels of gold 1Chr 18:10
all *m* of cunning men for every 1Chr 22:15
cunning men for every *m* of work 1Chr 22:15
for all *m* of measure and size 1Chr 23:29
of the LORD, according to their *m* 1Chr 24:19 4941
instruments of all *m* of service 1Chr 28:14
shall be with thee for all *m* of 1Chr 28:21
skilful man, for any *m* of service 1Chr 28:21
all *m* of precious stones, and 1Chr 29:2
for all *m* of work to be made by 1Chr 29:5
also to grave any *m* of graving 2Chr 2:14
after the *m* before the oracle 2Chr 4:20 4941
m of the nations of other lands 2Chr 13:9
And one spake saying after this *m* 2Chr 18:19 3541
and another saying after that *m* 2Chr 18:19
in their place after their *m* 2Chr 30:16 4941
you, nor persuade you on this *m* 2Chr 32:15
for all *m* of pleasant jewels 2Chr 32:27
and stalls for all *m* of beasts 2Chr 32:28
the work in any *m* of service 2Chr 34:13
said we unto them after this *m* Ezr 5:4
I answered them after the same *m* Neh 6:4 1697
m the fifth time with an open Neh 6:5 1697
assembly, according unto the *m* Neh 8:18 4941
and the fruit of all *m* of trees Neh 10:37
all *m* of burdens, which they Neh 13:15
all *m* of ware, and sold on the Neh 13:16
(for so was the king's *m* toward Est 1:13 1697
according to the *m* of the women Est 2:12 1881
soul abhorreth all *m* of meat Ps 107:18
be full, affording all *m* of store Ps 144:13 2177
are all *m* of pleasant fruits Song 7:13
the lambs feed after their *m* Is 5:17 1699
thee, after the *m* of Egypt Is 10:24 1870
lift it up after the *m* of Egypt Is 10:26 1870
dwell therein shall die in like *m* Is 51:6 3654
After this *m* will I mar the pride Jer 13:9 3541
hath been thy *m* from thy youth Jer 22:21 1870
shall remain after the *m* thereof Jer 30:18 4941
after the *m* of your fathers Eze 20:30 1870
after the *m* of the Babylonians of Eze 23:15 1823
them after the *m* of adulteresses Eze 23:45 4941
after the *m* of women that shed Eze 23:45 4941
no *m* of hurt was found upon him, Dan 6:23
pestilence after the *m* of Egypt Amos 4:10 1870
The *m* of Beer-sheba liveth Amos 8:14 1870
and healing all *m* of sickness Mt 4:23
all *m* of disease among the people Mt 4:23
shall say all *m* of evil against Mt 5:11
After this *m* therefore pray ye Mt 6:9 *3779*
What *m* of man is this, that even Mt 8:27 *4217*
out, and to heal all *m* of sickness Mt 10:1
of sickness and all *m* of disease Mt 10:1
All *m* of sin and blasphemy shall Mt 12:31
What *m* of man is this, that even Mk 4:41 *686*
see what *m* of stones and what Mk 13:1 *4217*
So ye in like *m*, when ye shall Mk 13:29 *3779*
cast in her mind what *m* of Lk 1:29 *4217*
What *m* of child shall this be Lk 1:66 *686*
for in the like *m* did their Lk 6:23
what *m* of woman this is that Lk 7:39 *4217*
to another, What *m* of man is this Lk 8:25 *686*
Ye know not what *m* of spirit ye Lk 9:55 *3634*
all *m* of herbs, and pass over Lk 11:42
and in like *m* the seven also Lk 20:31 *5615*
What *m* of communications are Lk 24:17
after the *m* of the purifying of Jn 2:6
What *m* of saying is this that he Jn 7:36
as the *m* of the Jews is to bury Jn 19:40 *1485*
shall so come in like *m* as ye Acts 1:11 *5158*
Wherein were all *m* of fourfooted Acts 10:12 *1485*
circumcised after the *m* of Moses Acts 15:1 *1485*
letters by them after this *m* Acts 15:23 *3592*
And Paul, as his *m* was, went in Acts 17:2 *1486*
after what *m* I have been with you Acts 20:18 *4458*
m of the law of the fathers Acts 22:3 *195*
And he wrote a letter after this *m* Acts 23:25 *5179*
It is not the *m* of the Romans to Acts 25:16 *1485*
I doubted of such *m* of questions Acts 25:20 *4012*
My *m* of life from my youth, which Acts 26:4 *981*
I speak after the *m* of men Rom 6:19 *442*
in me all *m* of concupiscence Rom 7:8
gift of God, one after this *m* 1Cor 7:7 *3779*
After the same *m* also he took the 1Cor 11:25 *5615*
If after the *m* of men I have 1Cor 15:32
were made sorry after a godly *m* 2Cor 7:9
livest after the *m* of Gentiles Gal 2:14 *1483*
I speak after the *m* of men Gal 3:15
as ye know what *m* of men we were 1Th 1:5 *3634*
m of entering in we had unto you 1Th 1:9 *3697*
In like *m* also, that women adorn 1Ti 2:9
m of life, purpose, faith, 2Ti 3:10 *72*
together, as the *m* of some is Heb 10:25 *1485*
forgetteth what *m* of man he was Jas 1:24 *3697*
or what *m* of time the Spirit of 1Pet 1:11 *4169*
ye holy in all *m* of conversation 1Pet 1:15

For after this *m* in the old time ... 1Pet 3:5 *3779*
what *m* of persons ought ye to be ... 2Pet 3:11 *4217*
what *m* of love the Father hath ... 1Jn 3:1 *4217*
the cities about them in like *m* ... Jude 7 *5158*
them, he must in this *m* be killed ... Rev 11:5 *3779*
all *m* vessels of ivory ... Rev 18:12
all *m* vessels of most precious ... Rev 18:12
with all *m* of precious stones ... Rev 21:19
which bare twelve *m* of fruits ... Rev 22:2

MANNERS
not walk in the *m* of the nation ... Lev 20:23 2708
day they do after the former *m* ... 2Kin 17:34 4941
but have done after the *m* of the ... Eze 11:12 4941
he their *m* in the wilderness ... Acts 13:18 *5159*
communications corrupt good *m* ... 1Cor 15:33 *2239*
in divers *m* spake in time past ... Heb 1:1 *4187*

MANOAH (*ma-no'-ah*) *Father of Samson.*
of the Danites, whose name was *M* ... Judg 13:2 4495
Then *M* intreated the LORD, and ... Judg 13:8 4495
God hearkened to the voice of *M* ... Judg 13:9 4495
but *M* her husband was not with ... Judg 13:9 4495
M arose, and went after his wife, ... Judg 13:11 4495
M said, Now let thy words come to ... Judg 13:12 4495
the angel of the LORD said unto *M* ... Judg 13:13 4495
M said unto the angel of the LORD ... Judg 13:15 4495
the angel of the LORD said unto *M* ... Judg 13:16 4495
For *M* knew not that he was an ... Judg 13:16 4495
M said unto the angel of the LORD ... Judg 13:17 4495
So *M* took a kid with a meat ... Judg 13:19 4495
and *M* and his wife looked on ... Judg 13:19 4495
And *M* and his wife looked on it, and ... Judg 13:20 4495
the LORD did no more appear to *M* ... Judg 13:21 4495
Then *M* knew that he was an angel ... Judg 13:21 4495
M said unto his wife, We shall ... Judg 13:22 4495
the buryingplace of *M* his father ... Judg 16:31 4495

MAN'S
the ground any more for *m* sake ... Gen 8:21 120
for the imagination of *m* heart is ... Gen 8:21 120
at the hand of every *m* brother ... Gen 9:5 120
Whoso sheddeth *m* blood, by man ... Gen 9:6 120
man, and every *m* hand against him ... Gen 16:12 376
for she is a *m* wife ... Gen 20:3 1167
We are all one *m* sons ... Gen 42:11 376
to restore every *m* money into his ... Gen 42:25 376
every *m* bundle of money was in ... Gen 42:35 376
every *m* money was in the mouth of ... Gen 43:21 376
put every *m* money in his sack's ... Gen 44:1 376
for we may not see the *m* face ... Gen 44:26 376
unto him, Who hath made *m* mouth ... Ex 4:11 120
But every *m* servant that is ... Ex 12:44 376
if one *m* ox hurt another's, that ... Ex 21:35 376
and shall feed in another *m* field ... Ex 22:5 312
it be stolen out of the *m* house ... Ex 22:7 376
Upon *m* flesh shall it not be ... Ex 30:32 120
offereth any *m* burnt offering ... Lev 7:8 376
if any *m* seed of copulation go ... Lev 15:16 376
adultery with another *m* wife ... Lev 20:10 376
every *m* hallowed things shall be ... Num 5:10 376
If any *m* wife go aside, and commit ... Num 5:12 376
write thou every *m* name upon his ... Num 17:2 376
come to pass, that the *m* rod ... Num 17:5 376
every *m* inheritance shall be in ... Num 33:54
is *m* life) to employ them in the ... Deut 20:19 120
she may go and be another *m* wife ... Deut 24:2 376
for he taketh a *m* life to pledge ... Deut 24:6
he put a trumpet in every *m* hand ... Judg 7:16
the LORD set every *m* sword ... Judg 7:22 376
of the *m* house where her lord was ... Judg 19:26 376
The *m* name with whom I wrought to ... Ruth 2:19 376
thou taken ought of any *m* hand ... 1Sa 12:4 376
every *m* sword was against his ... 1Sa 14:20 376
Let no *m* heart fail because of ... 1Sa 17:32 120
but took the poor *m* lamb, and ... 2Sa 12:4 376
came to a *m* house in Bahurim, ... 2Sa 17:18 376
which Amasa was a *m* son, whose ... 2Sa 17:25 376
out of the sea, like a *m* hand ... 1Kin 18:44 376
m heart to bring into the house ... 2Kin 12:4 376
which were on a *m* left hand at ... 2Kin 23:8 376
every great *m* house burnt he with ... 2Kin 25:9
do according to every *m* pleasure ... Est 1:8 376
are thy years as *m* days, ... Job 10:5 1397
I pray you, accept any *m* person ... Job 32:21 376
bread which strengtheneth *m* heart ... Ps 104:15 582
The rich *m* wealth is his strong ... Prov 10:15
the recompence of a *m* hands shall ... Prov 12:14 120
The ransom of a *m* life are his ... Prov 13:8 376
When a *m* ways please the LORD, he ... Prov 16:7 376
A *m* heart deviseth his way ... Prov 16:9 120
The words of a *m* mouth are as ... Prov 18:4 376
The rich *m* wealth is his strong ... Prov 18:11
A *m* gift maketh room for him, and ... Prov 18:16 120
A *m* belly shall be satisfied with ... Prov 18:20 376
are many devices in a *m* heart ... Prov 19:21 376
M goings are of the LORD ... Prov 20:24 1397
of a *m* friend by hearty counsel ... Prov 27:9
A *m* pride shall bring him low ... Prov 29:23 120
but every *m* judgment cometh from ... Prov 29:26 376
The wise *m* eyes are in his head ... Eccl 2:14
a *m* wisdom maketh his face to ... Eccl 8:1 120
a wise *m* heart discerneth both ... Eccl 8:5
the poor *m* wisdom is despised ... Eccl 9:16
A wise *m* heart is at his right ... Eccl 10:2
of a wise *m* mouth are gracious ... Eccl 10:12
in it with a *m* pen concerning ... Is 8:1 582
and every *m* heart shall melt ... Is 13:7 582
go from him, and become another *m* ... Jer 3:1 376
for every *m* word shall be his ... Jer 23:36 376
given thee cow's dung for *m* dung ... Eze 4:15 120
of a *m* hand under their wings ... Eze 10:8 120
every *m* sword shall be against ... Eze 38:21 376
the land, when any seeth a *m* bone ... Eze 39:15 120
in the *m* hand a measuring reed of ... Eze 40:5
Let his heart be changed from *m* ... Dan 4:16 606
came forth fingers of a *m* hand ... Dan 5:5 606
a *m* heart was given to it ... Dan 7:4 606
I heard a *m* voice between the ... Dan 8:16 120
a *m* uncle shall take him up, and ... Amos 6:10
let us not perish for this *m* life ... Jonah 1:14 376
a *m* enemies are the men of his ... Mic 7:6 376
a *m* foes shall be they of his own ... Mt 10:36 *444*
receive a righteous *m* reward ... Mt 10:41
one enter into a strong *m* house ... Mt 12:29
can enter into a strong *m* house ... Mk 3:27
If a *m* brother die, and leave his ... Mk 12:19 *5100*
as evil, for the Son of *m* sake ... Lk 6:22 *444*
for a *m* life consisteth not in ... Lk 12:15 *5100*
in that which is another *m* ... Lk 16:12 *245*
which fell from the rich *m* table ... Lk 16:21
If any *m* brother die, having a ... Lk 20:28 *5100*
thou also one of this *m* disciples ... Jn 18:17 *444*
to bring this *m* blood upon us ... Acts 5:28 *444*
their clothes at a young *m* feet ... Acts 7:58 *3494*
and we entered into the *m* house ... Acts 11:12 *435*
Of this *m* seed hath God according ... Acts 13:23
stone, graven by art and *m* device ... Acts 17:29 *444*
and entered into a certain *m* house ... Acts 18:7
I have coveted no *m* silver ... Acts 20:33 *3762*
no loss of any *m* life among you ... Acts 27:22
For if by one *m* offence death ... Rom 5:17
For as by one *m* disobedience many ... Rom 5:19 *444*
that judgest another *m* servant ... Rom 14:4 *245*
build upon another *m* foundation ... Rom 15:20 *245*
with enticing words of *m* wisdom ... 1Cor 2:4 *442*
the words which *m* wisdom teacheth ... 1Cor 2:13 *442*
Every *m* work shall be made ... 1Cor 3:13
every *m* work of what sort it is ... 1Cor 3:13
If any *m* work abide which he hath ... 1Cor 3:14
If any *m* work shall be burned, he ... 1Cor 3:15
judged of you, or of *m* judgment ... 1Cor 4:3 *442*
judged of another *m* conscience ... 1Cor 10:29
commending ourselves to every *m* ... 2Cor 4:2 *444*
not to boast in another *m* line of ... 2Cor 10:16 *245*
God accepteth no *m* person ... Gal 2:6 *444*
Though it be but a *m* covenant ... Gal 3:15 *444*
did we eat any *m* bread for nought ... 2Th 3:8
heart, this *m* religion is vain ... Jas 1:26
judgeth according to every *m* work ... 1Pet 1:17
the dumb ass speaking with *m* ... 2Pet 2:16 *444*

MANSERVANT
thy son, nor thy daughter, thy *m* ... Ex 20:10 5650
thy neighbour's wife, nor his *m* ... Ex 20:17 5650
shall push a *m* or a maidservant ... Ex 21:32 5650
son, nor thy daughter, nor thy *m* ... Deut 5:14 5650
that thy *m* and thy maidservant may ... Deut 5:14 5650
house, his field, or his *m* ... Deut 5:21 5650
son, and thy daughter, and thy *m* ... Deut 12:18 5650
son, and thy daughter, and thy *m* ... Deut 16:11 5650
son, and thy daughter, and thy *m* ... Deut 16:14 5650
of my *m* or of my maidservant ... Job 31:13 5650
That every man should let his *m* ... Jer 34:9 5650
that every one should let his *m* ... Jer 34:10 5650

MANSERVANT'S
And if he smite out his *m* tooth ... Ex 21:27 5650

MANSERVANTS
Beside their *m* and their ... Neh 7:67 5650

MANSIONS
In my Father's house are many *m* ... Jn 14:2 *3438*

MANSLAYER
which ye shall appoint for the *m* ... Num 35:6 7523
that the *m* die not, until he ... Num 35:12 7523

MANSLAYERS
and murderers of mothers, for *m* ... 1Ti 1:9 *409*

MANTLE
tent, she covered him with a *m* ... Judg 4:18 8063
laid hold upon the skirt of his *m* ... 1Sa 15:27 4598
and he is covered with a *m* ... 1Sa 28:14 4598
that he wrapped his face in his *m* ... 1Kin 19:13 155
by him, and cast his *m* upon him ... 1Kin 19:19 155
And Elijah took his *m*, and wrapped ... 2Kin 2:8 155
He took up also the *m* of Elijah ... 2Kin 2:13 155
he took the *m* of Elijah that fell ... 2Kin 2:14 155
thing, I rent my garment and my *m* ... Ezr 9:3 4598
rent my garment and my *m* ... Ezr 9:5 4598
Then Job arose, and rent his *m* ... Job 1:20 4598
and they rent every one his *m* ... Job 2:12 4598
their own confusion, as with a *m* ... Ps 109:29 4598

MANTLES
suits of apparel, and the *m* ... Is 3:22 4595

MANY
shalt be a father of *m* nations ... Gen 17:4 1995
for a father of *m* nations have I ... Gen 17:5 1995
in the Philistines' land *m* days ... Gen 21:34 7227
he made him a coat of *m* colours ... Gen 37:3
his coat of *m* colours that was on ... Gen 37:23
they sent the coat of *m* colours ... Gen 37:32
and mourned for his son *m* days ... Gen 37:34 7227
the people of the land now are *m* ... Ex 5:5 7227
LORD to gaze, and *m* of them perish ... Ex 19:21 7227
decline after *m* to wrest judgment ... Ex 23:2 7227
as *m* as were willing hearted, and ... Ex 35:22
have an issue of her blood *m* days ... Lev 15:25 7227
If there be yet *m* years behind ... Lev 25:51 7227
long upon the tabernacle *m* days ... Num 9:19 7227
unto the *m* thousands of Israel ... Num 10:36 7233
they be strong or weak, few or *m* ... Num 13:18 7227
the people, because they were *m* ... Num 22:3 7227
and his seed shall be in *m* waters ... Num 24:7 7227
To *m* thou shalt give the more ... Num 26:54 7227
thereof be divided between *m* ... Num 26:56 7227
from them that have *m* ... Num 35:8 7227
ye shall give *m*; but from ... Num 35:8 7235
times so *m* more as ye are ... Deut 1:11
So ye abode in Kadesh *m* days ... Deut 1:46 7227
and we compassed mount Seir *m* days ... Deut 2:1 7227
times past, a people great, and *m* ... Deut 2:10 7227
A people great, and *m*, and tall, as ... Deut 2:21 7227
beside unwalled towns a great *m* ... Deut 3:5 7235
hath cast out *m* nations before ... Deut 7:1 7227
and thou shalt lend unto *m* nations ... Deut 15:6 7227
thou shalt reign over *m* nations ... Deut 15:6 7227
him above these with *m* stripes ... Deut 25:3 7227
and thou shalt lend unto *m* nations ... Deut 28:12 7227
m evils and troubles shall befall ... Deut 31:17 7227
when *m* evils and troubles are ... Deut 31:21 7227
the years of *m* generations ... Deut 32:7
with horses and chariots very *m* ... Josh 11:4 7227
these *m* days unto this day ... Josh 22:3 7227
even as *m* of Israel as had not ... Judg 3:1
that are with thee are too *m* for ... Judg 7:2 7227
Gideon, The people are yet too *m* ... Judg 7:4 7227
for he had *m* wives ... Judg 8:30 7227
m were overthrown and wounded, ... Judg 9:40 7227
our country, which slew *m* of us ... Judg 16:24 7235
she that hath *m* children is waxed ... 1Sa 2:5 7227
m of the people with a great ... 1Sa 6:19
the LORD to save by *m* or by few ... 1Sa 14:6 7227
there be *m* servants now a days ... 1Sa 25:10 7231
m of the people also are fallen ... 2Sa 1:4 7235
that as *m* as came to the place ... 2Sa 2:23
rich man had exceeding *m* flocks ... 2Sa 12:2 7235
he drew me out of *m* waters ... 2Sa 22:17 7227
of Kabzeel, who had done *m* acts ... 2Sa 23:20 7227
people, how *m* soever they be, an ... 2Sa 24:3
Shimei dwelt in Jerusalem *m* days ... 1Kin 2:38 7227
Judah and Israel were *m*, as the ... 1Kin 4:20 7227
because they were exceeding *m* ... 1Kin 7:47 7230
Solomon loved *m* strange women ... 1Kin 11:1 7227
he, and her house, did eat *m* days ... 1Kin 17:15
And it came to pass after *m* days ... 1Kin 18:1 7227
for ye are *m* ... 1Kin 18:25 7227
How *m* times shall I adjure thee ... 1Kin 22:16
and her witchcrafts are so *m* ... 2Kin 9:22 7227
his brethren had not *m* children ... 1Chr 4:27 7227
For there fell down *m* slain ... 1Chr 5:22 7227
for they had *m* wives and sons ... 1Chr 7:4 7235
their father mourned *m* days ... 1Chr 7:22 7227
had *m* sons, and sons' sons, an ... 1Chr 8:40 7235
of Kabzeel, who had done *m* acts ... 1Chr 11:22 7227
times so *m* more as they be ... 1Chr 21:3
Jeush and Beriah had not *m* sons ... 1Chr 23:11 7235
the sons of Rehabiah were very *m* ... 1Chr 23:17 7235
for the LORD hath given me *m* sons ... 1Chr 28:5 7227
And he desired *m* wives ... 2Chr 11:23 1995
with thee to help, whether with *m* ... 2Chr 14:11 7227
a huge host, with very *m* chariots ... 2Chr 16:8 7235
How *m* times shall I adjure thee ... 2Chr 18:15
in the desert, and digged *m* wells ... 2Chr 26:10 7227
as *m* as were of a free heart ... 2Chr 29:31
For there were *m* in the ... 2Chr 30:17 7227
even *m* of Ephraim, and Manasseh, ... 2Chr 30:18 7227
m brought gifts unto the LORD to ... 2Chr 32:23 7227
But *m* of the priests and Levites ... Ezr 3:12 7227
and *m* shouted aloud for joy ... Ezr 3:12 7227
was builded these *m* years ago ... Ezr 5:11 7690
But the people are *m*, and it is a ... Ezr 10:13 7227
for we are *m* that have ... Ezr 10:13 7235
our sons, and our daughters, are *m* ... Neh 5:2 7227
Judah sent *m* letters unto Tobiah ... Neh 6:17 7235
For there were *m* in Judah sworn ... Neh 6:18 7227
man, and feared God above *m* ... Neh 7:2 7227
m times didst thou deliver them ... Neh 9:28 7227
Yet *m* years didst thou forbear ... Neh 9:30 7227
yet among *m* nations was there no ... Neh 13:26 7227
of his excellent majesty *m* days ... Est 1:4 7227
when *m* maidens were gathered ... Est 2:8 7227
m lay in sackcloth and ashes ... Est 4:3 7227
m of the people of the land ... Est 8:17 7227
Behold, thou hast instructed *m* ... Job 4:3 7227
m shall make suit unto thee ... Job 11:19 7227
How *m* are mine iniquities and sins ... Job 13:23
I have heard *m* such things ... Job 16:2 7227
m such things are with him ... Job 23:14 7227
Will he make *m* supplications unto ... Job 41:3 7235
m are they that rise up against ... Ps 3:1 7227
M there be which say of my soul, ... Ps 3:2 7227
There be *m* that say, Who will ... Ps 4:6 7227
me, he drew me out of *m* waters ... Ps 18:16 7227
M bulls have compassed me ... Ps 22:12 7227
for they are *m* ... Ps 25:19 7231
the LORD is upon *m* waters ... Ps 29:3 7227
For I have heard the slander of *m* ... Ps 31:13 7227
M sorrows shall be to the wicked ... Ps 32:10 7227
desireth life, and loveth *m* days ... Ps 34:12
M are the afflictions of the ... Ps 34:19 7227
than the riches of *m* wicked ... Ps 37:16 7227
m shall see it, and fear, and shall ... Ps 40:3 7227
M, O LORD my God, are thy ... Ps 40:5 7227
for there were *m* with me ... Ps 55:18 7227
for they be *m* that fight against ... Ps 56:2 7227
and his years as *m* generations ... Ps 61:6
I am as a wonder unto *m* ... Ps 71:7 7227
m a time turned he his anger away ... Ps 78:38 7235
than the noise of *m* waters ... Ps 93:4 7227
M times did he deliver them ... Ps 106:43 7227
wound the heads over *m* countries ... Ps 110:6 7227
How *m* are the days of thy servant ... Ps 119:84
M are my persecutors and mine ... Ps 119:157 7227
M a time have they afflicted me ... Ps 129:1 7227
M a time have they afflicted me ... Ps 129:2 7227
the years of thy life shall be *m* ... Prov 4:10 7235
though thou givest *m* gifts ... Prov 6:35 7235
For she hath cast down *m* wounded ... Prov 7:26 7227
m strong men have been slain by ... Prov 7:26 3605
The lips of the righteous feed *m* ... Prov 10:21 7227
but the rich hath *m* friends ... Prov 14:20 7227

M

Wealth maketh *m* friends	Prov 19:4	7227
M will intreat the favour of the	Prov 19:6	7227
There are *m* devices in a man's	Prov 19:21	7227
a land *m* are the princes thereof	Prov 28:2	7227
his eyes shall have *m* a curse	Prov 28:27	7227
M seek the ruler's favour	Prov 29:26	7227
M daughters have done virtuously,	Prov 31:29	7227
m words there are also divers	Eccl 5:7	7230
live *m* years, so that the days of	Eccl 6:3	7227
that the days of his years be *m*	Eccl 6:3	7227
Seeing there be *m* things that	Eccl 6:11	7235
they have sought out *m* inventions	Eccl 7:29	7227
thou shalt find it after *m* days	Eccl 11:1	7230
But if a man live *m* years	Eccl 11:8	7235
for they shall be *m*	Eccl 11:8	7235
out, and set in order *m* proverbs	Eccl 12:9	7235
of making *m* books there is no end	Eccl 12:12	7235
M waters cannot quench love,	Song 8:7	7227
yea, when ye make *m* prayers	Is 1:15	7235
m people shall go and say, Come ye	Is 2:3	7227
nations, and shall rebuke *m* people	Is 2:4	7227
Of a truth *m* houses shall be	Is 5:9	7227
waters of the river, strong and *m*	Is 8:7	7227
m among them shall stumble, and	Is 8:15	7227
Woe to the multitude of *m* people	Is 17:12	7227
rush like the rushing of *m* waters	Is 17:13	7227
city of David, that they are *m*	Is 22:9	7231
sing *m* songs, that thou mayest be	Is 23:16	7235
after *m* days shall they be	Is 24:22	7230
in chariots, because they are *m*	Is 31:1	7227
M days and years shall ye be	Is 32:10	
Seeing *m* things, but thou	Is 42:20	7227
As *m* were astonied at thee	Is 52:14	7227
So shall he sprinkle *m* nations	Is 52:15	7227
my righteous servant justify *m*	Is 53:11	7227
and he bare the sin of *m*, and made	Is 53:12	7227
the foundations of *m* generations	Is 58:12	
a joy of *m* generations	Is 60:15	
the desolations of *m* generations	Is 61:4	7227
the slain of the LORD shall be *m*	Is 66:16	7231
played the harlot with *m* lovers	Jer 3:1	7227
their transgressions are *m*	Jer 5:6	7231
she hath wrought lewdness with *m*	Jer 11:15	7227
M pastors have destroyed my	Jer 12:10	7227
And it came to pass after *m* days	Jer 13:6	7227
for our backslidings are *m*	Jer 14:7	7231
Behold, I will send for *m* fishers	Jer 16:16	7227
after will I send for *m* hunters	Jer 16:16	7227
For I heard the defaming of *m*	Jer 20:10	7227
m nations shall pass by this city	Jer 22:8	7227
For *m* nations and great kings	Jer 25:14	7227
then *m* nations and great kings	Jer 27:7	7227
both against *m* countries, and	Jer 28:8	7227
that they may continue *m* days	Jer 32:14	7227
that ye may live *m* days in the	Jer 35:7	7227
besides unto them *m* like words	Jer 36:32	7227
had remained there *m* days	Jer 37:16	7227
(for we are left but a few of *m*	Jer 42:2	7235
vain shalt thou use *m* medicines	Jer 46:11	7235
He made *m* to fall, yea, one fell	Jer 46:16	7235
m kings shall be raised up from	Jer 50:41	7227
thou that dwellest upon *m* waters	Jer 51:13	7227
for my sighs are *m*, and my heart	Lam 1:22	7227
Not to *m* people of a strange	Eze 3:6	7227
he seeth is for *m* days to come	Eze 12:27	7227
upon thee in the sight of *m* women	Eze 16:41	7227
with great wings and *m* feathers	Eze 17:7	7227
even without great power or *m*	Eze 17:9	7227
forts, to cut off *m* persons	Eze 17:17	7227
of branches by reason of *m* waters	Eze 19:10	7227
they have made her *m* widows in	Eze 22:25	7235
will cause *m* nations to come up	Eze 26:3	7227
of the people for *m* isles	Eze 27:3	7227
m isles were the merchandise of	Eze 27:15	7227
the seas, thou filledst *m* people	Eze 27:33	7227
thee with a company of *m* people	Eze 32:3	7227
also vex the hearts of *m* people	Eze 32:9	7227
I will make *m* people amazed at	Eze 32:10	7227
but we are *m*	Eze 33:24	7227
there were very *m* in the open	Eze 37:2	7227
and *m* people with thee	Eze 38:6	7227
After *m* days thou shalt be	Eze 38:8	7227
and is gathered out of *m* people	Eze 38:8	7227
thy bands, and *m* people with thee	Eze 38:9	7227
m people with thee, all of them	Eze 38:15	7227
m years that I would bring thee	Eze 38:17	
upon the *m* people that are with	Eze 38:22	7227
be known in the eyes of *m* nations	Eze 38:23	7227
in them in the sight of *m* nations	Eze 39:27	7227
was like a noise of *m* waters	Eze 43:2	7227
were very *m* trees on the one side	Eze 47:7	7227
of the great sea, exceeding *m*	Eze 47:10	7227
gave him *m* great gifts, and made	Dan 2:48	7690
and by peace shall destroy *m*	Dan 8:25	7227
for it shall be for *m* days	Dan 8:26	7227
the covenant with *m* for one week	Dan 9:27	7227
for yet the vision is for *m* days	Dan 10:14	
shall cast down *m* ten thousands	Dan 11:12	
in those times there shall *m*	Dan 11:14	7227
unto the isles, and shall take *m*	Dan 11:18	7227
and *m* shall fall down slain	Dan 11:26	7227
among the people shall instruct *m*	Dan 11:33	7227
by captivity, and by spoil, *m* days	Dan 11:33	
but *m* shall cleave to them with	Dan 11:34	7227
shall cause them to rule over *m*	Dan 11:39	7227
and with horsemen, and with *m* ships	Dan 11:40	7227
m countries shall be overthrown	Dan 11:41	7227
and utterly to make away *m*	Dan 11:44	7227
m of them that sleep in the dust	Dan 12:2	7227
they that turn *m* to righteousness	Dan 12:3	7227
m shall run to and fro, and	Dan 12:4	7227
M shall be purified, and made	Dan 12:10	7227
Thou shalt abide for me *m* days	Hos 3:3	7227
shall abide *m* days without a king	Hos 3:4	7227
Ephraim hath made *m* altars to sin	Hos 8:11	7235
to the years of *m* generations	Joel 2:2	
there shall be *m* dead bodies in	Amos 8:3	7227
m nations shall come, and say,	Mic 4:2	7227
And he shall judge among *m* people	Mic 4:3	7227
Now also *m* nations are gathered	Mic 4:11	7227
shalt beat in pieces *m* people	Mic 4:13	7227
m people as a dew from the LORD	Mic 5:7	7227
of *m* people as a lion among the	Mic 5:8	7227
they be quiet, and likewise *m*	Nah 1:12	7227
make thyself *m* as the cankerworm,	Nah 3:15	3513
make thyself *m* as the locusts	Nah 3:15	3513
thou hast spoiled *m* nations	Hab 2:8	7227
thy house by cutting off *m* people	Hab 2:10	7227
m nations shall be joined to the	Zec 2:11	7227
as I have done these so *m* years	Zec 7:3	
and the inhabitants of *m* cities	Zec 8:20	7227
m people and strong nations shall	Zec 8:22	7227
did turn *m* away from iniquity	Mal 2:6	7227
ye have caused *m* to stumble at	Mal 2:8	7227
But when he saw *m* of the	Mt 3:7	4183
m there be which go in thereat	Mt 7:13	4183
M will say to me in that day,	Mt 7:22	4183
thy name done *m* wonderful works	Mt 7:22	4183
That *m* shall come from the east	Mt 8:11	4183
they brought unto him *m* that were	Mt 8:16	4183
them an herd of *m* swine feeding	Mt 8:30	4183
m publicans and sinners came and	Mt 9:10	4183
are of more value than *m* sparrows	Mt 10:31	4183
he spake *m* things unto them in	Mt 13:3	4183
That *m* prophets and righteous men	Mt 13:17	4183
he did not *m* mighty works there	Mt 13:58	4183
as *m* as touched were made	Mt 14:36	3745
m others, and cast them down at	Mt 15:30	4183
unto them, How *m* loaves have ye	Mt 15:34	4214
and how *m* baskets ye took up	Mt 16:9	4214
and how *m* baskets ye took up	Mt 16:10	4214
suffer *m* things of the elders and	Mt 16:21	4183
But *m* that are first shall be	Mt 19:30	4183
for *m* be called, but few chosen	Mt 20:16	4183
to give his life a ransom for *m*	Mt 20:28	4183
as *m* as ye shall find, bid to the	Mt 22:9	3745
together all as *m* as they found	Mt 22:10	3745
For *m* are called, but few are	Mt 22:14	4183
For *m* shall come in my name,	Mt 24:5	4183
and shall deceive *m*	Mt 24:5	4183
then shall *m* be offended, and	Mt 24:10	4183
m false prophets shall rise	Mt 24:11	4183
and shall deceive *m*	Mt 24:11	4183
the love of *m* shall wax cold	Mt 24:12	4183
make thee ruler over *m* things	Mt 25:21	4183
make thee ruler over *m* things	Mt 25:23	4183
which is shed for *m* for the	Mt 26:28	4183
though *m* false witnesses came,	Mt 26:60	4183
Hearest thou not how *m* things	Mt 27:13	4214
for I have suffered *m* things this	Mt 27:19	4183
m bodies of the saints which	Mt 27:52	4183
the holy city, and appeared unto *m*	Mt 27:53	4183
m women were there beholding afar	Mt 27:55	4183
he healed *m* that were sick of	Mk 1:34	4183
diseases, and cast out *m* devils	Mk 1:34	4183
straightway *m* were gathered	Mk 2:2	4183
m publicans and sinners sat also	Mk 2:15	4183
for there were *m*, and they	Mk 2:15	4183
For he had healed *m*	Mk 3:10	4183
to touch him, as *m* as had plagues	Mk 3:10	3745
he taught them *m* things by	Mk 4:2	4183
with *m* such parables spake he the	Mk 4:33	4183
for we are *m*	Mk 5:9	4183
had suffered *m* things of *m*	Mk 5:26	4183
m hearing him were astonished,	Mk 6:2	4183
And they cast out *m* devils	Mk 6:13	4183
with oil *m* that were sick	Mk 6:13	4183
he heard him, he did *m* things	Mk 6:20	4183
for there were *m* coming and going,	Mk 6:31	4183
m knew him, and ran afoot thither	Mk 6:33	4183
he began to teach them *m* things	Mk 6:34	4183
unto them, How *m* loaves have ye	Mk 6:38	4214
as *m* as touched him were made	Mk 6:56	3745
m other things there be, which	Mk 7:4	4183
m other such like things ye do	Mk 7:8	4183
and *m* such like things do ye	Mk 7:13	4183
asked them, How *m* loaves have ye	Mk 8:5	4214
how *m* baskets full of fragments	Mk 8:19	4214
how *m* baskets full of fragments	Mk 8:20	4214
Son of man must suffer *m* things	Mk 8:31	4183
man, that he must suffer *m* things	Mk 9:12	4183
insomuch that *m* said, He is dead	Mk 9:26	4183
But *m* that are first shall be	Mk 10:31	4183
to give his life a ransom for *m*	Mk 10:45	4183
m charged him that he should hold	Mk 10:48	4183
m spread their garments in the	Mk 11:8	4183
and him they killed, and *m* others	Mk 12:5	4183
m that were rich cast in much	Mk 12:41	4183
For *m* shall come in my name,	Mk 13:6	4183
and shall deceive *m*	Mk 13:6	4183
testament, which is shed for *m*	Mk 14:24	4183
For *m* bare false witness against	Mk 14:56	4183
priests accused him of *m* things	Mk 15:3	4183
behold how *m* things they witness	Mk 15:4	4214
m other women which came up with	Mk 15:41	4183
Forasmuch as *m* have taken in hand	Lk 1:1	4183
m shall rejoice at his birth	Lk 1:14	4183
m of the children of Israel shall	Lk 1:16	4183
and rising again of *m* in Israel	Lk 2:34	4183
that the thoughts of *m* hearts	Lk 2:35	4183
m other things in his exhortation	Lk 3:18	4183
m widows were in Israel in the	Lk 4:25	4183
m lepers were in Israel in the	Lk 4:27	4183
And devils also came out of *m*	Lk 4:41	4183
m of his disciples went with him,	Lk 7:11	2425
he cured *m* of their infirmities	Lk 7:21	4183
unto *m* that were blind he gave	Lk 7:21	4183
unto thee, Her sins, which are *m*	Lk 7:47	4183
m others, which ministered unto	Lk 8:3	4183
because *m* devils were entered	Lk 8:30	4183
there was there an herd of *m*	Lk 8:32	2425
Son of man must suffer *m* things	Lk 9:22	4183
that *m* prophets and kings have	Lk 10:24	4183
and troubled about *m* things	Lk 10:41	4183
give him as *m* as he needeth	Lk 11:8	3745
provoke him to speak of *m* things	Lk 11:53	4119
are of more value than *m* sparrows	Lk 12:7	4183
much goods laid up for *m* years	Lk 12:19	4183
shall be beaten with *m* stripes	Lk 12:47	4183
for *m*, I say unto you, will seek	Lk 13:24	4183
made a great supper, and bade *m*	Lk 14:16	4183
not *m* days after the younger son	Lk 15:13	4183
How *m* hired servants of my	Lk 15:17	4214
these *m* years do I serve thee,	Lk 15:29	5118
But first must he suffer *m* things	Lk 17:25	4183
for *m* shall come in my name,	Lk 21:8	4183
m other things blasphemously	Lk 22:65	4183
he had heard *m* things of him	Lk 23:8	4183
he questioned with him in *m* words	Lk 23:9	2425
But as *m* as received him, to them	Jn 1:12	3745
they continued there not *m* days	Jn 2:12	4183
m believed in his name, when they	Jn 2:23	4183
m of the Samaritans of that city	Jn 4:39	4183
m more believed because of his	Jn 4:41	4183
but what are they among so *m*	Jn 6:9	5118
M therefore of his disciples,	Jn 6:60	4183
From that time *m* of his disciples	Jn 6:66	4183
m of the people believed on him,	Jn 7:31	4183
M of the people therefore, when	Jn 7:40	4183
I have *m* things to say and to	Jn 8:26	4183
these words, *m* believed on him	Jn 8:30	4183
m of them said, He hath a devil,	Jn 10:20	4183
M good works have I shewed you	Jn 10:32	4183
m resorted unto him, and said,	Jn 10:41	4183
And *m* believed on him there	Jn 10:42	4183
m of the Jews came to Martha and	Jn 11:19	4183
Then *m* of the Jews which came to	Jn 11:45	4183
for this man doeth *m* miracles	Jn 11:47	4183
m went out of the country up to	Jn 11:55	4183
of him *m* of the Jews went away	Jn 12:11	4183
done so *m* miracles before them	Jn 12:37	5118
rulers also *m* believed on him	Jn 12:42	4183
my Father's house are *m* mansions	Jn 14:2	4183
I have yet *m* things to say unto	Jn 16:12	4183
to as *m* as thou hast given him	Jn 17:2	
title then read *m* of the Jews	Jn 19:20	4183
m other signs truly did Jesus in	Jn 20:30	4183
and for all there were so *m*	Jn 21:11	5118
there are also *m* other things	Jn 21:25	4183
passion by *m* infallible proofs	Acts 1:3	4183
the Holy Ghost not *m* days hence	Acts 1:5	4183
even as *m* as the Lord our God	Acts 2:39	3745
with *m* other words did he testify	Acts 2:40	4119
m wonders and signs were done by	Acts 2:43	4183
as *m* as have spoken, have	Acts 3:24	3745
Howbeit *m* of them which heard the	Acts 4:4	4183
as *m* as were of the kindred of	Acts 4:6	3745
for as *m* as were possessors of	Acts 4:34	3745
upon as *m* as heard these things	Acts 5:11	
of the apostles were *m* signs	Acts 5:12	4183
and all, as *m* as obeyed him, were	Acts 5:36	3745
even as *m* as obeyed him, were	Acts 5:37	3745
came out of *m* that were possessed	Acts 8:7	4183
m taken with palsies, and that	Acts 8:7	4183
preached the gospel in *m* villages	Acts 8:25	4183
I have heard by *m* of this man	Acts 9:13	4183
after that *m* days were fulfilled,	Acts 9:23	2425
and *m* believed in the Lord	Acts 9:42	4183
that he tarried *m* days in Joppa	Acts 9:43	2425
found *m* that were come together	Acts 10:27	4183
as *m* as came with Peter, because	Acts 10:45	3745
where *m* were gathered together	Acts 12:12	2425
he was seen *m* days of them which	Acts 13:31	4119
m of the Jews and religious	Acts 13:43	4183
as *m* as were ordained to eternal	Acts 13:48	3745
to that city, and had taught *m*	Acts 14:21	2425
the brethren with *m* words	Acts 15:32	4183
of the Lord, with *m* others also	Acts 15:35	4183
And this did she *m* days	Acts 16:18	4183
they had laid *m* stripes upon them	Acts 16:23	4183
Therefore *m* of them believed	Acts 17:12	4183
m of the Corinthians hearing	Acts 18:8	4183
And *m* that believed came, and	Acts 19:18	4183
M of them also which used curious	Acts 19:19	2425
there were *m* lights in the upper	Acts 20:8	2425
with *m* tears, and temptations,	Acts 20:19	4183
And as we tarried there *m* days	Acts 21:10	4119
how *m* thousands of Jews there are	Acts 21:20	4214
I know that thou hast been of *m*	Acts 24:10	4183
Now after *m* years I came to bring	Acts 24:17	4119
stood round about, and laid *m*	Acts 25:7	4183
when they had been there *m* days	Acts 25:14	4119
that I ought to do *m* things	Acts 26:9	4183
m of the saints did I shut up in	Acts 26:10	4183
when we had sailed slowly *m* days	Acts 27:7	2425
sun nor stars in *m* days appeared	Acts 27:20	4119
also honoured us with *m* honours	Acts 28:10	4183
there came *m* to him into his	Acts 28:23	4119
For as *m* as have sinned without	Rom 2:12	3745
as *m* as have sinned in the law	Rom 2:12	3745
made thee a father of *m* nations	Rom 4:17	4183
become the father of *m* nations	Rom 4:18	4183
the offence of one *m* be dead	Rom 5:15	4183
Christ, hath abounded unto *m*	Rom 5:15	4183
but the free gift is of *m*	Rom 5:16	4183
disobedience *m* were made sinners	Rom 5:19	4183
of one shall *m* be made righteous	Rom 5:19	4183
that so *m* of us as were baptized	Rom 6:3	3745
For as *m* as are led by the Spirit	Rom 8:14	3745
be the firstborn among *m* brethren	Rom 8:29	4183
For as we have *m* members in one	Rom 12:4	4183
So we, being *m*, are one body in	Rom 12:5	4183

these *m* years to come unto you ... Rom 15:23 *4183*
she hath been a succourer of *m* ... Rom 16:2 *4183*
how that not *m* wise men after the ... 1Cor 1:26 *4183*
not *m* mighty, not *m* noble, are ... 1Cor 1:26 *4183*
Christ, yet have ye not *m* fathers ... 1Cor 4:15 *4183*
as there be gods *m*, and lords *m* ... 1Cor 8:5 *4183*
But with *m* of them God was not ... 1Cor 10:5 *4119*
For we being *m* are one bread, and ... 1Cor 10:17 *4183*
own profit, but the profit of *m* ... 1Cor 10:33 *4183*
For this cause *m* are weak ... 1Cor 11:30 *4183*
and sickly among you, and *m* sleep ... 1Cor 11:30 *2425*
hath *m* members, and all the ... 1Cor 12:12 *4183*
members of that one body, being *m* ... 1Cor 12:12 *4183*
the body is not one member, but *m* ... 1Cor 12:14 *4183*
But now are they *m* members ... 1Cor 12:20 *4183*
so *m* kinds of voices in the world ... 1Cor 14:10 *5118*
me, and there are *m* adversaries ... 1Cor 16:9 *4183*
upon us by the means of *m* persons ... 2Cor 1:11 *4183*
may be given by *m* on our behalf ... 2Cor 1:11 *4183*
I wrote unto you with *m* tears ... 2Cor 2:4 *4183*
which was inflicted of *m* ... 2Cor 2:6 *4119*
For we are not as *m*, which ... 2Cor 2:17 *4183*
of *m* redound to the glory of God ... 2Cor 4:15 *4119*
as poor, yet making *m* rich ... 2Cor 6:10 *4183*
proved diligent in *m* things ... 2Cor 8:22 *4183*
and your zeal hath provoked very *m* ... 2Cor 9:2 *4119*
also by *m* thanksgivings unto God ... 2Cor 9:12 *4183*
Seeing that *m* glory after the ... 2Cor 11:18 *4183*
that I shall bewail *m* which have ... 2Cor 12:21 *4183*
in the Jews' religion above *m* my ... Gal 1:14 *4183*
ye suffered so *m* things in vain ... Gal 3:4 *5118*
For as *m* as are of the works of ... Gal 3:10 *3745*
saith not, And to seeds, as of *m* ... Gal 3:16 *4183*
For as *m* of you as have been ... Gal 3:27 *3745*
for the desolate hath *m* more ... Gal 4:27 *4183*
As *m* as desire to make a fair ... Gal 6:12 *3745*
as *m* as walk according to this ... Gal 6:16 *3745*
m of the brethren in the Lord, ... Phil 1:14 *4119*
as *m* as be perfect, be thus ... Phil 3:15 *3745*
(For *m* walk, of whom I have told ... Phil 3:18 *4183*
for as *m* as have not seen my face ... Col 2:1 *3745*
Let as *m* servants as are under ... 1Ti 6:1 *3745*
into *m* foolish and hurtful lusts, ... 1Ti 6:9 *4183*
themselves through with *m* sorrows ... 1Ti 6:10 *4183*
profession before *m* witnesses ... 1Ti 6:12 *4183*
in how *m* things he ministered ... 2Ti 1:18 *3745*
heard of me among *m* witnesses ... 2Ti 2:2 *4183*
For there are *m* unruly and vain ... Titus 1:10 *4183*
in bringing *m* sons unto glory, to ... Heb 2:10 *4183*
Of whom we have *m* things to say ... Heb 5:11 *4183*
And they truly were *m* priests ... Heb 7:23 *4119*
offered to bear the sins of *m* ... Heb 9:28 *4183*
so *m* as the stars of the sky in ... Heb 11:12
you, and thereby *m* be defiled ... Heb 12:15 *4183*
be not *m* masters, knowing that we ... Jas 3:1 *4183*
For in *m* things we offend all ... Jas 3:2 *4183*
m shall follow their pernicious ... 2Pet 2:2 *4183*
even now are there *m* antichrists ... 1Jn 2:18 *4183*
because *m* false prophets are gone ... 1Jn 4:1 *4183*
For *m* deceivers are entered into ... 2Jn 7 *4183*
Having *m* things to write unto you ... 2Jn 12 *4183*
I had *m* things to write, but I ... 3Jn 13 *4183*
voice as the sound of *m* waters ... Rev 1:15 *4183*
as *m* as have not this doctrine, ... Rev 2:24 *3745*
As *m* as I love, I rebuke and ... Rev 3:19 *3745*
I heard the voice of *m* angels ... Rev 5:11 *4183*
m men died of the waters, because ... Rev 8:11 *4183*
of *m* horses running to battle ... Rev 9:9 *4183*
prophesy again before *m* peoples ... Rev 10:11 *4183*
cause that as *m* as would not ... Rev 13:15 *3745*
heaven, as the voice of *m* waters ... Rev 14:2 *4183*
whore that sitteth upon *m* waters ... Rev 17:1 *4183*
as *m* as trade by sea, stood afar ... Rev 18:17 *3745*
and as the voice of *m* waters ... Rev 19:6 *4183*
and on his head were *m* crowns ... Rev 19:12 *4183*

MAOCH (*ma'-ok*) *Father of Achish.*
him unto Achish, the son of *M* ... 1Sa 27:2 4582

MAON (*ma'-on*) See MAONITES.
1. A city in Judah.
M, Carmel, and Ziph, and Juttah, ... Josh 15:55 4584
And there was a man in *M*, whose ... 1Sa 25:2 4584
2. A descendant of Caleb.
And the son of Shammai was *M* ... 1Chr 2:45 4584
M was the father of Beth-zur ... 1Chr 2:45 4584
3. A wilderness in Judah.
men were in the wilderness of *M* ... 1Sa 23:24 4584
and abode in the wilderness of *M* ... 1Sa 23:25 4584
David in the wilderness of *M* ... 1Sa 23:25 4584

MAONITES (*ma'-on-ites*) See MEHUNIM. *An enemy tribe of Israel.*
also, and the Amalekites, and the *M* ... Judg 10:12 4584

MAR
neither shalt thou *m* the corners ... Lev 19:27 7843
lest I *m* mine own inheritance ... Ruth 4:6 7843
of your mice that *m* the land ... 1Sa 6:5 7843
m every good piece of land with ... 2Kin 3:19 3510
They *m* my path, they set forward ... Job 30:13 5420
will I *m* the pride of Judah ... Jer 13:9 7843

MARA (*ma'-rah*) *Another name for Naomi.*
Call me not Naomi, call me *M* ... Ruth 1:20 4755

MARAH (*ma'-rah*) *An Israelite encampment in the wilderness.*
And when they came to *M*, they ... Ex 15:23 4785
not drink of the waters of *M* ... Ex 15:23 4785
the name of it was called *M* ... Ex 15:23 4785
of Etham, and pitched in *M* ... Num 33:8 4785
And they removed from *M*, and came ... Num 33:9 4785

MARALAH (*mar'-a-lah*) *A city in Zebulun.*
went up toward the sea, and *M* ... Josh 19:11 4831

MARANATHA
Christ, let him be Anathema *M* ... 1Cor 16:22 *3134*

MARBLE
stones, and *m* stones in abundance ... 1Chr 29:2 7898
to silver rings and pillars of *m* ... Est 1:6 8338
and blue, and white, and black, *m* ... Est 1:6 8336
His legs are as pillars of *m* ... Song 5:15 8336
wood, and of brass, and iron, and *m* ... Rev 18:12 *3139*

MARCH
when thou didst *m* through the ... Ps 68:7 6805
for they shall *m* with an army ... Jer 46:22 3212
they shall *m* every one on his ... Joel 2:7 3212
which shall *m* through the breadth ... Hab 1:6 1980
Thou didst *m* through the land in ... Hab 3:12 6805

MARCHED
the Egyptians *m* after them ... Ex 14:10 5265

MARCHEDST
when thou *m* out of the field of ... Judg 5:4 6805

MARCUS (*mar'-cus*) See MARK. *Latin form of Mark.*
fellowprisoner saluteth you, and *M* ... Col 4:10 *3138*
M, Aristarchus, Demas, Lucas, my ... Philem 24 *3138*
and so doth *M* my son ... 1Pet 5:13 *3138*

MARDUK See MERODACH.

MAREAL See MARALAH.

MARESHAH
1. A city in Judah.
And Keilah, and Achzib, and *M* ... Josh 15:44 4762
And Gath, and *M*, and Ziph, ... 2Chr 11:8 4762
and came unto *M* ... 2Chr 14:9 4762
in the valley of Zephathah at *M* ... 2Chr 14:10 4762
Eliezer the son of Dodavah of *M* ... 2Chr 20:37 4762
heir unto thee, O inhabitant of *M* ... Mic 1:15 4762
2. Father of Hebron.
the sons of *M* the father of ... 1Chr 2:42 4762
3. A descendant of Shelah.
Lecah, and Laadah the father of *M* ... 1Chr 4:21 4762

MARINERS
of Zidon and Arvad were thy *m* ... Eze 27:8 7751
m were in thee to occupy thy ... Eze 27:9 4419
thy fairs, thy merchandise, thy *m* ... Eze 27:27 4419
And all that handle the oar, the *m* ... Eze 27:29 4419
Then the *m* were afraid, and cried ... Jonah 1:5 4419

MARISHES
the *m* thereof shall not be healed ... Eze 47:11 1360

MARK See MARCUS.
And the LORD set a *m* upon Cain ... Gen 4:15 226
that thou shalt *m* the place where ... Ruth 3:4 3045
thereof, as though I shot at a *m* ... 1Sa 20:20 4307
M ye now when Amnon's heart is ... 2Sa 13:28 7200
elders of the land, and said, *M* ... 1Kin 20:7 3045
him, Go, strengthen thyself, and *m* ... 1Kin 20:22 3045
thou set me as a *m* against thee ... Job 7:20 4645
to pieces, and set me up for his *m* ... Job 16:12 4307
m, and afterwards we will speak ... Job 18:2 995
M me, and be astonished, and lay ... Job 21:5 6437
M well, O Job, hearken unto me ... Job 33:31 7181
or canst thou *m* when the hinds do ... Job 39:1 8104
M the perfect man, and behold the ... Ps 37:37 8104
M ye well her bulwarks, consider ... Ps 48:13 7896
they *m* my steps, when they wait ... Ps 56:6 8104
shouldest *m* iniquities, O Lord, ... Ps 130:3 8104
set me as a *m* for the arrow ... Lam 3:12 4307
set a *m* upon the foreheads of the ... Eze 9:4 8420
near any man upon whom is the *m* ... Eze 9:6 8420
m well, and behold with thine eyes ... Eze 44:5 7760
m well the entering in of the ... Eze 44:5 7760
m them which cause divisions and ... Rom 16:17 *4648*
I press toward the *m* for the ... Phil 3:14 *4649*
m them which walk so as ye have ... Phil 3:17 *4648*
to receive a *m* in their right ... Rev 13:16 *5480*
or sell, save he that had the *m* ... Rev 13:17 *5480*
receive his *m* in his forehead, or ... Rev 14:9 *5480*
receiveth the *m* of his name ... Rev 14:11 *5480*
and over his image, and over his *m* ... Rev 15:2 *5480*
men which had the *m* of the beast ... Rev 16:2 *5480*
had received the *m* of the beast ... Rev 19:20 *5480*
his *m* upon their foreheads ... Rev 20:4 *5480*
Companion of Paul.
of John, whose surname was *M* ... Acts 12:12 *3138*
them John, whose surname was *M* ... Acts 12:25 *3138*
them John, whose surname was *M* ... Acts 15:37 *3138*
and so Barnabas took *M*, and sailed ... Acts 15:39 *3138*
Take *M*, and bring him with thee ... 2Ti 4:11 *3138*

MARKED
the LORD, that Eli *m* her mouth ... 1Sa 1:12 8104
Hast thou *m* the old way which ... Job 22:15 8104
which they had *m* for themselves ... Job 24:16 2856
yet thine iniquity is *m* before me ... Jer 2:22 3799
who hath *m* his word, and heard it ... Jer 23:18 7181
when he *m* how they chose out the ... Lk 14:7 *1907*

MARKEST
If I sin, then thou *m* me, and thou ... Job 10:14 8104

MARKET
men and vessels of brass in thy *m* ... Eze 27:13 4627
traded in thy *m* wheat of Minnith ... Eze 27:17 4627
cassia, and calamus, were in thy *m* ... Eze 27:19 4627
did sing of thee in thy *m* ... Eze 27:25 4627
And when they come from the *m* ... Mk 7:4 *58*
Jerusalem by the sheep *m* a pool ... Jn 5:2
in the *m* daily with them that met ... Acts 17:17 *58*

MARKETH
in the stocks, he *m* all my paths ... Job 33:11 8104
he *m* it out with a line ... Is 44:13 8388
he *m* it out with the compass, and ... Is 44:13 8388

MARKETPLACE
saw others standing idle in the *m* ... Mt 20:3 *58*
unto children sitting in the *m* ... Lk 7:32 *58*
them into the *m* unto the rulers ... Acts 16:19 *58*

MARKETPLACES
and love salutations in the *m* ... Mk 12:38 *58*

MARKETS
unto children sitting in the *m* ... Mt 11:16 *58*
And greetings in the *m*, and to be ... Mt 23:7 *58*
synagogues, and greetings in the *m* ... Lk 11:43 *58*
robes, and love greetings in the *m* ... Lk 20:46 *58*

MARKS
dead, nor print any *m* upon you ... Lev 19:28 7085
my body the *m* of the Lord Jesus ... Gal 6:17 *4742*

MAROTH (*ma'-roth*) *A city in Judah.*
For the inhabitant of *M* waited ... Mic 1:12 4796

MARRED
visage was so *m* more than any man ... Is 52:14 4893
and, behold, the girdle was *m* ... Jer 13:7 7843
was *m* in the hand of the potter ... Jer 18:4 7843
out, and *m* their vine branches ... Nah 2:2 7843
spilled, and the bottles will be *m* ... Mk 2:22 *622*

MARRIAGE
her raiment, and her duty of *m* ... Ex 21:10 5772
their maidens were not given to *m* ... Ps 78:63 1984
king, which made a *m* for his son ... Mt 22:2 *1062*
are ready: come unto the *m* ... Mt 22:4 *1062*
as ye shall find, bid to the *m* ... Mt 22:9 *1062*
neither marry, nor are given in *m* ... Mt 22:30 *1548*
drinking, marrying and giving in *m* ... Mt 24:38 *1547*
ready went in with him to the *m* ... Mt 25:10 *1062*
neither marry, nor are given in *m* ... Mk 12:25 *1061*
wives, they were given in *m* ... Lk 17:27 *1548*
world marry, and are given in *m* ... Lk 20:34 *1548*
neither marry, nor are given in *m* ... Lk 20:35 *1548*
there was a *m* in Cana of Galilee ... Jn 2:1 *1062*
and his disciples, to the *m* ... Jn 2:2 *1062*
that giveth her in *m* doeth well ... 1Cor 7:38 *1547*
giveth her not in *m* doeth better ... 1Cor 7:38 *1547*
M is honourable in all, and the ... Heb 13:4 *1062*
for the *m* of the Lamb is come, and ... Rev 19:7 *1062*
unto the *m* supper of the Lamb ... Rev 19:9 *1062*

MARRIAGES
And make ye *m* with us, and give ... Gen 34:9 2859
shalt thou make *m* with them ... Deut 7:3 2859
you, and shall make *m* with them ... Josh 23:12 2859

MARRIED
which *m* his daughters, and said, ... Gen 19:14 3947
if he were *m*, then his wife shall ... Ex 21:3
also be *m* unto a stranger ... Lev 22:12
the Ethiopian woman whom he had *m* ... Num 12:1 3947
for he had *m* an Ethiopian woman ... Num 12:1 3947
if they be *m* to any of the sons ... Num 36:3 802
were *m* unto their father's ... Num 36:11 802
they were *m* into the families of ... Num 36:12 802
with a woman *m* to an husband ... Deut 22:22 1166
m her, and it come to pass that ... Deut 24:1 1166
whom he *m* when he was threescore ... 1Chr 2:21 3947
m fourteen wives, and begat twenty ... 2Chr 13:21 5375
I Jews that had *m* wives of Ashdod ... Neh 13:23 3427
For an odious woman when she is *m* ... Prov 30:23 1166
than the children of the *m* wife ... Is 54:1 1166
in thee, and thy land shall be *m* ... Is 62:4 1166
for I am *m* unto you ... Jer 3:14 1166
hath *m* the daughter of a strange ... Mal 2:11 1166
the first, when he had *m* a wife ... Mt 22:25 *1060*
for he had *m* her ... Mk 6:17 *1060*
be *m* to another, she committeth ... Mk 10:12 *1060*
And another said, I have *m* a wife ... Lk 14:20 *1060*
they *m* wives, they were given in ... Lk 17:27 *1060*
she be *m* to another man, she ... Rom 7:3 *1096*
though she be *m* to another man ... Rom 7:3 *1096*
that ye should be *m* to another ... Rom 7:4 *1096*
unto the *m* I command, yet not I, ... 1Cor 7:10 *1060*
But he that is *m* careth for the ... 1Cor 7:33 *1060*
but she that is *m* careth for the ... 1Cor 7:34 *1060*
liberty to be *m* to whom she will ... 1Cor 7:39 *1060*

MARRIETH
For as a young man *m* a virgin ... Is 62:5 1166
whoso *m* her which is put away ... Mt 19:9 *1060*
m another, committeth adultery ... Lk 16:18 *1060*
whosoever *m* her that is put away ... Lk 16:18 *1060*

MARROW
and his bones are moistened with *m* ... Job 21:24 4221
soul shall be satisfied as with *m* ... Ps 63:5 2459
to thy navel, and *m* to thy bones ... Prov 3:8 8250
the lees, of fat things full of *m* ... Is 25:6 4229
and spirit, and of the joints and *m* ... Heb 4:12 *3452*

MARRY
m her, and raise up seed to thy ... Gen 38:8 2992
Let them *m* to whom they think ... Num 36:6 802
of their father shall they *m* ... Num 36:6 802
not *m* without unto a stranger ... Deut 25:5
virgin, so shall thy sons *m* thee ... Is 62:5 1166
whosoever shall *m* her that is ... Mt 5:32 *1060*
shall *m* another, committeth ... Mt 19:9 *1060*
his wife, it is not good to *m* ... Mt 19:10 *1060*
his brother shall *m* his wife ... Mt 22:24 *1918*
the resurrection they neither *m* ... Mt 22:30 *1060*
m another, committeth adultery ... Mk 10:11 *1060*
from the dead, they neither *m* ... Mk 12:25 *1060*
The children of this world *m* ... Lk 20:34 *1060*
from the dead, neither *m*, nor are ... Lk 20:35 *1060*
they cannot contain, let them *m* ... 1Cor 7:9 *1060*
it is better to *m* than to burn ... 1Cor 7:9 *1060*
But and if thou *m*, thou hast not ... 1Cor 7:28 *1060*
and if a virgin *m*, she hath not ... 1Cor 7:28 *1060*

he sinneth not: let them *m* 1Cor 7:36 *1060*
Forbidding to *m*, and commanding to 1Ti 4:3 *1060*
against Christ, they will *m* 1Ti 5:11 *1060*
that the younger women *m*, bear 1Ti 5:14 *1060*

MARRYING
our God in *m* strange wives Neh 13:27 3427
they were eating and drinking, *m* Mt 24:38 *1060*

MARS' (*marz*) *Refers to a landmark in Athens.*
Paul stood in the midst of *M* hill Acts 17:22 697

MARSENA (*mar'-se-nah*) *A prince of Media and Persia.*
Admatha, Tarshish, Meres, *M* Est 1:14 4826

MART
and she is a *m* of nations Is 23:3 5505

MARTHA (*mar'-thah*) *Sister of Lazarus.*
a certain woman named *M* received Lk 10:38 *3136*
But *M* was cumbered about much Lk 10:40 *3136*
and said unto her, *M*, *M* Lk 10:41 *3136*
the town of Mary and her sister *M* Jn 11:1 *3136*
Now Jesus loved *M*, and her sister, Jn 11:5 *3136*
And many of the Jews came to *M* Jn 11:19 *3136*
Then *M*, as soon as she heard that Jn 11:20 *3136*
Then said *M* unto Jesus, Lord, if Jn 11:21 *3136*
M saith unto him, I know that he Jn 11:24 *3136*
was in that place where *M* met him Jn 11:30 *3136*
M, the sister of him that was Jn 11:39 *3136*
a supper; and *M* served Jn 12:2 *3136*

MARTYR
blood of thy *m* Stephen was shed Acts 22:20 *3144*
wherein Antipas was my faithful *m* Rev 2:13 *3144*

MARTYRS
with the blood of the *m* of Jesus Rev 17:6 *3144*

MARVEL
a province, *m* not at the matter Eccl 5:8 8539
and all men did *m* Mk 5:20 *2296*
M not that I said unto thee, Ye Jn 3:7 *2296*
works than these, that ye may *m* Jn 5:20 *2296*
M not at this Jn 5:28 *2296*
I have done one work, and ye all *m* Jn 7:21 *2296*
men of Israel, why *m* ye at this Acts 3:12 *2296*
And no *m*; for Satan himself 2Cor 11:14 *2298*
I *m* that ye are so soon removed Gal 1:6 *2296*
M not, my brethren, if the world 1Jn 3:13 *2296*
unto me, Wherefore didst thou *m* Rev 17:7 *2296*

MARVELLED
and the men *m* one at another Gen 43:33 8539
They saw it, and so they *m* Ps 48:5 8539
When Jesus heard it, he *m* Mt 8:10 *2296*
But the men *m*, saying, What Mt 8:27 *2296*
the multitudes saw it, they *m* Mt 9:8 *2296*
and the multitudes *m*, saying, It Mt 9:33 *2296*
when the disciples saw it, they *m* Mt 21:20 *2296*
had heard these words, they *m* Mt 22:22 *2296*
that the governor *m* greatly Mt 27:14 *2296*
he *m* because of their unbelief Mk 6:6 *2296*
And they *m* at him Mk 12:17 *2296*
so that Pilate *m* Mk 15:5 *2296*
Pilate *m* if he were already dead Mk 15:44 *2296*
m that he tarried so long in the Lk 1:21 *2296*
And they *m* all Lk 1:63 *2296*
his mother *m* at those things Lk 2:33 *2296*
he *m* at him, and turned him about, Lk 7:9 *2296*
he *m* that he had not first washed Lk 11:38 *2296*
they *m* at his answer, and held Lk 20:26 *2296*
m that he talked with the woman Jn 4:27 *2296*
And the Jews *m*, saying, How Jn 7:15 *2296*
And they were all amazed and *m* Acts 2:7 *2296*
unlearned and ignorant men, they *m* Acts 4:13 *2296*

MARVELLOUS
Remember his *m* works that he hath 1Chr 16:12 6381
his *m* works among all nations 1Chr 16:24 6381
m things without number Job 5:9 6381
thou shewest thyself *m* upon me Job 10:16 6381
I will shew forth all thy *m* works Ps 9:1 6381
Shew thy *m* lovingkindness, O thou Ps 17:7 6395
his *m* kindness in a strong city Ps 31:21 6381
M things did he in the sight of Ps 78:12 6382
for he hath done *m* things Ps 98:1 6381
Remember his *m* works that he hath Ps 105:5 6381
it is *m* in our eyes Ps 118:23 6381
m are thy works Ps 139:14 6381
to do a *m* work among this people Is 29:14 6381
among this people, even a *m* work Is 29:14 6381
shall speak *m* things against the Dan 11:36 6381
will I shew unto him *m* things Mic 7:15 6381
If it be *m* in the eyes of the Zec 8:6 6381
should it also be *m* in mine eyes Zec 8:6 6381
doing, and it is *m* in our eyes Mt 21:42 *2298*
doing, and it is *m* in our eyes Mk 12:11 *2298*
them, Why herein is a *m* thing Jn 9:30 *2298*
out of darkness into his *m* light 1Pet 2:9 *2298*
sign in heaven, great and *m* Rev 15:1 *2298*
m are thy works, Lord God Rev 15:3 *2298*

MARVELLOUSLY
for he was *m* helped, till he was 2Chr 26:15 6381
God thundereth *m* with his voice Job 37:5 6381
heathen, and regard, and wonder *m* Hab 1:5 8539

MARVELS
before all thy people I will do *m* Ex 34:10 6381

MARY (*ma'-ry*)
1. Mother of Jesus.
begat Joseph the husband of *M* Mt 1:16 *3137*
When as his mother *M* was espoused Mt 1:18 *3137*
not to take unto thee *M* thy wife Mt 1:20 *3137*
the young child with *M* his mother Mt 2:11 *3137*
is not his mother called *M* Mt 13:55 *3137*
this the carpenter, the son of *M* Mk 6:3 *3137*
and the virgin's name was *M* Lk 1:27 *3137*
angel said unto her, Fear not, *M* Lk 1:30 *3137*
Then said *M* unto the angel, How Lk 1:34 *3137*
M said, Behold the handmaid of Lk 1:38 *3137*
M arose in those days, and went Lk 1:39 *3137*
heard the salutation of *M* Lk 1:41 *3137*
M said, My soul doth magnify the Lk 1:46 *3137*
M abode with her about three Lk 1:56 *3137*
To be taxed with *M* his espoused Lk 2:5 *3137*
they came with haste, and found *M* Lk 2:16 *3137*
But *M* kept all these things, and Lk 2:19 *3137*
said unto *M* his mother, Behold, Lk 2:34 *3137*
M the mother of Jesus, and with Acts 1:14 *3137*
2. A woman of Magdala.
Among which was *M* Magdalene Mt 27:56 *3137*
And there was *M* Magdalene, and the Mt 27:61 *3137*
came *M* Magdalene and the other Mt 28:1 *3137*
among whom was *M* Magdalene Mk 15:40 *3137*
M Magdalene and Mary the mother of Mk 15:47 *3137*
he appeared first to *M* Magdalene Mk 16:9 *3137*
M called Magdalene, out of whom Lk 8:2 *3137*
It was *M* Magdalene, and Joanna, and Lk 24:10 *3137*
wife of Cleophas, and *M* Magdalene Jn 19:25 *3137*
the week cometh *M* Magdalene early Jn 20:1 *3137*
But *M* stood without at the Jn 20:11 *3137*
Jesus saith unto her, *M* Jn 20:16 *3137*
M Magdalene came and told the Jn 20:18 *3137*
3. Mother of James and Joses.
M the mother of James and Joses, Mt 27:56 *3137*
Mary Magdalene, and the other *M* Mt 27:61 *3137*
the other *M* to see the sepulchre Mt 28:1 *3137*
M the mother of James the less and Mk 15:40 *3137*
M the mother of Joses beheld Mk 15:47 *3137*
M Magdalene, and Mary the mother Mk 16:1 *3137*
M the mother of James, and Salome, Mk 16:1 *3137*
M the mother of James, and other Lk 24:10 *3137*
4. Wife of Cleophas.
M the wife of Cleophas, and Mary Jn 19:25 *3137*
5. Sister of Lazarus.
And she had a sister called *M* Lk 10:39 *3137*
M hath chosen that good part, Lk 10:42 *3137*
of Bethany, the town of *M* Jn 11:1 *3137*
(It was that *M* which anointed the Jn 11:2 *3137*
of the Jews came to Martha and *M* Jn 11:19 *3137*
but *M* sat still in the house Jn 11:20 *3137*
called *M* her sister secretly, Jn 11:28 *3137*
and comforted her, when they saw *M* Jn 11:31 *3137*
Then when *M* was come where Jesus Jn 11:32 *3137*
many of the Jews which came to *M* Jn 11:45 *3137*
Then took *M* a pound of ointment Jn 12:3 *3137*
6. Mother of John Mark.
the house of *M* the mother of John Acts 12:12 *3137*
7. A Christian in Rome.
Greet *M*, who bestowed much labour Rom 16:6 *3137*

MASCHIL (*mas'-kil*) *A didactic poem.*
A Psalm of David, A *M* Ps 32:*t* 4905
To the chief Musician, *M*, for the Ps 42:*t* 4905
Musician for the sons of Korah, *M* Ps 44:*t* 4905
for the sons of Korah, A *M* Ps 45:*t* 4905
To the chief Musician, *M*, A Psalm Ps 52:*t* 4905
chief Musician upon Mahalath, *M* Ps 53:*t* 4905
the chief Musician on Neginoth, *M* Ps 54:*t* 4905
the chief Musician on Neginoth, *M* Ps 55:*t* 4905
M of Asaph Ps 74:*t* 4905
M of Asaph Ps 78:*t* 4905
Leannoth, *M* of Heman the Ezrahite Ps 88:*t* 4905
M of Ethan the Ezrahite Ps 89:*t* 4905
M of David Ps 142:*t* 4905

MASH (*mash*) *A son of Aram.*
Uz, and Hul, and Gether, and *M* Gen 10:23 4851

MASHAL (*ma'-shal*) *A Levitical city in Asher.*
M with her suburbs, and Abdon with 1Chr 6:74 4913

MASONS
cedar trees, and carpenters, and *m* 2Sa 5:11
And to *m*, and hewers of stone, and 2Kin 12:12 1443
carpenters, and builders, and *m* 2Kin 22:6 1443
and timber of cedars, with *m* 1Chr 14:1
he set *m* to hew wrought stones to 1Chr 22:2 2672
the house of the LORD, and hired *m* 2Chr 24:12 2672
They gave money also unto the *m* Ezr 3:7 2672

MASREKAH (*mas'-re-kah*) *A place in Edom.*
Samlah of *M* reigned in his stead Gen 36:36 4957
Samlah of *M* reigned in his stead 1Chr 1:47 4957

MASSA (*mas'-sah*) *A son of Ishmael.*
And Mishma, and Dumah, and *M* Gen 25:14 4854
Mishma, and Dumah, *M*, Hadad, and 1Chr 1:30 4854

MASSAH (*mas'-sah*) See MERIBAH. *A place in the wilderness where the Israelites murmured.*
he called the name of the place *M* Ex 17:7 4532
your God, as ye tempted him in *M* Deut 6:16 4532
And at Taberah, and at *M*, and at Deut 9:22 4532
one, whom thou didst prove at *M* Deut 33:8 4532

MAST
he that lieth upon the top of a *m* Prov 23:34 2260
could not well strengthen their *m* Is 33:23 8650

MASTER
under the thigh of Abraham his *m* Gen 24:9 113
ten camels of the camels of his *m* Gen 24:10 113
goods of his *m* were in his hand Gen 24:10 113
said, O LORD God of my *m* Abraham Gen 24:12 113
shew kindness unto my *m* Abraham Gen 24:12 113
hast shewed kindness unto my *m* Gen 24:14 113
be the LORD God of my *m* Abraham Gen 24:27 113
left destitute my *m* of his mercy Gen 24:27 113
LORD hath blessed my *m* greatly Gen 24:35 113
a son to my *m* when she was old Gen 24:36 113
my *m* made me swear, saying, Thou Gen 24:37 113
And I said unto my *m*, Peradventure Gen 24:39 113
said, O LORD God of my *m* Abraham Gen 24:42 113
the LORD God of my *m* Abraham Gen 24:48 113
deal kindly and truly with my *m* Gen 24:49 113
he said, Send me away unto my *m* Gen 24:54 113
me away that I may go to my *m* Gen 24:56 113
the servant had said, It is my *m* Gen 24:65 113
the house of his *m* the Egyptian Gen 39:2 113
his *m* saw that the LORD was with Gen 39:3 113
my *m* wotteth not what is with me Gen 39:8 113
when his *m* heard the words of his Gen 39:19 113
And Joseph's *m* took him, and put Gen 39:20 113
If his *m* have given him a wife, Ex 21:4 113
shall plainly say, I love my *m* Ex 21:5 113
Then his *m* shall bring him unto Ex 21:6 113
his *m* shall bore his ear through Ex 21:6 113
If she please not her *m*, who hath Ex 21:8 113
their *m* thirty shekels of silver Ex 21:32 113
then the *m* of the house shall be Ex 22:8 1167
m the servant which is escaped Deut 23:15 113
is escaped from his *m* unto thee Deut 23:15 113
and the servant said unto his *m* Judg 19:11 113
his *m* said unto him, We will not Judg 19:12 113
and spake to the *m* of the house Judg 19:22 1167
the *m* of the house, went out unto Judg 19:23 1167
up the arrows, and came to his *m* 1Sa 20:38 113
I should do this thing unto my *m* 1Sa 24:6 113
break away every man from his *m* 1Sa 25:10 113
of the wilderness to salute our *m* 1Sa 25:14 113
evil is determined against our *m* 1Sa 25:17 113
because ye have not kept your *m* 1Sa 26:16 113
he reconcile himself unto his *m* 1Sa 29:4 113
my *m* left me, because three days 1Sa 30:13 113
deliver me into the hands of my *m* 1Sa 30:15 113
for your *m* Saul is dead, and also 2Sa 2:7 113
and the LORD said, These have no *m* 1Kin 22:17 113
away thy *m* from thy head to day 2Kin 2:3 113
away thy *m* from thy head to day 2Kin 2:5 113
go, we pray thee, and seek thy *m* 2Kin 2:16 113
Syria, was a great man with his *m* 2Kin 5:1 113
that when my *m* goeth into the 2Kin 5:18 113
my *m* hath spared Naaman this 2Kin 5:20 113
My *m* hath sent me, saying, Behold 2Kin 5:22 113
he went in, and stood before his *m* 2Kin 5:25 113
and he cried, and said, Alas, *m* 2Kin 6:5 113
servant said unto him, Alas, my *m* 2Kin 6:15 113
eat and drink, and go to their *m* 2Kin 6:22 113
away, and they went to their *m* 2Kin 6:23 113
from Elisha, and came to his *m* 2Kin 8:14 113
smite the house of Ahab thy *m* 2Kin 9:7 113
Had Zimri peace, who slew his *m* 2Kin 9:31 113
behold, I conspired against my *m* 2Kin 10:9 113
Hath my *m* sent me to thy *m* 2Kin 18:27 113
his *m* hath sent to reproach the 2Kin 19:4 113
them, Thus shall ye say to your *m* 2Kin 19:6 113
He will fall to his *m* Saul to the 1Chr 12:19 113
Chenaniah the *m* of the song with 1Chr 15:27 8269
and the LORD said, These have no *m* 2Chr 18:16 113
and the servant is free from his *m* Job 3:19 113
on his *m* shall be honoured Prov 27:18 113
Accuse not a servant unto his *m* Prov 30:10 113
with the servant, so with his *m* Is 24:2 113
to my *m* the king of Assyria, and I Is 36:8 113
Hath my *m* sent me to thy *m* Is 36:12 113
his *m* hath sent to reproach the Is 37:4 113
Thus shall ye say unto your *m* Is 37:6 113
Ashpenaz the *m* of his eunuchs Dan 1:3 7227
m of the magicians, because I Dan 4:9 729
father, made *m* of the magicians, Dan 5:11 729
his father, and a servant his *m* Mal 1:6 113
and if I be a *m*, where is my fear Mal 1:6 113
the man that doeth this, the *m* Mal 2:12 5782
scribe came, and said unto him, *M* Mt 8:19 *1320*
Why eateth your *M* with publicans Mt 9:11 *1320*
The disciple is not above his *m* Mt 10:24 *1320*
the disciple that he be as his *m* Mt 10:25 *1320*
the *m* of the house Beelzebub Mt 10:25 *1320*
the Pharisees answered, saying, *M* Mt 12:38 *1320*
said, Doth not your *m* pay tribute Mt 17:24 *1320*
one came and said unto him, Good *M* Mt 19:16 *1320*
with the Herodians, saying, *M* Mt 22:16 *1320*
Saying, *M*, Moses said, If a man Mt 22:24 *1320*
M, which is the great commandment Mt 22:36 *1320*
for one is your *M*, even Christ Mt 23:8 *2519*
for one is your *M*, even Christ Mt 23:10 *2519*
The *M* saith, My time is at hand Mt 26:18 *1320*
betrayed him, answered and said, *M* Mt 26:25 *4461*
came to Jesus, and said, Hail, *m* Mt 26:49 *4461*
awake him, and say unto him, *M* Mk 4:38 *1320*
troublest thou the *M* any further Mk 5:35 *1320*
answered and said to Jesus, *M* Mk 9:5 *4461*
the multitude answered and said, *M* Mk 9:17 *1320*
And John answered him, saying, *M* Mk 9:38 *1320*
to him, and asked him, Good *M* Mk 10:17 *1320*
he answered and said unto him, *M* Mk 10:20 *1320*
Zebedee, come unto him, saying, *M* Mk 10:35 *1320*
to remembrance saith unto him, *M* Mk 11:21 *4461*
were come, they say unto him, *M* Mk 12:14 *1320*
M, Moses wrote unto us, If a Mk 12:19 *1320*
the scribe said unto him, Well, *M* Mk 12:32 *1320*
his disciples saith unto him, *M* Mk 13:1 *1320*
when the *m* of the house cometh Mk 13:35 *2962*
The *M* saith, Where is the Mk 14:14 *1320*
to him, and saith, *M*, *m* Mk 14:45 *4461*
be baptized, and said unto him, *M* Lk 3:12 *1320*
Simon answering said unto him, *M* Lk 5:5 *1988*
The disciple is not above his *m* Lk 6:40 *1320*
that is perfect shall be as his *m* Lk 6:40 *1320*
And he saith, *M*, say on Lk 7:40 *1320*
and awoke him, saying, *M*, *m* Lk 8:24 *1988*
they that were with him said, *M* Lk 8:45 *1988*
trouble not the *M* Lk 8:49 *1320*
him, Peter said unto Jesus, *M* Lk 9:33 *1988*
the company cried out, saying, *M* Lk 9:38 *1320*
And John answered and said, *M* Lk 9:49 *1988*
up, and tempted him, saying, *M* Lk 10:25 *1320*

the lawyers, and said unto him, *M* Lk 11:45 *1320*
of the company said unto him, *M* Lk 12:13 *1320*
When once the *m* of the house is Lk 13:25 *3617*
Then the *m* of the house being Lk 14:21 *3617*
their voices, and said, Jesus, *M* Lk 17:13 *1988*
ruler asked him, saying, Good *M* Lk 18:18 *1320*
the multitude said unto him, *M* Lk 19:39 *1320*
And they asked him, saying, *M* Lk 20:21 *1320*
Saying, *M*, Moses wrote unto us, Lk 20:28 *1320*
of the scribes answering said, *M* Lk 20:39 *1320*
And they asked him, saying, *M* Lk 21:7 *1320*
The *M* saith unto thee, Where is Lk 22:11 *1320*
is to say, being interpreted, *M* Jn 1:38 *1320*
unto him, Art thou a *m* of Israel Jn 3:10 *1320*
disciples prayed him, saying, *M* Jn 4:31 *4461*
They say unto him, *M*, this woman Jn 8:4 *1320*
disciples asked him, saying, *M* Jn 9:2 *4461*
His disciples say unto him, *M* Jn 11:8 *4461*
The *M* is come, and calleth for Jn 11:28 *1320*
Ye call me *M* and Lord Jn 13:13 *1320*
If I then, your Lord and *M* Jn 13:14 *1320*
which is to say, *M* Jn 20:16 *1320*
the centurion believed the *m* Acts 27:11 *2942*
to his own *m* he standeth or Rom 14:4 *2962*
that your *M* also is in heaven Eph 6:9 *2962*
that ye also have a *M* in heaven Col 4:1 *2962*

MASTERBUILDER
is given unto me, as a wise *m* 1Cor 3:10 753

MASTERIES
And if a man also strive for *m* 2Ti 2:5

MASTER'S
me to the house of my *m* brethren Gen 24:27 113
Sarah my *m* wife bare a son to my Gen 24:36 113
hath appointed out for my *m* son Gen 24:44 113
me in the right way to take my *m* Gen 24:48 113
and let her be thy *m* son's wife Gen 24:51 113
that his *m* wife cast her eyes Gen 39:7 113
refused, and said unto his *m* wife Gen 39:8 113
and her children shall be her *m* Ex 21:4 113
thy *m* servants that are come with 1Sa 29:10 113
I have given unto thy *m* son all 2Sa 9:9 113
that thy *m* son may have food to 2Sa 9:10 113
but Mephibosheth thy *m* son shall 2Sa 9:10 113
And I gave thee thy *m* house 2Sa 12:8 113
thy *m* wives into thy bosom, and 2Sa 12:8 113
king said, And where is thy *m* son 2Sa 16:3 113
sound of his *m* feet behind him 2Kin 6:32 113
seeing your *m* sons are with you 2Kin 10:2 113
best and meetest of your *m* sons 2Kin 10:3 113
throne, and fight for your *m* house 2Kin 10:3 113
the heads of the men your *m* sons 2Kin 10:6 113
of the least of my *m* servants 2Kin 18:24 113
his owner, and the ass his *m* crib Is 1:3 1167
of the least of my *m* servants Is 36:9 113
sanctified, and meet for the *m* use 2Ti 2:21 *1203*

MASTERS
look unto the hand of their *m* Ps 123:2 113
he refresheth the soul of his *m* Prov 25:13 113
fastened by the *m* of assemblies Eccl 12:11 1167
command them to say unto their *m* Jer 27:4 113
Thus shall ye say unto your *m* Jer 27:4 113
the needy, which say to their *m* Amos 4:1 113
No man can serve two *m* Mt 6:24 *2962*
Neither be ye called *m* Mt 23:10 *2519*
No servant can serve two *m* Lk 16:13 *2962*
which brought her *m* much gain by Acts 16:16 *2962*
when her *m* saw that the hope of Acts 16:19 *2962*
are your *m* according to the flesh Eph 6:5 *2962*
And, ye *m*, do the same things unto Eph 6:9 *2962*
your *m* according to the flesh Col 3:22 *2962*
M, give unto your servants that Col 4:1 *2962*
their own *m* worthy of all honour 1Ti 6:1 *1203*
And they that have believing *m* 1Ti 6:2 *1203*
to be obedient unto their own *m* Titus 2:9 *1203*
My brethren, be not many *m* Jas 3:1 *1320*
subject to your *m* with all fear 1Pet 2:18 *1203*

MASTERS'
which fill their *m* houses with Zeph 1:9 113
which fall from their *m* table Mt 15:27 *2962*

MASTERY
voice of them that shout for *m* Ex 32:18 1369
and the lions had the *m* of them Dan 6:24 6981
the *m* is temperate in all things 1Cor 9:25

MASTS
from Lebanon to make *m* for thee Eze 27:5 8650

MATE
be gathered, every one with her *m* Is 34:15 7468
shall fail, none shall want her *m* Is 34:16 7468

MATHUSALA (*ma-thu'-sa-lah*) See METHUSALAH. *Son of Enoch; ancestor of Jesus.*
Which was the son of *M*, which was Lk 3:37 *3103*

MATRED (*ma'-tred*) *Mother of Mehetabel.*
was Mehetabel, the daughter of *M* Gen 36:39 4308
was Mehetabel, the daughter of *M* 1Chr 1:50 4308

MATRI (*ma'-tri*) *An ancestral family of King Saul.*
the family of *M* was taken 1Sa 10:21 4309

MATRITE See MATRI.

MATRIX
the LORD all that openeth the *m* Ex 13:12 7358
the LORD all that openeth the *m* Ex 13:15 7358
All that openeth the *m* is mine Ex 34:19 7358
m among the children of Israel Num 3:12 7358
that openeth the *m* in all flesh Num 18:15 7358

MATTAN (*mat'-tan*)
1. A priest of Baal.
slew *M* the priest of Baal before 2Kin 11:18 4977
slew *M* the priest of Baal before 2Chr 23:17 4977
2. Father of Shephatiah.
Then Shephatiah the son of *M* Jer 38:1 4977

MATTANAH (*mat'-ta-nah*) *An encampment of Israel in the wilderness.*
the wilderness they went to *M* Num 21:18 4980
And from *M* to Nahaliel Num 21:19 4980

MATTANIAH (*mat-ta-ni'-ah*) See ZEDEKIAH.
1. Same as Zedekiah, king of Judah.
the king of Babylon made *M* his 2Kin 24:17 4983
2. A family of exiles.
M the son of Micah, the son of 1Chr 9:15 4983
the son of Jeiel, the son of *M* 2Chr 20:14 4983
M the son of Micha, the son of Neh 11:17 4983
son of Hashabiah, the son of *M* Neh 11:22 4983
Kadmiel, Sherebiah, Judah, and *M* Neh 12:8 4983
M, and Bakbukiah, Obadiah, Neh 12:25 4983
the son of Shemaiah, the son of *M* Neh 12:35 4983
3. A sanctuary servant.
Bukkiah, *M*, Uzziel, Shebuel, and 1Chr 25:4 4983
The ninth to *M*, he, his sons, and 1Chr 25:16 4983
4. A descendant of Asaph.
Zechariah, and *M* 2Chr 29:13 4983
5. A descendant of Elam.
M, Zechariah, and Jehiel, and Abdi, Ezr 10:26 4983
6. A descendant of Zattu.
Elioenai, Eliashib, *M*, and Ezr 10:27 4983
7. A descendant of Pahath-Moab.
and Chelal, Benaiah, Maaseiah, *M* Ezr 10:30 4983
8. A descendant of Bani.
M, Mattenai, and Jaasau, Ezr 10:37 4983
9. Father of Zaccur.
the son of Zaccur, the son of *M* Neh 13:13 4983

MATTATHA (*mat'-ta-thah*) See MATTATHAH. *A son of Nathan; ancestor of Jesus.*
of Menan, which was the son of *M* Lk 3:31 *3160*

MATTATHAH (*mat'-ta-thah*) See MATTATHA. *Married a foreigner in exile.*
Mattenai, *M*, Zabad, Eliphelet, Ezr 10:33 4992

MATTATHIAH See MATTATHIAS.

MATTATHIAS (*mat-ta-thi'-as*) See MATTITHIAH.
1. A son of Amos; ancestor of Jesus.
Which was the son of *M*, which was Lk 3:25 *3161*
2. A son of Semei; ancestor of Jesus.
of Maath, which was the son of *M* Lk 3:26 *3161*

MATTATTAH See MATTATHAH.

MATTENAI (*mat'-te-nahee*)
1. A descendant of Hashum.
M, Mattathah, Zabad, Eliphelet, Ezr 10:33 4982
2. A descendant of Bani.
Mattaniah, *M*, and Jaasau, Ezr 10:37 4982
3. A priest.
And of Joiarib, *M* Neh 12:19 4982

MATTER
and sware to him concerning that *m* Gen 24:9 1697
Is it a small *m* that thou hast Gen 30:15
When they have a *m*, they come Ex 18:16 1697
that every great *m* they shall Ex 18:22 1697
but every small *m* they shall Ex 18:22 1697
but every small *m* they judged Ex 18:26 1697
Keep thee far from a false *m* Ex 23:7 1697
that died about the *m* of Korah Num 16:49 1697
beguiled you in the *m* of Peor Num 25:18 1697
in the *m* of Cozbi, the daughter Num 25:18 1697
against the LORD in the *m* of Peor Num 31:16 1697
speak no more unto me of this *m* Deut 3:26 1697
If there arise a *m* too hard for Deut 17:8 1697
shall the *m* be established Deut 19:15 1697
and slayeth him, even so is this *m* Deut 22:26 1697
thou know how the *m* will fall Ruth 3:18 1697
But of the *m* of the kingdom, 1Sa 10:16 1697
And as touching the *m* which thou 1Sa 20:23 1697
only Jonathan and David knew the *m* 1Sa 20:39 1697
will hearken unto you in this *m* 1Sa 30:24 1697
said unto him, How went the *m* 2Sa 1:4 1697
for there is no *m* hid from the 2Sa 18:13 1697
then be ye angry for this *m* 2Sa 19:42 1697
and so they ended the *m* 2Sa 20:18 1697
The *m* is not so 2Sa 20:21 1697
all times, as the *m* shall require 1Kin 8:59 1697
save only in the *m* of Uriah the 1Kin 15:5 1697
for every *m* pertaining to God, and 1Chr 26:32 1697
the king in any *m* of the courses 1Chr 27:1 1697
and Levites concerning any *m* 2Chr 8:15 1697
year, and see that ye hasten the *m* 2Chr 24:5 1697
till the *m* came to Darius Ezr 5:5 2941
by letter concerning this *m* Ezr 5:5
pleasure to us concerning this *m* Ezr 5:17 1836
for this *m* belongeth unto thee Ezr 10:4 1697
God, trembling because of this *m* Ezr 10:9 1697
God for this *m* be turned from us Ezr 10:14 1697
Tikvah were employed about this *m* Ezr 10:15
the tenth month to examine the *m* Ezr 10:16 1697
might have *m* for an evil report Neh 6:13
inquisition was made of the *m* Est 2:23 1697
they had seen concerning this *m* Est 9:26 3602
the root of the *m* is found in me Job 19:28 1697
For I am full of *m* Job 32:18 4405
My heart is inditing a good *m* Ps 45:1 1697
encourage themselves in an evil *m* Ps 64:5 1697
faithful spirit concealeth the *m* Prov 11:13 1697
He that handleth a *m* wisely shall Prov 16:20 1697
a *m* separateth very friends Prov 17:9 1697
He that answereth a *m* before he Prov 18:13 1697
of kings is to search out a *m* Prov 25:2 1697
a province, marvel not at the *m* Eccl 5:8 2659
which hath wings shall tell the *m* Eccl 10:20 1697
the conclusion of the whole *m* Eccl 12:13 1697
for the *m* was not perceived Jer 38:27 1697
by his side, reported the *m* Eze 9:11 1697
this of thy whoredoms a small *m* Eze 16:20
So he consented to them in this *m* Dan 1:14 1697
earth that can shew the king's *m* Dan 2:10 4406
made known unto us the king's *m* Dan 2:23 4406
careful to answer thee in this *m* Dan 3:16 6600
This *m* is by the decree of the Dan 4:17 6600
Hitherto is the end of the *m* Dan 7:28 4406
but I kept the *m* in my heart Dan 7:28 4406
therefore understand the *m* Dan 9:23 1697
it much, and to blaze abroad the *m* Mk 1:45 *3056*
asked him again of the same *m* Mk 10:10
neither part nor lot in this *m* Acts 8:21 *3056*
the *m* from the beginning, and Acts 11:4
for to consider of this *m* Acts 15:6 *3056*
We will hear thee again of this *m* Acts 17:32
If it were a *m* of wrong or wicked Acts 18:14
have a *m* against any man, the law Acts 19:38 *3056*
will know the uttermost of your *m* Acts 24:22 *2596*
having a *m* against another, go to 1Cor 6:1 *4229*
yourselves to be clear in this *m* 2Cor 7:11 *4229*
as a *m* of bounty, and not as of 2Cor 9:5
they were, it maketh no *m* to me Gal 2:6 *1308*
and defraud his brother in any *m* 1Th 4:6 *4229*
how great a *m* a little fire Jas 3:5 *5208*

MATTERS
if any man have any *m* to do Ex 24:14 1697
being *m* of controversy within thy Deut 17:8 1697
and a man of war, and prudent in *m* 1Sa 16:18 1697
the *m* of the war unto the king 2Sa 11:19 1697
him, See, thy *m* are good and right 2Sa 15:3 1697
speakest thou any more of thy *m* 2Sa 19:29 1697
is over you in all *m* of the LORD 2Chr 19:11 1697
of Judah, for all the king's *m* 2Chr 19:11 1697
in all *m* concerning the people Neh 11:24 1697
whether Mordecai's *m* would stand Est 3:4 1697
the *m* of the fastings and their Est 9:31 1697
Esther confirmed these *m* of Purim Est 9:32 1697
not account of any of his *m* Job 33:13 1697
but they devise deceitful *m* Ps 35:20 1697
do I exercise myself in great *m* Ps 131:1 1419
And in all *m* of wisdom and Dan 1:20 1697
dream, and told the sum of the *m* Dan 7:1 4406
the weightier *m* of the law Mt 23:23
for I will be no judge of such *m* Acts 18:15
any thing concerning other *m* Acts 19:39
and there be judged of these *m* Acts 25:20
unworthy to judge the smallest *m* 1Cor 6:2
or as a busybody in other men's *m* 1Pet 4:15

MATTHAN (*mat'-than*) *Son of Eleazar; ancestor of Jesus.*
and Eleazar begat *M* Mt 1:15 *3157*
and *M* begat Jacob Mt 1:15 *3157*

MATTHAT (*mat'-that*)
1. Son of Levi; an ancestor of Jesus.
Which was the son of *M*, which was Lk 3:24 *3158*
2. Father of Jorim; an ancestor of Jesus.
of Jorim, which was the son of *M* Lk 3:29 *3158*

MATTHEW (*math'-ew*) See LEVI. *A disciple of Jesus.*
thence, he saw a man, named *M* Mt 9:9 *3156*
Thomas, and *M* the publican Mt 10:3 *3156*
and Philip, and Bartholomew, and *M* Mk 3:18 *3156*
M and Thomas, James the son of Lk 6:15 *3156*
and Thomas, Bartholomew, and *M* Acts 1:13 *3156*

MATTHIAS (*mat'-thias*) *Successor to Judas Iscariot as apostle.*
who was surnamed Justus, and *M* Acts 1:23 *3159*
and the lot fell upon *M* Acts 1:26 *3159*

MATTITHIAH (*mat-tith-i'-ah*) See MATTATHIAS.
1. A son of Shallum.
And *M*, one of the Levites, who was 1Chr 9:31 4993
2. A Levite gatekeeper.
and Benaiah, and Maaseiah, and *M* 1Chr 15:18 4993
And *M*, and Elipheleh, and Mikneiah, 1Chr 15:21 4993
and Shemiramoth, and Jehiel, and *M* 1Chr 16:5 4993
3. Son of Jeduthun.
and Jeshaiah, Hashabiah, and *M* 1Chr 25:3 4993
The fourteenth to *M*, he, his sons 1Chr 25:21 4993
4. Married a foreigner in exile.
Jeiel, *M*, Zabad, Zebina, Jadau, Ezr 10:43 4993
5. A priest who aided Ezra.
and beside him stood *M*, and Shema, Neh 8:4 4993

MATTOCK
his coulter, and his ax, and his *m* 1Sa 13:20 4281
that shall be digged with the *m* Is 7:25 4576

MATTOCKS
Yet they had a file for the *m* 1Sa 13:21 4281
with their *m* round about 2Chr 34:6 2719

MAUL
against his neighbour is a *m* Prov 25:18 4650

MAW
and the two cheeks, and the *m* Deut 18:3 6896

MAY
fowl that *m* fly above the earth Gen 1:20
We *m* eat of the fruit of the Gen 3:2
that they *m* breed abundantly in Gen 8:17
that I *m* remember the everlasting Gen 9:16
whose top *m* reach unto heaven Gen 11:4
that they *m* not understand one Gen 11:7
that it *m* be well with me for thy Gen 12:13
unto my maid; it *m* Gen 16:2 194
that I *m* obtain children Gen 16:2
that the LORD *m* bring upon Gen 18:19
out unto us, that we *m* know them Gen 19:5
that we *m* preserve seed of our Gen 19:32

M

that we *m* preserve seed of our ... Gen 19:34
that they *m* be a witness unto me, ... Gen 21:30
that I *m* bury my dead out of my ... Gen 23:4
That he *m* give me the cave of ... Gen 23:9
I pray thee, that I *m* drink ... Gen 24:14
that I *m* turn to the right hand, ... Gen 24:49
me away that I *m* go to my master ... Gen 24:56
and bring it to me, that I *m* eat ... Gen 27:4
that my soul *m* bless thee before ... Gen 27:4
me savoury meat, that I *m* eat ... Gen 27:7
it to thy father, that he *m* eat ... Gen 27:10
that he *m* bless thee before his ... Gen 27:10
venison, that thy soul *m* bless me ... Gen 27:19
that I *m* feel thee, my son, ... Gen 27:21
that my soul *m* bless thee ... Gen 27:25
venison, that thy soul *m* bless me ... Gen 27:31
that I *m* go in unto her ... Gen 29:21
that I *m* also have children by ... Gen 30:3
that I *m* go unto mine own place, ... Gen 30:25
that they *m* judge betwixt us both ... Gen 31:37
that I *m* find grace in thy sight ... Gen 32:5
that we *m* live, and not die ... Gen 42:2
that your words *m* be proved ... Gen 42:16
that we *m* live, and not die, both ... Gen 43:8
that he *m* send away your other ... Gen 43:14
that he *m* seek occasion against ... Gen 43:18
that I *m* set mine eyes upon him ... Gen 44:21
for we *m* not see the man's face, ... Gen 44:26 3201
that ye *m* dwell in the land of ... Gen 46:34
and give us seed, that we *m* live ... Gen 47:19
that I *m* tell you that which ... Gen 49:1
that she *m* nurse the child for ... Ex 2:7
call him, that he *m* eat bread ... Ex 2:20
that we *m* sacrifice to the LORD ... Ex 3:18
That they *m* believe that the LORD ... Ex 4:5
Let my son go, that he *m* serve me ... Ex 4:23
that they *m* hold a feast unto me ... Ex 5:1
that they *m* labour therein ... Ex 5:9
that I *m* lay my hand upon Egypt, ... Ex 7:4
that they *m* serve me in the ... Ex 7:16
water, that they *m* become blood ... Ex 7:19
that there *m* be blood throughout ... Ex 7:19
people go, that they *m* serve me ... Ex 8:1
that he *m* take away the frogs ... Ex 8:8
that they *m* do sacrifice unto the ... Ex 8:8
that they *m* remain in the river ... Ex 8:9
that it *m* become lice throughout ... Ex 8:16
people go, that they *m* serve me ... Ex 8:20
that ye *m* sacrifice to the LORD ... Ex 8:28
of flies *m* depart from Pharaoh ... Ex 8:29
people go, that they *m* serve me ... Ex 9:1
people go, that they *m* serve me ... Ex 9:13
that I *m* smite thee and thy people ... Ex 9:15
that my name *m* be declared ... Ex 9:16
that there *m* bc hail in all the ... Ex 9:22
that ye *m* know how that I am the ... Ex 10:2
people go, that they *m* serve me ... Ex 10:3
that they *m* serve the LORD their ... Ex 10:7
that they *m* come up upon the land ... Ex 10:12
that he *m* take away from me this ... Ex 10:17
that there *m* be darkness over the ... Ex 10:21
even darkness which *m* be felt ... Ex 10:21
that we *m* sacrifice unto the LORD ... Ex 10:25
that ye *m* know how that the LORD ... Ex 11:7
that my wonders *m* be multiplied ... Ex 11:9
that only *m* be done of you ... Ex 12:16
the LORD's law *m* be in thy mouth ... Ex 13:9
that the Egyptians *m* know that I ... Ex 14:4
that we *m* serve the Egyptians ... Ex 14:12
that the waters *m* come again upon ... Ex 14:26
that I *m* prove them, whether they ... Ex 16:4
that they *m* see the bread ... Ex 16:32
Give us water that we *m* drink ... Ex 17:2
of it, that the people *m* drink ... Ex 17:6
that the people *m* hear when I ... Ex 19:9
that thy days *m* be long upon the ... Ex 20:12
that his fear *m* be before your ... Ex 20:20
from mine altar, that he *m* die ... Ex 21:14
that the poor of thy people *m* eat ... Ex 23:11
that thine ox and thine ass *m* rest ... Ex 23:12
and the stranger, *m* be refreshed ... Ex 23:12
that I *m* dwell among them ... Ex 25:8
that the ark *m* be borne with them ... Ex 25:14
that the table *m* be borne with ... Ex 25:28
that they *m* give light over ... Ex 25:37
that the loops *m* take hold one of ... Ex 26:5
tent together, that it *m* be one ... Ex 26:11
that the net *m* be even to the ... Ex 27:5
that he *m* minister unto me in the ... Ex 28:1
that they *m* make Aaron's garments ... Ex 28:3
that he *m* minister unto me in the ... Ex 28:3
that he *m* minister unto me in the ... Ex 28:4
that it *m* be above the curious ... Ex 28:28
that it *m* be upon the mitre ... Ex 28:37
that Aaron *m* bear the iniquity of ... Ex 28:38
that they *m* be accepted before ... Ex 28:38
that they *m* minister unto me in ... Ex 28:41
that I *m* dwell among them ... Ex 29:46
that it *m* be a memorial unto the ... Ex 30:16
them, that they *m* be most holy ... Ex 30:29
that they *m* minister unto me in ... Ex 30:30
that they *m* make all that I have ... Ex 31:6
that ye *m* know that I am the LORD ... Ex 31:13
Six days *m* work be done ... Ex 31:15
that my wrath *m* wax hot against ... Ex 32:10
them, and that I *m* consume them ... Ex 32:10
that he *m* bestow upon you a ... Ex 32:29
that I *m* know what to do unto ... Ex 33:5
that I *m* know thee, that I *m* ... Ex 33:13
put in his heart that he *m* teach ... Ex 35:34
that he *m* minister unto me in the ... Ex 40:13
that they *m* minister unto me in ... Ex 40:15
m be used in any other use ... Lev 7:24
that the breast *m* be waved for a ... Lev 7:30

that ye *m* put difference between ... Lev 10:10
that ye *m* teach the children of ... Lev 10:11
Yet these *m* ye eat of every ... Lev 11:21
Even these of them ye *m* eat ... Lev 11:22
Of all meat which *m* be eaten ... Lev 11:34
all drink that *m* be drunk in ... Lev 11:34
if any beast, of which ye *m* eat ... Lev 11:39
between the beast that *m* be eaten ... Lev 11:47
and the beast that *m* not be eaten ... Lev 11:47
in water, that he *m* be clean ... Lev 14:8
m cover the mercy seat that is ... Lev 16:13
that ye *m* be clean from all your ... Lev 16:30
Israel *m* bring their sacrifices ... Lev 17:5
even that they *m* bring them unto ... Lev 17:5
any beast or fowl that *m* be eaten ... Lev 17:13
that it *m* yield unto you the ... Lev 19:25
for her *m* he be defiled ... Lev 21:3
whereby he *m* be made unclean, or ... Lev 22:5
man of whom he *m* take uncleanness ... Lev 22:5
she *m* not eat of an offering of ... Lev 22:12
that it *m* be an holy convocation ... Lev 23:21
That your generations *m* know that ... Lev 23:43
that it *m* be on the bread for a ... Lev 24:7
that he *m* return unto his ... Lev 25:27
then he *m* redeem it within a ... Lev 25:29
within a full year *m* he redeem it ... Lev 25:29
they *m* be redeemed, and they shall ... Lev 25:31
m the Levites redeem at any time ... Lev 25:32
of their cities *m* not be sold ... Lev 25:34
that he *m* live with thee ... Lev 25:35
that thy brother *m* live with thee ... Lev 25:36
he is sold he *m* be redeemed again ... Lev 25:48
one of his brethren *m* redeem him ... Lev 25:48
m redeem him, or any that is nigh ... Lev 25:49
him of his family *m* redeem him ... Lev 25:49
he be able, he *m* redeem himself ... Lev 25:49
that they *m* minister unto him ... Num 3:6
do unto them, that they *m* live ... Num 4:19
that the Nazarite *m* drink wine ... Num 6:20
that they *m* be to do the service ... Num 7:5
that they *m* execute the service ... Num 8:11
that we *m* not offer an offering ... Num 9:7
that they *m* be to you for a ... Num 10:10
Give us flesh, that we *m* eat ... Num 11:13
that they *m* stand there with thee ... Num 11:16
that they *m* eat a whole month ... Num 11:21
that they *m* search the land of ... Num 13:2
that ye *m* look upon it, and ... Num 15:39
That ye *m* remember, and do all my ... Num 15:40
that I *m* consume them in a moment ... Num 16:21
that I *m* consume them as in a ... Num 16:45
that they *m* be joined unto thee, ... Num 18:2
that he *m* bring her forth without ... Num 19:3
that we *m* smite them, and that I ... Num 22:6
that I *m* drive them out of the ... Num 22:6
that I *m* know what the LORD will ... Num 22:19
LORD *m* be turned away from Israel ... Num 25:4
Which *m* go out before them, and ... Num 27:17
which *m* go in before them, and ... Num 27:17
which *m* lead them out ... Num 27:17
and which *m* bring them in ... Num 27:17
children of Israel *m* be obedient ... Num 27:20
her husband *m* establish it ... Num 30:13
or her husband *m* make it void ... Num 30:13
Every thing that *m* abide the fire ... Num 31:23
on this side Jordan *m* be ours ... Num 32:32
manslayer, that he *m* flee thither ... Num 35:6
that the slayer *m* flee thither ... Num 35:11
person unawares *m* flee thither ... Num 35:15
a stone, wherewith he *m* die ... Num 35:17
of wood, wherewith he *m* die ... Num 35:18
any stone, wherewith a man *m* die ... Num 35:23
that the children of Israel *m* ... Num 36:8
of them for money, that ye *m* eat ... Deut 2:6
them for money, that ye *m* drink ... Deut 2:6
me meat for money, that I *m* eat ... Deut 2:28
water for money, that I *m* drink ... Deut 2:28
for to do them, that ye *m* live ... Deut 4:1
that ye *m* keep the commandments ... Deut 4:2
that they *m* learn to fear me all ... Deut 4:10
that they *m* teach their children ... Deut 4:10
that it *m* go well with thee, and ... Deut 4:40
that ye *m* learn them, and keep, and ... Deut 5:1
thy maidservant *m* rest as well as ... Deut 5:14
that thy days *m* be prolonged ... Deut 5:16
that it *m* go well with thee, in ... Deut 5:16
that they *m* do them in the land ... Deut 5:31
commanded you, that ye *m* live ... Deut 5:33
that it *m* be well with you, and ... Deut 5:33
that ye *m* prolong your days in ... Deut 5:33
and that thy days *m* be prolonged ... Deut 6:2
that it *m* be well with thee, and ... Deut 6:3
that ye *m* increase mightily, as ... Deut 6:3
that it *m* be well with thee, and ... Deut 6:18
that they *m* serve other gods ... Deut 7:4
ye observe to do, that ye *m* live ... Deut 8:1
that he *m* establish his covenant ... Deut 8:18
that he *m* perform the word which ... Deut 9:5
that I *m* destroy them, and blot ... Deut 9:14
the people, that they *m* go in ... Deut 10:11
that ye *m* be strong, and go in and ... Deut 11:8
that ye *m* prolong your days in ... Deut 11:9
that they *m* be as frontlets ... Deut 11:18
That your days *m* be multiplied ... Deut 11:21
the clean *m* eat thereof, as of ... Deut 12:15
that it *m* go well with thee, and ... Deut 12:25
that it *m* go well with thee, and ... Deut 12:28
that the LORD *m* turn from the ... Deut 13:17
not fins and scales ye *m* not eat ... Deut 14:10
But of all clean fowls ye *m* eat ... Deut 14:20
is in thy gates, that he *m* eat it ... Deut 14:21
that the LORD thy God *m* bless ... Deut 14:29
that he *m* learn to fear the LORD ... Deut 17:19
to the end that he *m* prolong his ... Deut 17:20

that every slayer *m* flee thither ... Deut 19:3
flee thither, that he *m* live ... Deut 19:4
avenger of blood, that he *m* die ... Deut 19:12
that it *m* go well with thee ... Deut 19:13
that he *m* not make the son of the ... Deut 21:16 3201
that it *m* be well with thee, and ... Deut 22:7
he *m* not put her away all his ... Deut 22:19 3201
he *m* not put her away all his ... Deut 22:29 3201
that the LORD thy God *m* bless ... Deut 23:20
out of his house, she *m* go ... Deut 24:2
m not take her again to be his ... Deut 24:4 3201
that he *m* sleep in his own ... Deut 24:13
that the LORD thy God *m* bless ... Deut 24:19
that the judges *m* judge them ... Deut 25:1
Forty stripes he *m* give him ... Deut 25:3
that thy days *m* be lengthened in ... Deut 25:15
that they *m* eat within thy gates, ... Deut 26:12
that ye *m* prosper in all that ye ... Deut 29:9
That he *m* establish thee to day ... Deut 29:13
that he *m* be unto thee a God, as ... Deut 29:13
that we *m* do all the words of ... Deut 29:29
it unto us, that we *m* hear it ... Deut 30:12
it unto us, that we *m* hear it ... Deut 30:13
that both thou and thy seed *m* live ... Deut 30:19
that ye *m* do unto them according ... Deut 31:5
m hear, and that they *m* learn ... Deut 31:12
m hear, and learn to fear the LORD ... Deut 31:13
that I *m* give him a charge ... Deut 31:14
that this song *m* be a witness for ... Deut 31:19
that it *m* be there for a witness ... Deut 31:26
that I *m* speak these words in ... Deut 31:28
afterward *m* ye go your way ... Josh 2:16
that ye *m* know the way by which ... Josh 3:4
all Israel, that they *m* know that ... Josh 3:7
That this *m* be a sign among you, ... Josh 4:6
now therefore we *m* not touch them ... Josh 9:19 3201
help me, that we *m* smite Gibeon ... Josh 10:4
that I *m* cast lots for you here ... Josh 18:6
that I *m* here cast lots for you ... Josh 18:8
unwittingly *m* flee thither ... Josh 20:3
that he *m* dwell among them ... Josh 20:4
But that it *m* be a witness ... Josh 22:27
that your children *m* not say to ... Josh 22:27
that we *m* say again, Behold the ... Josh 22:28
that we *m* fight against the ... Judg 1:3
through them I *m* prove Israel ... Judg 2:22
Bring out thy son, that he *m* die ... Judg 6:30
that God *m* hearken unto you ... Judg 9:7
that we *m* fight with the children ... Judg 11:6
alone two months, that I *m* go up ... Judg 11:37
She *m* not eat of any thing that ... Judg 13:14
come to pass we *m* do thee honour ... Judg 13:17
thy riddle, that we *m* hear it ... Judg 14:13
that he *m* declare unto us the ... Judg 14:15
that we *m* deliver thee into the ... Judg 15:12
by what means we *m* prevail ... Judg 16:5
that we *m* bind him to afflict him ... Judg 16:5
Samson, that he *m* make us sport ... Judg 16:25
Suffer me that I *m* feel the ... Judg 16:26
standeth, that I *m* lean upon them ... Judg 16:26
that I *m* be at once avenged of ... Judg 16:28
to sojourn where I *m* find a place ... Judg 17:9
that we *m* know whether our way ... Judg 18:5
that we *m* go up against them ... Judg 18:9
here, that thine heart *m* be merry ... Judg 19:9
thine house, that we *m* know him ... Judg 19:22
for the people, that they *m* do ... Judg 20:10
that we *m* put them to death, and ... Judg 20:13
Howbeit we *m* not give them wives ... Judg 21:18 3201
grant you that ye *m* find rest ... Ruth 1:9
that they *m* be your husbands ... Ruth 1:11
that she *m* glean them, and rebuke ... Ruth 2:16
that it *m* be well with thee ... Ruth 3:1
it, then tell me, that I *m* know ... Ruth 4:4
that his name *m* be famous in ... Ruth 4:14
that he *m* appear before the LORD, ... 1Sa 1:22
that I *m* eat a piece of bread ... 1Sa 2:36
it *m* save us out of the hand of ... 1Sa 4:3
and send it away, that it *m* go ... 1Sa 6:8
That we also *m* be like all the ... 1Sa 8:20
and that our king *m* judge us ... 1Sa 8:20
that he *m* save my people out of ... 1Sa 9:16
Up, that I *m* send thee away ... 1Sa 9:26
that I *m* shew thee the word of ... 1Sa 9:27
that I *m* thrust out all your ... 1Sa 11:2
that we *m* send messengers unto ... 1Sa 11:3
that we *m* put them to death ... 1Sa 11:12
that I *m* reason with you before ... 1Sa 12:7
that ye *m* perceive and see that ... 1Sa 12:17
it *m* be that the LORD will work ... 1Sa 14:6
that I *m* be avenged on mine ... 1Sa 14:24
that I *m* worship the LORD ... 1Sa 15:25
that I *m* worship the LORD thy God ... 1Sa 15:30
a man, that we *m* fight together ... 1Sa 17:10
that all the earth *m* know that ... 1Sa 17:46
that she *m* be a snare to him, and ... 1Sa 18:21
the Philistines *m* be against him ... 1Sa 18:21
me in the bed, that I *m* slay him ... 1Sa 19:15
that I *m* hide myself in the field ... 1Sa 20:5
the country, that I *m* dwell there ... 1Sa 27:5
that I *m* go to her, and enquire of ... 1Sa 28:7
that he *m* go again to his place ... 1Sa 29:4
that I *m* not go fight against the ... 1Sa 29:8
that they *m* lead them away, and ... 1Sa 30:22
that they *m* make a league with ... 2Sa 3:21
that they *m* dwell in a place of ... 2Sa 7:10
that it *m* continue for ever ... 2Sa 7:29
that I *m* shew him kindness for ... 2Sa 9:1
that I *m* shew the kindness of God ... 2Sa 9:3
master's son *m* have food to eat ... 2Sa 9:10
that he *m* be smitten, and die ... 2Sa 11:15
to me, that the child *m* live ... 2Sa 12:22
meat in my sight, that I *m* see it ... 2Sa 13:5
sight, that I *m* eat at her hand ... 2Sa 13:6

that I *m* eat of thine hand ... 2Sa 13:10
that we *m* kill him, for the life ... 2Sa 14:7
it *m* be that the king will ... 2Sa 14:15
that I *m* send thee to the king, ... 2Sa 14:32
seeing I go whither I *m*, return ... 2Sa 15:20
faint in the wilderness *m* drink ... 2Sa 16:2
that I *m* find grace in thy sight ... 2Sa 16:4
how much more now *m* this ... 2Sa 16:11
It *m* be that the LORD will look ... 2Sa 16:12
I *m* not tarry thus with thee ... 2Sa 18:14
that I *m* ride thereon, and go to ... 2Sa 19:26
that I *m* die in mine own city, and ... 2Sa 19:37
hither, that I *m* speak with thee ... 2Sa 20:16
that ye *m* bless the inheritance ... 2Sa 21:3
that I *m* know the number of the ... 2Sa 24:2
eyes of my lord the king *m* see it ... 2Sa 24:3
of them, that I *m* do it unto thee ... 2Sa 24:12
that the plague *m* be stayed from ... 2Sa 24:21
that my lord the king *m* get heat ... 1Kin 1:2
come up after him, that he *m* come ... 1Kin 1:35
That the LORD *m* continue his word ... 1Kin 2:4
that I *m* discern between good and ... 1Kin 3:9
That thine eyes *m* be open toward ... 1Kin 8:29
That they *m* fear thee all the ... 1Kin 8:40
of the earth *m* know thy name ... 1Kin 8:43
that they *m* know that this house, ... 1Kin 8:43
that they *m* have compassion on ... 1Kin 8:50
That thine eyes *m* be open unto ... 1Kin 8:52
That he *m* incline our hearts unto ... 1Kin 8:58
earth *m* know that the LORD is God ... 1Kin 8:60
that I *m* go to mine own country ... 1Kin 11:21
that David my servant *m* have a ... 1Kin 11:36
that I *m* answer this people ... 1Kin 12:6
ye that we *m* answer this people ... 1Kin 12:9
that my hand *m* be restored me ... 1Kin 13:6
I *m* not return with thee, nor go ... 1Kin 13:16 3201
that he *m* eat bread and drink ... 1Kin 13:18
Israel, that he *m* depart from me ... 1Kin 15:19
water in a vessel, that I *m* drink ... 1Kin 17:10
two sticks, that I *m* go in ... 1Kin 17:12
me and my son, that we *m* eat it ... 1Kin 17:12
peradventure we *m* find grass to ... 1Kin 18:5
that this people *m* know that thou ... 1Kin 18:37
but this thing I *m* not do ... 1Kin 20:9 3201
that I *m* have it for a garden of ... 1Kin 21:2
out, and stone him, that he *m* die ... 1Kin 21:10
by whom we *m* enquire of the LORD ... 1Kin 22:8
persuade Ahab, that he *m* go up ... 1Kin 22:20
that we *m* enquire of the LORD by ... 2Kin 3:11
with water, that ye *m* drink ... 2Kin 3:17
that I *m* run to the man of God, ... 2Kin 4:22
for the people, that they *m* eat ... 2Kin 4:41
unto the people, that they *m* eat ... 2Kin 4:42
Give the people, that they *m* eat ... 2Kin 4:43
m I not wash in them, and be clean ... 2Kin 5:12
a place there, where we *m* dwell ... 2Kin 6:2
and spy where he is, that I *m* send ... 2Kin 6:13
open his eyes, that he *m* see ... 2Kin 6:17
of these men, that they *m* see ... 2Kin 6:20
before them, that they *m* eat ... 2Kin 6:22
that we *m* eat him to day, and we ... 2Kin 6:28
Give thy son, that we *m* eat him ... 2Kin 6:29
now therefore come, that we *m* go ... 2Kin 7:9
that I *m* avenge the blood of my ... 2Kin 9:7
that they *m* eat their own dung, ... 2Kin 18:27
olive and of honey, that ye *m* live ... 2Kin 18:32
It *m* be the LORD thy God will ... 2Kin 19:4 194
all the kingdoms of the earth *m* ... 2Kin 19:19
that he *m* sum the silver which is ... 2Kin 22:4
evil, that it *m* not grieve me ... 1Chr 4:10
that they *m* gather themselves ... 1Chr 13:2
that ye *m* bring up the ark of the ... 1Chr 15:12
that we *m* give thanks to thy holy ... 1Chr 16:35
that thy name *m* be magnified for ... 1Chr 17:24
that it *m* be before thee for ever ... 1Chr 17:27
of them to me, that I *m* know it ... 1Chr 21:2
of them, that I *m* do it unto thee ... 1Chr 21:10
that I *m* build an altar therein ... 1Chr 21:22
that the plague *m* be stayed from ... 1Chr 21:22
that they *m* dwell in Jerusalem ... 1Chr 23:25
that ye *m* possess this good land, ... 1Chr 28:8
and knowledge, that I *m* go out ... 2Chr 1:10
That thine eyes *m* be open upon ... 2Chr 6:20
That they *m* fear thee, to walk in ... 2Chr 6:31
of the earth *m* know thy name ... 2Chr 6:33
m know that this house which I ... 2Chr 6:33
that my name *m* be there for ever ... 2Chr 7:16
What advice give ye that we *m* ... 2Chr 10:9
that they *m* know my service, and ... 2Chr 12:8
the same *m* be a priest of them ... 2Chr 13:9
Israel, that he *m* depart from me ... 2Chr 16:3
by whom we *m* enquire of the LORD ... 2Chr 18:7
king of Israel, that he *m* go up ... 2Chr 18:19
to them, that they *m* help me ... 2Chr 28:23
fierce wrath *m* turn away from us ... 2Chr 29:10
of his wrath *m* turn away from you ... 2Chr 30:8
that they *m* do according to the ... 2Chr 35:6
That search *m* be made in the book ... Ezr 4:15
That they *m* offer sacrifices of ... Ezr 6:10
which *m* judge all the people that ... Ezr 7:25
that our God *m* lighten our eyes, ... Ezr 9:8
that ye *m* be strong, and eat the ... Ezr 9:12
sepulchres, that I *m* build it ... Neh 2:5
that they *m* convey me over till I ... Neh 2:7
that he *m* give me timber to make ... Neh 2:8
the night they *m* be a guard to us ... Neh 4:22
up corn for them, that we *m* eat ... Neh 5:2
that they *m* gather together all ... Est 2:3
written that they *m* be destroyed ... Est 3:9
golden sceptre, that he *m* live ... Est 4:11
that he *m* do as Esther hath said ... Est 5:5
that Mordecai *m* be hanged thereon ... Est 5:14
that they *m* array the man withal ... Est 6:9
the king's ring, *m* no man reverse ... Est 8:8

It *m* be that my sons have sinned, ... Job 1:5 194
mourn *m* be exalted to safety ... Job 5:11
that I *m* take comfort a little, ... Job 10:20
let me alone, that I *m* speak ... Job 13:13
Turn from him, that he *m* rest ... Job 14:6
that ye *m* know there is a ... Job 19:29
Suffer me that I *m* speak ... Job 21:3
unto God, as he that is wise *m* be ... Job 22:2
He *m* prepare it, but the just ... Job 27:17
that God *m* know mine integrity ... Job 31:6
will speak, that I *m* be refreshed ... Job 32:20
That he *m* withdraw man from his ... Job 33:17
of iniquity *m* hide themselves ... Job 34:22
that Job *m* be tried unto the end ... Job 34:36
Thy wickedness *m* hurt a man as ... Job 35:8
thy righteousness *m* profit the ... Job 35:8
Every man *m* see it ... Job 36:25
man *m* behold it afar off ... Job 36:25
that all men *m* know his work ... Job 37:7
that they *m* do whatsoever he ... Job 37:12
abundance of waters *m* cover thee ... Job 38:34
send lightnings, that they *m* go ... Job 38:35
that the foot *m* crush them ... Job 39:15
that the wild beast *m* break them ... Job 39:15
That I *m* shew forth all thy ... Ps 9:14
that the nations *m* know ... Ps 9:20
that the poor *m* fall by his ... Ps 10:10
of the earth *m* no more oppress ... Ps 10:18
that they *m* privily shoot at the ... Ps 11:2
I *m* tell all my bones ... Ps 22:17
That I *m* publish with the voice ... Ps 26:7
that I *m* dwell in the house of ... Ps 27:4
weeping *m* endure for a night, but ... Ps 30:5
my glory *m* sing praise to thee ... Ps 30:12
many days, that he *m* see good ... Ps 34:12
that I *m* know how frail I am ... Ps 39:4
that I *m* recover strength, before ... Ps 39:13
me up, that I *m* requite them ... Ps 41:10
that ye *m* tell it to the ... Ps 48:13
that he *m* judge his people ... Ps 50:4
which thou hast broken *m* rejoice ... Ps 51:8
that I *m* walk before God in the ... Ps 56:13
that they *m* not see the sun ... Ps 58:8
consume them, that they *m* not be ... Ps 59:13
that it *m* be displayed because of ... Ps 60:4
That thy beloved *m* be delivered ... Ps 60:5
and truth, which *m* preserve him ... Ps 61:7
that I *m* daily perform my vows ... Ps 61:8
That they *m* shoot in secret at ... Ps 64:4
that he *m* dwell in thy courts ... Ps 65:4
That thy way *m* be known upon ... Ps 67:2
That thy foot *m* be dipped in the ... Ps 68:23
that they *m* dwell there, and have ... Ps 69:35
whereunto I *m* continually resort ... Ps 71:3
that I *m* declare all thy works ... Ps 73:28
who *m* stand in thy sight when ... Ps 76:7
that the name of Israel *m* be no ... Ps 83:4
that they *m* seek thy name, O LORD ... Ps 83:16
That men *m* know that thou, whose ... Ps 83:18
where she *m* lay her young, even ... Ps 84:3
that thy people *m* rejoice in thee ... Ps 85:6
that glory *m* dwell in our land ... Ps 85:9
that they which hate me *m* see it ... Ps 86:17
that we *m* apply our hearts unto ... Ps 90:12
that we *m* rejoice and be glad all ... Ps 90:14
that they *m* dwell with me ... Ps 101:6
that I *m* cut off all wicked doers ... Ps 101:8
a bound that they *m* not pass over ... Ps 104:9
that he *m* bring forth food out of ... Ps 104:14
That I *m* see the good of thy ... Ps 106:5
that I *m* rejoice in the gladness ... Ps 106:5
that I *m* glory with thine ... Ps 106:5
that they *m* prepare a city for ... Ps 107:36
which *m* yield fruits of increase ... Ps 107:37
That thy beloved *m* be delivered ... Ps 108:6
that he *m* cut off the memory of ... Ps 109:15
That they *m* know that this is thy ... Ps 109:27
that he *m* give them the heritage ... Ps 111:6
That he *m* set him with princes, ... Ps 113:8
with thy servant, that I *m* live ... Ps 119:17
that I *m* behold wondrous things ... Ps 119:18
that I *m* learn thy commandments ... Ps 119:73
come unto me, that I *m* live ... Ps 119:77
unto thy word, that I *m* live ... Ps 119:116
that I *m* know thy testimonies ... Ps 119:125
was on our side, now *m* Israel say ... Ps 124:1
from my youth, *m* Israel now say ... Ps 129:1
prison, that I *m* praise thy name ... Ps 142:7
That our sons *m* be as plants ... Ps 144:12
that our daughters *m* be as corner ... Ps 144:12
That our garners *m* be full ... Ps 144:13
that our sheep *m* bring forth ... Ps 144:13
That our oxen *m* be strong to ... Ps 144:14
that thy lips *m* keep knowledge ... Prov 5:2
That they *m* keep thee from the ... Prov 7:5
all the things that *m* be desired ... Prov 8:11
That I *m* cause those that love me ... Prov 8:21
that he *m* depart from hell ... Prov 15:24
that his heart *m* discover itself ... Prov 18:2
An inheritance *m* be gotten ... Prov 20:21
That thy trust *m* be in the LORD ... Prov 22:19
not what a day *m* bring forth ... Prov 27:1
glad, that I *m* answer him that ... Prov 27:11
any thing whereof it *m* be said ... Eccl 1:10
that he *m* give to him that is ... Eccl 2:26
which he *m* carry away in his hand ... Eccl 5:15
neither *m* he contend with him ... Eccl 6:10 3201
who *m* say unto him, What doest ... Eccl 8:4
the spices thereof *m* flow out ... Song 4:16
that we *m* seek him with thee ... Song 6:1
return, that we *m* look upon thee ... Song 6:13
that they *m* be placed alone in ... Is 5:8
that they *m* follow strong drink ... Is 5:11
hasten his work, that we *m* see it ... Is 5:19

nigh and come, that we *m* know it ... Is 5:19
that he *m* know to refuse the evil ... Is 7:15
that widows *m* be their prey, and ... Is 10:2
that they *m* rob the fatherless ... Is 10:2
be few, that a child *m* write them ... Is 10:19
that they *m* go into the gates of ... Is 13:2
or tail, branch or rush, *m* do ... Is 19:15
is shut up, that no man *m* come in ... Is 24:10
keepeth the truth *m* enter in ... Is 26:2
that he *m* make peace with me ... Is 27:5
ye *m* cause the weary to rest ... Is 28:12
that he *m* do his work, his ... Is 28:21
that they *m* add sin to sin ... Is 30:1
that it *m* be for the time to come ... Is 30:8
that he *m* be gracious unto you, ... Is 30:18
that he *m* have mercy upon you ... Is 30:18
that they *m* eat their own dung, ... Is 36:12
It *m* be the LORD thy God will ... Is 37:4
m know that thou art the LORD ... Is 37:20
That they *m* see, and know, and ... Is 41:20
that we *m* consider them, and know ... Is 41:22
that we *m* know that ye are gods ... Is 41:23
that we *m* be dismayed, and behold ... Is 41:23
the beginning, that we *m* know ... Is 41:26
and beforetime, that we *m* say ... Is 41:26
and look, ye blind, that ye *m* see ... Is 42:18
that they *m* be justified ... Is 43:9
that ye *m* know and believe me, and ... Is 43:10
that they *m* be ashamed ... Is 44:9
that it *m* remain in the house ... Is 44:13
That they *m* know from the rising ... Is 45:6
and compare me, that we *m* be like ... Is 46:5
they *m* forget, yet will I not ... Is 49:15
give place to me that I *m* dwell ... Is 49:20
hasteneth that he *m* be loosed ... Is 51:14
that I *m* plant the heavens, and ... Is 51:16
soul, Bow down, that we *m* go over ... Is 51:23
ye the LORD while he *m* be found ... Is 55:6
that it *m* give seed to the sower, ... Is 55:10
that men *m* bring unto thee the ... Is 60:11
and that their kings *m* be brought ... Is 60:11
my hands, that I *m* be glorified ... Is 60:21
that the nations *m* tremble at thy ... Is 64:2
that I *m* not destroy them all ... Is 65:8
That ye *m* suck, and be satisfied ... Is 66:11
that ye *m* milk out, and be ... Is 66:11
and give warning, that they *m* hear ... Jer 6:10
that they *m* provoke me to anger ... Jer 7:18
that it *m* be well unto you ... Jer 7:23
wise man, that *m* understand this ... Jer 9:12
that he *m* declare it, for what ... Jer 9:12
mourning women, that they *m* come ... Jer 9:17
cunning women, that they *m* come ... Jer 9:17
that our eyes *m* run down with ... Jer 9:18
them, that they *m* find it so ... Jer 10:18
That I *m* perform the oath which I ... Jer 11:5
that his name *m* be no more ... Jer 11:19
then *m* ye also do good, that are ... Jer 13:23 3201
thy face, that thy shame *m* appear ... Jer 13:26
that they *m* not hearken unto me ... Jer 16:12
works, that he *m* go up from us ... Jer 21:2
that I *m* repent me of the evil, ... Jer 26:3
that they *m* serve Nebuchadnezzar ... Jer 28:14
husbands, that they *m* bear sons ... Jer 29:6
that ye *m* be increased there, and ... Jer 29:6
that they *m* continue many days ... Jer 32:14
that they *m* fear me for ever, for ... Jer 32:39
Then *m* also my covenant be broken ... Jer 33:21
that ye *m* live many days in the ... Jer 35:7
It *m* be that the house of Judah ... Jer 36:3
that they *m* return every man from ... Jer 36:3
that I *m* forgive their iniquity ... Jer 36:3
It *m* be they will present their ... Jer 36:7
That the LORD thy God *m* shew us ... Jer 42:3
shew us the way wherein we *m* walk ... Jer 42:3
and the thing that we *m* do ... Jer 42:3
that it *m* be well with us, when ... Jer 42:6
that he *m* have mercy upon you, and ... Jer 42:12
that ye *m* know that my words ... Jer 44:29
that he *m* avenge him of his ... Jer 46:10
wings unto Moab, that it *m* flee ... Jer 48:9
that I *m* appoint over her ... Jer 49:19
that he *m* give rest to the land, ... Jer 50:34
that I *m* appoint over her ... Jer 50:44
pain, if so be she *m* be healed ... Jer 51:8
them drunken, that they *m* rejoice ... Jer 51:39
that I *m* comfort thee, O virgin ... Lam 2:13
if so be there *m* be hope ... Lam 3:29
That they *m* want bread and water, ... Eze 4:17
that your altars *m* be laid waste ... Eze 6:6
and your idols *m* be broken ... Eze 6:6
and your images *m* be cut down ... Eze 6:6
your works *m* be abolished ... Eze 6:6
that ye *m* have some that shall ... Eze 6:8
That they *m* walk in my statutes, ... Eze 11:20
it *m* be they will consider, ... Eze 12:3
that they *m* declare all their ... Eze 12:16
that her land *m* be desolate from ... Eze 12:19
That I *m* take the house of Israel ... Eze 14:5
That the house of Israel *m* go no ... Eze 14:11
but that they *m* be my people ... Eze 14:11
I *m* be their God, saith the Lord ... Eze 14:11
that no man *m* pass through ... Eze 14:15
that they *m* come unto thee on ... Eze 16:33
that they *m* see all thy nakedness ... Eze 16:37
that ye *m* know that I am the LORD ... Eze 20:20
That all flesh *m* know that I the ... Eze 21:5
it is furbished that it *m* glitter ... Eze 21:10
furbished, that it *m* be handled ... Eze 21:11
gates, that their heart *m* faint ... Eze 21:15
of the king of Babylon *m* come ... Eze 21:19
that the sword *m* come to Rabbath ... Eze 21:20
iniquity, that they *m* be taken ... Eze 21:23
midst of it, that her time *m* come ... Eze 22:3

that all women *m* be taught not to ... Eze 23:48
that the brass of it *m* be hot ... Eze 24:11
m burn, and that the filthiness of ... Eze 24:11
of it *m* be molten in it ... Eze 24:11
that the scum of it *m* be consumed ... Eze 24:11
that the Ammonites *m* not be ... Eze 25:10
kings, that they *m* behold thee ... Eze 28:17
that they *m* not be meat for them ... Eze 34:10
these slain, that they *m* live ... Eze 37:9
land, that the heathen *m* know me ... Eze 38:16
that they *m* cleanse the land ... Eze 39:12
that ye *m* eat flesh, and drink ... Eze 39:17
that they *m* be ashamed of their ... Eze 43:10
that they *m* keep the whole form ... Eze 43:11
husband, they *m* defile themselves ... Eze 44:25
that he *m* cause the blessing to ... Eze 44:30
that the bath *m* contain the tenth ... Eze 45:11
to the intent that the living *m* ... Dan 4:17
if it *m* be a lengthening of thy ... Dan 4:27
king establisheth *m* be changed ... Dan 6:15
idols, that they *m* be cut off ... Hos 8:4
where is any other that *m* save ... Hos 13:10
good, and not evil, that ye *m* live ... Amos 5:14
it *m* be that the LORD God of ... Amos 5:15
for we *m* not make mention of the ... Amos 6:10
moon be gone, that we *m* sell corn ... Amos 8:5
that we *m* set forth wheat, making ... Amos 8:5
That we *m* buy the poor for silver ... Amos 8:6
the door, that the posts *m* shake ... Amos 9:1
That they *m* possess the remnant ... Amos 9:12
of Esau *m* be cut off by slaughter ... Obad 9
that we *m* know for whose cause ... Jonah 1:7
that the sea *m* be calm unto us ... Jonah 1:11
that ye *m* know the righteousness ... Mic 6:5
That they *m* do evil with both ... Mic 7:3
that he *m* run that readeth it ... Hab 2:2
that he *m* set his nest on high, ... Hab 2:9
that he *m* be delivered from the ... Hab 2:9
it *m* be ye shall be hid in the ... Zeph 2:3 *194*
that I *m* assemble the kingdoms, ... Zeph 3:8
that they *m* all call upon the ... Zeph 3:9
that the fire *m* devour thy cedars ... Zec 11:1
But who *m* abide the day of his ... Mal 3:2
that they *m* offer unto the LORD ... Mal 3:3
that there *m* be meat in mine ... Mal 3:10
me word again, that I *m* come ... Mt 2:8
that they *m* see your good works, ... Mt 5:16
That ye *m* be the children of your ... Mt 5:45
that they *m* have glory of men ... Mt 6:2
That thine alms *m* be in secret ... Mt 6:4 *1410*
that they *m* be seen of men ... Mt 6:5
that they *m* appear unto men to ... Mt 6:16
But that ye *m* know that the Son ... Mt 9:6
If I *m* but touch his garment, I ... Mt 9:21
that they *m* go into the villages, ... Mt 14:15
every word *m* be established ... Mt 18:16
that I *m* have eternal life ... Mt 19:16
that these my two sons *m* sit ... Mt 20:21
Lord, that our eyes *m* be opened ... Mt 20:33
outside of them *m* be clean also ... Mt 23:26
That upon you *m* come all the ... Mt 23:35
if this cup *m* not pass away from ... Mt 26:42 *1410*
that I *m* preach there also ... Mk 1:38
But that ye *m* know that the Son ... Mk 2:10
That seeing they *m* see, and not ... Mk 4:12
and hearing they *m* hear, and not ... Mk 4:12
m lodge under the shadow of it ... Mk 4:32 *1410*
that we *m* enter into them ... Mk 5:12
on her, that she *m* be healed ... Mk 5:23
If I *m* touch but his clothes, I ... Mk 5:28
that they *m* go into the country ... Mk 6:36
that ye *m* keep your own tradition ... Mk 7:9
do that I *m* inherit eternal life ... Mk 10:17
him, Grant unto us that we *m* sit ... Mk 10:37
m forgive you your trespasses ... Mk 11:25
bring me a penny, that I *m* see it ... Mk 12:15
ye will ye *m* do them good ... Mk 14:7 *1410*
now from the cross, that we *m* see ... Mk 15:32
of many hearts *m* be revealed ... Lk 2:35
But that ye *m* know that the Son ... Lk 5:24
which enter in *m* see the light ... Lk 8:16
that they *m* go into the towns and ... Lk 9:12
which come in *m* see the light ... Lk 11:33
m be required of this generation ... Lk 11:50
they *m* open unto him immediately ... Lk 12:36
he *m* say unto thee, Friend, go up ... Lk 14:10
in, that my house *m* be filled ... Lk 14:23
they *m* receive me into their ... Lk 16:4
ye fail, they *m* receive you into ... Lk 16:9
that he *m* dip the tip of his ... Lk 16:24
that he *m* testify unto them, lest ... Lk 16:28
him, Make ready wherewith I *m* sup ... Lk 17:8
that I *m* receive my sight ... Lk 18:41
it *m* be they will reverence him ... Lk 20:13 *2481*
that the inheritance *m* be ours ... Lk 20:14
which are written *m* be fulfilled ... Lk 21:22
that ye *m* be accounted worthy to ... Lk 21:36
us the passover, that we *m* eat ... Lk 22:8
That ye *m* eat and drink at my ... Lk 22:30
that he *m* sift you as wheat ... Lk 22:31
that we *m* give an answer to them ... Jn 1:22
that his deeds *m* be made manifest ... Jn 3:21
he that reapeth *m* rejoice ... Jn 4:36
than these, that ye *m* marvel ... Jn 5:20
we buy bread, that these *m* eat ... Jn 6:5
every one of them *m* take a little ... Jn 6:7
shewest thou then, that we *m* see ... Jn 6:30
on him, *m* have everlasting life ... Jn 6:40
that a man *m* eat thereof, and not ... Jn 6:50
that thy disciples also *m* see the ... Jn 7:3
that ye *m* know, and believe, that ... Jn 10:38
that I *m* awake him out of sleep ... Jn 11:11
there, to the intent ye *m* believe ... Jn 11:15
also go, that we *m* die with him ... Jn 11:16
that they *m* believe that thou ... Jn 11:42
that ye *m* be the children of ... Jn 12:36
that the scripture *m* be fulfilled ... Jn 13:18
ye *m* believe that I am he ... Jn 13:19
where I am, there ye *m* be also ... Jn 14:3
that the Father *m* be glorified in ... Jn 14:13
that he *m* abide with you for ever ... Jn 14:16
But that the world *m* know that I ... Jn 14:31
that it *m* bring forth more fruit ... Jn 15:2
in my name, he *m* give it you ... Jn 15:16
ye *m* remember that I told you of ... Jn 16:4
receive, that your joy *m* be full ... Jn 16:24
that thy Son also *m* glorify thee ... Jn 17:1
hast given me, that they *m* be one ... Jn 17:11
That they all *m* be one ... Jn 17:21
that they also *m* be one in us ... Jn 17:21
that the world *m* believe that ... Jn 17:21
that they *m* be one, even as we ... Jn 17:22
that they *m* be made perfect in ... Jn 17:23
that the world *m* know that thou ... Jn 17:23
that they *m* behold my glory, ... Jn 17:24
thou hast loved me *m* be in them ... Jn 17:26
that ye *m* know that I find no ... Jn 19:4
That he *m* take part of this ... Acts 1:25
that your sins *m* be blotted out ... Acts 3:19
boldness they *m* speak thy word ... Acts 4:29
wonders *m* be done by the name of ... Acts 4:30
whom we *m* appoint over this ... Acts 6:3
he *m* receive the Holy Ghost ... Acts 8:19
of God *m* be purchased with money ... Acts 8:20
of thine heart *m* be forgiven thee ... Acts 8:22
M we know what this new doctrine, ... Acts 17:19 *1410*
we *m* give an account of this ... Acts 19:40 *1410*
that they *m* shave their heads ... Acts 21:24
all *m* know that those things, ... Acts 21:24
captain, *M* I speak unto thee ... Acts 21:37 *1832*
that they *m* set Paul on, and bring ... Acts 23:24
no man *m* deliver me unto them ... Acts 25:11 *1410*
that they *m* receive forgiveness ... Acts 26:18
that I *m* impart unto you some ... Rom 1:11
to the end ye *m* be established ... Rom 1:11
that I *m* be comforted together ... Rom 1:12
Because that which *m* be known of ... Rom 1:19
Let us do evil, that good *m* come ... Rom 3:8
that every mouth *m* be stopped ... Rom 3:19
all the world *m* become guilty ... Rom 3:19
in sin, that grace *m* abound ... Rom 6:1
that we *m* be also glorified ... Rom 8:17
be darkened, that they *m* not see ... Rom 11:10
If by any means I *m* provoke to ... Rom 11:14
mercy they also *m* obtain mercy ... Rom 11:31
that ye *m* prove what is that good ... Rom 12:2
that he *m* eat all things ... Rom 14:2
wherewith one *m* edify another ... Rom 14:19
That ye *m* with one mind and one ... Rom 15:6
that ye *m* abound in hope, through ... Rom 15:13
I have therefore whereof I *m* ... Rom 15:17
That I *m* be delivered from them ... Rom 15:31
m be accepted of the saints ... Rom 15:31
That I *m* come unto you with joy ... Rom 15:32
God, and *m* with you be refreshed ... Rom 15:32
that ye *m* be blameless in the day ... 1Cor 1:8
the Lord, that he *m* instruct him ... 1Cor 2:16
become a fool, that he *m* be wise ... 1Cor 3:18
that the spirit *m* be saved in the ... 1Cor 5:5
that ye *m* be a new lump, as ye ... 1Cor 5:7
that ye *m* give yourselves to ... 1Cor 7:5
Lord, how he *m* please the Lord ... 1Cor 7:32
world, how he *m* please his wife ... 1Cor 7:33
that she *m* be holy both in body ... 1Cor 7:34
how she *m* please her husband ... 1Cor 7:34
not that I *m* cast a snare upon ... 1Cor 7:35
that ye *m* attend upon the Lord ... 1Cor 7:35
I *m* make the gospel of Christ ... 1Cor 9:18
So run, that ye *m* obtain ... 1Cor 9:24
that ye *m* be able to bear it ... 1Cor 10:13
of many, that they *m* be saved ... 1Cor 10:33
m be made manifest among you ... 1Cor 11:19
but rather that ye *m* prophesy ... 1Cor 14:1
that the church *m* receive ... 1Cor 14:5
There are, it *m* be, so many kinds ... 1Cor 14:10
seek that ye *m* excel to the ... 1Cor 14:12
tongue pray that he *m* interpret ... 1Cor 14:13
For ye *m* all prophesy one by one, ... 1Cor 14:31 *1410*
m learn, and all *m* be comforted ... 1Cor 14:31
him, that God *m* be all in all ... 1Cor 15:28
it *m* chance of wheat, or of some ... 1Cor 15:37
it *m* be that I will abide, yea, ... 1Cor 16:6
that ye *m* bring me on my journey ... 1Cor 16:6
see that he *m* be with you without ... 1Cor 16:10
in peace, that he *m* come unto me ... 1Cor 16:11
that we *m* be able to comfort them ... 2Cor 1:4
means of many persons thanks *m* be ... 2Cor 1:11
that I *m* not overcharge you all ... 2Cor 2:5
of the power *m* be of God, and not ... 2Cor 4:7
absent, we *m* be accepted of him ... 2Cor 5:9
that every one *m* receive the ... 2Cor 5:10
that ye *m* have somewhat to answer ... 2Cor 5:12
so there *m* be a performance also ... 2Cor 8:11
m be a supply for their want ... 2Cor 8:14
also *m* be a supply for your want ... 2Cor 8:14
that there *m* be equality ... 2Cor 8:14
that, as I said, ye *m* be ready ... 2Cor 9:3
m abound to every good work ... 2Cor 9:8
that I *m* not be bold when I am ... 2Cor 10:2
That I *m* not seem as if I would ... 2Cor 10:9
that I *m* present you as a chaste ... 2Cor 11:2
that I *m* cut off occasion from ... 2Cor 11:12
they *m* be found even as we ... 2Cor 11:12
that I *m* boast myself a little ... 2Cor 11:16
power of Christ *m* rest upon me ... 2Cor 12:9
that they *m* glory in your flesh ... Gal 6:13
m give unto you the spirit of ... Eph 1:17
that ye *m* know what is the hope ... Eph 1:18
ye *m* understand my knowledge in ... Eph 3:4 *1410*
That Christ *m* dwell in your ... Eph 3:17
M be able to comprehend with all ... Eph 3:18
m grow up into him in all things, ... Eph 4:15
that he *m* have to give to him ... Eph 4:28
that it *m* minister grace unto the ... Eph 4:29
That it *m* be well with thee, and ... Eph 6:3
that ye *m* be able to stand ... Eph 6:11
that ye *m* be able to withstand in ... Eph 6:13
that utterance *m* be given unto me ... Eph 6:19
that I *m* open my mouth boldly, to ... Eph 6:19
that therein I *m* speak boldly ... Eph 6:20
that ye also *m* know my affairs ... Eph 6:21
that your love *m* abound yet more ... Phil 1:9
That ye *m* approve things that are ... Phil 1:10
that ye *m* be sincere and without ... Phil 1:10
That your rejoicing *m* be more ... Phil 1:26
I *m* hear of your affairs, that ye ... Phil 1:27
That ye *m* be blameless and ... Phil 2:15
that I *m* rejoice in the day of ... Phil 2:16
that I also *m* be of good comfort, ... Phil 2:19
ye *m* rejoice, and that I *m* be ... Phil 2:28
but dung, that I *m* win Christ, ... Phil 3:8
That I *m* know him, and the power ... Phil 3:10
if that I *m* apprehend that for ... Phil 3:12
that it *m* be fashioned like unto ... Phil 3:21
that *m* abound to your account ... Phil 4:17
that we *m* present every man ... Col 1:28
That I *m* make it manifest, as I ... Col 4:4
that ye *m* know how ye ought to ... Col 4:6
that ye *m* stand perfect and ... Col 4:12
To the end he *m* stablish your ... 1Th 3:13
That ye *m* walk honestly toward ... 1Th 4:12
that ye *m* have lack of nothing ... 1Th 4:12
that ye *m* be counted worthy of ... 2Th 1:5
Christ *m* be glorified in you ... 2Th 1:12
of the Lord *m* have free course ... 2Th 3:1
that we *m* be delivered from ... 2Th 3:2
with him, that he *m* be ashamed ... 2Th 3:14
Satan, that they *m* learn not to ... 1Ti 1:20
that we *m* lead a quiet and ... 1Ti 2:2
thy profiting *m* appear to all ... 1Ti 4:15
charge, that they *m* be blameless ... 1Ti 5:7
that it *m* relieve them that are ... 1Ti 5:16
all, that others also *m* fear ... 1Ti 5:20
that they *m* lay hold on eternal ... 1Ti 6:19
that I *m* be filled with joy ... 2Ti 1:4
m find mercy of the Lord in that ... 2Ti 1:18
that he *m* please him who hath ... 2Ti 2:4
that they *m* also obtain the ... 2Ti 2:10
that they *m* recover themselves ... 2Ti 2:26
That the man of God *m* be perfect ... 2Ti 3:17
I pray God that it *m* not be laid ... 2Ti 4:16
that he *m* be able by sound ... Titus 1:9
that they *m* be sound in the faith ... Titus 1:13
That they *m* teach the young women ... Titus 2:4
of the contrary part *m* be ashamed ... Titus 2:8
that they *m* adorn the doctrine of ... Titus 2:10
faith *m* become effectual by the ... Philem 6
that we *m* obtain mercy, and find ... Heb 4:16
that he *m* offer both gifts and ... Heb 5:1
as I *m* so say, Levi also, who ... Heb 7:9
that he *m* establish the second ... Heb 10:9
which cannot be shaken *m* remain ... Heb 12:27
whereby we *m* serve God acceptably ... Heb 12:28
So that we *m* boldly say, The Lord ... Heb 13:6
that they *m* do it with joy, and ... Heb 13:17
that I *m* be restored to you the ... Heb 13:19
that ye *m* be perfect and entire, ... Jas 1:4
Yea, a man *m* say, Thou hast faith ... Jas 2:18
mouths, that they *m* obey us ... Jas 3:3
that ye *m* consume it upon your ... Jas 4:3
for another, that ye *m* be healed ... Jas 5:16
the word, that ye *m* grow thereby ... 1Pet 2:2
they *m* by your good works, which ... 1Pet 2:12
that with well doing ye *m* put to ... 1Pet 2:15
they also *m* without the word be ... 1Pet 3:1
they *m* be ashamed that falsely ... 1Pet 3:16
For the time past of our life *m* ... 1Pet 4:3
that God in all things *m* be ... 1Pet 4:11
ye *m* be glad also with exceeding ... 1Pet 4:13
that he *m* exalt you in due time ... 1Pet 5:6
about, seeking whom he *m* devour ... 1Pet 5:8
I will endeavour that ye *m* be ... 2Pet 1:15
That ye *m* be mindful of the words ... 2Pet 3:2
be diligent that ye *m* be found of ... 2Pet 3:14
that ye also *m* have fellowship ... 1Jn 1:3
unto you, that your joy *m* be full ... 1Jn 1:4
we *m* have confidence, and not be ... 1Jn 2:28
that we *m* have boldness in the ... 1Jn 4:17
that ye *m* know that ye have ... 1Jn 5:13
that ye *m* believe on the name of ... 1Jn 5:13
that we *m* know him that is true, ... 1Jn 5:20
to face, that our joy *m* be full ... 2Jn 12
into prison, that ye *m* be tried ... Rev 2:10
that they *m* rest from their ... Rev 14:13
That ye *m* eat the flesh of kings, ... Rev 19:18
that they *m* have right to the ... Rev 22:14
m enter in through the gates into ... Rev 22:14

MAYEST

of the garden thou *m* freely eat ... Gen 2:16
but that thou *m* bury thy dead ... Gen 23:6
that thou *m* be a multitude of ... Gen 28:3
that thou *m* inherit the land ... Gen 28:4
that thou *m* come in unto me ... Gen 38:16
that thou *m* bring forth my people ... Ex 3:10
that thou *m* know that there is ... Ex 8:10
to the end thou *m* know that I am ... Ex 8:22
that thou *m* know that there is ... Ex 9:14
that thou *m* know how that the ... Ex 9:29
that thou *m* tell in the ears of ... Ex 10:2
that thou *m* bring the causes unto ... Ex 18:19
that thou *m* teach them ... Ex 24:12

that thou m bring in thither Ex 26:33
that m thou offer for a freewill Lev 22:23
that thou m use them for the Num 10:2
thou m be to us instead of eyes Num 10:31
from whence thou m see them Num 23:13
thou m curse me them from thence Num 23:27
that thou m inherit his land Deut 2:31
that thou m prolong thy days upon Deut 4:40
with thee, and that thou m go in Deut 6:18
thou m not consume them at once, Deut 7:22 3201
of whose hills thou m dig brass Deut 8:9
that thou m gather in thy corn, Deut 11:14
for thy cattle, that thou m eat Deut 11:15
Notwithstanding thou m kill Deut 12:15
Thou m not eat within thy gates Deut 12:17 3201
thou m eat flesh, whatsoever thy Deut 12:20
thou m not eat the life with the Deut 12:23
or thou m sell it unto an alien Deut 14:21
that thou m learn to fear the Deut 14:23
a foreigner thou m exact it again Deut 15:3
that thou m remember the day when Deut 16:3
Thou m not sacrifice the passover Deut 16:5 3201
thou follow, that thou m live Deut 16:20
thou m not set a stranger over Deut 17:15 3201
for thou m eat of them, and thou Deut 20:19
thou m not hide thyself Deut 22:3 3201
that thou m prolong thy days Deut 22:7
a stranger thou m lend upon usury Deut 23:20
then thou m eat grapes thy fill Deut 23:24
then thou m pluck the ears with Deut 23:25
that thou m be an holy people Deut 26:19
that thou m go in unto the land Deut 27:3
that thou m fear this glorious and Deut 28:58
all thy soul, that thou m live Deut 30:6
in thy heart, that thou m do it Deut 30:14
his judgments, that thou m live Deut 30:16
That thou m love the LORD thy God Deut 30:20
that thou m obey his voice, and Deut 30:20
that thou m cleave unto him Deut 30:20
that thou m dwell in the land Deut 30:20
that thou m observe to do Josh 1:7
that thou m prosper whithersoever Josh 1:7
that thou m observe to do Josh 1:8
then m thou do to them as thou Judg 9:33
that thou m go with us, and fight Judg 11:8
on your way, that thou m go home Judg 19:9
away, that thou m go in peace 1Sa 20:13
that thou m do to him as it shall 1Sa 24:4
that thou m make known unto me 1Sa 28:15
that thou m have strength, when 1Sa 28:22
that thou m reign over all that 2Sa 3:21
then m thou for me defeat the 2Sa 15:34
that thou m bring them down 2Sa 22:28
that thou m save thine own life, 1Kin 1:12
that thou m prosper in all that 1Kin 2:3
that thou m take away the 1Kin 2:31
that thou m hearken unto the 1Kin 8:29
that thou m recover him of his 2Kin 5:6
him, Thou m certainly recover 2Kin 8:10
that thou m keep the law of the 1Chr 22:12
and thou m add thereto 1Chr 22:14
that thou m judge my people, over 2Chr 1:11
that thou m carry me out of the 2Chr 18:33
That thou m buy speedily with Ezr 7:17
that thou m hear the prayer of Neh 1:6
that thou m be their king, Neh 6:6
me, that thou m be righteous Job 40:8
in a time when thou m be found Ps 32:6
whom thou m make princes in all Ps 45:16
That thou m give him rest from Ps 94:13
that thou m give them their meat Ps 104:27
with thee, that thou m be feared Ps 130:4
That thou m walk in the way of Prov 2:20
That thou m regard discretion, and Prov 5:2
that thou m be wise in thy latter Prov 19:20
that thou m be remembered Is 23:16
thou, that thou m be justified Is 43:26
that thou m know that I, the LORD Is 45:3
profit, if so be thou m prevail Is 47:12
that thou m be my salvation unto Is 49:6
That thou m say to the prisoners, Is 49:9
wickedness, that thou m be saved Jer 4:14
among my people, that thou m know Jer 6:27
cause, that thou m be bound up Jer 30:13
That thou m bear thine own shame, Eze 16:54
m be confounded in all that thou Eze 16:54
That thou m remember, and be Eze 16:63
that thou m look on their Hab 2:15
that thou m eat the passover Mk 14:12
that thou m be delivered from him Lk 12:58
for thou m be no longer steward Lk 16:2 1410
with all thine heart, thou m Acts 8:37 1832
m take knowledge of all these Acts 24:8
Because that thou m understand Acts 24:11
but if thou m be made free, use 1Cor 7:21 1410
thou m live long on the earth Eph 6:3
that thou m know how thou 1Ti 3:15
all things that thou m prosper 3Jn 2
in the fire, that thou m be rich Rev 3:18
that thou m be clothed, and that Rev 3:18
with eyesalve, that thou m see Rev 3:18

MAZZAROTH (maz'-za-roth) *The twelve signs of the Zodiac.*
thou bring forth M in his season Job 38:32 4216

ME See PREFACE.

MEADOW
and they fed in a m Gen 41:2 260
and they fed in a m Gen 41:18 260

MEADOWS
even out of the m of Gibeah Judg 20:33 4629

MEAH (me'-ah) *A tower on Jerusalem's wall.*
the tower of M they sanctified it Neh 3:1 3968
of Hananeel, and the tower of M Neh 12:39 3968

MEAL
quickly three measures of fine m Gen 18:6
part of an ephah of barley m Num 5:15 7058
and threescore measures of m 1Kin 4:22 7058
but an handful of m in a barrel 1Kin 17:12 7058
The barrel of m shall not waste, 1Kin 17:14 7058
And the barrel of m wasted not 1Kin 17:16 7058
But he said, Then bring m 2Kin 4:41 7058
on mules, and on oxen, and meat, m 1Chr 12:40 7058
Take the millstones, and grind m Is 47:2 7058
the bud shall yield no m Hos 8:7 7058
and hid in three measures of m Mt 13:33 224
and hid in three measures of m Lk 13:21 224

MEALTIME
At m come thou hither, and eat of Ruth 2:14

MEAN
What m these seven ewe lambs Gen 21:29
What m ye by this service Ex 12:26
What m the testimonies, and the Deut 6:20
What m ye by these stones Josh 4:6
come, saying, What m these stones Josh 4:21
And it came to pass in the m while 1Kin 18:45
he shall not stand before m men Prov 22:29 2823
the m man boweth down, and the Is 2:9 120
What m ye that ye beat my people Is 3:15
the m man shall be brought down, Is 5:15 120
and the sword, not of a m man Is 31:8 120
Know ye not what these things m Eze 17:12
What m ye, that ye use this Eze 18:2
the rising from the dead should m Mk 9:10 2076
In the m time, when there were Lk 12:1
In the m while his disciples Jn 4:31 3342
vision which he had seen should m Acts 10:17 1498
therefore what these things m Acts 17:20
What m ye to weep and to break Acts 21:13 4160
Cilicia, a citizen of no m city Acts 21:39 767
their thoughts the m while Rom 2:15 3342
For I m not that other men be 2Cor 8:13

MEANEST
What m thou by all this drove Gen 33:8
unto Ziba, What m thou by these 2Sa 16:2
not shew us what thou m by these Eze 37:18
and said unto him, What m thou Jonah 1:6

MEANETH
what m the heat of this great Deut 29:24
What m the noise of this great 1Sa 4:6
What m the noise of this tumult 1Sa 4:14
What m then this bleating of the 1Sa 15:14
Howbeit he m not so, neither doth Is 10:7 1819
But go ye and learn what that m Mt 9:13 2076
But if ye had known what this m Mt 12:7 2076
one to another, What m this Acts 2:12

MEANING
the vision, and sought for the m Dan 8:15 998
m to sail by the coasts of Asia Acts 27:2 3195
if I know not the m of the voice 1Cor 14:11 1411

MEANS
that will by no m clear the Ex 34:7
by no m clearing the guilty, Num 14:18
broken by the m of the pransings Judg 5:22
by what m we may prevail against Judg 16:5
yet doth he devise m, that his 2Sa 14:14 4284
they bring them out by their m 1Kin 10:29 3027
if by any m he be missing, then 1Kin 20:39
the kings of Syria, by their m 2Chr 1:17 3027
by this m thou shalt have no Ezr 4:16 6903
can by any m redeem his brother Ps 49:7
For by m of a whorish woman a man Prov 6:26 1157
the priests bear rule by their m Jer 5:31 3027
this hath been by your m Mal 1:9 3027
shalt by no m come out thence Mt 5:26 3361
they sought m to bring him in, and Lk 5:18
m he that was possessed of the Lk 8:36 4459
nothing shall by any m hurt you Lk 10:19 3364
But by what m he now seeth, we Jn 9:21 4459
by what m he is made whole Acts 4:9
I must by all m keep this feast Acts 18:21 3843
if by any m they might attain to Acts 27:12 4458
if by any m now at length I might Rom 1:10 4458
If by any m I may provoke to Rom 11:14 4458
But take heed lest by any m this 1Cor 8:9 4458
that I might by all m save some 1Cor 9:22 3843
lest that by any m, when I have 1Cor 9:27 4458
gift bestowed upon us by the m of 2Cor 1:11
But I fear, lest by any m 2Cor 11:3 4458
lest by any m I should run, or Gal 2:2 4458
If by any m I might attain unto Phil 3:11 4458
lest by some m the tempter have 1Th 3:5 4458
Let no man deceive you by any m 2Th 2:3 5158
give you peace always by all m 2Th 3:16 5158
that by m of death, for the Heb 9:15 1096
m of those miracles which he had Rev 13:14

MEANT
but God m it unto good, to bring Gen 50:20 2803
and asked what these things m Lk 15:26 1498
pass by, he asked what it m Lk 18:36 1498

MEARAH (me'-a-rah) *A place near Sidon.*
M that is beside the Sidonians, Josh 13:4 4632

MEASURE
of the curtains shall have one m Ex 26:2 4060
curtains shall be all of one m Ex 26:8 4060
in meteyard, in weight, or in m Lev 19:35 4884
ye shall m from without the city Num 35:5 4058
they shall m unto the cities Deut 21:2 4058
perfect and just m shalt thou have Deut 25:15 374
about two thousand cubits by m Josh 3:4 4060
both the cherubims were of one m 1Kin 6:25 4060
of them had one casting, one m 1Kin 7:37 4060
a m of fine flour be sold for a 2Kin 7:1 5429
So a m of fine flour was sold for 2Kin 7:16 5429
a m of fine flour for a shekel, 2Kin 7:18 5429
is fried, and for all manner of m 1Chr 23:29 4884
the first m was threescore cubits 2Chr 3:3 4060
The m thereof is longer than the Job 11:9 4055
and he weigheth the waters by m Job 28:25 4060
the m of my days, what it is Ps 39:4 4060
them tears to drink in great m Ps 80:5 7991
and opened her mouth without m Is 5:14 2706
In m, when it shooteth forth, Is 27:8 5432
the dust of the earth in a m Is 40:12 7991
therefore will I m their former Is 65:7 4058
but I will correct thee in m Jer 30:11 4941
of thee, but correct thee in m Jer 46:28 4941
the m of thy covetousness Jer 51:13 520
Thou shalt drink also water by m Eze 4:11 4884
and they shall drink water by m Eze 4:16 4884
they three were of one m Eze 40:10 4060
the posts had one m on this side Eze 40:10 4060
after the m of the first gate Eze 40:21 4060
were after the m of the gate that Eze 40:22 4060
about within and without, by m Eze 41:17 4060
and let them m the pattern Eze 43:10 4058
of this m shalt thou Eze 45:3 4060
shalt thou m the length of five Eze 45:3 4058
and the bath shall be of one m Eze 45:11 8506
the m thereof shall be after the Eze 45:11 4971
these four corners were of one m Eze 46:22 4060
east side ye shall m from Hauran Eze 47:18 4058
the scant m that is abominable Mic 6:10 374
To m Jerusalem, to see what is Zec 2:2 4058
and with what m ye mete, it shall Mt 7:2 3358
ye up then the m of your fathers Mt 23:32 3358
with what m ye mete, it shall be Mk 4:24 3358
amazed in themselves beyond m Mk 6:51 4053
And were beyond m astonished Mk 7:37 5249
And they were astonished out of m Mk 10:26 4057
good m, pressed down, and shaken Lk 6:38 3358
For with the same m that ye mete Lk 6:38 3358
not the Spirit by m unto him Jn 3:34 3358
dealt to every man the m of faith Rom 12:3 3358
that we were pressed out of m 2Cor 1:8 5236
not boast of things without our m 2Cor 10:13 280
but according to the m of the 2Cor 10:13 3358
a m to reach even unto you 2Cor 10:13 3358
not ourselves beyond our m 2Cor 10:14
boasting of things without our m 2Cor 10:15 280
more abundant, in stripes above m 2Cor 11:23 5234
m through the abundance of the 2Cor 12:7
lest I should be exalted above m 2Cor 12:7
how that beyond m I persecuted Gal 1:13 5236
to the m of the gift of Christ Eph 4:7 3358
unto the m of the stature of the Eph 4:13 3358
working in the m of every part Eph 4:16 3358
A m of wheat for a penny, and Rev 6:6 5518
m the temple of God, and the altar Rev 11:1 3354
the temple leave out, and m it not Rev 11:2 3354
had a golden reed to m the city Rev 21:15 3354
according to the m of a man Rev 21:17 3358

MEASURED
he m six measures of barley, and Ruth 3:15 4058
m them with a line, casting them 2Sa 8:2 4058
two lines m he to put to death 2Sa 8:2 4058
Who hath m the waters in the Is 40:12 4058
If heaven above can be m, and the Jer 31:37 4058
neither the sand of the sea m Jer 33:22 4058
so he m the breadth of the Eze 40:5 4058
m the threshold of the gate, Eze 40:6 4058
He m also the porch of the gate Eze 40:8 4058
Then m he the porch of the gate, Eze 40:9 4058
he m the breadth of the entry of Eze 40:11 4058
He m then the gate from the roof Eze 40:13 4058
Then he m the breadth from the Eze 40:19 4058
he m the length thereof, and the Eze 40:20 4058
he m from gate to gate an hundred Eze 40:23 4058
he m the posts thereof and the Eze 40:24 4058
he m from gate to gate toward the Eze 40:27 4058
he m the south gate according to Eze 40:28 4058
he m the gate according to these Eze 40:32 4058
m it according to these measures Eze 40:35 4058
So he m the court, an hundred Eze 40:47 4058
m each post of the porch, five Eze 40:48 4058
m the posts, six cubits broad on Eze 41:1 4058
he m the length thereof, forty Eze 41:2 4058
m the post of the door, two Eze 41:3 4058
So he m the length thereof, Eze 41:4 4058
After he m the wall of the house, Eze 41:5 4058
So he m the house, an hundred Eze 41:13 4058
he m the length of the building Eze 41:15 4058
the east, and m it round about Eze 42:15 4058
He m the east side with the Eze 42:16 4058
He m the north side, five hundred Eze 42:17 4058
He m the south side, five hundred Eze 42:18 4058
m five hundred reeds with the Eze 42:19 4058
He m it by the four sides Eze 42:20 4058
he m a thousand cubits, and he Eze 47:3 4058
Again he m a thousand, and brought Eze 47:4 4058
Again he m a thousand, and brought Eze 47:4 4058
Afterward he m a thousand Eze 47:5 4058
which cannot be m nor numbered Hos 1:10 4058
He stood, and m the earth Hab 3:6 4128
it shall be m to you again Mt 7:2 488
ye mete, it shall be m to you Mk 4:24 3354
withal it shall be m to you again Lk 6:38 488
he m the city with the reed, Rev 21:16 3354
he m the wall thereof, an hundred Rev 21:17 3354

MEASURES
quickly three *m* of fine meal Gen 18:6 5429
not have in thine house divers *m* Deut 25:14 374
it, he measured six *m* of barley Ruth 3:15
These six *m* of barley gave he me Ruth 3:17
five *m* of parched corn, and an 1Sa 25:18 5429
day was thirty *m* of fine flour 1Kin 4:22 3734
and threescore *m* of meal 1Kin 4:22 3734
m of wheat for food to his 1Kin 5:11 3734
and twenty *m* of pure oil 1Kin 5:11 3734
to the *m* of hewed stones, sawed 1Kin 7:9 4060
after the *m* of hewed stones, and 1Kin 7:11 4060
as would contain two *m* of seed 1Kin 18:32 5429
two *m* of barley for a shekel, in 2Kin 7:1 5429
two *m* of barley for a shekel 2Kin 7:16 5429
Two *m* of barley for a shekel, and 2Kin 7:18 5429
twenty thousand *m* of beaten wheat 2Chr 2:10 3734
and twenty thousand *m* of barley 2Chr 2:10 3734
and ten thousand *m* of wheat 2Chr 27:5 3734
and to an hundred *m* of wheat Ezr 7:22 3734
Who hath laid the *m* thereof Job 38:5 4461
Divers weights, and divers *m* Prov 20:10 374
lot, the portion of thy *m* from me Jer 13:25 4055
thereof according to these *m* Eze 40:24 4060
south gate according to these *m* Eze 40:28 4060
thereof, according to these *m* Eze 40:29 4060
the gate according to these *m* Eze 40:32 4060
were according to these *m* Eze 40:33 4060
measured it according to these *m* Eze 40:35 4060
these are the *m* of the altar Eze 43:13 4060
And these shall be the *m* thereof Eze 48:16 4060
four thousand and five hundred *m* Eze 48:30 4060
four thousand and five hundred *m* Eze 48:33 4060
round about eighteen thousand *m* Eze 48:35
one came to an heap of twenty *m* Hag 2:16
took, and hid in three *m* of meal Mt 13:33 *4568*
took and hid in three *m* of meal Lk 13:21 *4568*
And he said, An hundred *m* of oil Lk 16:6 *943*
And he said, An hundred *m* of wheat Lk 16:7 *2884*
three *m* of barley for a penny Rev 6:6 *5518*

MEASURING
the *m* line shall yet go forth Jer 31:39 4060
of flax in his hand, and a *m* reed Eze 40:3 4060
in the man's hand a *m* reed of six Eze 40:5 4060
made an end of *m* the inner house Eze 42:15 4060
the east side with the *m* reed Eze 42:16 4060
with the *m* reed round about Eze 42:16 4060
with the *m* reed round about Eze 42:17 4060
hundred reeds, with the *m* reed Eze 42:18 4060
hundred reeds with the *m* reed Eze 42:19 4060
a man with a *m* line in his hand Zec 2:1 4060
but they *m* themselves by 2Cor 10:12 *3354*

MEAT
to you it shall be for *m* Gen 1:29 402
have given every green herb for *m* Gen 1:30 402
that liveth shall be *m* for you Gen 9:3 402
there was set *m* before him to eat Gen 24:33
And make me savoury *m*, such as I Gen 27:4
me venison, and make me savoury *m* Gen 27:7
them savoury *m* for thy father Gen 27:9
and his mother made savoury *m* Gen 27:14
And she gave the savoury *m* Gen 27:17
And he also had made savoury *m* Gen 27:31
m for his father by the way Gen 45:23 4202
to the *m* offering of the morning Ex 29:41
burnt sacrifice, nor *m* offering Ex 30:9
burnt offering and the *m* offering Ex 40:29
when any will offer a *m* offering Lev 2:1
the remnant of the *m* offerings Lev 2:3
of a *m* offering baken in the oven Lev 2:4
if thy oblation be a *m* offering Lev 2:5
it is a *m* offering Lev 2:6
if thy oblation be a *m* offering Lev 2:7
thou shalt bring the *m* offering Lev 2:8
the *m* offering a memorial thereof Lev 2:9
the *m* offering shall be Aaron's Lev 2:10
No *m* offering, which ye shall Lev 2:11
every oblation of thy *m* offering Lev 2:13
to be lacking from thy *m* offering Lev 2:13
if thou offer a *m* offering of thy Lev 2:14
thou shalt offer for the *m* Lev 2:14
it is a *m* offering Lev 2:15
be the priest's, as a *m* offering Lev 5:13
this is the law of the *m* offering Lev 6:14
of the flour of the *m* offering Lev 6:15
which is upon the *m* offering Lev 6:15
flour for a *m* offering perpetual Lev 6:20
the baken pieces of the *m* Lev 6:21
For every *m* offering for the Lev 6:23
all the *m* offering that is baken Lev 7:9
every *m* offering, mingled with Lev 7:10
of the *m* offering, and of the sin Lev 7:37
a *m* offering mingled with oil Lev 9:4
And he brought the *m* offering Lev 9:17
left, Take the *m* offering that Lev 10:12
Of all *m* which may be eaten, that Lev 11:34 400
of fine flour for a *m* offering Lev 14:10
the *m* offering upon the altar Lev 14:20
mingled with oil for a *m* offering Lev 14:21
offering, with the *m* offering Lev 14:31
they shall eat of his *m* Lev 22:11 3899
she shall eat of her father's *m* Lev 22:13 3899
the *m* offering thereof shall be Lev 23:13
ye shall offer a new *m* offering Lev 23:16
the LORD, with their *m* offering Lev 23:18
a *m* offering, a sacrifice, and Lev 23:37
of the land shall be *m* for you Lev 25:6 402
all the increase thereof be *m* Lev 25:7 398
incense, and the daily *m* offering Num 4:16
their *m* offering, and their drink Num 6:15
shall offer also his *m* offering Num 6:17
mingled with oil for a *m* offering Num 7:13
mingled with oil for a *m* offering Num 7:19
mingled with oil for a *m* offering Num 7:25
mingled with oil for a *m* offering Num 7:31
mingled with oil for a *m* offering Num 7:37
mingled with oil for a *m* offering Num 7:43
mingled with oil for a *m* offering Num 7:49
mingled with oil for a *m* offering Num 7:55
mingled with oil for a *m* offering Num 7:61
mingled with oil for a *m* offering Num 7:67
mingled with oil for a *m* offering Num 7:73
mingled with oil for a *m* offering Num 7:79
twelve, with their *m* offering Num 7:87
young bullock with his *m* offering Num 8:8
a *m* offering of a tenth deal of Num 15:4
thou shalt prepare for a *m* Num 15:6
a *m* offering of three tenth deals Num 15:9
the LORD, with his *m* offering Num 15:24
every *m* offering of theirs, and Num 18:9
ephah of flour for a *m* offering Num 28:5
as the *m* offering of the morning Num 28:8
deals of flour for a *m* offering Num 28:9
deals of flour for a *m* offering Num 28:12
deals of flour for a *m* offering Num 28:12
for a *m* offering unto one lamb Num 28:13
their *m* offering shall be of Num 28:20
the *m* of the sacrifice made by Num 28:24 3899
when ye bring a new *m* offering Num 28:26
their *m* offering of flour mingled Num 28:28
his *m* offering, (they shall be Num 28:31
their *m* offering shall be of Num 29:3
his *m* offering, and the daily Num 29:6
his *m* offering, and their drink Num 29:6
their *m* offering shall be of Num 29:9
the *m* offering of it, and their Num 29:11
their *m* offering shall be of Num 29:14
his *m* offering, and his drink Num 29:16
their *m* offering and their drink Num 29:18
the *m* offering thereof, and their Num 29:19
their *m* offering and their drink Num 29:21
his *m* offering, and his drink Num 29:22
Their *m* offering and their drink Num 29:24
his *m* offering, and his drink Num 29:25
their *m* offering and their drink Num 29:27
his *m* offering, and his drink Num 29:28
their *m* offering and their drink Num 29:30
his *m* offering, and his drink Num 29:31
their *m* offering and their drink Num 29:33
his *m* offering, and his drink Num 29:34
Their *m* offering and their drink Num 29:37
his *m* offering, and his drink Num 29:38
for your *m* offerings, and for your Num 29:39
Ye shall buy *m* of them for money Deut 2:6 400
Thou shalt sell me *m* for money Deut 2:28 400
that they be not trees for *m* Deut 20:20 3978
thy carcase shall be *m* unto all Deut 28:26 3978
burnt offering or *m* offering Josh 22:23
for *m* offerings, or for Josh 22:29
gathered their *m* under my table Judg 1:7
took a kid with a *m* offering Judg 13:19
a *m* offering at our hands Judg 13:23
Out of the eater came forth *m* Judg 14:14 3978
fail to sit with the king at *m* 1Sa 20:5 398
the king sat him down to eat *m* 1Sa 20:24 3899
cometh not the son of Jesse to *m* 1Sa 20:27 3899
did eat no *m* the second day of 1Sa 20:34 3899
to eat *m* while it was yet day 2Sa 3:35 3899
him a mess of *m* from the king 2Sa 11:8
it did eat of his own *m*, and drank 2Sa 12:3 6595
sister Tamar come, and give me *m* 2Sa 13:5 3899
dress the *m* in my sight, that I 2Sa 13:5 1279
Amnon's house, and dress him *m* 2Sa 13:7 1279
Bring the *m* into the chamber, 2Sa 13:10 1279
m offerings, and the fat of the 1Kin 8:64
m offerings, and the fat of the 1Kin 8:64
the *m* of his table, and the 1Kin 10:5 3978
the strength of that *m* forty days 1Kin 19:8 396
when the *m* offering was offered, 2Kin 3:20
his *m* offering, and poured his 2Kin 16:13
and the evening *m* offering 2Kin 16:15
his *m* offering, with the burnt 2Kin 16:15
their *m* offering, and their drink 2Kin 16:15
and on mules, and on oxen, and *m* 1Chr 12:40 3978
and the wheat for the *m* offering 1Chr 21:23
for the fine flour for *m* offering 1Chr 23:29
the *m* offerings, and the fat 2Chr 7:7
the *m* of his table, and the 2Chr 9:4 3978
and *m*, and drink, and oil, unto them Ezr 3:7 3978
lambs, with their *m* offerings Ezr 7:17
and for the continual *m* offering Neh 10:33
they laid the *m* offerings Neh 13:5
house of God, with the *m* offering Neh 13:9
to touch are as my sorrowful *m* Job 6:7 3899
and the mouth taste his *m* Job 12:11 400
Yet his *m* in his bowels is turned Job 20:14 3899
There shall none of his *m* be left Job 20:21 400
and juniper roots for their *m* Job 30:4 3899
bread, and his soul dainty *m* Job 33:20 3978
words, as the mouth tasteth *m* Job 34:3 398
he giveth *m* in abundance Job 36:31 400
God, they wander for lack of *m* Job 38:41 400
My tears have been my *m* day Ps 42:3 3899
us like sheep appointed for *m* Ps 44:11 3978
Let them wander up and down for *m* Ps 59:15 398
They gave me also gall for my *m* Ps 69:21 1267
gavest him to be *m* to the people Ps 74:14 3978
heart by asking *m* for their lust Ps 78:18 400
he sent them *m* to the full Ps 78:25 6720
but while their *m* was yet in Ps 78:30 400
be *m* unto the fowls of the heaven Ps 79:2 3978
prey, and seek their *m* from God Ps 104:21 400
give them their *m* in due season Ps 104:27 400
soul abhorreth all manner of *m* Ps 107:18 400
He hath given *m* unto them that Ps 111:5 2964
givest them their *m* in due season Ps 145:15 400
Provideth her *m* in the summer Prov 6:8 3899
for they are deceitful *m* Prov 23:3 3899
a fool when he is filled with *m* Prov 30:22 3899
prepare their *m* in the summer Prov 30:25 3899
giveth *m* to her household, and a Prov 31:15 2964
thou hast offered a *m* offering Is 57:6
corn to be *m* for thine enemies Is 62:8 3978
and dust shall be the serpent's *m* Is 65:25 3899
of this people shall be *m* for the Jer 7:33 3978
be *m* for the fowls of heaven Jer 16:4 3978
m offerings, and incense, and Jer 17:26
carcases will I give to be *m* for Jer 19:7 3978
and to kindle *m* offerings Jer 33:18
m unto the fowls of the heaven Jer 34:20 3978
things for *m* to relieve the soul Lam 1:11 400
their *m* to relieve their souls Lam 1:19 400
they were their *m* in the Lam 4:10 1262
thy *m* which thou shalt eat shall Eze 4:10 3978
My *m* also which I gave thee, fine Eze 16:19 3899
I have given thee for *m* to the Eze 29:5 402
they became *m* to all the beasts Eze 34:5 402
my flock became *m* to every beast Eze 34:8 402
that they may not be *m* for them Eze 34:10 402
the *m* offering, and the sin Eze 42:13
They shall eat the *m* offering Eze 44:29
for a *m* offering, and for a burnt Eze 45:15
m offerings, and drink offerings, Eze 45:17
the *m* offering, and the burnt Eze 45:17
he shall prepare a *m* offering of Eze 45:24
and according to the *m* offering Eze 45:25
the *m* offering shall be an ephah Eze 46:5
the *m* offering for the lambs as Eze 46:5
And he shall prepare a *m* offering Eze 46:7
in the solemnities the *m* offering Eze 46:11
thou shalt prepare a *m* offering Eze 46:14
a *m* offering continually by a Eze 46:14
the *m* offering, and the oil, every Eze 46:15
they shall bake the *m* offering Eze 46:20
side, shall grow all trees for *m* Eze 47:12 3978
the fruit thereof shall be for *m* Eze 47:12 3978
a daily provision of the king's *m* Dan 1:5 6598
with the portion of the king's *m* Dan 1:8 6598
king, who hath appointed your *m* Dan 1:10 3978
of the portion of the king's *m* Dan 1:13 6598
eat the portion of the king's *m* Dan 1:15 6598
took away the portion of their *m* Dan 1:16 6598
much, and in it was *m* for all Dan 4:12 4203
much, and in it was *m* for all Dan 4:21 4203
of his *m* shall destroy him Dan 11:26 6598
their jaws, and I laid *m* unto them Hos 11:4 398
The *m* offering and the drink Joel 1:9
for the *m* offering and the drink Joel 1:13
Is not the *m* cut off before our Joel 1:16 400
even a *m* offering and a drink Joel 2:14
your *m* offerings, I will not Amos 5:22
is fat, and their *m* plenteous Hab 1:16 3978
and the fields shall yield no *m* Hab 3:17 400
or wine, or oil, or any *m* Hag 2:12 3978
and the fruit thereof, even his *m* Mal 1:12 400
that there may be *m* in mine house Mal 3:10 2964
his *m* was locusts and wild honey Mt 3:4 *5160*
Is not the life more than *m* Mt 6:25 *5160*
as Jesus sat at *m* in the house Mt 9:10
the workman is worthy of his *m* Mt 10:10 *5160*
and them which sat with him at *m* Mt 14:9
they took up of the broken *m* that Mt 15:37
to give them *m* in due season Mt 24:45 *5160*
I was an hungred, and ye gave me *m* Mt 25:35 *5315*
an hungred, and ye gave me no *m* Mt 25:42 *5315*
it on his head, as he sat at *m* Mt 26:7
as Jesus sat at *m* in his house Mk 2:15
they took up of the broken *m* that Mk 8:8
Simon the leper, as he sat at *m* Mk 14:3
unto the eleven as they sat at *m* Mk 16:14
and he that hath *m*, let him do Lk 3:11 *1033*
house, and sat down to *m* Lk 7:36
sat at *m* in the Pharisee's house Lk 7:37
they that sat at *m* with him began Lk 7:49
and he commanded to give her *m* Lk 8:55 *5315*
buy *m* for all this people Lk 9:13 *1033*
and he went in, and sat down to *m* Lk 11:37
The life is more than *m*, and the Lk 12:23 *5160*
and make them to sit down to *m* Lk 12:37
their portion of *m* in due season Lk 12:42 *4620*
of them that sit at *m* with thee Lk 14:10
at *m* with him heard these things Lk 14:15
the field, Go and sit down to *m* Lk 17:7
is greater, he that sitteth at *m* Lk 22:27
is not he that sitteth at *m* Lk 22:27
to pass, as he sat at *m* with them Lk 24:30
unto them, Have ye here any *m* Lk 24:41 *1034*
gone away unto the city to buy *m* Jn 4:8 *5160*
I have *m* to eat that ye know not Jn 4:32 *1035*
My *m* is to do the will of him Jn 4:34 *1033*
not for the *m* which perisheth Jn 6:27 *1035*
but for that *m* which endureth Jn 6:27 *1035*
For my flesh is *m* indeed, and my Jn 6:55 *1035*
them, Children, have ye any *m* Jn 21:5 *4371*
did eat their *m* with gladness Acts 2:46 *5160*
And when he had received *m* Acts 9:19 *5160*
he set *m* before them, and rejoiced Acts 16:34 *5132*
Paul besought them all to take *m* Acts 27:33 *5160*
I pray you to take some *m* Acts 27:34 *5160*
cheer, and they also took some *m* Acts 27:36 *5160*
thy brother be grieved with thy *m* Rom 14:15 *1033*
Destroy not him with thy *m* Rom 14:15 *1033*
For the kingdom of God is not *m* Rom 14:17 *1035*
For *m* destroy not the work of God Rom 14:20 *1033*
fed you with milk, and not with *m* 1Cor 3:2 *1033*
But *m* commendeth us not to God 1Cor 8:8 *1033*
sit at *m* in the idol's temple 1Cor 8:10
if *m* make my brother to offend, I 1Cor 8:13 *1033*
did all eat the same spiritual *m* 1Cor 10:3 *1033*
no man therefore judge you in *m* Col 2:16 *1035*
need of milk, and not of strong *m* Heb 5:12 *5160*

But strong m belongeth to them Heb 5:14 5160
morsel of m sold his birthright Heb 12:16 1035

MEATS
neither desire thou his dainty m Prov 23:6
into the draught, purging all m Mk 7:19 1033
abstain from m offered to idols Acts 15:29
M for the belly, and the belly for 1Cor 6:13 1033
for the belly, and the belly for m 1Cor 6:13 1033
and commanding to abstain from m 1Ti 4:3 1033
Which stood only in m and drinks, Heb 9:10 1033
not with m, which have not Heb 13:9 1033

MEBUNNAI (me-bun'-nahee) See SIBBECHAI. *A "mighty man" of David.*
Anethothite, M the Hushathite, 2Sa 23:27 4012

MECHERATHITE (me-ker'-ath-ite) *A family name of a "mighty man" of David.*
Hepher the M, Ahijah the Pelonite 1Chr 11:36 4382

MECONAH See MEKONAH.

MEDAD (me'-dad) *An elder of Israel.*
Eldad, and the name of the other M Num 11:26 4312
M do prophesy in the camp Num 11:27 4312

MEDAN (me'-dan) *A son of Abraham.*
bare him Zimran, and Jokshan, and M Gen 25:2 4091
she bare Zimran, and Jokshan, and M. 1Chr 1:32 4091

MEDDLE
M not with them Deut 2:5 1624
them not, nor m with them Deut 2:19 1624
why shouldest thou m to thy hurt 2Kin 14:10 1624
shouldest thou m to thine hurt 2Chr 25:19 1624
therefore m not with him that Prov 20:19 6148
m not with them that are given to Prov 24:21 6148

MEDDLED
contention, before it be m with Prov 17:14 1566

MEDDLETH
m with strife belonging not to Prov 26:17 5674

MEDDLING
forbear thee from m with God 2Chr 35:21
but every fool will be m Prov 20:3 1566

MEDE (meed) See MEDES, MEDIAN. *An inhabitant of Media.*
in the first year of Darius the M Dan 11:1 4075

MEDEBA (med'-e-bah) *A city in Reuben.*
Nophah, which reacheth unto M Num 21:30 4311
and all the plain of M unto Dibon Josh 13:9 4311
the river, and all the plain by M Josh 13:16 4311
who came and pitched before M 1Chr 19:7 4311
shall howl over Nebo, and over M Is 15:2 4311

MEDES (meeds)
Gozan, and in the cities of the M 2Kin 17:6 4074
Gozan, and in the cities of the M 2Kin 18:11 4074
that is in the province of the M Ezr 6:2 4074
the laws of the Persians and the M Est 1:19 4074
I will stir up the M against them Is 13:17 4074
Elam, and all the kings of the M Jer 25:25 4074
the spirit of the kings of the M Jer 51:11 4074
nations with the kings of the M Jer 51:28 4074
is divided, and given to the M Dan 5:28 4076
according to the law of the M Dan 6:8 4076
according to the law of the M Dan 6:12 4076
O king, that the law of the M Dan 6:15 4076
Ahasuerus, of the seed of the M Dan 9:1 4074
Parthians, and M, and Elamites, and Acts 2:9 3370

MEDIA (me'-de-ah) See MADAI, MEDE, MEDIAN. *A country north of Persia.*
the power of Persia and M, the Est 1:3 4074
the seven princes of Persia and M Est 1:14 4074
M say this day unto all the Est 1:18 4074
the chronicles of the kings of M Est 10:2 4074
besiege, O M Is 21:2 4074
two horns are the kings of M Dan 8:20 4074

MEDIAN (me'-de-an) See MEDE. *A native of Media.*
Darius the M took the kingdom, Dan 5:31 4077

MEDIATOR
by angels in the hand of a m Gal 3:19 3316
Now a m is not a Gal 3:20 3316
is not a m of one Gal 3:20
m between God and men 1Ti 2:5 3316
he is the m of a better covenant Heb 8:6 3316
he is the m of the new testament Heb 9:15 3316
to Jesus the m of the new Heb 12:24 3316

MEDICINE
A merry heart doeth good like a m Prov 17:22 1456
meat, and the leaf thereof for m Eze 47:12 8644

MEDICINES
thou hast no healing m Jer 30:13 7499
in vain shalt thou use many m Jer 46:11 7499

MEDITATE
Isaac went out to m in the field Gen 24:63
but thou shalt m therein day Josh 1:8 1897
and in his law doth he m day Ps 1:2 1897
m on thee in the night watches Ps 63:6 1897
I will m also of all thy work, and Ps 77:12 1897
I will m in thy precepts, and have Ps 119:15 7878
thy servant did m in thy statutes Ps 119:23 7878
and I will m in thy statutes Ps 119:48 7878
but I will m in thy precepts Ps 119:78 7878
that I might m in thy word Ps 119:148 7878
I m on all thy works Ps 143:5 1897
Thine heart shall m terror Is 33:18 1897
not to m before what ye shall Lk 21:14 4304
M upon these things 1Ti 4:15 3191

MEDITATION
consider my m Ps 5:1 1901
the m of my heart, be acceptable Ps 19:14 1902
the m of my heart shall be of Ps 49:3 1900
My m of him shall be sweet Ps 104:34 7879
it is my m all the day Ps 119:97 7881
for thy testimonies are my m Ps 119:99 7881

MEEK
(Now the man Moses was very m Num 12:3 6035
The m shall eat and be satisfied Ps 22:26 6035
The m will he guide in judgment Ps 25:9 6035
the m will he teach his way Ps 25:9 6035
But the m shall inherit the earth Ps 37:11 6035
to save all the m of the earth Ps 76:9 6035
The LORD lifteth up the m Ps 147:6 6035
beautify the m with salvation Ps 149:4 6035
equity for the m of the earth Is 11:4 6035
The m also shall increase their Is 29:19 6035
to preach good tidings unto the m Is 61:1 6035
and turn aside the way of the m Amos 2:7 6035
all ye m of the earth, which have Zeph 2:3 6035
Blessed are the m Mt 5:5 4239
for I am m and lowly in heart Mt 11:29 4235
thy King cometh unto thee, m Mt 21:5 4239
even the ornament of a m 1Pet 3:4 4239

MEEKNESS
because of truth and m and Ps 45:4 6037
seek righteousness, seek m Zeph 2:3 6038
or in love, and in the spirit of m 1Cor 4:21 4236
Paul myself beseech you by the m 2Cor 10:1 4236
M, temperance Gal 5:23 4236
such an one in the spirit of m Gal 6:1 4236
With all lowliness and m, with Eph 4:2 4236
kindness, humbleness of mind, m Col 3:12 4236
faith, love, patience, m 1Ti 6:11 4236
In m instructing those that 2Ti 2:25 4236
shewing all m unto all men Titus 3:2 4236
receive with m the engrafted word Jas 1:21 4240
his works with m of wisdom Jas 3:13 4240
of the hope that is in you with m 1Pet 3:15 4240

MEET
I will make him an help m for him Gen 2:18 5828
was not found an help m for him Gen 2:20 5828
m him after his return from the Gen 14:17 7125
he ran to m them from the tent Gen 18:2 7125
Lot seeing them rose up to m them Gen 19:1 7125
And the servant ran to m her Gen 24:17 7125
that walketh in the field to m us Gen 24:65 7125
son, that he ran to m him Gen 29:13 7125
and Leah went out to m him Gen 30:16 7125
Esau, and also he cometh to m thee Gen 32:6 7125
And Esau ran to m him Gen 33:4 7125
went up to m Israel his father, Gen 46:29 7125
behold, he cometh forth to m thee Ex 4:14 7125
Go into the wilderness to m Moses Ex 4:27 7125
Moses said, It is not m so to do Ex 8:26 3559
went out to m his father in law Ex 18:7 7125
out of the camp to m with God Ex 19:17 7125
If thou m thine enemy's ox or his Ex 23:4 6293
And there I will m with thee Ex 25:22 3259
where I will m you, to speak Ex 29:42 3259
there I will m with the children Ex 29:43 3259
where I will m with thee Ex 30:6 3259
where I will m with thee Ex 30:36 3259
where I will m with you Num 17:4 3259
he went out to m him unto a city Num 22:36 7125
the LORD will come to m me Num 23:3 7125
while I m the LORD yonder Num 23:15 7136
went forth to m them without the Num 31:13 7125
all that are m for the war Deut 3:18 1121
mountain, lest the pursuers m you Josh 2:16 6293
for the journey, and go to m them Josh 9:11 7125
And Jael went out to m Sisera Judg 4:18 7125
Sisera, Jael came out to m him Judg 4:22 7125
m for the necks of them that take Judg 5:30
and they came up to m them Judg 6:35 7125
of the doors of my house to m me Judg 11:31 7125
came out to m him with timbrels Judg 11:34 7125
saw him, he rejoiced to m him Judg 19:3 7125
that they m thee not in any other Ruth 2:22 6293
there shall m thee three men 1Sa 10:3 4672
that thou shalt m a company of 1Sa 10:5 6293
and Saul went out to m him 1Sa 13:10 7125
early to m Saul in the morning 1Sa 15:12 7125
and came and drew nigh to m David 1Sa 17:48 7125
the army to m the Philistine 1Sa 17:48 7125
to m king Saul, with tabrets, 1Sa 18:6 7125
which sent thee this day to m me 1Sa 25:32 7125
thou hadst hasted and come to m me 1Sa 25:34 7125
and they went forth to m David 1Sa 30:21 7125
to m the people that were with 1Sa 30:21 7125
of Saul came out to m David 2Sa 6:20 7125
it unto David, he sent to m them 2Sa 10:5 7125
came to m him with his coat rent 2Sa 15:32 7125
to Gilgal, to go to m the king 2Sa 19:15 7125
the men of Judah to m king David 2Sa 19:16 7125
to go down to m my lord the king 2Sa 19:20 7125
of Saul came down to m the king 2Sa 19:24 7125
come to Jerusalem to m the king 2Sa 19:25 7125
he came down to m me at Jordan 1Kin 2:8 7125
And the king rose up to m her 1Kin 2:19 7125
So Obadiah went to m Ahab 1Kin 18:16 7125
and Ahab went to m Elijah 1Kin 18:16 7125
go down to m Ahab king of Israel, 1Kin 21:18 7125
go up to m the messengers of the 2Kin 1:3 7125
him, There came a man up to m us 2Kin 1:6 7125
man was he which came up to m you 2Kin 1:7 7125
And they came to m him, and bowed 2Kin 2:15 7125
to m her, and say unto her, Is it 2Kin 4:26 7125
if thou m any man, salute him not 2Kin 4:29 4672
Wherefore he went again to m him 2Kin 4:31 7125
down from the chariot to m him 2Kin 5:21 7125
again from his chariot to m thee 2Kin 5:26 7125
m the man of God, and enquire of 2Kin 8:8 7125
So Hazael went to m him, and took 2Kin 8:9 7125
an horseman, and send to m them 2Kin 9:17 7125
went one on horseback to m him 2Kin 9:18 7125
the son of Rechab coming to m him 2Kin 10:15 7125
king Ahaz went to Damascus to m 2Kin 16:10 7125
And David went out to m them 1Chr 12:17 6440
And he sent to m them 1Chr 19:5 7125
And he went out to m Asa, and said 2Chr 15:2 6440
Hanani the seer went out to m him 2Chr 19:2 6440
it was not m for us to see the Ezr 4:14 749
let us m together in some one of Neh 6:2 3259
Let us m together in the house of Neh 6:10 3259
which were m to be given her, out Est 2:9 7200
They m with darkness in the Job 5:14 6298
Surely it is m to be said unto Job 34:31
he goeth on to m the armed men Job 39:21 7125
Therefore came I forth to m thee Prov 7:15 7125
that withholdeth more than is m Prov 11:24 3476
bear robbed of her whelps m a man Prov 17:12 6298
The rich and poor m together Prov 22:2 6298
and the deceitful man m together Prov 29:13 6298
Isaiah, Go forth now to m Ahaz Is 7:3 7125
for thee to m thee at thy coming Is 14:9 7125
m with the wild beasts of the Is 34:14 6298
I will not m thee as a man Is 47:3 6293
me as seemeth good and m unto you Jer 26:14 3477
it unto whom it seemed m unto me Jer 27:5 3474
went forth from Mizpah to m them Jer 41:6 7125
One post shall run to m another Jer 51:31 7125
and one messenger to m another Jer 51:31 7125
Is it m for any work Eze 15:4 6743
was whole, it was m for no work Eze 15:5 6213
shall it be m yet for any work Eze 15:5 6213
I will m them as a bear that is Hos 13:8 6298
unto thee, prepare to m thy God Amos 4:12 7125
another angel went out to m him Zec 2:3 7125
therefore fruits m for repentance Mt 3:8 514
whole city came out to m Jesus Mt 8:34 4877
and said, It is not m to take the Mt 15:26 2570
went forth to m the bridegroom Mt 25:1 529
go ye out to m him Mt 25:6 529
for it is not m to take the Mk 7:27 2570
there shall m you a man bearing a Mk 14:13 528
to m him that cometh against him Lk 14:31 528
It was m that we should make Lk 15:32 1163
the city, there shall a man m you Lk 22:10 4876
trees, and went forth to m him Jn 12:13 5222
do works m for repentance Acts 26:20 514
they came to m us as far as Appii Acts 28:15 529
of their error which was m Rom 1:27 1163
that am not m to be called an 1Cor 15:9 2425
if it be m that I go also, they 1Cor 16:4 514
Even as it is m for me to think Phil 1:7 1342
which hath made us m to be Col 1:12 2427
clouds, to m the Lord in the air 1Th 4:17 529
for you, brethren, as it is m 2Th 1:3 514
m for the master's use, and 2Ti 2:21 2173
bringeth forth herbs m for them Heb 6:7 2111
Yea, I think it m, as long as I 2Pet 1:13 1342

MEETEST
m of your master's sons, and set 2Kin 10:3 3477
Thou m him that rejoiceth and Is 64:5 6293

MEETETH
When Esau my brother m thee Gen 32:17 6298
when he m him, he shall slay him Num 35:19 6293
slay the murderer, when he m him Num 35:21 6293

MEETING
was afraid at the m of David 1Sa 21:1 7125
it is iniquity, even the solemn m Is 1:13 6116

MEGIDDO (me-ghid'-do) See MEGIDDON. *A city on the plain of Jezreel.*
the king of M, one Josh 12:21 4023
towns, and the inhabitants of M Josh 17:11 4023
towns, nor the inhabitants of M Judg 1:27 4023
in Taanach by the waters of M Judg 5:19 4023
to him pertained Taanach and M 1Kin 4:12 4023
wall of Jerusalem, and Hazor, and M 1Kin 9:15 4023
And he fled to M, and died there 2Kin 9:27 4023
and he slew him at M, when he had 2Kin 23:29 4023
him in a chariot dead from M 2Kin 23:30 4023
towns, Taanach and her towns, M 1Chr 7:29 4023
came to fight in the valley of M 2Chr 35:22 4023

MEGIDDON (me-ghid'-don) See ARMAGEDDON, MEGIDDO. *Same as Megiddo.*
of Hadadrimmon in the valley of M Zec 12:11 4023

MEHETABEEL (me-het'-a-be-el) See MEHETABEL. *Father of Delaiah.*
the son of Delaiah the son of M Neh 6:10 4105

MEHETABEL (me-het'-a-bel) See MEHETABEEL. *Wife of Hadar.*
and his wife's name was M, the Gen 36:39 4105
and his wife's name was M, the 1Chr 1:50 4105

MEHIDA (me-hi'-dah) *A family of exiles.*
of Bazluth, the children of M Ezr 2:52 4240
of Bazlith, the children of M Neh 7:54 4240

MEHIR (me'-hur) *A son of Chelub.*
the brother of Shuah begat M 1Chr 4:11 4243

MEHOLATHITE (me-ho'-lath-ite) *An inhabitant of a city in Issachar.*
given unto Adriel the M to wife 1Sa 18:19 4259
Adriel the son of Barzillai the M 2Sa 21:8 4259

MEHUJAEL (me-hu'-ja-el) *Son of Irad.*
and Irad begat M Gen 4:18 4232
and M begat Methusael Gen 4:18 4232

M

MEHUMAN (*me-hu'-man*) *A servant of King Ahasuerus.*
merry with wine, he commanded *M* ..... Est 1:10 4104

MEHUNIM (*me-hu'-nim*) See MAONITE, MEHUNIMS, MEUNIM. *A family of exiles.*
of Asnah, the children of *M* ..... Ezr 2:50 4586

MEHUNIMS (*me-hu'-nims*) See MEHUNIM. *A people who lived in Arabia.*
that dwelt in Gur-baal, and the *M* 2Chr 26:7 4586

ME-JARKON (*me-jar'-kon*) *A city in Dan.*
And *M*, and Rakkon, with the border ... Josh 19:46 4313

MEKERATHITE See MECHERATHITE.

MEKONAH (*me-ko'-nah*) *A city in Judah.*
And at Ziklag, and at *M*, and in the ..... Neh 11:28 4368

MELATIAH (*mel-a-ti'-ah*) *A repairer of Jerusalem's wall.*
them repaired *M* the Gibeonite ..... Neh 3:7 4424

MELCHI (*mel'-ki*) See MELCHI-SHUA, MELCHIZEDEK.
1. Son of Janna; ancestor of Jesus.
of Levi, which was the son of *M* ..... Lk 3:24 *3197*
2. Son of Addi; ancestor of Jesus.
Which was the son of *M*, which was .... Lk 3:28 *3197*

MELCHIAH (*mel-ki'-ah*) See MALCHIAH. *Father of Pashur.*
sent unto him Pashur the son of *M* ..... Jer 21:1 4441

MELCHISEDEC (*mel-kis'-e-dek*) See MELCHIZEDEK. *Greek form of Melchizedek.*
for ever after the order of *M* ..... Heb 5:6 *3198*
high priest after the order of *M* ..... Heb 5:10 *3198*
for ever after the order of *M* ..... Heb 6:20 *3198*
For this *M*, king of Salem, priest ..... Heb 7:1 *3198*
of his father, when *M* met him ..... Heb 7:10 *3198*
should rise after the order of *M* ..... Heb 7:11 *3198*
of *M* there ariseth another priest ..... Heb 7:15 *3198*
for ever after the order of *M* ..... Heb 7:17 *3198*
for ever after the order of *M* ..... Heb 7:21 *3198*

MELCHI-SHUA (*mel'-ki-shu'-ah*) See MALCHISHUA. *A son of King Saul.*
were Jonathan, and Ishui, and *M* 1Sa 14:49 4444
slew Jonathan, and Abinadab, and *M* ... 1Sa 31:2 4444

MELCHIZEDEK (*mel-kiz'-e-dek*) See MELCHISEDEC. *King and priest of Salem.*
M king of Salem brought forth ..... Gen 14:18 4442
for ever after the order of *M* ..... Ps 110:4 4442

MELEA (*mel'-e-ah*) *Son of Menan; an ancestor of Jesus.*
Which was the son of *M*, which was .... Lk 3:31 *3190*

MELECH (*me'-lek*) See EBED-MELECH, HAM-MELECH, NATHAN-MELECH, REGEM-MELECH. *A son of Micah.*
sons of Micah were, Pithon, and *M* 1Chr 8:35 4429
sons of Micah were, Pithon, and *M* 1Chr 9:41 4429

MELICHU See MELICU.

MELICU (*mel'-i-cu*) See MALLUCH. *A priest.*
Of *M*, Jonathan ..... Neh 12:14 4409

MELITA (*mel'-i-tah*) *A Mediterranean island.*
knew that the island was called *M* ..... Acts 28:1 *3194*

MELODY
make sweet *m*, sing many songs, ... Is 23:16 5059
thanksgiving, and the voice of *m* ..... Is 51:3 2172
will not hear the *m* of thy viols ..... Amos 5:23 2172
making *m* in your heart to the ..... Eph 5:19 5567

MELONS
the cucumbers, and the *m*, and the ..... Num 11:5 20

MELT
of Canaan shall *m* away ..... Ex 15:15 4127
these things, our hearts did *m* ..... Josh 2:11 4549
me made the heart of the people *m* ..... Josh 14:8 4529
heart of a lion, shall utterly *m* 2Sa 17:10 4549
Let them *m* away as waters which ..... Ps 58:7 3988
gnash with his teeth, and *m* away ..... Ps 112:10 4549
and every man's heart shall *m* ..... Is 13:7 4549
Egypt shall *m* in the midst of it ..... Is 19:1 4549
of hosts, Behold, I will *m* them ..... Jer 9:7 6884
and every heart shall *m*, and all ..... Eze 21:7 4549
to blow the fire upon it, to *m* it ..... Eze 22:20 5413
I will leave you there, and *m* you ..... Eze 22:20 5413
toucheth the land, and it shall *m* ..... Amos 9:5 4127
wine, and all the hills shall *m* ..... Amos 9:13 4127
quake at him, and the hills *m* ..... Nah 1:5 4127
shall *m* with fervent heat 2Pet 3:10 *3089*
shall *m* with fervent heat 2Pet 3:12 *5080*

MELTED
and when the sun waxed hot, it *m* ..... Ex 16:21 4549
passed over, that their heart *m* ..... Josh 5:1 4549
the hearts of the people *m* ..... Josh 7:5 4549
The mountains *m* from before the ..... Judg 5:5 5140
and, behold, the multitude *m* away 1Sa 14:16 4127
it is *m* in the midst of my bowels ..... Ps 22:14 4549
he uttered his voice, the earth *m* ..... Ps 46:6 4127
The hills *m* like wax at the ..... Ps 97:5 4549
their soul is *m* because of ..... Ps 107:26 4127
shall be *m* with their blood ..... Is 34:3 4549
ye shall be *m* in the midst ..... Eze 22:21 5413
As silver is *m* in the midst of ..... Eze 22:22 2046
so shall ye be *m* in the midst ..... Eze 22:22 5413

MELTETH
As a snail which *m*, let every one ..... Ps 58:8 8557
as wax *m* before the fire, so let ..... Ps 68:2 4549
My soul *m* for heaviness ..... Ps 119:28 1811
sendeth out his word, and *m* them ..... Ps 147:18 4549
The workman *m* a graven image, and .. Is 40:19 5258
the founder *m* in vain ..... Jer 6:29 6884
and the heart *m*, and the knees ..... Nah 2:10 4549

MELTING
As when the *m* fire burneth, the ..... Is 64:2 2003

MELZAR (*mel'-zar*) *Babylonian officer charged with Daniel and his companions.*
Then said Daniel to *M*, whom the ..... Dan 1:11 4453
Thus *M* took away the portion of ..... Dan 1:16 4453

MEMBER
or hath his privy *m* cut off ..... Deut 23:1
For the body is not one *m* 1Cor 12:14 *3196*
And if they were all one *m* 1Cor 12:19 *3196*
And whether one *m* suffer, all the 1Cor 12:26 *3196*
or one *m* be honoured, all the 1Cor 12:26 *3196*
Even so the tongue is a little *m* ..... Jas 3:5 *3196*

MEMBERS
and all my *m* are as a shadow ..... Job 17:7 3338
in thy book all my *m* were written ..... Ps 139:16
that one of thy *m* should perish ..... Mt 5:29 *3196*
that one of thy *m* should perish ..... Mt 5:30 *3196*
yield ye your *m* as instruments of ..... Rom 6:13 *3196*
dead, and your *m* as instruments of ..... Rom 6:13 *3196*
your *m* servants to uncleanness ..... Rom 6:19 *3196*
even so now yield your *m* servants ..... Rom 6:19 *3196*
did work in our *m* to bring forth ..... Rom 7:5 *3196*
But I see another law in my *m* ..... Rom 7:23 *3196*
the law of sin which is in my *m* ..... Rom 7:23 *3196*
For as we have many *m* in one body ... Rom 12:4 *3196*
all *m* have not the same office ..... Rom 12:4 *3196*
every one *m* one of another ..... Rom 12:5 *3196*
your bodies are the *m* of Christ 1Cor 6:15 *3196*
shall I then take the *m* of Christ 1Cor 6:15 *3196*
and make them the *m* of an harlot 1Cor 6:15 *3196*
the body is one, and hath many *m* 1Cor 12:12 *3196*
all the *m* of that one body, being 1Cor 12:12 *3196*
But now hath God set the *m* every 1Cor 12:18 *3196*
But now are they many *m*, yet but 1Cor 12:20 *3196*
much more those *m* of the body 1Cor 12:22 *3196*
those *m* of the body, which we 1Cor 12:23
but that the *m* should have the 1Cor 12:25 *3196*
suffer, all the *m* suffer with it 1Cor 12:26 *3196*
all the *m* rejoice with it 1Cor 12:26 *3196*
of Christ, and *m* in particular 1Cor 12:27 *3196*
for we are *m* one of another ..... Eph 4:25 *3196*
For we are *m* of his body, of his ..... Eph 5:30 *3196*
Mortify therefore your *m* which ..... Col 3:5 *3196*
so is the tongue among our *m* ..... Jas 3:6 *3196*
of your lusts that war in your *m* ..... Jas 4:1 *3196*

MEMORIAL
this is my *m* unto all generations ..... Ex 3:15 2143
day shall be unto you for a *m* ..... Ex 12:14 2146
for a *m* between thine eyes, that ..... Ex 13:9 2146
Write this for a *m* in a book ..... Ex 17:14 2146
of the ephod for stones of *m* unto ..... Ex 28:12 2146
upon his two shoulders for a *m* ..... Ex 28:12 2146
place, for a *m* before the LORD ..... Ex 28:29 2146
that it may be a *m* unto the ..... Ex 30:16 2146
for a *m* to the children of Israel ..... Ex 39:7 2146
burn the *m* of it upon the altar ..... Lev 2:2 234
the meat offering a *m* thereof ..... Lev 2:9 234
the priest shall burn the *m* of it ..... Lev 2:16 234
even a *m* thereof, and burn it on ..... Lev 5:12 234
a sweet savour, even the *m* of it ..... Lev 6:15 234
a *m* of blowing of trumpets, an ..... Lev 23:24 2146
it may be on the bread for a *m* ..... Lev 24:7 234
of jealousy, an offering of *m* ..... Num 5:15 2146
the offering of *m* in her hands ..... Num 5:18 2146
the offering, even the *m* thereof ..... Num 5:26 234
be to you for a *m* before your God ..... Num 10:10 2146
To be a *m* unto the children of ..... Num 16:40 2146
for a *m* for the children of ..... Num 31:54 2146
these stones shall be for a *m* ..... Josh 4:7 2146
have no portion, nor right, nor *m* ..... Neh 2:20 2146
nor the *m* of them perish from ..... Est 9:28 2143
their *m* is perished with them ..... Ps 9:6 2143
and thy *m*, O LORD, throughout all ..... Ps 135:13 2143
the LORD is his *m* ..... Hos 12:5 2143
for a *m* in the temple of the LORD ..... Zec 6:14 2146
hath done, be told for a *m* of her ..... Mt 26:13 *3422*
shall be spoken of for a *m* of her ..... Mk 14:9 *3422*
are come up for a *m* before God ..... Acts 10:4 *3422*

MEMORY
off the *m* of them from the earth ..... Ps 109:15 2143
utter the *m* of thy great goodness ..... Ps 145:7 2143
The *m* of the just is blessed ..... Prov 10:7 2143
for the *m* of them is forgotten ..... Eccl 9:5 2143
and made all their *m* to perish ..... Is 26:14 2143
if ye keep in *m* what I preached 1Cor 15:2

MEMPHIS (*mem'-fis*) See NOPH. *A city in Egypt.*
gather them up, *M* shall bury them ..... Hos 9:6 4644

MEMUCAN (*mem-u'-can*) *A prince of Media and Persia.*
Tarshish, Meres, Marsena, and *M* ..... Est 1:14 4462
M answered before the king and the .... Est 1:16 4462
did according to the word of *M* ..... Est 1:21 4462

MEN
then began *m* to call upon the ..... Gen 4:26 582
when *m* began to multiply on the ..... Gen 6:1 120
of *m* that they were fair ..... Gen 6:2 120
came in unto the daughters of *m* ..... Gen 6:4 120
became mighty *m* which were of old ... Gen 6:4 120
which were of old, *m* of renown ..... Gen 6:4 582
which the children of *m* builded ..... Gen 11:5 120
commanded his *m* concerning him ..... Gen 12:20 582
But the *m* of Sodom were wicked and . Gen 13:13 582
that which the young *m* have eaten ..... Gen 14:24
of the *m* which went with me ..... Gen 14:24 582
among the *m* of Abraham's house ..... Gen 17:23 582
all the *m* of his house, born in ..... Gen 17:27 582
and, lo, three *m* stood by him ..... Gen 18:2 582
the *m* rose up from thence, and ..... Gen 18:16 582
the *m* turned their faces from ..... Gen 18:22 582
the *m* of the city, even the *m* ..... Gen 19:4 582
Where are the *m* which came in to ..... Gen 19:5 582
only unto these *m* do nothing ..... Gen 19:8 582
But the *m* put forth their hand ..... Gen 19:10 582
they smote the *m* that were at the ..... Gen 19:11 582
the *m* said unto Lot, Hast thou ..... Gen 19:12 582
the *m* laid hold upon his hand, and ..... Gen 19:16 582
and the *m* were sore afraid ..... Gen 20:8 582
took two of his young *m* with him ..... Gen 22:3
And Abraham said unto his young *m* ..... Gen 22:5
Abraham returned unto his young *m* .. Gen 22:19
the daughters of the *m* of the ..... Gen 24:13 582
the *m* that were with him, and ..... Gen 24:54 582
and Abraham's servant, and his *m* ..... Gen 24:59 582
the *m* of the place asked him of ..... Gen 26:7 582
the *m* of the place should kill me ..... Gen 26:7 582
together all the *m* of the place ..... Gen 29:22 582
thee, and four hundred *m* with him ..... Gen 32:6 376
thou power with God and with *m* ..... Gen 32:28 582
came, and with him four hundred *m* .... Gen 33:1 376
if *m* should overdrive them one ..... Gen 33:13
the *m* were grieved, and they were ..... Gen 34:7 582
communed with the *m* of their city ..... Gen 34:20 582
These *m* are peaceable with us ..... Gen 34:21 582
Only herein will the *m* consent ..... Gen 34:22 582
Then he asked the *m* of that place ..... Gen 38:21 582
also the *m* of the place said ..... Gen 38:22 582
there was none of the *m* of the ..... Gen 39:11 582
called unto the *m* of her house ..... Gen 39:14 582
Egypt, and all the wise *m* thereof ..... Gen 41:8
we are true *m*, thy servants are ..... Gen 42:11
If ye be true *m*, let one of your ..... Gen 42:19
we said unto him, We are true *m* ..... Gen 42:31
shall I know that ye are true *m* ..... Gen 42:33
no spies, but that ye are true *m* ..... Gen 42:34
the *m* took that present, and they ..... Gen 43:15 582
of his house, Bring these *m* home ..... Gen 43:16 582
for these *m* shall dine with me at ..... Gen 43:16 582
brought the *m* into Joseph's house ..... Gen 43:17 582
the *m* were afraid, because they ..... Gen 43:18 582
brought the *m* into Joseph's house ..... Gen 43:24 582
the *m* marvelled one at another ..... Gen 43:33 582
the *m* were sent away, they and ..... Gen 44:3 582
steward, Up, follow after the *m* ..... Gen 44:4 582
the *m* are shepherds, for their ..... Gen 46:32 582
some of his brethren, even five *m* ..... Gen 47:2 582
if thou knowest any *m* of activity ..... Gen 47:6 582
but saved the *m* children alive ..... Ex 1:17
have saved the *m* children alive ..... Ex 1:18
two *m* of the Hebrews strove ..... Ex 2:13 582
for all the *m* are dead which ..... Ex 4:19 582
more work be laid upon the *m* ..... Ex 5:9 582
Pharaoh also called the wise *m* ..... Ex 7:11
let the *m* go, that they may serve ..... Ex 10:7 582
go now ye that are *m*, and serve ..... Ex 10:11 1397
for they said, We be all dead *m* ..... Ex 12:33
thousand on foot that were *m* ..... Ex 12:37 1397
the mighty *m* of Moab, trembling ..... Ex 15:15
said unto Joshua, Choose us out *m* ..... Ex 17:9 582
out of all the people able *m* ..... Ex 18:21 582
m of truth, hating covetousness ..... Ex 18:21 582
Moses chose able *m* out of all ..... Ex 18:25 582
if *m* strive together, and one ..... Ex 21:18 582
If *m* strive, and hurt a woman with ..... Ex 21:22 582
And ye shall be holy *m* unto me ..... Ex 22:31 582
he sent young *m* of the children ..... Ex 24:5
that day about three thousand *m* ..... Ex 32:28 376
in the year shall all your *m* ..... Ex 34:23 582
they came, both *m* and women ..... Ex 35:22 582
And all the wise *m*, that wrought ..... Ex 36:4
and five hundred and fifty *m* ..... Ex 38:26
of which *m* offer an offering made ..... Lev 7:25
have the *m* of the land done ..... Lev 18:27 582
whereof *m* bring an offering unto ..... Lev 27:9
which shall be devoted of *m* ..... Lev 27:29 120
the *m* that shall stand with you ..... Num 1:5 582
Aaron took these *m* which are ..... Num 1:17 582
princes of Israel, being twelve *m* ..... Num 1:44 376
commit any sin that *m* commit ..... Num 5:6 120
And there were certain *m*, who were ... Num 9:6 582
those *m* said unto him, We are ..... Num 9:7 582
Gather unto me seventy *m* of the ..... Num 11:16 376
gathered the seventy *m* of the ..... Num 11:24 376
remained two of the *m* in the camp ..... Num 11:26 582
of Moses, one of his young *m* ..... Num 11:28
above all the *m* which were upon ..... Num 12:3 120
Send thou *m*, that they may search ..... Num 13:2 582
all those *m* were heads of the ..... Num 13:3 582
These are the names of the *m* ..... Num 13:16 582
unto Rehob, as *m* come to Hamath ..... Num 13:21
But the *m* that went up with him ..... Num 13:31 582
in it are *m* of a great stature ..... Num 13:32 582
Because all those *m* which have ..... Num 14:22 582
And the *m*, which Moses sent to ..... Num 14:36 582
Even those *m* that did bring up ..... Num 14:37 582
which were of the *m* that went to ..... Num 14:38 582
of Peleth, sons of Reuben, took *m* ..... Num 16:1
in the congregation, *m* of renown ..... Num 16:2 582
thou put out the eyes of these *m* ..... Num 16:14 582
from the tents of these wicked *m* ..... Num 16:26 582
If these *m* die the common death ..... Num 16:29
die the common death of all *m* ..... Num 16:29 120
after the visitation of all *m* ..... Num 16:29 120
these *m* have provoked the LORD ..... Num 16:30 582
all the *m* that appertained unto ..... Num 16:32 120
fifty *m* that offered incense ..... Num 16:35 376
whether it be of *m* or beasts ..... Num 18:15 120
What *m* are these with thee ..... Num 22:9 582
If the *m* come to call thee, rise ..... Num 22:20 582
said unto Balaam, Go with the *m* ..... Num 22:35 582

Slay ye every one his *m* that were........ Num 25:5 582
devoured two hundred and fifty *m*......... Num 26:10 376
spoil, and all the prey, both of *m*.......... Num 31:11 120
the priest said unto the *m* of war......... Num 31:21 582
a tribute unto the LORD of the *m*.......... Num 31:28 582
which the *m* of war had caught........... Num 31:32 582
divided from the *m* that warred............ Num 31:42 582
have taken the sum of the *m* of............ Num 31:49 582
(For the *m* of war had taken spoil........ Num 31:53 582
Surely none of the *m* that came up...... Num 32:11 582
stead, an increase of sinful *m*.............. Num 32:14 582
These are the names of the *m*............... Num 34:17 582
And the names of the *m* are these........ Num 34:19 582
Take you wise *m*, and understanding... Deut 1:13 582
the chief of your tribes, wise *m*........... Deut 1:15 582
and said, We will send *m* before us....... Deut 1:22 582
and I took twelve *m* of you.................. Deut 1:23 582
m of this evil generation see............... Deut 1:35 582
the *m* of war were wasted out from..... Deut 2:14 582
when all the *m* of war were.................. Deut 2:16 582
time, and utterly destroyed the *m*......... Deut 2:34 4962
Heshbon, utterly destroying the *m*........ Deut 3:6 4962
for all the *m* that followed................... Deut 4:3 376
Certain *m*, the children of Belial.......... Deut 13:13 582
Then both the *m*, between whom the.. Deut 19:17 582
all the *m* of his city shall stone............ Deut 21:21 582
the *m* of her city shall stone her.......... Deut 22:21 582
there be a controversy between *m*......... Deut 25:1 582
When *m* strive together one with.......... Deut 25:11 582
say unto all the *m* of Israel with.......... Deut 27:14 376
with all the *m* of Israel......................... Deut 29:10 376
Then *m* shall say, Because they............. Deut 29:25
Gather the people together, *m*............... Deut 31:12 582
of them to cease from among *m*............ Deut 32:26 582
and let not his *m* be few...................... Deut 33:6 4962
armed, all the mighty *m* of valour......... Josh 1:14
of Shittim two *m* to spy secretly........... Josh 2:1 582
there came *m* in hither to night............ Josh 2:2 582
Bring forth the *m* that are come........... Josh 2:3 582
And the woman took the two *m*............. Josh 2:4 582
said thus, There came *m* unto me......... Josh 2:4 582
it was dark, that the *m* went out........... Josh 2:5 582
whither the *m* went I wot not............... Josh 2:5 582
the *m* pursued after them the way........ Josh 2:7 582
And she said unto the *m*, I know........... Josh 2:9 582
the *m* answered her, Our life for........... Josh 2:14 582
the *m* said unto her, We will be............ Josh 2:17 582
So the two *m* returned, and.................. Josh 2:23 582
m out of the tribes of Israel.................. Josh 3:12 376
Take you twelve *m* out of the............... Josh 4:2 582
Then Joshua called the twelve *m*.......... Josh 4:4 376
were males, even all the *m* of war........ Josh 5:4 582
all the people that were *m* of war........ Josh 5:6 582
and the mighty *m* of valour.................. Josh 6:2
compass the city, all ye *m* of war......... Josh 6:3 582
the armed *m* went before the............... Josh 6:9
the armed *m* went before them............ Josh 6:13
Joshua had said unto the two *m*........... Josh 6:22 582
the young *m* that were spies went......... Josh 6:23
Joshua sent *m* from Jericho to Ai,......... Josh 7:2 582
the *m* went up and viewed Ai................ Josh 7:2 582
two or three thousand *m* go up............ Josh 7:3 376
the people about three thousand *m*...... Josh 7:4 376
and they fled before the *m* of Ai........... Josh 7:4 582
the *m* of Ai smote of them about.......... Josh 7:5 582
of them about thirty and six *m*............. Josh 7:5 376
thousand mighty *m* of valour................ Josh 8:3 376
And he took about five thousand *m*....... Josh 8:12 376
the *m* of the city went out................... Josh 8:14 582
when the *m* of Ai looked behind............ Josh 8:20 582
turned again, and slew the *m* of Ai....... Josh 8:21 582
all that fell that day, both of *m*............ Josh 8:25 376
thousand, even all the *m* of Ai.............. Josh 8:25 582
to the *m* of Israel, We be come............. Josh 9:6 376
the *m* of Israel said unto the................ Josh 9:7 376
the *m* took of their victuals, and.......... Josh 9:14 582
all the *m* thereof were mighty.............. Josh 10:2 582
the *m* of Gibeon sent unto Joshua......... Josh 10:6 582
and all the mighty *m* of valour.............. Josh 10:7
set *m* by it for to keep them................. Josh 10:18 582
called for all the *m* of Israel................. Josh 10:24 376
the *m* of war which went with him........ Josh 10:24
among you three *m* for each tribe......... Josh 18:4 582
the *m* arose, and went away.................. Josh 18:8 582
the *m* went and passed through the..... Josh 18:9 582
the *m* of Jericho fought against............. Josh 24:11 1167
of them in Bezek ten thousand *m*.......... Judg 1:4 376
at that time about ten thousand *m*....... Judg 3:29 376
all lusty, and all *m* of valour................ Judg 3:29 376
six hundred *m* with an ox goad............ Judg 3:31 376
m of the children of Naphtali................. Judg 4:6 376
with ten thousand *m* at his feet............ Judg 4:10 376
and ten thousand *m* after him............... Judg 4:14 376
Gideon took ten *m* of his servants......... Judg 6:27 582
the *m* of the city, that he could............ Judg 6:27 582
when the *m* of the city arose................. Judg 6:28 582
Then the *m* of the city said unto............ Judg 6:30 582
their mouth, were three hundred *m*....... Judg 7:6 376
By the three hundred *m* that................. Judg 7:7 376
and retained those three hundred *m*..... Judg 7:8 376
the armed *m* that were in the host......... Judg 7:11
hundred *m* into three companies............ Judg 7:16 376
the hundred *m* that were with him,......... Judg 7:19 376
And the *m* of Israel gathered................ Judg 7:23 376
Then all the *m* of Ephraim..................... Judg 7:24 376
the *m* of Ephraim said unto him,............ Judg 8:1 376
the three hundred *m* that were............. Judg 8:4 376
And he said unto the *m* of Succoth........ Judg 8:5 582
the *m* of Penuel answered him as.......... Judg 8:8 582
the *m* of Succoth had answered him..... Judg 8:8 582
spake also unto the *m* of Penuel........... Judg 8:9 582
them, about fifteen thousand *m*............. Judg 8:10
twenty thousand *m* that drew sword..... Judg 8:10 376
a young man of the *m* of Succoth......... Judg 8:14 582

even threescore and seventeen *m*......... Judg 8:14 376
And he came unto the *m* of Succoth..... Judg 8:15 582
bread unto thy *m* that are weary.......... Judg 8:15 582
them he taught the *m* of Succoth.......... Judg 8:16 582
Penuel, and slew the *m* of the city........ Judg 8:17 582
What manner of *m* were they whom..... Judg 8:18 582
Then the *m* of Israel said unto.............. Judg 8:22 376
the ears of all the *m* of Shechem......... Judg 9:2 1167
the *m* of Shechem all these words........ Judg 9:3 1167
all the *m* of Shechem gathered............. Judg 9:6 1167
ye *m* of Shechem, that God may............ Judg 9:7 1167
king over the *m* of Shechem.................. Judg 9:18 1167
and devour the *m* of Shechem............... Judg 9:20 1167
come out from the *m* of Shechem.......... Judg 9:20 1167
Abimelech and the *m* of Shechem.......... Judg 9:23 1167
and the *m* of Shechem dealt.................. Judg 9:23 1167
upon the *m* of Shechem, which............. Judg 9:24 1167
the *m* of Shechem set liers in................ Judg 9:25 1167
the *m* of Shechem put their.................. Judg 9:26 1167
serve the *m* of Hamor the father........... Judg 9:28 582
the mountains as if they were *m*........... Judg 9:36 582
went out before the *m* of Shechem....... Judg 9:39 1167
when all the *m* of the tower of.............. Judg 9:46 1167
that all the *m* of the tower of............... Judg 9:47 1167
so that all the *m* of the tower of........... Judg 9:49 582
died also, about a thousand *m*.............. Judg 9:49 376
city, and thither fled all the *m*............. Judg 9:51 582
that *m* say not of me, A woman............ Judg 9:54
when the *m* of Israel saw that.............. Judg 9:55 376
all the evil of the *m* of Shechem.......... Judg 9:57 582
were gathered vain *m* to Jephthah........ Judg 11:3 582
the *m* of Ephraim gathered.................... Judg 12:1 376
together all the *m* of Gilead.................. Judg 12:4 582
the *m* of Gilead smote Ephraim,............. Judg 12:4 582
that the *m* of Gilead said unto............... Judg 12:5 582
for so used the young *m* to do.............. Judg 14:10
the *m* of the city said unto him............ Judg 14:18 582
and slew thirty *m* of them..................... Judg 14:19 376
the *m* of Judah said, Why are ye........... Judg 15:10 376
Then three thousand *m* of Judah........... Judg 15:11 376
and slew a thousand *m* therewith.......... Judg 15:15 376
an ass have I slain a thousand *m*......... Judg 15:16 376
Now there were *m* lying in wait............. Judg 16:9
Now the house was full of *m*................. Judg 16:27 582
the roof about three thousand *m*.......... Judg 16:27 376
family five *m* from their coasts............. Judg 18:2
m of valour, from Zorah, and from......... Judg 18:2
Then the five *m* departed, and came.... Judg 18:7 582
six hundred *m* appointed with............... Judg 18:11 376
Then answered the five *m* that.............. Judg 18:14 582
the six hundred *m* appointed with......... Judg 18:16 376
the five *m* that went to spy out............ Judg 18:17 582
m that were appointed with.................. Judg 18:17 376
the *m* that were in the houses.............. Judg 18:22 582
but the *m* of the place were................. Judg 19:16 582
the *m* of the city, certain sons.............. Judg 19:22 582
But the *m* would not hearken to............ Judg 19:25 582
the *m* of Gibeah rose against me,.......... Judg 20:5 1167
we will take ten *m* of an hundred........... Judg 20:10 582
So all the *m* of Israel were.................... Judg 20:11 376
sent *m* through all the tribe of.............. Judg 20:12 582
Now therefore deliver us the *m*............. Judg 20:13 582
six thousand *m* that drew sword,........... Judg 20:15 376
numbered seven hundred chosen *m*....... Judg 20:15 376
seven hundred chosen *m* lefthanded..... Judg 20:16 376
the *m* of Israel, beside Benjamin,........... Judg 20:17 376
thousand *m* that drew sword................. Judg 20:17 376
all these were *m* of war....................... Judg 20:17 376
the *m* of Israel went out to.................. Judg 20:20 376
the *m* of Israel put themselves in......... Judg 20:20 376
that day twenty and two thousand *m*.. Judg 20:21 376
the people the *m* of Israel.................... Judg 20:22 376
Israel again eighteen thousand *m*......... Judg 20:25 376
field, about thirty *m* of Israel.............. Judg 20:31 376
all the *m* of Israel rose up out.............. Judg 20:33 376
chosen *m* out of all Israel..................... Judg 20:34 376
and five thousand and an hundred *m*.... Judg 20:35 376
for the *m* of Israel gave place to.......... Judg 20:36 376
sign between the *m* of Israel................ Judg 20:38 376
when the *m* of Israel retired in............. Judg 20:39 376
kill of the *m* of Israel about................. Judg 20:39 376
when the *m* of Israel turned again......... Judg 20:41 376
the *m* of Benjamin were amazed............ Judg 20:41 376
m of Israel unto the way of the............ Judg 20:42 376
of Benjamin eighteen thousand *m*......... Judg 20:44 376
all these were *m* of valour.................... Judg 20:44 582
in the highways five thousand *m*........... Judg 20:45 376
and slew two thousand *m* of them.......... Judg 20:45 376
five thousand *m* that drew the.............. Judg 20:46 376
all these were *m* of valour.................... Judg 20:46 582
But six hundred *m* turned and fled....... Judg 20:47 376
the *m* of Israel turned again upon......... Judg 20:48 376
as well the *m* of every city, as............... Judg 20:48 4974
Now the *m* of Israel had sworn in.......... Judg 21:1 376
thousand *m* of the valiantest............... Judg 21:10 376
have I not charged the young *m*............ Ruth 2:9
that which the young *m* have drawn...... Ruth 2:9
glean, Boaz commanded his young *m*.. Ruth 2:15
shalt keep fast by my young *m*.............. Ruth 2:21
as thou followedst not young *m*........... Ruth 3:10
he took ten *m* of the elders of.............. Ruth 4:2 582
bows of the mighty *m* are broken......... 1Sa 2:4
m was very great before the LORD......... 1Sa 2:17
for *m* abhorred the offering of.............. 1Sa 2:17 582
with the LORD, and also with *m*............. 1Sa 2:26 582
the field about four thousand *m*............ 1Sa 4:2 376
strong, and quit yourselves like *m*......... 1Sa 4:9 582
quit yourselves like *m*, and fight........... 1Sa 4:9 582
when the *m* of Ashdod saw that it........... 1Sa 5:7 582
and he smote the *m* of the city.............. 1Sa 5:9 582
the *m* that died not were smitten......... 1Sa 5:12 582
And the *m* did so................................ 1Sa 6:10 582
the *m* of Beth-shemesh offered............. 1Sa 6:15 582
he smote the *m* of Beth-shemesh,......... 1Sa 6:19 376

thousand and threescore and ten *m*...... 1Sa 6:19 376
the *m* of Beth-shemesh said, Who......... 1Sa 6:20 582
the *m* of Kirjath-jearim came, and......... 1Sa 7:1 582
the *m* of Israel went out of.................... 1Sa 7:11 582
and your goodliest young *m*.................. 1Sa 8:16
Samuel said unto the *m* of Israel.......... 1Sa 8:22 582
then thou shalt find two *m* by.............. 1Sa 10:2 582
m going up to God to Beth-el................. 1Sa 10:3 582
there went with him a band of *m*.......... 1Sa 10:26
all the *m* of Jabesh said unto................ 1Sa 11:1 582
the tidings of the *m* of Jabesh.............. 1Sa 11:5 582
the *m* of Judah thirty thousand............ 1Sa 11:8 376
say unto the *m* of Jabesh-gilead.......... 1Sa 11:9 376
and shewed it to the *m* of Jabesh......... 1Sa 11:9 582
Therefore the *m* of Jabesh said,............ 1Sa 11:10 582
bring the *m*, that we may put them...... 1Sa 11:12 582
all the *m* of Israel rejoiced.................. 1Sa 11:15 582
him three thousand *m* of Israel............ 1Sa 13:2
When the *m* of Israel saw that............. 1Sa 13:6 376
with him, about six hundred *m*............. 1Sa 13:15 376
with him were about six hundred *m*..... 1Sa 14:2 376
we will pass over unto these *m*............ 1Sa 14:8 582
the *m* of the garrison answered............ 1Sa 14:12 582
made, was about twenty *m*, within....... 1Sa 14:14 376
Likewise all the *m* of Israel.................. 1Sa 14:22 376
the *m* of Israel were distressed............. 1Sa 14:24 376
and ten thousand *m* of Judah............... 1Sa 15:4 376
the *m* of Israel were gathered.............. 1Sa 17:2 376
the man went among *m* for an old........ 1Sa 17:12 582
all the *m* of Israel, were in the............. 1Sa 17:19 376
all the *m* of Israel, when they.............. 1Sa 17:24 376
the *m* of Israel said, Have ye................ 1Sa 17:25 376
spake to the *m* that stood by him......... 1Sa 17:26 582
heard when he spake unto the *m*........... 1Sa 17:28 582
the *m* of Israel and of Judah arose........ 1Sa 17:52 582
and Saul set him over the *m* of war..... 1Sa 18:5 582
David arose and went, he and his *m*.... 1Sa 18:27 582
of the Philistines two hundred *m*.......... 1Sa 18:27 376
if the young *m* have kept..................... 1Sa 21:4
vessels of the young *m* are holy............ 1Sa 21:5
Have I need of mad *m*, that ye.............. 1Sa 21:15
with him about four hundred *m*............ 1Sa 22:2 376
the *m* that were with him, (now........... 1Sa 22:6 582
the edge of the sword, both *m*............. 1Sa 22:19 376
David's *m* said unto him, Behold,......... 1Sa 23:3 582
his *m* went to Keilah, and fought.......... 1Sa 23:5 582
Keilah, to besiege David and his *m*........ 1Sa 23:8 582
Will the *m* of Keilah deliver me............. 1Sa 23:11 1167
Will the *m* of Keilah deliver me............. 1Sa 23:12 1167
my *m* into the hand of Saul.................... 1Sa 23:12 582
Then David and his *m*, which were......... 1Sa 23:13 582
his *m* were in the wilderness of............. 1Sa 23:24 582
also and his *m* went to seek him.......... 1Sa 23:25 582
his *m* on that side of the....................... 1Sa 23:26 582
his *m* compassed David and his *m*....... 1Sa 23:26 582
chosen *m* out of all Israel..................... 1Sa 24:2 376
his *m* upon the rocks of the wild........... 1Sa 24:2 582
his *m* remained in the sides of.............. 1Sa 24:3 582
the *m* of David said unto him,............... 1Sa 24:4 582
And he said unto his *m*, The LORD......... 1Sa 24:6 582
his *m* gat them up unto the hold.......... 1Sa 24:22 582
And David sent out ten young *m*.......... 1Sa 25:5
and David said unto the young *m*.......... 1Sa 25:5
Ask thy young *m*, and they will............. 1Sa 25:8
Wherefore let the young *m* find............ 1Sa 25:8
And when David's young *m* came........... 1Sa 25:9
my shearers, and give it unto *m*............ 1Sa 25:11 582
David's young *m* turned their way......... 1Sa 25:12
And David said unto his *m*, Gird ye...... 1Sa 25:13 582
after David about four hundred *m*......... 1Sa 25:13 376
one of the young *m* told Abigail............ 1Sa 25:14
But the *m* were very good unto us,....... 1Sa 25:15 582
his *m* came down against her.............. 1Sa 25:20 582
saw not the young *m* of my lord............ 1Sa 25:25
the young *m* that follow my lord........... 1Sa 25:27
chosen *m* of Israel with him.................. 1Sa 26:2 376
but if they be the children of *m*............ 1Sa 26:19 120
let one of the young *m* come over......... 1Sa 26:22
over with the six hundred *m* that.......... 1Sa 27:2 376
with Achish at Gath, he and his *m*......... 1Sa 27:3 582
his *m* went up, and invaded the............ 1Sa 27:8 582
with me to battle, thou and thy *m*........ 1Sa 28:1 582
two *m* with him, and they came to........ 1Sa 28:8 582
his *m* passed on in the rereward........... 1Sa 29:2 582
not be with the heads of these *m*......... 1Sa 29:4 582
his *m* rose up early to depart in........... 1Sa 29:11 582
his *m* were come to Ziklag on the......... 1Sa 30:1 582
his *m* came to the city, and,................. 1Sa 30:3 582
the six hundred *m* that were with......... 1Sa 30:9 376
pursued, he and four hundred *m*.......... 1Sa 30:10 376
them, save four hundred young *m*.......... 1Sa 30:17 376
David came to the two hundred *m*........ 1Sa 30:21 582
Then answered all the wicked *m*.......... 1Sa 30:22 376
m of Belial, of those that went.............. 1Sa 30:22
and his *m* were wont to haunt.............. 1Sa 30:31 582
the *m* of Israel fled from before............ 1Sa 31:1 582
and his armourbearer, and all his *m*...... 1Sa 31:6 582
when the *m* of Israel that were on......... 1Sa 31:7 582
saw that the *m* of Israel fled, and......... 1Sa 31:7 582
All the valiant *m* arose, and went......... 1Sa 31:12 376
likewise all the *m* that were with.......... 2Sa 1:11 582
David called one of the young *m*.......... 2Sa 1:15
his *m* that were with him did.............. 2Sa 2:3 582
the *m* of Judah came, and there............ 2Sa 2:4 582
That the *m* of Jabesh-gilead were......... 2Sa 2:4 582
unto the *m* of Jabesh-gilead................. 2Sa 2:5 582
Joab, Let the young *m* now arise........... 2Sa 2:14
the *m* of Israel, before the................... 2Sa 2:17 582
thee hold on one of the young *m*......... 2Sa 2:21
his *m* walked all that night................... 2Sa 2:29 582
of David's servants nineteen *m*............ 2Sa 2:30 376
of Benjamin, and of Abner's *m*............. 2Sa 2:31 582
hundred and threescore *m* died........... 2Sa 2:31 376
his *m* went all night, and they............. 2Sa 2:32 582

M

to Hebron, and twenty *m* with him	2Sa 3:20	582
the *m* that were with him a feast	2Sa 3:20	582
as a man falleth before wicked *m*	2Sa 3:34	1121
these *m* the sons of Zeruiah be	2Sa 3:39	582
Saul's son had two *m* that were	2Sa 4:2	582
when wicked *m* have slain a	2Sa 4:11	582
And David commanded his young *m*	2Sa 4:12	
his *m* went to Jerusalem unto the	2Sa 5:6	582
and David and his *m* burned them	2Sa 5:21	582
all the chosen *m* of Israel	2Sa 6:1	
Israel, as well to the women as *m*	2Sa 6:19	376
the great *m* that are in the earth	2Sa 7:9	
chasten him with the rod of *m*	2Sa 7:14	582
the stripes of the children of *m*	2Sa 7:14	120
Syrians two and twenty thousand *m*	2Sa 8:5	376
salt, being eighteen thousand *m*	2Sa 8:13	
because the *m* were greatly	2Sa 10:5	582
and of king Maacah a thousand *m*	2Sa 10:6	376
and of Ish-tob twelve thousand *m*	2Sa 10:6	376
and all the host of the mighty *m*	2Sa 10:7	
of all the choice *m* of Israel	2Sa 10:9	
let us play the *m* for our people	2Sa 10:12	2388
David slew the *m* of seven hundred	2Sa 10:18	
where he knew that valiant *m* were	2Sa 11:16	582
the *m* of the city went out, and	2Sa 11:17	582
Surely the *m* prevailed against us	2Sa 11:23	582
him, There were two *m* in one city	2Sa 12:1	582
said, Have out all *m* from me	2Sa 13:9	376
all the young *m* the king's sons	2Sa 13:32	
fifty *m* to run before him	2Sa 15:1	376
the hearts of the *m* of Israel	2Sa 15:6	582
two hundred *m* out of Jerusalem	2Sa 15:11	376
The hearts of the *m* of Israel are	2Sa 15:13	376
six hundred *m* which came after	2Sa 15:18	376
Gittite passed over, and all his *m*	2Sa 15:22	582
fruit for the young *m* to eat	2Sa 16:2	
all the mighty *m* were on his	2Sa 16:6	
his *m* went by the way, Shimei	2Sa 16:13	582
and all the people the *m* of Israel	2Sa 16:15	376
all the *m* of Israel, choose, his	2Sa 16:18	376
now choose out twelve thousand *m*	2Sa 17:1	376
thou knowest thy father and his *m*	2Sa 17:8	582
that they be mighty *m*	2Sa 17:8	
which be with him are valiant *m*	2Sa 17:10	1121
of all the *m* that are with him	2Sa 17:12	582
all the *m* of Israel said, The	2Sa 17:14	376
all the *m* of Israel with him	2Sa 17:24	376
that day of twenty thousand *m*	2Sa 18:7	
ten young *m* that bare Joab's	2Sa 18:15	
the *m* that lifted up their hand	2Sa 18:28	582
the heart of all the *m* of Judah	2Sa 19:14	376
came down with the *m* of Judah to	2Sa 19:16	376
a thousand *m* of Benjamin with him	2Sa 19:17	376
dead *m* before my lord the king	2Sa 19:28	582
any more the voice of singing *m*	2Sa 19:35	582
all the *m* of Israel came to the	2Sa 19:41	376
the *m* of Judah stolen thee away	2Sa 19:41	376
and all David's *m* with him	2Sa 19:41	582
all the *m* of Judah answered the	2Sa 19:42	376
of Judah answered the *m* of Israel	2Sa 19:42	376
the *m* of Israel answered the *m*	2Sa 19:43	376
the words of the *m* of Judah were	2Sa 19:43	376
than the words of the *m* of Israel	2Sa 19:43	376
but the *m* of Judah clave unto	2Sa 20:2	376
Assemble me the *m* of Judah within	2Sa 20:4	376
went to assemble the *m* of Judah	2Sa 20:5	
there went out after him Joab's *m*	2Sa 20:7	582
Pelethites, and all the mighty *m*	2Sa 20:7	
And one of Joab's *m* stood by him	2Sa 20:11	376
Let seven *m* of his sons be	2Sa 21:6	582
son from the *m* of Jabesh-gilead	2Sa 21:12	1167
Then the *m* of David sware unto	2Sa 21:17	582
of ungodly *m* made me afraid	2Sa 22:5	
that ruleth over *m* must be just	2Sa 23:3	120
of the mighty *m* whom David had	2Sa 23:8	
of the three mighty *m* with David	2Sa 23:9	
the *m* of Israel were gone away	2Sa 23:9	376
the three mighty *m* brake through	2Sa 23:16	
is not this the blood of the *m*	2Sa 23:17	582
things did these three mighty *m*	2Sa 23:17	
he slew two lionlike *m* of Moab	2Sa 23:20	
had the name among three mighty *m*	2Sa 23:22	
valiant *m* that drew the sword	2Sa 24:9	376
the *m* of Judah were five hundred	2Sa 24:9	376
were five hundred thousand *m*	2Sa 24:9	376
to Beer-sheba seventy thousand *m*	2Sa 24:15	376
fifty *m* to run before him	1Kin 1:5	376
the mighty *m* which belonged to	1Kin 1:8	
all the *m* of Judah the king's	1Kin 1:9	582
and Benaiah, and the mighty *m*	1Kin 1:10	
fell upon two *m* more righteous	1Kin 2:32	582
For he was wiser than all *m*	1Kin 4:31	120
and the levy was thirty thousand *m*	1Kin 5:13	376
all the *m* of Israel assembled	1Kin 8:2	376
hearts of all the children of *m*	1Kin 8:39	120
but they were *m* of war, and his	1Kin 9:22	582
Happy are thy *m*, happy are these	1Kin 10:8	582
they took *m* with them out of	1Kin 11:18	582
And he gathered *m* unto him	1Kin 11:24	582
Rehoboam consulted with the old *m*	1Kin 12:6	
forsook the counsel of the old *m*	1Kin 12:8	
consulted with the young *m* that	1Kin 12:8	
the young *m* that were grown up	1Kin 12:10	
after the counsel of the young *m*	1Kin 12:14	
and fourscore thousand chosen *m*	1Kin 12:21	
m passed by, and saw the carcase	1Kin 13:25	582
how I hid an hundred *m* of the	1Kin 18:13	376
are four hundred and fifty *m*	1Kin 18:22	376
Even by the young *m* of the	1Kin 20:14	
Then he numbered the young *m* of	1Kin 20:15	
the young *m* of the princes of the	1Kin 20:17	
There are *m* come out of Samaria	1Kin 20:17	582
So these young *m* of the princes	1Kin 20:19	
thousand of the *m* that were left	1Kin 20:30	376
Now the *m* did diligently observe	1Kin 20:33	582
And set two *m*, sons of Belial,	1Kin 21:10	582
the *m* of his city, even the	1Kin 21:11	582
And there came in two *m*, children	1Kin 21:13	582
the *m* of Belial witnessed against	1Kin 21:13	582
together, about four hundred *m*	1Kin 22:6	376
fifty *m* of the sons of the	2Kin 2:7	376
with thy servants fifty strong *m*	2Kin 2:16	
They sent therefore fifty *m*	2Kin 2:17	376
the *m* of the city said unto	2Kin 2:19	582
seven hundred *m* that drew swords	2Kin 3:26	376
I pray thee, one of the young *m*	2Kin 4:22	
they poured out for the *m* to eat	2Kin 4:40	582
I set this before an hundred *m*	2Kin 4:43	376
m of the sons of the prophets	2Kin 5:22	
and he let the *m* go, and they	2Kin 5:24	582
LORD, open the eyes of these *m*	2Kin 6:20	
there were four leprous *m* at the	2Kin 7:3	582
their young *m* wilt thou slay with	2Kin 8:12	
heads of the *m* your master's sons	2Kin 10:6	582
were with the great *m* of the city	2Kin 10:6	
in Jezreel, and all his great *m*	2Kin 10:11	
house, even two and forty *m*	2Kin 10:14	376
appointed fourscore *m* without	2Kin 10:24	376
If any of the *m* whom I have	2Kin 10:24	582
they took every man his *m* that	2Kin 11:9	582
they reckoned not with the *m*	2Kin 12:15	582
behold, they spied a band of *m*	2Kin 13:21	
of all the mighty *m* of wealth	2Kin 15:20	
Arieh, and with him fifty *m* of the	2Kin 15:25	376
of Assyria brought *m* from Babylon	2Kin 17:24	
And the *m* of Babylon made	2Kin 17:30	582
the *m* of Cuth made Nergal, and the	2Kin 17:30	582
the *m* of Hamath made Ashima,	2Kin 17:30	582
me to the *m* which sit on the wall	2Kin 18:27	582
said unto him, What said these *m*	2Kin 20:14	582
all the *m* of Judah and all the	2Kin 23:2	376
their places with the bones of *m*	2Kin 23:14	120
the *m* of the city told him, It is	2Kin 23:17	582
and all the mighty *m* of valour	2Kin 24:14	
all the *m* of might, even seven	2Kin 24:16	582
all the *m* of war fled by night by	2Kin 25:4	582
that was set over the *m* of war	2Kin 25:19	582
five *m* of them that were in the	2Kin 25:19	582
threescore *m* of the people of the	2Kin 25:19	376
of the armies, they and their *m*	2Kin 25:23	582
of a Maachathite, they and their *m*	2Kin 25:23	582
sware to them, and to their *m*	2Kin 25:24	582
ten *m* with him, and smote Gedaliah	2Kin 25:25	582
These are the *m* of Recah	1Chr 4:12	582
the *m* of Chozeba, and Joash, and	1Chr 4:22	582
sons of Simeon, five hundred *m*	1Chr 4:42	582
tribe of Manasseh, of valiant *m*	1Chr 5:18	
m able to bear buckler and sword,	1Chr 5:18	582
and of *m* an hundred thousand	1Chr 5:21	
mighty *m* of valour, famous *m*,	1Chr 5:24	582
they were valiant *m* of might in	1Chr 7:2	
all of them chief *m*	1Chr 7:3	
for war, six and thirty thousand *m*	1Chr 7:4	
Issachar were valiant *m* of might	1Chr 7:5	
their fathers, mighty *m* of valour	1Chr 7:7	
mighty *m* of valour, was twenty	1Chr 7:9	
fathers, mighty *m* of valour, were	1Chr 7:11	
whom the *m* of Gath that were born	1Chr 7:21	582
mighty *m* of valour, chief of the	1Chr 7:40	
was twenty and six thousand *m*	1Chr 7:40	582
by their generations, chief *m*	1Chr 8:28	
of Ulam were mighty *m* of valour	1Chr 8:40	582
All these *m* were chief of the	1Chr 9:9	582
very able *m* for the work of the	1Chr 9:13	1368
the *m* of Israel fled from before	1Chr 10:1	376
when all the *m* of Israel that	1Chr 10:7	376
They arose, all the valiant *m*	1Chr 10:12	376
of the mighty *m* whom David had	1Chr 11:10	
of the mighty *m* whom David had	1Chr 11:11	
I drink the blood of these *m* that	1Chr 11:19	582
he slew two lionlike *m* of Moab	1Chr 11:22	582
Also the valiant *m* of the armies	1Chr 11:26	
and they were among the mighty *m*	1Chr 12:1	
hold to the wilderness *m* of might	1Chr 12:8	582
m of war fit for the battle, that	1Chr 12:8	
they were all mighty *m* of valour	1Chr 12:21	
mighty *m* of valour for the war,	1Chr 12:25	
mighty *m* of valour, famous	1Chr 12:30	
Issachar, which were *m* that had	1Chr 12:32	582
All these *m* of war, that could	1Chr 12:38	582
let *m* say among the nations, The	1Chr 16:31	
the great *m* that are in the earth	1Chr 17:8	
Syrians two and twenty thousand *m*	1Chr 18:5	376
told David how the *m* were served	1Chr 19:5	582
for the *m* were greatly ashamed	1Chr 19:5	582
and all the host of the mighty *m*	1Chr 19:8	
m which fought in chariots	1Chr 19:18	
thousand *m* that drew sword	1Chr 21:5	376
ten thousand *m* that drew sword	1Chr 21:5	376
fell of Israel seventy thousand *m*	1Chr 21:14	376
all manner of cunning *m* for every	1Chr 22:15	
there were more chief *m* found of	1Chr 24:4	1397
there were sixteen chief *m* of the	1Chr 24:4	
for they were mighty *m* of valour	1Chr 26:6	
whose brethren were strong *m*	1Chr 26:7	1121
able *m* for strength for the	1Chr 26:8	376
had sons and brethren, strong *m*	1Chr 26:9	1121
porters, even among the chief *m*	1Chr 26:12	1397
m of valour, a thousand and seven	1Chr 26:30	1121
m of valour at Jazer of Gilead	1Chr 26:31	
m of valour, were two thousand and	1Chr 26:32	1121
officers, and with the mighty *m*	1Chr 28:1	
and with all the valiant *m*	1Chr 28:1	
all the princes, and the mighty *m*	1Chr 29:24	
ten thousand *m* to bear burdens,	2Chr 2:2	376
m that are with me in Judah	2Chr 2:7	
be put to him, with thy cunning *m*	2Chr 2:14	
with the cunning *m* of my lord	2Chr 2:14	
Wherefore all the *m* of Israel	2Chr 5:3	376
deed dwell with *m* on the earth	2Chr 6:18	120
the hearts of the children of *m*	2Chr 6:30	120
but they were *m* of war, and chief	2Chr 8:9	582
Happy are thy *m*, and happy are	2Chr 9:7	582
took counsel with the old *m* that	2Chr 10:6	
counsel which the old *m* gave him	2Chr 10:8	
took counsel with the young *m*	2Chr 10:8	
the young *m* that were brought up	2Chr 10:10	
forsook the counsel of the old *m*	2Chr 10:13	
after the advice of the young *m*	2Chr 10:14	
and fourscore thousand chosen *m*	2Chr 11:1	
with an army of valiant *m* of war	2Chr 13:3	
four hundred thousand chosen *m*	2Chr 13:3	376
eight hundred thousand chosen *m*	2Chr 13:3	376
being mighty *m* of valour	2Chr 13:3	
are gathered unto him vain *m*	2Chr 13:7	582
Then the *m* of Judah gave a shout	2Chr 13:15	376
as the *m* of Judah shouted, it	2Chr 13:15	376
five hundred thousand chosen *m*	2Chr 13:17	376
an army of *m* that bare targets	2Chr 14:8	
all these were mighty *m* of valour	2Chr 14:8	
the *m* of war, mighty *m* of	2Chr 17:13	582
mighty *m* of valour, were in	2Chr 17:13	
with him mighty *m* of valour three	2Chr 17:14	
thousand mighty *m* of valour	2Chr 17:16	
and with him armed *m* with bow	2Chr 17:17	
of prophets four hundred *m*	2Chr 18:5	376
for the band of *m* that came with	2Chr 22:1	582
took every man his *m* that were to	2Chr 23:8	582
came with a small company of *m*	2Chr 24:24	582
three hundred thousand choice *m*	2Chr 25:5	
m of valour out of Israel for an	2Chr 25:6	
Uzziah had an host of fighting *m*	2Chr 26:11	
m of valour were two thousand	2Chr 26:12	
engines, invented by cunning *m*	2Chr 26:15	
of the LORD, that were valiant *m*	2Chr 26:17	1121
one day, which were all valiant *m*	2Chr 28:6	1121
So the armed *m* left the captives	2Chr 28:14	
the *m* which were expressed by	2Chr 28:15	582
the *m* that were expressed by name	2Chr 31:19	582
his mighty *m* to stop the waters	2Chr 32:3	
off all the mighty *m* of valour	2Chr 32:21	
the *m* did the work faithfully	2Chr 34:12	582
all the *m* of Judah, and the	2Chr 34:30	376
and all the singing *m* and the	2Chr 35:25	
who slew their young *m* with the	2Chr 36:17	
let the *m* of his place help him	Ezr 1:4	582
The number of the *m* of the people	Ezr 2:2	582
The *m* of Netophah, fifty and six	Ezr 2:22	582
The *m* of Anathoth, an hundred	Ezr 2:23	582
The *m* of Michmas, an hundred	Ezr 2:27	582
The *m* of Beth-el and Ai, two	Ezr 2:28	582
among them two hundred singing *m*	Ezr 2:65	582
the fathers, who were ancient *m*	Ezr 3:12	
Thy servants the *m* on this side	Ezr 4:11	606
to cause these *m* to cease	Ezr 4:21	1400
of the *m* that make this building	Ezr 5:4	1400
the *m* that were the chief of them	Ezr 5:10	1400
expences be given unto these *m*	Ezr 6:8	1400
Israel chief *m* to go up with me	Ezr 7:28	582
and for Meshullam, chief *m*	Ezr 8:16	582
for Elnathan, *m* of understanding	Ezr 8:16	582
a very great congregation of *m*	Ezr 10:1	582
Then all the *m* of Judah and	Ezr 10:9	582
they made an end with all the *m*	Ezr 10:17	582
came, he and certain *m* of Judah	Neh 1:2	582
night, I and some few *m* with me	Neh 2:12	582
unto him builded the *m* of Jericho	Neh 3:2	582
the *m* of Gibeon, and of Mizpah,	Neh 3:7	582
the priests, the *m* of the plain	Neh 3:22	582
nor the *m* of the guard which	Neh 4:23	582
for other *m* have our lands and	Neh 5:5	582
of the *m* of the people of Israel	Neh 7:7	582
The *m* of Beth-lehem and Netophah,	Neh 7:26	582
The *m* of Anathoth, an hundred	Neh 7:27	582
The *m* of Beth-azmaveth, forty and	Neh 7:28	582
The *m* of Kirjath-jearim,	Neh 7:29	582
The *m* of Ramah and Gaba, six	Neh 7:30	582
The *m* of Michmas, an hundred and	Neh 7:31	582
The *m* of Beth-el and Ai, an	Neh 7:32	582
The *m* of the other Nebo, fifty and	Neh 7:33	582
hundred forty and five singing *m*	Neh 7:67	
before the congregation both of *m*	Neh 8:2	376
until midday, before the *m*	Neh 8:3	582
And the people blessed all the *m*	Neh 11:2	582
threescore and eight valiant *m*	Neh 11:6	
mighty *m* of valour, an hundred	Neh 11:14	
the son of one of the great *m*	Neh 11:14	
There dwelt *m* of Tyre also	Neh 13:16	582
Then the king said to the wise *m*	Est 1:13	
Then said his wise *m* and Zeresh	Est 6:13	
slew and destroyed five hundred *m*	Est 9:6	376
hundred *m* in Shushan the palace	Est 9:12	376
slew three hundred *m* at Shushan	Est 9:15	376
greatest of all the *m* of the east	Job 1:3	1121
and it fell upon the young *m*	Job 1:19	
when deep sleep falleth on *m*	Job 4:13	582
unto thee, O thou preserver of *m*	Job 7:20	120
thy lies make *m* hold their peace	Job 11:3	4962
For he knoweth vain *m*	Job 11:11	4962
the grayheaded and very aged *m*	Job 15:10	
Which wise *m* have told from their	Job 15:18	
Upright *m* shall be astonied at	Job 17:8	
way which wicked *m* have trodden	Job 22:15	4962
When *m* are cast down, then thou	Job 22:29	
M groan from out of the city, and	Job 24:12	4962
M shall clap their hands at him,	Job 27:23	
up, they are gone away from *m*	Job 28:4	582
The young *m* saw me, and hid	Job 29:8	
Unto me *m* gave ear, and waited, and	Job 29:21	
were driven forth from among *m*	Job 30:5	
of fools, yea, children of base *m*	Job 30:8	
If the *m* of my tabernacle said	Job 31:31	4962

So these three *m* ceased to answer	Job 32:1	582
in the mouth of these three *m*	Job 32:5	582
Great *m* are not always wise	Job 32:9	
when deep sleep falleth upon *m*	Job 33:15	582
Then he openeth the ears of *m*	Job 33:16	582
He looketh upon *m*, and if any say,	Job 33:27	582
Hear my words, O ye wise *m*	Job 34:2	
and walketh with wicked *m*	Job 34:8	582
unto me, ye *m* of understanding	Job 34:10	582
in pieces mighty *m* without number	Job 34:24	
He striketh them as wicked *m* in	Job 34:26	
Let *m* of understanding tell me,	Job 34:34	582
of his answers for wicked *m*	Job 34:36	582
because of the pride of evil *m*	Job 35:12	
magnify his work, which *m* behold	Job 36:24	582
that all *m* may know his work	Job 37:7	582
now *m* see not the bright light	Job 37:21	
M do therefore fear him	Job 37:24	582
he goeth on to meet the armed *m*	Job 39:21	
O ye sons of *m*, how long will ye	Ps 4:2	376
may know themselves to be but *m*	Ps 9:20	582
eyelids try, the children of *m*	Ps 11:4	120
fail from among the children of *m*	Ps 12:1	120
when the vilest *m* are exalted	Ps 12:8	
heaven upon the children of *m*	Ps 14:2	120
Concerning the works of *m*	Ps 17:4	120
From *m* which are thy hand, O LORD	Ps 17:14	4962
from *m* of the world, which have	Ps 17:14	4962
of ungodly *m* made me afraid	Ps 18:4	
seed from among the children of *m*	Ps 21:10	120
a reproach of *m*, and despised of	Ps 22:6	120
nor my life with bloody *m*	Ps 26:9	582
in thee before the sons of *m*	Ps 31:19	120
he beholdeth all the sons of *m*	Ps 33:13	120
of *m* put their trust under the	Ps 36:7	120
art fairer than the children of *m*	Ps 45:2	120
For he seeth that wise *m* die	Ps 49:10	
m will praise thee, when thou	Ps 49:18	
heaven upon the children of *m*	Ps 53:2	120
deceitful *m* shall not live out	Ps 55:23	582
set on fire, even the sons of *m*	Ps 57:4	120
judge uprightly, O ye sons of *m*	Ps 58:1	120
and save me from bloody *m*	Ps 59:2	582
Surely *m* of low degree are vanity	Ps 62:9	
m of high degree are a lie	Ps 62:9	376
all *m* shall fear, and shall	Ps 64:9	120
doing toward the children of *m*	Ps 66:5	120
Thou hast caused *m* to ride over	Ps 66:12	582
thou hast received gifts for *m*	Ps 68:18	120
m shall be blessed in him	Ps 72:17	
are not in trouble as other *m*	Ps 73:5	582
are they plagued like other *m*	Ps 73:5	120
none of the *m* of might have found	Ps 76:5	582
smote down the chosen *m* of Israel	Ps 78:31	
the tent which he placed among *m*	Ps 78:60	120
The fire consumed their young *m*	Ps 78:63	
But ye shall die like *m*, and fall	Ps 82:7	120
That *m* may know that thou, whose	Ps 83:18	
m have sought after my soul	Ps 86:14	
hast thou made all *m* in vain	Ps 89:47	
sayest, Return, ye children of *m*	Ps 90:3	120
they were but a few *m* in number	Ps 105:12	4962
Oh that *m* would praise the LORD	Ps 107:8	
works to the children of *m*	Ps 107:8	120
Oh that *m* would praise the LORD	Ps 107:15	
works to the children of *m*	Ps 107:15	120
Oh that *m* would praise the LORD	Ps 107:21	
works to the children of *m*	Ps 107:21	120
Oh that *m* would praise the LORD	Ps 107:31	
works to the children of *m*	Ps 107:31	120
he given to the children of *m*	Ps 115:16	120
said in my haste, All *m* are liars	Ps 116:11	120
when *m* rose up against us	Ps 124:2	120
from me therefore, ye bloody *m*	Ps 139:19	582
works with *m* that work iniquity	Ps 141:4	376
m shall speak of the might of thy	Ps 145:6	
to the sons of *m* his mighty acts	Ps 145:12	120
Both young *m*, and maidens	Ps 148:12	
old *m*, and children	Ps 148:12	
mayest walk in the way of good *m*	Prov 2:20	
and go not in the way of evil *m*	Prov 4:14	
M do not despise a thief, if he	Prov 6:30	
many strong *m* have been slain by	Prov 7:26	582
Unto you, O *m*, I call	Prov 8:4	376
delights were with the sons of *m*	Prov 8:31	120
Wise *m* lay up knowledge	Prov 10:14	
and the hope of unjust *m* perisheth	Prov 11:7	
and strong *m* retain riches	Prov 11:16	
wicked desireth the net of evil *m*	Prov 12:12	
walketh with wise *m* shall be wise	Prov 13:20	
the hearts of the children of *m*	Prov 15:11	120
of the LORD *m* depart from evil	Prov 16:6	
children are the crown of old *m*	Prov 17:6	
and bringeth him before great *m*	Prov 18:16	
Most *m* will proclaim every one	Prov 20:6	120
of young *m* is their strength	Prov 20:29	
beauty of old *m* is the grey head	Prov 20:29	
he shall not stand before mean *m*	Prov 22:29	
the transgressors among *m*	Prov 23:28	120
not thou envious against evil *m*	Prov 24:1	582
scorner is an abomination to *m*	Prov 24:9	120
not thyself because of evil *m*	Prov 24:19	
which the *m* of Hezekiah king of	Prov 25:1	582
stand not in the place of great *m*	Prov 25:6	
so for *m* to search their own	Prov 25:27	
seven *m* that can render a reason	Prov 26:16	
Evil *m* understand not judgment	Prov 28:5	582
of riotous *m* shameth his father	Prov 28:7	
When righteous *m* do rejoice	Prov 28:12	
wicked rise, *m* hide themselves	Prov 28:28	120
Scornful *m* bring a city into a	Prov 29:8	582
but wise *m* turn away wrath	Prov 29:8	
earth, and the needy from among *m*	Prov 30:14	120
was that good for the sons of *m*	Eccl 2:3	120
I gat me *m* singers and women	Eccl 2:8	
and the delights of the sons of *m*	Eccl 2:8	120
sons of *m* to be exercised in it	Eccl 3:10	120
that *m* should fear before him	Eccl 3:14	582
the estate of the sons of *m*	Eccl 3:18	120
the sons of *m* befalleth beasts	Eccl 3:19	120
the sun, and it is common among *m*	Eccl 6:1	120
for that is the end of all *m*	Eccl 7:2	120
mighty *m* which are in the city	Eccl 7:19	
the heart of the sons of *m* is	Eccl 8:11	120
that there be just *m*, unto whom	Eccl 8:14	
again, there be wicked *m*, to whom	Eccl 8:14	
of the sons of *m* is full of evil	Eccl 9:3	120
yet riches to *m* of understanding	Eccl 9:11	
nor yet favour to *m* of skill	Eccl 9:11	
so are the sons of *m* snared in an	Eccl 9:12	120
a little city, and few *m* within it	Eccl 9:14	582
The words of wise *m* are heard in	Eccl 9:17	
the strong *m* shall bow themselves	Eccl 12:3	582
threescore valiant *m* are about it	Song 3:7	
bucklers, all shields of mighty *m*	Song 4:4	
the haughtiness of *m* shall be	Is 2:11	582
of *m* shall be made low	Is 2:17	582
Thy *m* shall fall by the sword, and	Is 3:25	4962
m of Judah, judge, I pray you,	Is 5:3	376
the *m* of Judah his pleasant plant	Is 5:7	376
their honourable *m* are famished	Is 5:13	4962
m of strength to mingle strong	Is 5:22	582
the LORD have removed *m* far away	Is 6:12	120
a small thing for you to weary *m*	Is 7:13	582
and with bows shall *m* come thither	Is 7:24	
as *m* rejoice when they divide the	Is 9:3	
have no joy in their young *m*	Is 9:17	
and make *m* go over dryshod	Is 11:15	
shall dash the young *m* to pieces	Is 13:18	
where are thy wise *m*	Is 19:12	
here cometh a chariot of *m*	Is 21:9	376
the mighty *m* of the children of	Is 21:17	
thy slain *m* are not slain with	Is 22:2	
the quiver with chariots of *m*	Is 22:6	120
neither do I nourish up young *m*	Is 23:4	
earth are burned, and few *m* left	Is 24:6	582
Thy dead *m* shall live, together	Is 26:19	
word of the LORD, ye scornful *m*	Is 28:14	582
which *m* deliver to one that is	Is 29:11	
me is taught by the precept of *m*	Is 29:13	582
of their wise *m* shall perish	Is 29:14	
of their prudent *m* shall be hid	Is 29:14	
the poor among *m* shall rejoice in	Is 29:19	120
Now the Egyptians are *m*, and not	Is 31:3	120
his young *m* shall be discomfited	Is 31:8	
the wayfaring *m*, though fools,	Is 35:8	582
to the *m* that sit upon the wall	Is 36:12	582
O Lord, by these things *m* live	Is 38:16	
said unto him, What said these *m*	Is 39:3	582
the young *m* shall utterly fall	Is 40:30	
thee from the chief *m* thereof	Is 41:9	
worm Jacob, and ye *m* of Israel	Is 41:14	4962
therefore will I give *m* for thee	Is 43:4	120
and the workmen, they are of *m*	Is 44:11	120
that turneth wise *m* backward	Is 44:25	
m of stature, shall come over	Is 45:14	582
even to him shall *m* come	Is 45:24	
this, and shew yourselves *m*	Is 46:8	376
fear ye not the reproach of *m*	Is 51:7	582
his form more than the sons of *m*	Is 52:14	120
He is despised and rejected of *m*	Is 53:3	376
merciful *m* are taken away, none	Is 57:1	582
are in desolate places as dead *m*	Is 59:10	
that *m* may bring unto thee the	Is 60:11	
m, shall call you the Ministers	Is 61:6	
of the world *m* have not heard	Is 64:4	
look upon the carcases of the *m*	Is 66:24	582
saith the LORD to the *m* of Judah	Jer 4:3	376
ye *m* of Judah and inhabitants of	Jer 4:4	376
I will get me unto the great *m*	Jer 5:5	
sepulchre, they are all mighty *m*	Jer 5:16	
my people are found wicked *m*	Jer 5:26	
they set a trap, they catch *m*	Jer 5:26	582
the assembly of young *m* together	Jer 6:11	
set in array as *m* for war against	Jer 6:23	376
silver shall *m* call them, because	Jer 6:30	
The wise *m* are ashamed, they are	Jer 8:9	
a lodging place of wayfaring *m*	Jer 9:2	
an assembly of treacherous *m*	Jer 9:2	
neither can *m* hear the voice of	Jer 9:10	
the young *m* from the streets	Jer 9:21	
Even the carcases of *m* shall fall	Jer 9:22	120
all the wise *m* of the nations	Jer 10:7	
are all the work of cunning *m*	Jer 10:9	
and speak unto the *m* of Judah	Jer 11:2	376
is found among the *m* of Judah	Jer 11:9	376
the LORD of the *m* of Anathoth	Jer 11:21	582
the young *m* shall die by the	Jer 11:22	
bring evil upon the *m* of Anathoth	Jer 11:23	582
the young *m* a spoiler at noonday	Jer 15:8	
nor *m* have lent to me on usury	Jer 15:10	
neither shall *m* lament for them,	Jer 16:6	
Neither shall *m* tear themselves	Jer 16:7	
neither shall *m* give them the cup	Jer 16:7	
princes, the *m* of Judah, and the	Jer 17:25	376
go to, speak to the *m* of Judah	Jer 18:11	376
let their *m* be put to death	Jer 18:21	582
let their young *m* be slain by the	Jer 18:21	
sight of the *m* that go with thee	Jer 19:10	582
the king, with all his mighty *m*	Jer 26:21	
the king sent *m* into Egypt	Jer 26:22	582
certain *m* with him into Egypt	Jer 26:22	582
in the dance, both young *m*	Jer 31:13	
all the ways of the sons of *m*	Jer 32:19	120
and in Israel, and among other *m*	Jer 32:20	120
and the *m* of Judah, and the	Jer 32:32	376
M shall buy fields for money, and	Jer 32:44	
them with the dead bodies of *m*	Jer 33:5	120
I will give the *m* that have	Jer 34:18	582
Go and tell the *m* of Judah	Jer 35:13	376
Jerusalem, and upon the *m* of Judah	Jer 36:31	376
but wounded *m* among them	Jer 37:10	582
he weakeneth the hands of the *m*	Jer 38:4	582
these *m* have done evil in all	Jer 38:9	582
from hence thirty *m* with thee	Jer 38:10	582
Ebed-melech took the *m* with him	Jer 38:11	582
of these *m* that seek thy life	Jer 38:16	582
saw them, and all the *m* of war	Jer 39:4	582
of the *m* of whom thou art afraid	Jer 39:17	582
the fields, even they and their *m*	Jer 40:7	582
land, and had committed unto him *m*	Jer 40:7	582
of a Maachathite, they and their *m*	Jer 40:8	582
sware unto them and to their *m*	Jer 40:9	582
of the king, even ten *m* with him	Jer 41:1	582
the ten *m* that were with him, and	Jer 41:2	582
were found there, and the *m* of war	Jer 41:3	582
and from Samaria, even fourscore *m*	Jer 41:5	376
he, and the *m* that were with him	Jer 41:7	582
But ten *m* were found among them	Jer 41:8	582
cast all the dead bodies of the *m*	Jer 41:9	582
Then they took all the *m*, and went	Jer 41:12	582
escaped from Johanan with eight *m*	Jer 41:15	582
of Ahikam, even mighty *m* of war	Jer 41:16	582
So shall it be with all the *m*	Jer 42:17	582
son of Kareah, and all the proud *m*	Jer 43:2	582
m, and women, and children	Jer 43:6	1397
in the sight of the *m* of Judah	Jer 43:9	582
Then all the *m* which knew that	Jer 44:15	582
offerings unto her, without our *m*	Jer 44:19	582
unto all the people, to the *m*	Jer 44:20	1397
all the *m* of Judah that are in	Jer 44:27	376
and let the mighty *m* come forth	Jer 46:9	
Why are thy valiant *m* swept away	Jer 46:15	
Also her hired *m* are in the midst	Jer 46:21	
then the *m* shall cry, and all the	Jer 47:2	120
mighty and strong *m* for the war	Jer 48:14	582
his chosen young *m* are gone down	Jer 48:15	
mourn for the *m* of Kir-heres	Jer 48:31	582
like pipes for the *m* of Kir-heres	Jer 48:36	582
the heathen, and despised among *m*	Jer 49:15	120
m of Edom be as the heart of a	Jer 49:22	
Therefore her young *m* shall fall	Jer 49:26	
all the *m* of war shall be cut off	Jer 49:26	582
Kedar, and spoil the *m* of the east	Jer 49:28	1121
her young *m* fall in the streets	Jer 50:30	
all her *m* of war shall be cut off	Jer 50:30	582
her princes, and upon her wise *m*	Jer 50:35	
a sword is upon her mighty *m*	Jer 50:36	
and spare ye not her young *m*	Jer 51:3	
Surely I will fill thee with *m*	Jer 51:14	120
The mighty *m* of Babylon have	Jer 51:30	
the *m* of war are affrighted	Jer 51:32	582
and her mighty *m* are taken	Jer 51:56	
drunk her princes, and her wise *m*	Jer 51:57	
and her rulers, and her mighty *m*	Jer 51:57	
all the *m* of war fled, and went	Jer 52:7	582
and all the houses of the great *m*	Jer 52:13	
had the charge of the *m* of war	Jer 52:25	582
seven *m* of them that were near	Jer 52:25	582
threescore *m* of the people of the	Jer 52:25	376
my mighty *m* in the midst of me	Lam 1:15	
against me to crush my young *m*	Lam 1:15	
and my young *m* are gone into	Lam 1:18	
Is this the city that *m* call The	Lam 2:15	
my young *m* are fallen by the	Lam 2:21	
nor grieve the children of *m*	Lam 3:33	376
as blind *m* in the streets	Lam 4:14	
so that *m* could not touch their	Lam 4:14	
They took the young *m* to grind	Lam 5:13	
the young *m* from their musick	Lam 5:14	
your slain *m* before your idols	Eze 6:4	
when their slain *m* shall be among	Eze 6:13	
m of the ancients of the house of	Eze 8:11	376
were about five and twenty *m*	Eze 8:16	376
six *m* came from the way of the	Eze 9:2	582
the foreheads of the *m* that sigh	Eze 9:4	582
m which were before the house	Eze 9:6	582
door of the gate five and twenty *m*	Eze 11:1	376
these are the *m* that devise	Eze 11:2	582
the *m* of thy kindred, and all the	Eze 11:15	582
a few *m* of them from the sword	Eze 12:16	582
these *m* have set up their idols	Eze 14:3	582
Though these three *m*, Noah,	Eze 14:14	582
Though these three *m* were in it	Eze 14:16	582
Though these three *m* were in it	Eze 14:18	582
or will *m* take a pin of it to	Eze 15:3	
and madest to thyself images of *m*	Eze 16:17	2145
it devoured *m*	Eze 19:3	120
to catch the prey, and devoured *m*	Eze 19:6	120
of the great *m* that are slain	Eze 21:14	
thee into the hand of brutish *m*	Eze 21:31	582
In thee are *m* that carry tales to	Eze 22:9	582
all of them desirable young *m*	Eze 23:6	
that were the chosen *m* of Assyria	Eze 23:7	1121
all of them desirable young *m*	Eze 23:12	
for when she saw *m* pourtrayed	Eze 23:14	582
all of them desirable young *m*	Eze 23:23	
have sent for *m* to come from far	Eze 23:40	582
with the *m* of the common sort	Eze 23:42	582
And the righteous *m*, they shall	Eze 23:45	582
lips, and eat not the bread of *m*	Eze 24:17	582
your lips, nor eat the bread of *m*	Eze 24:22	582
I will deliver thee to the *m* of	Eze 25:4	1121
Unto the *m* of the east with the	Eze 25:10	1121
as *m* enter into a city wherein is	Eze 26:10	
wast inhabited of seafaring *m*	Eze 26:17	
thy wise *m*, O Tyrus, that were in	Eze 27:8	
the wise *m* thereof were in thee	Eze 27:9	
were in thine army, thy *m* of war	Eze 27:10	582
The *m* of Arvad with thine army	Eze 27:11	1121
they traded the persons of *m*	Eze 27:13	120
The *m* of Dedan were thy merchants	Eze 27:15	1121

merchandise, and all thy *m* of war	Eze 27:27	582
the *m* of the land that is in	Eze 30:5	1121
The young *m* of Aven and of	Eze 30:17	
in the midst of the children of *m*	Eze 31:14	120
the flock of my pasture, are *m*	Eze 34:31	120
his mountains with his slain *m*	Eze 35:8	
And I will multiply *m* upon you	Eze 36:10	120
I will cause *m* to walk upon you,	Eze 36:12	120
more henceforth bereave them of *m*	Eze 36:12	
you, Thou land devourest up *m*	Eze 36:13	120
thou shalt devour *m* no more	Eze 36:14	120
Neither will I cause *m* to hear in	Eze 36:15	
increase them with *m* like a flock	Eze 36:37	120
cities be filled with flocks of *m*	Eze 36:38	120
all the *m* that are upon the face	Eze 38:20	120
they shall sever out *m* of	Eze 39:14	582
horses and chariots, with mighty *m*	Eze 39:20	
and with all *m* of war	Eze 39:20	376
way of Hethlon, as *m* go to Zedad	Eze 47:15	
destroy all the wise *m* of Babylon	Dan 2:12	
that the wise *m* should be slain	Dan 2:13	
to slay the wise *m* of Babylon	Dan 2:14	
the rest of the wise *m* of Babylon	Dan 2:18	
to destroy the wise *m* of Babylon	Dan 2:24	
Destroy not the wise *m* of Babylon	Dan 2:24	
hath demanded cannot the wise *m*	Dan 2:27	
the children of *m* dwell, the	Dan 2:38	606
themselves with the seed of *m*	Dan 2:43	606
over all the wise *m* of Babylon	Dan 2:48	
these *m*, O king, have not	Dan 3:12	1400
brought these *m* before the king	Dan 3:13	1400
he commanded the most mighty *m*	Dan 3:20	1400
Then these *m* were bound in their	Dan 3:21	1400
those *m* that took up Shadrach	Dan 3:22	1400
And these three *m*, Shadrach,	Dan 3:23	1400
Did not we cast three *m* bound	Dan 3:24	1400
and said, Lo, I see four *m* loose	Dan 3:25	1400
gathered together, saw these *m*	Dan 3:27	1400
the wise *m* of Babylon before me	Dan 4:6	
High ruleth in the kingdom of *m*	Dan 4:17	606
up over it the basest of *m*	Dan 4:17	606
forasmuch as all the wise *m* of my	Dan 4:18	
That they shall drive thee from *m*	Dan 4:25	606
High ruleth in the kingdom of *m*	Dan 4:25	606
And they shall drive thee from *m*	Dan 4:32	606
High ruleth in the kingdom of *m*	Dan 4:32	606
and he was driven from *m*, and did	Dan 4:33	606
and said to the wise *m* of Babylon	Dan 5:7	
came in all the king's wise *m*	Dan 5:8	
And now the wise *m*, the	Dan 5:15	
he was driven from the sons of *m*	Dan 5:21	606
God ruled in the kingdom of *m*	Dan 5:21	606
Then said these *m*, We shall not	Dan 6:5	1400
Then these *m* assembled, and found	Dan 6:11	1400
Then these *m* assembled unto the	Dan 6:15	1400
they brought those *m* which had	Dan 6:24	1400
dominion of my kingdom *m* tremble	Dan 6:26	
to the *m* of Judah, and to the	Dan 9:7	376
for the *m* that were with me saw	Dan 10:7	582
of the sons of *m* touched my lips	Dan 10:16	120
But they like *m* have transgressed	Hos 6:7	120
in the multitude of thy mighty *m*	Hos 10:13	
Let the *m* that sacrifice kiss the	Hos 13:2	120
Hear this, ye old *m*, and give ear,	Joel 1:2	
withered away from the sons of *m*	Joel 1:12	120
They shall run like mighty *m*	Joel 2:7	
climb the wall like *m* of war	Joel 2:7	582
your old *m* shall dream dreams,	Joel 2:28	
your young *m* shall see visions	Joel 2:28	
Prepare war, wake up the mighty *m*	Joel 3:9	
let all the *m* of war draw near	Joel 3:9	582
and of your young *m* for Nazarites	Amos 2:11	
your young *m* have I slain with	Amos 4:10	
there remain ten *m* in one house	Amos 6:9	582
and young *m* faint for thirst	Amos 8:13	
All the *m* of thy confederacy have	Obad 7	582
the *m* that were at peace with	Obad 7	582
destroy the wise *m* out of Edom	Obad 8	
And thy mighty *m*, O Teman, shall	Obad 9	
Then were the *m* exceedingly	Jonah 1:10	582
For the *m* knew that he fled from	Jonah 1:10	582
Nevertheless the *m* rowed hard to	Jonah 1:13	582
Then the *m* feared the LORD	Jonah 1:16	582
by securely as *m* averse from war	Mic 2:8	
by reason of the multitude of *m*	Mic 2:12	120
shepherds, and eight principal *m*	Mic 5:5	120
nor waiteth for the sons of *m*	Mic 5:7	120
For the rich *m* thereof are full	Mic 6:12	
and there is none upright among *m*	Mic 7:2	120
are the *m* of his own house	Mic 7:6	582
of his mighty *m* is made red	Nah 2:3	
the valiant *m* are in scarlet	Nah 2:3	582
cast lots for her honourable *m*	Nah 3:10	
all her great *m* were bound in	Nah 3:10	
makest *m* as the fishes of the sea	Hab 1:14	120
punish the *m* that are settled on	Zeph 1:12	582
And I will bring distress upon *m*	Zeph 1:17	120
that they shall walk like blind *m*	Zeph 1:17	
m shall worship him, every one	Zeph 2:11	
ground bringeth forth, and upon *m*	Hag 1:11	120
walls for the multitude of *m*	Zec 2:4	120
for they are *m* wondered at	Zec 3:8	582
and Regem-melech, and their *m*	Zec 7:2	582
when *m* inhabited the south and the	Zec 7:7	
There shall yet old *m* and old	Zec 8:4	
for I set all *m* every one against	Zec 8:10	120
that ten *m* shall take hold out of	Zec 8:23	582
shall make the young *m* cheerful	Zec 9:17	
And they shall be as mighty *m*	Zec 10:5	
I will deliver the *m* every one	Zec 11:6	120
m shall dwell in it, and there	Zec 14:11	
there came wise *m* from the east	Mt 2:1	
he had privily called the wise *m*	Mt 2:7	
that he was mocked of the wise *m*	Mt 2:16	
diligently enquired of the wise *m*	Mt 2:16	
and I will make you fishers of *m*	Mt 4:19	*444*
when *m* shall revile you, and	Mt 5:11	
and to be trodden under foot of *m*	Mt 5:13	*444*
Neither do *m* light a candle, and	Mt 5:15	
Let your light so shine before *m*	Mt 5:16	*444*
commandments, and shall teach *m* so	Mt 5:19	*444*
that ye do not your alms before *m*	Mt 6:1	*444*
that they may have glory of *m*	Mt 6:2	*444*
that they may be seen of *m*	Mt 6:5	*444*
if ye forgive *m* their trespasses	Mt 6:14	*444*
ye forgive not *m* their trespasses	Mt 6:15	*444*
they may appear unto *m* to fast	Mt 6:16	*444*
thou appear not unto *m* to fast	Mt 6:18	*444*
ye would that *m* should do to you	Mt 7:12	*444*
Do *m* gather grapes of thorns, or	Mt 7:16	
But the *m* marvelled, saying, What	Mt 8:27	*444*
which had given such power unto *m*	Mt 9:8	*444*
Neither do *m* put new wine into	Mt 9:17	
two blind *m* followed him, crying,	Mt 9:27	
house, the blind *m* came to him	Mt 9:28	
But beware of *m*	Mt 10:17	*444*
hated of all *m* for my name's sake	Mt 10:22	
shall confess me before *m*	Mt 10:32	*444*
whosoever shall deny me before *m*	Mt 10:33	*444*
shall be forgiven unto *m*	Mt 12:31	*444*
shall not be forgiven unto *m*	Mt 12:31	*444*
idle word that *m* shall speak	Mt 12:36	*444*
The *m* of Nineveh shall rise in	Mt 12:41	*435*
righteous *m* have desired to see	Mt 13:17	
But while *m* slept, his enemy came	Mt 13:25	*444*
eaten were about five thousand *m*	Mt 14:21	*435*
when the *m* of that place had	Mt 14:35	*435*
doctrines the commandments of *m*	Mt 15:9	*444*
that did eat were four thousand *m*	Mt 15:38	*435*
Whom do *m* say that I the Son of	Mt 16:13	*444*
be of God, but those that be of *m*	Mt 16:23	*444*
be betrayed into the hands of *m*	Mt 17:22	*444*
All *m* cannot receive this saying,	Mt 19:11	
which were made eunuchs of *m*	Mt 19:12	*444*
With *m* this is impossible	Mt 19:26	*444*
two blind *m* sitting by the way	Mt 20:30	
from heaven, or of *m*	Mt 21:25	*444*
But if we shall say, Of *m*	Mt 21:26	*444*
miserably destroy those wicked *m*	Mt 21:41	
regardest not the person of *m*	Mt 22:16	*444*
works they do for to be seen of *m*	Mt 23:5	*444*
the markets, and to be called of *m*	Mt 23:7	*444*
the kingdom of heaven against *m*	Mt 23:13	*444*
outwardly appear righteous unto *m*	Mt 23:28	*444*
send unto you prophets, and wise *m*	Mt 23:34	
Though all *m* shall be offended	Mt 26:33	
did shake, and became as dead *m*	Mt 28:4	
make you to become fishers of *m*	Mk 1:17	*444*
unto him, All *m* seek for thee	Mk 1:37	
be forgiven unto the sons of *m*	Mk 3:28	*444*
and all *m* did marvel	Mk 5:20	
and preached that *m* should repent	Mk 6:12	
loaves were about five thousand *m*	Mk 6:44	*435*
doctrines the commandments of *m*	Mk 7:7	*444*
God, ye hold the tradition of *m*	Mk 7:8	*444*
within, out of the heart of *m*	Mk 7:21	*444*
these *m* with bread here in the	Mk 8:4	
I see *m* as trees, walking	Mk 8:24	*444*
them, Whom do *m* say that I am	Mk 8:27	*444*
God, but the things that be of *m*	Mk 8:33	*444*
is delivered into the hands of *m*	Mk 9:31	*444*
With *m* it is impossible, but not	Mk 10:27	*444*
John, was it from heaven, or of *m*	Mk 11:30	*444*
But if we shall say, Of *m*	Mk 11:32	*444*
for all *m* counted John, that he	Mk 11:32	
regardest not the person of *m*	Mk 12:14	*444*
hated of all *m* for my name's sake	Mk 13:13	
the young *m* laid hold on him	Mk 14:51	*3495*
to take away my reproach among *m*	Lk 1:25	*444*
earth peace, good will toward *m*	Lk 2:14	*444*
all *m* mused in their hearts of	Lk 3:15	
henceforth thou shalt catch *m*	Lk 5:10	*444*
m brought in a bed a man which	Lk 5:18	*435*
when *m* shall hate you, and when	Lk 6:22	*444*
when all *m* shall speak well of	Lk 6:26	*444*
ye would that *m* should do to you	Lk 6:31	*444*
shall *m* give into your bosom	Lk 6:38	
For of thorns *m* do not gather	Lk 6:44	
When the *m* were come unto him,	Lk 7:20	*435*
I liken the *m* of this generation	Lk 7:31	*444*
they were about five thousand *m*	Lk 9:14	*435*
there talked with him two *m*	Lk 9:30	*435*
the two *m* that stood with him	Lk 9:32	*435*
be delivered into the hands of *m*	Lk 9:44	*444*
with the *m* of this generation	Lk 11:31	*435*
The *m* of Nineve shall rise up in	Lk 11:32	*435*
the *m* that walk over them are not	Lk 11:44	*444*
for ye lade *m* with burdens	Lk 11:46	*444*
shall confess me before *m*	Lk 12:8	*444*
m shall be denied before the	Lk 12:9	*444*
ye yourselves like unto *m* that	Lk 12:36	*444*
to whom *m* have committed much, of	Lk 12:48	
all *m* that dwelt in Jerusalem	Lk 13:4	*444*
six days in which *m* ought to work	Lk 13:14	
That none of those *m* which were	Lk 14:24	*435*
but *m* cast it out	Lk 14:35	
which justify yourselves before *m*	Lk 16:15	*444*
m is abomination in the sight of	Lk 16:15	*444*
met him ten *m* that were lepers	Lk 17:12	*435*
there shall be two *m* in one bed	Lk 17:34	
Two *m* shall be in the field	Lk 17:36	
that *m* ought always to pray, and	Lk 18:1	
Two *m* went up into the temple to	Lk 18:10	*444*
that I am not as other *m* are	Lk 18:11	*444*
with *m* are possible with God	Lk 18:27	*444*
John, was it from heaven, or of *m*	Lk 20:4	*444*
But and if we say, Of *m*	Lk 20:6	*444*
should feign themselves just *m*	Lk 20:20	
saw the rich *m* casting their	Lk 21:1	
hated of all *m* for my name's sake	Lk 21:17	
the *m* that held Jesus mocked him,	Lk 22:63	*435*
Herod with his *m* of war set him	Lk 23:11	*4753*
two *m* stood by them in shining	Lk 24:4	*435*
into the hands of sinful *m*	Lk 24:7	*444*
and the life was the light of *m*	Jn 1:4	*444*
that all *m* through him might	Jn 1:7	
when *m* have well drunk, then that	Jn 2:10	
unto them, because he knew all *m*	Jn 2:24	
m loved darkness rather than	Jn 3:19	*444*
baptizeth, and all *m* come to him	Jn 3:26	
place where *m* ought to worship	Jn 4:20	
into the city, and saith to the *m*	Jn 4:28	*444*
other *m* laboured, and ye are	Jn 4:38	
That all *m* should honour the Son,	Jn 5:23	
I receive not honour from *m*	Jn 5:41	*444*
Jesus said, Make the *m* sit down	Jn 6:10	*444*
So the *m* sat down, in number	Jn 6:10	*435*
Then those *m*, when they had seen	Jn 6:14	*444*
the testimony of two *m* is true	Jn 8:17	*444*
all *m* will believe on him	Jn 11:48	
earth, will draw all *m* unto me	Jn 12:32	
of *m* more than the praise of God	Jn 12:43	*444*
By this shall all *m* know that ye	Jn 13:35	
m gather them, and cast them into	Jn 15:6	
manifested thy name unto the *m*	Jn 17:6	*444*
then, having received a band of *m*	Jn 18:3	
two *m* stood by them in white	Acts 1:10	*435*
Ye *m* of Galilee, why stand ye	Acts 1:11	*435*
M and brethren, this scripture	Acts 1:16	*435*
Wherefore of these *m* which have	Acts 1:21	
which knowest the hearts of all *m*	Acts 1:24	
at Jerusalem Jews, devout *m*	Acts 2:5	*435*
These *m* are full of new wine	Acts 2:13	
Ye *m* of Judaea, and all ye that	Acts 2:14	*435*
your young *m* shall see visions,	Acts 2:17	*3495*
your old *m* shall dream dreams	Acts 2:17	
Ye *m* of Israel, hear these words	Acts 2:22	*435*
M and brethren, let me freely	Acts 2:29	*435*
and to the rest of the apostles, *M*	Acts 2:37	*435*
and goods, and parted them to all *m*	Acts 2:45	
Ye *m* of Israel, why marvel ye at	Acts 3:12	*435*
the number of the *m* was about	Acts 4:4	*435*
name under heaven given among *m*	Acts 4:12	*444*
they were unlearned and ignorant *m*	Acts 4:13	*444*
What shall we do to these *m*	Acts 4:16	*444*
for all *m* glorified God for that	Acts 4:21	
thou hast not lied unto *m*	Acts 5:4	*444*
And the young *m* arose, wound him	Acts 5:6	
and the young *m* came in, and found	Acts 5:10	*3495*
to the Lord, multitudes both of *m*	Acts 5:14	*435*
the *m* whom ye put in prison are	Acts 5:25	*435*
ought to obey God rather than *m*	Acts 5:29	*444*
Ye *m* of Israel, take heed to	Acts 5:35	*435*
intend to do as touching these *m*	Acts 5:35	*444*
to whom a number of *m*, about four	Acts 5:36	*435*
unto you, Refrain from these *m*	Acts 5:38	*444*
this counsel or this work be of *m*	Acts 5:38	*444*
you seven *m* of honest report	Acts 6:3	*435*
Then they suborned *m*, which said,	Acts 6:11	*435*
And he said, *M*, brethren, and	Acts 7:2	*435*
devout *m* carried Stephen to his	Acts 8:2	*435*
into every house, and haling *m*	Acts 8:3	*435*
they were baptized, both *m*	Acts 8:12	*435*
way, whether they were *m* or women	Acts 9:2	*435*
the *m* which journeyed with him	Acts 9:7	*435*
there, they sent unto him two *m*	Acts 9:38	*435*
And now send *m* to Joppa, and call	Acts 10:5	*435*
the *m* which were sent from	Acts 10:17	*435*
him, Behold, three *m* seek thee	Acts 10:19	*435*
Then Peter went down to the *m*	Acts 10:21	*435*
wentest in to *m* uncircumcised	Acts 11:3	*435*
m already come unto the house	Acts 11:11	*435*
Send *m* to Joppa, and call for	Acts 11:13	*435*
And some of them were *m* of Cyprus	Acts 11:20	*435*
sent unto them, saying, Ye *m*	Acts 13:15	*435*
M of Israel, and ye that fear God,	Acts 13:16	*435*
M and brethren, children of the	Acts 13:26	*435*
Be it known unto you therefore, *m*	Acts 13:38	*435*
the chief *m* of the city, and	Acts 13:50	
down to us in the likeness of *m*	Acts 14:11	*444*
We also are *m* of like passions	Acts 14:15	*444*
certain *m* which came down from	Acts 15:1	
rose up, and said unto them, *M*	Acts 15:7	*435*
peace, James answered, saying, *M*	Acts 15:13	*435*
That the residue of *m* might seek	Acts 15:17	*444*
to send chosen *m* of their own	Acts 15:22	*435*
chief *m* among the brethren	Acts 15:22	*435*
to send chosen *m* unto you with	Acts 15:25	*435*
M that have hazarded their lives	Acts 15:26	*444*
These *m* are the servants of the	Acts 16:17	*444*
the magistrates, saying, These *m*	Acts 16:20	*444*
serjeants, saying, Let those *m* go	Acts 16:35	*444*
women which were Greeks, and of *m*	Acts 17:12	*435*
Ye *m* of Athens, I perceive that	Acts 17:22	*435*
of one blood all nations of *m* for	Acts 17:26	*444*
all *m* every where to repent	Acts 17:30	*444*
hath given assurance unto all *m*	Acts 17:31	
Howbeit certain *m* clave unto him	Acts 17:34	*435*
This fellow persuadeth *m* to	Acts 18:13	*444*
all the *m* were about twelve	Acts 19:7	*435*
and burned them before all *m*	Acts 19:19	
m of Macedonia, Paul's companions	Acts 19:29	
Ye *m* of Ephesus, what man is	Acts 19:35	*435*
ye have brought hither these *m*	Acts 19:37	*435*
I am pure from the blood of all *m*	Acts 20:26	
of your own selves shall *m* arise	Acts 20:30	*435*
We have four *m* which have a vow	Acts 21:23	*435*
Then Paul took the *m*, and the next	Acts 21:26	*435*
Crying out, *M* of Israel, help	Acts 21:28	*435*
that teacheth all *m* every where	Acts 21:28	
thousand *m* that were murderers	Acts 21:38	*435*
M, brethren, and fathers, hear ye	Acts 22:1	*435*

and delivering into prisons both *m* Acts 22:4 *435*
unto all *m* of what thou hast seen Acts 22:15 *444*
beholding the council, said, *M* Acts 23:1 *435*
he cried out in the council, *M* Acts 23:6 *435*
for him of them more than forty *m* Acts 23:21 *435*
offence toward God, and toward *m* Acts 24:16 *444*
principal *m* of the city, at Acts 25:23 *435*
all *m* which are here present with Acts 25:24 *435*
together, he said unto them, *M* Acts 28:17 *435*
and unrighteousness of *m*, who hold Rom 1:18 *444*
And likewise also the *m*, leaving Rom 1:27 *730*
m with *m* working that which is Rom 1:27 *730*
m with *m* working that which is Rom 1:27 *730*
God shall judge the secrets of *m* Rom 2:16 *444*
whose praise is not of *m*, but of Rom 2:29 *444*
and so death passed upon all *m* Rom 5:12 *444*
came upon all *m* to condemnation Rom 5:18 *444*
all *m* unto justification of life Rom 5:18 *444*
of *m* because of the infirmity of Rom 6:19 *442*
to myself seven thousand *m* Rom 11:4 *435*
but condescend to *m* of low estate Rom 12:16
honest in the sight of all *m* Rom 12:17 *444*
in you, live peaceably with all *m* Rom 12:18 *444*
to God, and approved of *m* Rom 14:18 *444*
is come abroad unto all *m* Rom 16:19
of God is wiser than *m* 1Cor 1:25 *444*
of God is stronger than *m* 1Cor 1:25 *444*
not many wise *m* after the flesh 1Cor 1:26
not stand in the wisdom of *m* 1Cor 2:5 *444*
are ye not carnal, and walk as *m* 1Cor 3:3 *444*
Therefore let no man glory in *m* 1Cor 3:21 *444*
of *m* above that which is written 1Cor 4:6
the world, and to angels, and to *m* 1Cor 4:9 *444*
For I would that all *m* were even 1Cor 7:7 *444*
be not ye the servants of *m* 1Cor 7:23 *444*
For though I be free from all *m* 1Cor 9:19
I am made all things to all *m* 1Cor 9:22
I speak as to wise *m* 1Cor 10:15
as I please all *m* in all things 1Cor 10:33
I speak with the tongues of *m* 1Cor 13:1 *444*
tongue speaketh not unto *m* 1Cor 14:2 *444*
speaketh unto *m* to edification 1Cor 14:3 *444*
but in understanding be *m* 1Cor 14:20 *5046*
With *m* of other tongues and other 1Cor 14:21
we are of all *m* most miserable 1Cor 15:19 *444*
If after the manner of *m* I have 1Cor 15:32 *444*
there is one kind of flesh of *m* 1Cor 15:39 *444*
in the faith, quit you like *m* 1Cor 16:13 *407*
hearts, known and read of all *m* 2Cor 3:2 *444*
terror of the Lord, we persuade *m* 2Cor 5:11 *444*
I mean not that other *m* be eased 2Cor 8:13
Lord, but also in the sight of *m* 2Cor 8:21 *444*
unto them, and unto all *m* 2Cor 9:13
Paul, an apostle, (not of *m* Gal 1:1 *444*
For do I now persuade *m*, or God Gal 1:10 *444*
or do I seek to please *m* Gal 1:10 *444*
for if I yet pleased *m*, I should Gal 1:10 *444*
I speak after the manner of *m* Gal 3:15 *444*
let us do good unto all *m* Gal 6:10
not made known unto the sons of *m* Eph 3:5 *444*
to make all *m* see what is the Eph 3:9
captive, and gave gifts unto *m* Eph 4:8 *444*
of doctrine, by the sleight of *m* Eph 4:14 *444*
So ought *m* to love their wives as Eph 5:28 *435*
as to the Lord, and not to *m* Eph 6:7 *444*
and was made in the likeness of *m* Phil 2:7 *444*
moderation be known unto all *m* Phil 4:5 *444*
deceit, after the tradition of *m* Col 2:8 *444*
commandments and doctrines of *m* Col 2:22 *444*
as to the Lord, and not unto *m* Col 3:23 *444*
as ye know what manner of *m* we 1Th 1:5
not as pleasing *m*, but God, which 1Th 2:4 *444*
Nor of *m* sought we glory, neither 1Th 2:6 *444*
received it not as the word of *m* 1Th 2:13 *444*
not God, and are contrary to all *m* 1Th 2:15 *444*
toward another, and toward all *m* 1Th 3:12
the weak, be patient toward all *m* 1Th 5:14
among yourselves, and to all *m* 1Th 5:15
from unreasonable and wicked *m* 2Th 3:2 *444*
for all *m* have not faith 2Th 3:2
of thanks, be made for all *m* 1Ti 2:1 *444*
Who will have all *m* to be saved 1Ti 2:4 *444*
and one mediator between God and *m* 1Ti 2:5 *444*
therefore that *m* pray every where 1Ti 2:8 *435*
God, who is the Saviour of all *m* 1Ti 4:10 *444*
and the younger *m* as brethren 1Ti 5:1
and some *m* they follow after 1Ti 5:24 *444*
disputings of *m* of corrupt minds 1Ti 6:5 *444*
which drown *m* in destruction and 1Ti 6:9 *444*
same commit thou to faithful *m* 2Ti 2:2 *444*
but be gentle unto all *m*, apt to 2Ti 2:24
For *m* shall be lovers of their 2Ti 3:2 *444*
m of corrupt minds, reprobate 2Ti 3:8 *444*
shall be manifest unto all *m* 2Ti 3:9
But evil *m* and seducers shall wax 2Ti 3:13 *444*
with me, but all *m* forsook me 2Ti 4:16
of hospitality, a lover of good *m* Titus 1:8
fables, and commandments of *m* Titus 1:14 *444*
That the aged *m* be sober, grave, Titus 2:2
Young *m* likewise exhort to be Titus 2:6
salvation hath appeared to all *m* Titus 2:11 *444*
shewing all meekness unto all *m* Titus 3:2 *444*
are good and profitable unto *m* Titus 3:8 *444*
high priest taken from among *m* is Heb 5:1 *444*
for *m* in things pertaining to God Heb 5:1 *444*
For *m* verily swear by the greater Heb 6:16 *444*
here *m* that die receive tithes Heb 7:8 *444*
For the law maketh *m* high priests Heb 7:28 *444*
is of force after *m* are dead Heb 9:17
is appointed unto *m* once to die Heb 9:27 *444*
Follow peace with all *m*, and Heb 12:14
spirits of just *m* made perfect Heb 12:23
that giveth to all *m* liberally Jas 1:5
Do not rich *m* oppress you Jas 2:6
and therewith curse we *m*, which Jas 3:9 *444*
Go to now, ye rich *m*, weep and Jas 5:1
stone, disallowed indeed of *m* 1Pet 2:4 *444*
the ignorance of foolish *m* 1Pet 2:15 *444*
Honour all *m* 1Pet 2:17
in the flesh to the lusts of *m* 1Pet 4:2 *444*
according to *m* in the flesh 1Pet 4:6 *444*
but holy *m* of God spake as they 2Pet 1:21 *444*
and perdition of ungodly *m* 2Pet 3:7 *444*
as some *m* count slackness 2Pet 3:9
I write unto you, young *m* 1Jn 2:13 *3495*
I have written unto you, young *m* 1Jn 2:14 *3495*
If we receive the witness of *m* 1Jn 5:9 *444*
hath good report of all *m* 3Jn 12
are certain *m* crept in unawares Jude 4 *444*
to this condemnation, ungodly *m* Jude 4
and the great *m*, and the rich *m* Rev 6:15
chief captains, and the mighty *m* Rev 6:15
many *m* died of the waters, Rev 8:11 *444*
but only those *m* which have not Rev 9:4 *444*
in those days shall *m* seek death Rev 9:6 *444*
faces were as the faces of *m* Rev 9:7 *444*
power was to hurt *m* five months Rev 9:10 *444*
for to slay the third part of *m* Rev 9:15 *444*
was the third part of *m* killed Rev 9:18 *444*
the rest of the *m* which were not Rev 9:20 *444*
were slain of *m* seven thousand Rev 11:13 *444*
on the earth in the sight of *m* Rev 13:13 *444*
These were redeemed from among *m* Rev 14:4 *444*
grievous sore upon the *m* which Rev 16:2 *444*
unto him to scorch *m* with fire Rev 16:8 *444*
m were scorched with great heat, Rev 16:9 *444*
not since *m* were upon the earth Rev 16:18 *444*
there fell upon *m* a great hail Rev 16:21 *444*
m blasphemed God because of the Rev 16:21 *444*
and slaves, and souls of *m* Rev 18:13 *444*
were the great *m* of the earth Rev 18:23
and the flesh of mighty *m* Rev 19:18
on them, and the flesh of all *m* Rev 19:18
the tabernacle of God is with *m* Rev 21:3 *444*

MENAHEM *(men'-a-hem) Son of Gadi.*
For *M* the son of Gadi went up 2Kin 15:14 4505
Then *M* smote Tiphsah, and all that 2Kin 15:16 4505
M the son of Gadi to reign over 2Kin 15:17 4505
M gave Pul a thousand talents of 2Kin 15:19 4505
M exacted the money of Israel, 2Kin 15:20 4505
And the rest of the acts of *M* 2Kin 15:21 4505
And *M* slept with his fathers 2Kin 15:22 4505
of Judah Pekahiah the son of *M* 2Kin 15:23 4505

MENAN *(me'-nan) Father of Melea; ancestor of Jesus.*
of Melea, which was the son of *M* Lk 3:31 *3104*

MEND
brass to *m* the house of the LORD 2Chr 24:12 2388

MENDING
their father, *m* their nets Mt 4:21 *2675*
were in the ship *m* their nets Mk 1:19 *2675*

MENE *(me'-ne) Part of "the handwriting on the wall".*
writing that was written, *M*, *M* Dan 5:25 4484
M; God hath numbered Dan 5:26 4484

MENI See MENAN.

MENNA See MENAN.

MENPLEASERS
Not with eyeservice, as *m* Eph 6:6 *441*
not with eyeservice, as *m* Col 3:22 *441*

MEN'S
the *m* feet that were with him Gen 24:32 582
Fill the *m* sacks with food, as Gen 44:1 582
serve gods, the work of *m* hands Deut 4:28 120
Wherefore hearest thou *m* words 1Sa 24:9 120
forsook the old *m* counsel that 1Kin 12:13
m bones shall be burnt upon thee 1Kin 13:2 120
no gods, but the work of *m* hands 2Kin 19:18 120
burned *m* bones upon them, and 2Kin 23:20 120
and gold, the work of *m* hands Ps 115:4 120
and gold, the work of *m* hands Ps 135:15 120
no gods, but the work of *m* hands Is 37:19 120
the mighty *m* hearts in Moab at Jer 48:41
because of *m* blood, and for the Hab 2:8 120
them afraid, because of *m* blood Hab 2:17 120
borne, and lay them on *m* shoulders Mt 23:4 *444*
are within full of dead *m* bones Mt 23:27
is not come to destroy *m* lives Lk 9:56 *444*
M hearts failing them for fear, Lk 21:26 *444*
is worshipped with *m* hands Acts 17:25 *444*
that is, of other *m* labours 2Cor 10:15
be partaker of other *m* sins 1Ti 5:22
Some *m* sins are open beforehand, 1Ti 5:24
as a busybody in other *m* matters 1Pet 4:15
having *m* persons in admiration Jude 16 *4283*

MENSERVANTS
sheep, and oxen, and he asses, and *m* Gen 12:16 5650
took sheep, and oxen, and *m* Gen 20:14 5650
herds, and silver, and gold, and *m* Gen 24:35 5650
cattle, and maidservants, and *m* Gen 30:43 5650
have oxen, and asses, flocks, and *m* Gen 32:5 5650
she shall not go out as the *m* do Ex 21:7 5650
and your daughters, and your *m* Deut 12:12 5650
And he will take your *m*, and your 1Sa 8:16 5650
and sheep, and oxen, and *m*, and 2Kin 5:26 5650
and shall begin to beat the *m* Lk 12:45 *3816*

MENSTEALERS
themselves with mankind, for *m* 1Ti 1:10 *405*

MENSTRUOUS
shalt cast them away as a *m* cloth Is 30:22 1739
is as a *m* woman among them Lam 1:17 5079
hath come near to a *m* woman Eze 18:6 5079

MENTION
make *m* of me unto Pharaoh, and Gen 40:14 2142
make no *m* of the name of other Ex 23:13 2142
neither make *m* of the names of Josh 23:7 2142
when he made *m* of the ark of God, 1Sa 4:18 2142
No *m* shall be made of coral, or Job 28:18 2142
I will make *m* of thy Ps 71:16 2142
I will make *m* of Rahab and Babylon Ps 87:4 2142
make *m* that his name is exalted Is 12:4 2142
every one that maketh *m* thereof Is 19:17 2142
only will we make *m* of thy name Is 26:13 2142
make *m* of the God of Israel, but Is 48:1 2142
mother hath he made *m* of my name Is 49:1 2142
ye that make *m* of the LORD Is 62:6 2142
I will *m* the lovingkindnesses of Is 63:7 2142
Make ye *m* to the nations Jer 4:16 2142
I said, I will not make *m* of him Jer 20:9 2142
of the LORD shall ye *m* no more Jer 23:36 2142
for we may not make *m* of the name Amos 6:10 2142
m of you always in my prayers Rom 1:9 *3417*
making *m* of you in my prayers Eph 1:16 *3417*
making *m* of you in our prayers 1Th 1:2 *3417*
making *m* of thee always in my Philem 4 *3417*
made *m* of the departing of the Heb 11:22 *3421*

MENTIONED
cities which are here *m* by name Josh 21:9 7121
These *m* by their names were 1Chr 4:38 935
who is *m* in the book of the kings 2Chr 20:34 5927
For thy sister Sodom was not *m* by Eze 16:56 8052
they shall not be *m* unto him Eze 18:22 2142
that he hath done shall not be *m* Eze 18:24 2142
committed shall be *m* unto him Eze 33:16 2142

MENUHOTH See MANAHETHITES.

MEONENIM *(me-on'-e-nim) A place near Shechem.*
come along by the plain of *M* Judg 9:37 6049

MEONOTHAI *(me-on'-o-thahee) Descendant of Judah.*
And *M* begat Ophrah 1Chr 4:14 4587

MEPHAATH *(mef'-a-ath) A Levitical city in Reuben.*
And Jahaza, and Kedemoth, and *M* Josh 13:18 4158
suburbs, and *M* with her suburbs Josh 21:37 4158
suburbs, and *M* with her suburbs 1Chr 6:79 4158
and upon Jahazah, and upon *M* Jer 48:21 4158

MEPHIBOSHETH *(me-fib'-o-sheth)* See MERIBBAAL.
1. Son of Jonathan.
And his name was *M* 2Sa 4:4 4648
Now when *M*, the son of Jonathan, 2Sa 9:6 4648
And David said, *M* 2Sa 9:6 4648
but *M* thy master's son shall eat 2Sa 9:10 4648
As for *M*, said the king, he shall 2Sa 9:11 4648
M had a young son, whose name was 2Sa 9:12 4648
of Ziba were servants unto *M* 2Sa 9:12 4648
So *M* dwelt in Jerusalem 2Sa 9:13 4648
Ziba the servant of *M* met him 2Sa 16:1 4648
are all that pertained unto *M* 2Sa 16:4 4648
M the son of Saul came down to 2Sa 19:24 4648
wentest not thou with me, *M* 2Sa 19:25 4648
M said unto the king, Yea, let 2Sa 19:30 4648
But the king spared *M*, the son of 2Sa 21:7 4648
2. Son of Rizpah.
she bare unto Saul, Armoni and *M* 2Sa 21:8 4648

MERAB *(me'-rab) Daughter of King Saul.*
the name of the firstborn *M* 1Sa 14:49 4764
David, Behold my elder daughter *M* 1Sa 18:17 4764
M Saul's daughter should have 1Sa 18:19 4764

MERAIAH *(mer-a-i'-ah) A priest.*
fathers: of Seraiah, *M* Neh 12:12 4811

MERAIOTH *(me-rah'-yoth)* See MEREMOTH.
1. An ancestor of Azariah.
Zerahiah, and Zerahiah begat *M* 1Chr 6:6 4812
M begat Amariah, and Amariah begat 1Chr 6:7 4812
M his son, Amariah his son, 1Chr 6:52 4812
the son of Azariah, the son of *M* Ezr 7:3 4812
2. Another ancestor of Azariah.
the son of Zadok, the son of *M* 1Chr 9:11 4812
the son of Zadok, the son of *M* Neh 11:11 4812
3. A priest in exile.
of *M*, Helkai Neh 12:15 4812

MERARI *(me-ra'-ri)* See MERARITES. *A son of Levi.*
Gershon, Kohath, and *M* Gen 46:11 4847
Gershon, and Kohath, and *M* Ex 6:16 4847
And the sons of *M* Ex 6:19 4847
Gershon, and Kohath, and *M* Num 3:17 4847
the sons of *M* by their families Num 3:20 4847
Of *M* was the family of the Num 3:33 4847
these are the families of *M* Num 3:33 4847
M was Zuriel the son of Abihail Num 3:35 4847
charge of the sons of *M* shall be Num 3:36 4847
As for the sons of *M*, thou shalt Num 4:29 4847
of the families of the sons of *M* Num 4:33 4847
of the families of the sons of *M* Num 4:42 4847
of the families of the sons of *M* Num 4:45 4847
oxen he gave unto the sons of *M* Num 7:8 4847
and the sons of *M* set forward Num 10:17 4847
of *M*, the family of the Merarites Num 26:57 4847
The children of *M* by their Josh 21:7 4847
the families of the children of *M* Josh 21:34 4847
children of *M* by their families Josh 21:40 4847
Gershon, Kohath, and *M* 1Chr 6:1 4847
Gershom, Kohath, and *M* 1Chr 6:16 4847
The sons of *M*; Mahli, and 1Chr 6:19 4847
The sons of *M*; Mahli, Libni 1Chr 6:29 4847
sons of *M* stood on the left hand 1Chr 6:44 4847
the son of Mushi, the son of *M* 1Chr 6:47 4847
Unto the sons of *M* were given by 1Chr 6:63 4847

M

the rest of the children of *M* 1Chr 6:77 4847
of Hashabiah, of the sons of *M* 1Chr 9:14 4847
Of the sons of *M* 1Chr 15:6 4847
of the sons of *M* their brethren 1Chr 15:17 4847
namely, Gershon, Kohath, and *M* 1Chr 23:6 4847
The sons of *M*; Mahli, and 1Chr 23:21 4847
The sons of *M* were Mahli and Mushi 1Chr 24:26 4847
The sons of *M* by Jaaziah 1Chr 24:27 4847
Also Hosah, of the children of *M* 1Chr 26:10 4847
of Kore, and among the sons of *M* 1Chr 26:19 4847
and of the sons of *M*, Kish the son 2Chr 29:12 4847
the Levites, of the sons of *M* 2Chr 34:12 4847
him Jeshaiah of the sons of *M* Ezr 8:19 4847

MERARITES (*me-ra'-rites*) *Descendants of Merari.*
of Merari, the family of the *M* Num 26:57 4848

MERATHAIM (*mer-a-tha'-im*) *A symbolic name for Babylon.*
Go up against the land of *M* Jer 50:21 4850

MERCHANDISE
thou shalt not make *m* of her Deut 21:14 6014
of Israel, and maketh *m* of him Deut 24:7 6014
For the *m* of it is better than Prov 3:14 5504
it is better than the *m* of silver Prov 3:14 5505
She perceiveth that her *m* is good Prov 31:18 5504
And her *m* and her hire shall be Is 23:18 5504
for her *m* shall be for them that Is 23:18 5504
m of Ethiopia and of the Sabeans, Is 45:14 5505
riches, and make a prey of thy *m* Eze 26:12 7404
were in thee to occupy thy *m* Eze 27:9 4627
isles were the *m* of thine hand Eze 27:15 5506
and made of cedar, among thy *m* Eze 27:24 4819
Thy riches, and thy fairs, thy *m* Eze 27:27 4627
and the occupiers of thy *m* Eze 27:27 4267
of thy riches and of thy *m* Eze 27:33 4627
in the depths of the waters thy *m* Eze 27:34 4627
By the multitude of thy *m* they Eze 28:16 7404
one to his farm, another to his *m* Mt 22:5 *1711*
my Father's house an house of *m* Jn 2:16 *1712*
with feigned words make *m* of you 2Pet 2:3
no man buyeth their *m* any more Rev 18:11 *1117*
The *m* of gold, and silver, and Rev 18:12 *1117*

MERCHANT
silver, current money with the *m* Gen 23:16
and delivereth girdles unto the *m* Prov 31:24 5503
with all powders of the *m* Song 3:6 7402
a commandment against the *m* city Is 23:11 3667
which art a *m* of the people for Eze 27:3 7402
Tarshish was thy *m* by reason of Eze 27:12 5503
Syria was thy *m* by reason of the Eze 27:16 5503
Damascus was thy *m* in the Eze 27:18 5503
Dedan was thy *m* in precious Eze 27:20 7402
He is a *m*, the balances of deceit Hos 12:7 3667
for all the *m* people are cut down Zeph 1:11 3667
of heaven is like unto a *m* man Mt 13:45 *1713*

MERCHANTMEN
Then there passed by Midianites *m* Gen 37:28 5503
Beside that he had of the *m* 1Kin 10:15 8446

MERCHANTS
and of the traffick of the spice *m* 1Kin 10:15 7402
the king's *m* received the linen 1Kin 10:28 5503
the king's *m* received the linen 2Chr 1:16 5503
that which chapmen and *m* brought 2Chr 9:14 5503
of the Nethinims, and of the *m* Neh 3:31 7402
repaired the goldsmiths and the *m* Neh 3:32 7402
So the *m* and sellers of all kind Neh 13:20 7402
shall they part him among the *m* Job 41:6 3669
thou whom the *m* of Zidon, that Is 23:2 5503
whose *m* are princes, whose Is 23:8 5503
thou hast laboured, even thy *m* Is 47:15 5503
he set it in a city of *m* Eze 17:4 7402
and Meshech, they were thy *m* Eze 27:13 7402
The men of Dedan were thy *m* Eze 27:15 7402
land of Israel, they were thy *m* Eze 27:17 7402
in these were they thy *m* Eze 27:21 5503
The *m* of Sheba and Raamah Eze 27:22 7402
Sheba and Raamah, they were thy *m* Eze 27:22 7402
the *m* of Sheba, Asshur, and Eze 27:23 7402
and Chilmad, were thy *m* Eze 27:23 7402
These were thy *m* in all sorts of Eze 27:24 7402
The *m* among the people shall hiss Eze 27:36 5503
the *m* of Tarshish, with all the Eze 38:13 5503
Thou hast multiplied thy *m* above Nah 3:16 7402
the *m* of the earth are waxed rich Rev 18:3 *1713*
the *m* of the earth shall weep and Rev 18:11 *1713*
The *m* of these things, which were Rev 18:15 *1713*
for thy *m* were the great men of Rev 18:23 *1713*

MERCHANTS'
She is like the *m* ships Prov 31:14 5503

MERCIES
worthy of the least of all the *m* Gen 32:10 2617
for his *m* are great 2Sa 24:14 7356
for very great are his *m* 1Chr 21:13 7356
remember the *m* of David thy 2Chr 6:42 2617
Yet thou in thy manifold *m* Neh 9:19 7356
m thou gavest them saviours Neh 9:27 7356
deliver them according to thy *m* Neh 9:28 7356
Remember, O LORD, thy tender *m* Ps 25:6 7356
not thou thy tender *m* from me Ps 40:11 7356
m blot out my transgressions Ps 51:1 7356
to the multitude of thy tender *m* Ps 69:16 7356
he in anger shut up his tender *m* Ps 77:9 7356
let thy tender *m* speedily prevent Ps 79:8 7356
I will sing of the *m* of the LORD Ps 89:1 2617
with lovingkindness and tender *m* Ps 103:4 7356
not the multitude of thy *m* Ps 106:7 2617
to the multitude of his *m* Ps 106:45 2617
Let thy *m* come also unto me, O Ps 119:41 2617
Let thy tender *m* come unto me Ps 119:77 7356
Great are thy tender *m*, O LORD Ps 119:156 7356
his tender *m* are over all his Ps 145:9 7356
but the tender *m* of the wicked Prov 12:10 7356
but with great *m* will I gather Is 54:7 7356
you, even the sure *m* of David Is 55:3 2617
on them according to his *m* Is 63:7 7356
thy bowels and of thy *m* toward me Is 63:15 7356
LORD, even lovingkindness and *m* Jer 16:5 7356
And I will shew *m* unto you Jer 42:12 7356
It is of the LORD's *m* that we are Lam 3:22 2617
to the multitude of his *m* Lam 3:32 2617
That they would desire *m* of the Dan 2:18 7359
To the Lord our God belong *m* Dan 9:9 7356
but for thy great *m* Dan 9:18 7356
and in lovingkindness, and in *m* Hos 2:19 7356
I am returned to Jerusalem with *m* Zec 1:16 7356
will give you the sure *m* of David Acts 13:34 *3741*
brethren, by the *m* of God Rom 12:1 *3628*
Jesus Christ, the Father of *m* 2Cor 1:3 *3628*
of the Spirit, if any bowels and *m* Phil 2:1 *3628*
God, holy and beloved, bowels of *m* Col 3:12 *3628*

MERCIES'
Nevertheless for thy great *m* sake Neh 9:31 7356
oh save me for thy *m* sake Ps 6:4 2617
save me for thy *m* sake Ps 31:16 2617
help, and redeem us for thy *m* sake Ps 44:26 2617

MERCIFUL
the LORD being *m* unto him Gen 19:16 2551
The LORD, The LORD God, *m* Ex 34:6 7349
(For the LORD thy God is a *m* God Deut 4:31 7349
Be *m*, O LORD, unto thy people Deut 21:8 3722
will be *m* unto his land, and to Deut 32:43 3722
With the *m* thou wilt shew thyself 2Sa 22:26 2623
thou wilt shew thyself *m* 2Sa 22:26 2616
the house of Israel are *m* kings 1Kin 20:31 2617
LORD your God is gracious and *m* 2Chr 30:9 7349
ready to pardon, gracious and *m* Neh 9:17 7349
for thou art a gracious and *m* God Neh 9:31 7349
With the *m* thou wilt shew thyself Ps 18:25 2623
thou wilt shew thyself *m* Ps 18:25 2616
redeem me, and be *m* unto me Ps 26:11 2603
He is ever *m*, and lendeth Ps 37:26 2603
I said, LORD, be *m* unto me Ps 41:4 2603
be *m* unto me, and raise me up, Ps 41:10 2603
Be *m* unto me, O God Ps 56:1 2603
Be *m* unto me, O God, be *m* Ps 57:1 2603
be not *m* to any wicked Ps 59:5 2603
God be *m* unto us, and bless us Ps 67:1 2603
Be *m* unto me, O Lord Ps 86:3 2603
The LORD is *m* and gracious, slow Ps 103:8 7349
yea, our God is *m* Ps 116:5 7355
For his *m* kindness is great Ps 117:2 2617
be *m* unto me according to thy Ps 119:58 2603
thy *m* kindness be for my comfort, Ps 119:76 2617
be *m* unto me, as thou usest to do Ps 119:132 2603
The *m* man doeth good to his own Prov 11:17 2617
m men are taken away, none Is 57:1 2617
for I am *m*, saith the LORD, and I Jer 3:12 2623
for he is gracious and *m*, slow to Joel 2:13 7349
thou art a gracious God, and *m* Jonah 4:2 7349
Blessed are the *m* Mt 5:7 *1655*
Be ye therefore *m*, as your Father Lk 6:36 *3629*
as your Father also is *m* Lk 6:36 *3629*
saying, God be *m* to me a sinner Lk 18:13 *2433*
brethren, that he might be a *m* Heb 2:17 *1655*
For I will be *m* to their Heb 8:12 *2436*

MERCURIUS (*mer-cu'-re-us*) *A Roman god.*
and Paul, *M*, because he was the Acts 14:12 *2060*

MERCY
and thou hast magnified thy *m* Gen 19:19 2617
left destitute my master of his *m* Gen 24:27 2617
was with Joseph, and shewed him *m* Gen 39:21 2617
give you *m* before the man Gen 43:14 7356
Thou in thy *m* hast led forth the Ex 15:13 2617
shewing *m* unto thousands of them Ex 20:6 2617
shalt make a *m* seat of pure gold Ex 25:17 3727
in the two ends of the *m* seat Ex 25:18 3727
even of the *m* seat shall ye make Ex 25:19 3727
covering the *m* seat with their Ex 25:20 3727
toward the *m* seat shall the faces Ex 25:20 3727
thou shalt put the *m* seat above Ex 25:21 3727
with thee from above the *m* seat Ex 25:22 3727
thou shalt put the *m* seat upon Ex 26:34 3727
before the *m* seat that is over Ex 30:6 3727
the *m* seat that is thereupon, and Ex 31:7 3727
shew *m* on whom I will shew *m* Ex 33:19 7355
Keeping *m* for thousands, Ex 34:7 2617
staves thereof, with the *m* seat Ex 35:12 3727
he made the *m* seat of pure gold Ex 37:6 3727
on the two ends of the *m* seat Ex 37:7 3727
out of the *m* seat made he the Ex 37:8 3727
with their wings over the *m* seat Ex 37:9 3727
even to the *m* seatward were the Ex 37:9 3727
staves thereof, and the *m* seat, Ex 39:35 3727
put the *m* seat above upon the ark Ex 40:20 3727
within the vail before the *m* seat Lev 16:2 3727
in the cloud upon the *m* seat Lev 16:2 3727
of the incense may cover the *m* Lev 16:13 3727
finger upon the *m* seat eastward Lev 16:14 3727
before the *m* seat shall he Lev 16:14 3727
and sprinkle it upon the *m* seat Lev 16:15 3727
and before the *m* seat Lev 16:15 3727
m seat that was upon the ark of Num 7:89 3727
is longsuffering, and of great *m* Num 14:18 2617
unto the greatness of thy *m* Num 14:19 2617
shewing *m* unto thousands of them Deut 5:10 2617
with them, nor shew *m* unto them Deut 7:2 2603
m with them that love him and keep Deut 7:9 2617
the *m* which he sware unto thy Deut 7:12 2617
of his anger, and shew thee *m* Deut 13:17 7356
the city, and we will shew thee *m* Judg 1:24 2617
But my *m* shall not depart away 2Sa 7:15 2617
m and truth be with thee 2Sa 15:20 2617
sheweth *m* to his anointed, unto 2Sa 22:51 2617
servant David my father great *m* 1Kin 3:6 2617
m with thy servants that walk 1Kin 8:23 2617
for his *m* endureth for ever 1Chr 16:34 2617
because his *m* endureth for ever 1Chr 16:41 2617
will not take my *m* away from him 1Chr 17:13 2617
and of the place of the *m* seat 1Chr 28:11 3727
great *m* unto David my father 2Chr 1:8 2617
for his *m* endureth for ever 2Chr 5:13 2617
shewest *m* unto thy servants, that 2Chr 6:14 2617
for his *m* endureth for ever 2Chr 7:3 2617
because his *m* endureth for ever, 2Chr 7:6 2617
for his *m* endureth for ever 2Chr 20:21 2617
for his *m* endureth for ever Ezr 3:11 2617
hath extended *m* unto me before Ezr 7:28 2617
but hath extended *m* unto us in Ezr 9:9 2617
m for them that love him and Neh 1:5 2617
grant him *m* in the sight of this Neh 1:11 7356
God, who keepest covenant and *m* Neh 9:32 2617
to the greatness of thy *m* Neh 13:22 2617
or for his land, or for *m* Job 37:13 2617
have *m* upon me, and hear my prayer Ps 4:1 2603
house in the multitude of thy *m* Ps 5:7 2617
Have *m* upon me, O LORD Ps 6:2 2603
Have *m* upon me, O LORD Ps 9:13 2603
But I have trusted in thy *m* Ps 13:5 2617
sheweth *m* to his anointed, to Ps 18:50 2617
through the *m* of the most High he Ps 21:7 2617
m shall follow me all the days of Ps 23:6 2617
according to thy *m* remember thou Ps 25:7 2617
All the paths of the LORD are *m* Ps 25:10 2617
thee unto me, and have *m* upon me Ps 25:16 2603
have *m* also upon me, and answer me Ps 27:7 2603
Hear, O LORD, and have *m* upon me Ps 30:10 2603
will be glad and rejoice in thy *m* Ps 31:7 2617
Have *m* upon me, O LORD, for I am Ps 31:9 2603
m shall compass him about Ps 32:10 2617
him, upon them that hope in his *m* Ps 33:18 2617
Let thy *m*, O LORD, be upon us, Ps 33:22 2617
Thy *m*, O LORD, is in the heavens Ps 36:5 2617
but the righteous sheweth *m* Ps 37:21 2603
Have *m* upon me, O God, according Ps 51:1 2603
I trust in the *m* of God for ever Ps 52:8 2617
God shall send forth his *m* Ps 57:3 2617
For thy *m* is great unto the Ps 57:10 2617
The God of my *m* shall prevent me Ps 59:10 2617
aloud of thy *m* in the morning Ps 59:16 2617
is my defence, and the God of my *m* Ps 59:17 2617
O prepare *m* and truth, which may Ps 61:7 2617
unto thee, O Lord, belongeth *m* Ps 62:12 2617
away my prayer, nor his *m* from me Ps 66:20 2617
in the multitude of thy *m* hear me Ps 69:13 2617
Is his *m* clean gone for ever Ps 77:8 2617
Shew us thy *m*, O LORD, and grant Ps 85:7 2617
M and truth are met together Ps 85:10 2617
plenteous in *m* unto all them that Ps 86:5 2617
For great is thy *m* toward me Ps 86:13 2617
longsuffering, and plenteous in *m* Ps 86:15 2617
O turn unto me, and have *m* upon me Ps 86:16 2603
M shall be built up for ever Ps 89:2 2617
m and truth shall go before thy Ps 89:14 2617
and my *m* shall be with him Ps 89:24 2617
My *m* will I keep for him for Ps 89:28 2617
O satisfy us early with thy *m* Ps 90:14 2617
thy *m*, O LORD, held me up Ps 94:18 2617
He hath remembered his *m* and his Ps 98:3 2617
his *m* is everlasting Ps 100:5 2617
I will sing of *m* and judgment Ps 101:1 2617
shalt arise, and have *m* upon Zion Ps 102:13 7355
slow to anger, and plenteous in *m* Ps 103:8 2617
so great is his *m* toward them Ps 103:11 2617
But the *m* of the LORD is from Ps 103:17 2617
for his *m* endureth for ever Ps 106:1 2617
for his *m* endureth for ever Ps 107:1 2617
For thy *m* is great above the Ps 108:4 2617
be none to extend *m* unto him Ps 109:12 2617
that he remembered not to shew *m* Ps 109:16 2617
because thy *m* is good, deliver Ps 109:21 2617
O save me according to thy *m* Ps 109:26 2617
thy name give glory, for thy *m* Ps 115:1 2617
because his *m* endureth for ever Ps 118:1 2617
that his *m* endureth for ever Ps 118:2 2617
that his *m* endureth for ever Ps 118:3 2617
that his *m* endureth for ever Ps 118:4 2617
for his *m* endureth for ever Ps 118:29 2617
earth, O LORD, is full of thy *m* Ps 119:64 2617
thy servant according unto thy *m* Ps 119:124 2617
God, until that he have *m* upon us Ps 123:2 2603
Have *m* upon us, O LORD, have Ps 123:3 2603
upon us, O LORD, have *m* upon us Ps 123:3 2603
for with the LORD there is *m* Ps 130:7 2617
for his *m* endureth for ever Ps 136:1 2617
for his *m* endureth for ever Ps 136:2 2617
for his *m* endureth for ever Ps 136:3 2617
for his *m* endureth for ever Ps 136:4 2617
for his *m* endureth for ever Ps 136:5 2617
for his *m* endureth for ever Ps 136:6 2617
for his *m* endureth for ever Ps 136:7 2617
for his *m* endureth for ever Ps 136:8 2617
for his *m* endureth for ever Ps 136:9 2617
for his *m* endureth for ever Ps 136:10 2617
for his *m* endureth for ever Ps 136:11 2617
for his *m* endureth for ever Ps 136:12 2617
for his *m* endureth for ever Ps 136:13 2617
for his *m* endureth for ever Ps 136:14 2617
for his *m* endureth for ever Ps 136:15 2617
for his *m* endureth for ever Ps 136:16 2617
for his *m* endureth for ever Ps 136:17 2617
for his *m* endureth for ever Ps 136:18 2617
for his *m* endureth for ever Ps 136:19 2617
for his *m* endureth for ever Ps 136:20 2617
for his *m* endureth for ever Ps 136:21 2617
for his *m* endureth for ever Ps 136:22 2617
for his *m* endureth for ever Ps 136:23 2617

for his *m* endureth for ever Ps 136:24 2617
for his *m* endureth for ever Ps 136:25 2617
for his *m* endureth for ever Ps 136:26 2617
thy *m*, O LORD, endureth for ever Ps 138:8 2617
of thy *m* cut off mine enemies, and Ps 143:12 2617
slow to anger, and of great *m* Ps 145:8 2617
him, in those that hope in his *m* Ps 147:11 2617
Let not *m* and truth forsake thee Prov 3:3 2617
but he that hath *m* on the poor Prov 14:21 2603
but *m* and truth shall be to them Prov 14:22 2617
honoureth him hath *m* on the poor Prov 14:31 2603
By *m* and truth iniquity is purged Prov 16:6 2617
M and truth preserve the king Prov 20:28 2617
and his throne is upholden by *m* Prov 20:28 2617
m findeth life, righteousness, and Prov 21:21 2617
and forsaketh them shall have *m* Prov 28:13 7355
neither shall have *m* on their Is 9:17 7355
For the LORD will have *m* on Jacob Is 14:1 7355
And in *m* shall the throne be Is 16:5 2617
made them will not have *m* on them Is 27:11 7355
that he may have *m* upon you Is 30:18 7355
thou didst shew them no *m* Is 47:6 7356
for he that hath *m* on them shall Is 49:10 7355
will have *m* upon his afflicted Is 49:13 7355
kindness will I have *m* on thee Is 54:8 7355
the LORD that hath *m* on thee Is 54:10 7355
LORD, and he will have *m* upon him Is 55:7 7355
in my favour have I had *m* on thee Is 60:10 7355
they are cruel, and have no *m* Jer 6:23 7355
not pity, nor spare, nor have *m* Jer 13:14 7355
neither have pity, nor have *m* Jer 21:7 7355
have *m* on his dwellingplaces Jer 30:18 7355
I will surely have *m* upon him Jer 31:20 7355
for his *m* endureth for ever Jer 33:11 2617
to return, and have *m* on them Jer 33:26 7355
you, that he may have *m* upon you Jer 42:12 7355
are cruel, and will not shew *m* Jer 50:42 7355
have *m* upon the whole house of Eze 39:25 7355
by shewing *m* to the poor Dan 4:27 2604
m to them that love him, and to Dan 9:4 2617
for I will no more have *m* upon Hos 1:6 7355
But I will have *m* upon the house Hos 1:7 7355
I will not have *m* upon her Hos 2:4 7355
I will have *m* upon her that had Hos 2:23 7355
upon her that had not obtained *m* Hos 2:23 7355
because there is no truth, nor *m* Hos 4:1 2617
For I desired *m*, and not sacrifice Hos 6:6 2617
in righteousness, reap in *m* Hos 10:12 2617
keep *m* and judgment, and wait on Hos 12:6 2617
in thee the fatherless findeth *m* Hos 14:3 7355
vanities forsake their own *m* Jonah 2:8 2617
but to do justly, and to love *m* Mic 6:8 2617
ever, because he delighteth in *m* Mic 7:18 2617
the *m* to Abraham, which thou hast Mic 7:20 2617
in wrath remember *m* Hab 3:2 7355
wilt thou not have *m* on Jerusalem Zec 1:12 7355
Execute true judgment, and shew *m* Zec 7:9 2617
for I have *m* upon them Zec 10:6 7355
for they shall obtain *m* Mt 5:7 *1653*
what that meaneth, I will have *m* Mt 9:13 *1656*
Thou son of David, have *m* on us Mt 9:27 *1653*
what this meaneth, I will have *m* Mt 12:7 *1656*
Have *m* on me, O Lord, thou son of Mt 15:22 *1653*
Lord, have *m* on my son Mt 17:15 *1653*
Have *m* on us, O Lord, thou son of Mt 20:30 *1653*
Have *m* on us, O Lord, thou son of Mt 20:31 *1653*
matters of the law, judgment, *m* Mt 23:23 *1656*
thou son of David, have *m* on me Mk 10:47 *1653*
Thou son of David, have *m* on me Mk 10:48 *1653*
his *m* is on them that fear him Lk 1:50 *1656*
Israel, in remembrance of his *m* Lk 1:54 *1656*
Lord had shewed great *m* upon her Lk 1:58 *1656*
To perform the *m* promised to our Lk 1:72 *1656*
Through the tender *m* of our God Lk 1:78 *1656*
he said, He that shewed *m* on him Lk 10:37 *1656*
have *m* on me, and send Lazarus, Lk 16:24 *1653*
said, Jesus, Master, have *m* on us Lk 17:13 *1653*
thou son of David, have *m* on me Lk 18:38 *1653*
Thou son of David, have *m* on me Lk 18:39 *1653*
I will have *m* on whom I will have Rom 9:15 *1653*
have *m* on whom I will have *m* Rom 9:15 *1653*
but of God that sheweth *m* Rom 9:16 *1653*
Therefore hath he *m* on whom he Rom 9:18 *1653*
on whom he will have *m* Rom 9:18
of his glory on the vessels of *m* Rom 9:23 *1656*
yet have now obtained *m* through Rom 11:30 *1653*
that through your *m* they also may Rom 11:31 *1656*
they also may obtain *m* Rom 11:31 *1653*
that he might have *m* upon all Rom 11:32 *1653*
he that sheweth *m*, with Rom 12:8 *1653*
might glorify God for his *m* Rom 15:9 *1656*
as one that hath obtained *m* of 1Cor 7:25 *1653*
ministry, as we have received *m* 2Cor 4:1 *1653*
this rule, peace be on them, and *m* Gal 6:16 *1656*
But God, who is rich in *m* Eph 2:4 *1656*
but God had *m* on him Phil 2:27 *1653*
Grace, *m*, and peace, from God our 1Ti 1:2 *1656*
but I obtained *m*, because I did 1Ti 1:13 *1653*
for this cause I obtained *m* 1Ti 1:16 *1653*
Grace, *m*, and peace, from God the 2Ti 1:2 *1656*
The Lord give *m* unto the house of 2Ti 1:16 *1656*
find *m* of the Lord in that day 2Ti 1:18 *1656*
Grace, *m*, and peace, from God the Titus 1:4 *1656*
according to his *m* he saved us Titus 3:5 *1656*
of grace, that we may obtain *m* Heb 4:16 *1656*
Moses' law died without *m* under Heb 10:28 *3628*
he shall have judgment without *m* Jas 2:13 *448*
that hath shewed no *m* Jas 2:13 *1656*
m rejoiceth against judgment Jas 2:13 *1656*
easy to be intreated, full of *m* Jas 3:17 *1656*
is very pitiful, and of tender *m* Jas 5:11 *3629*
m hath begotten us again unto a 1Pet 1:3 *1656*
which had not obtained *m* 1Pet 2:10 *1653*
but now have obtained *m* 1Pet 2:10 *1653*
Grace be with you, *m*, and peace, 2Jn 3 *1656*
M unto you, and peace, and love, be Jude 2 *1656*
looking for the *m* of our Lord Jude 21 *1656*

MERCYSEAT
of glory shadowing the *m* Heb 9:5 *2435*

MERED (*me'-red*) *A descendant of Judah.*
sons of Ezra were, Jether, and *M* 1Chr 4:17 4778
daughter of Pharaoh, which *M* took 1Chr 4:18 4778

MEREMOTH (*mer'-e-moth*) See MERAIOTH.
1. Son of Uriah the priest.
of *M* the son of Uriah the priest Ezr 8:33 4822
them repaired *M* the son of Urijah Neh 3:4 4822
After him repaired *M* the son of Neh 3:21 4822
2. Married a foreigner in exile.
Vaniah, *M*, Eliashib, Ezr 10:36 4822
3. A priest who renewed the covenant.
Harim, *M*, Obadiah, Neh 10:5 4822
Shechaniah, Rehum, *M*, Neh 12:3 4822

MERES (*me'-res*) *A prince of Media and Persia.*
Shethar, Admatha, Tarshish, *M* Est 1:14 4825

MERIBAH (*mer'-i-bah*) See MASSAH, MERIBAH-KADESH. *Same as Meribah-Kadesh.*
name of the place Massah, and *M* Ex 17:7 4809
This is the water of *M* Num 20:13 4809
against my word at the water of *M* Num 20:24 4809
that is the water of *M* in Kadesh Num 27:14 4809
didst strive at the waters of *M* Deut 33:8 4809
I proved thee at the waters of *M* Ps 81:7 4809

MERIBAH-KADESH (*mer'-i-bah-ka'-desh*) *A place between Zin and Sinai.*
of Israel at the waters of *M* Deut 32:51

MERIBATH-KADESH See MERIBAH-KADESH.

MERIB-BAAL (*me-rib'-ba-al*) See MEPHIBOSHETH. *Son of Jonathan.*
And the son of Jonathan was *M* 1Chr 8:34 4807
and *M* begat Micah 1Chr 8:34 4807
And the son of Jonathan was *M* 1Chr 9:40 4807
and *M* begat Micah 1Chr 9:40 4810

MERODACH (*mer'-o-dak*) See BERODACH, EVIL-MERODACH, MERODACH-BALADAN. *A Babylonian god of war.*
confounded, *M* is broken in pieces Jer 50:2 4781

MERODACH-BALADAN (*mer'-o-dak-bal'-a-dan*) See BERODACH-BALADAN. *A king of Babylon.*
At that time *M*, the son of Is 39:1 4757

MEROM (*me'-rom*) *A small lake north of the Sea of Chinneroth.*
together at the waters of *M* Josh 11:5 4792
them by the waters of *M* suddenly Josh 11:7 4792

MERONOTHITE (*me-ron'-o-thite*) *An inhabitant of a district of Zebulun.*
over the asses was Jehdeiah the *M* 1Chr 27:30 4824
the Gibeonite, and Jadon the *M* Neh 3:7 4824

MEROZ (*me'-roz*) *A place near Lake Merom.*
Curse ye *M*, said the angel of the Judg 5:23 4789

MERRILY
then go thou in *m* with the king Est 5:14 8056

MERRY
And they drank, and were *m* with him Gen 43:34 7937
and trode the grapes, and made *m* Judg 9:27 1974
to pass, when their hearts were *m* Judg 16:25 2896
night, and let thine heart be *m* Judg 19:6 3190
here, that thine heart may be *m* Judg 19:9 3190
they were making their hearts *m* Judg 19:22 3190
and drunk, and his heart was *m* Ruth 3:7 3190
Nabal's heart was *m* within him 1Sa 25:36 2896
when Amnon's heart is *m* with wine 2Sa 13:28 2896
eating and drinking, and making *m* 1Kin 4:20 8056
bread, and let thine heart be *m* 1Kin 21:7 3190
m in heart for the goodness that 2Chr 7:10 2896
heart of the king was *m* with wine Est 1:10 2896
A *m* heart maketh a cheerful Prov 15:13 8056
but he that is of a *m* heart hath Prov 15:15 2896
A *m* heart doeth good like a Prov 17:22 8056
to eat, and to drink, and to be *m* Eccl 8:15 8055
and drink thy wine with a *m* heart Eccl 9:7 2896
for laughter, and wine maketh *m* Eccl 10:19 8055
and the voice of them that make *m* Jer 30:19 7832
in the dances of them that make *m* Jer 31:4 7832
thine ease, eat, drink, and be *m* Lk 12:19 *2165*
and let us eat, and be *m* Lk 15:23 *2165*
And they began to be *m* Lk 15:24 *2165*
I might make *m* with my friends Lk 15:29 *2165*
It was meet that we should make *m* Lk 15:32 *2165*
Is any *m*? Jas 5:13 *2114*
rejoice over them, and make *m* Rev 11:10 *2165*

MERRYHEARTED
languisheth, all the *m* do sigh Is 24:7

MESECH (*me'-sek*) See MESHECH. *A tribe joined to Kedar.*
Woe is me, that I sojourn in *M* Ps 120:5 4902

MESHA (*me'-shah*)
1. A place in southeastern Arabia.
And their dwelling was from *M* Gen 10:30 4331
2. A king of Moab.
M king of Moab was a sheepmaster, 2Kin 3:4 4337
3. A son of Caleb.
M his firstborn, which was the 1Chr 2:42 4338
4. A son of Shaharaim.
his wife, Jobab, and Zibia, and *M* 1Chr 8:9 4331

MESHACH (*me'-shak*) *A companion of Daniel.*
and to Mishael, of *M* Dan 1:7 4335
the king, and he set Shadrach, *M* Dan 2:49 4336
province of Babylon, Shadrach, *M* Dan 3:12 4336
commanded to bring Shadrach, *M* Dan 3:13 4336
them, Is it true, O Shadrach, *M* Dan 3:14 4336
Shadrach, *M*, and Abed-nego, Dan 3:16 4336
was changed against Shadrach, *M* Dan 3:19 4336
in his army to bind Shadrach, *M* Dan 3:20 4336
men that took up Shadrach, *M* Dan 3:22 4336
And these three men, Shadrach, *M* Dan 3:23 4336
and spake, and said, Shadrach, *M* Dan 3:26 4336
Then Shadrach, *M*, and Abed-nego, Dan 3:26 4336
Blessed be the God of Shadrach, *M* Dan 3:28 4336
against the God of Shadrach, *M* Dan 3:29 4336
the king promoted Shadrach, *M* Dan 3:30 4336

MESHECH (*me'-shek*) See MESECH.
1. A son of Japheth.
Madai, and Javan, and Tubal, and *M* Gen 10:2 4902
Madai, and Javan, and Tubal, and *M* 1Chr 1:5 4902
2. A son of Shem.
and Uz, and Hul, and Gether, and *M* 1Chr 1:17 4902
3. Descendants of Meschech 1.
Javan, Tubal, and *M*, they were thy Eze 27:13 4902
There is *M*, Tubal, and all her Eze 32:26 4902
of Magog, the chief prince of *M* Eze 38:2 4902
O Gog, the chief prince of *M* Eze 38:3 4902
O Gog, the chief prince of *M* Eze 39:1 4902

MESHELEMIAH (*me-shel-e-mi'-ah*) See MESHULLAM, SHELEMIAH, SHALLUM. *Father of Zechariah.*
Zechariah the son of *M* was porter 1Chr 9:21 4920
Korhites was *M* the son of Kore 1Chr 26:1 4920
And the sons of *M* were, Zechariah 1Chr 26:2 4920
M had sons and brethren, strong 1Chr 26:9 4920

MESHEZABEEL (*me-shez'-a-be-el*)
1. Father of Berechiah.
son of Berechiah, the son of *M* Neh 3:4 4898
2. An Israelite who renewed the covenant.
M, Zadok, Jaddua, Neh 10:21 4898
And Pethahiah the son of *M* Neh 11:24 4898

MESHEZABEL See MESHEZABEEL.

MESHILLEMITH (*me-shil'-le-mith*) See MESHILLEMOTH. *A family of exiles.*
son of Meshullam, the son of *M* 1Chr 9:12 4921

MESHILLEMOTH (*me-shil'-le-moth*) See MESHILLEMITH.
1. Father of Berechiah.
Johanan, Berechiah the son of *M* 2Chr 28:12 4919
2. A family of exiles.
the son of Ahasai, the son of *M* Neh 11:13 4919

MESHOBAB (*me-sho'-bab*) *A chief of Simeon.*
And *M*, and Jamlech, and Joshah the 1Chr 4:34 4877

MESHULLAM (*me-shul'-lam*) See MESHELLEMIAH.
1. A scribe in Josiah's time.
the son of Azaliah, the son of *M* 2Kin 22:3 4918
2. A descendant of Jeconiah.
M, and Hananiah, and Shelomith 1Chr 3:19 4918
3. Head of a Gadite family.
their fathers were, Michael, and *M* 1Chr 5:13 4918
4. A Benjamite of the Elpaal family.
Zebadiah, and *M*, and 1Chr 8:17 4918
5. Father of Sallu.
Sallu the son of *M*, the son of 1Chr 9:7 4918
6. Son of Shephathiah.
M the son of Shephatiah, the son 1Chr 9:8 4918
7. Father of Hilkiah.
the son of Hilkiah, the son of *M* 1Chr 9:11 4918
the son of Hilkiah, the son of *M* Neh 11:11 4918
8. Son of Meshillemith.
the son of Jahzerah, the son of *M* 1Chr 9:12 4918
9. A Kohathite repairer of the wall.
and Zechariah and *M*, of the sons of 2Chr 34:12 4918
10. A clan leader with Ezra.
and for Zechariah, and for *M* Ezr 8:16 4918
11. A priest who accounted for the foreign wives.
and *M* and Shabbethai the Levite Ezr 10:15 4918
12. A son of Bani.
M, Malluch, and Adaiah, Jashub, and Ezr 10:29 4918
13. A son of Berechiah.
repaired *M* the son of Berechiah Neh 3:4 4918
After him repaired *M* the son of Neh 3:30 4918
of *M* the son of Berechiah Neh 6:18 4918
14. A son of Besodeiah.
Paseah, and *M* the son of Besodeiah Neh 3:6 4918
15. A Levite who aided Ezra.
and Hashbadana, Zechariah, and *M* Neh 8:4 4918
16. A priest who renewed the covenant.
M, Abijah, Mijamin, Neh 10:7 4918
17. A clan leader who renewed the covenant.
Magpiash, *M*, Hezir, Neh 10:20 4918
18. A family of exiles.
Sallu the son of *M*, the son of Neh 11:7 4918
19. A priest who dedicated the wall.
Of Ezra, *M* Neh 12:13 4918
And Azariah, Ezra, and *M*, Neh 12:33 4918
20. A descendant of Ginnethon.
of Ginnethon, *M* Neh 12:16 4918
21. A Levite gatekeeper.
and Bakbukiah, Obadiah, *M* Neh 12:25 4918

MESHULLEMETH (*me-shul'-le-meth*) *Mother of King Amon.*
And his mother's name was *M* 2Kin 21:19 4922

MESOBAITE (*me-so'-ba-ite*) *Family name of Jasiel.*
Eliel, and Obed, and Jasiel the *M* 1Chr 11:47 4677

MESOPOTAMIA (*mes-o-po-ta'-me-ah*) See ARAM, NAHARAIM. *Land between the Tigris and Euphrates Rivers.*

M

and he arose, and went to *M* .... Gen 24:10 763
the son of Beor of Pethor of *M* .... Deut 23:4 763
of Chushan-rishathaim king of *M* .... Judg 3:8 763
king of *M* into his hand .... Judg 3:10 763
chariots and horsemen out of *M* 1Chr 19:6 763
and Elamites, and the dwellers in *M* .... Acts 2:9 *3318*
father Abraham, when he was in *M* .... Acts 7:2 *3318*

MESS

but Benjamin's *m* was five times .... Gen 43:34 4864
there followed him a *m* of meat 2Sa 11:8 4864

MESSAGE

I have a *m* from God unto thee .... Judg 3:20 1697
pass, when Ben-hadad heard this *m* 1Kin 20:12 1697
He that sendeth a *m* by the hand .... Prov 26:6 1697
in the LORD's *m* unto the people .... Hag 1:13 4400
sent a *m* after him, saying, We .... Lk 19:14 *4242*
This then is the *m* which we have 1Jn 1:5 *1860*
For this is the *m* that ye heard 1Jn 3:11 *31*

MESSENGER

And they sent a *m* unto Joseph .... Gen 50:16 6680
the *m* answered and said, Israel is 1Sa 4:17 1319
But there came a *m* unto Saul 1Sa 23:27 4397
And charged the *m*, saying, When 2Sa 11:19 4397
So the *m* went, and came and shewed 2Sa 11:22 4397
the *m* said unto David, Surely the 2Sa 11:23 4397
Then David said unto the *m* 2Sa 11:25 4397
And there came a *m* to David 2Sa 15:13 5046
Then Jezebel sent a *m* unto Elijah 1Kin 19:2 4397
the *m* that was gone to call 1Kin 22:13 4397
And Elisha sent a *m* unto him 2Kin 5:10 4397
but ere the *m* came to him 2Kin 6:32 4397
look, when the *m* cometh, shut the 2Kin 6:32 4397
behold, the *m* came down unto him 2Kin 6:33 4397
The *m* came to them, but he cometh 2Kin 9:18 4397
And there came a *m*, and told him, ... 2Kin 10:8 4397
the *m* that went to call Micaiah 2Chr 18:12 4397
And there came a *m* unto Job .... Job 1:14 4397
If there be a *m* with him, an .... Job 33:23 4397
A wicked *m* falleth into mischief .... Prov 13:17 4397
therefore a cruel *m* shall be sent .... Prov 17:11 4397
so is a faithful *m* to them that .... Prov 25:13 6735
or deaf, as my *m* that I sent .... Is 42:19 4397
one *m* to meet another, to shew .... Jer 51:31 5046
from far, unto whom a *m* was sent .... Eze 23:40 4397
Then spake Haggai the LORD's *m* in .... Hag 1:13 4397
for he is the *m* of the LORD of .... Mal 2:7 4397
Behold, I will send my *m*, and he .... Mal 3:1 4397
even the *m* of the covenant, whom .... Mal 3:1 4397
I send my *m* before thy face, ... Mt 11:10 *32*
I send my *m* before thy face, ... Mk 1:2 *32*
I send my *m* before thy face, ... Lk 7:27 *32*
the *m* of Satan to buffet me, lest 2Cor 12:7 *32*
and fellow soldier, but your *m* .... Phil 2:25 *652*

MESSENGERS

Jacob sent *m* before him to Esau .... Gen 32:3 4397
the *m* returned to Jacob, saying, ... Gen 32:6 4397
Moses sent *m* from Kadesh unto the .... Num 20:14 4397
Israel sent *m* unto Sihon king of .... Num 21:21 4397
He sent *m* therefore unto Balaam .... Num 22:5 4397
Spake I not also to thy *m* which .... Num 24:12 4397
I sent *m* out of the wilderness of .... Deut 2:26 4397
she hid the *m* that we sent .... Josh 6:17 4397
because she hid the *m*, which .... Josh 6:25 4397
So Joshua sent *m*, and they ran .... Josh 7:22 4397
he sent *m* throughout all Manasseh .... Judg 6:35 4397
he sent *m* unto Asher, and unto .... Judg 6:35 4397
Gideon sent *m* throughout all .... Judg 7:24 4397
he sent *m* unto Abimelech privily, ... Judg 9:31 4397
Jephthah sent *m* unto the king of .... Judg 11:12 4397
answered unto the *m* of Jephthah .... Judg 11:13 4397
Jephthah sent *m* again unto the .... Judg 11:14 4397
Then Israel sent *m* unto the king .... Judg 11:17 4397
Israel sent *m* unto Sihon king of .... Judg 11:19 4397
they sent *m* to the inhabitants of 1Sa 6:21 4397
that we may send *m* unto all the 1Sa 11:3 4397
Then came the *m* to Gibeah of Saul 1Sa 11:4 4397
of Israel by the hands of *m* 1Sa 11:7 4397
And they said unto the *m* that came 1Sa 11:9 4397
the *m* came and shewed it to the 1Sa 11:9 4397
Wherefore Saul sent *m* unto Jesse 1Sa 16:19 4397
Saul also sent *m* unto David's 1Sa 19:11 4397
And when Saul sent *m* to take David 1Sa 19:14 4397
Saul sent the *m* again to see 1Sa 19:15 4397
when the *m* were come in, behold, ... 1Sa 19:16 4397
Saul sent *m* to take David 1Sa 19:20 4397
of God was upon the *m* of Saul 1Sa 19:20 4397
it was told Saul, he sent other *m* 1Sa 19:21 4397
Saul sent *m* again the third time, ... 1Sa 19:21 4397
Behold, David sent *m* out of the 1Sa 25:14 4397
and she went after the *m* of David 1Sa 25:42 4397
David sent *m* unto the men of 2Sa 2:5 4397
Abner sent *m* to David on his 2Sa 3:12 4397
David sent *m* to Ish-bosheth 2Sa 3:14 4397
he sent *m* after Abner, which 2Sa 3:26 4397
king of Tyre sent *m* to David 2Sa 5:11 4397
And David sent *m*, and took her 2Sa 11:4 4397
And Joab sent *m* to David, and said, ... 2Sa 12:27 4397
he sent *m* to Ahab king of Israel 1Kin 20:2 4397
the *m* came again, and said, Thus 1Kin 20:5 4397
he said unto the *m* of Ben-hadad 1Kin 20:9 4397
the *m* departed, and brought him 1Kin 20:9 4397
and he sent *m*, and said unto them, ... 2Kin 1:2 4397
go up to meet the *m* of the king 2Kin 1:3 4397
when the *m* turned back unto him, ... 2Kin 1:5 4397
Forasmuch as thou hast sent *m* to 2Kin 1:16 4397
the *m* returned, and told the king 2Kin 7:15 4397
Then Amaziah sent *m* to Jehoash 2Kin 14:8 4397
So Ahaz sent *m* to Tiglath-pileser 2Kin 16:7 4397
for he had sent *m* to So king of 2Kin 17:4 4397
he sent *m* again unto Hezekiah, ... 2Kin 19:9 4397
the letter of the hand of the *m* 2Kin 19:14 4397
By thy *m* thou hast reproached the 2Kin 19:23 4397
king of Tyre sent *m* to David 1Chr 14:1 4397
David sent *m* to comfort him 1Chr 19:2 4397
worse before Israel, they sent *m* 1Chr 19:16 4397
fathers sent to them by his *m* 2Chr 36:15 4397
But they mocked the *m* of God 2Chr 36:16 4397
I sent *m* unto them, saying, I am .... Neh 6:3 4397
wrath of a king is as *m* of death .... Prov 16:14 4397
then answer the *m* of the nation .... Is 14:32 4397
waters, saying, Go, ye swift *m* .... Is 18:2 4397
he sent *m* to Hezekiah, saying, ... Is 37:9 4397
the letter from the hand of the *m* .... Is 37:14 4397
performeth the counsel of his *m* .... Is 44:26 4397
and didst send thy *m* far off .... Is 57:9 6735
by the hand of the *m* which come .... Jer 27:3 4397
sent *m* unto them into Chaldea .... Eze 23:16 4397
In that day shall *m* go forth from .... Eze 30:9 4397
the voice of thy *m* shall no more .... Nah 2:13 4397
when the *m* of John were departed, ... Lk 7:24 *32*
And sent *m* before his face .... Lk 9:52 *32*
they are the *m* of the churches, ... 2Cor 8:23 *652*
when she had received the *m* .... Jas 2:25 *32*

MESSES

sent *m* unto them from before him .... Gen 43:34 4864

MESSIAH (*mes-si'-ah*) See MESSIAS. *The great Deliverer of Israel.*

to build Jerusalem unto the *M* the .... Dan 9:25 4899
and two weeks shall *M* be cut off .... Dan 9:26 4899

MESSIAS (*mes-si'-as*) See MESSIAH. *Greek form of Messiah.*

unto him, We have found the *M* .... Jn 1:41 *3323*
unto him, I know that *M* cometh .... Jn 4:25 *3323*

MET

way, and the angels of God *m* him .... Gen 32:1 6293
thou by all this drove which I *m* .... Gen 33:8 6298
God of the Hebrews hath *m* with us .... Ex 3:18 7136
in the inn, that the LORD *m* him .... Ex 4:24 6298
m him in the mount of God, and .... Ex 4:27 6298
God of the Hebrews hath *m* with us .... Ex 5:3 7122
they *m* Moses and Aaron, who stood .... Ex 5:20 6293
And God *m* Balaam .... Num 23:4 7136
And the LORD *m* Balaam, and put a .... Num 23:16 7136
Because they *m* you not with bread .... Deut 23:4 6923
How he *m* thee by the way, and .... Deut 25:18 7136
all these kings were *m* together .... Josh 11:5 3259
they *m* together in Asher on the .... Josh 17:10 6293
a company of prophets *m* him 1Sa 10:10 7125
and she *m* them 1Sa 25:20 6298
m together by the pool of Gibeon 2Sa 2:13 6298
the servant of Mephibosheth *m* him 2Sa 16:1 7135
Absalom *m* the servants of David 2Sa 18:9 7122
a lion *m* him by the way, and slew 1Kin 13:24 4672
in the way, behold, Elijah *m* him 1Kin 18:7 7125
m him in the portion of Naboth 2Kin 9:21 4672
Jehu *m* with the brethren of 2Kin 10:13 4672
Because they *m* not the children .... Neh 13:2 6923
Mercy and truth are *m* together .... Ps 85:10 6298
there *m* him a woman with the .... Prov 7:10 7125
and it came to pass, as he *m* them .... Jer 41:6 6298
flee from a lion, and a bear *m* him .... Amos 5:19 6293
there *m* him two possessed with .... Mt 8:28 *5221*
disciples, behold, Jesus *m* them .... Mt 28:9 *528*
immediately there *m* him out of .... Mk 5:2 *528*
in a place where two ways *m* .... Mk 11:4 *296*
there *m* him out of the city a .... Lk 8:27 *5221*
from the hill, much people *m* him .... Lk 9:37 *4876*
there *m* him ten men that were .... Lk 17:12 *528*
going down, his servants *m* him .... Jn 4:51 *528*
Jesus was coming, went and *m* him .... Jn 11:20 *5221*
in that place where Martha *m* him .... Jn 11:30 *5221*
this cause the people also *m* him .... Jn 12:18 *5221*
was coming in, Cornelius *m* him .... Acts 10:25 *4876*
with a spirit of divination *m* us .... Acts 16:16 *528*
daily with them that *m* with him .... Acts 17:17 *3909*
when he *m* with us at Assos, we .... Acts 20:14 *4820*
into a place where two seas *m* .... Acts 27:41
who *m* Abraham returning from the .... Heb 7:1 *4876*
father, when Melchisedec *m* him .... Heb 7:10 *4876*

METE

when they did *m* it with an omer, ... Ex 16:18 4058
m out the valley of Succoth .... Ps 60:6 4058
m out the valley of Succoth .... Ps 108:7 4058
and with what measure ye *m* .... Mt 7:2 *3354*
with what measure ye *m*, it shall .... Mk 4:24 *3354*
with the same measure that ye *m* .... Lk 6:38 *3354*

METED

a nation *m* out and trodden down, ... Is 18:2 6978
a nation *m* out and trodden under .... Is 18:7 6978
m out heaven with the span, and .... Is 40:12 8505

METEYARD

unrighteousness in judgment, in *m* .... Lev 19:35 4060

METHEG-AMMAH (*me'-theg-am'-mah*) *A place in Philistia.*

David took *M* out of the hand of 2Sa 8:1 4965

METHUSAEL (*me-thu'-sa-el*) *A descendant of Cain.*

and Mehujael begat *M* .... Gen 4:18 4967
and *M* begat Lamech .... Gen 4:18 4967

METHUSELAH (*me-thu'-se-lah*) See MATHUSALA. *Son of Enoch.*

sixty and five years, and begat *M* .... Gen 5:21 4968
he begat *M* three hundred years .... Gen 5:22 4968
M lived an hundred eighty and .... Gen 5:25 4968
M lived after he begat Lamech .... Gen 5:26 4968
all the days of *M* were nine .... Gen 5:27 4968
Henoch, *M*, Lamech, ... 1Chr 1:3 4968

METHUSHAEL See METHUSAEL.

MEUNIM (*me-u'-nim*) See MEHUNIM. *A family of exiles.*

of Besai, the children of *M* .... Neh 7:52 4586

MEUNITES See MEHUNIMS.

MEZAHAB (*mez'-a-hab*) *Grandmother of Mehetabel.*

of Matred, the daughter of *M* .... Gen 36:39 4314
of Matred, the daughter of *M* 1Chr 1:50 4314

MEZOBAITE See MESOBAITE.

MIAMIN (*mi'-a-min*) See MIJAMIN, MINIAMIN.

1. Married a foreigner in exile.

and Jeziah, and Malchiah, and *M* .... Ezr 10:25 4326

2. A priest with Zerubbabel.

M, Maadiah, Bilgah, ... Neh 12:5 4326

MIBHAR (*mib'-har*) *A "mighty man" of David.*

of Nathan, *M* the son of Haggeri, ... 1Chr 11:38 4006

MIBSAM (*mib'-sam*)

1. A son of Ishmael.

and Kedar, and Adbeel, and *M* .... Gen 25:13 4017
then Kedar, and Adbeel, and *M* 1Chr 1:29 4017

2. A son of Simeon.

M his son, Mishma his son 1Chr 4:25 4017

MIBZAR (*mib'-zar*) *A descendant of Esau.*

Duke Kenaz, duke Teman, duke *M* .... Gen 36:42 4014
Duke Kenaz, duke Teman, duke *M* 1Chr 1:53 4014

MICA See MICHA.

MICAH (*mi'-cah*) See MICAIAH, MICAH'S, MICHAH.

1. An Ephraimite who set up idols.

mount Ephraim, whose name was *M* .... Judg 17:1 4319
and they were in the house of *M* .... Judg 17:4 4319
the man *M* had an house of gods, ... Judg 17:5 4318
mount Ephraim to the house of *M* .... Judg 17:8 4318
M said unto him, Whence comest .... Judg 17:9 4319
M said unto him, Dwell with me, ... Judg 17:10 4319
And *M* consecrated the Levite .... Judg 17:12 4318
priest, and was in the house of *M* .... Judg 17:12 4318
Then said *M*, Now know I that the .... Judg 17:13 4318
mount Ephraim, to the house of *M* .... Judg 18:2 4318
When they were by the house of *M* .... Judg 18:3 4318
Thus and thus dealeth *M* with me .... Judg 18:4 4318
and came unto the house of *M* .... Judg 18:13 4318
Levite, even unto the house of *M* .... Judg 18:15 4318
a good way from the house of *M* .... Judg 18:22 4318
their faces, and said unto *M* .... Judg 18:23 4318
when *M* saw that they were too .... Judg 18:26 4318
took the things which *M* had made .... Judg 18:27 4318

2. Head of a Reubenite family.

M his son, Reaia his son, Baal 1Chr 5:5 4318

3. Son of Merib-baal.

and Merib-baal begat *M* 1Chr 8:34 4318
And the sons of *M* were, Pithon, and 1Chr 8:35 4318
and Merib-baal begat *M* 1Chr 9:40 4318
And the sons of *M* were, Pithon, and 1Chr 9:41 4318

4. A family of exiles.

Galal, and Mattaniah the son of *M* 1Chr 9:15 4316

5. A sanctuary servant.

M the first, and Jesiah the second 1Chr 23:20 4318

6. Father of Abdon.

of Shaphan, and Abdon the son of *M* 2Chr 34:20 4318

7. A prophet.

M the Morasthite prophesied in .... Jer 26:18 4320
M the Morasthite in the days of .... Mic 1:1 4318

MICAH'S (*mi'-cahs*) *Refers to Micah 1.*

And these went into *M* house .... Judg 18:18 4318
to *M* house were gathered together .... Judg 18:22 4318
they set them up *M* graven image .... Judg 18:31 4318

MICAIAH (*mi-ka-i'-ah*) See MICHA, MICHAIAH. *A prophet who foretold Ahab's fall.*

M the son of Imlah, by whom we 1Kin 22:8 4321
Hasten hither *M* the son of Imlah 1Kin 22:9 4321
was gone to call *M* spake unto him 1Kin 22:13 4321
M said, As the LORD liveth, what 1Kin 22:14 4321
And the king said unto him, *M* 1Kin 22:15 4321
smote *M* on the cheek, and said, ... 1Kin 22:24 4321
M said, Behold, thou shalt see in 1Kin 22:25 4321
the king of Israel said, Take *M* 1Kin 22:26 4321
M said, If thou return at all in 1Kin 22:28 4321
the same is *M* the son of Imla 2Chr 18:7 4321
Fetch quickly *M* the son of Imla 2Chr 18:8 4319
that went to call *M* spake to him 2Chr 18:12 4321
M said, As the LORD liveth, even 2Chr 18:13 4321
king, the king said unto him, *M* 2Chr 18:14 4318
smote *M* upon the cheek, and said, ... 2Chr 18:23 4321
M said, Behold, thou shalt see on 2Chr 18:24 4321
king of Israel said, Take ye *M* 2Chr 18:25 4321
M said, If thou certainly return 2Chr 18:27 4321

MICE

golden emerods, and five golden *m* 1Sa 6:4 5909
images of your *m* that mar the 1Sa 6:5 5909
and the coffer with the *m* of gold 1Sa 6:11 5909
And the golden *m*, according to the 1Sa 6:18 5909

MICHA (*mi'-cah*) See MICAH, MICAIAH.

1. Son of Mephibosheth.

had a young son, whose name was *M* .. 2Sa 9:12 4316

2. A Levite who renewed the covenant.

M, Rehob, Hashabiah, ... Neh 10:11 4316

3. A family of exiles.

And Mattaniah the son of *M* .... Neh 11:17 4316
son of Mattaniah, the son of *M* .... Neh 11:22 4316

MICHAEL (*mi'-ka-el*)

1. Father of Sethur.

of Asher, Sethur the son of *M* .... Num 13:13 4317

2. A Gadite who settled in Bashan.

house of their fathers were, *M* 1Chr 5:13 4317

3. Son of Jeshishai.
the son of Gilead, the son of *M* 1Chr 5:14 4317
4. Son of Baaseiah.
The son of *M*, the son of Baaseiah 1Chr 6:40 4317
5. A chief man of Issachar.
M, and Obadiah, and Joel, Ishiah, 1Chr 7:3 4317
6. A Benjamite in Jerusalem.
And *M*, and Ispah, and Joha, the sons. 1Chr 8:16 4317
7. A warrior in David's army.
and Jozabad, and Jediael, and *M* 1Chr 12:20 4317
8. Father of Omri.
of Issachar, Omri the son of *M* 1Chr 27:18 4317
9. A son of Jehoshaphat.
and Zechariah, and Azariah, and *M* 2Chr 21:2 4317
10. A family of exiles.
Zebadiah the son of *M*, and with Ezr 8:8 4317
11. Angelic messenger who came to Daniel.
but, lo, *M*, one of the chief Dan 10:13 4317
these things, but *M* your prince Dan 10:21 4317
And at that time shall *M* stand up Dan 12:1 4317
Yet *M* the archangel, when Jude 9 *3413*
M and his angels fought against Rev 12:7 *3413*

MICHAH (*mi'-cah*) See MICAH, MICHAIAH. *A sanctuary servant.*
sons of Uzziel; *M* 1Chr 24:24 4318
of the sons of *M* 1Chr 24:24 4318
The brother of *M* was Isshiah 1Chr 24:25 4318

MICHAIAH (*mi-ka-i'-ah*) See MICAH, MICAIAH.
1. Father of Achbor.
Shaphan, and Achbor the son of *M* 2Kin 22:12 4320
2. Wife of King Rehoboam.
His mother's name also was *M* the 2Chr 13:2 4322
3. A prince of Judah.
and to Nethaneel, and to *M* 2Chr 17:7 4322
4. A priest with Zerubbabel.
son of Mattaniah, the son of *M* Neh 12:35 4320
Eliakim, Maaseiah, Miniamin, *M* Neh 12:41 4320
5. Son of Gemariah.
When *M* the son of Gemariah, the Jer 36:11 4321
Then *M* declared unto them all the Jer 36:13 4321

MICHAL (*mi'-kal*) See EGLAH. *A wife of David.*
and the name of the younger *M* 1Sa 14:49 4324
M Saul's daughter loved David 1Sa 18:20 4324
Saul gave him *M* his daughter to 1Sa 18:27 4324
that *M* Saul's daughter loved him 1Sa 18:28 4324
M David's wife told him, saying, 1Sa 19:11 4324
So *M* let David down through a 1Sa 19:12 4324
M took an image, and laid it in 1Sa 19:13 4324
And Saul said unto *M*, Why hast 1Sa 19:17 4324
M answered Saul, He said unto me, 1Sa 19:17 4324
But Saul had given *M* his daughter 1Sa 25:44 4324
first bring *M* Saul's daughter 2Sa 3:13 4324
son, saying, Deliver me my wife *M* 2Sa 3:14 4324
M Saul's daughter looked through 2Sa 6:16 4324
M the daughter of Saul came out 2Sa 6:20 4324
And David said unto *M*, It was 2Sa 6:21 4324
Therefore *M* the daughter of Saul 2Sa 6:23 4324
the five sons of *M* the daughter 2Sa 21:8 4324
that *M* the daughter of Saul 1Chr 15:29 4324

MICHMAS (*mik'-mas*) See MICHMASH. *Home of some exiles.*
The men of *M*, an hundred twenty Ezr 2:27 4363
The men of *M*, an hundred and Neh 7:31 4363

MICHMASH (*mik'-mash*) See MICHMAS. *A city near Jerusalem.*
two thousand were with Saul in *M* 1Sa 13:2 4363
and they came up, and pitched in *M* 1Sa 13:5 4363
gathered themselves together at *M* 1Sa 13:11 4363
but the Philistines encamped in *M* 1Sa 13:16 4363
went out to the passage of *M* 1Sa 13:23 4363
situate northward over against *M* 1Sa 14:5 4363
that day from *M* to Aijalon 1Sa 14:31 4363
of Benjamin from Geba dwelt at *M* Neh 11:31 4363
at *M* he hath laid up his Is 10:28 4363

MICHMETHAH (*mik'-me-thah*) *A city between Ephraim and Manasseh.*
the sea to *M* on the north side Josh 16:6 4366
of Manasseh was from Asher to *M* Josh 17:7 4366

MICHMETHATH See MICHMETHAH.

MICHRI (*mik'-ri*) *Father of Uzzi.*
the son of Uzzi, the son of *M* 1Chr 9:8 4381

MICHTAM (*mik'-tam*) *A type of psalm.*
M of David Ps 16:*t* 4387
a *M* of David, when the Ps 56:*t* 4387
M of David, when he fled from Ps 57:*t* 4387
Musician, Altaschith, *M* of David Ps 58:*t* 4387
Musician, Altaschith, *M* of David Ps 59:*t* 4387
M of David, to teach Ps 60:*t* 4387

MICMASH See MICHMASH.

MICMETHAH See MICHMETHAH.

MICRI See MICHRI.

MIDDAY
to pass, when *m* was past, and they 1Kin 18:29 6672
gate from the morning until *m* Neh 8:3
At *m*, O king, I saw in the way a Acts 26:13

MIDDIN (*mid'-din*) *A city in the wilderness south of Judah.*
In the wilderness, Beth-arabah, *M* Josh 15:61 4081

MIDDLE
the *m* bar in the midst of the Ex 26:28 8432
he made the *m* bar to shoot Ex 36:33 8484
from the *m* of the river, and from Josh 12:2 8432
in the beginning of the *m* watch Judg 7:19 8484
people down by the *m* of the land Judg 9:37 2872
Samson took hold of the two *m* Judg 16:29 8432
out, as out of the *m* of a sling 1Sa 25:29 8432
cut off their garments in the *m* 2Sa 10:4 2677
the *m* was six cubits broad, and 1Kin 6:6 8484
The door for the *m* chamber was in 1Kin 6:8 8484
winding stairs into the *m* chamber 1Kin 6:8 8484
out of the *m* into the third 1Kin 6:8 8484
day did the king hallow the *m* of 1Kin 8:64 8432
was gone out into the *m* court 2Kin 20:4 8484
m of the court that was before 2Chr 7:7 8484
came in, and sat in the *m* gate Jer 39:3 8484
were a wheel in the *m* of a wheel Eze 1:16 8432
hath broken down the *m* wall of Eph 2:14 *3320*

MIDDLEMOST
than the *m* of the building Eze 42:5 8484
lowest and the *m* from the ground Eze 42:6 8484

MIDIAN (*mid'-e-an*) See MADIAN, MIDIANITE.
1. A son of Abraham.
and Jokshan, and Medan, and *M* Gen 25:2 4080
And the sons of *M* Gen 25:4 4080
and Jokshan, and Medan, and *M* 1Chr 1:32 4080
And the sons of *M* 1Chr 1:33 4080
2. A nation on the southern border of Israel.
who smote *M* in the field of Moab, Gen 36:35 4080
and dwelt in the land of *M* Ex 2:15 4080
Now the priest of *M* had seven Ex 2:16 4080
father in law, the priest of *M* Ex 3:1 4080
And the LORD said unto Moses in *M* Ex 4:19 4080
When Jethro, the priest of *M* Ex 18:1 4080
And Moab said unto the elders of *M* Num 22:4 4080
the elders of *M* departed with the Num 22:7 4080
people, and of a chief house in *M* Num 25:15 4080
the daughter of a prince of *M* Num 25:18 4080
and avenge the LORD of *M* Num 31:3 4080
And they slew the kings of *M* Num 31:8 4080
and Hur, and Reba, five kings of *M* Num 31:8 4080
took all the women of *M* captives Num 31:9 4080
Moses smote with the princes of *M* Josh 13:21 4080
into the hand of *M* seven years Judg 6:1 4080
the hand of *M* prevailed against Judg 6:2 4080
the host of *M* was beneath him in Judg 7:8 4080
bread tumbled into the host of *M* Judg 7:13 4080
his hand hath God delivered *M* Judg 7:14 4080
into your hand the host of *M* Judg 7:15 4080
winepress of Zeeb, and pursued *M* Judg 7:25 4080
into your hands the princes of *M* Judg 8:3 4080
Zebah and Zalmunna, kings of *M* Judg 8:5 4080
them, and took the two kings of *M* Judg 8:12 4080
delivered us from the hand of *M* Judg 8:22 4080
that was on the kings of *M* Judg 8:26 4080
Thus was *M* subdued before the Judg 8:28 4080
you out of the hand of *M* Judg 9:17 4080
And they arose out of *M*, and came 1Kin 11:18 4080
which smote *M* in the field of 1Chr 1:46 4080
his oppressor, as in the day of *M* Is 9:4 4080
of *M* at the rock of Oreb Is 10:26 4080
cover thee, the dromedaries of *M* Is 60:6 4080
of the land of *M* did tremble Hab 3:7 4080

MIDIANITE (*mid'-e-an-ite*) See MIDIANITES, MIDIANITISH. *A descendant of Midian.*
Hobab, the son of Raguel the *M* Num 10:29 4084

MIDIANITES (*mid'-e-an-ites*) See KENITES.
there passed by *M* merchantmen Gen 37:28 4084
the *M* sold him into Egypt unto Gen 37:36 4092
Vex the *M*, and smite them Num 25:17 4084
the children of Israel of the *M* Num 31:2 4084
war, and let them go against the *M* Num 31:3 4080
And they warred against the *M* Num 31:7 4080
because of the *M* the children of Judg 6:2 4080
had sown, that the *M* came up Judg 6:3 4080
impoverished because of the *M* Judg 6:6 4080
unto the LORD because of the *M* Judg 6:7 4080
winepress, to hide it from the *M* Judg 6:11 4080
us into the hands of the *M* Judg 6:13 4080
Israel from the hand of the *M* Judg 6:14 4080
thou shalt smite the *M* as one man Judg 6:16 4080
Then all the *M* and the Amalekites Judg 6:33 4080
so that the host of the *M* were on Judg 7:1 4080
me to give the *M* into their hands Judg 7:2 4080
deliver the *M* into thine hand Judg 7:7 4080
And the *M* and the Amalekites and all Judg 7:12 4080
Manasseh, and pursued after the *M* Judg 7:23 4080
saying, Come down against the *M* Judg 7:24 4080
And they took two princes of the *M* Judg 7:25 4080
thou wentest to fight with the *M* Judg 8:1 4080
Do unto them as unto the *M* Ps 83:9 4080

MIDIANITISH (*mid'-e-an-i'-tish*) *Belonging to the land of Midian.*
a *M* woman in the sight of Moses Num 25:6 4084
that was slain with the *M* woman Num 25:14 4084
the name of the *M* woman that was Num 25:15 4084

MIDNIGHT
About *m* will I go out into the Ex 11:4
that at *m* the LORD smote all the Ex 12:29
lay till *m*, and arose at *m* Judg 16:3
And it came to pass at *m*, that the Ruth 3:8
And she arose at *m*, and took my son 1Kin 3:20
the people shall be troubled at *m* Job 34:20
At *m* I will rise to give thanks Ps 119:62
at *m* there was a cry made, Behold Mt 25:6
house cometh, at even, or at *m* Mk 13:35 *3317*
friend, and shall go unto him at *m* Lk 11:5 *3317*
at *m* Paul and Silas prayed, and Acts 16:25 *3317*
and continued his speech until *m* Acts 20:7 *3317*
about *m* the shipmen deemed that Acts 27:27

MIDST
firmament in the *m* of the waters Gen 1:6 8432
life also in the *m* of the garden Gen 2:9 8432
which is in the *m* of the garden Gen 3:3 8432
these, and divided them in the *m* Gen 15:10 8432
Lot out of the *m* of the overthrow Gen 19:29 8432
a multitude in the *m* of the earth Gen 48:16 7130
of fire out of the *m* of a bush Ex 3:2 8432
unto him out of the *m* of the bush Ex 3:4 8432
which I will do in the *m* thereof Ex 3:20 7130
am the LORD in the *m* of the earth Ex 8:22 7130
will I go out into the *m* of Egypt Ex 11:4 8432
ground through the *m* of the sea Ex 14:16 8432
of Israel went into the *m* of the Ex 14:22 8432
in after them to the *m* of the sea Ex 14:23 8432
the Egyptians in the *m* of the sea Ex 14:27 8432
upon dry land in the *m* of the sea Ex 14:29 8432
on dry land in the *m* of the sea Ex 15:19 8432
sickness away from the *m* of thee Ex 23:25 7130
Moses out of the *m* of the cloud Ex 24:16 8432
went into the *m* of the cloud Ex 24:18 8432
the middle bar in the *m* of the Ex 26:28 8432
may be even to the *m* of the altar Ex 27:5 2677
the top of it, in the *m* thereof Ex 28:32 8432
I will not go up in the *m* of thee Ex 33:3 7130
up into the *m* of thee in a moment Ex 33:5 7130
be for a snare in the *m* of thee Ex 34:12 7130
thereof beneath unto the *m* of it Ex 38:4 2677
was an hole in the *m* of the robe Ex 39:23 8432
in the *m* of their uncleanness Lev 16:16 8432
the Levites in the *m* of the camp Num 2:17 8432
camps, in the *m* whereof I dwell Num 5:3 8432
and ran into the *m* of the Num 16:47 8432
cast it into the *m* of the burning Num 19:6 8432
passed through the *m* of the sea Num 33:8 8432
and the city shall be in the *m* Num 35:5 8432
with fire unto the *m* of heaven Deut 4:11 3820
unto you out of the *m* of the fire Deut 4:12 8432
in Horeb out of the *m* of the fire Deut 4:15 8432
speaking out of the *m* of the fire Deut 4:33 8432
from the *m* of another nation Deut 4:34 7130
words out of the *m* of the fire Deut 4:36 8432
mount out of the *m* of the fire Deut 5:4 8432
mount out of the *m* of the fire Deut 5:22 8432
out of the *m* of the darkness Deut 5:23 8432
voice out of the *m* of the fire Deut 5:24 8432
speaking out of the *m* of the fire Deut 5:26 8432
you in the mount out of the *m* of Deut 9:10 8432
you in the mount out of the *m* of Deut 10:4 8432
which he did in the *m* of Egypt Deut 11:3 8432
in the *m* of all Israel Deut 11:6 7130
the evil away from the *m* of thee Deut 13:5 7130
into the *m* of the street thereof Deut 13:16 8432
his children, in the *m* of Israel Deut 17:20 7130
thee a Prophet from the *m* of thee Deut 18:15 7130
for thee in the *m* of thy land Deut 19:2 8432
God walketh in the *m* of thy camp Deut 23:14 7130
the *m* of the children of Israel Deut 32:51 8432
on dry ground in the *m* of Jordan Josh 3:17 8432
you hence out of the *m* of Jordan Josh 4:3 8432
your God into the *m* of Jordan Josh 4:5 8432
stones out of the *m* of Jordan Josh 4:8 8432
twelve stones in the *m* of Jordan Josh 4:9 8432
the ark stood in the *m* of Jordan Josh 4:10 8432
come up out of the *m* of Jordan Josh 4:18 8432
accursed thing in the *m* of thee Josh 7:13 7130
in the earth in the *m* of my tent Josh 7:21 8432
them out of the *m* of the tent Josh 7:23 8432
night into the *m* of the valley Josh 8:13 8432
so they were in the *m* of Israel Josh 8:22 8432
stood still in the *m* of heaven Josh 10:13 2677
that is in the *m* of the river Josh 13:9 8432
that is in the *m* of the river Josh 13:16 8432
in the *m* between two tails Judg 15:4 8432
went in the *m* of the people Judg 18:20 7130
they destroyed in the *m* of them Judg 20:42 8432
they came into the *m* of the host 1Sa 11:11 8432
him in the *m* of his brethren 1Sa 16:13 7130
prophesied in the *m* of the house 1Sa 18:10 8432
fallen in the *m* of the battle 2Sa 1:25 8432
thither into the *m* of the house 2Sa 4:6 8432
in the *m* of the tabernacle that 2Sa 6:17 8432
was yet alive in the *m* of the oak 2Sa 18:14 3820
in blood in the *m* of the highway 2Sa 20:12 8432
he stood in the *m* of the ground 2Sa 23:12 8432
slew a lion in the *m* of a pit in 2Sa 23:20 8432
in the *m* of the river of Gad 2Sa 24:5 8432
thy servant is in the *m* of thy 1Kin 3:8 8432
one another in the *m* of the house 1Kin 6:27 8432
from the *m* of the furnace of iron 1Kin 8:51 8432
went out into the *m* of the battle 1Kin 20:39 7130
wound into the *m* of the chariot 1Kin 22:35 2436
they were in the *m* of Samaria 2Kin 6:20 8432
in the *m* of that parcel, and 1Chr 11:14 8432
set it in the *m* of the tent that 1Chr 16:1 8432
in the *m* hard by their buttocks 1Chr 19:4 2677
had set it in the *m* of the court 2Chr 6:13 8432
LORD in the *m* of the congregation 2Chr 20:14 8432
ran through the *m* of the land 2Chr 32:4 8432
till we come in the *m* among them Neh 4:11 8432
the *m* of the sea on the dry land Neh 9:11 8432
went out into the *m* of the city Est 4:1 8432
of his months is cut off in the *m* Job 21:21 2686
is melted in the *m* of my bowels Ps 22:14 8432
in the *m* of the congregation will Ps 22:22 8432
be carried into the *m* of the sea Ps 46:2 3820
God is in the *m* of her Ps 46:5 7130
O God, in the *m* of thy temple Ps 48:9 7130
also and sorrow are in the *m* of it Ps 55:10 7130
Wickedness is in the *m* thereof Ps 55:11 7130
into the *m* whereof they are Ps 57:6 8432
in the *m* of thy congregations Ps 74:4 7130
salvation in the *m* of the earth Ps 74:12 7130
it fall in the *m* of their camp Ps 78:28 7130
me not away in the *m* of my days Ps 102:24 2677
thou in the *m* of thine enemies Ps 110:2 7130
in the *m* of thee, O Jerusalem Ps 116:19 8432
and wonders into the *m* of thee Ps 135:9 8432
to pass through the *m* of it Ps 136:14 8432
upon the willows in the *m* thereof Ps 137:2 8432
Though I walk in the *m* of trouble Ps 138:7 7130

M

keep them in the *m* of thine heart........ Prov 4:21 8432
evil in the *m* of the congregation......... Prov 5:14 8432
in the *m* of the paths of judgment........ Prov 8:20 8432
in the *m* of fools is made known.......... Prov 14:33 7130
lieth down in the *m* of the sea............ Prov 23:34 3820
way of a ship in the *m* of the sea........ Prov 30:19 3820
the *m* thereof being paved with........... Song 3:10 8432
the *m* thereof by the spirit of............. Is 4:4 7130
and built a tower in the *m* of it........... Is 5:2 8432
alone in the *m* of the earth................. Is 5:8 7130
were torn in the *m* of the streets.......... Is 5:25 7130
I dwell in the *m* of a people of............ Is 6:5 8432
forsaking in the *m* of the land............. Is 6:12 7130
us, and set a king in the *m* of it.......... Is 7:6 8432
in the *m* of all the land.................... Is 10:23 7130
One of Israel in the *m* of thee............. Is 12:6 7130
the night in the *m* of the noonday......... Is 16:3 8432
Egypt shall melt in the *m* of it............ Is 19:1 7130
Egypt shall fail in the *m* thereof.......... Is 19:3 7130
perverse spirit in the *m* thereof.......... Is 19:14 7130
in the *m* of the land of Egypt.............. Is 19:19 8432
a blessing in the *m* of the land............ Is 19:24 7130
m of the land among the people............ Is 24:13 7130
m of the pit shall be taken in.............. Is 24:18 8432
forth his hands in the *m* of them.......... Is 25:11 7130
of mine hands, in the *m* of him............ Is 29:23 7130
shall reach to the *m* of the neck.......... Is 30:28 2673
fountains in the *m* of the valleys.......... Is 41:18 8432
go ye out of the *m* of her.................. Is 52:11 8432
away from the *m* of thee the yoke......... Is 58:9 8432
gardens behind one tree in the *m*.......... Is 66:17 8432
to flee out of the *m* of Jerusalem......... Jer 6:1 7130
wholly oppression in the *m* of her......... Jer 6:6 7130
habitation is in the *m* of deceit........... Jer 9:6 8432
be built in the *m* of my people............. Jer 12:16 8432
thou, O LORD, art in the *m* of us........... Jer 14:9 7130
leave them in the *m* of his days........... Jer 17:11 2677
them into the *m* of this city................ Jer 21:4 8432
diviners, that be in the *m* of you.......... Jer 29:8 7130
shall proceed from the *m* of them.......... Jer 30:21 7130
thence in the *m* of the people.............. Jer 37:12 8432
they came into the *m* of the city........... Jer 41:7 8432
cast them into the *m* of the pit............ Jer 41:7 8432
the *m* of her like fatted bullocks.......... Jer 46:21 7130
and a flame from the *m* of Sihon........... Jer 48:45
Remove out of the *m* of Babylon............ Jer 50:8 8432
people that are in the *m* of her............ Jer 50:37 8432
against them that dwell in the *m*........... Jer 51:1 3820
Flee out of the *m* of Babylon................ Jer 51:6 8432
people, go ye out of the *m* of her.......... Jer 51:45 8432
slain shall fall in the *m* of her............. Jer 51:47 8432
cast it into the *m* of Euphrates............. Jer 51:63 8432
were found in the *m* of the city............. Jer 52:25 8432
all my mighty men in the *m* of me.......... Lam 1:15 7130
and refuse in the *m* of the people.......... Lam 3:45 7130
blood of the just in the *m* of her........... Lam 4:13 7130
out of the *m* thereof as the.................. Eze 1:4 8432
amber, out of the *m* of the fire.............. Eze 1:4 8432
Also out of the *m* thereof came............... Eze 1:5 8432
a third part in the *m* of the city............. Eze 5:2 8432
cast them into the *m* of the fire.............. Eze 5:4 8432
set it in the *m* of the nations................. Eze 5:5 8432
the *m* of thee in the sight of the............. Eze 5:8 8432
eat the sons in the *m* of thee................. Eze 5:10 8432
they be consumed in the *m* of thee............ Eze 5:12 8432
slain shall fall in the *m* of you............... Eze 6:7 8432
shall be in the *m* of thee....................... Eze 7:4 8432
that are in the *m* of thee....................... Eze 7:9 8432
in the *m* of them stood Jaazaniah.............. Eze 8:11 8432
him, Go through the *m* of the city............. Eze 9:4 8432
through the *m* of Jerusalem, and............... Eze 9:4 8432
that be done in the *m* thereof.................. Eze 9:4 8432
had been in the *m* of a wheel................... Eze 10:10 8432
whom ye have laid in the *m* of it.............. Eze 11:7 8432
you forth out of the *m* of it.................... Eze 11:7 8432
bring you out of the *m* thereof................. Eze 11:9 8432
ye be the flesh in the *m* thereof............... Eze 11:11 8432
went up from the *m* of the city................. Eze 11:23 8432
thou dwellest in the *m* of a..................... Eze 12:2 8432
be consumed in the *m* thereof.................... Eze 13:14 8432
him off from the *m* of my people................ Eze 14:8 8432
from the *m* of my people Israel................. Eze 14:9 8432
of it, and the *m* of it is burned................ Eze 15:4 8432
of thy captives in the *m* of them................ Eze 16:53 8432
even with him in the *m* of Babylon............. Eze 17:16 8432
in the *m* of the land of Egypt................... Eze 20:8 8432
shall be in the *m* of the land................... Eze 21:32 8432
sheddeth blood in the *m* of it.................... Eze 22:3 8432
in the *m* of thee have they dealt................ Eze 22:7 8432
in the *m* of thee they commit.................... Eze 22:9 8432
which hath been in the *m* of thee............... Eze 22:13 8432
and lead, in the *m* of the furnace............... Eze 22:18 8432
you into the *m* of Jerusalem...................... Eze 22:19 8432
into the *m* of the furnace, to.................... Eze 22:20 8432
shall be melted in the *m* thereof................ Eze 22:21 8432
is melted in the *m* of the furnace............... Eze 22:22 8432
ye be melted in the *m* thereof................... Eze 22:22 8432
of her prophets in the *m* thereof................ Eze 22:25 8432
her many widows in the *m* thereof............... Eze 22:25 8432
Her princes in the *m* thereof are................ Eze 22:27 7130
they done in the *m* of mine house............... Eze 23:39 8432
For her blood is in the *m* of her................ Eze 24:7 8432
of nets in the *m* of the sea...................... Eze 26:5 8432
and thy dust in the *m* of the water.............. Eze 26:12 8432
is made in the *m* of thee......................... Eze 26:15 8432
borders are in the *m* of the seas................ Eze 27:4 3820
glorious in the *m* of the seas.................... Eze 27:25 3820
broken thee in the *m* of the seas................ Eze 27:26 3820
company which is in the *m* of thee.............. Eze 27:27 8432
shall fall into the *m* of the seas................ Eze 27:27 3820
the destroyed in the *m* of the sea.............. Eze 27:32 8432
in the *m* of thee shall fall....................... Eze 27:34 8432
seat of God, in the *m* of the seas............... Eze 28:2 3820
are slain in the *m* of the seas................... Eze 28:8 3820

down in the *m* of the stones of.................. Eze 28:14 8432
they have filled the *m* of thee................... Eze 28:16 8432
from the *m* of the stones of fire................ Eze 28:16 8432
forth a fire from the *m* of thee................. Eze 28:18 8432
be glorified in the *m* of thee.................... Eze 28:22 8432
wounded shall be judged in the *m*............... Eze 28:23 8432
that lieth in the *m* of his rivers................ Eze 29:3 8432
up out of the *m* of thy rivers.................... Eze 29:4 8432
the *m* of the countries that are.................. Eze 29:12 8432
of the mouth in the *m* of them................... Eze 29:21 8432
the *m* of the countries that are.................. Eze 30:7 8432
her cities shall be in the *m* of.................. Eze 30:7 8432
in the *m* of the children of men,................ Eze 31:14 8432
shadow in the *m* of the heathen................. Eze 31:17 8432
thou shalt lie in the *m* of the................... Eze 31:18 8432
They shall fall in the *m* of them............... Eze 32:20 8432
shall speak to him out of the *m*................. Eze 32:21 8432
the *m* of the slain with all her................... Eze 32:25 8432
he is put in the *m* of them that................. Eze 32:25 8432
in the *m* of the uncircumcised................... Eze 32:28 8432
he shall be laid in the *m* of the................. Eze 32:32 8432
ye have profaned in the *m* of them.............. Eze 36:23 8432
set me down in the *m* of the...................... Eze 37:1 8432
in the *m* of them for evermore.................. Eze 37:26 8432
be in the *m* of them for evermore............... Eze 37:28 8432
that dwell in the *m* of the land................. Eze 38:12 2872
in the *m* of my people Israel.................... Eze 39:7 8432
chamber to the highest by the *m*................ Eze 41:7 8484
where I will dwell in the *m* of................... Eze 43:7 8432
dwell in the *m* of them for ever................. Eze 43:9 8432
And the prince in the *m* of them................ Eze 46:10 8432
sanctuary shall be in the *m* of it............... Eze 48:8 8432
LORD shall be in the *m* thereof.................. Eze 48:10 8432
city shall be in the *m* thereof.................. Eze 48:15 8432
house shall be in the *m* thereof................ Eze 48:21 8432
being in the *m* of that which is.................. Eze 48:22 8432
the *m* of a burning fiery furnace................ Dan 3:6 1459
the *m* of a burning fiery furnace................ Dan 3:11 1459
the *m* of a burning fiery furnace................ Dan 3:15 1459
were cast into the *m* of the...................... Dan 3:21 1459
fell down bound into the *m* of the.............. Dan 3:23 1459
men bound into the *m* of the fire................ Dan 3:24 1459
walking in the *m* of the fire..................... Dan 3:25 1459
came forth of the *m* of the fire................. Dan 3:26 1459
a tree in the *m* of the earth..................... Dan 4:10 1459
in my spirit in the *m* of my body................ Dan 7:15 1459
in the *m* of the week he shall................... Dan 9:27 2677
of whoredoms is in the *m* of them.............. Hos 5:4 7130
the Holy One in the *m* of thee.................. Hos 11:9 7130
know that I am in the *m* of Israel.............. Joel 2:27 7130
off the judge from the *m* thereof............... Amos 2:3 7130
great tumults in the *m* thereof.................. Amos 3:9 7130
and the oppressed in the *m* thereof............ Amos 3:9 8432
calves out of the *m* of the stall................. Amos 6:4 8432
in the *m* of my people Israel..................... Amos 7:8 7130
in the *m* of the house of Israel.................. Amos 7:10 7130
the deep, in the *m* of the seas.................. Jonah 2:3 3824
the flock in the *m* of their fold.................. Mic 2:12 8432
of Jacob shall be in the *m* of..................... Mic 5:7 7130
be among the Gentiles in the *m* of.............. Mic 5:8 7130
thy horses out of the *m* of thee................. Mic 5:10 7130
images out of the *m* of thee...................... Mic 5:13 7130
thy groves out of the *m* of thee................. Mic 5:14 7130
down shall be in the *m* of thee.................. Mic 6:14 7130
in the wood, in the *m* of Carmel................. Mic 7:14 8432
people in the *m* of thee are women............. Nah 3:13 7130
no breath at all in the *m* of it.................. Hab 2:19 7130
thy work in the *m* of the years................... Hab 3:2 7130
in the *m* of the years make known............... Hab 3:2 7130
shall lie down in the *m* of her................... Zeph 2:14 8432
The just LORD is in the *m* thereof............... Zeph 3:5 7130
I will take away out of the *m* of................. Zeph 3:11 7130
in the *m* of thee an afflicted..................... Zeph 3:12 7130
the LORD, is in the *m* of thee..................... Zeph 3:15 7130
God in the *m* of thee is mighty................... Zeph 3:17 7130
will be the glory in the *m* of her................ Zec 2:5 8432
and I will dwell in the *m* of thee................ Zec 2:10 8432
and I will dwell in the *m* of thee................ Zec 2:11 8432
remain in the *m* of his house..................... Zec 5:4 8432
sitteth in the *m* of the ephah.................... Zec 5:7 8432
cast it into the *m* of the ephah.................. Zec 5:8 8432
will dwell in the *m* of Jerusalem................ Zec 8:3 8432
shall dwell in the *m* of Jerusalem............... Zec 8:8 8432
shall be divided in the *m* of thee............... Zec 14:1 7130
in the *m* thereof toward the east................ Zec 14:4 2677
forth as sheep in the *m* of wolves............... Mt 10:16 3319
ship was now in the *m* of the sea................ Mt 14:24 3319
him, and set him in the *m* of them.............. Mt 18:2 3319
name, there am I in the *m* of them.............. Mt 18:20 3319
the ship was in the *m* of the sea................ Mk 6:47 3319
through the *m* of the coasts of.................. Mk 7:31 3319
and set him in the *m* of them.................... Mk 9:36 3319
the high priest stood up in the *m*............... Mk 14:60 3319
sitting in the *m* of the doctors.................. Lk 2:46 3319
the *m* of them went his way...................... Lk 4:30 3319
the devil had thrown him in the *m*.............. Lk 4:35 3319
his couch into the *m* before Jesus.............. Lk 5:19 3319
Rise up, and stand forth in the *m*............... Lk 6:8 3319
passed through the *m* of Samaria................ Lk 17:11 3319
are in the *m* of it depart out..................... Lk 21:21 3319
a fire in the *m* of the hall........................ Lk 22:55 3319
of the temple was rent in the *m*................. Lk 23:45 3319
himself stood in the *m* of them.................. Lk 24:36 3319
Now about the *m* of the feast.................... Jn 7:14 3322
and when they had set her in the *m*............. Jn 8:3 3319
and the woman standing in the *m*................ Jn 8:9 3319
going through the *m* of them..................... Jn 8:59 3319
side one, and Jesus in the *m*.................... Jn 19:18 3319
came Jesus and stood in the *m*.................. Jn 20:19 3319
being shut, and stood in the *m*.................. Jn 20:26 3319
up in the *m* of the disciples..................... Acts 1:15 3319
he burst asunder in the *m*........................ Acts 1:18 3319
God did by him in the *m* of you.................. Acts 2:22 3319
when they had set them in the *m*................ Acts 4:7 3319

Paul stood in the *m* of Mars' hill................. Acts 17:22 3319
Paul stood forth in the *m* of them.............. Acts 27:21 3319
in the *m* of a crooked and perverse............. Phil 2:15 3319
in the *m* of the church will I...................... Heb 2:12 3319
And in the *m* of the seven.......................... Rev 1:13 3319
who walketh in the *m* of the seven.............. Rev 2:1 3319
which is in the *m* of the paradise............... Rev 2:7 3319
in the *m* of the throne, and round.............. Rev 4:6 3319
in the *m* of the throne and of the............... Rev 5:6 3319
in the *m* of the elders, stood a.................. Rev 5:6 3319
in the *m* of the four beasts say.................. Rev 6:6 3319
For the Lamb which is in the *m* of............... Rev 7:17 3319
flying through the *m* of heaven.................. Rev 8:13 3321
angel fly in the *m* of heaven...................... Rev 14:6 3321
fowls that fly in the *m* of heaven............... Rev 19:17 3321
In the *m* of the street of it, and.................. Rev 22:2 3319

MIDWIFE
that the *m* said unto her, Fear.................... Gen 35:17 3205
the *m* took and bound upon his hand.......... Gen 38:28 3205
office of a *m* to the Hebrew women............. Ex 1:16 3205

MIDWIVES
of Egypt spake to the Hebrew *m*................. Ex 1:15 3205
But the *m* feared God, and did not.............. Ex 1:17 3205
king of Egypt called for the *m*................... Ex 1:18 3205
the *m* said unto Pharaoh, Because............... Ex 1:19 3205
ere the *m* come in unto them..................... Ex 1:19 3205
God dealt well with the *m*......................... Ex 1:20 3205
to pass, because the *m* feared God.............. Ex 1:21 3205

MIGDAL EDER See EDAR.

MIGDAL-EL (*mig'-dal-el*) *A city in Naphtali.*
And Iron, and *M*, Horem, and...................... Josh 19:38 4027

MIGDAL-GAD (*mig'-dal-gad*) *A city in Judah.*
Zenan, and Hadashah, and *M*,..................... Josh 15:37 4028

MIGDOL (*mig'-dol*)
1. A place west of the Red Sea.
before Pi-hahiroth, between *M*.................... Ex 14:2 4024
and they pitched before *M*......................... Num 33:7 4024
2. A place in northern Egypt.
land of Egypt, which dwell at *M*.................. Jer 44:1 4024
ye in Egypt, and publish in *M*.................... Jer 46:14 4024

MIGHT
so I *m* have taken her to me to.................. Gen 12:19
that they *m* dwell together........................ Gen 13:6
O that Ishmael *m* live before thee.............. Gen 17:18
one of the people *m* lightly have................. Gen 26:10
I would it *m* be according to thy................. Gen 30:34
that they *m* conceive among the.................. Gen 30:41
that I *m* have sent thee away with.............. Gen 31:27
than that they *m* dwell together.................. Gen 36:7
that he *m* rid him out of their.................... Gen 37:22
because the Egyptians *m* not eat................. Gen 43:32 3201
thou art my firstborn, my *m*....................... Gen 49:3 3581
that I *m* shew these my signs..................... Ex 10:1
that they *m* send them out of the................ Ex 12:33
tent together, that it *m* be one.................. Ex 36:18
that it *m* be above the curious.................... Ex 39:21
that the breastplate *m* not be.................... Ex 39:21
mind of the LORD *m* be shewed them............ Lev 24:12
heathen, that I *m* be their God................... Lev 26:45
all that *m* do service in the........................ Num 4:37
of all that *m* do service in the.................... Num 4:41
people in thy *m* from among them............... Num 14:13 3581
that thence he *m* see the utmost................. Num 22:41
that he *m* deliver him into thy.................... Deut 2:30
thy works, and according to thy *m*.............. Deut 3:24 1369
that ye *m* do them in the land.................... Deut 4:14
voice, that he *m* instruct thee.................... Deut 4:36
That the slayer *m* flee thither.................... Deut 4:42
one of these cities he *m* live..................... Deut 4:42
that it *m* be well with them, and................ Deut 5:29
that ye *m* do them in the land.................... Deut 6:1
all thy soul, and with all thy *m*................... Deut 6:5 3966
that he *m* bring us in, to give us............... Deut 6:23
that he *m* preserve us alive, as.................. Deut 6:24
that he *m* make thee know that man........... Deut 8:3
that he *m* humble thee, and that he............ Deut 8:16
that he *m* prove thee, to do thee............... Deut 8:16
the *m* of mine hand hath gotten me............. Deut 8:17 6108
there shall be no *m* in thine hand............... Deut 28:32 410
that ye *m* know that I am the LORD............. Deut 29:6
that he *m* eat the increase of the.............. Deut 32:13
earth *m* know the hand of the LORD............. Josh 4:24
that ye *m* fear the LORD your God............... Josh 4:24
that he *m* destroy them utterly,................. Josh 11:20
that they *m* have no favour........................ Josh 11:20
but that he *m* destroy them, as.................. Josh 11:20
person at unawares *m* flee thither.............. Josh 20:9
that ye *m* rebel this day against................. Josh 22:16
m speak unto our children.......................... Josh 22:24
that we *m* do the service of the.................. Josh 22:27
that ye *m* possess their land...................... Josh 24:8
of the children of Israel *m* know.................. Judg 3:2
sun when he goeth forth in his *m*................ Judg 5:31 1369
him, and said, Go in this thy *m*.................. Judg 6:14 3581
and ten sons of Jerubbaal *m* come.............. Judg 9:24
he bowed himself with all his *m*.................. Judg 16:30 3581
that *m* put them to shame in any................ Judg 18:7
that she *m* return from the........................ Ruth 1:6
that they *m* bring from thence the.............. 1Sa 4:4
to meet him, that he *m* salute him.............. 1Sa 13:10
land, which a yoke of oxen *m* plow.............. 1Sa 14:14
that he *m* be the king's son in................... 1Sa 18:27
asked leave of me that he *m* run................. 1Sa 20:6
before the LORD with all his *m*.................... 2Sa 6:14 5797
that he *m* put them in array....................... 2Sa 10:10
any suit or cause *m* come unto me.............. 2Sa 15:4
LORD *m* bring evil upon Absalom.................. 2Sa 17:14
for they *m* not be seen to come.................. 2Sa 17:17 3201
that I *m* destroy them that hate.................. 2Sa 22:41
that he *m* fulfil the word of the................... 1Kin 2:27

for the throne where he *m* judge	1Kin 7:7	
that they *m* bring up the ark of	1Kin 8:1	
house, that my name *m* be therein	1Kin 8:16	
that he *m* perform his saying,	1Kin 12:15	
that he *m* not suffer any to go	1Kin 15:17	
all the acts of Asa, and all his *m*	1Kin 15:23	1369
Baasha, and what he did, and his *m*	1Kin 16:5	1369
his *m* that he shewed, are they	1Kin 16:27	1369
for himself that he *m* die	1Kin 19:4	
besides, that we *m* enquire of him	1Kin 22:7	
his *m* that he shewed, and how he	1Kin 22:45	1369
in heaven, *m* this thing be	2Kin 7:2	
in heaven, *m* such a thing be	2Kin 7:19	
to the intent that he *m* destroy	2Kin 10:19	
and all that he did, and all his *m*	2Kin 10:34	1369
and all that he did, and his *m*	2Kin 13:8	1369
his *m* wherewith he fought against	2Kin 13:12	1369
of Jehoash which he did, and his *m*	2Kin 14:15	1369
and all that he did, and his *m*	2Kin 14:28	1369
that his hand *m* be with him to	2Kin 15:19	
acts of Hezekiah, and all his *m*	2Kin 20:20	1369
that they *m* provoke me to anger	2Kin 22:17	
that no man *m* make his son or his	2Kin 23:10	
that he *m* perform the words of	2Kin 23:24	
all his soul, and with all his *m*	2Kin 23:25	3966
that he *m* not reign in Jerusalem	2Kin 23:33	
And all the men of *m*, even seven	2Kin 24:16	2428
and that thine hand *m* be with me	1Chr 4:10	
men of *m* in their generations	1Chr 7:2	2428
of Issachar were valiant men of *m*	1Chr 7:5	2428
hold to the wilderness men of *m*	1Chr 12:8	2428
before God with all their *m*	1Chr 13:8	5797
my *m* for the house of my God the	1Chr 29:2	3581
and in thine hand is power and *m*	1Chr 29:12	1369
With all his reign and his *m*	1Chr 29:30	1369
that *m* build an house for the	2Chr 2:12	
house in, that my name *m* be there	2Chr 6:5	
that my name *m* be there	2Chr 6:6	
that the LORD *m* perform his word,	2Chr 10:15	
that he *m* bring the kingdom again	2Chr 11:1	
to the intent that he *m* let none	2Chr 16:1	
besides, that we *m* enquire of him	2Chr 18:6	
hand is there not power and *m*	2Chr 20:6	1369
for we have no *m* against this	2Chr 20:12	3581
that he *m* deliver them into the	2Chr 25:20	
that they *m* be encouraged in the	2Chr 31:4	
that they *m* take the city	2Chr 32:18	
that he *m* know all that was in	2Chr 32:31	
that they *m* provoke me to anger	2Chr 34:25	
that they *m* give according to the	2Chr 35:12	
they *m* not depart from their	2Chr 35:15	
that he *m* fight with him, and	2Chr 35:22	
of Jeremiah *m* be accomplished	2Chr 36:22	
mouth of Jeremiah *m* be fulfilled	Ezr 1:1	
that we *m* write the names of the	Ezr 5:10	
that we *m* afflict ourselves	Ezr 8:21	
that we *m* buy corn, because of	Neh 5:3	
m exact of them money and corn	Neh 5:10	
that they *m* have matter for an	Neh 6:13	
report, that they *m* reproach me	Neh 6:13	
that they *m* be reckoned by	Neh 7:5	
that they *m* do with them as they	Neh 9:24	
that the same Levites *m* have the	Neh 10:37	
for none *m* enter into the king's	Est 4:2	
the acts of his power and of his *m*	Est 10:2	1369
Oh that I *m* have my request	Job 6:8	
that *m* lay his hand upon us both	Job 9:33	
Oh that one *m* plead for a man	Job 16:21	
Oh that I knew where I *m* find him	Job 23:3	
that I *m* come even to his seat	Job 23:3	
the righteous *m* dispute with him	Job 23:7	
whereto *m* the strength of their	Job 30:2	
That it *m* take hold of the ends	Job 38:13	
that the wicked *m* be shaken out	Job 38:13	
that I *m* destroy them that hate	Ps 18:40	
the LORD God *m* dwell among them	Ps 68:18	
none of the men of *m* have found	Ps 76:5	2428
generation to come *m* know them	Ps 78:6	
That they *m* set their hope in God	Ps 78:7	
m not be as their fathers, a	Ps 78:8	
That they *m* observe his statutes,	Ps 105:45	
that he *m* make his mighty power	Ps 106:8	
that they *m* go to a city of	Ps 107:7	
that he *m* even slay the broken in	Ps 109:16	
thrust sore at me that I *m* fall	Ps 118:13	
that I *m* not sin against thee	Ps 119:11	
that I *m* learn thy statutes	Ps 119:71	
evil way, that I *m* keep thy word	Ps 119:101	
that I *m* meditate in thy word	Ps 119:148	
of the *m* of thy terrible acts	Ps 145:6	5807
That I *m* make thee know the	Prov 22:21	
till I *m* see what was that good	Eccl 2:3	
that God *m* manifest them, and that	Eccl 3:18	
that they *m* see that they	Eccl 3:18	
findeth to do, do it with thy *m*	Eccl 9:10	3581
the spirit of counsel and *m*	Is 11:2	1369
that they *m* go, and fall backward,	Is 28:13	
that are near, acknowledge my *m*	Is 33:13	1369
names by the greatness of his *m*	Is 40:26	202
to them that have no *m* he	Is 40:29	202
that they *m* be called trees of	Is 61:3	
the LORD, that he *m* be glorified	Is 61:3	
that the mountains *m* flow down at	Is 64:1	
that I *m* weep day and night for	Jer 9:1	
that I *m* leave my people, and go	Jer 9:2	
let the mighty man glory in his *m*	Jer 9:23	1369
great, and thy name is great in *m*	Jer 10:6	1369
that they *m* be unto me for a	Jer 13:11	
them to know mine hand and my *m*	Jer 16:21	1369
neck stiff, that they *m* not hear	Jer 17:23	
that they *m* not hear my words	Jer 19:15	
or that my mother *m* have been my	Jer 20:17	
that ye *m* provoke me to anger	Jer 25:7	
Thus *m* we procure great evil	Jer 26:19	
that I *m* drive you out, and that	Jer 27:15	
you out, and that ye *m* perish	Jer 27:15	
that they *m* put us to death, and	Jer 43:3	
that ye *m* cut yourselves off, and	Jer 44:8	
that ye *m* be a curse and a	Jer 44:8	
bow of Elam, the chief of their *m*	Jer 49:35	1369
their *m* hath failed	Jer 51:30	1369
that he *m* water it by the furrows	Eze 17:7	
that it *m* bring forth branches,	Eze 17:8	
that it *m* bear fruit	Eze 17:8	
that it *m* be a goodly vine	Eze 17:8	
That the kingdom *m* be base	Eze 17:14	
that it *m* not lift itself up, but	Eze 17:14	
of his covenant it *m* stand	Eze 17:14	
that they *m* give him horses and	Eze 17:15	
that they *m* know that I am the	Eze 20:12	
that I *m* make them desolate	Eze 20:26	
to the end that they *m* know that	Eze 20:26	
That it *m* cause fury to come up	Eze 24:8	
which with their *m* are laid by	Eze 32:29	1369
they are ashamed of their *m*	Eze 32:30	1369
that ye *m* be a possession unto	Eze 36:3	
for to the intent that I *m* shew	Eze 40:4	
about, that they *m* have hold	Eze 41:6	
whom they *m* teach the learning and	Dan 1:4	
they *m* stand before the king	Dan 1:5	
that he *m* not defile himself	Dan 1:8	
for wisdom and *m* are his	Dan 2:20	1370
who hast given me wisdom and *m*	Dan 2:23	1370
that they *m* not serve nor worship	Dan 3:28	
that they *m* make known unto me	Dan 4:6	
the kingdom by the *m* of my power	Dan 4:30	8632
his concubines, *m* drink therein	Dan 5:2	
that the princes *m* give accounts	Dan 6:2	
that the purpose *m* not be changed	Dan 6:17	
that no beasts *m* stand before him	Dan 8:4	
that they *m* not obey thy voice	Dan 9:11	
our God, that we *m* turn from our	Dan 9:13	
girl for wine, that they *m* drink	Joel 3:3	
that ye *m* remove them far from	Joel 3:6	
that they *m* enlarge their border	Amos 1:13	
till he *m* see what would become	Jonah 4:5	
that it *m* be a shadow over his	Jonah 4:6	
the LORD, and of judgment, and of *m*	Mic 3:8	1369
and be confounded at all their *m*	Mic 7:16	1369
that I *m* rest in the day of	Hab 3:16	
unto Zerubbabel, saying, Not by *m*	Zec 4:6	2428
sought to go that they *m* walk to	Zec 6:7	
laid, that the temple *m* be built	Zec 8:9	
that I *m* break my covenant which	Zec 11:10	
that I *m* break the brotherhood	Zec 11:14	
that my covenant *m* be with Levi	Mal 2:4	
That he *m* seek a godly seed	Mal 2:15	
that it *m* be fulfilled which was	Mt 1:22	
that it *m* be fulfilled which was	Mt 2:15	
that it *m* be fulfilled which was	Mt 2:23	
That it *m* be fulfilled which was	Mt 4:14	
That it *m* be fulfilled which was	Mt 8:17	
so that no man *m* pass by that way	Mt 8:28	*2480*
that they *m* accuse him	Mt 12:10	
him, how they *m* destroy him	Mt 12:14	
That it *m* be fulfilled which was	Mt 12:17	
That it *m* be fulfilled which was	Mt 13:35	
besought him that they *m* only	Mt 14:36	
that it *m* be fulfilled which was	Mt 21:4	
afterward, that ye *m* believe him	Mt 21:32	
that they *m* receive the fruits of	Mt 21:34	
took counsel how they *m* entangle	Mt 22:15	
consulted that they *m* take Jesus	Mt 26:4	
For this ointment *m* have been	Mt 26:9	*1410*
of the prophets *m* be fulfilled	Mt 26:56	
that it *m* be fulfilled which was	Mt 27:35	
that they *m* accuse him	Mk 3:2	
him, how they *m* destroy him	Mk 3:6	
that he *m* send them forth to	Mk 3:14	
prayed him that he *m* be with him	Mk 5:18	
besought him that they *m* touch if	Mk 6:56	
that I *m* receive my sight	Mk 10:51	
if haply he *m* find any thing	Mk 11:13	
and sought how they *m* destroy him	Mk 11:18	
that he *m* receive from the	Mk 12:2	
how they *m* take him by craft	Mk 14:1	
For it *m* have been sold for more	Mk 14:5	*1410*
he sought how he *m* conveniently	Mk 14:11	
the hour *m* pass from him	Mk 14:35	
sweet spices, that they *m* come	Mk 16:1	
enemies *m* serve him without fear	Lk 1:74	
that they *m* cast him down	Lk 4:29	
m bring him in because of the	Lk 5:19	
that they *m* find an accusation	Lk 6:7	
another what they *m* do to Jesus	Lk 6:11	
saying, What *m* this parable be	Lk 8:9	
that seeing they *m* not see	Lk 8:10	
hearing they *m* not understand	Lk 8:10	
him that he *m* be with him	Lk 8:38	
his mouth, that they *m* accuse him	Lk 11:54	
that I *m* make merry with my	Lk 15:29	
ye *m* say unto this sycamine tree,	Lk 17:6	
that he *m* know how much every man	Lk 19:15	
that at my coming I *m* have	Lk 19:23	
And could not find what they *m* do	Lk 19:48	
that they *m* take hold of his	Lk 20:20	
that so they *m* deliver him unto	Lk 20:20	
sought how they *m* kill him	Lk 22:2	
how he *m* betray him unto them	Lk 22:4	
requiring that he *m* be crucified	Lk 23:23	
that he *m* bear it after Jesus	Lk 23:26	
that they *m* understand the	Lk 24:45	
all men through him *m* believe	Jn 1:7	
the world through him *m* be saved	Jn 3:17	
things I say, that ye *m* be saved	Jn 5:34	
come to me, that ye *m* have life	Jn 5:40	
that we *m* work the works of God	Jn 6:28	
that they *m* have to accuse him	Jn 8:6	
he, Lord, that I *m* believe on him	Jn 9:36	
that they which see not *m* see	Jn 9:39	
they which see *m* be made blind	Jn 9:39	
I am come that they *m* have life	Jn 10:10	
life, and that they *m* have it more	Jn 10:10	
my life, that I *m* take it again	Jn 10:17	
of God, that the Son of God *m* be	Jn 11:4	
shew it, that they *m* take him	Jn 11:57	
but that they *m* see Lazarus also,	Jn 12:9	
they *m* put Lazarus also to death	Jn 12:10	
Esaias the prophet *m* be fulfilled	Jn 12:38	
it is come to pass, ye *m* believe	Jn 14:29	
that my joy *m* remain in you, and	Jn 15:11	
you, and that your joy *m* be full	Jn 15:11	
that the word *m* be fulfilled that	Jn 15:25	
you, that in me ye *m* have peace	Jn 16:33	
that they *m* know thee the only	Jn 17:3	
that the scripture *m* be fulfilled	Jn 17:12	
that they *m* have my joy fulfilled	Jn 17:13	
that they also *m* be sanctified	Jn 17:19	
That the saying *m* be fulfilled	Jn 18:9	
but that they *m* eat the passover	Jn 18:28	
saying of Jesus *m* be fulfilled	Jn 18:32	
that the scripture *m* be fulfilled	Jn 19:24	
that the scripture *m* be fulfilled	Jn 19:28	
that their legs *m* be broken	Jn 19:31	
that they *m* be taken away	Jn 19:31	
he saith true, that ye *m* believe	Jn 19:35	
besought Pilate that he *m* take	Jn 19:38	
that ye *m* believe that Jesus is	Jn 20:31	
that believing ye *m* have life	Jn 20:31	
that he *m* go to his own place	Acts 1:25	
nothing how they *m* punish them	Acts 4:21	
by *m* overshadow some of them	Acts 5:15	
to the end they *m* not live	Acts 7:19	
that they *m* receive the Holy	Acts 8:15	
he *m* bring them bound unto	Acts 9:2	
that he *m* receive his sight	Acts 9:12	
that he *m* bring them bound unto	Acts 9:21	
besought that these words *m* be	Acts 13:42	
of men *m* seek after the Lord	Acts 15:17	
if haply they *m* feel after him,	Acts 17:27	
so that I *m* finish my course with	Acts 20:24	
that he *m* know wherefore they	Acts 22:24	
him of Paul, that he *m* loose him	Acts 24:26	
kept till I *m* send him to Caesar	Acts 25:21	
I *m* have somewhat to write	Acts 25:26	
This man *m* have been set at	Acts 26:32	*1410*
means they *m* attain to Phenice	Acts 27:12	*1410*
I *m* have a prosperous journey by	Rom 1:10	
that I *m* have some fruit among	Rom 1:13	
that he *m* be just, and the	Rom 3:26	
that he *m* be the father of all	Rom 4:11	
that righteousness *m* be imputed	Rom 4:11	
of faith, that it *m* be by grace	Rom 4:16	
to the end the promise *m* be sure	Rom 4:16	
that he *m* become the father of	Rom 4:18	
that the offence *m* abound	Rom 5:20	
even so *m* grace reign through	Rom 5:21	
the body of sin *m* be destroyed	Rom 6:6	
that it *m* appear sin, working	Rom 7:13	
m become exceeding sinful	Rom 7:13	
of the law *m* be fulfilled in us	Rom 8:4	
that he *m* be the firstborn among	Rom 8:29	
God according to election *m* stand	Rom 9:11	
that I *m* shew my power in thee,	Rom 9:17	
that my name *m* be declared	Rom 9:17	
that he *m* make known the riches	Rom 9:23	
Israel is, that they *m* be saved	Rom 10:1	
my flesh, and *m* save some of them	Rom 11:14	
off, that I *m* be graffed in	Rom 11:19	
that he *m* have mercy upon all	Rom 11:32	
that he *m* be Lord both of the	Rom 14:9	
of the scriptures *m* have hope	Rom 15:4	
that the Gentiles *m* glorify God	Rom 15:9	
of the Gentiles *m* be acceptable	Rom 15:16	
that we *m* know the things that	1Cor 2:12	
that ye *m* learn in us not to	1Cor 4:6	
that we also *m* reign with you	1Cor 4:8	
he that hath done this deed *m* be	1Cor 5:2	
unto all, that I *m* gain the more	1Cor 9:19	
as a Jew, that I *m* gain the Jews	1Cor 9:20	
that I *m* gain them that are under	1Cor 9:20	
that I *m* gain them that are	1Cor 9:21	
I as weak, that I *m* gain the weak	1Cor 9:22	
that I *m* by all means save some	1Cor 9:22	
that I *m* be partaker thereof with	1Cor 9:23	
by my voice I *m* teach others also	1Cor 14:19	
that ye *m* have a second benefit	2Cor 1:15	
but that ye *m* know the love which	2Cor 2:4	
that I *m* know the proof of you,	2Cor 2:9	
that the life also of Jesus *m* be	2Cor 4:10	
that the life also of Jesus *m* be	2Cor 4:11	
that the abundant grace *m* through	2Cor 4:15	
that mortality *m* be swallowed up	2Cor 5:4	
that we *m* be made the	2Cor 5:21	
that ye *m* receive damage by us in	2Cor 7:9	
sight of God *m* appear unto you	2Cor 7:12	
ye through his poverty *m* be rich	2Cor 8:9	
before, that the same *m* be ready	2Cor 9:5	
accepted, ye *m* well bear with him	2Cor 11:4	
myself that ye *m* be exalted	2Cor 11:7	
thrice, that it *m* depart from me	2Cor 12:8	
that he *m* deliver us from this	Gal 1:4	
that I *m* preach him among the	Gal 1:16	
that they *m* bring us into bondage	Gal 2:4	
of the gospel *m* continue with you	Gal 2:5	
that we *m* be justified by the	Gal 2:16	
the law, that I *m* live unto God	Gal 2:19	
m come on the Gentiles through	Gal 3:14	
that we *m* receive the promise of	Gal 3:14	
by faith of Jesus Christ *m* be	Gal 3:22	
that we *m* be justified by faith	Gal 3:24	
that we *m* receive the adoption of	Gal 4:5	

you, that ye *m* affect them ... Gal 4:17
he *m* gather together in one all ... Eph 1:10
all principality, and power, and *m* ... Eph 1:21 *1411*
That in the ages to come he *m* ... Eph 2:7
that he *m* reconcile both unto God ... Eph 2:16
powers in heavenly places *m* be ... Eph 3:10
to be strengthened with *m* by his ... Eph 3:16 *1411*
that ye *m* be filled with all the ... Eph 3:19
that he *m* fill all things ... Eph 4:10
That he *m* sanctify and cleanse it ... Eph 5:26
That he *m* present it to himself a ... Eph 5:27
Lord, and in the power of his *m* ... Eph 6:10 *2479*
that ye *m* know our affairs, and ... Eph 6:22
that he *m* comfort your hearts ... Eph 6:22
Though I *m* also have confidence ... Phil 3:4
whereof he *m* trust in the flesh ... Phil 3:4
If by any means I *m* attain unto ... Phil 3:11
to desire that ye *m* be filled ... Col 1:9
That ye *m* walk worthy of the Lord ... Col 1:10
Strengthened with all *m*, ... Col 1:11 *1411*
things he *m* have the preeminence ... Col 1:18
That their hearts *m* be comforted ... Col 2:2
that he *m* know your estate, and ... Col 4:8
when we *m* have been burdensome, ... 1Th 2:6 *1410*
the Gentiles that they *m* be saved ... 1Th 2:16
that we *m* see your face ... 1Th 3:10
m perfect that which is lacking ... 1Th 3:10
that he *m* be revealed in his time ... 2Th 2:6
the truth, that they *m* be saved ... 2Th 2:10
That they all *m* be damned who ... 2Th 2:12
that we *m* not be chargeable to ... 2Th 3:8
m shew forth all longsuffering ... 1Ti 1:16
me the preaching *m* be fully known ... 2Ti 4:17
and that all the Gentiles *m* hear ... 2Ti 4:17
that he *m* redeem us from all ... Titus 2:14
God *m* be careful to maintain good ... Titus 3:8
though I *m* be much bold in Christ ... Philem 8
that in thy stead he *m* have ... Philem 13
that through death he *m* destroy ... Heb 2:14
that he *m* be a merciful and ... Heb 2:17
we *m* have a strong consolation, ... Heb 6:18
they which are called *m* receive ... Heb 9:15
of God, ye *m* receive the promise ... Heb 10:36
they *m* have had opportunity to ... Heb 11:15
that they *m* obtain a better ... Heb 11:35
that we *m* be partakers of his ... Heb 12:10
unto the mount that *m* be touched ... Heb 12:18
that he *m* sanctify the people ... Heb 13:12
earnestly that it *m* not rain ... Jas 5:17
m be found unto praise and honour ... 1Pet 1:7
your faith and hope *m* be in God ... 1Pet 1:21
that he *m* bring us to God, being ... 1Pet 3:18
that they *m* be judged according ... 1Pet 4:6
that by these ye *m* be partakers ... 2Pet 1:4
which are greater in power and *m* ... 2Pet 2:11 *1411*
that they *m* be made manifest that ... 1Jn 2:19
that he *m* destroy the works of ... 1Jn 3:8
that we *m* live through him ... 1Jn 4:9
that we *m* be fellowhelpers to the ... 3Jn 8
and honour, and power, and *m* ... Rev 7:12 *2479*
eagle, that she *m* fly into the ... Rev 12:14
that he *m* cause her to be carried ... Rev 12:15
And that no man *m* buy or sell ... Rev 13:17 *1410*
kings of the east *m* be prepared ... Rev 16:12

MIGHTEST

that thou *m* know that the LORD he ... Deut 4:35
That thou *m* fear the LORD thy God ... Deut 6:2
wherewith thou *m* be bound to ... Judg 16:6
thee, wherewith thou *m* be bound ... Judg 16:10
tell me wherewith thou *m* be bound ... Judg 16:13
down that thou *m* see the battle ... 1Sa 17:28
that thou *m* bring them again unto ... Neh 9:29
that thou *m* still the enemy and ... Ps 8:2
that thou *m* be justified when ... Ps 51:4
that thou *m* answer the words of ... Prov 22:21
that thou *m* know the thoughts of ... Dan 2:30
thou *m* be profited by me ... Mt 15:5
thou *m* be profited by me ... Mk 7:11
That thou *m* know the certainty of ... Lk 1:4
that thou *m* receive thy sight, and ... Acts 9:17
That thou *m* be justified in thy ... Rom 3:4
m overcome when thou art judged ... Rom 3:4
that thou *m* charge some that they ... 1Ti 1:3
that thou by them *m* war a good ... 1Ti 1:18

MIGHTIER

for thou art much *m* than we ... Gen 26:16 6105
of Israel are more and *m* than we ... Ex 1:9 6099
a greater nation and *m* than they ... Num 14:12 6099
m than thou art, to bring thee in ... Deut 4:38 6099
nations greater and *m* than thou ... Deut 7:1 6099
m than thyself, cities great and ... Deut 9:1 6099
and I will make of thee a nation *m* ... Deut 9:14 6099
nations and *m* than yourselves ... Deut 11:23 6099
The LORD on high is *m* than the ... Ps 93:4 117
with him that is *m* than he ... Eccl 6:10 8623
that cometh after me is *m* than I ... Mt 3:11 *2478*
cometh one *m* than I after me ... Mk 1:7 *2478*
but one *m* than I cometh, the ... Lk 3:16 *2478*

MIGHTIES

who was one of the three *m* ... 1Chr 11:12 1368
and had the name among the three *m*. 1Chr 11:24 1368

MIGHTIEST

These things did these three *m* ... 1Chr 11:19 1368

MIGHTILY

thee, and that ye may increase *m* ... Deut 6:3 3966
twenty years he *m* oppressed the ... Judg 4:3 2393
of the LORD came *m* upon him ... Judg 14:6
of the LORD came *m* upon him ... Judg 15:14
he shall *m* roar upon his ... Jer 25:30
with sackcloth, and cry *m* unto God ... Jonah 3:8 2393
loins strong, fortify thy power *m* ... Nah 2:1 3966
For he *m* convinced the Jews, and ... Acts 18:28 *2159*
So *m* grew the word of God and ... Acts 19:20
working, which worketh in me *m* ... Col 1:29
he cried *m* with a strong voice, ... Rev 18:2

MIGHTY

the same became *m* men which were ... Gen 6:4 1368
began to be a *m* one in the earth ... Gen 10:8 1368
He was a *m* hunter before the LORD ... Gen 10:9 1368
Even as Nimrod the *m* hunter ... Gen 10:9 1368
m nation, and all the nations of ... Gen 18:18 6099
thou art a *m* prince among us ... Gen 23:6 430
the hands of the *m* God of Jacob ... Gen 49:24 46
multiplied, and waxed exceeding *m* ... Ex 1:7 6105
multiplied, and waxed very *m* ... Ex 1:20 6105
let you go, no, not by a *m* hand ... Ex 3:19 2389
there be no more *m* thunderings ... Ex 9:28 430
LORD turned a *m* strong west wind ... Ex 10:19 3966
they sank as lead in the *m* waters ... Ex 15:10 117
the *m* men of Moab, trembling ... Ex 15:15 352
great power, and with a *m* hand ... Ex 32:11 2389
nor honour the person of the *m* ... Lev 19:15 1419
for they are too *m* for me ... Num 22:6 6099
thy greatness, and thy *m* hand ... Deut 3:24 2389
and by war, and by a *m* hand ... Deut 4:34 2389
with his *m* power out of Egypt ... Deut 4:37 1419
thee out thence through a *m* hand ... Deut 5:15 2389
us out of Egypt with a *m* hand ... Deut 6:21 2389
brought you out with a *m* hand ... Deut 7:8 2389
the *m* hand, and the stretched out ... Deut 7:19 2389
is among you, a *m* God and terrible ... Deut 7:21 1419
destroy them with a *m* destruction ... Deut 7:23 1419
forth out of Egypt with a *m* hand ... Deut 9:26 2389
broughtest out by thy *m* power ... Deut 9:29 1419
Lord of lords, a great God, a *m* ... Deut 10:17 1368
his *m* hand, and his stretched out ... Deut 11:2 2389
became there a nation, great, *m* ... Deut 26:5 6099
forth out of Egypt with a *m* hand ... Deut 26:8 2389
And in all that *m* hand, and in all ... Deut 34:12 2389
all the *m* men of valour, and help ... Josh 1:14 1368
hand of the LORD, that it is *m* ... Josh 4:24 2389
thereof, and the *m* men of valour ... Josh 6:2 1368
thirty thousand *m* men of valour ... Josh 8:3 1368
Ai, and all the men thereof were *m* ... Josh 10:2 1368
him, and all the *m* men of valour ... Josh 10:7 1368
made me have dominion over the *m* ... Judg 5:13 1368
the pransings of their *m* ones ... Judg 5:22 47
help of the LORD against the *m* ... Judg 5:23 1368
with thee, thou *m* man of valour ... Judg 6:12 1368
Gileadite was a *m* man of valour ... Judg 11:1 1368
a *m* man of wealth, of the family ... Ruth 2:1 1368
The bows of the *m* men are broken ... 1Sa 2:4 1368
out of the hand of these *m* Gods ... 1Sa 4:8 117
a Benjamite, a *m* man of power ... 1Sa 9:1 1368
a *m* valiant man, and a man of war, ... 1Sa 16:18 1368
how are the *m* fallen ... 2Sa 1:19 1368
of the *m* is vilely cast away ... 2Sa 1:21 1368
the slain, from the fat of the *m* ... 2Sa 1:22 1368
How are the *m* fallen in the midst ... 2Sa 1:25 1368
How are the *m* fallen, and the ... 2Sa 1:27 1368
and all the host of the *m* men ... 2Sa 10:7 1368
all the *m* men were on his right ... 2Sa 16:6 1368
and his men, that they be *m* men ... 2Sa 17:8 1368
that thy father is a *m* man ... 2Sa 17:10 1368
the Pelethites, and all the *m* men ... 2Sa 20:7 1368
names of the *m* men whom David had ... 2Sa 23:8 1368
one of the three *m* men with David ... 2Sa 23:9 1368
the three *m* men brake through the ... 2Sa 23:16 1368
things did these three *m* men ... 2Sa 23:17 1368
the name among three *m* men ... 2Sa 23:22 1368
the *m* men which belonged to David ... 1Kin 1:8 1368
prophet, and Benaiah, and the *m* men . 1Kin 1:10 1368
Jeroboam was a *m* man of valour ... 1Kin 11:28 1368
he was also a *m* man in valour ... 2Kin 5:1 1368
even of all the *m* men of wealth ... 2Kin 15:20 1368
all the *m* men of valour, even ten ... 2Kin 24:14 1368
the *m* of the land, those carried ... 2Kin 24:15 193
he began to be *m* upon the earth ... 1Chr 1:10 1368
m men of valour, famous men, and ... 1Chr 5:24 1368
of their fathers, *m* men of valour ... 1Chr 7:7 1368
m men of valour, was twenty ... 1Chr 7:9 1368
m men of valour, were seventeen ... 1Chr 7:11 1368
m men of valour, chief of the ... 1Chr 7:40 1368
sons of Ulam were *m* men of valour ... 1Chr 8:40 1368
chief of the *m* men whom David had ... 1Chr 11:10 1368
of the *m* men whom David had ... 1Chr 11:11 1368
and they were among the *m* men ... 1Chr 12:1 1368
a *m* man among the thirty, and over ... 1Chr 12:4 1368
for they were all *m* men of valour ... 1Chr 12:21 1368
m men of valour for the war, ... 1Chr 12:25 1368
And Zadok, a young man *m* of valour ... 1Chr 12:28 1368
hundred, *m* men of valour, famous ... 1Chr 12:30 1368
and all the host of the *m* men ... 1Chr 19:8 1368
for they were men of valour ... 1Chr 26:6 1368
them *m* men of valour at Jazer of ... 1Chr 26:31 1368
who was *m* among the thirty, and ... 1Chr 27:6 1368
the officers, and with the *m* men ... 1Chr 28:1 1368
And all the princes, and the *m* men ... 1Chr 29:24 1368
thy *m* hand, and thy stretched out ... 2Chr 6:32 2389
chosen men, being *m* men of valour ... 2Chr 13:3 1368
But Abijah waxed *m*, and married ... 2Chr 13:21 2388
all these were *m* men of valour ... 2Chr 14:8 1368
of war, *m* men of valour, were in ... 2Chr 17:13 1368
with him *m* men of valour three ... 2Chr 17:14 1368
hundred thousand *m* men of valour ... 2Chr 17:16 1368
Eliada a *m* man of valour, and with ... 2Chr 17:17 1368
hired also an hundred thousand *m* ... 2Chr 25:6 1368
m men of valour were two thousand ... 2Chr 26:12 1368
that made war with *m* power ... 2Chr 26:13 2428
So Jotham became *m*, because he ... 2Chr 27:6 2388
a *m* man of Ephraim, slew Maaseiah ... 2Chr 28:7 1368
his *m* men to stop the waters of ... 2Chr 32:3 1368
cut off all the *m* men of valour ... 2Chr 32:21 1368
There have been *m* kings also over ... Ezr 4:20 8624
before all the king's *m* princes ... Ezr 7:28 1368
made, and unto the house of the *m* ... Neh 3:16 1368
as a stone into the *m* waters ... Neh 9:11 5794
our God, the great, the *m* ... Neh 9:32 1368
m men of valour, an hundred ... Neh 11:14 1368
mouth, and from the hand of the *m* ... Job 5:15 2389
Redeem me from the hand of the *m* ... Job 6:23 6184
wise in heart, and *m* in strength ... Job 9:4 533
spoiled, and overthroweth the *m* ... Job 12:19 386
weakeneth the strength of the *m* ... Job 12:21 650
become old, yea, are *m* in power ... Job 21:7 1396
But as for the *m* man, he had the ... Job 22:8 2220
draweth also the *m* with his power ... Job 24:22 47
the *m* shall be taken away without ... Job 34:20 47
in pieces *m* men without number ... Job 34:24 3524
out by reason of the arm of the *m* ... Job 35:9 7227
Behold, God is *m*, and despiseth ... Job 36:5 3524
he is *m* in strength and wisdom ... Job 36:5 3524
up himself, the *m* are afraid ... Job 41:25 410
and *m*, the LORD *m* in battle ... Ps 24:8 1368
Give unto the LORD, O ye *m* ... Ps 29:1
a *m* man is not delivered by much ... Ps 33:16 1368
sword upon thy thigh, O most *m* ... Ps 45:3 1368
The *m* God, even the LORD, hath ... Ps 50:1 410
thou thyself in mischief, O *m* man ... Ps 52:1 1368
the *m* are gathered against me ... Ps 59:3 5794
out his voice, and that a *m* voice ... Ps 68:33 5797
mine enemies wrongfully, are *m* ... Ps 69:4 6105
thou driedst up *m* rivers ... Ps 74:15 386
like a *m* man that shouteth by ... Ps 78:65 1368
in the congregation of the *m* ... Ps 82:1 410
who among the sons of the *m* can ... Ps 89:6 410
Thou hast a *m* arm ... Ps 89:13 1369
have laid help upon one that is *m* ... Ps 89:19 1368
the reproach of all the *m* people ... Ps 89:50 7227
than the *m* waves of the sea ... Ps 93:4 117
can utter the *m* acts of the LORD ... Ps 106:2 1369
make his *m* power to be known ... Ps 106:8 1369
His seed shall be *m* upon earth ... Ps 112:2 1368
Sharp arrows of the *m*, with coals ... Ps 120:4 1368
arrows are in the hand of a *m* man ... Ps 127:4 1368
and vowed unto the *m* God of Jacob .. Ps 132:2 46
habitation for the *m* God of Jacob ... Ps 132:5 46
great nations, and slew *m* kings ... Ps 135:10 6099
and shall declare thy *m* acts ... Ps 145:4 1369
to the sons of men his *m* acts ... Ps 145:12 1369
Praise him for his *m* acts ... Ps 150:2 1369
to anger is better than the *m* ... Prov 16:32 1368
cease, and parteth between the *m* ... Prov 18:18 6099
man scaleth the city of the *m* ... Prov 21:22 1368
For their redeemer is *m* ... Prov 23:11 2389
the wise more than ten *m* men ... Eccl 7:19 7989
bucklers, all shields of *m* men ... Song 4:4 1368
the *m* One of Israel, Ah, I will ... Is 1:24 46
The *m* man, and the man of war, the ... Is 3:2 1368
by the sword, and thy *m* in the war ... Is 3:25 1369
the *m* man shall be humbled, and ... Is 5:15 376
them that are *m* to drink wine ... Is 5:22 1368
Wonderful, Counsellor, The *m* God ... Is 9:6 1368
remnant of Jacob, unto the *m* God ... Is 10:21 1368
and Lebanon shall fall by a *m* one ... Is 10:34 117
with his *m* wind shall he shake ... Is 11:15 5868
called my *m* ones for mine anger ... Is 13:3 1368
like the rushing of *m* waters ... Is 17:12 3524
the *m* men of the children of ... Is 21:17 1368
thee away with a *m* captivity ... Is 22:17 1397
Behold, the Lord hath a *m* ... Is 28:2 2389
storm, as a flood of *m* waters ... Is 28:2 3524
the LORD, to the *m* One of Israel ... Is 30:29 6697
with the sword, not of a *m* man ... Is 31:8 376
LORD shall go forth as a *m* man ... Is 42:13 1368
sea, and a path in the *m* waters ... Is 43:16 5794
the prey be taken from the *m* ... Is 49:24 1368
of the *m* shall be taken away ... Is 49:25 1368
thy Redeemer, the *m* One of Jacob ... Is 49:26 46
thy Redeemer, the *m* One of Jacob ... Is 60:16 46
speak in righteousness, *m* to save ... Is 63:1 7227
it is a *m* nation, it is an ... Jer 5:15 386
sepulchre, they are all *m* men ... Jer 5:16 1368
neither let the *m* man glory in ... Jer 9:23 1368
as a *m* man that cannot save ... Jer 14:9 1368
is with me as a *m* terrible one ... Jer 20:11 1368
the king, with all his *m* men ... Jer 26:21 1368
the Great, the *M* God, the LORD of ... Jer 32:18 1368
Great in counsel, and *m* in work ... Jer 32:19 7227
m things, which thou knowest not ... Jer 33:3 1219
even *m* men of war, and the women, ... Jer 41:16 1397
their *m* ones are beaten down, and ... Jer 46:5 1368
flee away, nor the *m* man escape ... Jer 46:6 1368
and let the *m* men come forth ... Jer 46:9 1368
for the *m* man hath stumbled ... Jer 46:12 1368
man hath stumbled against the *m* ... Jer 46:12 1368
How say ye, We are *m* and strong ... Jer 48:14 1368
the *m* men's hearts in Moab at ... Jer 48:41 1368
m men of Edom be as the heart of ... Jer 49:22 1368
shall be as of a *m* expert man ... Jer 50:9 1368
a sword is upon her *m* men ... Jer 50:36 1368
The *m* men of Babylon have forborn ... Jer 51:30 1368
her *m* men are taken, every one of ... Jer 51:56 1368
and her rulers, and her *m* men ... Jer 51:57 1368
all my *m* men in the midst of me ... Lam 1:15 47
hath also taken the *m* of the land ... Eze 17:13 352
shall Pharaoh with his *m* army ... Eze 17:17 1419
Lord GOD, surely with a *m* hand ... Eze 20:33 2389
ye are scattered, with a *m* hand ... Eze 20:34 2389
hand of the *m* one of the heathen ... Eze 31:11 410
By the swords of the *m* will I ... Eze 32:12 1368
The strong among the *m* shall ... Eze 32:21 1368
with the *m* that are fallen of the ... Eze 32:27 1368
the *m* in the land of the living ... Eze 32:27 1368
a great company, and a *m* army ... Eze 38:15 7227
Ye shall eat the flesh of the *m* ... Eze 39:18 1368
horses and chariots, with *m* men ... Eze 39:20 1368
he commanded the most *m* men that ... Dan 3:20 1401

and how *m* are his wonders — Dan 4:3 — 8624
And his power shall be *m*, but not — Dan 8:24 — 6105
practise, and shall destroy the *m* — Dan 8:24 — 6099
the land of Egypt with a *m* hand — Dan 9:15 — 2389
a *m* king shall stand up, that — Dan 11:3 — 1368
with a very great and *m* army — Dan 11:25 — 6099
in the multitude of thy *m* men — Hos 10:13 — 1368
They shall run like *m* men — Joel 2:7 — 1368
Prepare war, wake up the *m* men — Joel 3:9 — 1368
cause thy *m* ones to come down — Joel 3:11 — 1368
shall the *m* deliver himself — Amos 2:14 — 1368
m shall flee away naked in that — Amos 2:16 — 1368
transgressions and your *m* sins — Amos 5:12 — 6099
and righteousness as a *m* stream — Amos 5:24 — 386
And thy *m* men, O Teman, shall be — Obad 9 — 1368
there was a *m* tempest in the sea, — Jonah 1:4 — 1419
shield of his *m* men is made red — Nah 2:3 — 1368
O *m* God, thou hast established — Hab 1:12 — 6697
the *m* man shall cry there — Zeph 1:14 — 1368
thy God in the midst of thee is *m* — Zeph 3:17 — 1368
made thee as the sword of a *m* man — Zec 9:13 — 1368
And they shall be as *m* men — Zec 10:5 — 1368
of Ephraim shall be like a *m* man — Zec 10:7 — 1368
because the *m* are spoiled — Zec 11:2 — 117
most of his *m* works were done — Mt 11:20 — *1411*
for if the *m* works, which were — Mt 11:21 — *1411*
for if the *m* works, which have — Mt 11:23 — *1411*
man this wisdom, and these *m* works — Mt 13:54 — *1411*
he did not many *m* works there — Mt 13:58 — *1411*
therefore *m* works do shew forth — Mt 14:2 — *1411*
that even such *m* works are — Mk 6:2 — *1411*
And he could there do no *m* work — Mk 6:5 — *1411*
therefore *m* works do shew forth — Mk 6:14 — *1411*
For he that is *m* hath done to me — Lk 1:49 — *1415*
put down the *m* from their seats — Lk 1:52 — *1413*
all amazed at the *m* power of God — Lk 9:43 — *3168*
for if the *m* works had been done — Lk 10:13 — *1411*
there arose a *m* famine in that — Lk 15:14 — *2478*
the *m* works that they had seen — Lk 19:37 — *1411*
which was a prophet *m* in deed — Lk 24:19 — *1415*
heaven as of a rushing *m* wind — Acts 2:2 — *972*
was *m* in words and in deeds — Acts 7:22 — *1415*
m in the scriptures, came to — Acts 18:24 — *1415*
Through *m* signs and wonders, by — Rom 15:19 — *1411*
men after the flesh, not many *m* — 1Cor 1:26 — *1415*
confound the things which are *m* — 1Cor 1:27 — *2478*
but *m* through God to the pulling — 2Cor 10:4 — *1415*
in signs, and wonders, and *m* deeds — 2Cor 12:12 — *1411*
is not weak, but is *m* in you — 2Cor 13:3 — *1414*
the same was *m* in me toward the — Gal 2:8 — *1754*
to the working of his *m* power — Eph 1:19 — *2479*
from heaven with his *m* angels — 2Th 1:7 — *1411*
therefore under the *m* hand of God — 1Pet 5:6 — *2900*
when she is shaken of a *m* wind — Rev 6:13 — *3173*
the chief captains, and the *m* men — Rev 6:15 — *1415*
I saw another *m* angel come down — Rev 10:1 — *2478*
so *m* an earthquake, and so great — Rev 16:18 — *5082*
great city Babylon, that *m* city — Rev 18:10 — *2478*
a *m* angel took up a stone like a — Rev 18:21 — *2478*
and as the voice of *m* thunderings — Rev 19:6 — *2478*
captains, and the flesh of *m* men — Rev 19:18 — *2478*

MIGRON (*mi'-gron*) *A city in Benjamin.*
a pomegranate tree which is in *M* — 1Sa 14:2 — 4051
come to Aiath, he is passed to *M* — Is 10:28 — 4051

MIJAMIN (*mij'-a-min*) See MIAMIN.
1. A priest in David's time.
to Malchijah, the sixth to *M* — 1Chr 24:9 — 4326
2. A priest who renewed the covenant.
Meshullam, Abijah, and *M* — Neh 10:7 — 4326

MIKLOTH (*mik'-loth*)
1. A Benjamite in Jerusalem.
And *M* begat Shimeah — 1Chr 8:32 — 4732
and Ahio, and Zechariah, and *M* — 1Chr 9:37 — 4732
And *M* begat Shimeam — 1Chr 9:38 — 4732
2. A ruler of David's guard.
his course was *M* also the ruler — 1Chr 27:4 — 4732

MIKNEIAH (*mik-ne-i'-ah*) *A Levite musician.*
and Mattithiah, and Elipheleh, and *M* — 1Chr 15:18 — 4737
And Mattithiah, and Elipheleh, and *M* — 1Chr 15:21 — 4737

MILALAI (*mil'-a-lahee*) *A priest who purified the wall.*
brethren, Shemaiah, and Azarael, *M* — Neh 12:36 — 4450

MILCAH (*mil'-cah*)
1. Daughter of Haran.
and the name of Nahor's wife, *M* — Gen 11:29 — 4435
of Haran, the father of *M* — Gen 11:29 — 4435
told Abraham, saying, Behold, *M* — Gen 22:20 — 4435
these eight *M* did bear to Nahor — Gen 22:23 — 4435
who was born to Bethuel, son of *M* — Gen 24:15 — 4435
daughter of Bethuel the son of *M* — Gen 24:24 — 4435
Nahor's son, whom *M* bare unto him — Gen 24:47 — 4435
2. A daughter of Zelophehad.
were Mahlah, Noah, and Hoglah, *M* — Num 26:33 — 4435
Mahlah, Noah, and Hoglah, and *M* — Num 27:1 — 4435
Mahlah, Tirzah, and Hoglah, and *M* — Num 36:11 — 4435
Mahlah, and Noah, Hoglah, *M* — Josh 17:3 — 4435

MILCH
Thirty *m* camels with their colts, — Gen 32:15 — 3243
a new cart, and take two *m* kine — 1Sa 6:7 — 5763
and took two *m* kine, and tied them — 1Sa 6:10 — 5763

MILCHAM See MILCOM.

MILCOM (*mil'-com*) See MALCHAM, MOLECH.
Chief god of the Ammonites.
after *M* the abomination of the — 1Kin 11:5 — 4445
M the god of the children of — 1Kin 11:33 — 4445
for *M* the abomination of the — 2Kin 23:13 — 4445

MILDEW
and with blasting, and with *m* — Deut 28:22 — 3420
there be pestilence, blasting, *m* — 1Kin 8:37 — 3420
if there be blasting, or *m* — 2Chr 6:28 — 3420
smitten you with blasting and *m* — Amos 4:9 — 3420
smote you with blasting and with *m* — Hag 2:17 — 3420

MILE
shall compel thee to go a *m* — Mt 5:41 — *3400*

MILETUM (*mi-le'-tum*) See MILETUS. *A city in the Roman province of Caria.*
Trophimus have I left at *M* sick — 2Ti 4:20 — *3399*

MILETUS (*mi-le-tus*) See MILETUM. *Same as Miletum.*
and the next day we came to *M* — Acts 20:15 — *3399*
from *M* he sent to Ephesus, and — Acts 20:17 — *3399*

MILK
And he took butter, and *m*, and the — Gen 18:8 — 2461
wine, and his teeth white with *m* — Gen 49:12 — 2461
large, unto a land flowing with *m* — Ex 3:8 — 2461
unto a land flowing with *m* — Ex 3:17 — 2461
give thee, a land flowing with *m* — Ex 13:5 — 2461
seethe a kid in his mother's *m* — Ex 23:19 — 2461
Unto a land flowing with *m* — Ex 33:3 — 2461
seethe a kid in his mother's *m* — Ex 34:26 — 2461
it, a land that floweth with *m* — Lev 20:24 — 2461
us, and surely it floweth with *m* — Num 13:27 — 2461
a land which floweth with *m* — Num 14:8 — 2461
out of a land that floweth with *m* — Num 16:13 — 2461
into a land that floweth with *m* — Num 16:14 — 2461
in the land that floweth with *m* — Deut 6:3 — 2461
seed, a land that floweth with *m* — Deut 11:9 — 2461
seethe a kid in his mother's *m* — Deut 14:21 — 2461
even a land that floweth with *m* — Deut 26:9 — 2461
a land that floweth with *m* — Deut 26:15 — 2461
thee, a land that floweth with *m* — Deut 27:3 — 2461
fathers, that floweth with *m* — Deut 31:20 — 2461
m of sheep, with fat of lambs, and — Deut 32:14 — 2461
us, a land that floweth with *m* — Josh 5:6 — 2461
And she opened a bottle of *m* — Judg 4:19 — 2461
He asked water, and she gave him *m* — Judg 5:25 — 2461
Hast thou not poured me out as *m* — Job 10:10 — 2461
His breasts are full of *m* — Job 21:24 — 2461
have goats' *m* enough for thy food — Prov 27:27 — 2461
of *m* bringeth forth butter — Prov 30:33 — 2461
honey and *m* are under thy tongue — Song 4:11 — 2461
I have drunk my wine with my *m* — Song 5:1 — 2461
rivers of waters, washed with *m* — Song 5:12 — 2461
of *m* that they shall give — Is 7:22 — 2461
them that are weaned from the *m* — Is 28:9 — 2461
m without money and without price — Is 55:1 — 2461
also suck the *m* of the Gentiles — Is 60:16 — 2461
that ye may *m* out, and be — Is 66:11 — 4711
give them a land flowing with *m* — Jer 11:5 — 2461
give them, a land flowing with *m* — Jer 32:22 — 2461
snow, they were whiter than *m* — Lam 4:7 — 2461
espied for them, flowing with *m* — Eze 20:6 — 2461
I had given them, flowing with *m* — Eze 20:15 — 2461
fruit, and they shall drink thy *m* — Eze 25:4 — 2461
and the hills shall flow with *m* — Joel 3:18 — 2461
I have fed you with *m*, and not — 1Cor 3:2 — *1051*
eateth not of the *m* of the flock — 1Cor 9:7 — *1051*
are become such as have need of *m* — Heb 5:12 — *1051*
For every one that useth *m* is — Heb 5:13 — *1051*
desire the sincere *m* of the word — 1Pet 2:2 — *1051*

MILL
maidservant that is behind the *m* — Ex 11:5 — 7347
women shall be grinding at the *m* — Mt 24:41 — *3459*

MILLET
and beans, and lentiles, and *m* — Eze 4:9 — 1764

MILLIONS
thou the mother of thousands of *m* — Gen 24:60 — 7233

MILLO (*mil'-lo*)
1. A fort near Shechem.
together, and all the house of *M* — Judg 9:6 — 4407
men of Shechem, and the house of *M* — Judg 9:20 — 4407
Shechem, and from the house of *M* — Judg 9:20 — 4407
2. A fort near Jerusalem.
And David built round about from *M* — 2Sa 5:9 — 4407
the LORD, and his own house, and *M* — 1Kin 9:15 — 4407
then did he build *M* — 1Kin 9:24 — 4407
Solomon built *M*, and repaired the — 1Kin 11:27 — 4407
and slew Joash in the house of *M* — 2Kin 12:20 — 4407
about, even from *M* round about — 1Chr 11:8 — 4407
repaired *M* in the city of David, — 2Chr 32:5 — 4407

MILLS
and gathered it, and ground it in *m* — Num 11:8 — 7347

MILLSTONE
nether or the upper *m* to pledge — Deut 24:6 — 7347
of a *m* upon Abimelech's head — Judg 9:53 — 7393
of a *m* upon him from the wall — 2Sa 11:21 — 7393
hard as a piece of the nether *m* — Job 41:24
a *m* were hanged about his neck — Mt 18:6
a *m* were hanged about his neck — Mk 9:42
a *m* were hanged about his neck — Lk 17:2
took up a stone like a great *m* — Rev 18:21 — *3458*
the sound of a *m* shall be heard — Rev 18:22 — *3458*

MILLSTONES
Take the *m*, and grind meal — Is 47:2 — 7347
of the bride, the sound of the *m* — Jer 25:10 — 7347

MINCING
m as they go, and making a — Is 3:16 — 2952

MIND
If it be your *m* that I should — Gen 23:8 — 5315
were a grief of *m* unto Isaac — Gen 26:35 — 7307
that the *m* of the LORD might be — Lev 24:12 — 6310
have not done them of mine own *m* — Num 16:28 — 3820
either good or bad of mine own *m* — Num 24:13 — 3820
m unto the place which the LORD — Deut 18:6 — 5315
failing of eyes, and sorrow of *m* — Deut 28:65 — 5315
them to *m* among all the nations — Deut 30:1 — 3824
which is in mine heart and in my *m* — 1Sa 2:35 — 5315
days ago, set not thy *m* on them — 1Sa 9:20 — 3820
it was in my *m* to build an house — 1Chr 22:7 — 3824
perfect heart and with a willing *m* — 1Chr 28:9 — 5315
for the people had a *m* to work — Neh 4:6 — 3820
But he is in one *m*, and who can — Job 23:13
Should it be according to thy *m* — Job 34:33 — 5973
forgotten as a dead man out of *m* — Ps 31:12 — 3820
he bringeth it with a wicked *m* — Prov 21:27
A fool uttereth all his *m* — Prov 29:11 — 7307
whose *m* is stayed on thee — Is 26:3 — 3336
bring it again to *m*, O ye — Is 46:8 — 3820
be remembered, nor come into *m* — Is 65:17 — 3820
neither shall it come to *m* — Jer 3:16 — 3820
yet my *m* could not be toward this — Jer 15:1 — 5315
it, neither came it into my *m* — Jer 19:5 — 3820
not, neither came it into my *m* — Jer 32:35 — 3820
them, and came it not into his *m* — Jer 44:21 — 3820
and let Jerusalem come into your *m* — Jer 51:50 — 3824
This I recall to my *m*, therefore — Lam 3:21 — 3820
the things that come into your *m* — Eze 11:5 — 7307
into your *m* shall not be at all — Eze 20:32 — 7307
her *m* was alienated from them — Eze 23:17 — 5315
then my *m* was alienated from her, — Eze 23:18 — 5315
like as my *m* was alienated from — Eze 23:18 — 5315
from whom thy *m* is alienated — Eze 23:22 — 5315
them from whom thy *m* is alienated — Eze 23:28 — 5315
time shall things come into thy *m* — Eze 38:10 — 3824
came into thy *m* upon thy bed — Dan 2:29
his *m* hardened in pride, he was — Dan 5:20 — 7307
Then shall his *m* change, and he — Hab 1:11 — 7307
all thy soul, and with all thy *m* — Mt 22:37 — *1271*
and clothed, and in his right *m* — Mk 5:15 — *4993*
all thy soul, and with all thy *m* — Mk 12:30 — *1271*
Peter called to *m* the word that — Mk 14:72 — *363*
cast in her *m* what manner of — Lk 1:29
Jesus, clothed, and in his right *m* — Lk 8:35 — *4993*
thy strength, and with all thy *m* — Lk 10:27 — *1271*
neither be ye of doubtful *m* — Lk 12:29
the word with all readiness of *m* — Acts 17:11 — 4288
the Lord with all humility of *m* — Acts 20:19
gave them over to a reprobate *m* — Rom 1:28 — *3563*
warring against the law of my *m* — Rom 7:23 — *3563*
So then with the *m* I myself serve — Rom 7:25 — *3563*
do *m* the things of the flesh — Rom 8:5 — *5426*
Because the carnal *m* is enmity — Rom 8:7 — *5427*
what is the *m* of the Spirit — Rom 8:27 — *5427*
who hath known the *m* of the Lord — Rom 11:34 — *3563*
by the renewing of your *m* — Rom 12:2 — *3563*
Be of the same *m* one toward — Rom 12:16 — *5426*
M not high things, but condescend — Rom 12:16 — *5426*
be fully persuaded in his own *m* — Rom 14:5 — *3563*
That ye may with one *m* and one — Rom 15:6 — *3661*
in some sort, as putting you in *m* — Rom 15:15 — *1878*
joined together in the same *m* — 1Cor 1:10 — *3563*
who hath known the *m* of the Lord — 1Cor 2:16 — *3563*
But we have the *m* of Christ — 1Cor 2:16 — *3563*
your fervent *m* toward me — 2Cor 7:7
For if there be first a willing *m* — 2Cor 8:12 — 4288
and declaration of your ready *m* — 2Cor 8:19 — 4288
I know the forwardness of your *m* — 2Cor 9:2 — 4288
be of good comfort, be of one *m* — 2Cor 13:11 — *5426*
desires of the flesh and of the *m* — Eph 2:3 — *1271*
walk, in the vanity of their *m* — Eph 4:17 — *3563*
renewed in the spirit of your *m* — Eph 4:23 — *3563*
with one *m* striving together for — Phil 1:27 — *5590*
being of one accord, of one *m* — Phil 2:2 — *5426*
but in lowliness of *m* let each — Phil 2:3 — *5012*
Let this *m* be in you, which was — Phil 2:5 — *5426*
rule, let us *m* the same thing — Phil 3:16 — *5426*
their shame, who *m* earthly things — Phil 3:19 — *5426*
they be of the same *m* in the Lord — Phil 4:2 — *5426*
enemies in your *m* by wicked works — Col 1:21 — *1271*
vainly puffed up by his fleshly *m* — Col 2:18 — *3563*
kindness, humbleness of *m* — Col 3:12
That ye be not soon shaken in *m* — 2Th 2:2 — *3563*
and of love, and of a sound *m* — 2Ti 1:7 — *4995*
but even their *m* and conscience is — Titus 1:15 — *3563*
Put them in *m* to be subject to — Titus 3:1 — *5279*
But without thy *m* would I do — Philem 14 — *1106*
I will put my laws into their *m* — Heb 8:10 — *1271*
gird up the loins of your *m* — 1Pet 1:13 — *1271*
Finally, be ye all of one *m* — 1Pet 3:8 — *3675*
likewise with the same *m* — 1Pet 4:1 — *1771*
filthy lucre, but of a ready *m* — 1Pet 5:2 — *4290*
here is the *m* which hath wisdom — Rev 17:9 — *3563*
These have one *m*, and shall give — Rev 17:13 — *1106*

MINDED
was stedfastly *m* to go with her — Ruth 1:18
that Joash was *m* to repair the — 2Chr 24:4
which are *m* of their own freewill — Ezr 7:13
was *m* to put her away privily — Mt 1:19 — *1014*
shore, into the which they were *m* — Acts 27:39 — *1014*
For to be carnally *m* is death — Rom 8:6 — *5427*
but to be spiritually *m* is life — Rom 8:6 — *5427*
I was *m* to come unto you before — 2Cor 1:15 — *1014*
When I therefore was thus *m* — 2Cor 1:17 — *1011*
that ye will be none otherwise *m* — Gal 5:10 — *5426*
as many as be perfect, be thus *m* — Phil 3:15 — *5426*
if in any thing ye be otherwise *m* — Phil 3:15 — *5426*
men likewise exhort to be sober *m* — Titus 2:6 — *4993*
A double *m* man is unstable in all — Jas 1:8 — *1374*
purify your hearts, ye double *m* — Jas 4:8 — *1374*

MINDFUL
Be ye *m* always of his covenant — 1Chr 16:15 — 2142
neither were *m* of thy wonders — Neh 9:17 — 2142
is man, that thou art *m* of him — Ps 8:4 — 2142
he will ever be *m* of his covenant — Ps 111:5 — 2142
The LORD hath been *m* of us — Ps 115:12 — 2142
hast not been *m* of the rock of — Is 17:10 — 2142
being *m* of thy tears, that I may — 2Ti 1:4 — *3403*
is man, that thou art *m* of him — Heb 2:6 — *3403*
if they had been *m* of that — Heb 11:15 — *3421*

That ye may be *m* of the words 2Pet 3:2 *3403*

MINDING
appointed, *m* himself to go afoot Acts 20:13 *3195*

MINDS
it, take advice, and speak your *m* Judg 19:30
men, and they be chafed in their *m* 2Sa 17:8 5315
And Jehu said, If it be your *m* 2Kin 9:15 5315
that whereupon they set their *m* Eze 24:25 5315
their heart, with despiteful *m* Eze 36:5 5315
made their *m* evil affected Acts 14:2 *5590*
come to him, they changed their *m* Acts 28:6
But their *m* were blinded 2Cor 3:14 *3540*
the *m* of them which believe not 2Cor 4:4 *3540*
so your *m* should be corrupted 2Cor 11:3 *3540*
hearts and *m* through Christ Jesus Phil 4:7 *3540*
disputings of men of corrupt *m* 1Ti 6:5 *3563*
men of corrupt *m*, reprobate 2Ti 3:8 *3563*
in their *m* will I write them Heb 10:16 *1271*
ye be wearied and faint in your *m* Heb 12:3 *5590*
your pure *m* by way of remembrance 2Pet 3:1 *1271*

MINE
I have lift up *m* hand unto the Gen 14:22
one born in my house is *m* heir Gen 15:3
eat, until I have told *m* errand Gen 24:33
I had done speaking in *m* heart Gen 24:45
that I may go unto *m* own place Gen 30:25
I provide for *m* own house also Gen 30:30
that I lifted up *m* eyes, and saw Gen 31:10
and my sleep departed from *m* eyes Gen 31:40
God hath seen *m* affliction Gen 31:42
and all that thou seest is *m* Gen 31:43
me he restored unto *m* office Gen 41:13
that I may set *m* eyes upon him Gen 44:21
came unto thee into Egypt, are *m* Gen 48:5
Reuben and Simeon, they shall be *m* Gen 48:5
m honour, be not thou united Gen 49:6
Egypt, and bring forth *m* armies Ex 7:4
I stretch forth *m* hand upon Egypt Ex 7:5
smite with the rod that is in *m* Ex 7:17
it is *m* Ex 13:2
with the rod of God in *m* hand Ex 17:9
was *m* help, and delivered me from Ex 18:4
for all the earth is *m* Ex 19:5
thou go up by steps unto *m* altar Ex 20:26
thou shalt take him from *m* altar Ex 21:14
For *m* Angel shall go before thee, Ex 23:23
m Angel shall go before thee Ex 32:34
And I will take away *m* hand Ex 33:23
All that openeth the matrix is *m* Ex 34:19
keep *m* ordinances, to walk Lev 18:4
shall ye keep *m* ordinance Lev 18:30
other people, that ye should be *m* Lev 20:26
shall therefore keep *m* ordinance Lev 22:9
for the land is *m* Lev 25:23
therefore the Levites shall be *m* Num 3:12
Because all the firstborn are *m* Num 3:13
m shall they be Num 3:13
and the Levites shall be *m* Num 3:45
and the Levites shall be *m* Num 8:14
of the children of Israel are *m* Num 8:17
but I will depart to *m* own land Num 10:30
who is faithful in all *m* house Num 12:7
LORD, as ye have spoken in *m* ears Num 14:28
have not done them of *m* own mind Num 16:28
of *m* heave offerings of all the Num 18:8
there were a sword in *m* hand Num 22:29
I took thee to curse *m* enemies Num 23:11
I called thee to curse *m* enemies Num 24:10
either good or bad of *m* own mind Num 24:13
the might of *m* hand hath gotten Deut 8:17
having the two tables in *m* hand Deut 10:3
hallowed things out of *m* house Deut 26:13
in the imagination of *m* heart Deut 29:19
For a fire is kindled in *m* anger Deut 32:22
I will spend *m* arrows upon them Deut 32:23
m hand take hold on judgment Deut 32:41
render vengeance to *m* enemies Deut 32:41
I will make *m* arrows drunk with Deut 32:42
word again as it was in *m* heart Josh 14:7
thou wilt save Israel by *m* hand Judg 6:36
thou wilt save Israel by *m* hand Judg 6:37
saying, *M* own hand hath saved me Judg 7:2
Zebah and Zalmunna into *m* hand Judg 8:7
children of Ammon into *m* hands Judg 11:30
hath not come a razor upon *m* head Judg 16:17
and spakest of also in *m* ears Judg 17:2
this man is come into *m* house Judg 19:23
lest I mar *m* own inheritance Ruth 4:6
m horn is exalted in the LORD 1Sa 2:1
mouth is enlarged over *m* enemies 1Sa 2:1
my priest, to offer upon *m* altar 1Sa 2:28
at *m* offering, which I have 1Sa 2:29
I shall not cut off from *m* altar 1Sa 2:33
to that which is in *m* heart 1Sa 2:35
walk before *m* anointed for ever 1Sa 2:35
bribe to blind *m* eyes therewith 1Sa 12:3
I may be avenged on *m* enemies 1Sa 14:24
how *m* eyes have been enlightened, 1Sa 14:29
end of the rod that was in *m* hand 1Sa 14:43
bleating of the sheep in *m* ears 1Sa 15:14
the LORD deliver thee into *m* hand 1Sa 17:46
Let not *m* hand be upon him, but 1Sa 18:17
me so, and sent away *m* enemy 1Sa 19:17
what is *m* iniquity? 1Sa 20:1
me five loaves of bread in *m* hand 1Sa 21:3
is no common bread under *m* hand 1Sa 21:4
hath delivered him into *m* hand 1Sa 23:7
stretch forth *m* hand against him 1Sa 24:6
to day into *m* hand in the cave 1Sa 24:10
but *m* eye spared thee 1Sa 24:10
put forth *m* hand against my lord 1Sa 24:10
evil nor transgression in *m* hand 1Sa 24:11
but *m* hand shall not be upon thee 1Sa 24:12
but *m* hand shall not be upon thee 1Sa 24:13
avenging myself with *m* own hand 1Sa 25:33
forth *m* hand against the LORD's 1Sa 26:11
or what evil is in *m* hand 1Sa 26:18
forth *m* hand against the LORD's 1Sa 26:23
much set by this day in *m* eyes 1Sa 26:24
thee keeper of *m* head for ever 1Sa 28:2
thou deliver them into *m* hand 2Sa 5:19
forth upon *m* enemies before me 2Sa 5:20
and will be base in *m* own sight 2Sa 6:22
shall I then go into *m* house 2Sa 11:11
and *m* husband is dead 2Sa 14:5
See, Joab's field is near *m* 2Sa 14:30 3027
LORD will look on *m* affliction 2Sa 16:12
shekels of silver in *m* hand 2Sa 18:12
yet would I not put forth *m* hand 2Sa 18:12
falsehood against *m* own life 2Sa 18:13
that I may die in *m* own city 2Sa 19:37
shall I be saved from *m* enemies 2Sa 22:4
have kept myself from *m* iniquity 2Sa 22:24
bow of steel is broken by *m* arms 2Sa 22:35
I have pursued *m* enemies, and 2Sa 22:38
given me the necks of *m* enemies 2Sa 22:41
bringeth me forth from *m* enemies 2Sa 22:49
my son to ride upon *m* own mule 1Kin 1:33
this day, *m* eyes even seeing it 1Kin 1:48
knowest that the kingdom was *m* 1Kin 2:15
for he is *m* elder brother 1Kin 2:22
Let it be neither *m* nor thine 1Kin 3:26
m eyes and *m* heart shall be 1Kin 9:3
eyes and *m* heart shall be there 1Kin 9:3
I heard in *m* own land of thy acts 1Kin 10:6
I came, and *m* eyes had seen it 1Kin 10:7
that I may go to *m* own country 1Kin 11:21
do that which is right in *m* eyes 1Kin 11:33
only which was right in *m* eyes 1Kin 14:8
Thy silver and thy gold is *m* 1Kin 20:3
even the goodliest, are *m* 1Kin 20:3
Hast thou found me, O *m* enemy 1Kin 21:20
I dwell among *m* own people 2Kin 4:13
Went not *m* heart with thee, when 2Kin 5:26
hath sent to take away *m* head 2Kin 6:32
time to them, saying, If ye be *m* 2Kin 10:6
that which is right in *m* eyes 2Kin 10:30
to all that was in *m* heart 2Kin 10:30
delivered Samaria out of *m* hand 2Kin 18:34
their country out of *m* hand 2Kin 18:35
deliver Jerusalem out of *m* hand 2Kin 18:35
thy tumult is come up into *m* ears 2Kin 19:28
for *m* own sake, and for my servant 2Kin 19:34
defend this city for *m* own sake 2Kin 20:6
are in *m* house have they seen 2Kin 20:15
the remnant of *m* inheritance 2Kin 21:14
m heart shall be knit unto you 1Chr 12:17
be come to betray me to *m* enemies 1Chr 12:17
there is no wrong in *m* hands 1Chr 12:17
thou deliver them into *m* hand 1Chr 14:10
broken in upon *m* enemies by *m* 1Chr 14:11
Saying, Touch not *m* anointed 1Chr 16:22
But I will settle him in *m* house 1Chr 17:14
I, O LORD God, and what is *m* house 1Chr 17:16
of the land into *m* hand 1Chr 22:18
I had in *m* heart to build an 1Chr 28:2
I have of *m* own proper good, of 1Chr 29:3
in the uprightness of *m* heart I 1Chr 29:17
Now *m* eyes shall be open, and *m* 2Chr 7:15
m ears attent unto the prayer 2Chr 7:15
m eyes and *m* heart shall be 2Chr 7:16
heard in *m* own land of thine acts 2Chr 9:5
I came, and *m* eyes had seen it 2Chr 9:6
Now it is in *m* heart to make a 2Chr 29:10
deliver their lands out of *m* hand 2Chr 32:13
deliver his people out of *m* hand 2Chr 32:14
able to deliver you out of *m* hand 2Chr 32:14
deliver his people out of *m* hand 2Chr 32:15
God deliver you out of *m* hand 2Chr 32:15
their people out of *m* hand 2Chr 32:17
deliver his people out of *m* hand 2Chr 32:17
my God put into *m* heart to gather Neh 7:5
womb, nor hid sorrow from *m* eyes Job 3:10
m ear received a little thereof Job 4:12
an image was before *m* eyes Job 4:16
and what is *m* end, that I should Job 6:11
m eye shall no more see good Job 7:7
and take away *m* iniquity Job 7:21
m own mouth shall condemn me Job 9:20
m own clothes shall abhor me Job 9:31
thou enquirest after *m* iniquity Job 10:6
not acquit me from *m* iniquity Job 10:14
therefore see thou *m* affliction Job 10:15
m eye hath seen all this, *m* Job 13:1
m ear hath heard and understood it Job 13:1
teeth, and put my life in *m* hand Job 13:14
maintain *m* own ways before him Job 13:15
How many are *m* iniquities Job 13:23
bag, and thou sewest up *m* iniquity Job 14:17
you, and shake *m* head at you Job 16:4
m enemy sharpeneth his eyes upon Job 16:9
Not for any injustice in *m* hands Job 16:17
but *m* eye poureth out tears unto Job 16:20
doth not *m* eye continue in their Job 17:2
M eye also is dim by reason of Job 17:7
If I wait, the grave is *m* house Job 17:13
m error remaineth with myself Job 19:4
m hope hath he removed like a Job 19:10
m acquaintance are verily Job 19:13
They that dwell in *m* house Job 19:15
the children's sake of *m* own body Job 19:17
m eyes shall behold, and not Job 19:27
not remove *m* integrity from me Job 27:5
Let *m* enemy be as the wicked, and Job 27:7
I made a covenant with *m* eyes Job 31:1
that God may know *m* integrity Job 31:6
and *m* heart walked after *m* eyes Job 31:7
any blot hath cleaved to *m* hands Job 31:7
If *m* heart have been deceived by Job 31:9
and would root out all *m* increase Job 31:12
Then let *m* arm fall from my Job 31:22
m arm be broken from the bone Job 31:22
because *m* hand had gotten much Job 31:25
by hiding *m* iniquity in my bosom Job 31:33
that *m* adversary had written a Job 31:35
and durst not shew you *m* opinion Job 32:6
I also will shew *m* opinion Job 32:10
part, I also will shew *m* opinion Job 32:17
thou hast spoken in *m* hearing Job 33:8
I will lay *m* hand upon my mouth Job 40:4
is under the whole heaven is *m* Job 41:11
but now *m* eye seeth thee Job 42:5
glory, and the lifter up of *m* head Ps 3:3
for thou hast smitten all *m* Ps 3:7
because of *m* enemies Ps 5:8
M eye is consumed because of Ps 6:7
old because of all *m* enemies Ps 6:7
Let all *m* enemies be ashamed and Ps 6:10
him that without cause is *m* enemy Ps 7:4
and lay *m* honour in the dust Ps 7:5
because of the rage of *m* enemies Ps 7:6
according to *m* integrity that is Ps 7:8
When *m* enemies are turned back, Ps 9:3
how long shall *m* enemy be exalted Ps 13:2
lighten *m* eyes, lest I sleep the Ps 13:3
Lest *m* enemy say, I have Ps 13:4
is the portion of *m* inheritance Ps 16:5
Thou hast proved *m* heart Ps 17:3
shall I be saved from *m* enemies Ps 18:3
and I kept myself from *m* iniquity Ps 18:23
bow of steel is broken by *m* arms Ps 18:34
I have pursued *m* enemies, and Ps 18:37
given me the necks of *m* enemies Ps 18:40
He delivereth me from *m* enemies Ps 18:48
me in the presence of *m* enemies Ps 23:5
let not *m* enemies triumph over me Ps 25:2
sake, O LORD, pardon *m* iniquity Ps 25:11
M eyes are ever toward the LORD Ps 25:15
Look upon *m* affliction and my pain Ps 25:18
Consider *m* enemies Ps 25:19
for I have walked in *m* integrity Ps 26:1
lovingkindness is before *m* eyes Ps 26:3
I will wash *m* hands in innocency Ps 26:6
me, I will walk in *m* integrity Ps 26:11
even *m* enemies and my foes, came Ps 27:2
now shall *m* head be lifted up Ps 27:6
up above *m* enemies round about me Ps 27:6
plain path, because of *m* enemies Ps 27:11
over unto the will of *m* enemies Ps 27:12
m eye is consumed with grief, yea Ps 31:9
faileth because of *m* iniquity Ps 31:10
a reproach among all *m* enemies Ps 31:11
and a fear to *m* acquaintance Ps 31:11
me from the hand of *m* enemies Ps 31:15
m iniquity have I not hid Ps 32:5
I will guide thee with *m* eye Ps 32:8
buckler, and stand up for *m* help Ps 35:2
prayer returned into *m* own bosom Ps 35:13
But in *m* adversity they rejoiced, Ps 35:15
Let not them that are *m* enemies Ps 35:19
together that rejoice at *m* hurt Ps 35:26
For *m* iniquities are gone over Ps 38:4
iniquities are gone over *m* head Ps 38:4
as for the light of *m* eyes Ps 38:10
For I will declare *m* iniquity Ps 38:18
But *m* enemies are lively, and they Ps 38:19
evil for good are *m* adversaries Ps 38:20
LORD, make me to know *m* end Ps 39:4
m age is as nothing before thee Ps 39:5
m ears hast thou opened Ps 40:6
m iniquities have taken hold upon Ps 40:12
are more than the hairs of *m* head Ps 40:12
M enemies speak evil of me, When Ps 41:5
m own familiar friend, in whom I Ps 41:9
because *m* enemy doth not triumph Ps 41:11
thou upholdest me in *m* integrity Ps 41:12
my bones, *m* enemies reproach me Ps 42:10
I will incline *m* ear to a parable Ps 49:4
every beast of the forest is *m* Ps 50:10
wild beasts of the field are *m* Ps 50:11 5978
for the world is *m*, and the Ps 50:12
Wash me throughly from *m* iniquity Ps 51:2
and blot out all *m* iniquities Ps 51:9
Behold, God is *m* helper Ps 54:4
shall reward evil unto *m* enemies Ps 54:5
m eye hath seen his desire upon Ps 54:7
seen his desire upon *m* enemies Ps 54:7
But it was thou, a man *m* equal Ps 55:13
my guide, and *m* acquaintance Ps 55:13
M enemies would daily swallow me Ps 56:2
then shall *m* enemies turn back Ps 56:9
Deliver me from *m* enemies Ps 59:1
me see my desire upon *m* enemies Ps 59:10
Gilead is *m*, and Manasseh is *m* Ps 60:7
also is the strength of *m* head Ps 60:7
m eyes fail while I wait for my Ps 69:3
are more than the hairs of *m* head Ps 69:4
being *m* enemies wrongfully, are Ps 69:4
deliver me because of *m* enemies Ps 69:18
m adversaries are all before thee Ps 69:19
For *m* enemies speak against me Ps 71:10
Thou holdest *m* eyes waking Ps 77:4
I commune with *m* own heart Ps 77:6
Thou hast put away *m* acquaintance Ps 88:8
M eye mourneth by reason of Ps 88:9
m acquaintance into darkness Ps 88:18
m arm also shall strengthen him Ps 89:21
M eye also shall see my desire on Ps 92:11
shall see my desire on *m* enemies Ps 92:11
m ears shall hear my desire of Ps 92:11

set no wicked thing before *m* eyes ... Ps 101:3
M eyes shall be upon the faithful ... Ps 101:6
M enemies reproach me all the day ... Ps 102:8
Saying, Touch not *m* anointed ... Ps 105:15
Gilead is *m* ... Ps 108:8
Manasseh is *m* ... Ps 108:8
also is the strength of *m* head ... Ps 108:8
of *m* adversaries from the LORD ... Ps 109:20
Let *m* adversaries be clothed with ... Ps 109:29
m eyes from tears, and my feet ... Ps 116:8
Thy word have I hid in *m* heart ... Ps 119:11
Open thou *m* eyes, that I may ... Ps 119:18
Turn away *m* eyes from beholding ... Ps 119:37
M eyes fail for thy word, saying ... Ps 119:82
have perished in *m* affliction ... Ps 119:92
hast made me wiser than *m* enemies ... Ps 119:98
I have inclined *m* heart to ... Ps 119:112
leave me not to *m* oppressors ... Ps 119:121
M eyes fail for thy salvation, and ... Ps 119:123
Rivers of waters run down *m* eyes ... Ps 119:136
because *m* enemies have forgotten ... Ps 119:139
M eyes prevent the night watches ... Ps 119:148
Consider *m* affliction, and deliver ... Ps 119:153
are my persecutors and *m* enemies ... Ps 119:157
I will lift up *m* eyes unto the ... Ps 121:1
Unto thee lift I up *m* eyes ... Ps 123:1
is not haughty, nor *m* eyes lofty ... Ps 131:1
I will not give sleep to *m* eyes ... Ps 132:4
or slumber to *m* eyelids ... Ps 132:4
ordained a lamp for *m* anointed ... Ps 132:17
against the wrath of *m* enemies ... Ps 138:7
m uprising, thou understandest my ... Ps 139:2
I count them *m* enemies ... Ps 139:22
But *m* eyes are unto thee, O GOD ... Ps 141:8
me, O LORD, from *m* enemies ... Ps 143:9
And of thy mercy cut off *m* enemies ... Ps 143:12
nor inclined *m* ear to them that ... Prov 5:13
Counsel is *m*, and sound wisdom ... Prov 8:14
my heart shall rejoice, even *m* ... Prov 23:15 589
I communed with *m* own heart ... Eccl 1:16
I said in *m* heart, Go to now, I ... Eccl 2:1
I sought in *m* heart to give ... Eccl 2:3
yet acquainting *m* heart with ... Eccl 2:3
whatsoever *m* eyes desired I kept ... Eccl 2:10
I said in *m* heart, God shall ... Eccl 3:17
I said in *m* heart concerning the ... Eccl 3:18
I applied *m* heart to know, and to ... Eccl 7:25
When I applied *m* heart to know ... Eccl 8:16
but *m* own vineyard have I not ... Song 1:6
My beloved is *m*, and I am his ... Song 2:16
my beloved's, and my beloved is *m* ... Song 6:3
My vineyard, which is *m*, is ... Song 8:12
I will hide *m* eyes from you ... Is 1:15
of your doings from before *m* eyes ... Is 1:16
I will ease me of *m* adversaries ... Is 1:24
and avenge me of *m* enemies ... Is 1:24
In *m* ears said the LORD of hosts ... Is 5:9
for *m* eyes have seen the King ... Is 6:5
O Assyrian, the rod of *m* anger ... Is 10:5
in their hand is *m* indignation ... Is 10:5
m anger in their destruction ... Is 10:25
called my mighty ones for *m* anger ... Is 13:3
Let *m* outcasts dwell with thee ... Is 16:4
m inward parts for Kir-haresh ... Is 16:11
my hands, and Israel *m* inheritance ... Is 19:25
it was revealed in *m* ears by the ... Is 22:14
his children, the work of *m* hands ... Is 29:23
tumult, is come up into *m* ears ... Is 37:29
city to save it for *m* own sake ... Is 37:35
M age is departed, and is removed ... Is 38:12
m eyes fail with looking upward ... Is 38:14
All that is in *m* house have they ... Is 39:4
m elect, in whom my soul ... Is 42:1
thou art *m* ... Is 43:1
thy transgressions for *m* own sake ... Is 43:25
servant's sake, and Israel *m* elect ... Is 45:4
I have polluted *m* inheritance ... Is 47:6
M idol hath done them, and my ... Is 48:5
name's sake will I defer *m* anger ... Is 48:9
For *m* own sake, even for *m* own ... Is 48:11
M hand also hath laid the ... Is 48:13
I will lift up *m* hand to the ... Is 49:22
he wakeneth *m* ear to hear as the ... Is 50:4
The Lord GOD hath opened *m* ear ... Is 50:5
who is *m* adversary? ... Is 50:8
This shall ye have of *m* hand ... Is 50:11
m arms shall judge the people ... Is 51:5
on *m* arm shall they trust ... Is 51:5
thee in the shadow of *m* hand ... Is 51:16
unto them will I give in *m* house ... Is 56:5
shall be accepted upon *m* altar ... Is 56:7
for *m* house shall be called an ... Is 56:7
up with acceptance on *m* altar ... Is 60:7
for I will tread them in *m* anger ... Is 63:3
day of vengeance is in *m* heart ... Is 63:4
therefore *m* own arm brought ... Is 63:5
tread down the people in *m* anger ... Is 63:6
m elect shall inherit it, and my ... Is 65:9
but did evil before *m* eyes ... Is 65:12
because they are hid from *m* eyes ... Is 65:16
m elect shall long enjoy the work ... Is 65:22
all those things hath *m* hand made ... Is 66:2
but they did evil before *m* eyes ... Is 66:4
made *m* heritage an abomination ... Jer 2:7
I will not cause *m* anger to fall ... Jer 3:12
you pastors according to *m* heart ... Jer 3:15
m anger and my fury shall be ... Jer 7:20
m eyes a fountain of tears, that ... Jer 9:1
hath my beloved to do in *m* house ... Jer 11:15
tried *m* heart toward thee ... Jer 12:3
I have forsaken *m* house ... Jer 12:7
I have left *m* heritage ... Jer 12:7
M heritage is unto me as a lion ... Jer 12:8
M heritage is unto me as a ... Jer 12:9
against all *m* evil neighbours ... Jer 12:14
m eye shall weep sore, and run ... Jer 13:17
Let *m* eyes run down with tears ... Jer 14:17
for a fire is kindled in *m* anger ... Jer 15:14
the joy and rejoicing of *m* heart ... Jer 15:16
For *m* eyes are upon all their ... Jer 16:17
is their iniquity hid from *m* eyes ... Jer 16:17
they have filled *m* inheritance ... Jer 16:18
I will cause them to know *m* hand ... Jer 16:21
ye have kindled a fire in *m* anger ... Jer 17:4
hand, so are ye in *m* hand ... Jer 18:6
But his word was in *m* heart as a ... Jer 20:9
M heart within me is broken ... Jer 23:9
For I will set *m* eyes upon them ... Jer 24:6
So Hanameel *m* uncle's son came to ... Jer 32:8
sight of Hanameel *m* uncle's son ... Jer 32:12
to me as a provocation of *m* anger ... Jer 32:31
I have driven them in *m* anger ... Jer 32:37
men, whom I have slain in *m* anger ... Jer 33:5
As *m* anger and my fury hath been ... Jer 42:18
m anger was poured forth, and was ... Jer 44:6
know whose words shall stand, *m* ... Jer 44:28
m heart shall mourn for the men ... Jer 48:31
Therefore *m* heart shall sound for ... Jer 48:36
m heart shall sound like pipes ... Jer 48:36
O ye destroyers of *m* heritage ... Jer 50:11
will stretch out *m* hand upon thee ... Jer 51:25
m eye, *m* eye runneth down with ... Lam 1:16
m elders gave up the ghost in the ... Lam 1:19
m heart is turned within me ... Lam 1:20
all *m* enemies have heard of my ... Lam 1:21
M eyes do fail with tears, my ... Lam 2:11
brought up hath *m* enemy consumed ... Lam 2:22
Remembering *m* affliction and my ... Lam 3:19
M eye runneth down with rivers of ... Lam 3:48
M eye trickleth down, and ceaseth ... Lam 3:49
M eye affecteth *m* heart ... Lam 3:51
M enemies chased me sore, like a ... Lam 3:52
Waters flowed over *m* head ... Lam 3:54
neither shall *m* eye spare ... Eze 5:11
Thus shall *m* anger be ... Eze 5:13
I will send *m* anger upon thee, and ... Eze 7:3
m eye shall not spare thee ... Eze 7:4
accomplish *m* anger upon thee ... Eze 7:8
m eye shall not spare, neither ... Eze 7:9
of the month, as I sat in *m* house ... Eze 8:1
and took me by a lock of *m* head ... Eze 8:3
So I lifted up *m* eyes the way ... Eze 8:5
m eye shall not spare, neither ... Eze 8:18
though they cry in *m* ears with a ... Eze 8:18
He cried also in *m* ears with a ... Eze 9:1
the others he said in *m* hearing ... Eze 9:5
m eye shall not spare, neither ... Eze 9:10
keep *m* ordinances, and do them ... Eze 11:20
through the wall with *m* hand ... Eze 12:7
m hand shall be upon the prophets ... Eze 13:9
an overflowing shower in *m* anger ... Eze 13:13
will I stretch out *m* hand upon it ... Eze 14:13
the Lord GOD, and thou becamest *m* ... Eze 16:8
m oil and *m* incense before them ... Eze 16:18
surely *m* oath that he hath ... Eze 17:19
Behold, all souls are *m* ... Eze 18:4
so also the soul of the son is *m* ... Eze 18:4
lifted up *m* hand unto the seed of ... Eze 20:5
when I lifted up *m* hand unto them ... Eze 20:5
that I lifted up *m* hand unto them ... Eze 20:6
Nevertheless *m* eye spared them ... Eze 20:17
Nevertheless I withdrew *m* hand ... Eze 20:22
I lifted up *m* hand unto them also ... Eze 20:23
up *m* hand to give it to them ... Eze 20:28
For in *m* holy mountain, in the ... Eze 20:40
for the which I lifted up *m* hand ... Eze 20:42
will also smite *m* hands together ... Eze 21:17
I will pour out *m* indignation ... Eze 21:31
Thou hast despised *m* holy things ... Eze 22:8
therefore I have smitten *m* hand ... Eze 22:13
so will I gather you in *m* anger ... Eze 22:20
and have profaned *m* holy things ... Eze 22:26
out *m* indignation upon them ... Eze 22:31
and they were *m*, and they bare sons ... Eze 23:4
played the harlot when she was *m* ... Eze 23:5
they done in the midst of *m* house ... Eze 23:39
hast set *m* incense and *m* oil ... Eze 23:41
will stretch out *m* hand upon thee ... Eze 25:7
also stretch out *m* hand upon Edom ... Eze 25:13
do in Edom according to *m* anger ... Eze 25:14
I will stretch out *m* hand upon ... Eze 25:16
hath said, My river is *m* own ... Eze 29:3
he hath said, The river is *m* ... Eze 29:9
stretch out *m* hand against thee ... Eze 35:3
and these two countries shall be *m* ... Eze 35:10
I have lifted up *m* hand, Surely ... Eze 36:7
But I had pity for *m* holy name ... Eze 36:21
but for *m* holy name's sake, which ... Eze 36:22
and they shall be one in *m* hand ... Eze 37:19
I have consumed them in *m* anger ... Eze 43:8
kept the charge of *m* holy things ... Eze 44:8
I lifted up *m* hand against them ... Eze 44:12
my statutes in all *m* assemblies ... Eze 44:24
the which I lifted up *m* hand to ... Eze 47:14
was at rest in *m* house, and ... Dan 4:4
the visions of *m* head in my bed ... Dan 4:10
lifted up *m* eyes unto heaven ... Dan 4:34
m understanding returned unto me ... Dan 4:34
m honour and brightness returned ... Dan 4:36
Then I lifted up *m* eyes, and saw ... Dan 8:3
Then I lifted up *m* eyes, and ... Dan 10:5
and my flax, *m* oil and my drink ... Hos 2:5
shall deliver her out of *m* hand ... Hos 2:10
m anger is kindled against them ... Hos 8:5
for the sacrifices of *m* offerings ... Hos 8:13
I will drive them out of *m* house ... Hos 9:15
m heart is turned within me, my ... Hos 11:8
execute the fierceness of *m* anger ... Hos 11:9
I gave thee a king in *m* anger ... Hos 13:11
shall be hid from *m* eyes ... Hos 13:14
for *m* anger is turned away from ... Hos 14:4
I will turn *m* hand against Ekron ... Amos 1:8
thence shall *m* hand take them ... Amos 9:2
I will set *m* eyes upon them for ... Amos 9:4
I cried by reason of *m* affliction ... Jonah 2:2
Rejoice not against me, O *m* enemy ... Mic 7:8
Then she that is *m* enemy shall ... Mic 7:10
m eyes shall behold her ... Mic 7:10
O LORD my God, *m* Holy One ... Hab 1:12
me to walk upon *m* high places ... Hab 3:19
stretch out *m* hand upon Judah ... Zeph 1:4
to pour upon them *m* indignation ... Zeph 3:8
dispersed, shall bring *m* offering ... Zeph 3:10
Because of *m* house that is waste ... Hag 1:9
silver is *m*, and the gold is *m* ... Hag 2:8
Then lifted I up *m* eyes, and saw ... Zec 1:18
I lifted up *m* eyes again, and ... Zec 2:1
I will shake *m* hand upon them, and ... Zec 2:9
I turned, and lifted up *m* eyes ... Zec 5:1
Then lifted I up *m* eyes, and ... Zec 5:9
And I turned, and lifted up *m* eyes ... Zec 6:1
it also be marvellous in *m* eyes ... Zec 8:6
I will encamp about *m* house ... Zec 9:8
for now have I seen with *m* eyes ... Zec 9:8
M anger was kindled against the ... Zec 10:3
Then I cut asunder *m* other staff ... Zec 11:14
I will open *m* eyes upon the house ... Zec 12:4
I will turn *m* hand upon the ... Zec 13:7
I be a father, where is *m* honour ... Mal 1:6
offer polluted bread upon *m* altar ... Mal 1:7
kindle fire on *m* altar for nought ... Mal 1:10
are gone away from *m* ordinances ... Mal 3:7
that there may be meat in *m* house ... Mal 3:10
And they shall be *m*, saith the ... Mal 3:17
heareth these sayings of *m* ... Mt 7:24 3450
that heareth these sayings of *m* ... Mt 7:26 3450
me to do what I will with *m* own ... Mt 20:15 1699
is not *m* to give, but it shall be ... Mt 20:23 1699
have received *m* own with usury ... Mt 25:27 1699
help thou *m* unbelief ... Mk 9:24 3450
on my left hand is not *m* to give ... Mk 10:40
thy salutation sounded in *m* ears ... Lk 1:44 3450
For *m* eyes have seen thy ... Lk 2:30 3450
for he is *m* only child ... Lk 9:38 3427
For a friend of *m* in his journey ... Lk 11:6 3450
saying, Avenge me of *m* adversary ... Lk 18:3 3450
have required *m* own with usury ... Lk 19:23 846
But those *m* enemies, which would ... Lk 19:27 3450
m hour is not yet come ... Jn 2:4 3450
I can of *m* own self do nothing ... Jn 5:30 1683
because I seek not *m* own will ... Jn 5:30 1699
from heaven, not to do *m* own will ... Jn 6:38 1699
and said, My doctrine is not *m* ... Jn 7:16 1699
And I seek not *m* own glory ... Jn 8:50 3450
made clay, and anointed *m* eyes ... Jn 9:11 3450
them, He put clay upon *m* eyes ... Jn 9:15 3450
is, and yet he hath opened *m* eyes ... Jn 9:30 3450
know my sheep, and am known of *m* ... Jn 10:14 1699
the word which ye hear is not *m* ... Jn 14:24 1699
for he shall receive of *m* ... Jn 16:14 1699
things that the Father hath are *m* ... Jn 16:15 1699
said I, that he shall take of *m* ... Jn 16:15 1699
all *m* are thine, and thine are ... Jn 17:10 1699
m are thine, and thine are *m* ... Jn 17:10 1699
which when I had fastened *m* eyes ... Acts 11:6
of Jesse, a man after *m* own heart ... Acts 13:22 3450
ye to weep and to break *m* heart ... Acts 21:13 3450
among *m* own nation at Jerusalem ... Acts 26:4 3450
the Gentiles, I magnify *m* office ... Rom 11:13 3450
for it is written, Vengeance is *m* ... Rom 12:19 1698
in the Lord, and his mother and *m* ... Rom 16:13 1700
Gaius *m* host, and of the whole ... Rom 16:23 3450
that I had baptized in *m* own name ... 1Cor 1:15 1699
yea, I judge not *m* own self ... 1Cor 4:3 1683
for the seal of *m* apostleship are ... 1Cor 9:2 1699
M answer to them that do examine ... 1Cor 9:3 1699
things, not seeking *m* own profit ... 1Cor 10:33 1683
of me Paul with *m* own hand ... 1Cor 16:21 1699
in perils by *m* own countrymen, in ... 2Cor 11:26
which concern *m* infirmities ... 2Cor 11:30 3450
not glory, but in *m* infirmities ... 2Cor 12:5 3450
many my equals in *m* own nation ... Gal 1:14 3450
written unto you with *m* own hand ... Gal 6:11 1699
Always in every prayer of *m* for ... Phil 1:4 3450
not having *m* own righteousness ... Phil 3:9 1699
of Paul with *m* own hand, which is ... 2Th 3:17 1699
m own son after the common faith ... Titus 1:4
him, that is, *m* own bowels ... Philem 12 1699
thee ought, put that on *m* account ... Philem 18 1699
have written it with *m* own hand ... Philem 19
I Jesus have sent *m* angel to ... Rev 22:16 3450

MINGLE

men of strength to *m* strong drink ... Is 5:22 4537
they shall *m* themselves with the ... Dan 2:43 6151

MINGLED

fire *m* with the hail, very ... Ex 9:24 3947
m with the fourth part of an hin ... Ex 29:40 1101
cakes of fine flour *m* with oil ... Lev 2:4 1101
fine flour unleavened, *m* with oil ... Lev 2:5 1101
m with oil, and dry, shall all the ... Lev 7:10 1101
unleavened cakes *m* with oil ... Lev 7:12 1101
cakes *m* with oil, of fine flour ... Lev 7:12 1101
and a meat offering *m* with oil ... Lev 9:4 1101
m with oil, and one log of oil ... Lev 14:10 1101
m with oil for a meat offering ... Lev 14:21 1101
not sow thy field with *m* seed ... Lev 19:19 3610
shall a garment *m* of linen ... Lev 19:19 3610
deals of fine flour *m* with oil ... Lev 23:13 1101
cakes of fine flour *m* with oil ... Num 6:15 1101
m with oil for a meat offering ... Num 7:13 1101
m with oil for a meat offering ... Num 7:19 1101

M

m with oil for a meat offering Num 7:25 1101
m with oil for a meat offering Num 7:31 1101
m with oil for a meat offering Num 7:37 1101
m with oil for a meat offering Num 7:43 1101
m with oil for a meat offering Num 7:49 1101
m with oil for a meat offering Num 7:55 1101
m with oil for a meat offering Num 7:61 1101
m with oil for a meat offering Num 7:67 1101
m with oil for a meat offering Num 7:73 1101
m with oil for a meat offering Num 7:79 1101
even fine flour *m* with oil Num 8:8 1101
of a tenth deal of flour *m* with Num 15:4 1101
two tenth deals of flour *m* with Num 15:6 1101
flour *m* with half an hin of oil Num 15:9 1101
m with the fourth part of an hin Num 28:5 1101
m with oil, and the drink offering Num 28:9 1101
m with oil, for one bullock Num 28:12 1101
offering, *m* with oil, for one ram Num 28:12 1101
m with oil for a meat offering Num 28:13 1101
shall be of flour *m* with oil Num 28:20 1101
meat offering of flour *m* with oil Num 28:28 1101
shall be of flour *m* with oil Num 29:3 1101
shall be of flour *m* with oil Num 29:9 1101
shall be of flour *m* with oil Num 29:14 1101
so that the holy seed have *m* Ezr 9:2 6148
and *m* my drink with weeping, Ps 102:9 4537
But were *m* among the heathen, and Ps 106:35 6148
she hath *m* her wine Prov 9:2 4537
drink of the wine which I have *m* Prov 9:5 4537
The LORD hath *m* a perverse spirit Is 19:14 4537
And all the *m* people, and all the Jer 25:20 6154
all the kings of the *m* people Jer 25:24 6154
upon all the *m* people that are in Jer 50:37 6154
and Lydia, and all the *m* people Eze 30:5 6154
him vinegar to drink *m* with gall Mt 27:34 3396
him to drink wine *m* with myrrh Mk 15:23
had *m* with their sacrifices Lk 13:1 3396
fire *m* with blood, and they were Rev 8:7 3396
were a sea of glass *m* with fire Rev 15:2 3396

MINIAMIN (*min'-e-a-min*) See MIAMIN.
1. A Levite.
And next him were Eden, and *M* 2Chr 31:15 4509
2. A priest with Zerubbabel.
of *M*, of Moadiah, Piltai Neh 12:17 4509
Eliakim, Maaseiah, *M*, Michaiah, Neh 12:41 4509

MINISH
Ye shall not *m* ought from your Ex 5:19 1639

MINISHED
Again, they are *m* and brought low Ps 107:39 4591

MINISTER
And Moses rose up, and his *m* Joshua Ex 24:13 8334
that he may *m* unto me in the Ex 28:1
that he may *m* unto me in the Ex 28:3
that he may *m* unto me in the Ex 28:4
And it shall be upon Aaron to *m* Ex 28:35 8334
that they may *m* unto me in the Ex 28:41
the altar to *m* in the holy place Ex 28:43 8334
to *m* unto me in the priest's Ex 29:1
to *m* in the holy place Ex 29:30 8334
to *m* to me in the priest's office Ex 29:44
they come near to the altar to *m* Ex 30:20 8334
that they may *m* unto me in the Ex 30:30
to *m* in the priest's office, Ex 31:10
to *m* in the priest's office Ex 35:19 8334
about the hem of the robe to *m* in Ex 39:26 8334
to *m* in the priest's office Ex 39:41 8334
that he may *m* unto me in the Ex 40:13
that they may *m* unto me in the Ex 40:15
m unto the LORD in the priest's Lev 7:35
whom he shall consecrate to *m* in Lev 16:32
and they shall *m* unto it, and shall Num 1:50 8334
to *m* in the priest's office Num 3:3
priest, that they may *m* unto him Num 3:6 8334
of the sanctuary wherewith they *m* Num 3:31 8334
thereof, wherewith they *m* unto it Num 4:9 8334
wherewith they *m* in the sanctuary Num 4:12 8334
wherewith they *m* about it Num 4:14 8334
But shall *m* with their brethren Num 8:26 8334
the congregation to *m* unto them Num 16:9 8334
joined unto thee, and *m* unto thee Num 18:2 8334
shall *m* before the tabernacle of Num 18:2
before the LORD to *m* unto him Deut 10:8 8334
the priest that standeth to *m* Deut 17:12 8334
to stand to *m* in the name of the Deut 18:5 8334
Then he shall *m* in the name of Deut 18:7 8334
thy God hath chosen to *m* unto him Deut 21:5 8334
Joshua the son of Nun, Moses' *m* Josh 1:1 8334
the child did *m* unto the LORD 1Sa 2:11 8334
stand to *m* because of the cloud 1Kin 8:11 8334
of God, and to *m* unto him for ever 1Chr 15:2 8334
certain of the Levites to *m* 1Chr 16:4 8334
to *m* before the ark continually, 1Chr 16:37 8334
to *m* unto him, and to bless in his 1Chr 23:13 8334
to *m* in the house of the LORD 1Chr 26:12 8334
stand to *m* by reason of the cloud 2Chr 5:14 8334
m before the priests, as the duty 2Chr 8:14 8334
which *m* unto the LORD, are the 2Chr 13:10 8334
they that *m* of the Levites 2Chr 23:6 8334
of the LORD, even vessels to *m* 2Chr 24:14 8335
him, and that ye should *m* unto him 2Chr 29:11 8334
and for peace offerings, to *m* 2Chr 31:2 8334
unto the priests that *m* in the Neh 10:36 8334
sanctuary, and the priests that *m* Neh 10:39 8334
he shall *m* judgment to the people Ps 9:8 1777
of Nebaioth shall *m* unto thee Is 60:7 8334
and their kings shall *m* unto thee Is 60:10 8334
and the Levites that *m* unto me Jer 33:22 8334
near to the LORD to *m* unto him Eze 40:46 8334
lay their garments wherein they *m* Eze 42:14 8334
to *m* unto me, saith the Lord GOD, Eze 43:19 8334
stand before them to *m* unto them Eze 44:11 8334
come near to me to *m* unto me Eze 44:15 8334
to *m* unto me, and they shall keep Eze 44:16 8334
whiles they *m* in the gates of the Eze 44:17 8334
to *m* in the sanctuary, he shall Eze 44:27 8334
come near to *m* unto the LORD Eze 45:4 8334
among you, let him be your *m* Mt 20:26 1249
to be ministered unto, but to *m* Mt 20:28 1247
in prison, and did not *m* unto thee Mt 25:44 1247
great among you, shall be your *m* Mk 10:43 1249
to be ministered unto, but to *m* Mk 10:45 1247
and he gave it again to the *m* Lk 4:20 5257
and they had also John to their *m* Acts 13:5 5257
to *m* or come unto him Acts 24:23 5256
this purpose, to make thee a *m* Acts 26:16 5257
For he is the *m* of God to thee Rom 13:4 1249
for he is the *m* of God, a Rom 13:4 1249
a *m* of the circumcision for the Rom 15:8 1249
That I should be the *m* of Jesus Rom 15:16 3011
Jerusalem to *m* unto the saints Rom 15:25 1247
their duty is also to *m* unto them Rom 15:27 3008
m about holy things live of the 1Cor 9:13 2038
sower both *m* bread for your food 2Cor 9:10 5524
is therefore Christ the *m* of sin Gal 2:17 1249
Whereof I was made a *m*, according Eph 3:7 1249
that it may *m* grace unto the Eph 4:29 1325
faithful *m* in the Lord, shall Eph 6:21 1249
is for you a faithful *m* of Christ Col 1:7 1249
whereof I Paul am made a *m* Col 1:23 1249
Whereof I am made a *m*, according Col 1:25 1249
beloved brother, and a faithful *m* Col 4:7 1249
m of God, and our fellowlabourer 1Th 3:2 1249
which *m* questions, rather than 1Ti 1:4 3930
shalt be a good *m* of Jesus Christ 1Ti 4:6 1249
sent forth to *m* for them who Heb 1:14 1248
ministered to the saints, and do *m* Heb 6:10 1247
A *m* of the sanctuary, and of the Heb 8:2 3011
but unto us they did *m* the things 1Pet 1:12 1247
even so *m* the same one to another 1Pet 4:10 1247
if any man *m*, let him do it as of 1Pet 4:11 1247

MINISTERED
Ithamar *m* in the priest's office Num 3:4
Eleazar his son *m* in the priest's Deut 10:6
But Samuel *m* before the LORD, 1Sa 2:18 8334
the child Samuel *m* unto the LORD 1Sa 3:1 8334
his servant that *m* unto him 2Sa 13:17 8334
cherished the king, and *m* to him 1Kin 1:4 8334
the Shunammite *m* unto the king 1Kin 1:15 8334
went after Elijah, and *m* unto him 1Kin 19:21 8334
vessels of brass wherewith they *m* 2Kin 25:14 8334
they *m* before the dwelling place 1Chr 6:32 8334
that *m* to the king by course 1Chr 28:1 8334
that *m* to Ahaziah, he slew them 2Chr 22:8 8334
king's servants that *m* unto him Est 2:2 8334
king's servants that *m* unto him Est 6:3 8334
vessels of brass wherewith they *m* Jer 52:18 8334
Because they *m* unto them before Eze 44:12 8334
off their garments wherein they *m* Eze 44:19 8334
thousand thousands *m* unto him Dan 7:10 8120
behold, angels came and *m* unto him Mt 4:11 1247
and she arose, and *m* unto them Mt 8:15 1247
Son of man came not to be *m* unto Mt 20:28 1247
and the angels *m* unto him Mk 1:13 1247
left her, and she *m* unto them Mk 1:31 1247
Son of man came not to be *m* unto Mk 10:45 1247
followed him, and *m* unto him Mk 15:41 1247
she arose and *m* unto them Lk 4:39 1247
which *m* unto him of their Lk 8:3 1247
As they *m* to the Lord, and fasted, Acts 13:2 3008
two of them that *m* unto him Acts 19:22 1247
hands have *m* unto my necessities Acts 20:34 5256
be the epistle of Christ *m* by us 2Cor 3:3 1247
and he that *m* to my wants Phil 2:25 3011
and bands having nourishment *m* Col 2:19 2023
things he *m* unto me at Ephesus 2Ti 1:18 1247
m unto me in the bonds of the Philem 13 1247
in that ye have *m* to the saints Heb 6:10 1247
For so an entrance shall be *m* 2Pet 1:11 2023

MINISTERETH
Now he that *m* seed to the sower 2Cor 9:10 2023
that *m* to you the Spirit, and Gal 3:5 2023

MINISTERING
had the charge of the *m* vessels 1Chr 9:28 5656
of the house, and *m* to the house Eze 44:11 8334
Jesus from Galilee, *m* unto him Mt 27:55 1247
Or ministry, let us wait on our *m* Rom 12:7 1248
m the gospel of God, that the Rom 15:16 2418
fellowship of the *m* to the saints 2Cor 8:4 1248
as touching the *m* to the saints 2Cor 9:1 1248
Are they not all *m* spirits, Heb 1:14 3010
And every priest standeth daily *m* Heb 10:11 3008

MINISTERS
and the attendance of his *m* 1Kin 10:5 8334
and the attendance of his *m* 2Chr 9:4 8334
or *m* of this house of God, it Ezr 7:24 6399
us *m* for the house of our God Ezr 8:17 8334
ye *m* of his, that do his pleasure Ps 103:21 8334
his *m* a flaming fire Ps 104:4 8334
shall call you the *M* of our God Is 61:6 8334
the Levites the priests, my *m* Jer 33:21 8334
they shall be *m* in my sanctuary Eze 44:11 8334
priests the *m* of the sanctuary Eze 45:4 8334
the *m* of the house, have for Eze 45:5 8334
where the *m* of the house shall Eze 46:24 8334
the priests, the LORD's *m* Joel 1:9 8334
howl, ye *m* of the altar Joel 1:13 8334
in sackcloth, ye *m* of my God Joel 1:13 8334
the *m* of the LORD, weep between Joel 2:17 8334
eyewitnesses, and *m* of the word Lk 1:2 5257
for they are God's *m*, attending Rom 13:6 3011
but *m* by whom ye believed, even 1Cor 3:5 1249
of us, as of the *m* of Christ 1Cor 4:1 5257
us able *m* of the new testament 2Cor 3:6 1249
ourselves as the *m* of God 2Cor 6:4 1249
his *m* also be transformed as the 2Cor 11:15 1249
as the *m* of righteousness 2Cor 11:15 1249
Are they *m* of Christ? 2Cor 11:23 1249
spirits, and his *m* a flame of fire Heb 1:7 3011

MINISTRATION
days of his *m* were accomplished Lk 1:23 3009
were neglected in the daily *m* Acts 6:1 1248
But if the *m* of death, written and 2Cor 3:7 1248
How shall not the *m* of the spirit 2Cor 3:8 1248
For if the *m* of condemnation be 2Cor 3:9 1248
be glory, much more doth the *m* of 2Cor 3:9 1248
this *m* they glorify God for your 2Cor 9:13 1248

MINISTRY
take all the instruments of *m* Num 4:12 8335
came to do the service of the *m* Num 4:47 5656
when David praised by their *m* 2Chr 7:6 3027
by the *m* of the prophets Hos 12:10 3027
and had obtained part of this *m* Acts 1:17 1248
That he may take part of this *m* Acts 1:25 1248
prayer, and to the *m* of the word Acts 6:4 1248
when they had fulfilled their *m* Acts 12:25 1248
my course with joy, and the *m* Acts 20:24 1248
among the Gentiles by his *m* Acts 21:19 1248
Or *m*, let us wait on our Rom 12:7 1248
themselves to the *m* of the saints 1Cor 16:15 1248
Therefore, seeing we have this *m* 2Cor 4:1 1248
to us the *m* of reconciliation 2Cor 5:18 1248
thing, that the *m* be not blamed 2Cor 6:3 1248
the saints, for the work of the *m* Eph 4:12 1248
Take heed to the *m* which thou Col 4:17 1248
faithful, putting me into the *m* 1Ti 1:12 1248
make full proof of thy *m* 2Ti 4:5 1248
he is profitable to me for the *m* 2Ti 4:11 1248
he obtained a more excellent *m* Heb 8:6 3009
and all the vessels of the *m* Heb 9:21 3009

MINJAMIN See MINIAMIN.

MINNI (*min'-ni*) *A district in Armenia.*
her the kingdoms of Ararat, *M* Jer 51:27 4508

MINNITH (*min'-nith*) *An Ammonite city.*
Aroer, even till thou come to *M* Judg 11:33 4511
traded in thy market wheat of *M* Eze 27:17 4511

MINSTREL
But now bring me a *m* 2Kin 3:15 5059
came to pass, when the *m* played 2Kin 3:15 5059

MINSTRELS
the ruler's house, and saw the *m* Mt 9:23 834

MINT
for ye pay tithe of *m* and anise and Mt 23:23 2238
for ye tithe *m* and rue and all Lk 11:42 2238

MIPHKAD (*mif'-kad*) *A gate of Jerusalem.*
over against the gate *M*, and to Neh 3:31 4663

MIRACLE
you, saying, Shew a *m* for you Ex 7:9 4159
not the *m* of the loaves Mk 6:52
man which shall do a *m* in my name Mk 9:39 1411
to have seen some *m* done by him Lk 23:8 4592
again the second *m* that Jesus did Jn 4:54 4592
had seen the *m* that Jesus did Jn 6:14 4592
unto him, and said, John did no *m* Jn 10:41 4592
heard that he had done this *m* Jn 12:18 4592
m hath been done by them is Acts 4:16 4592
on whom this *m* of healing was Acts 4:22 4592

MIRACLES
which have seen my glory, and my *m* Num 14:22 226
And his *m*, and his acts, which he Deut 11:3 226
seen, the signs, and those great *m* Deut 29:3 4159
where be all his *m* which our Judg 6:13 6381
This beginning of *m* did Jesus in Jn 2:11 4592
when they saw the *m* which he did Jn 2:23 4592
can do these *m* that thou doest Jn 3:2 4592
because they saw his *m* which he Jn 6:2 4592
seek me, not because ye saw the *m* Jn 6:26 4592
will he do more *m* than these Jn 7:31 4592
a man that is a sinner do such *m* Jn 9:16 4592
for this man doeth many *m* Jn 11:47 4592
he had done so many *m* before them Jn 12:37 4592
approved of God among you by *m* Acts 2:22 1411
wonders and *m* among the people Acts 6:8 4592
seeing the *m* which he did Acts 8:6 4592
and wondered, beholding the *m* Acts 8:13 1411
and Paul, declaring what *m* Acts 15:12 4592
God wrought special *m* by the Acts 19:11 1411
To another the working of *m* 1Cor 12:10 1411
thirdly teachers, after that *m* 1Cor 12:28 1411
are all workers of *m*? 1Cor 12:29 1411
worketh *m* among you, doeth he it Gal 3:5 1411
and wonders, and with divers *m* Heb 2:4 1411
m which he had power to do in the Rev 13:14 4592
the spirits of devils, working *m* Rev 16:14 4592
prophet that wrought *m* before him Rev 19:20 4592

MIRE
stamp them as the *m* of the street 2Sa 22:43 2916
Can the rush grow up without *m* Job 8:11 1207
He hath cast me into the *m* Job 30:19 2563
sharp pointed things upon the *m* Job 41:30 2916
I sink in deep *m*, where there is Ps 69:2 3121
Deliver me out of the *m*, and let Ps 69:14 2916
down like the *m* of the streets Is 10:6 2563
rest, whose waters cast up *m* Is 57:20 7516
dungeon there was no water, but *m* Jer 38:6 2916
so Jeremiah sunk in the *m* Jer 38:6 2916
thy feet are sunk in the *m* Jer 38:22 1206
down as the *m* of the streets Mic 7:10 2916
fine gold as the *m* of the streets Zec 9:3 2916
m of the streets in the battle Zec 10:5 2916
washed to her wallowing in the *m* 2Pet 2:22 1004

MIRIAM (*mir'-e-am*) See MARY.
1. Sister of Aaron.
M the prophetess, the sister of Ex 15:20 4813
M answered them, Sing ye to the Ex 15:21 4813
M and Aaron spake against Num 12:1 4813
Moses, and unto Aaron, and unto *M* Num 12:4 4813
tabernacle, and called Aaron and *M* Num 12:5 4813
M became leprous, white as snow Num 12:10 4813
and Aaron looked upon *M*, and, Num 12:10 4813
M was shut out from the camp Num 12:15 4813
not till *M* was brought in again Num 12:15 4813
M died there, and was buried there Num 20:1 4813
Aaron and Moses, and *M* their sister Num 26:59 4813
thy God did unto *M* by the way Deut 24:9 4813
Aaron, and Moses, and *M* 1Chr 6:3 4813
before thee Moses, Aaron, and *M* Mic 6:4 4813
2. A daughter of Ezra.
and she bare *M*, and Shammai, and 1Chr 4:17 4813

MIRMA (*mur'-mah*) *Son of Shaharaim.*
And Jeuz, and Shachia, and *M* 1Chr 8:10 4821

MIRMAH See MIRMA.

MIRTH
might have sent thee away with *m* Gen 31:27 8057
send portions, and to make great *m* Neh 8:12 8057
that wasted us required of us *m* Ps 137:3 8057
and the end of that *m* is heaviness Prov 14:13 8057
to now, I will prove thee with *m* Eccl 2:1 8057
and of *m*, What doeth it Eccl 2:2 8057
of fools is in the house of *m* Eccl 7:4 8057
Then I commended *m*, because a man Eccl 8:15 8057
The *m* of tabrets ceaseth, the Is 24:8 4885
the *m* of the land is gone Is 24:11 4885
of Jerusalem, the voice of *m* Jer 7:34 8342
and in your days, the voice of *m* Jer 16:9 8342
take from them the voice of *m* Jer 25:10 8342
should we then make *m*? Eze 21:10 7797
also cause all her *m* to cease Hos 2:11 4885

MIRY
horrible pit, out of the *m* clay Ps 40:2 3121
But the *m* places thereof and the Eze 47:11 1207
sawest the iron mixed with *m* clay Dan 2:41 2917
sawest iron mixed with *m* clay Dan 2:43 2917

MISCARRYING
give them a *m* womb and dry breasts Hos 9:14 7921

MISCHIEF
Lest peradventure *m* befall him Gen 42:4 611
if *m* befall him by the way in the Gen 42:38 611
m befall him, ye shall bring down Gen 44:29 611
from her, and yet no *m* follow Ex 21:22 611
And if any *m* follow, then thou Ex 21:23 611
For *m* did he bring them out, to Ex 32:12 7451
people, that they are set on *m* Ex 32:22 7451
secretly practised *m* against him 1Sa 23:9 7451
behold, thou art taken in thy *m* 2Sa 16:8 7451
beside the *m* that Hadad did 1Kin 11:25 7451
and see how this man seeketh *m* 1Kin 20:7 7451
light, some *m* will come upon us 2Kin 7:9 5771
But they thought to do me *m* Neh 6:2 7451
away the *m* of Haman the Agagite Est 8:3 7451
They conceive *m*, and bring forth Job 15:35 5999
iniquity, and hath conceived *m* Ps 7:14 5999
His *m* shall return upon his own Ps 7:16 5999
under his tongue is *m* and vanity Ps 10:7 5999
for thou beholdest *m* and spite, to Ps 10:14 5999
In whose hands is *m*, and their Ps 26:10 2154
but *m* is in their hearts Ps 28:3 7451
He deviseth *m* upon his bed Ps 36:4 205
Why boastest thou thyself in *m* Ps 52:1 7451
m also and sorrow are in the midst Ps 55:10 205
will ye imagine *m* against a man Ps 62:3 205
thee, which frameth *m* by a law Ps 94:20 5999
draw nigh that follow after *m* Ps 119:150 2154
let the *m* of their own lips cover Ps 140:9 5999
not, except they have done *m* Prov 4:16 7489
heart, he deviseth *m* continually Prov 6:14 7451
that be swift in running to *m* Prov 6:18 7451
It is as sport to a fool to do *m* Prov 10:23 2154
but he that seeketh *m*, it shall Prov 11:27 7451
the wicked shall be filled with *m* Prov 12:21 7451
A wicked messenger falleth into *m* Prov 13:17 7451
a perverse tongue falleth into *m* Prov 17:20 7451
and their lips talk of *m* Prov 24:2 5999
but the wicked shall fall into *m* Prov 24:16 7451
his heart shall fall into *m* Prov 28:14 7451
and *m* shall fall upon thee Is 47:11 1943
they conceive *m*, and bring forth Is 59:4 5999
M shall come upon *m* Eze 7:26 1943
these are the men that devise *m* Eze 11:2 205
kings' hearts shall be to do *m* Dan 11:27 4827
yet do they imagine *m* against me Hos 7:15 7451
O full of all subtilty and all *m* Acts 13:10 *4468*

MISCHIEFS
I will heap *m* upon them Deut 32:23 7451
Thy tongue deviseth *m* Ps 52:2 1942
Which imagine *m* in their heart Ps 140:2 7451

MISCHIEVOUS
they imagined a *m* device, which Ps 21:11 4209
that seek my hurt speak *m* things Ps 38:12 1942
evil shall be called a *m* person Prov 24:8 4209
the end of his talk is *m* madness Eccl 10:13 7451
man, he uttereth his *m* desire Mic 7:3 1942

MISERABLE
m comforters are ye all Job 16:2 5999
Christ, we are of all men most *m* 1Cor 15:19 *1652*
not that thou art wretched, and *m* Rev 3:17 *1652*

MISERABLY
He will *m* destroy those wicked Mt 21:41 *2560*

MISERIES
of her *m* all her pleasant things Lam 1:7 4788
howl for your *m* that shall come Jas 5:1 *5004*

MISERY
was grieved for the *m* of Israel Judg 10:16 5999
light given to him that is in *m* Job 3:20 6001
Because thou shalt forget thy *m* Job 11:16 5999
and remember his *m* no more Prov 31:7 5999
therefore the *m* of man is great Eccl 8:6 7451
mine affliction and my *m*, the Lam 3:19 4788
and *m* are in their ways Rom 3:16 *5004*

MISGAB (*mis'-gab*) *The mountainous area in Moab.*
M is confounded and dismayed Jer 48:1 4869

MISHAEL (*mish'-a-el*) See MISHAL.
1. A son of Uzziel.
M, and Elzaphan, and Zithri Ex 6:22 4332
Moses called *M* and Lev 10:4 4332
of Judah, Daniel, Hananiah, *M* Dan 1:6 4332
and to *M*, of Meshach Dan 1:7 4332
had set over Daniel, Hananiah, *M* Dan 1:11 4332
none like Daniel, Hananiah, *M* Dan 1:19 4332
the thing known to Hananiah, *M* Dan 2:17 4332
2. A priest who aided Ezra.
on his left hand, Pedaiah, and *M* Neh 8:4 4332

MISHAL (*mi'-shal*) See MISHAEL. *A Levitical city in Asher.*
M with her suburbs, Abdon with Josh 21:30 4861

MISHAM (*mi'-sham*) *Son of Elpaal.*
Eber, and *M*, and Shamed, who built 1Chr 8:12 4936

MISHEAL (*mish'-e-al*) *Same as Mishal.*
And Alammelech, and Amad, and *M* Josh 19:26 4861

MISHMA (*mish'-mah*) *A son of Ishmeal.*
And *M*, and Dumah, and Massa, Gen 25:14 4927
M, and Dumah, Massa, Hadad, and 1Chr 1:30 4927
son, Mibsam his son, *M* his son 1Chr 4:25 4927
And the sons of *M* 1Chr 4:26 4927

MISHMANNAH (*mish-man'-nah*) *A warrior in David's army.*
M the fourth, Jeremiah the fifth, 1Chr 12:10 4925

MISHRAITES (*mish'-ra-ites*) *A family of Kirjath-jearim.*
and the Shumathites, and the *M* 1Chr 2:53 4954

MISPAR See MIZPAR.

MISPERETH (*mis-pe'-reth*) See MIZPAR. *An exile with Ezra.*
Nahamani, Mordecai, Bilshan, *M* Neh 7:7 4559

MISREPHOTH-MAIM *Same as Zarephath.*
them unto great Zidon, and unto *M* Josh 11:8 4956
hill country from Lebanon unto *M* Josh 13:6 4956

MISS
at an hair breadth, and not *m* Judg 20:16 2398
If thy father at all *m* me 1Sa 20:6 6485

MISSED
and thou shalt be *m*, because thy 1Sa 20:18 6485
neither *m* we any thing, as long 1Sa 25:15 6485
so that nothing was *m* of all that 1Sa 25:21 6485

MISSING
was there ought *m* unto them 1Sa 25:7 6485
if by any means he be *m*, then 1Kin 20:39 6485

MIST
there went up a *m* from the earth Gen 2:6 108
immediately there fell on him a *m* Acts 13:11 887
to whom the *m* of darkness is 2Pet 2:17 *2217*

MISTRESS
her *m* was despised in her eyes Gen 16:4 1404
flee from the face of my *m* Sarai Gen 16:8 1404
said unto her, Return to thy *m* Gen 16:9 1404
the *m* of the house, fell sick 1Kin 17:17 1172
And she said unto her *m*, Would God 2Kin 5:3 1404
a maiden unto the hand of her *m* Ps 123:2 1404
an handmaid that is heir to her *m* Prov 30:23 1404
as with the maid, so with her *m* Is 24:2 1404
the *m* of witchcrafts, that Nah 3:4 1172

MISUSED
m his prophets, until the wrath 2Chr 36:16 8591

MITE
thou hast paid the very last *m* Lk 12:59 *3016*

MITES
poor widow, and she threw in two *m* Mk 12:42 *3016*
widow casting in thither two *m* Lk 21:2 *3016*

MITHCAH (*mith'-cah*) *An Israelite encampment in the wilderness.*
from Tarah, and pitched in *M* Num 33:28 4989
And they went from *M*, and pitched Num 33:29 4989

MITHCAK See MITHCAH.

MITHKAH See MITHCAH.

MITHNITE (*mith'-nite*) *Family name of Joshaphat.*
of Maachah, and Joshaphat the *M* 1Chr 11:43 4981

MITHREDATH (*mith'-re-dath*) *Treasurer for King Cyrus of Persia.*
by the hand of *M* the treasurer Ezr 1:8 4990
of Artaxerxes wrote Bishlam, *M* Ezr 4:7 4990

MITRE
a robe, and a broidered coat, a *m* Ex 28:4 4701
lace, that it may be upon the *m* Ex 28:37 4701
forefront of the *m* it shall be Ex 28:37 4701
shalt make the *m* of fine linen Ex 28:39 4701
shalt put the *m* upon his head Ex 29:6 4701
and put the holy crown upon the *m* Ex 29:6 4701
a *m* of fine linen, and goodly Ex 39:28 4701
to fasten it on high upon the *m* Ex 39:31 4701
he put the *m* upon his head Lev 8:9 4701
also upon the *m*, even upon his Lev 8:9 4701
with the linen *m* shall he be Lev 16:4 4701
them set a fair *m* upon his head Zec 3:5 6797
they set a fair *m* upon his head Zec 3:5 6797

MITYLENE (*mit-i-le'-ne*) *Major city of the island of Lesbos.*
we took him in, and came to *M* Acts 20:14 *3412*

MIXED
a *m* multitude went up also with Ex 12:38 6154
from Israel all the *m* multitude Neh 13:3 6154
they that go to seek *m* wine Prov 23:30 4469
dross, thy wine *m* with water Is 1:22 4107
sawest the iron *m* with miry clay Dan 2:41 6151
thou sawest iron *m* with miry clay Dan 2:43 6151
even as iron is not *m* with clay Dan 2:43 6151
he hath *m* himself among the Hos 7:8 1101
not being *m* with faith in them Heb 4:2 *4786*

MIXT
the *m* multitude that was among Num 11:4

MIXTURE
it is full of *m* Ps 75:8 4538
by night, and brought a *m* of myrrh Jn 19:39 *3395*
which is poured out without *m* Rev 14:10 *194*

MIZAR (*mi'-zar*) *A hill near Hermon.*
the Hermonites, from the hill *M* Ps 42:6 4706

MIZPAH (*miz'-pah*) See MIZPEH.
1. A city in Gad.
And *M*; for he said Gen 31:49 4709
2. A city in Benjamin.
with them Geba of Benjamin, and *M* 1Kin 15:22 4709
the men of Gibeon, and of *M* Neh 3:7 4709
3. A city in Judah.
there came to Gedaliah to *M* 2Kin 25:23 4709
Chaldees that were with him at *M* 2Kin 25:25 4709
and he built therewith Geba and *M* 2Chr 16:6 4709
Gedaliah the son of Ahikam to *M* Jer 40:6 4708
Then they came to Gedaliah to *M* Jer 40:8 4708
I will dwell at *M* to serve the Jer 40:10 4708
of Judah, to Gedaliah, unto *M* Jer 40:12 4708
the fields, came to Gedaliah to *M* Jer 40:13 4708
spake to Gedaliah in *M* secretly Jer 40:15 4709
Gedaliah the son of Ahikam to *M* Jer 41:1 4709
they did eat bread together in *M* Jer 41:1 4709
him, even with Gedaliah, at *M* Jer 41:3 4709
went forth from *M* to meet them Jer 41:6 4709
of the people that were in *M* Jer 41:10 4709
all the people that remained in *M* Jer 41:10 4709
away captive from *M* cast about Jer 41:14 4709
the son of Nethaniah, from *M* Jer 41:16 4709
because ye have been a snare on *M* Hos 5:1 4709
4. A district ruled by Shallum.
Colhozeh, the ruler of part of *M* Neh 3:15 4709
5. A place ruled by Ezer.
the son of Jeshua, the ruler of *M* Neh 3:19 4709

MIZPAR (*miz'-par*) See MISPERETH. *A clan leader with Zerubbabel.*
Reelaiah, Mordecai, Bilshan, *M* Ezr 2:2 4558

MIZPEH (*miz'-peh*) See MIZPAH, RAMATH-MIZPEH.
1. A valley near Mt. Hermon.
under Hermon in the land of *M* Josh 11:3 4709
and unto the valley of *M* eastward Josh 11:8 4708
2. A city in Judah.
And Dilean, and *M*, and Joktheel, Josh 15:38 4708
of Gilead, unto the LORD in *M* Judg 20:1 4709
of Israel were gone up to *M* Judg 20:3 4709
the men of Israel had sworn in *M* Judg 21:1 4709
that came not up to the LORD to *M* Judg 21:5 4709
that came not up to *M* to the LORD Judg 21:8 4709
said, Gather all Israel to *M* 1Sa 7:5 4708
And they gathered together to *M* 1Sa 7:6 4709
the children of Israel in *M* 1Sa 7:6 4708
were gathered together to *M* 1Sa 7:7 4708
the men of Israel went out of *M* 1Sa 7:11 4709
took a stone, and set it between *M* 1Sa 7:12 4709
to Beth-el, and Gilgal, and *M* 1Sa 7:16 4709
together unto the LORD to *M* 1Sa 10:17 4709
3. A city in Benjamin.
And *M*, and Chephirah, and Mozah, Josh 18:26 4708
4. A city in Gad.
together, and encamped in *M* Judg 10:17 4709
his words before the LORD in *M* Judg 11:11 4709
and passed over *M* of Gilead Judg 11:29 4708
from *M* of Gilead he passed over Judg 11:29 4708
Jephthah came to *M* unto his house Judg 11:34 4709
5. A city in Moab.
And David went thence to *M* of Moab. 1Sa 22:3 4708

MIZRAIM (*miz'-ra-im*) See ABEL-MIZRAIM. *Son of Ham.*
Cush, and *M*, and Phut, and Canaan Gen 10:6 4714
M begat Ludim, and Anamim, and Gen 10:13 4714
Cush, and *M*, Put, and Canaan 1Chr 1:8 4714
M begat Ludim, and Anamim, and 1Chr 1:11 4714

MIZZAH (*miz'-zah*) *Son of Reuel.*
Nahath, and Zerah, Shammah, and *M* Gen 36:13 4199
duke Zerah, duke Shammah, duke *M* Gen 36:17 4199
Nahath, Zerah, Shammah, and *M* 1Chr 1:37 4199

MNASON (*na'-son*) *A Christian in Jerusalem.*
brought with them one *M* of Cyprus Acts 21:16 *3416*

MOAB (*mo'-ab*)
1. A nation east of Israel.
smote Midian in the field of *M* Gen 36:35 4124

the mighty men of *M*, trembling Ex 15:15 4124
the wilderness which is before *M* Num 21:11 4124
is the border of *M*, between *M* Num 21:13 4124
Ar, and lieth upon the border of *M* Num 21:15 4124
that is in the country of *M* Num 21:20 4124
against the former king of *M* Num 21:26 4124
it hath consumed Ar of *M*, and the Num 21:28 4124
Woe to thee, *M* Num 21:29 4124
pitched in the plains of *M* on Num 22:1 4124
M was sore afraid of the people, Num 22:3 4124
M was distressed because of the Num 22:3 4124
M said unto the elders of Midian, Num 22:4 4124
And the elders of *M* and the elders Num 22:7 4124
the princes of *M* abode with Num 22:8 4124
the son of Zippor, king of *M* Num 22:10 4124
And the princes of *M* rose up Num 22:14 4124
and went with the princes of *M* Num 22:21 4124
out to meet him unto a city of *M* Num 22:36 4124
he, and all the princes of *M* Num 23:6 4124
Balak the king of *M* hath brought Num 23:7 4124
and the princes of *M* with him Num 23:17 4124
and shall smite the corners of *M* Num 24:17 4124
whoredom with the daughters of *M* Num 25:1 4124
of *M* by Jordan near Jericho Num 26:3 4124
of *M* by Jordan near Jericho Num 26:63 4124
unto the camp at the plains of *M* Num 31:12 4124
in Ije-abarim, in the border of *M* Num 33:44 4124
of *M* by Jordan near Jericho Num 33:48 4124
Abel-shittim in the plains of *M* Num 33:49 4124
in the plains of *M* by Jordan Num 33:50 4124
of *M* by Jordan near Jericho Num 35:1 4124
of *M* by Jordan near Jericho Num 36:13 4124
side Jordan, in the land of *M* Deut 1:5 4124
by the way of the wilderness of *M* Deut 2:8 4124
over through Ar, the coast of *M* Deut 2:18 4124
of Israel in the land of *M* Deut 29:1 4124
Nebo, which is in the land of *M* Deut 32:49 4124
of *M* unto the mountain of Nebo Deut 34:1 4124
LORD died there in the land of *M* Deut 34:5 4124
him in a valley in the land of *M* Deut 34:6 4124
in the plains of *M* thirty days Deut 34:8 4124
inheritance in the plains of *M* Josh 13:32 4124
the son of Zippor, king of *M* Josh 24:9 4124
the king of *M* against Israel Judg 3:12 4124
the king of *M* eighteen years Judg 3:14 4124
present unto Eglon the king of *M* Judg 3:15 4124
the present unto Eglon king of *M* Judg 3:17 4124
took the fords of Jordan toward *M* Judg 3:28 4124
they slew of *M* at that time about Judg 3:29 4124
So *M* was subdued that day under Judg 3:30 4124
gods of Zidon, and the gods of *M* Judg 10:6 4124
took not away the land of *M* Judg 11:15 4124
they sent unto the king of *M* Judg 11:17 4124
land of Edom, and the land of *M* Judg 11:18 4124
by the east side of the land of *M* Judg 11:18 4124
came not within the border of *M* Judg 11:18 4124
for Arnon was the border of *M* Judg 11:18 4124
the son of Zippor, king of *M* Judg 11:25 4124
to sojourn in the country of *M* Ruth 1:1 4124
they came into the country of *M* Ruth 1:2 4124
took them wives of the women of *M* Ruth 1:4 4125
return from the country of *M* Ruth 1:6 4124
M how that the LORD had visited Ruth 1:6 4124
returned out of the country of *M* Ruth 1:22 4124
Naomi out of the country of *M* Ruth 2:6 4124
again out of the country of *M* Ruth 4:3 4124
and into the hand of the king of *M* 1Sa 12:9 4124
enemies on every side, against *M* 1Sa 14:47 4124
David went thence to Mizpeh of *M* 1Sa 22:3 4124
and he said unto the king of *M* 1Sa 22:3 4124
brought them before the king of *M* 1Sa 22:4 4124
And he smote *M*, and measured them 2Sa 8:2 4124
Of Syria, and of *M*, and of the 2Sa 8:12 4124
he slew two lionlike men of *M* 2Sa 23:20 4124
for Chemosh, the abomination of *M* 1Kin 11:7 4124
Then *M* rebelled against Israel 2Kin 1:1 4124
Mesha king of *M* was a sheepmaster 2Kin 3:4 4124
that the king of *M* rebelled 2Kin 3:5 4124
The king of *M* hath rebelled 2Kin 3:7 4124
go with me against *M* to battle 2Kin 3:7 4124
deliver them into the hand of *M* 2Kin 3:10 4124
deliver them into the hand of *M* 2Kin 3:13 4124
now therefore, *M*, to the spoil 2Kin 3:23 4124
when the king of *M* saw that the 2Kin 3:26 4124
smote Midian in the field of *M* 1Chr 1:46 4124
Saraph, who had the dominion in *M* 1Chr 4:22 4124
children in the country of *M* 1Chr 8:8 4124
he slew two lionlike men of *M* 1Chr 11:22 4124
And he smote *M* 1Chr 18:2 4124
from Edom, and from *M*, and from the 1Chr 18:11 4124
this also, that the children of *M* 2Chr 20:1 4124
the children of Ammon and *M* 2Chr 20:10 4124
against the children of Ammon, *M* 2Chr 20:22 4124
Ammon and *M* stood up against the 2Chr 20:23 4124
of Ashdod, of Ammon, and of *M* Neh 13:23 4125
M is my washpot Ps 60:8 4124
of *M*, and the Hagarenes Ps 83:6 4124
M is my washpot Ps 108:9 4124
lay their hand upon Edom and *M* Is 11:14 4124
The burden of *M* Is 15:1 4124
the night Ar of *M* is laid waste Is 15:1 4124
the night Kir of *M* is laid waste Is 15:1 4124
M shall howl over Nebo, and over Is 15:2 4124
armed soldiers of *M* shall cry out Is 15:4 4124
My heart shall cry out for *M* Is 15:5 4124
gone round about the borders of *M* Is 15:8 4124
lions upon him that escapeth of *M* Is 15:9 4124
so the daughters of *M* shall be at Is 16:2 4124
mine outcasts dwell with thee, *M* Is 16:4 4124
We have heard of the pride of *M* Is 16:6 4124
Therefore shall *M* howl for *M* Is 16:7 4124
Therefore shall *M* howl for *M* Is 16:7 4124
shall sound like an harp for *M* Is 16:11 4124
when it is seen that *M* is weary Is 16:12 4124
concerning *M* since that time Is 16:13 4124
the glory of *M* shall be contemned Is 16:14 4124
M shall be trodden down under him Is 25:10 4124
and the children of Ammon, and *M* Jer 9:26 4124
Edom, and *M*, and the children of Jer 25:21 4124
king of Edom, and to the king of *M* Jer 27:3 4124
when all the Jews that were in *M* Jer 40:11 4124
Against *M* thus saith the LORD of Jer 48:1 4124
shall be no more praise of *M* Jer 48:2 4124
M is destroyed Jer 48:4 4124
Give wings unto *M*, that it may Jer 48:9 4124
M hath been at ease from his Jer 48:11 4124
M shall be ashamed of Chemosh, as Jer 48:13 4124
M is spoiled, and gone up out of Jer 48:15 4124
The calamity of *M* is near to come Jer 48:16 4124
for the spoiler of *M* shall come Jer 48:18 4124
M is confounded Jer 48:20 4124
it in Arnon, that *M* is spoiled, Jer 48:20 4124
all the cities of the land of *M* Jer 48:24 4124
The horn of *M* is cut off, and his Jer 48:25 4124
M also shall wallow in his vomit, Jer 48:26 4124
O ye that dwell in *M*, leave the Jer 48:28 4124
We have heard the pride of *M* Jer 48:29 4124
Therefore will I howl for *M* Jer 48:31 4124
and I will cry out for all *M* Jer 48:31 4124
field, and from the land of *M* Jer 48:33 4124
I will cause to cease in *M* Jer 48:35 4124
shall sound for *M* like pipes Jer 48:36 4124
upon all the housetops of *M* Jer 48:38 4124
for I have broken *M* like a vessel Jer 48:38 4124
how hath *M* turned the back with Jer 48:39 4124
so shall *M* be a derision and a Jer 48:39 4124
and shall spread his wings over *M* Jer 48:40 4124
the mighty men's hearts in *M* at Jer 48:41 4124
M shall be destroyed from being a Jer 48:42 4124
be upon thee, O inhabitant of *M* Jer 48:43 4124
I will bring upon it, even upon *M* Jer 48:44 4124
and shall devour the corner of *M* Jer 48:45 4124
Woe be unto thee, O *M* Jer 48:46 4124
captivity of *M* in the latter days Jer 48:47 4124
Thus far is the judgment of *M* Jer 48:47 4124
Because that *M* and Seir do say, Eze 25:8 4124
the side of *M* from the cities Eze 25:9 4124
I will execute judgments upon *M* Eze 25:11 4124
out of his hand, even Edom, and *M* Dan 11:41 4124
For three transgressions of *M* Amos 2:1 4124
But I will send a fire upon *M* Amos 2:2 4124
M shall die with tumult, with Amos 2:2 4124
what Balak king of *M* consulted Mic 6:5 4124
I have heard the reproach of *M* Zeph 2:8 4124
Surely *M* shall be as Sodom, and Zeph 2:9 4124
2. Son of Lot.
bare a son, and called his name *M* Gen 19:37 4124

MOABITE (*mo'-ab-ite*) See MOABITES, MOABITESS, MOABITISH. *An inhabitant of Moab.*
An Ammonite or *M* shall not enter Deut 23:3 4125
sons of Elnaam, and Ithmah the *M* 1Chr 11:46 4125
the *M* should not come into the Neh 13:1 4125

MOABITES (*mo'-ab-ites*)
the father of the *M* unto this day Gen 19:37 4124
was king of the *M* at that time Num 22:4 4124
said unto me, Distress not the *M* Deut 2:9 4124
but the *M* call them Emims Deut 2:11 4125
the *M* which dwell in Ar, did unto Deut 2:29 4125
your enemies the *M* into your hand Judg 3:28 4124
so the *M* became David's servants, 2Sa 8:2 4124
of Pharaoh, women of the *M* 1Kin 11:1 4125
Chemosh the god of the *M* 1Kin 11:33 4124
deliver the *M* also into your hand 2Kin 3:18 4124
when all the *M* heard that the 2Kin 3:21 4124
the *M* saw the water on the other 2Kin 3:22 4124
Israelites rose up and smote the *M* 2Kin 3:24 4124
they went forward smiting the *M* 2Kin 3:24 4124
the bands of the *M* invaded the 2Kin 13:20 4124
Chemosh the abomination of the *M* 2Kin 23:13 4124
of the Syrians, and bands of the *M* 2Kin 24:2 4124
the *M* became David's servants, and 1Chr 18:2 4124
Jebusites, the Ammonites, the *M* Ezr 9:1 4124

MOABITESS (*mo'-ab-i-tess*) *A female Moabite.*
So Naomi returned, and Ruth the *M* Ruth 1:22 4125
Ruth the *M* said unto Naomi, Let Ruth 2:2 4125
And Ruth the *M* said, He said unto Ruth 2:21 4125
must buy it also of Ruth the *M* Ruth 4:5 4125
Moreover Ruth the *M*, the wife of Ruth 4:10 4125
Jehozabad the son of Shimrith a *M* 2Chr 24:26 4125

MOABITISH (*mo'-ab-i-tish*) *Belonging to the Moabites.*
It is the *M* damsel that came back Ruth 2:6 4125

MOADIAH (*mo-ad-i'-ah*) See MAADIAH. *A priest.*
of Miniamin, of *M*, Piltai Neh 12:17 4153

MOCK
in an Hebrew unto us to *m* us Gen 39:14 6711
unto us, came in unto me to *m* me Gen 39:17 6711
mocketh another, do ye so *m* him Job 13:9 2048
and after that I have spoken, *m* on Job 21:3 3932
I will *m* when your fear cometh Prov 1:26 3932
Fools make a *m* at sin Prov 14:9 3887
me into their hand, and they *m* me Jer 38:19 5953
saw her, and did *m* at her sabbaths Lam 1:7 7832
be far from thee, shall *m* thee Eze 22:5 7046
deliver him to the Gentiles to *m* Mt 20:19 *1702*
And they shall *m* him, and shall Mk 10:34 *1702*
all that behold it begin to *m* him Lk 14:29 *1702*

MOCKED
one that *m* unto his sons in law Gen 19:14 6711
the ass, Because thou hast *m* me Num 22:29 5953
Samson, Behold, thou hast *m* me Judg 16:10 2048
Samson, Hitherto thou hast *m* me Judg 16:13 2048
thou hast *m* me these three times, Judg 16:15 2048
pass at noon, that Elijah *m* them 1Kin 18:27 2048
m him, and said unto him, Go up, 2Kin 2:23 7046
laughed them to scorn, and *m* them 2Chr 30:10 3932
But they *m* the messengers of God, 2Chr 36:16 3931
great indignation, and *m* the Jews Neh 4:1 3932
I am as one *m* of his neighbour, Job 12:4 7832
saw that he was *m* of the wise men Mt 2:16 *1702*
m him, saying, Hail, King of the Mt 27:29 *1702*
And after that they had *m* him Mt 27:31 *1702*
And when they had *m* him, they took Mk 15:20 *1702*
unto the Gentiles, and shall be *m* Lk 18:32 *1702*
And the men that held Jesus *m* him Lk 22:63 *1702*
m him, and arrayed him in a Lk 23:11 *1702*
And the soldiers also *m* him Lk 23:36 *1702*
resurrection of the dead, some *m* Acts 17:32 *5512*
God is not *m* Gal 6:7 *3456*

MOCKER
Wine is a *m*, strong drink is Prov 20:1 3887

MOCKERS
Are there not *m* with me Job 17:2 2049
With hypocritical *m* in feasts Ps 35:16 3934
Now therefore be ye not *m* Is 28:22 3887
sat not in the assembly of the *m* Jer 15:17 7832
should be *m* in the last time Jude 18 *1703*

MOCKEST
and when thou *m*, shall no man make. Job 11:3 3932

MOCKETH
or as one man *m* another, do ye so Job 13:9 2048
He *m* at fear, and is not Job 39:22 7832
Whoso *m* the poor reproacheth his Prov 17:5 3932
The eye that *m* at his father, and Prov 30:17 3932
in derision daily, every one *m* me Jer 20:7 3932

MOCKING
she had born unto Abraham, *m* Gen 21:9 6711
heathen, and a *m* to all countries Eze 22:4 7048
also the chief priests *m* him Mt 27:41 *1702*
m said among themselves with the Mk 15:31 *1702*
Others *m* said, These men are full Acts 2:13 *5512*

MOCKINGS
And others had trial of cruel *m* Heb 11:36 *1701*

MODERATELY
hath given you the former rain *m* Joel 2:23 6666

MODERATION
Let your *m* be known unto all men Phil 4:5 *1933*

MODEST
adorn themselves in *m* apparel 1Ti 2:9 *2887*

MOIST
of grapes, nor eat *m* grapes Num 6:3 3892

MOISTENED
and his bones are *m* with marrow Job 21:24 8248

MOISTURE
my *m* is turned into the drought Ps 32:4 3955
away, because it lacked *m* Lk 8:6 *2429*

MOLADAH (*mo-la'-dah*) *A city in Judah.*
Amam, and Shema, and *M*, Josh 15:26 4137
Beer-sheba, or Sheba, and *M* Josh 19:2 4137
And they dwelt at Beer-sheba, and *M* 1Chr 4:28 4137
And at Jeshua, and at *M*, and at Neh 11:26 4137

MOLE
lizard, and the snail, and the *m* Lev 11:30 8580

MOLECH (*mo'-lek*) See MALCHAM, MOLOCH. *An Ammonite god.*
seed pass through the fire to *M* Lev 18:21 4432
giveth any of his seed unto *M* Lev 20:2 4432
he hath given of his seed unto *M* Lev 20:3 4432
when he giveth of his seed unto *M* Lev 20:4 4432
him, to commit whoredom with *M* Lev 20:5 4432
is before Jerusalem, and for *M* 1Kin 11:7 4432
to pass through the fire to *M* 2Kin 23:10 4432
to pass through the fire unto *M* Jer 32:35 4432

MOLES
for himself to worship, to the *m* Is 2:20 2661

MOLID (*mo'-lid*) *A descendant of Jerahmeel.*
and she bare him Ahban, and *M* 1Chr 2:29 4140

MOLLIFIED
bound up, neither *m* with ointment Is 1:6 7401

MOLOCH (*mo'-loch*) See MILCHOM, MOLECH. *Same as Molech.*
borne the tabernacle of your *M* Amos 5:26 4432
ye took up the tabernacle of *M* Acts 7:43 *3434*

MOLTEN
after he had made it a *m* calf Ex 32:4 4541
they have made them a *m* calf Ex 32:8 4541
Thou shalt make thee no *m* gods Ex 34:17 4541
nor make to yourselves *m* gods Lev 19:4 4541
and destroy all their *m* images Num 33:52 4541
they have made them a *m* image Deut 9:12 4541
God, and had made you a *m* calf Deut 9:16 4541
that maketh any graven or *m* image Deut 27:15 4541
make a graven image and a *m* image Judg 17:3 4541
a graven image and a *m* image Judg 17:4 4541
and a graven image, and a *m* image Judg 18:14 4541
and the teraphim, and the *m* image Judg 18:17 4541
and the teraphim, and the *m* image Judg 18:18 4541
he made two chapiters of *m* brass 1Kin 7:16 3332
And he made a *m* sea, ten cubits 1Kin 7:23 3332
the laver were undersetters *m* 1Kin 7:30 3332
and their spokes, were all *m* 1Kin 7:33 3332
m images, to provoke me to anger, 1Kin 14:9 4541
their God, and made them *m* images 2Kin 17:16 4541
Also he made a *m* sea of ten 2Chr 4:2 3332
made also *m* images for Baalim 2Chr 28:2 4541
carved images, and the *m* images 2Chr 34:3 4541
the *m* images, he brake in pieces, 2Chr 34:4 4541

when they had made them a *m* calf	Neh 9:18	4541
brass is *m* out of the stone	Job 28:2	6694
strong, and as a *m* looking glass	Job 37:18	3332
Horeb, and worshipped the *m* image	Ps 106:19	4541
ornament of thy *m* images of gold	Is 30:22	4541
their *m* images are wind and	Is 41:29	5262
images, that say to the *m* images	Is 42:17	4541
or *m* a graven image that is	Is 44:10	5258
my *m* image, hath commanded them	Is 48:5	5262
for his *m* image is falsehood, and	Jer 10:14	5262
for his *m* image is falsehood, and	Jer 51:17	5262
filthiness of it may be *m* in it	Eze 24:11	5413
have made them *m* images of their	Hos 13:2	4541
mountains shall be *m* under him	Mic 1:4	4549
the graven image and the *m* image	Nah 1:14	4541
the *m* image, and a teacher of lies	Hab 2:18	4541

MOMENT

up into the midst of thee in a *m*	Ex 33:5	7281
that I may consume them in a *m*	Num 16:21	7281
that I may consume them as in a *m*	Num 16:45	7281
every morning, and try him every *m*	Job 7:18	7281
joy of the hypocrite but for a *m*	Job 20:5	7281
in a *m* go down to the grave	Job 21:13	7281
In a *m* shall they die, and the	Job 34:20	7281
For his anger endureth but a *m*	Ps 30:5	7281
into desolation, as in a *m*	Ps 73:19	7281
but a lying tongue is but for a *m*	Prov 12:19	7281
thyself as it were for a little *m*	Is 26:20	7281
I will water it every *m*	Is 27:3	7281
come to thee in a *m* in one day	Is 47:9	7281
For a small *m* have I forsaken	Is 54:7	7281
I hid my face from thee for a *m*	Is 54:8	7281
spoiled, and my curtains in a *m*	Jer 4:20	7281
that was overthrown as in a *m*	Lam 4:6	7281
and shall tremble at every *m*	Eze 26:16	7281
and they shall tremble at every *m*	Eze 32:10	7281
of the world in a *m* of time	Lk 4:5	4743
In a *m*, in the twinkling of an	1Cor 15:52	*823*
affliction, which is but for a *m*	2Cor 4:17	*3901*

MONEY

or bought with *m* of any stranger,	Gen 17:12	3701
and he that is bought with thy *m*	Gen 17:13	3701
all that were bought with his *m*	Gen 17:23	3701
bought with *m* of the stranger,	Gen 17:27	3701
for as much *m* as it is worth he	Gen 23:9	3701
I will give thee *m* for the field	Gen 23:13	3701
current *m* with the merchant	Gen 23:16	3701
and hath quite devoured also our *m*	Gen 31:15	3701
for an hundred pieces of *m*	Gen 33:19	7192
every man's *m* into his sack	Gen 42:25	3701
in the inn, he espied his *m*	Gen 42:27	3701
his brethren, My *m* is restored	Gen 42:28	3701
man's bundle of *m* was in his sack	Gen 42:35	3701
their father saw the bundles of *m*	Gen 42:35	3701
take double *m* in your hand	Gen 43:12	3701
the *m* that was brought again in	Gen 43:12	3701
they took double *m* in their hand	Gen 43:15	3701
Because of the *m* that was	Gen 43:18	3701
every man's *m* was in the mouth of	Gen 43:21	3701
of his sack, our *m* in full weight	Gen 43:21	3701
other *m* have we brought down in	Gen 43:22	3701
tell who put our *m* in our sacks	Gen 43:22	3701
I had your *m*	Gen 43:23	3701
put every man's *m* in his sack's	Gen 44:1	3701
of the youngest, and his corn *m*	Gen 44:2	3701
Behold, the *m*, which we found in	Gen 44:8	3701
Joseph gathered up all the *m* that	Gen 47:14	3701
Joseph brought the *m* into	Gen 47:14	3701
when *m* failed in the land of	Gen 47:15	3701
for the *m* faileth	Gen 47:15	3701
you for your cattle, if *m* fail	Gen 47:16	3701
my lord, how that our *m* is spent	Gen 47:18	3701
servant that is bought for *m*	Ex 12:44	3701
shall she go out free without *m*	Ex 21:11	3701
for he is his *m*	Ex 21:21	3701
there be laid on him a sum of *m*	Ex 21:30	
give *m* unto the owner of them	Ex 21:34	3701
live ox, and divide the *m* of it	Ex 21:35	3701
his neighbour *m* or stuff to keep	Ex 22:7	3701
he shall pay *m* according to the	Ex 22:17	3701
If thou lend *m* to any of my	Ex 22:25	3701
m of the children of Israel	Ex 30:16	3701
priest buy any soul with his *m*	Lev 22:11	3701
not give him thy *m* upon usury	Lev 25:37	3701
of the *m* that he was bought for	Lev 25:51	3701
the *m* of thy estimation unto it	Lev 27:15	3701
shall reckon unto him the *m*	Lev 27:18	3701
the *m* of thy estimation unto it	Lev 27:19	3701
And thou shalt give the *m*,	Num 3:48	3701
m of them that were over and above	Num 3:49	3701
children of Israel took he the *m*	Num 3:50	3701
Moses gave the *m* of them that	Num 3:51	3701
for the *m* of five shekels, after	Num 18:16	3701
Ye shall buy meat of them for *m*	Deut 2:6	3701
also buy water of them for *m*	Deut 2:6	3701
Thou shalt sell me meat for *m*	Deut 2:28	3701
and give me water for *m*, that I	Deut 2:28	3701
Then shalt thou turn it into *m*	Deut 14:25	3701
bind up the *m* in thine hand, and	Deut 14:25	3701
thou shalt bestow that *m* for	Deut 14:26	3701
shalt not sell her at all for *m*	Deut 21:14	3701
usury of *m*, usury of victuals,	Deut 23:19	3701
they took no gain of *m*	Judg 5:19	3701
her, and brought *m* in their hand	Judg 16:18	3701
he restored the *m* unto his mother	Judg 17:4	3701
give thee the worth of it in *m*	1Kin 21:2	3701
him, Give me thy vineyard for *m*	1Kin 21:6	3701
he refused to give thee for *m*	1Kin 21:15	3701
Is it a time to receive *m*	2Kin 5:26	3701
All the *m* of the dedicated things	2Kin 12:4	3701
even the *m* of every one that	2Kin 12:4	3701
the *m* that every man is set at,	2Kin 12:4	3701
all the *m* that cometh into any	2Kin 12:4	3701
no more *m* of your acquaintance	2Kin 12:7	3701
receive no more *m* of the people	2Kin 12:8	3701
the door put therein all the *m*	2Kin 12:9	3701
there was much *m* in the chest	2Kin 12:10	3701
told the *m* that was found in the	2Kin 12:10	3701
And they gave the *m*, being told,	2Kin 12:11	3701
of the *m* that was brought into	2Kin 12:13	3701
the *m* to be bestowed on workmen	2Kin 12:15	3701
The trespass *m* and sin *m* was	2Kin 12:16	3701
Menahem exacted the *m* of Israel	2Kin 15:20	3701
m that was delivered into their	2Kin 22:7	3701
the *m* that was found in the house	2Kin 22:9	3701
he taxed the land to give the *m*	2Kin 23:35	3701
gather of all Israel *m* to repair	2Chr 24:5	3701
they saw that there was much *m*	2Chr 24:11	3701
day, and gathered *m* in abundance	2Chr 24:11	3701
the rest of the *m* before the king	2Chr 24:14	3701
they delivered the *m* that was	2Chr 34:9	3701
when they brought out the *m* that	2Chr 34:14	3701
m that was found in the house of	2Chr 34:17	3701
They gave *m* also unto the masons,	Ezr 3:7	3701
buy speedily with this *m* bullocks	Ezr 7:17	3702
We have borrowed *m* for the king's	Neh 5:4	3701
servants, might exact of them *m*	Neh 5:10	3701
also the hundredth part of the *m*	Neh 5:11	3701
of the sum of the *m* that Haman	Est 4:7	3701
the fruits thereof without *m*	Job 31:39	3701
man also gave him a piece of *m*	Job 42:11	7192
putteth not out his *m* to usury	Ps 15:5	3701
He hath taken a bag of *m* with him	Prov 7:20	3701
is a defence, and *m* is a defence	Eccl 7:12	3701
but *m* answereth all things	Eccl 10:19	3701
bought me no sweet cane with *m*	Is 43:24	3701
and ye shall be redeemed without *m*	Is 52:3	3701
the waters, and he that hath no *m*	Is 55:1	3701
come, buy wine and milk without *m*	Is 55:1	3701
Wherefore do ye spend *m* for that	Is 55:2	3701
in Anathoth, and weighed him the *m*	Jer 32:9	3701
weighed him the *m* in the balances	Jer 32:10	3701
GOD, Buy thee the field for *m*	Jer 32:25	3701
Men shall buy fields for *m*	Jer 32:44	3701
We have drunken our water for *m*	Lam 5:4	3701
the prophets thereof divine for *m*	Mic 3:11	3701
received tribute *m* came to Peter	Mt 17:24	
thou shalt find a piece of *m*	Mt 17:27	*4715*
Shew me the tribute *m*	Mt 22:19	*3546*
in the earth, and hid his lord's *m*	Mt 25:18	*694*
have put my *m* to the exchangers	Mt 25:27	*694*
they gave large *m* unto the	Mt 28:12	*694*
So they took the *m*, and did as	Mt 28:15	*694*
no bread, no *m* in their purse	Mk 6:8	*5475*
people cast *m* into the treasury	Mk 12:41	*5475*
glad, and promised to give him *m*	Mk 14:11	*694*
scrip, neither bread, neither *m*	Lk 9:3	*694*
him, to whom he had given the *m*	Lk 19:15	*694*
not thou my *m* into the bank	Lk 19:23	*694*
glad, and covenanted to give him *m*	Lk 22:5	*694*
and the changers of *m* sitting	Jn 2:14	*2773*
and poured out the changers' *m*	Jn 2:15	*2772*
land, sold it, and brought the *m*	Acts 4:37	*5536*
Abraham bought for a sum of *m* of	Acts 7:16	*694*
was given, he offered them *m*	Acts 8:18	*5536*
Thy *m* perish with thee, because	Acts 8:20	*694*
of God may be purchased with *m*	Acts 8:20	*5536*
He hoped also that *m* should have	Acts 24:26	*5536*
For the love of *m* is the root of	1Ti 6:10	*5365*

MONEYCHANGERS

and overthrew the tables of the *m*	Mt 21:12	*2855*
and overthrew the tables of the *m*	Mk 11:15	*2855*

MONSTERS

Even the sea *m* draw out the	Lam 4:3	8577

MONTH

of Noah's life, in the second *m*	Gen 7:11	2320
the seventeenth day of the *m*	Gen 7:11	2320
the ark rested in the seventh *m*	Gen 8:4	2320
on the seventeenth day of the *m*	Gen 8:4	2320
continually until the tenth *m*	Gen 8:5	2320
in the tenth *m*, on the first day	Gen 8:5	
on the first day of the *m*	Gen 8:5	2320
and first year, in the first *m*	Gen 8:13	
the first day of the *m*	Gen 8:13	2320
And in the second *m*, on the seven	Gen 8:14	2320
seven and twentieth day of the *m*	Gen 8:14	2320
abode with him the space of a *m*	Gen 29:14	2320
This *m* shall be unto you the	Ex 12:2	2320
be the first *m* of the year to you	Ex 12:2	2320
In the tenth day of this *m* they	Ex 12:3	2320
the fourteenth day of the same *m*	Ex 12:6	2320
In the first *m*, on the fourteenth	Ex 12:18	
fourteenth day of the *m* at even	Ex 12:18	2320
and twentieth day of the *m* at even	Ex 12:18	2320
day came ye out in the *m* Abib	Ex 13:4	2320
shalt keep this service in this *m*	Ex 13:5	2320
m after their departing out of	Ex 16:1	2320
In the third *m*, when the children	Ex 19:1	2320
the time appointed of the *m* Abib	Ex 23:15	2320
thee, in the time of the *m* Abib	Ex 34:18	2320
for in the *m* Abib thou camest out	Ex 34:18	2320
the first *m* shalt thou set up the	Ex 40:2	2320
in the first *m* in the second year	Ex 40:17	2320
on the first day of the *m*	Ex 40:17	2320
that in the seventh *m*, on the	Lev 16:29	2320
m, on the tenth day of the *m*	Lev 16:29	2320
m at even is the LORD's passover	Lev 23:5	2320
same *m* is the feast of unleavened	Lev 23:6	2320
Israel, saying, In the seventh *m*	Lev 23:24	2320
in the first day of the *m*	Lev 23:24	2320
seventh *m* there shall be a day of	Lev 23:27	2320
in the ninth day of the *m* at even	Lev 23:32	2320
seventh *m* shall be the feast of	Lev 23:34	2320
fifteenth day of the seventh *m*	Lev 23:39	2320
celebrate it in the seventh *m*	Lev 23:41	2320
on the tenth day of the seventh *m*	Lev 25:9	2320
if it be from a *m* old even unto	Lev 27:6	2320
on the first day of the second *m*	Num 1:1	2320
on the first day of the second *m*	Num 1:18	2320
every male from a *m* old and upward	Num 3:15	2320
of all the males, from a *m* old	Num 3:22	2320
of all the males, from a *m* old	Num 3:28	2320
of all the males, from a *m* old	Num 3:34	2320
all the males from a *m* old	Num 3:39	2320
children of Israel from a *m* old	Num 3:40	2320
the number of names, from a *m* old	Num 3:43	2320
in the first *m* of the second year	Num 9:1	2320
In the fourteenth day of this *m*	Num 9:3	2320
m at even in the wilderness of	Num 9:5	2320
m at even they shall keep it	Num 9:11	2320
whether it were two days, or a *m*	Num 9:22	2320
the twentieth day of the second *m*	Num 10:11	2320
But even a whole *m*, until it come	Num 11:20	2320
that they may eat a whole *m*	Num 11:21	2320
from a *m* old shalt thou redeem	Num 18:16	2320
the desert of Zin in the first *m*	Num 20:1	2320
thousand, all males from a *m* old	Num 26:62	2320
m throughout the months of the	Num 28:14	2320
m is the passover of the LORD	Num 28:16	2320
day of this *m* is the feast	Num 28:17	2320
And in the seventh *m*, on the first	Num 29:1	2320
m, on the first day of the *m*	Num 29:1	2320
the burnt offering of the *m*	Num 29:6	2320
seventh *m* an holy convocation	Num 29:7	2320
seventh *m* ye shall have an holy	Num 29:12	2320
from Rameses in the first *m*	Num 33:3	2320
the fifteenth day of the first *m*	Num 33:3	2320
in the first day of the fifth *m*	Num 33:38	2320
fortieth year, in the eleventh *m*	Deut 1:3	2320
m, on the first day of the *m*	Deut 1:3	2320
Observe the *m* of Abib, and keep	Deut 16:1	2320
for in the *m* of Abib the LORD thy	Deut 16:1	2320
her father and her mother a full *m*	Deut 21:13	3391
on the tenth day of the first *m*	Josh 4:19	2320
of the *m* at even in the plains of	Josh 5:10	2320
which was the second day of the *m*	1Sa 20:27	2320
no meat the second day of the *m*	1Sa 20:34	2320
each man his *m* in a year made	1Kin 4:7	2320
table, every man in his *m*	1Kin 4:27	2320
ten thousand a *m* by courses	1Kin 5:14	2320
a *m* they were in Lebanon, and two	1Kin 5:14	2320
reign over Israel, in the *m* Zif	1Kin 6:1	2320
m Zif, which is the second *m*	1Kin 6:1	2320
of the LORD laid, in the *m* Zif	1Kin 6:37	3391
the eleventh year, in the *m* Bul	1Kin 6:38	3391
which is the eighth *m*	1Kin 6:38	2320
at the feast in the *m* Ethanim	1Kin 8:2	3391
which is the seventh *m*	1Kin 8:2	2320
ordained a feast in the eighth *m*	1Kin 12:32	2320
on the fifteenth day of the *m*	1Kin 12:32	2320
the fifteenth day of the eighth *m*	1Kin 12:33	2320
even in the *m* which he had	1Kin 12:33	2320
and he reigned a full *m* in Samaria	2Kin 15:13	3391
year of his reign, in the tenth *m*	2Kin 25:1	2320
in the tenth day of the *m*	2Kin 25:1	2320
m the famine prevailed in the	2Kin 25:3	2320
And in the fifth *m*, on the seventh	2Kin 25:8	2320
on the seventh day of the *m*	2Kin 25:8	2320
it came to pass in the seventh *m*	2Kin 25:25	2320
king of Judah, in the twelfth *m*	2Kin 25:27	2320
seven and twentieth day of the *m*	2Kin 25:27	2320
went over Jordan in the first *m*	1Chr 12:15	2320
went out *m* by *m* throughout	1Chr 27:1	2320
first *m* was Jashobeam the son of	1Chr 27:2	2320
of the host for the first *m*	1Chr 27:3	2320
the second *m* was Dodai an Ahohite	1Chr 27:4	2320
of the host for the third *m* was	1Chr 27:5	2320
fourth captain for the fourth *m*	1Chr 27:7	2320
fifth *m* was Shamhuth the Izrahite	1Chr 27:8	2320
m was Ira the son of Ikkesh the	1Chr 27:9	2320
seventh *m* was Helez the Pelonite	1Chr 27:10	2320
m was Sibbecai the Hushathite	1Chr 27:11	2320
m was Abiezer the Anetothite	1Chr 27:12	2320
m was Maharai the Netophathite	1Chr 27:13	2320
captain for the eleventh *m* was	1Chr 27:14	2320
m was Heldai the Netophathite	1Chr 27:15	2320
in the second day of the second *m*	2Chr 3:2	2320
feast which was in the seventh *m*	2Chr 5:3	2320
m he sent the people away into	2Chr 7:10	2320
at Jerusalem in the third *m*	2Chr 15:10	2320
year of his reign, in the first *m*	2Chr 29:3	2320
day of the first *m* to sanctify	2Chr 29:17	2320
on the eighth day of the *m* came	2Chr 29:17	2320
of the first *m* they made an end	2Chr 29:17	2320
keep the passover in the second *m*	2Chr 30:2	2320
unleavened bread in the second *m*	2Chr 30:13	2320
fourteenth day of the second *m*	2Chr 30:15	2320
In the third *m* they began to lay	2Chr 31:7	2320
and finished them in the seventh *m*	2Chr 31:7	2320
the fourteenth day of the first *m*	2Chr 35:1	2320
And when the seventh *m* was come	Ezr 3:1	2320
m began they to offer burnt	Ezr 3:6	2320
God at Jerusalem, in the second *m*	Ezr 3:8	2320
on the third day of the *m* Adar	Ezr 6:15	3393
the fourteenth day of the first *m*	Ezr 6:19	2320
came to Jerusalem in the fifth *m*	Ezr 7:8	2320
m began he to go up from Babylon	Ezr 7:9	2320
the fifth *m* came he to Jerusalem	Ezr 7:9	2320
on the twelfth day of the first *m*	Ezr 8:31	2320
It was the ninth *m*, on the	Ezr 10:9	2320
on the twentieth day of the *m*	Ezr 10:9	2320
the tenth *m* to examine the matter	Ezr 10:16	2320
by the first day of the first *m*	Ezr 10:17	2320
it came to pass in the *m* Chisleu	Neh 1:1	2320
And it came to pass in the *m* Nisan	Neh 2:1	2320
twenty and fifth day of the *m* Elul	Neh 6:15	
and when the seventh *m* came	Neh 7:73	2320
the first day of the seventh *m*	Neh 8:2	2320
in the feast of the seventh *m*	Neh 8:14	2320

fourth day of this *m* the children Neh 9:1 2320
his house royal in the tenth *m* Est 2:16 2320
which is the *m* Tebeth Est 2:16 2320
In the first *m*, that is Est 3:7 2320
the *m* Nisan, in the twelfth year Est 3:7 2320
m to *m*, to the twelfth *m* Est 3:7
that is, the *m* Adar Est 3:7 2320
the thirteenth day of the first *m* Est 3:12 2320
thirteenth day of the twelfth *m* Est 3:13 2320
which is the *m* Adar Est 3:13 2320
at that time in the third *m* Est 8:9 2320
the *m* Sivan, on the three and Est 8:9 2320
thirteenth day of the twelfth *m* Est 8:12 2320
which is the *m* Adar Est 8:12 2320
Now in the twelfth *m*, that is, Est 9:1 2320
the *m* Adar, on the thirteenth day Est 9:1 2320
fourteenth day also of the *m* Adar Est 9:15 2320
the thirteenth day of the *m* Adar Est 9:17 2320
of the *m* Adar a day of gladness Est 9:19 2320
the fourteenth day of the *m* Adar Est 9:21 2320
the *m* which was turned unto them Est 9:22 2320
Jerusalem captive in the fifth *m* Jer 1:3 2320
in her *m* they shall find her Jer 2:24 2320
fourth year, and in the fifth *m* Jer 28:1 2320
the same year in the seventh *m* Jer 28:17 2320
king of Judah, in the ninth *m* Jer 36:9 2320
in the winterhouse in the ninth *m* Jer 36:22 2320
king of Judah, in the tenth *m* Jer 39:1 2320
year of Zedekiah, in the fourth *m* Jer 39:2 2320
the ninth day of the *m* Jer 39:2 2320
it came to pass in the seventh *m* Jer 41:1 2320
year of his reign, in the tenth *m* Jer 52:4 2320
m, in the tenth day of the *m* Jer 52:4 2320
And in the fourth *m*, in the ninth Jer 52:6 2320
m, in the ninth day of the *m* Jer 52:6 2320
Now in the fifth *m*, in the tenth Jer 52:12 2320
m, in the tenth day of the *m* Jer 52:12 2320
king of Judah, in the twelfth *m* Jer 52:31 2320
five and twentieth day of the *m* Jer 52:31 2320
thirtieth year, in the fourth *m* Eze 1:1
in the fifth day of the *m* Eze 1:1 2320
In the fifth day of the *m* Eze 1:2 2320
in the sixth year, in the sixth *m* Eze 8:1
in the fifth day of the *m* Eze 8:1 2320
the seventh year, in the fifth *m* Eze 20:1
the tenth day of the *m* Eze 20:1 2320
in the ninth year, in the tenth *m* Eze 24:1 2320
in the tenth day of the *m* Eze 24:1 2320
year, in the first day of the *m* Eze 26:1 2320
In the tenth year, in the tenth *m* Eze 29:1
in the twelfth day of the *m* Eze 29:1 2320
and twentieth year, in the first *m* Eze 29:17
in the first day of the *m* Eze 29:17 2320
the eleventh year, in the first *m* Eze 30:20 2320
in the seventh day of the *m* Eze 30:20 2320
the eleventh year, in the third *m* Eze 31:1
in the first day of the *m* Eze 31:1 2320
twelfth year, in the twelfth *m* Eze 32:1 2320
in the first day of the *m* Eze 32:1 2320
in the fifteenth day of the *m* Eze 32:17 2320
of our captivity, in the tenth *m* Eze 33:21
in the fifth day of the *m* Eze 33:21 2320
year, in the tenth day of the *m* Eze 40:1 2320
In the first *m*, in the first day Eze 45:18
in the first day of the *m* Eze 45:18 2320
the *m* for every one that erreth Eze 45:20 2320
In the first *m*, in the fourteenth Eze 45:21
in the fourteenth day of the *m* Eze 45:21 2320
In the seventh *m*, in the Eze 45:25
in the fifteenth day of the *m* Eze 45:25 2320
and twentieth day of the first *m* Dan 10:4 2320
now shall a *m* devour them with Hos 5:7 2320
and the latter rain in the first *m* Joel 2:23
Darius the king, in the sixth *m* Hag 1:1 2320
m, in the first day of the *m* Hag 1:1 2320
and twentieth day of the sixth *m* Hag 1:15 2320
In the seventh *m*, in the one and Hag 2:1
the one and twentieth day of the *m* Hag 2:1 2320
and twentieth day of the ninth *m* Hag 2:10
and twentieth day of the ninth *m* Hag 2:18
four and twentieth day of the *m* Hag 2:20 2320
In the eighth *m*, in the second Zec 1:1 2320
twentieth day of the eleventh *m* Zec 1:7 2320
which is the *m* Sebat Zec 1:7 2320
in the fourth day of the ninth *m* Zec 7:1 2320
Should I weep in the fifth *m* Zec 7:3 2320
mourned in the fifth and seventh *m* Zec 7:5
The fast of the fourth *m*, and the Zec 8:19
shepherds also I cut off in one *m* Zec 11:8 3391
in the sixth *m* the angel Gabriel Lk 1:26 *3376*
and this is the sixth *m* with her Lk 1:36 *3376*
for an hour, and a day, and a *m* Rev 9:15 *3376*
and yielded her fruit every *m* Rev 22:2 *3376*

MONTHLY

the *m* prognosticators, stand up, Is 47:13 2320

MONTHS

came to pass about three *m* after Gen 38:24 2320
goodly child, she hid him three *m* Ex 2:2 3391
be unto you the beginning of *m* Ex 12:2 2320
and in the beginnings of your *m* Num 10:10 2320
in the beginnings of your *m* ye Num 28:11 2320
throughout the *m* of the year Num 28:14 2320
let me alone two *m*, that I may go Judg 11:37 2320
And he sent her away for two *m* Judg 11:38 2320
came to pass at the end of two *m* Judg 11:39 2320
and was there four whole *m* Judg 19:2 2320
abode in the rock Rimmon four *m* Judg 20:47 2320
of the Philistines seven *m* 1Sa 6:1 2320
was a full year and four *m* 1Sa 27:7 2320
of Judah was seven years and six *m* 2Sa 2:11 2320
over Judah seven years and six *m* 2Sa 5:5 2320
of Obed-edom the Gittite three *m* 2Sa 6:11 2320
to Jerusalem at the end of nine *m* 2Sa 24:8 2320
flee three *m* before thine enemies 2Sa 24:13 2320
were in Lebanon, and two *m* at home 1Kin 5:14 2320
(For six *m* did Joab remain there 1Kin 11:16 2320
over Israel in Samaria six *m* 2Kin 15:8 2320
he reigned three *m* in Jerusalem 2Kin 23:31 2320
he reigned in Jerusalem three *m* 2Kin 24:8 2320
he reigned seven years and six *m* 1Chr 3:4 2320
of Obed-edom in his house three *m* 1Chr 13:14 2320
or three *m* to be destroyed before 1Chr 21:12 2320
throughout all the *m* of the year 1Chr 27:1 2320
he reigned three *m* in Jerusalem 2Chr 36:2 2320
to reign, and he reigned three *m* 2Chr 36:9 2320
after that she had been twelve *m* Est 2:12 2320
six *m* with oil of myrrh, and six Est 2:12 2320
six *m* with sweet odours, and with Est 2:12 2320
not come into the number of the *m* Job 3:6 3391
am I made to possess *m* of vanity Job 7:3 3391
the number of his *m* are with thee Job 14:5 2320
when the number of his *m* is cut Job 21:21 2320
Oh that I were as in *m* past Job 29:2 3391
number the *m* that they fulfil Job 39:2 3391
seven *m* shall the house of Israel Eze 39:12 2320
end of seven *m* shall they search Eze 39:14 2320
new fruit according to his *m* Eze 47:12 2320
At the end of twelve *m* he walked Dan 4:29 3393
were yet three *m* to the harvest Amos 4:7 2320
conceived, and hid herself five *m* Lk 1:24 *3376*
Mary abode with her about three *m* Lk 1:56 *3376*
was shut up three years and six *m* Lk 4:25 *3376*
Say not ye, There are yet four *m* Jn 4:35 *5072*
up in his father's house three *m* Acts 7:20 *3376*
continued there a year and six *m* Acts 18:11 *3376*
boldly for the space of three *m* Acts 19:8 *3376*
And there abode three *m* Acts 20:3 *3376*
after three *m* we departed in a Acts 28:11 *3376*
Ye observe days, and *m*, and times, Gal 4:10 *3376*
was hid three *m* of his parents, Heb 11:23 *5150*
the space of three years and six *m* Jas 5:17 *3376*
they should be tormented five *m* Rev 9:5 *3376*
power was to hurt men five *m* Rev 9:10 *3376*
tread under foot forty and two *m* Rev 11:2 *3376*
him to continue forty and two *m* Rev 13:5 *3376*

MONUMENTS

the graves, and lodge in the *m* Is 65:4 5341

MOON

and, behold, the sun and the *m* Gen 37:9 3394
when thou seest the sun, and the *m* Deut 4:19 3394
them, either the sun, or *m* Deut 17:3 3394
things put forth by the *m* Deut 33:14 3391
and thou, *M*, in the valley of Josh 10:12 3394
the *m* stayed, until the people Josh 10:13 3394
Behold, to morrow is the new *m* 1Sa 20:5 2320
to David, To morrow is the new *m* 1Sa 20:18 2320
and when the new *m* was come 1Sa 20:24 2320
it is neither new *m*, nor sabbath 2Kin 4:23 2320
Baal, to the sun, and to the *m* 2Kin 23:5 3394
Behold even to the *m*, and it Job 25:5 3394
or the *m* walking in brightness Job 31:26 3394
the work of thy fingers, the *m* Ps 8:3 3394
sun and *m* endure, throughout all Ps 72:5 3394
peace so long as the *m* endureth Ps 72:7 3394
Blow up the trumpet in the new *m* Ps 81:3 2320
be established for ever as the *m* Ps 89:37 3394
He appointed the *m* for seasons Ps 104:19 3394
thee by day, nor the *m* by night Ps 121:6 3394
The *m* and stars to rule by night Ps 136:9 3394
Praise ye him, sun and *m* Ps 148:3 3394
the sun, or the light, or the *m* Eccl 12:2 3394
as the morning, fair as the *m* Song 6:10 3842
and their round tires like the *m* Is 3:18
the *m* shall not cause her light Is 13:10 3394
Then the *m* shall be confounded, Is 24:23 3842
Moreover the light of the *m* shall Is 30:26 3842
shall the *m* give light unto thee Is 60:19 3394
shall thy *m* withdraw itself Is 60:20 3391
that from one new *m* to another Is 66:23 2320
them before the sun, and the *m* Jer 8:2 3394
day, and the ordinances of the *m* Jer 31:35 3394
the *m* shall not give her light Eze 32:7 3394
of the new *m* it shall be opened Eze 46:1 2320
in the day of the new *m* it shall Eze 46:6 2320
the *m* shall be dark, and the stars Joel 2:10 3394
the *m* into blood, before the Joel 2:31 3394
the *m* shall be darkened, and the Joel 3:15 3394
When will the new *m* be gone Amos 8:5 2320
m stood still in their habitation Hab 3:11 3394
the *m* shall not give her light, Mt 24:29 *4582*
the *m* shall not give her light, Mk 13:24 *4582*
be signs in the sun, and in the *m* Lk 21:25 *4582*
the *m* into blood, before that Acts 2:20 *4582*
sun, and another glory of the *m* 1Cor 15:41 *4582*
of an holyday, or of the new *m* Col 2:16 *3561*
of hair, and the *m* became as blood Rev 6:12 *4582*
and the third part of the *m* Rev 8:12 *4582*
the *m* under her feet, and upon her Rev 12:1 *4582*
need of the sun, neither of the *m* Rev 21:23 *4582*

MOONS

in the sabbaths, in the new *m* 1Chr 23:31 2320
on the sabbaths, and on the new *m* 2Chr 2:4 2320
on the sabbaths, and on the new *m* 2Chr 8:13 2320
the sabbaths, and for the new *m* 2Chr 31:3 2320
burnt offering, both of the new *m* Ezr 3:5 2320
of the sabbaths, of the new *m* Neh 10:33 2320
the new *m* and sabbaths, the Is 1:13 2320
Your new *m* and your appointed Is 1:14 2320
in the feasts, and in the new *m* Eze 45:17 2320
in the sabbaths and in the new *m* Eze 46:3 2320
cease, her feast days, her new *m* Hos 2:11 2320

MORASTHITE (*mo'-ras-thite*) *Family name of Micah the prophet.*

Micah the *M* prophesied in the Jer 26:18 4183
Micah the *M* in the days of Jotham Mic 1:1 4183

MORDECAI (*mor'-de-cahee*) See MORDECAI'S.

1. A clan leader with Zerubbabel.

Nehemiah, Seraiah, Reelaiah, *M* Ezr 2:2 4782
Azariah, Raamiah, Nahamani, *M* Neh 7:7 4782

2. Cousin of Esther.

a certain Jew, whose name was *M* Est 2:5 4782
whom *M*, when her father and mother Est 2:7 4782
for *M* had charged her that she Est 2:10 4782
M walked every day before the Est 2:11 4782
of Abihail the uncle of *M* Est 2:15 4782
then *M* sat in the king's gate Est 2:19 4782
as *M* had charged her Est 2:20 4782
Esther did the commandment of *M* Est 2:20 4782
while *M* sat in the king's gate, Est 2:21 4782
And the thing was known to *M* Est 2:22 4782
But *M* bowed not, nor did him Est 3:2 4782
in the king's gate, said unto *M* Est 3:3 4782
when Haman saw that *M* bowed not Est 3:5 4782
scorn to lay hands on *M* alone Est 3:6 4782
had shewed him the people of *M* Est 3:6 4782
Ahasuerus, even the people of *M* Est 3:6 4782
When *M* perceived all that was Est 4:1 4782
M rent his clothes, and put on Est 4:1 4782
and she sent raiment to clothe *M* Est 4:4 4782
and gave him a commandment to *M* Est 4:5 4782
So Hatach went forth to *M* unto Est 4:6 4782
M told him of all that had Est 4:7 4782
and told Esther the words of *M* Est 4:9 4782
and gave him commandment unto *M* Est 4:10 4782
they told to *M* Esther's words Est 4:12 4782
Then *M* commanded to answer Esther Est 4:13 4782
bade them return *M* this answer Est 4:15 4782
So *M* went his way, and did Est 4:17 4782
Haman saw *M* in the king's gate Est 5:9 4782
was full of indignation against *M* Est 5:9 4782
so long as I see *M* the Jew Est 5:13 4782
king that *M* may be hanged thereon Est 5:14 4782
that *M* had told of Bigthana and Est 6:2 4782
hath been done to *M* for this Est 6:3 4782
hang *M* on the gallows that he had Est 6:4 4782
said, and do even so to *M* the Jew Est 6:10 4782
and the horse, and arrayed *M* Est 6:11 4782
M came again to the king's gate Est 6:12 4782
If *M* be of the seed of the Jews, Est 6:13 4782
high, which Haman had made for *M* Est 7:9 4782
that he had prepared for *M* Est 7:10 4782
And *M* came before the king Est 8:1 4782
from Haman, and gave it unto *M* Est 8:2 4782
Esther set *M* over the house of Est 8:2 4782
to *M* the Jew, Behold, I have Est 8:7 4782
that *M* commanded unto the Jews Est 8:9 4782
M went out from the presence of Est 8:15 4782
the fear of *M* fell upon them Est 9:3 4782
For *M* was great in the king's Est 9:4 4782
for this man *M* waxed greater and Est 9:4 4782
M wrote these things, and sent Est 9:20 4782
as *M* had written unto them Est 9:23 4782
M the Jew, wrote with all Est 9:29 4782
appointed, according as *M* the Jew Est 9:31 4782
declaration of the greatness of *M* Est 10:2 4782
For *M* the Jew was next unto king Est 10:3 4782

MORDECAI'S (*mor'-de-cahees*) *Refers to Mordecai 2.*

the king thereof in *M* name Est 2:22 4782
to see whether *M* matters would Est 3:4 4782

MORE

Now the serpent was *m* subtil than Gen 3:1
returned not again unto him any *m* Gen 8:12 5750
the ground any *m* for man's sake Gen 8:21 5750
smite any *m* every thing living Gen 8:21 5750
any *m* by the waters of a flood Gen 9:11 5750
neither shall there any *m* be a Gen 9:11 5750
the waters shall no *m* become a Gen 9:15 5750
thy name any *m* be called Abram Gen 17:5 5750
he loved also Rachel *m* than Leah Gen 29:30
name shall be called no *m* Jacob Gen 32:28 5750
he was *m* honourable than all the Gen 34:19 3513
shall not be called any *m* Jacob Gen 35:10 5750
For their riches were *m* than that Gen 36:7 7227
Joseph *m* than all his children Gen 37:3
loved him *m* than all his brethren Gen 37:4
and they hated him yet the *m* Gen 37:5 3254
him yet the *m* for his dreams Gen 37:8 3254
Behold, I have dreamed a dream *m* Gen 37:9 5750
She hath been *m* righteous than I Gen 38:26
And he knew her again no *m* Gen 38:26 5750
you, ye shall see my face no *m* Gen 44:23 3254
of the children of Israel are *m* Ex 1:9 7227
But the *m* they afflicted them, Ex 1:12 3651
the *m* they multiplied and grew Ex 1:12 3651
Ye shall no *m* give the people Ex 5:7 3254
Let there *m* work be laid upon the Ex 5:9
Pharaoh deal deceitfully any *m* in Ex 8:29 3254
there be no *m* mighty thunderings Ex 9:28
neither shall there be any *m* hail Ex 9:29 5750
were ceased, he sinned yet *m* Ex 9:34 3254
heed to thyself, see my face no *m* Ex 10:28 3254
I will see thy face again no *m* Ex 10:29 5750
I bring one plague *m* upon Pharaoh Ex 11:1
it, nor shall be like it any *m* Ex 11:6 3254
see them again no *m* for ever Ex 14:13 5750
did so, and gathered, some *m* Ex 16:17 7227
The rich shall not give *m* Ex 30:15 7235
The people bring much *m* than Ex 36:5 7235
m work for the offering of the Ex 36:6 5750
add the fifth part *m* thereto Lev 6:5 3254
or whatsoever hath *m* feet among Lev 11:42 7235
shall shut him up seven days *m* Lev 13:5 8145
that hath the scall seven days *m* Lev 13:33 8145
he shall shut it up seven days *m* Lev 13:54 8145
they shall no *m* offer their Lev 17:7 5750
you seven times *m* for your sins Lev 26:18 3254
I will bring seven times *m* Lev 26:21 3254

it shall not be redeemed any *m* Lev 27:20 5750
which are *m* than the Levites Num 3:46 5736
thereof, and shall serve no *m* Num 8:25 5750
that there be no wrath any *m* upon Num 18:5 5750
Balak sent yet again princes, *m* Num 22:15 7227
and *m* honourable than they Num 22:15
the LORD my God, to do less or *m* Num 22:18 1490
what the LORD will say unto me *m* Num 22:19 3254
thou shalt give the *m* inheritance Num 26:54 7235
to the *m* ye shall give the Num 33:54 7227
ye shall give the *m* inheritance Num 33:54 7235
times so many *m* as ye are Deut 1:11 3254
speak no *m* unto me of this matter Deut 3:26 5750
and he added no *m* Deut 5:22 3254
voice of the LORD our God any *m* Deut 5:25 3254
because ye were *m* in number than Deut 7:7 7230
heart, These nations are *m* than I Deut 7:17 7227
heart, and be no *m* stiffnecked Deut 10:16 5750
shall do no *m* any such wickedness Deut 13:11 3254
fear, and do no *m* presumptuously Deut 17:13 5750
henceforth return no *m* that way Deut 17:16 5750
let me see this great fire any *m* Deut 18:16 5750
thou add three cities *m* for thee Deut 19:9 5750
no *m* any such evil among you Deut 19:20 5750
a people *m* than thou, be not Deut 20:1 7227
Thou shalt see it no *m* again Deut 28:68 5750
I can no *m* go out and come in Deut 31:2 5750
how much *m* after my death Deut 31:27
remain any *m* courage in any man Josh 2:11 5750
was there spirit in them any *m* Josh 5:1 5750
children of Israel manna any *m* Josh 5:12 5750
neither will I be with you any *m* Josh 7:12 3254
they were *m* which died with Josh 10:11 7227
m drive out any of these nations Josh 23:13 3254
themselves *m* than their fathers Judg 2:19
they lifted up their heads no *m* Judg 8:28 3254
wherefore I will deliver you no *m* Judg 10:13 3254
LORD did no *m* appear to Manoah Judg 13:21 3254
Now shall I be *m* blameless than Judg 15:3
m than they which he slew in his Judg 16:30 7227
and what have I *m* Judg 18:24 5750
there yet any *m* sons in my womb Ruth 1:11
m also, if ought but death part Ruth 1:17 3254
for thou hast shewed *m* kindness Ruth 3:10
and her countenance was no *m* sad 1Sa 1:18 5750
Talk no *m* so exceeding proudly 1Sa 2:3 7235
m also, if thou hide any thing 1Sa 3:17 3254
they came no *m* into the coast of 1Sa 7:13
How much *m*, if haply the people 1Sa 14:30 637
answered, God do so and *m* also 1Sa 14:44 3254
Samuel came no *m* to see Saul 1Sa 15:35 3254
would let him go no *m* home to his 1Sa 18:2
can he have *m* but the kingdom 1Sa 18:8 5750
was yet the *m* afraid of David 1Sa 18:29 3254
that David behaved himself *m* 1Sa 18:30
LORD do so and much *m* to Jonathan 1Sa 20:13 3254
nothing of all this, less or *m* 1Sa 22:15 1490
how much *m* then if we come to 1Sa 23:3
Thou art *m* righteous than I 1Sa 24:17
m also do God unto the enemies of 1Sa 25:22 3254
she told him nothing, less or *m* 1Sa 25:36 1490
for I will no *m* do thee harm 1Sa 26:21 5750
to seek me any *m* in any coast of 1Sa 27:1 5750
he sought no *m* again for him 1Sa 27:4 3254
from me, and answereth me no *m* 1Sa 28:15
until they had no *m* power to weep 1Sa 30:4
and pursued after Israel no *m* 2Sa 2:28 5750
neither fought they any *m* 2Sa 2:28
m also, except, as the LORD hath 2Sa 3:9 3254
m also, if I taste bread, or 2Sa 3:35 3254
How much *m*, when wicked men have 2Sa 4:11
And David took him *m* concubines 2Sa 5:13 5750
I will yet be *m* vile than thus 2Sa 6:22
place of their own, and move no *m* 2Sa 7:10 5750
of wickedness afflict them any *m* 2Sa 7:10 3254
And what can David say *m* unto thee 2Sa 7:20 5750
help the children of Ammon any *m* 2Sa 10:19 5750
make thy battle *m* strong against 2Sa 11:25
and he shall not touch thee any *m* 2Sa 14:10
of blood to destroy any *m* 2Sa 14:11 7235
how much *m* now may this Benjamite 2Sa 16:11
the wood devoured *m* people that 2Sa 18:8 7235
m also, if thou be not captain of 2Sa 19:13 3254
I yet to cry any *m* unto the king 2Sa 19:28 5750
thou any *m* of thy matters 2Sa 19:29 5750
can I hear any *m* the voice of 2Sa 19:35 5750
we have also *m* right in David 2Sa 19:43
do us *m* harm than did Absalom 2Sa 20:6
Thou shalt go no *m* out with us to 2Sa 21:17 5750
He was *m* honourable than the 2Sa 23:23
m also, if Adonijah have not 1Kin 2:23 3254
who fell upon two men *m* righteous 1Kin 2:32
there was no *m* spirit in her 1Kin 10:5 5750
there came no *m* such abundance of 1Kin 10:10 5750
Ahab did *m* to provoke the LORD 1Kin 16:33 3254
m also, if I make not thy life as 1Kin 19:2 3254
m also, if the dust of Samaria 1Kin 20:10 3254
And he saw him no *m* 2Kin 2:12 5750
thence any *m* death or barren land 2Kin 2:21 5750
unto her, There is not a vessel *m* 2Kin 4:6 5750
are *m* than they that be with them 2Kin 6:16 7227
came no *m* into the land of Israel 2Kin 6:23
m also to me, if the head of 2Kin 6:31 3254
but they found no *m* of her than 2Kin 9:35
now therefore receive no *m* money 2Kin 12:7
receive no *m* money of the people 2Kin 12:8
the feet of Israel move any *m* out 2Kin 21:8 3254
Manasseh seduced them to do *m* 2Kin 21:9
not again any *m* out of his land 2Kin 24:7 5750
Jabez was *m* honourable than his 1Chr 4:9
he was *m* honourable than the two 1Chr 11:21
David took *m* wives at Jerusalem 1Chr 14:3 5750
and David begat *m* sons and 1Chr 14:3 5750
place, and shall be moved no *m* 1Chr 17:9 5750

of wickedness waste them any *m* 1Chr 17:9 3254
What can David speak *m* to thee 1Chr 17:18
help the children of Ammon any *m* 1Chr 19:19 5750
times so many *m* as they be 1Chr 21:3 3254
they shall no *m* carry the 1Chr 23:26
there were *m* chief men found of 1Chr 24:4 7227
there was no *m* spirit in her 2Chr 9:4 5750
I will put *m* to your yoke 2Chr 10:11 3254
there was no *m* war unto the five 2Chr 15:19
m than they could carry away 2Chr 20:25
to give thee much *m* than this 2Chr 25:9 7235
ye intend to add *m* to our sins 2Chr 28:13
trespass yet *m* against the LORD 2Chr 28:22 3254
for the Levites were *m* upright in 2Chr 29:34
for there be *m* with us than with 2Chr 32:7 7227
spake yet *m* against the LORD God 2Chr 32:16
Neither will I any *m* remove the 2Chr 33:8
but Amon trespassed *m* and *m* 2Chr 33:23 7235
but Amon trespassed *m* and *m* 2Chr 33:23
whatsoever *m* shall be needful for Ezr 7:20 7608
that we be no *m* a reproach Neh 2:17 5720
yet ye bring *m* wrath upon Israel Neh 13:18 3254
came they no *m* on the sabbath Neh 13:21
That Vashti come no *m* before king Est 1:19
she came in unto the king no *m* Est 2:14 5750
favour in his sight *m* than all Est 2:17
king's house, *m* than all the Jews Est 4:13
to do honour *m* than to myself Est 6:6 3148
dig for it *m* than for hid Job 3:21
mortal man be *m* just than God Job 4:17
shall a man be *m* pure than his Job 4:17
mine eye shall no *m* see good Job 7:7 7725
hath seen me shall see me no *m* Job 7:8
to the grave shall come up no *m* Job 7:9
He shall return no *m* to his house Job 7:10 5750
shall his place know him any *m* Job 7:10 5750
till the heavens be no *m*, they Job 14:12
How much *m* abominable and filthy Job 15:16
which saw him shall see him no *m* Job 20:9 3254
shall his place any *m* behold him Job 20:9 5750
mouth *m* than my necessary food Job 23:12
he shall be no *m* remembered Job 24:20 5750
were amazed, they answered no *m* Job 32:15 5750
but stood still, and answered no *m* Job 32:16 5750
the rich *m* than the poor Job 34:19 6440
not lay upon man *m* than right Job 34:23 5750
I will not offend any *m* Job 34:31
done iniquity, I will do no *m* Job 34:32
My righteousness is *m* than God's Job 35:2 3254
Who teacheth us *m* than the beasts Job 35:11
him, remember the battle, do no *m* Job 41:8 3254
end of Job *m* than his beginning Job 42:12
m than in the time that their Ps 4:7
man of the earth may no *m* oppress Ps 10:18
M to be desired are they than Ps 19:10
before I go hence, and be no *m* Ps 39:13
they are *m* than can be numbered Ps 40:5 6105
they are *m* than the hairs of mine Ps 40:12 6105
he lieth he shall rise up no *m* Ps 41:8 3254
Thou lovest evil *m* than good Ps 52:3
are *m* than the hairs of mine head Ps 69:4 7231
and will yet praise thee *m* and *m* Ps 71:14 3254
they have *m* than heart could wish Ps 73:7 5674
there is no *m* any prophet Ps 74:9 5750
Thou art *m* glorious and excellent Ps 76:4
and will he be favourable no *m* Ps 77:7
they sinned yet *m* against him by Ps 78:17
Israel may be no *m* in remembrance Ps 83:4
LORD loveth the gates of Zion *m* Ps 87:2
grave, whom thou rememberest no *m* Ps 88:5 5750
place thereof shall know it no *m* Ps 103:16 5750
earth, and let the wicked be no *m* Ps 104:35 5750
LORD shall increase you *m* and *m* Ps 115:14
I have *m* understanding than all Ps 119:99
I understand *m* than the ancients Ps 119:100
m than they that watch for the Ps 130:6
m than they that watch for the Ps 130:6
they are *m* in number than the Ps 139:18 7235
She is *m* precious than rubies Prov 3:15
the shining light, that shineth *m* Prov 4:18 1980
and *m* unto the perfect day Prov 4:18
passeth, so is the wicked no *m* Prov 10:25
that withholdeth *m* than is meet Prov 11:24
much *m* the wicked and the sinner Prov 11:31
The righteous is *m* excellent than Prov 12:26
how much *m* then the hearts of the Prov 15:11
A reproof entereth *m* into a wise Prov 17:10
how much *m* do his friends go far Prov 19:7
judgment is *m* acceptable to the Prov 21:3
how much *m*, when he bringeth it Prov 21:27
there is *m* hope of a fool than of Prov 26:12
a man afterwards shall find *m* Prov 28:23
there is *m* hope of a fool than of Prov 29:20
Surely I am *m* brutish than any Prov 30:2
and remember his misery no *m* Prov 31:7 5750
have gotten *m* wisdom than all Eccl 1:16
increased *m* than all that were Eccl 2:9
and why was I then *m* wise Eccl 2:15 3148
wise *m* than of the fool for ever Eccl 2:16 5973
can hasten hereunto, *m* than I Eccl 2:25 2351
m than the living which are yet Eccl 4:2 4480
who will no *m* be admonished Eccl 4:13 5750
be *m* ready to hear, than to give Eccl 5:1 7138
this hath *m* rest than the other Eccl 6:5
hath the wise *m* than the fool Eccl 6:8 3148
m than ten mighty men which are Eccl 7:19
I find *m* bitter than death the Eccl 7:26
neither have they any *m* a reward Eccl 9:5 5750
neither have they any *m* a portion Eccl 9:6 5750
of wise men are heard in quiet *m* Eccl 9:17
then must he put to *m* strength Eccl 10:10
remember thy love *m* than wine Song 1:4
What is thy beloved *m* than Song 5:9
what is thy beloved *m* than Song 5:9

Why should ye be stricken any *m* Is 1:5 5750
ye will revolt *m* and *m* Is 1:5
Bring no *m* vain oblations Is 1:13 5750
shall they learn war any *m* Is 2:4 5750
have been done *m* to my vineyard Is 5:4 5750
afterward did *m* grievously Is 9:1
shall no *m* again stay upon him Is 10:20 5750
I will make a man *m* precious than Is 13:12
for I will bring *m* upon Dimon Is 15:9 3254
be driven away, and be no *m* Is 19:7
there is no *m* strength Is 23:10 5750
he said, Thou shalt no *m* rejoice Is 23:12 5750
shall no *m* cover her slain Is 26:21 5750
thou shalt weep no *m* Is 30:19 1058
be removed into a corner any *m* Is 30:20 5750
shall be no *m* called liberal Is 32:5 5750
I shall behold man no *m* with the Is 38:11
thou shalt no *m* be called tender Is 47:1 3254
for thou shalt no *m* be called Is 47:5 3254
thou shalt no *m* drink it again Is 51:22 3254
shall no *m* come into thee the Is 52:1
was so marred *m* than any man Is 52:14
his form *m* than the sons of men Is 52:14
for *m* are the children of the Is 54:1 7227
reproach of thy widowhood any *m* Is 54:4 5750
should no *m* go over the earth Is 54:9 5750
as this day, and much *m* abundant Is 56:12 3499
Violence shall no *m* be heard in Is 60:18 5750
shall be no *m* thy light by day Is 60:19 5750
Thy sun shall no *m* go down Is 60:20 5750
Thou shalt no *m* be termed Is 62:4 5750
thy land any *m* be termed Desolate Is 62:4 5750
Surely I will no *m* give thy corn Is 62:8 5750
shall be no *m* heard in her Is 65:19 5750
There shall be no *m* thence an Is 65:20 5750
we will come no *m* unto thee Jer 2:31 5750
herself *m* than treacherous Judah Jer 3:11
the LORD, they shall say no *m* Jer 3:16 5750
neither shall that be done any *m* Jer 3:16 5750
neither shall they walk any *m* Jer 3:17 5750
it shall no *m* be called Tophet Jer 7:32 5750
to stretch forth my tent any *m* Jer 10:20 5750
his name may be no *m* remembered Jer 11:19 5750
LORD, that it shall no *m* be said Jer 16:14 5750
place shall no *m* be called Tophet Jer 19:6 5750
him, nor speak any *m* in his name Jer 20:9 5750
for he shall return no *m*, nor see Jer 22:10 5750
He shall not return thither any *m* Jer 22:11 5750
and shall see this land no *m* Jer 22:12 5750
David, and ruling any *m* in Judah Jer 22:30 5750
and they shall fear no *m*, nor be Jer 23:4 5750
LORD, that they shall no *m* say Jer 23:7 5750
of the LORD shall ye mention no *m* Jer 23:36 5750
and spue, and fall, and rise no *m* Jer 25:27
strangers shall no *m* serve Jer 30:8 5750
shall not sorrow any *m* at all Jer 31:12 3254
In those days they shall say no *m* Jer 31:29 5750
they shall teach no *m* every man Jer 31:34 5750
and I will remember their sin no *m* Jer 31:34 5750
nor thrown down any *m* for ever Jer 31:40 5750
be no *m* a nation before them Jer 33:24 5750
serve themselves of them any *m* Jer 34:10 5750
for there is no *m* bread in the Jer 38:9 5750
and ye shall see this place no *m* Jer 42:18 5750
that my name shall no *m* be named Jer 44:26 5750
because they are *m* than the Jer 46:23 7231
shall be no *m* praise of Moab Jer 48:2 5750
Is wisdom no *m* in Teman Jer 49:7 5750
it shall be no *m* inhabited for Jer 50:39 5750
not flow together any *m* unto him Jer 51:44 5750
the law is no *m* Lam 2:9
they were *m* ruddy in body than Lam 4:7
They shall no *m* sojourn there Lam 4:15 3254
he will no *m* regard them Lam 4:16 3254
he will no *m* carry thee away into Lam 4:22 3254
wickedness *m* than the nations Eze 5:6 4480
my statutes *m* than the countries Eze 5:6 4480
Because ye multiplied *m* than the Eze 5:7 4480
I will not do any *m* the like Eze 5:9 5750
m desolate than the wilderness Eze 6:14
they shall no *m* use it as a Eze 12:23 5750
For there shall be no *m* any vain Eze 12:24 5750
it shall be no *m* prolonged Eze 12:25 5750
of my words be prolonged any *m* Eze 12:28 5750
say unto you, The wall is no *m* Eze 13:15
they shall be no *m* in your hand Eze 13:21 5750
ye shall see no *m* vanity, nor Eze 13:23 5750
Israel may go no *m* astray from me Eze 14:11 5750
neither be polluted any *m* with Eze 14:11 5750
How much *m* when I send my four Eze 14:21 5750
is the vine tree *m* than any tree Eze 15:2
also shalt give no hire any *m* Eze 16:41 5750
be quiet, and will be no *m* angry Eze 16:42 5750
thou wast corrupted *m* than they Eze 16:47
thine abominations *m* than they Eze 16:51
committed *m* abominable than they Eze 16:52
they are *m* righteous than thou Eze 16:52
mouth any *m* because of thy shame Eze 16:63 5750
m to use this proverb in Israel Eze 18:3 5750
that his voice should no *m* be Eze 19:9 5750
my holy name no *m* with your gifts Eze 20:39 5750
it shall not return any *m* Eze 21:5 5750
it shall be no *m*, saith the Lord Eze 21:13
and it shall be no *m*, until he Eze 21:27
thou shalt be no *m* remembered Eze 21:32
this, she was *m* corrupt in her Eze 23:11
in her whoredoms *m* than her Eze 23:11
them, nor remember Egypt any *m* Eze 23:27 5750
purged from thy filthiness any *m* Eze 24:13 5750
thou shalt speak, and be no *m* dumb Eze 24:27 5750
of thy harps shall be no *m* heard Eze 26:13 5750
thou shalt be built no *m* Eze 26:14 5750
a terror, and thou shalt be no *m* Eze 26:21
a terror, and never shalt be any *m* Eze 27:36

and never shalt thou be any *m* Eze 28:19
there shall be no *m* a pricking Eze 28:24 5750
itself any *m* above the nations Eze 29:15 5750
that they shall no *m* rule over Eze 29:15
it shall be no *m* the confidence Eze 29:16 5750
there shall be no *m* a prince of Eze 30:13 5750
foot of man trouble them any *m* Eze 32:13 5750
was opened, and I was no *m* dumb Eze 33:22 5750
shepherds feed themselves any *m* Eze 34:10 5750
and they shall no *m* be a prey Eze 34:22 5750
they shall no *m* be a prey to the Eze 34:28 5750
they shall be no *m* consumed with Eze 34:29 5750
the shame of the heathen any *m* Eze 34:29 5750
thou shalt no *m* henceforth Eze 36:12 5750
thou shalt devour men no *m* Eze 36:14 5750
neither bereave thy nations any *m* Eze 36:14 5750
the shame of the heathen any *m* Eze 36:15 5750
the reproach of the people any *m* Eze 36:15 5750
cause thy nations to fall any *m* Eze 36:15 5750
that ye shall receive no *m* Eze 36:30 5750
and they shall be no *m* two nations Eze 37:22 5750
into two kingdoms any *m* at all Eze 37:22 5750
themselves any *m* with their idols Eze 37:23 5750
them pollute my holy name any *m* Eze 39:7 5750
left none of them any *m* there Eze 39:28 5750
I hide my face any *m* from them Eze 39:29 5750
was straitened *m* than the lowest Eze 42:6
the house of Israel no *m* defile Eze 43:7 5750
shall no *m* oppress my people Eze 45:8 5750
that I have *m* than any living Dan 2:30 4481
the furnace one seven times *m* Dan 3:19 5922
whose look was *m* stout than his Dan 7:20 5750
he shall continue *m* years than Dan 11:8
for I will no *m* have mercy upon Hos 1:6 5750
and shalt call me no *m* Baali Hos 2:16 5750
they shall no *m* be remembered by Hos 2:17 5750
of God *m* than burnt offerings Hos 6:6
mine house, I will love them no *m* Hos 9:15 3254
And now they sin *m* and *m* Hos 13:2
neither will we say any *m* to the Hos 14:3 5750
have I to do any *m* with idols Hos 14:8 5750
neither shall be any *m* after it Joel 2:2 3254
I will no *m* make you a reproach Joel 2:19 5750
strangers pass through her any *m* Joel 3:17 5750
she shall no *m* rise Amos 5:2 5750
will not again pass by them any *m* Amos 7:8 5750
not again any *m* at Beth-el Amos 7:13 5750
will not again pass by them any *m* Amos 8:2 5750
they shall no *m* be pulled up out Amos 9:15 5750
wherein are *m* than sixscore Jonah 4:11 7227
shall they learn war any *m* Mic 4:3 5750
thou shalt have no *m* soothsayers Mic 5:12
thou shalt no *m* worship the work Mic 5:13 5750
thee, I will afflict thee no *m* Nah 1:12 5750
that no *m* of thy name be sown Nah 1:14 5750
shall no *m* pass through thee Nah 1:15
messengers shall no *m* be heard Nah 2:13 5750
are *m* fierce than the evening Hab 1:8
man that is *m* righteous than he Hab 1:13
thou shalt no *m* be haughty Zeph 3:11
thou shalt not see evil any *m* Zeph 3:15 5750
shall pass through them any *m* Zec 9:8 5750
For I will no *m* pity the Zec 11:6 5750
and they shall no *m* be remembered Zec 13:2 5750
shall be no *m* utter destruction Zec 14:11 5750
m the Canaanite in the house of Zec 14:21 5750
regardeth not the offering any *m* Mal 2:13 5750
for whatsoever is *m* than these Mt 5:37 *4053*
only, what do ye *m* than others Mt 5:47 *4053*
Is not the life *m* than meat Mt 6:25 *4119*
shall he not much *m* clothe you Mt 6:30 *3123*
how much *m* shall your Father Mt 7:11 *3123*
It shall be *m* tolerable for the Mt 10:15 *414*
how much *m* shall they call them Mt 10:25 *3123*
ye are of *m* value than many Mt 10:31 *1308*
m than me is not worthy of me Mt 10:37 *5228*
m than me is not worthy of me Mt 10:37 *5228*
say unto you, and *m* than a prophet Mt 11:9 *4055*
It shall be *m* tolerable for Tyre Mt 11:22 *414*
That it shall be *m* tolerable for Mt 11:24 *414*
spirits *m* wicked than himself Mt 12:45
and he shall have *m* abundance Mt 13:12
he rejoiceth *m* of that sheep, Mt 18:13 *3123*
then take with thee one or two *m* Mt 18:16 *2089*
Wherefore they are no *m* twain Mt 19:6 *3765*
that they should have received *m* Mt 20:10 *4119*
but they cried the *m*, saying, Mt 20:31 *3185*
other servants *m* than the first Mt 21:36 *4119*
day forth ask him any *m* questions Mt 22:46 *3765*
ye make him twofold *m* the child Mt 23:15
gained beside them five talents *m* Mt 25:20 *243*
he shall presently give me *m* than Mt 26:53 *4119*
But they cried out the *m*, saying, Mt 27:23 *4057*
no *m* openly enter into the city Mk 1:45 *3370*
you that hear shall *m* be given Mk 4:24 *4369*
It shall be *m* tolerable for Sodom Mk 6:11 *414*
ye suffer him no *m* to do ought Mk 7:12 *3765*
but the *m* he charged them Mk 7:36 *3745*
so much the *m* a great deal they Mk 7:36 *3123*
ship with them *m* than one loaf Mk 8:14 *1508*
about, they saw no man any *m* Mk 9:8 *3765*
of him, and enter no *m* into him Mk 9:25 *3370*
so then they are no *m* twain Mk 10:8 *3765*
but he cried the *m* a great deal Mk 10:48 *3123*
is *m* than all whole burnt Mk 12:33 *4119*
this poor widow hath cast *m* in Mk 12:43 *4119*
for *m* than three hundred pence Mk 14:5 *1833*
I will drink no *m* of the fruit of Mk 14:25 *3765*
But he spake the *m* vehemently Mk 14:31 *3123*
they cried out the *m* exceedingly Mk 15:14 *4065*
Exact no *m* than that which is Lk 3:13 *4119*
But so much the *m* went there a Lk 5:15 *3123*
you, and much *m* than a prophet Lk 7:26 *4055*
We have no *m* but five loaves and Lk 9:13 *4119*
that it shall be *m* tolerable in Lk 10:12 *414*
But it shall be *m* tolerable for Lk 10:14 *414*
and whatsoever thou spendest *m* Lk 10:35 *4325*
how much *m* shall your heavenly Lk 11:13 *3123*
spirits *m* wicked than himself Lk 11:26
that have no *m* that they can do Lk 12:4 *4055*
ye are of *m* value than many Lk 12:7 *1308*
The life is *m* than meat, and the Lk 12:23 *4119*
the body is *m* than raiment Lk 12:23
how much *m* are ye better than the Lk 12:24 *3123*
how much *m* will he clothe you, O Lk 12:28 *3123*
much, of him they will ask the *m* Lk 12:48 *4055*
lest a *m* honourable man than thou Lk 14:8
m than over ninety and nine just Lk 15:7
am no *m* worthy to be called thy Lk 15:19 *3765*
am no *m* worthy to be called thy Lk 15:21 *3765*
manifold *m* in this present time Lk 18:30 *4179*
but he cried so much the *m* Lk 18:39 *3123*
Neither can they die any *m* Lk 20:36 *2089*
hath cast in *m* than they all Lk 21:3 *4119*
you, I will not any *m* eat thereof Lk 22:16 *3765*
in an agony he prayed *m* earnestly Lk 22:44 *1617*
And they were the *m* fierce Lk 23:5 *2001*
baptized *m* disciples than John, Jn 4:1 *4119*
many *m* believed because of his Jn 4:41 *4119*
sin no *m*, lest a worse thing come Jn 5:14 *3370*
the Jews sought the *m* to kill him Jn 5:18 *3123*
back, and walked no *m* with him Jn 6:66 *3765*
will he do *m* miracles than these Jn 7:31 *4119*
go, and sin no *m* Jn 8:11 *2001*
they might have it *m* abundantly Jn 10:10
walked no *m* openly among the Jews Jn 11:54 *2089*
of men *m* than the praise of God Jn 12:43 *3123*
while, and the world seeth me no *m* Jn 14:19 *2089*
that it may bring forth *m* fruit Jn 15:2 *4119*
no *m* can ye, except ye abide in Jn 15:4 *3761*
to my Father, and ye see me no *m* Jn 16:10 *2089*
she remembereth no *m* the anguish Jn 16:21 *2089*
when I shall no *m* speak unto you Jn 16:25 *2089*
now I am no *m* in the world, but Jn 17:11 *2089*
that saying, he was the *m* afraid Jn 19:8 *3123*
lovest thou me *m* than these Jn 21:15 *4119*
hearken unto you *m* than unto God Acts 4:19 *3123*
were the *m* added to the Lord Acts 5:14 *3123*
that the eunuch saw him no *m* Acts 8:39 *3765*
Saul increased the *m* in strength Acts 9:22 *3123*
now no *m* to return to corruption, Acts 13:34 *2001*
These were *m* noble than those in Acts 17:11
him the way of God *m* perfectly Acts 18:26 *197*
the *m* part knew not wherefore Acts 19:32 *4119*
of God, shall see my face no *m* Acts 20:25 *3765*
It is *m* blessed to give than to Acts 20:35 *3122*
they should see his face no *m* Acts 20:38 *3765*
to them, they kept the *m* silence Acts 22:2 *3123*
they were *m* than forty which had Acts 23:13 *4119*
m perfectly concerning him Acts 23:15 *197*
somewhat of him *m* perfectly Acts 23:20 *197*
for him of them *m* than forty men Acts 23:21 *4119*
I do the *m* cheerfully answer for Acts 24:10 *2115*
having *m* perfect knowledge of Acts 24:22 *197*
among them *m* than ten days Acts 25:6 *4119*
m than those things which were Acts 27:11 *3123*
the *m* part advised to depart Acts 27:12 *4119*
the creature *m* than the Creator Rom 1:25 *3844*
the things that are *m* excellent Rom 2:18
m abounded through my lie unto Rom 3:7
Much *m* then, being now justified Rom 5:9 *3123*
by the death of his Son, much *m* Rom 5:10 *3123*
much *m* the grace of God, and the Rom 5:15 *3123*
much *m* they which receive Rom 5:17 *3123*
abounded, grace did much *m* abound Rom 5:20
raised from the dead dieth no *m* Rom 6:9 *2089*
death hath no *m* dominion over him Rom 6:9 *3765*
Now then it is no *m* I that do it Rom 7:17 *2089*
it is no *m* I that do it, but sin Rom 7:20 *2089*
in all these things we are *m* than Rom 8:37 *5245*
grace, then is it no *m* of works Rom 11:6 *2089*
otherwise grace is no *m* grace Rom 11:6 *2089*
of works, then is it no *m* grace Rom 11:6 *2089*
otherwise work is no *m* work Rom 11:6 *2089*
how much *m* their fulness Rom 11:12 *3123*
how much *m* shall these, which be Rom 11:24 *3123*
not to think of himself *m* highly Rom 12:3 *3844*
therefore judge one another any *m* Rom 14:13 *2001*
I have written the *m* boldly unto Rom 15:15 *5112*
But now having no *m* place in Rom 15:23 *2001*
how much *m* things that pertain to 1Cor 6:3 *1065*
unto all, that I might gain the *m* 1Cor 9:19 *4119*
much *m* those members of the body, 1Cor 12:22 *3123*
which seem to be *m* feeble 1Cor 12:22 *3123*
these we bestow *m* abundant honour 1Cor 12:23 *4055*
parts have *m* abundant comeliness 1Cor 12:23 *4055*
having given *m* abundant honour to 1Cor 12:24 *4055*
shew I unto you a *m* excellent way 1Cor 12:31
speak with tongues *m* than ye all 1Cor 14:18 *3123*
but I laboured *m* abundantly than 1Cor 15:10 *4055*
and *m* abundantly to you-ward 2Cor 1:12 *4056*
I have *m* abundantly unto you 2Cor 2:4 *4056*
much *m* doth the ministration of 2Cor 3:9 *3123*
much *m* that which remaineth is 2Cor 3:11 *3123*
worketh for us a far *m* exceeding 2Cor 4:17
now henceforth know we him no *m* 2Cor 5:16 *2089*
so that I rejoiced the *m* 2Cor 7:7 *3123*
exceedingly the *m* joyed we for 2Cor 7:13 *3123*
is *m* abundant toward you, whilst 2Cor 7:15 *4056*
but being *m* forward, of his own 2Cor 8:17 *4707*
things, but now much *m* diligent 2Cor 8:22 *4707*
boast somewhat *m* of our authority 2Cor 10:8 *4055*
(I speak as a fool) I am *m* 2Cor 11:23 *5228*
in labours *m* abundant, in stripes 2Cor 11:23 *4056*
measure, in prisons *m* frequent 2Cor 11:23 *4056*
though the *m* abundantly I love 2Cor 12:15 *4056*
being *m* exceedingly zealous of Gal 1:14 *4056*
of the law, it is no *m* of promise Gal 3:18 *2089*
Wherefore thou art no *m* a servant Gal 4:7 *2089*
for the desolate hath many *m* Gal 4:27 *3123*
therefore ye are no *m* strangers Eph 2:19 *3765*
we henceforth be no *m* children Eph 4:14 *2001*
Let him that stole steal no *m* Eph 4:28 *2001*
that your love may abound yet *m* Phil 1:9 *3123*
m in knowledge and in all judgment Phil 1:9 *3123*
are much *m* bold to speak the word Phil 1:14 *4056*
in the flesh is *m* needful for you Phil 1:24 *316*
That your rejoicing may be *m* Phil 1:26
but now much *m* in my absence, Phil 2:12 *3123*
him therefore the *m* carefully Phil 2:28 *3123*
he might trust in the flesh, I *m* Phil 3:4 *3123*
endeavoured the *m* abundantly to 1Th 2:17 *4056*
please God, so ye would abound *m* 1Th 4:1 *3123*
God, so ye would abound *m* and *m* 1Th 4:1 *3123*
that ye increase *m* and *m* 1Th 4:10 *3123*
will increase unto *m* ungodliness 2Ti 2:16 *4119*
of pleasures *m* than lovers of God 2Ti 3:4 *3123*
to me, but how much *m* unto thee Philem 16 *3123*
thou wilt also do *m* than I say Philem 21 *5228*
a *m* excellent name than they Heb 1:4
the *m* earnest heed to the things Heb 2:1 *4056*
worthy of *m* glory than Moses Heb 3:3 *4119*
hath *m* honour than the house Heb 3:3 *4119*
willing *m* abundantly to shew unto Heb 6:17 *4054*
And it is yet far *m* evident Heb 7:15 *4055*
obtained a *m* excellent ministry Heb 8:6
iniquities will I remember no *m* Heb 8:12 *2089*
m perfect tabernacle, not made Heb 9:11
How much *m* shall the blood of Heb 9:14 *3123*
have had no *m* conscience of sins Heb 10:2 *2089*
iniquities will I remember no *m* Heb 10:17 *2089*
there is no *m* offering for sin Heb 10:18 *2089*
and so much the *m*, as ye see the Heb 10:25 *3123*
remaineth no *m* sacrifice for sins Heb 10:26 *2089*
a *m* excellent sacrifice than Cain Heb 11:4
And what shall I *m* say Heb 11:32 *2089*
not be spoken to them any *m* Heb 12:19 *4369*
much *m* shall not we escape, if we Heb 12:25 *3123*
Yet once *m* I shake not the earth Heb 12:26
And this word, Yet once *m*, Heb 12:27
But he giveth *m* grace Jas 4:6 *3187*
being much *m* precious than of 1Pet 1:7
We have also a *m* sure word of 2Pet 1:19
the last to be *m* than the first Rev 2:19 *4119*
my God, and he shall go no *m* out Rev 3:12 *2089*
no *m*, neither thirst any *m* Rev 7:16 *2089*
there come two woes *m* hereafter Rev 9:12 *2089*
their place found any *m* in heaven Rev 12:8 *2089*
buyeth their merchandise any *m* Rev 18:11 *3765*
thou shalt find them no *m* at all Rev 18:14 *3765*
and shall be found no *m* at all Rev 18:21 *2089*
be heard no *m* at all in thee Rev 18:22 *2089*
be, shall be found any *m* in thee Rev 18:22 *2089*
be heard no *m* at all in thee Rev 18:22 *2089*
shall shine no *m* at all in thee Rev 18:23 *2089*
be heard no *m* at all in thee Rev 18:23 *2089*
should deceive the nations no *m* Rev 20:3 *2089*
and there was no *m* sea Rev 21:1 *2089*
and there shall be no *m* death Rev 21:4 *2089*
neither shall there be any *m* pain Rev 21:4 *2089*
And there shall be no *m* curse Rev 22:3 *2089*

MOREH (*mo'-reh*)
1. A place in Ephraim.
of Sichem, unto the plain of *M* Gen 12:6 4176
Gilgal, beside the plains of *M* Deut 11:30 4176
2. A place in Issachar.
side of them, by the hill of *M* Judg 7:1 4176

MOREOVER
She said *m* unto him, We have both Gen 24:25
And say ye *m*, Behold, thy servant Gen 32:20 1571
M he kissed all his brethren, and Gen 45:15
They said *m* unto Pharaoh, For to Gen 47:4
M I have given to thee one Gen 48:22
M he said, I am the God of thy Ex 3:6
God said *m* unto Moses, Thus shalt Ex 3:15 5750
M the man Moses was very great in Ex 11:3
M thou shalt provide out of all Ex 18:21
M thou shalt make the tabernacle Ex 26:1
M the LORD spake unto Moses, Ex 30:22
M the soul that shall touch any Lev 7:21
M ye shall eat no manner of blood Lev 7:26
M he that goeth into the house Lev 14:46
M thou shalt not lie carnally Lev 18:20
M of the children of the Lev 25:45 1571
m we saw the children of Anak Num 13:28 1571
M thou hast not brought us into a Num 16:14 637
M it shall come to pass, that I Num 33:56
M ye shall take no satisfaction Num 35:31
m we have seen the sons of the Deut 1:28 1571
M your little ones, which ye said Deut 1:39
M the LORD thy God will send the Deut 7:20 1571
M all these curses shall come Deut 28:45
M he will bring upon thee all the Deut 28:60
M the children of Ammon passed Judg 10:9
M Ruth the Moabitess, the wife of Ruth 4:10 1571
M his mother made him a little 1Sa 2:19
M as for me, God forbid that I 1Sa 12:23 1571
M the Hebrews that were with the 1Sa 14:21
David said *m*, The LORD that 1Sa 17:37
And David sware *m*, and said, Thy 1Sa 20:3 5750
M, my father, see, yea, see the 1Sa 24:11
M the LORD will also deliver 1Sa 28:19 1571
M I will appoint a place for my 2Sa 7:10
I would *m* have given unto thee 2Sa 12:8 3254
Absalom said *m*, Oh that I were 2Sa 15:4
M Ahithophel said unto Absalom, 2Sa 17:1
M, if he be gotten into a city, 2Sa 17:13 518
M the Philistines had yet war 2Sa 21:15
m the king's servants came to 1Kin 1:47 1571
M thou knowest also what Joab the 1Kin 2:5 1571
He said *m*, I have somewhat to say 1Kin 2:14

The king said *m* to Shimei ... 1Kin 2:44
M concerning a stranger, that is ... 1Kin 8:41 1571
M the king made a great throne of ... 1Kin 10:18
M the LORD shall raise him up a ... 1Kin 14:14
M they reckoned not with the men, ... 2Kin 12:15
M Manasseh shed innocent blood ... 2Kin 21:16 1571
M the altar that was at Beth-el, ... 2Kin 23:15 1571
M the workers with familiar ... 2Kin 23:24 1571
m in time past, even when Saul ... 1Chr 11:2 1571
M they that were nigh them, even ... 1Chr 12:40 1571
M I will subdue all thine enemies ... 1Chr 17:10
M, Abishai the son Zeruiah slew ... 1Chr 18:12
M there are workmen with thee in ... 1Chr 22:15
M four thousand were porters ... 1Chr 23:5
M David and the captains of the ... 1Chr 25:1
M the sons of Obed-edom were, ... 1Chr 26:4
M I will establish his kingdom ... 1Chr 28:7
M, because I have set my ... 1Chr 29:3 5750
M the brasen altar, that Bezaleel ... 2Chr 1:5
Huram said *m*, Blessed be the LORD ... 2Chr 2:12
M he made an altar of brass, ... 2Chr 4:1
M the candlesticks with their ... 2Chr 4:20
M concerning the stranger, which ... 2Chr 6:32 1571
M Solomon hallowed the middle of ... 2Chr 7:7
M the king made a great throne of ... 2Chr 9:17
m he took away the high places and ... 2Chr 17:6 5750
M in Jerusalem did Jehoshaphat ... 2Chr 19:8 1571
M he made high places in the ... 2Chr 21:11 1571
M the LORD stirred up against ... 2Chr 21:16
M Jehoiada the priest delivered ... 2Chr 23:9
M Amaziah gathered Judah together ... 2Chr 25:5
M Uzziah built towers in ... 2Chr 26:9
M Uzziah had an host of fighting ... 2Chr 26:11
M he built cities in the ... 2Chr 27:4
M he burnt incense in the valley ... 2Chr 28:3
M all the vessels, which king ... 2Chr 29:19
M Hezekiah the king and the ... 2Chr 29:30
M he commanded the people that ... 2Chr 31:4
M he provided him cities, and ... 2Chr 32:29
M Josiah kept a passover unto the ... 2Chr 35:1
M all the chief of the priests, ... 2Chr 36:14 1571
M I make a decree what ye shall ... Ezr 6:8
M of Israel: of the sons ... Ezr 10:25
M I said unto the king, If it ... Neh 2:7
M the old gate repaired Jehoiada ... Neh 3:6
M the Nethinims dwelt in Ophel, ... Neh 3:26
M from the time that I was ... Neh 5:14 1571
M there were at my table an ... Neh 5:17
M in those days the nobles of ... Neh 6:17 1571
M thou leddest them in the day by ... Neh 9:12
M thou gavest them kingdoms and ... Neh 9:22
M the porters, Akkub, Talmon, and ... Neh 11:19
M the Levites: Jeshua ... Neh 12:8
Haman said *m*, Yea, Esther the ... Est 5:12 637
M Job continued his parable, and ... Job 27:1
M Job continued his parable, and ... Job 29:1
Elihu spake *m*, and said, ... Job 35:1
M the LORD answered Job, and said, ... Job 40:1
M by them is thy servant warned ... Ps 19:11 1571
M he refused the tabernacle of ... Ps 78:67
M he called for a famine upon the ... Ps 105:16
m I saw under the sun the place ... Eccl 3:16 5750
M the profit of the earth is for ... Eccl 5:9
M he hath not seen the sun, nor ... Eccl 6:5 1571
And *m*, because the preacher was ... Eccl 12:9 3148
M the LORD saith, Because the ... Is 3:16
M the LORD spake again unto Ahaz, ... Is 7:10
M the LORD said unto me, Take ... Is 8:1
M they that work in fine flax, and ... Is 19:9
M the multitude of thy strangers ... Is 29:5
M the light of the moon shall be ... Is 30:26
He said *m*, For there shall be ... Is 39:8
M the word of the LORD came unto ... Jer 1:11
M the word of the LORD came to me ... Jer 2:1
M thou shalt say unto them, Thus ... Jer 8:4
M I will deliver all the strength ... Jer 20:5
M I will take from them the voice ... Jer 25:10
M the word of the LORD came unto ... Jer 33:1
M the word of the LORD came to ... Jer 33:23
M Jeremiah said unto king ... Jer 37:18
M he put out Zedekiah's eyes, and ... Jer 39:7
M Johanan the son of Kareah, and ... Jer 40:13
M Jeremiah said unto all the ... Jer 44:24
M I will cause to cease in Moab, ... Jer 48:35
M he said unto me, Son of man, ... Eze 3:1
M he said unto me, Son of man, ... Eze 3:10
M take thou unto thee an iron pan ... Eze 4:3
M he said unto me, Son of man, ... Eze 4:16
M I will make thee waste, and a ... Eze 5:14
M the word of the LORD came unto ... Eze 7:1
M the spirit lifted me up, and ... Eze 11:1
M the word of the LORD came to me ... Eze 12:17
M thou hast taken thy sons and thy ... Eze 16:20
Thou hast *m* multiplied thy ... Eze 16:29
M the word of the LORD came unto ... Eze 17:11
M take thou up a lamentation for ... Eze 19:1
M also I gave them my sabbaths, ... Eze 20:12 1571
M the word of the LORD came unto ... Eze 20:45
M the word of the LORD came unto ... Eze 22:1
The LORD said *m* unto me ... Eze 23:36
M this they have done unto me ... Eze 23:38 5750
M the word of the LORD came unto ... Eze 28:11
M the word of the LORD came unto ... Eze 35:1
M the word of the LORD came unto ... Eze 36:16
M, thou son of man, take thee one ... Eze 37:16
M I will make a covenant of peace ... Eze 37:26
M, when ye shall divide by lot ... Eze 45:1
M the prince shall not take of ... Eze 46:18
M from the possession of the ... Eze 48:22
M the word of the LORD came unto ... Zec 4:8
He said *m*, This is their ... Zec 5:6
M when ye fast, be not, as the ... Mt 6:16 *1161*
M if thy brother shall trespass ... Mt 18:15 *1161*
m the dogs came and licked his ... Lk 16:21
m also my flesh shall rest in ... Acts 2:26 *2089*
M these six brethren accompanied ... Acts 11:12 *1161*
M ye see and hear, that not alone ... Acts 19:26 *2532*
M the law entered, that the ... Rom 5:20 *1161*
M whom he did predestinate, them ... Rom 8:30 *1161*
M it is required in stewards, ... 1Cor 4:2
M, brethren, I would not that ye ... 1Cor 10:1 *1161*
M, brethren, I declare unto you ... 1Cor 15:1 *1161*
M I call God for a record upon my ... 2Cor 1:23 *1161*
M, brethren, we do you to wit of ... 2Cor 8:1 *1161*
M he must have a good report of ... 1Ti 3:7 *1161*
M he sprinkled with blood both ... Heb 9:21 *1161*
m of bonds and imprisonment ... Heb 11:36 *1161*
M I will endeavour that ye may be ... 2Pet 1:15

MORESHETH See MORASTHITE.

MORESHETH-GATH (*mor'-e-sheth-gath*) See MORASTHITE. *A city in Judah.*
shalt thou give presents to *M* ... Mic 1:14 4182

MORIAH (*mo-ri'-ah*) *The Temple Mount.*
and get thee into the land of *M* ... Gen 22:2 4179
the LORD at Jerusalem in mount *M* ... 2Chr 3:1 4179

MORNING
and the *m* were the first day ... Gen 1:5 1242
the *m* were the second day ... Gen 1:8 1242
and the *m* were the third day ... Gen 1:13 1242
the *m* were the fourth day ... Gen 1:19 1242
and the *m* were the fifth day ... Gen 1:23 1242
and the *m* were the sixth day ... Gen 1:31 1242
And when the *m* arose, then the ... Gen 19:15 7837
the *m* to the place where he stood ... Gen 19:27 1242
Abimelech rose early in the *m* ... Gen 20:8 1242
And Abraham rose up early in the *m* ... Gen 21:14 1242
And Abraham rose up early in the *m* ... Gen 22:3 1242
and they rose up in the *m*, and he ... Gen 24:54 1242
And they rose up betimes in the *m* ... Gen 26:31 1242
And Jacob rose up early in the *m* ... Gen 28:18 1242
And it came to pass, that in the *m* ... Gen 29:25 1242
early in the *m* Laban rose up, and ... Gen 31:55 1242
Joseph came in unto them in the *m* ... Gen 40:6 1242
it came to pass in the *m* that his ... Gen 41:8 1242
As soon as the *m* was light ... Gen 44:3 1242
in the *m* he shall devour the prey ... Gen 49:27 1242
Get thee unto Pharaoh in the *m* ... Ex 7:15 1242
Moses, Rise up early in the *m* ... Ex 8:20 1242
Moses, Rise up early in the *m* ... Ex 9:13 1242
and when it was *m*, the east wind ... Ex 10:13 1242
nothing of it remain until the *m* ... Ex 12:10 1242
the *m* ye shall burn with fire ... Ex 12:10 1242
the door of his house until the *m* ... Ex 12:22 1242
that in the *m* watch the LORD ... Ex 14:24 1242
his strength when the *m* appeared ... Ex 14:27 1242
And in the *m*, then ye shall see ... Ex 16:7 1242
in the *m* bread to the full ... Ex 16:8 1242
in the *m* ye shall be filled with ... Ex 16:12 1242
in the *m* the dew lay round about ... Ex 16:13 1242
Let no man leave of it till the *m* ... Ex 16:19 1242
of them left of it until the *m* ... Ex 16:20 1242
And they gathered it every *m* ... Ex 16:21 1242
up for you to be kept until the *m* ... Ex 16:23 1242
And they laid it up till the *m* ... Ex 16:24 1242
Moses from the *m* unto the evening ... Ex 18:13 1242
stand by thee from *m* unto even ... Ex 18:14 1242
to pass on the third day in the *m* ... Ex 19:16 1242
my sacrifice remain until the *m* ... Ex 23:18 1242
LORD, and rose up early in the *m* ... Ex 24:4 1242
from evening to *m* before the LORD ... Ex 27:21 1242
of the bread, remain unto the *m* ... Ex 29:34 1242
lamb thou shalt offer in the *m* ... Ex 29:39 1242
to the meat offering of the *m* ... Ex 29:41 1242
thereon sweet incense every *m* ... Ex 30:7 1242
And be ready in the *m*, and come up ... Ex 34:2 1242
come up in the *m* unto mount Sinai ... Ex 34:2 1242
and Moses rose up early in the *m* ... Ex 34:4 1242
the passover be left unto the *m* ... Ex 34:25 1242
unto him free offerings every *m* ... Ex 36:3 1242
the altar all night unto the *m* ... Lev 6:9 1242
shall burn wood on it every *m* ... Lev 6:12 1242
perpetual, half of it in the *m* ... Lev 6:20 1242
not leave any of it until the *m* ... Lev 7:15 1242
the burnt sacrifice of the *m* ... Lev 9:17 1242
with thee all night until the *m* ... Lev 19:13 1242
the *m* before the LORD continually ... Lev 24:3 1242
shall leave none of it unto the *m* ... Num 9:12 1242
appearance of fire, until the *m* ... Num 9:15 1242
cloud abode from even unto the *m* ... Num 9:21 1242
the cloud was taken up in the *m* ... Num 9:21 1242
And they rose up early in the *m* ... Num 14:40 1242
And Balaam rose up in the *m* ... Num 22:13 1242
And Balaam rose up in the *m* ... Num 22:21 1242
lamb shalt thou offer in the *m* ... Num 28:4 1242
as the meat offering of the *m* ... Num 28:8 1242
the burnt offering in the *m* ... Num 28:23 1242
remain all night until the *m* ... Deut 16:4 1242
and thou shalt turn in the *m* ... Deut 16:7 1242
In the *m* thou shalt say, Would ... Deut 28:67 1242
shalt say, Would God it were *m* ... Deut 28:67 1242
And Joshua rose early in the *m* ... Josh 3:1 1242
And Joshua rose early in the *m* ... Josh 6:12 1242
In the *m* therefore ye shall be ... Josh 7:14 1242
So Joshua rose up early in the *m* ... Josh 7:16 1242
And Joshua rose up early in the *m* ... Josh 8:10 1242
of the city arose early in the *m* ... Judg 6:28 1242
put to death whilst it is yet *m* ... Judg 6:31 1242
And it shall be, that in the *m* ... Judg 9:33 1242
all the night, saying, In the *m* ... Judg 16:2 1242
when they arose early in the *m* ... Judg 19:5 1242
he arose early in the *m* on the ... Judg 19:8 1242
her all the night until the *m* ... Judg 19:25 1242
And her lord rose up in the *m* ... Judg 19:27 1242
of Israel rose up in the *m* ... Judg 20:19 1242
even from the *m* until now ... Ruth 2:7 1242
night, and it shall be in the *m* ... Ruth 3:13 1242
lie down until the *m* ... Ruth 3:13 1242
she lay at his feet until the *m* ... Ruth 3:14 1242
And they rose up in the *m* early ... 1Sa 1:19 1242
And Samuel lay until the *m* ... 1Sa 3:15 1242
they arose early on the morrow *m* ... 1Sa 5:4 1242
midst of the host in the *m* watch ... 1Sa 11:11 1242
and spoil them until the *m* light ... 1Sa 14:36 1242
rose early to meet Saul in the *m* ... 1Sa 15:12 1242
And the Philistine drew near *m* ... 1Sa 17:16 7925
And David rose up early in the *m* ... 1Sa 17:20 1242
take heed to thyself until the *m* ... 1Sa 19:2 1242
him, and to slay him in the *m* ... 1Sa 19:11 1242
And it came to pass in the *m* ... 1Sa 20:35 1242
m light any that pisseth against ... 1Sa 25:22 1242
m light any that pisseth against ... 1Sa 25:34 1242
less or more, until the *m* light ... 1Sa 25:36 1242
But it came to pass in the *m* ... 1Sa 25:37 1242
now rise up early in the *m* with ... 1Sa 29:10 1242
soon as ye be up early in the *m* ... 1Sa 29:10 1242
rose up early to depart in the *m* ... 1Sa 29:11 1242
surely then in the *m* the people ... 2Sa 2:27 1242
And it came to pass in the *m* ... 2Sa 11:14 1242
by the *m* light there lacked not ... 2Sa 17:22 1242
he shall be as the light of the *m* ... 2Sa 23:4 1242
riseth, even a *m* without clouds ... 2Sa 23:4 1242
For when David was up in the *m* ... 2Sa 24:11 1242
the *m* even to the time appointed ... 2Sa 24:15 1242
when I rose in the *m* to give my ... 1Kin 3:21 1242
when I had considered it in the *m* ... 1Kin 3:21 1242
him bread and flesh in the *m* ... 1Kin 17:6 1242
of Baal from *m* even until noon ... 1Kin 18:26 1242
And it came to pass in the *m* ... 2Kin 3:20 1242
And they rose up early in the *m* ... 2Kin 3:22 1242
if we tarry till the *m* light ... 2Kin 7:9 1242
in of the gate until the *m* ... 2Kin 10:8 1242
And it came to pass in the *m* ... 2Kin 10:9 1242
altar burn the *m* burnt offering ... 2Kin 16:15 1242
and when they arose early in the *m* ... 2Kin 19:35 1242
thereof every *m* pertained to them ... 1Chr 9:27 1242
the burnt offering continually *m* ... 1Chr 16:40 1242
And to stand every *m* to thank ... 1Chr 23:30 1242
and for the burnt offerings *m* ... 2Chr 2:4 1242
they burn unto the LORD every *m* ... 2Chr 13:11 1242
And they rose early in the *m* ... 2Chr 20:20 1242
offerings, to wit, for the *m* ... 2Chr 31:3 1242
the LORD, even burnt offerings *m* ... Ezr 3:3 1242
of the *m* till the stars appeared ... Neh 4:21 7837
gate from the *m* until midday ... Neh 8:3 216
them, and rose up early in the *m* ... Job 1:5 1242
are destroyed from *m* to evening ... Job 4:20 1242
thou shouldest visit him every *m* ... Job 7:18 1242
and thou shalt seek me in the *m* ... Job 7:21 7836
forth, thou shalt be as the *m* ... Job 11:17 1242
For the *m* is to them even as the ... Job 24:17 1242
When the *m* stars sang together, ... Job 38:7 1242
commanded the *m* since thy days ... Job 38:12 1242
are like the eyelids of the *m* ... Job 41:18 7837
My voice shalt thou hear in the *m* ... Ps 5:3 1242
in the *m* will I direct my prayer ... Ps 5:3 1242
a night, but joy cometh in the *m* ... Ps 30:5 1242
have dominion over them in the *m* ... Ps 49:14 1242
Evening, and *m*, and at noon, will I ... Ps 55:17 1242
sing aloud of thy mercy in the *m* ... Ps 59:16 1242
makest the outgoings of the *m* ... Ps 65:8 1242
plagued, and chastened every *m* ... Ps 73:14 1242
in the *m* shall my prayer prevent ... Ps 88:13 1242
in the *m* they are like grass ... Ps 90:5 1242
In the *m* it flourisheth, and ... Ps 90:6 1242
forth thy lovingkindness in the *m* ... Ps 92:2 1242
holiness from the womb of the *m* ... Ps 110:3 4891
I prevented the dawning of the *m* ... Ps 119:147
than they that watch for the *m* ... Ps 130:6 1242
than they that watch for the *m* ... Ps 130:6 1242
If I take the wings of the *m* ... Ps 139:9 7837
hear thy lovingkindness in the *m* ... Ps 143:8 1242
take our fill of love until the *m* ... Prov 7:18 1242
loud voice, rising early in the *m* ... Prov 27:14 1242
and thy princes eat in the *m* ... Eccl 10:16 1242
In the *m* sow thy seed, and in the ... Eccl 11:6 1242
she that looketh forth as the *m* ... Song 6:10 7837
them that rise up early in the *m* ... Is 5:11 1242
heaven, O Lucifer, son of the *m* ... Is 14:12 7837
in the *m* shalt thou make thy seed ... Is 17:11 1242
and before the *m* he is not ... Is 17:14 1242
The *m* cometh, and also the night ... Is 21:12 1242
for *m* by *m* shall it pass ... Is 28:19 1242
be thou their arm every *m* ... Is 33:2 1242
and when they arose early in the *m* ... Is 37:36 1242
I reckoned till *m*, that, as a ... Is 38:13 1242
he wakeneth *m* by *m*, he ... Is 50:4 1242
thy light break forth as the *m* ... Is 58:8 7837
They were as fed horses in the *m* ... Jer 5:8 7904
and let him hear the cry in the *m* ... Jer 20:16 1242
Execute judgment in the *m* ... Jer 21:12 1242
They are new every *m* ... Lam 3:23 1242
The *m* is come unto thee, O thou ... Eze 7:7 6843
the *m* is gone forth ... Eze 7:10 6843
in the *m* came the word of the ... Eze 12:8 1242
I spake unto the people in the *m* ... Eze 24:18 1242
I did in the *m* as I was commanded ... Eze 24:18 1242
until he came to me in the *m* ... Eze 33:22 1242
thou shalt prepare it every *m* ... Eze 46:13 1242
a meat offering for it every *m* ... Eze 46:14 1242
every *m* for a continual burnt ... Eze 46:15 1242
king arose very early in the *m* ... Dan 6:19 5053
the *m* which was told is true ... Dan 8:26 1242
going forth is prepared as the *m* ... Hos 6:3 7837
for your goodness is as a *m* cloud ... Hos 6:4 1242
in the *m* it burneth as a flaming ... Hos 7:6 1242
in a *m* shall the king of Israel ... Hos 10:15 7837
they shall be as the *m* cloud ... Hos 13:3 1242
as the *m* spread upon the ... Joel 2:2 7837
and bring your sacrifices every *m* ... Amos 4:4 1242
that maketh the *m* darkness ... Amos 4:13 7837

the shadow of death into the *m* .... Amos 5:8 1242
worm when the *m* rose the next day ... Jonah 4:7 7837
when the *m* is light, they .... Mic 2:1 1242
every *m* doth he bring his .... Zeph 3:5 1242
And in the *m*, It will be foul .... Mt 16:3 *4404*
the *m* to hire labourers into his .... Mt 20:1
Now in the *m* as he returned into .... Mt 21:18 *4405*
When the *m* was come, all the .... Mt 27:1 *4405*
And in the *m*, rising up a great .... Mk 1:35 *4404*
And in the *m*, as they passed by, ... Mk 11:20 *4404*
at the cockcrowing, or in the *m* .... Mk 13:35 *4404*
straightway in the *m* the chief .... Mk 15:1 *4404*
very early in the *m* the first day .... Mk 16:2
in the *m* to him in the temple .... Lk 21:38
of the week, very early in the *m* .... Lk 24:1
And And early in the *m* he came .... Jn 8:1
early in the *m* he came again into .... Jn 8:2
But when the *m* was now come .... Jn 21:4 *4405*
into the temple early in the *m* .... Acts 5:21
the prophets, from *m* till evening .... Acts 28:23 *4404*
And I will give him the *m* star .... Rev 2:28 *4407*
of David, and the bright and *m* star .... Rev 22:16 *3720*

MORROW

And it came to pass on the *m* .... Gen 19:34 4283
And he said, To *m* .... Ex 8:10 4279
to *m* shall this sign be .... Ex 8:23 4279
and from his people, to *m* .... Ex 8:29 4279
To *m* the LORD shall do this thing .... Ex 9:5 4279
the LORD did that thing on the *m* .... Ex 9:6 4283
to *m* about this time I will cause .... Ex 9:18 4279
to *m* will I bring the locusts .... Ex 10:4 4279
To *m* is the rest of the holy .... Ex 16:23 4279
to *m* I will stand on the top of .... Ex 17:9 4279
And it came to pass on the *m* .... Ex 18:13 4283
and sanctify them to day and to *m* .... Ex 19:10 4279
To *m* is a feast to the LORD .... Ex 32:5 4279
And they rose up early on the *m* .... Ex 32:6 4283
And it came to pass on the *m* .... Ex 32:30 4283
on the *m* also the remainder of it .... Lev 7:16 4283
same day ye offer it, and on the *m* .... Lev 19:6 4283
leave none of it until the *m* .... Lev 22:30 1242
on the *m* after the sabbath the .... Lev 23:11 4283
you from the *m* after the sabbath .... Lev 23:15 4283
Even unto the *m* after the seventh .... Lev 23:16 4283
Sanctify yourselves against to *m* .... Num 11:18 4279
To *m* turn you, and get you into .... Num 14:25 4279
Even to *m* the LORD will shew who .... Num 16:5 1242
in them before the LORD to *m* .... Num 16:7 4279
thou, and they, and Aaron, to *m* .... Num 16:16 4279
But on the *m* all the congregation .... Num 16:41 4283
that on the *m* Moses went into the .... Num 17:8 4283
And it came to pass on the *m* .... Num 22:41 1242
on the *m* after the passover the .... Num 33:3 4283
for to *m* the LORD will do wonders .... Josh 3:5 4279
land on the *m* after the passover .... Josh 5:11 4283
the manna ceased on the *m* after .... Josh 5:12 4283
Sanctify yourselves against to *m* .... Josh 7:13 4279
for to *m* about this time will I .... Josh 11:6 4279
that to *m* he will be wroth with .... Josh 22:18 4279
for he rose up early on the *m* .... Judg 6:38 4283
And it came to pass on the *m* .... Judg 9:42 4283
to *m* get you early on your way, ... Judg 19:9 4279
for to *m* I will deliver them into .... Judg 20:28 4279
And it came to pass on the *m* .... Judg 21:4 4279
of Ashdod arose early on the *m* 1Sa 5:3 4283
they arose early on the *m* morning 1Sa 5:4 4283
To *m* about this time I will send 1Sa 9:16 4279
to *m* I will let thee go, and will 1Sa 9:19 1242
the men of Jabesh-gilead, To *m* 1Sa 11:9 4279
To *m* we will come out unto you, ... 1Sa 11:10 4279
And it was so on the *m*, that Saul 1Sa 11:11 4283
And it came to pass on the *m* 1Sa 18:10 4283
night, to *m* thou shalt be slain 1Sa 19:11 4279
to *m* is the new moon, and I should 1Sa 20:5 4279
my father about to *m* any time 1Sa 20:12 4279
to David, To *m* is the new moon 1Sa 20:18 4279
And it came to pass on the *m* 1Sa 20:27 4283
to *m* shalt thou and thy sons be 1Sa 28:19 4279
And it came to pass on the *m* 1Sa 31:8 4283
to *m* I will let thee depart 2Sa 11:12 4279
in Jerusalem that day, and the *m* 2Sa 11:12 4283
of them by to *m* about this time 1Kin 19:2 4279
unto thee to *m* about this time 1Kin 20:6 4279
day, and we will eat my son to *m* 2Kin 6:28 4279
To *m* about this time shall a 2Kin 7:1 4279
shall be to *m* about this time in 2Kin 7:18 4279
And it came to pass on the *m* 2Kin 8:15 4283
me to Jezreel by to *m* this time 2Kin 10:6 4279
And it came to pass on the *m* 1Chr 10:8 4283
on the *m* after that day, even a 1Chr 29:21 4283
To *m* go ye down against them 2Chr 20:16 4279
to *m* go out against them 2Chr 20:17 4279
on the *m* she returned into the .... Est 2:14 1242
I will do to *m* as the king hath .... Est 5:8 4279
to *m* am I invited unto her also .... Est 5:12 4279
to *m* speak thou unto the king .... Est 5:14 1242
which are in Shushan to do to *m* .... Est 9:13 4279
come again, and to *m* I will give .... Prov 3:28 4279
Boast not thyself of to *m* .... Prov 27:1 4279
for to *m* we shall die .... Is 22:13 4279
to *m* shall be as this day, and .... Is 56:12 4279
And it came to pass on the *m* .... Jer 20:3 4283
gnaw not the bones till the *m* .... Zeph 3:3 1242
to *m* is cast into the oven, shall .... Mt 6:30 839
therefore no thought for the *m* .... Mt 6:34 839
for the *m* shall take thought for .... Mt 6:34 839
And on the *m*, when they were come .... Mk 11:12 *1887*
on the *m* when he departed, he .... Lk 10:35 839
to *m* is cast into the oven .... Lk 12:28 839
and I do cures to day and to *m* .... Lk 13:32 839
I must walk to day, and to *m* .... Lk 13:33 839
And it came to pass on the *m* .... Acts 4:5 839
On the *m*, as they went on their .... Acts 10:9 *1887*
on the *m* Peter went away with .... Acts 10:23 *1887*
the *m* after they entered into .... Acts 10:24 *1887*
them, ready to depart on the *m* .... Acts 20:7 *1887*
On the *m*, because he would have .... Acts 22:30 *1887*
he bring him down unto you to *m* .... Acts 23:15 *839*
down Paul to *m* into the council .... Acts 23:20 *839*
On the *m* they left the horsemen .... Acts 23:32 *1887*
without any delay on the *m* I sat .... Acts 25:17 *1836*
To *m*, said he, thou shalt hear .... Acts 25:22 *839*
And on the *m*, when Agrippa was .... Acts 25:23 *1887*
for to *m* we die 1Cor 15:32 *839*
To day or to *m* we will go into .... Jas 4:13 *839*
know not what shall be on the *m* .... Jas 4:14 *839*

MORSEL

And I will fetch a *m* of bread .... Gen 18:5 6595
thine heart with a *m* of bread .... Judg 19:5 6595
and dip thy *m* in the vinegar .... Ruth 2:14 6595
a *m* of bread, and shall say, Put 1Sa 2:36 3603
let me set a *m* of bread before 1Sa 28:22 6595
a *m* of bread in thine hand 1Kin 17:11 6595
Or have eaten my *m* myself alone .... Job 31:17 6595
Better is a dry *m*, and quietness .... Prov 17:1 6595
The *m* which thou hast eaten shalt .... Prov 23:8 6595
who for one *m* of meat sold his .... Heb 12:16 *1035*

MORSELS

He casteth forth his ice like *m* .... Ps 147:17 6595

MORTAL

Shall *m* man be more just than God .... Job 4:17 582
therefore reign in your *m* body .... Rom 6:12 *2349*
your *m* bodies by his Spirit that .... Rom 8:11 *2349*
this *m* must put on immortality 1Cor 15:53 *2349*
and this *m* shall have put on 1Cor 15:54 *2349*
be made manifest in our *m* flesh 2Cor 4:11 *2349*

MORTALITY

that *m* might be swallowed up of 2Cor 5:4 *2349*

MORTALLY

smite him *m* that he die, and .... Deut 19:11 5315

MORTAR

it in mills, or beat it in a *m* .... Num 11:8 4085
in a *m* among wheat with a pestle .... Prov 27:22 4388

MORTER

stone, and slime had they for *m* .... Gen 11:3 2563
bitter with hard bondage, in *m* .... Ex 1:14 2563
and he shall take other *m*, and .... Lev 14:42 6083
and all the *m* of the house .... Lev 14:45 6083
shall come upon princes as upon *m* .... Is 41:25 2563
daubed it with untempered *m* .... Eze 13:10
which daub it with untempered *m* .... Eze 13:11
ye have daubed with untempered *m* .... Eze 13:14
have daubed it with untempered *m* .... Eze 13:15
daubed them with untempered *m* .... Eze 22:28
go into clay, and tread the *m* .... Nah 3:14 2563

MORTGAGED

We have *m* our lands, vineyards, ... Neh 5:3 6148

MORTIFY

Spirit do *m* the deeds of the body .... Rom 8:13 *2289*
M therefore your members which .... Col 3:5 *3499*

MOSERA (*mo-se'-rah*) See MOSEROTH. *Where Aaron was buried.*
of the children of Jaakan to *M* .... Deut 10:6 4149

MOSERAH See MOSERA.

MOSEROTH (*mo-se'-roth*) See MOSERA. *An Israelite encampment in the wilderness.*
from Hashmonah, and encamped at *M* Num 33:30 4149
And they departed from *M*, and .... Num 33:31 4149

MOSES (*mo'-zez*) See MOSES'. *Led Israel out of Egypt.*
And she called his name *M* .... Ex 2:10 4872
when *M* was grown, that he went .... Ex 2:11 4872
M feared, and said, Surely this .... Ex 2:14 4872
this thing, he sought to slay *M* .... Ex 2:15 4872
But *M* fled from the face of .... Ex 2:15 4872
but *M* stood up and helped them, and .. Ex 2:17 4872
M was content to dwell with the .... Ex 2:21 4872
he gave *M* Zipporah his daughter .... Ex 2:21 4872
Now *M* kept the flock of Jethro .... Ex 3:1 4872
M said, I will now turn aside, and .... Ex 3:3 4872
of the bush, and said, *M*, *M* .... Ex 3:4 4872
And *M* hid his face .... Ex 3:6 4872
M said unto God, Who am I, that I .... Ex 3:11 4872
M said unto God, Behold, when I .... Ex 3:13 4872
And God said unto *M*, I AM THAT I ... Ex 3:14 4872
And God said moreover unto *M* .... Ex 3:15 4872
M answered and said, But, behold, ... Ex 4:1 4872
and *M* fled from before it .... Ex 4:3 4872
And the LORD said unto *M*, Put .... Ex 4:4 4872
M said unto the LORD, O my Lord, ... Ex 4:10 4872
of the LORD was kindled against *M* .... Ex 4:14 4872
M went and returned to Jethro his .... Ex 4:18 4872
And Jethro said to *M*, Go in peace .... Ex 4:18 4872
And the LORD said unto *M* in Midian ... Ex 4:19 4872
M took his wife and his sons, and .... Ex 4:20 4872
M took the rod of God in his hand .... Ex 4:20 4872
And the LORD said unto *M*, When .... Ex 4:21 4872
Go into the wilderness to meet *M* .... Ex 4:27 4872
M told Aaron all the words of the .... Ex 4:28 4872
And *M* and Aaron went and gathered .. Ex 4:29 4872
which the LORD had spoken unto *M* .... Ex 4:30 4872
And afterward *M* and Aaron went in, .. Ex 5:1 4872
unto them, Wherefore do ye, *M* .... Ex 5:4 4872
And they met *M* and Aaron .... Ex 5:20 4872
M returned unto the LORD, and said .... Ex 5:22 4872
Then the LORD said unto *M* .... Ex 6:1 4872
And God spake unto *M*, and said unto Ex 6:2 4872
M spake so unto the children of .... Ex 6:9 4872
not unto *M* for anguish of spirit .... Ex 6:9 4872
And the LORD spake unto *M*, saying, ... Ex 6:10 4872
M spake before the LORD, saying, ... Ex 6:12 4872
And the LORD spake unto *M* and unto. Ex 6:13 4872
and she bare him Aaron and *M* .... Ex 6:20 4872
These are that Aaron and *M* .... Ex 6:26 4872
these are that *M* and Aaron .... Ex 6:27 4872
spake unto *M* in the land of Egypt .... Ex 6:28 4872
That the LORD spake unto *M* .... Ex 6:29 4872
M said before the LORD, Behold, I .... Ex 6:30 4872
And the LORD said unto *M*, See, I .... Ex 7:1 4872
And *M* and Aaron did as the LORD .... Ex 7:6 4872
M was fourscore years old, and .... Ex 7:7 4872
And the LORD spake unto *M* and unto. Ex 7:8 4872
And *M* and Aaron went in unto .... Ex 7:10 4872
And the LORD said unto *M*, ... Ex 7:14 4872
And the LORD spake unto *M*, Say .... Ex 7:19 4872
And *M* and Aaron did so, as the LORD . Ex 7:20 4872
And the LORD spake unto *M*, Go unto . Ex 8:1 4872
And the LORD spake unto *M*, Say .... Ex 8:5 4872
Then Pharaoh called for *M* .... Ex 8:8 4872
M said unto Pharaoh, Glory over .... Ex 8:9 4872
And *M* and Aaron went out from .... Ex 8:12 4872
M cried unto the LORD because of .... Ex 8:12 4872
did according to the word of *M* .... Ex 8:13 4872
And the LORD said unto *M*, Say unto .. Ex 8:16 4872
And the LORD said unto *M*, Rise up .... Ex 8:20 4872
And Pharaoh called for *M* and for .... Ex 8:25 4872
M said, It is not meet so to do .... Ex 8:26 4872
M said, Behold, I go out from .... Ex 8:29 4872
M went out from Pharaoh, and .... Ex 8:30 4872
did according to the word of *M* .... Ex 8:31 4872
Then the LORD said unto *M* .... Ex 9:1 4872
And the LORD said unto *M* and unto .... Ex 9:8 4872
let *M* sprinkle it toward the .... Ex 9:8 4872
M sprinkled it up toward heaven .... Ex 9:10 4872
before *M* because of the boils .... Ex 9:11 4872
as the LORD had spoken unto *M* .... Ex 9:12 4872
And the LORD said unto *M*, Rise up .... Ex 9:13 4872
And the LORD said unto *M*, Stretch .... Ex 9:22 4872
M stretched forth his rod toward .... Ex 9:23 4872
And Pharaoh sent, and called for *M* .... Ex 9:27 4872
M said unto him, As soon as I am .... Ex 9:29 4872
M went out of the city from .... Ex 9:33 4872
as the LORD had spoken by *M* .... Ex 9:35 4872
And the LORD said unto *M*, Go in .... Ex 10:1 4872
And *M* and Aaron came in unto .... Ex 10:3 4872
And *M* and Aaron were brought again .. Ex 10:8 4872
M said, We will go with our young .... Ex 10:9 4872
And the LORD said unto *M*, Stretch .... Ex 10:12 4872
M stretched forth his rod over .... Ex 10:13 4872
Then Pharaoh called for *M* .... Ex 10:16 4872
And the LORD said unto *M*, Stretch .... Ex 10:21 4872
M stretched forth his hand toward .... Ex 10:22 4872
And Pharaoh called unto *M*, and said .. Ex 10:24 4872
M said, Thou must give us also .... Ex 10:25 4872
M said, Thou hast spoken well, I .... Ex 10:29 4872
And the LORD said unto *M*, Yet will .... Ex 11:1 4872
Moreover the man *M* was very great ... Ex 11:3 4872
M said, Thus saith the LORD, ... Ex 11:4 4872
And the LORD said unto *M*, Pharaoh .... Ex 11:9 4872
And *M* and Aaron did all these .... Ex 11:10 4872
LORD spake unto *M* .... Ex 12:1 4872
Then *M* called for all the elders .... Ex 12:21 4872
did as the LORD had commanded *M* .... Ex 12:28 4872
And he called for *M* and Aaron by .... Ex 12:31 4872
did according to the word of *M* .... Ex 12:35 4872
And the LORD said unto *M* and Aaron, Ex 12:43 4872
LORD commanded *M* .... Ex 12:50 4872
And the LORD spake unto *M*, saying, ... Ex 13:1 4872
M said unto the people, Remember .... Ex 13:3 4872
M took the bones of Joseph with .... Ex 13:19 4872
And the LORD spake unto *M*, saying, ... Ex 14:1 4872
And they said unto *M*, Because .... Ex 14:11 4872
M said unto the people, Fear ye .... Ex 14:13 4872
And the LORD said unto *M*, ... Ex 14:15 4872
M stretched out his hand over the .... Ex 14:21 4872
And the LORD said unto *M*, Stretch .... Ex 14:26 4872
M stretched forth his hand over .... Ex 14:27 4872
the LORD, and his servant *M* .... Ex 14:31 4872
Then sang *M* and the children of .... Ex 15:1 4872
So *M* brought Israel from the Red .... Ex 15:22 4872
And the people murmured against *M* ... Ex 15:24 4872
of Israel murmured against *M* .... Ex 16:2 4872
Then said the LORD unto *M* .... Ex 16:4 4872
And *M* and Aaron said unto all the .... Ex 16:6 4872
M said, This shall be, when the .... Ex 16:8 4872
M spake unto Aaron, Say unto all .... Ex 16:9 4872
And the LORD spake unto *M*, saying, ... Ex 16:11 4872
M said unto them, This is the .... Ex 16:15 4872
M said, Let no man leave of it .... Ex 16:19 4872
they hearkened not unto *M* .... Ex 16:20 4872
and *M* was wroth with them .... Ex 16:20 4872
the congregation came and told *M* .... Ex 16:22 4872
it up till the morning, as *M* bade .... Ex 16:24 4872
And *M* said, Eat that to day .... Ex 16:25 4872
And the LORD said unto *M*, How long .. Ex 16:28 4872
M said, This is the thing which .... Ex 16:32 4872
M said unto Aaron, Take a pot, and .... Ex 16:33 4872
As the LORD commanded *M*, so Aaron . Ex 16:34 4872
the people did chide with *M* .... Ex 17:2 4872
M said unto them, Why chide ye .... Ex 17:2 4872
and the people murmured against *M* .... Ex 17:3 4872
M cried unto the LORD, saying, ... Ex 17:4 4872
And the LORD said unto *M*, Go on .... Ex 17:5 4872
M did so in the sight of the .... Ex 17:6 4872
M said unto Joshua, Choose us out .... Ex 17:9 4872
Joshua did as *M* had said to him .... Ex 17:10 4872
and *M*, Aaron, and Hur went up to .... Ex 17:10 4872
when *M* held up his hand, that .... Ex 17:11 4872
And the LORD said unto *M*, Write .... Ex 17:14 4872
M built an altar, and called the .... Ex 17:15 4872
of all that God had done for *M* .... Ex 18:1 4872
sons and his wife unto *M* into the .... Ex 18:5 4872
And he said unto *M*, I thy father .... Ex 18:6 4872
M went out to meet his father in .... Ex 18:7 4872

M told his father in law all that	Ex 18:8	4872
that *M* sat to judge the people	Ex 18:13	4872
the people stood by *M* from the	Ex 18:13	4872
M said unto his father in law,	Ex 18:15	4872
So *M* hearkened to the voice of	Ex 18:24	4872
M chose able men out of all	Ex 18:25	4872
hard causes they brought unto *M*	Ex 18:26	4872
M let his father in law depart	Ex 18:27	4872
M went up unto God, and the LORD	Ex 19:3	4872
M came and called for the elders	Ex 19:7	4872
M returned the words of the	Ex 19:8	4872
And the LORD said unto *M*, Lo, I	Ex 19:9	4872
M told the words of the people	Ex 19:9	4872
And the LORD said unto *M*, Go unto	Ex 19:10	4872
M went down from the mount unto	Ex 19:14	4872
M brought forth the people out of	Ex 19:17	4872
M spake, and God answered him by a	Ex 19:19	4872
the LORD called *M* up to the top	Ex 19:20	4872
and *M* went up	Ex 19:20	4872
And the LORD said unto *M*, Go down,	Ex 19:21	4872
M said unto the LORD, The people	Ex 19:23	4872
So *M* went down unto the people,	Ex 19:25	4872
And they said unto *M*, Speak thou	Ex 20:19	4872
M said unto the people, Fear not	Ex 20:20	4872
M drew near unto the thick	Ex 20:21	4872
And the LORD said unto *M*, Thus	Ex 20:22	4872
And he said unto *M*, Come up unto	Ex 24:1	4872
M alone shall come near the LORD	Ex 24:2	4872
M came and told the people all the	Ex 24:3	4872
M wrote all the words of the LORD	Ex 24:4	4872
M took half of the blood, and put	Ex 24:6	4872
M took the blood, and sprinkled it	Ex 24:8	4872
Then went up *M*, and Aaron, Nadab,	Ex 24:9	4872
And the LORD said unto *M*, Come up	Ex 24:12	4872
M rose up, and his minister Joshua	Ex 24:13	4872
M went up into the mount of God	Ex 24:13	4872
M went up into the mount, and a	Ex 24:15	4872
M out of the midst of the cloud	Ex 24:16	4872
M went into the midst of the	Ex 24:18	4872
M was in the mount forty days and	Ex 24:18	4872
And the LORD spake unto *M*, saying,	Ex 25:1	4872
And the LORD spake unto *M*, saying,	Ex 30:11	4872
And the LORD spake unto *M*, saying,	Ex 30:17	4872
Moreover the LORD spake unto *M*	Ex 30:22	4872
And the LORD said unto *M*, Take	Ex 30:34	4872
And the LORD spake unto *M*, saying,	Ex 31:1	4872
And the LORD spake unto *M*, saying,	Ex 31:12	4872
And he gave unto *M*, when he had	Ex 31:18	4872
when the people saw that *M*	Ex 32:1	4872
for as for this *M*, the man that	Ex 32:1	4872
And the LORD said unto *M*, Go, get	Ex 32:7	4872
And the LORD said unto *M*, I have	Ex 32:9	4872
M besought the LORD his God, and	Ex 32:11	4872
M turned, and went down from the	Ex 32:15	4872
as they shouted, he said unto *M*	Ex 32:17	4872
M said unto Aaron, What did this	Ex 32:21	4872
for as for this *M*, the man that	Ex 32:23	4872
when *M* saw that the people were	Ex 32:25	4872
Then *M* stood in the gate of the	Ex 32:26	4872
did according to the word of *M*	Ex 32:28	4872
For *M* had said, Consecrate	Ex 32:29	4872
that *M* said unto the people, Ye	Ex 32:30	4872
M returned unto the LORD, and said	Ex 32:31	4872
And the LORD said unto *M*,	Ex 32:33	4872
And the LORD said unto *M*, Depart,	Ex 33:1	4872
For the LORD had said unto *M*	Ex 33:5	4872
M took the tabernacle, and pitched	Ex 33:7	4872
to pass, when *M* went out unto the	Ex 33:8	4872
his tent door, and looked after *M*	Ex 33:8	4872
as *M* entered into the tabernacle,	Ex 33:9	4872
and the LORD talked with *M*	Ex 33:9	4872
LORD spake unto *M* face to face	Ex 33:11	4872
M said unto the LORD, See, thou	Ex 33:12	4872
And the LORD said unto *M*, I will	Ex 33:17	4872
And the LORD said unto *M*, Hew thee	Ex 34:1	4872
M rose up early in the morning,	Ex 34:4	4872
M made haste, and bowed his head	Ex 34:8	4872
And the LORD said unto *M*, Write	Ex 34:27	4872
when *M* came down from mount Sinai	Ex 34:29	4872
that *M* wist not that the skin of	Ex 34:29	4872
all the children of Israel saw *M*	Ex 34:30	4872
And *M* called unto them	Ex 34:31	4872
and *M* talked with them	Ex 34:31	4872
till *M* had done speaking with	Ex 34:33	4872
But when *M* went in before the	Ex 34:34	4872
of Israel saw the face of *M*	Ex 34:35	4872
M put the vail upon his face	Ex 34:35	4872
M gathered all the congregation	Ex 35:1	4872
M spake unto all the congregation	Ex 35:4	4872
departed from the presence of *M*	Ex 35:20	4872
to be made by the hand of *M*	Ex 35:29	4872
M said unto the children of	Ex 35:30	4872
M called Bezaleel and Aholiab, and	Ex 36:2	4872
received of *M* all the offering	Ex 36:3	4872
And they spake unto *M*, saying, The	Ex 36:5	4872
M gave commandment, and they	Ex 36:6	4872
according to the commandment of *M*	Ex 38:21	4872
all that the LORD commanded *M*	Ex 38:22	4872
as the LORD commanded *M*	Ex 39:1	4872
as the LORD commanded *M*	Ex 39:5	4872
as the LORD commanded *M*	Ex 39:7	4872
as the LORD commanded *M*	Ex 39:21	4872
as the LORD commanded *M*	Ex 39:26	4872
as the LORD commanded *M*	Ex 39:29	4872
as the LORD commanded *M*	Ex 39:31	4872
to all that the LORD commanded *M*	Ex 39:32	4872
brought the tabernacle unto *M*	Ex 39:33	4872
to all that the LORD commanded *M*	Ex 39:42	4872
M did look upon all the work	Ex 39:43	4872
and *M* blessed them	Ex 39:43	4872
And the LORD spake unto *M*, saying,	Ex 40:1	4872
Thus did *M*	Ex 40:16	4872
M reared up the tabernacle, and	Ex 40:18	4872
as the LORD commanded *M*	Ex 40:19	4872
as the LORD commanded *M*	Ex 40:21	4872
as the LORD had commanded *M*	Ex 40:23	4872
as the LORD commanded *M*	Ex 40:25	4872
as the LORD commanded *M*	Ex 40:27	4872
as the LORD commanded *M*	Ex 40:29	4872
M and Aaron and his sons	Ex 40:31	4872
as the LORD commanded *M*	Ex 40:32	4872
So *M* finished the work	Ex 40:33	4872
M was not able to enter into the	Ex 40:35	4872
And the LORD called unto *M*	Lev 1:1	4872
And the LORD spake unto *M*, saying,	Lev 4:1	4872
And the LORD spake unto *M*, saying,	Lev 5:14	4872
And the LORD spake unto *M*, saying,	Lev 6:1	4872
And the LORD spake unto *M*, saying,	Lev 6:8	4872
And the LORD spake unto *M*, saying,	Lev 6:19	4872
And the LORD spake unto *M*, saying,	Lev 6:24	4872
And the LORD spake unto *M*, saying,	Lev 7:22	4872
And the LORD spake unto *M*, saying,	Lev 7:28	4872
LORD commanded *M* in mount Sinai	Lev 7:38	4872
And the LORD spake unto *M*, saying,	Lev 8:1	4872
M did as the LORD commanded him	Lev 8:4	4872
M said unto the congregation,	Lev 8:5	4872
M brought Aaron and his sons, and	Lev 8:6	4872
as the LORD commanded *M*	Lev 8:9	4872
M took the anointing oil, and	Lev 8:10	4872
M brought Aaron's sons, and put	Lev 8:13	4872
as the LORD commanded *M*	Lev 8:13	4872
M took the blood, and put it upon	Lev 8:15	4872
M burned it upon the altar	Lev 8:16	4872
as the LORD commanded *M*	Lev 8:17	4872
M sprinkled the blood upon the	Lev 8:19	4872
M burnt the head, and the pieces,	Lev 8:20	4872
M burnt the whole ram upon the	Lev 8:21	4872
as the LORD commanded *M*	Lev 8:21	4872
M took of the blood of it, and put	Lev 8:23	4872
M put of the blood upon the tip	Lev 8:24	4872
M sprinkled the blood upon the	Lev 8:24	4872
M took them from off their hands,	Lev 8:28	4872
M took the breast, and waved it	Lev 8:29	4872
as the LORD commanded *M*	Lev 8:29	4872
M took of the anointing oil, and	Lev 8:30	4872
M said unto Aaron and to his sons,	Lev 8:31	4872
LORD commanded by the hand of *M*	Lev 8:36	4872
that *M* called Aaron and his sons,	Lev 9:1	4872
they brought that which *M*	Lev 9:5	4872
M said, This is the thing which	Lev 9:6	4872
M said unto Aaron, Go unto the	Lev 9:7	4872
as the LORD commanded *M*	Lev 9:10	4872
as *M* commanded	Lev 9:21	4872
And *M* and Aaron went into the	Lev 9:23	4872
Then *M* said unto Aaron, This is	Lev 10:3	4872
M called Mishael and Elzaphan, and	Lev 10:4	4872
as *M* had said	Lev 10:5	4872
M said unto Aaron, and unto	Lev 10:6	4872
did according to the word of *M*	Lev 10:7	4872
spoken unto them by the hand of *M*	Lev 10:11	4872
M spake unto Aaron, and unto	Lev 10:12	4872
M diligently sought the goat of	Lev 10:16	4872
And Aaron said unto *M*, Behold,	Lev 10:19	4872
when *M* heard that, he was content	Lev 10:20	4872
And the LORD spake unto *M* and to	Lev 11:1	4872
And the LORD spake unto *M*, saying,	Lev 12:1	4872
the LORD spake unto *M*	Lev 13:1	4872
And the LORD spake unto *M*, saying,	Lev 14:1	4872
And the LORD spake unto *M* and unto.	Lev 14:33	4872
And the LORD spake unto *M* and to	Lev 15:1	4872
the LORD spake unto *M* after the	Lev 16:1	4872
And the LORD said unto *M*, Speak	Lev 16:2	4872
the LORD commanded *M*	Lev 16:34	4872
And the LORD spake unto *M*, saying,	Lev 17:1	4872
And the LORD spake unto *M*, saying,	Lev 18:1	4872
And the LORD spake unto *M*, saying,	Lev 19:1	4872
And the LORD spake unto *M*, saying,	Lev 20:1	4872
And the LORD said unto *M*, Speak	Lev 21:1	4872
And the LORD spake unto *M*, saying,	Lev 21:16	4872
M told it unto Aaron, and to his	Lev 21:24	4872
And the LORD spake unto *M*, saying,	Lev 22:1	4872
And the LORD spake unto *M*, saying,	Lev 22:17	4872
And the LORD spake unto *M*, saying,	Lev 22:26	4872
And the LORD spake unto *M*, saying,	Lev 23:1	4872
And the LORD spake unto *M*, saying,	Lev 23:9	4872
And the LORD spake unto *M*, saying,	Lev 23:23	4872
And the LORD spake unto *M*, saying,	Lev 23:26	4872
And the LORD spake unto *M*, saying,	Lev 23:33	4872
M declared unto the children of	Lev 23:44	4872
And the LORD spake unto *M*, saying,	Lev 24:1	4872
And they brought him unto *M*	Lev 24:11	4872
And the LORD spake unto *M*, saying,	Lev 24:13	4872
M spake to the children of Israel	Lev 24:23	4872
did as the LORD commanded *M*	Lev 24:23	4872
LORD spake unto *M* in mount Sinai	Lev 25:1	4872
in mount Sinai by the hand of *M*	Lev 26:46	4872
And the LORD spake unto *M*, saying,	Lev 27:1	4872
which the LORD commanded *M* for	Lev 27:34	4872
the LORD spake unto *M* in the	Num 1:1	4872
And *M* and Aaron took these men	Num 1:17	4872
As the LORD commanded *M*, so he	Num 1:19	4872
those that were numbered, which *M*	Num 1:44	4872
For the LORD had spoken unto *M*	Num 1:48	4872
to all that the LORD commanded *M*	Num 1:54	4872
And the LORD spake unto *M* and unto.	Num 2:1	4872
as the LORD commanded *M*	Num 2:33	4872
to all that the LORD commanded *M*	Num 2:34	4872
M in the day that the LORD spake	Num 3:1	4872
LORD spake with *M* in mount Sinai	Num 3:1	4872
And the LORD spake unto *M*, saying,	Num 3:5	4872
And the LORD spake unto *M*, saying,	Num 3:11	4872
the LORD spake unto *M* in the	Num 3:14	4872
M numbered them according to the	Num 3:16	4872
congregation eastward, shall be *M*	Num 3:38	4872
numbered of the Levites, which *M*	Num 3:39	4872
And the LORD said unto *M*, Number	Num 3:40	4872
M numbered, as the LORD commanded	Num 3:42	4872
And the LORD spake unto *M*, saying,	Num 3:44	4872
M took the redemption money of	Num 3:49	4872
M gave the money of them that	Num 3:51	4872
the LORD, as the LORD commanded *M*.	Num 3:51	4872
And the LORD spake unto *M* and unto.	Num 4:1	4872
And the LORD spake unto *M* and unto.	Num 4:17	4872
And the LORD spake unto *M*, saying,	Num 4:21	4872
And *M* and Aaron and the chief of the	Num 4:34	4872
of the congregation, which *M*	Num 4:37	4872
of the LORD by the hand of *M*	Num 4:37	4872
of the congregation, whom *M*	Num 4:41	4872
of the sons of Merari, whom *M*	Num 4:45	4872
word of the LORD by the hand of *M*	Num 4:45	4872
numbered of the Levites, whom *M*	Num 4:46	4872
were numbered by the hand of *M*	Num 4:49	4872
of him, as the LORD commanded *M*	Num 4:49	4872
And the LORD spake unto *M*, saying,	Num 5:1	4872
as the LORD spake unto *M*, so did	Num 5:4	4872
And the LORD spake unto *M*, saying,	Num 5:5	4872
And the LORD spake unto *M*, saying,	Num 5:11	4872
And the LORD spake unto *M*, saying,	Num 6:1	4872
And the LORD spake unto *M*, saying,	Num 6:22	4872
M had fully set up the tabernacle	Num 7:1	4872
And the LORD spake unto *M*, saying,	Num 7:4	4872
M took the wagons and the oxen, and.	Num 7:6	4872
And the LORD said unto *M*, They	Num 7:11	4872
And when *M* was gone into the	Num 7:89	4872
And the LORD spake unto *M*, saying,	Num 8:1	4872
as the LORD commanded *M*	Num 8:3	4872
which the LORD had shewed *M*	Num 8:4	4872
And the LORD spake unto *M*, saying,	Num 8:5	4872
And *M*, and Aaron, and all the	Num 8:20	4872
M concerning the Levites, so did	Num 8:20	4872
M concerning the Levites, so did	Num 8:22	4872
And the LORD spake unto *M*, saying,	Num 8:23	4872
the LORD spake unto *M* in the	Num 9:1	4872
M spake unto the children of	Num 9:4	4872
to all that the LORD commanded *M*	Num 9:5	4872
and they came before *M* and before	Num 9:6	4872
M said unto them, Stand still, and	Num 9:8	4872
And the LORD spake unto *M*, saying,	Num 9:9	4872
of the LORD by the hand of *M*	Num 9:23	4872
And the LORD spake unto *M*, saying,	Num 10:1	4872
of the LORD by the hand of *M*	Num 10:13	4872
M said unto Hobab, the son of	Num 10:29	4872
the ark set forward, that *M* said	Num 10:35	4872
And the people cried unto *M*	Num 11:2	4872
when *M* prayed unto the LORD, the	Num 11:2	4872
Then *M* heard the people weep	Num 11:10	4872
M also was displeased	Num 11:10	4872
M said unto the LORD, Wherefore	Num 11:11	4872
And the LORD said unto *M*, Gather	Num 11:16	4872
M said, The people, among whom I	Num 11:21	4872
And the LORD said unto *M*, Is the	Num 11:23	4872
M went out, and told the people	Num 11:24	4872
there ran a young man, and told *M*	Num 11:27	4872
the son of Nun, the servant of *M*	Num 11:28	4872
men, answered and said, My lord *M*	Num 11:28	4872
M said unto him, Enviest thou for	Num 11:29	4872
M gat him into the camp, he and	Num 11:30	4872
Aaron spake against *M* because of	Num 12:1	4872
the LORD indeed spoken only by *M*	Num 12:2	4872
(Now the man *M* was very meek,	Num 12:3	4872
And the LORD spake suddenly unto *M*.	Num 12:4	4872
My servant *M* is not so, who is	Num 12:7	4872
to speak against my servant *M*	Num 12:8	4872
And Aaron said unto *M*, Alas, my	Num 12:11	4872
M cried unto the LORD, saying,	Num 12:13	4872
And the LORD said unto *M*, If her	Num 12:14	4872
And the LORD spake unto *M*, saying,	Num 13:1	4872
M by the commandment of the LORD	Num 13:3	4872
which *M* sent to spy out the land	Num 13:16	4872
M called Oshea the son of Nun	Num 13:16	4872
M sent them to spy out the land	Num 13:17	4872
And they went and came to *M*	Num 13:26	4872
Caleb stilled the people before *M*	Num 13:30	4872
of Israel murmured against *M*	Num 14:2	4872
Then *M* and Aaron fell on their	Num 14:5	4872
And the LORD said unto *M*, How long	Num 14:11	4872
M said unto the LORD, Then the	Num 14:13	4872
And the LORD spake unto *M* and unto.	Num 14:26	4872
which *M* sent to search the land,	Num 14:36	4872
M told these sayings unto all the	Num 14:39	4872
M said, Wherefore now do ye	Num 14:41	4872
of the covenant of the LORD, and *M*	Num 14:44	4872
And the LORD spake unto *M*, saying,	Num 15:1	4872
And the LORD spake unto *M*, saying,	Num 15:17	4872
which the LORD hath spoken unto *M*	Num 15:22	4872
commanded you by the hand of *M*	Num 15:23	4872
the day that the LORD commanded *M*	Num 15:23	
sticks brought him unto *M*	Num 15:33	4872
And the LORD said unto *M*, The man	Num 15:35	4872
as the LORD commanded *M*	Num 15:36	4872
And the LORD spake unto *M*, saying,	Num 15:37	4872
And they rose up before *M*, with	Num 16:2	4872
themselves together against *M*	Num 16:3	4872
when *M* heard it, he fell upon his	Num 16:4	4872
M said unto Korah, Hear, I pray	Num 16:8	4872
M sent to call Dathan and Abiram,	Num 16:12	4872
M was very wroth, and said unto	Num 16:15	4872
M said unto Korah, Be thou and all	Num 16:16	4872
of the congregation with *M*	Num 16:18	4872
And the LORD spake unto *M* and unto.	Num 16:20	4872
And the LORD spake unto *M*, saying,	Num 16:23	4872
M rose up and went unto Dathan and.	Num 16:25	4872
M said, Hereby ye shall know that	Num 16:28	4872
And the LORD spake unto *M*, saying,	Num 16:36	4872
LORD said to him by the hand of *M*	Num 16:40	4872
of Israel murmured against *M*	Num 16:41	4872
was gathered against *M* and against	Num 16:42	4872
And *M* and Aaron came before the	Num 16:43	4872
And the LORD spake unto *M*, saying,	Num 16:44	4872
M said unto Aaron, Take a censer,	Num 16:46	4872
And Aaron took as *M* commanded	Num 16:47	4872
Aaron returned unto *M* unto the	Num 16:50	4872

And the LORD spake unto *M*, saying,	Num 17:1	4872
M spake unto the children of	Num 17:6	4872
M laid up the rods before the	Num 17:7	4872
that on the morrow *M* went into	Num 17:8	4872
M brought out all the rods from	Num 17:9	4872
And the LORD said unto *M*, Bring	Num 17:10	4872
And *M* did so	Num 17:11	4872
children of Israel spake unto *M*	Num 17:12	4872
And the LORD spake unto *M*, saying,	Num 18:25	4872
And the LORD spake unto *M* and unto.	Num 19:1	4872
themselves together against *M*	Num 20:2	4872
And the people chode with *M*	Num 20:3	4872
And *M* and Aaron went from the	Num 20:6	4872
And the LORD spake unto *M*, saying,	Num 20:7	4872
M took the rod from before the	Num 20:9	4872
And *M* and Aaron gathered the	Num 20:10	4872
M lifted up his hand, and with his	Num 20:11	4872
the LORD spake unto *M*	Num 20:12	4872
M sent messengers from Kadesh	Num 20:14	4872
the LORD spake unto *M*	Num 20:23	4872
M did as the LORD commanded	Num 20:27	4872
M stripped Aaron of his garments,	Num 20:28	4872
and *M* and Eleazar came down from	Num 20:28	4872
spake against God, and against *M*	Num 21:5	4872
Therefore the people came to *M*	Num 21:7	4872
And *M* prayed for the people	Num 21:7	4872
And the LORD said unto *M*, Make	Num 21:8	4872
M made a serpent of brass, and put	Num 21:9	4872
whereof the LORD spake unto *M*	Num 21:16	4872
M sent to spy out Jaazer, and they	Num 21:32	4872
And the LORD said unto *M*, Fear him	Num 21:34	4872
And the LORD said unto *M*, Take all	Num 25:4	4872
M said unto the judges of Israel,	Num 25:5	4872
woman in the sight of *M*, and in	Num 25:6	4872
And the LORD spake unto *M*, saying,	Num 25:10	4872
And the LORD spake unto *M*, saying,	Num 25:16	4872
that the LORD spake unto *M*	Num 26:1	4872
And *M* and Eleazar the priest spake	Num 26:3	4872
as the LORD commanded *M* and the	Num 26:4	4872
who strove against *M* and against	Num 26:9	4872
And the LORD spake unto *M*, saying,	Num 26:52	4872
unto Amram Aaron and *M*	Num 26:59	4872
are they that were numbered by *M*	Num 26:63	4872
was not a man of them whom *M*	Num 26:64	4872
And they stood before *M*, and before	Num 27:2	4872
M brought their cause before the	Num 27:5	4872
And the LORD spake unto *M*, saying,	Num 27:6	4872
judgment, as the LORD commanded *M*.	Num 27:11	4872
And the LORD said unto *M*, Get thee	Num 27:12	4872
M spake unto the LORD, saying,	Num 27:15	4872
And the LORD said unto *M*, Take	Num 27:18	4872
M did as the LORD commanded him	Num 27:22	4872
LORD commanded by the hand of *M*	Num 27:23	4872
And the LORD spake unto *M*, saying,	Num 28:1	4872
M told the children of Israel	Num 29:40	4872
to all that the LORD commanded *M*	Num 29:40	4872
M spake unto the heads of the	Num 30:1	4872
which the LORD commanded *M*	Num 30:16	4872
And the LORD spake unto *M*, saying,	Num 31:1	4872
M spake unto the people, saying,	Num 31:3	4872
M sent them to the war, a	Num 31:6	4872
as the LORD commanded *M*	Num 31:7	4872
and the prey, and the spoil, unto *M*	Num 31:12	4872
And *M*, and Eleazar the priest, and	Num 31:13	4872
M was wroth with the officers of	Num 31:14	4872
M said unto them, Have ye saved	Num 31:15	4872
law which the LORD commanded *M*	Num 31:21	4872
And the LORD spake unto *M*, saying,	Num 31:25	4872
And *M* and Eleazar the priest did as	Num 31:31	4872
did as the LORD commanded *M*	Num 31:31	4872
M gave the tribute, which was the	Num 31:41	4872
priest, as the LORD commanded *M*	Num 31:41	4872
which *M* divided from the men that	Num 31:42	4872
M took one portion of fifty, both	Num 31:47	4872
as the LORD commanded *M*	Num 31:47	4872
of hundreds, came near unto *M*	Num 31:48	4872
And they said unto *M*, Thy servants	Num 31:49	4872
And *M* and Eleazar the priest took	Num 31:51	4872
And *M* and Eleazar the priest took	Num 31:54	4872
of Reuben came and spake unto *M*	Num 32:2	4872
M said unto the children of Gad	Num 32:6	4872
M said unto them, If ye will do	Num 32:20	4872
children of Reuben spake unto *M*	Num 32:25	4872
So concerning them *M* commanded	Num 32:28	4872
M said unto them, If the children	Num 32:29	4872
M gave unto them, even to the	Num 32:33	4872
M gave Gilead unto Machir the son	Num 32:40	4872
their armies under the hand of *M*	Num 33:1	4872
And *M* wrote their goings out	Num 33:2	4872
the LORD spake unto *M* in the	Num 33:50	4872
And the LORD spake unto *M*, saying,	Num 34:1	4872
M commanded the children of	Num 34:13	4872
And the LORD spake unto *M*, saying,	Num 34:16	4872
the LORD spake unto *M* in the	Num 35:1	4872
And the LORD spake unto *M*, saying,	Num 35:9	4872
came near, and spake before *M*	Num 36:1	4872
M commanded the children of	Num 36:5	4872
Even as the LORD commanded *M*	Num 36:10	4872
LORD commanded by the hand of *M*	Num 36:13	4872
These be the words which *M* spake	Deut 1:1	4872
that *M* spake unto the children of	Deut 1:3	4872
began *M* to declare this law,	Deut 1:5	4872
Then *M* severed three cities on	Deut 4:41	4872
this is the law which *M* set	Deut 4:44	4872
which *M* spake unto the children	Deut 4:45	4872
who dwelt at Heshbon, whom *M*	Deut 4:46	4872
M called all Israel, and said unto	Deut 5:1	4872
M with the elders of Israel	Deut 27:1	4872
And *M* and the priests the Levites	Deut 27:9	4872
M charged the people the same day	Deut 27:11	4872
which the LORD commanded *M* to	Deut 29:1	4872
M called unto all Israel, and said	Deut 29:2	4872
M went and spake these words unto	Deut 31:1	4872
M called unto Joshua, and said	Deut 31:7	4872
M wrote this law, and delivered it	Deut 31:9	4872
M commanded them, saying, At the	Deut 31:10	4872
And the LORD said unto *M*, Behold,	Deut 31:14	4872
And *M* and Joshua went	Deut 31:14	4872
And the LORD said unto *M*, Behold,	Deut 31:16	4872
M therefore wrote this song the	Deut 31:22	4872
when *M* had made an end of writing	Deut 31:24	4872
That *M* commanded the Levites,	Deut 31:25	4872
M spake in the ears of all the	Deut 31:30	4872
M came and spake all the words of	Deut 32:44	4872
M made an end of speaking all	Deut 32:45	4872
spake unto *M* that selfsame day	Deut 32:48	4872
wherewith *M* the man of God	Deut 33:1	4872
M commanded us a law, even the	Deut 33:4	4872
M went up from the plains of Moab	Deut 34:1	4872
So *M* the servant of the LORD died	Deut 34:5	4872
M was an hundred and twenty years	Deut 34:7	4872
M in the plains of Moab thirty	Deut 34:8	4872
and mourning for *M* were ended	Deut 34:8	4872
for *M* had laid his hands upon him	Deut 34:9	4872
and did as the LORD commanded *M*	Deut 34:9	4872
since in Israel like unto *M*	Deut 34:10	4872
M shewed in the sight of all	Deut 34:12	4872
Now after the death of *M* the	Josh 1:1	4872
M my servant is dead	Josh 1:2	4872
given unto you, as I said unto *M*	Josh 1:3	4872
as I was with *M*, so I will be	Josh 1:5	4872
which *M* my servant commanded thee	Josh 1:7	4872
which *M* the servant of the LORD	Josh 1:13	4872
M gave you on this side Jordan	Josh 1:14	4872
which *M* the LORD's servant gave	Josh 1:15	4872
we hearkened unto *M* in all things	Josh 1:17	4872
be with thee, as he was with *M*	Josh 1:17	4872
may know that, as I was with *M*	Josh 3:7	4872
to all that *M* commanded Joshua	Josh 4:10	4872
of Israel, as *M* spake unto them	Josh 4:12	4872
they feared him, as they feared *M*	Josh 4:14	4872
As *M* the servant of the LORD	Josh 8:31	4872
in the book of the law of *M*	Josh 8:31	4872
the stones a copy of the law of *M*	Josh 8:32	4872
as *M* the servant of the LORD had	Josh 8:33	4872
a word of all that *M* commanded	Josh 8:35	4872
M to give you all the land	Josh 9:24	4872
as *M* the servant of the LORD	Josh 11:12	4872
the LORD commanded *M* his servant	Josh 11:15	4872
so did *M* command Joshua, and so	Josh 11:15	4872
of all that the LORD commanded *M*	Josh 11:15	4872
them, as the LORD commanded *M*	Josh 11:20	4872
to all that the LORD said unto *M*	Josh 11:23	4872
Them did *M* the servant of the	Josh 12:6	4872
M the servant of the LORD gave it	Josh 12:6	4872
which *M* gave them, beyond Jordan	Josh 13:8	4872
even as *M* the servant of the LORD	Josh 13:8	4872
for these did *M* smite, and cast	Josh 13:12	4872
M gave unto the tribe of the	Josh 13:15	4872
whom *M* smote with the princes of	Josh 13:21	4872
M gave inheritance unto the tribe	Josh 13:24	4872
M gave inheritance unto the half	Josh 13:29	4872
These are the countries which *M*	Josh 13:32	4872
Levi *M* gave not any inheritance	Josh 13:33	4872
LORD commanded by the hand of *M*	Josh 14:2	4872
For *M* had given the inheritance	Josh 14:3	4872
As the LORD commanded *M*, so the	Josh 14:5	4872
M the man of God concerning me	Josh 14:6	4872
Forty years old was I when *M* the	Josh 14:7	4872
M sware on that day, saying,	Josh 14:9	4872
the LORD spake this word unto *M*	Josh 14:10	4872
I was in the day that *M* sent me	Josh 14:11	4872
The LORD commanded *M* to give us	Josh 17:4	4872
which *M* the servant of the LORD	Josh 18:7	4872
I spake unto you by the hand of *M*	Josh 20:2	4872
M to give us cities to dwell in	Josh 21:2	4872
LORD commanded by the hand of *M*	Josh 21:8	4872
Ye have kept all that *M* the	Josh 22:2	4872
which *M* the servant of the LORD	Josh 22:4	4872
which *M* the servant of the LORD	Josh 22:5	4872
half of the tribe of Manasseh *M*	Josh 22:7	4872
word of the LORD by the hand of *M*	Josh 22:9	4872
in the book of the law of *M*	Josh 23:6	4872
I sent *M* also and Aaron, and I	Josh 24:5	4872
gave Hebron unto Caleb, as *M* said	Judg 1:20	4872
their fathers by the hand of *M*	Judg 3:4	4872
of Hobab the father in law of *M*	Judg 4:11	4872
It is the LORD that advanced *M*	1Sa 12:6	4872
the LORD, then the LORD sent *M*	1Sa 12:8	4872
as it is written in the law of *M*	1Kin 2:3	4872
which *M* put there at Horeb, when	1Kin 8:9	4872
by the hand of *M* thy servant	1Kin 8:53	4872
by the hand of *M* his servant	1Kin 8:56	4872
in the book of the law of *M*	2Kin 14:6	4872
brasen serpent that *M* had made	2Kin 18:4	4872
which the LORD commanded *M*	2Kin 18:6	4872
all that *M* the servant of the	2Kin 18:12	4872
that my servant *M* commanded them	2Kin 21:8	4872
according to all the law of *M*	2Kin 23:25	4872
Aaron, and *M*, and Miriam	1Chr 6:3	4872
according to all that *M* the	1Chr 6:49	4872
as *M* commanded according to the	1Chr 15:15	4872
which *M* made in the wilderness,	1Chr 21:29	4872
charged *M* with concerning Israel	1Chr 22:13	4872
of Amram; Aaron and *M*	1Chr 23:13	4872
Now concerning *M* the man of God	1Chr 23:14	4872
The sons of *M* were, Gershom, and	1Chr 23:15	4872
the son of Gershom, the son of *M*	1Chr 26:24	4872
which *M* the servant of the LORD	2Chr 1:3	4872
which *M* put therein at Horeb	2Chr 5:10	4872
according to the commandment of *M*	2Chr 8:13	4872
as it is written in the law of *M*	2Chr 23:18	4872
of *M* the servant of the LORD	2Chr 24:6	4872
M the servant of God laid upon	2Chr 24:9	4872
in the law in the book of *M*	2Chr 25:4	4872
to the law of *M* the man of God	2Chr 30:16	4872
the ordinances by the hand of *M*	2Chr 33:8	4872
of the law of the LORD given by *M*	2Chr 34:14	4872
word of the LORD by the hand of *M*	2Chr 35:6	4872
as it is written in the book of *M*	2Chr 35:12	4872
in the law of *M* the man of God	Ezr 3:2	4872
as it is written in the book of *M*	Ezr 6:18	4873
a ready scribe in the law of *M*	Ezr 7:6	4872
thou commandedst thy servant *M*	Neh 1:7	4872
thou commandedst thy servant *M*	Neh 1:8	4872
to bring the book of the law of *M*	Neh 8:1	4872
LORD had commanded by *M*	Neh 8:14	4872
by the hand of *M* thy servant	Neh 9:14	4872
was given by *M* the servant of God	Neh 10:29	4872
day they read in the book of *M* in	Neh 13:1	4872
like a flock by the hand of *M*	Ps 77:20	4872
A Prayer of *M*, the man of God	Ps 90:*t*	4872
M and Aaron among his priests, and	Ps 99:6	4872
He made known his ways unto *M*	Ps 103:7	4872
He sent *M* his servant	Ps 105:26	4872
They envied *M* also in the camp,	Ps 106:16	4872
had not *M* his chosen stood before	Ps 106:23	4872
went ill with *M* for their sakes	Ps 106:32	4872
he remembered the days of old, *M*	Is 63:11	4872
hand of *M* with his glorious arm	Is 63:12	4872
said the LORD unto me, Though *M*	Jer 15:1	4872
the law of *M* the servant of God	Dan 9:11	4872
As it is written in the law of *M*	Dan 9:13	4872
and I sent before thee *M*, Aaron,	Mic 6:4	4872
ye the law of *M* my servant	Mal 4:4	4872
offer the gift that *M* commanded	Mt 8:4	3475
there appeared unto them *M*	Mt 17:3	3475
one for thee, and one for *M*	Mt 17:4	3475
Why did *M* then command to give a	Mt 19:7	3475
M because of the hardness of your	Mt 19:8	3475
M said, If a man die, having no	Mt 22:24	3475
those things which *M* commanded	Mk 1:44	3475
For *M* said, Honour thy father and	Mk 7:10	3475
appeared unto them Elias with *M*	Mk 9:4	3475
one for thee, and one for *M*	Mk 9:5	3475
unto them, What did *M* command you	Mk 10:3	3475
M suffered to write a bill of	Mk 10:4	3475
M wrote unto us, If a man's	Mk 12:19	3475
have ye not read in the book of *M*	Mk 12:26	3475
to the law of *M* were accomplished	Lk 2:22	3475
according as *M* commanded	Lk 5:14	3475
with him two men, which were *M*	Lk 9:30	3475
one for thee, and one for *M*	Lk 9:33	3475
saith unto him, They have *M*	Lk 16:29	3475
said unto him, If they hear not *M*	Lk 16:31	3475
M wrote unto us, If any man's	Lk 20:28	3475
even *M* shewed at the bush, when	Lk 20:37	3475
And beginning at *M* and all the	Lk 24:27	3475
were written in the law of *M*	Lk 24:44	3475
For the law was given by *M*	Jn 1:17	3475
of whom *M* in the law, and the	Jn 1:45	3475
as *M* lifted up the serpent in the	Jn 3:14	3475
is one that accuseth you, even *M*	Jn 5:45	3475
For had ye believed *M*, ye would	Jn 5:46	3475
M gave you not that bread from	Jn 6:32	3475
Did not *M* give you the law, and	Jn 7:19	3475
M therefore gave unto you	Jn 7:22	3475
(not because it is of *M*, but of	Jn 7:22	3475
that the law of *M* should not be	Jn 7:23	3475
Now *M* in the law commanded us,	Jn 8:5	3475
We know that God spake unto *M*	Jn 9:29	3475
For *M* truly said unto the fathers	Acts 3:22	3475
speak blasphemous words against *M*	Acts 6:11	3475
the customs which *M* delivered us	Acts 6:14	3475
In which time *M* was born, and was	Acts 7:20	3475
M was learned in all the wisdom	Acts 7:22	3475
Then fled *M* at this saying, and	Acts 7:29	3475
When *M* saw it, he wondered at the	Acts 7:31	3475
Then *M* trembled, and durst not	Acts 7:32	3475
This *M* whom they refused, saying,	Acts 7:35	3475
This is that *M*, which said unto	Acts 7:37	3475
for as for this *M*, which brought	Acts 7:40	3475
he had appointed, speaking unto *M*	Acts 7:44	3475
not be justified by the law of *M*	Acts 13:39	3475
circumcised after the manner of *M*	Acts 15:1	3475
command them to keep the law of *M*	Acts 15:5	3475
For *M* of old time hath in every	Acts 15:21	3475
among the Gentiles to forsake *M*	Acts 21:21	3475
prophets and *M* did say should come	Acts 26:22	3475
Jesus, both out of the law of *M*	Acts 28:23	3475
death reigned from Adam to *M*	Rom 5:14	3475
For he saith to *M*, I will have	Rom 9:15	3475
For *M* describeth the	Rom 10:5	3475
First *M* saith, I will provoke you	Rom 10:19	3475
For it is written in the law of *M*	1Cor 9:9	3475
all baptized unto *M* in the cloud	1Cor 10:2	3475
face of *M* for the glory of his	2Cor 3:7	3475
And not as *M*, which put a vail	2Cor 3:13	3475
when *M* is read, the vail is upon	2Cor 3:15	3475
as Jannes and Jambres withstood *M*	2Ti 3:8	3475
as also *M* was faithful in all his	Heb 3:2	3475
worthy of more glory than *M*	Heb 3:3	3475
M verily was faithful in all his	Heb 3:5	3475
all that came out of Egypt by *M*	Heb 3:16	3475
of which tribe *M* spake nothing	Heb 7:14	3475
as *M* was admonished of God when	Heb 8:5	3475
For when *M* had spoken every	Heb 9:19	3475
By faith *M*, when he was born, was	Heb 11:23	3475
By faith *M*, when he was come to	Heb 11:24	3475
was the sight, that *M* said	Heb 12:21	3475
he disputed about the body of *M*	Jude 9	3475
the song of *M* the servant of God	Rev 15:3	3475

MOSES'

But *M* hands were heavy	Ex 17:12	4872
M father in law, heard of all	Ex 18:1	4872
M father in law, took Zipporah,	Ex 18:2	4872
M wife, after he had sent her	Ex 18:2	4872
M father in law, came with his	Ex 18:5	4872
M father in law, took a burnt	Ex 18:12	4872
to eat bread with *M* father in law	Ex 18:12	4872
when *M* father in law saw all that	Ex 18:14	4872

M father in law said unto him, Ex 18:17 4872
M anger waxed hot, and he cast the Ex 32:19 4872
two tables of testimony in *M* hand Ex 34:29 4872
that the skin of *M* face shone Ex 34:35 4872
ram of consecration it was *M* part Lev 8:29 4872
M father in law, We are Num 10:29 4872
son of Nun, *M* minister, saying, Josh 1:1 4872
M father in law, went up out of Judg 1:16 4872
and the Pharisees sit in *M* seat Mt 23:2 *3475*
but we are *M* disciples Jn 9:28 *3475*
He that despised *M* law died Heb 10:28 *3475*

MOST
was the priest of the *m* high God Gen 14:18 5945
be Abram of the *m* high God Gen 14:19 5945
And blessed be the *m* high God Gen 14:20 5945
the *m* high God, the possessor of Gen 14:22 5945
the holy place and the *m* holy Ex 26:33 6944
the testimony in the *m* holy place Ex 26:34 6944
and it shall be an altar *m* holy Ex 29:37 6944
it is *m* holy unto the LORD Ex 30:10 6944
them, that they may be *m* holy Ex 30:29 6944
it shall be unto you *m* holy Ex 30:36 6944
and it shall be an altar *m* holy Ex 40:10 6944
it is a thing *m* holy of the Lev 2:3 6944
it is a thing *m* holy of the Lev 2:10 6944
it is *m* holy, as is the sin Lev 6:17 6944
it is *m* holy Lev 6:25 6944
it is *m* holy Lev 6:29 6944
it is *m* holy Lev 7:1 6944
it is *m* holy Lev 7:6 6944
for it is *m* holy Lev 10:12 6944
holy place, seeing it is *m* holy Lev 10:17 6944
it is *m* holy Lev 14:13 6944
of his God, both of the *m* holy Lev 21:22 6944
for it is *m* holy unto him of the Lev 24:9 6944
thing is *m* holy unto the LORD Lev 27:28 6944
about the *m* holy things Num 4:4 6944
approach unto the *m* holy things Num 4:19 6944
be thine of the *m* holy things Num 18:9 6944
shall be *m* holy for thee and for Num 18:9 6944
In the *m* holy place shalt thou Num 18:10 6944
knew the knowledge of the *m* High Num 24:16 6944
When the *M* High divided to the Deut 32:8 6944
the *m* High uttered his voice 2Sa 22:14 6944
Was he not *m* honourable of three 2Sa 23:19
oracle, even for the *m* holy place 1Kin 6:16 6944
the *m* holy place, and for the 1Kin 7:50 6944
to the *m* holy place, even under 1Kin 8:6 6944
all the work of the place *m* holy 1Chr 6:49 6944
should sanctify the *m* holy things 1Chr 23:13 6944
And he made the *m* holy house 2Chr 3:8 6944
in the *m* holy house he made two 2Chr 3:10 6944
thereof for the *m* holy place 2Chr 4:22 6944
into the *m* holy place, even under 2Chr 5:7 6944
of the LORD, and the *m* holy things 2Chr 31:14 6944
not eat of the *m* holy things Ezr 2:63 6944
not eat of the *m* holy things Neh 7:65 6944
one of the king's *m* noble princes Est 6:9 6579
thou condemn him that is *m* just Job 34:17 3524
to the name of the LORD *m* high Ps 7:17 5945
praise to thy name, O thou *m* High Ps 9:2 5945
hast made him *m* blessed for ever Ps 21:6
through the mercy of the *m* High Ps 21:7 5945
O *m* mighty, with thy glory and thy Ps 45:3
of the tabernacles of the *m* High Ps 46:4 5945
For the LORD *m* high is terrible Ps 47:2 5945
and pay thy vows unto the *m* High Ps 50:14 5945
fight against me, O thou *m* High Ps 56:2 4971
I will cry unto God *m* high Ps 57:2 5945
is there knowledge in the *m* High Ps 73:11 5945
of the right hand of the *m* High Ps 77:10 5945
the *m* High in the wilderness Ps 78:17 5945
and provoked the *m* high God Ps 78:56 5945
of you are children of the *m* High Ps 82:6 5945
art the *m* high over all the earth Ps 83:18 5945
the *m* High shall abide under the Ps 91:1 5945
is my refuge, even the *m* High Ps 91:9 5945
praises unto thy name, O *m* High Ps 92:1 5945
LORD, art *m* high for evermore Ps 92:8
the counsel of the *m* High Ps 107:11 5945
M men will proclaim every one his Prov 20:6 7230
His head is as the *m* fine gold Song 5:11 3800
His mouth is *m* sweet Song 5:16
which hath a *m* vehement flame Song 8:6
I will be like the *m* High Is 14:14 5945
m upright, dost weigh the path of Is 26:7
an only son, *m* bitter lamentation Jer 6:26
I am against thee, O thou *m* proud Jer 50:31
the *m* proud shall stumble and fall Jer 50:32
man before the face of the *m* High Lam 3:35 5945
Out of the mouth of the *m* High Lam 3:38 5945
how is the *m* fine gold changed Lam 4:1 2896
for they are *m* rebellious Eze 2:7
and rulers clothed *m* gorgeously Eze 23:12
I will lay the land *m* desolate Eze 33:28
when I have laid the land *m* Eze 33:29
and I will make thee *m* desolate Eze 35:3
will I make mount Seir *m* desolate Eze 35:7 8077
unto me, This is the *m* holy place Eze 41:4 6944
LORD shall eat the *m* holy things Eze 42:13 6944
shall they lay the *m* holy things Eze 42:13 6944
round about shall be *m* holy Eze 43:12 6944
holy things, in the *m* holy place Eze 44:13 6944
the sanctuary and the *m* holy place Eze 45:3 6944
thing *m* holy by the border of the Eze 48:12 6944
he commanded the *m* mighty men Dan 3:20 2429
ye servants of the *m* high God Dan 3:26 5943
the living may know that the *m* Dan 4:17 5943
this is the decree of the *m* High Dan 4:24 5943
till thou know that the *m* High Dan 4:25 5943
until thou know that the *m* High Dan 4:32 5943
unto me, and I blessed the *m* High Dan 4:34 5943
O thou king, the *m* high God gave Dan 5:18 5943
till he knew that the *m* high God Dan 5:21 5943
But the saints of the *m* High Dan 7:18 5946
given to the saints of the *m* High Dan 7:22 5946
great words against the *m* High Dan 7:25 5943
wear out the saints of the *m* High Dan 7:25 5946
of the saints of the *m* High Dan 7:27 5945
prophecy, and to anoint the *m* Holy Dan 9:24 6944
and take the *m* fenced cities Dan 11:15
Thus shall he do in the *m* strong Dan 11:39 4581
return, but not to the *m* High Hos 7:16 5920
they called them to the *m* High Hos 11:7 5920
provoked him to anger *m* bitterly Hos 12:14 8563
the *m* upright is sharper than a Mic 7:4
m of his mighty works were done Mt 11:20 *4118*
Jesus, thou Son of the *m* high God Mk 5:7 *5310*
are *m* surely believed among us Lk 1:1
in order, *m* excellent Theophilus Lk 1:3 *2903*
which of them will love him *m* Lk 7:42 *4119*
that he, to whom he forgave *m* Lk 7:43 *4119*
Jesus, thou Son of God *m* high Lk 8:28 *5310*
Howbeit the *m* High dwelleth not Acts 7:48 *5310*
the servants of the *m* high God Acts 16:17 *5310*
Sorrowing *m* of all for the words Acts 20:38 *3122*
the *m* excellent governor Felix Acts 23:26 *2903*
places, *m* noble Felix, with all Acts 24:3 *2903*
that after the *m* straitest sect Acts 26:5
I am not mad, *m* noble Festus Acts 26:25 *2903*
be by two, or at the *m* by three 1Cor 14:27 *4119*
we are of all men *m* miserable 1Cor 15:19
M gladly therefore will I rather 2Cor 12:9 *2236*
Salem, priest of the *m* high God Heb 7:1 *5310*
yourselves on your *m* holy faith Jude 20 *40*
manner vessels of *m* precious wood Rev 18:12
was like unto a stone *m* precious Rev 21:11

MOTE
why beholdest thou the *m* that is Mt 7:3 *2595*
pull out the *m* out of thine eye Mt 7:4 *2595*
the *m* out of thy brother's eye Mt 7:5 *2595*
why beholdest thou the *m* that is Lk 6:41 *2595*
let me pull out the *m* that is in Lk 6:42 *2595*
see clearly to pull out the *m* Lk 6:42 *2595*

MOTH
which are crushed before the *m* Job 4:19 6211
as a garment that is *m* eaten Job 13:28 6211
He buildeth his house as a *m* Job 27:18 6211
beauty to consume away like a *m* Ps 39:11 6211
the *m* shall eat them up Is 50:9 6211
For the *m* shall eat them up like Is 51:8 6211
will I be unto Ephraim as a *m* Hos 5:12 6211
treasures upon earth, where *m* Mt 6:19 *4597*
where neither *m* nor rust doth Mt 6:20 *4597*
approacheth, neither *m* corrupteth Lk 12:33 *4597*

MOTHEATEN
corrupted, and your garments are *m* Jas 5:2 *4598*

MOTHER
a man leave his father and his *m* Gen 2:24 517
she was the *m* of all living Gen 3:20 517
and she shall be a *m* of nations Gen 17:16
but not the daughter of my *m* Gen 20:12 517
his *m* took him a wife out of the Gen 21:21 517
and to her *m* precious things Gen 24:53 517
her *m* said, Let the damsel abide Gen 24:55 517
be thou the *m* of thousands of Gen 24:60
her into his *m* Sarah's tent Gen 24:67 517
And Jacob said to Rebekah his *m* Gen 27:11 517
his *m* said unto him, Upon me be Gen 27:13 517
fetched, and brought them to his *m* Gen 27:14 517
his *m* made savoury meat, such as Gen 27:14 517
of Rebekah, Jacob's and Esau's *m* Gen 28:5 517
Jacob obeyed his father and his *m* Gen 28:7 517
and brought them unto his *m* Leah Gen 30:14 517
me, and the *m* with the children Gen 32:11 517
Shall I and thy *m* and thy brethren Gen 37:10 517
and he alone is left of his *m* Gen 44:20 517
maid went and called the child's *m* Ex 2:8 517
Honour thy father and thy *m* Ex 20:12 517
that smiteth his father, or his *m* Ex 21:15 517
that curseth his father, or his *m* Ex 21:17 517
father, or the nakedness of thy *m* Lev 18:7 517
she is thy *m* Lev 18:7 517
thy father, or daughter of thy *m* Lev 18:9 517
Ye shall fear every man his *m* Lev 19:3 517
m shall be surely put to death Lev 20:9 517
hath cursed his father or his *m* Lev 20:9 517
And if a man take a wife and her *m* Lev 20:14 517
near unto him, that is, for his *m* Lev 21:2 517
for his father, or for his *m* Lev 21:11 517
for his father, or for his *m* Num 6:7 517
whom her *m* bare to Levi in Egypt Num 26:59 517
Honour thy father and thy *m* Deut 5:16 517
If thy brother, the son of thy *m* Deut 13:6 517
her father and her *m* a full month Deut 21:13 517
his father, or the voice of his *m* Deut 21:18 517
his *m* lay hold on him, and bring Deut 21:19 517
father of the damsel, and her *m* Deut 22:15 517
light by his father or his *m* Deut 27:16 517
father, or the daughter of his *m* Deut 27:22 517
he that lieth with his *m* in law Deut 27:23 2859
said unto his father and to his *m* Deut 33:9 517
save alive my father, and my *m* Josh 2:13 517
shalt bring thy father, and thy *m* Josh 2:18 517
Rahab, and her father, and her *m* Josh 6:23 517
arose, that I arose a *m* in Israel Judg 5:7 517
The *m* of Sisera looked out at a Judg 5:28 517
brethren, even the sons of my *m* Judg 8:19 517
up, and told his father and his *m* Judg 14:2 517
his *m* said unto him, Is there Judg 14:3 517
his *m* knew not that it was of the Judg 14:4 517
down, and his father and his *m* Judg 14:5 517
father or his *m* what he had done Judg 14:6 517
and came to his father and *m* Judg 14:9 517
not told it my father nor my *m* Judg 14:16 517
And he said unto his *m*, The eleven Judg 17:2 517
his *m* said, Blessed be thou of Judg 17:2 517
shekels of silver to his *m* Judg 17:3 517
his *m* said, I had wholly Judg 17:3 517
he restored the money unto his *m* Judg 17:4 517
his *m* took two hundred shekels of Judg 17:4 517
and Orpah kissed her *m* in law Ruth 1:14 2545
that thou hast done unto thy *m* in Ruth 2:11 2545
hast left thy father and thy *m* Ruth 2:11 517
her *m* in law saw what she had Ruth 2:18 2545
her *m* in law said unto her, Where Ruth 2:19 2545
she shewed her *m* in law with whom Ruth 2:19 2545
and dwelt with her *m* in law Ruth 2:23 2545
Then Naomi her *m* in law said unto Ruth 3:1 2545
to all that her *m* in law bade her Ruth 3:6 2545
And when she came to her *m* in law Ruth 3:16 2545
Go not empty unto thy *m* in law Ruth 3:17 2545
Moreover his *m* made him a little 1Sa 2:19 517
so shall thy *m* be childless among 1Sa 15:33 517
of Moab, Let my father and my *m* 1Sa 22:3 517
sister to Zeruiah Joab's *m* 2Sa 17:25 517
the grave of my father and of my *m* 2Sa 19:37 517
destroy a city and a *m* in Israel 2Sa 20:19 517
his *m* bare him after Absalom 1Kin 1:6 517
unto Bath-sheba the *m* of Solomon 1Kin 1:11 517
to Bath-sheba the *m* of Solomon 1Kin 2:13 517
a seat to be set for the king's *m* 1Kin 2:19 517
king said unto her, Ask on, my *m* 1Kin 2:20 517
answered and said unto his *m* 1Kin 2:22 517
she is the *m* thereof 1Kin 3:27 517
And also Maachah his *m*, even her 1Kin 15:13 517
and delivered him unto his *m* 1Kin 17:23 517
pray thee, kiss my father and my *m* 1Kin 19:20 517
father, and in the way of his *m* 1Kin 22:52 517
like his father, and like his *m* 2Kin 3:2 517
and to the prophets of thy *m* 2Kin 3:13 517
said to a lad, Carry him to his *m* 2Kin 4:19 517
him, and brought him to his *m* 2Kin 4:20 517
the *m* of the child said, As the 2Kin 4:30 517
as the whoredoms of thy *m* Jezebel 2Kin 9:22 517
when Athaliah the *m* of Ahaziah 2Kin 11:1 517
the king of Babylon, he, and his *m* 2Kin 24:12 517
to Babylon, and the king's *m* 2Kin 24:15 517
she was the *m* of Onam 1Chr 2:26 517
his *m* called his name Jabez, 1Chr 4:9 517
Maachah the *m* of Asa the king 2Chr 15:16 517
for his *m* was his counsellor to 2Chr 22:3 517
But when Athaliah the *m* of 2Chr 22:10 517
for she had neither father nor *m* Est 2:7 517
m were dead, took for his own Est 2:7 517
to the worm, Thou art my *m* Job 17:14 517
my *m* forsake me, then the LORD Ps 27:10 517
as one that mourneth for his *m* Ps 35:14 517
and in sin did my *m* conceive me Ps 51:5 517
the sin of his *m* be blotted out Ps 109:14 517
and to be a joyful *m* of children Ps 113:9 517
a child that is weaned of his *m* Ps 131:2 517
and forsake not the law of thy *m* Prov 1:8 517
only beloved in the sight of my *m* Prov 4:3 517
and forsake not the law of thy *m* Prov 6:20 517
son is the heaviness of his *m* Prov 10:1 517
but a foolish man despiseth his *m* Prov 15:20 517
his father, and chaseth away his *m* Prov 19:26 517
Whoso curseth his father or his *m* Prov 20:20 517
despise not thy *m* when she is old Prov 23:22 517
thy *m* shall be glad, and she that Prov 23:25 517
Whoso robbeth his father or his *m* Prov 28:24 517
himself bringeth his *m* to shame Prov 29:15 517
father, and doth not bless their *m* Prov 30:11 517
and despiseth to obey his *m* Prov 30:17 517
prophecy that his *m* taught him Prov 31:1 517
with the crown wherewith his *m* Song 3:11 517
she is the only one of her *m* Song 6:9 517
that sucked the breasts of my *m* Song 8:1 517
there thy *m* brought thee forth Song 8:5 517
to cry, My father, and my *m* Is 8:4 517
from the bowels of my *m* hath he Is 49:1 517
transgressions is your *m* put away Is 50:1 517
As one whom his *m* comforteth Is 66:13 517
m of the young men a spoiler at Jer 15:8 517
Woe is me, my *m*, that thou hast Jer 15:10 517
for their father or for their *m* Jer 16:7 517
wherein my *m* bare me be blessed Jer 20:14 517
or that my *m* might have been my Jer 20:17 517
thy *m* that bare thee, into Jer 22:26 517
Your *m* shall be sore confounded Jer 50:12 517
an Amorite, and thy *m* an Hittite Eze 16:3 517
against thee, saying, As is the *m* Eze 16:44 517
your *m* was an Hittite, and your Eze 16:45 517
And say, What is thy *m* Eze 19:2 517
Thy *m* is like a vine in thy blood Eze 19:10 517
they set light by father and *m* Eze 22:7 517
two women, the daughters of one *m* Eze 23:2 517
but for father, or for *m*, or for Eze 44:25 517
Plead with your *m*, plead Hos 2:2 517
For their *m* hath played the Hos 2:5 517
night, and I will destroy thy *m* Hos 4:5 517
the *m* was dashed in pieces upon Hos 10:14 517
daughter riseth up against her *m* Mic 7:6 517
in law against her *m* in law Mic 7:6 2545
his *m* that begat him shall say Zec 13:3 517
his *m* that begat him shall thrust Zec 13:3 517
When as his *m* Mary was espoused Mt 1:18 *3384*
the young child with Mary his *m* Mt 2:11 *3384*
and take the young child and his *m* Mt 2:13 *3384*
his *m* by night, and departed into Mt 2:14 *3384*
and take the young child and his *m* Mt 2:20 *3384*
and took the young child and his *m* Mt 2:21 *3384*
house, he saw his wife's *m* laid Mt 8:14 *3994*
and the daughter against her *m* Mt 10:35 *3384*
in law against her *m* in law Mt 10:35 *3994*
He that loveth father or *m* more Mt 10:37 *3384*
to the people, behold, his *m* Mt 12:46 *3384*
one said unto him, Behold, thy *m* Mt 12:47 *3384*

him that told him, Who is my *m* .... Mt 12:48 3384
disciples, and said, Behold my *m* .... Mt 12:49 3384
is my brother, and sister, and *m* .... Mt 12:50 3384
is not his *m* called Mary .... Mt 13:55 3384
being before instructed of her *m* .... Mt 14:8 3384
and she brought it to her *m* .... Mt 14:11 3384
saying, Honour thy father and *m* .... Mt 15:4 3384
and, He that curseth father or *m* .... Mt 15:4 3384
shall say to his father or his *m* .... Mt 15:5 3384
And honour not his father or his *m* .... Mt 15:6 3384
shall a man leave father and *m* .... Mt 19:5 3384
Honour thy father and thy *m* .... Mt 19:19 3384
or sisters, or father, or *m* .... Mt 19:29 3384
Then came to him the *m* of .... Mt 20:20 3384
Magdalene, and Mary the *m* of James . Mt 27:56 3384
the *m* of Zebedee's children .... Mt 27:56 3384
But Simon's wife's *m* lay sick of .... Mk 1:30 3994
came then his brethren and his *m* .... Mk 3:31 3384
they said unto him, Behold, thy *m* .... Mk 3:32 3384
them, saying, Who is my *m* .... Mk 3:33 3384
about him, and said, Behold my *m* .... Mk 3:34 3384
is my brother, and my sister, and *m* .... Mk 3:35 3384
the *m* of the damsel, and them that .... Mk 5:40 3384
went forth, and said unto her *m* .... Mk 6:24 3384
and the damsel gave it to her *m* .... Mk 6:28 3384
said, Honour thy father and thy *m* .... Mk 7:10 3384
and, Whoso curseth father or *m* .... Mk 7:10 3384
man shall say to his father or *m* .... Mk 7:11 3384
do ought for his father or his *m* .... Mk 7:12 3384
shall a man leave his father and *m* .... Mk 10:7 3384
not, Honour thy father and *m* .... Mk 10:19 3384
or sisters, or father, or *m* .... Mk 10:29 3384
Mary the *m* of James the less and .... Mk 15:40 3384
Mary the *m* of Joses beheld where .... Mk 15:47
Magdalene, and Mary the *m* of James . Mk 16:1
that the *m* of my Lord should come .... Lk 1:43 3384
his *m* answered and said, Not so .... Lk 1:60 3384
his *m* marvelled at those things .... Lk 2:33 3384
them, and said unto Mary his *m* .... Lk 2:34 3384
and Joseph and his *m* knew not of it ... Lk 2:43 3384
his *m* said unto him, Son, why .... Lk 2:48 3384
but his *m* kept all these sayings .... Lk 2:51 3384
Simon's wife's *m* was taken with a .... Lk 4:38 3994
out, the only son of his *m* .... Lk 7:12 3384
And he delivered him to his *m* .... Lk 7:15 3384
Then came to him his *m* and his .... Lk 8:19 3384
him by certain which said, Thy *m* .... Lk 8:20 3384
answered and said unto them, My *m* .. Lk 8:21 3384
the father and the *m* of the maiden .... Lk 8:51 3384
the *m* against the daughter .... Lk 12:53 3384
and the daughter against the *m* .... Lk 12:53 3384
the *m* in law against her daughter .... Lk 12:53 3994
in law against her *m* in law .... Lk 12:53 3994
me, and hate not his father, and *m* .... Lk 14:26 3384
Honour thy father and thy *m* .... Lk 18:20 3384
and Joanna, and Mary the *m* of James Lk 24:10
and the *m* of Jesus was there .... Jn 2:1 3384
the *m* of Jesus saith unto him, ... Jn 2:3 3384
His *m* saith unto the servants, ... Jn 2:5 3384
down to Capernaum, he, and his *m* .... Jn 2:12 3384
Joseph, whose father and *m* we know . Jn 6:42 3384
stood by the cross of Jesus his *m* .... Jn 19:25 3384
When Jesus therefore saw his *m* .... Jn 19:26 3384
he loved, he saith unto his *m* .... Jn 19:26 3384
he to the disciple, Behold thy *m* .... Jn 19:27 3384
the women, and Mary the *m* of Jesus .. Acts 1:14 3384
the house of Mary the *m* of John .... Acts 12:12 3384
chosen in the Lord, and his *m* .... Rom 16:13 3384
is free, which is the *m* of us all .... Gal 4:26 3384
shall a man leave his father and *m* .... Eph 5:31 3384
Honour thy father and *m* .... Eph 6:2 3384
grandmother Lois, and thy *m* Eunice 2Ti 1:5 3384
Without father, without *m* .... Heb 7:3 282
THE *M* OF HARLOTS .... Rev 17:5 3384

MOTHER'S
told them of her *m* house these .... Gen 24:28 517
was comforted after his *m* death .... Gen 24:67 517
let thy *m* sons bow down to thee .... Gen 27:29 517
the house of Bethuel thy *m* father .... Gen 28:2 517
daughters of Laban thy *m* brother .... Gen 28:2 517
daughter of Laban his *m* brother .... Gen 29:10 517
the sheep of Laban his *m* brother .... Gen 29:10 517
the flock of Laban his *m* brother .... Gen 29:10 517
his brother Benjamin, his *m* son .... Gen 43:29 517
not seethe a kid in his *m* milk .... Ex 23:19 517
not seethe a kid in his *m* milk .... Ex 34:26 517
the nakedness of thy *m* sister .... Lev 18:13 517
for she is thy *m* near kinswoman .... Lev 18:13 517
or his *m* daughter, and see her .... Lev 20:17 517
the nakedness of thy *m* sister .... Lev 20:19 517
his *m* name was Shelomith, the .... Lev 24:11 517
when he cometh out of his *m* womb .... Num 12:12 517
not seethe a kid in his *m* milk .... Deut 14:21 517
to Shechem unto his *m* brethren .... Judg 9:1 517
of the house of his *m* father .... Judg 9:1 517
his *m* brethren spake of him in .... Judg 9:3 517
Nazarite unto God from my *m* womb .. Judg 16:17 517
Go, return each to her *m* house .... Ruth 1:8 517
the confusion of thy *m* nakedness 1Sa 20:30 517
whose *m* name was Zeruah, a widow .. 1Kin 11:26 517
And his *m* name was Naamah an 1Kin 14:21 517
And his *m* name was Naamah an 1Kin 14:31 517
his *m* name was Maachah, the 1Kin 15:2 517
his *m* name was Maachah, the 1Kin 15:10 517
his *m* name was Azubah the 1Kin 22:42 517
his *m* name was Athaliah, the 2Kin 8:26 517
And his *m* name was Zibiah of 2Kin 12:1 517
his *m* name was Jehoaddan of 2Kin 14:2 517
his *m* name was Jecholiah of 2Kin 15:2 517
his *m* name was Jerusha, the 2Kin 15:33 517
His *m* name also was Abi, the 2Kin 18:2 517
his *m* name was Hephzi-bah 2Kin 21:1 517
his *m* name was Meshullemeth, the 2Kin 21:19 517
his *m* name was Jedidah, the 2Kin 22:1 517
his *m* name was Hamutal, the 2Kin 23:31 517
his *m* name was Zebudah, the 2Kin 23:36 517
his *m* name was Nehushta, the 2Kin 24:8 517
his *m* name was Hamutal, the 2Kin 24:18 517
And his *m* name was Naamah an 2Chr 12:13 517
His *m* name also was Michaiah the 2Chr 13:2 517
his *m* name was Azubah the 2Chr 20:31 517
His *m* name also was Athaliah the 2Chr 22:2 517
His *m* name also was Zibiah of 2Chr 24:1 517
his *m* name was Jehoaddan of 2Chr 25:1 517
His *m* name also was Jecoliah of 2Chr 26:3 517
His *m* name also was Jerushah, the 2Chr 27:1 517
his *m* name was Abijah, the 2Chr 29:1 517
Naked came I out of my *m* womb .... Job 1:21 517
not up the doors of my *m* womb .... Job 3:10 517
I have guided her from my *m* womb .... Job 31:18 517
hope when I was upon my *m* breasts ... Ps 22:9 517
thou art my God from my *m* belly .... Ps 22:10 517
thou slanderest thine own *m* son .... Ps 50:20 517
and an alien unto my *m* children .... Ps 69:8 517
that took me out of my *m* bowels .... Ps 71:6 517
thou hast covered me in my *m* womb .. Ps 139:13 517
As he came forth of his *m* womb .... Eccl 5:15 517
my *m* children were angry with me .... Song 1:6 517
I had brought him into my *m* house .... Song 3:4 517
and bring thee into my *m* house .... Song 8:2 517
is the bill of your *m* divorcement .... Is 50:1 517
his *m* name was Hamutal the .... Jer 52:1 517
Thou art thy *m* daughter, that .... Eze 16:45 517
were so born from their *m* womb .... Mt 19:12 3384
Holy Ghost, even from his *m* womb .... Lk 1:15 3384
the second time into his *m* womb .... Jn 3:4 3384
his *m* sister, Mary the wife of .... Jn 19:25 3384
lame from his *m* womb was carried .... Acts 3:2 3384
being a cripple from his *m* womb .... Acts 14:8 3384
who separated me from my *m* womb ... Gal 1:15 3384

MOTHERS
and their queens thy nursing *m* .... Is 49:23
concerning their *m* that bare them .... Jer 16:3 517
They say to their *m*, Where is .... Lam 2:12 517
fatherless, our *m* are as widows .... Lam 5:3 517
and brethren, and sisters, and *m* .... Mk 10:30 3384
of fathers and murderers of *m* 1Ti 1:9 3389
The elder women as *m* 1Ti 5:2 3384

MOTHERS'
was poured out into their *m* bosom .... Lam 2:12 517

MOTIONS
the *m* of sins, which were by the .... Rom 7:5 3804

MOULDY
of their provision was dry and *m* .... Josh 9:5 5350
behold, it is dry, and it is *m* .... Josh 9:12 5350

MOUNT
goest unto Sephar a *m* of the east .... Gen 10:30 2022
And the Horites in their *m* Seir .... Gen 14:6 2042
In the *m* of the LORD it shall be .... Gen 22:14 2022
set his face toward the *m* Gilead .... Gen 31:21 2022
they overtook him in the *m* Gilead .... Gen 31:23 2022
had pitched his tent in the *m* .... Gen 31:25 2022
pitched in the *m* of Gilead .... Gen 31:25 2022
offered sacrifice upon the *m* .... Gen 31:54 2022
and tarried all night in the *m* .... Gen 31:54 2022
Thus dwelt Esau in *m* Seir .... Gen 36:8 2022
father of the Edomites in *m* Seir .... Gen 36:9 2022
went, and met him in the *m* of God .... Ex 4:27 2022
where he encamped at the *m* of God .... Ex 18:5 2022
there Israel camped before the *m* .... Ex 19:2 2022
of all the people upon *m* Sinai .... Ex 19:11 2022
that ye go not up into the *m* .... Ex 19:12 2022
whosoever toucheth the *m* shall be .... Ex 19:12 2022
long, they shall come up to the *m* .... Ex 19:13 2022
down from the *m* unto the people .... Ex 19:14 2022
and a thick cloud upon the *m* .... Ex 19:16 2022
stood at the nether part of the *m* .... Ex 19:17 2022
m Sinai was altogether on a smoke .... Ex 19:18 2022
the whole *m* quaked greatly .... Ex 19:18 2022
m Sinai, on the top of the *m* .... Ex 19:20 2022
Moses up to the top of the *m* .... Ex 19:20 2022
people cannot come up to *m* Sinai .... Ex 19:23 2022
saying, Set bounds about the *m* .... Ex 19:23 2022
Moses, Come up to me into the *m* .... Ex 24:12 2022
Moses went up into the *m* of God .... Ex 24:13 2022
And Moses went up into the *m* .... Ex 24:15 2022
and a cloud covered the *m* .... Ex 24:15 2022
of the LORD abode upon *m* Sinai .... Ex 24:16 2022
fire on the top of the *m* in the .... Ex 24:17 2022
cloud, and gat him up into the *m* .... Ex 24:18 2022
and Moses was in the *m* forty days .... Ex 24:18 2022
which was shewed thee in the *m* .... Ex 25:40 2022
which was shewed thee in the *m* .... Ex 26:30 2022
as it was shewed thee in the *m* .... Ex 27:8 2022
communing with him upon *m* Sinai .... Ex 31:18 2022
delayed to come down out of the *m* .... Ex 32:1 2022
turned, and went down from the *m* .... Ex 32:15 2022
and brake them beneath the *m* .... Ex 32:19 2022
of their ornaments by the *m* Horeb .... Ex 33:6 2022
up in the morning unto *m* Sinai .... Ex 34:2 2022
there to me in the top of the *m* .... Ex 34:2 2022
man be seen throughout all the *m* .... Ex 34:3 2022
nor herds feed before that *m* .... Ex 34:3 2022
morning, and went up unto *m* Sinai .... Ex 34:4 2022
when Moses came down from *m* Sinai Ex 34:29 2022
when he came down from the *m* .... Ex 34:29 2022
had spoken with him in *m* Sinai .... Ex 34:32 2022
LORD commanded Moses in *m* Sinai .... Lev 7:38 2022
LORD spake unto Moses in *m* Sinai .... Lev 25:1 2022
the children of Israel in *m* Sinai .... Lev 26:46 2022
the children of Israel in *m* Sinai .... Lev 27:34 2022
LORD spake with Moses in *m* Sinai .... Num 3:1 2022
they departed from the *m* of the .... Num 10:33 2022
from Kadesh, and came unto *m* Hor .... Num 20:22 2022
unto Moses and Aaron in *m* Hor .... Num 20:23 2022
son, and bring them up unto *m* Hor .... Num 20:25 2022
they went up into *m* Hor in the .... Num 20:27 2022
died there in the top of the *m* .... Num 20:28 2022
and Eleazar came down from the *m* .... Num 20:28 2022
they journeyed from *m* Hor by the .... Num 21:4 2022
Get thee up into this *m* Abarim .... Num 27:12 2022
which was ordained in *m* Sinai for .... Num 28:6 2022
and pitched in *m* Shapher .... Num 33:23 2022
And they removed from *m* Shapher .... Num 33:24 2022
from Kadesh, and pitched in *m* Hor .... Num 33:37 2022
m Hor at the commandment of the .... Num 33:38 2022
years old when he died in *m* Hor .... Num 33:39 2022
And they departed from *m* Hor .... Num 33:41 2022
ye shall point out for you *m* Hor .... Num 34:7 2022
From *m* Hor ye shall point out .... Num 34:8 2022
way of *m* Seir unto Kadesh-barnea .... Deut 1:2 2022
have dwelt long enough in this *m* .... Deut 1:6 2022
go to the *m* of the Amorites, and .... Deut 1:7 2022
we compassed *m* Seir many days .... Deut 2:1 2022
because I have given *m* Seir unto .... Deut 2:5 2022
the river of Arnon unto *m* Hermon .... Deut 3:8 2022
half *m* Gilead, and the cities .... Deut 3:12 2022
even unto *m* Sion which is Hermon, ... Deut 4:48 2022
m out of the midst of the fire .... Deut 5:4 2022
fire, and went not up into the *m* .... Deut 5:5 2022
m out of the midst of the fire .... Deut 5:22 2022
When I was gone up into the *m* to .... Deut 9:9 2022
then I abode in the *m* forty days .... Deut 9:9 2022
the LORD spake with you in the *m* .... Deut 9:10 2022
I turned and came down from the *m* ... Deut 9:15 2022
and the *m* burned with fire .... Deut 9:15 2022
brook that descended out of the *m* .... Deut 9:21 2022
and come up unto me into the *m* .... Deut 10:1 2022
the first, and went up into the *m* .... Deut 10:3 2022
the LORD spake unto you in the *m* .... Deut 10:4 2022
myself and came down from the *m* .... Deut 10:5 2022
And I stayed in the *m*, according .... Deut 10:10 2022
put the blessing upon *m* Gerizim .... Deut 11:29 2022
and the curse upon *m* Ebal .... Deut 11:29 2022
in *m* Ebal, and thou shalt plaister .... Deut 27:4 2022
These shall stand upon *m* Gerizim .... Deut 27:12 2022
shall stand upon *m* Ebal to curse .... Deut 27:13 2022
this mountain Abarim, unto *m* Nebo .... Deut 32:49 2022
die in the *m* whither thou goest .... Deut 32:50 2022
Aaron thy brother died in *m* Hor .... Deut 32:50 2022
he shined forth from *m* Paran .... Deut 33:2 2022
the LORD God of Israel in *m* Ebal .... Josh 8:30 2022
of them over against *m* Gerizim .... Josh 8:33 2022
half of them over against *m* Ebal .... Josh 8:33 2022
Even from the *m* Halak, that goeth .... Josh 11:17 2022
valley of Lebanon under *m* Hermon .... Josh 11:17 2022
the river Arnon unto *m* Hermon .... Josh 12:1 2022
And reigned in *m* Hermon, and in .... Josh 12:5 2022
of Lebanon even unto the *m* Halak .... Josh 12:7 2022
from Baal-gad under *m* Hermon unto .. Josh 13:5 2022
all *m* Hermon, and all Bashan unto .... Josh 13:11 2022
in the *m* of the valley, ... Josh 13:19 2022
out to the cities of *m* Ephron .... Josh 15:9 2022
from Baalah westward unto *m* Seir .... Josh 15:10 2022
along unto the side of *m* Jearim .... Josh 15:10 2022
and passed along to *m* Baalah .... Josh 15:11 2022
from Jericho throughout *m* Beth-el .... Josh 16:1 2022
if *m* Ephraim be too narrow for .... Josh 17:15 2022
even Timnath-serah in *m* Ephraim .... Josh 19:50 2022
Kedesh in Galilee in *m* Naphtali .... Josh 20:7 2022
and Shechem in *m* Ephraim .... Josh 20:7 2022
with her suburbs in *m* Ephraim .... Josh 21:21 2022
and I gave unto Esau *m* Seir .... Josh 24:4 2022
which is in *m* Ephraim, on the .... Josh 24:30 2022
which was given him in *m* Ephraim .... Josh 24:33 2022
would dwell in *m* Heres in Aijalon .... Judg 1:35 2022
in the *m* of Ephraim, on the north .... Judg 2:9 2022
Hivites that dwelt in *m* Lebanon .... Judg 3:3 2022
from *m* Baal-hermon unto the .... Judg 3:3 2022
went down with him from the *m* .... Judg 3:27 2022
Ramah and Beth-el in *m* Ephraim .... Judg 4:5 2022
saying, Go and draw toward *m* Tabor .. Judg 4:6 2022
of Abinoam was gone up to *m* Tabor ... Judg 4:12 2022
So Barak went down from *m* Tabor .... Judg 4:14 2022
and depart early from *m* Gilead .... Judg 7:3 2022
throughout all *m* Ephraim, saying, ... Judg 7:24 2022
and stood in the top of *m* Gerizim .... Judg 9:7 2022
Abimelech gat him up to *m* Zalmon .... Judg 9:48 2022
he dwelt in Shamir in *m* Ephraim .... Judg 10:1 2022
in the *m* of the Amalekites .... Judg 12:15 2022
And there was a man of *m* Ephraim .... Judg 17:1 2022
he came to *m* Ephraim to the house .... Judg 17:8 2022
who when they came to *m* Ephraim .... Judg 18:2 2022
they passed thence unto *m* Ephraim .... Judg 18:13 2022
on the side of *m* Ephraim, who .... Judg 19:1 2022
even, which was also of *m* Ephraim .... Judg 19:16 2022
toward the side of *m* Ephraim .... Judg 19:18 2022
of *m* Ephraim, and his name was 1Sa 1:1 2022
And he passed through *m* Ephraim 1Sa 9:4 2022
in *m* Beth-el, and a thousand were 1Sa 13:2 2022
had hid themselves in *m* Ephraim 1Sa 14:22 2022
and fell down slain in *m* Gilboa 1Sa 31:1 2022
his three sons fallen in *m* Gilboa 1Sa 31:8 2022
happened by chance upon *m* Gilboa 2Sa 1:6 2022
went up by the ascent of *m* Olivet 2Sa 15:30
was come to the top of the *m* 2Sa 15:32
but a man of *m* Ephraim, Sheba the 2Sa 20:21 2022
The son of Hur, in *m* Ephraim 1Kin 4:8 2022
built Shechem in *m* Ephraim 1Kin 12:25 2022
to me all Israel unto *m* Carmel 1Kin 18:19 2022
prophets together unto *m* Carmel 1Kin 18:20 2022
nights unto Horeb the *m* of God 1Kin 19:8 2022
stand upon the *m* before the LORD 1Kin 19:11 2022
he went from thence to *m* Carmel 2Kin 2:25 2022
unto the man of God to *m* Carmel 2Kin 4:25 2022
m Ephraim two young men of the 2Kin 5:22 2022
and they that escape out of *m* Zion 2Kin 19:31 2022
right hand of the *m* of corruption 2Kin 23:13 2022

that were there in the *m*, and sent 2Kin 23:16 2022
five hundred men, went to *m* Seir 1Chr 4:42 2022
and Senir, and unto *m* Hermon 1Chr 5:23 2022
Shechem in *m* Ephraim with her 1Chr 6:67 2022
and fell down slain in *m* Gilboa 1Chr 10:1 2022
and his sons fallen in *m* Gilboa 1Chr 10:8 2022
the LORD at Jerusalem in *m* Moriah 2Chr 3:1 2022
Abijah stood up upon *m* Zemaraim 2Chr 13:4 2022
Zemaraim, which is in *m* Ephraim 2Chr 13:4 2022
which he had taken from *m* Ephraim 2Chr 15:8 2022
from Beer-sheba to *m* Ephraim 2Chr 19:4 2022
m Seir, whom thou wouldest not 2Chr 20:10 2022
m Seir, which were come against 2Chr 20:22 2022
against the inhabitants of *m* Seir 2Chr 20:23 2022
in the *m* of the house of the LORD 2Chr 33:15 2022
saying, Go forth unto the *m* Neh 8:15 2022
camest down also upon *m* Sinai Neh 9:13 2022
excellency *m* up to the heavens Job 20:6 5927
Doth the eagle *m* up at thy Job 39:27 1361
is *m* Zion, on the sides of the Ps 48:2 2022
Let *m* Zion rejoice, let the Ps 48:11 2022
this *m* Zion, wherein thou hast Ps 74:2 2022
the *m* Zion which he loved Ps 78:68 2022
They *m* up to the heaven, they go Ps 107:26 5927
in the LORD shall be as *m* Zion Ps 125:1 2022
goats, that appear from *m* Gilead Song 4:1 2022
every dwelling place of *m* Zion Is 4:5 2022
hosts, which dwelleth in *m* Zion Is 8:18 2022
they shall *m* up like the lifting Is 9:18 55
his whole work upon *m* Zion Is 10:12 2022
the *m* of the daughter of Zion Is 10:32 2022
upon the *m* of the congregation Is 14:13 2022
unto the *m* of the daughter of Is 16:1 2022
of the LORD of hosts, the *m* Zion Is 18:7 2022
of hosts shall reign in *m* Zion Is 24:23 2022
LORD in the holy *m* at Jerusalem Is 27:13 2022
shall rise up as in *m* Perazim Is 28:21 2022
lay siege against thee with a *m* Is 29:3 4674
be, that fight against *m* Zion Is 29:8 2022
come down to fight for *m* Zion Is 31:4 2022
and they that escape out of *m* Zion Is 37:32 2022
they shall *m* up with wings as Is 40:31 5927
affliction from *m* Ephraim Jer 4:15 2022
cast a *m* against Jerusalem Jer 6:6 5550
upon the *m* Ephraim shall cry Jer 31:6 2022
shall be satisfied upon *m* Ephraim Jer 50:19 2022
Babylon should *m* up to heaven Jer 51:53 5927
it, and cast a *m* against it Eze 4:2 5550
wings to *m* up from the earth Eze 10:16 7311
against the gates, to cast a *m* Eze 21:22 5550
cast a *m* against thee, and lift up Eze 26:8 5550
man, set thy face against *m* Seir Eze 35:2 2022
O *m* Seir, I am against thee, and I Eze 35:3 2022
Thus will I make *m* Seir most Eze 35:7 2022
O *m* Seir, and all Idumea, even all Eze 35:15 2022
north shall come, and cast up a *m* Dan 11:15 5550
for in *m* Zion and in Jerusalem Joel 2:32 2022
out of the *m* of Esau Obad 8 2022
the *m* of Esau may be cut off by Obad 9 2022
But upon *m* Zion shall be Obad 17 2022
south shall possess the *m* of Esau Obad 19 2022
m Zion to judge the *m* of Esau Obad 21 2022
them in *m* Zion from henceforth Mic 4:7 2022
and the Holy One from *m* Paran Hab 3:3 2022
in that day upon the *m* of Olives Zec 14:4 2022
the *m* of Olives shall cleave in Zec 14:4 2022
unto the *m* of Olives, then sent Mt 21:1 3735
And as he sat upon the *m* of Olives Mt 24:3 3735
went out into the *m* of Olives Mt 26:30 3735
at the *m* of Olives, he sendeth Mk 11:1 3735
as he sat upon the *m* of Olives Mk 13:3 3735
went out into the *m* of Olives Mk 14:26 3735
at the *m* called the *m* of Lk 19:29 3735
called the *m* of Olives Lk 19:29
at the descent of the *m* of Olives Lk 19:37 3735
abode in the *m* that is called the Lk 21:37 3735
that is called the *m* of Olives Lk 21:37
he was wont, to the *m* of Olives Lk 22:39 3735
Jesus went unto the *m* of Olives Jn 8:1 3735
from the *m* called Olivet, which Acts 1:12 3735
to him in the wilderness of *m* Acts 7:30 3735
which spake to him in the *m* Sina Acts 7:38 3735
the one from the *m* Sinai, which Gal 4:24 3735
this Agar is *m* Sinai in Arabia Gal 4:25 3735
pattern shewed to thee in the *m* Heb 8:5 3735
unto the *m* that might be touched Heb 12:18 3735
But ye are come unto *m* Sion Heb 12:22 3735
we were with him in the holy *m* 2Pet 1:18 3735
lo, a Lamb stood on the *m* Sion Rev 14:1 3735

MOUNTAIN

unto a *m* on the east of Beth-el Gen 12:8 2022
they that remained fled to the *m* Gen 14:10 2022
escape to the *m*, lest thou be Gen 19:17 2022
and I cannot escape to the *m* Gen 19:19 2022
up out of Zoar, and dwelt in the *m* Gen 19:30 2022
desert, and came to the *m* of God Ex 3:1 2022
ye shall serve God upon this *m* Ex 3:12 2022
plant them in the *m* of thine Ex 15:17 2022
LORD called unto him out of the *m* Ex 19:3 2022
of the trumpet, and the *m* smoking Ex 20:18 2022
southward, and go up into the *m* Num 13:17 2022
gat them up into the top of the *m* Num 14:40 2022
the way of the *m* of the Amorites Deut 1:19 2022
come unto the *m* of the Amorites Deut 1:20 2022
they turned and went up into the *m* Deut 1:24 2022
Amorites, which dwelt in that *m* Deut 1:44 2022
have compassed this *m* long enough Deut 2:3 2022
is beyond Jordan, that goodly *m* Deut 3:25 2022
ye came near and stood under the *m* Deut 4:11 2022
the *m* burned with fire unto the Deut 4:11 2022
(for the *m* did burn with fire,) Deut 5:23 2022
Get thee up into this *m* Abarim Deut 32:49 2022
shall call the people unto the *m* Deut 33:19 2022
plains of Moab unto the *m* of Nebo Deut 34:1 2022
said unto them, Get you to the *m* Josh 2:16 2022
And they went, and came unto the *m* Josh 2:22 2022
returned, and descended from the *m* Josh 2:23 2022
the *m* of Israel, and the valley of Josh 11:16 2022
Now therefore give me this *m* Josh 14:12 2022
went up to the top of the *m* that Josh 15:8 2022
But the *m* shall be thine Josh 17:18 2022
came down to the end of the *m* Josh 18:16 2022
is Hebron, in the *m* of Judah Josh 20:7 2022
Canaanites, that dwelt in the *m* Judg 1:9 2022
out the inhabitants of the *m* Judg 1:19 2022
the children of Dan into the *m* Judg 1:34 2022
a trumpet in the *m* of Ephraim Judg 3:27 2022
stood on a *m* on the one side 1Sa 17:3 2022
stood on a *m* on the other side 1Sa 17:3 2022
remained in a *m* in the wilderness 1Sa 23:14 2022
Saul went on this side of the *m* 1Sa 23:26 2022
and his men on that side of the *m* 1Sa 23:26 2022
him up, and cast him upon some *m* 2Kin 2:16 2022
the *m* was full of horses and 2Kin 6:17 2022
thousand to hew in the *m*, and 2Chr 2:2 2022
thousand to be hewers in the *m* 2Chr 2:18 2022
surely the *m* falling cometh to Job 14:18 2022
my soul, Flee as a bird to your *m* Ps 11:1 2022
hast made my *m* to stand strong Ps 30:7 2042
our God, in the *m* of his holiness Ps 48:1 2022
of his sanctuary, even to this *m* Ps 78:54 2022
I will get me to the *m* of myrrh Song 4:6 2022
that the *m* of the LORD's house Is 2:2 2022
let us go up to the *m* of the LORD Is 2:3 2022
hurt nor destroy in all my holy *m* Is 11:9 2022
ye up a banner upon the high *m* Is 13:2 2022
in this *m* shall the LORD of hosts Is 25:6 2022
he will destroy in this *m* the Is 25:7 2022
For in this *m* shall the hand of Is 25:10 2022
as a beacon upon the top of a *m* Is 30:17 2022
there shall be upon every high *m* Is 30:25 2022
to come into the *m* of the LORD Is 30:29 2022
shall be exalted, and every *m* Is 40:4 2022
get thee up into the high *m* Is 40:9 2022
them will I bring to my holy *m* Is 56:7 2022
high *m* hast thou set thy bed Is 57:7 2022
land, and shall inherit my holy *m* Is 57:13 2022
the LORD, that forget my holy *m* Is 65:11 2022
hurt nor destroy in all my holy *m* Is 65:25 2022
beasts, to my holy *m* Jerusalem Is 66:20 2022
she is gone up upon every high *m* Jer 3:6 2022
they shall hunt them from every *m* Jer 16:16 2022
O my *m* in the field, I will give Jer 17:3 2042
the *m* of the house as the high Jer 26:18 2022
of justice, and *m* of holiness Jer 31:23 2022
they have gone from *m* to hill Jer 50:6 2022
I am against thee, O destroying *m* Jer 51:25 2022
and will make thee a burnt *m* Jer 51:25 2022
Because of the *m* of Zion, which Lam 5:18 2022
stood upon the *m* which is on the Eze 11:23 2022
and will plant it upon an high *m* Eze 17:22 2022
In the *m* of the height of Israel Eze 17:23 2022
For in mine holy *m* Eze 20:40 2022
in the *m* of the height of Israel, Eze 20:40 2022
thou wast upon the holy *m* of God Eze 28:14 2022
as profane out of the *m* of God Eze 28:16 2022
and set me upon a very high *m* Eze 40:2 2022
Upon the top of the *m* the whole Eze 43:12 2022
smote the image became a great *m* Dan 2:35 2906
cut out of the *m* without hands Dan 2:45 2906
thy city Jerusalem, thy holy *m* Dan 9:16 2022
my God for the holy *m* of my God Dan 9:20 2022
the seas in the glorious holy *m* Dan 11:45 2022
and sound an alarm in my holy *m* Joel 2:1 2022
God dwelling in Zion, my holy *m* Joel 3:17 2022
that are in the *m* of Samaria Amos 4:1 2022
and trust in the *m* of Samaria Amos 6:1 2022
as ye have drunk upon my holy *m* Obad 16 2022
the *m* of the house as the high Mic 3:12 2022
that the *m* of the house of the Mic 4:1 2022
let us go up to the *m* of the LORD Mic 4:2 2022
sea to sea, and from *m* to *m* Mic 7:12 2022
be haughty because of my holy *m* Zeph 3:11 2022
Go up to the *m*, and bring wood, and Hag 1:8 2022
Who art thou, O great *m* Zec 4:7 2022
the *m* of the LORD of hosts the Zec 8:3 2022
of the LORD of hosts the holy *m* Zec 8:3 2022
half of the *m* shall remove toward Zec 14:4 2022
him up into an exceeding high *m* Mt 4:8 3735
multitudes, he went up into a *m* Mt 5:1 3735
When he was come down from the *m* Mt 8:1 3735
he went up into a *m* apart to pray Mt 14:23 3735
and went up into a *m*, and sat down Mt 15:29 3735
them up into an high *m* apart Mt 17:1 3735
And as they came down from the *m* Mt 17:9 3735
seed, ye shall say unto this *m* Mt 17:20 3735
also if ye shall say unto this *m* Mt 21:21 3735
Galilee, into a *m* where Jesus had Mt 28:16 3735
And he goeth up into a *m*, and Mk 3:13 3735
he departed into a *m* to pray Mk 6:46 3735
an high *m* apart by themselves Mk 9:2 3735
And as they came down from the *m* Mk 9:9 3735
whosoever shall say unto this *m* Mk 11:23 3735
shall be filled, and every *m* Lk 3:5 3735
taking him up into an high *m* Lk 4:5 3735
that he went out into a *m* to pray Lk 6:12 3735
of many swine feeding on the *m* Lk 8:32 3735
and went up into a *m* to pray Lk 9:28 3735
Our fathers worshipped in this *m* Jn 4:20 3735
when ye shall neither in this *m* Jn 4:21 3735
And Jesus went up into a *m* Jn 6:3 3735
again into a *m* himself alone Jn 6:15 3735
if so much as a beast touch the *m* Heb 12:20 3735
and every *m* and island were moved Rev 6:14 3735
as it were a great *m* burning with Rev 8:8 3735
the spirit to a great and high *m* Rev 21:10 3735

MOUNTAINS

and the *m* were covered Gen 7:20 2022
the month, upon the *m* of Ararat Gen 8:4 2022
were the tops of the *m* seen Gen 8:5 2022
the *m* which I will tell thee of Gen 22:2 2022
them out, to slay them in the *m* Ex 32:12 2022
and the Amorites, dwell in the *m* Num 13:29 2022
out of the *m* of the east, saying, Num 23:7 2042
and pitched in the *m* of Abarim Num 33:47 2022
departed from the *m* of Abarim Num 33:48 2022
nor unto the cities in the *m* Deut 2:37 2022
their gods, upon the high *m* Deut 12:2 2022
on fire the foundations of the *m* Deut 32:22 2022
the chief things of the ancient *m* Deut 33:15 2042
m are gathered together against Josh 10:6 2022
that were on the north of the *m* Josh 11:2 2022
and the Jebusite in the *m* Josh 11:3 2022
and cut off the Anakims from the *m* Josh 11:21 2022
Anab, and from all the *m* of Judah Josh 11:21 2022
and from all the *m* of Israel Josh 11:21 2022
In the *m*, and in the valleys, and Josh 12:8 2022
And in the *m*, Shamir, and Jattir, Josh 15:48 2022
and went up through the *m* westward. Josh 18:12 2022
The *m* melted from before the LORD Judg 5:5 2022
them the dens which are in the *m* Judg 6:2 2022
wait for him in the top of the *m* Judg 9:25 2022
people down from the top of the *m* Judg 9:36 2022
of the *m* as if they were men Judg 9:36 2022
I may go up and down upon the *m* Judg 11:37 2022
bewailed her virginity upon the *m* Judg 11:38 2022
doth hunt a partridge in the *m* 1Sa 26:20 2022
Ye *m* of Gilboa, let there be no 2Sa 1:21 2022
thousand hewers in the *m* 1Kin 5:15 2022
a great and strong wind rent the *m* 1Kin 19:11 2022
am come up to the height of the *m* 2Kin 19:23 2022
as swift as the roes upon the *m* 1Chr 12:8 2022
all Israel scattered upon the *m* 2Chr 18:16 2022
high places in the *m* of Judah 2Chr 21:11 2022
also, and vine dressers in the *m* 2Chr 26:10 2022
he built cities in the *m* of Judah 2Chr 27:4 2022
Which removeth the *m*, and they Job 9:5 2022
are wet with the showers of the *m* Job 24:8 2022
he overturneth the *m* by the roots Job 28:9 2022
The range of the *m* is his pasture Job 39:8 2022
Surely the *m* bring him forth food Job 40:20 2022
righteousness is like the great *m* Ps 36:6 2042
though the *m* be carried into the Ps 46:2 2022
though the *m* shake with the Ps 46:3 2022
I know all the fowls of the *m* Ps 50:11 2022
his strength setteth fast the *m* Ps 65:6 2022
The *m* shall bring peace to the Ps 72:3 2022
the earth upon the top of the *m* Ps 72:16 2022
and excellent than the *m* of prey Ps 76:4 2042
the flame setteth the *m* on fire Ps 83:14 2022
His foundation is in the holy *m* Ps 87:1 2042
Before the *m* were brought forth, Ps 90:2 2022
the waters stood above the *m* Ps 104:6 2022
They go up by the *m* Ps 104:8 2022
The *m* skipped like rams, and the Ps 114:4 2022
Ye *m*, that ye skipped like rams Ps 114:6 2022
As the *m* are round about Ps 125:2 2022
that descended upon the *m* of Zion Ps 133:3 2042
touch the *m*, and they shall smoke Ps 144:5 2022
maketh grass to grow upon the *m* Ps 147:8 2022
M, and all hills Ps 148:9 2022
Before the *m* were settled, before Prov 8:25 2022
and herbs of the *m* are gathered Prov 27:25 2022
he cometh leaping upon the *m* Song 2:8 2022
a young hart upon the *m* of Bether Song 2:17 2022
from the *m* of the leopards Song 4:8 2042
a young hart upon the *m* of spices Song 8:14 2022
established in the top of the *m* Is 2:2 2022
And upon all the high *m*, and upon Is 2:14 2022
The noise of a multitude in the *m* Is 13:4 2022
upon my *m* tread him under foot Is 14:25 2022
chaff of the *m* before the wind Is 17:13 2022
he lifteth up an ensign on the *m* Is 18:3 2022
together unto the fowls of the *m* Is 18:6 2022
the walls, and of crying to the *m* Is 22:5 2022
the *m* shall be melted with their Is 34:3 2022
I come up to the height of the *m* Is 37:24 2022
and weighed the *m* in scales Is 40:12 2022
thou shalt thresh the *m*, and beat Is 41:15 2022
them shout from the top of the *m* Is 42:11 2022
I will make waste *m* and hills, and Is 42:15 2022
break forth into singing, ye *m* Is 44:23 2022
And I will make all my *m* a way Is 49:11 2022
and break forth into singing, O *m* Is 49:13 2022
How beautiful upon the *m* are the Is 52:7 2022
For the *m* shall depart, and the Is 54:10 2022
the *m* and the hills shall break Is 55:12 2022
that the *m* might flow down at thy Is 64:1 2022
the *m* flowed down at thy presence Is 64:3 2022
have burned incense upon the *m* Is 65:7 2022
out of Judah an inheritor of my *m* Is 65:9 2022
hills, and from the multitude of *m* Jer 3:23 2022
I beheld the *m*, and, lo, they Jer 4:24 2022
For the *m* will I take up a Jer 9:10 2022
your feet stumble upon the dark *m* Jer 13:16 2022
and from the plain, and from the *m* Jer 17:26 2022
plant vines upon the *m* of Samaria Jer 31:5 2022
Judah, and in the cities of the *m* Jer 32:44 2022
In the cities of the *m*, in the Jer 33:13 2022
Surely as Tabor is among the *m* Jer 46:18 2022
have turned them away on the *m* Jer 50:6 2022
they pursued us upon the *m* Lam 4:19 2022
thy face toward the *m* of Israel Eze 6:2 2022
Ye *m* of Israel, hear the word of Eze 6:3 2022
Thus saith the Lord GOD to the *m* Eze 6:3 2022
hill, in all the tops of the *m* Eze 6:13 2022
not the sounding again of the *m* Eze 7:7 2022
shall be on the *m* like doves of Eze 7:16 2022
And hath not eaten upon the *m* Eze 18:6 2022
but even hath eaten upon the *m* Eze 18:11 2022

That hath not eaten upon the *m* Eze 18:15 2022
be heard upon the *m* of Israel Eze 19:9 2022
and in thee they eat upon the *m* Eze 22:9 2022
upon the *m* and in all the valleys Eze 31:12 2022
I will lay thy flesh upon the *m* Eze 32:5 2022
thou swimmest, even to the *m* Eze 32:6 2022
the *m* of Israel shall be desolate Eze 33:28 2022
sheep wandered through all the *m* Eze 34:6 2022
feed them upon the *m* of Israel by Eze 34:13 2022
upon the high *m* of Israel shall Eze 34:14 2022
they feed upon the *m* of Israel Eze 34:14 2022
I will fill his *m* with his slain Eze 35:8 2022
spoken against the *m* of Israel Eze 35:12 2022
prophesy unto the *m* of Israel Eze 36:1 2022
Ye *m* of Israel, hear the word of Eze 36:1 2022
ye *m* of Israel, hear the word of Eze 36:4 2022
Thus saith the Lord GOD to the *m* Eze 36:4 2022
land of Israel, and say unto the *m* Eze 36:6 2022
O *m* of Israel, ye shall shoot Eze 36:8 2022
in the land upon the *m* of Israel Eze 37:22 2022
people, against the *m* of Israel Eze 38:8 2022
the *m* shall be thrown down, and Eze 38:20 2022
against him throughout all my *m* Eze 38:21 2022
bring thee upon the *m* of Israel Eze 39:2 2022
shalt fall upon the *m* of Israel Eze 39:4 2022
sacrifice upon the *m* of Israel Eze 39:17 2022
sacrifice upon the tops of the *m* Hos 4:13 2022
and they shall say to the *m* Hos 10:8 2022
as the morning spread upon the *m* Joel 2:2 2022
on the tops of *m* shall they leap Joel 2:5 2022
that the *m* shall drop down new Joel 3:18 2022
yourselves upon the *m* of Samaria Amos 3:9 2022
For, lo, he that formeth the *m* Amos 4:13 2022
the *m* shall drop sweet wine, and Amos 9:13 2022
went down to the bottoms of the *m* Jonah 2:6 2022
the *m* shall be molten under him, Mic 1:4 2022
established in the top of the *m* Mic 4:1 2022
Arise, contend thou before the *m* Mic 6:1 2022
Hear ye, O *m*, the LORD's Mic 6:2 2022
The *m* quake at him, and the hills Nah 1:5 2022
Behold upon the *m* the feet of him Nah 1:15 2022
people is scattered upon the *m* Nah 3:18 2022
the everlasting *m* were scattered Hab 3:6 2042
The *m* saw thee, and they trembled Hab 3:10 2022
upon the land, and upon the *m* Hag 1:11 2022
chariots out from between two *m* Zec 6:1 2022
and the *m* were *m* of brass Zec 6:1 2022
shall flee to the valley of the *m* Zec 14:5 2022
of the *m* shall reach unto Azal Zec 14:5 2022
And I hated Esau, and laid his *m* Mal 1:3 2022
and nine, and goeth into the *m* Mt 18:12 *3735*
be in Judaea flee into the *m* Mt 24:16 *3735*
night and day, he was in the *m* Mk 5:5 *3735*
m a great herd of swine feeding Mk 5:11 *3735*
that be in Judaea flee to the *m* Mk 13:14 *3735*
which are in Judaea flee to the *m* Lk 21:21 *3735*
shall they begin to say to the *m* Lk 23:30 *3735*
faith, so that I could remove *m* 1Cor 13:2 *3735*
they wandered in deserts, and in *m* Heb 11:38 *3735*
the dens and in the rocks of the *m* Rev 6:15 *3735*
And said to the *m* and rocks, Fall Rev 6:16 *3735*
away, and the *m* were not found Rev 16:20 *3735*
The seven heads are seven *m* Rev 17:9 *3735*

MOUNTED
m up from the earth in my sight Eze 10:19 7426

MOUNTING
for by the *m* up of Luhith with Is 15:5 4608

MOUNTS
Behold the *m*, they are come unto Jer 32:24 5550
which are thrown down by the *m* Jer 33:4 5550
him in the war, by casting up *m* Eze 17:17 5550

MOURN
and Abraham came to *m* for Sarah Gen 23:2 5594
How long wilt thou *m* for Saul 1Sa 16:1 56
with sackcloth, and *m* before Abner 2Sa 3:31 5594
prophet came to the city, to *m* 1Kin 13:29 5594
And all Israel shall *m* for him 1Kin 14:13 5594
m not, nor weep Neh 8:9 56
together to come to *m* with him Job 2:11 5110
that those which *m* may be exalted Job 5:11 6937
and his soul within him shall *m* Job 14:22 56
I *m* in my complaint, and make a Ps 55:2 7300
thou *m* at the last, when thy Prov 5:11 5098
wicked beareth rule, the people *m* Prov 29:2 584
a time to *m*, and a time to dance Eccl 3:4 5594
And her gates shall lament and *m* Is 3:26 56
of Kir-hareseth shall ye *m* Is 16:7 1897
The fishers also shall *m*, and all Is 19:8 578
I did *m* as a dove Is 38:14 1897
like bears, and *m* sore like doves Is 59:11 1897
to comfort all that *m* Is 61:2 57
appoint unto them that *m* in Zion Is 61:3 57
with her, all ye that *m* for her Is 66:10 56
For this shall the earth *m* Jer 4:28 56
How long shall the land *m* Jer 12:4 56
mine heart shall *m* for the men of Jer 48:31 1897
The ways of Zion do *m*, because Lam 1:4 57
buyer rejoice, nor the seller *m* Eze 7:12 56
The king shall *m*, and the prince Eze 7:27 56
yet neither shalt thou *m* nor weep Eze 24:16 5594
ye shall not *m* nor weep Eze 24:23 5594
and *m* one toward another Eze 24:23 5098
and I caused Lebanon to *m* for him Eze 31:15 6937
Therefore shall the land *m* Hos 4:3 56
people thereof shall *m* over it Hos 10:5 56
priests, the LORD's ministers, *m* Joel 1:9 56
of the shepherds shall *m*, and the Amos 1:2 56
every one *m* that dwelleth therein Amos 8:8 56
and all that dwell therein shall *m* Amos 9:5 56
pierced, and they shall *m* for him Zec 12:10 5594
And the land shall *m*, every family Zec 12:12 5594
Blessed are they that *m* Mt 5:4 *3996*
children of the bridechamber *m* Mt 9:15 *3996*
all the tribes of the earth *m* Mt 24:30 *2875*
for ye shall *m* and weep Lk 6:25 *3996*
Be afflicted, and *m*, and weep Jas 4:9 *3996*
earth shall weep and *m* over her Rev 18:11 *3996*

MOURNED
loins, and *m* for his son many days Gen 37:34 56
and the Egyptians *m* for him Gen 50:3 1058
there they *m* with a great and very Gen 50:10 5594
heard these evil tidings, they *m* Ex 33:4 56
and the people *m* greatly Num 14:39 56
they *m* for Aaron thirty days, Num 20:29 1058
nevertheless Samuel *m* for Saul 1Sa 15:35 56
And they *m*, and wept, and fasted 2Sa 1:12 5594
was dead, she *m* for her husband 2Sa 11:26 5594
David *m* for his son every day 2Sa 13:37 56
had a long time *m* for the dead 2Sa 14:2 56
they *m* over him, saying, Alas, my 1Kin 13:30 5594
and all Israel *m* for him, 1Kin 14:18 5594
Ephraim their father *m* many days 1Chr 7:22 56
Judah and Jerusalem *m* for Josiah 2Chr 35:24 56
for he *m* because of the Ezr 10:6 56
m certain days, and fasted, and Neh 1:4 56
m in the fifth and seventh month, Zec 7:5 5594
we have *m* unto you, and ye have Mt 11:17 *2354*
that had been with him, as they *m* Mk 16:10 *3996*
we have *m* to you, and ye have not Lk 7:32 *2354*
puffed up, and have not rather *m* 1Cor 5:2 *3996*

MOURNER
thee, feign thyself to be a *m* 2Sa 14:2 56

MOURNERS
as one that comforteth the *m* Job 29:25 57
the *m* go about the streets Eccl 12:5 5594
comforts unto him and to his *m* Is 57:18 57
be unto them as the bread of *m* Hos 9:4 205

MOURNETH
the king weepeth and *m* for Absalom 2Sa 19:1 56
as one that *m* for his mother Ps 35:14 57
Mine eye *m* by reason of Ps 88:9 1669
The earth *m* and fadeth away, the Is 24:4 56
The new wine *m*, the vine Is 24:7 56
The earth *m* and languisheth Is 33:9 56
and being desolate it *m* unto me Jer 12:11 56
Judah *m*, and the gates thereof Jer 14:2 56
because of swearing the land *m* Jer 23:10 56
The field is wasted, the land *m* Joel 1:10 56
as one *m* for his only son, and Zec 12:10 5594

MOURNFULLY
that we have walked *m* before the Mal 3:14 6941

MOURNING
The days of *m* for my father are Gen 27:41 60
down into the grave unto my son *m* Gen 37:35 57
when the days of his *m* were past Gen 50:4 1086
he made a *m* for his father seven Gen 50:10 60
saw the *m* in the floor of Atad, Gen 50:11 60
is a grievous *m* to the Egyptians Gen 50:11 60
I have not eaten thereof in my *m* Deut 26:14 205
weeping and *m* for Moses were ended Deut 34:8 60
And when the *m* was past, David 2Sa 11:27 60
mourner, and put on now *m* apparel 2Sa 14:2 60
turned into *m* unto all the people 2Sa 19:2 60
there was great *m* among the Jews Est 4:3 60
But Haman hasted to his house *m* Est 6:12 57
to joy, and from *m* into a good day Est 9:22 60
who are ready to raise up their *m* Job 3:8 3382
I went *m* without the sun Job 30:28 6937
My harp also is turned to *m* Job 30:31 60
turned for me my *m* into dancing Ps 30:11 4553
I go *m* all the day long Ps 38:6 6937
why go I *m* because of the Ps 42:9 6937
Why go I *m* because of the Ps 43:2 6937
is better to go to the house of *m* Eccl 7:2 60
of the wise is in the house of *m* Eccl 7:4 60
of hosts call to weeping, and to *m* Is 22:12 4553
and sorrow and *m* shall flee away Is 51:11 585
the days of thy *m* shall be ended Is 60:20 60
for ashes, the oil of joy for *m* Is 61:3 60
make thee *m*, as for an only son, Jer 6:26 60
ye, and call for the *m* women Jer 9:17 6969
Enter not into the house of *m* Jer 16:5 4798
men tear themselves for them in *m* Jer 16:7 60
for I will turn their *m* into joy Jer 31:13 60
in the daughter of Judah *m* Lam 2:5 8386
our dance is turned into *m* Lam 5:15 60
therein lamentations, and *m* Eze 2:10 1899
of the valleys, all of them *m* Eze 7:16 1993
make no *m* for the dead, bind the Eze 24:17 60
down to the grave I caused a *m* Eze 31:15 56
I Daniel was *m* three full weeks Dan 10:2 56
and with weeping, and with *m* Joel 2:12 4553
shall call the husbandman to *m* Amos 5:16 60
And I will turn your feasts into *m* Amos 8:10 60
make it as the *m* of an only son Amos 8:10 60
the dragons, and *m* as the owls Mic 1:8 60
not forth in the *m* of Beth-ezel Mic 1:11 4553
there be a great *m* in Jerusalem Zec 12:11 4553
as the *m* of Hadadrimmon in the Zec 12:11 4553
and weeping, and great *m*, Rachel Mt 2:18 *3602*
us your earnest desire, your *m* 2Cor 7:7 *3602*
let your laughter be turned to *m* Jas 4:9 *3997*
come in one day, death, and *m* Rev 18:8 *3997*

MOUSE
the weasel, and the *m*, and the Lev 11:29 5909
and the abomination, and the *m* Is 66:17 5909

MOUTH
which hath opened her *m* to Gen 4:11 6310
in her *m* was an olive leaf pluckt Gen 8:11 6310
the damsel, and enquire at her *m* Gen 24:57 6310
great stone was upon the well's *m* Gen 29:2 6310
the stone from the well's *m* Gen 29:3 6310
upon the well's *m* in his place Gen 29:3 6310
roll the stone from the well's *m* Gen 29:8 6310
the stone from the well's *m* Gen 29:10 6310
behold, it was in his sack's *m* Gen 42:27 6310
again in the *m* of your sacks Gen 43:12 6310
money was in the *m* of his sack Gen 43:21 6310
every man's money in his sack's *m* Gen 44:1 6310
in the sack's *m* of the youngest, Gen 44:2 6310
that it is my *m* that speaketh Gen 45:12 6310
unto him, Who hath made man's *m* Ex 4:11 6310
go, and I will be with thy *m* Ex 4:12 6310
unto him, and put words in his *m* Ex 4:15 6310
be with thy *m*, and with his *m* Ex 4:15 6310
shall be to thee instead of a *m* Ex 4:16 6310
the LORD's law may be in thy *m* Ex 13:9 6310
let it be heard out of thy *m* Ex 23:13 6310
With him will I speak *m* to *m* Num 12:8 6310
With him will I speak *m* to *m* Num 12:8 6310
thing, and the earth open her *m* Num 16:30 6310
And the earth opened her *m* Num 16:32 6310
the LORD opened the *m* of the ass Num 22:28 6310
the word that God putteth in my *m* Num 22:38 6310
the LORD put a word in Balaam's *m* Num 23:5 6310
which the LORD hath put in my *m* Num 23:12 6310
Balaam, and put a word in his *m* Num 23:16 6310
And the earth opened her *m* Num 26:10 6310
all that proceedeth out of his *m* Num 30:2 6310
hath proceeded out of your *m* Num 32:24 6310
to death by the *m* of witnesses Num 35:30 6310
the *m* of the LORD doth man live Deut 8:3 6310
how the earth opened her *m* Deut 11:6 6310
At the *m* of two witnesses, or Deut 17:6 6310
but at the *m* of one witness he Deut 17:6 6310
and will put my words in his *m* Deut 18:18 6310
at the *m* of two witnesses Deut 19:15 6310
or at the *m* of three witnesses, Deut 19:15 6310
thou hast promised with thy *m* Deut 23:23 6310
is very nigh unto thee, in thy *m* Deut 30:14 6310
hear, O earth, the words of my *m* Deut 32:1 6310
law shall not depart out of thy *m* Josh 1:8 6310
any word proceed out of your *m* Josh 6:10 6310
not counsel at the *m* of the LORD Josh 9:14 6310
stones upon the *m* of the cave Josh 10:18 6310
Open the *m* of the cave, and bring Josh 10:22 6310
laid great stones in the cave's *m* Josh 10:27 6310
putting their hand to their *m* Judg 7:6 6310
unto him, Where is now thy *m* Judg 9:38 6310
I have opened my *m* unto the LORD Judg 11:35 6310
hast opened thy *m* unto the LORD Judg 11:36 6310
which hath proceeded out of thy *m* Judg 11:36 6310
peace, lay thine hand upon thy *m* Judg 18:19 6310
the LORD, that Eli marked her *m* 1Sa 1:12 6310
my *m* is enlarged over mine 1Sa 2:1 6310
not arrogancy come out of your *m* 1Sa 2:3 6310
but no man put his hand to his *m* 1Sa 14:26 6310
and put his hand to his *m* 1Sa 14:27 6310
him, and delivered it out of his *m* 1Sa 17:35 6310
for thy *m* hath testified against 2Sa 1:16 6310
So Joab put the words in her *m* 2Sa 14:3 6310
words in the *m* of thine handmaid 2Sa 14:19 6310
a covering over the well's *m* 2Sa 17:19 6310
alone, there is tidings in his *m* 2Sa 18:25 6310
and fire out of his *m* devoured 2Sa 22:9 6310
the *m* of it within the chapiter 1Kin 7:31 6310
but the *m* thereof was round after 1Kin 7:31 6310
also upon the *m* of it were 1Kin 7:31 6310
with his *m* unto David my father 1Kin 8:15 6310
thou spakest also with thy *m* 1Kin 8:24 6310
hast disobeyed the *m* of the LORD 1Kin 13:21 6310
of the LORD in thy *m* is truth 1Kin 17:24 6310
every *m* which hath not kissed him 1Kin 19:18 6310
good unto the king with one *m* 1Kin 22:13 6310
in the *m* of all his prophets 1Kin 22:22 6310
the *m* of all these thy prophets 1Kin 22:23 6310
and put his *m* upon his *m* 2Kin 4:34 6310
and the judgments of his *m* 1Chr 16:12 6310
with his *m* to my father David 2Chr 6:4 6310
and spakest with thy *m*, and hast 2Chr 6:15 6310
in the *m* of all his prophets 2Chr 18:21 6310
in the *m* of these thy prophets 2Chr 18:22 6310
words of Necho from the *m* of God 2Chr 35:22 6310
speaking from the *m* of the LORD 2Chr 36:12 6310
of the LORD by the *m* of Jeremiah 2Chr 36:21 6310
by the *m* of Jeremiah might be 2Chr 36:22 6310
the word of the LORD by the *m* of Ezr 1:1 6310
not thy manna from their *m* Neh 9:20 6310
the word went out of the king's *m* Est 7:8 6310
After this opened Job his *m* Job 3:1 6310
poor from the sword, from their *m* Job 5:15 6310
hope, and iniquity stoppeth her *m* Job 5:16 6310
Therefore I will not refrain my *m* Job 7:11 6310
of thy *m* be like a strong wind Job 8:2 6310
Till he fill thy *m* with laughing Job 8:21 6310
mine own *m* shall condemn me Job 9:20 6310
and the *m* taste his meat Job 12:11 2441
For thy *m* uttereth thine iniquity Job 15:5 6310
Thine own *m* condemneth thee, and Job 15:6 6310
such words go out of thy *m* Job 15:13 6310
breath of his *m* shall he go away Job 15:30 6310
I would strengthen you with my *m* Job 16:5 6310
have gaped upon me with their *m* Job 16:10 6310
I intreated him with my *m* Job 19:16 6310
wickedness be sweet in his *m* Job 20:12 6310
but keep it still within his *m* Job 20:13 2441
and lay your hand upon your *m* Job 21:5 6310
I pray thee, the law from his *m* Job 22:22 6310
him, and fill my *m* with arguments Job 23:4 6310
his *m* more than my necessary food Job 23:12 6310
and laid their hand on their *m* Job 29:9 6310
cleaved to the roof of their *m* Job 29:10 2441
they opened their *m* wide as for Job 29:23 6310
or my *m* hath kissed my hand Job 31:27 6310
(Neither have I suffered my *m* to Job 31:30 2441
in the *m* of these three men Job 32:5 6310

Behold, now I have opened my *m* Job 33:2 6310
my tongue hath spoken in my *m* Job 33:2 2441
words, as the *m* tasteth meat Job 34:3 2441
doth Job open his *m* in vain Job 35:16 6310
the sound that goeth out of his *m* Job 37:2 6310
I will lay mine hand upon my *m* Job 40:4 6310
he can draw up Jordan into his *m* Job 40:23 6310
Out of his *m* go burning lamps, and Job 41:19 6310
and a flame goeth out of his *m* Job 41:21 6310
is no faithfulness in their *m* Ps 5:9 6310
Out of the *m* of babes and Ps 8:2 6310
His *m* is full of cursing and Ps 10:7 6310
that my *m* shall not transgress Ps 17:3 6310
with their *m* they speak proudly Ps 17:10 6310
and fire out of his *m* devoured Ps 18:8 6310
Let the words of my *m*, and the Ps 19:14 6310
Save me from the lion's *m* Ps 22:21 6310
whose *m* must be held in with bit Ps 32:9 5716
of them by the breath of his *m* Ps 33:6 6310
shall continually be in my *m* Ps 34:1 6310
opened their *m* wide against me Ps 35:21 6310
The words of his *m* are iniquity Ps 36:3 6310
The *m* of the righteous speaketh Ps 37:30 6310
a dumb man that openeth not his *m* Ps 38:13 6310
in whose *m* are no reproofs Ps 38:14 6310
I will keep my *m* with a bridle Ps 39:1 6310
I was dumb, I opened not my *m* Ps 39:9 6310
And he hath put a new song in my *m* Ps 40:3 6310
My *m* shall speak of wisdom Ps 49:3 6310
take my covenant in thy *m* Ps 50:16 6310
Thou givest thy *m* to evil Ps 50:19 6310
my *m* shall shew forth thy praise Ps 51:15 6310
give ear to the words of my *m* Ps 54:2 6310
The words of his *m* were smoother Ps 55:21 6310
their teeth, O God, in their *m* Ps 58:6 6310
they belch out with their *m* Ps 59:7 6310
For the sin of their *m* and the Ps 59:12 6310
they bless with their *m*, but they Ps 62:4 6310
my *m* shall praise thee with Ps 63:5 6310
but the *m* of them that speak lies Ps 63:11 6310
my *m* hath spoken, when I was in Ps 66:14 6310
I cried unto him with my *m* Ps 66:17 6310
not the pit shut her *m* upon me Ps 69:15 6310
Let my *m* be filled with thy Ps 71:8 6310
My *m* shall shew forth thy Ps 71:15 6310
They set their *m* against the Ps 73:9 6310
your ears to the words of my *m* Ps 78:1 6310
I will open my *m* in a parable Ps 78:2 6310
they did flatter him with their *m* Ps 78:36 6310
open thy *m* wide, and I will fill Ps 81:10 6310
with my *m* will I make known thy Ps 89:1 6310
satisfieth thy *m* with good things Ps 103:5 5716
and the judgments of his *m* Ps 105:5 6310
and all iniquity shall stop her *m* Ps 107:42 6310
For the *m* of the wicked and the Ps 109:2 6310
the *m* of the deceitful are opened Ps 109:2 6310
greatly praise the LORD with my *m* Ps 109:30 6310
all the judgments of thy *m* Ps 119:13 6310
word of truth utterly out of my *m* Ps 119:43 6310
The law of thy *m* is better unto Ps 119:72 6310
I keep the testimony of thy *m* Ps 119:88 6310
yea, sweeter than honey to my *m* Ps 119:103 6310
the freewill offerings of my *m* Ps 119:108 6310
I opened my *m*, and panted Ps 119:131 6310
Then was our *m* filled with Ps 126:2 6310
tongue cleave to the roof of my *m* Ps 137:6 2441
when they hear the words of thy *m* Ps 138:4 6310
Set a watch, O LORD, before my *m* Ps 141:3 6310
are scattered at the grave's *m* Ps 141:7 6310
Whose *m* speaketh vanity, and their Ps 144:8 6310
whose *m* speaketh vanity, and their Ps 144:11 6310
My *m* shall speak the praise of Ps 145:21 6310
high praises of God be in their *m* Ps 149:6 1627
out of his *m* cometh knowledge and Prov 2:6 6310
decline from the words of my *m* Prov 4:5 6310
Put away from thee a froward *m* Prov 4:24 6310
her *m* is smoother than oil Prov 5:3 2441
depart not from the words of my *m* Prov 5:7 6310
snared with the words of thy *m* Prov 6:2 6310
art taken with the words of thy *m* Prov 6:2 6310
man, walketh with a froward *m* Prov 6:12 6310
and attend to the words of my *m* Prov 7:24 6310
For my *m* shall speak truth Prov 8:7 2441
All the words of my *m* are in Prov 8:8 6310
and the evil way, and the froward *m* Prov 8:13 6310
covereth the *m* of the wicked Prov 10:6 6310
The *m* of a righteous man is a Prov 10:11 6310
covereth the *m* of the wicked Prov 10:11 6310
but the *m* of the foolish is near Prov 10:14 6310
The *m* of the just bringeth forth Prov 10:31 6310
but the *m* of the wicked speaketh Prov 10:32 6310
An hypocrite with his *m* Prov 11:9 6310
overthrown by the *m* of the wicked Prov 11:11 6310
but the *m* of the upright shall Prov 12:6 6310
with good by the fruit of his *m* Prov 12:14 6310
eat good by the fruit of his *m* Prov 13:2 6310
keepeth his *m* keepeth his life Prov 13:3 6310
In the *m* of the foolish is a rod Prov 14:3 6310
but the *m* of fools poureth out Prov 15:2 6310
but the *m* of fools feedeth on Prov 15:14 6310
hath joy by the answer of his *m* Prov 15:23 6310
but the *m* of the wicked poureth Prov 15:28 6310
his *m* transgresseth not in Prov 16:10 6310
heart of the wise teacheth his *m* Prov 16:23 6310
for his *m* craveth it of him Prov 16:26 6310
of a man's *m* are as deep waters Prov 18:4 6310
his *m* calleth for strokes Prov 18:6 6310
A fool's *m* is his destruction, and Prov 18:7 6310
satisfied with the fruit of his *m* Prov 18:20 6310
much as bring it to his *m* again Prov 19:24 6310
the *m* of the wicked devoureth Prov 19:28 6310
but afterwards his *m* shall be Prov 20:17 6310
Whoso keepeth his *m* and his tongue Prov 21:23 6310
The *m* of strange women is a deep Prov 22:14 6310
he openeth not his *m* in the gate Prov 24:7 6310
so is a parable in the *m* of fools Prov 26:7 6310
so is a parable in the *m* of fools Prov 26:9 6310
him to bring it again to his *m* Prov 26:15 6310
and a flattering *m* worketh ruin Prov 26:28 6310
praise thee, and not thine own *m* Prov 27:2 6310
she eateth, and wipeth her *m* Prov 30:20 6310
evil, lay thine hand upon thy *m* Prov 30:32 6310
Open thy *m* for the dumb in the Prov 31:8 6310
Open thy *m*, judge righteously, and Prov 31:9 6310
She openeth her *m* with wisdom Prov 31:26 6310
Be not rash with thy *m*, and let Eccl 5:2 6310
Suffer not thy *m* to cause thy Eccl 5:6 6310
the labour of man is for his *m* Eccl 6:7 6310
of a wise man's *m* are gracious Eccl 10:12 6310
the words of his *m* is foolishness Eccl 10:13 6310
kiss me with the kisses of his *m* Song 1:2 6310
His *m* is most sweet Song 5:16 2441
the roof of thy *m* like the best Song 7:9 2441
for the *m* of the LORD hath spoken Is 1:20 6310
opened her *m* without measure Is 5:14 6310
And he laid it upon my *m*, and said, Is 6:7 6310
shall devour Israel with open *m* Is 9:12 6310
and every *m* speaketh folly Is 9:17 6310
moved the wing, or opened the *m* Is 10:14 6310
the earth with the rod of his *m* Is 11:4 6310
by the *m* of the brooks, and every Is 19:7 6310
people draw near me with their *m* Is 29:13 6310
Egypt, and have not asked at my *m* Is 30:2 6310
for my *m* it hath commanded, and Is 34:16 6310
for the *m* of the LORD hath spoken Is 40:5 6310
gone out of my *m* in righteousness Is 45:23 6310
and they went forth out of my *m* Is 48:3 6310
he hath made my *m* like a sharp Is 49:2 6310
And I have put my words in thy *m* Is 51:16 6310
yet he opened not his *m* Is 53:7 6310
is dumb, so he openeth not his *m* Is 53:7 6310
neither was any deceit in his *m* Is 53:9 6310
be that goeth forth out of my *m* Is 55:11 6310
against whom make ye a wide *m* Is 57:4 6310
for the *m* of the LORD hath spoken Is 58:14 6310
words which I have put in thy *m* Is 59:21 6310
shall not depart out of thy *m* Is 59:21 6310
nor out of the *m* of thy seed Is 59:21 6310
nor out of the *m* of thy seed's Is 59:21 6310
which the *m* of the LORD shall Is 62:2 6310
forth his hand, and touched my *m* Jer 1:9 6310
I have put my words in thy *m* Jer 1:9 6310
will make my words in thy *m* fire Jer 5:14 6310
and is cut off from their *m* Jer 7:28 6310
to his neighbour with his *m* Jer 9:8 6310
who is he to whom the *m* of the Jer 9:12 6310
ear receive the word of his *m* Jer 9:20 6310
thou art near in their *m*, and far Jer 12:2 6310
the vile, thou shalt be as my *m* Jer 15:19 6310
and not out of the *m* of the LORD Jer 23:16 6310
shall speak with him *m* to *m* Jer 32:4 6310
shall speak with thee *m* to *m* Jer 34:3 6310
Baruch wrote from the *m* of Jer 36:4 6310
which thou hast written from my *m* Jer 36:6 6310
write all these words at his *m* Jer 36:17 6310
these words unto me with his *m* Jer 36:18 6310
Baruch wrote at the *m* of Jeremiah Jer 36:27 6310
who wrote therein from the *m* of Jer 36:32 6310
goeth forth out of our own *m* Jer 44:17 6310
shall no more be named in the *m* Jer 44:26 6310
in a book at the *m* of Jeremiah Jer 45:1 6310
nest in the sides of the hole's *m* Jer 48:28 6310
I will bring forth out of his *m* Jer 51:44 6310
have opened their *m* against thee Lam 2:16 6310
He putteth his *m* in the dust Lam 3:29 6310
Out of the *m* of the most High Lam 3:38 6310
to the roof of his *m* for thirst Lam 4:4 2441
open thy *m*, and eat that I give Eze 2:8 6310
So I opened my *m*, and he caused me Eze 3:2 6310
it was in my *m* as honey for Eze 3:3 6310
therefore hear the word at my *m* Eze 3:17 6310
cleave to the roof of thy *m* Eze 3:26 2441
with thee, I will open thy *m* Eze 3:27 6310
there abominable flesh into my *m* Eze 4:14 6310
by thy *m* in the day of thy pride Eze 16:56 6310
never open thy *m* any more because Eze 16:63 6310
to open the *m* in the slaughter, Eze 21:22 6310
In that day shall thy *m* be opened Eze 24:27 6310
of the *m* in the midst of them Eze 29:21 6310
thou shalt hear the word at my *m* Eze 33:7 6310
and had opened my *m*, until he came Eze 33:22 6310
my *m* was opened, and I was no more Eze 33:22 6310
for with their *m* they shew much Eze 33:31 6310
deliver my flock from their *m* Eze 34:10 6310
Thus with your *m* ye have boasted Eze 35:13 6310
m of the burning fiery furnace Dan 3:26 8651
the word was in the king's *m* Dan 4:31 6433
and laid upon the *m* of the den Dan 6:17 6433
it had three ribs in the *m* of it Dan 7:5 6433
a *m* speaking great things Dan 7:8 6433
a *m* that spake very great things, Dan 7:20 6433
came flesh nor wine in my *m* Dan 10:3 6310
then I opened my *m*, and spake, and Dan 10:16 6310
the names of Baalim out of her *m* Hos 2:17 6310
slain them by the words of my *m* Hos 6:5 6310
Set the trumpet to thy *m* Hos 8:1 2441
for it is cut off from your *m* Joel 1:5 6310
out of the *m* of the lion two legs Amos 3:12 6310
for the *m* of the LORD of hosts Mic 4:4 6310
tongue is deceitful in their *m* Mic 6:12 6310
keep the doors of thy *m* from her Mic 7:5 6310
shall lay their hand upon their *m* Mic 7:16 6310
even fall into the *m* of the eater Nah 3:12 6310
tongue be found in their *m* Zeph 3:13 6310
weight of lead upon the *m* thereof Zec 5:8 6310
words by the *m* of the prophets Zec 8:9 6310
take away his blood out of his *m* Zec 9:7 6310
shall consume away in their *m* Zec 14:12 6310
The law of truth was in his *m* Mal 2:6 6310
they should seek the law at his *m* Mal 2:7 6310
proceedeth out of the *m* of God Mt 4:4 4750
And he opened his *m*, and taught Mt 5:2 4750
of the heart the *m* speaketh Mt 12:34 4750
I will open my *m* in parables Mt 13:35 4750
draweth nigh unto me with their *m* Mt 15:8 4750
goeth into the *m* defileth a man Mt 15:11 4750
that which cometh out of the *m* Mt 15:11 4750
in at the *m* goeth into the belly Mt 15:17 4750
the *m* come forth from the heart Mt 15:18 4750
and when thou hast opened his *m* Mt 17:27 4750
that in the *m* of two or three Mt 18:16 4750
never read, Out of the *m* of babes Mt 21:16 4750
his *m* was opened immediately, and Lk 1:64 4750
As he spake by the *m* of his holy Lk 1:70 4750
which proceeded out of his *m* Lk 4:22 4750
of the heart his *m* speaketh Lk 6:45 4750
to catch something out of his *m* Lk 11:54 4750
Out of thine own *m* will I judge Lk 19:22 4750
For I will give you a *m* and wisdom Lk 21:15 4750
ourselves have heard of his own *m* Lk 22:71 4750
upon hyssop, and put it to his *m* Jn 19:29 4750
by the *m* of David spake before Acts 1:16 4750
by the *m* of all his prophets Acts 3:18 4750
which God hath spoken by the *m* of Acts 3:21 4750
Who by the *m* of thy servant David Acts 4:25 4750
shearer, so opened he not his *m* Acts 8:32 4750
Then Philip opened his *m*, and Acts 8:35 4750
Then Peter opened his *m*, and said, Acts 10:34 4750
at any time entered into my *m* Acts 11:8 4750
that the Gentiles by my *m* should Acts 15:7 4750
tell you the same things by *m* Acts 15:27 3056
Paul was now about to open his *m* Acts 18:14 4750
shouldest hear the voice of his *m* Acts 22:14 4750
by him to smite him on the *m* Acts 23:2 4750
Whose *m* is full of cursing and Rom 3:14 4750
that every *m* may be stopped, and Rom 3:19 4750
word is nigh thee, even in thy *m* Rom 10:8 4750
confess with thy *m* the Lord Jesus Rom 10:9 4750
with the *m* confession is made Rom 10:10 4750
one *m* glorify God, even the Rom 15:6 4750
Thou shalt not muzzle the *m* of 1Cor 9:9
our *m* is open unto you, our heart 2Cor 6:11 4750
In the *m* of two or three 2Cor 13:1 4750
proceed out of your *m*, but that Eph 4:29 4750
me, that I may open my *m* boldly Eph 6:19 4750
communication out of your *m* Col 3:8 4750
consume with the spirit of his *m* 2Th 2:8 4750
out of the *m* of the lion 2Ti 4:17 4750
Out of the same *m* proceedeth Jas 3:10 4750
neither was guile found in his *m* 1Pet 2:22 4750
their *m* speaketh great swelling Jude 16 4750
out of his *m* went a sharp Rev 1:16 4750
them with the sword of my *m* Rev 2:16 4750
hot, I will spue thee out of my *m* Rev 3:16 4750
For their power is in their *m* Rev 9:19 4750
shall be in thy *m* sweet as honey Rev 10:9 4750
it was in my *m* sweet as honey Rev 10:10 4750
fire proceedeth out of their *m* Rev 11:5 4750
his *m* water as a flood after the Rev 12:15 4750
woman, and the earth opened her *m* Rev 12:16 4750
the dragon cast out of his *m* Rev 12:16 4750
his *m* as the *m* of a lion Rev 13:2 4750
and his *m* as the *m* of a lion Rev 13:2 4750
him a *m* speaking great things Rev 13:5 4750
he opened his *m* in blasphemy Rev 13:6 4750
in their *m* was found no guile Rev 14:5 4750
come out of the *m* of the dragon Rev 16:13 4750
out of the *m* of the beast Rev 16:13 4750
out of the *m* of the false prophet Rev 16:13 4750
out of his *m* goeth a sharp sword, Rev 19:15 4750
sword proceeded out of his *m* Rev 19:21 4750

MOUTHS

which we found in our sacks' *m* Gen 44:8 6310
put it in their *m*, that this song Deut 31:19 6310
out of the *m* of their seed Deut 31:21 6310
They gaped upon me with their *m* Ps 22:13 6310
their meat was yet in their *m* Ps 78:30 6310
They have *m*, but they speak not Ps 115:5 6310
They have *m*, but they speak not Ps 135:16 6310
is there any breath in their *m* Ps 135:17 6310
kings shall shut their *m* at him Is 52:15 6310
have both spoken with your *m* Jer 44:25 6310
have opened their *m* against us Lam 3:46 6310
angel, and hath shut the lions' *m* Dan 6:22 6433
he that putteth not into their *m* Mic 3:5 6310
Whose *m* must be stopped, who Titus 1:11 *1993*
promises, stopped the *m* of lions Heb 11:33 4750
we put bits in the horses' *m* Jas 3:3 4750
and out of their *m* issued fire Rev 9:17 4750
which issued out of their *m* Rev 9:18 4750

MOVE

shall not a dog *m* his tongue Ex 11:7 2782
of all that *m* in the waters, and Lev 11:10 8318
but thou shalt not *m* a sickle Deut 23:25 5130
I will *m* them to jealousy with Deut 32:21
m him at times in the camp of Dan Judg 13:25 6470
place of their own, and *m* no more 2Sa 7:10 7264
m any more out of the land which 2Kin 21:8 5110
let no man *m* his bones 2Kin 23:18 5128
and with hammers, that it *m* not Jer 10:4 6328
they shall *m* out of their holes Mic 7:17 7264
but they themselves will not *m* Mt 23:4 *2795*
For in him we live, and *m*, and have Acts 17:28 *2795*
But none of these things *m* me Acts 20:24

MOVEABLE

the path of life, her ways are *m* Prov 5:6 5128

MOVED

the Spirit of God *m* upon the face Gen 1:2 7363
flesh died that *m* upon the earth Gen 7:21 7430
They have *m* me to jealousy with Deut 32:21

M

none *m* his tongue against any of Josh 10:21 2782
that she *m* him to ask of her Josh 15:18 5496
that she *m* him to ask of her Judg 1:14 5496
all the city was *m* about them Ruth 1:19 1949
only her lips *m*, but her voice 1Sa 1:13 5128
And the king was much *m*, and went 2Sa 18:33 7264
the foundations of heaven *m* 2Sa 22:8 7264
he *m* David against them to say, 2Sa 24:1 5496
shall be stable, that it be not *m* 1Chr 16:30 4131
place, and shall be *m* no more 1Chr 17:9 7264
God *m* them to depart from him 2Chr 18:31 5496
that they have *m* sedition within Ezr 4:15 5648
nor *m* for him, he was full of Est 5:9 2111
and is *m* out of his place Job 37:1 5425
they cannot be *m* Job 41:23 4131
in his heart, I shall not be *m* Ps 10:6 4131
trouble me rejoice when I am *m* Ps 13:4 4131
these things shall never be *m* Ps 15:5 4131
my right hand, I shall not be *m* Ps 16:8 4131
foundations also of the hills *m* Ps 18:7 7264
the most High he shall not be *m* Ps 21:7 4131
I said, I shall never be *m* Ps 30:6 4131
she shall not be *m* Ps 46:5 4131
raged, the kingdoms were *m* Ps 46:6 4131
suffer the righteous to be *m* Ps 55:22 4131
I shall not be greatly *m* Ps 62:2 4131
I shall not be *m* Ps 62:6 4131
and suffereth not our feet to be *m* Ps 66:9 4132
even Sinai itself was *m* at the Ps 68:8
m him to jealousy with their Ps 78:58
stablished, that it cannot be *m* Ps 93:1 4131
that it shall not be *m* Ps 96:10 4131
let the earth be *m* Ps 99:1 5120
Surely he shall not be *m* for ever Ps 112:6 4131
will not suffer thy foot to be *m* Ps 121:3 4132
of the righteous shall not be *m* Prov 12:3 4131
door, and my bowels were *m* for him Song 5:4 1993
the posts of the door *m* at the Is 6:4 5128
And his heart was *m*, and the heart Is 7:2 5128
of the wood are *m* with the wind Is 7:2 5128
and there was none that *m* the wing Is 10:14 5074
Hell from beneath is *m* for thee Is 14:9 7264
Egypt shall be *m* at his presence Is 19:1 5128
the earth is *m* exceedingly Is 24:19 4132
graven image, that shall not be *m* Is 40:20 4131
nails, that it should not be *m* Is 41:7 4131
and all the hills *m* lightly Jer 4:24 7043
And they shall drink, and be *m* Jer 25:16 1607
whose waters are *m* as the rivers Jer 46:7 1607
his waters are *m* like the rivers Jer 46:8 1607
The earth is *m* at the noise of Jer 49:21 7493
taking of Babylon the earth is *m* Jer 50:46 7493
he was *m* with choler against him, Dan 8:7
the south shall be *m* with choler Dan 11:11
he was *m* with compassion on them, Mt 9:36 *4697*
was *m* with compassion toward them Mt 14:14 *4697*
servant was *m* with compassion Mt 18:27 *4697*
they were *m* with indignation Mt 20:24 *23*
Jerusalem, all the city was *m* Mt 21:10 *4579*
m with compassion, put forth his Mk 1:41 *4697*
was *m* with compassion toward them Mk 6:34 *4697*
the chief priests *m* the people Mk 15:11 *383*
hand, that I should not be *m* Acts 2:25 *4531*
m with envy, sold Joseph into Acts 7:9 *2206*
m with envy, took unto them Acts 17:5 *2206*
And all the city was *m*, and the Acts 21:30 *2795*
be not *m* away from the hope of Col 1:23 *3334*
should be *m* by these afflictions 1Th 3:3 *4525*
m with fear, prepared an ark to Heb 11:7 *2125*
a kingdom which cannot be *m* Heb 12:28 *761*
as they were *m* by the Holy Ghost 2Pet 1:21 *5342*
island were *m* out of their places Rev 6:14 *2795*

MOVEDST
although thou *m* me against him, Job 2:3 5496

MOVER
a *m* of sedition among all the Acts 24:5 *2795*

MOVETH
and every living creature that *m* Gen 1:21 7430
thing that *m* upon the earth Gen 1:28 7430
upon all that *m* upon the earth, Gen 9:2 7430
creature that *m* in the waters Lev 11:46 7430
He *m* his tail like a cedar Job 40:17 2654
and every thing that *m* therein Ps 69:34 7430
the cup, when it *m* itself aright Prov 23:31 1980
every thing that liveth, which *m* Eze 47:9 8317

MOVING
the *m* creature that hath life Gen 1:20 8318
Every *m* thing that liveth shall Gen 9:3 7430
the *m* of my lips should asswage Job 16:5 5205
m his lips he bringeth evil to Prov 16:30 7169
waiting for the *m* of the water Jn 5:3 *2796*

MOWER
Wherewith the *m* filleth not his Ps 129:7 7114

MOWINGS
latter growth after the king's *m* Amos 7:1 1488

MOWN
down like rain upon the *m* grass Ps 72:6 1488

MOZA (*mo'-zah*)
1. A son of Caleb.
concubine, bare Haran, and *M* 1Chr 2:46 4162
2. Descendant of King Saul.
and Zimri begat *M*, 1Chr 8:36 4162
And *M* begat Binea 1Chr 8:37 4162
and Zimri begat *M* 1Chr 9:42 4162
And *M* begat Binea 1Chr 9:43 4162

MOZAH (*mo'-zah*) *A city in Benjamin.*
And Mizpeh, and Chephirah, and *M* Josh 18:26 4681

MUCH
for as *m* money as it is worth he Gen 23:9 7227
for thou art *m* mightier than we Gen 26:16 3966
had *m* cattle, and maidservants, and Gen 30:43 7227
Ask me never so *m* dowry and gift, Gen 34:12
as the sand of the sea, very *m* Gen 41:49 7235
five times so *m* as any of theirs Gen 43:34 7235
as *m* as they can carry, and put Gen 44:1 834
this day, to save *m* people alive Gen 50:20 7227
and herds, even very *m* cattle Ex 12:38 3515
It is a night to be *m* observed Ex 12:42
remained not so *m* as one of them Ex 14:28 5704
twice as *m* as they gather daily Ex 16:5 834
that gathered *m* had nothing over Ex 16:18 7235
they gathered twice as *m* bread Ex 16:22
and of sweet cinnamon half so *m* Ex 30:23 4276
The people bring *m* more than Ex 36:5 7235
all the work to make it, and too *m* Ex 36:7 3498
Aaron have, one as *m* as another Lev 7:10
scab spread *m* abroad in the skin Lev 13:7 6581
if it spread *m* abroad in the skin Lev 13:22 6581
if it be spread *m* abroad in the Lev 13:27 6581
But if the scall spread *m* in the Lev 13:35 6581
if he be poor, and cannot get so *m* Lev 14:21
unto them, Ye take too *m* upon you Num 16:3 7227
ye take too *m* upon you, ye sons Num 16:7 7227
out against him with *m* people Num 20:20 3515
the soul of the people was *m* Num 21:4 7114
and *m* people of Israel died Num 21:6 7227
not so *m* as a footbreadth Deut 2:5 5704
(for I know that ye have *m* cattle Deut 3:19 7227
Thou shalt carry *m* seed out into Deut 28:38 7227
how *m* more after my death Deut 31:27 7227
m people, even as the sand that Josh 11:4 7227
yet very *m* land to be possessed Josh 13:1 7235
of Judah was too *m* for them Josh 19:9 7227
Return with *m* riches unto your Josh 22:8 7227
your tents, and with very *m* cattle Josh 22:8 7227
with iron, and with very *m* raiment Josh 22:8 7235
for it grieveth me *m* for your Ruth 1:13 3966
then take as *m* as thy soul 1Sa 2:16
How *m* more, if haply the people 1Sa 14:30 637
a *m* greater slaughter among the 1Sa 14:30
so that his name was *m* set by 1Sa 18:30 3966
Saul's son delighted *m* in David 1Sa 19:2 3966
LORD do so and *m* more to Jonathan 1Sa 20:13 3254
how *m* more then if we come to 1Sa 23:3 637
as thy life was *m* set by this day 1Sa 26:24 1431
so let my life be *m* set by in the 1Sa 26:24 1431
How *m* more, when wicked men have 2Sa 4:11 637
king David took exceeding *m* brass 2Sa 8:8 7235
there came *m* people by the way of 2Sa 13:34 7227
so *m* praised as Absalom for his 2Sa 14:25 3966
how *m* more now may this Benjamite 2Sa 16:11 637
shall not be left so *m* as one 2Sa 17:12 1571
And the king was *m* moved, and went 2Sa 18:33
and understanding exceeding *m* 1Kin 4:29 7235
how *m* less this house that I have 1Kin 8:27 637
that bare spices, and very *m* gold 1Kin 10:2 7227
It is too *m* for you to go up to 1Kin 12:28 7227
how *m* rather then, when he saith 2Kin 5:13
but Jehu shall serve him *m* 2Kin 10:18 7235
there was *m* money in the chest 2Kin 12:10 7225
he wrought *m* wickedness in the 2Kin 21:6 7235
shed innocent blood very *m* 2Kin 21:16 7235
brought David very *m* brass 1Chr 18:8 7227
exceeding *m* spoil out of the city 1Chr 20:2 7235
brought *m* cedar wood to David 1Chr 22:4 7230
because thou hast shed *m* blood 1Chr 22:8 7227
Lebanon, as *m* as thou shalt need 2Chr 2:16 3605
how *m* less this house which I 2Chr 6:18 637
and they carried away very *m* spoil 2Chr 14:13 7235
was exceeding *m* spoil in them 2Chr 14:14 7235
he had *m* business in the cities 2Chr 17:13 7227
of the spoil, it was so *m* 2Chr 20:25 7227
they saw that there was *m* money 2Chr 24:11 7227
to give thee *m* more than this 2Chr 25:9 7235
thousand of them, and took *m* spoil 2Chr 25:13 7227
for he had *m* cattle, both in the 2Chr 26:10 7227
on the wall of Ophel he built *m* 2Chr 27:3 7230
So *m* did the children of Ammon 2Chr 27:5 1931
took also away *m* spoil from them, 2Chr 28:8 7227
m people to keep the feast of 2Chr 30:13 7227
was gathered *m* people together 2Chr 32:4 7227
of Assyria come, and find *m* water 2Chr 32:4 7227
how *m* less shall your God deliver 2Chr 32:15
Hezekiah had exceeding *m* riches 2Chr 32:27 7235
had given him substance very *m* 2Chr 32:29 7227
he wrought *m* evil in the sight of 2Chr 33:6 7235
transgressed very *m* after all the 2Chr 36:14 7227
and salt without prescribing how *m* Ezr 7:22 7227
many, and it is a time of *m* rain Ezr 10:13
is decayed, and there is *m* rubbish Neh 4:10 7235
they were *m* cast down in their Neh 6:16 3966
it yieldeth *m* increase unto the Neh 9:37 7235
shall there arise too *m* contempt Est 1:18 1767
How *m* less in them that dwell in Job 4:19 637
How *m* less shall I answer him, and Job 9:14
aged men, *m* elder than thy father Job 15:10 3524
How *m* more abominable and filthy Job 15:16
How *m* less man, that is a worm Job 25:6 637
and because mine hand had gotten *m* Job 31:25 3524
How *m* less to him that accepteth Job 34:19
Job twice as *m* as he had before Job 42:10 634
than gold, yea, than *m* fine gold Ps 19:10 7227
is not delivered by *m* strength Ps 33:16 7230
I will praise thee among *m* people Ps 35:18 6079
as *m* as in all riches Ps 119:14
I am afflicted very *m* Ps 119:107 3966
With her *m* fair speech she caused Prov 7:21 7230
m more the wicked and the sinner Prov 11:31 637
M food is in the tillage of the Prov 13:23 7230
but *m* increase is by the strength Prov 14:4 7230
of the righteous is *m* treasure Prov 15:6 7227
how *m* more then the hearts of the Prov 15:11 637
How *m* better is it to get wisdom Prov 16:16
m less do lying lips a prince Prov 17:7 637
how *m* more do his friends go far Prov 19:7 637
m less for a servant to have rule Prov 19:10 637
will not so *m* as bring it to his Prov 19:24 1571
how *m* more, when he bringeth it Prov 21:27 637
eat so *m* as is sufficient for Prov 25:16 1767
It is not good to eat *m* honey Prov 25:27 7235
For in *m* wisdom is *m* grief Eccl 1:18 7230
sweet, whether he eat little or *m* Eccl 5:12 7235
in darkness, and he hath *m* sorrow Eccl 5:17 7235
For he shall not *m* remember the Eccl 5:20 7235
Be not righteous over *m* Eccl 7:16 7235
Be not over *m* wicked, neither be Eccl 7:17 7235
but one sinner destroyeth *m* good Eccl 9:18 7235
By *m* slothfulness the building Eccl 10:18
m study is a weariness of the Eccl 12:12 7235
how *m* better is thy love than Song 4:10
hearkened diligently with *m* heed Is 21:7 7227
pile thereof is fire and *m* wood Is 30:33 7235
as this day, and *m* more abundant Is 56:12 3966
with nitre, and take thee *m* sope Jer 2:22 7235
thou about so *m* to change thy way Jer 2:36 3966
wine and summer fruits very *m* Jer 40:12 7335
How *m* more when I send my four Eze 14:21 637
how *m* less shall it be meet yet Eze 15:5 7227
might give him horses and *m* people Eze 17:15 7227
which art infamous and *m* vexed Eze 22:5 7227
it containeth *m* Eze 23:32 4767
and companies, and *m* people Eze 26:7 7227
with their mouth they shew *m* love Eze 33:31
were fair, and the fruit thereof *m* Dan 4:12 7690
were fair, and the fruit thereof *m* Dan 4:21 7690
unto it, Arise, devour *m* flesh Dan 7:5 7690
my cogitations *m* troubled me Dan 7:28 7690
a great army and with *m* riches Dan 11:13
face the people shall be *m* pained Joel 2:6
and also *m* cattle Jonah 4:11 7227
m pain is in all loins, and the Nah 2:10 2479
Ye have sown *m*, and bring in Hag 1:6 7235
Ye looked for *m*, and, lo, it came Hag 1:9 7235
have we spoken so *m* against thee Mal 3:13
be heard for their *m* speaking Mt 6:7 *4180*
Are ye not *m* better than they Mt 6:26 *3123*
shall he not *m* more clothe you, O Mt 6:30 *4183*
how *m* more shall your Father Mt 7:11 *4214*
how *m* more shall they call them Mt 10:25 *4214*
How *m* then is a man better than a Mt 12:12 *4214*
where they had not *m* earth Mt 13:5 *4183*
have so *m* bread in the wilderness Mt 15:33 *5118*
might have been sold for *m* Mt 26:9 *4183*
out, and began to publish it *m* Mk 1:45 *4183*
not so *m* as about the door Mk 2:2 *3366*
they could not so *m* as eat bread Mk 3:20 *3383*
ground, where it had not *m* earth Mk 4:5 *4183*
he besought him *m* that he would Mk 5:10 *4183*
m people gathered unto him Mk 5:21 *4183*
m people followed him, and Mk 5:24 *4183*
had no leisure so *m* as to eat Mk 6:31
saw *m* people, and was moved with Mk 6:34 *4183*
so *m* the more a great deal they Mk 7:36 *3123*
he was *m* displeased, and said unto Mk 10:14 *23*
they began to be *m* displeased Mk 10:41 *23*
and many that were rich cast in *m* Mk 12:41 *4183*
But so *m* the more went there a Lk 5:15 *3123*
Have ye not read so *m* as this Lk 6:3 *3761*
to sinners, to receive as *m* again Lk 6:34 *2470*
went with him, and *m* people Lk 7:11 *4183*
m people of the city was with her Lk 7:12 *2425*
you, and *m* more than a prophet Lk 7:26 *4055*
for she loved *m* Lk 7:47 *4183*
when *m* people were gathered Lk 8:4 *4183*
from the hill, *m* people met him Lk 9:37 *4183*
was cumbered about *m* serving Lk 10:40 *4183*
how *m* more shall your heavenly Lk 11:13 *4214*
thou hast *m* goods laid up for Lk 12:19 *4183*
how *m* more are ye better than the Lk 12:24 *4214*
how *m* more will he clothe you, O Lk 12:28 *4214*
For unto whomsoever *m* is given Lk 12:48 *4183*
of him shall be *m* required Lk 12:48 *4183*
and to whom men have committed *m* Lk 12:48 *4183*
How *m* owest thou unto my lord Lk 16:5 *4214*
to another, And how *m* owest thou Lk 16:7 *4214*
is least is faithful also in *m* Lk 16:10 *4183*
in the least is unjust also in *m* Lk 16:10 *4183*
would not lift up so *m* as his Lk 18:13 *3761*
but he cried so *m* the more Lk 18:39 *4183*
that he might know how *m* every Lk 19:15
to pass, as they were *m* perplexed Lk 24:4 *1280*
because there was *m* water there Jn 3:23 *4183*
Now there was *m* grass in the Jn 6:10 *4183*
of the fishes as *m* as they would Jn 6:11 *3745*
there was *m* murmuring among the Jn 7:12 *4183*
M people of the Jews therefore Jn 12:9 *4183*
On the next day *m* people that Jn 12:12 *4183*
it die, it bringeth forth *m* fruit Jn 12:24 *4183*
I will not talk *m* with you Jn 14:30 *4183*
the same bringeth forth *m* fruit Jn 15:5 *4183*
glorified, that ye bear *m* fruit Jn 15:8 *4183*
whether ye sold the land for so *m* Acts 5:8 *5118*
And she said, Yea, for so *m* Acts 5:8 *5118*
drew away *m* people after him Acts 5:37 *2425*
not so *m* as to set his foot on Acts 7:5
how *m* evil he hath done to thy Acts 9:13 *3745*
which gave *m* alms to the people, Acts 10:2 *4183*
m people was added unto the Lord Acts 11:24 *2425*
the church, and taught *m* people Acts 11:26 *2425*
faith, and that we must through *m* Acts 14:22 *4183*
when there had been *m* disputing Acts 15:7 *4183*
her masters *m* gain by soothsaying Acts 16:16 *4183*

for I have *m* people in this city ... Acts 18:10 *4183*
helped them *m* which had believed ... Acts 18:27 *4183*
We have not so *m* as heard whether ... Acts 19:2 *3761*
persuaded and turned away *m* people ... Acts 19:26 *2425*
and had given them *m* exhortation ... Acts 20:2 *4183*
m learning doth make thee mad ... Acts 26:24 *4183*
Now when *m* time was spent, and ... Acts 27:9 *2425*
m damage, not only of the lading ... Acts 27:10 *4183*
we had *m* work to come by the boat ... Acts 27:16 *3433*
as *m* as in me is, I am ready to ... Rom 1:15 *3588*
M every way: chiefly ... Rom 3:2 *4183*
M more then, being now justified ... Rom 5:9 *4183*
m more, being reconciled, we ... Rom 5:10 *4183*
m more the grace of God, and the ... Rom 5:15 *4183*
m more they which receive ... Rom 5:17 *4183*
abounded, grace did *m* more abound ... Rom 5:20 *5248*
endured with *m* longsuffering the ... Rom 9:22 *4183*
how *m* more their fulness ... Rom 11:12 *4124*
how *m* more shall these, which be ... Rom 11:24 *4124*
as *m* as lieth in you, live ... Rom 12:18 *3588*
m hindered from coming to you ... Rom 15:22 *5248*
Mary, who bestowed *m* labour on us ... Rom 16:6 *4183*
which laboured *m* in the Lord ... Rom 16:12 *4183*
and in fear, and in *m* trembling ... 1Cor 2:3 *4183*
so *m* as named among the Gentiles ... 1Cor 5:1 *3761*
how *m* more things that pertain to ... 1Cor 6:3 *3386*
m more those members of the body, ... 1Cor 12:22 *4183*
salute you *m* in the Lord, with ... 1Cor 16:19 *4183*
For out of *m* affliction and ... 2Cor 2:4 *4183*
m more doth the ministration of ... 2Cor 3:9 *4183*
m more that which remaineth is ... 2Cor 3:11 *4183*
in *m* patience, in afflictions, in ... 2Cor 6:4 *4183*
Praying us with *m* intreaty that ... 2Cor 8:4 *4183*
had gathered *m* had nothing over ... 2Cor 8:15 *4183*
but now *m* more diligent, upon the ... 2Cor 8:22 *4183*
are *m* more bold to speak the word ... Phil 1:14 *4056*
but now *m* more in my absence, ... Phil 2:12 *4183*
the Holy Ghost, and in *m* assurance ... 1Th 1:5 *4183*
received the word in *m* affliction ... 1Th 1:6 *4183*
gospel of God with *m* contention ... 1Th 2:2 *4183*
not given to *m* wine, not greedy ... 1Ti 3:8 *4183*
the coppersmith did me *m* evil ... 2Ti 4:14 *4183*
accusers, not given to *m* wine ... Titus 2:3 *4183*
though I might be *m* bold in ... Philem 8 *4183*
but how *m* more unto thee, both in ... Philem 16 *4214*
Being made so *m* better than the ... Heb 1:4 *5118*
By so *m* was Jesus made a surety ... Heb 7:22 *5118*
by how *m* also he is the mediator ... Heb 8:6 *3745*
How *m* more shall the blood of ... Heb 9:14 *4214*
so *m* the more, as ye see the day ... Heb 10:25 *5118*
Of how *m* sorer punishment, ... Heb 10:29 *4214*
shall we not *m* rather be in ... Heb 12:9 *4183*
if so *m* as a beast touch the ... Heb 12:20 *2579*
m more shall not we escape, if we ... Heb 12:25 *4183*
of a righteous man availeth *m* ... Jas 5:16 *4183*
being *m* more precious than of ... 1Pet 1:7 *4183*
through *m* wantonness, those that ... 2Pet 2:18
And I wept *m*, because no man was ... Rev 5:4 *4183*
was given unto him *m* incense ... Rev 8:3 *4183*
How *m* she hath glorified herself, ... Rev 18:7 *3745*
so *m* torment and sorrow give her ... Rev 18:7 *5118*
great voice of *m* people in heaven ... Rev 19:1 *4183*

MUFFLERS
and the bracelets, and the *m* ... Is 3:19 7479

MULBERRY
them over against the *m* trees ... 2Sa 5:23 1057
going in the tops of the *m* trees ... 2Sa 5:24 1057
them over against the *m* trees ... 1Chr 14:14 1057
going in the tops of the *m* trees ... 1Chr 14:15 1057

MULE
every man gat him up upon his *m* ... 2Sa 13:29 6505
And Absalom rode upon a *m*, and the .. 2Sa 18:9 6505
the *m* went under the thick boughs ... 2Sa 18:9 6505
the *m* that was under him went ... 2Sa 18:9 6505
my son to ride upon mine own *m* ... 1Kin 1:33 6506
to ride upon king David's *m* ... 1Kin 1:38 6506
him to ride upon the king's *m* ... 1Kin 1:44 6506
ye not as the horse, or as the *m* ... Ps 32:9 6505
the plague of the horse, of the *m* ... Zec 14:15 6505

MULES
found the *m* in the wilderness ... Gen 36:24 3222
armour, and spices, horses, and *m* ... 1Kin 10:25 6505
m alive, that we lose not all the ... 1Kin 18:5 6505
on asses, and on camels, and on *m* ... 1Chr 12:40 6505
harness, and spices, horses, and *m* ... 2Chr 9:24 6505
their *m*, two hundred forty and ... Ezr 2:66 6505
their *m*, two hundred forty and ... Neh 7:68 6505
on horseback, and riders on *m* ... Est 8:10 7409
So the posts that rode upon *m* ... Est 8:14 7409
and in litters, and upon *m* ... Is 66:20 6505
with horses and horsemen and *m* ... Eze 27:14 6505

MULES'
thy servant two *m* burden of earth ... 2Kin 5:17 6505

MULTIPLIED
and grew, and *m* exceedingly ... Gen 47:27 7235
and increased abundantly, and *m* ... Ex 1:7 7235
afflicted them, the more they *m* ... Ex 1:12 7235
and the people *m*, and waxed very ... Ex 1:20 7235
may be *m* in the land of Egypt ... Ex 11:9 7235
The LORD your God hath *m* you ... Deut 1:10 7235
and thy silver and thy gold is *m* ... Deut 8:13 7235
and all that thou hast is *m* ... Deut 8:13 7235
That your days may be *m*, and the ... Deut 11:21 7235
m his seed, and gave him Isaac ... Josh 24:3 7235
were *m* in the land of Gilead ... 1Chr 5:9 7235
If his children be *m*, it is for ... Job 27:14 7235
or if thy transgressions be *m* ... Job 35:6 7231
Their sorrows shall be *m* that ... Ps 16:4 7235
that hate me wrongfully are *m* ... Ps 38:19 7231
also, so that they are *m* greatly ... Ps 107:38 7235
For by me thy days shall be *m* ... Prov 9:11 7235
When the wicked are *m*, ... Prov 29:16 7235
Thou hast *m* the nation, and not ... Is 9:3 7235
transgressions are *m* before thee ... Is 59:12 7231
shall come to pass, when ye be *m* ... Jer 3:16 7235
Because ye *m* more than the ... Eze 5:7 1995
Ye have *m* your slain in this city ... Eze 11:6 7235
passed by, and *m* thy whoredoms ... Eze 16:25 7235
Thou hast moreover *m* thy ... Eze 16:29 7235
but thou hast *m* thine ... Eze 16:51 7235
may faint, and their ruins be *m* ... Eze 21:15 7235
Yet she *m* her whoredoms, in ... Eze 23:19 7235
the field, and his boughs were *m* ... Eze 31:5 7235
have *m* your words against me ... Eze 35:13 6280
Peace be *m* unto you ... Dan 4:1 7680
Peace be *m* unto you ... Dan 6:25 7680
m her silver and gold, which they ... Hos 2:8 7235
Judah hath *m* fenced cities ... Hos 8:14 7235
I have *m* visions, and used ... Hos 12:10 7235
Thou hast *m* thy merchants above ... Nah 3:16 7235
the number of the disciples was *m* ... Acts 6:1 *4129*
disciples *m* in Jerusalem greatly ... Acts 6:7 *4129*
the people grew and *m* in Egypt, ... Acts 7:17 *4129*
comfort of the Holy Ghost, were *m* ... Acts 9:31 *4129*
But the word of God grew and *m* ... Acts 12:24 *4129*
Grace unto you, and peace, be *m* ... 1Pet 1:2 *4129*
peace be *m* unto you through the ... 2Pet 1:2 *4129*
unto you, and peace, and love, be *m* ... Jude 2 *4129*

MULTIPLIEDST
Their children also *m* thou as the ... Neh 9:23 7235

MULTIPLIETH
m my wounds without cause ... Job 9:17 7235
us, and *m* his words against God ... Job 34:37 7235
he *m* words without knowledge ... Job 35:16 3527

MULTIPLY
them, saying, Be fruitful, and *m* ... Gen 1:22 7235
seas, and let fowl *m* in the earth ... Gen 1:22 7235
said unto them, Be fruitful, and *m* ... Gen 1:28 7235
said, I will greatly *m* thy sorrow ... Gen 3:16 7235
when men began to *m* on the face ... Gen 6:1 7231
be fruitful, and *m* upon the earth ... Gen 8:17 7235
said unto them, Be fruitful, and *m* ... Gen 9:1 7235
And you, be ye fruitful, and *m* ... Gen 9:7 7235
in the earth, and *m* therein ... Gen 9:7 7235
I will *m* thy seed exceedingly, ... Gen 16:10 7235
thee, and will *m* thee exceedingly ... Gen 17:2 7235
and will *m* him exceedingly ... Gen 17:20 7235
in multiplying I will *m* thy seed ... Gen 22:17 7235
seed to *m* as the stars of heaven ... Gen 26:4 7235
m thy seed for my servant ... Gen 26:24 7235
m thee, that thou mayest be a ... Gen 28:3 7235
be fruitful and *m* ... Gen 35:11 7235
m thee, and I will make of thee a ... Gen 48:4 7235
lest they *m*, and it come to pass, ... Ex 1:10 7235
m my signs and my wonders in the ... Ex 7:3 7235
beast of the field *m* against thee ... Ex 23:29 7227
I will *m* your seed as the stars ... Ex 32:13 7235
m you, and establish my covenant ... Lev 26:9 7235
thee, and bless thee, and *m* thee ... Deut 7:13 7235
to do, that ye may live, and *m* ... Deut 8:1 7235
And when thy herds and thy flocks *m*. Deut 8:13 7235
m thee, as he hath sworn unto thy ... Deut 13:17 7235
But he shall not *m* horses to ... Deut 17:16 7235
the end that he should *m* horses ... Deut 17:16 7235
shall he *m* wives to himself ... Deut 17:17 7235
he greatly *m* to himself silver ... Deut 17:17 7235
you to do you good, and to *m* you ... Deut 28:63 7235
good, and *m* thee above thy fathers ... Deut 30:5 7235
that thou mayest live and *m* ... Deut 30:16 7235
neither did all their family *m* ... 1Chr 4:27 7235
I shall *m* my days as the sand ... Job 29:18 7235
and I will *m* them, and they shall ... Jer 30:19 7235
so will I *m* the seed of David my ... Jer 33:22 7235
I have caused thee to *m* as the ... Eze 16:7 7233
I will *m* men upon you, all the ... Eze 36:10 7235
I will *m* upon you man and beast ... Eze 36:11 7235
I will *m* the fruit of the tree, ... Eze 36:30 7235
m them, and will set my sanctuary ... Eze 37:26 7235
at Gilgal *m* transgression ... Amos 4:4 7235
m your seed sown, and increase the ... 2Cor 9:10 *4129*
and multiplying I will *m* thee ... Heb 6:14 *4129*

MULTIPLYING
in *m* I will multiply thy seed as ... Gen 22:17 7235
thee, and *m* I will multiply thee ... Heb 6:14 *4129*

MULTITUDE
it shall not be numbered for *m* ... Gen 16:10 7230
that thou mayest be a *m* of people ... Gen 28:3 6951
and it is now increased unto a *m* ... Gen 30:30 7230
which cannot be numbered for *m* ... Gen 32:12 7230
I will make of thee a *m* of people ... Gen 48:4 6951
let them grow into a *m* in the ... Gen 48:16 7230
seed shall become a *m* of nations ... Gen 48:19 4393
a mixed *m* went up also with them ... Ex 12:38 7227
shalt not follow a *m* to do evil ... Ex 23:2 7227
According to the *m* of years thou ... Lev 25:16 7230
the mixt *m* that was among them ... Num 11:4 628
Gad had a very great *m* of cattle ... Num 32:1 7227
day as the stars of heaven for *m* ... Deut 1:10 7230
thee as the stars of heaven for *m* ... Deut 10:22 7230
were as the stars of heaven for *m* ... Deut 28:62 7230
that is upon the sea shore in *m* ... Josh 11:4 7230
army, with his chariots and his *m* ... Judg 4:7 1995
they came as grasshoppers for *m* ... Judg 6:5 7230
valley like grasshoppers for *m* ... Judg 7:12 7230
as the sand by the sea side for *m* ... Judg 7:12 7230
which is on the sea shore in *m* ... 1Sa 13:5 7230
the *m* melted away, and they went ... 1Sa 14:16 1995
even among the whole *m* of Israel ... 2Sa 6:19 1995
the sand that is by the sea for *m* ... 2Sa 17:11 7230
be numbered nor counted for *m* ... 1Kin 3:8 7230
the sand which is by the sea in *m* ... 1Kin 4:20 7230
not be told nor numbered for *m* ... 1Kin 8:5 7230
Hast thou seen all this great *m* ... 1Kin 20:13 1995
all this great *m* into thine hand ... 1Kin 20:28
they are as all the *m* of Israel ... 2Kin 7:13 1995
they are even as all the *m* of the ... 2Kin 7:13 1995
With the *m* of my chariots I am ... 2Kin 19:23 7393
with the remnant of the *m* ... 2Kin 25:11 1995
like the dust of the earth in *m* ... 2Chr 1:9 7227
not be told nor numbered for *m* ... 2Chr 5:6 7230
and ye be a great *m*, and there are ... 2Chr 13:8 1995
in thy name we go against this *m* ... 2Chr 14:11 1995
There cometh a great *m* against ... 2Chr 20:2 1995
by reason of this great *m* ... 2Chr 20:15 1995
they looked unto the *m*, and, ... 2Chr 20:24 1995
away a great *m* of them captives ... 2Chr 28:5
For a *m* of the people, even many ... 2Chr 30:18 4768
nor for all the *m* that is with ... 2Chr 32:7 1995
from Israel all the mixed *m* ... Neh 13:3 6154
the *m* of his children, and all the ... Est 5:11 7230
accepted of the *m* of his brethren ... Est 10:3 7230
Should not the *m* of words be ... Job 11:2 7230
Did I fear a great *m*, or did the ... Job 31:34 1995
m of years should teach wisdom ... Job 32:7 7230
the *m* of his bones with strong ... Job 33:19 7379
By reason of the *m* of oppressions ... Job 35:9 7230
He scorneth the *m* of the city ... Job 39:7 1995
thy house in the *m* of thy mercy ... Ps 5:7 7230
cast them out in the *m* of their ... Ps 5:10 7230
no king saved by the *m* of an host ... Ps 33:16 7230
for I had gone with the *m* ... Ps 42:4 5519
with a *m* that kept holyday ... Ps 42:4 1995
in the *m* of their riches ... Ps 49:6 7230
according unto the *m* of thy ... Ps 51:1 7230
the *m* of the bulls, with the ... Ps 68:30 5712
in the *m* of thy mercy hear me, in ... Ps 69:13 7230
to the *m* of thy tender mercies ... Ps 69:16 7230
unto the *m* of the wicked ... Ps 74:19 2416
In the *m* of my thoughts within me ... Ps 94:19 7230
let the *m* of isles be glad ... Ps 97:1 7227
not the *m* of thy mercies ... Ps 106:7 7230
according to the *m* of his mercies ... Ps 106:45 7230
I will praise him among the *m* ... Ps 109:30 7227
In the *m* of words there wanteth ... Prov 10:19 7230
but in the *m* of counsellors there ... Prov 11:14 7230
In the *m* of people is the king's ... Prov 14:28 7230
but in the *m* of counsellors they ... Prov 15:22 7230
There is gold, and a *m* of rubies ... Prov 20:15 7230
in *m* of counsellors there is ... Prov 24:6 7230
cometh through the *m* of business ... Eccl 5:3 7230
voice is known by *m* of words ... Eccl 5:3 7230
For in the *m* of dreams and many ... Eccl 5:7 7230
To what purpose is the *m* of your ... Is 1:11 7230
their *m* dried up with thirst ... Is 5:13 1995
and their glory, and their *m* ... Is 5:14 1995
The noise of a *m* in the mountains ... Is 13:4 1995
contemned, with all that great *m* ... Is 16:14 1995
Woe to the *m* of many people, ... Is 17:12 1995
Moreover the *m* of thy strangers ... Is 29:5 1995
the *m* of the terrible ones shall ... Is 29:5 1995
the *m* of all the nations that ... Is 29:7 1995
so shall the *m* of all the nations ... Is 29:8 1995
when a *m* of shepherds is called ... Is 31:4 4393
the *m* of the city shall be left ... Is 32:14 1995
By the *m* of my chariots am I come ... Is 37:24 7230
for the *m* of thy sorceries ... Is 47:9 7230
with the *m* of thy sorceries, ... Is 47:12 7230
wearied in the *m* of thy counsels ... Is 47:13 7230
The *m* of camels shall cover thee, ... Is 60:6 8229
according to the *m* of his ... Is 63:7 7230
hills, and from the *m* of mountains ... Jer 3:23 1995
there is a *m* of waters in the ... Jer 10:13 1995
they have called a *m* after thee ... Jer 12:6 4392
for the *m* of thine iniquity ... Jer 30:14 7230
for the *m* of thine iniquity ... Jer 30:15 7230
women that stood by, a great *m* ... Jer 44:15 6951
Behold, I will punish the *m* of No ... Jer 46:25 582
the *m* of their cattle a spoil ... Jer 49:32 527
there is a *m* of waters in the ... Jer 51:16 527
with the *m* of the waves thereof ... Jer 51:42 527
of Babylon, and the rest of the *m* ... Jer 52:15 527
for the *m* of her transgressions ... Lam 1:5 7230
according to the *m* of his mercies ... Lam 3:32 7230
them shall remain, nor of their *m* ... Eze 7:11 1995
wrath is upon all the *m* thereof ... Eze 7:12 1995
is touching the whole *m* thereof ... Eze 7:13 1995
wrath is upon all the *m* thereof ... Eze 7:14 1995
according to the *m* of his idols ... Eze 14:4 7230
height with the *m* of her branches ... Eze 19:11 7230
a voice of a *m* being at ease was ... Eze 23:42 1995
of the *m* of all kind of riches ... Eze 27:12 7230
the *m* of the wares of thy making ... Eze 27:16 7230
was thy merchant in the *m* of the ... Eze 27:18 7230
making, for the *m* of all riches ... Eze 27:18 7230
earth with the *m* of thy riches ... Eze 27:33 7230
By the *m* of thy merchandise they ... Eze 28:16 7230
by the *m* of thine iniquities ... Eze 28:18 7230
and he shall take her *m*, and take ... Eze 29:19 1995
and they shall take away her *m* ... Eze 30:4 1995
I will also make the *m* of Egypt ... Eze 30:10 1995
and I will cut off the *m* of No ... Eze 30:15 1995
king of Egypt, and to his *m* ... Eze 31:2 1995
long because of the *m* of waters ... Eze 31:5 7227
him fair by the *m* of his branches ... Eze 31:9 7230
This is Pharaoh and all his *m* ... Eze 31:18 1995
mighty will I cause thy *m* to fall ... Eze 32:12 1995
all the *m* thereof shall be ... Eze 32:12 1995
even for Egypt, and for all her *m* ... Eze 32:16 1995
of man, wail for the *m* of Egypt ... Eze 32:18 1995
all her *m* round about her grave, ... Eze 32:24 1995
midst of the slain with all her *m* ... Eze 32:25 1995
is Meshech, Tubal, and all her *m* ... Eze 32:26 1995
shall be comforted over all his *m* ... Eze 32:31 1995
sword, even Pharaoh and all his *m* ... Eze 32:32 1995
shall they bury Gog and all his *m* ... Eze 39:11 1995
shall be a very great *m* of fish ... Eze 47:9

his words like the voice of a *m* ... Dan 10:6 1995
assemble a *m* of great forces ... Dan 11:10 1995
and he shall set forth a great *m* ... Dan 11:11 1995
but the *m* shall be given into his ... Dan 11:11 1995
And when he hath taken away the *m* .. Dan 11:12 1995
shall set forth a *m* greater than ... Dan 11:13 1995
for the *m* of thine iniquity, and ... Hos 9:7 7230
according to the *m* of his fruit ... Hos 10:1 7230
in the *m* of thy mighty men ... Hos 10:13 7230
noise by reason of the *m* of men ... Mic 2:12
and there is a *m* of slain, and a ... Nah 3:3 7230
Because of the *m* of the whoredoms ... Nah 3:4 7230
without walls for the *m* of men ... Zec 2:4 7230
the whole *m* stood on the shore ... Mt 13:2 *3793*
Jesus unto the *m* in parables ... Mt 13:34 *3793*
Then Jesus sent the *m* away ... Mt 13:36 *3793*
put him to death, he feared the *m* ... Mt 14:5 *3793*
went forth, and saw a great *m* ... Mt 14:14 *3793*
send the *m* away, that they may go ... Mt 14:15 *3793*
he commanded the *m* to sit down on ... Mt 14:19 *3793*
and the disciples to the *m* ... Mt 14:19 *3793*
And he called the *m*, and said unto ... Mt 15:10 *3793*
Insomuch that the *m* wondered ... Mt 15:31 *3793*
said, I have compassion on the *m* ... Mt 15:32 *3793*
as to fill so great a *m* ... Mt 15:33 *3793*
he commanded the *m* to sit down on ... Mt 15:35 *3793*
and the disciples to the *m* ... Mt 15:36 *3793*
And he sent away the *m*, and took ... Mt 15:39 *3793*
And when they were come to the *m* ... Mt 17:14 *3793*
Jericho, a great *m* followed him ... Mt 20:29 *3793*
the *m* rebuked them, because they ... Mt 20:31 *3793*
a very great *m* spread their ... Mt 21:8 *3793*
the *m* said, This is Jesus the ... Mt 21:11 *3793*
hands on him, they feared the *m* ... Mt 21:46 *3793*
when the *m* heard this, they were ... Mt 22:33 *3793*
Then spake Jesus to the *m* ... Mt 23:1 *3793*
and with him a great *m* with swords ... Mt 26:47 *3793*
elders persuaded the *m* that they ... Mt 27:20 *3793*
and washed his hands before the *m* ... Mt 27:24 *3793*
all the *m* resorted unto him, and ... Mk 2:13 *3793*
a great *m* from Galilee followed ... Mk 3:7 *4128*
about Tyre and Sidon, a great *m* ... Mk 3:8 *4128*
wait on him because of the *m* ... Mk 3:9 *3793*
the *m* cometh together again, so ... Mk 3:20 *3793*
the *m* sat about him, and they said ... Mk 3:32 *3793*
was gathered unto him a great *m* ... Mk 4:1 *3793*
the whole *m* was by the sea on the ... Mk 4:1 *3793*
And when they had sent away the *m* .. Mk 4:36 *3793*
Thou seest the *m* thronging thee ... Mk 5:31 *3793*
And he took him aside from the *m* ... Mk 7:33 *3793*
those days the *m* being very great ... Mk 8:1 *3793*
I have compassion on the *m* ... Mk 8:2 *3793*
he saw a great *m* about them ... Mk 9:14 *3793*
And one of the *m* answered and said, .. Mk 9:17 *3793*
and with him a great *m* with swords ... Mk 14:43 *3793*
the *m* crying aloud began to ... Mk 15:8 *3793*
the whole *m* of the people were ... Lk 1:10 *4128*
there was with the angel a *m* of ... Lk 2:13 *4128*
Then said he to the *m* that came ... Lk 3:7 *3793*
they inclosed a great *m* of fishes ... Lk 5:6 *4128*
bring him in because of the *m* ... Lk 5:19 *3793*
a great *m* of people out of all ... Lk 6:17 *4128*
the whole *m* sought to touch him ... Lk 6:19 *3793*
Then the whole *m* of the country ... Lk 8:37 *4128*
the *m* throng thee and press thee, ... Lk 8:45 *3793*
and said unto him, Send the *m* away ... Lk 9:12 *3793*
the disciples to set before the *m* ... Lk 9:16 *3793*
an innumerable *m* of people ... Lk 12:1 *3461*
And hearing the *m* pass by, he ... Lk 18:36 *3793*
the whole *m* of the disciples ... Lk 19:37 *4128*
from among the *m* said unto him ... Lk 19:39 *3793*
unto them in the absence of the *m* ... Lk 22:6 *3793*
And while he yet spake, behold a *m* ... Lk 22:47 *3793*
the whole *m* of them arose, and led ... Lk 23:1 *4128*
lay a great *m* of impotent folk ... Jn 5:3 *4128*
away, a *m* being in that place ... Jn 5:13 *3793*
a great *m* followed him, because ... Jn 6:2 *3793*
to draw it for the *m* of fishes ... Jn 21:6 *4128*
the *m* came together, and were ... Acts 2:6 *4128*
the *m* of them that believed were ... Acts 4:32 *4128*
There came also a *m* out of the ... Acts 5:16 *4128*
the *m* of the disciples unto them ... Acts 6:2 *4128*
And the saying pleased the whole *m* ... Acts 6:5 *4128*
that a great *m* both of the Jews ... Acts 14:1 *4128*
But the *m* of the city was divided ... Acts 14:4 *4128*
Then all the *m* kept silence ... Acts 15:12 *4128*
they had gathered the *m* together ... Acts 15:30 *4128*
the *m* rose up together against ... Acts 16:22 *3793*
and of the devout Greeks a great *m* ... Acts 17:4 *4128*
evil of that way before the *m* ... Acts 19:9 *4128*
they drew Alexander out of the *m* ... Acts 19:33 *3793*
the *m* must needs come together ... Acts 21:22 *4128*
thing, some another, among the *m* ... Acts 21:34 *3793*
For the *m* of the people followed ... Acts 21:36 *4128*
and the *m* was divided ... Acts 23:7 *4128*
in the temple, neither with *m* ... Acts 24:18 *3793*
about whom all the *m* of the Jews ... Acts 25:24 *4128*
many as the stars of the sky in *m* ... Heb 11:12 *4128*
death, and shall hide a *m* of sins ... Jas 5:20 *4128*
charity shall cover the *m* of sins ... 1Pet 4:8 *4128*
this I beheld, and, lo, a great *m* ... Rev 7:9 *3793*
as it were the voice of a great *m* ... Rev 19:6 *3793*

MULTITUDES
draw her and all her *m* ... Eze 32:20 1995
M, *m* in the valley of ... Joel 3:14 1995
great *m* of people from Galilee ... Mt 4:25 *3793*
And seeing the *m*, he went up into ... Mt 5:1 *3793*
mountain, great *m* followed him ... Mt 8:1 *3793*
when Jesus saw great *m* about him ... Mt 8:18 *3793*
But when the *m* saw it, they ... Mt 9:8 *3793*
the *m* marvelled, saying, It was ... Mt 9:33 *3793*
But when he saw the *m*, he was ... Mt 9:36 *3793*
to say unto the *m* concerning John ... Mt 11:7 *3793*
great *m* followed him, and he ... Mt 12:15 *3793*
great *m* were gathered together ... Mt 13:2 *3793*
side, while he sent the *m* away ... Mt 14:22 *3793*
And when he had sent the *m* away ... Mt 14:23 *3793*
great *m* came unto him, having ... Mt 15:30 *3793*
And great *m* followed him ... Mt 19:2 *3793*
the *m* that went before, and that ... Mt 21:9 *3793*
same hour said Jesus to the *m* ... Mt 26:55 *3793*
great *m* came together to hear, and ... Lk 5:15 *3793*
And there went great *m* with him ... Lk 14:25 *3793*
the Lord, *m* both of men and women ... Acts 5:14 *4128*
But when the Jews saw the *m* ... Acts 13:45 *3793*
whore sitteth, are peoples, and *m* ... Rev 17:15 *3793*

MUNITION
that fight against her and her *m* ... Is 29:7 4685
keep the *m*, watch the way, make ... Nah 2:1 4694

MUNITIONS
defence shall be the *m* of rocks ... Is 33:16 4679

MUPPIM (*mup'-pim*) See SHUPPIM. *A son of Benjamin.*
Gera, and Naaman, Ehi, and Rosh, *M* .. Gen 46:21 4649

MURDER
places doth he *m* the innocent ... Ps 10:8 2026
the stranger, and *m* the fatherless ... Ps 94:6 7523
Will ye steal, *m*, and commit ... Jer 7:9 7523
priests *m* in the way by consent ... Hos 6:9 7523
Jesus said, Thou shalt do no *m* ... Mt 19:18 *5407*
who had committed *m* in the ... Mk 15:7 *5408*
made in the city, and for *m* ... Lk 23:19 *5408*
m was cast into prison, whom they ... Lk 23:25 *5408*
full of envy, *m*, debate, deceit, ... Rom 1:29 *5408*

MURDERER
iron, so that he die, he is a *m* ... Num 35:16 7523
the *m* shall surely be put to ... Num 35:16 7523
he may die, and he die, he is a *m* ... Num 35:17 7523
the *m* shall surely be put to ... Num 35:17 7523
he may die, and he die, he is a *m* ... Num 35:18 7523
the *m* shall surely be put to ... Num 35:18 7523
of blood himself shall slay the *m* ... Num 35:19 7523
for he is a *m* ... Num 35:21 7523
of blood shall slay the *m* ... Num 35:21 7523
the *m* shall be put to death by ... Num 35:30 7523
satisfaction for the life of a *m* ... Num 35:31 7523
See ye how this son of a *m* hath ... 2Kin 6:32 7523
The *m* rising with the light ... Job 24:14 7523
bring forth his children to the *m* ... Hos 9:13 2026
He was a *m* from the beginning, and ... Jn 8:44 *443*
desired a *m* to be granted unto ... Acts 3:14 *5406*
No doubt this man is a *m* ... Acts 28:4 *5406*
But let none of you suffer as a *m* ... 1Pet 4:15 *5406*
hateth his brother is a *m* ... 1Jn 3:15 *443*
ye know that no *m* hath eternal ... 1Jn 3:15 *443*

MURDERERS
the children of the *m* he slew not ... 2Kin 14:6 5221
lodged in it; but now *m* ... Is 1:21 7523
my soul is wearied because of *m* ... Jer 4:31 2026
his armies, and destroyed those *m* ... Mt 22:7 *5406*
have been now the betrayers and *m* ... Acts 7:52 *5406*
four thousand men that were *m* ... Acts 21:38 *4607*
for *m* of fathers and *m* of ... 1Ti 1:9 *3964*
m of mothers, for manslayers, ... 1Ti 1:9 *3389*
and the abominable, and *m*, and ... Rev 21:8 *5406*
sorcerers, and whoremongers, and *m* ... Rev 22:15 *5406*

MURDERS
heart proceed evil thoughts, *m* ... Mt 15:19 *5408*
adulteries, fornications, *m* ... Mk 7:21 *5408*
Envyings, *m*, drunkenness, ... Gal 5:21 *5408*
Neither repented they of their *m* ... Rev 9:21 *5408*

MURMUR
what are we, that ye *m* against us ... Ex 16:7 3885
murmurings which ye *m* against him ... Ex 16:8 3885
congregation, which *m* against me ... Num 14:27 3885
Israel, which they *m* against me ... Num 14:27 3885
the congregation to *m* against him ... Num 14:36 3885
is Aaron, that ye *m* against him ... Num 16:11 3885
whereby they *m* against you ... Num 17:5 3885
unto them, *M* not among yourselves ... Jn 6:43 *1111*
Neither *m* ye, as some of them ... 1Cor 10:10 *1111*

MURMURED
the people *m* against Moses, ... Ex 15:24 3885
of Israel *m* against Moses ... Ex 16:2 3885
the people *m* against Moses, and ... Ex 17:3 3885
of Israel *m* against Moses ... Num 14:2 3885
upward, which have *m* against me ... Num 14:29 3885
of Israel *m* against Moses ... Num 16:41 3885
ye *m* in your tents, and said, ... Deut 1:27 7279
m against the princes ... Josh 9:18 3885
But *m* in their tents, and ... Ps 106:25 7279
they that *m* shall learn doctrine ... Is 29:24 7279
they *m* against the goodman of the ... Mt 20:11 *1111*
And they *m* against her ... Mk 14:5 *1690*
Pharisees *m* against his disciples ... Lk 5:30 *1111*
And the Pharisees and scribes *m* ... Lk 15:2 *1234*
And when they saw it, they all *m* ... Lk 19:7 *1234*
The Jews then *m* at him, because ... Jn 6:41 *1111*
that his disciples *m* at it ... Jn 6:61 *1111*
m such things concerning him ... Jn 7:32 *1111*
murmur ye, as some of them also *m* ... 1Cor 10:10 *1111*

MURMURERS
These are *m*, complainers, walking ... Jude 16 *1113*

MURMURING
there was much *m* among the people .. Jn 7:12 *1112*
there arose a *m* of the Grecians ... Acts 6:1 *1112*

MURMURINGS
heareth your *m* against the LORD ... Ex 16:7 8519
m which ye murmur against him ... Ex 16:8 8519
your *m* are not against us, but ... Ex 16:8 8519
for he hath heard your *m* ... Ex 16:9 8519
I have heard the *m* of the ... Ex 16:12 8519
I have heard the *m* of the ... Num 14:27 8519
the *m* of the children of Israel ... Num 17:5 8519
quite take away their *m* from me ... Num 17:10 8519
Do all things without *m* and ... Phil 2:14 *1112*

MURRAIN
there shall be a very grievous *m* ... Ex 9:3 1698

MUSE
I *m* on the work of thy hands ... Ps 143:5 7878

MUSED
all men *m* in their hearts of John ... Lk 3:15 *1260*

MUSHI (*mu'-shi*) See MUSHITES. *A son of Merari.*
of Merari; Mahali and *M* ... Ex 6:19 4187
families; Mahli, and *M* ... Num 3:20 4187
Merari; Mahli, and *M* ... 1Chr 6:19 4187
The son of Mahli, the son of *M* ... 1Chr 6:47 4187
Merari; Mahli, and *M* ... 1Chr 23:21 4187
The sons of *M*; Mahli ... 1Chr 23:23 4187
sons of Merari were Mahli and *M* ... 1Chr 24:26 4187
The sons also of *M* ... 1Chr 24:30 4187

MUSHITES (*mu'-shites*) *The family of Mushi.*
Mahlites, and the family of the *M* ... Num 3:33 4188
the Mahlites, the family of the *M* ... Num 26:58 4188

MUSICAL
with *m* instruments of God ... 1Chr 16:42 7892
with the *m* instruments of David ... Neh 12:36 7892
as *m* instruments, and that of all ... Eccl 2:8 7705

MUSICIAN
To the chief *M* on Neginoth ... Ps 4:*t* 5329
To the chief *M* upon Nehiloth, A ... Ps 5:*t* 5329
To the chief *M* on Neginoth upon ... Ps 6:*t* 5329
To the chief *M* upon Gittith ... Ps 8:*t* 5329
To the chief *M* upon Muth-labben, ... Ps 9:*t* 5329
To the chief *M*, A Psalm of David ... Ps 11:*t* 5329
To the chief *M* upon Sheminith, A ... Ps 12:*t* 5329
To the chief *M*, A Psalm of David ... Ps 13:*t* 5329
To the chief *M*, A Psalm of David ... Ps 14:*t* 5329
To the chief *M*, A Psalm of David, ... Ps 18:*t* 5329
To the chief *M*, A Psalm of David ... Ps 19:*t* 5329
To the chief *M*, A Psalm of David ... Ps 20:*t* 5329
To the chief *M*, A Psalm of David ... Ps 21:*t* 5329
To the chief *M* upon Aijeleth ... Ps 22:*t* 5329
To the chief *M*, A Psalm of David ... Ps 31:*t* 5329
To the chief *M*, A Psalm of David, ... Ps 36:*t* 5329
To the chief *M*, even to Jeduthun, ... Ps 39:*t* 5329
To the chief *M*, A Psalm of David ... Ps 40:*t* 5329
To the chief *M*, A Psalm of David ... Ps 41:*t* 5329
To the chief *M*, Maschil, for the ... Ps 42:*t* 5329
To the chief *M* for the sons of ... Ps 44:*t* 5329
To the chief *M* upon Shoshannim, ... Ps 45:*t* 5329
To the chief *M* for the sons of ... Ps 46:*t* 5329
To the chief *M*, A Psalm for the ... Ps 47:*t* 5329
To the chief *M*, A Psalm for the ... Ps 49:*t* 5329
To the chief *M*, A Psalm of David, ... Ps 51:*t* 5329
To the chief *M*, Maschil, A Psalm ... Ps 52:*t* 5329
To the chief *M* upon Mahalath, ... Ps 53:*t* 5329
To the chief *M* on Neginoth ... Ps 54:*t* 5329
To the chief *M* on Neginoth ... Ps 55:*t* 5329
To the chief *M* upon ... Ps 56:*t* 5329
To the chief *M*, Altaschith, ... Ps 57:*t* 5329
To the chief *M*, Altaschith, ... Ps 58:*t* 5329
To the chief *M*, Altaschith, ... Ps 59:*t* 5329
To the chief *M* upon Shushan-eduth ... Ps 60:*t* 5329
To the chief *M* upon Neginah ... Ps 61:*t* 5329
To the chief *M*, to Jeduthun, A ... Ps 62:*t* 5329
To the chief *M*, A Psalm of David ... Ps 64:*t* 5329
To the chief *M*, A Psalm and Song ... Ps 65:*t* 5329
To the chief *M*, A Song or Psalm ... Ps 66:*t* 5329
To the chief *M* on Neginoth ... Ps 67:*t* 5329
To the chief *M*, A Psalm or Song ... Ps 68:*t* 5329
To the chief *M* upon Shoshannim, A ... Ps 69:*t* 5329
To the chief *M*, A Psalm of David, ... Ps 70:*t* 5329
To the chief *M*, Altaschith, A ... Ps 75:*t* 5329
To the chief *M* on Neginoth ... Ps 76:*t* 5329
To the chief *M*, to Jeduthun, A ... Ps 77:*t* 5329
To the chief *M* upon ... Ps 80:*t* 5329
To the chief *M* upon Gittith ... Ps 81:*t* 5329
To the chief *M* upon Gittith ... Ps 84:*t* 5329
To the chief *M*, A Psalm for the ... Ps 85:*t* 5329
chief *M* upon Mahalath Leannoth ... Ps 88:*t* 5329
To the chief *M*, A Psalm of David ... Ps 109:*t* 5329
To the chief *M*, A Psalm of David ... Ps 139:*t* 5329
To the chief *M*, A Psalm of David ... Ps 140:*t* 5329

MUSICIANS
And the voice of harpers, and *m* ... Rev 18:22 *3451*

MUSICK
joy, and with instruments of *m* ... 1Sa 18:6
the singers with instruments of *m* ... 1Chr 15:16 7892
and cymbals and instruments of *m* ... 2Chr 5:13 7892
with instruments of *m* of the LORD ... 2Chr 7:6 7892
the singers with instruments of *m* ... 2Chr 23:13 7892
could skill of instruments of *m* ... 2Chr 34:12 7892
of *m* shall be brought low ... Eccl 12:4 7892
I am their *m* ... Lam 3:63 4485
gate, the young men from their *m* ... Lam 5:14 5058
dulcimer, and all kinds of *m* ... Dan 3:5 2170
psaltery, and all kinds of *m* ... Dan 3:7 2170
and dulcimer, and all kinds of *m* ... Dan 3:10 2170
and dulcimer, and all kinds of *m* ... Dan 3:15 2170
of *m* brought before him ... Dan 6:18
to themselves instruments of *m* ... Amos 6:5 7892
nigh to the house, he heard *m* ... Lk 15:25 *4858*

MUSING
while I was *m* the fire burned ... Ps 39:3 1901

MUST
thy money, *m* needs be circumcised ... Gen 17:13
m I needs bring thy son again ... Gen 24:5

It *m* not be so done in our ... Gen 29:26
and said, Thou *m* come in unto me ... Gen 30:16
If it *m* be so now, do this ... Gen 43:11
time drew nigh that Israel *m* die ... Gen 47:29
for we *m* hold a feast unto the ... Ex 10:9
Thou *m* give us also sacrifices and ... Ex 10:25
for thereof *m* we take to serve ... Ex 10:26
not with what we *m* serve the LORD ... Ex 10:26
save that which every man *m* eat ... Ex 12:16
them the way wherein they *m* walk ... Ex 18:20
walk, and the work that they *m* do ... Ex 18:20
it *m* be put into water, and it ... Lev 11:32
seven days ye *m* eat unleavened ... Lev 23:6
so he *m* do after the law of his ... Num 6:21
Neither *m* the children of Israel ... Num 18:22
m we fetch you water out of this ... Num 20:10
M I not take heed to speak that ... Num 23:12
the LORD speaketh, that I *m* do ... Num 23:26
word again by what way we *m* go up ... Deut 1:22
But I *m* die in this land, I *m* ... Deut 4:22
But thou *m* eat them before the ... Deut 12:18
for thou *m* go with this people ... Deut 31:7
thy days approach that thou *m* die ... Deut 31:14
may know the way by which ye *m* go ... Josh 3:4
But that ye *m* turn away this day ... Josh 22:18
thou *m* offer it unto the LORD ... Judg 13:16
There *m* be an inheritance for ... Judg 21:17
thou *m* buy it also of Ruth the ... Ruth 4:5
was in mine hand, and, lo, I *m* die ... 1Sa 14:43
For we *m* needs die, and are as ... 2Sa 14:14
He that ruleth over men *m* be just ... 2Sa 23:3
touch them *m* be fenced with iron ... 2Sa 23:7
he sleepeth, and *m* be awaked ... 1Kin 18:27
thou *m* go to be with thy fathers ... 1Chr 17:11
LORD *m* be exceeding magnifical ... 1Chr 22:5
As thou hast said, so *m* we do ... Ezr 10:12
whose mouth *m* be held in with bit ... Ps 32:9
friends *m* shew himself friendly ... Prov 18:24
him, yet thou *m* do it again ... Prov 19:19
then *m* he put to more strength ... Eccl 10:10
m have a thousand, and those that ... Song 8:12
For precept *m* be upon precept, ... Is 28:10
they *m* needs be borne, because ... Jer 10:5
this is a grief, and I *m* bear it ... Jer 10:19
but ye *m* tread down with your ... Eze 34:18
but ye *m* foul the residue with ... Eze 34:18
how that he *m* go unto Jerusalem, ... Mt 16:21 *1163*
scribes that Elias *m* first come ... Mt 17:10 *1163*
for it *m* needs be that offences ... Mt 18:7 *318*
all these things *m* come to pass ... Mt 24:6 *1163*
be fulfilled, that thus it *m* be ... Mt 26:54 *1163*
but new wine *m* be put into new ... Mk 2:22
Son of man *m* suffer many things ... Mk 8:31 *1163*
scribes that Elias *m* first come ... Mk 9:11 *1163*
that he *m* suffer many things, and ... Mk 9:12
for such things *m* needs be ... Mk 13:7 *1163*
the gospel *m* first be published ... Mk 13:10 *1163*
but the scriptures *m* be fulfilled ... Mk 14:49 *2443*
wist ye not that I *m* be about my ... Lk 2:49 *1163*
I *m* preach the kingdom of God to ... Lk 4:43 *1163*
But new wine *m* be put into new ... Lk 5:38
The Son of man *m* suffer many ... Lk 9:22 *1163*
Nevertheless I *m* walk to day ... Lk 13:33 *1163*
ground, and I *m* needs go and see it ... Lk 14:18 *2192*
But first *m* he suffer many things ... Lk 17:25 *1163*
for to day I *m* abide at thy house ... Lk 19:5 *1163*
for these things *m* first come to ... Lk 21:9 *1163*
when the passover *m* be killed ... Lk 22:7 *1163*
m yet be accomplished in me ... Lk 22:37 *1163*
(For of necessity he *m* release ... Lk 23:17
The Son of man *m* be delivered ... Lk 24:7 *1163*
that all things *m* be fulfilled ... Lk 24:44 *1163*
unto thee, Ye *m* be born again ... Jn 3:7 *1163*
even so *m* the Son of man be ... Jn 3:14 *1163*
He *m* increase, but I ... Jn 3:30 *1163*
increase, but I *m* decrease ... Jn 3:30
he *m* needs go through Samaria ... Jn 4:4
him *m* worship him in spirit ... Jn 4:24 *1163*
I *m* work the works of him that ... Jn 9:4 *1163*
them also I *m* bring, and they ... Jn 10:16 *1163*
The Son of man *m* be lifted up ... Jn 12:34 *1163*
that he *m* rise again from the ... Jn 20:9 *1163*
this scripture *m* needs have been ... Acts 1:16 *1163*
m one be ordained to be a witness ... Acts 1:22 *1163*
Whom the heaven *m* receive until ... Acts 3:21 *1163*
among men, whereby we *m* be saved ... Acts 4:12 *1163*
shall be told thee what thou *m* do ... Acts 9:6 *1163*
he *m* suffer for my name's sake ... Acts 9:16 *1163*
faith, and that we *m* through much ... Acts 14:22 *1163*
Ye *m* be circumcised, and keep the ... Acts 15:24
Sirs, what *m* I do to be saved ... Acts 16:30 *1163*
that Christ *m* needs have suffered ... Acts 17:3 *1163*
I *m* by all means keep this feast ... Acts 18:21 *1163*
been there, I *m* also see Rome ... Acts 19:21 *1163*
the multitude *m* needs come ... Acts 21:22 *1163*
so *m* thou bear witness also at ... Acts 23:11 *1163*
thou *m* be brought before Caesar ... Acts 27:24 *1163*
Howbeit we *m* be cast upon a ... Acts 27:26 *1163*
Wherefore ye *m* needs be subject, ... Rom 13:5
for then *m* ye needs go out of the ... 1Cor 5:10 *3784*
For there *m* be also heresies ... 1Cor 11:19 *1163*
For he *m* reign, till he hath put ... 1Cor 15:25 *1163*
corruptible *m* put on incorruption ... 1Cor 15:53 *1163*
this mortal *m* put on immortality ... 1Cor 15:53
For we *m* all appear before the ... 2Cor 5:10 *1163*
If I *m* needs glory, I will glory ... 2Cor 11:30 *1163*
A bishop then *m* be blameless ... 1Ti 3:2 *1163*
Moreover he *m* have a good report ... 1Ti 3:7 *1163*
Likewise *m* the deacons be grave, ... 1Ti 3:8
Even so *m* their wives be grave, ... 1Ti 3:11
The husbandman that laboureth *m* ... 2Ti 2:6 *1163*
servant of the Lord *m* not strive ... 2Ti 2:24 *1163*
For a bishop *m* be blameless ... Titus 1:7 *1163*
Whose mouths *m* be stopped ... Titus 1:11 *1163*
that some *m* enter therein ... Heb 4:6
there *m* also of necessity be the ... Heb 9:16
For then *m* he often have suffered ... Heb 9:26 *1163*
to God *m* believe that he is ... Heb 11:6 *1163*
as they that *m* give account ... Heb 13:17
m begin at the house of God ... 1Pet 4:17
Knowing that shortly I *m* put off ... 2Pet 1:14
which *m* shortly come to pass ... Rev 1:1 *1163*
thee things which *m* be hereafter ... Rev 4:1 *1163*
Thou *m* prophesy again before many ... Rev 10:11 *1163*
he *m* in this manner be killed ... Rev 11:5 *1163*
sword *m* be killed with the sword ... Rev 13:10 *1163*
he *m* continue a short space ... Rev 17:10 *1163*
after that he *m* be loosed a ... Rev 20:3 *1163*
things which *m* shortly be done ... Rev 22:6 *1163*

MUSTARD
is like to a grain of *m* seed ... Mt 13:31 *4615*
have faith as a grain of *m* seed ... Mt 17:20 *4615*
It is like a grain of *m* seed ... Mk 4:31 *4615*
It is like a grain of *m* seed ... Lk 13:19 *4615*
ye had faith as a grain of *m* seed ... Lk 17:6 *4615*

MUSTERED
which *m* the people of the land, ... 2Kin 25:19 6633
who *m* the people of the land ... Jer 52:25 6633

MUSTERETH
the LORD of hosts *m* the host of ... Is 13:4 6485

MUTH-LABBEN (*muth-lab'-ben*) *A musical notation.*
To the chief Musician upon *M* ... Ps 9:*t* 4192

MUTTER
unto wizards that peep, and that *m* ... Is 8:19 1897

MUTTERED
your tongue hath *m* perverseness ... Is 59:3 1897

MUTUAL
you by the *m* faith both of you ... Rom 1:12

MUZZLE
Thou shalt not *m* the ox when he ... Deut 25:4 2629
Thou shalt not *m* the mouth of the ... 1Cor 9:9 *5392*
Thou shalt not *m* the ox that ... 1Ti 5:18 *5392*

MY See PREFACE.

MYRA (*mi'-rah*) *A city in Lycia.*
and Pamphylia, we came to *M* ... Acts 27:5 *3460*

MYRRH
bearing spicery and balm and *m* ... Gen 37:25 3910
and a little honey, spices, and *m* ... Gen 43:11 3910
of pure *m* five hundred shekels ... Ex 30:23 4753
to wit, six months with oil of *m* ... Est 2:12 4753
All thy garments smell of *m* ... Ps 45:8 4753
I have perfumed my bed with *m* ... Prov 7:17 4753
A bundle of *m* is my wellbeloved ... Song 1:13 4753
pillars of smoke, perfumed with *m* ... Song 3:6 4753
will get me to the mountain of *m* ... Song 4:6 4753
m and aloes, with all the chief ... Song 4:14 4753
have gathered my *m* with my spice ... Song 5:1 4753
and my hands dropped with *m* ... Song 5:5 4753
my fingers with sweet smelling *m* ... Song 5:5 4753
lilies, dropping sweet smelling *m* ... Song 5:13 4753
gold, and frankincense, and *m* ... Mt 2:11 *4666*
him to drink wine mingled with *m* ... Mk 15:23 *4669*
night, and brought a mixture of *m* ... Jn 19:39 *4666*

MYRTLE
m branches, and palm branches, and ... Neh 8:15 1918
cedar, the shittah tree, and the *m* ... Is 41:19 1918
brier shall come up the *m* tree ... Is 55:13 1918
he stood among the *m* trees that ... Zec 1:8 1918
stood among the *m* trees answered ... Zec 1:10 1918
LORD that stood among the *m* trees ... Zec 1:11 1918

MYSELF
and I hid *m* ... Gen 3:10
By *m* have I sworn, saith the LORD ... Gen 22:16
wings, and brought you unto *m* ... Ex 19:4
of Egypt I sanctified them for *m* ... Num 8:17
I the LORD will make *m* known unto ... Num 12:6
I am not able to bear you *m* alone ... Deut 1:9
How can I *m* alone bear your ... Deut 1:12
And I turned *m* and came down from ... Deut 10:5
at other times before, and shake *m* ... Judg 16:20
said, I cannot redeem it for *m* ... Ruth 4:6
I forced *m* therefore, and offered ... 1Sa 13:12
that I may hide *m* in the field ... 1Sa 20:5
from avenging *m* with mine own ... 1Sa 25:33
surely go forth with you *m* also ... 2Sa 18:2 589
have kept *m* from mine iniquity ... 2Sa 22:24
surely shew *m* unto him to day ... 1Kin 18:15
Jehoshaphat, I will disguise *m* ... 1Kin 22:30
I bow *m* in the house of Rimmon ... 2Kin 5:18
when I bow down *m* in the house of ... 2Kin 5:18
to *m* for an house of sacrifice ... 2Chr 7:12
Jehoshaphat, I will disguise *m* ... 2Chr 18:29
Then I consulted with *m*, and I ... Neh 5:7
that she had prepared but *m* ... Est 5:12
to do honour more than to *m* ... Est 6:6
yea, I would harden *m* in sorrow ... Job 6:10
thee, so that I am a burden to *m* ... Job 7:20
If I justify *m*, mine own mouth ... Job 9:20
off my heaviness, and comfort *m* ... Job 9:27
If I wash *m* with snow water, and ... Job 9:30
I will leave my complaint upon *m* ... Job 10:1
then I will not hide *m* from thee ... Job 13:20
mine error remaineth with *m* ... Job 19:4
Whom I shall see for *m*, and mine ... Job 19:27
Or have eaten my morsel *m* alone ... Job 31:17
or lifted up *m* when evil found ... Job 31:29
Wherefore I abhor *m*, and repent in ... Job 42:6
I kept *m* from mine iniquity ... Ps 18:23
I behaved *m* as though he had been ... Ps 35:14
then I would have hid *m* from him ... Ps 55:12
I *m* will awake early ... Ps 57:8
I will behave *m* wisely in a ... Ps 101:2
I *m* will awake early ... Ps 108:2
but I give *m* unto prayer ... Ps 109:4
I will delight *m* in thy statutes ... Ps 119:16
And I will delight *m* in thy ... Ps 119:47
and have comforted *m* ... Ps 119:52
do I exercise *m* in great matters ... Ps 131:1
I have behaved and quieted *m* ... Ps 131:2 5315
in mine heart to give *m* unto wine ... Eccl 2:3
I turned *m* to behold wisdom, and ... Eccl 2:12
I *m* perceived also that one event ... Eccl 2:14 589
have shewed *m* wise under the sun ... Eccl 2:19
now will I lift up *m* ... Is 33:10
I have been still, and refrained *m* ... Is 42:14
This people have I formed for *m* ... Is 43:21
spreadeth abroad the earth by *m* ... Is 44:24
I have sworn by *m*, the word is ... Is 45:23
I would comfort *m* against sorrow ... Jer 8:18
I *m* will fight against you with ... Jer 21:5 589
hear these words, I swear by *m* ... Jer 22:5
For I have sworn by *m*, saith the ... Jer 49:13
I the LORD will answer him by *m* ... Eze 14:7
made *m* known unto them in the ... Eze 20:5
sight I made *m* known unto them ... Eze 20:9
mine own, and I have made it for *m* ... Eze 29:3
I will make *m* known among them, ... Eze 35:11
I magnify *m*, and sanctify *m* ... Eze 38:23
neither did I anoint *m* at all ... Dan 10:3
bow *m* before the high God ... Mic 6:6
into my bones, and I trembled in *m* ... Hab 3:16
in the fifth month, separating *m* ... Zec 7:3
I *m* worthy to come unto thee ... Lk 7:7 *1683*
hands and my feet, that it is I *m* ... Lk 24:39
If I bear witness of *m*, my ... Jn 5:31 *1683*
of God, or whether I speak of *m* ... Jn 7:17 *1683*
and I am not come of *m*, but he ... Jn 7:28 *1683*
them, Though I bear record of *m* ... Jn 8:14 *1683*
I am one that bear witness of *m* ... Jn 8:18 *1683*
am he, and that I do nothing of *m* ... Jn 8:28 *1683*
neither came I of *m*, but he sent ... Jn 8:42 *1683*
Jesus answered, If I honour *m* ... Jn 8:54 *1683*
from me, but I lay it down of *m* ... Jn 10:18 *1683*
For I have not spoken of *m* ... Jn 12:49 *1683*
come again, and receive you unto *m* ... Jn 14:3 *1683*
I speak unto you I speak not of *m* ... Jn 14:10 *1683*
him, and will manifest *m* to him ... Jn 14:21 *1683*
And for their sakes I sanctify *m* ... Jn 17:19 *1683*
I *m* also am a man ... Acts 10:26
count I my life dear unto *m* ... Acts 20:24 *1683*
the more cheerfully answer for *m* ... Acts 24:10 *1683*
And herein do I exercise *m* ... Acts 24:16
I would also hear the man *m* ... Acts 25:22
I think *m* happy, king Agrippa, ... Acts 26:2 *1683*
because I shall answer for *m* this ... Acts 26:2
I verily thought with *m*, that I ... Acts 26:9 *1683*
the mind I *m* serve the law of God ... Rom 7:25
For I could wish that *m* were ... Rom 9:3 *846*
reserved to *m* seven thousand men ... Rom 11:4 *1683*
I *m* also am persuaded of you, my ... Rom 15:14
a succourer of many, and of *m* also ... Rom 16:2 *846*
For I know nothing by *m* ... 1Cor 4:4 *1683*
have in a figure transferred to *m* ... 1Cor 4:6 *1683*
that all men were even as I *m* ... 1Cor 7:7 *1683*
yet have I made *m* servant unto ... 1Cor 9:19 *1683*
others, I *m* should be a castaway ... 1Cor 9:27
But I determined this with *m* ... 2Cor 2:1 *1683*
Now I Paul *m* beseech you by the ... 2Cor 10:1
m that ye might be exalted ... 2Cor 11:7 *1683*
in all things I have kept *m* from ... 2Cor 11:9 *1683*
unto you, and so will I keep *m* ... 2Cor 11:9 *1683*
me, that I may boast *m* a little ... 2Cor 11:16
yet of *m* I will not glory, but in ... 2Cor 12:5 *1683*
except it be that I *m* was not ... 2Cor 12:13
I make *m* a transgressor ... Gal 2:18 *1683*
that I also *m* shall come shortly ... Phil 2:24
I count not *m* to have apprehended ... Phil 3:13
a partner, receive him as *m* ... Philem 17 *1691*

MYSIA (*miz'-ye-ah*) *A Roman province in Asia Minor.*
After they were come to *M* ... Acts 16:7 *3463*
they passing by *M* came down to ... Acts 16:8 *3463*

MYSTERIES
the *m* of the kingdom of heaven ... Mt 13:11 *3466*
know the *m* of the kingdom of God ... Lk 8:10 *3466*
and stewards of the *m* of God ... 1Cor 4:1 *3466*
of prophecy, and understand all *m* ... 1Cor 13:2 *3466*
in the spirit he speaketh *m* ... 1Cor 14:2 *3466*

MYSTERY
know the *m* of the kingdom of God ... Mk 4:11 *3466*
ye should be ignorant of this *m* ... Rom 11:25 *3466*
to the revelation of the *m* ... Rom 16:25 *3466*
we speak the wisdom of God in a *m* ... 1Cor 2:7 *3466*
Behold, I shew you a *m* ... 1Cor 15:51 *3466*
known unto us the *m* of his will ... Eph 1:9 *3466*
he made known unto me the *m* ... Eph 3:3 *3466*
my knowledge in the *m* of Christ) ... Eph 3:4 *3466*
what is the fellowship of the *m* ... Eph 3:9 *3466*
This is a great *m* ... Eph 5:32 *3466*
to make known the *m* of the gospel ... Eph 6:19 *3466*
Even the *m* which hath been hid ... Col 1:26 *3466*
of this *m* among the Gentiles ... Col 1:27 *3466*
acknowledgement of the *m* of God ... Col 2:2 *3466*
to speak the *m* of Christ ... Col 4:3 *3466*
For the *m* of iniquity doth ... 2Th 2:7 *3466*
Holding the *m* of the faith in a ... 1Ti 3:9 *3466*
great is the *m* of godliness ... 1Ti 3:16 *3466*
The *m* of the seven stars which ... Rev 1:20 *3466*
the *m* of God should be finished, ... Rev 10:7 *3466*
forehead was a name written, *M* ... Rev 17:5 *3466*
will tell thee the *m* of the woman ... Rev 17:7 *3466*

N

NAAM (*na'-am*) *A son of Caleb.*
Iru, Elah, and *N* ... 1Chr 4:15 5277

NAAMAH (*na'-a-mah*) See NAAMATHITE.
1. Sister of Tubal-cain.
and the sister of Tubal-cain was *N* ... Gen 4:22 5279
2. Mother of King Rehoboam.
mother's name was *N* an Ammonitess. 1Kin 14:21 5279
mother's name was *N* an Ammonitess. 1Kin 14:31 5279
mother's name was *N* an Ammonitess. 2Chr 12:13 5279
3. A city in Judah.
And Gederoth, Beth-dagon, and *N* ... Josh 15:41 5279

NAAMAN (*na'-a-man*) See NAAMAN'S, NAAMITES.
1. A son of Benjamin.
and Becher, and Ashbel, Gera, and *N* ... Gen 46:21 5283
2. A son of Bela.
And the sons of Bela were Ard and *N* ... Num 26:40 5283
and of *N*, the family of the ... Num 26:40 5283
And Abishua, and *N*, and Ahoah, ... 1Chr 8:4 5283
3. A son of Ehud.
And *N*, and Ahiah, and Gera, he ... 1Chr 8:7 5283
4. A Syrian captain.
Now *N*, captain of the host of the ... 2Kin 5:1 5283
sent *N* my servant to thee ... 2Kin 5:6 5283
So *N* came with his horses and with ... 2Kin 5:9 5283
But *N* was wroth, and went away, and 2Kin 5:11 5283
N said, Shall there not then, I ... 2Kin 5:17 5283
master hath spared *N* this Syrian ... 2Kin 5:20 5283
So Gehazi followed after *N* ... 2Kin 5:21 5283
when *N* saw him running after him, ... 2Kin 5:21 5283
N said, Be content, take two ... 2Kin 5:23 5283
of *N* shall cleave unto thee ... 2Kin 5:27 5283
was cleansed, saving *N* the Syrian ... Lk 4:27 *3497*

NAAMAN'S (*na'-a-mans*) *Refers fo Naaman 4.*
and she waited on *N* wife ... 2Kin 5:2 5283

NAAMATHITE (*na'-a-math-ite*) *Family name of Zophar.*
the Shuhite, and Zophar the *N* ... Job 2:11 5284
Then answered Zophar the *N* ... Job 11:1 5284
Then answered Zophar the *N* ... Job 20:1 5284
the Shuhite and Zophar the *N* went ... Job 42:9 5284

NAAMITES (*na'-a-mites*) *Descendants of Naaman 3.*
and of Naaman, the family of the *N* ... Num 26:40 5280

NAARAH (*na'-a-rah*) See NAARAN, NAARATH. *A wife of Ashur.*
Tekoa had two wives, Helah and *N* ... 1Chr 4:5 5292
N bare him Ahuzam, and Hepher, and. 1Chr 4:6 5292
These were the sons of *N* ... 1Chr 4:6 5292

NAARAI (*na'-a-rahee*) See PAARAI. *A "mighty man" of David.*
Carmelite, *N* the son of Ezbai, ... 1Chr 11:37 5293

NAARAN (*na'-a-ran*) *A city in Ephraim.*
the towns thereof, and eastward *N* ... 1Chr 7:28 5295

NAARATH (*na'-a-rath*) See NAARAH, NAARAN. *Same as Naaran.*
from Janohah to Ataroth, and to *N* ... Josh 16:7 5292

NAASHON (*na'-a-shon*) See NAHSHON. *Brother of Elisheba.*
of Amminadab, sister of *N* ... Ex 6:23 5177

NAASSON (*na'-as-son*) See NAASHON. *Father of Salmon.*
and Aminadab begat *N* ... Mt 1:4 *3476*
and *N* begat Salmon ... Mt 1:4 *3476*
of Salmon, which was the son of *N* ... Lk 3:32 *3476*

NABAJOTH See NABOTH.

NABAL (*na'-bal*) See NABAL'S. *A wife of David.*
Now the name of the man was *N* ... 1Sa 25:3 5037
that *N* did shear his sheep ... 1Sa 25:4 5037
Get you up to Carmel, and go to *N* ... 1Sa 25:5 5037
they spake to *N* according to all ... 1Sa 25:9 5037
N answered David's servants, and ... 1Sa 25:10 5037
But she told not her husband *N* ... 1Sa 25:19 5037
regard this man of Belial, even *N* ... 1Sa 25:25 5037
N is his name, and folly is with ... 1Sa 25:25 5037
seek evil to my lord, be as *N* ... 1Sa 25:26 5037
there had not been left unto *N* by ... 1Sa 25:34 5037
And Abigail came to *N* ... 1Sa 25:36 5037
days after, that the wine was gone out of *N* ... 1Sa 25:37 5037
days after, that the LORD smote *N* ... 1Sa 25:38 5037
when David heard that *N* was dead ... 1Sa 25:39 5037
of my reproach from the hand of *N* ... 1Sa 25:39 5037
wickedness of *N* upon his own head ... 1Sa 25:39 5037
the wife of *N* the Carmelite ... 1Sa 30:5 5037
the wife of *N* the Carmelite ... 2Sa 3:3 5037

NABAL'S (*na'-balz*)
N wife, saying, Behold, David ... 1Sa 25:14 5037
N heart was merry within him for ... 1Sa 25:36 5037
Abigail the Carmelitess, *N* wife ... 1Sa 27:3 5037
Abigail *N* wife the Carmelite ... 2Sa 2:2 5037

NABOTH (*na'-both*) *A Jezreelite of Issachar.*
that *N* the Jezreelite had a ... 1Kin 21:1 5022
And Ahab spake unto *N*, saying, ... 1Kin 21:2 5022
N said to Ahab, The LORD forbid ... 1Kin 21:3 5022
because of the word which *N* the ... 1Kin 21:4 5022
I spake unto *N* the Jezreelite ... 1Kin 21:6 5022
the vineyard of *N* the Jezreelite ... 1Kin 21:7 5022
were in his city, dwelling with *N* ... 1Kin 21:8 5022
set *N* on high among the people ... 1Kin 21:9 5022
set *N* on high among the people ... 1Kin 21:12 5022
against him, even against *N* ... 1Kin 21:13 5022
N did blaspheme God and the king ... 1Kin 21:13 5022
saying, *N* is stoned, and is dead ... 1Kin 21:14 5022
Jezebel heard that *N* was stoned ... 1Kin 21:15 5022
the vineyard of *N* the Jezreelite ... 1Kin 21:15 5022
for *N* is not alive, but dead ... 1Kin 21:15 5022
when Ahab heard that *N* was dead ... 1Kin 21:16 5022
the vineyard of *N* the Jezreelite ... 1Kin 21:16 5022
he is in the vineyard of *N* ... 1Kin 21:18 5022
of *N* shall dogs lick thy blood ... 1Kin 21:19 5022
the portion of *N* the Jezreelite ... 2Kin 9:21 5022
of the field of *N* the Jezreelite ... 2Kin 9:25 5022
seen yesterday the blood of *N* ... 2Kin 9:26 5022

NACHON See NACHON'S.

NACHON'S (*na'-kons*)
they came to *N* threshingfloor ... 2Sa 6:6 5225

NACHOR (*na'-kor*) See NAHOR.
1. Brother of Abraham.
of Abraham, and the father of *N* ... Josh 24:2 5152
2. Father of Thara; ancestor of Jesus.
of Thara, which was the son of *N* ... Lk 3:34 *3493*

NACON See NACHON'S.

NADAB (*na'-dab*)
1. Son of Aaron.
and she bare him *N*, and Abihu, ... Ex 6:23 5070
unto the LORD, thou, and Aaron, *N* ... Ex 24:1 5070
Then went up Moses, and Aaron, *N* ... Ex 24:9 5070
priest's office, even Aaron, *N* ... Ex 28:1 5070
And *N* and Abihu, the sons of Aaron, ... Lev 10:1 5070
N the firstborn, and Abihu, ... Num 3:2 5070
And *N* and Abihu died before the ... Num 3:4 5070
And unto Aaron was born *N*, and ... Num 26:60 5070
And *N* and Abihu died, when they ... Num 26:61 5070
N, and Abihu, Eleazar, and Ithamar ... 1Chr 6:3 5070
N, and Abihu, Eleazar, and Ithamar ... 1Chr 24:1 5070
But *N* and Abihu died before their ... 1Chr 24:2 5070
2. Son of King Jeroboam I.
N his son reigned in his stead ... 1Kin 14:20 5070
N the son of Jeroboam began to ... 1Kin 15:25 5070
for *N* and all Israel laid siege to ... 1Kin 15:27 5070
Now the rest of the acts of *N* ... 1Kin 15:31 5070
3. Great-grandson of Jerahmeel.
Shammai; *N*, and ... 1Chr 2:28 5070
And the sons of *N* ... 1Chr 2:30 5070
4. A descendant of King Saul.
and Zur, and Kish, and Baal, and *N* ... 1Chr 8:30 5070
and Kish, and Baal, and Ner, and *N* ... 1Chr 9:36 5070

NAGGAI See NAGGE.

NAGGE (*nag'-e*) See NEARIAH. *Father of Esli; ancestor of Jesus.*
of Esli, which was the son of *N* ... Lk 3:25 *3477*

NAHALAL (*na'-ha-lal*) *A Levitical city in Zebulun.*
her suburbs, *N* with her suburbs ... Josh 21:35 5096

NAHALIEL (*na-ha'-le-el*) *An Israelite encampment in the wilderness.*
And from Mattanah to *N* ... Num 21:19 5160
and from *N* to Bamoth ... Num 21:19 5160

NAHALLAL (*na'-hal-al*) See NAHALAL. *Same as Nahalal.*
Kattath, and *N*, and Shimron ... Josh 19:15 5096

NAHALOL (*na'-ha-lol*) *Same as Nahalal.*
Kitron, nor the inhabitants of *N* ... Judg 1:30 5096

NAHAM (*na'-ham*) See ISHBAH. *A descendant of Caleb.*
his wife Hodiah the sister of *N* ... 1Chr 4:19 5163

NAHAMANI (*na-ham'-a-ni*) *A ruling chief with Zerubbabel.*
Nehemiah, Azariah, Raamiah, *N* ... Neh 7:7 5167

NAHARAI (*na'-ha-rahee*) See NAHARI. *A "mighty man" of David.*
N the Berothite, the armourbearer ... 1Chr 11:39 5171

NAHARI (*na'-ha-ri*) See NAHARAI. *Same as Naharai.*
N the Beerothite, armourbearer to ... 2Sa 23:37 5171

NAHASH (*na'-hash*) See IR-NAHASH.
1. An Ammonite king.
Then *N* the Ammonite came up, and ... 1Sa 11:1 5176
all the men of Jabesh said unto *N* ... 1Sa 11:1 5176
N the Ammonite answered them, On ... 1Sa 11:2 5176
when ye saw that *N* the king of ... 1Sa 12:12 5176
2. Father of Shobi and Hanun.
kindness unto Hanun the son of *N* ... 2Sa 10:2 5176
that Shobi the son of *N* of Rabbah ... 2Sa 17:27 5176
that *N* the king of the children ... 1Chr 19:1 5176
kindness unto Hanun the son of *N* ... 1Chr 19:2 5176
3. Mother of Abigail.
in to Abigail the daughter of *N* ... 2Sa 17:25 5176

NAHATH (*na'-hath*) See TOHU.
1. A son of Reuel.
N, and Zerah, Shammah, and Mizzah ... Gen 36:13 5184
duke *N*, duke Zerah, duke Shammah, ... Gen 36:17 5184
N, Zerah, Shammah, and Mizzah ... 1Chr 1:37 5184
2. Son of Zophi.
Zophai his son, and *N* his son, ... 1Chr 6:26 5184
3. A Temple servant.
And Jehiel, and Azaziah, and *N* ... 2Chr 31:13 5184

NAHBI (*nah'-bi*) *A spy sent to the Promised Land.*
of Naphtali, *N* the son of Vophsi ... Num 13:14 5147

NAHOR (*na'-hor*) See NACHOR, NAHOR'S.
1. Grandfather of Abraham.
lived thirty years, and begat *N* ... Gen 11:22 5152
he begat *N* two hundred years ... Gen 11:23 5152
N lived nine and twenty years, and ... Gen 11:24 5152
N lived after he begat Terah an ... Gen 11:25 5152
Serug, *N*, Terah, ... 1Chr 1:26 5152
2. Son of Terah.
seventy years, and begat Abram, *N* ... Gen 11:26 5152
Terah begat Abram, *N*, and Haran ... Gen 11:27 5152
And Abram and *N* took them wives ... Gen 11:29 5152
born children unto thy brother *N* ... Gen 22:20 5152
these eight Milcah did bear to *N* ... Gen 22:23 5152
Mesopotamia, unto the city of *N* ... Gen 24:10 5152
son of Milcah, the wife of *N* ... Gen 24:15 5152
of Milcah, which she bare unto *N* ... Gen 24:24 5152
them, Know ye Laban the son of *N* ... Gen 29:5 5152
God of Abraham, and the God of *N* ... Gen 31:53 5152

NAHOR'S (*na'-hors*) *Refers to Nahor 2.*
and the name of *N* wife, Milcah, ... Gen 11:29 5152
N son, whom Milcah bare unto him ... Gen 24:47 5152

NAHSHON (*nah'-shon*) See NAASHON, NAASSON. *Son of Amminadab.*
N the son of Amminadab ... Num 1:7 5177
N the son of Amminadab shall be ... Num 2:3 5177
day was *N* the son of Amminadab ... Num 7:12 5177
of *N* the son of Amminadab ... Num 7:17 5177
over his host was *N* the son of ... Num 10:14 5177
And Amminadab begat *N*, and *N* ... Ruth 4:20 5177
begat *N*, and *N* begat Salmon, ... Ruth 4:20 5177
and Amminadab begat *N*, prince of ... 1Chr 2:10 5177
N begat Salma, and Salma begat ... 1Chr 2:11 5177

NAHUM (*na'-hum*) See NAUM. *A prophet who spoke against Nineveh.*
of the vision of *N* the Elkoshite ... Nah 1:1 5151

NAIL
Heber's wife took a *n* of the tent ... Judg 4:21 3489
smote the *n* into his temples, and ... Judg 4:21 3489
dead, and the *n* was in his temples ... Judg 4:22 3489
She put her hand to the *n* ... Judg 5:26 3489
to give us a *n* in his holy place, ... Ezr 9:8 3489
fasten him as a *n* in a sure place ... Is 22:23 3489
shall the *n* that is fastened in ... Is 22:25 3489
the corner, out of him the *n* ... Zec 10:4 3489

NAILING
out of the way, *n* it to his cross ... Col 2:14 *4338*

NAILS
shave her head, and pare her *n* ... Deut 21:12 6856
iron in abundance for the *n* for ... 1Chr 22:3 4548
the weight of the *n* was fifty ... 2Chr 3:9 4548
as *n* fastened by the masters of ... Eccl 12:11 4930
and he fastened it with *n*, that it ... Is 41:7 4548
they fasten it with *n* and with ... Jer 10:4 4548
and his *n* like birds' claws ... Dan 4:33 2953
were of iron, and his *n* of brass ... Dan 7:19 2953
in his hands the print of the *n* ... Jn 20:25 *2247*
my finger into the print of the *n* ... Jn 20:25 *2247*

NAIN (*nane*) *A city in Galilee.*
that he went into a city called *N* ... Lk 7:11 *3484*

NAIOTH (*nay'-yoth*) *A place in Ramah.*
he and Samuel went and dwelt in *N* ... 1Sa 19:18 5121
Behold, David is at *N* in Ramah ... 1Sa 19:19 5121
Behold, they be at *N* in Ramah ... 1Sa 19:22 5121
And he went thither to *N* in Ramah ... 1Sa 19:23 5121
until he came to *N* in Ramah ... 1Sa 19:23 5121
And David fled from *N* in Ramah ... 1Sa 20:1 5121

NAKED
And they were both *n*, the man and ... Gen 2:25 6174
and they knew that they were *n* ... Gen 3:7 5903
and I was afraid, because I was *n* ... Gen 3:10 5903
Who told thee that thou wast *n* ... Gen 3:11 5903
Moses saw that the people were *n* ... Ex 32:25 6544
(for Aaron had made them *n* unto ... Ex 32:25 6544
lay down *n* all that day and all ... 1Sa 19:24 6174
all that were *n* among them ... 2Chr 28:15 4636
for he made Judah *n*, and ... 2Chr 28:19 6544
N came I out of my mother's womb, ... Job 1:21 6174
and *n* shall I return thither ... Job 1:21 6174
stripped the *n* of their clothing ... Job 22:6 6174
They cause the *n* to lodge without ... Job 24:7 6174
him to go *n* without clothing ... Job 24:10 6174
Hell is *n* before him, and ... Job 26:6 6174
n shall he return to go as he ... Eccl 5:15 6174
And he did so, walking *n* and ... Is 20:2 6174
my servant Isaiah hath walked *n* ... Is 20:3 6174
captives, young and old, *n* ... Is 20:4 6174
when thou seest the *n*, that thou ... Is 58:7 6174
drunken, and shalt make thyself *n* ... Lam 4:21 6168
is grown, whereas thou wast *n* ... Eze 16:7 5903
of thy youth, when thou wast *n* ... Eze 16:22 5903
thy fair jewels, and leave thee *n* ... Eze 16:39 5903
hath covered the *n* with a garment ... Eze 18:7 5903
hath covered the *n* with a garment ... Eze 18:16 5903
thy labour, and shall leave thee *n* ... Eze 23:29 5903
Lest I strip her *n*, and set her as ... Hos 2:3 6174
shall flee away *n* in that day ... Amos 2:16 6174
and howl, I will go stripped and *n* ... Mic 1:8 6174
of Saphir, having thy shame *n* ... Mic 1:11 6181
Thy bow was made quite *n*, ... Hab 3:9 5783
N, and ye clothed me ... Mt 25:36 *1131*

or *n*, and clothed thee ... Mt 25:38 *1131*
n, and ye clothed me not ... Mt 25:43 *1131*
or athirst, or a stranger, or *n* ... Mt 25:44 *1131*
linen cloth cast about his *n* body ... Mk 14:51 *1131*
linen cloth, and fled from them *n* ... Mk 14:52 *1131*
coat unto him, (for he was *n* ... Jn 21:7 *1131*
they fled out of that house *n* ... Acts 19:16 *1131*
both hunger, and thirst, and are *n* ... 1Cor 4:11 *1130*
clothed we shall not be found *n* ... 2Cor 5:3 *1131*
but all things are *n* and opened ... Heb 4:13 *1131*
If a brother or sister be *n* ... Jas 2:15 *1131*
and poor, and blind, and *n* ... Rev 3:17 *1131*
his garments, lest he walk *n* ... Rev 16:15 *1131*
and shall make her desolate and *n* ... Rev 17:16 *1131*

NAKEDNESS

saw the *n* of his father, and told ... Gen 9:22 6172
covered the *n* of their father ... Gen 9:23 6172
and they saw not their father's *n* ... Gen 9:23 6172
to see the *n* of the land ye are ... Gen 42:9 6172
but to see the *n* of the land ye ... Gen 42:12 6172
that thy *n* be not discovered ... Ex 20:26 6172
linen breeches to cover their *n* ... Ex 28:42 6172
of kin to him, to uncover their *n* ... Lev 18:6 6172
The *n* of thy father ... Lev 18:7 6172
or the *n* of thy mother, shalt ... Lev 18:7 6172
thou shalt not uncover her *n* ... Lev 18:7 6172
The *n* of thy father's wife shalt ... Lev 18:8 6172
it is thy father's *n* ... Lev 18:8 6172
The *n* of thy sister, the daughter ... Lev 18:9 6172
even their *n* thou shalt not ... Lev 18:9 6172
The *n* of thy son's daughter, or ... Lev 18:10 6172
even their *n* thou shalt not ... Lev 18:10 6172
for theirs is thine own *n* ... Lev 18:10 6172
The *n* of thy father's wife's ... Lev 18:11 6172
thou shalt not uncover her *n* ... Lev 18:11 6172
the *n* of thy father's sister ... Lev 18:12 6172
the *n* of thy mother's sister ... Lev 18:13 6172
the *n* of thy father's brother ... Lev 18:14 6172
the *n* of thy daughter in law ... Lev 18:15 6172
thou shalt not uncover her *n* ... Lev 18:15 6172
the *n* of thy brother's wife ... Lev 18:16 6172
it is thy brother's *n* ... Lev 18:16 6172
not uncover the *n* of a woman ... Lev 18:17 6172
daughter, to uncover her *n* ... Lev 18:17 6172
to vex her, to uncover her *n* ... Lev 18:18 6172
unto a woman to uncover her *n* ... Lev 18:19 6172
hath uncovered his father's *n* ... Lev 20:11 6172
her *n*, and she see his *n* ... Lev 20:17 6172
he hath uncovered his sister's *n* ... Lev 20:17 6172
sickness, and shall uncover her *n* ... Lev 20:18 6172
the *n* of thy mother's sister ... Lev 20:19 6172
he hath uncovered his uncle's *n* ... Lev 20:20 6172
he hath uncovered his brother's *n* ... Lev 20:21 6172
in hunger, and in thirst, and in *n* ... Deut 28:48 5903
the confusion of thy mother's *n* ... 1Sa 20:30 6172
Thy *n* shall be uncovered, yea, ... Is 47:3 6172
her, because they have seen her *n* ... Lam 1:8 6172
skirt over thee, and covered thy *n* ... Eze 16:8 6172
thy *n* discovered through thy ... Eze 16:36 6172
and will discover thy *n* unto them ... Eze 16:37 6172
that they may see all thy *n* ... Eze 16:37 6172
they discovered their fathers' *n* ... Eze 22:10 6172
These discovered her *n* ... Eze 23:10 6172
whoredoms, and discovered her *n* ... Eze 23:18 6172
the *n* of thy whoredoms shall be ... Eze 23:29 6172
and my flax given to cover her *n* ... Hos 2:9 6172
and I will shew the nations thy *n* ... Nah 3:5 4626
that thou mayest look on their *n* ... Hab 2:15 4589
or persecution, or famine, or *n* ... Rom 8:35 *1132*
in fastings often, in cold and *n* ... 2Cor 11:27 *1132*
the shame of thy *n* do not appear ... Rev 3:18 *1132*

NAME

The *n* of the first is Pison ... Gen 2:11 8034
the *n* of the second river is ... Gen 2:13 8034
the *n* of the third river is ... Gen 2:14 8034
creature, that was the *n* thereof ... Gen 2:19 8034
And Adam called his wife's *n* Eve ... Gen 3:20 8034
called the *n* of the city ... Gen 4:17 8034
after the *n* of his son, Enoch ... Gen 4:17 8034
the *n* of the one was Adah, and the ... Gen 4:19 8034
the *n* of the other Zillah ... Gen 4:19 8034
And his brother's *n* was Jubal ... Gen 4:21 8034
bare a son, and called his *n* Seth ... Gen 4:25 8034
and he called his *n* Enos ... Gen 4:26 8034
to call upon the *n* of the LORD ... Gen 4:26 8034
them, and called their *n* Adam ... Gen 5:2 8034
and called his *n* Seth ... Gen 5:3 8034
And he called his *n* Noah, saying, ... Gen 5:29 8034
the *n* of one was Peleg ... Gen 10:25 8034
and his brother's *n* was Joktan ... Gen 10:25 8034
and let us make us a *n*, lest we be ... Gen 11:4 8034
Therefore is the *n* of it called ... Gen 11:9 8034
the *n* of Abram's wife was Sarai ... Gen 11:29 8034
the *n* of Nahor's wife, Milcah, ... Gen 11:29 8034
bless thee, and make thy *n* great ... Gen 12:2 8034
and called upon the *n* of the LORD ... Gen 12:8 8034
Abram called on the *n* of the LORD ... Gen 13:4 8034
an Egyptian, whose *n* was Hagar ... Gen 16:1 8034
son, and shalt call his *n* Ishmael ... Gen 16:11 8034
she called the *n* of the LORD that ... Gen 16:13 8034
and Abram called his son's *n* ... Gen 16:15 8034
Neither shall thy *n* any more be ... Gen 17:5 8034
but thy *n* shall be Abraham ... Gen 17:5 8034
thou shalt not call her *n* Sarai ... Gen 17:15 8034
Sarai, but Sarah shall her *n* be ... Gen 17:15 8034
and thou shalt call his *n* Isaac ... Gen 17:19 8034
Therefore the *n* of the city was ... Gen 19:22 8034
bare a son, and called his *n* Moab ... Gen 19:37 8034
a son, and called his *n* Ben-ammi ... Gen 19:38 8034
Abraham called the *n* of his son ... Gen 21:3 8034
called there on the *n* of the LORD ... Gen 21:33 8034
Abraham called the *n* of that ... Gen 22:14 8034
whose *n* was Reumah, she bare also ... Gen 22:24 8034
had a brother, and his *n* was Laban ... Gen 24:29 8034
took a wife, and her *n* was Keturah ... Gen 25:1 8034
and they called his *n* Esau ... Gen 25:25 8034
and his *n* was called Jacob ... Gen 25:26 8034
therefore was his *n* called Edom ... Gen 25:30 8034
he called the *n* of the well Esek ... Gen 26:20 8034
and he called the *n* of it Sitnah ... Gen 26:21 8034
he called the *n* of it Rehoboth ... Gen 26:22 8034
and called upon the *n* of the LORD ... Gen 26:25 8034
therefore the *n* of the city is ... Gen 26:33 8034
he called the *n* of that place ... Gen 28:19 8034
but the *n* of that city was called ... Gen 28:19 8034
the *n* of the elder was Leah, and ... Gen 29:16 8034
the *n* of the younger was Rachel ... Gen 29:16 8034
a son, and she called his *n* Reuben ... Gen 29:32 8034
and she called his *n* Simeon ... Gen 29:33 8034
therefore was his *n* called Levi ... Gen 29:34 8034
therefore she called his *n* Judah ... Gen 29:35 8034
therefore called she his *n* Dan ... Gen 30:6 8034
and she called his *n* Naphtali ... Gen 30:8 8034
and she called his *n* Gad ... Gen 30:11 8034
and she called his *n* Asher ... Gen 30:13 8034
and she called his *n* Issachar ... Gen 30:18 8034
and she called his *n* Zebulun ... Gen 30:20 8034
a daughter, and called her *n* Dinah ... Gen 30:21 8034
And she called his *n* Joseph ... Gen 30:24 8034
Therefore was the *n* of it called ... Gen 31:48 8034
he called the *n* of that place ... Gen 32:2 8034
he said unto him, What is thy *n* ... Gen 32:27 8034
Thy *n* shall be called no more ... Gen 32:28 8034
said, Tell me, I pray thee, thy *n* ... Gen 32:29 8034
it that thou dost ask after my *n* ... Gen 32:29 8034
Jacob called the *n* of the place ... Gen 32:30 8034
therefore the *n* of the place is ... Gen 33:17 8034
and the *n* of it was called ... Gen 35:8 8034
God said unto him, Thy *n* is Jacob ... Gen 35:10 8034
thy *n* shall not be called any ... Gen 35:10 8034
Jacob, but Israel shall be thy *n* ... Gen 35:10 8034
and he called his *n* Israel ... Gen 35:10 8034
Jacob called the *n* of the place ... Gen 35:15 8034
that she called his *n* Ben-oni ... Gen 35:18 8034
the *n* of his city was Dinhabah ... Gen 36:32 8034
the *n* of his city was Avith ... Gen 36:35 8034
the *n* of his city was Pau ... Gen 36:39 8034
his wife's *n* was Mehetabel, the ... Gen 36:39 8034
Adullamite, whose *n* was Hirah ... Gen 38:1 8034
Canaanite, whose *n* was Shuah ... Gen 38:2 8034
and he called his *n* Er ... Gen 38:3 8034
and she called his *n* Onan ... Gen 38:4 8034
and called his *n* Shelah ... Gen 38:5 8034
his firstborn, whose *n* was Tamar ... Gen 38:6 8034
therefore his *n* was called Pharez ... Gen 38:29 8034
and his *n* was called Zarah ... Gen 38:30 8034
Joseph's *n* Zaphnath-paaneah ... Gen 41:45 8034
Joseph called the *n* of the ... Gen 41:51 8034
the *n* of the second called he ... Gen 41:52 8034
shall be called after the *n* of ... Gen 48:6 8034
let my *n* be named on them, and the ... Gen 48:16 8034
the *n* of my fathers Abraham and ... Gen 48:16 8034
wherefore the *n* of it was called ... Gen 50:11 8034
of which the *n* of the one was ... Ex 1:15 8034
and the *n* of the other Puah ... Ex 1:15 8034
And she called his *n* Moses ... Ex 2:10 8034
a son, and he called his *n* Gershom ... Ex 2:22 8034
shall say to me, What is his *n* ... Ex 3:13 8034
this is my *n* for ever, and this is ... Ex 3:15 8034
came to Pharaoh to speak in thy *n* ... Ex 5:23 8034
by the *n* of God Almighty, but by ... Ex 6:3
but by my *n* JEHOVAH was I not ... Ex 6:3 8034
that my *n* may be declared ... Ex 9:16 8034
the LORD is his *n* ... Ex 15:3 8034
therefore the *n* of it was called ... Ex 15:23 8034
Israel called the *n* thereof Manna ... Ex 16:31 8034
he called the *n* of the place ... Ex 17:7 8034
called the *n* of it Jehovah-nissi ... Ex 17:15 8034
of which the *n* of the one was ... Ex 18:3 8034
the *n* of the other was Eliezer ... Ex 18:4 8034
Thou shalt not take the *n* of the ... Ex 20:7 8034
that taketh his *n* in vain ... Ex 20:7 8034
record my *n* I will come unto thee ... Ex 20:24 8034
no mention of the *n* of other gods ... Ex 23:13 8034
for my *n* is in him ... Ex 23:21 8034
every one with his *n* shall they ... Ex 28:21 8034
I have called by *n* Bezaleel the ... Ex 31:2 8034
thou hast said, I know thee by *n* ... Ex 33:12 8034
in my sight, and I know thee by *n* ... Ex 33:17 8034
I will proclaim the *n* of the LORD ... Ex 33:19 8034
and proclaimed the *n* of the LORD ... Ex 34:5 8034
whose *n* is Jealous, is a jealous ... Ex 34:14 8034
by *n* Bezaleel the son of Uri ... Ex 35:30 8034
of a signet, every one with his *n* ... Ex 39:14 8034
thou profane the *n* of thy God ... Lev 18:21 8034
shall not swear by my *n* falsely ... Lev 19:12 8034
thou profane the *n* of thy God ... Lev 19:12 8034
and to profane my holy *n* ... Lev 20:3 8034
and not profane the *n* of their God ... Lev 21:6 8034
holy *n* in those things which they ... Lev 22:2 8034
shall ye profane my holy *n* ... Lev 22:32 8034
son blasphemed the *n* of the LORD ... Lev 24:11 8034
his mother's *n* was Shelomith, the ... Lev 24:11 8034
blasphemeth the *n* of the LORD ... Lev 24:16 8034
he blasphemeth the *n* of the LORD ... Lev 24:16 8034
and by *n* ye shall reckon the ... Num 4:32 8034
they shall put my *n* upon the ... Num 6:27 8034
he called the *n* of the place ... Num 11:3 8034
the *n* of the one was Eldad ... Num 11:26 8034
and the *n* of the other Medad ... Num 11:26 8034
he called the *n* of that place ... Num 11:34 8034
thou every man's *n* upon his rod ... Num 17:2 8034
Aaron's *n* upon the rod of Levi ... Num 17:3 8034
he called the *n* of the place ... Num 21:3 8034
Now the *n* of the Israelite that ... Num 25:14 8034
the *n* of the Midianitish woman ... Num 25:15 8034
the *n* of the daughter of Asher ... Num 26:46 8034
the *n* of Amram's wife was ... Num 26:59 8034
Why should the *n* of our father be ... Num 27:4 8034
called it Nobah, after his own *n* ... Num 32:42 8034
and called them after his own *n* ... Deut 3:14 8034
Thou shalt not take the *n* of the ... Deut 5:11 8034
that taketh his *n* in vain ... Deut 5:11 8034
him, and shalt swear by his *n* ... Deut 6:13 8034
destroy their *n* from under heaven ... Deut 7:24 8034
blot out their *n* from under ... Deut 9:14 8034
unto him, and to bless in his *n* ... Deut 10:8 8034
thou cleave, and swear by his *n* ... Deut 10:20 8034
your tribes to put his *n* there ... Deut 12:5 8034
to cause his *n* to dwell there ... Deut 12:11 8034
his *n* there be too far from thee ... Deut 12:21 8034
shall choose to place his *n* there ... Deut 14:23 8034
shall choose to set his *n* there ... Deut 14:24 8034
shall choose to place his *n* there ... Deut 16:2 8034
shall choose to place his *n* in ... Deut 16:6 8034
hath chosen to place his *n* there ... Deut 16:11 8034
to minister in the *n* of the LORD ... Deut 18:5 8034
in the *n* of the LORD his God ... Deut 18:7 8034
which he shall speak in my *n* ... Deut 18:19 8034
presume to speak a word in my *n* ... Deut 18:20 8034
speak in the *n* of other gods ... Deut 18:20 8034
speaketh in the *n* of the LORD ... Deut 18:22 8034
and to bless in the *n* of the LORD ... Deut 21:5 8034
and bring up an evil *n* upon her ... Deut 22:14 8034
an evil *n* upon a virgin of Israel ... Deut 22:19 8034
n of his brother which is dead ... Deut 25:6 8034
that his *n* be not put out of ... Deut 25:6 8034
up unto his brother a *n* in Israel ... Deut 25:7 8034
his *n* shall be called in Israel, ... Deut 25:10 8034
shall choose to place his *n* there ... Deut 26:2 8034
he hath made, in praise, and in *n* ... Deut 26:19 8034
art called by the *n* of the LORD ... Deut 28:10 8034
fear this glorious and fearful *n* ... Deut 28:58 8034
blot out his *n* from under heaven ... Deut 29:20 8034
I will publish the *n* of the LORD ... Deut 32:3 8034
Wherefore the *n* of the place is ... Josh 5:9 8034
cut off our *n* from the earth ... Josh 7:9 8034
wilt thou do unto thy great *n* ... Josh 7:9 8034
Wherefore the *n* of that place was ... Josh 7:26 8034
of the *n* of the LORD thy God ... Josh 9:9 8034
the *n* of Hebron before was ... Josh 14:15 8034
the *n* of Debir before was ... Josh 15:15 8034
after the *n* of Dan their father ... Josh 19:47 8034
which are here mentioned by *n* ... Josh 21:9 8034
(now the *n* of Hebron before was ... Judg 1:10 8034
the *n* of Debir before was ... Judg 1:11 8034
the *n* of the city was called ... Judg 1:17 8034
(Now the *n* of the city before was ... Judg 1:23 8034
city, and called the *n* thereof Luz ... Judg 1:26 8034
which is the *n* thereof unto this ... Judg 1:26 8034
they called the *n* of that place ... Judg 2:5 8034
whose *n* he called Abimelech ... Judg 8:31 8034
the Danites, whose *n* was Manoah ... Judg 13:2 8034
he was, neither told he me his *n* ... Judg 13:6 8034
angel of the LORD, What is thy *n* ... Judg 13:17 8034
Why askest thou thus after my *n* ... Judg 13:18 8034
a son, and called his *n* Samson ... Judg 13:24 8034
called the *n* thereof En-hakkore ... Judg 15:19 8034
of Sorek, whose *n* was Delilah ... Judg 16:4 8034
mount Ephraim, whose *n* was Micah ... Judg 17:1 8034
they called the *n* of the city Dan ... Judg 18:29 8034
after the *n* of Dan their father, ... Judg 18:29 8034
howbeit the *n* of the city was ... Judg 18:29 8034
the *n* of the man was Elimelech, ... Ruth 1:2 8034
the *n* of his wife Naomi, and the ... Ruth 1:2 8034
the *n* of his two sons Mahlon and ... Ruth 1:2 8034
the *n* of the one was Orpah ... Ruth 1:4 8034
and the *n* of the other Ruth ... Ruth 1:4 8034
and his *n* was Boaz ... Ruth 2:1 8034
The man's *n* with whom I wrought ... Ruth 2:19 8034
to raise up the *n* of the dead ... Ruth 4:5 8034
to raise up the *n* of the dead ... Ruth 4:10 8034
that the *n* of the dead be not cut ... Ruth 4:10 8034
that his *n* may be famous in ... Ruth 4:14 8034
women her neighbours gave it a *n* ... Ruth 4:17 8034
and they called his *n* Obed ... Ruth 4:17 8034
his *n* was Elkanah, the son of ... 1Sa 1:1 8034
the *n* of the one was Hannah, and ... 1Sa 1:2 8034
the *n* of the other Peninnah ... 1Sa 1:2 8034
a son, and called his *n* Samuel ... 1Sa 1:20 8034
called the *n* of it Eben-ezer, ... 1Sa 7:12 8034
Now the *n* of his firstborn was ... 1Sa 8:2 8034
the *n* of his second, Abiah ... 1Sa 8:2 8034
whose *n* was Kish, the son of ... 1Sa 9:1 8034
whose *n* was Saul, a choice young ... 1Sa 9:2 8034
the *n* of the one was Bozez ... 1Sa 14:4 8034
and the *n* of the other Seneh ... 1Sa 14:4 8034
the *n* of the firstborn Merab, and ... 1Sa 14:49 8034
the *n* of the younger Michal ... 1Sa 14:49 8034
the *n* of Saul's wife was Ahinoam, ... 1Sa 14:50 8034
the *n* of the captain of his host ... 1Sa 14:50 8034
unto me him whom I *n* unto thee ... 1Sa 16:3 559
whose *n* was Jesse ... 1Sa 17:12 8034
Philistine of Gath, Goliath by *n* ... 1Sa 17:23 8034
in the *n* of the LORD of hosts ... 1Sa 17:45 8034
so that his *n* was much set by ... 1Sa 18:30 8034
both of us in the *n* of the LORD ... 1Sa 20:42 8034
his *n* was Doeg, an Edomite, the ... 1Sa 21:7 8034
my *n* out of my father's house ... 1Sa 24:21 8034
Now the *n* of the man was Nabal ... 1Sa 25:3 8034
the *n* of his wife Abigail ... 1Sa 25:3 8034
go to Nabal, and greet him in my *n* ... 1Sa 25:5 8034
all those words in the *n* of David ... 1Sa 25:9 8034
for as his *n* is, so is he ... 1Sa 25:25 8034
Nabal is his *n*, and folly is with ... 1Sa 25:25 8034
him up, whom I shall *n* unto thee ... 1Sa 28:8 559
whose *n* was Rizpah, the daughter ... 2Sa 3:7 8034
the *n* of the one was Baanah, and ... 2Sa 4:2 8034
the *n* of the other Rechab, the ... 2Sa 4:2 8034
And his *n* was Mephibosheth ... 2Sa 4:4 8034
Therefore he called the *n* of that ... 2Sa 5:20 8034

whose *n* is called by the *n* of	2Sa 6:2	8034
he called the *n* of the place	2Sa 6:8	
in the *n* of the LORD of hosts	2Sa 6:18	8034
and have made thee a great *n*	2Sa 7:9	8034
like unto the *n* of the great men	2Sa 7:9	8034
He shall build an house for my *n*	2Sa 7:13	8034
to himself, and to make him a *n*	2Sa 7:23	8034
let thy *n* be magnified for ever,	2Sa 7:26	8034
David gat him a *n* when he	2Sa 8:13	8034
Saul a servant whose *n* was Ziba	2Sa 9:2	8034
a young son, whose *n* was Micha	2Sa 9:12	8034
a son, and he called his *n* Solomon	2Sa 12:24	8034
and he called his *n* Jedidiah	2Sa 12:25	8034
city, and it be called after my *n*	2Sa 12:28	8034
a fair sister, whose *n* was Tamar	2Sa 13:1	8034
whose *n* was Jonadab, the son of	2Sa 13:3	8034
n nor remainder upon the earth	2Sa 14:7	8034
one daughter, whose *n* was Tamar	2Sa 14:27	8034
whose *n* was Shimei, the son of	2Sa 16:5	8034
whose *n* was Ithra an Israelite,	2Sa 17:25	8034
son to keep my *n* in remembrance	2Sa 18:18	8034
called the pillar after his own *n*	2Sa 18:18	8034
whose *n* was Sheba, the son of	2Sa 20:1	8034
Sheba the son of Bichri by *n*	2Sa 20:21	8034
them, and had the *n* among three	2Sa 23:18	8034
had the *n* among three mighty men	2Sa 23:22	8034
n of Solomon better than thy *n*	1Kin 1:47	8034
built unto the *n* of the LORD	1Kin 3:2	8034
the *n* of the LORD his God for the	1Kin 5:3	8034
unto the *n* of the LORD my God	1Kin 5:5	8034
he shall build an house unto my *n*	1Kin 5:5	8034
called the *n* thereof Jachin	1Kin 7:21	8034
called the *n* thereof Boaz	1Kin 7:21	8034
that my *n* might be therein	1Kin 8:16	8034
the *n* of the LORD God of Israel	1Kin 8:17	8034
heart to build an house unto my *n*	1Kin 8:18	8034
shall build the house unto my *n*	1Kin 8:19	8034
the *n* of the LORD God of Israel	1Kin 8:20	8034
hast said, My *n* shall be there	1Kin 8:29	8034
again to thee, and confess thy *n*	1Kin 8:33	8034
this place, and confess thy *n*	1Kin 8:35	8034
they shall hear of thy great *n*	1Kin 8:42	8034
of the earth may know thy *n*	1Kin 8:43	8034
have builded, is called by thy *n*	1Kin 8:43	8034
house that I have built for thy *n*	1Kin 8:44	8034
which I have built for thy *n*	1Kin 8:48	8034
to put my *n* there for ever	1Kin 9:3	8034
which I have hallowed for my *n*	1Kin 9:7	8034
concerning the *n* of the LORD	1Kin 10:1	8034
whose mother's *n* was Zeruah	1Kin 11:26	8034
have chosen me to put my *n* there	1Kin 11:36	8034
the house of David, Josiah by *n*	1Kin 13:2	8034
of Israel, to put his *n* there	1Kin 14:21	8034
his mother's *n* was Naamah an	1Kin 14:21	8034
his mother's *n* was Naamah an	1Kin 14:31	8034
And his mother's *n* was Maachah	1Kin 15:2	8034
And his mother's *n* was Maachah	1Kin 15:10	8034
called the *n* of the city which he	1Kin 16:24	8034
he built, after the *n* of Shemer	1Kin 16:24	8034
And call ye on the *n* of your gods	1Kin 18:24	8034
I will call on the *n* of the LORD	1Kin 18:24	8034
call on the *n* of your gods, but	1Kin 18:25	8034
called on the *n* of Baal from	1Kin 18:26	8034
saying, Israel shall be thy *n*	1Kin 18:31	8034
an altar in the *n* of the LORD	1Kin 18:32	8034
So she wrote letters in Ahab's *n*	1Kin 21:8	8034
is true in the *n* of the LORD	1Kin 22:16	8034
his mother's *n* was Azubah the	1Kin 22:42	8034
cursed them in the *n* of the LORD	2Kin 2:24	8034
call on the *n* of the LORD his God	2Kin 5:11	8034
And his mother's *n* was Athaliah	2Kin 8:26	8034
his mother's *n* was Zibiah of	2Kin 12:1	8034
his mother's *n* was Jehoaddan of	2Kin 14:2	8034
called the *n* of it Joktheel unto	2Kin 14:7	8034
the *n* of Israel from under heaven	2Kin 14:27	8034
his mother's *n* was Jecholiah of	2Kin 15:2	8034
And his mother's *n* was Jerusha	2Kin 15:33	8034
His mother's *n* also was Abi	2Kin 18:2	8034
his mother's *n* was Hephzi-bah	2Kin 21:1	8034
In Jerusalem will I put my *n*	2Kin 21:4	8034
Israel, will I put my *n* for ever	2Kin 21:7	8034
his mother's *n* was Meshullemeth,	2Kin 21:19	8034
And his mother's *n* was Jedidah	2Kin 22:1	8034
which I said, My *n* shall be there	2Kin 23:27	8034
And his mother's *n* was Hamutal	2Kin 23:31	8034
turned his *n* to Jehoiakim, and	2Kin 23:34	8034
And his mother's *n* was Zebudah	2Kin 23:36	8034
And his mother's *n* was Nehushta	2Kin 24:8	8034
and changed his *n* to Zedekiah	2Kin 24:17	8034
And his mother's *n* was Hamutal	2Kin 24:18	8034
the *n* of the one was Peleg	1Chr 1:19	8034
and his brother's *n* was Joktan	1Chr 1:19	8034
the *n* of his city was Dinhabah	1Chr 1:43	8034
the *n* of his city was Avith	1Chr 1:46	8034
the *n* of his city was Pai	1Chr 1:50	8034
his wife's *n* was Mehetabel, the	1Chr 1:50	8034
another wife, whose *n* was Atarah	1Chr 2:26	8034
the *n* of the wife of Abishur was	1Chr 2:29	8034
an Egyptian, whose *n* was Jarha	1Chr 2:34	8034
the *n* of their sister was	1Chr 4:3	8034
and his mother called his *n* Jabez	1Chr 4:9	8034
these written by *n* came in the	1Chr 4:41	8034
whose sister's *n* was Maachah	1Chr 7:15	8034
and the *n* of the second was	1Chr 7:15	8034
a son, and she called his *n* Peresh	1Chr 7:16	8034
the *n* of his brother was Sheresh	1Chr 7:16	8034
a son, and he called his *n* Beriah	1Chr 7:23	8034
whose wife's *n* was Maachah	1Chr 8:29	8034
whose wife's *n* was Maachah	1Chr 9:35	8034
them, and had a *n* among the three	1Chr 11:20	8034
had the *n* among the three	1Chr 11:24	8034
which were expressed by *n*	1Chr 12:31	8034
whose *n* is called on it	1Chr 13:6	8034
therefore they called the *n* of	1Chr 14:11	8034
the people in the *n* of the LORD	1Chr 16:2	8034
unto the LORD, call upon his *n*	1Chr 16:8	8034
Glory ye in his holy *n*	1Chr 16:10	8034
the LORD the glory due unto his *n*	1Chr 16:29	8034
we may give thanks to thy holy *n*	1Chr 16:35	8034
chosen, who were expressed by *n*	1Chr 16:41	8034
have made thee a *n* like the *n*	1Chr 17:8	8034
n of the great men that are in	1Chr 17:8	8034
to make thee a *n* of greatness	1Chr 17:21	8034
that thy *n* may be magnified for	1Chr 17:24	8034
he spake in the *n* of the LORD	1Chr 21:19	8034
unto the *n* of the LORD my God	1Chr 22:7	8034
not build an house unto my *n*	1Chr 22:8	8034
for his *n* shall be Solomon, and I	1Chr 22:9	8034
He shall build an house for my *n*	1Chr 22:10	8034
to be built to the *n* of the LORD	1Chr 22:19	8034
and to bless in his *n* for ever	1Chr 23:13	8034
shalt not build an house for my *n*	1Chr 28:3	8034
thee, and praise thy glorious *n*	1Chr 29:13	8034
thine holy *n* cometh of thine hand	1Chr 29:16	8034
an house for the *n* of the LORD	2Chr 2:1	8034
house to the *n* of the LORD my God	2Chr 2:4	8034
called the *n* of that on the right	2Chr 3:17	8034
the *n* of that on the left Boaz	2Chr 3:17	8034
in, that my *n* might be there	2Chr 6:5	8034
that my *n* might be there	2Chr 6:6	8034
the *n* of the LORD God of Israel	2Chr 6:7	8034
heart to build an house for my *n*	2Chr 6:8	8034
he shall build the house for my *n*	2Chr 6:9	8034
the *n* of the LORD God of Israel	2Chr 6:10	8034
thou wouldest put thy *n* there	2Chr 6:20	8034
and shall return and confess thy *n*	2Chr 6:24	8034
this place, and confess thy *n*	2Chr 6:26	8034
of the earth may know thy *n*	2Chr 6:33	8034
I have built is called by thy *n*	2Chr 6:33	8034
which I have built for thy *n*	2Chr 6:34	8034
which I have built for thy *n*	2Chr 6:38	8034
people, which are called by my *n*	2Chr 7:14	8034
that my *n* may be there for ever	2Chr 7:16	8034
which I have sanctified for my *n*	2Chr 7:20	8034
of Israel, to put his *n* there	2Chr 12:13	8034
his mother's *n* was Naamah an	2Chr 12:13	8034
His mother's *n* also was Michaiah	2Chr 13:2	8034
in thy *n* we go against this	2Chr 14:11	8034
truth to me in the *n* of the LORD	2Chr 18:15	8034
a sanctuary therein for thy *n*	2Chr 20:8	8034
(for thy *n* is in this house,) and	2Chr 20:9	8034
therefore the *n* of the same place	2Chr 20:26	8034
His mother's *n* was Azubah the	2Chr 20:31	8034
His mother's *n* also was Athaliah	2Chr 22:2	8034
His mother's *n* also was Zibiah of	2Chr 24:1	8034
His mother's *n* was Jehoaddan of	2Chr 25:1	8034
His mother's *n* also was Jecoliah	2Chr 26:3	8034
his *n* spread abroad even to the	2Chr 26:8	8034
And his *n* spread far abroad	2Chr 26:15	8034
His mother's *n* also was Jerushah,	2Chr 27:1	8034
LORD was there, whose *n* was Oded	2Chr 28:9	8034
which were expressed by *n* rose up	2Chr 28:15	8034
And his mother's *n* was Abijah	2Chr 29:1	8034
the men that were expressed by *n*	2Chr 31:19	8034
Jerusalem shall my *n* be for ever	2Chr 33:4	8034
Israel, will I put my *n* for ever	2Chr 33:7	8034
the *n* of the LORD God of Israel	2Chr 33:18	8034
turned his *n* to Jehoiakim	2Chr 36:4	8034
and was called after their *n*	Ezr 2:61	8034
Jerusalem in the *n* of the God of	Ezr 5:1	8036
whose *n* was Sheshbazzar, whom he	Ezr 5:14	8036
his *n* to dwell there destroy all	Ezr 6:12	8036
all of them were expressed by *n*	Ezr 8:20	8034
I have chosen to set my *n* there	Neh 1:9	8034
who desire to fear thy *n*	Neh 1:11	8034
wife, and was called after their *n*	Neh 7:63	8034
and blessed be thy glorious *n*	Neh 9:5	8034
and gavest him the *n* of Abraham	Neh 9:7	8034
So didst thou get thee a *n*	Neh 9:10	8034
whose *n* was Mordecai, the son of	Est 2:5	8034
her, and that she were called by *n*	Est 2:14	8034
the king thereof in Mordecai's *n*	Est 2:22	8034
in the *n* of king Ahasuerus was it	Est 3:12	8034
as it liketh you, in the king's *n*	Est 8:8	8034
which is written in the king's *n*	Est 8:8	8034
he wrote in the king Ahasuerus' *n*	Est 8:10	8034
days Purim after the *n* of Pur	Est 9:26	8034
the land of Uz, whose *n* was Job	Job 1:1	8034
blessed be the *n* of the LORD	Job 1:21	8034
he shall have no *n* in the street	Job 18:17	8034
And he called the *n* of the first	Job 42:14	8034
the *n* of the second, Kezia	Job 42:14	8034
the *n* of the third, Keren-happuch	Job 42:14	8034
that love thy *n* be joyful in thee	Ps 5:11	8034
to the *n* of the LORD most high	Ps 7:17	8034
is thy *n* in all the earth	Ps 8:1	8034
is thy *n* in all the earth	Ps 8:9	8034
I will sing praise to thy *n*	Ps 9:2	8034
hast put out their *n* for ever	Ps 9:5	8034
they that know thy *n* will put	Ps 9:10	8034
and sing praises unto thy *n*	Ps 18:49	8034
the *n* of the God of Jacob defend	Ps 20:1	8034
in the *n* of our God we will set	Ps 20:5	8034
the *n* of the LORD our God	Ps 20:7	8034
declare thy *n* unto my brethren	Ps 22:22	8034
the LORD the glory due unto his *n*	Ps 29:2	8034
we have trusted in his holy *n*	Ps 33:21	8034
and let us exalt his *n* together	Ps 34:3	8034
shall he die, and his *n* perish	Ps 41:5	8034
through thy *n* will we tread them	Ps 44:5	8034
long, and praise thy *n* for ever	Ps 44:8	8034
have forgotten the *n* of our God	Ps 44:20	8034
I will make thy *n* to be	Ps 45:17	8034
According to thy *n*, O God, so is	Ps 48:10	8034
and I will wait on thy *n*	Ps 52:9	8034
Save me, O God, by thy *n*, and	Ps 54:1	8034
I will praise thy *n*, O LORD	Ps 54:6	8034
heritage of those that fear thy *n*	Ps 61:5	8034
I sing praise unto thy *n* for ever	Ps 61:8	8034
I will lift up my hands in thy *n*	Ps 63:4	8034
Sing forth the honour of his *n*	Ps 66:2	8034
they shall sing to thy *n*	Ps 66:4	8034
unto God, sing praises to his *n*	Ps 68:4	8034
upon the heavens by his *n* JAH	Ps 68:4	8034
I will praise the *n* of God with a	Ps 69:30	8034
they that love his *n* shall dwell	Ps 69:36	8034
His *n* shall endure for ever	Ps 72:17	8034
his *n* shall be continued as long	Ps 72:17	8034
be his glorious *n* for ever	Ps 72:19	8034
place of thy *n* to the ground	Ps 74:7	8034
enemy blaspheme thy *n* for ever	Ps 74:10	8034
people have blasphemed thy *n*	Ps 74:18	8034
the poor and needy praise thy *n*	Ps 74:21	8034
for that thy *n* is near thy	Ps 75:1	8034
his *n* is great in Israel	Ps 76:1	8034
that have not called upon thy *n*	Ps 79:6	8034
salvation, for the glory of thy *n*	Ps 79:9	8034
us, and we will call upon thy *n*	Ps 80:18	8034
that the *n* of Israel may be no	Ps 83:4	8034
that they may seek thy *n*, O LORD	Ps 83:16	8034
whose *n* alone is JEHOVAH, art the	Ps 83:18	8034
and shall glorify thy *n*	Ps 86:9	8034
unite my heart to fear thy *n*	Ps 86:11	8034
I will glorify thy *n* for evermore	Ps 86:12	8034
and Hermon shall rejoice in thy *n*	Ps 89:12	8034
In thy *n* shall they rejoice all	Ps 89:16	8034
in my *n* shall his horn be exalted	Ps 89:24	8034
high, because he hath known my *n*	Ps 91:14	8034
and to sing praises unto thy *n*	Ps 92:1	8034
Sing unto the LORD, bless his *n*	Ps 96:2	8034
the LORD the glory due unto his *n*	Ps 96:8	8034
praise thy great and terrible *n*	Ps 99:3	8034
among them that call upon his *n*	Ps 99:6	8034
thankful unto him, and bless his *n*	Ps 100:4	8034
shall fear the *n* of the LORD	Ps 102:15	8034
To declare the *n* of the LORD in	Ps 102:21	8034
is within me, bless his holy *n*	Ps 103:1	8034
call upon his *n*	Ps 105:1	8034
Glory ye in his holy *n*	Ps 105:3	8034
to give thanks unto thy holy *n*	Ps 106:47	8034
let their *n* be blotted out	Ps 109:13	8034
holy and reverend is his *n*	Ps 111:9	8034
LORD, praise the *n* of the LORD	Ps 113:1	8034
Blessed be the *n* of the LORD from	Ps 113:2	8034
the LORD's *n* is to be praised	Ps 113:3	8034
us, but unto thy *n* give glory	Ps 115:1	8034
called I upon the *n* of the LORD	Ps 116:4	8034
and call upon the *n* of the LORD	Ps 116:13	8034
will call upon the *n* of the LORD	Ps 116:17	8034
but in the *n* of the LORD will I	Ps 118:10	8034
but in the *n* of the LORD I will	Ps 118:11	8034
for in the *n* of the LORD I will	Ps 118:12	8034
that cometh in the *n* of the LORD	Ps 118:26	8034
I have remembered thy *n*, O LORD,	Ps 119:55	8034
to do unto those that love thy *n*	Ps 119:132	8034
thanks unto the *n* of the LORD	Ps 122:4	8034
Our help is in the *n* of the LORD	Ps 124:8	8034
we bless you in the *n* of the LORD	Ps 129:8	8034
Praise ye the *n* of the LORD	Ps 135:1	8034
sing praises unto his *n*	Ps 135:3	8034
Thy *n*, O LORD, endureth for ever	Ps 135:13	8034
temple, and praise thy *n* for thy	Ps 138:2	8034
thy word above all thy *n*	Ps 138:2	8034
thine enemies take thy *n* in vain	Ps 139:20	8034
shall give thanks unto thy *n*	Ps 140:13	8034
prison, that I may praise thy *n*	Ps 142:7	8034
and I will bless thy *n* for ever	Ps 145:1	8034
and I will praise thy *n* for ever	Ps 145:2	8034
flesh bless his holy *n* for ever	Ps 145:21	8034
Let them praise the *n* of the LORD	Ps 148:5	8034
Let them praise the *n* of the LORD	Ps 148:13	8034
for his *n* alone is excellent	Ps 148:13	8034
them praise his *n* in the dance	Ps 149:3	8034
but the *n* of the wicked shall rot	Prov 10:7	8034
The *n* of the LORD is a strong	Prov 18:10	8034
Proud and haughty scorner is his *n*	Prov 21:24	8034
A good *n* is rather to be chosen	Prov 22:1	8034
his *n*, and what is his son's *n*	Prov 30:4	8034
take the *n* of my God in vain	Prov 30:9	8034
his *n* shall be covered with	Eccl 6:4	8034
A good *n* is better than precious	Eccl 7:1	8034
of thy good ointments thy *n* is as	Song 1:3	8034
only let us be called by thy *n*	Is 4:1	8034
son, and shall call his *n* Immanuel	Is 7:14	8034
Call his *n* Maher-shalal-hash-baz	Is 8:3	8034
his *n* shall be called Wonderful,	Is 9:6	8034
Praise the LORD, call upon his *n*	Is 12:4	8034
mention that his *n* is exalted	Is 12:4	8034
and cut off from Babylon the *n*	Is 14:22	8034
to the place of the *n* of the LORD	Is 18:7	8034
even the *n* of the LORD God of	Is 24:15	8034
exalt thee, I will praise thy *n*	Is 25:1	8034
desire of our soul is to thy *n*	Is 26:8	8034
will we make mention of thy *n*	Is 26:13	8034
of him, they shall sanctify my *n*	Is 29:23	8034
the *n* of the LORD cometh from far	Is 30:27	8034
the sun shall he call upon my *n*	Is 41:25	8034
that is my *n*	Is 42:8	8034
thee, I have called thee by thy *n*	Is 43:1	8034
every one that is called by my *n*	Is 43:7	8034
call himself by the *n* of Jacob	Is 44:5	8034
himself by the *n* of Israel	Is 44:5	8034
LORD, which call thee by thy *n*	Is 45:3	8034
I have even called thee by thy *n*	Is 45:4	8034
the LORD of hosts is his *n*	Is 47:4	8034
are called by the *n* of Israel	Is 48:1	8034
which swear by the *n* of the LORD	Is 48:1	8034
The LORD of hosts is his *n*	Is 48:2	8034
for how should my *n* be polluted	Is 48:11	8034
his *n* should not have been cut	Is 48:19	8034
hath he made mention of my *n*	Is 49:1	8034
him trust in the *n* of the LORD	Is 50:10	8034

The LORD of hosts is his *n*	Is 51:15	8034
my *n* continually every day is	Is 52:5	8034
my people shall know my *n*	Is 52:6	8034
the LORD of hosts is his *n*	Is 54:5	8034
it shall be to the LORD for a *n*	Is 55:13	8034
a *n* better than of sons and of	Is 56:5	8034
I will give them an everlasting *n*	Is 56:5	8034
him, and to love the *n* of the LORD	Is 56:6	8034
eternity, whose *n* is Holy	Is 57:15	8034
So shall they fear the *n* of the	Is 59:19	8034
unto the *n* of the LORD thy God,	Is 60:9	8034
thou shalt be called by a new *n*	Is 62:2	8034
the mouth of the LORD shall *n*	Is 62:2	8034
to make himself an everlasting *n*	Is 63:12	8034
to make thyself a glorious *n*	Is 63:14	8034
thy *n* is from everlasting	Is 63:16	8034
they were not called by thy *n*	Is 63:19	8034
to make thy *n* known to thine	Is 64:2	8034
is none that calleth upon thy *n*	Is 64:7	8034
that was not called by my *n*	Is 65:1	8034
ye shall leave your *n* for a curse	Is 65:15	8034
and call his servants by another *n*	Is 65:15	8034
shall your seed and your *n* remain	Is 66:22	8034
unto it, to the *n* of the LORD, to	Jer 3:17	8034
house, which is called by my *n*	Jer 7:10	8034
house, which is called by my *n*	Jer 7:11	8034
where I set my *n* at the first	Jer 7:12	8034
house, which is called by my *n*	Jer 7:14	8034
the house which is called by my *n*	Jer 7:30	8034
great, and thy *n* is great in might	Jer 10:6	8034
The LORD of hosts is his *n*	Jer 10:16	8034
families that call not on thy *n*	Jer 10:25	8034
The LORD called thy *n*, A green	Jer 11:16	8034
that his *n* may be no more	Jer 11:19	8034
Prophesy not in the *n* of the LORD	Jer 11:21	8034
of my people, to swear by my *n*	Jer 12:16	8034
unto me for a people, and for a *n*	Jer 13:11	8034
of us, and we are called by thy *n*	Jer 14:9	8034
prophets prophesy lies in my *n*	Jer 14:14	8034
prophets that prophesy in my *n*	Jer 14:15	8034
for I am called by thy *n*, O LORD	Jer 15:16	8034
shall know that my *n* is The LORD	Jer 16:21	8034
LORD hath not called thy *n* Pashur	Jer 20:3	8034
him, nor speak any more in his *n*	Jer 20:9	8034
this is his *n* whereby he shall be	Jer 23:6	8034
said, that prophesy lies in my *n*	Jer 23:25	8034
n by their dreams which they tell	Jer 23:27	8034
have forgotten my *n* for Baal	Jer 23:27	8034
the city which is called by my *n*	Jer 25:29	8034
prophesied in the *n* of the LORD	Jer 26:9	8034
us in the *n* of the LORD our God	Jer 26:16	8034
prophesied in the *n* of the LORD	Jer 26:20	8034
yet they prophesy a lie in my *n*	Jer 27:15	8034
prophesy falsely unto you in my *n*	Jer 29:9	8034
prophesy a lie unto you in my *n*	Jer 29:21	8034
have spoken lying words in my *n*	Jer 29:23	8034
thou hast sent letters in thy *n*	Jer 29:25	8034
The LORD of hosts is his *n*	Jer 31:35	8034
God, the LORD of hosts, is his *n*	Jer 32:18	8034
and hast made thee a *n*, as at this	Jer 32:20	8034
house, which is called by my *n*	Jer 32:34	8034
the LORD is his *n*	Jer 33:2	8034
And it shall be to me a *n* of joy	Jer 33:9	8034
this is the *n* wherewith she shall	Jer 33:16	
the house which is called by my *n*	Jer 34:15	8034
But ye turned and polluted my *n*	Jer 34:16	8034
whose *n* was Irijah, the son of	Jer 37:13	8034
unto us in the *n* of the LORD	Jer 44:16	8034
I have sworn by my great *n*	Jer 44:26	8034
that my *n* shall no more be named	Jer 44:26	8034
whose *n* is the LORD of hosts,	Jer 46:18	8034
whose *n* is the LORD of hosts	Jer 48:15	8034
and all ye that know his *n*	Jer 48:17	8034
the LORD of hosts is his *n*	Jer 50:34	8034
the LORD of hosts is his *n*	Jer 51:19	8034
whose *n* is the LORD of hosts	Jer 51:57	8034
his mother's *n* was Hamutal the	Jer 52:1	8034
I called upon thy *n*, O LORD, out	Lam 3:55	8034
the *n* thereof is called Bamah	Eze 20:29	8034
but pollute ye my holy *n* no more	Eze 20:39	8034
man, write thee the *n* of the day	Eze 24:2	8034
went, they profaned my holy *n*	Eze 36:20	8034
But I had pity for mine holy *n*	Eze 36:21	8034
And I will sanctify my great *n*	Eze 36:23	8034
So will I make my holy *n* known in	Eze 39:7	8034
them pollute my holy *n* any more	Eze 39:7	8034
also the *n* of the city shall be	Eze 39:16	8034
and will be jealous for my holy *n*	Eze 39:25	8034
of Israel for ever, and my holy *n*	Eze 43:7	8034
they have even defiled my holy *n*	Eze 43:8	8034
the *n* of the city from that day	Eze 48:35	8034
unto Daniel the *n* of Belteshazzar	Dan 1:7	8034
Blessed be the *n* of God for ever	Dan 2:20	8036
whose *n* was Belteshazzar, Art	Dan 2:26	8036
whose *n* was Belteshazzar,	Dan 4:8	8036
according to the *n* of my god	Dan 4:8	8036
whose *n* was Belteshazzar, was	Dan 4:19	8036
which spake in thy *n* to our kings	Dan 9:6	8034
the city which is called by thy *n*	Dan 9:18	8034
and thy people are called by thy *n*	Dan 9:19	8034
whose *n* was called Belteshazzar	Dan 10:1	8034
said unto him, Call his *n* Jezreel	Hos 1:4	8034
unto him, Call her *n* Lo-ruhamah	Hos 1:6	8034
Then said God, Call his *n* Lo-ammi	Hos 1:9	8034
no more be remembered by their *n*	Hos 2:17	8034
praise the *n* of the LORD your God	Joel 2:26	8034
whosoever shall call on the *n* of	Joel 2:32	8034
same maid, to profane my holy *n*	Amos 2:7	8034
LORD, The God of hosts, is his *n*	Amos 4:13	8034
The LORD is his *n*	Amos 5:8	8034
whose *n* is The God of hosts	Amos 5:27	8034
make mention of the *n* of the LORD	Amos 6:10	8034
The LORD is his *n*	Amos 9:6	8034
heathen, which are called by my *n*	Amos 9:12	8034
every one in the *n* of his god	Mic 4:5	8034
we will walk in the *n* of the LORD	Mic 4:5	8034
of the *n* of the LORD his God	Mic 5:4	8034
the man of wisdom shall see thy *n*	Mic 6:9	8034
that no more of thy *n* be sown	Nah 1:14	8034
the *n* of the Chemarims with the	Zeph 1:4	8034
all call upon the *n* of the LORD	Zeph 3:9	8034
shall trust in the *n* of the LORD	Zeph 3:12	8034
for I will make you a *n* and a	Zeph 3:20	8034
him that sweareth falsely by my *n*	Zec 5:4	8034
the man whose *n* is The BRANCH	Zec 6:12	8034
shall walk up and down in his *n*	Zec 10:12	8034
lies in the *n* of the LORD	Zec 13:3	8034
they shall call on my *n*, and I	Zec 13:9	8034
there be one LORD, and his *n* one	Zec 14:9	8034
you, O priests, that despise my *n*	Mal 1:6	8034
Wherein have we despised thy *n*	Mal 1:6	8034
my *n* shall be great among the	Mal 1:11	8034
shall be offered unto my *n*	Mal 1:11	8034
for my *n* shall be great among the	Mal 1:11	8034
my *n* is dreadful among the	Mal 1:14	8034
to heart, to give glory unto my *n*	Mal 2:2	8034
me, and was afraid before my *n*	Mal 2:5	8034
LORD, and that thought upon his *n*	Mal 3:16	8034
But unto you that fear my *n* shall	Mal 4:2	8034
and thou shalt call his *n* JESUS	Mt 1:21	*3686*
and they shall call his *n* Emmanuel	Mt 1:23	*3686*
and he called his *n* JESUS	Mt 1:25	*3686*
art in heaven, Hallowed be thy *n*	Mt 6:9	*3686*
have we not prophesied in thy *n*	Mt 7:22	*3686*
in thy *n* have cast out devils	Mt 7:22	*3686*
in thy *n* done many wonderful	Mt 7:22	*3686*
n of a prophet shall receive a	Mt 10:41	*3686*
a righteous man in the *n* of a	Mt 10:41	*3686*
water only in the *n* of a disciple	Mt 10:42	*3686*
in his *n* shall the Gentiles trust	Mt 12:21	*3686*
little child in my *n* receiveth me	Mt 18:5	*3686*
are gathered together in my *n*	Mt 18:20	*3686*
that cometh in the *n* of the Lord	Mt 21:9	*3686*
that cometh in the *n* of the Lord	Mt 23:39	*3686*
For many shall come in my *n*	Mt 24:5	*3686*
found a man of Cyrene, Simon by *n*	Mt 27:32	*3686*
them in the *n* of the Father	Mt 28:19	*3686*
And he asked him, What is thy *n*	Mk 5:9	*3686*
answered, saying, My *n* is Legion	Mk 5:9	*3686*
of the synagogue, Jairus by *n*	Mk 5:22	*3686*
(for his *n* was spread abroad	Mk 6:14	*3686*
one of such children in my *n*	Mk 9:37	*3686*
one casting out devils in thy *n*	Mk 9:38	*3686*
which shall do a miracle in my *n*	Mk 9:39	*3686*
a cup of water to drink in my *n*	Mk 9:41	*3686*
that cometh in the *n* of the Lord	Mk 11:9	*3686*
that cometh in the *n* of the Lord	Mk 11:10	*3686*
For many shall come in my *n*	Mk 13:6	*3686*
In my *n* shall they cast out	Mk 16:17	*3686*
of Aaron, and her *n* was Elisabeth	Lk 1:5	*3686*
and thou shalt call his *n* John	Lk 1:13	*3686*
to a man whose *n* was Joseph	Lk 1:27	*3686*
and the virgin's *n* was Mary	Lk 1:27	*3686*
a son, and shalt call his *n* JESUS	Lk 1:31	*3686*
and holy is his *n*	Lk 1:49	*3686*
after the *n* of his father	Lk 1:59	*3686*
kindred that is called by this *n*	Lk 1:61	*3686*
and wrote, saying, His *n* is John	Lk 1:63	*3686*
his *n* was called JESUS, which was	Lk 2:21	*3686*
in Jerusalem, whose *n* was Simeon	Lk 2:25	*3686*
you, and cast out your *n* as evil	Lk 6:22	*3686*
asked him, saying, What is thy *n*	Lk 8:30	*3686*
this child in my *n* receiveth me	Lk 9:48	*3686*
one casting out devils in thy *n*	Lk 9:49	*3686*
are subject unto us through thy *n*	Lk 10:17	*3686*
art in heaven, Hallowed be thy *n*	Lk 11:2	*3686*
that cometh in the *n* of the Lord	Lk 13:35	*3686*
that cometh in the *n* of the Lord	Lk 19:38	*3686*
for many shall come in my *n*	Lk 21:8	*3686*
whose *n* was Cleopas, answering	Lk 24:18	*3686*
in his *n* among all nations	Lk 24:47	*3686*
sent from God, whose *n* was John	Jn 1:6	*3686*
to them that believe on his *n*	Jn 1:12	*3686*
feast day, many believed in his *n*	Jn 2:23	*3686*
he hath not believed in the *n* of	Jn 3:18	*3686*
I am come in my Father's *n*	Jn 5:43	*3686*
another shall come in his own *n*	Jn 5:43	*3686*
and he calleth his own sheep by *n*	Jn 10:3	*3686*
works that I do in my Father's *n*	Jn 10:25	*3686*
that cometh in the *n* of the Lord	Jn 12:13	*3686*
Father, glorify thy *n*	Jn 12:28	*3686*
whatsoever ye shall ask in my *n*	Jn 14:13	*3686*
If ye shall ask any thing in my *n*	Jn 14:14	*3686*
whom the Father will send in my *n*	Jn 14:26	*3686*
shall ask of the Father in my *n*	Jn 15:16	*3686*
ye shall ask the Father in my *n*	Jn 16:23	*3686*
have ye asked nothing in my *n*	Jn 16:24	*3686*
At that day ye shall ask in my *n*	Jn 16:26	*3686*
I have manifested thy *n* unto the	Jn 17:6	*3686*
keep through thine own *n* those	Jn 17:11	*3686*
the world, I kept them in thy *n*	Jn 17:12	*3686*
I have declared unto them thy *n*	Jn 17:26	*3686*
The servant's *n* was Malchus	Jn 18:10	*3686*
ye might have life through his *n*	Jn 20:31	*3686*
the *n* of the Lord shall be saved	Acts 2:21	*3686*
in the *n* of Jesus Christ for the	Acts 2:38	*3686*
In the *n* of Jesus Christ of	Acts 3:6	*3686*
his *n* through faith in his *n*	Acts 3:16	*3686*
By what power, or by what *n*	Acts 4:7	*3686*
that by the *n* of Jesus Christ of	Acts 4:10	*3686*
for there is none other *n* under	Acts 4:12	*3686*
henceforth to no man in this *n*	Acts 4:17	*3686*
all nor teach in the *n* of Jesus	Acts 4:18	*3686*
by the *n* of thy holy child Jesus	Acts 4:30	*3686*
ye should not teach in this *n*	Acts 5:28	*3686*
not speak in the *n* of Jesus	Acts 5:40	*3686*
worthy to suffer shame for his *n*	Acts 5:41	*3686*
man's feet, whose *n* was Saul	Acts 7:58	*2564*
the *n* of Jesus Christ, they were	Acts 8:12	*3686*
in the *n* of the Lord Jesus	Acts 8:16	*3686*
to bind all that call on thy *n*	Acts 9:14	*3686*
to bear my *n* before the Gentiles,	Acts 9:15	*3686*
called on this *n* in Jerusalem	Acts 9:21	*3686*
at Damascus in the *n* of Jesus	Acts 9:27	*3686*
boldly in the *n* of the Lord Jesus	Acts 9:29	*3686*
that through his *n* whosoever	Acts 10:43	*3686*
be baptized in the *n* of the Lord	Acts 10:48	*3686*
a Jew, whose *n* was Bar-jesus	Acts 13:6	*3686*
the sorcerer (for so is his *n* by	Acts 13:8	*3686*
out of them a people for his *n*	Acts 15:14	*3686*
upon whom my *n* is called	Acts 15:17	*3686*
the *n* of our Lord Jesus Christ	Acts 15:26	*3686*
I command thee in the *n* of Jesus	Acts 16:18	*3686*
in the *n* of the Lord Jesus	Acts 19:5	*3686*
spirits the *n* of the Lord Jesus	Acts 19:13	*3686*
the *n* of the Lord Jesus was	Acts 19:17	*3686*
for the *n* of the Lord Jesus	Acts 21:13	*3686*
calling on the *n* of the Lord	Acts 22:16	*3686*
to the *n* of Jesus of Nazareth	Acts 26:9	*3686*
the island, whose *n* was Publius	Acts 28:7	*3686*
among all nations, for his *n*	Rom 1:5	*3686*
For the *n* of God is blasphemed	Rom 2:24	*3686*
that my *n* might be declared	Rom 9:17	*3686*
the *n* of the Lord shall be saved	Rom 10:13	*3686*
the Gentiles, and sing unto thy *n*	Rom 15:9	*3686*
the *n* of Jesus Christ our Lord	1Cor 1:2	*3686*
by the *n* of our Lord Jesus Christ	1Cor 1:10	*3686*
were ye baptized in the *n* of Paul	1Cor 1:13	*3686*
that I had baptized in mine own *n*	1Cor 1:15	*3686*
In the *n* of our Lord Jesus Christ	1Cor 5:4	*3686*
in the *n* of the Lord Jesus	1Cor 6:11	*3686*
every *n* that is named, not only	Eph 1:21	*3686*
the Father in the *n* of our Lord	Eph 5:20	*3686*
him a *n* which is above every *n*	Phil 2:9	*3686*
That at the *n* of Jesus every knee	Phil 2:10	*3686*
do all in the *n* of the Lord Jesus	Col 3:17	*3686*
That the *n* of our Lord Jesus	2Th 1:12	*3686*
in the *n* of our Lord Jesus Christ	2Th 3:6	*3686*
of all honour, that the *n* of God	1Ti 6:1	*3686*
Let every one that nameth the *n*	2Ti 2:19	*3686*
a more excellent *n* than they	Heb 1:4	*3686*
declare thy *n* unto my brethren	Heb 2:12	*3686*
which ye have shewed toward his *n*	Heb 6:10	*3686*
our lips giving thanks to his *n*	Heb 13:15	*3686*
n by the which ye are called	Jas 2:7	*3686*
have spoken in the *n* of the Lord	Jas 5:10	*3686*
him with oil in the *n* of the Lord	Jas 5:14	*3686*
be reproached for the *n* of Christ	1Pet 4:14	*3686*
on the *n* of his Son Jesus Christ	1Jn 3:23	*3686*
on the *n* of the Son of God	1Jn 5:13	*3686*
on the *n* of the Son of God	1Jn 5:13	*3686*
Greet the friends by *n*	3Jn 14	*3686*
and thou holdest fast my *n*	Rev 2:13	*3686*
and in the stone a new *n* written	Rev 2:17	*3686*
thou hast a *n* that thou livest	Rev 3:1	*3686*
out his *n* out of the book of life	Rev 3:5	*3686*
confess his *n* before my Father	Rev 3:5	*3686*
my word, and hast not denied my *n*	Rev 3:8	*3686*
write upon him the *n* of my God	Rev 3:12	*3686*
the *n* of the city of my God,	Rev 3:12	*3686*
and I will write upon him my new *n*	Rev 3:12	*3686*
his *n* that sat on him was Death,	Rev 6:8	*3686*
the *n* of the star is called	Rev 8:11	*3686*
whose *n* in the Hebrew tongue is	Rev 9:11	*3686*
Greek tongue hath his *n* Apollyon	Rev 9:11	*3686*
saints, and them that fear thy *n*	Rev 11:18	*3686*
upon his heads the *n* of blasphemy	Rev 13:1	*3686*
against God, to blaspheme his *n*	Rev 13:6	*3686*
or the *n* of the beast, or the	Rev 13:17	*3686*
the beast, or the number of his *n*	Rev 13:17	*3686*
having his Father's *n* written in	Rev 14:1	*3686*
receiveth the mark of his *n*	Rev 14:11	*3686*
mark, and over the number of his *n*	Rev 15:2	*3686*
thee, O Lord, and glorify thy *n*	Rev 15:4	*3686*
heat, and blasphemed the *n* of God	Rev 16:9	*3686*
upon her forehead was a *n* written	Rev 17:5	*3686*
and he had a *n* written, that no	Rev 19:12	*3686*
his *n* is called The Word of God	Rev 19:13	*3686*
and on his thigh a *n* written	Rev 19:16	*3686*
his *n* shall be in their foreheads	Rev 22:4	*3686*

NAMED

which he had *n* in the audience of	Gen 23:16	1696
said, Is not he rightly *n* Jacob	Gen 27:36	
and let my name be *n* on them	Gen 48:16	7121
house, *n* Rahab, and lodged there	Josh 2:1	8034
she *n* the child I-chabod, saying,	1Sa 4:21	7121
n Goliath, of Gath, whose height	1Sa 17:4	8034
n Abiathar, escaped, and fled	1Sa 22:20	8034
of Jacob, whom he *n* Israel	2Kin 17:34	8034
his sons were *n* of the tribe of	1Chr 23:14	7121
That which hath been is *n* already	Eccl 6:10	
But ye shall be *n* the Priests of	Is 61:6	7121
be *n* in the mouth of any man of	Jer 44:26	7121
whom the king *n* Belteshazzar	Dan 5:12	8036
which are *n* chief of the nations,	Amos 6:1	5344
O thou that art *n* the house of	Mic 2:7	559
n Matthew, sitting at the receipt	Mt 9:9	*3004*
n Joseph, who also himself was	Mt 27:57	*3686*
to a place which was *n* Gethsemane	Mk 14:32	*3686*
And there was one *n* Barabbas	Mk 15:7	*3004*
a certain priest *n* Zacharias	Lk 1:5	*3686*
a city of Galilee, *n* Nazareth,	Lk 1:26	*3686*
which was so *n* of the angel	Lk 2:21	*2564*
n Levi, sitting at the receipt of	Lk 5:27	*3686*
twelve, whom also he *n* apostles	Lk 6:13	*3687*
Simon, (whom he also *n* Peter	Lk 6:14	*3687*
behold, there came a man *n* Jairus	Lk 8:41	*3686*
a certain woman *n* Martha received	Lk 10:38	*3686*
was a certain beggar *n* Lazarus	Lk 16:20	*3686*
there was a man *n* Zacchaeus	Lk 19:2	*2564*
behold, there was a man *n* Joseph	Lk 23:50	*3686*

n Nicodemus, a ruler of the Jews Jn 3:1 3686
n Lazarus, of Bethany, the town Jn 11:1
n Caiaphas, being the high priest Jn 11:49
But a certain man n Ananias Acts 5:1 3686
n Gamaliel, a doctor of the law, Acts 5:34 3686
disciple at Damascus, n Ananias Acts 9:10 3686
vision a man n Ananias coming in Acts 9:12 3686
he found a certain man n Aeneas Acts 9:33 3686
a certain disciple n Tabitha Acts 9:36 3686
stood up one of them n Agabus Acts 11:28 3686
a damsel came to hearken, n Rhoda Acts 12:13 3686
n Timotheus, the son of a certain Acts 16:1 3686
And a certain woman n Lydia Acts 16:14 3686
Areopagite, and a woman n Damaris Acts 17:34 3686
And found a certain Jew n Aquila Acts 18:2 3686
n Justus, one that worshipped God Acts 18:7 3686
And a certain Jew n Apollos Acts 18:24 3686
For a certain man n Demetrius Acts 19:24 3686
a certain young man n Eutychus Acts 20:9 3686
a certain prophet, n Agabus Acts 21:10 3686
with a certain orator n Tertullus Acts 24:1
other prisoners unto one n Julius Acts 27:1 3686
gospel, not where Christ was n Rom 15:20 3687
so much as n among the Gentiles 1Cor 5:1 3687
dominion, and every name that is n Eph 1:21 3687
family in heaven and earth is n Eph 3:15 3687
let it not be once n among you Eph 5:3 3687

NAMELY
his offering be of the flocks, n Lev 1:10
Of the children of Joseph, n Num 1:32
cloud covered the tabernacle, n Num 9:15
Of the tribe of Joseph, n Num 13:11
n, Evi, and Rekem, and Zur, and Hur, Num 31:8
N, Bezer in the wilderness, in Deut 4:43
N, of the gods of the people Deut 13:7
n, the Hittites, and the Amorites, Deut 20:17
N, five lords of the Philistines, Judg 3:3
to the house of Jerubbaal, n Judg 8:35
they gave the cities of Judah, n 1Chr 6:57
given out of the half tribe, n 1Chr 6:61
gates of the house of the LORD, n 1Chr 9:23
courses among the sons of Levi, n 1Chr 23:6
n, of the sons of Jeshua the son Ezr 10:18
n, Zechariah the son of Jonathan, Neh 12:35
provinces of king Ahasuerus, n Est 8:12
I have seen under the sun, n Eccl 5:13
with a razor that is hired, n Is 7:20
the king sent men into Egypt, n Jer 26:22
n this, Thou shalt love thy Mk 12:31
n, Judas surnamed Barsabas, and Acts 15:22
comprehended in this saying, n Rom 13:9 1722

NAME'S
his people for his great n sake 1Sa 12:22 8034
of a far country for thy n sake 1Kin 8:41 8034
far country for thy great n sake 2Chr 6:32 8034
of righteousness for his n sake Ps 23:3 8034
For thy n sake, O LORD, pardon Ps 25:11 8034
therefore for thy n sake lead me Ps 31:3 8034
away our sins, for thy n sake Ps 79:9 8034
he saved them for his n sake Ps 106:8 8034
O GOD the Lord, for thy n sake Ps 109:21 8034
me, O LORD, for thy n sake Ps 143:11 8034
For my n sake will I defer mine Is 48:9 8034
that cast you out for my n sake Is 66:5 8034
us, do thou it for thy n sake Jer 14:7 8034
Do not abhor us, for thy n sake Jer 14:21 8034
But I wrought for my n sake Eze 20:9 8034
But I wrought for my n sake Eze 20:14 8034
hand, and wrought for my n sake Eze 20:22 8034
wrought with you for my n sake Eze 20:44 8034
Israel, but for mine holy n sake Eze 36:22 8034
be hated of all men for my n sake Mt 10:22 3686
children, or lands, for my n sake Mt 19:29 3686
of all nations for my n sake Mt 24:9 3686
be hated of all men for my n sake Mk 13:13 3686
kings and rulers for my n sake Lk 21:12 3686
be hated of all men for my n sake Lk 21:17 3686
they do unto you for my n sake Jn 15:21 3686
he must suffer for my n sake Acts 9:16 3686
are forgiven you for his n sake 1Jn 2:12 3686
for his n sake they went forth 3Jn 7 3686
for my n sake hast laboured, and Rev 2:3 3686

NAMES
Adam gave n to all cattle, and to Gen 2:20 8034
these are the n of the sons of Gen 25:13 8034
the sons of Ishmael, by their n Gen 25:13 8034
of Ishmael, and these are their n Gen 25:16 8034
he called their n after the n Gen 26:18 8034
These are the n of Esau's sons Gen 36:10 8034
these are the n of the dukes that Gen 36:40 8034
after their places, by their n Gen 36:40 8034
these are the n of the children Gen 46:8 8034
Now these are the n of the Ex 1:1 8034
these are the n of the sons of Ex 6:16 8034
grave on them the n of the Ex 28:9 8034
Six of their n on one stone Ex 28:10 8034
the other six n of the rest on Ex 28:10 8034
the n of the children of Israel Ex 28:11 8034
Aaron shall bear their n before Ex 28:12 8034
the n of the children of Israel Ex 28:21 8034
twelve, according to their n Ex 28:21 8034
Aaron shall bear the n of the Ex 28:29 8034
with the n of the children of Ex 39:6 8034
the n of the children of Israel Ex 39:14 8034
twelve, according to their n Ex 39:14 8034
with the number of their n Num 1:2 8034
these are the n of the men that Num 1:5 8034
which are expressed by their n Num 1:17 8034
according to the number of the n Num 1:18 8034
according to the number of the n Num 1:20 8034
according to the number of the n Num 1:22 8034
according to the number of the n Num 1:24 8034
according to the number of the n Num 1:26 8034
according to the number of the n Num 1:28 8034
according to the number of the n Num 1:30 8034
according to the number of the n Num 1:32 8034
according to the number of the n Num 1:34 8034
according to the number of the n Num 1:36 8034
according to the number of the n Num 1:38 8034
according to the number of the n Num 1:40 8034
according to the number of the n Num 1:42 8034
these are the n of the sons of Num 3:2 8034
These are the n of the sons of Num 3:3 8034
were the sons of Levi by their n Num 3:17 8034
these are the n of the sons of Num 3:18 8034
and take the number of their n Num 3:40 8034
males by the number of n, from a Num 3:43 8034
And these were their n Num 13:4 8034
These are the n of the men which Num 13:16 8034
the n of the daughters of Num 26:33 8034
according to the number of n Num 26:53 8034
according to the n of the tribes Num 26:55 8034
these are the n of his daughters Num 27:1 8034
(their n being changed,) and Num 32:38 8034
gave other n unto the cities Num 32:38 8034
These are the n of the men which Num 34:17 8034
the n of the men are these Num 34:19 8034
destroy the n of them out of that Deut 12:3 8034
these are the n of his daughters, Josh 17:3 8034
mention of the n of their gods Josh 23:7 8034
the n of his two daughters were 1Sa 14:49 8034
the n of his three sons that went 1Sa 17:13 8034
these be the n of those that were 2Sa 5:14 8034
These be the n of the mighty men 2Sa 23:8 8034
And these are their n 1Kin 4:8 8034
These mentioned by their n were 1Chr 4:38 8034
these be the n of the sons of 1Chr 6:17 8034
which are called by their n 1Chr 6:65 8034
whose n are these, Azrikam, 1Chr 8:38 8034
whose n are these, Azrikam, 1Chr 9:44 8034
Now these are the n of his 1Chr 14:4 8034
by number of n by their polls 1Chr 23:24 8034
What are the n of the men that Ezr 5:4 8036
We asked their n also, to certify Ezr 5:10 8036
that we might write the n of the Ezr 5:10 8036
whose n are these, Eliphelet, Ezr 8:13 8034
and all of them by their n Ezr 10:16 8034
nor take up their n into my lips Ps 16:4 8034
their lands after their own n Ps 49:11 8034
he calleth them all by their n Ps 147:4 8034
he calleth them all by n by the Is 40:26 8034
the n of them were Aholah the Eze 23:4 8034
Thus were their n Eze 23:4 8034
Now these are the n of the tribes Eze 48:1 8034
the n of the tribes of Israel Eze 48:31 8034
the prince of the eunuchs gave n Dan 1:7 8034
For I will take away the n of Hos 2:17 8034
that I will cut off the n of the Zec 13:2 8034
Now the n of the twelve apostles Mt 10:2 3686
because your n are written in Lk 10:20 3686
(the number of n together were Acts 1:15 3686
if it be a question of words and n Acts 18:15 3686
whose n are in the book of life Phil 4:3 3686
Thou hast a few n even in Sardis Rev 3:4 3686
whose n are not written in the Rev 13:8 3686
full of n of blasphemy, having Rev 17:3 3686
whose n were not written in the Rev 17:8 3686
n written thereon, which are the Rev 21:12 3686
which are the n of the twelve Rev 21:12
in them the n of the twelve Rev 21:14 3686

NAMETH
Let every one that n the name of 2Ti 2:19 3687

NAOMI (*na'-o-mee*) See NAOMI'S. *Mother-in-law of Ruth.*
and the name of his wife N Ruth 1:2 5281
N said unto her two daughters in Ruth 1:8 5281
N said, Turn again, my daughters Ruth 1:11 5281
them, and they said, Is this N Ruth 1:19 5281
she said unto them, Call me not N Ruth 1:20 5281
why then call ye me N, seeing the Ruth 1:21 5281
So N returned, and Ruth the Ruth 1:22 5281
N had a kinsman of her husband's, Ruth 2:1 5281
And Ruth the Moabitess said unto N Ruth 2:2 5281
with N out of the country of Moab Ruth 2:6 5281
N said unto her daughter in law, Ruth 2:20 5281
N said unto her, The man is near Ruth 2:20 5281
N said unto Ruth her daughter in Ruth 2:22 5281
Then N her mother in law said Ruth 3:1 5281
And he said unto the kinsman, N Ruth 4:3 5281
buyest the field of the hand of N Ruth 4:5 5281
and Mahlon's, of the hand of N Ruth 4:9 5281
And the women said unto N, Blessed Ruth 4:14 5281
N took the child, and laid it in Ruth 4:16 5281
saying, There is a son born to N Ruth 4:17 5281

NAOMI'S (*na'-o-meze*)
And Elimelech N husband died Ruth 1:3 5281

NAPHATH See DOR.

NAPHATH DOR See DOR.

NAPHETH See DOR.

NAPHISH (*na'-fish*) See NEPHISH. *A son of Ishmael.*
Hadar, and Tema, Jetur, N, and Gen 25:15 5305
Jetur, N, and Kedemah 1Chr 1:31 5305

NAPHTALI (*naf'-ta-li*) See NEPHTHALIM.
1. A son of Jacob.
and she called his name N Gen 30:8 5321
handmaid; Dan, and N Gen 35:25 5321
And the sons of N Gen 46:24 5321
N is a hind let loose Gen 49:21 5321
Dan, and N, Gad, and Asher Ex 1:4 5321
Dan, Joseph, and Benjamin, N 1Chr 2:2 5321
The sons of N 1Chr 7:13 5321
one gate of Asher, one gate of N Eze 48:34 5321
2. The tribe and land.
Of N; Ahira the son Num 1:15 5321
Of the children of N, throughout Num 1:42 5321
of them, even of the tribe of N Num 1:43 5321
Then the tribe of N Num 2:29 5321
N shall be Ahira the son of Enan Num 2:29 5321
Enan, prince of the children of N Num 7:78 5321
of N was Ahira the son of Enan Num 10:27 5321
Of the tribe of N, Nahbi the son Num 13:14 5321
Of the sons of N after their Num 26:48 5321
These are the families of N Num 26:50 5321
of the tribe of the children of N Num 34:28 5321
and Asher, and Zebulun, Dan, and N Deut 27:13 5321
And of Naphtali he said, O N Deut 33:23 5321
And all N, and the land of Ephraim, Deut 34:2 5321
lot came out to the children of N Josh 19:32 5321
even for the children of N Josh 19:32 5321
of N according to their families Josh 19:39 5321
Kedesh in Galilee in mount N Josh 20:7 5321
Asher, and out of the tribe of N Josh 21:6 5321
And out of the tribe of N, Kedesh Josh 21:32 5321
Neither did N drive out the Judg 1:33 5321
thousand men of the children of N Judg 4:6 5321
called Zebulun and N to Kedesh Judg 4:10 5321
N were a people that jeoparded Judg 5:18 5321
Asher, and unto Zebulun, and unto N Judg 6:35 5321
themselves together out of N Judg 7:23 5321
Ahimaaz was in N 1Kin 4:15 5321
a widow's son of the tribe of N 1Kin 7:14 5321
Cinneroth, with all the land of N 1Kin 15:20 5321
and Galilee, all the land of N 2Kin 15:29 5321
Asher, and out of the tribe of N 1Chr 6:62 5321
And out of the tribe of N 1Chr 6:76 5321
of N a thousand captains, and with 1Chr 12:34 5321
unto Issachar and Zebulun and N 1Chr 12:40 5321
of N, Jerimoth the son of Azriel 1Chr 27:19 5321
and all the store cities of N 2Chr 16:4 5321
Ephraim, and Simeon, even unto N 2Chr 34:6 5321
of Zebulun, and the princes of N Ps 68:27 5321
land of Zebulun and the land of N Is 9:1 5321
the west side, a portion for N Eze 48:3 5321
And by the border of N, from the Eze 48:4 5321

NAPHTUHIM (*naf'-too-him*) *Inhabitants of central Egypt.*
and Anamim, and Lehabim, and N Gen 10:13 5320

NAPKIN
which I have kept laid up in a n Lk 19:20 4676
his face was bound about with a n Jn 11:44 4676
And the n, that was about his head Jn 20:7 4676

NAPHTUHIM
and Anamim, and Lehabim, and N 1Chr 1:11 5320

NARCISSUS (*nar-sis'-sus*) *A Christian in Rome.*
that be of the household of N Rom 16:11 3488

NARROW
further, and stood in a n place Num 22:26 6862
mount Ephraim be too n for thee Josh 17:15 213
house he made windows of n lights 1Kin 6:4 331
and a strange woman is a n pit Prov 23:27 6862
shall even now be too n by reason Is 49:19 3334
there were n windows to the Eze 40:16 331
the n windows, and the galleries Eze 41:16 331
And there were n windows and palm Eze 41:26 331
n is the way, which leadeth unto Mt 7:14 2346

NARROWED
house he made n rests round about 1Kin 6:6 4052

NARROWER
the covering n than that he can Is 28:20 6887

NARROWLY
lookest n unto all my paths Job 13:27 8104
see thee shall n look upon thee Is 14:16

NATHAN (*na'-than*) See NATHAN-MELECH.
1. A son of David.
Shammuah, and Shobab, and N 2Sa 5:14 5416
Shimea, and Shobab, and N, and 1Chr 3:5 5416
and Shobab, N, and Solomon 1Chr 14:4 5416
Mattatha, which was the son of N Lk 3:31 3481
2. A prophet in David's court.
the king said unto N the prophet 2Sa 7:2 5416
N said to the king, Go, do all 2Sa 7:3 5416
the word of the LORD came unto N 2Sa 7:4 5416
so did N speak unto David 2Sa 7:17 5416
And the LORD sent N unto David 2Sa 12:1 5416
and he said to N, As the LORD 2Sa 12:5 5416
N said to David, Thou art the man 2Sa 12:7 5416
And David said unto N, I have 2Sa 12:13 5416
N said unto David, The LORD also 2Sa 12:13 5416
N departed unto his house 2Sa 12:15 5416
sent by the hand of N the prophet 2Sa 12:25 5416
N the prophet, and Shimei, and Rei, 1Kin 1:8 5416
But N the prophet, and Benaiah, and 1Kin 1:10 5416
Wherefore N spake unto Bath-sheba 1Kin 1:11 5416
N the prophet also came in 1Kin 1:22 5416
saying, Behold N the prophet 1Kin 1:23 5416
N said, My lord, O king, hast 1Kin 1:24 5416
N the prophet, and Benaiah the son 1Kin 1:32 5416
N the prophet anoint him there 1Kin 1:34 5416
N the prophet, and Benaiah the son 1Kin 1:38 5416
N the prophet, and Benaiah the son 1Kin 1:44 5416
N the prophet have anointed him 1Kin 1:45 5416
that David said to N the prophet 1Chr 17:1 5416
Then N said unto David, Do all 1Chr 17:2 5416
that the word of God came to N 1Chr 17:3 5416
so did N speak unto David 1Chr 17:15 5416
and in the book of N the prophet 1Chr 29:29 5416
in the book of N the prophet 2Chr 9:29 5416
the king's seer, and N the prophet 2Chr 29:25 5416
when N the prophet came unto him, Ps 51:t 5416

3. Father of Igal.
Igal the son of *N* of Zobah 2Sa 23:36 5416
4. Father of Azariah.
Azariah the son of *N* was over the 1Kin 4:5 5416
5. Father of Zebud.
Zabud the son of *N* was principal 1Kin 4:5 5416
6. Son of Attai.
And Attai begat *N* 1Chr 2:36 5416
and *N* begat Zabad 1Chr 2:36 5416
7. Brother of Joel.
Joel the brother of *N*, Mibhar the 1Chr 11:38 5416
8. A clan leader with Ezra.
Jarib, and for Elnathan, and for *N* Ezr 8:16 5416
9. Married a foreigner in exile.
And Shelemiah, and *N*, and Adaiah, Ezr 10:39 5416
10. A family leader.
family of the house of *N* apart Zec 12:12 5416

NATHANAEL (*na-than'-a-el*) See BARTHOLOMEW. *A disciple of Jesus.*
Philip findeth *N*, and saith unto Jn 1:45 *3482*
N said unto him, Can there any Jn 1:46 *3482*
Jesus saw *N* coming to him, and Jn 1:47 *3482*
N saith unto him, Whence knowest Jn 1:48 *3482*
N answered and saith unto him, Jn 1:49 *3482*
N of Cana in Galilee, and the sons Jn 21:2 *3482*

NATHAN-MELECH (*na'-than-me'-lek*) *A servant of King Josiah.*
the chamber of *N* the chamberlain 2Kin 23:11 5419

NATION
And I will make of thee a great *n* Gen 12:2 1471
And also that *n*, whom they shall Gen 15:14 1471
and I will make him a great *n* Gen 17:20 1471
surely become a great and mighty *n* Gen 18:18 1471
wilt thou slay also a righteous *n* Gen 20:4 1471
of the bondwoman will I make a *n* Gen 21:13 1471
for I will make him a great *n* Gen 21:18 1471
a *n* and a company of nations shall Gen 35:11 1471
will there make of thee a great *n* Gen 46:3 1471
land of Egypt since it became a *n* Ex 9:24 1471
kingdom of priests, and an holy *n* Ex 19:6 1471
strange *n* he shall have no power Ex 21:8 5971
and I will make of thee a great *n* Ex 32:10 1471
that this *n* is thy people Ex 33:13 1471
in all the earth, nor in any *n* Ex 34:10 1471
neither any of your own *n* Lev 18:26 249
not walk in the manners of the *n* Lev 20:23 1471
and will make of thee a greater *n* Num 14:12 1471
Surely this great *n* is a wise Deut 4:6 1471
For what *n* is there so great, who Deut 4:7 1471
what *n* is there so great, that Deut 4:8 1471
take him a *n* from the midst of Deut 4:34 1471
from the midst of another *n* Deut 4:34 1471
I will make of thee a *n* mightier Deut 9:14 1471
with a few, and became there a *n* Deut 26:5 1471
shall a *n* which thou knowest not Deut 28:33 5971
unto a *n* which neither thou nor Deut 28:36 1471
bring a *n* against thee from far Deut 28:49 1471
a *n* whose tongue thou shalt not Deut 28:49 1471
A *n* of fierce countenance, which Deut 28:50 1471
them to anger with a foolish *n* Deut 32:21 1471
For they are a *n* void of counsel, Deut 32:28 1471
what one *n* in the earth is like 2Sa 7:23 1471
liveth, there is no *n* or kingdom 1Kin 18:10 1471
took an oath of the kingdom and *n* 1Kin 18:10 1471
Howbeit every *n* made gods of 2Kin 17:29 1471
every *n* in their cities wherein 2Kin 17:29 1471
when they went from *n* to *n* 1Chr 16:20 1471
what one *n* in the earth is like 1Chr 17:21 1471
And *n* was destroyed of *n* 2Chr 15:6 1471
for no god of any *n* or kingdom 2Chr 32:15 1471
whether it be done against a *n* Job 34:29 1471
Blessed is the *n* whose God is the Ps 33:12 1471
my cause against an ungodly *n* Ps 43:1 1471
us cut them off from being a *n* Ps 83:4 1471
they went from one *n* to another Ps 105:13 1471
rejoice in the gladness of thy *n* Ps 106:5 1471
He hath not dealt so with any *n* Ps 147:20 1471
Righteousness exalteth a *n* Prov 14:34 1471
Ah sinful *n*, a people laden with Is 1:4 1471
n shall not lift up sword against Is 2:4 1471
shall not lift up sword against *n* Is 2:4 1471
Thou hast multiplied the *n* Is 9:3 1471
him against an hypocritical *n* Is 10:6 1471
answer the messengers of the *n* Is 14:32 1471
to a *n* scattered and peeled, to a Is 18:2 1471
a *n* meted out and trodden down, Is 18:2 1471
a *n* meted out and trodden under Is 18:7 1471
that the righteous *n* which Is 26:2 1471
Thou hast increased the *n* Is 26:15 1471
O LORD, thou hast increased the *n* Is 26:15 1471
to him whom the *n* abhorreth Is 49:7 1471
and give ear unto me, O my *n* Is 51:4 3816
thou shalt call a *n* that thou Is 55:5 1471
as a *n* that did righteousness, and Is 58:2 1471
For the *n* and kingdom that will Is 60:12 1471
and a small one a strong *n* Is 60:22 1471
unto a *n* that was not called by Is 65:1 1471
or shall a *n* be born at once Is 66:8 1471
Hath a *n* changed their gods, Jer 2:11 1471
be avenged on such a *n* as this Jer 5:9 1471
I will bring a *n* upon you from Jer 5:15 1471
mighty *n*, it is an ancient *n* Jer 5:15 1471
a *n* whose language thou knowest Jer 5:15 1471
be avenged on such a *n* as this Jer 5:29 1471
a great *n* shall be raised from Jer 6:22 1471
This is a *n* that obeyeth not the Jer 7:28 1471
be avenged on such a *n* as this Jer 9:9 1471
pluck up and destroy that *n* Jer 12:17 1471
I shall speak concerning a *n* Jer 18:7 1471
If that *n*, against whom I have Jer 18:8 1471
I shall speak concerning a *n* Jer 18:9 1471
the king of Babylon, and that *n* Jer 25:12 1471
shall go forth from *n* to *n* Jer 25:32 1471
it shall come to pass, that the *n* Jer 27:8 1471
that *n* will I punish, saith the Jer 27:8 1471
LORD hath spoken against the *n* Jer 27:13 1471
from being a *n* before me for ever Jer 31:36 1471
should be no more a *n* before them Jer 33:24 1471
let us cut it off from being a *n* Jer 48:2 1471
get you up unto the wealthy *n* Jer 49:31 1471
there shall be no *n* whither the Jer 49:36 1471
there cometh up a *n* against her Jer 50:3 1471
come from the north, and a great *n* Jer 50:41 1471
for a *n* that could not save us Lam 4:17 1471
to a rebellious *n* that hath Eze 2:3 1471
I will make them one *n* in the Eze 37:22 1471
a decree, That every people, *n* Dan 3:29 524
shall stand up out of the *n* Dan 8:22 1471
was a *n* even to that same time Dan 12:1 1471
For a *n* is come up upon my land, Joel 1:6 1471
I will raise up against you a *n* Amos 6:14 1471
n shall not lift up a sword Mic 4:3 1471
not lift up a sword against *n* Mic 4:3 1471
that was cast far off a strong *n* Mic 4:7 1471
Chaldeans, that bitter and hasty *n* Hab 1:6 1471
gather together, O *n* not desired Zeph 2:1 1471
coast, the *n* of the Cherethites Zeph 2:5 1471
people, and so is this *n* before me Hag 2:14 1471
have robbed me, even this whole *n* Mal 3:9 1471
given to a *n* bringing forth the Mt 21:43 *1484*
For *n* shall rise against *n*, Mt 24:7 *1484*
was a Greek, a Syrophenician by *n* Mk 7:26 *1085*
For *n* shall rise against *n*, Mk 13:8 *1484*
For he loveth our *n*, and he hath Lk 7:5 *1484*
N shall rise against *n*, and Lk 21:10 *1484*
this fellow perverting the *n* Lk 23:2 *1484*
and take away both our place and *n* Jn 11:48 *1484*
and that the whole *n* perish not Jn 11:50 *1484*
that Jesus should die for that *n* Jn 11:51 *1484*
And not for that *n* only, but that Jn 11:52 *1484*
Thine own *n* and the chief priests Jn 18:35 *1484*
men, out of every *n* under heaven Acts 2:5 *1484*
the *n* to whom they shall be in Acts 7:7 *1484*
among all the *n* of the Jews Acts 10:22 *1484*
or come unto one of another *n* Acts 10:28 *246*
But in every *n* he that feareth Acts 10:35 *1484*
unto this *n* by thy providence Acts 24:2 *1484*
of many years a judge unto this *n* Acts 24:10 *1484*
I came to bring alms to my *n* Acts 24:17 *1484*
among mine own *n* at Jerusalem Acts 26:4 *1484*
I had ought to accuse my *n* of Acts 28:19 *1484*
by a foolish *n* I will anger you Rom 10:19 *1484*
many my equals in mine own *n* Gal 1:14 *1085*
midst of a crooked and perverse *n* Phil 2:15 *1074*
a royal priesthood, an holy *n* 1Pet 2:9 *1484*
and tongue, and people, and *n* Rev 5:9 *1484*
dwell on the earth, and to every *n* Rev 14:6 *1484*

NATIONS
after their families, in their *n* Gen 10:5 1471
in their countries, and in their *n* Gen 10:20 1471
in their lands, after their *n* Gen 10:31 1471
their generations, in their *n* Gen 10:32 1471
by these were the *n* divided in Gen 10:32 1471
king of Elam, and Tidal king of *n* Gen 14:1 1471
of Elam, and with Tidal king of *n* Gen 14:9 1471
thou shalt be a father of many *n* Gen 17:4 1471
father of many *n* have I made thee Gen 17:5 1471
and I will make *n* of thee Gen 17:6 1471
and she shall be a mother of *n* Gen 17:16 1471
all the *n* of the earth shall be Gen 18:18 1471
all the *n* of the earth be blessed Gen 22:18 1471
princes according to their *n* Gen 25:16 523
Two *n* are in thy womb, and two Gen 25:23 1471
all the *n* of the earth be blessed Gen 26:4 1471
serve thee, and *n* bow down to thee Gen 27:29 3816
a company of *n* shall be of thee, Gen 35:11 1471
shall become a multitude of *n* Gen 48:19 1471
I will cast out the *n* before thee Ex 34:24 1471
for in all these the *n* are Lev 18:24 1471
as it spued out the *n* that were Lev 18:28 1471
then the *n* which have heard the Num 14:15 1471
shall not be reckoned among the *n* Num 23:9 1471
he shall eat up the *n* his enemies Num 24:8 1471
Amalek was the first of the *n* Num 24:20 1471
the fear of thee upon the *n* that Deut 2:25 5971
in the sight of the *n*, which Deut 4:6 5971
unto all *n* under the whole heaven Deut 4:19 5971
shall scatter you among the *n* Deut 4:27 5971
To drive out *n* from before thee Deut 4:38 1471
hath cast out many *n* before thee Deut 7:1 1471
seven *n* greater and mightier than Deut 7:1 1471
heart, These *n* are more than I Deut 7:17 1471
out those *n* before thee by little Deut 7:22 1471
As the *n* which the LORD Deut 8:20 1471
to go in to possess *n* greater Deut 9:1 1471
n the LORD doth drive them out Deut 9:4 1471
n the LORD thy God doth drive Deut 9:5 1471
out all these *n* from before you Deut 11:23 1471
and ye shall possess greater *n* Deut 11:23 1471
wherein the *n* which ye shall Deut 12:2 1471
cut off the *n* from before thee Deut 12:29 1471
How did these *n* serve their gods Deut 12:30 1471
above all the *n* that are upon the Deut 14:2 5971
and thou shalt lend unto many *n* Deut 15:6 1471
and thou shalt reign over many *n* Deut 15:6 1471
like as all the *n* that are about Deut 17:14 1471
after the abominations of those *n* Deut 18:9 1471
For these *n*, which thou shalt Deut 18:14 1471
LORD thy God hath cut off the *n* Deut 19:1 1471
are not of the cities of these *n* Deut 20:15 1471
above all *n* which he hath made Deut 26:19 1471
on high above all *n* of the earth Deut 28:1 1471
and thou shalt lend unto many *n* Deut 28:12 1471
among all *n* whither the LORD Deut 28:37 5971
among these *n* shalt thou find no Deut 28:65 1471
through the *n* which ye passed by Deut 29:16 1471
go and serve the gods of these *n* Deut 29:18 1471
Even all *n* shall say, Wherefore Deut 29:24 1471
call them to mind among all the *n* Deut 30:1 1471
and gather thee from all the *n* Deut 30:3 5971
destroy these *n* from before thee Deut 31:3 1471
to the *n* their inheritance Deut 32:8 1471
Rejoice, O ye *n*, with his people Deut 32:43 1471
the king of the *n* of Gilgal Josh 12:23 1471
unto all these *n* because of you Josh 23:3 1471
you by lot these *n* that remain Josh 23:4 1471
with all the *n* that I have cut Josh 23:4 1471
That ye come not among these *n* Josh 23:7 1471
out from before you great *n* Josh 23:9 1471
unto the remnant of these *n* Josh 23:12 1471
any of these *n* from before you Josh 23:13 1471
n which Joshua left when he died Judg 2:21 1471
Therefore the LORD left those *n* Judg 2:23 1471
Now these are the *n* which the Judg 3:1 1471
a king to judge us like all the *n* 1Sa 8:5 1471
we also may be like all the *n* 1Sa 8:20 1471
for those *n* were of old the 1Sa 27:8
to thee from Egypt, from the *n* 2Sa 7:23 1471
of all *n* which he subdued 2Sa 8:11 1471
his fame was in all *n* round about 1Kin 4:31 1471
Of the *n* concerning which the 1Kin 11:2 1471
n which the LORD cast out before 1Kin 14:24 1471
The *n* which thou hast removed, and 2Kin 17:26 1471
after the manner of the *n* whom 2Kin 17:33 1471
So these *n* feared the LORD, and 2Kin 17:41 1471
Hath any of the gods of the *n* 2Kin 18:33 1471
Have the gods of the *n* delivered 2Kin 19:12 1471
of Assyria have destroyed the *n* 2Kin 19:17 1471
to do more evil than did the *n* 2Kin 21:9 1471
the fear of him upon all *n* 1Chr 14:17 1471
his marvellous works among all *n* 1Chr 16:24 5971
and let men say among the *n* 1Chr 16:31 1471
by driving out *n* from before thy 1Chr 17:21 1471
that he brought from all these *n* 1Chr 18:11 1471
a proverb and a byword among all *n* 2Chr 7:20 5971
manner of the *n* of other lands 2Chr 13:9 5971
were the gods of the *n* of those 2Chr 32:13 1471
those *n* that my fathers utterly 2Chr 32:14 1471
As the gods of the *n* of other 2Chr 32:17 1471
sight of all *n* from thenceforth 2Chr 32:23 1471
the rest of the *n* whom the great Ezr 4:10 524
scatter you abroad among the *n* Neh 1:8 5971
thou gavest them kingdoms and *n* Neh 9:22 5971
yet among many *n* was there no Neh 13:26 1471
He increaseth the *n*, and Job 12:23 1471
he enlargeth the *n*, and Job 12:23 1471
all the *n* that forget God Ps 9:17 1471
that the *n* may know themselves to Ps 9:20 1471
all the kindreds of the *n* shall Ps 22:27 1471
and he is the governor among the *n* Ps 22:28 1471
under us, and the *n* under our feet Ps 47:3 3816
I will sing unto thee among the *n* Ps 57:9 3816
his eyes behold the *n* Ps 66:7 1471
thy saving health among all *n* Ps 67:2 1471
O let the *n* be glad and sing for Ps 67:4 3816
and govern the *n* upon earth Ps 67:4 3816
all *n* shall serve him Ps 72:11 1471
all *n* shall call him blessed Ps 72:17 1471
for thou shalt inherit all *n* Ps 82:8 1471
All *n* whom thou hast made shall Ps 86:9 1471
all the gods of the *n* are idols Ps 96:5 5971
their seed also among the *n* Ps 106:27 1471
They did not destroy the *n* Ps 106:34 5971
praises unto thee among the *n* Ps 108:3 3816
The LORD is high above all *n* Ps 113:4 1471
O praise the LORD, all ye *n* Ps 117:1 1471
All *n* compassed me about Ps 118:10 1471
Who smote great *n*, and slew mighty Ps 135:10 1471
people curse, *n* shall abhor him Prov 24:24 3816
and all *n* shall flow unto it Is 2:2 1471
And he shall judge among the *n* Is 2:4 1471
up an ensign to the *n* from far Is 5:26 1471
Jordan, in Galilee of the *n* Is 9:1 1471
to destroy and cut off *n* not a few Is 10:7 1471
shall set up an ensign for the *n* Is 11:12 1471
kingdoms of *n* gathered together Is 13:4 1471
he that ruled the *n* in anger Is 14:6 1471
thrones all the kings of the *n* Is 14:9 1471
ground, which didst weaken the *n* Is 14:12 1471
All the kings of the *n*, even all Is 14:18 1471
is stretched out upon all the *n* Is 14:26 1471
and to the rushing of *n*, that make Is 17:12 3816
The *n* shall rush like the rushing Is 17:13 3816
and she is a mart of *n* Is 23:3 1471
of the terrible *n* shall fear thee Is 25:3 1471
vail that is spread over all *n* Is 25:7 1471
the *n* that fight against Ariel Is 29:7 1471
the multitude of all the *n* be Is 29:8 1471
to sift the *n* with the sieve of Is 30:28 1471
of thyself the *n* were scattered Is 33:3 1471
Come near, ye *n*, to hear Is 34:1 1471
of the LORD is upon all *n* Is 34:2 1471
Hath any of the gods of the *n* Is 36:18 1471
Have the gods of the *n* delivered Is 37:12 1471
Assyria have laid waste all the *n* Is 37:18 776
the *n* are as a drop of a bucket, Is 40:15 1471
All *n* before him are as nothing Is 40:17 1471
gave the *n* before him, and made Is 41:2 1471
Let all the *n* be gathered Is 43:9 1471
holden, to subdue *n* before him Is 45:1 1471
ye that are escaped of the *n* Is 45:20 1471
holy arm in the eyes of all the *n* Is 52:10 1471
So shall he sprinkle many *n* Is 52:15 1471
n that knew not thee shall run Is 55:5 1471
those *n* shall be utterly wasted Is 60:12 1471
to spring forth before all the *n* Is 61:11 1471
that the *n* may tremble at thy Is 64:2 1471
come, that I will gather all *n* Is 66:18 1471
that escape of them unto the *n* Is 66:19 1471

N

the LORD out of all *n* upon horses Is 66:20 1471
thee a prophet unto the *n* Jer 1:5 1471
have this day set thee over the *n* Jer 1:10 1471
all the *n* shall be gathered unto Jer 3:17 1471
goodly heritage of the hosts of *n* Jer 3:19 1471
the *n* shall bless themselves in Jer 4:2 1471
Make ye mention to the *n* Jer 4:16 1471
Therefore hear, ye *n*, and know, O Jer 6:18 1471
for all these *n* are uncircumcised Jer 9:26 1471
would not fear thee, O King of *n* Jer 10:7 1471
among all the wise men of the *n* Jer 10:7 1471
the *n* shall not be able to abide Jer 10:10 1471
many *n* shall pass by this city, Jer 22:8 1471
against all these *n* round about Jer 25:9 1471
these *n* shall serve the king of Jer 25:11 1471
hath prophesied against all the *n* Jer 25:13 1471
For many *n* and great kings shall Jer 25:14 1471
at my hand, and cause all the *n* Jer 25:15 1471
hand, and made all the *n* to drink Jer 25:17 1471
hath a controversy with the *n* Jer 25:31 1471
a curse to all the *n* of the earth Jer 26:6 1471
all *n* shall serve him, and his son Jer 27:7 1471
and then many *n* and great kings Jer 27:7 1471
But the *n* that bring their neck Jer 27:11 1471
n within the space of two full Jer 28:11 1471
iron upon the neck of all these *n* Jer 28:14 1471
I will gather you from all the *n* Jer 29:14 1471
among all the *n* whither I have Jer 29:18 1471
n whither I have scattered thee Jer 30:11 1471
and shout among the chief of the *n* Jer 31:7 1471
Hear the word of the LORD, O ye *n* Jer 31:10 1471
before all the *n* of the earth Jer 33:9 1471
Judah, and against all the *n* Jer 36:2 1471
that were returned from all *n* Jer 43:5 1471
among all the *n* of the earth Jer 44:8 1471
The *n* have heard of thy shame, and Jer 46:12 1471
the *n* whither I have driven thee Jer 46:28 1471
Declare ye among the *n*, and Jer 50:2 1471
of great *n* from the north country Jer 50:9 1471
of the *n* shall be a wilderness Jer 50:12 1471
become a desolation among the *n* Jer 50:23 1471
and the cry is heard among the *n* Jer 50:46 1471
the *n* have drunken of her wine Jer 51:7 1471
therefore the *n* are mad Jer 51:7 1471
thee will I break in pieces the *n* Jer 51:20 1471
blow the trumpet among the *n* Jer 51:27 1471
prepare the *n* against her Jer 51:27 1471
Prepare against her the *n* with Jer 51:28 1471
an astonishment among the *n* Jer 51:41 1471
the *n* shall not flow together any Jer 51:44 1471
she that was great among the *n* Lam 1:1 1471
have set it in the midst of the *n* Eze 5:5 1471
into wickedness more than the *n* Eze 5:6 1471
the *n* that are round about you Eze 5:7 1471
to the judgments of the *n* that Eze 5:7 1471
of thee in the sight of the *n* Eze 5:8 1471
a reproach among the *n* that are Eze 5:14 1471
an astonishment unto the *n* that Eze 5:15 1471
escape the sword among the *n* Eze 6:8 1471
n whither they shall be carried Eze 6:9 1471
I shall scatter them among the *n* Eze 12:15 1471
The *n* also heard of him Eze 19:4 1471
Then the *n* set against him on Eze 19:8 1471
may not be remembered among the *n* Eze 25:10 1471
will cause many *n* to come up Eze 26:3 1471
it shall become a spoil to the *n* Eze 26:5 1471
upon thee, the terrible of the *n* Eze 28:7 1471
scatter the Egyptians among the *n* Eze 29:12 1471
exalt itself any more above the *n* Eze 29:15 1471
shall no more rule over the *n* Eze 29:15 1471
with him, the terrible of the *n* Eze 30:11 1471
scatter the Egyptians among the *n* Eze 30:23 1471
scatter the Egyptians among the *n* Eze 30:26 1471
his shadow dwelt all great *n* Eze 31:6 1471
strangers, the terrible of the *n* Eze 31:12 1471
I made the *n* to shake at the Eze 31:16 1471
art like a young lion of the *n* Eze 32:2 1471
bring thy destruction among the *n* Eze 32:9 1471
to fall, the terrible of the *n* Eze 32:12 1471
of the *n* shall lament her Eze 32:16 1471
and the daughters of the famous *n* Eze 32:18 1471
thou hast said, These two *n* Eze 35:10 1471
up men, and hast bereaved thy *n* Eze 36:13 1471
neither bereave thy *n* any more Eze 36:14 1471
thou cause thy *n* to fall any more Eze 36:15 1471
and they shall be no more two *n* Eze 37:22 1471
it is brought forth out of the *n* Eze 38:8 1471
that are gathered out of the *n* Eze 38:12 1471
be known in the eyes of many *n* Eze 38:23 1471
in them in the sight of many *n* Eze 39:27 1471
you it is commanded, O people, *n* Dan 3:4 524
of musick, all the people, the *n* Dan 3:7 524
the king, unto all people, *n* Dan 4:1 524
that he gave him, all people, *n* Dan 5:19 524
Darius wrote unto all people, *n* Dan 6:25 524
and a kingdom, that all people, *n* Dan 7:14 524
they have hired among the *n* Hos 8:10 1471
shall be wanderers among the *n* Hos 9:17 1471
I will also gather all *n*, and will Joel 3:2 1471
they have scattered among the *n* Joel 3:2 1471
which are named chief of the *n* Amos 6:1 1471
the house of Israel among all *n* Amos 9:9 1471
many *n* shall come, and say, Come, Mic 4:2 1471
and rebuke strong *n* afar off Mic 4:3 1471
Now also many *n* are gathered Mic 4:11 1471
The *n* shall see and be confounded Mic 7:16 1471
that selleth *n* through her Nah 3:4 1471
I will shew the *n* thy nakedness Nah 3:5 1471
spare continually to slay the *n* Hab 1:17 1471
but gathereth unto him all *n* Hab 2:5 1471
Because thou hast spoiled many *n* Hab 2:8 1471
he beheld, and drove asunder the *n* Hab 3:6 1471
of her, all the beasts of the *n* Zeph 2:14 1471
I have cut off the *n* Zeph 3:6 1471
determination is to gather the *n* Zeph 3:8 1471
I will shake all *n* Hag 2:7 1471
and the desire of all *n* shall come Hag 2:7 1471
me unto the *n* which spoiled you Zec 2:8 1471
many *n* shall be joined to the Zec 2:11 1471
all the *n* whom they knew not Zec 7:14 1471
strong *n* shall come to seek the Zec 8:22 1471
out of all languages of the *n* Zec 8:23 1471
the *n* that come against Jerusalem Zec 12:9 1471
For I will gather all *n* against Zec 14:2 1471
forth, and fight against those *n* Zec 14:3 1471
one that is left of all the *n* Zec 14:16 1471
the punishment of all *n* that come Zec 14:19 1471
all *n* shall call you blessed Mal 3:12 1471
hated of all *n* for my name's sake Mt 24:9 1484
world for a witness unto all *n* Mt 24:14 1484
him shall be gathered all *n* Mt 25:32 1484
Go ye therefore, and teach all *n* Mt 28:19 1484
of all *n* the house of prayer Mk 11:17 1484
first be published among all *n* Mk 13:10 1484
do the *n* of the world seek after Lk 12:30 1484
be led away captive into all *n* Lk 21:24 1484
and upon the earth distress of *n* Lk 21:25 1484
preached in his name among all *n* Lk 24:47 1484
seven *n* in the land of Chanaan Acts 13:19 1484
all *n* to walk in their own ways Acts 14:16 1484
hath made of one blood all *n* of Acts 17:26 1484
to the faith among all *n*, for his Rom 1:5 1484
have made thee a father of many *n* Rom 4:17 1484
might become the father of many *n* Rom 4:18 1484
made known to all *n* for the Rom 16:26 1484
In thee shall all *n* be blessed Gal 3:8 1484
him will I give power over the *n* Rev 2:26 1484
no man could number, of all *n* Rev 7:9 1484
again before many peoples, and *n* Rev 10:11 1484
n shall see their dead bodies Rev 11:9 1484
the *n* were angry, and thy wrath is Rev 11:18 1484
to rule all *n* with a rod of iron Rev 12:5 1484
all kindreds, and tongues, and *n* Rev 13:7 1484
because she made all *n* drink of Rev 14:8 1484
for all *n* shall come and worship Rev 15:4 1484
and the cities of the *n* fell Rev 16:19 1484
are peoples, and multitudes, and *n* Rev 17:15 1484
For all *n* have drunk of the wine Rev 18:3 1484
thy sorceries were all *n* deceived Rev 18:23 1484
with it he should smite the *n* Rev 19:15 1484
he should deceive the *n* no more Rev 20:3 1484
shall go out to deceive the *n* Rev 20:8 1484
the *n* of them which are saved Rev 21:24 1484
glory and honour of the *n* into it Rev 21:26 1484
were for the healing of the *n* Rev 22:2 1484

NATIVE

no more, nor see his *n* country Jer 22:10 4138

NATIVITY

father Terah in the land of his *n* Gen 11:28 4138
thy mother, and the land of thy *n* Ruth 2:11 4138
people, and to the land of our *n* Jer 46:16 4138
thy *n* is of the land of Canaan Eze 16:3 4138
And as for thy *n*, in the day thou Eze 16:4 4138
created, in the land of thy *n* Eze 21:30 4351
of Chaldea, the land of their *n* Eze 23:15 4138

NATURAL

not dim, nor his *n* force abated Deut 34:7 3893
n use into that which is against Rom 1:26 5446
leaving the *n* use of the woman, Rom 1:27 5446
without *n* affection, implacable, Rom 1:31
if God spared not the *n* branches Rom 11:21
these, which be the *n* branches Rom 11:24
But the *n* man receiveth not the 1Cor 2:14 5591
It is sown a *n* body 1Cor 15:44 5591
There is a *n* body, and there is a 1Cor 15:44 5591
is spiritual, but that which is *n* 1Cor 15:46 5591
Without *n* affection, 2Ti 3:3
beholding his *n* face in a glass Jas 1:23 1083
as *n* brute beasts, made to be 2Pet 2:12 5446

NATURALLY

who will *n* care for your state Phil 2:20 1103
but what they know *n*, as brute Jude 10 5447

NATURE

use into that which is against *n* Rom 1:26 5449
do by *n* the things contained in Rom 2:14 5449
not uncircumcision which is by *n* Rom 2:27 5449
the olive tree which is wild by *n* Rom 11:24 5449
to *n* into a good olive tree Rom 11:24 5449
Doth not even *n* itself teach you, 1Cor 11:14 5449
We who are Jews by *n*, and not Gal 2:15 5449
unto them which by *n* are no gods Gal 4:8 5449
were by *n* the children of wrath, Eph 2:3 5449
took not on him the *n* of angels Heb 2:16
setteth on fire the course of *n* Jas 3:6 1078
be partakers of the divine *n* 2Pet 1:4 5449

NAUGHT

but the water is *n*, and the ground 2Kin 2:19 7451
It is *n*, it is *n*, saith the Prov 20:14 7451

NAUGHTINESS

pride, and the *n* of thine heart 1Sa 17:28 7455
shall be taken in their own *n* Prov 11:6 1942
filthiness and superfluity of *n* Jas 1:21 2549

NAUGHTY

A *n* person, a wicked man, walketh Prov 6:12 1100
a liar giveth ear to a *n* tongue Prov 17:4 1942
the other basket had very *n* figs Jer 24:2 7451

NAUM (*na'-um*) See NAHUM. *Father of Amos; ancestor of Jesus.*

of Amos, which was the son of *N* Lk 3:25 3486

NAVEL

force is in the *n* of his belly Job 40:16 8306
It shall be health to thy *n* Prov 3:8 8270
Thy *n* is like a round goblet, Song 7:2 8326
thou wast born thy *n* was not cut Eze 16:4 8270

NAVES

their axletrees, and their *n* 1Kin 7:33 1354

NAVY

king Solomon made a *n* of ships in 1Kin 9:26 590
Hiram sent in the *n* his servants 1Kin 9:27 590
the *n* also of Hiram, that brought 1Kin 10:11 590
For the king had at sea a *n* of 1Kin 10:22 590
of Tharshish with the *n* of Hiram 1Kin 10:22 590
years came the *n* of Tharshish 1Kin 10:22 590

NAY

And he said, *N*; but thou didst Gen 18:15 3808
And they said, *N*; but we will Gen 19:2
N, my lord, hear me Gen 23:11 3808
And Jacob said, *N*, I pray thee, if Gen 33:10 408
And they said unto him, *N*, my lord Gen 42:10 3808
And he said unto them, *N*, but to Gen 42:12 3808
And he said, *N* Num 22:30 3808
And he said, *N*; but as captain Josh 5:14 3808
And the people said unto Joshua, *N* Josh 24:21 3808
If he said, *N* Judg 12:5 3808
unto them, and said unto them, *N* Judg 19:23 408
my brethren, *n*, I pray you Judg 19:23
n, my daughters; for it Ruth 1:13 408
then he would answer him, *N* 1Sa 2:16
N, my sons; for it is 1Sa 2:24 408
and they said, *N*; but we will 1Sa 8:19 3808
and ye have said unto him, *N* 1Sa 10:19
against you, ye said unto me, *N* 1Sa 12:12 3808
And she answered him, *N*, my 2Sa 13:12 408
And the king said to Absalom, *N* 2Sa 13:25 408
And Hushai said unto Absalom, *N* 2Sa 16:18 3808
And the king said unto Araunah, *N* 2Sa 24:24 3808
king, (for he will not say thee *n* 1Kin 2:17
I pray thee, say me not *n* 1Kin 2:20 6440
for I will not say thee *n* 1Kin 2:20
And he said, *N*; but I 1Kin 2:30 3808
And the other woman said, *N* 1Kin 3:22 3808
and the other saith, *N* 1Kin 3:23 3808
king of Israel said unto him, *N* 2Kin 3:13 408
And she said, *N*, my lord, thou man 2Kin 4:16 408
n, but let the shadow return 2Kin 20:10 3808
And king David said to Ornan, *N* 1Chr 21:24 3808
n, they were not at all ashamed, Jer 6:15 1571
n, they were not at all ashamed, Jer 8:12 1571
be, Yea, yea; *N*, *n* Mt 5:37 3756
But he said, *N*; lest while Mt 13:29 3756
I tell you, *N*; but rather Lk 12:51 3780
I tell you, *N*: but, except Lk 13:3 3780
I tell you, *N*: but, except Lk 13:5 3780
And he said, *N*, father Abraham Lk 16:30 3780
others said, *N*; but he Jn 7:12 3756
n verily; but let them Acts 16:37 3756
N: but by the law Rom 3:27 3780
N, I had not known sin, but by Rom 7:7 235
N, in all these things we are Rom 8:37 235
N but, O man, who art thou that Rom 9:20 3304
N, ye do wrong, and defraud, and 1Cor 6:8 235
N, much more those members of the 1Cor 12:22 235
there should be yea yea, and *n n* 2Cor 1:17 3756
word toward you was not yea and *n* 2Cor 1:18 3756
and Timotheus, was not yea and *n* 2Cor 1:19 3756
be yea; and your *n*, *n* Jas 5:12 3756

NAZARENE (*naz-a-reen'*) See NAZARENES. *Native to Nazareth.*

prophets, He shall be called a *N* Mt 2:23 3480

NAZARENES (*naz-a-reens'*)

a ringleader of the sect of the *N* Acts 24:5 3480

NAZARETH (*naz'-a-reth*) See NAZARENE. *A city in Galilee.*

came and dwelt in a city called *N* Mt 2:23 3478
And leaving *N*, he came and dwelt in Mt 4:13 3478
Jesus the prophet of *N* of Galilee Mt 21:11 3478
fellow was also with Jesus of *N* Mt 26:71 3478
that Jesus came from *N* of Galilee Mk 1:9 3478
to do with thee, thou Jesus of *N* Mk 1:24 3478
he heard that it was Jesus of *N* Mk 10:47 3478
And thou also wast with Jesus of *N* Mk 14:67 3478
Ye seek Jesus of *N*, which was Mk 16:6 3478
unto a city of Galilee, named *N* Lk 1:26 3478
Galilee, out of the city of *N* Lk 2:4 3478
into Galilee, to their own city *N* Lk 2:39 3478
went down with them, and came to *N*. Lk 2:51 3478
And he came to *N*, where he had Lk 4:16 3478
to do with thee, thou Jesus of *N* Lk 4:34 3478
him, that Jesus of *N* passeth by Lk 18:37 3478
unto him, Concerning Jesus of *N* Lk 24:19 3478
prophets, did write, Jesus of *N* Jn 1:45 3478
any good thing come out of *N* Jn 1:46 3478
They answered him, Jesus of *N* Jn 18:5 3478
And they said, Jesus of *N* Jn 18:7 3478
JESUS OF *N* THE Jn 19:19 3478
Jesus of *N*, a man approved of God Acts 2:22 3478
name of Jesus Christ of *N* rise up Acts 3:6 3478
by the name of Jesus Christ of *N* Acts 4:10 3478
that this Jesus of *N* shall Acts 6:14 3478
Jesus of *N* with the Holy Ghost Acts 10:38 3478
he said unto me, I am Jesus of *N* Acts 22:8 3478
to the name of Jesus of *N* Acts 26:9 3478

NAZARITE (*naz'-a-rite*) See NAZARITES. *Title applied to one making a special vow of abstention.*

themselves to vow a vow of a *N* Num 6:2 5139
And this is the law of the *N* Num 6:13 5139
the *N* shall shave the head of his Num 6:18 5139
put them upon the hands of the *N* Num 6:19 5139
after that the *N* may drink wine Num 6:20 5139
the law of the *N* who hath vowed Num 6:21 5139
be a *N* unto God from the womb Judg 13:5 5139
for the child shall be a *N* to God Judg 13:7 5139

for I have been a *N* unto God from...... Judg 16:17 5139

NAZARITES (*naz'-a-rites*)
Her *N* were purer than snow, they....... Lam 4:7 5139
and of your young men for *N*.............. Amos 2:11 5139
But ye gave the *N* wine to drink.......... Amos 2:12 5139

NEAH (*ne'-ah*) *A city in Zebulun.*
goeth out to Remmon-methoar to *N*.... Josh 19:13 5269

NEAPOLIS (*ne-ap'-o-lis*) *A Macedonian seaport.*
Samothracia, and the next day to *N*..... Acts 16:11 *3496*

NEAR
when he was come *n* to enter into........ Gen 12:11 7126
And Abraham drew *n*, and said, Wilt... Gen 18:23 5066
Lot, and came *n* to break the door....... Gen 19:9 5066
now, this city is *n* to flee unto............ Gen 19:20 7138
But Abimelech had not come *n* her....... Gen 20:4 7126
And Isaac said unto Jacob, Come *n*...... Gen 27:21 5066
Jacob went *n* unto Isaac his................. Gen 27:22 5066
And he said, Bring it *n* to me............... Gen 27:25 5066
And he brought it *n* to him.................. Gen 27:25 5066
Isaac said unto him, Come *n* now.......... Gen 27:26 5066
And he came *n*, and kissed him............ Gen 27:27 5066
brother, that Jacob went *n*.................. Gen 29:10 5066
until he came *n* to his brother............. Gen 33:3 5066
Then the handmaidens came *n*............. Gen 33:6 5066
also with her children came *n*............. Gen 33:7 5066
and after came Joseph *n* and Rachel,... Gen 33:7 5066
even before he came *n* unto them......... Gen 37:18 7126
they came *n* to the steward of.............. Gen 43:19 5066
Then Judah came *n* unto him............... Gen 44:18 5066
Come *n* to me, I pray you..................... Gen 45:4 5066
And they came *n*................................... Gen 45:4 5066
and thou shalt be *n* unto me................. Gen 45:10 7138
And he brought them *n* unto him.......... Gen 48:10 5066
hand, and brought them *n* unto him..... Gen 48:13 5066
and then let him come *n* and keep........ Ex 12:48 7126
Philistines, although that was *n*........... Ex 13:17 7138
not *n* the other all the night................ Ex 14:20 7126
of Israel, Come *n* before the Lord......... Ex 16:9 7126
which come *n* to the Lord,.................... Ex 19:22 5066
Moses drew *n* unto the thick................. Ex 20:21 5066
Moses alone shall come *n* the Lord........ Ex 24:2 5066
or when they come *n* unto the.............. Ex 28:43 5066
or when they come *n* to the altar......... Ex 30:20 5066
when they came *n* unto the altar.......... Ex 40:32 7126
and all the congregation drew *n*........... Lev 9:5 7126
Aaron, and said unto them, Come *n*..... Lev 10:4 7126
So they went *n*, and carried them......... Lev 10:5 7126
to any that is *n* of kin to him............... Lev 18:6 7607
she is thy father's *n* kinswoman.......... Lev 18:12 7607
she is thy mother's *n* kinswoman......... Lev 18:13 7607
for they are her *n* kinswomen.............. Lev 18:17 7608
for he uncovereth his *n* kin................. Lev 20:19 7607
that is *n* unto him, that is, for............ Lev 21:2 7138
Bring the tribe of Levi *n*..................... Num 3:6 7138
And the priest shall bring her *n*........... Num 5:16 7138
will cause him to come *n* unto him....... Num 16:5 7126
will he cause to come *n* unto him......... Num 16:5 7126
to bring you *n* to himself to do............ Num 16:9 7138
And he hath brought thee *n* to him..... Num 16:10 7138
come *n* to offer incense before............ Num 16:40 7126
Whosoever cometh any thing *n* unto... Num 17:13 7138
of Moab by Jordan *n* Jericho................ Num 26:3
of Moab by Jordan *n* Jericho................ Num 26:63
which are by Jordan *n* Jericho............. Num 31:12
of hundreds, came *n* unto Moses........... Num 31:48 5066
And they came *n* unto him, and said,.. Num 32:16 5066
of Moab by Jordan *n* Jericho................ Num 33:48
by Jordan, *n* Jericho, saying,............... Num 33:50
side Jordan *n* Jericho eastward........... Num 34:15
of Moab by Jordan *n* Jericho................ Num 35:1
of the sons of Joseph, came *n*.............. Num 36:1 5066
of Moab by Jordan *n* Jericho................ Num 36:13
ye came *n* unto me every one of........... Deut 1:22 7126
And ye came *n* and stood under the...... Deut 4:11 7126
fire,) that ye came *n* unto me............... Deut 5:23 7126
Go thou *n*, and hear all that the........... Deut 5:27 7126
n unto the altar of the Lord thy.......... Deut 16:21 681
the sons of Levi shall come *n*.............. Deut 21:5 5066
the wife of the one draweth *n* for......... Deut 25:11 7126
come not *n* unto it, that ye may............ Josh 3:4 7126
war which went with him, Come *n*........ Josh 10:24 7126
And they came *n*, and put their feet.... Josh 10:24 7126
the sea, all that lay *n* Ashdod............. Josh 15:46 3027
they came *n* before Eleazar the............ Josh 17:4 7126
n the hill that lieth on the................... Josh 18:13 5921
Then came *n* the heads of the............... Josh 21:1 5066
n to Micah's house were gathered........ Judg 18:22 5973
let us draw *n* to one of these............... Judg 19:13 7126
came *n* against the children of.............. Judg 20:24 7126
knew not that evil was *n* them............. Judg 20:34 5060
The man is *n* of kin unto us, one......... Ruth 2:20 7138
for thou art a *n* kinsman..................... Ruth 3:9
is true that I am thy *n* kinsman.......... Ruth 3:12
was with child, *n* to be delivered.......... 1Sa 4:19
the Philistines drew *n* to battle............ 1Sa 7:10 5066
Then Saul drew *n* to Samuel in the....... 1Sa 9:18 5066
the tribes of Israel to come *n*............... 1Sa 10:20 7126
to come *n* by their families.................. 1Sa 10:21 7126
Let us draw *n* hither unto God.............. 1Sa 14:36 7126
And Saul said, Draw ye *n* hither........... 1Sa 14:38 5066
And the Philistine drew *n* morning........ 1Sa 17:16 5066
he drew *n* to the Philistine.................. 1Sa 17:40 5066
came on and drew *n* unto David............ 1Sa 17:41 7126
when David came *n* to the people.......... 1Sa 30:21 5066
of the young men, and said, Go *n*......... 2Sa 1:15 5066
See, Joab's field is *n* mine.................... 2Sa 14:30 413
And he came apace, and drew *n*............ 2Sa 18:25 7126
the king is *n* of kin to us..................... 2Sa 19:42 7138
Come *n* hither, that I may speak.......... 2Sa 20:16 7126
And when he was come *n* unto her......... 2Sa 20:17 7126
the land of the enemy, far or *n*............. 1Kin 8:46 7138
all the people, Come *n* unto me............ 1Kin 18:30 5066
And all the people came *n* unto him..... 1Kin 18:30 5066
that Elijah the prophet came *n*............ 1Kin 18:36 5066
because it is *n* unto my house............... 1Kin 21:2 7138
the son of Chenaanah went *n*................ 1Kin 22:24 5066
but Gehazi came *n* to thrust her........... 2Kin 4:27 5066
And his servants came *n*, and spake...... 2Kin 5:13 5066
captives unto a land far off or *n*........... 2Chr 6:36 7138
the son of Chenaanah came *n*................ 2Chr 18:23 5066
that were *n* the Ethiopians................. 2Chr 21:16 3027
yourselves unto the Lord, come *n*......... 2Chr 29:31 5066
So Esther drew *n*, and touched the....... Est 5:2 7126
his decree drew *n* to be put in.............. Est 9:1 5060
as a prince would I go *n* unto him........ Job 31:37 7126
his soul draweth *n* unto the grave........ Job 33:22 7126
One is so *n* to another, that no............. Job 41:16 5066
for trouble is *n*................................... Ps 22:11 7138
lest they come *n* unto thee.................. Ps 32:9 7126
is good for me to draw *n* to God............ Ps 73:28 7132
for that thy name is *n* thy.................... Ps 75:1 7138
they draw *n* unto the gates of............... Ps 107:18 5060
Thou art *n*, O Lord.............................. Ps 119:151 7138
Let my cry come *n* before thee.............. Ps 119:169 7126
of Israel, a people *n* unto him.............. Ps 148:14 7138
through the street *n* her corner........... Prov 7:8 681
of the foolish is *n* destruction............... Prov 10:14 7138
that is *n* than a brother far off............. Prov 27:10 7138
and her time is *n* to come, and her....... Is 13:22 7138
that draweth *n* the time of her............. Is 26:17 7126
people draw *n* me with their mouth...... Is 29:13 5066
and, ye that are *n*, acknowledge my...... Is 33:13 7138
Come *n*, ye nations, to hear.................. Is 34:1 7126
let them come *n*................................... Is 41:1 5066
let us come *n* together to.................... Is 41:1 7126
of the earth were afraid, drew *n*........... Is 41:5 7126
draw *n* together, ye that are................ Is 45:20 5066
Tell ye, and bring them *n*..................... Is 45:21 5066
I bring *n* my righteousness.................. Is 46:13 7126
Come ye *n* unto me, hear ye this.......... Is 48:16 7126
He is *n* that justifieth me.................... Is 50:8 7138
let him come *n* to me.......................... Is 50:8 5066
My righteousness is *n*.......................... Is 51:5 7138
for it shall not come *n* thee................ Is 54:14 7126
call ye upon him while he is *n*.............. Is 55:6 7138
for my salvation is *n* to come............... Is 56:1 7138
But draw *n* hither, ye sons of the.......... Is 57:3 7126
is far off, and to him that is *n*............. Is 57:19 7138
by thyself, come not *n* to me................ Is 65:5 5066
thou art *n* in their mouth, and far....... Jer 12:2 7138
the kings of the north, far and *n*.......... Jer 25:26 7138
and I will cause him to draw *n*.............. Jer 30:21 7126
even unto the greatest, came *n*............ Jer 42:1 5066
and shield, and draw *n* to battle.......... Jer 46:3 5066
The calamity of Moab is *n* to come....... Jer 48:16 7138
of the land of Moab, far or *n*............... Jer 48:24 7138
that were *n* the king's person.............. Jer 52:25 7200
Thou drewest *n* in the day that I.......... Lam 3:57 7126
our end is *n*, our days are.................... Lam 4:18 7126
he that is *n* shall fall by the................ Eze 6:12 7138
is come, the day of trouble is *n*............ Eze 7:7 7138
time is come, the day draweth *n*.......... Eze 7:12 5060
charge over the city to draw *n*............. Eze 9:1 7126
but come not *n* any man upon whom.. Eze 9:6 5066
Which say, It is not *n*......................... Eze 11:3 7138
wife, neither hath come *n* to a.............. Eze 18:6 7126
hast caused thy days to draw *n*............. Eze 22:4 7126
Those that be *n*, and those that be....... Eze 22:5 7138
For the day is *n*, even the day of........... Eze 30:3 7138
even the day of the Lord is *n*................ Eze 30:3 7138
which come *n* to the Lord to................ Eze 40:46 7131
And they shall not come *n* unto me..... Eze 44:13 5066
nor to come *n* to any of my holy.......... Eze 44:13 5066
they shall come *n* to me to.................. Eze 44:15 7126
and they shall come *n* to my table........ Eze 44:16 7126
which shall come *n* to minister............. Eze 45:4 7131
time certain Chaldeans came *n*............. Dan 3:8 7127
Then Nebuchadnezzar came *n* to the... Dan 3:26 7127
Then they came *n*, and spake before...... Dan 6:12 7127
and they brought him *n* before him...... Dan 7:13 7127
I came *n* unto one of them that........... Dan 7:16 7127
So he came *n* where I stood................. Dan 8:17 681
and unto all Israel, that are *n*............. Dan 9:7 7138
let all the men of war draw *n*............... Joel 3:9 5066
is *n* in the valley of decision................ Joel 3:14 7138
the seat of violence to come *n*.............. Amos 6:3 5066
Lord is *n* upon all the heathen............. Obad 15 7138
The great day of the Lord is *n*............. Zeph 1:14 7138
it is *n*, and hasteth greatly.................. Zeph 1:14 7138
she drew not *n* to her God.................... Zeph 3:2 7126
I will come *n* to you to judgment......... Mal 3:5 7126
when the time of the fruit drew *n*......... Mt 21:34 *1448*
these things, know that it is *n*............. Mt 24:33 *1451*
leaves, ye know that summer is *n*.......... Mk 13:28 *1451*
Then drew *n* unto him all the.............. Lk 15:1 *1448*
and when he was come *n*, he asked....... Lk 18:40 *1448*
And when he was come *n*, he beheld.... Lk 19:41 *1448*
and the time draweth *n*........................ Lk 21:8 *1448*
drew *n* unto Jesus to kiss him.............. Lk 22:47 *1448*
and reasoned, Jesus himself drew *n*....... Lk 24:15 *1448*
was baptizing in Aenon *n* to Salim........ Jn 3:23 *1451*
n to the parcel of ground that............ Jn 4:5 *4139*
a country *n* to the wilderness.............. Jn 11:54 *1451*
as he drew *n* to behold it, the............. Acts 7:31 *4334*
the Spirit said unto Philip, Go *n*........... Acts 8:29 *4334*
he journeyed, he came *n* Damascus...... Acts 9:3 *1448*
together his kinsmen and *n* friends...... Acts 10:24 *316*
Then the chief captain came *n*............. Acts 21:33 *1448*
and we, or ever he come *n*, are.............. Acts 23:15 *1448*
that they drew *n* to some country......... Acts 27:27 *4317*
Let us draw *n* with a true heart........... Heb 10:22 *4334*

NEARER
there is a kinsman *n* than I................. Ruth 3:12 7138
salvation *n* than when we believed........ Rom 13:11 *1452*

NEARIAH (*ne-a-ri'-ah*) See Nagge.
1. A son of Shemiah.
and Igeal, and Bariah, and *N*................. 1Chr 3:22 5294
And the sons of *N*................................. 1Chr 3:23 5294
2. A son of Ishi.
for their captains Pelatiah, and *N*.......... 1Chr 4:42 5294

NEBAI (*ne'-bahee*) *A renewer of the covenant.*
Hariph, Anathoth, *N*,.............................. Neh 10:19 5109

NEBAIOTH (*ne-bah'-yoth*) See Nebajoth.
1. A son of Ishmael.
The firstborn of Ishmael, *N*..................... 1Chr 1:29 5032
2. Descendants of Ishmael.
the rams of *N* shall minister unto.......... Is 60:7 5032

NEBAJOTH (*ne-ba'-joth*) See Nebaioth. *Same as Nebaioth 1.*
the firstborn of Ishmael, *N*..................... Gen 25:13 5032
Abraham's son, the sister of *N*.............. Gen 28:9 5032
Ishmael's daughter, sister of *N*.............. Gen 36:3 5032

NEBALLAT (*ne-bal'-lat*) *A Benjamite city.*
Hadid, Zeboim, *N*,................................... Neh 11:34 5041

NEBAT (*ne'-bat*) *Father of King Jeroboam.*
And Jeroboam the son of *N*, an.............. 1Kin 11:26 5028
pass, when Jeroboam the son of *N*....... 1Kin 12:2 5028
unto Jeroboam the son of *N*.................. 1Kin 12:15 5028
of *N* reigned Abijam over Judah............. 1Kin 15:1 5028
house of Jeroboam the son of *N*........... 1Kin 16:3 5028
the way of Jeroboam the son of *N*........ 1Kin 16:26 5028
the sins of Jeroboam the son of *N*........ 1Kin 16:31 5028
house of Jeroboam the son of *N*........... 1Kin 21:22 5028
the way of Jeroboam the son of *N*........ 1Kin 22:52 5028
the sins of Jeroboam the son of *N*........ 2Kin 3:3 5028
house of Jeroboam the son of *N*........... 2Kin 9:9 5028
the sins of Jeroboam the son of *N*........ 2Kin 10:29 5028
the sins of Jeroboam the son of *N*........ 2Kin 13:2 5028
the sins of Jeroboam the son of *N*........ 2Kin 13:11 5028
the sins of Jeroboam the son of *N*........ 2Kin 14:24 5028
the sins of Jeroboam the son of *N*........ 2Kin 15:9 5028
the sins of Jeroboam the son of *N*........ 2Kin 15:18 5028
the sins of Jeroboam the son of *N*........ 2Kin 15:24 5028
the sins of Jeroboam the son of *N*........ 2Kin 15:28 5028
made Jeroboam the son of *N* king......... 2Kin 17:21 5028
place which Jeroboam the son of *N*....... 2Kin 23:15 5028
against Jeroboam the son of *N*.............. 2Chr 9:29 5028
pass, when Jeroboam the son of *N*....... 2Chr 10:2 5028
to Jeroboam the son of *N*..................... 2Chr 10:15 5028
Yet Jeroboam the son of *N*.................... 2Chr 13:6 5028

NEBO (*ne'-bo*) See Pisgah, Samgar-nebo.
1. A city in Reuben.
and Elealeh, and Shebam, and *N*........... Num 32:3 5015
And *N*, and Baal-meon, (their names... Num 32:38 5015
the mountains of Abarim, before *N*...... Num 33:47 5015
who dwelt in Aroer, even unto *N*.......... 1Chr 5:8 5015
Moab shall howl over *N*, and over......... Is 15:2 5015
Woe unto *N*... Jer 48:1 5015
And upon Dibon, and upon *N*................ Jer 48:22 5015
2. A mountain east of the Jordan.
mountain Abarim, unto mount *N*.......... Deut 32:49 5015
of Moab unto the mountain of *N*.......... Deut 34:1 5015
3. A city in Judah.
The children of *N*, fifty and two........... Ezr 2:29 5015
The men of the other *N*, fifty and......... Neh 7:33 5015
4. A Chaldean idol.
N stoopeth, their idols were upon......... Is 46:1 5015
5. Father of several who married foreigners.
Of the sons of *N*.................................... Ezr 10:43 5015

NEBO-SARSEKIM See Sarsechim.

NEBUCHADNEZZAR (*neb-u-kad-nez'-zar*) See Nebuchadrezzar. *King of Babylon.*
In his days *N* king of Babylon................ 2Kin 24:1 5019
At that time the servants of *N*.............. 2Kin 24:10 5019
N king of Babylon came against............ 2Kin 24:11 5019
that *N* king of Babylon came, he,........... 2Kin 25:1 5019
year of king *N* king of Babylon.............. 2Kin 25:8 5019
whom *N* king of Babylon had left,......... 2Kin 25:22 5019
and Jerusalem by the hand of *N*........... 1Chr 6:15 5019
him came up *N* king of Babylon............ 2Chr 36:6 5019
N also carried of the vessels of............. 2Chr 36:7 5019
the year was expired, king *N* sent........ 2Chr 36:10 5019
he also rebelled against king *N*........... 2Chr 36:13 5019
which *N* had brought forth out of......... Ezr 1:7 5019
whom *N* the king of Babylon had.......... Ezr 2:1 5019
the hand of *N* the king of Babylon........ Ezr 5:12 5020
which *N* took out of the temple............ Ezr 5:14 5020
which *N* took forth out of the............... Ezr 6:5 5020
whom *N* the king of Babylon had.......... Neh 7:6 5019
whom *N* the king of Babylon had.......... Est 2:6 5019
the hand of *N* the king of Babylon........ Jer 27:6 5019
the same *N* the king of Babylon............ Jer 27:8 5019
Which *N* king of Babylon took not,....... Jer 27:20 5019
that *N* king of Babylon took away.......... Jer 28:3 5019
so will I break the yoke of *N*................. Jer 28:11 5019
they may serve *N* king of Babylon......... Jer 28:14 5019
to all the people whom *N* had.............. Jer 29:1 5019
to *N* king of Babylon) saying................. Jer 29:3 5019
when *N* king of Babylon, and all............ Jer 34:1 5019
they brought him up to *N* king of......... Jer 39:5 5019
N king of Babylon unto Jerusalem......... Dan 1:1 5019
eunuchs brought them in before *N*........ Dan 1:18 5019
the second year of the reign of *N*.......... Dan 2:1 5019
N dreamed dreams, wherewith his......... Dan 2:1 5019
maketh known to the king *N* what........ Dan 2:28 5020
Then the king *N* fell upon his............... Dan 2:46 5020
N the king made an image of gold,........ Dan 3:1 5020
Then *N* the king sent to gather............. Dan 3:2 5020
image which *N* the king had set up....... Dan 3:2 5020
image that *N* the king had set up......... Dan 3:3 5020
the image that *N* had set up................. Dan 3:3 5020
image that *N* the king hath set up........ Dan 3:5 5020
image that *N* the king had set up......... Dan 3:7 5020
They spake and said to the king *N*........ Dan 3:9 5020

N

Then N in his rage and fury .... Dan 3:13 5020
N spake and said unto them, Is it .... Dan 3:14 5020
answered and said to the king, O N.... Dan 3:16 5020
Then was N full of fury, and the .... Dan 3:19 5020
Then N the king was astonied, and .... Dan 3:24 5020
Then N came near to the mouth of .... Dan 3:26 5020
Then N spake, and said, Blessed be .... Dan 3:28 5020
N the king, unto all people, ... Dan 4:1 5020
I N was at rest in mine house, and .... Dan 4:4 5020
This dream I king N have seen .... Dan 4:18 5020
All this came upon the king N.... Dan 4:28 5020
from heaven, saying, O king N .... Dan 4:31 5020
was the thing fulfilled upon N.... Dan 4:33 5020
at the end of the days I N lifted .... Dan 4:34 5020
Now I N praise and extol and honour.. Dan 4:37 5020
N had taken out of the temple .... Dan 5:2 5020
whom the king N thy father .... Dan 5:11 5020
God gave N thy father a kingdom .... Dan 5:18 5020

NEBUCHADREZZAR
(*neb-u-kad-rez'-zar*) See NEBUCHADNEZZAR. *Same as Nebuchadnezzar.*

for N king of Babylon maketh war .... Jer 21:2 5019
the hand of N king of Babylon .... Jer 21:7 5019
the hand of N king of Babylon .... Jer 22:25 5019
after that N king of Babylon had .... Jer 24:1 5019
first year of N king of Babylon .... Jer 25:1 5019
N the king of Babylon, my servant .... Jer 25:9 5019
the hand of N king of Babylon .... Jer 29:21 5019
was the eighteenth year of N .... Jer 32:1 5019
the hand of N king of Babylon .... Jer 32:28 5019
when N king of Babylon came up .... Jer 35:11 5019
whom N king of Babylon made king .... Jer 37:1 5019
came N king of Babylon and all his .... Jer 39:1 5019
Now N king of Babylon gave charge .... Jer 39:11 5019
take N the king of Babylon, my .... Jer 43:10 5019
the hand of N king of Babylon .... Jer 44:30 5019
which N king of Babylon smote in .... Jer 46:2 5019
how N king of Babylon should come .... Jer 46:13 5019
the hand of N king of Babylon .... Jer 46:26 5019
which N king of Babylon shall .... Jer 49:28 5019
for N king of Babylon hath taken .... Jer 49:30 5019
last this N king of Babylon hath .... Jer 50:17 5019
N the king of Babylon hath .... Jer 51:34 5019
that N king of Babylon came, he .... Jer 52:4 5019
year of N king of Babylon .... Jer 52:12 5019
whom N carried away captive .... Jer 52:28 5019
In the eighteenth year of N he .... Jer 52:29 5019
twentieth year of N Nebuzar-adan .... Jer 52:30 5019
upon Tyrus N king of Babylon .... Eze 26:7 5019
N king of Babylon caused his army .... Eze 29:18 5019
of Egypt unto N king of Babylon .... Eze 29:19 5019
by the hand of N king of Babylon .... Eze 30:10 5019

NEBUSHASBAN
(*neb-u-shas'-ban*) *A Babylonian prince.*

captain of the guard sent, and N .... Jer 39:13 5021

NEBUSHAZBAN
See NEBUSHASBAN.

NEBUZAR-ADAN
(*neb-u-zar'-a-dan*) *Commander of Nebuchadnezzar's army.*

king of Babylon, came N, captain 2Kin 25:8 5018
did N the captain of the guard 2Kin 25:11 5018
N captain of the guard took these 2Kin 25:20 5018
Then N the captain of the guard .... Jer 39:9 5018
But N the captain of the guard .... Jer 39:10 5018
to N the captain of the guard .... Jer 39:11 5018
So N the captain of the guard .... Jer 39:13 5018
after that N the captain of the .... Jer 40:1 5018
whom N the captain of the guard .... Jer 41:10 5018
every person that N the captain .... Jer 43:6 5018
king of Babylon, came N, captain .... Jer 52:12 5018
Then N the captain of the guard .... Jer 52:15 5018
But N the captain of the guard .... Jer 52:16 5018
So N the captain of the guard .... Jer 52:26 5018
year of Nebuchadrezzar N the .... Jer 52:30 5018

NEBUZARADAN
See NEBUZAR-ADAN.

NECESSARY

of his mouth more than my n food .... Job 23:12 2706
It was n that the word of God .... Acts 13:46 *316*
burden than these n things .... Acts 15:28 *1876*
us with such things as were n .... Acts 28:10
seem to be more feeble, are n 1Cor 12:22 *316*
it n to exhort the brethren 2Cor 9:5 *316*
Yet I supposed it n to send to .... Phil 2:25 *316*
to maintain good works for n uses .... Titus 3:14 *316*
It was therefore n that the .... Heb 9:23 *318*

NECESSITIES

hands have ministered unto my n .... Acts 20:34 *5532*
patience, in afflictions, in n 2Cor 6:4 *318*
infirmities, in reproaches, in n 2Cor 12:10 *318*

NECESSITY

(For of n he must release one .... Lk 23:17
Distributing to the n of saints .... Rom 12:13 *5532*
in his heart, having no n 1Cor 7:37 *318*
for n is laid upon me 1Cor 9:16 *318*
not grudgingly, or of n 2Cor 9:7 *318*
ye sent once and again unto my n .... Phil 4:16 *5532*
should not be as it were of n .... Philem 14 *318*
there is made of n a change also .... Heb 7:12 *318*
wherefore it is of n that this .... Heb 8:3 *316*
there must also of n be the death .... Heb 9:16 *318*

NECHO
(*ne'-ko*) See PHARAOH-NECHOH. *A king of Egypt.*

N king of Egypt came up to fight 2Chr 35:20 5224
words of N from the mouth of God 2Chr 35:22 5224
N took Jehoahaz his brother, and 2Chr 36:4 5224

NECK

and upon the smooth of his n .... Gen 27:16 6677
break his yoke from off thy n .... Gen 27:40 6677
and embraced him, and fell on his n .... Gen 33:4 6677
and put a gold chain about his n .... Gen 41:42 6677
upon his brother Benjamin's n .... Gen 45:14 6677
and Benjamin wept upon his n .... Gen 45:14 6677
and he fell on his n, and wept on .... Gen 46:29 6677
wept on his n a good while .... Gen 46:29 6677
be in the n of thine enemies .... Gen 49:8 6203
it, then thou shalt break his n .... Ex 13:13 6203
not, then shalt thou break his n .... Ex 34:20 6203
and wring off his head from his n .... Lev 5:8 6203
heifer's n there in the valley .... Deut 21:4 6203
put a yoke of iron upon thy n .... Deut 28:48 6677
thy rebellion, and thy stiff n .... Deut 31:27 6203
gate, and his n brake, and he died 1Sa 4:18 4665
like to the n of their fathers, ... 2Kin 17:14 6203
but he stiffened his n, and 2Chr 36:13 6203
the shoulder, and hardened their n .... Neh 9:29 6203
runneth upon him, even on his n .... Job 15:26 6677
he hath also taken me by my n .... Job 16:12 6203
thou clothed his n with thunder .... Job 39:19 6677
In his n remaineth strength, and .... Job 41:22 6677
speak not with a stiff n .... Ps 75:5 6677
thy head, and chains about thy n .... Prov 1:9 1621
bind them about thy n .... Prov 3:3 1621
unto thy soul, and grace to thy n .... Prov 3:22 1621
heart, and tie them about thy n .... Prov 6:21 1621
often reproved hardeneth his n .... Prov 29:1 6203
thy n with chains of gold .... Song 1:10 6677
Thy n is like the tower of David .... Song 4:4 6677
eyes, with one chain of thy n .... Song 4:9 6677
Thy n is as a tower of ivory .... Song 7:4 6677
he shall reach even to the n .... Is 8:8 6677
and his yoke from off thy n .... Is 10:27 6677
shall reach to the midst of the n .... Is 30:28 6677
thy n is an iron sinew, and thy .... Is 48:4 6203
thyself from the bands of thy n .... Is 52:2 6677
lamb, as if he cut off a dog's n .... Is 66:3 6202
their ear, but hardened their n .... Jer 7:26 6202
their ear, but made their n stiff .... Jer 17:23 6202
and yokes, and put them upon thy n ... Jer 27:2 6677
that will not put their n under .... Jer 27:8 6677
the nations that bring their n .... Jer 27:11 6677
from off the prophet Jeremiah's n .... Jer 28:10 6677
king of Babylon from the n of all .... Jer 28:11 6677
off the n of the prophet Jeremiah .... Jer 28:12 6677
upon the n of all these nations .... Jer 28:14 6677
break his yoke from off thy n .... Jer 30:8 6677
wreathed, and come up upon my n .... Lam 1:14 6677
thy hands, and a chain on thy n .... Eze 16:11 1627
have a chain of gold about his n .... Dan 5:7 6676
have a chain of gold about thy n .... Dan 5:16 6676
put a chain of gold about his n .... Dan 5:29 6676
but I passed over upon her fair n .... Hos 10:11 6676
the foundation unto the n .... Hab 3:13 6676
millstone were hanged about his n .... Mt 18:6 *5137*
millstone were hanged about his n .... Mk 9:42 *5137*
and ran, and fell on his n .... Lk 15:20 *5137*
millstone were hanged about his n .... Lk 17:2 *5137*
yoke upon the n of the disciples .... Acts 15:10 *5137*
wept sore, and fell on Paul's n .... Acts 20:37 *5137*

NECKS

feet upon the n of these kings .... Josh 10:24 6677
put their feet upon the n of them .... Josh 10:24 6677
meet for the n of them that take .... Judg 5:30 6677
that were on their camels' n .... Judg 8:21 6677
that were about their camels' n .... Judg 8:26 6677
given me the n of mine enemies 2Sa 22:41 6203
not hear, but hardened their n 2Kin 17:14 6203
their n to the work of their Lord .... Neh 3:5 6677
proudly, and hardened their n .... Neh 9:16 6203
but hardened their n, and in their .... Neh 9:17 6203
given me the n of mine enemies .... Ps 18:40 6203
and walk with stretched forth n .... Is 3:16 1627
they have hardened their n .... Jer 19:15 6203
Bring your n under the yoke of .... Jer 27:12 6677
Our n are under persecution .... Lam 5:5 6677
upon the n of them that are slain .... Eze 21:29 6677
which ye shall not remove your n .... Mic 2:3 6677
for my life laid down their own n .... Rom 16:4 *5137*

NECO
See NECHOH.

NECROMANCER

spirits, or a wizard, or a n .... Deut 18:11

NEDABIAH
(*ned-a-bi'-ah*) *Son of Jeconiah.*

Shenazar, Jecamiah, Hoshama, and N . 1Chr 3:18 5072

NEED

lend him sufficient for his n .... Deut 15:8 4270
Have I n of mad men, that ye have 1Sa 21:15 2638
Lebanon, as much as thou shalt n 2Chr 2:16 6878
Ye shall not n to fight in this 2Chr 20:17
And that which they have n of .... Ezr 6:9 2818
that he shall have no n of spoil .... Prov 31:11 2637
I have n to be baptized of thee, ... Mt 3:14 *5532*
knoweth what things ye have n of .... Mt 6:8 *5532*
ye have n of all these things .... Mt 6:32 *5535*
that be whole n not a physician .... Mt 9:12
said unto them, They n not depart .... Mt 14:16
say, The Lord hath n of them .... Mt 21:3 *5532*
what further n have we of .... Mt 26:65 *5532*
whole have no n of the physician .... Mk 2:17 *5532*
what David did, when he had n .... Mk 2:25 *5532*
ye that the Lord hath n of him .... Mk 11:3 *5532*
What n we any further witnesses .... Mk 14:63
that are whole n not a physician .... Lk 5:31
healed them that had n of healing .... Lk 9:11 *5532*
that ye have n of these things .... Lk 12:30 *5535*
persons, which n no repentance .... Lk 15:7
Because the Lord hath n of him .... Lk 19:31 *5532*
they said, The Lord hath n of him .... Lk 19:34 *5532*
What n we any further witness .... Lk 22:71
we have n of against the feast .... Jn 13:29 *5532*
to all men, as every man had n .... Acts 2:45 *5532*
every man according as he had n .... Acts 4:35 *5532*
business she hath n of you .... Rom 16:2 *5535*
n so require, let him do what he 1Cor 7:36 *3784*
the hand, I have no n of thee 1Cor 12:21 *5532*
to the feet, I have no n of you 1Cor 12:21 *5532*
For our comely parts have no n 1Cor 12:24 *5532*
or n we, as some others, epistles 2Cor 3:1 *5535*
both to abound and to suffer n .... Phil 4:12
your n according to his riches in .... Phil 4:19 *5532*
so that we n not to speak any 1Th 1:8
ye n not that I write unto you 1Th 4:9 *5532*
ye have no n that I write unto 1Th 5:1 *5532*
find grace to help in time of n .... Heb 4:16 *2121*
ye have n that one teach you .... Heb 5:12 *5532*
are become such as have n of milk .... Heb 5:12 *5532*
what further n was there that .... Heb 7:11 *5532*
For ye have n of patience .... Heb 10:36 *5532*
though now for a season, if n be 1Pet 1:6 *1163*
ye n not that any man teach you 1Jn 2:27
good, and seeth his brother have n 1Jn 3:17 *5532*
with goods, and have n of nothing .... Rev 3:17 *5532*
And the city had no n of the sun .... Rev 21:23 *5532*
they n no candle, neither light .... Rev 22:5

NEEDED

n not that any should testify of .... Jn 2:25
hands, as though he n any thing .... Acts 17:25 *4326*

NEEDEST

n not that any man should ask .... Jn 16:30

NEEDETH

And he said, What n it .... Gen 33:15
rise and give him as many as he n .... Lk 11:8 *5535*
He that is washed n not save to .... Jn 13:10
he may have to give to him that n .... Eph 4:28 *5532*
a workman that n not to be 2Ti 2:15 *422*
Who n not daily, as those high .... Heb 7:27

NEEDFUL

be n for the house of thy God .... Ezr 7:20 2819
But one thing is n .... Lk 10:42 *5532*
That it was n to circumcise them, ... Acts 15:5 *1163*
in the flesh is more n for you .... Phil 1:24 *316*
things which are n to the body .... Jas 2:16 *2006*
it was n for me to write unto you .... Jude 3 *318*

NEEDLE

to go through the eye of a n .... Mt 19:24 *4476*
to go through the eye of a n .... Mk 10:25 *4476*

NEEDLE'S

for a camel to go through a n eye .... Lk 18:25 *4476*

NEEDLEWORK

fine twined linen, wrought with n .... Ex 26:36
fine twined linen, wrought with n .... Ex 27:16 7551
thou shalt make the girdle of n .... Ex 28:39 7551
and fine twined linen, of n .... Ex 36:37 7551
for the gate of the court was n .... Ex 38:18 7551
blue, and purple, and scarlet, of n .... Ex 39:29 7551
a prey of divers colours of n .... Judg 5:30 7553
divers colours of n on both sides .... Judg 5:30 7553
unto the king in raiment of n .... Ps 45:14 7553

NEEDS

thy money, must n be circumcised .... Gen 17:13
sojourn, and he will n be a judge .... Gen 19:9
must I n bring thy son again unto .... Gen 24:5
though thou wouldest n be gone .... Gen 31:30
For we must n die, and are as 2Sa 14:14
they must n be borne, because .... Jer 10:5
for it must n be that offences .... Mt 18:7 *318*
for such things must n be .... Mk 13:7
a piece of ground, and I must n go .... Lk 14:18 *318*
he must n go through Samaria .... Jn 4:4
must n have been fulfilled .... Acts 1:16
that Christ must n have suffered .... Acts 17:3
multitude must n come together .... Acts 21:22 *3843*
Wherefore ye must n be subject .... Rom 13:5 *318*
for then must ye n go out of the 1Cor 5:10
If I must n glory, I will glory 2Cor 11:30

NEEDY

brother, to thy poor, and to thy n .... Deut 15:11 34
hired servant that is poor and n .... Deut 24:14 34
They turn the n out of the way .... Job 24:4 34
the light killeth the poor and n .... Job 24:14 34
For the n shall not alway be .... Ps 9:18 34
poor, for the sighing of the n .... Ps 12:5 34
the n from him that spoileth him .... Ps 35:10 34
bow, to cast down the poor and n .... Ps 37:14 34
But I am poor and n .... Ps 40:17 34
But I am poor and n .... Ps 70:5 34
shall save the children of the n .... Ps 72:4 34
deliver the n when he crieth .... Ps 72:12 34
He shall spare the poor and n .... Ps 72:13 34
and shall save the souls of the n .... Ps 72:13 34
let the poor and n praise thy name .... Ps 74:21 34
do justice to the afflicted and n .... Ps 82:3 7326
Deliver the poor and n .... Ps 82:4 34
for I am poor and n .... Ps 86:1 34
n man, that he might even slay .... Ps 109:16 34
For I am poor and n, and my heart .... Ps 109:22 34
lifteth the n out of the dunghill .... Ps 113:7 34
earth, and the n from among men .... Prov 30:14 34
plead the cause of the poor and n .... Prov 31:9 34
reacheth forth her hands to the n .... Prov 31:20 34
To turn aside the n from judgment .... Is 10:2 1800
the n shall lie down in safety .... Is 14:30 34
strength to the n in his distress .... Is 25:4 34
the poor, and the steps of the n .... Is 26:6 1800
even when the n speaketh right .... Is 32:7 34
n seek water, and there is none, ... Is 41:17 34
the right of the n do they not .... Jer 5:28 34
judged the cause of the poor and n .... Jer 22:16 34
the hand of the poor and n .... Eze 16:49 34
Hath oppressed the poor and n .... Eze 18:12 34
and have vexed the poor and n .... Eze 22:29 34
the poor, which crush the n .... Amos 4:1 34
this, O ye that swallow up the n .... Amos 8:4 34

the *n* for a pair of shoes........................ Amos 8:6 34

NEESINGS
By his *n* a light doth shine, and........... Job 41:18 5846

NEGEV See SOUTH.

NEGINAH (*neg'-i-nah*) See NEGINOTH. *A stringed instrument.*
To the chief Musician upon *N*............... Ps 61:*t* 5058

NEGINOTH (*neg'-i-noth*) See NEGINAH. *Same as Neginah.*
To the chief Musician on *N*................... Ps 4:*t* 5058
Musician on *N* upon Sheminith .... Ps 6:*t* 5058
To the chief Musician on *N*.................. Ps 54:*t* 5058
To the chief Musician on *N*.................. Ps 55:*t* 5058
To the chief Musician on *N*.................. Ps 67:*t* 5058
To the chief Musician on *N*.................. Ps 76:*t* 5058

NEGLECT
if he shall *n* to hear them, tell.............. Mt 18:17 *3878*
but if he *n* to hear the church,............... Mt 18:17 *3878*
N not the gift that is in thee, ... 1Ti 4:14 *272*
if we *n* so great salvation .... Heb 2:3 *272*

NEGLECTED
were *n* in the daily ministration............ Acts 6:1 *3865*

NEGLECTING
and humility, and *n* of the body .... Col 2:23 *857*

NEGLIGENT
My sons, be not now *n*.......................... 2Chr 29:11 7952
not be *n* to put you always in............... 2Pet 1:12 *272*

NEHELAM See NEHELAMITE.

NEHELAMITE (*ne-hel'-am-ite*) *Family name of Shemaiah.*
thou also speak to Shemaiah the *N*...... Jer 29:24 5161
LORD concerning Shemaiah the *N*........ Jer 29:31 5161
I will punish Shemaiah the *N*............... Jer 29:32 5161

NEHEMIAH (*ne-he-mi'-ah*)
1. A clan leader with Zerubbabel.
Jeshua, *N*, Seraiah, Reelaiah,................ Ezr 2:2 5166
came with Zerubbabel, Jeshua, *N* .... Neh 7:7 5166
2. Governor of Jerusalem.
The words of *N* the son of..................... Neh 1:1 5166
And *N*, which is the Tirshatha, and...... Neh 8:9 5166
Now those that sealed were, *N*............. Neh 10:1 5166
and in the days of *N* the governor........ Neh 12:26 5166
Zerubbabel, and in the days of *N*.......... Neh 12:47 5166
3. A rebuilder of Jerusalem's wall.
him repaired *N* the son of Azbuk.......... Neh 3:16 5166

NEHILOTH (*ne'-hi-loth*) *A musical choir or instrument.*
To the chief Musician upon *N*............... Ps 5:*t* 5155

NEHUM (*ne'-hum*) See REHUM. *A clan leader with Zerubbabel.*
Bilshan, Mispereth, Bigvai, *N*................ Neh 7:7 5149

NEHUSHTA (*ne-hush'-tah*) *Mother of King Jehoiachin.*
And his mother's name was *N*.............. 2Kin 24:8 5179

NEHUSHTAN (*ne-hush'-tan*) *Name given to the brazen serpents.*
and he called it *N*................................ 2Kin 18:4 5180

NEIEL (*ne-i'-el*) *A city in Asher.*
the north side of Beth-emek, and *N*...... Josh 19:27 5272

NEIGHBOUR
every woman shall borrow of her *n*....... Ex 3:22 7934
and let every man borrow of his *n*....... Ex 11:2 7453
and every woman of her *n*, jewels......... Ex 11:2 7468
his *n* next unto his house take it.......... Ex 12:4 7934
bear false witness against thy *n*.......... Ex 20:16 7453
come presumptuously upon his *n*.......... Ex 21:14 7453
unto his *n* money or stuff to keep......... Ex 22:7 7453
he shall pay double unto his *n*.............. Ex 22:9 7453
a man deliver unto his *n* an ass............. Ex 22:10 7453
And if a man borrow ought of his *n*....... Ex 22:14 7453
his companion, and every man his *n*...... Ex 32:27 7138
lie unto his *n* in that which was............ Lev 6:2 5997
violence, or hath deceived his *n*........... Lev 6:2 5997
Thou shalt not defraud thy *n*............... Lev 19:13 7453
shalt thou judge thy *n* .... Lev 19:15 5997
stand against the blood of thy *n*........... Lev 19:16 7453
shalt in any wise rebuke thy *n*.............. Lev 19:17 5997
thou shalt love thy *n* as thyself .... Lev 19:18 7453
if a man cause a blemish in his *n* .... Lev 24:19 5997
And if thou sell ought unto thy *n* .... Lev 25:14 5997
jubile thou shalt buy of thy *n* .... Lev 25:15 5997
which should kill his *n* unawares........... Deut 4:42 7453
bear false witness against thy *n*........... Deut 5:20 7453
ought unto his *n* shall release it .... Deut 15:2 7453
he shall not exact it of his *n*................ Deut 15:2 7453
Whoso killeth his *n* ignorantly............... Deut 19:4 7453
the wood with his *n* to hew wood........... Deut 19:5 7453
the helve, and lighteth upon his *n* .... Deut 19:5 7453
But if any man hate his *n*..................... Deut 19:11 7453
when a man riseth against his *n*........... Deut 22:26 7453
into the standing corn of thy *n*............ Deut 23:25 7453
be he that smiteth his *n* secretly .... Deut 27:24 7453
he smote his *n* unwittingly .... Josh 20:5 7453
off his shoe, and gave it to his *n*.......... Ruth 4:7 7453
and hath given it to a *n* of thine 1Sa 15:28 7453
thine hand, and given it to thy *n*.......... 1Sa 28:17 7453
eyes, and give them unto thy *n*............ 2Sa 12:11 7453
If any man trespass against his *n*........ 1Kin 8:31 7453
his *n* in the word of the LORD 1Kin 20:35 7453
If a man sin against his *n*.................... 2Chr 6:22 7453
I am as one mocked of his *n*................. Job 12:4 7453
God, as a man pleadeth for his *n*.......... Job 16:21 7453
speak vanity every one with his *n* .... Ps 12:2 7453
tongue, nor doeth evil to his *n*............. Ps 15:3 7453
up a reproach against his *n*.................. Ps 15:3 7138
Whoso privily slandereth his *n*.............. Ps 101:5 7453
Say not unto thy *n*, Go, and come........ Prov 3:28 7453
Devise not evil against thy *n*................ Prov 3:29 7453
with his mouth destroyeth his *n*........... Prov 11:9 7453
is void of wisdom despiseth his *n*......... Prov 11:12 7453
is more excellent than his *n*................. Prov 12:26 7453
poor is hated even of his own *n*............ Prov 14:20 7453
He that despiseth his *n* sinneth............ Prov 14:21 7453
A violent man enticeth his *n*................. Prov 16:29 7453
but his *n* cometh and searcheth him..... Prov 18:17 7453
the poor is separated from his *n*........... Prov 19:4 7453
his *n* findeth no favour in his............... Prov 21:10 7453
against thy *n* without cause .... Prov 24:28 7453
when thy *n* hath put thee to shame..... Prov 25:8 7453
thy cause with thy *n* himself................ Prov 25:9 7453
witness against his *n* is a maul .... Prov 25:18 7453
is the man that deceiveth his *n*........... Prov 26:19 7453
for better is a *n* that is near................. Prov 27:10 7934
A man that flattereth his *n*.................. Prov 29:5 7453
for this a man is envied of his *n*.......... Eccl 4:4 7453
by another, and every one by his *n* ...... Is 3:5 7453
and every one against his *n*................. Is 19:2 7453
They helped every one his *n*................. Is 41:6 7453
the *n* and his friend shall perish .... Jer 6:21 7934
judgment between a man and his *n* ...... Jer 7:5 7453
Take ye heed every one of his *n*........... Jer 9:4 7453
every *n* will walk with slanders .... Jer 9:4 7453
they will deceive every one his *n*......... Jer 9:5 7453
peaceably to his *n* with his mouth........ Jer 9:8 7453
and every one her *n* lamentation .... Jer 9:20 7468
they shall say every man to his *n*......... Jer 22:8 7453
they tell every man to his *n*................. Jer 23:27 7453
my words every one from his *n*............ Jer 23:30 7453
shall ye say every one to his *n*............ Jer 23:35 7453
teach no more every man his *n*............ Jer 31:34 7453
liberty every man to his *n*.................. Jer 34:15 7453
brother, and every man to his *n*.......... Jer 34:17 7453
the *n* cities thereof, saith the............. Jer 49:18 7934
the *n* cities thereof, saith the............. Jer 50:40 7934
unto him that giveth his *n* drink .... Hab 2:15 7453
every man his *n* under the vine........... Zec 3:10 7453
all men every one against his *n*........... Zec 8:10 7453
ye every man the truth to his *n*........... Zec 8:16 7453
evil in your hearts against his *n*......... Zec 8:17 7453
every one on the hand of his *n*........... Zec 14:13 7453
rise up against the hand of his *n* .... Zec 14:13 7453
been said, Thou shalt love thy *n*.......... Mt 5:43 *4139*
Thou shalt love thy *n* as thyself........... Mt 19:19 *4139*
Thou shalt love thy *n* as thyself........... Mt 22:39 *4139*
Thou shalt love thy *n* as thyself........... Mk 12:31 *4139*
and to love his *n* as himself .... Mk 12:33 *4139*
and thy *n* as thyself............................. Lk 10:27 *4139*
said unto Jesus, And who is my *n*......... Lk 10:29 *4139*
was *n* unto him that fell among .... Lk 10:36 *4139*
But he that did his *n* wrong................. Acts 7:27 *4139*
Thou shalt love thy *n* as thyself........... Rom 13:9 *4139*
Love worketh no ill to his *n* .... Rom 13:10 *4139*
his *n* for his good to edification .... Rom 15:2 *4139*
Thou shalt love thy *n* as thyself........... Gal 5:14 *4139*
speak every man truth with his *n* .... Eph 4:25 *4139*
shall not teach every man his *n*........... Heb 8:11 *4139*
Thou shalt love thy *n* as thyself........... Jas 2:8 *4139*

NEIGHBOUR'S
Thou shalt not covet thy *n* house.......... Ex 20:17 7453
thou shalt not covet thy *n* wife .... Ex 20:17 7453
ass, nor any thing that is thy *n*........... Ex 20:17 7453
put his hand unto his *n* goods.............. Ex 22:8 7453
not put his hand unto his *n* goods .... Ex 22:11 7453
all take thy *n* raiment to pledge .... Ex 22:26 7453
not lie carnally with thy *n* wife .... Lev 18:20 5997
adultery with his *n* wife, the................ Lev 20:10 7453
or buyest ought of thy *n* hand .... Lev 25:14 5997
shalt thou desire thy *n* wife................. Deut 5:21 7453
shalt thou covet thy *n* house................ Deut 5:21 7453
ass, or any thing that is thy *n*............ Deut 5:21 7453
shalt not remove thy *n* landmark.......... Deut 19:14 7453
he hath humbled his *n* wife .... Deut 22:24 7453
thou comest into thy *n* vineyard........... Deut 23:24 7453
a sickle unto thy *n* standing corn......... Deut 23:25 7453
he that removeth his *n* landmark.......... Deut 27:17 7453
if I have laid wait at my *n* door............ Job 31:9 7453
So he that goeth in to his *n* wife.......... Prov 6:29 7453
thy foot from thy *n* house................... Prov 25:17 7453
one neighed after his *n* wife .... Jer 5:8 7453
that useth his *n* service without........... Jer 22:13 7453
neither hath defiled his *n* wife.............. Eze 18:6 7453
mountains, and defiled his *n* wife.......... Eze 18:11 7453
hath not defiled his *n* wife .... Eze 18:15 7453
abomination with his *n* wife................. Eze 22:11 7453
and ye defile every one his *n* wife.......... Eze 33:26 7453
the men every one into his *n* hand....... Zec 11:6 7453

NEIGHBOURS
they heard that they were their *n*......... Josh 9:16 7138
the women her *n* gave it a name,.......... Ruth 4:17 7934
thee vessels abroad of all thy *n*............ 2Kin 4:3 7934
which speak peace to their *n*............... Ps 28:3 7453
but especially among my *n*................... Ps 31:11 7934
makest us a reproach to our *n*............. Ps 44:13 7934
We are become a reproach to our *n*..... Ps 79:4 7934
render unto our *n* sevenfold into........... Ps 79:12 7934
makest us a strife unto our *n*............... Ps 80:6 7934
he is a reproach to his *n*..................... Ps 89:41 7934
the LORD against all mine evil *n* .... Jer 12:14 7934
and his brethren, and his *n* .... Jer 49:10 7934
with the Egyptians thy *n*, great............ Eze 16:26 7934
gained of thy *n* by extortion................. Eze 22:12 7453
lovers, on the Assyrians her *n*.............. Eze 23:5 7138
doted upon the Assyrians her *n*............ Eze 23:12 7138
And her *n* and her cousins heard how.. Lk 1:58 *4040*
thy kinsmen, nor thy rich *n*................. Lk 14:12 *1069*
calleth together his friends and *n*......... Lk 15:6 *1069*
her *n* together, saying, Rejoice .... Lk 15:9 *1069*
The *n* therefore, and they which .... Jn 9:8 *1069*

NEIGHBOURS'
adultery with their *n* wives................... Jer 29:23 7453

NEIGHED
every one *n* after his neighbour's.......... Jer 5:8 6670

NEIGHING
sound of the *n* of his strong ones.......... Jer 8:16 4684

NEIGHINGS
seen thine adulteries, and thy *n*........... Jer 13:27 4684

NEITHER
n shall ye touch it, lest ye die .... Gen 3:3
n will I again smite any more .... Gen 8:21
n shall all flesh be cut off any............... Gen 9:11 3808
n shall there any more be a flood......... Gen 9:11 3808
N shall thy name any more be............... Gen 17:5 3808
n stay thou in all the plain.................. Gen 19:17 408
n didst thou tell me, *n* yet.................. Gen 21:26 3808
n do thou any thing unto him............... Gen 22:12 408
a virgin, *n* had any man known her....... Gen 24:16 3808
n is it time that the cattle .... Gen 29:7 3808
n hath he kept back any thing.............. Gen 39:9 3808
shall *n* be earing nor harvest................. Gen 45:6 369
n hearken to the voice of the............... Ex 4:8 3808
n hearken unto thy voice, that .... Ex 4:9 3808
n heretofore, nor since thou hast.......... Ex 4:10 1571
the LORD, *n* will I let Israel go .... Ex 5:2
n hast thou delivered thy people .... Ex 5:23 3808
n did he hearken unto them................. Ex 7:22 3808
n did he set his heart to this................ Ex 7:23 3808
n would he let the people go................ Ex 8:32 3808
n shall there be any more hail............... Ex 9:29 3808
n would he let the children of............... Ex 9:35 3808
which *n* thy fathers, nor thy................ Ex 10:6 3808
n after them shall be such.................... Ex 10:14 3808
n rose any from his place for............... Ex 10:23 3808
tarry, *n* had they prepared for.............. Ex 12:39
n shall ye break a bone thereof .... Ex 12:46 3808
n shall there be leaven seen with .... Ex 13:7 3808
n was there any worm therein.............. Ex 16:24 3808
n shall ye make unto you gods of......... Ex 20:23 3808
N shalt thou go up by steps unto .... Ex 20:26 3808
Thou shalt *n* vex a stranger, nor .... Ex 22:21 3808
n shalt thou lay upon him usury .... Ex 22:25 3808
n shall ye eat any flesh that is .... Ex 22:31 3808
n shalt thou speak in a cause to........... Ex 23:2 3808
N shalt thou countenance a poor.......... Ex 23:3 3808
n let it be heard out of thy.................. Ex 23:13 3808
n shall the fat of my sacrifice............... Ex 23:18 3808
n shall the people go up with him......... Ex 24:2 3808
n shall ye pour drink offering................ Ex 30:9 3808
n shall ye make any other like it........... Ex 30:32 3808
n is it the voice of them that............... Ex 32:18 369
n let any man be seen throughout......... Ex 34:3 408
n let the flocks nor herds feed .... Ex 34:3 408
n shall any man desire thy land,........... Ex 34:24 3808
n shall the sacrifice of the.................. Ex 34:25
he did *n* eat bread, nor drink................ Ex 34:28 3808
Let *n* man nor woman make.................. Ex 36:6 408
n shalt thou suffer the salt of............... Lev 2:13 3808
that ye eat *n* fat nor blood................... Lev 3:17 3808
n shall he put any frankincense............ Lev 5:11 3808
n shall it be imputed unto him.............. Lev 7:18 3808
your heads, *n* rend your clothes .... Lev 10:6 3808
n shall ye make yourselves.................... Lev 11:43 3808
n shall ye defile yourselves with........... Lev 11:44 3808
n shall any stranger that .... Lev 17:12 3808
n shall ye walk in their....................... Lev 18:3 3808
n shalt thou take her son's .... Lev 18:17 3808
N shalt thou take a wife to her............. Lev 18:18 3808
n shalt thou profane the name of......... Lev 18:21 3808
N shalt thou lie with any beast............. Lev 18:23 3808
n shall any woman stand before a .... Lev 18:23 3808
n any of your own nation, nor any......... Lev 18:26
n shalt thou gather the gleanings .... Lev 19:9
n shalt thou gather every grape .... Lev 19:10 3808
n deal falsely, *n* lie one .... Lev 19:11 3808
n shalt thou profane the name of......... Lev 19:12
defraud thy neighbour, *n* rob him .... Lev 19:13 3808
n shalt thou stand against the .... Lev 19:16 3808
n shall a garment mingled of................ Lev 19:19 3808
n shall ye use enchantment, nor........... Lev 19:26 3808
n shalt thou mar the corners of............ Lev 19:27 3808
n seek after wizards, to be.................. Lev 19:31 408
n shall they shave off the corner.......... Lev 21:5 3808
n shall they take a woman put .... Lev 21:7 3808
N shall he go in to any dead body .... Lev 21:11 3808
N shall he go out of the...................... Lev 21:12 3808
N shall he profane his seed among .... Lev 21:15 3808
n shall ye make any offering .... Lev 22:24 3808
N from a stranger's hand shall ye .... Lev 22:25 3808
N shall ye profane my holy name .... Lev 22:32 3808
And ye shall eat *n* bread, nor .... Lev 23:14 3808
n shalt thou gather any gleaning .... Lev 23:22 3808
thou shalt *n* sow thy field, nor............. Lev 25:4 3808
n gather the grapes of thy vine .... Lev 25:5 3808
n reap that which groweth of .... Lev 25:11 3808
n rear you up a standing image,............ Lev 26:1 3808
n shall ye set up any image of .... Lev 26:1 3808
n shall the sword go through your........ Lev 26:6 3808
n shall the trees of the land................ Lev 26:20 3808
n will I abhor them, to destroy............ Lev 26:44 3808
good or bad, *n* shall he change it .... Lev 27:33 3808
n take the sum of them among the .... Num 1:49 3808
n she be taken with the manner........... Num 5:13 3808
n shall he drink any liquor of.............. Num 6:3 3808
n ten days, nor twenty days .... Num 11:19 3808
n fear ye the people of the land........... Num 14:9 408
n shall any of them that provoked........ Num 14:23 3808
n have I hurt one of them.................... Num 16:15 3808
and the altar, that *n* they.................... Num 18:3
n shalt thou have any part among......... Num 18:20 3808
N must the children of Israel .... Num 18:22 3808
n shall ye pollute the holy................... Num 18:32 3808

N

n is there any water to drink Num 20:5 369
n will we drink of the water of Num 20:17 3808
is no bread, *n* is there any water Num 21:5 369
n the son of man, that he should Num 23:19
n hath he seen perverseness in Num 23:21 3808
n is there any divination against Num 23:23 3808
N curse them at all, nor bless Num 23:25 3808
not his enemy, *n* sought his harm Num 35:23 3808
N shall the inheritance remove Num 36:9 3808
fear not, *n* be discouraged Deut 1:21 408
Dread not, *n* be afraid of them Deut 1:29 3808
Say unto them, Go not up, *n* fight Deut 1:42 3808
n contend with them in battle Deut 2:9 408
I will *n* turn unto the right hand Deut 2:27 3808
n shall ye diminish ought from it Deut 4:2 3808
hands, wood and stone, which *n* see Deut 4:28 3808
n destroy thee, nor forget the Deut 4:31 3808
N shalt thou commit adultery Deut 5:18 3808
N shalt thou steal Deut 5:19 3808
N shalt thou bear false witness Deut 5:20 3808
N shalt thou desire thy Deut 5:21 3808
wife, *n* shalt thou covet thy Deut 5:21 3808
N shalt thou make marriages with Deut 7:3 3808
n shalt thou serve their gods Deut 7:16 3808
N shalt thou bring an abomination Deut 7:26 3808
not, *n* did thy fathers know Deut 8:3 3808
n did thy foot swell, these forty Deut 8:4 3808
I *n* did eat bread nor drink water Deut 9:9 3808
I did *n* eat bread, nor drink Deut 9:18 3808
n shall thine eye pity him Deut 13:8 3808
n shalt thou spare, *n* shalt Deut 13:8 3808
n shall there any thing of the Deut 16:4 3808
respect persons, *n* take a gift Deut 16:19 3808
N shalt thou set thee up any Deut 16:22 3808
N shall he multiply wives to Deut 17:17 3808
n shall he greatly multiply to Deut 17:17 3808
n let me see this great fire any Deut 18:16 3808
n be ye terrified because of them Deut 20:3 408
which is *n* eared nor sown, and Deut 21:4 3808
blood, *n* have our eyes seen it Deut 21:7 3808
n shall a man put on a woman's Deut 22:5 3808
n shall he be charged with any Deut 24:5 3808
n shall the sun go down upon it Deut 24:15 3808
n shall the children be put to Deut 24:16 3808
n have I forgotten them Deut 26:13 3808
n have I taken away ought thereof Deut 26:14 3808
unto a nation which *n* thou nor Deut 28:36 3808
but shalt *n* drink of the wine, Deut 28:39 3808
which *n* thou nor thy fathers have Deut 28:64 3808
n shall the sole of thy foot have Deut 28:65 3808
n have ye drunk wine or strong Deut 29:6 3808
N with you only do I make this Deut 29:14 3808
hidden from thee, *n* is it far off Deut 30:11 3808
N is it beyond the sea, that thou Deut 30:13 3808
not fail thee, *n* forsake thee Deut 31:6 3808
fear not, *n* be dismayed Deut 31:8 3808
n is there any understanding in Deut 32:28 369
n is there any that can deliver Deut 32:39 369
n did he acknowledge his brethren Deut 33:9 3808
be not afraid, *n* be thou dismayed Josh 1:9 408
n did there remain any more Josh 2:11 3808
n was there spirit in them any Josh 5:1 3808
n had the children of Israel Josh 5:12 3808
n shall any word proceed out of Josh 6:10 3808
n will I be with you any more, Josh 7:12 3808
Fear not, *n* be thou dismayed Josh 8:1 408
n left they any to breathe Josh 11:14 3808
n make mention of the names of Josh 23:7 3808
n serve them, nor bow yourselves Josh 23:7 3808
N did Manasseh drive out the Judg 1:27 3808
N did Ephraim drive out the Judg 1:29 3808
N did Zebulun drive out the Judg 1:30 3808
N did Asher drive out the Judg 1:31 3808
N did Naphtali drive out the Judg 1:33 3808
n delivered he them into the hand Judg 2:23 3808
Israel, *n* sheep, nor ox, nor ass Judg 6:4
n shall my son rule over you Judg 8:23 3808
N shewed they kindness to the Judg 8:35 3808
her he had *n* son nor daughter Judg 11:34 369
he was, *n* told he me his name Judg 13:6 3808
drink, *n* eat any unclean thing Judg 13:7 408
n let her drink wine or strong Judg 13:14 408
n would he have shewed us all Judg 13:23 3808
n will we any of us turn into his Judg 20:8 3808
n go from hence, but abide here Ruth 2:8
I have drunken *n* wine nor strong 1Sa 1:15 3808
n is there any rock like our God 1Sa 2:2 369
n was the word of the LORD yet 1Sa 3:7
answered not, *n* did she regard it 1Sa 4:20 3808
Therefore *n* the priests of Dagon, 1Sa 5:5 3808
n hast thou taken ought of any 1Sa 12:4 3808
that there was *n* sword nor spear 1Sa 13:22 3808
N hath the LORD chosen this 1Sa 16:8
N hath the LORD chosen this 1Sa 16:9
to meat, *n* yesterday, nor to day 1Sa 20:27 1571
for I have *n* brought my sword nor 1Sa 21:8
see that there is *n* evil nor 1Sa 24:11 369
n was there ought missing unto 1Sa 25:7 3808
n missed we any thing, as long as 1Sa 25:15 3808
man saw it, nor knew it, *n* awaked 1Sa 26:12 369
left *n* man nor woman alive, and 1Sa 27:9 3608
David saved *n* man nor woman alive 1Sa 27:11 3608
n by dreams, nor by Urim, nor by 1Sa 28:6 1571
n by prophets, nor by dreams 1Sa 28:15 1571
by God, that thou wilt *n* kill me 1Sa 30:15 518
n small nor great, *n* sons 1Sa 30:19 4480
n spoil, nor any thing that they 1Sa 30:19 4480
n let there be rain, upon you, 2Sa 1:21 408
no more, *n* fought they any more 2Sa 2:28 3808
n shall the children of 2Sa 7:10 3808
n is there any God beside thee, 2Sa 7:22 369
n did he eat bread with them 2Sa 12:17 3808
his brother Amnon *n* good nor bad 2Sa 13:22 3808
n name nor remainder upon the 2Sa 14:7 1115

n doth God respect any person 2Sa 14:14 3808
n if half of us die, will they 2Sa 18:3 518
that thou regardest *n* princes nor 2Sa 19:6 369
n do thou remember that which thy 2Sa 19:19 408
had *n* dressed his feet, nor 2Sa 19:24 3808
n have we inheritance in the son 2Sa 20:1 3808
n for us shalt thou kill any man 2Sa 21:4 369
suffered *n* the birds of the air 2Sa 21:10 3808
n will I offer burnt offerings 2Sa 24:24 3808
n hast asked riches for thyself, 1Kin 3:11 3808
n after thee shall any arise like 1Kin 3:12
Let it be *n* mine nor thine, but 1Kin 3:26
so that there is *n* adversary nor 1Kin 5:4 369
so that there was *n* hammer nor 1Kin 6:7 3808
n was the weight of the brass 1Kin 7:47 3808
n shall they come in unto you 1Kin 11:2 3808
n have we inheritance in the son 1Kin 12:16 3808
n will I eat bread nor drink 1Kin 13:8 3808
n will I eat bread nor drink 1Kin 13:16 3808
n of his kinsfolks, nor of his 1Kin 16:11
n shall the cruse of oil fail, 1Kin 17:14 3808
n did the cruse of oil fail, 1Kin 17:16 3808
sacrifice, that there was *n* voice 1Kin 18:29 369
Fight *n* with small nor great, 1Kin 22:31 3808
not see wind, *n* shall ye see rain 2Kin 3:17 3808
it is *n* new moon, nor sabbath 2Kin 4:23 3808
but there was *n* voice, nor 2Kin 4:31 369
n burnt offering nor sacrifice 2Kin 5:17 3808
not the way, *n* is this the city 2Kin 6:19 3808
n voice of man, but horses tied, 2Kin 7:10 369
n left he any of them 2Kin 10:14 3808
n to repair the breaches of the 2Kin 12:8 1115
N did he leave of the people to 2Kin 13:7 3808
n cast he them from his presence 2Kin 13:23 3808
n do they after their statutes, 2Kin 17:34 369
n shall ye fear other gods 2Kin 17:38 3808
N let Hezekiah make you trust in 2Kin 18:30 408
N will I make the feet of Israel 2Kin 21:8 3808
n after him arose there any like 2Kin 23:25 3808
n did all their family multiply, 1Chr 4:27 3808
n shall the children of 1Chr 17:9 3808
n is there any God beside thee, 1Chr 17:20 369
n would the Syrians help the 1Chr 19:19 3808
n was the number put in the 1Chr 27:24 3808
n yet hast asked long life 2Chr 1:11 3808
n shall there any after thee have 2Chr 1:12 3808
n chose I any man to be a ruler 2Chr 6:5 3808
n was there any such spice as the 2Chr 9:9 3808
N did Jeroboam recover strength 2Chr 13:20 3808
n know we what to do 2Chr 20:12 3808
n shall the children die for the 2Chr 25:4 3808
n shall it be for thine honour 2Chr 26:18 3808
n had the people gathered 2Chr 30:3 3808
on this manner, *n* yet believe him 2Chr 32:15 408
N will I any more remove the foot 2Chr 33:8 3808
declined *n* to the right hand, nor 2Chr 34:2 3808
n shall thine eyes see all the 2Chr 34:28 3808
n did all the kings of Israel 2Chr 35:18 3808
n take their daughters unto your Ezr 9:12 408
n is this a work of one day or Ezr 10:13 3808
n told I any man what my God had Neh 2:12 3808
n was there any beast with me, Neh 2:12 369
n had I as yet told it to the Neh 2:16 3808
n see, till we come in the midst Neh 4:11 3808
So *n* I, nor my brethren, nor my Neh 4:23 369
n is it in our power to redeem Neh 5:5 369
this wall, *n* bought we any land Neh 5:16 3808
n be ye sorry Neh 8:10 408
n be ye grieved Neh 8:11 408
n were mindful of thy wonders Neh 9:17 3808
n the pillar of fire by night, to Neh 9:19
N have our kings, our princes, Neh 9:34 3808
n turned they from their wicked Neh 9:35 3808
for she had *n* father nor mother, Est 2:7 369
n keep they the king's laws Est 3:8 369
n eat nor drink three days, night Est 4:16 408
n let the light shine upon it Job 3:4 408
n let it see the dawning of the Job 3:9 408
n had I rest, *n* was I quiet Job 3:26 3808
n is there any to deliver them Job 5:4 369
n doth trouble spring out of the Job 5:6 3808
n shalt thou be afraid of Job 5:21 3808
n shalt thou be afraid of the Job 5:22 408
n shall his place know him any Job 7:10 3808
n will he help the evil doers Job 8:20 3808
N is there any daysman betwixt us Job 9:33 3808
n shall his substance continue, Job 15:29 3808
n shall he prolong the perfection Job 15:29 3808
He shall *n* have son nor nephew Job 18:19 3808
n shall his place any more behold Job 20:9 3808
n is the rod of God upon them Job 21:9 3808
N have I gone back from the Job 23:12 3808
n hath he covered the darkness Job 23:17
n is it found in the land of the Job 28:13 3808
n shall silver be weighed for the Job 28:15 3808
n shall it be valued with pure Job 28:19 3808
(*N* have I suffered my mouth to Job 31:30 3808
n do the aged understand judgment Job 32:9
n will I answer him with your Job 32:14 3808
n let me give flattering titles Job 32:21 3808
n shall my hand be heavy upon Job 33:7 3808
n is there iniquity in me Job 33:9 3808
n will the Almighty pervert Job 34:12 3808
n will the Almighty regard it Job 35:13 3808
n can the number of his years be Job 36:26 3808
n regardeth he the crying of the Job 39:7 3808
n hath he imparted to her Job 39:17 3808
n turneth he back from the sword Job 39:22 3808
n believeth he that it is the Job 39:24 3808
n shall evil dwell with thee Ps 5:4 3808
anger, *n* chasten me in thy hot Ps 6:1
n wilt thou suffer thine Holy One Ps 16:10 3808
n did I turn again till they were Ps 18:37 3808
n hath he hid his face from him Ps 22:24 3808

n will I go in with dissemblers Ps 26:4 3808
n forsake me, O God of my Ps 27:9 408
n shall he deliver any by his Ps 33:17 3808
n let them wink with the eye that Ps 35:19
n be thou envious against the Ps 37:1 408
n chasten me in thy hot Ps 38:1
n is there any rest in my bones Ps 38:3 369
n did their own arm save them Ps 44:3 3808
my bow, *n* shall my sword save me Ps 44:6 3808
n have we dealt falsely in thy Ps 44:17 3808
n have our steps declined from Ps 44:18
n was it he that hated me that Ps 55:12 3808
n let the deep swallow me up, and Ps 69:15 408
n are they plagued like other men Ps 73:5 3808
n is there among us any that Ps 74:9 3808
promotion cometh *n* from the east Ps 75:6 3808
n were they stedfast in his Ps 78:37 3808
n shalt thou worship any strange Ps 81:9 3808
know not, *n* will they understand Ps 82:5 3808
n are there any works like unto Ps 86:8 369
n shall any plague come nigh thy Ps 91:10 3808
n doth a fool understand this Ps 92:6 3808
n shall the God of Jacob regard Ps 94:7 3808
n will he forsake his inheritance Ps 94:14 3808
n will he keep his anger for ever Ps 103:9 3808
n let there be any to favour his Ps 109:12 408
n speak they through their throat Ps 115:7 3808
n any that go down into silence Ps 115:17 3808
Israel shall *n* slumber nor sleep Ps 121:4 3804
N do they which go by say, The Ps 129:8 3808
n do I exercise myself in great Ps 131:1 3808
n is there any breath in their Ps 135:17 369
n take they hold of the paths of Prov 2:19
n be weary of his correction Prov 3:11 408
n of the desolation of the wicked Prov 3:25
n decline from the words of my Prov 4:5 408
n let her take thee with her Prov 6:25 408
n will he rest content, though Prov 6:35 3808
n will he go unto the wise Prov 15:12 3808
n oppress the afflicted in the Prov 22:22 3808
n desire thou his dainty meats Prov 23:6 408
men, *n* desire to be with them Prov 24:1 408
n be thou envious at the wicked Prov 24:19 408
n go into thy brother's house in Prov 27:10 408
I *n* learned wisdom, nor have the Prov 30:3 3808
give me *n* poverty nor riches Prov 30:8 408
n shall there be any remembrance Eccl 1:11 3808
he hath *n* child nor brother Eccl 4:8
n is his eye satisfied with Eccl 4:8 3808
n saith he, For whom do I labour, Eccl 4:8
n say thou before the angel, that Eccl 5:6 408
n may he contend with him that is Eccl 6:10 3808
n make thyself over wise Eccl 7:16 408
much wicked, *n* be thou foolish Eccl 7:17 408
n hath he power in the day of Eccl 8:8 369
n shall wickedness deliver those Eccl 8:8 3808
n shall he prolong his days, Eccl 8:13 3808
(for also there is that *n* day nor Eccl 8:16
n have they any more a reward Eccl 9:5 369
n have they any more a portion Eccl 9:6 369
n yet bread to the wise, nor yet Eccl 9:11 3808
n can the floods drown it Song 8:7 3808
n bound up, *n* mollified Is 1:6 3808
n doth the cause of the widow Is 1:23 3808
n shall they learn war any more Is 2:4 3808
n is there any end of their Is 2:7 3808
n is there any end of their Is 2:7 3808
my house is *n* bread nor clothing Is 3:7 369
n consider the operation of his Is 5:12 3808
n shall the girdle of their loins Is 5:27 3808
n be fainthearted for the two Is 7:4 408
stand, *n* shall it come to pass Is 7:7 3808
not ask, *n* will I tempt the LORD Is 7:12 3808
n fear ye their fear, nor be Is 8:12 3808
n do they seek the LORD of hosts Is 9:13 3808
n shall have mercy on their Is 9:17 3808
n doth his heart think so Is 10:7 3808
n reprove after the hearing of Is 11:3 3808
n shall it be dwelt in from Is 13:20 3808
n shall the Arabian pitch tent Is 13:20 3808
n shall the shepherds make their Is 13:20 3808
n shall there be shouting Is 16:10 3808
n shall respect that which his Is 17:8 3808
N shall there be any work for Is 19:15 3808
n had respect unto him that Is 22:11 3808
n do I nourish up young men, nor Is 23:4 3808
n have the inhabitants of the Is 26:18 1077
n is a cart wheel turned about Is 28:27 1077
n shall his face now wax pale Is 29:22 3808
One of Israel, *n* seek the LORD Is 31:1 3808
n shall any of the cords thereof Is 33:20 1077
n shall gallant ship pass thereby Is 33:21 3808
N let Hezekiah make you trust in Is 36:15 408
earth, fainteth not, *n* is weary Is 40:28 3808
n my praise to graven images Is 42:8
n were they obedient unto his law Is 42:24 3808
n shall the flame kindle upon Is 43:2 3808
n shall there be after me Is 43:10 3808
n consider the things of old Is 43:18 408
n hast thou honoured me with thy Is 43:23 3808
n hast thou filled me with the Is 43:24 3808
Fear ye not, *n* be afraid Is 44:8 408
heart, *n* is there knowledge nor Is 44:19 3808
n didst remember the latter end Is 47:7 3808
n shall I know the loss of Is 47:8 3808
n shall the heat nor sun smite Is 49:10 3808
rebellious, *n* turned away back Is 50:5 3808
n be ye afraid of their revilings Is 51:7 408
n is there any that taketh her by Is 51:18 369
n was any deceit in his mouth Is 53:9 3808
n be thou confounded Is 54:4 408
n shall the covenant of my peace Is 54:10 3808
n are your ways my ways, saith Is 55:8 3808
N let the son of the stranger, Is 56:3 408

n let the eunuch say, Behold, I	Is 56:3	408
ever, *n* will I be always wroth	Is 57:16	3808
n his ear heavy, that it cannot	Is 59:1	3808
n shall they cover themselves	Is 59:6	3808
n doth justice overtake us	Is 59:9	3808
n for brightness shall the moon	Is 60:19	3808
n shall thy moon withdraw itself	Is 60:20	3808
n shall thy land any more be	Is 62:4	3808
n hath the eye seen, O God,	Is 64:4	3808
n remember iniquity for ever	Is 64:9	408
my fame, *n* have seen my glory	Is 66:19	3808
n shall their fire be quenched	Is 66:24	3808
N said they, Where is the LORD	Jer 2:6	3808
n shall it come to mind	Jer 3:16	3808
n shall they remember it	Jer 3:16	3808
n shall they visit it	Jer 3:16	3808
n shall that be done any more	Jer 3:16	3808
n shall they walk any more after	Jer 3:17	3808
n will I turn back from it	Jer 4:28	3808
n shall evil come upon us	Jer 5:12	3808
n shall we see sword nor famine	Jer 5:12	3808
n understandest what they say	Jer 5:15	3808
N say they in their heart, Let us	Jer 5:24	3808
all ashamed, *n* could they blush	Jer 6:15	
n walk after other gods to your	Jer 7:6	3808
n lift up cry nor prayer for them	Jer 7:16	408
n make intercession to me	Jer 7:16	408
them not, *n* came it into my heart	Jer 7:31	3808
all ashamed, *n* could they blush	Jer 8:12	3808
n can men hear the voice of the	Jer 9:10	3808
obeyed my voice, *n* walked therein	Jer 9:13	3808
whom *n* they nor their fathers	Jer 9:16	3808
n let the mighty man glory in his	Jer 9:23	408
n also is it in them to do good	Jer 10:5	3808
n lift up a cry or prayer for	Jer 11:14	408
the sword, *n* shall ye have famine	Jer 14:13	3808
n have I commanded them, *n*	Jer 14:14	3808
I have *n* lent on usury, nor men	Jer 15:10	3808
n shalt thou have sons or	Jer 16:2	3808
n shall they be buried	Jer 16:4	3808
n go to lament nor bemoan them	Jer 16:5	408
n shall men lament for them, nor	Jer 16:6	3808
N shall men tear themselves for	Jer 16:7	3808
n shall men give them the cup of	Jer 16:7	3808
know not, *n* ye nor your fathers	Jer 16:13	
n is their iniquity hid from mine	Jer 16:17	3808
n shall cease from yielding fruit	Jer 17:8	3808
n have I desired the woeful day	Jer 17:16	3808
N carry forth a burden out of	Jer 17:22	3808
n do ye any work, but hallow ye	Jer 17:22	3808
n inclined their ear, but made	Jer 17:23	3808
n blot out their sin from thy	Jer 18:23	408
whom *n* they nor their fathers	Jer 19:4	3808
spake it, *n* came it into my mind	Jer 19:5	3808
n have pity, nor have mercy	Jer 21:7	3808
n shed innocent blood in this	Jer 22:3	408
ye not for the dead, *n* bemoan him	Jer 22:10	408
n shall they be lacking, saith	Jer 23:4	3808
lamented, *n* gathered, nor buried	Jer 25:33	3808
n hearken to your dreams which ye	Jer 29:8	408
n shall he behold the good that I	Jer 29:32	3808
n be dismayed, O Israel	Jer 30:10	408
thy voice, *n* walked in thy law	Jer 32:23	3808
n came it into my mind, that they	Jer 32:35	3808
N shall the priests the Levites	Jer 33:18	3808
n the sand of the sea measured	Jer 33:22	3808
not unto me, *n* inclined their ear	Jer 34:14	3808
n ye, nor your sons for ever	Jer 35:6	
N shall ye build house, nor sow	Jer 35:7	3808
n have we vineyard, nor field,	Jer 35:9	3808
n the king, nor any of his	Jer 36:24	
But *n* he, nor his servants, nor	Jer 37:2	3808
n will I give thee into the hand	Jer 38:16	518
n obey the voice of the LORD your	Jer 42:13	1115
n they, ye, nor your fathers	Jer 44:3	
n have they feared, nor walked in	Jer 44:10	3808
n hath he gone into captivity	Jer 48:11	3808
n shall a son of man dwell in it	Jer 49:18	3808
which have *n* gates nor bars,	Jer 49:31	3808
n shall it be dwelt in from	Jer 50:39	3808
n shall any son of man dwell	Jer 50:40	3808
n doth any son of man pass	Jer 51:43	3808
n man nor beast, but that it	Jer 51:62	1115
n be afraid of their words,	Eze 2:6	408
n be dismayed at their looks,	Eze 3:9	3808
n came there abominable flesh	Eze 4:14	3808
n have kept my judgments, *n*	Eze 5:7	3808
n shall mine eye spare, *n*	Eze 5:11	1571
spare thee, *n* will I have pity	Eze 7:4	3808
not spare, *n* will I have pity	Eze 7:9	3808
n shall there be wailing for them	Eze 7:11	3808
n shall any strengthen himself in	Eze 7:13	3808
their souls, *n* fill their bowels	Eze 7:19	3808
not spare, *n* will I have pity	Eze 8:18	3808
your eye spare, *n* have ye pity	Eze 9:5	408
n will I have pity, but I will	Eze 9:10	3808
n shall ye be the flesh in the	Eze 11:11	
n executed my judgments, but have	Eze 11:12	3808
n made up the hedge for the house	Eze 13:5	
n shall they be written in the	Eze 13:9	3808
n shall they enter into the land	Eze 13:9	3808
is no more, *n* they that daubed it	Eze 13:15	369
n be polluted any more with all	Eze 14:11	3808
deliver *n* sons nor daughters	Eze 14:16	518
deliver *n* sons nor daughters	Eze 14:18	3808
shall deliver *n* son nor daughter	Eze 14:20	518
n wast thou washed in water to	Eze 16:4	3808
shall not come, *n* shall it be so	Eze 16:16	3808
n did she strengthen the hand of	Eze 16:49	3808
N hath Samaria committed half of	Eze 16:51	3808
N shall Pharaoh with his mighty	Eze 17:17	3808
n hath lifted up his eyes to the	Eze 18:6	3808
n hath defiled his neighbour's	Eze 18:6	3808
n hath come near to a menstruous	Eze 18:6	3808
n hath taken any increase, that	Eze 18:8	3808
n hath lifted up his eyes to the	Eze 18:15	3808
N hath oppressed any, hath not	Eze 18:16	3808
n hath spoiled by violence, but	Eze 18:16	3808
n shall the father bear the	Eze 18:20	3808
n did they forsake the idols of	Eze 20:8	3808
n did I make an end of them in	Eze 20:17	3808
n observe their judgments, nor	Eze 20:18	408
n kept my judgments to do them,	Eze 20:21	3808
n have they shewed difference	Eze 22:26	3808
N left she her whoredoms brought	Eze 23:8	3808
n will I spare, *n* will I	Eze 24:14	3808
yet *n* shalt thou mourn nor weep,	Eze 24:16	3808
n shall thy tears run down	Eze 24:16	3808
n shall it be inhabited forty	Eze 29:11	3808
n shall it exalt itself any more	Eze 29:15	3808
n shoot up their top among the	Eze 31:14	3808
n their trees stand up in their	Eze 31:14	3808
n shall the foot of man trouble	Eze 32:13	3808
n shall the righteous be able to	Eze 33:12	3808
n have ye healed that which was	Eze 34:4	3808
n have ye bound up that which was	Eze 34:4	3808
n have ye brought again that	Eze 34:4	3808
n have ye sought that which was	Eze 34:4	3808
n did my shepherds search for my	Eze 34:8	3808
n shall the shepherds feed	Eze 34:10	3808
n shall the beast of the land	Eze 34:28	3808
n bear the shame of the heathen	Eze 34:29	3808
n bereave thy nations any more,	Eze 36:14	3808
N will I cause men to hear in	Eze 36:15	3808
n shalt thou bear the reproach of	Eze 36:15	3808
n shalt thou cause thy nations to	Eze 36:15	3808
n shall they be divided into two	Eze 37:22	3808
N shall they defile themselves	Eze 37:23	3808
and having *n* bars nor gates,	Eze 38:11	369
n cut down any out of the forests	Eze 39:10	3808
N will I hide my face any more	Eze 39:29	3808
n they, nor their kings, by their	Eze 43:7	
N shall they shave their heads,	Eze 44:20	3808
N shall any priest drink wine,	Eze 44:21	3808
N shall they take for their wives	Eze 44:22	3808
n shall the fruit thereof be	Eze 47:12	3808
n exchange, nor alienate the	Eze 48:14	3808
n were their coats changed, nor	Dan 3:27	3809
n was there any error or fault	Dan 6:4	3809
n were instruments of musick	Dan 6:18	3809
n was there any that could	Dan 8:4	369
N have we hearkened unto thy	Dan 9:6	3808
N have we obeyed the voice of the	Dan 9:10	3808
n came flesh nor wine in my mouth	Dan 10:3	3808
n did I anoint myself at all,	Dan 10:3	3808
n is there breath left in me	Dan 10:17	3808
n shall he stand, nor his arm	Dan 11:6	3808
n his chosen people, *n*	Dan 11:15	369
stand on his side, *n* be for him	Dan 11:17	3808
n in anger, nor in battle	Dan 11:20	3808
N shall he regard the God of his	Dan 11:37	3808
not my wife, *n* am I her husband	Hos 2:2	3808
n go ye up to Beth-aven, nor	Hos 4:15	408
n shall they be pleasing unto him	Hos 9:4	3808
n will we say any more to the	Hos 14:3	3808
n shall be any more after it,	Joel 2:2	3808
N shall one thrust another	Joel 2:8	3808
n shall the mighty deliver	Amos 2:14	3808
N shall he stand that handleth	Amos 2:15	3808
n shall he that rideth the horse	Amos 2:15	3808
n will I regard the peace	Amos 5:22	3808
prophet, *n* was I an prophet's son	Amos 7:14	3808
n shouldest thou have rejoiced	Obad 12	408
n shouldest thou have spoken	Obad 12	408
N shouldest thou have stood in	Obad 14	408
n shouldest thou have delivered	Obad 14	408
Let *n* man nor beast, herd nor	Jonah 3:7	369
not laboured, *n* madest it grow	Jonah 4:10	3808
n shall ye go haughtily	Mic 2:3	3808
n shall they learn war any more	Mic 4:3	3808
n understand they his counsel	Mic 4:12	3808
n keepeth at home, who enlargeth	Hab 2:5	3808
n shall fruit be in the vines	Hab 3:17	369
not do good, *n* will he do evil	Zeph 1:12	3808
N their silver nor their gold	Zeph 1:18	3808
n shall a deceitful tongue be	Zeph 3:13	3808
n was there any peace to him that	Zec 8:10	369
n shall seek the young one, nor	Zec 11:16	3808
n shall they wear a rough garment	Zec 13:4	3808
n do ye kindle fire on mine altar	Mal 1:10	3808
n will I accept an offering at	Mal 1:10	3808
n shall your vine cast her fruit	Mal 3:11	3808
leave them *n* root nor branch	Mal 4:1	
N do men light a candle, and put	Mt 5:15	3761
not at all; *n* by heaven	Mt 5:34	3383
his footstool: *n* by Jerusalem	Mt 5:35	3383
N shalt thou swear by thy head,	Mt 5:36	3383
n will your Father forgive your	Mt 6:15	3761
where *n* moth nor rust doth	Mt 6:20	3777
n do they reap, nor gather into	Mt 6:26	3761
they toil not, *n* do they spin	Mt 6:28	3761
n cast ye your pearls before	Mt 7:6	3366
n can a corrupt tree bring forth	Mt 7:18	3761
N do men put new wine into old	Mt 9:17	3761
Provide *n* gold, nor silver, nor	Mt 10:9	3361
n two coats, *n* shoes, nor	Mt 10:10	3366
For John came *n* eating nor	Mt 11:18	3383
n knoweth any man the Father,	Mt 11:27	3761
n for them which were with him,	Mt 12:4	3761
n shall any man hear his voice in	Mt 12:19	3761
n in this world, *n* in the	Mt 12:32	3777
hear not, *n* do they understand	Mt 13:13	3761
n remember the five loaves of the	Mt 16:9	3761
N the seven loaves of the four	Mt 16:10	3761
N tell I you by what authority I	Mt 21:27	3761
n carest thou for any man	Mt 22:16	
in the resurrection they *n* marry	Mt 22:30	3777
n durst any man from that day	Mt 22:46	3761
N be ye called masters	Mt 23:10	3366
for ye *n* go in yourselves,	Mt 23:13	3761
n suffer ye them that are	Mt 23:13	3756
N let him which is in the field	Mt 24:18	3361
the winter, *n* on the sabbath day	Mt 24:20	3366
for ye know *n* the day nor the	Mt 25:13	3383
n was any thing kept secret, but	Mk 4:22	3761
n could any man tame him	Mk 5:4	
n had they in the ship with them	Mk 8:14	
perceive ye not yet, *n* understand	Mk 8:17	3761
N go into the town, nor tell it	Mk 8:26	3366
n will your Father which is in	Mk 11:26	3761
N do I tell you by what authority	Mk 11:33	3761
her, and died, *n* left he any seed	Mk 12:21	3761
scriptures, *n* the power of God	Mk 12:24	3366
they *n* marry, nor are given in	Mk 12:25	3777
shall speak, *n* do ye premeditate	Mk 13:11	3366
n enter therein, to take any	Mk 13:15	3366
unto this time, *n* shall be	Mk 13:19	
n the Son, but the Father	Mk 13:32	3761
n wist they what to answer him	Mk 14:40	
But *n* so did their witness agree	Mk 14:59	3761
n understand I what thou sayest	Mk 14:68	3761
n said they any thing to any man	Mk 16:8	
n believed they them	Mk 16:13	3761
shall drink *n* wine nor strong	Lk 1:15	
to no man, *n* accuse any falsely	Lk 3:14	3366
n doth a corrupt tree bring forth	Lk 6:43	3761
Wherefore *n* thought I myself	Lk 7:7	3761
For John the Baptist came *n*	Lk 7:33	3383
n any thing hid, that shall not	Lk 8:17	3761
n abode in any house, but in the	Lk 8:27	
n could be healed of any,	Lk 8:43	3756
n staves, nor scrip	Lk 9:3	3383
nor scrip, *n* bread, *n* money	Lk 9:3	3383
n have two coats apiece	Lk 9:3	3383
Carry *n* purse, nor scrip, nor	Lk 10:4	3361
n under a bushel, but on a	Lk 11:33	3761
n hid, that shall not be known	Lk 12:2	
n for the body, what ye shall put	Lk 12:22	3366
for they *n* sow nor reap	Lk 12:24	3756
which *n* have storehouse nor barn	Lk 12:24	3756
drink, *n* be ye of doubtful mind	Lk 12:29	3361
approacheth, *n* moth corrupteth	Lk 12:33	3761
n did according to his will,	Lk 12:47	3366
n thy kinsmen, nor thy rich	Lk 14:12	3366
It is *n* fit for the land, nor yet	Lk 14:35	3777
n transgressed I at any time thy	Lk 15:29	3763
n can they pass to us, that would	Lk 16:26	3366
n will they be persuaded, though	Lk 16:31	3761
N shall they say, Lo here	Lk 17:21	3761
feared not God, *n* regarded man	Lk 18:2	3366
n knew they the things which were	Lk 18:34	
N tell I you by what authority I	Lk 20:8	3761
n acceptest thou the person of	Lk 20:21	
n marry, nor are given in	Lk 20:35	3777
N can they die any more	Lk 20:36	3777
Christ, nor Elias, *n* that prophet	Jn 1:25	
n cometh to the light, lest his	Jn 3:20	
thirst not, *n* come hither to draw	Jn 4:15	3366
when ye shall *n* in this mountain,	Jn 4:21	3777
Ye have *n* heard his voice at any	Jn 5:37	3777
n his disciples, they also took	Jn 6:24	3761
For *n* did his brethren believe in	Jn 7:5	3761
unto her, *N* do I condemn thee	Jn 8:11	3761
Ye *n* know me, nor my Father	Jn 8:19	3777
n came I of myself, but he sent	Jn 8:42	3761
N hath this man sinned, nor his	Jn 9:3	3777
n shall any man pluck them out of	Jn 10:28	
n he that is sent greater than he	Jn 13:16	3761
it seeth him not, *n* knoweth him	Jn 14:17	3761
be troubled, *n* let it be afraid	Jn 14:27	3366
N pray I for these alone, but for	Jn 17:20	3366
n wilt thou suffer thine Holy One	Acts 2:27	3761
n his flesh did see corruption	Acts 2:31	3761
N is there salvation in any other	Acts 4:12	
n said any of them that ought of	Acts 4:32	3761
N was there any among them that	Acts 4:34	3761
Thou hast *n* part nor lot in this	Acts 8:21	3756
sight, and *n* did eat nor drink	Acts 9:9	3756
which *n* our fathers nor we were	Acts 15:10	3777
n to observe, being Romans	Acts 16:21	3761
N is worshipped with men's hands,	Acts 17:25	3761
which are *n* robbers of churches,	Acts 19:37	3777
n count I my life dear unto	Acts 20:24	3761
n to walk after the customs	Acts 21:21	3366
resurrection, *n* angel, nor spirit	Acts 23:8	3366
saying that they would *n* eat nor	Acts 23:12	3383
that they will *n* eat nor drink	Acts 23:21	3383
they *n* found me in the temple	Acts 24:12	3777
n in the synagogues, nor in the	Acts 24:12	2228
N can they prove the things	Acts 24:13	2228
n with multitude, nor with tumult	Acts 24:18	3756
N against the law of the Jews,	Acts 25:8	3777
n against the temple, nor yet	Acts 25:8	3777
when *n* sun nor stars in many days	Acts 27:20	3383
We *n* received letters out of	Acts 28:21	3777
n any of the brethren that came	Acts 28:21	3777
him not as God, *n* were thankful	Rom 1:21	2228
n is that circumcision, which is	Rom 2:28	3761
n yet the deadness of Sarah's	Rom 4:19	
N yield ye your members as	Rom 6:13	3366
the law of God, *n* indeed can be	Rom 8:7	3761
that *n* death, nor life, nor	Rom 8:38	3777
N, because they are the seed of	Rom 9:7	3761
n having done any good or evil,	Rom 9:11	3366
It is good *n* to eat flesh, nor to	Rom 14:21	3361
n have entered into the heart of	1Cor 2:9	
n can he know them, because they	1Cor 2:14	
to bear it, *n* yet now are ye able	1Cor 3:2	
So then *n* is he that planteth any	1Cor 3:7	3777
any thing, *n* he that watereth	1Cor 3:7	3777
n with the leaven of malice and	1Cor 5:8	3366
n fornicators, nor idolaters, nor	1Cor 6:9	3777

N

for *n*, if we eat, are we the ... 1Cor 8:8 3777
n, if we eat not, are we the ... 1Cor 8:8 3777
n have I written these things, ... 1Cor 9:15
N be ye idolaters, as were some ... 1Cor 10:7 3366
N let us commit fornication, as ... 1Cor 10:8 3366
N let us tempt Christ, as some of ... 1Cor 10:9 3366
N murmur ye, as some of them also ... 1Cor 10:10 3366
n to the Jews, nor to the ... 1Cor 10:32
N was the man created for the ... 1Cor 11:9
Nevertheless *n* is the man without ... 1Cor 11:11 3777
n the woman without the man, in ... 1Cor 11:11 3777
custom, *n* the churches of God ... 1Cor 11:16 3761
n doth corruption inherit ... 1Cor 15:50 3761
n by man, but by Jesus Christ, and ... Gal 1:1 3761
For I *n* received it of man, ... Gal 1:12 3761
n was I taught it, but by the ... Gal 1:12 3777
N went I up to Jerusalem to them ... Gal 1:17 3761
But *n* Titus, who was with me, ... Gal 2:3 3761
There is *n* Jew nor Greek, there ... Gal 3:28 3756
there is *n* bond nor free ... Gal 3:28 3756
there is *n* male nor female ... Gal 3:28 3756
For in Jesus Christ *n* ... Gal 5:6 3777
For *n* they themselves who are ... Gal 6:13 3761
For in Christ Jesus *n* ... Gal 6:15 3777
N give place to the devil ... Eph 4:27 3383
N filthiness, nor foolish talking ... Eph 5:4
n is there respect of persons ... Eph 6:9
run in vain, *n* laboured in vain ... Phil 2:16 3761
Where there is *n* Greek nor Jew ... Col 3:11 3756
For *n* at any time used we ... 1Th 2:5 3777
n of you, nor yet of others, when ... 1Th 2:6 3777
n by spirit, nor by word, nor by ... 2Th 2:2 3383
N did we eat any man's bread for ... 2Th 3:8 3761
would not work, *n* should he eat ... 2Th 3:10 3366
N give heed to fables and endless ... 1Ti 1:4 3366
understanding *n* what they say ... 1Ti 1:7 3383
n be partaker of other men's sins ... 1Ti 5:22 3366
N is there any creature that is ... Heb 4:13
having *n* beginning of days, nor ... Heb 7:3 3383
N by the blood of goats and calves ... Heb 9:12 3761
Whereupon *n* the first testament ... Heb 9:18 3761
not, *n* hadst pleasure therein ... Heb 10:8 3761
with evil, *n* tempteth he any man ... Jas 1:13
variableness, *n* shadow of turning ... Jas 1:17 2228
n by heaven, *n* by the earth ... Jas 5:12 3383
by the earth, *n* by any other oath ... Jas 5:12 3383
n was guile found in his mouth ... 1Pet 2:22 3761
of their terror, *n* be troubled ... 1Pet 3:14 3366
N as being lords over God's ... 1Pet 5:3 3366
they make you that ye shall *n* be ... 2Pet 1:8 3756
n the things that are in the ... 1Jn 2:15 3366
hath not seen him, *n* known him ... 1Jn 3:6 3761
n he that loveth not his brother ... 1Jn 3:10
us not love in word, *n* in tongue ... 1Jn 3:18 3366
your house, *n* bid him God speed ... 2Jn 10 3366
n doth he himself receive the ... 3Jn 10 3777
that thou art *n* cold nor hot ... Rev 3:15 3777
n cold nor hot, I will spue thee ... Rev 3:16 3777
n under the earth, was able to ... Rev 5:3 3761
open the book, *n* to look thereon ... Rev 5:3 3761
read the book, *n* to look thereon ... Rev 5:4 3777
n the sea, nor the trees, till we ... Rev 7:3 3383
hunger no more, *n* thirst any more ... Rev 7:16 3761
n shall the sun light on them, ... Rev 7:16 3761
n any green thing, *n* any ... Rev 9:4
which *n* can see, nor hear, nor ... Rev 9:20 3777
N repented they of their murders, ... Rev 9:21
n was their place found any more ... Rev 12:8 3777
the beast, *n* his image ... Rev 20:4 3777
n had received his mark upon ... Rev 20:4
n sorrow, nor crying ... Rev 21:4 3777
n shall there be any more pain ... Rev 21:4
n of the moon, to shine in it ... Rev 21:23 3761
n whatsoever worketh abomination, ... Rev 21:27
no candle, *n* light of the sun ... Rev 22:5

NEKEB (*ne'-keb*) *A city in Naphtali.*
Allon to Zaanannim, and Adami, *N* ... Josh 19:33 5346

NEKODA (*ne-ko'-dah*)
1. A family of exiles.
of Rezin, the children of *N* ... Ezr 2:48 5353
of Rezin, the children of *N* ... Neh 7:50 5353
2. A family of uncertain origin.
of Tobiah, the children of *N* ... Ezr 2:60 5353
of Tobiah, the children of *N* ... Neh 7:62 5353

NEMUEL (*ne-mu'-el*) See JEMUEL, NEMUELITES.
1. Son of Eliab.
N, and Dathan, and Abiram ... Num 26:9 5241
2. A son of Simeon.
of *N*, the family of the ... Num 26:12 5241
The sons of Simeon were, *N* ... 1Chr 4:24 5241

NEMUELITES (*ne-mu'-el-ites*) *Descendants of Nemuel 2.*
of Nemuel, the family of the *N* ... Num 26:12 5242

NEPHEG (*ne'-feg*)
1. A son of Izhar.
Korah, and *N*, and Zichri ... Ex 6:21 5298
2. A son of David.
Ibhar also, and Elishua, and *N* ... 2Sa 5:15 5298
And Nogah, and *N*, and Japhia, ... 1Chr 3:7 5298
And Nogah, and *N*, and Japhia, ... 1Chr 14:6 5298

NEPHEW
have son nor *n* among his people ... Job 18:19 5220
name, and remnant, and son, and *n* ... Is 14:22 5220

NEPHEWS
And he had forty sons and thirty *n* ... Judg 12:14 1121
if any widow have children or *n* ... 1Ti 5:4 1549

NEPHILIM See GIANTS.

NEPHISH (*ne'-fish*) See NAPHISH. *Descendants of Naphish.*
the Hagarites, with Jetur, and *N* ... 1Chr 5:19 5305

NEPHISHESIM (*ne-fish'-e-sim*) See NEPHUSIM.
A family of exiles.
of Meunim, the children of *N* ... Neh 7:52 5300

NEPHISIM See NEPHUSIM.

NEPHTHALIM (*nef'-tha-lim*) See NAPHTALI.
Country and tribe of Naphtali.
in the borders of Zabulon and *N* ... Mt 4:13 3508
land of Zabulon, and the land of *N* ... Mt 4:15 3508

NEPHTOAH (*nef-to'-ah*) *A stream near Jerusalem.*
the fountain of the water of *N* ... Josh 15:9 5318
out to the well of waters of *N* ... Josh 18:15 5318

NEPHUSHESIM See NEPHISHESIM.

NEPHUSIM (*ne-fu'-sim*) See NEPHISHESIM. *A family of exiles.*
of Mehunim, the children of *N* ... Ezr 2:50 5304

NEPTHALIM
Of the tribe of *N* were sealed ... Rev 7:6 3508

NER (*nur*) *Grandfather of King Saul.*
his host was Abner, the son of *N* ... 1Sa 14:50 5369
N the father of Abner was the son ... 1Sa 14:51 5369
Saul lay, and Abner the son of *N* ... 1Sa 26:5 5369
people, and to Abner the son of *N* ... 1Sa 26:14 5369
But Abner the son of *N*, captain ... 2Sa 2:8 5369
And Abner the son of *N*, and the ... 2Sa 2:12 5369
the son of *N* came to the king ... 2Sa 3:23 5369
Thou knowest Abner the son of *N* ... 2Sa 3:25 5369
the blood of Abner the son of *N* ... 2Sa 3:28 5369
king to slay Abner the son of *N* ... 2Sa 3:37 5369
Israel, unto Abner the son of *N* ... 1Kin 2:5 5369
to wit, Abner the son of *N* ... 1Kin 2:32 5369
N begat Kish, and Kish begat Saul, ... 1Chr 8:33 5369
then Zur, and Kish, and Baal, and *N* ... 1Chr 9:36 5369
And *N* begat Kish ... 1Chr 9:39 5369
of Kish, and Abner the son of *N* ... 1Chr 26:28 5369

NERAIAH See NERIAH.

NEREUS (*ne'-re-us*) *A Christian acquaintance of Paul.*
Salute Philologus, and Julia, *N* ... Rom 16:15 3517

NERGAL (*nur'-gal*) See NERGAL-SHAREZER. *War god of Cuth.*
and the men of Cuth made *N* ... 2Kin 17:30 5370

NERGAL-SHAREZER (*nur'-gal-sha-re'-zur*)
1. A Babylonian prince.
and sat in the middle gate, even *N* ... Jer 39:3 5371
2. Another Babylonian prince.
Sarsechim, Rab-saris, *N*, Rab-mag ... Jer 39:3 5371
and Nebushasban, Rab-saris, and *N* ... Jer 39:13 5371

NERI (*ne'-ri*) *Father of Salathiel; ancestor of Jesus.*
Salathiel, which was the son of *N* ... Lk 3:27 3518

NERIAH (*ne-ri'-ah*) *Father of Baruch.*
purchase unto Baruch the son of *N* ... Jer 32:12 5374
purchase unto Baruch the son of *N* ... Jer 32:16 5374
called Baruch the son of *N* ... Jer 36:4 5374
Baruch the son of *N* did according ... Jer 36:8 5374
So Baruch the son of *N* took the ... Jer 36:14 5374
Baruch the scribe, the son of *N* ... Jer 36:32 5374
But Baruch the son of *N* setteth ... Jer 43:3 5374
prophet, and Baruch the son of *N* ... Jer 43:6 5374
spake unto Baruch the son of *N* ... Jer 45:1 5374
commanded Seraiah the son of *N* ... Jer 51:59 5374

NERO (*ne'-ro*) *Emperor of Rome.*
brought before *N* the second time ... 2Ti s 3505

NEST
and thou puttest thy *n* in a rock ... Num 24:21 7064
If a bird's *n* chance to be before ... Deut 22:6 7064
As an eagle stirreth up her *n* ... Deut 32:11 7064
Then I said, I shall die in my *n* ... Job 29:18 7064
command, and make her *n* on high ... Job 39:27 7064
and the swallow a *n* for herself ... Ps 84:3 7064
a bird that wandereth from her *n* ... Prov 27:8 7064
my hand hath found as a *n* the ... Is 10:14 7064
wandering bird cast out of the *n* ... Is 16:2 7064
shall the great owl make her *n* ... Is 34:15 7077
that makest thy *n* in the cedars ... Jer 22:23 7077
her *n* in the sides of the hole's ... Jer 48:28 7077
make thy *n* as high as the eagle ... Jer 49:16 7064
thou set thy *n* among the stars ... Obad 4 7064
that he may set his *n* on high ... Hab 2:9 7064

NESTS
Where the birds make their *n* ... Ps 104:17 7077
heaven made their *n* in his boughs ... Eze 31:6 7077
and the birds of the air have *n* ... Mt 8:20 2682
holes, and birds of the air have *n* ... Lk 9:58 2682

NET
upon the *n* shalt thou make four ... Ex 27:4 7568
that the *n* may be even to the ... Ex 27:5 7568
is cast into a *n* by his own feet ... Job 18:8 7568
and hath compassed me with his *n* ... Job 19:6 4685
in the *n* which they hid is their ... Ps 9:15 7568
when he draweth him into his *n* ... Ps 10:9 7568
shall pluck my feet out of the *n* ... Ps 25:15 7568
Pull me out of the *n* that they ... Ps 31:4 7568
they hid for me their *n* in a pit ... Ps 35:7 7568
let his *n* that he hath hid catch ... Ps 35:8 7568
have prepared a *n* for my steps ... Ps 57:6 7568
Thou broughtest us into the *n* ... Ps 66:11 4685
have spread a *n* by the wayside ... Ps 140:5 7568
Surely in vain the *n* is spread in ... Prov 1:17 7568
wicked desireth the *n* of evil men ... Prov 12:12 4686
spreadeth a *n* for his feet ... Prov 29:5 7568
that are taken in an evil *n* ... Eccl 9:12 4686
streets, as a wild bull in a *n* ... Is 51:20 4364
he hath spread a *n* for my feet ... Lam 1:13 7568
My *n* also will I spread upon him, ... Eze 12:13 7568
And I will spread my *n* upon him ... Eze 17:20 7568
and spread their *n* over him ... Eze 19:8 7568
my *n* over thee with a company of ... Eze 32:3 7568
they shall bring thee up in my *n* ... Eze 32:3 2764
Mizpah, and a *n* spread upon Tabor ... Hos 5:1 7568
go, I will spread my *n* upon them ... Hos 7:12 7568
every man his brother with a *n* ... Mic 7:2 2764
angle, they catch them in their *n* ... Hab 1:15 2764
they sacrifice unto their *n* ... Hab 1:16 2764
they therefore empty their *n* ... Hab 1:17 2764
brother, casting a *n* into the sea ... Mt 4:18 293
of heaven is like unto a *n* ... Mt 13:47 4522
brother casting a *n* into the sea ... Mk 1:16 293
at thy word I will let down the *n* ... Lk 5:5 1350
and their *n* brake ... Lk 5:6 1350
Cast the *n* on the right side of ... Jn 21:6 1350
dragging the *n* with fishes ... Jn 21:8 1350
drew the *n* to land full of great ... Jn 21:11 1350
so many, yet was not the *n* broken ... Jn 21:11 1350

NETAIM See PLANTS.

NETHANEAL See NETHANEEL.

NETHANEEL (*ne-than'-e-el*)
1. A son of Zuar.
N the son of Zuar ... Num 1:8 5417
N the son of Zuar shall be ... Num 2:5 5417
the second day *N* the son of Zuar ... Num 7:18 5417
the offering of *N* the son of Zuar ... Num 7:23 5417
of Issachar was *N* the son of Zuar ... Num 10:15 5417
2. A brother of David.
N the fourth, Raddai the fifth, ... 1Chr 2:14 5417
3. A priest who relocated the Ark.
Shebaniah, and Jehoshaphat, and *N* ... 1Chr 15:24 5417
4. A sanctuary servant.
Shemaiah the son of *N* the scribe ... 1Chr 24:6 5417
5. A son of Obed-edom.
Sacar the fourth, and *N* the fifth, ... 1Chr 26:4 5417
6. A prince of Judah.
Obadiah, and to Zechariah, and to *N* ... 2Chr 17:7 5417
7. A chief Levite.
Conaniah also, and Shemaiah and *N* ... 2Chr 35:9 5417
8. Married a foreigner in exile.
Elioenai, Maaseiah, Ishmael, *N* ... Ezr 10:22 5417
9. A priest with Zerubbabel.
of Jedaiah, *N* ... Neh 12:21 5417
10. A priest who dedicated the wall.
Milalai, Gilalai, Maai, *N* ... Neh 12:36 5417

NETHANEL See NETHANEEL.

NETHANIAH (*neth-a-ni'-ah*)
1. Father of Ishmael.
Mizpah, even Ishmael the son of *N* ... 2Kin 25:23 5418
month, that Ishmael the son of *N* ... 2Kin 25:25 5418
Mizpah, even Ishmael the son of *N* ... Jer 40:8 5418
Ishmael the son of *N* to slay thee ... Jer 40:14 5418
I will slay Ishmael the son of *N* ... Jer 40:15 5418
the son of *N* the son of Elishama ... Jer 41:1 5418
Then arose Ishmael the son of *N* ... Jer 41:2 5418
Ishmael the son of *N* went forth ... Jer 41:6 5418
Ishmael the son of *N* slew them ... Jer 41:7 5418
Ishmael the son of *N* filled it ... Jer 41:9 5418
Ishmael the son of *N* carried them ... Jer 41:10 5418
Ishmael the son of *N* had done ... Jer 41:11 5418
fight with Ishmael the son of *N* ... Jer 41:12 5418
But Ishmael the son of *N* escaped ... Jer 41:15 5418
from Ishmael the son of *N* ... Jer 41:16 5418
because Ishmael the son of *N* had ... Jer 41:18 5418
2. A sanctuary servant.
Zaccur, and Joseph, and *N*, and ... 1Chr 25:2 5418
The fifth to *N*, he, his sons, and ... 1Chr 25:12 5418
3. A Levite.
sent Levites, even Shemaiah, and *N* ... 2Chr 17:8 5418
4. Father of Jehudi.
princes sent Jehudi the son of *N* ... Jer 36:14 5418

NETHER
stood at the *n* part of the mount ... Ex 19:17 8482
No man shall take the *n* or the ... Deut 24:6 7347
upper springs, and the *n* springs ... Josh 15:19 8482
the coast of Beth-horon the *n* ... Josh 16:3 8481
south side of the *n* Beth-horon ... Josh 18:13 8481
upper springs and the *n* springs ... Judg 1:15 8482
built Gezer, and Beth-horon the *n* ... 1Kin 9:17 8481
who built Beth-horon the *n* ... 1Chr 7:24 8481
the upper, and Beth-horon the *n* ... 2Chr 8:5 8481
as a piece of the *n* millstone ... Job 41:24 8482
to the *n* parts of the earth, in ... Eze 31:14 8482
in the *n* parts of the earth ... Eze 31:16 8482
unto the *n* parts of the earth ... Eze 31:18 8482
unto the *n* parts of the earth, ... Eze 32:18 8482
into the *n* parts of the earth ... Eze 32:24 8482

NETHERMOST
The *n* chamber was five cubits ... 1Kin 6:6 8481

NETHINIM See NETHINIMS.

NETHINIMS (*neth'-in-ims*) *Assistants to the Levites.*
the priests, Levites, and the *N* ... 1Chr 9:2 5411
The *N*: the children of Ziha ... Ezr 2:43 5411
All the *N*, and the children of ... Ezr 2:58 5411
singers, and the porters, and the *N* ... Ezr 2:70 5411
singers, and the porters, and the *N* ... Ezr 7:7 5411
and Levites, singers, porters, *N* ... Ezr 7:24 5412
Iddo, and to his brethren the *N* ... Ezr 8:17 5411
Also of the *N*, whom David and the ... Ezr 8:20 5411
Levites, two hundred and twenty *N* ... Ezr 8:20 5411
Moreover the *N* dwelt in Ophel, ... Neh 3:26 5411

son unto the place of the *N* Neh 3:31 5411
The *N*: the children of Ziha Neh 7:46 5411
All the *N*, and the children of Neh 7:60 5411
and some of the people, and the *N* Neh 7:73 5411
the porters, the singers, the *N* Neh 10:28 5411
priests, and the Levites, and the *N* Neh 11:3 5411
But the *N* dwelt in Ophel Neh 11:21 5411
and Ziha and Gispa were over the *N* Neh 11:21 5411

NETOPHAH (*ne-to'-fah*) See NETOPHATHITE. *A city in Judah.*
The men of *N*, fifty and six Ezr 2:22 5199
The men of Beth-lehem and *N* Neh 7:26 5199

NETOPHATHI (*ne-to'-fa-thi*) See NETOPHATHITE. *An inhabitant of Netophah.*
and from the villages of *N* Neh 12:28 5200

NETOPHATHITE (*ne-to'-fa-thite*) See NETOPHATHI, NETOPHATHITES. *Same as Netophathi.*
Zalmon the Ahohite, Maharai the *N* 2Sa 23:28 5200
Heleb the son of Baanah, a *N* 2Sa 23:29 5200
the son of Tanhumeth the *N* 2Kin 25:23 5200
Maharai the *N*, Heled the son of 1Chr 11:30 5200
Heled the son of Baanah the *N* 1Chr 11:30 5200
the tenth month was Maharai the *N* 1Chr 27:13 5200
twelfth month was Heldai the *N* 1Chr 27:15 5200
and the sons of Ephai the *N* Jer 40:8 5200

NETOPHATHITES (*ne-to'-fa-thites*)
Beth-lehem, and the *N*, Ataroth, 1Chr 2:54 5200
dwelt in the villages of the *N* 1Chr 9:16 5200

NETS
n of checker work, and wreaths of 1Kin 7:17 7638
the wicked fall into their own *n* Ps 141:10 4365
woman, whose heart is snares and *n* Eccl 7:26 2764
they that spread *n* upon the Is 19:8 4364
of *n* in the midst of the sea Eze 26:5 2764
shalt be a place to spread *n* upon Eze 26:14 2764
be a place to spread forth *n* Eze 47:10 2764
And they straightway left their *n* Mt 4:20 1350
their father, mending their *n* Mt 4:21 1350
straightway they forsook their *n* Mk 1:18 1350
were in the ship mending their *n* Mk 1:19 1350
of them, and were washing their *n* Lk 5:2 1350
and let down your *n* for a draught Lk 5:4 1350

NETTLES
under the *n* they were gathered Job 30:7 2738
n had covered the face thereof, Prov 24:31 2738
shall come up in her palaces, *n* Is 34:13 7057
silver, *n* shall possess them Hos 9:6 7057
Gomorrah, even the breeding of *n* Zeph 2:9 2738

NETWORK
make for it a grate of *n* of brass Ex 27:4
of *n* under the compass thereof Ex 38:4
rows round about upon the one *n* 1Kin 7:18 7639
the belly which was by the *n* 1Kin 7:20 7639
rows of pomegranates for one *n* 1Kin 7:42 7639
chapiter was five cubits, with *n* Jer 52:22 7639
the *n* were an hundred round about Jer 52:23 7639

NETWORKS
and the two *n*, to cover the two 1Kin 7:41 7639
pomegranates for the two *n* 1Kin 7:42 7639
fine flax, and they that weave *n* Is 19:9 2355

NEVER
Ask me *n* so much dowry and gift, Gen 34:12
such as I *n* saw in all the land Gen 41:19 3808
it shall *n* go out Lev 6:13 3808
and upon which *n* came yoke Num 19:2 3808
For the poor shall *n* cease out of Deut 15:11 3808
I will *n* break my covenant with Judg 2:1
Is there *n* a woman among the Judg 14:3 369
green withs that were *n* dried Judg 16:7 3808
new ropes that *n* were occupied Judg 16:11 3808
shall *n* depart from thine house 2Sa 12:10
for he *n* prophesied good unto me, 2Chr 18:7 369
that there was *n* a son left him 2Chr 21:17
as infants which *n* saw light Job 3:16 3808
and make my hands *n* so clean Job 9:30 1253
soul, and *n* eateth with pleasure Job 21:25 3808
for I shall *n* be in adversity Ps 10:6 1755
he will *n* see it Ps 10:11
these things shall *n* be moved Ps 15:5
I said, I shall *n* be moved Ps 30:6
let me *n* be ashamed Ps 31:1 408
they shall *n* see light Ps 49:19
he shall *n* suffer the righteous Ps 55:22
of charmers, charming *n* so wisely Ps 58:5
let me *n* be put to confusion Ps 71:1
I will *n* forget thy precepts Ps 119:93
The righteous shall *n* be removed Prov 10:30
Hell and destruction are *n* full Prov 27:20 3808
the eyes of man are *n* satisfied Prov 27:20 3808
three things that are *n* satisfied Prov 30:15 3808
It shall *n* be inhabited, neither Is 13:20
of evildoers shall *n* be renowned Is 14:20
it shall *n* be built Is 25:2
dogs which can *n* have enough Is 56:11 3808
which shall *n* hold their peace Is 62:6 3808
thou *n* barest rule over them Is 63:19
confusion shall *n* be forgotten Jer 20:11
David shall *n* want a man to sit Jer 33:17 3808
n open thy mouth any more because Eze 16:63 3808
yet shalt thou *n* be found again Eze 26:21
a terror, and *n* shalt be any more Eze 27:36
and *n* shalt thou be any more Eze 28:19
which shall *n* be destroyed Dan 2:44
such as *n* was since there was a Dan 12:1 3808
and my people shall *n* be ashamed Joel 2:26
and my people shall *n* be ashamed Joel 2:27
Surely I will *n* forget any of Amos 8:7
shall fall, and *n* rise up again Amos 8:14 3808
and judgment doth *n* go forth Hab 1:4
I profess unto them, I *n* knew you Mt 7:23 3763
It was *n* so seen in Israel Mt 9:33 3763
have ye *n* read, Out of the mouth Mt 21:16 3763
Did ye *n* read in the scriptures, Mt 21:42 3763
of thee, yet will I *n* be offended Mt 26:33 3763
And he answered him to *n* a word Mt 27:14
We *n* saw it on this fashion Mk 2:12 3763
Have ye *n* read what David did, Mk 2:25 3763
the Holy Ghost hath *n* forgiveness Mk 3:29
the fire that *n* shall be quenched Mk 9:43 3756
the fire that *n* shall be quenched Mk 9:45 3756
a colt tied, whereon *n* man sat Mk 11:2
that man if he had *n* been born Mk 14:21 3756
yet thou *n* gavest me a kid, that Lk 15:29 3763
colt tied, whereon yet *n* man sat Lk 19:30 3762
barren, and the wombs that *n* bare Lk 23:29 3756
and the paps which *n* gave suck Lk 23:29 3756
wherein *n* man before was laid Lk 23:53 3764
I shall give him shall *n* thirst Jn 4:14
that cometh to me shall *n* hunger Jn 6:35 165
believeth on me shall *n* thirst Jn 6:35
man letters, having *n* learned Jn 7:15 3361
N man spake like this man Jn 7:46 3763
were *n* in bondage to any man Jn 8:33
my saying, he shall *n* see death Jn 8:51
he shall *n* taste of death Jn 8:52
and they shall *n* perish, neither Jn 10:28
and believeth in me shall *n* die Jn 11:26
Thou shalt *n* wash my feet Jn 13:8
wherein was *n* man yet laid Jn 19:41 3764
for I have *n* eaten any thing that Acts 10:14 3763
mother's womb, who *n* had walked Acts 14:8 3763
Charity *n* faileth 1Cor 13:8 3763
n able to come to the knowledge 2Ti 3:7 3368
can *n* with those sacrifices which Heb 10:1 3763
which can *n* take away sins Heb 10:11 3763
I will *n* leave thee, nor forsake Heb 13:5 3364
do these things, ye shall *n* fall 2Pet 1:10

NEVERTHELESS
n in the day when I visit I will Ex 32:34
N these shall ye not eat of them Lev 11:4 389
N a fountain or pit, wherein Lev 11:36 389
N the people be strong that dwell Num 13:28 657
n the ark of the covenant of the Num 14:44
n the firstborn of man shalt thou Num 18:15 389
N the Kenite shall be wasted, Num 24:22
n it shall be purified with the Num 31:23 389
N these ye shall not eat of them Deut 14:7 389
N the LORD thy God would not Deut 23:5
N the children of Israel expelled Josh 13:13
N my brethren that went up with Josh 14:8
n the inhabitants of Beth-shemesh Judg 1:33
N the LORD raised up judges, Judg 2:16
N the people refused to obey the 1Sa 8:19
n Samuel mourned for Saul 1Sa 15:35 3588
N Saul spake not any thing that 1Sa 20:26
n the lords favour thee not 1Sa 29:6
N David took the strong hold of 2Sa 5:7
N a lad saw them, and told Absalom 2Sa 17:18
n he would not drink thereof, but 2Sa 23:16
N thou shalt not build the house 1Kin 8:19 7535
N for David's sake did the LORD 1Kin 15:4 3588
n Asa's heart was perfect with 1Kin 15:14 7535
N in the time of his old age he 1Kin 15:23 7535
n the high places were not taken 1Kin 22:43 389
n, if thou see me when I am taken 2Kin 2:10
N he cleaved unto the sins of 2Kin 3:3 7535
N they departed not from the sins 2Kin 13:6 389
N the priests of the high places 2Kin 23:9 389
N David took the castle of Zion, 1Chr 11:5
N the king's word prevailed 1Chr 21:4
N they shall be his servants 2Chr 12:8 3588
n the heart of Asa was perfect 2Chr 15:17 7535
N there are good things found in 2Chr 19:3 61
N divers of Asher and Manasseh and 2Chr 30:11 389
N the people did sacrifice still 2Chr 33:17 61
N Josiah would not turn his face 2Chr 35:22
N we made our prayer unto our God Neh 4:9
N they were disobedient, and Neh 9:26
N for thy great mercies' sake Neh 9:31
n even him did outlandish women Neh 13:26 1571
N Haman refrained himself Est 5:10
n thou heardest the voice of my Ps 31:22 403
N man being in honour abideth not Ps 49:12
N I am continually with thee Ps 73:23
N they did flatter him with their Ps 78:36
N my lovingkindness will I not Ps 89:33
N he saved them for his name's Ps 106:8
N he regarded their affliction, Ps 106:44
n the counsel of the LORD, that Prov 19:21
n the poor man's wisdom is Eccl 9:16
N the dimness shall not be such Is 9:1 3588
N in those days, saith the LORD, Jer 5:18 1571
N the hand of Ahikam the son of Jer 26:24 389
N hear thou now this word that I Jer 28:7 389
N Elnathan and Delaiah Jer 36:25 1571
N if thou warn the righteous man, Eze 3:21
N I will remember my covenant Eze 16:60
N mine eye spared them from Eze 20:17
N I withdrew mine hand, and Eze 20:22
N, if thou warn the wicked of his Eze 33:9
N leave the stump of his roots in Dan 4:15 1297
N the men rowed hard to bring it Jonah 1:13
n for the oath's sake, and them Mt 14:9
n not as I will, but as thou wilt Mt 26:39 4133
n I say unto you, Hereafter shall Mt 26:64 4133
n not what I will, but what thou Mk 14:36 235
n at thy word I will let down the Lk 5:5 1161
N I must walk to day, and to Lk 13:33 4133
N when the Son of man cometh, Lk 18:8 4133
n not my will, but thine, be done Lk 22:42 4133
n let us go unto him Jn 11:15 235
N among the chief rulers also Jn 12:42
N I tell you the truth Jn 16:7 235
N he left not himself without Acts 14:17 2544
N the centurion believed the Acts 27:11 1161
N death reigned from Adam to Rom 5:14 235
N, brethren, I have written the Rom 15:15 1161
N, to avoid fornication, let 1Cor 7:2 1161
N such shall have trouble in the 1Cor 7:28 1161
N he that standeth stedfast in 1Cor 7:37 1161
N we have not used this power 1Cor 9:12 235
N neither is the man without the 1Cor 11:11 4133
N when it shall turn to the Lord, 2Cor 3:16 1161
N God, that comforteth those that 2Cor 7:6 235
n, being crafty, I caught you 2Cor 12:16 235
n I live; yet not I Gal 2:20 1161
N what saith the scripture Gal 4:30 235
N let every one of you in Eph 5:33 4133
N to abide in the flesh is more Phil 1:24 1161
N, whereto we have already Phil 3:16 4133
n I am not ashamed 2Ti 1:12 235
N the foundation of God standeth 2Ti 2:19 3305
n afterward it yieldeth the Heb 12:11 1161
N we, according to his promise, 2Pet 3:13 1161
N I have somewhat against thee, Rev 2:4 235

NEW
arose up a *n* king over Egypt Ex 1:8 2319
ye shall offer a *n* meat offering Lev 23:16 2319
forth the old because of the *n* Lev 26:10 2319
But if the LORD make a *n* thing Num 16:30 1278
when ye bring a *n* meat offering Num 28:26 2319
there that hath built a *n* house Deut 20:5 2319
When thou buildest a *n* house Deut 22:8 2319
When a man hath taken a *n* wife Deut 24:5 2319
to *n* gods that came newly up, Deut 32:17 2319
of wine, which we filled, were *n* Josh 9:13 2319
They chose *n* gods Judg 5:8 2319
they bound him with two *n* cords Judg 15:13 2319
he found a *n* jawbone of an ass, Judg 15:15 2961
If they bind me fast with *n* ropes Judg 16:11 2319
Delilah therefore took *n* ropes Judg 16:12 2319
Now therefore make a *n* cart 1Sa 6:7 2319
Behold, to morrow is the *n* moon 1Sa 20:5 2320
to David, To morrow is the *n* moon 1Sa 20:18 2320
when the *n* moon was come, the 1Sa 20:24 2320
set the ark of God upon a *n* cart 2Sa 6:3 2319
of Abinadab, drave the *n* cart 2Sa 6:3 2319
he being girded with a *n* sword 2Sa 21:16 2319
had clad himself with a *n* garment 1Kin 11:29 2319
Ahijah caught the *n* garment that 1Kin 11:30 2319
And he said, Bring me a *n* cruse 2Kin 2:20 2319
it is neither *n* moon, nor sabbath 2Kin 4:23 2320
in a *n* cart out of the house of 1Chr 13:7 2319
in the sabbaths, in the *n* moons 1Chr 23:31 2320
the sabbaths, and on the *n* moons 2Chr 2:4 2320
the sabbaths, and on the *n* moons 2Chr 8:13 2320
of the LORD, before the *n* court 2Chr 20:5 2319
the sabbaths, and for the *n* moons 2Chr 31:3 2320
offering, both of the *n* moons Ezr 3:5 2320
stones, and a row of *n* timber Ezr 6:4 2323
of the sabbaths, of the *n* moons Neh 10:33 2320
of the corn, of the *n* wine Neh 10:39 8492
the *n* wine, and the oil, which was Neh 13:5 8492
the *n* wine and the oil unto the Neh 13:12 8492
is ready to burst like *n* bottles Job 32:19 2319
Sing unto him a *n* song Ps 33:3 2319
he hath put a *n* song in my mouth, Ps 40:3 2319
Blow up the trumpet in the *n* moon Ps 81:3 2320
O sing unto the LORD a *n* song Ps 96:1 2319
O sing unto the LORD a *n* song Ps 98:1 2319
I will sing a *n* song unto thee, O Ps 144:9 2319
Sing unto the LORD a *n* song Ps 149:1 2319
shall burst out with *n* wine Prov 3:10 8492
there is no *n* thing under the sun Eccl 1:9 2319
it may be said, See, this is *n* Eccl 1:10 2319
all manner of pleasant fruits, *n* Song 7:13 2319
the *n* moons and sabbaths, the Is 1:13 2320
Your *n* moons and your appointed Is 1:14 2320
The *n* wine mourneth, the vine Is 24:7 8492
I will make thee a *n* sharp Is 41:15 2319
to pass, and *n* things do I declare Is 42:9 2319
Sing unto the LORD a *n* song Is 42:10 2319
Behold, I will do a *n* thing Is 43:19 2319
I have shewed thee *n* things from Is 48:6 2319
thou shalt be called by a *n* name Is 62:2 2319
As the *n* wine is found in the Is 65:8 8492
I create *n* heavens and a *n* earth Is 65:17 2319
For as the *n* heavens Is 66:22 2319
the *n* earth, which I will make, Is 66:22 2319
that from one *n* moon to another, Is 66:23 2320
of the *n* gate of the LORD's house Jer 26:10 2319
created a *n* thing in the earth Jer 31:22 2319
that I will make a *n* covenant Jer 31:31 2319
at the entry of the *n* gate of the Jer 36:10 2319
They are *n* every morning Lam 3:23 2319
I will put a *n* spirit within you Eze 11:19 2319
you a *n* heart and a *n* spirit Eze 18:31 2319
A *n* heart also will I give you, Eze 36:26 2319
a *n* spirit will I put within you Eze 36:26 2319
in the feasts, and in the *n* moons Eze 45:17 2320
in the day of the *n* moon it shall Eze 46:1 2320
in the sabbaths and in the *n* moons Eze 46:3 2320
in the day of the *n* moon it shall Eze 46:6 2320
it shall bring forth *n* fruit Eze 47:12 1069
her *n* moons, and her sabbaths, and Hos 2:11 2320
n wine take away the heart Hos 4:11 8492
the *n* wine shall fail in her Hos 9:2 8492
of wine, because of the *n* wine Joel 1:5
the *n* wine is dried up, the oil Joel 1:10 8492
mountains shall drop down *n* wine Joel 3:18
When will the *n* moon be gone Amos 8:5 2320
upon the corn, and upon the *n* wine Hag 1:11 8492
men cheerful, and *n* wine the maids Zec 9:17 8492
of *n* cloth unto an old garment Mt 9:16 46
Neither do men put *n* wine into Mt 9:17 3501

N

but they put *n* wine into Mt 9:17 *3501*
wine into *n* bottles Mt 9:17 *2537*
out of his treasure things *n* Mt 13:52 *2537*
is my blood of the *n* testament Mt 26:28 *2537*
until that day when I drink it *n* Mt 26:29 *2537*
And laid it in his own *n* tomb Mt 27:60 *2537*
what *n* doctrine is this Mk 1:27 *2537*
of *n* cloth on an old garment Mk 2:21 *46*
else the *n* piece that filled it Mk 2:21 *2537*
no man putteth *n* wine into old Mk 2:22 *3501*
else the *n* wine doth burst the Mk 2:22 *3501*
but *n* wine must be put into Mk 2:22 *3501*
wine must be put into *n* bottles Mk 2:22 *2537*
is my blood of the *n* testament Mk 14:24 *2537*
drink it *n* in the kingdom of God Mk 14:25 *2537*
they shall speak with *n* tongues Mk 16:17 *2537*
piece of a *n* garment upon an old Lk 5:36 *2537*
then both the *n* maketh a rent Lk 5:36 *2537*
of the *n* agreeth not with the old Lk 5:36 *2537*
no man putteth *n* wine into old Lk 5:37 *3501*
else the *n* wine will burst the Lk 5:37 *3501*
But *n* wine must be put into Lk 5:38 *3501*
wine must be put into *n* bottles Lk 5:38 *2537*
old wine straightway desireth *n* Lk 5:39 *2537*
This cup is the *n* testament in my Lk 22:20 *2537*
A *n* commandment I give unto you, Jn 13:34 *2537*
and in the garden a *n* sepulchre Jn 19:41 *2537*
These men are full of *n* wine Acts 2:13 *1098*
May we know what this *n* doctrine Acts 17:19 *2537*
to tell, or to hear some *n* thing Acts 17:21 *2537*
leaven, that ye may be a *n* lump 1Cor 5:7 *3501*
This cup is the *n* testament in my 1Cor 11:25 *2537*
able ministers of the *n* testament 2Cor 3:6 *2537*
be in Christ, he is a *n* creature 2Cor 5:17 *2537*
behold, all things are become *n* 2Cor 5:17 *2537*
uncircumcision, but a *n* creature Gal 6:15 *2537*
in himself of twain one *n* man Eph 2:15 *2537*
And that ye put on the *n* man Eph 4:24 *2537*
of an holyday, or of the *n* moon Col 2:16 *3561*
And have put on the *n* man, which Col 3:10 *3501*
when I will make a *n* covenant Heb 8:8 *2537*
A *n* covenant, he hath made the Heb 8:13 *2537*
the mediator of the *n* testament Heb 9:15 *2537*
By a *n* and living way, which he Heb 10:20 *4372*
the mediator of the *n* covenant Heb 12:24 *3501*
his promise, look for *n* heavens 2Pet 3:13 *2537*
a *n* earth, wherein dwelleth 2Pet 3:13 *2537*
I write no *n* commandment unto you 1Jn 2:7 *2537*
a *n* commandment I write unto you, 1Jn 2:8 *2537*
I wrote a *n* commandment unto thee 2Jn 5 *2537*
and in the stone a *n* name written Rev 2:17 *2537*
which is *n* Jerusalem, which Rev 3:12 *2537*
I will write upon him my *n* name Rev 3:12 *2537*
And they sung a *n* song, saying, Rev 5:9 *2537*
were a *n* song before the throne Rev 14:3 *2537*
I saw a *n* heaven and a *n* earth Rev 21:1 *2537*
n Jerusalem, coming down from God Rev 21:2 *2537*
said, Behold, I make all things *n* Rev 21:5 *2537*

NEWBORN
As *n* babes, desire the sincere 1Pet 2:2 *738*

NEWLY
not, to new gods that came *n* up Deut 32:17 7138
they had but *n* set the watch Judg 7:19 6965

NEWNESS
we also should walk in *n* of life Rom 6:4 *2538*
we should serve in *n* of spirit Rom 7:6 *2538*

NEWS
so is good *n* from a far country Prov 25:25 8052

NEXT
at this set time in the *n* year Gen 17:21 312
his neighbour *n* unto his house Ex 12:4 7138
those that do pitch *n* unto him Num 2:5
all that night, and all the *n* day Num 11:32 4283
that is *n* to him of his family Num 27:11 7138
which is *n* unto the slain man Deut 21:3 7138
that are *n* unto the slain man, Deut 21:6 7138
kin unto us, one of our *n* kinsmen Ruth 2:20
n unto him Abinadab, and the third 1Sa 17:13 4932
Israel, and I shall be *n* unto thee 1Sa 23:17 4932
unto the evening of the *n* day 1Sa 30:17 4283
and I said unto her on the *n* day 2Kin 6:29 312
Joel the chief, and Shapham the *n* 1Chr 5:12 4932
n to him Zechariah, Jeiel, and 1Chr 16:5 4932
n to him was Jehohanan the 2Chr 17:15
n him was Amasiah the son of 2Chr 17:16
n him was Jehozabad, and with him 2Chr 17:18
and Elkanah that was *n* to the king 2Chr 28:7 4932
and Shimei his brother was the *n* 2Chr 31:12 4932
n him were Eden, and Miniamin, and 2Chr 31:15
n unto him builded the men of Neh 3:2
n to them builded Zaccur the son Neh 3:2
n unto them repaired Meremoth the Neh 3:4
n unto them repaired Meshullam Neh 3:4
n unto them repaired Zadok the Neh 3:4
n unto them the Tekoites repaired Neh 3:5
n unto them repaired Melatiah the Neh 3:7
N unto him repaired Uzziel the Neh 3:8
N unto him also repaired Hananiah Neh 3:8
n unto them repaired Rephaiah the Neh 3:9
n unto them repaired Jedaiah the Neh 3:10
n unto him repaired Hattush the Neh 3:10
n unto him repaired Shallum the Neh 3:12
N unto him repaired Hashabiah, Neh 3:17
n to him repaired Ezer the son of Neh 3:19
n to them was Hanan the son of Neh 13:13
the *n* unto him was Carshena, Est 1:14 7138
the Jew was *n* unto king Ahasuerus Est 10:3 4932
when the morning rose the *n* day Jonah 4:7 4283
Now the *n* day, that followed the Mt 27:62 *1887*
them, Let us go into the *n* towns Mk 1:38 *2192*
came to pass, that on the *n* day Lk 9:37 *1836*
The *n* day John seeth Jesus coming Jn 1:29 *1887*
Again the *n* day after John stood, Jn 1:35 *1887*
On the *n* day much people that Jn 12:12 *1887*
put them in hold unto the *n* day Acts 4:3 *839*
the *n* day he shewed himself unto Acts 7:26 *1966*
be preached to them the *n* sabbath Acts 13:42 *3342*
the *n* sabbath day came almost the Acts 13:44 *2064*
the *n* day he departed with Acts 14:20 *1887*
and the *n* day to Neapolis Acts 16:11 *1966*
came the *n* day over against Chios Acts 20:15 *1966*
the *n* day we arrived at Samos, and Acts 20:15 *2087*
the *n* day we came to Miletus Acts 20:15 *2192*
the *n* day we that were of Paul's Acts 21:8 *1887*
the *n* day purifying himself with Acts 21:26 *2192*
the *n* day sitting on the judgment Acts 25:6 *1887*
the *n* day we touched at Sidon Acts 27:3 *2087*
the *n* day they lightened the ship Acts 27:18 *1836*
we came the *n* day to Puteoli Acts 28:13 *1206*

NEZIAH (*ne-zi'-ah*) *A family of exiles.*
The children of *N*, the children Ezr 2:54 5335
The children of *N*, the children Neh 7:56 5335

NEZIB (*ne'-zib*) *A city in Judah.*
And Jiphtah, and Ashnah, and *N* Josh 15:43 5334

NIBHAZ (*nib'-haz*) *A god of the Avites.*
And the Avites made *N* and Tartak, 2Kin 17:31 5026

NIBSHAN (*nib'-shan*) *A city in Judah.*
And *N*, and the city of Salt, and Josh 15:62 5044

NICANOR (*ni-ca'-nor*) *A leader in the Jerusalem church.*
and Philip, and Prochorus, and *N* Acts 6:5 *3527*

NICODEMUS (*nic-o-de'-mus*) *A Pharisee sympathetic to Jesus.*
a man of the Pharisees, named *N* Jn 3:1 *3530*
N saith unto him, How can a man Jn 3:4 *3530*
N answered and said unto him, How Jn 3:9 *3530*
N saith unto them, (he that came Jn 7:50 *3530*
And there came also *N*, which at Jn 19:39 *3530*

NICOLAITANES (*nic-o-la'-i-tans*) *A group condemned in Revelation.*
thou hatest the deeds of the *N* Rev 2:6 *3531*
that hold the doctrine of the *N* Rev 2:15 *3531*

NICOLAITANS See NICOLAITANES.

NICOLAS (*nic'-o-las*) *A leader in the Jerusalem church.*
and *N* a proselyte of Antioch Acts 6:5 *3532*

NICOLAUS See NICOLAS.

NICOPOLIS (*ni-cop'-o-lis*) *A city in Thrace.*
be diligent to come unto me to *N* Titus 3:12 *3533*
the Cretians, from *N* of Macedonia Titus *s* *3533*

NIGER (*ni'-jur*) See SIMEON. *A Christian teacher and prophet at Antioch.*
and Simeon that was called *N* Acts 13:1 *3526*

NIGH
the time drew *n* that Israel must Gen 47:29 7126
And he said, Draw not *n* hither Ex 3:5 7126
And when Pharaoh drew *n*, the Ex 14:10 7126
but they shall not come *n* Ex 24:2 5066
soon as he came *n* unto the camp Ex 32:19 7126
and they were afraid to come *n* him Ex 34:30 5066
all the children of Israel came *n* Ex 34:32 5066
sanctified in them that come *n* me Lev 10:3 7138
that is *n* unto him, which hath Lev 21:3 7138
n to offer the offerings of the Lev 21:21 5066
he shall not come *n* to offer the Lev 21:21 5066
nor come *n* unto the altar, Lev 21:23 5066
or any that is *n* of kin unto him Lev 25:49 7607
cometh *n* shall be put to death Num 1:51 7126
cometh *n* shall be put to death Num 3:10 7126
cometh *n* shall be put to death Num 3:38 7126
Israel come *n* unto the sanctuary Num 8:19 5066
only they shall not come *n* the Num 18:3 7126
shall not come *n* unto you Num 18:4 7126
cometh *n* shall be put to death Num 18:7 7126
come *n* the tabernacle of the Num 18:22 7126
I shall behold him, but not *n* Num 24:17 7126
unto all the places *n* thereunto Deut 1:7 7934
when thou comest *n* over against Deut 2:19 7126
who hath God so *n* unto them Deut 4:7 7126
n unto thee, or far off from thee Deut 13:7 7126
ye are come *n* unto the battle Deut 20:2 7126
When thou comest *n* unto a city to Deut 20:10 7126
if thy brother be not *n* unto thee Deut 22:2 7126
But the word is very *n* unto thee Deut 30:14 7126
were with him, went up, and drew *n* Josh 8:11 5066
drew *n* to meet David, that David 1Sa 17:48 7126
And Joab drew *n*, and the people 2Sa 10:13 5066
Wherefore approached ye so *n* unto 2Sa 11:20
why went ye *n* the wall 2Sa 11:21 5066
that when any man came *n* to him 2Sa 15:5 7126
David drew *n* that he should die 1Kin 2:1 7126
be *n* unto the LORD our God day and 1Kin 8:59 7126
Moreover they that were *n* them 1Chr 12:40 7126
n before the Syrians unto the 1Chr 19:14 5066
of the king Ahasuerus, both *n* Est 9:20 7126
they shall not come *n* unto him Ps 32:6 5060
The LORD is *n* unto them that are Ps 34:18 7126
Draw *n* unto my soul, and redeem it Ps 69:18 7126
my steps had well *n* slipped Ps 73:2 4952
salvation is *n* them that fear him Ps 85:9 7138
my life draweth *n* unto the grave Ps 88:3 5060
but it shall not come *n* thee Ps 91:7 5066
any plague come *n* thy dwelling Ps 91:10 7126
They draw *n* that follow after Ps 119:150 7126
The LORD is *n* unto all them that Ps 145:18 7138
come not *n* the door of her house Prov 5:8 7126
come not, nor the years draw *n* Eccl 12:1 5060
of the Holy One of Israel draw *n* Is 5:19 7126
LORD cometh, for it is *n* at hand Joel 2:1 7126
This people draweth *n* unto me Mt 15:8 *1448*
came *n* unto the sea of Galilee Mt 15:29 *3844*
when they drew *n* unto Jerusalem Mt 21:1 *1448*
leaves, ye know that summer is *n* Mt 24:32 *1451*
not come *n* unto him for the press Mk 2:4
Now there was there *n* unto the Mk 5:11 *4314*
and he was *n* unto the sea Mk 5:21 *3844*
And when they came *n* to Jerusalem Mk 11:1
come to pass, know that it is *n* Mk 13:29 *1451*
Now when he came *n* to the gate of Lk 7:12 *1448*
kingdom of God is come *n* unto you Lk 10:9 *1448*
kingdom of God is come *n* unto you Lk 10:11 *1448*
drew *n* to the house, he heard Lk 15:25 *1448*
as he was come *n* unto Jericho Lk 18:35 *1448*
because he was *n* to Jerusalem Lk 19:11 *1451*
when he was come *n* to Bethphage Lk 19:29 *1448*
And when he was come *n*, even now Lk 19:37 *1448*
that the desolation thereof is *n* Lk 21:20 *1448*
for your redemption draweth *n* Lk 21:28 *1448*
that summer is now *n* at hand Lk 21:30 *1451*
the kingdom of God is *n* at hand Lk 21:31 *1451*
feast of unleavened bread drew *n* Lk 22:1 *1448*
they drew *n* unto the village, Lk 24:28 *1448*
a feast of the Jews, was *n* Jn 6:4 *1451*
sea, and drawing *n* unto the ship Jn 6:19 *1451*
n unto the place where they did Jn 6:23 *1451*
Now Bethany was *n* unto Jerusalem Jn 11:18 *1451*
the Jews' passover was *n* at hand Jn 11:55 *1451*
was crucified was *n* to the city Jn 19:20 *1451*
for the sepulchre was *n* at hand Jn 19:42 *1451*
the time of the promise drew *n* Acts 7:17 *1448*
forasmuch as Lydda was *n* to Joppa Acts 9:38 *1451*
drew *n* unto the city, Peter went Acts 10:9 *1448*
was come *n* unto Damascus about Acts 22:6 *1448*
n whereunto was the city of Lasea Acts 27:8 *1451*
The word is *n* thee, even in thy Rom 10:8 *1451*
are made *n* by the blood of Christ Eph 2:13 *1451*
afar off, and to them that were *n* Eph 2:17 *1451*
indeed he was sick *n* unto death Phil 2:27 *3897*
of Christ he was *n* unto death Phil 2:30 *1448*
is rejected, and is *n* unto cursing Heb 6:8 *1451*
by the which we draw *n* unto God Heb 7:19 *1448*
Draw *n* to God, and he will draw Jas 4:8 *1448*
to God, and he will draw *n* to you Jas 4:8 *1448*
the coming of the Lord draweth *n* Jas 5:8 *1448*

NIGHT
Day, and the darkness he called *N* Gen 1:5 3915
to divide the day from the *n* Gen 1:14 3915
and the lesser light to rule the *n* Gen 1:16 3915
rule over the day and over the *n* Gen 1:18 3915
and day and *n* shall not cease Gen 8:22 3915
them, he and his servants, by *n* Gen 14:15 3915
servant's house, and tarry all *n* Gen 19:2
we will abide in the street all *n* Gen 19:2
men which came in to thee this *n* Gen 19:5 3915
their father drink wine that *n* Gen 19:33 3915
make him drink wine this *n* also Gen 19:34 3915
father drink wine that *n* also Gen 19:35 3915
came to Abimelech in a dream by *n* Gen 20:3 3915
were with him, and tarried all *n* Gen 24:54
LORD appeared unto him the same *n* Gen 26:24 3915
place, and tarried there all *n* Gen 28:11
thee to *n* for thy son's mandrakes Gen 30:15 3915
And he lay with her that *n* Gen 30:16 3915
Laban the Syrian in a dream by *n* Gen 31:24 3915
stolen by day, or stolen by *n* Gen 31:39 3915
consumed me, and the frost by *n* Gen 31:40 3915
tarried all *n* in the mount Gen 31:54
And he lodged there that same *n* Gen 32:13 3915
lodged that *n* in the company Gen 32:21 3915
And he rose up that *n*, and took his Gen 32:22 3915
them, each man his dream in one *n* Gen 40:5 3915
And we dreamed a dream in one *n* Gen 41:11 3915
Israel in the visions of the *n* Gen 46:2 3915
at *n* he shall divide the spoil Gen 49:27 6153
land all that day, and all that *n* Ex 10:13 3915
shall eat the flesh in that *n* Ex 12:8 3915
through the land of Egypt this *n* Ex 12:12 3915
And Pharaoh rose up in the *n* Ex 12:30 3915
he called for Moses and Aaron by *n* Ex 12:31 3915
It is a *n* to be much observed Ex 12:42 3915
this is that *n* of the LORD to be Ex 12:42 3915
by *n* in a pillar of fire, to give Ex 13:21 3915
to go by day and *n* Ex 13:21 3915
day, nor the pillar of fire by *n* Ex 13:22 3915
but it gave light by *n* to these Ex 14:20 3915
came not near the other all the *n* Ex 14:20 3915
by a strong east wind all that *n* Ex 14:21 3915
by day, and fire was on it by *n* Ex 40:38 3915
the altar all *n* unto the morning Lev 6:9 3915
the morning, and half thereof at *n* Lev 6:20 6153
n seven days, and keep the charge Lev 8:35 3915
the *n* hawk, and the cuckow, and the Lev 11:16 8464
with thee all *n* until the morning Lev 19:13
and the appearance of fire by *n* Num 9:16 3915
by *n* that the cloud was taken up Num 9:21 3915
dew fell upon the camp in the *n* Num 11:9 3915
up all that day, and all that *n* Num 11:32 3915
and the people wept that *n* Num 14:1 3915
and in a pillar of fire by *n* Num 14:14 3915
said unto them, Lodge here this *n* Num 22:8 3915
you, tarry ye also here this *n* Num 22:19 3915
And God came unto Balaam at *n* Num 22:20 3915
pitch your tents in, in fire by *n* Deut 1:33 3915
the *n* hawk, and the cuckow, and the Deut 14:15 8464
thee forth out of Egypt by *n* Deut 16:1 3915
remain all *n* until the morning Deut 16:4
not remain all *n* upon the tree Deut 21:23
that chanceth him by *n*, then Deut 23:10 3915
and thou shalt fear day and *n* Deut 28:66 3915
shalt meditate therein day and *n* Josh 1:8 3915
there came men in hither to *n* of Josh 2:2 3915

where ye shall lodge this *n* ... Josh 4:3 3915
of valour, and sent them away by *n* ... Josh 8:3 3915
lodged that *n* among the people ... Josh 8:9 3915
Joshua went that *n* into the midst ... Josh 8:13 3915
and went up from Gilgal all *n* ... Josh 10:9 3915
And it came to pass the same *n* ... Judg 6:25 3915
do it by day, that he did it by *n* ... Judg 6:27 3915
And God did so that *n* ... Judg 6:40 3915
And it came to pass the same *n* ... Judg 7:9 3915
Now therefore up by *n*, thou and ... Judg 9:32 3915
people that were with him, by *n* ... Judg 9:34 3915
laid wait for him all *n* in the ... Judg 16:2 3915
the city, and were quiet all the *n* ... Judg 16:2 3915
I pray thee, and tarry all *n* ... Judg 19:6
evening, I pray you tarry all *n* ... Judg 19:9
the man would not tarry that *n* ... Judg 19:10
of these places to lodge all *n* ... Judg 19:13
her all the *n* until the morning ... Judg 19:25 3915
house round about upon me by *n* ... Judg 20:5 3915
should have an husband also to *n* ... Ruth 1:12 3915
barley to *n* in the threshingfloor ... Ruth 3:2 3915
Tarry this *n*, and it shall be in ... Ruth 3:13 3915
every man his ox with him that *n* ... 1Sa 14:34 3915
down after the Philistines by *n* ... 1Sa 14:36 3915
and he cried unto the LORD all *n* ... 1Sa 15:11 3915
the LORD hath said to me this *n* ... 1Sa 15:16 3915
and David fled, and escaped that *n* ... 1Sa 19:10 3915
saying, If thou save not thy to *n* ... 1Sa 19:11 3915
naked all that day and all that *n* ... 1Sa 19:24 3915
were a wall unto us both by *n* ... 1Sa 25:16 3915
Abishai came to the people by *n* ... 1Sa 26:7 3915
and they came to the woman by *n* ... 1Sa 28:8 3915
bread all the day, nor all the *n* ... 1Sa 28:20 3915
they rose up, and went away that *n* ... 1Sa 28:25 3915
valiant men arose, and went all *n* ... 1Sa 31:12 3915
all that *n* through the plain ... 2Sa 2:29 3915
And Joab and his men went all *n* ... 2Sa 2:32 3915
them away through the plain all *n* ... 2Sa 4:7 3915
And it came to pass that *n* ... 2Sa 7:4 3915
in, and lay all *n* upon the earth ... 2Sa 12:16
and pursue after David this *n* ... 2Sa 17:1 3915
Lodge not this *n* in the plains of ... 2Sa 17:16 3915
not tarry one with thee this *n* ... 2Sa 19:7 3915
nor the beasts of the field by *n* ... 2Sa 21:10 3915
to Solomon in a dream by *n* ... 1Kin 3:5 3915
this woman's child died in the *n* ... 1Kin 3:19 3915
may be open toward this house *n* ... 1Kin 8:29 3915
unto the LORD our God day and *n* ... 1Kin 8:59 3915
and they came by *n*, and compassed ... 2Kin 6:14 3915
And the king arose in the *n* ... 2Kin 7:12 3915
and he rose by *n*, and smote the ... 2Kin 8:21 3915
And it came to pass that *n* ... 2Kin 19:35 3915
all the men of war fled by *n* by ... 2Kin 25:4 3915
employed in that work day and *n* ... 1Chr 9:33 3915
And it came to pass the same *n* ... 1Chr 17:3 3915
In that *n* did God appear unto ... 2Chr 1:7 3915
be open upon this house day and *n* ... 2Chr 6:20 3915
the LORD appeared to Solomon by *n* ... 2Chr 7:12 3915
and he rose up by *n*, and smote the ... 2Chr 21:9 3915
offerings and the fat until *n* ... 2Chr 35:14 3915
I pray before thee now, day and *n* ... Neh 1:6 3915
And I arose in the *n*, I and some ... Neh 2:12 3915
I went out by *n* by the gate of ... Neh 2:13 3915
went I up in the *n* by the brook ... Neh 2:15 3915
set a watch against them day and *n* ... Neh 4:9 3915
that in the *n* they may be a guard ... Neh 4:22 3915
in the *n* will they come to slay ... Neh 6:10 3915
in the *n* by a pillar of fire, to ... Neh 9:12 3915
neither the pillar of fire by *n* ... Neh 9:19 3915
nor drink three days, *n* or day ... Est 4:16 3915
On that *n* could not the king ... Est 6:1 3915
the *n* in which it was said, There ... Job 3:3 3915
As for that *n*, let darkness seize ... Job 3:6 3915
Lo, let that *n* be solitary ... Job 3:7 3915
from the visions of the *n* ... Job 4:13 3915
grope in the noonday as in the *n* ... Job 5:14 3915
shall I arise, and the *n* be gone ... Job 7:4 6153
They change the *n* into day ... Job 17:12 3915
chased away as a vision of the *n* ... Job 20:8 3915
needy, and in the *n* is as a thief ... Job 24:14 3915
until the day and *n* come to an end ... Job 26:10 2822
stealeth him away in the *n* ... Job 27:20 3915
the dew lay all *n* upon my branch ... Job 29:19
are pierced in me in the *n* season ... Job 30:17 3915
In a dream, in a vision of the *n* ... Job 33:15 3915
and he overturneth them in the *n* ... Job 34:25 3915
maker, who giveth songs in the *n* ... Job 35:10 3915
Desire not the *n*, when people are ... Job 36:20 3915
his law doth he meditate day and *n* ... Ps 1:2 3915
all the *n* make I my bed to swim ... Ps 6:6 3915
also instruct me in the *n* seasons ... Ps 16:7 3915
thou hast visited me in the *n* ... Ps 17:3 3915
n unto *n* sheweth knowledge ... Ps 19:2 3915
and in the *n* season, and am not ... Ps 22:2 3915
weeping may endure for a *n* ... Ps 30:5 6153
n thy hand was heavy upon me ... Ps 32:4 3915
tears have been my meat day and *n* ... Ps 42:3 3915
in the *n* his song shall be with ... Ps 42:8 3915
n they go about it upon the walls ... Ps 55:10 3915
meditate on thee in the *n* watches ... Ps 63:6
day is thine, the *n* also is thine ... Ps 74:16 3915
my sore ran in the *n*, and ceased ... Ps 77:2 3915
to remembrance my song in the *n* ... Ps 77:6 3915
all the *n* with a light of fire ... Ps 78:14 3915
I have cried day and *n* before thee ... Ps 88:1 3915
is past, and as a watch in the *n* ... Ps 90:4 3915
not be afraid for the terror by *n* ... Ps 91:5 3915
and thy faithfulness every *n* ... Ps 92:2 3915
Thou makest darkness, and it is *n* ... Ps 104:20 3915
and fire to give light in the *n* ... Ps 105:39 3915
thy name, O LORD, in the *n* ... Ps 119:55 3915
Mine eyes prevent the *n* watches ... Ps 119:148
thee by day, nor the moon by *n* ... Ps 121:6 3915
which by *n* stand in the house of ... Ps 134:1 3915
The moon and stars to rule by *n* ... Ps 136:9 3915
even the *n* shall be light about ... Ps 139:11 3915
but the *n* shineth as the day ... Ps 139:12 3915
evening, in the black and dark *n* ... Prov 7:9 3915
She riseth also while it is yet *n* ... Prov 31:15 3915
her candle goeth not out by *n* ... Prov 31:18 3915
heart taketh not rest in the *n* ... Eccl 2:23 3915
nor *n* seeth sleep with his eyes ... Eccl 8:16 3915
he shall lie all *n* betwixt my ... Song 1:13
By *n* on my bed I sought him whom ... Song 3:1 3915
thigh because of fear in the *n* ... Song 3:8 3915
my locks with the drops of the *n* ... Song 5:2 3915
shining of a flaming fire by *n* ... Is 4:5 3915
that continue until *n*, till wine ... Is 5:11 5399
Because in the *n* Ar of Moab is ... Is 15:1 3915
because in the *n* Kir of Moab is ... Is 15:1 3915
make thy shadow as the *n* in the ... Is 16:3 3915
the *n* of my pleasure hath he ... Is 21:4 5399
of Seir, Watchman, what of the *n* ... Is 21:11 3915
Watchman, what of the *n* ... Is 21:11 3915
The morning cometh, and also the *n* ... Is 21:12 3915
soul have I desired thee in the *n* ... Is 26:9 3915
any hurt it, I will keep it *n* ... Is 27:3 3915
it pass over, by day and by *n* ... Is 28:19 3915
shall be as a dream of a *n* vision ... Is 29:7 3915
as in the *n* when a holy solemnity ... Is 30:29 3915
shall not be quenched *n* nor day ... Is 34:10 3915
from day even to *n* wilt thou make ... Is 38:12 3915
from day even to *n* wilt thou make ... Is 38:13 3915
we stumble at noonday as in the *n* ... Is 59:10 5399
they shall not be shut day nor *n* ... Is 60:11 3915
never hold their peace day nor *n* ... Is 62:6 3915
Arise, and let us go by *n*, and let ... Jer 6:5 3915
n for the slain of the daughter ... Jer 9:1 3915
turneth aside to tarry for a *n* ... Jer 14:8
mine eyes run down with tears *n* ... Jer 14:17 3915
ye serve other gods day and *n* ... Jer 16:13 3915
and of the stars for a light by *n* ... Jer 31:35 3915
the day, and my covenant of the *n* ... Jer 33:20 3915
not be day and *n* in their season ... Jer 33:20 3915
my covenant be not with day and *n* ... Jer 33:25 3915
heat, and in the *n* to the frost ... Jer 36:30 3915
went forth out of the city by *n* ... Jer 39:4 3915
if thieves by *n*, they will ... Jer 49:9 3915
went forth out of the city by *n* ... Jer 52:7 3915
She weepeth sore in the *n* ... Lam 1:2 3915
run down like a river day and *n* ... Lam 2:18 3915
Arise, cry out in the *n* ... Lam 2:19 3915
unto Daniel in a *n* vision ... Dan 2:19 3916
In that *n* was Belshazzar the king ... Dan 5:30 3916
palace, and passed the *n* fasting ... Dan 6:18 956
and said, I saw in my vision by *n* ... Dan 7:2 3916
After this I saw in the *n* visions ... Dan 7:7 3916
I saw in the *n* visions, and ... Dan 7:13 6916
shall fall with thee in the *n* ... Hos 4:5 3915
their baker sleepeth all the *n* ... Hos 7:6 3915
lie all *n* in sackcloth, ye ... Joel 1:13
and maketh the day dark with *n* ... Amos 5:8 3915
came to thee, if robbers by *n* ... Obad 5 3915
up in a *n*, and perished in a *n* ... Jonah 4:10 3915
Therefore *n* shall be unto you ... Mic 3:6 3915
I saw by *n*, and behold a man ... Zec 1:8 3915
known to the LORD, not day, nor *n* ... Zec 14:7 3915
young child and his mother by *n* ... Mt 2:14 *3571*
of the *n* Jesus went unto them ... Mt 14:25 *3571*
be offended because of me this *n* ... Mt 26:31 *3571*
I say unto thee, That this *n* ... Mt 26:34 *3571*
day, lest his disciples come by *n* ... Mt 27:64 *3571*
Say ye, His disciples came by *n* ... Mt 28:13 *3571*
And should sleep, and rise *n* ... Mk 4:27 *3571*
And always, *n* and day, he was in ... Mk 5:5 *3571*
of the *n* he cometh unto them ... Mk 6:48 *3571*
be offended because of me this *n* ... Mk 14:27 *3571*
That this day, even in this *n* ... Mk 14:30 *3571*
watch over their flock by *n* ... Lk 2:8 *3571*
God with fastings and prayers *n* ... Lk 2:37 *3571*
Master, we have toiled all the *n* ... Lk 5:5 *3571*
continued all *n* in prayer to God ... Lk 6:12 *1273*
this *n* thy soul shall be required ... Lk 12:20 *3571*
in that *n* there shall be two men ... Lk 17:34 *3571*
n unto him, though he bear long ... Lk 18:7 *3571*
at *n* he went out, and abode in the ... Lk 21:37 *3571*
The same came to Jesus by *n* ... Jn 3:2 *3571*
them, (he that came to Jesus by *n* ... Jn 7:50 *3571*
the *n* cometh, when no man can ... Jn 9:4 *3571*
But if a man walk in the *n* ... Jn 11:10 *3571*
and it was *n* ... Jn 13:30 *3571*
at the first came to Jesus by *n* ... Jn 19:39 *3571*
that *n* they caught nothing ... Jn 21:3 *3571*
Lord by *n* opened the prison doors ... Acts 5:19 *3571*
the gates day and *n* to kill him ... Acts 9:24 *3571*
Then the disciples took him by *n* ... Acts 9:25 *3571*
the same *n* Peter was sleeping ... Acts 12:6 *3571*
vision appeared to Paul in the *n* ... Acts 16:9 *3571*
took them the same hour of the *n* ... Acts 16:33 *3571*
Paul and Silas by *n* unto Berea ... Acts 17:10 *3571*
Lord to Paul in the *n* by a vision ... Acts 18:9 *3571*
I ceased not to warn every one *n* ... Acts 20:31 *3571*
the *n* following the Lord stood by ... Acts 23:11 *3571*
at the third hour of the *n* ... Acts 23:23 *3571*
and brought him by *n* to Antipatris ... Acts 23:31 *3571*
instantly serving God day and *n* ... Acts 26:7 *3571*
by me this *n* the angel of God ... Acts 27:23 *3571*
when the fourteenth *n* was come ... Acts 27:27 *3571*
The *n* is far spent, the day is at ... Rom 13:12 *3571*
That the Lord Jesus the same *n* in ... 1Cor 11:23 *3571*
thrice I suffered shipwreck, a *n* ... 2Cor 11:25 *3574*
for labouring *n* and day, because ... 1Th 2:9 *3571*
N and day praying exceedingly that ... 1Th 3:10 *3571*
so cometh as a thief in the *n* ... 1Th 5:2 *3571*
we are not of the *n*, nor of ... 1Th 5:5 *3571*
they that sleep sleep in the *n* ... 1Th 5:7 *3571*
be drunken are drunken in the *n* ... 1Th 5:7 *3571*
wrought with labour and travail *n* ... 2Th 3:8 *3571*
in supplications and prayers *n* ... 1Ti 5:5 *3571*
of thee in my prayers *n* and day ... 2Ti 1:3 *3571*
will come as a thief in the *n* ... 2Pet 3:10 *3571*
and they rest not day and *n* ... Rev 4:8 *3571*
serve him day and *n* in his temple ... Rev 7:15 *3571*
part of it, and the *n* likewise ... Rev 8:12 *3571*
them before our God day and *n* ... Rev 12:10 *3571*
and they have no rest day nor *n* ... Rev 14:11 *3571*
day and *n* for ever and ever ... Rev 20:10 *3571*
for there shall be no *n* there ... Rev 21:25 *3571*
And there shall be no *n* there ... Rev 22:5 *3571*

NIGHTS

the earth forty days and forty *n* ... Gen 7:4 3915
the earth forty days and forty *n* ... Gen 7:12 3915
the mount forty days and forty *n* ... Ex 24:18 3915
the LORD forty days and forty *n* ... Ex 34:28 3915
the mount forty days and forty *n* ... Deut 9:9 3915
the end of forty days and forty *n* ... Deut 9:11 3915
the first, forty days and forty *n* ... Deut 9:18 3915
the LORD forty days and forty *n* ... Deut 9:25 3915
first time, forty days and forty *n* ... Deut 10:10 3915
any water, three days and three *n* ... 1Sa 30:12 3915
forty *n* unto Horeb the mount of ... 1Kin 19:8 3915
the ground seven days and seven *n* ... Job 2:13 3915
wearisome *n* are appointed to me ... Job 7:3 3915
and I am set in my ward whole *n* ... Is 21:8 3915
of the fish three days and three *n* ... Jonah 1:17 3915
had fasted forty days and forty *n* ... Mt 4:2 *3571*
three *n* in the whale's belly ... Mt 12:40 *3571*
three *n* in the heart of the earth ... Mt 12:40 *3571*

NILE See BROOKS, FLOOD, RIVER.

NIMRAH (*nim'-rah*) See BETH-NIMRAH. *A city in Gad.*

Ataroth, and Dibon, and Jazer, and *N* ... Num 32:3 5247

NIMRIM (*nim'-rim*) *A body of water on the border of Gad.*

the waters of *N* shall be desolate ... Is 15:6 5249
also of *N* shall be desolate ... Jer 48:34 5249

NIMROD (*nim'-rod*) *Son of Cush.*

And Cush begat *N* ... Gen 10:8 5248
Even as *N* the mighty hunter ... Gen 10:9 5248
And Cush begat *N* ... 1Chr 1:10 5248
the land of *N* in the entrances ... Mic 5:6 5248

NIMSHI (*nim'-shi*) *Grandfather of Jehu.*

Jehu the son of *N* shalt thou ... 1Kin 19:16 5250
son of Jehoshaphat the son of *N* ... 2Kin 9:2 5250
son of *N* conspired against Joram ... 2Kin 9:14 5250
the driving of Jehu the son of *N* ... 2Kin 9:20 5250
Jehoram against Jehu the son of *N* ... 2Chr 22:7 5250

NINE

that Adam lived were *n* hundred ... Gen 5:5 8672
the days of Seth were *n* hundred ... Gen 5:8 8672
the days of Enos were *n* hundred ... Gen 5:11 8672
the days of Cainan were *n* hundred ... Gen 5:14 8672
of Jared were *n* hundred sixty ... Gen 5:20 8672
n hundred sixty and *n* years ... Gen 5:27 8672
the days of Noah were *n* hundred ... Gen 9:29 8672
n years, and begat sons and ... Gen 11:19 8672
And Nahor lived *n* and twenty years ... Gen 11:24 8672
Abram was ninety years old and *n* ... Gen 17:1 8672
Abraham was ninety years old and *n* ... Gen 17:24 8672
n talents, and seven hundred and ... Ex 38:24 8672
be unto thee forty and *n* years ... Lev 25:8 8672
n thousand and three hundred ... Num 1:23 8672
n thousand and three hundred ... Num 2:13 8672
And on the fifth day *n* bullocks ... Num 29:26 8672
to give unto the *n* tribes ... Num 34:13 8672
n cubits was the length thereof ... Deut 3:11 8672
an inheritance unto the *n* tribes ... Josh 13:7 8672
hand of Moses, for the *n* tribes ... Josh 14:2 8672
all the cities are twenty and *n* ... Josh 15:32 8672
n cities with their villages ... Josh 15:44 8672
n cities with their villages ... Josh 15:54 8672
n cities out of those two tribes ... Josh 21:16 8672
for he had *n* hundred chariots of ... Judg 4:3 8672
even *n* hundred chariots of iron ... Judg 4:13 8672
Jerusalem at the end of *n* months ... 2Sa 24:8 8672
twenty and *n* years in Jerusalem ... 2Kin 14:2 8672
of Jabesh began to reign in the *n* ... 2Kin 15:13 8672
In the *n* and thirtieth year of ... 2Kin 15:17 8672
in Samaria over Israel *n* years ... 2Kin 17:1 8672
twenty and *n* years in Jerusalem ... 2Kin 18:2 8672
and Eliada, and Eliphelet, *n* ... 1Chr 3:8 8672
n hundred and fifty and six ... 1Chr 9:9 8672
twenty and *n* years in Jerusalem ... 2Chr 25:1 8672
twenty years old, and he reigned *n* ... 2Chr 29:1 8672
a thousand chargers of silver, *n* ... Ezr 1:9 8672
of Zattu, *n* hundred forty and five ... Ezr 2:8 8672
n hundred seventy and three ... Ezr 2:36 8672
in all an hundred thirty and *n* ... Ezr 2:42 8672
Senaah, three thousand *n* hundred ... Neh 7:38 8672
n hundred seventy and three ... Neh 7:39 8672
n parts to dwell in other cities ... Neh 11:1 8672
n hundred twenty and eight ... Neh 11:8 8672
doth he not leave the ninety and *n* ... Mt 18:12 *1768*
ninety and *n* which went not astray ... Mt 18:13 *1768*
n in the wilderness, and go after ... Lk 15:4 *1768*
n just persons, which need no ... Lk 15:7 *1768*
but where are the *n* ... Lk 17:17 *1767*

NINETEEN

n years, and begat sons and ... Gen 11:25
n cities with their villages ... Josh 19:38
lacked of David's servants *n* men ... 2Sa 2:30

NINETEENTH

which is the *n* year of king ... 2Kin 25:8
The *n* to Pethahiah, the twentieth ... 1Chr 24:16
The *n* to Mallothi, he, his sons ... 1Chr 25:26
month, which was the *n* year of ... Jer 52:12

NINETY
And Enos lived *n* years, and begat Gen 5:9 8673
Mahalaleel were eight hundred *n* Gen 5:17 8673
he begat Noah five hundred *n* Gen 5:30 8673
And when Abram was *n* years old Gen 17:1 8673
that is *n* years old, bear Gen 17:17 8673
And Abraham was *n* years old Gen 17:24 8673
Now Eli was *n* and eight years old 1Sa 4:15 8673
their brethren, six hundred and *n* 1Chr 9:6 8673
children of Ater of Hezekiah, *n* Ezr 2:16 8673
The children of Gibbar, *n* Ezr 2:20 8673
servants, were three hundred *n* Ezr 2:58 8673
twelve bullocks for all Israel, *n* Ezr 8:35 8673
children of Ater of Hezekiah, *n* Neh 7:21 8673
The children of Gibeon, *n* Neh 7:25 8673
servants, were three hundred *n* Neh 7:60 8673
And there were *n* and six Jer 52:23 8673
the days, three hundred and *n* days Eze 4:5 8673
n days shalt thou eat thereof Eze 4:9 8673
and the length thereof *n* cubits Eze 41:12 8673
a thousand two hundred and *n* days Dan 12:11 8673
astray, doth he not leave the *n* Mt 18:12 *1768*
more of that sheep, than of the *n* Mt 18:13 *1768*
one of them, doth not leave the *n* Lk 15:4 *1768*
that repenteth, more than over *n* Lk 15:7 *1768*

NINEVE (*nen'-e-ve*) See NINEVEH, NINEVITES. *Same as Nineveh.*
The men of *N* shall rise up in the Lk 11:32 *3535*

NINEVEH (*nin'-e-veh*) See NINEVE. *Capital of Assyria.*
went forth Asshur, and builded *N* Gen 10:11 5210
And Resen between *N* and Calah Gen 10:12 5210
went and returned, and dwelt at *N* 2Kin 19:36 5210
went and returned, and dwelt at *N* Is 37:37 5210
Arise, go to *N*, that great city, Jonah 1:2 5210
Arise, go unto *N*, that great city Jonah 3:2 5210
So Jonah arose, and went unto *N* Jonah 3:3 5210
Now *N* was an exceeding great city Jonah 3:3 5210
days, and *N* shall be overthrown Jonah 3:4 5210
So the people of *N* believed God Jonah 3:5 5210
For word came unto the king of *N* Jonah 3:6 5210
published through *N* by the decree Jonah 3:7 5210
And should not I spare *N*, that Jonah 4:11 5210
The burden of *N* Nah 1:1 5210
But *N* is of old like a pool of Nah 2:8 5210
thee, and say, *N* is laid waste Nah 3:7 5210
will make *N* a desolation, and dry Zeph 2:13 5210
The men of *N* shall rise in Mt 12:41 *3536*

NINEVITES (*nin'-e-vites*) *Inhabitants of Nineveh.*
as Jonas was a sign unto the *N* Lk 11:30 *3536*

NINTH
in the *n* day of the month at even Lev 23:32 8672
yet of old fruit until the *n* year Lev 25:22 8671
On the *n* day Abidan the son of Num 7:60 8671
In the *n* year of Hoshea the king 2Kin 17:6 8671
that is the *n* year of Hoshea king 2Kin 18:10 8672
pass in the *n* year of his reign 2Kin 25:1 8671
on the *n* day of the fourth month 2Kin 25:3 8672
Johanan the eighth, Elzabad the *n* 1Chr 12:12 8671
The *n* to Jeshua, the tenth to 1Chr 24:11 8671
The *n* to Mattaniah, he, his sons, 1Chr 25:16 8671
The *n* captain for the *n* month 1Chr 27:12 8671
for the *n* month was Abiezer the 1Chr 27:12 8671
n year of his reign was diseased 2Chr 16:12 8672
It was the *n* month, on the Ezr 10:9 8671
king of Judah, in the *n* month Jer 36:9 8671
in the winterhouse in the *n* month Jer 36:22 8671
In the *n* year of Zedekiah king of Jer 39:1 8671
the *n* day of the month, the city Jer 39:2 8672
pass in the *n* year of his reign Jer 52:4 8671
in the *n* day of the month, the Jer 52:6 8672
Again in the *n* year, in the tenth Eze 24:1 8671
and twentieth day of the *n* month Hag 2:10 8671
and twentieth day of the *n* month Hag 2:18 8671
in the fourth day of the *n* month Zec 7:1 8671
sixth and *n* hour, and did likewise Mt 20:5 *1766*
over all the land unto the *n* hour Mt 27:45 *1766*
about the *n* hour Jesus cried with Mt 27:46 *1766*
the whole land until the *n* hour Mk 15:33 *1766*
at the *n* hour Jesus cried with a Mk 15:34 *1766*
all the earth until the *n* hour Lk 23:44 *1766*
hour of prayer, being the *n* hour Acts 3:1 *1766*
n hour of the day an angel of God Acts 10:3 *1766*
at the *n* hour I prayed in my Acts 10:30 *1766*
the *n*, a topaz Rev 21:20 *1766*

NISAN (*ni'-san*) See ABIB. *First month of the Hebrew year.*
And it came to pass in the month *N* Neh 2:1 5212
first month, that is, the month *N* Est 3:7 5212

NISROCH (*nis'-rok*) *An Assyrian god.*
in the house of *N* his god 2Kin 19:37 5268
in the house of *N* his god Is 37:38 5268

NITRE
weather, and as vinegar upon *n* Prov 25:20 5427
For though thou wash thee with *n* Jer 2:22 5427

NO
But the dove found *n* rest for the Gen 8:9 3808
the waters shall *n* more become a Gen 9:15 3808
she had *n* child Gen 11:30 369
unto Lot, Let there be *n* strife Gen 13:8 408
to me thou hast given *n* seed Gen 15:3 3808
Abram's wife bare him *n* children Gen 16:1 3808
That thou wilt do us *n* hurt Gen 26:29 3808
that she bare Jacob *n* children Gen 30:1 369
my daughters, *n* man is with us Gen 31:50 369
name shall be called *n* more Jacob Gen 32:28 3808
Shed *n* blood, but cast him into Gen 37:22 3808
and lay *n* hand upon him Gen 37:22 3808
empty, there was *n* water in it Gen 37:24 3808
whether it be thy son's coat or *n* Gen 37:32 3808
There was *n* harlot in this place Gen 38:21 3808
that there was *n* harlot in this Gen 38:22 3808
And he knew her again *n* more Gen 38:26 3808
there is *n* interpreter of it Gen 40:8 369
without thee shall *n* man lift up Gen 41:44 3808
men, thy servants are *n* spies Gen 42:11 3808
we are *n* spies Gen 42:31 3808
shall I know that ye are *n* spies Gen 42:34 3808
you, ye shall see my face *n* more Gen 44:23 3808
there stood *n* man with him, while Gen 45:1 3808
for thy servants have *n* pasture Gen 47:4 369
there was *n* bread in all the land Gen 47:13 369
when he saw that there was *n* man Ex 2:12 369
of Egypt will not let you go, *n* Ex 3:19 3808
Ye shall *n* more give the people Ex 5:7 3808
There is *n* straw given unto thy Ex 5:16 369
for there shall *n* straw be given Ex 5:18 3808
that *n* swarms of flies shall be Ex 8:22 1115
of Israel were, was there *n* hail Ex 9:26 3808
be *n* more mighty thunderings Ex 9:28 3808
you go, and ye shall stay *n* longer Ex 9:28 3808
there were *n* such locusts as they Ex 10:14 3808
to thyself, see my face *n* more Ex 10:28 3808
I will see thy face again *n* more Ex 10:29 3808
n manner of work shall be done in Ex 12:16 3808
Seven days shall there be *n* Ex 12:19 3808
There shall *n* stranger eat Ex 12:43 3808
for *n* uncircumcised person shall Ex 12:48 3808
there shall *n* leavened bread be Ex 13:3 3808
there shall *n* leavened bread be Ex 13:7 3808
there were *n* graves in Egypt Ex 14:11 369
see them again *n* more for ever Ex 14:13 3808
the wilderness, and found *n* water Ex 15:22 3808
they will walk in my law, or *n* Ex 16:4 3808
that gathered little had *n* lack Ex 16:18 3808
Let *n* man leave of it till the Ex 16:19 408
let *n* man go out of his place on Ex 16:29 408
there was *n* water for the people Ex 17:1 369
Thou shalt have *n* other gods Ex 20:3 3808
nation he shall have *n* power Ex 21:8 3808
her, and yet *n* mischief follow Ex 21:22 3808
there shall *n* blood be shed for Ex 22:2 369
or driven away, *n* man seeing it Ex 22:10 369
And thou shalt take *n* gift Ex 23:8 3808
make *n* mention of the name of Ex 23:13 3808
Thou shalt make *n* covenant with Ex 23:32 3808
Ye shall offer *n* strange incense Ex 30:9 3808
that there be *n* plague among them Ex 30:12 3808
and *n* man did put on him his Ex 33:4 3808
for there shall *n* man see me Ex 33:20 3808
n man shall come up with thee, Ex 34:3 3808
that will by *n* means clear the Ex 34:7 3808
thou shalt worship *n* other god Ex 34:14 3808
shalt make thee *n* molten gods Ex 34:17 3808
Ye shall kindle *n* fire throughout Ex 35:3 3808
N meat offering, which ye shall Lev 2:11 3808
for ye shall burn *n* leaven Lev 2:11 3808
he shall put *n* oil upon it Lev 5:11 3808
n sin offering, whereof any of Lev 6:30 3808
Ye shall eat *n* manner of fat, of Lev 7:23 3808
but ye shall in *n* wise eat of it Lev 7:24 3808
ye shall eat *n* manner of blood Lev 7:26 3808
Whatsoever hath *n* fins nor scales Lev 11:12 369
she shall touch *n* hallowed thing Lev 12:4 3808
there be *n* white hairs therein, Lev 13:21 369
there be *n* white hair in the Lev 13:26 369
it be *n* lower than the other skin Lev 13:26 369
that there is *n* black hair in it Lev 13:31 369
and there be in it *n* yellow hair Lev 13:32 3808
there shall be *n* man in the Lev 16:17 3808
do *n* work at all, whether it be Lev 16:29 3808
they shall *n* more offer their Lev 17:7 3808
N soul of you shall eat blood, Lev 17:12 3808
the blood of *n* manner of flesh Lev 17:14 3808
Ye shall do *n* unrighteousness in Lev 19:15 3808
Ye shall do *n* unrighteousness in Lev 19:35 3808
that there be *n* wickedness among Lev 20:14 3808
him, which hath had *n* husband Lev 21:3 3808
N man that hath a blemish of the Lev 21:21
There shall *n* stranger eat of the Lev 22:10 3808
have *n* child, and is returned unto Lev 22:13 369
but there shall *n* stranger eat Lev 22:13 3808
there shall be *n* blemish therein Lev 22:21 3808
ye shall do *n* work therein Lev 23:3 3808
ye shall do *n* servile work Lev 23:7
ye shall do *n* servile work Lev 23:8
ye shall do *n* servile work Lev 23:21
Ye shall do *n* servile work Lev 23:25
ye shall do *n* work in that same Lev 23:28 3808
Ye shall do *n* manner of work Lev 23:31 3808
ye shall do *n* servile work Lev 23:35
ye shall do *n* servile work Lev 23:36
of the villages which have *n* wall Lev 25:31 369
Take thou *n* usury of him, or Lev 25:36 408
Ye shall make you *n* idols nor Lev 26:1 3808
ye shall have *n* power to stand Lev 26:37 3808
n man shall sanctify it Lev 27:26 3808
Notwithstanding *n* devoted thing Lev 27:28
that there be *n* wrath upon the Num 1:53 3808
of Sinai, and they had *n* children Num 3:4 3808
But if the man have *n* kinsman to Num 5:8 369
there be *n* witness against her, Num 5:13 369
he shall pour *n* oil upon it Num 5:15 3808
If *n* man have lain with thee, and Num 5:19 3808
shall drink *n* vinegar of wine, or Num 6:3 3808
shall *n* razor come upon his head Num 6:5 3808
LORD he shall come at *n* dead body Num 6:6 3808
that there be *n* plague among the Num 8:19 3808
thereof, and shall serve *n* more Num 8:25 3808
the charge, and shall do *n* service Num 8:26 3808
by *n* means clearing the guilty, Num 14:18 3808
that *n* stranger, which is not of Num 16:40 3808
that there be *n* wrath any more Num 18:5 3808
Thou shalt have *n* inheritance in Num 18:20 3808
of Israel they have *n* inheritance Num 18:23 3808
they shall have *n* inheritance Num 18:24 3808
ye shall bear *n* sin by reason of Num 18:32 3808
spot, wherein is *n* blemish Num 19:2 369
which hath *n* covering bound upon Num 19:15 369
there was *n* water for the Num 20:2
it is *n* place of seed, or of figs Num 20:5 3808
for there is *n* bread, neither is Num 21:5 369
where was *n* way to turn either to Num 22:26 369
Surely there is *n* enchantment Num 23:23 3808
the son of Hepher had *n* sons Num 26:33 3808
because there was *n* inheritance Num 26:62 3808
in his own sin, and had *n* sons Num 27:3 3808
his family, because he hath *n* son Num 27:4 369
If a man die, and have *n* son Num 27:8 369
And if he have *n* daughter, then ye Num 27:9 369
And if he have *n* brethren, then ye Num 27:10 369
And if his father have *n* brethren Num 27:11 369
as sheep which have *n* shepherd Num 27:17 369
ye shall do *n* manner of servile Num 28:18 3808
ye shall do *n* servile work Num 28:25
ye shall do *n* servile work Num 28:26
ye shall do *n* servile work Num 29:1
ye shall do *n* servile work, and ye Num 29:12
ye shall do *n* servile work Num 29:35
where was *n* water for the people Num 33:14 3808
Moreover ye shall take *n* Num 35:31 3808
ye shall take *n* satisfaction for Num 35:32 3808
which in that day had *n* knowledge Deut 1:39 3808
not give you of their land, *n* Deut 2:5
speak *n* more unto me of this Deut 3:26 408
the words, but saw *n* similitude Deut 4:12 369
for ye saw *n* manner of similitude Deut 4:15 3808
and he added *n* more Deut 5:22 3808
thou shalt make *n* covenant with Deut 7:2 3808
eye shall have *n* pity upon them Deut 7:16 3808
there shall *n* man be able to Deut 7:24 3808
keep his commandments, or *n* Deut 8:2 3808
drought, where there was *n* water Deut 8:15 369
Wherefore Levi hath *n* part nor Deut 10:9 3808
heart, and be *n* more stiffnecked Deut 10:16 3808
the heaven, that there be *n* rain Deut 11:17 3808
There shall *n* man be able to Deut 11:25 3808
forasmuch as he hath *n* part nor Deut 12:12 369
fear, and shall do *n* more any such Deut 13:11 3808
for he hath *n* part nor Deut 14:27 369
(because he hath *n* part nor Deut 14:29 369
there shall be *n* poor among you Deut 15:4 3808
thou shalt do *n* work with the Deut 15:19 3808
Thou shalt eat *n* leavened bread Deut 16:3 3808
there shall be *n* leavened bread Deut 16:4 3808
thou shalt do *n* work therein Deut 16:8 3808
fear, and do *n* more presumptuously Deut 17:13 3808
henceforth return *n* more that way Deut 17:16 3808
shall have *n* part nor inheritance Deut 18:1 3808
have *n* inheritance among their Deut 18:2 3808
shall henceforth commit *n* more Deut 19:20 3808
if it will make *n* peace with thee Deut 20:12 3808
if thou have *n* delight in her, Deut 21:14 3808
the damsel *n* sin worthy of death Deut 22:26 369
that he see *n* unclean thing in Deut 23:14 3808
There shall be *n* whore of the Deut 23:17 3808
to vow, it shall be *n* sin in thee Deut 23:22 3808
she find *n* favour in his eyes Deut 24:1 3808
N man shall take the nether or Deut 24:6 3808
have *n* child, the wife of the Deut 25:5 369
n man shall fray them away Deut 28:26 369
and *n* man shall save thee Deut 28:29 369
there shall be *n* might in thine Deut 28:32 369
nations shalt thou find *n* ease Deut 28:65 3808
Thou shalt see it *n* more again Deut 28:68 3808
bondwomen, and *n* man shall buy you Deut 28:68 369
I can *n* more go out and come in Deut 31:2 3808
there was *n* strange god with him Deut 32:12 369
children in whom is *n* faith Deut 32:20 3808
am he, and there is *n* god with me Deut 32:39 369
but *n* man knoweth of his Deut 34:6 3808
they had *n* power to flee this way Josh 8:20 3808
over which *n* man hath lift up any Josh 8:31 3808
there was *n* day like that before Josh 10:14 3808
and that they might have *n* favour Josh 11:20 1115
therefore they gave *n* part unto Josh 14:4 3808
had *n* sons, but daughters Josh 17:3 3808
the Levites have *n* part among you Josh 18:7 369
ye have *n* part in the LORD Josh 22:25 369
Ye have *n* part in the LORD Josh 22:27 369
n man hath been able to stand Josh 23:9 3808
n more drive out any of these Josh 23:13 3808
ye shall make *n* league with the Judg 2:2 3808
that thou shalt say, *N* Judg 4:20 369
they took *n* gain of money Judg 5:19 3808
left *n* sustenance for Israel, Judg 6:4 3808
they lifted up their heads *n* more Judg 8:28 3808
I will deliver you *n* more Judg 10:13 3808
and she knew *n* man Judg 11:39 3808
n razor shall come on his head Judg 13:5 3808
now drink *n* wine nor strong drink Judg 13:7 408
LORD did *n* more appear to Manoah Judg 13:21 3808
And they spake unto him, saying, *N* Judg 15:13 3808
days there was *n* king in Israel Judg 17:6 369
days there was *n* king in Israel Judg 18:1 369
there was *n* magistrate in the Judg 18:7 369
had *n* business with any man Judg 18:7 369
a place where there is *n* want of Judg 18:10 369
And there was *n* deliverer, because Judg 18:28 369
they had *n* business with any man Judg 18:28 369
when there was *n* king in Israel Judg 19:1 369
for there was *n* man that took Judg 19:15 369
there is *n* man that receiveth me Judg 19:18 369
there is *n* want of any thing Judg 19:19 369
There was *n* such deed done nor Judg 19:30 3808
that had known *n* man by lying Judg 21:12 3808
days there was *n* king in Israel Judg 21:25 369

but Hannah had *n* children	1Sa 1:2	369
there shall *n* razor come upon his	1Sa 1:11	3808
And Hannah answered and said, *N*	1Sa 1:15	3808
and her countenance was *n* more sad	1Sa 1:18	3808
Talk *n* more so exceeding proudly	1Sa 2:3	408
by strength shall *n* man prevail	1Sa 2:9	3808
for it is *n* good report that I	1Sa 2:24	3808
there was *n* open vision	1Sa 3:1	369
on which there hath come *n* yoke	1Sa 6:7	3808
they came *n* more into the coast	1Sa 7:13	3808
we saw that they were *n* where	1Sa 10:14	369
him, and brought him *n* presents	1Sa 10:27	3808
if there be *n* man to save us, we	1Sa 11:3	369
Now there was *n* smith found	1Sa 13:19	3808
for there is *n* restraint to the	1Sa 14:6	369
but *n* man put his hand to his	1Sa 14:26	369
Samuel came *n* more to see Saul	1Sa 15:35	3808
Let *n* man's heart fail because of	1Sa 17:32	408
but there was *n* sword in the hand	1Sa 17:50	369
would let him go *n* more home to	1Sa 18:2	3808
n, not when the LORD hath cut off	1Sa 20:15	
there is peace to thee, and *n* hurt	1Sa 20:21	369
did eat *n* meat the second day of	1Sa 20:34	3808
thou alone, and *n* man with thee	1Sa 21:1	369
Let *n* man know any thing of the	1Sa 21:2	408
There is *n* common bread under	1Sa 21:4	369
for there was *n* bread there but	1Sa 21:6	3808
for there is *n* other save that	1Sa 21:9	369
this shall be *n* grief unto thee	1Sa 25:31	3808
n man saw it, nor knew it,	1Sa 26:12	369
for I will *n* more do thee harm,	1Sa 26:21	3808
he sought *n* more again for him	1Sa 27:4	3808
there shall *n* punishment happen	1Sa 28:10	518
from me, and answereth me *n* more	1Sa 28:15	3808
there was *n* strength in him	1Sa 28:20	3808
for he had eaten *n* bread all the	1Sa 28:20	3808
I have found *n* fault in him since	1Sa 29:3	3808
until they had *n* more power to	1Sa 30:4	369
for he had eaten *n* bread, nor	1Sa 30:12	3808
of Gilboa, let there be *n* dew	2Sa 1:21	408
and pursued after Israel *n* more	2Sa 2:28	3808
n child unto the day of her death	2Sa 6:23	3808
of their own, and move *n* more	2Sa 7:10	3808
thing, and because he had *n* pity	2Sa 12:6	3808
for *n* such thing ought to be done	2Sa 13:12	3808
said unto him, There is *n* cause	2Sa 13:16	408
head there was *n* blemish in him	2Sa 14:25	3808
but there is *n* man deputed of the	2Sa 15:3	369
say, I have *n* delight in thee	2Sa 15:26	3808
for there is *n* matter hid from	2Sa 18:13	3808
I have *n* son to keep my name in	2Sa 18:18	369
day thou shalt bear *n* tidings	2Sa 18:20	3808
that thou hast *n* tidings ready	2Sa 18:22	369
We have *n* part in David, neither	2Sa 20:1	369
But Amasa took *n* heed to the	2Sa 20:10	3808
We will have *n* silver nor gold of	2Sa 21:4	369
Thou shalt go *n* more out with us	2Sa 21:17	3808
with clothes, but he gat *n* heat	1Kin 1:1	3808
because there was *n* house built	1Kin 3:2	3808
there was *n* stranger with us in	1Kin 3:18	369
And this said, *N*	1Kin 3:22	3808
child, and in *n* wise slay it	1Kin 3:26	408
child, and in *n* wise slay it	1Kin 3:27	3808
there was *n* stone seen	1Kin 6:18	369
I chose *n* city out of all the	1Kin 8:16	3808
there is *n* God like thee, in	1Kin 8:23	369
is shut up, and there is *n* rain	1Kin 8:35	3808
(for there is *n* man that sinneth	1Kin 8:46	369
Israel did Solomon make *n* bondmen	1Kin 9:22	3808
there was *n* more spirit in her	1Kin 10:5	3808
there came *n* more such abundance	1Kin 10:10	3808
there came *n* such almug trees,	1Kin 10:12	3808
Eat *n* bread, nor drink water, nor	1Kin 13:9	3808
Thou shalt eat *n* bread nor drink	1Kin 13:17	3808
Eat *n* bread, and drink *n* water	1Kin 13:22	408
Eat *n* bread, and drink *n* water	1Kin 13:22	408
there had been *n* rain in the land	1Kin 17:7	3808
that there was *n* breath left in	1Kin 17:17	3808
there is *n* nation or kingdom,	1Kin 18:10	518
it on wood, and put *n* fire under	1Kin 18:23	3808
it on wood, and put *n* fire under	1Kin 18:23	3808
your gods, but put *n* fire under	1Kin 18:25	3808
But there was *n* voice, nor any	1Kin 18:26	369
his face, and would eat *n* bread	1Kin 21:4	3808
so sad, that thou eatest *n* bread	1Kin 21:5	369
LORD said, These have *n* master	1Kin 22:17	3808
prophesy *n* good concerning me	1Kin 22:18	3808
There was then *n* king in Edom	1Kin 22:47	369
is it not because there is *n* God	2Kin 1:16	369
because he had *n* son	2Kin 1:17	3808
And he saw him *n* more	2Kin 2:12	3808
there was *n* water for the host,	2Kin 3:9	3808
answered, Verily she hath *n* child	2Kin 4:14	369
there was *n* harm in the pot	2Kin 4:41	3808
there is *n* God in all the earth	2Kin 5:15	369
said, Thy servant went *n* whither	2Kin 5:25	3808
So the bands of Syria came *n* more	2Kin 6:23	3808
behold, there was *n* man there	2Kin 7:5	369
and, behold, there was *n* man there	2Kin 7:10	369
but they found *n* more of her than	2Kin 9:35	3808
But Jehu took *n* heed to walk in	2Kin 10:31	3808
now therefore receive *n* more	2Kin 12:7	408
n more money of the people	2Kin 12:8	1115
brought *n* present to the king of	2Kin 17:4	3808
for they were *n* gods, but the	2Kin 19:18	3808
Howbeit there was *n* reckoning	2Kin 22:7	3808
that *n* man might make his son or	2Kin 23:10	1115
let *n* man move his bones	2Kin 23:18	408
him was there *n* king before him	2Kin 23:25	3808
there was *n* bread for the people	2Kin 25:3	3808
Now Sheshan had *n* sons, but	1Chr 2:34	3808
seeing there is *n* wrong in mine	1Chr 12:17	3808
He suffered *n* man to do them	1Chr 16:21	3808
and do my prophets *n* harm	1Chr 16:22	408
place, and shall be moved *n* more	1Chr 17:9	3808
and the iron, there is *n* number	1Chr 22:16	369
had *n* sons, but daughters	1Chr 23:22	3808
they shall *n* more carry the	1Chr 23:26	369
their father, and had *n* children	1Chr 24:2	3808
came Eleazar, who had *n* sons	1Chr 24:28	3808
n city among all the tribes of	2Chr 6:5	3808
there is *n* God like thee in the	2Chr 6:14	369
is shut up, and there is *n* rain	2Chr 6:26	3808
(for there is *n* man which sinneth	2Chr 6:36	369
up heaven that there be *n* rain	2Chr 7:13	3808
make *n* servants for his work	2Chr 8:9	3808
there was *n* more spirit in her	2Chr 9:4	3808
a priest of them that are *n* gods	2Chr 13:9	3808
he had *n* war in those years	2Chr 14:6	369
or with them that have *n* power	2Chr 14:11	369
in those times there was *n* peace	2Chr 15:5	369
there was *n* more war unto the	2Chr 15:19	3808
so that they made *n* war against	2Chr 17:10	3808
as sheep that have *n* shepherd	2Chr 18:16	369
LORD said, These have *n* master	2Chr 18:16	3808
for there is *n* iniquity with the	2Chr 19:7	369
for we have *n* might against this	2Chr 20:12	369
his people made *n* burning for him	2Chr 21:19	3808
So the house of Ahaziah had *n*	2Chr 22:9	369
for *n* god of any nation or	2Chr 32:15	3808
there was *n* passover like to that	2Chr 35:18	3808
people, till there was *n* remedy	2Chr 36:16	369
had *n* compassion upon young man	2Chr 36:17	3808
by this means thou shalt have *n*	Ezr 4:16	3809
should be *n* remnant nor escaping	Ezr 9:14	369
came thither, he did eat *n* bread	Ezr 10:6	3808
but there was *n* place for the	Neh 2:14	369
that we be *n* more a reproach	Neh 2:17	3808
but ye have *n* portion, nor right,	Neh 2:20	369
that there was *n* breach left	Neh 6:1	3808
There are *n* such things done as	Neh 6:8	3808
that there should *n* burden be	Neh 13:19	3808
came they *n* more on the sabbath	Neh 13:21	3808
nations was there *n* king like him	Neh 13:26	3808
That Vashti come *n* more before	Est 1:19	3808
she came in unto the king *n* more	Est 2:14	3808
Esther the queen did let *n* man	Est 5:12	3808
king's ring, may *n* man reverse	Est 8:8	369
n man could withstand them	Est 9:2	3808
let *n* joyful voice come therein	Job 3:7	408
he put *n* trust in his servants	Job 4:18	3808
there shall *n* evil touch thee	Job 5:19	3808
For now ye are *n* thing	Job 6:21	3808
mine eye shall *n* more see good	Job 7:7	3808
hath seen me shall see me *n* more	Job 7:8	3808
to the grave shall come up *n* more	Job 7:9	3808
He shall return *n* more to his	Job 7:10	3808
they flee away, they see *n* good	Job 9:25	3808
the ghost, and *n* eye had seen me	Job 10:18	3808
shall *n* man make thee ashamed	Job 11:3	369
N doubt but ye are the people, and	Job 12:2	551
a man, and there can be *n* opening	Job 12:14	3808
a wilderness where there is *n* way	Job 12:24	3808
ye are all physicians of *n* value	Job 13:4	457
till the heavens be *n* more	Job 14:12	1115
wherewith he can do *n* good	Job 15:3	3808
he putteth *n* trust in his saints	Job 15:15	3808
n stranger passed among them	Job 15:19	3808
in houses which *n* man inhabiteth	Job 15:28	3808
blood, and let my cry have *n* place	Job 16:18	408
he shall have *n* name in the	Job 18:17	3808
aloud, but there is *n* judgment	Job 19:7	369
servant, and he gave me *n* answer	Job 19:16	3808
saw him shall see him *n* more	Job 20:9	3808
therefore shall *n* man look for	Job 20:21	3808
N; but he would	Job 23:6	3808
that they have *n* covering in the	Job 24:7	369
saying, *N* eye shall see me	Job 24:15	3808
he shall be *n* more remembered	Job 24:20	3808
up, and *n* man is sure of life	Job 24:22	3808
thou the arm that hath *n* strength	Job 26:2	3808
counseled him that hath *n* wisdom	Job 26:3	3808
and destruction hath *n* covering	Job 26:6	369
is a path which *n* fowl knoweth	Job 28:7	3808
N mention shall be made of coral,	Job 28:18	3808
my calamity, they have *n* helper	Job 30:13	3808
and my sinews take *n* rest	Job 30:17	3808
because they had found *n* answer	Job 32:3	3808
n answer in the mouth of these	Job 32:5	369
were amazed, they answered *n* more	Job 32:15	3808
stood still, and answered *n* more	Job 32:16	3808
is as wine which hath *n* vent	Job 32:19	3808
There is *n* darkness, nor shadow	Job 34:22	369
done iniquity, I will do *n* more	Job 34:32	3808
where there is *n* straitness	Job 36:16	3808
n, not gold, nor all the forces	Job 36:19	3808
shalt thou come, but *n* further	Job 38:11	3808
rain on the earth, where *n* man is	Job 38:26	3808
wherein there is *n* man	Job 38:26	3808
but I will proceed *n* further	Job 40:5	3808
remember the battle, do *n* more	Job 41:8	408
that *n* air can come between them	Job 41:16	3808
that *n* thought can be withholden	Job 42:2	3808
in all the land were *n* women	Job 42:15	3808
There is *n* help for him in God	Ps 3:2	369
For there is *n* faithfulness in	Ps 5:9	369
there is *n* remembrance of thee	Ps 6:5	369
of the earth may *n* more oppress	Ps 10:18	1077
said in his heart, There is *n* God	Ps 14:1	369
there is none that doeth good, *n*	Ps 14:3	
workers of iniquity *n* knowledge	Ps 14:4	3808
There is *n* speech nor language,	Ps 19:3	369
But I am a worm, and *n* man	Ps 22:6	3808
of death, I will fear *n* evil	Ps 23:4	3808
in whose spirit there is *n* guile	Ps 32:2	369
which have *n* understanding	Ps 32:9	369
There is *n* king saved by the	Ps 33:16	369
for there is *n* want to them that	Ps 34:9	369
that there is *n* fear of God	Ps 36:1	369
There is *n* soundness in my flesh	Ps 38:3	369
there is *n* soundness in my flesh	Ps 38:7	369
and in whose mouth are *n* reproofs	Ps 38:14	369
before I go hence, and be *n* more	Ps 39:13	369
make *n* tarrying, O my God	Ps 40:17	408
he lieth he shall rise up *n* more	Ps 41:8	3808
I will take *n* bullock out of thy	Ps 50:9	3808
said in his heart, There is *n* God	Ps 53:1	369
there is none that doeth good, *n*	Ps 53:3	
workers of iniquity *n* knowledge	Ps 53:4	3808
in great fear, where *n* fear was	Ps 53:5	3808
Because they have *n* changes	Ps 55:19	369
and thirsty land, where *n* water is	Ps 63:1	1097
mire, where there is *n* standing	Ps 69:2	369
O LORD, make *n* tarrying	Ps 70:5	408
also, and him that hath *n* helper	Ps 72:12	369
For there are *n* bands in their	Ps 73:4	369
there is *n* more any prophet	Ps 74:9	369
and will he be favourable *n* more	Ps 77:7	3808
their widows made *n* lamentation	Ps 78:64	3808
There shall *n* strange god be in	Ps 81:9	3808
may be *n* more in remembrance	Ps 83:4	3808
n good thing will he withhold	Ps 84:11	3808
am as a man that hath *n* strength	Ps 88:4	369
whom thou rememberest *n* more	Ps 88:5	3808
There shall *n* evil befall thee,	Ps 91:10	3808
there is *n* unrighteousness in him	Ps 92:15	3808
I will set *n* wicked thing before	Ps 101:3	3808
and thy years shall have *n* end	Ps 102:27	3808
thereof shall know it *n* more	Ps 103:16	3808
and let the wicked be *n* more	Ps 104:35	369
He suffered *n* man to do them	Ps 105:14	3808
and do my prophets *n* harm	Ps 105:15	408
they found *n* city to dwell in	Ps 107:4	3808
wilderness, where there is *n* way	Ps 107:40	3808
They also do *n* iniquity	Ps 119:3	3808
but there was *n* man that would	Ps 142:4	369
n man cared for my soul	Ps 142:4	369
for in thy sight shall *n* man	Ps 143:2	3808
that there be *n* breaking in	Ps 144:14	369
that there be *n* complaining in	Ps 144:14	369
of man, in whom there is *n* help	Ps 146:3	369
out my hand, and *n* man regarded	Prov 1:24	369
if he have done thee *n* harm	Prov 3:30	3808
Which having *n* guide, overseer,	Prov 6:7	369
When there were *n* depths, I was	Prov 8:24	369
when there were *n* fountains	Prov 8:24	369
he addeth *n* sorrow with it	Prov 10:22	3808
passeth, so is the wicked *n* more	Prov 10:25	369
Where *n* counsel is, the people	Prov 11:14	369
There shall *n* evil happen to the	Prov 12:21	3808
pathway thereof there is *n* death	Prov 12:28	408
Where *n* oxen are, the crib is	Prov 14:4	369
seeing he hath *n* heart to it	Prov 17:16	369
a froward heart findeth *n* good	Prov 17:20	3808
the father of a fool hath *n* joy	Prov 17:21	3808
A fool hath *n* delight in	Prov 18:2	3808
findeth *n* favour in his eyes	Prov 21:10	3808
There is *n* wisdom nor	Prov 21:30	369
Make *n* friendship with an angry	Prov 22:24	408
For there shall be *n* reward to	Prov 24:20	3808
He that hath *n* rule over his own	Prov 25:28	369
Where *n* wood is, there the fire	Prov 26:20	657
so where there is *n* talebearer	Prov 26:20	369
wicked flee when *n* man pursueth	Prov 28:1	369
rain which leaveth *n* food	Prov 28:3	369
let *n* man stay him	Prov 28:17	408
and saith, It is *n* transgression	Prov 28:24	369
he rage or laugh, there is *n* rest	Prov 29:9	369
Where there is *n* vision, the	Prov 29:18	369
saith, I have done *n* wickedness	Prov 30:20	3808
The locusts have *n* king, yet go	Prov 30:27	369
against whom there is *n* rising up	Prov 30:31	510
and remember his misery *n* more	Prov 31:7	3808
he shall have *n* need of spoil	Prov 31:11	3808
there is *n* new thing under the	Eccl 1:9	369
There is *n* remembrance of former	Eccl 1:11	369
there was *n* profit under the sun	Eccl 2:11	369
For there is *n* remembrance of the	Eccl 2:16	369
so that *n* man can find out the	Eccl 3:11	1097
know that there is *n* good in them	Eccl 3:12	369
so that a man hath *n* preeminence	Eccl 3:19	369
and they had *n* comforter	Eccl 4:1	369
but they had *n* comforter	Eccl 4:1	369
yet is there *n* end of all his	Eccl 4:8	369
who will *n* more be admonished	Eccl 4:13	3808
There is *n* end of all the people,	Eccl 4:16	369
for he hath *n* pleasure in fools	Eccl 5:4	369
and also that he have *n* burial	Eccl 6:3	3808
told, yet hath he seen *n* good	Eccl 6:6	3808
Also take *n* heed unto all words	Eccl 7:21	808
shall feel *n* evil thing	Eccl 8:5	3808
There is *n* man that hath power	Eccl 8:8	369
there is *n* discharge in that war	Eccl 8:8	369
because a man hath *n* better thing	Eccl 8:15	369
n man knoweth either love or	Eccl 9:1	369
and let thy head lack *n* ointment	Eccl 9:8	408
for there is *n* work, nor device,	Eccl 9:10	369
yet *n* man remembered that same	Eccl 9:15	3808
and a babbler is *n* better	Eccl 10:11	369
the king, *n*, not in thy thought	Eccl 10:20	408
I have *n* pleasure in them	Eccl 12:1	369
making many books there is *n* end	Eccl 12:12	369
there is *n* spot in thee	Song 4:7	369
him, but he gave me *n* answer	Song 5:6	3808
sister, and she hath *n* breasts	Song 8:8	369
head there is *n* soundness in it	Is 1:6	369
Bring *n* more vain oblations	Is 1:13	3808
and as a garden that hath *n* water	Is 1:30	369
that they rain *n* rain upon it	Is 5:6	
to field, till there be *n* place	Is 5:8	675
because they have *n* knowledge	Is 5:13	1097
because there is *n* light in them	Is 8:20	369

and peace there shall be *n* end	Is 9:7	369
have *n* joy in their young men	Is 9:17	3808
n man shall spare his brother	Is 9:19	3808
up itself, as if it were *n* wood	Is 10:15	3808
shall *n* more again stay upon him	Is 10:20	3808
as a sheep that *n* man taketh up	Is 13:14	369
they shall have *n* pity on the	Is 13:18	3808
n feller is come up against us	Is 14:8	3808
faileth, there is *n* green thing	Is 15:6	3808
there shall be *n* singing, neither	Is 16:10	3808
tread out *n* wine in their presses	Is 16:10	3808
be driven away, and be *n* more	Is 19:7	369
waste, so that there is *n* house	Is 23:1	
there is *n* house, *n* entering in	Is 23:1	
there is *n* more strength	Is 23:10	369
Thou shalt *n* more rejoice, O thou	Is 23:12	3808
there also shalt thou have *n* rest	Is 23:12	3808
shut up, that *n* man may come in	Is 24:10	
palace of strangers to be *n* city	Is 25:2	
shall *n* more cover her slain	Is 26:21	3808
it is a people of *n* understanding	Is 27:11	3808
them will shew them *n* favour	Is 27:11	3808
so that there is *n* place clean	Is 28:8	1097
framed it, He had *n* understanding	Is 29:16	3808
help in vain, and to *n* purpose	Is 30:7	7385
But ye said, *N*	Is 30:16	3808
thou shalt weep *n* more	Is 30:19	3808
shall be *n* more called liberal	Is 32:5	3808
the cities, he regardeth *n* man	Is 33:8	3808
shall go *n* galley with oars	Is 33:21	1077
n one of these shall fail, none	Is 34:16	3808
N lion shall be there, nor any	Is 35:9	3808
for they were *n* gods, but the	Is 37:19	3808
I shall behold man *n* more with	Is 38:11	3808
n oblation chooseth a tree that	Is 40:20	3808
there is *n* searching of his	Is 40:28	369
to them that have *n* might he	Is 40:29	369
For I beheld, and there was *n* man	Is 41:28	369
there was *n* counsellor, that,	Is 41:28	369
before me there was *n* God formed	Is 43:10	3808
and beside me there is *n* saviour	Is 43:11	369
when there was *n* strange god	Is 43:12	369
Thou hast bought me *n* sweet cane	Is 43:24	3808
and beside me there is *n* God	Is 44:6	369
yea, there is *n* God	Is 44:8	369
he drinketh *n* water, and is faint	Is 44:12	3808
else, there is *n* God beside me	Is 45:5	369
or thy work, He hath *n* hands	Is 45:9	369
is none else, there is *n* God	Is 45:14	657
they have *n* knowledge that set up	Is 45:20	3808
there is *n* God else beside me	Is 45:21	369
there is *n* throne, O daughter of	Is 47:1	369
for thou shalt *n* more be called	Is 47:1	3808
for thou shalt *n* more be called	Is 47:5	3808
thou didst shew them *n* mercy	Is 47:6	3808
There is *n* peace, saith the LORD,	Is 48:22	369
when I came, was there *n* man	Is 50:2	369
or have I *n* power to deliver	Is 50:2	369
because there is *n* water	Is 50:2	369
in darkness, and hath *n* light	Is 50:10	369
thou shalt *n* more drink it again	Is 51:22	3808
shall *n* more come into thee the	Is 52:1	3808
thence, touch *n* unclean thing	Is 52:11	408
he hath *n* form nor comeliness	Is 53:2	3808
there is *n* beauty that we should	Is 53:2	3808
because he had done *n* violence	Is 53:9	3808
should *n* more go over the earth	Is 54:9	
N weapon that is formed against	Is 54:17	3808
waters, and he that hath *n* money	Is 55:1	369
and *n* man layeth it to heart	Is 57:1	369
saidst thou not, There is *n* hope	Is 57:10	
There is *n* peace, saith my God,	Is 57:21	369
soul, and thou takest *n* knowledge	Is 58:3	3808
there is *n* judgment in their	Is 59:8	369
and we grope as if we had *n* eyes	Is 59:10	369
him that there was *n* judgment	Is 59:15	369
And he saw that there was *n* man	Is 59:16	369
that there was *n* intercessor	Is 59:16	369
so that *n* man went through thee,	Is 60:15	369
Violence shall *n* more be heard in	Is 60:18	3808
The sun shall be *n* more thy light	Is 60:19	3808
Thy sun shall *n* more go down	Is 60:20	3808
Thou shalt *n* more be termed	Is 62:4	3808
And give him *n* rest, till he	Is 62:7	408
Surely I will *n* more give thy	Is 62:8	518
shall be *n* more heard in her	Is 65:19	3808
There shall be *n* more thence an	Is 65:20	3808
a land that *n* man passed through	Jer 2:6	3808
through, and where *n* man dwelt	Jer 2:6	3808
their gods, which are yet *n* gods	Jer 2:11	3808
cisterns, that can hold *n* water	Jer 2:13	3808
but thou saidst, There is *n* hope	Jer 2:25	
n; for I have loved	Jer 2:25	3808
they received *n* correction	Jer 2:30	3808
we will come *n* more unto thee	Jer 2:31	3808
and there hath been *n* latter rain	Jer 3:3	3808
the LORD, they shall say *n* more	Jer 3:16	3808
to do good they have *n* knowledge	Jer 4:22	3808
the heavens, and they had *n* light	Jer 4:23	369
I beheld, and, lo, there was *n* man	Jer 4:25	369
and sworn by them that are *n* gods	Jer 5:7	3808
they have *n* delight in it	Jer 6:10	3808
when there is *n* peace	Jer 6:14	369
they are cruel, and have *n* mercy	Jer 6:23	3808
that it shall *n* more be called	Jer 7:32	3808
in Tophet, till there be *n* place	Jer 7:32	369
n man repented him of his	Jer 8:6	369
when there is *n* peace	Jer 8:11	369
there shall be *n* grapes on the	Jer 8:13	369
looked for peace, but *n* good came	Jer 8:15	369
Is there *n* balm in Gilead	Jer 8:22	369
is there *n* physician there	Jer 8:22	369
there is *n* breath in them	Jer 10:14	3808
his name may be *n* more remembered	Jer 11:19	3808
there shall be *n* remnant of them	Jer 11:23	3808
because *n* man layeth it to heart	Jer 12:11	369
n flesh shall have peace	Jer 12:12	369
to the pits, and found *n* water	Jer 14:3	3808
for there was *n* rain in the earth	Jer 14:4	3808
it, because there was *n* grass	Jer 14:5	3808
fail, because there was *n* grass	Jer 14:6	369
there is *n* healing for us	Jer 14:19	369
for peace, and there is *n* good	Jer 14:19	369
that it shall *n* more be said	Jer 16:14	3808
things wherein there is *n* profit	Jer 16:19	369
unto himself, and they are *n* gods	Jer 16:20	3808
bear *n* burden on the sabbath day,	Jer 17:21	408
to bring in *n* burden through the	Jer 17:24	1115
sabbath day, to do *n* work therein	Jer 17:24	1115
And they said, There is *n* hope	Jer 18:12	
shall *n* more be called Tophet	Jer 19:6	3808
till there be *n* place to bury	Jer 19:11	369
do *n* wrong, do *n* violence to the	Jer 22:3	408
do *n* violence to the stranger,	Jer 22:3	408
for he shall return *n* more	Jer 22:10	3808
and shall see this land *n* more	Jer 22:12	3808
he a vessel wherein is *n* pleasure	Jer 22:28	363
for *n* man of his seed shall	Jer 22:30	3808
and they shall fear *n* more	Jer 23:4	3808
LORD, that they shall *n* more say	Jer 23:7	3808
N evil shall come upon you	Jer 23:17	3808
the LORD shall ye mention *n* more	Jer 23:36	3808
and I will do you *n* hurt	Jer 25:6	3808
and spue, and fall, and rise *n* more	Jer 25:27	3808
shall have *n* way to flee, nor the	Jer 25:35	4480
strangers shall *n* more serve	Jer 30:8	3808
thou hast *n* healing medicines	Jer 30:13	369
is Zion, whom *n* man seeketh after	Jer 30:17	369
those days they shall say *n* more	Jer 31:29	3808
they shall teach *n* more every man	Jer 31:34	3808
I will remember their sin *n* more	Jer 31:34	3808
that they should be *n* more a	Jer 33:24	
they said, We will drink *n* wine	Jer 35:6	3808
us, saying, Ye shall drink *n* wine	Jer 35:6	3808
to drink *n* wine all our days, we,	Jer 35:8	1115
let *n* man know where ye be	Jer 36:19	408
in the dungeon there was *n* water	Jer 38:6	369
for there is *n* more bread in the	Jer 38:9	369
Let *n* man know of these words, and	Jer 38:24	408
well to him, and do him *n* harm	Jer 39:12	408
Nethaniah, and *n* man shall know it	Jer 40:15	3808
slain Gedaliah, and *n* man knew it,	Jer 41:4	3808
Saying, *N*	Jer 42:14	3808
Egypt, where we shall see *n* war	Jer 42:14	3808
and ye shall see this place *n* more	Jer 42:18	3808
and *n* man dwelleth therein,	Jer 44:2	369
to burn *n* incense unto other gods	Jer 44:5	1115
and were well, and saw *n* evil	Jer 44:17	3808
that the LORD could *n* longer bear	Jer 44:22	3808
that my name shall *n* more be	Jer 44:26	518
in my sighing, and I find *n* rest	Jer 45:3	3808
There shall be *n* more praise of	Jer 48:2	369
city, and *n* city shall escape	Jer 48:8	3808
shouting shall be *n* shouting	Jer 48:33	3808
a vessel wherein is *n* pleasure	Jer 48:38	369
Hath Israel *n* sons	Jer 49:1	369
hath he *n* heir	Jer 49:1	369
Is wisdom *n* more in Teman	Jer 49:7	369
n man shall abide there, neither	Jer 49:18	3808
there shall *n* man abide there,	Jer 49:33	3808
there shall be *n* nation whither	Jer 49:36	3808
bow, shoot at her, spare *n* arrows	Jer 50:14	408
it shall be *n* more inhabited for	Jer 50:39	3808
so shall *n* man abide there,	Jer 50:40	3808
there is *n* breath in them	Jer 51:17	3808
a land wherein *n* man dwelleth	Jer 51:43	3808
so that there was *n* bread for the	Jer 52:6	3808
the heathen, she findeth *n* rest	Lam 1:3	3808
like harts that find *n* pasture	Lam 1:6	3808
she had *n* comforter	Lam 1:9	369
the law is *n* more	Lam 2:9	369
also find *n* vision from the LORD	Lam 2:9	3808
give thyself *n* rest	Lam 2:18	408
n man breaketh it unto them	Lam 4:4	369
moment, and *n* hands stayed on her	Lam 4:6	3808
They shall *n* more sojourn there	Lam 4:15	3808
he will *n* more regard them	Lam 4:16	3808
he will *n* more carry thee away	Lam 4:22	3808
we labour, and have *n* rest	Lam 5:5	3808
they shall *n* more use it as a	Eze 12:23	3808
For there shall be *n* more any	Eze 12:24	3808
it shall be *n* more prolonged	Eze 12:25	3808
and there was *n* peace	Eze 13:10	369
say unto you, The wall is *n* more	Eze 13:15	369
for her, and there is *n* peace	Eze 13:16	369
they shall be *n* more in your hand	Eze 13:21	3808
ye shall see *n* more vanity	Eze 13:23	3808
may go *n* more astray from me	Eze 14:11	3808
that *n* man may pass through	Eze 14:15	1097
was whole, it was meet for *n* work	Eze 15:5	3808
n reward is given unto thee,	Eze 16:34	3808
also shalt give *n* hire any more	Eze 16:41	3808
be quiet, and will be *n* more angry	Eze 16:42	3808
For I have *n* pleasure in the	Eze 18:32	3808
that his voice should *n* more be	Eze 19:9	3808
so that she hath *n* strong rod to	Eze 19:14	3808
holy name *n* more with your gifts	Eze 20:39	3808
it shall be *n* more, saith the	Eze 21:13	3808
and it shall be *n* more, until he	Eze 21:27	3808
thou shalt be *n* more remembered	Eze 21:32	3808
they have put *n* difference	Eze 22:26	3808
let *n* lot fall upon it	Eze 24:6	3808
make *n* mourning for the dead,	Eze 24:17	3808
shalt speak, and be *n* more dumb	Eze 24:27	3808
thy harps shall be *n* more heard	Eze 26:13	3808
thou shalt be built *n* more	Eze 26:14	3808
a terror, and thou shalt be *n* more	Eze 26:21	369
there is *n* secret that they can	Eze 28:3	3808
n God, in the hand of him that	Eze 28:9	3808
there shall be *n* more a pricking	Eze 28:24	3808
N foot of man shall pass through	Eze 29:11	3808
that they shall *n* more rule over	Eze 29:15	3808
it shall be *n* more the confidence	Eze 29:16	3808
yet had he *n* wages, nor his army,	Eze 29:18	3808
there shall be *n* more a prince of	Eze 30:13	3808
I have *n* pleasure in the death of	Eze 33:11	518
was opened, and I was *n* more dumb	Eze 33:22	3808
because there is *n* shepherd	Eze 34:5	1097
because there was *n* shepherd	Eze 34:8	369
they shall *n* more be a prey	Eze 34:22	3808
they shall *n* more be a prey to	Eze 34:28	3808
they shall be *n* more consumed	Eze 34:29	3808
thou shalt *n* more henceforth	Eze 36:12	3808
thou shalt devour men *n* more	Eze 36:14	3808
it, and lay *n* famine upon you	Eze 36:29	3808
that ye shall receive *n* more	Eze 36:30	3808
but there was *n* breath in them	Eze 37:8	369
they shall be *n* more two nations,	Eze 37:22	3808
take *n* wood out of the field	Eze 39:10	3808
the house of Israel *n* more defile	Eze 43:7	3808
n man shall enter in by it	Eze 44:2	3808
N stranger, uncircumcised in	Eze 44:9	3808
n wool shall come upon them,	Eze 44:17	3808
they shall come at *n* dead person	Eze 44:25	3808
sister that hath had *n* husband	Eze 44:25	3808
ye shall give them *n* possession	Eze 44:28	3808
my princes shall *n* more oppress	Eze 45:8	3808
Children in whom was *n* blemish	Dan 1:4	369
therefore there is *n* king	Dan 2:10	
that *n* place was found for them	Dan 2:35	
of the fire, and they have *n* hurt	Dan 3:25	3809
whose bodies the fire had *n* power	Dan 3:27	3809
because there is *n* other God that	Dan 3:29	3809
n secret troubleth thee, tell me	Dan 4:9	
and the king should have *n* damage	Dan 6:2	3809
That *n* decree nor statute which	Dan 6:15	
thee, O king, have I done *n* hurt	Dan 6:22	3809
n manner of hurt was found upon	Dan 6:23	
so that *n* beasts might stand	Dan 8:4	3808
there was *n* power in the ram to	Dan 8:7	3808
I ate *n* pleasant bread, neither	Dan 10:3	3808
there remained *n* strength in me	Dan 10:8	3808
and I retained *n* strength	Dan 10:8	3808
me, and I have retained *n* strength	Dan 10:16	3808
there remained *n* strength in me	Dan 10:17	3808
for I will *n* more have mercy upon	Hos 1:6	3808
and shalt call me *n* more Baali	Hos 2:16	3808
they shall *n* more be remembered	Hos 2:17	3808
land, because there is *n* truth	Hos 4:1	369
Yet let *n* man strive, nor reprove	Hos 4:4	408
that thou shalt be *n* priest to me	Hos 4:6	
it hath *n* stalk	Hos 8:7	369
the bud shall yield *n* meal	Hos 8:7	369
as a vessel wherein is *n* pleasure	Hos 8:8	369
house, I will love them *n* more	Hos 9:15	3808
dried up, they shall bear *n* fruit	Hos 9:16	1077
they shall say, We have *n* king	Hos 10:3	369
and thou shalt know *n* god but me	Hos 13:4	3808
for there is *n* saviour beside me	Hos 13:4	369
because they have *n* pasture	Joel 1:18	369
I will *n* more make you a reproach	Joel 2:19	3808
there shall *n* strangers pass	Joel 3:17	3808
the forest, when he hath *n* prey	Amos 3:4	369
the earth, where *n* gin is for him	Amos 3:5	369
she shall *n* more rise	Amos 5:2	3808
very dark, and *n* brightness in it	Amos 5:20	3808
and he shall say, *N*	Amos 6:10	657
I was *n* prophet, neither was I an	Amos 7:14	3808
they shall *n* more be pulled up	Amos 9:15	3808
for there is *n* answer of God	Mic 3:7	369
is there *n* king in thee	Mic 4:9	369
and thou shalt have *n* more	Mic 5:12	3808
thou shalt *n* more worship the	Mic 5:13	3808
there is *n* cluster to eat	Mic 7:1	369
thee, I will afflict thee *n* more	Nah 1:12	3808
that *n* more of thy name be sown	Nah 1:14	3808
for the wicked shall *n* more pass	Nah 1:15	3808
messengers shall *n* more be heard	Nah 2:13	3808
and *n* man gathereth them	Nah 3:18	369
There is *n* healing of thy bruise	Nah 3:19	369
that have *n* ruler over them	Hab 1:14	3808
there is *n* breath at all in the	Hab 2:19	369
and the fields shall yield *n* meat	Hab 3:17	3808
there shall be *n* herd in the	Hab 3:17	3808
that there shall be *n* inhabitant	Zeph 2:5	369
but the unjust knoweth *n* shame	Zeph 3:5	3808
destroyed, so that there is *n* man	Zeph 3:6	1097
thou shalt *n* more be haughty	Zeph 3:11	3808
the priests answered and said, *N*	Hag 2:12	3808
so that *n* man did lift up his	Zec 1:21	3808
And I said, *N*, my lord	Zec 4:5	3808
And I said, *N*, my lord	Zec 4:13	3808
that *n* man passed through nor	Zec 7:14	
days there was *n* hire for man	Zec 8:10	3808
and love *n* false oath	Zec 8:17	3808
n oppressor shall pass through	Zec 9:8	3808
out of the pit wherein is *n* water	Zec 9:11	3808
because there was *n* shepherd	Zec 10:2	369
For I will *n* more pity the	Zec 11:6	3808
they shall *n* more be remembered	Zec 13:2	3808
say, I am *n* prophet, I am an	Zec 13:5	3808
there shall be *n* more utter	Zec 14:11	3808
even upon them shall be *n* rain	Zec 14:17	3808
up, and come not, that have *n* rain	Zec 14:18	3808
in that day there shall be *n* more	Zec 14:21	3808
I have *n* pleasure in you, saith	Mal 1:10	639
shall in *n* wise pass from the law	Mt 5:18	*3364*
ye shall in *n* case enter into the	Mt 5:20	*3364*
Thou shalt by *n* means come out	Mt 5:26	*3364*
otherwise ye have *n* reward of	Mt 6:1	*3756*
N man can serve two masters	Mt 6:24	*3762*
Take *n* thought for your life,	Mt 6:25	*3361*

Therefore take *n* thought, saying, Mt 6:31 3361
Take therefore *n* thought for the Mt 6:34 3361
unto him, See thou tell *n* man Mt 8:4 3367
have not found so great faith, *n* Mt 8:10 3761
so that *n* man might pass by that Mt 8:28 3361
N man putteth a piece of new Mt 9:16 3762
saying, See that *n* man know it Mt 9:30 3762
as sheep having *n* shepherd Mt 9:36 3361
take *n* thought how or what ye Mt 10:19 3361
he shall in *n* wise lose his Mt 10:42 3364
n man knoweth the Son, but the Mt 11:27 3762
there shall *n* sign be given to it Mt 12:39 3756
because they had *n* deepness of Mt 13:5 3361
and because they had *n* root Mt 13:6 3361
there shall *n* sign be given unto Mt 16:4 3756
is because we have taken *n* bread Mt 16:7 3756
because ye have brought *n* bread Mt 16:8 3756
tell *n* man that he was Jesus the Mt 16:20 3762
up their eyes, they saw *n* man Mt 17:8 3762
saying, Tell the vision to *n* man Mt 17:9 3762
Wherefore they are *n* more twain Mt 19:6 3765
said, Thou shalt do *n* murder Mt 19:18 3756
Because *n* man hath hired us Mt 20:7 3762
said, Friend, I do thee *n* wrong Mt 20:13 3756
unto it, Let *n* fruit grow on thee Mt 21:19 3370
say that there is *n* resurrection Mt 22:23 3361
having *n* children, his brother Mt 22:24 3361
deceased, and, having *n* issue Mt 22:25 3361
n man was able to answer him a Mt 22:46 3762
call *n* man your father upon the Mt 23:9 3361
Take heed that *n* man deceive you Mt 24:4 3361
of the world to this time, *n* Mt 24:21
there should *n* flesh be saved Mt 24:22
of that day and hour knoweth *n* man Mt 24:36 3762
n, not the angels of heaven Mt 24:36 3761
lamps, and took *n* oil with them Mt 25:3 3756
an hungred, and ye gave me *n* meat Mt 25:42 3756
thirsty, and ye gave me *n* drink Mt 25:42 3756
temple, and ye laid *n* hold on me Mt 26:55 3756
insomuch that Jesus could *n* more Mk 1:45 3370
there was *n* room to receive them Mk 2:2 3370
n, not so much as about Mk 2:2
have *n* need of the physician Mk 2:17 3756
N man also seweth a piece of new Mk 2:21 3762
n man putteth new wine into old Mk 2:22 3762
N man can enter into a strong Mk 3:27 3762
because it had *n* depth of earth Mk 4:5 3361
and because it had *n* root, it Mk 4:6 3361
choked it, and it yielded *n* fruit Mk 4:7 3756
have *n* root in themselves, and so Mk 4:17 3756
how is it that ye have *n* faith Mk 4:40 3756
n man could bind him Mk 5:3 3762
n, not with chains Mk 5:3 3777
he suffered *n* man to follow him, Mk 5:37 3762
that *n* man should know it Mk 5:43 3367
he could there do *n* mighty work Mk 6:5 3762
n scrip, *n* bread, *n* money in Mk 6:8 3361
they had *n* leisure so much as to Mk 6:31 3761
ye suffer him *n* more to do ought Mk 7:12 3765
and would have *n* man know it Mk 7:24 3762
them that they should tell *n* man Mk 7:36 3367
There shall *n* sign be given unto Mk 8:12 1487
It is because we have *n* bread Mk 8:16 3756
ye, because ye have *n* bread Mk 8:17 3756
they should tell *n* man of him Mk 8:30 3367
so as *n* fuller on earth can white Mk 9:3 3756
they saw *n* man any more, save Mk 9:8 3762
them that they should tell *n* man Mk 9:9 3367
of him, and enter *n* more into him Mk 9:25 3370
for there is *n* man which shall do Mk 9:39 3756
so then they are *n* more twain Mk 10:8 3765
There is *n* man that hath left Mk 10:29 3762
N man eat fruit of thee hereafter Mk 11:14 3367
art true, and carest for *n* man Mk 12:14 3762
which say there is *n* resurrection Mk 12:18 3361
leave *n* children, that his Mk 12:19 3361
took a wife, and dying left *n* seed Mk 12:20 3756
the seven had her, and left *n* seed Mk 12:22 3756
n man after that durst ask him Mk 12:34 3762
take *n* thought beforehand what ye Mk 13:11 3361
days, *n* flesh should be saved Mk 13:20
day and that hour knoweth *n* man Mk 13:32 3762
n, not the angels Mk 13:32
I will drink *n* more of the fruit Mk 14:25 3765
And they had *n* child, because that Lk 1:7 3756
his kingdom there shall be *n* end Lk 1:33 3756
because there was *n* room for them Lk 2:7 3756
Exact *n* more than that which is Lk 3:13 3367
unto them, Do violence to *n* man Lk 3:14 3367
N prophet is accepted in his own Lk 4:24 3762
And he charged him to tell *n* man Lk 5:14 3367
N man putteth a piece of a new Lk 5:36 3762
n man putteth new wine into old Lk 5:37 3762
N man also having drunk old wine Lk 5:39 3762
have not found so great faith, *n* Lk 7:9 3761
thou gavest me *n* water for my Lk 7:44 3756
Thou gavest me *n* kiss Lk 7:45 3756
and these have *n* root, which for a Lk 8:13 3756
bring *n* fruit to perfection Lk 8:14 3756
N man, when he hath lighted a Lk 8:16 3762
ware *n* clothes, neither abode in Lk 8:27 3756
he suffered *n* man to go in, save Lk 8:51 3762
should tell *n* man what was done Lk 8:56 3367
We have *n* more but five loaves and Lk 9:13 3756
them to tell *n* man that thing Lk 9:21 3367
told *n* man in those days any of Lk 9:36 3762
N man, having put his hand to the Lk 9:62 3762
and salute *n* man by the way Lk 10:4 3367
n man knoweth who the Son is, but Lk 10:22 3762
n doubt the kingdom of God is Lk 11:20 686
there shall *n* sign be given it, Lk 11:29 3756
N man, when he hath lighted a Lk 11:33 3762
having *n* part dark, the whole Lk 11:36
after that have *n* more that they Lk 12:4

take ye *n* thought how or what Lk 12:11 3361
because I have *n* room where to Lk 12:17 3756
Take *n* thought for your life, Lk 12:22 3361
where *n* thief approacheth, Lk 12:33 3756
could in *n* wise lift up herself Lk 13:11 3361
persons, which need *n* repentance Lk 15:7 3756
and *n* man gave unto him Lk 15:16 3762
am *n* more worthy to be called thy Lk 15:19 3765
am *n* more worthy to be called thy Lk 15:21 3765
thou mayest be *n* longer steward Lk 16:2 3756
N servant can serve two masters Lk 16:13 3762
shall in *n* wise enter therein Lk 18:17 3364
There is *n* man that hath left Lk 18:29 3762
to give tribute unto Caesar, or *n* Lk 20:22 3756
and they left *n* children, and died Lk 20:31 3756
and he that hath *n* sword, let him Lk 22:36 3361
forth *n* hands against me Lk 22:53 3756
I find *n* fault in this man Lk 23:4 3762
have found *n* fault in this man Lk 23:14 3762
N, nor yet Herod Lk 23:15 235
I have found *n* cause of death in Lk 23:22 3762
N man hath seen God at any time Jn 1:18 3762
And he answered, *N* Jn 1:21 3756
indeed, in whom is *n* guile Jn 1:47 3756
saith unto him, They have *n* wine Jn 2:3 3756
for *n* man can do these miracles Jn 3:2 3762
n man hath ascended up to heaven, Jn 3:13 3762
n man receiveth his testimony Jn 3:32 3762
for the Jews have *n* dealings with Jn 4:9 3756
and said, I have *n* husband Jn 4:17 3756
hast well said, I have *n* husband Jn 4:17 3756
yet *n* man said, What seekest thou Jn 4:27 3762
that whereon ye bestowed *n* labour Jn 4:38 3756
that a prophet hath *n* honour in Jn 4:44 3756
answered him, Sir, I have *n* man Jn 5:7 3756
sin *n* more, lest a worse thing Jn 5:14 3370
For the Father judgeth *n* man Jn 5:22 3762
to me I will in *n* wise cast out Jn 6:37 3364
N man can come to me, except the Jn 6:44 3762
his blood, ye have *n* life in you Jn 6:53 3756
that *n* man can come unto me, Jn 6:65 3762
back, and walked *n* more with him Jn 6:66 3765
For there is *n* man that doeth any Jn 7:4 3762
Howbeit *n* man spake openly of him Jn 7:13 3762
n unrighteousness is in him Jn 7:18 3756
n man knoweth whence he is Jn 7:27 3762
but *n* man laid hands on him, Jn 7:30 3762
but *n* man laid hands on him Jn 7:44 3762
out of Galilee ariseth *n* prophet Jn 7:52 3756
hath *n* man condemned thee Jn 8:10 3762
She said, *N* man, Lord Jn 8:11 3762
go, and sin *n* more Jn 8:11 3370
I judge *n* man Jn 8:15 3762
and *n* man laid hands on him Jn 8:20 3762
my word hath *n* place in you Jn 8:37 3756
because there is *n* truth in him Jn 8:44 3756
night cometh, when *n* man can work Jn 9:4 3762
said, Whether he be a sinner or *n* Jn 9:25
were blind, ye should have *n* sin Jn 9:41 3756
N man taketh it from me, but I Jn 10:18 3762
n man is able to pluck them out Jn 10:29 3762
him, and said, John did *n* miracle Jn 10:41 3762
because there is *n* light in him Jn 11:10 3756
Jesus therefore walked *n* more Jn 11:54 3765
not, thou hast *n* part with me Jn 13:8 3756
Now *n* man at the table knew for Jn 13:28 3762
n man cometh unto the Father, but Jn 14:6 3762
and the world seeth me *n* more Jn 14:19 3765
n more can ye, except ye abide in Jn 15:4 3761
Greater love hath *n* man than this Jn 15:13 3762
but now they have *n* cloke for Jn 15:22 3756
to my Father, and ye see me *n* more Jn 16:10 3765
she remembereth *n* more the Jn 16:21 3765
your joy *n* man taketh from you Jn 16:22 3762
when I shall *n* more speak unto Jn 16:25 3765
plainly, and speakest *n* proverb Jn 16:29 3762
now I am *n* more in the world, but Jn 17:11 3765
I find in him *n* fault at all Jn 18:38 3762
know that I find *n* fault in him Jn 19:4 3762
for I find *n* fault in him Jn 19:6 3756
But Jesus gave him *n* answer Jn 19:9 3756
Thou couldest have *n* power at all Jn 19:11 3756
We have *n* king but Caesar Jn 19:15 3756
They answered him, *N* Jn 21:5 3756
and let *n* man dwell therein Acts 1:20 3361
But that it spread *n* further Acts 4:17 3361
henceforth to *n* man in this name Acts 4:17 3367
of the rest durst *n* man join Acts 5:13 3762
had opened, we found *n* man within Acts 5:23 3762
him none inheritance in it, *n* Acts 7:5
him, when as yet he had *n* child Acts 7:5 3756
and our fathers found *n* sustenance Acts 7:11 3756
that the eunuch saw him *n* more Acts 8:39 3765
hearing a voice, but seeing *n* man Acts 9:7 3367
eyes were opened, he saw *n* man Acts 9:8 3762
God is *n* respecter of persons Acts 10:34 3756
there was *n* small stir among the Acts 12:18 3756
though they found *n* cause of Acts 13:28 3367
the dead, now *n* more to return to Acts 13:34 3370
raised again, saw *n* corruption Acts 13:37 3756
which ye shall in *n* wise believe Acts 13:41 3364
Barnabas had *n* small dissension Acts 15:2 3756
put *n* difference between us and Acts 15:9 3762
to whom we gave *n* such Acts 15:24 3756
to lay upon you *n* greater burden Acts 15:28 3367
voice, saying, Do thyself *n* harm Acts 16:28 3367
n man shall set on thee to hurt Acts 18:10 3762
for I will be *n* judge of such Acts 18:15 3756
arose *n* small stir about that way Acts 19:23 3756
brought *n* small gain unto the Acts 19:24 3756
saying that they be *n* gods Acts 19:26 3756
there being *n* cause whereby we Acts 19:40 3367
of God, shall see my face *n* more Acts 20:25 3765
I have coveted *n* man's silver Acts 20:33 3762

they should see his face *n* more Acts 20:38 3765
that they observe *n* such thing Acts 21:25 3367
Cilicia, a citizen of *n* mean city Acts 21:39 3756
say that there is *n* resurrection Acts 23:8 3361
We find *n* evil in this man Acts 23:9 3762
See thou tell *n* man that thou Acts 23:22 3367
to the Jews have I done *n* wrong Acts 25:10 3762
n man may deliver me unto them Acts 25:11 3762
Of whom I have *n* certain thing to Acts 25:26 3756
n small tempest lay on us, all Acts 27:20 3756
for there shall be *n* loss of any Acts 27:22 3762
shewed us *n* little kindness Acts 28:2 3756
N doubt this man is a murderer, Acts 28:4
into the fire, and felt *n* harm Acts 28:5 3762
saw *n* harm come to him, they Acts 28:6 3367
because there was *n* cause of Acts 28:18 3367
confidence, *n* man forbidding him Acts 28:31 209
For there is *n* respect of persons Rom 2:11 3756
we better than they? *N* Rom 3:9 3756
in *n* wise: for we Rom 3:9 3843
There is none righteous, *n* Rom 3:10
there is none that doeth good, *n* Rom 3:12
There is *n* fear of God before Rom 3:18 3756
deeds of the law there shall *n* Rom 3:20
for there is *n* difference Rom 3:22 3756
for where *n* law is Rom 4:15 3756
there is *n* transgression Rom 4:15 3761
not imputed when there is *n* law Rom 5:13 3361
raised from the dead dieth *n* more Rom 6:9 3765
death hath *n* more dominion over Rom 6:9 3765
so that she is *n* adulteress Rom 7:3 3361
Now then it is *n* more I that do Rom 7:17 3765
my flesh,) dwelleth *n* good thing Rom 7:18 3756
it is *n* more I that do it, but Rom 7:20 3765
There is therefore now *n* Rom 8:1 3762
For there is *n* difference between Rom 10:12 3756
by them that are *n* people Rom 10:19 3756
then is it *n* more of works Rom 11:6 3765
otherwise grace is *n* more grace Rom 11:6 3765
of works, then is it *n* more grace Rom 11:6 3765
otherwise work is *n* more work Rom 11:6 3765
Recompense to *n* man evil for evil Rom 12:17 3367
For there is *n* power but of God Rom 13:1 3756
Owe *n* man any thing, but to love Rom 13:8 3367
Love worketh *n* ill to his Rom 13:10 3756
and *n* man dieth to himself Rom 14:7 3762
that *n* man put a stumblingblock Rom 14:13 3361
But now having *n* more place in Rom 15:23 3370
So that ye come behind in *n* gift 1Cor 1:7 3367
that there be *n* divisions among 1Cor 1:10 3361
That *n* flesh should glory in his 1Cor 1:29
the things of God knoweth *n* man 1Cor 2:11 3762
yet he himself is judged of *n* man 1Cor 2:15 3762
For other foundation can *n* man 1Cor 3:11 3762
Let *n* man deceive himself 1Cor 3:18 3367
Therefore let *n* man glory in men 1Cor 3:21 3367
that *n* one of you be puffed up 1Cor 4:6 3361
have *n* certain dwellingplace 1Cor 4:11 790
with such an one, *n* not to eat 1Cor 5:11
n, not one that shall be able to 1Cor 6:5
I have *n* commandment of the Lord 1Cor 7:25 3756
having *n* necessity, but hath 1Cor 7:37 3361
I will eat *n* flesh while the 1Cor 8:13 3364
sakes, *n* doubt, this is written 1Cor 9:10 1063
There hath *n* temptation taken you 1Cor 10:13 3756
Let *n* man seek his own, but every 1Cor 10:24 3367
asking *n* question for conscience 1Cor 10:25 3367
asking *n* question for conscience 1Cor 10:27 3367
we have *n* such custom, neither 1Cor 11:16 3756
that *n* man speaking by the Spirit 1Cor 12:3 3762
that *n* man can say that Jesus is 1Cor 12:3 3762
the hand, I have *n* need of thee 1Cor 12:21 3756
to the feet, I have *n* need of you 1Cor 12:21 3756
For our comely parts have *n* need 1Cor 12:24 3756
should be *n* schism in the body 1Cor 12:25 3361
easily provoked, thinketh *n* evil 1Cor 13:5 3756
for *n* man understandeth him 1Cor 14:2 3762
But if there be *n* interpreter 1Cor 14:28 3361
is *n* resurrection of the dead 1Cor 15:12 3756
But if there be *n* resurrection of 1Cor 15:13 3756
that there be *n* gatherings when I 1Cor 16:2 3361
Let *n* man therefore despise him 1Cor 16:11 3361
I had *n* rest in my spirit, 2Cor 2:13 3756
had *n* glory in this respect 2Cor 3:10 3761
know we *n* man after the flesh 2Cor 5:16 3762
now henceforth know we him *n* more 2Cor 5:16 3765
to be sin for us, who knew *n* sin 2Cor 5:21 3361
Giving *n* offence in any thing, 2Cor 6:3 3367
we have wronged *n* man, we have 2Cor 7:2 3762
n man, we have defrauded *n* man 2Cor 7:2 3762
Macedonia, our flesh had *n* rest 2Cor 7:5 3762
had gathered little had *n* lack 2Cor 8:15 3756
that *n* man should blame us in 2Cor 8:20 3361
wanted, I was chargeable to *n* man 2Cor 11:9 3762
n man shall stop me of this 2Cor 11:10
And *n* marvel 2Cor 11:14 3762
Therefore it is *n* great thing if 2Cor 11:15 3762
Let *n* man think me a fool 2Cor 11:16 3367
I pray to God that ye do *n* evil 2Cor 13:7
we gave place by subjection, *n* Gal 2:5
were, it maketh *n* matter to me Gal 2:6 3762
God accepteth *n* man's person Gal 2:6 3756
law shall *n* flesh be justified Gal 2:16
But that *n* man is justified by Gal 3:11 3762
n man disannulleth, or addeth Gal 3:15 3762
the law, it is *n* more of promise Gal 3:18 3765
is come, we are *n* longer under a Gal 3:25 3765
thou art *n* more a servant Gal 4:7 3765
them which by nature are *n* gods Gal 4:8 3361
is become of *n* effect unto you Gal 5:4 2673
against such there is *n* law Gal 5:23 3756
henceforth let *n* man trouble me Gal 6:17 3367
of promise, having *n* hope Eph 2:12 3361
therefore ye are *n* more strangers Eph 2:19 3765

we henceforth be *n* more children .... Eph 4:14 *3370*
Let him that stole steal *n* more........ Eph 4:28 *3370*
Let *n* corrupt communication .... Eph 4:29
that *n* whoremonger, nor unclean........ Eph 5:5 *3756*
Let *n* man deceive you with vain........ Eph 5:6 *3367*
have *n* fellowship with the........ Eph 5:11 *3361*
For *n* man ever yet hated his own........ Eph 5:29 *3762*
But made himself of *n* reputation........ Phil 2:7 *5013*
For I have *n* man likeminded, who........ Phil 2:20 *3762*
have *n* confidence in the flesh........ Phil 3:3 *3756*
n church communicated with me as..... Phil 4:15 *3762*
Let *n* man therefore judge you in........ Col 2:16 *3361*
Let *n* man beguile you of your........ Col 2:18 *3367*
there is *n* respect of persons........ Col 3:25 *3756*
when we could *n* longer forbear........ 1Th 3:1 *3370*
That *n* man should be moved by........ 1Th 3:3 *3367*
when I could *n* longer forbear, I 1Th 3:5 *3370*
That *n* man go beyond and defraud 1Th 4:6 *3361*
even as others which have *n* hope........ 1Th 4:13 *3361*
ye have *n* need that I write unto 1Th 5:1 *3756*
Let *n* man deceive you by any........ 2Th 2:3 *3361*
have *n* company with him, that he........ 2Th 3:14 *3361*
that they teach *n* other doctrine 1Ti 1:3 *3361*
n striker, not greedy of filthy 1Ti 3:3 *3361*
Let *n* man despise thy youth........ 1Ti 4:12 *3367*
Lay hands suddenly on *n* man 1Ti 5:22 *3367*
Drink *n* longer water, but use a........ 1Ti 5:23 *3370*
which *n* man can approach unto........ 1Ti 6:16 *3762*
whom *n* man hath seen, nor can see.... 1Ti 6:16 *3762*
N man that warreth entangleth........ 2Ti 2:4 *3762*
not about words to *n* profit........ 2Ti 2:14 *3762*
But they shall proceed *n* further........ 2Ti 3:9 *3756*
first answer *n* man stood with me........ 2Ti 4:16 *3762*
n striker, not given to filthy .... Titus 1:7 *3361*
having *n* evil thing to say of you .... Titus 2:8 *3367*
Let *n* man despise thee .... Titus 2:15 *3367*
To speak evil of *n* man .... Titus 3:2 *3367*
to be *n* brawlers, but gentle,........ Titus 3:2 *269*
n man taketh this honour unto .... Heb 5:4 *3756*
he could swear by *n* greater .... Heb 6:13 *3762*
of which *n* man gave attendance at ..... Heb 7:13 *3762*
then should *n* place have been........ Heb 8:7 *3756*
iniquities will I remember *n* more........ Heb 8:12 *3364*
otherwise it is of *n* strength at........ Heb 9:17 *3361*
shedding of blood is *n* remission........ Heb 9:22 *3756*
had *n* more conscience of sins .... Heb 10:2 *3367*
for sin thou hast had *n* pleasure........ Heb 10:6 *3756*
iniquities will I remember *n* more........ Heb 10:17 *3361*
there is *n* more offering for sin .... Heb 10:18 *3765*
there remaineth *n* more sacrifice........ Heb 10:26 *3765*
soul shall have *n* pleasure in him .... Heb 10:38 *3756*
Now *n* chastening for the present........ Heb 12:11
without which *n* man shall see the........ Heb 12:14 *3762*
for he found *n* place of........ Heb 12:17 *3756*
whereof they have *n* right to eat........ Heb 13:10 *3756*
here have we *n* continuing city .... Heb 13:14 *3756*
For the sun is *n* sooner risen........ Jas 1:11
Let *n* man say when he is tempted,...... Jas 1:13 *3367*
with whom is *n* variableness .... Jas 1:17 *3756*
Now if thou commit *n* adultery .... Jas 2:11 *3756*
mercy, that hath shewed *n* mercy........ Jas 2:13 *3361*
But the tongue can *n* man tame........ Jas 3:8 *3762*
so can *n* fountain both yield salt........ Jas 3:12 *3762*
Who did *n* sin, neither was guile........ 1Pet 2:22 *3756*
his lips that they speak *n* guile 1Pet 3:10 *3361*
That he *n* longer should live the........ 1Pet 4:2 *3370*
that *n* prophecy of the scripture........ 2Pet 1:20
in him is *n* darkness at all 1Jn 1:5 *3756*
If we say that we have *n* sin 1Jn 1:8 *3756*
I write *n* new commandment unto 1Jn 2:7 *3756*
they would *n* doubt have continued..... 1Jn 2:19
that *n* lie is of the truth 1Jn 2:21
is *n* lie, and even as it hath 1Jn 2:27 *3756*
and in him is *n* sin........ 1Jn 3:5 *3756*
children, let *n* man deceive you........ 1Jn 3:7 *3367*
ye know that *n* murderer hath........ 1Jn 3:15
N man hath seen God at any time........ 1Jn 4:12 *3762*
There is *n* fear in love 1Jn 4:18 *3756*
I have *n* greater joy than to hear........ 3Jn 4 *3756*
which *n* man knoweth saving he .... Rev 2:17 *3762*
that openeth, and *n* man shutteth .... Rev 3:7 *3762*
and shutteth, and *n* man openeth .... Rev 3:7 *3762*
open door, and *n* man can shut it .... Rev 3:8 *3762*
that *n* man take thy crown........ Rev 3:11 *3367*
my God, and he shall go *n* more out .... Rev 3:12 *3364*
n man in heaven, nor in earth,........ Rev 5:3 *3762*
because *n* man was found worthy to .... Rev 5:4 *3762*
which *n* man could number, of all .... Rev 7:9 *3762*
They shall hunger *n* more, neither........ Rev 7:16 *3756*
there should be time *n* longer .... Rev 10:6 *3756*
that *n* man might buy or sell,........ Rev 13:17 *3361*
n man could learn that song but........ Rev 14:3 *3762*
in their mouth was found *n* guile........ Rev 14:5 *3756*
they have *n* rest day nor night,........ Rev 14:11 *3756*
n man was able to enter into the .... Rev 15:8 *3762*
have received *n* kingdom as yet........ Rev 17:12 *3768*
am *n* widow, and shall see .... Rev 18:7 *3756*
and shall see *n* sorrow........ Rev 18:7 *3364*
for *n* man buyeth their........ Rev 18:11 *3762*
shalt find them *n* more at all........ Rev 18:14 *3364*
and shall be found *n* more at all........ Rev 18:21 *3364*
shall be heard *n* more at all in .... Rev 18:22 *3364*
n craftsman, of whatsoever craft........ Rev 18:22
be heard *n* more at all in thee........ Rev 18:22 *3364*
shall shine *n* more at all in thee .... Rev 18:23 *3364*
be heard *n* more at all in thee........ Rev 18:23 *3364*
that *n* man knew, but he himself .... Rev 19:12 *3762*
should deceive the nations *n* more........ Rev 20:3 *3361*
the second death hath *n* power .... Rev 20:6 *3756*
there was found *n* place for them .... Rev 20:11 *3756*
and there was *n* more sea .... Rev 21:1 *3756*
and there shall be *n* more death .... Rev 21:4 *3756*
And I saw *n* temple therein .... Rev 21:22 *3756*
the city had *n* need of the sun,........ Rev 21:23 *3756*
for there shall be *n* night there........ Rev 21:25 *3756*
there shall in *n* wise enter into .... Rev 21:27 *3364*
And there shall be *n* more curse........ Rev 22:3 *3756*
And there shall be *n* night there........ Rev 22:5 *3756*
and they need *n* candle, neither........ Rev 22:5
A city on the Nile.
I will punish the multitude of *N*........ Jer 46:25 4996
and will execute judgments in *N*........ Eze 30:14 4996
I will cut off the multitude of *N* .... Eze 30:15 4996
N shall be rent asunder, and Noph .... Eze 30:16 4996
Art thou better than populous *N*........ Nah 3:8 4996

NOADIAH (*no-a-di'-ah*)
1. Son of Binnui.
N the son of Binnui, Levites .... Ezr 8:33 5129
2. An opponent of Nehemiah.
works, and on the prophetess *N*........ Neh 6:14 5129

NOAH (*no'-ah*) See NOAH'S, NOE.
1. Son of Lamech; built the ark.
And he called his name *N*, saying, ... Gen 5:29 5146
he begat *N* five hundred ninety .... Gen 5:30 5146
N was five hundred years old........ Gen 5:32 5146
N begat Shem, Ham, and Japheth........ Gen 5:32 5146
But *N* found grace in the eyes of .... Gen 6:8 5146
These are the generations of *N*........ Gen 6:9 5146
N was a just man and perfect in .... Gen 6:9 5146
generations, and *N* walked with God ... Gen 6:9 5146
N begat three sons, Shem, Ham, and ... Gen 6:10 5146
And God said unto *N*, The end of .... Gen 6:13 5146
Thus did *N* .... Gen 6:22 5146
And the LORD said unto *N*, Come .... Gen 7:1 5146
N did according unto all that the........ Gen 7:5 5146
N was six hundred years old when .... Gen 7:6 5146
N went in, and his sons, and his........ Gen 7:7 5146
two unto *N* into the ark, the male........ Gen 7:9 5146
female, as God had commanded *N*........ Gen 7:9 5146
In the selfsame day entered *N* .... Gen 7:13 5146
and Ham, and Japheth, the sons of *N*.. Gen 7:13 5146
they went in unto *N* into the ark........ Gen 7:15 5146
N only remained alive, and they........ Gen 7:23 5146
And God remembered *N*, and every ..... Gen 8:1 5146
that *N* opened the window of the .... Gen 8:6 5146
so *N* knew that the waters were .... Gen 8:11 5146
N removed the covering of the ark........ Gen 8:13 5146
And God spake unto *N*, saying,........ Gen 8:15 5146
N went forth, and his sons, and his ...... Gen 8:18 5146
N builded an altar unto the LORD........ Gen 8:20 5146
And God blessed *N* and his sons, and.... Gen 9:1 5146
And God spake unto *N*, and to his........ Gen 9:8 5146
And God said unto *N*, This is the .... Gen 9:17 5146
And the sons of *N*, that went forth........ Gen 9:18 5146
These are the three sons of *N*........ Gen 9:19 5146
N began to be an husbandman, and ..... Gen 9:20 5146
N awoke from his wine, and knew .... Gen 9:24 5146
N lived after the flood three .... Gen 9:28 5146
all the days of *N* were nine........ Gen 9:29 5146
the generations of the sons of *N*........ Gen 10:1 5146
are the families of the sons of *N*........ Gen 10:32 5146
N, Shem, Ham, and Japheth 1Chr 1:4 5146
is as the waters of *N* unto me........ Is 54:9 5146
of *N* should no more go over the .... Is 54:9 5146
Though these three men, *N* .... Eze 14:14 5146
Though *N*, Daniel, and Job, were in ..... Eze 14:20 5146
By faith *N*, being warned of God........ Heb 11:7 *3575*
of God waited in the days of *N*........ 1Pet 3:20 *3575*
but saved *N* the eighth person, a........ 2Pet 2:5 *3575*
2. A daughter of Zelophehad.
of Zelophehad were Mahlah, and *N*...... Num 26:33 5270
Mahlah, *N*, and Hoglah, and Milcah, ... Num 27:1 5270
and Hoglah, and Milcah, and *N* .... Num 36:11 5270
of his daughters, Mahlah, and *N*........ Josh 17:3 5270

NOAH'S (*no'-ahz*) *Refers to Noah 1.*
the six hundredth year of *N* life........ Gen 7:11 5146
N wife, and the three wives of his .... Gen 7:13 5146

NO-AMON See No.

NOB (*nob*) *A Levitical city in Benjamin.*
Then came David to *N* to Ahimelech ... 1Sa 21:1 5011
saw the son of Jesse coming to *N*........ 1Sa 22:9 5011
house, the priests that were in *N*........ 1Sa 22:11 5011
And *N*, the city of the priests,........ 1Sa 22:19 5011
And at Anathoth, *N*, Ananiah,........ Neh 11:32 5011
yet shall he remain at *N* that day .... Is 10:32 5011

NOBAH (*no'-bah*) See KENAH, NOPHAH.
1. A Manassite who captured an Amorite city.
N went and took Kenath, and the .... Num 32:42 5025
villages thereof, and called it *N* .... Num 32:42 5025
2. A city in the Trachonitis.
dwelt in tents on the east of *N*........ Judg 8:11 5025

NOBLE
n Asnapper brought over, and set........ Ezr 4:10 3358
one of the king's most *n* princes........ Est 6:9 6579
Yet I had planted thee a *n* vine........ Jer 2:21
These were more *n* than those in........ Acts 17:11 *2104*
places, most *n* Felix, with all........ Acts 24:3 *2908*
said, I am not mad, most *n* Festus........ Acts 26:25 *2908*
not many mighty, not many *n*........ 1Cor 1:26 *2104*

NOBLEMAN
A certain *n* went into a far........ Lk 19:12
And there was a certain *n*, whose........ Jn 4:46 *937*
The *n* saith unto him, Sir, come .... Jn 4:49 *937*

NOBLES
upon the *n* of the children of .... Ex 24:11 678
the *n* of the people digged it, by........ Num 21:18 5081
over the *n* among the people........ Judg 5:13 117
to the *n* that were in his city,........ 1Kin 21:8 2715
the *n* who were the inhabitants in........ 1Kin 21:11 2715
captains of hundreds, and the *n* 2Chr 23:20 117
nor to the priests, nor to the *n*........ Neh 2:16 2715
but their *n* put not their necks .... Neh 3:5 117
and rose up, and said unto the *n*........ Neh 4:14 2715
And I said unto the *n*, and to the........ Neh 4:19 2715
with myself, and I rebuked the *n*........ Neh 5:7 2715
Moreover in those days the *n* of........ Neh 6:17 2715
heart to gather together the *n* .... Neh 7:5 2715
clave to their brethren, their *n*........ Neh 10:29 117
I contended with the *n* of Judah .... Neh 13:17 2715
power of Persia and Media, the *n*........ Est 1:3 6579
The *n* held their peace, and their .... Job 29:10 5057
Make their *n* like Oreb, and like........ Ps 83:11 5081
their *n* with fetters of iron .... Ps 149:8 3513
By me princes rule, and *n*, even........ Prov 8:16 5081
when thy king is the son of *n* .... Eccl 10:17 2715
may go into the gates of the *n*........ Is 13:2 5081
They shall call the *n* thereof to........ Is 34:12 2715
and have brought down all their *n* ...... Is 43:14 1281
their *n* have sent their little........ Jer 14:3 117
all the *n* of Judah and Jerusalem........ Jer 27:20 2715
their *n* shall be of themselves,........ Jer 30:21 117
Babylon slew all the *n* of Judah........ Jer 39:6 2715
the decree of the king and his *n*........ Jonah 3:7 1419
thy *n* shall dwell in the dust........ Nah 3:18 117

NOD (*nod*) *A land east of Eden.*
LORD, and dwelt in the land of *N* .... Gen 4:16 5113

NODAB (*no'-dab*) *Name of tribe east of the Jordan.*
with Jetur, and Nephish, and *N*........ 1Chr 5:19 5114

NOE (*no'-e*) See NOAH. *Greek form of Noah.*
But as the days of *N* were........ Mt 24:37 *3575*
until the day that *N* entered into .... Mt 24:38 *3575*
of Sem, which was the son of *N*........ Lk 3:36 *3575*
And as it was in the days of *N*........ Lk 17:26 *3575*
until the day that *N* entered into .... Lk 17:27 *3575*

NOGAH (*no'-gah*) *A son of David.*
And *N*, and Nepheg, and Japhia, ... 1Chr 3:7 5052
And *N*, and Nepheg, and Japhia, ... 1Chr 14:6 5052

NOHAH (*no'-hah*) *A son of Benjamin.*
N the fourth, and Rapha the fifth 1Chr 8:2 5119

NOISE
the *n* of the trumpet, and the........ Ex 20:18 6963
when Joshua heard the *n* of the........ Ex 32:17 6963
There is a *n* of war in the camp .... Ex 32:17 6963
but the *n* of them that sing do I........ Ex 32:18 6963
nor make any *n* with your voice,........ Josh 6:10 8085
the *n* of archers in the places of........ Judg 5:11 6963
heard the *n* of the shout, they 1Sa 4:6 6963
What meaneth the *n* of this great........ 1Sa 4:6 6963
Eli heard the *n* of the crying 1Sa 4:14 6963
What meaneth the *n* of this tumult...... 1Sa 4:14 6963
that the *n* that was in the host........ 1Sa 14:19 1995
Wherefore is this *n* of the city 1Kin 1:41 6963
This is the *n* that ye have heard........ 1Kin 1:45 6963
Syrians to hear a *n* of chariots........ 2Kin 7:6 6963
a *n* of horses, even the *n* of........ 2Kin 7:6 6963
Athaliah heard the *n* of the guard 2Kin 11:13 6963
making a *n* with psalteries and........ 1Chr 15:28 8085
heard the *n* of the people running 2Chr 23:12 6963
n of the shout of joy from the .... Ezr 3:13 6963
n of the weeping of the people........ Ezr 3:13 6963
and the *n* was heard afar off .... Ezr 3:13 6963
or the *n* of his tabernacle .... Job 36:29 8663
The *n* thereof sheweth concerning .... Job 36:33 7452
attentively the *n* of his voice........ Job 37:2 7267
play skilfully with a loud *n* .... Ps 33:3 8643
deep at the *n* of thy waterspouts........ Ps 42:7 6963
in my complaint, and make a *n* .... Ps 55:2 1949
they make a *n* like a dog, and go .... Ps 59:6 1993
and let them make a *n* like a dog........ Ps 59:14 1993
Which stilleth the *n* of the seas .... Ps 65:7 7588
the *n* of their waves, and the .... Ps 65:7 7588
Make a joyful *n* unto God, all ye .... Ps 66:1
make a joyful *n* unto the God of........ Ps 81:1
than the *n* of many waters........ Ps 93:4 6963
let us make a joyful *n* to the........ Ps 95:1
make a joyful *n* unto him with .... Ps 95:2
Make a joyful *n* unto the LORD........ Ps 98:4
make a loud *n*, and rejoice, and........ Ps 98:4 6476
make a joyful *n* before the LORD........ Ps 98:6
Make a joyful *n* unto the LORD........ Ps 100:1
of the warrior is with confused *n*........ Is 9:5
The *n* of a multitude in the........ Is 13:4 6963
a tumultuous *n* of the kingdoms of .... Is 13:4 6963
the grave, and the *n* of thy viols .... Is 14:11 1998
a *n* like the *n* of the seas........ Is 17:12 1993
the *n* of them that rejoice endeth .... Is 24:8 7588
that he who fleeth from the *n* of........ Is 24:18 6963
bring down the *n* of strangers........ Is 25:5 7588
and with earthquake, and great *n*........ Is 29:6 6963
abase himself for the *n* of them........ Is 31:4 1995
At the *n* of the tumult the people .... Is 33:3 6963
A voice of *n* from the city, a .... Is 66:6 7588
my heart maketh a *n* in me........ Jer 4:19 1993
flee for the *n* of the horsemen........ Jer 4:29 6963
the *n* of the bruit is come, and a .... Jer 10:22 6963
with the *n* of a great tumult he .... Jer 11:16 6963
A *n* shall come even to the ends .... Jer 25:31 7588
Pharaoh king of Egypt is but a *n*........ Jer 46:17 7588
At the *n* of the stamping of the........ Jer 47:3 6963
is moved at the *n* of their fall........ Jer 49:21 6963
at the cry the *n* thereof was........ Jer 49:21 6963
At the *n* of the taking of Babylon........ Jer 50:46 6963
a *n* of their voice is uttered........ Jer 51:55 7588
they have made a *n* in the house .... Lam 2:7 6963
I heard the *n* of their wings,........ Eze 1:24 6963
like the *n* of great waters, as........ Eze 1:24 6963
of speech, as the *n* of an host........ Eze 1:24 6963
I heard also the *n* of the wings........ Eze 3:13 6963
the *n* of the wheels over against .... Eze 3:13 6963
them, and a *n* of a great rushing........ Eze 3:13 6963
thereof, by the *n* of his roaring .... Eze 19:7 6963
shake at the *n* of the horsemen........ Eze 26:10 6963
I will cause the *n* of thy songs........ Eze 26:13 1995

and as I prophesied, there was a *n*... Eze 37:7 6963
voice was like a *n* of many waters... Eze 43:2 6963
Like the *n* of chariots on the... Joel 2:5 6963
like the *n* of a flame of fire... Joel 2:5 6963
away from me the *n* of thy songs... Amos 5:23 1995
they shall make great *n* by reason... Mic 2:12 1949
The *n* of a whip, and the *n* of... Nah 3:2 6963
that there shall be the *n* of a... Zeph 1:10 6963
and make a *n* as through wine... Zec 9:15 6963
and the people making a *n*,... Mt 9:23 *2350*
shall pass away with a great *n*... 2Pet 3:10 *4500*
as it were the *n* of thunder... Rev 6:1 *5456*

NOISED
his fame was *n* throughout all the... Josh 6:27
it was *n* that he was in the house... Mk 2:1 *191*
all these sayings were *n* abroad... Lk 1:65 *1255*
Now when this was *n* abroad... Acts 2:6

NOISOME
fowler, and from the *n* pestilence... Ps 91:3 1942
If I cause *n* beasts to pass... Eze 14:15 7451
the *n* beast, and the pestilence,... Eze 14:21 7451
and there fell a *n* and grievous... Rev 16:2 *2556*

NON (*non*) See NUN. *Son of Elishama.*
N his son, Jehoshuah his son... 1Chr 7:27 5126

NONE
n of us shall withhold from thee... Gen 23:6
this is *n* other but the house of... Gen 28:17 369
There is *n* greater in this house... Gen 39:9 369
there was *n* of the men of the... Gen 39:11 369
but there was *n* that could... Gen 41:8 369
there is *n* that can interpret it... Gen 41:15 369
but there was *n* that could... Gen 41:24 369
there is *n* so discreet and wise as... Gen 41:39 369
is *n* like unto the LORD our God... Ex 8:10 369
is *n* like me in all the earth... Ex 9:14 369
such as there was *n* like it in... Ex 9:24 3808
such as there was *n* like it... Ex 11:6 3808
n of you shall go out at the door... Ex 12:22 3808
I will put *n* of these diseases... Ex 15:26 3808
sabbath, in it there shall be *n*... Ex 16:26 3808
for to gather, and they found *n*... Ex 16:27 3808
n shall appear before me empty... Ex 23:15 3808
n shall appear before me empty... Ex 34:20 3808
N of you shall approach to any... Lev 18:6
There shall *n* be defiled for the... Lev 21:1 3808
ye shall leave *n* of it until the... Lev 22:30 3808
And if the man have *n* to redeem it... Lev 25:26 3808
down, and *n* shall make you afraid... Lev 26:6 369
ye shall flee when *n* pursueth you... Lev 26:17 369
they shall fall when *n* pursueth... Lev 26:36 369
before a sword, when *n* pursueth... Lev 26:37 369
N devoted, which shall be devoted... Lev 27:29
unto the sons of Kohath he gave *n*... Num 7:9 3808
They shall leave *n* of it unto the... Num 9:12 3808
until there was *n* left him alive... Num 21:35 1115
she bound her soul, of *n* effect... Num 30:8 6565
Surely *n* of the men that came up... Num 32:11
every city, we left *n* to remain... Deut 2:34 3808
we smote him until *n* was left to... Deut 3:3 1115
there is *n* else beside him... Deut 4:35 369
there is *n* else... Deut 4:39 369
Thou shalt have *n* other gods... Deut 5:7
will put *n* of the evil diseases... Deut 7:15 3808
cried, and there was *n* to save her... Deut 22:27 369
thou shalt have *n* to rescue them... Deut 28:31 369
shalt have *n* assurance of thy... Deut 28:66 3808
is gone, and there is *n* shut up... Deut 32:36 657
There is *n* like unto the God of... Deut 33:26 369
n went out, and *n* came in... Josh 6:1 369
so that they let *n* of them remain... Josh 8:22 1115
there shall *n* of you be freed... Josh 9:23 3808
n moved his tongue against any of... Josh 10:21 3808
he let *n* remain... Josh 10:28 3808
he let *n* remain in it... Josh 10:30 3808
until he had left him *n* remaining... Josh 10:33 1115
he left *n* remaining, according to... Josh 10:37 3808
he left *n* remaining... Josh 10:39 3808
he left *n* remaining, but utterly... Josh 10:40 3808
until they left them *n* remaining... Josh 11:8 1115
strength, Israel burned *n* of them... Josh 11:13 3808
There was *n* of the Anakims left... Josh 11:22 3808
of Levi he gave *n* inheritance... Josh 13:14 3808
he gave *n* inheritance among them... Josh 14:3 3808
But *n* answered... Judg 19:28 369
there came *n* to the camp from... Judg 21:8
there were *n* of the inhabitants... Judg 21:9
for there is *n* to redeem it... Ruth 4:4 369
There is *n* holy as the LORD... 1Sa 2:2 369
for there is *n* beside thee... 1Sa 2:2 369
did let *n* of his words fall to... 1Sa 3:19 3808
that there is *n* like him among... 1Sa 10:24 369
So *n* of the people tasted any... 1Sa 14:24 3808
David said, There is *n* like that... 1Sa 21:9 369
there is *n* that sheweth me that... 1Sa 22:8
there is *n* of you that is sorry... 1Sa 22:8 369
for there is *n* like thee, neither... 2Sa 7:22 369
there was *n* to part them, but the... 2Sa 14:6 369
n can turn to the right hand or... 2Sa 14:19 376
was *n* to be so much praised as... 2Sa 14:25
Beware that *n* touch the young man... 2Sa 18:12
looked, but there was *n* to save... 2Sa 22:42 369
so that there was *n* like thee... 1Kin 3:12 3808
is God, and that there is *n* else... 1Kin 8:60 369
n were of silver... 1Kin 10:21 369
there was *n* that followed the... 1Kin 12:20 3808
n was exempted... 1Kin 15:22 369
But there was *n* like unto Ahab,... 1Kin 21:25 3808
whom I stand, I will receive *n*... 2Kin 5:16
And one of his servants said, *N*... 2Kin 6:12 3808
and there shall be *n* to bury her... 2Kin 9:10 369
then let *n* go forth nor escape... 2Kin 9:15 408
until he left him *n* remaining... 2Kin 10:11 1115
let *n* be wanting... 2Kin 10:19
you *n* of the servants of the LORD... 2Kin 10:23
let *n* come forth... 2Kin 10:25 408
there was *n* left but the tribe of... 2Kin 17:18 3808
so that after him was *n* like him... 2Kin 18:5 3808
n remained, save the poorest sort... 2Kin 24:14 3808
N ought to carry the ark of God... 1Chr 15:2 3808
there is *n* like thee, neither is... 1Chr 17:20 369
And Eliezer had *n* other sons... 1Chr 23:17 3808
a shadow, and there is *n* abiding... 1Chr 29:15 369
such as *n* of the kings have had... 2Chr 1:12 3808
there were *n* such seen before in... 2Chr 9:11 3808
n were of silver... 2Chr 9:20 369
we have *n* inheritance in the son... 2Chr 10:16 3808
n go out or come in to Asa king... 2Chr 16:1 1115
so that *n* is able to withstand... 2Chr 20:6 369
fallen to the earth, and *n* escaped... 2Chr 20:24 369
But let *n* come into the house of... 2Chr 23:6 408
that *n* which was unclean in any... 2Chr 23:19 3808
found there *n* of the sons of Levi... Ezr 8:15 3808
n of us put off our clothes,... Neh 4:23 369
to the law; *n* did compel... Est 1:8 369
for *n* might enter into the king's... Est 4:2 369
that there is *n* like him in the... Job 1:8 369
that there is *n* like him in the... Job 2:3 369
and *n* spake a word unto him... Job 2:13 369
let it look for light, but have *n*... Job 3:9 369
there is *n* that can deliver out... Job 10:7 369
down, and *n* shall make thee afraid... Job 11:19 369
because it is *n* of his... Job 18:15 1097
There shall *n* of his meat be left... Job 20:21 369
and him that had *n* to help him... Job 29:12 3808
there was *n* of you that convinced... Job 32:12 369
But *n* saith, Where is God my... Job 35:10 3808
but *n* giveth answer, because of... Job 35:12 3808
N is so fierce that dare stir him... Job 41:10 3808
while there is *n* to deliver... Ps 7:2 369
his wickedness till thou find *n*... Ps 10:15 1077
there is *n* that doeth good... Ps 14:1 369
there is *n* that doeth good, no,... Ps 14:3 369
but there was *n* to save them... Ps 18:41 369
for there is *n* to help... Ps 22:11 369
n can keep alive his own soul... Ps 22:29 3808
let *n* that wait on thee be... Ps 25:3 3808
devices of the people of *n* effect... Ps 33:10 5106
n of them that trust in him shall... Ps 34:22 3808
n of his steps shall slide... Ps 37:31 3808
N of them can by any means redeem... Ps 49:7
pieces, and there be *n* to deliver... Ps 50:22 369
there is *n* that doeth good... Ps 53:1 369
there is *n* that doeth good, no,... Ps 53:3 369
to take pity, but there was *n*... Ps 69:20 369
and for comforters, but I found *n*... Ps 69:20 3808
let *n* dwell in their tents... Ps 69:25 408
for there is *n* to deliver him... Ps 71:11 369
there is *n* upon earth that I... Ps 73:25 3808
n of the men of might have found... Ps 76:5 3808
and there was *n* to bury them... Ps 79:3 369
and Israel would *n* of me... Ps 81:11 3808
gods there is *n* like unto thee... Ps 86:8 369
fell down, and there was *n* to help... Ps 107:12 369
Let there be *n* to extend mercy... Ps 109:12 408
when as yet there was *n* of them... Ps 139:16
counsel, and would *n* of my reproof... Prov 1:25 3808
They would *n* of my counsel... Prov 1:30 3808
N that go unto her return again,... Prov 2:19 3808
and choose *n* of his ways... Prov 3:31 408
twins, and *n* is barren among them... Song 4:2 369
together, and *n* shall quench them... Is 1:31 369
N shall be weary nor stumble... Is 5:27 369
n shall slumber nor sleep... Is 5:27 3808
away safe, and *n* shall deliver it... Is 5:29 369
there was *n* that moved the wing,... Is 10:14 3808
is persecuted, and *n* hindereth... Is 14:6 1097
n shall be alone in his appointed... Is 14:31 369
down, and *n* shall make them afraid... Is 17:2 369
so he shall open, and *n* shall shut... Is 22:22 369
and he shall shut, and *n* shall open... Is 22:22 369
n shall pass through it for ever... Is 34:10 369
but *n* shall be there, and all her... Is 34:12 369
shall fail, *n* shall want her mate... Is 34:16
needy seek water, and there is *n*... Is 41:17 369
there is *n* that sheweth, yea,... Is 41:26 369
there is *n* that declareth, yea,... Is 41:26 369
there is *n* that heareth your... Is 41:26 369
are for a prey, and *n* delivereth... Is 42:22 369
for a spoil, and *n* saith, Restore... Is 42:22 369
there is *n* that can deliver out... Is 43:13 369
n considereth in his heart,... Is 44:19 3808
I am the LORD, and there is *n* else... Is 45:5 369
west, that there is *n* beside me... Is 45:6 657
I am the LORD, and there is *n* else... Is 45:6 369
and there is *n* else, there is no... Is 45:14 369
and there is *n* else... Is 45:18 369
there is *n* beside me... Is 45:21 369
for I am God, and there is *n* else... Is 45:22 369
for I am God, and there is *n* else... Is 46:9 369
I am God, and there is *n* like me... Is 46:9 657
heart, I am, and *n* else beside me... Is 47:8 657
thou hast said, *N* seeth me... Is 47:10 369
heart, I am, and *n* else beside me... Is 47:10 657
n shall save thee... Is 47:15 369
I called, was there *n* to answer... Is 50:2 369
There is *n* to guide her among all... Is 51:18 369
n considering that the righteous... Is 57:1 369
N calleth for justice, nor any... Is 59:4 369
look for judgment, but there is *n*... Is 59:11 369
of the people there was *n* with me... Is 63:3
I looked, and there was *n* to help... Is 63:5 369
that there was *n* to uphold... Is 63:5 369
there is *n* that calleth upon thy... Is 64:7 369
when I called, *n* did answer... Is 66:4 369
burn that *n* can quench it because... Jer 4:4 369
they have *n* understanding... Jer 4:22 3808
and *n* shall fray them away... Jer 7:33 369
so that *n* can pass through them... Jer 9:10
that *n* passeth through... Jer 9:12 1997
and *n* shall gather them... Jer 9:22 369
as there is *n* like unto thee... Jer 10:6 369
there is *n* like unto thee... Jer 10:7 369
there is *n* to stretch forth my... Jer 10:20 369
be shut up, and *n* shall open them... Jer 13:19 369
and they shall have *n* to bury them... Jer 14:16 369
burn that *n* can quench it,... Jer 21:12 369
that *n* doth return from his... Jer 23:14 1115
is great, so that *n* is like it... Jer 30:7 369
quiet, and *n* shall make him afraid... Jer 30:10 369
There is *n* to plead thy cause,... Jer 30:13 369
that *n* should serve himself of... Jer 34:9 1115
that *n* should serve themselves of... Jer 34:10 1115
for unto this day they drink *n*... Jer 35:14 3808
He shall have *n* to sit upon the... Jer 36:30 3808
n of them shall remain or escape... Jer 42:17 3808
Judah, to leave you *n* to remain... Jer 44:7 1115
So that *n* of the remnant of Judah... Jer 44:14 3808
for *n* shall return but such as... Jer 44:14 3808
ease, and *n* shall make him afraid... Jer 46:27 369
n shall tread with shouting... Jer 48:33 3808
n shall gather up him that... Jer 49:5 369
and *n* shall dwell therein... Jer 50:3 3808
n shall return in vain... Jer 50:9 3808
sought for, and there shall be *n*... Jer 50:20 369
let *n* thereof escape... Jer 50:29 408
and fall, and *n* shall raise him up... Jer 50:32 369
that *n* shall remain in it,... Jer 51:62 1115
lovers she hath *n* to comfort her... Lam 1:2 369
because *n* come to the solemn... Lam 1:4 1997
of the enemy, and *n* did help her... Lam 1:7 369
there is *n* to comfort her... Lam 1:17 369
there is *n* to comfort me... Lam 1:21 369
anger *n* escaped nor remained... Lam 2:22 3808
there is *n* that doth deliver us... Lam 5:8 369
n of them shall remain, nor of... Eze 7:11 3808
but *n* goeth to the battle... Eze 7:14 369
seek peace, and there shall be *n*... Eze 7:25 369
There shall *n* of my words be... Eze 12:28 3808
N eye pitied thee, to do any of... Eze 16:5 3808
whereas *n* followeth thee to... Eze 16:34 3808
hath spoiled *n* by violence... Eze 18:7 3808
but I found *n*... Eze 22:30 3808
To the end that *n* of all the... Eze 31:14 3808
N of his sins that he hath... Eze 33:16 3808
that *n* shall pass through... Eze 33:28 369
n did search or seek after them... Eze 34:6 369
and *n* shall make them afraid... Eze 34:28 369
their land, and *n* made them afraid... Eze 39:26 369
have left *n* of them any more... Eze 39:28 3808
them all was found *n* like Daniel... Dan 1:19 3808
there is *n* other that can shew it... Dan 2:11 3809
n can stay his hand, or say unto... Dan 4:35 3809
could find *n* occasion nor fault... Dan 6:4 3809
there was *n* that could deliver... Dan 8:7 3808
the vision, but *n* understood it... Dan 8:27 369
there is *n* that holdeth with me... Dan 10:21 369
will, and *n* shall stand before him... Dan 11:16 369
to his end, and *n* shall help him... Dan 11:45 369
n of the wicked shall understand... Dan 12:10 3808
n shall deliver her out of mine... Hos 2:10 3808
take away, and *n* shall rescue him... Hos 5:14 369
there is *n* among them that... Hos 7:7 369
High, *n* at all would exalt him... Hos 11:7 3808
n iniquity in me that were sin... Hos 12:8 3808
I am the LORD your God, and *n* else... Joel 2:27 369
there is *n* to raise her up... Amos 5:2 369
there be *n* to quench it in... Amos 5:6 369
there is *n* understanding in him... Obad 7 369
Therefore thou shalt have *n* that... Mic 2:5 3808
n evil can come upon us... Mic 3:11 3808
and *n* shall make them afraid... Mic 4:4 369
in pieces, and *n* can deliver... Mic 5:8 369
there is *n* upright among men... Mic 7:2 369
but *n* shall look back... Nah 2:8 369
for there is *n* end of the store... Nah 2:9 369
whelp, and *n* made them afraid... Nah 2:11 369
there is *n* end of their corpses... Nah 3:3 369
I am, and there is *n* beside me... Zeph 2:15 657
streets waste, that *n* passeth by... Zeph 3:6 1097
man, that there is *n* inhabitant... Zeph 3:6 369
down, and *n* shall make them afraid... Zeph 3:13 369
clothe you, but there is *n* warm... Hag 1:6 369
let *n* of you imagine evil against... Zec 7:10 408
let *n* of you imagine evil in your... Zec 8:17 408
let *n* deal treacherously against... Mal 2:15 408
seeking rest, and findeth *n*... Mt 12:43 *3756*
God of *n* effect by your tradition... Mt 15:6 *208*
there is *n* good but one, that is,... Mt 19:17 *3762*
But found *n*: yea, though... Mt 26:60 *3756*
witnesses came, yet found they *n*... Mt 26:60 *3756*
Making the word of God of *n*... Mk 7:13 *208*
there is *n* good but one, that is,... Mk 10:18 *3762*
There is *n* other commandment... Mk 12:31 *3756*
and there is *n* other but he... Mk 12:32 *3756*
and found *n*.... Mk 14:55 *3756*
There is *n* of thy kindred that is... Lk 1:61 *3762*
let him impart to him that hath *n*... Lk 3:11 *3361*
But unto *n* of them was Elias sent... Lk 4:26 *3762*
n of them was cleansed, saving... Lk 4:27 *3762*
and finding *n*, he saith, I will... Lk 11:24 *3361*
sought fruit thereon, and found *n*... Lk 13:6 *3756*
fruit on this fig tree, and find *n*... Lk 13:7 *3756*
That *n* of those men which were... Lk 14:24 *3762*
n is good, save one, that is, God... Lk 18:19 *3762*
they understood *n* of these things... Lk 18:34 *3762*
that there was *n* other boat there... Jn 6:22 *3756*
yet *n* of you keepeth the law... Jn 7:19 *3762*
saw *n* but the woman, he said unto... Jn 8:10 *3367*
the works which *n* other man did... Jn 15:24 *3762*
n of you asketh me, Whither goest... Jn 16:5 *3762*

n of them is lost, but the son of Jn 17:12 *3762*
thou gavest me have I lost *n* Jn 18:9 *3762*
n of the disciples durst ask him, Jn 21:12 *3762*
said, Silver and gold have I *n* Acts 3:6 *3756*
for there is *n* other name under Acts 4:12 *3777*
he gave him *n* inheritance in it, Acts 7:5 *3756*
yet he was fallen upon *n* of them Acts 8:16 *3762*
that *n* of these things which ye Acts 8:24 *3367*
preaching the word to *n* but unto Acts 11:19 *3367*
cared for *n* of those things Acts 18:17 *3762*
But *n* of these things move me, Acts 20:24 *3762*
that he should forbid *n* of his Acts 24:23 *3367*
but if there be *n* of these things Acts 25:11 *3762*
they brought *n* accusation of such Acts 25:18 *3762*
saying *n* other things than those Acts 26:22 *3762*
for I am persuaded that *n* of Acts 26:26
There is *n* righteous, no, not one Rom 3:10 *3756*
There is *n* that understandeth, Rom 3:11 *3756*
there is *n* that seeketh after God Rom 3:11 *3756*
there is *n* that doeth good, no, Rom 3:12 *3756*
and the promise made of *n* effect Rom 4:14 *2673*
Spirit of Christ, he is *n* of his Rom 8:9 *3756*
word of God hath taken *n* effect Rom 9:6 *1601*
For *n* of us liveth to himself, and Rom 14:7 *3762*
God that I baptized *n* of you 1Cor 1:14 *3762*
Christ should be made of *n* effect 1Cor 1:17 *2758*
Which *n* of the princes of this 1Cor 2:8 *3762*
wives be as though they had *n* 1Cor 7:29 *3361*
that there is *n* other God but one 1Cor 8:4 *3762*
But I have used *n* of these things 1Cor 9:15 *3762*
Give *n* offence, neither to the 1Cor 10:32 *677*
world, and *n* of them is without 1Cor 14:10 *3762*
For we write *n* other things unto 2Cor 1:13 *3756*
But other of the apostles saw I *n* Gal 1:19 *3756*
make the promise of *n* effect Gal 3:17 *208*
that ye will be *n* otherwise Gal 5:10 *3762*
See that *n* render evil for evil 1Th 5:15
give *n* occasion to the adversary 1Ti 5:14 *3361*
But let *n* of you suffer as a 1Pet 4:15 *3387*
there is *n* occasion of stumbling 1Jn 2:10 *3756*
Fear *n* of those things which thou Rev 2:10 *3367*
will put upon you *n* other burden Rev 2:24 *3367*

NOON
these men shall dine with me at *n* Gen 43:16 6672
present against Joseph came at *n* Gen 43:25 6672
who lay on a bed at *n* 2Sa 4:5 6672
of Baal from morning even until *n* 1Kin 18:26 6672
And it came to pass at *n*, that 1Kin 18:27 6672
And they went out at *n* 1Kin 20:16 6672
he sat on her knees till *n* 2Kin 4:20 6672
Evening, and morning, and at *n* Ps 55:17 6672
makest thy flock to rest at *n* Song 1:7 6672
arise, and let us go up at *n* Jer 6:4 6672
cause the sun to go down at *n* Amos 8:9 6672
come nigh unto Damascus about *n* Acts 22:6 *3314*

NOONDAY
And thou shalt grope at *n*, as the Deut 28:29 6672
grope in the *n* as in the night Job 5:14 6672
age shall be clearer than the *n* Job 11:17 6672
light, and thy judgment as the *n* Ps 37:6 6672
the destruction that wasteth at *n* Ps 91:6 6672
the night in the midst of the *n* Is 16:3 6672
and thy darkness be as the *n* Is 58:10 6672
we stumble at *n* as in the night Is 59:10 6672
of the young men a spoiler at *n* Jer 15:8 6672
shall drive out Ashdod at the *n* Zeph 2:4 6672

NOONTIDE
the morning, and the shouting at *n* Jer 20:16

NOPH (*nof*) See MEMPHIS. *Same as Memphis.*
the princes of *N* are deceived Is 19:13 5297
Also the children of *N* and Jer 2:16 5297
Migdol, and at Tahpanhes, and at *N* Jer 44:1 5297
in Migdol, and publish in *N* Jer 46:14 5297
for *N* shall be waste and desolate Jer 46:19 5297
their images to cease out of *N* Eze 30:13 5297
N shall have distresses daily Eze 30:16 5297

NOPHAH (*no'-fah*) See NOBAH. *A city in Sihon.*
have laid them waste even unto *N* Num 21:30 5302

NOR
she lay down, *n* when she arose Gen 19:33
she lay down, *n* when she arose Gen 19:35
n with my son, *n* with my son's Gen 21:23
n angry with yourselves, that ye Gen 45:5 408
shall neither be earing *n* harvest Gen 45:6
n a lawgiver from between his Gen 49:10
me, *n* hearken unto my voice Ex 4:1 3808
n since thou hast spoken unto thy Ex 4:10 1571
n thy fathers' fathers have seen, Ex 10:6 3808
n shall be like it any more Ex 11:6 3808
n sodden at all with water, but Ex 12:9
n the pillar of fire by night, Ex 13:22
thyself to them, *n* serve them Ex 20:5 3808
n thy son, *n* thy daughter, thy Ex 20:10
n thy maidservant, *n* thy cattle Ex 20:10
n thy stranger that is within thy Ex 20:10
n his maidservant, *n* his ox, Ex 20:17
n his ass, *n* any thing that is Ex 20:17
vex a stranger, *n* oppress him Ex 22:21 3808
n curse the ruler of thy people Ex 22:28 3808
n serve them, *n* do after their Ex 23:24 3808
young, *n* be barren, in thy land Ex 23:26
with them, *n* with their gods Ex 23:32
n burnt sacrifice, *n* meat Ex 30:9
neither let the flocks *n* herds Ex 34:3 408
in all the earth, *n* in any nation Ex 34:10
neither eat bread, *n* drink water Ex 34:28 3808
Let neither man *n* woman make any Ex 36:6 408
n any honey, in any offering of Lev 2:11
that ye eat neither fat *n* blood Lev 3:17
Do not drink wine *n* strong drink Lev 10:9
n thy sons with thee, when ye go Lev 10:9
no fins *n* scales in the waters Lev 11:12
n cheweth the cud, are unclean Lev 11:26 369
n come into the sanctuary, until Lev 12:4 3808
n be in sight deeper than the Lev 13:34
wash them not, *n* bathe his flesh Lev 17:16 3808
n any stranger that sojourneth Lev 18:26
n make to yourselves molten gods Lev 19:4 3808
n put a stumblingblock before the Lev 19:14 3808
n honour the person of the mighty Lev 19:15 3808
n bear any grudge against the Lev 19:18 3808
all redeemed, *n* freedom given her Lev 19:20 3808
use enchantment, *n* observe times Lev 19:26 3808
n print any marks upon you Lev 19:28 3808
sister, *n* of thy father's sister Lev 20:19
n make any cuttings in their Lev 21:5 3808
his head, *n* rend his clothes Lev 21:10 3808
n defile himself for his father, Lev 21:11 3808
n profane the sanctuary of his Lev 21:12 3808
n come nigh unto the altar, Lev 21:23 3808
n make an offering by fire of Lev 22:22 3808
n parched corn, *n* green ears, Lev 23:14
thy field, *n* prune thy vineyard Lev 25:4 3808
n gather the grapes in it of thy Lev 25:11 3808
not sow, *n* gather in our increase Lev 25:20 3808
n lend him thy victuals for Lev 25:37 3808
make you no idols *n* graven image Lev 26:1
n change it, a good for a bad, or Lev 27:10 3808
n put frankincense thereon Num 5:15 3808
n eat moist grapes, or dried Num 6:3 3808
morning, *n* break any bone of it Num 9:12 3808
n two days, *n* five days, Num 11:19 3808
neither ten days, *n* twenty days Num 11:19 3808
that neither they, *n* ye also, die Num 18:3
to the right hand *n* to the left Num 20:17
them at all, *n* bless them at all Num 23:25 3808
your voice, *n* give ear unto you Deut 1:45 3808
them not, *n* meddle with them Deut 2:19 408
unto the right hand *n* to the left Deut 2:27
n unto any place of the river Deut 2:37
Jabbok, *n* unto the cities in the Deut 2:37
n unto whatsoever the LORD our Deut 2:37
see, *n* hear, *n* eat, *n* smell Deut 4:28 3808
n forget the covenant of thy Deut 4:31 3808
thyself unto them, *n* serve them Deut 5:9 3808
n thy son, *n* thy daughter, *n* Deut 5:14
n thy manservant, *n* thy Deut 5:14
n thine ox, *n* thine ass, *n* Deut 5:14
n any of thy cattle, *n* thy Deut 5:14
with them, *n* shew mercy unto them Deut 7:2 3808
n his daughter shalt thou take Deut 7:3 3808
n choose you, because ye were Deut 7:7 3808
n take it unto thee, lest thou be Deut 7:25
did eat bread *n* drink water Deut 9:9 3808
n drink water, because of all Deut 9:18 3808
him not, *n* hearkened to his voice Deut 9:23 3808
n to their wickedness, *n* to Deut 9:27
Wherefore Levi hath no part *n* Deut 10:9
not persons, *n* taketh reward Deut 10:17 3808
no part *n* inheritance with you Deut 12:12
n any of thy vows which thou Deut 12:17
n thy freewill offerings, or Deut 12:17
add thereto, *n* diminish from it Deut 12:32 3808
not known, thou, *n* thy fathers Deut 13:6
unto him, *n* hearken unto him Deut 13:8 3808
n make any baldness between your Deut 14:1 3808
n touch their dead carcase Deut 14:8 3808
for he hath no part *n* inheritance Deut 14:27
no part *n* inheritance with thee Deut 14:29
n shut thine hand from thy poor Deut 15:7 3808
n shear the firstling of thy Deut 15:19 3808
to the right hand, *n* to the left Deut 17:11
n cause the people to return to Deut 17:16 3808
shall have no part *n* inheritance Deut 18:1
n come to pass, that is the thing Deut 18:22 3808
which is neither eared *n* sown Deut 21:4 3808
n discover his father's skirt Deut 22:30 3808
n their prosperity all thy days Deut 23:6
n a sodomite of the sons of Deut 23:17 3808
the stranger, *n* of the fatherless Deut 24:17
n take a widow's raiment to Deut 24:17 3808
n given ought thereof for the Deut 26:14 3808
thou *n* thy fathers have known Deut 28:36
of the wine, *n* gather the grapes Deut 28:39 3808
n shew favour to the young Deut 28:50 3808
which neither thou *n* thy fathers Deut 28:64
n beareth, *n* any grass groweth Deut 29:23 3808
fear not, *n* be afraid of them Deut 31:6 408
not fail thee, *n* forsake thee Deut 31:6 3808
brethren, *n* knew his own children Deut 33:9 3808
n his natural force abated Deut 34:7 3808
not fail thee, *n* forsake thee Josh 1:5 3808
n make any noise with your voice, Josh 6:10 3808
n be dismayed, be strong and of Josh 10:25 408
Geshurites, *n* the Maachathites Josh 13:13 408
n rebel against us, in building Josh 22:19 408
burnt offering, *n* for sacrifice Josh 22:26 3808
burnt offerings, *n* for sacrifices Josh 22:28 3808
n cause to swear by them, neither Josh 23:7 3808
n bow yourselves unto them Josh 23:7 3808
with thy sword, *n* with thy bow Josh 24:12 3808
your transgressions *n* your sins Josh 24:19
n Taanach and her towns, *n* the Judg 1:27
n the inhabitants of Ibleam and Judg 1:27
n the inhabitants of Megiddo and Judg 1:27
n the inhabitants of Nahalol Judg 1:30
n the inhabitants of Zidon, *n* Judg 1:31
n of Achzib, *n* of Helbah, *n* Judg 1:31
n of Helbah, *n* of Aphik, *n* of Judg 1:31
n the inhabitants of Beth-anath Judg 1:33
n yet the works which he had done Judg 2:10 1571
n from their stubborn way Judg 2:19
neither sheep, *n* ox, *n* ass Judg 6:4
n the land of the children of Judg 11:15
her he had neither son *n* daughter Judg 11:34 176
and drink not wine *n* strong drink Judg 13:4
now drink no wine *n* strong drink Judg 13:7
drink, *n* eat any unclean thing Judg 13:14 408
n would as at this time have told Judg 13:23 3908
not told it my father *n* my mother Judg 14:16 3908
done *n* seen from the day that the Judg 19:30 3908
neither wine *n* strong drink 1Sa 1:15
sacrifice *n* offering for ever 1Sa 3:14
n any that come into Dagon's 1Sa 5:5
n oppressed us, neither hast thou 1Sa 12:4 3808
which cannot profit *n* deliver 1Sa 12:21 3808
that there was neither sword *n* 1Sa 13:22
of Israel will not lie *n* repent 1Sa 15:29 3808
meat, neither yesterday, *n* to day 1Sa 20:27 1571
not be established, *n* thy kingdom 1Sa 20:31
my sword *n* my weapons with me 1Sa 21:8 1571
n to all the house of my father 1Sa 22:15
evil *n* transgression in mine hand 1Sa 24:11
n offence of heart unto my lord, 1Sa 25:31
n knew it, neither awaked 1Sa 26:12 369
and left neither man *n* woman alive 1Sa 27:9
saved neither man *n* woman alive 1Sa 27:11
n by Urim, *n* by prophets 1Sa 28:6 1571
neither by prophets, *n* by dreams 1Sa 28:15 1571
n executedst his fierce wrath 1Sa 28:18 3808
all the day, *n* all the night 1Sa 28:20
n drunk any water, three days and 1Sa 30:12 3808
n deliver me into the hands of my 1Sa 30:15 518
to them, neither small *n* great 1Sa 30:19 5703
neither sons *n* daughters 1Sa 30:19 5703
n any thing that they had taken 1Sa 30:19 5703
upon you, *n* fields of offerings 2Sa 1:21
hand *n* to the left from following 2Sa 2:19
n thy feet put into fetters 2Sa 3:34 3808
brother Amnon neither good *n* bad 2Sa 13:22
name *n* remainder upon the earth 2Sa 14:7
neither princes *n* servants 2Sa 19:6
n trimmed his beard, *n* washed 2Sa 19:24 3808
n gold of Saul, *n* of his house 2Sa 21:4
n the beasts of the field by 2Sa 21:10
numbered *n* counted for multitude 1Kin 3:8
n hast asked the life of thine 1Kin 3:11 3808
Let it be neither mine *n* thine 1Kin 3:26
adversary *n* evil occurrent 1Kin 5:4 369
was neither hammer *n* axe *n* any 1Kin 6:7
be told *n* numbered for multitude 1Kin 8:5 3808
him not leave us, *n* forsake us 1Kin 8:57 408
n were seen unto this day 1Kin 10:12 3808
n fight against your brethren the 1Kin 12:24 3808
neither will I eat bread *n* drink 1Kin 13:8 3808
n drink water, *n* turn again by 1Kin 13:9 3808
with thee, *n* go in with thee 1Kin 13:16
neither will I eat bread *n* drink 1Kin 13:16 3808
eat no bread *n* drink water there 1Kin 13:17 3808
n turn again to go by the way 1Kin 13:17 3808
eaten the carcase, *n* torn the ass 1Kin 13:28 3808
his kinsfolks, *n* of his friends 1Kin 16:11
not be dew *n* rain these years 1Kin 17:1
was no voice, *n* any that answered 1Kin 18:26 369
n any to answer, *n* any that 1Kin 18:29 369
to answer, *n* any that regarded 1Kin 18:29 369
Hearken not unto him, *n* consent 1Kin 20:8 3808
Fight neither with small *n* great 1Kin 22:31
not look toward thee, *n* see thee 2Kin 3:14 518
it is neither new moon, *n* sabbath 2Kin 4:23 3808
was neither voice, *n* hearing 2Kin 4:31 369
n sacrifice unto other gods 2Kin 5:17
himself there, not once *n* twice 2Kin 6:10 3808
then let none go forth *n* escape 2Kin 9:15
n the children be put to death 2Kin 14:6 3808
n any left, *n* any helper for 2Kin 14:26 369
n bow yourselves to them, *n* 2Kin 17:35 3808
serve them, *n* sacrifice to them 2Kin 17:35 3808
n any that were before him 2Kin 18:5
and would not hear them, *n* do them 2Kin 18:12 3808
n shoot an arrow there, *n* come 2Kin 19:32 3808
shield, *n* cast a bank against it 2Kin 19:32
n in all his dominion, that 2Kin 20:13
n in all the days of the kings of 2Kin 23:22
Israel, *n* of the kings of Judah 2Kin 23:22
n offer burnt offerings without 1Chr 21:24
dread not, *n* be dismayed 1Chr 22:13 408
n any vessels of it for the 1Chr 23:26
fear not, *n* be dismayed 1Chr 28:20 408
n forsake thee, until thou hast 1Chr 28:20 3808
n the life of thine enemies, 2Chr 1:11
be told *n* numbered for multitude 2Chr 5:6 3808
in the heaven, *n* in the earth 2Chr 6:14
n fight against your brethren 2Chr 11:4 3808
n to him that came in, but great 2Chr 15:5
n respect of persons, *n* taking 2Chr 19:7
Be not afraid *n* dismayed by 2Chr 20:15 408
fear not, *n* be dismayed 2Chr 20:17 408
n in the ways of Asa king of 2Chr 21:12
have not burned incense *n* offered 2Chr 29:7 3808
be not afraid *n* dismayed for the 2Chr 32:7 408
n for all the multitude that is 2Chr 32:7
n persuade you on this manner, 2Chr 32:15 408
to the right hand, *n* to the left 2Chr 34:2
n seek their peace or their Ezr 9:12 3808
should be no remnant *n* escaping Ezr 9:14
did eat no bread, *n* drink water Ezr 10:6 3808
n the statutes, *n* the judgments Neh 1:7
n the judgments, which thou Neh 1:7
n to the priests, *n* to the Neh 2:16
n to the rulers, *n* to the rest Neh 2:16
n right, *n* memorial, in Neh 2:20
n my brethren, *n* my servants, Neh 4:23
n the men of the guard which Neh 4:23
n their seed, whether they were Neh 7:61
mourn not, *n* weep Neh 8:9 408
consume them, *n* forsake them Neh 9:31 3808
n our fathers, kept thy law, *n* Neh 9:34 3808
n take their daughters for our Neh 10:30 3808

n take their daughters unto your	Neh 13:25	518
she had neither father *n* mother	Est 2:7	
shewed her people *n* her kindred	Est 2:10	
shewed her kindred *n* her people	Est 2:20	
bowed not, *n* did him reverence	Est 3:2	3808
n did him reverence, then was	Est 3:5	
neither eat *n* drink three days,	Est 4:16	408
n moved for him, he was full of	Est 5:9	3808
n the memorial of them perish	Est 9:28	3808
not, *n* charged God foolishly	Job 1:22	3808
n hid sorrow from mine eyes	Job 3:10	
n let me alone till I swallow	Job 7:19	3808
n be raised out of their sleep	Job 14:12	3808
son *n* nephew among his people	Job 18:19	3808
n any remaining in his dwellings	Job 18:19	3808
n abide in the paths thereof	Job 24:13	3808
n my tongue utter deceit	Job 27:4	518
n the fierce lion passed by it	Job 28:8	3808
n regardeth the rich more than	Job 34:19	3808
n shadow of death, where the	Job 34:22	369
n all the forces of strength	Job 36:19	3808
n his power, *n* his comely	Job 41:12	
spear, the dart, *n* the habergeon	Job 41:26	
n standeth in the way of sinners,	Ps 1:1	3808
n sitteth in the seat of the	Ps 1:1	3808
n sinners in the congregation of	Ps 1:5	
n doeth evil to his neighbour,	Ps 15:3	3808
n taketh up a reproach against	Ps 15:3	3808
n taketh reward against the	Ps 15:5	3808
n take up their names into my	Ps 16:4	1077
There is no speech *n* language	Ps 19:3	369
For he hath not despised *n*	Ps 22:24	3808
unto vanity, *n* sworn deceitfully	Ps 24:4	3808
of my youth, *n* my transgressions	Ps 25:7	
n my life with bloody men	Ps 26:9	
n the operation of his hands, he	Ps 28:5	
n his seed begging bread	Ps 37:25	
n condemn him when he is judged	Ps 37:33	3808
n such as turn aside to lies	Ps 40:4	3808
n give to God a ransom for him	Ps 49:7	3808
n he goats out of thy folds	Ps 50:9	
n for my sin, O LORD	Ps 59:3	3808
my prayer, *n* his mercy from me	Ps 66:20	
n from the west, *n* from the	Ps 75:6	
from the west, *n* from the south	Ps 75:6	
n the day when he delivered them	Ps 78:42	
n the son of wickedness afflict	Ps 89:22	3808
n suffer my faithfulness to fail	Ps 89:33	3808
n alter the thing that is gone	Ps 89:34	3808
n for the arrow that flieth by	Ps 91:5	
N for the pestilence that walketh	Ps 91:6	
n for the destruction that	Ps 91:6	
n rewarded us according to our	Ps 103:10	3808
shall neither slumber *n* sleep	Ps 121:4	3808
thee by day, *n* the moon by night	Ps 121:6	
n he that bindeth sheaves his	Ps 129:7	
is not haughty, *n* mine eyes lofty	Ps 131:1	3808
of my house, *n* go up into my bed	Ps 132:3	
be no breaking in, *n* going out	Ps 144:14	369
n in the son of man, in whom	Ps 146:3	
to the right hand *n* to the left	Prov 4:27	
n inclined mine ear to them that	Prov 5:13	3808
n slumber to thine eyelids	Prov 6:4	
n the fields, *n* the highest	Prov 8:26	
n to strike princes for equity	Prov 17:26	
There is no wisdom *n*	Prov 21:30	369
n counsel against the LORD	Prov 21:30	369
n have the knowledge of the holy	Prov 30:3	
give me neither poverty *n* riches	Prov 30:8	
women, *n* thy ways to that which	Prov 31:3	
n for princes strong drink	Prov 31:4	408
n the ear filled with hearing	Eccl 1:8	3808
n any thing taken from it	Eccl 3:14	369
he hath neither child *n* brother	Eccl 4:8	
n he that loveth abundance with	Eccl 5:10	
seen the sun, *n* known any thing	Eccl 6:5	3808
also there is that neither day *n*	Eccl 8:16	
n device, *n* knowledge, *n*	Eccl 9:10	
n wisdom, in the grave, whither	Eccl 9:10	
n the battle to the strong,	Eccl 9:11	3808
the wise, *n* yet riches to men of	Eccl 9:11	3808
n yet favour to men of skill	Eccl 9:11	3808
n how the bones do grow in the	Eccl 11:5	
n the years draw nigh, when thou	Eccl 12:1	
n the clouds return after the	Eccl 12:2	
n awake my love, till he please	Song 2:7	518
n awake my love, till he please	Song 3:5	518
n awake my love, until he please	Song 8:4	
house is neither bread *n* clothing	Is 3:7	369
it shall not be pruned, *n* digged	Is 5:6	3808
be weary *n* stumble among them	Is 5:27	3808
none shall slumber *n* sleep	Is 5:27	3808
n the latchet of their shoes be	Is 5:27	3808
fear ye their fear, *n* be afraid	Is 8:12	3808
They shall not hurt *n* destroy in	Is 11:9	3808
n possess the land, *n* fill the	Is 14:21	
with the sword, *n* dead in battle	Is 22:2	3808
n bring forth children, neither	Is 23:4	3808
up young men, *n* bring up virgins	Is 23:4	
shall not be treasured *n* laid up	Is 23:18	3808
n break it with the wheel of his	Is 28:28	
n bruise it with his horsemen	Is 28:28	3808
n be an help *n* profit, but a	Is 30:5	3808
n abase himself for the noise of	Is 31:4	3808
n the churl said to be bountiful	Is 32:5	3808
shall not be quenched night *n* day	Is 34:10	
n any ravenous beast shall go up	Is 35:9	1077
n shoot an arrow there, *n* come	Is 37:33	3808
shields, *n* cast a bank against it	Is 37:33	3808
n in all his dominion, that	Is 39:2	
n the beasts thereof sufficient	Is 40:16	369
n lift up, *n* cause his voice to	Is 42:2	3808
shall not fail *n* be discouraged	Is 42:4	3808
n wearied thee with incense	Is 43:23	3808
they see not, *n* know	Is 44:9	1077
They have not known *n* understood	Is 44:18	
knowledge *n* understanding to say	Is 44:19	3808
n say, Is there not a lie in my	Is 44:20	3808
captives, not for price *n* reward	Is 45:13	3808
ye shall not be ashamed *n*	Is 45:17	3808
n save him out of his trouble	Is 46:7	3808
warm at, *n* fire to sit before it	Is 47:14	
not in truth, *n* in righteousness	Is 48:1	3808
off *n* destroyed from before me	Is 48:19	3808
They shall not hunger *n* thirst	Is 49:10	3808
shall the heat *n* sun smite them	Is 49:10	3808
n that his bread should fail	Is 51:14	3808
go out with haste, *n* go by flight	Is 52:12	3808
he hath no form *n* comeliness	Is 53:2	3808
be wroth with thee, *n* rebuke thee	Is 54:9	
me, *n* laid it to thy heart	Is 57:11	3808
n finding thine own pleasure, *n*	Is 58:13	
justice, *n* any pleadeth for truth	Is 59:4	369
n out of the mouth of thy seed,	Is 59:21	
n out of the mouth of thy seed's	Is 59:21	
shall not be shut day *n* night	Is 60:11	
wasting *n* destruction within thy	Is 60:18	
hold their peace day *n* night	Is 62:6	
n perceived by the ear, neither	Is 64:4	3808
be remembered, *n* come into mind	Is 65:17	3808
in her, *n* the voice of crying	Is 65:19	
n an old man that hath not filled	Is 65:20	
n bring forth for trouble	Is 65:23	3808
They shall not hurt *n* destroy in	Is 65:25	3808
people, not to fan, *n* to cleanse,	Jer 4:11	3808
n the judgment of their God	Jer 5:4	
shall we see sword *n* famine	Jer 5:12	
n to my law, but rejected it	Jer 6:19	
n your sacrifices sweet unto me	Jer 6:20	3808
into the field, *n* walk by the way	Jer 6:25	408
lift up cry *n* prayer for them	Jer 7:16	408
n commanded them in the day that	Jer 7:22	3808
n inclined their ear, but walked	Jer 7:24	3808
n inclined their ear, but	Jer 7:26	3808
their God, *n* receiveth correction	Jer 7:28	3808
n the valley of the son of Hinnom	Jer 7:32	
not be gathered, *n* be buried	Jer 8:2	3808
n figs on the fig tree, and the	Jer 8:13	369
whom neither they *n* their fathers	Jer 9:16	
n inclined their ear, but walked	Jer 11:8	3808
n spare, *n* have mercy, but	Jer 13:14	3808
n their sons, *n* their daughters	Jer 14:16	
n men have lent to me on usury	Jer 15:10	3808
of the mockers, *n* rejoiced	Jer 15:17	
go to lament *n* bemoan them	Jer 16:5	408
n cut themselves, *n* make	Jer 16:6	3808
neither ye *n* your fathers	Jer 16:13	
n bring it in by the gates of	Jer 17:21	
not hear, *n* receive instruction	Jer 17:23	1115
n counsel from the wise, *n* the	Jer 18:18	
whom neither they *n* their fathers	Jer 19:4	
n the kings of Judah, and have	Jer 19:4	
n spake it, neither came it into	Jer 19:5	3808
n The valley of the son of Hinnom	Jer 19:6	
n speak any more in his name	Jer 20:9	3808
neither have pity, *n* have mercy	Jer 21:7	3808
n the widow, neither shed	Jer 22:3	
no more, *n* see his native country	Jer 22:10	
n be dismayed, neither shall they	Jer 23:4	3808
I sent them not, *n* commanded them	Jer 23:32	3808
n inclined your ear to hear	Jer 25:4	3808
neither gathered, *n* buried	Jer 25:33	3808
n the principal of the flock to	Jer 25:35	
n to your diviners, *n* to your	Jer 27:9	
n to your enchanters, *n* to your	Jer 27:9	
n thrown down any more for ever	Jer 31:40	3808
neither ye, *n* your sons for ever	Jer 35:6	
n sow seed, *n* plant vineyard,	Jer 35:7	3808
n have any: but	Jer 35:7	3808
wives, our sons, *n* our daughters	Jer 35:8	
N to build houses for us to dwell	Jer 35:9	1115
we vineyard, *n* field, *n* seed	Jer 35:9	
your ear, *n* hearkened unto me	Jer 35:15	3808
n rent their garments, neither	Jer 36:24	3808
n any of his servants that heard	Jer 36:24	
n his servants, *n* the people of	Jer 37:2	
against you, *n* against this land	Jer 37:19	
n hear the sound of the trumpet,	Jer 42:14	3808
n have hunger of bread	Jer 42:14	3808
n any thing for the which he hath	Jer 42:21	
neither they, ye, *n* your fathers	Jer 44:3	
n inclined their ear to turn from	Jer 44:5	3808
n walked in my law	Jer 44:10	3808
n in my statutes, that I set	Jer 44:10	
n walked in his law	Jer 44:23	3808
n in his statutes, *n* in his	Jer 44:23	
statutes, *n* in his testimonies	Jer 44:23	
away, *n* the mighty man escape	Jer 46:6	408
which have neither gates *n* bars	Jer 49:31	3808
n any son of man dwell in it	Jer 49:33	3808
n Judah of his God, of the LORD	Jer 51:5	
n a stone for foundations	Jer 51:26	
remain in it, neither man *n* beast	Jer 51:62	
anger none escaped *n* remained	Lam 2:22	
n grieve the children of men	Lam 3:33	
n be dismayed at their looks,	Eze 2:6	408
n speakest to warn the wicked	Eze 3:18	3808
n from his wicked way, he shall	Eze 3:19	
n of their multitude, *n* of any	Eze 7:11	3808
buyer rejoice, *n* the seller mourn	Eze 7:12	408
be no more any vain vision *n*	Eze 12:24	
more vanity, *n* divine divinations	Eze 13:23	3808
deliver neither sons *n* daughters	Eze 14:16	508
deliver neither sons *n* daughters	Eze 14:18	
deliver neither son *n* daughter	Eze 14:20	518
salted at all, *n* swaddled at all	Eze 16:4	3808
n done after their abominations	Eze 16:47	
she *n* her daughters, as thou hast	Eze 16:48	
not received usury *n* increase	Eze 18:17	
n defile yourselves with their	Eze 20:18	408
n according to your corrupt	Eze 20:44	
n rained upon in the day of	Eze 22:24	3808
n remember Egypt any more	Eze 23:27	3808
neither shalt thou mourn *n* weep	Eze 24:16	3808
your lips, *n* eat the bread of men	Eze 24:22	3808
ye shall not mourn *n* weep	Eze 24:23	3808
n any grieving thorn of all that	Eze 28:24	
be brought together, *n* gathered	Eze 29:5	3808
n foot of beast shall pass	Eze 29:11	3808
n his army, for Tyrus, for the	Eze 29:18	
n any tree in the garden of God	Eze 31:8	
n the hoofs of beasts trouble	Eze 32:13	3808
n with their detestable things,	Eze 37:23	
n with any of their	Eze 37:23	
and having neither bars *n* gates	Eze 38:11	
n their kings, by their whoredom,	Eze 43:7	
n by the carcases of their kings	Eze 43:7	
n uncircumcised in flesh, shall	Eze 44:9	
n to come near to any of my holy	Eze 44:13	
n suffer their locks to grow long	Eze 44:20	3808
a widow, *n* her that is put away	Eze 44:22	
n alienate the firstfruits of the	Eze 48:14	3808
n with the wine which he drank	Dan 1:8	
n ruler, that asked such things	Dan 2:10	
n worship the golden image which	Dan 3:12	3809
n worship the golden image which	Dan 3:14	3809
n worship the golden image which	Dan 3:18	3809
n was an hair of their head	Dan 3:27	3809
n the smell of fire had passed on	Dan 3:27	3809
might not serve *n* worship any god	Dan 3:28	3809
n make known to the king the	Dan 5:8	
n let thy countenance be changed	Dan 5:10	408
which see not, *n* hear, *n* know	Dan 5:23	3809
could find none occasion *n* fault	Dan 6:4	3809
n the decree that thou hast	Dan 6:13	
That no decree *n* statute which	Dan 6:15	
came flesh *n* wine in my mouth	Dan 10:3	3808
n according to his dominion which	Dan 11:4	3808
neither shall he stand, *n* his arm	Dan 11:6	
neither in anger, *n* in battle	Dan 11:20	3808
not done, *n* his fathers' fathers	Dan 11:24	
n the desire of women	Dan 11:37	
desire of women, *n* regard any god	Dan 11:37	3808
n by sword, *n* by battle, by	Hos 1:7	
battle, by horses, *n* by horsemen	Hos 1:7	
cannot be measured *n* numbered	Hos 1:10	3808
n mercy, *n* knowledge of God in	Hos 4:1	369
no man strive, *n* reprove another	Hos 4:4	408
n your spouses when they commit	Hos 4:14	
n swear, The LORD liveth	Hos 4:15	408
you, *n* cure you of your wound	Hos 5:13	3808
God, *n* seek him for all this	Hos 7:10	3808
n enter into Gilgal, and pass not	Amos 5:5	3808
n a thirst for water, but of	Amos 8:11	3808
shall not overtake *n* prevent us	Amos 9:10	
n have laid hands on their	Obad 13	408
saying, Let neither man *n* beast	Jonah 3:7	
herd *n* flock, taste any thing	Jonah 3:7	
let them not feed, *n* drink water	Jonah 3:7	408
n waiteth for the sons of men	Mic 5:7	3808
the LORD, *n* enquired for him	Zeph 1:6	3808
Neither their silver *n* their gold	Zeph 1:18	1571
not do iniquity, *n* speak lies	Zeph 3:13	3808
n hearken unto me, saith the LORD	Zec 1:4	3808
n by power, but by my spirit,	Zec 4:6	3808
n the fatherless, the stranger,	Zec 7:10	
the stranger, *n* the poor	Zec 7:10	
no man passed through *n* returned	Zec 7:14	
for man, *n* any hire for beast	Zec 8:10	369
n heal that that is broken, *n*	Zec 11:16	3808
light shall not be clear, *n* dark	Zec 14:6	
to the LORD, not day, *n* night	Zec 14:7	3808
leave them neither root *n* branch	Mal 4:1	
N by the earth	Mt 5:35	*3383*
neither moth *n* rust doth corrupt	Mt 6:20	*3777*
do not break through *n* steal	Mt 6:20	*3761*
n yet for your body, what ye	Mt 6:25	*3366*
do they reap, *n* gather into barns	Mt 6:26	*3761*
n silver, *n* brass in your	Mt 10:9	*3366*
N scrip for your journey	Mt 10:10	*3361*
neither shoes, *n* yet staves	Mt 10:10	*3366*
n hear your words, when ye depart	Mt 10:14	*3366*
n the servant above his lord	Mt 10:24	*3761*
came neither eating *n* drinking	Mt 11:18	*3383*
He shall not strive, *n* cry	Mt 12:19	*3761*
scriptures, *n* the power of God	Mt 22:29	*3366*
n are given in marriage, but are	Mt 22:30	*3777*
to this time, no, *n* ever shall be	Mt 24:21	
for ye know neither the day *n* the	Mt 25:13	*3761*
n hear you, when ye depart thence	Mk 6:11	*3366*
n tell it to any in the town	Mk 8:26	*3366*
marry, *n* are given in marriage	Mk 12:25	*3777*
drink neither wine *n* strong drink	Lk 1:15	*2532*
n of a bramble bush gather they	Lk 6:44	*3761*
eating bread *n* drinking wine	Lk 7:33	*3383*
n scrip, neither bread, neither	Lk 9:3	*3383*
neither purse, *n* scrip, *n* shoes	Lk 10:4	*3361*
for they neither sow *n* reap	Lk 12:24	*3761*
neither have storehouse *n* barn	Lk 12:24	*3761*
n thy brethren, neither thy	Lk 14:12	*3364*
kinsmen, *n* thy rich neighbours	Lk 14:12	*3364*
the land, *n* yet for the dunghill	Lk 14:35	*3777*
go not after them, *n* follow them	Lk 17:23	*3364*
I fear not God, *n* regard man	Lk 18:4	*3756*
marry, *n* are given in marriage	Lk 20:35	*3777*
not be able to gainsay *n* resist	Lk 21:15	*3761*
will not answer me, *n* let me go	Lk 22:68	*2228*
No, *n* yet Herod	Lk 23:15	*3761*
n of the will of the flesh	Jn 1:13	*3761*
n of the will of man, but of God	Jn 1:13	*3761*
n Elias, neither that prophet	Jn 1:25	*3777*
n yet at Jerusalem, worship the	Jn 4:21	*3777*

N

at any time, *n* seen his shape ... Jn 5:37 *3777*
Ye neither know me, *n* my Father ... Jn 8:19 *3777*
this man sinned, *n* his parents ... Jn 9:3 *3777*
N consider that it is expedient ... Jn 11:50 *3761*
n understand with their heart, and ... Jn 12:40 *2532*
have not known the Father, *n* me ... Jn 16:3 *3761*
them not to speak at all *n* teach ... Acts 4:18 *3366*
neither part *n* lot in this matter ... Acts 8:21 *3761*
sight, and neither did eat *n* drink ... Acts 9:9 *3761*
n yet the voices of the prophets ... Acts 13:27 *2532*
fathers *n* we were able to bear ... Acts 15:10 *3777*
n yet blasphemers of your goddess ... Acts 19:37 *3777*
neither angel, *n* spirit ... Acts 23:8 *3383*
that they would neither eat *n* ... Acts 23:12
that they will neither eat *n* ... Acts 23:21
in the synagogues, *n* in the city ... Acts 24:12 *3777*
with multitude, *n* with tumult ... Acts 24:18 *3761*
n yet against Caesar, have I ... Acts 25:8 *3777*
when neither sun *n* stars in many ... Acts 27:20 *3383*
death, *n* life, *n* angels, *n* ... Rom 8:38 *3777*
n powers, *n* things present, *n* ... Rom 8:38 *3777*
N height, *n* depth, *n* any ... Rom 8:39 *3777*
n of him that runneth, but of God ... Rom 9:16 *3761*
n to drink wine, *n* any thing ... Rom 14:21 *3366*
n of the princes of this world, ... 1Cor 2:6 *3761*
n ear heard, neither have entered ... 1Cor 2:9
n idolaters, *n* adulterers, *n* ... 1Cor 6:9 *3777*
n abusers of themselves with ... 1Cor 6:9 *3777*
N thieves, *n* covetous, *n* ... 1Cor 6:10 *3777*
n revilers, *n* extortioners, ... 1Cor 6:10 *3756*
n to the Gentiles, *n* to the ... 1Cor 10:32 *2532*
n again the head to the feet, I ... 1Cor 12:21 *2228*
n handling the word of God ... 2Cor 4:2 *3366*
n for his cause that suffered ... 2Cor 7:12 *3761*
There is neither Jew *n* Greek ... Gal 3:28 *3761*
there is neither bond *n* free ... Gal 3:28 *3761*
there is neither male *n* female ... Gal 3:28 *3761*
flesh ye despised not, *n* rejected ... Gal 4:14 *3761*
any thing, *n* uncircumcision ... Gal 5:6 *3777*
n uncircumcision, but a new ... Gal 6:15 *3777*
filthiness, *n* foolish talking ... Eph 5:4 *2532*
n jesting, which are not ... Eph 5:4 *2228*
n unclean person, *n* covetous ... Eph 5:5 *2228*
there is neither Greek *n* Jew ... Col 3:11 *2532*
circumcision *n* uncircumcision, ... Col 3:11 *2532*
Barbarian, Scythian, bond *n* free ... Col 3:11
n of uncleanness ... 1Th 2:3 *3761*
n in guile ... 1Th 2:3 *3777*
n a cloke of covetousness ... 1Th 2:5 *3777*
N of men sought we glory, neither ... 1Th 2:6 *3777*
n yet of others, when we might ... 1Th 2:6 *3777*
not of the night, *n* of darkness ... 1Th 5:5 *3761*
n by word, *n* by letter as from ... 2Th 2:2 *3383*
they say, *n* whereof they affirm ... 1Ti 1:7 *3383*
n to usurp authority over the man ... 1Ti 2:12 *3761*
whom no man hath seen, *n* can see ... 1Ti 6:16 *3761*
n trust in uncertain riches, but ... 1Ti 6:17 *3366*
of our Lord, *n* of me his prisoner ... 2Ti 1:8 *3366*
beginning of days, *n* end of life ... Heb 7:3 *3383*
N yet that he should offer ... Heb 9:25 *3761*
n faint when thou art rebuked of ... Heb 12:5 *3366*
n unto blackness, and darkness, and ... Heb 12:18 *2532*
never leave thee, *n* forsake thee ... Heb 13:5
n unfruitful in the knowledge of ... 2Pet 1:8 *3761*
that thou art neither cold *n* hot ... Rev 3:15 *3777*
lukewarm, and neither cold *n* hot ... Rev 3:16 *3777*
n in earth, neither under the ... Rev 5:3 *3761*
n on the sea, *n* on any tree ... Rev 7:1 *3383*
n the trees, till we have sealed ... Rev 7:3 *3383*
the sun light on them, *n* any heat ... Rev 7:16 *3761*
neither can see, *n* hear, *n* walk ... Rev 9:20 *3777*
n of their sorceries, *n* of ... Rev 9:21 *3777*
fornication, *n* of their thefts ... Rev 9:21 *3777*
and they have no rest day *n* night ... Rev 14:11 *2532*
n crying, neither shall there be ... Rev 21:4 *3777*

NORTH

west, and to the east, and to the *n* ... Gen 28:14 6828
the *n* side there shall be twenty ... Ex 26:20 6828
shalt put the table on the *n* side ... Ex 26:35 6828
likewise for the *n* side in length ... Ex 27:11 6828
which is toward the *n* corner ... Ex 36:25 6828
for the *n* side the hangings were ... Ex 38:11 6828
be on the *n* side by their armies ... Num 2:25 6828
And this shall be your *n* border ... Num 34:7 6828
this shall be your *n* border ... Num 34:9 6828
on the *n* side two thousand cubits ... Num 35:5 6828
and pitched on the *n* side of Ai ... Josh 8:11 6828
that was on the *n* of the city ... Josh 8:13 6828
were on the *n* of the mountains ... Josh 11:2 6828
their border in the *n* quarter was ... Josh 15:5 6828
along by the *n* of Beth-arabah ... Josh 15:6 6828
which is Chesalon, on the *n* side ... Josh 15:10 6828
sea to Michmethah on the *n* side ... Josh 16:6 6828
was on the *n* side of the river ... Josh 17:9 6828
met together in Asher on the *n* ... Josh 17:10 6828
abide in their coasts on the *n* ... Josh 18:5 6828
their border on the *n* side was ... Josh 18:12 6828
the side of Jericho on the *n* side ... Josh 18:12 6828
the valley of the giants on the *n* ... Josh 18:16 6828
And was drawn from the *n*, and went . Josh 18:17 6828
of the border were at the *n* bay ... Josh 18:19 6828
it on the *n* side to Hannathon ... Josh 19:14 6828
toward the *n* side of Beth-emek ... Josh 19:27 6828
on the *n* side of the hill of ... Josh 24:30 6828
on the *n* side of the hill Gaash ... Judg 2:9 6828
were on the *n* side of them ... Judg 7:1 6828
which is on the *n* side of Beth-el ... Judg 21:19 6828
oxen, three looking toward the *n* ... 1Kin 7:25 6828
put it on the *n* side of the altar ... 2Kin 16:14 6828
porters, toward the east, west, *n* ... 1Chr 9:24 6828
oxen, three looking toward the *n* ... 2Chr 4:4 6828
out the *n* over the empty place ... Job 26:7 6828
and cold out of the *n* ... Job 37:9 4215
Fair weather cometh out of the *n* ... Job 37:22 6828
mount Zion, on the sides of the *n* ... Ps 48:2 6828
The *n* and the south thou hast ... Ps 89:12 6828
and from the west, from the *n* ... Ps 107:3 6828
The *n* wind driveth away rain ... Prov 25:23 6828
and turneth about unto the *n* ... Eccl 1:6 6828
toward the south, or toward the *n* ... Eccl 11:3 6828
Awake, O *n* wind ... Song 4:16 6828
in the sides of the *n* ... Is 14:13 6828
shall come from the *n* a smoke ... Is 14:31 6828
I have raised up one from the *n* ... Is 41:25 6828
I will say to the *n*, Give up ... Is 43:6 6828
and, lo, these from the *n* and from ... Is 49:12 6828
the face thereof is toward the *n* ... Jer 1:13 6828
Out of the *n* an evil shall break ... Jer 1:14 6828
families of the kingdoms of the *n* ... Jer 1:15 6828
proclaim these words toward the *n* ... Jer 3:12 6828
n to the land that I have given ... Jer 3:18 6828
for I will bring evil from the *n* ... Jer 4:6 6828
for evil appeareth out of the *n* ... Jer 6:1 6828
people cometh from the *n* country ... Jer 6:22 6828
commotion out of the *n* country ... Jer 10:22 6828
behold them that come from the *n* ... Jer 13:20 6828
of Israel from the land of the *n* ... Jer 16:15 6828
of Israel out of the *n* country ... Jer 23:8 6828
and take all the families of the *n* ... Jer 25:9 6828
And all the kings of the *n* ... Jer 25:26 6828
bring them from the *n* country ... Jer 31:8 6828
fall toward the *n* by the river ... Jer 46:6 6828
hosts hath a sacrifice in the *n* ... Jer 46:10 6828
it cometh out of the *n* ... Jer 46:20 6828
the hand of the people of the *n* ... Jer 46:24 6828
waters rise up out of the *n* ... Jer 47:2 6828
For out of the *n* there cometh up ... Jer 50:3 6828
great nations from the *n* country ... Jer 50:9 6828
a people shall come from the *n* ... Jer 50:41 6828
shall come unto her from the *n* ... Jer 51:48 6828
a whirlwind came out of the *n* ... Eze 1:4 6828
gate, that looketh toward the *n* ... Eze 8:3 6828
eyes now the way toward the *n* ... Eze 8:5 6828
up mine eyes the way toward the *n* ... Eze 8:5 6828
house which was toward the *n* ... Eze 8:14 6828
gate, which lieth toward the *n* ... Eze 9:2 6828
to the *n* shall be burned therein ... Eze 20:47 6828
all flesh from the south to the *n* ... Eze 21:4 6828
a king of kings, from the *n* ... Eze 26:7 6828
There be the princes of the *n* ... Eze 32:30 6828
of Togarmah of the *n* quarters ... Eze 38:6 6828
from thy place out of the *n* parts ... Eze 38:15 6828
thee to come up from the *n* parts ... Eze 39:2 6828
court that looked toward the *n* ... Eze 40:20 6828
against the gate toward the *n* ... Eze 40:23 6828
And he brought me to the *n* gate ... Eze 40:35 6828
up to the entry of the *n* gate ... Eze 40:40 6828
was at the side of the *n* gate ... Eze 40:44 6828
having the prospect toward the *n* ... Eze 40:44 6828
toward the *n* is for the priests ... Eze 40:46 6828
was left, one door toward the *n* ... Eze 41:11 6828
utter court, the way toward the *n* ... Eze 42:1 6828
before the building toward the *n* ... Eze 42:1 6828
an hundred cubits was the *n* door ... Eze 42:2 6828
and their doors toward the *n* ... Eze 42:4 6828
chambers which were toward the *n* ... Eze 42:11 6828
The *n* chambers and the south ... Eze 42:13 6828
He measured the *n* side, five ... Eze 42:17 6828
of the *n* gate before the house ... Eze 44:4 6828
entereth in by the way of the *n* ... Eze 46:9 6828
go forth by the way of the *n* gate ... Eze 46:9 6828
which looked toward the *n* ... Eze 46:19 6828
of the land toward the *n* side ... Eze 47:15 6828
the *n* northward, and the border of ... Eze 47:17 6828
And this is the *n* side ... Eze 47:17 6828
From the *n* end to the coast of ... Eze 48:1 6828
toward the *n* five and twenty ... Eze 48:10 6828
the *n* side four thousand and five ... Eze 48:16 6828
shall be toward the *n* two hundred ... Eze 48:17 6828
out of the city on the *n* side ... Eze 48:30 6828
of the *n* to make an agreement ... Dan 11:6 6828
the fortress of the king of the *n* ... Dan 11:7 6828
more years than the king of the *n* ... Dan 11:8 6828
him, even with the king of the *n* ... Dan 11:11 6828
the king of the *n* shall return ... Dan 11:13 6828
So the king of the *n* shall come ... Dan 11:15 6828
the king of the *n* shall come ... Dan 11:40 6828
out of the *n* shall trouble him ... Dan 11:44 6828
from the *n* even to the east, they ... Amos 8:12 6828
out his hand against the *n* ... Zeph 2:13 6828
and flee from the land of the *n* ... Zec 2:6 6828
go forth into the *n* country ... Zec 6:6 6828
these that go toward the *n* ... Zec 6:8 6828
my spirit in the *n* country ... Zec 6:8 6828
shall remove toward the *n* ... Zec 14:4 6828
and from the west, and from the *n* ... Lk 13:29 *1005*
toward the south west and *n* west ... Acts 27:12 *5566*
on the *n* three gates ... Rev 21:13 *1005*

NORTHERN

Shall iron break the *n* iron ... Jer 15:12 6828
far off from you the *n* army ... Joel 2:20 6830

NORTHWARD

from the place where thou art *n* ... Gen 13:14 6828
upon the side of the tabernacle *n* ... Ex 40:22 6828
of the altar *n* before the LORD ... Lev 1:11 6828
on the side of the tabernacle *n* ... Num 3:35 6828
turn you *n* ... Deut 2:3 6828
lift up thine eyes westward, and *n* ... Deut 3:27 6828
even unto the borders of Ekron *n* ... Josh 13:3 6828
from the valley of Achor, and so *n* ... Josh 15:7 6828
end of the valley of the giants *n* ... Josh 15:8 6828
went out unto the side of Ekron *n* ... Josh 15:11 6828
n it was Manasseh's, and the sea ... Josh 17:10 6828
the side over against Arabah *n* ... Josh 18:18 6828
to the side of Beth-hoglah *n* ... Josh 18:19 6828
themselves together, and went *n* ... Judg 12:1 6828
situate *n* over against Michmash ... 1Sa 14:5 6828
and his lot came out *n* ... 1Chr 26:14 6828
n four a day, southward four a ... 1Chr 26:17 6828
behold *n* at the gate of the altar ... Eze 8:5 6828
an hundred cubits eastward and *n* ... Eze 40:19 6828
me out of the way of the gate *n* ... Eze 47:2 6828
of Damascus, and the north *n* ... Eze 47:17 6828
the border of Damascus *n* ... Eze 48:1 6828
three gates *n*; one gate ... Eze 48:31 6828
the ram pushing westward, and *n* ... Dan 8:4 6828

NOSE

a lame, or he that hath a flat *n* ... Lev 21:18 2763
I will put my hook in thy *n* ... 2Kin 19:28 639
his *n* pierceth through snares ... Job 40:24 639
Canst thou put an hook into his *n* ... Job 41:2 639
the wringing of the *n* bringeth ... Prov 30:33 639
thy *n* is as the tower of Lebanon ... Song 7:4 639
and the smell of thy *n* like apples ... Song 7:8 639
The rings, and *n* jewels, ... Is 3:21 639
will I put my hook in thy *n* ... Is 37:29 639
These are a smoke in my *n* ... Is 65:5 639
they put the branch to their *n* ... Eze 8:17 639
they shall take away thy *n* ... Eze 23:25 639

NOSES

n have they, but they smell not ... Ps 115:6 639
stop the *n* of the passengers ... Eze 39:11

NOSTRILS

breathed into his *n* the breath of ... Gen 2:7 639
All in whose *n* was the breath of ... Gen 7:22 639
with the blast of thy *n* the ... Ex 15:8 639
until it come out at your *n* ... Num 11:20 639
went up a smoke out of his *n* ... 2Sa 22:9 639
the blast of the breath of his *n* ... 2Sa 22:16 639
breath of his *n* are they consumed ... Job 4:9 639
and the spirit of God is in my *n* ... Job 27:3 639
the glory of his *n* is terrible ... Job 39:20 5170
Out of his *n* goeth smoke, as out ... Job 41:20 5156
went up a smoke out of his *n* ... Ps 18:8 639
the blast of the breath of thy *n* ... Ps 18:15 639
man, whose breath is in his *n* ... Is 2:22 639
The breath of our *n*, the anointed ... Lam 4:20 639
your camps to come up unto your *n* ... Amos 4:10 639

NOT See PREFACE.

NOTABLE

the goat had a *n* horn between his ... Dan 8:5 2380
for it came up four *n* ones toward ... Dan 8:8 2380
And they had then a *n* prisoner ... Mt 27:16 *1978*
great and *n* day of the Lord come ... Acts 2:20 *2016*
for that indeed a *n* miracle hath ... Acts 4:16 *1110*

NOTE

n it in a book, that it may be ... Is 30:8 2710
who are of *n* among the apostles, ... Rom 16:7 *1978*
n that man, and have no company ... 2Th 3:14 *4593*

NOTED

is *n* in the scripture of truth ... Dan 10:21 7559

NOTHING

now *n* will be restrained from ... Gen 11:6
only unto these men do *n* ... Gen 19:8
we have done unto thee *n* but good ... Gen 26:29 7535
here also have I done *n* that they ... Gen 40:15
there shall *n* die of all that is ... Ex 9:4 3808
ye shall let *n* of it remain until ... Ex 12:10 3808
Ye shall eat *n* leavened ... Ex 12:20 3808
he that gathered much had *n* over ... Ex 16:18 3808
he shall go out free for *n* ... Ex 21:2 2600
if he have *n*, then he shall be ... Ex 22:3 369
There shall *n* cast their young, ... Ex 23:26 3808
n that is made of the vine tree ... Num 6:4 3808
there is *n* at all, beside this ... Num 11:6
touch *n* of theirs, lest ye be ... Num 16:26
Balak the son of Zippor, Let *n* ... Num 22:16 408
thou hast lacked *n* ... Deut 2:7 3808
shalt save alive *n* that breatheth ... Deut 20:16
unto the damsel thou shalt do *n* ... Deut 22:26
because he hath *n* left him in the ... Deut 28:55 3605
he left *n* undone of all that the ... Josh 11:15
such as before knew *n* thereof ... Judg 3:2 3808
This is *n* else save the sword of ... Judg 7:14 369
a kid, and he had *n* in his hand ... Judg 14:6
him every whit, and hid *n* from him ... 1Sa 3:18 3808
my father will do *n* either great ... 1Sa 20:2
thy servant knew *n* of all this ... 1Sa 22:15
so that *n* was missed of all that ... 1Sa 25:21
wherefore she told him *n*, less or ... 1Sa 25:36
there is *n* better for me than ... 1Sa 27:1 369
there was *n* lacking to them, ... 1Sa 30:19 3808
But the poor man had *n*, save one ... 2Sa 12:3
God of that which doth cost me *n* ... 2Sa 24:24 2600
they lacked *n* ... 1Kin 4:27
There was *n* in the ark save the ... 1Kin 8:9 369
it was *n* accounted of in the days ... 1Kin 10:21
And he answered, *N* ... 1Kin 11:22 3808
and looked, and said, There is *n* ... 1Kin 18:43
n but that which is true in the ... 1Kin 22:16 3808
earth *n* of the word of the LORD ... 2Kin 10:10 3808
there was *n* in his house, nor in ... 2Kin 20:13
there is *n* among my treasures ... 2Kin 20:15 1697
n shall be left, saith the LORD ... 2Kin 20:17
There was *n* in the ark save the ... 2Chr 5:10 369
there was *n* hid from Solomon ... 2Chr 9:2
it is *n* with thee to help, ... 2Chr 14:11
I adjure thee that thou say *n* but ... 2Chr 18:15 3808
Ye have *n* to do with us to build ... Ezr 4:3
this is *n* else but sorrow of ... Neh 2:2 369
their peace, and found *n* to answer ... Neh 5:8 3808
them, and will require *n* of them ... Neh 5:12 3808
unto them for whom *n* is prepared ... Neh 8:10 3808
wilderness, so that they lacked *n* ... Neh 9:21 3808
she required *n* but what Hegai the ... Est 2:15
Yet all this availeth me *n* ... Est 5:13 369

unto him, There is *n* done for him	Est 6:3	
let *n* fail of all that thou hast	Est 6:10	1697
they go to *n*, and perish	Job 6:18	8414
are but of yesterday, and know *n*	Job 8:9	3808
a liar, and make my speech *n* worth	Job 24:25	408
and hangeth the earth upon *n*	Job 26:7	1099
It profiteth a man *n* that he	Job 34:9	3808
hast tried me, and shalt find *n*	Ps 17:3	
there is *n* hid from the heat	Ps 19:6	369
and mine age is as *n* before thee	Ps 39:5	369
he dieth he shall carry *n* away	Ps 49:17	
and *n* shall offend them	Ps 119:165	369
there is *n* froward or perverse in	Prov 8:8	369
she is simple, and knoweth *n*	Prov 9:13	
Treasures of wickedness profit *n*	Prov 10:2	3808
the sluggard desireth, and hath *n*	Prov 13:4	369
maketh himself rich, yet hath *n*	Prov 13:7	
he beg in harvest, and have *n*	Prov 20:4	369
If thou hast *n* to pay, why should	Prov 22:27	369
There is *n* better for a man, than	Eccl 2:24	369
n can be put to it, nor any thing	Eccl 3:14	369
I perceive that there is *n* better	Eccl 3:22	369
a son, and there is *n* in his hand	Eccl 5:14	
shall take *n* of his labour, which	Eccl 5:15	
so that he wanteth *n* for his soul	Eccl 6:2	369
that man should find *n* after him	Eccl 7:14	
and all her princes shall be *n*	Is 34:12	657
there was *n* in his house, nor in	Is 39:2	
there is *n* among my treasures	Is 39:4	
n shall be left, saith the LORD	Is 39:6	
All nations before him are as *n*	Is 40:17	369
are counted to him less than *n*	Is 40:17	
That bringeth the princes to *n*	Is 40:23	
they shall be as *n*	Is 41:11	369
war against thee shall be as *n*	Is 41:12	369
Behold, ye are of *n*, and your work	Is 41:24	369
their works are *n*	Is 41:29	657
image that is profitable for *n*	Is 44:10	1115
anger, lest thou bring me to *n*	Jer 10:24	4591
marred, it was profitable for *n*	Jer 13:7	
this girdle, which is good for *n*	Jer 13:10	
there is *n* too hard for thee	Jer 32:17	
they have done *n* of all that thou	Jer 32:23	3808
hide *n* from me	Jer 38:14	
poor of the people, which had *n*	Jer 39:10	
I will keep *n* back from you	Jer 42:4	
let *n* of her be left	Jer 50:26	408
Is it *n* to you, all ye that pass	Lam 1:12	3808
their own spirit, and have seen *n*	Eze 13:3	1115
of the earth are reputed as *n*	Dan 4:35	3809
yea, and *n* shall escape them	Joel 2:3	3808
of his den, if he have taken *n*	Amos 3:4	1115
the earth, and have taken *n* at all	Amos 3:5	3808
Surely the Lord GOD will do *n*	Amos 3:7	
eyes in comparison of it as *n*	Hag 2:3	369
it is thenceforth good for *n*	Mt 5:13	*3762*
for there is *n* covered, that	Mt 10:26	*3762*
now three days, and have *n* to eat	Mt 15:32	
n shall be impossible unto you	Mt 17:20	*3762*
found *n* thereon, but leaves only,	Mt 21:19	*3762*
swear by the temple, it is *n*	Mt 23:16	*3762*
shall swear by the altar, it is *n*	Mt 23:18	*3762*
said unto him, Answerest thou *n*	Mt 26:62	*3762*
priests and elders, he answered *n*	Mt 27:12	*3762*
Have thou *n* to do with that just	Mt 27:19	*3367*
saw that he could prevail *n*	Mt 27:24	*3762*
him, See thou say *n* to any man	Mk 1:44	*3367*
For there is *n* hid, which shall	Mk 4:22	
was *n* bettered, but rather grew	Mk 5:26	*3367*
should take *n* for their journey	Mk 6:8	*3367*
for they have *n* to eat	Mk 6:36	
There is *n* from without a man,	Mk 7:15	*3762*
very great, and having *n* to eat	Mk 8:1	*3385*
me three days, and have *n* to eat	Mk 8:2	
This kind can come forth by *n*	Mk 9:29	*3762*
came to it, he found *n* but leaves	Mk 11:13	*3762*
Jesus, saying, Answerest thou *n*	Mk 14:60	*3762*
he held his peace, and answered *n*	Mk 14:61	*3762*
but he answered *n*	Mk 15:3	
again, saying, Answerest thou *n*	Mk 15:4	*3762*
But Jesus yet answered *n*	Mk 15:5	*3762*
For with God *n* shall be	Lk 1:37	
And in those days he did eat *n*	Lk 4:2	*3762*
all the night, and have taken *n*	Lk 5:5	*3762*
good, and lend, hoping for *n* again	Lk 6:35	*3367*
And when they had *n* to pay	Lk 7:42	*3361*
For *n* is secret, that shall not	Lk 8:17	*3756*
Take *n* for your journey, neither	Lk 9:3	*3367*
n shall by any means hurt you	Lk 10:19	*3762*
I have *n* to set before him	Lk 11:6	
For there is *n* covered, that	Lk 12:2	*3762*
And they said, *N*	Lk 22:35	*3762*
but he answered him *n*	Lk 23:9	*3762*
n worthy of death is done unto	Lk 23:15	*3762*
but this man hath done *n* amiss	Lk 23:41	*3762*
and said, A man can receive *n*	Jn 3:27	*3762*
thou hast *n* to draw with, and the	Jn 4:11	*3777*
you, The Son can do *n* of himself	Jn 5:19	*3762*
I can of mine own self do *n*	Jn 5:30	
that remain, that *n* be lost	Jn 6:12	
he hath given me I should lose *n*	Jn 6:39	
the flesh profiteth *n*	Jn 6:63	*3762*
boldly, and they say *n* unto him	Jn 7:26	*3762*
I am he, and that I do *n* of myself	Jn 8:28	*3762*
I honour myself, my honour is *n*	Jn 8:54	*3762*
were not of God, he could do *n*	Jn 9:33	*3762*
said unto them, Ye know *n* at all	Jn 11:49	*3756*
Perceive ye how ye prevail *n*	Jn 12:19	*3762*
world cometh, and hath *n* in me	Jn 14:30	*3762*
for without me ye can do *n*	Jn 15:5	*3762*
And in that day ye shall ask me *n*	Jn 16:23	*3762*
have ye asked *n* in my name	Jn 16:24	*3762*
and in secret have I said *n*	Jn 18:20	*3762*
and that night they caught *n*	Jn 21:3	*3762*
them, they could say *n* against it	Acts 4:14	*3762*
finding *n* how they might punish	Acts 4:21	*3367*
down, and go with them, doubting *n*	Acts 10:20	*3367*
for *n* common or unclean hath at	Acts 11:8	
bade me go with them, *n* doubting	Acts 11:12	*3367*
there spent their time in *n* else	Acts 17:21	*3762*
to be quiet, and to do *n* rashly	Acts 19:36	*3367*
how I kept back *n* that was	Acts 20:20	*3762*
informed concerning thee, are *n*	Acts 21:24	*3762*
that we will eat *n* until we have	Acts 23:14	*3367*
but to have *n* laid to his charge	Acts 23:29	*3367*
had committed *n* worthy of death	Acts 25:25	*3367*
This man doeth *n* worthy of death	Acts 26:31	*3762*
continued fasting, having taken *n*	Acts 27:33	*3367*
committed *n* against the people	Acts 28:17	*3762*
that there is *n* unclean of itself	Rom 14:14	*3762*
will bring to *n* the understanding	1Cor 1:19	*114*
For I know *n* by myself	1Cor 4:4	*3762*
Therefore judge *n* before the time	1Cor 4:5	*3385*
Circumcision is *n*, and	1Cor 7:19	*3762*
and uncircumcision is *n*	1Cor 7:19	*3762*
he knoweth *n* yet as he ought to	1Cor 8:2	*3762*
that an idol is *n* in the world	1Cor 8:4	*3762*
the gospel, I have *n* to glory of	1Cor 9:16	*3756*
and have not charity, I am *n*	1Cor 13:2	*3762*
not charity, it profiteth me *n*	1Cor 13:3	*3762*
as having *n*, and yet possessing	2Cor 6:10	*3367*
might receive damage by us in *n*	2Cor 7:9	*3367*
that had gathered much had *n* over	2Cor 8:15	*3756*
for in *n* am I behind the very	2Cor 12:11	*3762*
chiefest apostles, though I be *n*	2Cor 12:11	*3762*
For we can do *n* against the truth	2Cor 13:8	
in conference added *n* to me	Gal 2:6	*3762*
differeth *n* from a servant,	Gal 4:1	*3762*
Christ shall profit you *n*	Gal 5:2	*3762*
to be something, when he is *n*	Gal 6:3	*3367*
that in *n* I shall be ashamed, but	Phil 1:20	*3762*
And in *n* terrified by your	Phil 1:28	*3367*
Let *n* be done through strife or	Phil 2:3	*3367*
Be careful for *n*	Phil 4:6	*3367*
and that ye may have lack of *n*	1Th 4:12	*3367*
n to be refused, if it be	1Ti 4:4	*3762*
another, doing *n* by partiality	1Ti 5:21	*3367*
He is proud, knowing *n*, but	1Ti 6:4	*3367*
For we brought *n* into this world,	1Ti 6:7	*3762*
it is certain we can carry *n* out	1Ti 6:7	
defiled and unbelieving is *n* pure	Titus 1:15	*3762*
that *n* be wanting unto them	Titus 3:13	*3367*
But without thy mind would I do *n*	Philem 14	*3762*
he left *n* that is not put under	Heb 2:8	*3762*
spake *n* concerning priesthood	Heb 7:14	*3762*
For the law made *n* perfect	Heb 7:19	*3762*
be perfect and entire, wanting *n*	Jas 1:4	*3367*
let him ask in faith, *n* wavering	Jas 1:6	*3367*
forth, taking *n* of the Gentiles	3Jn 7	*3367*
with goods, and have need of *n*	Rev 3:17	*3762*

NOTICE

And all the people took *n* of it	2Sa 3:36	5234
bounty, whereof ye had *n* before	2Cor 9:5	*4293*

NOTWITHSTANDING

N they hearkened not unto Moses	Ex 16:20	
N, if he continue a day or two,	Ex 21:21	389
N the cities of the Levites, and	Lev 25:32	
N no devoted thing, that a man	Lev 27:28	389
N the children of Korah died not	Num 26:11	
N the land shall be divided by	Num 26:55	
N ye would not go up, but	Deut 1:26	
N thou mayest kill and eat flesh	Deut 12:15	7535
N, if the land of your possession	Josh 22:19	389
n the journey that thou takest	Judg 4:9	657
n yet Jotham the youngest son of	Judg 9:5	
N they hearkened not unto the	1Sa 2:25	
n, if there be in me iniquity,	1Sa 20:8	
n the princes of the Philistines	1Sa 29:9	389
N the king's word prevailed	2Sa 24:4	
N in thy days I will not do it	1Kin 11:12	389
N they would not hear, but	2Kin 17:14	
N the LORD turned not from the	2Kin 23:26	389
N thou shalt not build the house	2Chr 6:9	7535
N Hezekiah humbled himself for	2Chr 32:26	
n I have spoken unto you, rising	Jer 35:14	
N the children rebelled against	Eze 20:21	
N the land shall be desolate	Mic 7:13	
n, being warned of God in a dream	Mt 2:22	
n he that is least in the kingdom	Mt 11:11	
N, lest we should offend them, go	Mt 17:27	
n be ye sure of this, that the	Lk 10:11	*4133*
N in this rejoice not, that the	Lk 10:20	*4133*
N it pleased Silas to abide there	Acts 15:34	
N, that I be not further tedious	Acts 24:4	
n, every way, whether in pretence	Phil 1:18	*4133*
N ye have well done, that ye did	Phil 4:14	*4133*
N she shall be saved in	1Ti 2:15	
N the Lord stood with me, and	2Ti 4:17	
n ye give them not those things	Jas 2:16	
N I have a few things against	Rev 2:20	*235*

NOUGHT

thou therefore serve me for *n*	Gen 29:15	2600
there shall cleave *n* of the	Deut 13:17	
brother, and thou givest him *n*	Deut 15:9	3808
destroy you, and to bring you to *n*	Deut 28:63	8045
had brought their counsel to *n*	Neh 4:15	6565
and said, Doth Job fear God for *n*	Job 1:9	2600
of the wicked shall come to *n*	Job 8:22	369
the mountain falling cometh to *n*	Job 14:18	5034
a pledge from thy brother for *n*	Job 22:6	2600
the counsel of the heathen to *n*	Ps 33:10	6331
Thou sellest thy people for *n*	Ps 44:12	
ye have set at *n* all my counsel	Prov 1:25	6544
together, and it shall come to *n*	Is 8:10	6565
the terrible one is brought to *n*	Is 29:20	656
aside the just for a thing of *n*	Is 29:21	8414
be as nothing, and as a thing of *n*	Is 41:12	657
are of nothing, and your work of *n*	Is 41:24	659
I have spent my strength for *n*	Is 49:4	8414
Ye have sold yourselves for *n*	Is 52:3	2600
my people is taken away for *n*	Is 52:5	2600
and divination, and a thing of *n*	Jer 14:14	434
and Beth-el shall come to *n*	Amos 5:5	205
Ye which rejoice in a thing of *n*	Amos 6:13	
that would shut the doors for *n*	Mal 1:10	
kindle fire on mine altar for *n*	Mal 1:10	2600
many things, and be set at *n*	Mk 9:12	*1847*
with his men of war set him at *n*	Lk 23:11	*1848*
was set at *n* of you builders	Acts 4:11	*1848*
were scattered, and brought to *n*	Acts 5:36	*3762*
work be of men, it will come to *n*	Acts 5:38	*2647*
craft is in danger to be set at *n*	Acts 19:27	*557*
dost thou set at *n* thy brother	Rom 14:10	*1848*
to bring to *n* things that are	1Cor 1:28	*2673*
of this world, that come to *n*	1Cor 2:6	*2673*
did we eat any man's bread for *n*	2Th 3:8	*1432*
hour so great riches is come to *n*	Rev 18:17	*2049*

NOURISH

And there will I *n* thee	Gen 45:11	3557
I will *n* you, and your little ones	Gen 50:21	3557
that a man shall *n* a young cow	Is 7:21	2421
neither do I *n* up young men	Is 23:4	1431
an ash, and the rain doth *n* it	Is 44:14	1431

NOURISHED

Joseph *n* his father, and his	Gen 47:12	3557
lamb, which he had bought and *n* up	2Sa 12:3	2421
the LORD hath spoken, I have *n*	Is 1:2	1431
she *n* her whelps among young	Eze 19:2	7235
n up in his father's house three	Acts 7:20	*397*
him up, and *n* him for her own son	Acts 7:21	*397*
was *n* by the king's country	Acts 12:20	*5142*
n up in the words of faith and of	1Ti 4:6	*1789*
ye have *n* your hearts, as in a	Jas 5:5	*5142*
place, where she is *n* for a time	Rev 12:14	*5142*

NOURISHER

thy life, and a *n* of thine old age	Ruth 4:15	3557

NOURISHETH

but *n* and cherisheth it, even as	Eph 5:29	*1625*

NOURISHING

so *n* them three years, that at	Dan 1:5	1431

NOURISHMENT

and bands having *n* ministered	Col 2:19	*2023*

NOVICE

Not a *n*, lest being lifted up	1Ti 3:6	*3504*

NOW

This is *n* bone of my bones, and	Gen 2:23	6471
N the serpent was more subtil	Gen 3:1	
and *n*, lest he put forth his hand,	Gen 3:22	6258
n art thou cursed from the earth,	Gen 4:11	6258
N these are the generations of	Gen 10:1	
n nothing will be restrained from	Gen 11:6	6258
N these are the generations of	Gen 11:27	
N the LORD had said unto Abram,	Gen 12:1	
unto Sarai his wife, Behold *n*	Gen 12:11	4994
n therefore behold thy wife, take	Gen 12:19	6258
Lift up *n* thine eyes, and look	Gen 13:14	
Look *n* toward heaven, and tell the	Gen 15:5	4994
N Sarai Abram's wife bare him no	Gen 16:1	
Sarai said unto Abram, Behold *n*	Gen 16:2	4994
if *n* I have found favour in thy	Gen 18:3	4994
N Abraham and Sarah were old and	Gen 18:11	
I will go down *n*, and see whether	Gen 18:21	4994
answered and said, Behold *n*	Gen 18:27	4994
And he said, Behold *n*, I have	Gen 18:31	4994
And he said, Behold *n*, my lords,	Gen 19:2	4994
Behold *n*, I have two daughters	Gen 19:8	4994
n will we deal worse with thee,	Gen 19:9	6288
Behold *n*, thy servant hath found	Gen 19:19	4994
Behold *n*, this city is near to	Gen 19:20	4994
N therefore restore the man his	Gen 20:7	6258
N therefore swear unto me here by	Gen 21:23	6258
Take *n* thy son, thine only son	Gen 22:2	4994
for *n* I know that thou fearest	Gen 22:12	6258
if *n* thou do prosper my way which	Gen 24:42	4994
n if ye will deal kindly and truly	Gen 24:49	6258
N these are the generations of	Gen 25:12	
For *n* the LORD hath made room for	Gen 26:22	6258
Let there be *n* an oath betwixt us	Gen 26:28	4994
thou art *n* the blessed of the	Gen 26:29	6258
And he said, Behold *n*, I am old, I	Gen 27:2	4994
N therefore take, I pray thee,	Gen 27:3	6258
N therefore, my son, obey my	Gen 27:8	6258
Go *n* to the flock, and fetch me	Gen 27:9	4994
Isaac said unto him, Come near *n*	Gen 27:26	4994
n he hath taken away my blessing	Gen 27:36	6258
and what shall I do *n* unto thee	Gen 27:37	645
N therefore, my son, obey my	Gen 27:43	6258
n therefore my husband will love	Gen 29:32	6258
N this time will my husband be	Gen 29:34	
said, *N* will I praise the LORD	Gen 29:35	
n will my husband dwell with me,	Gen 30:20	6471
came, and it is *n* increased unto a	Gen 30:30	
n when shall I provide for mine	Gen 30:30	6258
Lift up *n* thine eyes, and see, all	Gen 31:12	4994
n arise, get thee out from this	Gen 31:13	6258
n then, whatsoever God hath said	Gen 31:16	6258
N Jacob had pitched his tent in	Gen 31:25	
thou hast *n* done foolishly in so	Gen 31:28	6258
And *n*, though thou wouldest needs	Gen 31:30	6258
N Rachel had taken the images, and	Gen 31:34	
thou hast sent me away *n* empty	Gen 31:42	6258
N therefore come thou, let us	Gen 31:44	6258
Laban, and stayed there until *n*	Gen 32:4	6258
and *n* I am become two bands	Gen 32:10	6258
if *n* I have found grace in thy	Gen 33:10	4994
Let me *n* leave with thee some of	Gen 33:15	4994

N

n his sons were with his cattle ... Gen 34:5
N the sons of Jacob were twelve ... Gen 35:22
N these are the generations of ... Gen 36:1
N Israel loved Joseph more than ... Gen 37:3
Come *n* therefore, and let us slay ... Gen 37:20 6258
know *n* whether it be thy son's ... Gen 37:32 4994
N therefore let Pharaoh look out ... Gen 41:33 6258
N when Jacob saw that there was ... Gen 42:1
surely *n* we had returned this ... Gen 43:10 6258
unto them, If it must be so *n* ... Gen 43:11 645
N also let it be according unto ... Gen 44:10 6258
N therefore when I come to thy ... Gen 44:30 6258
N therefore, I pray thee, let thy ... Gen 44:33 6258
N therefore be not grieved, nor ... Gen 45:5 6258
So *n* it was not you that sent me ... Gen 45:8 6258
N thou art commanded, this do ye ... Gen 45:19
N let me die, since I have seen ... Gen 46:30 6471
from our youth even until *n* ... Gen 46:34 6258
n therefore, we pray thee, let ... Gen 47:4 6258
If *n* I have found grace in thy ... Gen 47:29 4994
n thy two sons, Ephraim and ... Gen 48:5 6258
N the eyes of Israel were dim for ... Gen 48:10
If *n* I have found grace in your ... Gen 50:4 4994
N therefore let me go up, I pray ... Gen 50:5 6258
Joseph, Forgive, I pray thee *n* ... Gen 50:17 4994
and *n*, we pray thee, forgive the ... Gen 50:17 4994
N therefore fear ye not ... Gen 50:21 6258
N these are the names of the ... Ex 1:1
N there arose up a new king over ... Ex 1:8
N when Pharaoh heard this thing, ... Ex 2:15
N the priest of Midian had seven ... Ex 2:16
N Moses kept the flock of Jethro ... Ex 3:1
I will *n* turn aside, and see this ... Ex 3:3 4994
N therefore, behold, the cry of ... Ex 3:9 6258
Come *n* therefore, and I will send ... Ex 3:10 6258
n let us go, we beseech thee, ... Ex 3:18 6258
Put *n* thine hand into thy bosom ... Ex 4:6 4994
N therefore go, and I will be with ... Ex 4:12 6258
the people of the land *n* are many ... Ex 5:5 6258
Go therefore *n*, and work ... Ex 5:18 6258
N shalt thou see what I will do ... Ex 6:1 6258
n the magicians of Egypt, they ... Ex 7:11
For *n* I will stretch out my hand, ... Ex 9:15 6258
foundation thereof even until *n* ... Ex 9:18 6258
Send therefore *n*, and gather thy ... Ex 9:19 6258
go *n* ye that are men, and serve ... Ex 10:11 4994
N therefore forgive, I pray thee, ... Ex 10:17 6258
Speak *n* in the ears of the people ... Ex 11:2 4994
N the sojourning of the children ... Ex 12:40
N an omer is the tenth part of an ... Ex 16:36
N I know that the Lord is greater ... Ex 18:11 6258
Hearken *n* unto my voice, I will ... Ex 18:19 6258
N therefore, if ye will obey my ... Ex 19:5 6258
N these are the judgments which ... Ex 21:1
N this is that which thou shalt ... Ex 29:38
N therefore let me alone, that my ... Ex 32:10 6258
n I will go up unto the Lord ... Ex 32:30 6258
Yet *n*, if thou wilt forgive their ... Ex 32:32 6258
Therefore *n* go, lead the people ... Ex 32:34 6258
therefore *n* put off thy ornaments ... Ex 33:5 6258
N therefore, I pray thee, if I ... Ex 33:13 6258
in thy sight, shew me *n* thy way ... Ex 33:13 4994
If *n* I have found grace in thy ... Ex 34:9 4994
But *n* our soul is dried away ... Num 11:6 6258
thou shalt see *n* whether my word ... Num 11:23 6258
(*N* the man Moses was very meek, ... Num 12:3
And he said, Hear *n* my words ... Num 12:6 4994
unto the Lord, saying, Heal her *n* ... Num 12:13 4994
N the time was the time of the ... Num 13:20
(*N* Hebron was built seven years ... Num 13:22
N if thou shalt kill all this ... Num 14:15
And *n*, I beseech thee, let the ... Num 14:17 6258
people, from Egypt even until *n* ... Num 14:19 2008
have tempted me *n* these ten times ... Num 14:22 2088
(*N* the Amalekites and the ... Num 14:25
Wherefore *n* do ye transgress the ... Num 14:41 2088
N Korah, the son of Izhar, the ... Num 16:1
N they that died in the plague ... Num 16:49
and he said unto them, Hear *n* ... Num 20:10 4994
N shall this company lick up all ... Num 22:4 6258
Come *n* therefore, I pray thee, ... Num 22:6 6258
come *n*, curse me them ... Num 22:11 6258
N therefore, I pray you, tarry ye ... Num 22:19 6258
N he was riding upon his ass, and ... Num 22:22
hand, for *n* would I kill thee ... Num 22:29 6258
surely *n* also I had slain thee, ... Num 22:33 6258
n therefore, if it displease thee ... Num 22:34 6258
have I *n* any power at all to say ... Num 22:38 6258
Therefore *n* flee thou to thy ... Num 24:11 6258
And *n*, behold, I go unto my people ... Num 24:14 6258
I shall see him, but not *n* ... Num 24:17 6258
N the name of the Israelite that ... Num 25:14
N therefore kill every male among ... Num 31:17 6258
(*N* the half that pertained unto ... Num 31:43
N the children of Reuben and the ... Num 32:1
N rise up, said I, and get you ... Deut 2:13 6258
N therefore hearken, O Israel, ... Deut 4:1 6258
For ask *n* of the days that are ... Deut 4:32 4994
N therefore why should we die ... Deut 5:25 6258
N these are the commandments, the ... Deut 6:1
And *n*, Israel, what doth the Lord ... Deut 10:12 6258
n the Lord thy God hath made thee ... Deut 10:22 6258
And *n*, behold, I have brought the ... Deut 26:10 6258
N therefore write ye this song ... Deut 31:19 6258
which they go about, even *n* ... Deut 31:21 3117
See *n* that I, even I, am he, and ... Deut 32:39 6258
N after the death of Moses the ... Josh 1:1
n therefore arise, go over this ... Josh 1:2 6258
N therefore, I pray you, swear ... Josh 2:12 6258
N therefore take you twelve men ... Josh 3:12 6258
N all the people that came out ... Josh 5:5 3588
the host of the Lord am I *n* come ... Josh 5:14 6258
N Jericho was straitly shut up ... Josh 6:1
tell me *n* what thou hast done ... Josh 7:19 4994

n there was a valley between them ... Josh 8:11
n therefore make ye a league with ... Josh 9:6 6258
therefore *n* make ye a league with ... Josh 9:11 6258
but *n*, behold, it is dry, and it ... Josh 9:12 6258
N their cities were Gibeon, and ... Josh 9:17
n therefore we may not touch them ... Josh 9:19 6258
N therefore ye are cursed, and ... Josh 9:23 6258
And *n*, behold, we are in thine ... Josh 9:25 6258
N it came to pass, when ... Josh 10:1
N these are the kings of the land ... Josh 12:1
N Joshua was old and stricken in ... Josh 13:1
N therefore divide this land for ... Josh 13:7 6258
And *n*, behold, the Lord hath kept ... Josh 14:10 6258
and *n*, lo, I am this day fourscore ... Josh 14:10 6258
then, even so is my strength *n* ... Josh 14:11 6258
N therefore give me this mountain ... Josh 14:12 6258
N Manasseh had the land of ... Josh 17:8
N the cities of the tribe of the ... Josh 18:21
n the Lord your God hath given ... Josh 22:4 6258
therefore *n* return ye, and get you ... Josh 22:4 6258
N to the one half of the tribe of ... Josh 22:7
Let us *n* prepare to build us an ... Josh 22:26 4994
n ye have delivered the children ... Josh 22:31 227
N therefore fear the Lord, and ... Josh 24:14 6258
N therefore put away, said he, ... Josh 24:23 6258
N after the death of Joshua it ... Judg 1:1
N the children of Judah had ... Judg 1:8
(*n* the name of Hebron before was ... Judg 1:10
(*N* the name of the city before ... Judg 1:23
N these are the nations which the ... Judg 3:1
N Heber the Kenite, which was of ... Judg 4:11
but *n* the Lord hath forsaken us, ... Judg 6:13 6258
If *n* I have found grace in thy ... Judg 6:17 4994
let it *n* be dry only upon the ... Judg 6:39 4994
N therefore go to, proclaim in ... Judg 7:3 6258
What have I done *n* in comparison ... Judg 8:2 6258
Zalmunna *n* in thine hand, that we ... Judg 8:6 6258
N Zebah and Zalmunna were in ... Judg 8:10
Zalmunna *n* in thine hand, that we ... Judg 8:15 6258
N therefore, if ye have done ... Judg 9:16 6258
N therefore up by night, thou and ... Judg 9:32 6258
Where is *n* thy mouth, wherewith ... Judg 9:38 645
go out, I pray *n*, and fight with ... Judg 9:38 6258
N Jephthah the Gileadite was a ... Judg 11:1
unto me *n* when ye are in distress ... Judg 11:7 6258
Therefore we turn again to thee *n* ... Judg 11:8 6258
n therefore restore those lands ... Judg 11:13 6258
So *n* the Lord God of Israel hath ... Judg 11:23 6258
n art thou any thing better than ... Judg 11:25 6258
they unto him, Say *n* Shibboleth ... Judg 12:6 4994
woman, and said unto her, Behold *n* ... Judg 13:3 4994
N therefore beware, I pray thee, ... Judg 13:4 6258
n drink no wine nor strong drink, ... Judg 13:7 6258
N let thy words come to pass ... Judg 13:12 6258
n therefore get her for me to ... Judg 14:2 6258
I will *n* put forth a riddle unto ... Judg 14:12 4994
N shall I be more blameless than ... Judg 15:3 6471
n shall I die for thirst, and fall ... Judg 15:18 6258
N there were men lying in wait, ... Judg 16:9
n tell me, I pray thee, wherewith ... Judg 16:10 6258
N the house was full of men and ... Judg 16:27
n therefore I will restore it ... Judg 17:3 6258
N know I that the Lord will do me ... Judg 17:13 6258
n therefore consider what ye have ... Judg 18:14 6258
n the day draweth toward evening, ... Judg 19:9 4994
but I am *n* going to the house of ... Judg 19:18
N as they were making their ... Judg 19:22
them I will bring out *n*, and ... Judg 19:24 4994
(*N* the children of Benjamin heard ... Judg 20:3
But *n* this shall be the thing ... Judg 20:9 6258
N therefore deliver us the men, ... Judg 20:13 6258
N there was an appointed sign ... Judg 20:38
N the men of Israel had sworn in ... Judg 21:1
N it came to pass in the days ... Ruth 1:1
Let me *n* go to the field, and ... Ruth 2:2 4994
even from the morning until *n* ... Ruth 2:7 6258
n is not Boaz of our kindred, ... Ruth 3:2 6258
And *n*, my daughter, fear not ... Ruth 3:11 6258
n it is true that I am thy near ... Ruth 3:12 6258
N this was the manner in former ... Ruth 4:7
N these are the generations of ... Ruth 4:18
N there was a certain man of ... 1Sa 1:1
N Eli the priest sat upon a seat ... 1Sa 1:9
N Hannah, she spake in her heart ... 1Sa 1:13
N the sons of Eli were sons of ... 1Sa 2:12
but thou shalt give it me *n* ... 1Sa 2:16
N Eli was very old, and heard all ... 1Sa 2:22
but *n* the Lord saith, Be it far ... 1Sa 2:30 6258
N Samuel did not yet know the ... 1Sa 3:7
N Israel went out against the ... 1Sa 4:1
N Eli was ninety and eight years ... 1Sa 4:15
N therefore make a new cart, and ... 1Sa 6:7 6258
N the name of his firstborn was ... 1Sa 8:2
n make us a king to judge us like ... 1Sa 8:5 6258
N therefore hearken unto their ... 1Sa 8:9 6258
N there was a man of Benjamin, ... 1Sa 9:1
Take *n* one of the servants with ... 1Sa 9:3 4994
And he said unto him, Behold *n* ... 1Sa 9:6 4994
n let us go thither ... 1Sa 9:6 4994
for he that is *n* called a Prophet ... 1Sa 9:9 3117
make haste *n*, for he came to day ... 1Sa 9:12 6258
N therefore get you up ... 1Sa 9:13 6258
N the Lord had told Samuel in his ... 1Sa 9:15
N therefore present yourselves ... 1Sa 10:19 6258
And *n*, behold, the king walketh ... 1Sa 12:2 6258
N therefore stand still, that I ... 1Sa 12:7 6258
but *n* deliver us out of the hand ... 1Sa 12:10 6258
N therefore behold the king whom ... 1Sa 12:13 6258
N therefore stand and see this ... 1Sa 12:16 6258
come down *n* upon me to Gilgal ... 1Sa 13:12 6258
for *n* would the Lord have ... 1Sa 13:13 6258
But *n* thy kingdom shall not ... 1Sa 13:14 6258
N there was no smith found ... 1Sa 13:19
N it came to pass upon a day, ... 1Sa 14:1

that were with him, Number *n* ... 1Sa 14:17 4994
for had there not been *n* a much ... 1Sa 14:30 6258
N the sons of Saul were Jonathan, ... 1Sa 14:49
n therefore hearken thou unto the ... 1Sa 15:1 6258
N go and smite Amalek, and utterly ... 1Sa 15:3 6258
N therefore, I pray thee, pardon ... 1Sa 15:25 6258
yet honour me *n*, I pray thee, ... 1Sa 15:30 6258
N he was ruddy, and withal of a ... 1Sa 16:12
servants said unto him, Behold *n* ... 1Sa 16:15 4994
Let our lord *n* command thy ... 1Sa 16:16 4994
Provide me *n* a man that can play ... 1Sa 16:17 4994
N the Philistines gathered ... 1Sa 17:1
N David was the son of that ... 1Sa 17:12
Take *n* for thy brethren an ephah ... 1Sa 17:17 4994
N Saul, and they, and all the men ... 1Sa 17:19
And David said, What have I *n* done ... 1Sa 17:29 6258
n therefore be the king's son in ... 1Sa 18:22 6258
n therefore, I pray thee, take ... 1Sa 19:2 6258
and *n*, if I have found favour in ... 1Sa 20:29 6258
Wherefore *n* send and fetch him ... 1Sa 20:31 6258
find out *n* the arrows which I ... 1Sa 20:36 4994
N therefore what is under thine ... 1Sa 21:3 6258
N a certain man of the servants ... 1Sa 21:7
(*N* Saul abode in Gibeah under a ... 1Sa 22:6
that stood about him, Hear *n* ... 1Sa 22:7 4994
And Saul said, Hear *n*, thou son of ... 1Sa 22:12 4994
N therefore, O king, come down ... 1Sa 23:20 6258
And *n*, behold, I know well that ... 1Sa 24:20 6258
Swear *n* therefore unto me by the ... 1Sa 24:21 6258
N the name of the man was Nabal ... 1Sa 25:3
n I have heard that thou hast ... 1Sa 25:7 6258
n thy shepherds which were with ... 1Sa 25:7
there be many servants *n* a days ... 1Sa 25:10
N therefore know and consider what ... 1Sa 25:17 6258
N David had said, Surely in vain ... 1Sa 25:21
N therefore, my lord, as the Lord ... 1Sa 25:26 6258
n let thine enemies, and they that ... 1Sa 25:26 6258
n this blessing which thine ... 1Sa 25:27 6258
n therefore let me smite him, I ... 1Sa 26:8 6258
take thou *n* the spear that is at ... 1Sa 26:11 6258
n see where the king's spear is, ... 1Sa 26:16 6258
N therefore, I pray thee, let my ... 1Sa 26:19 6258
N therefore, let not my blood ... 1Sa 26:20 6258
I shall *n* perish one day by the ... 1Sa 27:1 6258
If I have *n* found grace in thine ... 1Sa 27:5 4994
N Samuel was dead, and all Israel ... 1Sa 28:3
N therefore, I pray thee, hearken ... 1Sa 28:22 6258
N the Philistines gathered ... 1Sa 29:1
Wherefore *n* return, and go in ... 1Sa 29:7 6258
Wherefore *n* rise up early in the ... 1Sa 29:10 6258
N the Philistines fought against ... 1Sa 31:1
N it came to pass after the death ... 2Sa 1:1
n the Lord shew kindness and truth ... 2Sa 2:6 6258
Therefore *n* let your hands be ... 2Sa 2:7 6258
Joab, Let the young men *n* arise ... 2Sa 2:14 4994
N there was long war between the ... 2Sa 3:1
N then do it ... 2Sa 3:18 6258
shall I not therefore *n* require ... 2Sa 4:11 6258
unto Nathan the prophet, See *n* ... 2Sa 7:2 4994
N therefore so shalt thou say ... 2Sa 7:8 6258
And *n*, O Lord God, the word that ... 2Sa 7:25 6258
And *n*, O Lord God, thou art that ... 2Sa 7:28 6258
Therefore *n* let it please thee to ... 2Sa 7:29 6258
N when Mephibosheth, the son of ... 2Sa 9:6
N Ziba had fifteen sons and twenty ... 2Sa 9:10
N therefore the sword shall never ... 2Sa 12:10 6258
But *n* he is dead, wherefore ... 2Sa 12:23 6258
N therefore gather the rest of ... 2Sa 12:28 6258
Go *n* to thy brother Amnon's house ... 2Sa 13:7 4994
N therefore, I pray thee, speak ... 2Sa 13:13 6258
Put *n* this woman out from me, and ... 2Sa 13:17 4994
but hold *n* thy peace, my sister ... 2Sa 13:20 6258
to the king, and said, Behold *n* ... 2Sa 13:24 4994
Nay, my son, let us not all *n* go ... 2Sa 13:25 4994
N Absalom had commanded his ... 2Sa 13:28
Mark ye *n* when Amnon's heart is ... 2Sa 13:28 4994
N therefore let not my lord the ... 2Sa 13:33 6258
N Joab the son of Zeruiah ... 2Sa 14:1
put on *n* mourning apparel, and ... 2Sa 14:2 4994
N therefore that I am come to ... 2Sa 14:15 6258
I will *n* speak unto the king ... 2Sa 14:15 4994
the king shall *n* be comfortable ... 2Sa 14:17 4994
Let my lord the king *n* speak ... 2Sa 14:18 4994
the king said unto Joab, Behold *n* ... 2Sa 14:21 4994
n therefore let me see the king's ... 2Sa 14:32 6258
so will I *n* also be thy servant ... 2Sa 15:34 6258
how much more *n* may this ... 2Sa 16:11 6258
Let me *n* choose out twelve ... 2Sa 17:1 4994
Call *n* Hushai the Archite also, ... 2Sa 17:5 4994
he is hid *n* in some pit, or in ... 2Sa 17:9 6258
N therefore send quickly, and tell ... 2Sa 17:16 6258
N Jonathan and Ahimaaz stayed by ... 2Sa 17:17
but *n* thou art worth ten thousand ... 2Sa 18:3 6258
therefore *n* it is better that ... 2Sa 18:3 6258
N Absalom in his lifetime had ... 2Sa 18:18
the son of Zadok, Let me *n* run ... 2Sa 18:19 4994
N therefore arise, go forth, and ... 2Sa 19:7 6258
thee from thy youth until *n* ... 2Sa 19:7 6258
n he is fled out of the land for ... 2Sa 19:9 6258
N therefore why speak ye not a ... 2Sa 19:10 6258
N Barzillai was a very aged man, ... 2Sa 19:32
N shall Sheba the son of Bichri ... 2Sa 20:6 6258
N Joab was over all the host of ... 2Sa 20:23
(*n* the Gibeonites were not of the ... 2Sa 21:2
N these be the last words of ... 2Sa 23:1
Go *n* through all the tribes of ... 2Sa 24:2 4994
N the Lord thy God add unto the ... 2Sa 24:3
and *n*, I beseech thee, O Lord, ... 2Sa 24:10 6258
n advise, and see what answer I ... 2Sa 24:13 6258
let us fall *n* into the hand of ... 2Sa 24:14 4994
stay *n* thine hand ... 2Sa 24:16 6258
N king David was old and stricken ... 1Kin 1:1
N therefore come, let me, I pray ... 1Kin 1:12 6258
And *n*, behold, Adonijah reigneth ... 1Kin 1:18 6258

and *n*, my lord the king, thou	1Kin 1:18	
N the days of David drew nigh	1Kin 2:1	
N therefore hold him not	1Kin 2:9	6258
n I ask one petition of thee,	1Kin 2:16	6258
N therefore, as the LORD liveth,	1Kin 2:24	6258
And *n*, O LORD my God, thou hast	1Kin 3:7	6258
But *n* the LORD my God hath given	1Kin 5:4	6258
N therefore command thou that	1Kin 5:6	6258
Therefore *n*, LORD God of Israel,	1Kin 8:25	6258
And *n*, O God of Israel, let thy	1Kin 8:26	6258
(*N* Hiram the king of Tyre had	1Kin 9:11	
N the weight of gold that came to	1Kin 10:14	
n therefore make thou the	1Kin 12:4	6258
n whereas my father did lade you	1Kin 12:11	6258
n see to thine own house, David	1Kin 12:16	6258
N shall the kingdom return to the	1Kin 12:26	6258
Intreat *n* the face of the LORD	1Kin 13:6	4994
N there dwelt an old prophet in	1Kin 13:11	
but what? even *n*.	1Kin 14:14	6258
N the rest of the acts of	1Kin 14:29	
N in the eighteenth year of king	1Kin 15:1	
N the rest of the acts of Abijam,	1Kin 15:7	
N the rest of the acts of Nadab,	1Kin 15:31	
N the rest of the acts of Baasha,	1Kin 16:5	
N the rest of the acts of Elah,	1Kin 16:14	
N the rest of the acts of Zimri,	1Kin 16:20	
N the rest of the acts of Omri	1Kin 16:27	
N by this I know that thou art a	1Kin 17:24	6258
(*N* Obadiah feared the LORD	1Kin 18:3	
n thou sayest, Go, tell thy lord,	1Kin 18:11	6258
n thou sayest, Go, tell thy lord,	1Kin 18:14	6258
N therefore send, and gather to me	1Kin 18:19	6258
And said to his servant, Go up *n*	1Kin 18:43	4994
n, O LORD, take away my life	1Kin 19:4	6258
servants said unto him, Behold *n*	1Kin 20:31	4994
N the men did diligently observe	1Kin 20:33	
Dost thou *n* govern the kingdom of	1Kin 21:7	6258
spake unto him, saying, Behold *n*	1Kin 22:13	4994
N therefore, behold, the LORD	1Kin 22:23	6258
N the rest of the acts of Ahab,	1Kin 22:39	
N the rest of the acts of	1Kin 22:45	
N therefore thus saith the LORD,	2Kin 1:4	
them, Why are ye *n* turned back	2Kin 1:5	2088
therefore let my life *n* be	2Kin 1:14	6258
N the rest of the acts of Ahaziah	2Kin 1:18	
And they said unto him, Behold *n*	2Kin 2:16	4994
N Jehoram the son of Ahab began	2Kin 3:1	
But *n* bring me a minstrel	2Kin 3:15	6258
n therefore, Moab, to the spoil	2Kin 3:23	6258
N there cried a certain woman of	2Kin 4:1	
said unto her husband, Behold *n*	2Kin 4:9	4994
Say *n* unto her, Behold, thou hast	2Kin 4:13	4994
Run *n*, I pray thee, to meet her,	2Kin 4:26	6258
N Naaman, captain of the host of	2Kin 5:1	
N when this letter is come unto	2Kin 5:6	6258
let him come *n* to me, and he shall	2Kin 5:8	4994
n I know that there is no God in	2Kin 5:15	4994
n therefore, I pray thee, take a	2Kin 5:15	6258
even *n* there be come to me from	2Kin 5:22	6258
said unto Elisha, Behold *n*	2Kin 6:1	4994
N therefore come, and let us fall	2Kin 7:4	6258
n therefore come, that we may go	2Kin 7:9	6258
I will *n* shew you what the	2Kin 7:12	4994
the man of God, and said, *N*	2Kin 7:19	
she left the land, even until *n*	2Kin 8:6	6258
It is false; tell us *n*	2Kin 9:12	4994
(*N* Joram had kept Ramoth-gilead,	2Kin 9:14	
N therefore take and cast him into	2Kin 9:26	6258
see *n* this cursed woman, and bury	2Kin 9:34	4994
N as soon as this letter cometh	2Kin 10:2	6258
N the king's sons, being seventy	2Kin 10:6	
Know *n* that there shall fall unto	2Kin 10:10	645
N therefore call unto me all the	2Kin 10:19	6258
N the rest of the acts of Jehu,	2Kin 10:34	
n therefore receive no more money	2Kin 12:7	6258
N the rest of the acts of	2Kin 13:8	
N Elisha was fallen sick of his	2Kin 13:14	
whereas *n* thou shalt smite Syria	2Kin 13:19	6258
N the rest of the acts of Jehoash	2Kin 14:15	
N they made a conspiracy against	2Kin 14:19	
N the rest of the acts of	2Kin 14:28	
N the rest of the acts of Jotham,	2Kin 15:36	
N the rest of the acts of Ahaz	2Kin 16:19	
N it came to pass in the third	2Kin 18:1	
N in the fourteenth year of king	2Kin 18:13	
Speak ye *n* to Hezekiah, Thus	2Kin 18:19	4994
N on whom dost thou trust, that	2Kin 18:20	6258
N, behold, thou trustest upon the	2Kin 18:21	6258
N therefore, I pray thee, give	2Kin 18:23	6258
Am I *n* come up without the LORD	2Kin 18:25	6258
N therefore, O LORD our God, I	2Kin 19:19	6258
n have I brought it to pass, that	2Kin 19:25	6258
remember *n* how I have walked	2Kin 20:3	4994
N the rest of the acts of	2Kin 21:17	
N the rest of the acts of Amon	2Kin 21:25	
(*n* she dwelt in Jerusalem in the	2Kin 22:14	
N the rest of the acts of Josiah,	2Kin 23:28	
N the rest of the acts of	2Kin 24:5	
(*n* the Chaldees were against the	2Kin 25:4	
N the rest of the people that	2Kin 25:11	
N the sons of Keturah, Abraham's	1Chr 1:32	
N these are the kings that	1Chr 1:43	
N Sheshan had no sons, but	1Chr 2:34	
N the sons of Caleb the brother	1Chr 2:42	
N these were the sons of David,	1Chr 3:1	
N the sons of Reuben the	1Chr 5:1	
N these are their dwelling places	1Chr 6:54	
N the sons of Issachar were, Tola	1Chr 7:1	
N Benjamin begat Bela his	1Chr 8:1	
N the first inhabitants that	1Chr 9:2	
N the Philistines fought against	1Chr 10:1	
N three of the thirty captains	1Chr 11:15	
N these are they that came to	1Chr 12:1	
N Hiram king of Tyre sent	1Chr 14:1	
N these are the names of his	1Chr 14:4	
N it came to pass, as David sat	1Chr 17:1	
N therefore thus shalt thou say	1Chr 17:7	6258
Therefore *n*, LORD, let the thing	1Chr 17:23	6258
And *n*, LORD, thou art God, and hast	1Chr 17:26	6258
N therefore let it please thee to	1Chr 17:27	6258
N after this it came to pass,	1Chr 18:1	
N when Tou king of Hamath heard	1Chr 18:9	
N it came to pass after this,	1Chr 19:1	
N when Joab saw that the battle	1Chr 19:10	
but *n*, I beseech thee, do away	1Chr 21:8	6258
N therefore advise thyself what	1Chr 21:12	6258
let me fall *n* into the hand of	1Chr 21:13	4994
It is enough, stay *n* thine hand	1Chr 21:15	6258
N Ornan was threshing wheat	1Chr 21:20	
I will therefore *n* make	1Chr 22:5	4994
N, my son, the LORD be with thee	1Chr 22:11	6258
N, behold, in my trouble I have	1Chr 22:14	
N set your heart and your soul to	1Chr 22:19	6258
N the Levites were numbered from	1Chr 23:3	
N concerning Moses the man of God	1Chr 23:14	
N these are the divisions of the	1Chr 24:1	
N the first lot came forth to	1Chr 24:7	
N the first lot came forth for	1Chr 25:9	
N the children of Israel after	1Chr 27:1	
N therefore, in the sight of all	1Chr 28:8	6258
Take heed *n*	1Chr 28:10	6258
N I have prepared with all my	1Chr 29:2	
N therefore, our God, we thank	1Chr 29:13	6258
n have I seen with joy thy people	1Chr 29:17	6258
N bless the LORD your God	1Chr 29:20	4994
N the acts of David the king,	1Chr 29:29	
N, O LORD God, let thy promise	2Chr 1:9	6258
Give me *n* wisdom and knowledge,	2Chr 1:10	6258
Send me *n* therefore a man cunning	2Chr 2:7	6258
n I have sent a cunning man,	2Chr 2:13	6258
N therefore the wheat, and the	2Chr 2:15	6258
N these are the things wherein	2Chr 3:3	
N it was in the heart of David my	2Chr 6:7	
N therefore, O LORD God of Israel	2Chr 6:16	6258
N then, O LORD God of Israel, let	2Chr 6:17	6258
N, my God, let, I beseech thee,	2Chr 6:40	6258
N therefore arise, O LORD God,	2Chr 6:41	6258
N when Solomon had made an end of	2Chr 7:1	
N mine eyes shall be open, and	2Chr 7:15	6258
For *n* have I chosen and sanctified	2Chr 7:16	6258
N all the work of Solomon was	2Chr 8:16	
N the weight of gold that came to	2Chr 9:13	
N the rest of the acts of Solomon	2Chr 9:29	
n therefore ease thou somewhat	2Chr 10:4	6258
man to your tents, O Israel, and *n*	2Chr 10:16	6258
N the acts of Rehoboam, first and	2Chr 12:15	
N in the eighteenth year of king	2Chr 13:1	
n ye think to withstand the	2Chr 13:8	6258
N for a long season Israel hath	2Chr 15:3	
N Jehoshaphat had riches and	2Chr 18:1	
N therefore, behold, the LORD	2Chr 18:22	6258
N the king of Syria had commanded	2Chr 18:30	
Wherefore *n* let the fear of the	2Chr 19:7	6258
And *n*, behold, the children of	2Chr 20:10	6258
N the rest of the acts of	2Chr 20:34	
N Jehoshaphat slept with his	2Chr 21:1	
N when Jehoram was risen up to	2Chr 21:4	
N when Athaliah heard the noise	2Chr 23:12	
N it came to pass, that at what	2Chr 24:11	
N after the death of Jehoiada	2Chr 24:17	
N concerning his sons, and the	2Chr 24:27	
N it came to pass, when the	2Chr 25:3	
N it came to pass, after that	2Chr 25:14	
abide *n* at home	2Chr 25:19	6258
N the rest of the acts of Amaziah	2Chr 25:26	
N after the time that Amaziah did	2Chr 25:27	
N the rest of the acts of Uzziah,	2Chr 26:22	
N the rest of the acts of Jotham,	2Chr 27:7	
n ye purpose to keep under the	2Chr 28:10	6258
N hear me therefore, and deliver	2Chr 28:11	6258
N the rest of his acts and of all	2Chr 28:26	
sanctify *n* yourselves, and	2Chr 29:5	6258
N it is in mine heart to make a	2Chr 29:10	6258
My sons, be not *n* negligent	2Chr 29:11	6258
N they began on the first day of	2Chr 29:17	
N ye have consecrated yourselves	2Chr 29:31	6258
N be ye not stiffnecked, as your	2Chr 30:8	6258
N when all this was finished, all	2Chr 31:1	
N therefore let not Hezekiah	2Chr 32:15	6258
N the rest of the acts of	2Chr 32:32	
N after this he built a wall	2Chr 33:14	
N the rest of the acts of	2Chr 33:18	
N in the eighteenth year of his	2Chr 34:8	
(*n* she dwelt in Jerusalem in the	2Chr 34:22	
serve *n* the LORD your God, and his	2Chr 35:3	6258
N the rest of the acts of Josiah,	2Chr 35:26	
N the rest of the acts of	2Chr 36:8	
N in the first year of Cyrus king	2Chr 36:22	
N in the first year of Cyrus king	Ezr 1:1	
N these are the children of the	Ezr 2:1	
N in the second year of their	Ezr 3:8	
N when the adversaries of Judah	Ezr 4:1	
Be it known *n* unto the king, that	Ezr 4:13	3705
N because we have maintenance	Ezr 4:14	3705
Give ye *n* commandment to cause	Ezr 4:21	3705
Take heed *n* that ye fail not to	Ezr 4:22	
N when the copy of king	Ezr 4:23	116
until *n* hath it been in building	Ezr 5:16	3705
N therefore, if it seem good to	Ezr 5:17	3705
N therefore, Tatnai, governor	Ezr 6:6	3705
N after these things, in the	Ezr 7:1	
N this is the copy of the letter	Ezr 7:11	
These are *n* the chief of their	Ezr 8:1	
N on the fourth day was the	Ezr 8:33	
N when these things were done,	Ezr 9:1	
n for a little space grace hath	Ezr 9:8	6258
And *n*, O our God, what shall we	Ezr 9:10	6258
N therefore give not your	Ezr 9:12	6258
N when Ezra had prayed, and when	Ezr 10:1	
yet *n* there is hope in Israel	Ezr 10:2	6258
N therefore let us make a	Ezr 10:3	6258
N therefore make confession unto	Ezr 10:11	6258
Let *n* our rulers of all the	Ezr 10:14	4994
Let thine ear *n* be attentive	Neh 1:6	4994
which I pray before thee *n*	Neh 1:6	3117
N these are thy servants and thy	Neh 1:10	
let *n* thine ear be attentive to	Neh 1:11	4994
N I had not been beforetime sad	Neh 2:1	
N the king had sent captains of	Neh 2:9	
N Tobiah the Ammonite was by him,	Neh 4:3	
Yet *n* our flesh is as the flesh	Neh 5:5	6258
N that which was prepared for me	Neh 5:18	
N it came to pass, when Sanballat	Neh 6:1	
n shall it be reported to the	Neh 6:7	6258
Come *n* therefore, and let us take	Neh 6:7	6258
N therefore, O God, strengthen my	Neh 6:9	6258
N it came to pass, when the wall	Neh 7:1	
N the city was large and great	Neh 7:4	
N in the twenty and fourth day of	Neh 9:1	
N therefore, our God, the great,	Neh 9:32	6258
N those that sealed were,	Neh 10:1	
N these are the chief of the	Neh 11:3	
N these are the priests and the	Neh 12:1	
N it came to pass, when they had	Neh 13:3	
N it came to pass in the days of	Est 1:1	
N in Shushan the palace there was	Est 2:5	
N when every maid's turn was come	Est 2:12	
N when the turn of Esther, the	Est 2:15	
N it came to pass, when they	Est 3:4	
N it came to pass on the third	Est 5:1	
N Haman was come into the outward	Est 6:4	
N Haman thought in his heart, To	Est 6:6	
N in the twelfth month, that is,	Est 9:1	
n what is thy petition	Est 9:12	
N there was a day when the sons	Job 1:6	
But put forth thine hand *n*	Job 1:11	4994
But put forth thine hand *n*	Job 2:5	4994
N when Job's three friends heard	Job 2:11	
For *n* should I have lain still and	Job 3:13	6258
But *n* it is come upon thee, and	Job 4:5	6258
N a thing was secretly brought to	Job 4:12	
Call *n*, if there be any that will	Job 5:1	4994
For *n* it would be heavier than	Job 6:3	6258
For *n* ye are no thing	Job 6:21	6258
N therefore be content, look upon	Job 6:28	6258
for *n* shall I sleep in the dust	Job 7:21	6258
surely *n* he would awake for thee,	Job 8:6	6258
N my days are swifter than a post	Job 9:25	
But ask *n* the beasts, and they	Job 12:7	4994
Hear *n* my reasoning, and hearken	Job 13:6	4994
Behold *n*, I have ordered my cause	Job 13:18	4994
for *n*, if I hold my tongue, I	Job 13:19	6258
For *n* thou numberest my steps	Job 14:16	6258
But *n* he hath made me weary	Job 16:7	6258
Also *n*, behold, my witness is in	Job 16:19	6258
Lay down *n*, put me in a surety	Job 17:3	4994
you all, do ye return, and come *n*	Job 17:10	4994
And where is *n* my hope	Job 17:15	645
Know *n* that God hath overthrown	Job 19:6	645
Oh that my words were *n* written	Job 19:23	645
Acquaint *n* thyself with him, and	Job 22:21	4994
And if it be not so *n*, who will	Job 24:25	645
But *n* they that are younger than	Job 30:1	6258
n am I their song, yea, I am	Job 30:9	6258
n my soul is poured out upon me	Job 30:16	6258
N Elihu had waited till Job had	Job 32:4	
N he hath not directed his words	Job 32:14	
n I have opened my mouth, my	Job 33:2	4994
If *n* thou hast understanding,	Job 34:16	
But *n*, because it is not so, he	Job 35:15	6258
n men see not the bright light	Job 37:21	6258
Gird up *n* thy loins like a man	Job 38:3	4994
Gird up thy loins *n* like a man	Job 40:7	4994
Deck thyself *n* with majesty	Job 40:10	4994
Behold *n* behemoth, which I made	Job 40:15	4994
Lo *n*, his strength is in his	Job 40:16	4994
but *n* mine eye seeth thee	Job 42:5	6258
take unto you *n* seven bullocks	Job 42:8	6258
Be wise *n* therefore, O ye kings	Ps 2:10	6258
n will I arise, saith the LORD	Ps 12:5	6258
They have *n* compassed us in our	Ps 17:11	6258
N know I that the LORD saveth his	Ps 20:6	6258
n shall mine head be lifted up	Ps 27:6	6258
I have been young, and *n* am old	Ps 37:25	
And *n*, Lord, what wait I for	Ps 39:7	6258
n that he lieth he shall rise up	Ps 41:8	
N consider this, ye that forget	Ps 50:22	4994
N also when I am old and	Ps 71:18	
But *n* they break down the carved	Ps 74:6	6258
heathen say, Where is *n* their God	Ps 115:2	4994
LORD *n* in the presence of all his	Ps 116:14	4994
LORD *n* in the presence of all his	Ps 116:18	4994
Let Israel *n* say, that his mercy	Ps 118:2	4994
Let the house of Aaron *n* say	Ps 118:3	4994
Let them *n* that fear the LORD say	Ps 118:4	4994
Save *n*, I beseech thee, O LORD	Ps 118:25	4994
I beseech thee, send *n* prosperity	Ps 118:25	4994
but *n* have I kept thy word	Ps 119:67	6258
companions' sakes, I will *n* say	Ps 122:8	4994
was on our side, *n* may Israel say	Ps 124:1	4994
from my youth, may Israel *n* say	Ps 129:1	4994
Hear me *n* therefore, O ye	Prov 5:7	6258
Do this *n*, my son, and deliver	Prov 6:3	645
N is she without, *n* in the	Prov 7:12	6471
Hearken unto me *n* therefore	Prov 7:24	6258
N therefore hearken unto me, O ye	Prov 8:32	6258
I said in mine heart, Go to *n*	Eccl 2:1	4994
seeing that which *n* is in the	Eccl 2:16	3528
That which hath been is *n*	Eccl 3:15	3528
and their envy, is *n* perished	Eccl 9:6	3528
for God *n* accepteth thy works	Eccl 9:7	3528
N there was found in it a poor	Eccl 9:15	

Remember *n* thy Creator in the	Eccl 12:1	
I will rise *n*, and go about the	Song 3:2	4994
n also thy breasts shall be as	Song 7:8	4994
Come *n*, and let us reason together	Is 1:18	4994
lodged in it; but *n* murderers	Is 1:21	6258
N will I sing to my wellbeloved a	Is 5:1	4994
And *n*, O inhabitants of Jerusalem,	Is 5:3	6258
And *n* go to	Is 5:5	6258
Go forth *n* to meet Ahaz, thou, and	Is 7:3	4994
And he said, Hear ye *n*, O house of	Is 7:13	4994
N therefore, behold, the Lord	Is 8:7	
But *n* the LORD hath spoken,	Is 16:14	6258
and let them tell thee *n*, and let	Is 19:12	4994
What aileth thee *n*, that thou art	Is 22:1	645
N therefore be ye not mockers,	Is 28:22	6258
Jacob shall not *n* be ashamed	Is 29:22	6258
neither shall his face *n* wax pale	Is 29:22	6258
N go, write it before them in a	Is 30:8	6258
N the Egyptians are men, and not	Is 31:3	
N will I rise, saith the LORD	Is 33:10	6258
n will I be exalted	Is 33:10	6258
n will I lift up myself	Is 33:10	6258
N it came to pass in the	Is 36:1	
Say ye *n* to Hezekiah, Thus saith	Is 36:4	4994
n on whom dost thou trust, that	Is 36:5	6258
N therefore give pledges, I pray	Is 36:8	6258
am I *n* come up without the LORD	Is 36:10	6258
N therefore, O LORD our God, save	Is 37:20	6258
n have I brought it to pass, that	Is 37:26	6258
And said, Remember *n*, O LORD, I	Is 38:3	4994
n will I cry like a travailing	Is 42:14	
But *n* thus saith the LORD that	Is 43:1	6258
n it shall spring forth	Is 43:19	6258
Yet *n* hear, O Jacob my servant	Is 44:1	6258
Therefore hear *n* this, thou that	Is 47:8	6258
Stand *n* with thine enchantments,	Is 47:12	4994
Let *n* the astrologers, the	Is 47:13	4994
They are created *n*, and not from	Is 48:7	6258
n the Lord GOD, and his Spirit,	Is 48:16	6258
And *n*, saith the LORD that formed	Is 49:5	6258
shall even *n* be too narrow by	Is 49:19	6258
Therefore hear *n* this, thou	Is 51:21	4994
N therefore, what have I here,	Is 52:5	6258
But *n*, O LORD, thou art our	Is 64:8	6258
n what hast thou to do in the way	Jer 2:18	6258
n also will I give sentence	Jer 4:12	6258
her hands, saying, Woe is me *n*	Jer 4:31	4994
streets of Jerusalem, and see *n*	Jer 5:1	4994
Hear *n* this, O foolish people, and	Jer 5:21	4994
Let us *n* fear the LORD our God,	Jer 5:24	4994
But go ye *n* unto my place which	Jer 7:12	4994
And *n*, because ye have done all	Jer 7:13	6258
he will *n* remember their iniquity	Jer 14:10	6258
let it come *n*	Jer 17:15	4994
N therefore go to, speak to the	Jer 18:11	6258
return ye *n* every one from his	Jer 18:11	4994
Ask ye *n* among the heathen, who	Jer 18:13	4994
N Pashur the son of Immer the	Jer 20:1	
Turn ye again *n* every one from	Jer 25:5	4994
N it came to pass, when Jeremiah	Jer 26:8	
Therefore *n* amend your ways and	Jer 26:13	6258
n have I given all these lands	Jer 27:6	6258
of the LORD's house shall *n*	Jer 27:16	6258
let them *n* make intercession to	Jer 27:18	4994
Nevertheless hear thou *n* this	Jer 28:7	4994
unto Hananiah the prophet, Hear *n*	Jer 28:15	4994
N these are the words of the	Jer 29:1	
N therefore why hast thou not	Jer 29:27	6258
Ask ye *n*, and see whether a man	Jer 30:6	4994
N when I had delivered the	Jer 32:16	
n therefore thus saith the LORD,	Jer 32:36	6258
N when all the princes, and all	Jer 34:10	
And ye were *n* turned, and had done	Jer 34:15	3117
Return ye *n* every man from his	Jer 35:15	4994
And they said unto him, Sit down *n*	Jer 36:15	4994
N it came to pass, when they had	Jer 36:16	
asked Baruch, saying, Tell us *n*	Jer 36:17	4994
N the king sat in the winterhouse	Jer 36:22	
Pray *n* unto the LORD our God for	Jer 37:3	4994
N Jeremiah came in and went out	Jer 37:4	
Where are *n* your prophets which	Jer 37:19	
Therefore hear *n*, I pray thee, O	Jer 37:20	6254
N when Ebed-melech the Ethiopian,	Jer 38:7	
Put *n* these old cast clouts and	Jer 38:12	4994
Declare unto us *n* what thou hast	Jer 38:25	4994
N Nebuchadrezzar king of Babylon	Jer 39:11	
N the word of the LORD came unto	Jer 39:15	
N the LORD hath brought it, and	Jer 40:3	
And *n*, behold, I loose thee this	Jer 40:4	6258
N while he was not yet gone back,	Jer 40:5	
N when all the captains of the	Jer 40:7	
N it came to pass in the seventh	Jer 41:1	
N the pit wherein Ishmael had	Jer 41:9	
N it came to pass, that when all	Jer 41:13	
n therefore hear the word of the	Jer 42:15	6258
n I have this day declared it to	Jer 42:21	
N therefore know certainly that	Jer 42:22	6258
Therefore *n* thus saith the LORD,	Jer 44:7	6258
Thou didst say, Woe is me *n*	Jer 45:3	4994
(*n* the Chaldeans were by the city	Jer 52:7	
N in the fifth month, in the	Jer 52:12	
N it came to pass in the	Eze 1:1	
N as I beheld the living	Eze 1:15	
n have I not eaten of that which	Eze 4:14	6258
N is the end come upon thee, and I	Eze 7:3	6258
N will I shortly pour out my fury	Eze 7:8	6258
lift up thine eyes *n* the way	Eze 8:5	4994
me, Son of man, dig *n* in the wall	Eze 8:8	4994
N the cherubims stood on the	Eze 10:3	
N when I passed by thee, and	Eze 16:8	
Say *n* to the rebellious house,	Eze 17:12	4994
N, lo, if he beget a son, that	Eze 18:14	
Hear *n*, O house of Israel	Eze 18:25	4994
N when she saw that she had	Eze 19:5	
And *n* she is planted in the	Eze 19:13	6258
N, thou son of man, wilt thou	Eze 22:2	
Will they *n* commit whoredoms with	Eze 23:43	6258
replenished, *n* she is laid waste	Eze 26:2	
N shall the isles tremble in the	Eze 26:18	6258
N, thou son of man, take up a	Eze 27:2	
N the hand of the LORD was upon	Eze 33:22	
places that are *n* inhabited	Eze 38:12	
N will I bring again the	Eze 39:25	6258
N the building that was before	Eze 41:12	
N the upper chambers were shorter	Eze 42:5	
N when he had made an end of	Eze 42:15	
N let them put away their	Eze 43:9	6258
N when the prince shall prepare a	Eze 46:12	3588
N when I had returned, behold, at	Eze 47:7	
N these are the names of the	Eze 48:1	
N among these were of the	Dan 1:6	
N God had brought Daniel into	Dan 1:9	
N at the end of the days that the	Dan 1:18	
unto me *n* what we desired of thee	Dan 2:23	3705
for thou hast *n* made known unto	Dan 2:23	3705
N if ye be ready that at what	Dan 3:15	3705
N thou, O Belteshazzar, declare	Dan 4:18	
N I Nebuchadnezzar praise and	Dan 4:37	3705
N the queen, by reason of the	Dan 5:10	
n let Daniel be called, and he	Dan 5:12	3705
n the wise men, the astrologers,	Dan 5:15	3705
n if thou canst read the writing,	Dan 5:16	3705
N, O king, establish the decree,	Dan 6:8	3705
N when Daniel knew that the	Dan 6:10	1768
N the king spake and said unto	Dan 6:16	116
N as he was speaking with me, I	Dan 8:18	
N that being broken, whereas four	Dan 8:22	
And *n*, O Lord our God, that hast	Dan 9:15	6258
N therefore, O our God, hear the	Dan 9:17	6258
I am *n* come forth to give thee	Dan 9:22	6258
for unto thee am I *n* sent	Dan 10:11	6258
N I am come to make thee	Dan 10:14	
n will I return to fight with the	Dan 10:20	6258
n will I shew thee the truth	Dan 11:2	6258
N when they shall fall, they	Dan 11:34	
N when she had weaned Lo-ruhamah,	Hos 1:8	
then was it better with me than *n*	Hos 2:7	6258
n will I discover her lewdness in	Hos 2:10	6258
n the LORD will feed them as a	Hos 4:16	6258
for *n*, O Ephraim, thou committest	Hos 5:3	
n shall a month devour them with	Hos 5:7	6258
n their own doings have beset	Hos 7:2	
n shall they be among the	Hos 8:8	
n will I gather them, and they	Hos 8:10	6258
n will he remember their iniquity	Hos 8:13	6258
n shall they be found faulty	Hos 10:2	6258
For *n* they shall say, We have no	Hos 10:3	6258
n they sin more and more, and have	Hos 13:2	6258
Therefore also *n*, saith the LORD,	Joel 2:12	6258
Therefore *n* shall they go captive	Amos 6:7	6258
N therefore hear thou the word of	Amos 7:16	6258
N the word of the LORD came unto	Jonah 1:1	
N the LORD had prepared a great	Jonah 1:17	
N Nineveh was an exceeding great	Jonah 3:3	
Therefore *n*, O LORD, take, I	Jonah 4:3	6258
N why dost thou cry out aloud	Mic 4:9	6258
for *n* shalt thou go forth out of	Mic 4:10	6258
N also many nations are gathered	Mic 4:11	6258
N gather thyself in troops, O	Mic 5:1	6258
for *n* shall he be great unto the	Mic 5:4	6258
Hear ye *n* what the LORD saith	Mic 6:1	4994
remember *n* what Balak king of	Mic 6:5	4994
n shall be their perplexity	Mic 7:4	6258
n shall she be trodden down as	Mic 7:10	6258
For *n* will I break his yoke from	Nah 1:13	6258
N therefore thus saith the LORD	Hag 1:5	6258
Speak *n* to Zerubbabel the son of	Hag 2:2	4994
and how do ye see it *n*	Hag 2:3	6258
Yet *n* be strong, O Zerubbabel,	Hag 2:4	6258
Ask *n* the priests concerning the	Hag 2:11	4994
And *n*, I pray you, consider from	Hag 2:15	4994
Consider *n* from this day and	Hag 2:18	4994
Turn ye *n* from your evil ways, and	Zec 1:4	4994
N Joshua was clothed with filthy	Zec 3:3	
Hear *n*, O Joshua the high priest,	Zec 3:8	4994
Lift up *n* thine eyes, and see what	Zec 5:5	4994
But *n* I will not be unto the	Zec 8:11	6258
for *n* have I seen with mine eyes	Zec 9:8	6258
offer it *n* unto thy governor	Mal 1:8	4994
And *n*, I pray you, beseech God	Mal 1:9	6258
And *n*, O ye priests, this	Mal 2:1	6258
house, and prove me *n* herewith	Mal 3:10	4994
n we call the proud happy	Mal 3:15	6258
N the birth of Jesus Christ was	Mt 1:18	*1161*
N all this was done, that it	Mt 1:22	*1161*
N when Jesus was born in	Mt 2:1	*1161*
n also the ax is laid unto the	Mt 3:10	*2236*
unto him, Suffer it to be so *n*	Mt 3:15	*737*
N when Jesus had heard that John	Mt 4:12	*1161*
N when Jesus saw great multitudes	Mt 8:18	*1161*
My daughter is even *n* dead	Mt 9:18	*737*
N the names of the twelve	Mt 10:2	*1161*
N when John had heard in the	Mt 11:2	*1161*
days of John the Baptist until *n*	Mt 11:12	*737*
place, and the time is *n* past	Mt 14:15	*2236*
But the ship was *n* in the midst	Mt 14:24	*2236*
continue with me *n* three days	Mt 15:32	*2236*
N in the morning as he returned	Mt 21:18	*1161*
N there were with us seven	Mt 22:25	*1161*
N learn a parable of the fig tree	Mt 24:32	*1161*
N when Jesus was in Bethany, in	Mt 26:6	*1161*
N the first day of the feast of	Mt 26:17	*1161*
N w the even was come, he sat	Mt 26:20	*1161*
and saith unto them, Sleep on *n*	Mt 26:45	*3063*
N he that betrayed him gave them	Mt 26:48	*1161*
that I cannot *n* pray to my Father	Mt 26:53	*737*
N the chief priests, and elders,	Mt 26:59	*1161*
n ye have heard his blasphemy	Mt 26:65	*3568*
N Peter sat without in the palace	Mt 26:69	*1161*
N at that feast the governor was	Mt 27:15	*1161*
let him *n* come down from the	Mt 27:42	*3568*
let him deliver him *n*, if he will	Mt 27:43	*3568*
N from the sixth hour there was	Mt 27:45	*1161*
N when the centurion, and they	Mt 27:54	*1161*
N the next day, that followed the	Mt 27:62	*1161*
N when they were going, behold,	Mt 28:11	*1161*
N after that John was put in	Mk 1:14	*1161*
N as he walked by the sea of	Mk 1:16	
the ship, so that it was *n* full	Mk 4:37	*2235*
N there was there nigh unto the	Mk 5:11	*1161*
And when the day was *n* far spent	Mk 6:35	*2236*
and *n* the time is far passed	Mk 6:35	*2236*
because they have *n* been with me	Mk 8:2	*2236*
N the disciples had forgotten to	Mk 8:14	*2532*
an hundredfold *n* in this time	Mk 10:30	*3568*
n the eventide was come, he went	Mk 11:11	*2236*
N there were seven brethren	Mk 12:20	*3767*
N the brother shall betray the	Mk 13:12	*1161*
N learn a parable of the fig tree	Mk 13:28	*1161*
and saith unto them, Sleep on *n*	Mk 14:41	*3063*
N at that feast he released unto	Mk 15:6	*1161*
Israel descend *n* from the cross	Mk 15:32	*3568*
n when the even was come, because	Mk 15:42	*2236*
N when Jesus was risen early the	Mk 16:9	*1161*
they both were *n* well stricken in	Lk 1:7	
N Elisabeth's full time came that	Lk 1:57	*1161*
Let us *n* go even unto Bethlehem,	Lk 2:15	*1211*
n lettest thou thy servant depart	Lk 2:29	*3568*
N his parents went to Jerusalem	Lk 2:41	*2532*
N in the fifteenth year of the	Lk 3:1	*1161*
n also the axe is laid unto the	Lk 3:9	*2236*
N when all the people were	Lk 3:21	*1161*
N when the sun was setting, all	Lk 4:40	*1161*
N when he had left speaking, he	Lk 5:4	*1161*
Blessed are ye that hunger *n*	Lk 6:21	*3568*
Blessed are ye that weep *n*	Lk 6:21	*3568*
Woe unto you that laugh *n*	Lk 6:25	*3568*
N when he had ended all his	Lk 7:1	*1161*
when he was *n* not far from the	Lk 7:6	*2236*
N when he came nigh to the gate	Lk 7:12	*1161*
N when the Pharisee which had	Lk 7:39	*1161*
N the parable is this	Lk 8:11	*1161*
N it came to pass on a certain	Lk 8:22	*2532*
N the man out of whom the devils	Lk 8:38	*1161*
N Herod the tetrarch heard of all	Lk 9:7	*1161*
Which *n* of these three, thinkest	Lk 10:36	*3767*
N it came to pass, as they went,	Lk 10:38	*1161*
the door is *n* shut, and my	Lk 11:7	*2236*
N do ye Pharisees make clean the	Lk 11:39	*3568*
for all things are *n* ready	Lk 14:17	*2236*
N his elder son was in the field	Lk 15:25	*1161*
but *n* he is comforted, and thou	Lk 16:25	*3568*
N when Jesus heard these things,	Lk 18:22	*1161*
even *n* at the descent of the	Lk 19:37	*2236*
but *n* they are hid from thine	Lk 19:42	*3568*
N that the dead are raised, even	Lk 20:37	*1161*
When they *n* shoot forth, ye see	Lk 21:30	*2236*
that summer is *n* nigh at hand	Lk 21:30	*2236*
N the feast of unleavened bread	Lk 22:1	*1161*
Then said he unto them, But *n*	Lk 22:36	*3568*
N when the centurion saw what was	Lk 23:47	*1161*
N upon the first day of the week,	Lk 24:1	*2532*
N Philip was of Bethsaida, the	Jn 1:44	*1161*
And he saith unto them, Draw out *n*	Jn 2:8	*3568*
hast kept the good wine until *n*	Jn 2:10	*737*
N when he was in Jerusalem at the	Jn 2:23	*1161*
N Jacob's well was there	Jn 4:6	*1161*
he whom thou *n* hast is not thy	Jn 4:18	*3568*
n is, when the true worshippers	Jn 4:23	*3568*
N we believe, not because of thy	Jn 4:42	*3765*
N after two days he departed	Jn 4:43	*1161*
as he was *n* going down, his	Jn 4:51	*2236*
N there is at Jerusalem by the	Jn 5:2	*1161*
knew that he had been *n* a long	Jn 5:6	*2236*
n is, when the dead shall hear	Jn 5:25	*3568*
N there was much grass in the	Jn 6:10	*1160*
And when even was *n* come, his	Jn 6:16	
And it was *n* dark, and Jesus was	Jn 6:17	*2236*
N the Jews' feast of tabernacles	Jn 7:2	*1161*
N about the midst of the feast	Jn 7:14	*2236*
N Moses in the law commanded us,	Jn 8:5	*1161*
But *n* ye seek to kill me, a man	Jn 8:40	*3568*
N we know that thou hast a devil	Jn 8:52	*3568*
how then doth he *n* see	Jn 9:19	*737*
But by what means he *n* seeth	Jn 9:21	*3568*
whereas I was blind, *n* I see	Jn 9:25	*737*
N we know that God heareth not	Jn 9:31	*1161*
but *n* ye say, We see	Jn 9:41	*3568*
N a certain man was sick, named	Jn 11:1	*1161*
N Jesus loved Martha, and her	Jn 11:5	*1161*
N Bethany was nigh unto Jerusalem	Jn 11:18	*1161*
But I know, that even *n*,	Jn 11:22	*3568*
N Jesus was not yet come into the	Jn 11:30	*1161*
N both the chief priests and the	Jn 11:57	*1161*
N is my soul troubled	Jn 12:27	*3568*
N is the judgment of this world	Jn 12:31	*3568*
n shall the prince of this world	Jn 12:31	*3568*
N before the feast of the	Jn 13:1	*1161*
the devil having *n* put into the	Jn 13:2	*2236*
him, What I do thou knowest not *n*	Jn 13:7	*737*
N I tell you before it come, that	Jn 13:19	*737*
N there was leaning on Jesus'	Jn 13:23	*1161*
N no man at the table knew for	Jn 13:28	*1161*
N is the Son of man glorified, and	Jn 13:31	*3568*
so *n* I say to you	Jn 13:33	*737*
I go, thou canst not follow me *n*	Jn 13:36	*3568*
Lord, why cannot I follow thee *n*	Jn 13:37	*737*
n I have told you before it come	Jn 14:29	*3568*
N ye are clean through the word	Jn 15:3	*2236*
but *n* they have no cloke for	Jn 15:22	*3568*
but *n* have they both seen and	Jn 15:24	*3568*
But *n* I go my way to him that	Jn 16:5	*3568*

you, but ye cannot bear them *n*	Jn 16:12	737
N Jesus knew that they were	Jn 16:19	3767
ye *n* therefore have sorrow	Jn 16:22	3568
n speakest thou plainly, and	Jn 16:29	3568
N are we sure that thou knowest	Jn 16:30	3568
answered them, Do ye *n* believe	Jn 16:31	737
is *n* come, that ye shall be	Jn 16:32	3568
And *n*, O Father, glorify thou me	Jn 17:5	3568
N they have known that all things	Jn 17:7	3568
n I am no more in the world, but	Jn 17:11	3765
And *n* come I to thee	Jn 17:13	3568
N Caiaphas was he, which gave	Jn 18:14	1161
N Annas had sent him bound unto	Jn 18:24	3767
but *n* is my kingdom not from	Jn 18:36	3568
N Barabbas was a robber	Jn 18:40	1161
n the coat was without seam,	Jn 19:23	1161
N there stood by the cross of	Jn 19:25	1161
all things were *n* accomplished	Jn 19:28	2236
N there was set a vessel full of	Jn 19:29	3767
N in the place where he was	Jn 19:41	1161
But when the morning was *n* come	Jn 21:4	2236
n they were not able to draw it	Jn 21:6	3765
N when Simon Peter heard that it	Jn 21:7	3767
the fish which ye have *n* caught	Jn 21:10	3568
This is *n* the third time that	Jn 21:14	2236
N this man purchased a field with	Acts 1:18	3767
N when this was noised abroad,	Acts 2:6	1161
shed forth this, which ye *n* see	Acts 2:33	3568
N when they heard this, they were	Acts 2:37	1161
N Peter and John went up together	Acts 3:1	1161
And *n*, brethren, I wot that	Acts 3:17	3568
for it was *n* eventide	Acts 4:3	2236
N when they saw the boldness of	Acts 4:13	1161
And *n*, Lord, behold their	Acts 4:29	3568
N when the high priest and the	Acts 5:24	1161
n I say unto you, Refrain from	Acts 5:38	3568
this land, wherein ye *n* dwell	Acts 7:4	3568
N there came a dearth over all	Acts 7:11	1161
n come, I will send thee into	Acts 7:34	3568
whom ye have been *n* the betrayers	Acts 7:52	3568
N when the apostles which were at	Acts 8:14	1161
N there was at Joppa a certain	Acts 9:36	1161
n send men to Joppa, and call for	Acts 10:5	3568
N while Peter doubted in himself	Acts 10:17	1161
N therefore are we all here	Acts 10:33	3568
N they which were scattered	Acts 11:19	3767
N about that time Herod the king	Acts 12:1	1161
N I know of a surety, that the	Acts 12:11	3568
N as soon as it was day, there	Acts 12:18	1161
N there were in the church that	Acts 13:1	1161
And *n*, behold, the hand of the	Acts 13:11	3568
N when Paul and his company loosed	Acts 13:13	1161
n no more to return to corruption	Acts 13:34	
N when the congregation was	Acts 13:43	1161
N therefore why tempt ye God, to	Acts 15:10	3568
N when they had gone throughout	Acts 16:6	1161
n therefore depart, and go in	Acts 16:36	3568
n do they thrust us out privily	Acts 16:37	3568
N when they had passed through	Acts 17:1	1161
N while Paul waited for them at	Acts 17:16	1161
but *n* commandeth all men every	Acts 17:30	3568
when Paul was *n* about to open his	Acts 18:14	1161
And *n*, behold, I go bound in the	Acts 20:22	3568
And *n*, behold, I know that ye all,	Acts 20:25	3568
And *n*, brethren, I commend you to	Acts 20:32	3568
N when we had discovered Cyprus,	Acts 21:3	1161
defence which I make *n* unto you	Acts 22:1	3568
And *n* why tarriest thou	Acts 22:16	3568
N therefore ye with the council	Acts 23:15	3568
n are they ready, looking for a	Acts 23:21	3568
things whereof they *n* accuse me	Acts 24:13	3568
N after many years I came to	Acts 24:17	1161
N when Festus was come into the	Acts 25:1	3767
n I stand and am judged for the	Acts 26:6	3568
unto whom *n* I send thee,	Acts 26:17	3568
N when much time was spent, and	Acts 27:9	1161
and when sailing was *n* dangerous	Acts 27:9	2235
the fast was *n* already past	Acts 27:9	2235
n I exhort you to be of good	Acts 27:22	3568
if by any means *n* at length I	Rom 1:10	2236
N I would not have you ignorant,	Rom 1:13	1161
N we know that what things soever	Rom 3:19	1161
But *n* the righteousness of God	Rom 3:21	3568
N to him that worketh is the	Rom 4:4	1161
not his own body *n* dead, when he	Rom 4:19	2236
N it was not written for his sake	Rom 4:23	1161
being *n* justified by his blood,	Rom 5:9	3568
by whom we have *n* received the	Rom 5:11	3568
N if we be dead with Christ, we	Rom 6:8	1161
even so *n* yield your members	Rom 6:19	3568
things whereof ye are *n* ashamed	Rom 6:21	3568
But *n* being made free from sin,	Rom 6:22	3570
But *n* we are delivered from the	Rom 7:6	3570
N then it is no more I that do it	Rom 7:17	3570
N if I do that I would not, it is	Rom 7:20	1161
There is therefore *n* no	Rom 8:1	3568
N if any man have not the Spirit	Rom 8:9	1161
in pain together until *n*	Rom 8:22	3568
N if the fall of them be the	Rom 11:12	1161
yet have *n* obtained mercy through	Rom 11:30	3568
so have these also *n* not believed	Rom 11:31	3568
that *n* it is high time to awake	Rom 13:11	2236
for *n* is our salvation nearer	Rom 13:11	3568
n walkest thou not charitably	Rom 14:15	3765
N the God of patience and	Rom 15:5	1161
N I say that Jesus Christ was a	Rom 15:8	1160
N the God of hope fill you with	Rom 15:13	1161
But *n* having no more place in	Rom 15:23	3570
But *n* I go unto Jerusalem to	Rom 15:25	3570
N I beseech you, brethren, for	Rom 15:30	1161
N the God of peace be with you	Rom 15:33	1161
N I beseech you, brethren, mark	Rom 16:17	1161
N to him that is of power to	Rom 16:25	1161
But *n* is made manifest, and by the	Rom 16:26	3568
N I beseech you, brethren, by the	1Cor 1:10	1161
N this I say, that every one of	1Cor 1:12	1161
N we have received, not the	1Cor 2:12	1161
it, neither yet *n* are ye able	1Cor 3:2	3568
N he that planteth and he that	1Cor 3:8	1161
N if any man build upon this	1Cor 3:12	1161
n if thou didst receive it, why	1Cor 4:7	2532
N ye are full, *n* ye are rich,	1Cor 4:8	2236
n ye are rich, ye have reigned as	1Cor 4:8	2236
N some are puffed up, as though I	1Cor 4:18	1161
But *n* I have written unto you not	1Cor 5:11	3570
N therefore there is utterly a	1Cor 6:7	2236
N the body is not for fornication	1Cor 6:13	1161
N concerning the things whereof	1Cor 7:1	1161
but *n* are they holy	1Cor 7:14	3568
N concerning virgins I have no	1Cor 7:25	1161
N as touching things offered unto	1Cor 8:1	1161
N they do it to obtain a	1Cor 9:25	3767
N these things were our examples,	1Cor 10:6	1161
N all these things happened unto	1Cor 10:11	1161
N I praise you, brethren, that ye	1Cor 11:2	1161
N in this that I declare unto you	1Cor 11:17	1161
N concerning spiritual gifts,	1Cor 12:1	1161
N there are diversities of gifts,	1Cor 12:4	1161
But *n* hath God set the members	1Cor 12:18	3570
But *n* are they many members, yet	1Cor 12:20	3568
N ye are the body of Christ, and	1Cor 12:27	1161
For *n* we see through a glass,	1Cor 13:12	737
n I know in part	1Cor 13:12	737
n abideth faith, hope, charity,	1Cor 13:13	3570
N, brethren, if I come unto you	1Cor 14:6	3570
N if Christ be preached that he	1Cor 15:12	1161
But *n* is Christ risen from the	1Cor 15:20	3570
N this I say, brethren, that	1Cor 15:50	1161
N concerning the collection for	1Cor 16:1	1161
N I will come unto you, when I	1Cor 16:5	1161
I will not see you *n* by the way	1Cor 16:7	737
N if Timotheus come, see that he	1Cor 16:10	1161
N he which stablisheth us with	2Cor 1:21	1161
N thanks be unto God, which	2Cor 2:14	1161
N the Lord is that Spirit	2Cor 3:17	1161
N he that hath wrought us for the	2Cor 5:5	1161
yet *n* henceforth know we him no	2Cor 5:16	3568
N then we are ambassadors for	2Cor 5:20	3767
behold, *n* is the accepted time	2Cor 6:2	3568
n is the day of salvation	2Cor 6:2	3568
N for a recompence in the same	2Cor 6:13	1161
N I rejoice, not that ye were	2Cor 7:9	3568
N therefore perform the doing of	2Cor 8:11	3570
that *n* at this time your	2Cor 8:14	3568
but *n* much more diligent, upon	2Cor 8:22	3570
N he that ministereth seed to the	2Cor 9:10	1161
N I Paul myself beseech you by	2Cor 10:1	1161
but *n* I forbear, lest any man	2Cor 12:6	
being absent *n* I write to them	2Cor 13:2	3568
N I pray to God that ye do no	2Cor 13:7	1161
we said before, so say I *n* again	Gal 1:9	737
For do I *n* persuade men, or God	Gal 1:10	737
N the things which I write unto	Gal 1:20	2236
persecuted us in times past *n*	Gal 1:23	3568
the life which I *n* live in the	Gal 2:20	3568
are ye *n* made perfect by the	Gal 3:3	3568
N to Abraham and his seed were the	Gal 3:16	1161
N a mediator is not a mediator of	Gal 3:20	1161
N I say, That the heir, as long	Gal 4:1	2236
But *n*, after that ye have known	Gal 4:9	3568
I desire to be present with you *n*	Gal 4:20	737
answereth to Jerusalem which *n* is	Gal 4:25	3568
N we, brethren, as Isaac was, are	Gal 4:28	1161
after the Spirit, even so it is *n*	Gal 4:29	3568
N the works of the flesh are	Gal 5:19	1161
the spirit that *n* worketh in the	Eph 2:2	3568
But *n* in Christ Jesus ye who	Eph 2:13	3570
N therefore ye are no more	Eph 2:19	3767
as it is *n* revealed unto his holy	Eph 3:5	3568
To the intent that *n* unto the	Eph 3:10	3568
N unto him that is able to do	Eph 3:20	1161
(*N* that he ascended, what is it	Eph 4:9	1161
but *n* are ye light in the Lord	Eph 5:8	3568
gospel from the first day until *n*	Phil 1:5	3568
so *n* also Christ shall be	Phil 1:20	3568
saw in me, and *n* hear to be in me	Phil 1:30	3568
but *n* much more in my absence,	Phil 2:12	3568
n tell you even weeping, that	Phil 3:18	3568
that *n* at the last your care of	Phil 4:10	2236
N ye Philippians know also, that	Phil 4:15	1161
N unto God and our Father be glory	Phil 4:20	1161
works, yet *n* hath he reconciled	Col 1:21	3570
Who *n* rejoice in my sufferings	Col 1:24	3568
but *n* is made manifest to his	Col 1:26	3570
But *n* ye also put off all these	Col 3:8	3570
But *n* when Timotheus came from	1Th 3:6	737
For *n* we live, if ye stand fast	1Th 3:8	3568
N God himself and our Father, and	1Th 3:11	1161
N we exhort you, brethren, warn	1Th 5:14	1161
N we beseech you, brethren, by	2Th 2:1	1161
n ye know what withholdeth that	2Th 2:6	3568
only he who *n* letteth will let,	2Th 2:7	737
N our Lord Jesus Christ himself,	2Th 2:16	1161
N we command you, brethren, in	2Th 3:6	1161
N them that are such we command	2Th 3:12	1161
N the Lord of peace himself give	2Th 3:16	1161
N the end of the commandment is	1Ti 1:5	1161
N unto the King eternal, immortal	1Ti 1:17	1161
N the Spirit speaketh expressly,	1Ti 4:1	1161
promise of the life that *n* is	1Ti 4:8	3568
N she that is a widow indeed, and	1Ti 5:5	1161
But is *n* made manifest by the	2Ti 1:10	3568
N as Jannes and Jambres withstood	2Ti 3:8	1161
For I am *n* ready to be offered,	2Ti 4:6	2236
n also a prisoner of Jesus Christ	Philem 9	3570
but *n* profitable to thee and to me	Philem 11	3570
Not *n* as a servant, but above a	Philem 16	3765
But *n* we see not yet all things	Heb 2:8	3568
N consider how great this man was	Heb 7:4	1161
N of the things which we have	Heb 8:1	1161
But *n* hath he obtained a more	Heb 8:6	3570
N that which decayeth and waxeth	Heb 8:13	1161
we cannot *n* speak particularly	Heb 9:5	3568
N when these things were thus	Heb 9:6	1161
n to appear in the presence of	Heb 9:24	3568
but *n* once in the end of the	Heb 9:26	3568
N where remission of these is,	Heb 10:18	1161
N the just shall live by faith	Heb 10:38	1161
N faith is the substance of	Heb 11:1	1161
But *n* they desire a better	Heb 11:16	3570
N no chastening for the present	Heb 12:11	1161
but *n* he hath promised, saying,	Heb 12:26	3568
N the God of peace, that brought	Heb 13:20	1161
N if thou commit no adultery, yet	Jas 2:11	
Go to *n*, ye that say, To day or	Jas 4:13	3568
But *n* ye rejoice in your	Jas 4:16	3568
Go to *n*, ye rich men, weep and	Jas 5:1	3568
though *n* for a season, if need be	1Pet 1:6	737
though *n* ye see him not, yet	1Pet 1:8	737
which are *n* reported unto you by	1Pet 1:12	3568
but are *n* the people of God	1Pet 2:10	3568
but *n* have obtained mercy	1Pet 2:10	3568
but are *n* returned unto the	1Pet 2:25	3568
even baptism doth also *n* save us	1Pet 3:21	3568
whose judgment *n* of a long time	2Pet 2:3	
beloved, I *n* write unto you	2Pet 3:1	2236
heavens and the earth, which are *n*	2Pet 3:7	3568
To him be glory both *n* and for	2Pet 3:18	3568
past, and the true light *n* shineth	1Jn 2:8	2236
is in darkness even until *n*	1Jn 2:9	737
even *n* are there many antichrists	1Jn 2:18	3568
And *n*, little children, abide in	1Jn 2:28	3568
n are we the sons of God, and it	1Jn 3:2	3568
even *n* already is it in the world	1Jn 4:3	3568
n I beseech thee, lady, not as	2Jn 5	3568
N unto him that is able to keep	Jude 24	1161
dominion and power, both *n*	Jude 25	3568
N is come salvation, and strength,	Rev 12:10	737

NUMBER

so that if a man can *n* the dust	Gen 13:16	4487
stars, if thou be able to *n* them	Gen 15:5	5608
and I being few in *n*, they shall	Gen 34:30	4557
for it was without *n*	Gen 41:49	4557
according to the *n* of the souls	Ex 12:4	4373
to the *n* of your persons	Ex 16:16	4557
the *n* of thy days I will fulfil	Ex 23:26	4557
children of Israel after their *n*	Ex 30:12	6485
then he shall *n* to himself seven	Lev 15:13	5608
then she shall *n* to herself seven	Lev 15:28	5608
sabbath shall ye *n* fifty days	Lev 23:16	5608
thou shalt *n* seven sabbaths of	Lev 25:8	5608
According to the *n* of years after	Lev 25:15	4557
according unto the *n* of years of	Lev 25:15	4557
for according to the *n* of the	Lev 25:16	4557
be according unto the *n* of years	Lev 25:50	4557
your cattle, and make you few in *n*	Lev 26:22	
with the *n* of their names, every	Num 1:2	4557
Aaron shall *n* them by their	Num 1:3	6485
according to the *n* of the names	Num 1:18	4557
according to the *n* of the names	Num 1:20	4557
according to the *n* of the names	Num 1:22	4557
according to the *n* of the names	Num 1:24	4557
according to the *n* of the names	Num 1:26	4557
according to the *n* of the names	Num 1:28	4557
according to the *n* of the names	Num 1:30	4557
according to the *n* of the names	Num 1:32	4557
according to the *n* of the names	Num 1:34	4557
according to the *n* of the names	Num 1:36	4557
according to the *n* of the names	Num 1:38	4557
according to the *n* of the names	Num 1:40	4557
according to the *n* of the names	Num 1:42	4557
shalt not *n* the tribe of Levi	Num 1:49	6485
N the children of Levi after the	Num 3:15	6485
old and upward shalt thou *n* them	Num 3:15	6485
to the *n* of all the males	Num 3:22	4557
In the *n* of all the males, from a	Num 3:28	4557
to the *n* of all the males	Num 3:34	4557
N all the firstborn of the males	Num 3:40	6485
take the *n* of their names	Num 3:40	4557
firstborn males by the *n* of names	Num 3:43	4557
wherewith the odd *n* of them is to	Num 3:48	5736
fifty years old shalt thou *n* them	Num 4:23	6485
thou shalt *n* them after their	Num 4:29	6485
fifty years old shalt thou *n* them	Num 4:30	6485
Aaron did *n* according to the	Num 4:37	6485
Aaron did *n* according to the	Num 4:41	6485
of you, according to your whole *n*	Num 14:29	4557
After the *n* of the days in which	Num 14:34	4557
According to the *n* that ye shall	Num 15:12	4557
to every one according to their *n*	Num 15:12	4557
the *n* of the fourth part of	Num 23:10	4557
according to the *n* of names	Num 26:53	4557
shall be according to their *n*	Num 29:18	4557
shall be according to their *n*	Num 29:21	4557
shall be according to their *n*	Num 29:24	4557
shall be according to their *n*	Num 29:27	4557
shall be according to their *n*	Num 29:30	4557
shall be according to their *n*	Num 29:33	4557
shall be according to their *n*	Num 29:37	4557
was in *n* three hundred thousand	Num 31:36	4557
left few in *n* among the heathen	Deut 4:27	4557
ye were more in *n* than any people	Deut 7:7	
weeks shalt thou *n* unto thee	Deut 16:9	5608
begin to *n* the seven weeks from	Deut 16:9	5608
to his fault, by a certain *n*	Deut 25:2	4557
And ye shall be left few in *n*	Deut 28:62	
the *n* of the children of Israel	Deut 32:8	4557
according unto the *n* of the	Josh 4:5	4557
according to the *n* of the tribes	Josh 4:8	4557
and their camels were without *n*	Judg 6:5	4557
the *n* of them that lapped,	Judg 7:6	4557

N

and their camels were without *n*.......... Judg 7:12 4557
them wives, according to their *n*.......... Judg 21:23 4557
according to the *n* of the lords............... 1Sa 6:4 4557
according to the *n* of all the.................. 1Sa 6:18 4557
N now, and see who is gone from us ... 1Sa 14:17 6485
went over by *n* twelve of Benjamin...... 2Sa 2:15 4557
six toes, four and twenty in *n*.............. 2Sa 21:20 4557
to say, Go, *n* Israel and Judah.............. 2Sa 24:1 4487
n ye the people, that I may know......... 2Sa 24:2 6485
I may know the *n* of the people............ 2Sa 24:2 4557
to *n* the people of Israel......................... 2Sa 24:4 6485
the *n* of the people unto the king.......... 2Sa 24:9 4662
according to the *n* of the tribes............. 1Kin 18:31 4557
n thee an army, like the army............... 1Kin 20:25 4487
whose *n* was in the days of David........ 1Chr 7:2 4557
the *n* of them, after their...................... 1Chr 7:9 3187
the *n* throughout the genealogy of........ 1Chr 7:40
this is the *n* of the mighty men............ 1Chr 11:11 4557
and provoked David to *n* Israel.............. 1Chr 21:1 4487
n Israel from Beer-sheba even to........... 1Chr 21:2 5608
bring the *n* of them to me, that I........... 1Chr 21:2 4557
of the *n* of the people unto David......... 1Chr 21:5 4662
brass, and the iron, there is no *n*.......... 1Chr 22:16 4557
their *n* by their polls, man by................ 1Chr 23:3 4557
by *n* of names by their polls.................. 1Chr 23:24 4557
moons, and on the set feasts, by *n*.......... 1Chr 23:31 4557
the *n* of the workmen according to....... 1Chr 25:1 4557
So the *n* of them, with their.................... 1Chr 25:7 4557
children of Israel after their *n*.............. 1Chr 27:1 4557
But David took not the *n* of them......... 1Chr 27:23 4557
the son of Zeruiah began to *n*................. 1Chr 27:24 4487
neither was the *n* put in the................... 1Chr 27:24 4557
the people were without *n* that............... 2Chr 12:3 4557
according to the *n* of their..................... 2Chr 26:11 4557
The whole *n* of the chief of the.............. 2Chr 26:12 4557
the *n* of the burnt offerings,.................... 2Chr 29:32 4557
a great *n* of priests sanctified................ 2Chr 30:24
to the *n* of thirty thousand, and............. 2Chr 35:7 4557
And this is the *n* of them........................ Ezr 1:9 4557
The *n* of the men of the people of.......... Ezr 2:2 4557
the daily burnt offerings by *n*................ Ezr 3:4 4557
according to the *n* of the tribes.............. Ezr 6:17 4510
By *n* and by weight of every one............ Ezr 8:34 4557
The *n*, I say, of the men of the............... Neh 7:7 4557
On that day the *n* of those that.............. Est 9:11 4557
according to the *n* of them all................. Job 1:5 4557
not come into the *n* of the months.......... Job 3:6 4557
marvellous things without *n*.................... Job 5:9 4557
yea, and wonders without *n*..................... Job 9:10 4557
the *n* of his months are with thee.......... Job 14:5 4557
the *n* of years is hidden to the.............. Job 15:20 4557
when the *n* of his months is cut............. Job 21:21 4557
Is there any *n* of his armies................... Job 25:3 4557
unto him the *n* of my steps.................... Job 31:37 4557
in pieces mighty men without *n*.............. Job 34:24 2714
neither can the *n* of his years be........... Job 36:26 4557
or because the *n* of thy days is.............. Job 38:21 4557
Who can *n* the clouds in wisdom........... Job 38:37 5608
Canst thou *n* the months that they........ Job 39:2 5608
So teach us to *n* our days........................ Ps 90:12 4487
When they were but a few men in *n*.... Ps 105:12 4557
caterpillers, and that without *n*............ Ps 105:34 4557
they are more in *n* than the sand........... Ps 139:18
He telleth the *n* of the stars................... Ps 147:4 4557
concubines, and virgins without *n*......... Song 6:8 4557
the residue of the *n* of archers.............. Is 21:17 4557
that bringeth out their host by *n*........... Is 40:26 4557
the drink offering unto that *n*............... Is 65:11 4507
will I *n* you to the sword........................ Is 65:12 4487
for according to the *n* of thy................. Jer 2:28 4557
have forgotten me days without *n*.......... Jer 2:32 4557
For according to the *n* of thy.................. Jer 11:13 4557
according to the *n* of the streets........... Jer 11:13 4557
Yet a small *n* that escape the................ Jer 44:28 4557
according to the *n* of the days............... Eze 4:4 4557
according to the *n* of the days............... Eze 4:5 4557
according to the *n* of the days............... Eze 4:9 4557
also take thereof a few in *n*................... Eze 5:3 4557
by books the *n* of the years................... Dan 9:2 4557
Yet the *n* of the children of.................... Hos 1:10 4557
my land, strong, and without *n*.............. Joel 1:6 4557
slain, and a great *n* of carcases............. Nah 3:3
a great *n* of people, blind....................... Mk 10:46 *3793*
being of the *n* of the twelve.................... Lk 22:3 *706*
down, in *n* about five thousand............... Jn 6:10 *706*
(the *n* of names together were............... Acts 1:15 *3793*
the *n* of the men was about five............. Acts 4:4 *706*
to whom a *n* of men, about four.............. Acts 5:36 *706*
when the *n* of the disciples was.............. Acts 6:1
the *n* of the disciples multiplied............. Acts 6:7 *706*
a great *n* believed, and turned................. Acts 11:21 *706*
faith, and increased in *n* daily................ Acts 16:5 *706*
Though the *n* of the children of............. Rom 9:27 *706*
dare not make ourselves of the *n*........... 2Cor 10:12 *1469*
the *n* under threescore years old............ 1Ti 5:9 *2639*
the *n* of them was ten thousand............. Rev 5:11 *706*
I heard the *n* of them which were.......... Rev 7:4 *706*
multitude, which no man could *n*............ Rev 7:9 *705*
the *n* of the army of the horsemen......... Rev 9:16 *706*
and I heard the *n* of them....................... Rev 9:16 *706*
the beast, or the *n* of his name.............. Rev 13:17 *706*
count the *n* of the beast.......................... Rev 13:18 *706*
for it is the *n* of a man........................... Rev 13:18 *706*
his *n* is six hundred threescore................ Rev 13:18 *706*
over the *n* of his name, stand on............ Rev 15:2 *706*
the *n* of whom is as the sand of.............. Rev 20:8 *706*

NUMBERED

then shall thy seed also be *n*.................. Gen 13:16 4487
it shall not be *n* for multitude............... Gen 16:10 5608
which cannot be *n* for multitude............. Gen 32:12 5608
passeth among them that are *n*.............. Ex 30:13 6485
passeth among them that are *n*.............. Ex 30:14 6485
were *n* of the congregation was an........ Ex 38:25 6485
for every one that went to be *n*............. Ex 38:26 6485
so he *n* them in the wilderness of.......... Num 1:19 6485
Those that were *n* of them...................... Num 1:21 6485
those that were *n* of them...................... Num 1:22 6485
Those that were *n* of them...................... Num 1:23 6485
Those that were *n* of them...................... Num 1:25 6485
Those that were *n* of them...................... Num 1:27 6485
Those that were *n* of them...................... Num 1:29 6485
Those that were *n* of them...................... Num 1:31 6485
Those that were *n* of them...................... Num 1:33 6485
Those that were *n* of them...................... Num 1:35 6485
Those that were *n* of them...................... Num 1:37 6485
Those that were *n* of them...................... Num 1:39 6485
Those that were *n* of them...................... Num 1:41 6485
Those that were *n* of them...................... Num 1:43 6485
n, which Moses and Aaron *n*.................. Num 1:44 6485
were *n* of the children of Israel............. Num 1:45 6485
Even all they that were *n* were.............. Num 1:46 6485
fathers were not *n* among them.............. Num 1:47 6485
and those that were *n* of them................ Num 2:4 6485
and those that were *n* thereof................ Num 2:6 6485
and those that were *n* thereof................ Num 2:8 6485
All that were *n* in the camp of................ Num 2:9 6485
and those that were *n* thereof................ Num 2:11 6485
and those that were *n* of them................ Num 2:13 6485
and those that were *n* of them................ Num 2:15 6485
All that were *n* in the camp of................ Num 2:16 6485
and those that were *n* of them................ Num 2:19 6485
and those that were *n* of them................ Num 2:21 6485
and those that were *n* of them................ Num 2:23 6485
All that were *n* of the camp of................ Num 2:24 6485
and those that were *n* of them................ Num 2:26 6485
and those that were *n* of them................ Num 2:28 6485
and those that were *n* of them................ Num 2:30 6485
All they that were *n* in the camp........... Num 2:31 6485
These are those which were *n* of............. Num 2:32 6485
all those that were *n* of the................... Num 2:32 6485
But the Levites were not *n* among.......... Num 2:33 6485
Moses *n* them according to the............... Num 3:16 6485
Those that were *n* of them...................... Num 3:22 6485
even those that were *n* of them.............. Num 3:22 6485
And those that were *n* of them............... Num 3:34 6485
All that were *n* of the Levites,............... Num 3:39 6485
Aaron *n* at the commandment of the...... Num 3:39 6485
And Moses *n*, as the LORD........................ Num 3:42 6485
of those that were *n* of them................. Num 3:43 6485
n the sons of the Kohathites................... Num 4:34 6485
those that were *n* of them by................. Num 4:36 6485
were *n* of the families of the................. Num 4:37 6485
those that were *n* of the sons of............. Num 4:38 6485
Even those that were *n* of them.............. Num 4:40 6485
These are they that were *n* of the.......... Num 4:41 6485
those that were *n* of the families............ Num 4:42 6485
Even those that were *n* of them.............. Num 4:44 6485
These be those that were *n* of the.......... Num 4:45 6485
Aaron *n* according to the word of.......... Num 4:45 6485
those that were *n* of the Levites............. Num 4:46 6485
and Aaron and the chief of Israel *n*....... Num 4:46 6485
Even those that were *n* of them.............. Num 4:48 6485
they were *n* by the hand of Moses.......... Num 4:49 6485
thus were they *n* of him, as the............. Num 4:49 6485
and were over them that were *n*............. Num 7:2 6485
and all that were *n* of you...................... Num 14:29 6485
they that were *n* of them were.............. Num 26:7 6485
to those that were *n* of them................. Num 26:18 6485
to those that were *n* of them................. Num 26:22 6485
to those that were *n* of them................. Num 26:25 6485
to those that were *n* of them................. Num 26:27 6485
and those that were *n* of them................ Num 26:34 6485
to those that were *n* of them................. Num 26:37 6485
they that were *n* of them were............... Num 26:41 6485
to those that were *n* of them................. Num 26:43 6485
to those that were *n* of them................. Num 26:47 6485
they that were *n* of them were............... Num 26:50 6485
These were the *n* of the children........... Num 26:51 6485
to those that were *n* of him.................. Num 26:54 6485
these are they that were *n* of the.......... Num 26:57 6485
those that were *n* of them were............. Num 26:62 6485
for they were not *n* among the............... Num 26:62 6485
are they that were *n* by Moses............... Num 26:63 6485
who *n* the children of Israel in.............. Num 26:63 6485
whom Moses and Aaron the priest *n*.... Num 26:64 6485
when they *n* the children of.................. Num 26:64 6485
n the people, and went up, he and........ Josh 8:10 6485
the children of Benjamin were *n*............ Judg 20:15 6485
which were *n* seven hundred chosen....... Judg 20:15 6485
were *n* four hundred thousand men...... Judg 20:17 6485
For the people were *n*, and, behold........ Judg 21:9 6485
when he *n* them in Bezek, the............... 1Sa 11:8 6485
Saul *n* the people that were.................. 1Sa 13:15 6485
And when they had *n*, behold,................ 1Sa 14:17 6485
n them in Telaim, two hundred.............. 1Sa 15:4 6485
David *n* the people that were with....... 2Sa 18:1 6485
after that he had *n* the people.............. 2Sa 24:10 5608
that cannot be *n* nor counted for.......... 1Kin 3:8 4487
not be told nor *n* for multitude............. 1Kin 8:5 4487
Then he *n* the young men of the............ 1Kin 20:15 6485
after them he *n* all the people,.............. 1Kin 20:15 6485
that Ben-hadad *n* the Syrians................. 1Kin 20:26 6485
And the children of Israel were *n*......... 1Kin 20:27 6485
the same time, and *n* all Israel.............. 2Kin 3:6 6485
that commanded the people to be *n*....... 1Chr 21:17 4487
Now the Levites were *n* from the........... 1Chr 23:3 5608
were *n* from twenty years old................ 1Chr 23:27 4557
Solomon *n* all the strangers that........... 2Chr 2:17 5608
David his father had *n* them.................. 2Chr 2:17 5608
not be told nor *n* for multitude............. 2Chr 5:6 4487
he *n* them from twenty years old........... 2Chr 25:5 6485
n them unto Sheshbazzar, the................ Ezr 1:8 5608
them, they are more than can be *n*........ Ps 40:5 5608
that which is wanting cannot be *n*......... Eccl 1:15 4487
ye have *n* the houses of Jerusalem......... Is 22:10 5608
he was *n* with the transgressors............ Is 53:12 4487
As the host of heaven cannot be *n*......... Jer 33:22 5608
God hath *n* thy kingdom, and................. Dan 5:26 4483
which cannot be measured nor *n*........... Hos 1:10 5608
very hairs of your head are all *n*.......... Mt 10:30 *705*
he was *n* with the transgressors............ Mk 15:28 *3049*
very hairs of your head are all *n*.......... Lk 12:7 *705*
For he was *n* with us, and had............... Acts 1:17 *2674*
he was *n* with the eleven apostles.......... Acts 1:26 *4785*

NUMBEREST

unto the LORD, when thou *n* them......... Ex 30:12 6485
among them, when thou *n* them............ Ex 30:12 6485
For now thou *n* my steps........................ Job 14:16 5608

NUMBERING

sea, very much, until he left *n*.............. Gen 41:49 5608
after the *n* wherewith David his............. 2Chr 2:17 5610

NUMBERS

these are the *n* of the bands that.......... 1Chr 12:23 4557
these are the *n* of them according......... 2Chr 17:14 6486
for I know not the *n* thereof.................. Ps 71:15 5615

NUN (*nun*) See NON. *Father of Joshua.*

his servant Joshua, the son of *N*........... Ex 33:11 5126
And Joshua the son of *N*, the................. Num 11:28 5126
of Ephraim, Oshea the son of *N*.............. Num 13:8 5126
Oshea the son of *N* Jehoshua.................. Num 13:16 5126
And Joshua the son of *N*, and Caleb.... Num 14:6 5126
Jephunneh, and Joshua the son of *N*... Num 14:30 5126
But Joshua the son of *N*, and Caleb...... Num 14:38 5126
Jephunneh, and Joshua the son of *N*... Num 26:65 5126
Take thee Joshua the son of *N*.............. Num 27:18 5126
Kenezite, and Joshua the son of *N*........ Num 32:12 5126
priest, and Joshua the son of *N*............ Num 32:28 5126
priest, and Joshua the son of *N*............ Num 34:17 5126
But Joshua the son of *N*, which............. Deut 1:38 5126
gave Joshua the son of *N* a charge......... Deut 31:23 5126
he, and Hoshea the son of *N*................. Deut 32:44 5126
Joshua the son of *N* was full of............ Deut 34:9 5126
spake unto Joshua the son of *N*............. Josh 1:1 5126
Joshua the son of *N* sent out of............. Josh 2:1 5126
and came to Joshua the son of *N*........... Josh 2:23 5126
Joshua the son of *N* called the.............. Josh 6:6 5126
priest, and Joshua the son of *N*............ Josh 14:1 5126
and before Joshua the son of *N*.............. Josh 17:4 5126
to Joshua the son of *N* among them...... Josh 19:49 5126
priest, and Joshua the son of *N*............ Josh 19:51 5126
and unto Joshua the son of *N*................ Josh 21:1 5126
things, that Joshua the son of *N*.......... Josh 24:29 5126
And Joshua the son of *N*, the................. Judg 2:8 5126
he spake by Joshua the son of *N*........... 1Kin 16:34 5126
of *N* unto that day had not the.............. Neh 8:17 5126

NURSE

Rebekah their sister, and her *n*............. Gen 24:59 3243
But Deborah Rebekah's *n* died.............. Gen 35:8 3243
call to thee a *n* of the Hebrew.............. Ex 2:7 3243
that she may *n* the child for thee.......... Ex 2:7 3243
n it for me, and I will give thee............. Ex 2:9 3243
in her bosom, and became *n* unto it..... Ruth 4:16 539
his *n* took him up, and fled................... 2Sa 4:4 539
they hid him, even him and his *n*.......... 2Kin 11:2 3243
put him and his *n* in a bedchamber....... 2Chr 22:11 3243
even as a *n* cherisheth her..................... 1Th 2:7 *5162*

NURSED

the woman took the child, and *n* it...... Ex 2:9 5134
daughters shall be *n* at thy side............ Is 60:4 539

NURSING

as a *n* father beareth the sucking.......... Num 11:12 539
And kings shall be thy *n* fathers............ Is 49:23 539
and their queens thy *n* mothers............ Is 49:23 3243

NURTURE

but bring them up in the *n*..................... Eph 6:4 *3809*

NUTS

little honey, spices, and myrrh, *n*........... Gen 43:11 992
I went down into the garden of *n*.......... Song 6:11 93

NYMPHA See NYMPHAS.

NYMPHAS (*nim'-fas*) *A Christian at Colosse.*

which are in Laodicea, and *N*................ Col 4:15 *3564*

O

O See PREFACE.

OAK
under the o which was by Shechem..... Gen 35:4 424
buried beneath Beth-el under an o..... Gen 35:8 437
and set it up there under an o..... Josh 24:26 427
sat under an o which was in..... Judg 6:11 424
it out unto him under the o..... Judg 6:19 424
the thick boughs of a great o..... 2Sa 18:9 424
and his head caught hold of the o..... 2Sa 18:9 424
I saw Absalom hanged in an o..... 2Sa 18:10 424
yet alive in the midst of the o..... 2Sa 18:14 424
and found him sitting under an o..... 1Kin 13:14 424
their bones under the o in Jabesh..... 1Chr 10:12 424
be as an o whose leaf fadeth..... Is 1:30 424
as a teil tree, and as an o..... Is 6:13 437
and taketh the cypress and the o..... Is 44:14 437
tree, and under every thick o..... Eze 6:13 424

OAKS
of the o which ye have desired..... Is 1:29 352
up, and upon all the o of Bashan..... Is 2:13 437
Of the o of Bashan have they made..... Eze 27:6 437
incense upon the hills, under o..... Hos 4:13 437
cedars, and he was strong as the o..... Amos 2:9 437
howl, O ye o of Bashan..... Zec 11:2 437

OAR
And all that handle the o, the..... Eze 27:29 4880

OARS
wherein shall go no galley with o..... Is 33:21 7885
of Bashan have they made thine o..... Eze 27:6 4880

OATH
shalt be clear from this my o..... Gen 24:8 7621
thou be clear from this my o..... Gen 24:41 423
thou shalt be clear from my o..... Gen 24:41 423
I will perform the o which I..... Gen 26:3 7621
Let there be now an o betwixt us..... Gen 26:28 423
Joseph took an o of the children..... Gen 50:25 7650
Then shall an o of the LORD be..... Ex 22:11 7621
a man shall pronounce with an o..... Lev 5:4 7621
priest shall charge her by an o..... Num 5:19 7650
the woman with an o of cursing..... Num 5:21 7621
an o among thy people, when the..... Num 5:21 7621
or swear an o to bind his soul..... Num 30:2 7621
her soul by a bond with an o..... Num 30:10 7621
every binding o to afflict the..... Num 30:13 7621
because he would keep the o which..... Deut 7:8 7621
the LORD thy God, and into his o..... Deut 29:12 423
do I make this covenant and this o..... Deut 29:14 423
o which thou hast made us swear..... Josh 2:17 7621
o which thou hast made us to..... Josh 2:20 7621
because of the o which we sware..... Josh 9:20 7621
For they had made a great o..... Judg 21:5 7621
for the people feared the o..... 1Sa 14:26 7621
charged the people with the o..... 1Sa 14:27 7650
charged the people with an o..... 1Sa 14:28 7650
LORD's o that was between them..... 2Sa 21:7 7621
thou not kept the o of the LORD..... 1Kin 2:43 7621
an o be laid upon him to cause..... 1Kin 8:31 423
the o come before thine altar in..... 1Kin 8:31 423
he took an o of the kingdom and..... 1Kin 18:10 7650
took an o of them in the house of..... 2Kin 11:4 7650
Abraham, and of his o unto Isaac..... 1Chr 16:16 7621
an o be laid upon him to make him..... 2Chr 6:22 423
the o come before thine altar in..... 2Chr 6:22 423
And all Judah rejoiced at the o..... 2Chr 15:15 7621
the priests, and took an o of them..... Neh 5:12 7650
into a curse, and into an o..... Neh 10:29 7621
with Abraham, and his o unto Isaac..... Ps 105:9 7621
and that in regard of the o of God..... Eccl 8:2 7621
sweareth, as he that feareth an o..... Eccl 9:2 7621
That I may perform the o which I..... Jer 11:5 7621
which hast despised the o in..... Eze 16:59 423
him, and hath taken an o of him..... Eze 17:13 423
whose o he despised, and whose..... Eze 17:16 423
Seeing he despised the o by..... Eze 17:18 423
surely mine o that he hath..... Eze 17:19 423
the o that is written in the law..... Dan 9:11 7621
and love no false o..... Zec 8:17 7621
an o to give her whatsoever she..... Mt 14:7 *3727*
And again he denied with an o..... Mt 26:72 *3727*
The o which he sware to our..... Lk 1:73 *3727*
God had sworn with an o to him..... Acts 2:30 *3727*
have bound themselves with an o..... Acts 23:21 *332*
an o for confirmation is to them..... Heb 6:16 *3727*
his counsel, confirmed it by an o..... Heb 6:17 *3727*
without an o he was made priest..... Heb 7:20 *3728*
priests were made without an o..... Heb 7:21 *3728*
but this with an o by him that..... Heb 7:21 *3728*
but the word of the o, which was..... Heb 7:28 *3728*
the earth, neither by any other o..... Jas 5:12 *3727*

OATH'S
nevertheless for the o sake..... Mt 14:9 *3727*
yet for his o sake, and for their..... Mk 6:26 *3727*

OATHS
sight, to them that have sworn o..... Eze 21:23 7621
according to the o of the tribes..... Hab 3:9 7621
perform unto the Lord thine o..... Mt 5:33 *3727*

OBADIAH (*o-ba-di'-ah*)
1. An officer in Ahab's court.
And Ahab called O, which was the..... 1Kin 18:3 5662
(Now O feared the LORD greatly..... 1Kin 18:3 5662
that O took an hundred prophets,..... 1Kin 18:4 5662
And Ahab said unto O, Go into the..... 1Kin 18:5 5662
O went another way by himself..... 1Kin 18:6 5662
as O was in the way, behold,..... 1Kin 18:7 5662
So O went to meet Ahab, and told..... 1Kin 18:16 5662
2. A descendant of David.
the sons of Arnan, the sons of O..... 1Chr 3:21 5662
3. A descendant of Tola.
Michael, and O, and Joel, Ishiah,..... 1Chr 7:3 5662
4. Son of Azel.
and Ishmael, and Sheariah, and O..... 1Chr 8:38 5662
and Ishmael, and Sheariah, and O..... 1Chr 9:44 5662
5. Son of Shemaiah.
O the son of Shemaiah, the son of..... 1Chr 9:16 5662
6. A warrior in David's army.
O the second, Eliab the third,..... 1Chr 12:9 5662
7. A prince of Zebulun.
Of Zebulun, Ishmaiah the son of O..... 1Chr 27:19 5662
8. A prince of Judah.
even to Ben-hail, and to O..... 2Chr 17:7 5662
9. A Levite in Josiah's time.
of them were Jahath and O, the..... 2Chr 34:12 5662
10. A clan leader with Ezra.
O the son of Jehiel, and with him..... Ezr 8:9 5662
11. A priest who renewed the covenant.
Harim, Meremoth, O,..... Neh 10:5 5662
12. A Temple gatekeeper.
Mattaniah, and Bakbukiah, O..... Neh 12:25 5662
13. A prophet.
The vision of O..... Obad 1 5662

OBAL (*o'-bal*) *A son of Joktan.*
And O, and Abimael, and Sheba,..... Gen 10:28 5745

OBED (*o'-bed*) See OBED-EDOM.
1. Father of Jesse.
and they called his name O..... Ruth 4:17 5744
begat Boaz, and Boaz begat O..... Ruth 4:21 5744
O begat Jesse, and Jesse begat..... Ruth 4:22 5744
And Boaz begat O, and O begat..... 1Chr 2:12 5744
and Booz begat O of Ruth..... Mt 1:5 *5601*
and O begat Jesse..... Mt 1:5 *5601*
of Jesse, which was the son of O..... Lk 3:32 *5601*
2. A descendant of Judah.
begat Ephlal, and Ephlal begat O..... 1Chr 2:37 5744
O begat Jehu, and Jehu begat..... 1Chr 2:38 5744
3. A "mighty man" of David.
Eliel, and O, and Jasiel the..... 1Chr 11:47 5744
4. A sanctuary servant.
Othni, and Rephael, and O, Elzabad,..... 1Chr 26:7 5744
5. Father of Azariah.
and Azariah the son of O, and..... 2Chr 23:1 5744

OBED-EDOM (*o''-bed-e'-dom*)
1. A Levite.
into the house of O the Gittite..... 2Sa 6:10 5654
of O the Gittite three months..... 2Sa 6:11 5654
and the LORD blessed O, and all his..... 2Sa 6:11 5654
LORD hath blessed the house of O..... 2Sa 6:12 5654
of O into the city of David with..... 2Sa 6:12 5654
into the house of O the Gittite..... 1Chr 13:13 5654
of O in his house three months..... 1Chr 13:14 5654
the LORD blessed the house of O..... 1Chr 13:14 5654
and O and Jehiah were doorkeepers..... 1Chr 15:24 5654
out of the house of O with joy..... 1Chr 15:25 5654
2. A priest who relocated the Ark.
and Elipheleh, and Mikneiah, and O..... 1Chr 15:18 5654
and Elipheleh, and Mikneiah, and O..... 1Chr 15:21 5654
Moreover the sons of O were..... 1Chr 26:4 5654
All these of the sons of O..... 1Chr 26:8 5654
were threescore and two of O..... 1Chr 26:8 5654
To O southward..... 1Chr 26:15 5654
3. Another priest who relocated the Ark.
and Eliab, and Benaiah, and O..... 1Chr 16:5 5654
O with their brethren, threescore..... 1Chr 16:38 5654
4. Son of Jeduthun.
O also the son of Jeduthun and..... 1Chr 16:38 5654
5. A Temple servant.
found in the house of God with O..... 2Chr 25:24 5654

OBEDIENCE
for o to the faith among all..... Rom 1:5 *5218*
so by the o of one shall many be..... Rom 5:19 *5218*
or of o unto righteousness..... Rom 6:16 *5218*
For your o is come abroad unto..... Rom 16:19 *5218*
to all nations for the o of faith..... Rom 16:26 *5218*
they are commanded to be under o..... 1Cor 14:34 *5293*
he remembereth the o of you all..... 2Cor 7:15 *5218*
every thought to the o of Christ..... 2Cor 10:5 *5218*
when your o is fulfilled..... 2Cor 10:6 *5218*
in thy o I wrote unto thee..... Philem 21 *5218*
yet learned he o by the things..... Heb 5:8 *5218*
of the Spirit, unto o and..... 1Pet 1:2 *5218*

OBEDIENT
hath said will we do, and be o..... Ex 24:7 8085
the children of Israel may be o..... Num 27:20 8085
shalt be o unto his voice..... Deut 4:30 8085
because ye would not be o unto..... Deut 8:20 8085
hear, they shall be o unto me..... 2Sa 22:45 8085
is a wise reprover upon an o ear..... Prov 25:12 8085
If ye be willing and o, ye shall..... Is 1:19 8085
neither were they o unto his law..... Is 42:24 8085
the priests were o to the faith..... Acts 6:7 *5219*
by me, to make the Gentiles o..... Rom 15:18 *5218*
whether ye be o in all things..... 2Cor 2:9 *5255*
be o to them that are your..... Eph 6:5 *5219*
became o unto death, even the..... Phil 2:8 *5255*
o to their own husbands, that the..... Titus 2:5 *5293*
Exhort servants to be o unto..... Titus 2:9 *5293*
As o children, not fashioning..... 1Pet 1:14 *5218*

OBEISANCE
about, and made o to my sheaf..... Gen 37:7 7812
and the eleven stars made o to me..... Gen 37:9 7812
bowed down their heads, and made o..... Gen 43:28 7812
meet his father in law, and did o..... Ex 18:7 7812
he fell to the earth, and did o..... 2Sa 1:2 7812
her face to the ground, and did o..... 2Sa 14:4 7812
man came nigh to him to do him o..... 2Sa 15:5 7812
bowed, and did o unto the king..... 1Kin 1:16 7812
of Judah, and made o to the king..... 2Chr 24:17 7812

OBEY
o my voice according to that..... Gen 27:8 8085
only o my voice, and go fetch me..... Gen 27:13 8085
Now therefore, my son, o my voice..... Gen 27:43 8085
that I should o his voice to let..... Ex 5:2 8085
if ye will o my voice indeed, and..... Ex 19:5 8085
o his voice, provoke him not..... Ex 23:21 8085
if thou shalt indeed o his voice..... Ex 23:22 8085
if ye o the commandments of the..... Deut 11:27 8085
if ye will not o the commandments..... Deut 11:28 8085
o his voice, and ye shall serve..... Deut 13:4 8085
which will not o the voice of his..... Deut 21:18 8085
he will not o our voice..... Deut 21:20 8085
Thou shalt therefore o the voice..... Deut 27:10 8085
because thou wouldest not o the..... Deut 28:62 8085
shalt o his voice according to..... Deut 30:2 8085
o the voice of the LORD, and do..... Deut 30:8 8085
and that thou mayest o his voice..... Deut 30:20 8085
we serve, and his voice will we o..... Josh 24:24 8085
refused to o the voice of Samuel..... 1Sa 8:19 8085
o his voice, and not rebel against..... 1Sa 12:14 8085
But if ye will not o the voice of..... 1Sa 12:15 8085
thou not o the voice of the LORD..... 1Sa 15:19 8085
to o is better than sacrifice, and..... 1Sa 15:22 8085
And refused to o, neither were..... Neh 9:17 8085
If they o and serve him, they..... Job 36:11 8085
But if they o not, they shall..... Job 36:12 8085
they hear of me, they shall o me..... Ps 18:44 8085
and despiseth to o his mother..... Prov 30:17 3349
children of Ammon shall o them..... Is 11:14 4928
O my voice, and I will be your God..... Jer 7:23 8085
O my voice, and do them, according..... Jer 11:4 8085
and protesting, saying, O my voice..... Jer 11:7 8085
But if they will not o, I will..... Jer 12:17 8085
that it o not my voice, then I..... Jer 18:10 8085
o the voice of the LORD your God..... Jer 26:13 8085
but o their father's commandment..... Jer 35:14 8085
O, I beseech thee, the voice of..... Jer 38:20 8085
we will o the voice of the LORD..... Jer 42:6 8085
when we o the voice of the LORD..... Jer 42:6 8085
neither o the voice of the LORD..... Jer 42:13 8085
dominions shall serve and o him..... Dan 7:27 8086
that they might not o thy voice..... Dan 9:11 8085
if ye will diligently o the voice..... Zec 6:15 8085
even the winds and the sea o him..... Mt 8:27 *5219*
unclean spirits, and they do o him..... Mk 1:27 *5219*
even the wind and the sea o him..... Mk 4:41 *5219*
the winds and water, and they o him..... Lk 8:25 *5219*
and it should o you..... Lk 17:6 *5219*
We ought to o God rather than men..... Acts 5:29 *3980*
God hath given to them that o him..... Acts 5:32 *3980*
To whom our fathers would not o..... Acts 7:39 *5255*
do not o the truth..... Rom 2:8 *544*
but o unrighteousness..... Rom 2:8 *3982*
that ye should o it in the lusts..... Rom 6:12 *5219*
ye yield yourselves servants to o..... Rom 6:16 *5218*
his servants ye are to whom ye o..... Rom 6:16 *5219*
that ye should not o the truth..... Gal 3:1 *3982*
that ye should not o the truth..... Gal 5:7 *3982*
o your parents in the Lord..... Eph 6:1 *5219*
o your parents in all things..... Col 3:20 *5219*
o in all things your masters..... Col 3:22 *5219*
that o not the gospel of our Lord..... 2Th 1:8 *5219*
if any man o not our word by this..... 2Th 3:14 *5219*
to o magistrates, to be ready to..... Titus 3:1 *3980*
unto all them that o him..... Heb 5:9 *5219*
O them that have the rule over..... Heb 13:17 *3982*
mouths, that they may o us..... Jas 3:3 *3982*
if any o not the word, they also..... 1Pet 3:1 *544*
them that o not the gospel of God..... 1Pet 4:17 *544*

OBEYED
because thou hast o my voice..... Gen 22:18 8085
Because that Abraham o my voice..... Gen 26:5 8085
And that Jacob o his father..... Gen 28:7 8085
because they o not the voice of..... Josh 5:6 8085
have o my voice in all that I..... Josh 22:2 8085
but ye have not o my voice..... Judg 2:2 8085
but ye have not o my voice..... Judg 6:10 8085
I have o the voice of the LORD,..... 1Sa 15:20 8085
the people, and o their voice..... 1Sa 15:24 8085
thine handmaid hath o thy voice..... 1Sa 28:21 8085
hast not o the voice of the LORD..... 1Kin 20:36 8085
Because they o not the voice of..... 2Kin 18:12 8085
and all Israel o him..... 1Chr 29:23 8085
they o the words of the LORD, and..... 2Chr 11:4 8085
have not o the voice of my..... Prov 5:13 8085
tree, and ye have not o my voice..... Jer 3:13 8085
have not o the voice of the LORD..... Jer 3:25 8085
them, and have not o my voice..... Jer 9:13 8085
Yet they o not, nor inclined..... Jer 11:8 8085
But they o not, neither inclined..... Jer 17:23 8085
but they o not thy voice, neither..... Jer 32:23 8085
of them any more, then they o..... Jer 34:10 8085
Thus have we o the voice of..... Jer 35:8 8085
we have dwelt in tents, and have o..... Jer 35:10 8085
Because ye have o the commandment..... Jer 35:18 8085
have not o his voice, therefore..... Jer 40:3 8085
but ye have not o the voice of..... Jer 42:21 8085
o not the voice of the LORD, to..... Jer 43:4 8085
for they o not the voice of the..... Jer 43:7 8085

have not *o* the voice of the LORD, Jer 44:23 8085
Neither have we *o* the voice of Dan 9:10 8085
for we *o* not his voice Dan 9:14 8085
She *o* not the voice Zeph 3:2 8085
o the voice of the LORD their God Hag 1:12 8085
and all, as many as *o* him, were Acts 5:36 *3982*
and all, even as many as *o* him Acts 5:37 *3982*
but ye have *o* from the heart that Rom 6:17 *5219*
they have not all *o* the gospel Rom 10:16 *5219*
my beloved, as ye have always *o* Phil 2:12 *5219*
receive for an inheritance, *o* Heb 11:8 *5219*
Even as Sarah *o* Abraham, calling 1Pet 3:6 *5219*

OBEYEDST
Because thou *o* not the voice of 1Sa 28:18 8085
youth, that thou *o* not my voice Jer 22:21 8085

OBEYETH
that *o* the voice of his servant, Is 50:10 8085
This is a nation that *o* not the Jer 7:28 8085
Cursed be the man that *o* not the Jer 11:3 8085

OBEYING
o the commandments of the LORD Judg 2:17 8085
as in *o* the voice of the LORD 1Sa 15:22 8085
in *o* the truth through the Spirit 1Pet 1:22 *5218*

OBIL (*o'-bil*) *An Ishmaelite camel driver.*
camels also was O the Ishmaelite 1Chr 27:30 179

OBJECT
have been here before thee, and *o* Acts 24:19 *2723*

OBLATION
if thou bring an *o* of a meat Lev 2:4 7133
if thy *o* be a meat offering baken Lev 2:5 7133
if thy *o* be a meat offering baken Lev 2:7 7133
As for the *o* of the firstfruits, Lev 2:12 7133
every *o* of thy meat offering Lev 2:13 7133
if his *o* be a sacrifice of peace Lev 3:1 7133
offer one out of the whole *o* for Lev 7:14 7133
unto the LORD shall bring his *o* Lev 7:29 7133
will offer his *o* for all his vows Lev 22:18 7133
every *o* of theirs, every meat Num 18:9 7133
brought an *o* for the LORD Num 31:50 7133
day, and shall do sacrifice and *o* Is 19:21 4503
o chooseth a tree that will not Is 40:20 8641
he that offereth an *o*, as if he Is 66:3 4503
they offer burnt offering and an *o* Jer 14:12 4503
every *o* of all, of every sort of Eze 44:30 8641
ye shall offer an *o* unto the LORD Eze 45:1 8641
over against the *o* of the holy Eze 45:6 8641
side of the *o* of the holy portion Eze 45:7 8641
before the *o* of the holy portion, Eze 45:7 8641
This is the *o* that ye shall offer Eze 45:13 8641
this *o* for the prince in Israel Eze 45:16 8641
The *o* that ye shall offer unto Eze 48:9 8641
the priests, shall be this holy *o* Eze 48:10 8641
this *o* of the land that is Eze 48:12 8642
in length over against the *o* of Eze 48:18 8641
against the *o* of the holy portion Eze 48:18 8641
All the *o* shall be five and twenty Eze 48:20 8641
shall offer the holy *o* foursquare Eze 48:20 8641
and on the other of the holy *o* Eze 48:21 8641
of the *o* toward the east border Eze 48:21 8641
and it shall be the holy *o* Eze 48:21 8641
that they should offer an *o* Dan 2:46 4541
about the time of the evening *o* Dan 9:21 4503
the *o* to cease, and for the Dan 9:27 4503

OBLATIONS
to offer their *o* unto the LORD Lev 7:38 7133
to distribute the *o* of the LORD 2Chr 31:14 8641
Bring no more vain *o* Is 1:13 4503
and the firstfruits of your *o* Eze 20:40 4864
of all, of every sort of your *o* Eze 44:30 8641

OBOTH (*o'-both*) *An Israelite encampment in the wilderness.*
set forward, and pitched in O Num 21:10 88
And they journeyed from O, and Num 21:11 88
from Punon, and pitched in O Num 33:43 88
And they departed from O, and Num 33:44 88

OBSCURE
shall be put out in *o* darkness Prov 20:20 380

OBSCURITY
of the blind shall see out of *o* Is 29:18 652
then shall thy light rise in *o* Is 58:10 2822
we wait for light, but behold *o* Is 59:9 2822

OBSERVATION
kingdom of God cometh not with *o* Lk 17:20 *3907*

OBSERVE
And ye shall *o* the feast of Ex 12:17 8104
therefore shall ye *o* this day in Ex 12:17 8104
ye shall *o* this thing for an Ex 12:24 8104
to *o* the sabbath throughout their Ex 31:16 6213
O thou that which I command thee Ex 34:11 8104
thou shalt *o* the feast of weeks, Ex 34:22 6213
ye use enchantment, nor *o* times Lev 19:26 6049
shall ye *o* all my statutes Lev 19:37 8104
shall ye *o* to offer unto me in Num 28:2 8104
Ye shall *o* to do therefore as the Deut 5:32 8104
O Israel, and *o* to do it Deut 6:3 8104
if we *o* to do all these Deut 6:25 8104
thee this day shall ye *o* to do Deut 8:1 8104
ye shall *o* to do all the statutes Deut 11:32 8104
which ye shall *o* to do in the Deut 12:1 8104
O and hear all these words which I Deut 12:28 8104
soever I command you, *o* to do it Deut 12:32 8104
to *o* to do all these commandments Deut 15:5 8104
O the month of Abib, and keep the Deut 16:1 8104
and thou shalt *o* and do these Deut 16:12 8104
Thou shalt *o* the feast of Deut 16:13 6213
thou shalt *o* to do according to Deut 17:10 8104
that thou *o* diligently, and do Deut 24:8 8104
them, so ye shall *o* to do Deut 24:8 8104
voice of the LORD thy God, to *o* Deut 28:1 8104
I command thee this day, to *o* Deut 28:13 8104
to *o* to do all his commandments Deut 28:15 8104
If thou wilt not *o* to do all the Deut 28:58 8104
o to do all the words of this law Deut 31:12 8104
command your children to *o* to do Deut 32:46 8104
that thou mayest *o* to do Josh 1:7 8104
night, that thou mayest *o* to do Josh 1:8 8104
that I commanded her let her *o* Judg 13:14 8104
Now the men did diligently *o* 1Kin 20:33 5172
ye shall *o* to do for evermore 2Kin 17:37 8104
only if they will *o* to do 2Kin 21:8 8104
shalt *o* my statutes and my 2Chr 7:17 8104
love him and *o* his commandments Neh 1:5 8104
Moses the servant of God, and to *o* Neh 10:29 8104
That they might *o* his statutes Ps 105:45 8104
will *o* these things, even they Ps 107:43 8104
I shall *o* it with my whole heart Ps 119:34 8104
and let thine eyes *o* my ways Prov 23:26 5341
the swallow *o* the time of their Jer 8:7 8104
neither *o* their judgments, nor Eze 20:18 8104
o my statutes, and do them Eze 37:24 8104
leopard by the way will I *o* them Hos 13:7 7789
They that *o* lying vanities Jonah 2:8 8104
they bid you *o*, that *o* Mt 23:3 *5083*
Teaching them to *o* all things Mt 28:20 *5083*
for us to receive, neither to *o* Acts 16:21 *4160*
that they *o* no such thing Acts 21:25 *5083*
Ye *o* days, and months, and times, Gal 4:10 *3906*
that thou *o* these things without 1Ti 5:21 *5442*

OBSERVED
but his father *o* the saying Gen 37:11 8104
It is a night to be much *o* unto Ex 12:42 8107
o of all the children of Israel Ex 12:42 8107
not *o* all these commandments, Num 15:22 6213
for they have *o* thy word, and kept Deut 33:9 8104
to pass, when Joab *o* the city 2Sa 11:16 8104
o times, and used enchantments, and 2Kin 21:6 6049
also he *o* times, and used 2Chr 33:6 6049
I have heard him, and *o* him Hos 14:8 7789
a just man and an holy, and *o* him Mk 6:20 *4933*
all these have I *o* from my youth Mk 10:20 *5442*

OBSERVER
or an *o* of times, or an enchanter Deut 18:10 6049

OBSERVERS
hearkened unto *o* of times Deut 18:14 6049

OBSERVEST
many things, but thou *o* not Is 42:20 8104

OBSERVETH
He that *o* the wind shall not sow Eccl 11:4 8104

OBSTINATE
his spirit, and made his heart *o* Deut 2:30 553
Because I knew that thou art *o* Is 48:4 7186

OBTAIN
be that I may *o* children by her Gen 16:2 1129
shall *o* favour of the LORD Prov 8:35 6329
they shall *o* joy and gladness, and Is 35:10 5381
they shall *o* gladness and joy Is 51:11 5381
o the kingdom by flatteries Dan 11:21 2388
for they shall *o* mercy Mt 5:7 *1653*
accounted worthy to *o* that world Lk 20:35 *5177*
your mercy they also may *o* mercy Rom 11:31 *1653*
So run, that ye may *o* 1Cor 9:24 *2638*
Now they do it to *o* a corruptible 1Cor 9:25 *2983*
but to *o* salvation by our Lord 1Th 5:9 *4047*
sakes, that they may also *o* the 2Ti 2:10 *5177*
of grace, that we may *o* mercy Heb 4:16 *2983*
that they might *o* a better Heb 11:35 *5177*
and desire to have, and cannot *o* Jas 4:2 *2013*

OBTAINED
after certain days *o* I leave of Neh 13:6 7592
him, and she *o* kindness of him Est 2:9 5375
Esther *o* favour in the sight of Est 2:15 5375
she *o* grace and favour in his Est 2:17 5375
that she *o* favour in his sight Est 5:2 5375
upon her that had not *o* mercy Hos 2:23 5375
had *o* part of this ministry Acts 1:17 *2975*
With a great sum *o* I this freedom Acts 22:28 *2932*
Having therefore *o* help of God Acts 26:22 *5177*
that they had *o* their purpose Acts 27:13 *2902*
Israel hath not *o* that which he Rom 11:7 *2013*
but the election hath *o* it Rom 11:7 *2013*
yet have now *o* mercy through Rom 11:30 *1653*
as one that hath *o* mercy of the 1Cor 7:25 *1653*
also we have *o* an inheritance Eph 1:11 *2820*
but I *o* mercy, because I did it 1Ti 1:13 *1653*
Howbeit for this cause I *o* mercy 1Ti 1:16 *1653*
as he hath by inheritance *o* a Heb 1:4 *2816*
endured, he *o* the promise Heb 6:15 *2013*
But now hath he *o* a more Heb 8:6 *5177*
having *o* eternal redemption for Heb 9:12 *2147*
by it the elders *o* a good report Heb 11:2 *3140*
by which he *o* witness that he was Heb 11:4 *3140*
o promises, stopped the mouths of Heb 11:33 *2013*
having *o* a good report through Heb 11:39 *3140*
which had not *o* mercy 1Pet 2:10 *1653*
but now have *o* mercy 1Pet 2:10 *1653*
to them that have *o* like precious 2Pet 1:1 *2975*

OBTAINETH
A good man *o* favour of the LORD Prov 12:2 6329
thing, and *o* favour of the LORD Prov 18:22 6329

OBTAINING
to the *o* of the glory of our Lord 2Th 2:14 *4047*

OCCASION
that he may seek *o* against us Gen 43:18 1556
do to them as thou shalt find *o* Judg 9:33 4672
that he sought an *o* against the Judg 14:4 8385
that thou do as *o* serve thee 1Sa 10:7 4672
o to the enemies of the LORD to 2Sa 12:14
which thou shalt have *o* to bestow Ezr 7:20 5308
in her *o* who can turn her away Jer 2:24 8385
ye shall not have *o* any more to Eze 18:3
princes sought to find *o* against Dan 6:4 5931
they could find none *o* nor fault Dan 6:4 5931
find any *o* against this Daniel Dan 6:5 5931
taking *o* by the commandment, Rom 7:8 *874*
taking *o* by the commandment, Rom 7:11 *874*
an *o* to fall in his brother's way Rom 14:13 *4625*
but give you *o* to glory on our 2Cor 5:12 *874*
but by *o* of the forwardness of 2Cor 8:8 *1223*
o from them which desire *o* 2Cor 11:12 *874*
not liberty for an *o* to the flesh Gal 5:13 *874*
give none *o* to the adversary to 1Ti 5:14 *874*
there is none *o* of stumbling in 1Jn 2:10 *4625*

OCCASIONED
I have *o* the death of all the 1Sa 22:22 5437

OCCASIONS
give *o* of speech against her, and Deut 22:14 5949
he hath given *o* of speech against Deut 22:17 5949
Behold, he findeth *o* against me Job 33:10 8569

OCCUPATION
you, and shall say, What is your *o* Gen 46:33 4639
unto his brethren, What is your *o* Gen 47:3 4639
What is thine *o* Jonah 1:8 4399
for by their *o* they were Acts 18:3 *5078*
with the workmen of like *o* Acts 19:25

OCCUPIED
All the gold that was *o* for the Ex 38:24 6213
with new ropes that never were *o* Judg 16:11
they *o* in thy fairs with emeralds Eze 27:16 5414
going to and fro *o* in thy fairs Eze 27:19 5414
they *o* with thee in lambs, and Eze 27:21 5503
they *o* in thy fairs with chief of Eze 27:22 5414
them that have been *o* therein Heb 13:9 *4043*

OCCUPIERS
the *o* of thy merchandise, and all Eze 27:27 6148

OCCUPIETH
how shall he that *o* the room of 1Cor 14:16 *378*

OCCUPY
were in thee to *o* thy merchandise Eze 27:9 6148
and said unto them, O till I come Lk 19:13 *4231*

OCCURRENT
is neither adversary nor evil *o* 1Kin 5:4 6294

OCHRAN See OCRAN.

OCRAN (*o'-cran*) *An Asherite who counted the people.*
Pagiel the son of O Num 1:13 5918
shall be Pagiel the son of O Num 2:27 5918
eleventh day Pagiel the son of O Num 7:72 5918
offering of Pagiel the son of O Num 7:77 5918
of Asher was Pagiel the son of O Num 10:26 5918

ODD
wherewith the *o* number of them is Num 3:48 5736

ODED (*o'-ded*)
1. Father of Azariah.
came upon Azariah the son of O 2Chr 15:1 5752
and the prophecy of O the prophet 2Chr 15:8 5752
2. A prophet of Samaria.
LORD was there, whose name was O 2Chr 28:9 5752

ODIOUS
had made themselves *o* to David 1Chr 19:6 887
For an *o* woman when she is Prov 30:23 8130

ODOUR
filled with the *o* of the ointment Jn 12:3 *3744*
you, an *o* of a sweet smell, a Phil 4:18 *3744*

ODOURS
smell the savour of your sweet *o* Lev 26:31 5207
bed which was filled with sweet *o* 2Chr 16:14 1314
myrrh, and six months with sweet *o* Est 2:12 1314
so shall they burn *o* for thee Jer 34:5
an oblation and sweet *o* unto him Dan 2:46 5208
harps, and golden vials full of *o* Rev 5:8 *2368*
And cinnamon, and *o*, and ointments, Rev 18:13 *2368*

OF See PREFACE.

OFF
from *o* the face of the earth Gen 7:4 5921
from *o* the earth continually Gen 8:3 5921
were dried up from *o* the earth Gen 8:7 5921
from *o* the face of the ground Gen 8:8 5921
mouth was an olive leaf pluckt *o* Gen 8:11
were abated from *o* the earth Gen 8:11 5921
were dried up from *o* the earth Gen 8:13 5921
cut *o* any more by the waters of a Gen 9:11
they left *o* to build the city Gen 11:8
shall be cut *o* from his people Gen 17:14
he left *o* talking with him, and Gen 17:22
over against him a good way *o* Gen 21:16
his eyes, and saw the place afar *o* Gen 22:4
Isaac, she lighted *o* the camel Gen 24:64 5921
break his yoke from *o* thy neck Gen 27:40 5921
And when they saw him afar *o* Gen 37:18
her widow's garments *o* from her Gen 38:14 5921
lift up thy head from *o* thee Gen 40:19 5921
shall eat thy flesh from *o* thee Gen 40:19 5921
Pharaoh took *o* his ring from his Gen 41:42
out of the city, and not yet far *o* Gen 44:4
And his sister stood afar *o* Ex 2:4
put *o* thy shoes from *o* thy feet Ex 3:5
cut *o* the foreskin of her son, and Ex 4:25
shalt be cut *o* from the earth Ex 9:15
soul shall be cut *o* from Israel Ex 12:15
even that soul shall be cut *o* Ex 12:19
took *o* their chariot wheels, that Ex 14:25

it, they removed, and stood afar o ... Ex 20:18
And the people stood afar o ... Ex 20:21
and I will cut them o ... Ex 23:23
and worship ye afar o ... Ex 24:1
even be cut o from his people ... Ex 30:33
even be cut o from his people ... Ex 30:38
be cut o from among his people ... Ex 31:14
Break o the golden earrings, ... Ex 32:2
all the people brake o the golden ... Ex 32:3
any gold, let them break it o ... Ex 32:24
therefore now put o thy ornaments ... Ex 33:5
afar o from the camp, and called ... Ex 33:7
with him, he took the vail o ... Ex 34:34
wring o his head, and burn it on ... Lev 1:15
it shall he take o hard by the ... Lev 3:9
he shall take o from it all the ... Lev 4:8
As it was taken o from the ... Lev 4:10
from o the sacrifice of peace ... Lev 4:31
wring o his head from his neck, ... Lev 5:8
And he shall put o his garments ... Lev 6:11
shall be cut o from his people ... Lev 7:20
shall be cut o from his people ... Lev 7:21
it shall be cut o from his people ... Lev 7:25
shall be cut o from his people ... Lev 7:27
o the sacrifices of their peace ... Lev 7:34
took them from o their hands ... Lev 8:28 5921
whose hair is fallen o his head ... Lev 13:40
o from the part of his head ... Lev 13:41
shave o all his hair, and wash ... Lev 14:8
shave all his hair o his head ... Lev 14:9
all his hair he shall shave o ... Lev 14:9
scrape o without the city into an ... Lev 14:41
from o the altar before the LORD ... Lev 16:12 5921
shall put o the linen garments ... Lev 16:23
be cut o from among his people ... Lev 17:4
be cut o from among his people ... Lev 17:9
will cut him o from among his ... Lev 17:10
eateth it shall be cut o ... Lev 17:14
be cut o from among their people ... Lev 18:29
be cut o from among his people ... Lev 19:8
will cut him o from among his ... Lev 20:3
his family, and will cut him o ... Lev 20:5
will cut him o from among his ... Lev 20:6
they shall be cut o in the sight ... Lev 20:17
be cut o from among their people ... Lev 20:18
neither shall they shave o the ... Lev 21:5
shall be cut o from my presence ... Lev 22:3
he shall be cut o from among his ... Lev 23:29
far o about the tabernacle of the ... Num 2:2
Cut ye not o the tribe of the ... Num 4:18
o the mercy seat that was upon ... Num 7:89 5921
body, or be in a journey afar o ... Num 9:10
be cut o from among his people ... Num 9:13
the cloud was taken up from o the ... Num 10:11 5921
departed from o the tabernacle ... Num 12:10 5921
be cut o from among his people ... Num 15:30
that soul shall utterly be cut o ... Num 15:31
put fire therein from o the altar ... Num 16:46 5921
soul shall be cut o from Israel ... Num 19:13
that soul shall be cut o from ... Num 19:20
o the land whereunto ye go over ... Deut 4:26 5921
destroy thee from o the face of ... Deut 6:15 5921
lest ye perish quickly from o the ... Deut 11:17 575
o the nations from before thee ... Deut 12:29
or far o from thee, from the one ... Deut 13:7
thy God hath cut o the nations ... Deut 19:1
which are very far o from thee ... Deut 20:15
shall strike o the heifer's neck ... Deut 21:4
of her captivity from o her ... Deut 21:13 5921
or hath his privy member cut o ... Deut 23:1
and loose his shoe from o his foot ... Deut 25:9 5921
Then thou shalt cut o her hand ... Deut 25:12
consumed thee from o the land ... Deut 28:21 5921
ye shall be plucked from o the ... Deut 28:63 5921
from thee, neither is it far o ... Deut 30:11
waters of Jordan shall be cut o ... Josh 3:13
salt sea, failed, and were cut o ... Josh 3:16
the waters of Jordan were cut o ... Josh 4:7
the waters of Jordan were cut o ... Josh 4:7
the reproach of Egypt from o you ... Josh 5:9 5921
Loose thy shoe from o thy foot ... Josh 5:15 5921
cut o our name from the earth ... Josh 7:9
they took them down o the trees ... Josh 10:27 5921
cut o the Anakims from the ... Josh 11:21
and she lighted o her ass ... Josh 15:18 5921
all the nations that I have cut o ... Josh 23:4
until ye perish from o this good ... Josh 23:13 5921
he have destroyed you from o this ... Josh 23:15 5921
o the good land which he hath ... Josh 23:16 5921
cut o his thumbs and his great ... Judg 1:6
thumbs and their great toes cut o ... Judg 1:7
and she lighted from o her ass ... Judg 1:14 5921
Sisera lighted down o his chariot ... Judg 4:15 5921
Sisera, she smote o his head ... Judg 5:26
up toward heaven from o the altar ... Judg 13:20 5921
his bands loosed from o his hands ... Judg 15:14 5921
he brake them from o his arms ... Judg 16:12 5921
she caused him to shave o the ... Judg 16:19
tribe cut o from Israel this day ... Judg 21:6
who hath not left o his kindness ... Ruth 2:20
a man plucked o his shoe, and gave ... Ruth 4:7
So he drew o his shoe ... Ruth 4:8
not cut o from among his brethren ... Ruth 4:10
come, that I will cut o thine arm ... 1Sa 2:31
I shall not cut o from mine altar ... 1Sa 2:33
that he fell from o the seat ... 1Sa 4:18 5921
were cut o upon the threshold ... 1Sa 5:4
will lighten his hand from o you ... 1Sa 6:5 5921
from o your gods, and from o ... 1Sa 6:5 5921
And David put them o him ... 1Sa 17:39 5921
him, and cut o his head therewith ... 1Sa 17:51
he stript o his clothes also, and ... 1Sa 19:24
But also thou shalt not cut o thy ... 1Sa 20:15
not when the LORD hath cut o the ... 1Sa 20:15

cut o the skirt of Saul's robe ... 1Sa 24:4
because he had cut o Saul's skirt ... 1Sa 24:5
for in that I cut o the skirt of ... 1Sa 24:11
wilt not cut o my seed after me ... 1Sa 24:21
she hasted, and lighted o the ass ... 1Sa 25:23 5921
on the top of an hill afar o ... 1Sa 26:13
how he hath cut o those that have ... 1Sa 28:9
And they cut o his head, and ... 1Sa 31:9
stripped o his armour, and sent ... 1Sa 31:9
cut o their hands and their feet, ... 2Sa 4:12
have cut o all thine enemies out ... 2Sa 7:9
shaved o the one half of their ... 2Sa 10:4
cut o their garments in the ... 2Sa 10:4
that David arose from o his bed ... 2Sa 11:2 5921
the shooters shot from o the wall ... 2Sa 11:24 5921
king's crown from o his head ... 2Sa 12:30 5921
tarried in a place that was far o ... 2Sa 15:17
I pray thee, and take o his head ... 2Sa 16:9
they cut o the head of Sheba the ... 2Sa 20:22
Then will I cut o Israel out of ... 1Kin 9:7
until he had cut o every male in ... 1Kin 11:16
of Jeroboam, even to cut it o ... 1Kin 13:34
to destroy it from o the face of ... 1Kin 13:34
will cut o from Jeroboam him that ... 1Kin 14:10
who shall cut o the house of ... 1Kin 14:14
that he left o building of Ramah, ... 1Kin 15:21
when Jezebel cut o the prophets ... 1Kin 18:4
himself as he that putteth it o ... 1Kin 20:11
will cut o from Ahab him that ... 1Kin 21:21
thou shalt not come down o that ... 2Kin 1:16
went, and stood to view afar o ... 2Kin 2:7
the man of God saw her afar o ... 2Kin 4:25
I will cut o from Ahab him that ... 2Kin 9:8
king Ahaz cut o the borders of ... 2Kin 16:17
and removed the laver from o them ... 2Kin 16:17 5921
took down the sea from o the ... 2Kin 16:17 5921
At that time did Hezekiah cut o ... 2Kin 18:16
will cast o this city Jerusalem ... 2Kin 23:27
have cut o all thine enemies from ... 1Chr 17:8
cut o their garments in the midst ... 1Chr 19:4
of their king from o his head ... 1Chr 20:2 5921
him, he will cast thee o for ever ... 1Chr 28:9
unto a land far o or near ... 2Chr 6:36
his sons had cast them o from ... 2Chr 11:14
that he left o building of Ramah, ... 2Chr 16:5
they stripped o for themselves ... 2Chr 20:25
to cut o the house of Ahab ... 2Chr 22:7
for he was cut o from the house ... 2Chr 26:21
which cut o all the mighty men of ... 2Chr 32:21
and the noise was heard afar o ... Ezr 3:13
plucked o the hair of my head and ... Ezr 9:3
me, none of us put o our clothes ... Neh 4:23
every one put them o for washing ... Neh 4:23
you, let us leave o this usury ... Neh 5:10
Jerusalem was heard even afar o ... Neh 12:43
plucked o their hair, and made ... Neh 13:25
And the king took o his ring ... Est 8:2
they lifted up their eyes afar o ... Job 2:12
or where were the righteous cut o ... Job 4:7
let loose his hand, and cut me o ... Job 6:9
Whose hope shall be cut o ... Job 8:14
I will leave o my heaviness ... Job 9:27
If he cut o, and shut up, or ... Job 11:10
Yea, thou castest o fear, and ... Job 15:4
He shall shake o his unripe grape ... Job 15:33
shall cast o his flower as the ... Job 15:33
past, my purposes are broken o ... Job 17:11
above shall his branch be cut o ... Job 18:16
his months is cut o in the midst ... Job 21:21
was not cut o before the darkness ... Job 23:17
cut o as the tops of the ears of ... Job 24:24
they left o speaking ... Job 32:15
people are cut o in their place ... Job 36:20
man may behold it afar o ... Job 36:25
and he smelleth the battle afar o ... Job 39:25
prey, and her eyes behold afar o ... Job 39:29
Why standest thou afar o, O LORD ... Ps 10:1
The LORD shall cut o all ... Ps 12:3
thou hast put o my sackcloth ... Ps 30:11
I am cut o from before thine eyes ... Ps 31:22
to cut o the remembrance of them ... Ps 34:16
he hath left o to be wise ... Ps 36:3
For evildoers shall be cut o ... Ps 37:9
be cursed of him shall be cut o ... Ps 37:22
seed of the wicked shall be cut o ... Ps 37:28
when the wicked are cut o ... Ps 37:34
end of the wicked shall be cut o ... Ps 37:38
and my kinsmen stand afar o ... Ps 38:11
why dost thou cast me o ... Ps 43:2
But thou hast cast o, and put us ... Ps 44:9
arise, cast us not o for ever ... Ps 44:23
cut them o in thy truth ... Ps 54:5
Lo, then would I wander far o ... Ps 55:7
O God, thou hast cast us o ... Ps 60:1
O God, which hadst cast us o ... Ps 60:10
them that are afar o upon the sea ... Ps 65:5
Cast me not o in the time of old ... Ps 71:9
why hast thou cast us o for ever ... Ps 74:1
of the wicked also will I cut o ... Ps 75:10
He shall cut o the spirit of ... Ps 76:12
Will the Lord cast o for ever ... Ps 77:7
let us cut them o from being a ... Ps 83:4
they are cut o from thy hand ... Ps 88:5
LORD, why castest thou o my soul ... Ps 88:14
thy terrors have cut me o ... Ps 88:16
But thou hast cast o and abhorred, ... Ps 89:38
for it is soon cut o, and we fly ... Ps 90:10
LORD will not cast o his people ... Ps 94:14
shall cut them o in their own ... Ps 94:23
the LORD our God shall cut them o ... Ps 94:23
his neighbour, him will I cut o ... Ps 101:5
that I may cut o all wicked doers ... Ps 101:8
thou, O God, who hast cast us o ... Ps 108:11
Let his posterity be cut o ... Ps 109:13

that he may cut o the memory of ... Ps 109:15
but the proud he knoweth afar o ... Ps 138:6
understandest my thought afar o ... Ps 139:2
of thy mercy cut o mine enemies ... Ps 143:12
shall be cut o from the earth ... Prov 2:22
therefore leave o contention ... Prov 17:14
expectation shall not be cut o ... Prov 23:18
expectation shall not be cut o ... Prov 24:14
hand of a fool cutteth o the feet ... Prov 26:6
that is near than a brother far o ... Prov 27:10
devour the poor from o the earth ... Prov 30:14
That which is far o, and exceeding ... Eccl 7:24
I have put o my coat ... Song 5:3
with the tongs from o the altar ... Is 6:6 5921
LORD will cut o from Israel head ... Is 9:14
and cut o nations not a few ... Is 10:7
be taken away from o thy shoulder ... Is 10:27 5921
and his yoke from o thy neck ... Is 10:27 5921
of Judah shall be cut o ... Is 11:13
cut o from Babylon the name, and ... Is 14:22
shall his yoke depart from o them ... Is 14:25 5921
depart from o their shoulders ... Is 14:25 5921
be baldness, and every beard cut o ... Is 15:2
them, and they shall flee far o ... Is 17:13
he shall both cut o the sprigs ... Is 18:5
the sackcloth from o thy loins ... Is 20:2 5921
put o thy shoe from thy foot ... Is 20:2
that was upon it shall be cut o ... Is 22:25
shall carry her afar o to sojourn ... Is 23:7
wipe away tears from o all faces ... Is 25:8 5921
he take away from o all the earth ... Is 25:8 5921
withered, they shall be broken o ... Is 27:11
that the LORD shall beat o from ... Is 27:12
that watch for iniquity are cut o ... Is 29:20
and Carmel shake o their fruits ... Is 33:9
Hear, ye that are far o, what I ... Is 33:13
the land that is very far o ... Is 33:17
the leaf falleth o from the vine ... Is 34:4
said in the cutting o of my days ... Is 38:10
I have cut o like a weaver my ... Is 38:12
he will cut me o with pining ... Is 38:12
it shall not be far o, and my ... Is 46:13
shalt not be able to put if o ... Is 47:11
for thee, that I cut thee not o ... Is 48:9
o nor destroyed from before me ... Is 48:19
to them that plucked o the hair ... Is 50:6
for he was cut o out of the land ... Is 53:8
sign that shall not be cut o ... Is 55:13
name, that shall not be cut o ... Is 56:5
didst send thy messengers far o ... Is 57:9
Peace, peace to him that is far o ... Is 57:19
but it is far o from us ... Is 59:11
and justice standeth afar o ... Is 59:14
lamb, as if he cut o a dog's neck ... Is 66:3
and Javan, to the isles afar o ... Is 66:19
is cut o from their mouth ... Jer 7:28
Cut o thine hair, O Jerusalem, and ... Jer 7:29
to cut o the children from ... Jer 9:21
let us cut him o from the land of ... Jer 11:19
the LORD, and not a God afar o ... Jer 23:23
till they be consumed from o the ... Jer 24:10 5921
o the prophet Jeremiah's neck ... Jer 28:10 5921
from o the neck of the prophet ... Jer 28:12 5921
thee from o the face of the earth ... Jer 28:16 5921
break his yoke from o thy neck ... Jer 30:8 5921
and declare it in the isles afar o ... Jer 31:10
I will also cast o all the seed ... Jer 31:37
chosen, he hath even cast them o ... Jer 33:24
So they left o speaking with him ... Jer 38:27
to cut o from you man and woman, ... Jer 44:7
that ye might cut yourselves o ... Jer 44:8
for evil, and to cut o all Judah ... Jer 44:11
But since we left o to burn ... Jer 44:18
I will save thee from afar o ... Jer 46:27
to cut o from Tyrus and Zidon ... Jer 47:4
Ashkelon is cut o with the ... Jer 47:5
let us cut it o from being a ... Jer 48:2
The horn of Moab is cut o ... Jer 48:25
of war shall be cut o in that day ... Jer 49:26
Flee, get you far o, dwell deep, ... Jer 49:30
Cut o the sower from Babylon, and ... Jer 50:16
of war shall be cut o in that day ... Jer 50:30
be not cut o in her iniquity ... Jer 51:6
remember the LORD afar o, and let ... Jer 51:50
against this place, to cut it o ... Jer 51:62
He hath cut o in his fierce anger ... Lam 2:3
The Lord hath cast o his altar ... Lam 2:7
removed my soul far o from peace ... Lam 3:17
the Lord will not cast o for ever ... Lam 3:31
They have cut o my life in the ... Lam 3:53
then I said, I am cut o ... Lam 3:54
He that is far o shall die of the ... Eze 6:12
should go far o from my sanctuary ... Eze 8:6
from o the threshold of the house ... Eze 10:18 5921
cast them far o among the heathen ... Eze 11:16
of the times that are far o ... Eze 12:27
I will cut him o from the midst ... Eze 14:8
famine upon it, and will cut o man ... Eze 14:13
so that I cut o man and beast from ... Eze 14:17
to cut o from it man and beast ... Eze 14:19
to cut o from it man and beast ... Eze 14:21
He cropped o the top of his young ... Eze 17:4
cut o the fruit thereof, that it ... Eze 17:9
forts, to cut o many persons ... Eze 17:17
I will crop o from the top of his ... Eze 17:22
That hath taken o his hand from ... Eze 18:17
and will cut o from thee the ... Eze 21:3
cut o from thee the righteous ... Eze 21:4
the diadem, and take o the crown ... Eze 21:26
pluck o thine own breasts ... Eze 23:34
I will cut thee o from the people ... Eze 25:7
hand upon Edom, and will cut o man ... Eze 25:13
I will cut o the Cherethims, and ... Eze 25:16
put o their broidered garments ... Eze 26:16

a sword upon thee, and cut o man Eze 29:8
I will cut o the multitude of No Eze 30:15
of the nations, have cut him o Eze 31:12
cut o from it him that passeth Eze 35:7
we are cut o for our parts Eze 37:11
they shall put o their garments Eze 44:19
cut o his branches Dan 4:14
shake o his leaves, and scatter Dan 4:14 575
break o thy sins by righteousness Dan 4:27
that are near, and that are far o Dan 9:7
two weeks shall Messiah be cut o Dan 9:26
because they have left o to take Hos 4:10
Israel hath cast o the thing that Hos 8:3
idols, that they may be cut o Hos 8:4
calf, O Samaria, hath cast thee o Hos 8:5
her king is cut o as the foam Hos 10:7
king of Israel utterly be cut o Hos 10:15
take o the yoke on their jaws Hos 11:4 5921
for it is cut o from your mouth Joel 1:5
the drink offering is cut o from Joel 1:9
the meat cut o before our eyes Joel 1:16
But I will remove far o from you Joel 2:20
to the Sabeans, to a people far o Joel 3:8
cut o the inhabitant from the Amos 1:5
I will cut o the inhabitant from Amos 1:8
the sword, and did cast o all pity Amos 1:11
I will cut o the judge from the Amos 2:3
horns of the altar shall be cut o Amos 3:14
leave o righteousness in the Amos 5:7
it from o the face of the earth Amos 9:8 5921
by night, (how art thou cut o Obad 5
of Esau may be cut o by slaughter Obad 9
and thou shalt be cut o for ever Obad 10
to cut o those of his that did Obad 14
ye pull o the robe with the Mic 2:8
pluck o their skin from o them Mic 3:2
and their flesh from o their bones Mic 3:2 5921
and flay their skin from o them Mic 3:3 5921
and rebuke strong nations afar o Mic 4:3
was cast far o a strong nation Mic 4:7
all thine enemies shall be cut o Mic 5:9
that I will cut o thy horses out Mic 5:10
I will cut o the cities of thy Mic 5:11
I will cut o witchcrafts out of Mic 5:12
graven images also will I cut o Mic 5:13
will I break his yoke from o thee Nah 1:13 5921
will I cut o the graven image Nah 1:14
he is utterly cut o Nah 1:15
I will cut o thy prey from the Nah 2:13
the sword shall cut thee o Nah 3:15
house by cutting o many people Hab 2:10
shall be cut o from the fold Hab 3:17
all things from o the land Zeph 1:2
will cut o man from o the land Zeph 1:3
I will cut o the remnant of Baal Zeph 1:4
they that bear silver are cut o Zeph 1:11
I have cut o the nations Zeph 3:6
dwelling should not be cut o Zeph 3:7
one that stealeth shall be cut o Zec 5:3
one that sweareth shall be cut o Zec 5:3
And they that are far o shall come Zec 6:15
I will cut o the pride of the Zec 9:6
I will cut o the chariot from Zec 9:10
and the battle bow shall be cut o Zec 9:10
as though I had not cast them o Zec 10:6
also I cut o in one month Zec 11:8
is to be cut o, let it be cut o Zec 11:9
not visit those that be cut o Zec 11:16
that I will cut o the names of Zec 13:2
two parts therein shall be cut o Zec 13:8
shall not be cut o from the city Zec 14:2
The LORD will cut o the man that Mal 2:12
right hand offend thee, cut it o Mt 5:30 1601
there was a good way o from them Mt 8:30 575
shake o the dust of your feet Mt 10:14 1621
thy foot offend thee, cut them o Mt 18:8 1581
high priest's, and smote o his ear Mt 26:51 851
But Peter followed him afar o Mt 26:58 575
they took the robe o from him Mt 27:31 1562
women were there beholding afar o Mt 27:55 575
But when he saw Jesus afar o Mk 5:6 575
shake o the dust under your feet Mk 6:11 1621
if thy hand offend thee, cut it o Mk 9:43 609
if thy foot offend thee, cut it o Mk 9:45 609
cut down branches o the trees Mk 11:8 1537
a fig tree afar o having leaves Mk 11:13
the high priest, and cut o his ear Mk 14:47 609
And Peter followed him afar o Mk 14:54 575
they took o the purple from him Mk 15:20 609
were also women looking on afar o Mk 15:40 575
shake o the very dust from your Lk 9:5 1575
on us, we do wipe o against you Lk 10:11 631
the other is yet a great way o Lk 14:32
But when he was yet a great way o Lk 15:20 568
torments, and seeth Abraham afar o Lk 16:23 575
were lepers, which stood afar o Lk 17:12
And the publican, standing afar o Lk 18:13
priest, and cut o his right ear Lk 22:50 851
And Peter followed afar o Lk 22:54
him from Galilee, stood afar o Lk 23:49
about fifteen furlongs o Jn 11:18 575
servant, and cut o his right ear Jn 18:10 609
his kinsman whose ear Peter cut o Jn 18:26 609
and to all that are afar o Acts 2:39
Put o thy shoes from thy feet Acts 7:33 3089
his chains fell o from his hands Acts 12:7 1601
But they shook o the dust of Acts 13:51 1621
magistrates rent o their clothes Acts 16:22 4048
cast o their clothes, and threw Acts 22:23 4496
cut o the ropes of the boat Acts 27:32 609
of the boat, and let her fall o Acts 27:32 1601
he shook o the beast into the Acts 28:5 660
some of the branches be broken o Rom 11:17 1575
then, The branches were broken o Rom 11:19 1575
of unbelief they were broken o Rom 11:20 1575
thou also shalt be cut o Rom 11:22 1581
cast o the works of darkness Rom 13:12 659
that I may cut o occasion from 2Cor 11:12 1581
were even cut o which trouble you Gal 5:12 609
o are made nigh by the blood of Eph 2:13 3112
peace to you which were afar o Eph 2:17
That ye put o concerning the Eph 4:22 659
in putting o the body of the sins Col 2:11 554
But now ye also put o all these Col 3:8 659
seeing that ye have put o the old Col 3:9 554
have cast o their first faith 1Ti 5:12 114
but having seen them afar o Heb 11:13
is blind, and cannot see afar o 2Pet 1:9
I must put o this my tabernacle 2Pet 1:14 595
Standing afar o for the fear of Rev 18:10 575
shall stand afar o for the fear Rev 18:15 575
as trade by sea, stood afar o Rev 18:17 575

OFFENCE

nor o of heart unto my lord, 1Sa 25:31 4383
for a rock of o to both the Is 8:14 4383
till they acknowledge their o Hos 5:15 816
thou art an o unto me Mt 16:23 4625
to that man by whom the o cometh Mt 18:7 4625
a conscience void of o toward God Acts 24:16 677
But not as the o, so also is the Rom 5:15 3900
For if through the o of one many Rom 5:15 3900
For if by one man's o death Rom 5:17 3900
Therefore as by the o of one Rom 5:18 3900
entered, that the o might abound Rom 5:20 3900
a stumblingstone and rock of o Rom 9:33 4625
for that man who eateth with o Rom 14:20 4348
Give none o, neither to the Jews, 1Cor 10:32 677
Giving no o in any thing, that 2Cor 6:3 4349
Have I committed an o in abasing 2Cor 11:7 266
then is the o of the cross ceased Gal 5:11 4625
without o till the day of Christ Phil 1:10 677
of stumbling, and a rock of o 1Pet 2:8 4625

OFFENCES

for yielding pacifieth great o Eccl 10:4 2399
Woe unto the world because of o Mt 18:7 4625
for it must needs be that o come Mt 18:7 4625
impossible but that o will come Lk 17:1 4625
Who was delivered for our o Rom 4:25 3900
is of many o unto justification Rom 5:16 3900
o contrary to the doctrine which Rom 16:17 4625

OFFEND

I will not o any more Job 34:31 2254
I should o against the generation Ps 73:15 898
and nothing shall o them Ps 119:165 4383
all that devour him shall o Jer 2:3 816
We o not, because they have Jer 50:7 816
the harlot, yet let not Judah o Hos 4:15 816
and he shall pass over, and o Hab 1:11 816
And if thy right eye o thee Mt 5:29 4624
And if thy right hand o thee Mt 5:30 4624
of his kingdom all things that o Mt 13:41 4625
lest we should o them, go thou Mt 17:27 4624
But whoso shall o one of these Mt 18:6 4624
if thy hand or thy foot o thee Mt 18:8 4624
And if thine eye o thee, pluck it Mt 18:9 4624
whosoever shall o one of these Mk 9:42 4624
And if thy hand o thee, cut it off Mk 9:43 4624
And if thy foot o thee, cut it off Mk 9:45 4624
And if thine eye o thee, pluck it Mk 9:47 4624
than that he should o one of Lk 17:2 4624
said unto them, Doth this o you Jn 6:61 4624
if meat make my brother to o 1Cor 8:13 4624
lest I make my brother to o 1Cor 8:13 4624
yet o in one point, he is guilty Jas 2:10 4417
For in many things we o all Jas 3:2 4417
If any man o not in word, the Jas 3:2 4417

OFFENDED

and what have I o thee, that thou Gen 20:9 2398
his baker had o their lord the Gen 40:1 2398
to Lachish, saying, I have o 2Kin 18:14 2398
for whereas we have o against the 2Chr 28:13 819
A brother o is harder to be won Prov 18:19 6586
What have I o against thee, or Jer 37:18 2398
vengeance, and hath greatly o Eze 25:12 816
but when he o in Baal, he died Hos 13:1 816
whosoever shall not be o in me Mt 11:6 4624
of the word, by and by he is o Mt 13:21 4624
And they were o in him Mt 13:57 4624
thou that the Pharisees were o Mt 15:12 4624
And then shall many be o, and shall Mt 24:10 4624
All ye shall be o because of me Mt 26:31 4624
men shall be o because of thee Mt 26:33 4624
yet will I never be o Mt 26:33 4624
sake, immediately they are o Mk 4:17 4624
And they were o at him Mk 6:3 4624
All ye shall be o because of me Mk 14:27 4624
unto him, Although all shall be o Mk 14:29 4624
whosoever shall not be o in me Lk 7:23 4624
unto you, that ye should not be o Jn 16:1 4624
have I o any thing at all Acts 25:8 264
thy brother stumbleth, or is o Rom 14:21 4624
who is o, and I burn not 2Cor 11:29 4624

OFFENDER

That make a man an o for a word Is 29:21 2398
For if I be an o, or have Acts 25:11 91

OFFENDERS

my son Solomon shall be counted o 1Kin 1:21 2400

OFFER

o him there for a burnt offering Gen 22:2 5927
Thou shalt not delay to o the Ex 22:29
Thou shalt not o the blood of my Ex 23:18 2076
thou shalt o every day a bullock Ex 29:36 6213
which thou shalt o upon the altar Ex 29:38 6213
lamb thou shalt o in the morning Ex 29:39 6213
other lamb thou shalt o at even Ex 29:39 6213
other lamb thou shalt o at even Ex 29:41 6213
Ye shall o no strange incense Ex 30:9 5927
Thou shalt not o the blood of my Ex 34:25 7819
Every one that did o an offering Ex 35:24 7311
let him o a male without blemish Lev 1:3 7126
he shall o it of his own Lev 1:3 7126
when any will o a meat offering Lev 2:1 7126
ye shall o them unto the LORD Lev 2:12 7126
thine offerings thou shalt o salt Lev 2:13 7126
if thou o a meat offering of thy Lev 2:14 7126
thou shalt o for the meat Lev 2:14 7126
offering, if he o it of the herd Lev 3:1 7126
he shall o it without blemish Lev 3:1 7126
he shall o of the sacrifice of Lev 3:3 7126
he shall o it without blemish Lev 3:6 7126
If he o a lamb for his offering, Lev 3:7 7126
then shall he o it before the Lev 3:7 7126
he shall o of the sacrifice of Lev 3:9 7126
then he shall o it before the Lev 3:12 7126
he shall o thereof his offering, Lev 3:14 7126
o a young bullock for the sin Lev 4:14 7126
who shall o that which is for the Lev 5:8 7126
he shall o the second for a burnt Lev 5:10 6213
Aaron shall o it before the LORD Lev 6:14 7126
which they shall o unto the LORD Lev 6:20 7126
o for a sweet savour unto the Lev 6:21 7126
anointed in his stead shall o it Lev 6:22 6213
he shall o of it all the fat Lev 7:3 7126
which he shall o unto the LORD Lev 7:11 7126
If he o it for a thanksgiving, Lev 7:12 7126
then he shall o with the Lev 7:12 7126
he shall o for his offering Lev 7:13 7126
of it he shall o one out of the Lev 7:14 7126
of which men o an offering made Lev 7:25 7126
the children of Israel to o their Lev 7:38 7126
and o them before the LORD Lev 9:2 7126
o thy sin offering, and thy burnt Lev 9:7 6213
o the offering of the people, and Lev 9:7 6213
Who shall o it before the LORD, Lev 12:7 7126
o him for a trespass offering, and Lev 14:12 7126
priest shall o the sin offering Lev 14:19 6213
the priest shall o the burnt Lev 14:20 5927
he shall o the one of the Lev 14:30 6213
And the priest shall o them Lev 15:15 6213
the priest shall o the one for a Lev 15:30 6213
Aaron shall o his bullock of the Lev 16:6 7126
fell, and o him for a sin offering Lev 16:9 6213
o his burnt offering, and the Lev 16:24 6213
to o an offering unto the LORD Lev 17:4 7126
which they o in the open field, Lev 17:5 2076
o them for peace offerings unto Lev 17:5 2076
they shall no more o their Lev 17:7 2076
to o it unto the LORD Lev 17:9 6213
if ye o a sacrifice of peace Lev 19:5 2076
ye shall o it at your own will Lev 19:5 2076
be eaten the same day ye o it Lev 19:6 2077
the bread of their God, they do o Lev 21:6 7126
to o the bread of his God Lev 21:17 7126
the priest shall come nigh to o Lev 21:21 7126
nigh to o the bread of his God Lev 21:21 7126
which they o unto the LORD Lev 22:15 7311
that will o his oblation for all Lev 22:18 7126
which they will o unto the LORD Lev 22:18 7126
Ye shall o at your own will a Lev 22:19
a blemish, that shall ye not o Lev 22:20 7126
ye shall not o these unto the Lev 22:22 7126
that mayest thou o for a freewill Lev 22:23 6213
Ye shall not o unto the LORD that Lev 22:24 7126
o the bread of your God of any of Lev 22:25 7126
when ye will o a sacrifice of Lev 22:29 2076
the LORD, o it at your own will Lev 22:29 2076
But ye shall o an offering made Lev 23:8 7126
ye shall o that day when ye wave Lev 23:12 6213
ye shall o a new meat offering Lev 23:16 7126
ye shall o with the bread seven Lev 23:18 7126
but ye shall o an offering made Lev 23:25 7126
o an offering made by fire unto Lev 23:27 7126
Seven days ye shall o an offering Lev 23:36 7126
ye shall o an offering made by Lev 23:36 7126
to o an offering made by fire Lev 23:37 7126
beast, of which they do not o a Lev 27:11 7126
the LORD, and o it upon the altar Num 5:25 7126
the priest shall o the one for a Num 6:11 6213
he shall o his offering unto the Num 6:14 7126
shall o his sin offering, and his Num 6:16 6213
And he shall o the ram for a Num 6:17 6213
the priest shall o also his meat Num 6:17 6213
They shall o their offering, each Num 7:11 7126
Zuar, prince of Issachar, did o Num 7:18 7126
of the children of Zebulun, did o Num 7:24
of the children of Reuben, did o Num 7:30
of the children of Simeon, did o Num 7:36
Aaron shall o the Levites before Num 8:11 5130
thou shalt o the one for a sin Num 8:12 6213
o them for an offering unto the Num 8:13 5130
them, and o them for an offering Num 8:15 5130
that we may not o an offering of Num 9:7 7126
o the third part of an hin of Num 15:7 7126
will o an offering made by fire, Num 15:14 6213
ye shall o up an heave offering Num 15:19 7311
Ye shall o up a cake of the first Num 15:20 7311
o one young bullock for a burnt Num 15:24 6213
come near to o incense before the Num 16:40
which they shall o unto the LORD Num 18:12 5414
of Israel o unto the LORD Num 18:19 7311
which they o as an heave offering Num 18:24 7311
then ye shall o up an heave Num 18:26 7311
Thus ye also shall o an heave Num 18:28 7311
o every heave offering of the Num 18:29 7311
shall ye observe to o unto me in Num 28:2 7126
which ye shall o unto the LORD Num 28:3 7126
lamb shalt thou o in the morning Num 28:4 6213
other lamb shalt thou o at even Num 28:4 6213

other lamb shalt thou o at even Num 28:8 6213
offering thereof, thou shalt o it Num 28:8 6213
of your months ye shall o a burnt Num 28:11 7126
But ye shall o a sacrifice made Num 28:19 7126
deals shall ye o for a bullock Num 28:20 6213
deal shalt thou o for every lamb Num 28:21 6213
Ye shall o these beside the burnt Num 28:23 6213
this manner ye shall o daily Num 28:24 6213
But ye shall o the burnt offering Num 28:27 7126
Ye shall o them beside the Num 28:31 6213
ye shall o a burnt offering for a Num 29:2 6213
But ye shall o a burnt offering Num 29:8 7126
ye shall o a burnt offering, a Num 29:13 7126
ye shall o twelve young bullocks Num 29:17
But ye shall o a burnt offering, Num 29:36 7126
thou o not thy burnt offerings in Deut 12:13 5927
there thou shalt o thy burnt Deut 12:14 5927
thou shalt o thy burnt offerings, Deut 12:27 6213
from them that o a sacrifice Deut 18:3 2076
thou shalt o burnt offerings Deut 27:6 5927
thou shalt o peace offerings, and Deut 27:7 2076
there they shall o sacrifices of Deut 33:19 2076
or if to o thereon burnt offering Josh 22:23 5927
or if to o peace offerings Josh 22:23 6213
had made an end to o the present Judg 3:18 7126
o a burnt sacrifice with the wood Judg 6:26 5927
I will o it up for a burnt Judg 11:31 5927
if thou wilt o a burnt offering, Judg 13:16 6213
thou must o it unto the LORD Judg 13:16 5927
to o a great sacrifice unto Dagon Judg 16:23 2076
went up to o unto the LORD the 1Sa 1:21 2076
husband to o the yearly sacrifice 1Sa 2:19 2076
to o upon mine altar, to burn 1Sa 2:28 5927
to o burnt offerings, and to 1Sa 10:8 5927
the LORD, I o thee three things 2Sa 24:12 5190
o up what seemeth good unto him 2Sa 24:22 5927
neither will I o burnt offerings 2Sa 24:24 5927
did Solomon o upon that altar 1Kin 3:4 5927
did Solomon o burnt offerings 1Kin 9:25 5927
upon thee shall he o the priests 1Kin 13:2 2076
o neither burnt offering nor 2Kin 5:17 6213
when they went in to o sacrifices 2Kin 10:24 6213
To o burnt offerings unto the 1Chr 16:40 5927
the LORD, I o thee three things 1Chr 21:10 5186
nor o burnt offerings without 1Chr 21:24 5927
to o all burnt sacrifices unto 1Chr 23:31 5927
that we should be able to o so 1Chr 29:14
here, to o willingly unto thee 1Chr 29:17
to o the burnt offerings of the 2Chr 23:18 5927
to o withal, and spoons, and 2Chr 24:14 5927
priests the sons of Aaron to o 2Chr 29:21 5927
Hezekiah commanded to o the burnt 2Chr 29:27 5927
to o unto the LORD, as it is 2Chr 35:12 7126
to o burnt offerings upon the 2Chr 35:16 5927
to o burnt offerings thereon, as Ezr 3:2 5927
o burnt offerings unto the LORD Ezr 3:6 5927
That they may o sacrifices of Ezr 6:10 7127
o them upon the altar of the Ezr 7:17 7127
o up for yourselves a burnt Job 42:8 5927
O the sacrifices of righteousness Ps 4:5 2076
offerings of blood will I not o Ps 16:4 5258
therefore will I o in his Ps 27:6 2076
O unto God thanksgiving Ps 50:14 2076
then shall they o bullocks upon Ps 51:19 5927
I will o unto thee burnt Ps 66:15 5927
I will o bullocks with goats Ps 66:15 6213
of Sheba and Seba shall o gifts Ps 72:10 7126
I will o to thee the sacrifice of Ps 116:17 2076
wentest thou up to o sacrifice Is 57:7 2076
the gods unto whom they o incense Jer 11:12
when they o burnt offering and an Jer 14:12 5927
before me to o burnt offerings Jer 33:18 5927
the place where they did o sweet Eze 6:13 5414
For when ye o your gifts, when ye Eze 20:31 5375
to o burnt offerings thereon, and Eze 43:18 5927
o a kid of the goats without Eze 43:22 7126
thou shalt o a young bullock Eze 43:23 7126
thou shalt o them before the LORD Eze 43:24 7126
they shall o them up for a burnt Eze 43:24 5927
when ye o my bread, the fat and Eze 44:7 7126
before me to o unto me the fat Eze 44:15 7126
he shall o his sin offering, Eze 44:27 7126
ye shall o an oblation unto the Eze 45:1 7311
is the oblation that ye shall o Eze 45:13 7311
ye shall o the tenth part of a Eze 45:14
o unto the LORD in the sabbath Eze 46:4 7126
offering which ye shall o of five Eze 48:8 7311
The oblation that ye shall o unto Eze 48:9 7311
ye shall o the holy oblation Eze 48:20 7311
that they should o an oblation Dan 2:46 5260
They shall not o wine offerings Hos 9:4 5258
o a sacrifice of thanksgiving Amos 4:5 6999
Though ye o me burnt offerings and Amos 5:22 5927
that which they o there is Hag 2:14 7126
Ye o polluted bread upon mine Mal 1:7 5066
if ye o the blind for sacrifice, Mal 1:8 5066
if ye o the lame and sick, is it Mal 1:8 5066
o it now unto thy governor Mal 1:8 7126
that they may o unto the LORD an Mal 3:3 5066
and then come and o thy gift Mt 5:24 4374
o the gift that Moses commanded, Mt 8:4 4374
o for thy cleansing those things, Mk 1:44 4374
to o a sacrifice according to Lk 2:24 *1325*
o for thy cleansing, according as Lk 5:14 4374
on the one cheek o also the other Lk 6:29 3930
an egg, will he o him a scorpion Lk 11:12 1929
to God, that he may o both gifts Heb 5:1 4374
also for himself, to o for sins Heb 5:3 4374
to o up sacrifice, first for his Heb 7:27 *399*
priest is ordained to o gifts Heb 8:3 4374
this man have somewhat also to o Heb 8:3 4374
that o gifts according to the law Heb 8:4 4374
that he should o himself often Heb 9:25 4374
By him therefore let us o the Heb 13:15 *399*
to o up spiritual sacrifices, 1Pet 2:5 *399*
that he should o it with the Rev 8:3 *1325*

OFFERED

o burnt offerings on the altar Gen 8:20 5927
o him up for a burnt offering in Gen 22:13 5927
Then Jacob o sacrifice upon the Gen 31:54 2076
o sacrifices unto the God of his Gen 46:1 2076
which o burnt offerings, and Ex 24:5 5927
o burnt offerings, and brought Ex 32:6 5927
every man that o Ex 35:22 5130
o an offering of gold Ex 35:22
o upon it the burnt offering and Ex 40:29 5927
burnt offering which he hath o Lev 7:8 7126
eaten the same day that it is o Lev 7:15 7133
o it for sin, as the first Lev 9:15 2398
o it according to the manner Lev 9:16 6213
o strange fire before the LORD, Lev 10:1 7126
have they o their sin offering Lev 10:19 7126
when they o before the LORD, and Lev 16:1 7126
when they o strange fire before Num 3:4 7126
over them that were numbered, o Num 7:2 7126
the princes o for dedicating of Num 7:10 7126
even the princes o their offering Num 7:10 7126
he that o his offering the first Num 7:12 7126
He o for his offering one silver Num 7:19 7126
prince of the children of Gad, o Num 7:42
of the children of Ephraim, o Num 7:48
On the eighth day o Gamaliel the Num 7:54
of the children of Benjamin, o Num 7:60
prince of the children of Dan, o Num 7:66
of the children of Asher, o Num 7:72
of the children of Naphtali, o Num 7:78
Aaron o them as an offering Num 8:21 5130
and fifty men that o incense Num 16:35 7126
for they o them before the LORD, Num 16:38 7126
they that were burnt had o Num 16:39 7126
And Balak o oxen and sheep, and sent Num 22:40 2076
Balaam o on every altar a bullock Num 23:2 5927
I have o upon every altar a Num 23:4 5927
o a bullock and a ram on every Num 23:14 5927
o a bullock and a ram on every Num 23:30 5927
when they o strange fire before Num 26:61 7126
offering unto the LORD shall be o Num 28:15 6213
it shall be o beside the Num 28:24 6213
that they o up to the LORD Num 31:52 7311
they o thereon burnt offerings Josh 8:31 5927
the people willingly o themselves Judg 5:2
that o themselves willingly among Judg 5:9
the second bullock was o upon the Judg 6:28 5927
o it upon a rock unto the LORD Judg 13:19 5927
o burnt offerings and peace Judg 20:26 5927
o burnt offerings and peace Judg 21:4 5927
when the time was that Elkanah o 1Sa 1:4 2076
that, when any man o sacrifice 1Sa 2:13 2076
o the kine a burnt offering unto 1Sa 6:14 5927
of Beth-shemesh o burnt offerings 1Sa 6:15 5927
o it for a burnt offering wholly 1Sa 7:9 5927
And he o the burnt offering 1Sa 13:9 5927
therefore, and o a burnt offering 1Sa 13:12 5927
David o burnt offerings and peace 2Sa 6:17 5927
from Giloh, while he o sacrifices 2Sa 15:12 2076
o burnt offerings and peace 2Sa 24:25 5927
o up burnt offerings 1Kin 3:15 5927
o peace offerings, and made a 1Kin 3:15 6213
o sacrifice before the LORD 1Kin 8:62 2076
Solomon o a sacrifice of peace 1Kin 8:63 2076
which he o unto the LORD, two and 1Kin 8:63 2076
for there he o burnt offerings, 1Kin 8:64 6213
in Judah, and he o upon the altar 1Kin 12:32 5927
So he o upon the altar which he 1Kin 12:33 5927
he o upon the altar, and burnt 1Kin 12:33 5927
for the people o and burnt incense 1Kin 22:43 2076
when the meat offering was o 2Kin 3:20 5927
o him for a burnt offering upon 2Kin 3:27 5927
to the altar, and o thereon 2Kin 16:12 5927
his sons o upon the altar of the 1Chr 6:49 6999
that they o seven bullocks and 1Chr 15:26 2076
they o burnt sacrifices and peace 1Chr 16:1 7126
o burnt offerings and peace 1Chr 21:26 5927
of the king's work, o willingly, 1Chr 29:6
for that they o willingly 1Chr 29:9
they o willingly to the LORD 1Chr 29:9
have willingly o all these things 1Chr 29:17
o burnt offerings unto the LORD, 1Chr 29:21 5927
o a thousand burnt offerings upon 2Chr 1:6 5927
such things as they o for the 2Chr 4:6 4639
all the people o sacrifices 2Chr 7:4 2076
king Solomon o a sacrifice of 2Chr 7:5 2076
for there he o burnt offerings, 2Chr 7:7 6213
Then Solomon o burnt offerings 2Chr 8:12 5927
they o unto the LORD the same 2Chr 15:11 2076
who willingly o himself unto the 2Chr 17:16
they o burnt offerings in the 2Chr 24:14 5927
nor o burnt offerings in the holy 2Chr 29:7 5927
beside all that was willingly o Ezr 1:6
o freely for the house of God to Ezr 2:68
they o burnt offerings thereon Ezr 3:3 5927
o the daily burnt offerings by Ezr 3:4
afterward o the continual burnt Ezr 3:5
of every one that willingly o a Ezr 3:5 5068
the place where they o sacrifices Ezr 6:3 1684
o at the dedication of this house Ezr 6:17 7127
freely o unto the God of Israel Ezr 7:15 5069
all Israel there present, had o Ezr 8:25 7311
o burnt offerings unto the God of Ezr 8:35 7126
they o a ram of the flock for Ezr 10:19
that willingly o themselves to Neh 11:2
that day they o great sacrifices Neh 12:43 2076
o burnt offerings according to Job 1:5 5927
thou hast o a meat offering Is 57:6 5927
as if he o swine's blood Is 66:3 5927
they have o incense unto Baal Jer 32:29 6999
they o there their sacrifices, and Eze 20:28 2076
oblation of the land that is o Eze 48:12 8641
the reproach o by him to cease Dan 11:18
Have ye o unto me sacrifices and Amos 5:25 5066
o a sacrifice unto the LORD, and Jonah 1:16 2076
incense shall be o unto my name Mal 1:11 5066
o sacrifice unto the idol, and Acts 7:41 *321*
have ye o to me slain beasts and Acts 7:42 4374
Ghost was given, he o them money, Acts 8:18 4374
ye abstain from meats o to idols Acts 15:29 *1494*
themselves from things o to idols Acts 21:25 *1494*
should be o for every one of them Acts 21:26 4374
as touching things o unto idols 1Cor 8:1 *1494*
are o in sacrifice unto idols 1Cor 8:4 *1494*
eat it as a thing o unto an idol 1Cor 8:7 *1494*
those things which are o to idols 1Cor 8:10 *1494*
or that which is o in sacrifice 1Cor 10:19 *1494*
This is o in sacrifice unto idols 1Cor 10:28 *1494*
if I be o upon the sacrifice and Phil 2:17 *4689*
For I am now ready to be o 2Ti 4:6 *4689*
flesh, when he had o up prayers Heb 5:7 4374
he did once, when he o up himself Heb 7:27
which he o for himself, and for Heb 9:7 4374
in which were o both gifts Heb 9:9
o himself without spot to God Heb 9:14 4374
So Christ was once o to bear the Heb 9:28 4374
those sacrifices which they o Heb 10:1 4374
they not have ceased to be o Heb 10:2 4374
which are o by the law Heb 10:8 4374
after he had o one sacrifice for Heb 10:12 4374
By faith Abel o unto God a more Heb 11:4 4374
when he was tried, o up Isaac Heb 11:17 4374
o up his only begotten son Heb 11:17 4374
when he had o Isaac his son upon Jas 2:21 *399*

OFFERETH

The priest that o it for sin Lev 6:26 2398
the priest that o any man's burnt Lev 7:8 7126
shall be the priest's that o it Lev 7:9 7126
same day that he o his sacrifice Lev 7:16 7126
it be imputed unto him that o it Lev 7:18 7126
He that o the sacrifice of his Lev 7:29 7126
that o the blood of the peace Lev 7:33 7126
that o a burnt offering or Lev 17:8 5926
for he o the bread of thy God Lev 21:8 7126
whosoever o a sacrifice of peace Lev 22:21 7126
Then shall he that o his offering Num 15:4 7126
Whoso o praise glorifieth me Ps 50:23 2076
he that o an oblation, as if he Is 66:3 5927
him that o in the high places, and Jer 48:35 5927
him that o an offering unto the Mal 2:12 5066

OFFERING

of the ground an o unto the LORD Gen 4:3 4503
had respect unto Abel and to his o Gen 4:4 4503
to his o he had not respect Gen 4:5 4503
offer him there for a burnt o Gen 22:2
and clave the wood for the burnt o Gen 22:3
took the wood of the burnt o Gen 22:6
where is the lamb for a burnt o Gen 22:7
himself a lamb for a burnt o Gen 22:8
a burnt o in the stead of his son Gen 22:13
and he poured a drink o thereon Gen 35:14
father in law, took a burnt o Ex 18:12
Israel, that they bring me an o Ex 25:2 8641
with his heart ye shall take my o Ex 25:2 8641
this is the o which ye shall take Ex 25:3 8641
it is a sin o Ex 29:14
it is a burnt o unto the LORD Ex 29:18
an o made by fire unto the LORD Ex 29:18
them for a wave o before the LORD Ex 29:24
them upon the altar for a burnt o Ex 29:25
it is an o made by fire unto the Ex 29:25
it for a wave o before the LORD Ex 29:26
sanctify the breast of the wave o Ex 29:27
and the shoulder of the heave o Ex 29:27 8641
for it is an heave o Ex 29:28 8641
it shall be an heave o from the Ex 29:28 8641
even their heave o unto the LORD Ex 29:28 8641
bullock for a sin o for atonement Ex 29:36
of an hin of wine for a drink o Ex 29:40
to the meat o of the morning Ex 29:41 4503
according to the drink o thereof Ex 29:41
an o made by fire unto the LORD Ex 29:41
o throughout your generations at Ex 29:42
nor burnt sacrifice, nor meat o Ex 30:9 4503
shall ye pour drink o thereon Ex 30:9
blood of the sin o of atonements Ex 30:10
shekel shall be the o of the LORD Ex 30:13 8641
shall give an o unto the LORD Ex 30:14 8641
when they give an o unto the LORD Ex 30:15 8641
to burn o made by fire unto the Ex 30:20
the altar of burnt o with all his Ex 30:28
the altar of burnt o with all his Ex 31:9
from among you an o unto the LORD Ex 35:5 8641
him bring it, an o of the LORD Ex 35:5 8641
The altar of burnt o, with his Ex 35:16
they brought the LORD's o to the Ex 35:21 8641
an o of gold unto the LORD Ex 35:22
one that did offer an o of silver Ex 35:24 8641
and brass brought the LORD's o Ex 35:24 8641
brought a willing o unto the LORD Ex 35:29
they received of Moses all the o Ex 36:3 8641
work for the o of the sanctuary Ex 36:6 8641
altar of burnt o of shittim wood Ex 38:1
place, even the gold of the o Ex 38:24 8573
the brass of the o was seventy Ex 38:29 8573
burnt o before the door of the Ex 40:6
anoint the altar of the burnt o Ex 40:10
he put the altar of burnt o by Ex 40:29
and offered upon it the burnt o Ex 40:29
and the meat o Ex 40:29 4503
of you bring an o unto the LORD Lev 1:2 7133
shall bring your o of the cattle Lev 1:2 7133
If his o be a burnt sacrifice of Lev 1:3 7133
hand upon the head of the burnt o Lev 1:4

And he shall flay the burnt o.... Lev 1:6
an o made by fire, of a sweet.... Lev 1:9
if his o be of the flocks, namely.... Lev 1:10 7133
an o made by fire, of a sweet.... Lev 1:13
for his o to the LORD be of fowls.... Lev 1:14 7133
shall bring his o of turtledoves.... Lev 1:14 7133
an o made by fire, of a sweet.... Lev 1:17
will offer a meat o unto the LORD.... Lev 2:1 7133
his o shall be of fine flour.... Lev 2:1 7133
to be an o made by fire, of a.... Lev 2:2
of a meat o baken in the oven.... Lev 2:4 4503
be a meat o baken in a pan.... Lev 2:5 4503
it is a meat o.... Lev 2:6 4503
a meat o baken in the frying pan.... Lev 2:7 4503
thou shalt bring the meat o that.... Lev 2:8 4503
the meat o a memorial thereof.... Lev 2:9 4503
it is an o made by fire, of a.... Lev 2:9
of the meat o shall be Aaron's.... Lev 2:10 4503
No meat o, which ye shall bring.... Lev 2:11 4503
in any o of the LORD made by fire.... Lev 2:11
every oblation of thy meat o.... Lev 2:13 4503
God to be lacking from thy meat o.... Lev 2:13 4503
if thou offer a meat o of thy.... Lev 2:14 4503
o of thy firstfruits green ears.... Lev 2:14 4503
it is a meat o.... Lev 2:15 4503
it is an o made by fire unto the.... Lev 2:16
be a sacrifice of peace o.... Lev 3:1
his hand upon the head of his o.... Lev 3:2 7133
of the peace o an o made.... Lev 3:3
it is an o made by fire, of a.... Lev 3:5
if his o for a sacrifice of peace.... Lev 3:6 7133
for a sacrifice of peace o unto.... Lev 3:6
If he offer a lamb for his o.... Lev 3:7 7133
his hand upon the head of his o.... Lev 3:8 7133
of the peace o an o made.... Lev 3:9
it is the food of the o made by.... Lev 3:11
if his o be a goat, then he shall.... Lev 3:12 7133
And he shall offer thereof his o.... Lev 3:14 7133
even an o made by fire unto the.... Lev 3:14
it is the food of the o made by.... Lev 3:16
blemish unto the LORD for a sin o.... Lev 4:3
of the altar of the burnt o.... Lev 4:7
fat of the bullock for the sin o.... Lev 4:8
upon the altar of the burnt o.... Lev 4:10
of the altar of the burnt o.... Lev 4:18
did with the bullock for a sin o.... Lev 4:20
it is a sin o for the.... Lev 4:21
he shall bring his o, a kid of.... Lev 4:23 7133
kill the burnt o before the LORD.... Lev 4:24
it is a sin o.... Lev 4:24
of the sin o with his finger.... Lev 4:25
the horns of the altar of burnt o.... Lev 4:25
bottom of the altar of burnt o.... Lev 4:25
then he shall bring his o.... Lev 4:28 7133
hand upon the head of the sin o.... Lev 4:29
slay the sin o in the place of.... Lev 4:29
in the place of the burnt o.... Lev 4:29
the horns of the altar of burnt o.... Lev 4:30
And if he bring a lamb for a sin o.... Lev 4:32 7133
hand upon the head of the sin o.... Lev 4:33
slay it for a sin o in the place.... Lev 4:33
place where they kill the burnt o.... Lev 4:33
of the sin o with his finger.... Lev 4:34
the horns of the altar of burnt o.... Lev 4:34
he shall bring his trespass o.... Lev 5:6 817
a kid of the goats, for a sin o.... Lev 5:6
one for a sin o, and the other for.... Lev 5:7
and the other for a burnt o.... Lev 5:7
that which is for the sin o first.... Lev 5:8
of the blood of the sin o upon.... Lev 5:9
it is a sin o.... Lev 5:9
offer the second for a burnt o.... Lev 5:10
o the tenth part of an ephah of.... Lev 5:11 7133
ephah of fine flour for a sin o.... Lev 5:11
for it is a sin o.... Lev 5:11
it is a sin o.... Lev 5:12
be the priest's, as a meat o.... Lev 5:13 4503
the sanctuary, for a trespass o.... Lev 5:15
with the ram of the trespass o.... Lev 5:16
thy estimation, for a trespass o.... Lev 5:18
It is a trespass o.... Lev 5:19
in the day of his trespass o.... Lev 6:5
his trespass o unto the LORD.... Lev 6:6
thy estimation, for a trespass o.... Lev 6:6
This is the law of the burnt o.... Lev 6:9
It is the burnt o, because of the.... Lev 6:9
with the burnt o on the altar.... Lev 6:10
lay the burnt o in order upon it.... Lev 6:12
And this is the law of the meat o.... Lev 6:14 4503
of the flour of the meat o.... Lev 6:15 4503
which is upon the meat o, and.... Lev 6:15 4503
it is most holy, as is the sin o.... Lev 6:17
and as the trespass o.... Lev 6:17
This is the o of Aaron and of his.... Lev 6:20 7133
fine flour for a meat o perpetual.... Lev 6:20 4503
o shalt thou offer for a sweet.... Lev 6:21 4503
For every meat o for the priest.... Lev 6:23 4503
This is the law of the sin o.... Lev 6:25
burnt o is killed shall the sin.... Lev 6:25
is killed shall the sin o be.... Lev 6:25
And no sin o, whereof any of the.... Lev 6:30
this is the law of the trespass o.... Lev 7:1
o shall they kill the trespass.... Lev 7:2
shall they kill the trespass o.... Lev 7:2
an o made by fire unto the LORD.... Lev 7:5
it is a trespass o.... Lev 7:5
o is, so is the trespass o.... Lev 7:7
that offereth any man's burnt o.... Lev 7:8
the burnt o which he hath offered.... Lev 7:8
all the meat o that is baken in.... Lev 7:9 4503
And every meat o, mingled with oil.... Lev 7:10 4503
he shall offer for his o leavened.... Lev 7:13 7133
for an heave o unto the LORD.... Lev 7:14 8641
the sacrifice of his o be a vow.... Lev 7:16 7133
be a vow, or a voluntary o.... Lev 7:16
of which men offer an o made by.... Lev 7:25
for a wave o before the LORD.... Lev 7:30
unto the priest for an heave o of.... Lev 7:32 8641
This is the law of the burnt o.... Lev 7:37
of the meat o.... Lev 7:37 4503
o, and of the trespass o.... Lev 7:37
oil, and a bullock for the sin o.... Lev 8:2
brought the bullock for the sin o.... Lev 8:14
head of the bullock for the sin o.... Lev 8:14
brought the ram for the burnt o.... Lev 8:18 5930
an o made by fire unto the LORD.... Lev 8:21
them for a wave o before the LORD.... Lev 8:27
on the altar upon the burnt o.... Lev 8:28
it is an o made by fire unto the.... Lev 8:28
it for a wave o before the LORD.... Lev 8:29
o, and a ram for a burnt o.... Lev 9:2
ye a kid of the goats for a sin o.... Lev 9:3
without blemish, for a burnt o.... Lev 9:3
a meat o mingled with oil.... Lev 9:4 4503
the altar, and offer thy sin o.... Lev 9:7
and thy burnt o.... Lev 9:7
offer the o of the people, and.... Lev 9:7 7133
and slew the calf of the sin o.... Lev 9:8
caul above the liver of the sin o.... Lev 9:10
And he slew the burnt o.... Lev 9:12
presented the burnt o unto him.... Lev 9:13
upon the burnt o on the altar.... Lev 9:14
And he brought the people's o.... Lev 9:15 7133
was the sin o for the people.... Lev 9:15
And he brought the burnt o.... Lev 9:16
And he brought the meat o, and took.... Lev 9:17 4503
for a wave o before the LORD.... Lev 9:21
came down from o of the sin.... Lev 9:22 6213
the sin o, and the burnt o.... Lev 9:22
upon the altar the burnt o.... Lev 9:24
Take the meat o that remaineth of.... Lev 10:12 4503
it for a wave o before the LORD.... Lev 10:15
sought the goat of the sin o.... Lev 10:16
eaten the sin o in the holy place.... Lev 10:17
day have they offered their sin o.... Lev 10:19
their burnt o before the LORD.... Lev 10:19
if I had eaten the sin o to day.... Lev 10:19
of the first year for a burnt o.... Lev 12:6
or a turtledove, for a sin o.... Lev 12:6
the one for the burnt o.... Lev 12:8
and the other for a sin o.... Lev 12:8
deals of fine flour for a meat o.... Lev 14:10
and offer him for a trespass o.... Lev 14:12
them for a wave o before the LORD.... Lev 14:12
the sin o and the burnt o.... Lev 14:13
for as the sin o is the priest's,.... Lev 14:13
so is the trespass o.... Lev 14:13
of the blood of the trespass o.... Lev 14:14
upon the blood of the trespass o.... Lev 14:17
the priest shall offer the sin o.... Lev 14:19
he shall kill the burnt o.... Lev 14:19
priest shall offer the burnt o.... Lev 14:20
the meat o upon the altar.... Lev 14:20 4503
lamb for a trespass o to be waved.... Lev 14:21
mingled with oil for a meat o.... Lev 14:21 4503
o, and the other a burnt o.... Lev 14:22
take the lamb of the trespass o.... Lev 14:24
them for a wave o before the LORD.... Lev 14:24
kill the lamb of the trespass o.... Lev 14:25
of the blood of the trespass o.... Lev 14:25
of the blood of the trespass o.... Lev 14:28
able to get, the one for a sin o.... Lev 14:31
and the other for a burnt o.... Lev 14:31
with the meat o.... Lev 14:31 4503
offer them, the one for a sin o.... Lev 15:15
and the other for a burnt o.... Lev 15:15
shall offer the one for a sin o.... Lev 15:30
and the other for a burnt o.... Lev 15:30
o, and a ram for a burnt o.... Lev 16:3
two kids of the goats for a sin o.... Lev 16:5
and one ram for a burnt o.... Lev 16:5
offer his bullock of the sin o.... Lev 16:6
fell, and offer him for a sin o.... Lev 16:9
bring the bullock of the sin o.... Lev 16:11
of the sin o which is for himself.... Lev 16:11
he kill the goat of the sin o.... Lev 16:15
come forth, and offer his burnt o.... Lev 16:24
the burnt o of the people, and.... Lev 16:24
the fat of the sin o shall he.... Lev 16:25
And the bullock for the sin o.... Lev 16:27
and the goat for the sin o.... Lev 16:27
to offer an o unto the LORD.... Lev 17:4 7133
offereth a burnt o or sacrifice.... Lev 17:8
his trespass o unto the LORD.... Lev 19:21
even a ram for a trespass o.... Lev 19:21
o before the LORD for his sin.... Lev 19:22
eat of an o of the holy things.... Lev 22:12 8641
offer unto the LORD for a burnt o.... Lev 22:18
or a freewill o in beeves or.... Lev 22:21
nor make an o by fire of them.... Lev 22:22
thou offer for a freewill o.... Lev 22:23
make any o thereof in your land.... Lev 22:24
an o made by fire unto the LORD.... Lev 22:27
But ye shall offer an o made by.... Lev 23:8
year for a burnt o unto the LORD.... Lev 23:12
the meat o thereof shall be two.... Lev 23:13 4503
an o made by fire unto the LORD.... Lev 23:13
the drink o thereof shall be of.... Lev 23:13
have brought an o unto your God.... Lev 23:14 7133
brought the sheaf of the wave o.... Lev 23:15
offer a new meat o unto the LORD.... Lev 23:16 4503
be for a burnt o unto the LORD.... Lev 23:18
unto the LORD, with their meat o.... Lev 23:18 4503
even an o made by fire, of sweet.... Lev 23:18
one kid of the goats for a sin o.... Lev 23:19
for a wave o before the LORD.... Lev 23:20
but ye shall offer an o made by.... Lev 23:25
offer an o made by fire unto the.... Lev 23:27
an o made by fire unto the LORD.... Lev 23:36
ye shall offer an o made by fire.... Lev 23:36
to offer an o made by fire unto.... Lev 23:37
by fire unto the LORD, a burnt o.... Lev 23:37
and a meat o.... Lev 23:37 4503
even an o made by fire unto the.... Lev 24:7
men bring an o unto the LORD.... Lev 27:9 7133
incense, and the daily meat o.... Num 4:16 4503
every o of all the holy things of.... Num 5:9 8641
and he shall bring her o for her.... Num 5:15 7133
for it is an o of jealousy.... Num 5:15 4503
an o of memorial, bringing.... Num 5:15 4503
put the o of memorial in her.... Num 5:18 4503
hands, which is the jealousy o.... Num 5:18 4503
o out of the woman's hand.... Num 5:25 4503
shall wave the o before the LORD,.... Num 5:25 4503
shall take an handful of the o.... Num 5:26 4503
shall offer the one for a sin o.... Num 6:11
and the other for a burnt o.... Num 6:11
the first year for a trespass o.... Num 6:12
shall offer his o unto the LORD.... Num 6:14 7133
without blemish for a burnt o.... Num 6:14
year without blemish for a sin o.... Num 6:14
with oil, and their meat o.... Num 6:15 4503
his sin o, and his burnt o.... Num 6:16
shall offer also his meat o.... Num 6:17 4503
and his drink o.... Num 6:17
them for a wave o before the LORD.... Num 6:20
of his o unto the LORD for his.... Num 6:21 7133
brought their o before the LORD.... Num 7:3 7133
offered their o before the altar.... Num 7:10 7133
Moses, They shall offer their o.... Num 7:11 7133
he that offered his o the first.... Num 7:12 7133
his o was one silver charger, the.... Num 7:13 7133
mingled with oil for a meat o.... Num 7:13 4503
of the first year, for a burnt o.... Num 7:15
One kid of the goats for a sin o.... Num 7:16
this was the o of Nahshon the son.... Num 7:17 7133
for his o one silver charger.... Num 7:19 7133
mingled with oil for a meat o.... Num 7:19 4503
of the first year, for a burnt o.... Num 7:21
One kid of the goats for a sin o.... Num 7:22
this was the o of Nethaneel the.... Num 7:23 7133
His o was one silver charger, the.... Num 7:25 7133
mingled with oil for a meat o.... Num 7:25 4503
of the first year, for a burnt o.... Num 7:27
One kid of the goats for a sin o.... Num 7:28
this was the o of Eliab the son.... Num 7:29 7133
His o was one silver charger of.... Num 7:31 7133
mingled with oil for a meat o.... Num 7:31 4503
of the first year, for a burnt o.... Num 7:33
One kid of the goats for a sin o.... Num 7:34
this was the o of Elizur the son.... Num 7:35 7133
His o was one silver charger, the.... Num 7:37 7133
mingled with oil for a meat o.... Num 7:37 4503
of the first year, for a burnt o.... Num 7:39
One kid of the goats for a sin o.... Num 7:40
this was the o of Shelumiel the.... Num 7:41 7133
His o was one silver charger of.... Num 7:43 7133
mingled with oil for a meat o.... Num 7:43 4503
of the first year, for a burnt o.... Num 7:45
One kid of the goats for a sin o.... Num 7:46
this was the o of Eliasaph the.... Num 7:47 7133
His o was one silver charger, the.... Num 7:49 7133
mingled with oil for a meat o.... Num 7:49 4503
of the first year, for a burnt o.... Num 7:51
One kid of the goats for a sin o.... Num 7:52
this was the o of Elishama the.... Num 7:53 7133
His o was one silver charger of.... Num 7:55 7133
mingled with oil for a meat o.... Num 7:55 4503
of the first year, for a burnt o.... Num 7:57
One kid of the goats for a sin o.... Num 7:58
this was the o of Gamaliel the.... Num 7:59 7133
His o was one silver charger, the.... Num 7:61 7133
mingled with oil for a meat o.... Num 7:61 4503
of the first year, for a burnt o.... Num 7:63
One kid of the goats for a sin o.... Num 7:64
this was the o of Abidan the son.... Num 7:65 7133
His o was one silver charger, the.... Num 7:67 7133
mingled with oil for a meat o.... Num 7:67 4503
of the first year, for a burnt o.... Num 7:69
One kid of the goats for a sin o.... Num 7:70
this was the o of Ahiezer the son.... Num 7:71 7133
His o was one silver charger, the.... Num 7:73 7133
mingled with oil for a meat o.... Num 7:73 4503
of the first year, for a burnt o.... Num 7:75
One kid of the goats for a sin o.... Num 7:76
this was the o of Pagiel the son.... Num 7:77 7133
His o was one silver charger, the.... Num 7:79 7133
mingled with oil for a meat o.... Num 7:79 4503
of the first year, for a burnt o.... Num 7:81
One kid of the goats for a sin o.... Num 7:82
this was the o of Ahira the son.... Num 7:83 7133
the burnt o were twelve bullocks.... Num 7:87
year twelve, with their meat o.... Num 7:87 4503
of the goats for sin o twelve.... Num 7:87
a young bullock with his meat o.... Num 8:8 4503
shalt thou take for a sin o.... Num 8:8
an o of the children of Israel.... Num 8:11 8573
shalt offer the one for a sin o.... Num 8:12
and the other for a burnt o.... Num 8:12
offer them for an o unto the LORD.... Num 8:13 8573
them, and offer them for an o.... Num 8:15 8573
them as an o before the LORD.... Num 8:21 8573
that we may not offer an o of the.... Num 9:7 7133
because he brought not the o of.... Num 9:13 7133
will make an o by fire unto the.... Num 15:3
by fire unto the LORD, a burnt o.... Num 15:3
a vow, or in a freewill o.... Num 15:3
his o unto the LORD bring a meat.... Num 15:4 7133
a meat o of a tenth deal of flour.... Num 15:4 4503
o shalt thou prepare with the.... Num 15:5
with the burnt o or sacrifice.... Num 15:5
a meat o two tenth deals of flour.... Num 15:6 4503

for a drink o thou shalt offer	Num 15:7	
preparest a bullock for a burnt o	Num 15:8	
o of three tenth deals of flour	Num 15:9	4503
for a drink o half an hin of wine	Num 15:10	
for an o made by fire, of a sweet	Num 15:10	
after this manner, in o	Num 15:13	7126
an o made by fire	Num 15:13	
and will offer an o made by fire	Num 15:14	
offer up an heave o unto the LORD	Num 15:19	8641
of your dough for an heave o	Num 15:20	8641
as ye do the heave o of the	Num 15:20	8641
an heave o in your generations	Num 15:21	8641
one young bullock for a burnt o	Num 15:24	
unto the LORD, with his meat o	Num 15:24	4503
and his drink o	Num 15:24	
one kid of the goats for a sin o	Num 15:24	
and they shall bring their o	Num 15:25	7133
their sin o before the LORD, for	Num 15:25	
of the first year for a sin o	Num 15:27	
LORD, Respect not thou their o	Num 16:15	4503
of theirs, every meat o of theirs	Num 18:9	4503
and every sin o of theirs	Num 18:9	
and every trespass o of theirs	Num 18:9	
the heave o of their gift, with	Num 18:11	8641
their fat for an o made by fire	Num 18:17	
offer as an heave o unto the LORD	Num 18:24	8641
up an heave o of it for the LORD	Num 18:26	8641
this your heave o shall be	Num 18:27	8641
heave o unto the LORD of all your	Num 18:28	8641
heave o to Aaron the priest	Num 18:28	8641
offer every heave o of the LORD	Num 18:29	8641
unto Balak, Stand by thy burnt o	Num 23:3	
Balak, Stand here by thy burnt o	Num 23:15	
behold, he stood by his burnt o	Num 23:17	
of Israel, and say unto them, My o	Num 28:2	7133
This is the o made by fire which	Num 28:3	
by day, for a continual burnt o	Num 28:3	
of an ephah of flour for a meat o	Num 28:5	4503
It is a continual burnt o	Num 28:6	
the drink o thereof shall be the	Num 28:7	
unto the LORD for a drink o	Num 28:7	
as the meat o of the morning, and	Num 28:8	4503
and as the drink o thereof	Num 28:8	
tenth deals of flour for a meat o	Num 28:9	4503
with oil, and the drink o thereof	Num 28:9	
is the burnt o of every sabbath	Num 28:10	
burnt o, and his drink o	Num 28:10	
offer a burnt o unto the LORD	Num 28:11	
tenth deals of flour for a meat o	Num 28:12	4503
tenth deals of flour for a meat o	Num 28:12	4503
oil for a meat o unto one lamb	Num 28:13	4503
for a burnt o of a sweet savour,	Num 28:13	
this is the burnt o of every	Num 28:14	
o unto the LORD shall be offered	Num 28:15	
burnt o, and his drink o	Num 28:15	
fire for a burnt o unto the LORD	Num 28:19	
their meat o shall be of flour	Num 28:20	4503
And one goat for a sin o, to make	Num 28:22	
beside the burnt o in the morning	Num 28:23	
which is for a continual burnt o	Num 28:23	
burnt o, and his drink o	Num 28:24	
bring a new meat o unto the LORD	Num 28:26	4503
o for a sweet savour unto the	Num 28:27	
their meat o of flour mingled	Num 28:28	4503
them beside the continual burnt o	Num 28:31	
and his meat o	Num 28:31	4503
ye shall offer a burnt o for a	Num 29:2	
their meat o shall be of flour	Num 29:3	4503
one kid of the goats for a sin o	Num 29:5	
Beside the burnt o of the month	Num 29:6	
of the month, and his meat o	Num 29:6	4503
and the daily burnt o	Num 29:6	
and his meat o	Num 29:6	4503
burnt o unto the LORD for a sweet	Num 29:8	
their meat o shall be of flour	Num 29:9	4503
One kid of the goats for a sin o	Num 29:11	
beside the sin o of atonement	Num 29:11	
and the continual burnt o	Num 29:11	
and the meat o of it	Num 29:11	4503
And ye shall offer a burnt o	Num 29:13	
their meat o shall be of flour	Num 29:14	4503
one kid of the goats for a sin o	Num 29:16	
beside the continual burnt o	Num 29:16	
his meat o	Num 29:16	4503
his meat o, and his drink o	Num 29:16	
And their meat o and their drink	Num 29:18	4503
one kid of the goats for a sin o	Num 29:19	
beside the continual burnt o	Num 29:19	
and the meat o thereof	Num 29:19	4503
And their meat o and their drink	Num 29:21	4503
And one goat for a sin o	Num 29:22	
beside the continual burnt o	Num 29:22	
and his meat o	Num 29:22	4503
and his drink o	Num 29:22	
Their meat o and their drink	Num 29:24	4503
one kid of the goats for a sin o	Num 29:25	
beside the continual burnt o	Num 29:25	
his meat o, and his drink	Num 29:25	4503
and his drink o	Num 29:25	
And their meat o and their drink	Num 29:27	4503
And one goat for a sin o	Num 29:28	
beside the continual burnt o	Num 29:28	
and his meat o	Num 29:28	4503
and his drink o	Num 29:28	
And their meat o and their drink	Num 29:30	4503
And one goat for a sin o	Num 29:31	
beside the continual burnt o	Num 29:31	
his meat o, and his drink	Num 29:31	4503
and his drink o	Num 29:31	
And their meat o and their drink	Num 29:33	4503
And one goat for a sin o	Num 29:34	
beside the continual burnt o	Num 29:34	
his meat o, and his drink	Num 29:34	4503
and his drink o	Num 29:34	

But ye shall offer a burnt o	Num 29:36	
Their meat o and their drink	Num 29:37	4503
And one goat for a sin o	Num 29:38	
beside the continual burnt o	Num 29:38	
and his meat o	Num 29:38	4503
and his drink o	Num 29:38	
for an heave o of the LORD	Num 31:29	8641
which was the LORD's heave o	Num 31:41	8641
all the gold of the o that they	Num 31:52	8641
the heave o of your hand, and all	Deut 12:11	8641
or heave o of thine hand	Deut 12:17	8641
of a freewill o of thine hand	Deut 16:10	
even a freewill o, according as	Deut 23:23	
thereon burnt o or meat	Josh 22:23	
or meat o, or if	Josh 22:23	4503
us an altar, not for burnt o	Josh 22:26	
I will offer it up for a burnt o	Judg 11:31	
and if thou wilt offer a burnt o	Judg 13:16	
Manoah took a kid with a meat o	Judg 13:19	4503
would not have received a burnt o	Judg 13:23	
a meat o at our hands, neither	Judg 13:23	4503
men abhorred the o of the LORD	1Sa 2:17	4503
ye at my sacrifice and at mine o	1Sa 2:29	4503
with sacrifice nor o for ever	1Sa 3:14	4503
any wise return him a trespass o	1Sa 6:3	
What shall be the trespass o	1Sa 6:4	
ye return him for a trespass o	1Sa 6:8	
the kine a burnt o unto the LORD	1Sa 6:14	
for a trespass o unto the LORD	1Sa 6:17	
a burnt o wholly unto the LORD	1Sa 7:9	
as Samuel was o up the burnt	1Sa 7:10	5927
up the burnt o	1Sa 7:10	
Bring hither a burnt o to me	1Sa 13:9	
And he offered the burnt o	1Sa 13:9	
an end of o the burnt	1Sa 13:10	5927
the burnt o, behold	1Sa 13:10	
therefore, and offered a burnt o	1Sa 13:12	
against me, let him accept an o	1Sa 26:19	4503
made an end of o burnt offerings	2Sa 6:18	5927
until the time of the o of the	1Kin 18:29	5927
of the o of the evening sacrifice	1Kin 18:36	5927
when the meat o was offered	2Kin 3:20	4503
him for a burnt o upon the wall	2Kin 3:27	
o nor sacrifice unto other gods	2Kin 5:17	
an end of o the burnt	2Kin 10:25	6213
the burnt o, that Jehu	2Kin 10:25	
And he burnt his burnt o and his	2Kin 16:13	
and his meat o	2Kin 16:13	4503
and poured his drink o	2Kin 16:13	
altar burn the morning burnt o	2Kin 16:15	
and the evening meat o	2Kin 16:15	4503
burnt sacrifice, and his meat o	2Kin 16:15	
with the burnt o of all the	2Kin 16:15	
of the land, and their meat o	2Kin 16:15	4503
it all the blood of the burnt o	2Kin 16:15	
upon the altar of the burnt o	1Chr 6:49	
an end of o the burnt offerings	1Chr 16:2	5927
bring an o, and come before him	1Chr 16:29	4503
the burnt o continually morning	1Chr 16:40	
wood, and the wheat for the meat o	1Chr 21:23	4503
by fire upon the altar of burnt o	1Chr 21:26	
and the altar of the burnt o	1Chr 21:29	
altar of the burnt o for Israel	1Chr 22:1	
and for the fine flour for meat o	1Chr 23:29	4503
the burnt o they washed in them	2Chr 4:6	
heaven, and consumed the burnt o	2Chr 7:1	
o according to the commandment of	2Chr 8:13	5927
the LORD, and the altar of burnt o	2Chr 29:18	
for a sin o for the kingdom, and	2Chr 29:21	
for the sin o before the king	2Chr 29:23	
king commanded that the burnt o	2Chr 29:24	
the sin o should be made for all	2Chr 29:24	
offer the burnt o upon the altar	2Chr 29:27	
And when the burnt o began	2Chr 29:27	
until the burnt o was finished	2Chr 29:28	
And when they had made an end of o	2Chr 29:29	5927
were for a burnt o to the LORD	2Chr 29:32	
drink offerings for every burnt o	2Chr 29:35	
o peace offerings, and making	2Chr 30:22	2076
busied in o of burnt offerings	2Chr 35:14	5927
beside the freewill o for the	Ezr 1:4	
offered the continual burnt o	Ezr 3:5	
a freewill o unto the LORD	Ezr 3:5	
for a sin o for all Israel,	Ezr 6:17	
with the freewill o of the people	Ezr 7:16	
o willingly for the house of	Ezr 7:16	
even the o of the house of our	Ezr 8:25	8641
the gold are a freewill o unto	Ezr 8:28	
twelve he goats for a sin o	Ezr 8:35	
this was a burnt o unto the LORD	Ezr 8:35	
and for the continual meat o	Neh 10:33	4503
and for the continual burnt o	Neh 10:33	
and the people, for the wood o	Neh 10:34	7133
shall bring the o of the corn	Neh 10:39	8641
the house of God, with the meat o	Neh 13:9	4503
And for the wood o, at times	Neh 13:31	7133
offer up for yourselves a burnt o	Job 42:8	
and o thou didst not desire	Ps 40:6	4503
burnt o and sin o hast thou	Ps 40:6	
thou delightest not in burnt o	Ps 51:16	
burnt o and whole burnt o	Ps 51:19	
bring an o, and come into his	Ps 96:8	4503
thereof sufficient for a burnt o	Is 40:16	
caused thee to serve with an o	Is 43:23	4503
shalt make his soul an o for sin	Is 53:10	
them hast thou poured a drink o	Is 57:6	
thou hast offered a meat o	Is 57:6	4503
I hate robbery for burnt o	Is 61:8	
the drink o unto that number	Is 65:11	
for an o unto the LORD out of all	Is 66:20	4503
an o in a clean vessel into the	Is 66:20	4503
to anger in o incense unto Baal	Jer 11:17	
and when they offer burnt o	Jer 14:12	
the provocation of their o	Eze 20:28	7133

where they washed the burnt o	Eze 40:38	
side, to slay thereon the burnt o	Eze 40:39	
sin o and the trespass o	Eze 40:39	
of hewn stone for the burnt o	Eze 40:42	
wherewith they slew the burnt o	Eze 40:42	
the tables was the flesh of the o	Eze 40:43	7133
most holy things, and the meat o	Eze 42:13	4503
sin o, and the trespass o	Eze 42:13	
GOD, a young bullock for a sin o	Eze 43:19	
the bullock also of the sin o	Eze 43:21	
goats without blemish for a sin o	Eze 43:22	
up for a burnt o unto the LORD	Eze 43:24	
every day a goat for a sin o	Eze 43:25	
they shall slay the burnt o	Eze 44:11	
he shall offer his sin o	Eze 44:27	
They shall eat the meat o	Eze 44:29	4503
sin o, and the trespass o	Eze 44:29	
for a meat o, and for a burnt	Eze 45:15	4503
and for a burnt o	Eze 45:15	
he shall prepare the sin o	Eze 45:17	
and the meat o	Eze 45:17	4503
and the burnt o	Eze 45:17	
take of the blood of the sin o	Eze 45:19	
of the land a bullock for a sin o	Eze 45:22	
prepare a burnt o to the LORD	Eze 45:23	
of the goats daily for a sin o	Eze 45:23	
he shall prepare a meat o of an	Eze 45:24	4503
days, according to the sin o	Eze 45:25	
according to the burnt o	Eze 45:25	
and according to the meat o	Eze 45:25	4503
priests shall prepare his burnt o	Eze 46:2	
the burnt o that the prince shall	Eze 46:4	
the meat o shall be an ephah for	Eze 46:5	4503
the meat o for the lambs as he	Eze 46:5	4503
And he shall prepare a meat o	Eze 46:7	4503
in the solemnities the meat o	Eze 46:11	4503
o or peace offerings voluntarily	Eze 46:12	
and he shall prepare his burnt o	Eze 46:12	
shalt daily prepare a burnt o	Eze 46:13	
a meat o for it every morning	Eze 46:14	4503
a meat o continually by a	Eze 46:14	4503
prepare the lamb, and the meat o	Eze 46:15	4503
morning for a continual burnt o	Eze 46:15	
trespass o and the sin o	Eze 46:20	
where they shall bake the meat o	Eze 46:20	4503
shall be the o which ye shall	Eze 48:8	8641
The meat o and the drink	Joel 1:9	4503
the drink o is cut off from the	Joel 1:9	
for the meat o and the drink	Joel 1:13	4503
the drink o is withholden from	Joel 1:13	
even a meat o and a drink	Joel 2:14	4503
a drink o unto the LORD your God	Joel 2:14	
my dispersed, shall bring mine o	Zeph 3:10	4503
will I accept an o at your hand	Mal 1:10	4503
offered unto my name, and a pure o	Mal 1:11	4503
thus ye brought an o	Mal 1:13	4503
him that offereth an o unto the	Mal 2:12	4503
he regardeth not the o any more	Mal 2:13	4503
the LORD an o in righteousness	Mal 3:3	4503
Then shall the o of Judah	Mal 3:4	4503
coming to him, and o him vinegar,	Lk 23:36	*4374*
until that an o should be offered	Acts 21:26	*4376*
that the o up of the Gentiles	Rom 15:16	*4376*
and hath given himself for us an o	Eph 5:2	*4376*
o thou wouldest not, but a body	Heb 10:5	*4376*
when he said, Sacrifice and o	Heb 10:8	*4376*
o for sin thou wouldest not	Heb 10:8	
the o of the body of Jesus Christ	Heb 10:10	*4376*
o oftentimes the same sacrifices,	Heb 10:11	*4374*
For by one o he hath perfected	Heb 10:14	*4376*
is, there is no more o for sin	Heb 10:18	*4376*

OFFERINGS

and offered burnt o on the altar	Gen 8:20	
us also sacrifices and burnt o	Ex 10:25	
sacrifice thereon thy burnt o	Ex 20:24	
burnt o, and thy peace o	Ex 20:24	
of Israel, which offered burnt o	Ex 24:5	
sacrificed peace o of oxen unto	Ex 24:5	2077
of the sacrifice of their peace o	Ex 29:28	
on the morrow, and offered burnt o	Ex 32:6	
o, and brought peace o	Ex 32:6	
yet unto him free o every morning	Ex 36:3	
of the meat o shall be Aaron's	Lev 2:3	
of the o of the LORD made by fire	Lev 2:3	
of the o of the LORD made by fire	Lev 2:10	
with all thine o thou shalt offer	Lev 2:13	7133
of the sacrifice of peace o	Lev 4:10	
fat of the sacrifice of peace o	Lev 4:26	
from off the sacrifice of peace o	Lev 4:31	
from the sacrifice of the peace o	Lev 4:35	
according to the o made by fire	Lev 4:35	
according to the o made by fire	Lev 5:12	
thereon the fat of the peace o	Lev 6:12	
portion of my o made by fire	Lev 6:17	
the o of the LORD made by fire	Lev 6:18	
law of the sacrifice of peace o	Lev 7:11	
of thanksgiving of his peace o	Lev 7:13	
the blood of the peace o	Lev 7:14	
of the sacrifice of his peace o	Lev 7:15	
o be eaten at all on the third	Lev 7:18	
flesh of the sacrifice of peace o	Lev 7:20	
flesh of the sacrifice of peace o	Lev 7:21	
the sacrifice of his peace o unto	Lev 7:29	
of the sacrifice of his peace o	Lev 7:29	
the o of the LORD made by fire	Lev 7:30	
of the sacrifices of your peace o	Lev 7:32	
offereth the blood of the peace o	Lev 7:33	
the sacrifices of their peace o	Lev 7:34	
out of the o of the LORD made by	Lev 7:35	
of the sacrifice of the peace o	Lev 7:37	
a bullock and a ram for peace o	Lev 9:4	
ram for a sacrifice of peace o	Lev 9:18	
and the burnt offering, and peace o	Lev 9:22	

of the o of the LORD made by fire	Lev 10:12	
peace o of the children of Israel	Lev 10:14	
the o made by fire of the fat	Lev 10:15	
them for peace o unto the LORD	Lev 17:5	2077
of peace o unto the LORD, ye	Lev 19:5	
for the o of the LORD made by	Lev 21:6	
the o of the LORD made by fire	Lev 21:21	
vows, and for all his freewill o	Lev 22:18	
offereth a sacrifice of peace o	Lev 22:21	
meat offering, and their drink o	Lev 23:18	
year for a sacrifice of peace o	Lev 23:19	
offering, a sacrifice, and drink o	Lev 23:37	
and beside all your freewill o	Lev 23:38	
o of the LORD made by fire by a	Lev 24:9	
ram without blemish for peace o	Num 6:14	
meat offering, and their drink o	Num 6:15	
of peace o unto the LORD, with	Num 6:17	
the sacrifice of the peace o	Num 6:18	
And for a sacrifice of peace o	Num 7:17	
And for a sacrifice of peace o	Num 7:23	
And for a sacrifice of peace o	Num 7:29	
And for a sacrifice of peace o	Num 7:35	
And for a sacrifice of peace o	Num 7:41	
And for a sacrifice of peace o	Num 7:47	
And for a sacrifice of peace o	Num 7:53	
And for a sacrifice of peace o	Num 7:59	
And for a sacrifice of peace o	Num 7:65	
And for a sacrifice of peace o	Num 7:71	
And for a sacrifice of peace o	Num 7:77	
And for a sacrifice of peace o	Num 7:83	
of the peace o were twenty	Num 7:88	
the trumpets over your burnt o	Num 10:10	
the sacrifices of your peace o	Num 10:10	
a vow, or peace o unto the LORD	Num 15:8	
o of all the hallowed things of	Num 18:8	8641
with all the wave o of the	Num 18:11	
All the heave o of the holy	Num 18:19	8641
their drink o shall be half an	Num 28:14	
without blemish) and their drink o	Num 28:31	
meat offering, and their drink o	Num 29:6	
offering of it, and their drink o	Num 29:11	
their drink o for the bullocks,	Num 29:18	
thereof, and their drink o	Num 29:19	
their drink o for the bullocks,	Num 29:21	
their drink o for the bullocks,	Num 29:24	
their drink o for the bullocks,	Num 29:27	
their drink o for the bullocks,	Num 29:30	
their drink o for the bullocks,	Num 29:33	
their drink o for the bullock,	Num 29:37	
your vows, and your freewill o	Num 29:39	
for your burnt o	Num 29:39	
and for your meat o	Num 29:39	4503
and for your drink o	Num 29:39	
and for your peace o	Num 29:39	
ye shall bring your burnt o	Deut 12:6	
heave o of your hand, and your	Deut 12:6	
and your vows, and your freewill o	Deut 12:6	
your burnt o, and your sacrifices,	Deut 12:11	
that thou offer not thy burnt o	Deut 12:13	
thou shalt offer thy burnt o	Deut 12:14	
thou vowest, nor thy freewill o	Deut 12:17	
And thou shalt offer thy burnt o	Deut 12:27	
they shall eat the o of the LORD	Deut 18:1	
thou shalt offer burnt o thereon	Deut 27:6	
And thou shalt offer peace o	Deut 27:7	
drank the wine of their drink o	Deut 32:38	
thereon burnt o unto the LORD	Josh 8:31	
the LORD, and sacrificed peace o	Josh 8:31	
or if to offer peace o thereon	Josh 22:23	2077
LORD before him with our burnt o	Josh 22:27	
sacrifices, and with our peace o	Josh 22:27	
our fathers made, not for burnt o	Josh 22:28	
to build an altar for burnt o	Josh 22:29	
for burnt o, for meat o	Josh 22:29	4503
until even, and offered burnt o	Judg 20:26	
and peace o before the LORD	Judg 20:26	
burnt o and peace o	Judg 21:4	
o made by fire of the children of	1Sa 2:28	
of all the o of Israel my people	1Sa 2:29	4503
of Beth-shemesh offered burnt o	1Sa 6:15	
down unto thee, to offer burnt o	1Sa 10:8	
sacrifice sacrifices of peace o	1Sa 10:8	
of peace o before the LORD	1Sa 11:15	
burnt offering to me, and peace o	1Sa 13:9	
LORD as great delight in burnt o	1Sa 15:22	
rain, upon you, nor fields of o	2Sa 1:21	8641
and David offered burnt o and peace	2Sa 6:17	
and peace o before the LORD	2Sa 6:17	
burnt o and peace o	2Sa 6:18	
neither will I offer burnt o unto	2Sa 24:24	
burnt o and peace o	2Sa 24:25	
a thousand burnt o did Solomon	1Kin 3:4	
the LORD, and offered up burnt o	1Kin 3:15	
o, and offered peace o	1Kin 3:15	
offered a sacrifice of peace o	1Kin 8:63	
for there he offered burnt o	1Kin 8:64	
and meat o	1Kin 8:64	4503
and the fat of the peace o	1Kin 8:64	
too little to receive the burnt o	1Kin 8:64	
and meat o	1Kin 8:64	4503
and the fat of the peace o	1Kin 8:64	
a year did Solomon offer burnt o	1Kin 9:25	
peace o upon the altar which he	1Kin 9:25	
in to offer sacrifices and burnt o	2Kin 10:24	
the blood of his peace o, upon	2Kin 16:13	
meat offering, and their drink o	2Kin 16:15	
sacrifices and peace o before God	1Chr 16:1	
burnt o and the peace o	1Chr 16:2	
To offer burnt o unto the LORD	1Chr 16:40	
thee the oxen also for burnt o	1Chr 21:23	
nor offer burnt o without cost	1Chr 21:24	
burnt o and peace o	1Chr 21:26	
and offered burnt o unto the LORD	1Chr 29:21	
lambs, with their drink o	1Chr 29:21	
a thousand burnt o upon it	2Chr 1:6	
and for the burnt o morning	2Chr 2:4	
for there he offered burnt o	2Chr 7:7	
and the fat of the peace o	2Chr 7:7	
not able to receive the burnt o	2Chr 7:7	
and the meat o	2Chr 7:7	4503
Then Solomon offered burnt o unto	2Chr 8:12	
to offer the burnt o of the LORD	2Chr 23:18	
they offered burnt o in the house	2Chr 24:14	
incense nor offered burnt o in	2Chr 29:7	
thank o into the house of the	2Chr 29:31	
brought in sacrifices and thank o	2Chr 29:31	
as were of a free heart burnt o	2Chr 29:31	
And the number of the burnt o	2Chr 29:32	
could not flay all the burnt o	2Chr 29:34	
And also the burnt o were in	2Chr 29:35	
with the fat of the peace o	2Chr 29:35	
the drink o for every burnt	2Chr 29:35	
brought in the burnt o into the	2Chr 30:15	
seven days, offering peace o	2Chr 30:22	2077
priests and Levites for burnt o	2Chr 31:2	
and for peace o	2Chr 31:2	
of his substance for the burnt o	2Chr 31:3	
the morning and evening burnt o	2Chr 31:3	
the burnt o for the sabbaths, and	2Chr 31:3	
the o into the house of the LORD	2Chr 31:10	8641
And brought in the o and the tithes	2Chr 31:12	8641
was over the freewill o of God	2Chr 31:14	8641
and sacrificed thereon peace o	2Chr 33:16	2077
and thank o, and commanded	2Chr 33:16	
and kids, all for the passover o	2Chr 35:7	
for the passover o two thousand	2Chr 35:8	
o five thousand small cattle	2Chr 35:9	
And they removed the burnt o	2Chr 35:12	
the other holy o sod they in pots	2Chr 35:13	
busied in offering of burnt o	2Chr 35:14	
to offer burnt o upon the altar	2Chr 35:16	
Israel, to offer burnt o thereon	Ezr 3:2	
they offered burnt o thereon unto	Ezr 3:3	
the LORD, even burnt o morning	Ezr 3:3	
the daily burnt o by number	Ezr 3:4	
to offer burnt o unto the LORD	Ezr 3:6	
for the burnt o of the God of	Ezr 6:9	
rams, lambs, with their meat o	Ezr 7:17	4503
and their drink o	Ezr 7:17	
offered burnt o unto the God of	Ezr 8:35	
and for the sin o to make an	Neh 10:33	
of our dough, and our o, and the	Neh 10:37	8641
for the treasures, for the o	Neh 12:44	8641
aforetime they laid the meat o	Neh 13:5	4503
and the o of the priests	Neh 13:5	4503
offered burnt o according to the	Job 1:5	
their drink o of blood will I not	Ps 16:4	
Remember all thy o, and accept thy	Ps 20:3	4503
for thy sacrifices or thy burnt o	Ps 50:8	
go into thy house with burnt o	Ps 66:13	
thee, the freewill o of my mouth	Ps 119:108	
I have peace o with me	Prov 7:14	
I am full of the burnt o of rams	Is 1:11	
the small cattle of thy burnt o	Is 43:23	
their burnt o and their sacrifices	Is 56:7	
your burnt o are not acceptable,	Jer 6:20	
pour out drink o unto other gods	Jer 7:18	5262
Put your burnt o unto your	Jer 7:21	
concerning burnt o or sacrifices	Jer 7:22	
from the south, bringing burnt o	Jer 17:26	
and sacrifices, and meat o	Jer 17:26	4503
with fire for burnt o unto Baal	Jer 19:5	
out drink o unto other gods	Jer 19:13	
out drink o unto other gods	Jer 32:29	
a man before me to offer burnt o	Jer 33:18	
and to kindle meat o	Jer 33:18	4503
and having cut themselves, with o	Jer 41:5	4503
and to pour out drink o unto her	Jer 44:17	
and to pour out drink o unto her	Jer 44:18	
and poured out drink o unto her	Jer 44:19	
and pour out drink o unto her	Jer 44:19	
and to pour out drink o unto her	Jer 44:25	
and poured out there their drink o	Eze 20:28	
and there will I require your o	Eze 20:40	8641
make it, to offer burnt o thereon	Eze 43:18	
make your burnt o upon the altar	Eze 43:27	
upon the altar, and your peace o	Eze 43:27	
a burnt offering, and for peace o	Eze 45:15	
the prince's part to give burnt o	Eze 45:17	
and meat o, and drink	Eze 45:17	4503
and drink o, in the	Eze 45:17	
burnt offering, and the peace o	Eze 45:17	
his burnt offering and his peace o	Eze 46:2	
burnt offering or peace o	Eze 46:12	
his burnt offering and his peace o	Eze 46:12	
of God more than burnt o	Hos 6:6	
for the sacrifices of mine o	Hos 8:13	1890
not offer wine o to the LORD	Hos 9:4	
and proclaim and publish the free o	Amos 4:5	
Though ye offer me burnt o	Amos 5:22	
and your meat o	Amos 5:22	4503
the peace o of your fat beasts	Amos 5:22	
o in the wilderness forty years,	Amos 5:25	4503
I come before him with burnt o	Mic 6:6	
In tithes and o	Mal 3:8	8641
is more than all whole burnt o	Mk 12:33	*3646*
cast in unto the o of God	Lk 21:4	*1435*
to bring alms to my nation, and o	Acts 24:17	*4376*
In burnt o and sacrifices for sin	Heb 10:6	*3646*
Sacrifice and offering and burnt o	Heb 10:8	*3646*

OFFICE

me he restored unto mine o	Gen 41:13	3653
When ye do the o of a midwife to	Ex 1:16	
unto me in the priest's o	Ex 28:1	
unto me in the priest's o	Ex 28:3	
unto me in the priest's o	Ex 28:4	
unto me in the priest's o	Ex 28:41	
unto me in the priest's o	Ex 29:1	
the priest's o shall be theirs	Ex 29:9	
minister to me in the priest's o	Ex 29:44	
unto me in the priest's o	Ex 30:30	
to minister in the priest's o	Ex 31:10	
to minister in the priest's o	Ex 35:19	
to minister in the priest's o	Ex 39:41	
unto me in the priest's o	Ex 40:13	
unto me in the priest's o	Ex 40:15	
unto the LORD in the priest's o	Lev 7:35	
priest's o in his father's stead	Lev 16:32	
to minister in the priest's o	Num 3:3	
ministered in the priest's o in	Num 3:4	
shall wait on their priest's o	Num 3:10	
to the o of Eleazar the son of	Num 4:16	6486
o for every thing of the altar	Num 18:7	
I have given your priest's o unto	Num 18:7	
in the priest's o in his stead	Deut 10:6	
o in the temple that Solomon	1Chr 6:10	
their o according to their order	1Chr 6:32	5656
seer did ordain in their set o	1Chr 9:22	
porters, were in their set o	1Chr 9:26	
had the set o over the things	1Chr 9:31	
Because their o was to wait on	1Chr 23:28	4612
Ithamar executed the priest's o	1Chr 24:2	
the priest's o unto the LORD	2Chr 11:14	
o by the hand of the Levites	2Chr 24:11	6486
of the priests, in their set o	2Chr 31:15	
for in their set o they	2Chr 31:18	
their o was to distribute unto	Neh 13:13	
and let another take his o	Ps 109:8	6486
to do the o of a priest unto me,	Eze 44:13	
o before God in the order of his	Lk 1:8	*2407*
to the custom of the priest's o	Lk 1:9	*2405*
of the Gentiles, I magnify mine o	Rom 11:13	*1248*
all members have not the same o	Rom 12:4	*4234*
If a man desire the o of a bishop	1Ti 3:1	*1984*
let them use the o of a deacon	1Ti 3:10	*1247*
For they that have used the o of	1Ti 3:13	*1247*
of Levi, who receive the o of the	Heb 7:5	*2405*

OFFICER

an o of Pharaoh's, and captain of	Gen 37:36	5631
an o of Pharaoh, captain of the	Gen 39:1	5631
and Zebul his o	Judg 9:28	6496
the son of Nathan was principal o	1Kin 4:5	5324
he was the only o which was in	1Kin 4:19	5333
the king of Israel called an o	1Kin 22:9	5631
appointed unto her a certain o	2Kin 8:6	5631
out of the city he took an o that	2Kin 25:19	5631
and the high priest's o came	2Chr 24:11	6496
the judge deliver thee to the o	Mt 5:25	*5257*
the judge deliver thee to the o	Lk 12:58	*4233*
the o cast thee into prison	Lk 12:58	*4233*

OFFICERS

was wroth against two of his o	Gen 40:2	5631
he asked Pharaoh's o that were	Gen 40:7	5631
let him appoint o over the land	Gen 41:34	6496
of the people, and their o	Ex 5:6	7860
the people went out, and their o	Ex 5:10	7860
the o of the children of Israel,	Ex 5:14	7860
Then the o of the children of	Ex 5:15	7860
the o of the children of Israel	Ex 5:19	7860
of the people, and o over them	Num 11:16	7860
was wroth with the o of the host	Num 31:14	6485
the o which were over thousands	Num 31:48	6485
over tens, and o among your tribes	Deut 1:15	7860
o shalt thou make thee in all thy	Deut 16:18	7860
the o shall speak unto the people	Deut 20:5	7860
the o shall speak further unto	Deut 20:8	7860
when the o have made an end of	Deut 20:9	7860
tribes, your elders, and your o	Deut 29:10	7860
elders of your tribes, and your o	Deut 31:28	7860
commanded the o of the people	Josh 1:10	7860
that the o went through the host	Josh 3:2	7860
all Israel, and their elders, and o	Josh 8:33	7860
for their judges, and for their o	Josh 23:2	7860
for their judges, and for their o	Josh 24:1	7860
your vineyards, and give to his o	1Sa 8:15	5631
the son of Nathan was over the o	1Kin 4:5	5324
had twelve o over all Israel	1Kin 4:7	5324
those o provided victual for king	1Kin 4:27	5324
unto the place where the o were	1Kin 4:28	
o which were over the work	1Kin 5:16	5324
These were the chief of the o	1Kin 9:23	5324
the o of the host, and said unto	2Kin 11:15	6485
the priest appointed o over the	2Kin 11:18	6486
and his princes, and his o	2Kin 24:12	5631
and the king's wives, and his o	2Kin 24:15	5631
and six thousand were o and judges	1Chr 23:4	7860
business over Israel, for o	1Chr 26:29	7860
were o among them of Israel on	1Chr 26:30	6486
their o that served the king in	1Chr 27:1	7860
king, and of his sons, with the o	1Chr 28:1	5631
the chief of king Solomon's o	2Chr 8:10	5324
of Israel called for one of his o	2Chr 18:8	5631
the Levites shall be o before you	2Chr 19:11	7860
Levites there were scribes, and o	2Chr 34:13	7860
to all the o of his house	Est 1:8	7227
let the king appoint o in all the	Est 2:3	6496
o of the king, helped the Jews	Est 9:3	6213
I will also make thy o peace	Is 60:17	6486
that ye should be o in the house	Jer 29:26	6496
chief priests sent o to take him	Jn 7:32	*5257*
Then came the o to the chief	Jn 7:45	*5257*
The o answered, Never man spake	Jn 7:46	*5257*
o from the chief priests and	Jn 18:3	*5257*
o of the Jews took Jesus, and	Jn 18:12	*5257*
o stood there, who had made a	Jn 18:18	*5257*
one of the o which stood by	Jn 18:22	*5257*
o saw him, they cried out, saying	Jn 19:6	*5257*
But when the o came, and found	Acts 5:22	*5257*
Then went the captain with the o	Acts 5:26	*5257*

OFFICES
thee, into one of the priests' o 1Sa 2:36
to their o in their service 1Chr 24:3 6486
And the priests waited on their o 2Chr 7:6 4931
Also Jehoiada appointed the o of 2Chr 23:18 6486
of my God, and for the o thereof Neh 13:14 4929

OFFSCOURING
Thou hast made us as the o Lam 3:45 5501
are the o of all things unto this 1Cor 4:13 *4067*

OFFSPRING
thine o as the grass of the earth Job 5:25 6631
their o before their eyes Job 21:8 6631
his o shall not be satisfied with Job 27:14 6631
yea, let my o be rooted out Job 31:8 6631
of his father's house, the o Is 22:24 6631
seed, and my blessing upon thine o Is 44:3 6631
the o of thy bowels like the Is 48:19 6631
and their o among the people Is 61:9 6631
of the LORD, and their o with them Is 65:23 6631
have said, For we are also his o Acts 17:28 *1085*
then as we are the o of God Acts 17:29 *1085*
the o of David, and the bright and Rev 22:16 *1085*

OFT
that as o as he passed by, he 2Kin 4:8 1767
How o is the candle of the wicked Job 21:17
how o cometh their destruction Job 21:17
How o did they provoke him in the Ps 78:40
Why do we and the Pharisees fast o Mt 9:14 *4183*
the fire, and o into the water Mt 17:15 *4178*
how o shall my brother sin Mt 18:21 *4212*
except they wash their hands o Mk 7:3 *4435*
I punished them o in every Acts 26:11 *4178*
do ye, as o as ye drink it, in 1Cor 11:25 *3740*
more frequent, in deaths o 2Cor 11:23 *4178*
for he o refreshed me, and was not 2Ti 1:16 *4178*
in the rain that cometh o upon it Heb 6:7 *4178*

OFTEN
that being o reproved hardeneth Prov 29:1
the LORD spake o one to another Mal 3:16
how o would I have gathered thy Mt 23:37 *4212*
he had been o bound with fetters Mk 5:4 *4178*
do the disciples of John fast o Lk 5:33 *4437*
how o would I have gathered thy Lk 13:34 *4212*
For as o as ye eat this bread, and 1Cor 11:26 *3740*
In journeyings o, in perils of 2Cor 11:26 *3740*
and painfulness, in watchings o 2Cor 11:27 *3740*
hunger and thirst, in fastings o 2Cor 11:27 *3740*
walk, of whom I have told you o Phil 3:18 *3740*
sake and thine o infirmities 1Ti 5:23 *4437*
that he should offer himself o Heb 9:25 *4178*
For then must he o have suffered Heb 9:26 *4178*
all plagues, as o as they will Rev 11:6 *3740*

OFTENER
wherefore he sent for him the o Acts 24:26 *4437*

OFTENTIMES
things worketh God o with man Job 33:29
For o also thine own heart Eccl 7:22
For o it had caught him Lk 8:29
that o I purposed to come unto Rom 1:13 *4178*
whom we have o proved diligent in 2Cor 8:22 *4178*
offering o the same sacrifices, Heb 10:11 *4178*

OFTTIMES
for o he falleth into the fire, Mt 17:15 *4178*
o it hath cast him into the fire, Mk 9:22 *4178*
for Jesus o resorted thither with Jn 18:2 *4178*

OG (*og*) *An Amorite king.*
O the king of Bashan went out Num 21:33 5747
the kingdom of O king of Bashan Num 32:33 5747
O the king of Bashan, which dwelt Deut 1:4 5747
O the king of Bashan came out Deut 3:1 5747
delivered into our hands O also Deut 3:3 5747
Argob, the kingdom of O in Bashan Deut 3:4 5747
of the kingdom of O in Bashan Deut 3:10 5747
For only O king of Bashan Deut 3:11 5747
Bashan, being the kingdom of O Deut 3:13 5747
the land of O king of Bashan, two Deut 4:47 5747
O the king of Bashan, came out Deut 29:7 5747
them as he did to Sihon and to O Deut 31:4 5747
the other side Jordan, Sihon and O Josh 2:10 5747
to O king of Bashan, which was at Josh 9:10 5747
the coast of O king of Bashan, Josh 12:4 5747
All the kingdom of O in Bashan Josh 13:12 5747
the kingdom of O king of Bashan Josh 13:30 5747
of the kingdom of O in Bashan Josh 13:31 5747
Amorites, and of O king of Bashan 1Kin 4:19 5747
the land of O king of Bashan Neh 9:22 5747
O king of Bashan, and all the Ps 135:11 5747
And O the king of Bashan Ps 136:20 5747

OH
O let not the LORD be angry, and I Gen 18:30 4994
O let not the Lord be angry, and I Gen 18:32 4994
And Lot said unto them, O, not so, Gen 19:18 4994
O, let me escape thither, (is it Gen 19:20 4994
O my lord, let thy servant, I Gen 44:18 994
unto the LORD, and said, O Ex 32:31 577
O my Lord, if the LORD be with us Judg 6:13 994
O my Lord, wherewith shall I save Judg 6:15 994
O my lord, as thy soul liveth, my 1Sa 1:26 994
O that I were made judge in the 2Sa 15:4
O that one would give me drink of 2Sa 23:15
O that thou wouldest bless me 1Chr 4:10 518
O that one would give me drink of 1Chr 11:17
O that I might have my request Job 6:8
O that I had given up the ghost, Job 10:18
But o that God would speak, and Job 11:5
O that ye would altogether hold Job 13:5 994
O that thou wouldest hide me in Job 14:13 994
O that one might plead for a man Job 16:21 994
O that my words were now written Job 19:23
o that they were printed in a Job 19:23
O that I knew where I might find Job 23:3
O that I were as in months past, Job 29:2
O that we had of his flesh Job 31:31
O that one would hear me Job 31:35
o save me for thy mercies' sake Ps 6:4
O let the wickedness of the Ps 7:9 4994
O that the salvation of Israel Ps 14:7
O how great is thy goodness, Ps 31:19
O that the salvation of Israel Ps 53:6
O that I had wings like a dove Ps 55:6
O that my people had hearkened Ps 81:13 3863
O that men would praise the LORD Ps 107:8
O that men would praise the LORD Ps 107:15
O that men would praise the LORD Ps 107:21
O that men would praise the LORD Ps 107:31
O that thou wouldest rend the Is 64:1 3863
O that my head were waters, and Jer 9:1
O that I had in the wilderness a Jer 9:2
early and sending them, saying, O Jer 44:4 4994

OHAD (*o'-had*) *A son of Simeon.*
Jemuel, and Jamin, and O, and Jachin. Gen 46:10 161
Jemuel, and Jamin, and O, and Jachin. Ex 6:15 161

OHEL (*o'-hel*) *A son of Zerubbabel.*
And Hashubah, and O, and Berechiah, 1Chr 3:20 169

OHOLAH See AHOLAH.

OHOLIAB See AHOLIAB.

OHOLIBAH See AHOLIBAH.

OHOLIBAMAH See AHOLIBAMAH.

OIL
poured o upon the top of it Gen 28:18 8081
thereon, and he poured o thereon Gen 35:14 8081
O for the light, spices for Ex 25:6 8081
the light, spices for anointing o Ex 25:6 8081
that they bring thee pure o olive Ex 27:20 8081
cakes unleavened tempered with o Ex 29:2 8081
wafers unleavened anointed with o Ex 29:2 8081
shalt thou take the anointing o Ex 29:7 8081
the altar, and of the anointing o Ex 29:21 8081
fourth part of an hin of beaten o Ex 29:40 8081
sanctuary, and of o olive an hin Ex 30:24 8081
make it an o of holy ointment Ex 30:25 8081
it shall be an holy anointing o Ex 30:25 8081
o unto me throughout your Ex 30:31 8081
And the anointing o, and sweet Ex 31:11 8081
o for the light, and spices for Ex 35:8 8081
light, and spices for anointing o Ex 35:8 8081
with the o for the light, Ex 35:14 8081
and his staves, and the anointing o Ex 35:15 8081
o for the light, and for the Ex 35:28 8081
the light, and for the anointing o Ex 35:28 8081
And he made the holy anointing o Ex 37:29 8081
thereof, and the o for light, Ex 39:37 8081
golden altar, and the anointing o Ex 39:38 8081
thou shalt take the anointing o Ex 40:9 8081
and he shall pour o upon it Lev 2:1 8081
of the o thereof, with all the Lev 2:2 8081
of fine flour mingled with o Lev 2:4 8081
unleavened wafers anointed with o Lev 2:4 8081
flour unleavened, mingled with o Lev 2:5 8081
it in pieces, and pour o thereon Lev 2:6 8081
be made of fine flour with o Lev 2:7 8081
And thou shalt put o upon it Lev 2:15 8081
thereof, and part of the o thereof Lev 2:16 8081
he shall put no o upon it Lev 5:11 8081
of the o thereof, and all the Lev 6:15 8081
In a pan it shall be made with o Lev 6:21 8081
meat offering, mingled with o Lev 7:10 8081
unleavened cakes mingled with o Lev 7:12 8081
with o, and cakes mingled with o Lev 7:12 8081
the garments, and the anointing o Lev 8:2 8081
And Moses took the anointing o Lev 8:10 8081
the anointing o upon Aaron's head Lev 8:12 8081
And Moses took of the anointing o Lev 8:30 8081
and a meat offering mingled with o Lev 9:4 8081
for the anointing o of the LORD Lev 10:7 8081
mingled with o, and one log of o Lev 14:10 8081
offering, and the log of o Lev 14:12 8081
shall take some of the log of o Lev 14:15 8081
in the o that is in his left hand Lev 14:16 8081
shall sprinkle of the o with his Lev 14:16 8081
of the rest of the o that is in Lev 14:17 8081
the remnant of the o that is in Lev 14:18 8081
with o for a meat offering Lev 14:21 8081
a meat offering, and a log of o Lev 14:21 8081
offering, and the log of o Lev 14:24 8081
the priest shall pour of the o Lev 14:26 8081
his right finger some of the o Lev 14:27 8081
the priest shall put of the o Lev 14:28 8081
the rest of the o that is in the Lev 14:29 8081
head the anointing o was poured Lev 21:10 8081
o of his God is upon him Lev 21:12 8081
of fine flour mingled with o Lev 23:13 8081
pure o olive beaten for the light Lev 24:2 8081
all the o vessels thereof, Num 4:9 8081
pertaineth the o for the light Num 4:16 8081
meat offering, and the anointing o Num 4:16 8081
he shall pour no o upon it Num 5:15 8081
of fine flour mingled with o Num 6:15 8081
unleavened bread anointed with o Num 6:15 8081
with o for a meat offering Num 7:13 8081
with o for a meat offering Num 7:19 8081
with o for a meat offering Num 7:25 8081
with o for a meat offering Num 7:31 8081
with o for a meat offering Num 7:37 8081
with o for a meat offering Num 7:43 8081
with o for a meat offering Num 7:49 8081
with o for a meat offering Num 7:55 8081
with o for a meat offering Num 7:61 8081
with o for a meat offering Num 7:67 8081
with o for a meat offering Num 7:73 8081
with o for a meat offering Num 7:79 8081
even fine flour mingled with o Num 8:8 8081
of it was as the taste of fresh o Num 11:8 8081
the fourth part of an hin of o Num 15:4 8081
the third part of an hin of o Num 15:6 8081
mingled with half an hin of o Num 15:9 8081
All the best of the o, and all the Num 18:12 8081
fourth part of an hin of beaten o Num 28:5 8081
a meat offering, mingled with o Num 28:9 8081
a meat offering, mingled with o Num 28:12 8081
a meat offering, mingled with o Num 28:12 8081
deal of flour mingled with o for Num 28:13 8081
shall be of flour mingled with o Num 28:20 8081
offering of flour mingled with o Num 28:28 8081
shall be of flour mingled with o Num 29:3 8081
shall be of flour mingled with o Num 29:9 8081
shall be of flour mingled with o Num 29:14 8081
was anointed with the holy o Num 35:25 8081
thy corn, and thy wine, and thine o Deut 7:13 3323
a land of o olive, and honey Deut 8:8 8081
thy corn, and thy wine, and thine o Deut 11:14 3323
corn, or of thy wine, or of thy o Deut 12:17 3323
corn, of thy wine, and of thine o Deut 14:23 3323
corn, of thy wine, and of thine o Deut 18:4 3323
not anoint thyself with the o Deut 28:40 8081
thee either corn, wine, or o Deut 28:51 3323
rock, and o out of the flinty rock Deut 32:13 8081
and let him dip his foot in o Deut 33:24 8081
Then Samuel took a vial of o 1Sa 10:1 8081
fill thine horn with o, and go, I 1Sa 16:1 8081
Then Samuel took the horn of o 1Sa 16:13 8081
he had not been anointed with o 2Sa 1:21 8081
and anoint not thyself with o 2Sa 14:2 8081
horn of o out of the tabernacle 1Kin 1:39 8081
and twenty measures of pure o 1Kin 5:11 8081
barrel, and a little o in a cruse 1Kin 17:12 8081
neither shall the cruse of o fail 1Kin 17:14 8081
neither did the cruse of o fail 1Kin 17:16 8081
in the house, save a pot of o 2Kin 4:2 8081
And the o stayed 2Kin 4:6 8081
And he said, Go, sell the o 2Kin 4:7 8081
take this box of o in thine hand 2Kin 9:1 8081
Then take the box of o, and pour 2Kin 9:3 8081
and he poured the o on his head 2Kin 9:6 8081
and vineyards, a land of o olive 2Kin 18:32 3323
fine flour, and the wine, and the o 1Chr 9:29 8081
bunches of raisins, and wine, and o 1Chr 12:40 8081
over the cellars of o was Joash 1Chr 27:28 8081
and twenty thousand baths of o 2Chr 2:10 8081
the wheat, and the barley, the o 2Chr 2:15 8081
and store of victual, and of o 2Chr 11:11 8081
firstfruits of corn, wine, and o 2Chr 31:5 3323
increase of corn, and wine, and o 2Chr 32:28 3323
and meat, and drink, and o, unto Ezr 3:7 8081
heaven, wheat, salt, wine, and o Ezr 6:9 4887
wine, and to an hundred baths of o Ezr 7:22 4887
of the corn, the wine, and the o Neh 5:11 3323
manner of trees, of wine and of o Neh 10:37 3323
corn, of the new wine, and the o Neh 10:39 3323
the corn, the new wine, and the o Neh 13:5 3323
the o unto the treasuries Neh 13:12 3323
wit, six months with o of myrrh Est 2:12 8081
Which make o within their walls, Job 24:11 6671
rock poured me out rivers of o Job 29:6 8081
thou anointest my head with o Ps 23:5 8081
hath anointed thee with the o of Ps 45:7 8081
his words were softer than o Ps 55:21 8081
with my holy o have I anointed Ps 89:20 8081
I shall be anointed with fresh o Ps 92:10 8081
o to make his face to shine, and Ps 104:15 8081
water, and like o into his bones Ps 109:18 8081
it shall be an excellent o Ps 141:5 8081
and her mouth is smoother than o Prov 5:3 8081
wine and o shall not be rich Prov 21:17 8081
o in the dwelling of the wise Prov 21:20 8081
and the myrtle, and the o tree Is 41:19 8081
the o of joy for mourning, the Is 61:3 8081
for wheat, and for wine, and for o Jer 31:12 3323
ye wine, and summer fruits, and o Jer 40:10 8081
of wheat, and of barley, and of o Jer 41:8 8081
thee, and I anointed thee with o Eze 16:9 8081
eat fine flour, and honey, and o Eze 16:13 8081
and thou hast set mine o and mine Eze 16:18 8081
I gave thee, fine flour, and o Eze 16:19 8081
hast set mine incense and mine o Eze 23:41 8081
and Pannag, and honey, and o Eze 27:17 8081
cause their rivers to run like o Eze 32:14 8081
ordinance of o, the bath of o Eze 45:14 8081
ram, and an hin of o for an ephah Eze 45:24 8081
offering, and according to the o Eze 45:25 8081
give, and an hin of o to an ephah Eze 46:5 8081
unto, and an hin of o to an ephah Eze 46:7 8081
give, and an hin of o to an ephah Eze 46:11 8081
and the third part of an hin of o Eze 46:14 8081
and the meat offering, and the o Eze 46:15 8081
water, my wool and my flax, mine o Hos 2:5 8081
I gave her corn, and wine, and o Hos 2:8 3323
the corn, and the wine, and the o Hos 2:22 3323
and o is carried into Egypt Hos 12:1 8081
is dried up, the o languisheth Joel 1:10 3323
will send you corn, and wine, and o Joel 2:19 3323
shall overflow with wine and o Joel 2:24 3323
with ten thousands of rivers of o Mic 6:7 8081
thou shalt not anoint thee with o Mic 6:15 8081
upon the new wine, and upon the o Hag 1:11 3323
bread, or pottage, or wine, or o Hag 2:12 8081
the golden o out of themselves Zec 4:12
lamps, and took no o with them Mt 25:3 *1637*
But the wise took o in their Mt 25:4 *1637*
unto the wise, Give us of your o Mt 25:8 *1637*
anointed with o many that were Mk 6:13 *1637*
My head with o thou didst not Lk 7:46 *1637*
bound up his wounds, pouring in o Lk 10:34 *1637*

he said, An hundred measures of o Lk 16:6 *1637*
hath anointed thee with the o of Heb 1:9 *1637*
anointing him with o in the name Jas 5:14 *1637*
and see thou hurt not the o Rev 6:6 *1637*
and frankincense, and wine, and o Rev 18:13 *1637*

OILED

of bread, and one cake of o bread Ex 29:23 8081
cake, and a cake of o bread Lev 8:26 8081

OINTMENT

shalt make it an oil of holy o Ex 30:25 4888
an o compound after the art of Ex 30:25 7545
and the spices, and the precious o 2Kin 20:13 8081
priests made the o of the spices 1Chr 9:30 4842
he maketh the sea like a pot of o Job 41:31 4841
like the precious o upon the head Ps 133:2 8081
O and perfume rejoice the heart Prov 27:9 8081
the o of his right hand, which Prov 27:16 8081
name is better than precious o Eccl 7:1 8081
and let thy head lack no o Eccl 9:8 8081
Dead flies cause the o of the Eccl 10:1 8081
thy name is as o poured forth Song 1:3 8081
up, neither mollified with o Is 1:6 8081
and the spices, and the precious o Is 39:2 8081
thou wentest to the king with o Is 57:9 8081
alabaster box of very precious o Mt 26:7 *3464*
For this o might have been sold Mt 26:9 *3464*
she hath poured this o on my body Mt 26:12 *3464*
of o of spikenard very precious Mk 14:3 *3464*
Why was this waste of the o made Mk 14:4 *3464*
brought an alabaster box of o Lk 7:37 *3464*
feet, and anointed them with the o Lk 7:38 *3464*
hath anointed my feet with o Lk 7:46 *3464*
which anointed the Lord with o Jn 11:2 *3464*
Mary a pound of o of spikenard Jn 12:3 *3464*
filled with the odour of the o Jn 12:3 *3464*
Why was not this o sold for three Jn 12:5 *3464*

OINTMENTS

of the savour of thy good o thy Song 1:3 8081
smell of thine o than all spices Song 4:10 8081
themselves with the chief o Amos 6:6 8081
returned, and prepared spices and o Lk 23:56 *3464*
And cinnamon, and odours, and o Rev 18:13 *3464*

OLD

And Noah was five hundred years o Gen 5:32 1121
became mighty men which were of o Gen 6:4 5769
Noah was six hundred years o when Gen 7:6 1121
Shem was an hundred years o Gen 11:10 1121
five years o when he departed out Gen 12:4 1121
me an heifer of three years o Gen 15:9 8027
and a she goat of three years o Gen 15:9 8027
and a ram of three years o Gen 15:9 8027
shalt be buried in a good o age Gen 15:15 7872
was fourscore and six years o Gen 16:16 1121
And when Abram was ninety years o Gen 17:1 1121
he that is eight days o shall be Gen 17:12 1121
him that is an hundred years o Gen 17:17 1121
Sarah, that is ninety years o Gen 17:17 1323
And Abraham was ninety years o Gen 17:24 1121
his son was thirteen years o Gen 17:25 1121
Now Abraham and Sarah were o Gen 18:11 2205
After I am waxed o shall I have Gen 18:12 1086
pleasure, my lord being o also Gen 18:12 2204
a surety bear a child, which am o Gen 18:13 2204
compassed the house round, both o Gen 19:4 2205
unto the younger, Our father is o Gen 19:31 2204
bare Abraham a son in his o age Gen 21:2 2208
his son Isaac being eight days o Gen 21:4 1121
And Abraham was an hundred years o Gen 21:5 1121
have born him a son in his o age Gen 21:7 2208
and seven and twenty years o Gen 23:1 2416
And Abraham was o, and well Gen 24:1 2204
a son to my master when she was o Gen 24:36 2209
ghost, and died in a good o age Gen 25:8 7872
an o man, and full of years Gen 25:8 2205
Isaac was forty years o when he Gen 25:20 1121
years o when she bare them Gen 25:26 1121
Esau was forty years o when he Gen 26:34 1121
to pass, that when Isaac was o Gen 27:1 2204
And he said, Behold now, I am o Gen 27:2 2204
gathered unto his people, being o Gen 35:29 2205
Joseph, being seventeen years o Gen 37:2 1121
he was the son of his o age Gen 37:3 2208
Joseph was thirty years o when he Gen 41:46 1121
the o man of whom ye spake Gen 43:27 2205
o man, and a child of his o age Gen 44:20 2208
said unto Jacob, How o art thou Gen 47:8
as a lion, and as an o lion Gen 49:9 3833
being an hundred and ten years o Gen 50:26 1121
And Moses was fourscore years o Ex 7:7 1121
Aaron fourscore and three years o Ex 7:7 1121
go with our young and with our o Ex 10:9 2205
are numbered, from twenty years o Ex 30:14 1121
be numbered, from twenty years o Ex 38:26 1121
It is an o leprosy in the skin of Lev 13:11 3462
and honour the face of the o man Lev 19:32 2205
eat yet of o fruit until the Lev 25:22 3465
in ye shall eat of the o store Lev 25:22 3465
And ye shall eat o store Lev 26:10 3462
bring forth the o because of the Lev 26:10 3465
years o even unto sixty years o Lev 27:3 1121
o even unto twenty years o Lev 27:5 1121
month o even unto five years o Lev 27:6 1121
And if it be from sixty years o Lev 27:7 1121
From twenty years o and upward, Num 1:3 1121
of the names, from twenty years o Num 1:18 1121
every male from twenty years o Num 1:20 1121
every male from twenty years o Num 1:22 1121
of the names, from twenty years o Num 1:24 1121
of the names, from twenty years o Num 1:26 1121
of the names, from twenty years o Num 1:28 1121
of the names, from twenty years o Num 1:30 1121
of the names, from twenty years o Num 1:32 1121
of the names, from twenty years o Num 1:34 1121
of the names, from twenty years o Num 1:36 1121
of the names, from twenty years o Num 1:38 1121
of the names, from twenty years o Num 1:40 1121
of the names, from twenty years o Num 1:42 1121
fathers, from twenty years o Num 1:45 1121
every male from a month o Num 3:15 1121
of all the males, from a month o Num 3:22 1121
of all the males, from a month o Num 3:28 1121
of all the males, from a month o Num 3:34 1121
all the males from a month o Num 3:39 1121
children of Israel from a month o Num 3:40 1121
number of names, from a month o Num 3:43 1121
From thirty years o and upward Num 4:3 1121
upward even until fifty years o Num 4:3 1121
From thirty years o and upward Num 4:23 1121
years o shalt thou number them Num 4:23 1121
From thirty years o and upward Num 4:30 1121
years o shalt thou number them Num 4:30 1121
From thirty years o and upward Num 4:35 1121
and upward even unto fifty years o Num 4:35 1121
From thirty years o and upward Num 4:39 1121
and upward even unto fifty years o Num 4:39 1121
From thirty years o and upward Num 4:43 1121
and upward even unto fifty years o Num 4:43 1121
From thirty years o and upward Num 4:47 1121
and upward even unto fifty years o Num 4:47 1121
from twenty and five years o Num 8:24 1121
whole number, from twenty years o Num 14:29 1121
from a month o shalt thou redeem Num 18:16 1121
of Israel, from twenty years o Num 26:2 1121
the people, from twenty years o Num 26:4 1121
all males from a month o Num 26:62 1121
out of Egypt, from twenty years o Num 32:11 1121
three years o when he died in Num 33:39 1121
giants dwelt therein in o time Deut 2:20 6440
Thy raiment waxed not o upon thee Deut 8:4 1086
which they of o time have set in Deut 19:14 7223
not regard the person of the o Deut 28:50 2205
clothes are not waxen o upon you Deut 29:5 1086
shoe is not waxen o upon thy foot Deut 29:5 1086
and twenty years o this day Deut 31:2 1121
Remember the days of o, consider Deut 32:7 5769
and twenty years o when he died Deut 34:7 1121
they did eat of the o corn of the Josh 5:11 5669
eaten of the o corn of the land Josh 5:12 5669
both man and woman, young and o Josh 6:21 5288
took o sacks upon their asses, and Josh 9:4 1087
their asses, and wine bottles, o Josh 9:4 1087
o shoes and clouted upon their Josh 9:5 1087
feet, and o garments upon them Josh 9:5 1087
our shoes are become o by reason Josh 9:13 1086
Now Joshua was o and stricken in Josh 13:1 2204
LORD said unto him, Thou art o Josh 13:1 2204
Forty years o was I when Moses Josh 14:7 1121
day fourscore and five years o Josh 14:10 1121
round about, that Joshua waxed o Josh 23:1 2204
and said unto them, I am o Josh 23:2 2204
other side of the flood in o time Josh 24:2 5769
being an hundred and ten years o Josh 24:29 1121
being an hundred and ten years o Judg 2:8 1121
second bullock of seven years o Judg 6:25
son of Joash died in a good o age Judg 8:32 7872
there came an o man from his work Judg 19:16 2205
the o man said, Whither goest Judg 19:17 2205
the o man said, Peace be with Judg 19:20 2205
master of the house, the o man Judg 19:22 2205
for I am too o to have an husband Ruth 1:12 2204
and a nourisher of thine o age Ruth 4:15 7872
Now Eli was very o, and heard all 1Sa 2:22 2204
not be an o man in thine house 1Sa 2:31 2205
there shall not be an o man in 1Sa 2:32 2205
Eli was ninety and eight years o 1Sa 4:15 1121
for he was an o man, and heavy 1Sa 4:18 2204
came to pass, when Samuel was o 1Sa 8:1 2204
said unto him, Behold, thou art o 1Sa 8:5 2204
and I am o and grayheaded 1Sa 12:2 2204
for an o man in the days of Saul 1Sa 17:12 2204
for those nations were of o the 1Sa 27:8 5769
And she said, An o man cometh up 1Sa 28:14 2205
Saul's son was forty years o when 2Sa 2:10 1121
He was five years o when the 2Sa 4:4 1121
years o when he began to reign 2Sa 5:4 1121
aged man, even fourscore years o 2Sa 19:32 1121
I am this day fourscore years o 2Sa 19:35 1121
They were wont to speak in o time 2Sa 20:18 7223
Now king David was o and stricken 1Kin 1:1 2204
and the king was very o 1Kin 1:15 2204
came to pass, when Solomon was o 1Kin 11:4 2209
Rehoboam consulted with the o men 1Kin 12:6 2205
forsook the counsel of the o men 1Kin 12:8 2205
forsook the o men's counsel that 1Kin 12:13 2205
dwelt an o prophet in Beth-el 1Kin 13:11 2205
city where the o prophet dwelt 1Kin 13:25 2205
the o prophet came to the city, 1Kin 13:29 2205
one years o when he began to 1Kin 14:21 1121
o age he was diseased in his feet 1Kin 15:23 2209
five years o when he began to 1Kin 22:42 1121
no child, and her husband is o 2Kin 4:14 2204
two years o was he when he began 2Kin 8:17 1121
twenty years o was Ahaziah when 2Kin 8:26 1121
Seven years o was Jehoash when he 2Kin 11:21 1121
five years o when he began to 2Kin 14:2 1121
which was sixteen years o 2Kin 14:21 1121
Sixteen years o was he when he 2Kin 15:2 1121
twenty years o was he when he 2Kin 15:33 1121
Twenty years o was Ahaz when he 2Kin 16:2 1121
five years o was he when he began 2Kin 18:2 1121
years o when he began to reign 2Kin 21:1 1121
two years o when he began to 2Kin 21:19 1121
years o when he began to reign 2Kin 22:1 1121
three years o when he began to 2Kin 23:31 1121
five years o when he began to 2Kin 23:36 1121
years o when he began to reign 2Kin 24:8 1121
one years o when he began to 2Kin 24:18 1121
when he was threescore years o 1Chr 2:21 1121
they of Ham had dwelt there of o 1Chr 4:40 6440
So when David was o and full of 1Chr 23:1 2204
were numbered from twenty years o 1Chr 23:27 1121
of them from twenty years o 1Chr 27:23 1121
And he died in a good o age 1Chr 29:28 7872
the o men that had stood before 2Chr 10:6 2205
counsel which the o men gave him 2Chr 10:8 2205
forsook the counsel of the o men 2Chr 10:13 2205
forty years o when he began to 2Chr 12:13 1121
five years o when he began to 2Chr 20:31 1121
two years o when he began to 2Chr 21:5 1121
two years o was he when he began 2Chr 21:20 1121
two years o was Ahaziah when he 2Chr 22:2 1121
Joash was seven years o when he 2Chr 24:1 1121
But Jehoiada waxed o, and was full 2Chr 24:15 2204
thirty years o was he when he 2Chr 24:15 1121
five years o when he began to 2Chr 25:1 1121
numbered them from twenty years o 2Chr 25:5 1121
Uzziah, who was sixteen years o 2Chr 26:1 1121
Sixteen years o was Uzziah when 2Chr 26:3 1121
five years o when he began to 2Chr 27:1 1121
twenty years o when he began to 2Chr 27:8 1121
Ahaz was twenty years o when he 2Chr 28:1 1121
he was five and twenty years o 2Chr 29:1 1121
of males, from three years o 2Chr 31:16 1121
the Levites from twenty years o 2Chr 31:17 1121
years o when he began to reign 2Chr 33:1 1121
twenty years o when he began to 2Chr 33:21 1121
years o when he began to reign 2Chr 34:1 1121
three years o when he began to 2Chr 36:2 1121
five years o when he began to 2Chr 36:5 1121
years o when he began to reign 2Chr 36:9 1121
twenty years o when he began to 2Chr 36:11 1121
o man, or him that stooped for 2Chr 36:17 2205
the Levites, from twenty years o Ezr 3:8 1121
within the same of o time Ezr 4:15 5957
of o time hath made insurrection Ezr 4:19 5957
Moreover the o gate repaired Neh 3:6 3465
their clothes waxed not o Neh 9:21 1086
of Ephraim, and above the o gate Neh 12:39 3465
Asaph of o there were chief of Neh 12:46 6924
perish, all Jews, both young and o Est 3:13 2205
The o lion perisheth for lack of Job 4:11
root thereof wax o in the earth Job 14:8 2204
Knowest thou not this of o Job 20:4 5703
do the wicked live, become o Job 21:7 6275
Hast thou marked the o way which Job 22:15 5769
in whom o age was perished Job 30:2
I am young, and ye are very o Job 32:6 3453
So Job died, being o and full of Job 42:17 2205
it waxeth o because of all mine Ps 6:7 6275
for they have been ever of o Ps 25:6 5769
my bones waxed o through my Ps 32:3 1086
I have been young, and now am o Ps 37:25 2204
in their days, in the times of o Ps 44:1 6924
them, even he that abideth of o Ps 55:19 6924
of heavens, which were of o Ps 68:33 6924
me not off in the time of o age Ps 71:9 2209
Now also when I am o and Ps 71:18 2209
which thou hast purchased of o Ps 74:2 6924
For God is my King of o, working Ps 74:12 6924
I have considered the days of o Ps 77:5 6924
I will remember thy wonders of o Ps 77:11 6924
I will utter dark sayings of o Ps 78:2 6924
still bring forth fruit in o age Ps 92:14 7872
Thy throne is established of o Ps 93:2 227
Of o hast thou laid the Ps 102:25 6440
them shall wax o like a garment Ps 102:26 1086
I remembered thy judgments of o Ps 119:52 5769
I have known of o that thou hast Ps 119:152 6924
I remember the days of o Ps 143:5 6924
o men, and children Ps 148:12 2205
of his way, before his works of o Prov 8:22 227
children are the crown of o men Prov 17:6 2205
the beauty of o men is the grey Prov 20:29 2205
and when he is o, he will not Prov 22:6 2204
Remove not the o landmark Prov 23:10 5769
not thy mother when she is o Prov 23:22 2204
it hath been already of o time Eccl 1:10 5769
a poor and a wise child than an o Eccl 4:13 2205
of pleasant fruits, new and o Song 7:13 3465
Zoar, an heifer of three years o Is 15:5 7992
Ethiopians captives, young and o Is 20:4 2205
walls for the water of the o pool Is 22:11 3465
thy counsels of o are Is 25:1 7350
o lion, the viper and fiery flying Is 30:6 3918
For Tophet is ordained of o Is 30:33 865
neither consider the things of o Is 43:18 6931
And even to your o age I am he Is 46:4 2209
Remember the former things of o Is 46:9 5769
they all shall wax o as a garment Is 50:9 1086
earth shall wax o like a garment Is 51:6 1086
days, in the generations of o Is 51:9 5769
not I held my peace even of o Is 57:11 5769
shall build the o waste places Is 58:12 5769
And they shall build the o wastes Is 61:4 5769
and carried them all the days of o Is 63:9 5769
Then he remembered the days of o Is 63:11 5769
nor an o man that hath not filled Is 65:20 2205
shall die an hundred years o Is 65:20 1121
hundred years o shall be accursed Is 65:20 1121
For of o time I have broken thy Jer 2:20 5769
and see, and ask for the o paths Jer 6:16 5769
before thee of o prophesied both Jer 28:8 5769
LORD hath appeared of o unto me Jer 31:3 7350
both young men and o together Jer 31:13 2205
and took thence o cast clouts Jer 38:11 1094
o rotten rags, and let them down Jer 38:11 1094
Put now these o cast clouts Jer 38:12 1094
be inhabited, as in the days of o Jer 46:26 6924
as an heifer of three years o Jer 48:34 7992
thee will I break in pieces o Jer 51:22 2205

twenty years o when he began to ... Jer 52:1 1121
that she had in the days of o ... Lam 1:7 6924
he had commanded in the days of o ... Lam 2:17 6924
the o lie on the ground in the ... Lam 2:21 2205
flesh and my skin hath he made o ... Lam 3:4 1086
places, as they that be dead of o ... Lam 3:6 5769
renew our days as of o ... Lam 5:21 6924
Slay utterly o and young, both ... Eze 9:6 2205
unto her that was o in adulteries ... Eze 23:43 1087
to destroy it for the o hatred ... Eze 25:15 5769
pit, with the people of o time ... Eze 26:20 5769
earth, in places desolate of o ... Eze 26:20 5769
settle you after your o estates ... Eze 36:11 6927
in o time by my servants the ... Eze 38:17 6931
about threescore and two years o ... Dan 5:31 1247
ye o men, and give ear, all ye ... Joel 1:2 2205
your o men shall dream dreams, ... Joel 2:28 2205
will build it as in the days of o ... Amos 9:11 5769
goings forth have been from of o ... Mic 5:2 6924
with calves of a year o ... Mic 6:6 1121
and Gilead, as in the days of o ... Mic 7:14 5769
our fathers from the days of o ... Mic 7:20 6924
But Nineveh is of o like a pool ... Nah 2:8 3117
where the lion, even the o lion ... Nah 2:11
There shall yet o men ... Zec 8:4 2205
o women dwell in the streets of ... Zec 8:4 2205
the LORD, as in the days of o ... Mal 3:4 5769
coasts thereof, from two years o ... Mt 2:16 *1332*
it was said by them of o time ... Mt 5:21 *744*
it was said by them of o time ... Mt 5:27 *744*
hath been said by them of o time ... Mt 5:33 *744*
of new cloth unto an o garment ... Mt 9:16 *3820*
men put new wine into o bottles ... Mt 9:17 *3820*
of his treasure things new and o ... Mt 13:52 *3820*
of new cloth on an o garment ... Mk 2:21 *3820*
it up taketh away from the o ... Mk 2:21 *3820*
putteth new wine into o bottles ... Mk 2:22 *3820*
for I am an o man, and my wife ... Lk 1:18 *4246*
also conceived a son in her o age ... Lk 1:36 *1094*
And when he was twelve years o ... Lk 2:42
piece of a new garment upon an o ... Lk 5:36 *3820*
of the new agreeth not with the o ... Lk 5:36 *3820*
putteth new wine into o bottles ... Lk 5:37 *3820*
No man also having drunk o wine ... Lk 5:39 *3820*
for he saith, The o is better ... Lk 5:39 *3820*
that one of the o prophets was ... Lk 9:8 *744*
that one of the o prophets is ... Lk 9:19 *744*
yourselves bags which wax not o ... Lk 12:33 *3822*
can a man be born when he is o ... Jn 3:4 *1088*
Thou art not yet fifty years o ... Jn 8:57
but when thou shalt be o, thou ... Jn 21:18 *1095*
your o men shall dream dreams ... Acts 2:17 *4245*
the man was above forty years o ... Acts 4:22
And when he was full forty years o ... Acts 7:23 *5550*
For Moses of o time hath in every ... Acts 15:21 *744*
an o disciple, with whom we ... Acts 21:16 *744*
he was about an hundred years o ... Rom 4:19 *1541*
that our o man is crucified with ... Rom 6:6 *3820*
Purge out therefore the o leaven ... 1Cor 5:7 *3820*
keep the feast, not with o leaven ... 1Cor 5:8 *3820*
in the reading of the o testament ... 2Cor 3:14 *3820*
o things are passed away ... 2Cor 5:17 *744*
the former conversation the o man ... Eph 4:22 *3820*
put off the o man with his deeds ... Col 3:9 *3820*
o wives' fables, and exercise ... 1Ti 4:7 *1126*
number under threescore years o ... 1Ti 5:9
all shall wax o as doth a garment ... Heb 1:11 *3822*
he hath made the first o ... Heb 8:13 *3822*
waxeth o is ready to vanish away ... Heb 8:13 *1095*
in the o time the holy women also ... 1Pet 3:5 *4218*
he was purged from his o sins ... 2Pet 1:9 *3819*
not in o time by the will of man ... 2Pet 1:21 *4218*
And spared not the o world ... 2Pet 2:5 *744*
word of God the heavens were of o ... 2Pet 3:5 *1597*
but an o commandment which ye had ... 1Jn 2:7 *3820*
The o commandment is the word ... 1Jn 2:7 *3820*
who were before of o ordained to ... Jude 4 *3819*
that o serpent, called the Devil, ... Rev 12:9 *744*
that o serpent, which is the ... Rev 20:2 *744*

OLDNESS

not in the o of the letter ... Rom 7:6 *3821*

OLIVE

mouth was an o leaf pluckt off ... Gen 8:11 2132
pure oil o beaten for the light ... Ex 27:20 2132
the sanctuary, and of oil o an hin ... Ex 30:24 2132
pure oil o beaten for the light ... Lev 24:2 2132
o trees, which thou plantedst not ... Deut 6:11 2132
a land of oil o, and honey ... Deut 8:8 2132
When thou beatest thine o tree ... Deut 24:20 2132
Thou shalt have o trees ... Deut 28:40 2132
for thine o shall cast his fruit ... Deut 28:40 2132
and they said unto the o tree ... Judg 9:8 2132
But the o tree said unto them, ... Judg 9:9 2132
he made two cherubims of o tree ... 1Kin 6:23 8081
oracle he made doors of o tree ... 1Kin 6:31 8081
The two doors also were of o tree ... 1Kin 6:32 8081
of the temple posts of o tree ... 1Kin 6:33 8081
and vineyards, a land of oil o ... 2Kin 18:32 2132
And over the o trees and the ... 1Chr 27:28 2132
fetch o branches, and pine ... Neh 8:15 2132
cast off his flower as the o ... Job 15:33 2132
But I am like a green o tree in ... Ps 52:8 2132
thy children like o plants round ... Ps 128:3 2132
it, as the shaking of an o tree ... Is 17:6 2132
be as the shaking of an o tree ... Is 24:13 2132
called thy name, A green o tree ... Jer 11:16 2132
his beauty shall be as the o tree ... Hos 14:6 2132
your o trees increased, the ... Amos 4:9 2132
the labour of the o shall fail ... Hab 3:17 2132
the o tree, hath not brought ... Hag 2:19 2132
two o trees by it, one upon the ... Zec 4:3 2132
What are these two o trees upon ... Zec 4:11 2132
What be these two o branches ... Zec 4:12 2132
off, and thou, being a wild o tree ... Rom 11:17 *65*
the root and fatness of the o tree ... Rom 11:17 *1636*
o tree which is wild by nature ... Rom 11:24 *65*
to nature into a good o tree ... Rom 11:24 *2565*
be graffed into their own o tree ... Rom 11:24 *1636*
tree, my brethren, bear o berries ... Jas 3:12 *1636*
These are the two o trees ... Rev 11:4 *1636*

OLIVES

corn, with the vineyards and o ... Judg 15:5 2132
thou shalt tread the o, but thou ... Mic 6:15 2132
in that day upon the mount of O ... Zec 14:4 2132
the mount of O shall cleave in ... Zec 14:4 2132
to Bethphage, unto the mount of O ... Mt 21:1 *1636*
And as he sat upon the mount of O ... Mt 24:3 *1636*
they went out into the mount of O ... Mt 26:30 *1636*
and Bethany, at the mount of O ... Mk 11:1 *1636*
of O over against the temple ... Mk 13:3 *1636*
they went out into the mount of O ... Mk 14:26 *1636*
the mount called the mount of O ... Lk 19:29 *1636*
at the descent of the mount of O ... Lk 19:37 *1636*
that is called the mount of O ... Lk 21:37 *1636*
as he was wont, to the mount of O ... Lk 22:39 *1636*
Jesus went unto the mount of O ... Jn 8:1 *1636*

OLIVET See MOUNT, OLIVES. *Hills east of Jerusalem.*

went up by the ascent of mount O ... 2Sa 15:30 2132
Jerusalem from the mount called O ... Acts 1:12 *1638*

OLIVEYARD

with thy vineyard, and with thy o ... Ex 23:11 2132

OLIVEYARDS

o which ye planted not do ye eat ... Josh 24:13 2132
and your vineyards, and your o ... 1Sa 8:14 2132
and to receive garments, and o ... 2Kin 5:26 2132
lands, their vineyards, their o ... Neh 5:11 2132
wells digged, vineyards, and o ... Neh 9:25 2132

OLYMPAS (*o-lim'-pas*) *A Christian acquaintance of Paul.*

Nereus, and his sister, and O ... Rom 16:15 *3632*

OMAR (*o'-mar*) *A son of Eliphaz.*

the sons of Eliphaz were Teman, O ... Gen 36:11 201
duke Teman, duke O, duke Zepho, ... Gen 36:15 201
Teman, and O, Zephi, and Gatam, ... 1Chr 1:36 201

OMEGA (*o'-me-gah*) *Last letter of Greek alphabet; a title applied to Jesus.*

I am Alpha and O, the beginning and .. Rev 1:8 *5598*
Saying, I am Alpha and O, the ... Rev 1:11 *5598*
I am Alpha and O, the beginning and ... Rev 21:6 *5598*
I am Alpha and O, the beginning and ... Rev 22:13 *5598*

OMER

an o for every man, according to ... Ex 16:16 6016
when they did mete it with an o ... Ex 16:18 6016
Fill an o of it to be kept for ... Ex 16:32 6016
put an o full of manna therein, ... Ex 16:33 6016
Now an o is the tenth part of an ... Ex 16:36 6016

OMERS

as much bread, two o for one man ... Ex 16:22 6016

OMITTED

have o the weightier matters of ... Mt 23:23 *863*

OMNIPOTENT

for the Lord God o reigneth ... Rev 19:6 *3841*

OMRI (*om'-ri*)

1. A king of Israel.

wherefore all Israel made O ... 1Kin 16:16 6018
O went up from Gibbethon, and all ... 1Kin 16:17 6018
and half followed O ... 1Kin 16:21 6018
O prevailed against the people ... 1Kin 16:22 6018
so Tibni died, and O reigned ... 1Kin 16:22 6018
began O to reign over Israel ... 1Kin 16:23 6018
But O wrought evil in the eyes of ... 1Kin 16:25 6018
of the acts of O which he did ... 1Kin 16:27 6018
So O slept with his fathers, and ... 1Kin 16:28 6018
the son of O to reign over Israel ... 1Kin 16:29 6018
Ahab the son of O reigned over ... 1Kin 16:29 6018
Ahab the son of O did evil in the ... 1Kin 16:30 6018
the daughter of O king of Israel ... 2Kin 8:26 6018
was Athaliah the daughter of O ... 2Chr 22:2 6018
For the statutes of O are kept ... Mic 6:16 6018

2. Son of Becher.

and Eliezer, and Elioenai, and O ... 1Chr 7:8 6018

3. A descendant of Pharez.

the son of Ammihud, the son of O ... 1Chr 9:4 6018

4. A ruler of Issachar.

of Issachar, O the son of Michael ... 1Chr 27:18 6018

ON (*on*)

1. A preposition.

o the seventh day God ended his ... Gen 2:2
he rested o the seventh day from ... Gen 2:2
shall be taken o him sevenfold ... Gen 4:15
land of Nod, o the east of Eden ... Gen 4:16
multiply o the face of the earth ... Gen 6:1 5921
that he had made man o the earth ... Gen 6:6
o the seventeenth day of the ... Gen 8:4
o the first day of the month, ... Gen 8:5
for the waters were o the face of ... Gen 8:9 5921
o the seven and twentieth day of ... Gen 8:14
burnt offerings o the altar ... Gen 8:20
a mountain o the east of Beth-el ... Gen 12:8
o the west, and Hai o the east ... Gen 12:8
going o still toward the south ... Gen 12:9
he went o his journeys from the ... Gen 13:3
there Abram called o the name of ... Gen 13:4
which is o the left hand of ... Gen 14:15
And Abram fell o his face ... Gen 17:3 5921
after that ye shall pass o ... Gen 18:5
with them to bring them o the way ... Gen 18:16
rise up early, and go o your ways ... Gen 19:2
And it came to pass o the morrow ... Gen 19:34
o me and o my kingdom a great sin ... Gen 20:9 5921
putting it o her shoulder, and the ... Gen 21:14 5921
called there o the name of the ... Gen 21:33
Then o the third day Abraham ... Gen 22:4
laid him o the altar upon the ... Gen 22:9 5921
And he said, Speak o ... Gen 24:33
with her pitcher o her shoulder ... Gen 24:45 5921
his hand took hold o Esau's heel ... Gen 25:26
a ladder set up o the earth ... Gen 28:12
God ascending and descending o it ... Gen 28:12
bread to eat, and raiment to put o ... Gen 28:20
Then Jacob went o his journey ... Gen 29:1
it was told Laban o the third day ... Gen 31:22
And Jacob went o his way, and the ... Gen 32:1
O this manner shall ye speak unto ... Gen 32:19
fell o his neck, and kissed him ... Gen 33:4 5921
and I will lead o softly, ... Gen 33:14
that day o his way unto Seir ... Gen 33:16
it came to pass o the third day ... Gen 34:25
of many colours that was o him ... Gen 37:23 5921
that he spilled it o the ground ... Gen 38:9
put o the garments of her ... Gen 38:19
But think o me when it shall be ... Gen 40:14
had three white baskets o my head ... Gen 40:16 5921
thee, and shall hang thee o a tree ... Gen 40:19 5921
himself, and said, Set o bread ... Gen 43:31
they set o for him by himself, and ... Gen 43:32
they fell before him o the ground ... Gen 44:14
evil that shall come o my father ... Gen 44:34
he fell o his neck, and wept o ... Gen 46:29 5921
and let my name be named o them ... Gen 48:16
they shall be o the head of ... Gen 49:26
o the crown of the head of him ... Gen 49:26
Come o, let us deal wisely with ... Ex 1:10
And she had compassion o him ... Ex 2:6 5921
and looked o their burdens ... Ex 2:11
And he said, Cast it o the ground ... Ex 4:3
And he cast it o the ground ... Ex 4:3
it came to pass o the day when ... Ex 6:28
frogs shall come up both o thee ... Ex 8:4
LORD did that thing o the morrow ... Ex 9:6 5921
strike it o the two side posts and ... Ex 12:7 5921
o the upper door post of the ... Ex 12:7 5921
girded, your shoes o your feet ... Ex 12:11
o the fourteenth day of the month ... Ex 12:18
o the two side posts, the LORD ... Ex 12:23 5921
o his throne unto the firstborn ... Ex 12:29 5921
thousand o foot that were men ... Ex 12:37
o dry ground through the midst of ... Ex 14:16
wall unto them o their right hand ... Ex 14:22
their right hand, and o their left ... Ex 14:22
wall unto them o their right hand ... Ex 14:29
their right hand, and o their left ... Ex 14:29
sorrow shall take hold o the ... Ex 15:14
o dry land in the midst of the ... Ex 15:19
o the fifteenth day of the second ... Ex 16:1
that o the sixth day they shall ... Ex 16:5
as the hoar frost o the ground ... Ex 16:14 5921
that o the sixth day they ... Ex 16:22
but o the seventh day, which is ... Ex 16:26
went out some of the people o the ... Ex 16:27
therefore he giveth you o the ... Ex 16:29
of his place o the seventh day ... Ex 16:29
people rested o the seventh day ... Ex 16:30 5921
Go o before the people, and take ... Ex 17:5
to morrow I will stand o the top ... Ex 17:9 5921
the one o the one side ... Ex 17:12
the other o the other side ... Ex 17:12
And it came to pass o the morrow ... Ex 18:13
and how I bare you o eagles' wings ... Ex 19:4 5921
it came to pass o the third day ... Ex 19:16
Sinai was altogether o a smoke ... Ex 19:18
Sinai, o the top of the mount ... Ex 19:20 413
If there be laid o him a sum of ... Ex 21:30 5921
o the eighth day thou shalt give ... Ex 22:30
o the seventh day thou shalt rest ... Ex 23:12
blood he sprinkled o the altar ... Ex 24:6 5921
and sprinkled it o the people ... Ex 24:8 5921
o the top of the mount in the ... Ex 24:17
And make one cherub o the one end ... Ex 25:19
the other cherub o the other end ... Ex 25:19
cherubims o the two ends thereof ... Ex 25:19
stretch forth their wings o high ... Ex 25:20
that are o the four feet thereof ... Ex 25:26 5921
o the edge of the one curtain ... Ex 26:10 5921
a cubit o the one side ... Ex 26:13
a cubit o the other side of that ... Ex 26:13
of the tabernacle o this side ... Ex 26:13
side and o that side, to cover it ... Ex 26:13
twenty boards o the south side ... Ex 26:18
o the north side there shall be ... Ex 26:20
over against the table o the side ... Ex 26:35 5921
put the table o the north side ... Ex 26:35 5921
for the breadth of the court o ... Ex 27:12
the breadth of the court o the ... Ex 27:13
o the other side shall be ... Ex 27:15
o the behalf of the children of ... Ex 27:21 5921
grave o them the names of the ... Ex 28:9 5921
Six of their names o one stone ... Ex 28:10 5921
of the rest o the other stone ... Ex 28:10 5921
shalt put the two rings o the two ... Ex 28:23 5921
are o the ends of the breastplate ... Ex 28:24 413
put them o the shoulderpieces of ... Ex 28:25 5921
shalt put them o the two sides of ... Ex 28:27 5921
thou shalt put it o a blue lace ... Ex 28:37 5921
sons, and put the bonnets o them ... Ex 29:9
stead shall put them o seven days ... Ex 29:30
o the seventh day he rested, and ... Ex 31:17
they rose up early o the morrow ... Ex 32:6
were written o both their sides ... Ex 32:15
o the one side and o the other ... Ex 32:15
that they are set o mischief ... Ex 32:22
and said, Who is o the LORD's side ... Ex 32:26
And it came to pass o the morrow ... Ex 32:30

O

and no man did put o him his	Ex 33:4	
will shew mercy o whom I will	Ex 33:19	
but o the seventh day thou shalt	Ex 34:21	
them, he put a vail o his face	Ex 34:33	5921
but o the seventh day there shall	Ex 35:2	
he made loops of blue o the edge	Ex 36:11	5921
o the two ends of the mercy seat	Ex 37:7	
One cherub o the end o this side	Ex 37:8	
o the other end o that side	Ex 37:8	
cherubims o the two ends thereof	Ex 37:8	
spread out their wings o high	Ex 37:9	
thereof o the four corners of it	Ex 38:2	5921
rings o the sides of the altar	Ex 38:7	5921
o the south side southward the	Ex 38:9	
o this hand and that hand, were	Ex 38:15	
he put them o the shoulders of	Ex 39:7	5921
o the ends of the breastplate	Ex 39:17	5921
put them o the shoulderpieces of	Ex 39:18	5921
put them o the two ends of the	Ex 39:19	5921
which was o the side of the ephod	Ex 39:19	413
put them o the two sides of the	Ex 39:20	5921
to fasten it o high upon the	Ex 39:31	
O the first day of the first	Ex 40:2	
o the first day of the month,	Ex 40:17	
ark, and set the staves o the ark	Ex 40:20	5921
o the side of the tabernacle	Ex 40:24	5921
fire was o it by night, in the	Ex 40:38	
is o the fire which is upon the	Lev 1:8	5921
priest shall burn all o the altar	Lev 1:9	
he shall kill it o the side of	Lev 1:11	5921
o the wood that is o the fire	Lev 1:12	5921
his head, and burn it o the altar	Lev 1:15	
beside the altar o the east part	Lev 1:16	
but they shall not be burnt o the	Lev 2:12	413
and the fat that is o them	Lev 3:4	5921
it o the altar upon the burnt	Lev 3:5	
upon the wood that is o the fire	Lev 3:5	5921
burn him o the wood with fire	Lev 4:12	5921
burn it o the altar, according to	Lev 5:12	
shall put o his linen garment	Lev 6:10	
the burnt offering o the altar	Lev 6:10	5921
put o other garments, and carry	Lev 6:11	
burn wood o it every morning	Lev 6:12	
and the fat that is o them	Lev 7:4	5921
o the morrow also the remainder	Lev 7:16	
o the third day shall be burnt	Lev 7:17	
be eaten at all o the third day	Lev 7:18	
one wafer, and put them o the fat	Lev 8:26	5921
burnt them o the altar upon the	Lev 8:28	
it came to pass o the eighth day	Lev 9:1	
the burnt offering o the altar	Lev 9:14	
shouted, and fell o their faces	Lev 9:24	5921
the beasts that are o the earth	Lev 11:2	5921
of beasts that go o all four	Lev 11:27	5921
that o which such water cometh	Lev 11:34	5921
the priest shall look o the	Lev 13:3	
and the priest shall look o him	Lev 13:3	
shall look o him the seventh day	Lev 13:5	
the priest shall look o him again	Lev 13:6	
But if the priest look o it	Lev 13:21	
But if the priest look o it	Lev 13:26	
if the priest look o the plague	Lev 13:31	
priest shall look o the plague	Lev 13:32	
the priest shall look o the scall	Lev 13:34	
Then the priest shall look o him	Lev 13:36	
o the plague o the seventh day	Lev 13:51	
priest shall look o the plague	Lev 13:55	
But it shall be o the seventh day	Lev 14:9	
o the eighth day he shall take	Lev 14:10	
he shall bring them o the eighth	Lev 14:23	5921
And he shall look o the plague	Lev 14:37	
he that sitteth o any thing	Lev 15:6	5921
o the eighth day he shall take to	Lev 15:14	
And if it be o her bed	Lev 15:23	5921
or o any thing whereon she	Lev 15:23	5921
o the eighth day she shall take	Lev 15:29	
He shall put o the holy linen	Lev 16:4	
flesh in water, and so put them o	Lev 16:4	
o which the lot fell to be the	Lev 16:10	5921
which he put o when he went into	Lev 16:23	
put o his garments, and come forth	Lev 16:24	
o the tenth day of the month, ye	Lev 16:29	
For o that day shall the priest	Lev 16:30	
shall put o the linen clothes,	Lev 16:32	
day ye offer it, and o the morrow	Lev 19:6	
be eaten at all o the third day	Lev 19:7	
thing that creepeth o the ground	Lev 20:25	
consecrated to put o the garments	Lev 21:10	
O the same day it shall be eaten	Lev 22:30	
o the fifteenth day of the same	Lev 23:6	
o the morrow after the sabbath	Lev 23:11	
shall proclaim o the selfsame day	Lev 23:21	
Also o the tenth day of this	Lev 23:27	
O the first day shall be an holy	Lev 23:35	
o the eighth day shall be an holy	Lev 23:36	
o the first day shall be a	Lev 23:39	
o the eighth day shall be a	Lev 23:39	
ye shall take you o the first day	Lev 23:40	
six o a row, upon the pure table	Lev 24:6	
that it may be o the bread for a	Lev 24:7	
o the tenth day of the seventh	Lev 25:9	
o the first day of the second	Num 1:1	
o the first day of the second	Num 1:18	
o the east side toward the rising	Num 2:3	
O the south side shall be the	Num 2:10	
O the west side shall be the	Num 2:18	
of the camp of Dan shall be o the	Num 2:25	5921
they shall wait o their priest's	Num 3:10	
for o the day that I smote all	Num 3:13	
o the side of the tabernacle	Num 3:29	5921
these shall pitch o the side of	Num 3:35	5921
skins, and shall put them o a bar	Num 4:12	5921
o the seventh day shall he shave	Num 6:9	
o the eighth day he shall bring	Num 6:10	
O this wise ye shall bless the	Num 6:23	
it came to pass o the day that	Num 7:1	
offering, each prince o his day	Num 7:11	
O the second day Nethaneel the	Num 7:18	
O the third day Eliab the son of	Num 7:24	
O the fourth day Elizur the son	Num 7:30	
O the fifth day Shelumiel the son	Num 7:36	
O the sixth day Eliasaph the son	Num 7:42	
O the seventh day Elishama the	Num 7:48	
O the eighth day offered Gamaliel	Num 7:54	
O the ninth day Abidan the son of	Num 7:60	
O the tenth day Ahiezer the son	Num 7:66	
O the eleventh day Pagiel the son	Num 7:72	
O the twelfth day Ahira the son	Num 7:78	
o the day that I smote every	Num 8:17	
they kept the passover o the	Num 9:5	
not keep the passover o that day	Num 9:6	
Moses and before Aaron o that day	Num 9:6	
o the day that the tabernacle was	Num 9:15	
then the camps that lie o the	Num 10:5	
then the camps that lie o the	Num 10:6	
it came to pass o the twentieth	Num 10:11	
were a day's journey o this side	Num 11:31	
a day's journey o the other side	Num 11:31	
Aaron fell o their faces before	Num 14:5	5921
Dathan, and Abiram, o every side	Num 16:27	
But o the morrow all the	Num 16:41	
put o incense, and go quickly unto	Num 16:46	
he put o incense, and made an	Num 16:47	
that o the morrow Moses went into	Num 17:8	
himself with it o the third day	Num 19:12	
o the seventh day he shall be	Num 19:12	
upon the unclean o the third day	Num 19:19	
and o the seventh day	Num 19:19	
o the seventh day he shall purify	Num 19:19	
thing else, go through o my feet	Num 20:19	
pitched o the other side of Arnon	Num 21:13	
o this side Jordan by Jericho	Num 22:1	
a wall being o this side	Num 22:24	
and a wall o that side	Num 22:24	
his head, and fell flat o his face	Num 22:31	
And it came to pass o the morrow	Num 22:41	
Balaam offered o every altar a	Num 23:2	
a bullock and a ram o every altar	Num 23:14	
a bullock and a ram o every altar	Num 23:30	
And when he looked o Amalek	Num 24:20	
he looked o the Kenites, and took	Num 24:21	
o the sabbath day two lambs of	Num 28:9	
o the seventh day ye shall have	Num 28:25	
o the first day of the month, ye	Num 29:1	
ye shall have o the tenth day of	Num 29:7	
o the fifteenth day of the	Num 29:12	
o the second day ye shall offer	Num 29:17	
o the third day eleven bullocks,	Num 29:20	
o the fourth day ten bullocks,	Num 29:23	
o the fifth day nine bullocks,	Num 29:26	
o the sixth day eight bullocks,	Num 29:29	
o the seventh day seven bullocks,	Num 29:32	
O the eighth day ye shall have a	Num 29:35	
her o the day that he heard it	Num 30:8	5921
them void o the day he heard them	Num 30:12	
and your captives o the third day	Num 31:19	
and o the seventh day	Num 31:19	
your clothes o the seventh day	Num 31:24	
with them o yonder side Jordan	Num 32:19	
to us o this side Jordan eastward	Num 32:19	
o this side Jordan may be ours	Num 32:32	
o the fifteenth day of the first	Num 33:3	
o the morrow after the passover	Num 33:3	
of Akrabbim, and pass o to Zin	Num 34:4	
shall go o to Hazar-addar	Num 34:4	
and pass o to Azmon	Num 34:4	
the border shall go o to Ziphron	Num 34:9	
to Riblah, o the east side of Ain	Num 34:11	
o this side Jordan near Jericho	Num 34:15	
city o the east side two thousand	Num 35:5	
o the south side two thousand	Num 35:5	
o the west side two thousand	Num 35:5	
o the north side two thousand	Num 35:5	
three cities o this side Jordan	Num 35:14	
Israel o this side Jordan in the	Deut 1:1	
o the first day of the month,	Deut 1:3	
O this side Jordan, in the land	Deut 1:5	
when ye had girded o every man	Deut 1:41	
I will pass through o my feet	Deut 2:28	
land that was o this side Jordan	Deut 3:8	
o the day that the LORD spake	Deut 4:15	
of any beast that is o the earth	Deut 4:17	
thing that creepeth o the ground	Deut 4:18	
o this side Jordan toward the	Deut 4:41	
O this side Jordan, in the valley	Deut 4:46	
which were o this side Jordan	Deut 4:47	
all the plain o this side Jordan	Deut 4:49	
of thy house, and o thy gates	Deut 6:9	
the silver or gold that is o them	Deut 7:25	5921
o them was written according to	Deut 9:10	5921
I will write o the tables the	Deut 10:2	5921
he wrote o the tables, according	Deut 10:4	5921
Are they not o the other side	Deut 11:30	
o the seventh day shall be a	Deut 16:8	
and his mother lay hold o him	Deut 21:19	
death, and thou hang him o a tree	Deut 21:22	5921
a man put o a woman's garment	Deut 22:5	
or o the ground, whether they be	Deut 22:6	5921
not betrothed, and lay hold o her	Deut 22:28	
shall be, when evening cometh o	Deut 23:11	
looked o our affliction, and our	Deut 26:7	
it shall be o the day when ye	Deut 27:2	
o high above all nations of the	Deut 28:1	5921
these blessings shall come o thee	Deut 28:2	5921
o them that hate thee, which	Deut 30:7	5921
them, beareth them o her wings	Deut 32:11	5921
He made him ride o the high	Deut 32:13	5921
set o fire the foundations of the	Deut 32:22	
and mine hand take hold o judgment	Deut 32:41	
and in his excellency o the sky	Deut 33:26	
Moses gave you o this side Jordan	Josh 1:14	
you o this side Jordan toward the	Josh 1:15	
that were o the other side Jordan	Josh 2:10	
his blood shall be o our head	Josh 2:19	
firm o dry ground in the midst of	Josh 3:17	
passed over o dry ground, until	Josh 3:17	
O that day the LORD magnified	Josh 4:14	
o the tenth day of the first	Josh 4:19	
came over this Jordan o dry land	Josh 4:22	
which were o the side of Jordan	Josh 5:1	
and kept the passover o the	Josh 5:10	
o the morrow after the passover	Josh 5:11	
the manna ceased o the morrow	Josh 5:12	
Joshua fell o his face to the	Josh 5:14	413
he said unto the people, Pass o	Josh 6:7	
pass o before the ark of the LORD	Josh 6:7	413
horns passed o before the LORD	Josh 6:8	413
the ark, the priests going o	Josh 6:9	
of the LORD went o continually	Josh 6:13	413
of the LORD, the priests going o	Josh 6:13	413
it came to pass o the seventh day	Josh 6:15	
only o that day they compassed	Josh 6:15	
o the east side of Beth-el, and	Josh 7:2	
dwelt o the other side Jordan	Josh 7:7	
that ye shall set the city o fire	Josh 8:8	
and Ai, o the west side of Ai	Josh 8:9	
pitched o the north side of Ai	Josh 8:11	
o the west side of the city	Josh 8:12	
that was o the north of the city	Josh 8:13	
their liers in wait o the west of	Josh 8:13	
and hasted and set the city o fire	Josh 8:19	
some o this side, and some o that	Josh 8:22	
fallen o the edge of the sword	Josh 8:24	
he hanged o a tree until eventide	Josh 8:29	5921
stood o this side the ark	Josh 8:33	
o that side before the priests	Josh 8:33	
which were o this side Jordan	Josh 9:1	
o the day we came forth to go	Josh 9:12	
unto their cities o the third day	Josh 9:17	
them, and hanged them o five trees	Josh 10:26	5921
which took it o the second day,	Josh 10:32	
And they took it o that day	Josh 10:35	
to the kings that were o the	Josh 11:2	
in the borders of Dor o the west	Josh 11:2	
And to the Canaanite o the east	Josh 11:3	
o the west, and to the Amorite, and	Josh 11:3	
possessed their land o the other	Josh 12:1	
and all the plain o the east	Josh 12:1	
the sea of Chinneroth o the east	Josh 12:3	
even the salt sea o the east	Josh 12:3	
o this side Jordan o the west	Josh 12:7	
that is o the bank of the river	Josh 13:16	5921
edge of the sea of Chinnereth o	Josh 13:27	
o the other side Jordan, by	Josh 13:32	
an half tribe o the other side	Josh 14:3	
And Moses sware o that day	Josh 14:9	
ascended up o the south side unto	Josh 15:3	
which is o the south side of the	Josh 15:7	
o the north side, and went down to	Josh 15:10	
and passed o to Timnah	Josh 15:10	
the water of Jericho o the east	Josh 16:1	
o the east side was Ataroth-addar	Josh 16:5	
to Michmethah o the north side	Josh 16:6	
passed by it o the east to	Josh 16:6	
which were o the other side	Josh 17:5	
the border went along o the right	Josh 17:7	413
but Tappuah o the border of	Josh 17:8	413
was o the north side of the river	Josh 17:9	
met together in Asher o the north	Josh 17:10	
and in Issachar o the east	Josh 17:10	
abide in their coast o the south	Josh 18:5	
abide in their coasts o the north	Josh 18:5	
beyond Jordan o the east, which	Josh 18:7	
their border o the north side was	Josh 18:12	
side of Jericho o the north side	Josh 18:12	
near the hill that lieth o the	Josh 18:13	
and the border went out o the west	Josh 18:15	
valley of the giants o the north	Josh 18:16	
to the side of Jebusi o the south	Josh 18:16	
the border of it o the east side	Josh 18:20	
from thence passeth o along o	Josh 19:13	
the border compasseth it o the	Josh 19:14	
out to Cabul o the left hand	Josh 19:27	
to Zebulun o the south side	Josh 19:34	
reacheth to Asher o the west side	Josh 19:34	
o the other side Jordan by	Josh 20:8	
gave you o the other side Jordan	Josh 22:4	
o this side Jordan westward	Josh 22:7	
wrath fell o all the congregation	Josh 22:20	5921
Your fathers dwelt o the other	Josh 24:2	
which dwelt o the other side	Josh 24:8	
o the other side of the flood	Josh 24:14	
o the other side of the flood	Josh 24:15	
o the north side of the hill of	Josh 24:30	
the sword, and set the city o fire	Judg 1:8	
o the north side of the hill	Judg 2:9	
was fallen down dead o the earth	Judg 3:25	
chariot, and fled away o his feet	Judg 4:15	
Howbeit Sisera fled away o his	Judg 4:17	
So God subdued o that day Jabin	Judg 4:23	
the son of Abinoam o that day	Judg 5:1	
Speak, ye that ride o white asses	Judg 5:10	
he was sent o foot into the	Judg 5:15	
Asher continued o the sea shore	Judg 5:17	
of needlework o both sides	Judg 5:30	
Therefore o that day he called	Judg 6:32	
if the dew be o the fleece only,	Judg 6:37	5921
for he rose up early o the morrow	Judg 6:38	
there was dew o all the ground	Judg 6:40	5921
were o the north side of them	Judg 7:1	
And he said unto them, Look o me	Judg 7:17	
also o every side of all the camp	Judg 7:18	

Zeeb to Gideon o the other side .... Judg 7:25
in tents o the east of Nobah .... Judg 8:11
that were o their camels' necks .... Judg 8:21
that was o the kings of Midian .... Judg 8:26 5921
of all their enemies o every side .... Judg 8:34
The trees went forth o a time to .... Judg 9:8
And it came to pass o the morrow .... Judg 9:42
laid it o his shoulder, and said .... Judg 9:48 5921
set the hold o fire upon them .... Judg 9:49
sons that rode o thirty ass colts .... Judg 10:4 5921
o the other side Jordan in the .... Judg 10:8
pitched o the other side of Arnon .... Judg 11:18
that rode o threescore and ten ass .... Judg 12:14 5921
and no razor shall come o his head .... Judg 13:5 5921
and Manoah and his wife looked o .... Judg 13:19
And Manoah and his wife looked o it .. Judg 13:20
fell o their faces to the ground .... Judg 13:20 5921
went o eating, and came to his .... Judg 14:9
it came to pass o the seventh day .... Judg 14:15
it came to pass o the seventh day .... Judg 14:17
men of the city said unto him o .... Judg 14:18
when he had set the brands o fire .... Judg 15:5
called o the LORD, and said, Thou .... Judg 15:18 413
o which it was borne up, of the .... Judg 16:29 5921
o the side of mount Ephraim .... Judg 19:1
it came to pass o the fourth day .... Judg 19:5
morning o the fifth day to depart .... Judg 19:8
morrow get you early o your way .... Judg 19:9
And they passed o and went their .... Judg 19:14
laid hold o his concubine, and .... Judg 19:29
of Benjamin o the third day .... Judg 20:30
also they set o fire all the .... Judg 20:48
And it came to pass o the morrow .... Judg 21:4
is o the north side of Beth-el .... Judg 21:19
o the east side of the highway .... Judg 21:19
and o the south of Lebonah .... Judg 21:19
they went o the way to return .... Ruth 1:7
her hap was to light o a part of .... Ruth 2:3
Let thine eyes be o the field .... Ruth 2:9
Then she fell o her face, and .... Ruth 2:10 5921
of barley, and laid it o her .... Ruth 3:15 5921
look o the affliction of thine 1Sa 1:11
And the child Samuel grew o 1Sa 2:26
two sons, o Hophni and Phinehas 1Sa 2:34 413
Ashdod arose early o the morrow 1Sa 5:3
arose early o the morrow morning 1Sa 5:4
tread o the threshold of Dagon in 1Sa 5:5 5921
was o you all, and o your lords 1Sa 6:4
o which there hath come no yoke, ... 1Sa 6:7 5921
put them o the great stone 1Sa 6:15 413
fasted o that day, and said there, ... 1Sa 7:6
o that day upon the Philistines 1Sa 7:10
days ago, set not thy mind o them 1Sa 9:20
o whom is all the desire of 1Sa 9:20
Is it not o thee, and o all thy 1Sa 9:20
o before us, (and he passed o 1Sa 9:27
Then shalt thou go o forward from 1Sa 10:3
O this condition will I make a 1Sa 11:2
of the LORD fell o the people 1Sa 11:7 5921
it was so o the morrow, that Saul 1Sa 11:11
hand of your enemies o every side 1Sa 12:11
is o the sea shore in multitude 1Sa 13:5 5921
that is o the other side 1Sa 14:1
was a sharp rock o the one side 1Sa 14:4
a sharp rock o the other side 1Sa 14:4
they went o beating down one 1Sa 14:16
host of the Philistines went o 1Sa 14:19
I may be avenged o mine enemies 1Sa 14:24
calves, and slew them o the ground 1Sa 14:32
Be ye o one side, and I and 1Sa 14:40
my son will be o the other side 1Sa 14:40
all his enemies o every side 1Sa 14:47
and is gone about, and passed o 1Sa 15:12
And he said unto him, Say o 1Sa 15:16
And the LORD sent thee o a journey 1Sa 15:18
were come, that he looked o Eliab 1Sa 16:6
Look not o his countenance 1Sa 16:7 413
or o the height of his stature 1Sa 16:7
for man looketh o the outward 1Sa 16:7
but the LORD looketh o the heart 1Sa 16:7
who is a cunning player o an harp 1Sa 16:16
o a mountain o the one side 1Sa 17:3 413
o a mountain o the other side 1Sa 17:3 413
And the Philistine came o and drew 1Sa 17:41
And it came to pass o the morrow 1Sa 18:10
O this manner spake David 1Sa 18:24
was upon him also, and he went o 1Sa 19:23
three arrows o the side thereof 1Sa 20:20
the arrows are o this side of 1Sa 20:21
And it came to pass o the morrow 1Sa 20:27
fell o his face to the ground, and 1Sa 20:41
scrabbled o the doors of the gate 1Sa 21:13 5921
slew o that day fourscore and five 1Sa 22:18
which is o the south of Jeshimon 1Sa 23:19
for ye have compassion o me 1Sa 23:21
in the plain o the south of 1Sa 23:24 413
Saul went o this side of the 1Sa 23:26
his men o that side of the 1Sa 23:26
of the cave, and went o his way 1Sa 24:7
Gird ye o every man his sword 1Sa 25:13
they girded o every man his sword 1Sa 25:13
and David also girded o his sword 1Sa 25:13
and he railed o them 1Sa 25:14
of figs, and laid them o asses 1Sa 25:18 5921
unto her servants, Go o before me 1Sa 25:19
it was so, as she rode o the ass 1Sa 25:20 5921
and fell before David o her face 1Sa 25:23 5921
bowed herself o her face to the 1Sa 25:41
stood o the top of an hill afar 1Sa 26:13 5921
So David went o his way, and Saul 1Sa 26:25
Lest they should tell o us 1Sa 27:11 5921
put o other raiment, and he went, ... 1Sa 28:8
straightway all along o the earth 1Sa 28:20
when thou goest o thy way 1Sa 28:22

Philistines passed o by hundreds 1Sa 29:2
his men passed o in the rereward 1Sa 29:2
come to Ziklag o the third day 1Sa 30:1
them away, and went o their way 1Sa 30:2
the men of Israel that were o the 1Sa 31:7
they that were o the other side 1Sa 31:7
And it came to pass o the morrow 1Sa 31:8
came even to pass o the third day 2Sa 1:2
the bracelet that was o his arm 2Sa 1:10 5921
David took hold o his clothes 2Sa 1:11
who put o ornaments of gold upon 2Sa 1:24
the one o the one side of the 2Sa 2:13 5921
the other o the other side of the 2Sa 2:13 5921
lay thee hold o one of the young 2Sa 2:21
stood o the top of an hill 2Sa 2:25 5921
messengers to David o his behalf 2Sa 3:12
Let it rest o the head of Joab, ... 2Sa 3:29 5921
and o all his father's house 2Sa 3:29 413
leper, or that leaneth o a staff 2Sa 3:29
or that falleth o the sword 2Sa 3:29
who lay o a bed at noon 2Sa 4:5
house, he lay o his bed in his 2Sa 4:7 5921
And David said o that day, ... 2Sa 5:8
And David went o, and grew great, ... 2Sa 5:10
Israel played before the LORD o 2Sa 6:5
even o harps, and 2Sa 6:5
o psalteries, and o timbrels, and 2Sa 6:5
and o cornets, and o cymbals 2Sa 6:5
and o cornets, and o cymbals 2Sa 6:5
were o the servants of Hadadezer 2Sa 8:7 413
a son, which is lame o his feet 2Sa 9:3
he fell o his face, and did 2Sa 9:6 5921
and was lame o both his feet 2Sa 9:13
at even he went out to lie o his 2Sa 11:13
it came to pass o the seventh day 2Sa 12:18
it was set o David's head 2Sa 12:30 5921
unto him, Lay thee down o thy bed 2Sa 13:5 5921
And Tamar put ashes o her head 2Sa 13:19 5921
of divers colours that was o her 2Sa 13:19 5921
her, and laid her hand o her head 2Sa 13:19 5921
her head, and went o crying 2Sa 13:19
his garments, and lay o the earth 2Sa 13:31
put o now mourning apparel, and 2Sa 14:2
speak o this manner unto him 2Sa 14:3
she fell o her face to the ground 2Sa 14:4 5921
O king, the iniquity be o me 2Sa 14:9 5921
be o me, and o my father's house 2Sa 14:9 5921
And he said, Say o 2Sa 14:12
are as water spilt o the ground 2Sa 14:14
fell to the ground o his face 2Sa 14:22 413
because the hair was heavy o him 2Sa 14:26 5921
go and set it o fire 2Sa 14:30
servants set the field o fire 2Sa 14:30
thy servants set my field o fire 2Sa 14:31
bowed himself o his face to the 2Sa 14:33 5921
o this manner did Absalom to all 2Sa 15:6
his servants passed o beside him 2Sa 15:18
Gath, passed o before the king 2Sa 15:18
said, If thou passest o with me 2Sa 15:33
the king's household to ride o 2Sa 16:2
o his right hand and o his left 2Sa 16:6
LORD will look o mine affliction 2Sa 16:12
Shimei went along o the hill's 2Sa 16:13
as the dew falleth o the ground 2Sa 17:12 5921
Then the king went o to Gilgal 2Sa 19:40
and Chimham went o with him 2Sa 19:40
he had put o was girded unto him 2Sa 20:8
all the people went o after Joab 2Sa 20:13
of the air to rest o them by day 2Sa 21:10 5921
that had o every hand six fingers 2Sa 21:20
o every foot six toes, four and 2Sa 21:20
I will call o the LORD, who is 2Sa 22:4
thou also hast lifted me up o 2Sa 22:49
the man who was raised up o high 2Sa 23:1
o the right side of the city that 2Sa 24:5
his servants coming o toward him 2Sa 24:20
king o his face upon the ground 2Sa 24:20
tell them who shall sit o the 1Kin 1:20 5921
who should sit o the throne of my 1Kin 1:27 5921
also Solomon sitteth o the throne 1Kin 1:46 5921
one to sit o my throne this day 1Kin 1:48 5921
caught hold o the horns of the 1Kin 1:50
he hath caught hold o the horns 1Kin 1:51
he) a man o the throne of Israel 1Kin 2:4 5921
in his shoes that were o his feet 1Kin 2:5
And she said, Say o 1Kin 2:14
all Israel set their faces o me 1Kin 2:15 5921
And she said unto him, Say o 1Kin 2:16
sat down o his throne, and caused 1Kin 2:19 5921
and she sat o his right hand 1Kin 2:19
And the king said unto her, Ask o 1Kin 2:20
set me o the throne of David my 1Kin 2:24 5921
caught hold o the horns of the 1Kin 2:28
that o the day thou goest out, and 1Kin 2:37
o the day thou goest out, and 1Kin 2:42
him a son to sit o his throne 1Kin 3:6 5921
the region o this side the river 1Kin 4:24
over all the kings o this side 1Kin 4:24
he had peace o all sides round 1Kin 4:24
the sand that is o the sea shore 1Kin 4:29 5921
which were about him o every side 1Kin 5:3
hath given me rest o every side 1Kin 5:4
they rested o the house with 1Kin 6:10
he covered them o the inside with 1Kin 6:15
cubits o the sides of the house 1Kin 6:16
that lay o forty five pillars, ... 1Kin 7:3
so o the outside toward the great 1Kin 7:9 5704
of the bases was o this manner 1Kin 7:28
o the borders that were between 1Kin 7:29 5921
o the top of the base the ledges 1Kin 7:35 5921
For o the plates of the ledges 1Kin 7:36 5921
o the borders thereof, he graved 1Kin 7:36 5921
he put five bases o the right 1Kin 7:39 5921
five o the left side of the house 1Kin 7:39 5921

he set the sea o the right side 1Kin 7:39
were o the top of the two pillars 1Kin 7:41 5921
bases, and ten lavers o the bases 1Kin 7:43 5921
five o the right side, and five o 1Kin 7:49
five o the left, before the 1Kin 7:49
sit o the throne of Israel, as 1Kin 8:20 5921
or o earth beneath, who keepest 1Kin 8:23 5921
to sit o the throne of Israel 1Kin 8:25 5921
will God indeed dwell o the earth 1Kin 8:27 5921
they may have compassion o them 1Kin 8:50
from kneeling o his knees with 1Kin 8:54 5921
O the eighth day he sent the 1Kin 8:66
o the shore of the Red sea, in 1Kin 9:26 5921
to set thee o the throne of 1Kin 10:9 5921
there were stays o either 1Kin 10:19
side o the place of the seat 1Kin 10:19 413
lions stood there o the one side 1Kin 10:20
o the other upon the six steps 1Kin 10:20
the new garment that was o him 1Kin 11:30 5921
o the fifteenth day of the month, ... 1Kin 12:32
the altar, saying, Lay hold o him 1Kin 13:4
o every high hill, and under every 1Kin 14:23 5921
as soon as he sat o his throne 1Kin 16:11 5921
built o the hill, and called the 1Kin 16:24 853
fell o his face, and said, Art 1Kin 18:7 5921
it in pieces, and lay it o wood 1Kin 18:23 5921
other bullock, and lay it o wood 1Kin 18:23 5921
call ye o the name of your gods, ... 1Kin 18:24
I will call o the name of the 1Kin 18:24
call o the name of your gods, but 1Kin 18:25
called o the name of Baal from 1Kin 18:26
in pieces, and laid him o the wood 1Kin 18:33 5921
pour it o the burnt sacrifice, and 1Kin 18:33 5921
burnt sacrifice, and o the wood 1Kin 18:33 5921
saw it, they fell o their faces 1Kin 18:39 5921
the hand of the LORD was o Elijah 1Kin 18:46 413
was a cake baken o the coals 1Kin 19:6
him, Go, return o thy way to the 1Kin 19:15
Let not him that girdeth o his 1Kin 20:11
the king of Syria escaped o an 1Kin 20:20 5921
thee, put sackcloth o our loins 1Kin 20:31
girded sackcloth o their loins 1Kin 20:32
put ropes o their heads, and came 1Kin 20:32
set Naboth o high among the 1Kin 21:9
set Naboth o high among the 1Kin 21:12
of Judah sat each o his throne 1Kin 22:10 5921
having put o their robes, in a 1Kin 22:10
saw the LORD sitting o his throne 1Kin 22:19 5921
standing by him o his right hand 1Kin 22:19
o his right hand and o his left 1Kin 22:19
one said o this manner 1Kin 22:20
and another said o that manner 1Kin 22:20
and smote Micaiah o the cheek 1Kin 22:24 5921
but put thou o thy robes 1Kin 22:30
that bed o which thou art gone up 2Kin 1:4
that bed o which thou art gone up 2Kin 1:6
he sat o the top of an hill 2Kin 1:9 5921
fell o his knees before Elijah, ... 2Kin 1:13 5921
that bed o which thou art gone up 2Kin 1:16
And they two went o 2Kin 2:6
they two went over o dry ground 2Kin 2:8
to pass, as they still went o 2Kin 2:11
of Elijah doth rest o Elisha 2Kin 2:15 5921
he turned back, and looked o them 2Kin 2:24
which poured water o the hands of 2Kin 3:11 5921
that were able to put o armour 2Kin 3:21
the Moabites saw the water o the 2Kin 3:22
o every good piece of land cast 2Kin 3:25
And it fell o a day, that Elisha 2Kin 4:8
chamber, I pray thee, o the wall 2Kin 4:10
And it fell o a day, that he came 2Kin 4:11
child was grown, it fell o a day 2Kin 4:18
he sat o her knees till noon, and 2Kin 4:20 5921
laid him o the bed of the man of 2Kin 4:21 5921
And Gehazi passed o before them 2Kin 4:31
Set o the great pot, and seethe 2Kin 4:38
she waited o Naaman's wife 2Kin 5:2
call o the name of the LORD his 2Kin 5:11
there, and he leaneth o my hand 2Kin 5:18 5921
and I said unto her o the next day 2Kin 6:29
shall stand o him this day 2Kin 6:31 5921
Then a lord o whose hand the king 2Kin 7:2 5921
the king appointed the lord o 2Kin 7:17 5921
strong holds wilt thou set o fire 2Kin 8:12
And it came to pass o the morrow 2Kin 8:15
in water, and spread it o his face 2Kin 8:15 5921
pour it o his head, and say, Thus 2Kin 9:3 5921
and he poured the oil o his head 2Kin 9:6 413
put it under him o the top of the 2Kin 9:13 413
a watchman o the tower in Jezreel 2Kin 9:17 5921
So there went one o horseback to 2Kin 9:18
he sent out a second o horseback 2Kin 9:19
window, and said, Who is o my side 2Kin 9:32 854
o the wall, and o the horses 2Kin 9:33 413
set him o his father's throne, and 2Kin 10:3 5921
he lighted o Jehonadab the son of 2Kin 10:15 854
shall sit o the throne of Israel 2Kin 10:30 5921
in o the sabbath shall even be 2Kin 11:5
you that go forth o the sabbath 2Kin 11:7
were to come in o the sabbath 2Kin 11:9
that should go out o the sabbath 2Kin 11:9
And they laid hands o her 2Kin 11:16
he sat o the throne of the kings 2Kin 11:19 5921
o the right side as one cometh 2Kin 12:9
money to be bestowed o workmen 2Kin 12:15
revived, and stood up o his feet 2Kin 13:21 5921
them, and had compassion o them 2Kin 13:23
burnt incense o the high places 2Kin 14:4
And they brought him o horses 2Kin 14:20 5921
incense still o the high places 2Kin 15:4
Thy sons shall sit o the throne 2Kin 15:12 5921
o the hills, and under every green 2Kin 16:4 5921
put it o the north side of the 2Kin 16:14 5921
thou puttest o me will I bear 2Kin 18:14 5921

Now o whom dost thou trust, that 2Kin 18:20 5921
o which if a man lean, it will go 2Kin 18:21 5921
Egypt unto all that trust o him 2Kin 18:21 5921
if thou be able o thy part to set 2Kin 18:23
put thy trust o Egypt for 2Kin 18:24 5921
of the people that are o the wall 2Kin 18:26 5921
to the men which sit o the wall 2Kin 18:27 5921
and lifted up thine eyes o high 2Kin 19:22
as the grass o the house tops, and 2Kin 19:26
o the third day thou shalt go up 2Kin 20:5
laid it o the boil, and he 2Kin 20:7 5921
which were o a man's left hand at 2Kin 23:8 5921
the altars that were o the top of 2Kin 23:12 5921
which were o the right hand of 2Kin 23:13
o the ninth day of the fourth 2Kin 25:3
o the seventh day of the month, 2Kin 25:8
o the seven and twentieth day of 2Kin 25:27
Jabez called o the God of Israel, 1Chr 4:10
then they waited o their office 1Chr 6:32
who stood o his right hand, even 1Chr 6:39 5921
of Merari stood o the left hand 1Chr 6:44 5921
o the altar of incense, and were 1Chr 6:49 5921
o the other side Jordan by 1Chr 6:78 5921
o the east side of Jordan, were 1Chr 6:78
he fell likewise o the sword 1Chr 10:5 5921
And it came to pass o the morrow 1Chr 10:8
o thy side, thou son of Jesse 1Chr 12:18
o the other side of Jordan, of 1Chr 12:37
Naphtali, brought bread o asses 1Chr 12:40
o camels, and o mules, and o oxen 1Chr 12:40
whose name is called o it 1Chr 13:6
his kingdom was lifted up o high 1Chr 14:2
with psalteries o Alamoth 1Chr 15:20 5921
with harps o the Sheminith to 1Chr 15:21 5921
Then o that day David delivered 1Chr 16:7
were o the servants of Hadarezer 1Chr 18:7 5921
six o each hand, and six o each 1Chr 20:6
be o me, and o my father's house 1Chr 21:17
but not o thy people, that they 1Chr 21:17
not given you rest o every side 1Chr 22:18
their office was to wait o the 1Chr 23:28
o the set feasts, by number, 1Chr 23:31
o this side Jordan westward in 1Chr 26:30
our days o the earth are as a 1Chr 29:15 5921
o the morrow after that day, even 1Chr 29:21
drink before the LORD o that day 1Chr 29:22
Then Solomon sat o the throne of 1Chr 29:23 5921
o any king before him in Israel 1Chr 29:25 5921
o the sabbaths, and o the new 2Chr 2:4
o the solemn feasts of the LORD 2Chr 2:4
and graved cherubims o the walls 2Chr 3:7 5921
and they stood o their feet 2Chr 3:13 5921
the chapiter that was o the top 2Chr 3:15 5921
put them o the heads of the 2Chr 3:16 5921
and put them o the chains 2Chr 3:16
one o the right hand, and the 2Chr 3:17
hand, and the other o the left 2Chr 3:17
of that o the right hand Jachin 2Chr 3:17
the name of that o the left Boaz 2Chr 3:17
put five o the right hand, and 2Chr 4:6
five o the left, to wash in them 2Chr 4:6
five o the right hand, and five o 2Chr 4:7
right hand, and five o the left 2Chr 4:7
five o the right side 2Chr 4:8
and five o the left 2Chr 4:8
he set the sea o the right side 2Chr 4:10
the chapiters which were o the 2Chr 4:12 5921
were o the top of the pillars 2Chr 4:12 5921
pomegranates o the two wreaths 2Chr 4:13
of pomegranates o each wreath 2Chr 4:13
am set o the throne of Israel, as 2Chr 6:10 5921
deed dwell with men o the earth 2Chr 6:18 5921
priests waited o their offices 2Chr 7:6
o the three and twentieth day of 2Chr 7:10
laid hold o other gods, and 2Chr 7:22
the LORD o the altar of the LORD 2Chr 8:12 5921
o the sabbaths, and o the new 2Chr 8:13
o the solemn feasts, three times 2Chr 8:13
in thee to set thee o his throne 2Chr 9:8 5921
stays o each side of the sitting 2Chr 9:18
lions stood there o the one side 2Chr 9:19
o the other upon the six steps 2Chr 9:19
came to Rehoboam o the third day 2Chr 10:12
Come again to me o the third day 2Chr 10:12
Judah and Benjamin o his side 2Chr 11:12
hath given us rest o every side 2Chr 14:7
for we rest o thee, and in thy 2Chr 14:11 5921
hast relied o the king of Syria 2Chr 16:7 5921
not relied o the LORD thy God, 2Chr 16:7 5921
thou didst rely o the LORD 2Chr 16:8 5921
These waited o the king, beside 2Chr 17:19
sat either of them o his throne 2Chr 18:9 5921
heaven standing o his right hand 2Chr 18:18
right hand and o his left 2Chr 18:18 5921
thou shalt see o that day when 2Chr 18:24
but put thou o thy robes 2Chr 18:29
beyond the sea o this side Syria 2Chr 20:2
Israel with a loud voice o high 2Chr 20:19
o the fourth day they assembled 2Chr 20:26
the fear of God was o all the 2Chr 20:29 5921
of you entering o the sabbath 2Chr 23:4
were to come in o the sabbath 2Chr 23:8
that were to go out o the sabbath 2Chr 23:8
So they laid hands o her 2Chr 23:15
the priest, and slew him o his bed 2Chr 24:25 5921
to be o the towers and upon the 2Chr 26:15 5921
o the wall of Ophel he built much 2Chr 27:3
o the hills, and under every green 2Chr 28:4 5921
Now they began o the first day of 2Chr 29:17
o the eighth day of the month 2Chr 29:17
them o the altar of the LORD 2Chr 29:21 5921
and sprinkled it o the altar 2Chr 29:22
o the fourteenth day of the 2Chr 30:15
nor persuade you o this manner 2Chr 32:15
to rail o the LORD God of Israel 2Chr 32:17
of Jerusalem that were o the wall 2Chr 32:18 5921
and guided them o every side 2Chr 32:22
o the west side of Gihon, in the 2Chr 33:14
that were o high above them, he 2Chr 34:4
they killed the passover o the 2Chr 35:1
he had compassion o his people 2Chr 36:15 5921
and o his dwelling place 2Chr 36:15 5921
the rest that are o this side the Ezr 4:10
the men o this side the river Ezr 4:11
no portion o this side the river Ezr 4:16
governor o this side the river, Ezr 5:3
governor o this side the river, Ezr 5:6
which were o this side the river, Ezr 5:6
walls, and this work goeth fast o Ezr 5:8
governor o this side the river, Ezr 6:13
this house was finished o the Ezr 6:15 5705
o the first day of the fifth Ezr 7:9
from the river of Ahava o the Ezr 8:31
Now o the fourth day was the Ezr 8:33
to the governors o this side the Ezr 8:36
o the twentieth day of the month Ezr 10:9
Then I went o to the gate of the Neh 2:14 413
governor o this side the river Neh 3:7
a thousand cubits o the wall unto Neh 3:13
o the higher places, I even set Neh 4:13
They which builded o the wall Neh 4:17
guard to us, and labour o the day Neh 4:22
o the prophetess Noadiah, and the Neh 6:14
and Maaseiah, o his right hand Neh 8:4 5921
o his left hand, Pedaiah, and Neh 8:4
o the second day were gathered Neh 8:13
o the eighth day was a solemn Neh 8:18
o all his servants, and o all the Neh 9:10
midst of the sea o the dry land Neh 9:11
o our kings, o our princes, and Neh 9:32
o our priests, and o our prophets Neh 9:32
o our fathers, and o all thy Neh 9:32
o all thy people, since the time Neh 9:32
o the sabbath day to sell Neh 10:31
o the sabbath, or o the holy day Neh 10:31
whereof one went o the right hand Neh 12:31
O that day they read in the book Neh 13:1
winepresses o the sabbath Neh 13:15
into Jerusalem o the sabbath day Neh 13:15
sold o the sabbath unto the Neh 13:16
be brought in o the sabbath day Neh 13:19
so again, I will lay hands o you Neh 13:21
came they no more o the sabbath Neh 13:21
sat o the throne of his kingdom Est 1:2 5921
O the seventh day, when the heart Est 1:10
for she was fair to look o Est 1:11
o the morrow she returned into Est 2:14
to lay hand o the king Ahasuerus Est 2:21
they were both hanged o a tree Est 2:23 5921
to lay hands o Mordecai alone Est 3:6
were the king's scribes called o Est 3:12
put o sackcloth with ashes, and Est 4:1
it came to pass o the third day Est 5:1
that Esther put o her royal Est 5:1
O that night could not the king Est 6:1
to lay hand o the king Ahasuerus Est 6:2
o the gallows that he had Est 6:4 5921
bring him o horseback through the Est 6:9
brought him o horseback through Est 6:11
o the second day at the banquet Est 7:2
So they hanged Haman o the Est 7:10 5921
O that day did the king Ahasuerus Est 8:1
o the three and twentieth day Est 8:9
o horseback, and riders o mules Est 8:10
avenge themselves o their enemies Est 8:13
and pressed o by the king's Est 8:14
o the thirteenth day of the same, Est 9:1
to lay hand o such as sought Est 9:2
but o the spoil laid they not Est 9:10
O that day the number of those Est 9:11
gathered themselves together o Est 9:15
but o the prey they laid not Est 9:15
laid not their hands o the prey Est 9:16
O the thirteenth day of the month Est 9:17
o the fourteenth day of the same Est 9:17
o the thirteenth day thereof Est 9:18
and o the fourteenth thereof Est 9:18
o the fifteenth day of the same Est 9:18
should be hanged o the gallows Est 9:25 5921
all that he hath o every side Job 1:10
when deep sleep falleth o men Job 4:13 5921
To set up o high those that be Job 5:11
he passeth o also, but I perceive Job 9:11
speak, and let come o me what will Job 13:13
even o his neck, upon the thick Job 15:26
collops of fat o his flanks Job 15:27
o my eyelids is the shadow of Job 16:16 5921
in heaven, and my record is o high Job 16:19
also shall hold o his way Job 17:9
make him afraid o every side Job 18:11
He hath destroyed me o every side Job 19:10
after that I have spoken, mock o Job 21:3
trembling taketh hold o my flesh Job 21:6
O the left hand, where he doth Job 23:9
hideth himself o the right hand Job 23:9
the worm shall feed sweetly o him Job 24:20
it, but the just shall put it o Job 27:17
Terrors take hold o him as waters Job 27:20
and laid their hand o their mouth Job 29:9
I put o righteousness, and it Job 29:14
If I laughed o them, they Job 29:24 413
of the Almighty from o high Job 31:2
have yet to speak o God's behalf Job 36:2
with kings are they o the throne Job 36:7
that which should be set o thy Job 36:16
and justice take hold o thee Job 36:17
to the snow, Be thou o the earth Job 37:6
To cause it to rain o the earth Job 38:26 5921
o the wilderness, wherein there Job 38:26 5921
she lifteth up herself o high Job 39:18
he goeth o to meet the armed men Job 39:21
command, and make her nest o high Job 39:27
abideth o the rock, upon the crag Job 39:28
Look o every one that is proud, Job 40:12
To the chief Musician o Neginoth Ps 4:t
To the chief Musician o Neginoth Ps 6:t
therefore return thou o high Ps 7:7
The wicked walk o every side Ps 12:8
a crown of pure gold o his head Ps 21:3
He trusted o the LORD that he Ps 22:8 413
none that wait o thee be ashamed Ps 25:3
o thee do I wait all the day Ps 25:5
for I wait o thee Ps 25:21
Wait o the LORD Ps 27:14
wait, I say, o the LORD Ps 27:14
fear was o every side Ps 31:13
LORD, how long wilt thou look o Ps 35:17
Wait o the LORD, and keep his way, Ps 37:34
o the sides of the north, the Ps 48:2
death shall feed o them Ps 49:14
and I will wait o thy name Ps 52:9
To the chief Musician o Neginoth Ps 54:t
To the chief Musician o Neginoth Ps 55:t
among them that are set o fire Ps 57:4
meditate o thee in the night Ps 63:6
little hills rejoice o every side Ps 65:12
went through the flood o foot Ps 66:6
To the chief Musician o Neginoth Ps 67:t
Thou hast ascended o high Ps 68:18
goeth o still in his trespasses Ps 68:21
the players o instruments Ps 68:25
Let not them that wait o thee Ps 69:6
O God, set me up o high Ps 69:29
and comfort me o every side Ps 71:21
Lift not up your horn o high Ps 75:5
To the chief Musician o Neginoth Ps 76:t
And he led them o safely, so that Ps 78:53
they have laid Jerusalem o heaps Ps 79:1
appointed, o our solemn feast day Ps 81:3
they walk o in darkness Ps 82:5
setteth the mountains o fire Ps 83:14
o instruments shall be there Ps 87:7
I will set him o high, because he Ps 91:14
see my desire o mine enemies Ps 92:11
The LORD o high is mightier than Ps 93:4
He looketh o the earth, and it Ps 104:32
the poor o high from affliction Ps 107:41
LORD our God, who dwelleth o high Ps 113:5
The LORD is o my side Ps 118:6
I thought o my ways, and turned my Ps 119:59
judgment o them that persecute me Ps 119:84
and anguish have taken hold o me Ps 119:143
been the LORD who was o our side Ps 124:1
been the LORD who was o our side Ps 124:2
I looked o my right hand, and Ps 142:4
I meditate o all thy works Ps 143:5
I muse o the work of thy hands Ps 143:5
Let thine eyes look right o Prov 4:25
her steps take hold o hell Prov 5:5
o a seat in the high places of Prov 9:14 5921
who go right o their ways Prov 9:15
but he that hath mercy o the poor Prov 14:21
him hath mercy o the poor Prov 14:31
of fools feedeth o foolishness Prov 15:14
but wait o the LORD, and he shall Prov 20:22
but the simple pass o, and are Prov 22:3
but the simple pass o, and are Prov 27:12
so he that waiteth o his master Prov 27:18
and to lay hold o folly, till I Eccl 2:3
Then I looked o all the works Eccl 2:11
o the labour that I had laboured Eccl 2:11
o the side of their oppressors Eccl 4:1
The flowers appear o the earth Song 2:12
By night o my bed I sought him Song 3:1 5921
how shall I put it o Song 5:3
o all hills that shall be digged Is 7:25
have mercy o their fatherless Is 9:17
he shall snatch o the right hand Is 9:20 5921
he shall eat o the left hand, and Is 9:20 5921
o Jerusalem, I will punish the Is 10:12
shall play o the hole of the asp Is 11:8 5921
his hand o the cockatrice' den Is 11:8 5921
no pity o the fruit of the womb Is 13:18
the LORD will have mercy o Jacob Is 14:1
o all their heads shall be Is 15:2
o the tops of their houses, and in Is 15:3 5921
Moab is weary o the high place Is 16:12 5921
dwellers o the earth, see ye, Is 18:3
up an ensign o the mountains Is 18:3
him out an sepulchre o high Is 22:16
the windows from o high are open Is 24:18
of the high ones that are o high Is 24:21
a feast of wines o the lees Is 25:6
of wines o the lees well refined Is 25:6
whose mind is stayed o thee Is 26:3
down them that dwell o high Is 26:5 4791
women come, and set them o fire Is 27:11
them will not have mercy o them Is 27:11
which are o the head of the fat Is 28:1
which is o the head of the fat Is 28:4 5921
a man can stretch himself o it Is 28:20
and as an ensign o an hill Is 30:17 5921
stay o horses, and trust in Is 31:1 5921
the young lion roaring o his prey Is 31:4 5921
be poured upon us from o high Is 32:15
hail, coming down o the forest Is 32:19
for he dwelleth o high Is 33:5
He shall dwell o high Is 33:16
now o whom dost thou trust, that Is 36:5 5921
of this broken reed, o Egypt Is 36:6 5921
if thou be able o thy part to set Is 36:8
put thy trust o Egypt for Is 36:9 5921

of the people that are o the wall Is 36:11 5921
and lifted up thine eyes o high Is 37:23
as the grass o the housetops, and Is 37:27
Lift up your eyes o high, and Is 40:26
it hath set him o fire round Is 42:25
He feedeth o ashes Is 44:20
of Babylon, sit o the ground Is 47:1 5921
he will do his pleasure o Babylon Is 48:14
his arm shall be o the Chaldeans Is 48:14
hath mercy o them shall lead them Is 49:10
compassion o the son of her womb Is 49:15
an ornament, and bind them o thee Is 49:18
o mine arm shall they trust Is 51:5 413
put o strength, O arm of the LORD Is 51:9
put o thy strength, O Zion Is 52:1
put o thy beautiful garments, O Is 52:1
the LORD hath laid o him the Is 53:6
o the right hand and o the left Is 54:3
kindness will I have mercy o thee Is 54:8
the LORD that hath mercy o thee Is 54:10
son of man that layeth hold o it Is 56:2
he went o frowardly in the way of Is 57:17
your voice to be heard o high Is 58:4
doing thy pleasure o my holy day Is 58:13
For he put o righteousness as a Is 59:17
and he put o the garments of Is 59:17
up with acceptance o mine altar Is 60:7 5921
my favour have I had mercy o thee Is 60:10
that the LORD hath bestowed o us Is 63:7
which he hath bestowed o them Is 63:7
of the Gentiles is o his way Jer 4:7
avenged o such a nation as this Jer 5:9
avenged o such a nation as this Jer 5:29
They shall lay hold o bow Jer 6:23
the enemy and fear is o every side Jer 6:25
up a lamentation o high places Jer 7:29 5921
shall be no grapes o the vine Jer 8:13
nor figs o the fig tree, and the Jer 8:13
astonishment hath taken hold o me Jer 8:21
avenged o such a nation as this Jer 9:9
families that call not o thy name Jer 10:25
let me see thy vengeance o them Jer 11:20
return, and have compassion o them Jer 12:15
of the LORD, and put it o my loins Jer 13:2 5921
thine abominations o the hills in Jer 13:27 5921
I have neither lent o usury Jer 15:10
nor men have lent to me o usury Jer 15:10
As the partridge sitteth o eggs Jer 17:11
bear no burden o the sabbath day, Jer 17:21
of your houses o the sabbath day Jer 17:22
of this city o the sabbath day Jer 17:24
o horses, they, and their princes, Jer 17:25
of Jerusalem o the sabbath day Jer 17:27
he wrought a work o the wheels Jer 18:3 5921
And it came to pass o the morrow Jer 20:3
of many, fear o every side Jer 20:10
we shall take our revenge o him Jer 20:10
let me see thy vengeance o them Jer 20:12
o horses, he, and his servants, and Jer 22:4
they shall be driven o, and fall Jer 23:12
I begin to bring evil o the city Jer 25:29
The LORD shall roar from o high Jer 25:30
man with his hands o his loins Jer 30:6 5921
have mercy o his dwellingplaces Jer 30:18
children's teeth are set o edge Jer 31:29
his teeth shall be set o edge Jer 31:30
set fire o this city, and burn it Jer 32:29
to return, and have mercy o them Jer 33:26
there was a fire o the hearth Jer 36:22
the fire that was o the hearth Jer 36:23 413
in the fire that was o the hearth Jer 36:23 5921
say, Thy friends have set thee o Jer 38:22
Neriah setteth thee o against us Jer 43:3
a shepherd putteth o his garment Jer 43:12
spears, and put o the brigandines Jer 46:4
and he hath settled o his lees Jer 48:11 413
there is sorrow o the sea Jer 49:23
flee, and fear hath seized o her Jer 49:24
unto them, Fear is o every side Jer 49:29
turned them away o the mountains Jer 50:6
and he shall feed o Carmel Jer 50:19
and six pomegranates o a side Jer 52:23
and her tears are o her cheeks Lam 1:2 5921
the old lie o the ground in the Lam 2:21
moment, and no hands stayed o her Lam 4:6
their wings o their four sides Eze 1:8 5921
face of a lion, o the right side Eze 1:10 413
the face of an ox o the left side Eze 1:10
two, which covered o this side Eze 1:23
two, which covered o that side Eze 1:23
and I fell o my face Eze 3:23 5921
lie again o thy right side, and Eze 4:6 5921
shall be o the mountains like Eze 7:16 413
Now the cherubims stood o the Eze 10:3 5921
is o the east side of the city Eze 11:23
thy hands, and a chain o thy neck Eze 16:11 5921
And I put a jewel o thy forehead Eze 16:12 5921
o every one that passed by Eze 16:15
o every side for thy whoredom Eze 16:33
children's teeth are set o edge Eze 18:2
the nations set against him o Eze 19:8
either o the right hand Eze 21:16
or o the left, whithersoever thy Eze 21:16
she doted o her lovers Eze 23:5 413
o the Assyrians her neighbours, Eze 23:5 413
with all o whom she doted Eze 23:7
them against thee o every side Eze 23:22
Set o a pot, set it o, and also Eze 24:3
Heap o wood, kindle the fire, Eze 24:10
put o thy shoes upon thy feet, and Eze 24:17
cities which are o his frontiers Eze 25:9
terror to be o all that haunt it Eze 26:17
the sword upon her o every side Eze 28:23
the deep set him up o high with Eze 31:4

and can play well o an instrument Eze 33:32
and swallowed you up o every side Eze 36:3
and will gather them o every side Eze 37:21
And I will send a fire o Magog Eze 39:6
go forth, and shall set o fire Eze 39:9
passengers o the east of the sea Eze 39:11
gather yourselves o every side to Eze 39:17
the frame of a city o the south Eze 40:2
behold a wall o the outside of Eze 40:5
eastward were three o this side Eze 40:10
and three o that side Eze 40:10
o this side and o that side Eze 40:10
was one cubit o this side Eze 40:12
space was one cubit o that side Eze 40:12
were six cubits o this side Eze 40:12
and six cubits o that side Eze 40:12
thereof were three o this side Eze 40:21
o this side and three o that side Eze 40:21
one o this side, and another o Eze 40:26
o this side, and o that side Eze 40:34
o this side, and o that side Eze 40:37
gate were two tables o this side Eze 40:39
and two tables o that side Eze 40:39
o the other side, which was at Eze 40:40 413
Four tables were o this side Eze 40:41
and four tables o that side Eze 40:41
porch, five cubits o this side Eze 40:48
and five cubits o that side Eze 40:48
gate was three cubits o this side Eze 40:48
and three cubits o that side Eze 40:48
one o this side, and another o Eze 40:49
six cubits broad o the one side Eze 41:1
six cubits broad o the other side Eze 41:1
were five cubits o the one side Eze 41:2
five cubits o the other side Eze 41:2
about the house o every side Eze 41:5
about the house o every side Eze 41:10
galleries thereof o the one side Eze 41:15
o the other side, an hundred Eze 41:15
round about o their three stories Eze 41:16
the palm tree o the one side Eze 41:19
the palm tree o the other side Eze 41:19
made, and o the wall of the temple Eze 41:20
And there were made o them Eze 41:25 413
o the doors of the temple, Eze 41:25 413
palm trees o the one side and o Eze 41:26
o the sides of the porch, and upon Eze 41:26 413
toward the utter court o the Eze 42:7
was the entry o the east side Eze 42:9
shall put o other garments, and Eze 42:14
put it o the four horns of it, and Eze 43:20 5921
o the four corners of the settle, Eze 43:20 413
o the second day thou shalt offer Eze 43:22
they shall put o other garments Eze 44:19
be for the prince o the one side Eze 45:7
o the other side of the oblation Eze 45:7
but o the sabbath it shall be Eze 46:1
as he did o the sabbath day Eze 46:12
there was a place o the two sides Eze 46:19
ran out waters o the right side Eze 47:2
o the one side and o the other Eze 47:7
o this side and o that side, Eze 47:12
o the east side four thousand and Eze 48:16
o the one side and o the other of Eze 48:21 5921
out of the city o the north side Eze 48:30
smell of fire had passed o them Dan 3:27
set his heart o Daniel to deliver Dan 6:14 5922
and it raised up itself o one side Dan 7:5
o the face of the whole earth Dan 8:5
I was in a deep sleep o my face Dan 8:18 5921
was I in a deep sleep o my face Dan 10:9
she shall not stand o his side Dan 11:17
And arms shall stand o his part Dan 11:31
the one o this side of the bank Dan 12:5
the other o that side of the bank Dan 12:5
set their heart o their iniquity Hos 4:8 413
ye have been a snare o Mizpah Hos 5:1
if we follow o to know the LORD Hos 6:3
thereof that rejoiced o it Hos 10:5 5921
shall come up o their altars Hos 10:8 5921
and to the hills, Fall o us Hos 10:8 5921
take off the yoke o their jaws Hos 11:4 5921
sword shall abide o his cities Hos 11:6
Ephraim feedeth o wind, and Hos 12:1
wait o thy God continually Hos 12:6
Like the noise of chariots o the Joel 2:5 5921
shall march every one o his ways Joel 2:7
that whosoever shall call o the Joel 2:32
send a fire o the wall of Gaza Amos 1:7
send a fire o the wall of Tyrus Amos 1:10
the earth o the head of the poor Amos 2:7
and leaned his hand o the wall Amos 5:19 5921
thou stoodest o the other side Obad 11
o the day of thy brother in the Obad 12
o their affliction in the day of Obad 13
nor have laid hands o their Obad 13
saviours shall come up o mount Obad 21
put o sackcloth, from the Jonah 3:5
sat o the east side of the city, Jonah 4:5
Thou hast had pity o the gourd Jonah 4:10 5921
the LORD o the head of them Mic 2:13
take vengeance o his adversaries Nah 1:2
and canst not look o iniquity Hab 1:13 413
that he may set his nest o high Hab 2:9
mayest look o their nakedness Hab 2:15 5921
spewing shall be o thy glory Hab 2:16 5921
and lifted up his hands o high Hab 3:10
To the chief singer o my stringed Hab 3:19
those that leap o the threshold Zeph 1:9 5921
men that are settled o their lees Zeph 1:12 5921
thou not have mercy o Jerusalem Zec 1:12
o the cities of Judah, against Zec 1:12
as o this side according to it Zec 5:3
as o that side according to it Zec 5:3

the riders o horses shall be Zec 10:5
o the right hand and o the left Zec 12:6 5921
they shall call o my name Zec 13:9
is before Jerusalem o the east Zec 14:4
one o the hand of his neighbour Zec 14:13
fire o mine altar for nought Mal 1:10
of Jesus Christ was o this wise Mt 1:18 *3779*
while he thought o these things Mt 1:20 *1760*
setteth him o a pinnacle of the Mt 4:5 *1909*
going o from thence, he saw other Mt 4:21
A city that is set o an hill Mt 5:14 *1883*
a bushel, but o a candlestick Mt 5:15 *1909*
That whosoever looketh o a woman Mt 5:28
smite thee o thy right cheek Mt 5:39 *1909*
maketh his sun to rise o the evil Mt 5:45 *1909*
o the good, and sendeth rain Mt 5:45
and sendeth rain o the just Mt 5:45 *1909*
the just and o the unjust Mt 5:45
your body, what ye shall put o Mt 6:25 *1746*
sick of the palsy, lying o a bed Mt 9:2 *1909*
power o earth to forgive sins Mt 9:6 *1909*
son of David, have mercy o us Mt 9:27
was moved with compassion o them Mt 9:36 *4012*
one of them shall not fall o the Mt 10:29 *1909*
I am come to send peace o earth Mt 10:34 *1909*
At that time Jesus went o the Mt 12:1
how that o the sabbath days the Mt 12:5
lawful to heal o the sabbath days Mt 12:10
fall into a pit o the sabbath day Mt 12:11
day, will he not lay hold o it Mt 12:11
to do well o the sabbath days Mt 12:12
whole multitude stood o the shore Mt 13:2 *1909*
For Herod had laid hold o John Mt 14:3
they followed him o foot out of Mt 14:13 *3979*
multitude to sit down o the grass Mt 14:19 *1909*
went unto them, walking o the sea Mt 14:25 *1909*
saw him walking o the sea Mt 14:26 *1909*
bid me come unto thee o the water Mt 14:28 *1909*
the ship, he walked o the water Mt 14:29 *1909*
unto him, saying, Have mercy o me Mt 15:22
I have compassion o the multitude Mt 15:32 *1909*
to sit down o the ground Mt 15:35 *1909*
whatsoever thou shalt bind o Mt 16:19 *1909*
whatsoever thou shalt loose o Mt 16:19 *1909*
they fell o their face, and were Mt 17:6 *1909*
Lord, have mercy o my son Mt 17:15
Whatsoever ye shall bind o earth Mt 18:18 *1909*
whatsoever ye shall loose o earth Mt 18:18 *1909*
o earth as touching any thing Mt 18:19 *1909*
and he laid hands o him, and took Mt 18:28
compassion o thy fellowservant Mt 18:33
even as I had pity o thee Mt 18:33
he should put his hands o them Mt 19:13 *2007*
And he laid his hands o them Mt 19:15 *2007*
the one o thy right hand Mt 20:21 *1537*
and the other o the left Mt 20:21 *1537*
but to sit o my right hand, and o Mt 20:23 *1537*
out, saying, Have mercy o us Mt 20:30
the more, saying, Have mercy o us Mt 20:31
So Jesus had compassion o them Mt 20:34
put o them their clothes, and they Mt 21:7 *1883*
unto it, Let no fruit grow o thee Mt 21:19 *1537*
let us seize o his inheritance Mt 21:38
whosoever shall fall o this stone Mt 21:44 *1909*
but o whomsoever it shall fall, Mt 21:44 *1909*
they sought to lay hands o him Mt 21:46
which had not o a wedding garment Mt 22:11 *1746*
O these two commandments hang all Mt 22:40 *1722*
Sit thou o my right hand, till I Mt 22:44 *1537*
lay them o men's shoulders Mt 23:4 *1909*
Let him which is o the housetop Mt 24:17 *1909*
neither o the sabbath day Mt 24:20 *1722*
set the sheep o his right hand Mt 25:33 *1537*
but the goats o the left Mt 25:33 *1537*
say unto them o his right hand Mt 25:34 *1537*
also unto them o the left hand Mt 25:41 *1537*
Not o the feast day, lest there Mt 26:5 *1722*
ointment, and poured it o his head Mt 26:7 *1909*
poured this ointment o my body Mt 26:12 *1909*
fell o his face, and prayed, Mt 26:39 *1909*
and saith unto them, Sleep o now Mt 26:45
came they, and laid hands o Jesus Mt 26:50 *1909*
temple, and ye laid no hold o me Mt 26:55
they that had laid hold o Jesus Mt 26:57
sitting o the right hand of power Mt 26:64 *1537*
was set down o the judgment seat Mt 27:19 *1909*
blood be o us, and o our children Mt 27:25 *1909*
him, and put o him a scarlet robe Mt 27:28 *4060*
the reed, and smote him o the head Mt 27:30 *1519*
him, and put his own raiment o him Mt 27:31 *1746*
one o the right hand, and another Mt 27:38 *1537*
right hand, and another o the left Mt 27:38 *1537*
with vinegar, and put it o a reed Mt 27:48 *4060*
straightway o the sabbath day he Mk 1:21
power o earth to forgive sins Mk 2:10 *1909*
We never saw it o this fashion Mk 2:12
of new cloth o an old garment Mk 2:21 *1909*
the corn fields o the sabbath day Mk 2:23 *1722*
why do they o the sabbath day Mk 2:24 *1722*
would heal him o the sabbath day Mk 3:2
to do good o the sabbath days Mk 3:4
round about o them with anger Mk 3:5
o him because of the multitude Mk 3:9 *4342*
they went out to lay hold o him Mk 3:21
he looked round about o them Mk 3:34
was by the sea o the land Mk 4:1 *1909*
some fell o stony ground, where Mk 4:5 *1909*
other fell o good ground, and did Mk 4:8 *1519*
which are sown o stony ground Mk 4:16 *1909*
they which are sown o good ground Mk 4:20 *1909*
and not to be set o a candlestick Mk 4:21 *1909*
of the ship, asleep o a pillow Mk 4:38 *1909*
and hath had compassion o thee Mk 5:19
thee, come and lay thy hands o her Mk 5:23 *2007*

Context	Reference	Strong's No.
and not put o two coats	Mk 6:9	1746
that Herod o his birthday made a	Mk 6:21	
the sea, and he alone o the land	Mk 6:47	1909
I have compassion o the multitude	Mk 8:2	1909
people to sit down o the ground	Mk 8:6	1909
and when he had spit o his eyes	Mk 8:23	1519
looked o his disciples, he	Mk 8:33	
so as no fuller o earth can white	Mk 9:3	1909
he fell o the ground, and wallowed	Mk 9:20	1909
any thing, have compassion o us	Mk 9:22	1909
is not against us is o our part	Mk 9:40	5228
one o thy right hand, and the	Mk 10:37	1537
the other o thy left hand, in thy	Mk 10:37	1537
But to sit o my right hand	Mk 10:40	1537
o my left hand is not mine to	Mk 10:40	1537
son of David, have mercy o me	Mk 10:47	
son of David, have mercy o me	Mk 10:48	
and cast their garments o him	Mk 11:7	1911
o the morrow, when they were come	Mk 11:12	
And they sought to lay hold o him	Mk 12:12	
Sit thou o my right hand, till I	Mk 12:36	1537
let him that is o the housetop	Mk 13:15	1909
Not o the feast day, lest there	Mk 14:2	1722
the box, and poured it o his head	Mk 14:3	2596
she hath wrought a good work o me	Mk 14:6	1722
fell o the ground, and prayed that	Mk 14:35	1909
and saith unto them, Sleep o now	Mk 14:41	
And they laid their hands o him	Mk 14:46	1909
and the young men laid hold o him	Mk 14:51	
sitting o the right hand of power	Mk 14:62	1537
And some began to spit o him	Mk 14:65	1716
they smote him o the head with a	Mk 15:19	
him, and put his own clothes o him	Mk 15:20	1746
the one o his right hand, and the	Mk 15:27	1537
hand, and the other o his left	Mk 15:27	1537
they that passed by railed o him	Mk 15:29	
of vinegar, and put it o a reed	Mk 15:36	4060
also women looking o afar off	Mk 15:40	
man sitting o the right side	Mk 16:5	1722
they shall lay hands o the sick	Mk 16:18	1909
sat o the right hand of God	Mk 16:19	1537
an angel of the Lord standing o	Lk 1:11	1537
the days wherein he looked o me	Lk 1:25	1896
his mercy is o them that fear him	Lk 1:50	
that o the eighth day they came	Lk 1:59	1722
fear came o all that dwelt round	Lk 1:65	1909
from o high hath visited us	Lk 1:78	
o earth peace, good will toward	Lk 2:14	1909
set him o a pinnacle of the	Lk 4:9	1909
the synagogue o the sabbath day	Lk 4:16	1722
the synagogue were fastened o him	Lk 4:20	
taught them o the sabbath days	Lk 4:31	1722
his hands o every one of them	Lk 4:40	
who seeing Jesus fell o his face	Lk 5:12	1909
it came to pass o a certain day	Lk 5:17	1722
it came to pass o the second	Lk 6:1	1722
lawful to do o the sabbath days	Lk 6:2	1722
to pass also o another sabbath	Lk 6:6	1722
he would heal o the sabbath day	Lk 6:7	1722
Is it lawful o the sabbath days	Lk 6:9	
up his eyes o his disciples	Lk 6:20	1519
unto him that smiteth thee o the	Lk 6:29	1909
and laid the foundation o a rock	Lk 6:48	1909
saw her, he had compassion o her	Lk 7:13	1909
And there came a fear o all	Lk 7:16	
And he saith, Master, say o	Lk 7:40	
other fell o good ground, and	Lk 8:8	1519
They o the rock are they, which,	Lk 8:13	1909
But that o the good ground are	Lk 8:15	1722
but setteth it o a candlestick	Lk 8:16	1909
it came to pass o a certain day	Lk 8:22	1722
down a storm of wind o the lake	Lk 8:23	1519
many swine feeding o the mountain	Lk 8:32	1722
that o the next day, when they	Lk 9:37	1722
of your city, which cleaveth o us	Lk 10:11	
you power to tread o serpents	Lk 10:19	1883
he passed by o the other side	Lk 10:31	
the place, came and looked o him	Lk 10:32	
passed by o the other side	Lk 10:32	
saw him, he had compassion o him	Lk 10:33	
set him o his own beast, and	Lk 10:34	1909
o the morrow when he departed, he	Lk 10:35	1909
said, He that shewed mercy o him	Lk 10:37	3326
but o a candlestick, that they	Lk 11:33	1909
for the body, what ye shall put o	Lk 12:22	1746
am come to send fire o the earth	Lk 12:49	1519
I am come to give peace o earth	Lk 12:51	1722
seeking fruit o this fig tree	Lk 13:7	1722
of the synagogues o the sabbath	Lk 13:10	1722
And he laid his hands o her	Lk 13:13	2007
had healed o the sabbath day	Lk 13:14	
healed, and not o the sabbath day	Lk 13:14	
doth not each one of you o the	Lk 13:15	
from this bond o the sabbath day	Lk 13:16	
to eat bread o the sabbath day	Lk 14:1	
lawful to heal o the sabbath day	Lk 14:3	
pull him out o the sabbath day	Lk 14:5	1722
he layeth it o his shoulders,	Lk 15:5	1909
fell o his neck, and kissed him	Lk 15:20	1909
the best robe, and put it o him	Lk 15:22	1746
o his hand, and shoes o his feet	Lk 15:22	1519
Father Abraham, have mercy o me	Lk 16:24	
Jesus, Master, have mercy o us	Lk 17:13	
fell down o his face at his feet,	Lk 17:16	1909
shall he find faith o the earth	Lk 18:8	1909
entreated, and spitted o	Lk 18:32	1716
son of David, have mercy o me	Lk 18:38	
son of David, have mercy o me	Lk 18:39	
and keep thee in o every side	Lk 19:43	3840
that o one of those days, as he	Lk 20:1	1722
but o whomsoever it shall fall,	Lk 20:18	1909
hour sought to lay hands o him	Lk 20:19	1909
Sit thou o my right hand,	Lk 20:42	1537
they shall lay their hands o you	Lk 21:12	1909
which are coming o the earth	Lk 21:26	1904
For as a snare shall it come o	Lk 21:35	1909
o the face of the whole earth	Lk 21:35	1909
me is with me o the table	Lk 22:21	1909
sit o thrones judging the twelve	Lk 22:30	1909
him, they struck him o the face	Lk 22:64	
shall the Son of man sit o the	Lk 22:69	1537
o him they laid the cross, that	Lk 23:26	2007
say to the mountains, Fall o us	Lk 23:30	1909
one o the right hand	Lk 23:33	1537
and the other o the left	Lk 23:33	1537
which were hanged railed o him	Lk 23:39	
and the sabbath drew o	Lk 23:54	2020
be endued with power from o high	Lk 24:49	
to them that believe o his name	Jn 1:12	1519
descending, and remaining o him	Jn 1:33	1909
and his disciples believed o him	Jn 2:11	1519
He that believeth o him is not	Jn 3:18	1519
He that believeth o the Son hath	Jn 3:36	1519
the wrath of God abideth o him	Jn 3:36	1909
his journey, sat thus o the well	Jn 4:6	1909
your eyes, and look o the fields	Jn 4:35	
of that city believed o him for	Jn 4:39	1519
o the same day was the sabbath	Jn 5:9	1722
these things o the sabbath day	Jn 5:16	1722
believeth o him that sent me,	Jn 5:24	
he did o them that were diseased	Jn 6:2	1909
they see Jesus walking o the sea	Jn 6:19	1909
when the people which stood o the	Jn 6:22	
when they had found him o the	Jn 6:25	
that ye believe o him whom he	Jn 6:29	1519
he that believeth o me shall	Jn 6:35	1519
seeth the Son, and believeth o him	Jn 6:40	1519
He that believeth o me hath	Jn 6:47	1519
ye o the sabbath day circumcise a	Jn 7:22	1722
If a man o the sabbath day	Jn 7:23	1722
whit whole o the sabbath day	Jn 7:23	1722
but no man laid hands o him	Jn 7:30	1909
many of the people believed o him	Jn 7:31	1519
He that believeth o me, as the	Jn 7:38	1519
that believe o him should receive	Jn 7:39	1519
but no man laid hands o him	Jn 7:44	1909
of the Pharisees believed o him	Jn 7:48	1519
his finger wrote o the ground	Jn 8:6	1519
down, and wrote o the ground	Jn 8:8	1519
and no man laid hands o him	Jn 8:20	
these words, many believed o him	Jn 8:30	1519
those Jews which believed o him	Jn 8:31	
he spat o the ground, and made	Jn 9:6	5476
thou believe o the Son of God	Jn 9:35	1519
Lord, that I might believe o him	Jn 9:36	1519
And many believed o him there	Jn 10:42	1519
which Jesus did, believed o him	Jn 11:45	1519
alone, all men will believe o him	Jn 11:48	1519
went away, and believed o Jesus	Jn 12:11	1519
O the next day much people that	Jn 12:12	
cometh, sitting o an ass's colt	Jn 12:15	1909
them, yet they believed not o him	Jn 12:37	1519
rulers also many believed o him	Jn 12:42	1519
and said, He that believeth o me	Jn 12:44	1519
not o me, but o him that sent me	Jn 12:44	1519
that whosoever believeth o me	Jn 12:46	1519
disciples looked one o another	Jn 13:22	1519
Now there was leaning o Jesus'	Jn 13:23	1722
He then lying o Jesus' breast	Jn 13:25	1909
unto you, He that believeth o me	Jn 14:12	1519
because they believe not o me	Jn 16:9	1519
I have glorified thee o the earth	Jn 17:4	1909
believe o me through their word	Jn 17:20	1519
put it o his head	Jn 19:2	2007
they put o him a purple robe,	Jn 19:2	4016
o either side one, and Jesus in	Jn 19:18	1782
a title, and put it o the cross	Jn 19:19	1909
upon the cross o the sabbath day	Jn 19:31	1722
They shall look o him whom they	Jn 19:37	1519
had said this, he breathed o them	Jn 20:22	1720
o this wise shewed he himself	Jn 21:1	
now come, Jesus stood o the shore	Jn 21:4	1519
Cast the net o the right side of	Jn 21:6	1519
which also leaned o his breast at	Jn 21:20	1909
And o my servants and o my	Acts 2:18	1909
that whosoever shall call o the	Acts 2:21	1941
for he is o my right hand, that I	Acts 2:25	1537
up Christ to sit o his throne	Acts 2:30	1909
Sit thou o my right hand,	Acts 2:34	1537
him with John, said, Look o us	Acts 3:4	1519
or why look ye so earnestly o us	Acts 3:12	1909
And they laid hands o them	Acts 4:3	
And it came to pass o the morrow	Acts 4:5	1909
o whom this miracle of healing	Acts 4:22	1909
great fear came o all them that	Acts 5:5	1909
the streets, and laid them o beds	Acts 5:15	1909
laid their hands o the apostles	Acts 5:18	1909
whom ye slew and hanged o a tree	Acts 5:30	1909
they laid their hands o them	Acts 6:6	2007
council, looking stedfastly o him	Acts 6:15	1519
not so much as to set his foot o	Acts 7:5	
And God spake o this wise, That	Acts 7:6	
they gnashed o him with their	Acts 7:54	1909
Jesus standing o the right hand	Acts 7:55	1537
standing o the right hand of God	Acts 7:56	1537
Then laid they their hands o them	Acts 8:17	1909
Simon saw that through laying o	Acts 8:18	1936
that o whomsoever I lay hands, he	Acts 8:19	2007
And as they went o their way	Acts 8:36	2596
he went o his way rejoicing	Acts 8:39	
in, and putting his hand o him	Acts 9:12	2007
to bind all that call o thy name	Acts 9:14	
and putting his hands o him said	Acts 9:17	1909
called o this name in Jerusalem	Acts 9:21	1941
And when he looked o him, he was	Acts 10:4	
that waited o him continually	Acts 10:7	4342
O the morrow, as they went o	Acts 10:9	
While Peter thought o the vision	Acts 10:19	4012
o the morrow Peter went away with	Acts 10:23	
whom they slew and hanged o a tree	Acts 10:39	1909
the Holy Ghost fell o all them	Acts 10:44	1909
because that o the Gentiles also	Acts 10:45	1909
o them, as o us at the beginning	Acts 11:15	1909
who believed o the Lord Jesus	Acts 11:17	1909
and he smote Peter o the side	Acts 12:7	
thyself, and bind o thy sandals	Acts 12:8	5265
passed o through one street	Acts 12:10	
and laid their hands o them	Acts 13:3	2007
Holy Ghost, set his eyes o him	Acts 13:9	1519
there fell o him a mist and a	Acts 13:11	1909
the synagogue o the sabbath day	Acts 13:14	
exhortation for the people, say o	Acts 13:15	
he said o this wise, I will give	Acts 13:34	
fell o sleep, and was laid unto	Acts 13:36	
voice, Stand upright o thy feet	Acts 14:10	1909
to the Lord, o whom they believed	Acts 14:23	1519
being brought o their way by the	Acts 15:3	
o the sabbath we went out of the	Acts 16:13	
Believe o the Lord Jesus Christ,	Acts 16:31	1909
and set all the city o an uproar	Acts 17:5	
dwell o all the face of the earth	Acts 17:26	1909
believed o the Lord with all his	Acts 18:8	
no man shall set o thee to hurt	Acts 18:10	2007
that they should believe o him	Acts 19:4	1519
that is, o Christ Jesus	Acts 19:4	1519
them, the Holy Ghost came o them	Acts 19:6	1909
the evil spirit was leaped o them	Acts 19:16	1909
and fear fell o them all, and the	Acts 19:17	1909
ready to depart o the morrow	Acts 20:7	
And Paul went down, and fell o him	Acts 20:10	1968
fell o Paul's neck, and kissed him	Acts 20:37	1909
we left it o the left hand, and	Acts 21:3	
and they all brought us o our way	Acts 21:5	1909
and we kneeled down o the shore	Acts 21:5	1909
four men which have a vow o them	Acts 21:23	1909
the people, and laid hands o him	Acts 21:27	1909
licence, Paul stood o the stairs	Acts 21:40	1909
calling o the name of the Lord	Acts 22:16	1941
them that believed o thee	Acts 22:19	1909
O the morrow, because he would	Acts 22:30	
by him to smite him o the mouth	Acts 23:2	
beasts, that they may set Paul o	Acts 23:24	1913
O the morrow they left the	Acts 23:32	
the next day sitting o the	Acts 25:6	1909
without any delay o the morrow I	Acts 25:17	1909
morrow I sat o the judgment seat	Acts 25:17	1909
o the morrow, when Agrippa was	Acts 25:23	
and no small tempest lay o us	Acts 27:20	1945
And while the day was coming o	Acts 27:33	
some o boards, and some o broken	Acts 27:44	1909
sticks, and laid them o the fire	Acts 28:3	1909
the heat, and fastened o his hand	Acts 28:3	2510
venomous beast hang o his hand	Acts 28:4	1537
prayed, and laid his hands o him	Acts 28:8	2007
not, but believeth o him that	Rom 4:5	1909
if we believe o him that raised	Rom 4:24	1909
I will have mercy o whom I will	Rom 9:15	
I will have compassion o whom I	Rom 9:15	
mercy o whom he will have mercy	Rom 9:18	
his glory o the vessels of mercy	Rom 9:23	1909
whosoever believeth o him shall	Rom 9:33	1909
is of faith speaketh o this wise	Rom 10:6	
Whosoever believeth o him shall	Rom 10:11	1909
How then shall they call o him in	Rom 10:14	1941
o them which fell, severity	Rom 11:22	1909
let us wait o our ministering	Rom 12:7	1722
or he that teacheth, o teaching	Rom 12:7	1722
he that exhorteth, o exhortation	Rom 12:8	1722
heap coals of fire o his head	Rom 12:20	1909
let us put o the armour of light	Rom 13:12	1746
But put ye o the Lord Jesus	Rom 13:14	1746
that reproached thee fell o me	Rom 15:3	1909
and to be brought o my way	Rom 15:24	
who bestowed much labour o us	Rom 16:6	1519
I am glad therefore o your behalf	Rom 16:19	1909
thank my God always o your behalf	1Cor 1:4	4012
ought the woman to have power o	1Cor 11:10	1909
so falling down o his face he	1Cor 14:25	1909
must put o incorruption, and this	1Cor 15:53	1746
mortal must put o immortality	1Cor 15:53	1746
shall have put o incorruption	1Cor 15:54	1746
shall have put o immortality	1Cor 15:54	1746
that ye may bring me o my journey	1Cor 16:6	
for that which was lacking o your	1Cor 16:17	
may be given by many o our behalf	2Cor 1:11	5228
be brought o my way toward Judaea	2Cor 1:16	
We are troubled o every side	2Cor 4:8	1722
occasion to glory o our behalf	2Cor 5:12	5228
o the right hand and o the left,	2Cor 6:7	
but we were troubled o every side	2Cor 7:5	1722
o the churches of Macedonia	2Cor 8:1	1722
and of our boasting o your behalf	2Cor 8:24	5228
Do ye look o things after the	2Cor 10:7	991
if a man smite you o the face	2Cor 11:20	1519
every one that hangeth o a tree	Gal 3:13	1909
come o the Gentiles through Jesus	Gal 3:14	1519
into Christ have put o Christ	Gal 3:27	1746
to this rule, peace be o them	Gal 6:16	1909
in heaven, and which are o earth	Eph 1:10	1909
saith, When he ascended up o high	Eph 4:8	5311
And that ye put o the new man	Eph 4:24	1746
thou mayest live long o the earth	Eph 6:3	1909
Put o the whole armour of God,	Eph 6:11	1746
having o the breastplate of	Eph 6:14	1746
Christ, not only to believe o him	Phil 1:29	1519
not every man o his own things	Phil 2:4	
but every man also o the things	Phil 2:4	
but God had mercy o him	Phil 2:27	
not o him only, but o me also,	Phil 2:27	
any praise, think o these things	Phil 4:8	
where Christ sitteth o the right	Col 3:1	1722
Set your affection o things above	Col 3:2	

not o things o the earth — Col 3:2 — *1909*
o the children of disobedience — Col 3:6 — *1909*
have put o the new man, which is — Col 3:10 — *1746*
Put o therefore, as the elect of — Col 3:12 — *1746*
all these things put o charity — Col 3:14
putting o the breastplate of — 1Th 5:8 — *1746*
o them that know not God, and that — 2Th 1:8
believe o him to life everlasting — 1Ti 1:16 — *1909*
which went before o thee, that — 1Ti 1:18 — *1909*
believed o in the world, received — 1Ti 3:16
with the laying o of the hands of — 1Ti 4:14
Lay hands suddenly o no man — 1Ti 5:22 — *2007*
faith, lay hold o eternal life, — 1Ti 6:12 — *1949*
they may lay hold o eternal life — 1Ti 6:19 — *1949*
thee by the putting o of my hands — 2Ti 1:6 — *1936*
with them that call o the Lord — 2Ti 2:22 — *1941*
Which he shed o us abundantly — Titus 3:6 — *1909*
lawyer and Apollos o their journey — Titus 3:13
ought, put that o mine account — Philem 18 — *1677*
sat down o the right hand of the — Heb 1:3 — *1722*
right hand of the Majesty o high — Heb 1:3 — *1722*
Sit o my right hand, until I make — Heb 1:13 — *1537*
For verily he took not o him the — Heb 2:16 — *1949*
but he took o him the seed of — Heb 2:16 — *1949*
of the seventh day o this wise — Heb 4:4
have compassion o the ignorant — Heb 5:2
o them that are out of the way — Heb 5:2
let us go o unto perfection — Heb 6:1
baptisms, and of laying o of hands — Heb 6:2 — *1936*
who is set o the right hand of — Heb 8:1 — *1722*
For if he were o earth, he should — Heb 8:4 — *1909*
imposed o them until the time of — Heb 9:10
sat down o the right hand of God — Heb 10:12 — *1722*
strangers and pilgrims o the earth — Heb 11:13 — *1909*
refused him that spake o earth — Heb 12:25 — *1909*
setteth o fire the course of — Jas 3:6
and it is set o fire of hell — Jas 3:6
not what shall be o the morrow — Jas 4:14
lived in pleasure o the earth — Jas 5:5 — *1909*
it rained not o the earth by the — Jas 5:17 — *1909*
And if ye call o the Father — 1Pet 1:17 — *1941*
he that believeth o him shall not — 1Pet 2:6 — *1909*
sins in his own body o the tree — 1Pet 2:24 — *1909*
gold, or of putting o of apparel — 1Pet 3:3 — *1745*
is o the right hand of God — 1Pet 3:22 — *1722*
o their part he is evil spoken of — 1Pet 4:14 — *2596*
but o your part he is glorified — 1Pet 4:14 — *2596*
let him glorify God o this behalf — 1Pet 4:16 — *1722*
being o fire shall be dissolved — 2Pet 3:12
That we should believe o the name — 1Jn 3:23
He that believeth o the Son of — 1Jn 5:10 — *1519*
o the name of the Son of God — 1Jn 5:13 — *1519*
that ye may believe o the name of — 1Jn 5:13 — *1519*
whom if thou bring forward o — 3Jn 6
yourselves o your most holy faith — Jude 20
in the Spirit o the Lord's day — Rev 1:10 — *1722*
I will come o thee as a thief, and — Rev 3:3 — *1909*
heaven, and one sat o the throne — Rev 4:2 — *1909*
they had o their heads crowns of — Rev 4:4 — *1909*
to him that sat o the throne — Rev 4:9 — *1909*
before him that sat o the throne — Rev 4:10 — *1909*
sat o the throne a book written — Rev 5:1 — *1909*
o the backside, sealed with seven — Rev 5:1 — *1909*
and we shall reign o the earth — Rev 5:10 — *1909*
o the earth, and under the earth, — Rev 5:13 — *1722*
he that sat o him had a bow — Rev 6:2 — *1909*
he that sat o him had a pair of — Rev 6:5 — *1909*
his name that sat o him was Death — Rev 6:8 — *1883*
avenge our blood o them that — Rev 6:10 — *575*
them that dwell o the earth — Rev 6:10 — *1909*
the mountains and rocks, Fall o us — Rev 6:16 — *1909*
of him that sitteth o the throne — Rev 6:16 — *1909*
I saw four angels standing o the — Rev 7:1 — *1909*
wind should not blow o the earth — Rev 7:1 — *1909*
nor o the sea, nor o any tree — Rev 7:1 — *1909*
before the throne o their faces — Rev 7:11 — *1909*
he that sitteth o the throne — Rev 7:15 — *1909*
shall the sun light o them — Rev 7:16 — *1909*
o their heads were as it were — Rev 9:7 — *1909*
vision, and them that sat o them — Rev 9:17 — *1909*
sea, and his left foot o the earth — Rev 10:2 — *1909*
them that dwelt o the earth — Rev 11:10 — *1909*
sat before God o their seats — Rev 11:16 — *1909*
fire come down from heaven o the — Rev 13:13 — *1519*
deceiveth them that dwell o the — Rev 13:14 — *1909*
to them that dwell o the earth — Rev 13:14 — *1909*
a Lamb stood o the mount Sion, and — Rev 14:1 — *1909*
unto them that dwell o the earth — Rev 14:6 — *1909*
having o his head a golden crown, — Rev 14:14 — *1909*
voice to him that sat o the cloud — Rev 14:15 — *1909*
he that sat o the cloud thrust in — Rev 14:16 — *1909*
thrust in his sickle o the earth — Rev 14:16 — *1909*
stand o the sea of glass, having — Rev 15:2 — *1909*
they that dwell o the earth shall — Rev 17:8 — *1909*
o which the woman sitteth — Rev 17:9 — *1909*
And they cast dust o their heads — Rev 18:19 — *1909*
for God hath avenged you o her — Rev 18:20 — *1537*
God that sat o the throne — Rev 19:4 — *1909*
o his head were many crowns — Rev 19:12 — *1909*
he hath o his vesture and o his — Rev 19:16 — *1909*
and of them that sit o them — Rev 19:18 — *1909*
against him that sat o the horse — Rev 19:19 — *1909*
And he laid hold o the dragon — Rev 20:2
o such the second death hath no — Rev 20:6 — *1909*
they went up o the breadth of the — Rev 20:9 — *1909*
throne, and him that sat o it — Rev 20:11 — *1909*
O the east three gates — Rev 21:13 — *575*
o the north three gates — Rev 21:13 — *575*
o the south three gates — Rev 21:13 — *575*
and o the west three gates — Rev 21:13 — *575*
o either side of the river, was — Rev 22:2 — *1909*

2. Capital of Lower Egypt.
of Poti-pherah priest of O — Gen 41:45 — 204
priest of O bare unto him — Gen 41:50 — 204
priest of O bare unto him — Gen 46:20 — 204

3. Son of Peleth.
Abiram, the sons of Eliab, and O — Num 16:1 — 203

ONAM (*o'-nam*)
1. A son of Shobal.
Manahath, and Ebal, Shepho, and O — Gen 36:23 — 208
Manahath, and Ebal, Shephi, and O — 1Chr 1:40 — 208
2. A son of Jerahmeel.
she was the mother of O — 1Chr 2:26 — 208
And the sons of O were, Shammai, — 1Chr 2:28 — 208

ONAN (*o'-nan*) *A son of Judah.*
and she called his name O — Gen 38:4 — 209
And Judah said unto O, Go in unto — Gen 38:8 — 209
O knew that the seed should not — Gen 38:9 — 209
Er, and O, and Shelah, and Pharez, — Gen 46:12 — 209
O died in the land of Canaan — Gen 46:12 — 209
The sons of Judah were Er and O — Num 26:19 — 209
O died in the land of Canaan — Num 26:19 — 209
Er, and O, and Shelah — 1Chr 2:3 — 209

ONCE
and I will speak yet but this o — Gen 18:32 — 6471
I pray thee, my sin only this o — Ex 10:17 — 6471
atonement upon the horns of it o — Ex 30:10 — 259
o in the year shall he make — Ex 30:10 — 259
for all their sins o a year — Lev 16:34 — 259
Moses, and said, Let us go up at o — Num 13:30
thou mayest not consume them at o — Deut 7:22 — 4118
war, and go round about the city o — Josh 6:3 — 259
the city, going about it o — Josh 6:11 — 259
day they compassed the city o — Josh 6:14 — 259
me, and I will speak but this o — Judg 6:39 — 6471
but this o with the fleece — Judg 6:39 — 6471
saying, Come up this o, for he — Judg 16:18 — 6471
me, I pray thee, only this o — Judg 16:28 — 6471
that I may be at o avenged of the — Judg 16:28
the spear even to the earth at o — 1Sa 26:8
o in three years came the navy of — 1Kin 10:22 — 259
himself there, not o nor twice — 2Kin 6:10 — 259
every three years o came the — 2Chr 9:21 — 259
o in ten days store of all sorts — Neh 5:18 — 996
without Jerusalem o or twice — Neh 13:20 — 6471
For God speaketh o, yea twice, — Job 33:14 — 259
O have I spoken — Job 40:5 — 259
God hath spoken o — Ps 62:11 — 259
work thereof at o with axes — Ps 74:6
thy sight when o thou art angry — Ps 76:7 — 227
O have I sworn by my holiness — Ps 89:35 — 259
in his ways shall fall at o — Prov 28:18 — 259
I will destroy and devour at o — Is 42:14 — 3162
or shall a nation be born at o — Is 66:8 — 6471
inhabitants of the land at this o — Jer 10:18 — 6471
when shall it o be — Jer 13:27 — 5750
I will this o cause them to know, — Jer 16:21 — 6471
Yet o, it is a little while, and I — Hag 2:6 — 259
When o the master of the house is — Lk 13:25
And they cried out all at o — Lk 23:18 — *3826*
that he died, he died unto sin o — Rom 6:10 — *2178*
For I was alive without the law o — Rom 7:9 — *4218*
above five hundred brethren at o — 1Cor 15:6 — *2178*
o was I stoned, thrice I suffered — 2Cor 11:25 — *530*
the faith which o he destroyed — Gal 1:23 — *4218*
let it not be o named among you, — Eph 5:3 — *3366*
even in Thessalonica ye sent o — Phil 4:16 — *530*
come unto you, even I Paul, o — 1Th 2:18 — *530*
for those who were o enlightened — Heb 6:4 — *530*
for this he did o, when he — Heb 7:27 — *2178*
high priest alone o every year — Heb 9:7 — *530*
entered in o into the holy place — Heb 9:12 — *2178*
but now o in the end of the world — Heb 9:26 — *530*
it is appointed unto men o to die — Heb 9:27 — *530*
So Christ was o offered to bear — Heb 9:28 — *530*
because that the worshippers o — Heb 10:2 — *530*
body of Jesus Christ o for all — Heb 10:10 — *2178*
Yet o more I shake not the earth — Heb 12:26 — *530*
Yet o more, signifieth the — Heb 12:27 — *530*
also hath o suffered for sins — 1Pet 3:18 — *530*
when o the longsuffering of God — 1Pet 3:20 — *530*
was o delivered unto the saints — Jude 3 — *530*
though ye o knew this, how that — Jude 5 — *530*

ONE
be gathered together unto o place — Gen 1:9 — 259
he took o of his ribs, and closed — Gen 2:21 — 259
and they shall be o flesh — Gen 2:24 — 259
tree to be desired to make o wise — Gen 3:6
the man is become as o of us — Gen 3:22 — 259
that every o that findeth me — Gen 4:14
the name of the o was Adah — Gen 4:19 — 259
every o after his tongue, after — Gen 10:5 — 376
to be a mighty o in the earth — Gen 10:8
the name of o was Peleg — Gen 10:25 — 259
of o language, and of o speech — Gen 11:1 — 259
they said o to another, Go to, — Gen 11:3 — 376
said, Behold, the people is o — Gen 11:6 — 259
and they have all o language — Gen 11:6 — 259
not understand o another's speech — Gen 11:7 — 376
themselves the o from the other — Gen 13:11 — 376
there came o that had escaped, and — Gen 14:13
o born in my house is mine heir — Gen 15:3
laid each piece o against another — Gen 15:10
This o fellow came in to sojourn, — Gen 19:9 — 259
But he seemed as o that mocked — Gen 19:14
to flee unto, and it is a little o — Gen 19:20
thither, (is it not a little o — Gen 19:20
the child under o of the shrubs — Gen 21:15 — 259
o of the mountains which I will — Gen 22:2 — 259
and if they give not thee o — Gen 24:41
the o people shall be stronger — Gen 25:23
o of the people might lightly — Gen 26:10 — 259
Ahuzzath o of his friends, and — Gen 26:26
morning, and sware o to another — Gen 26:31 — 376
cursed be every o that curseth — Gen 27:29
father, Hast thou but o blessing — Gen 27:38 — 259
also of you both in o day — Gen 27:45 — 259
every o that is not speckled and — Gen 30:33 — 3605
every o that had some white in it — Gen 30:35
when we are absent o from another — Gen 31:49 — 376
If Esau come to the o company — Gen 32:8 — 259
men should overdrive them o day — Gen 33:13 — 259
sister to o that is uncircumcised — Gen 34:14 — 376
you, and we will become o people — Gen 34:16 — 259
to be o people, if every male — Gen 34:22 — 259
they said o to another, Behold, — Gen 37:19 — 376
that the o put out his hand — Gen 38:28
each man his dream in o night — Gen 40:5 — 259
ears of corn came up upon o stalk — Gen 41:5 — 259
And we dreamed a dream in o night — Gen 41:11 — 259
seven ears came up in o stalk — Gen 41:22 — 259
The dream of Pharaoh is o — Gen 41:25 — 259
the dream is o — Gen 41:26 — 259
Can we find such a o as this is — Gen 41:38
Why do ye look o upon another — Gen 42:1
We are all o man's sons — Gen 42:11 — 259
the sons of o man in the land of — Gen 42:13 — 259
day with our father, and o is not — Gen 42:13 — 259
Send o of you, and let him fetch — Gen 42:16 — 259
let o of your brethren be bound — Gen 42:19 — 259
they said o to another, We are — Gen 42:21 — 376
as o of them opened his sack to — Gen 42:27 — 259
saying o to another, What is this — Gen 42:28 — 376
o is not, and the youngest is this — Gen 42:32 — 259
leave o of your brethren here — Gen 42:33 — 259
and the men marvelled o at another — Gen 43:33 — 376
child of his old age, a little o — Gen 44:20
the o went out from me, and I said — Gen 44:28 — 259
o end of the borders of Egypt — Gen 47:21
that o told Joseph, Behold, thy — Gen 48:1
o told Jacob, and said, Behold, — Gen 48:2
thee o portion above thy brethren — Gen 48:22 — 259
as o of the tribes of Israel — Gen 49:16 — 259
every o according to his blessing — Gen 49:28 — 376
the name of the o was Shiphrah — Ex 1:15 — 259
This is o of the Hebrews' — Ex 2:6
an Hebrew, o of his brethren — Ex 2:11
Eleazar Aaron's son took him o of — Ex 6:25
there remained not o — Ex 8:31 — 259
the children of Israel died not o — Ex 9:6 — 259
there was not o of the cattle of — Ex 9:7 — 259
that o cannot be able to see the — Ex 10:5
there remained not o locust in — Ex 10:19 — 259
They saw not o another, neither — Ex 10:23 — 376
Yet will I bring o plague more — Ex 11:1 — 259
eat unleavened bread, until the o — Ex 12:18 — 259
house where there was not o dead — Ex 12:30
In o house shall it be eaten — Ex 12:46 — 259
he shall be as o that is born in — Ex 12:48
O law shall be to him that is — Ex 12:49 — 259
and captains over every o of them — Ex 14:7
so that the o came not near the — Ex 14:20 — 2088
remained not so much as o of them — Ex 14:28 — 259
they said o to another, It is — Ex 16:15 — 376
much bread, two omers for o man — Ex 16:22 — 259
his hands, the o on the o side — Ex 17:12 — 2088
the name of the o was Gershom — Ex 18:3 — 259
and I judge between o and another, — Ex 18:16 — 376
o smite another with a stone, or — Ex 21:18
if o man's ox hurt another's, — Ex 21:35
out from before thee in o year — Ex 23:29 — 259
the people answered with o voice — Ex 24:3 — 259
shall be in the o side of it — Ex 25:12 — 259
And make o cherub on the o end — Ex 25:19 — 259
faces shall look o to another — Ex 25:20
the candlestick out of the o side — Ex 25:32 — 259
a knop and a flower in o branch — Ex 25:33 — 259
all it shall be o beaten work of — Ex 25:36 — 259
The length of o curtain shall be — Ex 26:2 — 259
the breadth of o curtain four — Ex 26:2 — 259
every o of the curtains shall — Ex 26:2
the curtains shall have o measure — Ex 26:2 — 259
be coupled together o to another — Ex 26:3 — 802
shall be coupled o to another — Ex 26:3 — 802
o curtain from the selvedge in — Ex 26:4 — 259
shalt thou make in the o curtain — Ex 26:5 — 259
loops may take hold o of another — Ex 26:5 — 802
and it shall be o tabernacle — Ex 26:6 — 259
The length of o curtain shall be — Ex 26:8 — 259
the breadth of o curtain four — Ex 26:8
shall be all of o measure — Ex 26:8 — 259
o curtain that is outmost in the — Ex 26:10 — 259
tent together, that it may be o — Ex 26:11 — 259
And a cubit on the o side, and a — Ex 26:13
shall be the breadth of o board — Ex 26:16 — 259
tenons shall there be in o board — Ex 26:17 — 259
set in order o against another — Ex 26:17 — 802
two sockets under o board for his — Ex 26:19 — 259
two sockets under o board — Ex 26:21 — 259
above the head of it unto o ring — Ex 26:24 — 259
two sockets under o board — Ex 26:25 — 259
of the o side of the tabernacle — Ex 26:26 — 259
an hundred cubits long for o side — Ex 27:9 — 259
The hangings of o side of the — Ex 27:14
Six of their names on o stone — Ex 28:10 — 259
every o with his name shall they — Ex 28:21 — 376
Take o young bullock, and two rams — Ex 29:1 — 259
thou shalt put them into o basket — Ex 29:3 — 259
Thou shalt also take o ram — Ex 29:15 — 259
o loaf of bread, and o cake of — Ex 29:23 — 259
o wafer out of the basket of the — Ex 29:23 — 259
The o lamb thou shalt offer in — Ex 29:39 — 259
with the o lamb a tenth deal of — Ex 29:40 — 259
every o that passeth among them — Ex 30:13
Every o that passeth among them — Ex 30:14
every o that defileth it shall — Ex 31:14
on the o side and on the other — Ex 32:15
that every o which sought the — Ex 33:7
o call thee, and thou eat of his — Ex 34:15
every o whose heart stirred him — Ex 35:21

O

every o whom his spirit made ... Ex 35:21
Every o that did offer an ... Ex 35:24
even every o whose heart stirred ... Ex 36:2
The length of o curtain was ... Ex 36:9 259
the breadth of o curtain four ... Ex 36:9
the curtains were all of o size ... Ex 36:9 259
the five curtains o unto another ... Ex 36:10 259
he coupled o unto another ... Ex 36:10 259
of o curtain from the selvedge in ... Ex 36:11 259
Fifty loops made he in o curtain ... Ex 36:12 259
the loops held o curtain to ... Ex 36:12 259
coupled the curtains o unto ... Ex 36:13 259
so it became o tabernacle ... Ex 36:13 259
The length of o curtain was ... Ex 36:15 259
was the breadth of o curtain ... Ex 36:15 259
eleven curtains were of o size ... Ex 36:15 259
tent together, that it might be o ... Ex 36:18 259
and the breadth of a board o cubit ... Ex 36:21
O board had two tenons ... Ex 36:22
equally distant o from another ... Ex 36:22 259
two sockets under o board for his ... Ex 36:24 259
two sockets under o board ... Ex 36:26 259
at the head thereof, to o ring ... Ex 36:29 259
of the o side of the tabernacle ... Ex 36:31 259
from the o end to the other ... Ex 36:33
two rings upon the o side of it ... Ex 37:3 259
o cubit and a half the breadth ... Ex 37:6
beaten out of o piece made he ... Ex 37:7
O cherub on the end on this side, ... Ex 37:8 259
with their faces o to another ... Ex 37:9 376
out of the o side thereof ... Ex 37:18
fashion of almonds in o branch ... Ex 37:19 259
all of it was o beaten work of ... Ex 37:22 259
The hangings of the o side of the ... Ex 38:14
for every o that went to be ... Ex 38:26
every o with his name, according ... Ex 39:14 376
if any o of the common people sin ... Lev 4:27 5315
he shall be guilty in o of these ... Lev 5:4 259
be guilty in o of these things ... Lev 5:5 259
o for a sin offering, and the ... Lev 5:7 259
that he hath sinned in o of these ... Lev 5:13 259
every o that toucheth them shall ... Lev 6:18
there is o law for them ... Lev 7:7 259
Aaron have, o as much as another ... Lev 7:10 376
of it he shall offer o out of the ... Lev 7:14 259
he took o unleavened cake, and a ... Lev 8:26 259
o wafer, and put them on the fat, ... Lev 8:26 259
every o that toucheth them shall ... Lev 11:26 259
the o for the burnt offering, and ... Lev 12:8 259
or unto o of his sons the priests ... Lev 13:2 259
o of the birds be killed in an ... Lev 14:5 259
o ewe lamb of the first year ... Lev 14:10 259
mingled with oil, and o log of oil ... Lev 14:10 259
the priest shall take o he lamb ... Lev 14:12 259
then he shall take o lamb for a ... Lev 14:21 259
o tenth deal of fine flour ... Lev 14:21 259
the o shall be a sin offering, and ... Lev 14:22 259
offer the o of the turtledoves ... Lev 14:30 259
the o for a sin offering, and the ... Lev 14:31 259
he shall kill the o of the birds ... Lev 14:50 259
the o for a sin offering, and the ... Lev 15:15 259
offer the o for a sin offering ... Lev 15:30 259
o ram for a burnt offering ... Lev 16:5 259
o lot for the LORD, and the other ... Lev 16:8 259
shall o carry forth without the ... Lev 16:27
whether it be o of your own ... Lev 16:29
whether it be o of your own ... Lev 17:15
that ye commit not any o of these ... Lev 18:30
Therefore every o that eateth it ... Lev 19:8
falsely, neither lie o to another ... Lev 19:11 376
be unto you as o born among you ... Lev 19:34
For every o that curseth his ... Lev 20:9 376
it and her young both in o day ... Lev 22:28 259
o young bullock, and two rams ... Lev 23:18 259
Then ye shall sacrifice o kid of ... Lev 23:19 259
tenth deals shall be in o cake ... Lev 24:5 259
Ye shall have o manner of law ... Lev 24:22 259
as for o of your own country ... Lev 24:22
ye shall not oppress o another ... Lev 25:14 376
not therefore oppress o another ... Lev 25:17 376
ye shall not rule o over another ... Lev 25:46 376
o of his brethren may redeem him ... Lev 25:48 259
shall bake your bread in o oven ... Lev 26:26 259
And they shall fall o upon another ... Lev 26:37 376
every o head of the house of his ... Num 1:4 376
o thousand and five hundred ... Num 1:41 259
each o was for the house of his ... Num 1:44 259
o thousand and four hundred and ... Num 2:16 259
o thousand and five hundred ... Num 2:28 259
every o after their families, ... Num 2:34 376
them every o to his service ... Num 4:19 376
every o that entereth into the ... Num 4:30
every o that entereth into the ... Num 4:35
every o that entereth into the ... Num 4:39
every o that entereth into the ... Num 4:43
every o that came to do the ... Num 4:47
every o according to his service, ... Num 4:49 376
every o that hath an issue, and ... Num 5:2
offer the o for a sin offering ... Num 6:11 259
o he lamb of the first year ... Num 6:14 259
o ewe lamb of the first year ... Num 6:14 259
o ram without blemish for peace ... Num 6:14 259
o unleavened cake out of the ... Num 6:19 259
o unleavened wafer, and shall put ... Num 6:19 259
the princes, and for each o an ox ... Num 7:3
his offering was o silver charger ... Num 7:13 259
o silver bowl of seventy shekels, ... Num 7:13 259
O spoon of ten shekels of gold, ... Num 7:14 259
O young bullock, o ram ... Num 7:15 259
o lamb of the first year, for a ... Num 7:15 259
O kid of the goats for a sin ... Num 7:16 259
for his offering o silver charger ... Num 7:19 259
o silver bowl of seventy shekels, ... Num 7:19 259
O spoon of gold of ten shekels, ... Num 7:20 259
O young bullock, o ram ... Num 7:21 259
o lamb of the first year, for a ... Num 7:21 259
O kid of the goats for a sin ... Num 7:22 259
His offering was o silver charger ... Num 7:25 259
o silver bowl of seventy shekels, ... Num 7:25 259
O golden spoon of ten shekels, ... Num 7:26 259
O young bullock, o ram ... Num 7:27 259
o lamb of the first year, for a ... Num 7:27 259
O kid of the goats for a sin ... Num 7:28 259
His offering was o silver charger ... Num 7:31 259
o silver bowl of seventy shekels, ... Num 7:31 259
O golden spoon of ten shekels, ... Num 7:32 259
O young bullock, o ram ... Num 7:33 259
o lamb of the first year, for a ... Num 7:33 259
O kid of the goats for a sin ... Num 7:34 259
His offering was o silver charger ... Num 7:37 259
o silver bowl of seventy shekels, ... Num 7:37 259
O golden spoon of ten shekels, ... Num 7:38 259
O young bullock, o ram ... Num 7:39 259
o lamb of the first year, for a ... Num 7:39 259
O kid of the goats for a sin ... Num 7:40 259
His offering was o silver charger ... Num 7:43 259
o silver bowl of seventy shekels, ... Num 7:43 259
O golden spoon of ten shekels, ... Num 7:44 259
O young bullock, o ram ... Num 7:45 259
o lamb of the first year, for a ... Num 7:45 259
O kid of the goats for a sin ... Num 7:46 259
His offering was o silver charger ... Num 7:49 259
o silver bowl of seventy shekels, ... Num 7:49 259
O golden spoon of ten shekels, ... Num 7:50 259
O young bullock, o ram ... Num 7:51 259
o lamb of the first year, for a ... Num 7:51 259
O kid of the goats for a sin ... Num 7:52 259
His offering was o silver charger ... Num 7:55 259
o silver bowl of seventy shekels, ... Num 7:55 259
O golden spoon of ten shekels, ... Num 7:56 259
O young bullock, o ram ... Num 7:57 259
o lamb of the first year, for a ... Num 7:57 259
O kid of the goats for a sin ... Num 7:58 259
His offering was o silver charger ... Num 7:61 259
o silver bowl of seventy shekels, ... Num 7:61 259
O golden spoon of ten shekels, ... Num 7:62 259
O young bullock, o ram ... Num 7:63 259
o lamb of the first year, for a ... Num 7:63 259
O kid of the goats for a sin ... Num 7:64 259
His offering was o silver charger ... Num 7:67 259
o silver bowl of seventy shekels, ... Num 7:67 259
O golden spoon of ten shekels, ... Num 7:68 259
O young bullock, o ram ... Num 7:69 259
o lamb of the first year, for a ... Num 7:69 259
O kid of the goats for a sin ... Num 7:70 259
His offering was o silver charger ... Num 7:73 259
o silver bowl of seventy shekels, ... Num 7:73 259
O golden spoon of ten shekels, ... Num 7:74 259
O young bullock, o ram ... Num 7:75 259
o lamb of the first year, for a ... Num 7:75 259
O kid of the goats for a sin ... Num 7:76 259
His offering was o silver charger ... Num 7:79 259
o silver bowl of seventy shekels, ... Num 7:79 259
O golden spoon of ten shekels, ... Num 7:80 259
O young bullock, o ram ... Num 7:81 259
o lamb of the first year, for a ... Num 7:81 259
O kid of the goats for a sin ... Num 7:82 259
then he heard the voice of o ... Num 7:89
offer the o for a sin offering ... Num 8:12 259
ye shall have o ordinance ... Num 9:14 259
if they blow but with o trumpet ... Num 10:4 259
Ye shall not eat o day, nor two ... Num 11:19 259
camp, the name of the o was Eldad ... Num 11:26 259
o of his young men, answered and ... Num 11:28
Let her not be as o dead, of whom ... Num 12:12
every o a ruler among them ... Num 13:2
a branch with o cluster of grapes ... Num 13:23 259
they said o to another, Let us ... Num 14:4 376
kill all this people as o man ... Num 14:15 259
offering or sacrifice, for o lamb ... Num 15:5 259
for o bullock, or for o ram ... Num 15:11 259
so shall ye do to every o ... Num 15:12 259
O ordinance shall be both for you ... Num 15:15 259
O law and o manner shall be for ... Num 15:16 259
offer o young bullock for a burnt ... Num 15:24 259
o kid of the goats for a sin ... Num 15:24 259
Ye shall have o law for him that ... Num 15:29 259
every o of them, and the LORD is ... Num 16:3
I have not taken o ass from them ... Num 16:15 259
neither have I hurt o of them ... Num 16:15 259
shall o man sin, and wilt thou be ... Num 16:22 259
take of every o of them a rod ... Num 17:2
for o rod shall be for the head ... Num 17:3 259
every o of their princes gave him ... Num 17:6
a rod apiece, for each prince o ... Num 17:6 259
every o that is clean in thy ... Num 18:11
every o that is clean in thine ... Num 18:13
o shall slay her before his face ... Num 19:3
o shall burn the heifer in his ... Num 19:5
whosoever toucheth o that is ... Num 19:16
o slain, or o dead, or a grave ... Num 19:18
that every o that is bitten, when ... Num 21:8
Slay ye every o his men that were ... Num 25:5 376
o of the children of Israel came ... Num 25:6 376
to every o shall his inheritance ... Num 26:54 376
The o lamb shalt thou offer in ... Num 28:4 259
part of an hin for the o lamb ... Num 28:7 259
o ram, seven lambs of the first ... Num 28:11 259
mingled with oil, for o bullock ... Num 28:12 259
mingled with oil, for o ram ... Num 28:12 259
for a meat offering unto o lamb ... Num 28:13 259
o kid of the goats for a sin ... Num 28:15 259
o ram, and seven lambs of the ... Num 28:19 259
o goat for a sin offering, to ... Num 28:22 259
o ram, seven lambs of the first ... Num 28:27 259
three tenth deals unto o bullock ... Num 28:28 259
two tenth deals unto o ram ... Num 28:28 259
A several tenth deal unto o lamb ... Num 28:29 259
o kid of the goats, to make an ... Num 28:30 259
o young bullock, o ram, and ... Num 29:2 259
o tenth deal for o lamb ... Num 29:4 259
And o tenth deal for o lamb ... Num 29:4 259
o kid of the goats for a sin ... Num 29:5 259
o young bullock, o ram, and ... Num 29:8 259
o ram, and seven lambs of the ... Num 29:8 259
and two tenth deals to o ram ... Num 29:9 259
A several tenth deal for o lamb ... Num 29:10 259
O kid of the goats for a sin ... Num 29:11 259
o kid of the goats for a sin ... Num 29:16 259
o kid of the goats for a sin ... Num 29:19 259
o goat for a sin offering ... Num 29:22 259
o kid of the goats for a sin ... Num 29:25 259
o goat for a sin offering ... Num 29:28 259
o goat for a sin offering ... Num 29:31 259
o goat for a sin offering ... Num 29:34 259
o bullock, o ram, seven lambs ... Num 29:36 259
o goat for a sin offering ... Num 29:38 259
o soul of five hundred, both of ... Num 31:28 259
thou shalt take o portion of ... Num 31:30 259
threescore and o thousand asses, ... Num 31:34 259
tribute was threescore and o ... Num 31:39 259
Moses took o portion of fifty, ... Num 31:47 259
and there lacketh not o man of us ... Num 31:49
ye shall take o prince of every ... Num 34:18 259
every o shall give of his cities ... Num 35:8 376
that every o that killeth any ... Num 35:15
but o witness shall not testify ... Num 35:30 259
for every o of the children of ... Num 36:7 376
shall be wife unto o of the ... Num 36:8 259
from o tribe to another tribe ... Num 36:9
but every o of the tribes of the ... Num 36:9 376
came near unto me every o of you ... Deut 1:22
twelve men of you, o of a tribe ... Deut 1:23 259
Surely there shall not o of these ... Deut 1:35 376
there was not o city too strong ... Deut 2:36
are alive every o of you this day ... Deut 4:4
ask from the o side of heaven ... Deut 4:32
that fleeing unto o of these ... Deut 4:42 259
The LORD our God is o LORD ... Deut 6:4 259
shall choose in o of thy tribes ... Deut 12:14 259
from the o end of the earth even ... Deut 13:7
shalt hear say in o of thy cities ... Deut 13:12 259
be among you a poor man of o of ... Deut 15:7 259
but at the mouth of o witness he ... Deut 17:6 259
o from among thy brethren shalt ... Deut 17:15
any o that maketh his son or his ... Deut 18:10
shall flee unto o of those cities ... Deut 19:5 259
fleeth into o of these cities ... Deut 19:11 259
O witness shall not rise up ... Deut 19:15 259
If o be found slain in the land ... Deut 21:1
o beloved, and another hated, and ... Deut 21:15 259
he shall choose in o of thy gates ... Deut 23:16 259
he shall be free at home o year ... Deut 24:5 259
o of them die, and have no child, ... Deut 25:5 259
strive together o with another ... Deut 25:11 259
the wife of the o draweth near ... Deut 25:11 259
shall come out against thee o way ... Deut 28:7 259
shalt go out o way against them ... Deut 28:25 259
toward her young o that cometh ... Deut 28:57
from the o end of the earth even ... Deut 28:64 259
How should o chase a thousand, and ... Deut 32:30 259
every o shall receive of thy ... Deut 33:3
and thy Urim be with thy holy o ... Deut 33:8
and with Israel, with o accord ... Josh 9:2 259
as o of the royal cities, and ... Josh 10:2 259
land did Joshua take at o time ... Josh 10:42 259
The king of Jericho, o ... Josh 12:9 259
of Ai, which is beside Beth-el, o ... Josh 12:9 259
The king of Jerusalem, o ... Josh 12:10 259
the king of Hebron, o ... Josh 12:10 259
The king of Jarmuth, o ... Josh 12:11 259
the king of Lachish, o ... Josh 12:11 259
The king of Eglon, o ... Josh 12:12 259
the king of Gezer, o ... Josh 12:12 259
The king of Debir, o ... Josh 12:13 259
the king of Geder, o ... Josh 12:13 259
The king of Hormah, o ... Josh 12:14 259
the king of Arad, o ... Josh 12:14 259
The king of Libnah, o ... Josh 12:15 259
the king of Adullam, o ... Josh 12:15 259
The king of Makkedah, o ... Josh 12:16 259
the king of Beth-el, o ... Josh 12:16 259
The king of Tappuah, o ... Josh 12:17 259
the king of Hepher, o ... Josh 12:17 259
The king of Aphek, o ... Josh 12:18 259
the king of Lasharon, o ... Josh 12:18 259
The king of Madon, o ... Josh 12:19 259
the king of Hazor, o ... Josh 12:19 259
The king of Shimron-meron, o ... Josh 12:20 259
the king of Achshaph, o ... Josh 12:20 259
The king of Taanach, o ... Josh 12:21 259
the king of Megiddo, o ... Josh 12:21 259
The king of Kedesh, o ... Josh 12:22 259
the king of Jokneam of Carmel, o ... Josh 12:22 259
of Dor in the coast of Dor, o ... Josh 12:23 259
king of the nations of Gilgal, o ... Josh 12:23 259
The king of Tirzah, o ... Josh 12:24 259
all the kings thirty and o ... Josh 12:24 259
even to the o half of the ... Josh 13:31
Why hast thou given me but o lot ... Josh 17:14 259
o portion to inherit, seeing I am ... Josh 17:14 259
thou shalt not have o lot only ... Josh 17:17 259
when he that doth flee unto o of ... Josh 20:4 259
These cities were every o with ... Josh 21:42
Now to the o half of the tribe of ... Josh 22:7
each o was an head of the house ... Josh 22:14 376
O man of you shall chase a ... Josh 23:10 259
that not o thing hath failed of ... Josh 23:14 259
not o thing hath failed thereof ... Josh 23:14 259
smite the Midianites as o man ... Judg 6:16 259
they said o to another, Who hath ... Judg 6:29 376
because o hath cast down his ... Judg 6:31
Every o that lappeth of the water ... Judg 7:5

likewise every o that boweth down ... Judg 7:5
each o resembled the children of ... Judg 8:18 259
you, or that o reign over you ... Judg 9:2 259
and ten persons, upon o stone ... Judg 9:5 259
upon o stone, and have made ... Judg 9:18 259
of Gilead said o to another ... Judg 10:18 376
thou art o of them that trouble ... Judg 11:35 259
was buried in o of the cities of ... Judg 12:7
we will give thee every o of us ... Judg 16:5 376
of the o with his right hand, and ... Judg 16:29 259
and consecrated o of his sons ... Judg 17:5 259
man was unto him as o of his sons ... Judg 17:11 259
a priest unto the house of o man ... Judg 18:19 259
let us draw near to o of these ... Judg 19:13 259
was gathered together as o man ... Judg 20:1 259
And all the people arose as o man ... Judg 20:8 259
the city, knit together as o man ... Judg 20:11 259
every o could sling stones at an ... Judg 20:16
of which o goeth up to the house ... Judg 20:31 259
to day o tribe lacking in Israel ... Judg 21:3 259
There is o tribe cut off from ... Judg 21:6 259
What o is there of the tribes of ... Judg 21:8 259
the name of the o was Orpah ... Ruth 1:4 259
like unto o of thine handmaidens ... Ruth 2:13 259
unto us, o of our next kinsmen ... Ruth 2:20
up before o could know another ... Ruth 3:14
unto whom he said, Ho, such a o ... Ruth 4:1 492
the name of the o was Hannah ... 1Sa 1:2 259
o ephah of flour, and a bottle of ... 1Sa 1:24 259
If o man sin against another, the ... 1Sa 2:25
in o day they shall die both of ... 1Sa 2:34 259
that every o that is left in ... 1Sa 2:36
into o of the priests' offices, ... 1Sa 2:36 259
o that heareth it shall tingle ... 1Sa 3:11
for o plague was on you all, and ... 1Sa 6:4 259
for Ashdod o, for Gaza o ... 1Sa 6:17 259
o, for Askelon o, for Gath o ... 1Sa 6:17 259
for Ekron o ... 1Sa 6:17 259
Take now o of the servants with ... 1Sa 9:3 259
o carrying three kids, and another ... 1Sa 10:3 259
then the people said o to another ... 1Sa 10:11 376
o of the same place answered and ... 1Sa 10:12 376
and they came out with o consent ... 1Sa 11:7 259
Saul reigned o year ... 1Sa 13:1
o company turned unto the way ... 1Sa 13:17 259
was a sharp rock on the o side ... 1Sa 14:4 2088
and the name of the o was Bozez ... 1Sa 14:4 259
The forefront of the o was ... 1Sa 14:5 259
went on beating down o another ... 1Sa 14:16
Then answered o of the people ... 1Sa 14:28
unto all Israel, Be ye on o side ... 1Sa 14:40 259
there shall not o hair of his ... 1Sa 14:45
Then answered o of the servants, ... 1Sa 16:18 259
stood on a mountain on the o side ... 1Sa 17:3 2088
o bearing a shield went before ... 1Sa 17:7
Philistine shall be as o of them ... 1Sa 17:36 259
the women answered o another as ... 1Sa 18:7
son in law in the o of the twain ... 1Sa 18:21
o said, Behold, they be at Naioth ... 1Sa 19:22
o from the face of the earth ... 1Sa 20:15 376
and they kissed o another, and wept ... 1Sa 20:41 376
wept o with another, until David ... 1Sa 20:41 376
did they not sing o to another of ... 1Sa 21:11
every o that was in distress, and ... 1Sa 22:2 376
every o that was in debt, and ... 1Sa 22:2 376
every o that was discontented, ... 1Sa 22:2 376
Jesse give every o of you fields ... 1Sa 22:7
o of the sons of Ahimelech the ... 1Sa 22:20 259
But o of the young men told ... 1Sa 25:14 259
for there came o of the people in ... 1Sa 26:15 259
as when o doth hunt a partridge ... 1Sa 26:20
let o of the young men come over ... 1Sa 26:22 259
I shall now perish o day by the ... 1Sa 27:1 259
of whom they sang o to another in ... 1Sa 29:5
David called o of the young men, ... 2Sa 1:15 259
the o on the o side of the pool ... 2Sa 2:13 428
the o on the o side of the pool ... 2Sa 2:13 2088
they caught every o his fellow by ... 2Sa 2:16 376
thee hold on o of the young men ... 2Sa 2:21 259
after Abner, and became o troop ... 2Sa 2:25 259
o from following his brother ... 2Sa 2:27 376
but o thing I require of thee, ... 2Sa 3:13 259
of Joab o that hath an issue ... 2Sa 3:29
the name of the o was Baanah ... 2Sa 4:2 259
When o told me, saying, Behold, ... 2Sa 4:10
to every o a cake of bread, and a ... 2Sa 6:19 376
departed every o to his house ... 2Sa 6:19 376
as o of the vain fellows ... 2Sa 6:20 259
what o nation in the earth is ... 2Sa 7:23 259
with o full line to keep alive ... 2Sa 8:2
my table, as o of the king's sons ... 2Sa 9:11 259
shaved off the o half of their ... 2Sa 10:4
o said, Is not this Bath-sheba, ... 2Sa 11:3
devoureth o as well as another ... 2Sa 11:25 2088
him, There were two men in o city ... 2Sa 12:1 259
the o rich, and the other poor ... 2Sa 12:1 259
save o little ewe lamb, which he ... 2Sa 12:3 259
thou shalt be as o of the fools ... 2Sa 13:13 259
and there is not o of them left ... 2Sa 13:30 259
but the o smote the other, and ... 2Sa 14:6 259
there shall not o hair of thy son ... 2Sa 14:11
speak o word unto my lord the ... 2Sa 14:12
this thing as o which is faulty ... 2Sa 14:13
o daughter, whose name was Tamar ... 2Sa 14:27 259
Thy servant is of o of the tribes ... 2Sa 15:2 259
o told David, saying, Ahithophel ... 2Sa 15:31
shall not be left so much as o ... 2Sa 17:12 259
until there be not o small stone ... 2Sa 17:13 1571
o of them that was not gone over ... 2Sa 17:22 259
Israel fled every o to his tent ... 2Sa 18:17 376
not tarry o with thee this night ... 2Sa 19:7 376
Judah, even as the heart of o man ... 2Sa 19:14 259
o of Joab's men stood by him, and ... 2Sa 20:11 376
when he saw that every o that ... 2Sa 20:12

I am o of them that are peaceable ... 2Sa 20:19
hundred, whom he slew at o time ... 2Sa 23:8 259
o of the three mighty men with ... 2Sa 23:9
Oh that o would give me drink of ... 2Sa 23:15
of Joab was o of the thirty ... 2Sa 23:24
choose thee o of them, that I may ... 2Sa 24:12 259
which hath given o to sit on my ... 1Kin 1:48
now I ask o petition of thee, ... 1Kin 2:16 259
I desire o small petition of thee ... 1Kin 2:20 259
the o woman said, O my lord, I and ... 1Kin 3:17 259
I and this woman dwell in o house ... 1Kin 3:17 259
The o saith, This is my son that ... 1Kin 3:23 2063
in two, and give half to the o ... 1Kin 3:25 259
Solomon's provision for o day was ... 1Kin 4:22 259
was the o wing of the cherub ... 1Kin 6:24 259
from the uttermost part of the o ... 1Kin 6:24
were of o measure and o size ... 1Kin 6:25 259
The height of the o cherub was ... 1Kin 6:26 259
of the o touched the ... 1Kin 6:27 259
touched the o wall ... 1Kin 6:27
their wings touched o another in ... 1Kin 6:27 3671
leaves of the o door were folding ... 1Kin 6:34 259
o side of the floor to the other ... 1Kin 7:7
the height of the o chapiter was ... 1Kin 7:16 259
seven for the o chapiter, and ... 1Kin 7:17 259
round about upon the o network ... 1Kin 7:18 259
from the o brim to the other ... 1Kin 7:23
cubits was the length of o base ... 1Kin 7:27 259
to the four corners of o base ... 1Kin 7:34 259
to the proportion of every o ... 1Kin 7:36 376
all of them had o casting ... 1Kin 7:37 259
o measure, and o size ... 1Kin 7:37 259
o laver contained forty baths ... 1Kin 7:38 259
o of the ten bases o laver ... 1Kin 7:38 259
of pomegranates for o network ... 1Kin 7:42 259
o sea, and twelve oxen under the ... 1Kin 7:44 259
there hath not failed o word of ... 1Kin 8:56 259
every o that passeth by it shall ... 1Kin 9:8
o year was six hundred threescore ... 1Kin 10:14 259
shekels of gold went to o target ... 1Kin 10:16 259
pound of gold went to o shield ... 1Kin 10:17 259
lions stood there on the o side ... 1Kin 10:20 2088
but will give o tribe to thy son ... 1Kin 11:13 259
(But he shall have o tribe for my ... 1Kin 11:32 259
unto his son will I give o tribe ... 1Kin 11:36 259
And he set the o in Beth-el ... 1Kin 12:29 259
went to worship before the o ... 1Kin 12:30 259
he became o of the priests of the ... 1Kin 13:33
o years old when he began to ... 1Kin 14:21 259
o years reigned he in Jerusalem ... 1Kin 15:10 259
he left him not o that pisseth ... 1Kin 16:11
Ahab went o way by himself, and ... 1Kin 18:6 259
let them choose o bullock for ... 1Kin 18:23 259
of Baal, Choose you o bullock for ... 1Kin 18:25 259
let not o of them escape ... 1Kin 18:40 376
not thy life as the life of o of ... 1Kin 19:2 259
And they slew every o his man ... 1Kin 20:20 376
they pitched o over against the ... 1Kin 20:29 259
hundred thousand footmen in o day ... 1Kin 20:29 259
Jehoshaphat, There is yet o man ... 1Kin 22:8 259
good unto the king with o mouth ... 1Kin 22:13 259
be like the word of o of them ... 1Kin 22:13 259
o said on this manner, and another ... 1Kin 22:20
Hearken, O people, every o of you ... 1Kin 22:28
o washed the chariot in the pool ... 1Kin 22:38
o of the king of Israel's ... 2Kin 3:11 259
and they have smitten o another ... 2Kin 3:23 376
o of the young men, and o of the ... 2Kin 4:22 259
o went out into the field to ... 2Kin 4:39 259
o went in, and told his lord, ... 2Kin 5:4
o said, Be content, I pray thee, ... 2Kin 6:3 259
But as o was felling a beam, the ... 2Kin 6:5 259
o of his servants said, None, my ... 2Kin 6:12 259
they said o to another, Why sit ... 2Kin 7:3 376
they said o to another, Lo, the ... 2Kin 7:6 376
the camp, they went into o tent ... 2Kin 7:8 259
Then they said o to another ... 2Kin 7:9 376
o of his servants answered and ... 2Kin 7:13 259
he reigned o year in Jerusalem ... 2Kin 8:26 259
Elisha the prophet called o of ... 2Kin 9:1 259
o said unto him, Is all well ... 2Kin 9:11
So there went o on horseback to ... 2Kin 9:18
was full from o end to another ... 2Kin 10:21 6310
even the money of every o that ... 2Kin 12:4
on the right side as o cometh ... 2Kin 12:9 376
let us look o another in the face ... 2Kin 14:8
looked o another in the face at ... 2Kin 14:11
and reigned forty and o years ... 2Kin 14:23 259
Carry thither o of the priests ... 2Kin 17:27 259
Then o of the priests whom they ... 2Kin 17:28 259
of o captain of the least of my ... 2Kin 18:24 259
every o of his fig tree, and drink ... 2Kin 18:31 376
drink ye every o the waters of ... 2Kin 18:31 376
even against the Holy O of Israel ... 2Kin 19:22
Jerusalem from o end to another ... 2Kin 21:16
thirty and o years in Jerusalem ... 2Kin 22:1 259
of every o according to his ... 2Kin 23:35 376
o years old when he began to ... 2Kin 24:18 259
o sea, and the bases which Solomon ... 2Kin 25:16 259
The height of the o pillar was ... 2Kin 25:17 259
the name of the o was Peleg ... 1Chr 1:19 259
o of the Levites, who was the ... 1Chr 9:31
of o that had a familiar spirit ... 1Chr 10:13
hundred slain by him at o time ... 1Chr 11:11 259
who was o of the three mighties ... 1Chr 11:12
Oh that o would give me drink of ... 1Chr 11:17
o of the least was over an ... 1Chr 12:14 259
war, seven thousand and o hundred ... 1Chr 12:25
of o heart to make David king ... 1Chr 12:38 259
And he dealt to every o of Israel ... 1Chr 16:3 376
to every o a loaf of bread, and a ... 1Chr 16:3 376
from o kingdom to another people ... 1Chr 16:20
from o tabernacle to another ... 1Chr 17:5
what o nation in the earth is ... 1Chr 17:21 259

choose thee o of them, that I may ... 1Chr 21:10 259
they were in o reckoning, ... 1Chr 23:11 259
by lot, o sort with another ... 1Chr 24:5 428
o of the Levites, wrote them ... 1Chr 24:6
o principal household being taken ... 1Chr 24:6 259
Eleazar, and o taken for Ithamar ... 1Chr 24:6
The o and twentieth to Jachin, the ... 1Chr 24:17 259
The o and twentieth to Hothir, he, ... 1Chr 25:28 259
having wards o against another, ... 1Chr 26:12
o of the brethren of David ... 1Chr 27:18
o hundred thousand talents of ... 1Chr 29:7
o wing of the ... 2Chr 3:11 259
of the o cherub was five ... 2Chr 3:11
o wing of the other cherub was ... 2Chr 3:12
o on the right hand, and the other ... 2Chr 3:17 259
O sea, and twelve oxen under it ... 2Chr 4:15 259
trumpeters and singers were as o ... 2Chr 5:13 259
to make o sound to be heard in ... 2Chr 5:13 259
when every o shall know his own ... 2Chr 6:29
to every o that passeth by it ... 2Chr 7:21
the o half of the greatness of ... 2Chr 9:6
Solomon in o year was six hundred ... 2Chr 9:13 259
of beaten gold went to o target ... 2Chr 9:15 259
shekels of gold went to o shield ... 2Chr 9:16 259
lions stood there on the o side ... 2Chr 9:19
for Rehoboam was o and forty years ... 2Chr 12:13 259
his fathers, and died in the o ... 2Chr 16:13 259
Jehoshaphat, There is yet o man ... 2Chr 18:7 259
called for o of his officers ... 2Chr 18:8 259
good to the king with o assent ... 2Chr 18:12 259
be like o of theirs, and speak ... 2Chr 18:12 259
o spake saying after this manner, ... 2Chr 18:19
every o helped to destroy another ... 2Chr 20:23
he reigned o year in Jerusalem ... 2Chr 22:2 259
let us see o another in the face ... 2Chr 25:17
they saw o another in the face, ... 2Chr 25:21
o of the king's captains ... 2Chr 26:11
and twenty thousand in o day ... 2Chr 28:6 259
hand of God was to give them o ... 2Chr 30:12 259
for every o that was not clean ... 2Chr 30:17
The good LORD pardon every o ... 2Chr 30:18
even unto every o that entereth ... 2Chr 31:16
Ye shall worship before o altar ... 2Chr 32:12 259
and he reigned in Jerusalem o ... 2Chr 34:1 259
was buried in o of the sepulchres ... 2Chr 35:24
Zedekiah was o and twenty years ... 2Chr 36:11 259
and Judah, every o unto his city ... Ezr 2:1 376
and Gaba, six hundred twenty and o ... Ezr 2:26 259
o thousand drams of gold, and five ... Ezr 2:69
o hundred priests' garments ... Ezr 2:69
together as o man to Jerusalem ... Ezr 3:1 259
of every o that willingly offered ... Ezr 3:5
and they were delivered unto o ... Ezr 5:14
every o to his place, and place ... Ezr 6:5
By number and by weight of every o ... Ezr 8:34
were assembled unto me every o ... Ezr 9:4
from o end to another with their ... Ezr 9:11
o of the sons of Elam, answered ... Ezr 10:2
is this a work of o day or two ... Ezr 10:13 259
o of my brethren, came, he and ... Neh 1:2 259
the son of o of the apothecaries ... Neh 3:8
every o over against his house ... Neh 3:28 376
the wall, every o unto his work ... Neh 4:15 376
every o with ... Neh 4:17
with o of his hands ... Neh 4:17 259
every o had his sword girded by ... Neh 4:18 376
upon the wall, o far from another ... Neh 4:19
Let every o with his servant ... Neh 4:22 376
saving that every o put them off ... Neh 4:23 376
usury, every o of his brother ... Neh 5:7 376
prepared for me daily was o ox ... Neh 5:18 259
let us meet together in some o of ... Neh 6:2
every o in his watch, and every ... Neh 7:3 376
every o to be over against his ... Neh 7:3 376
to Judah, every o unto his city ... Neh 7:6 376
and Gaba, six hundred twenty and o ... Neh 7:30 259
and Ono, seven hundred twenty and o ... Neh 7:37 259
which took o of the daughters of ... Neh 7:63
as o man into the street that was ... Neh 8:1 259
every o upon the roof of his ... Neh 8:16 376
God o fourth part of the day ... Neh 9:3
every o having knowledge, and ... Neh 10:28
to bring o of ten to dwell in ... Neh 11:1 259
o in his possession in their ... Neh 11:3 376
the son of o of the great men ... Neh 11:14
every o in his inheritance ... Neh 11:20 376
whereof o went on the right hand ... Neh 12:31
were fled every o to his field ... Neh 13:10 376
o of the sons of Joiada, the son ... Neh 13:28 259
Levites, every o in his business ... Neh 13:30 376
being diverse o from another ... Est 1:7 3627
and women, in o day, even upon the ... Est 3:13 259
o of the king's chamberlains, ... Est 4:5
there is o law of his to put him ... Est 4:11 259
of o of the king's most noble ... Est 6:9 376
o of the chamberlains, said ... Est 7:9 259
Upon o day in all the provinces ... Est 8:12 259
of sending portions o to another ... Est 9:19 376
of sending portions o to another ... Est 9:22 376
o that feared God, and eschewed ... Job 1:1
in their houses, every o his day ... Job 1:4 376
o that feareth God, and escheweth ... Job 1:8
o that feareth God, and escheweth ... Job 2:3
Thou speakest as o of the foolish ... Job 2:10 259
they came every o from his own ... Job 2:11 376
and they rent every o his mantle ... Job 2:12 376
man, and envy slayeth the silly o ... Job 5:2
concealed the words of the Holy O ... Job 6:10
the speeches of o that is ... Job 6:26
cannot answer him o of a thousand ... Job 9:3 259
This is o thing, therefore I said ... Job 9:22 259
I am as o mocked of his neighbour ... Job 12:4
or as o man mocketh another, do ... Job 13:9
open thine eyes upon such an o ... Job 14:3

O

of an unclean? not o	Job 14:4	259
Oh that o might plead for a man	Job 16:21	
for I cannot find o wise man	Job 17:10	
me unto him as o of his enemies	Job 19:11	
O dieth in his full strength,	Job 21:23	
But he is in o mind, and who can	Job 23:13	259
They reap every o his corn in the	Job 24:6	
if o know them, they are in the	Job 24:17	
as o that comforteth the mourners	Job 29:25	
did not o fashion us in the womb	Job 31:15	259
Oh that o would hear me	Job 31:35	
o among a thousand, to shew unto	Job 33:23	259
behold every o that is proud, and	Job 40:11	
Look on every o that is proud	Job 40:12	
shall not o be cast down even at	Job 41:9	
O is so near to another, that no	Job 41:16	259
They are joined o to another	Job 41:17	376
o would think the deep to be	Job 41:32	
every o an earring of gold	Job 42:11	376
vanity every o with his neighbour	Ps 12:2	376
none that doeth good, no, not o	Ps 14:3	259
thine Holy O to see corruption	Ps 16:10	
O thing have I desired of the	Ps 27:4	259
doth every o speak of his glory	Ps 29:9	
For this shall every o that is	Ps 32:6	
not o of them is broken	Ps 34:20	259
as o that mourneth for his mother	Ps 35:14	
thou afraid when o is made rich	Ps 49:16	376
altogether such an o as thyself	Ps 50:21	
Every o of them is gone back	Ps 53:3	
none that doeth good, no, not o	Ps 53:3	259
let every o of them pass away	Ps 58:8	
every o that sweareth by him	Ps 63:11	
inward thought of every o of them	Ps 64:6	376
an o as goeth on still in his	Ps 68:21	
till every o submit himself with	Ps 68:30	
power to every o that is to come	Ps 71:18	
the harp, O thou Holy O of Israel	Ps 71:22	
As a dream when o awaketh	Ps 73:20	
he putteth down o, and setteth up	Ps 75:7	
and limited the Holy O of Israel	Ps 78:41	
the Lord awaked as o out of sleep	Ps 78:65	
fall like o of the princes	Ps 82:7	259
consulted together with o consent	Ps 83:5	
every o of them in Zion appeareth	Ps 84:7	
in pieces, as o that is slain	Ps 89:10	
the Holy O of Israel is our king	Ps 89:18	
spakest in vision to thy holy o	Ps 89:19	
laid help upon o that is mighty	Ps 89:19	
I have exalted o chosen out of	Ps 89:19	
went from o nation to another	Ps 105:13	
from o kingdom to another people	Ps 105:13	
there was not o feeble person	Ps 105:37	
there was not o of them left	Ps 106:11	259
so is every o that trusteth in	Ps 115:8	
and every o of thy righteous	Ps 119:160	
as o that findeth great spoil	Ps 119:162	
Blessed is every o that feareth	Ps 128:1	
so is every o that trusteth in	Ps 135:18	
Sing us o of the songs of Zion	Ps 137:3	
grave's mouth, as when o cutteth	Ps 141:7	
O generation shall praise thy	Ps 145:4	
let us all have o purse	Prov 1:14	259
of every o that is greedy of gain	Prov 1:19	
happy is every o that retaineth	Prov 3:18	
poverty come as o that travelleth	Prov 6:11	
Can o go upon hot coals, and his	Prov 6:28	376
by him, as o brought up with him	Prov 8:30	
loveth not o that reproveth him	Prov 15:12	
Every o that is proud in heart is	Prov 16:5	
is as when o letteth out water	Prov 17:14	
reprove o that hath understanding	Prov 19:25	
proclaim every o his own goodness	Prov 20:6	376
but of every o that is hasty only	Prov 21:5	
Be not thou o of them that strike	Prov 22:26	
poverty come as o that travelleth	Prov 24:34	
is like o that taketh a dog by	Prov 26:17	
O generation passeth away, and	Eccl 1:4	
o event happeneth to them all	Eccl 2:14	259
even o thing befalleth them	Eccl 3:19	2088
as the o dieth, so dieth the	Eccl 3:19	2088
yea, they have all o breath	Eccl 3:19	259
All go unto o place	Eccl 3:20	259
There is o alone, and there is not	Eccl 4:8	259
Two are better than o	Eccl 4:9	259
the o will lift up his fellow	Eccl 4:10	259
but how can o be warm alone	Eccl 4:11	259
if o prevail against him, two	Eccl 4:12	259
it is good and comely for o to eat	Eccl 5:18	
do not all go to o place	Eccl 6:6	259
God also hath set the o over	Eccl 7:14	2088
the preacher, counting o by o	Eccl 7:27	259
o man among a thousand have I	Eccl 7:28	259
there is a time wherein o man	Eccl 8:9	
there is o event to the righteous	Eccl 9:2	259
that there is o event unto all	Eccl 9:3	259
but o sinner destroyeth much good	Eccl 9:18	259
to every o that he is a fool	Eccl 10:3	
foolish wearieth every o of them	Eccl 10:15	
which are given from o shepherd	Eccl 12:11	259
for why should I be as o that	Song 1:7	
me, Rise up, my love, my fair o	Song 2:10	
Arise, my love, my fair o	Song 2:13	
whereof every o bear twins	Song 4:2	
my heart with o of thine eyes	Song 4:9	259
with o chain of thy neck	Song 4:9	259
whereof every o beareth twins	Song 6:6	259
there is not o barren among them	Song 6:6	259
My dove, my undefiled is but o	Song 6:9	259
she is the only o of her mother	Song 6:9	259
she is the choice o of her that	Song 6:9	259
his eyes as o that found favour	Song 8:10	
every o for the fruit thereof was	Song 8:11	376
the Holy O of Israel unto anger	Is 1:4	
every o loveth gifts, and	Is 1:23	
of hosts, the mighty O of Israel	Is 1:24	
be upon every o that is proud	Is 2:12	
upon every o that is lifted up	Is 2:12	
which they made each o for	Is 2:20	
every o by another, and every o	Is 3:5	376
women shall take hold of o man	Is 4:1	259
even every o that is written	Is 4:3	
of vineyard shall yield o bath	Is 5:10	259
of the Holy O of Israel draw nigh	Is 5:19	
the word of the Holy O of Israel	Is 5:24	
if o look unto the land, behold	Is 5:30	
each o had six wings	Is 6:2	259
o cried unto another, and said,	Is 6:3	
Then flew o of the seraphims unto	Is 6:6	259
honey shall every o eat that is	Is 7:22	
and tail, branch and rush, in o day	Is 9:14	259
for every o is an hypocrite and an	Is 9:17	
as o gathereth eggs that are left	Is 10:14	
a fire, and his Holy O for a flame	Is 10:17	
his thorns and his briers in o day	Is 10:17	259
the Holy O of Israel, in truth	Is 10:20	
Lebanon shall fall by a mighty o	Is 10:34	
for great is the Holy O of Israel	Is 12:6	
they shall be amazed o at another	Is 13:8	376
flee every o into his own land	Is 13:14	
Every o that is found shall be	Is 13:15	
every o that is joined unto them	Is 13:15	
glory, every o in his own house	Is 14:18	376
What shall o then answer the	Is 14:32	
every o shall howl, weeping	Is 15:3	
howl for Moab, every o shall howl	Is 16:7	
respect to the Holy O of Israel	Is 17:7	
fight every o against his brother	Is 19:2	376
every o against his neighbour	Is 19:2	376
every o that maketh mention	Is 19:17	
o shall be called, The city of	Is 19:18	259
send them a saviour, and a great o	Is 19:20	
according to the days of o king	Is 23:15	259
and ye shall be gathered o by o	Is 27:12	259
Lord hath a mighty and strong o	Is 28:2	
as of o that hath a familiar	Is 29:4	
men deliver to o that is learned	Is 29:11	
rejoice in the Holy O of Israel	Is 29:19	
For the terrible o is brought to	Is 29:20	
and sanctify the Holy O of Jacob	Is 29:23	
cause the Holy O of Israel to	Is 30:11	
thus saith the Holy O of Israel	Is 30:12	
Lord GOD, the Holy O of Israel	Is 30:15	
O thousand shall flee at the	Is 30:17	259
shall flee at the rebuke of o	Is 30:17	259
as when o goeth with a pipe to	Is 30:29	
LORD, to the mighty O of Israel	Is 30:29	
not unto the Holy O of Israel	Is 31:1	
not o of the stakes thereof shall	Is 33:20	
gathered, every o with her mate	Is 34:15	
no o of these shall fail, none	Is 34:16	259
of o captain of the least of my	Is 36:9	259
and eat ye every o of his vine	Is 36:16	376
every o of his fig tree, and drink	Is 36:16	376
drink ye every o the waters of	Is 36:16	376
even against the Holy O of Israel	Is 37:23	
saith the Holy O	Is 40:25	
not o faileth	Is 40:26	376
They helped every o his neighbour	Is 41:6	376
every o said to his brother, Be	Is 41:6	376
redeemer, the Holy O of Israel	Is 41:14	
glory in the Holy O of Israel	Is 41:16	
the Holy O of Israel hath created	Is 41:20	
I have raised up o from the north	Is 41:25	
I will give to Jerusalem o that	Is 41:27	
the Holy O of Israel, thy Saviour	Is 43:3	
Even every o that is called by my	Is 43:7	
redeemer, the Holy O of Israel	Is 43:14	
I am the LORD, your Holy O	Is 43:15	
O shall say, I am the LORD's	Is 44:5	
the Holy O of Israel, and his	Is 45:11	
Surely, shall o say, in the LORD	Is 45:24	
o shall cry unto him, yet can he	Is 46:7	
is his name, the Holy O of Israel	Is 47:4	
come to thee in a moment in o day	Is 47:9	259
wander every o to his quarter	Is 47:15	376
Redeemer, the Holy O of Israel	Is 48:17	
Redeemer of Israel, and his Holy O	Is 49:7	
the Holy O of Israel, and he shall	Is 49:7	
Redeemer, the mighty O of Jacob	Is 49:26	
turned every o to his own way	Is 53:6	376
thy Redeemer the Holy O of Israel	Is 54:5	
every o that thirsteth, come ye	Is 55:1	
God, and for the Holy O of Israel	Is 55:5	
every o that keepeth the sabbath	Is 56:6	
every o for his gain, from his	Is 56:11	376
each o walking in his uprightness	Is 57:2	
lofty O that inhabiteth eternity,	Is 57:15	
God, and to the Holy O of Israel	Is 60:9	
The Zion of the Holy O of Israel	Is 60:14	
Redeemer, the mighty O of Jacob	Is 60:16	
A little o shall become a	Is 60:22	
a small o a strong nation	Is 60:22	
and o saith, Destroy it not	Is 65:8	
be made to bring forth in o day	Is 66:8	259
As o whom his mother comforteth,	Is 66:13	376
behind o tree in the midst	Is 66:17	259
that from o new moon to another,	Is 66:23	
from o sabbath to another, shall	Is 66:23	
they shall set every o his throne	Jer 1:15	376
and I will take you o of a city	Jer 3:14	259
every o that goeth out thence	Jer 5:6	
every o neighed after his	Jer 5:8	376
shall feed every o in his place	Jer 6:3	376
every o is given to covetousness	Jer 6:13	
priest every o dealeth falsely	Jer 6:13	
every o turned to his course, as	Jer 8:6	
for every o from the least even	Jer 8:10	
priest every o dealeth falsely	Jer 8:10	
ye heed every o of his neighbour	Jer 9:4	376
deceive every o his neighbour	Jer 9:5	376
o speaketh peaceably to his	Jer 9:8	
every o her neighbour lamentation	Jer 9:20	
for o cutteth a tree out of the	Jer 10:3	
but walked every o in the	Jer 11:8	376
the o end of the land even to the	Jer 12:12	
will dash them o against another	Jer 13:14	376
yet every o of them doth curse me	Jer 15:10	
ye walk every o after the	Jer 16:12	376
ye now every o from his evil way	Jer 18:11	376
and we will every o do the	Jer 18:12	376
every o that passeth thereby	Jer 18:16	
every o that passeth thereby	Jer 19:8	
they shall eat every o the flesh	Jer 19:9	376
as o breaketh a potter's vessel,	Jer 19:11	
daily, every o mocketh me	Jer 20:7	
is with me as a mighty terrible o	Jer 20:11	
thee, every o with his weapons	Jer 22:7	376
they say unto every o that	Jer 23:17	
words every o from his neighbour	Jer 23:30	376
ye say every o to his neighbour	Jer 23:35	376
every o to his brother, What hath	Jer 23:35	376
O basket had very good figs, even	Jer 24:2	259
now every o from his evil way	Jer 25:5	376
o with another, and all the	Jer 25:26	376
o end of the earth even unto the	Jer 25:33	
the chastisement of a cruel o	Jer 30:14	
every o of them, shall go into	Jer 30:16	
But every o shall die for his own	Jer 31:30	376
to give every o according to his	Jer 32:19	376
And I will give them o heart	Jer 32:39	259
o way, that they may fear me for	Jer 32:39	259
heard that every o should let his	Jer 34:10	376
every o his maidservant, go free,	Jer 34:10	376
every o to his brother, and every	Jer 34:17	376
into o of the chambers, and give	Jer 35:2	259
return every o from his evil way	Jer 36:7	
words, they were afraid both o	Jer 36:16	376
o of the eunuchs which was in the	Jer 38:7	376
to fall, yea, o fell upon another	Jer 46:16	376
every o that goeth by it shall be	Jer 49:17	
every o that goeth by Babylon	Jer 50:13	
shall turn every o to his own people	Jer 50:16	376
flee every o to his own land	Jer 50:16	376
against the Holy O of Israel	Jer 50:29	
every o put in array, like a man	Jer 50:42	
sin against the Holy O of Israel	Jer 51:5	
let us go every o into his own	Jer 51:9	376
O post shall run to meet another,	Jer 51:31	
o messenger to meet another, to	Jer 51:31	
that his city is taken at o end	Jer 51:31	
a rumour shall both come o year	Jer 51:46	
every o of their bows is broken	Jer 51:56	
Zedekiah was o and twenty years	Jer 52:1	259
o sea, and twelve brasen bulls	Jer 52:20	259
the height of o pillar was	Jer 52:21	259
the height of o chapiter was five	Jer 52:22	259
every o had four faces, and every	Eze 1:6	259
faces, and every o had four wings	Eze 1:6	259
wings were joined o to another	Eze 1:9	802
they went every o straight	Eze 1:9	376
o were joined o to another	Eze 1:11	376
they went every o straight	Eze 1:12	376
behold o wheel upon the earth by	Eze 1:15	259
and they four had o likeness	Eze 1:16	259
straight, the o toward the other	Eze 1:23	802
every o had two, which covered on	Eze 1:23	376
every o had two, which covered on	Eze 1:23	376
I heard a voice of o that spake	Eze 1:28	
creatures that touched o another	Eze 3:13	802
turn thee from o side to another	Eze 4:8	
fitches, and put them in o vessel	Eze 4:9	259
be astonied o with another, and	Eze 4:17	376
every o for his iniquity	Eze 7:16	376
o man among them was clothed with	Eze 9:2	259
o cherub stretched forth his hand	Eze 10:7	
cherubims, o wheel by o cherub	Eze 10:9	259
they four had o likeness	Eze 10:10	259
And every o had four faces	Eze 10:14	259
every o stood at the door of the	Eze 10:19	
Every o had four faces apiece, and	Eze 10:21	259
apiece, and every o four wings	Eze 10:21	259
they went every o straight	Eze 10:22	376
into your mind, every o of them	Eze 11:5	
And I will give them o heart	Eze 11:19	259
o built up a wall, and, lo, others	Eze 13:10	
For every o of the house of	Eze 14:7	376
they shall go out from o fire	Eze 15:7	
on every o that passed by	Eze 16:15	
feet to every o that passed by	Eze 16:25	
every o that useth proverbs shall	Eze 16:44	
top of his young twigs a tender o	Eze 17:22	
the like to any o of these things	Eze 18:10	259
every o according to his ways,	Eze 18:30	376
And she brought up o of her whelps	Eze 19:3	259
Go ye, serve ye every o his idols	Eze 20:39	376
Go thee o way or other, either on	Eze 21:16	
shall come forth out of o land	Eze 21:19	259
every o were in thee to their	Eze 22:6	376
o hath committed abomination with	Eze 22:11	
women, the daughters of o mother	Eze 23:2	259
that they took both o way	Eze 23:13	259
and mourn o toward another	Eze 24:23	376
of the mighty o of the heathen	Eze 31:11	
judge you every o after his ways	Eze 33:20	376
that o that had escaped out of	Eze 33:21	
speak, saying, Abraham was o	Eze 33:24	259
ye defile every o his neighbour's	Eze 33:26	376
speak o to another	Eze 33:30	2297
every o to his brother, saying,	Eze 33:30	376
of o that hath a pleasant voice	Eze 33:32	
I will set up o shepherd over	Eze 34:23	259

son of man, take thee o stick	Eze 37:16	259
them o to another into o stick	Eze 37:17	259
they shall become o in thine hand	Eze 37:17	259
of Judah, and make them o stick	Eze 37:19	259
and they shall be o in mine hand	Eze 37:19	259
I will make them o nation in the	Eze 37:22	259
o king shall be king to them all	Eze 37:22	259
and they all shall have o shepherd	Eze 37:24	259
am the LORD, the Holy O in Israel	Eze 39:7	
breadth of the building, o reed	Eze 40:5	259
and the height, o reed	Eze 40:5	259
the gate, which was o reed broad	Eze 40:6	259
the gate, which was o reed broad	Eze 40:6	259
o reed long, and o reed broad	Eze 40:7	259
of the gate within was o reed	Eze 40:7	259
porch of the gate within, o reed	Eze 40:8	259
they three were of o measure	Eze 40:10	259
the posts had o measure on this	Eze 40:10	259
chambers was o cubit on this side	Eze 40:12	259
the space was o cubit on that	Eze 40:12	259
o little chamber to the roof of	Eze 40:13	
o on this side, and another on	Eze 40:26	259
as o goeth up to the entry of the	Eze 40:40	259
and an half broad, and o cubit high	Eze 40:42	259
o at the side of the east gate	Eze 40:44	259
o on this side, and another on	Eze 40:49	259
six cubits broad on the o side	Eze 41:1	
were five cubits on the o side	Eze 41:2	
o over another, and thirty in	Eze 41:6	
o door toward the north, and	Eze 41:11	259
galleries thereof on the o side	Eze 41:15	
the palm tree on the o side	Eze 41:19	
the appearance of the o as the	Eze 41:21	
two leaves for the o door	Eze 41:24	259
and palm trees on the o side	Eze 41:26	
breadth inward, a way of o cubit	Eze 42:4	259
as o goeth into them from the	Eze 42:9	
the east, as o entereth into them	Eze 42:12	
cubits, and the breadth o cubit	Eze 43:14	259
cubits, and the breadth o cubit	Eze 43:14	
be for the prince on the o side	Eze 45:7	
be over against o of the portions	Eze 45:7	259
and the bath shall be of o measure	Eze 45:11	259
o lamb out of the flock, out of	Eze 45:15	259
the month for every o that erreth	Eze 45:20	376
o shall then open him the gate	Eze 46:12	
going forth o shall shut the gate	Eze 46:12	
inheritance to o of his servants	Eze 46:17	259
four corners were of o measure	Eze 46:22	259
very many trees on the o side	Eze 47:7	
inherit it, o as well as another	Eze 47:14	376
as o goeth to Hamath, Hazar-enan,	Eze 48:1	
in length as o of the other parts	Eze 48:8	259
be for the prince, on the o side	Eze 48:21	
o gate of Reuben	Eze 48:31	259
o gate of Judah, o gate of Levi	Eze 48:31	259
o gate of Joseph	Eze 48:32	259
o gate of Benjamin	Eze 48:32	259
o gate of Dan	Eze 48:32	259
o gate of Simeon	Eze 48:33	259
o gate of Issachar	Eze 48:33	259
o gate of Zebulun	Eze 48:33	259
o gate of Gad, o gate of Asher,	Eze 48:34	259
o gate of Naphtali	Eze 48:34	259
there is but o decree for you	Dan 2:9	2298
shall not cleave o to another	Dan 2:43	1836
o seven times more than it was	Dan 3:19	2298
an holy o came down from heaven	Dan 4:13	
was astonied for o hour, and his	Dan 4:19	2298
an holy o coming down from heaven	Dan 4:23	
his knees smote o against another	Dan 5:6	1668
the sea, diverse o from another	Dan 7:3	1668
and it raised up itself on o side	Dan 7:5	2298
o like the Son of man came with	Dan 7:13	
I came near unto o of them that	Dan 7:16	2298
but o was higher than the other,	Dan 8:3	259
out of o of them came forth a	Dan 8:9	259
Then I heard o saint speaking, and	Dan 8:13	259
the covenant with many for o week	Dan 9:27	259
kingdom of Persia withstood me o	Dan 10:13	259
o of the chief princes, came to	Dan 10:13	259
o like the similitude of the sons	Dan 10:16	
touched me o like the appearance	Dan 10:18	
be strong, and o of his princes	Dan 11:5	
shall o stand up in his estate	Dan 11:7	
o shall certainly come, and	Dan 11:10	
they shall speak lies at o table	Dan 11:27	259
every o that shall be found	Dan 12:1	
the o on this side of the bank of	Dan 12:5	259
o said to the man clothed in	Dan 12:6	
and appoint themselves o head	Hos 1:11	259
every o that dwelleth therein	Hos 4:3	
the Holy O in the midst of thee	Hos 11:9	
shall march every o on his ways	Joel 2:7	376
Neither shall o thrust another	Joel 2:8	376
shall walk every o in his path	Joel 2:8	1397
shall o take up a snare from the	Amos 3:5	
I caused it to rain upon o city	Amos 4:7	259
o piece was rained upon, and the	Amos 4:7	259
three cities wandered unto o city	Amos 4:8	259
there remain ten men in o house	Amos 6:9	259
will o plow there with oxen	Amos 6:12	
every o mourn that dwelleth	Amos 8:8	
to the end that every o of the	Obad 9	376
even thou wast as o of them	Obad 11	259
they said every o to his fellow	Jonah 1:7	376
turn every o from his evil way	Jonah 3:8	376
In that day shall o take up a	Mic 2:4	
every o in the name of his god	Mic 4:5	376
There is o come out of thee, that	Nah 1:11	
they shall justle o against	Nah 2:4	
O LORD my God, mine Holy O	Hab 1:12	6918
the Holy O from mount Paran	Hab 3:3	6918
every o from his place, even all	Zeph 2:11	376
every o that passeth by her shall	Zeph 2:15	
LORD, to serve him with o consent	Zeph 3:9	259
In the seventh month, in the o	Hag 2:1	259
If o bear holy flesh in the skirt	Hag 2:12	
If o that is unclean by a dead	Hag 2:13	
when o came to an heap of twenty	Hag 2:16	
when o came to the pressfat for	Hag 2:16	
every o by the sword of his	Hag 2:22	376
upon o stone shall be seven eyes	Zec 3:9	259
iniquity of that land in o day	Zec 3:9	259
o upon the right side of the bowl	Zec 4:3	259
for every o that stealeth shall	Zec 5:3	
every o that sweareth shall be	Zec 5:3	
men every o against his neighbour	Zec 8:10	376
the inhabitants of o city shall	Zec 8:21	259
to every o grass in the field	Zec 10:1	376
every o into his neighbour's hand	Zec 11:6	376
the o I called Beauty, and the	Zec 11:7	259
also I cut off in o month	Zec 11:8	259
eat every o the flesh of another	Zec 11:9	802
neither shall seek the young o	Zec 11:16	
as o mourneth for his only son,	Zec 12:10	
as o that is in bitterness for	Zec 12:10	
be ashamed every o of his vision	Zec 13:4	376
o shall say unto him, What are	Zec 13:6	
But it shall be o day which shall	Zec 14:7	259
there be o LORD, and his name o	Zec 14:9	259
they shall lay hold every o on	Zec 14:13	376
that every o that is left of all	Zec 14:16	
o shall take you away with it	Mal 2:3	
Have we not all o father	Mal 2:10	259
hath not o God created us	Mal 2:10	259
And did not he make o	Mal 2:15	259
And wherefore o	Mal 2:15	259
for o covereth violence with his	Mal 2:16	
Every o that doeth evil is good	Mal 2:17	
the LORD spake often o to another	Mal 3:16	376
The voice of o crying in the	Mt 3:3	
Till heaven and earth pass, o jot	Mt 5:18	*1520*
or o tittle shall in no	Mt 5:18	*3391*
o of these least commandments	Mt 5:19	*3391*
o of thy members should perish	Mt 5:29	*1520*
o of thy members should perish	Mt 5:30	*1520*
not make o hair white or black	Mt 5:36	*3391*
for either he will hate the o	Mt 6:24	*1520*
or else he will hold to the o	Mt 6:24	*1520*
can add o cubit unto his stature	Mt 6:27	*1520*
was not arrayed like o of these	Mt 6:29	*1520*
For every o that asketh receiveth	Mt 7:8	
Not every o that saith unto me,	Mt 7:21	
every o that heareth these	Mt 7:26	
taught them as o having authority	Mt 7:29	
o of them shall not fall on the	Mt 10:29	*1520*
shall give to drink unto o of	Mt 10:42	*1520*
That in this place is o greater	Mt 12:6	
you, that shall have o sheep	Mt 12:11	*1520*
unto him o possessed with a devil	Mt 12:22	
Or else how can o enter into a	Mt 12:29	*5100*
Then o said unto him, Behold, thy	Mt 12:47	*5100*
When any o heareth the word of	Mt 13:19	
it not, then cometh the wicked o	Mt 13:19	
are the children of the wicked o	Mt 13:38	
when he had found o pearl of	Mt 13:46	*1520*
Jeremias, or o of the prophets	Mt 16:14	*1520*
o for thee, and o for Moses, and	Mt 17:4	*3391*
and o for Moses, and o for Elias	Mt 17:4	*3391*
whoso shall receive o such little	Mt 18:5	*1520*
But whoso shall offend o of these	Mt 18:6	*1520*
to enter into life with o eye	Mt 18:9	*3442*
not o of these little ones	Mt 18:10	*1520*
o of them be gone astray, doth he	Mt 18:12	*1520*
that o of these little ones	Mt 18:14	*1520*
then take with thee o or two more	Mt 18:16	*1520*
o was brought unto him, which	Mt 18:24	*1520*
found o of his fellowservants,	Mt 18:28	*1520*
o his brother their trespasses	Mt 18:35	
and they twain shall be o flesh	Mt 19:5	*3391*
are no more twain, but o flesh	Mt 19:6	*3391*
o came and said unto him, Good	Mt 19:16	*1520*
there is none good but o, that is	Mt 19:17	*1520*
every o that hath forsaken houses	Mt 19:29	
last have wrought but o hour	Mt 20:12	*3391*
But he answered o of them	Mt 20:13	*1520*
the o on thy right hand, and the	Mt 20:21	*1520*
them, I also will ask you o thing	Mt 21:24	*1520*
took his servants, and beat o	Mt 21:35	*3739*
o to his farm, another to his	Mt 22:5	
Then o of them, which was a	Mt 22:35	*1520*
move them with o of their fingers	Mt 23:4	
for o is your Master, even Christ	Mt 23:8	*1520*
for o is your Father, which is in	Mt 23:9	*1520*
for o is your Master, even Christ	Mt 23:10	*1520*
sea and land to make o proselyte	Mt 23:15	*1520*
be left here o stone upon another	Mt 24:2	
and shall betray o another	Mt 24:10	*240*
and shall hate o another	Mt 24:10	*240*
from o end of heaven to the other	Mt 24:31	
the o shall be taken, and the	Mt 24:40	*1520*
the o shall be taken, and the	Mt 24:41	*1520*
unto o he gave five talents	Mt 25:15	
to another two, and to another o	Mt 25:15	*1520*
But he that had received o went	Mt 25:18	*1520*
had received the o talent came	Mt 25:24	*1520*
For unto every o that hath shall	Mt 25:29	
separate them o from another	Mt 25:32	*240*
as ye have done it unto o of the	Mt 25:40	*1520*
it not to o of the least of these	Mt 25:45	*1520*
Then o of the twelve, called	Mt 26:14	*1520*
that o of you shall betray me	Mt 26:21	*1520*
began every o of them to say unto	Mt 26:22	
could ye not watch with me o hour	Mt 26:40	*3391*
o of the twelve, came, and with	Mt 26:47	*1520*
o of them which were with Jesus	Mt 26:51	*1520*
Surely thou also art o of them	Mt 26:73	
o on the right hand, and another	Mt 27:38	*1520*
And straightway o of them ran	Mt 27:48	*1520*
The voice of o crying in the	Mk 1:3	
There cometh o mightier than I	Mk 1:7	
them as o that had authority	Mk 1:22	
who thou art, the Holy O of God	Mk 1:24	
bringing o sick of the palsy,	Mk 2:3	
said o to another, What manner of	Mk 4:41	*240*
there cometh o of the rulers of	Mk 5:22	*1520*
prophet, or as o of the prophets	Mk 6:15	*1520*
Hearken unto me every o of you	Mk 7:14	
bring unto him o that was deaf	Mk 7:32	
ship with them more than o loaf	Mk 8:14	*1520*
and others, O of the prophets	Mk 8:28	*1520*
o for thee, and o for Moses, and	Mk 9:5	*3391*
and o for Elias	Mk 9:5	
questioning o with another what	Mk 9:10	
o of the multitude answered and	Mk 9:17	*1520*
and he was as o dead	Mk 9:26	
Whosoever shall receive o of such	Mk 9:37	*1520*
we saw o casting out devils in	Mk 9:38	*5100*
whosoever shall offend o of these	Mk 9:42	*1520*
the kingdom of God with o eye	Mk 9:47	*3442*
For every o shall be salted with	Mk 9:49	
have peace o with another	Mk 9:50	*240*
And they twain shall be o flesh	Mk 10:8	*3391*
are no more twain, but o flesh	Mk 10:8	
the way, there came o running	Mk 10:17	*1520*
there is none good but o, that is	Mk 10:18	*1520*
unto him, O thing thou lackest	Mk 10:21	*1520*
o on thy right hand, and the other	Mk 10:37	*1520*
I will also ask of you o question	Mk 11:29	*1520*
Having yet therefore o son	Mk 12:6	*1520*
o of the scribes came, and having	Mk 12:28	*1520*
The Lord our God is o Lord	Mk 12:29	*1520*
for there is o God	Mk 12:32	*1520*
o of his disciples saith unto him	Mk 13:1	*1520*
not be left o stone upon another	Mk 13:2	
o of the twelve, went unto the	Mk 14:10	*1520*
O of you which eateth with me	Mk 14:18	*1520*
and to say unto him o by o	Mk 14:19	*1520*
It is o of the twelve, that	Mk 14:20	*1520*
couldest not thou watch o hour	Mk 14:37	*3391*
o of the twelve, and with him a	Mk 14:43	*1520*
o of them that stood by drew a	Mk 14:47	*1520*
there cometh o of the maids of	Mk 14:66	*3391*
that stood by, This is o of them	Mk 14:69	
Peter, Surely thou art o of them	Mk 14:70	
he released unto them o prisoner	Mk 15:6	*1520*
there was o named Barabbas, which	Mk 15:7	
they compel o Simon a Cyrenian,	Mk 15:21	*5100*
the o on his right hand, and the	Mk 15:27	*1520*
o ran and filled a spunge full of	Mk 15:36	*1520*
every o into his own city	Lk 2:3	
the shepherds said o to another	Lk 2:15	*240*
And there was o Anna, a prophetess	Lk 2:36	
The voice of o crying in the	Lk 3:4	
but o mightier than I cometh, the	Lk 3:16	
the Holy O of God	Lk 4:34	
laid his hands on every o of them	Lk 4:40	*1520*
And he entered into o of the ships	Lk 5:3	*1520*
unto them, I will ask you o thing	Lk 6:9	*5100*
communed o with another what they	Lk 6:11	*240*
the o cheek offer also the other	Lk 6:29	
but every o that is perfect shall	Lk 6:40	
me soldiers, and I say unto o	Lk 7:8	*5129*
calling o to another, and saying,	Lk 7:32	*240*
o of the Pharisees desired him	Lk 7:36	*5100*
the o owed five hundred pence, and	Lk 7:41	*1520*
saying o to another, What manner	Lk 8:25	*240*
For he had o only daughter, about	Lk 8:42	
there cometh o from the ruler of	Lk 8:49	*5100*
that o of the old prophets was	Lk 9:8	*1520*
that o of the old prophets is	Lk 9:19	*5100*
o for thee, and o for Moses, and	Lk 9:33	*3391*
and o for Elias	Lk 9:33	*3391*
o at all things which Jesus did	Lk 9:43	*3956*
we saw o casting out devils in	Lk 9:49	*5100*
But o thing is needful	Lk 10:42	*1520*
o of his disciples said unto him,	Lk 11:1	*5100*
every o that is indebted to us	Lk 11:4	
For every o that asketh receiveth	Lk 11:10	
Then answered o of the lawyers,	Lk 11:45	*5100*
burdens with o of your fingers	Lk 11:46	*1520*
that they trode o upon another	Lk 12:1	*240*
not o of them is forgotten before	Lk 12:6	*1520*
o of the company said unto him,	Lk 12:13	*5100*
can add to his stature o cubit	Lk 12:25	*1520*
was not arrayed like o of these	Lk 12:27	*1520*
shall be five in o house divided	Lk 12:52	*1520*
he was teaching in o of the	Lk 13:10	*3391*
doth not each o of you on the	Lk 13:15	
Then said o unto him, Lord, are	Lk 13:23	*5100*
as he went into the house of o of	Lk 14:1	*5100*
when o of them that sat at meat	Lk 14:15	*5100*
they all with o consent began to	Lk 14:18	*3391*
sheep, if he lose o of them	Lk 15:4	*1520*
over o sinner that repenteth	Lk 15:7	*1520*
of silver, if she lose o piece	Lk 15:8	*3391*
God over o sinner that repenteth	Lk 15:10	*1520*
make me as o of thy hired	Lk 15:19	*1520*
he called o of the servants, and	Lk 15:26	*1520*
So he called every o of his	Lk 16:5	*1520*
for either he will hate the o	Lk 16:13	*1520*
or else he will hold to the o	Lk 16:13	*1520*
than o tittle of the law to fail	Lk 16:17	*3391*
but if o went unto them from the	Lk 16:30	*5100*
though o rose from the dead	Lk 16:31	*5100*
offend o of these little ones	Lk 17:2	*1520*
o of them, when he saw that he	Lk 17:15	*1520*
when ye shall desire to see o of	Lk 17:22	*3391*
out of the o part under heaven	Lk 17:24	
there shall be two men in o bed	Lk 17:34	*3391*
the o shall be taken, and the	Lk 17:34	*1520*

O

the o shall be taken, and the Lk 17:35 3391
the o shall be taken, and the Lk 17:36 1520
the o a Pharisee, and the other a Lk 18:10 1520
for every o that exalteth himself Lk 18:14
none is good, save o, that is, Lk 18:19 1520
him, Yet lackest thou o thing Lk 18:22 1520
That unto every o which hath Lk 19:26
in thee o stone upon another Lk 19:44
that on o of those days, as he Lk 20:1 3391
them, I will also ask you o thing Lk 20:3 1520
not be left o stone upon another Lk 21:6
him sell his garment, and buy o Lk 22:36
o of the twelve, went before them Lk 22:47 1520
o of them smote the servant of Lk 22:50 1520
about the space of o hour after Lk 22:59 3391
as o that perverteth the people Lk 23:14
release o unto them at the feast Lk 23:17 1520
away, they laid hold upon o Simon Lk 23:26 5100
o on the right hand, and the other Lk 23:33
o of the malefactors which were Lk 23:39 1520
these that ye have o to another Lk 24:17 240
the o of them, whose name was Lk 24:18 1520
they said o to another, Did not Lk 24:32 240
I am the voice of o crying in the Jn 1:23
but there standeth o among you Jn 1:26
O of the two which heard John Jn 1:40 1520
so is every o that is born of the Jn 3:8
For every o that doeth evil Jn 3:20
said the disciples o to another Jn 4:33 240
O soweth, and another reapeth Jn 4:37 243
which receive honour o of another Jn 5:44 240
there is o that accuseth you, Jn 5:45
that every o of them may take a Jn 6:7
O of his disciples, Andrew, Simon Jn 6:8 1520
save that o whereinto his Jn 6:22 1520
that every o which seeth the Son, Jn 6:40
twelve, and o of you is a devil Jn 6:70 1520
betray him, being o of the twelve Jn 6:71 1520
unto them, I have done o work Jn 7:21 1520
Jesus by night, being o of them,) Jn 7:50 1520
own conscience, went out o by o Jn 8:9 1520
I am o that bear witness of Jn 8:18
we have o Father, even God Jn 8:41 1520
there is o that seeketh and Jn 8:50
o thing I know, that, whereas I Jn 9:25 1520
the eyes of o that was born blind Jn 9:32
and there shall be o fold Jn 10:16 3391
fold, and o shepherd Jn 10:16 1520
I and my Father are o Jn 10:30 1520
o of them, named Caiaphas, being Jn 11:49 1520
that o man should die for the Jn 11:50 1520
he should gather together in o Jn 11:52 1520
but Lazarus was o of them that Jn 12:2 1520
Then saith o of his disciples, Jn 12:4 1520
my words, hath o that judgeth him Jn 12:48
ought to wash o another's feet Jn 13:14 240
that o of you shall betray me Jn 13:21 1520
the disciples looked o on another Jn 13:22 240
Jesus' bosom o of his disciples Jn 13:23 1520
unto you, That ye love o another Jn 13:34 240
you, that ye also love o another Jn 13:34 240
if ye have love o to another Jn 13:35 240
That ye love o another, as I Jn 15:12 240
you, that ye love o another Jn 15:17 240
hast given me, that they may be o Jn 17:11 1520
That they all may be o Jn 17:21 1520
that they also may be o in us Jn 17:21 1520
they may be o, even as we are o Jn 17:22 1520
they may be made perfect in o Jn 17:23 1520
that it was expedient that o man Jn 18:14 1520
Art not thou also o of this man's Jn 18:17
o of the officers which stood by Jn 18:22 1520
not thou also o of his disciples Jn 18:25
O of the servants of the high Jn 18:26 1520
Every o that is of the truth Jn 18:37
unto you o at the passover Jn 18:39 1520
others with him, on either side o Jn 19:18
But o of the soldiers with a Jn 19:34 1520
the o at the head, and the other Jn 20:12 1520
o of the twelve, called Didymus, Jn 20:24 1520
if they should be written every o Jn 21:25 1520
continued with o accord in prayer Acts 1:14 3661
must o be ordained to be a Acts 1:22 1520
they were all with o accord in Acts 2:1 3661
all with o accord in o place Acts 2:1
saying o to another, Behold, are Acts 2:7 240
saying o to another, What meaneth Acts 2:12 243
thine Holy O to see corruption Acts 2:27
be baptized every o of you in the Acts 2:38
daily with o accord in the temple Acts 2:46 3661
But ye denied the Holy O and the Acts 3:14
in turning away every o of you Acts 3:26
their voice to God with o accord Acts 4:24 3661
that believed were of o heart Acts 4:32
heart and of o soul Acts 4:32 3391
they were all with o accord in Acts 5:12 3661
and they were healed every o Acts 5:16
Then came o and told them, saying, Acts 5:25 5100
stood there up o in the council Acts 5:34 5100
seeing o of them suffer wrong, he Acts 7:24 5100
and would have set them at o again Acts 7:26 1515
why do ye wrong o to another Acts 7:26 240
of the coming of the Just O Acts 7:52
and ran upon him with o accord Acts 7:57 3661
the people with o accord gave Acts 8:6 3661
out that himself was some great o Acts 8:9
house of Judas for o called Saul Acts 9:11
in Joppa with o Simon a tanner Acts 9:43 5100
o that feared God with all his Acts 10:2
men to Joppa, and call for o Simon Acts 10:5
He lodgeth with o Simon a tanner Acts 10:6 5100
o that feareth God, and of good Acts 10:22
or come unto o of another nation Acts 10:28
he is lodged in the house of o Acts 10:32
there stood up o of them named Acts 11:28 1520
and passed on through o street Acts 12:10 3391
they came with o accord to him Acts 12:20 3661
behold, there cometh o after me Acts 13:25
thine Holy O to see corruption Acts 13:35
us, being assembled with o accord Acts 15:25 3661
in asunder o from the other Acts 15:39 240
there is another king, o Jesus Acts 17:7
hath made of o blood all nations Acts 17:26 1520
he be not far from every o of us Acts 17:27 1520
o that worshipped God, whose Acts 18:7
with o accord against Paul Acts 18:12 3661
daily in the school of o Tyrannus Acts 19:9 5100
there were seven sons of o Sceva Acts 19:14
they rushed with o accord into Acts 19:29 3661
Some therefore cried o thing Acts 19:32 3303
all with o voice about the space Acts 19:34 3391
let them implead o another Acts 19:38 240
ceased not to warn every o night Acts 20:31 1520
had taken our leave o of another Acts 21:6 240
and abode with them o day Acts 21:7 3391
which was o of the seven Acts 21:8
with them o Mnason of Cyprus Acts 21:16 5100
be offered for every o of them Acts 21:26 1520
And some cried o thing, some Acts 21:34
o Ananias, a devout man according Acts 22:12 5100
know his will, and see that Just O Acts 22:14
that the o part were Sadducees Acts 23:6 1520
Then Paul called o of the Acts 23:17 1520
Except it be for this o voice Acts 24:21 3391
of o Jesus, which was dead, whom Acts 25:19 5100
prisoners unto o named Julius Acts 27:1
o Aristarchus, a Macedonian of Acts 27:2
a fire, and received us every o Acts 28:2
after o day the south wind blew, Acts 28:13 3391
after that Paul had spoken o word Acts 28:25 1520
to every o that believeth Rom 1:16
in their lust o toward another Rom 1:27 240
or else excusing o another Rom 2:15 240
not a Jew, which is o outwardly Rom 2:28
he is a Jew, which is o inwardly Rom 2:29
is none righteous, no, not o Rom 3:10 1520
none that doeth good, no, not o Rom 3:12 1520
Seeing it is o God, which shall Rom 3:30 1520
for a righteous man will o die Rom 5:7 5100
as by o man sin entered into the Rom 5:12 1520
the offence of o many be dead Rom 5:15 1520
gift by grace, which is by o man Rom 5:15 1520
And not as it was by o that sinned Rom 5:16 1520
judgment was by o to condemnation Rom 5:16 1520
For if by o man's offence death Rom 5:17 1520
man's offence death reigned by o Rom 5:17 1520
shall reign in life by o, Jesus Rom 5:17 1520
o judgment came upon all men to Rom 5:18 1520
o the free gift came upon all men Rom 5:18 1520
For as by o man's disobedience Rom 5:19 1520
so by the obedience of o shall Rom 5:19 1520
Rebecca also had conceived by o Rom 9:10 1520
lump to make o vessel unto honour Rom 9:21
to every o that believeth Rom 10:4 3956
as we have many members in o body Rom 12:4 1520
are o body in Christ Rom 12:5 1520
and every o members Rom 12:5 1520
members o of another Rom 12:5 240
Be kindly affectioned o to o Rom 12:10 240
in honour preferring o another Rom 12:10 240
of the same mind o toward another Rom 12:16 240
any thing, but to love o another Rom 13:8 240
For o believeth that he may eat Rom 14:2
O man esteemeth o day above Rom 14:5
man esteemeth o day above another Rom 14:5
So then every o of us shall give Rom 14:12
judge o another any more Rom 14:13 240
things wherewith o may edify Rom 14:19 240
Let every o of us please his Rom 15:2
grant you to be likeminded o Rom 15:5 240
That ye may with o mind Rom 15:6 3661
o mouth glorify God, even the Rom 15:6 1520
Wherefore receive ye o another Rom 15:7 240
able also to admonish o another Rom 15:14 240
Salute o another with an holy Rom 16:16 240
that every o of you saith, I am 1Cor 1:12
For while o saith, I am of Paul 1Cor 3:4 5100
and he that watereth are o 1Cor 3:8 1520
that no o of you be puffed up for 1Cor 4:6 1520
puffed up for o against another 1Cor 4:6 1520
that o should have his father's 1Cor 5:1 5100
To deliver such a o unto Satan 1Cor 5:5
with such an o, no not to eat 1Cor 5:11
not o that shall be able to judge 1Cor 6:5
ye go to law o with another 1Cor 6:7 1438
is joined to an harlot is o body 1Cor 6:16 1520
two, saith he, shall be o flesh 1Cor 6:16 3391
joined unto the Lord is o spirit 1Cor 6:17 1520
Defraud ye not o the other 1Cor 7:5 240
o after this manner, and another 1Cor 7:7
as the Lord hath called every o 1Cor 7:17
as o that hath obtained mercy of 1Cor 7:25
there is none other God but o 1Cor 8:4 1520
But to us there is but o God 1Cor 8:6 1520
o Lord Jesus Christ, by whom are 1Cor 8:6 1520
but o receiveth the prize 1Cor 9:24 1520
not as o that beateth the air 1Cor 9:26
fell in o day three and twenty 1Cor 10:8 3391
many are o bread, and o body 1Cor 10:17 1520
are all partakers of that o bread 1Cor 10:17 1520
for that is even all o as if she 1Cor 11:5 1520
together therefore into o place 1Cor 11:20
For in eating every o taketh 1Cor 11:21
o is hungry, and another is 1Cor 11:21
to eat, tarry o for another 1Cor 11:33 240
For to o is given by the Spirit 1Cor 12:8
But all these worketh that o 1Cor 12:11 1520
For as the body is o, and hath 1Cor 12:12 1520
and all the members of that o body 1Cor 12:12 1520
being many, are o body 1Cor 12:12 1520
For by o Spirit are we all 1Cor 12:13 1520
are we all baptized into o body 1Cor 12:13 1520
all made to drink into o Spirit 1Cor 12:13 1520
For the body is not o member 1Cor 12:14 1520
every o of them in the body 1Cor 12:18 1520
And if they were all o member 1Cor 12:19 1520
they many members, yet but o body 1Cor 12:20 1520
have the same care o for another 1Cor 12:25 240
whether o member suffer, all the 1Cor 12:26 1520
or o member be honoured, all the 1Cor 12:26 1520
be come together into o place 1Cor 14:23
there come in o that believeth 1Cor 14:24 5100
or o unlearned, he is convinced 1Cor 14:24
every o of you hath a psalm, hath 1Cor 14:26
and let o interpret 1Cor 14:27 1520
For ye may all prophesy o by o 1Cor 14:31 1520
as of o born out of due time 1Cor 15:8
but there is o kind of flesh of 1Cor 15:39 243
the glory of the celestial is o 1Cor 15:40 2087
There is o glory of the sun, and 1Cor 15:41 243
for o star differeth from another 1Cor 15:41
o of you lay by him in store 1Cor 16:2
to every o that helpeth with us, 1Cor 16:16
Greet ye o another with an holy 1Cor 16:20 240
lest perhaps such a o should be 2Cor 2:7
To the o we are the savour of 2Cor 2:16
that every o may receive the 2Cor 5:10
that if o died for all, then were 2Cor 5:14 1520
Let such an o think this, that 2Cor 10:11
I have espoused you to o husband 2Cor 11:2 1520
received I forty stripes save o 2Cor 11:24 3391
such an o caught up to the third 2Cor 12:2
Of such an o will I glory 2Cor 12:5
be of good comfort, be of o mind 2Cor 13:11
Greet o another with an holy kiss 2Cor 13:12 240
Cursed is every o that continueth Gal 3:10
Cursed is every o that hangeth on Gal 3:13
but as of o, And to thy seed, Gal 3:16 1520
a mediator of o, but God is o Gal 3:20 1520
for ye are all o in Christ Jesus Gal 3:28 1520
the o by a bondmaid, the other by Gal 4:22 1520
the o from the mount Sinai, which Gal 4:24 3391
but by love serve o another Gal 5:13 240
the law is fulfilled in o word Gal 5:14 1520
devour o another, take heed that Gal 5:15 240
ye be not consumed o of another Gal 5:15 240
are contrary the o to the other Gal 5:17 240
o another, envying o another Gal 5:26 240
restore such an o in the spirit Gal 6:1
Bear ye o another's burdens, and Gal 6:2 240
in o all things in Christ Eph 1:10
our peace, who hath made both o Eph 2:14 1520
in himself of twain o new man Eph 2:15 1520
unto God in o body by the cross Eph 2:16 1520
by o Spirit unto the Father Eph 2:18 1520
forbearing o another in love Eph 4:2 240
There is o body, and o Spirit, Eph 4:4 1520
o Spirit, even as ye are called Eph 4:4 1520
called in o hope of your calling Eph 4:4 3391
O Lord Eph 4:5 1520
Lord, o faith Eph 4:5 3391
faith, o baptism Eph 4:5 1520
O God and Father of all, who is Eph 4:6 1520
But unto every o of us is given Eph 4:7 1520
for we are members o of another Eph 4:25 240
And be ye kind o to another Eph 4:32 240
forgiving o another, even as God Eph 4:32 1438
Submitting yourselves o to o Eph 5:21 240
and they two shall be o flesh Eph 5:31 3391
Nevertheless let every o of you Eph 5:33
The o preach Christ of contention Phil 1:16 3303
that ye stand fast in o spirit Phil 1:27 1520
with o mind striving together for Phil 1:27 3391
the same love, being of o accord Phil 2:2 4861
accord, of o mind Phil 2:2
but this o thing I do, forgetting Phil 3:13 1520
Lie not o to another, seeing that Col 3:9 240
Forbearing o another, and Col 3:13 240
another, and forgiving o another Col 3:13 1438
also ye are called in o body Col 3:15 1520
admonishing o another in psalms Col 3:16 1438
beloved brother, who is o of you Col 4:9
Epaphras, who is o of you Col 4:12
and charged every o of you 1Th 2:11 1520
abound in love o toward another 1Th 3:12 240
That every o of you should know 1Th 4:4
taught of God to love o another 1Th 4:9 240
Wherefore comfort o another with 1Th 4:18 240
edify o another, even as also ye 1Th 5:11 1520
the charity of every o of you all 2Th 1:3 1520
For there is o God 1Ti 2:5 1520
o mediator between God and men, 1Ti 2:5 1520
blameless, the husband of o wife 1Ti 3:2 3391
O that ruleth well his own house, 1Ti 3:4 1520
deacons be the husbands of o wife 1Ti 3:12 3391
having been the wife of o man 1Ti 5:9 1520
preferring o before another 1Ti 5:21
Let every o that nameth the name 2Ti 2:19
blameless, the husband of o wife Titus 1:6 3391
O of themselves, even a prophet Titus 1:12 5100
hateful, and hating o another Titus 3:3 240
being such an o as Paul the aged, Philem 9
But o in a certain place Heb 2:6 5100
who are sanctified are all of o Heb 2:11 1520
But exhort o another daily, while Heb 3:13 1438
ye have need that o teach you Heb 5:12
For every o that useth milk is Heb 5:13
we desire that every o of you do Heb 6:11
after he had offered o sacrifice Heb 10:12 3391
For by o offering he hath Heb 10:14 3391
let us consider o another to Heb 10:24 240
but exhorting o another Heb 10:25

- Therefore sprang there even of *o* ... Heb 11:12 *1520*
- who for *o* morsel of meat sold his ... Heb 12:16 *3391*
- city, but we seek *o* to come ... Heb 13:14
- law, and yet offend in *o* point ... Jas 2:10 *1520*
- *o* of you say unto them, Depart in ... Jas 2:16 *5100*
- believest that there is *o* God ... Jas 2:19 *1520*
- Speak not evil *o* of another ... Jas 4:11 *240*
- There is *o* lawgiver, who is able ... Jas 4:12 *1520*
- Grudge not *o* against another, ... Jas 5:9 *240*
- Confess your faults *o* to another ... Jas 5:16 *240*
- pray *o* for another, that ye may ... Jas 5:16 *240*
- from the truth, and *o* convert him ... Jas 5:19 *5100*
- see that ye love *o* another with a ... 1Pet 1:22 *240*
- Finally, be ye all of *o* mind ... 1Pet 3:8 *3675*
- having compassion *o* of another ... 1Pet 3:8
- Use hospitality *o* to another ... 1Pet 4:9 *240*
- so minister the same *o* to another ... 1Pet 4:10 *1438*
- of you be subject *o* to another ... 1Pet 5:5 *240*
- Greet ye *o* another with a kiss of ... 1Pet 5:14 *240*
- be not ignorant of this *o* thing ... 2Pet 3:8 *1520*
- that *o* day is with the Lord as a ... 2Pet 3:8 *3391*
- and a thousand years as *o* day ... 2Pet 3:8 *3391*
- we have fellowship *o* with another ... 1Jn 1:7 *3391*
- ye have overcome the wicked *o* ... 1Jn 2:13
- and ye have overcome the wicked *o* ... 1Jn 2:14
- have an unction from the Holy *O* ... 1Jn 2:20
- ye know that every *o* that doeth ... 1Jn 2:29
- that we should love *o* another ... 1Jn 3:11 *240*
- as Cain, who was of that wicked *o* ... 1Jn 3:12
- love *o* another, as he gave us ... 1Jn 3:23 *240*
- Beloved, let us love *o* another ... 1Jn 4:7 *240*
- every *o* that loveth is born of ... 1Jn 4:7
- we ought also to love *o* another ... 1Jn 4:11 *240*
- If we love *o* another, God ... 1Jn 4:12 *240*
- every *o* that loveth him that ... 1Jn 5:1
- and these three are *o* ... 1Jn 5:7 *1520*
- and these three agree in *o* ... 1Jn 5:8 *1520*
- that wicked *o* toucheth him not ... 1Jn 5:18
- beginning, that we love *o* another ... 2Jn 5 *240*
- *o* like unto the Son of man ... Rev 1:13
- I will give unto every *o* of you ... Rev 2:23
- in heaven, and *o* sat on the throne ... Rev 4:2
- *o* of the elders saith unto me ... Rev 5:5 *1520*
- having every *o* of them harps, and ... Rev 5:8
- the Lamb opened *o* of the seals ... Rev 6:1 *3391*
- *o* of the four beasts saying, Come ... Rev 6:1 *1520*
- that they should kill *o* another ... Rev 6:4 *240*
- were given unto every *o* of them ... Rev 6:11
- *o* of the elders answered, saying ... Rev 7:13 *1520*
- *O* woe is past ... Rev 9:12 *3391*
- and shall send gifts *o* to another ... Rev 11:10 *240*
- I saw *o* of his heads as it were ... Rev 13:3 *3391*
- upon the cloud *o* sat like unto ... Rev 14:14
- *o* of the four beasts gave unto ... Rev 15:7 *1520*
- there came *o* of the seven angels ... Rev 17:1 *1520*
- *o* is, and the other is not yet ... Rev 17:10 *1520*
- as kings *o* hour with the beast ... Rev 17:12 *3391*
- These have *o* mind, and shall give ... Rev 17:13 *3391*
- shall her plagues come in *o* day ... Rev 18:8 *3391*
- for in *o* hour is thy judgment ... Rev 18:10 *3391*
- For in *o* hour so great riches is ... Rev 18:17 *3391*
- for in *o* hour is she made ... Rev 18:19
- there came unto me *o* of the seven ... Rev 21:9 *1520*
- every several gate was of *o* pearl ... Rev 21:21 *1520*

ONE'S

- of death than the day of *o* birth ... Eccl 7:1
- every *o* bands were loosed ... Acts 16:26

ONES

- wealth, and all their little *o* ... Gen 34:29
- we, and thou, and also our little *o* ... Gen 43:8
- land of Egypt for your little *o* ... Gen 45:19
- their father, and their little *o* ... Gen 46:5
- and for food for your little *o* ... Gen 47:24
- only their little *o*, and their ... Gen 50:8
- nourish you, and your little *o* ... Gen 50:21
- will let you go, and your little *o* ... Ex 10:10
- let your little *o* also go with ... Ex 10:24
- But your little *o*, which ye said ... Num 14:31
- captives, and their little *o* ... Num 31:9
- every male among the little *o* ... Num 31:17
- and cities for our little *o* ... Num 32:16
- our little *o* shall dwell in the ... Num 32:17
- you cities for your little *o* ... Num 32:24
- Our little *o*, our wives, our ... Num 32:26
- Moreover your little *o*, which ye ... Deut 1:39
- and the women, and the little *o* ... Deut 2:34
- But your wives, and your little *o* ... Deut 3:19
- But the women, and the little *o* ... Deut 20:14
- ground, whether they be young *o* ... Deut 22:6
- Your little *o*, your wives, and thy ... Deut 29:11
- Your wives, your little *o* ... Josh 1:14
- with the women, and the little *o* ... Josh 8:35
- the pransings of their mighty *o* ... Judg 5:22
- and departed, and put the little *o* ... Judg 18:21
- all the little *o* that were with ... 2Sa 15:22
- children of Jacob, his chosen *o* ... 1Chr 16:13
- the LORD, with their little *o* ... 2Chr 20:13
- genealogy of all their little *o* ... 2Chr 31:18
- way for us, and for our little *o* ... Ezr 8:21
- would assault them, both little *o* ... Est 8:11
- forth their little *o* like a flock ... Job 21:11
- when his young *o* cry unto God ... Job 38:41
- they bring forth their young *o* ... Job 39:3
- Their young *o* are in good liking, ... Job 39:4
- is hardened against her young *o* ... Job 39:16
- Her young *o* also suck up blood ... Job 39:30
- the poor may fall by his strong *o* ... Ps 10:10
- and consulted against thy hidden *o* ... Ps 83:3
- thy little *o* against the stones ... Ps 137:9
- How long, ye simple *o*, will ye ... Prov 1:22
- And beheld among the simple *o* ... Prov 7:7
- of the fat *o* shall strangers eat ... Is 5:17
- send among his fat *o* leanness ... Is 10:16
- the high *o* of stature shall be ... Is 10:33
- their young *o* shall lie down ... Is 11:7
- I have commanded my sanctified *o* ... Is 13:3
- called my mighty *o* for mine anger ... Is 13:3
- even all the chief *o* of the earth ... Is 14:9
- of the high *o* that are on high ... Is 24:21
- *o* is as a storm against the wall ... Is 25:4
- terrible *o* shall be brought low ... Is 25:5
- the multitude of the terrible *o* ... Is 29:5
- be troubled, ye careless *o* ... Is 32:11
- their valiant *o* shall cry without ... Is 33:7
- the heart of the contrite *o* ... Is 57:15
- also taught the wicked *o* thy ways ... Jer 2:33
- of the neighing of his strong *o* ... Jer 8:16
- sent their little *o* to the waters ... Jer 14:3
- their mighty *o* are beaten down, ... Jer 46:5
- her little *o* have caused a cry to ... Jer 48:4
- of the head of the tumultuous *o* ... Jer 48:45 1121
- they give suck to their young *o* ... Lam 4:3
- demand by the word of the holy *o* ... Dan 4:17
- for it came up four notable *o* ... Dan 8:8
- kingdom, and upright *o* with him ... Dan 11:17
- cause thy mighty *o* to come down ... Joel 3:11
- he, These are the two anointed *o* ... Zec 4:14
- turn mine hand upon the little *o* ... Zec 13:7
- drink unto one of these little *o* ... Mt 10:42
- little *o* which believe in me ... Mt 18:6
- despise not one of these little *o* ... Mt 18:10
- of these little *o* should perish ... Mt 18:14
- these little *o* that believe in me ... Mk 9:42
- their great *o* exercise authority ... Mk 10:42
- offend one of these little *o* ... Lk 17:2

ONESIMUS (*o-nes'-i-mus*) *A Christian of Colosse.*

- With *O*, a faithful and beloved ... Col 4:9 *3682*
- the Colossians by Tychicus and *O* ... Col *s* *3682*
- I beseech thee for my son *O* ... Philem 10 *3682*
- from Rome to Philemon, by *O* ... Philem *s* *3682*

ONESIPHORUS (*o-ne-sif'-o-rus*) *A Christian of Ephesus.*

- give mercy unto the house of *O* ... 2Ti 1:16 *3683*
- and Aquila, and the household of *O* ... 2Ti 4:19 *3683*

ONIONS

- melons, and the leeks, and the *o* ... Num 11:5 1211

ONLY

- his heart was *o* evil continually ... Gen 6:5 7535
- Noah *o* remained alive, and they ... Gen 7:23 389
- Save *o* that which the young men ... Gen 14:24
- *o* unto these men do nothing ... Gen 19:8
- thine *o* son Isaac, whom thou ... Gen 22:2 3173
- thy son, thine *o* son from me ... Gen 22:12 3162
- not withheld thy son, thine *o* son ... Gen 22:16 3173
- *o* bring not my son thither again ... Gen 24:8
- *o* obey my voice, and go fetch me ... Gen 27:13
- *O* herein will the men consent ... Gen 34:22 389
- *o* let us consent unto them, and ... Gen 34:23 389
- *o* in the throne will I be greater ... Gen 41:40 7535
- *O* the land of the priests bought ... Gen 47:22 7535
- except the land of the priests *o* ... Gen 47:26 905
- *o* their little ones, and their ... Gen 50:8 7535
- they may remain in the river *o* ... Ex 8:9
- they shall remain in the river *o* ... Ex 8:11 7535
- *o* ye shall not go very far away ... Ex 8:28
- *O* in the land of Goshen, where ... Ex 9:26 7535
- my sin *o* this once, and intreat ... Ex 10:17
- take away from me this death *o* ... Ex 10:17
- *o* let your flocks and your herds ... Ex 10:24
- that *o* may be done of you ... Ex 12:16
- *o* he shall pay for the loss of ... Ex 21:19 7535
- any god, save unto the LORD *o* ... Ex 22:20 905
- For that is his covering *o* ... Ex 22:27 905
- *O* he shall not go in unto the ... Lev 21:23 389
- *O* the firstling of the beasts, ... Lev 27:26 389
- *O* thou shalt not number the tribe ... Num 1:49 389
- the LORD indeed spoken *o* by Moses ... Num 12:2 7535
- *O* rebel not ye against the LORD, ... Num 14:9 389
- *o* they shall not come nigh the ... Num 18:3 389
- I will *o*, without doing any thing ... Num 20:19 7535
- but *o* the word that I shalt speak ... Num 22:35
- *O* the gold, and the silver, the ... Num 31:22 389
- *o* to the family of the tribe of ... Num 36:6 389
- *o* I will pass through on my feet ... Deut 2:28 7535
- *O* the cattle we took for a prey ... Deut 2:35 7535
- *O* unto the land of the children ... Deut 2:37 7535
- For *o* Og king of Bashan remained ... Deut 3:11 7535
- *O* take heed to thyself, and keep ... Deut 4:9 7535
- *o* ye heard a voice ... Deut 4:12 2108
- that man doth not live by bread *o* ... Deut 8:3 905
- *O* the LORD had a delight in thy ... Deut 10:15 7535
- *O* ye shall not eat the blood ... Deut 12:16 7535
- *O* be sure that thou eat not the ... Deut 12:23 7535
- *O* thy holy things which thou hast ... Deut 12:26 7535
- *O* if thou carefully hearken unto ... Deut 15:5 7535
- *O* thou shalt not eat the blood ... Deut 15:23 7535
- *O* the trees which thou knowest ... Deut 20:20 7535
- then the man *o* that lay with her ... Deut 22:25 905
- and thou shalt be above *o*, and thou ... Deut 28:13 7535
- and thou shalt be *o* oppressed ... Deut 28:29 389
- and thou shalt be *o* oppressed ... Deut 28:33 389
- Neither with you *o* do I make this ... Deut 29:14 905
- *O* be thou strong and very ... Josh 1:7 7535
- *o* the LORD thy God be with thee, ... Josh 1:17 7535
- *o* be strong and of a good courage ... Josh 1:18 7535
- *o* on that day they compassed the ... Josh 6:15 7535
- *o* Rahab the harlot shall live, ... Josh 6:17 7535
- *o* the silver, and the gold, and the ... Josh 6:24 7535
- *o* the spoil thereof, and the ... Josh 8:2 7535
- *O* the cattle and the spoil of that ... Josh 8:27 7535
- burned none of them, save Hazor *o* ... Josh 11:13 905
- *o* in Gaza, in Gath, and in Ashdod, ... Josh 11:22 7535
- *o* divide thou it by lot unto the ... Josh 13:6 7535
- *O* unto the tribe of Levi he gave ... Josh 13:14 7535
- thou shalt not have one lot *o* ... Josh 17:17
- *O* that the generations of the ... Judg 3:2 7535
- and if the dew be on the fleece *o* ... Judg 6:37 905
- it now be dry *o* upon the fleece ... Judg 6:39 905
- for it was dry upon the fleece *o* ... Judg 6:40 905
- deliver us *o*, we pray thee, this ... Judg 10:15 389
- and she was his *o* child ... Judg 11:34 3173
- *o* this once, O God, that I may be ... Judg 16:28 389
- *o* lodge not in the street ... Judg 19:20 7535
- *o* her lips moved, but her voice ... 1Sa 1:13 7535
- *o* the LORD establish his word ... 1Sa 1:23 389
- *o* the stump of Dagon was left to ... 1Sa 5:4 7535
- unto the LORD, and serve him *o* ... 1Sa 7:3 905
- Ashtaroth, and served the LORD *o* ... 1Sa 7:4 905
- *O* fear the LORD, and serve him in ... 1Sa 12:24 389
- *o* be thou valiant for me, and ... 1Sa 18:17 389
- thou shalt not *o* while yet I live ... 1Sa 20:14
- *o* Jonathan and David knew the ... 1Sa 20:39 389
- for Amnon *o* is dead ... 2Sa 13:32 905
- for Amnon *o* is dead ... 2Sa 13:33 905
- and I will smite the king *o* ... 2Sa 17:2 905
- deliver him *o*, and I will depart ... 2Sa 20:21
- returned after him *o* to spoil ... 2Sa 23:10 389
- *O* the people sacrificed in high ... 1Kin 3:2 7535
- *o* he sacrificed and burnt incense ... 1Kin 3:3 7535
- he was the *o* officer which was in ... 1Kin 4:19 259
- (for thou, even thou *o*, knowest ... 1Kin 8:39 905
- David, but the tribe of Judah *o* ... 1Kin 12:20 905
- to do that *o* which was right in ... 1Kin 14:8 7535
- for he *o* of Jeroboam shall come ... 1Kin 14:13 905
- save *o* in the matter of Uriah the ... 1Kin 15:5 7535
- unto the people, I, even I *o* ... 1Kin 18:22 905
- and I, even I *o*, am left ... 1Kin 19:10 905
- and I, even I *o*, am left ... 1Kin 19:14 905
- save *o* with the king of Israel ... 1Kin 22:31 905
- *o* in Kir-haraseth left they the ... 2Kin 3:25
- but the worshippers of Baal *o* ... 2Kin 10:23 905
- left but the tribe of Judah *o* ... 2Kin 17:18 905
- art the LORD God, even thou *o* ... 2Kin 19:19 905
- *o* if they will observe to do ... 2Kin 21:8 7535
- *O* the LORD give thee wisdom and ... 1Chr 22:12
- save *o* to burn sacrifice before ... 2Chr 2:6
- (for thou *o* knowest the hearts of ... 2Chr 6:30
- save *o* with the king of Israel ... 2Chr 18:30 905
- yet unto the LORD their God *o* ... 2Chr 33:17 7535
- *O* Jonathan the son of Asahel and ... Ezr 10:15 389
- hath not done wrong to the king *o* ... Est 1:16 905
- *o* upon himself put not forth ... Job 1:12 3535
- I *o* am escaped alone to tell thee ... Job 1:15 7535
- I *o* am escaped alone to tell thee ... Job 1:16 7535
- I *o* am escaped alone to tell thee ... Job 1:17 7535
- I *o* am escaped alone to tell thee ... Job 1:19 7535
- *O* do not two things unto me ... Job 13:20 389
- a nation, or against a man *o* ... Job 34:29 3162
- *o* makest me dwell in safety ... Ps 4:8 910
- Against thee, thee *o*, have I ... Ps 51:4 905
- He *o* is my rock and my salvation ... Ps 62:2 389
- They *o* consult to cast him down ... Ps 62:4 389
- My soul, wait thou *o* upon God ... Ps 62:5 389
- He *o* is my rock and my salvation ... Ps 62:6 389
- righteousness, even of thine *o* ... Ps 71:16 905
- who *o* doeth wondrous things ... Ps 72:18 905
- *O* with thine eyes shalt thou ... Ps 91:8 7535
- *o* beloved in the sight of my ... Prov 4:3 3173
- Let them be *o* thine own, and not ... Prov 5:17
- desire of the righteous is *o* good ... Prov 11:23 389
- *O* by pride cometh contention ... Prov 13:10 7535
- of the lips tendeth *o* to penury ... Prov 14:23 389
- An evil man seeketh *o* rebellion ... Prov 17:11 389
- diligent tend *o* to plenteousness ... Prov 21:5 389
- every one that is hasty *o* to want ... Prov 21:5 389
- this *o* have I found, that God ... Eccl 7:29 905
- she is the *o* one of her mother, ... Song 6:9
- *o* let us be called by thy name, ... Is 4:1 7535
- but by thee *o* will we make ... Is 26:13 905
- it shall be a vexation *o* to ... Is 28:19 7535
- thou art the LORD, even thou *o* ... Is 37:20 905
- *O* acknowledge thine iniquity, ... Jer 3:13 389
- thee mourning, as for an *o* son ... Jer 6:26 3173
- the children of Judah have *o* done ... Jer 32:30 389
- *o* provoked me to anger with the ... Jer 32:30 389
- an *o* evil, behold, is come ... Eze 7:5 259
- they *o* shall be delivered, but ... Eze 14:16 905
- but they *o* shall be delivered ... Eze 14:18 905
- they shall *o* poll their heads ... Eze 44:20 3697
- You *o* have I known of all the ... Amos 3:2 7535
- it as the mourning of an *o* son ... Amos 8:10 3173
- as one mourneth for his *o* son ... Zec 12:10 3173
- God, and him *o* shalt thou serve ... Mt 4:10 *3441*
- And if ye salute your brethren *o* ... Mt 5:47 *3440*
- but speak the word *o*, and my ... Mt 8:8 *3440*
- water *o* in the name of a disciple ... Mt 10:42 *3440*
- with him, but *o* for the priests ... Mt 12:4 *3441*
- *o* touch the hem of his garment ... Mt 14:36 *3440*
- they saw no man, save Jesus *o* ... Mt 17:8 *3441*
- nothing thereon, but leaves *o* ... Mt 21:19 *3440*
- ye shall not *o* do this which is ... Mt 21:21 *3440*
- angels of heaven, but my Father *o* ... Mt 24:36 *3441*
- who can forgive sins but God *o* ... Mk 2:7 *1520*
- Be not afraid, *o* believe ... Mk 5:36 *3440*
- for their journey, save a staff *o* ... Mk 6:8 *3440*
- save Jesus *o* with themselves ... Mk 9:8 *3441*
- God, and him *o* shalt thou serve ... Lk 4:8 *3441*
- the *o* son of his mother, and she ... Lk 7:12 *3439*
- For he had one *o* daughter ... Lk 8:42 *3439*
- believe *o*, and she shall be made ... Lk 8:50 *3440*
- for he is mine *o* child ... Lk 9:38 *3439*
- him, Art thou *o* a stranger in ... Lk 24:18 *3441*
- the glory as of the *o* begotten of ... Jn 1:14 *3439*
- the *o* begotten Son, which is in ... Jn 1:18 *3439*
- that he gave his *o* begotten Son ... Jn 3:16 *3439*
- name of the *o* begotten Son of God ... Jn 3:18 *3439*
- because he not *o* had broken the ... Jn 5:18 *3440*
- the honour that cometh from God *o* ... Jn 5:44 *3441*

And not for that nation o, but ... Jn 11:52 3440
they came not for Jesus' sake o ... Jn 12:9 3440
unto him, Lord, not my feet o ... Jn 13:9 3440
might know thee the o true God ... Jn 17:3 3441
o they were baptized in the name ... Acts 8:16 3440
word to none but unto the Jews o ... Acts 11:19 3440
knowing o the baptism of John ... Acts 18:25 3440
So that not o this our craft is ... Acts 19:27 3440
for I am ready not to be bound o ... Acts 21:13 3440
save o that they keep themselves ... Acts 21:25 3440
I would to God, that not o thou ... Acts 26:29 3440
not o of the lading and ship, but ... Acts 27:10 3440
not o do the same, but have ... Rom 1:32 3440
Is he the God of the Jews o ... Rom 3:29 3440
then upon the circumcision o ... Rom 4:9
who are not of the circumcision o ... Rom 4:12 3440
not to that o which is of the law ... Rom 4:16 3440
And not o so, but we glory in ... Rom 5:3 3440
And not o so, but we also joy in ... Rom 5:11 3440
not o they, but ourselves also, ... Rom 8:23 3440
And not o this ... Rom 9:10 3440
he hath called, not of the Jews o ... Rom 9:24 3440
not o for wrath, but also for ... Rom 13:5 3440
unto whom not o I give thanks ... Rom 16:4 3441
To God o wise, be glory through ... Rom 16:27 3441
o in the Lord ... 1Cor 7:39 3440
Or I o and Barnabas, have not we ... 1Cor 9:6 3441
or came it unto you o ... 1Cor 14:36 3441
If in this life o we have hope in ... 1Cor 15:19 3440
And not by his coming o, but by ... 2Cor 7:7 3440
not o to do, but also to be ... 2Cor 8:10 3440
And not that o, but who was also ... 2Cor 8:19 3440
not o in the sight of the Lord, ... 2Cor 8:21 3440
of this service not o supplieth ... 2Cor 9:12 3440
But they had heard o, That he ... Gal 1:23 3440
O they would that we should ... Gal 2:10 3440
This o would I learn of you, ... Gal 3:2 3440
not o when I am present with you ... Gal 4:18 3440
o use not liberty for an occasion ... Gal 5:13 3440
o lest they should suffer ... Gal 6:12 3440
not o in this world, but also in ... Eph 1:21 3440
O let your conversation be as it ... Phil 1:27 3440
not o to believe on him, but also ... Phil 1:29 3440
obeyed, not as in my presence o ... Phil 2:12 3440
and not on him o, but on me also, ... Phil 2:27 3440
giving and receiving, but ye o ... Phil 4:15 3441
These o are my fellow workers ... Col 4:11 3441
came not unto you in word o ... 1Th 1:5 3440
of the Lord not o in Macedonia ... 1Th 1:8 3440
unto you, not the gospel of God o ... 1Th 2:8 3440
o he who now letteth will let, ... 2Th 2:7 3440
the o wise God, be honour and ... 1Ti 1:17 3441
not o idle, but tattlers also and ... 1Ti 5:13 3440
o Potentate, the King of kings, ... 1Ti 6:15 3441
Who o hath immortality, dwelling ... 1Ti 6:16 3441
there are not o vessels of gold ... 2Ti 2:20 3440
and not to me o, but unto all them ... 2Ti 4:8 3440
O Luke is with me ... 2Ti 4:11 3441
Which stood o in meats and drinks, ... Heb 9:10 3440
offered up his o begotten son ... Heb 11:17 3439
once more I shake not the earth o ... Heb 12:26 3440
of the word, and not hearers o ... Jas 1:22 3440
is justified, and not by faith o ... Jas 2:24 3440
not o to the good and gentle, but ... 1Pet 2:18 3440
and not for ours o, but also for ... 1Jn 2:2 3440
because that God sent his o ... 1Jn 4:9 3439
not by water o, but by water and ... 1Jn 5:6 3440
and not I o, but also all they ... 2Jn 1 3441
and denying the o Lord God ... Jude 4 3441
To the o wise God our Saviour, be ... Jude 25 3441
but o those men which have not ... Rev 9:4 3441
for thou o art holy ... Rev 15:4 3441

ONO (*o'-no*)
1. A city in Benjamin.
and Shamed, who built O ... 1Chr 8:12 207
The children of Lod, Hadid, and O ... Ezr 2:33 207
The children of Lod, Hadid, and O ... Neh 7:37 207
Lod, and O, the valley of ... Neh 11:35 207
2. A valley near Jerusalem.
of the villages in the plain of O ... Neh 6:2 207

ONWARD
went o in all their journeys ... Ex 40:36

ONYCHA
thee sweet spices, stacte, and o ... Ex 30:34 7827

ONYX
there is bdellium and the o stone ... Gen 2:12 7718
O stones, and stones to be set in ... Ex 25:7 7718
And thou shalt take two o stones ... Ex 28:9 7718
the fourth row a beryl, and an o ... Ex 28:20 7718
o stones, and stones to be set for ... Ex 35:9 7718
And the rulers brought o stones ... Ex 35:27 7718
they wrought o stones inclosed in ... Ex 39:6 7718
And the fourth row, a beryl, an o ... Ex 39:13 7718
o stones, and stones to be set, ... 1Chr 29:2 7718
of Ophir, with the precious o ... Job 28:16 7718
and the diamond, the beryl, the o ... Eze 28:13 7718

OPEN
in the o firmament of heaven ... Gen 1:20 6440
herself, and sat in an o place ... Gen 38:14 5869
And if a man shall o a pit ... Ex 21:33 6605
bird loose into the o field ... Lev 14:7 6440
out of the city into the o fields ... Lev 14:53 6440
which they offer in the o field ... Lev 17:5 6440
instead of such as o every womb ... Num 8:16 6363
thing, and the earth o her mouth ... Num 16:30 6475
every o vessel, which hath no ... Num 19:15 6605
with a sword in the o fields ... Num 19:16 6440
man whose eyes are o hath said ... Num 24:3 8365
a trance, but having his eyes o ... Num 24:4 1540
man whose eyes are o hath said ... Num 24:15 8365
a trance, but having his eyes o ... Num 24:16 1540
But thou shalt o thine hand wide ... Deut 15:8 6605
Thou shalt o thine hand wide unto ... Deut 15:11 6605
o unto thee, then it shall be, ... Deut 20:11 6605
The LORD shall o unto thee his ... Deut 28:12 6605
and they left the city o, and ... Josh 8:17 6605
O the mouth of the cave, and bring ... Josh 10:22 6605
there was no o vision ... 1Sa 3:1 6555
are encamped in the o fields ... 2Sa 11:11 6440
carved with knops and o flowers ... 1Kin 6:18 6358
o flowers, within and without ... 1Kin 6:29 6358
o flowers, and overlaid them with ... 1Kin 6:32 6358
and palm trees and o flowers ... 1Kin 6:35 6358
That thine eyes may be o toward ... 1Kin 8:29 6605
That thine eyes may be o unto the ... 1Kin 8:52 6605
o his eyes, that he may see ... 2Kin 6:17 6491
o the eyes of these men, that ... 2Kin 6:20 6491
Then o the door, and flee, and ... 2Kin 9:3 6605
And he said, O the window eastward ... 2Kin 13:17 6605
o, LORD, thine eyes, and see ... 2Kin 19:16 6491
eyes may be o upon this house day ... 2Chr 6:20 6605
I beseech thee, thine eyes be o ... 2Chr 6:40 6605
Now mine eyes shall be o, and mine ... 2Chr 7:15 6605
now be attentive, and thine eyes o ... Neh 1:6 6605
time with an o letter in his hand ... Neh 6:5 6605
speak, and o his lips against thee ... Job 11:5 6605
dost thou o thine eyes upon such ... Job 14:3 6491
I will o my lips and answer ... Job 32:20 6605
men in the o sight of others ... Job 34:26 4725
doth Job o his mouth in vain ... Job 35:16 6475
Who can o the doors of his face ... Job 41:14 6605
their throat is an o sepulchre ... Ps 5:9 6605
his ears are o unto their cry ... Ps 34:15
I will o my dark saying upon the ... Ps 49:4 6605
O Lord, o thou my lips ... Ps 51:15 6605
I will o my mouth in a parable ... Ps 78:2 6605
o thy mouth wide, and I will fill ... Ps 81:10
O to me the gates of ... Ps 118:19 6605
O thou mine eyes, that I may ... Ps 119:18 1540
but a fool layeth o his folly ... Prov 13:16 6566
o thine eyes, and thou shalt be ... Prov 20:13 6491
O rebuke is better than secret ... Prov 27:5 1540
O thy mouth for the dumb in the ... Prov 31:8 6605
O thy mouth, judge righteously, ... Prov 31:9 6605
O to me, my sister, my love, my ... Song 5:2 6605
I rose up to o to my beloved ... Song 5:5 6605
shall devour Israel with o mouth ... Is 9:12 3605
so he shall o, and none shall shut ... Is 22:22 6605
and he shall shut, and none shall o ... Is 22:22 6605
the windows from on high are o ... Is 24:18 6605
O ye the gates, that the ... Is 26:2 6605
doth he o and break the clods of ... Is 28:24 6605
o thine eyes, O LORD, and see ... Is 37:17 6491
I will o rivers in high places, ... Is 41:18 6605
To o the blind eyes, to bring out ... Is 42:7 6491
to o before him the two leaved ... Is 45:1 6605
let the earth o, and let them ... Is 45:8 6605
thy gates shall be o continually ... Is 60:11 6605
Their quiver is as an o sepulchre ... Jer 5:16 6605
fall as dung upon the o field ... Jer 9:22 6440
be shut up, and none shall o them ... Jer 13:19 6605
and custom, and that which was o ... Jer 32:11 1540
and this evidence which is o ... Jer 32:14 1540
for thine eyes are o upon all the ... Jer 32:19 6491
utmost border, o her storehouses ... Jer 50:26 6605
o thy mouth, and eat that I give ... Eze 2:8 6475
I will o thy mouth, and thou shalt ... Eze 3:27 6605
thou wast cast out in the o field ... Eze 16:5 6440
never o thy mouth any more ... Eze 16:63 6610
to o the mouth in the slaughter, ... Eze 21:22 6605
I will o the side of Moab from ... Eze 25:9 6605
thou shalt fall upon the o fields ... Eze 29:5 6440
cast thee forth upon the o field ... Eze 32:4 6440
him that is in the o field will I ... Eze 33:27 6440
were very many in the o valley ... Eze 37:2 6440
I will o your graves, and cause ... Eze 37:12 6605
Thou shalt fall upon the o field ... Eze 39:5 6440
one shall then o him the gate ... Eze 46:12 6605
his windows being o in his ... Dan 6:10 6606
o thine eyes, and behold our ... Dan 9:18 6491
be set wide o unto thine enemies ... Nah 3:13 6605
O thy doors, O Lebanon, that the ... Zec 11:1 6605
I will o mine eyes upon the house ... Zec 12:4 6491
if I will not o you the windows ... Mal 3:10 6605
I will o my mouth in parables ... Mt 13:35 455
saying, Lord, Lord, o to us ... Mt 25:11 455
they may o unto him immediately ... Lk 12:36 455
saying, Lord, Lord, o unto us ... Lk 13:25 455
Hereafter ye shall see heaven o ... Jn 1:51 455
Can a devil o the eyes of the ... Jn 10:21 455
and seeing the prison doors o ... Acts 16:27 455
Paul was now about to o his mouth ... Acts 18:14 455
against any man, the law is o ... Acts 19:38 71
To o their eyes, and to turn them ... Acts 26:18 455
Their throat is an o sepulchre ... Rom 3:13 455
with o face beholding as in a ... 2Cor 3:18 343
our mouth is o unto you, our ... 2Cor 6:11 455
that I may o my mouth boldly, to ... Eph 6:19
that God would o unto us a door ... Col 4:3 455
Some men's sins are o beforehand ... 1Ti 5:24 4271
afresh, and put him to an o shame ... Heb 6:6 3856
his ears are o unto their prayers ... 1Pet 3:12
I have set before thee an o door ... Rev 3:8 455
o the door, I will come in to him ... Rev 3:20 455
Who is worthy to o the book ... Rev 5:2 455
the earth, was able to o the book ... Rev 5:3 455
no man was found worthy to o ... Rev 5:4 455
hath prevailed to o the book ... Rev 5:5 455
book, and to o the seals thereof ... Rev 5:9 455
had in his hand a little book o ... Rev 10:2 455
take the little book which is o ... Rev 10:8 455

OPENED
then your eyes shall be o ... Gen 3:5 6491
And the eyes of them both were o ... Gen 3:7 6491
which hath o her mouth to receive ... Gen 4:11 6475
and the windows of heaven were o ... Gen 7:11 6605
that Noah o the window of the ark ... Gen 8:6 6605
God o her eyes, and she saw a well ... Gen 21:19 6491
Leah was hated, he o her womb ... Gen 29:31 6605
hearkened to her, and o her womb ... Gen 30:22 6605
Joseph o all the storehouses, and ... Gen 41:56 6605
as one of them o his sack to give ... Gen 42:27 6605
that we o our sacks, and, behold, ... Gen 43:21 6605
ground, and o every man his sack ... Gen 44:11 6605
And when she had o it, she saw the ... Ex 2:6 6605
And the earth o her mouth, and ... Num 16:32 6605
the LORD o the mouth of the ass, ... Num 22:28 6605
Then the LORD o the eyes of ... Num 22:31 1540
And the earth o her mouth, and ... Num 26:10 6605
how the earth o her mouth ... Deut 11:6 6475
he o not the doors of the parlour ... Judg 3:25 6605
they took a key, and o them ... Judg 3:25 6605
she o a bottle of milk, and gave ... Judg 4:19 6605
for I have o my mouth unto the ... Judg 11:35 6475
if thou hast o thy mouth unto the ... Judg 11:36 6475
o the doors of the house, and went ... Judg 19:27 6605
o the doors of the house of the ... 1Sa 3:15 6605
times, and the child o his eyes ... 2Kin 4:35 6491
the LORD o the eyes of the young ... 2Kin 6:17 6491
the LORD o their eyes, and they ... 2Kin 6:20 6491
And he o the door, and fled ... 2Kin 9:10 6605
And he o it ... 2Kin 13:17 6605
because they o not to him ... 2Kin 15:16 6605
o the doors of the house of the ... 2Chr 29:3 6605
be o until the sun be hot ... Neh 7:3 6605
Ezra o the book in the sight of ... Neh 8:5 6605
and when he o it, all the people ... Neh 8:5 6605
not be o till after the sabbath ... Neh 13:19 6605
After this o Job his mouth, and ... Job 3:1 6605
they o their mouth wide as for ... Job 29:23 6473
but I o my doors to the traveller ... Job 31:32 6605
Behold, now I have o my mouth ... Job 33:2 6605
gates of death been o unto thee ... Job 38:17 1540
they o their mouth wide against ... Ps 35:21
I was dumb, I o not my mouth ... Ps 39:9 6605
mine ears hast thou o ... Ps 40:6 3738
above, and o the doors of heaven, ... Ps 78:23 6605
He o the rock, and the waters ... Ps 105:41 6605
The earth o and swallowed up ... Ps 106:17 6605
of the deceitful are o against me ... Ps 109:2 6605
I o my mouth, and panted ... Ps 119:131 6473
I o to my beloved ... Song 5:6 6605
o her mouth without measure ... Is 5:14 6473
or o the mouth, or peeped ... Is 10:14 6475
that o not the house of his ... Is 14:17 6605
the eyes of the blind shall be o ... Is 35:5 6491
time that thine ear was not o ... Is 48:8 6605
The Lord GOD hath o mine ear ... Is 50:5 6605
afflicted, yet he o not his mouth ... Is 53:7 6605
for unto thee have I o my cause ... Jer 20:12 1540
The LORD hath o his armoury ... Jer 50:25 6605
All thine enemies have o their ... Lam 2:16 6475
All our enemies have o their ... Lam 3:46 6475
Chebar, that the heavens were o ... Eze 1:1 6605
So I o my mouth, and he caused me ... Eze 3:2 6605
hast o thy feet to every one that ... Eze 16:25 6589
be o to him which is escaped ... Eze 24:27 6605
had o my mouth, until he came to ... Eze 33:22 6605
and my mouth was o, and I was no ... Eze 33:22 6605
LORD, when I have o your graves ... Eze 37:13 6605
shall be shut, it shall not be o ... Eze 44:2 6605
but on the sabbath it shall be o ... Eze 46:1 6605
day of the new moon it shall be o ... Eze 46:1 6605
was set, and the books were o ... Dan 7:10 6606
then I o my mouth, and spake, and ... Dan 10:16 6605
gates of the rivers shall be o ... Nah 2:6 6605
fountain o to the house of David ... Zec 13:1 6605
when they had o their treasures, ... Mt 2:11 455
lo, the heavens were o unto him ... Mt 3:16 455
he o his mouth, and taught them, ... Mt 5:2 455
knock, and it shall be o unto you ... Mt 7:7 455
him that knocketh it shall be o ... Mt 7:8 455
And their eyes were o ... Mt 9:30 455
and when thou hast o his mouth ... Mt 17:27 455
him, Lord, that our eyes may be o ... Mt 20:33 455
And the graves were o ... Mt 27:52 455
the water, he saw the heavens o ... Mk 1:10 4977
him, Ephphatha, that is, Be o ... Mk 7:34 1272
And straightway his ears were o ... Mk 7:35 1272
And his mouth was o immediately ... Lk 1:64 455
and praying, the heaven was o ... Lk 3:21 455
And when he had o the book ... Lk 4:17 380
knock, and it shall be o unto you ... Lk 11:9 455
him that knocketh it shall be o ... Lk 11:10 455
And their eyes were o, and they ... Lk 24:31 1272
while he o to us the scriptures ... Lk 24:32 1272
Then o he their understanding, ... Lk 24:45 1272
unto him, How were thine eyes o ... Jn 9:10 455
made the clay, and o his eyes ... Jn 9:14 455
of him, that he hath o thine eyes ... Jn 9:17 455
or who hath o his eyes, we know ... Jn 9:21 455
how o he thine eyes ... Jn 9:26 455
he is, and yet he hath o mine eyes ... Jn 9:30 455
o the eyes of one that was born ... Jn 9:32 455
which o the eyes of the blind, ... Jn 11:37 455
Lord by night o the prison doors ... Acts 5:19 455
but when we had o, we found no ... Acts 5:23 455
said, Behold, I see the heavens o ... Acts 7:56 455
shearer, so o he not his mouth ... Acts 8:32 455
Then Philip o his mouth, and began ... Acts 8:35 455
and when his eyes were o, he saw ... Acts 9:8 455
And she o her eyes ... Acts 9:40 455
And saw heaven o, and a certain ... Acts 10:11 455
Then Peter o his mouth, and said, ... Acts 10:34 455
which o to them of his own accord ... Acts 12:10 455
she o not the gate for gladness, ... Acts 12:14 455
and when they had o the door ... Acts 12:16 455
how he had o the door of faith ... Acts 14:27 455

whose heart the Lord o, that she Acts 16:14 *1272*
immediately all the doors were o Acts 16:26 *455*
door and effectual is o unto me 1Cor 16:9 *455*
a door was o unto me of the Lord, 2Cor 2:12 *455*
o unto the eyes of him with whom Heb 4:13 *5136*
behold, a door was o in heaven Rev 4:1 *455*
when the Lamb o one of the seals Rev 6:1 *455*
when he had o the second seal, I Rev 6:3 *455*
when he had o the third seal, I Rev 6:5 *455*
when he had o the fourth seal, I Rev 6:7 *455*
when he had o the fifth seal, I Rev 6:9 *455*
when he had o the sixth seal Rev 6:12 *455*
when he had o the seventh seal, Rev 8:1 *455*
And he o the bottomless pit Rev 9:2 *455*
the temple of God was o in heaven Rev 11:19 *455*
woman, and the earth o her mouth Rev 12:16 *455*
he o his mouth in blasphemy Rev 13:6 *455*
of the testimony in heaven was o Rev 15:5 *455*
And I saw heaven o, and behold a Rev 19:11 *455*
and the books were o Rev 20:12 *455*
and another book was o, which is Rev 20:12 *455*

OPENEST
thou o thine hand, they are Ps 104:28 6605
Thou o thine hand, and satisfiest Ps 145:16 6605

OPENETH
whatsoever o the womb among the Ex 13:2 6363
the LORD all that o the matrix Ex 13:12 6363
to the LORD all that o the matrix Ex 13:15 6363
All that o the matrix is mine Ex 34:19 6363
of all the firstborn that o the Num 3:12 6363
Every thing that o the matrix in Num 18:15 6363
he o his eyes, and he is not Job 27:19 6491
Then he o the ears of men, and Job 33:16 1540
He o also their ear to discipline Job 36:10 1540
o their ears in oppression Job 36:15 1540
a dumb man that o not his mouth Ps 38:13 6605
The LORD o the eyes of the blind Ps 146:8 6491
but he that o wide his lips shall Prov 13:3 6589
he o not his mouth in the gate Prov 24:7 6605
She o her mouth with wisdom Prov 31:26 6605
is dumb, so he o not his mouth Is 53:7 6605
the fire all that o the womb Eze 20:26 6363
Every male that o the womb shall Lk 2:23 *1272*
To him the porter o Jn 10:3 *455*
hath the key of David, he that o Rev 3:7 *455*
and shutteth, and no man o Rev 3:7 *455*

OPENING
the o thereof every morning 1Chr 9:27 4668
up a man, and there can be no o Job 12:14 6605
the o of my lips shall be right Prov 8:6 4669
o the ears, but he heareth not Is 42:20 6491
the o of the prison to them that Is 61:1 6495
I will give thee the o of the Eze 29:21 6610
O and alleging, that Christ must Acts 17:3 *1272*

OPENINGS
concourse, in the o of the gates Prov 1:21 6607

OPENLY
that was o by the way side Gen 38:21 5879
his righteousness hath he o Ps 98:2
himself shall reward thee o Mt 6:4
in secret shall reward thee o Mt 6:6
in secret, shall reward thee o Mt 6:18
no more o enter into the city Mk 1:45 *5320*
And he spake that saying o Mk 8:32 *3954*
he himself seeketh to be known o Jn 7:4
he also up unto the feast, not o Jn 7:10 *5320*
Howbeit no man spake o of him for Jn 7:13 *3954*
walked no more o among the Jews Jn 11:54 *3954*
him, I spake o to the world Jn 18:20 *3954*
up the third day, and shewed him o Acts 10:40 *1717*
They have beaten us o uncondemned Acts 16:37 *1219*
powers, he made a shew of them o Col 2:15

OPERATION
nor the o of his hands, he shall Ps 28:5 4639
consider the o of his hands Is 5:12 4639
through the faith of the o of God Col 2:12 *1753*

OPERATIONS
And there are diversities of o 1Cor 12:6 *1755*

OPHEL (*o'-fel*) *A fortified place near Jerusalem.*
and on the wall of O he built much 2Chr 27:3 6077
fish gate, and compassed about O 2Chr 33:14 6077
Moreover the Nethinims dwelt in O Neh 3:26 6077
out, even unto the wall of O Neh 3:27 6077
But the Nethinims dwelt in O Neh 11:21 6077

OPHIR (*o'-fur*)
1. A son of Joktan.
And O, and Havilah, and Jobab Gen 10:29 211
And O, and Havilah, and Jobab 1Chr 1:23 211
2. A place in southern Arabia.
And they came to O, and fetched 1Kin 9:28 211
Hiram, that brought gold from O 1Kin 10:11 211
brought in from O great plenty of 1Kin 10:11 211
of Tharshish to go to O for gold 1Kin 22:48 211
talents of gold, of the gold of O 1Chr 29:4 211
with the servants of Solomon to O 2Chr 8:18 211
which brought gold from O 2Chr 9:10 211
the gold of O as the stones of Job 22:24 211
be valued with the gold of O Job 28:16 211
did stand the queen in gold of O Ps 45:9 211
a man than the golden wedge of O Is 13:12 211

OPHNI (*of'-ni*) *A place in Benjamin.*
And Chephar-haammonai, and O Josh 18:24 6078

OPHRAH (*of'-rah*) See APHRAH.
1. A city in Benjamin.
And Avim, and Parah, and O, Josh 18:23 6084
unto the way that leadeth to O 1Sa 13:17 6084
2. A city in Manasseh.
sat under an oak which was in O Judg 6:11 6084
it is yet in O of the Abi-ezrites Judg 6:24 6084
and put it in his city, even in O Judg 8:27 6084
father, in O of the Abi-ezrites Judg 8:32 6084
went unto his father's house at O Judg 9:5 6084
3. Head of a family in Judah.
And Meonothai begat O 1Chr 4:14 6084

OPINION
and durst not shew you mine o Job 32:6 1843
I also will shew mine o Job 32:10 1843
my part, I also will shew mine o Job 32:17 1843

OPINIONS
How long halt ye between two o 1Kin 18:21 5587

OPPORTUNITY
time he sought o to betray him Mt 26:16 *2120*
sought o to betray him unto them Lk 22:6 *2120*
As we have therefore o, let us do Gal 6:10 *2540*
also careful, but ye lacked o Phil 4:10 *170*
might have had o to have returned Heb 11:15 *2540*

OPPOSE
those that o themselves 2Ti 2:25 *475*

OPPOSED
when they o themselves, and Acts 18:6 *498*

OPPOSEST
hand thou o thyself against me Job 30:21 7852

OPPOSETH
Who o and exalteth himself above 2Th 2:4 *480*

OPPOSITIONS
o of science falsely so called 1Ti 6:20 *477*

OPPRESS
wherewith the Egyptians o them Ex 3:9 3905
neither vex a stranger, nor o him Ex 22:21 3905
Also thou shalt not o a stranger Ex 23:9 3905
hand, ye shall not o one another Lev 25:14 3238
shall not therefore o one another Lev 25:17 3238
thou shalt not o him Deut 23:16 3238
Thou shalt not o an hired servant Deut 24:14 6231
and the Maonites, did o you Judg 10:12 3905
unto thee that thou shouldest o Job 10:3 6231
man of the earth may no more o Ps 10:18 6206
From the wicked that o me Ps 17:9 7703
let not the proud o me Ps 119:122 6231
neither o the afflicted in the Prov 22:22 1792
I will feed them that o thee with Is 49:26 3238
If ye o not the stranger, the Jer 7:6 6231
and I will punish all that o them Jer 30:20 3905
princes shall no more o my people Eze 45:8 3238
he loveth to o Hos 12:7 6231
which o the poor, which crush the Amos 4:1 6231
so they o a man and his house, Mic 2:2 6231
And o not the widow, nor the Zec 7:10 6231
against those that o the hireling Mal 3:5 6231
Do not rich men o you, and draw Jas 2:6 *2616*

OPPRESSED
and thou shalt be only o and Deut 28:29 6231
and thou shalt be only o and Deut 28:33 6231
by reason of them that o them Judg 2:18 3905
mightily o the children of Israel Judg 4:3 3905
out of the hand of all that o you Judg 6:9 3905
vexed and o the children of Israel Judg 10:8 7533
kingdoms, and of them that o you 1Sa 10:18 3905
whom have I o 1Sa 12:3 7533
hast not defrauded us, nor o us 1Sa 12:4 7533
because the king of Syria o them 2Kin 13:4 3905
But Hazael king of Syria o Israel 2Kin 13:22 3905
Asa o some of the people the same 2Chr 16:10 7533
Because he hath o and hath Job 20:19 7533
they make the o to cry Job 35:9
also will be a refuge for the o Ps 9:9 1790
To judge the fatherless and the o Ps 10:18 1790
O let not the o return ashamed Ps 74:21 1790
and judgment for all that are o Ps 103:6 6231
Their enemies also o them Ps 106:42 3905
executeth judgment for the o Ps 146:7 6231
the tears of such as were o Eccl 4:1 6231
seek judgment, relieve the o Is 1:17 2541
And the people shall be o, every Is 3:5 5065
no more rejoice, O thou o virgin Is 23:12 6231
O LORD, I am o Is 38:14 6234
the Assyrian o them without cause Is 52:4 6231
He was o, and he was afflicted, Is 53:7 5065
burdens, and to let the o go free Is 58:6 7533
children of Judah were o together Jer 50:33 6231
And hath not o any, but hath Eze 18:7 3238
Hath o the poor and needy, hath Eze 18:12 3238
Neither hath o any, hath not Eze 18:16 3238
his father, because he cruelly o Eze 18:18 6231
yea, they have o the stranger Eze 22:29 6231
Ephraim is o and broken in Hos 5:11 6231
the o in the midst thereof Amos 3:9 6217
him, and avenged him that was o Acts 7:24 *2669*
all that were o of the devil Acts 10:38 *2616*

OPPRESSETH
land against the enemy that o you Num 10:9 6887
he fighting daily o me Ps 56:1 3905
He that o the poor reproacheth Prov 14:31 6231
He that o the poor to increase Prov 22:16 6231
A poor man that o the poor is Prov 28:3 6231

OPPRESSING
of our nativity, from the o sword Jer 46:16 3238
for fear of the o sword they Jer 50:16 3238
filthy and polluted, to the o city Zeph 3:1 3238

OPPRESSION
I have also seen the o wherewith Ex 3:9 3906
and our labour, and our o Deut 26:7 3906
for he saw the o of Israel 2Kin 13:4 3906
and openeth their ears in o Job 36:15 3906
For the o of the poor, for the Ps 12:5 7701
because of the o of the enemy Ps 42:9 3906
because of the o of the enemy Ps 43:2 3906
our affliction and our o Ps 44:24 3906
because of the o of the wicked Ps 55:3 6125
Trust not in o, and become not Ps 62:10 6233
and speak wickedly concerning o Ps 73:8 6233
minished and brought low through o Ps 107:39 6115
Deliver me from the o of man Ps 119:134 6233
If thou seest the o of the poor Eccl 5:8 6233
Surely o maketh a wise man mad Eccl 7:7 6233
looked for judgment, but behold o Is 5:7 4939
despise this word, and trust in o Is 30:12 6233
thou shalt be far from o Is 54:14 6233
away from our God, speaking o Is 59:13 6233
she is wholly o in the midst of Jer 6:6 6233
to shed innocent blood, and for o Jer 22:17 6233
they dealt by o with the stranger Eze 22:7 6233
people of the land have used o Eze 22:29 6233
of the people's inheritance by o Eze 46:18 3238

OPPRESSIONS
By reason of the multitude of o Job 35:9 6217
considered all the o that are Eccl 4:1 6217
he that despiseth the gain of o Is 33:15 4642

OPPRESSOR
they hear not the voice of the o Job 3:18 5065
of years is hidden to the o Job 15:20 6184
and shall break in pieces the o Ps 72:4 6231
Envy thou not the o, and choose Prov 3:31
understanding is also a great o Prov 28:16 4642
of his shoulder, the rod of his o Is 9:4 5065
and say, How hath the o ceased Is 14:4 5065
day because of the fury of the o Is 51:13 6693
and where is the fury of the o Is 51:13 6693
spoiled out of the hand of the o Jer 21:12 6231
spoiled out of the hand of the o Jer 22:3 6216
of the fierceness of the o Jer 25:38 3238
no o shall pass through them any Zec 9:8 5065
bow, out of him every o together Zec 10:4 5065

OPPRESSORS
with God, and the heritage of o Job 27:13 6184
me, and o seek after my soul Ps 54:3 6184
leave me not to mine o Ps 119:121 6231
side of their o there was power Eccl 4:1 6231
my people, children are their o Is 3:12 5065
and they shall rule over their o Is 14:2 5065
the o are consumed out of the Is 16:4 7429
unto the LORD because of the o Is 19:20 3905

OR
o if thou depart to the right Gen 13:9
o bought with money of any Gen 17:12
made his journey prosperous o not Gen 24:21
to the right hand, o to the left Gen 24:49 176
cannot speak unto thee bad o good Gen 24:50 176
He that toucheth this man o his Gen 26:11
thou be my very son Esau o not Gen 27:21
Give me children, o else I die Gen 30:1
Is there yet any portion o Gen 31:14
not to Jacob either good o bad Gen 31:24 5704
not to Jacob either good o bad Gen 31:29 5704
stolen by day, o stolen by night Gen 31:39
o unto their children which they Gen 31:43 176
o if thou shalt take other wives Gen 31:50
o shalt thou indeed have dominion Gen 37:8
whether it be thy son's coat o no Gen 37:32
to lie by her, o to be with her Gen 39:10
o foot in all the land of Egypt Gen 41:44
o else by the life of Pharaoh Gen 42:16
of thy lord's house silver o gold Gen 44:8 176
o how shall we clear ourselves Gen 44:16
Have ye a father, o a brother Gen 44:19 176
o who maketh the dumb, o deaf, Ex 4:11 176
o the seeing, o the blind Ex 4:11 176
with pestilence, o with the sword Ex 5:3 176
o in the herbs of the field, Ex 10:15
his tongue, against man o beast Ex 11:7 5704
from the sheep, o from the goats Ex 12:5
be a stranger, o born in the land Ex 12:19
they will walk in my law, o no Ex 16:4
Is the LORD among us, o not Ex 17:7
mount, o touch the border of it Ex 19:12
surely be stoned, o shot through Ex 19:13
whether it be beast o man Ex 19:13 176
o any likeness of any thing that Ex 20:4
o that is in the earth beneath, Ex 20:4
o that is in the water under the Ex 20:4
have born him sons o daughters Ex 21:4 176
to the door, o unto the door post Ex 21:6 176
o his mother, shall be surely put Ex 21:15
o if he be found in his hand, he Ex 21:16
o his mother, shall surely be put Ex 21:17
o with his fist, and he die not, Ex 21:18 176
o his maid, with a rod, and he die Ex 21:20 176
if he continue a day o two Ex 21:21 176
o the eye of his maid, that it Ex 21:26 176
o his maidservant's tooth Ex 21:27 176
If an ox gore a man o a woman Ex 21:28 176
he hath killed a man o a woman Ex 21:29 176
a son, o have gored a daughter, Ex 21:31 176
push a manservant o a maidservant Ex 21:32 176
o if a man shall dig a pit, and Ex 21:33 176
an ox o an ass fall therein Ex 21:33 176
O if it be known that the ox hath Ex 21:36 176
o a sheep, and kill it, o sell it Ex 22:1 176
whether it be ox, o ass, o sheep Ex 22:4 5704
whether it be ox, o ass, o sheep Ex 22:4 5704
a field o vineyard to be eaten Ex 22:5 176
o the standing corn, o the field Ex 22:6 176
neighbour money o stuff to keep Ex 22:7 176
o for any manner of lost thing, Ex 22:9
o an ox, o a sheep, o any beast Ex 22:10 176
o be hurt, o driven away, no man Ex 22:10 176
o die, the owner thereof being Ex 22:14 176

any widow, o fatherless child ... Ex 22:22
enemy's ox o his ass going astray ... Ex 23:4 176
o when they come near unto the ... Ex 28:43 176
o of the bread, remain unto the ... Ex 29:34
o when they come near to the ... Ex 30:20 176
o whosoever putteth any of it ... Ex 30:33
thy cattle, whether ox o sheep ... Ex 34:19
o of the goats, for a burnt ... Lev 1:10 176
turtledoves, o of young pigeons ... Lev 1:14 176
o unleavened wafers anointed with ... Lev 2:4
whether it be a male o female ... Lev 3:1
male o female, he shall offer it ... Lev 3:6 176
O if his sin, wherein he hath ... Lev 4:23 176
O if his sin, which he hath ... Lev 4:28 176
he hath seen o known of it ... Lev 5:1 176
O if a soul touch any unclean ... Lev 5:2 176
o a carcase of unclean cattle, o ... Lev 5:2 176
O if he touch the uncleanness of ... Lev 5:3 176
O if a soul swear, pronouncing ... Lev 5:4 176
o to do good, whatsoever it be ... Lev 5:4 176
a lamb o a kid of the goats, for ... Lev 5:6 176
o two young pigeons, unto the ... Lev 5:7 176
o two young pigeons, then he that ... Lev 5:11 176
o in fellowship, o in a thing ... Lev 6:2 176
o hath deceived his neighbour ... Lev 6:2 176
O have found that which was lost, ... Lev 6:3 176
o the thing which he hath ... Lev 6:4 176
o that which was delivered him to ... Lev 6:4 176
o the lost thing which he found, ... Lev 6:4 176
O all that about which he hath ... Lev 6:5 176
o a voluntary offering, it shall ... Lev 7:16 176
o any unclean beast, o any ... Lev 7:21 176
of ox, o of sheep, o of goat ... Lev 7:23
whether it be of fowl o of beast ... Lev 7:26
o of them that divide the hoof ... Lev 11:4
o raiment, o skin, o sack, ... Lev 11:32 176
o ranges for pots, they shall be ... Lev 11:35
Nevertheless a fountain o pit ... Lev 11:36
o whatsoever hath more feet among ... Lev 11:42 5704
o for a daughter, she shall bring ... Lev 12:6
o a turtledove, for a sin ... Lev 12:6 176
that hath born a male o a female ... Lev 12:7 176
two turtles, o two young pigeons ... Lev 12:8 176
o bright spot, and it be in the ... Lev 13:2 176
o unto one of his sons the ... Lev 13:2 176
O if the raw flesh turn again, and ... Lev 13:16 176
o a bright spot, white, and ... Lev 13:19 176
O if there be any flesh, in the ... Lev 13:24 176
spot, somewhat reddish, o white ... Lev 13:24 176
If a man o woman have a plague ... Lev 13:29 176
plague upon the head o the beard ... Lev 13:29 176
a leprosy upon the head o beard ... Lev 13:30 176
If a man also o a woman have in ... Lev 13:38 176
o bald forehead, a white reddish ... Lev 13:42 176
bald head, o his bald forehead ... Lev 13:42 176
o in his bald forehead, as the ... Lev 13:43 176
garment, o a linen garment ... Lev 13:47 176
Whether it be in the warp, o woof ... Lev 13:48 176
of linen, o of woollen ... Lev 13:48 176
o in any thing made of skin ... Lev 13:48 176
greenish o reddish in the garment ... Lev 13:49 176
o in the skin, either in the warp ... Lev 13:49 176
o in the woof, o in any thing of ... Lev 13:49 176
o in the woof, o in a skin, o ... Lev 13:51 176
o woof, in woollen o in linen ... Lev 13:52 176
o any thing of skin, wherein the ... Lev 13:52 176
o in the woof, o in any thing of ... Lev 13:53 176
it be bare within o without ... Lev 13:55 176
o out of the skin, o out of the ... Lev 13:56 176
of the warp, o out of the woof ... Lev 13:56 176
o in the woof, o in any thing of ... Lev 13:57 176
o woof, o whatsoever thing of ... Lev 13:58 176
in a garment of woollen o linen ... Lev 13:59 176
o woof, o any thing of skins, to ... Lev 13:59 176
o to pronounce it unclean ... Lev 13:59 176
o two young pigeons, such as he ... Lev 14:22 176
o of the young pigeons, such as ... Lev 14:30 176
strakes, greenish o reddish ... Lev 14:37 176
o his flesh be stopped from his ... Lev 15:3 176
o two young pigeons, and come ... Lev 15:14 176
o on any thing whereon she ... Lev 15:23 176
o if it run beyond the time of ... Lev 15:25 176
o two young pigeons, and bring ... Lev 15:29 176
o a stranger that sojourneth ... Lev 16:29
o lamb, o goat, in the camp, o ... Lev 17:3 176
o of the strangers which sojourn ... Lev 17:8
a burnt offering o sacrifice ... Lev 17:8 176
o of the strangers that sojourn ... Lev 17:10
o of the strangers that sojourn ... Lev 17:13
catcheth any beast o fowl that ... Lev 17:13 176
o that which was torn with beasts ... Lev 17:15
o a stranger, he shall both wash ... Lev 17:15
o the nakedness of thy mother, ... Lev 18:7
o daughter of thy mother, whether ... Lev 18:9 176
o born abroad, even their ... Lev 18:9 176
o of thy daughter's daughter, ... Lev 18:10 176
o her daughter's daughter, to ... Lev 18:17
meteyard, in weight, o in measure ... Lev 19:35
o of the strangers that sojourn ... Lev 20:2
one that curseth his father o his ... Lev 20:9
cursed his father o his mother ... Lev 20:9
o his mother's daughter, and see ... Lev 20:17 176
o by fowl, o by any manner of ... Lev 20:25
A man also o woman that hath a ... Lev 20:27 176
o that is a wizard, shall surely ... Lev 20:27
a wife that is a whore, o profane ... Lev 21:7
for his father, o for his mother ... Lev 21:11
o a divorced woman, o profane, ... Lev 21:14
o an harlot, these shall he not ... Lev 21:14
o a lame, o he that hath a flat ... Lev 21:18 176
nose, o any thing superfluous, ... Lev 21:18 176
O a man that is brokenfooted, o ... Lev 21:19 176
O crookbackt, o a dwarf, o that ... Lev 21:20 176
o that hath a blemish in his eye, ... Lev 21:20
o be scurvy, o scabbed, o hath ... Lev 21:20 176
a leper, o hath a running issue ... Lev 22:4 176
o a man whose seed goeth from him ... Lev 22:4 176
O whosoever toucheth any creeping ... Lev 22:5 176
o a man of whom he may take ... Lev 22:5 176
o is torn with beasts, he shall ... Lev 22:8
o an hired servant, shall not eat ... Lev 22:10
o divorced, and have no child, and ... Lev 22:13
O suffer them to bear the ... Lev 22:16
o of the strangers in Israel, ... Lev 22:18
of the sheep, o of the goats ... Lev 22:19
o a freewill offering in beeves ... Lev 22:21 176
offering in beeves o sheep ... Lev 22:21
o broken, o maimed, o having a ... Lev 22:22 176
o scurvy, o scabbed, ye shall ... Lev 22:22 176
Either a bullock o a lamb that ... Lev 22:23
o lacking in his parts, that ... Lev 22:23
o crushed, o broken, o cut ... Lev 22:24
o a sheep, o a goat, is brought ... Lev 22:27 176
And whether it be cow o ewe ... Lev 22:28 176
o buyest ought of thy neighbour's ... Lev 25:14 176
he be a stranger, o a sojourner ... Lev 25:35
thou no usury of him, o increase ... Lev 25:36
if a sojourner o stranger wax ... Lev 25:47
the stranger o sojourner by thee ... Lev 25:47
o to the stock of the stranger's ... Lev 25:47
o his uncle's son, may redeem him ... Lev 25:49 176
o any that is nigh of kin unto ... Lev 25:49
o if he be able, he may redeem ... Lev 25:49 176
o if your soul abhor my judgments ... Lev 26:15
for a bad, o a bad for a good ... Lev 27:10 176
it, whether it be good o bad ... Lev 27:12
it, whether it be good o bad ... Lev 27:14
o if he have sold the field to ... Lev 27:20
whether it be ox, o sheep ... Lev 27:26 176
o if it be not redeemed, then it ... Lev 27:27
shall be sold o redeemed ... Lev 27:28
o of the fruit of the tree, is ... Lev 27:30
the herd, o of the flock, even of ... Lev 27:32
search whether it be good o bad ... Lev 27:33
When a man o woman shall commit ... Num 5:6 176
o if the spirit of jealousy come ... Num 5:14 176
O when the spirit of jealousy ... Num 5:30 176
When either man o woman shall ... Num 6:2 176
o vinegar of strong drink, ... Num 6:3
nor eat moist grapes, o dried ... Num 6:3
o for his mother, for his brother ... Num 6:7
o for his sister, when they die ... Num 6:7
o two young pigeons, to the ... Num 6:10 176
If any man of you o of your ... Num 9:10
o be in a journey afar off, yet ... Num 9:10 176
whether it was by day o by night ... Num 9:21
O whether it were two days, o a ... Num 9:22
o a year, that the cloud tarried ... Num 9:22 176
o beat it in a mortar, and baked ... Num 11:8 176
o shall all the fish of the sea ... Num 11:22
come to pass unto thee o not ... Num 11:23
be strong o weak, few o many ... Num 13:18
in, whether it be good o bad ... Num 13:19
in tents, o in strong holds ... Num 13:19
land is, whether it be fat o lean ... Num 13:20
there be wood therein, o not ... Num 13:20
o would God we had died in this ... Num 14:2
o a sacrifice in performing a vow ... Num 15:3 176
o in a freewill offering, o in ... Num 15:3 176
LORD, of the herd, o of the flock ... Num 15:3 176
the burnt offering o sacrifice ... Num 15:5 176
O for a ram, thou shalt prepare ... Num 15:6 176
o for a sacrifice in performing a ... Num 15:8 176
o peace offerings unto the LORD ... Num 15:8 176
o for one ram ... Num 15:11
one ram, o for a lamb, o a kid ... Num 15:11 176
o whosoever be among you in your ... Num 15:14 176
the land, o a stranger, the same ... Num 15:30
o given us inheritance of fields ... Num 16:14
o if they be visited after the ... Num 16:29 176
whether it be of men o beasts ... Num 18:15 176
o the firstling of a sheep ... Num 18:17
o the firstling of a goat, thou ... Num 18:17 176
o a dead body, o a bone of a man ... Num 19:16
o a grave, shall be unclean seven ... Num 19:16
o one slain ... Num 19:18
one slain, o one dead, o a grave ... Num 19:18 176
o of figs, o of vines, o of ... Num 20:5
o through the vineyards, neither ... Num 20:17
the fields, o into the vineyards ... Num 21:22
LORD my God, to do less o more ... Num 22:18 176
to the right hand o to the left ... Num 22:26
o how shall I defy, whom the LORD ... Num 23:8
to do either good o bad of mine ... Num 24:13 176
o swear an oath to bind his soul ... Num 30:2 176
o of her bonds wherewith she hath ... Num 30:5
o uttered ought out of her lips, ... Num 30:6 176
o bound her soul by a bond with ... Num 30:10 176
o concerning the bond of her soul ... Num 30:12 176
o her husband may make it void ... Num 30:13
o all her bonds, which are upon ... Num 30:14 176
on yonder side Jordan, o forward ... Num 32:19
O if he smite him with an hand ... Num 35:18 176
o hurl at him by laying of wait, ... Num 35:20 176
O in enmity smite him with his ... Num 35:21 176
o have cast upon him any thing ... Num 35:22 176
O with any stone, wherewith a man ... Num 35:23 176
God is there in heaven o in earth ... Deut 3:24
the likeness of male o female ... Deut 4:16 176
o the likeness of any thing, ... Deut 4:23
o the likeness of any thing, and ... Deut 4:25
o hath been heard like it ... Deut 4:32 176
O hath God assayed to go and take ... Deut 4:34 176
o any likeness of any thing that ... Deut 5:8
o that is in the earth beneath, ... Deut 5:8
o that is in the waters beneath ... Deut 5:8
field, o his manservant, o his ... Deut 5:21
o his ass, o any thing that is ... Deut 5:21
to the right hand o to the left ... Deut 5:32
be male o female barren among you ... Deut 7:14
among you, o among your cattle ... Deut 7:14
the silver o gold that is on them ... Deut 7:25
keep his commandments, o no ... Deut 8:2
o for the uprightness of thine ... Deut 9:5
o of thy wine, o of thy oil, o ... Deut 12:17
o the firstlings of thy herds o ... Deut 12:17
o heave offering of thine hand ... Deut 12:17
o a dreamer of dreams, and giveth ... Deut 13:1 176
and giveth thee a sign o a wonder ... Deut 13:1 176
the sign o the wonder come to ... Deut 13:2
prophet, o that dreamer of dreams ... Deut 13:3 176
o that dreamer of dreams, shall ... Deut 13:5 176
o thy son, o thy daughter, o ... Deut 13:6
o thy friend, which is as thine ... Deut 13:6 176
o far off from thee, from the one ... Deut 13:7 176
o of them that divide the cloven ... Deut 14:7 176
o thou mayest sell it unto an ... Deut 14:21 176
o if the place be too far from ... Deut 14:24
o for sheep, o for wine, o for ... Deut 14:26
o for whatsoever thy soul ... Deut 14:26
his neighbour, o of his brother ... Deut 15:2
o an Hebrew woman, be sold unto ... Deut 15:12 176
o blind, o have any ill blemish, ... Deut 15:21 176
o sheep, wherein is blemish, o ... Deut 17:1
man o woman, that hath wrought ... Deut 17:2
o moon, o any of the host of ... Deut 17:3 176
bring forth that man o that woman ... Deut 17:5 176
gates, even that man o that woman ... Deut 17:5 176
o three witnesses, shall he that ... Deut 17:6 176
o unto the judge, even that man ... Deut 17:12 176
to the right hand, o to the left ... Deut 17:20
whether it be ox o sheep ... Deut 18:3
o his daughter to pass through ... Deut 18:10
o that useth divination ... Deut 18:10
o an observer of times ... Deut 18:10
o an enchanter, o a witch, ... Deut 18:10
O a charmer, o a consulter with ... Deut 18:11
o a wizard, o a necromancer ... Deut 18:11
o that shall speak in the name of ... Deut 18:20
o for any sin, in any sin that he ... Deut 19:15
o at the mouth of three witnesses ... Deut 19:15
o the voice of his mother, and ... Deut 21:18
ox o his sheep go astray, and hide ... Deut 22:1 176
o if thou know him not, then thou ... Deut 22:2
ass o his ox fall down by the way ... Deut 22:4 176
o on the ground, whether they be ... Deut 22:6 176
o eggs, and the dam sitting upon ... Deut 22:6 176
o upon the eggs, thou shalt not ... Deut 22:6 176
o hath his privy member cut off, ... Deut 23:1
An Ammonite o Moabite shall not ... Deut 23:3
o the price of a dog, into the ... Deut 23:18
o if the latter husband die, ... Deut 24:3 176
No man shall take the nether o ... Deut 24:6
merchandise of him, o selleth him ... Deut 24:7
o of thy strangers that are in ... Deut 24:14
maketh any graven o molten image ... Deut 27:15
light by his father o his mother ... Deut 27:16
o the daughter of his mother ... Deut 27:22 176
o to the left, to go after other ... Deut 28:14
o oil, o the increase of thy ... Deut 28:51
o flocks of thy sheep, until he ... Deut 28:51
have ye drunk wine o strong drink ... Deut 29:6
o woman, o family, o tribe, ... Deut 29:18 176
and there is none shut up, o left ... Deut 32:36
to the right hand o to the left ... Josh 1:7
for us, o for our adversaries ... Josh 5:13
but let about two o three ... Josh 7:3 176
not a man left in Ai o Beth-el ... Josh 8:17
power to flee this way o that way ... Josh 8:20
let none of them remain o escape ... Josh 8:22
like that before it o after it ... Josh 10:14
Beer-sheba, o Sheba, and Moladah, ... Josh 19:2
o if in transgression against the ... Josh 22:22
o if to offer thereon burnt ... Josh 22:23
burnt offering o meat offering ... Josh 22:23
o if to offer peace offerings ... Josh 22:23
o to our generations in time to ... Josh 22:28
o for sacrifices, beside the ... Josh 22:29
to the right hand o to the left ... Josh 23:6
o the gods of the Amorites, in ... Josh 24:15
their fathers did keep it, o not ... Judg 2:22
was there a shield o spear seen ... Judg 5:8
to every man a damsel o two ... Judg 5:30
o that one reign over you ... Judg 9:2
o did he ever fight against them, ... Judg 11:25
let her drink wine o strong drink ... Judg 13:14
o among all my people, that thou ... Judg 14:3
but he told not his father o his ... Judg 14:6
o that thou be a priest unto a ... Judg 18:19 176
all night, in Gibeah, o in Ramah ... Judg 19:13 176
my brother, o shall I cease ... Judg 20:28
when their fathers o their ... Judg 21:22 176
o to return from following after ... Ruth 1:16
young men, whether poor o rich ... Ruth 3:10
o kettle, o caldron, o pot ... 1Sa 2:14 176
to the right hand o to the left ... 1Sa 6:12
o whose ass have I taken ... 1Sa 12:3
o whom have I defrauded ... 1Sa 12:3
o of whose hand have I received ... 1Sa 12:3
Hebrews make them swords o spears ... 1Sa 13:19 176
the LORD to save by many o by few ... 1Sa 14:6 176
o any valiant man, he took him ... 1Sa 14:52
o on the height of his stature ... 1Sa 16:7
o my father's family in Israel, ... 1Sa 18:18
do nothing either great o small ... 1Sa 20:2 176
o what if thy father answer thee ... 1Sa 20:10 176
o the third day, and, behold, if ... 1Sa 20:12
hand, o what there is present ... 1Sa 21:3 176
under thine hand spear o sword ... 1Sa 21:8 176
o sheweth unto me that my son ... 1Sa 22:8
nothing of all this, less o more ... 1Sa 22:15 176
o that my lord hath avenged ... 1Sa 25:31

she told him nothing, less o more	1Sa 25:36	
o his day shall come to die	1Sa 26:10	176
o he shall descend into battle,	1Sa 26:10	
o what evil is in mine hand	1Sa 26:18	
o these years, and I have found no	1Sa 29:3	176
not any, either great o small	1Sa 30:2	
to thy right hand o to thy left	2Sa 2:21	176
o that is a leper, o that	2Sa 3:29	
o that falleth on the sword, o	2Sa 3:29	
o ought else, till the sun be	2Sa 3:35	176
o to the left from ought that my	2Sa 14:19	
suit o cause might come unto me	2Sa 15:4	
shall be, whether in death o life	2Sa 15:21	
some pit, o in some other place	2Sa 17:9	176
taste what I eat o what I drink	2Sa 19:35	854
o hath he given us any gift	2Sa 19:42	
I should swallow up o destroy	2Sa 20:20	
o wilt thou flee three months	2Sa 24:13	
o that there be three days'	2Sa 24:13	
know not how to go out o come in	1Kin 3:7	
o on earth beneath, who keepest	1Kin 8:23	
o if there be caterpiller	1Kin 8:37	
o by all thy people Israel, which	1Kin 8:38	
the land of the enemy, far o near	1Kin 8:46	176
ye o your children, and will not	1Kin 9:6	
o come in to Asa king of Judah	1Kin 15:17	
there is no nation o kingdom	1Kin 18:10	
o he is pursuing, o he is in a	1Kin 18:27	
o peradventure he sleepeth, and	1Kin 18:27	
o whether they be come out for	1Kin 20:18	
o else thou shalt pay a talent of	1Kin 20:39	176
o, if it seem good to thee, I	1Kin 21:2	176
o else, if it please thee, I will	1Kin 21:6	
to battle, o shall I forbear	1Kin 22:6	
to battle, o shall we forbear	1Kin 22:15	
some mountain, o into some valley	2Kin 2:16	176
any more death o barren land	2Kin 2:21	
o to the captain of the host	2Kin 4:13	176
barnfloor, o out of the winepress	2Kin 6:27	176
out to him two o three eunuchs	2Kin 9:32	
o vessels of silver, of the money	2Kin 12:13	
have smitten five o six times	2Kin 13:19	176
o after their ordinances, o	2Kin 17:34	
degrees, o go back ten degrees	2Kin 20:9	
to the right hand o to the left	2Kin 22:2	
o his daughter to pass through	2Kin 23:10	
o three months to be destroyed	1Chr 21:12	
o else three days the sword of	1Chr 21:12	
o honour, nor the life of thine	2Chr 1:11	
blasting, o mildew, locusts, o	2Chr 6:28	
whatsoever sore o whatsoever	2Chr 6:28	
Then what prayer o what	2Chr 6:29	
o of all thy people Israel, when	2Chr 6:29	
unto a land far off o near	2Chr 6:36	176
o if I command the locusts to	2Chr 7:13	
o if I send pestilence among my	2Chr 7:13	
o concerning the treasures	2Chr 8:15	
o with them that have no power	2Chr 14:11	
o great, whether man o woman	2Chr 15:13	5704
o come in to Asa king of Judah	2Chr 16:1	
to battle, o shall I forbear	2Chr 18:5	
to battle, o shall I forbear	2Chr 18:14	
Fight ye not with small o great	2Chr 18:30	854
o pestilence, o famine, we stand	2Chr 20:9	
o famine, we stand before this	2Chr 20:9	
for no god of any nation o	2Chr 32:15	
upon young man o maiden, old man,	2Chr 36:17	
o him that stooped for age	2Chr 36:17	
o ministers of this house of God,	Ezr 7:24	
tribute, o custom, upon them	Ezr 7:24	
death, o to banishment, o to	Ezr 7:26	2006
of goods, o to imprisonment	Ezr 7:26	
nor seek their peace o their	Ezr 9:12	
is this a work of one day o two	Ezr 10:13	
not whither I went, o what I did	Neh 2:16	
o shall they be sold unto us	Neh 5:8	
people of the land bring ware o	Neh 10:31	
on the sabbath, o on the holy day	Neh 10:31	
without Jerusalem once o twice	Neh 13:20	
unto your sons, o for yourselves	Neh 13:25	
whosoever, whether man o woman	Est 4:11	
nor drink three days, night o day	Est 4:16	
o how can I endure to see the	Est 8:6	
o what is thy request further	Est 9:12	
o why the breasts that I should	Job 3:12	
O with princes that had gold, who	Job 3:15	176
O as an hidden untimely birth I	Job 3:16	176
o where were the righteous cut	Job 4:7	
o loweth the ox over his fodder	Job 6:5	
o is there any taste in the white	Job 6:6	
o is my flesh of brass	Job 6:12	
o, Give a reward for me of your	Job 6:22	
O, Deliver me from the enemy's	Job 6:23	
o, Redeem me from the hand of the	Job 6:23	
o a whale, that thou settest a	Job 7:12	
o doth the Almighty pervert	Job 8:3	
o seest thou as man seeth	Job 10:4	
o gather together, then who can	Job 11:10	
O speak to the earth, and it shall	Job 12:8	176
o as one man mocketh another, do	Job 13:9	
o let me speak, and answer thou me	Job 13:22	176
o with speeches wherewith he can	Job 15:3	
o wast thou made before the hills	Job 15:7	
o what emboldeneth thee that thou	Job 16:3	176
o is it gain to him, that thou	Job 22:3	
O darkness, that thou canst not	Job 22:11	176
o how can he be clean that is	Job 25:4	
the precious onyx, o the sapphire	Job 28:16	
be made of coral, o of pearls	Job 28:18	
o if my foot hath hasted to	Job 31:5	
o if I have laid wait at my	Job 31:9	
my manservant o of my maidservant	Job 31:13	
o have caused the eyes of the	Job 31:16	
O have eaten my morsel myself	Job 31:17	
o any poor without covering	Job 31:19	
o have said to the fine gold,	Job 31:24	
o the moon walking in brightness	Job 31:26	
o my mouth hath kissed my hand	Job 31:27	
o lifted up myself when evil	Job 31:29	
o did the contempt of families	Job 31:34	
o that the furrows likewise	Job 31:38	
o have caused the owners thereof	Job 31:39	
o that answered his words	Job 32:12	
O who hath disposed the whole	Job 34:13	
a nation, o against a man only	Job 34:29	
refuse, o whether thou choose	Job 34:33	
o if thy transgressions be	Job 35:6	
o what receiveth he of thine hand	Job 35:7	176
o who can say, Thou hast wrought	Job 36:23	
o the noise of his tabernacle	Job 36:29	
o for his land, o for mercy	Job 37:13	
o who hath stretched the line	Job 38:5	176
o who laid the corner stone	Job 38:6	176
O who shut up the sea with doors,	Job 38:8	
o hast thou walked in the search	Job 38:16	
o hast thou seen the doors of the	Job 38:17	
o because the number of thy days	Job 38:21	
o hast thou seen the treasures of	Job 38:22	
o a way for the lightning of	Job 38:25	
o who hath begotten the drops of	Job 38:28	176
o loose the bands of Orion	Job 38:31	176
o canst thou guide Arcturus with	Job 38:32	
o who hath given understanding to	Job 38:36	176
o who can stay the bottles of	Job 38:37	
o fill the appetite of the young	Job 38:39	
o canst thou mark when the hinds	Job 39:1	
o knowest thou the time when they	Job 39:2	
o who hath loosed the bands of	Job 39:5	
serve thee, o abide by thy crib	Job 39:9	
o will he harrow the valleys	Job 39:10	
o wilt thou leave thy labour to	Job 39:11	
o wings and feathers unto the	Job 39:13	
o that the wild beast may break	Job 39:15	
o canst thou thunder with a voice	Job 40:9	
o his tongue with a cord which	Job 41:1	
o bore his jaw through with a	Job 41:2	
o wilt thou bind him for thy	Job 41:5	
o his head with fish spears	Job 41:7	
o who can come to him with his	Job 41:13	
out of a seething pot o caldron	Job 41:20	
o who is a rock save our God	Ps 18:31	176
o who shall stand in his holy	Ps 24:3	
o as the mule, which have no	Ps 32:9	
he had been my friend o brother	Ps 35:14	
o stretched out our hands to a	Ps 44:20	
sacrifices o thy burnt offerings	Ps 50:8	
o drink the blood of goats	Ps 50:13	
o that thou shouldest take my	Ps 50:16	
chief Musician, A Song o Psalm	Ps 66:t	
on Neginoth, A Psalm o Song	Ps 67:t	
Musician, A Psalm o Song of David	Ps 68:t	
an ox o bullock that hath horns	Ps 69:31	
A Psalm o Song of Asaph	Ps 75:t	
Neginoth, A Psalm o Song of Asaph	Ps 76:t	
A Song o Psalm of Asaph	Ps 83:t	
A Psalm o Song for the sons of	Ps 87:t	
A Song o Psalm for the sons of	Ps 88:t	
o thy faithfulness in destruction	Ps 88:11	
o to thy faithfulness round about	Ps 89:8	
o ever thou hadst formed the	Ps 90:2	
A Psalm o Song for the sabbath	Ps 92:t	
o who will stand up for me	Ps 94:16	
A Song o Psalm of David	Ps 108:t	
o what shall be done unto thee,	Ps 120:3	
o in things too high for me	Ps 131:1	
o slumber to mine eyelids,	Ps 132:4	
o whither shall I flee from thy	Ps 139:7	
o the son of man, that thou	Ps 144:3	
no guide, overseer, o ruler,	Prov 6:7	
o as a fool to the correction of	Prov 7:22	
froward o perverse in them	Prov 8:8	
beginning, o ever the earth was	Prov 8:23	
curseth his father o his mother	Prov 20:20	
o of them that are sureties for	Prov 22:26	
o as he that lieth upon the top	Prov 23:34	
robbeth his father o his mother	Prov 28:24	
man, whether he rage o laugh	Prov 29:9	
up into heaven, o descended	Prov 30:4	
o lest I be poor, and steal, and	Prov 30:9	
o if thou hast thought evil, lay	Prov 30:32	
he shall be a wise man o a fool	Eccl 2:19	176
o who else can hasten hereunto,	Eccl 2:25	
whether he eat little o much	Eccl 5:12	
no man knoweth either love o	Eccl 9:1	
o toward the north, in the place	Eccl 11:3	
shall prosper, either this o that	Eccl 11:6	176
o whether they both shall be	Eccl 11:6	
o the light, o the moon, o the	Eccl 12:2	
O ever the silver cord be loosed,	Eccl 12:6	5704
o the golden bowl be broken, o	Eccl 12:6	
o the wheel broken at the cistern	Eccl 12:6	
it be good, o whether it be evil	Eccl 12:14	
is like a roe o a young hart	Song 2:9	176
be thou like a roe o a young hart	Song 2:17	176
O ever I was aware, my soul made	Song 6:12	
be thou like to a roe o to a	Song 8:14	176
o of lambs, o of he goats	Is 1:11	
the depth, o in the height above	Is 7:11	176
o opened the mouth, o peeped	Is 10:14	
o shall the saw magnify itself	Is 10:15	
o as if the staff should lift up	Is 10:15	
two o three berries in the top of	Is 17:6	
four o five in the outmost	Is 17:6	
either the groves, o the images	Is 17:8	
the head o tail, branch o rush	Is 19:15	
O let him take hold of my	Is 27:5	176
o is he slain according to the	Is 27:7	
o as when a thirsty man dreameth,	Is 29:8	
o shall the thing framed say of	Is 29:16	
o to take water withal out of the	Is 30:14	
Like a crane o a swallow, so did	Is 38:14	
o being his counsellor hath	Is 40:13	
o what likeness will ye compare	Is 40:18	
ye liken me, o shall I be equal	Is 40:25	
o declare us things for to come	Is 41:22	
o do evil, that we may be	Is 41:23	
o deaf, as my messenger that I	Is 42:19	
o let them hear, and say, It is	Is 43:9	
o molten a graven image that is	Is 44:10	
o thy work, He hath no hands	Is 45:9	
o to the woman, What hast thou	Is 45:10	
o the lawful captive delivered	Is 49:24	
o which of my creditors is it to	Is 50:1	176
o have I no power to deliver	Is 50:2	
hast thou been afraid o feared	Is 57:11	
o shall a nation be born at once	Is 66:8	
o what hast thou to do in the way	Jer 2:18	
ornaments, o a bride her attire	Jer 2:32	
burnt offerings o sacrifices	Jer 7:22	
lift up a cry o prayer for them	Jer 11:14	
But I was like a lamb o an ox	Jer 11:19	
his skin, o the leopard his spots	Jer 13:23	
o can the heavens give showers	Jer 14:22	
o who shall bemoan thee	Jer 15:5	
o who shall go aside to ask how	Jer 15:5	
sons o daughters in this place	Jer 16:2	176
their father o for their mother	Jer 16:7	
o what is our iniquity	Jer 16:10	
o what is our sin that we have	Jer 16:10	
o shall the cold flowing waters	Jer 18:14	
o that my mother might have been	Jer 20:17	
o who shall enter into our	Jer 21:13	
o, Ah sister	Jer 22:18	
o, Ah his glory	Jer 22:18	
o the prophet, o a priest, shall	Jer 23:33	176
is desolate without man o beast	Jer 32:43	
being an Hebrew o an Hebrewess	Jer 34:9	
had read three o four leaves	Jer 36:23	
o against thy servants, o	Jer 37:18	
o go wheresoever it seemeth	Jer 40:5	176
o whether it be evil, we will	Jer 42:6	
none of them shall remain o	Jer 42:17	
there, shall escape o remain	Jer 44:14	
words shall stand, mine, o theirs	Jer 44:28	
of the land of Moab, far o near	Jer 48:24	
o whether they will forbear, (for	Eze 2:5	
o whether they will forbear	Eze 2:7	
o whether they will forbear	Eze 3:11	
of itself, o is torn in pieces	Eze 4:14	
o of the stranger that sojourneth	Eze 14:7	
O if I bring a sword upon that	Eze 14:17	176
O if I send a pestilence into	Eze 14:19	176
o than a branch which is among	Eze 15:2	
o will men take a pin of it to	Eze 15:3	
even without great power o many	Eze 17:9	
o shall he break the covenant, and	Eze 17:15	
Go thee one way o other, either	Eze 21:16	
o on the left, whithersoever thy	Eze 21:16	
o can thine hands be strong, in	Eze 22:14	
none did search o seek after them	Eze 34:6	
o a widow that had a priest	Eze 44:22	
o for mother, o for son, o for	Eze 44:25	
o for sister that hath had no	Eze 44:25	
o torn, whether it be fowl o	Eze 44:31	
a voluntary burnt offering o	Eze 46:12	
o astrologer, o Chaldean	Dan 2:10	
o the interpretation thereof,	Dan 4:19	
o say unto him, What doest thou	Dan 4:35	
any error o fault found in him	Dan 6:4	
of any God o man for thirty days	Dan 6:7	
any God o man within thirty days	Dan 6:12	
o ever they came at the bottom of	Dan 6:24	
be as the former, o as the latter	Dan 11:29	
o even in the days of your	Joel 1:2	
two legs, o a piece of an ear	Amos 3:12	176
So two o three cities wandered	Amos 4:8	
o went into the house, and leaned	Amos 5:19	
o their border greater than your	Amos 6:2	
o with ten thousands of rivers of	Mic 6:7	
o pottage, o wine, o oil, o	Hag 2:12	
went out o came in because of the	Zec 8:10	
with thee, o accept thy person	Mal 1:8	176
o receiveth it with good will at	Mal 2:13	
o, Where is the God of judgment	Mal 2:17	176
destroy the law, o the prophets	Mt 5:17	2228
one jot o one tittle shall in no	Mt 5:18	2228
not make one hair white o black	Mt 5:36	2228
o else he will hold to the one,	Mt 6:24	2228
shall eat, o what ye shall drink	Mt 6:25	
o, What shall we drink	Mt 6:31	2228
o, Wherewithal shall we be	Mt 6:31	2228
O how wilt thou say to thy	Mt 7:4	2228
O what man is there of you, whom	Mt 7:9	2228
O if he ask a fish, will he give	Mt 7:10	2532
of thorns, o figs of thistles	Mt 7:16	2228
o to say, Arise, and walk	Mt 9:5	2228
city o town ye shall enter	Mt 10:11	2228
depart out of that house o city	Mt 10:14	2228
thought how o what ye shall speak	Mt 10:19	2228
He that loveth father o mother	Mt 10:37	2228
he that loveth son o daughter	Mt 10:37	2228
come, o do we look for another	Mt 11:3	2228
O have ye not read in the law,	Mt 12:5	2228
every city o house divided	Mt 12:25	2228
O else how can one enter into a	Mt 12:29	2228
o else make the tree corrupt, and	Mt 12:33	2228
for when tribulation o	Mt 13:21	2228
He that curseth father o mother	Mt 15:4	2228
say to his father o his mother	Mt 15:5	2228
not his father o his mother	Mt 15:6	2228
Jeremias, o one of the prophets	Mt 16:14	2228
o what shall a man give in	Mt 16:26	2228

the earth take custom o tribute Mt 17:25 2228
own children, o of strangers Mt 17:25 2228
thy hand o thy foot offend thee Mt 18:8 2228
to enter into life halt o maimed Mt 18:8 2228
hands o two feet to be cast into Mt 18:8 2228
take with thee one o two more Mt 18:16 2228
that in the mouth of two o three Mt 18:16 2228
For where two o three are Mt 18:20 2228
o brethren, o sisters, o father Mt 19:29 2228
o mother, o wife, o children, Mt 19:29 2228
o lands, for my name's sake, Mt 19:29 2228
from heaven, o of men Mt 21:25 2228
give tribute unto Caesar, o not Mt 22:17 2228
o the temple that sanctifieth the Mt 23:17 2228
o the altar that sanctifieth the Mt 23:19 2228
you, Lo, here is Christ, o there Mt 24:23 2228
o thirsty, and gave thee drink Mt 25:37 2228
o naked, and clothed thee Mt 25:38 2228
O when saw we thee sick, o in Mt 25:39 2228
o in prison, and came unto thee Mt 25:39 2228
o athirst, o a stranger, o Mt 25:44 2228
o sick, o in prison, and did not Mt 25:44 2228
o Jesus which is called Christ Mt 27:17 2228
o to say, Arise, and take up thy Mk 2:9 2228
on the sabbath days, o to do evil Mk 3:4 2228
to save life, o to kill Mk 3:4 2228
Who is my mother, o my brethren Mk 3:33 2228
when affliction o persecution Mk 4:17 2228
put under a bushel, o under a bed Mk 4:21 2228
o with what comparison shall we Mk 4:30 2228
prophet, o as one of the prophets Mk 6:15 2228
o cities, o country, they laid Mk 6:56 2228
and, Whoso curseth father o mother Mk 7:10 2228
shall say to his father o mother Mk 7:11 2228
ought for his father o his mother Mk 7:12 2228
O what shall a man give in Mk 8:37 2228
o brethren, o sisters, o father Mk 10:29 2228
o mother, o wife, o children, Mk 10:29 2228
o lands, for my sake, and the Mk 10:29 2228
was it from heaven, o of men Mk 11:30 2228
to give tribute to Caesar, o not Mk 12:14 2228
we give, o shall we not give Mk 12:15 2228
o, lo, he is there Mk 13:21 2228
at even, o at midnight, o at the Mk 13:35 2228
the cockcrowing, o in the morning Mk 13:35 2228
turtledoves, o two young pigeons Lk 2:24 2228
whether he were the Christ, o not Lk 3:15 2228
o to say, Rise up and walk Lk 5:23 2228
days to do good, o to do evil Lk 6:9 2228
to save life, o to destroy it Lk 6:9 2228
o look we for another Lk 7:19 2228
o look we for another Lk 7:20 2228
vessel, o putteth it under a bed Lk 8:16 2228
and lose himself, o be cast away Lk 9:25 2228
o if he ask a fish, will he for a Lk 11:11 2228
O if he shall ask an egg, will he Lk 11:12 2228
take ye no thought how o what Lk 12:11 2228
shall answer, o what ye shall say Lk 12:11 2228
me a judge o a divider over you Lk 12:14 2228
o what ye shall drink, neither be Lk 12:29 2228
o come in the third watch, and Lk 12:38 2532
parable unto us, o even to all Lk 12:41 2228
O those eighteen, upon whom the Lk 13:4 2228
his ox o his ass from the stall Lk 13:15 2228
an ass o an ox fallen into a pit Lk 14:5 2228
thou makest a dinner o a supper Lk 14:12 2228
O what king, going to make war Lk 14:31 2228
O else, while the other is yet a Lk 14:32 1161
o else he will hold to the one, Lk 16:13 2228
servant plowing o feeding cattle Lk 17:7 2228
o, lo there Lk 17:21 2228
o, see there Lk 17:23 2228
o even as this publican Lk 18:11 2228
o parents, o brethren, o wife, Lk 18:29 2228
o children, for the kingdom of Lk 18:29 2228
o who is he that gave thee this Lk 20:2 2228
was it from heaven, o of men Lk 20:4 2228
to give tribute unto Caesar, o no Lk 20:22 2228
at meat, o he that serveth Lk 22:27 2228
containing two o three firkins Jn 2:6 2228
o, Why talkest thou with her Jn 4:27 2228
twenty o thirty furlongs, they Jn 6:19 2228
o whether I speak of myself Jn 7:17 2228
Have any of the rulers o of the Jn 7:48 2228
o his parents, that he was born Jn 9:2 2228
o who hath opened his eyes, we Jn 9:21 2228
said, Whether he be a sinner o no Jn 9:25 2228
o, that he should give something Jn 13:29 2228
o else believe me for the very Jn 14:11 1161
o did others tell it thee of me Jn 18:34 2228
to know the times o the seasons Acts 1:7 2228
o why look ye so earnestly on us, Acts 3:12 2228
as though by our own power o Acts 3:12 2228
o by what name, have ye done this Acts 4:7 2228
of lands o houses sold them Acts 4:34 2228
counsel o this work be of men Acts 5:38 2228
o what is the place of my rest Acts 7:49 2228
of himself, o of some other man Acts 8:34 2228
whether they were men o women Acts 9:2 2532
thing that is common o unclean Acts 10:14 2228
o come unto one of another nation Acts 10:28 2228
not call any man common o unclean Acts 10:28 2228
for nothing common o unclean hath Acts 11:8 2228
to tell, o to hear some new thing Acts 17:21 2532
o silver, o stone, graven by art Acts 17:29 2228
matter of wrong o wicked lewdness Acts 18:14 2228
the sick handkerchiefs o aprons Acts 19:12 2228
man's silver, o gold, o apparel Acts 20:33 2228
but if a spirit o an angel hath Acts 23:9 2228
o ever he come near, are ready to Acts 23:15 4253
charge worthy of death o of bonds Acts 23:29 2228
O else let these same here say, Acts 24:20 2228
to minister o come unto him Acts 24:23 2228
o have committed any thing worthy Acts 25:11 2532
worthy of death o of bonds Acts 26:31 2228
o fallen down dead suddenly Acts 28:6 2228
o customs of our fathers, yet was Acts 28:17 2228
shewed o spake any harm of thee Acts 28:21 2228
O despisest thou the riches of Rom 2:4 2228
the mean while accusing o else Rom 2:15 2228
o what profit is there of Rom 3:1 2228
o upon the uncircumcision also Rom 4:9 2228
circumcision, o in uncircumcision Rom 4:10 2228
o to his seed, through the law, Rom 4:13 2228
o of obedience unto righteousness Rom 6:16 2228
o distress, o persecution, o Rom 8:35 2228
o nakedness, o peril, o sword Rom 8:35 2228
having done any good o evil Rom 9:11 2228
O, Who shall descend into the Rom 10:7 2228
o who hath been his counsellor Rom 11:34 2228
O who hath first given to him, and Rom 11:35 2228
O ministry, let us wait on our Rom 12:7 1535
o he that teacheth, on teaching Rom 12:7 1535
O he that exhorteth, on Rom 12:8 1535
own master he standeth o falleth Rom 14:4 2228
o die, we are the Lord's Rom 14:8 5037
o why dost thou set at nought thy Rom 14:10 2228
o an occasion to fall in his Rom 14:13 2228
o is offended, o is made weak Rom 14:21 2228
o were ye baptized in the name of 1Cor 1:13 2228
excellency of speech o of wisdom 1Cor 2:1 2228
o Apollos, o Cephas, o the 1Cor 3:22 1535
o life, o death, o things 1Cor 3:22 1535
things present, o things to come 1Cor 3:22 1535
of you, o of man's judgment 1Cor 4:3 2228
o in love, and in the spirit of 1Cor 4:21 2228
o with the covetous 1Cor 5:10 2228
o extortioners, o with idolaters 1Cor 5:10 2228
o covetous, o an idolater, o a 1Cor 5:11 2228
o a drunkard, o an extortioner 1Cor 5:11 2228
o be reconciled to her husband 1Cor 7:11 2228
A brother o a sister is not under 1Cor 7:15 2228
o how knowest thou, O man, 1Cor 7:16 2228
whether in heaven o in earth 1Cor 8:5 1535
O I only and Barnabas, have not we 1Cor 9:6 2228
o who feedeth a flock, and eateth 1Cor 9:7 2228
o saith not the law the same also 1Cor 9:8 2228
O saith he it altogether for our 1Cor 9:10 2228
o that which is offered in 1Cor 10:19 2228
o drink, o whatsoever ye do, do 1Cor 10:31 1535
Every man praying o prophesying 1Cor 11:4 2228
o prophesieth with her head 1Cor 11:5 2228
for a woman to be shorn o shaven 1Cor 11:6 2228
o despise ye the church of God, 1Cor 11:22 2228
whether we be Jews o Gentiles 1Cor 12:13 1535
whether we be bond o free 1Cor 12:13 1535
o one member be honoured, all the 1Cor 12:26 1535
brass, o a tinkling cymbal 1Cor 13:1 2228
o by knowledge, o by prophesying 1Cor 14:6 2228
o by doctrine 1Cor 14:6 2228
giving sound, whether pipe o harp 1Cor 14:7 1535
be known what is piped o harped 1Cor 14:7 2228
o unbelievers, will they not say 1Cor 14:23 2228
o one unlearned, he is convinced 1Cor 14:24 2228
o at the most by three, and that 1Cor 14:27 2228
the prophets speak two o three 1Cor 14:29 2228
o came it unto you only 1Cor 14:36 2228
o spiritual, let him acknowledge 1Cor 14:37 2228
whether it were I o they, so we 1Cor 15:11 1535
of wheat, o of some other grain 1Cor 15:37 2228
o whether we be comforted, it is 2Cor 1:6 1535
than what ye read o acknowledge 2Cor 1:13 2228
o the things that I purpose, do I 2Cor 1:17 2228
o need we, as some others, 2Cor 3:1 2228
o letters of commendation from 2Cor 3:1 2228
that, whether present o absent 2Cor 5:9 1535
done, whether it be good o bad 2Cor 5:10 1535
o whether we be sober, it is for 2Cor 5:13 1535
o what part hath he that 2Cor 6:15 2228
o our brethren be enquired of, 2Cor 8:23 1535
not grudgingly, o of necessity 2Cor 9:7 2228
o compare ourselves with some 2Cor 10:12 2228
o if ye receive another spirit, 2Cor 11:4 2228
o another gospel, which ye have 2Cor 11:4 2228
o whether out of the body, I 2Cor 12:2 1535
o out of the body, I cannot tell 2Cor 12:3 1535
me to be, o that he heareth of me 2Cor 12:6 2228
In the mouth of two o three 2Cor 13:1 2532
o an angel from heaven, preach Gal 1:8 2228
For do I now persuade men, o God Gal 1:10 2228
o do I seek to please men Gal 1:10 2228
I should run, o had run, in vain Gal 2:2 2228
o by the hearing of faith Gal 3:2 2228
o by the hearing of faith Gal 3:5 2228
disannulleth, o addeth thereto Gal 3:15 2228
o rather are known of God, how Gal 4:9 1161
above all that we ask o think Eph 3:20 2228
o covetousness, let it not be Eph 5:3 2228
o wrinkle, o any such thing Eph 5:27 2228
Lord, whether he be bond o free Eph 6:8 1535
o in truth, Christ is preached Phil 1:18 1535
whether it be by life, o by death Phil 1:20 1535
o else be absent, I may hear of Phil 1:27 1535
done through strife o vainglory Phil 2:3 2228
o dominions Col 1:16 1535
o principalities, o powers Col 1:16 1535
in earth, o things in heaven Col 1:20 1535
o in drink, o in respect of an Col 2:16 2228
o of the new moon, o of the Col 2:16 2228
whatsoever ye do in word o deed Col 3:17 2228
o joy, o crown of rejoicing 1Th 2:19 2228
o joy, o crown of rejoicing 1Th 2:19 2228
us, that, whether we wake o sleep 1Th 5:10 1535
o be troubled, neither by spirit, 2Th 2:2 3383
called God, o that is worshipped 2Th 2:4 2228
whether by word, o our epistle 2Th 2:15 1535
o gold, o pearls, o costly 1Ti 2:9 2228
any widow have children o nephews 1Ti 5:4 2228
If any man o woman that believeth 1Ti 5:16 2228
but before two o three witnesses 1Ti 5:19 2228
not accused of riot o unruly Titus 1:6 2228
o Tychicus, be diligent to come Titus 3:12 2228
o oweth thee ought, put that on Philem 18 2228
o the son of man, that thou Heb 2:6 2228
mercy under two o three witnesses Heb 10:28 2228
o profane person, as Esau, who Heb 12:16 2228
o thrust through with a dart Heb 12:20 2228
o sit here under my footstool Jas 2:3 2228
If a brother o sister be naked, Jas 2:15 2228
To day o to morrow we will go Jas 4:13 2228
we shall live, and do this, o that Jas 4:15 2228
o what manner of time the Spirit 1Pet 1:11 2228
O unto governors, as unto them 1Pet 2:14 1535
o of putting on of apparel 1Pet 3:3 2228
for evil, o railing for railing 1Pet 3:9 2228
o as a thief, o as an evildoer, 1Pet 4:15 2228
o as a busybody in other men's 1Pet 4:15 2228
o else I will come unto thee Rev 2:5 1161
o else I will come unto thee Rev 2:16 1161
I would thou wert cold o hot Rev 3:15 2228
right hand, o in their foreheads Rev 13:16 2228
And that no man might buy o sell Rev 13:17 2228
o the name of the beast, o the Rev 13:17 2228
in his forehead, o in his hand, Rev 14:9 2228
their foreheads, o in their hands Rev 20:4 2532
abomination, o maketh a lie Rev 21:27 2532

ORACLE

man had enquired at the o of God 2Sa 16:23 1697
both of the temple and of the o 1Kin 6:5 1687
for it within, even for the o 1Kin 6:16 1687
the o he prepared in the house 1Kin 6:19 1687
the o in the forepart was twenty 1Kin 6:20 1687
the chains of gold before the o 1Kin 6:21 1687
by the o he overlaid with gold 1Kin 6:22 1687
And within the o he made two 1Kin 6:23 1687
for the entering of the o he made 1Kin 6:31 1687
and five on the left, before the o 1Kin 7:49 1687
into the o of the house, to the 1Kin 8:6 1687
in the holy place before the o 1Kin 8:8 1687
And he made chains, as in the o 2Chr 3:16 1687
after the manner before the o 2Chr 4:20 1687
to the o of the house, into the 2Chr 5:7 1687
seen from the ark before the o 2Chr 5:9 1687
up my hands toward thy holy o Ps 28:2 1687

ORACLES

the lively o to give unto us Acts 7:38 3051
them were committed the o of God Rom 3:2 3051
first principles of the o of God Heb 5:12 3051
let him speak as the o of God 1Pet 4:11 3051

ORATION

throne, and made an o unto them Acts 12:21 1215

ORATOR

artificer, and the eloquent o Is 3:3 3908
with a certain o named Tertullus, Acts 24:1 4489

ORCHARD

plants are an o of pomegranates Song 4:13 6508

ORCHARDS

I made me gardens and o, and I Eccl 2:5 6508

ORDAIN

seer did o in their set office 1Chr 9:22 3245
Also I will o a place for my 1Chr 17:9 7760
LORD, thou wilt o peace for us Is 26:12 8239
And so o I in all churches 1Cor 7:17 1299
o elders in every city, as I had Titus 1:5 2525

ORDAINED

which was o in mount Sinai for a Num 28:6 6213
Jeroboam o a feast in the eighth 1Kin 12:32 6213
o a feast unto the children of 1Kin 12:33 6213
had o to burn incense in the high 2Kin 23:5 5414
he o him priests for the high 2Chr 11:15 5975
singing, as it was o by David 2Chr 23:18
with the instruments o by David 2Chr 29:27
The Jews o, and took upon them, and Est 9:27 6965
sucklings hast thou o strength Ps 8:2 3245
and the stars, which thou hast o Ps 8:3 3559
This he o in Joseph for a Ps 81:5 7760
I have o a lamp for mine anointed Ps 132:17 6186
For Tophet is o of old Is 30:33 6186
I o thee a prophet unto the Jer 1:5 5414
whom the king had o to destroy Dan 2:24 4483
thou hast o them for judgment Hab 1:12 7760
he o twelve, that they should be Mk 3:14 4160
o you, that ye should go and bring Jn 15:16 5087
must one be o to be a witness Acts 1:22 1096
o of God to be the Judge of quick Acts 10:42 3724
as many as were o to eternal life Acts 13:48 5021
when they had o them elders in Acts 14:23 5500
that were o of the apostles and Acts 16:4 2919
by that man whom he hath o Acts 17:31 3724
commandment, which was o to life Rom 7:10
the powers that be are o of God Rom 13:1 5021
which God o before the world unto 1Cor 2:7 4304
Even so hath the Lord o that they 1Cor 9:14 1299
it was o by angels in the hand of Gal 3:19 1299
which God hath before o that we Eph 2:10 4282
Whereunto I am o a preacher 1Ti 2:7 5087
o the first bishop of the church 2Ti s 5500
o the first bishop of the church Titus s 5500
priest taken from among men is o Heb 5:1 2525
high priest is o to offer gifts Heb 8:3 2525
Now when these things were thus o Heb 9:6 2680
of old o to this condemnation Jude 4 4270

ORDAINETH

he o his arrows against the Ps 7:13 6466

ORDER

there, and laid the wood in o Gen 22:9
set in o one against another Ex 26:17 7947

his sons shall o it from evening ... Ex 27:21 6186
with the lamps to be set in o ... Ex 39:37 4634
set in o the things that are to ... Ex 40:4 6186
that are to be set in o upon it ... Ex 40:4 6187
he set the bread in o upon it ... Ex 40:23 6186
lay the wood in o upon the fire ... Lev 1:7 6186
in o upon the wood that is on the ... Lev 1:8 6186
the priest shall lay them in o on ... Lev 1:12 6186
the burnt offering in o upon it ... Lev 6:12 6186
shall Aaron o it from the evening ... Lev 24:3 6186
He shall o the lamps upon the ... Lev 24:4 6186
sabbath he shall set it in o ... Lev 24:8 6186
she had laid in o upon the roof ... Josh 2:6 6186
How shall we o the child, and how ... Judg 13:12 4941
city, and put his household in o ... 2Sa 17:23 6680
And he put the wood in o, and cut ... 1Kin 18:33 6186
he said, Who shall o the battle ... 1Kin 20:14 631
the LORD, Set thine house in o ... 2Kin 20:1 6680
and the priests of the second o ... 2Kin 23:4
their office according to their o ... 1Chr 6:32 4941
we sought him not after the due o ... 1Chr 15:13 4941
according to the o commanded unto ... 1Chr 23:31 4941
according to the o of the king ... 1Chr 25:2 3027
to the king's o to Asaph, ... 1Chr 25:6 3027
according to the o of David his ... 2Chr 8:14 4941
set they in o upon the pure table ... 2Chr 13:11
house of the LORD was set in o ... 2Chr 29:35 3559
shadow of death, without any o ... Job 10:22 5468
I would o my cause before him, and ... Job 23:4 6186
me, set thy words in o before me ... Job 33:5 6186
for we cannot o our speech by ... Job 37:19 6186
be reckoned up in o unto thee ... Ps 40:5 6186
set them in o before thine eyes ... Ps 50:21 6186
ever after the o of Melchizedek ... Ps 110:4 1700
O my steps in thy word ... Ps 119:133 3559
out, and set in o many proverbs ... Eccl 12:9 8626
and upon his kingdom, to o it ... Is 9:7 3559
the LORD, Set thine house in o ... Is 38:1 6680
declare it, and set it in o for me ... Is 44:7 6186
O ye the buckler and shield, and ... Jer 46:3 6186
one over another, and thirty in o ... Eze 41:6 6471
o a declaration of those things ... Lk 1:1 *1299*
first, to write unto thee in o ... Lk 1:3 *2517*
before God in the o of his course ... Lk 1:8 *5010*
and expounded it by o unto them ... Acts 11:4 *2517*
of Galatia and Phrygia in o ... Acts 18:23 *2517*
rest will I set in o when I come ... 1Cor 11:34 *1299*
things be done decently and in o ... 1Cor 14:40 *5010*
But every man in his own o ... 1Cor 15:23 *5001*
as I have given o to the churches ... 1Cor 16:1 *1299*
joying and beholding your o ... Col 2:5 *5010*
that thou shouldest set in o the ... Titus 1:5 *1930*
ever after the o of Melchisedec ... Heb 5:6 *5010*
priest after the o of Melchisedec ... Heb 5:10 *5010*
ever after the o of Melchisedec ... Heb 6:20 *5010*
rise after the o of Melchisedec ... Heb 7:11 *5010*
be called after the o of Aaron ... Heb 7:11 *5010*
ever after the o of Melchisedec ... Heb 7:17 *5010*
ever after the o of Melchisedec ... Heb 7:21 *5010*

ORDERED
top of this rock, in the o place ... Judg 6:26 4634
o in all things, and sure ... 2Sa 23:5 6186
Behold now, I have o my cause ... Job 13:18 6186
of a good man are o by the LORD ... Ps 37:23 3559

ORDERETH
to him that o his conversation ... Ps 50:23 7760

ORDERINGS
These were the o of them in their ... 1Chr 24:19 6486

ORDERLY
that thou thyself also walkest o ... Acts 21:24 *4748*

ORDINANCE
keep it a feast by an o for ever ... Ex 12:14 2708
your generations by an o for ever ... Ex 12:17 2708
this thing for an o to thee ... Ex 12:24 2706
This is the o of the passover ... Ex 12:43 2708
Thou shalt therefore keep this o ... Ex 13:10 2708
made for them a statute and an o ... Ex 15:25 4941
Therefore shall ye keep mine o ... Lev 18:30 4931
They shall therefore keep mine o ... Lev 22:9 4931
to the o of the passover, and ... Num 9:14 2708
ye shall have one o, both for the ... Num 9:14 2708
for an o for ever throughout your ... Num 10:8 2708
One o shall be both for you of ... Num 15:15 2708
an o for ever in your generations ... Num 15:15 2708
and to thy sons, by an o for ever ... Num 18:8 2706
This is the o of the law which ... Num 19:2 2708
This is the o of the law which ... Num 31:21 2708
them a statute and an o in Shechem ... Josh 24:25 4941
an o for Israel unto this day ... 1Sa 30:25 4941
This is an o for ever to Israel ... 2Chr 2:4
with fire according to the o ... 2Chr 35:13 4941
day, and made them an o in Israel ... 2Chr 35:25 2706
after the o of David king of ... Ezr 3:10 3027
and the o that he gave them ... Ps 99:7 2706
the laws, changed the o, broken ... Is 24:5 2706
and forsook not the o of their God ... Is 58:2 4941
Concerning the o of oil, the bath ... Eze 45:14 2706
by a perpetual o unto the LORD ... Eze 46:14 2708
is it that we have kept his o ... Mal 3:14 4931
the power, resisteth the o of God ... Rom 13:2 *1296*
o of man for the Lord's sake ... 1Pet 2:13 *2937*

ORDINANCES
And thou shalt teach them o ... Ex 18:20 2706
neither shall ye walk in their o ... Lev 18:3 2708
do my judgments, and keep mine o ... Lev 18:4 2708
according to all the o of the ... Num 9:12 2708
their statutes, or after their o ... 2Kin 17:34 4941
And the statutes, and the o ... 2Kin 17:37 4941
the o by the hand of Moses ... 2Chr 33:8 4941
Also we made o for us, to charge ... Neh 10:32 4687
Knowest thou the o of heaven ... Job 38:33 2708
this day according to thine o ... Ps 119:91 4941
they ask of me the o of justice ... Is 58:2 4941
the o of the moon and of the stars ... Jer 31:35 2708
If those o depart from before me ... Jer 31:36 2706
not appointed the o of heaven ... Jer 33:25 2708
in my statutes, and keep mine o ... Eze 11:20 4941
thereof, and all the o thereof ... Eze 43:11 2708
thereof, and all the o thereof ... Eze 43:11 2708
These are the o of the altar in ... Eze 43:18 2708
the o of the house of the LORD ... Eze 44:5 2708
ye are gone away from mine o ... Mal 3:7 2706
and o of the Lord blameless ... Lk 1:6 *1345*
me in all things, and keep the o ... 1Cor 11:2 *3862*
of commandments contained in o ... Eph 2:15 *1378*
of o that was against us, which ... Col 2:14 *1378*
in the world, are ye subject to o ... Col 2:20 *1379*
had also o of divine service ... Heb 9:1 *1345*
and divers washings, and carnal o ... Heb 9:10 *1345*

ORDINARY
and have diminished thine o food ... Eze 16:27 2706

OREB (*o'-reb*)
1. A prince of Midian.
two princes of the Midianites, O ... Judg 7:25 6157
they slew O upon the rock O, ... Judg 7:25 6157
Midian, and brought the heads of O ... Judg 7:25 6157
hands the princes of Midian, O ... Judg 8:3 6157
Make their nobles like O, and like ... Ps 83:11 6157
2. A rock east of the Jordan.
of Midian at the rock of O ... Is 10:26 6157

OREN (*o'-ren*) *A son of Jerahmeel.*
Ram the firstborn, and Bunah, and O .. 1Chr 2:25 767

ORGAN
all such as handle the harp and o ... Gen 4:21 5748
and rejoice at the sound of the o ... Job 21:12 5748
my o into the voice of them that ... Job 30:31 5748

ORGANS
with stringed instruments and o ... Ps 150:4 5748

ORION (*o'-ri'-on*) *A constellation of stars.*
Which maketh Arcturus, O, and ... Job 9:9 3685
Pleiades, or loose the bands of O ... Job 38:31 3685
that maketh the seven stars and O ... Amos 5:8 3685

ORNAMENT
For they shall be an o of grace ... Prov 1:9 3880
give to thine head an o of grace ... Prov 4:9 3880
an o of fine gold, so is a wise ... Prov 25:12 2481
the o of thy molten images of ... Is 30:22 642
thee with them all, as with an o ... Is 49:18 5716
As for the beauty of his o ... Eze 7:20 5716
even the o of a meek and quiet ... 1Pet 3:4

ORNAMENTS
and no man did put on him his o ... Ex 33:4 5716
now put off thy o from thee ... Ex 33:5 5716
of their o by the mount Horeb ... Ex 33:6 5716
took away the o that were on ... Judg 8:21 7720
beside o, and collars, and purple ... Judg 8:26 7720
who put on o of gold upon your ... 2Sa 1:24 5716
their tinkling o about their feet ... Is 3:18 5914
the o of the legs, and the ... Is 3:20 6807
bridegroom decketh himself with o ... Is 61:10 6287
Can a maid forget her o, or a ... Jer 2:32 5716
thou deckest thee with o of gold ... Jer 4:30 5716
and thou art come to excellent o ... Eze 16:7 5716
I decked thee also with o ... Eze 16:11 5716
eyes, and deckedst thyself with o ... Eze 23:40 5716

ORNAN (*or'-nan*) See ARAUNAH. *A Jebusite prince.*
threshingfloor of O the Jebusite ... 1Chr 21:15 771
threshingfloor of O the Jebusite ... 1Chr 21:18 771
O turned back, and saw the angel ... 1Chr 21:20 771
Now O was threshing wheat ... 1Chr 21:20 771
And as David came to O, O ... 1Chr 21:21 771
Then David said to O, Grant me ... 1Chr 21:22 771
O said unto David, Take it to ... 1Chr 21:23 771
And king David said to O, Nay ... 1Chr 21:24 771
So David gave to O for the place ... 1Chr 21:25 771
threshingfloor of O the Jebusite ... 1Chr 21:28 771
threshingfloor of O the Jebusite ... 2Chr 3:1 771

ORPAH (*or'-pah*) *Daughter-in-law of Naomi.*
the name of the one was O ... Ruth 1:4 6204
O kissed her mother in law ... Ruth 1:14 6204

ORPHANS
We are o and fatherless, our ... Lam 5:3 3490

OSEE (*o'-see*) See HOSEA, JOSHUA, OSHEA. *Greek form of Hoshea.*
As he saith also in O, I will ... Rom 9:25 *5617*

OSHEA (*o-she'-ah*) See HOSHEA, OSEE. *Same as Joshua, son of Nun.*
of Ephraim, O the son of Nun ... Num 13:8 1954
Moses called O the son of Nun ... Num 13:16 1954

OSNAPPAR See ASNAPPER.

OSPRAY
eagle, and the ossifrage, and the o ... Lev 11:13 5822
eagle, and the ossifrage, and the o ... Deut 14:12 5822

OSSIFRAGE
the eagle, and the o, and the ... Lev 11:13 6538
the eagle, and the o, and the ... Deut 14:12 6538

OSTRICH
or wings and feathers unto the o ... Job 39:13 5133

OSTRICHES
like the o in the wilderness ... Lam 4:3 3283

OTHER
Adah, and the name of the o Zillah ... Gen 4:19 8145
And he stayed yet o seven days ... Gen 8:10 312
And he stayed yet o seven days ... Gen 8:12 312
themselves the one from the o ... Gen 13:11 251
that are with thee, and with all o ... Gen 20:16
be stronger than the o people ... Gen 25:23
this is none o but the house of ... Gen 28:17
serve with me yet seven o years ... Gen 29:27 312
served with him yet seven o years ... Gen 29:30 312
or if thou shalt take o wives ... Gen 31:50
then the o company which is left ... Gen 32:8
seven o kine came up after them ... Gen 41:3 312
stood by the o kine upon the ... Gen 41:3
seven o kine came up after them, ... Gen 41:19 312
he may send away your o brother ... Gen 43:14 312
o money have we brought down in ... Gen 43:22 312
Egypt even to the o end thereof ... Gen 47:21
and the name of the o Puah ... Ex 1:15 8145
was turned again as his o flesh ... Ex 4:7
came not near the o all the night ... Ex 14:20 2088
side, and the o on the ... Ex 17:12 259
on the o side ... Ex 17:12 2088
And the name of the o was Eliezer ... Ex 18:4 259
they asked each o of their ... Ex 18:7 7453
shalt have no o gods before me ... Ex 20:3 312
no mention of the name of o gods ... Ex 23:13 312
and two rings in the o side of it ... Ex 25:12 8145
the o cherub on the ... Ex 25:19 259
cherub on the o end ... Ex 25:19 2088
the candlestick out of the o side ... Ex 25:32 8145
made like almonds in the o branch ... Ex 25:33 259
o five curtains shall be coupled ... Ex 26:3
a cubit on the o side of that ... Ex 26:13 2088
of the o side of the tabernacle ... Ex 26:27 8145
on the o side shall be hangings ... Ex 27:15 8145
the o six names of the rest on ... Ex 28:10
names of the rest on the o stone ... Ex 28:10
the o two ends of the two ... Ex 28:25
two o rings of gold thou shalt ... Ex 28:27
against the o coupling thereof ... Ex 28:27
And thou shalt take the o ram ... Ex 29:19 8145
the o lamb thou shalt offer at ... Ex 29:39 8145
the o lamb thou shalt offer at ... Ex 29:41 8145
shall ye make any o like it ... Ex 30:32
on the o were they written ... Ex 32:15 2088
For thou shalt worship no o god ... Ex 34:14 312
the o five curtains he coupled ... Ex 36:10
for the o side of the tabernacle, ... Ex 36:25 8145
of the o side of the tabernacle ... Ex 36:32 8145
boards from the one end to the o ... Ex 36:33 8145
two rings upon the o side of it ... Ex 37:3 8145
cherub on the o end on that side ... Ex 37:8
out of the o side thereof ... Ex 37:18 8145
for the o side of the court gate, ... Ex 38:15 8145
And they made two o golden rings ... Ex 39:20
against the o coupling thereof ... Ex 39:20
the o for a burnt offering ... Lev 5:7 259
put on o garments, and carry forth ... Lev 6:11 312
beasts, may be used in any o use ... Lev 7:24
And he brought the o ram, the ram ... Lev 8:22 8145
But all o flying creeping things, ... Lev 11:23
and the o for a sin offering ... Lev 12:8 259
and it be no lower than the o skin ... Lev 13:26
and the o a burnt offering ... Lev 14:22 259
the o for a burnt offering, with ... Lev 14:31 259
And they shall take o stones ... Lev 14:42 312
and he shall take o morter ... Lev 14:42 312
the o for a burnt offering ... Lev 15:15 259
the o for a burnt offering ... Lev 15:30 259
the o lot for the scapegoat ... Lev 16:8 259
beside the o in her life time ... Lev 18:18
have separated you from o people ... Lev 20:24
and have severed you from o people ... Lev 20:26
the o shall not rule with rigour ... Lev 25:53
the o for a burnt offering, and ... Num 6:11 259
the o for a burnt offering, unto ... Num 8:12 259
the o did set up the tabernacle ... Num 10:21
Eldad, and the name of the o Medad ... Num 11:26 8145
a day's journey on the o side ... Num 11:31 3541
and pitched on the o side of Arnon ... Num 21:13 5676
he went not, as at o times ... Num 24:1 312
the o lamb shalt thou offer at ... Num 28:4 8145
the o lamb shalt thou offer at ... Num 28:8 8145
gave o names unto the cities ... Num 32:38 312
the o tribes of the children of ... Num 36:3 259
the one side of heaven unto the o ... Deut 4:32
shalt have none o gods before me ... Deut 5:7 312
Ye shall not go after o gods ... Deut 6:14 312
me, that they may serve o gods ... Deut 7:4 312
thy God, and walk after o gods ... Deut 8:19 312
and ye turn aside, and serve o gods ... Deut 11:16 312
you this day, to go after o gods ... Deut 11:28 312
Are they not on the o side Jordan ... Deut 11:30 5676
saying, Let us go after o gods ... Deut 13:2 312
saying, Let us go and serve o gods ... Deut 13:6 312
even unto the o end of the earth ... Deut 13:7
saying, Let us go and serve o gods ... Deut 13:13 312
And hath gone and served o gods ... Deut 17:3 312
shall speak in the name of o gods ... Deut 18:20 312
to go after o gods to serve them ... Deut 28:14 312
and there shalt thou serve o gods ... Deut 28:36 312
end of the earth even unto the o ... Deut 28:64
and there thou shalt serve o gods ... Deut 28:64 312
For they went and served o gods ... Deut 29:26 312
be drawn away, and worship o gods ... Deut 30:17 312
that they are turned unto o gods ... Deut 31:18 312
then will they turn unto o gods ... Deut 31:20 312
that were on the o side Jordan ... Josh 2:10 5676
and dwelt on the o side Jordan ... Josh 7:7 5676
the o issued out of the city ... Josh 8:22 428
all o they took in battle ... Josh 11:19
possessed their land on the o ... Josh 12:1 5676
on the o side Jordan eastward ... Josh 13:27 5676
on the o side Jordan, by Jericho, ... Josh 13:32 5676
half tribe on the o side Jordan ... Josh 14:3 5676
which were on the o side Jordan ... Josh 17:5 5676
on the o side Jordan by Jericho ... Josh 20:8 5676

Context	Reference	Strong's
out of the o half tribe of	Josh 21:27	
gave you on the o side Jordan	Josh 22:4	5676
but unto the o half thereof gave	Josh 22:7	
and have gone and served o gods	Josh 23:16	312
Your fathers dwelt on the o side	Josh 24:2	5676
and they served o gods	Josh 24:2	312
from the o side of the flood	Josh 24:3	5676
which dwelt on the o side Jordan	Josh 24:8	5676
served on the o side of the flood	Josh 24:14	5676
were on the o side of the flood	Josh 24:15	5676
forsake the LORD, to serve o gods	Josh 24:16	312
land of Egypt, and followed o gods	Judg 2:12	312
they went a whoring after o gods	Judg 2:17	312
in following o gods to serve them	Judg 2:19	312
let all the o people go every man	Judg 7:7	
to Gideon on the o side Jordan	Judg 7:25	5676
the two o companies ran upon all	Judg 9:44	
of Israel that were on the o side	Judg 10:8	5676
forsaken me, and served o gods	Judg 10:13	312
and pitched on the o side of Arnon	Judg 11:18	5676
me, that came unto me the o day	Judg 13:10	
become weak, and be like any o man	Judg 16:17	
will go out as at o times before	Judg 16:20	
hand, and of the o with his left	Judg 16:29	259
against Gibeah, as at o times	Judg 20:30	
people, and kill, as at o times	Judg 20:31	
the o to Gibeah in the field,	Judg 20:31	259
Orpah, and the name of the o Ruth	Ruth 1:4	8145
they meet thee not in any o field	Ruth 2:22	312
and the name of the o Peninnah	1Sa 1:2	8145
and stood, and called as at o times	1Sa 3:10	
forsaken me, and served o gods	1Sa 8:8	312
garrison, that is on the o side	1Sa 14:1	5676
and a sharp rock on the o side	1Sa 14:4	2088
Bozez, and the name of the o Seneh	1Sa 14:4	259
the o southward over against	1Sa 14:5	259
my son will be on the o side	1Sa 14:40	259
stood on a mountain on the o side	1Sa 17:3	2088
with his hand, as at o times	1Sa 18:10	
he sent o messengers, and they	1Sa 19:21	312
sat upon his seat, as at o times	1Sa 20:25	
for there is no o save that here	1Sa 21:9	312
David went over to the o side	1Sa 26:13	5676
LORD, saying, Go, serve o gods	1Sa 26:19	312
put on o raiment, and he went, and	1Sa 28:8	312
they drave before those o cattle	1Sa 30:20	
were on the o side of the valley	1Sa 31:7	5676
that were on the o side Jordan	1Sa 31:7	5676
with o delights, who put on	2Sa 1:24	
the o on the	2Sa 2:13	428
on the o side of the pool	2Sa 2:13	2088
and the name of the o Rechab	2Sa 4:2	8145
the one rich, and the o poor	2Sa 12:1	259
the o that thou didst unto me	2Sa 13:16	312
them, but the one smote the o	2Sa 14:6	259
in some pit, or in some o place	2Sa 17:9	
o instruments of the oxen for	2Sa 24:22	
And the o woman said, Nay	1Kin 3:22	312
and the o saith, Nay	1Kin 3:23	2063
half to the one, and half to the o	1Kin 3:25	259
But the o said, Let it be neither	1Kin 3:26	2063
five cubits the o wing of the	1Kin 6:24	8145
part of the o were ten cubits	1Kin 6:24	3671
the o cherub was ten cubits	1Kin 6:25	8145
and so was it of the o cherub	1Kin 6:26	8145
o cherub touched the o wall	1Kin 6:27	8145
leaves of the o door were folding	1Kin 6:34	8145
the o pillars and the thick beam	1Kin 7:6	
one side of the floor to the o	1Kin 7:7	
the height of the o chapiter was	1Kin 7:16	8145
and seven for the o chapiter	1Kin 7:17	8145
and so did he for the o chapiter	1Kin 7:18	8145
round about upon the o chapiter	1Kin 7:20	8145
cubits from the one brim to the o	1Kin 7:23	
you, but go and serve o gods	1Kin 9:6	312
and have taken hold upon o gods	1Kin 9:9	312
on the o upon the six steps	1Kin 10:20	2088
away his heart after o gods	1Kin 11:4	312
he should not go after o gods	1Kin 11:10	312
Beth-el, and the o put he in Dan	1Kin 12:29	259
hast gone and made thee o gods	1Kin 14:9	312
and I will dress the o bullock	1Kin 18:23	259
one over against the o seven days	1Kin 20:29	428
on the o side as red as blood	2Kin 3:22	5048
nor sacrifice unto o gods	2Kin 5:17	312
the o priests, and said unto them,	2Kin 12:7	
of Egypt, and had feared o gods	2Kin 17:7	312
saying, Ye shall not fear o gods	2Kin 17:35	312
and ye shall not fear o gods	2Kin 17:37	312
neither shall ye fear o gods	2Kin 17:38	312
have burned incense unto o gods	2Kin 22:17	312
on the o side Jordan by Jericho,	1Chr 6:78	5676
o of their brethren, of the sons	1Chr 9:32	
on the o side of Jordan, of the	1Chr 12:37	5676
And Eliezer had none o sons	1Chr 23:17	312
the o wing was likewise five	2Chr 3:11	312
to the wing of the o cherub	2Chr 3:11	312
one wing of the o cherub was five	2Chr 3:12	259
the o wing was five cubits also,	2Chr 3:12	312
to the wing of the o cherub	2Chr 3:12	312
right hand, and the o on the left	2Chr 3:17	259
you, and shall go and serve o gods	2Chr 7:19	312
of Egypt, and laid hold on o gods	2Chr 7:22	312
on the o upon the six steps	2Chr 9:19	2088
manner of the nations of o lands	2Chr 13:9	
with them o beside the Ammonites,	2Chr 20:1	
o ten thousand left alive did the	2Chr 25:12	
to burn incense unto o gods	2Chr 28:25	312
ended, and until the o priests had	2Chr 29:34	
took counsel to keep o seven days	2Chr 30:23	312
they kept o seven days with	2Chr 30:23	
unto all the people of o lands	2Chr 32:13	
As the gods of the nations of o	2Chr 32:17	
and from the hand of all o	2Chr 32:22	
o of the Levites, all that could	2Chr 34:12	
have burned incense unto o gods	2Chr 34:25	312
but the o holy offerings sod they	2Chr 35:13	
and ten, and o vessels a thousand	Ezr 1:10	312
The children of the o Elam	Ezr 2:31	312
Pahath-moab, repaired the o piece	Neh 3:11	8145
earnestly repaired the o piece	Neh 3:20	8145
the o half of them held both the	Neh 4:16	
with the o hand held a weapon	Neh 4:17	259
for o men have our lands and	Neh 5:5	312
The men of the o Nebo, fifty and	Neh 7:33	312
The children of the o Elam	Neh 7:34	312
nine parts to dwell in o cities	Neh 11:1	
the o company of them that gave	Neh 12:38	8145
with o things for the purifying	Est 2:12	
But the o Jews that were in the	Est 9:16	7605
it withereth before any o herb	Job 8:12	
are taken out of the way as all o	Job 24:24	
They are not in trouble as o men	Ps 73:5	
are they plagued like o men	Ps 73:5	
and peace have kissed each o	Ps 85:10	
as the one dieth, so dieth the o	Eccl 3:19	2088
this hath more rest than the o	Eccl 6:5	2088
set the one over against the o	Eccl 7:14	2088
o lords besides thee have had	Is 26:13	
have, after thou hast lost the o	Is 49:20	
have burned incense unto o gods	Jer 1:16	312
walk after o gods to your hurt	Jer 7:6	312
walk after o gods whom ye know	Jer 7:9	312
out drink offerings unto o gods	Jer 7:18	312
they went after o gods to serve	Jer 11:10	312
even to the o end of the land	Jer 12:12	
their heart, and walk after o gods	Jer 13:10	312
LORD, and have walked after o gods	Jer 16:11	312
there shall ye serve o gods day	Jer 16:13	312
burned incense in it unto o gods	Jer 19:4	312
out drink offerings unto o gods	Jer 19:13	312
their God, and worshipped o gods	Jer 22:9	312
the o basket had very naughty	Jer 24:2	259
go not after o gods to serve them	Jer 25:6	312
even unto the o end of the earth	Jer 25:33	
day, and in Israel, and among o men	Jer 32:20	
out drink offerings unto o gods	Jer 32:29	312
go not after o gods to serve them	Jer 35:15	312
they were afraid both one and o	Jer 36:16	7453
burn incense, and to serve o gods	Jer 44:3	312
to burn no incense unto o gods	Jer 44:5	312
burning incense unto o gods in	Jer 44:8	312
had burned incense unto o gods	Jer 44:15	312
straight, the one toward the o	Eze 1:23	269
from o women in thy whoredoms	Eze 16:34	
Go thee one way or o, either on	Eze 21:16	
the o threshold of the gate,	Eze 40:6	259
and on the o side, which was at	Eze 40:40	312
and six cubits broad on the o side	Eze 41:1	6311
and five cubits on the o side	Eze 41:2	6311
on the one side and on the o side	Eze 41:15	6311
the palm tree on the o side	Eze 41:19	6311
one as the appearance of the o	Eze 41:21	
and two leaves for the o door	Eze 41:24	312
on the one side and on the o side	Eze 41:26	6311
and shall put on o garments	Eze 42:14	312
and they shall put on o garments	Eze 44:19	312
on the o side of the oblation of	Eze 45:7	2088
trees on the one side and on the o	Eze 47:7	2088
in length as one of the o parts	Eze 48:8	
on the o of the holy oblation, and	Eze 48:21	2088
there is none o that can shew it	Dan 2:11	321
shall not be left to o people	Dan 2:44	321
their o garments, and were cast	Dan 3:21	
because there is no o God that	Dan 3:29	321
of the o which came up, and before	Dan 7:20	317
but one was higher than the o	Dan 8:3	8145
and, behold, there stood o two	Dan 12:5	312
the o on that side of the bank of	Dan 12:5	259
of Israel, who look to o gods	Hos 3:1	312
O Israel, for joy, as o people	Hos 9:1	
where is any o that may save thee	Hos 13:10	
that thou stoodest on the o side	Obad 11	5048
the o upon the left side thereof	Zec 4:3	259
Beauty, and the o I called Bands	Zec 11:7	259
Then I cut asunder mine o staff	Zec 11:14	8145
he saw o two brethren, James the	Mt 4:21	243
cheek, turn to him the o also	Mt 5:39	*243*
will hate the one, and love the o	Mt 6:24	*2087*
hold to the one, and despise the o	Mt 6:24	*2087*
to depart unto the o side	Mt 8:18	*4008*
when he was come to the o side	Mt 8:28	*4008*
was restored whole, like as the o	Mt 12:13	*243*
seven o spirits more wicked than	Mt 12:45	*2087*
But o fell into good ground, and	Mt 13:8	*243*
to go before him unto the o side	Mt 14:22	*4008*
disciples were come to the o side	Mt 16:5	*4008*
the o on the left, in thy kingdom	Mt 20:21	*1520*
he sent o servants more than the	Mt 21:36	*243*
his vineyard unto o husbandmen	Mt 21:41	*243*
Again, he sent forth o servants	Mt 22:4	*243*
and not to leave the o undone	Mt 23:23	*2548*
from one end of heaven to the o	Mt 24:31	*1565*
one shall be taken, and the o left	Mt 24:40	*1520*
one shall be taken, and the o left	Mt 24:41	*1520*
Afterward came also the o virgins	Mt 25:11	*3062*
same, and made them o five talents	Mt 25:16	*243*
two, he also gained o two	Mt 25:17	*243*
brought o five talents, saying,	Mt 25:20	*243*
I have gained two o talents	Mt 25:22	*243*
the o Mary, sitting over against	Mt 27:61	*243*
the o Mary to see the sepulchre	Mt 28:1	*243*
hand was restored whole as the o	Mk 3:5	*243*
o fell on good ground, and did	Mk 4:8	*243*
the lusts of o things entering in	Mk 4:19	*3062*
Let us pass over unto the o side	Mk 4:35	*4008*
were also with him o little ships	Mk 4:36	*243*
over unto the o side of the sea	Mk 5:1	*4008*
again by ship unto the o side	Mk 5:21	*4008*
to go to the o side before unto	Mk 6:45	*4008*
many o things there be, which	Mk 7:4	*243*
many o such like things ye do	Mk 7:8	*243*
ship again departed to the o side	Mk 8:13	*4008*
the o on thy left hand, in thy	Mk 10:37	*1520*
There is none o commandment	Mk 12:31	*243*
and there is none o but he	Mk 12:32	*243*
right hand, and the o on his left	Mk 15:27	*1520*
many o women which came up with	Mk 15:41	*243*
many o things in his exhortation	Lk 3:18	*2087*
kingdom of God to o cities also	Lk 4:43	*2087*
which were in the o ship	Lk 5:7	*2087*
hand was restored whole as the o	Lk 6:10	*243*
on the one cheek offer also the o	Lk 6:29	*243*
hundred pence, and the o fifty	Lk 7:41	*2087*
o fell on good ground, and sprang	Lk 8:8	*2087*
over unto the o side of the lake	Lk 8:22	*4008*
the Lord appointed o seventy also	Lk 10:1	*2087*
him, he passed by on the o side	Lk 10:31	*492*
him, and passed by on the o side	Lk 10:32	*492*
taketh to him seven o spirits	Lk 11:26	*2087*
and not to leave the o undone	Lk 11:42	*2548*
while the o is yet a great way	Lk 14:32	*846*
will hate the one, and love the o	Lk 16:13	*2087*
hold to the one, and despise the o	Lk 16:13	*2087*
shineth unto the o part under	Lk 17:24	
be taken, and the o shall be left	Lk 17:34	*2087*
one shall be taken, and the o left	Lk 17:35	*2087*
one shall be taken, and the o left	Lk 17:36	*2087*
a Pharisee, and the o a publican	Lk 18:10	*2087*
thee, that I am not as o men are	Lk 18:11	*3062*
house justified rather than the o	Lk 18:14	*1565*
many o things blasphemously spake	Lk 22:65	*2087*
right hand, and the o on the left	Lk 23:33	*3739*
But the o answering rebuked him,	Lk 23:40	*2087*
o women that were with them,	Lk 24:10	*3062*
o men laboured, and ye are entered	Jn 4:38	*243*
the people which stood on the o	Jn 6:22	*4008*
that there was none o boat there	Jn 6:22	*243*
(Howbeit there came o boats from	Jn 6:23	*243*
him on the o side of the sea	Jn 6:25	*4008*
but climbeth up some o way	Jn 10:1	*237*
o sheep I have, which are not of	Jn 10:16	*243*
the works which none o man did	Jn 15:24	*243*
Then went out that o disciple	Jn 18:16	*243*
of the o which was crucified with	Jn 19:32	*243*
to the o disciple, whom Jesus	Jn 20:2	*243*
that o disciple, and came to the	Jn 20:3	*243*
the o disciple did outrun Peter,	Jn 20:4	*243*
Then went in also that o disciple	Jn 20:8	*243*
the o at the feet, where the body	Jn 20:12	*1520*
The o disciples therefore said	Jn 20:25	*243*
many o signs truly did Jesus in	Jn 20:30	*243*
and two o of his disciples	Jn 21:2	*243*
the o disciples came in a little	Jn 21:8	*243*
there are also many o things	Jn 21:25	*243*
and began to speak with o tongues	Acts 2:4	*2087*
with many o words did he testify	Acts 2:40	*2087*
is there salvation in any o	Acts 4:12	*243*
for there is none o name under	Acts 4:12	*2087*
the o apostles answered and said,	Acts 5:29	
of himself, or of some o man	Acts 8:34	*2087*
and Barnabas, and certain o of them	Acts 15:2	*243*
in asunder one from the o	Acts 15:39	*240*
security of Jason, and of the o	Acts 17:9	*3062*
o some, He seemeth to be a setter	Acts 17:18	
any thing concerning o matters	Acts 19:39	*2087*
the o Pharisees, he cried out in	Acts 23:6	*2087*
saying none o things than those	Acts 26:22	*1622*
certain o prisoners unto one	Acts 27:1	*2087*
also, even as among o Gentiles	Rom 1:13	*3062*
nor any o creature, shall be able	Rom 8:39	*2087*
and if there be any o commandment	Rom 13:9	*2087*
know not whether I baptized any o	1Cor 1:16	*243*
For o foundation can no man lay	1Cor 3:11	*243*
Defraud ye not one the o, except	1Cor 7:5	*240*
that there is none o God but one	1Cor 8:4	*2087*
a wife, as well as o apostles	1Cor 9:5	*3062*
say, not thine own, but of the o	1Cor 10:29	*2087*
taketh before o his own supper	1Cor 11:21	
well, but the o is not edified	1Cor 14:17	*2087*
is written, With men of o tongues	1Cor 14:21	*2084*
o lips will I speak unto this	1Cor 14:21	*2087*
two or three, and let the o judge	1Cor 14:29	*243*
of wheat, or of some o grain	1Cor 15:37	*3062*
we write none o things unto you	2Cor 1:13	*243*
to the o the savour of life unto	2Cor 2:16	3739
I mean not that o men be eased	2Cor 8:13	*243*
that is, of o men's labours	2Cor 10:15	*245*
I robbed o churches, taking wages	2Cor 11:8	*243*
ye were inferior to o churches	2Cor 12:13	*3062*
have sinned, and to all o, that,	2Cor 13:2	*3062*
preach any o gospel unto you than	Gal 1:8	
If any man preach any o gospel	Gal 1:9	
But o of the apostles saw I none,	Gal 1:19	*2087*
the o Jews dissembled likewise	Gal 2:13	*3062*
a bondmaid, the o by a freewoman	Gal 4:22	*1520*
are contrary the one to the o	Gal 5:17	*240*
Which in o ages was not made	Eph 3:5	*2087*
walk not as o Gentiles walk	Eph 4:17	*3062*
the palace, and in all o places	Phil 1:13	*3062*
But the o of love, knowing that I	Phil 1:17	
esteem o better than themselves	Phil 2:3	*240*
If any o man thinketh that he	Phil 3:4	*243*
with o my fellowlabourers, whose	Phil 4:3	*3062*
you all toward each o aboundeth	2Th 1:3	*240*
that they teach no o doctrine	1Ti 1:3	*2085*
if there be any o thing that is	1Ti 1:10	*2087*
be partaker of o men's sins	1Ti 5:22	*245*
the earth, neither by any o oath	Jas 5:12	*243*
as a busybody in o men's matters	1Pet 4:15	*244*
as they do also the o scriptures	2Pet 3:16	*3062*
I will put upon you none o burden	Rev 2:24	*243*

o voices of the trumpet of the Rev 8:13 3062
one is, and the o is not yet come Rev 17:10 243

OTHERS
and out of the earth shall o grow Job 8:19 312
and let o bow down upon her Job 31:10 312
number, and set o in their stead Job 34:24 312
wicked men in the open sight of o Job 34:26
and leave their wealth to o Ps 49:10 312
thou give thine honour unto o Prov 5:9 312
thyself likewise hast cursed o Eccl 7:22 312
saith, Yet will I gather o to him Is 56:8
houses shall be turned unto o Jer 6:12 312
will I give their wives unto o Jer 8:10 312
to the o he said in mine hearing, Eze 9:5 428
they have made o to hope that Eze 13:6
o daubed it with untempered Eze 13:10
which was diverse from all the o Dan 7:19
up, even for o beside those Dan 11:4 312
only, what do ye more than o Mt 5:47
blind, dumb, maimed, and many o Mt 15:30 2087
and o, Jeremias, or one of the Mt 16:14 2087
saw o standing idle in the Mt 20:3 243
found o standing idle, and saith Mt 20:6 243
o cut down branches from the Mt 21:8 243
o smote him with the palms of Mt 26:67 3588
He saved o Mt 27:42 243
O said, That it is Elias Mk 6:15 243
o said, That it is a prophet, or Mk 6:15 243
and o, One of the prophets Mk 8:28 243
o cut down branches off the trees Mk 11:8 243
and him they killed, and many o Mk 12:5 243
and will give the vineyard unto o Mk 12:9 243
with the scribes, He saved o Mk 15:31 243
of o that sat down with them Lk 5:29 243
steward, and Susanna, and many o Lk 8:3 2087
but to o in parables Lk 8:10 3062
and of o, that one of the old Lk 9:8 243
o say, that one of the old Lk 9:19 243
And o, tempting him, sought of him Lk 11:16 2087
were righteous, and despised o Lk 18:9 3062
and shall give the vineyard to o Lk 20:16 243
And there were also two o, Lk 23:32 3062
derided him, saying, He saved o Lk 23:35 243
prepared, and certain o with them Lk 24:1
o said, Nay Jn 7:12 243
O said, This is the Christ Jn 7:41 243
o said, He is like him Jn 9:9 243
O said, How can a man that is a Jn 9:16 243
O said, These are not the words Jn 10:21 243
o said, An angel spake to him Jn 12:29 243
or did o tell it thee of me Jn 18:34 243
two o with him, on either side Jn 19:18 3062
O mocking said, These men are Acts 2:13 2087
of the Lord, with many o also Acts 15:35 2087
o said, We will hear thee again Acts 17:32 3588
named Damaris, and o with them Acts 17:34 2087
o also, which had diseases in the Acts 28:9 3062
If I be not an apostle unto o 1Cor 9:2 243
If o be partakers of this power 1Cor 9:12 243
means, when I have preached to o 1Cor 9:27 243
by my voice I might teach o also 1Cor 14:19 243
or need we, as some o, epistles 2Cor 3:1
occasion of the forwardness of o 2Cor 8:8 2087
the children of wrath, even as o Eph 2:3 3062
every man also on the things of o Phil 2:4 2087
neither of you, nor yet of o 1Th 2:6 243
even as o which have no hope 1Th 4:13 3062
let us not sleep, as do o 1Th 5:6 3062
before all, that o also may fear 1Ti 5:20 3062
who shall be able to teach o also 2Ti 2:2 2087
place every year with blood of o Heb 9:25 245
o were tortured, not accepting Heb 11:35 243
o had trial of cruel mockings and Heb 11:36 2087
o save with fear, pulling them Jude 23 3739

OTHERWISE
O I should have wrought falsehood 2Sa 18:13 176
O it shall come to pass, when my 1Kin 1:21
passover o than it was written 2Chr 30:18 3808
lest o they should rejoice over Ps 38:16
o ye have no reward of your Mt 6:1 1490
if o, then both the new maketh a Lk 5:36 1490
o grace is no more grace Rom 11:6 1893
o work is no more work Rom 11:6 1893
o thou also shalt be cut off Rom 11:22 1893
if o, yet as a fool receive me, 2Cor 11:16 1490
that ye will be none o minded Gal 5:10 243
and if in any thing ye be o minded Phil 3:15 2088
and they that are o cannot be hid 1Ti 5:25 247
If any man teach o, and consent 1Ti 6:3 2085
o it is of no strength at all Heb 9:17 1893

OTHNI (*oth'-ni*) *A son of Shemiah.*
O, and Rephael, and Obed, Elzabad, 1Chr 26:7 6273

OTHNIEL (*oth'-ne-el*)
1. A brother of Caleb.
O the son of Kenaz, the brother Josh 15:17 6274
O the son of Kenaz, Caleb's Judg 1:13 6274
even O the son of Kenaz, Caleb's Judg 3:9 6274
And O the son of Kenaz died Judg 3:11 6274
O, and Seraiah 1Chr 4:13 6274
and the sons of O 1Chr 4:13 6274
2. Tribe or family of Othniel 1.
was Heldai the Netophathite, of O 1Chr 27:15 6274

OUCHES
make them to be set in o of gold Ex 28:11 4865
And thou shalt make o of gold Ex 28:13 4865
the wreathen chains to the o Ex 28:14 4865
thou shalt fasten in the two o Ex 28:25 4865
onyx stones inclosed in o of gold Ex 39:6 4865
they were inclosed in o of gold Ex 39:13 4865
And they made two o of gold Ex 39:16 4865
chains they fastened in the two o Ex 39:18 4865

OUGHT
unto me that o not to be done Gen 20:9 3972
which thing o not to be done Gen 34:7
and he knew not o he had, save the Gen 39:6 3972
there is not o left in the sight Gen 47:18
ye shall not diminish o thereof Ex 5:8
yet not o of your work shall be Ex 5:11 1697
Ye shall not minish o from your Ex 5:19
thou shalt not carry forth o of Ex 12:46
And if a man borrow o of his Ex 22:14
And if o of the flesh of the Ex 29:34
things which o not to be done Lev 4:2
things which o not to be done Lev 4:27
whosoever beareth o of the Lev 11:25
if o remain until the third day, Lev 19:6
if thou sell o unto thy neighbour Lev 25:14 4465
or buyest o of thy neighbour's Lev 25:14
if o be committed by ignorance Num 15:24
soul that doeth o presumptuously Num 15:30
or uttered o out of her lips, Num 30:6
shall ye diminish o from it Deut 4:2
o unto his neighbour shall Deut 15:2
neither have I taken away o Deut 26:14
nor given o thereof for the dead Deut 26:14
There failed not o of any good Josh 21:45 1697
if o but death part thee and me Ruth 1:17
thou taken o of any man's hand 1Sa 12:4 3972
ye have not found o in my hand 1Sa 12:5 3972
was there o missing unto them 1Sa 25:7 3972
we will not give them o of the 1Sa 30:22
or o else, till the sun be down 2Sa 3:35 3972
for no such thing o to be done in 2Sa 13:12
said, Whosoever saith o unto thee 2Sa 14:10
from o that my lord the king hath 2Sa 14:19
to know what Israel o to do 1Chr 12:32
None o to carry the ark of God 1Chr 15:2
O ye not to know that the LORD 2Chr 13:5
o ye not to walk in the fear of Neh 5:9
unto him that o to be feared Ps 76:11
thy brother hath o against thee Mt 5:23 5100
And if any man say o unto you Mt 21:3 5100
these o ye to have done, and not Mt 23:23 1163
ye suffer him no more to do o for Mk 7:12 3762
him, he asked him if he saw o Mk 8:23 5100
forgive, if ye have o against any Mk 11:25 5100
prophet, standing where it o not Mk 13:14 1163
these o ye to have done, and not Lk 11:42 1163
in the same hour what ye o to say Lk 12:12 1163
six days in which men o to work Lk 13:14 1163
o not this woman, being a Lk 13:16 1163
that men o always to pray, and not Lk 18:1 1163
O not Christ to have suffered Lk 24:26 1163
the place where men o to worship Jn 4:20 1163
Hath any man brought him o to eat Jn 4:33
ye also o to wash one another's Jn 13:14 3784
a law, and by our law he o to die Jn 19:7 3784
that o of the things which he Acts 4:32 5100
We o to obey God rather than men Acts 5:29 1163
we o not to think that the Acts 17:29 3784
ye o to be quiet, and to do Acts 19:36 1163
ye o to support the weak, and to Acts 20:35 1163
saying that they o not to Acts 21:21
Who o to have been here before Acts 24:19 1163
object, if they had o against me Acts 24:19 5100
seat, where I o to be judged Acts 25:10 1163
crying that he o not to live any Acts 25:24 1163
that I o to do many things Acts 26:9 1163
not that I had o to accuse my Acts 28:19 5100
what we should pray for as we o Rom 8:26 1163
more highly than he o to think Rom 12:3 1163
We then that are strong o to bear Rom 15:1 3784
nothing yet as he o to know 1Cor 8:2 1163
For a man indeed o not to cover 1Cor 11:7 3784
For this cause o the woman to 1Cor 11:10 3784
from them of whom I o to rejoice 2Cor 2:3 1163
ye o rather to forgive him 2Cor 2:7
for I o to have been commended of 2Cor 12:11 3784
for the children o not to lay up 2Cor 12:14 3784
So o men to love their wives as Eph 5:28 3784
may speak boldly, as I o to speak Eph 6:20 1163
make it manifest, as I o to speak Col 4:4 1163
know how ye o to answer every man Col 4:6 1163
received of us how ye o to walk 1Th 4:1 1163
know how ye o to follow us 2Th 3:7 1163
speaking things which they o not 1Ti 5:13 1163
teaching things which they o not Titus 1:11 1163
wronged thee, or oweth thee o Philem 18 5100
Therefore we o to give the more Heb 2:1 1163
And by reason hereof he o, as for Heb 5:3 3784
for the time ye o to be teachers Heb 5:12 3784
these things o not so to be Jas 3:10 5534
For that ye o to say, If the Lord Jas 4:15
of persons o ye to be in all holy 2Pet 3:11 1163
in him o himself also so to walk 1Jn 2:6 3784
we o to lay down our lives for 1Jn 3:16 3784
we o also to love one another 1Jn 4:11 3784
We therefore o to receive such, 3Jn 8 3784

OUGHTEST
what thou o to do unto him 1Kin 2:9
Thou o therefore to have put my Mt 25:27 1163
shall tell thee what thou o to do Acts 10:6 1163
o to behave thyself in the house 1Ti 3:15 1163

OUR See PREFACE.

OURS
herdmen, saying, The water is o Gen 26:20
taken from our father, that is o Gen 31:16
and every beast of theirs be o Gen 34:23
on this side Jordan may be o Num 32:32
ye that Ramoth in Gilead is o 1Kin 22:3
high places are o in possession Eze 36:2
and the inheritance shall be o Mk 12:7 2257
that the inheritance may be o Lk 20:14 2257
Christ our Lord, both theirs and o 1Cor 1:2 2257
even as ye also are o in the day 2Cor 1:14 2257
let o also learn to maintain good Titus 3:14 2251
and not for o only, but also for 1Jn 2:2 2251

OURSELVES
bow down o to thee to the earth Gen 37:10
or how shall we clear o Gen 44:16
But we o will go ready armed Num 32:17 587
cattle we took for a prey unto o Deut 2:35
cities, we took for a prey to o Deut 3:7
and we will discover o unto them 1Sa 14:8
let us behave o valiantly for our 1Chr 19:13
but we o together will build unto Ezr 4:3 587
we might afflict o before our God Ezr 8:21
to charge o yearly with the third Neh 10:32
let us know among o what is good Job 34:4
Let us take to o the houses of Ps 83:12
he that hath made us, and not we o Ps 100:3 587
let us solace o with loves Prov 7:18
and under falsehood have we hid o Is 28:15
we will fill o with strong drink Is 56:12
let us join o to the LORD in a Jer 50:5
for we o have heard of his own Lk 22:71
for we have heard him o, and know Jn 4:42
But we will give o continually to Acts 6:4
We have bound o under a great Acts 23:14 1438
but o also, which have the Rom 8:23
even we o groan within Rom 8:23
groan within o, waiting for Rom 8:23 1438
of the weak, and not to please o Rom 15:1 1438
For if we would judge o, we 1Cor 11:31 1438
we o are comforted of God 2Cor 1:4
we had the sentence of death in o 2Cor 1:9 1438
that we should not trust in o 2Cor 1:9 1438
Do we begin again to commend o 2Cor 3:1 1438
of o to think any thing as of 2Cor 3:5 1438
to think any thing as of o 2Cor 3:5 1438
of the truth commending o to 2Cor 4:2 1438
For we preach not o, but Christ 2Cor 4:5 1438
o your servants for Jesus' sake 2Cor 4:5 1438
we commend not o again unto you 2Cor 5:12 1438
For whether we be beside o 2Cor 5:13
o as the ministers of God 2Cor 6:4 1438
let us cleanse o from all 2Cor 7:1 1438
we dare not make o of the number 2Cor 10:12 1438
or compare o with some that 2Cor 10:12 1438
stretch not o beyond our measure 2Cor 10:14 1438
ye that we excuse o unto you 2Cor 12:19
we o also are found sinners, is Gal 2:17
behaved o among you that believe 1Th 2:10
So that we o glory in you in the 2Th 1:4 846
for we behaved not o disorderly 2Th 3:7
but to make o an ensample unto 2Th 3:9 1438
For we o also were sometimes Titus 3:3 2249
the assembling of o together Heb 10:25 1438
that we have no sin, we deceive o 1Jn 1:8 1438

OUT See PREFACE.

OUTCAST
because they called thee an O Jer 30:17 5080

OUTCASTS
together the o of Israel Ps 147:2 1760
and shall assemble the o of Israel Is 11:12 1760
hide the o Is 16:3 5080
Let mine o dwell with thee, Moab Is 16:4 5080
the o in the land of Egypt, and Is 27:13 5080
gathereth the o of Israel saith Is 56:8 1760
the o of Elam shall not come Jer 49:36 5080

OUTER
was heard even to the o court Eze 10:5 2435
shall be cast out into o darkness Mt 8:12 1857
away, and cast him into o darkness Mt 22:13 1857
servant into o darkness Mt 25:30 1857

OUTGOINGS
the o of it were at the sea Josh 17:9 8444
the o of it shall be thine Josh 17:18 8444
the o of the border were at the Josh 18:19 8444
the o thereof are in the valley Josh 19:14 8444
the o of their border were at Josh 19:22 8444
the o thereof are at the sea from Josh 19:29 8444
the o thereof were at Jordan Josh 19:33 8444
thou makest the o of the morning Ps 65:8 4161

OUTLANDISH
even him did o women cause to sin Neh 13:26 5237

OUTLIVED
days of the elders that o Joshua Judg 2:7

OUTMOST
curtain that is o in the coupling Ex 26:10 7020
o coast of the salt sea eastward Num 34:3 7097
out unto the o parts of heaven Deut 30:4 7097
four or five in the o fruitful Is 17:6

OUTRAGEOUS
Wrath is cruel, and anger is o Prov 27:4 7858

OUTRUN
and the other disciple did o Peter Jn 20:4

OUTSIDE
Phurah his servant unto the o of Judg 7:11 7097
when I come to the o of the camp Judg 7:17 7097
came unto the o of the camp in Judg 7:19 7097
so on the o toward the great 1Kin 7:9 2351
behold a wall on the o of the Eze 40:5 2351
ye make clean the o of the cup Mt 23:25 1855
that the o of them may be clean Mt 23:26 1623
make clean the o of the cup Lk 11:39 1855

OUTSTRETCHED
a mighty hand, and with an o arm Deut 26:8 5186
fight against you with an o hand Jer 21:5 5186
by my great power and by my o arm Jer 27:5 5186

O

OUTWARD
o a thousand cubits round about ... Num 35:4 2435
man looketh on the o appearance ... 1Sa 16:7 5869
for the o business over Israel ... 1Chr 26:29 2435
had the oversight of the o ... Neh 11:16 2435
the o court of the king's house ... Est 6:4 2435
brought he me into the o court ... Eze 40:17 2435
the gate of the o court that ... Eze 40:20 2435
thereof were toward the o court ... Eze 40:34 2435
o sanctuary which looketh toward ... Eze 44:1 2435
which indeed appear beautiful o ... Mt 23:27 *1855*
which is o in the flesh ... Rom 2:28
but though our o man perish ... 2Cor 4:16 *1854*
on things after the o appearance ... 2Cor 10:7 *4383*
adorning let it not be that o ... 1Pet 3:3 *1855*

OUTWARDLY
Even so ye also o appear ... Mt 23:28 *1855*
he is not a Jew, which is one o ... Rom 2:28

OUTWENT
o them, and came together unto him ... Mk 6:33 *4281*

OVEN
of a meat offering baken in the o ... Lev 2:4 8574
offering that is baken in the o ... Lev 7:9 8574
whether it be o, or ranges for ... Lev 11:35 8574
shall bake your bread in one o ... Lev 26:26 8574
o in the time of thine anger ... Ps 21:9 8574
Our skin was black like an o ... Lam 5:10 8574
as an o heated by the baker, who ... Hos 7:4 8574
made ready their heart like an o ... Hos 7:6 8574
They are all hot as an o, and have ... Hos 7:7 8574
cometh, that shall burn as an o ... Mal 4:1 8574
and to morrow is cast into the o ... Mt 6:30 *2823*
and to morrow is cast into the o ... Lk 12:28 *2823*

OVENS
upon thy people, and into thine o ... Ex 8:3 8574

OVER
And to rule o the day and o the ... Gen 1:18
o the night, and to divide the ... Gen 1:18
dominion o the fish of the sea ... Gen 1:26
o the fowl of the air, and o ... Gen 1:26
o the cattle, and o all the ... Gen 1:26
o all the earth, and o every ... Gen 1:26
o every creeping thing that ... Gen 1:26
have dominion o the fish of the ... Gen 1:28
o the fowl of the air, and o ... Gen 1:28
o every living thing that moveth ... Gen 1:28
husband, and he shall rule o thee ... Gen 3:16
desire, and thou shalt rule o him ... Gen 4:7
made a wind to pass o the earth ... Gen 8:1 5921
when I bring a cloud o the earth ... Gen 9:14 5921
sat her down o against him a good ... Gen 21:16 5048
she sat o against him, and lift up ... Gen 21:16 5048
that ruled o all that he had, Put ... Gen 24:2
all o like an hairy garment ... Gen 25:25
be lord o thy brethren, and let ... Gen 27:29
passed o the river, and set his ... Gen 31:21 5674
will not pass o this heap to thee ... Gen 31:52 5674
thou shalt not pass o this heap ... Gen 31:52 5674
my staff I passed o this Jordan ... Gen 32:10 5674
Pass o before me, and put a space ... Gen 32:16 5674
So went the present o before him ... Gen 32:21 5674
sons, and passed o the ford Jabbok ... Gen 32:22 5674
them, and sent them o the brook ... Gen 32:23 5674
the brook, and sent o that he had ... Gen 32:23 5674
as he passed o Penuel the sun ... Gen 32:31 5674
he passed o before them, and bowed ... Gen 33:3 5674
pass o before his servant ... Gen 33:14 5674
any king o the children of Israel ... Gen 36:31
him, Shalt thou indeed reign o us ... Gen 37:8 5921
thou indeed have dominion o us ... Gen 37:8
he made him overseer o his house ... Gen 39:4 5921
o all that he had, that the LORD ... Gen 39:5 5921
set him o the land of Egypt ... Gen 41:33 5921
him appoint officers o the land ... Gen 41:34 5921
Thou shalt be o my house, and ... Gen 41:40 5921
I have set thee o all the land of ... Gen 41:41 5921
he made him ruler o all the land ... Gen 41:43 5921
Joseph went out o all the land of ... Gen 41:45 5921
the famine was o all the face of ... Gen 41:56 5921
was the governor o the land ... Gen 42:6 5921
he is governor o all the land of ... Gen 45:26 5921
then make them rulers o my cattle ... Gen 47:6 5921
the famine prevailed o them ... Gen 47:20 5921
Joseph made it a law o the land ... Gen 47:26 5921
whose branches run o the wall ... Gen 49:22 5921
there arose up a new king o Egypt ... Ex 1:8 5921
Therefore they did set o them ... Ex 1:11 5921
thee a prince and a judge o us ... Ex 2:14 5921
taskmasters had set o them ... Ex 5:14 5921
hand with thy rod o the streams ... Ex 8:5 5921
o the rivers, and o the ponds, ... Ex 8:5 5921
his hand o the waters of Egypt ... Ex 8:6 5921
said unto Pharaoh, Glory o me ... Ex 8:9 5921
Stretch out thine hand o the land ... Ex 10:12 5921
forth his rod o the land of Egypt ... Ex 10:13 5921
the locusts went up o all the ... Ex 10:14 5921
be darkness o the land of Egypt ... Ex 10:21 5921
see the blood, I will pass o you ... Ex 12:13 5921
the LORD will pass o the door ... Ex 12:23 5921
who passed o the houses of the ... Ex 12:27 5921
and the sea, o against Baal-zephon ... Ex 14:2 6440
captains o every one of them ... Ex 14:7 5921
stretch out thine hand o the sea ... Ex 14:16 5921
stretched out his hand o the sea ... Ex 14:21 5921
Stretch out thine hand o the sea ... Ex 14:26 5921
forth his hand o the sea, and the ... Ex 14:27 5921
till thy people pass o, O LORD, ... Ex 15:16 5764
O LORD, till the people pass o ... Ex 15:16 5764
that gathered much had nothing o ... Ex 16:18 5736
that which remaineth o lay up for ... Ex 16:23 5736
and place such o them, to be ... Ex 18:21 5921
and made them heads o the people ... Ex 18:25 5921
O against the border shall the ... Ex 25:27 5980
they may give light o against it ... Ex 25:37
shall hang o the backside of the ... Ex 26:12 5921
it shall hang o the sides of the ... Ex 26:13 5921
the candlestick o against the ... Ex 26:35 5227
o against the other coupling ... Ex 28:27 5980
seat that is o the testimony ... Ex 30:6 5921
for the tent o the tabernacle ... Ex 36:14 5921
with their wings o the mercy seat ... Ex 37:9 5980
O against the border were the ... Ex 37:14 5980
o against the other coupling ... Ex 39:20 5980
abroad the tent o the tabernacle ... Ex 40:19 5921
o against the table, on the side ... Ex 40:24 5227
taken up from o the tabernacle ... Ex 40:36 5921
an earthen vessel o running water ... Lev 14:5 5921
was killed o the running water ... Lev 14:6 5921
an earthen vessel o running water ... Lev 14:50 5921
confess o him all the iniquities ... Lev 16:21 5921
shalt not rule o him with rigour ... Lev 25:43
but o your brethren the children ... Lev 25:46
rule one o another with rigour ... Lev 25:46
with rigour o him in thy sight ... Lev 25:53
I will even appoint o you terror ... Lev 26:16
that hate you shall reign o you ... Lev 26:17
o the tabernacle of testimony ... Num 1:50 5921
o all the vessels thereof, and ... Num 1:50 5921
o all things that belong to it ... Num 1:50 5921
chief o the chief of the Levites ... Num 3:32
money of them that were o ... Num 3:49 5736
shall spread o it a cloth wholly ... Num 4:6 4605
him, and he be jealous o his wife ... Num 5:30
were o them that were numbered, ... Num 7:2 5975
light o against the candlestick ... Num 8:2
thereof o against the candlestick ... Num 8:3
trumpets o your burnt offerings ... Num 10:10 5921
o the sacrifices of your peace ... Num 10:10
o his host was Nahshon the son of ... Num 10:14 5921
o the host of the tribe of the ... Num 10:15 5921
o the host of the tribe of the ... Num 10:16 5921
o his host was Elizur the son of ... Num 10:18 5921
o the host of the tribe of the ... Num 10:19 5921
o the host of the tribe of the ... Num 10:20 5921
o his host was Elishama the son ... Num 10:22 5921
o the host of the tribe of the ... Num 10:23 5921
o the host of the tribe of the ... Num 10:24 5921
o his host was Ahiezer the son of ... Num 10:25 5921
o the host of the tribe of the ... Num 10:26 5921
o the host of the tribe of the ... Num 10:27 5921
of the people, and officers o them ... Num 11:16
and that thy cloud standeth o them ... Num 14:14 5921
thyself altogether a prince o us ... Num 16:13 5921
earth, and they abide o against me ... Num 22:5
he was head o a people, and of a ... Num 25:15
set a man o the congregation, ... Num 27:16 5921
with the captains o thousands ... Num 31:14
thousands, and captains o hundreds ... Num 31:14
were o thousands of the host ... Num 31:48
and bring us not o Jordan ... Num 32:5 5674
o into the land which the LORD ... Num 32:7 5674
armed o Jordan before the LORD ... Num 32:21 5674
But thy servants will pass o ... Num 32:27 5674
will pass with you o Jordan ... Num 32:29 5674
will not pass o with you armed ... Num 32:30 5674
We will pass o armed before the ... Num 32:32 5674
When ye are passed o Jordan into ... Num 33:51 5674
When ye be come o Jordan into the ... Num 35:10 5674
in the plain o against the Red ... Deut 1:1 4136
and I will make them rulers o you ... Deut 1:13
known, and made them heads o you ... Deut 1:15 5921
captains o thousands, and captains ... Deut 1:15
thousands, and captains o hundreds ... Deut 1:15
hundreds, and captains o fifties ... Deut 1:15
o fifties, and captains o tens ... Deut 1:15
get you o the brook Zered ... Deut 2:13 5674
we went o the brook Zered ... Deut 2:13 5674
we were come o the brook Zered ... Deut 2:14 5674
Thou art to pass o through Ar ... Deut 2:18 5674
when thou comest nigh o against ... Deut 2:19 4136
and pass o the river Arnon ... Deut 2:24 5674
until I shall pass o Jordan into ... Deut 2:29 5674
ye shall pass o armed before your ... Deut 3:18 5674
I pray thee, let me go o, and see ... Deut 3:25 5674
thou shalt not go o this Jordan ... Deut 3:27 5674
for he shall go o before this ... Deut 3:28 5674
in the valley o against Beth-peor ... Deut 3:29 4136
whither ye go o to possess it ... Deut 4:14 5674
that I should not go o Jordan ... Deut 4:21 5674
this land, I must not go o Jordan ... Deut 4:22 5674
but ye shall go o, and possess ... Deut 4:22 5674
ye go o Jordan to possess it ... Deut 4:26 5674
in the valley o against Beth-peor ... Deut 4:46 4136
art to pass o Jordan this day ... Deut 9:1 5674
is he which goeth o before thee ... Deut 9:3 5674
in the champaign o against Gilgal ... Deut 11:30 4136
For ye shall pass o Jordan to go ... Deut 11:31 5674
But when ye go o Jordan, and dwell ... Deut 12:10 5674
thou shalt reign o many nations ... Deut 15:6
but they shall not reign o thee ... Deut 15:6
shalt say, I will set a king o me ... Deut 17:14 5921
in any wise set him king o thee ... Deut 17:15 5921
shalt thou set king o thee ... Deut 17:15 5921
mayest not set a stranger o thee ... Deut 17:15 5921
shall wash their hands o the ... Deut 21:6 5921
shalt not go o the boughs again ... Deut 24:20
on the day when ye shall pass o ... Deut 27:2 5674
this law, when thou art passed o ... Deut 27:3 5674
shall be when ye be gone o Jordan ... Deut 27:4 5674
people, when ye are come o Jordan ... Deut 27:12 5674
thy heaven that is o thy head ... Deut 28:23 5921
king which thou shalt set o thee ... Deut 28:36 5921
rejoiced o you to do you good ... Deut 28:63 5921
will rejoice o you to destroy you ... Deut 28:63 5921
again rejoice o thee for good ... Deut 30:9 5921
as he rejoiced o thy fathers ... Deut 30:9 5921
Who shall go o the sea for us, and ... Deut 30:13 5674
whither thou passest o Jordan to ... Deut 30:18 5674
Thou shalt not go o this Jordan ... Deut 31:2 5674
he will go o before thee, and he ... Deut 31:3 5674
Joshua, he shall go o before thee ... Deut 31:3 5674
ye go o Jordan to possess it ... Deut 31:13 5674
o the door of the tabernacle ... Deut 31:15 5921
her nest, fluttereth o her young ... Deut 32:11 5921
whither ye go o Jordan to possess ... Deut 32:47 5674
that is o against Jericho ... Deut 32:49
that is o against Jericho ... Deut 34:1
but thou shalt not go o thither ... Deut 34:4 5674
land of Moab, o against Beth-peor ... Deut 34:6 4136
go o this Jordan, thou, and all ... Josh 1:2 5674
days ye shall pass o this Jordan ... Josh 1:11 5674
from the mountain, and passed o ... Josh 2:23 5674
lodged there before they passed o ... Josh 3:1 5674
and pass o before the people ... Josh 3:6 5674
passeth o before you into Jordan ... Josh 3:11 5674
their tents, to pass o Jordan ... Josh 3:14 5674
the people passed o right against ... Josh 3:16 5674
Israelites passed o on dry ground ... Josh 3:17 5674
people were passed clean o Jordan ... Josh 3:17 5674
people were clean passed o Jordan ... Josh 4:1 5674
and ye shall carry them o with you ... Josh 4:3 5674
Pass o before the ark of the LORD ... Josh 4:5 5674
when it passed o Jordan, the ... Josh 4:7 5674
carried them o with them unto the ... Josh 4:8 5674
and the people hasted and passed o ... Josh 4:10 5674
the people were clean passed o ... Josh 4:11 5674
that the ark of the LORD passed o ... Josh 4:11 5674
passed o armed before the ... Josh 4:12 5674
prepared for war passed o before ... Josh 4:13 5674
flowed o all his banks, as they ... Josh 4:18 5921
Israel came o this Jordan on dry ... Josh 4:22 5674
you, until ye were passed o ... Josh 4:23 5674
before us, until we were gone o ... Josh 4:23 5674
of Israel, until we were passed o ... Josh 5:1 5674
there stood a man o against him ... Josh 5:13 5048
all brought this people o Jordan ... Josh 7:7 5674
they raised o him a great heap of ... Josh 7:26 5921
o which no man hath lift up any ... Josh 8:31 5921
half of them o against mount ... Josh 8:33 413
half of them o against mount Ebal ... Josh 8:33
the great sea o against Lebanon ... Josh 9:1
the border went o from thence ... Josh 18:13 5674
which is o against the going up ... Josh 18:17 5227
side o against Arabah northward ... Josh 18:18 4136
o against the land of Canaan ... Josh 22:11
then pass ye o unto the land of ... Josh 22:19 5674
And ye went o Jordan, and came unto ... Josh 24:11 5674
and suffered not a man to pass o ... Judg 3:28 5674
o the nobles among the people ... Judg 5:13
me have dominion o the mighty ... Judg 5:13
were gathered together, and went o ... Judg 6:33 5674
came to Jordan, and passed o ... Judg 8:4 5674
said unto Gideon, Rule thou o us ... Judg 8:22
unto them, I will not rule o you ... Judg 8:23
neither shall my son rule o you ... Judg 8:23
the LORD shall rule o you ... Judg 8:23
and ten persons, reign o you ... Judg 9:2
o you, or that one reign o you ... Judg 9:2
on a time to anoint a king o them ... Judg 9:8 5921
the olive tree, Reign thou o us ... Judg 9:8 5921
and go to be promoted o the trees ... Judg 9:9 5921
tree, Come thou, and reign o us ... Judg 9:10 5921
and go to be promoted o the trees ... Judg 9:11 5921
vine, Come thou, and reign o us ... Judg 9:12 5921
and go to be promoted o the trees ... Judg 9:13 5921
bramble, Come thou, and reign o us ... Judg 9:14 5921
in truth ye anoint me king o you ... Judg 9:15 5921
king o the men of Shechem, ... Judg 9:18 5921
had reigned three years o Israel ... Judg 9:22 5921
brethren, and went o to Shechem ... Judg 9:26 5674
o Jordan to fight also against ... Judg 10:9 5674
he shall be head o all the ... Judg 10:18
be our head o all the inhabitants ... Judg 11:8
made him head and captain o them ... Judg 11:11 5921
Jephthah, and he passed o Gilead ... Judg 11:29 5674
passed o Mizpeh of Gilead, and ... Judg 11:29 5674
o unto the children of Ammon ... Judg 11:29 5674
So Jephthah passed o unto the ... Judg 11:32 5674
Wherefore passedst thou o to ... Judg 12:1 5674
passed o against the children of ... Judg 12:3 5674
were escaped said, Let me go o ... Judg 12:5 5674
Philistines had dominion o Israel ... Judg 14:4
the Philistines are rulers o us ... Judg 15:11
came o against Jebus, which is ... Judg 19:10 5227
we will pass o to Gibeah ... Judg 19:12 5674
ease o against Gibeah toward the ... Judg 20:43 5227
that was set o the reapers ... Ruth 2:5 5921
was set o the reapers answered ... Ruth 2:6 5921
thy skirt o thine handmaid ... Ruth 3:9 5921
mouth is enlarged o mine enemies ... 1Sa 2:1 5921
he made his sons judges o Israel ... 1Sa 8:1
that I should not reign o them ... 1Sa 8:7 5921
the king that shall reign o them ... 1Sa 8:9 5921
the king that shall reign o you ... 1Sa 8:11
appoint him captains o thousands ... 1Sa 8:12
and captains o fifties ... 1Sa 8:12
but we will have a king o us ... 1Sa 8:19 5921
to be captain o my people Israel ... 1Sa 9:16 5921
this same shall reign o my people ... 1Sa 9:17
to be captain o his inheritance ... 1Sa 10:1 5921
him, Nay, but set a king o us ... 1Sa 10:19 5921
that said, Shall Saul reign o us ... 1Sa 11:12 5921
me, and have made a king o you ... 1Sa 12:1 5921
but a king shall reign o us ... 1Sa 12:12 5921
the LORD hath set a king o you ... 1Sa 12:13 5921
also the king that reigneth o you ... 1Sa 12:14 5921
he had reigned two years o Israel ... 1Sa 13:1 5921
some of the Hebrews went o Jordan ... 1Sa 13:7 5674
him to be captain o his people ... 1Sa 13:14 5921

let us go *o* to the Philistines'	1Sa 14:1	5674
o unto the Philistines' garrison	1Sa 14:4	5674
northward *o* against Michmash	1Sa 14:5	4136
other southward *o* against Gibeah	1Sa 14:5	4136
let us go *o* unto the garrison of	1Sa 14:6	5674
we will pass *o* unto these men, and	1Sa 14:8	5674
battle passed *o* unto Beth-aven	1Sa 14:23	5674
So Saul took the kingdom *o* Israel	1Sa 14:47	5921
thee to be king *o* his people	1Sa 15:1	5921
his people, *o* Israel	1Sa 15:1	
to Shur, that is *o* against Egypt	1Sa 15:7	
LORD anointed thee king *o* Israel	1Sa 15:17	5921
thee from being king *o* Israel	1Sa 15:26	5921
he had made Saul king *o* Israel	1Sa 15:35	5921
him from reigning *o* Israel	1Sa 16:1	5921
So David prevailed *o* the	1Sa 17:50	4480
Saul set him *o* the men of war, and	1Sa 18:5	5921
made him his captain *o* a thousand	1Sa 18:13	
standing as appointed *o* them	1Sa 19:20	5921
and he became a captain *o* them	1Sa 22:2	5921
which was set *o* the servants of	1Sa 22:9	5921
and thou shalt be king *o* Israel	1Sa 23:17	5921
appointed thee ruler *o* Israel	1Sa 25:30	
Then David went *o* to the other	1Sa 26:13	5674
let one of the young men come *o*	1Sa 26:22	5674
he passed *o* with the six hundred	1Sa 27:2	5674
could not go *o* the brook Besor	1Sa 30:10	5674
o Saul and *o* Jonathan his son	2Sa 1:17	5921
daughters of Israel, weep *o* Saul	2Sa 1:24	413
David king *o* the house of Judah	2Sa 2:4	5921
have anointed me king *o* them	2Sa 2:7	5921
and brought him *o* to Mahanaim	2Sa 2:8	5674
And made him king *o* Gilead	2Sa 2:9	413
o the Ashurites, and *o* Jezreel,	2Sa 2:9	1591
o Ephraim, and *o* Benjamin, and	2Sa 2:9	5921
and *o* all Israel	2Sa 2:9	5921
when he began to reign *o* Israel	2Sa 2:10	5921
o the house of Judah was seven	2Sa 2:11	5921
went *o* by number twelve of	2Sa 2:15	5674
the plain, and passed *o* Jordan	2Sa 2:29	5674
up the throne of David *o* Israel	2Sa 3:10	5921
o Judah, from Dan even to	2Sa 3:10	5921
in times past to be king *o* you	2Sa 3:17	5921
that thou mayest reign *o* all that	2Sa 3:21	
And the king lamented *o* Abner	2Sa 3:33	413
all the people wept again *o* him	2Sa 3:34	5921
hanged them up *o* the pool in	2Sa 4:12	5921
past, when Saul was king *o* us	2Sa 5:2	5921
thou shalt be a captain *o* Israel	2Sa 5:2	5921
they anointed David king *o* Israel	2Sa 5:3	5921
he reigned *o* Judah seven years	2Sa 5:5	5921
and three years *o* all Israel	2Sa 5:5	5921
had established him king *o* Israel	2Sa 5:12	5921
had anointed David king *o* Israel	2Sa 5:17	5921
come upon them *o* against the	2Sa 5:23	4136
to appoint me ruler *o* the people	2Sa 6:21	5921
the people of the LORD, *o* Israel	2Sa 6:21	5921
be ruler *o* my people, *o* Israel	2Sa 7:8	5921
judges to be *o* my people Israel	2Sa 7:11	5921
LORD of hosts is the God *o* Israel	2Sa 7:26	5921
And David reigned *o* all Israel	2Sa 8:15	5921
the son of Zeruiah was *o* the host	2Sa 8:16	5921
was *o* both the Cherethites	2Sa 8:18	
together, and passed *o* Jordan	2Sa 10:17	5674
I anointed thee king *o* Israel	2Sa 12:7	5921
David said to Ittai, Go and pass *o*	2Sa 15:22	5674
And Ittai the Gittite passed *o*	2Sa 15:22	5674
voice, and all the people passed *o*	2Sa 15:23	5674
himself passed *o* the brook Kidron	2Sa 15:23	5674
and all the people passed *o*	2Sa 15:23	5674
let me go *o*, I pray thee, and take	2Sa 16:9	5674
on the hill's side *o* against him	2Sa 16:13	5980
wilderness, but speedily pass *o*	2Sa 17:16	5674
a covering *o* the well's mouth	2Sa 17:19	5921
They be gone *o* the brook of water	2Sa 17:20	5674
and pass quickly *o* the water	2Sa 17:21	5674
with him, and they passed *o* Jordan	2Sa 17:22	5674
them that was not gone *o* Jordan	2Sa 17:22	5674
And Absalom passed *o* Jordan	2Sa 17:24	5674
and captains of hundreds *o* them	2Sa 18:1	5921
o the face of all the country	2Sa 18:8	5921
the roof *o* the gate unto the wall	2Sa 18:24	413
went up to the chamber *o* the gate	2Sa 18:33	5921
And Absalom, whom we anointed *o* us	2Sa 19:10	5921
to conduct the king *o* Jordan	2Sa 19:15	5674
they went *o* Jordan before the	2Sa 19:17	6743
there went *o* a ferry boat to	2Sa 19:18	5674
to carry *o* the king's household	2Sa 19:18	5674
the king, as he was come *o* Jordan	2Sa 19:18	5674
that I am this day king *o* Israel	2Sa 19:22	5921
went *o* Jordan with the king, to	2Sa 19:31	5674
the king, to conduct him *o* Jordan	2Sa 19:31	5674
Barzillai, Come thou *o* with me	2Sa 19:33	5674
little way *o* Jordan with the king	2Sa 19:36	5674
let him go *o* with my lord the	2Sa 19:37	5674
Chimham shall go *o* with me	2Sa 19:38	
And all the people went *o* Jordan	2Sa 19:39	
And when the king was come *o*	2Sa 19:39	
David's men with him, *o* Jordan	2Sa 19:41	
be thrown to thee *o* the wall	2Sa 20:21	1157
Now Joab was *o* all the host of	2Sa 20:23	413
of Jehoiada was *o* the Cherethites	2Sa 20:23	5921
Cherethites and *o* the Pelethites	2Sa 20:23	5921
And Adoram was *o* the tribute	2Sa 20:24	5921
by my God have I leaped *o* a wall	2Sa 22:30	
He that ruleth *o* men must be just	2Sa 23:3	
And David set him *o* his guard	2Sa 23:23	413
And they passed *o* Jordan, and	2Sa 24:5	5674
anoint him there king *o* Israel	1Kin 1:34	5921
him to be ruler *o* Israel and *o*	1Kin 1:35	5921
be ruler *o* Israel and *o* Judah	1Kin 1:35	5921
reigned *o* Israel were forty years	1Kin 2:11	5921
Jehoiada in his room *o* the host	1Kin 2:35	5921
passest *o* the brook Kidron, thou	1Kin 2:37	5674
Solomon was king *o* all Israel	1Kin 4:1	5921
son of Jehoiada was *o* the host	1Kin 4:4	5921
son of Nathan was *o* the officers	1Kin 4:5	5921
Ahishar was *o* the household	1Kin 4:6	5921
the son of Abda was *o* the tribute	1Kin 4:6	5921
had twelve officers *o* all Israel	1Kin 4:7	5921
Solomon reigned *o* all kingdoms	1Kin 4:21	
For he had dominion *o* all the	1Kin 4:24	
o all the kings on this side the	1Kin 4:24	
a wise son *o* this great people	1Kin 5:7	5921
and Adoniram was *o* the levy	1Kin 5:14	5921
officers which were *o* the work	1Kin 5:16	5921
which ruled *o* the people that	1Kin 5:16	
year of Solomon's reign *o* Israel	1Kin 6:1	5921
o against the belly which was by	1Kin 7:20	5980
eastward *o* against the south	1Kin 7:39	4136
two wings *o* the place of the ark	1Kin 8:7	413
David to be *o* my people Israel	1Kin 8:16	5921
that were *o* Solomon's work	1Kin 9:23	5921
which bare rule *o* the people that	1Kin 9:23	
him, and became captain *o* a band	1Kin 11:24	
Israel, and reigned *o* Syria	1Kin 11:25	5921
he made him ruler *o* all the	1Kin 11:28	
and shalt be king *o* Israel	1Kin 11:37	5921
o all Israel was forty years	1Kin 11:42	5921
of Judah, Rehoboam reigned *o* them	1Kin 12:17	5921
Adoram, who was *o* the tribute	1Kin 12:18	5921
and made him king *o* all Israel	1Kin 12:20	5921
and they mourned *o* him, saying,	1Kin 13:30	5921
I should be king *o* this people	1Kin 14:2	5921
thee prince *o* my people Israel	1Kin 14:7	5921
raise him up a king *o* Israel	1Kin 14:14	5921
of Nebat reigned Abijam *o* Judah	1Kin 15:1	5921
of Israel reigned Asa *o* Judah	1Kin 15:9	5921
o Israel in the second year of	1Kin 15:25	5921
reigned *o* Israel two years	1Kin 15:25	5921
to reign *o* all Israel in Tirzah	1Kin 15:33	5921
thee prince *o* my people Israel	1Kin 16:2	5921
to reign *o* Israel in Tirzah	1Kin 16:8	5921
king *o* Israel that day in the	1Kin 16:16	5921
the king's house *o* him with fire	1Kin 16:18	5921
began Omri to reign *o* Israel	1Kin 16:23	5921
the son of Omri to reign *o* Israel	1Kin 16:29	5921
o Israel in Samaria twenty	1Kin 16:29	5921
anoint Hazael to be king *o* Syria	1Kin 19:15	5921
thou anoint to be king *o* Israel	1Kin 19:16	5921
they pitched one *o* against the	1Kin 20:29	5227
that had rule *o* his chariots	1Kin 22:31	
o Judah in the fourth year of	1Kin 22:41	5921
to reign *o* Israel in Samaria the	1Kin 22:51	5921
and reigned two years *o* Israel	1Kin 22:51	5921
they two went *o* on dry ground	2Kin 2:8	5674
to pass, when they were gone *o*	2Kin 2:9	5674
and Elisha went *o*	2Kin 2:14	5674
to reign *o* Israel in Samaria the	2Kin 3:1	5921
and strike his hand *o* the place	2Kin 5:11	413
that thou shalt be king *o* Syria	2Kin 8:13	5921
and made a king *o* themselves	2Kin 8:20	5921
So Joram went *o* to Zair, and all	2Kin 8:21	5674
have anointed thee king *o* Israel	2Kin 9:3	5921
king *o* the people of the LORD	2Kin 9:6	413
people of the LORD, even *o* Israel	2Kin 9:6	413
have anointed thee king *o* Israel	2Kin 9:12	413
began Ahaziah to reign *o* Judah	2Kin 9:29	5921
And he that was *o* the house	2Kin 10:5	5921
house, and he that was *o* the city	2Kin 10:5	5921
unto him that was *o* the vestry	2Kin 10:22	5921
the time that Jehu reigned *o*	2Kin 10:36	5921
And Athaliah did reign *o* the land	2Kin 11:3	5921
and fetched the rulers *o* hundreds	2Kin 11:4	
the captains *o* the hundreds did	2Kin 11:9	
to the captains *o* hundreds did	2Kin 11:10	
officers *o* the house of the LORD	2Kin 11:18	5921
And he took the rulers *o* hundreds	2Kin 11:19	
to reign *o* Israel in Samaria	2Kin 13:1	5921
to reign *o* Israel in Samaria	2Kin 13:10	5921
wept *o* his face, and said, O my	2Kin 13:14	5921
the king's son was *o* the house	2Kin 15:5	5921
the son of Jeroboam reign *o*	2Kin 15:8	5921
the son of Gadi to reign *o* Israel	2Kin 15:17	5921
to reign *o* Israel in Samaria	2Kin 15:23	5921
to reign *o* Israel in Samaria	2Kin 15:27	5921
in Samaria *o* Israel nine years	2Kin 17:1	5921
which was *o* the household, and	2Kin 18:18	5921
which was *o* the household, and	2Kin 18:37	5921
which was *o* the household, and	2Kin 19:2	5921
I will stretch *o* Jerusalem the	2Kin 21:13	5921
that was set *o* the men of war	2Kin 25:19	5921
even *o* them he made Gedaliah the	2Kin 25:22	5921
reigned *o* the children of Israel	1Chr 1:43	
of Gad dwelt *o* against them	1Chr 5:11	5048
set *o* the service of song in the	1Chr 6:31	5921
in Jerusalem, *o* against them	1Chr 8:32	5048
were *o* the work of the service,	1Chr 9:19	5921
being *o* the host of the LORD,	1Chr 9:19	5921
was the ruler *o* them in time past	1Chr 9:20	5921
were *o* the chambers and treasuries	1Chr 9:26	5921
had the set office *o* the things	1Chr 9:31	5921
were *o* the shewbread, to prepare	1Chr 9:32	5921
o against their brethren	1Chr 9:38	5048
shalt be ruler *o* my people Israel	1Chr 11:2	5921
they anointed David king *o* Israel	1Chr 11:3	5921
and David set him *o* his guard	1Chr 11:25	5921
among the thirty, and *o* the thirty	1Chr 12:4	5921
one of the least was *o* an hundred	1Chr 12:14	
and the greatest *o* a thousand	1Chr 12:14	
These are they that went *o* Jordan	1Chr 12:15	5674
to make David king *o* all Israel	1Chr 12:38	5921
had confirmed him king *o* Israel	1Chr 14:2	5921
was anointed king *o* all Israel	1Chr 14:8	5921
come upon them *o* against the	1Chr 14:14	4136
and the captains *o* thousands	1Chr 15:25	
be ruler *o* my people Israel	1Chr 17:7	5921
judges to be *o* my people Israel	1Chr 17:10	5921
So David reigned *o* all Israel	1Chr 18:14	5921
the son of Zeruiah was *o* the host	1Chr 18:15	5921
of Jehoiada was *o* the Cherethites	1Chr 18:17	5921
all Israel, and passed *o* Jordan	1Chr 19:17	5674
hand stretched out *o* Jerusalem	1Chr 21:16	5921
of his kingdom *o* Israel for ever	1Chr 22:10	5921
Solomon his son king *o* Israel	1Chr 23:1	5921
These likewise cast lots *o*	1Chr 24:31	5980
even the principal fathers *o*	1Chr 24:31	5980
Ahijah was *o* the treasures of the	1Chr 26:20	5921
o the treasures of the dedicated	1Chr 26:20	
which were *o* the treasures of the	1Chr 26:22	5921
his brethren were *o* all the	1Chr 26:26	5921
fathers, the captains *o* thousands	1Chr 26:26	
for the outward business *o* Israel	1Chr 26:29	5921
made rulers *o* the Reubenites	1Chr 26:32	5921
O the first course for the first	1Chr 27:2	5921
o the course of the second month	1Chr 27:4	5921
Furthermore *o* the tribes of	1Chr 27:16	5921
o the king's treasures was	1Chr 27:25	5921
o the storehouses in the fields,	1Chr 27:25	5921
o them that did the work of the	1Chr 27:26	5921
o the vineyards was Shimei the	1Chr 27:27	5921
o the increase of the vineyards	1Chr 27:27	5921
o the olive trees and the sycomore	1Chr 27:28	5921
o the cellars of oil was Joash	1Chr 27:28	5921
o the herds that fed in Sharon	1Chr 27:29	5921
o the herds that were in the	1Chr 27:29	5921
O the camels also was Obil the	1Chr 27:30	5921
o the asses was Jehdeiah the	1Chr 27:30	5921
o the flocks was Jaziz the	1Chr 27:31	5921
the captains *o* the thousands, and	1Chr 28:1	
captains *o* the hundreds	1Chr 28:1	
the stewards *o* all the substance	1Chr 28:1	
to be king *o* Israel for ever	1Chr 28:4	5921
me to make me king *o* all Israel	1Chr 28:4	5921
the kingdom of the LORD *o* Israel	1Chr 28:5	5921
given to the house of my God, *o*	1Chr 29:3	5921
of thee, and thou reignest *o* all	1Chr 29:12	4605
son of Jesse reigned *o* all Israel	1Chr 29:26	5921
reigned *o* Israel was forty years	1Chr 29:27	5921
and the times that went *o* him	1Chr 29:30	5674
o Israel, and *o* all the	1Chr 29:30	5921
for thou hast made me king *o* a	2Chr 1:9	5921
o whom I have made thee king	2Chr 1:11	5921
congregation, and reigned *o* Israel	2Chr 1:13	5921
he hath made thee king *o* them	2Chr 2:11	5921
the east end, *o* against the south	2Chr 4:10	4136
wings *o* the place of the ark	2Chr 5:8	5921
to be a ruler *o* my people Israel	2Chr 6:5	5921
David to be *o* my people Israel	2Chr 6:6	5921
deliver them *o* before their	2Chr 6:36	6440
that bare rule *o* the people	2Chr 8:10	
made he thee king *o* them, to do	2Chr 9:8	5921
he reigned *o* all the kings from	2Chr 9:26	
o all Israel forty years	2Chr 9:30	5921
of Judah, Rehoboam reigned *o* them	2Chr 10:17	5921
Hadoram that was *o* the tribute	2Chr 10:18	5921
began Abijah to reign *o* Judah	2Chr 13:1	5921
o Israel to David for ever	2Chr 13:5	5921
Amariah the chief priest is *o* you	2Chr 19:11	5921
rulest not thou *o* all the	2Chr 20:6	
them to rejoice *o* their enemies	2Chr 20:27	
And Jehoshaphat reigned *o* Judah	2Chr 20:31	5921
and Athaliah reigned *o* the land	2Chr 22:12	5921
hundreds that were set *o* the host	2Chr 23:14	
and made them captains *o* thousands	2Chr 25:5	
and captains *o* hundreds	2Chr 25:5	
his son was *o* the king's house	2Chr 26:21	5921
o which Cononiah the Levite was	2Chr 31:12	5921
was *o* the freewill offerings of	2Chr 31:14	5921
set captains of war *o* the people	2Chr 32:6	5921
o yourselves to die by famine	2Chr 32:11	
Also they were *o* the bearers of	2Chr 34:13	5921
Eliakim his brother king *o* Judah	2Chr 36:4	5921
Zedekiah his brother king *o* Judah	2Chr 36:10	5921
great and noble Asnapper brought *o*	Ezr 4:10	1541
mighty kings also *o* Jerusalem	Ezr 4:20	5922
which have ruled *o* all countries	Ezr 4:20	
are increased *o* our head, and our	Ezr 9:6	4605
me *o* till I come into Judah	Neh 2:7	5674
even *o* against his house	Neh 3:10	5048
unto the place *o* against the	Neh 3:16	5048
another piece *o* against the going	Neh 3:19	5048
Hashub *o* against their house	Neh 3:23	5048
o against the turning of the wall	Neh 3:25	5048
unto the place *o* against the	Neh 3:26	5048
o against the great tower that	Neh 3:27	5048
every one *o* against his house	Neh 3:28	5048
son of Immer *o* against his house	Neh 3:29	5048
Berechiah *o* against his chamber	Neh 3:30	5048
o against the gate Miphkad, and to	Neh 3:31	5048
servants bare rule *o* the people	Neh 5:15	5921
of the palace, charge *o* Jerusalem	Neh 7:2	5921
every one to be *o* against his	Neh 7:3	5048
that they had the dominion *o* them	Neh 9:28	
hast set *o* us because of our sins	Neh 9:37	5921
they have dominion *o* our bodies	Neh 9:37	5921
o our cattle, at their pleasure,	Neh 9:37	5921
of Senuah was second *o* the city	Neh 11:9	5921
Gispa were *o* the Nethinims	Neh 11:21	5921
the singers were *o* the business	Neh 11:22	5048
which was *o* the thanksgiving, he	Neh 12:8	5921
were *o* against them in the	Neh 12:9	5048
their brethren *o* against them	Neh 12:24	5980
man of God, ward *o* against ward	Neh 12:24	5980
which was *o* against them, they	Neh 12:37	5048
gave thanks went *o* against them	Neh 12:38	4136
that time were some appointed *o*	Neh 12:44	5921
made treasurers *o* the treasuries	Neh 13:13	5921
and God made him king *o* all Israel	Neh 13:26	5921
o an hundred and seven and twenty	Est 1:1	
that were *o* every province	Est 3:12	5921
o against the king's house	Est 5:1	5227

o against the gate of the house Est 5:1 5227
set Mordecai o the house of Haman Est 8:2 5921
Jews hoped to have power o them Est 9:1
had rule o them that hated them Est 9:1
or loweth the ox o his fodder Job 6:5 5921
that thou settest a watch o me Job 7:12 5921
dost thou not watch o my sin Job 14:16 5921
turned me o into the hands of the Job 16:11 5921
out the north o the empty place Job 26:7 5921
given him a charge o the earth Job 34:13
he is a king o all the children Job 41:34 5921
comforted him o all the evil that Job 42:11 5921
dominion o the works of thy hands Ps 8:6
who is lord o us Ps 12:4
shall mine enemy be exalted o me Ps 13:2 5921
by my God have I leaped o a wall Ps 18:29
let them not have dominion o me Ps 19:13
my cup runneth o Ps 23:5
let not mine enemies triumph o me Ps 25:2
Deliver me not o unto the will of Ps 27:12
not made my foes to rejoice o me Ps 30:1
enemies wrongfully rejoice o me Ps 35:19
and let them not rejoice o me Ps 35:24
iniquities are gone o mine head Ps 38:4 5674
they should rejoice o me Ps 38:16
mine enemy doth not triumph o me Ps 41:11 5921
and thy billows are gone o me Ps 42:7 5921
is a great King o all the earth Ps 47:2 5921
God reigneth o the heathen Ps 47:8 5921
dominion o them in the morning Ps 49:14
o Edom will I cast out my shoe Ps 60:8 5921
also are covered o with corn Ps 65:13 5848
caused men to ride o our heads Ps 66:12
his excellency is o Israel Ps 68:34 5921
their life o to the pestilence Ps 78:50 5462
He gave his people o also unto Ps 78:62 5462
art the most high o all the earth Ps 83:18 5921
Thy fierce wrath goeth o me Ps 88:16 5674
give his angels charge o thee Ps 91:11
For the wind passeth o it Ps 103:16 5674
and his kingdom ruleth o all Ps 103:19
a bound that they may not pass o Ps 104:9 5674
they that hated them ruled o them Ps 106:41
o Edom will I cast out my shoe Ps 108:9 5921
o Philistia will I triumph Ps 108:9
Set thou a wicked man o him Ps 109:6 5921
wound the heads o many countries Ps 110:6 5921
he hath not given me o unto death Ps 118:18 5414
any iniquity have dominion o me Ps 119:133
the stream had gone o our soul Ps 124:4 5674
proud waters had gone o our soul Ps 124:5 5674
mercies are o all his works Ps 145:9 5921
rule o a son that causeth shame Prov 17:2
a servant to have rule o princes Prov 19:10
glory to pass o a transgression Prov 19:11 5921
and bringeth the wheel o them Prov 20:26 5921
The rich ruleth o the poor Prov 22:7
it was all grown o with thorns Prov 24:31 5927
He that hath no rule o his own Prov 25:28
a wicked ruler o the poor people Prov 28:15 5921
was king o Israel in Jerusalem Eccl 1:12 5921
yet shall he have rule o all my Eccl 2:19
set the one o against the other Eccl 7:14 5980
Be not righteous o much Eccl 7:16 7235
neither make thyself o wise Eccl 7:16 3148
Be not o much wicked, neither be Eccl 7:17 7235
o the spirit to retain the spirit Eccl 8:8
ruleth o another to his own hurt Eccl 8:9
and his banner o me was love Song 2:4 5921
the winter is past, the rain is o Song 2:11 2498
and babes shall rule o them Is 3:4
oppressors, and women rule o them Is 3:12
shall come up o all his channels Is 8:7 5921
and go o all his banks Is 8:7 5921
he shall overflow and go o Is 8:8 5674
They are gone o the passage Is 10:29 5674
he shake his hand o the river Is 11:15 5921
streams, and make men go o dryshod Is 11:15 1869
and they shall rule o their Is 14:2
shall howl o Nebo, and o Medeba Is 15:2 5921
out, they are gone o the sea Is 16:8 5674
the Egyptians will I give o into Is 19:4 5534
a fierce king shall rule o them Is 19:4
of hosts, which he shaketh o it Is 19:16 5921
which is o the house, and say, Is 22:15 5921
of Zidon, that pass o the sea Is 23:2 5674
Pass ye o to Tarshish Is 23:6 5674
stretched out his hand o the sea Is 23:11 5921
arise, pass o to Chittim Is 23:12 5674
of the covering cast o all people Is 25:7 5921
vail that is spread o all nations Is 25:7 5921
thee have had dominion o us Is 26:13
by morning shall it pass o Is 28:19 5674
passing o he will preserve it Is 31:5
he shall pass o to his strong Is 31:9 5674
the unclean shall not pass o it Is 35:8 5674
son, which was o the house Is 36:3 5921
that was o the household, and Is 36:22 5921
who was o the household, and Is 37:2 5921
spreadeth it o with gold, and Is 40:19
judgment is passed o from my God Is 40:27 5674
him, and made him rule o kings Is 41:2
stature, shall come o unto thee Is 45:14 5674
in chains they shall come o Is 45:14 5674
the thigh, pass o the rivers Is 47:2 5674
a way for the ransomed to pass o Is 51:10 5674
soul, Bow down, that we may go o Is 51:23 5674
the street, to them that went o Is 51:23 5674
they that rule o them make them Is 52:5
should no more go o the earth Is 54:9 5674
bridegroom rejoiceth o the bride Is 62:5 5921
so shall thy God rejoice o thee Is 62:5 5921
thou never barest rule o them Is 63:19
this day set thee o the nations Jer 1:10 5921
o the kingdoms, to root out, and Jer 1:10 5921
For pass o the isles of Chittim, Jer 2:10 5674
shall watch o their cities Jer 5:6 5921
roar, yet can they not pass o it Jer 5:22 5674
Also I set watchmen o you Jer 6:17 5921
be captains, and as chief o thee Jer 13:21 5921
I will appoint o them four kinds, Jer 15:3 5921
I will set up shepherds o them Jer 23:4 5921
like as I have watched o them Jer 31:28 5921
so will I watch o them, to build, Jer 31:28 5921
line shall yet go forth o against Jer 31:39 5048
I will rejoice o them to do them Jer 32:41 5921
be rulers o the seed of Abraham Jer 33:26 413
governor o the cities of Judah Jer 40:5
that he had set o them Gedaliah Jer 40:11 5921
had made governor o the land Jer 41:2
departed to go o to the Ammonites Jer 41:10 5674
spread his royal pavilion o them Jer 43:10 5921
I will watch o them for evil, and Jer 44:27 5921
thy plants are gone o the sea Jer 48:32 5674
and shall spread his wings o Moab Jer 48:40 413
man, that I may appoint o her Jer 49:19 413
and spread his wings o Bozrah Jer 49:22 5921
man, that I may appoint o her Jer 50:44 413
thine enemy to rejoice o thee Lam 2:17 5921
Waters flowed o mine head Lam 3:54 5921
Servants have ruled o us Lam 5:8
were lifted up o against them Eze 1:20 5980
were lifted up o against them Eze 1:21 5980
stretched forth o their heads Eze 1:22 5921
firmament that was o their heads Eze 1:25 5921
above the firmament that was o Eze 1:26 5921
of the wheels o against them Eze 3:13 5980
charge o the city to draw near Eze 9:1
o them as it were a sapphire Eze 10:1 5921
and scatter them o the city Eze 10:2 5921
stood o the threshold of the Eze 10:4 5921
house, and stood o the cherubims Eze 10:18 5921
God of Israel was o them above Eze 10:19 5921
God of Israel was o them above Eze 11:22 5921
and I spread my skirt o thee Eze 16:8 5921
have stretched out my hand o thee Eze 16:27 5921
and spread their net o him Eze 19:8 5921
poured out, will I rule o you Eze 20:33
for thee, and lament o thee Eze 27:32 5921
shall no more rule o the nations Eze 29:15 5921
net o thee with a company of many Eze 32:3 5921
of heaven will I make dark o thee Eze 32:8 5921
be comforted o all his multitude Eze 32:31 5921
I will set up one shepherd o them Eze 34:23 5921
my servant shall be king o them Eze 37:24 5921
by the side of the gates o Eze 40:18 5980
was o against the gate toward the Eze 40:23 5048
one o another, and thirty in order Eze 41:6 413
o against the separate place Eze 41:15
o against the door, cieled with Eze 41:16 5048
was o against the separate place Eze 42:1 5048
O against the twenty cubits which Eze 42:3 5048
o against the pavement which was Eze 42:3 5048
without o against the chambers Eze 42:7 5980
o against the separate place, and Eze 42:10
place, and o against the building Eze 42:10
o against the oblation of the Eze 45:6 5980
the length shall be o against one Eze 45:7 5980
but shall go forth o against it Eze 46:9 5226
a river that I could not pass o Eze 47:5 5674
river that could not be passed o Eze 47:5 5674
till a man come o against Hamath Eze 47:20 5227
o against the border of the Eze 48:13 5980
in the breadth o against the five Eze 48:15
the residue in length o against Eze 48:18 5980
it shall be o against the Eze 48:18 5980
o against the five and twenty Eze 48:21
westward o against the five and Eze 48:21
o against the portions for the Eze 48:21 5980
of the eunuchs had set o Daniel Dan 1:11 5921
hath made thee ruler o them all Dan 2:38
shall bear rule o all the earth Dan 2:39
made him ruler o the whole Dan 2:48 5922
chief of the governors o all the Dan 2:48 5922
o the affairs of the province of Dan 2:49 5922
o the affairs of the province of Dan 3:12 5921
and let seven times pass o him Dan 4:16 5922
setteth up o it the basest of men Dan 4:17 5922
till seven times pass o him Dan 4:23 5922
and seven times shall pass o thee Dan 4:25 5922
and seven times shall pass o thee Dan 4:32 5922
wrote o against the candlestick Dan 5:5 6903
men, and that he appointeth o it Dan 5:21 5922
to set o the kingdom an hundred Dan 6:1 5922
which should be o the whole Dan 6:1
And o these three presidents Dan 6:2 5924
to set him o the whole realm Dan 6:3 5922
which was made king o the realm Dan 9:1 5921
shall cause them to rule o many Dan 11:39
and shall overflow and pass o Dan 11:40 5674
power o the treasures of gold Dan 11:43
o all the precious things of Dan 11:43
people thereof shall mourn o it Hos 10:5 5921
but I passed o upon her fair neck Hos 10:11 5674
Yea, he had power o the angel Hos 12:4 413
the heathen should rule o them Joel 2:17
o the children of Judah in the Obad 12
billows and thy waves passed o me Jonah 2:3 5674
and made it to come up o Jonah Jonah 4:6 5921
it might be a shadow o his head Jonah 4:6 5921
sun shall go down o the prophets Mic 3:6 5921
and the day shall be dark o them Mic 3:6 5921
the LORD shall reign o them in Mic 4:7 5921
thee shall clap the hands o thee Nah 3:19 5921
mind change, and he shall pass o Hab 1:11 5674
things, that have no ruler o them Hab 1:14
Behold, it is laid o with gold Hab 2:19
he will rejoice o thee with joy Zeph 3:17 5921
he will joy o thee with singing Zeph 3:17 5921
Therefore the heaven o you is Hag 1:10 5921
which lifted up their horn o the Zec 1:21 413
o the face of the whole earth Zec 5:3 5921
And the LORD shall be seen o them Zec 9:14 5921
shall be king o all the earth Zec 14:9 5921
stood o where the young child was Mt 2:9 *1883*
entered into a ship, and passed o Mt 9:1 *1276*
have gone o the cities of Israel Mt 10:23 *5055*
And when they were gone o, they Mt 14:34 *1276*
Gentiles exercise dominion o them Mt 20:25
Go into the village o against you Mt 21:2 *561*
hath made ruler o his household Mt 24:45 *1909*
make him ruler o all his goods Mt 24:47 *1909*
hast been faithful o a few things Mt 25:21 *1909*
make thee ruler o many things Mt 25:21 *1909*
hast been faithful o a few things Mt 25:23 *1909*
make thee ruler o many things Mt 25:23 *1909*
set up o his head his accusation Mt 27:37 *1883*
o all the land unto the ninth Mt 27:45 *1909*
sitting o against the sepulchre Mt 27:61 *561*
Let us pass o unto the other side Mk 4:35 *1330*
they came o unto the other side Mk 5:1
when Jesus was passed o again by Mk 5:21 *1276*
gave them power o unclean spirits Mk 6:7
And when they had passed o Mk 6:53 *1276*
which are accounted to rule o the Mk 10:42
Gentiles exercise lordship o them Mk 10:42
into the village o against you Mk 11:2 *2713*
Jesus sat o against the treasury, Mk 12:41 *2713*
of Olives o against the temple Mk 13:3 *2713*
of his accusation was written o Mk 15:26 *1924*
there was darkness o the whole Mk 15:33 *1909*
which stood o against him Mk 15:39
he shall reign o the house of Lk 1:33 *1909*
keeping watch o their flock by Lk 2:8 *1909*
give his angels charge o thee Lk 4:10 *4012*
And he stood o her, and rebuked the Lk 4:39 *1883*
and shaken together, and running o Lk 6:38 *5240*
Let us go o unto the other side Lk 8:22 *1330*
which is o against Galilee Lk 8:26 *495*
authority o all devils, and to Lk 9:1 *1909*
o all the power of the enemy Lk 10:19 *1909*
pass o judgment and the love of Lk 11:42 *3928*
the men that walk o them are not Lk 11:44 *1883*
me a judge or a divider o you Lk 12:14 *1909*
shall make ruler o his household Lk 12:42 *1909*
make him ruler o all that he hath Lk 12:44 *1909*
o one sinner that repenteth Lk 15:7 *1909*
more than o ninety Lk 15:7 *1909*
God o one sinner that repenteth Lk 15:10 *1909*
not have this man to reign o us Lk 19:14 *1909*
have thou authority o ten cities Lk 19:17 *1883*
him, Be thou also o five cities Lk 19:19 *1883*
not that I should reign o them Lk 19:27 *1909*
ye into the village o against you Lk 19:30 *2713*
he beheld the city, and wept o it Lk 19:41 *1909*
Gentiles exercise lordship o them Lk 22:25
written o him in letters of Greek Lk 23:38 *1909*
there was a darkness o all the Lk 23:44 *1909*
Jesus went o the sea of Galilee Jn 6:1 *4008*
barley loaves, which remained o Jn 6:13 *4052*
went o the sea toward Capernaum Jn 6:17 *4008*
hast given him power o all flesh Jn 17:2
his disciples o the brook Cedron Jn 18:1 *4008*
we may appoint o this business Acts 6:3 *1909*
and he made him governor o Egypt Acts 7:10 *1909*
a dearth o all the land of Egypt Acts 7:11 *1909*
And were carried o into Sychem Acts 7:16 *3346*
made thee a ruler and a judge o us Acts 7:27 *1909*
and made great lamentation o him Acts 8:2 *1909*
Come o into Macedonia, and help us Acts 16:9 *1224*
went o all the country of Galatia Acts 18:23 *1330*
took upon them to call o them Acts 19:13 *1909*
And when he had gone o those parts Acts 20:2 *1330*
came the next day o against Chios Acts 20:15 *481*
o the which the Holy Ghost hath Acts 20:28 *1722*
a ship sailing o unto Phenicia Acts 21:2 *1276*
had sailed o the sea of Cilicia Acts 27:5 *1277*
scarce were come o against Cnidus Acts 27:7 *2596*
under Crete, o against Salmone Acts 27:7 *2596*
God gave them o to a reprobate Rom 1:28 *3860*
even o them that had not sinned Rom 5:14 *1909*
death hath no more dominion o him Rom 6:9
sin shall not have dominion o you Rom 6:14
o a man as long as he liveth Rom 7:1
flesh Christ came, who is o all Rom 9:5 *1909*
not the potter power o the clay Rom 9:21
for the same Lord o all is rich Rom 10:12
rise to reign o the Gentiles Rom 15:12
but hath power o his own will 1Cor 7:37 *4012*
be partakers of this power o you 1Cor 9:12
we have dominion o your faith 2Cor 1:24
which put a vail o his face 2Cor 3:13 *1909*
had gathered much had nothing o 2Cor 8:15 *4121*
For I am jealous o you with godly 2Cor 11:2
gave him to be the head o all Eph 1:22 *5228*
themselves o unto lasciviousness Eph 4:19 *3860*
openly, triumphing o them in it Col 2:15
we were comforted o you in all 1Th 3:7 *1909*
are o you in the Lord, and 1Th 5:12 *4291*
nor to usurp authority o the man 1Ti 2:12
didst set him o the works of thy Heb 2:7 *1909*
Christ as a son o his own house Heb 3:6 *1909*
o it the cherubims of glory Heb 9:5 *5231*
an high priest o the house of God Heb 10:21 *1909*
them which have the rule o you Heb 13:7
them that have the rule o you Heb 13:17
all them that have the rule o you Heb 13:24
and let them pray o him, anointing Jas 5:14 *1909*
of the Lord are o the righteous 1Pet 3:12 *1909*
as being lords o God's heritage 1Pet 5:3 *2634*
themselves o to fornication Jude 7 *1608*
will I give power o the nations Rev 2:26 *1909*

power was given unto them o the Rev 6:8 *1909*
And they had a king o them Rev 9:11 *1909*
have power o waters to turn them Rev 11:6 *1909*
the earth shall rejoice o them Rev 11:10 *1909*
was given him o all kindreds Rev 13:7 *1909*
the altar, which had power o fire Rev 14:18 *1909*
gotten the victory o the beast Rev 15:2 *1537*
o his image, and o his mark, and Rev 15:2 *1537*
o the number of his name, stand Rev 15:2 *1537*
which hath power o these plagues Rev 16:9 *1909*
which reigneth o the kings of the Rev 17:18 *1909*
earth shall weep and mourn o her Rev 18:11 *1909*
Rejoice o her, thou heaven, and ye Rev 18:20 *1909*

OVERCAME
o them, and prevailed against them Acts 19:16 *2634*
me in my throne, even as I also o Rev 3:21 *3528*
they o him by the blood of the Rev 12:11 *3528*

OVERCHARGE
that I may not o you all 2Cor 2:5 *1912*

OVERCHARGED
your hearts be o with surfeiting Lk 21:34 *925*

OVERCOME
Gad, a troop shall o him Gen 49:19 1464
but he shall o at the last Gen 49:19 1464
of them that cry for being o Ex 32:18 2476
for we are well able to o it Num 13:30 3201
I shall be able to o them Num 22:11 3898
Ahaz, but could not o him 2Kin 16:5 3898
eyes from me, for they have o me Song 6:5 7292
of them that are o with wine Is 28:1 1986
and like a man whom wine hath o Jer 23:9 5674
o him, he taketh from him all his Lk 11:22 *3528*
I have o the world Jn 16:33 *3528*
mightest o when thou art judged Rom 3:4 *3528*
Be not o of evil, but o Rom 12:21 *3528*
for of whom a man is o, of the 2Pet 2:19 *2274*
are again entangled therein, and o 2Pet 2:20 *2274*
because ye have o the wicked one 1Jn 2:13 *3528*
you, and ye have o the wicked one 1Jn 2:14 *3528*
little children, and have o them 1Jn 4:4 *3528*
war against them, and shall o them Rev 11:7 *3528*
war with the saints, and to o them Rev 13:7 *3528*
Lamb, and the Lamb shall o them Rev 17:14 *3528*

OVERCOMETH
is born of God o the world 1Jn 5:4 *3528*
is the victory that o the world 1Jn 5:4 *3528*
Who is he that o the world 1Jn 5:5 *3528*
To him that o will I give to eat Rev 2:7 *3528*
He that o shall not be hurt of Rev 2:11 *3528*
To him that o will I give to eat Rev 2:17 *3528*
And he that o, and keepeth my works Rev 2:26 *3528*
He that o, the same shall be Rev 3:5 *3528*
Him that o will I make a pillar Rev 3:12 *3528*
To him that o will I grant to sit Rev 3:21 *3528*
He that o shall inherit all Rev 21:7 *3528*

OVERDRIVE
and if men should o them one day Gen 33:13 1849

OVERFLOW
the water of the Red sea to o Deut 11:4 6687
waters, where the floods o me Ps 69:2 7857
Let not the waterflood o me Ps 69:15 7857
he shall o and go over, he shall Is 8:8 7857
shall o with righteousness Is 10:22 7857
waters shall o the hiding place Is 28:17 7857
the rivers, they shall not o thee Is 43:2 7857
shall o the land, and all that is Jer 47:2 7857
and one shall certainly come, and o Dan 11:10 7857
destroy him, and his army shall o Dan 11:26 7857
into the countries, and shall o Dan 11:40 7857
and the fats shall o with wine Joel 2:24 7783
for the press is full, the fats o Joel 3:13 7783

OVERFLOWED
gushed out, and the streams o Ps 78:20 7857
being o with water, perished 2Pet 3:6 *2626*

OVERFLOWETH
(for Jordan o all his banks all Josh 3:15 4390

OVERFLOWING
He bindeth the floods from o Job 28:11 1065
a watercourse for the o of waters Job 38:25 7858
as a flood of mighty waters o Is 28:2 7857
when the o scourge shall pass Is 28:15 7857
when the o scourge shall pass Is 28:18 7857
as an o stream, shall reach to Is 30:28 7857
the north, and shall be an o flood Jer 47:2 7857
there shall be an o shower Eze 13:11 7857
there shall be an o shower in Eze 13:13 7857
o rain, and great hailstones, fire Eze 38:22 7857
the o of the water passed by Hab 3:10 2230

OVERFLOWN
when it had o all his banks 1Chr 12:15 4390
foundation was o with a flood Job 22:16 3332
shall they be o from before him Dan 11:22 7857

OVERLAID
of shittim wood o with gold Ex 26:32 6823
he o the boards with gold, and Ex 36:34 6823
the bars, and o the bars with gold Ex 36:34 6823
shittim wood, and o them with gold Ex 36:36 6823
he o their chapiters and their Ex 36:38 6823
he o it with pure gold within and Ex 37:2 6823
shittim wood, and o them with gold Ex 37:4 6823
he o it with pure gold, and made Ex 37:11 6823
o them with gold, to bear the Ex 37:15 6823
he o it with pure gold, both the Ex 37:26 6823
shittim wood, and o them with gold Ex 37:28 6823
and he o it with brass Ex 38:2 6823
wood, and o them with brass Ex 38:6 6823
o their chapiters, and filleted Ex 38:28 6823
because she o it 1Kin 3:19 7901
and he o it with pure gold 1Kin 6:20 6823
So Solomon o the house within 1Kin 6:21 6823
and he o it with gold 1Kin 6:21 6823
And the whole house he o with gold 1Kin 6:22 6823
was by the oracle he o with gold 1Kin 6:22 6823
he o the cherubims with gold 1Kin 6:28 6823
floor of the house he o with gold 1Kin 6:30 6823
o them with gold, and spread gold 1Kin 6:32 6823
ivory, and o it with the best gold 1Kin 10:18 6823
Hezekiah king of Judah had o 2Kin 18:16 6823
he o it within with pure gold 2Chr 3:4 6823
which he o with fine gold, and set 2Chr 3:5 2645
He o also the house, the beams, 2Chr 3:7 2645
he o it with fine gold, amounting 2Chr 3:8 2645
he o the upper chambers with gold 2Chr 3:9 2645
image work, and o them with gold 2Chr 3:10 6823
o the doors of them with brass 2Chr 4:9 6823
of ivory, and o it with pure gold 2Chr 9:17 6823
as bright ivory o with sapphires Song 5:14 5968
covenant o round about with gold Heb 9:4 *4028*

OVERLAY
thou shalt o it with pure gold, Ex 25:11 6823
within and without shalt thou o it Ex 25:11 6823
shittim wood, and o them with gold Ex 25:13 6823
thou shalt o it with pure gold, Ex 25:24 6823
o them with gold, that the table Ex 25:28 6823
thou shalt o the boards with gold Ex 26:29 6823
thou shalt o the bars with gold Ex 26:29 6823
o them with gold, and their hooks Ex 26:37 6823
thou shalt o it with brass Ex 27:2 6823
wood, and o them with brass Ex 27:6 6823
thou shalt o it with pure gold, Ex 30:3 6823
shittim wood, and o them with gold Ex 30:5 6823
to o the walls of the houses 1Chr 29:4 2902

OVERLAYING
the o of their chapiters of Ex 38:17 6826
the o of their chapiters and their Ex 38:19 6826

OVERLIVED
days of the elders that o Joshua Josh 24:31

OVERMUCH
be swallowed up with o sorrow 2Cor 2:7 *4055*

OVERPASS
they o the deeds of the wicked Jer 5:28 5674

OVERPAST
until these calamities be o Ps 57:1 5674
until the indignation be o Is 26:20 5674

OVERPLUS
restore the o unto the man to Lev 25:27 5736

OVERRAN
the way of the plain, and o Cushi 2Sa 18:23 5674

OVERRUNNING
But with an o flood he will make Nah 1:8 5674

OVERSEE
were appointed to o the vessels 1Chr 9:29
thousand and six hundred to o them 2Chr 2:2 5329

OVERSEER
he made him o over his house, and Gen 39:4 6485
he had made him o in his house Gen 39:5 6485
the son of Zichri was their o Neh 11:9 6496
their o was Zabdiel, the son of Neh 11:14 6496
The o also of the Levites at Neh 11:22 6496
sang loud, with Jezrahiah their o Neh 12:42 6496
Which having no guide, o, or Prov 6:7 7860

OVERSEERS
six hundred o to set the people a 2Chr 2:18 5329
were o under the hand of Cononiah 2Chr 31:13 6496
the o of them were Jahath and 2Chr 34:12 6485
were o of all that wrought the 2Chr 34:13 5329
it into the hand of the o 2Chr 34:17 6485
the Holy Ghost hath made you o Acts 20:28 *1985*

OVERSHADOW
power of the Highest shall o thee Lk 1:35 *1982*
passing by might o some of them Acts 5:15 *1982*

OVERSHADOWED
behold, a bright cloud o them Mt 17:5 *1982*
And there was a cloud that o them Mk 9:7 *1982*
there came a cloud, and o them Lk 9:34 *1982*

OVERSIGHT
peradventure it was an o Gen 43:12 4870
have the o of them that keep the Num 3:32 6486
the o of all the tabernacle, and Num 4:16 6486
that had the o of the house of 2Kin 12:11 6485
that have the o of the house of 2Kin 22:5 6485
that have the o of the house of 2Kin 22:9 6485
their children had the o of the 1Chr 9:23 5921
the o of the house of the LORD 2Chr 34:10 6485
had the o of the outward business Neh 11:16 5921
having the o of the chamber of Neh 13:4 5414
among you, taking the o thereof 1Pet 5:2 *1983*

OVERSPREAD
and of them was the whole earth o Gen 9:19 5310

OVERSPREADING
for the o of abominations he Dan 9:27 3671

OVERTAKE
and when thou dost o them, say Gen 44:4 5381
said, I will pursue, I will o Ex 15:9 5381
o him, because the way is long, Deut 19:6 5381
o thee, if thou shalt hearken Deut 28:2 5381
shall come upon thee, and o thee Deut 28:15 5381
o thee, till thou be destroyed Deut 28:45 5381
for ye shall o them Josh 2:5 5381
shall I o them 1Sa 30:8 5381
for thou shalt surely o them 1Sa 30:8 5381
lest he o us suddenly, and bring 2Sa 15:14 5381
us, neither doth justice o us Is 59:9 5381
shall o you there in the land of Jer 42:16 5381
lovers, but she shall not o them Hos 2:7 5381
of iniquity did not o them Hos 10:9 5381
evil shall not o nor prevent us Amos 9:10 5066
the plowman shall o the reaper Amos 9:13 5066
that day should o you as a thief 1Th 5:4 *2638*

OVERTAKEN
pursued mine enemies, and o them Ps 18:37 5381
if a man be o in a fault Gal 6:1 *4301*

OVERTAKETH
the sword of thine enemies o thee 1Chr 21:12 5381

OVERTHREW
he o those cities, and all the Gen 19:25 2015
when he o the cities in the which Gen 19:29 2015
the LORD o the Egyptians in the Ex 14:27 5287
which the LORD o in his anger Deut 29:23 2015
But o Pharaoh and his host in the Ps 136:15 5286
shall be as when God o Sodom Is 13:19 4114
be as the cities which the LORD o Jer 20:16 2015
As God o Sodom and Jer 50:40 4114
some of you, as God o Sodom Amos 4:11 4114
o the tables of the moneychangers Mt 21:12 *2690*
o the tables of the moneychangers Mk 11:15 *2690*
changers' money, and o the tables Jn 2:15 *390*

OVERTHROW
also, that I will not o this city Gen 19:21 2015
Lot out of the midst of the o Gen 19:29 2018
but thou shalt utterly o them Ex 23:24 2040
ye shall o their altars, and break Deut 12:3 5422
therein, like the o of Sodom Deut 29:23 4114
and to spy it out, and to o it 2Sa 10:3 2015
strong against the city, and o it 2Sa 11:25 2040
unto thee for to search, and to o 1Chr 19:3 2015
to o them in the wilderness Ps 106:26 5307
To o their seed also among the Ps 106:27 5307
who have purposed to o my goings Ps 140:4 1760
hunt the violent man to o him Ps 140:11 4073
to o the righteous in judgment Prov 18:5 5186
As in the o of Sodom and Gomorrah Jer 49:18 4114
I will o the throne of kingdoms, Hag 2:22 2015
I will o the chariots, and those Hag 2:22 2015
if it be of God, ye cannot o it Acts 5:39 *2647*
and o the faith of some 2Ti 2:18 *396*
ashes condemned them with an o 2Pet 2:6 *2692*

OVERTHROWETH
away spoiled, and o the mighty Job 12:19 5557
but wickedness o the sinner Prov 13:6 5557
but God o the wicked for their Prov 21:12 5557
and he o the words of the Prov 22:12 5557
but he that receiveth gifts o it Prov 29:4 2040

OVERTHROWN
of thine excellency thou hast o Ex 15:7 2040
fled before him, and many were o Judg 9:40 5307
some of them be o at the first 2Sa 17:9 5307
and the Ethiopians were o, that 2Chr 14:13 5307
Know now that God hath o me Job 19:6 5791
judges are o in stony places Ps 141:6 8058
but it is o by the mouth of the Prov 11:11 2040
The wicked are o, and are not Prov 12:7 2015
house of the wicked shall be o Prov 14:11 8045
it is desolate, as o by strangers Is 1:7 4114
but let them be o before thee Jer 18:23 3782
that was o as in a moment, and no Lam 4:6 2015
and many countries shall be o Dan 11:41 3782
I have o some of you, as God Amos 4:11 2015
forty days, and Nineveh shall be o Jonah 3:4 2015
for they were o in the wilderness 1Cor 10:5 *2693*

OVERTOOK
they o him in the mount Gilead Gen 31:23 1692
Then Laban o Jacob Gen 31:25 5381
he o them, and he spake unto them Gen 44:6 5381
o them encamping by the sea, Ex 14:9 5381
and o the children of Dan Judg 18:22 1692
but the battle o them Judg 20:42 1692
o him in the plains of Jericho 2Kin 25:5 5381
o Zedekiah in the plains of Jer 39:5 5381
o Zedekiah in the plains of Jer 52:8 5381
all her persecutors o her between Lam 1:3 5381

OVERTURN
them out, and they o the earth Job 12:15 2015
I will o, o, o Eze 21:27 5754

OVERTURNED
o it, that the tent lay along Judg 7:13 2015

OVERTURNETH
which o them in his anger Job 9:5 2015
he o the mountains by the roots Job 28:9 2015
he o them in the night, so that Job 34:25 2015

OVERWHELM
ye o the fatherless, and ye dig a Job 6:27 5307

OVERWHELMED
come upon me, and horror hath o me Ps 55:5 3680
cry unto thee, when my heart is o Ps 61:2 5848
I complained, and my spirit was o Ps 77:3 5848
but the sea o their enemies Ps 78:53 3680
of the afflicted, when he is o Ps 102:*t* 5848
Then the waters had o us, the Ps 124:4 7857
When my spirit was o within me Ps 142:3 5848
is my spirit o within me Ps 143:4 5848

OWE
O no man any thing, but to love Rom 13:8 *3784*

OWED
which o him ten thousand talents Mt 18:24 *3781*
which o him an hundred pence Mt 18:28 *3784*
the one o five hundred pence, and Lk 7:41 *3784*

OWEST
saying, Pay me that thou o ... Mt 18:28 3784
How much o thou unto my lord ... Lk 16:5 3784
he to another, And how much o thou ... Lk 16:7 3784
o unto me even thine own self ... Philem 19 4359

OWETH
or o thee ought, put that on mine ... Philem 18 3784

OWL
And the o, and the night hawk, and ... Lev 11:16
And the little o, and the cormorant ... Lev 11:17 3563
and the cormorant, and the great o ... Lev 11:17 3244
And the o, and the night hawk, and ... Deut 14:15
The little o, and the great ... Deut 14:16 3563
and the great o ... Deut 14:16 3244
I am like an o of the desert ... Ps 102:6 3563
the o also and the raven shall ... Is 34:11 3244
the screech o also shall rest ... Is 34:14 3917
shall the great o make her nest ... Is 34:15 7091

OWLS
to dragons, and a companion to o ... Job 30:29
o shall dwell there, and satyrs ... Is 13:21
of dragons, and a court for o ... Is 34:13
honour me, the dragons and the o ... Is 43:20
the o shall dwell therein ... Jer 50:39
the dragons, and mourning as the o ... Mic 1:8

OWN
So God created man in his o image ... Gen 1:27
and begat a son in his o likeness ... Gen 5:3 249
servants, born in his o house ... Gen 14:14 249
o bowels shall be thine heir ... Gen 15:4 249
that I may go unto mine o place ... Gen 30:25
I provide for mine o house also ... Gen 30:30
he put his o flocks by themselves ... Gen 30:40
and four parts shall be your o ... Gen 47:24
the fault is in thine o people ... Ex 5:16
he went his way into his o land ... Ex 18:27
and the dead shall be his o ... Ex 21:36
of the best of his o field ... Ex 22:5
and of the best of his o vineyard ... Ex 22:5
whom thou swarest by thine o self ... Ex 32:13
he shall offer it of his o ... Lev 1:3
His o hands shall bring the ... Lev 7:30
into the palm of his o left hand ... Lev 14:15 3548
into the palm of his o left hand ... Lev 14:26 3548
it be one of your o country ... Lev 16:29 249
it be one of your o country ... Lev 17:15 249
for theirs is thine o nakedness ... Lev 18:10
neither any of your o nation ... Lev 18:26 249
ye shall offer it at your o will ... Lev 19:5
a virgin of his o people to wife ... Lev 21:14
Ye shall offer at your o will a ... Lev 22:19
the LORD, offer it at your o will ... Lev 22:29
as for one of your o country ... Lev 24:22 249
That which groweth of its o ... Lev 25:5
and shall return unto his o family ... Lev 25:41
tents, every man by his o camp ... Num 1:52
and every man by his o standard ... Num 1:52
shall pitch by his o standard ... Num 2:2
but I will depart to mine o land ... Num 10:30
we were in our o sight as ... Num 13:33
ye seek not after your o heart ... Num 15:39
your o heart and your o eyes ... Num 15:39
have not done them of mine o mind ... Num 16:28
sinners against their o souls ... Num 16:38
either good or bad of mine o mind ... Num 24:13
but died in his o sin, and had no ... Num 27:3
called it Nobah, after his o name ... Num 32:42
keep himself to his o inheritance ... Num 36:9
and called them after his o name ... Deut 3:14
whatsoever is right in his o eyes ... Deut 12:8
friend, which is as thine o soul ... Deut 13:6
shalt bring it unto thine o house ... Deut 22:2
thy fill at thine o pleasure ... Deut 23:24
he may sleep in his o raiment ... Deut 24:13
be put to death for his o sin ... Deut 24:16
eat the fruit of thine o body ... Deut 28:53
brethren, nor knew his o children ... Deut 33:9
put it even among their o stuff ... Josh 7:11
his o city, and unto his o house ... Josh 20:6
ceased not from their o doings ... Judg 2:19
Mine o hand hath saved me ... Judg 7:2
went and dwelt in his o house ... Judg 8:29
which was right in his o eyes ... Judg 17:6
which was right in his o eyes ... Judg 21:25
lest I mar mine o inheritance ... Ruth 4:6
And they went unto their o home ... 1Sa 2:20
and let it go again to his o place ... 1Sa 5:11
of his o coast to Beth-shemesh ... 1Sa 6:9
him a man after his o heart ... 1Sa 13:14
Philistines went to their o place ... 1Sa 14:46
thou wast little in thine o sight ... 1Sa 15:17
Jonathan loved him as his o soul ... 1Sa 18:1
he loved him as his o soul ... 1Sa 18:3
loved him as he loved his o soul ... 1Sa 20:17
son of Jesse to thine o confusion ... 1Sa 20:30
thyself with thine o hand ... 1Sa 25:26
avenging myself with mine o hand ... 1Sa 25:33
of Nabal upon his o head ... 1Sa 25:39
him in Ramah, even in his o city ... 1Sa 28:3
in his o house upon his bed ... 2Sa 4:11
and will be base in mine o sight ... 2Sa 6:22
may dwell in a place of their o ... 2Sa 7:10
and according to thine o heart ... 2Sa 7:21
o meat, and drank of his o cup ... 2Sa 12:3
of his o flock and of his o herd ... 2Sa 12:4
against thee out of thine o house ... 2Sa 12:11
then he came to his o house ... 2Sa 12:20
said, Let him turn to his o house ... 2Sa 14:24
Absalom returned to his o house ... 2Sa 14:24
go to battle in thine o person ... 2Sa 17:11
falsehood against mine o life ... 2Sa 18:13
the pillar after his o name ... 2Sa 18:18
that did eat at thine o table ... 2Sa 19:28
again in peace unto his o house ... 2Sa 19:30
that I may die in mine o city ... 2Sa 19:37
and he returned unto his o place ... 2Sa 19:39
and slew him with his o spear ... 2Sa 23:21
thou mayest save thine o life ... 1Kin 1:12
my son to ride upon mine o mule ... 1Kin 1:33
this word against his o life ... 1Kin 2:23
to Anathoth, unto thine o fields ... 1Kin 2:26
return his blood upon his o head ... 1Kin 2:32
he was buried in his o house in ... 1Kin 2:34
blood shall be upon thine o head ... 1Kin 2:37
thy wickedness upon thine o head ... 1Kin 2:44
an end of building his o house ... 1Kin 3:1
his o house thirteen years ... 1Kin 7:1
man the plague of his o heart ... 1Kin 8:38
his o house, and Millo, and the ... 1Kin 9:15
heard in mine o land of thy acts ... 1Kin 10:6
turned and went to her o country ... 1Kin 10:13 249
to wife the sister of his o wife ... 1Kin 11:19
that I may go to mine o country ... 1Kin 11:21
seekest to go to thine o country ... 1Kin 11:22
now see to thine o house, David ... 1Kin 12:16
he had devised of his o heart ... 1Kin 12:33
laid his carcase in his o grave ... 1Kin 13:30
get thee to thine o house ... 1Kin 14:12
abode, and laid him upon his o bed ... 1Kin 17:19
and every man to his o country ... 1Kin 22:36
and he took hold of his o clothes ... 2Kin 2:12 249
him, and returned to their o land ... 2Kin 3:27
I dwell among mine o people ... 2Kin 4:13
his o hallowed things, and all the ... 2Kin 12:18
be put to death for his o sin ... 2Kin 14:6
carried away out of their o land ... 2Kin 17:23
every nation made gods of their o ... 2Kin 17:29
the LORD, and served their o gods ... 2Kin 17:33
that they may eat their o dung ... 2Kin 18:27
drink their o piss with you ... 2Kin 18:27
eat ye every man of his o vine ... 2Kin 18:31
away to a land like your o land ... 2Kin 18:32
and shall return to his o land ... 2Kin 19:7
fall by the sword in his o land ... 2Kin 19:7
city, to save it, for mine o sake ... 2Kin 19:34
defend this city for mine o sake ... 2Kin 20:6
in the garden of his o house ... 2Kin 21:18
and slew the king in his o house ... 2Kin 21:23
and buried him in his o sepulchre ... 2Kin 23:30
and slew him with his o spear ... 1Chr 11:23
and according to thine o heart ... 1Chr 17:19
went to redeem to be his o people ... 1Chr 17:21
thou make thine o people for ever ... 1Chr 17:22
God, I have of mine o proper good ... 1Chr 29:3
of thine o have we given thee ... 1Chr 29:14
of thine hand, and is all thine o ... 1Chr 29:16
his way upon his o head ... 2Chr 6:23
every one shall know his o sore ... 2Chr 6:29
his o grief, and shall spread ... 2Chr 6:29
of the LORD, and in his o house ... 2Chr 7:11
of the LORD, and his o house, ... 2Chr 8:1
in mine o land of thine acts ... 2Chr 9:5
and went away to her o land ... 2Chr 9:12
now, David, see to thine o house ... 2Chr 10:16
buried him in his o sepulchres ... 2Chr 16:14
his o servants conspired against ... 2Chr 24:25 249
every man shall die for his o sin ... 2Chr 25:4
their o people out of thine hand ... 2Chr 25:15
possession, into their o cities ... 2Chr 31:1
with shame of face to his o land ... 2Chr 32:21
they that came forth of his o ... 2Chr 32:21
and they buried him in his o house ... 2Chr 33:20
him, and slew him in his o house ... 2Chr 33:24
which are minded of their o ... Ezr 7:13
their reproach upon their o head ... Neh 4:4
them out of thine o heart ... Neh 6:8
much cast down in their o eyes ... Neh 6:16
should bear rule in his o house ... Est 1:22
dead, took for his o daughter ... Est 2:7
should return upon his o head ... Est 9:25
came every one from his o place ... Job 2:11
the wise in their o craftiness ... Job 5:13
mine o mouth shall condemn me ... Job 9:20
mine o clothes shall abhor me ... Job 9:31
maintain mine o ways before him ... Job 13:15
Thine o mouth condemneth thee, and ... Job 15:6
thine o lips testify against thee ... Job 15:6
his o counsel shall cast him down ... Job 18:7
is cast into a net by his o feet ... Job 18:8
children's sake of mine o body ... Job 19:17
perish for ever like his o dung ... Job 20:7
he was righteous in his o eyes ... Job 32:1
thine o right hand can save thee ... Job 40:14
commune with your o heart upon ... Ps 4:4
let them fall by their o counsels ... Ps 5:10
shall return upon his o head ... Ps 7:16
shall come down upon his o pate ... Ps 7:16
they hid is their o foot taken ... Ps 9:15
snared in the work of his o hands ... Ps 9:16
our lips are our o ... Ps 12:4
He that sweareth to his o hurt ... Ps 15:4
They are inclosed in their o fat ... Ps 17:10 249
thee according to thine o heart ... Ps 20:4
LORD, in thine o strength ... Ps 21:13
and none can keep alive his o soul ... Ps 22:29
hath chosen for his o inheritance ... Ps 33:12
prayer returned into mine o bosom ... Ps 35:13
flattereth himself in his o eyes ... Ps 36:2
shall enter into their o heart ... Ps 37:15
mine o familiar friend, in whom I ... Ps 41:9
in possession by their o sword ... Ps 44:3
neither did their o arm save them ... Ps 44:3
forget also thine o people ... Ps 45:10
their lands after their o names ... Ps 49:11
slanderest thine o mother's son ... Ps 50:20
So they shall make their o tongue ... Ps 64:8
and God, even our o God, shall ... Ps 67:6
Arise, O God, plead thine o cause ... Ps 74:22
I commune with mine o heart ... Ps 77:6
for he gave them their o desire ... Ps 78:29
But made his o people to go forth ... Ps 78:52
them up unto their o hearts' lust ... Ps 81:12
they walked in their o counsels ... Ps 81:12
bring upon them their o iniquity ... Ps 94:23
them off in their o wickedness ... Ps 94:23
they defiled with their o works ... Ps 106:39
a whoring with their o inventions ... Ps 106:39
he abhorred his o inheritance ... Ps 106:40
themselves with their o confusion ... Ps 109:29
not the works of thine o hands ... Ps 138:8
of their o lips cover them ... Ps 140:9
the wicked fall into their o nets ... Ps 141:10 249
they lay wait for their o blood ... Prov 1:18
lurk privily for their o lives ... Prov 1:18
eat of the fruit of their o way ... Prov 1:31
and be filled with their o devices ... Prov 1:31
not unto thine o understanding ... Prov 3:5
Be not wise in thine o eyes ... Prov 3:7
waters out of thine o cistern ... Prov 5:15
waters out of thine o well ... Prov 5:15
Let them be only thine o, and not ... Prov 5:17 249
His o iniquities shall take the ... Prov 5:22 249
doeth it destroyeth his o soul ... Prov 6:32
against me wrongeth his o soul ... Prov 8:36
shall fall by his o wickedness ... Prov 11:5
be taken in their o naughtiness ... Prov 11:6
man doeth good to his o soul ... Prov 11:17
is cruel troubleth his o flesh ... Prov 11:17
evil pursueth it to his o death ... Prov 11:19
He that troubleth his o house ... Prov 11:29
of a fool is right in his o eyes ... Prov 12:15
heart knoweth his o bitterness ... Prov 14:10 5315
shall be filled with his o ways ... Prov 14:14
is hated even of his o neighbour ... Prov 14:20
of gain troubleth his o house ... Prov 15:27
instruction despiseth his o soul ... Prov 15:32
of a man are clean in his o eyes ... Prov 16:2
as an high wall in his o conceit ... Prov 18:11
first in his o cause seemeth just ... Prov 18:17
getteth wisdom loveth his o soul ... Prov 19:8
commandment keepeth his o soul ... Prov 19:16
anger sinneth against his o soul ... Prov 20:2
proclaim every one his o goodness ... Prov 20:6
a man then understand his o way ... Prov 20:24
of a man is right in his o eyes ... Prov 21:2
cease from thine o wisdom ... Prov 23:4
search their o glory is not glory ... Prov 25:27
o spirit is like a city that is ... Prov 25:28
lest he be wise in his o conceit ... Prov 26:5
thou a man wise in his o conceit ... Prov 26:12
The sluggard is wiser in his o ... Prov 26:16
praise thee, and not thine o mouth ... Prov 27:2
a stranger, and not thine o lips ... Prov 27:2
Thine o friend, and thy father's ... Prov 27:10
shall fall himself into his o pit ... Prov 28:10
rich man is wise in his o conceit ... Prov 28:11
trusteth in his o heart is a fool ... Prov 28:26
with a thief hateth his o soul ... Prov 29:24
that are pure in their o eyes ... Prov 30:12
let her o works praise her in the ... Prov 31:31
I communed with mine o heart ... Eccl 1:16
man should rejoice in his o works ... Eccl 3:22
together, and eateth his o flesh ... Eccl 4:5
For oftentimes also thine o heart ... Eccl 7:22
ruleth over another to his o hurt ... Eccl 8:9
but mine o vineyard have I not ... Song 1:6
worship the work of their o hands ... Is 2:8
that which their o fingers have ... Is 2:8
saying, We will eat our o bread ... Is 4:1
o bread, and wear our o apparel ... Is 4:1
that are wise in their o eyes ... Is 5:21
and prudent in their o sight ... Is 5:21
every man the flesh of his o arm ... Is 9:20
every man turn to his o people ... Is 13:14
and flee every one into his o land ... Is 13:14
and set them in their o land ... Is 14:1
glory, every one in his o house ... Is 14:18
her o feet shall carry her afar ... Is 23:7
which your o hands have made unto ... Is 31:7
that they may eat their o dung ... Is 36:12
drink their o piss with you ... Is 36:12
one the waters of his o cistern ... Is 36:16
away to a land like your o land ... Is 36:17
a rumour, and return to his o land ... Is 37:7
fall by the sword in his o land ... Is 37:7
city to save it for mine o sake ... Is 37:35
transgressions for mine o sake ... Is 43:25
and they are their o witnesses ... Is 44:9
o sake, even for mine o sake ... Is 48:11
oppress thee with their o flesh ... Is 49:26
be drunken with their o blood ... Is 49:26
turned every one to his o way ... Is 53:6
they all look to their o way ... Is 56:11
not thyself from thine o flesh ... Is 58:7
him, not doing thine o ways ... Is 58:13
nor finding thine o pleasure ... Is 58:13
nor speaking thine o words ... Is 58:13
therefore mine o arm brought ... Is 63:5
not good, after their o thoughts ... Is 65:2
they have chosen their o ways ... Is 66:3
the works of their o hands ... Jer 1:16 249
Thine o wickedness shall correct ... Jer 2:19
your o sword hath devoured your ... Jer 2:30
to the confusion of their o faces ... Jer 7:19
the imagination of their o heart ... Jer 9:14
we will walk after our o devices ... Jer 18:12
they shall dwell in their o land ... Jer 23:8
speak a vision of their o heart ... Jer 23:16
the imagination of his o heart ... Jer 23:17
of the deceit of their o heart ... Jer 23:26

of your hands to your o hurt	Jer 25:7	
to the works of their o hands	Jer 25:14	
let remain still in their o land	Jer 27:11	
shall be builded upon her o heap	Jer 30:18	
come again to their o border	Jer 31:17	
one shall die for his o iniquity	Jer 31:30	
return to Egypt into their o land	Jer 37:7	
you to return to your o land	Jer 42:12	
your o wickedness, and the	Jer 44:9	
goeth forth out of our o mouth	Jer 44:17	
let us go again to our o people	Jer 46:16	
flee every one to his o land	Jer 50:16	
go every one into his o country	Jer 51:9	
away captive out of his o land	Jer 52:27	
have sodden their o children	Lam 4:10	
their way upon their o heads	Eze 11:21	
prophesy out of their o hearts	Eze 13:2	
that follow their o spirit	Eze 13:3	
prophesy out of their o heart	Eze 13:17	
house of Israel in their o heart	Eze 14:5	
o souls by their righteousness	Eze 14:14	
o souls by their righteousness	Eze 14:20	
thee polluted in thine o blood	Eze 16:6	
didst trust in thine o beauty	Eze 16:15	
bear thine o shame for thy sins	Eze 16:52	
thou mayest bear thine o shame	Eze 16:54	
will I recompense upon his o head	Eze 17:19	
I polluted them in their o gifts	Eze 20:26	
o sight for all your evils that	Eze 20:43	
their o way have I recompensed	Eze 22:31	
and pluck off thine o breasts	Eze 23:34	
hath said, My river is mine o	Eze 29:3	
moment, every man for his o life	Eze 32:10	
blood shall be upon his o head	Eze 33:4	
he trust to his o righteousness	Eze 33:13	
will bring them to their o land	Eze 34:13	
of Israel dwelt in their o land	Eze 36:17	
they defiled it by their o way	Eze 36:17	
will bring you into your o land	Eze 36:24	
ye remember your o evil ways	Eze 36:31	
your o sight for your iniquities	Eze 36:31	
and confounded for your o ways	Eze 36:32	
I shall place you in your o land	Eze 37:14	
and bring them into their o land	Eze 37:21	
gathered them unto their o land	Eze 39:28	
out of his o possession	Eze 46:18	
any god, except their o God	Dan 3:28	
king sealed it with his o signet	Dan 6:17	
be mighty, but not by his o power	Dan 8:24	
defer not, for thine o sake	Dan 9:19	
and shall return into his o land	Dan 11:9	
shall do according to his o will	Dan 11:16	7522
but a prince for his o behalf	Dan 11:18	
without his o reproach he shall	Dan 11:18	
toward the fort of his o land	Dan 11:19	
exploits, and return to his o land	Dan 11:28	
now their o doings have beset	Hos 7:2	
shall be ashamed of his o counsel	Hos 10:6	
them, because of their o counsels	Hos 11:6	
to their o understanding, all of	Hos 13:2	
your recompence upon your o head	Joel 3:4	
your recompence upon your o head	Joel 3:7	
to us horns by our o strength	Amos 6:13	
away captive out of their o land	Amos 7:11	
shall return upon thine o head	Obad 15	
vanities forsake their o mercy	Jonah 2:8	
are the men of his o house	Mic 7:6	
ye run every man unto his o house	Hag 1:9	
and set there upon her o base	Zec 5:11	
their o shepherds pity them not	Zec 11:5	
be inhabited again in her o place	Zec 12:6	
his o son that serveth him	Mal 3:17	
into their o country another way	Mt 2:12	
the beam that is in thine o eye	Mt 7:3	
behold, a beam is in thine o eye	Mt 7:4	
out the beam out of thine o eye	Mt 7:5	
over, and came into his o city	Mt 9:1	2398
shall be they of his o household	Mt 10:36	
he was come into his o country	Mt 13:54	
o country, and in his o house	Mt 13:57	
whole world, and lose his o soul	Mt 16:26	
of their o children, or of	Mt 17:25	
me to do what I will with mine o	Mt 20:15	
who called his o servants	Mt 25:14	2398
have received mine o with usury	Mt 25:27	
put his o raiment on him, and led	Mt 27:31	
And laid it in his o new tomb	Mt 27:60	
and came into his o country	Mk 6:1	
honour, but in his o country	Mk 6:4	
his o kin, and in his o house	Mk 6:4	
that ye may keep your o tradition	Mk 7:9	
away fasting to their o houses	Mk 8:3	
whole world, and lose his o soul	Mk 8:36	
put his o clothes on him, and led	Mk 15:20	2398
he departed to his o house	Lk 1:23	
and returned to her o house	Lk 1:56	
taxed, every one into his o city	Lk 2:3	2398
pierce through thy o soul also	Lk 2:35	
Galilee, to their o city Nazareth	Lk 2:39	
is accepted in his o country	Lk 4:24	
lay, and departed to his o house	Lk 5:25	
him a great feast in his o house	Lk 5:29	
the beam that is in thine o eye	Lk 6:41	2398
the beam that is in thine o eye	Lk 6:42	
first the beam out of thine o eye	Lk 6:42	
tree is known by his o fruit	Lk 6:44	2398
Return to thine o house, and shew	Lk 8:39	
when he shall come in his o glory	Lk 9:26	
wine, and set him on his o beast	Lk 10:34	2398
his o life also, he cannot be my	Lk 14:26	1438
give you that which is your o	Lk 16:12	
shall not God avenge his o elect	Lk 18:7	
Out of thine o mouth will I judge	Lk 19:22	
have required mine o with usury	Lk 19:23	
know of your o selves that summer	Lk 21:30	
have heard of his o mouth	Lk 22:71	1438
He came unto his o	Jn 1:11	
and his o received him not	Jn 1:11	
first findeth his o brother Simon	Jn 1:41	
believed because of his o word	Jn 4:41	
hath no honour in his o country	Jn 4:44	2398
I can of mine o self do nothing	Jn 5:30	
because I seek not mine o will	Jn 5:30	
another shall come in his o name	Jn 5:43	2398
heaven, not to do mine o will	Jn 6:38	
of himself seeketh his o glory	Jn 7:18	2398
every man went unto his o house	Jn 7:53	
convicted by their o conscience	Jn 8:9	
a lie, he speaketh of his o	Jn 8:44	2398
And I seek not mine o glory	Jn 8:50	
and he calleth his o sheep by name	Jn 10:3	2398
when he putteth forth his o sheep	Jn 10:4	2398
whose o the sheep are not, seeth	Jn 10:12	2398
having loved his o which were in	Jn 13:1	2398
world, the world would love his o	Jn 15:19	2398
be scattered, every man to his o	Jn 16:32	2398
glorify thou me with thine o self	Jn 17:5	4572
keep through thine o name those	Jn 17:11	
Thine o nation and the chief	Jn 18:35	
disciple took her unto his o home	Jn 19:27	2398
went away again unto their o home	Jn 20:10	1438
Father hath put in his o power	Acts 1:7	2398
that he might go to his o place	Acts 1:25	2398
them speak in his o language	Acts 2:6	2398
hear we every man in our o tongue	Acts 2:8	2398
as though by our o power or	Acts 3:12	2398
go, they went to their o company	Acts 4:23	2398
which he possessed was his o	Acts 4:32	2398
it remained, was it not thine o	Acts 5:4	
sold, was it not in thine o power	Acts 5:4	
and nourished him for her o son	Acts 7:21	1438
in the works of their o hands	Acts 7:41	
opened to them of his o accord	Acts 12:10	848
Jesse, a man after mine o heart	Acts 13:22	
after he had served his o	Acts 13:36	2398
nations to walk in their o ways	Acts 14:16	848
to send chosen men of their o	Acts 15:22	
also of your o poets have said	Acts 17:28	2596
Your blood be upon your o heads	Acts 18:6	
hath purchased with his o blood	Acts 20:28	2398
Also of your o selves shall men	Acts 20:30	
girdle, and bound his o hands	Acts 21:11	848
him of their o superstition	Acts 25:19	2398
among mine o nation at Jerusalem	Acts 26:4	
o hands the tackling of the ship	Acts 27:19	849
whole years in his o hired house	Acts 28:30	2398
the lusts of their o hearts	Rom 1:24	
to dishonour their o bodies	Rom 1:24	
not his o body now dead, when he	Rom 4:19	1438
God sending his o Son in the	Rom 8:3	1438
He that spared not his o Son	Rom 8:32	2398
establish their o righteousness	Rom 10:3	2398
graffed into their o olive tree	Rom 11:24	2398
should be wise in your o conceits	Rom 11:25	1438
Be not wise in your o conceits	Rom 12:16	1438
to his o master he standeth or	Rom 14:4	2398
be fully persuaded in his o mind	Rom 14:5	2398
my life laid down their o necks	Rom 16:4	1438
Jesus Christ, but their o belly	Rom 16:18	1438
I had baptized in mine o name	1Cor 1:15	
his o reward according to his o	1Cor 3:8	2398
reward according to his o labour	1Cor 3:8	2398
the wise in their o craftiness	1Cor 3:19	
yea, I judge not mine o self	1Cor 4:3	1683
labour, working with our o hands	1Cor 4:12	2398
also raise up us by his o power	1Cor 6:14	848
sinneth against his o body	1Cor 6:18	2398
have of God, and ye are not your o	1Cor 6:19	1438
let every man have his o wife	1Cor 7:2	1438
let every woman have her o husband	1Cor 7:2	2398
wife hath not power of her o body	1Cor 7:4	2398
hath not power of his o body	1Cor 7:4	2398
And this I speak for your o profit	1Cor 7:35	846
but hath power over his o will	1Cor 7:37	2398
warfare any time at his o charges	1Cor 9:7	2398
Let no man seek his o, but every	1Cor 10:24	1438
Conscience, I say, not thine o	1Cor 10:29	1438
things, not seeking mine o profit	1Cor 10:33	1683
taketh before other his o supper	1Cor 11:21	2398
unseemly, seeketh not her o	1Cor 13:5	1438
But every man in his o order	1Cor 15:23	2398
him, and to every seed his o body	1Cor 15:38	2398
of me Paul with mine o hand	1Cor 16:21	1699
are straitened in your o bowels	2Cor 6:12	
gave their o selves to the Lord	2Cor 8:5	
of his o accord he went unto you	2Cor 8:17	830
in perils by mine o countrymen	2Cor 11:26	
prove your o selves	2Cor 13:5	
Know ye not your o selves	2Cor 13:5	
many my equals in mine o nation	Gal 1:14	
have plucked out your o eyes	Gal 4:15	
let every man prove his o work	Gal 6:4	1438
every man shall bear his o burden	Gal 6:5	2398
written unto you with mine o hand	Gal 6:11	
after the counsel of his o will	Eph 1:11	848
set him at his o right hand in	Eph 1:20	848
yourselves unto your o husbands	Eph 5:22	2398
their o husbands in every thing	Eph 5:24	2398
their wives as their o bodies	Eph 5:28	1438
no man ever yet hated his o flesh	Eph 5:29	1438
not every man on his o things	Phil 2:4	1438
work out your o salvation with	Phil 2:12	1438
For all seek their o, not the	Phil 2:21	
not having mine o righteousness	Phil 3:9	1699
yourselves unto your o husbands	Col 3:18	2398
of God only, but also our o souls	1Th 2:8	1438
like things of your o countrymen	1Th 2:14	2398
their o prophets, and have	1Th 2:15	2398
quiet, and to do your o business	1Th 4:11	2398
and to work with your o hands	1Th 4:11	2398
they work, and eat their o bread	2Th 3:12	1438
of Paul with mine o hand, which	2Th 3:17	
Timothy, my o son in the faith	1Ti 1:2	1103
One that ruleth well his o house	1Ti 3:4	2398
know not how to rule his o house	1Ti 3:5	2398
children and their o houses well	1Ti 3:12	2398
But if any provide not for his o	1Ti 5:8	2398
for those of his o house, he hath	1Ti 5:8	2398
o masters worthy of all honour	1Ti 6:1	2398
but according to his o purpose	2Ti 1:9	2398
shall be lovers of their o selves	2Ti 3:2	
but after their o lusts shall	2Ti 4:3	2398
mine o son after the common faith	Titus 1:4	1103
even a prophet of their o	Titus 1:12	2398
obedient to their o husbands	Titus 2:5	2398
be obedient unto their o masters	Titus 2:9	2398
him, that is, mine o bowels	Philem 12	
have written it with mine o hand	Philem 19	
unto me even thine o self besides	Philem 19	4572
Ghost, according to his o will	Heb 2:4	
Christ as a son over his o house	Heb 3:6	848
also hath ceased from his o works	Heb 4:10	848
sacrifice, first for his o sins	Heb 7:27	2398
but by his o blood he entered in	Heb 9:12	2398
us after their o pleasure	Heb 12:10	848
the people with his o blood	Heb 13:12	2398
he is drawn away of his o lust	Jas 1:14	2398
Of his o will begat he us with	Jas 1:18	
only, deceiving your o selves	Jas 1:22	
tongue, but deceiveth his o heart	Jas 1:26	848
Who his o self bare our sins in	1Pet 2:24	848
sins in his o body on the tree	1Pet 2:24	
in subjection to your o husbands	1Pet 3:1	2398
subjection unto their o husbands	1Pet 3:5	2398
perish in their o corruption	2Pet 2:12	848
o deceivings while they feast	2Pet 2:13	848
is turned to his o vomit again	2Pet 2:22	2398
walking after their o lusts	2Pet 3:3	2398
unto their o destruction	2Pet 3:16	2398
fall from your o stedfastness	2Pet 3:17	2398
Because his o works were evil, and	1Jn 3:12	
but left their o habitation	Jude 6	2398
sea, foaming out their o shame	Jude 13	1438
walking after their o lusts	Jude 16	848
walk after their o ungodly lusts	Jude 18	1438
us from our sins in his o blood	Rev 1:5	848

OWNER

but the o of the ox shall be quit	Ex 21:28	1167
it hath been testified to his o	Ex 21:29	1167
his o also shall be put to death	Ex 21:29	1167
The o of the pit shall make it	Ex 21:34	1167
and give money unto the o of them	Ex 21:34	1167
his o hath not kept him in	Ex 21:36	1167
the o of it shall accept thereof,	Ex 22:11	1167
restitution unto the o thereof	Ex 22:12	1167
the o thereof being not with it,	Ex 22:14	1167
But if the o thereof be with it,	Ex 22:15	1167
of Shemer, o of the hill, Samaria	1Kin 16:24	113
The ox knoweth his o, and the ass	Is 1:3	7069
the o of the ship, more than	Acts 27:11	3490

OWNERS

or have caused the o thereof to	Job 31:39	1167
away the life of the o thereof	Prov 1:19	1167
good is there to the o thereof	Eccl 5:11	1167
riches kept for the o thereof to	Eccl 5:13	1167
the o thereof said unto them, Why	Lk 19:33	2962

OWNETH

he that o the house shall come and	Lev 14:35	
bind the man that o this girdle	Acts 21:11	2076

OX

nor his maidservant, nor his o	Ex 20:17	7794
If an o gore a man or a woman,	Ex 21:28	7794
then the o shall be surely stoned	Ex 21:28	7794
the owner of the o shall be quit	Ex 21:28	7794
But if the o were wont to push	Ex 21:29	7794
the o shall be stoned, and his	Ex 21:29	7794
If the o shall push a manservant	Ex 21:32	7794
silver, and the o shall be stoned	Ex 21:32	7794
an o or an ass fall therein	Ex 21:33	7794
if one man's o hurt another's,	Ex 21:35	7794
then they shall sell the live o	Ex 21:35	7794
the dead o also they shall divide	Ex 21:35	
Or if it be known that the o hath	Ex 21:36	7794
he shall surely pay o for o	Ex 21:36	7794
If a man shall steal an o	Ex 22:1	7794
shall restore five oxen for an o	Ex 22:1	7794
his hand alive, whether it be o	Ex 22:4	7794
of trespass, whether it be for o	Ex 22:9	7794
his neighbour an ass, or an o	Ex 22:10	7794
enemy's o or his ass going astray	Ex 23:4	7794
that thine o and thine ass may	Ex 23:12	7794
whether o or sheep, that is male	Ex 34:19	7794
shall eat no manner of fat, of o	Lev 7:23	7794
of Israel, that killeth an o	Lev 17:3	7794
whether it be o, or sheep	Lev 27:26	7794
the princes, and for each one an o	Num 7:3	7794
as the o licketh up the grass of	Num 22:4	7794
nor thy maidservant, nor thine o	Deut 5:14	7794
or his maidservant, his o	Deut 5:21	7794
the o, the sheep, and the goat,	Deut 14:4	7794
and the pygarg, and the wild o	Deut 14:5	8377
whether it be o or sheep	Deut 18:3	7794
o or his sheep go astray, and hide	Deut 22:1	7794
ass or his o fall down by the way	Deut 22:4	7794
Thou shalt not plow with an o	Deut 22:10	7794
Thou shalt not muzzle the o when	Deut 25:4	7794
Thine o shall be slain before	Deut 28:31	7794
young and old, and o	Josh 6:21	7794
six hundred men with an o goad	Judg 3:31	1241
for Israel, neither sheep, nor o	Judg 6:4	7794

O

whose *o* have I taken 1Sa 12:3 7794
Bring me hither every man his *o* 1Sa 14:34 7794
man his *o* with him that night 1Sa 14:34 7794
and woman, infant and suckling, *o* 1Sa 15:3 7794
prepared for me daily was one *o* Neh 5:18 7794
or loweth the *o* over his fodder Job 6:5 7794
take the widow's *o* for a pledge Job 24:3 7794
he eateth grass as an *o* Job 40:15 1241
an *o* or bullock that hath horns Ps 69:31 7794
of an *o* that eateth grass Ps 106:20 7794
as an *o* goeth to the slaughter, Prov 7:22 7794
is by the strength of the *o* Prov 14:4 7794
where love is, than a stalled *o* Prov 15:17 7794
The *o* knoweth his owner, and the Is 1:3 7794
lion shall eat straw like the *o* Is 11:7 1241
forth thither the feet of the *o* Is 32:20 7794
He that killeth an *o* is as if he Is 66:3 7794
or an *o* that is brought to the Jer 11:19 441
the face of an *o* on the left side Eze 1:10 7794
his *o* or his ass from the stall Lk 13:15 *1016*
an ass or an *o* fallen into a pit Lk 14:5 *1016*
the *o* that treadeth out the corn 1Cor 9:9 *1016*
Thou shalt not muzzle the *o* that 1Ti 5:18 *1016*

OXEN
and he had sheep, and *o*, and he Gen 12:16 1241
And Abimelech took sheep, and *o* Gen 20:14 1241
And Abraham took sheep and *o* Gen 21:27 1241
And I have *o*, and asses, flocks, and Gen 32:5 7794
They took their sheep, and their *o* Gen 34:28 1241
upon the camels, upon the *o* Ex 9:3 1241
offerings, thy sheep, and thine *o* Ex 20:24 1241
he shall restore five *o* for an ox Ex 22:1 1241
shalt thou do with thine *o* Ex 22:30 7794
offerings of *o* unto the LORD Ex 24:5 6499
six covered wagons, and twelve *o* Num 7:3 1241
And Moses took the wagons and the *o* Num 7:6 1241
four *o* he gave unto the sons of Num 7:7 1241
eight *o* he gave unto the sons of Num 7:8 1241
of peace offerings, two *o* Num 7:17 1241
of peace offerings, two *o* Num 7:23 1241
of peace offerings, two *o* Num 7:29 1241
of peace offerings, two *o* Num 7:35 1241
of peace offerings, two *o* Num 7:41 1241
of peace offerings, two *o* Num 7:47 1241
of peace offerings, two *o* Num 7:53 1241
of peace offerings, two *o* Num 7:59 1241
of peace offerings, two *o* Num 7:65 1241
of peace offerings, two *o* Num 7:71 1241
of peace offerings, two *o* Num 7:77 1241
of peace offerings, two *o* Num 7:83 1241
All the *o* for the burnt offering Num 7:87 1241
all the *o* for the sacrifice of Num 7:88 1241
And Balak offered *o* and sheep, and Num 22:40 1241
and prepare me here seven *o* Num 23:1 6499
thy soul lusteth after, for *o* Deut 14:26 1241
sons, and his daughters, and his *o* Josh 7:24 7794
And he took a yoke of *o*, and hewed 1Sa 11:7 1241
so shall it be done unto his *o* 1Sa 11:7 1241
which a yoke of *o* might plow 1Sa 14:14
the spoil, and took sheep, and *o* 1Sa 14:32 1241
best of the sheep, and of the *o* 1Sa 15:9 1241
the lowing of the *o* which I hear 1Sa 15:14 1241
the best of the sheep and of the *o* 1Sa 15:15 1241
took of the spoil, sheep and *o* 1Sa 15:21 1241
children and sucklings, and *o* 1Sa 22:19 7794
and took away the sheep, and the *o* 1Sa 27:9 1241
for the *o* shook it 2Sa 6:6 1241
gone six paces, he sacrificed *o* 2Sa 6:13 7794
here be *o* for burnt sacrifice, and 2Sa 24:22 1241
instruments of the *o* for wood 2Sa 24:22 1241
the *o* for fifty shekels of silver 2Sa 24:24 1241
And Adonijah slew sheep and *o* 1Kin 1:9 1241
And he hath slain *o* and fat cattle 1Kin 1:19 7794
down this day, and hath slain *o* 1Kin 1:25 7794
Ten fat *o*, and twenty *o* out of 1Kin 4:23 1241
It stood upon twelve *o*, three 1Kin 7:25 1241
between the ledges were lions, *o* 1Kin 7:29 1241
o were certain additions made of 1Kin 7:29 1241
sea, and twelve *o* under the sea 1Kin 7:44 1241
the ark, sacrificing sheep and *o* 1Kin 8:5 1241
LORD, two and twenty thousand *o* 1Kin 8:63 1241
with twelve yoke of *o* before him 1Kin 19:19
And he left the *o*, and ran after 1Kin 19:20 1241
from him, and took a yoke of *o* 1Kin 19:21 1241
with the instruments of the *o* 1Kin 19:21 1241
and vineyards, and sheep, and *o* 2Kin 5:26 1241
the brasen *o* that were under it 2Kin 16:17 1241
on camels, and on mules, and on *o* 1Chr 12:40 1241
of raisins, and wine, and oil, and *o* 1Chr 12:40 1241
for the *o* stumbled 1Chr 13:9 1241
I give thee the *o* also for burnt 1Chr 21:23 1241
under it was the similitude of *o* 2Chr 4:3 1241
Two rows of *o* were cast, when it 2Chr 4:3 1241
It stood upon twelve *o*, three 2Chr 4:4 1241
One sea, and twelve *o* under it 2Chr 4:15 1241
the ark, sacrificed sheep and *o* 2Chr 5:6 1241
of twenty and two thousand *o* 2Chr 7:5 1241
they had brought, seven hundred *o* 2Chr 15:11 1241
o for him in abundance, and for 2Chr 18:2 1241
things were six hundred *o* 2Chr 29:33 1241
also brought in the tithe of *o* 2Chr 31:6 1241
small cattle, and three hundred *o* 2Chr 35:8 1241
small cattle, and five hundred *o* 2Chr 35:9 1241
And so did they with the *o* 2Chr 35:12 1241
camels, and five hundred yoke of *o* Job 1:3 1241
The *o* were plowing, and the asses Job 1:14 1241
camels, and a thousand yoke of *o* Job 42:12 1241
All sheep and *o*, yea, and the Ps 8:7 504
That our *o* may be strong to Ps 144:14 441
Where no *o* are, the crib is clean Prov 14:4 5091
be for the sending forth of *o* Is 7:25 7794
behold joy and gladness, slaying *o* Is 22:13 1241
The *o* likewise and the young asses Is 30:24 504
the husbandman and his yoke of *o* Jer 51:23
shall make thee to eat grass as *o* Dan 4:25 8450
shall make thee to eat grass as *o* Dan 4:32 8450
from men, and did eat grass as *o* Dan 4:33 8450
they fed him with grass like *o* Dan 5:21 8450
will one plow there with *o* Amos 6:12 1241
my *o* and my fatlings are killed, Mt 22:4 *5022*
I have bought five yoke of *o* Lk 14:19 *1016*
in the temple those that sold *o* Jn 2:14 *1016*
temple, and the sheep, and the *o* Jn 2:15 *1016*
was before their city, brought *o* Acts 14:13 *5022*
Doth God take care for *o* 1Cor 9:9 *1016*

OZEM (*o'-zem*)
1. Son of Jesse.
O the sixth, David the seventh 1Chr 2:15 684
2. Son of Jerahmeel.
and Bunah, and Oren, and O, and 1Chr 2:25 684

OZIAS (*o-zi'-as*) See UZZIAH. *Son of Joram; ancestor of Jesus.*
and Joram begat O Mt 1:8 *3604*
And O begat Joatham Mt 1:9 *3604*

OZNI (*oz'-ni*) See OZNITES. *A son of Gad.*
Of O, the family of the Oznites Num 26:16 244

OZNITES (*oz'-nites*) *Descendants of Ozni.*
Of Ozni, the family of the O Num 26:16 244

P

PAARAI (*pa'-ar-ahee*) See NOARAI. *A "mighty man" of David.*
the Carmelite, P the Arbite, 2Sa 23:35 6474

PACATIANA (*pa-ca-she-a'-nah*) *A region of Phrygia in Asia Minor.*
is the chiefest city of Phrygia P 1Ti s *3818*

PACES
ark of the LORD had gone six *p* 2Sa 6:13 6806

PACIFIED
Then was the king's wrath *p* Est 7:10 7918
when I am *p* toward thee for all Eze 16:63 3722

PACIFIETH
A gift in secret *p* anger Prov 21:14 3711
for yielding *p* great offences Eccl 10:4 3240

PACIFY
but a wise man will *p* it Prov 16:14 3722

PADAN (*pa'-dan*) See PADAN-ARAM. *Same as Padan-aram.*
And as for me, when I came from P Gen 48:7 6307

PADAN-ARAM (*pa''-dan-a'-ram*) *The plains of Mesopotamia.*
of Bethuel the Syrian of P Gen 25:20 6307
Arise, go to P, to the house of Gen 28:2 6307
and he went to P unto Laban Gen 28:5 6307
Jacob, and sent him away to P Gen 28:6 6307
and his mother, and was gone to P Gen 28:7 6307
getting, which he had gotten in P Gen 31:18 6307
of Canaan, when he came from P Gen 33:18 6307
again, when he came out of P Gen 35:9 6307
which were born to him in P Gen 35:26 6307
which she bare unto Jacob in P Gen 46:15 6307

PADDLE
shalt have a *p* upon thy weapon Deut 23:13 3489

PADON (*pa'-don*) *A family of exiles.*
of Siaha, the children of P Ezr 2:44 6303
of Sia, the children of P Neh 7:47 6303

PAGIEL (*pa'-ghe-el*) *An Asherite who counted the people.*
P the son of Ocran Num 1:13 6295
Asher shall be P the son of Ocran Num 2:27 6295
eleventh day P the son of Ocran Num 7:72 6295
offering of P the son of Ocran Num 7:77 6295
of Asher was P the son of Ocran Num 10:26 6295

PAHATH-MOAB (*pa''-hath-mo'-ab*)
1. A family of exiles.
The children of P, of the Ezr 2:6 6355
And of the sons of P Ezr 10:30 6355
of Harim, and Hashub the son of P Neh 3:11 6355
The children of P, of the Neh 7:11 6355
2. Another family of exiles.
Of the sons of P Ezr 8:4 6355
3. A family who renewed the covenant.
Parosh, P, Elam, Zatthu, Bani, Neh 10:14 6355

PAI (*pa'-i*) See PAU. *A city in Edom.*
and the name of his city was P 1Chr 1:50 6464

PAID
and custom, was *p* unto them Ezr 4:20 3052
so he *p* the fare thereof, and went Jonah 1:3 5414
till thou hast *p* the uttermost Mt 5:26 *591*
till thou hast *p* the very last Lk 12:59 *591*

PAIN
his flesh upon him shall have *p* Job 14:22 3510
travaileth with *p* all his days Job 15:20
also with *p* upon his bed, and the Job 33:19 4341
of his bones with strong *p* Job 33:19
Look upon mine affliction and my *p* Ps 25:18 5999
took hold upon them there, and *p* Ps 48:6 2427
they shall be in *p* as a woman Is 13:8 2342
are my loins filled with *p* Is 21:3 2479
the time of her delivery, is in *p* Is 26:17 2342
with child, we have been in *p* Is 26:18 2342
before her *p* came, she was Is 66:7 2256
hath taken hold of us, and *p* Jer 6:24 2427
they have put themselves to *p* Jer 12:13 2470
Why is my *p* perpetual, and my Jer 15:18 3511
the *p* as of a woman in travail Jer 22:23 2427
it shall fall with *p* upon the Jer 30:23 2342
take balm for her *p*, if so be she Jer 51:8 4341
great *p* shall be in Ethiopia, Eze 30:4 2479
great *p* shall come upon them, as Eze 30:9 2479
Sin shall have great *p*, and No Eze 30:16 2342
Be in *p*, and labour to bring forth Mic 4:10 2342
much *p* is in all loins, and the Nah 2:10 2479
travaileth in *p* together until Rom 8:22
they gnawed their tongues for *p* Rev 16:10 *4192*
neither shall there be any more *p* Rev 21:4 *4192*

PAINED
My heart is sore *p* within me Ps 55:4 2342
be sorely *p* at the report of Tyre Is 23:5 2342
I am *p* at my very heart Jer 4:19 3176
face the people shall be much *p* Joel 2:6 2342
in birth, and *p* to be delivered Rev 12:2 *928*

PAINFUL
to know this, it was too *p* for me Ps 73:16 5999

PAINFULNESS
In weariness and *p*, in watchings 2Cor 11:27 *3449*

PAINS
for her *p* came upon her 1Sa 4:19 6735
the *p* of hell gat hold upon me Ps 116:3 4712
up, having loosed the *p* of death Acts 2:24 *5604*
God of heaven because of their *p* Rev 16:11 *4192*

PAINTED
she *p* her face, and tired her head 2Kin 9:30
with cedar, and *p* with vermilion Jer 22:14 4886

PAINTEDST
p thy eyes, and deckedst thyself Eze 23:40 3583

PAINTING
thou rentest thy face with *p* Jer 4:30 6320

PAIR
and the poor for a *p* of shoes Amos 2:6
and the needy for a *p* of shoes Amos 8:6
A *p* of turtledoves, or two young Lk 2:24 *2201*
had a *p* of balances in his hand Rev 6:5 *2218*

PALACE
into the *p* of the king's house 1Kin 16:18 759
hard by the *p* of Ahab king of 1Kin 21:1 1964
in the *p* of the king's house, 2Kin 15:25 759
in the *p* of the king of Babylon 2Kin 20:18 1964
for the *p* is not for man, but for 1Chr 29:1 1002
these things, and to build the *p* 1Chr 29:19 1002
of the LORD, and to the king's *p* 2Chr 9:11 1004
maintenance from the king's *p* Ezr 4:14 1964
in the *p* that is in the province Ezr 6:2 1002
year, as I was in Shushan the *p* Neh 1:1 1002
p which appertained to the house Neh 2:8 1002
and Hananiah the ruler of the *p* Neh 7:2 1002
which was in Shushan the *p* Est 1:2 1002
were present in Shushan the *p* Est 1:5 1002
of the garden of the king's *p* Est 1:5 1055
young virgins unto Shushan the *p* Est 2:3 1002
Now in Shushan the *p* there was a Est 2:5 1002
together unto Shushan the *p* Est 2:8 1002
decree was given in Shushan the *p* Est 3:15 1002
his wrath went into the *p* garden Est 7:7 1055
p garden into the place of the Est 7:8 1055
decree was given at Shushan the *p* Est 8:14 1002
And in Shushan the *p* the Jews slew Est 9:6 1002
the *p* was brought before the king Est 9:11 1002
five hundred men in Shushan the *p* Est 9:12 1002
shall enter into the king's *p* Ps 45:15 1964
after the similitude of a *p* Ps 144:12 1964
will build upon her a *p* of silver Song 8:9 2918
a *p* of strangers to be no city Is 25:2 759
in the *p* of the king of Babylon Is 39:7 1964
the *p* shall remain after the Jer 30:18 759
in them to stand in the king's *p* Dan 1:4 1964
house, and flourishing in my *p* Dan 4:4 1965
the *p* of the kingdom of Babylon Dan 4:29 1965
of the wall of the king's *p* Dan 5:5 1965
Then the king went to his *p* Dan 6:18 1965
that I was at Shushan in the *p* Dan 8:2 1002
of his *p* between the seas in the Dan 11:45 643
and ye shall cast them into the *p* Amos 4:3 2038
and the *p* shall be dissolved Nah 2:6 1964

unto the *p* of the high priest, Mt 26:3 833
afar off unto the high priest's *p* Mt 26:58 833
Now Peter sat without in the *p* Mt 26:69 833
even into the *p* of the high Mk 14:54 833
And as Peter was beneath in the *p* Mk 14:66 833
a strong man armed keepeth his *p* Lk 11:21 833
into the *p* of the high priest Jn 18:15 833
Christ are manifest in all the *p* Phil 1:13 4232

PALACES
burnt all the *p* thereof with fire 2Chr 36:19 759
and cassia, out of the ivory *p* Ps 45:8 1964
is known in her *p* for a refuge Ps 48:3 759
well her bulwarks, consider her *p* Ps 48:13 759
built his sanctuary like high *p* Ps 78:69 759
walls, and prosperity within thy *p* Ps 122:7 759
with her hands, and is in kings' *p* Prov 30:28 1964
and dragons in their pleasant *p* Is 13:22 1964
they raised up the *p* thereof Is 23:13 759
Because the *p* shall be forsaken Is 32:14 759
And thorns shall come up in her *p* Is 34:13 759
by night, and let us destroy her *p* Jer 6:5 759
windows, and is entered into our *p* Jer 9:21 759
shall devour the *p* of Jerusalem Jer 17:27 759
shall consume the *p* of Ben-hadad Jer 49:27 759
he hath swallowed up all her *p* Lam 2:5 759
of the enemy the walls of her *p* Lam 2:7 759
And he knew their desolate *p* Eze 19:7 759
and they shall set their *p* in thee Eze 25:4 2918
and it shall devour the *p* thereof Hos 8:14 759
shall devour the *p* of Ben-hadad Amos 1:4 759
which shall devour the *p* thereof Amos 1:7 759
which shall devour the *p* thereof Amos 1:10 759
shall devour the *p* of Bozrah Amos 1:12 759
and it shall devour the *p* thereof Amos 1:14 759
it shall devour the *p* of Kirioth Amos 2:2 759
shall devour the *p* of Jerusalem Amos 2:5 759
Publish in the *p* at Ashdod Amos 3:9 759
in the *p* in the land of Egypt, and Amos 3:9 759
up violence and robbery in their *p* Amos 3:10 759
thee, and thy *p* shall be spoiled Amos 3:11 759
of Jacob, and hate his *p* Amos 6:8 759
and when he shall tread in our *p* Mic 5:5 759

PALAL (*pa'-lal*) *A rebuilder of Jerusalem's wall.*
P the son of Uzai, over against Neh 3:25 6420

PALE
neither shall his face now wax *p* Is 29:22 2357
And I looked, and behold a *p* horse Rev 6:8 5515

PALENESS
and all faces are turned into *p* Jer 30:6 3420

PALESTINA (*pal-es-ti'-nah*) See PALESTINE, PHILISTIA. *The west coast of Canaan.*
take hold on the inhabitants of *P* Ex 15:14 6429
Rejoice not thou, whole *P* Is 14:29 6429
thou, whole *P*, art dissolved Is 14:31 6429

PALESTINE (*pal'-es-tine*) See PALESTINA. *Same as Palestina.*
and Zidon, and all the coasts of *P* Joel 3:4 6429

PALLU (*pal'-lu*) See PALLUITES, PHALLU. *A son of Reuben.*
Hanoch, and *P*, Hezron, and Carmi Ex 6:14 6396
of *P*, the family of the Palluites Num 26:5 6396
And the sons of *P* Num 26:8 6396
of Israel were, Hanoch, and *P* 1Chr 5:3 6396

PALLUITES (*pal'-lu-ites*) *Descendants of Pallu.*
of Pallu, the family of the *P* Num 26:5 6384

PALM
and threescore and ten *p* trees Ex 15:27 8558
pour it into the *p* of his own Lev 14:15 3709
into the *p* of his own left hand Lev 14:26 3709
goodly trees, branches of *p* trees Lev 23:40 8558
and threescore and ten *p* trees Num 33:9 8558
of Jericho, the city of *p* trees Deut 34:3 8558
of *p* trees with the children of Judg 1:16 8558
and possessed the city of *p* trees Judg 3:13 8558
she dwelt under the *p* tree of Judg 4:5 8560
p trees and open flowers, within 1Kin 6:29 8561
p trees and open flowers, and 1Kin 6:32 8561
cherubims, and upon the *p* trees 1Kin 6:32 8561
and *p* trees and open flowers 1Kin 6:35 8561
p trees, according to the 1Kin 7:36 8561
fine gold, and set thereon *p* trees 2Chr 3:5 8561
to Jericho, the city of *p* trees 2Chr 28:15 8558
p branches, and branches of thick Neh 8:15 8558
shall flourish like the *p* tree Ps 92:12 8558
thy stature is like to a *p* tree Song 7:7 8558
said, I will go up to the *p* tree Song 7:8 8558
They are upright as the *p* tree Jer 10:5 8560
and upon each post were *p* trees Eze 40:16 8561
and their arches, and their *p* trees Eze 40:22 8561
and it had *p* trees, one on this Eze 40:26 8561
p trees were upon the posts Eze 40:31 8561
p trees were upon the posts Eze 40:34 8561
p trees were upon the posts Eze 40:37 8561
toward the *p* tree on the one side Eze 41:19 8561
the *p* tree on the other side Eze 41:19 8561
p trees made, and on the wall of Eze 41:20 8561
p trees, like as were made upon Eze 41:25 8561
p trees on the one side and on the Eze 41:26 8561
the *p* tree also, and the apple Joel 1:12 8558
Took branches of *p* trees, and went Jn 12:13 5404
Jesus with the *p* of his hand Jn 18:22 4475

PALMERWORM
That which the *p* hath left hath Joel 1:4 1501
and the caterpiller, and the *p* Joel 2:25 1501
increased, the *p* devoured them Amos 4:9 1501

PALMS
both the *p* of his hands were cut 1Sa 5:4 3709
the feet, and the *p* of her hands 2Kin 9:35 3709
thee upon the *p* of my hands Is 49:16 3709
knees and upon the *p* of my hands Dan 10:10 3709
him with the *p* of their hands Mt 26:67 4474
him with the *p* of their hands Mk 14:65 4475
white robes, and *p* in their hands Rev 7:9 5404

PALSIES
and many taken with *p*, and that Acts 8:7 3886

PALSY
lunatick, and those that had the *p* Mt 4:24 3885
lieth at home sick of the *p* Mt 8:6 3885
to him a man sick of the *p* Mt 9:2 3885
faith said unto the sick of the *p* Mt 9:2 3885
saith he to the sick of the *p* Mt 9:6 3885
him, bringing one sick of the *p* Mk 2:3 3885
bed wherein the sick of the *p* lay Mk 2:4 3885
he said unto the sick of the *p* Mk 2:5 3885
to say to the sick of the *p* Mk 2:9 3885
(he saith to the sick of the *p* Mk 2:10 3885
a man which was taken with a *p* Lk 5:18 3886
(he said unto the sick of the *p* Lk 5:24 3886
eight years, and was sick of the *p* Acts 9:33 3886

PALTI (*pal'-ti*) *A spy sent to the Promised Land.*
of Benjamin, *P* the son of Raphu Num 13:9 6406

PALTIEL (*pal'-te-el*) See PHALTIEL. *A chief of Issachar.*
of Issachar, *P* the son of Azzan Num 34:26 6409

PALTITE (*pal'-tite*) See PELONITE. *A resident of Beth-palet.*
Helez the *P*, Ira the son of 2Sa 23:26 6407

PAMPHYLIA (*pam-fil'-e-ah*) *A province of Asia Minor.*
Phrygia, and *P*, in Egypt, and in Acts 2:10 3828
Paphos, they came to Perga in *P* Acts 13:13 3828
Pisidia, they came to *P* Acts 14:24 3828
who departed from them from *P* Acts 15:38 3828
over the sea of Cilicia and *P* Acts 27:5 3828

PAN
be a meat offering baken in a *p* Lev 2:5 4227
offering baken in the frying *p* Lev 2:7 4227
In a *p* it shall be made with oil Lev 6:21 4227
in the fryingpan, and in the *p* Lev 7:9 4227
And he struck it into the *p* 1Sa 2:14 3595
And she took a *p*, and poured them 2Sa 13:9 4958
for that which is baked in the *p* 1Chr 23:29 4227
take thou unto thee an iron *p* Eze 4:3 4227

PANGS
p and sorrows shall take hold of Is 13:8 6735
p have taken hold upon me, as the Is 21:3 6735
upon me, as the *p* of a woman that Is 21:3 6735
in pain, and crieth out in her *p* Is 26:17 2256
thou be when *p* come upon thee Jer 22:23 2256
as the heart of a woman in her *p* Jer 48:41 6887
as the heart of a woman in her *p* Jer 49:22 6887
p as of a woman in travail Jer 50:43 2427
for *p* have taken thee as a woman Mic 4:9 2427

PANNAG (*pan'-nag*) *A place on the Damascus-Baalbeck road.*
thy market wheat of Minnith, and *P* Eze 27:17 6436

PANS
thou shalt make his *p* to receive Ex 27:3 5518
it in a mortar, and baked it in *p* Num 11:8 6517
things that were made in the *p* 1Chr 9:31 2281
in pots, and in caldrons, and in *p* 2Chr 35:13 6745

PANT
That *p* after the dust of the Amos 2:7 7602

PANTED
I opened my mouth, and *p* Ps 119:131 7602
My heart *p*, fearfulness Is 21:4 8582

PANTETH
My heart *p*, my strength faileth Ps 38:10 5503
As the hart *p* after the water Ps 42:1 6165
so *p* my soul after thee, O God Ps 42:1 6165

PAPER
The *p* reeds by the brooks, by the Is 19:7 6169
you, I would not write with *p* 2Jn 12 5489

PAPHOS (*pa'-fos*) *Capital of Cyprus.*
had gone through the isle unto *P* Acts 13:6 3974
Paul and his company loosed from *P* Acts 13:13 3974

PAPS
Egyptians for the *p* of thy youth Eze 23:21 7699
the *p* which thou hast sucked Lk 11:27 3149
the *p* which never gave suck Lk 23:29 3149
girt about the *p* with a golden Rev 1:13 3149

PARABLE
And he took up his *p*, and said, Num 23:7 4912
And he took up his *p*, and said, Num 23:18 4912
And he took up his *p*, and said, Num 24:3 4912
And he took up his *p*, and said, Num 24:15 4912
on Amalek, he took up his *p* Num 24:20 4912
on the Kenites, and took up his *p* Num 24:21 4912
And he took up his *p*, and said, Num 24:23 4912
Moreover Job continued his *p* Job 27:1 4912
Moreover Job continued his *p* Job 29:1 4912
I will incline mine ear to a *p* Ps 49:4 4912
I will open my mouth in a *p* Ps 78:2 4912
so is a *p* in the mouth of fools Prov 26:7 4912
so is a *p* in the mouth of fools Prov 26:9 4912
speak a *p* unto the house of Eze 17:2 4912
utter a *p* unto the rebellious Eze 24:3 4912
shall one take up a *p* against you Mic 2:4 4912
all these take up a *p* against him Hab 2:6 4912
ye therefore the *p* of the sower Mt 13:18 3850
Another *p* put he forth unto them, Mt 13:24 3850
Another *p* put he forth unto them, Mt 13:31 3850
Another *p* spake he unto them Mt 13:33 3850
without a *p* spake he not unto Mt 13:34 3850
Declare unto us the *p* of the Mt 13:36 3850
unto him, Declare unto us this *p* Mt 15:15 3850
Hear another *p* Mt 21:33 3850
Now learn a *p* of the fig tree Mt 24:32 3850
the twelve asked of him the *p* Mk 4:10 3850
unto them, Know ye not this *p* Mk 4:13 3850
But without a *p* spake he not unto Mk 4:34 3850
asked him concerning the *p* Mk 7:17 3850
he had spoken the *p* against them Mk 12:12 3850
Now learn a *p* of the fig tree Mk 13:28 3850
And he spake also a *p* unto them Lk 5:36 3850
And he spake a *p* unto them Lk 6:39 3850
of every city, he spake by a *p* Lk 8:4 3850
him, saying, What might this *p* be Lk 8:9 3850
Now the *p* is this Lk 8:11 3850
And he spake a *p* unto them Lk 12:16 3850
speakest thou this *p* unto us Lk 12:41 3850
He spake also this *p* Lk 13:6 3850
he put forth a *p* to those which Lk 14:7 3850
And he spake this *p* unto them Lk 15:3 3850
he spake a *p* unto them to this Lk 18:1 3850
he spake this *p* unto certain Lk 18:9 3850
things, he added and spake a *p* Lk 19:11 3850
he to speak to the people this *p* Lk 20:9 3850
he had spoken this *p* against them Lk 20:19 3850
And he spake to them a *p* Lk 21:29 3850
This *p* spake Jesus unto them Jn 10:6 3942

PARABLES
say of me, Doth he not speak *p* Eze 20:49 4912
spake many things unto them in *p* Mt 13:3 3850
Why speakest thou unto them in *p* Mt 13:10 3850
Therefore speak I to them in *p* Mt 13:13 3850
Jesus unto the multitude in *p* Mt 13:34 3850
saying, I will open my mouth in *p* Mt 13:35 3850
when Jesus had finished these *p* Mt 13:53 3850
and Pharisees had heard his *p* Mt 21:45 3850
and spake unto them again by *p* Mt 22:1 3850
unto him, and said unto them in *p* Mk 3:23 3850
he taught them many things by *p* Mk 4:2 3850
all these things are done in *p* Mk 4:11 3850
and how then will ye know all *p* Mk 4:13 3850
with many such *p* spake he the Mk 4:33 3850
he began to speak unto them by *p* Mk 12:1 3850
but to others in *p* Lk 8:10 3850

PARADISE
To day shalt thou be with me in *p* Lk 23:43 3857
How that he was caught up into *p* 2Cor 12:4 3857
is in the midst of the *p* of God Rev 2:7 3857

PARAH (*pa'-rah*) *A city in Benjamin.*
And Avim, and *P*, and Ophrah, Josh 18:23 6511

PARAMOURS
For she doted upon their *p* Eze 23:20 6370

PARAN (*pa'-ran*) *A wilderness south of Canaan.*
he dwelt in the wilderness of *P* Gen 21:21 6290
rested in the wilderness of *P* Num 10:12 6290
and pitched in the wilderness of *P* Num 12:16 6290
them from the wilderness of *P* Num 13:3 6290
Israel, unto the wilderness of *P* Num 13:26 6290
against the Red sea, between *P* Deut 1:1 6290
he shined forth from mount *P* Deut 33:2 6290
went down to the wilderness of *P* 1Sa 25:1 6290
arose out of Midian, and came to *P* 1Kin 11:18 6290
they took men with them out of *P* 1Kin 11:18 6290
and the Holy One from mount *P* Hab 3:3 6290

PARBAR (*par'-bar*) *A place near the Temple in Jerusalem.*
At *P* westward, four at the 1Chr 26:18 6503
four at the causeway, and two at *P* 1Chr 26:18 6503

PARCEL
And he bought a *p* of a field Gen 33:19 2513
in a *p* of ground which Jacob Josh 24:32 2513
of Moab, selleth a *p* of land Ruth 4:3 2513
where was a *p* of ground full of 1Chr 11:13 2513
themselves in the midst of that *p* 1Chr 11:14 2513
near to the *p* of ground that Jn 4:5 5564

PARCHED
nor *p* corn, nor green ears, until Lev 23:14 7039
p corn in the selfsame day Josh 5:11
and he reached her *p* corn, and she Ruth 2:14 7039
brethren an ephah of this *p* corn 1Sa 17:17 7039
and five measures of *p* corn 1Sa 25:18 7039
p corn, and beans, and lentiles, and 2Sa 17:28 7039
beans, and lentiles, and *p* pulse, 2Sa 17:28 7039
the *p* ground shall become a pool, Is 35:7 8273
but shall inhabit the *p* places in Jer 17:6 2788

PARCHMENTS
the books, but especially the *p* 2Ti 4:13 3200

PARDON
for he will not *p* your Ex 23:21 5375
p our iniquity and our sin, and Ex 34:9 5545
P, I beseech thee, the iniquity Num 14:19 5545
p my sin, and turn again with me, 1Sa 15:25 5375
this thing the LORD *p* thy servant 2Kin 5:18 5545
the LORD *p* thy servant in this 2Kin 5:18 5545
which the LORD would not *p* 2Kin 24:4 5545
saying, The good LORD *p* every one 2Chr 30:18 3722
but thou art a God ready to *p* Neh 9:17 5547
dost thou not *p* my transgression Job 7:21 5375
sake, O LORD, *p* mine iniquity Ps 25:11 5545
our God, for he will abundantly *p* Is 55:7 5545
and I will *p* it Jer 5:1 5545
How shall I *p* thee for this Jer 5:7 5545
I will *p* all their iniquities, Jer 33:8 5545
for I will *p* them whom I reserve Jer 50:20 5545

PARDONED
I have p according to thy word ... Num 14:20 5545
that her iniquity is p ... Is 40:2 7521
thou hast not p ... Lam 3:42 5545

PARDONETH
that p iniquity, and passeth by ... Mic 7:18 5375

PARE
shave her head, and p her nails ... Deut 21:12 6213

PARENTS
shall rise up against their p ... Mt 10:21 *1118*
shall rise up against their p ... Mk 13:12 *1118*
when the p brought in the child ... Lk 2:27 *1118*
Now his p went to Jerusalem every ... Lk 2:41 *1118*
And her p were astonished ... Lk 8:56 *1118*
no man that hath left house, or p ... Lk 18:29 *1118*
And ye shall be betrayed both by p ... Lk 21:16 *1118*
who did sin, this man, or his p ... Jn 9:2 *1118*
hath this man sinned, nor his p ... Jn 9:3 *1118*
until they called the p of him ... Jn 9:18 *1118*
His p answered them and said, We ... Jn 9:20 *1118*
These words spake his p, because ... Jn 9:22 *1118*
Therefore said his p, He is of ... Jn 9:23 *1118*
of evil things, disobedient to p ... Rom 1:30 *1118*
ought not to lay up for the p ... 2Cor 12:14 *1118*
but the p for the children ... 2Cor 12:14 *1118*
Children, obey your p in the Lord ... Eph 6:1 *1118*
obey your p in all things ... Col 3:20 *1118*
at home, and to requite their p ... 1Ti 5:4 *4269*
blasphemers, disobedient to p ... 2Ti 3:2 *1118*
was hid three months of his p ... Heb 11:23 *3962*

PARLOUR
and he was sitting in a summer p ... Judg 3:20 5944
shut the doors of the p upon him ... Judg 3:23 5944
the doors of the p were locked ... Judg 3:24 5944
he opened not the doors of the p ... Judg 3:25 5944
and brought them into the p ... 1Sa 9:22 3957

PARLOURS
and of the inner p thereof ... 1Chr 28:11 2315

PARMASHTA (*par-mash'-tah*) *A son of Haman.*
And P, and Arisai, and Aridai, and ... Est 9:9 6534

PARMENAS (*par'-me-nas*) *A leader in the Jerusalem church.*
and Nicanor, and Timon, and P ... Acts 6:5 *3937*

PARNACH (*par'-nak*) *A Zebulunite who apportioned the Promised Land.*
Zebulun, Elizaphan the son of P ... Num 34:25 6535

PAROSH (*pa'-rosh*) See PHAROSH.
1. A family of exiles.
The children of P, two thousand ... Ezr 2:3 6551
The children of P, two thousand ... Neh 7:8 6551
2. Married a foreigner in exile.
of the sons of P ... Ezr 10:25 6551
3. Father of Pedaiah.
After him Pedaiah the son of P ... Neh 3:25 6551
4. A family who renewed the covenant.
P, Pahath-moab, Elam, Zatthu, ... Neh 10:14 6551

PARSHANDATHA (*par-shan'-da-thah*) *A son of Haman.*
And P, and Dalphon, and Aspatha, ... Est 9:7 6577

PART
take up the fifth p of the land ... Gen 41:34
give the fifth p unto Pharaoh ... Gen 47:24
Pharaoh should have the fifth p ... Gen 47:26
omer is the tenth p of an ephah ... Ex 16:36
at the nether p of the mount ... Ex 19:17
and it shall be thy p ... Ex 29:26 4490
fourth p of an hin of beaten oil ... Ex 29:40
the fourth p of an hin of wine ... Ex 29:40
it beside the altar on the east p ... Lev 1:16
Thou shalt p it in pieces, and ... Lev 2:6 6626
p of the beaten corn thereof, and ... Lev 2:16
p of the oil thereof, with all ... Lev 2:16
for his offering the tenth p of ... Lev 5:11
and shall add the fifth p thereto ... Lev 5:16
add the fifth p more thereto ... Lev 6:5
the tenth p of an ephah of fine ... Lev 6:20
have the right shoulder for his p ... Lev 7:33 4940
of consecration it was Moses' p ... Lev 8:29 4940
every thing whereupon any p of ... Lev 11:35
if any p of their carcase fall ... Lev 11:37
any p of their carcase fall ... Lev 11:38
the p of his head toward his face ... Lev 13:41
put the fifth p thereof unto it ... Lev 22:14
be of wine, the fourth p of a hin ... Lev 23:13
then he shall add a fifth p ... Lev 27:13
then he shall add the fifth p of ... Lev 27:15
sanctify unto the LORD some p of ... Lev 27:16
then he shall add the fifth p of ... Lev 27:19
shall add a fifth p of it thereto ... Lev 27:27
add thereto the fifth p thereof ... Lev 27:31
add unto it the fifth p thereof ... Num 5:7
the tenth p of an ephah of barley ... Num 5:15
the fourth p of an hin of oil ... Num 15:4
the fourth p of an hin of wine ... Num 15:5
with the third p of an hin of oil ... Num 15:6
the third p of an hin of wine ... Num 15:7
shalt thou have any p among them ... Num 18:20 2506
I am thy p and thine inheritance ... Num 18:20 2506
LORD, even a tenth p of the tithe ... Num 18:26
the hallowed p thereof out of it ... Num 18:29
see the utmost p of the people ... Num 22:41
number of the fourth p of Israel ... Num 23:10
see but the utmost p of them ... Num 23:13
a tenth p of an ephah of flour ... Num 28:5
fourth p of an hin of beaten oil ... Num 28:5
p of an hin for the one lamb ... Num 28:7
the third p of an hin unto a ram, ... Num 28:14
a fourth p of an hin unto a lamb ... Num 28:14
Wherefore Levi hath no p nor ... Deut 10:9 2506
forasmuch as he hath no p nor ... Deut 12:12 2506
for he hath no p nor inheritance ... Deut 14:27 2506
(because he hath no p nor ... Deut 14:29 2506
shall have no p nor inheritance ... Deut 18:1 2506
provided the first p for himself ... Deut 33:21
therefore they gave no p unto the ... Josh 14:4 2506
uttermost p of the south coast ... Josh 15:1
sea at the uttermost p of Jordan ... Josh 15:5
a p among the children of Judah ... Josh 15:13 2506
the Levites have no p among you ... Josh 18:7 2506
for the p of the children of ... Josh 19:9 2506
ye have no p in the LORD ... Josh 22:25 2506
to come, Ye have no p in the LORD ... Josh 22:27 2506
also, if ought but death p thee ... Ruth 1:17 6504
her hap was to light on a p of ... Ruth 2:3 2513
unto thee the p of a kinsman ... Ruth 3:13
let him do the kinsman's p ... Ruth 3:13
not do the p of a kinsman to thee ... Ruth 3:13
then will I do the p of a kinsman ... Ruth 3:13
fourth p of a shekel of silver ... 1Sa 9:8
p of Gibeah under a pomegranate ... 1Sa 14:2
our p shall be to deliver him ... 1Sa 23:20
but as his p is that goeth down ... 1Sa 30:24 2506
so shall his p be that tarrieth ... 1Sa 30:24 2506
they shall p alike ... 1Sa 30:24 2505
and there was none to p them ... 2Sa 14:6 5337
David sent forth a third p of the ... 2Sa 18:2
a third p under the hand of ... 2Sa 18:2
a third p under the hand of Ittai ... 2Sa 18:2
and said, We have no p in David ... 2Sa 20:1 2506
from the uttermost p of the one ... 1Kin 6:24
p of the other were ten cubits ... 1Kin 6:24
posts were a fifth p of the wall ... 1Kin 6:31
tree, a fourth p of the wall ... 1Kin 6:33
the fourth p of a cab of dove's ... 2Kin 6:25
uttermost p of the camp of Syria ... 2Kin 7:5
to the uttermost p of the camp ... 2Kin 7:8
A third p of you that enter in on ... 2Kin 11:5
a third p shall be at the gate of ... 2Kin 11:6
a third p at the gate behind the ... 2Kin 11:6
if thou be able on thy p to set ... 2Kin 18:23
for hitherto the greatest p of ... 1Chr 12:29
A third p of you entering on the ... 2Chr 23:4
a third p shall be at the king's ... 2Chr 23:5
a third p at the gate of the ... 2Chr 23:5
inner p of the house of the LORD ... 2Chr 29:16
the uttermost p of the heaven ... Neh 1:9
ruler of the half p of Jerusalem ... Neh 3:9 6418
ruler of the half p of Jerusalem ... Neh 3:12 6418
the ruler of p of Beth-haccerem ... Neh 3:14 6418
the ruler of p of Mizpah ... Neh 3:15 6418
ruler of the half p of Beth-zur ... Neh 3:16 6418
the half p of Keilah, in his p ... Neh 3:17 6418
the ruler of the half p of Keilah ... Neh 3:18 6418
also the hundredth p of the money ... Neh 5:11
their God one fourth p of the day ... Neh 9:3
another fourth p they confessed ... Neh 9:3
p of a shekel for the service of ... Neh 10:32
I said, I will answer also my p ... Job 32:17 2506
shall they p him among the ... Job 41:6 2673
their inward p is very wickedness ... Ps 5:9
They p my garments among ... Ps 22:18 2505
in the hidden p thou shalt make ... Ps 51:6
The LORD taketh my p with them ... Ps 118:7
nor the highest p of the dust of ... Prov 8:26
in the habitable p of his earth ... Prov 8:31
shall have p of the inheritance ... Prov 17:2 2505
p of the rivers of Egypt, and for ... Is 7:18
From the uttermost p of the earth ... Is 24:16
If thou be able on thy p to set ... Is 36:8
He burneth p thereof in the fire ... Is 44:16 2677
with p thereof he eateth flesh ... Is 44:16 2677
I have burned p of it in the fire ... Is 44:19 2677
by measure, the sixth p of an hin ... Eze 4:11
third p in the midst of the city ... Eze 5:2
and thou shalt take a third p ... Eze 5:2
a third p thou shalt scatter in ... Eze 5:2
A third p of thee shall die with ... Eze 5:12
a third p shall fall by the sword ... Eze 5:12
a third p into all the winds ... Eze 5:12
and leave but the sixth p of thee ... Eze 39:2
contain the tenth p of an homer ... Eze 45:11
the ephah the tenth p of an homer ... Eze 45:11
the sixth p of an ephah of an ... Eze 45:13
ye shall give the sixth p of an ... Eze 45:13
tenth p of a bath out of the cor ... Eze 45:14
p to give burnt offerings ... Eze 45:17
the sixth p of an ephah, and the ... Eze 46:14
the third p of an hin of oil, to ... Eze 46:14
with p of the vessels of the ... Dan 1:2 7117
feet p of iron and p of clay ... Dan 2:33 4481
p of potters' clay ... Dan 2:41 4481
p of iron, the kingdom shall be ... Dan 2:41 4481
toes of the feet were p of iron ... Dan 2:42 4481
p of clay, so the kingdom shall ... Dan 2:42 4481
the king saw the p of the hand ... Dan 5:5 6447
Then was the p of the hand sent ... Dan 5:24 6447
And arms shall stand on his p ... Dan 11:31 2506
his hinder p toward the utmost ... Joel 2:20
the great deep, and did eat up a p ... Amos 7:4 2506
the third p through the fire ... Zec 13:9
was in the hinder p of the ship ... Mk 4:38
is not against us is on our p ... Mk 9:40
from the uttermost p of the earth ... Mk 13:27
to the uttermost p of heaven ... Mk 13:27
and Mary hath chosen that good p ... Lk 10:42 *3310*
full of light, having no p dark ... Lk 11:36 *3313*
but your inward p is full of ... Lk 11:39
out of the one p under heaven ... Lk 17:24
unto the other p under heaven ... Lk 17:24
thee not, thou hast no p with me ... Jn 13:8 *3313*
four parts, to every soldier a p ... Jn 19:23 *3313*
unto the uttermost p of the earth ... Acts 1:8
had obtained p of this ministry ... Acts 1:17 *2819*
he may take p of this ministry ... Acts 1:25 *2819*
kept back p of the price, his ... Acts 5:2
to it, and brought a certain p ... Acts 5:2 *3313*
to keep back p of the price of ... Acts 5:3
Thou hast neither p nor lot in ... Acts 8:21 *3310*
p held with the Jews ... Acts 14:4
and p with the apostles ... Acts 14:4
chief city of that p of Macedonia ... Acts 16:12 *3310*
the more p knew not wherefore ... Acts 19:32
that the one p were Sadducees ... Acts 23:6 *3313*
were of the Pharisees' p arose ... Acts 23:9 *3313*
the more p advised to depart ... Acts 27:12
but the hinder p was broken with ... Acts 27:41 *4403*
that blindness in p is happened ... Rom 11:25 *3313*
honour to that p which lacked ... 1Cor 12:24
For we know in p, and we prophesy ... 1Cor 13:9 *3313*
know in p, and we prophesy in p ... 1Cor 13:9 *3313*
which is in p shall be done away ... 1Cor 13:10 *3313*
now I know in p ... 1Cor 13:12 *3313*
of whom the greater p remain unto ... 1Cor 15:6 *4119*
on your p they have supplied ... 1Cor 16:17
also ye have acknowledged us in p ... 2Cor 1:14 *3313*
he hath not grieved me, but in p ... 2Cor 2:5 *3313*
or what p hath he that believeth ... 2Cor 6:15 *3310*
working in the measure of every p ... Eph 4:16 *3313*
of the contrary p may be ashamed ... Titus 2:8
likewise took p of the same ... Heb 2:14 *3348*
Abraham gave a tenth p of all ... Heb 7:2 *3307*
on their p he is evil spoken of, ... 1Pet 4:14
but on your p he is glorified ... 1Pet 4:14
over the fourth p of the earth ... Rev 6:8
the third p of trees was burnt up ... Rev 8:7 *3310*
the third p of the sea became ... Rev 8:8
the third p of the creatures ... Rev 8:9
the third p of the ships were ... Rev 8:9
upon the third p of the rivers ... Rev 8:10
the third p of the waters became ... Rev 8:11
the third p of the sun was ... Rev 8:12
the third p of the moon, and the ... Rev 8:12
moon, and the third p of the stars ... Rev 8:12
so as the third p of them was ... Rev 8:12
day shone not for a third p of it ... Rev 8:12
for to slay the third p of men ... Rev 9:15
was the third p of men killed ... Rev 9:18
the tenth p of the city fell, and ... Rev 11:13
third p of the stars of heaven ... Rev 12:4
holy is he that hath p in the ... Rev 20:6 *3313*
shall have their p in the lake ... Rev 21:8 *3313*
his p out of the book of life ... Rev 22:19 *3313*

PARTAKER
hast been p with adulterers ... Ps 50:18 2506
in hope should be p of his hope ... 1Cor 9:10 *3348*
that I might be p thereof with ... 1Cor 9:23 *4791*
For if I by grace be a p, why am ... 1Cor 10:30 *3348*
neither be p of other men's sins ... 1Ti 5:22 *2841*
but be thou p of the afflictions ... 2Ti 1:8 *4777*
must be first p of the fruits ... 2Ti 2:6 *3335*
also a p of the glory that shall ... 1Pet 5:1 *2844*
God speed is p of his evil deeds ... 2Jn 11 *2841*

PARTAKERS
we would not have been p with ... Mt 23:30 *2844*
made p of their spiritual things ... Rom 15:27 *2841*
If others be p of this power over ... 1Cor 9:12 *3348*
at the altar are p with the altar ... 1Cor 9:13 *4829*
for we are all p of that one ... 1Cor 10:17 *3348*
of the sacrifices p of the altar ... 1Cor 10:18 *2844*
ye cannot be p of the Lord's ... 1Cor 10:21 *3348*
knowing, that as ye are p of the ... 2Cor 1:7 *2844*
p of his promise in Christ by the ... Eph 3:6 *4830*
Be not ye therefore p with them ... Eph 5:7 *4830*
gospel, ye all are p of my grace ... Phil 1:7 *4791*
to be p of the inheritance of the ... Col 1:12 *3310*
and beloved, p of the benefit ... 1Ti 6:2 *482*
as the children are p of flesh ... Heb 2:14 *2841*
p of the heavenly calling, ... Heb 3:1 *3353*
For we are made p of Christ ... Heb 3:14 *3353*
were made p of the Holy Ghost, ... Heb 6:4 *3353*
chastisement, whereof all are p ... Heb 12:8 *3353*
we might be p of his holiness ... Heb 12:10 *3335*
inasmuch as ye are p of Christ's ... 1Pet 4:13 *2841*
might be p of the divine nature ... 2Pet 1:4 *2844*
that ye be not p of her sins ... Rev 18:4 *4790*

PARTAKEST
with them p of the root and ... Rom 11:17

PARTED
and from thence it was p, and ... Gen 2:10 6504
of fire, and p them both asunder ... 2Kin 2:11 6504
waters, they p hither and thither ... 2Kin 2:14 2673
By what way is the light p ... Job 38:24 2505
among the nations, and p my land ... Joel 3:2 2505
p his garments, casting lots ... Mt 27:35 *1266*
They p my garments among ... Mt 27:35 *1266*
they p his garments, casting lots ... Mk 15:24 *1266*
they p his raiment, and cast lots ... Lk 23:34 *1266*
he was p from them, and carried up ... Lk 24:51 *1339*
They p my raiment among them, and ... Jn 19:24 *1266*
p them to all men, as every man ... Acts 2:45 *1266*

PARTETH
Whatsoever p the hoof, and is ... Lev 11:3 6536
And every beast that p the hoof ... Deut 14:6 6536
to cease, and p between the mighty ... Prov 18:18 6504

PARTHIANS (*par-the'-uns*) *Inhabitants of Parthia, now Iran.*
P, and Medes, and Elamites, and the ... Acts 2:9 *3934*

PARTIAL
ways, but have been p in the law ... Mal 2:9
Are ye not then p in yourselves ... Jas 2:4 *1252*

PARTIALITY
another, doing nothing by p ... 1Ti 5:21 4346
mercy and good fruits, without p ... Jas 3:17 87

PARTICULAR
body of Christ, and members in p ... 1Cor 12:27 3313
let every one of you in p so love ... Eph 5:33

PARTICULARLY
he declared p what things God had ... Acts 21:19
of which we cannot now speak p ... Heb 9:5

PARTIES
the cause of both p shall come ... Ex 22:9

PARTING
Babylon stood at the p of the way ... Eze 21:21 517

PARTITION
he made a p by the chains of gold ... 1Kin 6:21 5674
the middle wall of p between us ... Eph 2:14 5418

PARTLY
be p strong, and p broken ... Dan 2:42 7118
and I p believe it ... 1Cor 11:18
P, whilst ye were made a ... Heb 10:33
and p, whilst ye became companions ... Heb 10:33 1161

PARTNER
Whoso is p with a thief hateth ... Prov 29:24 2505
do enquire of Titus, he is my p ... 2Cor 8:23 2844
If thou count me therefore a p ... Philem 17 2844

PARTNERS
And they beckoned unto their p ... Lk 5:7 3353
Zebedee, which were p with Simon ... Lk 5:10 2844

PARTRIDGE
doth hunt a p in the mountains ... 1Sa 26:20 7124
As the p sitteth on eggs, and ... Jer 17:11 7124

PARTS
four p shall be your own, for ... Gen 47:24 3027
hand, and thou shalt see my back p ... Ex 33:23
Aaron's sons, shall lay the p ... Lev 1:8 5409
superfluous or lacking in his p ... Lev 22:23
on the east p shall go forward ... Num 10:5
in the uttermost p of the camp ... Num 11:1
And divide the prey into two p ... Num 31:27
thee to inherit, into three p ... Deut 19:3
out unto the outmost p of heaven ... Deut 30:4
they shall divide it into seven p ... Josh 18:5 2506
describe the land into seven p ... Josh 18:6 2506
by cities into seven p in a book ... Josh 18:9 2506
had emerods in their secret p ... 1Sa 5:9 2506
said, We have ten p in the king ... 2Sa 19:43
throughout all the p thereof ... 1Kin 6:38 1697
and all their hinder p were inward ... 1Kin 7:25
of Israel divided into two p ... 1Kin 16:21 2677
two p of all you that go forth on ... 2Kin 11:7 3027
and all their hinder p were inward ... 2Chr 4:4
nine p to dwell in other cities ... Neh 11:1 3027
Lo, these are p of his ways ... Job 26:14 7098
hath put wisdom in the inward p ... Job 38:36
I will not conceal his p, nor his ... Job 41:12 905
the uttermost p of the earth for ... Ps 2:8
desirest truth in the inward p ... Ps 51:6
go into the lower p of the earth ... Ps 63:9
p are afraid at thy tokens ... Ps 65:8
smote his enemies in the hinder p ... Ps 78:66
which divided the Red sea into p ... Ps 136:13 1506
in the uttermost p of the sea ... Ps 139:9
in the lowest p of the earth ... Ps 139:15
into the innermost p of the belly ... Prov 18:8
all the inward p of the belly ... Prov 20:27
stripes the inward p of the belly ... Prov 20:30
into the innermost p of the belly ... Prov 26:22
LORD will discover their secret p ... Is 3:17
mine inward p for Kir-haresh ... Is 16:11
shout, ye lower p of the earth ... Is 44:23
will put my law in their inward p ... Jer 31:33
and passed between the p thereof ... Jer 34:18 1335
passed between the p of the calf ... Jer 34:19 1335
thee in the low p of the earth ... Eze 26:20
to the nether p of the earth ... Eze 31:14
in the nether p of the earth ... Eze 31:16
unto the nether p of the earth ... Eze 31:18
unto the nether p of the earth ... Eze 32:18
into the nether p of the earth ... Eze 32:24
we are cut off for our p ... Eze 37:11 2506
from thy place out of the north p ... Eze 38:15 3411
thee to come up from the north p ... Eze 39:2 3411
in length as one of the other p ... Eze 48:8 2506
two p therein shall be cut off and ... Zec 13:8 6310
aside into the p of Galilee ... Mt 2:22
p of the earth to hear the wisdom ... Mt 12:42
and came into the p of Dalmanutha ... Mk 8:10 3313
for she came from the utmost p of ... Lk 11:31
took his garments, and made four p ... Jn 19:23 3313
in the p of Libya about Cyrene ... Acts 2:10 3313
And when he had gone over those p ... Acts 20:2 3313
having no more place in these p ... Rom 15:23 2825
our uncomely p have more abundant ... 1Cor 12:23
For our comely p have no need ... 1Cor 12:24
into the lower p of the earth ... Eph 4:9 3313
city was divided into three p ... Rev 16:19 3313

PARUAH (*par'-u-ah*) *Father of Jehoshaphat.*
Jehoshaphat the son of P, in ... 1Kin 4:17 6515

PARVAIM (*par-va'-im*) *A place rich in gold.*
and the gold was gold of P ... 2Chr 3:6 6516

PARZITES See PHARZITES.

PASACH (*pa'-sak*) *A son of Japhet.*
P, and Bimhal, and Ashvath ... 1Chr 7:33 6457

PAS-DAMMIM (*pas-dam'-mim*) *A place in Judah.*
He was with David at P, and there ... 1Chr 11:13 6450

PASEAH (*pa-se'-ah*) See PHASEAH.
1. A son of Eshton.
And Eshton begat Beth-rapha, and P ... 1Chr 4:12 6454
2. A family of exiles.
of Uzza, the children of P ... Ezr 2:49 6454
3. Father of Jehoiada.
repaired Jehoiada the son of P ... Neh 3:6 6454

PASHUR (*pash'-ur*)
1. Head of a priestly family.
the son of Jeroham, the son of P ... 1Chr 9:12 6583
The children of P, a thousand two ... Ezr 2:38 6583
And of the sons of P ... Ezr 10:22 6583
The children of P, a thousand two ... Neh 7:41 6583
son of Zechariah, the son of P ... Neh 11:12 6583
2. A priest who renewed the covenant.
P, Amariah, Malchijah ... Neh 10:3 6583
3. A son of Immer.
Now P the son of Immer the priest ... Jer 20:1 6583
Then P smote Jeremiah the prophet ... Jer 20:2 6583
that P brought forth Jeremiah out ... Jer 20:3 6583
LORD hath not called thy name P ... Jer 20:3 6583
And thou, P, and all that dwell in ... Jer 20:6 6583
Mattan, and Gedaliah the son of P ... Jer 38:1 6583
4. A son of Melchiah/Malchiah.
unto him P the son of Melchiah ... Jer 21:1 6583
P the son of Malchiah, heard the ... Jer 38:1 6583

PASS
in process of time it came to p ... Gen 4:3
and it came to p, when they were ... Gen 4:8
and it shall come to p, that every ... Gen 4:14
And it came to p, when men began ... Gen 6:1
it came to p after seven days ... Gen 7:10
made a wind to p over the earth ... Gen 8:1 5674
it came to p at the end of forty ... Gen 8:6
it came to p in the six hundredth ... Gen 8:13
And it shall come to p, when I ... Gen 9:14
And it came to p, as they ... Gen 11:2
And it came to p, when he was come ... Gen 12:11
Therefore it shall come to p ... Gen 12:12
And it came to p, that, when Abram ... Gen 12:14
it came to p in the days of ... Gen 14:1
And it came to p, that, when the ... Gen 15:17
p not away, I pray thee, from thy ... Gen 18:3 5674
after that ye shall p on ... Gen 18:5 5674
And it came to p, when they had ... Gen 19:17
And it came to p, when God ... Gen 19:29
it came to p on the morrow, that ... Gen 19:34
And it came to p, when God caused ... Gen 20:13
it came to p at that time, that ... Gen 21:22
it came to p after these things ... Gen 22:1
it came to p after these things ... Gen 22:20
And let it come to p, that the ... Gen 24:14
And it came to p, before he had ... Gen 24:15
And it came to p, as the camels ... Gen 24:22
And it came to p, when he saw the ... Gen 24:30
and it shall come to p, that when ... Gen 24:43
And it came to p, that, when ... Gen 24:52
it came to p after the death of ... Gen 25:11
And it came to p, when he had been ... Gen 26:8
it came to p the same day, that ... Gen 26:32
And it came to p, that when Isaac ... Gen 27:1
And it came to p, as soon as Isaac ... Gen 27:30
it shall come to p when thou ... Gen 27:40
And it came to p, when Jacob saw ... Gen 29:10
And it came to p, when Laban heard ... Gen 29:13
it came to p in the evening, that ... Gen 29:23
And it came to p, that in the ... Gen 29:25
And it came to p, when Rachel had ... Gen 30:25
I will p through all thy flock to ... Gen 30:32 5674
And it came to p, whensoever the ... Gen 30:41
it came to p at the time that the ... Gen 31:10
that I will not p over this heap ... Gen 31:52 5674
thou shalt not p over this heap ... Gen 31:52 5674
P over before me, and put a space ... Gen 32:16 5674
p over before his servant ... Gen 33:14 5674
it came to p on the third day ... Gen 34:25
And it came to p, when she was in ... Gen 35:17
And it came to p, as her soul was ... Gen 35:18
And it came to p, when Israel ... Gen 35:22
And it came to p, when Joseph was ... Gen 37:23
it came to p at that time, that ... Gen 38:1
and it came to p, when he went in ... Gen 38:9
it came to p about three months ... Gen 38:24
it came to p in the time of her ... Gen 38:27
And it came to p, when she ... Gen 38:28
And it came to p, as he drew back ... Gen 38:29
it came to p from the time that ... Gen 39:5
it came to p after these things ... Gen 39:7
And it came to p, as she spake to ... Gen 39:10
it came to p about this time ... Gen 39:11
And it came to p, when she saw ... Gen 39:13
And it came to p, when he heard ... Gen 39:15
And it came to p, as I lifted up ... Gen 39:18
And it came to p, when his master ... Gen 39:19
it came to p after these things ... Gen 40:1
it came to p the third day, which ... Gen 40:20
it came to p at the end of two ... Gen 41:1
it came to p in the morning that ... Gen 41:8
And it came to p, as he ... Gen 41:13
and God will shortly bring it to p ... Gen 41:32 6213
it came to p as they emptied ... Gen 42:35
And it came to p, when they had ... Gen 43:2
And it came to p, when we came to ... Gen 43:21
it came to p when we came up unto ... Gen 44:24
It shall come to p, when he seeth ... Gen 44:31
And it shall come to p, when ... Gen 46:33
shall come to p in the increase ... Gen 47:24
it came to p after these things ... Gen 48:1
meant it unto good, to bring to p ... Gen 50:20 6213
they multiply, and it come to p ... Ex 1:10
And it came to p, because the ... Ex 1:21
it came to p in those days, when ... Ex 2:11
it came to p in process of time ... Ex 2:23
and it shall come to p, that, when ... Ex 3:21
And it shall come to p, if they ... Ex 4:8
And it shall come to p, if they ... Ex 4:9
it came to p by the way in the ... Ex 4:24
it came to p on the day when the ... Ex 6:28
For I will p through the land of ... Ex 12:12 5674
I will p over you, and the plague ... Ex 12:13 6452
For the LORD will p through to ... Ex 12:23 5674
the LORD will p over the door ... Ex 12:23 6452
And it shall come to p, when ye be ... Ex 12:25
And it shall come to p, when your ... Ex 12:26
And it came to p, that at midnight ... Ex 12:29
it came to p at the end of the ... Ex 12:41
the selfsame day it came to p ... Ex 12:41
it came to p the selfsame day ... Ex 12:51
And it came to p, when Pharaoh ... Ex 13:15
And it came to p, when Pharaoh had ... Ex 13:17
And it came to p, that in the ... Ex 14:24
till thy people p over, O LORD ... Ex 15:16 5674
O LORD, till the people p over ... Ex 15:16 5674
And it shall come to p, that on ... Ex 16:5
And it came to p, as Aaron spake ... Ex 16:10
And it came to p, that at even the ... Ex 16:13
And it came to p, that on the ... Ex 16:22
And it came to p, that there went ... Ex 16:27
And it came to p, when Moses held ... Ex 17:11
it came to p on the morrow, that ... Ex 18:13
it came to p on the third day in ... Ex 19:16
and it shall come to p, when he ... Ex 22:27
And it came to p, as soon as he ... Ex 32:19
it came to p on the morrow, that ... Ex 32:30
And it came to p, that every one ... Ex 33:7
And it came to p, when Moses went ... Ex 33:8
And it came to p, as Moses entered ... Ex 33:9
all my goodness p before thee ... Ex 33:19 5674
And it shall come to p, while my ... Ex 33:22
thee with my hand while I p by ... Ex 33:22 5674
And it came to p, when Moses came ... Ex 34:29
it came to p in the first month ... Ex 40:17
it came to p on the eighth day ... Lev 9:1
seed p through the fire to Molech ... Lev 18:21 5674
water, then it shall come to p ... Num 5:27
it came to p on the day that ... Num 7:1
it came to p on the twentieth day ... Num 10:11
And it came to p, when the ark set ... Num 10:35
shall come to p unto thee or not ... Num 11:23
and it came to p, that, when the ... Num 11:25
And it came to p, as he had made ... Num 16:31
And it came to p, when the ... Num 16:42
And it shall come to p, that the ... Num 17:5
And it came to p, that on the ... Num 17:8
Let us p, I pray thee, through ... Num 20:17 5674
we will not p through the fields ... Num 20:17 5674
unto him, Thou shalt not p by me ... Num 20:18 5674
and it shall come to p, that every ... Num 21:8
it upon a pole, and it came to p ... Num 21:9
Let me p through thy land ... Num 21:22 5674
Israel to p through his border ... Num 21:23 5674
it came to p on the morrow, that ... Num 22:41
it came to p after the plague ... Num 26:1
of their father to p unto them ... Num 27:7 5674
to p unto his daughter ... Num 27:8 5674
But thy servants will p over ... Num 32:27 5674
will p with you over Jordan ... Num 32:29 5674
will not p over with you armed ... Num 32:30 5674
We will p over armed before the ... Num 32:32 5674
then it shall come to p, that ... Num 33:55
Moreover it shall come to p ... Num 33:56
of Akrabbim, and p on to Zin ... Num 34:4 5674
to Hazar-addar, and p on to Azmon ... Num 34:4 5674
it came to p in the fortieth year ... Deut 1:3
Ye are to p through the coast of ... Deut 2:4 5674
So it came to p, when all the men ... Deut 2:16
Thou art to p over through Ar ... Deut 2:18 5674
and p over the river Arnon ... Deut 2:24 5674
Let me p through thy land ... Deut 2:27 5674
only I will p through on my feet ... Deut 2:28 5674
until I shall p over Jordan into ... Deut 2:29 5674
Heshbon would not let us p by him ... Deut 2:30 5674
ye shall p over armed before your ... Deut 3:18 5674
And it came to p, when ye heard ... Deut 5:23
Wherefore it shall come to p ... Deut 7:12
Thou art to p over Jordan this ... Deut 9:1 5674
it came to p at the end of forty ... Deut 9:11
And it shall come to p, if ye ... Deut 11:13
And it shall come to p, when the ... Deut 11:29
For ye shall p over Jordan to go ... Deut 11:31 5674
the sign or the wonder come to p ... Deut 13:2
daughter to p through the fire ... Deut 18:10 5674
And it shall come to p, that ... Deut 18:19
thing follow not, nor come to p ... Deut 18:22
it come to p that she find no ... Deut 24:1
be on the day when ye shall p ... Deut 27:2 5674
And it shall come to p, if thou ... Deut 28:1
But it shall come to p, if thou ... Deut 28:15
And it shall come to p, that as ... Deut 28:63
And it come to p, when he heareth ... Deut 29:19
And it shall come to p, when all ... Deut 30:1
And it shall come to p, when many ... Deut 31:21
And it came to p, when Moses had ... Deut 31:24
servant of the LORD it came to p ... Josh 1:1
P through the host, and command ... Josh 1:11 5674
days ye shall p over this Jordan ... Josh 1:11 5674
but ye shall p before your ... Josh 1:14 5674
it came to p about the time of ... Josh 2:5
it came to p after three days ... Josh 3:2
and p over before the people ... Josh 3:6 5674
And it shall come to p, as soon as ... Josh 3:13
And it came to p, when the people ... Josh 3:14
to p over Jordan, and the priests ... Josh 3:14 5674
And it came to p, when all the ... Josh 4:1
P over before the ark of the LORD ... Josh 4:5 5674
And it came to p, when all the ... Josh 4:11
And it came to p, when the priests ... Josh 4:18

And it came to p, when all the .... Josh 5:1
And it came to p, when they had.......... Josh 5:8
And it came to p, when Joshua was...... Josh 5:13
And it shall come to p, that when......... Josh 6:5
P on, and compass the city, and let...... Josh 6:7 5674
let him that is armed p on before.......... Josh 6:7 5674
And it came to p, when Joshua had....... Josh 6:8
it came to p on the seventh day,.......... Josh 6:15
it came to p at the seventh time,.......... Josh 6:16
and it came to p, when the people........ Josh 6:20
and it shall come to p, when they......... Josh 8:5
and it came to p, when the king of........ Josh 8:14
And it came to p, when Israel had......... Josh 8:24
And it came to p, when all the............. Josh 9:1
it came to p at the end of three............ Josh 9:16
Now it came to p, when .... Josh 10:1
And it came to p, as they fled............... Josh 10:11
And it came to p, when Joshua and....... Josh 10:20
And it came to p, when they.................. Josh 10:24
it came to p at the time of the............... Josh 10:27
And it came to p, when Jabin king......... Josh 11:1
And it came to p, as she came unto....... Josh 15:18
Yet it came to p, when the.................... Josh 17:13
all came to p... Josh 21:45 935
then p ye over unto the land of.............. Josh 22:19 5674
it came to p a long time after................ Josh 23:1
all are come to p unto you..................... Josh 23:14
Therefore it shall come to p.................. Josh 23:15
it came to p after these things,............. Josh 24:29
the death of Joshua it came to p.......... Judg 1:1
And it came to p, when she came to...... Judg 1:14
And it came to p, when Israel was........ Judg 1:28
And it came to p, when the angel.......... Judg 2:4
And it came to p, when the judge.......... Judg 2:19
And it came to p, when he was come.. Judg 3:27
and suffered not a man to p over.......... Judg 3:28 5674
And it came to p, when the.................... Judg 6:7
it came to p the same night, that.......... Judg 6:25
it came to p the same night, that.......... Judg 7:9
And it came to p, as soon as................. Judg 8:33
it came to p on the morrow, that........... Judg 9:42
it came to p in process of time,............. Judg 11:4
I pray thee, p through thy land.............. Judg 11:17 5674
and Israel said unto him, Let us p........ Judg 11:19 5674
not Israel to p through his coast........... Judg 11:20 5674
And it came to p, when he saw her,...... Judg 11:35
it came to p at the end of two................ Judg 11:39
said, Now let thy words come to p......... Judg 13:12 935
come to p we may do thee honour.......... Judg 13:17 935
For it came to p, when the flame........... Judg 13:20
And it came to p, when they saw........... Judg 14:11
it came to p on the seventh day,........... Judg 14:15
it came to p on the seventh day,........... Judg 14:17
But it came to p within a while............. Judg 15:1
And it came to p, when he had made.. Judg 15:17
And it came to p afterward.................... Judg 16:4
And it came to p, when she pressed...... Judg 16:16
And it came to p, when their................. Judg 16:25
it came to p in those days, when.......... Judg 19:1
it came to p on the fourth day,.............. Judg 19:5
we will p over to Gibeah....................... Judg 19:12 5674
why is this come to p in Israel.............. Judg 21:3
it came to p on the morrow, that........... Judg 21:4
Now it came to p in the days when........ Ruth 1:1
And it came to p, when they were......... Ruth 1:19
it came to p at midnight, that............... Ruth 3:8
And it came to p, as she continued....... 1Sa 1:12
Wherefore it came to p, when the.......... 1Sa 1:20
And it shall come to p, that every......... 1Sa 2:36
it came to p at that time, when............. 1Sa 3:2
And it came to p, when he made............ 1Sa 4:18
And it came to p, as the ark of............... 1Sa 5:10
And it came to p, while the ark.............. 1Sa 7:2
And it came to p, when Samuel was....... 1Sa 8:1
that he saith cometh surely to p............ 1Sa 9:6
it came to p about the spring of............. 1Sa 9:26
Bid the servant p on before us.............. 1Sa 9:27 5674
and it shall come to p, when thou......... 1Sa 10:5
those signs came to p that day.............. 1Sa 10:9
And it came to p, when all that............. 1Sa 10:11
and it came to p, that they which.......... 1Sa 11:11
And it came to p, that as soon as.......... 1Sa 13:10
So it came to p in the day of................. 1Sa 13:22
Now it came to p upon a day................. 1Sa 14:1
we will p over unto these men, and....... 1Sa 14:8 5674
And it came to p, while Saul................. 1Sa 14:19
And it came to p, when they were.......... 1Sa 16:6
and made him p before Samuel.............. 1Sa 16:8 5674
Then Jesse made Shammah to p by....... 1Sa 16:9 5674
of his sons to p before Samuel.............. 1Sa 16:10 5674
and it shall come to p, when the........... 1Sa 16:16
And it came to p, when the evil............. 1Sa 16:23
And it came to p, when the.................... 1Sa 17:48
And it came to p, when he had made.. 1Sa 18:1
it came to p as they came, when............ 1Sa 18:6
it came to p on the morrow, that........... 1Sa 18:10
But it came to p at the time when......... 1Sa 18:19
and it came to p, after they went.......... 1Sa 18:30
it came to p on the morrow, which........ 1Sa 20:27
it came to p in the morning, that.......... 1Sa 20:35
And it came to p, when Abiathar........... 1Sa 23:6
and it shall come to p, if he be............. 1Sa 23:23
And it came to p, when Saul was.......... 1Sa 24:1
And it came to p afterward................... 1Sa 24:5
And it came to p, when David had......... 1Sa 24:16
And it shall come to p, when the........... 1Sa 25:30
But it came to p in the morning............ 1Sa 25:37
it came to p about ten days after........... 1Sa 25:38
it came to p in those days, that............ 1Sa 28:1
And it came to p, when David and......... 1Sa 30:1
it came to p on the morrow, when.......... 1Sa 31:8
Now it came to p after the death........... 2Sa 1:1
It came even to p on the third............... 2Sa 1:2
And it came to p after this.................... 2Sa 2:1
and it came to p, that as many as.......... 2Sa 2:23
And it came to p, while there was......... 2Sa 3:6
and it came to p, as she made.............. 2Sa 4:4
And it came to p, when the king............ 2Sa 7:1
And it came to p that night.................. 2Sa 7:4
And after this it came to p.................. 2Sa 8:1
And it came to p after this.................... 2Sa 10:1
And it came to p, after the year............ 2Sa 11:1
it came to p in an eveningtide,.............. 2Sa 11:2
it came to p in the morning, that........... 2Sa 11:14
And it came to p, when Joab................. 2Sa 11:16
it came to p on the seventh day,........... 2Sa 12:18
made them p through the brickkiln....... 2Sa 12:31 5674
And it came to p after this.................... 2Sa 13:1
it came to p after two full years............ 2Sa 13:23
And it came to p, while they were......... 2Sa 13:30
And it came to p, as soon as he............. 2Sa 13:36
And it came to p after this.................... 2Sa 15:1
it came to p after forty years,............... 2Sa 15:7
David said to Ittai, Go and p over......... 2Sa 15:22 5674
And it came to p, that when David......... 2Sa 15:32
And it came to p, when Hushai the........ 2Sa 16:16
and it will come to p, when some........... 2Sa 17:9
wilderness, but speedily p over............. 2Sa 17:16 5674
And it came to p, after they were......... 2Sa 17:21
and p quickly over the water................ 2Sa 17:21 5674
And it came to p, when David was......... 2Sa 17:27
And it came to p, when he was come.. 2Sa 19:25
And it came to p after this.................... 2Sa 21:18
Otherwise it shall come to p................. 1Kin 1:21
it came to p at the end of three............. 1Kin 2:39
it came to p the third day after.............. 1Kin 3:18
And it came to p, when Hiram heard...... 1Kin 5:7
it came to p in the four hundred............ 1Kin 6:1
And it came to p, when the priests........ 1Kin 8:10
And it came to p, when Solomon had.. 1Kin 9:1
it came to p at the end of twenty.......... 1Kin 9:10
For it came to p, when Solomon............ 1Kin 11:4
For it came to p, when David was.......... 1Kin 11:15
it came to p at that time when.............. 1Kin 11:29
And it came to p, when Jeroboam.......... 1Kin 12:2
And it came to p, when all Israel.......... 1Kin 12:20
And it came to p, when king................. 1Kin 13:4
And it came to p, as they sat at............ 1Kin 13:20
And it came to p, after he had............. 1Kin 13:23
And it came to p, after he had............. 1Kin 13:31
Samaria, shall surely come to p............ 1Kin 13:32
it came to p in the fifth year of............. 1Kin 14:25
And it came to p, when Baasha............. 1Kin 15:21
And it came to p, when he reigned,....... 1Kin 15:29
And it came to p, when he began to...... 1Kin 16:11
And it came to p, when Zimri saw......... 1Kin 16:18
And it came to p, as if it had................. 1Kin 16:31
it came to p after a while, that.............. 1Kin 17:7
it came to p after these things,............. 1Kin 17:17
it came to p after many days,................ 1Kin 18:1
between them to p throughout it.......... 1Kin 18:6 5674
And it shall come to p, as soon as......... 1Kin 18:12
And it came to p, when Ahab saw.......... 1Kin 18:17
And it came to p at noon, that.............. 1Kin 18:27
And it came to p, when midday was...... 1Kin 18:29
it came to p at the time of the.............. 1Kin 18:36
it came to p at the seventh time,........... 1Kin 18:44
it came to p in the mean while,............. 1Kin 18:45
And it shall come to p, that him............ 1Kin 19:17
And it came to p, when Ben-hadad......... 1Kin 20:12
it came to p at the return of the........... 1Kin 20:26
it came to p after these things,............. 1Kin 21:1
And it came to p, when Jezebel............ 1Kin 21:15
And it came to p, when Ahab heard....... 1Kin 21:16
And it came to p, when Ahab heard....... 1Kin 21:27
it came to p in the third year................ 1Kin 22:2
And it came to p, when the.................. 1Kin 22:32
And it came to p, when the.................. 1Kin 22:33
And it came to p, when the LORD.......... 2Kin 2:1
And it came to p, when they were......... 2Kin 2:9
And it came to p, as they still............... 2Kin 2:11
But it came to p, when Ahab was.......... 2Kin 3:5
And it came to p, when the.................. 2Kin 3:15
it came to p in the morning, when......... 2Kin 3:20
And it came to p, when the vessels....... 2Kin 4:6
And it came to p, when the man of....... 2Kin 4:25
And it came to p, as they were............. 2Kin 4:40
And it came to p, when the king of....... 2Kin 5:7
that thou p not such a place............... 2Kin 6:9 5674
And it came to p, when they were......... 2Kin 6:20
And it came to p after this.................. 2Kin 6:24
And it came to p, when the king........... 2Kin 6:30
it came to p as the man of God............. 2Kin 7:18
it came to p at the seven years'............. 2Kin 8:3
And it came to p, as he was................. 2Kin 8:5
it came to p on the morrow, that........... 2Kin 8:15
And it came to p, when Joram saw........ 2Kin 9:22
And it came to p, when the letter.......... 2Kin 10:7
it came to p in the morning, that........... 2Kin 10:9
And it came to p, as soon as he............. 2Kin 10:25
And it came to p, as they were............. 2Kin 13:21
And it came to p, as soon as the........... 2Kin 14:5
And so it came to p............................. 2Kin 15:12
made his son to p through the.............. 2Kin 16:3 5674
daughters to p through the fire............ 2Kin 17:17 5674
Now it came to p in the third................ 2Kin 18:1
it came to p in the fourth year.............. 2Kin 18:9
And it came to p, when king................. 2Kin 19:1
now have I brought it to p.................... 2Kin 19:25
And it came to p that night.................. 2Kin 19:35
And it came to p, as he was................. 2Kin 19:37
And it came to p, afore Isaiah was........ 2Kin 20:4
he made his son p through the............ 2Kin 21:6 5674
it came to p in the eighteenth............... 2Kin 22:3
And it came to p, when the king........... 2Kin 22:11
to p through the fire to Molech............ 2Kin 23:10 5674
LORD it came to p in Jerusalem........... 2Kin 24:20
it came to p in the ninth year of............ 2Kin 25:1
But it came to p in the seventh............. 2Kin 25:25
it came to p in the seven and............... 2Kin 25:27
it came to p on the morrow, when......... 1Chr 10:8
And it came to p, when God helped...... 1Chr 15:26
And it came to p, as the ark of............... 1Chr 15:29
Now it came to p, as David sat in......... 1Chr 17:1
it came to p the same night, that......... 1Chr 17:3
And it shall come to p, when thy.......... 1Chr 17:11
Now after this it came to p.................. 1Chr 18:1
Now it came to p after this.................. 1Chr 19:1
And it came to p, that after the............ 1Chr 20:1
And it came to p after this.................. 1Chr 20:4
And it came to p, when the priests....... 2Chr 5:11
It came even to p, as the..................... 2Chr 5:13
it came to p at the end of twenty.......... 2Chr 8:1
And it came to p, when Jeroboam......... 2Chr 10:2
And it came to p, when Rehoboam........ 2Chr 12:1
And it came to p, that in the................ 2Chr 12:2
of Judah shouted, it came to p............ 2Chr 13:15
And it came to p, when Baasha............. 2Chr 16:5
And it came to p, when the.................. 2Chr 18:31
For it came to p, that, when the........... 2Chr 18:32
It came to p after this also,................. 2Chr 20:1
And it came to p, that in process.......... 2Chr 21:19
And it came to p, that, when Jehu......... 2Chr 22:8
And it came to p after this.................. 2Chr 24:4
Now it came to p, that at what.............. 2Chr 24:11
it came to p at the end of the............... 2Chr 24:23
Now it came to p, when the.................. 2Chr 25:3
Now it came to p, after that................. 2Chr 25:14
And it came to p, as he talked............. 2Chr 25:16
he caused his children to p.................. 2Chr 33:6 5674
And it came to p, when the king........... 2Chr 34:19
it came to p in the month Chisleu......... Neh 1:1
And it came to p, when I heard............. Neh 1:4
it came to p in the month Nisan,........... Neh 2:1
the beast that was under me to p.......... Neh 2:14 5674
But it came to p, that when.................. Neh 4:1
But it came to p, that when.................. Neh 4:7
And it came to p, that when the............ Neh 4:12
And it came to p, when our enemies...... Neh 4:15
it came to p from that time forth........... Neh 4:16
Now it came to p, when Sanballat,........ Neh 6:1
And it came to p, that when all............. Neh 6:16
Now it came to p, when the wall........... Neh 7:1
Now it came to p, when they had.......... Neh 13:3
And it came to p, that when the............ Neh 13:19
Now it came to p in the days of............ Est 1:1
So it came to p, when the king's........... Est 2:8
Now it came to p, when they spake....... Est 3:4
Now it came to p on the third day......... Est 5:1
the stream of brooks they p away......... Job 6:15 5674
remember it as waters that p away....... Job 11:16 5674
his bounds that he cannot p................. Job 14:5 5674
fenced up my way that I cannot p.......... Job 19:8 5674
troubled at midnight, and p away.......... Job 34:20 5674
and he shall bring it to p...................... Ps 37:5 6213
who bringeth wicked devices to p......... Ps 37:7 6213
let every one of them p away............... Ps 58:8 1980
sea, and caused them to p through....... Ps 78:13 5674
so that all they which p by the............. Ps 80:12 5674
All that p by the way spoil him............ Ps 89:41 5674
a bound that they may not p over......... Ps 104:9 5674
made Israel to p through the............... Ps 136:14 5674
made a decree which shall not p.......... Ps 148:6 5674
p not by it, turn from it, and.............. Prov 4:15 5674
by it, turn from it, and p away............ Prov 4:15 5674
should not p his commandment............ Prov 8:29 5674
his lips he bringeth evil to p.............. Prov 16:30 3615
it is his glory to p over a.................... Prov 19:11 5674
but the simple p on, and are............... Prov 22:3 5674
but the simple p on, and are............... Prov 27:12 5674
shall come to p in the last days........... Is 2:2
And it shall come to p, that................. Is 3:24
And it shall come to p, that he............. Is 4:3
it came to p in the days of Ahaz........... Is 7:1
stand, neither shall it come to p........... Is 7:7
And it shall come to p in that day........ Is 7:18
And it shall come to p in that day........ Is 7:21
And it shall come to p, for the............. Is 7:22
And it shall come to p in that day........ Is 7:23
And he shall p through Judah............... Is 8:8 2498
And they shall p through it................... Is 8:21 5674
and it shall come to p, that when......... Is 8:21
Wherefore it shall come to p................ Is 10:12
And it shall come to p in that day........ Is 10:20
And it shall come to p in that day........ Is 10:27
And it shall come to p in that day........ Is 11:11
it shall come to p in the day................ Is 14:3
thought, so shall it come to p.............. Is 14:24
And it shall come to p, when it is......... Is 16:12
And in that day it shall come to p........ Is 17:4
whirlwinds in the south p through........ Is 21:1 2498
And it shall come to p, that thy........... Is 22:7
And it shall come to p in that day........ Is 22:20
that p over the sea, have..................... Is 23:2 5674
P ye over to Tarshish......................... Is 23:6 5674
P through thy land as a river, O........... Is 23:10 5674
arise, p over to Chittim...................... Is 23:12 5674
And it shall come to p in that day........ Is 23:15
it shall come to p after the end............ Is 23:17
And it shall come to p, that he............. Is 24:18
And it shall come to p in that day........ Is 24:21
And it shall come to p in that day........ Is 27:12
And it shall come to p in that day........ Is 27:13
scourge shall p through, it shall.......... Is 28:15 5674
scourge shall p through, then ye......... Is 28:18 5674
by morning shall it p over................... Is 28:19 5674
and bring to p his act, his.................. Is 28:21 5674
where the grounded staff shall p.......... Is 30:32 4569
he shall p over to his strong................ Is 31:9 5674
shall gallant ship p thereby................ Is 33:21 5674
none shall p through it for ever............ Is 34:10 5674
the unclean shall not p over it............. Is 35:8 5674

Now it came to *p* in the … Is 36:1
And it came to *p*, when king … Is 37:1
now have I brought it to *p* … Is 37:26
And it came to *p*, as he was … Is 37:38
the former things are come to *p* … Is 42:9
it, I will also bring it to *p* … Is 46:11
the thigh, *p* over the rivers … Is 47:2 5674
them suddenly, and they came to *p* … Is 48:3
it came to *p* I shewed it thee … Is 48:5
a way for the ransomed to *p* over … Is 51:10 5674
And it shall come to *p*, that … Is 65:24
And it shall come to *p*, that from … Is 66:23
For *p* over the isles of Chittim, … Jer 2:10 5674
And it came to *p* through the … Jer 3:9
And it shall come to *p*, when ye be … Jer 3:16
And it shall come to *p* at that day … Jer 4:9
And it shall come to *p*, when ye … Jer 5:19
decree, that it cannot *p* it … Jer 5:22 5674
roar, yet can they not *p* over it … Jer 5:22 5674
given them shall *p* away from them … Jer 8:13 5674
so that none can *p* through them … Jer 9:10 5674
And it shall come to *p*, after that … Jer 12:15
And it shall come to *p*, if they … Jer 12:16
it came to *p* after many days, … Jer 13:6
And it shall come to *p*, if they … Jer 15:2
I will make thee to *p* with thine … Jer 15:14 5674
And it shall come to *p*, when thou … Jer 16:10
And it shall come to *p*, if ye … Jer 17:24
it came to *p* on the morrow, that … Jer 20:3
many nations shall *p* by this city … Jer 22:8 5674
And it shall come to *p*, when … Jer 25:12
Now it came to *p*, when Jeremiah … Jer 26:8
And it shall come to *p*, that the … Jer 27:8
it came to *p* the same year, in … Jer 28:1
of the prophet shall come to *p* … Jer 28:9
it shall come to *p* in that day … Jer 30:8
And it shall come to *p*, that like … Jer 31:28
thou hast spoken is come to *p* … Jer 32:24
their daughters to *p* through the … Jer 32:35 5674
shall the flocks *p* again under … Jer 33:13 5674
But it came to *p*, when … Jer 35:11
it came to *p* in the fourth year … Jer 36:1
it came to *p* in the fifth year of … Jer 36:9
Now it came to *p*, when they had … Jer 36:16
And it came to *p*, that when Jehudi … Jer 36:23
And it came to *p*, that when the … Jer 37:11
And it came to *p*, that when … Jer 39:4
Now it came to *p* in the seventh … Jer 41:1
it came to *p* the second day after … Jer 41:4
and it came to *p*, as he met them, … Jer 41:6
Now it came to *p*, that when all … Jer 41:13
and it shall come to *p*, that … Jer 42:4
it came to *p* after ten days, that … Jer 42:7
Then it shall come to *p*, that the … Jer 42:16
And it came to *p*, that when … Jer 43:1
come to *p* in the latter days … Jer 49:39
doth any son of man *p* thereby … Jer 51:43 5674
LORD it came to *p* in Jerusalem … Jer 52:3
it came to *p* in the ninth year of … Jer 52:4
it came to *p* in the seven and … Jer 52:31
nothing to you, all ye that *p* by … Lam 1:12 5674
All that *p* by clap their hands at … Lam 2:15 5674
he that saith, and it cometh to *p* … Lam 3:37
our prayer should not *p* through … Lam 3:44 5674
also shall *p* through unto thee … Lam 4:21 5674
Now it came to *p* in the thirtieth … Eze 1:1
it came to *p* at the end of seven … Eze 3:16
cause it to *p* upon thine head and … Eze 5:1 5674
in the sight of all that *p* by … Eze 5:14 5674
blood shall *p* through thee … Eze 5:17 5674
it came to *p* in the sixth year, … Eze 8:1
And it came to *p*, while they were … Eze 9:8
And it came to *p*, that when he had … Eze 10:6
And it came to *p*, when I … Eze 11:13
I shall speak shall come to *p* … Eze 12:25 6213
beasts to *p* through the land … Eze 14:15 5674
that no man may *p* through because … Eze 14:15 5674
to *p* through the fire for them … Eze 16:21 5674
it came to *p* after all thy … Eze 16:23
it came to *p* in the seventh year, … Eze 20:1
in that they caused to *p* through … Eze 20:26 5674
your sons to *p* through the fire … Eze 20:31 5674
will cause you to *p* under the rod … Eze 20:37 5674
cometh, and shall be brought to *p* … Eze 21:7
to *p* for them through the fire, … Eze 23:37 5674
it shall come to *p*, and I will do … Eze 24:14
it came to *p* in the eleventh year … Eze 26:1
No foot of man shall *p* through it … Eze 29:11 5674
foot of beast shall *p* through it … Eze 29:11 5674
it came to *p* in the seven and … Eze 29:17
it came to *p* in the eleventh year … Eze 30:20
it came to *p* in the eleventh year … Eze 31:1
it came to *p* in the twelfth year, … Eze 32:1
It came to *p* also in the twelfth … Eze 32:17
Whom dost thou *p* in beauty … Eze 32:19
it came to *p* in the twelfth year … Eze 33:21
that none shall *p* through … Eze 33:28 5674
And when this cometh to *p*, (lo, it … Eze 33:33
caused me to *p* by them round … Eze 37:2 5674
It shall also come to *p*, that at … Eze 38:10
it shall come to *p* at the same … Eze 38:18
And it shall come to *p* in that day … Eze 39:11
that *p* through the land, when any … Eze 39:15 5674
And it shall come to *p*, that when … Eze 44:17
caused me to *p* by the four … Eze 46:21 5674
a river that I could not *p* over … Eze 47:5 5674
And it shall come to *p*, that every … Eze 47:9
And it shall come to *p*, that the … Eze 47:10
And it shall come to *p*, that ye … Eze 47:22
And it shall come to *p*, that in … Eze 47:23
what should come to *p* hereafter … Dan 2:29
to thee what shall come to *p* … Dan 2:29
what shall come to *p* hereafter … Dan 2:45
and let seven times *p* over him … Dan 4:16 2499
till seven times *p* over him … Dan 4:23 2499
and seven times shall *p* over thee … Dan 4:25 2499
and seven times shall *p* over thee … Dan 4:32 2499
dominion, which shall not *p* away … Dan 7:14 5709
and it came to *p*, when I saw, that … Dan 8:2
And it came to *p*, when I, even I … Dan 8:15
come, and overflow, and *p* through … Dan 11:10 5674
and shall overflow and *p* over … Dan 11:40 5674
And it shall come to *p* at that day … Hos 1:5
and it shall come to *p*, that in … Hos 1:10
And it shall come to *p* in that day … Hos 2:21
And it shall come to *p* afterward … Joel 2:28
And it shall come to *p*, that … Joel 2:32
strangers *p* through her any more … Joel 3:17 5674
And it shall come to *p* in that day … Joel 3:18
Gilgal, and *p* not to Beer-sheba … Amos 5:5 5674
for I will *p* through thee, saith … Amos 5:17 5674
P ye unto Calneh, and see … Amos 6:2 5674
And it shall come to *p*, if there … Amos 6:9
And it came to *p*, that when they … Amos 7:2
will not again *p* by them any more … Amos 7:8 5674
will not again *p* by them any more … Amos 8:2 5674
And it shall come to *p* in that day … Amos 8:9
And it came to *p*, when the sun did … Jonah 4:8
P ye away, thou inhabitant of … Mic 1:11 5674
p by securely as men averse from … Mic 2:8 5674
and their king shall *p* before them … Mic 2:13 5674
the last days it shall come to *p* … Mic 4:1
And it shall come to *p* in that day … Mic 5:10
cut down, when he shall *p* through … Nah 1:12 5674
shall no more *p* through thee … Nah 1:15 5674
And it shall come to *p*, that all … Nah 3:7
mind change, and he shall *p* over … Hab 1:11 5674
it shall come to *p* in the day of … Zeph 1:8
And it shall come to *p* in that day … Zeph 1:10
it shall come to *p* at that time … Zeph 1:12
before the day *p* as the chaff … Zeph 2:2 5674
thine iniquity to *p* from thee … Zec 3:4 5674
And this shall come to *p*, if ye … Zec 6:15
it came to *p* in the fourth year … Zec 7:1
Therefore it is come to *p* … Zec 7:13
And it shall come to *p*, that as ye … Zec 8:13
It shall yet come to *p*, that … Zec 8:20
In those days it shall come to *p* … Zec 8:23
no oppressor shall *p* through them … Zec 9:8 5674
he shall *p* through the sea with … Zec 10:11 5674
And it shall come to *p* in that day … Zec 12:9
And it shall come to *p* in that day … Zec 13:2
spirit to *p* out of the land … Zec 13:2 5674
And it shall come to *p*, that when … Zec 13:3
And it shall come to *p* in that day … Zec 13:4
And it shall come to *p*, that in … Zec 13:8
And it shall come to *p* in that day … Zec 14:6
but it shall come to *p*, that at … Zec 14:7
And it shall come to *p* in that day … Zec 14:13
And it shall come to *p*, that every … Zec 14:16
unto you, Till heaven and earth *p* … Mt 5:18 *3928*
shall in no wise *p* from the law … Mt 5:18 *3928*
And it came to *p*, when Jesus had … Mt 7:28
that no man might *p* by that way … Mt 8:28 *3928*
And it came to *p*, as Jesus sat at … Mt 9:10
And it came to *p*, when Jesus had … Mt 11:1
And it came to *p*, that when Jesus … Mt 13:53
And it came to *p*, that when Jesus … Mt 19:1
all these things must come to *p* … Mt 24:6
you, This generation shall not *p* … Mt 24:34 *3928*
Heaven and earth shall *p* away … Mt 24:35 *3928*
but my words shall not *p* away … Mt 24:35 *3928*
And it came to *p*, when Jesus had … Mt 26:1
possible, let this cup *p* from me … Mt 26:39 *3928*
this cup may not *p* away from me … Mt 26:42 *3928*
it came to *p* in those days, that … Mk 1:9
And it came to *p*, that, as Jesus … Mk 2:15
And it came to *p*, that he went … Mk 2:23
And it came to *p*, as he sowed, … Mk 4:4
Let us *p* over unto the other side … Mk 4:35 *1330*
which he saith shall come to *p* … Mk 11:23
shall see these things come to *p* … Mk 13:29
that this generation shall not *p* … Mk 13:30 *3928*
Heaven and earth shall *p* away … Mk 13:31 *3928*
but my words shall not *p* away … Mk 13:31 *3928*
the hour might *p* from him … Mk 14:35 *3928*
And it came to *p*, that while he … Lk 1:8
And it came to *p*, that, as soon as … Lk 1:23
And it came to *p*, that, when … Lk 1:41
And it came to *p*, that on the … Lk 1:59
it came to *p* in those days, that … Lk 2:1
And it came to *p*, as the angels … Lk 2:15
see this thing which is come to *p* … Lk 2:15
And it came to *p*, that after three … Lk 2:46
were baptized, it came to *p*, … Lk 3:21
And it came to *p*, that, as the … Lk 5:1
And it came to *p*, when he was in a … Lk 5:12
it came to *p* on a certain day, as … Lk 5:17
it came to *p* on the second … Lk 6:1
it came to *p* also on another … Lk 6:6
it came to *p* in those days, that … Lk 6:12
it came to *p* the day after, that … Lk 7:11
And it came to *p* afterward … Lk 8:1
Now it came to *p* on a certain day … Lk 8:22
And it came to *p*, that, when Jesus … Lk 8:40
And it came to *p*, as he was alone … Lk 9:18
it came to *p* about an eight days … Lk 9:28
And it came to *p*, as they departed … Lk 9:33
And it came to *p*, that on the next … Lk 9:37
And it came to *p*, when the time … Lk 9:51
And it came to *p*, that, as they … Lk 9:57
Now it came to *p*, as they went, … Lk 10:38
And it came to *p*, that, as he was … Lk 11:1
And it came to *p*, when the devil … Lk 11:14
And it came to *p*, as he spake … Lk 11:27
p over judgment and the love of … Lk 11:42 *3928*
and it cometh to *p* … Lk 12:55
And it came to *p*, as he went into … Lk 14:1
easier for heaven and earth to *p* … Lk 16:17 *3928*
And it came to *p*, that the beggar … Lk 16:22
would *p* from hence to you cannot … Lk 16:26 *1224*
neither can they *p* to us, that … Lk 16:26 *1276*
And it came to *p*, as he went to … Lk 17:11
And it came to *p*, that, as they … Lk 17:14
And it came to *p*, that as he was … Lk 18:35
And hearing the multitude *p* by … Lk 18:36 *1279*
for he was to *p* that way … Lk 19:4 *1330*
And it came to *p*, that when he was … Lk 19:15
And it came to *p*, when he was come … Lk 19:29
And it came to *p*, that on one of … Lk 20:1
when these things shall come to *p* … Lk 21:7
these things must first come to *p* … Lk 21:9
these things begin to come to *p* … Lk 21:28
ye see these things come to *p* … Lk 21:31
This generation shall not *p* away … Lk 21:32 *3928*
Heaven and earth shall *p* away … Lk 21:33 *3928*
but my words shall not *p* away … Lk 21:33 *3928*
these things that shall come to *p* … Lk 21:36
And it came to *p*, as they were … Lk 24:4
at that which was come to *p* … Lk 24:12
And it came to *p*, that, while they … Lk 24:15
are come to *p* there in these days … Lk 24:18
And it came to *p*, as he sat at … Lk 24:30
And it came to *p*, while he blessed … Lk 24:51
come, that, when it is come to *p* … Jn 13:19
have told you before it come to *p* … Jn 14:29
that, when it is come to *p* … Jn 14:29
But this cometh to *p*, that the … Jn 15:25
shall come to *p* in the last days … Acts 2:17
And it shall come to *p*, that … Acts 2:21
And it shall come to *p*, that every … Acts 3:23
it came to *p* on the morrow, that … Acts 4:5
And it came to *p*, as Peter passed … Acts 9:32 *1330*
it came to *p* in those days, that … Acts 9:37
And it came to *p*, that he tarried … Acts 9:43
And it came to *p*, that a whole … Acts 11:26
which came to *p* in the days of … Acts 11:28
And it came to *p* in Iconium … Acts 14:1
And it came to *p*, as we went to … Acts 16:16
he was disposed to *p* into Achaia … Acts 18:27 *1330*
And it came to *p*, that, while … Acts 19:1
And it came to *p*, that after we … Acts 21:1
And it came to *p*, that, as I made … Acts 22:6
And it came to *p*, that, when I was … Acts 22:17
And so it came to *p*, that they … Acts 27:44
And it came to *p*, that the father … Acts 28:8
And it came to *p*, that after three … Acts 28:17
And it shall come to *p*, that in … Rom 9:26
if she *p* the flower of her age, … 1Cor 7:36 *5230*
then shall be brought to *p* the … 1Cor 15:54
when I shall *p* through Macedonia … 1Cor 16:5 *1330*
for I do *p* through Macedonia … 1Cor 16:5 *1330*
to *p* by you into Macedonia, and to … 2Cor 1:16 *1330*
even as it came to *p*, and ye know … 1Th 3:4
of the grass he shall *p* away … Jas 1:10 *3928*
p the time of your sojourning … 1Pet 1:17 *390*
shall *p* away with a great noise … 2Pet 3:10 *3928*
which must shortly come to *p* … Rev 1:1

PASSAGE

give Israel *p* through his border … Num 20:21 5674
at the *p* of the children of … Josh 22:11 1552
went out to the *p* of Michmash … 1Sa 13:23 4569
They are gone over the *p* … Is 10:29 4569

PASSAGES

took the *p* of Jordan before the … Judg 12:5 4569
and slew him at the *p* of Jordan … Judg 12:6 4569
And between the *p*, by which … 1Sa 14:4 4569
in Bashan, and cry from the *p* … Jer 22:20 5676
that the *p* are stopped, and the … Jer 51:32 4569

PASSED

Abram *p* through the land unto the … Gen 12:6 5674
a burning lamp that *p* between … Gen 15:17 5674
p over the river, and set his face … Gen 31:21 5674
my staff I *p* over this Jordan … Gen 32:10 5674
sons, and *p* over the ford Jabbok … Gen 32:22 5674
as he *p* over Penuel the sun rose … Gen 32:31 5674
he *p* over before them, and bowed … Gen 33:3 5674
Then there *p* by Midianites … Gen 37:28 5674
who *p* over the houses of the … Ex 12:27 6452
the LORD *p* by before him, and … Ex 34:6 5674
which we *p* through to search it, … Num 14:7 5674
left, until we have *p* thy borders … Num 20:17 5674
p through the midst of the sea … Num 33:8 5674
When ye are *p* over Jordan into … Num 33:51 5674
when we *p* by from our brethren … Deut 2:8 5674
p by the way of the wilderness of … Deut 2:8 5674
of this law, when thou art *p* over … Deut 27:3 5674
through the nations which ye *p* by … Deut 29:16 5674
p over, and came to Joshua the son … Josh 2:23 5674
lodged there before they *p* over … Josh 3:1 5674
for ye have not *p* this way … Josh 3:4 5674
the people *p* over right against … Josh 3:16 5674
Israelites *p* over on dry ground … Josh 3:17 5674
people were *p* clean over Jordan … Josh 3:17 5674
people were clean *p* over Jordan … Josh 4:1 5674
when it *p* over Jordan, the waters … Josh 4:7 5674
and the people hasted and *p* over … Josh 4:10 5674
all the people were clean *p* over … Josh 4:11 5674
that the ark of the LORD *p* over … Josh 4:11 5674
p over armed before the children … Josh 4:12 5674
war *p* over before the LORD unto … Josh 4:13 5674
before you, until ye were *p* over … Josh 4:23 5674
of Israel, until we were *p* over … Josh 5:1 5674
rams' horns *p* on before the LORD … Josh 6:8 5674
Then Joshua *p* from Makkedah, and … Josh 10:29 5674
Joshua *p* from Libnah, and all … Josh 10:31 5674
from Lachish Joshua *p* unto Eglon … Josh 10:34 5674
p along to Zin, and ascended up on … Josh 15:3 5674
p along to Hezron, and went up to … Josh 15:3 5674
From thence it *p* toward Azmon … Josh 15:4 5674

and *p* along by the north of	Josh 15:6	5674
the border *p* toward the waters of	Josh 15:7	5674
p along unto the side of mount	Josh 15:10	5674
Beth-shemesh, and *p* on to Timnah	Josh 15:10	5674
p along to mount Baalah, and went	Josh 15:11	5674
p by it on the east to Janohah	Josh 16:6	5674
p through the land, and described	Josh 18:9	5674
p along toward the side over	Josh 18:18	5674
the border *p* along to the side of	Josh 18:19	5674
all the people through whom we *p*	Josh 24:17	5674
p beyond the quarries, and escaped	Judg 3:26	5674
p over, he, and the three hundred	Judg 8:4	5674
Ammon *p* over Jordan to fight also	Judg 10:9	5674
he *p* over Gilead, and Manasseh, and	Judg 11:29	5674
p over Mizpeh of Gilead, and from	Judg 11:29	5674
from Mizpeh of Gilead he *p* over	Judg 11:29	5674
So Jephthah *p* over unto the	Judg 11:32	5674
p over against the children of	Judg 12:3	5674
they *p* thence unto mount Ephraim,	Judg 18:13	5674
And they *p* on and went their way	Judg 19:14	5674
he *p* through mount Ephraim, and	1Sa 9:4	5674
p through the land of Shalisha,	1Sa 9:4	5674
then they *p* through the land of	1Sa 9:4	5674
he *p* through the land of the	1Sa 9:4	5674
pass on before us, (and he *p* on	1Sa 9:27	5674
the battle *p* over unto Beth-aven	1Sa 14:23	5674
p on, and gone down to Gilgal	1Sa 15:12	5674
he *p* over with the six hundred	1Sa 27:2	5674
the Philistines *p* on by hundreds	1Sa 29:2	5674
his men *p* on in the rereward with	1Sa 29:2	5674
p over Jordan, and went through	2Sa 2:29	5674
p over Jordan, and came to Helam	2Sa 10:17	5674
all his servants *p* on beside him	2Sa 15:18	5674
from Gath, *p* on before the king	2Sa 15:18	5674
And Ittai the Gittite *p* over	2Sa 15:22	5674
voice, and all the people *p* over	2Sa 15:23	5674
himself *p* over the brook Kidron	2Sa 15:23	5674
and all the people *p* over	2Sa 15:23	5674
with him, and they *p* over Jordan	2Sa 17:22	5674
Absalom *p* over Jordan, he and all	2Sa 17:24	5674
they *p* over Jordan, and pitched in	2Sa 24:5	5674
And, behold, men *p* by, and saw the	1Kin 13:25	5674
And, behold, the LORD *p* by	1Kin 19:11	5674
and Elijah *p* by him, and cast his	1Kin 19:19	5674
And as the king *p* by, he cried	1Kin 20:39	5674
on a day, that Elisha *p* to Shunem	2Kin 4:8	5674
so it was, that as oft as he *p* by	2Kin 4:8	5674
Gehazi *p* on before them, and laid	2Kin 4:31	5674
he *p* by upon the wall, and the	2Kin 6:30	5674
there *p* by a wild beast that was	2Kin 14:9	5674
p over Jordan, and came upon them,	1Chr 19:17	5674
king Solomon *p* all the kings of	2Chr 9:22	1431
there *p* by a wild beast that was	2Chr 25:18	5674
So the posts *p* from city to city	2Chr 30:10	5674
Then a spirit *p* before my face	Job 4:15	2498
They are *p* away as the swift	Job 9:26	2498
and no stranger *p* among them	Job 15:19	5674
it, nor the fierce lion *p* by it	Job 28:8	5710
was before him his thick clouds *p*	Ps 18:12	5674
Yet he *p* away, and, lo, he was not	Ps 37:36	5674
assembled, they *p* by together	Ps 48:4	5674
our days are *p* away in thy wrath	Ps 90:9	6437
but a little that I *p* from them	Song 3:4	5674
come to Aiath, he is *p* to Migron	Is 10:28	5674
my judgment is *p* over from my God	Is 40:27	5674
He pursued them, and *p* safely	Is 41:3	5674
a land that no man *p* through	Jer 2:6	5674
and the holy flesh is *p* from thee	Jer 11:15	5674
p between the parts thereof,	Jer 34:18	5674
which *p* between the parts of the	Jer 34:19	5674
he hath *p* the time appointed	Jer 46:17	5674
when I *p* by thee, and saw thee	Eze 16:6	5674
Now when I *p* by thee, and looked	Eze 16:8	5674
on every one that *p* by	Eze 16:15	5674
thy feet to every one that *p* by	Eze 16:25	5674
in the sight of all that *p* by	Eze 36:34	5674
a river that could not be *p* over	Eze 47:5	5674
the smell of fire had *p* on them	Dan 3:27	5709
palace, and *p* the night fasting	Dan 6:18	
but I *p* over upon her fair neck	Hos 10:11	5674
billows and thy waves *p* over me	Jonah 2:3	5674
have *p* through the gate, and are	Mic 2:13	5674
not thy wickedness *p* continually	Nah 3:19	5674
the overflowing of the water *p* by	Hab 3:10	5674
that no man *p* through nor	Zec 7:14	5674
p over, and came into his own city	Mt 9:1	*1276*
as Jesus *p* forth from thence, he	Mt 9:9	*3855*
when they heard that Jesus *p* by	Mt 20:30	*3855*
they that *p* by reviled him,	Mt 27:39	*3899*
And as he *p* by, he saw Levi the	Mk 2:14	*3855*
when Jesus was *p* over again by	Mk 5:21	*1276*
place, and now the time is far *p*	Mk 6:35	
the sea, and would have *p* by them	Mk 6:48	*3928*
And when they had *p* over, they	Mk 6:53	*1276*
thence, and *p* through Galilee	Mk 9:30	*3899*
And in the morning, as they *p* by	Mk 11:20	*3899*
one Simon a Cyrenian, who *p* by	Mk 15:21	*3855*
they that *p* by railed on him,	Mk 15:29	*3899*
he *p* by on the other side	Lk 10:31	*492*
on him, and *p* by on the other side	Lk 10:32	*492*
that he *p* through the midst of	Lk 17:11	*1330*
entered and *p* through Jericho	Lk 19:1	*1330*
but is *p* from death unto life	Jn 5:24	*3327*
the midst of them, and so *p* by	Jn 8:59	*3855*
And as Jesus *p* by, he saw a man	Jn 9:1	*3855*
as Peter *p* throughout all	Acts 9:32	*1330*
out, and *p* on through one street	Acts 12:10	*4281*
after they had *p* throughout	Acts 14:24	*1330*
they *p* through Phenice and Samaria	Acts 15:3	*1330*
Now when they had *p* through	Acts 17:1	*1353*
For as I *p* by, and beheld your	Acts 17:23	*1330*
Paul having *p* through the upper	Acts 19:1	*1330*
when he had *p* through Macedonia	Acts 19:21	*1330*
so death *p* upon all men, for that	Rom 5:12	*1330*
cloud, and all *p* through the sea	1Cor 10:1	*1330*
old things are *p* away	2Cor 5:17	*3928*
that is *p* into the heavens, Jesus	Heb 4:14	*1330*
By faith they *p* through the Red	Heb 11:29	*1224*
we have *p* from death unto life	1Jn 3:14	*3327*
and the first earth were *p* away	Rev 21:1	*3928*
for the former things are *p* away	Rev 21:4	*565*

PASSEDST

Wherefore *p* thou over to fight	Judg 12:1	5674

PASSENGERS

To call *p* who go right on their	Prov 9:15	
the valley of the *p* on the east	Eze 39:11	5674
it shall stop the noses of the *p*	Eze 39:11	5674
the land to bury with the *p* those	Eze 39:14	5674
the *p* that pass through the land,	Eze 39:15	5674

PASSEST

all the kingdoms whither thou *p*	Deut 3:21	5674
whither thou *p* over Jordan to go	Deut 30:18	5674
If thou *p* on with me, then thou	2Sa 15:33	5674
p over the brook Kidron, thou	1Kin 2:37	5674
When thou *p* through the waters, I	Is 43:2	5674

PASSETH

every one that *p* among them that	Ex 30:13	5674
Every one that *p* among them that	Ex 30:14	5674
come to pass, while my glory *p* by	Ex 33:22	5674
of whatsoever *p* under the rod	Lev 27:32	5674
p over before you into Jordan	Josh 3:11	5674
p along unto the borders of Archi	Josh 16:2	5674
from thence *p* on along on the	Josh 19:13	5674
every one that *p* by it shall be	1Kin 9:8	5674
which *p* by us continually	2Kin 4:9	5674
of every one that *p* the account	2Kin 12:4	5674
to every one that *p* by it	2Chr 7:21	5674
he *p* on also, but I perceive him	Job 9:11	2498
for ever against him, and he *p*	Job 14:20	1980
my welfare *p* away as a cloud	Job 30:15	5674
but the wind *p*, and cleanseth them	Job 37:21	5674
whatsoever *p* through the paths of	Ps 8:8	5674
a wind that *p* away, and cometh not	Ps 78:39	1980
For the wind *p* over it, and it is	Ps 103:16	5674
days are as a shadow that *p* away	Ps 144:4	5674
As the whirlwind *p*, so is the	Prov 10:25	5674
He that *p* by, and meddleth with	Prov 26:17	5674
One generation *p* away, and another	Eccl 1:4	1980
shall be as chaff that *p* away	Is 29:5	5674
a wilderness, that none *p* through	Jer 9:12	5674
that *p* away by the wind of the	Jer 13:24	5674
every one that *p* thereby shall be	Jer 18:16	5674
every one that *p* thereby shall be	Jer 19:8	5674
and cut off from it him that *p* out	Eze 35:7	5674
and as the early dew that *p* away	Hos 13:3	1980
p by the transgression of the	Mic 7:18	5674
every one that *p* by her shall	Zeph 2:15	5674
streets waste, that none *p* by	Zeph 3:6	5674
army, because of him that *p* by	Zec 9:8	5674
him, that Jesus of Nazareth *p* by	Lk 18:37	*3928*
the fashion of this world *p* away	1Cor 7:31	*3855*
which *p* knowledge, that ye might	Eph 3:19	*5235*
which *p* all understanding, shall	Phil 4:7	*5242*
And the world *p* away, and the lust	1Jn 2:17	*3855*

PASSING

We are *p* from Beth-lehem-judah	Judg 19:18	5674
wonderful, *p* the love of women	2Sa 1:26	
people had done *p* out of the city	2Sa 15:24	5674
of Israel was *p* by upon the wall	2Kin 6:26	5674
Who *p* through the valley of Baca	Ps 84:6	5674
P through the street near her	Prov 7:8	5674
p over he will preserve it	Is 31:5	5674
p through the land to bury with	Eze 39:14	5674
But he *p* through the midst of	Lk 4:30	*1330*
p by might overshadow some of	Acts 5:15	*2064*
p through he preached in all the	Acts 8:40	*1330*
they *p* by Mysia came down to	Acts 16:8	*3928*
And, hardly *p* it, came unto a	Acts 27:8	*3881*

PASSION

his *p* by many infallible proofs	Acts 1:3	*3958*

PASSIONS

also are men of like *p* with you	Acts 14:15	*3663*
a man subject to like *p* as we are	Jas 5:17	*3663*

PASSOVER

it is the LORD's *p*	Ex 12:11	6453
to your families, and kill the *p*	Ex 12:21	6453
is the sacrifice of the LORD's *p*	Ex 12:27	6453
This is the ordinance of the *p*	Ex 12:43	6453
and will keep the *p* to the LORD	Ex 12:48	6453
of the *p* be left unto the morning	Ex 34:25	6453
month at even is the LORD's *p*	Lev 23:5	6453
the *p* at his appointed season	Num 9:2	6453
that they should keep the *p*	Num 9:4	6453
they kept the *p* on the fourteenth	Num 9:5	6453
could not keep the *p* on that day	Num 9:6	6453
he shall keep the *p* unto the LORD	Num 9:10	6453
of the *p* they shall keep it	Num 9:12	6453
and forbeareth to keep the *p*	Num 9:13	6453
and will keep the *p* unto the LORD	Num 9:14	6453
to the ordinance of the *p*	Num 9:14	6453
first month is the *p* of the LORD	Num 28:16	6453
on the morrow after the *p* the	Num 33:3	6453
keep the *p* unto the LORD thy God	Deut 16:1	6453
the *p* unto the LORD thy God	Deut 16:2	6453
the *p* within any of thy gates	Deut 16:5	6453
shalt sacrifice the *p* at even	Deut 16:6	6453
kept the *p* on the fourteenth day	Josh 5:10	6453
land on the morrow after the *p*	Josh 5:11	6453
Keep the *p* unto the LORD your God	2Kin 23:21	6453
a *p* from the days of the judges	2Kin 23:22	6453
wherein this *p* was holden to the	2Kin 23:23	6453
to keep the *p* unto the LORD God	2Chr 30:1	6453
to keep the *p* in the second month	2Chr 30:2	6453
they should come to keep the *p*	2Chr 30:5	6453
Then they killed the *p* on the	2Chr 30:15	6453
yet did they eat the *p* otherwise	2Chr 30:18	6453
Moreover Josiah kept a *p* unto the	2Chr 35:1	6453
and they killed the *p* on the	2Chr 35:1	6453
So kill the *p*, and sanctify	2Chr 35:6	6453
and kids, all for the *p* offerings	2Chr 35:7	6453
for the *p* offerings two thousand	2Chr 35:8	6453
gave unto the Levites for *p*	2Chr 35:9	6453
And they killed the *p*, and the	2Chr 35:11	6453
they roasted the *p* with fire	2Chr 35:13	6453
the same day, to keep the *p*	2Chr 35:16	6453
present kept the *p* at that time	2Chr 35:17	6453
there was no *p* like to that kept	2Chr 35:18	6453
keep such a *p* as Josiah kept	2Chr 35:18	6453
reign of Josiah was this *p* kept	2Chr 35:19	6453
of the captivity kept the *p* upon	Ezr 6:19	6453
killed the *p* for all the children	Ezr 6:20	6453
of the month, ye shall have the *p*	Eze 45:21	6453
two days is the feast of the *p*	Mt 26:2	*3957*
we prepare for thee to eat the *p*	Mt 26:17	*3957*
I will keep the *p* at thy house	Mt 26:18	*3957*
and they made ready the *p*	Mt 26:19	*3957*
two days was the feast of the *p*	Mk 14:1	*3957*
bread, when they killed the *p*	Mk 14:12	*3957*
that thou mayest eat the *p*	Mk 14:12	*3957*
shall eat the *p* with my disciples	Mk 14:14	*3957*
and they made ready the *p*	Mk 14:16	*3957*
every year at the feast of the *p*	Lk 2:41	*3957*
drew nigh, which is called the *P*	Lk 22:1	*3957*
when the *p* must be killed	Lk 22:7	*3957*
saying, Go and prepare us the *p*	Lk 22:8	*3957*
shall eat the *p* with my disciples	Lk 22:11	*3957*
and they made ready the *p*	Lk 22:13	*3957*
this *p* with you before I suffer	Lk 22:15	*3957*
the Jews' *p* was at hand, and Jesus	Jn 2:13	*3957*
when he was in Jerusalem at the *p*	Jn 2:23	*3957*
And the *p*, a feast of the Jews,	Jn 6:4	*3957*
the Jews' *p* was nigh at hand	Jn 11:55	*3957*
up to Jerusalem before the *p*	Jn 11:55	*3957*
days before the *p* came to Bethany	Jn 12:1	*3957*
Now before the feast of the *p*	Jn 13:1	*3957*
but that they might eat the *p*	Jn 18:28	*3957*
release unto you one at the *p*	Jn 18:39	*3957*
it was the preparation of the *p*	Jn 19:14	*3957*
For even Christ our *p* is	1Cor 5:7	*3957*
Through faith he kept the *p*	Heb 11:28	*3957*

PASSOVERS

the *p* for every one that was not	2Chr 30:17	6453

PAST

the days of his mourning were *p*	Gen 50:4	5674
to push with his horn in time *p*	Ex 21:29	8032
ox hath used to push in time *p*	Ex 21:36	8032
way, until we be *p* thy borders	Num 21:22	5674
Emims dwelt therein in times *p*	Deut 2:10	
ask now of the days that are *p*	Deut 4:32	7223
and hated him not in times *p*	Deut 4:42	8032
whom he hated not in time *p*	Deut 19:4	8032
as he hated him not in time *p*	Deut 19:6	8032
the bitterness of death is *p*	1Sa 15:32	5493
in his presence, as in times *p*	1Sa 19:7	8032
in times *p* to be king over you	2Sa 3:17	8032
Also in time *p*, when Saul was	2Sa 5:2	8032
And when the mourning was *p*	2Sa 11:27	5493
a little *p* the top of the hill	2Sa 16:1	5674
came to pass, when midday was *p*	1Kin 18:29	5674
was the ruler over them in time *p*	1Chr 9:20	
And moreover in time *p*, even when	1Chr 11:2	8032
doeth great things *p* finding out	Job 9:10	369
me secret, until thy wrath be *p*	Job 14:13	7725
My days are *p*, my purposes are	Job 17:11	5674
Oh that I were as in months *p*	Job 29:2	6924
are but as yesterday when it is *p*	Ps 90:4	5674
and God requireth that which is *p*	Eccl 3:15	7291
For, lo, the winter is *p*, the	Song 2:11	5674
The harvest is *p*, the summer is	Jer 8:20	5674
place, and the time is now *p*	Mt 14:15	*3928*
And when the sabbath was *p*	Mk 16:1	*1230*
And when the voice was *p*, Jesus	Lk 9:36	*1096*
When they were *p* the first	Acts 12:10	*1330*
Who in times *p* suffered all	Acts 14:16	*3944*
the fast was now already *p*	Acts 27:9	*3928*
the remission of sins that are *p*	Rom 3:25	*4266*
For as ye in times *p* have not	Rom 11:30	
and his ways *p* finding out	Rom 11:33	*421*
in time *p* in the Jews' religion	Gal 1:13	
p now preacheth the faith which	Gal 1:23	
as I have also told you in time *p*	Gal 5:21	*4302*
Wherein in time *p* ye walked	Eph 2:2	
times *p* in the lusts of our flesh	Eph 2:3	
in time *p* Gentiles in the flesh	Eph 2:11	
Who being *p* feeling have given	Eph 4:19	*524*
the resurrection is *p* already	2Ti 2:18	*1096*
Which in time *p* was to thee	Philem 11	
in time *p* unto the fathers by the	Heb 1:1	*3819*
of a child when she was *p* age	Heb 11:11	*3844*
Which in time *p* were not a people	1Pet 2:10	
For the time *p* of our life may	1Pet 4:3	*3928*
because the darkness is *p*	1Jn 2:8	*3855*
One woe is *p*	Rev 9:12	*565*
The second woe is *p*	Rev 11:14	*565*

PASTOR

from being a *p* to follow thee	Jer 17:16	7462

PASTORS

the *p* also transgressed against	Jer 2:8	7462
I will give you *p* according to	Jer 3:15	7462
For the *p* are become brutish, and	Jer 10:21	7462
Many *p* have destroyed my vineyard	Jer 12:10	7462
The wind shall eat up all thy *p*	Jer 22:22	7462
Woe be unto the *p* that destroy	Jer 23:1	7462
against the *p* that feed my people	Jer 23:2	7462
and some, *p* and teachers	Eph 4:11	*4166*

PASTURE
have no p for their flocks ... Gen 47:4 4829
to seek p for their flocks ... 1Chr 4:39 4829
And they found fat p and good, and ... 1Chr 4:40 4829
because there was p there for ... 1Chr 4:41 4829
range of the mountains is his p ... Job 39:8 4829
smoke against the sheep of thy p ... Ps 74:1 4830
sheep of thy p will give thee ... Ps 79:13 4830
and we are the people of his p ... Ps 95:7 4830
his people, and the sheep of his p ... Ps 100:3 4830
joy of wild asses, a p of flocks ... Is 32:14 4829
and scatter the sheep of my p ... Jer 23:1 4830
for the LORD hath spoiled their p ... Jer 25:36 4830
become like harts that find no p ... Lam 1:6 4829
I will feed them in a good p ... Eze 34:14 4829
in a fat p shall they feed upon ... Eze 34:14 4829
you to have eaten up the good p ... Eze 34:18 4829
And ye my flock, the flock of my p ... Eze 34:31 4830
According to their p, so were ... Hos 13:6 4830
perplexed, because they have no p ... Joel 1:18 4829
and shall go in and out, and find p ... Jn 10:9 3542

PASTURES
oxen, and twenty oxen out of the p ... 1Kin 4:23 7471
maketh me to lie down in green p ... Ps 23:2 4999
drop upon the p of the wilderness ... Ps 65:12 4999
The p are clothed with flocks ... Ps 65:13 3733
shall thy cattle feed in large p ... Is 30:23 3733
their p shall be in all high ... Is 49:9 4830
your feet the residue of your p ... Eze 34:18 4829
out of the fat p of Israel ... Eze 45:15 4945
devoured the p of the wilderness ... Joel 1:19 4999
devoured the p of the wilderness ... Joel 1:20 4999
for the p of the wilderness do ... Joel 2:22 4999

PATARA (*pat'-a-rah*) *A city in Lycia in Asia Minor.*
Rhodes, and from thence unto P ... Acts 21:1 3959

PATE
shall come down upon his own p ... Ps 7:16 6936

PATH
by the way, an adder in the p ... Gen 49:17 734
stood in a p of the vineyards ... Num 22:24 4934
There is a p which no fowl ... Job 28:7 5410
They mar my p, they set forward ... Job 30:13 5410
He maketh a p to shine after him ... Job 41:32 5410
Thou wilt shew me the p of life ... Ps 16:11 734
O LORD, and lead me in a plain p ... Ps 27:11 734
thy p in the great waters, and thy ... Ps 77:19 7635
go in the p of thy commandments ... Ps 119:35 5410
my feet, and a light unto my p ... Ps 119:105 5410
Thou compassest my p and my lying ... Ps 139:3 734
within me, then thou knewest my p ... Ps 142:3 5410
refrain thy foot from their p ... Prov 1:15 5410
yea, every good p ... Prov 2:9 4570
not into the p of the wicked ... Prov 4:14 734
But the p of the just is as the ... Prov 4:18 734
Ponder the p of thy feet, and let ... Prov 4:26 4570
shouldest ponder the p of life ... Prov 5:6 734
dost weigh the p of the just ... Is 26:7 4570
the way, turn aside out of the p ... Is 30:11 734
taught him in the p of judgment ... Is 40:14 734
sea, and a p in the mighty waters ... Is 43:16 5410
shall walk every one in his p ... Joel 2:8 4546

PATHROS (*path'-ros*) See PATHRUSIM. *A name for Upper Egypt.*
Assyria, and from Egypt, and from P ... Is 11:11 6624
at Noph, and in the country of P ... Jer 44:1 6624
dwelt in the land of Egypt, in P ... Jer 44:15 6624
them to return into the land of P ... Eze 29:14 6624
And I will make P desolate ... Eze 30:14 6624

PATHRUS See PATHROS.

PATHRUSIM (*path-ru'-sim*) *A descendant of Mizraim.*
And P, and Casluhim, (out of whom ... Gen 10:14 6625
And P, and Casluhim, (of whom came ... 1Chr 1:12 6625

PATHS
The p of their way are turned ... Job 6:18 734
So are the p of all that forget ... Job 8:13 734
and lookest narrowly unto all my p ... Job 13:27 734
and he hath set darkness in my p ... Job 19:8 5410
nor abide in the p thereof ... Job 24:13 5410
the stocks, he marketh all my p ... Job 33:11 734
know the p to the house thereof ... Job 38:20 5410
passeth through the p of the seas ... Ps 8:8 734
me from the p of the destroyer ... Ps 17:4 734
Hold up my goings in thy p ... Ps 17:5 4570
he leadeth me in the p of ... Ps 23:3 4570
teach me thy p ... Ps 25:4 734
All the p of the LORD are mercy ... Ps 25:10 734
and thy p drop fatness ... Ps 65:11 4570
He keepeth the p of judgment ... Prov 2:8 734
Who leave the p of uprightness, ... Prov 2:13 734
and they froward in their p ... Prov 2:15 4570
death, and her p unto the dead ... Prov 2:18 4570
take they hold of the p of life ... Prov 2:19 734
keep the p of the righteous ... Prov 2:20 734
him, and he shall direct thy p ... Prov 3:6 734
and all her p are peace ... Prov 3:17 5410
I have led thee in right p ... Prov 4:11 4570
her ways, go not astray in her p ... Prov 7:25 5410
by the way in the places of the p ... Prov 8:2 5410
in the midst of the p of judgment ... Prov 8:20 5410
ways, and we will walk in his p ... Is 2:3 734
err, and destroy the way of thy p ... Is 3:12 734
I will lead them in p that they ... Is 42:16 5410
The restorer of p to dwell in ... Is 58:12 5410
and destruction are in their p ... Is 59:7 4546
they have made them crooked p ... Is 59:8 5410
and see, and ask for the old p ... Jer 6:16 5410
in their ways from the ancient p ... Jer 18:15 7635
the ancient p, to walk in p ... Jer 18:15 5410
stone, he hath made my p crooked ... Lam 3:9 5410
that she shall not find her p ... Hos 2:6 5410
ways, and we will walk in his p ... Mic 4:2 734
of the Lord, make his p straight ... Mt 3:3 5147
of the Lord, make his p straight ... Mk 1:3 5147
of the Lord, make his p straight ... Lk 3:4 5147
And make straight p for your feet ... Heb 12:13 5163

PATHWAY
in the p thereof there is no ... Prov 12:28

PATIENCE
have p with me, and I will pay ... Mt 18:26 3114
Have p with me, and I will pay ... Mt 18:29 3114
it, and bring forth fruit with p ... Lk 8:15 5281
In your p possess ye your souls ... Lk 21:19 5281
that tribulation worketh p ... Rom 5:3 5281
And p, experience ... Rom 5:4 5281
then do we with p wait for it ... Rom 8:25 5281
our learning, that we through p ... Rom 15:4 5281
Now the God of p and consolation ... Rom 15:5 5281
the ministers of God, in much p ... 2Cor 6:4 5281
were wrought among you in all p ... 2Cor 12:12 5281
to his glorious power, unto all p ... Col 1:11 5281
p of hope in our Lord Jesus ... 1Th 1:3 5281
in the churches of God for your p ... 2Th 1:4 5281
godliness, faith, love, p ... 1Ti 6:11 5281
faith, longsuffering, charity, p ... 2Ti 3:10 5281
sound in faith, in charity, in p ... Titus 2:2 5281
faith and p inherit the promises ... Heb 6:12 3115
For ye have need of p, that ... Heb 10:36 5281
let us run with p the race that ... Heb 12:1 5281
trying of your faith worketh p ... Jas 1:3 5281
But let p have her perfect work, ... Jas 1:4 5281
the earth, and hath long p for it ... Jas 5:7 3114
of suffering affliction, and of p ... Jas 5:10 3115
Ye have heard of the p of Job ... Jas 5:11 5281
and to temperance p ... 2Pet 1:6 5281
and to p godliness ... 2Pet 1:6 5281
p of Jesus Christ, was in the ... Rev 1:9 5281
works, and thy labour, and thy p ... Rev 2:2 5281
And hast borne, and hast p, and for ... Rev 2:3 5281
and service, and faith, and thy p ... Rev 2:19 5281
thou hast kept the word of my p ... Rev 3:10 5281
Here is the p and the faith of the ... Rev 13:10 5281
Here is the p of the saints ... Rev 14:12 5281

PATIENT
the p in spirit is better than ... Eccl 7:8 750
To them who by p continuance in ... Rom 2:7 5281
p in tribulation ... Rom 12:12 5278
the weak, be p toward all men ... 1Th 5:14 3114
into the p waiting for Christ ... 2Th 3:5 5281
but p, not a brawler, not ... 1Ti 3:3 1933
unto all men, apt to teach, p ... 2Ti 2:24 420
Be p therefore, brethren, unto ... Jas 5:7 3114
Be ye also p ... Jas 5:8 3114

PATIENTLY
in the LORD, and wait p for him ... Ps 37:7 2342
I waited p for the LORD ... Ps 40:1 6960
I beseech thee to hear me p ... Acts 26:3 3116
And so, after he had p endured ... Heb 6:15 3114
your faults, ye shall take it p ... 1Pet 2:20 5278
and suffer for it, ye take it p ... 1Pet 2:20 5278

PATMOS (*pat'-mos*) *An island off the west coast of Asia Minor.*
was in the isle that is called P ... Rev 1:9 3963

PATRIARCH
speak unto you of the p David ... Acts 2:29 3966
unto whom even the p Abraham gave. Heb 7:4 3966

PATRIARCHS
and Jacob begat the twelve p ... Acts 7:8 3966
And the p, moved with envy, sold ... Acts 7:9 3966

PATRIMONY
which cometh of the sale of his p ... Deut 18:8

PATROBAS (*pat'-ro-bas*) *A Christian in Rome.*
Asyncritus, Phlegon, Hermas, P ... Rom 16:14 3969

PATTERN
after the p of the tabernacle, and ... Ex 25:9 8403
the p of all the instruments ... Ex 25:9 8403
that thou make them after their p ... Ex 25:40 8403
according unto the p which the ... Num 8:4 4758
Behold the p of the altar of the ... Josh 22:28 8403
the p of it, according to all the ... 2Kin 16:10 8403
his son the p of the porch ... 1Chr 28:11 8403
the p of all that he had by the ... 1Chr 28:12 8403
gold for the p of the chariot of ... 1Chr 28:18 8403
me, even all the works of this p ... 1Chr 28:19 8403
and let them measure the p ... Eze 43:10 8508
for a p to them which should ... 1Ti 1:16 5296
shewing thyself a p of good works ... Titus 2:7 5179
the p shewed to thee in the mount ... Heb 8:5 5179

PATTERNS
therefore necessary that the p of ... Heb 9:23 5262

PAU (*pa'-u*) See PAI. *City of King Hagar of Edom.*
and the name of his city was P ... Gen 36:39 6464

PAUL (*pawl*) See PAUL'S, PAULUS, SAUL. *The apostle to the Gentiles.*
Then Saul, (who also is called P ... Acts 13:9 3972
Now when P and his company loosed.. Acts 13:13 3972
Then P stood up, and beckoning ... Acts 13:16 3972
religious proselytes followed P ... Acts 13:43 3972
things which were spoken by P ... Acts 13:45 3972
Then P and Barnabas waxed bold, and Acts 13:46 3972
and raised persecution against P ... Acts 13:50 3972
The same heard P speak ... Acts 14:9 3972
the people saw what P had done ... Acts 14:11 3972
and P, Mercurius, because he was ... Acts 14:12 3972
when the apostles, Barnabas and P ... Acts 14:14 3972
the people, and, having stoned P ... Acts 14:19 3972
When therefore P and Barnabas had ... Acts 15:2 3972
with them, they determined that P ... Acts 15:2 3972
and gave audience to Barnabas and P.. Acts 15:12 3972
own company to Antioch with P ... Acts 15:22 3972
with our beloved Barnabas and P ... Acts 15:25 3972
P also and Barnabas continued in ... Acts 15:35 3972
some days after P said unto ... Acts 15:36 3972
But P thought not good to take ... Acts 15:38 3972
P chose Silas, and departed, being ... Acts 15:40 3972
Him would P have to go forth with ... Acts 16:3 3972
vision appeared to P in the night ... Acts 16:9 3972
the things which were spoken of P ... Acts 16:14 3972
The same followed P and us, and ... Acts 16:17 3972
But P, being grieved, turned and ... Acts 16:18 3972
gains was gone, they caught P ... Acts 16:19 3972
And at midnight P and Silas prayed, ... Acts 16:25 3972
But P cried with a loud voice, ... Acts 16:28 3972
trembling, and fell down before P ... Acts 16:29 3972
the prison told this saying to P ... Acts 16:36 3972
But P said unto them, They have ... Acts 16:37 3972
And P, as his manner was, went in ... Acts 17:2 3972
believed, and consorted with P ... Acts 17:4 3972
brethren immediately sent away P ... Acts 17:10 3972
of God was preached of P at Berea ... Acts 17:13 3972
the brethren sent away P to go as ... Acts 17:14 3972
they that conducted P brought him ... Acts 17:15 3972
Now while P waited for them at ... Acts 17:16 3972
Then P stood in the midst of ... Acts 17:22 3972
So P departed from among them ... Acts 17:33 3972
After these things P departed ... Acts 18:1 3972
P was pressed in the spirit, and ... Acts 18:5 3972
Then spake the Lord to P in the ... Acts 18:9 3972
with one accord against P ... Acts 18:12 3972
when P was now about to open his ... Acts 18:14 3972
P after this tarried there yet a ... Acts 18:18 3972
P having passed through the upper ... Acts 19:1 3972
Then said P, John verily baptized ... Acts 19:4 3972
when P had laid his hands upon ... Acts 19:6 3972
miracles by the hands of P ... Acts 19:11 3972
you by Jesus whom P preacheth ... Acts 19:13 3972
said, Jesus I know, and P I know ... Acts 19:15 3972
P purposed in the spirit, when he ... Acts 19:21 3972
this P hath persuaded and turned ... Acts 19:26 3972
when P would have entered in unto ... Acts 19:30 3972
P called unto him the disciples, ... Acts 20:1 3972
P preached unto them, ready to ... Acts 20:7 3972
as P was long preaching, he sunk ... Acts 20:9 3972
P went down, and fell on him, and ... Acts 20:10 3972
there intending to take in P ... Acts 20:13 3972
For P had determined to sail by ... Acts 20:16 3972
who said to P through the Spirit, ... Acts 21:4 3972
Then P answered, What mean ye to ... Acts 21:13 3972
the day following P went in with ... Acts 21:18 3972
Then P took the men, and the next ... Acts 21:26 3972
whom they supposed that P had ... Acts 21:29 3972
and they took P, and drew him out ... Acts 21:30 3972
soldiers, they left beating of P ... Acts 21:32 3972
as P was to be led into the ... Acts 21:37 3972
But P said, I am a man which am a ... Acts 21:39 3972
P stood on the stairs, and ... Acts 21:40 3972
P said unto the centurion that ... Acts 22:25 3972
P said, But I was free born ... Acts 22:28 3972
to appear, and brought P down ... Acts 22:30 3972
And P, earnestly beholding the ... Acts 23:1 3972
Then said P unto him, God shall ... Acts 23:3 3972
Then said P, I wist not, brethren ... Acts 23:5 3972
But when P perceived that the one ... Acts 23:6 3972
fearing lest P should have been ... Acts 23:10 3972
him, and said, Be of good cheer, P ... Acts 23:11 3972
nor drink till they had killed P ... Acts 23:12 3972
eat nothing until we have slain P ... Acts 23:14 3972
into the castle, and told P ... Acts 23:16 3972
Then P called one of the ... Acts 23:17 3972
P the prisoner called me unto him ... Acts 23:18 3972
down P to morrow into the council ... Acts 23:20 3972
beasts, that they may set P on ... Acts 23:24 3972
as it was commanded them, took P ... Acts 23:31 3972
presented P also before him ... Acts 23:33 3972
informed the governor against P ... Acts 24:1 3972
Then P, after that the governor ... Acts 24:10 3972
commanded a centurion to keep P ... Acts 24:23 3972
which was a Jewess, he sent for P ... Acts 24:24 3972
should have been given him of P ... Acts 24:26 3972
the Jews a pleasure, left P bound ... Acts 24:27 3972
the Jews informed him against P ... Acts 25:2 3972
that P should be kept at Caesarea ... Acts 25:4 3972
seat commanded P to be brought ... Acts 25:6 3972
and grievous complaints against P ... Acts 25:7 3972
the Jews a pleasure, answered P ... Acts 25:9 3972
Then said P, I stand at Caesar's ... Acts 25:10 3972
whom P affirmed to be alive ... Acts 25:19 3972
But when P had appealed to be ... Acts 25:21 3972
commandment P was brought forth ... Acts 25:23 3972
Then Agrippa said unto P, Thou ... Acts 26:1 3972
Then P stretched forth the hand, ... Acts 26:1 3972
Festus said with a loud voice, P ... Acts 26:24 3972
Then Agrippa said unto P, Almost ... Acts 26:28 3972
P said, I would to God, that not ... Acts 26:29 3972
sail into Italy, they delivered P ... Acts 27:1 3972
And Julius courteously entreated P ... Acts 27:3 3972
already past, P admonished them, ... Acts 27:9 3972
things which were spoken by P ... Acts 27:11 3972
But after long abstinence P stood ... Acts 27:21 3972
Saying, Fear not, P ... Acts 27:24 3972
P said to the centurion and to the ... Acts 27:31 3972
P besought them all to take meat, ... Acts 27:33 3972
the centurion, willing to save P ... Acts 27:43 3972
when P had gathered a bundle of ... Acts 28:3 3972
to whom P entered in, and prayed, ... Acts 28:8 3972
whom when P saw, he thanked God, ... Acts 28:15 3972
but P was suffered to dwell by ... Acts 28:16 3972
that after three days P called ... Acts 28:17 3972
after that P had spoken one word, ... Acts 28:25 3972

P dwelt two whole years in his Acts 28:30 *3972*
P, a servant of Jesus Christ, Rom 1:1 *3972*
P, called to be an apostle of 1Cor 1:1 *3972*
every one of you saith, I am of *P* 1Cor 1:12 *3972*
was *P* crucified for you 1Cor 1:13 *3972*
were ye baptized in the name of *P* 1Cor 1:13 *3972*
For while one saith, I am of *P* 1Cor 3:4 *3972*
Who then is *P*, and who is Apollos, 1Cor 3:5 *3972*
Whether *P*, or Apollos, or Cephas, 1Cor 3:22 *3972*
of me *P* with mine own hand 1Cor 16:21 *3972*
P, an apostle of Jesus Christ by 2Cor 1:1 *3972*
Now I *P* myself beseech you by the 2Cor 10:1 *3972*
P, an apostle, (not of men, Gal 1:1 *3972*
I *P* say unto you, that if ye be Gal 5:2 *3972*
P, an apostle of Jesus Christ by Eph 1:1 *3972*
For this cause I *P*, the prisoner Eph 3:1 *3972*
P and Timotheus, the servants of Phil 1:1 *3972*
P, an apostle of Jesus Christ by Col 1:1 *3972*
whereof I *P* am made a minister Col 1:23 *3972*
salutation by the hand of me *P* Col 4:18 *3972*
P, and Silvanus, and Timotheus, 1Th 1:1 *3972*
have come unto you, even I *P* 1Th 2:18 *3972*
P, and Silvanus, and Timotheus, 2Th 1:1 *3972*
The salutation of *P* with mine own 2Th 3:17 *3972*
P, an apostle of Jesus Christ by 1Ti 1:1 *3972*
P, an apostle of Jesus Christ by 2Ti 1:1 *3972*
when *P* was brought before Nero 2Ti *s* *3972*
P, a servant of God, and an Titus 1:1 *3972*
P, a prisoner of Jesus Christ, and Philem 1 *3972*
being such an one as *P* the aged Philem 9 *3972*
I *P* have written it with mine own Philem 19 *3972*
even as our beloved brother *P* 2Pet 3:15 *3972*

PAUL'S (*pawls*)
P companions in travel, they Acts 19:29 *3972*
all wept sore, and fell on *P* neck Acts 20:37 *3972*
that were of *P* company departed Acts 21:8 *3972*
come unto us, he took *P* girdle Acts 21:11 *3972*
when *P* sister's son heard of Acts 23:16 *3972*
Festus declared *P* cause unto the Acts 25:14 *3972*

PAULUS See Paul. *A Roman proconsul.*
deputy of the country, Sergius *P* Acts 13:7 *3972*

PAVED
were a *p* work of a sapphire stone Ex 24:10 3840
midst thereof being *p* with love Song 3:10 7528

PAVEMENT
it, and put it upon a *p* of stones 2Kin 16:17 4837
faces to the ground upon the *p* 2Chr 7:3 7531
gold and silver, upon a *p* of red Est 1:6 7531
a *p* made for the court round Eze 40:17 7531
thirty chambers were upon the *p* Eze 40:17 7531
the *p* by the side of the gates Eze 40:18 7531
of the gates was the lower *p* Eze 40:18 7531
over against the *p* which was for Eze 42:3 7531
in a place that is called the *P* Jn 19:13 *3037*

PAVILION
his *p* round about him were dark Ps 18:11 5521
trouble he shall hide me in his *p* Ps 27:5 5520
in a *p* from the strife of tongues Ps 31:20 5521
spread his royal *p* over them Jer 43:10 8237

PAVILIONS
made darkness *p* round about him 2Sa 22:12 5521
he and the kings in the *p* 1Kin 20:12 5521
drinking himself drunk in the *p* 1Kin 20:16 5521

PAW
me out of the *p* of the lion 1Sa 17:37 3027
out of the *p* of the bear, he will 1Sa 17:37 3027

PAWETH
He *p* in the valley, and rejoiceth Job 39:21 2658

PAWS
And whatsoever goeth upon his *p* Lev 11:27 3709

PAY
only he shall *p* for the loss of Ex 21:19 5414
and he shall *p* as the judges Ex 21:22 5414
he shall surely *p* ox for ox Ex 21:36 7999
thief be found, let him *p* double Ex 22:7 7999
he shall *p* double unto his Ex 22:9 7999
he shall *p* money according to the Ex 22:17 8254
thy water, then I will *p* for it Num 20:19
God, thou shalt not slack to *p* it Deut 23:21 7999
p my vow, which I have vowed unto 2Sa 15:7 7999
thou shalt *p* a talent of silver 1Kin 20:39 8254
p thy debt, and live thou and thy 2Kin 4:7 7999
make to *p* tribute until this day 2Chr 8:8 5927
the children of Ammon *p* unto him 2Chr 27:5 7725
again, then will they not *p* toll Ezr 4:13 5415
I will *p* ten thousand talents of Est 3:9 8254
that Haman had promised to *p* to Est 4:7 8254
thee, and thou shalt *p* thy vows Job 22:27 7999
I will *p* my vows before them that Ps 22:25 7999
p thy vows unto the most High Ps 50:14 7999
I will *p* thee my vows, Ps 66:13 7999
Vow, and *p* unto the Lord your God Ps 76:11 7999
I will *p* my vows unto the Lord Ps 116:14 7999
I will *p* my vows unto the Lord Ps 116:18 7999
he hath given will he *p* him again Prov 19:17 7999
If thou hast nothing to *p* Prov 22:27 7999
a vow unto God, defer not to *p* it Eccl 5:4 7999
p that which thou hast vowed Eccl 5:4 7999
that thou shouldest vow and not *p* Eccl 5:5 7999
I will *p* that that I have vowed Jonah 2:9 7999
Doth not your master *p* tribute Mt 17:24 *5055*
But forasmuch as he had not to *p* Mt 18:25 *591*
with me, and I will *p* thee all Mt 18:26 *591*
saying, *P* me that thou owest Mt 18:28 *591*
with me, and I will *p* thee all Mt 18:29 *591*
prison, till he should *p* the debt Mt 18:30 *591*
till he should *p* all that was due Mt 18:34 *591*
for ye *p* tithe of mint and anise Mt 23:23 *586*
And when they had nothing to *p* Lk 7:42 *591*

for this cause *p* ye tribute also Rom 13:6 *5055*

PAYED
this day have I *p* my vows Prov 7:14 7999
tithes, *p* tithes in Abraham Heb 7:9 *1183*

PAYETH
wicked borroweth, and *p* not again Ps 37:21 7999

PAYMENT
all that he had, and *p* to be made Mt 18:25 *591*

PEACE
thou shalt go to thy fathers in *p* Gen 15:15 7965
man wondering at her held his *p* Gen 24:21 2790
good, and have sent thee away in *p* Gen 26:29 7965
and they departed from him in *p* Gen 26:31 7965
again to my father's house in *p* Gen 28:21 7965
Jacob held his *p* until they were Gen 34:5 2790
shall give Pharaoh an answer of *p* Gen 41:16 7965
And he said, *P* be to you, fear not Gen 43:23 7965
get you up in *p* unto your father Gen 44:17 7965
And Jethro said to Moses, Go in *p* Ex 4:18 7965
for you, and ye shall hold your *p* Ex 14:14 2790
shall also go to their place in *p* Ex 18:23 7965
thy *p* offerings, thy sheep, and Ex 20:24 8002
sacrificed *p* offerings of oxen Ex 24:5 8002
sacrifice of their *p* offerings Ex 29:28 8002
offerings, and brought *p* offerings Ex 32:6 8002
be a sacrifice of *p* offering Lev 3:1 8002
p offering an offering made by Lev 3:3 8002
of *p* offering unto the Lord be of Lev 3:6 8002
p offering an offering made by Lev 3:9 8002
of the sacrifice of *p* offerings Lev 4:10 8002
of the sacrifice of *p* offerings Lev 4:26 8002
off the sacrifice of *p* offerings Lev 4:31 8002
the sacrifice of the *p* offerings Lev 4:35 8002
the fat of the *p* offerings Lev 6:12 8002
of the sacrifice of *p* offerings Lev 7:11 8002
thanksgiving of his *p* offerings Lev 7:13 8002
the blood of the *p* offerings Lev 7:14 8002
his *p* offerings for thanksgiving Lev 7:15 8002
p offerings be eaten at all on Lev 7:18 8002
of the sacrifice of *p* offerings Lev 7:20 8002
of the sacrifice of *p* offerings Lev 7:21 8002
p offerings unto the Lord shall Lev 7:29 8002
the sacrifice of his *p* offerings Lev 7:29 8002
sacrifices of your *p* offerings Lev 7:32 8002
the blood of the *p* offerings Lev 7:33 8002
sacrifices of their *p* offerings Lev 7:34 8002
the sacrifice of the *p* offerings Lev 7:37 8002
bullock and a ram for *p* offerings Lev 9:4 8002
for a sacrifice of *p* offerings Lev 9:18 8002
burnt offering, and *p* offerings Lev 9:22 8002
And Aaron held his *p* Lev 10:3 1826
of *p* offerings of the children of Lev 10:14 8002
offer them for *p* offerings unto Lev 17:5 8002
of *p* offerings unto the Lord Lev 19:5 8002
offereth a sacrifice of *p* Lev 22:21 8002
for a sacrifice of *p* offerings Lev 23:19 8002
And I will give *p* in the land Lev 26:6 7965
without blemish for *p* offerings Num 6:14 8002
of *p* offerings unto the Lord Num 6:17 8002
the sacrifice of the *p* offerings Num 6:18 8002
upon thee, and give thee *p* Num 6:26 7965
And for a sacrifice of *p* offerings Num 7:17 8002
And for a sacrifice of *p* offerings Num 7:23 8002
And for a sacrifice of *p* offerings Num 7:29 8002
And for a sacrifice of *p* offerings Num 7:35 8002
And for a sacrifice of *p* offerings Num 7:41 8002
And for a sacrifice of *p* offerings Num 7:47 8002
And for a sacrifice of *p* offerings Num 7:53 8002
And for a sacrifice of *p* offerings Num 7:59 8002
And for a sacrifice of *p* offerings Num 7:65 8002
And for a sacrifice of *p* offerings Num 7:71 8002
And for a sacrifice of *p* offerings Num 7:77 8002
And for a sacrifice of *p* offerings Num 7:83 8002
of the *p* offerings were twenty Num 7:88 8002
sacrifices of your *p* offerings Num 10:10 8002
or *p* offerings unto the Lord Num 15:8 8002
I give unto him my covenant of *p* Num 25:12 7965
and for your *p* offerings Num 29:39 8002
father shall hold his *p* at her Num 30:4 2790
held his *p* at her in the day that Num 30:7 2790
heard it, and held his *p* at her Num 30:11 2790
hold his *p* at her from day to day Num 30:14 2790
because he held his *p* at her in Num 30:14 2790
king of Heshbon with words of *p* Deut 2:26 7965
it, then proclaim *p* unto it Deut 20:10 7965
be, if it make thee answer of *p* Deut 20:11 7965
And if it will make no *p* with thee Deut 20:12 7999
Thou shalt not seek their *p* nor Deut 23:6 7965
And thou shalt offer *p* offerings Deut 27:7 8002
his heart, saying, I shall have *p* Deut 29:19 7965
Lord, and sacrificed *p* offerings Josh 8:31 8002
And Joshua made *p* with them Josh 9:15 7965
of Gibeon had made *p* with Israel Josh 10:1 7999
for it hath made *p* with Joshua Josh 10:4 7999
camp to Joshua at Makkedah in *p* Josh 10:21 7965
p with the children of Israel Josh 11:19 7999
or if to offer *p* offerings Josh 22:23 8002
and with our *p* offerings Josh 22:27 8002
for there was *p* between Jabin the Judg 4:17 7965
said unto him, *P* be unto thee Judg 6:23 7965
saying, When I come again in *p* Judg 8:9 7965
when I return in *p* from the Judg 11:31 7965
priest said unto them, Go in *p* Judg 18:6 7965
And they said unto him, Hold thy *p* Judg 18:19 2790
the old man said, *P* be with thee Judg 19:20 7965
p offerings before the Lord Judg 20:26 8002
burnt offerings and *p* offerings Judg 21:4 8002
Eli answered and said, Go in *p* 1Sa 1:17 7965
there was *p* between Israel and the 1Sa 7:14 7965
sacrifices of *p* offerings 1Sa 10:8 8002
But he held his *p* 1Sa 10:27 2790
of *p* offerings before the Lord 1Sa 11:15 8002

offering to me, and *p* offerings 1Sa 13:9 8002
thy servant shall have *p* 1Sa 20:7 7965
away, that thou mayest go in *p* 1Sa 20:13 7965
for there is *p* to thee, and no 1Sa 20:21 7965
Jonathan said to David, Go in *p* 1Sa 20:42 7965
P be both to thee 1Sa 25:6 7965
p be to thine house 1Sa 25:6 7965
p be unto all that thou hast 1Sa 25:6 7965
Go up in *p* to thine house 1Sa 25:35 7965
Wherefore now return, and go in *p* 1Sa 29:7 7965
and he went in *p* 2Sa 3:21 7965
him away, and he was gone in *p* 2Sa 3:22 7965
sent him away, and he is gone in *p* 2Sa 3:23 7965
p offerings before the Lord 2Sa 6:17 8002
p offerings, he blessed the 2Sa 6:18 8002
they made *p* with Israel, and 2Sa 10:19 7999
but hold now thy *p*, my sister 2Sa 13:20 2790
the king said unto him, Go in *p* 2Sa 15:9 7965
return into the city in *p* 2Sa 15:27 7965
so all the people shall be in *p* 2Sa 17:3 7965
until the day he came again in *p* 2Sa 19:24 7965
again in *p* unto his own house 2Sa 19:30 7965
burnt offerings and *p* offerings 2Sa 24:25 8002
and shed the blood of war in *p* 1Kin 2:5 7965
head go down to the grave in *p* 1Kin 2:6 7965
shall there be *p* for ever from 1Kin 2:33 7965
offered *p* offerings, and made a 1Kin 3:15 8002
he had *p* on all sides round about 1Kin 4:24 7965
there was *p* between Hiram and 1Kin 5:12 7965
a sacrifice of *p* offerings 1Kin 8:63 8002
and the fat of the *p* offerings 1Kin 8:64 8002
and the fat of the *p* offerings 1Kin 8:64 8002
p offerings upon the altar which 1Kin 9:25 8002
Whether they be come out for *p* 1Kin 20:18 7965
every man to his house in *p* 1Kin 22:17 7965
of affliction, until I come in *p* 1Kin 22:27 7965
said, If thou return at all in *p* 1Kin 22:28 7965
Jehoshaphat made *p* with the king 1Kin 22:44 7999
hold ye your *p* 2Kin 2:3 2814
hold ye your *p* 2Kin 2:5 2814
And he said unto him, Go in *p* 2Kin 5:19 7965
of good tidings, and we hold our *p* 2Kin 7:9 2814
them, and let him say, Is it *p* 2Kin 9:17 7965
Thus saith the king, Is it *p* 2Kin 9:18 7965
said, What hast thou to do with *p* 2Kin 9:18 7965
Thus saith the king, Is it *p* 2Kin 9:19 7965
What hast thou to do with *p* 2Kin 9:19 7965
saw Jehu, that he said, Is it *p* 2Kin 9:22 7965
And he answered, What *p*, so long 2Kin 9:22 7965
the gate, she said, Had Zimri *p* 2Kin 9:31 7965
the blood of his *p* offerings 2Kin 16:13 8002
But the people held their *p* 2Kin 18:36 2790
And he said, Is it not good, if *p* 2Kin 20:19 7965
be gathered into thy grave in *p* 2Kin 22:20 7965
p, *p* be unto thee, and *p* 1Chr 12:18 7965
thee, and *p* be to thine helpers 1Chr 12:18 7965
and *p* offerings before God 1Chr 16:1 8002
the *p* offerings, he blessed the 1Chr 16:2 8002
they made *p* with David, and became 1Chr 19:19 7999
p offerings, and called upon the 1Chr 21:26 8002
be Solomon, and I will give *p* 1Chr 22:9 7965
and the fat of the *p* offerings 2Chr 7:7 8002
was no *p* to him that went out 2Chr 15:5 7965
every man to his house in *p* 2Chr 18:16 7965
affliction, until I return in *p* 2Chr 18:26 7965
If thou certainly return in *p* 2Chr 18:27 7965
to his house in *p* to Jerusalem 2Chr 19:1 7965
with the fat of the *p* offerings 2Chr 29:35 8002
offering *p* offerings, and making 2Chr 30:22 8002
for *p* offerings, to minister, and 2Chr 31:2 8002
and sacrificed thereon *p* offerings 2Chr 33:16 8002
be gathered to thy grave in *p* 2Chr 34:28 7965
unto the rest beyond the river, *P* Ezr 4:17 8001
Unto Darius the king, all *p* Ezr 5:7 8001
of the God of heaven, perfect *p* Ezr 7:12
nor seek their *p* or their wealth Ezr 9:12 7965
Then held they their *p*, and found Neh 5:8 2790
the people, saying, Hold your *p* Neh 8:11 2013
holdest thy *p* at this time Est 4:14 2790
of Ahasuerus, with words of *p* Est 9:30 7965
speaking *p* to all his seed Est 10:3 7965
the field shall be at *p* with thee Job 5:23 7999
that thy tabernacle shall be in *p* Job 5:24 7965
thy lies make men hold their *p* Job 11:3 2790
ye would altogether hold your *p* Job 13:5 2790
Hold your *p*, let me alone, that I Job 13:13 2790
now thyself with him, and be at *p* Job 22:21 7999
he maketh *p* in his high places Job 25:2 7965
The nobles held their *p*, and their Job 29:10 6963
hold thy *p*, and I will speak Job 33:31 2790
hold thy *p*, and I shall teach thee Job 33:33 2790
I will both lay me down in *p* Ps 4:8 7965
unto him that was at *p* with me Ps 7:4 7999
which speak *p* to their neighbours Ps 28:3 7965
Lord will bless his people with *p* Ps 29:11 7965
seek *p*, and pursue it Ps 34:14 7965
For they speak not *p* Ps 35:20 7965
themselves in the abundance of *p* Ps 37:11 7965
for the end of that man is *p* Ps 37:37 7965
dumb with silence, I held my *p* Ps 39:2 2814
hold not thy *p* at my tears Ps 39:12 2790
in *p* from the battle that was Ps 55:18 7965
against such as be at *p* with him Ps 55:20 7965
shall bring *p* to the people Ps 72:3 7965
abundance of *p* so long as the Ps 72:7 7965
hold not thy *p*, and be not still, Ps 83:1 2790
he will speak *p* unto his people Ps 85:8 7965
and *p* have kissed each other Ps 85:10 7965
Hold not thy *p*, O God of my Ps 109:1 2790
Great *p* have they which love thy Ps 119:165 7965
long dwelt with him that hateth *p* Ps 120:6 7965
I am for *p* Ps 120:7 7965
Pray for the *p* of Jerusalem Ps 122:6 7965
P be within thy walls, and Ps 122:7 7965

I will now say, P be within thee Ps 122:8 7965
but p shall be upon Israel Ps 125:5 7965
children, and p upon Israel Ps 128:6 7965
He maketh p in thy borders, and Ps 147:14 7965
of days, and long life, and p Prov 3:2 7965
and all her paths are p Prov 3:17 7965
I have p offerings with me Prov 7:14 8002
of understanding holdeth his p Prov 11:12 2790
to the counsellors of p is joy Prov 12:20 7965
his enemies to be at p with him Prov 16:7 7999
a fool, when he holdeth his p Prov 17:28 2790
a time of war, and a time of p Eccl 3:8 7965
Father, The Prince of P Is 9:6 7965
p there shall be no end, upon the Is 9:7 7965
Thou wilt keep him in perfect p Is 26:3 7965
LORD, thou wilt ordain p for us Is 26:12 7965
that he may make p with me Is 27:5 7965
and he shall make p with me Is 27:5 7965
work of righteousness shall be p Is 32:17 7965
the ambassadors of p shall weep Is 33:7 7965
But they held their p, and Is 36:21 2790
for p I had great bitterness Is 38:17 7965
moreover, For there shall be p Is 39:8 7965
I have long time holden my p Is 42:14 2814
I make p, and create evil Is 45:7 7965
then had thy p been as a river, Is 48:18 7965
There is no p, saith the LORD, Is 48:22 7965
good tidings, that publisheth p Is 52:7 7965
of our p was upon him Is 53:5 7965
the covenant of my p be removed Is 54:10 7965
shall be the p of thy children Is 54:13 7965
with joy, and be led forth with p Is 55:12 7965
He shall enter into p Is 57:2 7965
have not I held my p even of old Is 57:11 2814
P, p to him that is far off, Is 57:19 7965
There is no p, saith my God, to Is 57:21 7965
The way of p they know not Is 59:8 7965
goeth therein shall not know p Is 59:8 7965
I will also make thy officers p Is 60:17 7965
Zion's sake will I not hold my p Is 62:1 2814
never hold their p day nor night Is 62:6 2814
wilt thou hold thy p, and afflict Is 64:12 2814
I will extend p to her like a Is 66:12 7965
saying, Ye shall have p Jer 4:10 7965
I cannot hold my p, because thou Jer 4:19 2790
people slightly, saying, P, p Jer 6:14 7965
when there is no p Jer 6:14 7965
people slightly, saying, P, p Jer 8:11 7965
when there is no p Jer 8:11 7965
We looked for p, but no good came Jer 8:15 7965
and if in the land of p, wherein Jer 12:5 7965
no flesh shall have p Jer 12:12 7965
give you assured p in this place Jer 14:13 7965
we looked for p, and there is no Jer 14:19 7965
taken away my p from this people Jer 16:5 7965
LORD hath said, Ye shall have p Jer 23:17 7965
prophet which prophesieth of p Jer 28:9 7965
seek the p of the city whither I Jer 29:7 7965
the p thereof shall ye have p Jer 29:7 7965
saith the LORD, thoughts of p Jer 29:11 7965
trembling, of fear, and not of p Jer 30:5 7965
unto them the abundance of p Jer 33:6 7965
But thou shalt die in p Jer 34:5 7965
shall go forth from thence in p Jer 43:12 7965
removed my soul far off from p Lam 3:17 7965
and they shall seek p, and there Eze 7:25 7965
have seduced my people, saying, P Eze 13:10 7965
and there was no p Eze 13:10 7965
p for her, and there is no p Eze 13:16 7965
make with them a covenant of p Eze 34:25 7965
make a covenant of p with them Eze 37:26 7965
the altar, and your p offerings Eze 43:27 8002
and for p offerings, to make Eze 45:15 8002
and the p offerings, to make Eze 45:17 8002
his p offerings, and he shall Eze 46:2 8002
a voluntary burnt offering or p Eze 46:12 8002
his p offerings, as he did on the Eze 46:12 8002
P be multiplied unto you Dan 4:1 8001
P be multiplied unto you Dan 6:25 8001
heart, and by p shall destroy many Dan 8:25 7962
p be unto thee, be strong, yea, Dan 10:19 7965
neither will I regard the p Amos 5:22 8002
the men that were at p with thee Obad 7 7965
bite with their teeth, and cry, P Mic 3:5 7965
And this man shall be the p Mic 5:5 7965
good tidings, that publisheth p Nah 1:15 7965
Hold thy p at the presence of the Zeph 1:7 2013
and in this place will I give p Hag 2:9 7965
the counsel of p shall be between Zec 6:13 7965
neither was there any p to him Zec 8:10 7965
of truth and p in your gates Zec 8:16 7965
therefore love the truth and p Zec 8:19 7965
he shall speak p unto the heathen Zec 9:10 7965
was with him of life and p Mal 2:5 7965
he walked with me in p and equity, Mal 2:6 7965
worthy, let your p come upon it Mt 10:13 *1515*
worthy, let your p return to you Mt 10:13 *1515*
that I am come to send p on earth Mt 10:34 *1515*
I came not to send p, but a sword Mt 10:34 *1515*
because they should hold their p Mt 20:31 4623
But Jesus held his p Mt 26:63 4623
rebuked him, saying, Hold thy p Mk 1:25 5392
But they held their p Mk 3:4 4623
the wind, and said unto the sea, P Mk 4:39 4623
go in p, and be whole of thy Mk 5:34 *1515*
But they held their p Mk 9:34 4623
and have p one with another Mk 9:50 *1518*
him that he should hold his p Mk 10:48 4623
But he held his p, and answered Mk 14:61 4623
guide our feet into the way of p Lk 1:79 *1515*
God in the highest, and on earth p Lk 2:14 *1515*
thou thy servant depart in p Lk 2:29 *1515*
rebuked him, saying, Hold thy p Lk 4:35 *5392*
go in p Lk 7:50 *1515*
go in p Lk 8:48 *1515*
first say, P be to this house Lk 10:5 *1515*
And if the son of p be there Lk 10:6 *1515*
your p shall rest upon it Lk 10:6 *1515*
his palace, his goods are in p Lk 11:21 *1515*
that I am come to give p on earth Lk 12:51 *1515*
And they held their p Lk 14:4 *2270*
and desireth conditions of p Lk 14:32 *1515*
him, that he should hold his p Lk 18:39 *4263*
p in heaven, and glory in the Lk 19:38 *1515*
if these should hold their p Lk 19:40 *4623*
things which belong unto thy p Lk 19:42 *1515*
at his answer, and held their p Lk 20:26 *4601*
and saith unto them, P be unto you Lk 24:36 *1515*
P I leave with you, my p I Jn 14:27 *1515*
you, that in me ye might have p Jn 16:33 *1515*
and saith unto them, P be unto you Jn 20:19 *1515*
to them again, P be unto you Jn 20:21 *1515*
the midst, and said, P be unto you Jn 20:26 *1515*
preaching p by Jesus Christ Acts 10:36 *1515*
these things, they held their p Acts 11:18 *2270*
with the hand to hold their p Acts 12:17 *4601*
their friend, desired p Acts 12:20 *1515*
And after they had held their p Acts 15:13 *4601*
they were let go in p from the Acts 15:33 *1515*
now therefore depart, and go in p Acts 16:36 *1515*
but speak, and hold not thy p Acts 18:9 *4623*
p from God our Father, and the Rom 1:7 *1515*
But glory, honour, and p, to every Rom 2:10 *1515*
the way of p have they not known Rom 3:17 *1515*
we have p with God through our Rom 5:1 *1515*
spiritually minded is life and p Rom 8:6 *1515*
them that preach the gospel of p Rom 10:15 *1515*
but righteousness, and p, and joy Rom 14:17 *1515*
after the things which make for p Rom 14:19 *1515*
p in believing, that ye may Rom 15:13 *1515*
Now the God of p be with you all Rom 15:33 *1515*
the God of p shall bruise Satan Rom 16:20 *1515*
Grace be unto you, and p, from God 1Cor 1:3 *1515*
but God hath called us to p 1Cor 7:15 *1515*
by, let the first hold his p 1Cor 14:30 *4601*
the author of confusion, but of p 1Cor 14:33 *1515*
but conduct him forth in p 1Cor 16:11 *1515*
p from God our Father, and from 2Cor 1:2 *1515*
be of one mind, live in p 2Cor 13:11 *1518*
of love and p shall be with you 2Cor 13:11 *1515*
p from God the Father, and from Gal 1:3 *1515*
of the Spirit is love, joy, p Gal 5:22 *1515*
p be on them, and mercy, and upon Gal 6:16 *1515*
Grace be to you, and p, from God Eph 1:2 *1515*
For he is our p, who hath made Eph 2:14 *1515*
of twain one new man, so making p Eph 2:15 *1515*
preached p to you which were afar Eph 2:17 *1515*
of the Spirit in the bond of p Eph 4:3 *1515*
preparation of the gospel of p Eph 6:15 *1515*
P be to the brethren, and love Eph 6:23 *1515*
Grace be unto you, and p, from God Phil 1:2 *1515*
the p of God, which passeth all Phil 4:7 *1515*
the God of p shall be with you Phil 4:9 *1515*
Grace be unto you, and p, from God Col 1:2 *1515*
having made p through the blood Col 1:20 *1517*
let the p of God rule in your Col 3:15 *1515*
Grace be unto you, and p, from God 1Th 1:1 *1515*
For when they shall say, P 1Th 5:3 *1515*
And be at p among yourselves 1Th 5:13 *1518*
the very God of p sanctify you 1Th 5:23 *1515*
Grace unto you, and p, from God 2Th 1:2 *1515*
Now the Lord of p himself give 2Th 3:16 *1515*
give you p always by all means 2Th 3:16 *1515*
Grace, mercy, and p, from God our 1Ti 1:2 *1515*
Grace, mercy, and p, from God the 2Ti 1:2 *1515*
righteousness, faith, charity, p 2Ti 2:22 *1515*
Grace, mercy, and p, from God the Titus 1:4 *1515*
Grace to you, and p, from God our Philem 3 *1515*
of Salem, which is, King of p Heb 7:2 *1515*
she had received the spies with p Heb 11:31 *1515*
Follow p with all men, and Heb 12:14 *1515*
Now the God of p, that brought Heb 13:20 *1515*
of you say unto them, Depart in p Jas 2:16 *1515*
sown in p of them that make p Jas 3:18 *1515*
Grace unto you, and p, be 1Pet 1:2 *1515*
let him seek p, and ensue it 1Pet 3:11 *1515*
P be with you all that are in 1Pet 5:14 *1515*
p be multiplied unto you through 2Pet 1:2 *1515*
that ye may be found of him in p 2Pet 3:14 *1515*
Grace be with you, mercy, and p 2Jn 3 *1515*
P be to thee 3Jn 14 *1515*
Mercy unto you, and p, and love, be Jude 2 *1515*
Grace be unto you, and p, from him Rev 1:4 *1515*
thereon to take p from the earth Rev 6:4 *1515*

PEACEABLE
These men are p with us Gen 34:21 8003
I am one of them that are p 2Sa 20:19 7999
the land was wide, and quiet, and p 1Chr 4:40 7961
shall dwell in a p habitation Is 32:18 7965
the p habitations are cut down Jer 25:37 7965
p life in all godliness and 1Ti 2:2 *2272*
afterward it yieldeth the p fruit Heb 12:11 *1516*
from above is first pure, then p Jas 3:17 *1516*

PEACEABLY
and could not speak p unto him Gen 37:4 7965
restore those lands again p Judg 11:13 7965
Rimmon, and to call p unto them Judg 21:13 7965
coming, and said, Comest thou p 1Sa 16:4 7965
And he said, P 1Sa 16:5 7965
And she said, Comest thou p 1Kin 2:13 7965
And he said, P 1Kin 2:13 7965
If ye be come p unto me to help 1Chr 12:17 7965
one speaketh p to his neighbour Jer 9:8 7965
but he shall come in p, and obtain Dan 11:21 7962
He shall enter p even upon the Dan 11:24 7962
lieth in you, live p with all men Rom 12:18 *1518*

PEACEMAKERS
Blessed are the p Mt 5:9 *1518*

PEACOCKS
and silver, ivory, and apes, and p 1Kin 10:22 8500
and silver, ivory, and apes, and p 2Chr 9:21 8500
thou the goodly wings unto the p Job 39:13 7443

PEARL
he had found one p of great price Mt 13:46 *3135*
every several gate was of one p Rev 21:21 *3135*

PEARLS
shall be made of coral, or of p Job 28:18 1378
cast ye your p before swine Mt 7:6 *3135*
a merchant man, seeking goodly p Mt 13:45 *3135*
with broided hair, or gold, or p 1Ti 2:9 *3135*
with gold and precious stones and p Rev 17:4 *3135*
and precious stones, and of p Rev 18:12 *3135*
gold, and precious stones, and p Rev 18:16 *3135*
And the twelve gates were twelve p Rev 21:21 *3135*

PECULIAR
then ye shall be a p treasure Ex 19:5 5459
to be a p people unto himself Deut 14:2 5459
thee this day to be his p people Deut 26:18 5459
and Israel for his p treasure Ps 135:4 5459
the p treasure of kings and of the Eccl 2:8 5459
and purify unto himself a p people Titus 2:14 *4041*
an holy nation, a p people 1Pet 2:9

PEDAHEL (ped'-a-hel) *A Naphtalite who apportioned the Promised Land.*
of Naphtali, P the son of Ammihud Num 34:28 6300

PEDAHZUR (pe-dah'-zur) *Father of Gamaliel.*
Gamaliel the son of P Num 1:10 6301
shall be Gamaliel the son of P Num 2:20 6301
day offered Gamaliel the son of P Num 7:54 6301
offering of Gamaliel the son of P Num 7:59 6301
was Gamaliel the son of P Num 10:23 6301

PEDAIAH (pe-dah'-yah)
1. Grandfather of King Josiah.
the daughter of P of Rumah 2Kin 23:36 6305
2. Descendant of Jeconiah.
Malchiram also, and P, and Shenazar 1Chr 3:18 6305
And the sons of P were, Zerubbabel 1Chr 3:19 6305
3. Father of Joel.
of Manasseh, Joel the son of P 1Chr 27:20 6305
4. Son of Parosh.
After him P the son of Parosh Neh 3:25 6305
5. A priest who aided Ezra.
and on his left hand, P, and Neh 8:4 6305
the scribe, and of the Levites, P Neh 13:13 6305
6. A family of exiles.
the son of Joed, the son of P Neh 11:7 6305

PEDIGREES
they declared their p after their Num 1:18 3205

PEELED
to a nation scattered and p Is 18:2 4178
hosts of a people scattered and p Is 18:7 4178
bald, and every shoulder was p Eze 29:18 4803

PEEP
spirits, and unto wizards that p Is 8:19 6850

PEEPED
wing, or opened the mouth, or p Is 10:14 6850

PEKAH (pe'-kah) *A king of Israel.*
But P the son of Remaliah, a 2Kin 15:25 6492
P the son of Remaliah began to 2Kin 15:27 6492
In the days of P king of Israel 2Kin 15:29 6492
against P the son of Remaliah 2Kin 15:30 6492
And the rest of the acts of P 2Kin 15:31 6492
In the second year of P the son 2Kin 15:32 6492
Syria, and P the son of Remaliah 2Kin 15:37 6492
In the seventeenth year of P the 2Kin 16:1 6492
P son of Remaliah king of Israel 2Kin 16:5 6492
For P the son of Remaliah slew in 2Chr 28:6 6492
P the son of Remaliah, king of Is 7:1 6492

PEKAHIAH (pe-ka-hi'-ah) *Son of King Menahem.*
P his son reigned in his stead 2Kin 15:22 6494
P the son of Menahem began to 2Kin 15:23 6494
And the rest of the acts of P 2Kin 15:26 6494

PEKOD (pe'-kod) *Symbolic name for Chaldea.*
and against the inhabitants of P Jer 50:21 6489
and all the Chaldeans, P, and Shoa Eze 23:23 6489

PELAIAH (pel-a-i'-ah)
1. A son of Elioenai.
were, Hodaiah, and Eliashib, and P 1Chr 3:24 6411
2. A priest who aided Ezra.
Azariah, Jozabad, Hanan, P Neh 8:7 6411
3. A Levite who renewed the covenant.
Shebaniah, Hodijah, Kelita, P Neh 10:10 6411

PELALIAH (pel-a-li'-ah) *A family of exiles.*
the son of Jeroham, the son of P Neh 11:12 6421

PELATIAH (pel-a-ti'-ah)
1. Son of Hananiah.
of Hananiah; P, and Jesaiah 1Chr 3:21 6410
2. A Simeonite captain.
Seir, having for their captains P 1Chr 4:42 6410
3. A family who renewed the covenant.
P, Hanan, Anaiah, Neh 10:22 6410
4. Son of Benaiah.
P the son of Benaiah, princes of Eze 11:1 6410
that P the son of Benaiah died Eze 11:13 6410

PELEG (pe'-leg) See PHALEG. *A son of Eber.*
the name of one was P Gen 10:25 6389
four and thirty years, and begat P Gen 11:16 6389
after he begat P four hundred Gen 11:17 6389
P lived thirty years, and begat Gen 11:18 6389
P lived after he begat Reu two Gen 11:19 6389

the name of the one was *P* ... 1Chr 1:19 6389
Eber, *P*, Reu, ... 1Chr 1:25 6389

PELET (*pe'-let*) See Beth-palet.
1. A son of Jahdai.
Jotham, and Gesham, and *P* ... 1Chr 2:47 6404
2. A captain in David's army.
and Jeziel, and *P*, the sons of ... 1Chr 12:3 6404

PELETH (*pe'-leth*)
1. Father of On.
of Eliab, and On, the son of *P* ... Num 16:1 6431
of Jonathan; *P*, and Zaza ... 1Chr 2:33 6431

PELETHITES (*pel'-e-thites*) *A company of David's bodyguards.*
both the Cherethites and the *P* ... 2Sa 8:18 6432
all the Cherethites, and all the *P* ... 2Sa 15:18 6432
men, and the Cherethites, and the *P* ... 2Sa 20:7 6432
the Cherethites and over the *P* ... 2Sa 20:23 6432
and the Cherethites, and the *P* ... 1Kin 1:38 6432
and the Cherethites, and the *P* ... 1Kin 1:44 6432
was over the Cherethites and the *P* ... 1Chr 18:17 6432

PELICAN
And the swan, and the *p*, and the ... Lev 11:18 6893
And the *p*, and the gier eagle, and ... Deut 14:17 6893
I am like a *p* of the wilderness ... Ps 102:6 6893

PELONITE (*pel'-o-nite*) See Paltite.
1. Family name of Helez.
the Harorite, Helez the *P* ... 1Chr 11:27 6397
the seventh month was Helez the *P* ... 1Chr 27:10 6397
2. Family name of Ahijah.
the Mecherathite, Ahijah the *P* ... 1Chr 11:36 6397

PELUSIUM See Sin.

PEN
that handle the *p* of the writer ... Judg 5:14 7626
they were graven with an iron *p* ... Job 19:24 5842
my tongue is the *p* of a ready ... Ps 45:1 5842
in it with a man's *p* concerning ... Is 8:1 2747
the *p* of the scribes is in vain ... Jer 8:8 5842
Judah is written with a *p* of iron ... Jer 17:1 5842
not with ink and *p* write unto thee ... 3Jn 13 *2563*

PENCE
which owed him an hundred *p* ... Mt 18:28 *1220*
for more than three hundred *p* ... Mk 14:5 *1220*
the one owed five hundred *p* ... Lk 7:41 *1220*
he departed, he took out two *p* ... Lk 10:35 *1220*
ointment sold for three hundred *p* ... Jn 12:5 *1220*

PENIEL (*pe-ni'-el*) See Penuel. *Same as Penuel.*
called the name of the place *P* ... Gen 32:30 6439

PENINNAH (*pe-nin'-nah*) *A wife of Elkanah.*
and the name of the other *P* ... 1Sa 1:2 6444
P had children, but Hannah had no ... 1Sa 1:2 6444
offered, he gave to *P* his wife ... 1Sa 1:4 6444

PENKNIFE
four leaves, he cut it with the *p* ... Jer 36:23 8593

PENNY
with the labourers for a *p* a day ... Mt 20:2 *1220*
hour, they received every man a *p* ... Mt 20:9 *1220*
likewise received every man a *p* ... Mt 20:10 *1220*
not thou agree with me for a *p* ... Mt 20:13 *1220*
And they brought unto him a *p* ... Mt 22:19 *1220*
bring me a *p*, that I may see it ... Mk 12:15 *1220*
Shew me a *p* ... Lk 20:24 *1220*
say, A measure of wheat for a *p* ... Rev 6:6 *1220*
three measures of barley for a *p* ... Rev 6:6 *1220*

PENNYWORTH
go and buy two hundred *p* of bread ... Mk 6:37 *1220*
Two hundred *p* of bread is not ... Jn 6:7 *1220*

PENTECOST (*pen'-te-cost*) *Greek name for Passover.*
when the day of *P* was fully come ... Acts 2:1 *4005*
to be at Jerusalem the day of *P* ... Acts 20:16 *4005*
I will tarry at Ephesus until *P* ... 1Cor 16:8 *4005*

PENUEL (*pe-nu'-el*) See Peniel.
1. Where Jacob wrestled God.
as he passed over *P* the sun rose ... Gen 32:31 6439
And he went up thence to *P* ... Judg 8:8 6439
the men of *P* answered him as the ... Judg 8:8 6439
he spake also unto the men of *P* ... Judg 8:9 6439
And he beat down the tower of *P* ... Judg 8:17 6439
2. Father of Gedor.
P the father of Gedor, and Ezer ... 1Chr 4:4 6439
3. A son of Shashak.
And Iphedeiah, and *P*, the sons of ... 1Chr 8:25 6439

PENURY
of the lips tendeth only to *p* ... Prov 14:23 4270
but she of her *p* hath cast in all ... Lk 21:4 *5303*

PEOPLE
the *p* is one, and they have all ... Gen 11:6 5971
and the women also, and the *p* ... Gen 14:16 5971
soul shall be cut off from his *p* ... Gen 17:14 5971
kings of *p* shall be of her ... Gen 17:16 5971
all the *p* from every quarter ... Gen 19:4 5971
himself to the *p* of the land ... Gen 23:7 5971
the sons of my *p* give I it thee ... Gen 23:11 5971
himself before the *p* of the land ... Gen 23:12 5971
the audience of the *p* of the land ... Gen 23:13 5971
and was gathered to his *p* ... Gen 25:8 5971
and was gathered unto his *p* ... Gen 25:17 5971
womb, and two manner of *p* shall be ... Gen 25:23 3816
the one *p* shall be stronger than ... Gen 25:23 3816
be stronger than the other *p* ... Gen 25:23 3816
one of the *p* might lightly have ... Gen 26:10 5971
And Abimelech charged all his *p* ... Gen 26:11 5971
Let *p* serve thee, and nations bow ... Gen 27:29 5971
thou mayest be a multitude of *p* ... Gen 28:3 5971
the land of the *p* of the east ... Gen 29:1 1121
he divided the *p* that was with ... Gen 32:7 5971
with you, and we will become one *p* ... Gen 34:16 5971
for to dwell with us, to be one *p* ... Gen 34:22 5971
all the *p* that were with him ... Gen 35:6 5971
died, and was gathered unto his *p* ... Gen 35:29 5971
thy word shall all my *p* be ruled ... Gen 41:40 5971
the *p* cried to Pharaoh for bread ... Gen 41:55 5971
sold to all the *p* of the land ... Gen 42:6 5971
And as for the *p*, he removed them ... Gen 47:21 5971
Then Joseph said unto the *p* ... Gen 47:23 5971
make of thee a multitude of *p* ... Gen 48:4 5971
he also shall become a *p*, and he ... Gen 48:19 5971
shall the gathering of the *p* be ... Gen 49:10 5971
Dan shall judge his *p*, as one of ... Gen 49:16 5971
I am to be gathered unto my *p* ... Gen 49:29 5971
ghost, and was gathered unto his *p* ... Gen 49:33 5971
is this day, to save much *p* alive ... Gen 50:20 5971
And he said unto his *p*, Behold, ... Ex 1:9 5971
the *p* of the children of Israel ... Ex 1:9 5971
the *p* multiplied, and waxed very ... Ex 1:20 5971
And Pharaoh charged all his *p* ... Ex 1:22 5971
of my *p* which are in Egypt ... Ex 3:7 5971
p the children of Israel out of ... Ex 3:10 5971
brought forth the *p* out of Egypt ... Ex 3:12 5971
I will give this *p* favour in the ... Ex 3:21 5971
shall be thy spokesman unto the *p* ... Ex 4:16 5971
that he shall not let the *p* go ... Ex 4:21 5971
the signs in the sight of the *p* ... Ex 4:30 5971
And the *p* believed ... Ex 4:31 5971
Lord God of Israel, Let my *p* go ... Ex 5:1 5971
let the *p* from their works ... Ex 5:4 5971
the *p* of the land now are many, ... Ex 5:5 5971
same day the taskmasters of the *p* ... Ex 5:6 5971
give the *p* straw to make brick ... Ex 5:7 5971
the taskmasters of the *p* went out ... Ex 5:10 5971
officers, and they spake to the *p* ... Ex 5:10 5971
So the *p* were scattered abroad ... Ex 5:12 5971
but the fault is in thine own *p* ... Ex 5:16 5971
thou so evil entreated this *p* ... Ex 5:22 5971
name, he hath done evil to this *p* ... Ex 5:23 5971
hast thou delivered thy *p* at all ... Ex 5:23 5971
And I will take you to me for a *p* ... Ex 6:7 5971
my *p* the children of Israel, out ... Ex 7:4 5971
he refuseth to let the *p* go ... Ex 7:14 5971
me unto thee, saying, Let my *p* go ... Ex 7:16 5971
Thus saith the Lord, Let my *p* go ... Ex 8:1 5971
of thy servants, and upon thy *p* ... Ex 8:3 5971
up both on thee, and upon thy *p* ... Ex 8:4 5971
the frogs from me, and from my *p* ... Ex 8:8 5971
and I will let the *p* go, that they ... Ex 8:8 5971
and for thy servants, and for thy *p* ... Ex 8:9 5971
from thy servants, and from thy *p* ... Ex 8:11 5971
Thus saith the Lord, Let my *p* go ... Ex 8:20 5971
if thou wilt not let my *p* go ... Ex 8:21 5971
upon thy servants, and upon thy *p* ... Ex 8:21 5971
of Goshen, in which my *p* dwell ... Ex 8:22 5971
between my *p* and thy *p* ... Ex 8:23 5971
from his servants, and from his *p* ... Ex 8:29 5971
the *p* go to sacrifice to the Lord ... Ex 8:29 5971
from his servants, and from his *p* ... Ex 8:31 5971
neither would he let the *p* go ... Ex 8:32 5971
God of the Hebrews, Let my *p* go ... Ex 9:1 5971
and he did not let the *p* go ... Ex 9:7 5971
God of the Hebrews, Let my *p* go ... Ex 9:13 5971
upon thy servants, and upon thy *p* ... Ex 9:14 5971
thee and thy *p* with pestilence ... Ex 9:15 5971
thou thyself against my *p* ... Ex 9:17 5971
and I and my *p* are wicked ... Ex 9:27 5971
let my *p* go, that they may serve ... Ex 10:3 5971
if thou refuse to let my *p* go ... Ex 10:4 5971
Speak now in the ears of the *p* ... Ex 11:2 5971
the Lord gave the *p* favour in the ... Ex 11:3 5971
and in the sight of the *p* ... Ex 11:3 5971
all the *p* that follow thee ... Ex 11:8 5971
And the *p* bowed the head and ... Ex 12:27 5971
and get you forth from among my *p* ... Ex 12:31 5971
Egyptians were urgent upon the *p* ... Ex 12:33 5971
the *p* took their dough before it ... Ex 12:34 5971
the Lord gave the *p* favour in the ... Ex 12:36 5971
And Moses said unto the *p*, ... Ex 13:3 5971
when Pharaoh had let the *p* go ... Ex 13:17 5971
Lest peradventure the *p* repent ... Ex 13:17 5971
But God led the *p* about, through ... Ex 13:18 5971
fire by night, from before the *p* ... Ex 13:22 5971
the king of Egypt that the *p* fled ... Ex 14:5 5971
servants was turned against the *p* ... Ex 14:5 5971
chariot, and took his *p* with him ... Ex 14:6 5971
And Moses said unto the *p*, Fear ye ... Ex 14:13 5971
the *p* feared the Lord, and ... Ex 14:31 5971
the *p* which thou hast redeemed ... Ex 15:13 5971
The *p* shall hear, and be afraid ... Ex 15:14 5971
till thy *p* pass over, O Lord, ... Ex 15:16 5971
till the *p* pass over, which thou ... Ex 15:16 5971
the *p* murmured against Moses, ... Ex 15:24 5971
the *p* shall go out and gather a ... Ex 16:4 5971
the *p* on the seventh day for to ... Ex 16:27 5971
So the *p* rested on the seventh ... Ex 16:30 5971
was no water for the *p* to drink ... Ex 17:1 5971
Wherefore the *p* did chide with ... Ex 17:2 5971
the *p* thirsted there for water ... Ex 17:3 5971
the *p* murmured against Moses, and ... Ex 17:3 5971
What shall I do unto this *p* ... Ex 17:4 5971
unto Moses, Go on before the *p* ... Ex 17:5 5971
out of it, that the *p* may drink ... Ex 17:6 5971
his *p* with the edge of the sword ... Ex 17:13 5971
for Moses, and for Israel his *p* ... Ex 18:1 5971
who hath delivered the *p* from ... Ex 18:10 5971
that Moses sat to judge the *p* ... Ex 18:13 5971
the *p* stood by Moses from the ... Ex 18:13 5971
law saw all that he did to the *p* ... Ex 18:14 5971
thing that thou doest to the *p* ... Ex 18:14 5971
all the *p* stand by thee from ... Ex 18:14 5971
Because the *p* come unto me to ... Ex 18:15 5971
thou, and this *p* that is with thee ... Ex 18:18 5971
Be thou for the *p* to God-ward ... Ex 18:19 5971
provide out of all the *p* able men ... Ex 18:21 5971
them judge the *p* at all seasons ... Ex 18:22 5971
all this *p* shall also go to their ... Ex 18:23 5971
and made them heads over the *p* ... Ex 18:25 5971
they judged the *p* at all seasons ... Ex 18:26 5971
treasure unto me above all *p* ... Ex 19:5 5971
and called for the elders of the *p* ... Ex 19:7 5971
all the *p* answered together, and ... Ex 19:8 5971
the words of the *p* unto the Lord ... Ex 19:8 5971
that the *p* may hear when I speak ... Ex 19:9 5971
the words of the *p* unto the Lord ... Ex 19:9 5971
said unto Moses, Go unto the *p* ... Ex 19:10 5971
of all the *p* upon mount Sinai ... Ex 19:11 5971
set bounds unto the *p* round about ... Ex 19:12 5971
down from the mount unto the *p* ... Ex 19:14 5971
and sanctified the *p* ... Ex 19:14 5971
And he said unto the *p*, Be ready ... Ex 19:15 5971
so that all the *p* that was in the ... Ex 19:16 5971
Moses brought forth the *p* out of ... Ex 19:17 5971
unto Moses, Go down, charge the *p* ... Ex 19:21 5971
The *p* cannot come up to mount ... Ex 19:23 5971
the *p* break through to come up ... Ex 19:24 5971
So Moses went down unto the *p* ... Ex 19:25 5971
all the *p* saw the thunderings, and ... Ex 20:18 5971
and when the *p* saw it, they ... Ex 20:18 5971
And Moses said unto the *p*, Fear ... Ex 20:20 5971
the *p* stood afar off, and Moses ... Ex 20:21 5971
any of my *p* that is poor by thee ... Ex 22:25 5971
nor curse the ruler of thy *p* ... Ex 22:28 5971
that the poor of thy *p* may eat ... Ex 23:11 5971
will destroy all the *p* to whom ... Ex 23:27 5971
shall the *p* go up with him ... Ex 24:2 5971
told the *p* all the words of the ... Ex 24:3 5971
all the *p* answered with one voice ... Ex 24:3 5971
and read in the audience of the *p* ... Ex 24:7 5971
blood, and sprinkled it on the *p* ... Ex 24:8 5971
shall even be cut off from his *p* ... Ex 30:33 5971
shall even be cut off from his *p* ... Ex 30:38 5971
shall be cut off from among his *p* ... Ex 31:14 5971
when the *p* saw that Moses delayed ... Ex 32:1 5971
the *p* gathered themselves ... Ex 32:1 5971
all the *p* brake off the golden ... Ex 32:3 5971
the *p* sat down to eat and to drink ... Ex 32:6 5971
for thy *p*, which thou broughtest ... Ex 32:7 5971
unto Moses, I have seen this *p* ... Ex 32:9 5971
and, behold, it is a stiffnecked *p* ... Ex 32:9 5971
thy wrath wax hot against thy *p* ... Ex 32:11 5971
repent of this evil against thy *p* ... Ex 32:12 5971
which he thought to do unto his *p* ... Ex 32:14 5971
noise of the *p* as they shouted ... Ex 32:17 5971
Aaron, What did this *p* unto thee ... Ex 32:21 5971
thou knowest the *p*, that they are ... Ex 32:22 5971
Moses saw that the *p* were naked ... Ex 32:25 5971
there fell of the *p* that day ... Ex 32:28 5971
that Moses said unto the *p* ... Ex 32:30 5971
this *p* have sinned a great sin ... Ex 32:31 5971
lead the *p* unto the place of ... Ex 32:34 5971
And the Lord plagued the *p* ... Ex 32:35 5971
the *p* which thou hast brought up ... Ex 33:1 5971
for thou art a stiffnecked *p* ... Ex 33:3 5971
when the *p* heard these evil ... Ex 33:4 5971
of Israel, Ye are a stiffnecked *p* ... Ex 33:5 5971
that all the *p* rose up, and stood ... Ex 33:8 5971
all the *p* saw the cloudy pillar ... Ex 33:10 5971
and all the *p* rose up and ... Ex 33:10 5971
sayest unto me, Bring up this *p* ... Ex 33:12 5971
that this nation is thy *p* ... Ex 33:13 5971
thy *p* have found grace in thy ... Ex 33:16 5971
shall we be separated, I and thy *p* ... Ex 33:16 5971
from all the *p* that are upon the ... Ex 33:16 5971
for it is a stiffnecked *p* ... Ex 34:9 5971
before all thy *p* I will do ... Ex 34:10 5971
all the *p* among which thou art ... Ex 34:10 5971
The *p* bring much more than enough ... Ex 36:5 5971
So the *p* were restrained from ... Ex 36:6 5971
sin according to the sin of the *p* ... Lev 4:3 5971
common *p* sin through ignorance ... Lev 4:27 5971
soul shall be cut off from his *p* ... Lev 7:20 5971
soul shall be cut off from his *p* ... Lev 7:21 5971
it shall be cut off from his *p* ... Lev 7:25 5971
soul shall be cut off from his *p* ... Lev 7:27 5971
for thyself, and for the *p* ... Lev 9:7 5971
and offer the offering of the *p* ... Lev 9:7 5971
was the sin offering for the *p* ... Lev 9:15 5971
offerings, which was for the *p* ... Lev 9:18 5971
lifted up his hand toward the *p* ... Lev 9:22 5971
and came out, and blessed the *p* ... Lev 9:23 5971
the Lord appeared unto all the *p* ... Lev 9:23 5971
which when all the *p* saw, they ... Lev 9:24 5971
before all the *p* I will be ... Lev 10:3 5971
and lest wrath come upon all the *p* ... Lev 10:6 5712
sin offering, that is for the *p* ... Lev 16:15 5971
and the burnt offering of the *p* ... Lev 16:24 5971
for himself, and for the *p* ... Lev 16:24 5971
for all the *p* of the congregation ... Lev 16:33 5971
shall be cut off from among his *p* ... Lev 17:4 5971
shall be cut off from among his *p* ... Lev 17:9 5971
will cut him off from among his *p* ... Lev 17:10 5971
be cut off from among their *p* ... Lev 18:29 5971
shall be cut off from among his *p* ... Lev 19:8 5971
down as a talebearer among thy *p* ... Lev 19:16 5971
against the children of thy *p* ... Lev 19:18 5971
the *p* of the land shall stone him ... Lev 20:2 5971
will cut him off from among his *p* ... Lev 20:3 5971
if the *p* of the land do any ways ... Lev 20:4 5971
with Molech, from among their *p* ... Lev 20:5 5971
will cut him off from among his *p* ... Lev 20:6 5971
cut off in the sight of their *p* ... Lev 20:17 5971
be cut off from among their *p* ... Lev 20:18 5971
have separated you from other *p* ... Lev 20:24 5971
and have severed you from other *p* ... Lev 20:26 5971
defiled for the dead among his *p* ... Lev 21:1 5971
being a chief man among his *p* ... Lev 21:4 5971

a virgin of his own *p* to wife	Lev 21:14	5971
he profane his seed among his *p*	Lev 21:15	5971
shall be cut off from among his *p*	Lev 23:29	5971
will I destroy from among his *p*	Lev 23:30	5971
be your God, and ye shall be my *p*	Lev 26:12	5971
a curse and an oath among thy *p*	Num 5:21	5971
shall be a curse among her *p*	Num 5:27	5971
shall be cut off from among his *p*	Num 9:13	5971
when the *p* complained, it	Num 11:1	5971
And the *p* cried unto Moses	Num 11:2	5971
the *p* went about, and gathered it,	Num 11:8	5971
Then Moses heard the *p* weep	Num 11:10	5971
the burden of all this *p* upon me	Num 11:11	5971
Have I conceived all this *p*	Num 11:12	5971
flesh to give unto all this *p*	Num 11:13	5971
not able to bear all this *p* alone	Num 11:14	5971
knowest to be the elders of the *p*	Num 11:16	5971
the burden of the *p* with thee	Num 11:17	5971
And say thou unto the *p*, Sanctify	Num 11:18	5971
And Moses said, The *p*, among whom	Num 11:21	5971
told the *p* the words of the LORD,	Num 11:24	5971
men of the elders of the *p*	Num 11:24	5971
all the LORD's *p* were prophets	Num 11:29	5971
the *p* stood up all that day, and	Num 11:32	5971
LORD was kindled against the *p*	Num 11:33	5971
the LORD smote the *p* with a very	Num 11:33	5971
they buried the *p* that lusted	Num 11:34	5971
And the *p* journeyed from	Num 11:35	5971
the *p* journeyed not till Miriam	Num 12:15	5971
afterward the *p* removed from	Num 12:16	5971
the *p* that dwelleth therein,	Num 13:18	5971
Nevertheless the *p* be strong that	Num 13:28	5971
Caleb stilled the *p* before Moses	Num 13:30	5971
not able to go up against the *p*	Num 13:31	5971
all the *p* that we saw in it are	Num 13:32	5971
and the *p* wept that night	Num 14:1	5971
neither fear ye the *p* of the land	Num 14:9	5971
How long will this *p* provoke me	Num 14:11	5971
p in thy might from among them	Num 14:13	5971
that thou LORD art among this *p*	Num 14:14	5971
shalt kill all this *p* as one man	Num 14:15	5971
p into the land which he sware	Num 14:16	5971
the iniquity of this *p* according	Num 14:19	5971
and as thou hast forgiven this *p*	Num 14:19	5971
and the *p* mourned greatly	Num 14:39	5971
seeing all the *p* were in	Num 15:26	5971
shall be cut off from among his *p*	Num 15:30	5971
Ye have killed the *p* of the LORD	Num 16:41	5971
the plague was begun among the *p*	Num 16:47	5971
and made an atonement for the *p*	Num 16:47	5971
and the *p* abode in Kadesh	Num 20:1	5971
the *p* chode with Moses, and spake,	Num 20:3	5971
came out against him with much *p*	Num 20:20	5971
shall be gathered unto his *p*	Num 20:24	5971
shall be gathered unto his *p*	Num 20:26	5971
deliver this *p* into my hand	Num 21:2	5971
the soul of the *p* was much	Num 21:4	5971
the *p* spake against God, and	Num 21:5	5971
sent fiery serpents among the *p*	Num 21:6	5971
and they bit the *p*	Num 21:6	5971
and much *p* of Israel died	Num 21:6	5971
Therefore the *p* came to Moses	Num 21:7	5971
And Moses prayed for the *p*	Num 21:7	5971
unto Moses, Gather the *p* together	Num 21:16	5971
the nobles of the *p* digged it	Num 21:18	5971
Sihon gathered all his *p* together	Num 21:23	5971
thou art undone, O *p* of Chemosh	Num 21:29	5971
against them, he, and all his *p*	Num 21:33	5971
him into thy hand, and all his *p*	Num 21:34	5971
him, and his sons, and all his *p*	Num 21:35	5971
And Moab was sore afraid of the *p*	Num 22:3	5971
the land of the children of his *p*	Num 22:5	5971
there is a *p* come out from Egypt	Num 22:5	5971
I pray thee, curse me this *p*	Num 22:6	5971
there is a *p* come out of Egypt,	Num 22:11	5971
thou shalt not curse the *p*	Num 22:12	5971
I pray thee, curse me this *p*	Num 22:17	5971
see the utmost part of the *p*	Num 22:41	5971
the *p* shall dwell alone, and shall	Num 23:9	5971
the *p* shall rise up as a great	Num 23:24	5971
And now, behold, I go unto my *p*	Num 24:14	5971
p shall do to thy *p* in the	Num 24:14	5971
the *p* began to commit whoredom	Num 25:1	5971
they called the *p* unto the	Num 25:2	5971
the *p* did eat, and bowed down to	Num 25:2	5971
Take all the heads of the *p*	Num 25:4	5971
he was head over a *p*, and of a	Num 25:15	523
Take the sum of the *p*, from	Num 26:4	
also shalt be gathered unto thy *p*	Num 27:13	5971
shalt thou be gathered unto thy *p*	Num 31:2	5971
And Moses spake unto the *p*	Num 31:3	5971
and ye shall destroy all this *p*	Num 32:15	5971
was no water for the *p* to drink	Num 33:14	5971
The *p* is greater and taller than	Deut 1:28	5971
And command thou the *p*, saying, Ye	Deut 2:4	5971
a *p* great, and many, and tall, as	Deut 2:10	5971
consumed and dead from among the *p*	Deut 2:16	5971
A *p* great, and many, and tall, as	Deut 2:21	5971
out against us, he and all his *p*	Deut 2:32	5971
him, and his sons, and all his *p*	Deut 2:33	5971
out against us, he and all his *p*	Deut 3:1	5971
I will deliver him, and all his *p*	Deut 3:2	5971
the king of Bashan, and all his *p*	Deut 3:3	5971
he shall go over before this *p*	Deut 3:28	5971
is a wise and understanding *p*	Deut 4:6	5971
unto me, Gather me the *p* together	Deut 4:10	5971
to be unto him a *p* of inheritance	Deut 4:20	5971
Did ever *p* hear the voice of God	Deut 4:33	5971
the voice of the words of this *p*	Deut 5:28	5971
of the gods of the *p* which are	Deut 6:14	5971
For thou art an holy *p* unto the	Deut 7:6	5971
to be a special *p* unto himself	Deut 7:6	5971
above all *p* that are upon the	Deut 7:6	5971
ye were more in number than any *p*	Deut 7:7	5971
for ye were the fewest of all *p*	Deut 7:7	5971
Thou shalt be blessed above all *p*	Deut 7:14	5971
thou shalt consume all the *p*	Deut 7:16	5971
all the *p* of whom thou art afraid	Deut 7:19	5971
A *p* great and tall, the children	Deut 9:2	5971
for thou art a stiffnecked *p*	Deut 9:6	5971
for thy *p* which thou hast brought	Deut 9:12	5971
me, saying, I have seen this *p*	Deut 9:13	5971
and, behold, it is a stiffnecked *p*	Deut 9:13	5971
O Lord GOD, destroy not thy *p*	Deut 9:26	5971
unto the stubbornness of this *p*	Deut 9:27	5971
Yet they are thy *p* and thine	Deut 9:29	5971
take thy journey before the *p*	Deut 10:11	5971
after them, even you above all *p*	Deut 10:15	5971
of the gods of the *p* which are	Deut 13:7	5971
afterwards the hand of all the *p*	Deut 13:9	5971
For thou art an holy *p* unto the	Deut 14:2	5971
to be a peculiar *p* unto himself	Deut 14:2	5971
for thou art an holy *p* unto the	Deut 14:21	5971
judge the *p* with just judgment	Deut 16:18	5971
afterward the hands of all the *p*	Deut 17:7	5971
all the *p* shall hear, and fear, and	Deut 17:13	5971
nor cause the *p* to return to	Deut 17:16	5971
be the priest's due from the *p*	Deut 18:3	5971
a *p* more than thou, be not afraid	Deut 20:1	5971
approach and speak unto the *p*	Deut 20:2	5971
officers shall speak unto the *p*	Deut 20:5	5971
shall speak further unto the *p*	Deut 20:8	5971
an end of speaking unto the *p*	Deut 20:9	5971
of the armies to lead the *p*	Deut 20:9	5971
that all the *p* that is found	Deut 20:11	5971
But of the cities of these *p*	Deut 20:16	5971
O LORD, unto thy *p* Israel	Deut 21:8	5971
unto thy *p* of Israel's charge	Deut 21:8	5971
heaven, and bless thy *p* Israel	Deut 26:15	5971
this day to be his peculiar *p*	Deut 26:18	5971
an holy *p* unto the LORD thy God	Deut 26:19	5971
elders of Israel commanded the *p*	Deut 27:1	5971
become the *p* of the LORD thy God	Deut 27:9	5971
Moses charged the *p* the same day	Deut 27:11	5971
upon mount Gerizim to bless the *p*	Deut 27:12	5971
all the *p* shall answer and say,	Deut 27:15	5971
all the *p* shall say, Amen	Deut 27:16	5971
all the *p* shall say, Amen	Deut 27:17	5971
all the *p* shall say, Amen	Deut 27:18	5971
all the *p* shall say, Amen	Deut 27:19	5971
all the *p* shall say, Amen	Deut 27:20	5971
all the *p* shall say, Amen	Deut 27:21	5971
all the *p* shall say, Amen	Deut 27:22	5971
all the *p* shall say, Amen	Deut 27:23	5971
all the *p* shall say, Amen	Deut 27:24	5971
all the *p* shall say, Amen	Deut 27:25	5971
all the *p* shall say, Amen	Deut 27:26	5971
thee an holy *p* unto himself	Deut 28:9	5971
all *p* of the earth shall see that	Deut 28:10	5971
shall be given unto another *p*	Deut 28:32	5971
shall scatter thee among all *p*	Deut 28:64	5971
thee to day for a *p* unto himself	Deut 29:13	5971
for thou must go with this *p* unto	Deut 31:7	5971
Gather the *p* together, men, and	Deut 31:12	5971
this *p* will rise up, and go a	Deut 31:16	5971
requite the LORD, O foolish *p*	Deut 32:6	5971
he set the bounds of the *p*	Deut 32:8	5971
For the LORD's portion is his *p*	Deut 32:9	5971
with those which are not a *p*	Deut 32:21	5971
For the LORD shall judge his *p*	Deut 32:36	5971
Rejoice, O ye nations, with his *p*	Deut 32:43	5971
unto his land, and to his *p*	Deut 32:43	5971
of this song in the ears of the *p*	Deut 32:44	5971
up, and be gathered unto thy *p*	Deut 32:50	5971
Hor, and was gathered unto his *p*	Deut 32:50	5971
Yea, he loved the *p*	Deut 33:3	5971
Jeshurun, when the heads of the *p*	Deut 33:5	5971
of Judah, and bring him unto his *p*	Deut 33:7	5971
the *p* together to the ends of the	Deut 33:17	5971
call the *p* unto the mountain	Deut 33:19	5971
he came with the heads of the *p*	Deut 33:21	5971
O *p* saved by the LORD, the shield	Deut 33:29	5971
this Jordan, thou, and all this *p*	Josh 1:2	5971
for unto this *p* shalt thou divide	Josh 1:6	5971
commanded the officers of the *p*	Josh 1:10	5971
the host, and command the *p*	Josh 1:11	5971
And they commanded the *p*, saying,	Josh 3:3	5971
And Joshua said unto the *p*	Josh 3:5	5971
and pass over before the *p*	Josh 3:6	5971
covenant, and went before the *p*	Josh 3:6	5971
when the *p* removed from their	Josh 3:14	5971
ark of the covenant before the *p*	Josh 3:14	5971
the *p* passed over right against	Josh 3:16	5971
until all the *p* were passed clean	Josh 3:17	1471
when all the *p* were clean passed	Josh 4:1	1471
Take you twelve men out of the *p*	Josh 4:2	5971
Joshua to speak unto the *p*	Josh 4:10	5971
the *p* hasted and passed over	Josh 4:10	5971
when all the *p* were clean passed	Josh 4:11	5971
priests, in the presence of the *p*	Josh 4:11	5971
the *p* came up out of Jordan on	Josh 4:19	5971
That all the *p* of the earth might	Josh 4:24	5971
All the *p* that came out of Egypt,	Josh 5:4	5971
Now all the *p* that came out were	Josh 5:5	5971
but all the *p* that were born in	Josh 5:5	5971
till all the *p* that were men of	Josh 5:6	1471
had done circumcising all the *p*	Josh 5:8	1471
all the *p* shall shout with a	Josh 6:5	5971
the *p* shall ascend up every man	Josh 6:5	5971
And he said unto the *p*, Pass on,	Josh 6:7	5971
when Joshua had spoken unto the *p*	Josh 6:8	5971
And Joshua had commanded the *p*	Josh 6:10	5971
trumpets, Joshua said unto the *p*	Josh 6:16	5971
So the *p* shouted when the priests	Josh 6:20	5971
when the *p* heard the sound of the	Josh 6:20	5971
the *p* shouted with a great shout,	Josh 6:20	5971
so that the *p* went up into the	Josh 6:20	5971
unto him, Let not all the *p* go up	Josh 7:3	5971
make not all the *p* to labour	Josh 7:3	5971
of the *p* about three thousand men	Josh 7:4	5971
the hearts of the *p* melted	Josh 7:5	5971
at all brought this *p* over Jordan	Josh 7:7	5971
Up, sanctify the *p*, and say,	Josh 7:13	5971
take all the *p* of war with thee,	Josh 8:1	5971
thy hand the king of Ai, and his *p*	Josh 8:1	5971
Joshua arose, and all the *p* of war	Josh 8:3	5971
all the *p* that are with me, will	Josh 8:5	5971
lodged that night among the *p*	Josh 8:9	5971
in the morning, and numbered the *p*	Josh 8:10	5971
of Israel, before the *p* to Ai	Josh 8:10	5971
And all the *p*, even the	Josh 8:11	5971
even the *p* of war that were with	Josh 8:11	
And when they had set the *p*	Josh 8:13	5971
Israel to battle, he and all his *p*	Josh 8:14	5971
all the *p* that were in Ai were	Josh 8:16	5971
the *p* that fled to the wilderness	Josh 8:20	5971
they should bless the *p* of Israel	Josh 8:33	5971
all the *p* of war with him, and all	Josh 10:7	5971
stayed, until the *p* had avenged	Josh 10:13	1471
all the *p* returned to the camp to	Josh 10:21	5971
and Joshua smote him and his *p*	Josh 10:33	5971
all their hosts with them, much *p*	Josh 11:4	5971
all the *p* of war with him,	Josh 11:7	5971
me made the heart of the *p* melt	Josh 14:8	5971
to inherit, seeing I am a great *p*	Josh 17:14	5971
them, If thou be a great *p*	Josh 17:15	5971
saying, Thou art a great *p*	Josh 17:17	5971
And Joshua said unto all the *p*	Josh 24:2	5971
the *p* answered and said, God	Josh 24:16	5971
among all the *p* through whom we	Josh 24:17	5971
out from before us all the *p*	Josh 24:18	5971
And Joshua said unto the *p*	Josh 24:19	5971
the *p* said unto Joshua, Nay	Josh 24:21	5971
And Joshua said unto the *p*	Josh 24:22	5971
the *p* said unto Joshua, The LORD	Josh 24:24	5971
a covenant with the *p* that day	Josh 24:25	5971
And Joshua said unto all the *p*	Josh 24:27	5971
So Joshua let the *p* depart	Josh 24:28	5971
and they went and dwelt among the *p*	Judg 1:16	5971
that the *p* lifted up their voice,	Judg 2:4	5971
And when Joshua had let the *p* go	Judg 2:6	5971
the *p* served the LORD all the	Judg 2:7	5971
of the gods of the *p* that were	Judg 2:12	5971
he said, Because that this *p* hath	Judg 2:20	1471
he sent away the *p* that bare the	Judg 3:18	5971
all the *p* that were with him,	Judg 4:13	5971
when the *p* willingly offered	Judg 5:2	5971
themselves willingly among the *p*	Judg 5:9	5971
then shall the *p* of the LORD go	Judg 5:11	5971
over the nobles among the *p*	Judg 5:13	5971
after thee, Benjamin, among thy *p*	Judg 5:14	5971
Naphtali were a *p* that jeoparded	Judg 5:18	5971
all the *p* that were with him,	Judg 7:1	5971
The *p* that are with thee are too	Judg 7:2	5971
to, proclaim in the ears of the *p*	Judg 7:3	5971
And there returned of the *p* twenty	Judg 7:3	5971
Gideon, The *p* are yet too many	Judg 7:4	5971
brought down the *p* unto the water	Judg 7:5	5971
but all the rest of the *p* bowed	Judg 7:6	5971
let all the other *p* go every man	Judg 7:7	5971
So the *p* took victuals in their	Judg 7:8	5971
bread unto the *p* that follow me	Judg 8:5	5971
would to God this *p* were under my	Judg 9:29	5971
the *p* that is with thee, and lie	Judg 9:32	5971
the *p* that is with him come out	Judg 9:33	5971
all the *p* that were with him, by	Judg 9:34	5971
the *p* that were with him, from	Judg 9:35	5971
And when Gaal saw the *p*, he said	Judg 9:36	5971
there come *p* down from the top of	Judg 9:36	5971
See there come *p* down by the	Judg 9:37	5971
is not this the *p* that thou hast	Judg 9:38	5971
that the *p* went out into the	Judg 9:42	5971
And he took the *p*, and divided them	Judg 9:43	5971
the *p* were come forth out of the	Judg 9:43	5971
all the *p* that were in the fields	Judg 9:44	
slew the *p* that was therein, and	Judg 9:45	5971
all the *p* that were with him	Judg 9:48	5971
said unto the *p* that were with	Judg 9:48	5971
all the *p* likewise cut down every	Judg 9:49	5971
And the *p* and princes of Gilead	Judg 10:18	5971
the *p* made him head and captain	Judg 11:11	5971
Sihon gathered all his *p* together	Judg 11:20	5971
all his *p* into the hand of Israel	Judg 11:21	5971
Amorites from before his *p* Israel	Judg 11:23	5971
my *p* were at great strife with	Judg 12:2	5971
thy brethren, or among all my *p*	Judg 14:3	5971
riddle unto the children of my *p*	Judg 14:16	5971
riddle to the children of her *p*	Judg 14:17	5971
And when the *p* saw him, they	Judg 16:24	5971
upon all the *p* that were therein	Judg 16:30	5971
saw the *p* that were therein, how	Judg 18:7	5971
go, ye shall come unto a *p* secure	Judg 18:10	5971
and went in the midst of the *p*	Judg 18:20	5971
unto a *p* that were at quiet and	Judg 18:27	5971
And the chief of all the *p*	Judg 20:2	5971
in the assembly of the *p* of God	Judg 20:2	5971
all the *p* arose as one man,	Judg 20:8	5971
to fetch victual for the *p*	Judg 20:10	5971
Among all this *p* there were seven	Judg 20:16	5971
And the *p* the men of Israel	Judg 20:22	5971
children of Israel, and all the *p*	Judg 20:26	5971
Benjamin went out against the *p*	Judg 20:31	5971
and they began to smite of the *p*	Judg 20:31	5971
the *p* came to the house of God,	Judg 21:2	5971
that the *p* rose early, and built	Judg 21:4	5971
For the *p* were numbered, and,	Judg 21:9	5971
the *p* repented them for Benjamin,	Judg 21:15	5971
his *p* in giving them bread	Ruth 1:6	5971
will return with thee unto thy *p*	Ruth 1:10	5971
in law is gone back unto her *p*	Ruth 1:15	5971
thy *p* shall be my *p*, and thy	Ruth 1:16	5971
art come unto a *p* which thou	Ruth 2:11	5971

for all the city of my *p* doth ... Ruth 3:11 5971
and before the elders of my *p* ... Ruth 4:4 5971
the elders, and unto all the *p* ... Ruth 4:9 5971
all the *p* that were in the gate, ... Ruth 4:11 5971
priest's custom with the *p* was ... 1Sa 2:13 5971
your evil dealings by all this *p* ... 1Sa 2:23 5971
make the LORD's *p* to transgress ... 1Sa 2:24 5971
all the offerings of Israel my *p* ... 1Sa 2:29 5971
when the *p* were come into the ... 1Sa 4:3 5971
So the *p* sent to Shiloh, that ... 1Sa 4:4 5971
a great slaughter among the *p* ... 1Sa 4:17 5971
Israel to us, to slay us and our *p* ... 1Sa 5:10 5971
that it slay us not, and our *p* ... 1Sa 5:11 5971
them, did they not let the *p* go ... 1Sa 6:6
he smote of the *p* fifty thousand ... 1Sa 6:19 5971
the *p* lamented, because the LORD ... 1Sa 6:19 5971
of the *p* with a great slaughter ... 1Sa 6:19 5971
Hearken unto the voice of the *p* ... 1Sa 8:7 5971
the *p* that asked of him a king ... 1Sa 8:10 5971
Nevertheless the *p* refused to ... 1Sa 8:19 5971
heard all the words of the *p* ... 1Sa 8:21 5971
he was higher than any of the *p* ... 1Sa 9:2 5971
of the *p* to day in the high place ... 1Sa 9:12 5971
for the *p* will not eat until he ... 1Sa 9:13 5971
to be captain over my *p* Israel ... 1Sa 9:16 5971
that he may save my *p* out of the ... 1Sa 9:16 5971
for I have looked upon my *p* ... 1Sa 9:16 5971
this same shall reign over my *p* ... 1Sa 9:17 5971
I said, I have invited the *p* ... 1Sa 9:24 5971
then the *p* said one to another, ... 1Sa 10:11 5971
Samuel called the *p* together unto ... 1Sa 10:17 5971
and when he stood among the *p* ... 1Sa 10:23 5971
any of the *p* from his shoulders ... 1Sa 10:23 5971
And Samuel said to all the *p* ... 1Sa 10:24 5971
is none like him among all the *p* ... 1Sa 10:24 5971
And all the *p* shouted, and said, ... 1Sa 10:24 5971
Then Samuel told the *p* the manner ... 1Sa 10:25 5971
And Samuel sent all the *p* away ... 1Sa 10:25 5971
the tidings in the ears of the *p* ... 1Sa 11:4 5971
all the *p* lifted up their voices, ... 1Sa 11:4 5971
What aileth the *p* that they weep ... 1Sa 11:5 5971
fear of the LORD fell on the *p* ... 1Sa 11:7 5971
that Saul put the *p* in three ... 1Sa 11:11 5971
the *p* said unto Samuel, Who is he ... 1Sa 11:12 5971
Then said Samuel to the *p* ... 1Sa 11:14 5971
And all the *p* went to Gilgal ... 1Sa 11:15 5971
And Samuel said unto the *p* ... 1Sa 12:6 5971
all the *p* greatly feared the LORD ... 1Sa 12:18 5971
all the *p* said unto Samuel, Pray ... 1Sa 12:19 5971
And Samuel said unto the *p* ... 1Sa 12:20 5971
his *p* for his great name's sake ... 1Sa 12:22 5971
the LORD to make you his *p* ... 1Sa 12:22 5971
the rest of the *p* he sent every ... 1Sa 13:2 5971
the *p* were called together after ... 1Sa 13:4 5971
p as the sand which is on the sea ... 1Sa 13:5 5971
(for the *p* were distressed,) ... 1Sa 13:6 5971
then the *p* did hide themselves ... 1Sa 13:6 5971
all the *p* followed him trembling ... 1Sa 13:7 5971
the *p* were scattered from him ... 1Sa 13:8 5971
that the *p* were scattered from me ... 1Sa 13:11 5971
him to be captain over his *p* ... 1Sa 13:14 5971
Saul numbered the *p* that were ... 1Sa 13:15 5971
the *p* that were present with them ... 1Sa 13:16 5971
any of the *p* that were with Saul ... 1Sa 13:22 5971
the *p* that were with him were ... 1Sa 14:2 5971
the *p* knew not that Jonathan was ... 1Sa 14:3 5971
in the field, and among all the *p* ... 1Sa 14:15 5971
unto the *p* that were with him ... 1Sa 14:17 5971
all the *p* that were with him ... 1Sa 14:20 5971
for Saul had adjured the *p* ... 1Sa 14:24 5971
So none of the *p* tasted any food ... 1Sa 14:24 5971
when the *p* were come into the ... 1Sa 14:26 5971
for the *p* feared the oath ... 1Sa 14:26 5971
charged the *p* with the oath ... 1Sa 14:27 5971
Then answered one of the *p* ... 1Sa 14:28 5971
charged the *p* with an oath ... 1Sa 14:28 5971
And the *p* were faint ... 1Sa 14:28 5971
if haply the *p* had eaten freely ... 1Sa 14:30 5971
and the *p* were very faint ... 1Sa 14:31 5971
the *p* flew upon the spoil, and ... 1Sa 14:32 5971
the *p* did eat them with the blood ... 1Sa 14:32 5971
the *p* sin against the LORD, in ... 1Sa 14:33 5971
Disperse yourselves among the *p* ... 1Sa 14:34 5971
all the *p* brought every man his ... 1Sa 14:34 5971
hither, all the chief of the *p* ... 1Sa 14:38 5971
among all the *p* that answered him ... 1Sa 14:39 5971
the *p* said unto Saul, Do what ... 1Sa 14:40 5971
but the *p* escaped ... 1Sa 14:41 5971
the *p* said unto Saul, Shall ... 1Sa 14:45 5971
So the *p* rescued Jonathan, that ... 1Sa 14:45 5971
anoint thee to be king over his *p* ... 1Sa 15:1 5971
And Saul gathered the *p* together ... 1Sa 15:4 5971
utterly destroyed all the *p* with ... 1Sa 15:8 5971
the *p* spared Agag, and the best of ... 1Sa 15:9 5971
for the *p* spared the best of the ... 1Sa 15:15 5971
But the *p* took of the spoil, ... 1Sa 15:21 5971
because I feared the *p*, and obeyed ... 1Sa 15:24 5971
thee, before the elders of my *p* ... 1Sa 15:30 5971
the *p* answered him after this ... 1Sa 17:27 5971
the *p* answered him again after ... 1Sa 17:30 5971
in the sight of all the *p* ... 1Sa 18:5 5971
went out and came in before the *p* ... 1Sa 18:13 5971
called all the *p* together to war ... 1Sa 23:8 5971
the *p* pitched round about him ... 1Sa 26:5 5971
and Abishai came to the *p* by night ... 1Sa 26:7 5971
the *p* lay round about him ... 1Sa 26:7 5971
And David cried to the *p*, and to ... 1Sa 26:14 5971
for there came one of the *p* in to ... 1Sa 26:15 5971
He hath made his *p* Israel utterly ... 1Sa 27:12 5971
the *p* that were with him lifted ... 1Sa 30:4 5971
for the *p* spake of stoning him, ... 1Sa 30:6 5971
the soul of all the *p* was grieved ... 1Sa 30:6 5971
to meet the *p* that were with him ... 1Sa 30:21 5971
and when David came near to the *p* ... 1Sa 30:21 5971

of their idols, and among the *p* ... 1Sa 31:9 5971
That the *p* are fled from the ... 2Sa 1:4 5971
many of the *p* also are fallen and ... 2Sa 1:4 5971
for the *p* of the LORD, and for the ... 2Sa 1:12 5971
ere thou bid the *p* return from ... 2Sa 2:26 5971
the *p* had gone up every one from ... 2Sa 2:27 5971
all the *p* stood still, and pursued ... 2Sa 2:28 5971
had gathered all the *p* together ... 2Sa 2:30 5971
p Israel out of the hand of the ... 2Sa 3:18 5971
to all the *p* that were with him, ... 2Sa 3:31 5971
and all the *p* wept ... 2Sa 3:32 5971
all the *p* wept again over him ... 2Sa 3:34 5971
when all the *p* came to cause ... 2Sa 3:35 5971
all the *p* took notice of it, and ... 2Sa 3:36 5971
the king did pleased all the *p* ... 2Sa 3:36 5971
For all the *p* and all Israel ... 2Sa 3:37 5971
thee, Thou shalt feed my *p* Israel ... 2Sa 5:2 5971
kingdom for his *p* Israel's sake ... 2Sa 5:12 5971
went with all the *p* that were ... 2Sa 6:2 5971
he blessed the *p* in the name of ... 2Sa 6:18 5971
And he dealt among all the *p* ... 2Sa 6:19 5971
So all the *p* departed every one ... 2Sa 6:19 5971
me ruler over the *p* of the LORD ... 2Sa 6:21 5971
I commanded to feed my *p* Israel ... 2Sa 7:7 5971
the sheep, to be ruler over my *p* ... 2Sa 7:8 5971
appoint a place for my *p* Israel ... 2Sa 7:10 5971
judges to be over my *p* Israel ... 2Sa 7:11 5971
nation in the earth is like thy *p* ... 2Sa 7:23 5971
went to redeem for a *p* to himself ... 2Sa 7:23 5971
for thy land, before thy *p* ... 2Sa 7:23 5971
hast confirmed to thyself thy *p* ... 2Sa 7:24 5971
to be a *p* unto thee for ever ... 2Sa 7:24 5971
and justice unto all his *p* ... 2Sa 8:15 5971
the rest of the *p* he delivered ... 2Sa 10:10 5971
and let us play the men for our *p* ... 2Sa 10:12 5971
the *p* that were with him, unto ... 2Sa 10:13 5971
how Joab did, and how the *p* did ... 2Sa 11:7 5971
there fell some of the *p* of the ... 2Sa 11:17 5971
gather the rest of the *p* together ... 2Sa 12:28 5971
David gathered all the *p* together ... 2Sa 12:29 5971
forth the *p* that were therein ... 2Sa 12:31 5971
all the *p* returned unto Jerusalem ... 2Sa 12:31 5971
there came much *p* by the way of ... 2Sa 13:34 5971
such a thing against the *p* of God ... 2Sa 14:13 5971
it is because the *p* have made me ... 2Sa 14:15 5971
for the *p* increased continually ... 2Sa 15:12 5971
all the *p* after him, and tarried ... 2Sa 15:17 5971
voice, and all the *p* passed over ... 2Sa 15:23 5971
all the *p* passed over, toward the ... 2Sa 15:23 5971
until all the *p* had done passing ... 2Sa 15:24 5971
all the *p* that was with him ... 2Sa 15:30 5971
and all the *p* and all the mighty ... 2Sa 16:6 5971
all the *p* that were with him, ... 2Sa 16:14 5971
all the *p* the men of Israel, came ... 2Sa 16:15 5971
but whom the LORD, and this *p* ... 2Sa 16:18 5971
all the *p* that are with him shall ... 2Sa 17:2 5971
bring back all the *p* unto thee ... 2Sa 17:3 5971
so all the *p* shall be in peace ... 2Sa 17:3 5971
war, and will not lodge with the *p* ... 2Sa 17:8 5971
among the *p* that follow Absalom ... 2Sa 17:9 5971
all the *p* that are with him ... 2Sa 17:16 5971
all the *p* that were with him, and ... 2Sa 17:22 5971
for the *p* that were with him, to ... 2Sa 17:29 5971
The *p* is hungry, and weary, and ... 2Sa 17:29 5971
numbered the *p* that were with him ... 2Sa 18:1 5971
of the *p* under the hand of Joab ... 2Sa 18:2 5971
And the king said unto the *p* ... 2Sa 18:2 5971
But the *p* answered, Thou shalt ... 2Sa 18:3 5971
all the *p* came out by hundreds and ... 2Sa 18:4 5971
all the *p* heard when the king ... 2Sa 18:5 5971
So the *p* went out into the field ... 2Sa 18:6 5971
Where the *p* of Israel were slain ... 2Sa 18:7 5971
the wood devoured more *p* that day ... 2Sa 18:8 5971
the *p* returned from pursuing ... 2Sa 18:16 5971
for Joab held back the *p* ... 2Sa 18:16 5971
into mourning unto all the *p* ... 2Sa 19:2 5971
for the *p* heard say that day how ... 2Sa 19:2 5971
the *p* gat them by stealth that ... 2Sa 19:3 5971
as *p* being ashamed steal away ... 2Sa 19:3 5971
And they told unto all the *p* ... 2Sa 19:8 5971
all the *p* came before the king ... 2Sa 19:8 5971
And all the *p* were at strife ... 2Sa 19:9 5971
all the *p* went over Jordan ... 2Sa 19:39 5971
all the *p* of Judah conducted the ... 2Sa 19:40 5971
and also half the *p* of Israel ... 2Sa 19:40 5971
saw that all the *p* stood still ... 2Sa 20:12 5971
all the *p* went on after Joab, to ... 2Sa 20:13 376
all the *p* that were with Joab ... 2Sa 20:15 5971
went unto all the *p* in her wisdom ... 2Sa 20:22 5971
the afflicted *p* thou wilt save ... 2Sa 22:28 5971
me from the strivings of my *p* ... 2Sa 22:44 5971
a *p* which I knew not shall serve ... 2Sa 22:44 5971
that bringeth down the *p* under me ... 2Sa 22:48 5971
the *p* returned after him only to ... 2Sa 23:10 5971
the *p* fled from the Philistines ... 2Sa 23:11 5971
to Beer-sheba, and number ye the *p* ... 2Sa 24:2 5971
I may know the number of the *p* ... 2Sa 24:2 5971
the LORD thy God add unto the *p* ... 2Sa 24:3 5971
king, to number the *p* of Israel ... 2Sa 24:4 5971
the number of the *p* unto the king ... 2Sa 24:9 5971
after that he had numbered the *p* ... 2Sa 24:10 5971
there died of the *p* from Dan even ... 2Sa 24:15 5971
to the angel that destroyed the *p* ... 2Sa 24:16 5971
he saw the angel that smote the *p* ... 2Sa 24:17 5971
plague may be stayed from the *p* ... 2Sa 24:21 5971
and all the *p* said, God save king ... 1Kin 1:39 5971
all the *p* came up after him, and ... 1Kin 1:40 5971
the *p* piped with pipes, and ... 1Kin 1:40 5971
Only the *p* sacrificed in high ... 1Kin 3:2 5971
of thy *p* which thou hast chosen ... 1Kin 3:8 5971
which thou hast chosen, a great *p* ... 1Kin 3:8 5971
heart to judge thy *p*, that I may ... 1Kin 3:9 5971
to judge this thy so great a *p* ... 1Kin 3:9 5971
there came of all *p* to hear the ... 1Kin 4:34 5971

a wise son over this great *p* ... 1Kin 5:7 5971
which ruled over the *p* that ... 1Kin 5:16 5971
and will not forsake my *p* Israel ... 1Kin 6:13 5971
forth my *p* Israel out of Egypt ... 1Kin 8:16 5971
David to be over my *p* Israel ... 1Kin 8:16 5971
thy servant, and of thy *p* Israel ... 1Kin 8:30 5971
When thy *p* Israel be smitten down ... 1Kin 8:33 5971
forgive the sin of thy *p* Israel ... 1Kin 8:34 5971
thy servants, and of thy *p* Israel ... 1Kin 8:36 5971
given to thy *p* for an inheritance ... 1Kin 8:36 5971
any man, or by all thy *p* Israel ... 1Kin 8:38 5971
that is not of thy *p* Israel ... 1Kin 8:41 5971
that all *p* of the earth may know ... 1Kin 8:43 5971
to fear thee, as do thy *p* Israel ... 1Kin 8:43 5971
If thy *p* go out to battle against ... 1Kin 8:44 5971
forgive thy *p* that have sinned ... 1Kin 8:50 5971
For they be thy *p*, and thine ... 1Kin 8:51 5971
the supplication of thy *p* Israel ... 1Kin 8:52 5971
from among all the *p* of the earth ... 1Kin 8:53 5971
hath given rest unto his *p* Israel ... 1Kin 8:56 5971
the cause of his *p* Israel at all ... 1Kin 8:59 5971
That all the *p* of the earth may ... 1Kin 8:60 5971
the eighth day he sent the *p* away ... 1Kin 8:66 5971
his servant, and for Israel his *p* ... 1Kin 8:66 5971
a proverb and a byword among all *p* ... 1Kin 9:7 5971
all the *p* that were left of the ... 1Kin 9:20 5971
the *p* that wrought in the work ... 1Kin 9:23 5971
And the *p* departed ... 1Kin 12:5 5971
advise that I may answer this *p* ... 1Kin 12:6 5971
be a servant unto this *p* this day ... 1Kin 12:7 5971
give ye that we may answer this *p* ... 1Kin 12:9 5971
unto this *p* that spake unto thee ... 1Kin 12:10 5971
all the *p* came to Rehoboam the ... 1Kin 12:12 5971
the king answered the *p* roughly ... 1Kin 12:13 5971
the king hearkened not unto the *p* ... 1Kin 12:15 5971
the *p* answered the king, saying, ... 1Kin 12:16 5971
and to the remnant of the *p* ... 1Kin 12:23 5971
If this *p* go up to do sacrifice ... 1Kin 12:27 5971
this *p* turn again unto their lord ... 1Kin 12:27 5971
for the *p* went to worship before ... 1Kin 12:30 5971
priests of the lowest of the *p* ... 1Kin 12:31 5971
the *p* priests of the high places ... 1Kin 13:33 5971
that I should be king over this *p* ... 1Kin 14:2 5971
I exalted thee from among the *p* ... 1Kin 14:7 5971
made thee prince over my *p* Israel ... 1Kin 14:7 5971
made thee prince over my *p* Israel ... 1Kin 16:2 5971
hast made my *p* Israel to sin, to ... 1Kin 16:2 5971
the *p* were encamped against ... 1Kin 16:15 5971
the *p* that were encamped heard ... 1Kin 16:16 5971
Then were the *p* of Israel divided ... 1Kin 16:21 5971
half of the *p* followed Tibni the ... 1Kin 16:21 5971
But the *p* that followed Omri ... 1Kin 16:22 5971
Omri prevailed against the *p* that ... 1Kin 16:22 5971
And Elijah came unto all the *p* ... 1Kin 18:21 5971
the *p* answered him not a word ... 1Kin 18:21 5971
Then said Elijah unto the *p* ... 1Kin 18:22 5971
all the *p* answered and said, It is ... 1Kin 18:24 5971
And Elijah said unto all the *p* ... 1Kin 18:30 5971
all the *p* came near unto him ... 1Kin 18:30 5971
that this *p* may know that thou ... 1Kin 18:37 5971
And when all the *p* saw it, they ... 1Kin 18:39 5971
of the oxen, and gave unto the *p* ... 1Kin 19:21 5971
all the *p* said unto him, Hearken ... 1Kin 20:8 5971
for all the *p* that follow me ... 1Kin 20:10 5971
after them he numbered all the *p* ... 1Kin 20:15 5971
his life, and thy *p* for his *p* ... 1Kin 20:42 5971
and set Naboth on high among the *p* ... 1Kin 21:9 5971
and set Naboth on high among the *p* ... 1Kin 21:12 5971
Naboth, in the presence of the *p* ... 1Kin 21:13 5971
as thou art, my *p* as thy *p* ... 1Kin 22:4 5971
And he said, Hearken, O *p*, every ... 1Kin 22:28 5971
for the *p* offered and burnt ... 1Kin 22:43 5971
as thou art, my *p* as thy *p* ... 2Kin 3:7 5971
I dwell among mine own *p* ... 2Kin 4:13 5971
and he said, Pour out for the *p* ... 2Kin 4:41 5971
And he said, Give unto the *p* ... 2Kin 4:42 5971
He said again, Give the *p* ... 2Kin 4:43 5971
the LORD, and said, Smite this *p* ... 2Kin 6:18 1471
the *p* looked, and, behold, he had ... 2Kin 6:30 5971
the *p* went out, and spoiled the ... 2Kin 7:16 5971
the *p* trode upon him in the gate, ... 2Kin 7:17 5971
for the *p* trode upon him in the ... 2Kin 7:20 5971
the *p* fled into their tents ... 2Kin 8:21 5971
thee king over the *p* of the LORD ... 2Kin 9:6 5971
and stood, and said to all the *p* ... 2Kin 10:9 5971
Jehu gathered all the *p* together ... 2Kin 10:18 5971
noise of the guard and of the *p* ... 2Kin 11:13 5971
she came to the *p* into the temple ... 2Kin 11:13 5971
all the *p* of the land rejoiced, ... 2Kin 11:14 5971
the LORD and the king and the *p* ... 2Kin 11:17 5971
that they should be the LORD's *p* ... 2Kin 11:17 5971
between the king also and the *p* ... 2Kin 11:17 5971
all the *p* of the land went into ... 2Kin 11:18 5971
guard, and all the *p* of the land ... 2Kin 11:19 5971
all the *p* of the land rejoiced, ... 2Kin 11:20 5971
the *p* still sacrificed and burnt ... 2Kin 12:3 5971
to receive no more money of the *p* ... 2Kin 12:8 5971
Neither did he leave of the *p* to ... 2Kin 13:7 5971
as yet the *p* did sacrifice and ... 2Kin 14:4 5971
all the *p* of Judah took Azariah, ... 2Kin 14:21 5971
the *p* sacrificed and burnt incense ... 2Kin 15:4 5971
house, judging the *p* of the land ... 2Kin 15:5 5971
him, and smote him before the *p* ... 2Kin 15:10 5971
the *p* sacrificed and burned ... 2Kin 15:35 5971
carried the *p* of it captive to ... 2Kin 16:9
offering of all the *p* of the land ... 2Kin 16:15 5971
of the *p* that are on the wall ... 2Kin 18:26 5971
But the *p* held their peace, and ... 2Kin 18:36 5971
tell Hezekiah the captain of my *p* ... 2Kin 20:5 5971
the *p* of the land slew all them ... 2Kin 21:24 5971
the *p* of the land made Josiah his ... 2Kin 21:24 5971
the door have gathered of the *p* ... 2Kin 22:4 5971
of the LORD for me, and for the *p* ... 2Kin 22:13 5971
and the prophets, and all the *p* ... 2Kin 23:2 5971

all the *p* stood to the covenant 2Kin 23:3 5971
graves of the children of the *p* 2Kin 23:6 5971
And the king commanded all the *p* 2Kin 23:21 5971
the *p* of the land took Jehoahaz 2Kin 23:30 5971
and the gold of the *p* of the land 2Kin 23:35 5971
poorest sort of the *p* of the land 2Kin 24:14 5971
no bread for the *p* of the land 2Kin 25:3 5971
Now the rest of the *p* that were 2Kin 25:11 5971
which mustered the *p* of the land 2Kin 25:19 5971
threescore men of the *p* of the 2Kin 25:19 5971
as for the *p* that remained in the 2Kin 25:22 5971
And all the *p*, both small and great 2Kin 25:26 5971
the gods of the *p* of the land 1Chr 5:25 5971
unto their idols, and to the *p* 1Chr 10:9 5971
thee, Thou shalt feed my *p* Israel 1Chr 11:2 5971
shalt be ruler over my *p* Israel 1Chr 11:2 5971
the *p* fled from before the 1Chr 11:13 5971
right in the eyes of all the *p* 1Chr 13:4 5971
on high, because of his *p* Israel 1Chr 14:2 5971
he blessed the *p* in the name of 1Chr 16:2 5971
make known his deeds among the *p* 1Chr 16:8 5971
and from one kingdom to another *p* 1Chr 16:20 5971
all the gods of the *p* are idols 1Chr 16:26 5971
the LORD, ye kindreds of the *p* 1Chr 16:28 5971
And all the *p* said, Amen, and 1Chr 16:36 5971
all the *p* departed every man to 1Chr 16:43 5971
whom I commanded to feed my *p* 1Chr 17:6 5971
be ruler over my *p* Israel 1Chr 17:7 5971
ordain a place for my *p* Israel 1Chr 17:9 5971
judges to be over my *p* Israel 1Chr 17:10 5971
in the earth is like thy *p* Israel 1Chr 17:21 5971
went to redeem to be his own *p* 1Chr 17:21 5971
out nations from before thy *p* 1Chr 17:21 5971
For thy *p* Israel didst thou make 1Chr 17:22 5971
thou make thine own *p* for ever 1Chr 17:22 5971
and justice among all his *p* 1Chr 18:14 5971
and the king of Maachah and his *p* 1Chr 19:7 5971
the rest of the *p* he delivered 1Chr 19:11 5971
ourselves valiantly for our *p* 1Chr 19:13 5971
the *p* that were with him drew 1Chr 19:14 5971
brought out the *p* that were in it 1Chr 20:3 5971
all the *p* returned to Jerusalem 1Chr 20:3 5971
to Joab and to the rulers of the *p* 1Chr 21:2 5971
The LORD make his *p* an hundred 1Chr 21:3 5971
of the number of the *p* unto David 1Chr 21:5 5971
commanded the *p* to be numbered 1Chr 21:17 5971
but not on thy *p*, that they 1Chr 21:17 5971
plague may be stayed from the *p* 1Chr 21:22 5971
before the LORD, and before his *p* 1Chr 22:18 5971
Israel hath given rest unto his *p* 1Chr 23:25 5971
Hear me, my brethren, and my *p* 1Chr 28:2 5971
all the *p* will be wholly at thy 1Chr 28:21 5971
Then the *p* rejoiced, for that 1Chr 29:9 5971
But who am I, and what is my *p* 1Chr 29:14 5971
and now have I seen with joy thy *p* 1Chr 29:17 5971
thoughts of the heart of thy *p* 1Chr 29:18 5971
a *p* like the dust of the earth in 2Chr 1:9 5971
go out and come in before this *p* 2Chr 1:10 5971
for who can judge this thy *p* 2Chr 1:10 5971
that thou mayest judge my *p* 2Chr 1:11 5971
Because the LORD hath loved his *p* 2Chr 2:11 5971
overseers to set the *p* a work 2Chr 2:18 5971
my *p* out of the land of Egypt I 2Chr 6:5 5971
to be a ruler over my *p* Israel 2Chr 6:5 5971
David to be over my *p* Israel 2Chr 6:6 5971
thy servant, and of thy *p* Israel 2Chr 6:21 5971
if thy *p* Israel be put to the 2Chr 6:24 5971
forgive the sin of thy *p* Israel 2Chr 6:25 5971
thy servants, and of thy *p* Israel 2Chr 6:27 5971
unto thy *p* for an inheritance 2Chr 6:27 5971
any man, or of all thy *p* Israel 2Chr 6:29 5971
which is not of thy *p* Israel 2Chr 6:32 5971
that all *p* of the earth may know 2Chr 6:33 5971
fear thee, as doth thy *p* Israel 2Chr 6:33 5971
If thy *p* go out to war against 2Chr 6:34 5971
forgive thy *p* which have sinned 2Chr 6:39 5971
all the *p* offered sacrifices 2Chr 7:4 5971
all the *p* dedicated the house of 2Chr 7:5 5971
sent the *p* away into their tents 2Chr 7:10 5971
and to Solomon, and to Israel his *p* 2Chr 7:10 5971
if I send pestilence among my *p* 2Chr 7:13 5971
If my *p*, which are called by my 2Chr 7:14 5971
As for all the *p* that were left 2Chr 8:7 5971
fifty, that bare rule over the *p* 2Chr 8:10 5971
And the *p* departed 2Chr 10:5 5971
ye me to return answer to this *p* 2Chr 10:6 5971
saying, If thou be kind to this *p* 2Chr 10:7 5971
we may return answer to this *p* 2Chr 10:9 5971
answer the *p* that spake unto thee 2Chr 10:10 5971
all the *p* came to Rehoboam on the 2Chr 10:12 5971
the king hearkened not unto the *p* 2Chr 10:15 5971
the *p* answered the king, saying, 2Chr 10:16 5971
the *p* were without number that 2Chr 12:3 5971
his *p* slew them with a great 2Chr 13:17 5971
the *p* that were with him pursued 2Chr 14:13 5971
some of the *p* the same time 2Chr 16:10 5971
cities of Judah, and taught the *p* 2Chr 17:9 5971
for the *p* that he had with him, 2Chr 18:2 5971
thou art, and my *p* as thy *p* 2Chr 18:3 5971
And he said, Hearken, all ye *p* 2Chr 18:27 5971
the *p* from Beer-sheba to mount 2Chr 19:4 5971
of this land before thy *p* Israel 2Chr 20:7 5971
when he had consulted with the *p* 2Chr 20:21 5971
his *p* came to take away the spoil 2Chr 20:25 5971
for as yet the *p* had not prepared 2Chr 20:33 5971
plague will the LORD smite thy *p* 2Chr 21:14 5971
his *p* made no burning for him, 2Chr 21:19 5971
all the *p* shall be in the courts 2Chr 23:5 5971
but all the *p* shall keep the 2Chr 23:6 5971
And he set all the *p*, every man 2Chr 23:10 5971
heard the noise of the *p* running 2Chr 23:12 5971
she came to the *p* into the house 2Chr 23:12 5971
all the *p* of the land rejoiced, 2Chr 23:13 5971
between him, and between all the *p* 2Chr 23:16 5971
that they should be the LORD's *p* 2Chr 23:16 5971
Then all the *p* went to the house 2Chr 23:17 5971
nobles, and the governors of the *p* 2Chr 23:20 5971
all the *p* of the land, and brought 2Chr 23:20 5971
all the *p* of the land rejoiced 2Chr 23:21 5971
all the *p* rejoiced, and brought in 2Chr 24:10 5971
priest, which stood above the *p* 2Chr 24:20 5971
of the *p* from among the *p* 2Chr 24:23 5971
himself, and led forth his *p* 2Chr 25:11 5971
sought after the gods of the *p* 2Chr 25:15 5971
their own *p* out of thine hand 2Chr 25:15 5971
Then all the *p* of Judah took 2Chr 26:1 5971
house, judging the *p* of the land 2Chr 26:21 5971
And the *p* did yet corruptly 2Chr 27:2 5971
Hezekiah rejoiced, and all the *p* 2Chr 29:36 5971
that God had prepared the *p* 2Chr 29:36 5971
neither had the *p* gathered 2Chr 30:3 5971
assembled at Jerusalem much *p* to 2Chr 30:13 5971
For a multitude of the *p*, even 2Chr 30:18 5971
to Hezekiah, and healed the *p* 2Chr 30:20 5971
Levites arose and blessed the *p* 2Chr 30:27 5971
Moreover he commanded the *p* that 2Chr 31:4 5971
blessed the LORD, and his *p* Israel 2Chr 31:8 5971
Since the *p* began to bring the 2Chr 31:10
for the LORD hath blessed his *p* 2Chr 31:10 5971
was gathered much *p* together 2Chr 32:4 5971
he set captains of war over the *p* 2Chr 32:6 5971
the *p* rested themselves upon the 2Chr 32:8 5971
unto all the *p* of other lands 2Chr 32:13 5971
deliver his *p* out of mine hand 2Chr 32:14 5971
to deliver his *p* out of mine hand 2Chr 32:15 5971
their *p* out of mine hand, so 2Chr 32:17 5971
deliver his *p* out of mine hand 2Chr 32:17 5971
in the Jews' speech unto the *p* of 2Chr 32:18 5971
the gods of the *p* of the earth 2Chr 32:19 5971
spake to Manasseh, and to his *p* 2Chr 33:10 5971
Nevertheless the *p* did sacrifice 2Chr 33:17 5971
But the *p* of the land slew all 2Chr 33:25 5971
the *p* of the land made Josiah his 2Chr 33:25 5971
and the Levites, and all the *p* 2Chr 34:30 5971
LORD your God, and his *p* Israel, 2Chr 35:3 5971
fathers of your brethren the *p* 2Chr 35:5
And Josiah gave to the *p*, of the 2Chr 35:7
princes gave willingly unto the *p* 2Chr 35:8 5971
of the families of the *p*, to 2Chr 35:12
them speedily among all the *p* 2Chr 35:13
Then the *p* of the land took 2Chr 36:1 5971
chief of the priests, and the *p* 2Chr 36:14 5971
he had compassion on his *p* 2Chr 36:15 5971
of the LORD arose against his *p* 2Chr 36:16 5971
is there among you of all his *p* 2Chr 36:23 5971
is there among you of all his *p* Ezr 1:3 5971
of the men of the *p* of Israel Ezr 2:2 5971
and the Levites, and some of the *p* Ezr 2:70 5971
the *p* gathered themselves Ezr 3:1 5971
of the *p* of those countries Ezr 3:3 5971
all the *p* shouted with a great Ezr 3:11 5971
So that the *p* could not discern Ezr 3:13 5971
the noise of the weeping of the *p* Ezr 3:13 5971
for the *p* shouted with a loud Ezr 3:13 5971
Then the *p* of the land weakened Ezr 4:4 5971
the hands of the *p* of Judah Ezr 4:4 5971
carried the *p* away into Babylon Ezr 5:12 5972
there destroy all kings and *p* Ezr 6:12 5972
that all they of the *p* of Israel Ezr 7:13 5972
the freewill offering of the *p* Ezr 7:16 5972
which may judge all the *p* that Ezr 7:25 5972
and I viewed the *p*, and the priests Ezr 8:15 5971
and they furthered the *p*, and the Ezr 8:36 5971
The *p* of Israel, and the priests, Ezr 9:1 5971
from the *p* of the lands, doing Ezr 9:1 5971
with the *p* of those lands Ezr 9:2 5971
filthiness of the *p* of the lands Ezr 9:11 5971
with the *p* of these abominations Ezr 9:14 5971
for the *p* wept very sore Ezr 10:1 5971
wives of the *p* of the land Ezr 10:2 5971
all the *p* sat in the street of Ezr 10:9 5971
yourselves from the *p* of the land Ezr 10:11 5971
But the *p* are many, and it is a Ezr 10:13 5971
these are thy servants and thy *p* Neh 1:10 5971
for the *p* had a mind to work Neh 4:6 5971
I even set the *p* after their Neh 4:13 5971
rulers, and to the rest of the *p* Neh 4:14 5971
rulers, and to the rest of the *p* Neh 4:19 5971
the same time said I unto the *p* Neh 4:22 5971
And there was a great cry of the *p* Neh 5:1 5971
the *p* did according to this Neh 5:13 5971
me were chargeable unto the *p* Neh 5:15 5971
servants bare rule over the *p* Neh 5:15 5971
the bondage was heavy upon this *p* Neh 5:18 5971
all that I have done for this *p* Neh 5:19 5971
but the *p* were few therein, and Neh 7:4 5971
nobles, and the rulers, and the *p* Neh 7:5 5971
of the men of the *p* of Israel was Neh 7:7 5971
that which the rest of the *p* gave Neh 7:72 5971
and the singers, and some of the *p* Neh 7:73 5971
all the *p* gathered themselves Neh 8:1 5971
the ears of all the *p* were Neh 8:3 5971
the book in the sight of all *p* Neh 8:5 5971
(for he was above all the *p* Neh 8:5 5971
he opened it, all the *p* stood up Neh 8:5 5971
all the *p* answered, Amen, Amen, Neh 8:6 5971
caused the *p* to understand the Neh 8:7 5971
the *p* stood in their place Neh 8:7 5971
and the Levites that taught the *p* Neh 8:9 5971
said unto all the *p* Neh 8:9 5971
For all the *p* wept, when they Neh 8:9 5971
So the Levites stilled all the *p* Neh 8:11 5971
all the *p* went their way to eat, Neh 8:12 5971
chief of the fathers of all the *p* Neh 8:13 5971
So the *p* went forth, and brought Neh 8:16 5971
and on all the *p* of his land Neh 9:10 5971
the *p* of the land, that they Neh 9:24 5971
the hand of the *p* of the lands Neh 9:30 5971
on our fathers, and on all thy *p* Neh 9:32 5971
The chief of the *p* Neh 10:14 5971
And the rest of the *p*, the priests Neh 10:28 5971
p of the lands unto the law of Neh 10:28 5971
daughters unto the *p* of the land Neh 10:30 5971
if the *p* of the land bring ware Neh 10:31 5971
priests, the Levites, and the *p* Neh 10:34 5971
the rulers of the *p* dwelt at Neh 11:1 5971
the rest of the *p* also cast lots Neh 11:1 5971
the *p* blessed all the men, that Neh 11:2 5971
in all matters concerning the *p* Neh 11:24 5971
themselves, and purified the *p* Neh 12:30 5971
the half of the *p* upon the wall Neh 12:38 5971
of Moses in the audience of the *p* Neh 13:1 5971
to the language of each *p* Neh 13:24 5971
p that were present in Shushan Est 1:5 5971
the crown royal, to shew the *p* Est 1:11 5971
to all the *p* that are in all the Est 1:16 5971
to every *p* after their language, Est 1:22 5971
to the language of every *p* Est 1:22 5971
not shewed her *p* nor her kindred Est 2:10 5971
yet shewed her kindred nor her *p* Est 2:20 5971
had shewed him the *p* of Mordecai Est 3:6 5971
Ahasuerus, even the *p* of Mordecai Est 3:6 5971
is a certain *p* scattered abroad Est 3:8 5971
dispersed among the *p* in all the Est 3:8 5971
their laws are diverse from all *p* Est 3:8 5971
the *p* also, to do with them as it Est 3:11 5971
to the rulers of every *p* of every Est 3:12 5971
to every *p* after their language Est 3:12 5971
province was published unto all *p* Est 3:14 5971
make request before him for her *p* Est 4:8 5971
the *p* of the king's provinces, do Est 4:11 5971
petition, and my *p* at my request Est 7:3 5971
For we are sold, I and my *p* Est 7:4 5971
evil that shall come unto my *p* Est 8:6 5971
unto every *p* after their language Est 8:9 5971
to perish, all the power of the *p* Est 8:11 5971
province was published unto all *p* Est 8:13 5971
many of the *p* of the land became Est 8:17 5971
the fear of them fell upon all *p* Est 9:2 5971
seeking the wealth of his *p* Est 10:3 5971
No doubt but ye are the *p* Job 12:2 5971
the chief of the *p* of the earth Job 12:24 5971
made me also a byword of the *p* Job 17:6 5971
have son nor nephew among his *p* Job 18:19 5971
the *p* shall be troubled at Job 34:20 5971
reign not, lest the *p* be ensnared Job 34:30 5971
when *p* are cut off in their place Job 36:20 5971
For by them judgeth he the *p* Job 36:31 5971
the *p* imagine a vain thing Ps 2:1 3816
be afraid of ten thousands of *p* Ps 3:6 5971
thy blessing is upon thy *p* Ps 3:8 5971
of the *p* compass thee about Ps 7:7 3816
The LORD shall judge the *p* Ps 7:8 5971
judgment to the *p* in uprightness Ps 9:8 3816
declare among the *p* his doings Ps 9:11 5971
who eat up my *p* as they eat bread Ps 14:4 5971
back the captivity of his *p* Ps 14:7 5971
thou wilt save the afflicted *p* Ps 18:27 5971
me from the strivings of the *p* Ps 18:43 5971
a *p* whom I have not known shall Ps 18:43 5971
me, and subdueth the *p* under me Ps 18:47 5971
of men, and despised of the *p* Ps 22:6 5971
unto a *p* that shall be born Ps 22:31 5971
Save thy *p*, and bless thine Ps 28:9 5971
will give strength unto his *p* Ps 29:11 5971
LORD will bless his *p* with peace Ps 29:11 5971
devices of the *p* of none effect Ps 33:10 5971
the *p* whom he hath chosen for his Ps 33:12 5971
I will praise thee among much *p* Ps 35:18 5971
how thou didst afflict the *p* Ps 44:2 3816
Thou sellest thy *p* for nought Ps 44:12 5971
a shaking of the head among the *p* Ps 44:14 3816
whereby the *p* fall under thee Ps 45:5 5971
forget also thine own *p*, and thy Ps 45:10 5971
even the rich among the *p* shall Ps 45:12 5971
therefore shall the *p* praise thee Ps 45:17 5971
O clap your hands, all ye *p* Ps 47:1 5971
He shall subdue the *p* under us Ps 47:3 5971
The princes of the *p* are gathered Ps 47:9 5971
even the *p* of the God of Abraham Ps 47:9 5971
Hear this, all ye *p* Ps 49:1 5971
earth, that he may judge his *p* Ps 50:4 *2992*
Hear, O my *p*, and I will speak Ps 50:7 5971
who eat up my *p* as they eat bread Ps 53:4 5971
back the captivity of his *p* Ps 53:6 5971
in thine anger cast down the *p* Ps 56:7 5971
praise thee, O Lord, among the *p* Ps 57:9 5971
Slay them not, lest my *p* forget Ps 59:11 5971
hast shewed thy *p* hard things Ps 60:3 5971
ye *p*, pour out your heart before Ps 62:8 5971
waves, and the tumult of the *p* Ps 65:7 3816
O bless our God, ye *p*, and make Ps 66:8 5971
Let the *p* praise thee, O God Ps 67:3 5971
let all the *p* praise thee Ps 67:3 5971
shalt judge the *p* righteously Ps 67:4 5971
Let the *p* praise thee, O God Ps 67:5 5971
let all the *p* praise thee Ps 67:5 5971
thou wentest forth before thy *p* Ps 68:7 5971
I will bring my *p* again from the Ps 68:22
bulls, with the calves of the *p* Ps 68:30 5971
scatter thou the *p* that delight Ps 68:30 5971
strength and power unto his *p* Ps 68:35 5971
judge thy *p* with righteousness Ps 72:2 5971
shall bring peace to the *p* Ps 72:3 5971
He shall judge the poor of the *p* Ps 72:4 5971
Therefore his *p* return hither Ps 73:10 5971
the *p* inhabiting the wilderness Ps 74:14 5971
LORD, and that the foolish *p* have Ps 74:18 5971
declared thy strength among the *p* Ps 77:14 5971
with thine arm redeemed thy *p* Ps 77:15 5971
Thou leddest thy *p* like a flock Ps 77:20 5971
Give ear, O my *p*, to my law Ps 78:1 5971

can he provide flesh for his *p*	Ps 78:20	5971
But made his own *p* to go forth	Ps 78:52	5971
He gave his *p* over also unto the	Ps 78:62	5971
brought him to feed Jacob his *p*	Ps 78:71	5971
So we thy *p* and sheep of thy	Ps 79:13	5971
angry against the prayer of thy *p*	Ps 80:4	5971
Hear, O my *p*, and I will testify	Ps 81:8	5971
But my *p* would not hearken to my	Ps 81:11	5971
Oh that my *p* had hearkened unto	Ps 81:13	5971
crafty counsel against thy *p*	Ps 83:3	5971
forgiven the iniquity of thy *p*	Ps 85:2	5971
that thy *p* may rejoice in thee	Ps 85:6	5971
he will speak peace unto his *p*	Ps 85:8	5971
count, when he writeth up the *p*	Ps 87:6	5971
Blessed is the *p* that know the	Ps 89:15	5971
exalted one chosen out of the *p*	Ps 89:19	5971
the reproach of all the mighty *p*	Ps 89:50	5971
They break in pieces thy *p*	Ps 94:5	5971
ye brutish among the *p*	Ps 94:8	5971
the LORD will not cast off his *p*	Ps 94:14	5971
we are the *p* of his pasture, and	Ps 95:7	5971
It is a *p* that do err in their	Ps 95:10	5971
heathen, his wonders among all *p*	Ps 96:3	5971
the LORD, O ye kindreds of the *p*	Ps 96:7	5971
he shall judge the *p* righteously	Ps 96:10	5971
and the *p* with his truth	Ps 96:13	5971
and all the *p* see his glory	Ps 97:6	5971
the world, and the *p* with equity	Ps 98:9	5971
let the *p* tremble	Ps 99:1	5971
and he is high above all the *p*	Ps 99:2	5971
we are his *p*, and the sheep of his	Ps 100:3	5971
the *p* which shall be created	Ps 102:18	5971
When the *p* are gathered together,	Ps 102:22	5971
make known his deeds among the *p*	Ps 105:1	5971
from one kingdom to another *p*	Ps 105:13	5971
even the ruler of the *p*, and let	Ps 105:20	5971
And he increased his *p* greatly	Ps 105:24	5971
turned their heart to hate his *p*	Ps 105:25	5971
The *p* asked, and he brought quails	Ps 105:40	
he brought forth his *p* with joy	Ps 105:43	5971
inherited the labour of the *p*	Ps 105:44	3816
that thou bearest unto thy *p*	Ps 106:4	5971
of the LORD kindled against his *p*	Ps 106:40	5971
and let all the *p* say, Amen	Ps 106:48	5971
also in the congregation of the *p*	Ps 107:32	5971
praise thee, O LORD, among the *p*	Ps 108:3	5971
Thy *p* shall be willing in the day	Ps 110:3	5971
He hath shewed his *p* the power of	Ps 111:6	5971
He sent redemption unto his *p*	Ps 111:9	5971
even with the princes of his *p*	Ps 113:8	5971
from a *p* of strange language	Ps 114:1	5971
now in the presence of all his *p*	Ps 116:14	5971
now in the presence of all his *p*	Ps 116:18	5971
praise him, all ye *p*	Ps 117:1	528
p from henceforth even for ever	Ps 125:2	5971
an heritage unto Israel his *p*	Ps 135:12	5971
For the LORD will judge his *p*	Ps 135:14	5971
To him which led his *p* through	Ps 136:16	5971
who subdueth my *p* under me	Ps 144:2	5971
Happy is that *p*, that is in such	Ps 144:15	5971
yea, happy is that *p*, whose God	Ps 144:15	5971
Kings of the earth, and all *p*	Ps 148:11	3816
also exalteth the horn of his *p*	Ps 148:14	5971
of Israel, a *p* near unto him	Ps 148:14	5971
the LORD taketh pleasure in his *p*	Ps 149:4	5971
and punishments upon the *p*	Ps 149:7	3816
Where no counsel is, the *p* fall	Prov 11:14	5971
corn, the *p* shall curse him	Prov 11:26	3816
In the multitude of *p* is the	Prov 14:28	5971
but in the want of *p* is the	Prov 14:28	3816
but sin is a reproach to any *p*	Prov 14:34	3816
him shall the *p* curse, nations	Prov 24:24	5971
is a wicked ruler over the poor *p*	Prov 28:15	5971
are in authority, the *p* rejoice	Prov 29:2	5971
wicked beareth rule, the *p* mourn	Prov 29:2	5971
there is no vision, the *p* perish	Prov 29:18	5971
The ants are a *p* not strong	Prov 30:25	5971
There is no end of all the *p*	Eccl 4:16	5971
he still taught the *p* knowledge	Eccl 12:9	5971
not know, my *p* doth not consider	Is 1:3	5971
a *p* laden with iniquity, a seed	Is 1:4	5971
law of our God, ye *p* of Gomorrah	Is 1:10	5971
many *p* shall go and say, Come ye,	Is 2:3	5971
nations, and shall rebuke many *p*	Is 2:4	5971
forsaken thy *p* the house of Jacob	Is 2:6	5971
the *p* shall be oppressed, every	Is 3:5	5971
make me not a ruler of the *p*	Is 3:7	5971
As for my *p*, children are their	Is 3:12	5971
O my *p*, they which lead thee	Is 3:12	5971
plead, and standeth to judge the *p*	Is 3:13	5971
with the ancients of his *p*	Is 3:14	5971
ye that beat my *p* to pieces	Is 3:15	5971
Therefore my *p* are gone into	Is 5:13	5971
of the LORD kindled against his *p*	Is 5:25	5971
the midst of a *p* of unclean lips	Is 6:5	5971
And he said, Go, and tell this *p*	Is 6:9	5971
Make the heart of this *p* fat	Is 6:10	5971
was moved, and the heart of his *p*	Is 7:2	5971
be broken, that it be not a *p*	Is 7:8	5971
bring upon thee, and upon thy *p*	Is 7:17	5971
Forasmuch as this *p* refuseth the	Is 8:6	5971
Associate yourselves, O ye *p*	Is 8:9	5971
not walk in the way of this *p*	Is 8:11	5971
all them to whom this *p* shall say	Is 8:12	5971
should not a *p* seek unto their	Is 8:19	5971
The *p* that walked in darkness	Is 9:2	5971
all the *p* shall know, even	Is 9:9	5971
For the *p* turneth not unto him	Is 9:13	5971
of this *p* cause them to err	Is 9:16	5971
the *p* shall be as the fuel of the	Is 9:19	5971
the right from the poor of my *p*	Is 10:2	5971
against the *p* of my wrath will I	Is 10:6	5971
have removed the bounds of the *p*	Is 10:13	5971
as a nest the riches of the *p*	Is 10:14	5971
For though thy *p* Israel be as the	Is 10:22	5971
O my *p* that dwellest in Zion, be	Is 10:24	5971
stand for an ensign of the *p*	Is 11:10	5971
to recover the remnant of his *p*	Is 11:11	5971
highway for the remnant of his *p*	Is 11:16	5971
declare his doings among the *p*	Is 12:4	5971
mountains, like as of a great *p*	Is 13:4	5971
shall every man turn to his own *p*	Is 13:14	5971
the *p* shall take them, and bring	Is 14:2	5971
He who smote the *p* in wrath with	Is 14:6	5971
thy land, and slain thy *p*	Is 14:20	5971
the poor of his *p* shall trust in	Is 14:32	5971
Woe to the multitude of many *p*	Is 17:12	5971
to a *p* terrible from their	Is 18:2	5971
LORD of hosts of a *p* scattered	Is 18:7	5971
from a *p* terrible from their	Is 18:7	5971
saying, Blessed be Egypt my *p*	Is 19:25	5971
spoiling of the daughter of my *p*	Is 22:4	5971
this *p* was not, til the Assyrian	Is 23:13	5971
And it shall be, as with the *p*	Is 24:2	5971
the haughty *p* of the earth do	Is 24:4	5971
the midst of the land among the *p*	Is 24:13	5971
shall the strong *p* glorify thee	Is 25:3	5971
unto all *p* a feast of fat things	Is 25:6	5971
of the covering cast over all *p*	Is 25:7	5971
the rebuke of his *p* shall he take	Is 25:8	5971
ashamed for their envy at the *p*	Is 26:11	5971
Come, my *p*, enter thou into thy	Is 26:20	5971
for it is a *p* of no understanding	Is 27:11	5971
beauty, unto the residue of his *p*	Is 28:5	5971
tongue will he speak to this *p*	Is 28:11	5971
that rule this *p* which is in	Is 28:14	5971
Forasmuch as this *p* draw near me	Is 29:13	5971
do a marvellous work among this *p*	Is 29:14	5971
of a *p* that could not profit them	Is 30:5	5971
to a *p* that shall not profit them	Is 30:6	5971
That this is a rebellious *p*	Is 30:9	5971
For the *p* shall dwell in Zion at	Is 30:19	5971
bindeth up the breach of his *p*	Is 30:26	5971
be a bridle in the jaws of the *p*	Is 30:28	5971
Upon the land of my *p* shall come	Is 32:13	5971
my *p* shall dwell in a peaceable	Is 32:18	5971
noise of the tumult the *p* fled	Is 33:3	5971
the *p* shall be as the burnings of	Is 33:12	5971
Thou shalt not see a fierce *p*	Is 33:19	5971
a *p* of a deeper speech than thou	Is 33:19	5971
the *p* that dwell therein shall be	Is 33:24	5971
and hearken, ye *p*	Is 34:1	3816
upon the *p* of my curse, to	Is 34:5	5971
in the ears of the *p* that are on	Is 36:11	5971
Comfort ye, comfort ye my *p*	Is 40:1	5971
surely the *p* is grass	Is 40:7	5971
let the *p* renew their strength	Is 41:1	3816
giveth breath unto the *p* upon it	Is 42:5	5971
give thee for a covenant of the *p*	Is 42:6	5971
But this is a *p* robbed and spoiled	Is 42:22	5971
men for thee, and *p* for thy life	Is 43:4	3816
forth the blind *p* that have eyes	Is 43:8	5971
and let the *p* be assembled	Is 43:9	3816
the desert, to give drink to my *p*	Is 43:20	5971
This *p* have I formed for myself	Is 43:21	5971
since I appointed the ancient *p*	Is 44:7	5971
I was wroth with my *p*, I have	Is 47:6	5971
and hearken, ye *p*, from far	Is 49:1	3816
give thee for a covenant of the *p*	Is 49:8	5971
for the LORD hath comforted his *p*	Is 49:13	5971
and set up my standard to the *p*	Is 49:22	5971
Hearken unto me, my *p*	Is 51:4	5971
to rest for a light of the *p*	Is 51:4	5971
and mine arms shall judge the *p*	Is 51:5	5971
the *p* in whose heart is my law	Is 51:7	5971
and say unto Zion, Thou art my *p*	Is 51:16	5971
that pleadeth the cause of his *p*	Is 51:22	5971
My *p* went down aforetime into	Is 52:4	5971
that my *p* is taken away for	Is 52:5	5971
Therefore my *p* shall know my name	Is 52:6	5971
for the LORD hath comforted his *p*	Is 52:9	5971
of my *p* was he stricken	Is 53:8	5971
given him for a witness to the *p*	Is 55:4	3816
a leader and commander to the *p*	Is 55:4	3816
utterly separated me from his *p*	Is 56:3	5971
an house of prayer for all *p*	Is 56:7	5971
out of the way of my *p*	Is 57:14	5971
shew my *p* their transgression, and	Is 58:1	5971
earth, and gross darkness the *p*	Is 60:2	3816
Thy *p* also shall be all righteous	Is 60:21	5971
and their offspring among the *p*	Is 61:9	5971
prepare ye the way of the *p*	Is 62:10	5971
lift up a standard for the *p*	Is 62:10	5971
they shall call them, The holy *p*	Is 62:12	5971
of the *p* there was none with me	Is 63:3	5971
tread down the *p* in mine anger	Is 63:6	5971
For he said, Surely they are my *p*	Is 63:8	5971
the days of old, Moses, and his *p*	Is 63:11	5971
so didst thou lead thy *p*, to make	Is 63:14	5971
The *p* of thy holiness have	Is 63:18	5971
we beseech thee, we are all thy *p*	Is 64:9	5971
all the day unto a rebellious *p*	Is 65:2	5971
A *p* that provoketh me to anger	Is 65:3	5971
for my *p* that have sought me	Is 65:10	5971
a rejoicing, and her *p* a joy	Is 65:18	5971
in Jerusalem, and joy in my *p*	Is 65:19	5971
of a tree are the days of my *p*	Is 65:22	5971
and against the *p* of the land	Jer 1:18	5971
but my *p* have changed their glory	Jer 2:11	5971
For my *p* have committed two evils	Jer 2:13	5971
wherefore say my *p*, We are lords	Jer 2:31	5971
yet my *p* have forgotten me days	Jer 2:32	5971
thou hast greatly deceived this *p*	Jer 4:10	5971
time shall it be said to this *p*	Jer 4:11	5971
toward the daughter of my *p*	Jer 4:11	5971
For my *p* is foolish, they have	Jer 4:22	5971
in thy mouth fire, and this *p* wood	Jer 5:14	5971
Hear now this, O foolish *p*	Jer 5:21	5971
But this *p* hath a revolting and a	Jer 5:23	5971
For among my *p* are found wicked	Jer 5:26	5971
and my *p* love to have it so	Jer 5:31	5971
of the daughter of my *p* slightly	Jer 6:14	5971
I will bring evil upon this *p*	Jer 6:19	5971
lay stumblingblocks before this *p*	Jer 6:21	5971
a *p* cometh from the north country	Jer 6:22	5971
O daughter of my *p*, gird thee	Jer 6:26	5971
a tower and a fortress among my *p*	Jer 6:27	5971
for the wickedness of my *p* Israel	Jer 7:12	5971
pray not thou for this *p*, neither	Jer 7:16	5971
be your God, and ye shall be my *p*	Jer 7:23	5971
the carcases of this *p* shall be	Jer 7:33	5971
Why then is this *p* of Jerusalem	Jer 8:5	5971
but my *p* know not the judgment of	Jer 8:7	5971
of the daughter of my *p* slightly	Jer 8:11	5971
the cry of the daughter of my *p*	Jer 8:19	5971
of the daughter of my *p* am I hurt	Jer 8:21	5971
of the daughter of my *p* recovered	Jer 8:22	5971
the slain of the daughter of my *p*	Jer 9:1	5971
that I might leave my *p*, and go	Jer 9:2	5971
I do for the daughter of my *p*	Jer 9:7	5971
I will feed them, even this *p*	Jer 9:15	5971
For the customs of the *p* are vain	Jer 10:3	5971
so shall ye be my *p*, and I will be	Jer 11:4	5971
pray not thou for this *p*, neither	Jer 11:14	5971
caused my *p* Israel to inherit	Jer 12:14	5971
diligently learn the ways of my *p*	Jer 12:16	5971
they taught my *p* to swear by Baal	Jer 12:16	5971
be built in the midst of my *p*	Jer 12:16	5971
This evil *p*, which refuse to hear	Jer 13:10	5971
they might be unto me for a *p*	Jer 13:11	5971
Thus saith the LORD unto this *p*	Jer 14:10	5971
not for this *p* for their good	Jer 14:11	5971
the *p* to whom they prophesy shall	Jer 14:16	5971
p is broken with a great breach	Jer 14:17	5971
mind could not be toward this *p*	Jer 15:1	5971
of children, I will destroy my *p*	Jer 15:7	5971
unto this *p* a fenced brasen wall	Jer 15:20	5971
taken away my peace from this *p*	Jer 16:5	5971
shalt shew this *p* all these words	Jer 16:10	5971
the gate of the children of the *p*	Jer 17:19	5971
Because my *p* hath forgotten me,	Jer 18:15	5971
and take of the ancients of the *p*	Jer 19:1	5971
Even so will I break this *p*	Jer 19:11	5971
and said to all the *p*,	Jer 19:14	5971
Judah, and his servants, and the *p*	Jer 21:7	5971
unto this *p* thou shalt say, Thus	Jer 21:8	5971
thy *p* that enter in by these	Jer 22:2	5971
he, and his servants, and his *p*	Jer 22:4	5971
the pastors that feed my *p*	Jer 23:2	5971
caused my *p* Israel to err	Jer 23:13	5971
had caused my *p* to hear my words,	Jer 23:22	5971
Which think to cause my *p* to	Jer 23:27	5971
cause my *p* to err by their lies,	Jer 23:32	5971
shall not profit this *p* at all	Jer 23:32	5971
And when this *p*, or the prophet,	Jer 23:33	5971
prophet, and the priest, and the *p*	Jer 23:34	5971
and they shall be my *p*, and I will	Jer 24:7	5971
p of Judah in the fourth year of	Jer 25:1	5971
spake unto all the *p* of Judah	Jer 25:2	5971
and his princes, and all his *p*	Jer 25:19	5971
And all the mingled *p*, and all the	Jer 25:20	
p that dwell in the desert	Jer 25:24	
all the *p* heard Jeremiah speaking	Jer 26:7	5971
him to speak unto all the *p*	Jer 26:8	5971
all the *p* took him, saying, Thou	Jer 26:8	5971
all the *p* were gathered against	Jer 26:9	5971
unto the princes and to all the *p*	Jer 26:11	5971
all the princes and to all the *p*	Jer 26:12	5971
all the *p* unto the priests and to	Jer 26:16	5971
to all the assembly of the *p*	Jer 26:17	5971
and spake to all the *p* of Judah	Jer 26:18	5971
into the graves of the common *p*	Jer 26:23	5971
hand of the *p* to put him to death	Jer 26:24	5971
of Babylon, and serve him and his *p*	Jer 27:12	5971
Why will ye die, thou and thy *p*	Jer 27:13	5971
to the priests and to all this *p*	Jer 27:16	5971
of the priests and of all the *p*	Jer 28:1	5971
in the presence of all the *p* that	Jer 28:5	5971
ears, and in the ears of all the *p*	Jer 28:7	5971
in the presence of all the *p*	Jer 28:11	5971
makest this *p* to trust in a lie	Jer 28:15	5971
to all the *p* whom Nebuchadnezzar	Jer 29:1	5971
of all the *p* that dwelleth in	Jer 29:16	5971
all the *p* that are at Jerusalem	Jer 29:25	5971
have a man to dwell among this *p*	Jer 29:32	5971
the good that I will do for my *p*	Jer 29:32	5971
the captivity of my *p* Israel	Jer 30:3	5971
And ye shall be my *p*, and I will be	Jer 30:22	5971
of Israel, and they shall be my *p*	Jer 31:1	5971
The *p* which were left of the	Jer 31:2	5971
ye, and say, O LORD, save thy *p*	Jer 31:7	5971
my *p* shall be satisfied with my	Jer 31:14	5971
their God, and they shall be my *p*	Jer 31:33	5971
hast brought forth thy *p* Israel	Jer 32:21	5971
And they shall be my *p*, and I will	Jer 32:38	5971
all this great evil upon this *p*	Jer 32:42	5971
thou not what this *p* have spoken	Jer 33:24	5971
thus they have despised my *p*	Jer 33:24	5971
of his dominion, and all the *p*	Jer 34:1	5971
all the *p* which were at Jerusalem	Jer 34:8	5971
all the princes, and all the *p*	Jer 34:10	5971
all the *p* of the land, which	Jer 34:19	5971
but this *p* hath not hearkened	Jer 35:16	5971
p in the LORD's house upon the	Jer 36:6	5971
hath pronounced against this *p*	Jer 36:7	5971
LORD to all the *p* in Jerusalem	Jer 36:9	5971
to all the *p* that came from the	Jer 36:9	5971
house, in the ears of all the *p*	Jer 36:10	5971
the book in the ears of the *p*	Jer 36:13	5971
hast read in the ears of the *p*	Jer 36:14	5971
nor the *p* of the land, did	Jer 37:2	5971
came in and went out among the *p*	Jer 37:4	5971

thence in the midst of the *p*	Jer 37:12	5971
thy servants, or against this *p*	Jer 37:18	5971
had spoken unto all the *p*	Jer 38:1	5971
city, and the hands of all the *p*	Jer 38:4	5971
seeketh not the welfare of this *p*	Jer 38:4	5971
house, and the houses of the *p*	Jer 39:8	5971
the *p* that remained in the city	Jer 39:9	5971
the rest of the *p* that remained	Jer 39:9	5971
guard left of the poor of the *p*	Jer 39:10	5971
so he dwelt among the *p*	Jer 39:14	5971
and dwell with him among the *p*	Jer 40:5	5971
dwelt with him among the *p* that	Jer 40:6	5971
of the *p* that were in Mizpah	Jer 41:10	5971
all the *p* that remained in Mizpah	Jer 41:10	5971
that when all the *p* which were	Jer 41:13	5971
So all the *p* that Ishmael had	Jer 41:14	5971
all the remnant of the *p* whom he	Jer 41:16	5971
all the *p* from the least even	Jer 42:1	5971
all the *p* from the least even to	Jer 42:8	5971
p all the words of the LORD their	Jer 43:1	5971
of the forces, and all the *p*	Jer 43:4	5971
even all the *p* that dwelt in the	Jer 44:15	5971
Then Jeremiah said unto all the *p*	Jer 44:20	5971
to all the *p* which had given him	Jer 44:20	5971
the *p* of the land, did not the	Jer 44:21	5971
Jeremiah said unto all the *p*	Jer 44:24	5971
and let us go again to our own *p*	Jer 46:16	5971
the hand of the *p* of the north	Jer 46:24	5971
shall be destroyed from being a *p*	Jer 48:42	5971
the *p* of Chemosh perisheth	Jer 48:46	5971
his *p* dwell in his cities	Jer 49:1	5971
My *p* hath been lost sheep	Jer 50:6	5971
shall turn every one to his *p*	Jer 50:16	5971
upon all the mingled *p* that are	Jer 50:37	
a *p* shall come from the north, and	Jer 50:41	5971
My *p*, go ye out of the midst of	Jer 51:45	5971
the *p* shall labour in vain, and	Jer 51:58	5971
no bread for the *p* of the land	Jer 52:6	5971
certain of the poor of the *p*	Jer 52:15	5971
the residue of the *p* that	Jer 52:15	5971
who mustered the *p* of the land	Jer 52:25	5971
men of the *p* of the land, that	Jer 52:25	5971
This is the *p* whom Nebuchadrezzar	Jer 52:28	5971
sit solitary, that was full of *p*	Lam 1:1	5971
when her *p* fell into the hand of	Lam 1:7	5971
All her *p* sigh, they seek bread	Lam 1:11	5971
hear, I pray you, all *p*, and	Lam 1:18	5971
of the daughter of my *p*	Lam 2:11	5971
I was a derision to all my *p*	Lam 3:14	5971
and refuse in the midst of the *p*	Lam 3:45	5971
of the daughter of my *p*	Lam 3:48	5971
daughter of my *p* is become cruel	Lam 4:3	5971
p is greater than the punishment	Lam 4:6	5971
of the daughter of my *p*	Lam 4:10	5971
sent to a *p* of a strange speech	Eze 3:5	5971
Not to many *p* of a strange speech	Eze 3:6	5971
unto the children of thy *p*	Eze 3:11	5971
the hands of the *p* of the land	Eze 7:27	5971
son of Benaiah, princes of the *p*	Eze 11:1	5971
I will even gather you from the *p*	Eze 11:17	5971
and they shall be my *p*, and I will	Eze 11:20	5971
And say unto the *p* of the land	Eze 12:19	5971
not be in the assembly of my *p*	Eze 13:9	5971
because they have seduced my *p*	Eze 13:10	5971
against the daughters of thy *p*	Eze 13:17	5971
Will ye hunt the souls of my *p*	Eze 13:18	5971
among my *p* for handfuls of barley	Eze 13:19	5971
lying to my *p* that hear your lies	Eze 13:19	5971
deliver my *p* out of your hand, and	Eze 13:21	5971
deliver my *p* out of your hand	Eze 13:23	5971
him off from the midst of my *p*	Eze 14:8	5971
him from the midst of my *p* Israel	Eze 14:9	5971
but that they may be my *p*	Eze 14:11	5971
p to pluck it up by the roots	Eze 17:9	5971
might give him horses and much *p*	Eze 17:15	5971
which is not good among his *p*	Eze 18:18	5971
I will bring you out from the *p*	Eze 20:34	5971
you into the wilderness of the *p*	Eze 20:35	5971
when I bring you out from the *p*	Eze 20:41	5971
for it shall be upon my *p*	Eze 21:12	5971
of the sword shall be upon my *p*	Eze 21:12	5971
The *p* of the land have used	Eze 22:29	5971
wheels, and with an assembly of *p*	Eze 23:24	5971
I spake unto the *p* in the morning	Eze 24:18	5971
the *p* said unto me, Wilt thou not	Eze 24:19	5971
and I will cut thee off from the *p*	Eze 25:7	5971
Edom by the hand of my *p* Israel	Eze 25:14	5971
that was the gates of the *p*	Eze 26:2	5971
and companies, and much *p*	Eze 26:7	5971
he shall slay thy *p* by the sword	Eze 26:11	5971
with the *p* of old time, and shall	Eze 26:20	5971
merchant of the *p* for many isles	Eze 27:3	5971
of the seas, thou filledst many *p*	Eze 27:33	5971
among the *p* shall hiss at thee	Eze 27:36	5971
the *p* shall be astonished at thee	Eze 28:19	5971
the house of Israel from the *p*	Eze 28:25	5971
the *p* whither they were scattered	Eze 29:13	5971
and Lydia, and all the mingled *p*	Eze 30:5	
his *p* with him, the terrible of	Eze 30:11	5971
all the *p* of the earth are gone	Eze 31:12	5971
thee with a company of many *p*	Eze 32:3	5971
also vex the hearts of many *p*	Eze 32:9	5971
I will make many *p* amazed at thee	Eze 32:10	5971
speak to the children of thy *p*	Eze 33:2	5971
if the *p* of the land take a man	Eze 33:2	5971
blow the trumpet, and warn the *p*	Eze 33:3	5971
trumpet, and the *p* be not warned	Eze 33:6	5971
say unto the children of thy *p*	Eze 33:12	5971
Yet the children of thy *p* say	Eze 33:17	5971
the children of thy *p* still are	Eze 33:30	5971
come unto thee as the *p* cometh	Eze 33:31	5971
and they sit before thee as my *p*	Eze 33:31	5971
I will bring them out from the *p*	Eze 34:13	5971
the house of Israel, are my *p*	Eze 34:30	5971
and are an infamy of the *p*	Eze 36:3	5971
your fruit to my *p* of Israel	Eze 36:8	5971
walk upon you, even my *p* Israel	Eze 36:12	5971
the reproach of the *p* any more	Eze 36:15	5971
them, These are the *p* of the LORD	Eze 36:20	5971
and ye shall be my *p*, and I will be	Eze 36:28	5971
Behold, O my *p*, I will open your	Eze 37:12	5971
I have opened your graves, O my *p*	Eze 37:13	5971
of thy *p* shall speak unto thee	Eze 37:18	5971
so shall they be my *p*, and I will	Eze 37:23	5971
their God, and they shall be my *p*	Eze 37:27	5971
and many *p* with thee	Eze 38:6	5971
and is gathered out of many *p*	Eze 38:8	5971
thy bands, and many *p* with thee	Eze 38:9	5971
upon the *p* that are gathered out	Eze 38:12	5971
In that day when my *p* of Israel	Eze 38:14	5971
many *p* with thee, all of them	Eze 38:15	5971
come up against my *p* of Israel	Eze 38:16	5971
upon the many *p* that are with him	Eze 38:22	5971
bands, and the *p* that is with thee	Eze 39:4	5971
known in the midst of my *p* Israel	Eze 39:7	5971
all the *p* of the land shall bury	Eze 39:13	5971
brought them again from the *p*	Eze 39:27	5971
those things which are for the *p*	Eze 42:14	5971
and the sacrifice for the *p*	Eze 44:11	5971
into the utter court to the *p*	Eze 44:19	5971
the *p* with their garments	Eze 44:19	5971
they shall teach my *p* the	Eze 44:23	5971
shall no more oppress my *p*	Eze 45:8	5971
away your exactions from my *p*	Eze 45:9	5971
All the *p* of the land shall give	Eze 45:16	5971
for all the *p* of the land a	Eze 45:22	5971
Likewise the *p* of the land shall	Eze 46:3	5971
But when the *p* of the land shall	Eze 46:9	5971
that my *p* be not scattered every	Eze 46:18	5971
utter court, to sanctify the *p*	Eze 46:20	5971
shall boil the sacrifice of the *p*	Eze 46:24	5971
shall not be left to other *p*	Dan 2:44	5972
To you it is commanded, O *p*	Dan 3:4	5972
when all the *p* heard the sound of	Dan 3:7	5972
and all kinds of musick, all the *p*	Dan 3:7	5972
I make a decree, That every *p*	Dan 3:29	5972
the king, unto all *p*, nations, and	Dan 4:1	5972
majesty that he gave him, all *p*	Dan 5:19	5972
Then king Darius wrote unto all *p*	Dan 6:25	5972
glory, and a kingdom, that all *p*	Dan 7:14	5972
shall be given to the *p* of the	Dan 7:27	5972
destroy the mighty and the holy *p*	Dan 8:24	5971
and to all the *p* of the land	Dan 9:6	5971
that hast brought thy *p* forth out	Dan 9:15	5971
thy *p* are become a reproach to	Dan 9:16	5971
thy *p* are called by thy name	Dan 9:19	5971
my sin and the sin of my *p* Israel	Dan 9:20	5971
weeks are determined upon thy *p*	Dan 9:24	5971
the *p* of the prince that shall	Dan 9:26	5971
befall thy *p* in the latter days	Dan 10:14	5971
also the robbers of thy *p* shall	Dan 11:14	5971
withstand, neither his chosen *p*	Dan 11:15	5971
become strong with a small *p*	Dan 11:23	1471
but the *p* that do know their God	Dan 11:32	5971
among the *p* shall instruct many	Dan 11:33	5971
for the children of thy *p*	Dan 12:1	5971
at that time thy *p* shall be	Dan 12:1	5971
scatter the power of the holy *p*	Dan 12:7	5971
for ye are not my *p*, and I will	Hos 1:9	5971
said unto them, Ye are not my *p*	Hos 1:10	5971
were not my *p*, Thou art my *p*	Hos 2:23	5971
for thy *p* are as they that strive	Hos 4:4	5971
My *p* are destroyed for lack of	Hos 4:6	5971
They eat up the sin of my *p*	Hos 4:8	5971
And there shall be, like *p*	Hos 4:9	5971
My *p* ask counsel at their stocks	Hos 4:12	5971
therefore the *p* that doth not	Hos 4:14	5971
I returned the captivity of my *p*	Hos 6:11	5971
he hath mixed himself among the *p*	Hos 7:8	5971
O Israel, for joy, as other *p*	Hos 9:1	5971
for the *p* thereof shall mourn	Hos 10:5	5971
the *p* shall be gathered against	Hos 10:10	5971
shall a tumult arise among thy *p*	Hos 10:14	5971
my *p* are bent to backsliding from	Hos 11:7	5971
a great *p* and a strong	Joel 2:2	5971
as a strong *p* set in battle array	Joel 2:5	5971
face the *p* shall be much pained	Joel 2:6	5971
Gather the *p*, sanctify the	Joel 2:16	5971
and let them say, Spare thy *p*	Joel 2:17	5971
should they say among the *p*	Joel 2:17	5971
for his land, and pity his *p*	Joel 2:18	5971
will answer and say unto his *p*	Joel 2:19	5971
my *p* shall never be ashamed	Joel 2:26	5971
my *p* shall never be ashamed	Joel 2:27	5971
plead with them there for my *p*	Joel 3:2	5971
And they have cast lots for my *p*	Joel 3:3	5971
to the Sabeans, to a *p* far off	Joel 3:8	1471
LORD will be the hope of his *p*	Joel 3:16	5971
the *p* of Syria shall go into	Amos 1:5	5971
the city, and the *p* not be afraid	Amos 3:6	5971
in the midst of my *p* Israel	Amos 7:8	5971
me, Go, prophesy unto my *p* Israel	Amos 7:15	5971
end is come upon my *p* of Israel	Amos 8:2	5971
All the sinners of my *p* shall die	Amos 9:10	5971
the captivity of my *p* of Israel	Amos 9:14	5971
entered into the gate of my *p* in	Obad 13	5971
and of what *p* art thou	Jonah 1:8	5971
So the *p* of Nineveh believed God	Jonah 3:5	582
Hear, all ye *p*	Mic 1:2	5971
he is come unto the gate of my *p*	Mic 1:9	5971
hath changed the portion of my *p*	Mic 2:4	5971
Even of late my *p* is risen up as	Mic 2:8	5971
The women of my *p* have ye cast	Mic 2:9	5971
even be the prophet of this *p*	Mic 2:11	5971
Who also eat the flesh of my *p*	Mic 3:3	5971
the prophets that make my *p* err	Mic 3:5	5971
and *p* shall flow unto it	Mic 4:1	5971
And he shall judge among many *p*	Mic 4:3	5971
For all *p* will walk every one in	Mic 4:5	5971
thou shalt beat in pieces many *p*	Mic 4:13	5971
of many *p* as a dew from the LORD	Mic 5:7	5971
p as a lion among the beasts of	Mic 5:8	5971
hath a controversy with his *p*	Mic 6:2	5971
O my *p*, what have I done unto	Mic 6:3	5971
O my *p*, remember now what Balak	Mic 6:5	5971
shall bear the reproach of my *p*	Mic 6:16	5971
Feed thy *p* with thy rod, the	Mic 7:14	5971
thy *p* in the midst of thee are	Nah 3:13	5971
thy *p* is scattered upon the	Nah 3:18	5971
and heapeth unto him all *p*	Hab 2:5	5971
remnant of the *p* shall spoil thee	Hab 2:8	5971
thy house by cutting off many *p*	Hab 2:10	5971
p shall labour in the very fire	Hab 2:13	5971
the *p* shall weary themselves for	Hab 2:13	3816
forth for the salvation of thy *p*	Hab 3:13	5971
when he cometh up unto the *p*	Hab 3:16	5971
all the merchant *p* are cut down	Zeph 1:11	5971
whereby they have reproached my *p*	Zeph 2:8	5971
residue of my *p* shall spoil them	Zeph 2:9	5971
the remnant of my *p* shall possess	Zeph 2:9	1471
the *p* of the LORD of hosts	Zeph 2:10	5971
I turn to the *p* a pure language	Zeph 3:9	5971
of thee an afflicted and poor *p*	Zeph 3:12	5971
a praise among all *p* of the earth	Zeph 3:20	5971
LORD of hosts, saying, This *p* say	Hag 1:2	5971
with all the remnant of the *p*	Hag 1:12	5971
the *p* did fear before the LORD	Hag 1:12	5971
in the LORD'S message unto the *p*	Hag 1:13	5971
of all the remnant of the *p*	Hag 1:14	5971
and to the residue of the *p*	Hag 2:2	5971
all ye *p* of the land, saith the	Hag 2:4	5971
Haggai, and said, So is this *p*	Hag 2:14	5971
in that day, and shall be my *p*	Zec 2:11	5971
Speak unto all the *p* of the land	Zec 7:5	5971
remnant of this *p* in these days	Zec 8:6	5971
I will save my *p* from the east	Zec 8:7	5971
and they shall be my *p*, and I will	Zec 8:8	5971
of this *p* as in the former days	Zec 8:11	5971
p to possess all these things	Zec 8:12	5971
to pass, that there shall come *p*	Zec 8:20	5971
Yea, many *p* and strong nations	Zec 8:22	5971
in that day as the flock of his *p*	Zec 9:16	5971
And I will sow them among the *p*	Zec 10:9	5971
which I had made with all the *p*	Zec 11:10	5971
unto all the *p* round about	Zec 12:2	5971
a burdensome stone for all *p*	Zec 12:3	5971
though all the *p* of the earth be	Zec 12:3	1471
horse of the *p* with blindness	Zec 12:4	5971
devour all the *p* round about	Zec 12:6	5971
I will say, It is my *p*	Zec 13:9	5971
the residue of the *p* shall not be	Zec 14:2	5971
the *p* that have fought against	Zec 14:12	5971
The *p* against whom the LORD hath	Mal 1:4	5971
and base before all the *p*	Mal 2:9	5971
shall save his *p* from their sins	Mt 1:21	*2992*
and scribes of the *p* together	Mt 2:4	*2992*
that shall rule my *p* Israel	Mt 2:6	*2992*
The *p* which sat in darkness saw	Mt 4:16	*2992*
all manner of disease among the *p*	Mt 4:23	*2992*
p that were taken with divers	Mt 4:24	
multitudes of *p* from Galilee	Mt 4:25	
the *p* were astonished at his	Mt 7:28	*3793*
and the *p* making a noise	Mt 9:23	*3793*
But when the *p* were put forth, he	Mt 9:25	*3793*
and every disease among the *p*	Mt 9:35	*2992*
all the *p* were amazed, and said	Mt 12:23	*3793*
While he yet talked to the *p*	Mt 12:46	*3793*
when the *p* had heard thereof	Mt 14:13	*3793*
This *p* draweth nigh unto me with	Mt 15:8	*2992*
the elders of the *p* came unto him	Mt 21:23	*2992*
we fear the *p*	Mt 21:26	*3793*
scribes, and the elders of the *p*	Mt 26:3	*2992*
there be an uproar among the *p*	Mt 26:5	*2992*
chief priests and elders of the *p*	Mt 26:47	*2992*
elders of the *p* took counsel	Mt 27:1	*2992*
to release unto the *p* a prisoner	Mt 27:15	*3793*
Then answered all the *p*, and said	Mt 27:25	*2992*
steal him away, and say unto the *p*	Mt 27:64	*2992*
side, much *p* gathered unto him	Mk 5:21	*3793*
much *p* followed him, and thronged	Mk 5:24	*3793*
the *p* saw them departing, and many	Mk 6:33	*3793*
when he came out, saw much *p*	Mk 6:34	*3793*
while he sent away the *p*	Mk 6:45	*3793*
This *p* honoureth me with their	Mk 7:6	*2992*
he had called all the *p* unto him	Mk 7:14	*3793*
entered into the house from the *p*	Mk 7:17	*3793*
he commanded the *p* to sit down on	Mk 8:6	*3793*
and they did set them before the *p*	Mk 8:6	*3793*
when he had called the *p* unto him	Mk 8:34	*3793*
And straightway all the *p*, when	Mk 9:15	*3793*
that the *p* came running together	Mk 9:25	*3793*
the *p* resort unto him again	Mk 10:1	*3793*
disciples and a great number of *p*	Mk 10:46	*3793*
because all the *p* was astonished	Mk 11:18	*3793*
they feared the *p*	Mk 11:32	*2992*
lay hold on him, but feared the *p*	Mk 12:12	*3793*
the common *p* heard him gladly	Mk 12:37	*3793*
beheld how the *p* cast money into	Mk 12:41	*3793*
lest there be an uproar of the *p*	Mk 14:2	*2992*
But the chief priests moved the *p*	Mk 15:11	*3793*
Pilate, willing to content the *p*	Mk 15:15	*3793*
the whole multitude of the *p* were	Lk 1:10	*2992*
to make ready a *p* prepared for	Lk 1:17	*2992*
the *p* waited for Zacharias, and	Lk 1:21	*2992*
he hath visited and redeemed his *p*	Lk 1:68	*2992*
p by the remission of their sins	Lk 1:77	*2992*
joy, which shall be to all *p*	Lk 2:10	*2992*
prepared before the face of all *p*	Lk 2:31	*2992*
and the glory of thy *p* Israel	Lk 2:32	*2992*
the *p* asked him, saying, What	Lk 3:10	*3793*
as the *p* were in expectation, and	Lk 3:15	*2992*
preached he unto the *p*	Lk 3:18	*2992*

Now when all the p were baptized... Lk 3:21 2992
the p sought him, and came unto... Lk 4:42 3793
as the p pressed upon him to hear... Lk 5:1 3793
taught the p out of the ship... Lk 5:3 3793
multitude of p out of all Judaea... Lk 6:17 2992
sayings in the audience of the p... Lk 7:1 2992
said unto the p that followed him... Lk 7:9 3793
went with him, and much p... Lk 7:11 3793
much p of the city was with her... Lk 7:12 3793
and, That God hath visited his p... Lk 7:16 2992
speak unto the p concerning John... Lk 7:24 3793
all the p that heard him, and the... Lk 7:29 2992
when much p were gathered... Lk 8:4 3793
the p gladly received him... Lk 8:40 3793
But as he went the p thronged him... Lk 8:42 3793
unto him before all the p for... Lk 8:47 2992
And the p, when they knew it,... Lk 9:11 3793
go and buy meat for all this p... Lk 9:13 2992
saying, Whom say the p that I am... Lk 9:18 3793
from the hill, much p met him... Lk 9:37 3793
and the p wondered... Lk 11:14 3793
when the p were gathered thick... Lk 11:29 3793
an innumerable multitude of p... Lk 12:1 3793
And he said also to the p, When ye... Lk 12:54 3793
sabbath day, and said unto the p... Lk 13:14 3793
all the p rejoiced for all the... Lk 13:17 3793
and all the p, when they saw it,... Lk 18:43 2992
the chief of the p sought to... Lk 19:47 2992
for all the p were very attentive... Lk 19:48 2992
as he taught the p in the temple... Lk 20:1 2992
all the p will stone us... Lk 20:6 2992
he to speak to the p this parable... Lk 20:9 2992
and they feared the p... Lk 20:19 2992
hold of his words before the p... Lk 20:26 2992
the p he said unto his disciples... Lk 20:45 2992
in the land, and wrath upon this p... Lk 21:23 2992
all the p came early in the... Lk 21:38 2992
for they feared the p... Lk 22:2 2992
it was day, the elders of the p... Lk 22:66 2992
to the chief priests and to the p... Lk 23:4 3793
saying, He stirreth up the p... Lk 23:5 2992
priests and the rulers and the p... Lk 23:13 2992
me, as one that perverteth the p... Lk 23:14 2992
followed him a great company of p... Lk 23:27 2992
And the p stood beholding... Lk 23:35 2992
all the p that came together to... Lk 23:48 3793
and word before God and all the p... Lk 24:19 2992
when the p which stood on the... Jn 6:22 3793
When the p therefore saw that... Jn 6:24 3793
among the p concerning him... Jn 7:12 3793
but he deceiveth the p... Jn 7:12 3793
The p answered and said, Thou hast... Jn 7:20 3793
many of the p believed on him, and... Jn 7:31 3793
The Pharisees heard that the p... Jn 7:32 3793
Many of the p therefore, when... Jn 7:40 3793
among the p because of him... Jn 7:43 3793
But this p who knoweth not the... Jn 7:49 3793
and all the p came unto him... Jn 8:2 2992
but because of the p which stand... Jn 11:42 3793
that one man should die for the p... Jn 11:50 2992
Much p of the Jews therefore knew... Jn 12:9 3793
On the next day much p that were... Jn 12:12 3793
The p therefore that was with him... Jn 12:17 3793
For this cause the p also met him... Jn 12:18 3793
The p therefore, that stood by,... Jn 12:29 3793
The p answered him, We have heard... Jn 12:34 3793
that one man should die for the p... Jn 18:14 2992
and having favour with all the p... Acts 2:47 2992
all the p saw him walking and... Acts 3:9 2992
all the p ran together unto them... Acts 3:11 2992
saw it, he answered unto the p... Acts 3:12 2992
be destroyed from among the p... Acts 3:23 2992
And as they spake unto the p... Acts 4:1 2992
grieved that they taught the p... Acts 4:2 2992
unto them, Ye rulers of the p... Acts 4:8 2992
all, and to all the p of Israel... Acts 4:10 2992
it spread no further among the p... Acts 4:17 2992
punish them, because of the p... Acts 4:21 2992
the p imagine vain things... Acts 4:25 2992
the p of Israel, were gathered... Acts 4:27 2992
and wonders wrought among the p... Acts 5:12 2992
but the p magnified them... Acts 5:13 2992
the p all the words of this life... Acts 5:20 2992
in the temple, and teaching the p... Acts 5:25 2992
for they feared the p, lest they... Acts 5:26 2992
had in reputation among all the p... Acts 5:34 2992
and drew away much p after him... Acts 5:37 2992
wonders and miracles among the p... Acts 6:8 2992
And they stirred up the p, and the... Acts 6:12 2992
the p grew and multiplied in Egypt... Acts 7:17 2992
of my p which is in Egypt... Acts 7:34 2992
the p with one accord gave heed... Acts 8:6 3793
and bewitched the p of Samaria... Acts 8:9 1484
which gave much alms to the p... Acts 10:2 2992
Not to all the p, but unto... Acts 10:41 2992
commanded us to preach unto the p... Acts 10:42 2992
much p was added unto the Lord... Acts 11:24 3793
with the church, and taught much p... Acts 11:26 3793
to bring him forth to the p... Acts 12:4 2992
expectation of the p of the Jews... Acts 12:11 2992
the p gave a shout, saying, It is... Acts 12:22 1218
any word of exhortation for the p... Acts 13:15 2992
The God of this p of Israel chose... Acts 13:17 2992
exalted the p when they dwelt as... Acts 13:17 2992
repentance to all the p of Israel... Acts 13:24 2992
who are his witnesses unto the p... Acts 13:31 2992
when the p saw what Paul had done... Acts 14:11 3793
have done sacrifice with the p... Acts 14:13 3793
clothes, and ran in among the p... Acts 14:14 3793
scarce restrained they the p... Acts 14:18 3793
and Iconium, who persuaded the p... Acts 14:19 3793
take out of them a p for his name... Acts 15:14 2992
sought to bring them out to the p... Acts 17:5 1218
And they troubled the p and the... Acts 17:8 3793
thither also, and stirred up the p... Acts 17:13 3793
for I have much p in this city... Acts 18:10 2992
of repentance, saying unto the p... Acts 19:4 2992
persuaded and turned away much p... Acts 19:26 3793
would have entered in unto the p... Acts 19:30 1218
have made his defence unto the p... Acts 19:33 1218
the townclerk had appeased the p... Acts 19:35 3793
the temple, stirred up all the p... Acts 21:27 3793
all men every where against the p... Acts 21:28 2992
was moved, and the p ran together... Acts 21:30 2992
for the violence of the p... Acts 21:35 3793
multitude of the p followed after... Acts 21:36 2992
suffer me to speak unto the p... Acts 21:39 2992
beckoned with the hand unto the p... Acts 21:40 2992
speak evil of the ruler of thy p... Acts 23:5 2992
any man, neither raising up the p... Acts 24:12 3793
Delivering thee from the p... Acts 26:17 2992
and should shew light unto the p... Acts 26:23 2992
the barbarous p shewed us no... Acts 28:2
committed nothing against the p... Acts 28:17 2992
Saying, Go unto this p, and say,... Acts 28:26 2992
heart of this p is waxed gross... Acts 28:27 2992
my p, which were not my p... Rom 9:25 2992
said unto them, Ye are not my p... Rom 9:26 2992
to jealousy by them that are no p... Rom 10:19 1484
a disobedient and gainsaying p... Rom 10:21 2992
then, Hath God cast away his p... Rom 11:1 2992
cast away his p which he foreknew... Rom 11:2 2992
Rejoice, ye Gentiles, with his p... Rom 15:10 2992
and laud him, all ye p... Rom 15:11 2992
The p sat down to eat and drink,... 1Cor 10:7 2992
lips will I speak unto this p... 1Cor 14:21 2992
their God, and they shall be my p... 2Cor 6:16 2992
purify unto himself a peculiar p... Titus 2:14 2992
for the sins of the p... Heb 2:17 2992
therefore a rest to the p of God... Heb 4:9 2992
hereof he ought, as for the p... Heb 5:3 2992
of the p according to the law... Heb 7:5 2992
under it the p received the law... Heb 7:11 2992
a God, and they shall be to me a p... Heb 8:10 2992
and for the errors of the p... Heb 9:7 2992
to all the p according to the law... Heb 9:19 2992
both the book, and all the p... Heb 9:19 2992
again, The Lord shall judge his p... Heb 10:30 2992
affliction with the p of God... Heb 11:25 2992
sanctify the p with his own blood... Heb 13:12 2992
an holy nation, a peculiar p... 1Pet 2:9 2992
Which in time past were not a p... 1Pet 2:10 2992
but are now the p of God... 1Pet 2:10 2992
false prophets also among the p... 2Pet 2:1 2992
having saved the p out of the... Jude 5 2992
of every kindred, and tongue, and p... Rev 5:9 2992
of all nations, and kindreds, and p... Rev 7:9 2992
And they of the p and kindreds and... Rev 11:9 2992
and kindred, and tongue, and p... Rev 14:6 2992
saying, Come out of her, my p... Rev 18:4 2992
a great voice of much p in heaven... Rev 19:1 3793
with them, and they shall be his p... Rev 21:3 2992

PEOPLE'S

And he brought the p offering... Lev 9:15 5971
the p inheritance by oppression... Eze 46:18 5971
For this p heart is waxed gross,... Mt 13:15 2992
his own sins, and then for the p... Heb 7:27 2992

PEOPLES

must prophesy again before many p... Rev 10:11 2992
where the whore sitteth, are p... Rev 17:15 2992

PEOR (*pe'-or*) See BAAL-PEOR, BETH-PEOR, PEOR'S.

1. A Moabite god.

beguiled you in the matter of P... Num 25:18 6465
the LORD in the matter of P... Num 31:16 6465
iniquity of P too little for us... Josh 22:17 6465

2. A mountain.

brought Balaam unto the top of P... Num 23:28 6465

PEOR'S

the day of the plague for P sake... Num 25:18 6465

PERADVENTURE

P there be fifty righteous within... Gen 18:24 194
P there shall lack five of the... Gen 18:28 194
P there shall be forty found... Gen 18:29 194
P there shall thirty be found... Gen 18:30 194
P there shall be twenty found... Gen 18:31 194
P ten shall be found there... Gen 18:32 194
P the woman will not be willing... Gen 24:5 194
P the woman will not follow me... Gen 24:39 194
My father p will feel me, and I... Gen 27:12 194
P thou wouldest take by force thy... Gen 31:31 6435
p he will accept of me... Gen 32:20 194
Lest p he die also, as his... Gen 38:11
Lest p mischief befall him... Gen 42:4
p it was an oversight... Gen 43:12 194
lest p I see the evil that shall... Gen 44:34
they said, Joseph will p hate us... Gen 50:15 3863
Lest p the people repent when... Ex 13:17
p I shall make an atonement for... Ex 32:30 194
p I shall prevail, that we may... Num 22:6 194
p I shall be able to overcome... Num 22:11 194
p the LORD will come to meet me... Num 23:3 194
p it will please God that thou... Num 23:27 194
the Hivites, P ye dwell among us... Josh 9:7 194
p he will lighten his hand from... 1Sa 6:5 194
p he can shew us our way that we... 1Sa 9:6 194
p we may find grass to save the... 1Kin 18:5 194
or p he sleepeth, and must be... 1Kin 18:27 194
p he will save thy life... 1Kin 20:31 194
lest p the Spirit of the LORD... 2Kin 2:16
P he will be enticed, and we shall... Jer 20:10 194
yet p for a good man some would... Rom 5:7 5029
if God p will give them... 2Ti 2:25 3379

PERAZIM (*per'-a-zim*) *Where David defeated the Philistines.*

LORD shall rise up as in mount P... Is 28:21

PERCEIVE

hath not given you an heart to p... Deut 29:4 3045
This day we p that the LORD is... Josh 22:31 3045
that ye may p and see that your... 1Sa 12:17 3045
for this day I p, that if Absalom... 2Sa 19:6 3045
I p that this is an holy man of... 2Kin 4:9 3045
passeth on also, but I p him not... Job 9:11 995
and backward, but I cannot p him... Job 23:8 3045
to p the words of understanding... Prov 1:2
Wherefore I p that there is... Eccl 3:22 7200
and see ye indeed, but p not... Is 6:9 3045
a deeper speech than thou canst p... Is 33:19 8085
ye shall see, and shall not p... Mt 13:14 1492
seeing they may see, and not p... Mk 4:12 1492
Do ye not p, that whatsoever... Mk 7:18 3539
p ye not yet, neither understand... Mk 8:17 3539
for I p that virtue is gone out... Lk 8:46 1097
I p that thou art a prophet... Jn 4:19 2334
P ye how ye prevail nothing... Jn 12:19 2334
For I p that thou art in the gall... Acts 8:23 3708
Of a truth I p that God is no... Acts 10:34 2638
I p that in all things ye are too... Acts 17:22 2334
I p that this voyage will be with... Acts 27:10 2334
and seeing ye shall see, and not p... Acts 28:26 1492
for I p that the same epistle... 2Cor 7:8 991
Hereby p we the love of God,... 1Jn 3:16 1097

PERCEIVED

he p not when she lay down, nor... Gen 19:33 3045
he p not when she lay down, nor... Gen 19:35 3045
when Gideon p that he was an... Judg 6:22 7200
Eli p that the LORD had called... 1Sa 3:8 995
Saul p that it was Samuel, and he... 1Sa 28:14 3045
David p that the LORD had... 2Sa 5:12 3045
David p that the child was dead... 2Sa 12:19 995
p that the king's heart was... 2Sa 14:1 3045
p that it was not the king of... 1Kin 22:33 7200
David p that the LORD had... 1Chr 14:2 3045
p that it was not the king of... 2Chr 18:32 7200
I p that God had not sent him... Neh 6:12 5234
for they p that this work was... Neh 6:16 3045
I p that the portions of the... Neh 13:10 3045
When Mordecai p all that was done... Est 4:1 3045
Hast thou p the breadth of the... Job 38:18 995
I p that this also is vexation of... Eccl 1:17 3045
I myself p also that one event... Eccl 2:14 3045
nor p by the ear, neither hath... Is 64:4 238
counsel of the LORD, and hath p... Jer 23:18 7200
for the matter was not p... Jer 38:27 8085
Which when Jesus p, he said unto... Mt 16:8 1097
they p that he spake of them... Mt 21:45 1097
But Jesus p their wickedness, and... Mt 22:18 1097
immediately when Jesus p in his... Mk 2:8 1921
they p that he had seen a vision... Lk 1:22 1921
But when Jesus p their thoughts... Lk 5:22 1921
hid from them, that they p it not... Lk 9:45 143
for they p that he had spoken... Lk 20:19 1097
But he p their craftiness, and... Lk 20:23 2657
therefore p that they would come... Jn 6:15 1097
p that they were unlearned and... Acts 4:13 2638
But when Paul p that the one part... Acts 23:6 1097
Whom I p to be accused of... Acts 23:29 2147
p the grace that was given unto... Gal 2:9 1097

PERCEIVEST

when thou p not in him the lips... Prov 14:7 3045
but p not the beam that is in... Lk 6:41 2657

PERCEIVETH

low, but he p it not of them... Job 14:21 995
once, yea twice, yet man p it not... Job 33:14 7789
She p that her merchandise is... Prov 31:18 2938

PERCEIVING

p that he had answered them well,... Mk 12:28 1492
p the thought of their heart,... Lk 9:47 1492
p that he had faith to be healed,... Acts 14:9 1492

PERDITION

of them is lost, but the son of p... Jn 17:12 684
is to them an evident token of p... Phil 1:28 684
of sin be revealed, the son of p... 2Th 2:3 684
drown men in destruction and p... 1Ti 6:9 684
not of them who draw back unto p... Heb 10:39 684
of judgment and p of ungodly men... 2Pet 3:7 684
the bottomless pit, and go into p... Rev 17:8 684
is of the seven, and goeth into p... Rev 17:11 684

PERES (*pe'-res*) *Portion of "the handwriting on the wall."*

P; Thy kingdom is... Dan 5:28 6537

PERESH (*pe'-resh*) *A son of Machir.*

a son, and she called his name P... 1Chr 7:16 6570

PEREZ (*pe'-rez*) See PEREZ-UZZAH, PHARES.

1. An ancestor of Jashobeam.

Of the children of P was the... 1Chr 27:3 6557

2. A son of Judah; same as Pharez.

Mahalaleel, of the children of P... Neh 11:4 6557
All the sons of P that dwelt at... Neh 11:6 6557

PEREZITES See PHARZITES.

PEREZ-UZZA (*pe'-rez-uz'-zah*) See PEREZ-UZZAH. *Where Uzza died.*

place is called P to this day... 1Chr 13:11 6560

PEREZ-UZZAH (*pe''-rez-uz'-zah*) See PEREZ-UZZA. *Same as Perez-uzza.*

name of the place P to this day... 2Sa 6:8 6560

PERFECT

p in his generations, and Noah... Gen 6:9 8549
walk before me, and be thou p... Gen 17:1 8549
it shall be p to be accepted... Lev 22:21 8549

Thou shalt be *p* with the LORD thy Deut 18:13 8549
a *p* and just weight, a *p* Deut 25:15 8003
He is the Rock, his work is *p* Deut 32:4 8549
LORD God of Israel, Give a *p* lot 1Sa 14:41 8549
As for God, his way is *p* 2Sa 22:31 8549
and he maketh my way *p* 2Sa 22:33 8549
be *p* with the LORD our God 1Kin 8:61 8003
his heart was not *p* with the LORD 1Kin 11:4 8003
his heart was not *p* with the LORD 1Kin 15:3 8003
was *p* with the LORD all his days 1Kin 15:14 8003
thee in truth and with a *p* heart 2Kin 20:3 8003
came with a *p* heart to Hebron, to 1Chr 12:38 8003
and serve him with a *p* heart 1Chr 28:9 8003
because with *p* heart they offered 1Chr 29:9 8003
unto Solomon my son a *p* heart 1Chr 29:19 8003
made he of gold, and that *p* gold 2Chr 4:21 4357
heart of Asa was *p* all his days 2Chr 15:17 8003
them whose heart is *p* toward him 2Chr 16:9 8003
faithfully, and with a *p* heart 2Chr 19:9 8003
the LORD, but not with a *p* heart 2Chr 25:2 8003
p peace, and at such a time Ezr 7:12 1585
and that man was *p* and upright, and Job 1:1 8535
none like him in the earth, a *p* Job 1:8 8535
none like him in the earth, a *p* Job 2:3 8535
God will not cast away a *p* man Job 8:20 8535
if I say, I am *p*, it shall also Job 9:20 8535
Though I were *p*, yet would I not Job 9:21 8535
I said it, He destroyeth the *p* Job 9:22 8535
him, that thou makest thy ways *p* Job 22:3 8552
he that is *p* in knowledge is with Job 36:4 8549
of him which is *p* in knowledge Job 37:16 8549
As for God, his way is *p* Ps 18:30 8549
with strength, and maketh my way *p* Ps 18:32 8549
The law of the LORD is *p*, Ps 19:7 8549
Mark the *p* man, and behold the Ps 37:37 8535
they may shoot in secret at the *p* Ps 64:4 8535
behave myself wisely in a *p* way Ps 101:2 8549
within my house with a *p* heart Ps 101:2 8537
he that walketh in a *p* way Ps 101:6 8549
The LORD will *p* that which Ps 138:8 1584
I hate them with *p* hatred Ps 139:22 8503
land, and the *p* shall remain in it Prov 2:21 8549
more and more unto the *p* day Prov 4:18 3559
of the *p* shall direct his way Prov 11:5 8549
the harvest, when the bud is *p* Is 18:5 8552
Thou wilt keep him in *p* peace Is 26:3
thee in truth and with a *p* heart Is 38:3 8003
who is blind as he that is *p* Is 42:19 7999
for it was *p* through my Eze 16:14 3632
thou hast said, I am of *p* beauty Eze 27:3 3632
they have made thy beauty *p* Eze 27:11 3634
full of wisdom, and *p* in beauty Eze 28:12 3632
Thou wast *p* in thy ways from the Eze 28:15 8549
Be ye therefore *p*, even as your Mt 5:48 5046
Father which is in heaven is *p* Mt 5:48 5046
said unto him, If thou wilt be *p* Mt 19:21 5046
having had *p* understanding of all Lk 1:3 199
but every one that is *p* shall be Lk 6:40 2675
that they may be made *p* in one Jn 17:23 5048
p soundness in the presence of Acts 3:16 3647
taught according to the *p* manner Acts 22:3 195
having more *p* knowledge of that Acts 24:22 197
is that good, and acceptable, and *p* Rom 12:2 5046
wisdom among them that are *p* 1Cor 2:6 5046
But when that which is *p* is come 1Cor 13:10 5046
my strength is made *p* in weakness 2Cor 12:9 5048
Be *p*, be of good comfort, be of 2Cor 13:11 2675
are ye now made *p* by the flesh Gal 3:3 2005
of the Son of God, unto a *p* man Eph 4:13 5046
attained, either were already *p* Phil 3:12 5048
Let us therefore, as many as be *p* Phil 3:15 5046
every man *p* in Christ Jesus Col 1:28 5046
in prayers, that ye may stand *p* Col 4:12 5046
might *p* that which is lacking in 1Th 3:10 2675
That the man of God may be *p* 2Ti 3:17 739
salvation *p* through sufferings Heb 2:10 5048
And being made *p*, he became the Heb 5:9 5048
For the law made nothing *p* Heb 7:19 5048
make him that did the service *p* Heb 9:9 5048
more *p* tabernacle, not made with Heb 9:11 5046
make the comers thereunto *p* Heb 10:1 5048
without us should not be made *p* Heb 11:40 5048
to the spirits of just men made *p* Heb 12:23 5048
Make you *p* in every good work to Heb 13:21 2675
But let patience have her *p* work Jas 1:4 5046
that ye may be *p* Jas 1:4 5046
every *p* gift is from above, and Jas 1:17 5046
looketh into the *p* law of liberty Jas 1:25 5046
and by works was faith made *p* Jas 2:22 5048
not in word, the same is a *p* man Jas 3:2 5046
have suffered a while, make you *p* 1Pet 5:10 2675
Herein is our love made *p* 1Jn 4:17 5048
but *p* love casteth out fear 1Jn 4:18 5046
feareth is not made *p* in love 1Jn 4:18 5048
not found thy works *p* before God Rev 3:2 4137

PERFECTED
So the house of the LORD was *p* 2Chr 8:16 8003
and the work was *p* by them 2Chr 24:13
thy builders have *p* thy beauty Eze 27:4 3634
and sucklings thou hast *p* praise Mt 21:16 2675
and the third day I shall be *p* Lk 13:32 5048
he hath *p* for ever them that are Heb 10:14 5048
him verily is the love of God *p* 1Jn 2:5 5048
in us, and his love is *p* in us 1Jn 4:12 5048

PERFECTING
p holiness in the fear of God 2Cor 7:1 2005
For the *p* of the saints, for the Eph 4:12 2677

PERFECTION
thou find out the Almighty unto *p* Job 11:7 8503
the *p* thereof upon the earth Job 15:29 4512
darkness, and searcheth out all *p* Job 28:3 8503
the *p* of beauty, God hath shined Ps 50:2 4359
I have seen an end of all *p* Ps 119:96 8502
their *p* for the multitude of thy Is 47:9 8537
that men call The *p* of beauty Lam 2:15 3632
this life, and bring no fruit to *p* Lk 8:14 5052
and this also we wish, even your *p* 2Cor 13:9 2676
of Christ, let us go on unto *p* Heb 6:1 5051
If therefore *p* were by the Heb 7:11 5050

PERFECTLY
days ye shall consider it *p* Jer 23:20 998
many as touched were made *p* whole Mt 14:36 1295
unto him the way of God more *p* Acts 18:26 197
something more *p* concerning him Acts 23:15 197
enquire somewhat of him more *p* Acts 23:20 197
but that ye be *p* joined together 1Cor 1:10 2675
For yourselves know *p* that the 1Th 5:2 199

PERFECTNESS
charity, which is the bond of *p* Col 3:14 5047

PERFORM
I will *p* the oath which I sware Gen 26:3 6965
not able to *p* it thyself alone Ex 18:18 6213
that enter in to *p* the service Num 4:23 6633
which he commanded you to *p* Deut 4:13 6213
that he may *p* the word which the Deut 9:5 6965
of thy lips thou shalt keep and *p* Deut 23:23 6213
p the duty of an husband's Deut 25:5
he will not *p* the duty of my Deut 25:7
that if he will *p* unto thee the Ruth 3:13
In that day I will *p* against Eli 1Sa 3:12 6965
p the request of his handmaid 2Sa 14:15 6213
then will I *p* my word with thee, 1Kin 6:12 6965
LORD, that he might *p* his saying 1Kin 12:15 6965
to *p* the words of this covenant 2Kin 23:3 6965
that he might *p* the words of the 2Kin 23:24 6965
that the LORD might *p* his word 2Chr 10:15 6965
to *p* the words of the covenant 2Chr 34:31 6213
to *p* my request, let the king and Est 5:8 6213
hands cannot *p* their enterprise Job 5:12
which they are not able to *p* Ps 21:11
ever, that I may daily *p* my vows Ps 61:8 7999
I have sworn, and I will *p* it Ps 119:106 6965
heart to *p* thy statutes alway Ps 119:112 6213
of the LORD of hosts will *p* this Is 9:7 6213
vow a vow unto the LORD, and *p* it Is 19:21 7999
and shall *p* all my pleasure Is 44:28 7999
for I will hasten my word to *p* it Jer 1:12 6213
That I may *p* the oath which I Jer 11:5 6965
the LORD *p* thy words which thou Jer 28:6 6965
p my good word toward you, in Jer 29:10 6965
that I will *p* that good thing Jer 33:14 6965
We will surely *p* our vows that we Jer 44:25 6213
your vows, and surely *p* your vows Jer 44:25 6213
will I say the word, and will *p* it Eze 12:25 6213
Thou wilt *p* the truth to Jacob, Mic 7:20 5414
thy solemn feasts, *p* thy vows Nah 1:15 7999
but shalt *p* unto the Lord thine Mt 5:33 591
To *p* the mercy promised to our Lk 1:72 4160
promised, he was able also to *p* Rom 4:21 4160
but how to *p* that which is good I Rom 7:18 2716
Now therefore *p* the doing of it 2Cor 8:11 2005
will *p* it until the day of Jesus Phil 1:6 2005

PERFORMANCE
for there shall be a *p* of those Lk 1:45 5050
so there may be a *p* also out of 2Cor 8:11 2005

PERFORMED
hath not *p* my commandments 1Sa 15:11 6965
I have *p* the commandment of the 1Sa 15:13 6965
and they *p* all that the king 2Sa 21:14 6213
the LORD hath *p* his word that he 1Kin 8:20 6965
The LORD therefore hath *p* his 2Chr 6:10 6965
to his seed, and hast *p* thy words Neh 9:8 6965
because she hath not *p* the Est 1:15 6213
half of the kingdom it shall be *p* Est 5:6 6213
and it shall be *p*, even to the Est 7:2 6213
and unto thee shall the vow be *p* Ps 65:1 7999
that when the Lord hath *p* his Is 10:12 1214
till he have *p* the thoughts of Jer 23:20 6965
until he have *p* the intents of Jer 30:24 6965
which have not *p* the words of the Jer 34:18 6965
his sons not to drink wine, are *p* Jer 35:14 6965
Jonadab the son of Rechab have *p* Jer 35:16 6965
LORD shall be *p* against Babylon Jer 51:29 6965
it, and *p* it, saith the LORD Eze 37:14 6213
day that these things shall be *p* Lk 1:20 1096
when they had *p* all things Lk 2:39 5055
When therefore I have *p* this Rom 15:28 2005

PERFORMETH
that *p* not this promise, even Neh 5:13 6965
For he *p* the thing that is Job 23:14 7999
unto God that *p* all things for me Ps 57:2 1584
p the counsel of his messengers Is 44:26 7999

PERFORMING
or a sacrifice in *p* a vow Num 15:3 6381
or for a sacrifice in *p* a vow Num 15:8 6381

PERFUME
And thou shalt make it a *p* Ex 30:35 7004
as for the *p* which thou shalt Ex 30:37 7004
Ointment and *p* rejoice the heart Prov 27:9 7004

PERFUMED
I have *p* my bed with myrrh, aloes Prov 7:17 5130
p with myrrh and frankincense, Song 3:6 6999

PERFUMES
ointment, and didst increase thy *p* Is 57:9 7547

PERGA (*pur'-gah*) *Capital of Pamphylia.*
they came to *P* in Pamphylia Acts 13:13 4011
But when they departed from *P* Acts 13:14 4011
they had preached the word in *P* Acts 14:25 4011

PERGAMOS (*pur'-ga-mos*) *A city in Mysia in Asia Minor.*
and unto Smyrna, and unto *P* Rev 1:11 4010
angel of the church in *P* write Rev 2:12 4010

PERGAMUM See PERGAMOS.

PERHAPS
if *p* the thought of thine heart Acts 8:22 686
lest *p* such a one should be 2Cor 2:7 3381
For *p* he therefore departed for a Philem 15 5029

PERIDA (*per-i'-dah*) *A family of exiles.*
of Sophereth, the children of *P* Neh 7:57 6514

PERIL
We gat our bread with the *p* of Lam 5:9
or famine, or nakedness, or *p* Rom 8:35 2794

PERILOUS
the last days *p* times shall come 2Ti 3:1 5467

PERILS
in *p* of waters 2Cor 11:26 2794
in *p* of robbers 2Cor 11:26 2794
in *p* by mine own countrymen 2Cor 11:26 2794
in *p* by the heathen 2Cor 11:26 2794
in *p* in the city 2Cor 11:26 2794
in *p* in the wilderness 2Cor 11:26 2794
in *p* in the sea 2Cor 11:26 2794
in *p* among false brethren 2Cor 11:26 2794

PERISH
that the land *p* not through the Gen 41:36 3772
LORD to gaze, and many of them *p* Ex 19:21 5307
or the eye of his maid, that it *p* Ex 21:26 7843
ye shall *p* among the heathen, and Lev 26:38 6
we die, we *p*, we all *p* Num 17:12 6
end shall be that he *p* for ever Num 24:20 8
Eber, and he also shall *p* for ever Num 24:24 8
that ye shall soon utterly *p* from Deut 4:26 6
this day that ye shall surely *p* Deut 8:19 6
before your face, so shall ye *p* Deut 8:20 6
lest ye *p* quickly from off the Deut 11:17 6
A Syrian ready to *p* was my father Deut 26:5 6
and until thou *p* quickly Deut 28:20 6
shall pursue thee until thou *p* Deut 28:22 6
this day, that ye shall surely *p* Deut 30:18 6
until ye *p* from off this good Josh 23:13 6
ye shall *p* quickly from off the Josh 23:16 6
So let all thine enemies *p* Judg 5:31 6
shall descend into battle, and *p* 1Sa 26:10 5595
I shall now *p* one day by the hand 1Sa 27:1 5595
the whole house of Ahab shall *p* 2Kin 9:8 6
to kill, and to cause to *p* Est 3:13 6
and if I *p*, I *p* Est 4:16 6
destroyed, to be slain, and to *p* Est 7:4 6
to slay, and to cause to *p* Est 8:11 6
of them *p* from their seed Est 9:28 5486
Let the day *p* wherein I was born, Job 3:3 6
By the blast of God they *p* Job 4:9 6
they *p* for ever without any Job 4:20 6
they go to nothing, and *p* Job 6:18 6
and the hypocrite's hope shall *p* Job 8:13 6
shall *p* from the earth, and he Job 18:17 6
Yet he shall *p* for ever like his Job 20:7 6
that was ready to *p* came upon me Job 29:13 6
If I have seen any *p* for want of Job 31:19 6
All flesh shall *p* together Job 34:15 1478
they shall *p* by the sword, and Job 36:12 5674
the way of the ungodly shall *p* Ps 1:6 6
ye *p* from the way, when his wrath Ps 2:12 6
shall fall and *p* at thy presence Ps 9:3 6
of the poor shall not *p* for ever Ps 9:18 6
But the wicked shall *p*, and the Ps 37:20 6
When shall he die, and his name *p* Ps 41:5 6
the fool and the brutish person *p* Ps 49:10 6
he is like the beasts that *p* Ps 49:12 1820
not, is like the beasts that *p* Ps 49:20 1820
so let the wicked *p* at the Ps 68:2 6
that are far from thee shall *p* Ps 73:27 6
they *p* at the rebuke of thy Ps 80:16 6
let them be put to shame, and *p* Ps 83:17 6
for, lo, thine enemies shall *p* Ps 92:9 6
They shall *p*, but thou shalt Ps 102:26 6
the desire of the wicked shall *p* Ps 112:10 6
in that very day his thoughts *p* Ps 146:4 6
expectation of the wicked shall *p* Prov 10:28 6
dieth, his expectation shall *p* Prov 11:7 6
and when the wicked *p*, there is Prov 11:10 6
and he that speaketh lies shall *p* Prov 19:9 6
A false witness shall *p* Prov 21:28 6
but when they *p*, the righteous Prov 28:28 6
there is no vision, the people *p* Prov 29:18 6544
drink unto him that is ready to *p* Prov 31:6 6
those riches *p* by evil travail Eccl 5:14 6
and made all their memory to *p* Is 26:14 6
ready to *p* in the land of Assyria Is 27:13 6
wisdom of their wise men shall *p* Is 29:14 6
that strive with thee shall *p* Is 41:11 6
that will not serve thee shall *p* Is 60:12 6
the heart of the king shall *p* Jer 4:9 6
neighbour and his friend shall *p* Jer 6:21 6
even they shall *p* from the earth Jer 10:11 7
of their visitation they shall *p* Jer 10:15 6
law shall not *p* from the priest Jer 18:18 6
drive you out, and ye should *p* Jer 27:10 6
drive you out, and that ye might *p* Jer 27:15 6
and the remnant in Judah *p* Jer 40:15 6
the valley also shall *p*, and the Jer 48:8 6
of their visitation they shall *p* Jer 51:18 6
the law shall *p* from the priest Eze 7:26 6
thee to *p* out of the countries Eze 25:7 6
his fellows should not *p* with the Dan 2:18 7
of the Philistines shall *p* Amos 1:8 6
the flight shall *p* from the swift Amos 2:14 6
and the houses of ivory shall *p* Amos 3:15 6

P

will think upon us, that we *p* not Jonah 1:6 6
let us not *p* for this man's life, Jonah 1:14 6
his fierce anger, that we *p* not Jonah 3:9 6
and the king shall *p* from Gaza Zec 9:5 6
that one of thy members should *p* Mt 5:29 *622*
that one of thy members should *p* Mt 5:30 *622*
Lord, save us: we *p* Mt 8:25 *622*
runneth out, and the bottles *p* Mt 9:17 *622*
one of these little ones should *p* Mt 18:14 *622*
the sword shall *p* with the sword Mt 26:52 *622*
Master, carest thou not that we *p* Mk 4:38 *622*
spilled, and the bottles shall *p* Lk 5:37 *622*
him, saying, Master, master, we *p* Lk 8:24 *622*
repent, ye shall all likewise *p* Lk 13:3 *622*
repent, ye shall all likewise *p* Lk 13:5 *622*
that a prophet *p* out of Jerusalem Lk 13:33 *622*
and to spare, and I *p* with hunger Lk 15:17 *622*
shall not an hair of your head *p* Lk 21:18 *622*
believeth in him should not *p* Jn 3:15 *622*
believeth in him should not *p* Jn 3:16 *622*
and they shall never *p*, neither Jn 10:28 *622*
and that the whole nation *p* not Jn 11:50 *622*
unto him, Thy money *p* with thee Acts 8:20
ye despisers, and wonder, and *p* Acts 13:41 *853*
law shall also *p* without law Rom 2:12 *622*
is to them that *p* foolishness 1Cor 1:18 *622*
shall the weak brother *p*, for 1Cor 8:11 *622*
that are saved, and in them that *p* 2Cor 2:15 *622*
but though our outward man *p* 2Cor 4:16 *1311*
Which all are to *p* with the using Col 2:22 *5356*
of unrighteousness in them that *p* 2Th 2:10 *622*
They shall *p*; but thou Heb 1:11 *622*
shall utterly *p* in their own 2Pet 2:12 *2704*
not willing that any should *p* 2Pet 3:9 *622*

PERISHED
and they *p* from among the Num 16:33 6
Heshbon is *p* even unto Dibon, and Num 21:30 6
that man *p* not alone in his Josh 22:20 1478
fallen, and the weapons of war *p* 2Sa 1:27 6
Remember, I pray thee, who ever *p* Job 4:7 6
profit me, in whom old age was *p* Job 30:2 6
their memorial is *p* with them Ps 9:6 6
the heathen are *p* out of his land Ps 10:16 6
Which *p* at En-dor Ps 83:10 8045
then have *p* in mine affliction Ps 119:92 6
hatred, and their envy, is now *p* Eccl 9:6 6
truth is *p*, and is cut off from Jer 7:28 6
riches that he hath gotten are *p* Jer 48:36 6
is counsel *p* from the prudent Jer 49:7 6
my hope is *p* from the LORD Lam 3:18 6
the harvest of the field is *p* Joel 1:11 6
up in a night, and *p* in a night Jonah 4:10 6
is thy counsellor *p* Mic 4:9 6
The good man is *p* out of the Mic 7:2 6
into the sea, and *p* in the waters Mt 8:32 *599*
which *p* between the altar and the Lk 11:51 *622*
after him: he also *p* Acts 5:37 *622*
are fallen asleep in Christ are *p* 1Cor 15:18 *622*
By faith the harlot Rahab *p* not Heb 11:31 *4881*
being overflowed with water, *p* 2Pet 3:6 *622*
p in the gainsaying of Core Jude 11 *622*

PERISHETH
The old lion *p* for lack of prey, Job 4:11 6
and the hope of unjust men *p* Prov 11:7 6
man that *p* in his righteousness Eccl 7:15 6
The righteous *p*, and no man layeth Is 57:1 6
declare it, for what the land *p* Jer 9:12 6
the people of Chemosh *p* Jer 48:46 6
Labour not for the meat which *p* Jn 6:27 *622*
the grace of the fashion of it *p* Jas 1:11 *622*
more precious than of gold that *p* 1Pet 1:7 *622*

PERISHING
and his life from *p* by the sword Job 33:18 5674

PERIZZITE (*per'-iz-zite*) See PERIZZITES. *A tribe in Judah.*
the *P* dwelled then in the land Gen 13:7 6522
Amorite, and the Hittite, and the *P* Ex 33:2 6522
and the Hittite, and the *P* Ex 34:11 6522
the Amorite, the Canaanite, the *P* Josh 9:1 6522
Amorite, and the Hittite, and the *P* Josh 11:3 6522

PERIZZITES (*per'-iz-zites*)
And the Hittites, and the *P* Gen 15:20 6522
among the Canaanites and the *P* Gen 34:30 6522
and the Amorites, and the *P* Ex 3:8 6522
and the Amorites, and the *P* Ex 3:17 6522
and the Hittites, and the *P* Ex 23:23 6522
and the Canaanites, and the *P* Deut 7:1 6522
the Canaanites, and the *P* Deut 20:17 6522
and the Hivites, and the *P* Josh 3:10 6522
and the Canaanites, the *P* Josh 12:8 6522
there in the land of the *P* Josh 17:15 6522
you, the Amorites, and the *P* Josh 24:11 6522
and the *P* into their hand Judg 1:4 6522
they slew the Canaanites and the *P* Judg 1:5 6522
Hittites, and Amorites, and *P* Judg 3:5 6522
left of the Amorites, Hittites, *P* 1Kin 9:20 6522
and the Amorites, and the *P* 2Chr 8:7 6522
Canaanites, the Hittites, the *P* Ezr 9:1 6522
Hittites, the Amorites, and the *P* Neh 9:8 6522

PERJURED
for *p* persons, and if there be any 1Ti 1:10 *1965*

PERMISSION
But I speak this by *p*, and not of 1Cor 7:6 *4774*

PERMIT
a while with you, if the Lord *p* 1Cor 16:7 *2010*
And this will we do, if God *p* Heb 6:3 *2010*

PERMITTED
Thou art *p* to speak for thyself Acts 26:1 *2010*
for it is not *p* unto them to 1Cor 14:34 *2010*

PERNICIOUS
And many shall follow their *p* ways 2Pet 2:2 *684*

PERPETUAL
is with you, for *p* generations Gen 9:12 5769
shall be theirs for a *p* statute Ex 29:9 5769
a *p* incense before the LORD Ex 30:8 8548
generations, for a *p* covenant Ex 31:16 5769
It shall be a *p* statute for your Lev 3:17 5769
fine flour for a meat offering *p* Lev 6:20 8548
LORD made by fire by a *p* statute Lev 24:9 5769
for it is their *p* possession Lev 25:34 5769
it shall be a *p* statute unto them Num 19:21 5769
destructions are come to a *p* end Ps 9:6 5331
thy feet unto the *p* desolations Ps 74:3 5331
he put them to a *p* reproach Ps 78:66 5769
bound of the sea by a *p* decree Jer 5:22 5769
slidden back by a *p* backsliding Jer 8:5 5331
Why is my pain *p*, and my wound Jer 15:18 5331
land desolate, and a *p* hissing Jer 18:16 5769
a *p* shame, which shall not be Jer 23:40 5769
and an hissing, and *p* desolations Jer 25:9 5769
and will make it *p* desolations Jer 25:12 5769
cities thereof shall be *p* wastes Jer 49:13 5769
in a *p* covenant that shall not be Jer 50:5 5769
may rejoice, and sleep a *p* sleep Jer 51:39 5769
and they shall sleep a *p* sleep Jer 51:57 5769
Because thou hast had a *p* hatred Eze 35:5 5769
I will make thee *p* desolations Eze 35:9 5769
by a *p* ordinance unto the LORD Eze 46:14 5769
scattered, the *p* hills did bow Hab 3:6 5769
and saltpits, and a *p* desolation Zeph 2:9 5769

PERPETUALLY
and mine heart shall be there *p* 1Kin 9:3
and mine heart shall be there *p* 2Chr 7:16
all pity, and his anger did tear *p* Amos 1:11 5703

PERPLEXED
but the city Shushan was *p* Est 3:15 943
the herds of cattle are *p* Joel 1:18 943
and he was *p*, because that it was Lk 9:7 *1280*
as they were much *p* thereabout Lk 24:4 *1280*
we are *p*, but not in despair 2Cor 4:8 *639*

PERPLEXITY
of *p* by the Lord GOD of hosts in Is 22:5 3998
now shall be their *p* Mic 7:4 3998
earth distress of nations, with *p* Lk 21:25 *640*

PERSECUTE
Why do ye *p* me as God, and are not Job 19:22 7291
Why *p* we him, seeing the root of Job 19:28 7291
save me from all them that *p* me Ps 7:1 7291
Let the enemy *p* my soul, and take Ps 7:5 7291
in his pride doth *p* the poor Ps 10:2 1814
enemies, and from them that *p* me Ps 31:15 7291
the way against them that *p* me Ps 35:3 7291
let the angel of the LORD *p* them Ps 35:6 7291
For they *p* him whom thou hast Ps 69:26 7291
p and take him Ps 71:11 7291
So *p* them with thy tempest, and Ps 83:15 7291
judgment on them that *p* me Ps 119:84 7291
they *p* me wrongfully Ps 119:86 7291
Let them be confounded that *p* me Jer 17:18 7291
I will *p* them with the sword, Jer 29:18
P and destroy them in anger from Lam 3:66 7291
p you, and shall say all manner of Mt 5:11 *1377*
despitefully use you, and *p* you Mt 5:44 *1377*
But when they *p* you in this city, Mt 10:23 *1377*
and *p* them from city to city Mt 23:34 *1377*
some of them they shall slay and *p* Lk 11:49 *1559*
p you, delivering you up to the Lk 21:12 *1377*
And therefore did the Jews *p* Jesus Jn 5:16 *1377*
me, they will also *p* you Jn 15:20 *1377*
Bless them which *p* you Rom 12:14 *1377*

PERSECUTED
them that hate thee, which *p* thee Deut 30:7 7291
but *p* the poor and needy man, that Ps 109:16 7291
Princes have *p* me without a cause Ps 119:161 7291
For the enemy hath *p* my soul Ps 143:3 7291
ruled the nations in anger, is *p* Is 14:6 4783
hast covered with anger, and *p* us Lam 3:43 7291
are *p* for righteousness' sake Mt 5:10 *1377*
for so *p* they the prophets which Mt 5:12 *1377*
If they have *p* me, they will also Jn 15:20 *1377*
prophets have not your fathers *p* Acts 7:52 *1377*
I *p* this way unto the death, Acts 22:4 *1377*
I *p* them even unto strange cities Acts 26:11 *1377*
being *p*, we suffer it 1Cor 4:12 *1377*
because I *p* the church of God 1Cor 15:9 *1377*
P, but not forsaken 2Cor 4:9 *1377*
measure I *p* the church of God Gal 1:13 *1377*
That he which *p* us in times past Gal 1:23 *1377*
p him that was born after the Gal 4:29 *1377*
their own prophets, and have *p* us 1Th 2:15 *1559*
he *p* the woman which brought Rev 12:13 *1377*

PERSECUTEST
him, Saul, Saul, why *p* thou me Acts 9:4 *1377*
Lord said, I am Jesus whom thou *p* Acts 9:5 *1377*
me, Saul, Saul, why *p* thou me Acts 22:7 *1377*
am Jesus of Nazareth, whom thou *p* Acts 22:8 *1377*
tongue, Saul, Saul, why *p* thou me Acts 26:14 *1377*
he said, I am Jesus whom thou *p* Acts 26:15 *1377*

PERSECUTING
Concerning zeal, *p* the church Phil 3:6 *1377*

PERSECUTION
Our necks are under *p* Lam 5:5 7291
for when tribulation or *p* ariseth Mt 13:21 *1375*
when affliction or *p* ariseth for Mk 4:17 *1375*
at that time there was a great *p* Acts 8:1 *1375*
the *p* that arose about Stephen Acts 11:19 *2347*
raised *p* against Paul and Barnabas Acts 13:50 *1375*
tribulation, or distress, or *p* Rom 8:35 *1375*
why do I yet suffer *p* Gal 5:11 *1377*
suffer *p* for the cross of Christ Gal 6:12 *1377*
in Christ Jesus shall suffer *p* 2Ti 3:12 *1377*

PERSECUTIONS
and children, and lands, with *p* Mk 10:30 *1375*
reproaches, in necessities, in *p* 2Cor 12:10 *1375*
patience and faith in all your *p* 2Th 1:4 *1375*
P, afflictions, which came unto 2Ti 3:11 *1375*
what *p* I endured 2Ti 3:11 *1375*

PERSECUTOR
was before a blasphemer, and a *p* 1Ti 1:13 *1376*

PERSECUTORS
their *p* thou threwest into the Neh 9:11 7291
his arrows against the *p* Ps 7:13 1814
Many are my *p* and mine enemies Ps 119:157 7291
deliver me from my *p* Ps 142:6 7291
visit me, and revenge me of my *p* Jer 15:15 7291
therefore my *p* shall stumble, and Jer 20:11 7291
all her *p* overtook her between Lam 1:3 7291
Our *p* are swifter than the eagles Lam 4:19 7291

PERSEVERANCE
and watching thereunto with all *p* Eph 6:18 *4343*

PERSIA (*per'-she-ah*) See ELAM, PERSIAN. *An ancient world power located in present-day Iran.*
the reign of the kingdom of *P* 2Chr 36:20 6539
the first year of Cyrus king of *P* 2Chr 36:22 6539
up the spirit of Cyrus king of *P* 2Chr 36:22 6539
Thus saith Cyrus king of *P* 2Chr 36:23 6539
the first year of Cyrus king of *P* Ezr 1:1 6539
up the spirit of Cyrus king of *P* Ezr 1:1 6539
Thus saith Cyrus king of *P* Ezr 1:2 6539
of *P* bring forth by the hand of Ezr 1:8 6539
that they had of Cyrus king of *P* Ezr 3:7 6539
the king of *P* hath commanded us Ezr 4:3 6539
all the days of Cyrus king of *P* Ezr 4:5 6539
the reign of Darius king of *P* Ezr 4:5 6539
unto Artaxerxes king of *P* Ezr 4:7 6539
of the reign of Darius king of *P* Ezr 4:24 6540
Darius, and Artaxerxes king of *P* Ezr 6:14 6540
the reign of Artaxerxes king of *P* Ezr 7:1 6539
us in the sight of the kings of *P* Ezr 9:9 6539
the power of *P* and Media, the Est 1:3 6539
Memucan, the seven princes of *P* Est 1:14 6539
Likewise shall the ladies of *P* Est 1:18 6539
of the kings of Media and *P* Est 10:2 6539
They of *P* and of Lud and of Phut Eze 27:10 6539
P, Ethiopia, and Libya with them Eze 38:5 6539
horns are the kings of Media and *P* Dan 8:20 6539
of *P* a thing was revealed unto Dan 10:1 6539
the kingdom of *P* withstood me one Dan 10:13 6539
there with the kings of *P* Dan 10:13 6539
to fight with the prince of *P* Dan 10:20 6539
stand up yet three kings in *P* Dan 11:2 6539

PERSIAN (*per'-she-un*) *A native of Persia.*
to the reign of Darius the *P* Neh 12:22 6542
and in the reign of Cyrus the *P* Dan 6:28 6523

PERSIANS (*per'-she-uns*) See ELAMITES.
written among the laws of the *P* Est 1:19 6539
and given to the Medes and *P* Dan 5:28 6540
to the law of the Medes and *P* Dan 6:8 6540
to the law of the Medes and *P* Dan 6:12 6540
P is, That no decree nor statute Dan 6:15 6540

PERSIS (*pur'-sis*) *A Christian in Rome.*
Salute the beloved *P*, which Rom 16:12 *4069*

PERSON
And Joseph was a goodly *p*, and well Gen 39:6
uncircumcised *p* shall eat thereof Ex 12:48
not respect the *p* of the poor Lev 19:15 6440
nor honour the *p* of the mighty Lev 19:15 6440
the LORD, and that *p* be guilty Num 5:6 5315
for an unclean *p* they shall take Num 19:17
a clean *p* shall take hyssop, and Num 19:18
the clean *p* shall sprinkle upon Num 19:19
whatsoever the unclean *p* toucheth Num 19:22
whosoever hath killed any *p* Num 31:19 5315
which killeth any *p* at unawares Num 35:11 5315
any *p* unawares may flee thither Num 35:15 5315
Whoso killeth any *p*, the murderer Num 35:30 5315
against any *p* to cause him to die Num 35:30 5315
the clean *p* shall eat it alike, Deut 15:22
reward to slay an innocent *p* Deut 27:25 5315
shall not regard the *p* of the old Deut 28:50 6440
that killeth any *p* unawares Josh 20:3 5315
that whosoever killeth any *p* at Josh 20:9 5315
of Israel a goodlier *p* than he 1Sa 9:2 376
prudent in matters, and a comely *p* 1Sa 16:18 376
thy voice, and have accepted thy *p* 1Sa 25:35 6440
men have slain a righteous *p* in 2Sa 4:11 376
neither doth God respect any *p* 2Sa 14:14 5315
thou go to battle in thine own *p* 2Sa 17:11 6440
Will ye accept his *p* Job 13:8 6440
and he shall save the humble *p* Job 22:29
I pray you, accept any man's *p* Job 32:21 6440
whose eyes a vile *p* is contemned Ps 15:4
the fool and the brutish *p* perish Ps 49:10
I will not know a wicked *p* Ps 101:4
one feeble *p* among their tribes Ps 105:37
A naughty *p*, a wicked man, Prov 6:12 120
to accept the *p* of the wicked Prov 18:5 6440
shall be called a mischievous *p* Prov 24:8 1167
of any *p* shall flee to the pit Prov 28:17 5315
The vile *p* shall be no more Is 32:5
For the vile *p* will speak villany Is 32:6
every *p* that Nebuzar-adan the Jer 43:6 5315
them that were near the king's *p* Jer 52:25 6440
field, to the lothing of thy *p* Eze 16:5 5315
take any *p* from among them, he is Eze 33:6 5315
at no dead *p* to defile themselves Eze 44:25 120

estate shall stand up a vile p Dan 11:21
with thee, or accept thy p Mal 1:8 6440
thou regardest not the p of men Mt 22:16 4383
of the blood of this just p Mt 27:24
thou regardest not the p of men Mk 12:14 4383
acceptest thou the p of any Lk 20:21 4383
among yourselves that wicked p 1Cor 5:13
forgave I it in the p of Christ 2Cor 2:10 4383
God accepteth no man's p Gal 2:6 4383
no whoremonger, nor unclean p Eph 5:5
and the express image of his p Heb 1:3 5287
be any fornicator, or profane p Heb 12:16
but saved Noah the eighth p 2Pet 2:5

PERSONS
said unto Abram, Give me the p Gen 14:21 5315
all the p of his house, and his Gen 36:6 5315
according to the number of your p Ex 16:16 5315
the p shall be for the LORD by Lev 27:2 5315
upon the p that were there, and Num 19:18 5315
of five hundred, both of the p Num 31:28 120
one portion of fifty, of the p Num 31:30 120
thirty and two thousand p in all Num 31:35
the p were sixteen thousand Num 31:40
tribute was thirty and two p Num 31:40
And sixteen thousand p Num 31:46
shall not respect p in judgment Deut 1:17 6440
a terrible, which regardeth not p Deut 10:17 6440
Egypt with threescore and ten p Deut 10:22 5315
thou shalt not respect p, neither Deut 16:19 6440
which are threescore and ten p Judg 9:2 376
Abimelech hired vain and light p Judg 9:4 582
being threescore and ten p Judg 9:5 376
his sons, threescore and ten p Judg 9:18 376
the men of Israel about thirty p Judg 20:39 376
bidden, which were about thirty p 1Sa 9:22 376
five p that did wear a linen 1Sa 22:18 376
all the p of thy father's house 1Sa 22:22 5315
the king's sons, being seventy p 2Kin 10:6 376
king's sons, and slew seventy p 2Kin 10:7 376
LORD our God, nor respect of p 2Chr 19:7 6440
you, if ye do secretly accept p Job 13:10 6440
accepteth not the p of princes Job 34:19 6440
I have not sat with vain p Ps 26:4 4962
accept the p of the wicked Ps 82:2 6440
vain p is void of understanding Prov 12:11
to have respect of p in judgment Prov 24:23 6440
vain p shall have poverty enough Prov 28:19
To have respect of p is not good Prov 28:21 6440
eight hundred thirty and two p Jer 52:29 5315
seven hundred forty and five p Jer 52:30 5315
all the p were four thousand and Jer 52:30 5315
not the p of the priests, they Lam 4:16 6440
building forts, to cut off many p Eze 17:17 5315
they traded the p of men and Eze 27:13 5315
p that cannot discern between Jonah 4:11 120
are light and treacherous p Zeph 3:4 582
will he regard your p Mal 1:9 6440
than over ninety and nine just p Lk 15:7
that God is no respecter of p Acts 10:34 4381
the Jews, and with the devout p Acts 17:17
there is no respect of p with God Rom 2:11 4382
upon us by the means of many p 2Cor 1:11 4383
is there respect of p with him Eph 6:9 4382
and there is no respect of p Col 3:25 4382
for liars, for perjured p 1Ti 1:10 678
Lord of glory, with respect of p Jas 2:1 4382
But if ye have respect to p Jas 2:9 4380
who without respect of p judgeth 1Pet 1:17 678
what manner of p ought ye to be 2Pet 3:11
having men's p in admiration Jude 16 4383

PERSUADE
the LORD said, Who shall p Ahab 1Kin 22:20 6601
the LORD, and said, I will p him 1Kin 22:21 6601
And he said, Thou shalt p him 1Kin 22:22 6601
Doth not Hezekiah p you to give 2Chr 32:11 5496
nor p you on this manner, neither 2Chr 32:15 5496
Beware lest Hezekiah p you Is 36:18 5496
governor's ears, we will p him Mt 28:14 3982
the terror of the Lord, we p men 2Cor 5:11 3982
For do I now p men, or God Gal 1:10 3982

PERSUADED
p him to go up with him to 2Chr 18:2 5496
By long forbearing is a prince p Prov 25:15 6601
elders p the multitude that they Mt 27:20 3982
prophets, neither will they be p Lk 16:31 3982
for they be p that John was a Lk 20:6 3982
p them to continue in the grace Acts 13:43 3982
who p the people, and, having Acts 14:19 3982
and p the Jews and the Greeks Acts 18:4 3982
all Asia, this Paul hath p Acts 19:26 3982
And when he would not be p Acts 21:14 3982
for I am p that none of these Acts 26:26 3982
And being fully p that, what he Rom 4:21 4135
For I am p, that neither death, Rom 8:38 3982
man be fully p in his own mind Rom 14:5 4135
am p by the Lord Jesus, that Rom 14:14 3982
And I myself also am p of you Rom 15:14 3982
and I am p that in thee also 2Ti 1:5 3982
am p that he is able to keep that 2Ti 1:12 3982
we are p better things of you, and Heb 6:9 3982
were p of them, and embraced them, Heb 11:13 3982

PERSUADEST
Paul, Almost thou p me to be a Acts 26:28 3982

PERSUADETH
not unto Hezekiah, when he p you 2Kin 18:32 5496
This fellow p men to worship God Acts 18:13 374

PERSUADING
p the things concerning the Acts 19:8 3982
p them concerning Jesus, both out Acts 28:23 3982

PERSUASION
This p cometh not of him that Gal 5:8 3988

PERTAIN
that p unto the LORD, having his Lev 7:20
which p unto the LORD, even that Lev 7:21
if I leave of all that p to him 1Sa 25:22
in those things which p to God Rom 15:17
more things that p to this life 1Cor 6:3
us all things that p unto life 2Pet 1:3

PERTAINED
(Now the half that p unto the Num 31:43
a hill that p to Phinehas his son Josh 24:33
that p unto Joash the Abi-ezrite Judg 6:11
was missed of all that p unto him 1Sa 25:21
which p to Ish-bosheth the son of 2Sa 2:15
master's son all that p to Saul 2Sa 9:9 1961
are all that p unto Mephibosheth 2Sa 16:4
to him p Sochoh, and all the land 1Kin 4:10
to him p Taanach and Megiddo, and 1Kin 4:12
to him p the towns of Jair the 1Kin 4:13
to him also p the region of Argob 1Kin 4:13
made all the vessels that p unto 1Kin 7:48
all that p to the king of Egypt 2Kin 24:7
thereof every morning p to them 1Chr 9:27
that p to the children of 1Chr 11:31
fenced cities which p to Judah 2Chr 12:4
that p to the children of Israel 2Chr 34:33

PERTAINETH
get that which p to his cleansing Lev 14:32
priest p the oil for the light Num 4:16
not wear that which p unto a man Deut 22:5 3627
wherefore Ziklag p unto the kings 1Sa 27:6 1961
Obed-edom, and all that p unto him 2Sa 6:12
to whom p the adoption, and the Rom 9:4
are spoken p to another tribe Heb 7:13 3348

PERTAINING
were p unto the children of Josh 13:31
for every matter p to God 1Chr 26:32
things p to the kingdom of God Acts 1:3 4012
as p to the flesh, hath found Rom 4:1
of things p to this life, set 1Cor 6:4
high priest in things p to God Heb 2:17
for men in things p to God Heb 5:1
perfect, as p to the conscience Heb 9:9

PERUDA (*per'-u-dah*) See PERIDA. *A family of exiles.*
of Sophereth, the children of P Ezr 2:55 6514

PERVERSE
because thy way is p before me Num 22:32 3399
they are a p and crooked Deut 32:5 6141
Thou son of the p rebellious 1Sa 20:30 5753
cannot my taste discern p things Job 6:30 1942
perfect, it shall also prove me p Job 9:20 6140
and p lips put far from thee Prov 4:24 3891
is nothing froward or p in them Prov 8:8 6141
but he that is of a p heart shall Prov 12:8 5753
but he that is p in his ways Prov 14:2 3868
he that hath a p tongue falleth Prov 17:20 2015
than he that is p in his lips Prov 19:1 6141
thine heart shall utter p things Prov 23:33 8419
than he that is p in his ways Prov 28:6 6141
but he that is p in his ways Prov 28:18 6140
The LORD hath mingled a p spirit Is 19:14 5773
p generation, how long shall I be Mt 17:17 1294
p generation, how long shall I be Lk 9:41 1294
men arise, speaking p things Acts 20:30 1294
p nation, among whom ye shine as Phil 2:15 1294
P disputings of men of corrupt 1Ti 6:5 3859

PERVERSELY
that which thy servant did p the 2Sa 19:19 5753
We have sinned, and have done p 1Kin 8:47 5753
for they dealt p with me without Ps 119:78 5791

PERVERSENESS
neither hath he seen p in Israel Num 23:21 5999
but the p of transgressors shall Prov 11:3 5558
but p therein is a breach in the Prov 15:4 5558
word, and trust in oppression and p Is 30:12 3868
lies, your tongue hath muttered p Is 59:3 5766
of blood, and the city full of p Eze 9:9 4297

PERVERT
p the words of the righteous Deut 16:19 5557
Thou shalt not p the judgment of Deut 24:17 5186
Doth God p judgment Job 8:3 5791
or doth the Almighty p justice Job 8:3 5791
will the Almighty p judgment Job 34:12 5791
bosom to p the ways of judgment Prov 17:23 5186
p the judgment of any of the Prov 31:5 8138
abhor judgment, and p all equity Mic 3:9 6140
wilt thou not cease to p the Acts 13:10 1294
would p the gospel of Christ Gal 1:7 3344

PERVERTED
and took bribes, and p judgment 1Sa 8:3 5186
p that which was right, and it Job 33:27 5753
and thy knowledge, it hath p thee Is 47:10 7725
for they have p their way Jer 3:21 5753
for ye have p the words of the Jer 23:36 2015

PERVERTETH
p the words of the righteous Ex 23:8 5557
Cursed be he that p the judgment Deut 27:19 5186
but he that p his ways shall be Prov 10:9 6140
The foolishness of man p his way Prov 19:3 5557
unto me, as one that p the people Lk 23:14 654

PERVERTING
violent p of judgment and justice Eccl 5:8
We found this fellow p the nation Lk 23:2 1294

PESTILENCE
lest he fall upon us with p Ex 5:3 1698
smite thee and thy people with p Ex 9:15 1698
I will send the p among you Lev 26:25 1698
I will smite them with the p Num 14:12 1698
shall make the p cleave unto thee Deut 28:21 1698
be three days' p in thy land 2Sa 24:13 1698
So the LORD sent a p upon Israel 2Sa 24:15 1698
in the land famine, if there be p 1Kin 8:37 1698
the sword of the LORD, even the p 1Chr 21:12 1698
So the LORD sent p upon Israel 1Chr 21:14 1698
dearth in the land, if there be p 2Chr 6:28 1698
or if I send p among my people 2Chr 7:13 1698
us, as the sword, judgment, or p 2Chr 20:9 1698
but gave their life over to the p Ps 78:50 1698
the fowler, and from the noisome p Ps 91:3 1698
Nor for the p that walketh in Ps 91:6 1698
and by the famine, and by the p Jer 14:12 1698
they shall die of a great p Jer 21:6 1698
are left in this city from the p Jer 21:7 1698
and by the famine, and by the p Jer 21:9 1698
the sword, the famine, and the p Jer 24:10 1698
and with the famine, and with the p Jer 27:8 1698
sword, by the famine, and by the p Jer 27:13 1698
of war, and of evil, and of p Jer 28:8 1698
the sword, the famine, and the p Jer 29:17 1698
with the famine, and with the p Jer 29:18 1698
and of the famine, and of the p Jer 32:24 1698
and by the famine, and by the p Jer 32:36 1698
the LORD, to the sword, to the p Jer 34:17 1698
sword, by the famine, and by the p Jer 38:2 1698
sword, by the famine, and by the p Jer 42:17 1698
sword, by the famine, and by the p Jer 42:22 1698
sword, by the famine, and by the p Jer 44:13 1698
part of thee shall die with the p Eze 5:12 1698
and p and blood shall pass through Eze 5:17 1698
sword, by the famine, and by the p Eze 6:11 1698
is far off shall die of the p Eze 6:12 1698
The sword is without, and the p Eze 7:15 1698
famine and p shall devour him Eze 7:15 1698
from the famine, and from the p Eze 12:16 1698
Or if I send a p into that land Eze 14:19 1698
and the noisome beast, and the p Eze 14:21 1698
For I will send into her p Eze 28:23 1698
in the caves shall die of the p Eze 33:27 1698
I will plead against him with p Eze 38:22 1698
the p after the manner of Egypt Amos 4:10 1698
Before him went the p, and burning Hab 3:5 1698

PESTILENCES
and there shall be famines, and p Mt 24:7 3061
divers places, and famines, and p Lk 21:11 3061

PESTILENT
we have found this man a p fellow Acts 24:5 3061

PESTLE
in a mortar among wheat with a p Prov 27:22 5940

PETER (*pe'-tur*) See CEPHAS, PETER'S, SIMON. *A disciple of Jesus.*
saw two brethren, Simon called P Mt 4:18 4074
The first, Simon, who is called P Mt 10:2 4074
P answered him and said, Lord, if Mt 14:28 4074
when P was come down out of the Mt 14:29 4074
Then answered P and said unto him, Mt 15:15 4074
Simon P answered and said, Thou Mt 16:16 4074
also unto thee, That thou art P Mt 16:18 4074
Then P took him, and began to Mt 16:22 4074
But he turned, and said unto P Mt 16:23 4074
And after six days Jesus taketh P Mt 17:1 4074
Then answered P, and said unto Mt 17:4 4074
received tribute money came to P Mt 17:24 4074
P saith unto him, Of strangers Mt 17:26 4074
Then came P to him, and said, Lord Mt 18:21 4074
Then answered P and said unto him, Mt 19:27 4074
P answered and said unto him, Mt 26:33 4074
P said unto him, Though I should Mt 26:35 4074
And he took with him P and the two Mt 26:37 4074
them asleep, and saith unto P Mt 26:40 4074
But P followed him afar off unto Mt 26:58 4074
Now P sat without in the palace Mt 26:69 4074
they that stood by, and said to P Mt 26:73 4074
P remembered the word of Jesus, Mt 26:75 4074
And Simon he surnamed P Mk 3:16 4074
no man to follow him, save P Mk 5:37 4074
P answereth and saith unto him, Mk 8:29 4074
P took him, and began to rebuke Mk 8:32 4074
on his disciples, he rebuked P Mk 8:33 4074
six days Jesus taketh with him P Mk 9:2 4074
P answered and said to Jesus, Mk 9:5 4074
Then P began to say unto him, Lo, Mk 10:28 4074
P calling to remembrance saith Mk 11:21 4074
Olives over against the temple, P Mk 13:3 4074
But P said unto him, Although all Mk 14:29 4074
And he taketh with him P and James Mk 14:33 4074
them sleeping, and saith unto P Mk 14:37 4074
P followed him afar off, even Mk 14:54 4074
as P was beneath in the palace, Mk 14:66 4074
when she saw P warming himself, Mk 14:67 4074
that stood by said again to P Mk 14:70 4074
P called to mind the word that Mk 14:72 4074
P that he goeth before you into Mk 16:7 4074
When Simon P saw it, he fell down Lk 5:8 4074
Simon, (whom he also named P Lk 6:14 4074
When all denied, P and they that Lk 8:45 4074
suffered no man to go in, save P Lk 8:51 4074
P answering said, The Christ of Lk 9:20 4074
after these sayings, he took P Lk 9:28 4074
But P and they that were with him Lk 9:32 4074
P said unto Jesus, Master, it is Lk 9:33 4074
Then P said unto him, Lord, Lk 12:41 4074
Then P said, Lo, we have left all Lk 18:28 4074
And he sent P and John, saying, Go Lk 22:8 4074
And he said, I tell thee, P Lk 22:34 4074
And P followed afar off Lk 22:54 4074

together, P sat down among them ... Lk 22:55 4074
And P said, Man, I am not ... Lk 22:58 4074
P said, Man, I know not what thou ... Lk 22:60 4074
the Lord turned, and looked upon P ... Lk 22:61 4074
P remembered the word of the Lord ... Lk 22:61 4074
P went out, and wept bitterly ... Lk 22:62 4074
Then arose P, and ran unto the ... Lk 24:12 4074
the city of Andrew and P ... Jn 1:44 4074
Then Simon P answered him, Lord, ... Jn 6:68 4074
Then cometh he to Simon P ... Jn 13:6 4074
P saith unto him, Lord, dost thou ... Jn 13:6 4074
P saith unto him, Thou shalt ... Jn 13:8 4074
Simon P saith unto him, Lord, not ... Jn 13:9 4074
Simon P therefore beckoned to him ... Jn 13:24 4074
Simon P said unto him, Lord, ... Jn 13:36 4074
P said unto him, Lord, why cannot ... Jn 13:37 4074
Then Simon P having a sword drew ... Jn 18:10 4074
Then said Jesus unto P, Put up ... Jn 18:11 4074
Simon P followed Jesus, and so did ... Jn 18:15 4074
But P stood at the door without ... Jn 18:16 4074
kept the door, and brought in P ... Jn 18:16 4074
damsel that kept the door unto P ... Jn 18:17 4074
P stood with them, and warmed ... Jn 18:18 4074
And Simon P stood and warmed ... Jn 18:25 4074
his kinsman whose ear P cut off ... Jn 18:26 4074
P then denied again ... Jn 18:27 4074
she runneth, and cometh to Simon P ... Jn 20:2 4074
P therefore went forth, and that ... Jn 20:3 4074
the other disciple did outrun P ... Jn 20:4 4074
Then cometh Simon P following him ... Jn 20:6 4074
There were together Simon P ... Jn 21:2 4074
Simon P saith unto them, I go a ... Jn 21:3 4074
whom Jesus loved saith unto P ... Jn 21:7 4074
Now when Simon P heard that it ... Jn 21:7 4074
Simon P went up, and drew the net ... Jn 21:11 4074
had dined, Jesus saith to Simon P ... Jn 21:15 4074
P was grieved because he said ... Jn 21:17 4074
Then P, turning about, seeth the ... Jn 21:20 4074
P seeing him saith to Jesus, Lord ... Jn 21:21 4074
an upper room, where abode both P ... Acts 1:13 4074
in those days P stood up in the ... Acts 1:15 4074
But P, standing up with the ... Acts 2:14 4074
in their heart, and said unto P ... Acts 2:37 4074
Then P said unto them, Repent, and ... Acts 2:38 4074
Now P and John went up together ... Acts 3:1 4074
Who seeing P and John about to go ... Acts 3:3 4074
And P, fastening his eyes upon him ... Acts 3:4 4074
Then P said, Silver and gold have ... Acts 3:6 4074
lame man which was healed held P ... Acts 3:11 4074
when P saw it, he answered unto ... Acts 3:12 4074
Then P, filled with the Holy ... Acts 4:8 4074
when they saw the boldness of P ... Acts 4:13 4074
But P and John answered and said ... Acts 4:19 4074
But P said, Ananias, why hath ... Acts 5:3 4074
P answered unto her, Tell me ... Acts 5:8 4074
Then P said unto her, How is it ... Acts 5:9 4074
of P passing by might overshadow ... Acts 5:15 4074
Then P and the other apostles ... Acts 5:29 4074
of God, they sent unto them P ... Acts 8:14 4074
But P said unto him, Thy money ... Acts 8:20 4074
as P passed throughout all ... Acts 9:32 4074
P said unto him, Aeneas, Jesus ... Acts 9:34 4074
had heard that P was there ... Acts 9:38 4074
Then P arose and went with them ... Acts 9:39 4074
But P put them all forth, and ... Acts 9:40 4074
and when she saw P, she sat up ... Acts 9:40 4074
for one Simon, whose surname is P ... Acts 10:5 4074
P went up upon the housetop to ... Acts 10:9 4074
came a voice to him, Rise, P ... Acts 10:13 4074
But P said, Not so, Lord ... Acts 10:14 4074
Now while P doubted in himself ... Acts 10:17 4074
Simon, which was surnamed P ... Acts 10:18 4074
While P thought on the vision, ... Acts 10:19 4074
Then P went down to the men which ... Acts 10:21 4074
on the morrow P went away with ... Acts 10:23 4074
as P was coming in, Cornelius met ... Acts 10:25 4074
But P took him up, saying, Stand ... Acts 10:26 4074
hither Simon, whose surname is P ... Acts 10:32 4074
Then P opened his mouth, and said, ... Acts 10:34 4074
While P yet spake these words, ... Acts 10:44 4074
as many as came with P, because ... Acts 10:45 4074
Then answered P, ... Acts 10:46 4074
when P was come up to Jerusalem, ... Acts 11:2 4074
But P rehearsed the matter from ... Acts 11:4 4074
a voice saying unto me, Arise, P ... Acts 11:7 4074
for Simon, whose surname is P ... Acts 11:13 4074
proceeded further to take P also ... Acts 12:3 4074
P therefore was kept in prison ... Acts 12:5 4074
the same night P was sleeping ... Acts 12:6 4074
he smote P on the side, and raised ... Acts 12:7 4074
when P was come to himself, he ... Acts 12:11 4074
as P knocked at the door of the ... Acts 12:13 4074
told how P stood before the gate ... Acts 12:14 4074
But P continued knocking ... Acts 12:16 4074
soldiers, what was become of P ... Acts 12:18 4074
P rose up, and said unto them, Men ... Acts 15:7 4074
I went up to Jerusalem to see P ... Gal 1:18 4074
of the circumcision was unto P ... Gal 2:7 4074
in P to the apostleship of the ... Gal 2:8 4074
But when P was come to Antioch, I ... Gal 2:11 4074
I said unto P before them all, If ... Gal 2:14 4074
P, an apostle of Jesus Christ, to ... 1Pet 1:1 4074
Simon P, a servant and an apostle ... 2Pet 1:1 4074

PETER'S (*pe'-turz*)
when Jesus was come into P house ... Mt 8:14 4074
him, was Andrew, Simon P brother ... Jn 1:40 4074
Simon P brother, saith unto him, ... Jn 6:8 4074
And when she knew P voice, she ... Acts 12:14 4074

PETHAHIAH (*peth-a-hi'-ah*)
1. A sanctuary servant.
The nineteenth to P, the ... 1Chr 24:16 6611
2. Married a foreigner.
Kelaiah, (the same is Kelita,) P ... Ezr 10:23 6611
3. A Levite who helped Ezra.
Hodijah, Shebaniah, and P ... Neh 9:5 6611
4. An aide to Nehemiah.
P the son of Meshezabeel, of the ... Neh 11:24 6611

PETHOR (*pe'-thor*) *A city in Mesopotamia.*
unto Balaam the son of Beor to P ... Num 22:5 6604
son of Beor of P of Mesopotamia ... Deut 23:4 6604

PETHUEL *Father of Joel the prophet.*
that came to Joel the son of P ... Joel 1:1 6602

PETITION
thy p that thou hast asked of him ... 1Sa 1:17 7596
me my p which I asked of him ... 1Sa 1:27 7596
And now I ask one p of thee ... 1Kin 2:16 7596
I desire one small p of thee ... 1Kin 2:20 7596
banquet of wine, What is thy p ... Est 5:6 7596
answered Esther, and said, My p ... Est 5:7 7596
it please the king to grant my p ... Est 5:8 7596
banquet of wine, What is thy p ... Est 7:2 7596
let my life be given me at my p ... Est 7:3 7596
now what is thy p ... Est 9:12 7596
that whosoever shall ask a p of ... Dan 6:7 1159
p of any God or man within thirty ... Dan 6:12
but maketh his p three times a ... Dan 6:13 1159

PETITIONS
the LORD fulfil all thy p ... Ps 20:5 4862
have the p that we desired of him ... 1Jn 5:15 155

PEULLETHAI See PEULTHAI.

PEULTHAI (*pe-ul'-thahee*) *A sanctuary servant.*
the seventh, P the eighth ... 1Chr 26:5 6469

PHALEC (*fa'-lek*) See PELEG. *Father of Ragau; ancestor of Jesus.*
of Ragau, which was the son of P ... Lk 3:35 5317

PHALLU (*fal'-lu*) *Son of Reuben.*
Hanoch, and P, and Hezron ... Gen 46:9 6396

PHALTI (*fal'-ti*) See PHALTIEL. *Son of Laish.*
to P the son of Laish, which was ... 1Sa 25:44 6406

PHALTIEL (*fal'-te-el*) See PHALTI. *Same as Phalti.*
even from P the son of Laish ... 2Sa 3:15 6409

PHANUEL (*fan-u'-el*) *Mother of Anna.*
a prophetess, the daughter of P ... Lk 2:36 5323

PHARAOH (*fa'-ra-o*) See PHARAOH'S, PHARAOH-HOPHRA, PHARAOH-NECHO.
1. Ruler of Egypt in Abraham's time.
The princes also of P saw her ... Gen 12:15 6547
and commended her before P ... Gen 12:15 6547
And the LORD plagued P and his ... Gen 12:17 6547
P called Abram, and said, What is ... Gen 12:18 6547
P commanded his men concerning ... Gen 12:20 6547
2. Ruler of Egypt in Joseph's time.
and Potiphar, an officer of P ... Gen 39:1 6547
P was wroth against two of his ... Gen 40:2 6547
days shall P lift up thine head ... Gen 40:13 6547
me, and make mention of me unto P ... Gen 40:14 6547
of all manner of bakemeats for P ... Gen 40:17 6547
Yet within three days shall P ... Gen 40:19 6547
of two full years, that P dreamed ... Gen 41:1 6547
So P awoke ... Gen 41:4 6547
P awoke, and, behold, it was a ... Gen 41:7 6547
and P told them his dream ... Gen 41:8 6547
that could interpret them unto P ... Gen 41:8 6547
spake the chief butler unto P ... Gen 41:9 6547
P was wroth with his servants, and ... Gen 41:10 6547
Then P sent and called Joseph, and ... Gen 41:14 6547
his raiment, and came in unto P ... Gen 41:14 6547
P said unto Joseph, I have ... Gen 41:15 6547
And Joseph answered P, saying, It ... Gen 41:16 6547
God shall give P an answer of ... Gen 41:16 6547
P said unto Joseph, In my dream, ... Gen 41:17 6547
And Joseph said unto P ... Gen 41:25 6547
The dream of P is one ... Gen 41:25 6547
God hath shewed P what he is ... Gen 41:25 6547
thing which I have spoken unto P ... Gen 41:28 6547
is about to do he sheweth unto P ... Gen 41:28 6547
dream was doubled unto P twice ... Gen 41:32 6547
Now therefore let P look out a ... Gen 41:33 6547
Let P do this, and let him appoint ... Gen 41:34 6547
lay up corn under the hand of P ... Gen 41:35 6547
thing was good in the eyes of P ... Gen 41:37 6547
P said unto his servants, Can we ... Gen 41:38 6547
P said unto Joseph, Forasmuch as ... Gen 41:39 6547
P said unto Joseph, See, I have ... Gen 41:41 6547
P took off his ring from his hand ... Gen 41:42 6547
P said unto Joseph, I am Pharaoh, ... Gen 41:44 6547
And P called Joseph's name ... Gen 41:45 6547
he stood before P king of Egypt ... Gen 41:46 6547
went out from the presence of P ... Gen 41:46 6547
the people cried to P for bread ... Gen 41:55 6547
P said unto all the Egyptians, Go ... Gen 41:55 6547
By the life of P ye shall not go ... Gen 42:15 6547
the life of P surely ye are spies ... Gen 42:16 6547
for thou art even as P ... Gen 44:18 6547
Egyptians and the house of P heard ... Gen 45:2 6547
and he hath made me a father to P ... Gen 45:8 6547
and it pleased P well, and his ... Gen 45:16 6547
P said unto Joseph, Say unto thy ... Gen 45:17 6547
according to the commandment of P ... Gen 45:21 6547
in the wagons which P had sent to ... Gen 46:5 6547
house, I will go up, and shew P ... Gen 46:31 6547
when P shall call you, and shall ... Gen 46:33 6547
Then Joseph came and told P ... Gen 47:1 6547
men, and presented them unto P ... Gen 47:2 6547
P said unto his brethren, What is ... Gen 47:3 6547
And they said unto P, Thy servants ... Gen 47:3 6547
They said moreover unto P ... Gen 47:4 6547
P spake unto Joseph, saying, Thy ... Gen 47:5 6547
his father, and set him before P ... Gen 47:7 6547
and Jacob blessed P ... Gen 47:7 6547
P said unto Jacob, How old art ... Gen 47:8 6547
And Jacob said unto P, The days of ... Gen 47:9 6547
And Jacob blessed P ... Gen 47:10 6547
and went out from before P ... Gen 47:10 6547
of Rameses, as P had commanded ... Gen 47:11 6547
our land will be servants unto P ... Gen 47:19 6547
all the land of Egypt for P ... Gen 47:20 6547
had a portion assigned them of P ... Gen 47:22 6547
their portion which P gave them ... Gen 47:22 6547
you this day and your land for P ... Gen 47:23 6547
shall give the fifth part unto P ... Gen 47:24 6547
that P should have the fifth part ... Gen 47:26 6547
Joseph spake unto the house of P ... Gen 50:4 6547
I pray you, in the ears of P ... Gen 50:4 6547
P said, Go up, and bury thy father ... Gen 50:6 6547
him went up all the servants of P ... Gen 50:7 6547
in the sight of P king of Egypt ... Acts 7:10 5328
kindred was made known unto P ... Acts 7:13 5328
3. Ruler of Egypt during Moses' infancy.
they built for P treasure cities, ... Ex 1:11 6547
And the midwives said unto P ... Ex 1:19 6547
P charged all his people, saying, ... Ex 1:22 6547
the daughter of P came down to ... Ex 2:5 6547
4. Ruler of Egypt during Moses' adulthood.
Now when P heard this thing, he ... Ex 2:15 6547
But Moses fled from the face of P ... Ex 2:15 6547
5. Ruler of Egypt when Moses returned to Egypt.
and I will send thee unto P ... Ex 3:10 6547
Who am I, that I should go unto P ... Ex 3:11 6547
do all those wonders before P ... Ex 4:21 6547
And thou shalt say unto P, Thus ... Ex 4:22 6547
Moses and Aaron went in, and told P ... Ex 5:1 6547
P said, Who is the LORD, that I ... Ex 5:2 6547
P said, Behold, the people of the ... Ex 5:5 6547
P commanded the same day the ... Ex 5:6 6547
the people, saying, Thus saith P ... Ex 5:10 6547
of Israel came and cried unto P ... Ex 5:15 6547
way, as they came forth from P ... Ex 5:20 6547
to be abhorred in the eyes of P ... Ex 5:21 6547
For since I came to P to speak in ... Ex 5:23 6547
thou see what I will do to P ... Ex 6:1 6547
speak unto P king of Egypt, that ... Ex 6:11 6547
how then shall P hear me, who am ... Ex 6:12 6547
unto P king of Egypt, to bring ... Ex 6:13 6547
which spake to P king of Egypt ... Ex 6:27 6547
speak thou unto P king of Egypt ... Ex 6:29 6547
how shall P hearken unto me ... Ex 6:30 6547
See, I have made thee a god to P ... Ex 7:1 6547
thy brother shall speak unto P ... Ex 7:2 6547
But P shall not hearken unto you, ... Ex 7:4 6547
years old, when they spake unto P ... Ex 7:7 6547
When P shall speak unto you, ... Ex 7:9 6547
Take thy rod, and cast it before P ... Ex 7:9 6547
And Moses and Aaron went in unto P. ... Ex 7:10 6547
Aaron cast down his rod before P ... Ex 7:10 6547
Then P also called the wise men ... Ex 7:11 6547
Get thee unto P in the morning ... Ex 7:15 6547
in the river, in the sight of P ... Ex 7:20 6547
P turned and went into his house, ... Ex 7:23 6547
LORD spake unto Moses, Go unto P ... Ex 8:1 6547
Then P called for Moses and Aaron, ... Ex 8:8 6547
And Moses said unto P, Glory over ... Ex 8:9 6547
and Aaron went out from P ... Ex 8:12 6547
which he had brought against P ... Ex 8:12 6547
But when P saw that there was ... Ex 8:15 6547
Then the magicians said unto P ... Ex 8:19 6547
in the morning, and stand before P ... Ex 8:20 6547
of flies into the house of P ... Ex 8:24 6547
P called for Moses and for Aaron, ... Ex 8:25 6547
P said, I will let you go, that ... Ex 8:28 6547
swarms of flies may depart from P ... Ex 8:29 6547
but let not P deal deceitfully ... Ex 8:29 6547
And Moses went out from P, and ... Ex 8:30 6547
the swarms of flies from P ... Ex 8:31 6547
P hardened his heart at this time ... Ex 8:32 6547
said unto Moses, Go in unto P ... Ex 9:1 6547
P sent, and, behold, there was not ... Ex 9:7 6547
And the heart of P was hardened ... Ex 9:7 6547
the heaven in the sight of P ... Ex 9:8 6547
of the furnace, and stood before P ... Ex 9:10 6547
the LORD hardened the heart of P ... Ex 9:12 6547
in the morning, and stand before P ... Ex 9:13 6547
servants of P made his servants ... Ex 9:20 6547
P sent, and called for Moses and ... Ex 9:27 6547
Moses went out of the city from P ... Ex 9:33 6547
when P saw that the rain and the ... Ex 9:34 6547
And the heart of P was hardened ... Ex 9:35 6547
said unto Moses, Go in unto P ... Ex 10:1 6547
And Moses and Aaron came in unto P ... Ex 10:3 6547
himself, and went out from P ... Ex 10:6 6547
Aaron were brought again unto P ... Ex 10:8 6547
Then P called for Moses and Aaron ... Ex 10:16 6547
And he went out from P, and ... Ex 10:18 6547
P called unto Moses, and said, Go ... Ex 10:24 6547
P said unto him, Get thee from me ... Ex 10:28 6547
I bring one plague more upon P ... Ex 11:1 6547
from the firstborn of P that ... Ex 11:5 6547
went out from P in a great anger ... Ex 11:8 6547
P shall not hearken unto you ... Ex 11:9 6547
did all these wonders before P ... Ex 11:10 6547
from the firstborn of P that sat ... Ex 12:29 6547
P rose up in the night, he, and ... Ex 12:30 6547
when P would hardly let us go, ... Ex 13:15 6547
when P had let the people go, ... Ex 13:17 6547
For P will say of the children of ... Ex 14:3 6547
and I will be honoured upon P ... Ex 14:4 6547
and the heart of P and of his ... Ex 14:5 6547
the heart of P king of Egypt ... Ex 14:8 6547
all the horses and chariots of P ... Ex 14:9 6547
when P drew nigh, the children of ... Ex 14:10 6547
and I will get me honour upon P ... Ex 14:17 6547
I have gotten me honour upon P ... Ex 14:18 6547

all the host of P that came into ... Ex 14:28 6547
For the horse of P went in with ... Ex 15:19 6547
delivered me from the sword of P ... Ex 18:4 6547
all that the LORD had done unto P ... Ex 18:8 6547
and out of the hand of P, who ... Ex 18:10 6547
great and sore, upon Egypt, upon P ... Deut 6:22 6547
from the hand of P king of Egypt ... Deut 7:8 6547
what the LORD thy God did unto P ... Deut 7:18 6547
of Egypt unto P the king of Egypt ... Deut 11:3 6547
eyes in the land of Egypt unto P ... Deut 29:2 6547
to do in the land of Egypt to P ... Deut 34:11 6547
and P hardened their hearts ... 1Sa 6:6 6547
under the hand of P king of Egypt ... 2Kin 17:7 6547
shewedst signs and wonders upon P ... Neh 9:10 6547
midst of thee, O Egypt, upon P ... Ps 135:9 6547
But overthrew P and his host in ... Ps 136:15 6547
For the scripture saith unto P ... Rom 9:17 5328

6. Ruler of Egypt in Solomon's time.
affinity with P king of Egypt ... 1Kin 3:1 6547
For P king of Egypt had gone up, ... 1Kin 9:16 6547
together with the daughter of P ... 1Kin 11:1 6547
to Egypt, unto P king of Egypt ... 1Kin 11:18 6547
great favour in the sight of P ... 1Kin 11:19 6547
household among the sons of P ... 1Kin 11:20 6547
host was dead, Hadad said to P ... 1Kin 11:21 6547
Then P said unto him, But what ... 1Kin 11:22 6547
brought up the daughter of P out ... 2Chr 8:11 6547

7. Ruler of Egypt in Isaiah's time.
of P is become brutish ... Is 19:11 6547
how say ye unto P, I am the son ... Is 19:11 6547
themselves in the strength of P ... Is 30:2 6547
the strength of P be your shame ... Is 30:3 6547
so is P king of Egypt to all that ... Is 36:6 6547

8. Ruler of Egypt in Jeremiah's time.
so is P king of Egypt unto all ... 2Kin 18:21 6547
gave the silver and the gold to P ... 2Kin 23:35 6547
according to the commandment of P ... 2Kin 23:35 6547
sons of Bithiah the daughter of P ... 1Chr 4:18 6547
P king of Egypt, and his servants, ... Jer 25:19 6547
P king of Egypt is but a noise ... Jer 46:17 6547
punish the multitude of No, and P ... Jer 46:25 6547
even P, and all them that trust in ... Jer 46:25 6547
before that P smote Gaza ... Jer 47:1 6547
Neither shall P with his mighty ... Eze 17:17 6547
thy face against P king of Egypt ... Eze 29:2 6547
P king of Egypt, the great dragon ... Eze 29:3 6547
broken the arm of P king of Egypt ... Eze 30:21 6547
I am against P king of Egypt, and ... Eze 30:22 6547
the arms of P shall fall down ... Eze 30:25 6547
speak unto P king of Egypt, and to ... Eze 31:2 6547
This is P and all his multitude, ... Eze 31:18 6547
a lamentation for P king of Egypt ... Eze 32:2 6547
P shall see them, and shall be ... Eze 32:31 6547
over all his multitude, even P ... Eze 32:31 6547
are slain with the sword, even P ... Eze 32:32 6547

PHARAOH-HOPHRA (*fa''-ra-o-hof'-rah*) *Same as Pharaoh 8.*
I will give P king of Egypt into ... Jer 44:30 6548

PHARAOH-NECHO (*fa''-ra-o-ne'-ko*) See PHARAOH-NECHOH. *Egyptian ruler during Josiah's time.*
the army of P king of Egypt ... Jer 46:2 6549

PHARAOH-NECHOH (*fa''-ra-o-ne'-ko*) See PHARAOH-NECHO. *Same as Pharaoh-necho.*
In his days P king of Egypt went ... 2Kin 23:29 6549
P put him in bands at Riblah in ... 2Kin 23:33 6549
P made Eliakim the son of Josiah ... 2Kin 23:34 6549
his taxation, to give it unto P ... 2Kin 23:35 6549

PHARAOH'S (*fa'-ra-oze*)
the woman was taken into P house ... Gen 12:15 6547
unto Potiphar, an officer of P ... Gen 37:36 6547
he asked P officers that were ... Gen 40:7 6547
And P cup was in my hand ... Gen 40:11 6547
and pressed them into P cup ... Gen 40:11 6547
and I gave the cup into P hand ... Gen 40:11 6547
shalt deliver P cup into his hand ... Gen 40:13 6547
third day, which was P birthday ... Gen 40:20 6547
and he gave the cup into P hand ... Gen 40:21 6547
fame thereof was heard in P house ... Gen 45:16 6547
brought the money into P house ... Gen 47:14 6547
so the land became P ... Gen 47:20 6547
my lord, and we will be P servants ... Gen 47:25 6547
priests only, which became not P ... Gen 47:26 6547
said his sister to P daughter ... Ex 2:7 6547
P daughter said to her, Go ... Ex 2:8 6547
P daughter said unto her, Take ... Ex 2:9 6547
she brought him unto P daughter ... Ex 2:10 6547
which P taskmasters had set over ... Ex 5:14 6547
And I will harden P heart, and ... Ex 7:3 6547
And he hardened P heart, that he ... Ex 7:13 6547
P heart is hardened, he refuseth ... Ex 7:14 6547
P heart was hardened, neither did ... Ex 7:22 6547
P heart was hardened, and he ... Ex 8:19 6547
P servants said unto him, How ... Ex 10:7 6547
were driven out from P presence ... Ex 10:11 6547
But the LORD hardened P heart ... Ex 10:20 6547
But the LORD hardened P heart ... Ex 10:27 6547
Egypt, in the sight of P servants ... Ex 11:3 6547
and the LORD hardened P heart ... Ex 11:10 6547
And I will harden P heart, that he ... Ex 14:4 6547
of the sea, even all P horses ... Ex 14:23 6547
P chariots and his host hath he ... Ex 15:4 6547
We were P bondmen in Egypt ... Deut 6:21 6547
they were in Egypt in P house ... 1Sa 2:27 6547
took P daughter, and brought her ... 1Kin 3:1 6547
made also an house for P daughter ... 1Kin 7:8 6547
But P daughter came up out of the ... 1Kin 9:24 6547
whom Tahpenes weaned in P house ... 1Kin 11:20 6547
Genubath was in P household among ... 1Kin 11:20 6547
a company of horses in P chariots ... Song 1:9 6547
Then P army was come forth out of ... Jer 37:5 6547
P army, which is come forth to ... Jer 37:7 6547
from Jerusalem for fear of P army ... Jer 37:11 6547
the entry of P house in Tahpanhes ... Jer 43:9 6547
but I will break P arms, and he ... Eze 30:24 6547
P daughter took him up, and ... Acts 7:21 5328
be called the son of P daughter ... Heb 11:24 5328

PHARES (*fa'-rez*) See PHAREZ. *Same as Pharez.*
And Judas begat P and Zara of ... Mt 1:3 5329
and P begat Esrom ... Mt 1:3 5329
of Esrom, which was the son of P ... Lk 3:33 5329

PHAREZ (*fa'-rez*) See PEREZ, PHARES, PHARZITES. *A son of Judah.*
therefore his name was called P ... Gen 38:29 6557
Er, and Onan, and Shelah, and P ... Gen 46:12 6557
And the sons of P were Hezron ... Gen 46:12 6557
of P, the family of the Pharzites ... Num 26:20 6557
And the sons of P were ... Num 26:21 6557
thy house be like the house of P ... Ruth 4:12 6557
these are the generations of P ... Ruth 4:18 6557
P begat Hezron, ... Ruth 4:18 6557
his daughter in law bare him P ... 1Chr 2:4 6557
The sons of P ... 1Chr 2:5 6557
P, Hezron, and Carmi, and Hur, and ... 1Chr 4:1 6557
children of P the son of Judah ... 1Chr 9:4 6557

PHARISAIC See PHARISEES.

PHARISEE (*far'-i-see*) See PHARISEE'S, PHARISEES. *A member of a Jewish sect.*
Thou blind P, cleanse first that ... Mt 23:26 5330
Now when the P which had bidden ... Lk 7:39 5330
a certain P besought him to dine ... Lk 11:37 5330
And when the P saw it, he ... Lk 11:38 5330
the one a P, and the other a ... Lk 18:10 5330
The P stood and prayed thus with ... Lk 18:11 5330
there up one in the council, a P ... Acts 5:34 5330
I am a P, the son of a P ... Acts 23:6 5330
sect of our religion I lived a P ... Acts 26:5 5330
as touching the law, a P ... Phil 3:5 5330

PHARISEE'S (*far'-i-seze*)
And he went into the P house ... Lk 7:36 5330
Jesus sat at meat in the P house ... Lk 7:37 5330

PHARISEES (*far'-i-seze*) See PHARISEES'. *A Jewish sect.*
But when he saw many of the P ... Mt 3:7 5330
righteousness of the scribes and P ... Mt 5:20 5330
And when the P saw it, they said ... Mt 9:11 5330
the P fast oft, but thy disciples ... Mt 9:14 5330
But the P said, He casteth out ... Mt 9:34 5330
But when the P saw it, they said ... Mt 12:2 5330
Then the P went out, and held a ... Mt 12:14 5330
But when the P heard it, they ... Mt 12:24 5330
of the P answered, saying, Master ... Mt 12:38 5330
Then came to Jesus scribes and P ... Mt 15:1 5330
thou that the P were offended ... Mt 15:12 5330
The P also with the Sadducees ... Mt 16:1 5330
and beware of the leaven of the P ... Mt 16:6 5330
beware of the leaven of the P ... Mt 16:11 5330
but of the doctrine of the P ... Mt 16:12 5330
The P also came unto him, ... Mt 19:3 5330
P had heard his parables, they ... Mt 21:45 5330
Then went the P, and took counsel ... Mt 22:15 5330
But when the P had heard that he ... Mt 22:34 5330
While the P were gathered ... Mt 22:41 5330
and the P sit in Moses' seat ... Mt 23:2 5330
But woe unto you, scribes and P ... Mt 23:13 5330
Woe unto you, scribes and P ... Mt 23:14 5330
Woe unto you, scribes and P ... Mt 23:15 5330
Woe unto you, scribes and P ... Mt 23:23 5330
Woe unto you, scribes and P ... Mt 23:25 5330
Woe unto you, scribes and P ... Mt 23:27 5330
Woe unto you, scribes and P ... Mt 23:29 5330
P came together unto Pilate, ... Mt 27:62 5330
P saw him eat with publicans and ... Mk 2:16 5330
of John and of the P used to fast ... Mk 2:18 5330
of John and of the P fast, but thy ... Mk 2:18 5330
the P said unto him, Behold, why ... Mk 2:24 5330
the P went forth, and straightway ... Mk 3:6 5330
Then came together unto him the P ... Mk 7:1 5330
For the P, and all the Jews, ... Mk 7:3 5330
Then the P and scribes asked him, ... Mk 7:5 5330
the P came forth, and began to ... Mk 8:11 5330
beware of the leaven of the P ... Mk 8:15 5330
the P came to him, and asked him, ... Mk 10:2 5330
send unto him certain of the P ... Mk 12:13 5330
was teaching, that there were P ... Lk 5:17 5330
the P began to reason, saying, ... Lk 5:21 5330
P murmured against his disciples, ... Lk 5:30 5330
likewise the disciples of the P ... Lk 5:33 5330
certain of the P said unto them ... Lk 6:2 5330
P watched him, whether he would ... Lk 6:7 5330
But the P and lawyers rejected the ... Lk 7:30 5330
one of the P desired him that he ... Lk 7:36 5330
Now do ye P make clean the ... Lk 11:39 5330
But woe unto you, P ... Lk 11:42 5330
Woe unto you, P ... Lk 11:43 5330
Woe unto you, scribes and P ... Lk 11:44 5330
and the P began to urge him ... Lk 11:53 5330
Beware ye of the leaven of the P ... Lk 12:1 5330
day there came certain of the P ... Lk 13:31 5330
the house of one of the chief P ... Lk 14:1 5330
spake unto the lawyers and P ... Lk 14:3 5330
And the P and scribes murmured, ... Lk 15:2 5330
the P also, who were covetous, ... Lk 16:14 5330
And when he was demanded of the P ... Lk 17:20 5330
some of the P from among the ... Lk 19:39 5330
which were sent were of the P ... Jn 1:24 5330
There was a man of the P, named ... Jn 3:1 5330
the P had heard that Jesus made ... Jn 4:1 5330
The P heard that the people ... Jn 7:32 5330
and the P and the chief priests ... Jn 7:32 5330
to the chief priests and P ... Jn 7:45 5330
Then answered them the P, Are ye ... Jn 7:47 5330
or of the P believed on him ... Jn 7:48 5330
P brought unto him a woman taken ... Jn 8:3 5330
The P therefore said unto him, ... Jn 8:13 5330
They brought to the P him that ... Jn 9:13 5330
Then again the P also asked him ... Jn 9:15 5330
Therefore said some of the P ... Jn 9:16 5330
some of the P which were with him ... Jn 9:40 5330
of them went their ways to the P ... Jn 11:46 5330
the P a council, and said, What do ... Jn 11:47 5330
the P had given a commandment, ... Jn 11:57 5330
The P therefore said among ... Jn 12:19 5330
but because of the P they did not ... Jn 12:42 5330
from the chief priests and P ... Jn 18:3 5330
the sect of the P which believed ... Acts 15:5 5330
were Sadducees, and the other P ... Acts 23:6 5330
arose a dissension between the P ... Acts 23:7 5330
but the P confess both ... Acts 23:8 5330

PHARISEES' (*far'-i-seez*)
that were of the P part arose ... Acts 23:9 5330

PHAROSH (*fa'-rosh*) *A family of exiles.*
of Shechaniah, of the sons of P ... Ezr 8:3 6551

PHARPAR (*far'-par*) *A river near Damascus.*
Are not Abana and P, rivers of ... 2Kin 5:12 6554

PHARZITES (*far'-zites*) *Descendants of Pharez.*
of Pharez, the family of the P ... Num 26:20 6558

PHASEAH (*fa-se'-ah*) See PASEAH. *A family of exiles.*
of Uzza, the children of P ... Neh 7:51 6454

PHEBE (*fe'-be*) *A Christian acquaintance of Paul.*
I commend unto you P our sister ... Rom 16:1 5402
sent by P servant of the church ... Rom s 5402

PHENICE (*fe-ni'-se*) See PHENICIA.
1. Same as Phenecia.
Stephen travelled as far as P ... Acts 11:19 5403
the church, they passed through P ... Acts 15:3 5403
2. A harbor on Crete.
any means they might attain to P ... Acts 27:12 5405

PHENICIA (*fe-nish'-e-ah*) See PHENICE. *Coastal region of northern Palestine.*
a ship sailing over unto P ... Acts 21:2 5403

PHICHOL *The commander of Abimelech's army.*
P the chief captain of his host ... Gen 21:22 6369
P the chief captain of his host, ... Gen 21:32 6369
P the chief captain of his army ... Gen 26:26 6369

PHICOL (*fi'-col*) See PHICHOL. *A Philistine commander.*

PHILADELPHIA (*fil-a-del'-fe-ah*) *A city in Lydia in Asia Minor.*
and unto Sardis, and unto P ... Rev 1:11 5359
angel of the church in P write ... Rev 3:7 5359

PHILEMON (*fi-le'-mon*) *A recipient of a New Testament epistle.*
unto P our dearly beloved, and ... Philem 1 5371
Written from Rome to P, by ... Philem s 5371

PHILETUS (*fi-le'tus*) *A false Christian teacher.*
of whom is Hymenaeus and P ... 2Ti 2:17 5372

PHILIP (*fil'-ip*) See PHILIP'S.
1. An apostle.
P, and Bartholomew ... Mt 10:3 5376
and P, and Bartholomew, ... Mk 3:18 5376
his brother, James and John, P ... Lk 6:14 5376
forth into Galilee, and findeth P ... Jn 1:43 5376
Now P was of Bethsaida, the city ... Jn 1:44 5376
P findeth Nathanael, and saith ... Jn 1:45 5376
P saith unto him, Come and see ... Jn 1:46 5376
him, Before that P called thee ... Jn 1:48 5376
come unto him, he saith unto P ... Jn 6:5 5376
P answered him, Two hundred ... Jn 6:7 5376
The same came therefore to P ... Jn 12:21 5376
P cometh and telleth Andrew ... Jn 12:22 5376
and again Andrew and P tell Jesus ... Jn 12:22 5376
P saith unto him, Lord, shew us ... Jn 14:8 5376
and yet hast thou not known me, P ... Jn 14:9 5376
and James, and John, and Andrew, P ... Acts 1:13 5376
2. A son of Herod the Great.
his brother P tetrarch of Ituraea ... Lk 3:1 5376
3. The evangelist.
faith and of the Holy Ghost, and P ... Acts 6:5 5376
Then P went down to the city of ... Acts 8:5 5376
unto those things which P spake ... Acts 8:6 5376
But when they believed P ... Acts 8:12 5376
was baptized, he continued with P ... Acts 8:13 5376
angel of the Lord spake unto P ... Acts 8:26 5376
Then the Spirit said unto P ... Acts 8:29 5376
P ran thither to him, and heard ... Acts 8:30 5376
he desired P that he would come ... Acts 8:31 5376
And the eunuch answered P, and said ... Acts 8:34 5376
Then P opened his mouth, and began ... Acts 8:35 5376
P said, If thou believest with ... Acts 8:37 5376
down both into the water, both P ... Acts 8:38 5376
Spirit of the Lord caught away P ... Acts 8:39 5376
But P was found at Azotus ... Acts 8:40 5376
the house of P the evangelist ... Acts 21:8 5376

PHILIPPI (*fil-ip'-pi*) See PHILIPPIANS.
1. A town in northern Palestine.
into the coasts of Caesarea P ... Mt 16:13 5375
into the towns of Caesarea P ... Mk 8:27 5375
2. A Macedonian city.
And from thence to P, which is the ... Acts 16:12 5375
we sailed away from P after the ... Acts 20:6 5375
was written from P by Stephanus ... 1Cor s 5375
Corinthians was written from P ... 2Cor s 5375
in Christ Jesus which are at P ... Phil 1:1 5375
entreated, as ye know, at P ... 1Th 2:2 5375

PHILIPPIANS (*fil-ip'-pe-uns*) *Residents of Philippi 2.*
Now ye *P* know also, that in the Phil 4:15 *5374*
It was written to the *P* from Rome Phil s

PHILIP'S (*fil'-ips*) *Refers to Philip 2.*
sake, his brother *P* wife Mt 14:3 *5376*
sake, his brother *P* wife Mk 6:17 *5376*
for Herodias his brother *P* wife Lk 3:19 *5376*

PHILISTIA (*fil-is'-te-ah*) See PALESTINE, PHILISTINE. *Land of the Philistines.*
P, triumph thou because of me Ps 60:8 6429
behold *P*, and Tyre, with Ethiopia Ps 87:4 6429
over *P* will I triumph Ps 108:9 6429

PHILISTIM (*fil-is'-tim*) See PHILISTINES. *Descendents of Casluhim.*
and Casluhim, (out of whom came *P*... Gen 10:14 6430

PHILISTINE (*fil-is'-tin*) See PHILISTINES. *An inhabitant of Philistia.*
am not I a *P*, and ye servants to 1Sa 17:8 6430
the *P* said, I defy the armies of 1Sa 17:10 6430
Israel heard those words of the *P* 1Sa 17:11 6430
the *P* drew near morning and 1Sa 17:16 6430
the *P* of Gath, Goliath by name, 1Sa 17:23 6430
to the man that killeth this *P* 1Sa 17:26 6430
for who is this uncircumcised *P* 1Sa 17:26 6430
will go and fight with this *P* 1Sa 17:32 6430
against this *P* to fight with him 1Sa 17:33 6430
this uncircumcised *P* shall be as 1Sa 17:36 6430
me out of the hand of this *P* 1Sa 17:37 6430
and he drew near to the *P* 1Sa 17:40 6430
the *P* came on and drew near unto 1Sa 17:41 6430
when the *P* looked about, and saw 1Sa 17:42 6430
the *P* said unto David, Am I a dog 1Sa 17:43 6430
the *P* cursed David by his gods 1Sa 17:43 6430
the *P* said to David, Come to me, 1Sa 17:44 6430
Then said David to the *P*, Thou 1Sa 17:45 6430
it came to pass, when the *P* arose 1Sa 17:48 6430
ran toward the army to meet the *P* 1Sa 17:48 6430
smote the *P* in his forehead, that 1Sa 17:49 6430
prevailed over the *P* with a sling 1Sa 17:50 6430
and with a stone, and smote the *P* 1Sa 17:50 6430
David ran, and stood upon the *P* 1Sa 17:51 6430
And David took the head of the *P* 1Sa 17:54 6430
saw David go forth against the *P* 1Sa 17:55 6430
from the slaughter of the *P* 1Sa 17:57 6430
the head of the *P* in his hand 1Sa 17:57 6430
from the slaughter of the *P* 1Sa 18:6 6430
life in his hand, and slew the *P* 1Sa 19:5 6430
said, The sword of Goliath the *P* 1Sa 21:9 6430
him the sword of Goliath the *P* 1Sa 22:10 6430
succoured him, and smote the *P* 2Sa 21:17 6430

PHILISTINES (*fil-is'-tinz*) See PHILISTIM, PHILISTINES'.
returned into the land of the *P* Gen 21:32 6430
king of the *P* unto Gerar Gen 26:1 6430
of the *P* looked out at a window Gen 26:8 6430
and the *P* envied him Gen 26:14 6430
the *P* had stopped them, and filled Gen 26:15 6430
for the *P* had stopped them after Gen 26:18 6430
the way of the land of the *P* Ex 13:17 6430
sea even unto the sea of the *P* Ex 23:31 6430
all the borders of the *P*, and all Josh 13:2 6430
five lords of the *P* Josh 13:3 6430
Namely, five lords of the *P* Judg 3:3 6430
which slew of the *P* six hundred Judg 3:31 6430
of Ammon, and the gods of the *P* Judg 10:6 6430
sold them into the hands of the *P* Judg 10:7 6430
children of Ammon, and from the *P* Judg 10:11 6430
the hand of the *P* forty years Judg 13:1 6430
Israel out of the hand of the *P* Judg 13:5 6430
Timnath of the daughters of the *P* Judg 14:1 6430
Timnath of the daughters of the *P* Judg 14:2 6430
a wife of the uncircumcised *P* Judg 14:3 6430
sought an occasion against the *P* Judg 14:4 6430
for at that time the *P* had Judg 14:4 6430
I be more blameless than the *P* Judg 15:3 6430
into the standing corn of the *P* Judg 15:5 6430
Then the *P* said, Who hath done Judg 15:6 6430
the *P* came up, and burnt her and Judg 15:6 6430
Then the *P* went up, and pitched in Judg 15:9 6430
not that the *P* are rulers over us Judg 15:11 6430
thee into the hand of the *P* Judg 15:12 6430
the *P* shouted against him Judg 15:14 6430
in the days of the *P* twenty years Judg 15:20 6430
lords of the *P* came up unto her Judg 16:5 6430
Then the lords of the *P* brought Judg 16:8 6430
The *P* be upon thee, Samson Judg 16:9 6430
The *P* be upon thee, Samson Judg 16:12 6430
The *P* be upon thee, Samson Judg 16:14 6430
and called for the lords of the *P* Judg 16:18 6430
lords of the *P* came up unto her Judg 16:18 6430
The *P* be upon thee, Samson Judg 16:20 6430
But the *P* took him, and put out Judg 16:21 6430
Then the lords of the *P* gathered Judg 16:23 6430
all the lords of the *P* were there Judg 16:27 6430
avenged of the *P* for my two eyes Judg 16:28 6430
said, Let me die with the *P* Judg 16:30 6430
went out against the *P* to battle 1Sa 4:1 6430
and the *P* pitched in Aphek 1Sa 4:1 6430
the *P* put themselves in array 1Sa 4:2 6430
Israel was smitten before the *P* 1Sa 4:2 6430
smitten us to day before the *P* 1Sa 4:3 6430
when the *P* heard the noise of the 1Sa 4:6 6430
the *P* were afraid, for they said 1Sa 4:7 6430
quit yourselves like men, O ye *P* 1Sa 4:9 6430
the *P* fought, and Israel was 1Sa 4:10 6430
said, Israel is fled before the *P* 1Sa 4:17 6430
the *P* took the ark of God, and 1Sa 5:1 6430
When the *P* took the ark of God, 1Sa 5:2 6430
all the lords of the *P* unto them 1Sa 5:8 6430
together all the lords of the *P* 1Sa 5:11 6430
the country of the *P* seven months 1Sa 6:1 6430
the *P* called for the priests and 1Sa 6:2 6430
the number of the lords of the *P* 1Sa 6:4 6430
the lords of the *P* went after 1Sa 6:12 6430
five lords of the *P* had seen it 1Sa 6:16 6430
the *P* returned for a trespass 1Sa 6:17 6430
the *P* belonging to the five lords 1Sa 6:18 6430
The *P* have brought again the ark 1Sa 6:21 6430
you out of the hand of the *P* 1Sa 7:3 6430
when the *P* heard that the 1Sa 7:7 6430
the lords of the *P* went up 1Sa 7:7 6430
it, they were afraid of the *P* 1Sa 7:7 6430
save us out of the hand of the *P* 1Sa 7:8 6430
the *P* drew near to battle against 1Sa 7:10 6430
thunder on that day upon the *P* 1Sa 7:10 6430
out of Mizpeh, and pursued the *P* 1Sa 7:11 6430
So the *P* were subdued, and they 1Sa 7:13 6430
the *P* all the days of Samuel 1Sa 7:13 6430
the cities which the *P* had taken 1Sa 7:14 6430
deliver out of the hands of the *P* 1Sa 7:14 6430
people out of the hand of the *P* 1Sa 9:16 6430
where is the garrison of the *P* 1Sa 10:5 6430
Hazor, and into the hand of the *P* 1Sa 12:9 6430
of the *P* that was in Geba 1Sa 13:3 6430
and the *P* heard of it 1Sa 13:3 6430
had smitten a garrison of the *P* 1Sa 13:4 6430
was had in abomination with the *P* 1Sa 13:4 6430
the *P* gathered themselves 1Sa 13:5 6430
that the *P* gathered themselves 1Sa 13:11 6430
The *P* will come down now upon me 1Sa 13:12 6430
but the *P* encamped in Michmash 1Sa 13:16 6430
camp of the *P* in three companies 1Sa 13:17 6430
for the *P* said, Lest the Hebrews 1Sa 13:19 6430
the Israelites went down to the *P* 1Sa 13:20 6430
the garrison of the *P* went out to 1Sa 13:23 6430
unto the garrison of the *P* 1Sa 14:11 6430
the *P* said, Behold, the Hebrews 1Sa 14:11 6430
was in the host of the *P* went on 1Sa 14:19 6430
were with the *P* before that time 1Sa 14:21 6430
when they heard that the *P* fled 1Sa 14:22 6430
greater slaughter among the *P* 1Sa 14:30 6430
they smote the *P* that day from 1Sa 14:31 6430
us go down after the *P* by night 1Sa 14:36 6430
God, Shall I go down after the *P* 1Sa 14:37 6430
Saul went up from following the *P* 1Sa 14:46 6430
the *P* went to their own place 1Sa 14:46 6430
kings of Zobah, and against the *P* 1Sa 14:47 6430
the *P* all the days of Saul 1Sa 14:52 6430
Now the *P* gathered together their 1Sa 17:1 6430
the battle in array against the *P* 1Sa 17:2 6430
the *P* stood on a mountain on the 1Sa 17:3 6430
champion out of the camp of the *P* 1Sa 17:4 6430
of Elah, fighting with the *P* 1Sa 17:19 6430
the *P* had put the battle in array 1Sa 17:21 6430
name, out of the armies of the *P* 1Sa 17:23 6430
P this day unto the fowls of the 1Sa 17:46 6430
when the *P* saw their champion was 1Sa 17:51 6430
and shouted, and pursued the *P* 1Sa 17:52 6430
the wounded of the *P* fell down by 1Sa 17:52 6430
returned from chasing after the *P* 1Sa 17:53 6430
let the hand of the *P* be upon him 1Sa 18:17 6430
hand of the *P* may be against him 1Sa 18:21 6430
but an hundred foreskins of the *P* 1Sa 18:25 6430
David fall by the hand of the *P* 1Sa 18:25 6430
slew of the *P* two hundred men 1Sa 18:27 6430
the princes of the *P* went forth 1Sa 18:30 6430
went out, and fought with the *P* 1Sa 19:8 6430
the *P* fight against Keilah, and 1Sa 23:1 6430
Shall I go and smite these *P* 1Sa 23:2 6430
unto David, Go, and smite the *P* 1Sa 23:2 6430
against the armies of the *P* 1Sa 23:3 6430
deliver the *P* into thine hand 1Sa 23:4 6430
to Keilah, and fought with the *P* 1Sa 23:5 6430
for the *P* have invaded the land 1Sa 23:27 6430
David, and went against the *P* 1Sa 23:28 6430
was returned from following the *P* 1Sa 24:1 6430
escape into the land of the *P* 1Sa 27:1 6430
country of the *P* was a full year 1Sa 27:7 6430
dwelleth in the country of the *P* 1Sa 27:11 6430
that the *P* gathered their armies 1Sa 28:1 6430
the *P* gathered themselves 1Sa 28:4 6430
when Saul saw the host of the *P* 1Sa 28:5 6430
for the *P* make war against me, and 1Sa 28:15 6430
with thee into the hand of the *P* 1Sa 28:19 6430
of Israel into the hand of the *P* 1Sa 28:19 6430
Now the *P* gathered together all 1Sa 29:1 6430
the lords of the *P* passed on by 1Sa 29:2 6430
Then said the princes of the *P* 1Sa 29:3 6430
said unto the princes of the *P* 1Sa 29:3 6430
the princes of the *P* were wroth 1Sa 29:4 6430
princes of the *P* said unto him 1Sa 29:4 6430
displease not the lords of the *P* 1Sa 29:7 6430
the princes of the *P* have said 1Sa 29:9 6430
to return into the land of the *P* 1Sa 29:11 6430
And the *P* went up to Jezreel 1Sa 29:11 6430
taken out of the land of the *P* 1Sa 30:16 6430
Now the *P* fought against Israel 1Sa 31:1 6430
of Israel fled from before the *P* 1Sa 31:1 6430
the *P* followed hard upon Saul and 1Sa 31:2 6430
the *P* slew Jonathan, and Abinadab, 1Sa 31:2 6430
the *P* came and dwelt in them 1Sa 31:7 6430
when the *P* came to strip the 1Sa 31:8 6430
the land of the *P* round about 1Sa 31:9 6430
that which the *P* had done to Saul 1Sa 31:11 6430
the daughters of the *P* rejoice 2Sa 1:20 6430
for an hundred foreskins of the *P* 2Sa 3:14 6430
Israel out of the hand of the *P* 2Sa 3:18 6430
But when the *P* heard that they 2Sa 5:17 6430
all the *P* came up to seek David 2Sa 5:17 6430
The *P* also came and spread 2Sa 5:18 6430
saying, Shall I go up to the *P* 2Sa 5:19 6430
deliver the *P* into thine hand 2Sa 5:19 6430
the *P* came up yet again, and 2Sa 5:22 6430
thee, to smite the host of the *P* 2Sa 5:24 6430
smote the *P* from Geba until thou 2Sa 5:25 6430
to pass, that David smote the *P* 2Sa 8:1 6430
out of the hand of the *P* 2Sa 8:1 6430
children of Ammon, and of the *P* 2Sa 8:12 6430
us out of the hand of the *P* 2Sa 19:9 6430
where the *P* had hanged them 2Sa 21:12 6430
when the *P* had slain Saul in 2Sa 21:12 6430
Moreover the *P* had yet war again 2Sa 21:15 6430
with him, and fought against the *P* 2Sa 21:15 6430
again a battle with the *P* at Gob 2Sa 21:18 6430
again a battle in Gob with the *P* 2Sa 21:19 6430
when they defied the *P* that were 2Sa 23:9 6430
smote the *P* until his hand was 2Sa 23:10 6430
the *P* were gathered together into 2Sa 23:11 6430
and the people fled from the *P* 2Sa 23:11 6430
and defended it, and slew the *P* 2Sa 23:12 6430
the troop of the *P* pitched in the 2Sa 23:13 6430
the garrison of the *P* was then in 2Sa 23:14 6430
brake through the host of the *P* 2Sa 23:16 6430
the river unto the land of the *P* 1Kin 4:21 6430
which belonged to the *P* 1Kin 15:27 6430
which belonged to the *P* 1Kin 16:15 6430
in the land of the *P* seven years 2Kin 8:2 6430
returned out of the land of the *P* 2Kin 8:3 6430
He smote the *P*, even unto Gaza, 2Kin 18:8 6430
and Casluhim, (of whom came the *P* 1Chr 1:12 6430
Now the *P* fought against Israel 1Chr 10:1 6430
of Israel fled from before the *P* 1Chr 10:1 6430
the *P* followed hard after Saul, 1Chr 10:2 6430
the *P* slew Jonathan, and Abinadab, 1Chr 10:2 6430
the *P* came and dwelt in them 1Chr 10:7 6430
when the *P* came to strip the 1Chr 10:8 6430
the land of the *P* round about 1Chr 10:9 6430
all that the *P* had done to Saul 1Chr 10:11 6430
there the *P* were gathered 1Chr 11:13 6430
the people fled from before the *P* 1Chr 11:13 6430
and delivered it, and slew the *P* 1Chr 11:14 6430
the host of the *P* encamped in the 1Chr 11:15 6430
brake through the host of the *P* 1Chr 11:18 6430
when he came with the *P* against 1Chr 12:19 6430
for the lords of the *P* upon 1Chr 12:19 6430
when the *P* heard that David was 1Chr 14:8 6430
all the *P* went up to seek David 1Chr 14:8 6430
the *P* came and spread themselves 1Chr 14:9 6430
Shall I go up against the *P* 1Chr 14:10 6430
the *P* yet again spread themselves 1Chr 14:13 6430
thee to smite the host of the *P* 1Chr 14:15 6430
the *P* from Gibeon even to Gazer 1Chr 14:16 6430
to pass, that David smote the *P* 1Chr 18:1 6430
towns out of the hand of the *P* 1Chr 18:1 6430
children of Ammon, and from the *P* 1Chr 18:11
arose war at Gezer with the *P* 1Chr 20:4 6430
And there was war again with the *P* 1Chr 20:5 6430
river even unto the land of the *P* 2Chr 9:26 6430
Also some of the *P* brought 2Chr 17:11 6430
Jehoram the spirit of the *P* 2Chr 21:16 6430
forth and warred against the *P* 2Chr 26:6 6430
about Ashdod, and among the *P* 2Chr 26:6 6430
And God helped him against the *P* 2Chr 26:7 6430
The *P* also had invaded the cities 2Chr 28:18 6430
when the *P* took him in Gath Ps 56:t 6430
the *P* with the inhabitants of Ps 83:7 6430
and are soothsayers like the *P* Is 2:6 6430
Syrians before, and the *P* behind Is 9:12 6430
of the *P* toward the west Is 11:14 6430
the kings of the land of the *P* Jer 25:20 6430
the prophet against the *P* Jer 47:1 6430
that cometh to spoil all the *P* Jer 47:4 6430
for the LORD will spoil the *P* Jer 47:4 6430
hate thee, the daughters of the *P* Eze 16:27 6430
about her, the daughters of the *P* Eze 16:57 6430
Because the *P* have dealt by Eze 25:15 6430
stretch out mine hand upon the *P* Eze 25:16 6430
the remnant of the *P* shall perish Amos 1:8 6430
then go down to Gath of the *P* Amos 6:2 6430
the *P* from Caphtor, and the Amos 9:7 6430
and they of the plain the *P* Obad 19 6430
O Canaan, the land of the *P* Zeph 2:5 6430
I will cut off the pride of the *P* Zec 9:6 6430

PHILISTINES' (*fil-is'-tinz*)
sojourned in the *P* land many days Gen 21:34 6430
let us go over to the *P* garrison 1Sa 14:1 6430
to go over unto the *P* garrison 1Sa 14:4 6430
the *P* garrison was then at 1Chr 11:16 6430

PHILOLOGUS (*fil-ol'-o-gus*) *A Christian in Rome.*
Salute *P*, and Julia, Nereus, and Rom 16:15 5378

PHILOSOPHERS
Then certain *p* of the Epicureans, Acts 17:18 *5386*

PHILOSOPHY
lest any man spoil you through *p* Col 2:8 *5385*

PHINEHAS (*fin'-e-has*) See PHINEHAS'.
1. A son of Eleazar.
and she bare him *P* Ex 6:25 6372
And when *P*, the son of Eleazar, Num 25:7 6372
P, the son of Eleazar, the son of Num 25:11 6372
P the son of Eleazar the priest, Num 31:6 6372
P the son of Eleazar the priest, Josh 22:13 6372
when *P* the priest, and the princes Josh 22:30 6372
P the son of Eleazar the priest Josh 22:31 6372
P the son of Eleazar the priest, Josh 22:32 6372
hill that pertained to *P* his son Josh 24:33 6372
And *P*, the son of Eleazar, the son Judg 20:28 6372
Eleazar begat *P* 1Chr 6:4 6372
P begat Abishua 1Chr 6:4 6372
P his son, Abishua his son, 1Chr 6:50 6372
P the son of Eleazar was the 1Chr 9:20 6372
The son of Abishua, the son of *P* Ezr 7:5 6372
Of the sons of *P* Ezr 8:2 6372
Then stood up *P*, and executed Ps 106:30 6372

2. A son of Eli.
the two sons of Eli, Hophni and P ... 1Sa 1:3 6372
upon thy two sons, on Hophni and P ... 1Sa 2:34 6372
the two sons of Eli, Hophni and P ... 1Sa 4:4 6372
the two sons of Eli, Hophni and P ... 1Sa 4:11 6372
and thy two sons also, Hophni and P ... 1Sa 4:17 6372
I-chabod's brother, the son of P ... 1Sa 14:3 6372
3. Father of Eleazar.
with him was Eleazar the son of P ... Ezr 8:33 6372

PHINEHAS' *(fin'-e-has) Refers to Phinehas 2.*
P wife, was with child, near to ... 1Sa 4:19 6372

PHLEGON *(fle'-gon) A Christian in Rome.*
Salute Asyncritus, P, Hermas, ... Rom 16:14 *5393*

PHOENIX See PHENICE.

PHRYGIA *(frij'-e-ah) A Roman province in Asia Minor.*
P, and Pamphylia, in Egypt, and in ... Acts 2:10 *5435*
when they had gone throughout P ... Acts 16:6 *5435*
P in order, strengthening all the ... Acts 18:23 *5435*
the chiefest city of P Pacatiana ... 1Ti s *5435*

PHURAH *(fu'-rah) A servant of Gideon.*
go thou with P thy servant down ... Judg 7:10 6513
Then went he down with P his ... Judg 7:11 6513

PHUT *(fut)* See PUT.
1. A son of Ham.
Mizraim, and P, and Canaan ... Gen 10:6 6316
2. Land of Phut's descendants.
of P were in thine army, thy men ... Eze 27:10 6316

PHUVAH *(fu'-vah)* See PUAH. *A son of Issachar.*
Tola, and P, and Job, and Shimron ... Gen 46:13 6312

PHYGELLUS *(fi-jel'-lus) An unfaithful Christian.*
of whom are P and Hermogenes ... 2Ti 1:15 *5436*

PHYGELUS See PHYGELLUS.

PHYLACTERIES
they make broad their p, and ... Mt 23:5 *5440*

PHYSICIAN
is there no p there ... Jer 8:22 7495
They that be whole need not a p ... Mt 9:12 *2395*
are whole have no need of the p ... Mk 2:17 *2395*
say unto me this proverb, P ... Lk 4:23 *2395*
They that are whole need not a p ... Lk 5:31 *2395*
Luke, the beloved p, and Demas, ... Col 4:14 *2395*

PHYSICIANS
the p to embalm his father ... Gen 50:2 7495
and the p embalmed Israel ... Gen 50:2 7495
not to the LORD, but to the p ... 2Chr 16:12 7495
of lies, ye are all p of no value ... Job 13:4 7495
suffered many things of many p ... Mk 5:26 *2395*
had spent all her living upon p ... Lk 8:43 *2395*

PI-BESETH *A city in Egypt.*
of P shall fall by the sword ... Eze 30:17 6364

PICK
of the valley shall p it out ... Prov 30:17 5365

PICTURES
you, and destroy all their p ... Num 33:52 4906
apples of gold in p of silver ... Prov 25:11 4906
Tarshish, and upon all pleasant p ... Is 2:16 7914

PIECE
laid each p one against another ... Gen 15:10 1335
beaten out of one p made he them ... Ex 37:7 4749
of a whole p shalt thou make them ... Num 10:2
a certain woman cast a p of a ... Judg 9:53 6400
crouch to him for a p of silver ... 1Sa 2:36 95
that I may eat a p of bread ... 1Sa 2:36 6595
they gave him a p of a cake of ... 1Sa 30:12 6400
a good p of flesh, and a flagon of ... 2Sa 6:19 829
did not a woman cast a p of a ... 2Sa 11:21 6400
where was a p of ground full of ... 2Sa 23:11 2513
mar every good p of land with ... 2Kin 3:19 2513
on every good p of land cast ... 2Kin 3:25 2513
a good p of flesh, and a flagon of ... 1Chr 16:3 829
Pahath-moab, repaired the other p ... Neh 3:11 4060
another p over against the going ... Neh 3:19 4060
earnestly repaired the other p ... Neh 3:20 4060
Urijah the son of Koz another p ... Neh 3:21 4060
the son of Henadad another p ... Neh 3:24 4060
the Tekoites repaired another p ... Neh 3:27 4060
sixth son of Zalaph, another p ... Neh 3:30 4060
as hard as a p of the nether ... Job 41:24 6400
man also gave him a p of money ... Job 42:11
a man is brought to a p of bread ... Prov 6:26 3603
for for a p of bread that man ... Prov 28:21 6595
thy temples are like a p of a ... Song 4:3 6400
As a p of a pomegranate are thy ... Song 6:7 6400
a p of bread out of the bakers' ... Jer 37:21 3603
into it, even every good p ... Eze 24:4 5409
bring it out p by p ... Eze 24:6 5409
lion two legs, or a p of an ear ... Amos 3:12 915
one p was rained upon ... Amos 4:7
the p whereupon it rained not ... Amos 4:7
No man putteth a p of new cloth ... Mt 9:16 *1915*
thou shalt find a p of money ... Mt 17:27
No man also seweth a p of new ... Mk 2:21 *1915*
else the new p that filled it up ... Mk 2:21 *4138*
No man putteth a p of a new ... Lk 5:36 *1915*
the p that was taken out of the ... Lk 5:36 *1915*
him, I have bought a p of ground ... Lk 14:18
of silver, if she lose one p ... Lk 15:8 *1406*
have found the p which I had lost ... Lk 15:9 *1406*
they gave him a p of a broiled ... Lk 24:42 *3313*

PIECES
lamp that passed between those p ... Gen 15:17 1506
brother a thousand p of silver ... Gen 20:16
father, for an hundred p of money ... Gen 33:19
for twenty p of silver ... Gen 37:28
Joseph is without doubt rent in p ... Gen 37:33
and I said, Surely he is torn in p ... Gen 44:28
he gave three hundred p of silver ... Gen 45:22
LORD, hath dashed in p the enemy ... Ex 15:6
If it be torn in p, then let him ... Ex 22:13
And thou shalt cut the ram in p ... Ex 29:17 5409
his legs, and put them unto his p ... Ex 29:17 5409
offering, and cut it into his p ... Lev 1:6 5409
And he shall cut it into his p ... Lev 1:12 5409
Thou shalt part it in p, and pour ... Lev 2:6 6595
the baken p of the meat offering ... Lev 6:21 6595
And he cut the ram into p ... Lev 8:20 5409
and Moses burnt the head, and the p ... Lev 8:20 5409
unto him, with the p thereof ... Lev 9:13 5409
for an hundred p of silver ... Josh 24:32
ten p of silver out of the house ... Judg 9:4
of us eleven hundred p of silver ... Judg 16:5
with her bones, into twelve p ... Judg 19:29 5409
my concubine, and cut her in p ... Judg 20:6
of the LORD shall be broken to p ... 1Sa 2:10
yoke of oxen, and hewed them in p ... 1Sa 11:7
Samuel hewed Agag in p before the ... 1Sa 15:33
on him, and rent it in twelve p ... 1Kin 11:30 7168
said to Jeroboam, Take thee ten p ... 1Kin 11:31 7168
for themselves, and cut it in p ... 1Kin 18:23
in order, and cut the bullock in p ... 1Kin 18:33
brake in p the rocks before the ... 1Kin 19:11
clothes, and rent them in two p ... 2Kin 2:12 7168
silver, and six thousand p of gold ... 2Kin 5:5
sold for fourscore p of silver ... 2Kin 6:25
dove's dung for five p of silver ... 2Kin 6:25
images brake they in p thoroughly ... 2Kin 11:18
brake in p the brasen serpent ... 2Kin 18:4
And he brake in p the images ... 2Kin 23:14
cut in p all the vessels of gold ... 2Kin 24:13
LORD, did the Chaldees break in p ... 2Kin 25:13
his altars and his images in p ... 2Chr 23:17
that they all were broken in p ... 2Chr 25:12
cut in p the vessels of the house ... 2Chr 28:24
Judah, and brake the images in p ... 2Chr 31:1
the molten images, he brake in p ... 2Chr 34:4
me by my neck, and shaken me to p ... Job 16:12
soul, and break me in p with words ... Job 19:2
He shall break in p mighty men ... Job 34:24
bones are as strong p of brass ... Job 40:18
them in p like a potter's vessel ... Ps 2:9
soul like a lion, rending it in p ... Ps 7:2
forget God, lest I tear you in p ... Ps 50:22
arrows, let them be as cut in p ... Ps 58:7
submit himself with p of silver ... Ps 68:30 7518
and shall break in p the oppressor ... Ps 72:4
the heads of leviathan in p ... Ps 74:14
Thou hast broken Rahab in p ... Ps 89:10
They break in p thy people ... Ps 94:5
to bring a thousand p of silver ... Song 8:11
ye that ye beat my people to p ... Is 3:15
and ye shall be broken in p ... Is 8:9
and ye shall be broken in p ... Is 8:9
and ye shall be broken in p ... Is 8:9
be dashed to p before their eyes ... Is 13:16
shall dash the young men to p ... Is 13:18
vessel that is broken in p ... Is 30:14
I will break in p the gates of ... Is 45:2
out thence shall be torn in p ... Jer 5:6
that breaketh the rock in p ... Jer 23:29
Merodach is broken in p ... Jer 50:2
her images are broken in p ... Jer 50:2
will I break in p the nations ... Jer 51:20
thee will I break in p the horse ... Jer 51:21
will I break in p the chariot ... Jer 51:21
thee also will I break in p man ... Jer 51:22
with thee will I break in p old ... Jer 51:22
will I break in p the young man ... Jer 51:22
I will also break in p with thee ... Jer 51:23
will I break in p the husbandman ... Jer 51:23
thee will I break in p captains ... Jer 51:23
aside my ways, and pulled me in p ... Lam 3:11
dieth of itself, or is torn in p ... Eze 4:14
for p of bread, to slay the souls ... Eze 13:19 6595
Gather the p thereof into it, ... Eze 24:4 5409
thereof, ye shall be cut in p ... Dan 2:5 1917
iron and clay, and brake them to p ... Dan 2:34
and the gold, broken to p together ... Dan 2:35
forasmuch as iron breaketh in p ... Dan 2:40
all these, shall it break in p ... Dan 2:40
people, but it shall break in p ... Dan 2:44
and that it brake in p the iron ... Dan 2:45
and Abed-nego, shall be cut in p ... Dan 3:29 1917
brake all their bones in p or ... Dan 6:24
it devoured and brake in p ... Dan 7:7
which devoured, brake in p ... Dan 7:19
tread it down, and break it in p ... Dan 7:23
her to me for fifteen p of silver ... Hos 3:2
of Samaria shall be broken in p ... Hos 8:6
was dashed in p upon her children ... Hos 10:14
infants shall be dashed in p ... Hos 13:16
thereof shall be beaten to p ... Mic 1:7
their bones, and chop them in p ... Mic 3:3
thou shalt beat in p many people ... Mic 4:13
treadeth down, and teareth in p ... Mic 5:8
He that dasheth in p is come up ... Nah 2:1
The lion did tear in p enough for ... Nah 2:12
children also were dashed in p at ... Nah 3:10
for my price thirty p of silver ... Zec 11:12
And I took the thirty p of silver ... Zec 11:13
the fat, and tear their claws in p ... Zec 11:16
with it shall be cut in p ... Zec 12:3
with him for thirty p of silver ... Mt 26:15
brought again the thirty p of ... Mt 27:3
he cast down the p of silver in ... Mt 27:5
chief priests took the silver p ... Mt 27:6
they took the thirty p of silver ... Mt 27:9
him, and the fetters broken in p ... Mk 5:4
what woman having ten p of silver ... Lk 15:8 *1406*
it fifty thousand p of silver ... Acts 19:19
have been pulled in p of them ... Acts 23:10 *1288*
and some on broken p of the ship ... Acts 27:44

PIERCE
p them through with his arrows ... Num 24:8 4272
it will go into his hand, and p it ... 2Kin 18:21 5344
it will go into his hand, and p it ... Is 36:6 5344
a sword shall p through thy own ... Lk 2:35 *1330*

PIERCED
off his head, when she had p ... Judg 5:26 4272
My bones are p in me in the night ... Job 30:17 5365
they p my hands and my feet ... Ps 22:16 738
look upon me whom they have p ... Zec 12:10 1856
soldiers with a spear p his side ... Jn 19:34 *3572*
shall look on him whom they p ... Jn 19:37 *1574*
p themselves through with many ... 1Ti 6:10 *4044*
see him, and they also which p him ... Rev 1:7 *1574*

PIERCETH
his nose p through snares ... Job 40:24 5344

PIERCING
punish leviathan the p serpent ... Is 27:1 1281
p even to the dividing asunder of ... Heb 4:12 *1338*

PIERCINGS
speaketh like the p of a sword ... Prov 12:18 4094

PIETY
learn first to shew p at home ... 1Ti 5:4 *2151*

PIGEON
and a turtledove, and a young p ... Gen 15:9 1469
a burnt offering, and a young p ... Lev 12:6 3123

PIGEONS
of turtledoves, or of young p ... Lev 1:14 3123
two turtledoves, or two young p ... Lev 5:7 3123
two turtledoves, or two young p ... Lev 5:11 3123
bring two turtles, or two young p ... Lev 12:8 3123
two turtledoves, or two young p ... Lev 14:22 3123
turtledoves, or of the young p ... Lev 14:30 3123
two turtledoves, or two young p ... Lev 15:14 3123
her two turtles, or two young p ... Lev 15:29 3123
bring two turtles, or two young p ... Num 6:10 3123
of turtledoves, or two young p ... Lk 2:24 *4058*

PI-HAHIROTH *A wilderness encampment.*
that they turn and encamp before P ... Ex 14:2 6367
encamping by the sea, beside P ... Ex 14:9 6367
Etham, and turned again unto P ... Num 33:7 6367
And they departed from before P ... Num 33:8 6367

PILATE *(pi'-lut) A Roman procurator of Judea.*
him to Pontius P the governor ... Mt 27:2 *4091*
Then said P unto him, Hearest ... Mt 27:13 *4091*
P said unto them, Whom will ye ... Mt 27:17 *4091*
P saith unto them, What shall I ... Mt 27:22 *4091*
When P saw that he could prevail ... Mt 27:24 *4091*
He went to P, and begged the body ... Mt 27:58 *4091*
Then P commanded the body to be ... Mt 27:58 *4091*
and Pharisees came together unto P ... Mt 27:62 *4091*
P said unto them, Ye have a watch ... Mt 27:65 *4091*
him away, and delivered him to P ... Mk 15:1 *4091*
P asked him, Art thou the King of ... Mk 15:2 *4091*
P asked him again, saying, ... Mk 15:4 *4091*
so that P marvelled ... Mk 15:5 *4091*
But P answered them, saying, Will ... Mk 15:9 *4091*
P answered and said again unto ... Mk 15:12 *4091*
Then P said unto them, Why, what ... Mk 15:14 *4091*
And so P, willing to content the ... Mk 15:15 *4091*
came, and went in boldly unto P ... Mk 15:43 *4091*
P marvelled if he were already ... Mk 15:44 *4091*
Pontius P being governor of ... Lk 3:1 *4091*
whose blood P had mingled with ... Lk 13:1 *4091*
of them arose, and led him unto P ... Lk 23:1 *4091*
P asked him, saying, Art thou the ... Lk 23:3 *4091*
Then said P to the chief priests ... Lk 23:4 *4091*
When P heard of Galilee, he asked ... Lk 23:6 *4091*
robe, and sent him again to P ... Lk 23:11 *4091*
And the same day P and Herod were ... Lk 23:12 *4091*
And P, when he had called together ... Lk 23:13 *4091*
P therefore, willing to release ... Lk 23:20 *4091*
P gave sentence that it should be ... Lk 23:24 *4091*
This man went unto P, and begged ... Lk 23:52 *4091*
P then went out unto them, and ... Jn 18:29 *4091*
Then said P unto them, Take ye ... Jn 18:31 *4091*
Then P entered into the judgment ... Jn 18:33 *4091*
P answered, Am I a Jew ... Jn 18:35 *4091*
P therefore said unto him, Art ... Jn 18:37 *4091*
P saith unto him, What is truth ... Jn 18:38 *4091*
Then P therefore took Jesus, and ... Jn 19:1 *4091*
P therefore went forth again, and ... Jn 19:4 *4091*
P saith unto them, Behold the man ... Jn 19:5
P saith unto them, Take ye him, ... Jn 19:6 *4091*
When P therefore heard that ... Jn 19:8 *4091*
Then saith P unto him, Speakest ... Jn 19:10 *4091*
from thenceforth P sought to ... Jn 19:12 *4091*
When P therefore heard that ... Jn 19:13 *4091*
P saith unto them, Shall I ... Jn 19:15 *4091*
P wrote a title, and put it on the ... Jn 19:19 *4091*
chief priests of the Jews to P ... Jn 19:21 *4091*
P answered, What I have written I ... Jn 19:22 *4091*
besought P that their legs might ... Jn 19:31 *4091*
besought P that he might take ... Jn 19:38 *4091*
and P gave him leave ... Jn 19:38 *4091*
denied him in the presence of P ... Acts 3:13 *4091*
both Herod, and Pontius P ... Acts 4:27 *4091*
yet desired they P that he should ... Acts 13:28 *4091*
who before Pontius P witnessed a ... 1Ti 6:13 *4091*

PILDASH (pil'-dash) *A son of Nahor.*
And Chesed, and Hazo, and P, and ... Gen 22:22 6394

PILE
the p thereof is fire and much ... Is 30:33 4071
even make the p for fire great ... Eze 24:9 4071

PILEHA (pil'-e-hah) *A renewer of the covenant.*
Hallohesh, P, Shobek, ... Neh 10:24 6401

PILGRIMAGE
the years of my p are an hundred ... Gen 47:9 4033
my fathers in the days of their p ... Gen 47:9 4033
of Canaan, the land of their p ... Ex 6:4 4033
my songs in the house of my p ... Ps 119:54 4033

PILGRIMS
were strangers and p on the earth ... Heb 11:13 3927
I beseech you as strangers and p ... 1Pet 2:11 3927

PILHA See PILEHA.

PILLAR
him, and she became a p of salt ... Gen 19:26 5333
his pillows, and set it up for a p ... Gen 28:18 4676
stone, which I have set for a p ... Gen 28:22 4676
where thou anointedst the p ... Gen 31:13 4676
a stone, and set it up for a p ... Gen 31:45 4676
this heap, and behold this p ... Gen 31:51 4676
this p be witness, that I will ... Gen 31:52 4676
heap and this p unto me, for harm ... Gen 31:52 4676
Jacob set up a p in the place ... Gen 35:14 4676
with him, even a p of stone ... Gen 35:14 4678
Jacob set a p upon her grave ... Gen 35:20 4676
that is the p of Rachel's grave ... Gen 35:20 4678
them by day in a p of a cloud ... Ex 13:21 5982
and by night in a p of fire ... Ex 13:21 5982
away the p of the cloud by day ... Ex 13:22 5982
nor the p of fire by night, from ... Ex 13:22 5982
the p of the cloud went from ... Ex 14:19 5982
Egyptians through the p of fire ... Ex 14:24 5982
the cloudy p descended, and stood ... Ex 33:9 5982
p stand at the tabernacle door ... Ex 33:10 5982
came down in the p of the cloud ... Num 12:5 5982
by daytime in a p of a cloud ... Num 14:14 5982
and in a p of fire by night ... Num 14:14 5982
the tabernacle in a p of a cloud ... Deut 31:15 5982
the p of the cloud stood over the ... Deut 31:15 5982
of the p that was in Shechem ... Judg 9:6 5324
out of the city with a p of smoke ... Judg 20:40 5982
and reared up for himself a p ... 2Sa 18:18 4678
he called the p after his own ... 2Sa 18:18 4678
and he set up the right p, and ... 1Kin 7:21 5982
and he set up the left p, and ... 1Kin 7:21 5982
behold, the king stood by a p ... 2Kin 11:14 5982
And the king stood by a p, and made .. 2Kin 23:3 5982
of the one p was eighteen cubits ... 2Kin 25:17 5982
the second p with wreathen work ... 2Kin 25:17 5982
stood at his p at the entering in ... 2Chr 23:13 5982
them in the day by a cloudy p ... Neh 9:12 5982
and in the night by a p of fire ... Neh 9:12 5982
the p of the cloud departed not ... Neh 9:19 5982
neither the p of fire by night, ... Neh 9:19 5982
spake unto them in the cloudy p ... Ps 99:7 5982
a p at the border thereof to the ... Is 19:19 4676
day a defenced city, and an iron p ... Jer 1:18 5982
the height of one p was eighteen ... Jer 52:21 5982
The second p also and the ... Jer 52:22 5982
church of the living God, the p ... 1Ti 3:15 4769
make a p in the temple of my God ... Rev 3:12 4769

PILLARS
altar under the hill, and twelve p ... Ex 24:4 4676
thou shalt hang it upon four p of ... Ex 26:32 5982
hanging five p of shittim wood ... Ex 26:37 5982
And the twenty p thereof and their ... Ex 27:10 5982
the hooks of the p and their ... Ex 27:10 5982
cubits long, and his twenty p ... Ex 27:11 5982
the hooks of the p and their ... Ex 27:11 5982
their p ten, and their sockets ten ... Ex 27:12 5982
their p three, and their sockets ... Ex 27:14 5982
their p three, and their sockets ... Ex 27:15 5982
their p shall be four, and their ... Ex 27:16 5982
All the p round about the court ... Ex 27:17 5982
and his boards, his bars, his p ... Ex 35:11 5982
The hangings of the court, his p ... Ex 35:17 5982
thereunto four p of shittim wood ... Ex 36:36 5982
the five p of it with their hooks ... Ex 36:38 5982
Their p were twenty, and their ... Ex 38:10 5982
the hooks of the p and their ... Ex 38:10 5982
their p were twenty, and their ... Ex 38:11 5982
the hooks of the p and their ... Ex 38:11 5982
of fifty cubits, their p ten ... Ex 38:12 5982
the hooks of the p and their ... Ex 38:12 5982
their p three, and their sockets ... Ex 38:14 5982
their p three, and their sockets ... Ex 38:15 5982
sockets for the p were of brass ... Ex 38:17 5982
the hooks of the p and their ... Ex 38:17 5982
all the p of the court were ... Ex 38:17 5982
their p were four, and their ... Ex 38:19 5982
shekels he made hooks for the p ... Ex 38:28 5982
his boards, his bars, and his p ... Ex 39:33 5982
The hangings of the court, his p ... Ex 39:40 5982
bars thereof, and reared up his p ... Ex 40:18 5982
the p thereof, and the sockets ... Num 3:36 5982
the p of the court round about, ... Num 3:37 5982
the p thereof, and sockets thereof ... Num 4:31 5982
the p of the court round about, ... Num 4:32 5982
their altars, and break their p ... Deut 12:3 4676
and they set him between the p ... Judg 16:25 5982
p whereupon the house standeth ... Judg 16:26 5982
p upon which the house stood ... Judg 16:29 5982
for the p of the earth are the ... 1Sa 2:8 4690
cubits, upon four rows of cedar p ... 1Kin 7:2 5982
with cedar beams upon the p ... 1Kin 7:2 5982
beams, that lay on forty five p ... 1Kin 7:3 5982
And he made a porch of p ... 1Kin 7:6 5982
and the other p and the thick beam ... 1Kin 7:6 5982
For he cast two p of brass ... 1Kin 7:15 5982
to set upon the tops of the p ... 1Kin 7:16 5982
which were upon the top of the p ... 1Kin 7:17 5982
And he made the p, and two rows ... 1Kin 7:18 5982
that were upon the top of the p ... 1Kin 7:19 5982
the chapiters upon the two p had ... 1Kin 7:20 5982
he set up the p in the porch of ... 1Kin 7:21 5982
the top of the p was lily work ... 1Kin 7:22 5982
so was the work of the p finished ... 1Kin 7:22 5982
The two p, and the two bowls of ... 1Kin 7:41 5982
that were on the top of the two p ... 1Kin 7:41 5982
which were upon the top of the p ... 1Kin 7:41 5982
chapiters that were upon the p ... 1Kin 7:42 5982
trees p for the house of the LORD ... 1Kin 10:12 4552
from the p which Hezekiah king of ... 2Kin 18:16 547
the p of brass that were in the ... 2Kin 25:13 5982
The two p, one sea, and the bases ... 2Kin 25:16 5982
made the brasen sea, and the p ... 1Chr 18:8 5982
before the house two p of thirty ... 2Chr 3:15 5982
and put them on the heads of the p ... 2Chr 3:16 5982
he reared up the p before the ... 2Chr 3:17 5982
To wit, the two p, and the pommels ... 2Chr 4:12 5982
were on the top of the two p ... 2Chr 4:12 5982
which were on the top of the p ... 2Chr 4:12 5982
chapiters which were upon the p ... 2Chr 4:13 5982
to silver rings and p of marble ... Est 1:6 5982
place, and the p thereof tremble ... Job 9:6 5982
The p of heaven tremble, and are ... Job 26:11 5982
I bear up the p of it ... Ps 75:3 5982
she hath hewn out her seven p ... Prov 9:1 5982
of the wilderness like p of smoke ... Song 3:6 8490
He made the p thereof of silver, ... Song 3:10 5982
His legs are as p of marble ... Song 5:15 5982
LORD of hosts concerning the p ... Jer 27:19 5982
Also the p of brass that were in ... Jer 52:17 5982
The two p, one sea, and twelve ... Jer 52:20 5982
And concerning the p, the height ... Jer 52:21 5982
there were p by the posts, one on ... Eze 40:49 5982
p as the p of the courts ... Eze 42:6 5982
blood, and fire, and p of smoke ... Joel 2:30 8490
and John, who seemed to be p ... Gal 2:9 4769
the sun, and his feet as p of fire ... Rev 10:1 4769

PILLED
p white strakes in them, and made ... Gen 30:37 6478
he had p before the flocks in the ... Gen 30:38 6478

PILLOW
put a p of goats' hair for his ... 1Sa 19:13 3523
with a p of goats' hair for his ... 1Sa 19:16 3523
part of the ship, asleep on a p ... Mk 4:38 4344

PILLOWS
that place, and put them for his p ... Gen 28:11 4763
stone that he had put for his p ... Gen 28:18 4763
women that sew p to all armholes ... Eze 13:18 3704
Behold, I am against your p ... Eze 13:20 3704

PILOTS
that were in thee, were thy p ... Eze 27:8 2259
thy mariners, and thy p, thy ... Eze 27:27 2259
at the sound of the cry of thy p ... Eze 27:28 2259
all the p of the sea, shall come ... Eze 27:29 2259

PILTAI (pil'-tahee) *A priest.*
of Miniamin, of Moadiah, P ... Neh 12:17 6408

PIN
And she fastened it with the p ... Judg 16:14 3489
went away with the p of the beam ... Judg 16:14 3489
or will men take a p of it to ... Eze 15:3 3489

PINE
p away in their iniquity in your ... Lev 26:39 4743
shall they p away with them ... Lev 26:39 4743
p branches, and myrtle branches, ... Neh 8:15
the desert the fir tree, and the p ... Is 41:19 8410
the p tree, and the box together, ... Is 60:13 8410
for these p away, stricken ... Lam 4:9 2100
but ye shall p away for your ... Eze 24:23 4743
we p away in them, how should we ... Eze 33:10 4743

PINETH
with his teeth, and p away ... Mk 9:18 3583

PINING
will cut me off with p sickness ... Is 38:12 1803

PINNACLE
setteth him on a p of the temple ... Mt 4:5 4419
set him on a p of the temple, and ... Lk 4:9 4419

PINON
Aholibamah, duke Elah, duke P ... Gen 36:41 6373
Aholibamah, duke Elah, duke P ... 1Chr 1:52 6373

PINS
thereof, and all the p thereof ... Ex 27:19 3489
all the p of the court, shall be ... Ex 27:19 3489
The p of the tabernacle, and the ... Ex 35:18 3489
the p of the court, and their ... Ex 35:18 3489
all the p of the tabernacle, and ... Ex 38:20 3489
all the p of the tabernacle, and ... Ex 38:31 3489
all the p of the court round ... Ex 38:31 3489
court gate, his cords, and his p ... Ex 39:40 3489
and their sockets, and their p ... Num 3:37 3489
and their sockets, and their p ... Num 4:32 3489
and the wimples, and the crisping p ... Is 3:22

PIPE
a psaltery, and a tabret, and a p ... 1Sa 10:5 2485
and the viol, the tabret, and p ... Is 5:12 2485
as when one goeth with a p to ... Is 30:29 2485
giving sound, whether p or harp ... 1Cor 14:7 836

PIPED
him, and the people p with pipes ... 1Kin 1:40 2490
We have p unto you, and ye have ... Mt 11:17 832
We have p unto you, and ye have ... Lk 7:32 832
it be known what is p or harped ... 1Cor 14:7 832

PIPERS
of harpers, and musicians, and of p ... Rev 18:22 834

PIPES
him, and the people piped with p ... 1Kin 1:40 2485
heart shall sound for Moab like p ... Jer 48:36 2485
like p for the men of Kir-heres ... Jer 48:36 2485
of thy p was prepared in thee in ... Eze 28:13 5345
seven p to the seven lamps, which ... Zec 4:2 4166
p empty the golden oil out of ... Zec 4:12 6804

PIRAM (pi'-ram) *An Amorite king.*
unto P king of Jarmuth, and unto ... Josh 10:3 6502

PIRATHON (pir'-a-thon) See PIRATHONITE. *A place in Ephraim.*
was buried in P in the land of ... Judg 12:15 6552

PIRATHONITE (pir'-a-thon-ite) *An inhabitant of Pirathon.*
him Abdon the son of Hillel, a P ... Judg 12:13 6553
the son of Hillel the P died ... Judg 12:15 6553
Benaiah the P, Hiddai of the ... 2Sa 23:30 6553
of Benjamin, Benaiah the P ... 1Chr 11:31 6553
eleventh month was Benaiah the P ... 1Chr 27:14 6553

PISGAH (piz'-gah) *A mountain peak in Moab.*
country of Moab, to the top of P ... Num 21:20 6449
field of Zophim, to the top of P ... Num 23:14 6449
Get thee up into the top of P ... Deut 3:27 6449
the plain, under the springs of P ... Deut 4:49 6449
mountain of Nebo, to the top of P ... Deut 34:1 6449

PISHON See PISON.

PISIDIA (pi-sid'-e-ah) *A Roman province in Asia Minor.*
Perga, they came to Antioch in P ... Acts 13:14 4099
they had passed throughout P ... Acts 14:24 4099

PISIDIAN ANTIOCH See PISIDIA.

PISON (pi'-son) *A river of Eden.*
The name of the first is P ... Gen 2:11 6376

PISPA See PISPAH.

PISPAH (piz'-pah) *A son of Jether.*
Jephunneh, and P, and Ara ... 1Chr 7:38 6462

PISS
and drink their own p with you ... 2Kin 18:27 7890
and drink their own p with you ... Is 36:12 7890

PISSETH
light any that p against the wall ... 1Sa 25:22 8366
light any that p against the wall ... 1Sa 25:34 8366
him that p against the wall ... 1Kin 14:10 8366
him not one that p against a wall ... 1Kin 16:11 8366
Ahab him that p against the wall ... 1Kin 21:21 8366
Ahab him that p against the wall ... 2Kin 9:8 8366

PIT
slay him, and cast him into some p ... Gen 37:20 953
but cast him into this p that is ... Gen 37:22 953
took him, and cast him into a p ... Gen 37:24 953
the p was empty, there was no ... Gen 37:24 953
and lifted up Joseph out of the p ... Gen 37:28 953
And Reuben returned unto the p ... Gen 37:29 953
behold, Joseph was not in the p ... Gen 37:29 953
And if a man shall open a p ... Ex 21:33 953
or if a man shall dig a p ... Ex 21:33 953
The owner of the p shall make it ... Ex 21:34 953
Nevertheless a fountain or p ... Lev 11:36 953
and they go down quick into the p ... Num 16:30 7585
them, went down alive into the p ... Num 16:33 7585
Behold, he is hid now in some p ... 2Sa 17:9 6354
him into a great p in the wood ... 2Sa 18:17 6354
the midst of a p in time of snow ... 2Sa 23:20 953
slew them at the p of the ... 2Kin 10:14 953
slew a lion in a p in a snowy day ... 1Chr 11:22 953
ye dig a p for your friend ... Job 6:27
go down to the bars of the p ... Job 17:16 7585
keepeth back his soul from the p ... Job 33:18 7845
him from going down to the p ... Job 33:24 7845
his soul from going into the p ... Job 33:28 7845
To bring back his soul from the p ... Job 33:30 7845
He made a p, and digged it, and is ... Ps 7:15 953
sunk down in the p that they made ... Ps 9:15 7845
like them that go down into the p ... Ps 28:1 953
I should not go down to the p ... Ps 30:3 953
my blood, when I go down to the p ... Ps 30:9 7845
they hid for me their net in a p ... Ps 35:7 7845
me up also out of an horrible p ... Ps 40:2 953
down into the p of destruction ... Ps 55:23 875
they have digged a p before me ... Ps 57:6 7882
let not the p shut her mouth upon ... Ps 69:15 875
with them that go down into the p ... Ps 88:4 953
Thou hast laid me in the lowest p ... Ps 88:6 953
until the p be digged for the ... Ps 94:13 7845
unto them that go down into the p ... Ps 143:7 953
as those that go down into the p ... Prov 1:12 953
of strange women is a deep p ... Prov 22:14 7745
and a strange woman is a narrow p ... Prov 23:27 875
Whoso diggeth a p shall fall ... Prov 26:27 7845
shall fall himself into his own p ... Prov 28:10 7816
of any person shall flee to the p ... Prov 28:17 953
He that diggeth a p shall fall ... Eccl 10:8 1475
to hell, to the sides of the p ... Is 14:15 953
go down to the stones of the p ... Is 14:19 953
Fear, and the p, and the snare, are ... Is 24:17 6354
of the fear shall fall into the p ... Is 24:18 6354
up out of the midst of the p ... Is 24:18 6354
prisoners are gathered in the p ... Is 24:22 953
to take water withal out of the p ... Is 30:14 1360
it from the p of corruption ... Is 38:17 7845
the p cannot hope for thy truth ... Is 38:18 953
to the hole of the p whence ye ... Is 51:1 953
that he should not die in the p ... Is 51:14 7845
they have digged a p for my soul ... Jer 18:20 7745
they have digged a p to take me ... Jer 18:22

cast them into the midst of the p	Jer 41:7	953
Now the p wherein Ishmael had	Jer 41:9	953
Fear, and the p, and the snare,	Jer 48:43	6354
the fear shall fall into the p	Jer 48:44	6354
the p shall be taken in the snare	Jer 48:44	6354
he was taken in their p, and they	Eze 19:4	7845
he was taken in their p	Eze 19:8	7845
with them that descend into the p	Eze 26:20	953
with them that go down to the p	Eze 26:20	953
shall bring thee down to the p	Eze 28:8	7845
with them that go down to the p	Eze 31:14	953
with them that descend into the p	Eze 31:16	953
with them that go down into the p	Eze 32:18	953
are set in the sides of the p	Eze 32:23	953
with them that go down to the p	Eze 32:24	953
with them that go down to the p	Eze 32:25	953
with them that go down to the p	Eze 32:29	953
with them that go down to the p	Eze 32:30	953
out of the p wherein is no water	Zec 9:11	953
if it fall into a p on the	Mt 12:11	*999*
an ass or an ox fallen into a p	Lk 14:5	*5421*
given the key of the bottomless p	Rev 9:1	*5421*
And he opened the bottomless p	Rev 9:2	*5421*
there arose a smoke out of the p	Rev 9:2	*5421*
by reason of the smoke of the p	Rev 9:2	*5421*
is the angel of the bottomless p	Rev 9:11	
p shall make war against them	Rev 11:7	
ascend out of the bottomless p	Rev 17:8	
the key of the bottomless p	Rev 20:1	
And cast him into the bottomless p	Rev 20:3	

PITCH

p it within and without with p	Gen 6:14	3724
and daubed it with slime and with p	Ex 2:3	2203
of Israel shall p their tents	Num 1:52	2583
But the Levites shall p round	Num 1:53	2583
shall p by his own standard	Num 2:2	2583
of the congregation shall they p	Num 2:2	2583
Judah p throughout their armies	Num 2:3	2583
those that do p next unto him	Num 2:5	2583
those which p by him shall be the	Num 2:12	2583
of the Gershonites shall p behind	Num 3:23	2583
of the sons of Kohath shall p on	Num 3:29	2583
these shall p on the side of the	Num 3:35	2583
out a place to p your tents in	Deut 1:33	2583
of Jordan, did Joshua p in Gilgal	Josh 4:20	6965
shall the Arabian p tent there	Is 13:20	167
thereof shall be turned into p	Is 34:9	2203
thereof shall become burning p	Is 34:9	2203
they shall p their tents against	Jer 6:3	8628

PITCHED

p his tent, having Beth-el on the	Gen 12:8	5186
plain, and p his tent toward Sodom	Gen 13:12	167
p his tent in the valley of Gerar	Gen 26:17	2583
of the LORD, and p his tent there	Gen 26:25	5186
Now Jacob had p his tent in the	Gen 31:25	8628
brethren p in the mount of Gilead	Gen 31:25	8628
p his tent before the city	Gen 33:18	2583
of the LORD, and p in Rephidim	Ex 17:1	2583
Sinai, and had p in the wilderness	Ex 19:2	2583
p it without the camp, afar off	Ex 33:7	5186
and when the tabernacle is to be p	Num 1:51	2583
so they p by their standards, and	Num 2:34	2583
children of Israel p their tents	Num 9:17	2583
commandment of the LORD they p	Num 9:18	2583
p in the wilderness of Paran	Num 12:16	2583
Israel set forward, and p in Oboth	Num 21:10	2583
Oboth, and p at Ije-abarim, in the	Num 21:11	2583
and p in the valley of Zared	Num 21:12	2583
p on the other side of Arnon,	Num 21:13	2583
p in the plains of Moab on this	Num 22:1	2583
from Rameses, and p in Succoth	Num 33:5	2583
p in Etham, which is in the edge	Num 33:6	2583
and they p before Migdol	Num 33:7	2583
of Etham, and p in Marah	Num 33:8	2583
and they p there	Num 33:9	2583
p in the wilderness of Sinai	Num 33:15	2583
Sinai, and p at Kibroth-hattaavah	Num 33:16	2583
from Hazeroth, and p in Rithmah	Num 33:18	2583
Rithmah, and p at Rimmon-parez	Num 33:19	2583
from Rimmon-parez, and p in Libnah	Num 33:20	2583
from Libnah, and p at Rissah	Num 33:21	2583
from Rissah, and p in Kehelathah	Num 33:22	2583
Kehelathah, and p in mount Shapher	Num 33:23	2583
from Haradah, and p in Makheloth	Num 33:25	2583
from Tahath, and p at Tarah	Num 33:27	2583
from Tarah, and p in Mithcah	Num 33:28	2583
from Mithcah, and p in Hashmonah	Num 33:29	2583
Moseroth, and p in Bene-jaakan	Num 33:31	2583
Hor-hagidgad, and p in Jotbathah	Num 33:33	2583
p in the wilderness of Zin, which	Num 33:36	2583
p in mount Hor, in the edge of	Num 33:37	2583
from mount Hor, and p in Zalmonah	Num 33:41	2583
from Zalmonah, and p in Punon	Num 33:42	2583
from Punon, and p in Oboth	Num 33:43	2583
p in Ije-abarim, in the border of	Num 33:44	2583
from Iim, and p in Dibon-gad	Num 33:45	2583
p in the mountains of Abarim,	Num 33:47	2583
p in the plains of Moab by Jordan	Num 33:48	2583
And they p by Jordan, from	Num 33:49	2583
p on the north side of Ai	Josh 8:11	2583
p together at the waters of Merom	Josh 11:5	2583
p his tent unto the plain of	Judg 4:11	5186
p in the valley of Jezreel	Judg 6:33	2583
p beside the well of Harod	Judg 7:1	2583
p on the other side of Arnon, but	Judg 11:18	2583
p in Jahaz, and fought against	Judg 11:20	2583
p in Judah, and spread themselves	Judg 15:9	2583
p in Kirjath-jearim, in Judah	Judg 18:12	2583
to battle, and p beside Eben-ezer	1Sa 4:1	2583
and the Philistines p in Aphek	1Sa 4:1	2583
p in Michmash, eastward from	1Sa 13:5	2583
p between Shochoh and Azekah, in	1Sa 17:1	2583
p by the valley of Elah, and set	1Sa 17:2	2583
Saul p in the hill of Hachilah,	1Sa 26:3	2583
to the place where Saul had p	1Sa 26:5	2583
the people p round about him	1Sa 26:5	2583
together, and came and p in Shunem	1Sa 28:4	2583
together, and they p in Gilboa	1Sa 28:4	2583
the Israelites p by a fountain	1Sa 29:1	2583
that David had p for it	2Sa 6:17	5186
Absalom p in the land of Gilead	2Sa 17:26	2583
p in the valley of Rephaim	2Sa 23:13	2583
p in Aroer, on the right side of	2Sa 24:5	2583
the children of Israel p before	1Kin 20:27	2583
they p one over against the other	1Kin 20:29	2583
Jerusalem, and p against it	2Kin 25:1	2583
ark of God, and p for it a tent	1Chr 15:1	5186
the tent that David had p for it	1Chr 16:1	5186
who came and p before Medeba	1Chr 19:7	2583
for he had p a tent for it at	2Chr 1:4	5186
p against it, and built forts	Jer 52:4	2583
true tabernacle, which the Lord p	Heb 8:2	*4078*

PITCHER

whom I shall say, Let down thy p	Gen 24:14	3537
with her p upon her shoulder	Gen 24:15	3537
down to the well, and filled her p	Gen 24:16	3537
drink a little water of thy p	Gen 24:17	3537
let down her p upon her hand, and	Gen 24:18	3537
emptied her p into the trough, and	Gen 24:20	3537
a little water of thy p to drink	Gen 24:43	3537
forth with her p on her shoulder	Gen 24:45	3537
let down her p from her shoulder,	Gen 24:46	3537
or the p be broken at the	Eccl 12:6	3537
you a man bearing a p of water	Mk 14:13	*2765*
meet you, bearing a p of water	Lk 22:10	*2765*

PITCHERS

in every man's hand, with empty p	Judg 7:16	3537
and lamps within the p	Judg 7:16	3537
brake the p that were in their	Judg 7:19	3537
blew the trumpets, and brake the p	Judg 7:20	3537
are they esteemed as earthen p	Lam 4:2	5035

PITHOM (*pi'-thom*) *A city in Lower Egypt.*

for Pharaoh treasure cities, P	Ex 1:11	6619

PITHON (*pi'-thon*) *A son of Micah.*

And the sons of Micah were, P	1Chr 8:35	6377
And the sons of Micah were, P	1Chr 9:41	6377

PITIED

He made them also to be p of all	Ps 106:46	7356
of Jacob, and hath not p	Lam 2:2	2550
hath thrown down, and hath not p	Lam 2:17	2550
thou hast killed, and not p	Lam 2:21	2550
thou hast slain, thou hast not p	Lam 3:43	2550
None eye p thee, to do any of	Eze 16:5	2347

PITIETH

Like as a father p his children	Ps 103:13	7355
so the LORD p them that fear him	Ps 103:13	7355
eyes, and that which your soul p	Eze 24:21	4263

PITIFUL

The hands of the p women have	Lam 4:10	7362
that the Lord is very p, and of	Jas 5:11	*4184*
another, love as brethren, be p	1Pet 3:8	*2155*

PITS

rocks, and in high places, and in p	1Sa 13:6	953
The proud have digged p for me	Ps 119:85	7882
into deep p, that they rise not	Ps 140:10	
through a land of deserts and of p	Jer 2:6	7745
they came to the p, and found no	Jer 14:3	1356
of the LORD, was taken in their p	Lam 4:20	7825

PITY

eye shall have no p upon them	Deut 7:16	2347
neither shall thine eye p him	Deut 13:8	2347
Thine eye shall not p him	Deut 19:13	2347
And thine eye shall not p	Deut 19:21	2347
hand, thine eye shall not p her	Deut 25:12	2347
thing, and because he had no p	2Sa 12:6	2550
To him that is afflicted p should	Job 6:14	2617
Have p upon me, have p upon me	Job 19:21	2603
and I looked for some to take p	Ps 69:20	5110
He that hath p upon the poor	Prov 19:17	2603
it for him that will p the poor	Prov 28:8	2603
they shall have no p on the fruit	Is 13:18	7355
in his p he redeemed them	Is 63:9	2551
I will not p, nor spare, nor have	Jer 13:14	2550
For who shall have p upon thee	Jer 15:5	2550
not spare them, neither have p	Jer 21:7	2550
spare, neither will I have any p	Eze 5:11	2550
spare thee, neither will I have p	Eze 7:4	2550
not spare, neither will I have p	Eze 7:9	2550
not spare, neither will I have p	Eze 8:18	2550
your eye spare, neither have ye p	Eze 9:5	2550
not spare, neither will I have p	Eze 9:10	2550
But I had p for mine holy name,	Eze 36:21	2550
for his land, and p his people	Joel 2:18	2550
the sword, and did cast off all p	Amos 1:11	7356
Thou hast had p on the gourd	Jonah 4:10	2347
and their own shepherds p them not	Zec 11:5	2550
For I will no more p the	Zec 11:6	2550
even as I had p on thee	Mt 18:33	*1653*

PLACE

be gathered together unto one p	Gen 1:9	4725
the land unto the p of Sichem	Gen 12:6	4725
unto the p where his tent had	Gen 13:3	4725
Unto the p of the altar, which he	Gen 13:4	4725
look from the p where thou art	Gen 13:14	4725
not spare the p for the fifty	Gen 18:24	4725
spare all the p for their sakes	Gen 18:26	4725
and Abraham returned unto his p	Gen 18:33	4725
city, bring them out of this p	Gen 19:12	4725
For we will destroy this p	Gen 19:13	4725
said, Up, get you out of this p	Gen 19:14	4725
p where he stood before the LORD	Gen 19:27	4725
the fear of God is not in this p	Gen 20:11	4725
at every p whither we shall come,	Gen 20:13	4725
he called that p Beer-sheba	Gen 21:31	4725
went unto the p of which God had	Gen 22:3	4725
his eyes, and saw the p afar off	Gen 22:4	4725
they came to the p which God had	Gen 22:9	4725
the name of that p Jehovah-jireh	Gen 22:14	4725
the men of the p asked him of his	Gen 26:7	4725
the men of the p should kill me	Gen 26:7	4725
And he lighted upon a certain p	Gen 28:11	4725
he took of the stones of that p	Gen 28:11	4725
and lay down in that p to sleep	Gen 28:11	4725
Surely the LORD is in this p	Gen 28:16	4725
and said, How dreadful is this p	Gen 28:17	4725
called the name of that p Beth-el	Gen 28:19	4725
upon the well's mouth in his p	Gen 29:3	4725
together all the men of the p	Gen 29:22	4725
that I may go unto mine own p	Gen 30:25	4725
departed, and returned unto his p	Gen 31:55	4725
the name of that p Mahanaim	Gen 32:2	4725
called the name of the p Peniel	Gen 32:30	4725
name of the p is called Succoth	Gen 33:17	4725
altar, and called the p El-beth-el	Gen 35:7	4725
in the p where he talked with him	Gen 35:13	4725
in the p where he talked with him	Gen 35:14	4725
of the p where God spake with him	Gen 35:15	4725
herself, and sat in an open p	Gen 38:14	6607
Then he asked the men of that p	Gen 38:21	4725
There was no harlot in this p	Gen 38:21	
and also the men of the p said	Gen 38:22	4725
there was no harlot in this p	Gen 38:22	
a p where the king's prisoners	Gen 39:20	4725
the p where Joseph was bound	Gen 40:3	4725
head, and restore thee unto thy p	Gen 40:13	3653
whom God hath given me in this p	Gen 48:9	
for am I in the p of God	Gen 50:19	
for the p whereon thou standest	Ex 3:5	4725
unto the p of the Canaanites, and	Ex 3:8	4725
any from his p for three days	Ex 10:23	8478
LORD brought you out from this p	Ex 13:3	
of thine inheritance, in the p	Ex 15:17	4349
abide ye every man in his p	Ex 16:29	8478
out of his p on the seventh day	Ex 16:29	4725
called the name of the p Massah	Ex 17:7	4725
p such over them, to be rulers of	Ex 18:21	7760
shall also go to their p in peace	Ex 18:23	4725
thee a p whither he shall flee	Ex 21:13	4725
into the p which I have prepared	Ex 23:20	4725
unto you between the holy p	Ex 26:33	
the testimony in the most holy p	Ex 26:34	
when he goeth in unto the holy p	Ex 28:29	
unto the holy p before the LORD	Ex 28:35	
altar to minister in the holy p	Ex 28:43	
to minister in the holy p	Ex 29:30	
and seethe his flesh in the holy p	Ex 29:31	4725
and sweet incense for the holy p	Ex 31:11	
lead the people unto the p of	Ex 32:34	
said, Behold, there is a p by me	Ex 33:21	4725
to do service in the holy p	Ex 35:19	
in all the work of the holy p	Ex 38:24	
to do service in the holy p	Ex 39:1	
to do service in the holy p	Ex 39:41	
east part, by the p of the ashes	Lev 1:16	4725
without the camp unto a clean p	Lev 4:12	4725
kill it in the p where they kill	Lev 4:24	4725
in the p of the burnt offering	Lev 4:29	4725
the p where they kill the burnt	Lev 4:33	4725
without the camp unto a clean p	Lev 6:11	4725
shall it be eaten in the holy p	Lev 6:16	4725
In the p where the burnt offering	Lev 6:25	4725
in the holy p shall it be eaten,	Lev 6:26	4725
it was sprinkled in the holy p	Lev 6:27	4725
to reconcile withal in the holy p	Lev 6:30	
In the p where they kill the	Lev 7:2	4725
it shall be eaten in the holy p	Lev 7:6	4725
And ye shall eat it in the holy p	Lev 10:13	4725
shall ye eat in a clean p	Lev 10:14	4725
the sin offering in the holy p	Lev 10:17	4725
not brought in within the holy p	Lev 10:18	
have eaten it in the holy p	Lev 10:18	
in the p of the boil there be a	Lev 13:19	4725
if the bright spot stay in his p	Lev 13:23	8478
if the bright spot stay in his p	Lev 13:28	8478
the p where he shall kill the sin	Lev 14:13	4725
the burnt offering, in the holy p	Lev 14:13	4725
upon the p of the blood of the	Lev 14:28	4725
an unclean p without the city	Lev 14:40	4725
the city into an unclean p	Lev 14:41	4725
put them in the p of those stones	Lev 14:42	8478
out of the city into an unclean p	Lev 14:45	4725
holy p within the vail before the	Lev 16:2	
shall Aaron come into the holy p	Lev 16:3	
make an atonement for the holy p	Lev 16:16	
make an atonement in the holy p	Lev 16:17	
an end of reconciling the holy p	Lev 16:20	
on when he went into the holy p	Lev 16:23	
flesh with water in the holy p	Lev 16:24	4725
to make atonement in the holy p	Lev 16:27	
they shall eat it in the holy p	Lev 24:9	4725
every man in his p by their	Num 2:17	3027
in the p where the cloud abode,	Num 9:17	4725
In the first p went the standard	Num 10:14	
unto the p of which the LORD said	Num 10:29	4725
search out a resting p for them	Num 10:33	
called the name of the p Taberah	Num 11:3	4725
name of that p Kibroth-hattaavah	Num 11:34	4725
The p was called the brook Eshcol	Num 13:24	4725
will go up unto the p which the	Num 14:40	4725
In the most holy p shalt thou eat	Num 18:10	
And ye shall eat it in every p	Num 18:31	4725
up without the camp in a clean p	Num 19:9	4725
to bring us in unto this evil p	Num 20:5	4725
it is no p of seed, or of figs,	Num 20:5	4725
called the name of the p Hormah	Num 21:3	4725
further, and stood in a narrow p	Num 22:26	4725

P

And he went to an high *p*	Num 23:3	
pray thee, with me unto another *p*	Num 23:13	4725
I will bring thee unto another *p*	Num 23:27	4725
Therefore now flee thou to thy *p*	Num 24:11	4725
up, and went and returned to his *p*	Num 24:25	4725
in the holy *p* shalt thou cause	Num 28:7	
the *p* was a *p* for cattle	Num 32:1	4725
we have brought them unto their *p*	Num 32:17	4725
be in the *p* where his lot falleth	Num 33:54	
went, until ye came into this *p*	Deut 1:31	4725
to search you out a *p* to pitch	Deut 1:33	4725
nor unto any *p* of the river	Deut 2:37	3027
Egypt, until ye came unto this *p*	Deut 9:7	4725
until ye came into this *p*	Deut 11:5	4725
Every *p* whereon the soles of your	Deut 11:24	4725
the names of them out of that *p*	Deut 12:3	4725
But unto the *p* which the LORD	Deut 12:5	4725
Then there shall be a *p* which the	Deut 12:11	4725
in every *p* that thou seest	Deut 12:13	4725
But in the *p* which the LORD shall	Deut 12:14	4725
p which the LORD thy God shall	Deut 12:18	4725
If the *p* which the LORD thy God	Deut 12:21	4725
go unto the *p* which the LORD	Deut 12:26	4725
in the *p* which he shall choose to	Deut 14:23	4725
shall choose to *p* his name there	Deut 14:23	7931
or if the *p* be too far from thee,	Deut 14:24	4725
shalt go unto the *p* which the	Deut 14:25	4725
the *p* which the LORD shall choose	Deut 15:20	4725
in the *p* which the LORD shall	Deut 16:2	4725
shall choose to *p* his name there	Deut 16:2	7931
But at the *p* which the LORD thy	Deut 16:6	4724
God shall choose to *p* his name in	Deut 16:6	7931
eat it in the *p* which the LORD	Deut 16:7	4725
in the *p* which the LORD thy God	Deut 16:11	4725
hath chosen to *p* his name there	Deut 16:11	7931
the *p* which the LORD shall choose	Deut 16:15	4725
in the *p* which he shall choose	Deut 16:16	4725
get thee up into the *p* which the	Deut 17:8	4725
which they of that *p* which the	Deut 17:10	4725
the *p* which the LORD shall choose	Deut 18:6	4725
city, and unto the gate of his *p*	Deut 21:19	4725
Thou shalt have a *p* also without	Deut 23:12	4725
in that *p* which he shall choose	Deut 23:16	4725
shalt go unto the *p* which the	Deut 26:2	4725
shall choose to *p* his name there	Deut 26:2	7931
And he hath brought us into this *p*	Deut 26:9	4725
and putteth it in a secret *p*	Deut 27:15	
And when ye came unto this *p*	Deut 29:7	4725
in the *p* which he shall choose	Deut 31:11	4725
Every *p* that the sole of your	Josh 1:3	4725
then ye shall remove from your *p*	Josh 3:3	4725
out of the *p* where the priests'	Josh 4:3	
and leave them in the lodging *p*	Josh 4:3	
them unto the *p* where they lodged	Josh 4:8	
in the *p* where the feet of the	Josh 4:9	
of Jordan returned unto their *p*	Josh 4:18	4725
Wherefore the name of the *p* is	Josh 5:9	4725
for the *p* whereon thou standest	Josh 5:15	4725
the name of that *p* was called	Josh 7:26	4725
arose quickly out of their *p*	Josh 8:19	4725
in the *p* which he should choose	Josh 9:27	4725
city unto them, and give him a *p*	Josh 20:4	4725
called the name of that *p* Bochim	Judg 2:5	4725
of this rock, in the ordered *p*	Judg 6:26	4634
people go every man unto his *p*	Judg 7:7	4725
man in his *p* round about the camp	Judg 7:21	8478
departed every man unto his *p*	Judg 9:55	4725
thee, through thy land into my *p*	Judg 11:19	4725
and called that *p* Ramath-lehi	Judg 15:17	4725
an hollow *p* that was in the jaw	Judg 15:19	
sojourn where he could find a *p*	Judg 17:8	
to sojourn where I may find a *p*	Judg 17:9	
and what makest thou in this *p*	Judg 18:3	
a *p* where there is no want of any	Judg 18:10	4725
that *p* Mahaneh-dan unto this day	Judg 18:12	4725
the men of the *p* were Benjamites	Judg 19:16	4725
rose up, and gat him unto his *p*	Judg 19:28	4725
p where they put themselves in	Judg 20:22	4725
of Israel rose up out of their *p*	Judg 20:33	4725
Israel gave *p* to the Benjamites	Judg 20:36	4725
a *p* which is on the north side of	Judg 21:19	
forth out of the *p* where she was	Ruth 1:7	4725
mark the *p* where he shall lie	Ruth 3:4	4725
and from the gate of his *p*	Ruth 4:10	4725
when Eli was laid down in his *p*	1Sa 3:2	4725
Samuel went and lay down in his *p*	1Sa 3:9	4725
Dagon, and set him in his *p* again	1Sa 5:3	4725
and let it go again to his own *p*	1Sa 5:11	4725
we shall send it to his *p*	1Sa 6:2	4725
the people to day in the high *p*	1Sa 9:12	
he go up to the high *p* to eat	1Sa 9:13	
them, for to go up to the high *p*	1Sa 9:14	
go up before me unto the high *p*	1Sa 9:19	
p among them that were bidden	1Sa 9:22	4725
from the high *p* into the city	1Sa 9:25	
from the high *p* with a psaltery	1Sa 10:5	
And one of the same *p* answered	1Sa 10:12	
he came to the high *p*	1Sa 10:13	
and made them dwell in this *p*	1Sa 12:8	4725
then we will stand still in our *p*	1Sa 14:9	8478
Philistines went to their own *p*	1Sa 14:46	4725
and, behold, he set him up a *p*	1Sa 15:12	3027
morning, and abide in a secret *p*	1Sa 19:2	
come to the *p* where thou didst	1Sa 20:19	4725
side, and David's *p* was empty	1Sa 20:25	4725
month, that David's *p* was empty	1Sa 20:27	4725
when the lad was come to the *p* of	1Sa 20:37	4725
arose out of a *p* toward the south	1Sa 20:41	
my servants to such and such a *p*	1Sa 21:2	4725
see his *p* where his haunt is, and	1Sa 23:22	4725
called that *p* Sela-hammahlekoth	1Sa 23:28	4725
came to the *p* where Saul had	1Sa 26:5	4725
David beheld the *p* where Saul lay	1Sa 26:5	4725
way, and Saul returned to his *p*	1Sa 26:25	4725
let them give me a *p* in some town	1Sa 27:5	4725
that he may go again to his *p*	1Sa 29:4	4725
wherefore that *p* was called	2Sa 2:16	4725
down there, and died in the same *p*	2Sa 2:23	8478
to the *p* where Asahel fell down	2Sa 2:23	4725
the name of that *p* Baal-perazim	2Sa 5:20	4725
of the *p* Perez-uzzah to this day	2Sa 6:8	4725
of the LORD, and set it in his *p*	2Sa 6:17	4725
appoint a *p* for my people Israel	2Sa 7:10	4725
may dwell in a *p* of their own	2Sa 7:10	8478
that he assigned Uriah unto a *p*	2Sa 11:16	4725
tarried in a *p* that was far off	2Sa 15:17	1004
return to thy *p*, and abide with	2Sa 15:19	4725
surely in what *p* my lord the king	2Sa 15:21	4725
in some pit, or in some other *p*	2Sa 17:9	4725
in some *p* where he shall be found	2Sa 17:12	4725
called unto this day, Absalom's *p*	2Sa 18:18	3027
and he returned unto his own *p*	2Sa 19:39	4725
me forth also into a large *p*	2Sa 22:20	
burned with fire in the same *p*	2Sa 23:7	7675
for that was the great high *p*	1Kin 3:4	
even unto the *p* that is beyond	1Kin 4:12	
brought they unto the *p* where the	1Kin 4:28	4725
the *p* that thou shalt appoint me	1Kin 5:9	4725
oracle, even for the most holy *p*	1Kin 6:16	
the inner house, the most holy *p*	1Kin 7:50	
covenant of the LORD unto his *p*	1Kin 8:6	4725
of the house, to the most holy *p*	1Kin 8:6	
two wings over the *p* of the ark	1Kin 8:7	4725
in the holy *p* before the oracle	1Kin 8:8	
were come out of the holy *p*	1Kin 8:10	
a settled *p* for thee to abide in	1Kin 8:13	
I have set there a *p* for the ark	1Kin 8:21	4725
even toward the *p* of which thou	1Kin 8:29	4725
servant shall make toward this *p*	1Kin 8:29	4725
they shall pray toward this *p*	1Kin 8:30	4725
thou in heaven thy dwelling *p*	1Kin 8:30	4725
if they pray toward this *p*	1Kin 8:35	4725
thou in heaven thy dwelling *p*	1Kin 8:39	4349
thou in heaven thy dwelling *p*	1Kin 8:43	4349
in heaven thy dwelling *p*, and	1Kin 8:49	4349
either side on the *p* of the seat	1Kin 10:19	4725
build an high *p* for Chemosh	1Kin 11:7	
bread nor drink water in this *p*	1Kin 13:8	4725
drink water with thee in this *p*	1Kin 13:16	4725
bread and drunk water in the *p*	1Kin 13:22	4725
away, every man out of his *p*	1Kin 20:24	4725
In the *p* where dogs licked the	1Kin 21:19	4725
in a void *p* in the entrance of	1Kin 22:10	4725
and strike his hand over the *p*	2Kin 5:11	4725
the *p* where we dwell with thee is	2Kin 6:1	4725
beam, and let us make us a *p* there	2Kin 6:2	4725
And he shewed him the *p*	2Kin 6:6	4725
such a *p* shall be my camp	2Kin 6:8	4725
that thou pass not such a *p*	2Kin 6:9	4725
p which the man of God told him	2Kin 6:10	4725
LORD against this *p* to destroy it	2Kin 18:25	4725
I will bring evil upon this *p*	2Kin 22:16	4725
shall be kindled against this *p*	2Kin 22:17	4725
what I spake against this *p*	2Kin 22:19	4725
which I will bring upon this *p*	2Kin 22:20	4725
the high *p* which Jeroboam the son	2Kin 23:15	
the high *p* he brake down	2Kin 23:15	
and burned the high *p*	2Kin 23:15	
p of the tabernacle of the	1Chr 6:32	
all the work of the *p* most holy	1Chr 6:49	
wherefore that *p* is called	1Chr 13:11	4725
the name of that *p* Baal-perazim	1Chr 14:11	4725
prepared a *p* for the ark of God,	1Chr 15:1	4725
up the ark of the LORD unto his *p*	1Chr 15:3	4725
the *p* that I have prepared for it	1Chr 15:12	
strength and gladness are in his *p*	1Chr 16:27	4725
in the high *p* that was at Gibeon	1Chr 16:39	
ordain a *p* for my people Israel	1Chr 17:9	4725
and they shall dwell in their *p*	1Chr 17:9	8478
to Ornan, Grant me the *p* of this	1Chr 21:22	4725
p six hundred shekels of gold by	1Chr 21:25	4725
season in the high *p* at Gibeon	1Chr 21:29	
and the charge of the holy *p*	1Chr 23:32	
of the *p* of the mercy seat,	1Chr 28:11	1004
went to the high *p* that was at	2Chr 1:3	
up from Kirjath-jearim to the *p*	2Chr 1:4	
from his journey to the high *p*	2Chr 1:13	
in the *p* that David had prepared	2Chr 3:1	4725
doors thereof for the most holy *p*	2Chr 4:22	
covenant of the LORD unto his *p*	2Chr 5:7	4725
the house, into the most holy *p*	2Chr 5:7	
their wings over the *p* of the ark	2Chr 5:8	4725
were come out of the holy *p*	2Chr 5:11	
a *p* for thy dwelling for ever	2Chr 6:2	4349
upon the *p* whereof thou hast said	2Chr 6:20	4725
thy servant prayeth toward this *p*	2Chr 6:20	4725
they shall make toward this *p*	2Chr 6:21	4725
hear thou from thy dwelling *p*	2Chr 6:21	4725
yet if they pray toward this *p*	2Chr 6:26	4725
thou from heaven thy dwelling *p*	2Chr 6:30	4349
heavens, even from thy dwelling *p*	2Chr 6:33	4349
heavens, even from thy dwelling *p*	2Chr 6:39	4349
the prayer that is made in this *p*	2Chr 6:40	4725
O LORD God, into thy resting *p*	2Chr 6:41	
have chosen this *p* to myself for	2Chr 7:12	4725
the prayer that is made in this *p*	2Chr 7:15	4725
on each side of the sitting *p*	2Chr 9:18	4725
they sat in a void *p* at the	2Chr 18:9	
the name of the same *p* was called	2Chr 20:26	4725
it, and carried it to his *p* again	2Chr 24:11	4725
the filthiness out of the holy *p*	2Chr 29:5	
the holy *p* unto the God of Israel	2Chr 29:7	
in their *p* after their manner	2Chr 30:16	5977
came up to his holy dwelling *p*	2Chr 30:27	
I will bring evil upon this *p*	2Chr 34:24	4725
shall be poured out upon this *p*	2Chr 34:25	4725
heardest his words against this *p*	2Chr 34:27	4725
that I will bring upon this *p*	2Chr 34:28	4725
And the king stood in his *p*	2Chr 34:31	5977
stand in the holy *p* according to	2Chr 35:5	
and the priests stood in their *p*	2Chr 35:10	5977
the sons of Asaph were in their *p*	2Chr 35:15	4612
his people, and on his dwelling *p*	2Chr 36:15	
in any *p* where he sojourneth	Ezr 1:4	4725
let the men of his *p* help him	Ezr 1:4	4725
of God to set it up in his *p*	Ezr 2:68	4349
house of God be builded in his *p*	Ezr 5:15	870
builded, the *p* where they offered	Ezr 6:3	870
at Jerusalem, every one to his *p*	Ezr 6:5	870
p them in the house of God	Ezr 6:5	5182
build this house of God in his *p*	Ezr 6:7	870
Iddo the chief at the *p* Casiphia	Ezr 8:17	4725
at the *p* Casiphia, that they	Ezr 8:17	4725
to give us a nail in his holy *p*	Ezr 9:8	4725
will bring them unto the *p* that I	Neh 1:9	4725
the *p* of my fathers' sepulchres,	Neh 2:3	1004
but there was no *p* for the beast	Neh 2:14	4725
unto the *p* over against the	Neh 3:16	
unto the *p* over against the water	Neh 3:26	
son unto the *p* of the Nethinims	Neh 3:31	1004
In what *p* therefore ye hear the	Neh 4:20	4725
and the people stood in their *p*	Neh 8:7	5977
And they stood up in their *p*	Neh 9:3	5977
together, and set them in their *p*	Neh 13:11	5977
her maids unto the best *p* of the	Est 2:9	
arise to the Jews from another *p*	Est 4:14	4725
into the *p* of the banquet of wine	Est 7:8	1004
came every one from his own *p*	Job 2:11	4725
they are consumed out of their *p*	Job 6:17	4725
shall his *p* know him any more	Job 7:10	4725
heap, and seeth the *p* of stones	Job 8:17	1004
If he destroy him from his *p*	Job 8:18	4725
the dwelling *p* of the wicked	Job 8:22	
shaketh the earth out of her *p*	Job 9:6	4725
the rock is removed out of his *p*	Job 14:18	4725
my blood, and let my cry have no *p*	Job 16:18	4725
the rock be removed out of his *p*	Job 18:4	4725
this is the *p* of him that knoweth	Job 18:21	4725
neither shall his *p* any more	Job 20:9	4725
out the north over the empty *p*	Job 26:7	8414
a storm hurleth him out of his *p*	Job 27:21	4725
and shall hiss him out of his *p*	Job 27:23	4725
a *p* for gold where they fine it	Job 28:1	4725
of it are the *p* of sapphires	Job 28:6	4725
where is the *p* of understanding	Job 28:12	4725
where is the *p* of understanding	Job 28:20	4725
and he knoweth the *p* thereof	Job 28:23	4725
out of the strait into a broad *p*	Job 36:16	
people are cut off in their *p*	Job 36:20	8478
and is moved out of his *p*	Job 37:1	4725
And brake up for it my decreed *p*	Job 38:10	
the dayspring to know his *p*	Job 38:12	4725
darkness, where is the *p* thereof	Job 38:19	4725
crag of the rock, and the strong *p*	Job 39:28	
tread down the wicked in their *p*	Job 40:12	8478
He made darkness his secret *p*	Ps 18:11	
me forth also into a large *p*	Ps 18:19	4800
or who shall stand in his holy *p*	Ps 24:3	4725
the *p* where thine honour dwelleth	Ps 26:8	4725
My foot standeth in an even *p*	Ps 26:12	
Thou art my hiding *p*	Ps 32:7	
From the *p* of his habitation he	Ps 33:14	4349
shalt diligently consider his *p*	Ps 37:10	4725
broken us in the *p* of dragons	Ps 44:19	4725
the holy *p* of the tabernacles of	Ps 46:4	
pluck thee out of thy dwelling *p*	Ps 52:5	
us out into a wealthy *p*	Ps 66:12	
them, as in Sinai, in the holy *p*	Ps 68:17	
p of thy name to the ground	Ps 74:7	
and his dwelling *p* in Zion	Ps 76:2	
and laid waste his dwelling *p*	Ps 79:7	
thee in the secret *p* of thunder	Ps 81:7	
our dwelling *p* in all generations	Ps 90:1	
p of the most High shall abide	Ps 91:1	
the *p* thereof shall know it no	Ps 103:16	4725
the *p* which thou hast founded for	Ps 104:8	4725
me, and set me in a large *p*	Ps 118:5	
Thou art my hiding *p* and my shield	Ps 119:114	
Until I find out a *p* for the LORD	Ps 132:5	4725
in the chief *p* of concourse	Prov 1:21	
children shall have a *p* of refuge	Prov 14:26	
eyes of the LORD are in every *p*	Prov 15:3	4725
spoil not his resting *p*	Prov 24:15	
stand not in the *p* of great men	Prov 25:6	4725
a man that wandereth from his *p*	Prov 27:8	4725
hasteth to his *p* where he arose	Eccl 1:5	4725
unto the *p* from whence the rivers	Eccl 1:7	4725
under the sun the *p* of judgment	Eccl 3:16	4725
the *p* of righteousness, that	Eccl 3:16	4725
All go unto one *p*	Eccl 3:20	4725
do not all go to one *p*	Eccl 6:6	4725
and gone from the *p* of the holy	Eccl 8:10	4725
up against thee, leave not thy *p*	Eccl 10:4	4725
dignity, and the rich sit in low *p*	Eccl 10:6	
in the *p* where the tree falleth,	Eccl 11:3	4725
every dwelling *p* of mount Zion	Is 4:5	
for a *p* of refuge, and for a	Is 4:6	
to field, till there be no *p*	Is 5:8	4725
that day, that every *p* shall be	Is 7:23	4725
earth shall remove out of her *p*	Is 13:13	4725
them, and bring them to their *p*	Is 14:2	4725
that Moab is weary on the high *p*	Is 16:12	
p like a clear heat upon herbs	Is 18:4	
to the *p* of the name of the LORD	Is 18:7	4725
fasten him as a nail in a sure *p*	Is 22:23	4725
fastened in the sure *p* be removed	Is 22:25	4725
strangers, as the heat in a dry *p*	Is 25:5	
the LORD cometh out of his *p* to	Is 26:21	4725
so that there is no *p* clean	Is 28:8	4725
shall overflow the hiding *p*	Is 28:17	
barley and the rie in their *p*	Is 28:25	1367
in every *p* where the grounded	Is 30:32	

be as an hiding p from the wind ... Is 32:2
as rivers of water in a dry p ... Is 32:2
the city shall be low in a low p ... Is 32:19
his p of defence shall be the ... Is 33:16
be unto us a p of broad rivers ... Is 33:21 4725
and find for herself a p of rest ... Is 34:14
the solitary p shall be glad for ... Is 35:1
secret, in a dark p of the earth ... Is 45:19 4725
carry him, and set him in his p ... Is 46:7 8478
from his p shall he not remove ... Is 46:7 4725
I will p salvation in Zion for ... Is 46:13 5414
The p is too strait for me ... Is 49:20 4725
give p to me that I may dwell ... Is 49:20 4725
Enlarge the p of thy tent ... Is 54:2 4725
mine house and within my walls a p ... Is 56:5 3027
I dwell in the high and holy p ... Is 57:15
to beautify the p of my sanctuary ... Is 60:13 4725
I will make the p of my feet ... Is 60:13 4725
the valley of Achor a p for the ... Is 65:10
and where is the p of my rest ... Is 66:1 4725
his p to make thy land desolate ... Jer 4:7 4725
the fruitful p was a wilderness, ... Jer 4:26
shall feed every one in his p ... Jer 6:3 3027
will cause you to dwell in this p ... Jer 7:3 4725
shed not innocent blood in this p ... Jer 7:6 4725
I cause you to dwell in this p ... Jer 7:7 4725
now unto my p which was in Shiloh ... Jer 7:12 4725
unto the p which I gave to you and ... Jer 7:14 4725
shall be poured out upon this p ... Jer 7:20 4725
in Tophet, till there be no p ... Jer 7:32 4725
a lodging p of wayfaring men ... Jer 9:2
from the p where I had hid it ... Jer 13:7 4725
give you assured peace in this p ... Jer 14:13 4725
have sons or daughters in this p ... Jer 16:2 4725
daughters that are born in this p ... Jer 16:3 4725
cease out of this p in your eyes ... Jer 16:9 4725
is the p of our sanctuary ... Jer 17:12 4725
come from another p be forsaken ... Jer 18:14
I will bring evil upon this p ... Jer 19:3 4725
me, and have estranged this p ... Jer 19:4 4725
have filled this p with the blood ... Jer 19:4 4725
that this p shall no more be ... Jer 19:6 4725
of Judah and Jerusalem in this p ... Jer 19:7 4725
till there be no p to bury ... Jer 19:11 4725
Thus will I do unto this p ... Jer 19:12 4725
be defiled as the p of Tophet ... Jer 19:13 4725
shed innocent blood in this p ... Jer 22:3 4725
which went forth out of this p ... Jer 22:11 4725
But he shall die in the p whither ... Jer 22:12 4725
whom I have sent out of this p ... Jer 24:5 4725
up, and restore them to this p ... Jer 27:22 4725
will I bring again into this p ... Jer 28:3 4725
of Babylon took away from this p ... Jer 28:3 4725
I will bring again to this p ... Jer 28:4 4725
captive, from Babylon into this p ... Jer 28:6 4725
causing you to return to this p ... Jer 29:10 4725
the p whence I caused you to be ... Jer 29:14 4725
will bring them again unto this p ... Jer 32:37 4725
there shall be heard in this p ... Jer 33:10 4725
Again in this p, which is ... Jer 33:12 4725
for hunger in the p where he is ... Jer 38:9 8478
pronounced this evil upon this p ... Jer 40:2 4725
and ye shall see this p no more ... Jer 42:18 4725
in the p whither ye desire to go ... Jer 42:22 4725
that I will punish you in this p ... Jer 44:29 4725
a dwelling p for dragons, an ... Jer 51:37 4725
thou hast spoken against this p ... Jer 51:62 4725
the glory of the LORD from his p ... Eze 3:12 4725
the p where they did offer sweet ... Eze 6:13 4725
and they shall pollute my secret p ... Eze 7:22
but to the p whither the head ... Eze 10:11 4725
thou shalt remove from thy p ... Eze 12:3 4725
to another p in their sight ... Eze 12:3 4725
also built unto thee an eminent p ... Eze 16:24
thee an high p in every street ... Eze 16:24
high p at every head of the way ... Eze 16:25
p in the head of every way ... Eze 16:31
thine high p in every street ... Eze 16:31
shall throw down thine eminent p ... Eze 16:39
surely in the p where the king ... Eze 17:16 4725
is the high p whereunto ye go ... Eze 20:29
and choose thou a p, choose it at ... Eze 21:19 3027
in the p where thou wast created ... Eze 21:30 4725
It shall be a p for the spreading ... Eze 26:5
thou shalt be a p to spread nets ... Eze 26:14
I shall p you in your own land ... Eze 37:14 3241
and I will p them, and multiply ... Eze 37:26 5414
from thy p out of the north parts ... Eze 38:15 4725
Gog a p there of graves in Israel ... Eze 39:11 4725
unto me, This is the most holy p ... Eze 41:4
that which was left was the p of ... Eze 41:9 1004
were toward the p that was left ... Eze 41:11
the breadth of the p that was ... Eze 41:11 4725
that was before the separate p at ... Eze 41:12
and the separate p, and the ... Eze 41:13
of the separate p toward the east ... Eze 41:14
separate p which was behind it ... Eze 41:15
was over against the separate p ... Eze 42:1
east, over against the separate p ... Eze 42:10
which are before the separate p ... Eze 42:13
for the p is holy ... Eze 42:13 4725
the holy p into the utter court ... Eze 42:14
the sanctuary and the profane p ... Eze 42:20
the p of my throne ... Eze 43:7 4725
the p of the soles of my feet, ... Eze 43:7 4725
be the higher p of the altar ... Eze 43:13
in the appointed p of the house ... Eze 43:21
holy things, in the most holy p ... Eze 44:13
the sanctuary and the most holy p ... Eze 45:3
it shall be a p for their houses, ... Eze 45:4 4725
an holy p for the sanctuary ... Eze 45:4
there was a p on the two sides ... Eze 46:19 4725
This is the p where the priests ... Eze 46:20 4725
they shall be a p to spread forth ... Eze 47:10
shall be a profane p for the city ... Eze 48:15
that no p was found for them ... Dan 2:35 870
the p of his sanctuary was cast ... Dan 8:11 4349
they shall p the abomination that ... Dan 11:31 5414
that in the p where it was said ... Hos 1:10 4725
feed them as a lamb in a large p ... Hos 4:16
I will go and return to my p ... Hos 5:15 4725
Tyrus, is planted in a pleasant p ... Hos 9:13
I will p them in their houses, ... Hos 11:11 3427
in the p of the breaking forth of ... Hos 13:13
the p whither ye have sold them ... Joel 3:7 4725
be many dead bodies in every p ... Amos 8:3 4725
LORD cometh forth out of his p ... Mic 1:3 4725
that are poured down a steep p ... Mic 1:4
an utter end of the p thereof ... Nah 1:8 4725
the feeding p of the young lions, ... Nah 2:11 4725
their p is not known where they ... Nah 3:17 4725
the remnant of Baal from this p ... Zeph 1:4 4725
worship him, every one from his p ... Zeph 2:11 4725
a p for beasts to lie down in ... Zeph 2:15
in this p will I give peace, ... Hag 2:9 4725
and he shall grow up out of his p ... Zec 6:12 8478
I will bring them again to p them ... Zec 10:6 3427
p shall not be found for them ... Zec 10:10
be inhabited again in her own p ... Zec 12:6 8478
lifted up, and inhabited in her p ... Zec 14:10 8478
gate unto the p of the first gate ... Zec 14:10 4725
in every p incense shall be ... Mal 1:11 4725
down a steep p into the sea ... Mt 8:32
He said unto them, Give p ... Mt 9:24 402
That in this p is one greater ... Mt 12:6 5602
by ship into a desert p apart ... Mt 14:13 5117
him, saying, This is a desert p ... Mt 14:15 5117
of that p had knowledge of him ... Mt 14:35 5117
Remove hence to yonder p ... Mt 17:20
the prophet, stand in the holy p ... Mt 24:15 5117
them unto a p called Gethsemane ... Mt 26:36 5564
Put up again thy sword into his p ... Mt 26:52 5117
come unto a p called Golgotha ... Mt 27:33 5117
that is to say, a p of a skull, ... Mt 27:33 5117
see the p where the Lord lay ... Mt 28:6 5117
and departed into a solitary p ... Mk 1:35 5117
down a steep p into the sea ... Mk 5:13
In what p soever ye enter into a ... Mk 6:10 3699
abide till ye depart from that p ... Mk 6:10 1564
yourselves apart into a desert p ... Mk 6:31 5117
into a desert p by ship privately ... Mk 6:32 5117
him, and said, This is a desert p ... Mk 6:35 5117
without in a p where two ways met ... Mk 11:4
digged a p for the winefat, and ... Mk 12:1
they came to a p which was named ... Mk 14:32 5564
bring him unto the p Golgotha ... Mk 15:22 5117
interpreted, The p of a skull ... Mk 15:22 5117
behold the p where they laid him ... Mk 16:6 5117
he found the p where it was ... Lk 4:17 5117
p of the country round about ... Lk 4:37 5117
departed and went into a desert p ... Lk 4:42 5117
down a steep p into the lake ... Lk 8:33
p belonging to the city called ... Lk 9:10 5117
for we are here in a desert p ... Lk 9:12 5117
his face into every city and p ... Lk 10:1 5117
a Levite, when he was at the p ... Lk 10:32 5117
as he was praying in a certain p ... Lk 11:1 5117
candle, putteth it in a secret p ... Lk 11:33
and say to thee, Give this man p ... Lk 14:9 5117
also come into this p of torment ... Lk 16:28 5117
And when Jesus came to the p ... Lk 19:5 5117
And when he was at the p, he said ... Lk 22:40 5117
beginning from Galilee to this p ... Lk 23:5 5602
And when they were come to the p ... Lk 23:33 5117
that in Jerusalem is the p where ... Jn 4:20 5117
away, a multitude being in that p ... Jn 5:13 5117
Now there was much grass in the p ... Jn 6:10 5117
the p where they did eat bread ... Jn 6:23 5117
because my word hath no p in you ... Jn 8:37 5562
p where John at first baptized ... Jn 10:40 5117
still in the same p where he was ... Jn 11:6 5117
but was in that p where Martha ... Jn 11:30 5117
the p where the dead was laid ... Jn 11:41
come and take away both our p ... Jn 11:48 5117
I go to prepare a p for you ... Jn 14:2 5117
And if I go and prepare a p for you ... Jn 14:3 5117
which betrayed him, knew the p ... Jn 18:2 5117
a p that is called the Pavement ... Jn 19:13 5117
a p called the p of a skull ... Jn 19:17 5117
for the p where Jesus was ... Jn 19:20 5117
Now in the p where he was ... Jn 19:41 5117
wrapped together in a p by itself ... Jn 20:7 5117
that he might go to his own p ... Acts 1:25 5117
were all with one accord in one p ... Acts 2:1
the p was shaken where they were ... Acts 4:31 5117
words against this holy p ... Acts 6:13 5117
of Nazareth shall destroy this p ... Acts 6:14 5117
come forth, and serve me in this p ... Acts 7:7 5117
for the p where thou standest is ... Acts 7:33 5117
or what is the p of my rest ... Acts 7:49 5117
The p of the scripture which he ... Acts 8:32 4042
departed, and went into another p ... Acts 12:17 5117
both we, and they of that p ... Acts 21:12 1786
the people, and the law, and this p ... Acts 21:28 5117
and hath polluted this holy p ... Acts 21:28 5117
was entered into the p of hearing ... Acts 25:23 201
came unto a p which is called The ... Acts 27:8 5117
falling into a p where two seas ... Acts 27:41 5117
that in the p where it was said ... Rom 9:26 5117
but rather give p unto wrath ... Rom 12:19 5117
having no more p in these parts ... Rom 15:23 5117
with all that in every p call ... 1Cor 1:2 5117
have no certain dwellingplace p ... 1Cor 4:11 5117
together therefore into one p ... 1Cor 11:20
be come together into one p ... 1Cor 14:23
of his knowledge by us in every p ... 2Cor 2:14 5117
To whom we gave p by subjection ... Gal 2:5 1502
Neither give p to the devil ... Eph 4:27 5117
but also in every p your faith to ... 1Th 1:8 5117
But one in a certain p testified ... Heb 2:6
For he spake in a certain p of ... Heb 4:4
And in this p again, If they shall ... Heb 4:5
As he saith also in another p ... Heb 5:6
then should no p have been sought ... Heb 8:7 5117
entered in once into the holy p ... Heb 9:12
priest entereth into the holy p ... Heb 9:25
a p which he should after receive ... Heb 11:8 5117
for he found no p of repentance ... Heb 12:17 5117
him, Sit thou here in a good p ... Jas 2:3
forth at the same p sweet water ... Jas 3:11 3692
a light that shineth in a dark p ... 2Pet 1:19 5117
thy candlestick out of his p ... Rev 2:5 5117
she hath a p prepared of God ... Rev 12:6 5117
neither was their p found any ... Rev 12:8 5117
into the wilderness, into her p ... Rev 12:14 5117
a p called in the Hebrew tongue ... Rev 16:16 5117
and there was found no p for them ... Rev 20:11 5117

PLACED

he p at the east of the garden of ... Gen 3:24 7931
Joseph p his father and his ... Gen 47:11 3427
he p in Beth-el the priests of ... 1Kin 12:32 5975
p them in Halah and in Habor by ... 2Kin 17:6 3427
p them in the cities of Samaria ... 2Kin 17:24 3427
p in the cities of Samaria, know ... 2Kin 17:26 3427
which he p in the chariot cities, ... 2Chr 1:14 3240
p them in the temple, five on the ... 2Chr 4:8 3240
he p forces in all the fenced ... 2Chr 17:2 5414
old, since man was p upon earth ... Job 20:4 7760
the tent which he p among men ... Ps 78:60 7931
that they may be p alone in the ... Is 5:8 3427
which have p the sand for the ... Jer 5:22 776
he p it by great waters, and set ... Eze 17:5 3947

PLACES

thee in all p whither thou goest ... Gen 28:15
to their families, after their p ... Gen 36:40 4725
in all p where I record my name I ... Ex 20:24 4725
border shall the rings be for p ... Ex 25:27 1004
rings of gold for p for the bars ... Ex 26:29 1004
they shall be for p for the ... Ex 30:4 1004
of gold to be p for the bars ... Ex 36:34 1004
the p for the staves to bear the ... Ex 37:14 1004
to be p for the staves to bear it ... Ex 37:27 1004
of brass, to be p for the staves ... Ex 38:5 1004
And I will destroy your high p ... Lev 26:30
the lords of the high p of Arnon ... Num 21:28
him up into the high p of Baal ... Num 22:41
quite pluck down all their high p ... Num 33:52
unto all the p nigh thereunto, in ... Deut 1:7
shall utterly destroy all the p ... Deut 12:2 4725
ride on the high p of the earth ... Deut 32:13
shalt tread upon their high p ... Deut 33:29
they abode in their p in the camp ... Josh 5:8 8478
archers in the p of drawing water ... Judg 5:11
death in the high p of the field ... Judg 5:18
one of these p to lodge all night ... Judg 19:13 4725
Israel came forth out of their p ... Judg 20:33 4725
and judged Israel in all those p ... 1Sa 7:16 4725
and in rocks, and in high p ... 1Sa 13:6
lurking p where he hideth himself ... 1Sa 23:23
to all the p where David himself ... 1Sa 30:31 4725
Israel is slain upon thy high p ... 2Sa 1:19
thou wast slain in thine high p ... 2Sa 1:25
In all the p wherein I have ... 2Sa 7:7
and setteth me upon my high p ... 2Sa 22:34
be afraid out of their close p ... 2Sa 22:46
the people sacrificed in high p ... 1Kin 3:2
and burnt incense in high p ... 1Kin 3:3
And he made an house of high p ... 1Kin 12:31
of the high p which he had made ... 1Kin 12:32
p that burn incense upon thee ... 1Kin 13:2
high p which are in the cities of ... 1Kin 13:32
the people priests of the high p ... 1Kin 13:33
one of the priests of the high p ... 1Kin 13:33
For they also built them high p ... 1Kin 14:23
But the high p were not removed ... 1Kin 15:14
the high p were not taken away ... 1Kin 22:43
burnt incense yet in the high p ... 1Kin 22:43
But the high p were not taken ... 2Kin 12:3
and burnt incense in the high p ... 2Kin 12:3
Howbeit the high p were not taken ... 2Kin 14:4
and burnt incense on the high p ... 2Kin 14:4
that the high p were not removed ... 2Kin 15:4
burnt incense still on the high p ... 2Kin 15:4
the high p were not removed ... 2Kin 15:35
incense still in the high p ... 2Kin 15:35
and burnt incense in the high p ... 2Kin 16:4
them high p in all their cities ... 2Kin 17:9
burnt incense in all the high p ... 2Kin 17:11
p which the Samaritans had made ... 2Kin 17:29
of them priests of the high p ... 2Kin 17:32
them in the houses of the high p ... 2Kin 17:32
He removed the high p, and brake ... 2Kin 18:4
is not that he, whose high p ... 2Kin 18:22
up all the rivers of besieged p ... 2Kin 19:24
p which Hezekiah his father had ... 2Kin 21:3
the high p in the cities of Judah ... 2Kin 23:5
in the p round about Jerusalem ... 2Kin 23:5
defiled the high p where the ... 2Kin 23:8
brake down the high p of the ... 2Kin 23:8
the priests of the high p came ... 2Kin 23:9
the high p that were before ... 2Kin 23:13
filled their p with the bones of ... 2Kin 23:14 4725
high p that were in the cities of ... 2Kin 23:19
all the priests of the high p ... 2Kin 23:20
p throughout their castles in ... 1Chr 6:54
of Israel, because the p are holy ... 2Chr 8:11
him priests for the high p ... 2Chr 11:15
the strange gods, and the high p ... 2Chr 14:3
the cities of Judah the high p ... 2Chr 14:5
But the high p were not taken ... 2Chr 15:17
moreover he took away the high p ... 2Chr 17:6

P

Howbeit the high *p* were not taken ... 2Chr 20:33
Moreover he made high *p* in the ... 2Chr 21:11
and burnt incense in the high *p* ... 2Chr 28:4
city of Judah he made high *p* to ... 2Chr 28:25
groves, and threw down the high *p* ... 2Chr 31:1
Hezekiah taken away his high *p* ... 2Chr 32:12
For he built again the high *p* ... 2Chr 33:3
did sacrifice still in the high *p* ... 2Chr 33:17
the *p* wherein he built high ... 2Chr 33:19 4725
p wherein he built high *p* ... 2Chr 33:19
and Jerusalem from the high *p* ... 2Chr 34:3
From all *p* whence ye shall return ... Neh 4:12 4725
I in the lower *p* behind the wall ... Neh 4:13 4725
the wall, and on the higher *p* ... Neh 4:13
the Levites out of all their *p* ... Neh 12:27 4725
built desolate *p* for themselves ... Job 3:14 2723
shall be hid in his secret *p* ... Job 20:26
are the dwelling *p* of the wicked ... Job 21:28 168
he maketh peace in his high *p* ... Job 25:2
into dens, and remain in their *p* ... Job 37:8 4585
in the lurking *p* of the villages ... Ps 10:8
in the secret *p* doth he murder ... Ps 10:8
are fallen unto me in pleasant *p* ... Ps 16:6
a young lion lurking in secret *p* ... Ps 17:12
and setteth me upon my high *p* ... Ps 18:33
and be afraid out of their close *p* ... Ps 18:45
ever, and their dwelling *p* to all ... Ps 49:11
art terrible out of thy holy *p* ... Ps 68:35
thou didst set them in slippery *p* ... Ps 73:18
for the dark *p* of the earth are ... Ps 74:20
him to anger with their high *p* ... Ps 78:58
hand are the deep *p* of the earth ... Ps 95:4
works in all *p* of his dominion ... Ps 103:22 4725
ran in the dry *p* like a river ... Ps 105:41
also out of their desolate *p* ... Ps 109:10
he shall fill the *p* with the dead ... Ps 110:6
earth, in the seas, and all deep *p* ... Ps 135:6
judges are overthrown in stony *p* ... Ps 141:6 3027
She standeth in the top of high *p* ... Prov 8:2
by the way in the *p* of the paths ... Prov 8:2 1004
upon the highest *p* of the city ... Prov 9:3
a seat in the high *p* of the city ... Prov 9:14
in the secret *p* of the stairs ... Song 2:14
the waste *p* of the fat ones shall ... Is 5:17
Bajith, and to Dibon, the high *p* ... Is 15:2
dwellings, and in quiet resting *p* ... Is 32:18
is it not he, whose high *p* ... Is 36:7
all the rivers of the besieged *p* ... Is 37:25
straight, and the rough *p* plain ... Is 40:4
I will open rivers in high *p* ... Is 41:18
raise up the decayed *p* thereof ... Is 44:26
and make the crooked *p* straight ... Is 45:2
and hidden riches of secret *p* ... Is 45:3
pastures shall be in all high *p* ... Is 49:9
For thy waste and thy desolate *p* ... Is 49:19
he will comfort all her waste *p* ... Is 51:3
together, ye waste *p* of Jerusalem ... Is 52:9
thee shall build the old waste *p* ... Is 58:12
ride upon the high *p* of the earth ... Is 58:14
we are in desolate *p* as dead men ... Is 59:10
up thine eyes unto the high *p* ... Jer 3:2
A voice was heard upon the high *p* ... Jer 3:21
A dry wind of the high *p* in the ... Jer 4:11
from those *p* shall come unto me ... Jer 4:12
and seek in the broad *p* thereof ... Jer 5:1
take up a lamentation on high *p* ... Jer 7:29
have built the high *p* of Tophet ... Jer 7:31
which remain in all the *p* whither ... Jer 8:3 4725
all high *p* through the wilderness ... Jer 12:12
weep in secret *p* for your pride ... Jer 13:17
asses did stand in the high *p* ... Jer 14:6
the spoil, and thy high *p* for sin ... Jer 17:3
the parched *p* in the wilderness ... Jer 17:6
from the *p* about Jerusalem, and ... Jer 17:26 5439
built also the high *p* of Baal ... Jer 19:5
the pleasant *p* of the wilderness ... Jer 23:10
secret *p* that I shall not see him ... Jer 23:24
in all *p* whither I shall drive ... Jer 24:9 4725
house as the high *p* of a forest ... Jer 26:18
from all the *p* whither I have ... Jer 29:14 4725
And they built the high *p* of Baal ... Jer 32:35
in the *p* about Jerusalem, and in ... Jer 32:44
in the *p* about Jerusalem, and in ... Jer 33:13
of all *p* whither they were driven ... Jer 40:12 4725
prey in all *p* whither thou goest ... Jer 45:5 4725
him that offereth in the high *p* ... Jer 48:35
I have uncovered his secret *p* ... Jer 49:10
destroyed his *p* of the assembly ... Lam 2:6
He hath set me in dark *p*, as they ... Lam 3:6
in wait, and as a lion in secret *p* ... Lam 3:10
and I will destroy your high *p* ... Eze 6:3
the high *p* shall be desolate ... Eze 6:6
their holy *p* shall be defiled ... Eze 7:24
deckedst thy high *p* with divers ... Eze 16:16
and shall break down thy high *p* ... Eze 16:39
drop thy word toward the holy *p* ... Eze 21:2
in *p* desolate of old, with them ... Eze 26:20
will deliver them out of all *p* ... Eze 34:12 4725
the inhabited *p* of the country ... Eze 34:13
the *p* round about my hill a ... Eze 34:26
even the ancient high *p* are ours ... Eze 36:2
I the LORD build the ruined *p* ... Eze 36:36
desolate *p* that are now inhabited ... Eze 38:12
the steep *p* shall fall, and every ... Eze 38:20
of their kings in their high *p* ... Eze 43:7
it was made with boiling *p* under ... Eze 46:23
These are the *p* of them that boil ... Eze 46:24 1004
But the miry *p* thereof and the ... Eze 47:11
the fattest *p* of the province ... Dan 11:24
the pleasant *p* for their silver, ... Hos 9:6
The high *p* also of Aven, the sin ... Hos 10:8
and want of bread in all your *p* ... Amos 4:6 4725
upon the high *p* of the earth ... Amos 4:13
the high *p* of Isaac shall be ... Amos 7:9
upon the high *p* of the earth ... Mic 1:3
and what are the high *p* of Judah ... Mic 1:5
house as the high *p* of the forest ... Mic 3:12
make me to walk upon mine high *p* ... Hab 3:19
I will give thee *p* to walk among ... Zec 3:7
return and build the desolate *p* ... Mal 1:4
a man, he walketh through dry *p* ... Mt 12:43 *5117*
Some fell upon stony *p*, where ... Mt 13:5
received the seed into stony *p* ... Mt 13:20
and earthquakes, in divers *p* ... Mt 24:7 *5117*
city, but was without in desert *p* ... Mk 1:45 *5117*
shall be earthquakes in divers *p* ... Mk 13:8 *5117*
a man, he walketh through dry *p* ... Lk 11:24 *5117*
earthquakes shall be in divers *p* ... Lk 21:11 *5117*
We accept it always, and in all *p* ... Acts 24:3 *3837*
blessings in heavenly *p* in Christ ... Eph 1:3
own right hand in the heavenly *p* ... Eph 1:20
in heavenly *p* in Christ Jesus ... Eph 2:6
powers in heavenly *p* might be ... Eph 3:10
spiritual wickedness in high *p* ... Eph 6:12
all the palace, and in all other *p* ... Phil 1:13
into the holy *p* made with hands ... Heb 9:24
island were moved out of their *p* ... Rev 6:14 *5117*

PLAGUE

I bring one *p* more upon Pharaoh ... Ex 11:1 5061
the *p* shall not be upon you to ... Ex 12:13 5063
that there be no *p* among them ... Ex 30:12 5063
his flesh like the *p* of leprosy ... Lev 13:2 5061
on the *p* in the skin of the flesh ... Lev 13:3 5061
the hair in the *p* is turned white ... Lev 13:3 5061
the *p* in sight be deeper than the ... Lev 13:3 5061
his flesh, it is a *p* of leprosy ... Lev 13:3 5061
up him that hath the *p* seven days ... Lev 13:4 5061
if the *p* in his sight be at a ... Lev 13:5 5061
the *p* spread not in the skin ... Lev 13:5 5061
if the *p* be somewhat dark ... Lev 13:6 5061
the *p* spread not in the skin ... Lev 13:6 5061
When the *p* of leprosy is in a man ... Lev 13:9 5061
the skin of him that hath the *p* ... Lev 13:12 5061
him clean that hath the *p* ... Lev 13:13 5061
if the *p* be turned into white ... Lev 13:17 5061
him clean that hath the *p* ... Lev 13:17 5061
it is a *p* of leprosy broken out ... Lev 13:20 5061
it is a *p* ... Lev 13:22 5061
it is the *p* of leprosy ... Lev 13:25 5061
it is the *p* of leprosy ... Lev 13:27 5061
If a man or woman have a *p* upon ... Lev 13:29 5061
Then the priest shall see the *p* ... Lev 13:30 5061
priest look on the *p* of the scall ... Lev 13:31 5061
the *p* of the scall seven days ... Lev 13:31 5061
the priest shall look on the *p* ... Lev 13:32 5061
his *p* is in his head ... Lev 13:44 5061
And the leper in whom the *p* is ... Lev 13:45 5061
All the days wherein the *p* shall ... Lev 13:46 5061
also that the *p* of leprosy is in ... Lev 13:47 5061
if the *p* be greenish or reddish ... Lev 13:49 5061
it is a *p* of leprosy, and shall be ... Lev 13:49 5061
the priest shall look upon the *p* ... Lev 13:50 5061
up it that hath the *p* seven days ... Lev 13:50 5061
look on the *p* on the seventh day ... Lev 13:51 5061
if the *p* be spread in the garment ... Lev 13:51 5061
the *p* is a fretting leprosy ... Lev 13:51 5061
thing of skin, wherein the *p* is ... Lev 13:52 5061
the *p* be not spread in the ... Lev 13:53 5061
wash the thing wherein the *p* is ... Lev 13:54 5061
And the priest shall look on the *p* ... Lev 13:55 5061
if the *p* have not changed his ... Lev 13:55 5061
colour, and the *p* be not spread ... Lev 13:55 5061
the *p* be somewhat dark after the ... Lev 13:56 5061
it is a spreading *p* ... Lev 13:57
that wherein the *p* is with fire ... Lev 13:57 5061
if the *p* be departed from them, ... Lev 13:58 5061
This is the law of the *p* of ... Lev 13:59 5061
if the *p* of leprosy be healed in ... Lev 14:3 5061
him in whom is the *p* of leprosy ... Lev 14:32 5061
I put the *p* of leprosy in a house ... Lev 14:34 5061
is as it were a *p* in the house ... Lev 14:35 5061
priest go into it to see the *p* ... Lev 14:36 5061
And he shall look on the *p* ... Lev 14:37 5061
if the *p* be in the walls of the ... Lev 14:37 5061
if the *p* be spread in the walls ... Lev 14:39 5061
away the stones in which the *p* is ... Lev 14:40 5061
if the *p* come again, and break out ... Lev 14:43 5061
if the *p* be spread in the house, ... Lev 14:44 5061
the *p* hath not spread in the ... Lev 14:48 5061
clean, because the *p* is healed ... Lev 14:48 5061
for all manner of *p* of leprosy ... Lev 14:54 5061
that there be no *p* among the ... Num 8:19 5063
the people with a very great *p* ... Num 11:33 4347
died by the *p* before the LORD ... Num 14:37 4046
the *p* is begun ... Num 16:46 5063
the *p* was begun among the people ... Num 16:47 5063
and the *p* was stayed ... Num 16:48 4046
in the *p* were fourteen thousand ... Num 16:49 4046
and the *p* was stayed ... Num 16:50 4046
So the *p* was stayed from the ... Num 25:8 4046
that died in the *p* were twenty ... Num 25:9 4046
the day of the *p* for Peor's sake ... Num 25:18 4046
And it came to pass after the *p* ... Num 26:1 4046
Peor, and there was a *p* among the ... Num 31:16 4046
Take heed in the *p* of leprosy ... Deut 24:8 5061
Also every sickness, and every *p* ... Deut 28:61 4347
although there was a *p* in the ... Josh 22:17 5063
for one *p* was on you all, and on ... 1Sa 6:4 4046
that the *p* may be stayed from the ... 2Sa 24:21 4046
the *p* was stayed from Israel ... 2Sa 24:25 4046
whatsoever *p*, whatsoever sickness ... 1Kin 8:37 5061
every man the *p* of his own heart ... 1Kin 8:38 5061
that the *p* may be stayed from the ... 1Chr 21:22 4046
with a great *p* will the LORD ... 2Chr 21:14 4046
his face, and *p* them that hate him ... Ps 89:23 5063
neither shall any *p* come nigh thy ... Ps 91:10 5061
and the *p* brake in upon them ... Ps 106:29 4046
and so the *p* was stayed ... Ps 106:30 4046
this shall be the *p* wherewith the ... Zec 14:12 4046
And so shall be the *p* of the horse ... Zec 14:15 4046
be in these tents, as this *p* ... Zec 14:15 4046
there shall be the *p*, wherewith ... Zec 14:18 4046
that she was healed of that *p* ... Mk 5:29 *3148*
go in peace, and be whole of thy *p* ... Mk 5:34 *3148*
God because of the *p* of the hail ... Rev 16:21 *4127*
for the *p* thereof was exceeding ... Rev 16:21 *4127*

PLAGUED

And the LORD *p* Pharaoh and his ... Gen 12:17 5060
the LORD *p* the people, because ... Ex 32:35 5062
I *p* Egypt, according to that ... Josh 24:5 5062
thy people, that they should be *p* ... 1Chr 21:17 4046
neither are they *p* like other men ... Ps 73:5 5060
all the day long have I been *p* ... Ps 73:14 5060

PLAGUES

his house with great *p* because of ... Gen 12:17 5061
send all my *p* upon thine heart ... Ex 9:14 4046
I will bring seven times more *p* ... Lev 26:21 4347
LORD will make thy *p* wonderful ... Deut 28:59 4347
p of thy seed, even great *p* ... Deut 28:59 4347
when they see the *p* of that land ... Deut 29:22 4347
with all the *p* in the wilderness ... 1Sa 4:8 4347
hiss because of all the *p* thereof ... Jer 19:8 4347
shall hiss at all the *p* thereof ... Jer 49:17 4347
astonished, and hiss at all her *p* ... Jer 50:13 4347
O death, I will be thy *p* ... Hos 13:14 1698
to touch him, as many as had *p* ... Mk 3:10 *3148*
many of their infirmities and *p* ... Lk 7:21 *3148*
p yet repented not of the works ... Rev 9:20 *4127*
and to smite the earth with all *p* ... Rev 11:6 *4127*
angels having the seven last *p* ... Rev 15:1 *4127*
of the temple, having the seven *p* ... Rev 15:6 *4127*
till the seven *p* of the seven ... Rev 15:8 *4127*
which hath power over these *p* ... Rev 16:9 *4127*
and that ye receive not of her *p* ... Rev 18:4 *4127*
shall her *p* come in one day ... Rev 18:8 *4127*
vials full of the seven last *p* ... Rev 21:9 *4127*
God shall add unto him the *p* that ... Rev 22:18 *4127*

PLAIN

that they found a *p* in the land ... Gen 11:2 1237
of Sichem, unto the *p* of Moreh ... Gen 12:6 436
and beheld all the *p* of Jordan ... Gen 13:10 3603
Lot chose him all the *p* of Jordan ... Gen 13:11 3603
dwelled in the cities of the *p* ... Gen 13:12 3603
came and dwelt in the *p* of Mamre ... Gen 13:18 436
for he dwelt in the *p* of Mamre ... Gen 14:13 436
neither stay thou in all the *p* ... Gen 19:17 3603
those cities, and all the *p* ... Gen 19:25 3603
and toward all the land of the *p* ... Gen 19:28 3603
God destroyed the cities of the *p* ... Gen 19:29 3603
and Jacob was a *p* man, dwelling in ... Gen 25:27 8535
in the *p* over against the Red sea ... Deut 1:1 6160
places nigh thereunto, in the *p* ... Deut 1:7 6160
the way of the *p* from Elath ... Deut 2:8 6160
All the cities of the *p*, and all ... Deut 3:10 4334
The *p* also, and Jordan, and the ... Deut 3:17 6160
even unto the sea of the *p* ... Deut 3:17 6160
in the *p* country, of the ... Deut 4:43 4334
all the *p* on this side Jordan ... Deut 4:49 6160
even unto the sea of the *p* ... Deut 4:49 6160
the *p* of the valley of Jericho ... Deut 34:3 3603
came down toward the sea of the *p* ... Josh 3:16 6160
at a time appointed, before the *p* ... Josh 8:14 6160
Goshen, and the valley, and the *p* ... Josh 11:16 6160
Hermon, and all the *p* on the east ... Josh 12:1 6160
And from the *p* to the sea of ... Josh 12:3 6160
east, and unto the sea of the *p* ... Josh 12:3 6160
all the *p* of Medeba unto Dibon ... Josh 13:9 4334
the river, and all the *p* by Medeba ... Josh 13:16 4334
all her cities that are in the *p* ... Josh 13:17 4334
And all the cities of the *p* ... Josh 13:21 4334
the *p* out of the tribe of Reuben ... Josh 20:8 4334
his tent unto the *p* of Zaanaim ... Judg 4:11 436
by the *p* of the pillar that was ... Judg 9:6 436
come along by the *p* of Meonenim ... Judg 9:37 436
unto the *p* of the vineyards, with ... Judg 11:33 58
thou shalt come to the *p* of Tabor ... 1Sa 10:3 436
in the *p* on the south of Jeshimon ... 1Sa 23:24 6160
all that night through the *p* ... 2Sa 2:29 6160
them away through the *p* all night ... 2Sa 4:7 6160
tarry in the *p* of the wilderness ... 2Sa 15:28 6160
Ahimaaz ran by the way of the *p* ... 2Sa 18:23 3603
In the *p* of Jordan did the king ... 1Kin 7:46 3603
us fight against them in the *p* ... 1Kin 20:23 4334
will fight against them in the *p* ... 1Kin 20:25 4334
of Hamath unto the sea of the *p* ... 2Kin 14:25 6160
king went the way toward the *p* ... 2Kin 25:4 6160
In the *p* of Jordan did the king ... 2Chr 4:17 3603
the priests, the men of the *p* ... Neh 3:22 3603
of the villages in the *p* of Ono ... Neh 6:2 1237
both out of the *p* country round ... Neh 12:28 3603
O LORD, and lead me in a *p* path ... Ps 27:11 4334
They are all *p* to him that ... Prov 8:9 5228
way of the righteous is made *p* ... Prov 15:19 5549
he hath made *p* the face thereof ... Is 28:25 7737
straight, and the rough places *p* ... Is 40:4 1237
land of Benjamin, and from the *p* ... Jer 17:26 8219
of the valley, and rock of the *p* ... Jer 21:13 4334
and he went out the way of the *p* ... Jer 39:4 6160
the *p* shall be destroyed, as the ... Jer 48:8 4334
is come upon the *p* country ... Jer 48:21 4334
and they went by the way of the *p* ... Jer 52:7 6160
me, Arise, go forth into the *p* ... Eze 3:22 1237
I arose, and went forth into the *p* ... Eze 3:23 1237
to the vision that I saw in the *p* ... Eze 8:4 1237
he set it up in the *p* of Dura ... Dan 3:1 1236
the inhabitant from the *p* of Aven ... Amos 1:5 1237
they of the *p* the Philistines ... Obad 19 8219
make it *p* upon tables, that he ... Hab 2:2 874
Zerubbabel thou shalt become a *p* ... Zec 4:7 4334

men inhabited the south and the *p* ... Zec 7:7 8219
a *p* from Geba to Rimmon south of ... Zec 14:10 6160
tongue was loosed, and he spake *p* ... Mk 7:35 *3723*
down with them, and stood in the *p* ... Lk 6:17

PLAINLY
And if the servant shall *p* say ... Ex 21:5 559
all the words of this law very *p* ... Deut 27:8 874
Did I *p* appear unto the house of ... 1Sa 2:27 1540
He told us *p* that the asses were ... 1Sa 10:16 5046
us hath been *p* read before me ... Ezr 4:18 6568
shall be ready to speak *p* ... Is 32:4 6703
If thou be the Christ, tell us *p* ... Jn 10:24 *3954*
Then said Jesus unto them *p* ... Jn 11:14 *3954*
I shall shew you *p* of the Father ... Jn 16:25 *3954*
unto him, Lo, now speakest thou *p* ... Jn 16:29 *3954*
p that they seek a country ... Heb 11:14 *1718*

PLAINNESS
hope, we use great *p* of speech ... 2Cor 3:12 *3954*

PLAINS
unto him in the *p* of Mamre ... Gen 18:1 436
pitched in the *p* of Moab on this ... Num 22:1 6160
priest spake with them in the *p* ... Num 26:3 6160
the children of Israel in the *p* ... Num 26:63 6160
unto the camp at the *p* of Moab ... Num 31:12 6160
pitched in the *p* of Moab by ... Num 33:48 6160
Abel-shittim in the *p* of Moab ... Num 33:49 6160
Moses in the *p* of Moab by Jordan ... Num 33:50 6160
LORD spake unto Moses in the *p* of ... Num 35:1 6160
the children of Israel in the *p* ... Num 36:13 6160
Gilgal, beside the *p* of Moreh ... Deut 11:30 436
Moses went up from the *p* of Moab ... Deut 34:1 6160
in the *p* of Moab thirty days ... Deut 34:8 6160
unto battle, to the *p* of Jericho ... Josh 4:13 6160
month at even in the *p* of Jericho ... Josh 5:10 6160
of the *p* south of Chinneroth, and ... Josh 11:2 6160
and in the valleys, and in the *p* ... Josh 12:8 6160
for inheritance in the *p* of Moab ... Josh 13:32 6160
night in the *p* of the wilderness ... 2Sa 17:16 6160
overtook him in the *p* of Jericho ... 2Kin 25:5 6160
trees that were in the low *p* was ... 1Chr 27:28 8219
are in the low *p* in abundance ... 2Chr 9:27 8219
in the low country, and in the *p* ... 2Chr 26:10 4334
Zedekiah in the *p* of Jericho ... Jer 39:5 6160
Zedekiah in the *p* of Jericho ... Jer 52:8 6160

PLAISTER
morter, and shall *p* the house ... Lev 14:42 2902
stones, and *p* them with *p* ... Deut 27:2 7874
thou shalt *p* them with *p* ... Deut 27:4 7874
lay it for a *p* upon the boil, and ... Is 38:21 4799
the candlestick upon the *p* of the ... Dan 5:5 1528

PLAISTERED
the house, and after it is *p* ... Lev 14:43 2902
the house, after the house was *p* ... Lev 14:48 2902

PLAITING
outward adorning of *p* the hair ... 1Pet 3:3 *1708*

PLANES
he fitteth it with *p*, and he ... Is 44:13 4741

PLANETS
sun, and to the moon, and to the *p* ... 2Kin 23:5 4208

PLANKS
floor of the house with *p* of fir ... 1Kin 6:15 6763
there were thick *p* upon the face ... Eze 41:25 6086
chambers of the house, and thick *p* ... Eze 41:26 5646

PLANT
every *p* of the field before it ... Gen 2:5 7880
p them in the mountain of thine ... Ex 15:17 5193
Thou shalt not *p* thee a grove of ... Deut 16:21 5193
thou shalt *p* a vineyard, and shalt ... Deut 28:30 5193
Thou shalt *p* vineyards, and dress ... Deut 28:39 5193
my people Israel, and will *p* them ... 2Sa 7:10 5193
p vineyards, and eat the fruits ... 2Kin 19:29 5193
my people Israel, and will *p* them ... 1Chr 17:9 5193
and bring forth boughs like a *p* ... Job 14:9 5194
p vineyards, which may yield ... Ps 107:37 5193
a time to *p*, and a time to pluck ... Eccl 3:2 5193
the men of Judah his pleasant *p* ... Is 5:7 5194
shalt thou *p* pleasant plants ... Is 17:10 5193
day shalt thou make thy *p* to grow ... Is 17:11 5194
p vineyards, and eat the fruit ... Is 37:30 5193
I will *p* in the wilderness the ... Is 41:19 5414
that I may *p* the heavens, and lay ... Is 51:16 5193
grow up before him as a tender *p* ... Is 53:2
and they shall *p* vineyards ... Is 65:21 5193
they shall not *p*, and another eat ... Is 65:22 5193
to throw down, to build, and to *p* ... Jer 1:10 5193
p of a strange vine unto me ... Jer 2:21
a kingdom, to build and to *p* it ... Jer 18:9 5193
and I will *p* them, and not pluck ... Jer 24:6 5193
p gardens, and eat the fruit of ... Jer 29:5 5193
p gardens, and eat the fruit of ... Jer 29:28 5193
Thou shalt yet *p* vines upon the ... Jer 31:5 5193
the planters shall *p*, and shall ... Jer 31:5 5193
over them, to build, and to *p* ... Jer 31:28 5193
I will *p* them in this land ... Jer 32:41 5193
nor *p* vineyard, nor have any ... Jer 35:7 5193
pull you down, and I will *p* you ... Jer 42:10 5193
will *p* it upon an high mountain ... Eze 17:22 8362
the height of Israel will I *p* it ... Eze 17:23 8362
build houses, and *p* vineyards ... Eze 28:26 5193
raise up for them a *p* of renown ... Eze 34:29 4302
and *p* that that was desolate ... Eze 36:36 5193
he shall *p* the tabernacles of his ... Dan 11:45 5193
and they shall *p* vineyards ... Amos 9:14 5193
I will *p* them upon their land, and ... Amos 9:15 5193
and they shall *p* vineyards ... Zeph 1:13 5193
But he answered and said, Every *p* ... Mt 15:13 *5451*

PLANTATION
water it by the furrows of her *p* ... Eze 17:7 4302

PLANTED
the LORD God *p* a garden eastward ... Gen 2:8 5193
an husbandman, and he *p* a vineyard ... Gen 9:20 5193
Abraham *p* a grove in Beer-sheba, ... Gen 21:33 5193
shall have *p* all manner of trees ... Lev 19:23 5193
lign aloes which the LORD hath *p* ... Num 24:6 5193
man is he that hath *p* a vineyard ... Deut 20:6 5193
which ye *p* not do ye eat ... Josh 24:13 5193
a tree *p* by the rivers of water ... Ps 1:3 8362
cast out the heathen, and *p* it ... Ps 80:8 5193
which thy right hand hath *p* ... Ps 80:15 5193
Those that be *p* in the house of ... Ps 92:13 8362
He that *p* the ear, shall he not ... Ps 94:9 5193
of Lebanon, which he hath *p* ... Ps 104:16 5193
I *p* me vineyards ... Eccl 2:4 5193
I *p* trees in them of all kind of ... Eccl 2:5 5193
time to pluck up that which is *p* ... Eccl 3:2 5193
p it with the choicest vine, and ... Is 5:2 5193
Yea, they shall not be *p* ... Is 40:24 5193
Yet I had *p* thee a noble vine, ... Jer 2:21 5193
the LORD of hosts, that *p* thee ... Jer 11:17 5193
Thou hast *p* them, yea, they have ... Jer 12:2 5193
be as a tree *p* by the waters ... Jer 17:8 8362
which I have *p* I will pluck up ... Jer 45:4 5193
land, and *p* it in a fruitful field ... Eze 17:5
It was *p* in a good soil by great ... Eze 17:8 8362
Yea, behold, being *p*, shall it ... Eze 17:10 8362
in thy blood, *p* by the waters ... Eze 19:10 8362
now she is *p* in the wilderness, ... Eze 19:13 8362
Tyrus, is *p* in a pleasant place ... Hos 9:13 8362
ye have *p* pleasant vineyards, but ... Amos 5:11 5193
my heavenly Father hath not *p* ... Mt 15:13 *5452*
which *p* a vineyard, and hedged it ... Mt 21:33 *5452*
A certain man *p* a vineyard ... Mk 12:1 *5452*
had a fig tree *p* in his vineyard ... Lk 13:6 *5452*
the root, and be thou *p* in the sea ... Lk 17:6 *5452*
they bought, they sold, they *p* ... Lk 17:28 *5452*
A certain man *p* a vineyard ... Lk 20:9 *5452*
For if we have been *p* together in ... Rom 6:5 *4854*
I have *p*, Apollos watered ... 1Cor 3:6 *5452*

PLANTEDST
and olive trees, which thou *p* not ... Deut 6:11 5193
heathen with thy hand, and *p* them ... Ps 44:2 5193

PLANTERS
the *p* shall plant, and shall eat ... Jer 31:5 5193

PLANTETH
of her hands she *p* a vineyard ... Prov 31:16 5192
he *p* an ash, and the rain doth ... Is 44:14 5192
neither is he that *p* any thing ... 1Cor 3:7 *5452*
Now he that *p* and he that watereth ... 1Cor 3:8 *5452*
who *p* a vineyard, and eateth not ... 1Cor 9:7 *5452*

PLANTING
land for ever, the branch of my *p* ... Is 60:21 4302
the *p* of the LORD, that he might ... Is 61:3 4302

PLANTINGS
the field, and as *p* of a vineyard ... Mic 1:6 4302

PLANTS
and those that dwelt among *p* ... 1Chr 4:23 5194
olive *p* round about thy table ... Ps 128:3 8363
be as *p* grown up in their youth ... Ps 144:12 5195
Thy *p* are an orchard of ... Song 4:13 7973
down the principal *p* thereof ... Is 16:8 8291
shalt thou plant pleasant *p* ... Is 17:10 5194
thy *p* are gone over the sea, they ... Jer 48:32 5189
rivers running round about his *p* ... Eze 31:4 4302

PLAT
and I will requite thee in this *p* ... 2Kin 9:26 2513
and cast him into the *p* of ground ... 2Kin 9:26 2513

PLATE
thou shalt make a *p* of pure gold ... Ex 28:36 6731
they made the *p* of the holy crown ... Ex 39:30 6731
did he put the golden *p*, the ... Lev 8:9 6731

PLATES
did beat the gold into thin *p* ... Ex 39:3 6341
let them make them broad *p* for a ... Num 16:38 6341
they were made broad *p* for a ... Num 16:39
four brasen wheels, and *p* of brass ... 1Kin 7:30 5633
For on the *p* of the ledges ... 1Kin 7:36 3871
Silver spread into *p* is brought ... Jer 10:9

PLATTED
when they had *p* a crown of thorns ... Mt 27:29 *4120*
p a crown of thorns, and put it ... Mk 15:17 *4120*
the soldiers *p* a crown of thorns, ... Jn 19:2 *4120*

PLATTER
outside of the cup and of the *p* ... Mt 23:25 *3953*
that which is within the cup and *p* ... Mt 23:26 *3953*
the outside of the cup and the *p* ... Lk 11:39 *4094*

PLAY
eat and to drink, and rose up to *p* ... Ex 32:6 6711
to *p* the whore in her father's ... Deut 22:21
that he shall *p* with his hand ... 1Sa 16:16 5059
me now a man that can *p* well ... 1Sa 16:17 5059
to *p* the mad man in my presence ... 1Sa 21:15
men now arise, and *p* before us ... 2Sa 2:14 7832
will I *p* before the LORD ... 2Sa 6:21 7832
let us *p* the men for our people, ... 2Sa 10:12
all the beasts of the field *p* ... Job 40:20 7832
Wilt thou *p* with him as with a ... Job 41:5 7832
p skilfully with a loud noise ... Ps 33:3 5059
whom thou hast made to *p* therein ... Ps 104:26 7832
shall *p* on the hole of the asp ... Is 11:8 8173
can *p* well on an instrument ... Eze 33:32 5059
thou shalt not *p* the harlot ... Hos 3:3
p the harlot, yet let not Judah ... Hos 4:15
to eat and drink, and rose up to *p* ... 1Cor 10:7 *3815*

PLAYED
daughter in law hath *p* the harlot ... Gen 38:24
his concubine *p* the whore against ... Judg 19:2
took an harp, and *p* with his hand ... 1Sa 16:23 5059
answered one another as they *p* ... 1Sa 18:7 7832
David *p* with his hand, as at ... 1Sa 18:10 5059
and David *p* with his hand ... 1Sa 19:9 5059
I have *p* the fool, and have erred ... 1Sa 26:21
all the house of Israel *p* before ... 2Sa 6:5 7832
came to pass, when the minstrel *p* ... 2Kin 3:15 5059
all Israel *p* before God with all ... 1Chr 13:8 7832
but thou hast *p* the harlot with ... Jer 3:1
tree, and there hath *p* the harlot ... Jer 3:6
but went and *p* the harlot also ... Jer 3:8
Thou hast *p* the whore also with ... Eze 16:28
thou hast *p* the harlot with them, ... Eze 16:28
Aholah *p* the harlot when she was ... Eze 23:5
wherein she had *p* the harlot in ... Eze 23:19
their mother hath *p* the harlot ... Hos 2:5

PLAYEDST
p the harlot because of thy ... Eze 16:15
and *p* the harlot thereupon ... Eze 16:16

PLAYER
who is a cunning *p* on an harp ... 1Sa 16:16 5059

PLAYERS
the *p* on instruments followed ... Ps 68:25 5059
As well the singers as the *p* on ... Ps 87:7 2490

PLAYETH
in unto a woman that *p* the harlot ... Eze 23:44

PLAYING
profane herself by *p* the whore ... Lev 21:9
that is cunning in *p*, and a ... 1Sa 16:18 5059
saw king David dancing and *p* ... 1Chr 15:29 7832
were the damsels *p* with timbrels ... Ps 68:25
tree thou wanderest, *p* the harlot ... Jer 2:20
thee to cease from *p* the harlot ... Eze 16:41
girls *p* in the streets thereof ... Zec 8:5 7832

PLEA
blood and blood, between *p* and *p* ... Deut 17:8 1779

PLEAD
against him, Will ye *p* for Baal ... Judg 6:31 7378
he that will *p* for him, let him ... Judg 6:31 7378
let him *p* for himself, because ... Judg 6:31 7378
Let Baal *p* against him, because ... Judg 6:32 7378
p my cause, and deliver me out of ... 1Sa 24:15 7378
who shall set me a time to *p* ... Job 9:19
Who is he that will *p* with me ... Job 13:19 7378
Oh that one might *p* for a man ... Job 16:21 3198
me, and *p* against me my reproach ... Job 19:5 3198
Will he *p* against me with his ... Job 23:6 7378
P my cause, O LORD, with them ... Ps 35:1 7378
p my cause against an ungodly ... Ps 43:1 7378
Arise, O God, *p* thine own cause ... Ps 74:22 7378
P my cause, and deliver me ... Ps 119:154 7378
For the LORD will *p* their cause ... Prov 22:23 7378
he shall *p* their cause with thee ... Prov 23:11 7378
p the cause of the poor and needy ... Prov 31:9 1777
the fatherless, *p* for the widow ... Is 1:17 7378
The LORD standeth up to *p* ... Is 3:13 7378
let us *p* together ... Is 43:26 8199
will the LORD *p* with all flesh ... Is 66:16 8199
Wherefore I will yet *p* with you ... Jer 2:9 7378
your children's children will I *p* ... Jer 2:9 7378
Wherefore will ye *p* with me ... Jer 2:29 7378
I will *p* with thee, because thou ... Jer 2:35 8199
thou, O LORD, when I *p* with thee ... Jer 12:1 7378
nations, he will *p* with all flesh ... Jer 25:31 8199
There is none to *p* thy cause ... Jer 30:13 1777
he shall throughly *p* their cause ... Jer 50:34 7378
I will *p* thy cause, and take ... Jer 51:36 7378
will *p* with him there for his ... Eze 17:20 8199
there will I *p* with you face to ... Eze 20:35 8199
of Egypt, so will I *p* with you ... Eze 20:36 8199
I will *p* against him with ... Eze 38:22 8199
P with your mother, *p* ... Hos 2:2 7378
will *p* with them there for my ... Joel 3:2 8199
people, and he will *p* with Israel ... Mic 6:2 3198
against him, until he *p* my cause ... Mic 7:9 7378

PLEADED
that hath *p* the cause of my ... 1Sa 25:39 7378
thou hast *p* the causes of my soul ... Lam 3:58 7378
Like as I *p* with your fathers in ... Eze 20:36 8199

PLEADETH
as a man *p* for his neighbour ... Job 16:21
thy God that *p* the cause of his ... Is 51:22 7378
for justice, nor any *p* for truth ... Is 59:4 8199

PLEADINGS
and hearken to the *p* of my lips ... Job 13:6 7379

PLEASANT
every tree that is *p* to the sight ... Gen 2:9 2530
and that it was *p* to the eyes ... Gen 3:6 8378
good, and the land that it was *p* ... Gen 49:15 5276
p in their lives, and in their ... 2Sa 1:23 5273
very *p* hast thou been unto me ... 2Sa 1:26 5276
whatsoever is *p* in thine eyes ... 1Kin 20:6 4261
the situation of this city is *p* ... 2Kin 2:19 2896
and for all manner of *p* jewels ... 2Chr 32:27 2532
are fallen unto me in *p* places ... Ps 16:6 5273
the *p* harp with the psaltery ... Ps 81:2 5273
Yea, they despised the *p* land ... Ps 106:24 2532
how *p* it is for brethren to dwell ... Ps 133:1 5273
for it is *p* ... Ps 135:3 5273
knowledge is *p* unto thy soul ... Prov 2:10 5276
be as the loving hind and *p* roe ... Prov 5:19 2580
and bread eaten in secret is *p* ... Prov 9:17 5276
the words of the pure are *p* words ... Prov 15:26 5278
P words are as an honeycomb, ... Prov 16:24 5278
For it is a *p* thing if thou keep ... Prov 22:18 5273

with all precious and p riches ... Prov 24:4 5273
a p thing it is for the eyes to ... Eccl 11:7 2896
thou art fair, my beloved, yea, p ... Song 1:16 5273
of pomegranates, with p fruits ... Song 4:13 4022
his garden, and eat his p fruits ... Song 4:16 4022
how p art thou, O love, for ... Song 7:6 5276
gates are all manner of p fruits ... Song 7:13 4022
Tarshish, and upon all p pictures ... Is 2:16 2532
and the men of Judah his p plant ... Is 5:7 8191
and dragons in their p palaces ... Is 13:22 6027
shalt thou plant p plants ... Is 17:10 2532
for the teats, for the p fields ... Is 32:12 2531
and all thy borders of p stones ... Is 54:12 2656
all our p things are laid waste ... Is 64:11 4261
children, and give thee a p land ... Jer 3:19 2532
they have made my p portion a ... Jer 12:10 2532
the p places of the wilderness ... Jer 23:10 4999
and ye shall fall like a p vessel ... Jer 25:34 2532
is he a p child ... Jer 31:20 8191
of her miseries all her p things ... Lam 1:7 4262
his hand upon all her p things ... Lam 1:10 4621
they have given their p things ... Lam 1:11 4622
slew all that were p to the eye ... Lam 2:4 4622
walls, and destroy thy p houses ... Eze 26:12 2532
song of one that hath a p voice ... Eze 33:32 3303
the east, and toward the p land ... Dan 8:9 6643
I ate no p bread, neither came ... Dan 10:3 2530
with precious stones, and p things ... Dan 11:38 2530
the p places for their silver, ... Hos 9:6 4621
Tyrus, is planted in a p place ... Hos 9:13 5116
the treasure of all p vessels ... Hos 13:15 2532
your temples my goodly p things ... Joel 3:5 4261
ye have planted p vineyards ... Amos 5:11 2531
ye cast out from their p houses ... Mic 2:9 8588
glory out of all the p furniture ... Nah 2:9 2532
for they laid the p land desolate ... Zec 7:14 2532
Jerusalem be p unto the LORD, as ... Mal 3:4 6148

PLEASANTNESS
Her ways are ways of p, and all ... Prov 3:17 5278

PLEASE
If she p not her master, who hath ... Ex 21:8
peradventure it will p God that ... Num 23:27
but if it p my father to do thee ... 1Sa 20:13 3190
Therefore now let it p thee to ... 2Sa 7:29 2894
or else, if it p thee, I will ... 1Kin 21:6 2655
Now therefore let it p thee to ... 1Chr 17:27 2894
p them, and speak good words to ... 2Chr 10:7 7521
If it p the king, and if thy ... Neh 2:5 2895
If it p the king, let letters be ... Neh 2:7 2895
If it p the king, let there go a ... Est 1:19 2895
If it p the king, let it be ... Est 3:9 2895
if it p the king to grant my ... Est 5:8 2895
if it p the king, let my life be ... Est 7:3 2895
If it p the king, and if I have ... Est 8:5 2896
If it p the king, let it be ... Est 9:13 2896
that it would p God to destroy me ... Job 6:9 2894
children shall seek to p the poor ... Job 20:10 7521
This also shall p the LORD better ... Ps 69:31 3190
When a man's ways p the LORD ... Prov 16:7 7521
up, nor awake my love, till he p ... Song 2:7 2654
up, nor awake my love, till he p ... Song 3:5 2654
up, nor awake my love, until he p ... Song 8:4 2654
they p themselves in the children ... Is 2:6 5606
shall accomplish that which I p ... Is 55:11 2654
and choose the things that p me ... Is 56:4 2654
do always those things that p him ... Jn 8:29 *701*
are in the flesh cannot p God ... Rom 8:8 *700*
the weak, and not to p ourselves ... Rom 15:1 *700*
Let every one of us p his ... Rom 15:2 *700*
the Lord, how he may p the Lord ... 1Cor 7:32 *700*
the world, how he may p his wife ... 1Cor 7:33 *700*
world, how she may p her husband ... 1Cor 7:34 *700*
Even as I p all men in all things ... 1Cor 10:33 *700*
or do I seek to p men ... Gal 1:10 *700*
they p not God, and are contrary ... 1Th 2:15 *700*
to p God, so ye would abound more ... 1Th 4:1 *700*
that he may p him who hath chosen ... 2Ti 2:4 *700*
to p them well in all things ... Titus 2:9
faith it is impossible to p him ... Heb 11:6 *2100*

PLEASED
of Canaan p not Isaac his father ... Gen 28:8
of God, and thou wast p with me ... Gen 33:10 7521
And their words p Hamor, and ... Gen 34:18
it p Pharaoh well, and his ... Gen 45:16
when Balaam saw that it p the ... Num 24:1 2895
And the saying p me well ... Deut 1:23
of Manasseh spake, it p them ... Josh 22:30
the thing p the children of ... Josh 22:33
If the LORD were p to kill us ... Judg 13:23 2654
and she p Samson well ... Judg 14:7
because it hath p the LORD to ... 1Sa 12:22 2974
told Saul, and the thing p him ... 1Sa 18:20
it p David well to be the king's ... 1Sa 18:26
took notice of it, and it p them ... 2Sa 3:36
the king did p all the people ... 2Sa 3:36
the saying p Absalom well, and all ... 2Sa 17:4
this day, then it had p thee well ... 2Sa 19:6
And the speech p the Lord, that ... 1Kin 3:10
desire which he was p to do ... 1Kin 9:1 2654
and they p him not ... 1Kin 9:12
And the thing p the king and all ... 2Chr 30:4
So it p the king to send me ... Neh 2:6 3190
And the saying p the king and the ... Est 1:21
And the thing p the king ... Est 2:4
And the maiden p him, and she ... Est 2:9
And the thing p Haman ... Est 5:14 3190
Be p, O LORD, to deliver me ... Ps 40:13 7521
Then shalt thou be p with the ... Ps 51:19 2654
he hath done whatsoever he hath p ... Ps 115:3 2654
Whatsoever the LORD p, that did ... Ps 135:6 2654
The LORD is well p for his ... Is 42:21 2654
Yet it p the LORD to bruise him ... Is 53:10 2654
It p Darius to set over the ... Dan 6:1 8232
O LORD, hast done as it p thee ... Jonah 1:14 2654
Will the LORD be p with thousands ... Mic 6:7 7521
will he be p with thee, or accept ... Mal 1:8 7521
beloved Son, in whom I am well p ... Mt 3:17 *2106*
in whom my soul is well p ... Mt 12:18 *2106*
danced before them, and p Herod ... Mt 14:6 *700*
beloved Son, in whom I am well p ... Mt 17:5 *2106*
beloved Son, in whom I am well p ... Mk 1:11 *2106*
p Herod and them that sat with him ... Mk 6:22 *700*
in thee I am well p ... Lk 3:22 *2106*
the saying p the whole multitude ... Acts 6:5 *700*
And because he saw it p the Jews ... Acts 12:3 *701*
Then p it the apostles and elders, ... Acts 15:22 *1380*
Notwithstanding it p Silas to ... Acts 15:34 *1380*
For even Christ p not himself ... Rom 15:3 *700*
For it hath p them of Macedonia ... Rom 15:26 *2106*
It hath p them verily ... Rom 15:27 *2106*
it p God by the foolishness of ... 1Cor 1:21 *2106*
she be p to dwell with him, let ... 1Cor 7:12 *4909*
if he be p to dwell with her, let ... 1Cor 7:13 *4909*
many of them God was not well p ... 1Cor 10:5 *2106*
in the body, as it hath p him ... 1Cor 12:18 *2309*
giveth it a body as it hath p him ... 1Cor 15:38 *2309*
for if I yet p men, I should not ... Gal 1:10 *700*
But when it p God, who separated ... Gal 1:15 *2106*
For it p the Father that in him ... Col 1:19 *2106*
had this testimony, that he p God ... Heb 11:5 *2100*
such sacrifices God is well p ... Heb 13:16 *2100*
beloved Son, in whom I am well p ... 2Pet 1:17 *2106*

PLEASETH
do to her as it p thee ... Gen 16:6
dwell where it p thee ... Gen 20:15
for she p me well ... Judg 14:3
let the maiden which p the king ... Est 2:4
whoso p God shall escape from her ... Eccl 7:26
for he doeth whatsoever p him ... Eccl 8:3 2654

PLEASING
I be p in his eyes, let it be ... Est 8:5 2896
neither shall they be p unto him ... Hos 9:4 6148
worthy of the Lord unto all p ... Col 1:10 *699*
for this is well p unto the Lord ... Col 3:20 *700*
not as p men, but God, which ... 1Th 2:4 *700*
things that are p in his sight ... 1Jn 3:22 *701*

PLEASURE
I am waxed old shall I have p ... Gen 18:12 5730
grapes thy fill at thine own p ... Deut 23:24 5315
heart, and hast p in uprightness ... 1Chr 29:17 7521
let the king send his p to us ... Ezr 5:17 7470
God of your fathers, and do his p ... Ezr 10:11 7522
and over our cattle, at their p ... Neh 9:37 7522
do according to every man's p ... Est 1:8 7522
For what p hath he in his house ... Job 21:21 2656
his soul, and never eateth with p ... Job 21:25 2896
Is it any p to the Almighty, that ... Job 22:3 2656
a God that hath p in wickedness ... Ps 5:4 2655
which hath p in the prosperity of ... Ps 35:27 2655
Do good in thy good p unto Zion ... Ps 51:18 7522
thy servants take p in her stones ... Ps 102:14 7521
ministers of his, that do his p ... Ps 103:21 7522
To bind his princes at his p ... Ps 105:22 5315
of all them that have p therein ... Ps 111:2 2656
he taketh not p in the legs of a ... Ps 147:10 7521
The LORD taketh p in them that ... Ps 147:11 7521
the LORD taketh p in his people ... Ps 149:4 7521
He that loveth p shall be a poor ... Prov 21:17 8057
with mirth, therefore enjoy p ... Eccl 2:1 2896
for he hath no p in fools ... Eccl 5:4 2656
shalt say, I have no p in them ... Eccl 12:1 2656
the night of my p hath he turned ... Is 21:4 2837
and shall perform all my p ... Is 44:28 2656
stand, and I will do all my p ... Is 46:10 2656
he will do his p on Babylon ... Is 48:14 2656
the p of the LORD shall prosper ... Is 53:10 2656
in the day of your fast ye find p ... Is 58:3 2656
from doing thy p on my holy day ... Is 58:13 2656
own ways, nor finding thine own p ... Is 58:13 2656
snuffeth up the wind at her p ... Jer 2:24
is he a vessel wherein is no p ... Jer 22:28 2656
he had set at liberty at their p ... Jer 34:16 5315
like a vessel wherein is no p ... Jer 48:38 2656
with whom thou hast taken p ... Eze 16:37 6148
Have I any p at all that the ... Eze 18:23 2654
For I have no p in the death of ... Eze 18:32 2654
I have no p in the death of the ... Eze 33:11 2654
as a vessel wherein is no p ... Hos 8:8 2656
and I will take p in it, and I will ... Hag 1:8 7521
I have no p in you, saith the ... Mal 1:10 2656
good p to give you the kingdom ... Lk 12:32 *2106*
willing to shew the Jews a p ... Acts 24:27 *5485*
willing to do the Jews a p ... Acts 25:9 *5485*
but have p in them that do them ... Rom 1:32 *4909*
Therefore I take p in infirmities ... 2Cor 12:10 *2106*
to the good p of his will ... Eph 1:5 *2107*
according to his good p which he ... Eph 1:9 *2107*
to will and to do of his good p ... Phil 2:13 *2107*
all the good p of his goodness ... 2Th 1:11 *2107*
but had p in unrighteousness ... 2Th 2:12 *2106*
But she that liveth in p is dead ... 1Ti 5:6 *4684*
for sin thou hast had no p ... Heb 10:6 *2106*
not, neither hadst p therein ... Heb 10:8 *2106*
my soul shall have no p in him ... Heb 10:38 *2106*
chastened us after their own p ... Heb 12:10
Ye have lived in p on the earth ... Jas 5:5 *5171*
as they that count it p to riot ... 2Pet 2:13 *2237*
for thy p they are and were ... Rev 4:11 *2307*

PLEASURES
prosperity, and their years in p ... Job 36:11 5273
hand there are p for evermore ... Ps 16:11 5273
them drink of the river of thy p ... Ps 36:8 5730
this, thou that art given to p ... Is 47:8 5719
p of this life, and bring no fruit ... Lk 8:14 *2237*
lovers of p more than lovers of ... 2Ti 3:4 *5569*
serving divers lusts and p ... Titus 3:3 *2237*
than to enjoy the p of sin for a ... Heb 11:25

PLEDGE
she said, Wilt thou give me a p ... Gen 38:17 6162
he said, What p shall I give thee ... Gen 38:18 6162
to receive his p from the woman's ... Gen 38:20 6162
take thy neighbour's raiment to p ... Ex 22:26 2254
or the upper millstone to p ... Deut 24:6 2254
for he taketh a man's life to p ... Deut 24:6 2254
go into his house to fetch his p ... Deut 24:10 5667
bring out the p abroad unto thee ... Deut 24:11 5667
thou shalt not sleep with his p ... Deut 24:12 5667
p again when the sun goeth down ... Deut 24:13 5667
nor take a widow's raiment to p ... Deut 24:17 2254
brethren fare, and take their p ... 1Sa 17:18 6161
For thou hast taken a p from thy ... Job 22:6 2254
they take the widow's ox for a p ... Job 24:3 2254
breast, and take a p of the poor ... Job 24:9 2254
take a p of him for a strange ... Prov 20:16 2254
take a p of him for a strange ... Prov 27:13 2254
hath restored to the debtor his p ... Eze 18:7 2258
violence, hath not restored the p ... Eze 18:12 2258
any, hath not withholden the p ... Eze 18:16 2258
If the wicked restore the p ... Eze 33:15 2258
clothes laid to p by every altar ... Amos 2:8 2254

PLEDGES
give p to my lord the king of ... 2Kin 18:23 6148
Now therefore give p, I pray thee ... Is 36:8 6148

PLEIADES *(ple'-ya-dez) A constellation of stars.*
maketh Arcturus, Orion, and P ... Job 9:9 3598
bind the sweet influences of P ... Job 38:31 3598

PLENTEOUS
of Egypt in the seven p years ... Gen 41:34 7647
in the seven p years the earth ... Gen 41:47 7647
LORD shall make thee p in goods ... Deut 28:11 3498
p in every work of thine hand ... Deut 30:9 3498
gold at Jerusalem as p as stones ... 2Chr 1:15
p in mercy unto all them that ... Ps 86:5 7227
and p in mercy and truth ... Ps 86:15 7227
slow to anger, and p in mercy ... Ps 103:8 7227
and with him is p redemption ... Ps 130:7 7235
earth, and it shall be fat and p ... Is 30:23 8082
portion is fat, and their meat p ... Hab 1:16 1277
disciples, The harvest truly is p ... Mt 9:37 *4180*

PLENTEOUSNESS
And the seven years of p, that was ... Gen 41:53 7647
of the diligent tend only to p ... Prov 21:5 4195

PLENTIFUL
Thou, O God, didst send a p rain ... Ps 68:9 5071
away, and joy out of the p field ... Is 16:10 3759
And I brought you into a p country ... Jer 2:7 3759
is taken from the p field ... Jer 48:33 3759

PLENTIFULLY
how hast thou p declared the ... Job 26:3 7230
p rewardeth the proud doer ... Ps 31:23 3499
certain rich man brought forth p ... Lk 12:16 *2164*

PLENTY
the earth, and p of corn and wine ... Gen 27:28 7230
p throughout all the land of ... Gen 41:29 7647
all the p shall be forgotten in ... Gen 41:30 7647
the p shall not be known in the ... Gen 41:31 7647
pit, wherein there is p of water ... Lev 11:36 4723
from Ophir great p of almug trees ... 1Kin 10:11 7235
had enough to eat, and have left p ... 2Chr 31:10 7230
and thou shalt have p of silver ... Job 22:25 8443
in judgment, and in p of justice ... Job 37:23 7230
shall thy barns be filled with p ... Prov 3:10 7647
his land shall have p of bread ... Prov 28:19 7646
for then had we p of victuals ... Jer 44:17 7646
And ye shall eat in p, and be ... Joel 2:26 398

PLOTTETH
The wicked p against the just, and ... Ps 37:12 2161

PLOUGH
man, having put his hand to the p ... Lk 9:62 *723*

PLOW
Thou shalt not p with an ox ... Deut 22:10 2790
which a yoke of oxen might p ... 1Sa 14:14
I have seen, they that p iniquity ... Job 4:8 2790
will not p by reason of the cold ... Prov 20:4 2790
Doth the plowman p all day to sow ... Is 28:24 2790
Judah shall p, and Jacob shall ... Hos 10:11 2790
will one p there with oxen ... Amos 6:12 2790
he that ploweth should p in hope ... 1Cor 9:10 *722*

PLOWED
If ye had not p with my heifer, ... Judg 14:18 2790
The plowers p upon my back ... Ps 129:3 2790
Zion shall be p like a field ... Jer 26:18 2790
Ye have p wickedness, ye have ... Hos 10:13 2790
for your sake be p as a field ... Mic 3:12 2790

PLOWERS
The p plowed upon my back ... Ps 129:3 2790

PLOWETH
that he that p should plow in ... 1Cor 9:10

PLOWING
who was p with twelve yoke of ... 1Kin 19:19 2790
Job, and said, The oxen were p ... Job 1:14 2790
the p of the wicked, is sin ... Prov 21:4 5215
having a servant p or feeding ... Lk 17:7 *722*

PLOWMAN
Doth the p plow all day to sow ... Is 28:24 2790
that the p shall overtake the ... Amos 9:13 2790

PLOWMEN
sons of the alien shall be your p.......... Is 61:5 406
the p were ashamed, they covered.......... Jer 14:4 406

PLOWSHARES
shall beat their swords into p.......... Is 2:4 855
Beat your p into swords, and your.......... Joel 3:10 855
shall beat their swords into p.......... Mic 4:3 855

PLUCK
he shall p away his crop with his.......... Lev 1:16 5493
quite p down all their high.......... Num 33:52 8045
then thou mayest p the ears with.......... Deut 23:25 6998
Then will I p them up by the.......... 2Chr 7:20 5428
They p the fatherless from the.......... Job 24:9 1497
for he shall p my feet out of the.......... Ps 25:15 3318
p thee out of thy dwelling place,.......... Ps 52:5 5255
p it out of thy bosom.......... Ps 74:11 3615
which pass by the way do p her.......... Ps 80:12 717
a time to p up that which is.......... Eccl 3:2 6131
I will p them out of their land,.......... Jer 12:14 5428
p out the house of Judah from.......... Jer 12:14 5428
not obey, I will utterly p up.......... Jer 12:17 5428
and concerning a kingdom, to p up.......... Jer 18:7 5428
hand, yet would I p thee thence.......... Jer 22:24 5423
will plant them, and not p them up.......... Jer 24:6 5428
I have watched over them, to p up.......... Jer 31:28 5428
I will plant you, and not p you up.......... Jer 42:10 5428
which I have planted I will p up.......... Jer 45:4 5428
to p it up by the roots thereof.......... Eze 17:9 5375
and p off thine own breasts.......... Eze 23:34 5423
who p off their skin from off.......... Mic 3:2 1497
I will p up thy groves out of the.......... Mic 5:14 5428
p it out, and cast it from thee.......... Mt 5:29 *1808*
began to p the ears of corn, and.......... Mt 12:1 *5089*
p it out, and cast it from thee.......... Mt 18:9 *1807*
they went, to p the ears of corn.......... Mk 2:23 *5089*
thine eye offend thee, p it out.......... Mk 9:47 *1544*
any man p them out of my hand.......... Jn 10:28 *726*
no man is able to p them out of.......... Jn 10:29 *726*

PLUCKED
p it out of his bosom, and, behold.......... Ex 4:7 3318
ye shall be p from off the land.......... Deut 28:63 5255
a man p off his shoe, and gave it.......... Ruth 4:7 8025
p the spear out of the Egyptian's.......... 2Sa 23:21 1497
p the spear out of the Egyptian's.......... 1Chr 11:23 1497
p off the hair of my head and of.......... Ezr 9:3 4803
p off their hair, and made them.......... Neh 13:25 4803
p the spoil out of his teeth.......... Job 29:17 7993
to them that p off the hair.......... Is 50:6 4803
for the wicked are not p away.......... Jer 6:29 5423
after that I have p them out I.......... Jer 12:15 5428
it shall not be p up, nor thrown.......... Jer 31:40 5428
But she was p up in fury, she was.......... Eze 19:12 5428
till the wings thereof were p.......... Dan 7:4 4804
the first horns p up by the roots.......... Dan 7:8 6132
for his kingdom shall be p up.......... Dan 11:4 5428
a firebrand p out of the burning.......... Amos 4:11 5337
this a brand p out of the fire.......... Zec 3:2 5337
chains had been p asunder by him.......... Mk 5:4 *1288*
his disciples p the ears of corn,.......... Lk 6:1 *5089*
Be thou p up by the root, and be.......... Lk 17:6 *1610*
ye would have p out your own eyes.......... Gal 4:15 *1846*
twice dead, p up by the roots.......... Jude 12 *1610*

PLUCKETH
but the foolish p it down with.......... Prov 14:1 2040

PLUCKT
her mouth was an olive leaf p off.......... Gen 8:11 2965

PLUMBLINE
stood upon a wall made by a p.......... Amos 7:7 594
with a p in his hand.......... Amos 7:7 594
And I said, A p.......... Amos 7:8 594
I will set a p in the midst of my.......... Amos 7:8 594

PLUMMET
the p of the house of Ahab.......... 2Kin 21:13 4949
line, and righteousness to the p.......... Is 28:17 4949
shall see the p in the hand of.......... Zec 4:10

PLUNGE
Yet shalt thou p me in the ditch,.......... Job 9:31 2881

POCHERETH (*po-ke'-reth*) *A family of exiles.*
the children of P of Zebaim.......... Ezr 2:57 6380
the children of P of Zebaim.......... Neh 7:59 6380

POETS
also of your own p have said.......... Acts 17:28 *4163*

POINT
Behold, I am at the p to die.......... Gen 25:32 1980
ye shall p out for you mount Hor.......... Num 34:7 8376
From mount Hor ye shall p out.......... Num 34:8 8376
ye shall p out your east border.......... Num 34:10 184
iron, and with the p of a diamond.......... Jer 17:1 6856
I have set the p of the sword.......... Eze 21:15 19
daughter lieth at the p of death.......... Mk 5:23 *2079*
for he was at the p of death.......... Jn 4:47 *3195*
whole law, and yet offend in one p.......... Jas 2:10

POINTED
he spreadeth sharp p things upon.......... Job 41:30 2742

POINTS
evil, that in all p as he came.......... Eccl 5:16 5980
but was in all p tempted like as.......... Heb 4:15

POISON
with the p of serpents of the.......... Deut 32:24 2534
Their wine is the p of dragons.......... Deut 32:33 2534
the p whereof drinketh up my.......... Job 6:4 2534
He shall suck the p of asps.......... Job 20:16 7219
p is like the p of a serpent.......... Ps 58:4 2534
adders' p is under their lips.......... Ps 140:3 2534
the p of asps is under their lips.......... Rom 3:13 *2447*
an unruly evil, full of deadly p.......... Jas 3:8 *2447*

POLE
fiery serpent, and set it upon a p.......... Num 21:8 5251
of brass, and put it upon a p.......... Num 21:9 5251

POLICY
through his p also he shall cause.......... Dan 8:25 7922

POLISHED
p after the similitude of a.......... Ps 144:12 2404
he hid me, and made me a p shaft.......... Is 49:2 1305
feet like in colour to p brass.......... Dan 10:6 7044

POLISHING
rubies, their p was of sapphire.......... Lam 4:7 1508

POLL
take five shekels apiece by the p.......... Num 3:47 1538
they shall only p their heads.......... Eze 44:20 3697
p thee for thy delicate children.......... Mic 1:16 1494

POLLED
when he p his head, (for it was.......... 2Sa 14:26 1548
at every year's end that he p it.......... 2Sa 14:26 1548
heavy on him, therefore he p it.......... 2Sa 14:26 1548

POLLS
names, every male by their p.......... Num 1:2 1538
years old and upward, by their p.......... Num 1:18 1538
number of the names, by their p.......... Num 1:20 1538
number of the names, by their p.......... Num 1:22 1538
and their number by their p.......... 1Chr 23:3 1538
by number of names by their p.......... 1Chr 23:24 1538

POLLUTE
neither shall ye p the holy.......... Num 18:32 2490
So ye shall not p the land.......... Num 35:33 2610
is called by my name, to p it.......... Jer 7:30 2930
and they shall p it.......... Eze 7:21 2490
they shall p my secret place.......... Eze 7:22 2490
will ye p me among my people for.......... Eze 13:19 2490
ye p yourselves with all your.......... Eze 20:31 2930
but p ye my holy name no more.......... Eze 20:39 2490
I will not let them p my holy.......... Eze 39:7 2490
to be in my sanctuary, to p it.......... Eze 44:7 2490
they shall p the sanctuary of.......... Dan 11:31 2490

POLLUTED
thy tool upon it, thou hast p it.......... Ex 20:25 2490
p it, according to the word of.......... 2Kin 23:16 2930
p the house of the LORD which he.......... 2Chr 36:14 2930
therefore were they, as p.......... Ezr 2:62 1351
therefore were they, as p.......... Neh 7:64 1351
and the land was p with blood.......... Ps 106:38 2610
I have p mine inheritance, and.......... Is 47:6 2490
for how should my name be p.......... Is 48:11 2490
How canst thou say, I am not p.......... Jer 2:23 2930
shall not that land be greatly p.......... Jer 3:1 2610
thou hast p the land with thy.......... Jer 3:2 2610
p my name, and caused every man.......... Jer 34:16 2490
he hath p the kingdom and the.......... Lam 2:2 2490
they have p themselves with blood.......... Lam 4:14 1351
behold, my soul hath not been p.......... Eze 4:14 2930
neither be p any more with all.......... Eze 14:11 2930
saw thee p in thine own blood, I.......... Eze 16:6 947
and bare, and wast p in thy blood.......... Eze 16:22 947
not be p before the heathen.......... Eze 20:9 2490
and my sabbaths they greatly p.......... Eze 20:13 2490
not be p before the heathen.......... Eze 20:14 2490
in my statutes, but p my sabbaths.......... Eze 20:16 2490
they p my sabbaths.......... Eze 20:21 2490
that it should not be p in the.......... Eze 20:22 2490
had p my sabbaths, and their eyes.......... Eze 20:24 2490
I p them in their own gifts, in.......... Eze 20:26 2930
Are ye p after the manner of your.......... Eze 20:30 2930
she was p with them, and her mind.......... Eze 23:17 2930
thou art p with their idols.......... Eze 23:30 2930
idols wherewith they had p it.......... Eze 36:18 2930
work iniquity, and is p with blood.......... Hos 6:8 6121
all that eat thereof shall be p.......... Hos 9:4 2930
and thou shalt die in a p land.......... Amos 7:17 2931
because it is p, it shall destroy.......... Mic 2:10 2930
Woe to her that is filthy and p.......... Zeph 3:1 1351
her priests have p the sanctuary.......... Zeph 3:4 2490
Ye offer p bread upon mine altar.......... Mal 1:7 1351
and ye say, Wherein have we p thee.......... Mal 1:7 1351
say, The table of the LORD is p.......... Mal 1:12 1351
temple, and hath p this holy place.......... Acts 21:28 *2840*

POLLUTING
keepeth the sabbath from p it.......... Is 56:2 2490
keepeth the sabbath from p it.......... Is 56:6 2490

POLLUTION
her that was set apart for p.......... Eze 22:10 2931

POLLUTIONS
that they abstain from p of idols.......... Acts 15:20 *234*
the p of the world through the.......... 2Pet 2:20 *3393*

POLLUX *A Roman god.*
isle, whose sign was Castor and P.......... Acts 28:11 *1359*

POMEGRANATE
A golden bell and a p, a golden.......... Ex 28:34 7416
p, a golden bell and a p.......... Ex 28:34 7416
A bell and a p, a bell and a.......... Ex 39:26 7416
and a p, a bell and a p.......... Ex 39:26 7416
part of Gibeah under a p tree.......... 1Sa 14:2 7416
a piece of a p within thy locks.......... Song 4:3 7416
As a piece of a p are thy temples.......... Song 6:7 7416
spiced wine of the juice of my p.......... Song 8:2 7416
the p tree, the palm tree also,.......... Joel 1:12 7416
vine, and the fig tree, and the p.......... Hag 2:19 7416

POMEGRANATES
of it thou shalt make p of blue.......... Ex 28:33 7416
the hems of the robe p of blue.......... Ex 39:24 7416
the p upon the hem of the robe.......... Ex 39:25 7416
robe, round about between the p.......... Ex 39:25 7416
and they brought of the p, and of.......... Num 13:23 7416
or of figs, or of vines, or of p.......... Num 20:5 7416

and vines, and fig trees, and p.......... Deut 8:8 7416
that were upon the top, with p.......... 1Kin 7:18 7416
the two pillars had p also above.......... 1Kin 7:20
the p were two hundred in rows.......... 1Kin 7:20 7416
four hundred p for the two.......... 1Kin 7:42 7416
two rows of p for one network.......... 1Kin 7:42 7416
p upon the chapiter round about,.......... 2Kin 25:17 7416
and made an hundred p, and put them 2Chr 3:16 7416
four hundred p on the two wreaths.......... 2Chr 4:13 7416
two rows of p on each wreath, to.......... 2Chr 4:13 7416
Thy plants are an orchard of p.......... Song 4:13 7416
vine flourished, and the p budded.......... Song 6:11 7416
grape appear, and the p bud forth.......... Song 7:12 7416
p upon the chapiters round about,.......... Jer 52:22 7416
the p were like unto these.......... Jer 52:22 7416
were ninety and six p on a side.......... Jer 52:23 7416
all the p upon the network were.......... Jer 52:23 7416

POMMELS
To wit, the two pillars, and the p.......... 2Chr 4:12 1543
two wreaths to cover the two p of.......... 2Chr 4:12 1543
to cover the two p of the.......... 2Chr 4:13 1543

POMP
and their multitude, and their p.......... Is 5:14 7588
Thy p is brought down to the.......... Is 14:11 1347
I will also make the p of the.......... Eze 7:24 1347
the p of her strength shall cease.......... Eze 30:18 1347
they shall spoil the p of Egypt.......... Eze 32:12 1347
the p of her strength shall cease.......... Eze 33:28 1347
come, and Bernice, with great p.......... Acts 25:23 *5325*

PONDER
P the path of thy feet, and let.......... Prov 4:26 6424
thou shouldest p the path of life.......... Prov 5:6 6424

PONDERED
things, and p them in her heart.......... Lk 2:19 *4820*

PONDERETH
the LORD, and he p all his goings.......... Prov 5:21 6424
but the LORD p the hearts.......... Prov 21:2 8505
doth not he that p the heart.......... Prov 24:12 8505

PONDS
their rivers, and upon their p.......... Ex 7:19 98
over the rivers, and over the p.......... Ex 8:5 98
that make sluices and p for fish.......... Is 19:10 99

PONTIUS (*pon'-she-us*) *The family name of Pilate.*
delivered him to P Pilate the.......... Mt 27:2 *4194*
P Pilate being governor of Judaea.......... Lk 3:1 *4194*
P Pilate, with the Gentiles, and.......... Acts 4:27 *4194*
who before P Pilate witnessed a.......... 1Ti 6:13 *4194*

PONTUS (*pon'-tus*) *A Roman province in Asia Minor.*
and in Judaea, and Cappadocia, in P.......... Acts 2:9 *4195*
Jew named Aquila, born in P.......... Acts 18:2 *4195*
strangers scattered throughout P.......... 1Pet 1:1 *4195*

POOL
met together by the p of Gibeon.......... 2Sa 2:13 1295
the one on the one side of the p.......... 2Sa 2:13 1295
other on the other side of the p.......... 2Sa 2:13 1295
them up over the p in Hebron.......... 2Sa 4:12 1295
the chariot in the p of Samaria.......... 1Kin 22:38 1295
by the conduit of the upper p.......... 2Kin 18:17 1295
all his might, and how he made a p.......... 2Kin 20:20 1295
the fountain, and to the king's p.......... Neh 2:14 1295
the wall of the p of Siloah by.......... Neh 3:15 1295
to the p that was made, and unto.......... Neh 3:16 1295
p in the highway of the fuller's.......... Is 7:3 1295
the waters of the lower p.......... Is 22:9 1295
walls for the water of the old p.......... Is 22:11 1295
parched ground shall become a p.......... Is 35:7 98
by the conduit of the upper p in.......... Is 36:2 1295
make the wilderness a p of water.......... Is 41:18 98
is of old like a p of water.......... Nah 2:8 1295
Jerusalem by the sheep market a p.......... Jn 5:2 *2861*
at a certain season into the p.......... Jn 5:4 *2861*
is troubled, to put me into the p.......... Jn 5:7 *2861*
him, Go, wash in the p of Siloam.......... Jn 9:7 *2861*
unto me, Go to the p of Siloam.......... Jn 9:11 *2861*

POOLS
and upon all their p of water.......... Ex 7:19 4723
the rain also filleth the p.......... Ps 84:6 1293
I made me p of water, to water.......... Eccl 2:6 1295
for the bittern, and p of water.......... Is 14:23 98
islands, and I will dry up the p.......... Is 42:15 98

POOR
other kine came up after them, p.......... Gen 41:19 1800
of my people that is p by thee.......... Ex 22:25 6041
countenance a p man in his cause.......... Ex 23:3 1800
judgment of thy p in his cause.......... Ex 23:6 34
that the p of thy people may eat.......... Ex 23:11 34
the p shall not give less than.......... Ex 30:15 1800
And if he be p, and cannot get so.......... Lev 14:21 1800
thou shalt leave them for the p.......... Lev 19:10 6041
not respect the person of the p.......... Lev 19:15 1800
thou shalt leave them unto the p.......... Lev 23:22 6041
If thy brother be waxen p.......... Lev 25:25 4134
And if thy brother be waxen p.......... Lev 25:35 4134
that dwelleth by thee be waxen p.......... Lev 25:39 4134
that dwelleth by him wax p.......... Lev 25:47 4134
there shall be no p among you.......... Deut 15:4 34
If there be among you a p man of.......... Deut 15:7 34
thine hand from thy p brother.......... Deut 15:7 34
eye be evil against thy p brother.......... Deut 15:9 34
For the p shall never cease out.......... Deut 15:11 34
wide unto thy brother, to thy p.......... Deut 15:11 6041
And if the man be p, thou shalt.......... Deut 24:12 6041
an hired servant that is p.......... Deut 24:14 6041
for he is p, and setteth his heart.......... Deut 24:15 6041
my family is p in Manasseh.......... Judg 6:15 1800
not young men, whether p or rich.......... Ruth 3:10 1800

P

The LORD maketh *p*, and maketh rich. 1Sa 2:7 3423
raiseth up the *p* out of the dust 1Sa 2:8 1800
in law, seeing that I am a *p* man 1Sa 18:23 7326
the one rich, and the other *p* 2Sa 12:1 7326
But the *p* man had nothing, save 2Sa 12:3 7326
but took the *p* man's lamb 2Sa 12:4 7326
of the guard left of the *p* of the 2Kin 25:12 1803
one to another, and gifts to the *p* Est 9:22 34
he saveth the *p* from the sword Job 5:15 34
So the *p* hath hope, and iniquity Job 5:16 1800
shall seek to please the *p* Job 20:10 1800
oppressed and hath forsaken the *p* Job 20:19 1800
the *p* of the earth hide Job 24:4 6035
breast, and take a pledge of the *p* Job 24:9 6041
with the light killeth the *p* Job 24:14 6041
I delivered the *p* that cried Job 29:12 6041
I was a father to the *p* Job 29:16 34
was not my soul grieved for the *p* Job 30:25 34
withheld the *p* from their desire Job 31:16 1800
or any *p* without covering Job 31:19 34
the rich more than the *p* Job 34:19 1800
the cry of the *p* to come unto him Job 34:28 1800
but giveth right to the *p* Job 36:6 6041
the *p* in his affliction, and Job 36:15 6041
the expectation of the *p* shall Ps 9:18 6041
in his pride doth persecute the *p* Ps 10:2 6041
are privily set against the *p* Ps 10:8 2489
he lieth in wait to catch the *p* Ps 10:9 6041
he doth catch the *p*, when he Ps 10:9 6041
that the *p* may fall by his strong Ps 10:10 2489
the *p* committeth himself unto Ps 10:14 2489
For the oppression of the *p* Ps 12:5 6041
have shamed the counsel of the *p* Ps 14:6 6041
This *p* man cried, and the LORD Ps 34:6 6041
which deliverest the *p* from him Ps 35:10 6041
is too strong for him, yea, the *p* Ps 35:10 6041
their bow, to cast down the *p* Ps 37:14 6041
But I am *p* and needy Ps 40:17 6041
is he that considereth the *p* Ps 41:1 1800
Both low and high, rich and *p* Ps 49:2 34
of thy goodness for the *p* Ps 68:10 6041
But I am *p* and sorrowful Ps 69:29 6041
For the LORD heareth the *p* Ps 69:33 34
But I am *p* and needy Ps 70:5 6041
and thy *p* with judgment Ps 72:2 6041
shall judge the *p* of the people Ps 72:4 6041
the *p* also, and him that hath no Ps 72:12 6041
He shall spare the *p* and needy, and Ps 72:13 1800
congregation of thy *p* for ever Ps 74:19 6041
let the *p* and needy praise thy Ps 74:21 6041
Defend the *p* and fatherless Ps 82:3 1800
Deliver the *p* and needy Ps 82:4 1800
for I am *p* and needy Ps 86:1 6041
Yet setteth he the *p* on high from Ps 107:41 34
shew mercy, but persecuted the *p* Ps 109:16 6041
For I am *p* and needy, and my heart Ps 109:22 6041
stand at the right hand of the *p* Ps 109:31 34
dispersed, he hath given to the *p* Ps 112:9 34
raiseth up the *p* out of the dust Ps 113:7 1800
I will satisfy her *p* with bread Ps 132:15 34
afflicted, and the right of the *p* Ps 140:12 34
He becometh *p* that dealeth with a Prov 10:4 7326
of the *p* is their poverty Prov 10:15 1800
there is that maketh himself *p* Prov 13:7 7326
but the *p* heareth not rebuke Prov 13:8 7326
food is in the tillage of the *p* Prov 13:23 7326
The *p* is hated even of his own Prov 14:20 7326
but he that hath mercy on the *p* Prov 14:21
the *p* reproacheth his Maker Prov 14:31 1800
honoureth him hath mercy on the *p* Prov 14:31 34
Whoso mocketh the *p* reproacheth Prov 17:5 7326
The *p* useth intreaties Prov 18:23 7326
Better is the *p* that walketh in Prov 19:1 7326
but the *p* is separated from his Prov 19:4 1800
the brethren of the *p* do hate him Prov 19:7 7326
upon the *p* lendeth unto the LORD Prov 19:17 1800
a *p* man is better than a liar Prov 19:22 7326
his ears at the cry of the *p* Prov 21:13 1800
loveth pleasure shall be a *p* man Prov 21:17 4270
The rich and *p* meet together Prov 22:2 7326
The rich ruleth over the *p* Prov 22:7 7326
he giveth of his bread to the *p* Prov 22:9 1800
the *p* to increase his riches Prov 22:16 1800
Rob not the *p*, because he is *p* Prov 22:22 1800
A *p* man that oppresseth the Prov 28:3 7326
p is like a sweeping rain which Prov 28:3 1800
Better is the *p* that walketh in Prov 28:6 7326
it for him that will pity the *p* Prov 28:8 1800
but the *p* that hath understanding Prov 28:11 1800
a wicked ruler over the *p* people Prov 28:15 1800
giveth unto the *p* shall not lack Prov 28:27 7326
considereth the cause of the *p* Prov 29:7 1800
The *p* and the deceitful man meet Prov 29:13 7326
that faithfully judgeth the *p* Prov 29:14 1800
or lest I be *p*, and steal, and take Prov 30:9 3423
to devour the *p* from off the Prov 30:14 6041
and plead the cause of the *p* Prov 31:9 6041
stretcheth out her hand to the *p* Prov 31:20 6041
Better is a *p* and a wise child Eccl 4:13 4542
is born in his kingdom becometh *p* Eccl 4:14 7326
seest the oppression of the *p* Eccl 5:8 7326
what hath the *p*, that knoweth to Eccl 6:8 6041
was found in it a *p* wise man Eccl 9:15 4542
no man remembered that same *p* man Eccl 9:15 4542
nevertheless the *p* man's wisdom Eccl 9:16 4542
the spoil of the *p* is in your Is 3:14 6041
and grind the faces of the *p* Is 3:15 6041
the right from the *p* of my people Is 10:2 6041
be heard unto Laish, O *p* Anathoth Is 10:30 6041
shall he judge the *p*, and reprove Is 11:4 1800
the firstborn of the *p* shall feed Is 14:30 1800
the *p* of his people shall trust Is 14:32 6041
hast been a strength to the *p* Is 25:4 1800
it down, even the feet of the *p* Is 26:6 6041
the *p* among men shall rejoice in Is 29:19 34
to destroy the *p* with lying words Is 32:7
When the *p* and needy seek water, Is 41:17 6041
that thou bring the *p* that are Is 58:7 6041
I look, even to him that is *p* Is 66:2 6041
of the souls of the *p* innocents Jer 2:34 34
I said, Surely these are *p* Jer 5:4 1800
the *p* from the hand of evildoers Jer 20:13 34
He judged the cause of the *p* Jer 22:16 6041
guard left of the *p* of the people Jer 39:10 1800
of the *p* of the land, of them Jer 40:7 1803
certain of the *p* of the people Jer 52:15 1803
p of the land for vinedressers Jer 52:16 1803
she strengthen the hand of the *p* Eze 16:49 6041
Hath oppressed the *p* and needy, Eze 18:12 6041
taken off his hand from the *p* Eze 18:17 6041
robbery, and have vexed the *p* Eze 22:29 6041
by shewing mercy to the *p* Dan 4:27 6033
the *p* for a pair of shoes Amos 2:6 34
of the earth on the head of the *p* Amos 2:7 1800
of Samaria, which oppress the *p* Amos 4:1 1800
as your treading is upon the *p* Amos 5:11 1800
they turn aside the *p* in the gate Amos 5:12 34
even to make the *p* of the land to Amos 8:4
That we may buy the *p* for silver Amos 8:6 1800
was as to devour the *p* secretly Hab 3:14 6041
p people, and they shall trust in Zeph 3:12 1800
the stranger, nor the *p* Zec 7:10 6041
even you, O *p* of the flock Zec 11:7 6041
so the *p* of the flock that waited Zec 11:11 6041
Blessed are the *p* in spirit Mt 5:3 4434
the *p* have the gospel preached to Mt 11:5 4434
that thou hast, and give to the *p* Mt 19:21 4434
sold for much, and given to the *p* Mt 26:9 4434
For ye have the *p* always with you Mt 26:11 4434
thou hast, and give to the *p* Mk 10:21 4434
And there came a certain *p* widow Mk 12:42 4434
That this *p* widow hath cast more Mk 12:43 4434
and have been given to the *p* Mk 14:5 4434
For ye have the *p* with you always Mk 14:7 4434
me to preach the gospel to the *p* Lk 4:18 4434
and said, Blessed be ye *p* Lk 6:20 4434
to the *p* the gospel is preached Lk 7:22 4434
thou makest a feast, call the *p* Lk 14:13 4434
city, and bring in hither the *p* Lk 14:21 4434
hast, and distribute unto the *p* Lk 18:22 4434
half of my goods I give to the *p* Lk 19:8 4434
he saw also a certain *p* widow Lk 21:2 3998
that this *p* widow hath cast in Lk 21:3 4434
hundred pence, and given to the *p* Jn 12:5 4434
said, not that he cared for the *p* Jn 12:6 4434
For the *p* always ye have with you Jn 12:8 4434
he should give something to the *p* Jn 13:29 4434
p saints which are at Jerusalem Rom 15:26 4434
bestow all my goods to feed the *p* 1Cor 13:3
as *p*, yet making many rich 2Cor 6:10 4434
yet for your sakes he became *p* 2Cor 8:9 4433
he hath given to the *p* 2Cor 9:9 3993
that we should remember the *p* Gal 2:10 4434
in also a *p* man in vile raiment Jas 2:2 4434
and say to the *p*, Stand thou there Jas 2:3 4434
Hath not God chosen the *p* of this Jas 2:5 4434
But ye have despised the *p* Jas 2:6 4434
art wretched, and miserable, and *p* Rev 3:17 4434
both small and great, rich and *p* Rev 13:16 4434

POORER
But if he be *p* than thy Lev 27:8 4134

POOREST
save the *p* sort of the people of 2Kin 24:14 1803

POPLAR
And Jacob took him rods of green *p* Gen 30:37 3839

POPLARS
upon the hills, under oaks and *p* Hos 4:13 3839

POPULOUS
a nation, great, mighty, and *p* Deut 26:5 7227
Art thou better than *p* No Nah 3:8 527

PORATHA (*por'-a-thah*) *A son of Haman.*
And *P*, and Adalia, and Aridatha, Est 9:8 6334

PORCH
Ehud went forth through the *p* Judg 3:23 4528
the *p* before the temple of the 1Kin 6:3 197
And he made a *p* of pillars 1Kin 7:6 197
and the *p* was before them 1Kin 7:6 197
Then he made a *p* for the throne 1Kin 7:7 197
judge, even the *p* of judgment 1Kin 7:7 197
had another court within the *p* 1Kin 7:8 197
taken to wife, like unto this *p* 1Kin 7:8 197
LORD, and for the *p* of the house 1Kin 7:12 197
were of lily work in the *p* 1Kin 7:19 197
pillars in the *p* of the temple 1Kin 7:21 197
his son the pattern of the *p* 1Chr 28:11 197
the *p* that was in the front of 2Chr 3:4 197
which he had built before the *p* 2Chr 8:12 197
that was before the *p* of the LORD 2Chr 15:8 197
have shut up the doors of the *p* 2Chr 29:7 197
came they to the *p* of the LORD 2Chr 29:17 197
temple of the LORD, between the *p* Eze 8:16 197
threshold of the gate by the *p* of Eze 40:7 197
also the *p* of the gate within Eze 40:8 197
measured he the *p* of the gate Eze 40:9 197
the *p* of the gate was inward Eze 40:9 197
p of the inner gate were fifty Eze 40:15 197
in the *p* of the gate were two Eze 40:39 197
which was at the *p* of the gate Eze 40:40 197
brought me to the *p* of the house Eze 40:48 197
and measured each post of the *p* Eze 40:48 197
length of the *p* was twenty cubits Eze 40:49 197
upon the face of the *p* without Eze 41:25 197
other side, on the sides of the *p* Eze 41:26 197
by the way of the *p* of that gate Eze 44:3 197
way of the *p* of that gate without Eze 46:2 197
by the way of the *p* of that gate Eze 46:8 197
of the LORD, weep between the *p* Joel 2:17 197
when he was gone out into the *p* Mt 26:71 4440
And he went out into the *p* Mk 14:68 4259
in the temple in Solomon's *p* Jn 10:23 4745
in the *p* that is called Solomon's Acts 3:11 4745
with one accord in Solomon's *p* Acts 5:12 4745

PORCHES
temple, and the *p* of the court Eze 41:15 197
tongue Bethesda, having five *p* Jn 5:2 4745

PORCIUS (*por'-she-us*) *Family name of Festus.*
But after two years *P* Festus came Acts 24:27 4201

PORT
the dragon well, and to the dung *p* Neh 2:13 8179

PORTER
and the watchman called unto the *p* 2Sa 18:26 7778
and called unto the *p* of the city 2Kin 7:10 7778
the son of Meshelemiah was *p* of 1Chr 9:21 7778
the *p* toward the east, was over 2Chr 31:14 7778
work, and commanded the *p* to watch Mk 13:34 2377
To him the *p* openeth Jn 10:3 2377

PORTERS
And he called the *p* 2Kin 7:11 7778
the *p* were, Shallum, and Akkub, and 1Chr 9:17 7778
they were *p* in the companies of 1Chr 9:18 7778
p in the gates were two hundred 1Chr 9:22 7778
In four quarters were the *p* 1Chr 9:24 7778
these Levites, the four chief *p* 1Chr 9:26 7778
and Obed-edom, and Jeiel, the *p* 1Chr 15:18 7778
son of Jeduthun and Hosah to be *p* 1Chr 16:38 7778
And the sons of Jeduthun were *p* 1Chr 16:42 8179
Moreover four thousand were *p* 1Chr 23:5 7778
Concerning the divisions of the *p* 1Chr 26:1 7778
these were the divisions of the *p* 1Chr 26:12 7778
of the *p* among the sons of Kore 1Chr 26:19 7778
the *p* also by their courses at 2Chr 8:14 7778
Levites, shall be *p* of the doors 2Chr 23:4 7778
he set the *p* at the gates of the 2Chr 23:19 7778
were scribes, and officers, and *p* 2Chr 34:13 7778
the *p* waited at every gate 2Chr 35:15 7778
The children of the *p* Ezr 2:42 7778
people, and the singers, and the *p* Ezr 2:70 7778
Levites, and the singers, and the *p* Ezr 7:7 7778
priests and Levites, singers, *p* Ezr 7:24 8652
the *p*; Shallum, and Telem Ezr 10:24 7778
I had set up the doors, and the *p* Neh 7:1 7778
The *p*: the children of Shallum Neh 7:45 7778
priests, and the Levites, and the *p* Neh 7:73 7778
the priests, the Levites, the *p* Neh 10:28 7778
priests that minister, and the *p* Neh 10:39 7778
Moreover the *p*, Akkub, Talmon, and Neh 11:19 7778
were *p* keeping the ward at the Neh 12:25 7778
the *p* kept the ward of their God, Neh 12:45 7778
portions of the singers and the *p* Neh 12:47 7778
Levites, and the singers, and the *p* Neh 13:5 7778

PORTION
the *p* of the men which went with Gen 14:24 2506
let them take their *p* Gen 14:24 2506
Is there yet any *p* or inheritance Gen 31:14 2506
for the priests had a *p* assigned Gen 47:22 2706
did eat their *p* which Pharaoh Gen 47:22 2706
to thee one *p* above thy brethren Gen 48:22 7926
p of my offerings made by fire Lev 6:17 2506
This is the *p* of the anointing of Lev 7:35
thou shalt take one *p* of fifty Num 31:30 270
which was the *p* of them that went Num 31:36 2506
half, Moses took one *p* of fifty Num 31:47 270
a double *p* of all that he hath Deut 21:17 6310
For the LORD's *p* is his people Deut 32:9 2506
in a *p* of the lawgiver, was he Deut 33:21 2513
one *p* to inherit, seeing I am a Josh 17:14 2256
Out of the *p* of the children of Josh 19:9 2256
unto Hannah he gave a worthy *p* 1Sa 1:5 4490
Bring the *p* which I gave thee, of 1Sa 9:23 4490
saying, What *p* have we in David 1Kin 12:16 2506
let a double *p* of thy spirit be 2Kin 2:9 6310
eat Jezebel in the *p* of Jezreel 2Kin 9:10 2506
met him in the *p* of Naboth the 2Kin 9:21 2513
cast him in the *p* of the field of 2Kin 9:25 2513
In the *p* of Jezreel shall dogs 2Kin 9:36 2506
of the field in the *p* of Jezreel 2Kin 9:37 2506
saying, What *p* have we in David 2Chr 10:16 2506
For Ahaz took away a *p* out of the 2Chr 28:21 2505
He appointed also the king's *p* of 2Chr 31:3 4521
to give the *p* of the priests 2Chr 31:4 4521
his daily *p* for their service in 2Chr 31:16 1697
have no *p* on this side the river Ezr 4:16 2508
but ye have no *p*, nor right, nor Neh 2:20 2506
that a certain *p* should be for Neh 11:23
and the porters, every day his *p* Neh 12:47 1697
This is the *p* of a wicked man Job 20:29 2506
their *p* is cursed in the earth Job 24:18 2513
how little a *p* is heard of him Job 26:14 1697
This is the *p* of a wicked man Job 27:13 2506
For what *p* of God is there from Job 31:2 2506
this shall be the *p* of their cup Ps 11:6 4521
The LORD is the *p* of mine Ps 16:5 4490
which have their *p* in this life Ps 17:14 2506
they shall be a *p* for foxes Ps 63:10 4521
of my heart, and my *p* for ever Ps 73:26 2506
Thou art my *p*, O LORD Ps 119:57 2506
my *p* in the land of the living Ps 142:5 2506
household, and a *p* to her maidens Prov 31:15 2706
this was my *p* of all my labour Eccl 2:10 2506
shall he leave it for his *p* Eccl 2:21 2506
for that is his *p* Eccl 3:22 2506
for it is his *p* Eccl 5:18 2506
to eat thereof, and to take his *p* Eccl 5:19 2506
neither have they any more a *p* Eccl 9:6 2506
for that is thy *p* in this life Eccl 9:9 2506

Give a *p* to seven, and also to Eccl 11:2 2506
This is the *p* of them that spoil Is 17:14 2506
I divide him a *p* with the great Is 53:12
stones of the stream is thy *p* Is 57:6 2506
they shall rejoice in their *p* Is 61:7 2506
The *p* of Jacob is not like them Jer 10:16 2506
they have trodden my *p* under foot Jer 12:10 2513
pleasant *p* a desolate wilderness Jer 12:10 2513
the *p* of thy measures from me, Jer 13:25 4490
The *p* of Jacob is not like them Jer 51:19 2506
every day a *p* until the day of Jer 52:34 1697
The LORD is my *p*, saith my soul Lam 3:24 2506
the LORD, an holy *p* of the land Eze 45:1
The holy *p* of the land shall be Eze 45:4
the oblation of the holy *p* Eze 45:6
a *p* shall be for the prince on Eze 45:7
of the oblation of the holy *p* Eze 45:7
before the oblation of the holy *p* Eze 45:7
a *p* for Dan Eze 48:1
unto the west side, a *p* for Asher Eze 48:2
the west side, a *p* for Naphtali Eze 48:3
the west side, a *p* for Manasseh Eze 48:4
the west side, a *p* for Ephraim Eze 48:5
the west side, a *p* for Reuben Eze 48:6
unto the west side, a *p* for Judah Eze 48:7
the oblation of the holy *p* shall Eze 48:18
the oblation of the holy *p* Eze 48:18
side, Benjamin shall have a *p* Eze 48:23
west side, Simeon shall have a *p* Eze 48:24
unto the west side, Issachar a *p* Eze 48:25
unto the west side, Zebulun a *p* Eze 48:26
side unto the west side, Gad a *p* Eze 48:27
with the *p* of the king's meat Dan 1:8 6598
eat of the *p* of the king's meat Dan 1:13 6598
did eat the *p* of the king's meat Dan 1:15 6598
took away the *p* of their meat Dan 1:16 6598
let his *p* be with the beasts in Dan 4:15 2508
let his *p* be with the beasts of Dan 4:23 2508
they that feed of the *p* of his Dan 11:26 6598
hath changed the *p* of my people Mic 2:4 2506
because by them their *p* is fat Hab 1:16 2506
Judah his *p* in the holy land Zec 2:12 2506
appoint him his *p* with the Mt 24:51 *3313*
to give them their *p* of meat in Lk 12:42 *4620*
him his *p* with the unbelievers Lk 12:46 *3313*
give me the *p* of goods that Lk 15:12 *3313*

PORTIONS
They shall have like *p* to eat Deut 18:8 2506
And there fell ten *p* to Manasseh Josh 17:5 2256
all her sons and her daughters, *p* 1Sa 1:4 4490
to give *p* to all the males among 2Chr 31:19 4490
send *p* unto them for whom nothing Neh 8:10 4490
to eat, and to drink, and to send *p* Neh 8:12 4490
the *p* of the law for the priests Neh 12:44 4521
gave the *p* of the singers and the Neh 12:47 4521
I perceived that the *p* of the Neh 13:10 4521
of sending *p* one to another Est 9:19 4490
of sending *p* one to another, and Est 9:22 4490
be over against one of the *p* Eze 45:7 2506
Joseph shall have two *p* Eze 47:13 2256
over against the *p* for the prince Eze 48:21 2506
inheritance, and these are their *p* Eze 48:29 4256
a month devour them with their *p* Hos 5:7 2506

POSSESS
thy seed shall *p* the gate of his Gen 22:17 3423
let thy seed *p* the gate of those Gen 24:60 3423
I will give it unto you to *p* it Lev 20:24 3423
Let us go up at once, and *p* it Num 13:30 3423
and his seed shall *p* it Num 14:24 3423
of his family, and he shall *p* it Num 27:11 3423
I have given you the land to *p* it Num 33:53 3423
p the land which the LORD sware Deut 1:8 3423
p it, as the LORD God of thy Deut 1:21 3423
I give it, and they shall *p* it Deut 1:39 3423
begin to *p* it, and contend with Deut 2:24 3423
begin to *p*, that thou mayest Deut 2:31 3423
hath given you this land to *p* it Deut 3:18 3423
until they also *p* the land which Deut 3:20 3423
p the land which the LORD God of Deut 4:1 3423
in the land whither ye go to *p* it Deut 4:5 3423
land whither ye go over to *p* it Deut 4:14 3423
go over, and *p* that good land Deut 4:22 3423
ye go over Jordan to *p* it Deut 4:26 3423
land which I give them to *p* it Deut 5:31 3423
days in the land which ye shall *p* Deut 5:33 3423
in the land whither ye go to *p* it Deut 6:1 3423
p the good land which the LORD Deut 6:18 3423
land whither thou goest to *p* it Deut 7:1 3423
p the land which the LORD sware Deut 8:1 3423
to go in to *p* nations greater and Deut 9:1 3423
hath brought me in to *p* this land Deut 9:4 3423
dost thou go to *p* their land Deut 9:5 3423
to *p* it for thy righteousness Deut 9:6 3423
p the land which I have given you Deut 9:23 3423
p the land, which I sware unto Deut 10:11 3423
p the land, whither ye go to Deut 11:8 3423
the land, whither ye go to *p* it Deut 11:8 3423
whither thou goest in to *p* it Deut 11:10 3423
the land, whither ye go to *p* it Deut 11:11 3423
ye shall *p* greater nations and Deut 11:23 3423
land whither thou goest to *p* it Deut 11:29 3423
to *p* the land which the LORD your Deut 11:31 3423
God giveth you, and ye shall *p* it Deut 11:31 3423
thy fathers giveth thee to *p* it Deut 12:1 3423
ye shall *p* served their gods Deut 12:2 3423
whither thou goest to *p* them Deut 12:29 3423
thee for an inheritance to *p* it Deut 15:4 3423
God giveth thee, and shalt *p* it Deut 17:14 3423
these nations, which thou shalt *p* Deut 18:14 3423
LORD thy God giveth thee to *p* it Deut 19:2 3423
LORD thy God giveth thee to *p* it Deut 19:14 3423
LORD thy God giveth thee to *p* it Deut 21:1 3423
land whither thou goest to *p* it Deut 23:20 3423
thee for an inheritance to *p* it Deut 25:19 3423
land, whither thou goest to *p* it Deut 28:21 3423
land whither thou goest to *p* it Deut 28:63 3423
possessed, and thou shalt *p* it Deut 30:5 3423
land whither thou goest to *p* it Deut 30:16 3423
passest over Jordan to go to *p* it Deut 30:18 3423
before thee, and thou shalt *p* them Deut 31:3 3423
whither ye go over Jordan to *p* it Deut 31:13 3423
whither ye go over Jordan to *p* it Deut 32:47 3423
p thou the west and the south Deut 33:23 3423
Jordan, to go in to *p* the land Josh 1:11 3423
LORD your God giveth you to *p* it Josh 1:11 3423
are ye slack to go to *p* the land Josh 18:3 3423
ye shall *p* their land, as the Josh 23:5 3423
unto Esau mount Seir, to *p* it Josh 24:4 3423
hand, that ye might *p* their land Josh 24:8 3423
his inheritance to *p* the land Judg 2:6 3423
Israel, and shouldest thou *p* it Judg 11:23 3423
Wilt not thou *p* that which Judg 11:24 3423
Chemosh thy god giveth thee to *p* Judg 11:24 3423
from before us, them will we *p* Judg 11:24 3423
to go, and to enter to *p* the land Judg 18:9 3423
whither he is gone down to *p* it 1Kin 21:18 3423
that ye may *p* this good land, and 1Chr 28:8 3423
land, unto which ye go to *p* it Ezr 9:11 3423
them that they should go in to *p* Neh 9:15 3423
that they should go in to *p* it Neh 9:23 3423
So am I made to *p* months of Job 7:3 5157
makest me to *p* the iniquities of Job 13:26 3423
the house of Israel shall *p* them Is 14:2 5157
nor *p* the land, nor fill the face Is 14:21 3423
and the bittern shall *p* it Is 34:11 3423
they shall *p* it for ever, from Is 34:17 3423
his trust in me shall *p* the land Is 57:13 5157
land they shall *p* the double Is 61:7 3423
their fathers, and they shall *p* it Jer 30:3 3423
they shall *p* their houses Eze 7:24 3423
and shall ye *p* the land Eze 33:25 3423
and shall ye *p* the land Eze 33:26 3423
shall be mine, and we will *p* it Eze 35:10 3423
and they shall *p* thee, and thou Eze 36:12 3423
p the kingdom for ever, even for Dan 7:18 2631
silver, nettles shall *p* them Hos 9:6 3423
to *p* the land of the Amorite Amos 2:10 3423
That they may *p* the remnant of Amos 9:12 3423
Jacob shall *p* their possessions Obad 17 3423
south shall *p* the mount of Esau Obad 19 3423
they shall *p* the fields of Obad 19 3423
and Benjamin shall *p* Gilead Obad 19
shall *p* that of the Canaanites Obad 20
shall *p* the cities of the south Obad 20 423
to *p* the dwellingplaces that are Hab 1:6 423
remnant of my people shall *p* them Zeph 2:9 5157
this people to *p* all these things Zec 8:12 5157
I give tithes of all that I *p* Lk 18:12 *2932*
In your patience *p* ye your souls Lk 21:19 *2932*
to *p* his vessel in sanctification 1Th 4:4 *2932*

POSSESSED
p his land from Arnon unto Jabbok Num 21:24 3423
and they *p* his land Num 21:35 3423
which we *p* at that time, from Deut 3:12 3423
they *p* his land, and the land of Deut 4:47 3423
into the land which thy fathers *p* Deut 30:5 3423
they also have *p* the land which Josh 1:15 3423
p their land on the other side Josh 12:1 3423
yet very much land to be *p* Josh 13:1 3423
p it, and dwelt therein, and called Josh 19:47 3423
and they *p* it, and dwelt therein Josh 21:43 3423
possession, whereof they were *p* Josh 22:9 270
and *p* the city of palm trees Judg 3:13 3423
so Israel *p* all the land of the Judg 11:21 3423
they *p* all the coasts of the Judg 11:22 3423
they *p* Samaria, and dwelt in the 2Kin 17:24 3423
so they *p* the land of Sihon, and Neh 9:22 3423
p the land, and thou subduedst Neh 9:24 3423
p houses full of all goods, wells Neh 9:25 3423
For thou hast *p* my reins Ps 139:13 7069
The LORD *p* me in the beginning of Prov 8:22 7069
have *p* it but a little while Is 63:18 3423
shall be *p* again in this land Jer 32:15 7069
And they came in, and *p* it Jer 32:23 3423
that the saints *p* the kingdom Dan 7:22 2631
and those which were *p* with devils Mt 4:24 *1139*
him many that were *p* with devils Mt 8:16 *1139*
there met him two *p* with devils Mt 8:28 *1139*
befallen to the *p* of the devils Mt 8:33 *1139*
to him a dumb man *p* with a devil Mt 9:32 *1139*
unto him one *p* with a devil Mt 12:22 *1139*
and them that were *p* with devils Mk 1:32 *1139*
see him that was *p* with the devil Mk 5:15 *1139*
to him that was *p* with the devil Mk 5:16 *1139*
he that had been *p* with the devil Mk 5:18 *1139*
was *p* of the devils was healed Lk 8:36 *1139*
the things which he *p* was his own Acts 4:32 *5224*
out of many that were *p* with them Acts 8:7 *2192*
a certain damsel *p* with a spirit Acts 16:16 *2192*
that buy, as though they *p* not 1Cor 7:30 *2722*

POSSESSEST
p it, and dwellest therein Deut 26:1 3423

POSSESSETH
that *p* an inheritance in any Num 36:8 3423
of the things which he *p* Lk 12:15 *5224*

POSSESSING
nothing, and yet *p* all things 2Cor 6:10 *2722*

POSSESSION
of Canaan, for an everlasting *p* Gen 17:8 272
give me a *p* of a buryingplace Gen 23:4 272
a *p* of a buryingplace amongst you Gen 23:9 272
Unto Abraham for a *p* in the Gen 23:18 4736
made sure unto Abraham for a *p* of Gen 23:20 272
For he had *p* of flocks, and Gen 26:14 4735
p of herds, and great store of Gen 26:14 4735
in the land of their *p* Gen 36:43 272
gave them a *p* in the land of Gen 47:11 272
after thee for an everlasting *p* Gen 48:4 272
Hittite for a *p* of a buryingplace Gen 49:30 272
bought with the field for a *p* of Gen 50:13 272
which I give to you for a *p* Lev 14:34 272
in a house of the land of your *p* Lev 14:34 272
shall return every man unto his *p* Lev 25:10 272
shall return every man unto his *p* Lev 25:13 272
in all the land of your *p* ye Lev 25:24 272
and hath sold away some of his *p* Lev 25:25 272
that he may return unto his *p* Lev 25:27 272
and he shall return unto his *p* Lev 25:28 272
houses of the cities of their *p* Lev 25:32 272
was sold, and the city of his *p* Lev 25:33 272
p among the children of Israel Lev 25:33 272
for it is their perpetual *p* Lev 25:34 272
unto the *p* of his fathers shall Lev 25:41 272
and they shall be your *p* Lev 25:45 272
you, to inherit them for a *p* Lev 25:46 272
some part of a field of his *p* Lev 27:16 272
the *p* thereof shall be the Lev 27:21 272
is not of the fields of his *p* Lev 27:22 272
whom the *p* of the land did belong Lev 27:24 272
beast, and of the field of his *p* Lev 27:28 272
And Edom shall be a *p* Num 24:18 3424
also shall be a *p* for his enemies Num 24:18 3424
According to the lot shall the *p* Num 26:56 5159
Give unto us therefore a *p* among Num 27:4 272
a *p* of an inheritance among their Num 27:7 272
given unto thy servants for a *p* Num 32:5 272
shall be your *p* before the LORD Num 32:22 272
them the land of Gilead for a *p* Num 32:29 272
that the *p* of our inheritance on Num 32:32 272
of their *p* cities to dwell in Num 35:2 272
the *p* of the children of Israel Num 35:8 272
return into the land of his *p* Num 35:28 272
mount Seir unto Esau for a *p* Deut 2:5 3425
give thee of their land for a *p* Deut 2:9 3425
unto the children of Lot for a *p* Deut 2:9 3425
Israel did unto the land of his *p* Deut 2:12 3425
of the children of Ammon any *p* Deut 2:19 3425
unto the children of Lot for a *p* Deut 2:19 3425
ye return every man unto his *p* Deut 3:20 3425
the substance that was in their *p* Deut 11:6 7272
the children of Israel for a *p* Deut 32:49 272
return unto the land of your *p* Josh 1:15 3425
it for a *p* unto the Reubenites Josh 12:6 3425
a *p* according to their divisions Josh 12:7 3425
this was the *p* of the half tribe Josh 13:29
the son of Jephunneh for his *p* Josh 21:12 272
of the Levites within the *p* of Josh 21:41 272
tents, and unto the land of your *p* Josh 22:4 272
Moses had given *p* in Bashan Josh 22:7
of Gilead, to the land of their *p* Josh 22:9 272
if the land of your *p* be unclean Josh 22:19 272
the land of the *p* of the LORD Josh 22:19 272
dwelleth, and take *p* among us Josh 22:19 270
take *p* of the vineyard of Naboth 1Kin 21:15 3423
the Jezreelite, to take *p* of it 1Kin 21:16 3423
Hast thou killed, and also taken *p* 1Kin 21:19 3423
p of the king, and of his sons, 1Chr 28:1 4735
left their suburbs and their *p* 2Chr 11:14 272
to come to cast us out of thy *p* 2Chr 20:11 3425
returned, every man to his *p* 2Chr 31:1 272
one in his *p* in their cities Neh 11:3 272
parts of the earth for thy *p* Ps 2:8 272
the land in *p* by their own sword Ps 44:3 3423
may dwell there, and have it in *p* Ps 69:35 3423
ourselves the houses of God in *p* Ps 83:12 3423
shall have good things in *p* Prov 28:10 5157
also make it a *p* for the bittern Is 14:23 4180
unto us is this land given in *p* Eze 11:15 4181
to the men of the east for a *p* Eze 25:4 4181
Ammonites, and will give them in *p* Eze 25:10 4181
ancient high places are ours in *p* Eze 36:2 4181
that ye might be a *p* unto the Eze 36:3 4181
appointed my land into their *p* Eze 36:5 4181
ye shall give them no *p* in Israel Eze 44:28 272
I am their *p* Eze 44:28 272
for a *p* for twenty chambers Eze 45:5 272
ye shall appoint the *p* of the Eze 45:6 272
of the *p* of the city, before the Eze 45:7 272
before the *p* of the city, from Eze 45:7 272
the land shall be his *p* in Israel Eze 45:8 272
shall be their *p* by inheritance Eze 46:16 272
to thrust them out of their *p* Eze 46:18 272
sons inheritance out of his own *p* Eze 46:18 272
scattered every man from his *p* Eze 46:18 272
with the *p* of the city Eze 48:20 272
of the *p* of the city, over Eze 48:21 272
from the *p* of the Levites Eze 48:22 272
from the *p* of the city, being in Eze 48:22 272
with Sapphira his wife, sold a *p* Acts 5:1 *2933*
he would give it to him for a *p* Acts 7:5 *2697*
Jesus into the *p* of the Gentiles Acts 7:45 *2697*
the redemption of the purchased *p* Eph 1:14 *4047*

POSSESSIONS
ye therein, and get you *p* therein Gen 34:10 270
and they had *p* therein, and grew, Gen 47:27 270
they shall have *p* among you in Num 32:30 270
in Maon, whose *p* were in Carmel 1Sa 25:2 4639
And their *p* and habitations were, 1Chr 7:28 272
in their *p* in their cities were 1Chr 9:2 272
p of flocks and herds in abundance 2Chr 32:29 4735
also I had great *p* of great Eccl 2:7 4735
of Jacob shall possess their *p* Obad 17 4180
for he had great *p* Mt 19:22 *2933*
for he had great *p* Mk 10:22 *2933*
And sold their *p* and goods, and Acts 2:45 *2933*
In the same quarters were *p* of Acts 28:7 *5564*

POSSESSOR
high God, p of heaven and earth Gen 14:19 7069
the p of heaven and earth, Gen 14:22 7069

POSSESSORS
Whose p slay them, and hold Zec 11:5 7069
for as many as were p of lands or Acts 4:34 *2935*

POSSIBLE
but with God all things are p Mt 19:26 *1415*
insomuch that, if it were p Mt 24:24 *1415*
saying, O my Father, if it be p Mt 26:39 *1415*
all things are p to him that Mk 9:23 *1415*
for with God all things are p Mk 10:27 *1415*
wonders, to seduce, if it were p Mk 13:22 *1415*
and prayed that, if it were p Mk 14:35 *1415*
all things are p unto thee Mk 14:36 *1415*
with men are p with God Lk 18:27 *1415*
because it was not p that he Acts 2:24 *1415*
he hasted, if it were p for him Acts 20:16 *1415*
they were minded, if it were p Acts 27:39 *1410*
If it be p, as much as lieth in Rom 12:18 *1415*
record, that, if it had been p Gal 4:15 *1415*
For it is not p that the blood of Heb 10:4 *102*

POST
on the upper door p of the houses Ex 12:7 4947
to the door, or unto the door p Ex 21:6 4201
by a p of the temple of the LORD 1Sa 1:9 4201
Now my days are swifter than a p Job 9:25 7323
One p shall run to meet another, Jer 51:31 7323
even unto the p of the court Eze 40:14 352
upon each p were palm trees Eze 40:16 352
and measured each p of the porch Eze 40:48 352
and measured the p of the door Eze 41:3 352
their p by my posts, and the wall Eze 43:8 4201
shall stand by the p of the gate Eze 46:2 4201

POSTERITY
to preserve you a p in the earth Gen 45:7 7611
If any man of you or of your p Num 9:10 1755
I will take away the p of Baasha 1Kin 16:3 310
of Baasha, and the p of his house 1Kin 16:3 310
thee, and will take away thy p 1Kin 21:21 310
yet their p approve their sayings Ps 49:13 310
Let his p be cut off Ps 109:13 319
and not to his p, nor according to Dan 11:4 319
hooks, and your p with fishhooks Amos 4:2 319

POSTS
and strike it on the two side p Ex 12:7 4201
the two side p with the blood Ex 12:22 4201
the lintel, and on the two side p Ex 12:23 4201
them upon the p of thy house Deut 6:9 4201
upon the door p of thine house Deut 11:20 4201
gate of the city, and the two p Judg 16:3 4201
side p were a fifth part of the 1Kin 6:31 4201
of the temple p of olive tree 1Kin 6:33 4201
p were square, with the windows 1Kin 7:5 4201
also the house, the beams, the p 2Chr 3:7 5592
So the p went with the letters 2Chr 30:6 7323
So the p passed from city to city 2Chr 30:10 7323
the letters were sent by p into Est 3:13 7323
The p went out, being hastened by Est 3:15 7323
and sent letters by p on horseback Est 8:10 7323
So the p that rode upon mules and Est 8:14 7323
waiting at the p of my doors Prov 8:34 4201
the p of the door moved at the Is 6:4 520
the p hast thou set up thy Is 57:8 4201
the p thereof, two cubits Eze 40:9 352
the p had one measure on this Eze 40:10 352
He made also p of threescore Eze 40:14 352
to their p within the gate round Eze 40:16 352
the p thereof and the arches Eze 40:21 352
and he measured the p thereof Eze 40:24 352
on that side, upon the p thereof Eze 40:26 352
the p thereof, and the arches Eze 40:29 352
trees were upon the p thereof Eze 40:31 352
the p thereof, and the arches Eze 40:33 352
trees were upon the p thereof Eze 40:34 352
the p thereof, and the arches Eze 40:36 352
the p thereof were toward the Eze 40:37 352
trees were upon the p thereof Eze 40:37 352
were by the p of the gates Eze 40:38 352
and there were pillars by the p Eze 40:49 352
to the temple, and measured the p Eze 41:1 352
The door p, and the narrow windows Eze 41:16 5592
The p of the temple were squared, Eze 41:21 4201
thresholds, and their post by my p Eze 43:8 4201
and put it upon the p of the house Eze 45:19 4201
upon the p of the gate of the Eze 45:19 4201
of the door, that the p may shake Amos 9:1 5592

POT
Moses said unto Aaron, Take a p Ex 16:33 6803
and if it be sodden in a brasen p Lev 6:28 3627
and he put the broth in a p Judg 6:19 6517
pan, or kettle, or caldron, or p 1Sa 2:14 6517
in the house, save a p of oil 2Kin 4:2 610
his servant, Set on the great p 2Kin 4:38 5518
shred them into the p of pottage 2Kin 4:39 5518
of God, there is death in the p 2Kin 4:40 5518
And he cast it into the p 2Kin 4:41 5518
And there was no harm in the p 2Kin 4:41 5518
as out of a seething p or caldron Job 41:20 1731
maketh the deep to boil like a p Job 41:31 5518
the sea like a p of ointment Job 41:31
The fining p is for silver, and Prov 17:3 4715
As the fining p for silver Prov 27:21 4715
the crackling of thorns under a p Eccl 7:6 5518
and I said, I see a seething p Jer 1:13 5518
Set on a p, set it on, and also Eze 24:3 5518
to the p whose scum is therein, Eze 24:6 5518
chop them in pieces, as for the p Mic 3:3 5518
every p in Jerusalem and in Judah Zec 14:21 5518
was the golden p that had manna Heb 9:4 *4713*

POTENTATE
who is the blessed and only P 1Ti 6:15 *1413*

POTIPHAR (*pot'i-far*) *A captain of Pharaoh's guard.*
sold him into Egypt unto P Gen 37:36 6318
and P, an officer of Pharaoh, Gen 39:1 6318

POTI-PHERAH *Priest of On.*
the daughter of P priest of On Gen 41:45 6319
of P priest of On bare unto him Gen 41:50 6319
of P priest of On bare unto him Gen 46:20 6319

POTS
Egypt, when we sat by the flesh p Ex 16:3 5518
the vessels of the altar, the p Ex 38:3 5518
it be oven, or ranges for p Lev 11:35
And the p, and the shovels, and the 1Kin 7:45 5518
And the p, and the shovels, and the 2Kin 25:14 5518
And Huram made the p, and the 2Chr 4:11 5518
The p also, and the shovels, and 2Chr 4:16 5518
holy offerings sod they in p 2Chr 35:13 5518
Before your p can feel the thorns Ps 58:9 5518
Though ye have lien among the p Ps 68:13 8240
hands were delivered from the p Ps 81:6 1731
of the Rechabites p full of wine Jer 35:5 1375
the p in the LORD's house shall Zec 14:20 5518
as the washing of cups, and p Mk 7:4 *3582*
of men, as the washing of p Mk 7:8 *3582*

POTSHERD
he took him a p to scrape himself Job 2:8 2789
My strength is dried up like a p Ps 22:15 2789
a p covered with silver dross Prov 26:23 2789
Let the p strive with the Is 45:9 2789

POTSHERDS
strive with the p of the earth Is 45:9 2789

POTTAGE
And Jacob sod p Gen 25:29 5138
I pray thee, with that same red p Gen 25:30
gave Esau bread and p of lentiles Gen 25:34 5138
seethe p for the sons of the 2Kin 4:38 5138
and shred them into the pot of p 2Kin 4:39 5138
as they were eating of the p 2Kin 4:40 5138
his skirt do touch bread, or p Hag 2:12 5138

POTTER
morter, and as the p treadeth clay Is 41:25 3335
we are the clay, and thou our p Is 64:8 3335
was marred in the hand of the p Jer 18:4 3335
seemed good to the p to make it Jer 18:4 3335
cannot I do with you as this p Jer 18:6 3335
the work of the hands of the p Lam 4:2 3335
said unto me, Cast it unto the p Zec 11:13 3335
cast them to the p in the house Zec 11:13 3335
Hath not the p power over the Rom 9:21 *2763*
as the vessels of a p shall they Rev 2:27 *2764*

POTTER'S
them in pieces like a p vessel Ps 2:9 3335
shall be esteemed as the p clay Is 29:16 3335
Arise, and go down to the p house Jer 18:2 3335
Then I went down to the p house Jer 18:3 3335
as the clay is in the p hand Jer 18:6 3335
get a p earthen bottle, and take Jer 19:1 3335
city, as one breaketh a p vessel Jer 19:11 3335
and bought with them the p field Mt 27:7 *2763*
And gave them for the p field Mt 27:10 *2763*

POTTERS
These were the p, and those that 1Chr 4:23 3335

POTTERS'
p vessel that is broken in pieces Is 30:14 3335
the feet and toes, part of p clay Dan 2:41 6353

POUND
three p of gold went to one 1Kin 10:17 4488
and five thousand p of silver Ezr 2:69 4488
thy p hath gained ten pounds Lk 19:16 *3414*
thy p hath gained five pounds Lk 19:18 *3414*
Lord, behold, here is thy p Lk 19:20 *3414*
stood by, Take from him the p Lk 19:24 *3414*
Then took Mary a p of ointment of Jn 12:3 *3046*
aloes, about an hundred p weight Jn 19:39 *3046*

POUNDS
and two hundred p of silver Neh 7:71 4488
gold, and two thousand p of silver Neh 7:72 4488
servants, and delivered them ten p Lk 19:13 *3414*
Lord, thy pound hath gained ten p Lk 19:16 *3414*
thy pound hath gained five p Lk 19:18 *3414*
and give it to him that hath ten p Lk 19:24 *3414*
unto him, Lord, he hath ten p Lk 19:25 *3414*

POUR
river, and p it upon the dry land Ex 4:9 8210
p it upon his head, and anoint him Ex 29:7 3332
p all the blood beside the bottom Ex 29:12 8210
neither shall ye p drink offering Ex 30:9 5258
he shall p oil upon it, and put Lev 2:1 3332
it in pieces, and p oil thereon Lev 2:6 3332
shall p all the blood of the Lev 4:7 8210
shall p out all the blood at the Lev 4:18 8210
shall p out his blood at the Lev 4:25 8210
shall p out all the blood thereof Lev 4:30 8210
shall p out all the blood thereof Lev 4:34 8210
p it into the palm of his own Lev 14:15 3332
in the priest's hand he shall p Lev 14:18 5414
the priest shall p of the oil Lev 14:26 3332
they shall p out the dust that Lev 14:41 8210
he shall even p out the blood Lev 17:13 8210
he shall p no oil upon it, nor Num 5:15 3332
He shall p the water out of his Num 24:7 5140
ye shall p it upon the earth as Deut 12:16 8210
thou shalt p it upon the earth as Deut 12:24 8210
thou shalt p it upon the ground Deut 15:23 8210
this rock, and p out the broth Judg 6:20 8210
p it on the burnt sacrifice, and 1Kin 18:33 3332
shalt p out into all those 2Kin 4:4 3332
P out for the people, that they 2Kin 4:41 3332
p it on his head, and say, Thus 2Kin 9:3 3332
they p down rain according to the Job 36:27 2212
things, I p out my soul in me Ps 42:4 8210
p out your heart before him Ps 62:8 8210
P out thine indignation upon them Ps 69:24 8210
P out thy wrath upon the heathen Ps 79:6 8210
I will p out my spirit unto you, Prov 1:23 5042
For I will p water upon him that Is 44:3 3332
I will p my spirit upon thy seed, Is 44:3 3332
above, and let the skies p down Is 45:8 5140
I will p it out upon the children Jer 6:11 8210
to p out drink offerings unto Jer 7:18 5258
P out thy fury upon the heathen Jer 10:25 8210
for I will p their wickedness Jer 14:16 8210
p out their blood by the force of Jer 18:21 5064
to p out drink offerings unto her Jer 44:17 5258
to p out drink offerings unto her Jer 44:18 5258
p out drink offerings unto her, Jer 44:19 5258
to p out drink offerings unto her Jer 44:25 5258
p out thine heart like water Lam 2:19 8210
Now will I shortly p out my fury Eze 7:8 8210
p out my fury upon it in blood, Eze 14:19 8210
I will p out my fury upon them, Eze 20:8 8210
I would p out my fury upon them Eze 20:13 8210
I would p out my fury upon them, Eze 20:21 8210
I will p out mine indignation Eze 21:31 8210
it on, and also p water into it Eze 24:3 3332
I will p my fury upon Sin, the Eze 30:15 8210
therefore I will p out my wrath Hos 5:10 8210
that I will p out my spirit upon Joel 2:28 8210
those days will I p out my spirit Joel 2:29 8210
I will p down the stones thereof Mic 1:6 5064
to p upon them mine indignation, Zeph 3:8 8210
I will p upon the house of David, Zec 12:10 8210
p you out a blessing, that there Mal 3:10 7324
I will p out of my Spirit upon Acts 2:17 *1632*
on my handmaidens I will p out in Acts 2:18 *1632*
p out the vials of the wrath of Rev 16:1 *1632*

POURED
and p oil upon the top of it Gen 28:18 3332
he p a drink offering thereon Gen 35:14 5258
and he p oil thereon Gen 35:14 3332
the rain was not p upon the earth Ex 9:33 5413
man's flesh shall it not be p Ex 30:32 3251
place, where the ashes are p out Lev 4:12 8211
where the ashes are p out shall Lev 4:12 8211
he p of the anointing oil upon Lev 8:12 3332
p the blood at the bottom of the Lev 8:15 3332
p out the blood at the bottom of Lev 9:9 3332
head the anointing oil was p Lev 21:10 3332
to be p unto the LORD for a drink Num 28:7 5258
of thy sacrifices shall be p out Deut 12:27 8210
but have p out my soul before the 1Sa 1:15 8210
p it out before the LORD, and 1Sa 7:6 8210
p it upon his head, and kissed him 1Sa 10:1 3332
a pan, and p them out before him 2Sa 13:9 3332
but p it out unto the LORD 2Sa 23:16 5258
that are upon it shall be p out 1Kin 13:3 8210
the ashes p out from the altar, 1Kin 13:5 8210
which p water on the hands of 2Kin 3:11 3332
and she p out 2Kin 4:5 3332
So they p out for the men to eat 2Kin 4:40 3332
he p the oil on his head, and said 2Kin 9:6 3332
and p his drink offering, and 2Kin 16:13 5258
but p it out to the LORD, 1Chr 11:18 5258
my wrath shall not be p out upon 2Chr 12:7 5413
of the LORD that is p out upon us 2Chr 34:21 5413
shall be p out upon this place 2Chr 34:25 5413
my roarings are p out like the Job 3:24 5413
Hast thou not p me out as milk, Job 10:10 5413
the rock p me out rivers of oil Job 29:6 6694
And now my soul is p out upon me Job 30:16 8210
I am p out like water, and all my Ps 22:14 8210
grace is p into thy lips Ps 45:2 3332
The clouds p out water Ps 77:17 2229
I p out my complaint before him Ps 142:2 8210
thy name is as ointment p forth Song 1:3 7324
they p out a prayer when thy Is 26:16 6694
For the LORD hath p out upon you Is 29:10 5258
Until the spirit be p upon us Is 32:15 6168
Therefore he hath p upon him the Is 42:25 8210
because he hath p out his soul Is 53:12 6168
them hast thou p a drink offering Is 57:6 8210
my fury shall be p out upon this Jer 7:20 5413
have p out drink offerings unto Jer 19:13 5258
p out drink offerings unto other Jer 32:29 5258
my fury hath been p forth upon Jer 42:18 5413
shall my fury be p forth upon you Jer 42:18 5413
my fury and mine anger was p forth Jer 44:6 5413
p out drink offerings unto her, Jer 44:19 5258
he p out his fury like fire Lam 2:4 8210
my liver is p upon the earth, for Lam 2:11 8210
when their soul was p out into Lam 2:12 8210
p out in the top of every street Lam 4:1 8210
he hath p out his fierce anger, Lam 4:11 8210
Because thy filthiness was p out Eze 16:36 8210
p out there their drink offerings Eze 20:28 5258
out arm, and with fury p out Eze 20:33 8210
out arm, and with fury p out Eze 20:34 8210
LORD have p out my fury upon you Eze 22:22 8210
Therefore have I p out mine Eze 22:31 8210
p their whoredom upon her Eze 23:8 8210
she p it not upon the ground, to Eze 24:7 8210
Wherefore I p my fury upon them Eze 36:18 8210
for I have p out my spirit upon Eze 39:29 8210
therefore the curse is p upon us Dan 9:11 5413
shall be p upon the desolate Dan 9:27 5413
that are p down a steep place Mic 1:4 5064
his fury is p out like fire, and Nah 1:6 5413
blood shall be p out as dust Zeph 1:17 8210

p it on his head, as he sat at ... Mt 26:7 *2708*
For in that she hath p this ... Mt 26:12 *906*
the box, and p it on his head ... Mk 14:3 *2708*
p out the changers' money, and ... Jn 2:15 *1632*
that on the Gentiles also was p ... Acts 10:45 *1632*
which is p out without mixture ... Rev 14:10 *2767*
p out his vial upon the earth ... Rev 16:2 *1632*
the second angel p out his vial ... Rev 16:3 *1632*
the third angel p out his vial ... Rev 16:4 *1632*
the fourth angel p out his vial ... Rev 16:8 *1632*
the fifth angel p out his vial ... Rev 16:10 *1632*
the sixth angel p out his vial ... Rev 16:12 *1632*
the seventh angel p out his vial ... Rev 16:17 *1632*

POUREDST
p out thy fornications on every ... Eze 16:15 8210

POURETH
He p contempt upon princes, and ... Job 12:21 8210
he p out my gall upon the ground ... Job 16:13 8210
but mine eye p out tears unto God ... Job 16:20 1811
and he p out of the same ... Ps 75:8 5064
p out his complaint before the ... Ps 102:t 8210
He p contempt upon princes, and ... Ps 107:40 8210
mouth of fools p out foolishness ... Prov 15:2 5042
of the wicked p out evil things ... Prov 15:28 5042
p them out upon the face of the ... Amos 5:8 8210
p them out upon the face of the ... Amos 9:6 8210
After that he p water into a ... Jn 13:5 *906*

POURING
the residue of Israel in thy p ... Eze 9:8 8210
p in oil and wine, and set him on ... Lk 10:34

POURTRAY
thee, and p upon it the city, even ... Eze 4:1 2710

POURTRAYED
p upon the wall round about ... Eze 8:10 2707
when she saw men p upon the wall ... Eze 23:14 2707
of the Chaldeans p with vermilion ... Eze 23:14 2710

POVERTY
and all that thou hast, come to p ... Gen 45:11 3423
So shall thy p come as one that ... Prov 6:11 7389
of the poor is their p ... Prov 10:15 7389
than is meet, but it tendeth to p ... Prov 11:24 4270
P and shame shall be to him that ... Prov 13:18 7389
not sleep, lest thou come to p ... Prov 20:13 3423
and the glutton shall come to p ... Prov 23:21 3423
So shall thy p come as one that ... Prov 24:34 7389
vain persons shall have p enough ... Prov 28:19 7389
not that p shall come upon him ... Prov 28:22 2639
give me neither p nor riches ... Prov 30:8 7389
Let him drink, and forget his p ... Prov 31:7 7389
their deep p abounded unto the ... 2Cor 8:2 *4432*
ye through his p might be rich ... 2Cor 8:9 *4432*
thy works, and tribulation, and p ... Rev 2:9 *4432*

POWDER
it in the fire, and ground it to p ... Ex 32:20 1854
shall make the rain of thy land p ... Deut 28:24 80
Kidron, and stamped it small to p ... 2Kin 23:6 6083
cast the p thereof upon the ... 2Kin 23:6 6083
place, and stamped it small to p ... 2Kin 23:15 6083
beaten the graven images into p ... 2Chr 34:7 1854
fall, it will grind him to p ... Mt 21:44 *3039*
fall, it will grind him to p ... Lk 20:18 *3039*

POWDERS
with all p of the merchant ... Song 3:6 81

POWER
ye know that with all my p I have ... Gen 31:6 3581
It is in the p of my hand to do ... Gen 31:29 410
as a prince hast thou p with God ... Gen 32:28 8280
dignity, and the excellency of p ... Gen 49:3 5794
thee up, for to shew in thee my p ... Ex 9:16 3581
O LORD, is become glorious in p ... Ex 15:6 3581
strange nation he shall have no p ... Ex 21:8 4910
of the land of Egypt with great p ... Ex 32:11 3581
I will break the pride of your p ... Lev 26:19 5797
ye shall have no p to stand ... Lev 26:37 8617
let the p of my LORD be great, ... Num 14:17 3581
have I now any p at all to say ... Num 22:38 3201
with his mighty p out of Egypt ... Deut 4:37 3581
And thou say in thine heart, My p ... Deut 8:17 3581
that giveth thee p to get wealth ... Deut 8:18 3581
broughtest out by thy mighty p ... Deut 9:29 3581
he seeth that their p is gone ... Deut 32:36 3027
they had no p to flee this way or ... Josh 8:20 3027
a great people, and hast great p ... Josh 17:17 3581
a Benjamite, a mighty man of p ... 1Sa 9:1 2428
until they had no more p to weep ... 1Sa 30:4 3581
God is my strength and p ... 2Sa 22:33 2428
of the land of Egypt with great p ... 2Kin 17:36 3581
their inhabitants were of small p ... 2Kin 19:26 3027
Joab led forth the p of the army ... 1Chr 20:1 2428
LORD, is the greatness, and the p ... 1Chr 29:11 1369
and in thine hand is p and might ... 1Chr 29:12 3581
many, or with them that have no p ... 2Chr 14:11 3581
and in thine hand is there not p ... 2Chr 20:6 3581
no p to keep still the kingdom ... 2Chr 22:9 3581
for God hath p to help, and to ... 2Chr 25:8 3581
that made war with mighty p ... 2Chr 26:13 3581
all his p with him,) unto ... 2Chr 32:9 4475
made them to cease by force and p ... Ezr 4:23 2429
but his p and his wrath is against ... Ezr 8:22 5797
thou hast redeemed by thy great p ... Neh 1:10 3581
is it in our p to redeem them ... Neh 5:5 3027
the p of Persia and Media, the ... Est 1:3 2428
all the p of the people and ... Est 8:11 2428
Jews hoped to have p over them ... Est 9:1 7980
And all the acts of his p and of ... Est 10:2 8633
all that he hath is in thy p ... Job 1:12 3027
and in war from the p of the sword ... Job 5:20 3027
become old, yea, are mighty in p ... Job 21:7 2428
plead against me with his great p ... Job 23:6 3581
also the mighty with his p ... Job 24:22 3581
thou helped him that is without p ... Job 26:2 3581
He divideth the sea with his p ... Job 26:12 3581
of his p who can understand ... Job 26:14 1369
Behold, God exalteth by his p ... Job 36:22 3581
he is excellent in p, and in ... Job 37:23 3581
not conceal his parts, nor his p ... Job 41:12 1369
so will we sing and praise thy p ... Ps 21:13 1369
my darling from the p of the dog ... Ps 22:20 3027
I have seen the wicked in great p ... Ps 37:35 6184
my soul from the p of the grave ... Ps 49:15 3027
scatter them by thy p ... Ps 59:11 2428
But I will sing of thy p ... Ps 59:16 5797
that p belongeth unto God ... Ps 62:11 5797
To see thy p and thy glory, so as ... Ps 63:2 5797
being girded with p ... Ps 65:6 1369
thy p shall thine enemies submit ... Ps 66:3 5797
He ruleth by his p for ever ... Ps 66:7 1369
strength and p unto his people ... Ps 68:35 8592
thy p to every one that is to ... Ps 71:18 1369
by his p he brought in the south ... Ps 78:26 5797
to the greatness of thy p ... Ps 79:11 2220
Who knoweth the p of thine anger ... Ps 90:11 5797
make his mighty p to be known ... Ps 106:8 1369
be willing in the day of thy p ... Ps 110:3 2428
his people the p of his works ... Ps 111:6 3581
of thy kingdom, and talk of thy p ... Ps 145:11 1369
Great is our Lord, and of great p ... Ps 147:5 3581
him in the firmament of his p ... Ps 150:1 5797
when it is in the p of thine hand ... Prov 3:27 410
life are in the p of the tongue ... Prov 18:21 3027
of their oppressors there was p ... Eccl 4:1 3581
hath given him p to eat thereof ... Eccl 5:19 7980
giveth him not p to eat thereof ... Eccl 6:2 7980
the word of a king is, there is p ... Eccl 8:4 7983
There is no man that hath p over ... Eccl 8:8 7989
neither hath he p in the day of ... Eccl 8:8 7983
their inhabitants were of small p ... Is 37:27 3027
might, for that he is strong in p ... Is 40:26 3581
He giveth p to the faint ... Is 40:29 3581
and horse, the army and the p ... Is 43:17 5808
from the p of the flame ... Is 47:14 3027
or have I no p to deliver ... Is 50:2 3581
He hath made the earth by his p ... Jer 10:12 3581
upon the ground, by my great p ... Jer 27:5 3581
and the earth by thy great p ... Jer 32:17 3581
He hath made the earth by his p ... Jer 51:15 3581
even without great p or many ... Eze 17:9 2220
in thee to their p to shed blood ... Eze 22:6 2220
pride of her p shall come down ... Eze 30:6 5797
hath given thee a kingdom, p ... Dan 2:37 2632
whose bodies the fire had no p ... Dan 3:27 7981
the kingdom by the might of my p ... Dan 4:30 2632
Daniel from the p of the lions ... Dan 6:27 3028
ran unto him in the fury of his p ... Dan 8:6 3581
there was no p in the ram to ... Dan 8:7 3581
of the nation, but not in his p ... Dan 8:22 3581
his p shall be mighty ... Dan 8:24 3581
but not by his own p ... Dan 8:24 3581
shall not retain the p of the arm ... Dan 11:6 3581
And he shall stir up his p ... Dan 11:25 3581
But he shall have p over the ... Dan 11:43 4910
scatter the p of the holy people ... Dan 12:7 3027
by his strength he had p with God ... Hos 12:3 8280
he had p over the angel, and ... Hos 12:4 7786
them from the p of the grave ... Hos 13:14 3027
it is in the p of their hand ... Mic 2:1 410
But truly I am full of p by the ... Mic 3:8 3581
is slow to anger, and great in p ... Nah 1:3 3581
strong, fortify thy p mightily ... Nah 2:1 3581
imputing this his p unto his god ... Hab 1:11 3581
be delivered from the p of evil ... Hab 2:9 3709
and there was the hiding of his p ... Hab 3:4 5797
saying, Not by might, nor by p ... Zec 4:6 3581
and he will smite her p in the sea ... Zec 9:4 2428
thine is the kingdom, and the p ... Mt 6:13 *1411*
hath p on earth to forgive sins ... Mt 9:6 *1849*
which had given such p unto men ... Mt 9:8 *1849*
he gave them p against unclean ... Mt 10:1 *1849*
the scriptures, nor the p of God ... Mt 22:29 *1411*
in the clouds of heaven with p ... Mt 24:30 *1411*
sitting on the right hand of p ... Mt 26:64 *1411*
All p is given unto me in heaven ... Mt 28:18 *1849*
hath p on earth to forgive sins ... Mk 2:10 *1849*
to have p to heal sicknesses, and ... Mk 3:15 *1849*
gave them p over unclean spirits ... Mk 6:7 *1849*
the kingdom of God come with p ... Mk 9:1 *1411*
scriptures, neither the p of God ... Mk 12:24 *1411*
coming in the clouds with great p ... Mk 13:26 *1411*
sitting on the right hand of p ... Mk 14:62 *1411*
p of Elias, to turn the hearts of ... Lk 1:17 *1411*
the p of the Highest shall ... Lk 1:35 *1411*
All this p will I give thee, and ... Lk 4:6 *1849*
Jesus returned in the p of the ... Lk 4:14 *1411*
for his word was with p ... Lk 4:32 *1849*
p he commandeth the unclean ... Lk 4:36 *1411*
the p of the Lord was present to ... Lk 5:17 *1411*
hath p upon earth to forgive sins ... Lk 5:24 *1849*
together, and gave them p and ... Lk 9:1 *1411*
all amazed at the mighty p of God ... Lk 9:43 *3168*
I give unto you p to tread on ... Lk 10:19 *1849*
and over all the p of the enemy ... Lk 10:19 *1411*
killed hath p to cast into hell ... Lk 12:5 *1849*
they might deliver him unto the p ... Lk 20:20 *746*
of man coming in a cloud with p ... Lk 21:27 *1411*
your hour, and the p of darkness ... Lk 22:53 *1849*
on the right hand of the p of God ... Lk 22:69 *1411*
ye be endued with p from on high ... Lk 24:49 *1411*
to them gave he p to become the ... Jn 1:12 *1849*
I have p to lay it down, and I ... Jn 10:18 *1849*
I have p to take it again ... Jn 10:18 *1849*
hast given him p over all flesh ... Jn 17:2 *1849*
not that I have p to crucify thee ... Jn 19:10 *1849*
and have p to release thee ... Jn 19:10 *1849*
have no p at all against me ... Jn 19:11 *1849*
the Father hath put in his own p ... Acts 1:7 *1849*
But ye shall receive p, after ... Acts 1:8 *1411*
as though by our own p or ... Acts 3:12 *1411*
the midst, they asked, By what p ... Acts 4:7 *1411*
with great p gave the apostles ... Acts 4:33 *1411*
sold, was it not in thine own p ... Acts 5:4 *1849*
And Stephen, full of faith and p ... Acts 6:8 *1411*
This man is the great p of God ... Acts 8:10 *1411*
Saying, Give me also this p ... Acts 8:19 *1849*
with the Holy Ghost and with p ... Acts 10:38 *1411*
from the p of Satan unto God, ... Acts 26:18 *1849*
to be the Son of God with p ... Rom 1:4 *1411*
for it is the p of God unto ... Rom 1:16 *1411*
that are made, even his eternal p ... Rom 1:20 *1411*
that I might shew my p in thee ... Rom 9:17 *1411*
not the potter p over the clay ... Rom 9:21 *1849*
his wrath, and to make his p known ... Rom 9:22 *1415*
For there is no p but of God ... Rom 13:1 *1849*
therefore resisteth the p ... Rom 13:2 *1849*
thou then not be afraid of the p ... Rom 13:3 *1849*
through the p of the Holy Ghost ... Rom 15:13 *1411*
by the p of the Spirit of God ... Rom 15:19 *1411*
Now to him that is of p to ... Rom 16:25 *1410*
are saved it is the p of God ... 1Cor 1:18 *1411*
and Greeks, Christ the p of God ... 1Cor 1:24 *1411*
of the Spirit and of p ... 1Cor 2:4 *1411*
of men, but in the p of God ... 1Cor 2:5 *1411*
which are puffed up, but the p ... 1Cor 4:19 *1411*
of God is not in word, but in p ... 1Cor 4:20 *1411*
with the p of our Lord Jesus ... 1Cor 5:4 *1411*
not be brought under the p of any ... 1Cor 6:12 *1850*
also raise up us by his own p ... 1Cor 6:14 *1411*
wife hath not p of her own body ... 1Cor 7:4 *1850*
hath not p of his own body ... 1Cor 7:4 *1850*
but hath p over his own will, and ... 1Cor 7:37 *1849*
Have we not p to eat and to drink ... 1Cor 9:4 *1849*
Have we not p to lead about a ... 1Cor 9:5 *1849*
have not we p to forbear working ... 1Cor 9:6 *1849*
be partakers of this p over you ... 1Cor 9:12 *1849*
we have not used this p ... 1Cor 9:12 *1849*
I abuse not my p in the gospel ... 1Cor 9:18 *1849*
have p on her head because of the ... 1Cor 11:10 *1849*
all rule and all authority and p ... 1Cor 15:24 *1411*
it is raised in p ... 1Cor 15:43 *1411*
excellency of the p may be of God ... 2Cor 4:7 *1411*
word of truth, by the p of God ... 2Cor 6:7 *1411*
For to their p, I bear record, ... 2Cor 8:3 *1411*
beyond their p they were willing ... 2Cor 8:3 *1411*
that the p of Christ may rest ... 2Cor 12:9 *1411*
yet he liveth by the p of God ... 2Cor 13:4 *1411*
him by the p of God toward you ... 2Cor 13:4 *1411*
according to the p which the Lord ... 2Cor 13:10 *1849*
of his p to us-ward who believe ... Eph 1:19 *1411*
to the working of his mighty p ... Eph 1:19 *2904*
Far above all principality, and p ... Eph 1:21 *1849*
to the prince of the p of the air ... Eph 2:2 *1849*
by the effectual working of his p ... Eph 3:7 *1411*
according to the p that worketh ... Eph 3:20 *1411*
Lord, and in the p of his might ... Eph 6:10 *2904*
the p of his resurrection, and the ... Phil 3:10 *1411*
according to his glorious p ... Col 1:11 *2904*
us from the p of darkness ... Col 1:13 *1849*
the head of all principality and p ... Col 2:10 *1849*
you in word only, but also in p ... 1Th 1:5 *1411*
Lord, and from the glory of his p ... 2Th 1:9 *2479*
and the work of faith with p ... 2Th 1:11 *1411*
the working of Satan with all p ... 2Th 2:9 *1411*
Not because we have not p ... 2Th 3:9 *1849*
whom be honour and p everlasting ... 1Ti 6:16 *2904*
but of p, and of love, and of a ... 2Ti 1:7 *1411*
gospel according to the p of God ... 2Ti 1:8 *1411*
but denying the p thereof ... 2Ti 3:5 *1411*
all things by the word of his p ... Heb 1:3 *1411*
him that had the p of death ... Heb 2:14 *2904*
but after the p of an endless ... Heb 7:16 *1411*
Who are kept by the p of God ... 1Pet 1:5 *1411*
According as his divine p hath ... 2Pet 1:3 *1411*
when we made known unto you the p ... 2Pet 1:16 *1411*
angels, which are greater in p ... 2Pet 2:11 *2479*
glory and majesty, dominion and p ... Jude 25 *1849*
will I give p over the nations ... Rev 2:26 *1849*
to receive glory and honour and p ... Rev 4:11 *1411*
Lamb that was slain to receive p ... Rev 5:12 *1411*
and honour, and glory, and p ... Rev 5:13 *2904*
p was given to him that sat ... Rev 6:4
p was given unto them over the ... Rev 6:8 *1849*
and thanksgiving, and honour, and p ... Rev 7:12 *1411*
and unto them was given p, as the ... Rev 9:3 *1849*
the scorpions of the earth have p ... Rev 9:3 *1849*
their p was to hurt men five ... Rev 9:10 *1849*
For their p is in their mouth, and ... Rev 9:19 *1849*
I will give p unto my two ... Rev 11:3
These have p to shut heaven, that ... Rev 11:6 *1849*
have p over waters to turn them ... Rev 11:6 *1849*
hast taken to thee thy great p ... Rev 11:17 *1411*
our God, and the p of his Christ ... Rev 12:10 *1849*
and the dragon gave him his p ... Rev 13:2 *1411*
which gave p unto the beast ... Rev 13:4 *1849*
p was given unto him to continue ... Rev 13:5 *1849*
p was given him over all kindreds ... Rev 13:7 *1849*
he exerciseth all the p of the ... Rev 13:12 *1849*
of those miracles which he had p ... Rev 13:14 *1325*
he had p to give life unto the ... Rev 13:15 *1325*
the altar, which had p over fire ... Rev 14:18 *1849*
the glory of God, and from his p ... Rev 15:8 *1411*
p was given unto him to scorch ... Rev 16:8
which hath p over these plagues ... Rev 16:9 *1849*
but receive p as kings one hour ... Rev 17:12 *1849*
one mind, and shall give their p ... Rev 17:13 *1411*
down from heaven, having great p ... Rev 18:1 *1849*
and glory, and honour, and p ... Rev 19:1 *1411*
such the second death hath no p ... Rev 20:6 *1849*

POWERFUL
The voice of the LORD is *p* ...... Ps 29:4 3581
say they, are weighty and *p* 2Cor 10:10 *2478*
the word of God is quick, and *p* ...... Heb 4:12 *1756*

POWERS
the *p* of the heavens shall be ...... Mt 24:29 *1411*
the *p* that are in heaven shall be ...... Mk 13:25 *1411*
and unto magistrates, and *p* ...... Lk 12:11 *1849*
for the *p* of heaven shall be ...... Lk 21:26 *1411*
angels, nor principalities, nor *p* ...... Rom 8:38 *1411*
soul be subject unto the higher *p* ...... Rom 13:1 *1849*
the *p* that be are ordained of God ...... Rom 13:1 *1849*
p in heavenly places might be ...... Eph 3:10 *1849*
against principalities, against *p* ...... Eph 6:12 *1849*
or principalities, or *p* ...... Col 1:16 *1849*
spoiled principalities and *p* ...... Col 2:15 *1849*
be subject to principalities and *p* ...... Titus 3:1 *1849*
the *p* of the world to come, ... Heb 6:5 *1411*
p being made subject unto him 1Pet 3:22 *1411*

PRACTICES
have exercised with covetous *p* 2Pet 2:14

PRACTISE
to *p* wicked works with men that ...... Ps 141:4 5953
to *p* hypocrisy, and to utter error ...... Is 32:6 6213
and shall prosper, and *p*, and shall ...... Dan 8:24 6213
the morning is light, they *p* it ...... Mic 2:1 6213

PRACTISED
secretly *p* mischief against him 1Sa 23:9 2790
and it *p*, and prospered ...... Dan 8:12 6213

PRAETORIUM (*pre-to'-re-um*) *Palace of the Roman procurator in Jerusalem.*
him away into the hall, called P ...... Mk 15:16 *4232*

PRAISE
she said, Now will I *p* the LORD ...... Gen 29:35 3034
art he whom thy brethren shall *p* ...... Gen 49:8 3034
be holy to *p* the LORD withal ...... Lev 19:24 1974
He is thy *p*, and he is thy God, ... Deut 10:21 8416
nations which he hath made, in *p* ...... Deut 26:19 8416
P ye the LORD for the avenging of ...... Judg 5:2 1288
I will sing *p* to the LORD God of ...... Judg 5:3
thank and *p* the LORD God of Israel 1Chr 16:4 1984
thy holy name, and glory in thy *p* 1Chr 16:35 8416
made, said David, to *p* therewith 1Chr 23:5 1984
p the LORD, and likewise at even 1Chr 23:30 1984
to give thanks and to *p* the LORD 1Chr 25:3 1984
thee, and *p* thy glorious name 1Chr 29:13 1984
the king had made to *p* the LORD 2Chr 7:6 3034
Levites to their charges, to *p* 2Chr 8:14 1984
stood up to *p* the LORD God of 2Chr 20:19 1984
that should *p* the beauty of 2Chr 20:21 1984
the army, and to say, *P* the LORD 2Chr 20:21 3034
when they began to sing and to *p* 2Chr 20:22 8416
and such as taught to sing *p* 2Chr 23:13 1984
commanded the Levites to sing *p* 2Chr 29:30 1984
to *p* in the gates of the tents of 2Chr 31:2 1984
cymbals, to *p* the LORD, after the ...... Ezr 3:10 1984
exalted above all blessing and *p* ...... Neh 9:5 8416
brethren over against them, to *p* ...... Neh 12:24 1984
of the singers, and songs of *p* ...... Neh 12:46 8416
I will *p* the LORD according to ...... Ps 7:17 3034
will sing *p* to the name of the ...... Ps 7:17
I will *p* thee, O LORD, with my ...... Ps 9:1 3034
I will sing *p* to thy name ...... Ps 9:2
That I may shew forth all thy *p* ...... Ps 9:14 8416
so will we sing and *p* thy power ...... Ps 21:13 2167
of the congregation will I *p* thee ...... Ps 22:22 1984
Ye that fear the LORD, *p* him ...... Ps 22:23 1984
My *p* shall be of thee in the ...... Ps 22:25 8416
they shall *p* the LORD that seek ...... Ps 22:26 1984
and with my song will I *p* him ...... Ps 28:7 3034
shall the dust *p* thee ...... Ps 30:9 3034
that my glory may sing *p* to thee ...... Ps 30:12
for *p* is comely for the upright ...... Ps 33:1 8416
P the LORD with harp ...... Ps 33:2 3034
his *p* shall continually be in my ...... Ps 34:1 8416
I will *p* thee among much people ...... Ps 35:18 1984
of thy *p* all the day long ...... Ps 35:28 8416
in my mouth, even *p* unto our God ...... Ps 40:3 8416
God, with the voice of joy and *p* ...... Ps 42:4 8426
for I shall yet *p* him for the ...... Ps 42:5 3034
for I shall yet *p* him, who is the ...... Ps 42:11 3034
yea, upon the harp will I *p* thee ...... Ps 43:4 3034
for I shall yet *p* him, who is the ...... Ps 43:5 3034
day long, and *p* thy name for ever ...... Ps 44:8 3034
shall the people *p* thee for ever ...... Ps 45:17 3034
so is thy *p* unto the ends of the ...... Ps 48:10 8416
his soul, and men will *p* thee ...... Ps 49:18 3034
Whoso offereth *p* glorifieth me ...... Ps 50:23 8426
my mouth shall shew forth thy *p* ...... Ps 51:15 8416
I will *p* thee for ever, because ...... Ps 52:9 3034
I will *p* thy name, O LORD ...... Ps 54:6 3034
In God I will *p* his word, in God ...... Ps 56:4 1984
In God will I *p* his word ...... Ps 56:10 1984
in the LORD will I *p* his word ...... Ps 56:10 1984
I will sing and give *p* ...... Ps 57:7 2167
I will *p* thee, O Lord, among the ...... Ps 57:9 3034
So will I sing *p* unto thy name ...... Ps 61:8
than life, my lips shall *p* thee ...... Ps 63:3 7623
my mouth shall *p* thee with joyful ...... Ps 63:5 1984
P waiteth for thee, O God in Sion ...... Ps 65:1 8416
make his *p* glorious ...... Ps 66:2 8416
the voice of his *p* to be heard ...... Ps 66:8 8416
Let the people *p* thee, O God ...... Ps 67:3 3034
let all the people *p* thee ...... Ps 67:3 3034
Let the people *p* thee, O God ...... Ps 67:5 3034
let all the people *p* thee ...... Ps 67:5 3034
I will *p* the name of God with a ...... Ps 69:30 1984
Let the heaven and earth *p* him ...... Ps 69:34 1984
my *p* shall be continually of thee ...... Ps 71:6 8416
Let my mouth be filled with thy *p* ...... Ps 71:8 8416
will yet *p* thee more and more ...... Ps 71:14 8416
I will also *p* thee with the ...... Ps 71:22 3034
let the poor and needy *p* thy name ...... Ps 74:21 1984
the wrath of man shall *p* thee ...... Ps 76:10 3034
forth thy *p* to all generations ...... Ps 79:13 8416
I will *p* thee, O Lord my God, ... Ps 86:12 3034
shall the dead arise and *p* thee ...... Ps 88:10 3034
the heavens shall *p* thy wonders ...... Ps 89:5 3034
loud noise, and rejoice, and sing *p* ...... Ps 98:4
Let them *p* thy great and terrible ...... Ps 99:3 3034
A Psalm of *p* ...... Ps 100:*t* 8426
and into his courts with *p* ...... Ps 100:4 8416
shall be created shall *p* the LORD ...... Ps 102:18 1984
in Zion, and his *p* in Jerusalem ...... Ps 102:21 8416
I will sing *p* to my God while I ...... Ps 104:33
P ye the LORD ...... Ps 104:35 1984
P ye the LORD ...... Ps 105:45 1984
P ye the LORD ...... Ps 106:1 1984
who can shew forth all his *p* ...... Ps 106:2 8416
they sang his *p* ...... Ps 106:12 8416
holy name, and to triumph in thy *p* ...... Ps 106:47 8416
P ye the LORD ...... Ps 106:48 1984
Oh that men would *p* the LORD for ...... Ps 107:8 3034
Oh that men would *p* the LORD for ...... Ps 107:15 3034
Oh that men would *p* the LORD for ...... Ps 107:21 3034
Oh that men would *p* the LORD for ...... Ps 107:31 3034
p him in the assembly of the ...... Ps 107:32 1984
I will sing and give *p*, even with ...... Ps 108:1 2167
I will *p* thee, O LORD, among the ...... Ps 108:3 3034
Hold not thy peace, O God of my *p* ...... Ps 109:1 8416
I will greatly *p* the LORD with my ...... Ps 109:30 3034
I will *p* him among the multitude ...... Ps 109:30 1984
P ye the LORD ...... Ps 111:1 1984
I will *p* the LORD with my whole ...... Ps 111:1 3034
his *p* endureth for ever ...... Ps 111:10 8416
P ye the LORD ...... Ps 112:1 1984
P ye the LORD ...... Ps 113:1 1984
P, O ye servants of the LORD, ... Ps 113:1 1984
p the name of the LORD ...... Ps 113:1 1984
P ye the LORD ...... Ps 113:9 1984
The dead *p* not the LORD, neither ...... Ps 115:17 1984
P the LORD ...... Ps 115:18 1984
P ye the LORD ...... Ps 116:19 1984
O *p* the LORD, all ye nations ...... Ps 117:1 1984
p him, all ye people ...... Ps 117:1 7623
P ye the LORD ...... Ps 117:2 1984
into them, and I will *p* the LORD ...... Ps 118:19 3034
I will *p* thee ...... Ps 118:21 3034
Thou art my God, and I will *p* thee ...... Ps 118:28 3034
I will *p* thee with uprightness of ...... Ps 119:7 3034
Seven times a day do I *p* thee ...... Ps 119:164 1984
My lips shall utter *p*, when thou ...... Ps 119:171 8416
my soul live, and it shall *p* thee ...... Ps 119:175 1984
P ye the LORD ...... Ps 135:1 1984
P ye the name of the LORD ...... Ps 135:1 1984
p him, O ye servants of the LORD ...... Ps 135:1 1984
P the LORD ...... Ps 135:3 1984
P ye the LORD ...... Ps 135:21 1984
I will *p* thee with my whole heart ...... Ps 138:1 3034
the gods will I sing *p* unto thee ...... Ps 138:1 2167
p thy name for thy lovingkindness ...... Ps 138:2 3034
kings of the earth shall *p* thee ...... Ps 138:4 3034
I will *p* thee ...... Ps 139:14 3034
of prison, that I may *p* thy name ...... Ps 142:7 3034
David's Psalm of *p* ...... Ps 145:*t* 8416
I will *p* thy name for ever and ...... Ps 145:2 1984
shall *p* thy works to another ...... Ps 145:4 7623
All thy works shall *p* thee ...... Ps 145:10 3034
shall speak the *p* of the LORD ...... Ps 145:21 8416
P ye the LORD ...... Ps 146:1 1984
P the LORD, O my soul ...... Ps 146:1 1984
While I live will I *p* the LORD ...... Ps 146:2 1984
P ye the LORD ...... Ps 146:10 1984
P ye the LORD ...... Ps 147:1 1984
and *p* is comely ...... Ps 147:1 8416
sing *p* upon the harp unto our God ...... Ps 147:7
P the LORD, O Jerusalem ...... Ps 147:12 7623
p thy God, O Zion ...... Ps 147:12 1984
P ye the LORD ...... Ps 147:20 1984
P ye the LORD ...... Ps 148:1 1984
P ye the LORD from the heavens ...... Ps 148:1 1984
p him in the heights ...... Ps 148:1 1984
P ye him, all his angels ...... Ps 148:2 1984
p ye him, all his hosts ...... Ps 148:2 1984
P ye him, sun and moon ...... Ps 148:3 1984
p him, all ye stars of light ...... Ps 148:3 1984
P him, ye heavens of heavens, and ...... Ps 148:4 1984
Let them *p* the name of the LORD ...... Ps 148:5 1984
P the LORD from the earth, ye ...... Ps 148:7 1984
Let them *p* the name of the LORD ...... Ps 148:13 1984
people, the *p* of all his saints ...... Ps 148:14 8416
P ye the LORD ...... Ps 148:14 1984
P ye the LORD ...... Ps 149:1 1984
his *p* in the congregation of ...... Ps 149:1 8416
Let them *p* his name in the dance ...... Ps 149:3 1984
P ye the LORD ...... Ps 149:9 1984
P ye the LORD ...... Ps 150:1 1984
P God in his sanctuary ...... Ps 150:1 1984
p him in the firmament of his ...... Ps 150:1 1984
P him for his mighty acts ...... Ps 150:2 1984
p him according to his excellent ...... Ps 150:2 1984
P him with the sound of the ...... Ps 150:3 1984
p him with the psaltery and harp ...... Ps 150:3 1984
P him with the timbrel and dance ...... Ps 150:4 1984
p him with stringed instruments ...... Ps 150:4 1984
P him upon the loud cymbals ...... Ps 150:5 1984
p him upon the high sounding ...... Ps 150:5 1984
thing that hath breath *p* the LORD ...... Ps 150:6 1984
P ye the LORD ...... Ps 150:6 1984
Let another man *p* thee, and not ...... Prov 27:2 1984
so is a man to his *p* ...... Prov 27:21 4110
that forsake the law *p* the wicked ...... Prov 28:4 1984
her own works *p* her in the gates ...... Prov 31:31 1984
shalt say, O LORD, I will *p* thee ...... Is 12:1 3034
P the LORD, call upon his name, ... Is 12:4 3034
exalt thee, I will *p* thy name ...... Is 25:1 3034
For the grave cannot *p* thee ...... Is 38:18 3034
the living, he shall *p* thee ...... Is 38:19 3034
neither my *p* to graven images ...... Is 42:8 8416
his *p* from the end of the earth, ... Is 42:10 8416
declare his *p* in the islands ...... Is 42:12 8416
they shall shew forth my *p* ...... Is 43:21 8416
for my *p* will I refrain for thee, ... Is 48:9 8416
walls Salvation, and thy gates *P* ...... Is 60:18 8416
the garment of *p* for the spirit ...... Is 61:3 8416
p to spring forth before all the ...... Is 61:11 8416
make Jerusalem a *p* in the earth ...... Is 62:7 8416
it shall eat it, and *p* the LORD ...... Is 62:9 1984
people, and for a name, and for a *p* ...... Jer 13:11 8416
for thou art my *p* ...... Jer 17:14 8416
and bringing sacrifices of *p* ...... Jer 17:26 8426
Sing unto the LORD, *p* ye the LORD ...... Jer 20:13 1984
p ye, and say, O LORD, save thy ...... Jer 31:7 1984
shall be to me a name of joy, a *p* ...... Jer 33:9 8416
shall say, *P* the LORD of hosts ...... Jer 33:11 3034
of *p* into the house of the LORD ...... Jer 33:11 8426
There shall be no more *p* of Moab ...... Jer 48:2 8416
How is the city of *p* not left ...... Jer 49:25 8416
how is the *p* of the whole earth ...... Jer 51:41 8416
p thee, O thou God of my fathers, ... Dan 2:23 7624
Now I Nebuchadnezzar *p* and extol ...... Dan 4:37 7624
p the name of the LORD your God, ... Joel 2:26 1984
and the earth was full of his *p* ...... Hab 3:3 8416
and I will get them *p* and fame in ...... Zeph 3:19 8416
a *p* among all people of the earth ...... Zeph 3:20 8416
sucklings thou hast perfected *p* ...... Mt 21:16 *136*
when they saw it, gave *p* unto God ...... Lk 18:43 *136*
p God with a loud voice for all ...... Lk 19:37 *134*
and said unto him, Give God the *p* ...... Jn 9:24 *1391*
For they loved the *p* of men more ...... Jn 12:43 *1391*
of men more than the *p* of God ...... Jn 12:43 *1391*
whose *p* is not of men, but of God ...... Rom 2:29 *1868*
and thou shalt have *p* of the same ...... Rom 13:3 *1868*
P the Lord, all ye Gentiles ...... Rom 15:11 *134*
shall every man have *p* of God 1Cor 4:5 *1868*
Now I *p* you, brethren, that ye 1Cor 11:2 *1867*
I declare unto you I *p* you not 1Cor 11:17 *1867*
shall I *p* you in this 1Cor 11:22 *1867*
I *p* you not 1Cor 11:22 *1868*
brother, whose *p* is in the gospel 2Cor 8:18 *1868*
To the *p* of the glory of his ...... Eph 1:6 *1868*
should be to the *p* of his glory ...... Eph 1:12 *1868*
unto the *p* of his glory ...... Eph 1:14 *1868*
unto the glory and *p* of God ...... Phil 1:11 *1868*
any virtue, and if there be any *p* ...... Phil 4:8 *1868*
church will I sing *p* unto thee ...... Heb 2:12 *5214*
sacrifice of *p* to God continually ...... Heb 13:15 *133*
with fire, might be found unto *p* 1Pet 1:7 *1868*
for the *p* of them that do well 1Pet 2:14 *1868*
Jesus Christ, to whom be *p* 1Pet 4:11 *1391*
P our God, all ye his servants, ... Rev 19:5 *134*

PRAISED
people saw him, they *p* their god ...... Judg 16:24 1984
much *p* as Absalom for his beauty 2Sa 14:25 1984
the LORD, who is worthy to be *p* 2Sa 22:4 1984
is the LORD, and greatly to be *p* 1Chr 16:25 1984
people said, Amen, and *p* the LORD 1Chr 16:36 1984
four thousand *p* the LORD with the 1Chr 23:5 1984
p the LORD, saying, For he is 2Chr 5:13 1984
p the LORD, saying, For he is 2Chr 7:3 3034
when David *p* by their ministry 2Chr 7:6 1984
the priests *p* the LORD day by day 2Chr 30:21 1984
great shout, when they *p* the LORD ...... Ezr 3:11 1984
said, Amen, and *p* the LORD ...... Neh 5:13 1984
the LORD, who is worthy to be *p* ...... Ps 18:3 1984
greatly to be *p* in the city of ...... Ps 48:1 1984
and daily shall he be *p* ...... Ps 72:15 1288
LORD is great, and greatly to be *p* ...... Ps 96:4 1984
same the LORD's name is to be *p* ...... Ps 113:3 1984
is the LORD, and greatly to be *p* ...... Ps 145:3 1984
feareth the LORD, she shall be *p* ...... Prov 31:30 1984
Wherefore I *p* the dead which are ...... Eccl 4:2 7623
and the concubines, and they *p* her ...... Song 6:9 1984
house, where our fathers *p* thee ...... Is 64:11 1984
I blessed the most High, and I *p* ...... Dan 4:34 7624
p the gods of gold, and of silver, ... Dan 5:4 7624
thou hast *p* the gods of silver, ... Dan 5:23 7624
loosed, and he spake, and *p* God ...... Lk 1:64 *2127*

PRAISES
in holiness, fearful in *p* ...... Ex 15:11 8416
they sang *p* with gladness, and 2Chr 29:30 1984
Sing *p* to the LORD, which ...... Ps 9:11
heathen, and sing *p* unto thy name ...... Ps 18:49
that inhabitest the *p* of Israel ...... Ps 22:3 8416
I will sing *p* unto the LORD ...... Ps 27:6
Sing *p* to God, sing *p* ...... Ps 47:6
p unto our King, sing *p* ...... Ps 47:6
sing ye *p* with understanding ...... Ps 47:7
I will render *p* unto thee ...... Ps 56:12 8426
Sing unto God, sing *p* to his name ...... Ps 68:4
O sing *p* unto the Lord ...... Ps 68:32
I will sing *p* to the God of Jacob ...... Ps 75:9
to come the *p* of the LORD ...... Ps 78:4 8416
to sing *p* unto thy name, O most ...... Ps 92:1
I will sing *p* unto thee among the ...... Ps 108:3
sing *p* unto his name ...... Ps 135:3
strings will I sing *p* unto thee ...... Ps 144:9
I will sing *p* unto my God while I ...... Ps 146:2
it is good to sing *p* unto our God ...... Ps 147:1
let them sing *p* unto him with the ...... Ps 149:3
Let the high *p* of God be in their ...... Ps 149:6
shew forth the *p* of the LORD ...... Is 60:6 8416
the *p* of the LORD, according to ...... Is 63:7 8416
Silas prayed, and sang *p* unto God ...... Acts 16:25
that ye should shew forth the *p* 1Pet 2:9 *703*

PRAISETH
her husband also, and he *p* her … Prov 31:28 1984

PRAISING
make one sound to be heard in *p* … 2Chr 5:13 1984
p the king, she came to the … 2Chr 23:12 1984
they sang together by course in *p* … Ezr 3:11 1984
they will be still *p* thee … Ps 84:4 1984
of the heavenly host *p* God … Lk 2:13 *134*
p God for all the things that … Lk 2:20 *134*
were continually in the temple, *p* … Lk 24:53 *134*
P God, and having favour with all … Acts 2:47 *134*
walking, and leaping, and *p* God … Acts 3:8 *134*
people saw him walking and *p* God … Acts 3:9 *134*

PRANSING
of the wheels, and of the *p* horses … Nah 3:2 1725

PRANSINGS
broken by the means of the *p* … Judg 5:22 1726
the *p* of their mighty ones … Judg 5:22 1726

PRATING
but a *p* fool shall fall … Prov 10:8 8193
but a *p* fool shall fall … Prov 10:10 8193
p against us with malicious words … 3Jn 10 *5396*

PRAY
I *p* thee, thou art my sister … Gen 12:13 4994
I *p* thee, between me and thee, and … Gen 13:8 4994
thyself, I *p* thee, from me … Gen 13:9 4994
I *p* thee, go in unto my maid … Gen 16:2 4994
I *p* thee, from thy servant … Gen 18:3 4994
I *p* you, be fetched, and wash your … Gen 18:4 4994
I *p* you, into your servant's … Gen 19:2 4994
I *p* you, brethren, do not so … Gen 19:7 4994
I *p* you, bring them out unto you, … Gen 19:8 4994
a prophet, and he shall *p* for thee … Gen 20:7 6419
wilt give it, I *p* thee, hear me … Gen 23:13 3863
I *p* thee, thy hand under my thigh … Gen 24:2 4994
I *p* thee, send me good speed this … Gen 24:12 4994
I *p* thee, that I may drink … Gen 24:14 4994
I *p* thee, drink a little water of … Gen 24:17 4994
tell me, I *p* thee … Gen 24:23 4994
I *p* thee, a little water of thy … Gen 24:43 4994
unto her, Let me drink, I *p* thee … Gen 24:45 4994
I *p* thee, with that same red … Gen 25:30 4994
I *p* thee, thy weapons, thy quiver … Gen 27:3 4994
I *p* thee, sit and eat of my … Gen 27:19 4994
I *p* thee, that I may feel thee, … Gen 27:21 4994
I *p* thee, of thy son's mandrakes … Gen 30:14 4994
I *p* thee, if I have found favour … Gen 30:27 4994
I *p* thee, from the hand of my … Gen 32:11 4994
said, Tell me, I *p* thee, thy name … Gen 32:29 4994
I *p* thee, if now I have found … Gen 33:10 4994
I *p* thee, my blessing that is … Gen 33:11 4994
I *p* thee, pass over before his … Gen 33:14 4994
I *p* you give her him to wife … Gen 34:8 4994
I *p* you, this dream which I have … Gen 37:6 4994
I *p* thee, see whether it be well … Gen 37:14 4994
I *p* thee, where they feed their … Gen 37:16 4994
I *p* thee, let me come in unto … Gen 38:16 4994
I *p* thee, whose are these, the … Gen 38:25 4994
tell me them, I *p* you … Gen 40:8 4994
I *p* thee, unto me, and make … Gen 40:14 4994
I *p* thee, speak a word in my … Gen 44:18 4994
I *p* thee, let thy servant abide … Gen 44:33 4994
Come near to me, I *p* you … Gen 45:4 4994
we *p* thee, let thy servants dwell … Gen 47:4 4994
I *p* thee, thy hand under my thigh … Gen 47:29 4994
bury me not, I *p* thee, in Egypt … Gen 47:29 4994
I *p* thee, unto me, and I will … Gen 48:9 4994
I *p* you, in the ears of Pharaoh, … Gen 50:4 4994
I *p* thee, and bury my father, and I … Gen 50:5 4994
I *p* thee now, the trespass of thy … Gen 50:17 577
we *p* thee, forgive the trespass … Gen 50:17 4994
I *p* thee, by the hand of him whom … Ex 4:13 4994
I *p* thee, and return unto my … Ex 4:18 4994
we *p* thee, three days' journey … Ex 5:3 4994
I *p* thee, my sin only this once, … Ex 10:17 4994
I *p* thee, out of thy book which … Ex 32:32 4994
I *p* thee, if I have found grace … Ex 33:13 4994
my Lord, I *p* thee, go among us … Ex 34:9 4994
he said, Leave us not, I *p* thee … Num 10:31 4994
I *p* thee, out of hand, if I have … Num 11:15 4994
Hear, I *p* you, ye sons of Levi … Num 16:8 4994
I *p* you, from the tents of these … Num 16:26 4994
I *p* thee, through thy country … Num 20:17 4994
p unto the LORD, that he take … Num 21:7 6419
I *p* thee, curse me this people … Num 22:6 4994
I *p* thee, hinder thee from coming … Num 22:16 4994
I *p* thee, curse me this people … Num 22:17 4994
I *p* you, tarry ye also here this … Num 22:19 4994
I *p* thee, with me unto another … Num 23:13 4994
I *p* thee, I will bring thee unto … Num 23:27 4994
I *p* thee, let me go over, and see … Deut 3:25 4994
I *p* you, swear unto me by the … Josh 2:12 4994
I *p* thee, glory to the LORD God … Josh 7:19 4994
we *p* thee, the entrance into the … Judg 1:24 4994
I *p* thee, a little water to drink … Judg 4:19 4994
I *p* thee, until I come unto thee, … Judg 6:18 4994
I *p* thee, but this once with the … Judg 6:39 4994
I *p* you, loaves of bread unto the … Judg 8:5 4994
I *p* you, in the ears of all the … Judg 9:2 4994
I *p* now, and fight with them … Judg 9:38 4994
us only, we *p* thee, this day … Judg 10:15 4994
I *p* thee, pass through thy land … Judg 11:17 4994
we *p* thee, through thy land into … Judg 11:19 4994
I *p* thee, and drink not wine nor … Judg 13:4 4994
I *p* thee, let us detain thee, … Judg 13:15 4994
her, I *p* thee, instead of her … Judg 15:2 4994
I *p* thee, wherein thy great … Judg 16:6 4994
I *p* thee, wherewith thou mightest … Judg 16:10 4994
I *p* thee, and strengthen me … Judg 16:28 4994
I *p* thee, only this once, O God, … Judg 16:28 4994
we *p* thee, of God, that we may … Judg 18:5 4994
I *p* thee, and tarry all night, and … Judg 19:6 4994
Comfort thine heart, I *p* thee … Judg 19:8 4994
evening, I *p* you tarry all night … Judg 19:9 4994
I *p* thee, and let us turn in into … Judg 19:11 4994
I *p* you, do not so wickedly … Judg 19:23 4994
I *p* you, let me glean and gather … Ruth 2:7 4994
I *p* thee, into one of the … 1Sa 2:36 4994
I *p* thee hide it not from me … 1Sa 3:17 4994
I will *p* for you unto the LORD … 1Sa 7:5 6419
I *p* thee, where the seer's house … 1Sa 9:18 4994
I *p* thee, what Samuel said unto … 1Sa 10:15 4994
P for thy servants unto the LORD … 1Sa 12:19 6419
the LORD in ceasing to *p* for you … 1Sa 12:23 6419
I *p* you, how mine eyes have been … 1Sa 14:29 4994
I *p* thee, pardon my sin, and turn … 1Sa 15:25 4994
I *p* thee, before the elders of my … 1Sa 15:30 4994
I *p* thee, stand before me … 1Sa 16:22 4994
I *p* thee, take heed to thyself … 1Sa 19:2 4994
And he said, Let me go, I *p* thee … 1Sa 20:29 4994
I *p* thee, and see my brethren … 1Sa 20:29 4994
I *p* thee, come forth, and be with … 1Sa 22:3 4994
I *p* you, prepare yet, and know and … 1Sa 23:22 4994
I *p* thee, whatsoever cometh to … 1Sa 25:8 4994
I *p* thee, speak in thine audience … 1Sa 25:24 4994
I *p* thee, regard this man of … 1Sa 25:25 4994
I *p* thee, forgive the trespass of … 1Sa 25:28 4994
I *p* thee, with the spear even to … 1Sa 26:8 4994
I *p* thee, take thou now the spear … 1Sa 26:11 4994
I *p* thee, let my lord the king … 1Sa 26:19 4994
I *p* thee, divine unto me by the … 1Sa 28:8 4994
I *p* thee, hearken thou also unto … 1Sa 28:22 4994
I *p* thee, bring me hither the … 1Sa 30:7 4994
I *p* thee, tell me … 2Sa 1:4 4994
I *p* thee, upon me, and slay me … 2Sa 1:9 4994
heart to *p* this prayer unto thee … 2Sa 7:27 6419
I *p* thee, let my sister Tamar … 2Sa 13:5 4994
I *p* thee, let Tamar my sister … 2Sa 13:6 4994
I *p* thee, speak unto the king … 2Sa 13:13 4994
I *p* thee, let my brother Amnon go … 2Sa 13:26 4994
I *p* thee, feign thyself to be a … 2Sa 14:2 4994
I *p* thee, let the king remember … 2Sa 14:11 4994
I *p* thee, speak one word unto my … 2Sa 14:12 4994
I *p* thee, the thing that I shall … 2Sa 14:18 4994
I *p* thee, let me go and pay my vow … 2Sa 15:7 4994
I *p* thee, turn the counsel of … 2Sa 15:31 4994
I *p* thee, and take off his head … 2Sa 16:9 4994
I *p* thee, also run after Cushi … 2Sa 18:22 4994
I *p* thee, turn back again, that I … 2Sa 19:37 4994
I *p* you, unto Joab, Come near … 2Sa 20:16 4994
I *p* thee, be against me, and … 2Sa 24:17 4994
I *p* thee, give thee counsel, that … 1Kin 1:12 4994
I *p* thee, unto Solomon the king, … 1Kin 2:17 4994
I *p* thee, say me not nay … 1Kin 2:20
I *p* thee, be verified, which thou … 1Kin 8:26 4994
when they shall *p* toward this … 1Kin 8:30 6419
thee, and confess thy name, and *p* … 1Kin 8:33 6419
if they *p* toward this place, and … 1Kin 8:35 6419
shall come and *p* toward this house … 1Kin 8:42 6419
shall *p* unto the LORD toward the … 1Kin 8:44 6419
p unto thee toward their land, … 1Kin 8:48 6419
p for me, that my hand may be … 1Kin 13:6 6419
I *p* thee, and disguise thyself, … 1Kin 14:2 4994
I *p* thee, a little water in a … 1Kin 17:10 4994
I *p* thee, a morsel of bread in … 1Kin 17:11 4994
I *p* thee, let this child's soul … 1Kin 17:21 4994
I *p* thee, kiss my father and my … 1Kin 19:20 4994
I *p* you, and see how this man … 1Kin 20:7 4994
I *p* thee, put sackcloth on our … 1Kin 20:31 4994
saith, I *p* thee, let me live … 1Kin 20:32 4994
of the LORD, Smite me, I *p* thee … 1Kin 20:35 4994
man, and said, Smite me, I *p* thee … 1Kin 20:37 4994
I *p* thee, at the word of the LORD … 1Kin 22:5 4994
I *p* thee, be like the word of one … 1Kin 22:13 4994
I *p* thee, let my life, and the … 2Kin 1:13 4994
unto Elisha, Tarry here, I *p* thee … 2Kin 2:2 4994
him, Elisha, tarry here, I *p* thee … 2Kin 2:4 4994
unto him, Tarry, I *p* thee, here … 2Kin 2:6 4994
I *p* thee, let a double portion of … 2Kin 2:9 4994
we *p* thee, and seek thy master … 2Kin 2:16 4994
I *p* thee, the situation of this … 2Kin 2:19 4994
chamber, I *p* thee, on the wall … 2Kin 4:10 4994
I *p* thee, one of the young men, … 2Kin 4:22 4994
I *p* thee, to meet her, and say … 2Kin 4:26 4994
I *p* you, and see how he seeketh a … 2Kin 5:7 4994
I *p* thee, take a blessing of thy … 2Kin 5:15 4994
I *p* thee, be given to thy servant … 2Kin 5:17 4994
I *p* thee, a talent of silver, and … 2Kin 5:22 4994
we *p* thee, unto Jordan, and take … 2Kin 6:2 4994
I *p* thee, and go with thy servants … 2Kin 6:3 4994
I *p* thee, open his eyes, that he … 2Kin 6:17 4994
people, I *p* thee, with blindness … 2Kin 6:18 4994
I *p* thee, five of the horses that … 2Kin 7:13 4994
I *p* thee, all the great things … 2Kin 8:4 4994
I *p* thee, give pledges to my lord … 2Kin 18:23 4994
I *p* thee, to thy servants in the … 2Kin 18:26 4994
in his heart to *p* before thee … 1Chr 17:25 6419
I *p* thee, O LORD my God, be on me … 1Chr 21:17 4994
return and confess thy name, and *p* … 2Chr 6:24 6419
yet if they *p* toward this place, … 2Chr 6:26 6419
if they come and *p* in this house … 2Chr 6:32 6419
they *p* unto thee toward this city … 2Chr 6:34
p unto thee in the land of their … 2Chr 6:37 2603
p toward their land, which thou … 2Chr 6:38 6419
shall humble themselves, and *p* … 2Chr 7:14 6419
I *p* thee, at the word of the LORD … 2Chr 18:4 4994
I *p* thee, be like one of theirs, … 2Chr 18:12 4994
p for the life of the king, and of … Ezr 6:10 6739
which I *p* before thee now, day and … Neh 1:6 6419
I *p* thee, thy servant this day, … Neh 1:11 4994
I *p* you, let us leave off this … Neh 5:10 4994
I *p* you, to them, even this day, … Neh 5:11 4994
I *p* thee, who ever perished, … Job 4:7 4994
I *p* you, let it not be iniquity … Job 6:29 4994
I *p* thee, of the former age, and … Job 8:8 4994
should we have, if we *p* unto him … Job 21:15 6293
I *p* thee, the law from his mouth, … Job 22:22 4994
I *p* you, accept any man's person, … Job 32:21 4994
I *p* thee, hear my speeches, and … Job 33:1 4994
He shall *p* unto God, and he will … Job 33:26 6279
and my servant Job shall *p* for you … Job 42:8 6419
for unto thee will I *p* … Ps 5:2 6419
p unto thee in a time when thou … Ps 32:6 6419
and morning, and at noon, will I *p* … Ps 55:17 7878
I *p* thee, thy merciful kindness … Ps 119:76 7592
P for the peace of Jerusalem … Ps 122:6 7592
I *p* you, betwixt me and my … Is 5:3 4994
shall come to his sanctuary to *p* … Is 16:12 6419
saying, Read this, I *p* thee … Is 29:11 4994
saying, Read this, I *p* thee … Is 29:12 4994
I *p* thee, to my master the king … Is 36:8 4994
I *p* thee, unto thy servants in … Is 36:11 4994
p unto a god that cannot save … Is 45:20 6419
Therefore *p* not thou for this … Jer 7:16 6419
Therefore *p* not thou for this … Jer 11:14 6419
P not for this people for their … Jer 14:11 6419
I *p* thee, of the LORD for us … Jer 21:2 4994
and *p* unto the LORD for it … Jer 29:7 6419
p unto me, and I will hearken unto … Jer 29:12 6419
I *p* thee, that is in Anathoth, … Jer 32:8 4994
P now unto the LORD our God for … Jer 37:3 6419
I *p* thee, O my lord the king … Jer 37:20 4994
I *p* thee, be accepted before thee … Jer 37:20 4994
I *p* thee, and I will slay Ishmael … Jer 40:15 4994
p for us unto the LORD thy God, … Jer 42:2 6419
I will *p* unto the LORD your God … Jer 42:4 6419
P for us unto the LORD our God … Jer 42:20 6419
I *p* you, all people, and behold my … Lam 1:18 4994
I *p* you, and hear what is the word … Eze 33:30 4994
we *p* thee, for whose cause this … Jonah 1:8 4994
I *p* thee, O LORD, was not this my … Jonah 4:2 577
I *p* you, O heads of Jacob, and ye … Mic 3:1 4994
I *p* you, ye heads of the house of … Mic 3:9 4994
I *p* you, consider from this day … Hag 2:15 4994
their men, to *p* before the LORD, … Zec 7:2 2470
go speedily to *p* before the LORD … Zec 8:21 2470
and to *p* before the LORD … Zec 8:22 2470
I *p* you, beseech God that he will … Mal 1:9 4994
p for them which despitefully use … Mt 5:44 *4336*
for they love to *p* standing in … Mt 6:5 *4336*
p to thy Father which is in … Mt 6:6 *4336*
But when ye *p*, use not vain … Mt 6:7 *4336*
After this manner therefore *p* ye … Mt 6:9 *4336*
P ye therefore the Lord of the … Mt 9:38 *1189*
up into a mountain apart to *p* … Mt 14:23 *4336*
put his hands on them, and *p* … Mt 19:13 *4336*
But *p* ye that your flight be not … Mt 24:20 *4336*
ye here, while I go and *p* yonder … Mt 26:36 *4336*
Watch and *p*, that ye enter not … Mt 26:41 *4336*
that I cannot now *p* to my Father … Mt 26:53 *3870*
they began to *p* him to depart out … Mk 5:17 *3870*
I *p* thee, come and lay thy hands … Mk 5:23
he departed into a mountain to *p* … Mk 6:46 *4336*
soever ye desire, when ye *p* … Mk 11:24 *4336*
p ye that your flight be not in … Mk 13:18 *4336*
Take ye heed, watch and *p* … Mk 13:33 *4336*
Sit ye here, while I shall *p* … Mk 14:32 *4336*
Watch ye and *p*, lest ye enter into … Mk 14:38 *4336*
he went out into a mountain to *p* … Lk 6:12 *4336*
p for them which despitefully use … Lk 6:28 *4336*
and went up into a mountain to *p* … Lk 9:28 *4336*
p ye therefore the Lord of the … Lk 10:2 *1189*
unto him, Lord, teach us to *p* … Lk 11:1 *4336*
And he said unto them, When ye *p* … Lk 11:2 *4336*
I *p* thee have me excused … Lk 14:18 *2065*
I *p* thee have me excused … Lk 14:19 *2065*
I *p* thee therefore, father, that … Lk 16:27 *2065*
end, that men ought always to *p* … Lk 18:1 *4336*
men went up into the temple to *p* … Lk 18:10 *4336*
and *p* always, that ye may be … Lk 21:36 *1189*
them, *P* that ye enter not into … Lk 22:40 *4336*
rise and *p*, lest ye enter into … Lk 22:46 *4336*
I will *p* the Father, and he shall … Jn 14:16 *2065*
that I will *p* the Father for you … Jn 16:26 *2065*
I *p* for them … Jn 17:9 *2065*
I *p* not for the world, but for … Jn 17:9 *2065*
I *p* not that thou shouldest take … Jn 17:15 *2065*
Neither *p* I for these alone, but … Jn 17:20 *2065*
p God, if perhaps the thought of … Acts 8:22 *1189*
P ye to the Lord for me, that … Acts 8:24 *1189*
I *p* thee, of whom speaketh the … Acts 8:34 *1189*
to *p* about the sixth hour … Acts 10:9 *4336*
I *p* thee that thou wouldest hear … Acts 24:4 *3870*
Wherefore I *p* you to take some … Acts 27:34 *3870*
what we should *p* for as we ought … Rom 8:26 *4336*
that a woman *p* unto God uncovered … 1Cor 11:13 *4336*
tongue *p* that he may interpret … 1Cor 14:13 *4336*
For if I *p* in an unknown tongue, … 1Cor 14:14 *4336*
I will *p* with the spirit, and I … 1Cor 14:15 *4336*
I will *p* with the understanding … 1Cor 14:15 *4336*
we *p* you in Christ's stead, be ye … 2Cor 5:20 *1189*
Now I *p* to God that ye do no evil … 2Cor 13:7 *2172*
And this I *p*, that your love may … Phil 1:9 *4336*
it, do not cease to *p* for you … Col 1:9 *4336*
P without ceasing … 1Th 5:17 *4336*
I *p* God your whole spirit and soul … 1Th 5:23
Brethren, *p* for us … 1Th 5:25 *4336*
also we *p* always for you, that … 2Th 1:11 *4336*
p for us, that the word of the … 2Th 3:1 *4336*
therefore that men *p* every where … 1Ti 2:8 *4336*
I *p* God that it may not be laid … 2Ti 4:16
P for us … Heb 13:18 *4336*
let him *p* … Jas 5:13 *4336*
and let them *p* over him, anointing … Jas 5:14 *4336*
p one for another, that ye may be … Jas 5:16 *2172*
do not say that he shall *p* for it … 1Jn 5:16 *2065*

P

PRAYED

Context	Reference	Number
So Abraham p unto God	Gen 20:17	6419
when Moses p unto the LORD, the	Num 11:2	6419
And Moses p for the people	Num 21:7	6419
I p for Aaron also the same time	Deut 9:20	6419
I p therefore unto the LORD, and	Deut 9:26	6419
p unto the LORD, and wept sore	1Sa 1:10	6419
For this child I p	1Sa 1:27	6419
And Hannah p, and said, My heart	1Sa 2:1	6419
And Samuel p unto the LORD	1Sa 8:6	6419
them twain, and p unto the LORD	2Kin 4:33	6419
And Elisha p, and said, LORD, I	2Kin 6:17	6419
Elisha p unto the LORD, and said	2Kin 6:18	6419
Hezekiah p before the LORD, and	2Kin 19:15	6419
That which thou hast p to me	2Kin 19:20	6419
wall, and p unto the LORD, saying	2Kin 20:2	6419
But Hezekiah p for them, saying	2Chr 30:18	6419
prophet Isaiah the son of Amoz, p	2Chr 32:20	6419
to the death, and p unto the LORD	2Chr 32:24	6419
And p unto him	2Chr 33:13	6419
Now when Ezra had p, and when he	Ezr 10:1	6419
p before the God of heaven	Neh 1:4	6419
So I p to the God of heaven	Neh 2:4	6419
when he p for his friends	Job 42:10	6419
Hezekiah p unto the LORD, saying	Is 37:15	6419
Whereas thou hast p to me against	Is 37:21	6419
the wall, and p unto the LORD	Is 38:2	6419
I p unto the LORD, saying	Jer 32:16	6419
his knees three times a day, and p	Dan 6:10	6739
I p unto the LORD my God, and made	Dan 9:4	6419
Then Jonah p unto the LORD his	Jonah 2:1	6419
he p unto the LORD, and said, I	Jonah 4:2	6419
and fell on his face, and p	Mt 26:39	4336
away again the second time, and p	Mt 26:42	4336
p the third time, saying the same	Mt 26:44	4336
into a solitary place, and there p	Mk 1:35	4336
p him that he might be with him	Mk 5:18	3870
p that, if it were possible, the	Mk 14:35	4336
And again he went away, and p	Mk 14:39	4336
p him that he would thrust out a	Lk 5:3	2065
himself into the wilderness, and p	Lk 5:16	4336
And as he p, the fashion of his	Lk 9:29	4336
p thus with himself, God, I thank	Lk 18:11	4336
But I have p for thee, that thy	Lk 22:32	1189
cast, and kneeled down, and p	Lk 22:41	4336
in an agony he p more earnestly	Lk 22:44	4336
mean while his disciples p him	Jn 4:31	2065
And they p, and said, Thou, Lord	Acts 1:24	4336
And when they had p, the place was	Acts 4:31	1189
and when they had p, they laid	Acts 6:6	4336
p for them, that they might	Acts 8:15	4336
all forth, and kneeled down, and p	Acts 9:40	4336
to the people, and p to God alway	Acts 10:2	1189
at the ninth hour I p in my house	Acts 10:30	4336
Then p they him to tarry certain	Acts 10:48	2065
And when they had fasted and p	Acts 13:3	4336
and had p with fasting, they	Acts 14:23	4336
p him, saying, Come over into	Acts 16:9	3870
And at midnight Paul and Silas p	Acts 16:25	4336
kneeled down, and p with them all	Acts 20:36	4336
kneeled down on the shore, and p	Acts 21:5	4336
even while I p in the temple, I	Acts 22:17	4336
p me to bring this young man unto	Acts 23:18	2065
to whom Paul entered in, and p	Acts 28:8	4336
he p earnestly that it might not	Jas 5:17	4336
he p again, and the heaven gave	Jas 5:18	4336

PRAYER

Context	Reference	Number
heart to pray this p unto thee	2Sa 7:27	8605
respect unto the p of thy servant	1Kin 8:28	8605
hearken unto the cry and to the p	1Kin 8:28	8605
p which thy servant shall make	1Kin 8:29	8605
What p and supplication soever be	1Kin 8:38	8605
Then hear thou in heaven their p	1Kin 8:45	8605
Then hear thou their p and their	1Kin 8:49	8605
made an end of praying all this p	1Kin 8:54	8605
said unto him, I have heard thy p	1Kin 9:3	8605
wherefore lift up thy p for the	2Kin 19:4	8605
thy father, I have heard thy p	2Kin 20:5	8605
therefore to the p of thy servant	2Chr 6:19	8605
the p which thy servant prayeth	2Chr 6:19	8605
to hearken unto the p which thy	2Chr 6:20	8605
Then what p or what supplication	2Chr 6:29	8605
thou from the heavens their p	2Chr 6:35	8605
from thy dwelling place, their p	2Chr 6:39	8605
the p that is made in this place	2Chr 6:40	8605
said unto him, I have heard thy p	2Chr 7:12	8605
mine ears attent unto the p that	2Chr 7:15	8605
their p came up to his holy	2Chr 30:27	8605
his p unto his God, and the words	2Chr 33:18	8605
His p also, and how God was	2Chr 33:19	8605
mayest hear the p of thy servant	Neh 1:6	8605
attentive to the p of thy servant	Neh 1:11	8605
to the p of thy servants, who	Neh 1:11	8605
we made our p unto our God	Neh 4:9	6419
to begin the thanksgiving in p	Neh 11:17	8605
fear, and restrainest p before God	Job 15:4	7878
also my p is pure	Job 16:17	8605
Thou shalt make thy p unto him	Job 22:27	6279
have mercy upon me, and hear my p	Ps 4:1	8605
will I direct my p unto thee	Ps 5:3	
the LORD will receive my p	Ps 6:9	8605
A P of David	Ps 17:t	8605
unto my cry, give ear unto my p	Ps 17:1	8605
my p returned into mine own bosom	Ps 35:13	8605
Hear my p, O LORD, and give ear	Ps 39:12	8605
my p unto the God of my life	Ps 42:8	8605
Hear my p, O God	Ps 54:2	8605
Give ear to my p, O God	Ps 55:1	8605
attend unto my p	Ps 61:1	8605
Hear my voice, O God, in my p	Ps 64:1	7879
O thou that hearest p, unto thee	Ps 65:2	8605
attended to the voice of my p	Ps 66:19	8605
which hath not turned away my p	Ps 66:20	8605
my p is unto thee, O LORD, in an	Ps 69:13	8605
p also shall be made for him	Ps 72:15	6419
angry against the p of thy people	Ps 80:4	8605
O LORD God of hosts, hear my p	Ps 84:8	8605
A P of David	Ps 86:t	8605
Give ear, O LORD, unto my p	Ps 86:6	8605
Let my p come before thee	Ps 88:2	8605
morning shall my p prevent thee	Ps 88:13	8605
A P of Moses, the man of God	Ps 90:t	8605
A P of the afflicted, when he is	Ps 102:t	8605
Hear my p, O LORD, and let my cry	Ps 102:1	8605
regard the p of the destitute	Ps 102:17	8605
and not despise their p	Ps 102:17	8605
but I give myself unto p	Ps 109:4	8605
and let his p become sin	Ps 109:7	8605
Let my p be set forth before thee	Ps 141:2	8605
for yet my p also shall be in	Ps 141:5	8605
A P when he was in the cave	Ps 142:t	8605
Hear my p, O LORD, give ear to my	Ps 143:1	8605
but the p of the upright is his	Prov 15:8	8605
he heareth the p of the righteous	Prov 15:29	8605
even his p shall be abomination	Prov 28:9	8605
they poured out a p when thy	Is 26:16	3908
wherefore lift up thy p for the	Is 37:4	8605
thy father, I have heard thy p	Is 38:5	8605
make them joyful in my house of p	Is 56:7	8605
an house of p for all people	Is 56:7	8605
lift up cry nor p for them	Jer 7:16	8605
lift up a cry or p for them	Jer 11:14	8605
and shout, he shutteth out my p	Lam 3:8	8605
that our p should not pass	Lam 3:44	8605
unto the Lord God, to seek by p	Dan 9:3	8605
yet made we not our p before the	Dan 9:13	2470
hear the p of thy servant, and his	Dan 9:17	8605
Yea, whiles I was speaking in p	Dan 9:21	8605
my p came in unto thee, into	Jonah 2:7	8605
A p of Habakkuk the prophet upon	Hab 3:1	8605
this kind goeth not out but by p	Mt 17:21	4335
shall be called the house of p	Mt 21:13	4335
whatsoever ye shall ask in p	Mt 21:22	4335
and for a pretence make long p	Mt 23:14	4336
come forth by nothing, but by p	Mk 9:29	4335
of all nations the house of p	Mk 11:17	4335
for thy p is heard	Lk 1:13	1162
continued all night in p to God	Lk 6:12	4335
My house is the house of p	Lk 19:46	4335
And when he rose up from p	Lk 22:45	4335
continued with one accord in p	Acts 1:14	4335
into the temple at the hour of p	Acts 3:1	4335
give ourselves continually to p	Acts 6:4	4335
thy p is heard, and thine alms are	Acts 10:31	4335
but p was made without ceasing of	Acts 12:5	4335
where p was wont to be made	Acts 16:13	4335
it came to pass, as we went to p	Acts 16:16	4335
p to God for Israel is, that they	Rom 10:1	1162
continuing instant in p	Rom 12:12	4335
give yourselves to fasting and p	1Cor 7:5	4335
also helping together by p for us	2Cor 1:11	1162
And by their p for you, which long	2Cor 9:14	1162
Praying always with all p	Eph 6:18	4335
Always in every p of mine for you	Phil 1:4	1162
to my salvation through your p	Phil 1:19	1162
but in every thing by p and	Phil 4:6	4335
Continue in p, and watch in the	Col 4:2	4335
by the word of God and p	1Ti 4:5	1783
the p of faith shall save the	Jas 5:15	2171
The effectual fervent p of a	Jas 5:16	1162
therefore sober, and watch unto p	1Pet 4:7	4335

PRAYERS

Context	Reference	Number
The p of David the son of Jesse	Ps 72:20	8605
yea, when ye make many p, I will	Is 1:15	8605
and for a pretence make long p	Mk 12:40	4336
with fastings and p night and day	Lk 2:37	1162
of John fast often, and make p	Lk 5:33	1162
houses, and for a shew make long p	Lk 20:47	4336
and in breaking of bread, and in p	Acts 2:42	4335
And he said unto him, Thy p	Acts 10:4	4335
mention of you always in my p	Rom 1:9	4335
with me in your p to God for me	Rom 15:30	4335
making mention of you in my p	Eph 1:16	4335
labouring fervently for you in p	Col 4:12	4335
making mention of you in our p	1Th 1:2	4335
first of all, supplications, p	1Ti 2:1	4335
supplications and p night and day	1Ti 5:5	4335
remembrance of thee in my p night	2Ti 1:3	1162
mention of thee always in my p	Philem 4	4335
your p I shall be given unto you	Philem 22	4335
flesh, when he had offered up p	Heb 5:7	1162
that your p be not hindered	1Pet 3:7	4335
and his ears are open unto their p	1Pet 3:12	1162
odours, which are the p of saints	Rev 5:8	4335
he should offer it with the p of	Rev 8:3	4335
came with the p of the saints	Rev 8:4	4335

PRAYEST

Context	Reference	Number
And when thou p, thou shalt not be	Mt 6:5	4336
But thou, when thou p, enter into	Mt 6:6	4336

PRAYETH

Context	Reference	Number
which thy servant p before thee	1Kin 8:28	6419
which thy servant p before thee	2Chr 6:19	6419
thy servant p toward this place	2Chr 6:20	6419
p unto it, and saith, Deliver me	Is 44:17	6419
for, behold, he p	Acts 9:11	4336
But every woman that p or	1Cor 11:5	4336
in an unknown tongue, my spirit p	1Cor 14:14	4336

PRAYING

Context	Reference	Number
she continued p before the LORD	1Sa 1:12	6419
by thee here, p unto the LORD	1Sa 1:26	6419
made an end of p all this prayer	1Kin 8:54	6419
when Solomon had made an end of p	2Chr 7:1	6419
men assembled, and found Daniel p	Dan 6:11	1156
And whiles I was speaking, and p	Dan 9:20	6419
And when ye stand p, forgive, if	Mk 11:25	4336
multitude of the people were p	Lk 1:10	4336
Jesus also being baptized, and p	Lk 3:21	4336
came to pass, as he was alone p	Lk 9:18	4336
as he was p in a certain place	Lk 11:1	4336
I was in the city of Joppa p	Acts 11:5	4336
many were gathered together p	Acts 12:12	4336
Every man p or prophesying	1Cor 11:4	4336
P us with much intreaty that we	2Cor 8:4	1189
P always with all prayer and	Eph 6:18	4336
Jesus Christ, p always for you	Col 1:3	4336
Withal p also for us, that God	Col 4:3	4336
day p exceedingly that we might	1Th 3:10	1189
holy faith, p in the Holy Ghost	Jude 20	4336

PREACH

Context	Reference	Number
to p of thee at Jerusalem	Neh 6:7	7121
to p good tidings unto the meek	Is 61:1	1319
p unto it the preaching that I	Jonah 3:2	7121
From that time Jesus began to p	Mt 4:17	2784
And as ye go, p, saying, The	Mt 10:7	2784
that p ye upon the housetops	Mt 10:27	2784
to teach and to p in their cities	Mt 11:1	2784
p the baptism of repentance for	Mk 1:4	2784
towns, that I may p there also	Mk 1:38	2784
he might send them forth to p	Mk 3:14	2784
p the gospel to every creature	Mk 16:15	2784
me to p the gospel to the poor	Lk 4:18	2097
to p deliverance to the captives	Lk 4:18	2784
To p the acceptable year of the	Lk 4:19	2784
I must p the kingdom of God to	Lk 4:43	2097
he sent them to p the kingdom of	Lk 9:2	2784
go thou and p the kingdom of God	Lk 9:60	1229
not to teach and p Jesus Christ	Acts 5:42	2097
commanded us to p unto the people	Acts 10:42	2784
p unto you that ye should turn	Acts 14:15	2097
in every city them that p him	Acts 15:21	2784
Holy Ghost to p the word in Asia	Acts 16:6	2980
us for to p the gospel unto them	Acts 16:10	2097
whom I p unto you, is Christ	Acts 17:3	2605
I am ready to p the gospel to you	Rom 1:15	2097
is, the word of faith, which we p	Rom 10:8	2784
And how shall they p, except they	Rom 10:15	2784
them that p the gospel of peace	Rom 10:15	2097
so have I strived to p the gospel	Rom 15:20	2097
to baptize, but to p the gospel	1Cor 1:17	2097
But we p Christ crucified, unto	1Cor 1:23	2784
p the gospel should live of the	1Cor 9:14	2605
For though I p the gospel	1Cor 9:16	2097
is unto me, if I p not the gospel	1Cor 9:16	2097
when I p the gospel, I may make	1Cor 9:18	2097
it were I or they, so we p	1Cor 15:11	2784
to Troas to p Christ's gospel	2Cor 2:12	
For we p not ourselves, but	2Cor 4:5	2784
To p the gospel in the regions	2Cor 10:16	2097
p any other gospel unto you than	Gal 1:8	2097
If any man p any other gospel	Gal 1:9	2097
that I might p him among the	Gal 1:16	2097
which I p among the Gentiles	Gal 2:2	2784
if I yet p circumcision, why do I	Gal 5:11	2784
that I should p among the	Eph 3:8	2097
Some indeed p Christ even of envy	Phil 1:15	2784
The one p Christ of contention	Phil 1:16	2605
Whom we p, warning every man, and	Col 1:28	2605
P the word	2Ti 4:2	2784
the everlasting gospel to p unto	Rev 14:6	2097

PREACHED

Context	Reference	Number
I have p righteousness in the	Ps 40:9	1319
poor have the gospel p to them	Mt 11:5	2097
p in all the world for a witness	Mt 24:14	2784
shall be p in the whole world	Mt 26:13	2784
And p, saying, There cometh one	Mk 1:7	2784
And he p in their synagogues	Mk 1:39	2784
and he p the word unto them	Mk 2:2	2980
out, and p that men should repent	Mk 6:12	2784
this gospel shall be p throughout	Mk 14:9	2784
p every where, the Lord working	Mk 16:20	2784
exhortation p he unto the people	Lk 3:18	2097
he p in the synagogues of Galilee	Lk 4:44	2784
to the poor the gospel is p	Lk 7:22	2097
that time the kingdom of God is p	Lk 16:16	2097
p the gospel, the chief priests	Lk 20:1	2097
remission of sins should be p in	Lk 24:47	2784
which before was p unto you	Acts 3:20	4296
p through Jesus the resurrection	Acts 4:2	2605
of Samaria, and p Christ unto them	Acts 8:5	2784
p the word of the Lord, returned	Acts 8:25	2980
p the gospel in many villages of	Acts 8:25	2097
scripture, and p unto him Jesus	Acts 8:35	2097
through he p in all the cities	Acts 8:40	2097
straightway he p Christ in the	Acts 9:20	2784
how he had p boldly at Damascus	Acts 9:27	3954
after the baptism which John p	Acts 10:37	2784
they p the word of God in the	Acts 13:5	2605
When John had first p before his	Acts 13:24	4296
that through this man is p unto	Acts 13:38	2605
be p to them the next sabbath	Acts 13:42	2980
And there they p the gospel	Acts 14:7	2097
when they had p the gospel to	Acts 14:21	2097
when they had p the word in Perga	Acts 14:25	2980
we have p the word of the Lord	Acts 15:36	2605
of God was p of Paul at Berea	Acts 17:13	2605
because he p unto them Jesus, and	Acts 17:18	2097
Paul p unto them, ready to depart	Acts 20:7	1256
I have fully p the gospel of	Rom 15:19	4137
means, when I have p to others	1Cor 9:27	2784
you the gospel which I p unto you	1Cor 15:1	2097
keep in memory what I p unto you	1Cor 15:2	2097
Now if Christ be p that he rose	1Cor 15:12	2784
who was p among you by us, even	2Cor 1:19	2784
another Jesus, whom we have not p	2Cor 11:4	2784
because I have p to you the	2Cor 11:7	2097
that which we have p unto you	Gal 1:8	2097
was p of me is not after man	Gal 1:11	2097
p before the gospel unto Abraham	Gal 3:8	4283

infirmity of the flesh I p the ... Gal 4:13 2097
p peace to you which were afar ... Eph 2:17 2097
or in truth, Christ is p ... Phil 1:18 2605
which was p to every creature ... Col 1:23 2784
we p unto you the gospel of God ... 1Th 2:9 2784
p unto the Gentiles, believed on ... 1Ti 3:16 2784
For unto us was the gospel p ... Heb 4:2 2097
but the word p did not profit ... Heb 4:2 189
first p entered not in because of ... Heb 4:6 2097
unto you by them that have p the ... 1Pet 1:12 2097
which by the gospel is p unto you ... 1Pet 1:25 2097
p unto the spirits in prison ... 1Pet 3:19 2784
p also to them that are dead ... 1Pet 4:6 2097

PREACHER
The words of the P, the son of ... Eccl 1:1 6953
Vanity of vanities, saith the P ... Eccl 1:2 6953
I the P was king over Israel in ... Eccl 1:12 6953
this have I found, saith the p ... Eccl 7:27 6953
Vanity of vanities, saith the p ... Eccl 12:8 6953
moreover, because the p was wise ... Eccl 12:9 6953
The p sought to find out ... Eccl 12:10 6953
how shall they hear without a p ... Rom 10:14 2784
Whereunto I am ordained a p ... 1Ti 2:7 2783
Whereunto I am appointed a p ... 2Ti 1:11 2783
a p of righteousness, bringing in ... 2Pet 2:5 2783

PREACHEST
thou that p a man should not ... Rom 2:21 2784

PREACHETH
adjure you by Jesus whom Paul p ... Acts 19:13 2784
if he that cometh p another Jesus ... 2Cor 11:4 2784
now p the faith which once he ... Gal 1:23 2097

PREACHING
unto it the p that I bid thee ... Jonah 3:2 7150
p in the wilderness of Judaea, ... Mt 3:1 2784
p the gospel of the kingdom, and ... Mt 4:23 2784
p the gospel of the kingdom, and ... Mt 9:35 2784
they repented at the p of Jonas ... Mt 12:41 2782
p the gospel of the kingdom of ... Mk 1:14 2784
p the baptism of repentance for ... Lk 3:3 2784
every city and village, p and ... Lk 8:1 2784
p the gospel, and healing every ... Lk 9:6 2097
they repented at the p of Jonas ... Lk 11:32 2782
went every where p the word ... Acts 8:4 2097
p the things concerning the ... Acts 8:12 2097
Israel, p peace by Jesus Christ ... Acts 10:36 2097
p the word to none but unto the ... Acts 11:19 2980
the Grecians, p the Lord Jesus ... Acts 11:20 2097
p the word of the Lord, with many ... Acts 15:35 2097
and as Paul was long p, he sunk ... Acts 20:9 1256
I have gone p the kingdom of God ... Acts 20:25 2784
P the kingdom of God, and teaching ... Acts 28:31 2784
the p of Jesus Christ, according ... Rom 16:25 2782
For the p of the cross is to them ... 1Cor 1:18 3056
of p to save them that believe ... 1Cor 1:21 2782
my p was not with enticing words ... 1Cor 2:4 2782
be not risen, then is our p vain ... 1Cor 15:14 2782
also in p the gospel of Christ ... 2Cor 10:14
that by me the p might be fully ... 2Ti 4:17 2782
manifested his word through p ... Titus 1:3 2782

PRECEPT
For p must be upon p, ... Is 28:10 6673
p upon p; line upon line ... Is 28:10 6673
LORD was unto them p upon p ... Is 28:13 6673
p upon p; line upon line ... Is 28:13 6673
me is taught by the p of men ... Is 29:13 4687
of your heart he wrote you this p ... Mk 10:5 1785
p to all the people according to ... Heb 9:19 1785

PRECEPTS
sabbath, and commandedst them p ... Neh 9:14 4687
us to keep thy p diligently ... Ps 119:4 6490
I will meditate in thy p, and have ... Ps 119:15 6490
me to understand the way of thy p ... Ps 119:27 6490
Behold, I have longed after thy p ... Ps 119:40 6490
for I seek thy p ... Ps 119:45 6490
This I had, because I kept thy p ... Ps 119:56 6490
thee, and of them that keep thy p ... Ps 119:63 6490
keep thy p with my whole heart ... Ps 119:69 6490
but I will meditate in thy p ... Ps 119:78 6490
but I forsook not thy p ... Ps 119:87 6490
I will never forget thy p ... Ps 119:93 6490
for I have sought thy p ... Ps 119:94 6490
ancients, because I keep thy p ... Ps 119:100 6490
Through thy p I get understanding ... Ps 119:104 6490
yet I erred not from thy p ... Ps 119:110 6490
Therefore I esteem all thy p ... Ps 119:128 6490
so will I keep thy p ... Ps 119:134 6490
yet do not I forget thy p ... Ps 119:141 6490
Consider how I love thy p ... Ps 119:159 6490
I have kept thy p and thy ... Ps 119:168 6490
for I have chosen thy p ... Ps 119:173 6490
your father, and kept all his p ... Jer 35:18 4687
even by departing from thy p ... Dan 9:5 4687

PRECIOUS
brother and to her mother p things ... Gen 24:53 4030
for the p things of heaven, for ... Deut 33:13 4022
for the p fruits brought forth by ... Deut 33:14 4022
for the p things put forth by the ... Deut 33:14 4022
for the p things of the lasting ... Deut 33:15 4022
for the p things of the earth and ... Deut 33:16 4022
of the LORD was p in those days ... 1Sa 3:1 3368
because my soul was p in thine ... 1Sa 26:21 3365
talent of gold with the p stones ... 2Sa 12:30 3368
and very much gold, and p stones ... 1Kin 10:2 3368
very great store, and p stones ... 1Kin 10:10 3368
of almug trees, and p stones ... 1Kin 10:11 3368
thy servants, be p in thy sight ... 2Kin 1:13 3365
let my life now be p in thy sight ... 2Kin 1:14 3365
all the house of his p things ... 2Kin 20:13 5238
the p ointment, and all the house ... 2Kin 20:13 2896
there were p stones in it ... 1Chr 20:2 3368
and all manner of p stones ... 1Chr 29:2 3368
they with whom p stones were ... 1Chr 29:8
house with p stones for beauty ... 2Chr 3:6 3368
and gold in abundance, and p stones ... 2Chr 9:1 3368
great abundance, and p stones ... 2Chr 9:9 3368
brought algum trees and p stones ... 2Chr 9:10 3368
p jewels, which they stripped off ... 2Chr 20:25 2530
of p things, with fenced cities ... 2Chr 21:3 4030
for p stones, and for spices, and ... 2Chr 32:27 3368
with p things, beside all that ... Ezr 1:6 4030
vessels of fine copper, p as gold ... Ezr 8:27 2530
and his eye seeth every p thing ... Job 28:10 3366
gold of Ophir, with the p onyx ... Job 28:16 3368
the redemption of their soul is p ... Ps 49:8 3365
p shall their blood be in his ... Ps 72:14 3365
P in the sight of the LORD is the ... Ps 116:15 3368
forth and weepeth, bearing p seed ... Ps 126:6 4901
It is like the p ointment upon ... Ps 133:2 2896
How p also are thy thoughts unto ... Ps 139:17 3365
We shall find all p substance ... Prov 1:13 3368
She is more p than rubies ... Prov 3:15 3368
will hunt for the p life ... Prov 6:26 3368
substance of a diligent man is p ... Prov 12:27 3368
A gift is as a p stone in the ... Prov 17:8 2580
lips of knowledge are a p jewel ... Prov 20:15 3366
the chambers be filled with all p ... Prov 24:4 3368
name is better than p ointment ... Eccl 7:1 2896
make a man more p than fine gold ... Is 13:12 3365
stone, a p corner stone, a sure ... Is 28:16 3368
them the house of his p things ... Is 39:2 5238
the p ointment, and all the house ... Is 39:2 2896
Since thou wast p in my sight ... Is 43:4 3365
take forth the p from the vile ... Jer 15:19 3368
all the p things thereof, and all ... Jer 20:5 3366
The p sons of Zion, comparable to ... Lam 4:2 3368
taken the treasure and p things ... Eze 22:25 3366
in p clothes for chariots ... Eze 27:20 2667
all spices, and with all p stones ... Eze 27:22 3368
every p stone was thy covering, ... Eze 28:13 3368
with their p vessels of silver and ... Dan 11:8 2532
with p stones, and pleasant things ... Dan 11:38 3368
over all the p things of Egypt ... Dan 11:43 2530
alabaster box of very p ointment ... Mt 26:7 927
of ointment of spikenard very p ... Mk 14:3 4185
p stones, wood, hay, stubble ... 1Cor 3:12 5093
for the p fruit of the earth ... Jas 5:7 5093
being much more p than of gold ... 1Pet 1:7 5093
But with the p blood of Christ, ... 1Pet 1:19 5093
of men, but chosen of God, and p ... 1Pet 2:4 1784
a chief corner stone, elect, p ... 1Pet 2:6 1784
therefore which believe he is p ... 1Pet 2:7 5092
like p faith with us through the ... 2Pet 1:1 2472
us exceeding great and p promises ... 2Pet 1:4 5093
p stones and pearls, having a ... Rev 17:4 5093
p stones, and of pearls, and fine ... Rev 18:12 5093
all manner vessels of most p wood ... Rev 18:12 5093
with gold, and p stones, and pearls ... Rev 18:16 5093
was like unto a stone most p ... Rev 21:11 5093
with all manner of p stones ... Rev 21:19 5093

PREDESTINATE
he also did p to be conformed to ... Rom 8:29 4309
Moreover whom he did p, them he ... Rom 8:30 4309

PREDESTINATED
Having p us unto the adoption of ... Eph 1:5 4309
being p according to the purpose ... Eph 1:11 4309

PREEMINENCE
a man hath no p above a beast ... Eccl 3:19 4195
in all things he might have the p ... Col 1:18 4409
loveth to have the p among them ... 3Jn 9 5383

PREFER
if I p not Jerusalem above my ... Ps 137:6 5927

PREFERRED
he p her and her maids unto the ... Est 2:9 8138
Daniel was p above the presidents ... Dan 6:3 5330
cometh after me is p before me ... Jn 1:15 1096
coming after me is p before me ... Jn 1:27 1096
cometh a man which is p before me ... Jn 1:30 1096

PREFERRING
in honour p one another ... Rom 12:10 4285
without p one before another ... 1Ti 5:21 4299

PREMEDITATE
ye shall speak, neither do ye p ... Mk 13:11 3191

PREPARATION
will therefore now make p for it ... 1Chr 22:5 3559
torches in the day of his p ... Nah 2:3 3559
that followed the day of the p ... Mt 27:62 3904
was come, because it was the p ... Mk 15:42 3904
And that day was the p, and the ... Lk 23:54 3904
it was the p of the passover, and ... Jn 19:14 3904
therefore, because it was the p ... Jn 19:31 3904
because of the Jews' p day ... Jn 19:42 3904
with the p of the gospel of peace ... Eph 6:15 2091

PREPARATIONS
The p of the heart in man, and the ... Prov 16:1 4633

PREPARE
I will p him an habitation ... Ex 15:2
shall p that which they bring in ... Ex 16:5 3559
thou p with the burnt offering or ... Num 15:5 6213
thou shalt p for a meat offering ... Num 15:6 6213
to the number that ye shall p ... Num 15:12 6213
p me here seven oxen and seven ... Num 23:1 3559
p me here seven bullocks and seven ... Num 23:29 3559
Thou shalt p thee a way, and ... Deut 19:3 3559
people, saying, P you victuals ... Josh 1:11 3559
Let us now p to build us an altar ... Josh 22:26 6213
p your hearts unto the LORD, and ... 1Sa 7:3 3559
p yet, and know and see his place ... 1Sa 23:22 3559
P thy chariot, and get thee down, ... 1Kin 18:44 631
shewbread, to p it every sabbath ... 1Chr 9:32 3559
and p their heart unto thee ... 1Chr 29:18 3559
Even to p me timber in abundance ... 2Chr 2:9 3559
Then Hezekiah commanded to p ... 2Chr 31:11 3559
p yourselves by the houses of ... 2Chr 35:4 3559
p your brethren, that they may do ... 2Chr 35:6 3559
banquet that I shall p for them ... Est 5:8 6213
p thyself to the search of their ... Job 8:8 3559
If thou p thine heart, and stretch ... Job 11:13 3559
dust, and p raiment as the clay ... Job 27:16 3559
He may p it, but the just shall ... Job 27:17 3559
thou wilt p their heart, thou ... Ps 10:17 3559
p themselves without my fault ... Ps 59:4 3559
O p mercy and truth, which may ... Ps 61:7 4487
that they may p a city for ... Ps 107:36 3559
P thy work without, and make it ... Prov 24:27 3559
yet they p their meat in the ... Prov 30:25 3559
P slaughter for his children for ... Is 14:21 3559
P the table, watch in the ... Is 21:5 6186
P ye the way of the LORD, make ... Is 40:3 6437
workman to p a graven image ... Is 40:20 3559
ye up, p the way, take up the ... Is 57:14 6437
p ye the way of the people ... Is 62:10 6437
that p a table for that troop, and ... Is 65:11 6186
P ye war against her ... Jer 6:4 6942
p them for the day of slaughter ... Jer 12:3 6942
I will p destroyers against thee, ... Jer 22:7 6942
say ye, Stand fast, and p thee ... Jer 46:14 3559
up the watchmen, p the ambushes ... Jer 51:12 3559
p the nations against her, call ... Jer 51:27 6942
P against her the nations with ... Jer 51:28 6942
thou shalt p thy bread therewith ... Eze 4:15 6213
p thee stuff for removing, and ... Eze 12:3 6213
I will p thee unto blood, and ... Eze 35:6 6213
p for thyself, thou, and all thy ... Eze 38:7 3559
Seven days shalt thou p every day ... Eze 43:25 6213
they shall also p a young bullock ... Eze 43:25 3559
he shall p the sin offering, and ... Eze 45:17 3559
shall the prince p for himself ... Eze 45:22 3559
days of the feast he shall p a ... Eze 45:23 3559
he shall p a meat offering of an ... Eze 45:24 3559
the priests shall p his burnt ... Eze 46:2 3559
he shall p a meat offering, an ... Eze 46:7 3559
Now when the prince shall p a ... Eze 46:12 3559
he shall p his burnt offering and ... Eze 46:12 3559
Thou shalt daily p a burnt ... Eze 46:13 3559
thou shalt p it every morning ... Eze 46:13 3559
thou shalt p a meat offering for ... Eze 46:14 3559
Thus shall they p the lamb ... Eze 46:15 3559
P war, wake up the mighty men, ... Joel 3:9 6942
p to meet thy God, O Israel ... Amos 4:12 3559
they even p war against him ... Mic 3:5 6942
he shall p the way before me ... Mal 3:1 6437
P ye the way of the Lord, make ... Mt 3:3 2090
which shall p thy way before thee ... Mt 11:10 2680
Where wilt thou that we p for ... Mt 26:17 2090
which shall p thy way before thee ... Mk 1:2 2680
P ye the way of the Lord, make ... Mk 1:3 2090
p that thou mayest eat the ... Mk 14:12 2090
face of the Lord to p his ways ... Lk 1:76 2090
P ye the way of the Lord, make ... Lk 3:4 2090
which shall p thy way before thee ... Lk 7:27 2680
p us the passover, that we may ... Lk 22:8 2090
him, Where wilt thou that we p ... Lk 22:9 2090
I go to p a place for you ... Jn 14:2 2090
p a place for you, I will come ... Jn 14:3 2090
who shall p himself to the battle ... 1Cor 14:8 3903
But withal p me also a lodging ... Philem 22 2090

PREPARED
for I have p the house, and room ... Gen 24:31 6437
and the bread, which she had p ... Gen 27:17 6213
neither had they p for themselves ... Ex 12:39 6213
into the place which I have p ... Ex 23:20 3559
the city of Sihon be built and p ... Num 21:27 3559
I have p seven altars, and I have ... Num 23:4 6186
whom he had p of the children of ... Josh 4:4 3559
About forty thousand p for war ... Josh 4:13 2502
this, that Absalom p him chariots ... 2Sa 15:1 6213
he p him chariots and horsemen, and ... 1Kin 1:5 6213
so they p timber and stones to ... 1Kin 5:18 3559
the oracle he p in the house ... 1Kin 6:19 3559
he p great provision for them ... 2Kin 6:23 3739
for their brethren had p for them ... 1Chr 12:39 3559
p a place for the ark of God, and ... 1Chr 15:1 3559
his place, which he had p for it ... 1Chr 15:3 3559
the place that I have p for it ... 1Chr 15:12 3559
David p iron in abundance for the ... 1Chr 22:3 3559
So David p abundantly before his ... 1Chr 22:5 3559
in my trouble I have p for the ... 1Chr 22:14 3559
timber also and stone have I p ... 1Chr 22:14 3559
Now I have p with all my might ... 1Chr 29:2 3559
that I have p for the holy house ... 1Chr 29:3 3559
have p to build thee an house for ... 1Chr 29:16 3559
place which David had p for it ... 2Chr 1:4 3559
in the place that David had p in ... 2Chr 3:1 3559
p unto the day of the foundation ... 2Chr 8:16 3559
because he p not his heart to ... 2Chr 12:14 3559
divers kinds of spices p by the ... 2Chr 16:14 7543
thousand ready p for the war ... 2Chr 17:18 2502
hast p thine heart to seek God ... 2Chr 19:3 3559
p their hearts unto the God of ... 2Chr 20:33 3559
Uzziah p for them throughout all ... 2Chr 26:14 3559
because he p his ways before the ... 2Chr 27:6 3559
in his transgression, have we p ... 2Chr 29:19 3559
people, that God had p the people ... 2Chr 29:36 3559
and they p them, ... 2Chr 31:11 3559
So the service was p, and the ... 2Chr 35:10 3559
the Levites p for themselves ... 2Chr 35:14 3559
brethren the Levites p for them ... 2Chr 35:15 3559
of the LORD was p the same day ... 2Chr 35:16 3559
when Josiah had p the temple ... 2Chr 35:20 3559
For Ezra had p his heart to seek ... Ezr 7:10 3559
Now that which was p for me daily ... Neh 5:18 6213
also fowls were p for me, and once ... Neh 5:18 6213

unto them for whom nothing is *p*	Neh 8:10	3559
he had *p* for him a great chamber,	Neh 13:5	6213
the banquet that I have *p* for him	Est 5:4	6213
to the banquet that Esther had *p*	Est 5:5	6213
banquet that she had *p* but myself	Est 5:12	6213
the gallows that he had *p* for him	Est 6:4	3559
the banquet that Esther had *p*	Est 6:14	6213
that he had *p* for Mordecai	Est 7:10	3559
he *p* it, yea, and searched it out	Job 28:27	3559
when I *p* my seat in the street	Job 29:7	3559
He hath also *p* for him the	Ps 7:13	3559
he hath *p* his throne for judgment	Ps 9:7	3559
They have *p* a net for my steps	Ps 57:6	3559
hast *p* of thy goodness for the	Ps 68:10	3559
thou hast *p* the light and the sun	Ps 74:16	3559
The LORD hath *p* his throne in the	Ps 103:19	3559
When he *p* the heavens, I was	Prov 8:27	3559
Judgments are *p* for scorners	Prov 19:29	3559
The horse is *p* against the day of	Prov 21:31	3559
yea, for the king it is *p*	Is 30:33	3559
what he hath *p* for him that	Is 64:4	6213
a table *p* before it, whereupon	Eze 23:41	6186
of thy pipes was *p* in thee in the	Eze 28:13	3559
Be thou *p*, and prepare for thyself	Eze 38:7	3559
for ye have *p* lying and corrupt	Dan 2:9	2164
and gold, which they *p* for Baal	Hos 2:8	6213
going forth is *p* as the morning	Hos 6:3	3559
Now the LORD had *p* a great fish	Jonah 1:17	4487
And the LORD God *p* a gourd	Jonah 4:6	4487
But God *p* a worm when the morning	Jonah 4:7	4487
that God *p* a vehement east wind	Jonah 4:8	4487
and the defence shall be *p*	Nah 2:5	3559
for the LORD hath *p* a sacrifice	Zeph 1:7	3559
for whom it is *p* of my Father	Mt 20:23	2090
Behold, I have *p* my dinner	Mt 22:4	2090
inherit the kingdom *p* for you	Mt 25:34	2090
p for the devil and his angels	Mt 25:41	2090
be given to them for whom it is *p*	Mk 10:40	2090
a large upper room furnished and *p*	Mk 14:15	2092
ready a people *p* for the Lord	Lk 1:17	2680
Which thou hast *p* before the face	Lk 2:31	2090
p not himself, neither did	Lk 12:47	2090
and *p* spices and ointments	Lk 23:56	2090
the spices which they had *p*	Lk 24:1	2090
which he had afore *p* unto glory	Rom 9:23	4282
God hath *p* for them that love him	1Cor 2:9	2090
use, and *p* unto every good work	2Ti 2:21	2090
not, but a body hast thou *p* me	Heb 10:5	2675
p an ark to the saving of his	Heb 11:7	2680
for he hath *p* for them a city	Heb 11:16	2090
trumpets *p* themselves to sound	Rev 8:6	2090
like unto horses *p* unto battle	Rev 9:7	2090
which were *p* for an hour, and a	Rev 9:15	2090
where she hath a place *p* of God	Rev 12:6	2090
the kings of the east might be *p*	Rev 16:12	2090
p as a bride adorned for her	Rev 21:2	2090

PREPAREDST

Thou *p* room before it, and didst	Ps 80:9	6437

PREPAREST

when thou *p* a bullock for a burnt	Num 15:8	6213
Thou *p* a table before me in the	Ps 23:5	6186
thou *p* them corn, when thou hast	Ps 65:9	3559

PREPARETH

That *p* his heart to seek God, the	2Chr 30:19	3559
vanity, and their belly *p* deceit	Job 15:35	3559
who *p* rain for the earth, who	Ps 147:8	3559

PREPARING

in *p* him a chamber in the courts	Neh 13:7	6213
of Noah, while the ark was a *p*	1Pet 3:20	2680

PRESBYTERY

laying on of the hands of the *p*	1Ti 4:14	4244

PRESCRIBED

grievousness which they have *p*	Is 10:1	3789

PRESCRIBING

oil, and salt without *p* how much	Ezr 7:22	3792

PRESENCE

the *p* of the LORD God amongst the	Gen 3:8	6440
went out from the *p* of the LORD	Gen 4:16	6440
in the *p* of all his brethren	Gen 16:12	6440
in the *p* of the sons of my people	Gen 23:11	5869
in the *p* of the children of Heth	Gen 23:18	5869
he died in the *p* of all his	Gen 25:18	6440
from the *p* of Isaac his father	Gen 27:30	6440
went out from the *p* of Pharaoh	Gen 41:46	6440
for they were troubled at his *p*	Gen 45:3	6440
for why should we die in thy *p*	Gen 47:15	5048
were driven out from Pharaoh's *p*	Ex 10:11	5869
My *p* shall go with thee, and I	Ex 33:14	6440
If thy *p* go not with me, carry us	Ex 33:15	6440
departed from the *p* of Moses	Ex 35:20	6440
soul shall be cut off from my *p*	Lev 22:3	6440
Aaron went from the *p* of the	Num 20:6	6440
unto him in the *p* of the elders	Deut 25:9	5869
priests, in the *p* of the people	Josh 4:11	6440
which he wrote in the *p* of the	Josh 8:32	6440
David avoided out of his *p* twice	1Sa 18:11	6440
David to Saul, and he was in his *p*	1Sa 19:7	6440
he slipped away out of Saul's *p*	1Sa 19:10	6440
to play the mad man in my *p*	1Sa 21:15	5921
I not serve in the *p* of his son	2Sa 16:19	6440
I have served in thy father's *p*	2Sa 16:19	6440
so will I be in thy *p*	2Sa 16:19	6440
went out from the *p* of the king	2Sa 24:4	6440
And she came into the king's *p*	1Kin 1:28	6440
the *p* of all the congregation of	1Kin 8:22	5048
fled from the *p* of king Solomon	1Kin 12:2	6440
in the *p* of the people, saying,	1Kin 21:13	5048
the *p* of Jehoshaphat the king of	2Kin 3:14	6440
he went out from his *p* a leper as	2Kin 5:27	6440
cast he them from his *p* as yet	2Kin 13:23	6440
he had cast them out from his *p*	2Kin 24:20	6440
of them that were in the king's *p*	2Kin 25:19	6440
Glory and honour are in his *p*	1Chr 16:27	6440
sing out at the *p* of the LORD	1Chr 16:33	6440
Aaron in the *p* of David the king	1Chr 24:31	6440
the *p* of all the congregation of	2Chr 6:12	5048
the earth sought the *p* of Solomon	2Chr 9:23	6440
from the *p* of Solomon the king	2Chr 10:2	6440
before this house, and in thy *p*	2Chr 20:9	6440
the altars of Baalim in his *p*	2Chr 34:4	6440
not been beforetime sad in his *p*	Neh 2:1	6440
in the *p* of Ahasuerus the king	Est 1:10	6440
Mordecai went out from the *p* of	Est 8:15	6440
went forth from the *p* of the LORD	Job 1:12	6440
forth from the *p* of the LORD	Job 2:7	6440
Therefore am I troubled at his *p*	Job 23:15	6440
shall fall and perish at thy *p*	Ps 9:3	6440
in thy *p* is fulness of joy	Ps 16:11	6440
my sentence come forth from thy *p*	Ps 17:2	6440
me in the *p* of mine enemies	Ps 23:5	5048
of thy *p* from the pride of man	Ps 31:20	6440
Cast me not away from thy *p*	Ps 51:11	6440
the wicked perish at the *p* of God	Ps 68:2	6440
also dropped at the *p* of God	Ps 68:8	6440
itself was moved at the *p* of God	Ps 68:8	6440
before his *p* with thanksgiving	Ps 95:2	6440
like wax at the *p* of the LORD	Ps 97:5	6440
at the *p* of the LORD of the whole	Ps 97:5	6440
come before his *p* with singing	Ps 100:2	6440
at the *p* of the Lord	Ps 114:7	6440
at the *p* of the God of Jacob	Ps 114:7	6440
now in the *p* of all his people	Ps 116:14	5048
now in the *p* of all his people	Ps 116:18	5048
whither shall I flee from thy *p*	Ps 139:7	6440
the upright shall dwell in thy *p*	Ps 140:13	6440
Go from the *p* of a foolish man,	Prov 14:7	5048
surety in the *p* of his friend	Prov 17:18	6440
thyself in the *p* of the king	Prov 25:6	6440
p of the prince whom thine eyes	Prov 25:7	6440
strangers devour it in your *p*	Is 1:7	5048
of Egypt shall be moved at his *p*	Is 19:1	6440
and the angel of his *p* saved them	Is 63:9	6440
might flow down at thy *p*,	Is 64:1	6440
the nations may tremble at thy *p*	Is 64:2	6440
mountains flowed down at thy *p*	Is 64:3	6440
broken down at the *p* of the LORD	Jer 4:26	6440
will ye not tremble at my *p*	Jer 5:22	6440
fathers, and cast you out of my *p*	Jer 23:39	6440
in the *p* of the priests and of all	Jer 28:1	5869
Hananiah in the *p* of the priests	Jer 28:5	5869
in the *p* of all the people that	Jer 28:5	5869
spake in the *p* of all the people	Jer 28:11	5869
in the *p* of the witnesses that	Jer 32:12	5869
he had cast them out from his *p*	Jer 52:3	6440
of the earth, shall shake at my *p*	Eze 38:20	6440
answered in the *p* of the king	Dan 2:27	6925
Tarshish from the *p* of the LORD	Jonah 1:3	6440
Tarshish from the *p* of the LORD	Jonah 1:3	6440
he fled from the *p* of the LORD	Jonah 1:10	6440
and the earth is burned at his *p*	Nah 1:5	6440
peace at the *p* of the Lord GOD	Zeph 1:7	6440
that stand in the *p* of God	Lk 1:19	1799
We have eaten and drunk in thy *p*	Lk 13:26	1799
p of them that sit at meat with	Lk 14:10	1799
there is joy in the *p* of the	Lk 15:10	1799
Jesus in the *p* of his disciples	Jn 20:30	1799
and denied him in the *p* of Pilate	Acts 3:13	4383
soundness in the *p* of you all	Acts 3:16	561
shall come from the *p* of the Lord	Acts 3:19	4383
from the *p* of the council	Acts 5:41	4383
thanks to God in *p* of them all	Acts 27:35	1799
no flesh should glory in his *p*	1Cor 1:29	1799
who in *p* am base among you, but	2Cor 10:1	4383
but his bodily *p* is weak, and his	2Cor 10:10	3952
obeyed, not as in my *p* only	Phil 2:12	3952
from you for a short time in *p*	1Th 2:17	4383
Are not even ye in the *p* of our	1Th 2:19	1715
from the *p* of the Lord, and from	2Th 1:9	4383
to appear in the *p* of God for us	Heb 9:24	4383
you faultless before the *p* of his	Jude 24	2714
brimstone in the *p* of the holy	Rev 14:10	1799
angels, and in the *p* of the Lamb	Rev 14:10	1799

PRESENT

his hand a *p* for Esau his brother	Gen 32:13	4503
it is a *p* sent unto my lord Esau	Gen 32:18	4503
with the *p* that goeth before me	Gen 32:20	4503
So went the *p* over before him	Gen 32:21	4503
then receive my *p* at my hand	Gen 33:10	4503
and carry down the man a *p*	Gen 43:11	4503
And the men took that *p*, and they	Gen 43:15	4503
they made ready the *p* against	Gen 43:25	4503
they brought him the *p* which was	Gen 43:26	4503
p thyself there to me in the top	Ex 34:2	5324
p the man that is to be made	Lev 14:11	5975
p them before the LORD at the	Lev 16:7	5975
then he shall *p* himself before	Lev 27:8	5975
then he shall *p* the beast before	Lev 27:11	5975
p them before Aaron the priest,	Num 3:6	5975
p yourselves in the tabernacle of	Deut 31:14	3320
a *p* unto Eglon the king of Moab	Judg 3:15	4503
he brought the *p* unto Eglon king	Judg 3:17	4503
he had made an end to offer the *p*	Judg 3:18	4503
away the people that bare the *p*	Judg 3:18	4503
unto thee, and bring forth my *p*	Judg 6:18	4503
there is not a *p* to bring to the	1Sa 9:7	8670
Now therefore *p* yourselves before	1Sa 10:19	3320
the people that were *p* with him	1Sa 13:15	4672
the people that were *p* with them	1Sa 13:16	4672
in mine hand, or what there is *p*	1Sa 21:3	4672
Behold a *p* for you of the spoil	1Sa 30:26	1293
three days, and be thou here *p*	2Sa 20:4	5975
given it for a *p* unto his	1Kin 9:16	7964
And they brought every man his *p*	1Kin 10:25	4503
have sent unto thee a *p* of silver	1Kin 15:19	7810
were numbered, and were all *p*	1Kin 20:27	3557
Take a *p* in thine hand, and go,	2Kin 8:8	4503
took a *p* with him, even of every	2Kin 8:9	4503
sent it for a *p* to the king of	2Kin 16:8	7810
brought no *p* to the king of	2Kin 17:4	4503
Make an agreement with me by a *p*	2Kin 18:31	1293
sent letters and a *p* unto Hezekiah	2Kin 20:12	4503
joy thy people, which are *p* here	1Chr 29:17	4672
that were *p* were sanctified	2Chr 5:11	4672
And they brought every man his *p*	2Chr 9:24	4503
all that were *p* with him bowed	2Chr 29:29	4672
children of Israel that were *p* at	2Chr 30:21	4672
all Israel that were *p* went out	2Chr 31:1	4672
all that were *p* in Jerusalem	2Chr 34:32	4672
that were *p* in Israel to serve	2Chr 34:33	4672
offerings, for all that were *p*	2Chr 35:7	4672
children of Israel that were *p*	2Chr 35:17	4672
all Judah and Israel that were *p*	2Chr 35:18	4672
his lords, and all Israel there *p*	Ezr 8:25	4672
that were *p* in Shushan the palace	Est 1:5	4672
the Jews that are *p* in Shushan	Est 4:16	4672
to *p* themselves before the LORD	Job 1:6	3320
to *p* themselves before the LORD	Job 2:1	3320
them to *p* himself before the LORD	Job 2:1	3320
a very *p* help in trouble	Ps 46:1	4672
In that time shall the *p* be	Is 18:7	7862
Make an agreement with me by a *p*	Is 36:16	1293
sent letters and a *p* to Hezekiah	Is 39:1	4503
It may be they will *p* their	Jer 36:7	5307
unto whom ye sent me to *p* your	Jer 42:9	5307
thee for a *p* horns of ivory	Eze 27:15	814
for we do not *p* our supplications	Dan 9:18	5307
Assyria for a *p* to king Jareb	Hos 10:6	4503
Jerusalem, to *p* him to the Lord	Lk 2:22	3936
of the Lord was *p* to heal them	Lk 5:17	
There were *p* at that season some	Lk 13:1	3918
manifold more in this *p* time	Lk 18:30	3918
unto you, being yet *p* with you	Jn 14:25	3306
are we all here *p* before God	Acts 10:33	3918
and all the elders were *p*	Acts 21:18	3854
all men which are here *p* with us	Acts 25:24	4840
every one, because of the *p* rain	Acts 28:2	2186
for to will is *p* with me	Rom 7:18	3873
would do good, evil is *p* with me	Rom 7:21	3873
this *p* time are not worthy to be	Rom 8:18	3568
nor powers, nor things *p*	Rom 8:38	1764
Even so then at this *p* time also	Rom 11:5	3568
that ye *p* your bodies a living	Rom 12:1	3936
or life, or death, or things *p*	1Cor 3:22	1764
Even unto this *p* hour we both	1Cor 4:11	737
but *p* in spirit, have judged	1Cor 5:3	3918
already, as though I were *p*	1Cor 5:3	3918
this is good for the *p* distress	1Cor 7:26	1764
greater part remain unto this *p*	1Cor 15:6	737
by Jesus, and shall *p* us with you	2Cor 4:14	3936
body, and to be *p* with the Lord	2Cor 5:8	1736
whether *p* or absent, we may be	2Cor 5:9	1736
when I am *p* with that confidence	2Cor 10:2	3918
we be also in deed when we are *p*	2Cor 10:11	3918
that I may *p* you as a chaste	2Cor 11:2	3936
And when I was *p* with you, and	2Cor 11:9	3918
and foretell you, as if I were *p*	2Cor 13:2	3918
lest being *p* I should use	2Cor 13:10	3918
deliver us from this *p* evil world	Gal 1:4	1764
and not only when I am *p* with you	Gal 4:18	3918
I desire to be *p* with you now	Gal 4:20	3918
That he might *p* it to himself a	Eph 5:27	3936
to *p* you holy and unblameable and	Col 1:22	3936
that we may *p* every man perfect	Col 1:28	3936
me, having loved this *p* world	2Ti 4:10	3568
and godly, in this *p* world	Titus 2:12	3568
was a figure for the time then *p*	Heb 9:9	1764
for the *p* seemeth to be joyous	Heb 12:11	3918
and be established in the *p* truth	2Pet 1:12	3918
to *p* you faultless before the	Jude 24	2476

PRESENTED

to Goshen, and *p* himself unto him	Gen 46:29	7200
five men, and *p* them unto Pharaoh	Gen 47:2	3322
when it is *p* unto the priest, he	Lev 2:8	7126
in the day when he *p* them to	Lev 7:35	7126
Aaron's sons *p* unto him the blood	Lev 9:12	4672
they *p* the burnt offering unto	Lev 9:13	4672
Aaron's sons *p* unto him the blood	Lev 9:18	4672
shall be *p* alive before the LORD,	Lev 16:10	5975
p themselves in the tabernacle of	Deut 31:14	3320
they *p* themselves before God	Josh 24:1	3320
unto him under the oak, and *p* it	Judg 6:19	5066
p themselves in the assembly of	Judg 20:2	3320
evening, and *p* himself forty days	1Sa 17:16	3320
I *p* my supplication before the	Jer 38:26	5307
there they *p* the provocation of	Eze 20:28	5414
treasures, they *p* unto him gifts	Mt 2:11	4374
the saints and widows, *p* her alive	Acts 9:41	3936
governor, *p* Paul also before him	Acts 23:33	3936

PRESENTING

p my supplication before the LORD	Dan 9:20	5307

PRESENTLY

them not fail to burn the fat *p*	1Sa 2:16	3117
A fool's wrath is *p* known	Prov 12:16	3117
p the fig tree withered away	Mt 21:19	3916
he shall *p* give me more than	Mt 26:53	3936
Him therefore I hope to send *p*	Phil 2:23	1824

PRESENTS

despised him, and brought him no *p*	1Sa 10:27	4503
they brought *p*, and served Solomon	1Kin 4:21	4503
became his servant, and gave him *p*	2Kin 17:3	4503
Judah brought to Jehoshaphat *p*	2Chr 17:5	4503
Philistines brought Jehoshaphat *p*	2Chr 17:11	4503
p to Hezekiah king of Judah	2Chr 32:23	4030
shall kings bring *p* unto thee	Ps 68:29	7862
and of the isles shall bring *p*	Ps 72:10	4503

bring *p* unto him that ought to be Ps 76:11 7862
thou give *p* to Moresheth-gath Mic 1:14 7964

PRESERVE
that we may *p* seed of our father Gen 19:32 2421
that we may *p* seed of our father Gen 19:34 2421
did send me before you to *p* life Gen 45:5 4241
God sent me before you to *p* you a Gen 45:7 7760
always, that he might *p* us alive Deut 6:24 2421
thou shalt *p* them from this Ps 12:7 5341
P me, O God Ps 16:1 8104
Let integrity and uprightness *p* me Ps 25:21 5341
thou shalt *p* me from trouble Ps 32:7 5341
and thy truth continually *p* me Ps 40:11 5341
The LORD will *p* him, and keep him Ps 41:2 8104
mercy and truth, which may *p* him Ps 61:7 5341
p my life from fear of the enemy Ps 64:1 5341
p thou those that are appointed Ps 79:11 3498
P my soul Ps 86:2 8104
The LORD shall *p* thee from all Ps 121:7 8104
he shall *p* thy soul Ps 121:7 8104
The LORD shall *p* thy going out Ps 121:8 8104
p me from the violent man Ps 140:1 5341
p me from the violent man Ps 140:4 5341
Discretion shall *p* thee, Prov 2:11 8104
her not, and she shall *p* thee Prov 4:6 8104
the lips of the wise shall *p* them Prov 14:3 8104
Mercy and truth *p* the king Prov 20:28 5341
The eyes of the LORD *p* knowledge Prov 22:12 5341
and passing over he will *p* it Is 31:5 4422
and I will *p* thee, and give thee Is 49:8 5341
children, I will *p* them alive Jer 49:11 2421
shall lose his life shall *p* it Lk 17:33 *2225*
will *p* me unto his heavenly 2Ti 4:18 *4982*

PRESERVED
God face to face, and my life is *p* Gen 32:30 5337
p us in all the way wherein we Josh 24:17 8104
LORD hath given us, who hath *p* us 1Sa 30:23 8104
the LORD *p* David whithersoever he 2Sa 8:6 3467
the LORD *p* David whithersoever he 2Sa 8:14 3467
Thus the LORD *p* David 1Chr 18:6 3467
Thus the LORD *p* David 1Chr 18:13 3467
thy visitation hath *p* my spirit Job 10:12 8104
as in the days when God *p* me Job 29:2 8104
they are *p* for ever Ps 37:28 8104
and to restore the *p* of Israel Is 49:6 5336
Egypt, and by a prophet was he *p* Hos 12:13 8104
into new bottles, and both are *p* Mt 9:17 *4933*
and both are *p* Lk 5:38 *4933*
body be *p* blameless unto the 1Th 5:23 *5083*
p in Jesus Christ, and called Jude 1 *5083*

PRESERVER
I do unto thee, O thou *p* of men Job 7:20 5314

PRESERVEST
is therein, and thou *p* them all Neh 9:6 2421
O LORD, thou *p* man and beast Ps 36:6 3467

PRESERVETH
He *p* not the life of the wicked Job 36:6 2421
for the LORD *p* the faithful Ps 31:23 5341
he *p* the souls of his saints Ps 97:10 8104
The LORD *p* the simple Ps 116:6 8104
The LORD *p* all them that love him Ps 145:20 8104
The LORD *p* the strangers Ps 146:9 8104
and *p* the way of his saints Prov 2:8 8104
that keepeth his way *p* his soul Prov 16:17 8104

PRESIDENTS
And over these three *p* Dan 6:2 5632
Daniel was preferred above the *p* Dan 6:3 5632
Then the *p* and princes sought to Dan 6:4 5632
Then these *p* and princes assembled Dan 6:6 5632
All the *p* of the kingdom, the Dan 6:7 5632

PRESS
for the *p* is full, the fats Joel 3:13 1660
out fifty vessels out of the *p* Hag 2:16 6333
not come nigh unto him for the *p* Mk 2:4 *3793*
of Jesus, came in the *p* behind Mk 5:27 *3793*
of him, turned him about in the *p* Mk 5:30 *3793*
could not come at him for the *p* Lk 8:19 *3793*
p thee, and sayest thou, Who Lk 8:45 *598*
and could not for the *p*, because Lk 19:3 *3793*
I *p* toward the mark for the prize Phil 3:14 *1377*

PRESSED
And he *p* upon them greatly Gen 19:3 6484
they *p* sore upon the man, even Gen 19:9 6484
p them into Pharaoh's cup, and I Gen 40:11 7818
when she *p* him daily with her Judg 16:16 6693
And he *p* him 2Sa 13:25 6555
But Absalom *p* him, that he let 2Sa 13:27 6555
p on by the king's commandment Est 8:14 1765
there were their breasts *p* Eze 23:3 4600
I am *p* under you, as a cart is Amos 2:13 5781
as a cart is *p* that is full of Amos 2:13 5781
insomuch that they *p* upon him for Mk 3:10 *1968*
as the people *p* upon him to hear Lk 5:1 *1945*
p down, and shaken together, and Lk 6:38 *4085*
Paul was *p* in the spirit, and Acts 18:5 *4912*
that we were *p* out of measure, 2Cor 1:8 *916*

PRESSES
thy *p* shall burst out with new Prov 3:10 3342
tread out no wine in their *p* Is 16:10 3342

PRESSETH
fast in me, and thy hand *p* me sore Ps 38:2 5181
preached, and every man *p* into it Lk 16:16 *971*

PRESSFAT
when one came to the *p* for to Hag 2:16 3342

PRESUME
which shall *p* to speak a word in Deut 18:20 2102
that durst *p* in his heart to do Est 7:5 4390

PRESUMED
But they *p* to go up unto the hill Num 14:44 6075

PRESUMPTUOUS
back thy servant also from *p* sins Ps 19:13 2086
P are they, selfwilled, they are 2Pet 2:10 *5113*

PRESUMPTUOUSLY
But if a man come *p* upon his Ex 21:14 2102
But the soul that doeth ought *p* Num 15:30 3027
LORD, and went *p* up into the hill Deut 1:43 2102
And the man that will do *p* Deut 17:12 2087
hear, and fear, and do no more *p* Deut 17:13 2102
but the prophet hath spoken it *p* Deut 18:22 2087

PRETENCE
and for a *p* make long prayer Mt 23:14 *4392*
for a *p* make long prayers Mk 12:40 *4392*
every way, whether in *p*, or in Phil 1:18 *4392*

PREVAIL
cubits upward did the waters *p* Gen 7:20 1396
peradventure I shall *p*, that we Num 22:6 3201
what means we may *p* against him Judg 16:5 3201
for by strength shall no man *p* 1Sa 2:9 1396
but if I *p* against him, and kill 1Sa 17:9 3201
things, and also shalt still *p* 1Sa 26:25 3201
shalt persuade him, and *p* also 1Kin 22:22 3201
let not man *p* against thee 2Chr 14:11 6113
entice him, and thou shalt also *p* 2Chr 18:21 3201
thou shalt not *p* against him Est 6:13 3201
they shall *p* against him, as a Job 15:24 8630
and the robber shall *p* against him Job 18:9 2388
let not man *p* Ps 9:19 5810
said, With our tongue will we *p* Ps 12:4 1396
Iniquities *p* against me Ps 65:3 1396
if one *p* against him, two shall Eccl 4:12 8630
it, but could not *p* against it Is 7:1 3898
but he shall not *p* Is 16:12 3201
he shall *p* against his enemies Is 42:13 1396
to profit, if so be thou mayest *p* Is 47:12 6206
but they shall not *p* against thee Jer 1:19 3201
themselves, yet can they not *p* Jer 5:22 3201
but they shall not *p* against thee Jer 15:20 3201
we shall *p* against him, and we Jer 20:10 3201
stumble, and they shall not *p* Jer 20:11 3201
deal against them, and shall *p* Dan 11:7 2388
of hell shall not *p* against it Mt 16:18 *2729*
saw that he could *p* nothing Mt 27:24 *5623*
Perceive ye how ye *p* nothing Jn 12:19 *5623*

PREVAILED
And the waters *p*, and were Gen 7:18 1396
the waters *p* exceedingly upon the Gen 7:19 1396
the waters *p* upon the earth an Gen 7:24 1396
with my sister, and I have *p* Gen 30:8 3201
he saw that he *p* not against him Gen 32:25 3201
with God and with men, and hast *p* Gen 32:28 3201
because the famine *p* over them Gen 47:20 2388
have *p* above the blessings of my Gen 49:26 1396
held up his hand, that Israel *p* Ex 17:11 1396
he let down his hand, Amalek *p* Ex 17:11 1396
the hand of the house of Joseph *p* Judg 1:35 3513
and his hand *p* against Judg 3:10 5810
p against Jabin the king of Judg 4:24 7186
hand of Midian *p* against Israel Judg 6:2 5810
So David *p* over the Philistine 1Sa 17:50 2388
Surely the men *p* against us 2Sa 11:23 1396
the king's word *p* against Joab 2Sa 24:4 2388
Omri *p* against the people that 1Kin 16:22 2388
month the famine *p* in the city 2Kin 25:3 2388
For Judah *p* above his brethren, 1Chr 5:2 1396
the king's word *p* against Joab 1Chr 21:4 2388
to Hamath-zobah, and *p* against it 2Chr 8:3 2388
time, and the children of Judah *p* 2Chr 13:18 553
the Ammonites, and *p* against them 2Chr 27:5 2388
enemy say, I have *p* against him Ps 13:4 3201
yet they have not *p* against me Ps 129:2 3201
art stronger than I, and hast *p* Jer 20:7 3201
thee on, and have *p* against thee Jer 38:22 3201
are desolate, because the enemy *p* Lam 1:16 1396
the saints, and *p* against them Dan 7:21 3202
he had power over the angel, and *p* Hos 12:4 3201
deceived thee, and *p* against thee Obad 7 3201
of them and of the chief priests *p* Lk 23:23 *2729*
p against them, so that they fled Acts 19:16 *2480*
grew the word of God and *p* Acts 19:20 *2480*
hath *p* to open the book, and to Rev 5:5 *3528*
And *p* not Rev 12:8 *2480*

PREVAILEST
Thou *p* for ever against him, and Job 14:20 8630

PREVAILETH
my bones, and it *p* against them Lam 1:13 7287

PREVENT
Why did the knees *p* me Job 3:12 6923
The God of my mercy shall *p* me Ps 59:10 6923
thy tender mercies speedily *p* us Ps 79:8 6923
morning shall my prayer *p* thee Ps 88:13 6923
Mine eyes *p* the night watches, Ps 119:148 6923
evil shall not overtake nor *p* us Amos 9:10 6923
shall not *p* them which are asleep 1Th 4:15 *5348*

PREVENTED
the snares of death *p* me 2Sa 22:6 6923
They *p* me in the day of my 2Sa 22:19 6923
the days of affliction *p* me Job 30:27 6923
Who hath *p* me, that I should Job 41:11 6923
the snares of death *p* me Ps 18:5 6923
They *p* me in the day of my Ps 18:18 6923
I *p* the dawning of the morning, Ps 119:147 6923
they *p* with their bread him that Is 21:14 6923
come into the house, Jesus *p* him Mt 17:25 *4399*

PREVENTEST
For thou *p* him with the blessings Ps 21:3 6923

PREY
from the *p*, my son, thou art gone Gen 49:9 2964
the morning he shall devour the *p* Gen 49:27 5706
and our children should be a *p* Num 14:3 957
ones, which ye said should be a *p* Num 14:31 957
lie down until he eat of the *p* Num 23:24 2964
took all the spoil, and all the *p* Num 31:11 4455
brought the captives, and the *p* Num 31:12 4455
the sum of the *p* that was taken Num 31:26 4455
divide the *p* into two parts Num 31:27 4455
being the rest of the *p* which the Num 31:32 957
ones, which ye said should be a *p* Deut 1:39 957
we took for a *p* unto ourselves Deut 2:35 962
we took for a *p* to ourselves Deut 3:7 962
ye take for a *p* unto yourselves Josh 8:2 962
took for a *p* unto themselves Josh 8:27 962
took for a *p* unto themselves Josh 11:14 962
have they not divided the *p* Judg 5:30 7998
to Sisera a *p* of divers colours, Judg 5:30 7998
a *p* of divers colours of Judg 5:30 7998
every man the earrings of his *p* Judg 8:24 7998
every man the earrings of his *p* Judg 8:25 7998
and they shall become a *p* and a 2Kin 21:14 957
give them for a *p* in the land of Neh 4:4 961
to take the spoil of them for a *p* Est 3:13 962
to take the spoil of them for a *p* Est 8:11 962
but on the *p* they laid not their Est 9:15 961
laid not their hands on the *p* Est 9:16 961
old lion perisheth for lack of *p* Job 4:11 2964
the eagle that hasteth to the *p* Job 9:26 400
rising betimes for a *p* Job 24:5 2964
Wilt thou hunt the *p* for the lion Job 38:39 2964
From thence she seeketh the *p* Job 39:29 400
as a lion that is greedy of his *p* Ps 17:12 2963
excellent than the mountains of *p* Ps 76:4 2964
young lions roar after their *p* Ps 104:21 2964
given us as a *p* to their teeth Ps 124:6 2964
She also lieth in wait as for a *p* Prov 23:28 2863
shall roar, and lay hold of the *p* Is 5:29 2964
that widows may be their *p* Is 10:2 7998
take the spoil, and to take the *p* Is 10:6 957
the young lion roaring on his *p* Is 31:4 2964
then is the *p* of a great spoil Is 33:23 5706
the lame take the *p* Is 33:23 957
they are for a *p*, and none Is 42:22 957
Shall the *p* be taken from the Is 49:24 4455
the *p* of the terrible shall be Is 49:25 4455
from evil maketh himself a *p* Is 59:15 7997
life shall be unto him for a *p* Jer 21:9 7998
all that *p* upon thee will I give Jer 30:16 962
upon thee will I give for a *p* Jer 30:16 7998
he shall have his life for a *p* Jer 38:2 7998
life shall be for a *p* unto thee Jer 39:18 7998
a *p* in all places whither thou Jer 45:5 7998
hands of the strangers for a *p* Eze 7:21 957
and it learned to catch the *p* Eze 19:3 2964
lion, and learned to catch the *p* Eze 19:6 2964
a roaring lion ravening the *p* Eze 22:25 2964
are like wolves ravening the *p* Eze 22:27 2964
make a *p* of thy merchandise Eze 26:12 962
and take her spoil, and take her *p* Eze 29:19 957
because my flock became a *p* Eze 34:8 957
and they shall no more be a *p* Eze 34:22 957
no more be a *p* to the heathen Eze 34:28 957
are forsaken, which became a *p* Eze 36:4 957
minds, to cast it out for a *p* Eze 36:5 957
To take a spoil, and to take a *p* Eze 38:12 957
gathered thy company to take a *p* Eze 38:13 957
he shall scatter among them the *p* Dan 11:24 961
in the forest, when he hath no *p* Amos 3:4 2964
and filled his holes with *p* Nah 2:12 2964
will cut off thy *p* from the earth Nah 2:13 2964
the *p* departeth not Nah 3:1 2964
the day that I rise up to the *p* Zeph 3:8 5706

PRICE
thou shalt increase the *p* thereof Lev 25:16 4736
thou shalt diminish the *p* of it Lev 25:16 4736
the *p* of his sale shall be Lev 25:50 3701
p of his redemption out of the Lev 25:51
him again the *p* of his redemption Lev 25:52
or the *p* of a dog, into the house Deut 23:18 4242
will surely buy it of thee at a *p* 2Sa 24:24 4242
received the linen yarn at a *p* 1Kin 10:28 4242
shalt grant it me for the full *p* 1Chr 21:22 3701
will verily buy it for the full *p* 1Chr 21:24 3701
received the linen yarn at a *p* 2Chr 1:16 4242
Man knoweth not the *p* thereof Job 28:13 6187
be weighed for the *p* thereof Job 28:15 4242
for the *p* of wisdom is above Job 28:18 4901
increase thy wealth by their *p* Ps 44:12 4242
Wherefore is there a *p* in the Prov 17:16 4242
the goats are the *p* of the field Prov 27:26 4242
for her *p* is far above rubies Prov 31:10 4377
not for *p* nor reward, saith the Is 45:13 4242
milk without money and without *p* Is 55:1 4242
I give to the spoil without *p* Jer 15:13 4242
If ye think good, give me my *p* Zec 11:12 7939
So they weighed for my *p* thirty Zec 11:12 7939
a goodly *p* that I was prised at Zec 11:13 3365
he had found one pearl of great *p* Mt 13:46 *4186*
because it is the *p* of blood Mt 27:6 *5092*
the *p* of him that was valued, Mt 27:9 *5092*
And kept back part of the *p* Acts 5:2 *5092*
back part of the *p* of the land Acts 5:3 *5092*
and they counted the *p* of them Acts 19:19 *5092*
For ye are bought with a *p* 1Cor 6:20 *5092*
Ye are bought with a *p* 1Cor 7:23 *5092*
is in the sight of God of great *p* 1Pet 3:4 *4185*

PRICES
brought the p of the things that Acts 4:34 *5092*

PRICKED
grieved, and I was p in my reins Ps 73:21 8150
they were p in their heart, and Acts 2:37 *2669*

PRICKING
there shall be no more a p brier Eze 28:24 3992

PRICKS
of them shall be p in your eyes Num 33:55 7899
for thee to kick against the p Acts 9:5 *2759*
for thee to kick against the p Acts 26:14 *2759*

PRIDE
I will break the p of your power Lev 26:19 1347
I know thy p, and the naughtiness 1Sa 17:28 2087
himself for the p of his heart 2Chr 32:26 1363
his purpose, and hide p from man Job 33:17 1466
because of the p of evil men Job 35:12 1347
His scales are his p, shut up Job 41:15 1346
a king over all the children of p Job 41:34 7830
The wicked in his p doth Ps 10:2 1346
through the p of his countenance, Ps 10:4 1363
of thy presence from the p of man Ps 31:20 7407
not the foot of p come against me Ps 36:11 1346
let them even be taken in their p Ps 59:12 1347
Therefore p compasseth them about Ps 73:6 1346
p, and arrogancy, and the evil way, Prov 8:13 1344
When p cometh, then cometh shame Prov 11:2 2087
Only by p cometh contention Prov 13:10 2087
of the foolish is a rod of p Prov 14:3 1346
P goeth before destruction, and an Prov 16:18 1347
A man's p shall bring him low Prov 29:23 1346
of Samaria, that say in the p Is 9:9 1346
We have heard of the p of Moab Is 16:6 1347
even of his haughtiness, and his p Is 16:6 1347
it, to stain the p of all glory Is 23:9 1347
he shall bring down their p Is 25:11 1346
Woe to the crown of p, to the Is 28:1 1348
The crown of p, the drunkards of Is 28:3 1348
manner will I mar the p of Judah Jer 13:9 1347
and the great p of Jerusalem Jer 13:9 1347
weep in secret places for your p Jer 13:17 1466
We have heard the p of Moab Jer 48:29 1347
and his arrogancy, and his p Jer 48:29 1347
the p of thine heart, O thou that Jer 49:16 2087
rod hath blossomed, p hath budded Eze 7:10 2087
iniquity of thy sister Sodom, p Eze 16:49 1347
by thy mouth in the day of thy p Eze 16:56 1347
the p of her power shall come Eze 30:6 1347
those that walk in p he is able Dan 4:37 1466
up, and his mind hardened in p Dan 5:20 2103
the p of Israel doth testify to Hos 5:5 1347
the p of Israel testifieth to his Hos 7:10 1347
The p of thine heart hath Obad 3 2087
This shall they have for their p Zeph 2:10 1347
thee them that rejoice in thy p Zeph 3:11 1346
cut off the p of the Philistines Zec 9:6 1347
the p of Assyria shall be brought Zec 10:11 1347
for the p of Jordan is spoiled Zec 11:3 1347
an evil eye, blasphemy, p Mk 7:22 *5243*
lest being lifted up with p he 1Ti 3:6 *5187*
the p of life, is not of the 1Jn 2:16 *212*

PRIEST
he was the p of the most high God Gen 14:18 3548
daughter of Poti-pherah p of On Gen 41:45 3548
Poti-pherah p of On bare unto him Gen 41:50 3548
Poti-pherah p of On bare unto him Gen 46:20 3548
Now the p of Midian had seven Ex 2:16 3548
father in law, the p of Midian Ex 3:1 3548
the p of Midian, Moses' father in Ex 18:1 3548
that son that is p in his stead Ex 29:30 3548
the holy garments for Aaron the p Ex 31:10 3548
the holy garments for Aaron the p Ex 35:19 3548
of Ithamar, son to Aaron the p Ex 38:21 3548
the holy garments for Aaron the p Ex 39:41 3548
the sons of Aaron the p shall put Lev 1:7 3548
the p shall burn all on the altar Lev 1:9 3548
the p shall lay them in order on Lev 1:12 3548
the p shall bring it all, and burn Lev 1:13 3548
the p shall bring it unto the Lev 1:15 3548
the p shall burn it upon the Lev 1:17 3548
the p shall burn the memorial of Lev 2:2 3548
when it is presented unto the p Lev 2:8 3548
the p shall take from the meat Lev 2:9 3548
the p shall burn the memorial of Lev 2:16 3548
the p shall burn it upon the Lev 3:11 3548
the p shall burn them upon the Lev 3:16 3548
If the p that is anointed do sin Lev 4:3 3548
the p that is anointed shall take Lev 4:5 3548
the p shall dip his finger in the Lev 4:6 3548
the p shall put some of the blood Lev 4:7 3548
the p shall burn them upon the Lev 4:10 3548
the p that is anointed shall Lev 4:16 3548
the p shall dip his finger in Lev 4:17 3548
the p shall make an atonement for Lev 4:20 3548
the p shall take of the blood of Lev 4:25 3548
the p shall make an atonement for Lev 4:26 3548
the p shall take of the blood Lev 4:30 3548
the p shall burn it upon the Lev 4:31 3548
the p shall make an atonement for Lev 4:31 3548
the p shall take of the blood of Lev 4:34 3548
the p shall burn them upon the Lev 4:35 3548
the p shall make an atonement for Lev 4:35 3548
the p shall make an atonement for Lev 5:6 3548
And he shall bring them unto the p Lev 5:8 3548
the p shall make an atonement for Lev 5:10 3548
Then shall he bring it to the p Lev 5:12 3548
the p shall take his handful of Lev 5:12 3548
the p shall make an atonement for Lev 5:13 3548
thereto, and give it unto the p Lev 5:16 3548
the p shall make an atonement for Lev 5:16 3548
a trespass offering, unto the p Lev 5:18 3548
the p shall make an atonement for Lev 5:18 3548
a trespass offering, unto the p Lev 6:6 3548
the p shall make an atonement for Lev 6:7 3548
the p shall put on his linen Lev 6:10 3548
the p shall burn wood on it every Lev 6:12 3548
the p of his sons that is Lev 6:22 3548
for the p shall be wholly burnt Lev 6:23 3548
The p that offereth it for sin Lev 6:26 3548
the p shall burn them upon the Lev 7:5 3548
the p that maketh atonement Lev 7:7 3548
the p that offereth any man's Lev 7:8 3548
even the p shall have to himself Lev 7:8 3548
the p shall burn the fat upon the Lev 7:31 3548
p for an heave offering of the Lev 7:32 3548
have given them unto Aaron the p Lev 7:34 3548
of the congregation, unto the p Lev 12:6 3548
the p shall make an atonement for Lev 12:8 3548
shall be brought unto Aaron the p Lev 13:2 3548
the p shall look on the plague in Lev 13:3 3548
the p shall look on him, and Lev 13:3 3548
then the p shall shut up him that Lev 13:4 3548
the p shall look on him the Lev 13:5 3548
then the p shall shut him up Lev 13:5 3548
the p shall look on him again the Lev 13:6 3548
the p shall pronounce him clean Lev 13:6 3548
seen of the p for his cleansing Lev 13:7 3548
he shall be seen of the p again Lev 13:7 3548
if the p see that, behold, the Lev 13:8 3548
then the p shall pronounce him Lev 13:8 3548
he shall be brought unto the p Lev 13:9 3548
And the p shall see him Lev 13:10 3548
the p shall pronounce him unclean Lev 13:11 3548
foot, wheresoever the p looketh Lev 13:12 3548
Then the p shall consider Lev 13:13 3548
the p shall see the raw flesh, and Lev 13:15 3548
white, he shall come unto the p Lev 13:16 3548
And the p shall see him Lev 13:17 3548
then the p shall pronounce him Lev 13:17 3548
reddish, and it be shewed to the p Lev 13:19 3548
And if, when the p seeth it Lev 13:20 3548
the p shall pronounce him unclean Lev 13:20 3548
But if the p look on it, and, Lev 13:21 3548
then the p shall shut him up Lev 13:21 3548
then the p shall pronounce him Lev 13:22 3548
the p shall pronounce him clean Lev 13:23 3548
Then the p shall look upon it Lev 13:25 3548
wherefore the p shall pronounce Lev 13:25 3548
But if the p look on it, and, Lev 13:26 3548
then the p shall shut him up Lev 13:26 3548
the p shall look upon him the Lev 13:27 3548
then the p shall pronounce him Lev 13:27 3548
the p shall pronounce him clean Lev 13:28 3548
Then the p shall see the plague Lev 13:30 3548
then the p shall pronounce him Lev 13:30 3548
if the p look on the plague of Lev 13:31 3548
then the p shall shut up him that Lev 13:31 3548
in the seventh day the p shall Lev 13:32 3548
the p shall shut up him that hath Lev 13:33 3548
in the seventh day the p shall Lev 13:34 3548
then the p shall pronounce him Lev 13:34 3548
Then the p shall look on him Lev 13:36 3548
the p shall not seek for yellow Lev 13:36 3548
the p shall pronounce him clean Lev 13:37 3548
Then the p shall look Lev 13:39 3548
Then the p shall look upon it Lev 13:43 3548
the p shall pronounce him utterly Lev 13:44 3548
and shall be shewed unto the p Lev 13:49 3548
the p shall look upon the plague, Lev 13:50 3548
if the p shall look, and, behold, Lev 13:53 3548
Then the p shall command that Lev 13:54 3548
the p shall look on the plague, Lev 13:55 3548
And if the p look, and, behold, the Lev 13:56 3548
He shall be brought unto the p Lev 14:2 3548
the p shall go forth out of the Lev 14:3 3548
the p shall look, and, behold, if Lev 14:3 3548
Then shall the p command to take Lev 14:4 3548
the p shall command that one of Lev 14:5 3548
the p that maketh him clean shall Lev 14:11 3548
the p shall take one he lamb, and Lev 14:12 3548
the p shall take some of the Lev 14:14 3548
the p shall put it upon the tip Lev 14:14 3548
the p shall take some of the log Lev 14:15 3548
the p shall dip his right finger Lev 14:16 3548
p put upon the tip of the right Lev 14:17 3548
the p shall make an atonement for Lev 14:18 3548
the p shall offer the sin Lev 14:19 3548
the p shall offer the burnt Lev 14:20 3548
the p shall make an atonement for Lev 14:20 3548
day for his cleansing unto the p Lev 14:23 3548
the p shall take the lamb of the Lev 14:24 3548
the p shall wave them for a wave Lev 14:24 3548
the p shall take some of the Lev 14:25 3548
the p shall pour of the oil into Lev 14:26 3548
the p shall sprinkle with his Lev 14:27 3548
the p shall put of the oil that Lev 14:28 3548
the p shall make an atonement for Lev 14:31 3548
house shall come and tell the p Lev 14:35 3548
Then the p shall command that Lev 14:36 3548
before the p go into it to see Lev 14:36 3548
afterward the p shall go in to Lev 14:36 3548
Then the p shall go out of the Lev 14:38 3548
the p shall come again the Lev 14:39 3548
Then the p shall command that Lev 14:40 3548
Then the p shall come and look, and Lev 14:44 3548
if the p shall come in, and look Lev 14:48 3548
then the p shall pronounce the Lev 14:48 3548
and give them unto the p Lev 15:14 3548
the p shall offer them, the one Lev 15:15 3548
the p shall make an atonement for Lev 15:15 3548
pigeons, and bring them unto the p Lev 15:29 3548
the p shall offer the one for a Lev 15:30 3548
the p shall make an atonement for Lev 15:30 3548
the p make an atonement for you Lev 16:30
And the p, whom he shall anoint, Lev 16:32 3548
of the congregation, unto the p Lev 17:5 3548
the p shall sprinkle the blood Lev 17:6 3548
the p shall make an atonement for Lev 19:22 3548
And the daughter of any p, if she Lev 21:9 3548
is the high p among his brethren Lev 21:10 3548
of the seed of Aaron the p shall Lev 21:21 3548
a sojourner of the p, or an hired Lev 22:10 3548
But if the p buy any soul with Lev 22:11 3548
it unto the p with the holy thing Lev 22:14 3548
of your harvest unto the p Lev 23:10 3548
the sabbath the p shall wave it Lev 23:11 3548
the p shall wave them with the Lev 23:20 3548
be holy to the LORD for the p Lev 23:20 3548
present himself before the p Lev 27:8 3548
and the p shall value him Lev 27:8 3548
that vowed shall the p value him Lev 27:8 3548
present the beast before the p Lev 27:11 3548
the p shall value it, whether it Lev 27:12 3548
as thou valuest it, who art the p Lev 27:12 3548
then the p shall estimate it, Lev 27:14 3548
as the p shall estimate it, so Lev 27:14 3548
then the p shall reckon unto him Lev 27:18 3548
Then the p shall reckon unto him Lev 27:23 3548
present them before Aaron the p Num 3:6 3548
Eleazar the son of Aaron the p Num 3:32 3548
the p pertaineth the oil for the Num 4:16 3548
of Ithamar the son of Aaron the p Num 4:28 3548
of Ithamar the son of Aaron the p Num 4:33 3548
unto the LORD, even to the p Num 5:8 3548
which they bring unto the p Num 5:9 3548
whatsoever any man giveth the p Num 5:10 3548
the man bring his wife unto the p Num 5:15 3548
the p shall bring her near, and Num 5:16 3548
the p shall take holy water in an Num 5:17 3548
the tabernacle the p shall take Num 5:17 3548
the p shall set the woman before Num 5:18 3548
the p shall have in his hand the Num 5:18 3548
the p shall charge her by an oath Num 5:19 3548
Then the p shall charge the woman Num 5:21 3548
the p shall say unto the woman, Num 5:21 3548
the p shall write these curses in Num 5:23 3548
Then the p shall take the Num 5:25 3548
the p shall take an handful of Num 5:26 3548
the p shall execute upon her all Num 5:30 3548
or two young pigeons, to the p Num 6:10 3548
the p shall offer the one for a Num 6:11 3548
the p shall bring them before the Num 6:16 3548
the p shall offer also his meat Num 6:17 3548
the p shall take the sodden Num 6:19 3548
the p shall wave them for a wave Num 6:20 3548
this is holy for the p, with the Num 6:20 3548
of Ithamar the son of Aaron the p Num 7:8 3548
the p shall make an atonement for Num 15:25 3548
the p shall make an atonement for Num 15:28 3548
Eleazar the son of Aaron the p Num 16:37 3548
Eleazar the p took the brasen Num 16:39 3548
heave offering to Aaron the p Num 18:28 3548
shall give her unto Eleazar the p Num 19:3 3548
Eleazar the p shall take of her Num 19:4 3548
the p shall take cedar wood, and Num 19:6 3548
Then the p shall wash his clothes Num 19:7 3548
the p shall be unclean until the Num 19:7 3548
Eleazar, the son of Aaron the p Num 25:7 3548
Eleazar, the son of Aaron the p Num 25:11 3548
Eleazar the son of Aaron the p Num 26:1 3548
Eleazar the p spake with them in Num 26:3 3548
by Moses and Eleazar the p Num 26:63 3548
Moses and Aaron the p numbered Num 26:64 3548
Moses, and before Eleazar the p Num 27:2 3548
And set him before Eleazar the p Num 27:19 3548
shall stand before Eleazar the p Num 27:21 3548
and set him before Eleazar the p Num 27:22 3548
Phinehas the son of Eleazar the p Num 31:6 3548
unto Moses, and Eleazar the p Num 31:12 3548
And Moses, and Eleazar the p Num 31:13 3548
Eleazar the p said unto the men Num 31:21 3548
of beast, thou, and Eleazar the p Num 31:26 3548
and give it unto Eleazar the p Num 31:29 3548
Eleazar the p did as the LORD Num 31:31 3548
offering, unto Eleazar the p Num 31:41 3548
Eleazar the p took the gold of Num 31:51 3548
Eleazar the p took the gold of Num 31:54 3548
unto Moses, and to Eleazar the p Num 32:2 3548
Moses commanded Eleazar the p Num 32:28 3548
Aaron the p went up into mount Num 33:38 3548
Eleazar the p, and Joshua the son Num 34:17 3548
it unto the death of the high p Num 35:25 3548
until the death of the high p Num 35:28 3548
p the slayer shall return into Num 35:28 3548
land, until the death of the p Num 35:32 3548
will not hearken unto the p that Deut 17:12 3548
give unto the p the shoulder Deut 18:3 3548
that the p shall approach and Deut 20:2 3548
thou shalt go unto the p that Deut 26:3 3548
the p shall take the basket out Deut 26:4 3548
of Canaan, which Eleazar the p Josh 14:1 3548
came near before Eleazar the p Josh 17:4 3548
inheritances, which Eleazar the p Josh 19:51 3548
p that shall be in those days Josh 20:6 3548
of the Levites unto Eleazar the p Josh 21:1 3548
and the children of Aaron the p Josh 21:4 3548
the p Hebron with her suburbs Josh 21:13 3548
Phinehas the son of Eleazar the p Josh 22:13 3548
And when Phinehas the p, and the Josh 22:30 3548
the p said unto the children of Josh 22:31 3548
Phinehas the son of Eleazar the p Josh 22:32 3548
one of his sons, who became his p Judg 17:5 3548
me, and be unto me a father and a p Judg 17:10 3548
and the young man became his p Judg 17:12 3548
seeing I have a Levite to my p Judg 17:13 3548
and hath hired me, and I am his p Judg 18:4 3548
the p said unto them, Go in peace Judg 18:6 3548
the p stood in the entering of Judg 18:17 3548
Then said the p unto them Judg 18:18 3548

us, and be to us a father and a *p* Judg 18:19 3548
be a *p* unto the house of one man Judg 18:19 3548
or that thou be a *p* unto a tribe Judg 18:19 3548
my gods which I made, and the *p* Judg 18:24 3548
the *p* which he had, and came unto Judg 18:27 3548
Now Eli the *p* sat upon a seat by 1Sa 1:9 3548
unto the LORD before Eli the *p* 1Sa 2:11 3548
brought up the *p* took for himself 1Sa 2:14 3548
Give flesh to roast for the *p* 1Sa 2:15 3548
the tribes of Israel to be my *p* 1Sa 2:28 3548
I will raise me up a faithful *p* 1Sa 2:35 3548
of Eli, the LORD's *p* in Shiloh 1Sa 14:3 3548
while Saul talked unto the *p* 1Sa 14:19 3548
and Saul said unto the *p*, Withdraw 1Sa 14:19 3548
Then said the *p*, Let us draw near 1Sa 14:36 3548
David to Nob to Ahimelech the *p* 1Sa 21:1 3548
David said unto Ahimelech the *p* 1Sa 21:2 3548
the *p* answered David, and said 1Sa 21:4 3548
And David answered the *p*, and said 1Sa 21:5 3548
So the *p* gave him hallowed bread 1Sa 21:6 3548
the *p* said, The sword of Goliath 1Sa 21:9 3548
king sent to call Ahimelech the *p* 1Sa 22:11 3548
and he said to Abiathar the *p* 1Sa 23:9 3548
And David said to Abiathar the *p* 1Sa 30:7 3548
king said also unto Zadok the *p* 2Sa 15:27 3548
Zeruiah, and with Abiathar the *p* 1Kin 1:7 3548
But Zadok the *p*, and Benaiah the 1Kin 1:8 3548
of the king, and Abiathar the *p* 1Kin 1:19 3548
of the host, and Abiathar the *p* 1Kin 1:25 3548
me thy servant, and Zadok the *p* 1Kin 1:26 3548
David said, Call me Zadok the *p* 1Kin 1:32 3548
And let Zadok the *p* and Nathan the 1Kin 1:34 3548
So Zadok the *p*, and Nathan the 1Kin 1:38 3548
Zadok the *p* took an horn of oil 1Kin 1:39 3548
the son of Abiathar the *p* came 1Kin 1:42 3548
hath sent with him Zadok the *p* 1Kin 1:44 3548
And Zadok the *p* and Nathan the 1Kin 1:45 3548
for him, and for Abiathar the *p* 1Kin 2:22 3548
unto Abiathar the *p* said the king 1Kin 2:26 3548
from being *p* unto the LORD 1Kin 2:27 3548
Zadok the *p* did the king put in 1Kin 2:35 3548
Azariah the son of Zadok the *p* 1Kin 4:2 3548
that Jehoiada the *p* commanded 2Kin 11:9 3548
and came to Jehoiada the *p* 2Kin 11:9 3548
the *p* give king David's spears 2Kin 11:10 3548
But Jehoiada the *p* commanded the 2Kin 11:15 3548
For the *p* had said, Let her not 2Kin 11:15 3548
slew Mattan the *p* of Baal before 2Kin 11:18 3548
the *p* appointed officers over the 2Kin 11:18 3548
Jehoiada the *p* instructed him 2Kin 12:2 3548
Jehoash called for Jehoiada the *p* 2Kin 12:7 3548
But Jehoiada the *p* took a chest 2Kin 12:9 3548
scribe and the high *p* came up 2Kin 12:10 3548
the *p* the fashion of the altar 2Kin 16:10 3548
Urijah the *p* built an altar 2Kin 16:11 3548
so Urijah the *p* made it against 2Kin 16:11 3548
king Ahaz commanded Urijah the *p* 2Kin 16:15 3548
Thus did Urijah the *p*, according 2Kin 16:16 3548
Go up to Hilkiah the high *p* 2Kin 22:4 3548
Hilkiah the high *p* said unto 2Kin 22:8 3548
Hilkiah the *p* hath delivered me a 2Kin 22:10 3548
the king commanded Hilkiah the *p* 2Kin 22:12 3548
So Hilkiah the *p*, and Ahikam, and 2Kin 22:14 3548
king commanded Hilkiah the high *p* 2Kin 23:4 3548
in the book that Hilkiah the *p* 2Kin 23:24 3548
guard took Seraiah the chief *p* 2Kin 25:18 3548
and Zephaniah the second *p* 2Kin 25:18 3548
And Zadok the *p*, and his brethren 1Chr 16:39 3548
and the princes, and Zadok the *p* 1Chr 24:6 3548
the son of Jehoiada, a chief *p* 1Chr 27:5 3548
chief governor, and Zadok to be *p* 1Chr 29:22 3548
the same may be a *p* of them that 2Chr 13:9 3548
true God, and without a teaching *p* 2Chr 15:3 3548
Amariah the chief *p* is over you 2Chr 19:11 3548
the wife of Jehoiada the *p* 2Chr 22:11 3548
that Jehoiada the *p* had commanded 2Chr 23:8 3548
for Jehoiada the *p* dismissed not 2Chr 23:8 3548
Moreover Jehoiada the *p* delivered 2Chr 23:9 3548
Then Jehoiada the *p* brought out 2Chr 23:14 3548
For the *p* said, Slay her not in 2Chr 23:14 3548
slew Mattan the *p* of Baal before 2Chr 23:17 3548
all the days of Jehoiada the *p* 2Chr 24:2 3548
the son of Jehoiada the *p* 2Chr 24:20 3548
of the sons of Jehoiada the *p* 2Chr 24:25 3548
Azariah the *p* went in after him 2Chr 26:17 3548
And Azariah the chief *p*, and all 2Chr 26:20 3548
Azariah the chief *p* of the house 2Chr 31:10 3548
they came to Hilkiah the high *p* 2Chr 34:9 3548
Hilkiah the *p* found a book of the 2Chr 34:14 3548
Hilkiah the *p* hath given me a 2Chr 34:18 3548
till there stood up a *p* with Urim Ezr 2:63 3548
the son of Aaron the chief *p* Ezr 7:5 3548
Artaxerxes gave unto Ezra the *p* Ezr 7:11 3548
king of kings, unto Ezra the *p* Ezr 7:12 3549
river, that whatsoever Ezra the *p* Ezr 7:21 3548
Meremoth the son of Uriah the *p* Ezr 8:33 3548
And Ezra the *p* stood up, and said Ezr 10:10 3548
And Ezra the *p*, with certain chief Ezr 10:16 3548
Then Eliashib the high *p* rose up Neh 3:1 3548
the house of Eliashib the high *p* Neh 3:20 3548
till there stood up a *p* with Urim Neh 7:65 3548
Ezra the *p* brought the law before Neh 8:2 3548
Ezra the *p* the scribe, and the Neh 8:9 3548
the *p* the son of Aaron shall be Neh 10:38 3548
the governor, and of Ezra the *p* Neh 12:26 3548
And before this, Eliashib the *p* Neh 13:4 3548
the treasuries, Shelemiah the *p* Neh 13:13 3548
the son of Eliashib the high *p* Neh 13:28 3548
Thou art a *p* for ever after the Ps 110:4 3548
witnesses to record, Uriah the *p* Is 8:2 3548
as with the people, so with the *p* Is 24:2 3548
the *p* and the prophet have erred Is 28:7 3548
the *p* every one dealeth falsely Jer 6:13 3548
the *p* every one dealeth falsely Jer 8:10 3548
the *p* go about into a land that Jer 14:18 3548
law shall not perish from the *p* Jer 18:18 3548
Now Pashur the son of Immer the *p* Jer 20:1 3548
the son of Maaseiah the *p* Jer 21:1 3548
For both prophet and *p* are profane Jer 23:11 3548
people, or the prophet, or a *p* Jer 23:33 3548
And as for the prophet, and the *p* Jer 23:34 3548
the son of Maaseiah the *p* Jer 29:25 3548
The LORD hath made thee *p* in the Jer 29:26 3548
in the stead of Jehoiada the *p* Jer 29:26 3548
Zephaniah the *p* read this letter Jer 29:29 3548
the *p* to the prophet Jeremiah Jer 37:3 3548
guard took Seraiah the chief *p* Jer 52:24 3548
and Zephaniah the second *p* Jer 52:24 3548
of his anger the king and the *p* Lam 2:6 3548
shall the *p* and the prophet be Lam 2:20 3548
came expressly unto Ezekiel the *p* Eze 1:3 3548
the law shall perish from the *p* Eze 7:26 3548
to do the office of a *p* unto me Eze 44:13 3547
Neither shall any *p* drink wine Eze 44:21 3548
or a widow that had a *p* before Eze 44:22 3548
the *p* the first of your dough Eze 44:30 3548
the *p* shall take of the blood of Eze 45:19 3548
as they that strive with the *p* Hos 4:4 3548
that thou shalt be no *p* to me Hos 4:6 3547
shall be, like people, like *p* Hos 4:9 3548
Then Amaziah the *p* of Beth-el Amos 7:10 3548
the son of Josedech, the high *p* Hag 1:1 3548
the son of Josedech, the high *p* Hag 1:12 3548
the son of Josedech, the high *p* Hag 1:14 3548
the son of Josedech, the high *p* Hag 2:2 3548
son of Josedech, the high *p* Hag 2:4 3548
p standing before the angel of Zec 3:1 3548
Hear now, O Joshua the high *p* Zec 3:8 3548
the son of Josedech, the high *p* Zec 6:11 3548
he shall be a *p* upon his throne Zec 6:13 3548
go thy way, shew thyself to the *p* Mt 8:4 2409
unto the palace of the high *p* Mt 26:3 749
him away to Caiaphas the high *p* Mt 26:57 749
And the high *p* arose, and said unto Mt 26:62 749
And the high *p* answered and said Mt 26:63 749
Then the high *p* rent his clothes Mt 26:65 749
go thy way, shew thyself to the *p* Mk 1:44 2409
the days of Abiathar the high *p* Mk 2:26 749
and staves, from the chief *p* Mk 14:43 749
and smote a servant of the high *p* Mk 14:47 749
they led Jesus away to the high *p* Mk 14:53 749
into the palace of the high *p* Mk 14:54 749
the high *p* stood up in the midst Mk 14:60 749
Again the high *p* asked him Mk 14:61 749
Then the high *p* rent his clothes Mk 14:63 749
one of the maids of the high *p* Mk 14:66 749
a certain *p* named Zacharias, of Lk 1:5 2409
but go, and shew thyself to the *p* Lk 5:14 2409
came down a certain *p* that way Lk 10:31 2409
smote the servant of the high *p* Lk 22:50 749
being the high *p* that same year Jn 11:49 749
but being high *p* that year Jn 11:51 749
was the high *p* that same year Jn 18:13 749
was known unto the high *p* Jn 18:15 749
into the palace of the high *p* Jn 18:15 749
which was known unto the high *p* Jn 18:16 749
The high *p* then asked Jesus of Jn 18:19 749
Answerest thou the high *p* so Jn 18:22 749
bound unto Caiaphas the high *p* Jn 18:24 749
One of the servants of the high *p* Jn 18:26 749
And Annas the high *p*, and Caiaphas Acts 4:6 749
were of the kindred of the high *p* Acts 4:6 748
Then the high *p* rose up, and all Acts 5:17 749
But the high *p* came, and they that Acts 5:21 749
Now when the high *p* and the Acts 5:24 749
and the high *p* asked them Acts 5:27 749
Then said the high *p*, Are these Acts 7:1 749
of the Lord, went unto the high *p* Acts 9:1 749
Then the *p* of Jupiter, which was Acts 14:13 2409
As also the high *p* doth bear me Acts 22:5 749
the high *p* Ananias commanded them Acts 23:2 749
said, Revilest thou God's high *p* Acts 23:4 749
brethren, that he was the high *p* Acts 23:5 749
high *p* descended with the elders Acts 24:1 749
Then the high *p* and the chief of Acts 25:2 749
faithful high *p* in things Heb 2:17 749
High *P* of our profession, Christ Heb 3:1 749
then that we have a great high *p* Heb 4:14 749
For we have not an high *p* which Heb 4:15 749
For every high *p* taken from among Heb 5:1 749
not himself to be made an high *p* Heb 5:5 749
Thou art a *p* for ever after the Heb 5:6 2409
Called of God an high *p* after the Heb 5:10 749
made an high *p* for ever after the Heb 6:20 749
p of the most high God, who met Heb 7:1 2409
abideth a *p* continually Heb 7:3 2409
need was there that another *p* Heb 7:11 2409
there ariseth another *p* Heb 7:15 2409
Thou art a *p* for ever after the Heb 7:17 2409
not without an oath he was made *p* Heb 7:20
Thou art a *p* for ever after the Heb 7:21 2409
For such an high *p* became us Heb 7:26 749
We have such an high *p*, who is Heb 8:1 749
For every high *p* is ordained to Heb 8:3 749
on earth, he should not be a *p* Heb 8:4 2409
the high *p* alone once every year Heb 9:7 749
an high *p* of good things to come Heb 9:11 749
as the high *p* entereth into the Heb 9:25 749
And every *p* standeth daily Heb 10:11 2409
having an high *p* over the house Heb 10:21 2409
sanctuary by the high *p* for sin Heb 13:11 749

PRIESTHOOD

p throughout their generations Ex 40:15 3550
and seek ye the *p* also Num 16:10 3550
shall bear the iniquity of your *p* Num 18:1 3550
the covenant of an everlasting *p* Num 25:13 3550
for the *p* of the LORD is their Josh 18:7 3550
they, as polluted, put from the *p* Ezr 2:62 3550
they, as polluted, put from the *p* Neh 7:64 3550
because they have defiled the *p* Neh 13:29 3550
and the covenant of the *p* Neh 13:29 3550
who receive the office of the *p* Heb 7:5 2405
were by the Levitical *p*, (for Heb 7:11 2420
For the *p* being changed, there is Heb 7:12 2420
Moses spake nothing concerning *p* Heb 7:14 2420
ever, hath an unchangeable *p* Heb 7:24 2420
up a spiritual house, an holy *p* 1Pet 2:5 2406
a chosen generation, a royal *p* 1Pet 2:9 2406

PRIEST'S

minister unto me in the *p* office Ex 28:1 3547
minister unto me in the *p* office Ex 28:3 3547
minister unto me in the *p* office Ex 28:4 3547
minister unto me in the *p* office Ex 28:41 3547
minister unto me in the *p* office Ex 29:1 3547
the *p* office shall be theirs for Ex 29:9 3550
to minister to me in the *p* office Ex 29:44 3547
minister unto me in the *p* office Ex 30:30 3547
sons, to minister in the *p* office Ex 31:10 3547
sons, to minister in the *p* office Ex 35:19 3547
to minister in the *p* office Ex 39:41 3547
minister unto me in the *p* office Ex 40:13 3547
minister unto me in the *p* office Ex 40:15 3547
and the remnant shall be the *p* Lev 5:13 3548
shall be the *p* that offereth it Lev 7:9 3548
it shall be the *p* that sprinkleth Lev 7:14 3548
unto the LORD in the *p* office Lev 7:35 3547
for as the sin offering is the *p* Lev 14:13 3548
of the oil that is in the *p* hand Lev 14:18 3548
rest of the oil that is in the *p* Lev 14:29 3548
p office in his father's stead Lev 16:32 3547
If the *p* daughter also be married Lev 22:12 3548
But if the *p* daughter be a widow Lev 22:13 3548
possession thereof shall be the *p* Lev 27:21 3548
to minister in the *p* office Num 3:3 3547
Ithamar ministered in the *p* Num 3:4 3547
they shall wait on their *p* office Num 3:10 3550
p office for every thing of the Num 18:7 3550
I have given your *p* office unto Num 18:7 3550
in the *p* office in his stead Deut 10:6 3547
this shall be the *p* due from the Deut 18:3 3548
the *p* heart was glad, and he took Judg 18:20 3548
the *p* custom with the people was 1Sa 2:13 3548
the *p* servant came, while the 1Sa 2:13 3548
the *p* servant came, and said to 1Sa 2:15 3548
the *p* office in the temple that 1Chr 6:10 3547
and Ithamar executed the *p* office 1Chr 24:2 3547
the *p* office unto the LORD 2Chr 11:14 3547
the high *p* officer came and 2Chr 24:11 3548
of your oblations, shall be the *p* Eze 44:30 3548
For the *p* lips should keep Mal 2:7 3548
and struck a servant of the high *p* Mt 26:51 749
afar off unto the high *p* palace Mt 26:58 749
that while he executed the *p* Lk 1:8 2407
to the custom of the *p* office Lk 1:9 2405
brought him into the high *p* house Lk 22:54 749
it, and smote the high *p* servant Jn 18:10 749

PRIESTS

the land of the *p* bought he not Gen 47:22 3548
for the *p* had a portion assigned Gen 47:22 3548
except the land of the *p* only Gen 47:26 3548
shall be unto me a kingdom of *p* Ex 19:6 3548
And let the *p* also, which come Ex 19:22 3548
but let not the *p* and the people Ex 19:24 3548
and the *p*, Aaron's sons, shall Lev 1:5 3548
And the *p*, Aaron's sons, shall lay Lev 1:8 3548
and the *p*, Aaron's sons, shall Lev 1:11 3548
bring it to Aaron's sons the *p* Lev 2:2 3548
Aaron's sons the *p* shall sprinkle Lev 3:2 3548
among the *p* shall eat thereof Lev 6:29 3548
among the *p* shall eat thereof Lev 7:6 3548
or unto one of his sons the *p* Lev 13:2 3548
shall make an atonement for the *p* Lev 16:33 3548
Speak unto the *p* the sons of Lev 21:1 3548
the *p* which were anointed, whom Num 3:3 3548
And the sons of Aaron, the *p* Num 10:8 3548
shalt come unto the *p* the Levites Deut 17:9 3548
which is before the *p* the Levites Deut 17:18 3548
The *p* the Levites, and all the Deut 18:1 3548
before the LORD, before the *p* Deut 19:17 3548
the *p* the sons of Levi shall come Deut 21:5 3548
the *p* the Levites shall teach you Deut 24:8 3548
the *p* the Levites spake unto all Deut 27:9 3548
it unto the *p* the sons of Levi Deut 31:9 3548
the *p* the Levites bearing it Josh 3:3 3548
And Joshua spake unto the *p* Josh 3:6 3548
thou shalt command the *p* that Josh 3:8 3548
p that bear the ark of the LORD Josh 3:13 3548
the *p* bearing the ark of the Josh 3:14 3548
the feet of the *p* that bare the Josh 3:15 3548
the *p* that bare the ark of the Josh 3:17 3548
the *p* which bare the ark of the Josh 4:9 3548
For the *p* which bare the ark Josh 4:10 3548
of the LORD passed over, and the *p* Josh 4:11 3548
Command the *p* that bear the ark Josh 4:16 3548
Joshua therefore commanded the *p* Josh 4:17 3548
when the *p* that bare the ark of Josh 4:18 3548
seven *p* shall bear before the ark Josh 6:4 3548
the *p* shall blow with the Josh 6:4 3548
the son of Nun called the *p* Josh 6:6 3548
let seven *p* bear seven trumpets Josh 6:6 3548
that the seven *p* bearing the Josh 6:8 3548
the *p* that blew with the trumpets Josh 6:9 3548
the *p* going on, and blowing with Josh 6:9 3548
the *p* took up the ark of the LORD Josh 6:12 3548
seven *p* bearing seven trumpets of Josh 6:13
the *p* going on, and blowing with Josh 6:13 3548
when the *p* blew with the trumpets Josh 6:16 3548
when the *p* blew with the trumpets Josh 6:20 3548
side before the *p* the Levites Josh 8:33 3548
of the children of Aaron, the *p* Josh 21:19 3548

P

his sons were *p* to the tribe of	Judg 18:30	3548
the *p* of the LORD, were there	1Sa 1:3	3548
Therefore neither the *p* of Dagon	1Sa 5:5	3548
the Philistines called for the *p*	1Sa 6:2	3548
house, the *p* that were in Nob	1Sa 22:11	3548
Turn, and slay the *p* of the LORD	1Sa 22:17	3548
to fall upon the *p* of the LORD	1Sa 22:17	3548
Turn thou, and fall upon the *p*	1Sa 22:18	3548
turned, and he fell upon the *p*	1Sa 22:18	3548
And Nob, the city of the *p*	1Sa 22:19	3548
that Saul had slain the LORD's *p*	1Sa 22:21	3548
the son of Abiathar, were the *p*	2Sa 8:17	3548
with thee Zadok and Abiathar the *p*	2Sa 15:35	3548
it to Zadok and Abiathar the *p*	2Sa 15:35	3548
unto Zadok and to Abiathar the *p*	2Sa 17:15	3548
to Zadok and to Abiathar the *p*	2Sa 19:11	3548
and Zadok and Abiathar were the *p*	2Sa 20:25	3548
and Zadok and Abiathar were the *p*	1Kin 4:4	3548
came, and the *p* took up the ark	1Kin 8:3	3548
tabernacle, even those did the *p*	1Kin 8:4	3548
the *p* brought in the ark of the	1Kin 8:6	3548
when the *p* were come out of the	1Kin 8:10	3548
So that the *p* could not stand to	1Kin 8:11	3548
made *p* of the lowest of the	1Kin 12:31	3548
he placed in Beth-el the *p* of the	1Kin 12:32	3548
p of the high places that burn	1Kin 13:2	3548
the people *p* of the high places	1Kin 13:33	3548
one of the *p* of the high places	1Kin 13:33	3548
men, and his kinsfolks, and his *p*	2Kin 10:11	3548
all his servants, and all his *p*	2Kin 10:19	3548
And Jehoash said to the *p*, All the	2Kin 12:4	3548
Let the *p* take it to them, every	2Kin 12:5	3548
year of king Jehoash the *p* had	2Kin 12:6	3548
the priest, and the other *p*	2Kin 12:7	3548
the *p* consented to receive no	2Kin 12:8	3548
the *p* that kept the door put	2Kin 12:9	3548
Carry thither one of the *p* whom	2Kin 17:27	3548
Then one of the *p* whom they had	2Kin 17:28	3548
of them *p* of the high places	2Kin 17:32	3548
scribe, and the elders of the *p*	2Kin 19:2	3548
of Jerusalem with him, and the *p*	2Kin 23:2	3548
the *p* of the second order, and the	2Kin 23:4	3548
And he put down the idolatrous *p*	2Kin 23:5	
he brought all the *p* out of the	2Kin 23:8	3548
where the *p* had burned incense	2Kin 23:8	3548
Nevertheless the *p* of the high	2Kin 23:9	3548
he slew all the *p* of the high	2Kin 23:20	3548
were, the Israelites, the *p*	1Chr 9:2	3548
And of the *p*; Jedaiah	1Chr 9:10	3548
some of the sons of the *p* made	1Chr 9:30	3548
and with them also to the *p*	1Chr 13:2	3548
for Zadok and Abiathar the *p*	1Chr 15:11	3548
So the *p* and the Levites	1Chr 15:14	3548
and Benaiah, and Eliezer, the *p*	1Chr 15:24	3548
Jahaziel the *p* with trumpets	1Chr 16:6	3548
the priest, and his brethren the *p*	1Chr 16:39	3548
the son of Abiathar, were the *p*	1Chr 18:16	3548
the princes of Israel, with the *p*	1Chr 23:2	3548
the chief of the fathers of the *p*	1Chr 24:6	3548
the chief of the fathers of the *p*	1Chr 24:31	3548
Also for the courses of the *p*	1Chr 28:13	3548
And, behold, the courses of the *p*	1Chr 28:21	3548
the sea was for the *p* to wash in	2Chr 4:6	3548
he made the court of the *p*	2Chr 4:9	3548
the tabernacle, these did the *p*	2Chr 5:5	3548
the *p* brought in the ark of the	2Chr 5:7	3548
when the *p* were come out of the	2Chr 5:11	3548
(for all the *p* that were present	2Chr 5:11	3548
twenty *p* sounding with trumpets	2Chr 5:12	3548
So that the *p* could not stand to	2Chr 5:14	3548
let thy *p*, O LORD God, be clothed	2Chr 6:41	3548
the *p* could not enter into the	2Chr 7:2	3548
the *p* waited on their offices	2Chr 7:6	3548
the *p* sounded trumpets before	2Chr 7:6	3548
courses of the *p* to their service	2Chr 8:14	3548
praise and minister before the *p*	2Chr 8:14	3548
of the king unto the *p* and Levites	2Chr 8:15	3548
And the *p* and the Levites that were	2Chr 11:13	3548
he ordained him *p* for the high	2Chr 11:15	3548
ye not cast out the *p* of the LORD	2Chr 13:9	3548
have made you *p* after the manner	2Chr 13:9	3548
and the *p*, which minister unto the	2Chr 13:10	3548
his *p* with sounding trumpets to	2Chr 13:12	3548
the *p* sounded with the trumpets	2Chr 13:14	3548
with them Elishama and Jehoram, *p*	2Chr 17:8	3548
set of the Levites, and of the *p*	2Chr 19:8	3548
entering on the sabbath, of the *p*	2Chr 23:4	3548
the house of the LORD, save the *p*	2Chr 23:6	3548
by the hand of the *p* the Levites	2Chr 23:18	3548
And he gathered together the *p*	2Chr 24:5	3548
with him fourscore *p* of the LORD	2Chr 26:17	3548
but to the *p* the sons of Aaron,	2Chr 26:18	3548
and while he was wroth with the *p*	2Chr 26:19	3548
the *p* in the house of the LORD	2Chr 26:19	3548
the chief priest, and all the *p*	2Chr 26:20	3548
And he brought in the *p* and the	2Chr 29:4	3548
the *p* went into the inner part of	2Chr 29:16	3548
he commanded the *p* the sons of	2Chr 29:21	3548
the *p* received the blood, and	2Chr 29:22	3548
the *p* killed them, and they made	2Chr 29:24	3548
David, and the *p* with the trumpets	2Chr 29:26	3548
But the *p* were too few, so that	2Chr 29:34	3548
until the other *p* had sanctified	2Chr 29:34	3548
to sanctify themselves than the *p*	2Chr 29:34	3548
because the *p* had not sanctified	2Chr 30:3	3548
and the *p* and the Levites were	2Chr 30:15	3548
the *p* sprinkled the blood, which	2Chr 30:16	3548
the *p* praised the LORD day by day	2Chr 30:21	3548
a great number of *p* sanctified	2Chr 30:24	3548
congregation of Judah, with the *p*	2Chr 30:25	3548
Then the *p* the Levites arose and	2Chr 30:27	3548
appointed the courses of the *p*	2Chr 31:2	3548
according to his service, the *p*	2Chr 31:2	3548
to give the portion of the *p*	2Chr 31:4	3548
Hezekiah questioned with the *p*	2Chr 31:9	3548
Shecaniah, in the cities of the *p*	2Chr 31:15	3548
Both to the genealogy of the *p* by	2Chr 31:17	3548
Also of the sons of Aaron the *p*	2Chr 31:19	3548
to all the males among the *p*	2Chr 31:19	3548
bones of the *p* upon their altars	2Chr 34:5	3548
of Jerusalem, and the *p*, and the	2Chr 34:30	3548
he set the *p* in their charges, and	2Chr 35:2	3548
unto the people, to the *p*	2Chr 35:8	3548
gave unto the *p* for the passover	2Chr 35:8	3548
the *p* stood in their place, and	2Chr 35:10	3548
the *p* sprinkled the blood from	2Chr 35:11	3548
for themselves, and for the *p*	2Chr 35:14	3548
because the *p* the sons of Aaron	2Chr 35:14	3548
for the *p* the sons of Aaron	2Chr 35:14	3548
passover as Josiah kept, and the *p*	2Chr 35:18	3548
Moreover all the chief of the *p*	2Chr 36:14	3548
of Judah and Benjamin, and the *p*	Ezr 1:5	3548
The *p*: the children of	Ezr 2:36	3548
And of the children of the *p*	Ezr 2:61	3548
So the *p*, and the Levites, and some	Ezr 2:70	3548
of Jozadak, and his brethren the *p*	Ezr 3:2	3548
remnant of their brethren the *p*	Ezr 3:8	3548
they set the *p* in their apparel	Ezr 3:10	3548
But many of the *p* and Levites and	Ezr 3:12	3548
of the *p* which are at Jerusalem	Ezr 6:9	3549
And the children of Israel, the *p*	Ezr 6:16	3549
they set the *p* in their divisions	Ezr 6:18	3549
For the *p* and the Levites were	Ezr 6:20	3548
and for their brethren the *p*	Ezr 6:20	3548
children of Israel, and of the *p*	Ezr 7:7	3548
the people of Israel, and of his *p*	Ezr 7:13	3549
of the people, and of the *p*	Ezr 7:16	3549
you, that touching any of the *p*	Ezr 7:24	3549
and I viewed the people, and the *p*	Ezr 8:15	3548
twelve of the chief of the *p*	Ezr 8:24	3548
them before the chief of the *p*	Ezr 8:29	3548
So took the *p* and the Levites the	Ezr 8:30	3548
The people of Israel, and the *p*	Ezr 9:1	3548
have we, our kings, and our *p*	Ezr 9:7	3548
arose Ezra, and made the chief *p*	Ezr 10:5	3548
among the sons of the *p* there	Ezr 10:18	3548
told it to the Jews, nor to the *p*	Neh 2:16	3548
rose up with his brethren the *p*	Neh 3:1	3548
And after him repaired the *p*	Neh 3:22	3548
the horse gate repaired the *p*	Neh 3:28	3548
Then I called the *p*, and took an	Neh 5:12	3548
The *p*: the children of	Neh 7:39	3548
And of the *p*: the children	Neh 7:63	3548
So the *p*, and the Levites, and the	Neh 7:73	3548
fathers of all the people, the *p*	Neh 8:13	3548
on our princes, and on our *p*	Neh 9:32	3548
our kings, our princes, our *p*	Neh 9:34	3548
and our princes, Levites, and *p*	Neh 9:38	3548
these were the *p*	Neh 10:8	3548
And the rest of the people, the *p*	Neh 10:28	3548
And we cast the lots among the *p*	Neh 10:34	3548
unto the *p* that minister in the	Neh 10:36	3548
of wine and of oil, unto the *p*	Neh 10:37	3548
the *p* that minister, and the	Neh 10:39	3548
cities, to wit, Israel, the *p*	Neh 11:3	3548
Of the *p*: Jedaiah	Neh 11:10	3548
the residue of Israel, of the *p*	Neh 11:20	3548
Now these are the *p* and the	Neh 12:1	3548
These were the chief of the *p*	Neh 12:7	3548
And in the days of Joiakim were *p*	Neh 12:12	3548
also the *p*, to the reign of	Neh 12:22	3548
And the *p* and the Levites purified	Neh 12:30	3548
And the *p*; Eliakim	Neh 12:41	3548
the portions of the law for the *p*	Neh 12:44	3548
for Judah rejoiced for the *p*	Neh 12:44	3548
and the offerings of the *p*	Neh 13:5	3548
and appointed the wards of the *p*	Neh 13:30	3548
Their *p* fell by the sword	Ps 78:64	3548
Moses and Aaron among his *p*	Ps 99:6	3548
Let thy *p* be clothed with	Ps 132:9	3548
also clothe her *p* with salvation	Ps 132:16	3548
the elders of the *p* covered with	Is 37:2	3548
shall be named the P of the LORD	Is 61:6	3548
And I will also take of them for *p*	Is 66:21	3548
of the *p* that were in Anathoth in	Jer 1:1	3548
thereof, against the *p* thereof	Jer 1:18	3548
The *p* said not, Where is the LORD	Jer 2:8	3548
kings, their princes, and their *p*	Jer 2:26	3548
the *p* shall be astonished, and the	Jer 4:9	3548
the *p* bear rule by their means	Jer 5:31	3548
princes, and the bones of the *p*	Jer 8:1	3548
sit upon David's throne, and the *p*	Jer 13:13	3548
and of the ancients of the *p*	Jer 19:1	3548
So the *p* and the prophets and all	Jer 26:7	3548
unto all the people, that the *p*	Jer 26:8	3548
Then spake the *p* and the prophets	Jer 26:11	3548
and all the people unto the *p*	Jer 26:16	3548
Also I spake to the *p* and to all	Jer 27:16	3548
LORD, in the presence of the *p*	Jer 28:1	3548
Hananiah in the presence of the *p*	Jer 28:5	3548
away captives, and to the *p*	Jer 29:1	3548
the priest, and to all the *p*	Jer 29:25	3548
the soul of the *p* with fatness	Jer 31:14	3548
kings, their princes, their *p*	Jer 32:32	3548
Neither shall the *p* the Levites	Jer 33:18	3548
and with the Levites the *p*	Jer 33:21	3548
Jerusalem, the eunuchs, and the *p*	Jer 34:19	3548
forth into captivity with his *p*	Jer 48:7	3548
shall go into captivity, and his *p*	Jer 49:3	3548
her *p* sigh, her virgins are	Lam 1:4	3548
my *p* and mine elders gave up the	Lam 1:19	3548
and the iniquities of her *p*	Lam 4:13	3548
not the persons of the *p*, they	Lam 4:16	3548
Her *p* have violated my law, and	Eze 22:26	3548
is toward the south, is for the *p*	Eze 40:45	3548
is toward the north is for the *p*	Eze 40:46	3548
where the *p* that approach unto	Eze 42:13	3548
When the *p* enter therein, then	Eze 42:14	3548
thou shalt give to the *p* the	Eze 43:19	3548
the *p* shall cast salt upon them,	Eze 43:24	3548
the *p* shall make your burnt	Eze 43:27	3548
But the *p* the Levites, the sons	Eze 44:15	3548
The *p* shall not eat of any thing	Eze 44:31	3548
of the land shall be for the *p*	Eze 45:4	3548
the *p* shall prepare his burnt	Eze 46:2	3548
into the holy chambers of the *p*	Eze 46:19	3548
the *p* shall boil the trespass	Eze 46:20	3548
And for them, even for the *p*	Eze 48:10	3548
It shall be for the *p* that are	Eze 48:11	3548
the *p* the Levites shall have five	Eze 48:13	3548
Hear ye this, O *p*	Hos 5:1	3548
so the company of *p* murder in the	Hos 6:9	3548
the *p* thereof that rejoiced on it	Hos 10:5	3649
the *p*, the LORD's ministers,	Joel 1:9	3548
Gird yourselves, and lament, ye *p*	Joel 1:13	3548
Let the *p*, the ministers of the	Joel 2:17	3548
the *p* thereof teach for hire, and	Mic 3:11	3548
name of the Chemarims with the *p*	Zeph 1:4	3548
her *p* have polluted the sanctuary	Zeph 3:4	3548
Ask now the *p* concerning the law,	Hag 2:11	3548
the *p* answered and said, No	Hag 2:12	3548
the *p* answered and said, It shall	Hag 2:13	3548
to speak unto the *p* which were in	Zec 7:3	3548
people of the land, and to the *p*	Zec 7:5	3548
the LORD of hosts unto you, O *p*	Mal 1:6	3548
And now, O ye *p*, this commandment	Mal 2:1	3548
he had gathered all the chief *p*	Mt 2:4	749
were with him, but only for the *p*	Mt 12:4	*2409*
the *p* in the temple profane the	Mt 12:5	*2409*
things of the elders and chief *p*	Mt 16:21	749
be betrayed unto the chief *p*	Mt 20:18	749
And when the chief *p* and scribes	Mt 21:15	749
come into the temple, the chief *p*	Mt 21:23	749
And when the chief *p* and Pharisees	Mt 21:45	749
assembled together the chief *p*	Mt 26:3	749
Iscariot, went unto the chief *p*	Mt 26:14	749
and staves, from the chief *p*	Mt 26:47	749
Now the chief *p*, and elders, and	Mt 26:59	749
morning was come, all the chief *p*	Mt 27:1	749
pieces of silver to the chief *p*	Mt 27:3	749
the chief *p* took the silver	Mt 27:6	749
he was accused of the chief *p*	Mt 27:12	749
But the chief *p* and elders	Mt 27:20	749
also the chief *p* mocking him	Mt 27:41	749
of the preparation, the chief *p*	Mt 27:62	749
shewed unto the chief *p* all the	Mt 28:11	749
not lawful to eat but for the *p*	Mk 2:26	*2409*
of the elders, and of the chief *p*	Mk 8:31	749
be delivered unto the chief *p*	Mk 10:33	749
chief *p* heard it, and sought how	Mk 11:18	749
there come to him the chief *p*	Mk 11:27	749
and the chief *p* and the scribes	Mk 14:1	749
the twelve, went unto the chief *p*	Mk 14:10	749
were assembled all the chief *p*	Mk 14:53	749
And the chief *p* and all the council	Mk 14:55	749
in the morning the chief *p* held a	Mk 15:1	749
the chief *p* accused him of many	Mk 15:3	749
p had delivered him for envy	Mk 15:10	749
But the chief *p* moved the people,	Mk 15:11	749
Likewise also the chief *p* mocking	Mk 15:31	749
and Caiaphas being the high *p*	Lk 3:2	749
lawful to eat but for the *p* alone	Lk 6:4	*2409*
rejected of the elders and chief *p*	Lk 9:22	749
Go shew yourselves unto the *p*	Lk 17:14	*2409*
But the chief *p* and the scribes and	Lk 19:47	749
preached the gospel, the chief *p*	Lk 20:1	749
And the chief *p* and the scribes the	Lk 20:19	749
And the chief *p* and scribes sought	Lk 22:2	749
way, and communed with the chief *p*	Lk 22:4	749
Then Jesus said unto the chief *p*	Lk 22:52	749
of the people and the chief *p*	Lk 22:66	749
Then said Pilate to the chief *p*	Lk 23:4	749
And the chief *p* and scribes stood	Lk 23:10	749
had called together the chief *p*	Lk 23:13	749
them and of the chief *p* prevailed	Lk 23:23	749
And how the chief *p* and our rulers	Lk 24:20	749
of John, when the Jews sent *p*	Jn 1:19	*2409*
the chief *p* sent officers to take	Jn 7:32	749
came the officers to the chief *p*	Jn 7:45	749
Then gathered the chief *p*	Jn 11:47	749
Now both the chief *p* and the	Jn 11:57	749
But the chief *p* consulted that	Jn 12:10	749
men and officers from the chief *p*	Jn 18:3	749
the chief *p* have delivered thee	Jn 18:35	749
When the chief *p* therefore	Jn 19:6	749
The chief *p* answered, We have no	Jn 19:15	749
Then said the chief *p* of the Jews	Jn 19:21	749
they spake unto the people, the *p*	Acts 4:1	*2409*
and reported all that the chief *p*	Acts 4:23	749
the chief *p* heard these things,	Acts 5:24	749
a great company of the *p* were	Acts 6:7	*2409*
p to bind all that call on thy	Acts 9:14	749
bring them bound unto the chief *p*	Acts 9:21	749
Sceva, a Jew, and chief of the *p*	Acts 19:14	749
bands, and commanded the chief *p*	Acts 22:30	749
And they came to the chief *p*	Acts 23:14	749
I was at Jerusalem, the chief *p*	Acts 25:15	749
authority from the chief *p*	Acts 26:10	749
and commission from the chief *p*	Acts 26:12	749
(For those *p* were made without an	Heb 7:21	*2409*
And they truly were many *p*	Heb 7:23	*2409*
not daily, as those high *p*	Heb 7:27	749
men high *p* which have infirmity	Heb 7:28	749
seeing that there are *p* that	Heb 8:4	*2409*
the *p* went always into the first	Heb 9:6	*2409*
kings and *p* unto God and his Father	Rev 1:6	*2409*
made us unto our God kings and *p*	Rev 5:10	*2409*
power, but they shall be *p* of God	Rev 20:6	*2409*

PRIESTS'

place where the *p* feet stood firm	Josh 4:3	3548
the soles of the *p* feet were	Josh 4:18	3548

thee, into one of the *p* offices 1Sa 2:36 3548
it was the *p* 2Kin 12:16 3548
silver, and one hundred *p* garments Ezr 2:69 3548
five hundred and thirty *p* garments Neh 7:70 3548
and threescore and seven *p* garments Neh 7:72 3548
certain of the *p* sons with Neh 12:35 3548

PRINCE
thou art a mighty *p* among us Gen 23:6 5387
for as a *p* hast thou power with Gen 32:28
p of the country, saw her, he Gen 34:2 5387
And he said, Who made thee a *p* Ex 2:14 8269
each *p* on his day, for the Num 7:11 5387
of Zuar, *p* of Issachar, did offer Num 7:18 5387
p of the children of Zebulun, did Num 7:24 5387
p of the children of Reuben, did Num 7:30 5387
p of the children of Simeon, did Num 7:36 5387
p of the children of Gad, offered Num 7:42 5387
p of the children of Ephraim, Num 7:48 5387
p of the children of Manasseh Num 7:54 5387
p of the children of Benjamin, Num 7:60 5387
p of the children of Dan, offered Num 7:66 5387
p of the children of Asher, Num 7:72 5387
p of the children of Naphtali, Num 7:78 5387
thyself altogether a *p* over us Num 16:13 8323
him a rod apiece, for each *p* one Num 17:6 5387
a *p* of a chief house among the Num 25:14 5387
the daughter of a *p* of Midian Num 25:18 5387
shall take one *p* of every tribe Num 34:18 5387
the *p* of the tribe of the Num 34:22 5387
The *p* of the children of Joseph, Num 34:23 5387
the *p* of the tribe of the Num 34:24 5387
the *p* of the tribe of the Num 34:25 5387
the *p* of the tribe of the Num 34:26 5387
the *p* of the tribe of the Num 34:27 5387
the *p* of the tribe of the Num 34:28 5387
princes, of each chief house a *p* Josh 22:14 5387
Know ye not that there is a *p* 2Sa 3:38 8269
but I will make him *p* all the 1Kin 11:34 5387
made thee *p* over my people Israel 1Kin 14:7 5057
made thee *p* over my people Israel 1Kin 16:2 5057
p of the children of Judah 1Chr 2:10 5387
he was *p* of the Reubenites 1Chr 5:6 5387
unto Sheshbazzar, the *p* of Judah Ezr 1:8 5387
say, Where is the house of the *p* Job 21:28 5081
as a *p* would I go near unto him Job 31:37 5057
is the destruction of the *p* Prov 14:28 7333
much less do lying lips a *p* Prov 17:7 5081
will intreat the favour of the *p* Prov 19:6 5081
the *p* whom thine eyes have seen Prov 25:7 5081
long forbearing is a *p* persuaded Prov 25:15 7101
The *p* that wanteth understanding Prov 28:16 5057
Father, The *P* of Peace Is 9:6 8269
And this Seraiah was a quiet *p* Jer 51:59 8269
the *p* shall be clothed with Eze 7:27 5387
concerneth the *p* in Jerusalem Eze 12:10 5387
the *p* that is among them shall Eze 12:12 5387
thou, profane wicked *p* of Israel Eze 21:25 5387
of man, say unto the *p* of Tyrus Eze 28:2 5057
no more a *p* of the land of Egypt Eze 30:13 5387
my servant David a *p* among them Eze 34:24 5387
David shall be their *p* for ever Eze 37:25 5387
the chief *p* of Meshech and Tubal, Eze 38:2 5387
the chief *p* of Meshech and Tubal Eze 38:3 5387
the chief *p* of Meshech and Tubal Eze 39:1 5387
It is for the *p* Eze 44:3 5387
the *p*, he shall sit in it to eat Eze 44:3 5387
be for the *p* on the one side Eze 45:7 5387
this oblation for the *p* in Israel Eze 45:16 5387
shall the *p* prepare for himself Eze 45:22 5387
the *p* shall enter by the way of Eze 46:2 5387
the burnt offering that the *p* Eze 46:4 5387
when the *p* shall enter, he shall Eze 46:8 5387
the *p* in the midst of them, when Eze 46:10 5387
Now when the *p* shall prepare a Eze 46:12 5387
If the *p* give a gift unto any of Eze 46:16 5387
after, it shall return to the *p* Eze 46:17 5387
Moreover the *p* shall not take of Eze 46:18 5387
And the residue shall be for the *p* Eze 48:21 5387
against the portions for the *p* Eze 48:21 5387
of Benjamin, shall be for the *p* Eze 48:22 5387
Unto whom the *p* of the eunuchs Dan 1:7 8269
p of the eunuchs that he might Dan 1:8 8269
love with the *p* of the eunuchs Dan 1:9 8269
the *p* of the eunuchs said unto Dan 1:10 8269
whom the *p* of the eunuchs had set Dan 1:11 8269
then the *p* of the eunuchs brought Dan 1:18 8269
himself even to the *p* of the host Dan 8:11 8269
stand up against the *P* of princes Dan 8:25 8269
the *P* shall be seven weeks Dan 9:25 5057
the people of the *p* that shall Dan 9:26 5057
But the *p* of the kingdom of Dan 10:13 8269
to fight with the *p* of Persia Dan 10:20 8269
the *p* of Grecia shall come Dan 10:20 8269
these things, but Michael your *p* Dan 10:21 8269
but a *p* for his own behalf shall Dan 11:18 7101
also the *p* of the covenant Dan 11:22 5057
the great *p* which standeth for Dan 12:1 8269
without a king, and without a *p* Hos 3:4 8269
the *p* asketh, and the judge asketh Mic 7:3 8269
through the *p* of the devils Mt 9:34 758
by Beelzebub the *p* of the devils Mt 12:24 758
by the *p* of the devils casteth he Mk 3:22 758
now shall the *p* of this world be Jn 12:31 758
for the *p* of this world cometh, Jn 14:30 758
because the *p* of this world is Jn 16:11 758
And killed the *P* of life, whom God Acts 3:15 747
with his right hand to be a *P* Acts 5:31 747
according to the *p* of the power Eph 2:2 758
the *p* of the kings of the earth Rev 1:5 758

PRINCE'S
thy feet with shoes, O *p* daughter Song 7:1 5081
it shall be the *p* part to give Eze 45:17 5387
the midst of that which is the *p* Eze 48:22 5387

PRINCES
The *p* also of Pharaoh saw her, and Gen 12:15 8269
twelve *p* shall he beget, and I Gen 17:20 5387
twelve *p* according to their Gen 25:16 5387
p of the tribes of their fathers, Num 1:16 5387
the *p* of Israel, being twelve men Num 1:44 5387
That the *p* of Israel, heads of Num 7:2 5387
who were the *p* of the tribes, and Num 7:2 5387
a wagon for two of the *p*, and for Num 7:3 5387
the *p* offered for dedicating of Num 7:10 5387
even the *p* offered their offering Num 7:10 5387
was anointed, by the *p* of Israel Num 7:84 5387
but with one trumpet, then the *p* Num 10:4 5387
fifty *p* of the assembly, famous Num 16:2 5387
of all their *p* according to the Num 17:2 5387
every one of their *p* gave him a Num 17:6 5387
The *p* digged the well, the nobles Num 21:18 8269
the *p* of Moab abode with Balaam Num 22:8 8269
and said unto the *p* of Balak Num 22:13 8269
the *p* of Moab rose up, and they Num 22:14 8269
And Balak sent yet again *p* Num 22:15 8269
ass, and went with the *p* of Moab Num 22:21 8269
Balaam went with the *p* of Balak Num 22:35 8269
to the *p* that were with him Num 22:40 8269
he, and all the *p* of Moab Num 23:6 8269
and the *p* of Moab with him Num 23:17 8269
the priest, and before the *p* Num 27:2 5387
all the *p* of the congregation, Num 31:13 5387
unto the *p* of the congregation, Num 32:2 5387
before Moses, and before the *p* Num 36:1 5387
the *p* of the congregation sware Josh 9:15 5387
because the *p* of the congregation Josh 9:18 5387
murmured against the *p* Josh 9:18 5387
But all the *p* said unto all the Josh 9:19 5387
the *p* said unto them, Let them Josh 9:21 5387
as the *p* had promised them Josh 9:21 5387
Moses smote with the *p* of Midian Josh 13:21 5387
the son of Nun, and before the *p* Josh 17:4 5387
And with him ten *p*, of each chief Josh 22:14 5387
the *p* of the congregation and Josh 22:30 5387
of Eleazar the priest, and the *p* Josh 22:32 5387
give ear, O ye *p* Judg 5:3 7336
the *p* of Issachar were with Judg 5:15 8269
they took two *p* of the Midianites Judg 7:25 8269
into your hands the *p* of Midian Judg 8:3 8269
the *p* of Succoth said, Are the Judg 8:6 8269
unto him the *p* of Succoth Judg 8:14 8269
p of Gilead said one to another, Judg 10:18 8269
the dunghill, to set them among *p* 1Sa 2:8 5081
Then the *p* of the Philistines 1Sa 18:30 8269
Then said the *p* of the 1Sa 29:3 8269
unto the *p* of the Philistines 1Sa 29:3 8269
the *p* of the Philistines were 1Sa 29:4 8269
the *p* of the Philistines said 1Sa 29:4 8269
notwithstanding the *p* of the 1Sa 29:9 8269
the *p* of the children of Ammon 2Sa 10:3 8269
regardest neither *p* nor servants 2Sa 19:6 8269
And these were the *p* which he had 1Kin 4:2 8269
of war, and his servants, and his *p* 1Kin 9:22 8269
men of the *p* of the provinces 1Kin 20:14 8269
men of the *p* of the provinces 1Kin 20:15 8269
the young men of the *p* of the 1Kin 20:17 8269
So these young men of the *p* of 1Kin 20:19 8269
as the manner was, and the *p* 2Kin 11:14 8269
mother, and his servants, and his *p* 2Kin 24:12 8269
away all Jerusalem, and all the *p* 2Kin 24:14 8269
names were *p* in their families 1Chr 4:38 5387
men of valour, chief of the *p* 1Chr 7:40 5387
But the *p* of the children of 1Chr 19:3 8269
David also commanded all the *p* of 1Chr 22:17 8269
together all the *p* of Israel 1Chr 23:2 8269
them before the king, and the *p* 1Chr 24:6 8269
These were the *p* of the tribes of 1Chr 27:22 8269
assembled all the *p* of Israel 1Chr 28:1 8269
the *p* of the tribes, and the 1Chr 28:1 8269
also the *p* and all the people will 1Chr 28:21 8269
p of the tribes of Israel, and the 1Chr 29:6 8269
And all the *p*, and the mighty men, 1Chr 29:24 8269
to the *p* of Judah, that were 2Chr 12:5 8269
Whereupon the *p* of Israel 2Chr 12:6 8269
of his reign he sent to his *p* 2Chr 17:7 8269
and divers also of the *p* of Israel 2Chr 21:4 8269
Jehoram went forth with his *p* 2Chr 21:9 8269
of Ahab, and found the *p* of Judah 2Chr 22:8 8269
at the entering in, and the *p* 2Chr 23:13 8269
And all the *p* and all the people 2Chr 24:10 8269
of Jehoiada came the *p* of Judah 2Chr 24:17 8269
destroyed all the *p* of the people 2Chr 24:23 8269
and the spoil before the *p* 2Chr 28:14 8269
house of the king, and of the *p* 2Chr 28:21 8269
the *p* commanded the Levites to 2Chr 29:30 8269
king had taken counsel, and his *p* 2Chr 30:2 8269
his *p* throughout all Israel and 2Chr 30:6 8269
of the king and of the *p*, by the 2Chr 30:12 8269
the *p* gave to the congregation a 2Chr 30:24 8269
the *p* came and saw the heaps, they 2Chr 31:8 8269
He took counsel with his *p* 2Chr 32:3 8269
ambassadors of the *p* of Babylon 2Chr 32:31 8269
his *p* gave willingly unto the 2Chr 35:8 8269
of the king, and of his *p* 2Chr 36:18 8269
and before all the king's mighty *p* Ezr 7:28 8269
the *p* had appointed for the Ezr 8:20 8269
the *p* came to me, saying, The Ezr 9:1 8269
yea, the hand of the *p* and rulers Ezr 9:2 8269
according to the counsel of the *p* Ezr 10:8 8269
upon us, on our kings, on our *p* Neh 9:32 8269
Neither have our kings, our *p* Neh 9:34 8269
and our *p*, Levites, and priests, Neh 9:38 8269
Then I brought up the *p* of Judah Neh 12:31 8269
and half of the *p* of Judah Neh 12:32 8269
he made a feast unto all his *p* Est 1:3 8269
p of the provinces, being before Est 1:3 8269
the people and the *p* her beauty Est 1:11 8269
and Memucan, the seven *p* of Persia Est 1:14 8269
answered before the king and the *p* Est 1:16 8269
king only, but also to all the *p* Est 1:16 8269
this day unto all the king's *p* Est 1:18 8269
saying pleased the king and the *p* Est 1:21 8269
made a great feast unto all his *p* Est 2:18 8269
all the *p* that were with him Est 3:1 8269
he had advanced him above the *p* Est 5:11 8269
of one of the king's most noble *p* Est 6:9 8269
Or with *p* that had gold, who Job 3:15 8269
He leadeth *p* away spoiled, and Job 12:19 3548
He poureth contempt upon *p* Job 12:21 5081
The *p* refrained talking, and laid Job 29:9 8269
and to *p*, Ye are ungodly Job 34:18 5081
accepteth not the persons of *p* Job 34:19 8269
mayest make *p* in all the earth Ps 45:16 8269
The *p* of the people are gathered Ps 47:9 5081
the *p* of Judah and their council, Ps 68:27 8269
the *p* of Zebulun Ps 68:27 8269
and the *p* of Naphtali Ps 68:27 8269
P shall come out of Egypt Ps 68:31 2831
He shall cut off the spirit of *p* Ps 76:12 5057
men, and fall like one of the *p* Ps 82:7 8269
yea, all their *p* as Zebah Ps 83:11 5257
To bind his *p* at his pleasure Ps 105:22 8269
He poureth contempt upon *p* Ps 107:40 5081
That he may set him with *p* Ps 113:8 5081
even with the *p* of his people Ps 113:8 5081
LORD than to put confidence in *p* Ps 118:9 5081
P also did sit and speak against Ps 119:23 8269
P have persecuted me without a Ps 119:161 8269
Put not your trust in *p*, nor in Ps 146:3 5081
p, and all judges of the earth Ps 148:11 8269
kings reign, and *p* decree justice Prov 8:15 7336
By me *p* rule, and nobles, even all Prov 8:16 8269
good, nor to strike *p* for equity Prov 17:26 5081
for a servant to have rule over *p* Prov 19:10 8269
of a land many are the *p* thereof Prov 28:2 8269
nor for *p* strong drink Prov 31:4 7336
p walking as servants upon the Eccl 10:7 8269
and thy *p* eat in the morning Eccl 10:16 8269
thy *p* eat in due season, for Eccl 10:17 8269
Thy *p* are rebellious, and Is 1:23 8269
will give children to be their *p* Is 3:4 8269
of his people, and the *p* thereof Is 3:14 8269
Are not my *p* altogether kings Is 10:8 8269
Surely the *p* of Zoan are fools, Is 19:11 8269
The *p* of Zoan are become fools, Is 19:13 8269
the *p* of Noph are deceived Is 19:13 8269
arise, ye *p*, and anoint the shield Is 21:5 8269
city, whose merchants are *p* Is 23:8 8269
For his *p* were at Zoan, and his Is 30:4 8269
his *p* shall be afraid of the Is 31:9 8269
and *p* shall rule in judgment Is 32:1 8269
all her *p* shall be nothing Is 34:12 8269
That bringeth the *p* to nothing Is 40:23 7336
shall come upon *p* as upon morter Is 41:25 5461
profaned the *p* of the sanctuary Is 43:28 8269
p also shall worship, because of Is 49:7 8269
of Judah, against the *p* thereof Jer 1:18 8269
they, their kings, their *p* Jer 2:26 8269
perish, and the heart of the *p* Jer 4:9 8269
of Judah, and the bones of his *p* Jer 8:1 8269
p sitting upon the throne of Jer 17:25 8269
and on horses, they, and their *p* Jer 17:25 8269
and the *p* of Judah, with the Jer 24:1 8269
the king of Judah, and his *p* Jer 24:8 8269
the *p* thereof, to make them a Jer 25:18 8269
Egypt, and his servants, and his *p* Jer 25:19 8269
When the *p* of Judah heard these Jer 26:10 8269
and the prophets unto the *p* Jer 26:11 8269
spake Jeremiah unto all the *p* Jer 26:12 8269
Then said the *p* and all the people Jer 26:16 8269
all his mighty men, and all the *p* Jer 26:21 8269
the *p* of Judah and Jerusalem, and Jer 29:2 8269
anger, they, their kings, their *p* Jer 32:32 8269
Now when all the *p*, and all the Jer 34:10 8269
The *p* of Judah Jer 34:19 8269
the *p* of Jerusalem, the eunuchs, Jer 34:19 8269
his *p* will I give into the hand Jer 34:21 8269
which was by the chamber of the *p* Jer 35:4 8269
all the *p* sat there, even Jer 36:12 8269
the son of Hananiah, and all the *p* Jer 36:12 8269
Therefore all the *p* sent Jehudi Jer 36:14 8269
Then said the *p* unto Baruch Jer 36:19 8269
in the ears of all the *p* which Jer 36:21 8269
Jeremiah, and brought him to the *p* Jer 37:14 8269
Wherefore the *p* were wroth with Jer 37:15 8269
Therefore the *p* said unto the Jer 38:4 8269
unto the king of Babylon's *p* Jer 38:17 8269
forth to the king of Babylon's *p* Jer 38:18 8269
forth to the king of Babylon's *p* Jer 38:22 8269
But if the *p* hear that I have Jer 38:25 8269
Then came all the *p* unto Jeremiah Jer 38:27 8269
all the *p* of the king of Babylon Jer 39:3 8269
of the *p* of the king of Babylon Jer 39:3 8269
and all the king of Babylon's *p* Jer 39:13 7227
the *p* of the king, even ten men Jer 41:1 7227
our fathers, our kings, and our *p* Jer 44:17 8269
fathers, your kings, and your *p* Jer 44:21 8269
his priests and his *p* together Jer 48:7 8269
and his priests and his *p* together Jer 49:3 8269
from thence the king and the *p* Jer 49:38 8269
of Babylon, and upon her *p* Jer 50:35 8269
And I will make drunk her *p* Jer 51:57 8269
also all the *p* of Judah in Riblah Jer 52:10 8269
her *p* are become like harts that Lam 1:6 8269
the kingdom and the *p* thereof Lam 2:2 8269
her *p* are among the Gentiles Lam 2:9 8269
P are hanged up by their hand Lam 5:12 8269
son of Benaiah, *p* of the people Eze 11:1 8269
the *p* thereof, and led them with Eze 17:12 8269
a lamentation for the *p* of Israel Eze 19:1 5387
shall be upon all the *p* of Israel Eze 21:12 5387
the *p* of Israel, every one were Eze 22:6 5387

Her *p* in the midst thereof are Eze 22:27 8269
heads, all of them *p* to look to Eze 23:15 7991
Then all the *p* of the sea shall Eze 26:16 5387
all the *p* of Kedar, they occupied Eze 27:21 5387
is Edom, her kings, and all her *p* Eze 32:29 5387
There be the *p* of the north Eze 32:30 5257
the blood of the *p* of the earth Eze 39:18 5387
my *p* shall no more oppress my Eze 45:8 5387
Let it suffice you, O *p* of Israel Eze 45:9 5387
of the king's seed, and of the *p* Dan 1:3 6579
sent to gather together the *p* Dan 3:2 324
Then the *p*, the governors, and Dan 3:3 324
And the *p*, governors, and captains, Dan 3:27 324
that the king, and his *p*, his Dan 5:2 7261
and the king, and his *p*, his wives, Dan 5:3 7261
kingdom an hundred and twenty *p* Dan 6:1 324
that the *p* might give accounts Dan 6:2 324
above the presidents and *p* Dan 6:3 324
p sought to find occasion against Dan 6:4 324
p assembled together to the king, Dan 6:6 324
kingdom, the governors, and the *p* Dan 6:7 324
stand up against the Prince of *p* Dan 8:25 8269
in thy name to our kings, our *p* Dan 9:6 8269
of face, to our kings, to our *p* Dan 9:8 8269
lo, Michael, one of the chief *p* Dan 10:13 8269
shall be strong, and one of his *p* Dan 11:5 8269
Egypt their gods, with their *p* Dan 11:8 5257
The *p* of Judah were like them Hos 5:10 8269
and the *p* with their lies Hos 7:3 8269
In the day of our king the *p* have Hos 7:5 8269
their *p* shall fall by the sword Hos 7:16 8269
they have made *p*, and I knew it Hos 8:4 8269
for the burden of the king of *p* Hos 8:10 8269
all their *p* are revolters Hos 9:15 8269
thou saidst, Give me a king and *p* Hos 13:10 8269
his *p* together, saith the LORD Amos 1:15 8269
slay all the *p* thereof with him Amos 2:3 8269
ye *p* of the house of Israel Mic 3:1 7101
p of the house of Israel, that Mic 3:9 7101
the *p* shall be a scorn unto them Hab 1:10 7336
that I will punish the *p* Zeph 1:8 8269
Her *p* within her are roaring Zeph 3:3 8269
not the least among the *p* of Juda Mt 2:6 *2232*
Ye know that the *p* of the Mt 20:25 758
nor of the *p* of this world, that 1Cor 2:6 758
Which none of the *p* of this world 1Cor 2:8 758

PRINCESS
p among the provinces, how is she Lam 1:1 8282

PRINCESSES
And he had seven hundred wives, *p* 1Kin 11:3 8282

PRINCIPAL
Take thou also unto thee *p* spices Ex 30:23 7218
he shall even restore it in the *p* Lev 6:5 7218
his trespass with the *p* thereof Num 5:7 7218
the son of Nathan was *p* officer 1Kin 4:5 3548
the *p* scribe of the host, which 2Kin 25:19 8269
one *p* household being taken for 1Chr 24:6 1
even the *p* fathers over against 1Chr 24:31 7218
of Asaph, was the *p* to begin the Neh 11:17 7218
Wisdom is the *p* thing Prov 4:7 7225
broken down the *p* plants thereof Is 16:8 8291
cummin, and cast in the *p* wheat Is 28:25 7795
in the ashes, ye *p* of the flock Jer 25:34 117
nor the *p* of the flock to escape Jer 25:35 117
an howling of the *p* of the flock Jer 25:36 117
the *p* scribe of the host, who Jer 52:25 8269
seven shepherds, and eight *p* men Mic 5:5 5257
p men of the city, at Festus' Acts 25:23

PRINCIPALITIES
for your *p* shall come down, even Jer 13:18 4761
nor life, nor angels, nor *p* Rom 8:38 *746*
To the intent that now unto the *p* Eph 3:10 *746*
flesh and blood, but against *p* Eph 6:12 *746*
be thrones, or dominions, or *p* Col 1:16 *746*
And having spoiled *p* and powers, he Col 2:15 *746*
them in mind to be subject to *p* Titus 3:1 *746*

PRINCIPALITY
Far above all *p*, and power, and Eph 1:21 *746*
him, which is the head of all *p* Col 2:10 *746*

PRINCIPLES
the first *p* of the oracles of God Heb 5:12 *4747*
Therefore leaving the *p* of the Heb 6:1 *746*

PRINT
dead, nor *p* any marks upon you Lev 19:28 5414
thou settest a *p* upon the heels Job 13:27 2707
in his hands the *p* of the nails Jn 20:25 *5179*
my finger into the *p* of the nails Jn 20:25 *5179*

PRINTED
oh that they were *p* in a book Job 19:23 2710

PRISCA (*pris'-cah*) See PRISCILLA. *Same as Priscilla.*
Salute P and Aquila, and the 2Ti 4:19 *4251*

PRISCILLA (*pris-sil'-lah*) See PRISCA. *Wife of Aquila and co-worker of Paul.*
come from Italy, with his wife P Acts 18:2 *4252*
thence into Syria, and with him P Acts 18:18 *4252*
P had heard, they took him unto Acts 18:26 *4252*
Greet P and Aquila my helpers in Rom 16:3 *4252*
P salute you much in the Lord, 1Cor 16:19 *4252*

PRISED
price that I was *p* at of them Zec 11:13 3365

PRISON
took him, and put him into the *p* Gen 39:20
and he was there in the *p* Gen 39:20
the sight of the keeper of the *p* Gen 39:21
the keeper of the *p* committed to Gen 39:22
the prisoners that were in the *p* Gen 39:22
The keeper of the *p* looked not to Gen 39:23
captain of the guard, into the *p* Gen 40:3
Egypt, which were bound in the *p* Gen 40:5
brother, and ye shall be kept in *p* Gen 42:16
be bound in the house of your *p* Gen 42:19 4929
and he did grind in the *p* house Judg 16:21 631
for Samson out of the *p* house Judg 16:25 631
king, Put this fellow in the *p* 1Kin 22:27
shut him up, and bound him in *p* 2Kin 17:4
Jehoiachin king of Judah out of *p* 2Kin 25:27
And changed his *p* garments 2Kin 25:29 3608
the seer, and put him in a *p* house 2Chr 16:10 4115
king, Put this fellow in the *p* 2Chr 18:26
that was by the court of the *p* Neh 3:25 4307
and they stood still in the *p* gate Neh 12:39 4307
Bring my soul out of *p*, that I Ps 142:7 4525
For out of *p* he cometh to reign Eccl 4:14
pit, and shall be shut up in the *p* Is 24:22 4525
out the prisoners from the *p* Is 42:7 4525
in darkness out of the *p* house Is 42:7 3608
and they are hid in *p* houses Is 42:22 3608
He was taken from *p* and from Is 53:8 6115
the opening of the *p* to them that Is 61:1 6495
that thou shouldest put him in *p* Jer 29:26 4115
was shut up in the court of the *p* Jer 32:2 4307
p according to the word of the Jer 32:8 4307
that sat in the court of the *p* Jer 32:12 4307
yet shut up in the court of the *p* Jer 33:1 4307
for they had not put him into *p* Jer 37:4
put him in *p* in the house of Jer 37:15 612
for they had made that the *p* Jer 37:15 3608
people, that ye have put me in *p* Jer 37:18
Jeremiah into the court of the *p* Jer 37:21 4307
remained in the court of the *p* Jer 37:21 4307
that was in the court of the *p* Jer 38:6 4307
remained in the court of the *p* Jer 38:13 4307
abode in the court of the *p* until Jer 38:28 4307
out of the court of the *p* Jer 39:14 4307
was shut up in the court of the *p* Jer 39:15 4307
put him in *p* till the day of his Jer 52:11
and brought him forth out of *p* Jer 52:31 3608
And changed his *p* garments Jer 52:33 3608
heard that John was cast into *p* Mt 4:12 *3860*
officer, and thou be cast into *p* Mt 5:25 *5438*
in the *p* the works of Christ Mt 11:2 *1201*
put him in *p* for Herodias' sake, Mt 14:3 *5438*
sent, and beheaded John in the *p* Mt 14:10 *5438*
but went and cast him into *p* Mt 18:30 *5438*
I was in *p*, and ye came unto me Mt 25:36 *5438*
Or when saw we thee sick, or in *p* Mt 25:39 *5438*
sick, and in *p*, and ye visited me Mt 25:43 *5438*
or naked, or sick, or in *p* Mt 25:44 *5438*
Now after that John was put in *p* Mk 1:14 *3860*
bound him in *p* for Herodias' sake Mk 6:17 *5438*
he went and beheaded him in the *p* Mk 6:27 *5438*
all, that he shut up John in *p* Lk 3:20 *5438*
and the officer cast thee into *p* Lk 12:58 *5438*
to go with thee, both into *p* Lk 22:33 *5438*
and for murder, was cast into *p* Lk 23:19 *5438*
and murder was cast into *p* Lk 23:25 *5438*
For John was not yet cast into *p* Jn 3:24 *5438*
and put them in the common *p* Acts 5:18 *5084*
Lord by night opened the *p* doors Acts 5:19 *5438*
sent to the *p* to have them Acts 5:21 *1201*
came, and found them not in the *p* Acts 5:22 *5438*
The *p* truly found we shut with Acts 5:23 *1201*
the men whom ye put in *p* are Acts 5:25 *5438*
men and women committed them to *p* Acts 8:3 *5438*
apprehended him, he put him in *p* Acts 12:4 *5438*
Peter therefore was kept in *p* Acts 12:5 *5438*
before the door kept the *p* Acts 12:6 *5438*
him, and a light shined in the *p* Acts 12:7 *3612*
Lord had brought him out of the *p* Acts 12:17 *5438*
upon them, they cast them into *p* Acts 16:23 *5438*
thrust them into the inner *p* Acts 16:24 *5438*
foundations of the *p* were shaken Acts 16:26 *1201*
the keeper of the *p* awaking out Acts 16:27 *1200*
sleep, and seeing the *p* doors open Acts 16:27 *5438*
the keeper of the *p* told this Acts 16:36 *1200*
Romans, and have cast us into *p* Acts 16:37 *5438*
And they went out of the *p* Acts 16:40 *5438*
of the saints did I shut up in *p* Acts 26:10 *5438*
and preached unto the spirits in *p* 1Pet 3:19 *5438*
shall cast some of you into *p* Rev 2:10 *5438*
shall be loosed out of his *p* Rev 20:7 *5438*

PRISONER
sighing of the *p* come before thee Ps 79:11 616
To hear the groaning of the *p* Ps 102:20 615
to release unto the people a *p* Mt 27:15 *1198*
And they had then a notable *p* Mt 27:16 *1198*
feast he released unto them one *p* Mk 15:6 *1198*
Paul the *p* called me unto him, and Acts 23:18 *1198*
to me unreasonable to send a *p* Acts 25:27 *1198*
yet was I delivered *p* from Acts 28:17 *1198*
the *p* of Jesus Christ for you Eph 3:1 *1198*
the *p* of the Lord, beseech you Eph 4:1 *1198*
of our Lord, nor of me his *p* 2Ti 1:8 *1198*
a *p* of Jesus Christ, and Timothy Philem 1 *1198*
now also a *p* of Jesus Christ Philem 9 *1198*

PRISONERS
where the king's *p* were bound Gen 39:20 615
all the *p* that were in the prison Gen 39:22 615
Israel, and took some of them *p* Num 21:1 7628
There the *p* rest together Job 3:18 615
the poor, and despiseth not his *p* Ps 69:33 615
The LORD looseth the *p* Ps 146:7 631
they shall bow down under the *p* Is 10:4 616
opened not the house of his *p* Is 14:17 615
Assyria lead away the Egyptians *p* Is 20:4 7628
as *p* are gathered in the pit, and Is 24:22 616
bring out the *p* from the prison Is 42:7 616
That thou mayest say to the *p* Is 49:9 631
his feet all the *p* of the earth Lam 3:34 615
p out of the pit wherein is no Zec 9:11 615
to the strong hold, ye *p* of hope Zec 9:12 615
and the *p* heard them Acts 16:25 *1198*
that the *p* had been fled Acts 16:27 *1198*
certain other *p* unto one named Acts 27:1 *1202*
counsel was to kill the *p* Acts 27:42 *1202*
the *p* to the captain of the guard Acts 28:16 *1198*

PRISONS
up to the synagogues, and into *p* Lk 21:12 *5438*
and delivering into *p* both men Acts 22:4 *5438*
in *p* more frequent, in deaths oft 2Cor 11:23 *5438*

PRIVATE
is of any *p* interpretation 2Pet 1:20 *2398*

PRIVATELY
the disciples came unto him *p* Mt 24:3
into a desert place by ship *p* Mk 6:32
house, his disciples asked him *p* Mk 9:28
and John and Andrew asked him *p* Mk 13:3
went aside *p* into a desert place Lk 9:10
him unto his disciples, and said *p* Lk 10:23
hand, and went with him aside *p* Acts 23:19
but *p* to them which were of Gal 2:2

PRIVILY
sent messengers unto Abimelech *p* Judg 9:31 8649
off the skirt of Saul's robe *p* 1Sa 24:4 3909
his eyes are *p* set against the Ps 10:8 6845
that they may *p* shoot at the Ps 11:2 652
net that they have laid *p* for me Ps 31:4 2934
they commune of laying snares *p* Ps 64:5 2934
Whoso *p* slandereth his neighbour, Ps 101:5 5643
have they *p* laid a snare for me Ps 142:3 2934
let us lurk *p* for the innocent Prov 1:11
they lurk *p* for their own lives Prov 1:18
was minded to put her away *p* Mt 1:19 *2977*
when he had *p* called the wise men Mt 2:7 *2977*
and now do they thrust us out *p* Acts 16:37 *2977*
who came in *p* to spy out our Gal 2:4 *3922*
who *p* shall bring in damnable 2Pet 2:1 *3918*

PRIVY
or hath his *p* member cut off, Deut 23:1 8212
which thine heart is *p* to 1Kin 2:44 3045
entereth into their *p* chambers Eze 21:14 2314
his wife also being *p* to it Acts 5:2 *4894*

PRIZE
run all, but one receiveth the *p* 1Cor 9:24 *1017*
p of the high calling of God in Phil 3:14 *1017*

PROCEED
that *p* out of the candlestick Ex 25:35 3318
any word *p* out of your mouth Josh 6:10 3318
which shall *p* out of thy bowels, 2Sa 7:12 3318
but I will *p* no further Job 40:5 3254
I will *p* to do a marvellous work Is 29:14 3254
for a law shall *p* from me Is 51:4 3318
for they *p* from evil to evil, and Jer 9:3 3318
out of them shall *p* thanksgiving Jer 30:19 3318
their governor shall *p* from the Jer 30:21 3318
dignity shall *p* of themselves Hab 1:7 3318
But those things which *p* out of Mt 15:18 *1607*
out of the heart *p* evil thoughts Mt 15:19 *1831*
p evil thoughts, adulteries, Mk 7:21 *1607*
communication *p* out of your mouth Eph 4:29 *1607*
But they shall *p* no further 2Ti 3:9 *4298*

PROCEEDED
then whatsoever *p* out of her lips Num 30:12 4161
which hath *p* out of your mouth Num 32:24 3318
which hath *p* out of thy mouth Judg 11:36 3318
Elihu also *p*, and said, Job 36:1 3254
words which *p* out of his mouth Lk 4:22 *1607*
for I *p* forth and came from God Jn 8:42 *1831*
he *p* further to take Peter also Acts 12:3 *4369*
And out of the throne *p* lightnings Rev 4:5 *1607*
which sword *p* out of his mouth Rev 19:21 *1607*

PROCEEDETH
The thing *p* from the LORD Gen 24:50 3318
to all that *p* out of his mouth Num 30:2 3318
but by every word that *p* out of Deut 8:3 4161
Wickedness *p* from the wicked 1Sa 24:13 3318
an error which *p* from the ruler Eccl 10:5 3318
mouth of the most High *p* not evil Lam 3:38 3318
therefore wrong judgment *p* Hab 1:4 3318
but by every word that *p* out of Mt 4:4 *1607*
which *p* from the Father, he shall Jn 15:26 *1607*
Out of the same mouth *p* blessing Jas 3:10 *1831*
fire *p* out of their mouth, and Rev 11:5 *1607*

PROCEEDING
p out of the throne of God and of Rev 22:1 *1607*

PROCESS
in *p* of time it came to pass, Gen 4:3 7093
in *p* of time the daughter of Gen 38:12 7235
And it came to pass in *p* of time Ex 2:23 7227
And it came to pass in *p* of time Judg 11:4
came to pass, that in *p* of time 2Chr 21:19

PROCHORUS (*prok'-o-rus*) *A leader in the Jerusalem church.*
the Holy Ghost, and Philip, and P Acts 6:5 *4402*

PROCLAIM
I will *p* the name of the LORD Ex 33:19 7121
which ye shall *p* to be holy Lev 23:2 7121
which ye shall *p* in their seasons Lev 23:4 7121
ye shall *p* on the selfsame day, Lev 23:21 7121
which ye shall *p* to be holy Lev 23:37 7121
p liberty throughout all the land Lev 25:10 7121
against it, then *p* peace unto it Deut 20:10 7121
p in the ears of the people, Judg 7:3 7121
P a fast, and set Naboth on high 1Kin 21:9 7121
P a solemn assembly for Baal 2Kin 10:20 6942
p in all their cities, and in Neh 8:15 5674
p before him, Thus shall it be Est 6:9 7121

Most men will *p* every one his own ... Prov 20:6 7121
to *p* liberty to the captives, and ... Is 61:1 7121
To *p* the acceptable year of the ... Is 61:2 7121
p these words toward the north, ... Jer 3:12 7121
p there this word, and say, Hear ... Jer 7:2 7121
P all these words in the cities ... Jer 11:6 7121
p there the words that I shall ... Jer 19:2 7121
Jerusalem, to *p* liberty unto them ... Jer 34:8 7121
I *p* a liberty for you, saith the ... Jer 34:17 7121
P ye this among the Gentiles ... Joel 3:9 7121
of thanksgiving with leaven, and *p* ... Amos 4:5 7121

PROCLAIMED
there, and *p* the name of the LORD ... Ex 34:5 7121
LORD passed by before him, and *p* ... Ex 34:6 7121
it to be *p* throughout the camp ... Ex 36:6 5674
They *p* a fast, and set Naboth on ... 1Kin 21:12 7121
And they *p* it ... 2Kin 10:20 7121
God *p*, who *p* these words ... 2Kin 23:16 7121
p these things that thou hast ... 2Kin 23:17 7121
p a fast throughout all Judah ... 2Chr 20:3 7121
Then I *p* a fast there, at the ... Ezr 8:21 7121
p before him, Thus shall it be ... Est 6:11 7121
the LORD hath *p* unto the end of ... Is 62:11 8085
that they *p* a fast before the ... Jer 36:9 7121
p a fast, and put on sackcloth, ... Jonah 3:5 7121
And he caused it to be *p* and ... Jonah 3:7 2199
shall be *p* upon the housetops ... Lk 12:3 *2784*

PROCLAIMETH
the heart of fools *p* foolishness ... Prov 12:23 7121

PROCLAIMING
in *p* liberty every man to his ... Jer 34:15 7121
in *p* liberty, every one to his ... Jer 34:17 7121
strong angel *p* with a loud voice ... Rev 5:2 *2784*

PROCLAMATION
and Aaron made *p*, and said, To ... Ex 32:5 7121
Asa made a *p* throughout all Judah ... 1Kin 15:22 8085
there went a *p* throughout the ... 1Kin 22:36 7440
they made a *p* through Judah and ... 2Chr 24:9 6963
to make *p* throughout all Israel ... 2Chr 30:5
that he made a *p* throughout all ... 2Chr 36:22
that he made a *p* throughout all ... Ezr 1:1
they made *p* throughout Judah and ... Ezr 10:7
made a *p* concerning him, that he ... Dan 5:29 3745

PROCURE
Thus might we *p* great evil ... Jer 26:19 6213
the prosperity that I *p* unto it ... Jer 33:9 6213

PROCURED
Hast thou not *p* this unto thyself ... Jer 2:17 6213
thy doings have *p* these things ... Jer 4:18 6213

PROCURETH
diligently seeketh good *p* favour ... Prov 11:27 1245

PRODUCE
P your cause, saith the LORD ... Is 41:21 7126

PROFANE
neither shalt thou *p* the name of ... Lev 18:21 2490
neither shalt thou *p* the name of ... Lev 19:12 2490
sanctuary, and to *p* my holy name ... Lev 20:3 2490
among his people, to *p* himself ... Lev 21:4 2490
not *p* the name of their God ... Lev 21:6 2490
take a wife that is a whore, or *p* ... Lev 21:7 2491
if she *p* herself by playing the ... Lev 21:9 2490
nor *p* the sanctuary of his God ... Lev 21:12 2490
widow, or a divorced woman, or *p* ... Lev 21:14 2491
Neither shall he *p* his seed among ... Lev 21:15 2490
that he *p* not my sanctuaries ... Lev 21:23 2490
that they *p* not my holy name in ... Lev 22:2 2490
and die therefore, if they *p* it ... Lev 22:9 2490
they shall not *p* the holy things ... Lev 22:15 2490
Neither shall ye *p* my holy name ... Lev 22:32 2490
that ye do, and *p* the sabbath day ... Neh 13:17 2490
For both prophet and priest are *p* ... Jer 23:11 2610
p wicked prince of Israel, whose ... Eze 21:25 2491
difference between the holy and *p* ... Eze 22:26 2455
day into my sanctuary to *p* it ... Eze 23:39 2490
I will *p* my sanctuary, the ... Eze 24:21 2490
as *p* out of the mountain of God ... Eze 28:16 2490
the sanctuary and the *p* place ... Eze 42:20 2455
difference between the holy and *p* ... Eze 44:23 2455
shall be a *p* place for the city, ... Eze 48:15 2455
the same maid, to *p* my holy name ... Amos 2:7 2490
in the temple *p* the sabbath ... Mt 12:5 *953*
hath gone about to *p* the temple ... Acts 24:6 *953*
and for sinners, for unholy and *p* ... 1Ti 1:9 *952*
But refuse *p* and old wives' fables ... 1Ti 4:7 *952*
to thy trust, avoiding *p* and vain ... 1Ti 6:20 *952*
But shun *p* and vain babblings ... 2Ti 2:16 *952*
or *p* person, as Esau, who for one ... Heb 12:16 *952*

PROFANED
because he hath *p* the hallowed ... Lev 19:8 2490
thou hast *p* his crown by casting ... Ps 89:39 2490
Therefore I have *p* the princes of ... Is 43:28 2490
things, and hast *p* my sabbaths ... Eze 22:8 2490
law, and have *p* mine holy things ... Eze 22:26 2490
my sabbaths, and I am *p* among them. Eze 22:26 2490
same day, and have *p* my sabbaths ... Eze 23:38 2490
my sanctuary, when it was *p* ... Eze 25:3 2490
they *p* my holy name, when they ... Eze 36:20 2490
of Israel had *p* among the heathen ... Eze 36:21 2490
which ye have *p* among the heathen ... Eze 36:22 2490
which was *p* among the heathen, ... Eze 36:23 2490
which ye have *p* in the midst of ... Eze 36:23 2490
But ye have *p* it, in that ye say, ... Mal 1:12 2490
for Judah hath *p* the holiness of ... Mal 2:11 2490

PROFANENESS
is *p* gone forth into all the land ... Jer 23:15 2613

PROFANETH
the whore, she *p* her father ... Lev 21:9 2490

PROFANING
upon Israel by *p* the sabbath ... Neh 13:18 2490
by *p* the covenant of our fathers ... Mal 2:10 2490

PROFESS
I *p* this day unto the LORD thy ... Deut 26:3 5046
And then will I *p* unto them ... Mt 7:23 *3670*
They *p* that they know God ... Titus 1:16 *3670*

PROFESSED
they glorify God for your *p* ... 2Cor 9:13 *3671*
hast *p* a good profession before ... 1Ti 6:12 *3670*

PROFESSING
P themselves to be wise, they ... Rom 1:22 5335
But (which becometh women *p* ... 1Ti 2:10 *1861*
Which some *p* have erred ... 1Ti 6:21 *1861*

PROFESSION
a good *p* before many witnesses ... 1Ti 6:12 *3671*
Apostle and High Priest of our *p* ... Heb 3:1 *3671*
of God, let us hold fast our *p* ... Heb 4:14 *3671*
Let us hold fast the *p* of our ... Heb 10:23 *3671*

PROFIT
what *p* shall this birthright do ... Gen 25:32
What *p* is it if we slay our ... Gen 37:26 1215
which cannot *p* nor deliver ... 1Sa 12:21 3276
for the king's *p* to suffer them ... Est 3:8 7737
what *p* should we have, if we pray ... Job 21:15 3276
the strength of their hands *p* me ... Job 30:2
What *p* shall I have, if I be ... Job 35:3 3276
may *p* the son of man ... Job 35:8
What *p* is there in my blood, when ... Ps 30:9 1215
Treasures of wickedness *p* nothing ... Prov 10:2 3276
Riches *p* not in the day of wrath ... Prov 11:4 3276
In all labour there is *p* ... Prov 14:23 4195
What *p* hath a man of all his ... Eccl 1:3 3504
there was no *p* under the sun ... Eccl 2:11 3504
What *p* hath he that worketh in ... Eccl 3:9 3504
Moreover the *p* of the earth is ... Eccl 5:9 3504
what *p* hath he that hath laboured ... Eccl 5:16 3504
by it there is *p* to them that see ... Eccl 7:11 3148
of a people that could not *p* them ... Is 30:5 3276
nor be an help nor *p* ... Is 30:5 3276
to a people that shall not *p* them ... Is 30:6 3276
delectable things shall not *p* ... Is 44:9 3276
if so be thou shalt be able to *p* ... Is 47:12 3276
thy God which teacheth thee to *p* ... Is 48:17 3276
for they shall not *p* thee ... Is 57:12 3276
walked after things that do not *p* ... Jer 2:8 3276
glory for that which doth not *p* ... Jer 2:11 3276
in lying words, that cannot *p* ... Jer 7:8 3276
to pain, but shall not *p* ... Jer 12:13 3276
and things wherein there is no *p* ... Jer 16:19 3276
shall not *p* this people at all ... Jer 23:32 3276
what *p* is it that we have kept ... Mal 3:14 1215
For what shall it *p* a man ... Mk 8:36 *5623*
or what *p* is there of ... Rom 3:1 *5622*
And this I speak for your own *p* ... 1Cor 7:35 *4851*
own *p*, but the *p* of many ... 1Cor 10:33 *4851*
is given to every man to *p* withal ... 1Cor 12:7 *4851*
with tongues, what shall I *p* you ... 1Cor 14:6 *5623*
Christ shall *p* you nothing ... Gal 5:2 *5623*
strive not about words to no *p* ... 2Ti 2:14 *5539*
the word preached did not *p* them ... Heb 4:2 *5623*
but he for our *p*, that we might ... Heb 12:10 *4851*
What doth it *p*, my brethren, ... Jas 2:14 *3786*
what doth it *p* ... Jas 2:16 *3786*

PROFITABLE
Can a man be *p* unto God, as he ... Job 22:2 5532
is wise may be *p* unto himself ... Job 22:2 5532
but wisdom is *p* to direct ... Eccl 10:10 3504
image that is *p* for nothing ... Is 44:10 3276
was marred, it was *p* for nothing ... Jer 13:7 6743
for it is *p* for thee that one of ... Mt 5:29 *4851*
for it is *p* for thee that one of ... Mt 5:30 *4851*
back nothing that was *p* unto you ... Acts 20:20 *4851*
godliness is *p* unto all things ... 1Ti 4:8 *5624*
is *p* for doctrine, for reproof, ... 2Ti 3:16 *5624*
for he is *p* to me for the ... 2Ti 4:11 *2173*
things are good and *p* unto men ... Titus 3:8 *5624*
unprofitable, but now *p* to thee ... Philem 11 *2173*

PROFITED
which was right, and it *p* me not ... Job 33:27 7737
thou mightest be *p* by me ... Mt 15:5 *5623*
For what is a man *p*, if he shall ... Mt 16:26 *5623*
thou mightest be *p* by me ... Mk 7:11 *5623*
p in the Jews' religion above ... Gal 1:14 *4298*
which have not *p* them that have ... Heb 13:9 *5623*

PROFITETH
It *p* a man nothing that he should ... Job 34:9 5532
What *p* the graven image that the ... Hab 2:18 3276
the flesh *p* nothing ... Jn 6:63 *5623*
For circumcision verily *p* ... Rom 2:25 *5623*
have not charity, it *p* me nothing ... 1Cor 13:3 *5623*
For bodily exercise *p* little ... 1Ti 4:8

PROFITING
that thy *p* may appear to all ... 1Ti 4:15 *4297*

PROFOUND
revolters are *p* to make slaughter ... Hos 5:2 6009

PROGENITORS
above the blessings of my *p* unto ... Gen 49:26 2029

PROGNOSTICATORS
the stargazers, the monthly *p* ... Is 47:13 3045

PROLONG
ye shall not *p* your days upon it, ... Deut 4:26 748
that thou mayest *p* thy days upon ... Deut 4:40 748
that ye may *p* your days in the ... Deut 5:33 748
that ye may *p* your days in the ... Deut 11:9 748
to the end that he may *p* his days ... Deut 17:20 748
and that thou mayest *p* thy days ... Deut 22:7 748
that ye shall not *p* your days ... Deut 30:18 748
ye shall *p* your days in the land ... Deut 32:47 748
mine end, that I should *p* my life ... Job 6:11 748
neither shall he *p* the perfection ... Job 15:29 5186
Thou wilt *p* the king's life ... Ps 61:6 3254
covetousness shall *p* his days ... Prov 28:16 748
neither shall he *p* his days ... Eccl 8:13 748
see his seed, he shall *p* his days ... Is 53:10 748

PROLONGED
that thy days may be *p*, and that ... Deut 5:16 748
and that thy days may be *p* ... Deut 6:2 748
the state thereof shall be *p* ... Prov 28:2 748
hundred times, and his days be *p* ... Eccl 8:12 748
come, and her days shall not be *p* ... Is 13:22 4900
of Israel, saying, The days are *p* ... Eze 12:22 748
it shall be no more *p* ... Eze 12:25 4900
none of my words be *p* any more ... Eze 12:28 4900
their lives were *p* for a season ... Dan 7:12

PROLONGETH
The fear of the LORD *p* days ... Prov 10:27 3254
that *p* his life in his wickedness ... Eccl 7:15 748

PROMISE
and ye shall know my breach of *p* ... Num 14:34
failed one word of all his good *p* ... 1Kin 8:56 1697
let thy *p* unto David my father be ... 2Chr 1:9 1697
should do according to this *p* ... Neh 5:12 1697
that performeth not this *p* ... Neh 5:13 1697
people did according to this *p* ... Neh 5:13 1697
doth his *p* fail for evermore ... Ps 77:8 562
For he remembered his holy *p* ... Ps 105:42 1697
I send the *p* of my Father upon ... Lk 24:49 *1860*
but wait for the *p* of the Father ... Acts 1:4 *1860*
Father the *p* of the Holy Ghost ... Acts 2:33 *1860*
For the *p* is unto you, and to your ... Acts 2:39 *1860*
when the time of the *p* drew nigh ... Acts 7:17 *1860*
p raised unto Israel a Saviour ... Acts 13:23 *1860*
how that the *p* which was made ... Acts 13:32 *1860*
ready, looking for a *p* from thee ... Acts 23:21 *1860*
p made of God unto our fathers ... Acts 26:6 *1860*
Unto which *p* our twelve tribes, ... Acts 26:7
For the *p*, that he should be the ... Rom 4:13 *1860*
the *p* made of none effect ... Rom 4:14 *1860*
to the end the *p* might be sure to ... Rom 4:16 *1860*
at the *p* of God through unbelief ... Rom 4:20 *1860*
but the children of the *p* are ... Rom 9:8 *1860*
For this is the word of *p* ... Rom 9:9 *1860*
that we might receive the *p* of ... Gal 3:14 *1860*
should make the *p* of none effect ... Gal 3:17 *1860*
be of the law, it is no more of *p* ... Gal 3:18 *1860*
but God gave it to Abraham by *p* ... Gal 3:18 *1860*
come to whom the *p* was made ... Gal 3:19 *1861*
that the *p* by faith of Jesus ... Gal 3:22 *1860*
seed, and heirs according to the *p* ... Gal 3:29 *1860*
but he of the freewoman was by *p* ... Gal 4:23 *1860*
Isaac was, are the children of *p* ... Gal 4:28 *1860*
sealed with that holy Spirit of *p* ... Eph 1:13 *1860*
strangers from the covenants of *p* ... Eph 2:12 *1860*
partakers of his *p* in Christ by ... Eph 3:6 *1860*
is the first commandment with *p* ... Eph 6:2 *1860*
having *p* of the life that now is, ... 1Ti 4:8 *1860*
according to the *p* of life which ... 2Ti 1:1 *1860*
a *p* being left us of entering ... Heb 4:1 *1860*
For when God made *p* to Abraham ... Heb 6:13 *1861*
endured, he obtained the *p* ... Heb 6:15 *1860*
to shew unto the heirs of *p* the ... Heb 6:17 *1860*
the *p* of eternal inheritance ... Heb 9:15 *1860*
of God, ye might receive the *p* ... Heb 10:36 *1860*
he sojourned in the land of *p* ... Heb 11:9 *1860*
the heirs with him of the same *p* ... Heb 11:9 *1860*
through faith, received not the *p* ... Heb 11:39 *1860*
While they *p* them liberty, they ... 2Pet 2:19 *1861*
Where is the *p* of his coming ... 2Pet 3:4 *1860*
is not slack concerning his *p* ... 2Pet 3:9 *1860*
we, according to his *p*, look for ... 2Pet 3:13 *1862*
this is the *p* that he hath ... 1Jn 2:25 *1860*

PROMISED
give you, according as he hath *p* ... Ex 12:25 1696
the place which the LORD hath *p* ... Num 14:40 559
and bless you, as he hath *p* you ... Deut 1:11 1696
God of thy fathers hath *p* thee ... Deut 6:3 1696
into the land which he *p* them ... Deut 9:28 1696
as the LORD thy God *p* him ... Deut 10:9 1696
thy border, as he hath *p* thee ... Deut 12:20 1696
God blesseth thee, as he *p* thee ... Deut 15:6 1696
he *p* to give unto thy fathers ... Deut 19:8 1696
which thou hast *p* with thy mouth ... Deut 23:23 1696
people, as he hath *p* thee ... Deut 26:18 1696
God of thy fathers hath *p* thee ... Deut 27:3 1696
as the princes had *p* them ... Josh 9:21 1696
unto your brethren, as he *p* them ... Josh 22:4 1696
the LORD your God hath *p* unto you ... Josh 23:5 1696
for you, as he hath *p* you ... Josh 23:10 1696
which the LORD your God *p* you ... Josh 23:15 1696
thou hast *p* this goodness unto ... 2Sa 7:28 1696
hath made me an house, as he *p* ... 1Kin 2:24 1696
gave Solomon wisdom, as he *p* him ... 1Kin 5:12 1696
throne of Israel, as the LORD *p* ... 1Kin 8:20 1696
according to all that he *p* ... 1Kin 8:56 1696
which he *p* by the hand of Moses ... 1Kin 8:56 1696
as I *p* to David thy father, ... 1Kin 9:5 1696
as he *p* him to give him alway a ... 2Kin 8:19 559
hast *p* this goodness unto thy ... 1Chr 17:26 1696
throne of Israel, as the LORD *p* ... 2Chr 6:10 1696
father that which thou hast *p* him ... 2Chr 6:15 1696
father that which thou hast *p* him ... 2Chr 6:16 1696
as he *p* to give a light to him and ... 2Chr 21:7 559
thou hadst *p* to their fathers ... Neh 9:23 559
p to pay to the king's treasuries ... Est 4:7 559
all the good that I have *p* them ... Jer 32:42 1696

P

I have p unto the house of Israel ... Jer 33:14 1696
Whereupon he p with an oath to ... Mt 14:7 *3670*
were glad, and p to give him money ... Mk 14:11 *1861*
the mercy p to our fathers ... Lk 1:72
And he p, and sought opportunity to ... Lk 22:6 *1843*
yet he p that he would give it to ... Acts 7:5 *1861*
(Which he had p afore by his ... Rom 1:2 *4279*
persuaded that, what he had p ... Rom 4:21 *1861*
lie, p before the world began ... Titus 1:2 *1861*
(for he is faithful that p ... Heb 10:23 *1861*
she judged him faithful who had p ... Heb 11:11 *1861*
but now he hath p, saying, Yet ... Heb 12:26 *1861*
which the Lord hath p to them ... Jas 1:12 *1861*
he hath p to them that love him ... Jas 2:5 *1861*
is the promise that he hath p us ... 1Jn 2:25 *1861*

PROMISEDST
David my father that thou p him ... 1Kin 8:24 1696
David my father that thou p him ... 1Kin 8:25 1696
p them that they should go in to ... Neh 9:15 559

PROMISES
and the service of God, and the p ... Rom 9:4 *1860*
to confirm the p made unto the ... Rom 15:8 *1860*
For all the p of God in him are ... 2Cor 1:20 *1860*
therefore these p dearly beloved ... 2Cor 7:1 *1860*
and his seed were the p made ... Gal 3:16 *1860*
the law then against the p of God ... Gal 3:21 *1860*
faith and patience inherit the p ... Heb 6:12 *1860*
and blessed him that had the p ... Heb 7:6 *1860*
was established upon better p ... Heb 8:6 *1860*
faith, not having received the p ... Heb 11:13 *1860*
he that had received the p ... Heb 11:17 *1860*
wrought righteousness, obtained p ... Heb 11:33 *1860*
us exceeding great and precious p ... 2Pet 1:4 *1862*

PROMISING
his wicked way, by p him life ... Eze 13:22 2421

PROMOTE
For I will p thee unto very great ... Num 22:17 3513
able indeed to p thee to honour ... Num 22:37 3513
I thought to p thee unto great ... Num 24:11 3513
p Haman the son of Hammedatha the. Est 3:1 1431
Exalt her, and she shall p thee ... Prov 4:8 7311

PROMOTED
go to be p over the trees ... Judg 9:9 5128
go to be p over the trees ... Judg 9:11 5128
go to be p over the trees ... Judg 9:13 5128
things wherein the king had p him ... Est 5:11 1431
Then the king p Shadrach, Meshach ... Dan 3:30 6744

PROMOTION
For p cometh neither from the ... Ps 75:6 7311
but shame shall be the p of fools ... Prov 3:35 7311

PRONOUNCE
that a man shall p with an oath ... Lev 5:4 981
look on him, and p him unclean ... Lev 13:3
the priest shall p him clean ... Lev 13:6
the priest shall p him unclean ... Lev 13:8
and the priest shall p him unclean ... Lev 13:11
he shall p him clean that hath ... Lev 13:13
raw flesh, and p him to be unclean ... Lev 13:15
then the priest shall p him clean ... Lev 13:17
the priest shall p him unclean ... Lev 13:20
the priest shall p him unclean ... Lev 13:22
and the priest shall p him clean ... Lev 13:23
the priest shall p him unclean ... Lev 13:25
the priest shall p him unclean ... Lev 13:27
and the priest shall p him clean ... Lev 13:28
the priest shall p him unclean ... Lev 13:30
then the priest shall p him clean ... Lev 13:34
and the priest shall p him clean ... Lev 13:37
the priest shall p him utterly ... Lev 13:44
to p it clean, or to p it ... Lev 13:59
shall p him clean, and shall let ... Lev 14:7
priest shall p the house clean ... Lev 14:48
he could not frame to p it right ... Judg 12:6 1696

PRONOUNCED
but that he p this prophecy ... Neh 6:12 1696
hath p evil against thee, for the ... Jer 11:17 1696
Wherefore hath the LORD p all ... Jer 16:10 1696
nation, against whom I have p ... Jer 18:8 1696
the evil that I have p against it ... Jer 19:15 1696
words which I have p against it ... Jer 25:13 1696
evil that he hath p against you ... Jer 26:13 1696
evil which he had p against them ... Jer 26:19 1696
for I have p the word, saith the ... Jer 34:5 1696
evil that I have p against them ... Jer 35:17 1696
LORD hath p against this people ... Jer 36:7 1696
He p all these words unto me with ... Jer 36:18 7126
evil that I have p against them ... Jer 36:31 1691
The LORD thy God hath p this evil ... Jer 40:2 1691

PRONOUNCING
p with his lips to do evil, or to ... Lev 5:4 981

PROOF
that I might know the p of you ... 2Cor 2:9 *1382*
the p of your love, and of our ... 2Cor 8:24 *1732*
Since ye seek a p of Christ ... 2Cor 13:3 *1382*
But ye know the p of him, that, ... Phil 2:22 *1382*
make full p of thy ministry ... 2Ti 4:5 *4135*

PROOFS
his passion by many infallible p ... Acts 1:3 *5039*

PROPER
my God, I have of mine own p good ... 1Chr 29:3 5459
field is called in their p tongue ... Acts 1:19 *2398*
every man hath his p gift of God ... 1Cor 7:7 *2398*
because they saw he was a p child ... Heb 11:23 *791*

PROPHECIES
but whether there be p, they ... 1Cor 13:8 *4394*
according to the p which went ... 1Ti 1:18 *4394*

PROPHECY
in the p of Ahijah the Shilonite, ... 2Chr 9:29 5016
the p of Oded the prophet, he ... 2Chr 15:8 5016
he pronounced this p against me ... Neh 6:12 5016
Agur the son of Jakeh, even the p ... Prov 30:1 4853
the p that his mother taught him ... Prov 31:1 4853
and to seal up the vision and p ... Dan 9:24 5030
them is fulfilled the p of Esaias ... Mt 13:14 *4394*
that is given to us, whether p ... Rom 12:6 *4394*
to another p ... 1Cor 12:10 *4394*
And though I have the gift of p ... 1Cor 13:2 *4394*
thee, which was given thee by p ... 1Ti 4:14 *4394*
have also a more sure word of p ... 2Pet 1:19 *4397*
that no p of the scripture is of ... 2Pet 1:20 *4394*
For the p came not in old time by ... 2Pet 1:21 *4394*
that hear the words of this p ... Rev 1:3 *4394*
rain not in the days of their p ... Rev 11:6 *4394*
of Jesus is the spirit of p ... Rev 19:10 *4394*
the sayings of the p of this book ... Rev 22:7 *4394*
the sayings of the p of this book ... Rev 22:10 *4394*
the words of the p of this book ... Rev 22:18 *4394*
the words of the book of this p ... Rev 22:19 *4394*

PROPHESIED
spirit rested upon them, they p ... Num 11:25 5012
and they p in the camp ... Num 11:26 5012
and he p among them ... 1Sa 10:10 5012
he p among the prophets, then the ... 1Sa 10:11 5012
he p in the midst of the house ... 1Sa 18:10 5012
of Saul, and they also p ... 1Sa 19:20 5012
messengers, and they p likewise ... 1Sa 19:21 5012
the third time, and they p also ... 1Sa 19:21 5012
him also, and he went on, and p ... 1Sa 19:23 5012
p before Samuel in like manner, ... 1Sa 19:24 5012
they p until the time of the ... 1Kin 18:29 5012
and all the prophets p before them ... 1Kin 22:10 5012
And all the prophets p so, saying, ... 1Kin 22:12 5012
which p according to the order of ... 1Chr 25:2 5012
who p with a harp, to give thanks ... 1Chr 25:3 5012
for he never p good unto me ... 2Chr 18:7 5012
and all the prophets p before them ... 2Chr 18:9 5012
And all the prophets p so, saying, ... 2Chr 18:11 5012
of Mareshah p against Jehoshaphat ... 2Chr 20:37 5012
p unto the Jews that were in ... Ezr 5:1 5013
me, and the prophets p by Baal ... Jer 2:8 5012
that Jeremiah p these things ... Jer 20:1 5012
friends, to whom thou hast p lies ... Jer 20:6 5012
they p in Baal, and caused my ... Jer 23:13 5012
not spoken to them, yet they p ... Jer 23:21 5012
which Jeremiah hath p against all ... Jer 25:13 5012
Why hast thou p in the name of ... Jer 26:9 5012
for he hath p against this city, ... Jer 26:11 5012
Micah the Morasthite p in the ... Jer 26:18 5012
that p in the name of the LORD ... Jer 26:20 5012
who p against this city and ... Jer 26:20 5012
thy words which thou hast p ... Jer 28:6 5012
before thee of old p both against ... Jer 28:8 5012
that Shemaiah hath p unto you ... Jer 29:31 5012
your prophets which p unto you ... Jer 37:19 5012
And it came to pass, when I p ... Eze 11:13 5012
So I p as I was commanded ... Eze 37:7 5012
and as I p, there was a noise, and ... Eze 37:7 5012
So I p as he commanded me, and the .. Eze 37:10 5012
which p in those days many years ... Eze 38:17 5012
one of his vision, when he hath p ... Zec 13:4 5012
Lord, have we not p in thy name ... Mt 7:22 *4395*
prophets and the law p until John ... Mt 11:13 *4395*
Well hath Esaias p of you ... Mk 7:6 *4395*
filled with the Holy Ghost, and p ... Lk 1:67 *4395*
he p that Jesus should die for ... Jn 11:51 *4395*
and they spake with tongues, and p ... Acts 19:6 *4395*
tongues, but rather that ye p ... 1Cor 14:5 *4395*
who p of the grace that should ... 1Pet 1:10 *4395*
p of these, saying, Behold, the ... Jude 14 *4395*

PROPHESIETH
The prophet which p of peace ... Jer 28:9 5012
he p of the times that are far ... Eze 12:27 5012
thrust him through when he p ... Zec 13:3 5012
or p with her head uncovered ... 1Cor 11:5 *4395*
But he that p speaketh unto men ... 1Cor 14:3 *4395*
but he that p edifieth the church ... 1Cor 14:4 *4395*
for greater is he that p than he ... 1Cor 14:5 *4395*

PROPHESY
Eldad and Medad do p in the camp ... Num 11:27 5012
and they shall p ... 1Sa 10:5 5012
thee, and thou shalt p with them ... 1Sa 10:6 5012
for he doth not p good concerning ... 1Kin 22:8 5012
he would p no good concerning me ... 1Kin 22:18 5012
Jeduthun, who should p with harps ... 1Chr 25:1 5012
that he would not p good unto me ... 2Chr 18:17 5012
P not unto us right things, speak ... Is 30:10 2372
unto us smooth things, p deceits ... Is 30:10 2372
The prophets p falsely, and the ... Jer 5:31 5012
P not in the name of the LORD, ... Jer 11:21 5012
The prophets p lies in my name ... Jer 14:14 5012
they p unto you a false vision and ... Jer 14:14 5012
the prophets that p in my name ... Jer 14:15 5012
the people to whom they p shall ... Jer 14:16 5012
the LORD had sent him to p ... Jer 19:14 5012
of the prophets that p unto you ... Jer 23:16 5012
that p lies in my name, saying, I ... Jer 23:25 5012
heart of the prophets that p lies ... Jer 23:26 5012
against them that p false dreams ... Jer 23:32 5012
Therefore p thou against them all ... Jer 25:30 5012
sent me to p against this house ... Jer 26:12 5012
For they p a lie unto you, to ... Jer 27:10 5012
for they p a lie unto you ... Jer 27:14 5012
yet they p a lie in my name ... Jer 27:15 5012
and the prophets that p unto you ... Jer 27:15 5012
of your prophets that p unto you ... Jer 27:16 5012
for they p a lie unto you ... Jer 27:16 5012
For they p falsely unto you in my ... Jer 29:9 5012
which p a lie unto you in my name ... Jer 29:21 5012
up, saying, Wherefore dost thou p ... Jer 32:3 5012
and thou shalt p against it ... Eze 4:7 5012
of Israel, and p against them, ... Eze 6:2 5012
p against them, p, O son ... Eze 11:4 5012
p against the prophets of Israel ... Eze 13:2 5012
the prophets of Israel that p ... Eze 13:2 5012
that p out of their own hearts ... Eze 13:2 5012
which p concerning Jerusalem ... Eze 13:16 5012
which p out of their own heart ... Eze 13:17 5012
and p thou against them, ... Eze 13:17 5012
p against the forest of the south ... Eze 20:46 5012
p against the land of Israel, ... Eze 21:2 5012
Son of man, p, and say, Thus saith ... Eze 21:9 5012
Thou therefore, son of man, p ... Eze 21:14 5012
And thou, son of man, p and say, ... Eze 21:28 5012
the Ammonites, and p against them ... Eze 25:2 5012
against Zidon, and p against it, ... Eze 28:21 5012
p against him, and against all ... Eze 29:2 5012
Son of man, p and say, Thus saith ... Eze 30:2 5012
p against the shepherds of Israel ... Eze 34:2 5012
the shepherds of Israel, p ... Eze 34:2 5012
mount Seir, and p against it, ... Eze 35:2 5012
p unto the mountains of Israel, ... Eze 36:1 5012
Therefore p and say, Thus saith ... Eze 36:3 5012
P therefore concerning the land ... Eze 36:6 5012
P upon these bones, and say unto ... Eze 37:4 5012
P unto the wind, p, son of ... Eze 37:9 5012
Therefore p and say unto them, ... Eze 37:12 5012
and Tubal, and p against him, ... Eze 38:2 5012
Therefore, son of man, p and say ... Eze 38:14 5012
p against Gog, and say, Thus saith ... Eze 39:1 5012
sons and your daughters shall p ... Joel 2:28 5012
the prophets, saying, P not ... Amos 2:12 5012
GOD hath spoken, who can but p ... Amos 3:8 5012
and there eat bread, and p there ... Amos 7:12 5012
But p not again any more at ... Amos 7:13 5012
me, Go, p unto my people Israel ... Amos 7:15 5012
P not against Israel, and drop not ... Amos 7:16 5012
P ye not, say they to them that ... Mic 2:6 5197
ye not, say they to them that p ... Mic 2:6 5197
they shall not p to them, that ... Mic 2:6 5197
I will p unto thee of wine and of ... Mic 2:11 5197
pass, that when any shall yet p ... Zec 13:3 5197
well did Esaias p of you ... Mt 15:7 *4395*
P unto us, thou Christ, Who is he ... Mt 26:68 *4395*
buffet him, and to say unto him, P ... Mk 14:65 *4395*
the face, and asked him, saying, P ... Lk 22:64 *4395*
sons and your daughters shall p ... Acts 2:17 *4395*
and they shall p ... Acts 2:18 *4395*
daughters, virgins, which did p ... Acts 21:9 *4395*
let us p according to the ... Rom 12:6
we know in part, and we p in part ... 1Cor 13:9 *4395*
gifts, but rather that ye may p ... 1Cor 14:1 *4395*
But if all p, and there come in ... 1Cor 14:24 *4395*
For ye may all p one by one ... 1Cor 14:31 *4395*
Wherefore, brethren, covet to p ... 1Cor 14:39 *4395*
Thou must p again before many ... Rev 10:11 *4395*
they shall p a thousand two ... Rev 11:3 *4395*

PROPHESYING
And when he had made an end of p ... 1Sa 10:13 5012
saw the company of the prophets p ... 1Sa 19:20 5012
the p of Haggai the prophet ... Ezr 6:14 5017
Every man praying or p, having ... 1Cor 11:4 *4395*
or by knowledge, or by p ... 1Cor 14:6 *4394*
but p serveth not for them that ... 1Cor 14:22 *4394*

PROPHESYINGS
Despise not p ... 1Th 5:20 *4394*

PROPHET
for he is a p, and he shall pray ... Gen 20:7 5030
Aaron thy brother shall be thy p ... Ex 7:1 5030
If there be a p among you ... Num 12:6 5030
If there arise among you a p ... Deut 13:1 5030
hearken unto the words of that p ... Deut 13:3 5030
And that p, or that dreamer of ... Deut 13:5 5030
thee a P from the midst of thee ... Deut 18:15 5030
I will raise them up a P from ... Deut 18:18 5030
But the p, which shall presume to ... Deut 18:20 5030
other gods, even that p shall die ... Deut 18:20 5030
When a p speaketh in the name of ... Deut 18:22 5030
spoken, but the p hath spoken it ... Deut 18:22 5030
there arose not a p since in ... Deut 34:10 5030
That the LORD sent a p unto the ... Judg 6:8 5030
established to be a p of the LORD ... 1Sa 3:20 5030
for he that is now called a P was ... 1Sa 9:9 5030
the p Gad said unto David, Abide ... 1Sa 22:5 5030
the king said unto Nathan the p ... 2Sa 7:2 5030
sent by the hand of Nathan the p ... 2Sa 12:25 5030
of the LORD came unto the p Gad ... 2Sa 24:11 5030
son of Jehoiada, and Nathan the p ... 1Kin 1:8 5030
But Nathan the p, and Benaiah, and ... 1Kin 1:10 5030
Nathan the p also came in ... 1Kin 1:22 5030
king, saying, Behold Nathan the p ... 1Kin 1:23 5030
Zadok the priest, and Nathan the p ... 1Kin 1:32 5030
Nathan the p anoint him there ... 1Kin 1:34 5030
Zadok the priest, and Nathan the p ... 1Kin 1:38 5030
Zadok the priest, and Nathan the p ... 1Kin 1:44 5030
Nathan the p have anointed him ... 1Kin 1:45 5030
that the p Ahijah the Shilonite ... 1Kin 11:29 5030
there dwelt an old p in Beth-el ... 1Kin 13:11 5030
I am a p also as thou art ... 1Kin 13:18 5030
unto the p that brought him back ... 1Kin 13:20 5030
for the p whom he had brought ... 1Kin 13:23 5030
in the city where the old p dwelt ... 1Kin 13:25 5030
when the p that brought him back ... 1Kin 13:26 5030
the p took up the carcase of the ... 1Kin 13:29 5030
the old p came to the city, to ... 1Kin 13:29 5030
behold, there is Ahijah the p ... 1Kin 14:2 5030
hand of his servant Ahijah the p ... 1Kin 14:18 5030
also by the hand of the p Jehu ... 1Kin 16:7 5030
against Baasha by Jehu the p ... 1Kin 16:12 5030
I only, remain a p of the LORD ... 1Kin 18:22 5030
that Elijah the p came near ... 1Kin 18:36 5030

thou anoint to be p in thy room	1Kin 19:16	5030
there came a p unto Ahab king of	1Kin 20:13	5030
the p came to the king of Israel,	1Kin 20:22	5030
So the p departed, and waited for	1Kin 20:38	5030
not here a p of the LORD besides	1Kin 22:7	5030
Is there not here a p of the LORD	2Kin 3:11	5030
with the p that is in Samaria	2Kin 5:3	5030
know that there is a p in Israel	2Kin 5:8	5030
if the p had bid thee do some	2Kin 5:13	5030
the p that is in Israel, telleth	2Kin 6:12	5030
Elisha the p called one of the	2Kin 9:1	5030
man, even the young man the p	2Kin 9:4	5030
Jonah, the son of Amittai, the p	2Kin 14:25	5030
to Isaiah the p the son of Amoz	2Kin 19:2	5030
the p Isaiah the son of Amoz came	2Kin 20:1	5030
Isaiah the p cried unto the LORD	2Kin 20:11	5030
Isaiah the p unto king Hezekiah	2Kin 20:14	5030
with the bones of the p that came	2Kin 23:18	5030
that David said to Nathan the p	1Chr 17:1	5030
and in the book of Nathan the p	1Chr 29:29	5030
in the book of Nathan the p	2Chr 9:29	5030
came Shemaiah the p to Rehoboam	2Chr 12:5	5030
in the book of Shemaiah the p	2Chr 12:15	5030
in the story of the p Iddo	2Chr 13:22	5030
and the prophecy of Oded the p	2Chr 15:8	5030
not here a p of the LORD besides	2Chr 18:6	5030
writing to him from Elijah the p	2Chr 21:12	5030
Amaziah, and he sent unto him a p	2Chr 25:15	5030
Then the p forbare, and said, I	2Chr 25:16	5030
first and last, did Isaiah the p	2Chr 26:22	5030
But a p of the LORD was there,	2Chr 28:9	5030
the king's seer, and Nathan the p	2Chr 29:25	5030
the p Isaiah the son of Amoz,	2Chr 32:20	5030
in the vision of Isaiah the p	2Chr 32:32	5030
from the days of Samuel the p	2Chr 35:18	5030
p speaking from the mouth of the	2Chr 36:12	5030
Then the prophets, Haggai the p	Ezr 5:1	5029
the prophesying of Haggai the p	Ezr 6:14	5029
when Nathan the p came unto him	Ps 51:t	5030
there is no more any p	Ps 74:9	5030
man of war, the judge, and the p	Is 3:2	5030
the p that teacheth lies, he is	Is 9:15	5030
the p have erred through strong	Is 28:7	5030
unto Isaiah the p the son of Amoz	Is 37:2	5030
Isaiah the p the son of Amoz came	Is 38:1	5030
Isaiah the p unto king Hezekiah	Is 39:3	5030
thee a p unto the nations	Jer 1:5	5030
from the p even unto the priest	Jer 6:13	5030
from the p even unto the priest	Jer 8:10	5030
yea, both the p and the priest go	Jer 14:18	5030
the wise, nor the word from the p	Jer 18:18	5030
Then Pashur smote Jeremiah the p	Jer 20:2	5030
For both p and priest are profane	Jer 23:11	5030
The p that hath a dream, let him	Jer 23:28	5030
And when this people, or the p	Jer 23:33	5030
And as for the p, and the priest,	Jer 23:34	5030
Thus shalt thou say to the p	Jer 23:37	5030
The which Jeremiah the p spake	Jer 25:2	5030
Hananiah the son of Azur the p	Jer 28:1	5030
p Jeremiah said unto the p	Jer 28:5	5030
Even the p Jeremiah said, Amen	Jer 28:6	5030
The p which prophesieth of peace,	Jer 28:9	5030
word of the p shall come to pass	Jer 28:9	5030
then shall the p be known	Jer 28:9	5030
Then Hananiah the p took the yoke	Jer 28:10	5030
from off the p Jeremiah's neck	Jer 28:10	5030
the p Jeremiah went his way	Jer 28:11	5030
the LORD came unto Jeremiah the p	Jer 28:12	
after that Hananiah the p had	Jer 28:12	5030
off the neck of the p Jeremiah	Jer 28:12	5030
Then said the p Jeremiah unto	Jer 28:15	5030
Jeremiah unto Hananiah the p	Jer 28:15	5030
So Hananiah the p died the same	Jer 28:17	5030
p sent from Jerusalem unto the	Jer 29:1	5030
is mad, and maketh himself a p	Jer 29:26	5012
which maketh himself a p to you	Jer 29:27	5012
in the ears of Jeremiah the p	Jer 29:29	5030
Jeremiah the p was shut up in the	Jer 32:2	5030
Then Jeremiah the p spake all	Jer 34:6	5030
that Jeremiah the p commanded him	Jer 36:8	5030
the scribe and Jeremiah the p	Jer 36:26	5030
which he spake by the p Jeremiah	Jer 37:2	5030
the priest to the p Jeremiah	Jer 37:3	5030
of the LORD unto the p Jeremiah	Jer 37:6	5030
and he took Jeremiah the p	Jer 37:13	5030
they have done to Jeremiah the p	Jer 38:9	5030
Jeremiah the p out of the dungeon	Jer 38:10	5030
took Jeremiah the p unto him into	Jer 38:14	5030
And said unto Jeremiah the p	Jer 42:2	5030
Jeremiah the p said unto them	Jer 42:4	5030
son of Shaphan, and Jeremiah the p	Jer 43:6	5030
The word that Jeremiah the p	Jer 45:1	5030
the p against the Gentiles	Jer 46:1	5030
the LORD spake to Jeremiah the p	Jer 46:13	5030
the p against the Philistines	Jer 47:1	5030
p against Elam in the beginning	Jer 49:34	5030
the Chaldeans by Jeremiah the p	Jer 50:1	5030
The word which Jeremiah the p	Jer 51:59	5030
the p be slain in the sanctuary	Lam 2:20	5030
there hath been a p among them	Eze 2:5	5030
shall they seek a vision of the p	Eze 7:26	5030
his face, and cometh to the p	Eze 14:4	5030
cometh to a p to enquire of him	Eze 14:7	5030
if the p be deceived when he hath	Eze 14:9	5030
I the LORD have deceived that p	Eze 14:9	5030
the punishment of the p shall be	Eze 14:10	5030
that a p hath been among them	Eze 33:33	5030
the LORD came to Jeremiah the p	Dan 9:2	5030
the p also shall fall with thee	Hos 4:5	5030
the p is a fool, the spiritual	Hos 9:7	5030
but the p is a snare of a fowler	Hos 9:8	5030
by a p the LORD brought Israel	Hos 12:13	5030
Egypt, and by a p was he preserved	Hos 12:13	5030
and said to Amaziah, I was no p	Amos 7:14	5030
even be the p of this people	Mic 2:11	5197
which Habakkuk the p did see	Hab 1:1	5030
of Habakkuk the p upon Shigionoth	Hab 3:1	5030
the p unto Zerubbabel the son of	Hag 1:1	5030
word of the LORD by Haggai the p	Hag 1:3	5030
God, and the words of Haggai the p	Hag 1:12	5030
word of the LORD by the p Haggai	Hag 2:1	5030
word of the LORD by Haggai the p	Hag 2:10	5030
Berechiah, the son of Iddo the p	Zec 1:1	5030
Berechiah, the son of Iddo the p	Zec 1:7	5030
But he shall say, I am no p	Zec 13:5	5030
I will send you Elijah the p	Mal 4:5	5030
was spoken of the Lord by the p	Mt 1:22	4396
for thus it is written by the p	Mt 2:5	4396
was spoken of the Lord by the p	Mt 2:15	4396
which was spoken by Jeremy the p	Mt 2:17	4396
was spoken of by the p Esaias	Mt 3:3	4396
which was spoken by Esaias the p	Mt 4:14	4396
which was spoken by Esaias the p	Mt 8:17	4396
He that receiveth a p in the name	Mt 10:41	4396
of a p shall receive a prophet's	Mt 10:41	4396
for to see? A p?	Mt 11:9	4396
I say unto you, and more than a p	Mt 11:9	4396
which was spoken by Esaias the p	Mt 12:17	4396
it, but the sign of the p Jonas	Mt 12:39	4396
which was spoken by the p	Mt 13:35	4396
A p is not without honour, save	Mt 13:57	4396
because they counted him as a p	Mt 14:5	4396
it, but the sign of the p Jonas	Mt 16:4	4396
which was spoken by the p	Mt 21:4	4396
This is Jesus the p of Nazareth	Mt 21:11	4396
for all hold John as a p	Mt 21:26	4396
because they took him for a p	Mt 21:46	4396
spoken of by Daniel the p	Mt 24:15	4396
which was spoken by Jeremy the p	Mt 27:9	4396
which was spoken by the p	Mt 27:35	4396
A p is not without honour, but in	Mk 6:4	4396
And others said, That it is a p	Mk 6:15	4396
John, that he was a p indeed	Mk 11:32	4396
spoken of by Daniel the p	Mk 13:14	4396
be called the p of the Highest	Lk 1:76	4396
book of the words of Esaias the p	Lk 3:4	4396
unto him the book of the p Esaias	Lk 4:17	4396
No p is accepted in his own	Lk 4:24	4396
in the time of Eliseus the p	Lk 4:27	4396
That a great p is risen up among	Lk 7:16	4396
for to see? A p?	Lk 7:26	4396
unto you, and much more than a p	Lk 7:26	4396
a greater p than John the Baptist	Lk 7:28	4396
saying, This man, if he were a p	Lk 7:39	4396
it, but the sign of Jonas the p	Lk 11:29	4396
that a p perish out of Jerusalem	Lk 13:33	4396
be persuaded that John was a p	Lk 20:6	4396
which was a p mighty in deed and	Lk 24:19	4396
Art thou that p	Jn 1:21	4396
of the Lord, as said the p Esaias	Jn 1:23	4396
Christ, nor Elias, neither that p	Jn 1:25	4396
Sir, I perceive that thou art a p	Jn 4:19	4396
that a p hath no honour in his	Jn 4:44	4396
This is of a truth that p that	Jn 6:14	4396
said, Of a truth this is the P	Jn 7:40	4396
for out of Galilee ariseth no p	Jn 7:52	4396
He said, He is a p	Jn 9:17	4396
Esaias the p might be fulfilled	Jn 12:38	4396
which was spoken by the p Joel	Acts 2:16	4396
Therefore being a p, and knowing	Acts 2:30	4396
A p shall the Lord your God raise	Acts 3:22	4396
soul, which will not hear that p	Acts 3:23	4396
A p shall the Lord your God raise	Acts 7:37	4396
as saith the p,	Acts 7:48	4396
in his chariot read Esaias the p	Acts 8:28	4396
and heard him read the p Esaias	Acts 8:30	4396
thee, of whom speaketh the p this	Acts 8:34	4396
a certain sorcerer, a false p	Acts 13:6	5578
fifty years, until Samuel the p	Acts 13:20	4396
came down from Judaea a certain p	Acts 21:10	4396
by Esaias the p unto our fathers	Acts 28:25	4396
any man think himself to be a p	1Cor 14:37	4396
even a p of their own, said, The	Titus 1:12	4396
voice forbad the madness of the p	2Pet 2:16	4396
out of the mouth of the false p	Rev 16:13	5578
with him the false p that wrought	Rev 19:20	5578
the beast and the false p are	Rev 20:10	5578

PROPHETESS

And Miriam the p, the sister of	Ex 15:20	5031
And Deborah, a p, the wife of	Judg 4:4	5031
Asahiah, went unto Huldah the p	2Kin 22:14	5031
appointed, went to Huldah the p	2Chr 34:22	5031
on the p Noadiah, and the rest of	Neh 6:14	5031
And I went unto the p	Is 8:3	5031
And there was one Anna, a p	Lk 2:36	4398
which calleth herself a p	Rev 2:20	4398

PROPHET'S

prophet, neither was I an p son	Amos 7:14	5030
prophet shall receive a p reward	Mt 10:41	4396

PROPHETS

that all the LORD's people were p	Num 11:29	5030
thou shalt meet a company of p	1Sa 10:5	5030
behold, a company of p met him	1Sa 10:10	5030
behold, he prophesied among the p	1Sa 10:11	5030
Is Saul also among the p	1Sa 10:11	5030
proverb, Is Saul also among the p	1Sa 10:12	5030
the company of the p prophesying	1Sa 19:20	5030
say, Is Saul also among the p	1Sa 19:24	5030
by dreams, nor by Urim, nor by p	1Sa 28:6	5030
me no more, neither by p, nor by	1Sa 28:15	5030
Jezebel cut off the p of the LORD	1Kin 18:4	5030
that Obadiah took an hundred p	1Kin 18:4	5030
Jezebel slew the p of the LORD	1Kin 18:13	5030
the LORD's p by fifty in a cave	1Kin 18:13	5030
the p of Baal four hundred and	1Kin 18:19	5030
the p of the groves four hundred,	1Kin 18:19	5030
gathered the p together unto	1Kin 18:20	5030
but Baal's p are four hundred and	1Kin 18:22	5030
And Elijah said unto the p of Baal	1Kin 18:25	5030
unto them, Take the p of Baal	1Kin 18:40	5030
slain all the p with the sword	1Kin 19:1	5030
slain thy p with the sword	1Kin 19:10	5030
slain thy p with the sword	1Kin 19:14	5030
p said unto his neighbour in the	1Kin 20:35	5030
him that he was of the p	1Kin 20:41	5030
of Israel gathered the p together	1Kin 22:6	5030
all the p prophesied before them	1Kin 22:10	5030
all the p prophesied so, saying,	1Kin 22:12	5030
the words of the p declare good	1Kin 22:13	5030
spirit in the mouth of all his p	1Kin 22:22	5030
in the mouth of all these thy p	1Kin 22:23	5030
the sons of the p that were at	2Kin 2:3	5030
the sons of the p that were at	2Kin 2:5	5030
men of the sons of the p went	2Kin 2:7	5030
when the sons of the p which were	2Kin 2:15	5030
get thee to the p of thy father	2Kin 3:13	5030
and to the p of thy mother	2Kin 3:13	5030
of the sons of the p unto Elisha	2Kin 4:1	5030
the sons of the p were sitting	2Kin 4:38	5030
pottage for the sons of the p	2Kin 4:38	5030
young men of the sons of the p	2Kin 5:22	5030
the sons of the p said unto	2Kin 6:1	5030
one of the children of the p	2Kin 9:1	5030
the blood of my servants the p	2Kin 9:7	5030
call unto me all the p of Baal	2Kin 10:19	5030
and against Judah, by all the p	2Kin 17:13	5030
sent to you by my servants the p	2Kin 17:13	5030
said by all his servants the p	2Kin 17:23	5030
LORD spake by his servants the p	2Kin 21:10	5030
him, and the priests, and the p	2Kin 23:2	5030
he spake by his servants the p	2Kin 24:2	5030
mine anointed, and do my p no harm	1Chr 16:22	5030
together of p four hundred men	2Chr 18:5	5030
all the p prophesied before them	2Chr 18:9	5030
all the p prophesied so, saying,	2Chr 18:11	5030
the words of the p declare good	2Chr 18:12	5030
spirit in the mouth of all his p	2Chr 18:21	5030
in the mouth of these thy p	2Chr 18:22	5030
believe his p, so shall ye	2Chr 20:20	5030
Yet he sent p to them, to bring	2Chr 24:19	5030
commandment of the LORD by his p	2Chr 29:25	5030
his words, and misused his p	2Chr 36:16	5030
Then the p, Haggai the prophet,	Ezr 5:1	5029
with them were the p of God	Ezr 5:2	5029
commanded by thy servants the p	Ezr 9:11	5030
thou hast also appointed p to	Neh 6:7	5030
Noadiah, and the rest of the p	Neh 6:14	5030
slew thy p which testified	Neh 9:26	5030
them by thy spirit in thy p	Neh 9:30	5030
and on our priests, and on our p	Neh 9:32	5030
mine anointed, and do my p no harm	Ps 105:15	5030
the p and your rulers, the seers	Is 29:10	5030
and to the p, Prophesy not unto us	Is 30:10	2374
the p prophesied by Baal, and	Jer 2:8	5030
and their priests, and their p	Jer 2:26	5030
own sword hath devoured your p	Jer 2:30	5030
astonished, and the p shall wonder	Jer 4:9	5030
the p shall become wind, and the	Jer 5:13	5030
The p prophesy falsely, and the	Jer 5:31	5030
unto you all my servants the p	Jer 7:25	5030
priests, and the bones of the p	Jer 8:1	5030
throne, and the priests, and the p	Jer 13:13	5030
the p say unto them, Ye shall not	Jer 14:13	5030
The p prophesy lies in my name	Jer 14:14	5030
the p that prophesy in my name	Jer 14:15	5030
famine shall those p be consumed	Jer 14:15	5030
me is broken because of the p	Jer 23:9	5030
seen folly in the p of Samaria	Jer 23:13	5030
I have seen also in the p of	Jer 23:14	5030
LORD of hosts concerning the p	Jer 23:15	5030
for from the p of Jerusalem is	Jer 23:15	5030
of the p that prophesy unto you	Jer 23:16	5030
I have not sent these p, yet they	Jer 23:21	5030
I have heard what the p said	Jer 23:25	5030
heart of the p that prophesy lies	Jer 23:26	5030
they are p of the deceit of their	Jer 23:26	5030
behold, I am against the p	Jer 23:30	5030
Behold, I am against the p	Jer 23:31	5030
unto you all his servants the p	Jer 25:4	5030
to the words of my servants the p	Jer 26:5	5030
So the priests and the p and all	Jer 26:7	5030
people, that the priests and the p	Jer 26:8	5030
the p unto the princes and to all	Jer 26:11	5030
unto the priests and to the p	Jer 26:16	5030
hearken not ye to your p, nor to	Jer 27:9	5030
of the p that speak unto you	Jer 27:14	5030
the p that prophesy unto you	Jer 27:15	5030
of your p that prophesy unto you	Jer 27:16	5030
But if they be p, and if the word	Jer 27:18	5030
The p that have been before me and	Jer 28:8	5030
and to the priests, and to the p	Jer 29:1	5030
Let not your p and your diviners,	Jer 29:8	5030
hath raised us up p in Babylon	Jer 29:15	5030
unto them by my servants the p	Jer 29:19	5030
their priests, and their p	Jer 32:32	5030
unto you all my servants the p	Jer 35:15	5030
Where are now your p which	Jer 37:19	5030
unto you all my servants the p	Jer 44:4	5030
her p also find no vision from	Lam 2:9	5030
Thy p have seen vain and foolish	Lam 2:14	5030
For the sins of her p, and the	Lam 4:13	5030
prophesy against the p of Israel	Eze 13:2	5030
Woe unto the foolish p, that	Eze 13:3	5030
thy p are like the foxes in the	Eze 13:4	5030
be upon the p that see vanity	Eze 13:9	5030
the p of Israel which prophesy	Eze 13:16	5030
of her p in the midst thereof	Eze 22:25	5030
her p have daubed them with	Eze 22:28	5030
by my servants the p of Israel	Eze 38:17	5030
hearkened unto thy servants the p	Dan 9:6	5030

before us by his servants the *p* ... Dan 9:10 5030
have I hewed them by the *p* ... Hos 6:5 5030
I have also spoken by the *p* ... Hos 12:10 5030
by the ministry of the *p* ... Hos 12:10 5030
And I raised up of your sons for *p* ... Amos 2:11 5030
and commanded the *p*, saying, ... Amos 2:12 5030
secret unto his servants the *p* ... Amos 3:7 5030
the *p* that make my people err ... Mic 3:5 5030
the sun shall go down over the *p* ... Mic 3:6 5030
the *p* thereof divine for money ... Mic 3:11 5030
Her *p* are light and treacherous ... Zeph 3:4 5030
unto whom the former *p* have cried ... Zec 1:4 5030
and the *p*, do they live for ever ... Zec 1:5 5030
I commanded my servants the *p* ... Zec 1:6 5030
of the LORD of hosts, and to the *p* ... Zec 7:3 5030
LORD hath cried by the former *p* ... Zec 7:7 5030
in his spirit by the former *p* ... Zec 7:12 5030
these words by the mouth of the *p* ... Zec 8:9 5030
and also I will cause the *p* ... Zec 13:2 5030
that the *p* shall be ashamed every ... Zec 13:4 5030
which was spoken by the *p* ... Mt 2:23 *4396*
they the *p* which were before you ... Mt 5:12 *4396*
come to destroy the law, or the *p* ... Mt 5:17 *4396*
for this is the law and the *p* ... Mt 7:12 *4396*
Beware of false *p*, which come to ... Mt 7:15 *5578*
For all the *p* and the law ... Mt 11:13 *4396*
I say unto you, That many *p* ... Mt 13:17 *4396*
others, Jeremias, or one of the *p* ... Mt 16:14 *4396*
hang all the law and the *p* ... Mt 22:40 *4396*
ye build the tombs of the *p* ... Mt 23:29 *4396*
with them in the blood of the *p* ... Mt 23:30 *4396*
of them which killed the *p* ... Mt 23:31 *4396*
behold, I send unto you *p* ... Mt 23:34 *4396*
thou that killest the *p*, and ... Mt 23:37 *4396*
And many false *p* shall rise ... Mt 24:11 *5578*
arise false Christs, and false *p* ... Mt 24:24 *5578*
of the *p* might be fulfilled ... Mt 26:56 *4396*
As it is written in the *p* ... Mk 1:2 *4396*
is a prophet, or as one of the *p* ... Mk 6:15 *4396*
and others, One of the *p* ... Mk 8:28 *4396*
false *p* shall rise, and shall shew ... Mk 13:22 *5578*
spake by the mouth of his holy *p* ... Lk 1:70 *4396*
did their fathers unto the *p* ... Lk 6:23 *4396*
did their fathers to the false *p* ... Lk 6:26 *5578*
one of the old *p* was risen again ... Lk 9:8 *4396*
one of the old *p* is risen again ... Lk 9:19 *4396*
For I tell you, that many *p* ... Lk 10:24 *4396*
ye build the sepulchres of the *p* ... Lk 11:47 *4396*
wisdom of God, I will send them *p* ... Lk 11:49 *4396*
That the blood of all the *p* ... Lk 11:50 *4396*
and Isaac, and Jacob, and all the *p* ... Lk 13:28 *4396*
Jerusalem, which killest the *p* ... Lk 13:34 *4396*
The law and the *p* were until John ... Lk 16:16 *4396*
him, They have Moses and the *p* ... Lk 16:29 *4396*
If they hear not Moses and the *p* ... Lk 16:31 *4396*
things that are written by the *p* ... Lk 18:31 *4396*
all that the *p* have spoken ... Lk 24:25 *4396*
beginning at Moses and all the *p* ... Lk 24:27 *4396*
in the law of Moses, and in the *p* ... Lk 24:44 *4396*
whom Moses in the law, and the *p* ... Jn 1:45 *4396*
It is written in the *p*, And they ... Jn 6:45 *4396*
Abraham is dead, and the *p* ... Jn 8:52 *4396*
and the *p* are dead ... Jn 8:53 *4396*
shewed by the mouth of all his *p* ... Acts 3:18 *4396*
his holy *p* since the world began ... Acts 3:21 *4396*
all the *p* from Samuel and those ... Acts 3:24 *4396*
Ye are the children of the *p* ... Acts 3:25 *4396*
is written in the book of the *p* ... Acts 7:42 *4396*
Which of the *p* have not your ... Acts 7:52 *4396*
To him give all the *p* witness ... Acts 10:43 *4396*
in these days came *p* from ... Acts 11:27 *4396*
that was at Antioch certain *p* ... Acts 13:1 *4396*
the *p* the rulers of the synagogue ... Acts 13:15 *4396*
nor yet the voices of the *p* which ... Acts 13:27 *4396*
you, which is spoken of in the *p* ... Acts 13:40 *4396*
to this agree the words of the *p* ... Acts 15:15 *4396*
being *p* also themselves, exhorted ... Acts 15:32 *4396*
written in the law and in the *p* ... Acts 24:14 *4396*
things than those which the *p* ... Acts 26:22 *4396*
Agrippa, believest thou the *p* ... Acts 26:27 *4396*
the law of Moses, and out of the *p* ... Acts 28:23 *4396*
by his *p* in the holy scriptures ... Rom 1:2 *4396*
witnessed by the law and the *p* ... Rom 3:21 *4396*
Lord, they have killed thy *p* ... Rom 11:3 *4396*
and by the scriptures of the *p* ... Rom 16:26 *4397*
first apostles, secondarily *p* ... 1Cor 12:28 *4396*
are all *p*? ... 1Cor 12:29 *4396*
Let the *p* speak two or three, and ... 1Cor 14:29 *4396*
the *p* are subject to the *p* ... 1Cor 14:32 *4396*
foundation of the apostles and *p* ... Eph 2:20 *4396*
holy apostles and *p* by the Spirit ... Eph 3:5 *4396*
and some, *p* ... Eph 4:11 *4396*
the Lord Jesus, and their own *p* ... 1Th 2:15 *4396*
past unto the fathers by the *p* ... Heb 1:1 *4396*
also, and Samuel, and of the *p* ... Heb 11:32 *4396*
Take, my brethren, the *p*, who ... Jas 5:10 *4396*
salvation the *p* have enquired ... 1Pet 1:10 *4396*
But there were false *p* also among ... 2Pet 2:1 *5578*
were spoken before by the holy *p* ... 2Pet 3:2 *4396*
because many false *p* are gone out ... 1Jn 4:1 *5578*
declared to his servants the *p* ... Rev 10:7 *4396*
because these two *p* tormented ... Rev 11:10 *4396*
reward unto thy servants the *p* ... Rev 11:18 *4396*
shed the blood of saints and *p* ... Rev 16:6 *4396*
heaven, and ye holy apostles and *p* ... Rev 18:20 *4396*
in her was found the blood of *p* ... Rev 18:24 *4396*
the Lord God of the holy *p* sent ... Rev 22:6 *4396*
and of thy brethren the *p* ... Rev 22:9 *4396*

PROPITIATION
be a *p* through faith in his blood ... Rom 3:25 *2435*
And he is the *p* for our sins ... 1Jn 2:2 *2434*
his Son to be the *p* for our sins ... 1Jn 4:10 *2434*

PROPORTION
according to the *p* of every one ... 1Kin 7:36 4626
nor his power, nor his comely *p* ... Job 41:12 6187
according to the *p* of faith ... Rom 12:6 *356*

PROSELYTE
compass sea and land to make one *p* ... Mt 23:15 *4339*
and Nicolas a *p* of Antioch ... Acts 6:5 *4339*

PROSELYTES
and strangers of Rome, Jews and *p* ... Acts 2:10 *4339*
religious *p* followed Paul and ... Acts 13:43 *4339*

PROSPECT
their *p* was toward the south ... Eze 40:44 6440
having the *p* toward the north ... Eze 40:44 6440
whose *p* is toward the south, is ... Eze 40:45 6440
the chamber whose *p* is toward the ... Eze 40:46 6440
gate whose *p* is toward the east ... Eze 42:15 6440
gate whose *p* is toward the east ... Eze 43:4 6440

PROSPER
his angel with thee, and *p* thy way ... Gen 24:40 6743
if now thou do *p* my way which I ... Gen 24:42 6743
all that he did to *p* in his hand ... Gen 39:3 6743
he did, the LORD made it to *p* ... Gen 39:23 6743
but it shall not *p* ... Num 14:41 6743
and thou shalt not *p* in thy ways ... Deut 28:29 6743
that ye may *p* in all that ye do ... Deut 29:9 7919
that thou mayest *p* whithersoever ... Josh 1:7 7919
that thou mayest *p* in all that ... 1Kin 2:3 7919
Go up to Ramoth-gilead, and *p* ... 1Kin 22:12 6743
And he answered him, Go, and *p* ... 1Kin 22:15 6743
p thou, and build the house of the ... 1Chr 22:11 6743
Then shalt thou *p*, if thou takest ... 1Chr 22:13 6743
for ye shall not *p* ... 2Chr 13:12 6743
Go up to Ramoth-gilead, and *p* ... 2Chr 18:11 6743
And he said, Go ye up, and *p* ... 2Chr 18:14 6743
his prophets, so shall ye *p* ... 2Chr 20:20 6743
of the LORD, that ye cannot *p* ... 2Chr 24:20 6743
the LORD, God made him to *p* ... 2Chr 26:5 6743
and *p*, I pray thee, thy servant ... Neh 1:11 6743
The God of heaven, he will *p* us ... Neh 2:20 6743
The tabernacles of robbers *p* ... Job 12:6 7951
and whatsoever he doeth shall *p* ... Ps 1:3 6743
the ungodly, who *p* in the world ... Ps 73:12 7951
they shall *p* that love thee ... Ps 122:6 7951
covereth his sins shall not *p* ... Prov 28:13 6743
thou knowest not whether shall *p* ... Eccl 11:6 3787
of the LORD shall *p* in his hand ... Is 53:10 6743
is formed against thee shall *p* ... Is 54:17 6743
it shall *p* in the thing whereto I ... Is 55:11 6743
and thou shalt not *p* in them ... Jer 2:37 6743
of the fatherless, yet they *p* ... Jer 5:28 6743
therefore they shall not *p* ... Jer 10:21 7919
doth the way of the wicked *p* ... Jer 12:1 6743
for they shall not *p* ... Jer 20:11 7919
man that shall not *p* in his days ... Jer 22:30 6743
for no man of his seed shall *p* ... Jer 22:30 6743
and a King shall reign and *p* ... Jer 23:5 7919
the Chaldeans, ye shall not *p* ... Jer 32:5 6743
are the chief, her enemies *p* ... Lam 1:5 7919
thou didst *p* into a kingdom ... Eze 16:13 6743
Shall it *p*? ... Eze 17:9 6743
behold, being planted, shall it *p* ... Eze 17:10 6743
Shall he *p*? ... Eze 17:15 6743
destroy wonderfully, and shall *p* ... Dan 8:24 6743
cause craft to *p* in his hand ... Dan 8:25 6743
but it shall not *p* ... Dan 11:27 6743
shall *p* till the indignation be ... Dan 11:36 6743
all things that thou mayest *p* ... 3Jn 2 *2137*

PROSPERED
seeing the LORD hath *p* my way ... Gen 24:56 6743
hand of the children of Israel *p* ... Judg 4:24 1980
the people did, and how the war *p* ... 2Sa 11:7 7965
he *p* whithersoever he went forth ... 2Kin 18:7 7919
instead of David his father, and *p* ... 1Chr 29:23 6743
So they built and *p* ... 2Chr 14:7 6743
did it with all his heart, and *p* ... 2Chr 31:21 6743
Hezekiah *p* in all his works ... 2Chr 32:30 6743
they *p* through the prophesying of ... Ezr 6:14 6744
himself against him, and hath *p* ... Job 9:4 7999
So this Daniel *p* in the reign of ... Dan 6:28 6744
and it practised, and *p* ... Dan 8:12 6743
him in store, as God hath *p* him ... 1Cor 16:2 *2137*

PROSPERETH
fast on, and *p* in their hands ... Ezr 5:8 6744
because of him who *p* in his way ... Ps 37:7 6743
whithersoever it turneth, it *p* ... Prov 17:8 7919
be in health, even as thy soul *p* ... 3Jn 2 *2137*

PROSPERITY
nor their *p* all thy days for ever ... Deut 23:6 2896
ye say to him that liveth in *p* ... 1Sa 25:6
p exceedeth the fame which I ... 1Kin 10:7 2896
in *p* the destroyer shall come ... Job 15:21 7965
they shall spend their days in *p* ... Job 36:11 2896
in my *p* I said, I shall never be ... Ps 30:6 7961
pleasure in the *p* of his servant ... Ps 35:27 7965
when I saw the *p* of the wicked ... Ps 73:3 7965
LORD, I beseech thee, send now *p* ... Ps 118:25 6743
walls, and *p* within thy palaces ... Ps 122:7 7962
the *p* of fools shall destroy them ... Prov 1:32 7962
In the day of *p* be joyful ... Eccl 7:14 2896
I spake unto thee in thy *p* ... Jer 22:21 7962
for all the *p* that I procure unto ... Jer 33:9 7965
I forgat *p* ... Lam 3:17 2896
My cities through *p* shall yet be ... Zec 1:17 2896
Jerusalem was inhabited and in *p* ... Zec 7:7 7961

PROSPEROUS
had made his journey *p* or not ... Gen 24:21 6743
with Joseph, and he was a *p* man ... Gen 39:2 6743
then thou shalt make thy way *p* ... Josh 1:8 6743
our way which we go shall be *p* ... Judg 18:5 6743
habitation of thy righteousness *p* ... Job 8:6 7999
him, and he shall make his way *p* ... Is 48:15 6743
For the seed shall be *p* ... Zec 8:12 7965
now at length I might have a *p* ... Rom 1:10 *2137*

PROSPEROUSLY
in his own house, he *p* effected ... 2Chr 7:11 6743
majesty ride *p* because of truth ... Ps 45:4 6743

PROSTITUTE
Do not *p* thy daughter, to cause ... Lev 19:29 2490

PROTECTION
rise up and help you, and be your *p* ... Deut 32:38 5643

PROTEST
The man did solemnly *p* unto us ... Gen 43:3 5749
howbeit yet *p* solemnly unto them, ... 1Sa 8:9 5749
I *p* by your rejoicing which I ... 1Cor 15:31 *3513*

PROTESTED
p unto thee, saying, Know for a ... 1Kin 2:42 5749
For I earnestly *p* unto your ... Jer 11:7 5749
angel of the LORD *p* unto Joshua ... Zec 3:6 5749

PROTESTING
unto this day, rising early and *p* ... Jer 11:7 5749

PROUD
the *p* helpers do stoop under him ... Job 9:13 7293
he smiteth through the *p* ... Job 26:12 7293
here shall thy *p* waves be stayed ... Job 38:11 1347
and behold every one that is *p* ... Job 40:11 1343
Look on every one that is *p* ... Job 40:12 1343
the tongue that speaketh *p* things ... Ps 12:3 1419
plentifully rewardeth the *p* doer ... Ps 31:23 1346
trust, and respecteth not the *p* ... Ps 40:4 7295
the *p* are risen against me, and ... Ps 86:14 2086
render a reward to the *p* ... Ps 94:2 1343
a *p* heart will not I suffer ... Ps 101:5 7342
rebuked the *p* that are cursed ... Ps 119:21 2086
The *p* have had me greatly in ... Ps 119:51 2086
The *p* have forged a lie against ... Ps 119:69 2086
Let the *p* be ashamed ... Ps 119:78 2086
The *p* have digged pits for me, ... Ps 119:85 2086
let not the *p* oppress me ... Ps 119:122 2086
and with the contempt of the *p* ... Ps 123:4 1349
Then the *p* waters had gone over ... Ps 124:5 2121
but the *p* he knoweth afar off ... Ps 138:6 1364
The *p* have hid a snare for me, and ... Ps 140:5 1343
A *p* look, a lying tongue, and ... Prov 6:17 7311
will destroy the house of the *p* ... Prov 15:25 1343
Every one that is *p* in heart is ... Prov 16:5 1362
to divide the spoil with the *p* ... Prov 16:19 1343
a *p* heart, and the plowing of the ... Prov 21:4 7342
P and haughty scorner is his name, ... Prov 21:24 2086
who dealeth in *p* wrath ... Prov 21:24 2087
He that is of a *p* heart stirreth ... Prov 28:25 7342
is better than the *p* in spirit ... Eccl 7:8 1362
shall be upon every one that is *p* ... Is 2:12 1343
the arrogancy of the *p* to cease ... Is 13:11 2086
he is very *p* ... Is 16:6 1341
be not *p* ... Jer 13:15 1341
son of Kareah, and all the *p* men ... Jer 43:2 2086
(he is exceeding *p*) his loftiness ... Jer 48:29 1343
she hath been *p* against the LORD ... Jer 50:29 2102
I am against thee, O thou most *p* ... Jer 50:31 2087
the most *p* shall stumble and fall, ... Jer 50:32 2087
by wine, he is a *p* man, neither ... Hab 2:5 3093
And now we call the *p* happy ... Mal 3:15 2086
and all the *p*, yea, and all that do ... Mal 4:1 2086
he hath scattered the *p* in the ... Lk 1:51 *5244*
haters of God, despiteful, *p* ... Rom 1:30 *5244*
He is *p*, knowing nothing, but ... 1Ti 6:4 *5187*
own selves, covetous, boasters, *p* ... 2Ti 3:2 *5244*
he saith, God resisteth the *p* ... Jas 4:6 *5244*
for God resisteth the *p*, and ... 1Pet 5:5 *5244*

PROUDLY
they dealt *p* he was above them ... Ex 18:11 *2102*
Talk no more so exceeding *p* ... 1Sa 2:3 1364
that they dealt *p* against them ... Neh 9:10 *2102*
But they and our fathers dealt *p* ... Neh 9:16 *2102*
yet they dealt *p*, and hearkened ... Neh 9:29 *2102*
with their mouth they speak *p* ... Ps 17:10 1348
which speak grievous things *p* ... Ps 31:18 1346
himself *p* against the ancient ... Is 3:5 7292
spoken *p* in the day of distress ... Obad 12 1431

PROVE
rate every day, that I may *p* them ... Ex 16:4 5254
for God is come to *p* you, and that ... Ex 20:20 5254
to *p* thee, to know what was in ... Deut 8:2 5254
thee, and that he might *p* thee ... Deut 8:16 5254
one, whom thou didst *p* at Massah ... Deut 33:8 5254
That through them I may *p* Israel ... Judg 2:22 5254
to *p* Israel by them, even as many ... Judg 3:1 5254
they were to *p* Israel by them, to ... Judg 3:4 5254
let me *p*, I pray thee, but this ... Judg 6:39 5254
she came to *p* him with hard ... 1Kin 10:1 5254
she came to *p* Solomon with hard ... 2Chr 9:1 5254
it shall also *p* me perverse ... Job 9:20
Examine me, O LORD, and *p* me ... Ps 26:2 5254
I will *p* thee with mirth, ... Eccl 2:1 5254
P thy servants, I beseech thee, ... Dan 1:12 5254
p me now herewith, saith the LORD ... Mal 3:10 974
yoke of oxen, and I go to *p* them ... Lk 14:19 *1381*
And this he said to *p* him ... Jn 6:6 *3985*
Neither can they *p* the things ... Acts 24:13 *3936*
Paul, which they could not *p* ... Acts 25:7 *584*
that ye may *p* what is that good, ... Rom 12:2 *1381*
to *p* the sincerity of your love ... 2Cor 8:8 *1381*
p your own selves ... 2Cor 13:5 *1381*
But let every man *p* his own work ... Gal 6:4 *1381*
P all things ... 1Th 5:21 *1381*

PROVED
Hereby ye shall be *p* ... Gen 42:15 974
prison, that your words may be *p* ... Gen 42:16 974
an ordinance, and there he *p* them ... Ex 15:25 5254

for he had not p it ... 1Sa 17:39 5254
for I have not p them ... 1Sa 17:39 5254
Thou hast p mine heart ... Ps 17:3 974
For thou, O God, hast p us ... Ps 66:10 974
I p thee at the waters of Meribah ... Ps 81:7 974
tempted me, p me, and saw my work .. Ps 95:9 974
All this have I p by wisdom ... Eccl 7:23 5254
this matter, and p them ten days ... Dan 1:14 5254
for we have before p both Jews ... Rom 3:9 4256
p diligent in many things ... 2Cor 8:22 1381
And let these also first be p ... 1Ti 3:10 1381
p me, and saw my works forty years ... Heb 3:9 1381

PROVENDER
p enough, and room to lodge in ... Gen 24:25 4554
p for the camels, and water to ... Gen 24:32 4554
sack to give his ass p in the inn ... Gen 42:27 4554
and he gave their asses p ... Gen 43:24 4554
is both straw and p for our asses ... Judg 19:19 4554
house, and gave p unto the asses ... Judg 19:21 1101
ear the ground shall eat clean p ... Is 30:24 1098

PROVERB
shalt become an astonishment, a p ... Deut 28:37 4912
Therefore it became a p, Is Saul ... 1Sa 10:12 4912
As saith the p of the ancients, ... 1Sa 24:13 4912
and Israel shall be a p and a ... 1Kin 9:7 4912
sight, and will make it to be a p ... 2Chr 7:20 4912
and I became a p to them ... Ps 69:11 4912
To understand a p, and the ... Prov 1:6 4912
p against the king of Babylon ... Is 14:4 4912
hurt, to be a reproach and a p ... Jer 24:9 4912
what is that p that ye have in ... Eze 12:22 4912
I will make this p to cease ... Eze 12:23 4912
no more use it as a p in Israel ... Eze 12:23 4911
and will make him a sign and a p ... Eze 14:8 4912
shall use this p against thee ... Eze 16:44 4911
that ye use this p concerning the ... Eze 18:2 4911
any more to use this p in Israel ... Eze 18:3 4911
a taunting p against him, and say, ... Hab 2:6 2420
Ye will surely say unto me this p ... Lk 4:23 3850
thou plainly, and speakest no p ... Jn 16:29 3942
unto them according to the true p ... 2Pet 2:22 3942

PROVERBS
they that speak in p say, Come ... Num 21:27 4911
And he spake three thousand p ... 1Kin 4:32 4912
The P of Solomon the son of David ... Prov 1:1 4912
The p of Solomon ... Prov 10:1 4912
These are also p of Solomon ... Prov 25:1 4912
out, and set in order many p ... Eccl 12:9 4912
every one that useth p shall use ... Eze 16:44 4911
have I spoken unto you in p ... Jn 16:25 3942
shall no more speak unto you in p ... Jn 16:25 3942

PROVETH
for the LORD your God p you ... Deut 13:3 5254

PROVIDE
God will p himself a lamb for a ... Gen 22:8 7200
now when shall I p for mine own ... Gen 30:30 6213
Moreover thou shalt p out of all ... Ex 18:21 2372
P me now a man that can play well ... 1Sa 16:17 7200
whom David my father did p ... 2Chr 2:7 3559
can he p flesh for his people ... Ps 78:20 3559
P neither gold, nor silver, nor ... Mt 10:9 2532
p yourselves bags which wax not ... Lk 12:33 4160
p them beasts, that they may set ... Acts 23:24 3936
P things honest in the sight of ... Rom 12:17 4306
But if any p not for his own, and ... 1Ti 5:8 4306

PROVIDED
he p the first part for himself, ... Deut 33:21 7200
for I have p me a king among his ... 1Sa 16:1 7200
he had p the king of sustenance ... 2Sa 19:32
which p victuals for the king and ... 1Kin 4:7
those officers p victual for king ... 1Kin 4:27
Moreover he p him cities, and ... 2Chr 32:29 6213
corn, when thou hast so p for it ... Ps 65:9 3559
things be, which thou hast p ... Lk 12:20 2090
God having p some better thing ... Heb 11:40 4265

PROVIDENCE
done unto this nation by thy p ... Acts 24:2 4307

PROVIDETH
Who p for the raven his food ... Job 38:41 3559
P her meat in the summer, and ... Prov 6:8 3559

PROVIDING
P for honest things, not only in ... 2Cor 8:21 4306

PROVINCE
of the p that went up out of the ... Ezr 2:1 4082
that we went into the p of Judea ... Ezr 5:8 4083
that is in the p of the Medes ... Ezr 6:2 4082
find in all the p of Babylon ... Ezr 7:16 4082
in the p are in great affliction ... Neh 1:3 4082
These are the children of the p ... Neh 7:6 4082
of the p that dwelt in Jerusalem ... Neh 11:3 4082
into every p according to the ... Est 1:22 4082
governors that were over every p ... Est 3:12 4082
every p according to the writing ... Est 3:12 4082
to be given in every p was ... Est 3:14 4082
And in every p, whithersoever the ... Est 4:3 4082
unto every p according to the ... Est 8:9 4082
p that would assault them, both ... Est 8:11 4082
to be given in every p was ... Est 8:13 4082
And in every p, and in every city, ... Est 8:17 4082
generation, every family, every p ... Est 9:28 4082
of judgment and justice in a p ... Eccl 5:8 4082
ruler over the whole p of Babylon ... Dan 2:48 4083
the affairs of the p of Babylon ... Dan 2:49 4083
of Dura, in the p of Babylon ... Dan 3:1 4083
the affairs of the p of Babylon ... Dan 3:12 4083
and Abed-nego, in the p of Babylon ... Dan 3:30 4082
palace, which is in the p of Elam ... Dan 8:2 4082
upon the fattest places of the p ... Dan 11:24 4082
letter, he asked of what p he was ... Acts 23:34 1885
when Festus was come into the p ... Acts 25:1 1885

PROVINCES
young men of the princes of the p ... 1Kin 20:14 4082
young men of the princes of the p ... 1Kin 20:15 4082
princes of the p went out first ... 1Kin 20:17 4082
of the p came out of the city ... 1Kin 20:19 4082
city, and hurtful unto kings and p ... Ezr 4:15 4083
an hundred and seven and twenty p ... Est 1:1 4082
the nobles and princes of the p ... Est 1:3 4082
all the p of the king Ahasuerus ... Est 1:16 4082
letters into all the king's p ... Est 1:22 4082
in all the p of his kingdom ... Est 2:3 4082
and he made a release to the p ... Est 2:18 4082
in all the p of thy kingdom ... Est 3:8 4082
by posts into all the king's p ... Est 3:13 4082
and the people of the king's p ... Est 4:11 4082
which are in all the king's p ... Est 8:5 4082
rulers of the p which are from ... Est 8:9 4082
an hundred twenty and seven p ... Est 8:9 4082
in all the p of king Ahasuerus ... Est 8:12 4082
all the p of the king Ahasuerus ... Est 9:2 4082
And all the rulers of the p ... Est 9:3 4082
went out throughout all the p ... Est 9:4 4082
done in the rest of the king's p ... Est 9:12 4082
p gathered themselves together ... Est 9:16 4082
all the p of the king Ahasuerus ... Est 9:20 4082
seven p of the kingdom of ... Est 9:30 4082
treasure of kings and of the p ... Eccl 2:8 4082
nations, and princess among the p ... Lam 1:1 4082
him on every side from the p ... Eze 19:8 4082
and all the rulers of the p ... Dan 3:2 4082
and all the rulers of the p ... Dan 3:3 4082

PROVING
p that this is very Christ ... Acts 9:22 4822
P what is acceptable unto the ... Eph 5:10 1381

PROVISION
and to give them p for the way ... Gen 42:25 6720
and gave them p for the way ... Gen 45:21 6720
all the bread of their p was dry ... Josh 9:5 6718
our bread we took hot for our p ... Josh 9:12 6679
man his month in a year made p ... 1Kin 4:7 3557
Solomon's p for one day was ... 1Kin 4:22 3899
And he prepared great p for them ... 2Kin 6:23 3740
for the which I have made p ... 1Chr 29:19 3559
I will abundantly bless her p ... Ps 132:15 6718
them a daily p of the king's meat ... Dan 1:5 1697
make not p for the flesh, to ... Rom 13:14 4307

PROVOCATION
by his p wherewith he provoked ... 1Kin 15:30 3708
for the p wherewith thou hast ... 1Kin 21:22 3708
not mine eye continue in their p ... Job 17:2 4784
not your heart, as in the p ... Ps 95:8 4808
been to me as a p of mine anger ... Jer 32:31 3708
presented the p of their offering ... Eze 20:28 3708
not your hearts, as in the p ... Heb 3:8 3894
not your hearts, as in the p ... Heb 3:15 3894

PROVOCATIONS
because of all the p that ... 2Kin 23:26 3708
of Egypt, and had wrought great p ... Neh 9:18 5007
to thee, and they wrought great p ... Neh 9:26 5007

PROVOKE
him, and obey his voice, p him not ... Ex 23:21 4843
How long will this people p me ... Num 14:11 5006
LORD thy God, to p him to anger ... Deut 4:25
of the LORD, to p him to anger ... Deut 9:18
p me, and break my covenant ... Deut 31:20 5006
to p him to anger through the ... Deut 31:29
I will p them to anger with a ... Deut 32:21
to p me to anger, and hast cast me ... 1Kin 14:9
to p me to anger with their sins ... 1Kin 16:2
to p the LORD God of Israel to ... 1Kin 16:26
Ahab did more to p the LORD God ... 1Kin 16:33
things to p the LORD to anger ... 2Kin 17:11
of the LORD, to p him to anger ... 2Kin 17:17
of the LORD, to p him to anger ... 2Kin 21:6
that they might p me to anger ... 2Kin 22:17
had made to p the LORD to anger ... 2Kin 23:19
of the LORD, to p him to anger ... 2Chr 33:6
that they might p me to anger ... 2Chr 34:25
they that p God are secure ... Job 12:6 7264
How oft did they p him in the ... Ps 78:40 4784
to p the eyes of his glory ... Is 3:8 4784
gods, that they may p me to anger ... Jer 7:18
Do they p me to anger ... Jer 7:19
do they not p themselves to the ... Jer 7:19
p me to anger in offering incense ... Jer 11:17
p me not to anger with the works ... Jer 25:6
that ye might p me to anger with ... Jer 25:7
unto other gods, to p me to anger ... Jer 32:29
they have done to p me to anger ... Jer 32:32
have committed to p me to anger ... Jer 44:3
In that ye p me unto wrath with ... Jer 44:8
and have returned to p me to anger ... Eze 8:17
thy whoredoms, to p me to anger ... Eze 16:26
to p him to speak of many things ... Lk 11:53 653
I will p you to jealousy by them ... Rom 10:19 3863
for to p them to jealousy ... Rom 11:11 3863
If by any means I may p to ... Rom 11:14 3863
Do we p the Lord to jealousy ... 1Cor 10:22 3863
p not your children to wrath ... Eph 6:4 3949
p not your children to anger, ... Col 3:21 2042
some, when they had heard, did p ... Heb 3:16 3893
one another to p unto love ... Heb 10:24 3948

PROVOKED
any of them that p me see it ... Num 14:23 5006
that these men have p the LORD ... Num 16:30 5006
Also in Horeb ye p the LORD to ... Deut 9:8
ye p the LORD to wrath ... Deut 9:22
They p him to jealousy with ... Deut 32:16 3707
abominations p they him to anger ... Deut 32:16
they have p me to anger with ... Deut 32:21
unto them, and p the LORD to anger ... Judg 2:12
And her adversary also p her sore ... 1Sa 1:6 3707
house of the LORD, so she p her ... 1Sa 1:7 3707
they p him to jealousy with their ... 1Kin 14:22
p the LORD God of Israel to anger ... 1Kin 15:30
wherewith thou hast p me to anger ... 1Kin 21:22
p to anger the LORD God of Israel ... 1Kin 22:53
have p me to anger, since the day ... 2Kin 21:15
that Manasseh had p him withal ... 2Kin 23:26 3707
and p David to number Israel ... 1Chr 21:1 5496
p to anger the LORD God of his ... 2Chr 28:25
p the God of heaven unto wrath ... Ezr 5:12 7265
for they have p thee to anger ... Neh 4:5
p the most high God, and kept not ... Ps 78:56 4784
For they p him to anger with ... Ps 78:58
but p him at the sea, even at the ... Ps 106:7 4784
Thus they p him to anger with ... Ps 106:29
Because they p his spirit ... Ps 106:33 4784
but they p him with their counsel ... Ps 106:43 4784
they have p the Holy One of ... Is 1:4 5006
Why have they p me to anger with ... Jer 8:19
p me to anger with the work of ... Jer 32:30
Ephraim p him to anger most ... Hos 12:14
when your fathers p me to wrath ... Zec 8:14
not her own, is not easily p ... 1Cor 13:5 3947
and your zeal hath p very many ... 2Cor 9:2 2042

PROVOKEDST
how thou p the LORD thy God to ... Deut 9:7

PROVOKETH
whoso p him to anger sinneth ... Prov 20:2 5674
A people that p me to anger ... Is 65:3
of jealousy, which p to jealousy ... Eze 8:3

PROVOKING
because of the p of his sons ... Deut 32:19 3707
their groves, p the LORD to anger ... 1Kin 14:15
in p him to anger with the work ... 1Kin 16:7
in p the LORD God of Israel to ... 1Kin 16:13
sinned yet more against him by p ... Ps 78:17 4784
p one another, envying one ... Gal 5:26 4292

PRUDENCE
king a wise son, endued with p ... 2Chr 2:12 7922
I wisdom dwell with p, and find ... Prov 8:12 6195
toward us in all wisdom and p ... Eph 1:8 5428

PRUDENT
p in matters, and a comely person, ... 1Sa 16:18 995
but a p man covereth shame ... Prov 12:16 6175
A p man concealeth knowledge ... Prov 12:23 6175
Every p man dealeth with ... Prov 13:16 6175
The wisdom of the p is to ... Prov 14:8 6175
but the p man looketh well to his ... Prov 14:15 6175
but the p are crowned with ... Prov 14:18 6175
he that regardeth reproof is p ... Prov 15:5 6191
wise in heart shall be called p ... Prov 16:21 995
The heart of the p getteth ... Prov 18:15 995
a p wife is from the LORD ... Prov 19:14 7919
A p man foreseeth the evil, and ... Prov 22:3 6175
A p man foreseeth the evil, and ... Prov 27:12 6175
judge, and the prophet, and the p ... Is 3:2 7080
own eyes, and p in their own sight ... Is 5:21 995
for I am p ... Is 10:13 995
of their p men shall be hid ... Is 29:14 995
is counsel perished from the p ... Jer 49:7 995
p, and he shall know them ... Hos 14:9 995
Therefore the p shall keep ... Amos 5:13 7919
these things from the wise and p ... Mt 11:25 4908
these things from the wise and p ... Lk 10:21 4908
country, Sergius Paulus, a p man ... Acts 13:7 4908
the understanding of the p ... 1Cor 1:19 4908

PRUDENTLY
Behold, my servant shall deal p ... Is 52:13 7919

PRUNE
years thou shalt p thy vineyard ... Lev 25:3 2168
sow thy field, nor p thy vineyard ... Lev 25:4 2168

PRUNED
it shall not be p, nor digged ... Is 5:6 2167

PRUNINGHOOKS
and their spears into p ... Is 2:4 4211
both cut off the sprigs with p ... Is 18:5 4211
swords, and your p into spears ... Joel 3:10 4211
and their spears into p ... Mic 4:3 4211

PSALM
day David delivered first this p ... 1Chr 16:7
A P of David, when he fled from ... Ps 3:t 4210
on Neginoth, A P of David ... Ps 4:t 4210
upon Nehiloth, A P of David ... Ps 5:t 4210
upon Sheminith, A P of David ... Ps 6:t 4210
upon Gittith, A P of David ... Ps 8:t 4210
upon Muth-labben, A P of David ... Ps 9:t 4210
the chief Musician, A P of David ... Ps 11:t
upon Sheminith, A P of David ... Ps 12:t 4210
the chief Musician, A P of David ... Ps 13:t 4210
the chief Musician, A P of David ... Ps 14:t
A P of David ... Ps 15:t 4210
A P of David, the servant of the ... Ps 18:t 4210
the chief Musician, A P of David ... Ps 19:t 4210
the chief Musician, A P of David ... Ps 20:t 4210
the chief Musician, A P of David ... Ps 21:t 4210
Aijeleth Shahar, A P of David ... Ps 22:t 4210
A P of David ... Ps 23:t 4210
A P of David ... Ps 24:t
A P of David ... Ps 25:t
A P of David ... Ps 26:t
A P of David ... Ps 27:t
A P of David ... Ps 28:t
A P of David ... Ps 29:t 4210
A P and Song at the dedication of ... Ps 30:t 4210
the chief Musician, A P of David ... Ps 31:t 4210
A P of David, A Maschil ... Ps 32:t

P

A P of David, when he changed his...... Ps 34:t
A P of David...... Ps 35:t
A P of David, the servant of the...... Ps 36:t
A P of David...... Ps 37:t
A P of David, to bring to...... Ps 38:t 4210
even to Jeduthun, A P of David...... Ps 39:t 4210
the chief Musician, A P of David...... Ps 40:t 4210
the chief Musician, A P of David...... Ps 41:t 4210
A P for the sons of Korah...... Ps 47:t 4210
A Song and P for the sons of Korah...... Ps 48:t 4210
A P for the sons of Korah...... Ps 49:t 4210
A P of Asaph...... Ps 50:t 4210
A P of David, when Nathan the...... Ps 51:t 4210
A P of David, when Doeg the...... Ps 52:t
Mahalath, Maschil, A P of David...... Ps 53:t
A P of David, when the Ziphims...... Ps 54:t
Neginoth, Maschil, A P of David...... Ps 55:t
upon Neginah, A P of David...... Ps 61:t
to Jeduthun, A P of David...... Ps 62:t 4210
A P of David, when he was in the...... Ps 63:t 4210
the chief Musician, A P of David...... Ps 64:t 4210
To the chief Musician, A P...... Ps 65:t 4210
the chief Musician, A Song or P...... Ps 66:t 4210
Musician on Neginoth, A P or Song...... Ps 67:t 4210
Musician, A P or Song of David...... Ps 68:t 4210
upon Shoshannim, A P of David...... Ps 69:t
A P of David, to bring to...... Ps 70:t
A P for Solomon...... Ps 72:t 4210
A P of Asaph...... Ps 73:t 4210
Altaschith, A P or Song of Asaph...... Ps 75:t 4210
on Neginoth, A P or Song of Asaph...... Ps 76:t 4210
to Jeduthun, A P of Asaph...... Ps 77:t 4210
A P of Asaph...... Ps 79:t 4210
Shoshannim-Eduth, A P of Asaph...... Ps 80:t 4210
upon Gittith, A P of Asaph...... Ps 81:t
Take a p, and bring hither the...... Ps 81:2 2172
A P of Asaph...... Ps 82:t 4210
A Song or P of Asaph...... Ps 83:t 4210
A P for the sons of Korah...... Ps 84:t 4210
A P for the sons of Korah...... Ps 85:t 4210
A P or Song for the sons of Korah...... Ps 87:t 4210
A Song or P for the sons of Korah...... Ps 88:t 4210
A P or Song for the sabbath day...... Ps 92:t 4210
A P...... Ps 98:t 4210
the harp, and the voice of a p...... Ps 98:5 2172
A P of praise...... Ps 100:t 4210
A P of David...... Ps 101:t 4210
A P of David...... Ps 103:t
A Song or P of David...... Ps 108:t 4210
the chief Musician, A P of David...... Ps 109:t 4210
A P of David...... Ps 110:t 4210
A P of David...... Ps 138:t
the chief Musician, A P of David...... Ps 139:t 4210
the chief Musician, A P of David...... Ps 140:t 4210
A P of David...... Ps 141:t 4210
A P of David...... Ps 143:t 4210
A P of David...... Ps 144:t
David's P of praise...... Ps 145:t
is also written in the second p...... Acts 13:33 5568
he saith also in another p...... Acts 13:35
every one of you hath a p...... 1Cor 14:26 5568

PSALMIST
Jacob, and the sweet p of Israel...... 2Sa 23:1 2158

PSALMS
sing p unto him, talk ye of all...... 1Chr 16:9 2167
a joyful noise unto him with p...... Ps 95:2 2158
Sing unto him, sing p unto him...... Ps 105:2 2167
himself saith in the book of P...... Lk 20:42 5568
and in the prophets, and in the p...... Lk 24:44 5568
it is written in the book of P...... Acts 1:20 5568
Speaking to yourselves in p...... Eph 5:19 5568
and admonishing one another in p...... Col 3:16 5568
let him sing p...... Jas 5:13 5567

PSALTERIES
fir wood, even on harps, and on p...... 2Sa 6:5 5035
harps also and p for singers...... 1Kin 10:12 5035
singing, and with harps, and with p...... 1Chr 13:8 5035
with instruments of musick, p...... 1Chr 15:16 5035
and Benaiah, with p on Alamoth...... 1Chr 15:20 5035
cymbals, making a noise with p...... 1Chr 15:28 5035
and Jeiel with p and with harps...... 1Chr 16:5 3627
prophesy with harps, with p...... 1Chr 25:1 5035
of the LORD, with cymbals, p...... 1Chr 25:6 5035
white linen, having cymbals and p...... 2Chr 5:12 5035
palace, and harps and p for singers...... 2Chr 9:11 5035
And they came to Jerusalem with p...... 2Chr 20:28 5035
of the LORD with cymbals, with p...... 2Chr 29:25 5035
and with singing, with cymbals, p...... Neh 12:27 5035

PSALTERY
down from the high place with a p...... 1Sa 10:5 5035
sing unto him with the p and an...... Ps 33:2 5035
awake, p and harp...... Ps 57:8 5035
will also praise thee with the p...... Ps 71:22 3627
the pleasant harp with the p...... Ps 81:2 5035
of ten strings, and upon the p...... Ps 92:3 5035
Awake, p and harp...... Ps 108:2 5035
upon a p and an instrument of ten...... Ps 144:9 5035
praise him with the p and harp...... Ps 150:3 5035
cornet, flute, harp, sackbut, p...... Dan 3:5 6460
cornet, flute, harp, sackbut, p...... Dan 3:7 6460
cornet, flute, harp, sackbut, p...... Dan 3:10 6460
cornet, flute, harp, sackbut, p...... Dan 3:15 6460

PTOLEMAIS (*tol-e-ma'-is*) See ACCHO. *A seaport between Carmel and Tyre.*
course from Tyre, we came to P...... Acts 21:7 4424

PUA (*pu'ah*) See PUAH. *A son of Issachar.*
of P, the family of the Punites...... Num 26:23 6312

PUAH (*pu'-ah*) See PHUVAH, PUA, PUNITES.
1. Same as Pua.
sons of Issachar were, Tola, and P...... 1Chr 7:1 6312
2. Father of Tola.
defend Israel Tola the son of P...... Judg 10:1 6312
3. A Hebrew midwife in Egypt.
and the name of the other P...... Ex 1:15 6326

PUBLICAN
Thomas, and Matthew the p...... Mt 10:3 5057
thee as an heathen man and a p...... Mt 18:17 5057
things he went forth, and saw a p...... Lk 5:27 5057
one a Pharisee, and the other a p...... Lk 18:10 5057
adulterers, or even as this p...... Lk 18:11 5057
And the p, standing afar off,...... Lk 18:13 5057

PUBLICANS
do not even the p the same...... Mt 5:46 5057
do not even the p so...... Mt 5:47 5057
meat in the house, behold, many p...... Mt 9:10 5057
Why eateth your Master with p...... Mt 9:11 5057
and a winebibber, a friend of p...... Mt 11:19 5057
Verily I say unto you, That the p...... Mt 21:31 5057
but the p and the harlots believed...... Mt 21:32 5057
sat at meat in his house, many p...... Mk 2:15 5057
and Pharisees saw him eat with p...... Mk 2:16 5057
that he eateth and drinketh with p...... Mk 2:16 5057
Then came also p to be baptized...... Lk 3:12 5057
and there was a great company of p...... Lk 5:29 5057
Why do ye eat and drink with p...... Lk 5:30 5057
people that heard him, and the p...... Lk 7:29 5057
and a winebibber, a friend of p...... Lk 7:34 5057
Then drew near unto him all the p...... Lk 15:1 5057
which was the chief among the p...... Lk 19:2 754

PUBLICK
willing to make her a p example...... Mt 1:19 3856

PUBLICKLY
convinced the Jews, and that p...... Acts 18:28 1219
shewed you, and have taught you p...... Acts 20:20 1219

PUBLISH
Because I will p the name of the...... Deut 32:3 7121
to p it in the house of their...... 1Sa 31:9 1319
p it not in the streets of...... 2Sa 1:20 1319
And that they should p and proclaim...... Neh 8:15 8085
That I may p with the voice of...... Ps 26:7 8085
ye in Judah, and p in Jerusalem...... Jer 4:5 8085
p against Jerusalem, that...... Jer 4:16 8085
Jacob, and p it in Judah, saying,...... Jer 5:20 8085
p ye, praise ye, and say, O LORD,...... Jer 31:7 8085
p in Migdol, and p in Noph...... Jer 46:14 8085
ye among the nations, and p...... Jer 50:2 8085
p, and conceal not...... Jer 50:2 8085
P in the palaces at Ashdod, and in...... Amos 3:9 8085
proclaim and p the free offerings...... Amos 4:5 8085
went out, and began to p it much...... Mk 1:45 2784
began to p in Decapolis how great...... Mk 5:20 2784

PUBLISHED
be p throughout all his empire...... Est 1:20 8085
that it should be p according to...... Est 1:22 1696
province was p unto all people...... Est 3:14 1540
province was p unto all people...... Est 8:13 1540
the company of those that p it...... Ps 68:11 1319
p through Nineveh by the decree...... Jonah 3:7 559
the more a great deal they p it...... Mk 7:36 2784
must first be p among all nations...... Mk 13:10 2784
p throughout the whole city how...... Lk 8:39 2784
which was p throughout all Judaea...... Acts 10:37 1096
the word of the Lord was p...... Acts 13:49 1308

PUBLISHETH
good tidings, that p peace...... Is 52:7 8085
tidings of good, that p salvation...... Is 52:7 8085
p affliction from mount Ephraim...... Jer 4:15 8085
good tidings, that p peace...... Nah 1:15 8085

PUBLIUS (*pub'-le-us*) *A chief man on Melita.*
of the island, whose name was P...... Acts 28:7 4196
that the father of P lay sick of...... Acts 28:8 4196

PUDENS (*pu'-denz*) *A Christian in Rome.*
Eubulus greeteth thee, and P...... 2Ti 4:21 4227

PUFFED
that no one of you be p up for...... 1Cor 4:6 5448
Now some are p up, as though I...... 1Cor 4:18 5448
the speech of them which are p up...... 1Cor 4:19 5448
And ye are p up, and have not...... 1Cor 5:2 5448
vaunteth not itself, is not p up...... 1Cor 13:4 5448
vainly p up by his fleshly mind,...... Col 2:18 5448

PUFFETH
for all his enemies, he p at them...... Ps 10:5 6315
in safety from him that p at him...... Ps 12:5 6315
Knowledge p up, but charity...... 1Cor 8:1 5448

PUHITES (*pu'-hites*) *A family descended from Caleb.*
the Ithrites, and the P, and the...... 1Chr 2:53 6336

PUL (*pul*)
1. Same as Tiglath-pileser.
P the king of Assyria came...... 2Kin 15:19 6322
Menahem gave P a thousand talents...... 2Kin 15:19 6322
the spirit of P king of Assyria...... 1Chr 5:26 6322
2. A place near Libya.
unto the nations, to Tarshish, P...... Is 66:19 6322

PULL
he could not p it in again to him...... 1Kin 13:4 7725
P me out of the net that they...... Ps 31:4 3318
thy state shall he p thee down...... Is 22:19 2040
to p down, and to destroy, and to...... Jer 1:10 5422
p them out like sheep for the...... Jer 12:3 5423
to p down, and to destroy it...... Jer 18:7 5422
build them, and not p them down...... Jer 24:6 2040
not p you down, and I will plant...... Jer 42:10 2040
shall he not p up the roots...... Eze 17:9 5423
ye p off the robe with the...... Mic 2:8 6584
Let me p out the mote out of...... Mt 7:4 1544
let me p out the mote that is in...... Lk 6:42 1544
to p out the mote that is in thy...... Lk 6:42 1544
I will p down my barns, and build...... Lk 12:18 2507
will not straightway p him out on...... Lk 14:5 385

PULLED
p her in unto him into the ark...... Gen 8:9 4026
p Lot into the house to them, and...... Gen 19:10 935
let timber be p down from his...... Ezr 6:11 5256
aside my ways, and p me in pieces...... Lam 3:11 6582
they shall no more be p up out of...... Amos 9:15 5428
p away the shoulder, and stopped...... Zec 7:11 5414
have been p in pieces of them...... Acts 23:10 1288

PULLING
God to the p down of strong holds...... 2Cor 10:4 2506
with fear, p them out of the fire...... Jude 23 726

PULPIT
the scribe stood upon a p of wood...... Neh 8:4 4026

PULSE
beans, and lentiles, and parched p...... 2Sa 17:28
and let them give us p to eat...... Dan 1:12 2235
and gave them p...... Dan 1:16 2235

PUNISH
then I will p you seven times...... Lev 26:18 3256
will p you yet seven times for...... Lev 26:24 5221
Also to p the just is not good,...... Prov 17:26 6064
I will p the fruit of the stout...... Is 10:12 6485
I will p the world for their evil...... Is 13:11 6485
that the LORD shall p the host of...... Is 24:21 6485
to p the inhabitants of the earth...... Is 26:21 6485
strong sword shall p leviathan...... Is 27:1 6485
that I will p all them which are...... Jer 9:25 6485
of hosts, Behold, I will p them...... Jer 11:22 6485
thou say when he shall p thee...... Jer 13:21 6485
But I will p you according to the...... Jer 21:14 6485
the LORD, I will even p that man...... Jer 23:34 6485
that I will p the king of Babylon...... Jer 25:12 6485
of Babylon, that nation will I p...... Jer 27:8 6485
I will p Shemaiah the Nehelamite,...... Jer 29:32 6485
I will p all that oppress them...... Jer 30:20 6485
And I will p him and his seed and...... Jer 36:31 6485
For I will p them that dwell in...... Jer 44:13 6485
that I will p you in this place,...... Jer 44:29 6485
I will p the multitude of No, and...... Jer 46:25 6485
I will p the king of Babylon and...... Jer 50:18 6485
I will p Bel in Babylon, and I...... Jer 51:44 6485
I will p them for their ways, and...... Hos 4:9 6485
I will not p your daughters when...... Hos 4:14 6485
will p Jacob according to his...... Hos 12:2 6485
therefore I will p you for all...... Amos 3:2 6485
that I will p the princes...... Zeph 1:8 6485
I p all those that leap on the...... Zeph 1:9 6485
p the men that are settled on...... Zeph 1:12 6485
As I thought to p you, when your...... Zec 8:14 7489
nothing how they might p them...... Acts 4:21 2849

PUNISHED
he shall be surely p...... Ex 21:20 5358
a day or two, he shall not be p...... Ex 21:21 5358
he shall be surely p, according...... Ex 21:22 6064
p us less than our iniquities...... Ezr 9:13 2820
an iniquity to be p by the judges...... Job 31:11
an iniquity to be p by the judge...... Job 31:28
When the scorner is p, the simple...... Prov 21:11 6064
but the simple pass on, and are p...... Prov 22:3 6064
but the simple pass on, and are p...... Prov 27:12 6064
of Egypt, as I have p Jerusalem...... Jer 44:13 6485
as I have p the king of Assyria...... Jer 50:18 6485
be cut off, howsoever I p them...... Zeph 3:7 6485
the shepherds, and I p the goats...... Zec 10:3 6485
bound unto Jerusalem, for to be p...... Acts 22:5 5097
I p them oft in every synagogue,...... Acts 26:11 5097
Who shall be p with everlasting...... 2Th 1:9 1349
unto the day of judgment to be p...... 2Pet 2:9 2849

PUNISHMENT
My p is greater than I can bear...... Gen 4:13 5771
accept of the p of their iniquity...... Lev 26:41 5771
accept of the p of their iniquity...... Lev 26:43 5771
there shall no p happen to thee...... 1Sa 28:10 5771
a strange p to the workers of...... Job 31:3
man of great wrath shall suffer p...... Prov 19:19 6066
a man for the p of his sins...... Lam 3:39 2399
For the p of the iniquity of the...... Lam 4:6 5771
than the p of the sin of Sodom...... Lam 4:6 2403
The p of thine iniquity is...... Lam 4:22 5771
bear the p of their iniquity...... Eze 14:10 5771
the p of the prophet shall be...... Eze 14:10 5771
p of him that seeketh unto him...... Eze 14:10 5771
will not turn away the p thereof...... Amos 1:3
will not turn away the p thereof...... Amos 1:6
will not turn away the p thereof...... Amos 1:9
will not turn away the p thereof...... Amos 1:11
will not turn away the p thereof...... Amos 1:13
will not turn away the p thereof...... Amos 2:1
will not turn away the p thereof...... Amos 2:4
will not turn away the p thereof...... Amos 2:6
This shall be the p of Egypt...... Zec 14:19 2403
the p of all nations that come...... Zec 14:19 2403
shall go away into everlasting p...... Mt 25:46 2851
to such a man is this p, which...... 2Cor 2:6 2009
Of how much sorer p, suppose ye,...... Heb 10:29 5098
by him for the p of evildoers...... 1Pet 2:14 1557

PUNISHMENTS
wrath bringeth the p of the sword...... Job 19:29 5771
the heathen, and p upon the people...... Ps 149:7 5771

PUNITES (*pu'-nites*) *Descendents of Pua.*
of Pua, the family of the P...... Num 26:23 6324

PUNON (*pu'-non*) *An Edomite city.*
from Zalmonah, and pitched in P...... Num 33:42 6325
And they departed from P, and...... Num 33:43 6325

PUR (*pur*) See PURIM. *Same as Purim.*
of king Ahasuerus, they cast P ... Est 3:7 6332
to destroy them, and had cast P ... Est 9:24 6332
days Purim after the name of P ... Est 9:26 6332

PURAH See PHURAH.

PURCHASE
The p of the field and of the cave ... Gen 49:32 4736
if a man p of the Levites, then ... Lev 25:33 1350
So I took the evidence of the p ... Jer 32:11 4736
I gave the evidence of the p unto ... Jer 32:12 4736
that subscribed the book of the p ... Jer 32:12 4736
evidences, this evidence of the p ... Jer 32:14 4736
p unto Baruch the son of Neriah ... Jer 32:16 4736
p to themselves a good degree ... 1Ti 3:13 4046

PURCHASED
Abraham p of the sons of Heth ... Gen 25:10 7069
pass over, which thou hast p ... Ex 15:16 7069
have I p to be my wife, to raise ... Ruth 4:10 7069
which thou hast p of old ... Ps 74:2 7069
which his right hand had p ... Ps 78:54 7069
Now this man p a field with the ... Acts 1:18 2932
gift of God may be p with money ... Acts 8:20 2932
which he hath p with his own ... Acts 20:28 4046
redemption of the p possession ... Eph 1:14 4047

PURE
thou shalt overlay it with p gold ... Ex 25:11 2889
shalt make a mercy seat of p gold ... Ex 25:17 2889
thou shalt overlay it with p gold ... Ex 25:24 2889
of p gold shalt thou make them ... Ex 25:29 2889
make a candlestick of p gold ... Ex 25:31 2889
be one beaten work of p gold ... Ex 25:36 2889
thereof, shall be of p gold ... Ex 25:38 2889
Of a talent of p gold shall he ... Ex 25:39 2889
that they bring thee p oil olive ... Ex 27:20 2134
two chains of p gold at the ends ... Ex 28:14 2889
ends of wreathen work of p gold ... Ex 28:22 2889
thou shalt make a plate of p gold ... Ex 28:36 2889
thou shalt overlay it with p gold ... Ex 30:3 2889
of p myrrh five hundred shekels ... Ex 30:23 1865
sweet spices with p frankincense ... Ex 30:34 2134
apothecary, tempered together, p ... Ex 30:35 2889
the p candlestick with all his ... Ex 31:8 2889
he overlaid it with p gold within ... Ex 37:2 2889
he made the mercy seat of p gold ... Ex 37:6 2889
And he overlaid it with p gold ... Ex 37:11 2889
covers to cover withal, of p gold ... Ex 37:16 2889
he made the candlestick of p gold ... Ex 37:17 2889
it was one beaten work of p gold ... Ex 37:22 2889
and his snuffdishes, of p gold ... Ex 37:23 2889
Of a talent of p gold made he it ... Ex 37:24 2889
And he overlaid it with p gold ... Ex 37:26 2889
the p incense of sweet spices ... Ex 37:29 2889
ends, of wreathen work of p gold ... Ex 39:15 2889
And they made bells of p gold ... Ex 39:25 2889
plate of the holy crown of p gold ... Ex 39:30 2889
The p candlestick, with the lamps ... Ex 39:37 2889
that they bring unto thee p oil ... Lev 24:2 2134
the p candlestick before the LORD ... Lev 24:4 2888
upon the p table before the LORD ... Lev 24:6 2888
thou shalt put p frankincense ... Lev 24:7 2134
drink the p blood of the grape ... Deut 32:14 2561
With the p thou wilt shew thyself ... 2Sa 22:27 2889
thou wilt shew thyself p ... 2Sa 22:27 1305
and twenty measures of p oil ... 1Kin 5:11 3795
and he overlaid it with p gold ... 1Kin 6:20 5462
the house within with p gold ... 1Kin 6:21 5462
And the candlesticks of p gold ... 1Kin 7:49 5462
spoons, and the censers of p gold ... 1Kin 7:50 5462
forest of Lebanon were of p gold ... 1Kin 10:21 5462
Also p gold for the fleshhooks ... 1Chr 28:17 2889
he overlaid it within with p gold ... 2Chr 3:4 2889
before the oracle, of p gold ... 2Chr 4:20 5462
spoons, and the censers, of p gold ... 2Chr 4:22 5462
ivory, and overlaid it with p gold ... 2Chr 9:17 2889
forest of Lebanon were of p gold ... 2Chr 9:20 5462
they in order upon the p table ... 2Chr 13:11 2889
together, all of them were p ... Ezr 6:20 2889
a man be more p than his maker ... Job 4:17 2891
If thou wert p and upright ... Job 8:6 2134
thou hast said, My doctrine is p ... Job 11:4 2134
also my prayer is p ... Job 16:17 2134
the stars are not p in his sight ... Job 25:5 2141
shall it be valued with p gold ... Job 28:19 2889
The words of the LORD are p words ... Ps 12:6 2889
With the p thou wilt shew thyself ... Ps 18:26 2889
thou wilt shew thyself p ... Ps 18:26 1305
the commandment of the LORD is p ... Ps 19:8 1249
a crown of p gold on his head ... Ps 21:3 6337
hath clean hands, and a p heart ... Ps 24:4 1249
Thy word is very p ... Ps 119:140 6884
words of the p are pleasant words ... Prov 15:26 2889
heart clean, I am p from my sin ... Prov 20:9 2891
his doings, whether his work be p ... Prov 20:11 2134
but as for the p, his work is ... Prov 21:8 2134
Every word of God is p ... Prov 30:5 6884
that are p in their own eyes ... Prov 30:12 2889
hair of his head like the p wool ... Dan 7:9 5343
Shall I count them p with the ... Mic 6:11 2135
I turn to the people a p language ... Zeph 3:9 1305
unto my name, and a p offering ... Mal 1:11 2889
Blessed are the p in heart ... Mt 5:8 2513
that I am p from the blood of all ... Acts 20:26 2513
All things indeed are p ... Rom 14:20 2513
are just, whatsoever things are p ... Phil 4:8 53
is charity out of a p heart ... 1Ti 1:5 2513
of the faith in a p conscience ... 1Ti 3:9 2513
keep thyself p ... 1Ti 5:22 53
my forefathers with p conscience ... 2Ti 1:3 2513
call on the Lord out of a p heart ... 2Ti 2:22 2513
Unto the p all things are p ... Titus 1:15 2513
and unbelieving is nothing p ... Titus 1:15 2513
and our bodies washed with p water ... Heb 10:22 2513
P religion and undefiled before ... Jas 1:27 2513
that is from above is first p ... Jas 3:17 53
another with a p heart fervently ... 1Pet 1:22 2513
p minds by way of remembrance ... 2Pet 3:1 1506
himself, even as he is p ... 1Jn 3:3 53
the seven plagues, clothed in p ... Rev 15:6 2513
and the city was p gold, like unto ... Rev 21:18 2513
the street of the city was p gold ... Rev 21:21 2513
he shewed me a p river of water ... Rev 22:1 2513

PURELY
p purge away thy dross, and take ... Is 1:25 1252

PURENESS
delivered by the p of thine hands ... Job 22:30 1252
He that loveth p of heart ... Prov 22:11 2890
By p, by knowledge, by ... 2Cor 6:6 54

PURER
Her Nazarites were p than snow ... Lam 4:7 2141
Thou art of p eyes than to behold ... Hab 1:13 2889

PURGE
twelfth year he began to p Judah ... 2Chr 34:3 2891
P me with hyssop, and I shall be ... Ps 51:7 2398
thou shalt p them away ... Ps 65:3 3722
p away our sins, for thy name's ... Ps 79:9 3722
purely p away thy dross, and take ... Is 1:25 6884
I will p out from among you the ... Eze 20:38 1305
thus shalt thou cleanse and p it ... Eze 43:20 3722
Seven days shall they p the altar ... Eze 43:26 3722
shall fall, to try them, and to p ... Dan 11:35 1305
p them as gold and silver, that ... Mal 3:3 2212
and he will throughly p his floor ... Mt 3:12 1245
and he will throughly p his floor ... Lk 3:17 1245
P out therefore the old leaven ... 1Cor 5:7 1571
therefore p himself from these ... 2Ti 2:21 1571
p your conscience from dead works ... Heb 9:14 2511

PURGED
of Eli's house shall not be p ... 1Sa 3:14 3722
his reign, when he had p the land ... 2Chr 34:8 2891
By mercy and truth iniquity is p ... Prov 16:6 3722
shall have p the blood of ... Is 4:4 1740
is taken away, and thy sin p ... Is 6:7 3722
not be p from you till ye die ... Is 22:14 3722
shall the iniquity of Jacob be p ... Is 27:9 3722
because I have p thee ... Eze 24:13 2891
and thou wast not p ... Eze 24:13 2891
thou shalt not be p from thy ... Eze 24:13 2891
when he had by himself p our sins ... Heb 1:3 4160
are by the law p with blood ... Heb 9:22 2511
once p should have had no more ... Heb 10:2 2508
that he was p from his old sins ... 2Pet 1:9 2512

PURGETH
that beareth fruit, he p it ... Jn 15:2 2508

PURGING
out into the draught, p all meats ... Mk 7:19 2511

PURIFICATION
it is a p for sin ... Num 19:9 2403
of the burnt heifer of p for sin ... Num 19:17 2403
to the p of the sanctuary ... 2Chr 30:19 2893
their God, and the ward of the p ... Neh 12:45 2893
their things for p be given them ... Est 2:3 8562
gave her her things for p ... Est 2:9 8562
when the days of her p according ... Lk 2:22 2512
accomplishment of the days of p ... Acts 21:26 49

PURIFICATIONS
the days of their p accomplished ... Est 2:12 4795

PURIFIED
p the altar, and poured the blood ... Lev 8:15 2398
And the Levites were p, and they ... Num 8:21 2398
nevertheless it shall be p with ... Num 31:23 2398
for she was p from her ... 2Sa 11:4 6942
and the Levites were p together ... Ezr 6:20 2891
and the Levites p themselves ... Neh 12:30 2891
p the people, and the gates, and ... Neh 12:30 2891
a furnace of earth, p seven times ... Ps 12:6 2212
Many shall be p, and made white ... Dan 12:10 1305
Asia found me p in the temple ... Acts 24:18 48
heavens should be p with these ... Heb 9:23 2511
Seeing ye have p your souls in ... 1Pet 1:22 48

PURIFIER
sit as a refiner and p of silver ... Mal 3:3 2891

PURIFIETH
p not himself, defileth the ... Num 19:13 2398
hath this hope in him p himself ... 1Jn 3:3 48

PURIFY
He shall p himself with it on the ... Num 19:12 2398
but if he p not himself the third ... Num 19:12 2398
seventh day he shall p himself ... Num 19:19 2398
unclean, and shall not p himself ... Num 19:20 2398
p both yourselves and your ... Num 31:19 2398
p all your raiment, and all that ... Num 31:20 2398
of breakings they p themselves ... Job 41:25 2398
p themselves in the gardens ... Is 66:17 2891
they purge the altar and p it ... Eze 43:26 2891
he shall p the sons of Levi, and ... Mal 3:3 2891
the passover, to p themselves ... Jn 11:55 48
p thyself with them, and be at ... Acts 21:24 48
p unto himself a peculiar people ... Titus 2:14 2511
p your hearts, ye double minded ... Jas 4:8 48

PURIFYING
in the blood of her p three ... Lev 12:4 2893
the days of her p be fulfilled ... Lev 12:4 2892
in the blood of her p threescore ... Lev 12:5 2893
the days of her p are fulfilled ... Lev 12:6 2892
Sprinkle water of p upon them ... Num 8:7 2403
in the p of all holy things, and ... 1Chr 23:28 2893
things for the p of the women ... Est 2:12 8562
the manner of the p of the Jews ... Jn 2:6 2512
disciples and the Jews about p ... Jn 3:25 2512
and them, p their hearts by faith ... Acts 15:9 2511
the next day p himself with them ... Acts 21:26 48
sanctifieth to the p of the flesh ... Heb 9:13 2514

PURIM (*pu'-rim*) See PUR. *A Jewish festival celebrating the deliverance from Haman.*
days P after the name of Pur ... Est 9:26 6332
that these days of P should not ... Est 9:28 6332
confirm this second letter of P ... Est 9:29 6332
of P in their times appointed ... Est 9:31 6332
confirmed these matters of P ... Est 9:32 6332

PURITY
in spirit, in faith, in p ... 1Ti 4:12 47
younger as sisters, with all p ... 1Ti 5:2 47

PURLOINING
Not p, but shewing all good ... Titus 2:10 3557

PURPLE
And blue, and p, and scarlet, and ... Ex 25:4 713
fine twined linen, and blue, and p ... Ex 26:1 713
shalt make a vail of blue, and p ... Ex 26:31 713
door of the tent, of blue, and p ... Ex 26:36 713
of twenty cubits, of blue, and p ... Ex 27:16 713
shall take gold, and blue, and p ... Ex 28:5 713
ephod of gold, of blue, and of p ... Ex 28:6 713
even of gold, of blue, and p ... Ex 28:8 713
of gold, of blue, and of p ... Ex 28:15 713
pomegranates of blue, and of p ... Ex 28:33 713
And blue, and p, and scarlet, and ... Ex 35:6 713
with whom was found blue, and p ... Ex 35:23 713
had spun, both of blue, and of p ... Ex 35:25 713
the embroiderer, in blue, and in p ... Ex 35:35 713
fine twined linen, and blue, and p ... Ex 36:8 713
And he made a vail of blue, and p ... Ex 36:35 713
the tabernacle door of blue, and p ... Ex 36:37 713
was needlework, of blue, and p ... Ex 38:18 713
an embroiderer in blue, and in p ... Ex 38:23 713
And of the blue, and p, and scarlet ... Ex 39:1 713
the ephod of gold, blue, and p ... Ex 39:2 713
work it in the blue, and in the p ... Ex 39:3 713
of gold, blue, and p, and scarlet ... Ex 39:5 713
of gold, blue, and p, and scarlet ... Ex 39:8 713
robe pomegranates of blue, and p ... Ex 39:24 713
fine twined linen, and blue, and p ... Ex 39:29 713
and spread a p cloth thereon ... Num 4:13 713
p raiment that was on the kings ... Judg 8:26 713
and in brass, and in iron, and in p ... 2Chr 2:7 710
in stone, and in timber, in p ... 2Chr 2:14 713
And he made the vail of blue, and p ... 2Chr 3:14 713
p to silver rings and pillars of ... Est 1:6 713
with a garment of fine linen and p ... Est 8:15 713
her clothing is silk and p ... Prov 31:22 713
of gold, the covering of it of p ... Song 3:10 713
and the hair of thine head like p ... Song 7:5 713
blue and p is their clothing ... Jer 10:9 713
p from the isles of Elishah was ... Eze 27:7 713
in thy fairs with emeralds, p ... Eze 27:16 713
And they clothed him with p ... Mk 15:17 4209
him, they took off the p from him ... Mk 15:20 4209
rich man, which was clothed in p ... Lk 16:19 4209
head, and they put on him a p robe ... Jn 19:2 4210
crown of thorns, and the p robe ... Jn 19:5 4210
woman named Lydia, a seller of p ... Acts 16:14 4211
And the woman was arrayed in p ... Rev 17:4 4209
and of pearls, and fine linen, and p ... Rev 18:12 4209
was clothed in fine linen, and p ... Rev 18:16 4210

PURPOSE
some of the handfuls of p for her ... Ruth 2:16 7997
I p to build an house unto the ... 1Kin 5:5 559
now ye p to keep under the ... 2Chr 28:10 559
them, to frustrate their p ... Ezr 4:5 6098
which they had made for the p ... Neh 8:4 1697
he may withdraw man from his p ... Job 33:17 4639
Every p is established by counsel ... Prov 20:18 4284
a time to every p under the ... Eccl 3:1 2656
there is a time there for every p ... Eccl 3:17 2656
Because to every p there is time ... Eccl 8:6 2656
To what p is the multitude of ... Is 1:11
This is the p that is purposed ... Is 14:26 6098
shall help in vain, and to no p ... Is 30:7 7385
To what p cometh there to me ... Jer 6:20
which I p to do unto them because ... Jer 26:3 2803
evil which I p to do unto them ... Jer 36:3 2803
and hath conceived a p against you ... Jer 49:30 4284
for every p of the LORD shall be ... Jer 51:29 4284
that the p might not be changed ... Dan 6:17 6640
saying, To what p is this waste ... Mt 26:8
that with p of heart they would ... Acts 11:23 4286
appeared unto thee for this p ... Acts 26:16
that they had obtained their p ... Acts 27:13 4286
save Paul, kept them from their p ... Acts 27:43 1013
are the called according to his p ... Rom 8:28 4286
that the p of God according to ... Rom 9:11 4286
Even for this same p have I ... Rom 9:17
or the things that I p ... 2Cor 1:17 1011
do I p according to the flesh ... 2Cor 1:17 1011
p of him who worketh all things ... Eph 1:11 4286
According to the eternal p which ... Eph 3:11 4286
have sent unto you for the same p ... Eph 6:22
have sent unto you for the same p ... Col 4:8
works, but according to his own p ... 2Ti 1:9 4286
my doctrine, manner of life, p ... 2Ti 3:10 4286
For this p the Son of God was ... 1Jn 3:8

PURPOSED
that he was p to fight against ... 2Chr 32:2 6440
I am p that my mouth shall not ... Ps 17:3 2161
who have p to overthrow my goings ... Ps 140:4 2803
and as I have p, so shall it stand ... Is 14:24 3289
that is p upon the whole earth ... Is 14:26 3289
For the LORD of hosts hath p ... Is 14:27 3289
LORD of hosts hath p upon Egypt ... Is 19:12 3289
The LORD of hosts hath p it ... Is 23:9 3289
I have p it, I will also do it ... Is 46:11 3335

I have spoken it, I have *p* it ... Jer 4:28 2161
that he hath *p* against the ... Jer 49:20 2803
that he hath *p* against the land ... Jer 50:45 2803
The LORD hath *p* to destroy the ... Lam 2:8 2803
But Daniel *p* in his heart that he ... Dan 1:8 7760
Paul *p* in the spirit, when he had ... Acts 19:21 *5087*
he *p* to return through Macedonia ... Acts 20:3 *1096*
oftentimes I *p* to come unto you ... Rom 1:13 *4388*
which he hath *p* in himself ... Eph 1:9 *4388*
he *p* in Christ Jesus our Lord ... Eph 3:11 *4160*

PURPOSES
my *p* are broken off, even the ... Job 17:11 2154
Without counsel *p* are ... Prov 15:22 4284
shall be broken in the *p* thereof ... Is 19:10 8356
and his *p*, that he hath purposed ... Jer 49:20 4284
and his *p*, that he hath purposed ... Jer 50:45 4284

PURPOSETH
according as he *p* in his heart ... 2Cor 9:7 *4255*

PURPOSING
comfort himself, *p* to kill thee ... Gen 27:42

PURSE
let us all have one *p* ... Prov 1:14 3599
no bread, no money in their *p* ... Mk 6:8 *2223*
Carry neither *p*, nor scrip, nor ... Lk 10:4 *905*
them, When I sent you without *p* ... Lk 22:35 *905*
them, But now, he that hath a *p* ... Lk 22:36 *905*

PURSES
nor silver, nor brass in your *p* ... Mt 10:9 *2223*

PURSUE
they did not *p* after the sons of ... Gen 35:5 7291
The enemy said, I will *p*, I will ... Ex 15:9 7291
avenger of the blood *p* the slayer ... Deut 19:6 7291
they shall *p* thee until thou ... Deut 28:22 7291
come upon thee, and shall *p* thee ... Deut 28:45 7291
p after them quickly ... Josh 2:5 7291
called together to *p* after them ... Josh 8:16 7291
but *p* after your enemies, and ... Josh 10:19 7291
the avenger of blood *p* after him ... Josh 20:5 7291
after whom dost thou *p* ... 1Sa 24:14 7291
Yet a man is risen to *p* thee ... 1Sa 25:29 7291
my lord thus *p* after his servant ... 1Sa 26:18 7291
Shall I *p* after this troop ... 1Sa 30:8 7291
And he answered him, *P* ... 1Sa 30:8 7291
arise and *p* after David this night ... 2Sa 17:1 7291
p after him, lest he get him ... 2Sa 20:6 7291
to *p* after Sheba the son of ... 2Sa 20:7 7291
to *p* after Sheba the son of ... 2Sa 20:13 7291
thine enemies, while they *p* thee ... 2Sa 24:13 7291
wilt thou *p* the dry stubble ... Job 13:25 7291
they *p* my soul as the wind ... Job 30:15 7291
seek peace, and *p* it ... Ps 34:14 7291
shall they that *p* you be swift ... Is 30:16 7291
the sword shall *p* thee ... Jer 48:2 3212
unto blood, and blood shall *p* thee ... Eze 35:6 7291
blood, even blood shall *p* thee ... Eze 35:6 7291
the enemy shall *p* him ... Hos 8:3 7291
because he did *p* his brother with ... Amos 1:11 7291
and darkness shall *p* his enemies ... Nah 1:8 7291

PURSUED
and eighteen, and *p* them unto Dan ... Gen 14:14 7291
p them unto Hobah, which is on ... Gen 14:15 7291
p after him seven days' journey ... Gen 31:23 7291
thou hast so hotly *p* after me ... Gen 31:36 1814
he *p* after the children of Israel ... Ex 14:8 7291
But the Egyptians *p* after them ... Ex 14:9 7291
And the Egyptians *p*, and went in ... Ex 14:23 7291
overflow them as they *p* after you ... Deut 11:4 7291
the men *p* after them the way to ... Josh 2:7 7291
as soon as they which *p* after ... Josh 2:7 7291
they *p* after Joshua, and were ... Josh 8:16 7291
the city open, and *p* after Israel ... Josh 8:17 7291
the Egyptians *p* after your ... Josh 24:6 7291
they *p* after him, and caught him, ... Judg 1:6 7291
But Barak *p* after the chariots, ... Judg 4:16 7291
And, behold, as Barak *p* Sisera ... Judg 4:22 7291
and *p* after the Midianites ... Judg 7:23 7291
p Midian, and brought the heads of ... Judg 7:25 7291
he *p* after them, and took the two ... Judg 8:12 7291
p hard after them unto Gidom, and ... Judg 20:45 1692
p the Philistines, and smote them, ... 1Sa 7:11 7291
p the Philistines, until thou ... 1Sa 17:52 7291
that, he *p* after David in the ... 1Sa 23:25 7291
But David *p*, he and four hundred ... 1Sa 30:10 7291
And Asahel *p* after Abner ... 2Sa 2:19 7291
also and Abishai *p* after Abner ... 2Sa 2:24 7291
p after Israel no more, neither ... 2Sa 2:28 7291
Abishai his brother *p* after Sheba ... 2Sa 20:10 7291
I have *p* mine enemies, and ... 2Sa 22:38 7291
and Israel *p* them ... 1Kin 20:20 7291
of the Chaldees *p* after the king ... 2Kin 25:5 7291
Abijah *p* after Jeroboam, and took ... 2Chr 13:19 7291
were with him *p* them unto Gerar ... 2Chr 14:13 7291
I have *p* mine enemies, and ... Ps 18:37 7291
He *p* them, and passed safely ... Is 41:3 7291
the Chaldeans' army *p* after them ... Jer 39:5 7291
of the Chaldeans *p* after the king ... Jer 52:8 7291
they *p* us upon the mountains, ... Lam 4:19 1814

PURSUER
without strength before the *p* ... Lam 1:6 7291

PURSUERS
the mountain, lest the *p* meet you ... Josh 2:16 7291
days, until the *p* be returned ... Josh 2:16 7291
until the *p* were returned ... Josh 2:22 7291
the *p* sought them throughout all ... Josh 2:22 7291
wilderness turned back upon the *p* ... Josh 8:20 7291

PURSUETH
and ye shall flee when none *p* you ... Lev 26:17 7291
and they shall fall when none *p* ... Lev 26:36 7291
were before a sword, when none *p* ... Lev 26:37 7291
so he that *p* evil *p* it to ... Prov 11:19 7291
evil *p* it to his own death ... Prov 11:19
Evil *p* sinners ... Prov 13:21 7291
he *p* them with words, yet they ... Prov 19:7 7291
The wicked flee when no man *p* ... Prov 28:1 7291

PURSUING
were with him, faint, yet *p* them ... Judg 8:4 7291
I am *p* after Zebah and Zalmunna, ... Judg 8:5 7291
Saul returned from *p* after David ... 1Sa 23:28 7291
David and Joab came from *p* a troop ... 2Sa 3:22
returned from *p* after Israel ... 2Sa 18:16 7291
either he is talking, or he is *p* ... 1Kin 18:27 7873
that they turned back from *p* him ... 1Kin 22:33 310
they turned back again from *p* him ... 2Chr 18:32 310

PURTENANCE
his legs, and with the *p* thereof ... Ex 12:9 7130

PUSH
to *p* with his horn in time past ... Ex 21:29 5056
If the ox shall *p* a manservant or ... Ex 21:32 5055
ox hath used to *p* in time past ... Ex 21:36 5056
with them he shall *p* the people ... Deut 33:17 5055
these shalt thou *p* the Syrians ... 1Kin 22:11 5055
With these thou shalt *p* Syria ... 2Chr 18:10 5055
they *p* away my feet, and they ... Job 30:12 7971
thee will we *p* down our enemies ... Ps 44:5 5055
the king of the south *p* at him ... Dan 11:40 5055

PUSHED
p all the diseased with your ... Eze 34:21 5055

PUSHING
I saw the ram *p* westward, and ... Dan 8:4 5055

PUT (*put*) See PHUT.
1. A verb.
there he *p* the man whom he had ... Gen 2:8 7760
p him into the garden of Eden to ... Gen 2:15 3240
I will *p* enmity between thee and ... Gen 3:15 7896
lest he *p* forth his hand, and take ... Gen 3:22 7971
then he *p* forth his hand, and took ... Gen 8:9 7971
But the men *p* forth their hand, ... Gen 19:10 7971
ruled over all that he had, *P* ... Gen 24:2 7760
the servant *p* his hand under the ... Gen 24:9 7760
I *p* the earring upon her face, and ... Gen 24:47 7760
wife shall surely be *p* to death ... Gen 26:11
p them upon Jacob her younger son ... Gen 27:15 3847
she *p* the skins of the kids of ... Gen 27:16 3847
p them for his pillows, and lay ... Gen 28:11 7760
that he had *p* for his pillows ... Gen 28:18 7760
bread to eat, and raiment to *p* on ... Gen 28:20 3847
p the stone again upon the well's ... Gen 29:3 7725
he *p* his own flocks by themselves ... Gen 30:40 7896
p them not unto Laban's cattle ... Gen 30:40 7896
were feeble, he *p* them not in ... Gen 30:42 7760
p them in the camel's furniture, ... Gen 31:34 7760
p a space betwixt drove and drove ... Gen 32:16 7760
he *p* the handmaids and their ... Gen 33:2 7760
P away the strange gods that are ... Gen 35:2 5493
p sackcloth upon his loins, and ... Gen 37:34 7760
she *p* her widow's garments off ... Gen 38:14 5493
her, and *p* on the garments of her ... Gen 38:19 3847
that the one *p* out his hand ... Gen 38:28 5414
that he had he *p* into his hand ... Gen 39:4 5414
p him into the prison, a place ... Gen 39:20 5414
he *p* them in ward in the house of ... Gen 40:3 5414
they should *p* me into the dungeon ... Gen 40:15 7760
p me in ward in the captain of ... Gen 41:10 5414
p it upon Joseph's hand, and ... Gen 41:42 5414
p a gold chain about his neck ... Gen 41:42 7760
he *p* them all together into ward ... Gen 42:17 622
we cannot tell who *p* our money in ... Gen 43:22 7760
p every man's money in his sack's ... Gen 44:1 7760
p my cup, the silver cup, in the ... Gen 44:2 7760
Joseph shall *p* his hand upon ... Gen 46:4 7896
have found grace in thy sight, *p* ... Gen 47:29 7760
p thy right hand upon his head ... Gen 48:18 7760
he was *p* in a coffin in Egypt ... Gen 50:26 3455
pitch, and *p* the child therein ... Ex 2:3 7760
p off thy shoes from off thy feet ... Ex 3:5 5394
ye shall *p* them upon your sons, ... Ex 3:22 7760
P forth thine hand, and take it by ... Ex 4:4 7971
he *p* forth his hand, and caught it ... Ex 4:4 7971
P now thine hand into thy bosom ... Ex 4:6 935
he *p* his hand into his bosom ... Ex 4:6 935
P thine hand into thy bosom again ... Ex 4:7 7725
he *p* his hand into his bosom ... Ex 4:7 7725
unto him, and *p* words in his mouth ... Ex 4:15 7760
which I have *p* in thine hand ... Ex 4:21 7760
to *p* a sword in their hand to ... Ex 5:21 5414
I will *p* a division between my ... Ex 8:23 7760
doth *p* a difference between the ... Ex 11:7
even the first day ye shall *p* ... Ex 12:15 7673
I will *p* none of these diseases ... Ex 15:26 7760
p an omer full of manna therein, ... Ex 16:33 5414
p it under him, and he sat thereon ... Ex 17:12 7760
for I will utterly *p* out the ... Ex 17:14 4229
mount shall be surely *p* to death ... Ex 19:12
die, shall be surely *p* to death ... Ex 21:12
shall surely be *p* to death ... Ex 21:15
he shall surely be *p* to death ... Ex 21:16
shall surely be *p* to death ... Ex 21:17
owner also shall be *p* to death ... Ex 21:29
shall *p* in his beast, and shall ... Ex 22:5 7971
to see whether he have *p* his hand ... Ex 22:8 7971
that he hath not *p* his hand unto ... Ex 22:11 7971
beast shall surely be *p* to death ... Ex 22:19
p not thine hand with the wicked ... Ex 23:1 7896
of the blood, and *p* it in basons ... Ex 24:6 7760
p them in the four corners ... Ex 25:12 5414
thou shalt *p* the staves into the ... Ex 25:14 935
thou shalt *p* into the ark the ... Ex 25:16 5414
thou shalt *p* the mercy seat above ... Ex 25:21 5414
in the ark thou shalt *p* the ... Ex 25:21 5414
p the rings in the four corners ... Ex 25:26 5414
p the taches into the loops, and ... Ex 26:11 935
thou shalt *p* the mercy seat upon ... Ex 26:34 5414
thou shalt *p* the table on the ... Ex 26:35 5414
thou shalt *p* it under the compass ... Ex 27:5 5414
staves shall be *p* into the rings ... Ex 27:7 935
thou shalt *p* the two stones upon ... Ex 28:12 7760
shalt *p* the two rings on the two ... Ex 28:23 5414
thou shalt *p* the two wreathen ... Ex 28:24 5414
p them on the shoulderpieces of ... Ex 28:25 5414
thou shalt *p* them upon the two ... Ex 28:26 7760
shalt *p* them on the two sides of ... Ex 28:27 5414
thou shalt *p* in the breastplate ... Ex 28:30 5414
thou shalt *p* it on a blue lace, ... Ex 28:37 7760
thou shalt *p* them upon Aaron thy ... Ex 28:41 3847
thou shalt *p* them into one basket ... Ex 29:3 5414
p upon Aaron the coat, and the ... Ex 29:5 3847
thou shalt *p* the mitre upon his ... Ex 29:6 7760
p the holy crown upon the mitre ... Ex 29:6 5414
his sons, and *p* coats upon them ... Ex 29:8 3847
sons, and *p* the bonnets on them ... Ex 29:9 2280
his sons shall *p* their hands upon ... Ex 29:10 5564
p it upon the horns of the altar ... Ex 29:12 5414
his sons shall *p* their hands upon ... Ex 29:15 5564
p them unto his pieces, and unto ... Ex 29:17 5414
his sons shall *p* their hands upon ... Ex 29:19 5564
p it upon the tip of the right ... Ex 29:20 5414
thou shalt *p* all in the hands of ... Ex 29:24 7760
stead shall *p* them on seven days ... Ex 29:30 3847
thou shalt *p* it before the vail ... Ex 30:6 5414
thou shalt *p* it between the ... Ex 30:18 5414
thou shalt *p* water therein ... Ex 30:18 5414
p of it before the testimony in ... Ex 30:36 5414
are wise hearted I have *p* wisdom ... Ex 31:6 5414
it shall surely be *p* to death ... Ex 31:14
he shall surely be *p* to death ... Ex 31:15
P every man his sword by his side ... Ex 32:27 7760
no man did *p* on him his ornaments ... Ex 33:4 7896
therefore now *p* off thy ornaments ... Ex 33:5 3381
that I will *p* thee in a clift of ... Ex 33:22 7760
them, he *p* a vail on his face ... Ex 34:33 5414
Moses *p* the vail upon his face ... Ex 34:35 7725
work therein shall be *p* to death ... Ex 35:2
he hath *p* in his heart that he ... Ex 35:34 5414
man, in whom the LORD *p* wisdom ... Ex 36:1 5414
whose heart the LORD had *p* wisdom ... Ex 36:2 5414
he *p* the staves into the rings by ... Ex 37:5 935
p the rings upon the four corners ... Ex 37:13 5414
he *p* the staves into the rings on ... Ex 38:7 935
he *p* them on the shoulders of the ... Ex 39:7 7760
p the two rings in the two ends ... Ex 39:16 5414
they *p* the two wreathen chains of ... Ex 39:17 5414
p them on the shoulderpieces of ... Ex 39:18 5414
p them on the two ends of the ... Ex 39:19 7760
p them on the two sides of the ... Ex 39:20 5414
gold, and *p* the bells between the ... Ex 39:25 5414
thou shalt *p* therein the ark of ... Ex 40:3 7760
p the hanging of the door to the ... Ex 40:5 7760
altar, and shalt *p* water therein ... Ex 40:7 5414
thou shalt *p* upon Aaron the holy ... Ex 40:13 3847
p in the bars thereof, and reared ... Ex 40:18 5414
p the covering of the tent above ... Ex 40:19 7760
p the testimony into the ark, and ... Ex 40:20 5114
p the mercy seat above upon the ... Ex 40:20 5114
he *p* the table in the tent of the ... Ex 40:22 5114
he *p* the candlestick in the tent ... Ex 40:24 7760
he *p* the golden altar in the tent ... Ex 40:26 7760
he *p* the altar of burnt offering ... Ex 40:29 7760
p water there, to wash withal ... Ex 40:30 5414
he shall *p* his hand upon the head ... Lev 1:4 5564
shall *p* fire upon the altar ... Lev 1:7 5414
it, and *p* frankincense thereon ... Lev 2:1 5414
thou shalt *p* oil upon it, and lay ... Lev 2:15 5414
the priest shall *p* some of the ... Lev 4:7 5414
he shall *p* some of the blood upon ... Lev 4:18 5414
p it upon the horns of the altar ... Lev 4:25 5414
p it upon the horns of the altar ... Lev 4:30 5414
p it upon the horns of the altar ... Lev 4:34 5414
he shall *p* no oil upon it, ... Lev 5:11 7760
upon it, neither shall he *p* any ... Lev 5:11 5414
the priest shall *p* on his linen ... Lev 6:10 3847
shall he *p* upon his flesh ... Lev 6:10 3847
he shall *p* them beside the altar ... Lev 6:10 7760
he shall *p* off his garments, and ... Lev 6:11 6584
p on other garments, and carry ... Lev 6:11 3847
it shall not be *p* out ... Lev 6:12 3518
he *p* upon him the coat, and girded ... Lev 8:7 5414
p the ephod upon him, and he ... Lev 8:7 5414
he *p* the breastplate upon him ... Lev 8:8 7760
also he *p* in the breastplate the ... Lev 8:8 5414
he *p* the mitre upon his head ... Lev 8:9 7760
did he *p* the golden plate, the ... Lev 8:9 7760
p coats upon them, and girded them ... Lev 8:13 3847
girdles, and *p* bonnets upon them ... Lev 8:13 2280
p it upon the horns of the altar ... Lev 8:15 5414
p it upon the tip of Aaron's ... Lev 8:23 5414
Moses *p* of the blood upon the tip ... Lev 8:24 5414
p them on the fat, and upon the ... Lev 8:26 7760
he *p* all upon Aaron's hands, and ... Lev 8:27 5414
p it upon the horns of the altar, ... Lev 9:9 5414
they *p* the fat upon the breasts, ... Lev 9:20 7760
p fire therein, and *p* incense ... Lev 10:1 5414
p incense thereon, and offered ... Lev 10:1 7760
that ye may *p* difference between ... Lev 10:10
is done, it must be *p* into water ... Lev 11:32 935
if any water be *p* upon the seed ... Lev 11:38 5414
he shall *p* a covering upon his ... Lev 13:45
the priest shall *p* it upon the ... Lev 14:14 5414
p upon the tip of the right ear ... Lev 14:17 5414
p it upon the tip of the right ... Lev 14:25 5414
the priest shall *p* of the oil ... Lev 14:28 5414
in the priest's hand he shall *p* ... Lev 14:29 5414
I *p* the plague of leprosy in a ... Lev 14:34 5414
p them in the place of those ... Lev 14:42 935
she shall be *p* apart seven days ... Lev 15:19 5079

He shall *p* on the holy linen coat	Lev 16:4	3847
flesh in water, and so *p* them on	Lev 16:4	3847
he shall *p* the incense upon the	Lev 16:13	5414
p it upon the horns of the altar	Lev 16:18	5414
shall *p* off the linen garments,	Lev 16:23	6584
which he *p* on when he went into	Lev 16:23	3847
p on his garments, and come forth,	Lev 16:24	3847
shall *p* on the linen clothes,	Lev 16:32	3847
as long as she is *p* apart for her	Lev 18:19	5079
nor *p* a stumblingblock before the	Lev 19:14	5414
they shall not be *p* to death	Lev 19:20	
he shall surely be *p* to death	Lev 20:2	
mother shall be surely *p* to death	Lev 20:9	
shall surely be *p* to death	Lev 20:10	
them shall surely be *p* to death	Lev 20:11	
them shall surely be *p* to death	Lev 20:12	
they shall surely be *p* to death	Lev 20:13	
he shall surely be *p* to death	Lev 20:15	
they shall surely be *p* to death	Lev 20:16	
Ye shall therefore *p* difference	Lev 20:25	
shall surely be *p* to death	Lev 20:27	
a woman *p* away from her husband	Lev 21:7	1644
consecrated to *p* on the garments	Lev 21:10	3847
then he shall *p* the fifth part	Lev 22:14	3254
thou shalt *p* pure frankincense	Lev 24:7	5414
they *p* him in ward, that the mind	Lev 24:12	3240
he shall surely be *p* to death	Lev 24:16	
of the LORD, shall be *p* to death	Lev 24:16	
man shall surely be *p* to death	Lev 24:17	
a man, he shall be *p* to death	Lev 24:21	
shall *p* ten thousand to flight	Lev 26:8	
but shall surely be *p* to death	Lev 27:29	
cometh nigh shall be *p* to death	Num 1:51	
cometh nigh shall be *p* to death	Num 3:10	
cometh nigh shall be *p* to death	Num 3:38	
shall *p* thereon the covering of	Num 4:6	5414
shall *p* in the staves thereof	Num 4:6	7760
p thereon the dishes, and the	Num 4:7	5414
shall *p* in the staves thereof	Num 4:8	7760
And they shall *p* it and all the	Num 4:10	5414
skins, and shall *p* it upon a bar	Num 4:10	5414
shall *p* to the staves thereof	Num 4:11	7725
p them in a cloth of blue, and	Num 4:12	5414
skins, and shall *p* them on a bar	Num 4:12	5414
they shall *p* upon it all the	Num 4:14	5414
skins, and *p* to the staves of it	Num 4:14	7760
that they *p* out of the camp every	Num 5:2	7971
male and female shall ye *p* out	Num 5:3	7971
without the camp shall ye *p* them	Num 5:3	7971
p them out without the camp	Num 5:4	7971
nor *p* frankincense thereon	Num 5:15	5414
take, and *p* it into the water	Num 5:17	5414
p the offering of memorial in her	Num 5:18	5414
p it in the fire which is under	Num 6:18	5414
shall *p* them upon the hands of	Num 6:19	5414
they shall *p* my name upon the	Num 6:27	7760
p their hands upon the Levites	Num 8:10	5564
upon thee, and will *p* it upon them	Num 11:17	7760
that the LORD would *p* his spirit	Num 11:29	5414
they *p* him in ward, because it	Num 15:34	3240
man shall be surely *p* to death	Num 15:35	
that they *p* upon the fringe of	Num 15:38	5414
p fire therein, and *p* incense in	Num 16:7	5414
p incense in them before the LORD	Num 16:7	7760
wilt thou *p* out the eyes of these	Num 16:14	5365
p incense in them, and bring ye	Num 16:17	5414
p fire in them, and laid incense	Num 16:18	5414
p fire therein from off the altar	Num 16:46	5414
p on incense, and go quickly unto	Num 16:46	7760
he *p* on incense, and made an	Num 16:47	5414
cometh nigh shall be *p* to death	Num 18:7	
shall be *p* thereto in a vessel	Num 19:17	5414
p them upon Eleazar his son	Num 20:26	3847
p them upon Eleazar his son	Num 20:28	3847
p it upon a pole, and it came to	Num 21:9	7760
the LORD *p* a word in Balaam's	Num 23:5	7760
which the LORD hath *p* in my mouth	Num 23:12	7760
p a word in his mouth, and said,	Num 23:16	7760
thou shalt *p* some of thine honour	Num 27:20	5414
shall surely be *p* to death	Num 35:16	
shall surely be *p* to death	Num 35:17	
shall surely be *p* to death	Num 35:18	
him shall surely be *p* to death	Num 35:21	
the murderer shall be *p* to death	Num 35:30	
but he shall be surely *p* to death	Num 35:31	
shall be *p* to the inheritance of	Num 36:3	3254
be *p* unto the inheritance of the	Num 36:4	3254
I begin to *p* the dread of thee	Deut 2:25	5414
will *p* none of the evil diseases	Deut 7:15	7760
the LORD thy God will *p* out those	Deut 7:22	5394
thou shalt *p* them in the ark	Deut 10:2	7760
p the tables in the ark which I	Deut 10:5	7760
that thou shalt *p* the blessing	Deut 11:29	5414
your tribes to *p* his name there	Deut 12:5	7760
in all that ye *p* your hand unto	Deut 12:7	4916
p his name there be too far from	Deut 12:21	7760
of dreams, shall be *p* to death	Deut 13:5	
So shalt thou *p* the evil away	Deut 13:5	1197
first upon him to *p* him to death	Deut 13:9	
to *p* the sickle to the corn	Deut 16:9	
is worthy of death be *p* to death	Deut 17:6	
he shall not be *p* to death	Deut 17:6	
first upon him to *p* him to death	Deut 17:7	
So thou shalt *p* the evil away	Deut 17:7	1197
thou shalt *p* away the evil from	Deut 17:12	1197
will *p* my words in his mouth	Deut 18:18	5414
but thou shalt *p* away the guilt	Deut 19:13	1197
so shalt thou *p* the evil away	Deut 19:19	1197
So shalt thou *p* away the guilt of	Deut 21:9	1197
she shall *p* the raiment of her	Deut 21:13	5493
so shalt thou *p* evil away from	Deut 21:21	1197
death, and he be to be *p* to death	Deut 21:22	
neither shall a man *p* on a	Deut 22:5	3847
he may not *p* her away all his	Deut 22:19	7971

so shalt thou *p* evil away from	Deut 22:21	1197
so shalt thou *p* away evil from	Deut 22:22	1197
so thou shalt *p* away evil from	Deut 22:24	1197
he may not *p* her away all his	Deut 22:29	7971
shalt not *p* any in thy vessel	Deut 23:24	5414
thou shalt *p* evil away from among	Deut 24:7	1197
The fathers shall not be *p* to	Deut 24:16	
be *p* to death for the fathers	Deut 24:16	
every man shall be *p* to death for	Deut 24:16	
his name be not *p* out of Israel	Deut 25:6	4229
shalt *p* it in a basket, and shalt	Deut 26:2	7760
he shall *p* a yoke of iron upon	Deut 28:48	5414
the LORD thy God will *p* all these	Deut 30:7	5414
p it in their mouths, that this	Deut 31:19	7760
p it in the side of the ark of	Deut 31:26	7760
two *p* ten thousand to flight,	Deut 32:30	
they shall *p* incense before thee,	Deut 33:10	7760
things *p* forth by the moon	Deut 33:14	1645
him, he shall be *p* to death	Josh 1:18	
they *p* into the treasury of the	Josh 6:24	5414
and *p* dust upon their heads	Josh 7:6	5927
they have *p* it even among their	Josh 7:11	7760
p your feet upon the necks of	Josh 10:24	7760
p their feet upon the necks of	Josh 10:24	7760
that they *p* the Canaanites to	Josh 17:13	5414
he *p* darkness between you and the	Josh 24:7	7760
p away the gods which your	Josh 24:14	5493
Now therefore *p* away, said he,	Josh 24:23	5493
that they *p* the Canaanites to	Judg 1:28	7760
Ehud *p* forth his left hand, and	Judg 3:21	7971
She *p* her hand to the nail, and	Judg 5:26	7971
the flesh he *p* in a basket	Judg 6:19	7760
he *p* the broth in a pot, and	Judg 6:19	7760
Then the angel of the LORD *p*	Judg 6:21	7971
let him be *p* to death whilst it	Judg 6:31	
I will *p* a fleece of wool in the	Judg 6:37	3322
he *p* a trumpet in every man's	Judg 7:16	5414
p it in his city, even in Ophrah	Judg 8:27	3322
p your trust in my shadow	Judg 9:15	
the men of Shechem *p* their	Judg 9:26	
p them to the hold, and set the	Judg 9:49	7760
they *p* away the strange gods from	Judg 10:16	5493
I *p* my life in my hands, and	Judg 12:3	7760
I will now *p* forth a riddle unto	Judg 14:12	2330
P forth thy riddle, that we may	Judg 14:13	2330
thou hast *p* forth a riddle unto	Judg 14:16	2330
p a firebrand in the midst	Judg 15:4	7760
p forth his hand, and took it, and	Judg 15:15	7971
p them upon his shoulders, and	Judg 16:3	7760
p out his eyes, and brought him	Judg 16:21	5365
that might *p* them to shame in any	Judg 18:7	3637
p the little ones and the cattle	Judg 18:21	7760
that we may *p* them to death, and	Judg 20:13	
death, and *p* away evil from Israel	Judg 20:13	1197
the men of Israel *p* themselves in	Judg 20:20	
p themselves in array the first	Judg 20:22	
p themselves in array against	Judg 20:30	
and *p* themselves in array at	Judg 20:33	
He shall surely be *p* to death	Judg 21:5	
p thy raiment upon thee, and get	Ruth 3:3	7760
p away thy wine from thee	1Sa 1:14	5493
P me, I pray thee, into one of	1Sa 2:36	5596
the Philistines *p* themselves in	1Sa 4:2	
p the jewels of gold, which ye	1Sa 6:8	7760
p them on the great stone	1Sa 6:15	7760
then *p* away the strange gods and	1Sa 7:3	5493
of Israel did *p* away Baalim	1Sa 7:4	5493
your asses, and *p* them to his work	1Sa 8:16	6213
that Saul *p* the people in three	1Sa 11:11	7760
that we may *p* them to death	1Sa 11:12	
not a man be *p* to death this day	1Sa 11:13	
but no man *p* his hand to his	1Sa 14:26	5381
wherefore he *p* forth the end of	1Sa 14:27	7971
and *p* his hand to his mouth	1Sa 14:27	7725
had *p* the battle in array	1Sa 17:21	
he *p* an helmet of brass upon his	1Sa 17:38	5414
And David *p* them off him	1Sa 17:39	5493
p them in a shepherd's bag which	1Sa 17:40	7760
David *p* his hand in his bag, and	1Sa 17:49	7971
but he *p* his armour in his tent	1Sa 17:54	7760
For he did *p* his life in his hand	1Sa 19:5	7760
p a pillow of goats' hair for his	1Sa 19:13	7760
to *p* hot bread in the day when it	1Sa 21:6	7760
p forth their hand to fall upon	1Sa 22:17	7971
I will not *p* forth mine hand	1Sa 24:10	7971
Saul had *p* away those that had	1Sa 28:3	5493
p on other raiment, and he went,	1Sa 28:8	3847
I have *p* my life in my hand, and	1Sa 28:21	7760
they *p* his armour in the house of	1Sa 31:10	7760
who *p* on ornaments of gold upon	2Sa 1:24	5927
nor thy feet *p* into fetters	2Sa 3:34	5056
Uzzah *p* forth his hand to the ark	2Sa 6:6	7971
whom I *p* away before thee	2Sa 7:15	5493
lines measured he to *p* to death	2Sa 8:2	
Then David *p* garrisons in Syria	2Sa 8:6	7760
And he *p* garrisons in Edom	2Sa 8:14	7760
all Edom *p* he garrisons, and all	2Sa 8:14	7760
p the battle in array at the	2Sa 10:8	
p them in array against the	2Sa 10:9	
that he might *p* them in array	2Sa 10:10	
The LORD also hath *p* away thy sin	2Sa 12:13	5674
p them under saws, and under	2Sa 12:31	7760
P now this woman out from me, and	2Sa 13:17	7971
Tamar *p* ashes on her head, and	2Sa 13:19	3947
p on now mourning apparel, and	2Sa 14:2	3847
So Joab *p* the words in her mouth	2Sa 14:3	7760
he *p* all these words in the mouth	2Sa 14:19	7760
he *p* forth his hand, and took him,	2Sa 15:5	7971
p his household in order, and	2Sa 17:23	
yet would I not *p* forth mine hand	2Sa 18:12	7971
not Shimei be *p* to death for this	2Sa 19:21	
shall there any man be *p* to death	2Sa 19:22	
p them in ward, and fed them, but	2Sa 20:3	5414
he had *p* on was girded unto him	2Sa 20:8	5414

were *p* to death in the days of	2Sa 21:9	
p the blood of war upon his	1Kin 2:5	5414
I will not *p* thee to death with	1Kin 2:8	
shall be *p* to death this day	1Kin 2:24	
not at this time *p* thee to death	1Kin 2:26	
the king *p* Benaiah the son of	1Kin 2:35	5414
king *p* in the room of Abiathar	1Kin 2:35	5414
until the LORD *p* them under the	1Kin 5:3	5414
he *p* five bases on the right side	1Kin 7:39	5414
did he *p* among the treasures of	1Kin 7:51	5414
which Moses *p* there at Horeb,	1Kin 8:9	3240
to *p* my name there for ever	1Kin 9:3	7760
the king *p* them in the house of	1Kin 10:17	5414
which God had *p* in his heart	1Kin 10:24	5414
have chosen me to *p* my name there	1Kin 11:36	7760
his heavy yoke which he *p* upon us	1Kin 12:4	5414
thy father did *p* upon us lighter	1Kin 12:9	5414
Beth-el, and the other *p* he in Dan	1Kin 12:29	5414
that he *p* forth his hand from the	1Kin 13:4	7971
which he *p* forth against him,	1Kin 13:4	7971
of Israel, to *p* his name there	1Kin 14:21	7760
it on wood, and *p* no fire under	1Kin 18:23	7760
it on wood, and *p* no fire under	1Kin 18:23	7760
of your gods, but *p* no fire under	1Kin 18:25	7760
he *p* the wood in order, and cut	1Kin 18:33	6186
p his face between his knees,	1Kin 18:42	7760
they shall *p* it in their hand, and	1Kin 20:6	7760
p captains in their rooms	1Kin 20:24	7760
p sackcloth on our loins, and	1Kin 20:31	7760
p ropes on their heads, and came	1Kin 20:32	
p sackcloth upon his flesh, and	1Kin 21:27	7760
having *p* on their robes, in a	1Kin 22:10	3847
the LORD hath *p* a lying spirit in	1Kin 22:23	5414
P this fellow in the prison, and	1Kin 22:27	7760
but *p* thou on thy robes	1Kin 22:30	3847
me a new cruse, and *p* salt therein	2Kin 2:20	7760
for he *p* away the image of Baal	2Kin 3:2	5493
all that were able to *p* on armour	2Kin 3:21	2296
p his mouth upon his mouth, and	2Kin 4:34	7760
he *p* out his hand, and took it	2Kin 6:7	7971
p it under him on the top of the	2Kin 9:13	7760
p their heads in baskets, and sent	2Kin 10:7	7760
p the crown upon him, and gave him	2Kin 11:12	5414
p therein all the money that was	2Kin 12:9	5414
they *p* up in bags, and told the	2Kin 12:10	6695
P thine hand upon the bow	2Kin 13:16	7392
And he *p* his hand upon it	2Kin 13:16	7760
Elisha *p* his hands upon the	2Kin 13:16	7760
The fathers shall not be *p* to	2Kin 14:6	4191
nor the children be *p* to death	2Kin 14:6	4191
but every man shall be *p* to death	2Kin 14:6	4191
Judah was *p* to the worse before	2Kin 14:12	
p it on the north side of the	2Kin 16:14	5414
p it upon a pavement of stones	2Kin 16:17	5414
p them in the houses of the high	2Kin 17:29	3240
p them in Halah and in Habor by	2Kin 18:11	5148
p thy trust on Egypt for chariots	2Kin 18:24	
therefore I will *p* my hook in thy	2Kin 19:28	7760
In Jerusalem will I *p* my name	2Kin 21:4	7760
will I *p* my name for ever	2Kin 21:7	7760
he *p* down the idolatrous priests,	2Kin 23:5	7673
in Jerusalem, did Josiah *p* away	2Kin 23:24	1197
Pharaoh-nechoh *p* him in bands at	2Kin 23:33	
p the land to a tribute of an	2Kin 23:33	
p out the eyes of Zedekiah, and	2Kin 25:7	5786
because they *p* their trust in him	1Chr 5:20	
they *p* his armour in the house of	1Chr 10:10	7760
have *p* their lives in jeopardy	1Chr 11:19	5414
they *p* to flight all them of the	1Chr 12:15	7760
Uzza *p* forth his hand to hold the	1Chr 13:9	7971
because he *p* his hand to the ark	1Chr 13:10	7971
Then David *p* garrisons in	1Chr 18:6	7760
And he *p* garrisons in Edom	1Chr 18:13	7760
p the battle in array before the	1Chr 19:9	
p them in array against the	1Chr 19:10	
were *p* to the worse before Israel	1Chr 19:16	
So when David had *p* the battle in	1Chr 19:17	
were *p* to the worse before Israel	1Chr 19:19	
he *p* up his sword again into the	1Chr 21:27	7725
number *p* in the account of the	1Chr 27:24	5927
he *p* before the tabernacle of the	2Chr 1:5	7760
device which shall be *p* to him	2Chr 2:14	5414
p them on the heads of the	2Chr 3:16	5414
and *p* them on the chains	2Chr 3:16	5414
p five on the right hand, and five	2Chr 4:6	5414
p he among the treasures of the	2Chr 5:1	5414
which Moses *p* therein at Horeb	2Chr 5:10	5414
And in it have I *p* the ark	2Chr 6:11	7760
thou wouldest *p* thy name there	2Chr 6:20	7760
if thy people Israel be *p* to the	2Chr 6:24	
the king *p* them in the house of	2Chr 9:16	5414
that God had *p* in his heart	2Chr 9:23	5414
his heavy yoke that he *p* upon us	2Chr 10:4	5414
that thy father did *p* upon us	2Chr 10:9	5414
my father *p* a heavy yoke upon you	2Chr 10:11	6006
I will *p* more to your yoke	2Chr 10:11	3254
p captains in them, and store of	2Chr 11:11	5414
every several city he *p* shields	2Chr 11:12	
of Israel, to *p* his name there	2Chr 12:13	7760
p away the abominable idols out	2Chr 15:8	5674
of Israel should be *p* to death	2Chr 15:13	
seer, and *p* him in a prison house	2Chr 16:10	5414
beside those whom the king *p* in	2Chr 17:19	5414
the LORD hath *p* a lying spirit in	2Chr 18:22	5414
P this fellow in the prison, and	2Chr 18:26	7760
but *p* thou on thy robes	2Chr 18:29	3847
slain, and *p* him and his nurse in a	2Chr 22:11	5414
the house, he shall be *p* to death	2Chr 23:7	
p upon him the crown, and gave him	2Chr 23:11	5414
Judah was *p* to the worse before	2Chr 25:22	
p out the lamps, and have not	2Chr 29:7	3518
will I *p* my name for ever	2Chr 33:7	7760
p captains of war in all the	2Chr 33:14	7760
they *p* it in the hand of the	2Chr 34:10	5414

P the holy ark in the house which	2Chr 35:3	5414
p him in the second chariot that	2Chr 35:24	7392
the king of Egypt *p* him down at	2Chr 36:3	5493
p them in his temple at Babylon	2Chr 36:7	5414
p it also in writing, saying,	2Chr 36:22	
p it also in writing, saying,	Ezr 1:1	
had *p* them in the house of his	Ezr 1:7	5414
polluted, *p* from the priesthood	Ezr 2:62	
that shall *p* to their hand to	Ezr 6:12	7972
which hath *p* such a thing as this	Ezr 7:27	5414
our God to *p* away all the wives	Ezr 10:3	3318
they would *p* away their wives	Ezr 10:19	3318
p in my heart to do at Jerusalem	Neh 2:12	5414
but their nobles *p* not their	Neh 3:5	935
none of us *p* off our clothes,	Neh 4:23	6584
every one *p* them off for washing	Neh 4:23	7973
that would have *p* me in fear	Neh 6:14	
sent letters to *p* me in fear	Neh 6:19	
my God *p* into mine heart to	Neh 7:5	5414
polluted, *p* from the priesthood	Neh 7:64	
p on sackcloth with ashes, and	Est 4:1	3847
one law of his to *p* him to death	Est 4:11	
that Esther *p* on her royal	Est 5:1	3847
besought him with tears to *p* away	Est 8:3	5674
drew near to be *p* in execution	Est 9:1	
But *p* forth thine hand now, and	Job 1:11	7971
only upon himself *p* not forth	Job 1:12	7971
But *p* forth thine hand now, and	Job 2:5	7971
he *p* no trust in his servants	Job 4:18	
p it far away, and let not	Job 11:14	
teeth, and *p* my life in mine hand	Job 13:14	7760
p me in a surety with thee	Job 17:3	
of the wicked shall be *p* out	Job 18:5	1846
candle shall be *p* out with him	Job 18:6	1846
He hath *p* my brethren far from me	Job 19:13	
is the candle of the wicked *p* out	Job 21:17	1846
thou shalt *p* away iniquity far	Job 22:23	
but he would *p* strength in me	Job 23:6	7760
it, but the just shall *p* it on	Job 27:17	3847
I *p* on righteousness, and it	Job 29:14	3847
Who hath *p* wisdom in the inward	Job 38:36	7896
Canst thou *p* an hook into his	Job 41:2	7760
they that *p* their trust in him	Ps 2:12	
and *p* your trust in the LORD	Ps 4:5	
Thou hast *p* gladness in my heart,	Ps 4:7	5414
But let all those that *p* their	Ps 5:11	
my God, in thee do I *p* my trust	Ps 7:1	
thou hast *p* all things under his	Ps 8:6	7896
thou hast *p* out their name for	Ps 9:5	4229
name will *p* their trust in thee	Ps 9:10	
P them in fear, O LORD	Ps 9:20	7896
In the LORD *p* I my trust	Ps 11:1	
for in thee do I *p* my trust	Ps 16:1	
by thy right hand them which *p*	Ps 17:7	
I did not *p* away his statutes	Ps 18:22	5493
for I *p* my trust in thee	Ps 25:20	
p not thy servant away in anger	Ps 27:9	5186
thou hast *p* off my sackcloth, and	Ps 30:11	6605
IN thee, O LORD, do I *p* my trust	Ps 31:1	
the lying lips be *p* to silence	Ps 31:18	
p to shame that seek after my	Ps 35:4	
therefore the children of men *p*	Ps 36:7	
he hath *p* a new song in my mouth,	Ps 40:3	5414
p to shame that wish me evil	Ps 40:14	
hast *p* them to shame that hated	Ps 44:7	
hast cast off, and *p* us to shame	Ps 44:9	
thou hast *p* them to shame,	Ps 53:5	
He hath *p* forth his hands against	Ps 55:20	7971
word, in God I have *p* my trust	Ps 56:4	
p thou my tears into thy bottle	Ps 56:8	5414
In God have I *p* my trust	Ps 56:11	
p to confusion, that desire my	Ps 70:2	
In thee, O LORD, do I *p* my trust	Ps 71:1	
let me never be *p* to confusion	Ps 71:1	
I have *p* my trust in the Lord GOD	Ps 73:28	7896
he *p* them to a perpetual reproach	Ps 78:66	5414
yea, let them be *p* to shame	Ps 83:17	
Thou hast *p* away mine	Ps 88:8	7368
and friend hast thou *p* far from me	Ps 88:18	7368
LORD than to *p* confidence in man	Ps 118:8	
than to *p* confidence in princes	Ps 118:9	
O LORD, *p* me not to shame	Ps 119:31	
lest the righteous *p* forth their	Ps 125:3	7971
P not your trust in princes, nor	Ps 146:3	
P away from thee a froward mouth,	Prov 4:24	5493
and perverse lips *p* far from thee	Prov 4:24	7368
understanding *p* forth her voice	Prov 8:1	5414
lamp of the wicked shall be *p* out	Prov 13:9	1846
his lamp shall be *p* out in	Prov 20:20	1846
p a knife to thy throat, if thou	Prov 23:2	7760
of the wicked shall be *p* out	Prov 24:20	1846
P not forth thyself in the	Prov 25:6	1921
than that thou shouldest be *p*	Prov 25:7	
neighbour hath *p* thee to shame	Prov 25:8	
that heareth it *p* thee to shame	Prov 25:10	
them that *p* their trust in him	Prov 30:5	
nothing can be *p* to it, nor any	Eccl 3:14	3254
then must he *p* to more strength	Eccl 10:10	1396
p away evil from thy flesh	Eccl 11:10	5674
I have *p* off my coat	Song 5:3	6584
how shall I *p* it on	Song 5:3	3847
My beloved *p* in his hand by the	Song 5:4	7971
p away the evil of your doings	Is 1:16	5493
that *p* darkness for light, and	Is 5:20	7760
that *p* bitter for sweet, and sweet	Is 5:20	7760
I have *p* down the inhabitants	Is 10:13	3381
the weaned child shall *p* his hand	Is 11:8	1911
p off thy shoe from thy foot	Is 20:2	2502
p thy trust on Egypt for chariots	Is 36:9	
therefore will I *p* my hook in thy	Is 37:29	7760
I have *p* my spirit upon him	Is 42:1	5414
P me in remembrance	Is 43:26	
shalt not be able to *p* if off	Is 47:11	3722
divorcement, whom I have *p* away	Is 50:1	7971
is your mother *p* away	Is 50:1	7971
p on strength, O arm of the LORD	Is 51:9	3847
I have *p* my words in thy mouth,	Is 51:16	7760
But I will *p* it into the hand of	Is 51:23	7760
p on thy strength, O Zion	Is 52:1	3847
p on thy beautiful garments, O	Is 52:1	3847
he hath *p* him to grief	Is 53:10	
for thou shalt not be *p* to shame	Is 54:4	
For he *p* on righteousness as a	Is 59:17	3847
he *p* on the garments of vengeance	Is 59:17	3847
words which I have *p* in thy mouth	Is 59:21	7760
where is he that *p* his holy	Is 63:11	7760
Then the LORD *p* forth his hand,	Jer 1:9	7971
I have *p* my words in thy mouth	Jer 1:9	5414
If a man *p* away his wife, and she	Jer 3:1	7971
adultery I had *p* her away	Jer 3:8	7971
How shall I *p* thee among the	Jer 3:19	7896
if thou wilt *p* away thine	Jer 4:1	5493
P your burnt offerings unto your	Jer 7:21	5595
LORD our God hath *p* us to silence	Jer 8:14	
they have *p* themselves to pain,	Jer 12:13	
p it upon thy loins, and *p* it	Jer 13:1	7760
thy loins, and *p* it not in water	Jer 13:1	7760
of the LORD, and *p* it on my loins	Jer 13:2	7760
and let their men be *p* to death	Jer 18:21	2026
p him in the stocks that were in	Jer 20:2	5414
that if ye *p* me to death, ye	Jer 26:15	
all Judah *p* him at all to death	Jer 26:19	
the king sought to *p* him to death	Jer 26:21	
of the people to *p* him to death	Jer 26:24	
yokes, and *p* them upon thy neck,	Jer 27:2	5414
that will not *p* their neck under	Jer 27:8	5414
I have *p* a yoke of iron upon the	Jer 28:14	5414
thou shouldest *p* him in prison	Jer 29:26	5414
I will *p* my law in their inward	Jer 31:33	5414
p them in an earthen vessel, that	Jer 32:14	5414
but I will *p* my fear in their	Jer 32:40	5414
they had not *p* him into prison	Jer 37:4	5414
p him in prison in the house of	Jer 37:15	5414
that ye have *p* me in prison	Jer 37:18	5414
thee, let this man be *p* to death	Jer 38:4	
heard that they had *p* Jeremiah in	Jer 38:7	5414
P now these old cast clouts and	Jer 38:12	7760
thou not surely *p* me to death	Jer 38:15	
I will not *p* thee to death,	Jer 38:16	
we will not *p* thee to death	Jer 38:25	
Moreover he *p* out Zedekiah's eyes	Jer 39:7	5786
thou hast *p* thy trust in me	Jer 39:18	
p them in your vessels, and dwell	Jer 40:10	7760
that they might *p* us to death	Jer 43:3	
spears, and *p* on the brigandines	Jer 46:4	3847
p up thyself into thy scabbard,	Jer 47:6	622
P yourselves in array against	Jer 50:14	
upon horses, every one *p* in array	Jer 50:42	
Then he *p* out the eyes of	Jer 52:11	5786
p him in prison till the day of	Jer 52:11	5411
p them to death in Riblah in the	Jer 52:27	
they shall *p* bands upon thee, and	Eze 3:25	5414
p them in one vessel, and make	Eze 4:9	5414
he *p* forth the form of an hand,	Eze 8:3	7971
they *p* the branch to their nose	Eze 8:17	7971
p it into the hands of him that	Eze 10:7	5414
I will *p* a new spirit within you	Eze 11:19	5414
p the stumblingblock of their	Eze 14:3	5414
I *p* bracelets upon thy hands, and	Eze 16:11	5414
I *p* a jewel on thy forehead, and	Eze 16:12	5414
which I had *p* upon thee, saith	Eze 16:14	7760
p forth a riddle, and speak a	Eze 17:2	2330
they *p* him in ward in chains, and	Eze 19:9	5414
they have *p* no difference between	Eze 22:26	
which *p* bracelets upon their	Eze 23:42	5414
p on thy shoes upon thy feet, and	Eze 24:17	7760
p off their broidered garments	Eze 26:16	6584
But I will *p* hooks in thy jaws,	Eze 29:4	5414
I will *p* a fear in the land of	Eze 30:13	5414
to *p* a roller to bind it, to make	Eze 30:21	7760
and *p* my sword in his hand	Eze 30:24	5414
when I shall *p* my sword into the	Eze 30:25	5414
And when I shall *p* thee out	Eze 32:7	3518
he is *p* in the midst of them that	Eze 32:25	5414
a new spirit will I *p* within you	Eze 36:26	5414
I will *p* my spirit within you, and	Eze 36:27	5414
p breath in you, and ye shall live	Eze 37:6	5414
shall *p* my spirit in you, and ye	Eze 37:14	5414
will *p* them with him, even with	Eze 37:19	5414
p hooks into thy jaws, and I will	Eze 38:4	5414
shall *p* on other garments, and	Eze 42:14	3847
Now let them *p* away their	Eze 43:9	7368
p it on the four horns of it, and	Eze 43:20	5414
they shall *p* off their garments	Eze 44:19	6584
they shall *p* on other garments	Eze 44:19	3847
a widow, nor her that is *p* away	Eze 44:22	1644
p it upon the posts of the house,	Eze 45:19	5414
and whom he would he *p* down	Dan 5:19	8214
p a chain of gold about his neck,	Dan 5:29	
let her therefore *p* away her	Hos 2:2	5493
P ye in the sickle, for the	Joel 3:13	7971
Ye that *p* far away the evil day,	Amos 6:3	
p on sackcloth, from the greatest	Jonah 3:5	3847
I will *p* them together as the	Mic 2:12	7760
p ye not confidence in a guide	Mic 7:5	
where they have been *p* to shame	Zeph 3:19	
to *p* it into a bag with holes	Hag 1:6	
was minded to *p* her away privily	Mt 1:19	*630*
p it under a bushel, but on a	Mt 5:15	*5087*
Whosoever shall *p* away his wife	Mt 5:31	*630*
whosoever shall *p* away his wife	Mt 5:32	*630*
for your body, what ye shall *p* on	Mt 6:25	*1749*
Jesus *p* forth his hand, and	Mt 8:3	*1614*
for that which is *p* in to fill it	Mt 9:16	
Neither do men *p* new wine into	Mt 9:17	*906*
but they *p* new wine into new	Mt 9:17	*906*
But when the people were *p* forth	Mt 9:25	*1544*
and cause them to be *p* to death	Mt 10:21	*2289*
I will *p* my Spirit upon him, and	Mt 12:18	*5087*
Another parable *p* he forth unto	Mt 13:24	*3908*
Another parable *p* he forth unto	Mt 13:31	*3908*
p him in prison for Herodias'	Mt 14:3	*5087*
when he would have *p* him to death	Mt 14:5	*615*
Is it lawful for a man to *p* away	Mt 19:3	*630*
together, let not man *p* asunder	Mt 19:6	*5562*
of divorcement, and to *p* her away	Mt 19:7	*630*
suffered you to *p* away your wives	Mt 19:8	*630*
Whosoever shall *p* away his wife	Mt 19:9	*630*
is *p* away doth commit adultery	Mt 19:9	*630*
that he should *p* his hands on	Mt 19:13	*2007*
p on them their clothes, and they	Mt 21:7	*2007*
he had *p* the Sadducees to silence	Mt 22:34	
have *p* my money to the exchangers	Mt 25:27	*906*
P up again thy sword into his	Mt 26:52	*654*
against Jesus, to *p* him to death	Mt 26:59	*2289*
against Jesus to *p* him to death	Mt 27:1	*2289*
for to *p* them into the treasury	Mt 27:6	*906*
him, and *p* on him a scarlet robe	Mt 27:28	*4060*
they *p* it upon his head, and a	Mt 27:29	*2007*
p his own raiment on him, and led	Mt 27:31	*1746*
p it on a reed, and gave him to	Mt 27:48	*4060*
after that John was *p* in prison	Mk 1:14	*3860*
p forth his hand, and touched him,	Mk 1:41	*1614*
wine must be *p* into new bottles	Mk 2:22	*906*
brought to be *p* under a bushel	Mk 4:21	*5087*
But when he had *p* them all out	Mk 5:40	*1544*
and not *p* on two coats	Mk 6:9	*1746*
him to *p* his hand upon him	Mk 7:32	*2007*
p his fingers into his ears, and	Mk 7:33	*906*
p his hands upon him, he asked	Mk 8:23	*2007*
After that he *p* his hands again	Mk 8:25	*2007*
for a man to *p* away his wife	Mk 10:2	*630*
of divorcement, and to *p* her away	Mk 10:4	*630*
together, let not man *p* asunder	Mk 10:9	*5562*
Whosoever shall *p* away his wife	Mk 10:11	*630*
a woman shall *p* away her husband	Mk 10:12	*630*
p his hands upon them, and blessed	Mk 10:16	*5087*
shall cause them to be *p* to death	Mk 13:12	*2289*
him by craft, and *p* him to death	Mk 14:1	*615*
against Jesus to *p* him to death	Mk 14:55	*2289*
thorns, and *p* it about his head,	Mk 15:17	*4060*
p his own clothes on him, and led	Mk 15:20	*1746*
p it on a reed, and gave him to	Mk 15:36	*4060*
He hath *p* down the mighty from	Lk 1:52	*2507*
he *p* forth his hand, and touched	Lk 5:13	*1614*
wine must be *p* into new bottles	Lk 5:38	*906*
he *p* them all out, and took her by	Lk 8:54	*1544*
having *p* his hand to the plough,	Lk 9:62	*1911*
for the body, what ye shall *p* on	Lk 12:22	*1746*
he *p* forth a parable to those	Lk 14:7	*3004*
the best robe, and *p* it on him	Lk 15:22	*1746*
p a ring on his hand, and shoes on	Lk 15:22	*1325*
do, that, when I am *p* out of the	Lk 16:4	*3179*
that is *p* away from her husband	Lk 16:18	*630*
scourge him, and *p* him to death	Lk 18:33	*615*
shall they cause to be *p* to death	Lk 21:16	*2289*
led with him to be *p* to death	Lk 23:32	*337*
troubled, to *p* me into the pool	Jn 5:7	*906*
He *p* clay upon mine eyes, and I	Jn 9:15	*2007*
he should be *p* out of the	Jn 9:22	
together for to *p* him to death	Jn 11:53	*615*
bag, and bare what was *p* therein	Jn 12:6	*906*
might *p* Lazarus also to death	Jn 12:10	*615*
lest they should be *p* out of the	Jn 12:42	*1096*
the devil having now *p* into the	Jn 13:2	*906*
They shall *p* you out of the	Jn 16:2	*4160*
P up thy sword into the sheath	Jn 18:11	*906*
for us to *p* any man to death	Jn 18:31	*615*
p it on his head, and they *p* on	Jn 19:2	*2007*
they *p* on him a purple robe,	Jn 19:2	*4016*
a title, and *p* it on the cross	Jn 19:19	*5087*
p it upon hyssop, and *p* it to	Jn 19:29	*4060*
upon hyssop, and *p* it to his mouth	Jn 19:29	*4374*
p my finger into the print of the	Jn 20:25	*906*
Father hath *p* in his own power	Acts 1:7	*5087*
p them in hold unto the next day	Acts 4:3	*5087*
p them in the common prison	Acts 5:18	*5087*
the men whom ye *p* in prison are	Acts 5:25	*5087*
commanded to *p* the apostles forth	Acts 5:34	*4160*
P off thy shoes from thy feet	Acts 7:33	*3089*
But Peter *p* them all forth, and	Acts 9:40	*1544*
he *p* him in prison, and delivered	Acts 12:4	*5087*
that they should be *p* to death	Acts 12:19	*520*
but seeing ye *p* it from you	Acts 13:46	*683*
p no difference between us and	Acts 15:9	*1252*
to *p* a yoke upon the neck of the	Acts 15:10	*2007*
and when they were *p* to death	Acts 26:10	*337*
and he *p* us therein	Acts 27:6	*1688*
let us *p* on the armour of light	Rom 13:12	*1746*
But *p* ye on the Lord Jesus Christ	Rom 13:14	*1746*
that no man *p* a stumblingblock or	Rom 14:13	*5087*
Therefore *p* away from among	1Cor 5:13	*1808*
not the husband *p* away his wife	1Cor 7:11	*863*
with him, let him not *p* her away	1Cor 7:12	*863*
a man, I *p* away childish things	1Cor 13:11	*2673*
he shall have *p* down all rule	1Cor 15:24	*2673*
till he hath *p* all enemies under	1Cor 15:25	*5087*
For he hath *p* all things under	1Cor 15:27	*5293*
saith all things are *p* under him	1Cor 15:27	*5293*
which did *p* all things under him	1Cor 15:27	*5293*
him that *p* all things under him	1Cor 15:28	*5293*
must *p* on incorruption, and this	1Cor 15:53	*1746*
this mortal must *p* on immortality	1Cor 15:53	*1746*
shall have *p* on incorruption	1Cor 15:54	*1746*
shall have *p* on immortality	1Cor 15:54	*1746*
which *p* a vail over his face,	2Cor 3:13	*5087*
which *p* the same earnest care	2Cor 8:16	*132*
into Christ have *p* on Christ	Gal 3:27	*174*
hath *p* all things under his feet,	Eph 1:22	*529*
That ye *p* off concerning the	Eph 4:22	*65*
that ye *p* on the new man, which	Eph 4:24	*174*

be *p* away from you, with all ... Eph 4:31 *142*
P on the whole armour of God, ... Eph 6:11 *1746*
But now ye also *p* off all these ... Col 3:8 *659*
seeing that ye have *p* off the old ... Col 3:9 *554*
have *p* on the new man, which is ... Col 3:10 *1746*
P on therefore, as the elect of ... Col 3:12 *1746*
all these things *p* on charity ... Col 3:14
to be *p* in trust with the gospel ... 1Th 2:4 *4160*
which some having *p* away ... 1Ti 1:19 *683*
If thou *p* the brethren in ... 1Ti 4:6 *5294*
Wherefore I *p* thee in remembrance ... 2Ti 1:6 *363*
Of these things *p* them in ... 2Ti 2:14 *5279*
P them in mind to be subject to ... Titus 3:1 *5279*
ought, *p* that on mine account ... Philem 18 *1677*
p in subjection the world to come ... Heb 2:5 *5293*
Thou hast *p* all things in ... Heb 2:8 *5293*
For in that he *p* all in ... Heb 2:8 *5293*
nothing that is not *p* under him ... Heb 2:8 *506*
not yet all things *p* under him ... Heb 2:8 *5293*
again, I will *p* my trust in him ... Heb 2:13 *3982*
afresh, and *p* him to an open shame ... Heb 6:6 *3856*
I will *p* my laws into their mind, ... Heb 8:10 *1325*
to *p* away sin by the sacrifice of ... Heb 9:26 *115*
I will *p* my laws into their ... Heb 10:16 *1325*
we *p* bits in the horses' mouths, ... Jas 3:3 *906*
may *p* to silence the ignorance of ... 1Pet 2:15 *5392*
being *p* to death in the flesh, ... 1Pet 3:18 *2289*
I will not be negligent to *p* you ... 2Pet 1:12 *5279*
I must *p* off this my tabernacle ... 2Pet 1:14 *595*
I will therefore *p* you in ... Jude 5 *5279*
I will *p* upon you none other ... Rev 2:24 *906*
dead bodies to be *p* in graves ... Rev 11:9 *5087*
For God hath *p* in their hearts to ... Rev 17:17 *1325*
2. Descendant of Put 3.
P and Lubim were thy helpers ... Nah 3:9 6316
3. Son of Ham.
Cush, and Mizraim, *P*, and Canaan ... 1Chr 1:8 6319

PUTEOLI (*pu-te'-o-li*) *A seaport in Italy.*
and we came the next day to *P* ... Acts 28:13 *4223*

PUTHITES See PUHITES.

PUTIEL (*pu'-te-el*) *Father-in-law of Eleazar.*
one of the daughters of *P* to wife ... Ex 6:25 6317

PUTRIFYING
wounds, and bruises, and *p* sores ... Is 1:6 2961

PUTTEST
thou *p* thy nest in a rock ... Num 24:21 7760
all that thou *p* thine hands unto ... Deut 12:18 4916
all that thou *p* thine hand unto ... Deut 15:10 4916
that which thou *p* on me will I ... 2Kin 18:14 5414
Thou *p* my feet also in the stocks ... Job 13:27 7760
Thou *p* away all the wicked of the ... Ps 119:119 7673
that *p* thy bottle to him, and ... Hab 2:15 5596

PUTTETH
or whosoever *p* any of it upon a ... Ex 30:33 5414
the word that God *p* in my mouth ... Num 22:38 7760
p forth her hand, and taketh him ... Deut 25:11 7971
and *p* it in a secret place ... Deut 27:15 7760
boast himself as he that *p* it off ... 1Kin 20:11 6605
he *p* no trust in his saints ... Job 15:15
He *p* forth his hand upon the rock ... Job 28:9 7971
He *p* my feet in the stocks, he ... Job 33:11 7760
He that *p* not out his money to ... Ps 15:5 5414
he *p* down one, and setteth up ... Ps 75:7 8213
but he that *p* his trust in the ... Prov 28:25
but whoso *p* his trust in the LORD ... Prov 29:25
The fig tree *p* forth her green ... Song 2:13 2590
but he that *p* his trust in me ... Is 57:13
as a shepherd *p* on his garment ... Jer 43:12 5844
He *p* his mouth in the dust ... Lam 3:29 5414
p the stumblingblock of his ... Eze 14:4 7760
p the stumblingblock of his ... Eze 14:7 7760
he that *p* not into their mouths, ... Mic 3:5 5414
No man *p* a piece of new cloth ... Mt 9:16 *1911*
p forth leaves, ye know that ... Mt 24:32 *1631*
no man *p* new wine into old ... Mk 2:22 *906*
immediately he *p* in the sickle ... Mk 4:29 *649*
p forth leaves, ye know that ... Mk 13:28 *1631*
No man *p* a piece of a new garment ... Lk 5:36 *1911*
no man *p* new wine into old ... Lk 5:37 *906*
a vessel, or *p* it under a bed ... Lk 8:16 *5087*
p it in a secret place, neither ... Lk 11:33 *5087*
Whosoever *p* away his wife, and ... Lk 16:18 *630*
when he *p* forth his own sheep, he ... Jn 10:4 *1544*

PUTTING
p it on her shoulder, and the ... Gen 21:14 7760
p them upon the head of the goat, ... Lev 16:21 5414
p their hand to their mouth, were ... Judg 7:6
the *p* forth of the finger, and ... Is 58:9 7971
saith that he hateth *p* away ... Mal 2:16 7971
p his hand on him, that he might ... Acts 9:12 *2007*
p his hands on him said, Brother ... Acts 9:17 *2007*
multitude, the Jews *p* him forward ... Acts 19:33 *4261*
as *p* you in mind, because of the ... Rom 15:15 *1878*
Wherefore *p* away lying, speak ... Eph 4:25 *659*
in *p* off the body of the sins of ... Col 2:11 *555*
p on the breastplate of faith and ... 1Th 5:8 *1746*
faithful, *p* me into the ministry ... 1Ti 1:12 *5087*
in thee by the *p* on of my hands ... 2Ti 1:6 *1936*
of gold, or of *p* on of apparel ... 1Pet 3:3 *1745*
p away of the filth of the flesh ... 1Pet 3:21 *595*
to stir you up by *p* you in ... 2Pet 1:13 *5279*

PUVAH See PUA.

PUVVAH See PHUVAH.

PYGARG
deer, and the wild goat, and the *p* ... Deut 14:5 1787

PYRRHUS Not in KJV.

Q

QUAILS
pass, that at even the *q* came up ... Ex 16:13 7958
brought *q* from the sea, and let ... Num 11:31 7958
next day, and they gathered the *q* ... Num 11:32 7958
The people asked, and he brought *q* ... Ps 105:40 7958

QUAKE
The earth shall *q* before them ... Joel 2:10 7264
The mountains *q* at him, and the ... Nah 1:5 7493
and the earth did *q*, and the rocks ... Mt 27:51 *4579*
said, I exceedingly fear and *q* ... Heb 12:21 *1790*

QUAKED
and the whole mount *q* greatly ... Ex 19:18 2729
also trembled, and the earth *q* ... 1Sa 14:15 7264

QUAKING
Son of man, eat thy bread with *q* ... Eze 12:18 7494
but a great *q* fell upon them, so ... Dan 10:7 2731

QUANTITY
the issue, all vessels of small *q* ... Is 22:24

QUARREL
shall avenge the *q* of my covenant ... Lev 26:25 5359
see how he seeketh a *q* against me ... 2Kin 5:7 579
Herodias had a *q* against him ... Mk 6:19 *1758*
if any man have a *q* against any ... Col 3:13 *3437*

QUARRIES
from the *q* that were by Gilgal ... Judg 3:19 6456
tarried, and passed beyond the *q* ... Judg 3:26 6456

QUARTER
all the people from every *q* ... Gen 19:4 7098
Then your south *q* shall be from ... Num 34:3 6285
their border in the north *q* was ... Josh 15:5 6285
this was the west *q* ... Josh 18:14 6285
the south *q* was from the end of ... Josh 18:15 6285
shall wander every one to his *q* ... Is 47:15 5676
one for his gain, from his *q* ... Is 56:11 7098
and they came to him from every *q* ... Mk 1:45 *3836*

QUARTERS
seen with thee in all thy *q* ... Ex 13:7 1366
upon the four *q* of thy vesture ... Deut 22:12 3671
In four *q* were the porters, ... 1Chr 9:24 7307
winds from the four *q* of heaven ... Jer 49:36 7098
house of Togarmah of the north *q* ... Eze 38:6 3411
as Peter passed throughout all *q* ... Acts 9:32
of the Jews which were in those *q* ... Acts 16:3 *5117*
In the same *q* were possessions of ... Acts 28:7 *5117*
are in the four *q* of the earth ... Rev 20:8 *1137*

QUARTUS (*quar'-tus*) *A Christian in Rome.*
city saluteth you, and *Q* a brother ... Rom 16:23 *2890*

QUATERNIONS
delivered him to four *q* of ... Acts 12:4 *5069*

QUEEN
when the *q* of Sheba heard of the ... 1Kin 10:1 4436
when the *q* of Sheba had seen all ... 1Kin 10:4 4436
of spices as these which the *q* of ... 1Kin 10:10 4436
the *q* of Sheba all her desire ... 1Kin 10:13 4436
the sister of Tahpenes the *q* ... 1Kin 11:19 1377
even her he removed from being *q* ... 1Kin 15:13 1377
the king and the children of the *q* ... 2Kin 10:13 1377
when the *q* of Sheba heard of the ... 2Chr 9:1 4436
when the *q* of Sheba had seen the ... 2Chr 9:3 4436
the *q* of Sheba gave king Solomon ... 2Chr 9:9 4436
to the *q* of Sheba all her desire ... 2Chr 9:12 4436
king, he removed her from being *q* ... 2Chr 15:16 1377
(the *q* also sitting by him,) For ... Neh 2:6 7694
Also Vashti the *q* made a feast ... Est 1:9 4436
To bring Vashti the *q* before the ... Est 1:11 4436
But the *q* Vashti refused to come ... Est 1:12 4436
the *q* Vashti according to law ... Est 1:15 4436
Vashti the *q* hath not done wrong ... Est 1:16 4436
For this deed of the *q* shall come ... Est 1:17 4436
the *q* to be brought in before him ... Est 1:17 4436
have heard of the deed of the *q* ... Est 1:18 4436
the king be *q* instead of Vashti ... Est 2:4 4427
made her *q* instead of Vashti ... Est 2:17 4427
who told it unto Esther the *q* ... Est 2:22 4436
Then was the *q* exceedingly ... Est 4:4 4436
the *q* standing in the court ... Est 5:2 4436
her, What wilt thou, *q* Esther ... Est 5:3 4436
Esther the *q* did let no man come ... Est 5:12 4436
came to banquet with Esther the *q* ... Est 7:1 4436
What is thy petition, *q* Esther ... Est 7:2 4436
Then Esther the *q* answered ... Est 7:3 4436
and said unto Esther the *q* ... Est 7:5 4436
afraid before the king and the *q* ... Est 7:6 4436
for his life to Esther the *q* ... Est 7:7 4436
Will he force the *q* also before ... Est 7:8 4436
the Jews' enemy unto Esther the *q* ... Est 8:1 4436
Ahasuerus said unto Esther the *q* ... Est 8:7 4436
the king said unto Esther the *q* ... Est 9:12 4436
Then Esther the *q*, the daughter ... Est 9:29 4436
Esther the *q* had enjoined them, ... Est 9:31 4436
did stand the *q* in gold of Ophir ... Ps 45:9 7694
to make cakes to the *q* of heaven ... Jer 7:18 4446
Say unto the king and to the *q* ... Jer 13:18 1377
that Jeconiah the king, and the *q* ... Jer 29:2 1377
burn incense unto the *q* of heaven ... Jer 44:17 4446
burn incense to the *q* of heaven ... Jer 44:18 4446
burned incense to the *q* of heaven ... Jer 44:19 4446
burn incense to the *q* of heaven ... Jer 44:25 4446
Now the *q*, by reason of the words ... Dan 5:10 4433
the *q* spake and said, O king, live ... Dan 5:10 4433
The *q* of the south shall rise up ... Mt 12:42 *938*
The *q* of the south shall rise up ... Lk 11:31 *938*
under Candace *q* of the Ethiopians ... Acts 8:27 *938*
she saith in her heart, I sit a *q* ... Rev 18:7 *938*

QUEENS
There are threescore *q*, and ... Song 6:8 4436
yea, the *q* and the concubines, and ... Song 6:9 4436
their *q* thy nursing mothers ... Is 49:23 8282

QUENCH
so they shall *q* my coal which is ... 2Sa 14:7 3518
that thou *q* not the light of ... 2Sa 21:17 3518
the wild asses *q* their thirst ... Ps 104:11 7665
Many waters cannot *q* love ... Song 8:7 3518
together, and none shall *q* them ... Is 1:31 3518
the smoking flax shall he not *q* ... Is 42:3 3518
burn that none can *q* it because ... Jer 4:4 3518
fire, and burn that none can *q* it ... Jer 21:12 3518
there be none to *q* it in Beth-el ... Amos 5:6 3518
and smoking flax shall he not *q* ... Mt 12:20 *4570*
to *q* all the fiery darts of the ... Eph 6:16 *4570*
Q not the Spirit ... 1Th 5:19 *4570*

QUENCHED
unto the LORD, the fire was *q* ... Num 11:2 8257
this place, and shall not be *q* ... 2Kin 22:17 3518
this place, and shall not be *q* ... 2Chr 34:25 3518
they are *q* as the fire of thorns ... Ps 118:12 1846
It shall not be *q* night nor day ... Is 34:10 3518
are extinct, they are *q* as tow ... Is 43:17 3518
neither shall their fire be *q* ... Is 66:24 3518
it shall burn, and shall not be *q* ... Jer 7:20 3518
Jerusalem, and it shall not be *q* ... Jer 17:27 3518
the flaming flame shall not be *q* ... Eze 20:47 3518
it shall not be *q* ... Eze 20:48 3518
the fire that never shall be *q* ... Mk 9:43 *762*
dieth not, and the fire is not *q* ... Mk 9:44 *4570*
the fire that never shall be *q* ... Mk 9:45 *762*
dieth not, and the fire is not *q* ... Mk 9:46 *4570*
dieth not, and the fire is not *q* ... Mk 9:48 *4570*
Q the violence of fire, escaped ... Heb 11:34 *4570*

QUESTION
which was a lawyer, asked him a *q* ... Mt 22:35
forth, and began to *q* with him ... Mk 8:11 *4802*
the scribes, What *q* ye with them ... Mk 9:16 *4802*
I will also ask of you one *q* ... Mk 11:29 *3056*
after that durst ask him any *q* ... Mk 12:34
durst not ask him any *q* at all ... Lk 20:40
Then there arose a *q* between some ... Jn 3:25 *2214*
apostles and elders about this *q* ... Acts 15:2 *2213*
But if it be a *q* of words ... Acts 18:15 *2213*
called in *q* for this day's uproar ... Acts 19:40 *1458*
of the dead I am called in *q* ... Acts 23:6 *2919*
I am called in *q* by you this day ... Acts 24:21 *2919*
asking no *q* for conscience sake ... 1Cor 10:25
asking no *q* for conscience sake ... 1Cor 10:27

QUESTIONED
Then Hezekiah *q* with the priests ... 2Chr 31:9 1875
that they *q* among themselves ... Mk 1:27 *4802*
Then he *q* with him in many words ... Lk 23:9 *1905*

QUESTIONING
q one with another what the ... Mk 9:10 *4802*
them, and the scribes *q* with them ... Mk 9:14 *4802*

QUESTIONS
she came to prove him with hard *q* ... 1Kin 10:1 2420
And Solomon told her all her *q* ... 1Kin 10:3 1697
Solomon with hard *q* at Jerusalem ... 2Chr 9:1 2420
And Solomon told her all her *q* ... 2Chr 9:2 1697
that day forth ask him any more *q* ... Mt 22:46
hearing them, and asking them *q* ... Lk 2:46 *1905*
to be accused of *q* of their law ... Acts 23:29 *2213*
But had certain *q* against him of ... Acts 25:19 *2213*
I doubted of such manner of *q* ... Acts 25:20 *2214*
q which are among the Jews ... Acts 26:3 *2213*
genealogies, which minister *q* ... 1Ti 1:4 *2214*
nothing, but doting about *q* ... 1Ti 6:4 *2214*
But foolish and unlearned *q* avoid ... 2Ti 2:23 *2214*
But avoid foolish *q*, and ... Titus 3:9 *2214*

QUICK
there be *q* raw flesh in the ... Lev 13:10 4241
the *q* flesh that burneth have a ... Lev 13:24 4241
and they go down *q* into the pit ... Num 16:30 2416
and let them go down *q* into hell ... Ps 55:15 2416
Then they had swallowed us up *q* ... Ps 124:3 2416
shall make him of *q* understanding ... Is 11:3
of God to be the Judge of *q* ... Acts 10:42 *2198*
Christ, who shall judge the *q* ... 2Ti 4:1 *2198*
For the word of God is *q*, and ... Heb 4:12 *2198*
him that is ready to judge the *q* ... 1Pet 4:5 *2198*

Q

QUICKEN
shalt q me again, and shalt bring ... Ps 71:20 2421
q us, and we will call upon thy ... Ps 80:18 2421
q thou me according to thy word ... Ps 119:25 2421
and q thou me in thy way ... Ps 119:37 2421
q me in thy righteousness ... Ps 119:40 2421
Q me after thy lovingkindness ... Ps 119:88 2421
q me, O LORD, according unto thy ... Ps 119:107 2421
q me according to thy judgment ... Ps 119:149 2421
q me according to thy word ... Ps 119:154 2421
q me according to thy judgments ... Ps 119:156 2421
q me, O LORD, according to thy ... Ps 119:159 2421
Q me, O LORD, for thy name's sake ... Ps 143:11 2421
also q your mortal bodies by his ... Rom 8:11 2227

QUICKENED
for thy word hath q me ... Ps 119:50 2421
for with them thou hast q me ... Ps 119:93 2421
that which thou sowest is not q ... 1Cor 15:36 2227
And you hath he q, who were dead ... Eph 2:1
hath q us together with Christ, (... Eph 2:5 4806
hath he q together with him, ... Col 2:13 4806
in the flesh, but q by the Spirit ... 1Pet 3:18 2227

QUICKENETH
raiseth up the dead, and q them ... Jn 5:21 2227
even so the Son q whom he will ... Jn 5:21 2227
It is the spirit that q ... Jn 6:63 2227
who q the dead, and calleth those ... Rom 4:17 2227
who q all things, and before ... 1Ti 6:13 2227

QUICKENING
the last Adam was made a q spirit ... 1Cor 15:45 2227

QUICKLY
Make ready q three measures of ... Gen 18:6 4116
it that thou hast found it so q ... Gen 27:20 4116
aside q out of the way which I ... Ex 32:8 4118
go q unto the congregation, and ... Num 16:46 4120
drive them out, and destroy them q ... Deut 9:3 4118
Arise, get thee down q from hence ... Deut 9:12 4118
they are q turned aside out of ... Deut 9:12 4118
ye had turned aside q out of the ... Deut 9:16 4118
lest ye perish q from off the ... Deut 11:17 4120
destroyed, and until thou perish q ... Deut 28:20 4118
pursue after them q ... Josh 2:5 4118
the ambush arose q out of their ... Josh 8:19 4120
come up to us q, and save us, and ... Josh 10:6 4120
ye shall perish q from off the ... Josh 23:16 4120
they turned q out of the way ... Judg 2:17 4118
days, then thou shalt go down q ... 1Sa 20:19 3966
Now therefore send q, and tell ... 2Sa 17:16 4120
but they went both of them away q ... 2Sa 17:18 4120
Arise, and pass q over the water ... 2Sa 17:21 4120
Come down q ... 2Kin 1:11 4120
Fetch q Micaiah the son of Imla ... 2Chr 18:8 4116
a threefold cord is not q broken ... Eccl 4:12 4120
Agree with thine adversary q ... Mt 5:25 5035
And go q, and tell his disciples ... Mt 28:7 5035
And they departed q from the ... Mt 28:8 5035
And they went out q, and fled from ... Mk 16:8 5035
Go out q into the streets and ... Lk 14:21 5030
him, Take thy bill, and sit down q ... Lk 16:6 5030
as she heard that, she arose q ... Jn 11:29 5035
unto him, That thou doest, do q ... Jn 13:27 5032
raised him up, saying, Arise up q ... Acts 12:7
get thee q out of Jerusalem ... Acts 22:18
or else I will come unto thee q ... Rev 2:5 5035
or else I will come unto thee q ... Rev 2:16 5035
Behold, I come q ... Rev 3:11 5035
behold, the third woe cometh q ... Rev 11:14 5035
Behold, I come q ... Rev 22:7 5035
And, behold, I come q ... Rev 22:12 5035
things saith, Surely I come q ... Rev 22:20 5035

QUICKSANDS
lest they should fall into the q ... Acts 27:17 4950

QUIET
were q all the night, saying, In ... Judg 16:2 2790
the manner of the Zidonians, q ... Judg 18:7 8252
unto a people that were at q ... Judg 18:27 8252
rejoiced, and the city was in q ... 2Kin 11:20 8252
good, and the land was wide, and q ... 1Chr 4:40 8252
his days the land was q ten years ... 2Chr 14:1 8252
and the kingdom was q before him ... 2Chr 14:5 8252
So the realm of Jehoshaphat was q ... 2Chr 20:30 8252
and the city was q, after that ... 2Chr 23:21 8252
I have lain still and been q ... Job 3:13 8252
had I rest, neither was I q ... Job 3:26 5117
being wholly at ease and q ... Job 21:23 7961
them that are q in the land ... Ps 35:20 7282
are they glad because they be q ... Ps 107:30 8367
shall be q from fear of evil ... Prov 1:33 7599
q more than the cry of him that ... Eccl 9:17 5183
say unto him, Take heed, and be q ... Is 7:4 8252
whole earth is at rest, and is q ... Is 14:7 8252
dwellings, and in q resting places ... Is 32:18 7600
see Jerusalem a q habitation ... Is 33:20 7600
and shall be in rest, and be q ... Jer 30:10 7599
how long will it be ere thou be q ... Jer 47:6 8252
How can it be q, seeing the LORD ... Jer 47:7 8252
it cannot be q ... Jer 49:23 8252
And this Seraiah was a q prince ... Jer 51:59 4496
depart from thee, and I will be q ... Eze 16:42 8252
Though they be q, and likewise ... Nah 1:12 8003
spoken against, ye ought to be q ... Acts 19:36 2687
And that ye study to be q, and to ... 1Th 4:11 2270
that we may lead a q and peaceable ... 1Ti 2:2 2263
q spirit, which is in the sight ... 1Pet 3:4 2272

QUIETED
q myself, as a child that is ... Ps 131:2 1826
toward the north country have q ... Zec 6:8 5117

QUIETETH
when he q the earth by the south ... Job 37:17 8252

QUIETLY
in the gate to speak with him q ... 2Sa 3:27 7987
q wait for the salvation of the ... Lam 3:26

QUIETNESS
the country was in q forty years ... Judg 8:28 8252
q unto Israel in his days ... 1Chr 22:9 8253
he shall not feel q in his belly ... Job 20:20 7961
When he giveth q, who then can ... Job 34:29 8252
q therewith, than an house full ... Prov 17:1 7962
Better is an handful with q ... Eccl 4:6 5183
in q and in confidence shall be ... Is 30:15 8252
and the effect of righteousness q ... Is 32:17 8252
that by thee we enjoy great q ... Acts 24:2 1515
Christ, that with q they work ... 2Th 3:12 2271

QUIRINIUS See CYRENIUS.

QUIT
then shall he that smote him be q ... Ex 21:19 5352
the owner of the ox shall be q ... Ex 21:28 5355
then we will be q of thine oath ... Josh 2:20 5355
q yourselves like men, O ye ... 1Sa 4:9 1961
q yourselves like men, and fight ... 1Sa 4:9
q you like men, be strong ... 1Cor 16:13 407

QUITE
hath q devoured also our money ... Gen 31:15
q break down their images ... Ex 23:24
thou shalt q take away their ... Num 17:10 3615
q pluck down all their high ... Num 33:52
sent him away, and he is q gone ... 2Sa 3:24
and is wisdom driven q from me ... Job 6:13 5080
Thy bow was made q naked, ... Hab 3:9 6181

QUIVER
I pray thee, thy weapons, thy q ... Gen 27:3 8522
The q rattleth against him, the ... Job 39:23 827
man that hath his q full of them ... Ps 127:5 827
Elam bare the q with chariots of ... Is 22:6 827
in his q hath he hid me ... Is 49:2 827
Their q is as an open sepulchre, ... Jer 5:16 827
of his q to enter into my reins ... Lam 3:13 827

QUIVERED
my lips q at the voice ... Hab 3:16 6750

R

RAAMA See RAAMAH.

RAAMAH (ra'-a-mah)
1. A son of Cush.
Seba, and Havilah, and Sabtah, and R. Gen 10:7 7484
and the sons of R ... Gen 10:7 7484
Seba, and Havilah, and Sabta, and R ... 1Chr 1:9 7484
And the sons of R ... 1Chr 1:9 7484
2. A place in Arabia.
The merchants of Sheba and R ... Eze 27:22 7484

RAAMIAH (ra-a-mi'-ah) *A clan leader in exile.*
Jeshua, Nehemiah, Azariah, R ... Neh 7:7 7485

RAAMSES (ra-am'-seze) See RAMESES. *An Egyptian city.*
treasure cities, Pithom and R ... Ex 1:11 7486

RABBAH (rab'-bah) See RABBATH.
1. An Ammonite city.
unto Aroer that is before R ... Josh 13:25 7237
children of Ammon, and besieged R ... 2Sa 11:1 7237
Joab fought against R of the ... 2Sa 12:26 7237
and said, I have fought against R ... 2Sa 12:27 7237
the people together, and went to R ... 2Sa 12:29 7237
of R of the children of Ammon ... 2Sa 17:27 7237
of Ammon, and came and besieged R .. 1Chr 20:1 7237
And Joab smote R, and destroyed it ... 1Chr 20:1 7237
to be heard in R of the Ammonites ... Jer 49:2 7237
cry, ye daughters of R, gird you ... Jer 49:3 7237
I will make R a stable for camels ... Eze 25:5 7237
kindle a fire in the wall of R ... Amos 1:14 7237
2. A city in Judah.
which is Kirjath-jearim, and R ... Josh 15:60 7237

RABBATH (rab'-bath) See RABBAH. *Same as Rabbah 1.*
is it not in R of the children of ... Deut 3:11 7237
may come to R of the Ammonites ... Eze 21:20 7237

RABBI (rab'-bi) See RABBONI. *A Jewish title meaning "teacher."*
and to be called of men, R, R ... Mt 23:7 4461
But be not ye called R ... Mt 23:8 4461
They said unto him, R, (which is ... Jn 1:38 4461
answered and saith unto him, R ... Jn 1:49 4461
by night, and said unto him, R ... Jn 3:2 4461
unto John, and said unto him, R ... Jn 3:26 4461
of the sea, they said unto him, R ... Jn 6:25 4461

RABBITH (rab'-bith) *A city in Issachar.*
And R, and Kishion, and Abez, ... Josh 19:20 7245

RABBONI (rab-bo'-ni) See RABBI. *A Jewish title of respect.*
herself, and saith unto him, R ... Jn 20:16 4462

RAB-MAG *A Babylonian prince.*
Rab-saris, Nergal-sharezer, R ... Jer 39:3 7248
Rab-saris, and Nergal-sharezer, R ... Jer 39:13 7248

RAB-SARIS
1. A Babylonian prince.
Samgar-nebo, Sarsechim, R ... Jer 39:3 7249
the guard sent, and Nebushasban, R ... Jer 39:13 7249
2. An Assyrian officer.
king of Assyria sent Tartan and R ... 2Kin 18:17 7249

RAB-SHAKEH (rab'-sha-keh) See RABSHAKEH. *An Assyrian officer.*
R from Lachish to king Hezekiah ... 2Kin 18:17 7262
R said unto them, Speak ye now to ... 2Kin 18:19 7262
and Shebna, and Joah, unto R ... 2Kin 18:26 7262
But R said unto them, Hath my ... 2Kin 18:27 7262
Then R stood and cried with a loud ... 2Kin 18:28 7262
rent, and told him the words of R ... 2Kin 18:37 7262
God will hear all the words of R ... 2Kin 19:4 7262
So R returned, and found the king ... 2Kin 19:8 7262

RABSHAKEH (rab'-sha-keh) See RAB-SHAKEH. *Same as Rab-shakeh.*
the king of Assyria sent R from ... Is 36:2 7262
R said unto them, Say ye now to ... Is 36:4 7262
Eliakim and Shebna and Joah unto R ... Is 36:11 7262
But R said, Hath my master sent ... Is 36:12 7262
Then R stood, and cried with a ... Is 36:13 7262
rent, and told him the words of R ... Is 36:22 7262
thy God will hear the words of R ... Is 37:4 7262
So R returned, and found the king ... Is 37:8 7262

RACA (ra'-cah) *A Jewish term of disrespect.*
shall say to his brother, R ... Mt 5:22 4469

RACAL See RACHAL.

RACE
as a strong man to run a r ... Ps 19:5 734
that the r is not to the swift, ... Eccl 9:11 4793
they which run in a r run all ... 1Cor 9:24 4712
the r that is set before us ... Heb 12:1 73

RACHAB (ra'kab) See RAHAB. *Same as Rahab; ancestor of Jesus.*
And Salmon begat Booz of R ... Mt 1:5 4477

RACHAL (ra'-kal) *A city in Judah.*
And to them which were in R ... 1Sa 30:29 7403

RACHEL (ra'-chel) See RACHEL'S, RAHEL. *Wife of Jacob.*
R his daughter cometh with the ... Gen 29:6 7354
R came with her father's sheep ... Gen 29:9 7354
when Jacob saw R the daughter of ... Gen 29:10 7354
And Jacob kissed R, and lifted up ... Gen 29:11 7354
Jacob told R that he was her ... Gen 29:12 7354
and the name of the younger was R ... Gen 29:16 7354
but R was beautiful and well ... Gen 29:17 7354
And Jacob loved R ... Gen 29:18 7354
years for R thy younger daughter ... Gen 29:18 7354
And Jacob served seven years for R ... Gen 29:20 7354
did not I serve with thee for R ... Gen 29:25 7354
he gave him R his daughter to ... Gen 29:28 7354
Laban gave to R his daughter ... Gen 29:29 7354
And he went in also unto R ... Gen 29:30 7354
he loved also R more than Leah, ... Gen 29:30 7354
but R was barren ... Gen 29:31 7354
when R saw that she bare Jacob no ... Gen 30:1 7354
no children, R envied her sister ... Gen 30:1 7354
anger was kindled against R ... Gen 30:2 7354
R said, God hath judged me, and ... Gen 30:6 7354
R said, With great wrestlings ... Gen 30:8 7354
Then R said to Leah, Give me, I ... Gen 30:14 7354
R said, Therefore he shall lie ... Gen 30:15 7354
And God remembered R, and God ... Gen 30:22 7354
when R had born Joseph, that ... Gen 30:25 7354
And Jacob sent and called R ... Gen 31:4 7354
And R and Leah answered and said ... Gen 31:14 7354
R had stolen the images that were ... Gen 31:19 7354
knew not that R had stolen them ... Gen 31:32 7354
Now R had taken the images, and ... Gen 31:34 7354
the children unto Leah, and unto R ... Gen 33:1 7354
Leah and her children after, and R ... Gen 33:2 7354
and after came Joseph near and R ... Gen 33:7 7354
R travailed, and she had hard ... Gen 35:16 7354
R died, and was buried in the way ... Gen 35:19 7354
The sons of R ... Gen 35:24 7354
The sons of R Jacob's wife ... Gen 46:19 7354
These are the sons of R, which ... Gen 46:22 7354
Laban gave unto R his daughter ... Gen 46:25 7354
R died by me in the land of ... Gen 48:7 7354
is come into thine house like R ... Ruth 4:11 7354
R weeping for her children, and ... Mt 2:18 4478

RACHEL'S (ra'-chelz)
Bilhah R maid conceived again, and ... Gen 30:7 7354
tent, and entered into R tent ... Gen 31:33 7354
pillar of R grave unto this day ... Gen 35:20 7354
And the sons of Bilhah, R handmaid ... Gen 35:25 7354
by R sepulchre in the border of ... 1Sa 10:2 7354

RADDAI (*rad'-dahee*) *Son of Jesse.*
the fourth, *R* the fifth, 1Chr 2:14 7288

RAFTERS
house are cedar, and our *r* of fir Song 1:17 7351

RAGAU (*ra'-gaw*) See REU. *Father of Saruch; ancestor of Jesus.*
of Saruch, which was the son of *R* Lk 3:35 *4466*

RAGE
So he turned and went away in a *r* 2Kin 5:12 2534
coming in, and thy *r* against me 2Kin 19:27 7264
Because thy *r* against me and thy 2Kin 19:28 7264
for he was in a *r* with him 2Chr 16:10 2197
ye have slain them in a *r* that 2Chr 28:9 2197
the ground with fierceness and *r* Job 39:24 7267
Cast abroad the *r* of thy wrath Job 40:11 5678
Why do the heathen *r*, and the Ps 2:1 7283
because of the *r* of mine enemies Ps 7:6 5678
For jealousy is the *r* of a man Prov 6:34 2534
man, whether he *r* or laugh Prov 29:9 7264
coming in, and thy *r* against me Is 37:28 7264
Because thy *r* against me, and thy Is 37:29 7264
and *r*, ye chariots Jer 46:9 1984
Then Nebuchadnezzar in his *r* Dan 3:13 7266
sword for the *r* of their tongue Hos 7:16 2195
chariots shall *r* in the streets Nah 2:4 1984
hast said, Why did the heathen *r* Acts 4:25 *5433*

RAGED
The heathen *r*, the kingdoms were Ps 46:6 1993

RAGETH
but the fool *r*, and is confident Prov 14:16 5674

RAGGED
and into the tops of the *r* rocks Is 2:21

RAGING
Thou rulest the *r* of the sea Ps 89:9 1348
is a mocker, strong drink is *r* Prov 20:1 1993
and the sea ceased from her *r* Jonah 1:15 2197
the wind and the *r* of the water Lk 8:24 *2830*
R waves of the sea, foaming out Jude 13 *66*

RAGS
shall clothe a man with *r* Prov 23:21 7168
righteousnesses are as filthy *r* Is 64:6 899
old cast clouts and old rotten *r* Jer 38:11 4418
rotten *r* under thine armholes Jer 38:12 4418

RAGUEL (*ra-gu'-el*) *Father-in-law of Moses.*
the son of *R* the Midianite, Num 10:29 7467

RAHAB (*ra'-hab*) See RACHAB.
1. A Jericho woman who befriended the spies.
into an harlot's house, named *R* Josh 2:1 7343
the king of Jericho sent unto *R* Josh 2:3 7343
only *R* the harlot shall live, she Josh 6:17 7343
spies went in, and brought out *R* Josh 6:23 7343
Joshua saved *R* the harlot alive, Josh 6:25 7343
By faith the harlot *R* perished Heb 11:31 *4460*
Likewise also was not *R* the Jas 2:25 *4460*
2. A symbolic name for Egypt.
I will make mention of *R* and Ps 87:4 7294
Thou hast broken *R* in pieces Ps 89:10 7294
Art thou not it that hath cut *R* Is 51:9 7294

RAHAM (*ra'-ham*) *Son of Shema.*
And Shema begat *R*, the father of 1Chr 2:44 7357

RAHEL (*ra'-hel*) See RACHEL. *Same as Rachel.*
R weeping for her children Jer 31:15 7354

RAIL
He wrote also letters to *r* on the 2Chr 32:17 2778

RAILED
and he *r* on them 1Sa 25:14 5860
And they that passed by *r* on him Mk 15:29 *987*
which were hanged *r* on him Lk 23:39 *987*

RAILER
covetous, or an idolater, or a *r* 1Cor 5:11 *3060*

RAILING
evil for evil, or *r* for *r* 1Pet 3:9 *3059*
bring not *r* accusation against 2Pet 2:11 *989*
bring against him a *r* accusation Jude 9 *988*

RAILINGS
whereof cometh envy, strife, *r* 1Ti 6:4 *988*

RAIMENT
silver, and jewels of gold, and *r* Gen 24:53 899
Rebekah took goodly *r* of her Gen 27:15 899
and he smelled the smell of his *r* Gen 27:27 899
me bread to eat, and *r* to put on, Gen 28:20 899
shaved himself, and changed his *r* Gen 41:14 8071
he gave each man changes of *r* Gen 45:22 8071
of silver, and five changes of *r* Gen 45:22 8071
silver, and jewels of gold, and *r* Ex 3:22 8071
silver, and jewels of gold, and *r* Ex 12:35 8071
her food, her *r*, and her duty of Ex 21:10 3682
for ox, for ass, for sheep, for *r* Ex 22:9 8008
take thy neighbour's *r* to pledge Ex 22:26 8008
only, it is his *r* for his skin Ex 22:27 8071
it be any vessel of wood, or *r* Lev 11:32 899
And purify all your *r*, and all that Num 31:20 899
Thy *r* waxed not old upon thee, Deut 8:4 8071
stranger, in giving him food and *r* Deut 10:18 8071
she shall put the *r* of her Deut 21:13 8071
and so shalt thou do with his *r* Deut 22:3 8071
that he may sleep in his own *r* Deut 24:13 8008
nor take a widow's *r* to pledge Deut 24:17 899
and with iron, and with very much *r* Josh 22:8 8008
under his *r* upon his right thigh Judg 3:16 4055
purple *r* that was on the kings of Judg 8:26 899
put thy *r* upon thee, and get thee Ruth 3:3 8071
himself, and put on other *r* 1Sa 28:8 899
of gold, and ten changes of *r* 2Kin 5:5 899
thence silver, and gold, and *r* 2Kin 7:8 899
silver, and vessels of gold, and *r* 2Chr 9:24 8008
she sent *r* to clothe Mordecai, and Est 4:4 899
dust, and prepare *r* as the clay Job 27:16 4403
unto the king in *r* of needlework Ps 45:14 7553
as the *r* of those that are slain, Is 14:19 3830
and I will stain all my *r* Is 63:3 4403
thy *r* was of fine linen, and silk, Eze 16:13 4403
will clothe thee with change of *r* Zec 3:4 4254
John had his *r* of camel's hair Mt 3:4 *1742*
than meat, and the body than *r* Mt 6:25 *1742*
And why take ye thought for *r* Mt 6:28 *1742*
A man clothed in soft *r* Mt 11:8 *2440*
his *r* was white as the light Mt 17:2 *2440*
from him, and put his own *r* on him Mt 27:31 *2440*
lightning, and his *r* white as snow Mt 28:3 *1742*
his *r* became shining, exceeding Mk 9:3 *2440*
A man clothed in soft *r* Lk 7:25 *2440*
his *r* was white and glistering Lk 9:29 *2441*
which stripped him of his *r* Lk 10:30 *2441*
meat, and the body is more than *r* Lk 12:23 *1742*
And they parted his *r*, and cast Lk 23:34 *2440*
They parted my *r* among them Jn 19:24 *2440*
and blasphemed, he shook his *r* Acts 18:6 *2440*
kept the *r* of them that slew him Acts 22:20 *2440*
r let us be therewith content 1Ti 6:8 *4629*
come in also a poor man in vile *r* Jas 2:2 *2066*
same shall be clothed in white *r* Rev 3:5 *2440*
and white *r*, that thou mayest be Rev 3:18 *2440*
sitting, clothed in white *r* Rev 4:4 *2440*

RAIN
not caused it to *r* upon the earth Gen 2:5 4305
I will cause it to *r* upon the Gen 7:4 4305
the *r* was upon the earth forty Gen 7:12 1653
the *r* from heaven was restrained Gen 8:2 1653
it to *r* a very grievous hail Ex 9:18 4305
the *r* was not poured upon the Ex 9:33 4306
And when Pharaoh saw that the *r* Ex 9:34 4306
I will *r* bread from heaven for Ex 16:4 4305
I will give you *r* in due season Lev 26:4 1653
drinketh water of the *r* of heaven Deut 11:11 4306
That I will give you the *r* of Deut 11:14 4306
in his due season, the first *r* Deut 11:14 4456
and the latter *r* Deut 11:14 3138
up the heaven, that there be no *r* Deut 11:17 4306
the heaven to give the *r* unto thy Deut 28:12 4306
make the *r* of thy land powder Deut 28:24 4306
My doctrine shall drop as the *r* Deut 32:2 4306
as the small *r* upon the tender Deut 32:2 8164
and he shall send thunder and *r* 1Sa 12:17 4306
LORD sent thunder and *r* that day 1Sa 12:18 4306
be no dew, neither let there be *r* 2Sa 1:21 4306
earth by clear shining after *r* 2Sa 23:4 4306
is shut up, and there is no *r* 1Kin 8:35 4306
give *r* upon thy land, which thou 1Kin 8:36 4306
not be dew nor *r* these years 1Kin 17:1 4306
there had been no *r* in the land 1Kin 17:7 1653
the LORD sendeth *r* upon the earth 1Kin 17:14 1653
I will send *r* upon the earth 1Kin 18:1 4306
is a sound of abundance of *r* 1Kin 18:41 1653
down, that the *r* stop thee not 1Kin 18:44 1653
and wind, and there was a great *r* 1Kin 18:45 1653
see wind, neither shall ye see *r* 2Kin 3:17 1653
is shut up, and there is no *r* 2Chr 6:26 4306
send *r* upon thy land, which thou 2Chr 6:27 4306
shut up heaven that there be no *r* 2Chr 7:13 4306
this matter, and for the great *r* Ezr 10:9 1653
many, and it is a time of much *r* Ezr 10:13 1653
Who giveth *r* upon the earth, and Job 5:10 4306
shall *r* it upon him while he is Job 20:23 4305
When he made a decree for the *r* Job 28:26 4306
they waited for me as for the *r* Job 29:23 4306
mouth wide as for the latter *r* Job 29:23 4456
they pour down *r* according to the Job 36:27 4306
likewise to the small *r*, and to Job 37:6 1653
to the great *r* of his strength Job 37:6 1653
To cause it to *r* on the earth Job 38:26 4305
Hath the *r* a father Job 38:28 4306
Upon the wicked he shall *r* snares Ps 11:6 4305
O God, didst send a plentiful *r* Ps 68:9 1653
down like *r* upon the mown grass Ps 72:6 4306
the *r* also filleth the pools Ps 84:6 4175
He gave them hail for *r*, and Ps 105:32 1653
he maketh lightnings for the *r* Ps 135:7 4306
who prepareth *r* for the earth Ps 147:8 4306
is as a cloud of the latter *r* Prov 16:15 4456
is like clouds and wind without *r* Prov 25:14 1653
The north wind driveth away *r* Prov 25:23 1653
as *r* in harvest, so honour is not Prov 26:1 4306
sweeping *r* which leaveth no food Prov 28:3 4306
If the clouds be full of *r* Eccl 11:3 1653
nor the clouds return after the *r* Eccl 12:2 1653
is past, the *r* is over and gone Song 2:11 1653
for a covert from storm and from *r* Is 4:6 4306
that they *r* no *r* upon it Is 5:6 4305
that they *r* no *r* upon it Is 5:6 4306
shall he give the *r* of thy seed Is 30:23 4306
an ash, and the *r* doth nourish it Is 44:14 1653
For as the *r* cometh down, and the Is 55:10 1653
and there hath been no latter *r* Jer 3:3 4456
the LORD our God, that giveth *r* Jer 5:24 1653
he maketh lightnings with *r* Jer 10:13 4306
for there was no *r* in the earth Jer 14:4 1653
of the Gentiles that can cause *r* Jer 14:22 1653
he maketh lightnings with *r* Jer 51:16 4306
is in the cloud in the day of *r* Eze 1:28 1653
I will *r* upon him, and upon his Eze 38:22 4305
are with him, and overflowing *r* Eze 38:22 1653
and he shall come unto us as the *r* Hos 6:3 1653
latter and former *r* unto the earth Hos 6:3 3384
come and *r* righteousness upon you Hos 10:12 3384
given you the former *r* moderately Joel 2:23 4175
cause to come down for you the *r* Joel 2:23 1653
the former *r*, and the latter Joel 2:23 4175
the latter *r* in the first month Joel 2:23 4456
I have withholden the *r* from you Amos 4:7 1653
and I caused it to *r* upon one city Amos 4:7 4305
caused it not to *r* upon another Amos 4:7 4305
Ask ye of the LORD *r* in the time Zec 10:1 4306
in the time of the latter *r* Zec 10:1 4456
clouds, and give them showers of *r* Zec 10:1 4306
even upon them shall be no *r* Zec 14:17 4306
up, and come not, that have no *r* Zec 14:18
sendeth *r* on the just and on the Mt 5:45 *1026*
the *r* descended, and the floods Mt 7:25 *1028*
the *r* descended, and the floods Mt 7:27 *1028*
gave us *r* from heaven, and Acts 14:17 *5205*
one, because of the present *r* Acts 28:2 *5205*
in the *r* that cometh oft upon it Heb 6:7 *5205*
he receive the early and latter *r* Jas 5:7 *5205*
earnestly that it might not *r* Jas 5:17 *1026*
again, and the heaven gave *r* Jas 5:18 *5205*
that it *r* not in the days of Rev 11:6

RAINBOW
there was a *r* round about the Rev 4:3 *2463*
a *r* was upon his head, and his Rev 10:1 *2463*

RAINED
Then the LORD *r* upon Sodom Gen 19:24 4305
the LORD *r* hail upon the land of Ex 9:23 4305
had *r* down manna upon them to eat Ps 78:24 4305
He *r* flesh also upon them as dust Ps 78:27 4305
nor *r* upon in the day of Eze 22:24 1656
one piece was *r* upon, and the Amos 4:7 4305
piece whereupon it *r* not withered Amos 4:7 4305
Lot went out of Sodom it *r* fire Lk 17:29 *1026*
it *r* not on the earth by the Jas 5:17 *1026*

RAINY
dropping in a very *r* day and a Prov 27:15 5464

RAISE
her, and *r* up seed to thy brother Gen 38:8 6965
Thou shalt not *r* a false report Ex 23:1 5375
The LORD thy God will *r* up unto Deut 18:15 6965
I will *r* them up a Prophet from Deut 18:18 6965
r up unto his brother a name in Deut 25:7 6965
r thereon a great heap of stones, Josh 8:29 6965
to *r* up the name of the dead upon Ruth 4:5 6965
to *r* up the name of the dead upon Ruth 4:10 6965
I will *r* me up a faithful priest, 1Sa 2:35 6965
I will *r* up evil against thee out 2Sa 12:11 6965
to *r* him up from the earth 2Sa 12:17 6965
Moreover the LORD shall *r* him up 1Kin 14:14 6965
that I will *r* up thy seed after 1Chr 17:11 6965
who are ready to *r* up their Job 3:8 5782
r up their way against me, and Job 19:12 5549
they *r* up against me the ways of Job 30:12 5549
r me up, that I may requite them Ps 41:10 6965
shall *r* up a cry of destruction Is 15:5 5782
I will *r* forts against thee Is 29:3 6965
I will *r* up the decayed places Is 44:26 6965
to *r* up the tribes of Jacob Is 49:6 6965
thou shalt *r* up the foundations Is 58:12 6965
they shall *r* up the former Is 61:4 6965
that I will *r* unto David a Jer 23:5 6965
whom I will *r* up unto them Jer 30:9 6965
For, lo, I will *r* and cause to Jer 50:9 5782
and fall, and none shall *r* him up Jer 50:32 6965
I will *r* up against Babylon, and Jer 51:1 5782
I will *r* up thy lovers against Eze 23:22 5782
I will *r* up for them a plant of Eze 34:29 6965
in the third day he will *r* us up Hos 6:2 6965
I will *r* them out of the place Joel 3:7 5782
there is none to *r* her up Amos 5:2 6965
I will *r* up against you a nation, Amos 6:14 6965
In that day will I *r* up the Amos 9:11 6965
I will *r* up his ruins, and I will Amos 9:11 6965
then shall we *r* against him seven Mic 5:5 6965
and there are that *r* up strife Hab 1:3 5375
I *r* up the Chaldeans, that bitter Hab 1:6 6965
I will *r* up a shepherd in the Zec 11:16 6965
to *r* up children unto Abraham Mt 3:9 *1453*
r the dead, cast out devils Mt 10:8 *1453*
r up seed unto his brother Mt 22:24 *450*
r up seed unto his brother Mk 12:19 *1817*
to *r* up children unto Abraham Lk 3:8 *1453*
r up seed unto his brother Lk 20:28 *1817*
and in three days I will *r* it up Jn 2:19 *1453*
but should *r* it up again at the Jn 6:39 *450*
I will *r* him up at the last day Jn 6:40 *450*
I will *r* him up at the last day Jn 6:44 *450*
I will *r* him up at the last day Jn 6:54 *450*
he would *r* up Christ to sit on Acts 2:30 *450*
r up unto you of your brethren Acts 3:22 *450*
r up unto you of your brethren Acts 7:37 *450*
you, that God should *r* the dead Acts 26:8 *1453*
will also *r* up us by his own 1Cor 6:14 *1825*
Jesus shall *r* up us also by Jesus 2Cor 4:14 *1453*
that God was able to *r* him up Heb 11:19 *1453*
sick, and the Lord shall *r* him up Jas 5:15 *1453*

RAISED
for this cause have I *r* thee up Ex 9:16 5975
whom he *r* up in their stead, them Josh 5:7 6965
they *r* over him a great heap of Josh 7:26 6965
Nevertheless the LORD *r* up judges Judg 2:16 6965
when the LORD *r* them up judges, Judg 2:18 6965
the LORD *r* up a deliverer to the Judg 3:9 6965
the LORD *r* them up a deliverer, Judg 3:15 6965
and the man who was *r* up on high 2Sa 23:1 6965
king Solomon *r* a levy out of all 1Kin 5:13 5927
of the levy which king Solomon *r* 1Kin 9:15 5927
r it up to the towers, and another 2Chr 32:5 5927
r it up a very great height, and 2Chr 33:14 1361
all them whose spirit God had *r* Ezr 1:5 5782
nor be *r* out of their sleep Job 14:12 5782
I *r* thee up under the apple tree Song 8:5 5782
it hath *r* up from their thrones Is 14:9 6965

they *r* up the palaces thereof... Is 23:13 6209
Who *r* up the righteous man from... Is 41:2 5782
I have *r* up one from the north,... Is 41:25 5782
I have *r* him up in righteousness,... Is 45:13 5782
a great nation shall be *r* from... Jer 6:22 5782
a great whirlwind shall be *r* up... Jer 25:32 5782
The LORD hath *r* us up prophets in... Jer 29:15 6965
many kings shall be *r* up from the... Jer 50:41 5782
the LORD hath *r* up the spirit of... Jer 51:11 5782
it *r* up itself on one side, and it... Dan 7:5 6966
I *r* up of your sons for prophets,... Amos 2:11 6965
for he is *r* up out of his holy... Zec 2:13 5782
r up thy sons, O Zion, against... Zec 9:13 5782
Then Joseph being *r* from sleep... Mt 1:24 *1326*
the deaf hear, the dead are *r* up... Mt 11:5 *1453*
and be *r* again the third day... Mt 16:21 *1453*
the third day he shall be *r* again... Mt 17:23 *1453*
hath *r* up an horn of salvation... Lk 1:69 *1453*
the deaf hear, the dead are *r*... Lk 7:22 *1453*
be slain, and be *r* the third day... Lk 9:22 *1453*
Now that the dead are *r*, even... Lk 20:37 *1453*
dead, whom he *r* from the dead... Jn 12:1 *1453*
whom he had *r* from the dead... Jn 12:9 *1453*
r him from the dead, bare record... Jn 12:17 *1453*
Whom God hath *r* up, having loosed... Acts 2:24 *450*
This Jesus hath God *r* up, whereof... Acts 2:32 *450*
whom God hath *r* from the dead... Acts 3:15 *1453*
having *r* up his Son Jesus, sent... Acts 3:26 *450*
whom God *r* from the dead, even by... Acts 4:10 *1453*
The God of our fathers *r* up Jesus... Acts 5:30 *1453*
Him God *r* up the third day, and... Acts 10:40 *1453*
r him up, saying, Arise up... Acts 12:7 *1453*
he *r* up unto them David to be... Acts 13:22 *1453*
promise *r* unto Israel a Saviour... Acts 13:23 *1453*
But God *r* him from the dead... Acts 13:30 *1453*
in that he hath *r* up Jesus again... Acts 13:33 *450*
that he *r* him up from the dead... Acts 13:34 *450*
But he, whom God *r* again, saw no... Acts 13:37 *1453*
r persecution against Paul and... Acts 13:50 *1892*
in that he hath *r* him from the... Acts 17:31 *450*
if we believe on him that *r* up... Rom 4:24 *1453*
was *r* again for our justification... Rom 4:25 *1453*
that like as Christ was *r* up from... Rom 6:4 *1453*
Knowing that Christ being *r* from... Rom 6:9 *1453*
to him who is *r* from the dead... Rom 7:4 *1453*
But if the Spirit of him that *r*... Rom 8:11 *1453*
he that *r* up Christ from the dead... Rom 8:11 *1453*
same purpose have I *r* thee up... Rom 9:17 *1825*
that God hath *r* him from the dead... Rom 10:9 *1453*
And God hath both *r* up the Lord... 1Cor 6:14 *1453*
of God that he *r* up Christ... 1Cor 15:15 *1453*
whom he *r* not up, if so be that... 1Cor 15:15 *1453*
rise not, then is not Christ *r*... 1Cor 15:16 *1453*
And if Christ be not *r*, your faith... 1Cor 15:17 *1453*
will say, How are the dead *r* up... 1Cor 15:35 *1453*
it is *r* in incorruption... 1Cor 15:42 *1453*
it is *r* in glory... 1Cor 15:43 *1453*
it is *r* in power... 1Cor 15:43 *1453*
it is *r* a spiritual body... 1Cor 15:44 *1453*
the dead shall be *r* incorruptible... 1Cor 15:52 *1453*
Knowing that he which *r* up the... 2Cor 4:14 *1453*
Father, who *r* him from the dead... Gal 1:1 *1453*
when he *r* him from the dead, and... Eph 1:20 *1453*
hath *r* us up together, and made us... Eph 2:6 *4891*
who hath *r* him from the dead... Col 2:12 *1453*
whom he *r* from the dead, even... 1Th 1:10 *1453*
r from the dead according to my... 2Ti 2:8 *1453*
their dead *r* to life again... Heb 11:35 *386*
that *r* him up from the dead, and... 1Pet 1:21 *1453*

RAISER
a *r* of taxes in the glory of the... Dan 11:20 5674

RAISETH
He *r* up the poor out of the dust,... 1Sa 2:8 6965
When he *r* up himself, the mighty... Job 41:25 7613
r the stormy wind, which lifteth... Ps 107:25 5975
He *r* up the poor out of the dust,... Ps 113:7 6965
r up all those that be bowed down... Ps 145:14 2210
the LORD *r* them that are bowed... Ps 146:8 2210
For as the Father *r* up the dead... Jn 5:21 *1453*
but in God which *r* the dead... 2Cor 1:9 *1453*

RAISING
who ceaseth from *r* after he hath... Hos 7:4 5872
neither *r* up the people, neither... Acts 24:12

RAISINS
corn, and an hundred clusters of *r*... 1Sa 25:18 6778
of figs, and two clusters of *r*... 1Sa 30:12 6778
bread, and an hundred bunches of *r*... 2Sa 16:1 6778
cakes of figs, and bunches of *r*... 1Chr 12:40 6778

RAKEM (*ra'-kem*) *Son of Sheresh.*
and his sons were Ulam and R... 1Chr 7:16 7552

RAKKATH (*rah'-kath*) *A city in Naphtali.*
are Ziddim, Zer, and Hammath, R... Josh 19:35 7557

RAKKON (*rak'-kon*) *A city in Dan.*
And Me-jarkon, and R, with the... Josh 19:46 7542

RAM (*ram*)
1. Father of Aminadab.
And Hezron begat R... Ruth 4:19 7410
and R begat Amminadab... Ruth 4:19 7410
Jerahmeel, and R, and Chelubai... 1Chr 2:9 7410
And R begat Amminadab... 1Chr 2:10 7410
2. Son of Jerahmeel.
R the firstborn, and Bunah, and... 1Chr 2:25 7410
the sons of R the firstborn of... 1Chr 2:27 7410
3. Head of Elihu's family.
the Buzite, of the kindred of R... Job 32:2 7410
4. Male sheep.
a *r* of three years old, and a... Gen 15:9 352
behold behind him a *r* caught in a... Gen 22:13 352
and Abraham went and took the *r*... Gen 22:13 352
Thou shalt also take one *r*... Ex 29:15 352
hands upon the head of the *r*... Ex 29:15 352
And thou shalt slay the *r*, and thou... Ex 29:16 352
And thou shalt cut the *r* in pieces... Ex 29:17 352
burn the whole *r* upon the altar... Ex 29:18 352
And thou shalt take the other *r*... Ex 29:19 352
hands upon the head of the *r*... Ex 29:19 352
Then shalt thou kill the *r*... Ex 29:20 352
thou shalt take of the *r* the fat... Ex 29:22 352
for it is a *r* of consecration... Ex 29:22 352
of the *r* of Aaron's consecration... Ex 29:26 352
of the *r* of the consecration,... Ex 29:27 352
take the *r* of the consecration... Ex 29:31 352
sons shall eat the flesh of the *r*... Ex 29:32 352
a *r* without blemish out of the... Lev 5:15 352
the *r* of the trespass offering... Lev 5:16 352
he shall bring a *r* without... Lev 5:18 352
a *r* without blemish out of the... Lev 6:6 352
he brought the *r* for the burnt... Lev 8:18 352
hands upon the head of the *r*... Lev 8:18 352
And he cut the *r* into pieces... Lev 8:20 352
burnt the whole *r* upon the altar... Lev 8:21 352
other ram, the *r* of consecration... Lev 8:22 352
hands upon the head of the *r*... Lev 8:22 352
for of the *r* of consecration it... Lev 8:29 352
a *r* for a burnt offering, without... Lev 9:2 352
a *r* for peace offerings, to... Lev 9:4 352
the *r* for a sacrifice of peace... Lev 9:18 352
fat of the bullock and of the *r*... Lev 9:19 352
and a *r* for a burnt offering... Lev 16:3 352
one *r* for a burnt offering... Lev 16:5 352
even a *r* for a trespass offering... Lev 19:21 352
an atonement for him with the *r*... Lev 19:22 352
beside the *r* of the atonement,... Num 5:8 352
one *r* without blemish for peace... Num 6:14 352
he shall offer the *r* for a... Num 6:17 352
take the sodden shoulder of the *r*... Num 6:19 352
One young bullock, one *r*, one... Num 7:15 352
One young bullock, one *r*, one... Num 7:21 352
One young bullock, one *r*, one... Num 7:27 352
One young bullock, one *r*, one... Num 7:33 352
One young bullock, one *r*, one... Num 7:39 352
One young bullock, one *r*, one... Num 7:45 352
One young bullock, one *r*, one... Num 7:51 352
One young bullock, one *r*, one... Num 7:57 352
One young bullock, one *r*, one... Num 7:63 352
One young bullock, one *r*, one... Num 7:69 352
One young bullock, one *r*, one... Num 7:75 352
One young bullock, one *r*, one... Num 7:81 352
Or for a *r*, thou shalt prepare... Num 15:6 352
for one bullock, or for one *r*... Num 15:11 352
on every altar a bullock and a *r*... Num 23:2 352
upon every altar a bullock and a *r*... Num 23:4 352
a bullock and a *r* on every altar... Num 23:14 352
a bullock and a *r* on every altar... Num 23:30 352
two young bullocks, and one *r*... Num 28:11 352
mingled with oil, for one *r*... Num 28:12 352
the third part of an hin unto a *r*... Num 28:14 352
two young bullocks, and one *r*... Num 28:19 352
and two tenth deals for a *r*... Num 28:20 352
two young bullocks, one *r*... Num 28:27 352
two tenth deals unto one *r*... Num 28:28 352
one young bullock, one *r*, and... Num 29:2 352
and two tenth deals for a *r*... Num 29:3 352
one young bullock, one *r*, and... Num 29:8 352
and two tenth deals to one *r*... Num 29:9 352
deals to each *r* of the two rams... Num 29:14 352
one bullock, one *r*, seven lambs... Num 29:36 352
for the bullock, for the *r*... Num 29:37 352
they offered a *r* of the flock for... Ezr 10:19 352
a *r* out of the flock without... Eze 43:23 352
a *r* out of the flock, without... Eze 43:25 352
a bullock, and an ephah for a *r*... Eze 45:24 352
blemish, and a *r* without blemish... Eze 46:4 352
shall be an ephah for a *r*... Eze 46:5 352
blemish, and six lambs, and a *r*... Eze 46:6 352
a bullock, and an ephah for a *r*... Eze 46:7 352
to a bullock, and an ephah to a *r*... Eze 46:11 352
the river a *r* which had two horns... Dan 8:3 352
I saw the *r* pushing westward, and... Dan 8:4 352
he came to the *r* that had two... Dan 8:6 352
I saw him come close unto the *r*... Dan 8:7 352
against him, and smote the *r*... Dan 8:7 352
in the *r* to stand before him... Dan 8:7 352
deliver the *r* out of his hand... Dan 8:7 352
The *r* which thou sawest having... Dan 8:20 352

RAMA (*ra-mah*) See RAMAH. *Same as Ramah 1.*
In R was there a voice heard,... Mt 2:18 *4471*

RAMAH (*ra'-mah*) See RAMA, RAMATH.
1. A city in Benjamin.
Gibeon, and R, and Beeroth,... Josh 18:25 7414
palm tree of Deborah between R... Judg 4:5 7414
all night, in Gibeah, or in R... Judg 19:13 7414
went up against Judah, and built R... 1Kin 15:17 7414
that he left off building of R... 1Kin 15:21 7414
and they took away the stones of R... 1Kin 15:22 7414
came up against Judah, and built R... 2Chr 16:1 7414
that he left off building of R... 2Chr 16:5 7414
they carried away the stones of R... 2Chr 16:6 7414
The children of R and Gaba, six... Ezr 2:26 7414
The men of R and Gaba, six hundred... Neh 7:30 7414
Hazor, R, Gittaim,... Neh 11:33 7414
R is afraid,... Is 10:29 7414
the guard had let him go from R... Jer 40:1 7414
in Gibeah, and the trumpet in R... Hos 5:8 7414
2. A city in Naphtali.
And then the coast turneth to R... Josh 19:29 7414
And Adamah, and R, and Hazor,... Josh 19:36 7414
3. A city in Ephraim.
and came to their house to R... 1Sa 1:19 7414
And Elkanah went to R to his house... 1Sa 2:11 7414
And his return was to R... 1Sa 7:17 7414
and came to Samuel unto R... 1Sa 8:4 7414
Then Samuel went to R... 1Sa 15:34 7414
So Samuel rose up, and went to R... 1Sa 16:13 7414
escaped, and came to Samuel to R... 1Sa 19:18 7414
Behold, David is at Naioth in R... 1Sa 19:19 7414
Then went he also to R, and came... 1Sa 19:22 7414
Behold, they be at Naioth in R... 1Sa 19:22 7414
And he went thither to Naioth in R... 1Sa 19:23 7414
until he came to Naioth in R... 1Sa 19:23 7414
And David fled from Naioth in R... 1Sa 20:1 7414
abode in Gibeah under a tree in R... 1Sa 22:6 7414
and buried him in his house at R... 1Sa 25:1 7414
lamented him, and buried him in R... 1Sa 28:3 7414
A voice was heard in R,... Jer 31:15 7414
4. A short form of Ramoth-Gilead.
the Syrians had given him at R... 2Kin 8:29 7414
wounds which were given him at R... 2Chr 22:6 7414

RAMATH (*ra-math*) *A city in Simeon.*
to Baalath-beer, R of the south... Josh 19:8 7418

RAMATHAIM-ZOPHIM (*ram-a-tha''-im-zo'-fim*) *A city on Mt. Ephraim.*
Now there was a certain man of R... 1Sa 1:1 7436

RAMATHITE (*ra'-math-ite*) *An inhabitant of Ramah 1.*
the vineyards was Shimei the R... 1Chr 27:27 7435

RAMATH-LEHI (*ra''-math-le'-hi*) *A place in Judah.*
his hand, and called that place R... Judg 15:17 7437

RAMATH MIZPAH See RAMATH-MIZPEH.

RAMATH-MIZPEH (*ra''-math-miz'-peh*) *A city in Gad.*
And from Heshbon unto R, and... Josh 13:26 7434

RAMESES (*ram'-e-seze*) See RAAMSES. *A city in Goshen.*
of the land, in the land of R... Gen 47:11 7486
journeyed from R to Succoth... Ex 12:37 7486
from R in the first month... Num 33:3 7486
children of Israel removed from R... Num 33:5 7486

RAMIAH (*ra'-mi-ah*) *Married a foreigner while in exile.*
R, and Jeziah, and Malchiah, and... Ezr 10:25 7422

RAMOTH (*ra'-moth*) See JARMUTH, RAMAH, RAMOTH-GILEAD, REMETH.
1. A Levitical city in Gad.
R in Gilead, of the Gadites... Deut 4:43 7216
R in Gilead out of the tribe of... Josh 20:8 7216
R in Gilead with her suburbs, to... Josh 21:38 7216
R in Gilead with her suburbs, and... 1Chr 6:80 7216
2. A Levitical city in Issachar.
R with her suburbs, and Anem with... 1Chr 6:73 7216
3. Married a foreigner in exile.
and Adaiah, Jashub, and Sheal, and R. Ezr 10:29 3406
4. A city in Simeon.
and to them which were in south R... 1Sa 30:27 7418
5. Same as Ramoth-gilead.
Know ye that R in Gilead is ours,... 1Kin 22:3 7216

RAMOTH-GILEAD (*ra''-moth-ghil'-e-ad*) *A city in Gad.*
The son of Geber, in R... 1Kin 4:13 7433
thou go with me to battle to R... 1Kin 22:4 7433
Shall I go against R to battle... 1Kin 22:6 7433
prophesied so, saying, Go up to R... 1Kin 22:12 7433
shall we go against R to battle... 1Kin 22:15 7433
that he may go up and fall at R... 1Kin 22:20 7433
the king of Judah went up to R... 1Kin 22:29 7433
against Hazael king of Syria in R... 2Kin 8:28 7433
of oil in thine hand, and go to R... 2Kin 9:1 7433
young man the prophet, went to R... 2Kin 9:4 7433
(Now Joram had kept R, he and all... 2Kin 9:14 7433
him to go up with him to R... 2Chr 18:2 7433
Judah, Wilt thou go with me to R... 2Chr 18:3 7433
them, Shall we go to R to battle... 2Chr 18:5 7433
prophesied so, saying, Go up to R... 2Chr 18:11 7433
shall we go to R to battle... 2Chr 18:14 7433
that he may go up and fall at R... 2Chr 18:19 7433
the king of Judah went up to R... 2Chr 18:28 7433
against Hazael king of Syria at R... 2Chr 22:5 7433

RAMOTH NEGEV See RAMOTH-GILEAD.

RAMPART
therefore he made the *r* and the... Lam 2:8 2426
whose *r* was the sea, and her wall... Nah 3:8 2426

RAM'S
make a long blast with the *r* horn... Josh 6:5 3104

RAMS
the *r* which leaped upon the... Gen 31:10 6260
all the *r* which leap upon the... Gen 31:12 6260
the *r* of thy flock have I not... Gen 31:38 352
two hundred ewes, and twenty *r*... Gen 32:14 352
and two *r* without blemish,... Ex 29:1 352
with the bullock and the two *r*... Ex 29:3 352
and goats' hair, and red skins of *r*... Ex 35:23 352
for the sin offering, and two *r*... Lev 8:2 352
and one young bullock, and two *r*... Lev 23:18 352
peace offerings, two oxen, five *r*... Num 7:17 352
peace offerings, two oxen, five *r*... Num 7:23 352
peace offerings, two oxen, five *r*... Num 7:29 352
peace offerings, two oxen, five *r*... Num 7:35 352
peace offerings, two oxen, five *r*... Num 7:41 352
peace offerings, two oxen, five *r*... Num 7:47 352
peace offerings, two oxen, five *r*... Num 7:53 352
peace offerings, two oxen, five *r*... Num 7:59 352
peace offerings, two oxen, five *r*... Num 7:65 352
peace offerings, two oxen, five *r*... Num 7:71 352
peace offerings, two oxen, five *r*... Num 7:77 352
peace offerings, two oxen, five *r*... Num 7:83 352
the *r* twelve, the lambs of the... Num 7:87 352
the *r* sixty, the he goats sixty,... Num 7:88 352
me here seven oxen and seven *r*... Num 23:1 352
me here seven bullocks and seven *r*... Num 23:29 352

thirteen young bullocks, two *r* Num 29:13 352
deals to each ram of the two *r* Num 29:14 352
twelve young bullocks, two *r* Num 29:17 352
for the bullocks, for the *r* Num 29:18 352
third day eleven bullocks, two *r* Num 29:20 352
for the bullocks, for the *r* Num 29:21 352
fourth day ten bullocks, two *r* Num 29:23 352
for the bullocks, for the *r* Num 29:24 352
fifth day nine bullocks, two *r* Num 29:26 352
for the bullocks, for the *r* Num 29:27 352
sixth day eight bullocks, two *r* Num 29:29 352
for the bullocks, for the *r* Num 29:30 352
seventh day seven bullocks, two *r* Num 29:32 352
for the bullocks, for the *r* Num 29:33 352
r of the breed of Bashan, and Deut 32:14 352
and to hearken than the fat of *r* 1Sa 15:22 352
lambs, and an hundred thousand *r* 2Kin 3:4 352
offered seven bullocks and seven *r* 1Chr 15:26 352
a thousand bullocks, a thousand *r* 1Chr 29:21 352
with a young bullock and seven *r* 2Chr 13:9 352
seven thousand and seven hundred *r* 2Chr 17:11 352
seven bullocks, and seven *r* 2Chr 29:21 352
when they had killed the *r* 2Chr 29:22 352
and ten bullocks, an hundred *r* 2Chr 29:32 352
of, both young bullocks, and *r* Ezr 6:9 1798
hundred bullocks, two hundred *r* Ezr 6:17 1798
with this money bullocks, *r* Ezr 7:17 1798
for all Israel, ninety and six *r* Ezr 8:35 352
you now seven bullocks and seven *r* Job 42:8 352
fatlings, with the incense of *r* Ps 66:15 352
The mountains skipped like *r* Ps 114:4 352
mountains, that ye skipped like *r* Ps 114:6 352
full of the burnt offerings of *r* Is 1:11 352
with the fat of the kidneys of *r* Is 34:6 352
the *r* of Nebaioth shall minister Is 60:7 352
slaughter, like *r* with he goats Jer 51:40 352
set battering *r* against it round Eze 4:2 3733
battering *r* against the gates Eze 21:22 3733
occupied with thee in lambs, and *r* Eze 27:21 352
cattle and cattle, between the *r* Eze 34:17 352
of the princes of the earth, of *r* Eze 39:18 352
seven *r* without blemish daily the Eze 45:23 352
be pleased with thousands of *r* Mic 6:7 352

RAMS'
r skins dyed red, and badgers' Ex 25:5 352
for the tent of *r* skins dyed red Ex 26:14 352
r skins dyed red, and badgers' Ex 35:7 352
for the tent of *r* skins dyed red Ex 36:19 352
the covering of *r* skins dyed red Ex 39:34 352
the ark seven trumpets of *r* horns Josh 6:4 3104
of *r* horns before the ark of the Josh 6:6 3104
bearing the seven trumpets of *r* Josh 6:8 3104
bearing seven trumpets of *r* horns Josh 6:13 3104

RAN
he *r* to meet them from the tent Gen 18:2 7323
Abraham *r* unto the herd, and Gen 18:7 7323
And the servant *r* to meet her Gen 24:17 7323
r again unto the well to draw Gen 24:20 7323
And the damsel *r*, and told them of Gen 24:28 7323
Laban *r* out unto the man, unto Gen 24:29 7323
and she *r* and told her father Gen 29:12 7323
that he *r* to meet him, and Gen 29:13 7323
Esau *r* to meet him, and embraced Gen 33:4 7323
the fire *r* along upon the ground Ex 9:23 1980
there *r* a young man, and told Num 11:27 7323
and *r* into the midst of the Num 16:47 7323
and they *r* unto the tent Josh 7:22 7323
and they *r* as soon as he had Josh 8:19 7323
and all the host *r*, and cried, and Judg 7:21 7323
And Jotham *r* away, and fled, and Judg 9:21 7323
the two other companies *r* upon Judg 9:44 6584
And the woman made haste, and *r* Judg 13:10 7323
he *r* unto Eli, and said, Here am I 1Sa 3:5 7323
there *r* a man of Benjamin out of 1Sa 4:12 7323
And they *r* and fetched him thence 1Sa 10:23 7323
r into the army, and came and 1Sa 17:22 7323
r toward the army to meet the 1Sa 17:48 7323
Therefore David *r*, and stood upon 1Sa 17:51 7323
And as the lad *r*, he shot an arrow 1Sa 20:36 7323
bowed himself unto Joab, and *r* 2Sa 18:21 7323
Then Ahimaaz *r* by the way of the 2Sa 18:23 7323
two of the servants of Shimei *r* 1Kin 2:39 1272
the water *r* round about the altar 1Kin 18:35 7323
r before Ahab to the entrance of 1Kin 18:46 7323
r after Elijah, and said, Let me 1Kin 19:20 7323
the blood *r* out of the wound into 1Kin 22:35 3332
the brook that *r* through the 2Chr 32:4 7857
my sore *r* in the night, and ceased Ps 77:2 5064
they *r* in the dry places like a Ps 105:41 1980
that *r* down upon the beard, even Ps 133:2 3331
sent these prophets, yet they *r* Jer 23:21 7323
And the living creatures *r* Eze 1:14 7519
there *r* out waters on the right Eze 47:2 6379
r unto him in the fury of his Dan 8:6 7323
the whole herd of swine *r* Mt 8:32 3729
And straightway one of them *r* Mt 27:48 5143
when he saw Jesus afar off, he *r* Mk 5:6 5143
the herd *r* violently down a steep Mk 5:13 3729
r afoot thither out of all cities Mk 6:33 4936
r through that whole region round Mk 6:55 4063
And one *r* and filled a spunge full Mk 15:36 5143
the herd *r* violently down a steep Lk 8:33 3729
saw him, and had compassion, and *r* Lk 15:20 5143
he *r* before, and climbed up into a Lk 19:4 4390
Peter, and *r* unto the sepulchre Lk 24:12 5143
So they *r* both together Jn 20:4 5143
all the people *r* together unto Acts 3:11 4936
r upon him with one accord, Acts 7:57 3729
Philip *r* thither to him, and heard Acts 8:30 4370
the gate for gladness, but *r* in Acts 12:14 1532
r in among the people, crying out Acts 14:14 1530
moved, and the people *r* together Acts 21:30 4890
centurions, and *r* down unto them Acts 21:32 2701

seas met, they *r* the ship aground Acts 27:41 2027
r greedily after the error of Jude 11 1632

RANG
shout, so that the earth *r* again 1Sa 4:5 1949
so that the city *r* again 1Kin 1:45 1949

RANGE
The *r* of the mountains is his Job 39:8 3491

RANGES
or *r* for pots, they shall be Lev 11:35 3600
and he that cometh within the *r* 2Kin 11:8 7713
Have her forth without the *r* 2Kin 11:15 7713
them, Have her forth of the *r* 2Chr 23:14 7713

RANGING
As a roaring lion, and a *r* bear Prov 28:15 8264

RANK
of corn came up upon one stalk, *r* Gen 41:5 1277
thin ears devoured the seven *r* Gen 41:7 1277
shall set forth in the second *r* Num 2:16
shall go forward in the third *r* Num 2:24
thousand, which could keep *r* 1Chr 12:33 5737
men of war, that could keep *r* 1Chr 12:38 4634

RANKS
was against light in three *r* 1Kin 7:4 6471
was against light in three *r* 1Kin 7:5 6471
and they shall not break their *r* Joel 2:7 734
And they sat down in *r*, by Mk 6:40 4237

RANSOM
then he shall give for the *r* of Ex 21:30 6306
a *r* for his soul unto the LORD Ex 30:12 3724
I have found a *r* Job 33:24 3724
then a great *r* cannot deliver Job 36:18 3724
nor give to God a *r* for him Ps 49:7 3724
He will not regard any *r* Prov 6:35 3724
The *r* of a man's life are his Prov 13:8 3724
shall be a *r* for the righteous Prov 21:18 3724
I gave Egypt for thy *r*, Ethiopia Is 43:3 3724
I will *r* them from the power of Hos 13:14 6299
and to give his life a *r* for many Mt 20:28 3083
and to give his life a *r* for many Mk 10:45 3083
Who gave himself a *r* for all 1Ti 2:6 487

RANSOMED
the *r* of the LORD shall return, Is 35:10 6299
sea a way for the *r* to pass over Is 51:10 1350
r him from the hand of him that Jer 31:11 1350

RAPHA (*ra'-fah*) See BETH-RAPHA, REPHAIAH.
1. Son of Benjamin.
Nohah the fourth, and *R* the fifth 1Chr 8:2 7498
2. A member of Saul's family.
R was his son, Eleasah his son, 1Chr 8:37 7498

RAPHAIN See RAPHA.

RAPHU (*ra'-fu*) *A Benjamite spy sent to the Promised Land.*
of Benjamin, Palti the son of *R* Num 13:9 7505

RARE
it is a *r* thing that the king Dan 2:11 3358

RASE
R it, *r* it, even to the Ps 137:7 6168

RASH
Be not *r* with thy mouth, and let Eccl 5:2 926
The heart also of the *r* shall Is 32:4 4116

RASHLY
to be quiet, and to do nothing *r* Acts 19:36 4312

RASOR
like a sharp *r*, working Ps 52:2 8593

RATE
and gather a certain *r* every day Ex 16:4 1697
and mules, a *r* year by year 1Kin 10:25 1697
a daily *r* for every day, all the 2Kin 25:30 1697
Even after a certain *r* every day 2Chr 8:13 1697
and mules, a *r* year by year 2Chr 9:24 1697

RATHER
if we have not *r* done it for fear Josh 22:24
hath not David *r* sent his 2Sa 10:3
how much *r* then, when he saith to 2Kin 5:13
and death *r* than my life Job 7:15
he justified himself *r* than God Job 32:2
thou chosen *r* than affliction Job 36:21
and lying *r* than to speak Ps 52:3
I had *r* be a doorkeeper in the Ps 84:10 977
knowledge *r* than choice gold Prov 8:10 408
to get understanding *r* to be Prov 16:16
r than a fool in his folly Prov 17:12 408
A good name is *r* to be chosen Prov 22:1
and loving favour *r* than silver Prov 22:1
death shall be chosen *r* than life Jer 8:3
But go *r* to the lost sheep of the Mt 10:6 3123
but *r* fear him which is able to Mt 10:28 3123
r than having two hands or two Mt 18:8 2228
r than having two eyes to be cast Mt 18:9 2228
but go ye *r* to them that sell, and Mt 25:9 3123
but that *r* a tumult was made, he Mt 27:24 3123
bettered, but *r* grew worse, Mk 5:26 3123
that he should *r* release Barabbas Mk 15:11 3123
but *r* rejoice, because your names Lk 10:20 3123
But he said, Yea *r*, blessed are Lk 11:28 3304
But *r* give alms of such things as Lk 11:41 4133
But *r* seek ye the kingdom of God Lk 12:31 4133
but *r* division Lk 12:51 2228
will not *r* say unto him, Make Lk 17:8
house justified *r* than the other Lk 18:14
men loved darkness *r* than light Jn 3:19 3123
We ought to obey God *r* than men Acts 5:29 3123
And not *r*, (as we be slanderously Rom 3:8
It is Christ that died, yea *r* Rom 8:34 3123
but *r* through their fall Rom 11:11

but *r* give place unto wrath Rom 12:19
but judge this *r*, that no man put Rom 14:13 3123
puffed up, and have not *r* mourned 1Cor 5:2 3123
Why do ye not *r* take wrong 1Cor 6:7 3123
why do ye not *r* suffer yourselves 1Cor 6:7 3123
mayest be made free, use it *r* 1Cor 7:21 3123
this power over you, are not we *r* 1Cor 9:12 3123
but *r* that ye may prophesy 1Cor 14:1 3123
tongues, but *r* that ye prophesied 1Cor 14:5 3123
Yet in the church I had *r* speak 1Cor 14:19 2309
ye ought *r* to forgive him 2Cor 2:7 3123
of the spirit be *r* glorious 2Cor 3:8 3123
willing *r* to be absent from the 2Cor 5:8 3123
will I *r* glory in my infirmities 2Cor 12:9 3123
or *r* are known of God, how turn Gal 4:9 3123
but *r* let him labour, working Eph 4:28 3123
but *r* giving of thanks Eph 5:4 3123
of darkness, but *r* reprove them Eph 5:11 3123
unto me have fallen out *r* unto Phil 1:12 3123
r than godly edifying which is in 1Ti 1:4 3123
exercise thyself *r* unto godliness 1Ti 4:7
but *r* do them service, because 1Ti 6:2 3123
for love's sake I *r* beseech thee Philem 9 3123
Choosing *r* to suffer affliction Heb 11:25 3123
shall we not much *r* be in Heb 12:9 3123
but let it *r* be healed Heb 12:13 3123
I beseech you the *r* to do this Heb 13:19 4056
Wherefore the *r*, brethren, give 2Pet 1:10 3123

RATTLETH
The quiver *r* against him, the Job 39:23 7439

RATTLING
the noise of the *r* of the wheels Nah 3:2 7494

RAVEN
And he sent forth a *r*, which went Gen 8:7 6158
Every *r* after his kind Lev 11:15 6158
And every *r* after his kind, Deut 14:14 6158
Who provideth for the *r* his food Job 38:41 6158
locks are bushy, and black as a *r* Song 5:11 6158
also and the *r* shall dwell in it Is 34:11 6158

RAVENING
upon me with their mouths, as a *r* Ps 22:13 2963
like a roaring lion *r* the prey Eze 22:25 2963
are like wolves *r* the prey Eze 22:27 2963
but inwardly they are *r* wolves Mt 7:15 727
but your inward part is full of *r* Lk 11:39 724

RAVENOUS
nor any *r* beast shall go up Is 35:9 6530
Calling a *r* bird from the east, Is 46:11 5861
unto the *r* birds of every sort Eze 39:4 5861

RAVENS
the *r* to feed thee there 1Kin 17:4 6158
the *r* brought him bread and flesh 1Kin 17:6 6158
food, and to the young *r* which cry Ps 147:9 6158
the *r* of the valley shall pick it Prov 30:17 6158
Consider the *r* Lk 12:24 2876

RAVIN
Benjamin shall *r* as a wolf Gen 49:27 2963
with prey, and his dens with *r* Nah 2:12 2966

RAVISHED
be thou *r* always with her love Prov 5:19 7686
be *r* with a strange woman, and Prov 5:20 7686
Thou hast *r* my heart, my sister, Song 4:9 3823
thou hast *r* my heart with one of Song 4:9 3823
be spoiled, and their wives *r* Is 13:16 7693
They *r* the women in Zion, and the Lam 5:11 6031
the houses rifled, and the women *r* Zec 14:2 7693

RAW
Eat not of it *r*, nor sodden at Ex 12:9 4995
there be quick *r* flesh in the Lev 13:10 2416
But when *r* flesh appeareth in him Lev 13:14 2416
the priest shall see the *r* flesh Lev 13:15 2416
for the *r* flesh is unclean Lev 13:15 2416
Or if the *r* flesh turn again, and Lev 13:16 2416
have sodden flesh of thee, but *r* 1Sa 2:15 2416

RAZOR
shall no *r* come upon his head Num 6:5
no *r* shall come on his head Judg 13:5 4177
hath not come a *r* upon mine head Judg 16:17 4177
there shall no *r* come upon his 1Sa 1:11 4177
Lord shave with a *r* that is hired Is 7:20 8593
knife, take thee a barber's *r* Eze 5:1 8593

REACH
whose top may *r* unto heaven Gen 11:4
boards shall *r* from end to end Ex 26:28 1272
even unto the thighs they shall *r* Ex 28:42 1961
shall *r* unto the vintage Lev 26:5 5381
the vintage shall *r* unto the Lev 26:5 5381
shall *r* unto the side of the sea Num 34:11 4229
shall *r* from the wall of the city Num 35:4
his head *r* unto the clouds Job 20:6 5060
he shall *r* even to the neck Is 8:8 5060
shall *r* to the midst of the neck, Is 30:28 5060
they *r* even to the sea of Jazer Jer 48:32 5060
the mountains shall *r* unto Azal Zec 14:5 5060
R hither thy finger, and behold my Jn 20:27 5342
r hither thy hand, and thrust it Jn 20:27 5342
a measure to *r* even unto you 2Cor 10:13 2185

REACHED
and the top of it *r* to heaven Gen 28:12 5060
r to Dabbasheth, and *r* to Josh 19:11 6293
he *r* her parched corn, and she did Ruth 2:14 6642
the height thereof *r* unto heaven Dan 4:11 4291
whose height *r* unto the heaven, Dan 4:20 4291
as though we *r* not unto you 2Cor 10:14 2185
For her sins have *r* unto heaven Rev 18:5 190

R

REACHETH
unto Nophah, which *r* unto Medeba ..... Num 21:30
And the coast *r* to Tabor, and ..... Josh 19:22 6293
r to Carmel westward, and to ..... Josh 19:26 6293
r to Zebulun, and to the valley of ..... Josh 19:27 6293
r to Zebulun on the south side, ... Josh 19:34 6293
r to Asher on the west side, and ..... Josh 19:34 6293
in a rage that *r* up unto heaven 2Chr 28:9 5060
faithfulness *r* unto the clouds ..... Ps 36:5
thy truth *r* unto the clouds ..... Ps 108:4
she *r* forth her hands to the ..... Prov 31:20 7971
whereas the sword *r* unto the soul ..... Jer 4:10 5060
because it *r* unto thine heart ..... Jer 4:18 5060
for her judgment *r* unto heaven ..... Jer 51:9 5060
r unto heaven, and thy dominion to ..... Dan 4:22 4291

REACHING
r to the wall of the house 2Chr 3:11 5060
r to the wing of the other cherub 2Chr 3:11 5060
r to the wall of the house 2Chr 3:12 5060
r forth unto those things which ..... Phil 3:13 *1901*

READ
r in the audience of the people ..... Ex 24:7 7121
he shall *r* therein all the days ..... Deut 17:19 7121
thou shalt *r* this law before all ..... Deut 31:11 7121
afterward he *r* all the words of ..... Josh 8:34 7121
which Joshua *r* not before all the ..... Josh 8:35 7121
king of Israel had *r* the letter 2Kin 5:7 7121
hand of the messengers, and *r* it 2Kin 19:14 7121
the book to Shaphan, and he *r* it 2Kin 22:8 7121
Shaphan *r* it before the king 2Kin 22:10 7121
which the king of Judah hath *r* 2Kin 22:16 7121
he *r* in their ears all the words 2Kin 23:2 7121
Shaphan *r* it before the king 2Chr 34:18 7121
have *r* before the king of Judah 2Chr 34:24 7121
he *r* in their ears all the words 2Chr 34:30 7121
us hath been plainly *r* before me ..... Ezr 4:18 7123
letter was *r* before Rehum ..... Ezr 4:23 7123
he *r* therein before the street ..... Neh 8:3 7121
So they *r* in the book in the law ..... Neh 8:8 7121
he *r* in the book of the law of ..... Neh 8:18 7121
r in the book of the law of the ..... Neh 9:3 7121
On that day they *r* in the book of ..... Neh 13:1 7121
they were *r* before the king ..... Est 6:1 7121
saying, *R* this, I pray thee ..... Is 29:11 7121
saying, *R* this, I pray thee ..... Is 29:12 7121
out of the book of the LORD, and *r* ..... Is 34:16 7121
hand of the messengers, and *r* it ..... Is 37:14 7121
Zephaniah the priest *r* this ..... Jer 29:29 7121
r in the roll, which thou hast ..... Jer 36:6 7121
also thou shalt *r* them in the ..... Jer 36:6 7121
Then *r* Baruch in the book the ..... Jer 36:10 7121
when Baruch *r* the book in the ..... Jer 36:13 7121
hast *r* in the ears of the people ..... Jer 36:14 7121
Sit down now, and *r* it in our ears ..... Jer 36:15 7121
So Baruch *r* it in their ears ..... Jer 36:15 7121
Jehudi *r* it in the ears of the ..... Jer 36:21 7121
Jehudi had *r* three or four leaves ..... Jer 36:23 7121
see, and shalt *r* all these words ..... Jer 51:61 7121
Whosoever shall *r* this writing ..... Dan 5:7 7123
but they could not *r* the writing ..... Dan 5:8 7123
that they should *r* this writing ..... Dan 5:15 7123
now if thou canst *r* the writing ..... Dan 5:16 7123
yet I will *r* the writing unto the ..... Dan 5:17 7123
Have ye not *r* what David did, ... Mt 12:3 *314*
Or have ye not *r* in the law ..... Mt 12:5 *314*
and said unto them, Have ye not *r* ..... Mt 19:4 *314*
have ye never *r*, Out of the mouth ..... Mt 21:16 *314*
Did ye never *r* in the scriptures, ... Mt 21:42 *314*
have ye not *r* that which was ..... Mt 22:31 *314*
Have ye never *r* what David did, ... Mk 2:25 *314*
have ye not *r* this scripture ..... Mk 12:10 *314*
have ye not *r* in the book of ..... Mk 12:26 *314*
sabbath day, and stood up for to *r* ..... Lk 4:16 *314*
Have ye not *r* so much as this, ... Lk 6:3 *314*
This title then *r* many of the ..... Jn 19:20 *314*
his chariot *r* Esaias the prophet ..... Acts 8:28 *314*
heard him *r* the prophet Esaias, ... Acts 8:30 *314*
the scripture which he *r* was this ..... Acts 8:32 *314*
which are *r* every sabbath day ..... Acts 13:27 *314*
being *r* in the synagogues every ..... Acts 15:21 *314*
Which when they had *r*, they ..... Acts 15:31 *314*
the governor had *r* the letter ..... Acts 23:34 *314*
than what ye *r* or acknowledge 2Cor 1:13 *314*
our hearts, known and *r* of all men 2Cor 3:2 *314*
unto this day, when Moses is *r* 2Cor 3:15 *314*
Whereby, when ye *r*, ye may ..... Eph 3:4 *314*
when this epistle is *r* among you ..... Col 4:16 *314*
cause that it be *r* also in the ..... Col 4:16 *314*
that ye likewise *r* the epistle ..... Col 4:16 *314*
be *r* unto all the holy brethren 1Th 5:27 *314*
to *r* the book, neither to look ..... Rev 5:4 *314*

READEST
how *r* thou ..... Lk 10:26 *314*
Understandest thou what thou *r* ..... Acts 8:30 *314*

READETH
tables, that he may run that *r* it ..... Hab 2:2 7121
stand in the holy place, (whoso *r* ..... Mt 24:15 *314*
not, (let him that *r* understand ..... Mk 13:14 *314*
Blessed is he that *r*, and they ..... Rev 1:3 *314*

READINESS
the word with all *r* of mind ..... Acts 17:11 *4288*
that as there was a *r* to will 2Cor 8:11 *4288*
having in a *r* to revenge all 2Cor 10:6 *2092*

READING
caused them to understand the *r* ..... Neh 8:8 4744
r in the book the words of the ..... Jer 36:8 7121
hast made an end of *r* this book ..... Jer 51:63 7121
after the *r* of the law and the ..... Acts 13:15 *320*
in the *r* of the old testament 2Cor 3:14 *320*
Till I come, give attendance to *r* 1Ti 4:13 *320*

READY
Make *r* quickly three measures of ..... Gen 18:6 4116
men home, and slay, and make *r* ..... Gen 43:16 3559
they made *r* the present against ..... Gen 43:25 3559
And Joseph made *r* his chariot ..... Gen 46:29 631
he made *r* his chariot, and took ..... Ex 14:6 631
they be almost *r* to stone me ..... Ex 17:4 5750
be *r* against the third day ..... Ex 19:11 3559
Be *r* against the third day ..... Ex 19:15 3559
be *r* in the morning, and come up ..... Ex 34:2 3559
But we ourselves will go *r* armed ..... Num 32:17 2363
ye were *r* to go up into the hill ..... Deut 1:41 1951
A Syrian *r* to perish was my ..... Deut 26:5
from the city, but be ye all *r* ..... Josh 8:4 3559
made *r* a kid, and unleavened cakes ..... Judg 6:19
shall have made *r* a kid for thee ..... Judg 13:15
of wine, and five sheep *r* dressed 1Sa 25:18
Behold, thy servants are *r* to do 2Sa 15:15
that thou hast no tidings *r* 2Sa 18:22 4672
was built of stone made *r* before 1Kin 6:7 8003
And Joram said, Make *r* 2Kin 9:21 631
And his chariot was made *r* 2Kin 9:21 631
that were *r* armed to the war 1Chr 12:23
eight hundred, *r* armed to the war 1Chr 12:24
had made *r* for the building 1Chr 28:2 3559
fourscore thousand *r* prepared for 2Chr 17:18
they made *r* for themselves 2Chr 35:14 3559
he was a *r* scribe in the law of ..... Ezr 7:6 4106
but thou art a God *r* to pardon ..... Neh 9:17
they should be *r* against that day ..... Est 3:14 6264
that the Jews should be *r* against ..... Est 8:13 6264
who are *r* to raise up their ..... Job 3:8 6264
He that is *r* to slip with his ..... Job 12:5 3559
day of darkness is *r* at his hand ..... Job 15:23 3559
as a king *r* to the battle ..... Job 15:24 6264
which are *r* to become heaps ..... Job 15:28 6257
extinct, the graves are *r* for me ..... Job 17:1
shall be *r* at his side ..... Job 18:12 3559
that was *r* to perish came upon me ..... Job 29:13
it is *r* to burst like new bottles ..... Job 32:19
hath bent his bow, and made it *r* ..... Ps 7:12 3559
they make *r* their arrow upon the ..... Ps 11:2 3559
when thou shalt make *r* thine ..... Ps 21:12 3559
For I am *r* to halt, and my sorrow ..... Ps 38:17 3559
tongue is the pen of a *r* writer ..... Ps 45:1 4106
Lord, art good, and *r* to forgive ..... Ps 86:5
r to die from my youth up ..... Ps 88:15
and those that are *r* to be slain ..... Prov 24:11 4131
unto him that is *r* to perish ..... Prov 31:6
of God, and be more *r* to hear ..... Eccl 5:1 7138
were *r* to perish in the land of ..... Is 27:13
be to you as a breach *r* to fall ..... Is 30:13
shall be *r* to speak plainly ..... Is 32:4 4116
The LORD was *r* to save me ..... Is 38:20
saying, It is *r* for the sodering ..... Is 41:7 2896
as if he were *r* to destroy ..... Is 51:13 3559
the trumpet, even to make all *r* ..... Eze 7:14 3559
Now if ye be *r* that at what time ..... Dan 3:15 6263
For they have made *r* their heart ..... Hos 7:6 7126
are killed, and all things are *r* ..... Mt 22:4 *2092*
to his servants, The wedding is *r* ..... Mt 22:8 *2092*
Therefore be ye also *r* ..... Mt 24:44 *2092*
they that were *r* went in with him ..... Mt 25:10 *2092*
and they made *r* the passover ..... Mt 26:19 *2090*
there make *r* for us ..... Mk 14:15 *2090*
and they made *r* the passover ..... Mk 14:16 *2090*
The spirit truly is *r*, but the ..... Mk 14:38 *4289*
to make *r* a people prepared for ..... Lk 1:17 *2090*
unto him, was sick, and *r* to die ..... Lk 7:2 *3195*
the Samaritans, to make *r* for him ..... Lk 9:52 *2090*
Be ye therefore *r* also ..... Lk 12:40 *2092*
for all things are now *r* ..... Lk 14:17 *2092*
Make *r* wherewith I may sup, and ..... Lk 17:8 *2090*
there make *r* ..... Lk 22:12 *2090*
and they made *r* the passover ..... Lk 22:13 *2090*
I am *r* to go with thee, both into ..... Lk 22:33 *2092*
but your time is alway *r* ..... Jn 7:6 *2092*
but while they made *r*, he fell ..... Acts 10:10 *3903*
r to depart on the morrow ..... Acts 20:7 *3195*
for I am *r* not to be bound only, ... Acts 21:13 *2093*
he come near, are *r* to kill him ..... Acts 23:15 *2092*
and now are they *r*, looking for a ..... Acts 23:21 *2092*
Make *r* two hundred soldiers to go ..... Acts 23:23 *2090*
I am *r* to preach the gospel to ..... Rom 1:15 *4289*
and declaration of your *r* mind 2Cor 8:19 *4288*
that Achaia was *r* a year ago 2Cor 9:2 *3903*
that, as I said, ye may be *r* 2Cor 9:3 *3903*
before, that the same might be *r* 2Cor 9:5 *2092*
line of things made *r* to our hand 2Cor 10:16 *2092*
third time I am *r* to come to you 2Cor 12:14 *2093*
r to distribute, willing to 1Ti 6:18 *2130*
For I am now *r* to be offered, and 2Ti 4:6 *4689*
to be *r* to every good work, ... Titus 3:1 *2092*
waxeth old is *r* to vanish away ..... Heb 8:13 *1451*
through faith unto salvation *r* to 1Pet 1:5 *2092*
be *r* always to give an answer to 1Pet 3:15 *2092*
him that is *r* to judge the quick 1Pet 4:5 *2093*
for filthy lucre, but of a *r* mind 1Pet 5:2 *4289*
which remain, that are *r* to die ..... Rev 3:2 *3195*
woman which was *r* to be delivered ..... Rev 12:4 *3195*
and his wife hath made herself *r* ..... Rev 19:7 *2090*

REAIA (*re-ah'-yah*) *Grandfather of Beerah.*
his son, *R* his son, Baal his son, ... 1Chr 5:5 7211

REAIAH (*re-ah'-yah*) See REAIA.
1. Son of Shobal.
R the son of Shobal begat Jahath 1Chr 4:2 7211
2. A family of exiles.
of Gahar, the children of *R* ..... Ezr 2:47 7211
The children of *R*, the children ..... Neh 7:50 7211

REALM
So the *r* of Jehoshaphat was quiet 2Chr 20:30 4438
his priests and Levites, in my *r* ..... Ezr 7:13 4437
wrath against the *r* of the king ..... Ezr 7:23 4437
that were in all his *r* ..... Dan 1:20 4438
to set him over the whole *r* ..... Dan 6:3 4437
king over the *r* of the Chaldeans ..... Dan 9:1 4438
up all against the *r* of Grecia ..... Dan 11:2 4438

REAP
when ye *r* the harvest of your ..... Lev 19:9 7114
thou shalt not wholly *r* the ..... Lev 19:9
shall *r* the harvest thereof, then ..... Lev 23:10 7114
when ye *r* the harvest of your ..... Lev 23:22 7114
of thy harvest thou shalt not *r* ..... Lev 25:5 7114
neither *r* that which groweth of ..... Lev 25:11 7114
be on the field that they do *r* ..... Ruth 2:9 7114
to *r* his harvest, and to make his 1Sa 8:12 7114
and in the third year sow ye, and *r* 2Kin 19:29 7114
and sow wickedness, *r* the same ..... Job 4:8 7114
They *r* every one his corn in the ..... Job 24:6 7114
that sow in tears shall *r* in joy ..... Ps 126:5 7114
soweth iniquity shall *r* vanity ..... Prov 22:8 7114
regardeth the clouds shall not *r* ..... Eccl 11:4 7114
and in the third year sow ye, and *r* ..... Is 37:30 7114
sown wheat, but shall *r* thorns ..... Jer 12:13 7114
they shall *r* the whirlwind ..... Hos 8:7 7114
in righteousness, *r* in mercy ..... Hos 10:12 7114
shalt sow, but thou shalt not *r* ..... Mic 6:15 7114
they sow not, neither do they *r* ..... Mt 6:26 *2325*
that I *r* where I sowed not ..... Mt 25:26 *2325*
for they neither sow nor *r* ..... Lk 12:24 *2325*
I sent you to *r* that whereon ye ..... Jn 4:38 *2325*
if we shall *r* your carnal things 1Cor 9:11 *2325*
sparingly shall *r* also sparingly 2Cor 9:6 *2325*
shall *r* also bountifully 2Cor 9:6 *2325*
man soweth, that shall he also *r* ..... Gal 6:7 *2325*
shall of the flesh *r* corruption ..... Gal 6:8 *2325*
of the Spirit *r* life everlasting ..... Gal 6:8 *2325*
for in due season we shall *r* ..... Gal 6:9 *2325*
cloud, Thrust in thy sickle, and *r* ..... Rev 14:15 *2325*
the time is come for thee to *r* ..... Rev 14:15 *2325*

REAPED
wickedness, ye have *r* iniquity ..... Hos 10:13 7114
who have *r* down your fields ..... Jas 5:4 *270*
r are entered into the ears of ..... Jas 5:4 *2325*
and the earth was *r* ..... Rev 14:16 *2325*

REAPER
the plowman shall overtake the *r* ..... Amos 9:13 7114

REAPERS
gleaned in the field after the *r* ..... Ruth 2:3 7114
Beth-lehem, and said unto the *r* ..... Ruth 2:4 7114
servant that was set over the *r* ..... Ruth 2:5 7114
that was set over the *r* answered ..... Ruth 2:6 7114
gather after the *r* among the ..... Ruth 2:7 7114
And she sat beside the *r* ..... Ruth 2:14 7114
went out to his father to the *r* 2Kin 4:18 7114
of harvest I will say to the *r* ..... Mt 13:30 *2327*
and the *r* are the angels ..... Mt 13:39 *2327*

REAPEST
corners of thy field when thou *r* ..... Lev 23:22 7114
r that thou didst not sow ..... Lk 19:21 *2325*

REAPETH
corn, and *r* the ears with his arm ..... Is 17:5 7114
he that *r* receiveth wages, and ..... Jn 4:36 *2325*
he that *r* may rejoice together ..... Jn 4:36 *2325*
true, One soweth, and another *r* ..... Jn 4:37 *2325*

REAPING
they of Beth-shemesh were *r* their 1Sa 6:13 7114
r where thou hast not sown, and ..... Mt 25:24 *2325*
not down, and *r* that I did not sow ..... Lk 19:22 *2325*

REAR
thou shalt *r* up the tabernacle ..... Ex 26:30 6965
neither *r* you up a standing image ..... Lev 26:1 6965
r an altar unto the LORD in the 2Sa 24:18 6965
wilt thou *r* it up in three days ..... Jn 2:20 *1453*

REARED
that the tabernacle was *r* up ..... Ex 40:17 6965
Moses *r* up the tabernacle, and ..... Ex 40:18 6965
bars thereof, and *r* up his pillars ..... Ex 40:18 6965
he *r* up the court round about the ..... Ex 40:33 6965
was *r* up the cloud covered the ..... Num 9:15 6965
r up for himself a pillar, which 2Sa 18:18 5324
he *r* up an altar for Baal in the 1Kin 16:32 6965
he *r* up altars for Baal, and made 2Kin 21:3 6965
he *r* up the pillars before the 2Chr 3:17 6965
he *r* up altars for Baalim, and 2Chr 33:3 6965

REASON
by *r* of that famine following ..... Gen 41:31 6440
Canaan fainted by *r* of the famine ..... Gen 47:13 6440
Israel sighed by *r* of the bondage ..... Ex 2:23 4480
up unto God by *r* of the bondage ..... Ex 2:23 4480
cry by *r* of their taskmasters ..... Ex 3:7 6440
by *r* of the swarm of flies ..... Ex 8:24 6440
be unclean by *r* of a dead body ..... Num 9:10
given them by *r* of the anointing ..... Num 18:8
ye shall bear no sin by *r* of it ..... Num 18:32 5921
ye were afraid by *r* of the fire ..... Deut 5:5 6440
that is not clean by *r* of ..... Deut 23:10
old by *r* of the very long journey ..... Josh 9:13
by *r* of them that oppressed them ..... Judg 2:18
that I may *r* with you before the 1Sa 12:7 8199
this is the *r* of the levy which 1Kin 9:15 1697
his eyes were set by *r* of his age 1Kin 14:4
to minister by *r* of the cloud 2Chr 5:14 6440
by *r* of this great multitude 2Chr 20:15 6440
by *r* of the sickness day by day 2Chr 21:15 4480
fell out by *r* of his sickness 2Chr 21:19 5973
are blackish by *r* of the ice ..... Job 6:16 4480
choose out my words to *r* with him ..... Job 9:14
and I desire to *r* with God ..... Job 13:3 3198
Should he *r* with unprofitable ..... Job 15:3 3198
eye also is dim by *r* of sorrow ..... Job 17:7

by *r* of his highness I could not ... Job 31:23
By *r* of the multitude of ... Job 35:9
they cry out by *r* of the arm of ... Job 35:9
order our speech by *r* of darkness ... Job 37:19 6440
by *r* of breakings they purify ... Job 41:25
I have roared by *r* of the ... Ps 38:8
by *r* of the enemy and avenger ... Ps 44:16 6440
man that shouteth by *r* of wine ... Ps 78:65
eye mourneth by *r* of affliction ... Ps 88:9 4480
if by *r* of strength they be ... Ps 90:10
By *r* of the voice of my groaning ... Ps 102:5
will not plow by *r* of the cold ... Prov 20:4
seven men that can render a *r* ... Prov 26:16 2940
the *r* of things, and to know the ... Eccl 7:25 2808
let us *r* together, saith the LORD ... Is 1:18 3198
narrow by *r* of the inhabitants ... Is 49:19
of branches by *r* of many waters ... Eze 19:10
terrors by *r* of the sword shall ... Eze 21:12 413
By *r* of the abundance of his ... Eze 26:10
Tarshish was thy merchant by *r* of ... Eze 27:12
Syria was thy merchant by *r* of ... Eze 27:16
thy wisdom by *r* of thy brightness ... Eze 28:17 5921
same time my *r* returned unto me ... Dan 4:36 4486
by *r* of the words of the king and ... Dan 5:10 6903
sacrifice by *r* of transgression ... Dan 8:12
I cried by *r* of mine affliction ... Jonah 2:2
by *r* of the multitude of men ... Mic 2:12
why *r* ye among yourselves, ... Mt 16:8 *1260*
Why *r* ye these things in your ... Mk 2:8 *1260*
it, he saith unto them, Why *r* ye ... Mk 8:17 *1260*
and the Pharisees began to *r* ... Lk 5:21 *1260*
them, What *r* ye in your hearts ... Lk 5:22 *1260*
the sea arose by *r* of a great ... Jn 6:18
Because that by *r* of him many of ... Jn 12:11 *1223*
It is not *r* that we should leave ... Acts 6:2 *701*
r would that I should bear with ... Acts 18:14 *3056*
but by *r* of him who hath ... Rom 8:20 *1223*
by *r* of the glory that excelleth ... 2Cor 3:10 *1752*
by *r* hereof he ought, as for the ... Heb 5:3 *1223*
even those who by *r* of use have ... Heb 5:14 *1223*
to continue by *r* of death ... Heb 7:23
to every man that asketh you a *r* ... 1Pet 3:15 *3056*
by *r* of whom the way of truth ... 2Pet 2:2 *1223*
by *r* of the other voices of the ... Rev 8:13 *1537*
by *r* of the smoke of the pit ... Rev 9:2 *1537*
in the sea by *r* of her costliness ... Rev 18:19 *1537*

REASONABLE
unto God, which is your *r* service ... Rom 12:1 *3050*

REASONED
they *r* among themselves, saying, ... Mt 16:7 *1260*
they *r* with themselves, saying, ... Mt 21:25 *1260*
that they so *r* within themselves ... Mk 2:8 *1260*
they *r* among themselves, saying, ... Mk 8:16 *1260*
they *r* with themselves, saying, ... Mk 11:31 *3049*
they *r* with themselves, saying, ... Lk 20:5 *4817*
they *r* among themselves, saying, ... Lk 20:14 *1260*
while they communed together and *r* .. Lk 24:15 *4802*
three sabbath days *r* with them ... Acts 17:2 *1256*
he *r* in the synagogue every ... Acts 18:4 *1256*
the synagogue, and *r* with the Jews ... Acts 18:19 *1256*
as he *r* of righteousness, ... Acts 24:25 *1256*

REASONING
Hear now my *r*, and hearken to the ... Job 13:6 8433
there, and *r* in their hearts, ... Mk 2:6 *1260*
and having heard them *r* together ... Mk 12:28 *4802*
Then there arose a *r* among them ... Lk 9:46 *1261*
had great *r* among themselves ... Acts 28:29 *4803*

REASONS
I gave ear to your *r*, whilst ye ... Job 32:11 8394
bring forth your strong *r* ... Is 41:21

REBA (*re'-bah*) *A king of Midian.*
and Rekem, and Zur, and Hur, and *R* .. Num 31:8 7254
and Rekem, and Zur, and Hur, and *R* .. Josh 13:21 7254

REBECCA (*re-bek'-kah*) See REBEKAH. *Greek form of Rebekah.*
but when *R* also had conceived by ... Rom 9:10 *4479*

REBEKAH (*re-bek'-kah*) See REBECCA, REBEKAH'S. *Wife of Isaac.*
And Bethuel begat *R* ... Gen 22:23 7259
R came out, who was born to ... Gen 24:15 7259
R had a brother, and his name was ... Gen 24:29 7259
heard the words of *R* his sister ... Gen 24:30 7259
R came forth with her pitcher on ... Gen 24:45 7259
R is before thee, take her, and go ... Gen 24:51 7259
and raiment, and gave them to *R* ... Gen 24:53 7259
And they called *R*, and said unto ... Gen 24:58 7259
And they sent away *R* their sister ... Gen 24:59 7259
And they blessed *R*, and said unto ... Gen 24:60 7259
R arose, and her damsels, and they ... Gen 24:61 7259
and the servant took *R*, and went ... Gen 24:61 7259
R lifted up her eyes, and when she ... Gen 24:64 7259
mother Sarah's tent, and took *R* ... Gen 24:67 7259
years old when he took *R* to wife ... Gen 25:20 7259
of him, and *R* his wife conceived ... Gen 25:21 7259
but *R* loved Jacob ... Gen 25:28 7259
of the place should kill me for *R* ... Gen 26:7 7259
was sporting with *R* his wife ... Gen 26:8 7259
grief of mind unto Isaac and to *R* ... Gen 26:35 7259
R heard when Isaac spake to Esau ... Gen 27:5 7259
R spake unto Jacob her son, ... Gen 27:6 7259
And Jacob said to *R* his mother ... Gen 27:11 7259
R took goodly raiment of her ... Gen 27:15 7259
Esau her elder son were told to *R* ... Gen 27:42 7259
R said to Isaac, I am weary of my ... Gen 27:46 7259
the Syrian, the brother of *R* ... Gen 28:5 7259
they buried Isaac and *R* his wife ... Gen 49:31 7259

REBEKAH'S (*re-bek'-kahz*)
brother, and that he was *R* son ... Gen 29:12 7259
But Deborah *R* nurse died, and she ... Gen 35:8 7259

REBEL
Only *r* not ye against the LORD, ... Num 14:9 4775
doth *r* against thy commandment ... Josh 1:18 4784
that ye might *r* this day against ... Josh 22:16 4775
seeing ye *r* to day against the ... Josh 22:18 4775
but *r* not against the LORD ... Josh 22:19 4775
nor *r* against us, in building you ... Josh 22:19 4775
that we should *r* against the LORD ... Josh 22:29 4775
not *r* against the commandment of ... 1Sa 12:14 4784
but *r* against the commandment of ... 1Sa 12:15 4784
will ye *r* against the king ... Neh 2:19 4775
that thou and the Jews think to *r* ... Neh 6:6 4775
of those that *r* against the light ... Job 24:13 4775
But if ye refuse and *r*, ye shall ... Is 1:20 4784
and wine, and they *r* against me ... Hos 7:14 5493

REBELLED
and in the thirteenth year they *r* ... Gen 14:4 4775
because ye *r* against my word at ... Num 20:24 4784
For ye *r* against my commandment ... Num 27:14 4784
but *r* against the commandment of ... Deut 1:26 4784
but *r* against the commandment of ... Deut 1:43 4784
then ye *r* against the commandment ... Deut 9:23 4784
So Israel *r* against the house of ... 1Kin 12:19 6586
Then Moab *r* against Israel after ... 2Kin 1:1 6586
that the king of Moab *r* against ... 2Kin 3:5 6586
king of Moab hath *r* against me ... 2Kin 3:7 6586
he *r* against the king of Assyria, ... 2Kin 18:7 4775
then he turned and *r* against him ... 2Kin 24:1 4775
that Zedekiah *r* against the king ... 2Kin 24:20 4775
Israel *r* against the house of ... 2Chr 10:19 6856
up, and hath *r* against his lord ... 2Chr 13:6 4775
And he also *r* against king ... 2Chr 36:13 4775
r against thee, and cast thy law ... Neh 9:26 4775
for they have *r* against thee ... Ps 5:10 4784
they *r* not against his word ... Ps 105:28 4784
Because they *r* against the words ... Ps 107:11 4784
and they have *r* against me ... Is 1:2 6586
But they *r*, and vexed his holy ... Is 63:10 4784
that Zedekiah *r* against the king ... Jer 52:3 4775
for I have *r* against his ... Lam 1:18 4784
for I have grievously *r* ... Lam 1:20 4784
We have transgressed and have *r* ... Lam 3:42 4784
nation that hath *r* against me ... Eze 2:3 4775
But he *r* against him in sending ... Eze 17:15 4775
But they *r* against me, and would ... Eze 20:8 4784
But the house of Israel *r* against ... Eze 20:13 4784
the children *r* against me ... Eze 20:21 4784
and have done wickedly, and have *r* ... Dan 9:5 4775
though we have *r* against him ... Dan 9:9 4775
for she hath *r* against her God ... Hos 13:16 4784

REBELLEST
trust, that thou *r* against me ... 2Kin 18:20 4775
trust, that thou *r* against me ... Is 36:5 4775

REBELLION
For I know thy *r*, and thy stiff ... Deut 31:27 4805
if it be in *r*, or if in ... Josh 22:22 4779
For *r* is as the sin of witchcraft ... 1Sa 15:23 4805
against kings, and that *r* and ... Ezr 4:19 4776
in their *r* appointed a captain to ... Neh 9:17 4805
For he addeth *r* unto his sin ... Job 34:37 6588
An evil man seeketh only *r* ... Prov 17:11 4805
hast taught *r* against the LORD ... Jer 28:16 5627
he hath taught *r* against the LORD ... Jer 29:32 5627

REBELLIOUS
ye have been *r* against the LORD ... Deut 9:7 4784
Ye have been *r* against the LORD ... Deut 9:24 4784
r son, which will not obey the ... Deut 21:18 4784
This our son is stubborn and *r* ... Deut 21:20 4784
ye have been *r* against the LORD ... Deut 31:27 4784
Thou son of the perverse *r* woman ... 1Sa 20:30 4780
unto Jerusalem, building the *r* ... Ezr 4:12 4779
know that this city is a *r* city ... Ezr 4:15 4779
let not the *r* exalt themselves ... Ps 66:7 5637
but the *r* dwell in a dry land ... Ps 68:6 5637
yea, for the *r* also, that the ... Ps 68:18 5637
a stubborn and *r* generation ... Ps 78:8 4784
Thy princes are *r*, and companions ... Is 1:23 5637
Woe to the *r* children, saith the ... Is 30:1 5637
That this is a *r* people, lying ... Is 30:9 4805
opened mine ear, and I was not *r* ... Is 50:5 4784
hands all the day unto a *r* people ... Is 65:2 5637
she hath been *r* against me ... Jer 4:17 4784
hath a revolting and a *r* heart ... Jer 5:23 5637
to a *r* nation that hath rebelled ... Eze 2:3 4775
forbear, (for they are a *r* house ... Eze 2:5 4805
looks, though they be a *r* house ... Eze 2:6 4805
for they are most *r* ... Eze 2:7 4805
Be not thou *r* like that ... Eze 2:8 4805
like that *r* house ... Eze 2:8 4805
looks, though they be a *r* house ... Eze 3:9 4805
for they are a *r* house ... Eze 3:26 4805
for they are a *r* house ... Eze 3:27 4805
in the midst of a *r* house ... Eze 12:2 4805
for they are a *r* house ... Eze 12:2 4805
though they be a *r* house ... Eze 12:3 4805
the *r* house, said unto thee, What ... Eze 12:9 4805
O *r* house, will I say the word, ... Eze 12:25 4805
Say now to the *r* house, Know ye ... Eze 17:12 4805
utter a parable unto the *r* house ... Eze 24:3 4805
And thou shalt say to the *r* ... Eze 44:6 4805

REBELS
be kept for a token against the *r* ... Num 17:10 4805
he said unto them, Hear now, ye *r* ... Num 20:10 4784
purge out from among you the *r* ... Eze 20:38 4775

REBUKE
shalt in any wise *r* thy neighbour ... Lev 19:17 3198
upon thee cursing, vexation, and *r* ... Deut 28:20 4045
she may glean them, and *r* her not ... Ruth 2:16 1605
day is a day of trouble, and of *r* ... 2Kin 19:3 8433
our fathers look thereon, and *r* it ... 1Chr 12:17 3198
r me not in thine anger, neither ... Ps 6:1 3198
world were discovered at thy *r* ... Ps 18:15 1606
O LORD, *r* me not in thy wrath ... Ps 38:1 3198
R the company of spearmen, the ... Ps 68:30 1605
At thy *r*, O God of Jacob, both ... Ps 76:6 1606
at the *r* of thy countenance ... Ps 80:16 1606
At thy *r* they fled ... Ps 104:7 1606
r a wise man, and he will love ... Prov 9:8 3198
but a scorner heareth not *r* ... Prov 13:1 1606
but the poor heareth not *r* ... Prov 13:8 1606
But to them that *r* him shall be ... Prov 24:25 3198
Open *r* is better than secret love ... Prov 27:5 8433
better to hear the *r* of the wise ... Eccl 7:5 1606
nations, and shall *r* many people ... Is 2:4 3198
but God shall *r* them, and they ... Is 17:13 1605
the *r* of his people shall he take ... Is 25:8 2781
shall flee at the *r* of one ... Is 30:17 1606
at the *r* of five shall ye flee ... Is 30:17 1606
day is a day of trouble, and of *r* ... Is 37:3 8433
at my *r* I dry up the sea, I make ... Is 50:2 1606
of the LORD, the *r* of thy God ... Is 51:20 1606
be wroth with thee, nor *r* thee ... Is 54:9 1605
his *r* with flames of fire ... Is 66:15 1606
for thy sake I have suffered *r* ... Jer 15:15 2781
shall be desolate in the day of *r* ... Hos 5:9 8433
r strong nations afar off ... Mic 4:3 3198
said unto Satan, The LORD *r* thee ... Zec 3:2 1605
that hath chosen Jerusalem *r* thee ... Zec 3:2 1605
I will *r* the devourer for your ... Mal 3:11 1605
Peter took him, and began to *r* him ... Mt 16:22 *2008*
Peter took him, and began to *r* him ... Mk 8:32 *2008*
trespass against thee, *r* him ... Lk 17:3 *2008*
unto him, Master, *r* thy disciples ... Lk 19:39 *2008*
the sons of God, without *r* ... Phil 2:15 *298*
R not an elder, but intreat him ... 1Ti 5:1 *1969*
Them that sin *r* before all ... 1Ti 5:20 *1651*
reprove, *r*, exhort with all ... 2Ti 4:2 *2008*
Wherefore *r* them sharply, that ... Titus 1:13 *1651*
exhort, and *r* with all authority ... Titus 2:15 *1651*
but said, The Lord *r* thee ... Jude 9 *2008*
As many as I love, I *r* and chasten ... Rev 3:19 *1651*

REBUKED
my hands, and *r* thee yesternight ... Gen 31:42 3198
and his father *r* him, and said unto ... Gen 37:10 1605
I *r* the nobles, and the rulers, and ... Neh 5:7 7378
Thou hast *r* the heathen, thou ... Ps 9:5 1605
He *r* the Red sea also, and it was ... Ps 106:9 1605
Thou hast *r* the proud that are ... Ps 119:21 1605
arose, and *r* the winds and the sea ... Mt 8:26 *2008*
And Jesus *r* the devil ... Mt 17:18 *2008*
and the disciples *r* them ... Mt 19:13 *2008*
And the multitude *r* them, because ... Mt 20:31 *2008*
And Jesus *r* him, saying, Hold thy ... Mk 1:25 *2008*
r the wind, and said unto the sea, ... Mk 4:39 *2008*
he *r* Peter, saying, Get thee ... Mk 8:33 *2008*
he *r* the foul spirit, saying unto ... Mk 9:25 *2008*
his disciples *r* those that ... Mk 10:13 *2008*
And Jesus *r* him, saying, Hold thy ... Lk 4:35 *2008*
he stood over her, and *r* the fever ... Lk 4:39 *2008*
r the wind and the raging of the ... Lk 8:24 *2008*
Jesus *r* the unclean spirit, and ... Lk 9:42 *2008*
r them, and said, Ye know not what ... Lk 9:55 *2008*
his disciples saw it, they *r* them ... Lk 18:15 *2008*
And they which went before *r* him ... Lk 18:39 *2008*
But the other answering *r* him ... Lk 23:40 *2008*
nor faint when thou art *r* of him ... Heb 12:5 *1651*
But was *r* for his iniquity ... 2Pet 2:16

REBUKER
I have been a *r* of them all ... Hos 5:2 4148

REBUKES
When thou with *r* dost correct man ... Ps 39:11 8433
anger and in fury and in furious *r* ... Eze 5:15 8433
upon them with furious *r* ... Eze 25:17 8433

REBUKETH
he that *r* a wicked man getteth ... Prov 9:7 3198
He that *r* a man afterwards shall ... Prov 28:23 3198
They hate him that *r* in the gate ... Amos 5:10 3198
He *r* the sea, and maketh it dry, ... Nah 1:4 1605

REBUKING
at the *r* of the LORD, at the ... 2Sa 22:16 1606
he *r* them suffered them not to ... Lk 4:41 *2008*

RECALL
This I *r* to my mind, therefore ... Lam 3:21 7725

RECEIPT
sitting at the *r* of custom ... Mt 9:9 *5058*
sitting at the *r* of custom ... Mk 2:14 *5058*
Levi, sitting at the *r* of custom ... Lk 5:27 *5058*

RECEIVE
to *r* thy brother's blood from thy ... Gen 4:11 3947
then *r* my present at my hand ... Gen 33:10 3947
to *r* his pledge from the woman's ... Gen 38:20 3947
make his pans to *r* his ashes ... Ex 27:3 1878
thou shalt *r* them of their hands, ... Ex 29:25 3947
which ye *r* of the children of ... Num 18:28 3947
mount to *r* the tables of stone ... Deut 9:9 3947
every one shall *r* of thy words ... Deut 33:3 5375
which thou shalt *r* of their hands ... 1Sa 10:4 3947
Though I should *r* a thousand ... 2Sa 18:12 8254
there, and thou shalt *r* them ... 1Kin 5:9 5375
little to *r* the burnt offerings ... 1Kin 8:64 3557
whom I stand, I will *r* none ... 2Kin 5:16 3947
Is it a time to *r* money ... 2Kin 5:26 3947
to *r* garments, and oliveyards, and ... 2Kin 5:26 3947
now therefore *r* no more money of ... 2Kin 12:7 3947
the priests consented to *r* no ... 2Kin 12:8 3947
not able to *r* the burnt offerings ... 2Chr 7:7 3557
shall we *r* good at the hand of ... Job 2:10 6901
of God, and shall we not *r* evil ... Job 2:10 6901
R, I pray thee, the law from his ... Job 22:22 3947
they shall *r* of the Almighty ... Job 27:13 3947
the LORD will *r* my prayer ... Ps 6:9 3947

He shall *r* the blessing from the	Ps 24:5	5375
for he shall *r* me	Ps 49:15	3947
and afterward *r* me to glory	Ps 73:24	3947
When I shall *r* the congregation I	Ps 75:2	3947
To *r* the instruction of wisdom,	Prov 1:3	3947
My son, if thou wilt *r* my words	Prov 2:1	3947
Hear, O my son, and *r* my sayings	Prov 4:10	3947
R my instruction, and not silver	Prov 8:10	3947
wise in heart will *r* commandments	Prov 10:8	3947
r instruction, that thou mayest	Prov 19:20	6901
Should I *r* comfort in these	Is 57:6	5162
they have refused to *r* correction	Jer 5:3	3947
let your ear *r* the word of his	Jer 9:20	3947
might not hear, nor *r* instruction	Jer 17:23	3947
not hearkened to *r* instruction	Jer 32:33	3947
Will ye not *r* instruction to	Jer 35:13	3947
speak unto thee *r* in thine heart	Eze 3:10	3947
when thou shalt *r* thy sisters	Eze 16:61	3947
that ye shall *r* no more reproach	Eze 36:30	3947
ye shall *r* of me gifts and rewards	Dan 2:6	6902
Ephraim shall *r* shame, and Israel	Hos 10:6	3947
all iniquity, and *r* us graciously	Hos 14:2	3947
he shall *r* of you his standing	Mic 1:11	3947
fear me, thou wilt *r* instruction	Zeph 3:7	3947
shall not be room enough to *r* it	Mal 3:10	
And whosoever shall not *r* you	Mt 10:14	*1209*
shall *r* a prophet's reward	Mt 10:41	*2983*
shall *r* a righteous man's reward	Mt 10:41	*2983*
The blind *r* their sight, and the	Mt 11:5	*308*
And if ye will *r* it, this is Elias	Mt 11:14	*1209*
whoso shall *r* one such little	Mt 18:5	*1209*
All men cannot *r* this saying	Mt 19:11	*5562*
He that is able to *r* it	Mt 19:12	*5562*
let him *r* it	Mt 19:12	*5562*
shall *r* an hundredfold, and shall	Mt 19:29	*2983*
is right, that shall ye *r*	Mt 20:7	*2983*
in prayer, believing, ye shall *r*	Mt 21:22	*2983*
that they might *r* the fruits of	Mt 21:34	*2983*
therefore ye shall *r* the greater	Mt 23:14	*2983*
that there was no room to *r* them	Mk 2:2	*5562*
immediately *r* it with gladness	Mk 4:16	*2983*
r it, and bring forth fruit, some	Mk 4:20	*3858*
And whosoever shall not *r* you	Mk 6:11	*1209*
Whosoever shall *r* one of such	Mk 9:37	*1209*
and whosoever shall *r* me,	Mk 9:37	*1209*
Whosoever shall not *r* the kingdom	Mk 10:15	*1209*
But he shall *r* an hundredfold now	Mk 10:30	*2983*
Lord, that I might *r* my sight	Mk 10:51	*308*
ye pray, believe that ye *r* them	Mk 11:24	*2983*
servant, that he might *r* from the	Mk 12:2	*2983*
these shall *r* greater damnation	Mk 12:40	*2983*
lend to them of whom ye hope to *r*	Lk 6:34	*618*
to sinners, to *r* as much again	Lk 6:34	*618*
they hear, *r* the word with joy	Lk 8:13	*1209*
And whosoever will not *r* you	Lk 9:5	*1209*
Whosoever shall *r* this child in	Lk 9:48	*1209*
whosoever shall *r* me receiveth	Lk 9:48	*1209*
And they did not *r* him, because	Lk 9:53	*1209*
city ye enter, and they *r* you	Lk 10:8	*1209*
they *r* you not, go your ways out	Lk 10:10	*1209*
they may *r* me into their houses	Lk 16:4	*1209*
they may *r* you into everlasting	Lk 16:9	*1209*
Whosoever shall not *r* the kingdom	Lk 18:17	*1209*
Who shall not *r* manifold more in	Lk 18:30	*618*
said, Lord, that I may *r* my sight	Lk 18:41	*308*
Jesus said unto him, *R* thy sight	Lk 18:42	*308*
to *r* for himself a kingdom	Lk 19:12	*2983*
the same shall *r* greater	Lk 20:47	*2983*
for we *r* the due reward of our	Lk 23:41	*618*
and ye *r* not our witness	Jn 3:11	*2983*
and said, A man can *r* nothing	Jn 3:27	*2983*
But I *r* not testimony from man	Jn 5:34	*2983*
I *r* not honour from men	Jn 5:41	*2983*
my Father's name, and ye *r* me not	Jn 5:43	*2983*
in his own name, him ye will *r*	Jn 5:43	*2983*
which *r* honour one of another, and	Jn 5:44	*2983*
on the sabbath day *r* circumcision	Jn 7:23	*2983*
they that believe on him should *r*	Jn 7:39	*2983*
come again, and *r* you unto myself	Jn 14:3	*3880*
whom the world cannot *r*, because	Jn 14:17	*2983*
for he shall *r* of mine, and shall	Jn 16:14	*2983*
ask, and ye shall *r*, that your joy	Jn 16:24	*2983*
unto them, *R* ye the Holy Ghost	Jn 20:22	*2983*
But ye shall *r* power, after that	Acts 1:8	*2983*
ye shall *r* the gift of the Holy	Acts 2:38	*2983*
expecting to *r* something of them	Acts 3:5	*2983*
Whom the heaven must *r* until the	Acts 3:21	*1209*
saying, Lord Jesus, *r* my spirit	Acts 7:59	*1209*
that they might *r* the Holy Ghost	Acts 8:15	*2983*
hands, he may *r* the Holy Ghost	Acts 8:19	*2983*
on him, that he might *r* his sight	Acts 9:12	*308*
that thou mightest *r* thy sight	Acts 9:17	*308*
in him shall *r* remission of sins	Acts 10:43	*2983*
which are not lawful for us to *r*	Acts 16:21	*3858*
exhorting the disciples to *r* him	Acts 18:27	*588*
is more blessed to give than to *r*	Acts 20:35	*2983*
me, Brother Saul, *r* thy sight	Acts 22:13	*308*
for they will not *r* thy testimony	Acts 22:18	*3858*
that they may *r* forgiveness of	Acts 26:18	*2983*
they which *r* abundance of grace	Rom 5:17	*2983*
they that resist shall *r* to	Rom 13:2	*2983*
that is weak in the faith *r* ye	Rom 14:1	*4355*
Wherefore *r* ye one another, as	Rom 15:7	*4355*
That ye *r* her in the Lord, as	Rom 16:2	*4327*
every man shall *r* his own reward	1Cor 3:8	*2983*
thereupon, he shall *r* a reward	1Cor 3:14	*2983*
hast thou that thou didst not *r*	1Cor 4:7	*2983*
now if thou didst *r* it, why dost	1Cor 4:7	*2983*
that the church may *r* edifying	1Cor 14:5	*2983*
that every one may *r* the things	2Cor 5:10	*2865*
beseech you also that ye *r* not	2Cor 6:1	*1209*
and I will *r* you,	2Cor 6:17	*1523*
R us; we have wronged	2Cor 7:2	*5562*
that ye might *r* damage by us in	2Cor 7:9	*2210*
intreaty that we would *r* the gift	2Cor 8:4	*1209*
or if ye *r* another spirit, which	2Cor 11:4	*2983*
if otherwise, yet as a fool *r* me	2Cor 11:16	*1209*
that we might *r* the promise of	Gal 3:14	*2983*
that we might *r* the adoption of	Gal 4:5	*618*
the same shall he *r* of the Lord	Eph 6:8	*2865*
R him therefore in the Lord with	Phil 2:29	*4327*
that of the Lord ye shall *r* the	Col 3:24	*618*
r for the wrong which he hath	Col 3:25	*2865*
if he come unto you, *r* him	Col 4:10	*1209*
Against an elder *r* not an	1Ti 5:19	*3858*
thou therefore *r* him, that is,	Philem 12	*4355*
thou shouldest *r* him for ever	Philem 15	*568*
a partner, *r* him as myself	Philem 17	*4355*
of Levi, who *r* the office of the	Heb 7:5	*2983*
And here men that die *r* tithes	Heb 7:8	*2983*
might *r* the promise of eternal	Heb 9:15	*2983*
of God, ye might *r* the promise	Heb 10:36	*2865*
should after *r* for an inheritance	Heb 11:8	*2983*
he shall *r* any thing of the Lord	Jas 1:7	*2983*
he shall *r* the crown of life,	Jas 1:12	*2983*
r with meekness the engrafted	Jas 1:21	*1209*
knowing that we shall *r* the	Jas 3:1	*2983*
r not, because ye ask amiss, that	Jas 4:3	*2983*
until he *r* the early and latter	Jas 5:7	*2983*
ye shall *r* a crown of glory that	1Pet 5:4	*2865*
And shall *r* the reward of	2Pet 2:13	*2865*
we *r* of him, because we keep his	1Jn 3:22	*2983*
If we *r* the witness of men, the	1Jn 5:9	*2983*
but that we *r* a full reward	2Jn 8	*618*
r him not into your house,	2Jn 10	*2983*
We therefore ought to *r* such	3Jn 8	*618*
doth he himself *r* the brethren	3Jn 10	*1926*
to *r* glory and honour and power	Rev 4:11	*2983*
Lamb that was slain to *r* power	Rev 5:12	*2983*
to *r* a mark in their right hand,	Rev 13:16	*1325*
r his mark in his forehead, or in	Rev 14:9	*2983*
but *r* power as kings one hour	Rev 17:12	*2983*
that ye *r* not of her plagues	Rev 18:4	*2983*

RECEIVED

r in the same year an hundredfold	Gen 26:12	4672
he *r* them at their hand, and	Ex 32:4	3947
they *r* of Moses all the offering,	Ex 36:3	3947
after that let her be *r* in again	Num 12:14	622
I have *r* commandment to bless	Num 23:20	3947
fathers, have *r* their inheritance	Num 34:14	3947
Manasseh have *r* their inheritance	Num 34:14	3947
the half tribe have *r* their	Num 34:15	3947
of the tribe whereunto they are *r*	Num 36:3	1961
of the tribe whereunto they are *r*	Num 36:4	1961
and the Gadites have *r* their	Josh 13:8	3947
had not yet *r* their inheritance	Josh 18:2	2505
have *r* their inheritance beyond	Josh 18:7	3947
would not have *r* a burnt offering	Judg 13:23	3947
or of whose hand have I *r* any	1Sa 12:3	3947
So David *r* of her hand that which	1Sa 25:35	3947
the king's merchants *r* the linen	1Kin 10:28	3947
Hezekiah *r* the letter of the hand	2Kin 19:14	3947
Then David *r* them, and made them	1Chr 12:18	6901
the king's merchants *r* the linen	2Chr 1:16	3947
and it *r* and held three thousand	2Chr 4:5	2388
and the priests *r* the blood	2Chr 29:22	6901
which they *r* of the hand of the	2Chr 30:16	
but he *r* it not	Est 4:4	6901
mine ear *r* a little thereof	Job 4:12	3947
thou hast *r* gifts for men	Ps 68:18	3947
looked upon it, and *r* instruction	Prov 24:32	3947
Hezekiah *r* the letter from the	Is 37:14	3947
for she hath *r* of the LORD's hand	Is 40:2	3947
they *r* no correction	Jer 2:30	3947
that hath not *r* usury nor	Eze 18:17	3947
she *r* not correction	Zeph 3:2	3947
freely ye have *r*, freely give	Mt 10:8	*2983*
This is he which *r* seed by the	Mt 13:19	*4687*
But he that *r* the seed into stony	Mt 13:20	*4687*
He also that *r* seed among the	Mt 13:22	*4687*
But he that *r* seed into the good	Mt 13:23	*4687*
they that *r* tribute money came to	Mt 17:24	*2983*
hour, they *r* every man a penny	Mt 20:9	*2983*
that they should have *r* more	Mt 20:10	*2983*
they likewise *r* every man a penny	Mt 20:10	*2983*
And when they had *r* it, they	Mt 20:11	*2983*
and immediately their eyes *r* sight	Mt 20:34	*308*
Then he that had *r* the five	Mt 25:16	*2983*
And likewise he that had *r* two	Mt 25:17	
But he that had *r* one went	Mt 25:18	*2983*
so he that had *r* five talents	Mt 25:20	*2983*
also that had *r* two talents came	Mt 25:22	*2983*
Then he which had *r* the one	Mt 25:24	*2983*
should have *r* mine own with usury	Mt 25:27	*2865*
be, which they have *r* to hold	Mk 7:4	*3880*
And immediately he *r* his sight	Mk 10:52	*308*
but he *r* it not	Mk 15:23	*2983*
he was *r* up into heaven, and sat	Mk 16:19	*353*
for ye have *r* your consolation	Lk 6:24	*568*
returned, the people gladly *r* him	Lk 8:40	*588*
he *r* them, and spake unto them of	Lk 9:11	*1209*
was come that he should be *r* up	Lk 9:51	*354*
named Martha *r* him into her house	Lk 10:38	*5264*
calf, because he hath *r* him safe	Lk 15:27	*618*
And immediately he *r* his sight	Lk 18:43	*308*
and came down, and *r* him joyfully	Lk 19:6	*5264*
having *r* the kingdom, then he	Lk 19:15	*2983*
his own, and his own *r* him not	Jn 1:11	*3880*
But as many as *r* him, to them	Jn 1:12	*2983*
And of his fulness have all we *r*	Jn 1:16	*2983*
He that hath *r* his testimony hath	Jn 3:33	*2983*
Galilee, the Galilaeans *r* him	Jn 4:45	*1209*
willingly *r* him into the ship	Jn 6:21	*2983*
and I went and washed, and I *r* sight	Jn 9:11	*308*
asked him how he had *r* his sight	Jn 9:15	*308*
r his sight, until they called	Jn 9:18	*308*
of him that had *r* his sight	Jn 9:18	*308*
commandment have I *r* of my Father	Jn 10:18	*2983*
He then having *r* the sop went	Jn 13:30	*2983*
and they have *r* them, and have	Jn 17:8	*2983*
having *r* a band of men and	Jn 18:3	*2983*
Jesus therefore had *r* the vinegar	Jn 19:30	*2983*
a cloud *r* him out of their sight	Acts 1:9	*5274*
having *r* of the Father the	Acts 2:33	*2983*
Then they that gladly *r* his word	Acts 2:41	*588*
feet and ancle bones *r* strength	Acts 3:7	*4732*
who *r* the lively oracles to give	Acts 7:38	*1209*
Who have *r* the law by the	Acts 7:53	*2983*
Samaria had *r* the word of God	Acts 8:14	*1209*
on them, and they *r* the Holy Ghost	Acts 8:17	*2983*
he *r* sight forthwith, and arose,	Acts 9:18	*308*
And when he had *r* meat, he was	Acts 9:19	*2983*
the vessel was *r* up again into	Acts 10:16	*353*
which have *r* the Holy Ghost as	Acts 10:47	*2983*
had also *r* the word of God	Acts 11:1	*1209*
they were *r* of the church, and of	Acts 15:4	*588*
having *r* such a charge, thrust	Acts 16:24	*2983*
Whom Jason hath *r*	Acts 17:7	*5264*
in that they *r* the word with all	Acts 17:11	*1209*
Have ye *r* the Holy Ghost since ye	Acts 19:2	*2983*
which I have *r* of the Lord Jesus,	Acts 20:24	*2983*
the brethren *r* us gladly	Acts 21:17	*1209*
from whom also I *r* letters unto	Acts 22:5	*1209*
having *r* authority from the chief	Acts 26:10	*2983*
r us every one, because of the	Acts 28:2	*4355*
who *r* us, and lodged us three days	Acts 28:7	*324*
We neither *r* letters out of	Acts 28:21	*1209*
r all that came in unto him,	Acts 28:30	*588*
By whom we have *r* grace and	Rom 1:5	*2983*
he *r* the sign of circumcision, a	Rom 4:11	*2983*
whom we have now *r* the atonement	Rom 5:11	*2983*
For ye have not *r* the spirit of	Rom 8:15	*2983*
but ye have *r* the Spirit of	Rom 8:15	*2983*
for God hath *r* him	Rom 14:3	*4355*
as Christ also *r* us to the glory	Rom 15:7	*4355*
Now we have *r*, not the spirit of	1Cor 2:12	*2983*
glory, as if thou hadst not *r* it	1Cor 4:7	*2983*
For I have *r* of the Lord that	1Cor 11:23	*3880*
unto you, which also ye have *r*	1Cor 15:1	*3880*
first of all that which I also *r*	1Cor 15:3	*3880*
this ministry, as we have *r* mercy	2Cor 4:1	*1653*
with fear and trembling ye *r* him	2Cor 7:15	*1209*
spirit, which ye have not *r*	2Cor 11:4	*2983*
Of the Jews five times *r* I forty	2Cor 11:24	*2983*
unto you than that ye have *r*	Gal 1:9	*3880*
For I neither *r* it of man	Gal 1:12	*3880*
R ye the Spirit by the works of	Gal 3:2	*2983*
but *r* me as an angel of God, even	Gal 4:14	*1209*
which ye have both learned, and *r*	Phil 4:9	*3880*
having *r* of Epaphroditus the	Phil 4:18	*1209*
As ye have therefore *r* Christ	Col 2:6	*3880*
(touching whom ye *r* commandments	Col 4:10	*2983*
which thou hast *r* in the Lord	Col 4:17	*3880*
having *r* the word in much	1Th 1:6	*1209*
when ye *r* the word of God which	1Th 2:13	*3880*
ye *r* it not as the word of men,	1Th 2:13	*1209*
that as ye have *r* of us how ye	1Th 4:1	*3880*
because they *r* not the love of	2Th 2:10	*1209*
the tradition which he *r* of us	2Th 3:6	*3880*
on in the world, *r* up into glory	1Ti 3:16	*353*
which God hath created to be *r*	1Ti 4:3	*3336*
if it be *r* with thanksgiving	1Ti 4:4	*2983*
disobedience *r* a just recompence	Heb 2:2	*2983*
from them *r* tithes of Abraham	Heb 7:6	*1183*
for under it the people *r* the law	Heb 7:11	*3549*
have *r* the knowledge of the truth	Heb 10:26	*2983*
r strength to conceive seed	Heb 11:11	*2983*
not having *r* the promises, but	Heb 11:13	*2983*
he that had *r* the promises	Heb 11:17	*324*
whence also he *r* him in a figure	Heb 11:19	*2865*
when she had *r* the spies with	Heb 11:31	*1209*
Women *r* their dead raised to life	Heb 11:35	*2983*
through faith, *r* not the promise	Heb 11:39	*2865*
when she had *r* the messengers, and	Jas 2:25	*5264*
from your vain conversation *r* by	1Pet 1:18	
As every man hath *r* the gift	1Pet 4:10	*2983*
For he *r* from God the Father	2Pet 1:17	*2983*
ye have *r* of him abideth in you	1Jn 2:27	*2983*
as we have *r* a commandment from	2Jn 4	*2983*
even as I *r* of my Father	Rev 2:27	*2983*
therefore how thou hast *r*	Rev 3:3	*2983*
which have *r* no kingdom as yet	Rev 17:12	*2983*
that had *r* the mark of the beast	Rev 19:20	*2983*
neither had *r* his mark upon their	Rev 20:4	

RECEIVEDST

in thy lifetime *r* thy good things	Lk 16:25	*618*

RECEIVER

where is the *r*	Is 33:18	8254

RECEIVETH

is no man that *r* me to house	Judg 19:18	622
or what *r* he of thine hand	Job 35:7	3947
is instructed, he *r* knowledge	Prov 21:11	3947
but he that *r* gifts overthroweth	Prov 29:4	
LORD their God, nor *r* correction	Jer 7:28	3947
or *r* it with good will at your	Mal 2:13	3947
For every one that asketh *r*	Mt 7:8	*2983*
He that *r* you *r* me, and he	Mt 10:40	*1209*
r me *r* him that sent me	Mt 10:40	*1209*
He that *r* a prophet in the name	Mt 10:41	*2983*
he that *r* a righteous man in the	Mt 10:41	*2983*
the word, and anon with joy *r* it	Mt 13:20	*2983*
such little child in my name *r* me	Mt 18:5	*1209*
of such children in my name, *r* me	Mk 9:37	*1209*
r not me, but him that sent me	Mk 9:37	*1209*
this child in my name *r* me	Lk 9:48	*1209*
receive me *r* him that sent me	Lk 9:48	*1209*
For every one that asketh *r*	Lk 11:10	*2983*
saying, This man *r* sinners	Lk 15:2	*4327*
and no man *r* his testimony	Jn 3:32	*2983*

And he that reapeth *r* wages Jn 4:36 *2983*
r not my words, hath one that Jn 12:48 *2983*
r whomsoever I send *r* me Jn 13:20 *2983*
r me *r* him that sent me Jn 13:20 *2983*
But the natural man *r* not the 1Cor 2:14 *1209*
race run all, but one *r* the prize 1Cor 9:24 *2983*
is dressed, *r* blessing from God Heb 6:7 *3335*
but there he *r* them, of whom it Heb 7:8
who *r* tithes, payed tithes in Heb 7:9 *2983*
and scourgeth every son whom he *r* Heb 12:6 *3858*
preeminence among them, *r* us not 3Jn 9 *1926*
man knoweth saving he that *r* it Rev 2:17 *2983*
whosoever *r* the mark of his name Rev 14:11 *2983*

RECEIVING
in not *r* at his hands that which 2Kin 5:20 3947
r a commandment unto Silas and Acts 17:15 *2983*
r in themselves that recompence Rom 1:27 *618*
what shall the *r* of them be Rom 11:15 *4356*
with me as concerning giving and *r* Phil 4:15 *3028*
Wherefore we *r* a kingdom which Heb 12:28 *3880*
R the end of your faith, even the 1Pet 1:9 *2865*

RECHAB (*re'-kab*) See RECHABITES.
1. A son of Rimmon.
and the name of the other *R* 2Sa 4:2 7394
sons of Rimmon the Beerothite, *R* 2Sa 4:5 7394
and *R* and Baanah his brother 2Sa 4:6 7394
And David answered *R* 2Sa 4:9 7394
2. Founder of the Rechabites.
the son of *R* coming to meet him 2Kin 10:15 7394
went, and Jehonadab the son of *R* 2Kin 10:23 7394
for Jonadab the son of *R* our Jer 35:6 7394
R our father in all that he hath Jer 35:8 7394
The words of Jonadab the son of *R* Jer 35:14 7394
R have performed the commandment Jer 35:16 7394
Jonadab the son of *R* shall not Jer 35:19 7394
3. A descendant of Hemath.
the father of the house of *R* 1Chr 2:55 7394
4. Father of Malchiah.
repaired Malchiah the son of *R* Neh 3:14 7394

RECHABITES (*rek'-ab-ites*) *Descendants of Rechab 2.*
Go unto the house of the *R* Jer 35:2 7397
sons, and the whole house of the *R* Jer 35:3 7397
house of the *R* pots full of wine Jer 35:5 7397
said unto the house of the *R* Jer 35:18 7397

RECHAH *A family of Judah.*
These are the men of *R* 1Chr 4:12 7397

RECKON
he shall *r* with him that bought Lev 25:50 2803
then the priest shall *r* unto him Lev 27:18 2803
Then the priest shall *r* unto him Lev 27:23 2803
and by name ye shall *r* the Num 4:32 6485
they shall *r* unto him seven days Eze 44:26 5608
And when he had begun to *r* Mt 18:24 *4868*
Likewise *r* ye also yourselves to Rom 6:11 *3049*
For I *r* that the sufferings of Rom 8:18 *3049*

RECKONED
offering shall be *r* unto you Num 18:27 2803
shall not be *r* among the nations Num 23:9 2803
Beeroth also was *r* to Benjamin 2Sa 4:2 2803
Moreover they *r* not with the men, 2Kin 12:15 2803
not to be *r* after the birthright 1Chr 5:1 3187
of their generations was *r* 1Chr 5:7 3187
All these were *r* by genealogies 1Chr 5:17 3187
r in all by their genealogies 1Chr 7:5 3187
were *r* by their genealogies 1Chr 7:7 3187
all Israel were *r* by genealogies 1Chr 9:1 3187
These were *r* by their genealogy 1Chr 9:22 3187
to all that were *r* by genealogies 2Chr 31:19 3187
those that were *r* by genealogy Ezr 2:62 3187
with him were *r* by genealogy of Ezr 8:3 3187
that they might be *r* by genealogy Neh 7:5 3187
those that were *r* by genealogy Neh 7:64 3187
they cannot be *r* up in order unto Ps 40:5
I *r* till morning, that, as a lion Is 38:13 7737
he was *r* among the transgressors Lk 22:37 *3049*
is the reward not *r* of grace Rom 4:4 *3049*
for we say that faith was *r* to Rom 4:9 *3049*
How was it then *r* Rom 4:10 *3049*

RECKONETH
servants cometh, and *r* with them Mt 25:19

RECKONING
Howbeit there was no *r* made with 2Kin 22:7 2803
therefore they were in one *r* 1Chr 23:11 6486

RECOMMENDED
from whence they had been *r* to Acts 14:26 *3860*
being *r* by the brethren unto the Acts 15:40 *3860*

RECOMPENCE
To me belongeth vengeance, and *r* Deut 32:35 8005
for vanity shall be his *r* Job 15:31 8545
with vengeance, even God with a *r* Is 35:4 1576
his adversaries, *r* to his enemies Is 59:18 1576
to the islands he will repay *r* Is 59:18 1576
that rendereth *r* to his enemies Is 66:6 1576
he will render unto her a *r* Jer 51:6 1576
Render unto them a *r*, O LORD, Lam 3:64 1576
are come, the days of *r* are come Hos 9:7 7966
will ye render me a *r* Joel 3:4 1576
return your *r* upon your own head Joel 3:4 1576
will return your *r* upon your own Joel 3:7 1576
thee again, and a *r* be made thee Lk 14:12 *468*
receiving in themselves that *r* of Rom 1:27 *489*
stumblingblock, and a *r* unto them Rom 11:9 *468*
Now for a *r* in the same, (I speak 2Cor 6:13 *489*
received a just *r* of reward Heb 2:2 *3405*
which hath great *r* of reward Heb 10:35 *3405*
respect unto the *r* of the reward Heb 11:26 *3405*

RECOMPENCES
the year of *r* for the controversy Is 34:8 7966
for the LORD God of *r* shall Jer 51:56 1578

RECOMPENSE
he shall *r* his trespass with the Num 5:7 7725
no kinsman to *r* the trespass unto Num 5:8 7725
The LORD *r* thy work, and a full Ruth 2:12 7999
why should the king *r* it me with 2Sa 19:36 1580
he will *r* it, whether thou refuse Job 34:33 7999
the *r* of a man's hands shall be Prov 12:14
Say not thou, I will *r* evil Prov 20:22 7999
will not keep silence, but will *r* Is 65:6 7999
even *r* into their bosom, Is 65:6
first I will *r* their iniquity and Jer 16:18 7999
I will *r* them according to their Jer 25:14 7999
r her according to her work Jer 50:29 7999
will *r* upon thee all thine Eze 7:3 5414
but I will *r* thy ways upon thee, Eze 7:4 5414
will *r* thee for all thine Eze 7:8 5414
I will *r* thee according to thy Eze 7:9 5414
but I will *r* their way upon their Eze 9:10 5414
I will *r* their way upon their own Eze 11:21 5414
therefore I also will *r* thy way Eze 16:43 5414
even it will I *r* upon his own Eze 17:19 5414
they shall *r* your lewdness upon Eze 23:49 5414
to his doings will he *r* him Hos 12:2 7725
and if ye *r* me, swiftly and Joel 3:4 1580
for they cannot *r* thee Lk 14:14 *467*
R to no man evil for evil Rom 12:17 *591*
God to *r* tribulation to them that 2Th 1:6 *467*
belongeth unto me, I will *r* Heb 10:30 *467*

RECOMPENSED
the trespass be *r* unto the LORD Num 5:8 7725
of my hands hath he *r* me 2Sa 22:21 7725
LORD hath *r* me according to my 2Sa 22:25 7725
of my hands hath he *r* me Ps 18:20 7725
the LORD *r* me according to my Ps 18:24 7725
righteous shall be *r* in the earth Prov 11:31 7999
Shall evil be *r* for good Jer 18:20 7999
own way have I *r* upon their heads Eze 22:31 5414
for thou shalt be *r* at the Lk 14:14 *467*
it shall be *r* unto him again Rom 11:35 *467*

RECOMPENSEST
r the iniquity of the fathers Jer 32:18 7999

RECOMPENSING
by *r* his way upon his own head 2Chr 6:23 5414

RECONCILE
of the congregation to *r* withal Lev 6:30 3722
he *r* himself unto his master 1Sa 29:4 7521
so shall ye *r* the house Eze 45:20 3722
that he might *r* both unto God in Eph 2:16 *604*
by him to *r* all things unto Col 1:20 *604*

RECONCILED
first be *r* to thy brother, and Mt 5:24 *1259*
we were *r* to God by the death of Rom 5:10 *2644*
of his Son, much more, being *r* Rom 5:10 *2644*
unmarried, or be *r* to her husband 1Cor 7:11 *2644*
who hath *r* us to himself by Jesus 2Cor 5:18 *2644*
in Christ's stead, be ye *r* to God 2Cor 5:20 *2644*
wicked works, yet now hath he *r* Col 1:21 *604*

RECONCILIATION
sanctified it, to make *r* upon it Lev 8:15 3722
they made *r* with their blood upon 2Chr 29:24 2398
to make *r* for them, saith the Eze 45:15 3722
to make *r* for the house of Israel Eze 45:17 3722
to make *r* for iniquity, and to Dan 9:24 3722
given to us the ministry of *r* 2Cor 5:18 *2643*
committed unto us the word of *r* 2Cor 5:19 *2643*
to make *r* for the sins of the Heb 2:17 *2433*

RECONCILING
made an end of *r* the holy place Lev 16:20 3722
of them be the *r* of the world Rom 11:15 *2643*
r the world unto himself, not 2Cor 5:19 *2644*

RECORD
in all places where I *r* my name I Ex 20:24 2142
earth to *r* this day against you, Deut 30:19 5749
heaven and earth to *r* against them Deut 31:28 5749
the ark of the LORD, and to *r* 1Chr 16:4 2142
and therein was a *r* thus written Ezr 6:2 1799
is in heaven, and my *r* is on high Job 16:19 7717
unto me faithful witnesses to *r* Is 8:2 5749
And this is the *r* of John, when Jn 1:19 *3141*
And John bare *r*, saying, I saw the Jn 1:32 *3140*
bare *r* that this is the Son of Jn 1:34 *3140*
him, Thou bearest *r* of thyself Jn 8:13 *3140*
thy *r* is not true Jn 8:13 *3141*
them, Though I bear *r* of myself Jn 8:14 *3140*
yet my *r* is true Jn 8:14 *3141*
raised him from the dead, bare *r* Jn 12:17 *3140*
And he that saw it bare *r*, and his Jn 19:35 *3140*
and his *r* is true Jn 19:35 *3141*
I take you to *r* this day, that I Acts 20:26 *3143*
For I bear them *r* that they have Rom 10:2 *3140*
I call God for a *r* upon my soul 2Cor 1:23 *3144*
For to their power, I bear *r* 2Cor 8:3 *3140*
for I bear you *r*, that, if it had Gal 4:15 *3140*
For God is my *r*, how greatly I Phil 1:8 *3144*
For I bear him *r*, that he hath a Col 4:13 *3140*
are three that bear *r* in heaven 1Jn 5:7 *3140*
the *r* that God gave of his Son 1Jn 5:10 *3141*
And this is the *r*, that God hath 1Jn 5:11 *3141*
yea, and we also bear *r* 3Jn 12 *3140*
and ye know that our *r* is true 3Jn 12 *3141*
Who bare *r* of the word of God, and Rev 1:2 *3140*

RECORDED
were *r* chief of the fathers Neh 12:22 3789

RECORDER
the son of Ahilud was *r* 2Sa 8:16 2142
the son of Ahilud was *r* 2Sa 20:24 2142
the son of Ahilud, the *r* 1Kin 4:3 2142
and Joah the son of Asaph the *r* 2Kin 18:18 2142
and Joah the son of Asaph the *r* 2Kin 18:37 2142
Jehoshaphat the son of Ahilud, *r* 1Chr 18:15 2142
and Joah the son of Joahaz the *r* 2Chr 34:8 2142
and Joah, Asaph's son, the *r* Is 36:3 2142
and Joah, the son of Asaph, the *r* Is 36:22 2142

RECORDS
the book of the *r* of thy fathers Ezr 4:15 1799
thou find in the book of the *r* Ezr 4:15 1799
the book of *r* of the chronicles Est 6:1 2146

RECOUNT
He shall *r* his worthies Nah 2:5 2142

RECOVER
ye not *r* them within that time Judg 11:26 5337
them, and without fail *r* all 1Sa 30:8 5337
as he went to *r* his border at the 2Sa 8:3 7725
whether I shall *r* of this disease 2Kin 1:2 2421
for he would *r* him of his leprosy 2Kin 5:3 622
that thou mayest *r* him of his 2Kin 5:6 622
unto me to *r* a man of his leprosy 2Kin 5:7 622
over the place, and *r* the leper 2Kin 5:11 622
Shall I *r* of this disease 2Kin 8:8 2421
Shall I *r* of this disease 2Kin 8:9 2421
unto him, Thou mayest certainly *r* 2Kin 8:10 2421
me that thou shouldest surely *r* 2Kin 8:14 2421
Neither did Jeroboam *r* strength 2Chr 13:20 6113
that they could not *r* themselves 2Chr 14:13 4241
O spare me, that I may *r* strength Ps 39:13 1082
to *r* the remnant of his people Is 11:11 7069
so wilt thou *r* me, and make me to Is 38:16 2492
upon the boil, and he shall *r* Is 38:21 2421
will *r* my wool and my flax given Hos 2:9 5337
on the sick, and they shall *r* Mk 16:18
that they may *r* themselves out of 2Ti 2:26 *366*

RECOVERED
David *r* all that the Amalekites 1Sa 30:18 5337
David *r* all 1Sa 30:19 7725
ought of the spoil that we have *r* 1Sa 30:22 5337
him, and *r* the cities of Israel 2Kin 13:25 7725
how he *r* Damascus, and Hamath, 2Kin 14:28 7725
king of Syria *r* Elath to Syria 2Kin 16:6 7725
and laid it on the boil, and he *r* 2Kin 20:7 2421
sick, and was *r* of his sickness Is 38:9 2421
that he had been sick, and was *r* Is 39:1 2388
of the daughter of my people *r* Jer 8:22 5927
he had *r* from Ishmael the son of Jer 41:16 7725

RECOVERING
r of sight to the blind, to set Lk 4:18 *309*

RED *The sea dividing Egypt and Arabia.*
And the first came out *r*, all over Gen 25:25 132
thee, with that same *r* pottage Gen 25:30 122
His eyes shall be *r* with wine Gen 49:12 2447
and cast them into the *R* sea Ex 10:19 5488
of the wilderness of the *R* sea Ex 13:18 5488
also are drowned in the *R* sea Ex 15:4 5488
brought Israel from the *R* sea Ex 15:22 5488
R sea even unto the sea of the Ex 23:31 5488
And rams' skins dyed *r*, and Ex 25:5 119
the tent of rams' skins dyed *r* Ex 26:14 119
And rams' skins dyed *r*, and Ex 35:7 119
r skins of rams, and badgers' Ex 35:23 119
the tent of rams' skins dyed *r* Ex 36:19 119
covering of rams' skins dyed *r* Ex 39:34 119
by the way of the *R* sea Num 14:25 5488
thee a *r* heifer without spot Num 19:2 122
mount Hor by the way of the *R* sea Num 21:4 5488
LORD, What he did in the *R* sea Num 21:14 5492
Elim, and encamped by the *R* sea Num 33:10 5488
And they removed from the *R* sea Num 33:11 5488
the plain over against the *R* sea Deut 1:1 5489
by the way of the *R* sea Deut 1:40 5488
by the way of the *R* sea, as the Deut 2:1 5488
R sea to overflow them as they Deut 11:4 5488
up the water of the *R* sea for you Josh 2:10 5488
LORD your God did to the *R* sea Josh 4:23 5488
and horsemen unto the *R* sea Josh 24:6 5488
the wilderness unto the *R* sea Judg 11:16 5488
Eloth, on the shore of the *R* sea 1Kin 9:26 5488
on the other side as *r* as blood 2Kin 3:22 122
heardest their cry by the *R* sea Neh 9:9 5488
and silver, upon a pavement of *r* Est 1:6 923
there is a cup, and the wine is *r* Ps 75:8 2560
him at the sea, even at the *R* sea Ps 106:7 5488
He rebuked the *R* sea also Ps 106:9 5488
and terrible things by the *R* sea Ps 106:22 5488
divided the *R* sea into parts Ps 136:13 5488
Pharaoh and his host in the *R* sea Ps 136:15 5488
thou upon the wine when it is *r* Prov 23:31 119
though they be *r* like crimson Is 1:18 119
ye unto her, A vineyard of *r* wine Is 27:2 2561
art thou *r* in thine apparel Is 63:2 122
thereof was heard in the *R* sea Jer 49:21 5488
of his mighty men is made *r* Nah 2:3 119
a man riding upon a *r* horse Zec 1:8 122
and behind him were there *r* horses Zec 1:8 122
the first chariot were *r* horses Zec 6:2 122
for the sky is *r* Mt 16:2 *4449*
for the sky is *r* and lowring Mt 16:3 *4449*
land of Egypt, and in the *R* sea Acts 7:36 *2281*
through the *R* sea as by dry land Heb 11:29 *2281*
went out another horse that was *r* Rev 6:4 *4450*
and behold a great *r* dragon Rev 12:3 *4450*

REDDISH
bright spot, white, and somewhat *r* Lev 13:19 125
a white bright spot, somewhat *r* Lev 13:24 125
or bald forehead, a white *r* sore Lev 13:42 125
sore be white *r* in his bald head Lev 13:43 125
be greenish or *r* in the garment Lev 13:49 125
hollow strakes, greenish or *r* Lev 14:37 125

REDEEM
I will *r* you with a stretched out Ex 6:6 1350
an ass thou shalt *r* with a lamb Ex 13:13 6299
and if thou wilt not *r* it, then Ex 13:13 6299
among thy children shalt thou *r* Ex 13:13 6299
the firstborn of my children I *r* Ex 13:15 6299
an ass thou shalt *r* with a lamb Ex 34:20 6299
and if thou *r* him not, then shalt Ex 34:20 6299
of thy sons thou shalt *r* Ex 34:20 6299
and if any of his kin come to *r* it Lev 25:25 1350
then shall he *r* that which his Lev 25:25 1350
And if the man have none to *r* it Lev 25:26 1350
and himself be able to *r* it Lev 25:26 1353
then he may *r* it within a whole Lev 25:29 1353
within a full year may he *r* it Lev 25:29 1353
may the Levites *r* at any time Lev 25:32 1353
one of his brethren may *r* him Lev 25:48 1350
or his uncle's son, may *r* him Lev 25:49 1350
unto him of his family may *r* him Lev 25:49 1350
if he be able, he may *r* himself Lev 25:49 1353
But if he will at all *r* it Lev 27:13 1350
sanctified it will *r* his house Lev 27:15 1350
the field will in any wise *r* it Lev 27:19 1350
And if he will not *r* the field Lev 27:20 1350
then he shall *r* it according to Lev 27:27 6299
will at all *r* ought of his tithes Lev 27:31 1350
of man shalt thou surely *r* Num 18:15 6299
of unclean beasts shalt thou *r* Num 18:15 6299
from a month old shalt thou *r* Num 18:16 6299
of a goat, thou shalt not *r* Num 18:17 6299
If thou wilt *r* it Ruth 4:4 1350
r it: but if thou wilt Ruth 4:4 6299
but if thou wilt not *r* it Ruth 4:4 1350
there is none to *r* it beside thee Ruth 4:4 1350
And he said, I will *r* it Ruth 4:4 1350
I cannot *r* it for myself, lest I Ruth 4:6 1350
r thou my right to thyself Ruth 4:6 1350
for I cannot *r* it Ruth 4:6 1350
whom God went to *r* for a people 2Sa 7:23 6299
whom God went to *r* to be his own 1Chr 17:21 6299
is it in our power to *r* them Neh 5:5
famine he shall *r* thee from death Job 5:20 6299
R me from the hand of the mighty Job 6:23 6299
R Israel, O God, out of all his Ps 25:22 6299
r me, and be merciful unto me Ps 26:11 6299
r us for thy mercies' sake Ps 44:26 6299
can by any means *r* his brother Ps 49:7 6299
But God will *r* my soul from the Ps 49:15 6299
Draw nigh unto my soul, and *r* it Ps 69:18 1350
He shall *r* their soul from deceit Ps 72:14 1350
he shall *r* Israel from all his Ps 130:8 6299
at all, that it cannot *r* Is 50:2 6304
I will *r* thee out of the hand of Jer 15:21 6299
I will *r* them from death Hos 13:14 1350
there the LORD shall *r* thee from Mic 4:10 1350
To *r* them that were under the law Gal 4:5 *1805*
that he might *r* us from all Titus 2:14 *3084*

REDEEMED
The angel which *r* me from all Gen 48:16 1350
the people which thou hast *r* Ex 15:13 1350
then shall he let her be *r* Ex 21:8 6299
to an husband, and not at all *r* Lev 19:20 6299
if it be not *r* within the space Lev 25:30 1350
they may be *r*, and they shall go Lev 25:31 1353
that he is sold he may be *r* again Lev 25:48 1353
if he be not *r* in these years, Lev 25:54 1350
man, it shall not be *r* any more Lev 27:20 1350
or if it be not *r*, then it shall Lev 27:27 1350
possession, shall be sold or *r* Lev 27:28 1350
be devoted of men, shall be *r* Lev 27:29 6299
it shall not be *r* Lev 27:33 1350
are to be *r* of the two hundred Num 3:46 6302
the odd number of them is to be *r* Num 3:48 6302
them that were *r* by the Levites Num 3:49 6306
of them that were *r* unto Aaron Num 3:51 6306
those that are to be *r* from a Num 18:16 6299
r you out of the house of bondmen Deut 7:8 6299
which thou hast *r* through thy Deut 9:26 6299
r you out of the house of bondage Deut 13:5 6299
Egypt, and the LORD thy God *r* thee Deut 15:15 6299
people Israel, whom thou hast *r* Deut 21:8 6299
and the LORD thy God *r* thee thence Deut 24:18 6299
who hath *r* my soul out of all 2Sa 4:9 6299
that hath *r* my soul out of all 1Kin 1:29 6299
whom thou hast *r* out of Egypt 1Chr 17:21 6299
whom thou hast *r* by thy great Neh 1:10 6299
have *r* our brethren the Jews Neh 5:8 7069
thou hast *r* me, O LORD God of Ps 31:5 6299
and my soul, which thou hast *r* Ps 71:23 6299
inheritance, which thou hast *r* Ps 74:2 1350
hast with thine arm *r* thy people Ps 77:15 1350
r them from the hand of the enemy Ps 106:10 1350
Let the *r* of the LORD say so, Ps 107:2 1350
whom he hath *r* from the hand of Ps 107:2 1350
hath *r* us from our enemies Ps 136:24 6561
Zion shall be *r* with judgment Is 1:27 6299
who *r* Abraham, concerning the Is 29:22 6299
but the *r* shall walk there Is 35:9 1350
for I have *r* thee, I have called Is 43:1 1350
for I have *r* thee Is 44:22 1350
for the LORD hath *r* Jacob Is 44:23 1350
The LORD hath *r* his servant Jacob Is 48:20 1350
Therefore the *r* of the LORD shall Is 51:11 6299
ye shall be *r* without money Is 52:3 1350
his people, he hath *r* Jerusalem Is 52:9 1350
holy people, The *r* of the LORD Is 62:12 1350
and the year of my *r* is come Is 63:4 1350
his love and in his pity he *r* them Is 63:9 1350
For the LORD hath *r* Jacob Jer 31:11 6299
thou hast *r* my life Lam 3:58 1350
though I have *r* them, yet they Hos 7:13 6299
r thee out of the house of Mic 6:4 6299
for I have *r* them Zec 10:8 6299
he hath visited and *r* his people, Lk 1:68
he which should have *r* Israel Lk 24:21 *3084*
Christ hath *r* us from the curse Gal 3:13 *1805*
not *r* with corruptible things 1Pet 1:18 *3084*
hast *r* us to God by thy blood out Rev 5:9 *59*
which were *r* from the earth Rev 14:3 *59*
These were *r* from among men, Rev 14:4 *59*

REDEEMEDST
which thou *r* to thee from Egypt, 2Sa 7:23 6299

REDEEMER
For I know that my *r* liveth Job 19:25 1350
O LORD, my strength, and my *r* Ps 19:14 1350
rock, and the high God their *r* Ps 78:35 1350
For their *r* is mighty Prov 23:11 1350
thee, saith the LORD, and thy *r* Is 41:14 1350
Thus saith the LORD, your *r* Is 43:14 1350
and his *r* the LORD of hosts Is 44:6 1350
Thus saith the LORD, thy *r* Is 44:24 1350
As for our *r*, the LORD of hosts Is 47:4 1350
Thus saith the LORD, thy *R* Is 48:17 1350
the *R* of Israel, and his Holy One, Is 49:7 1350
the LORD am thy Saviour and thy *R* Is 49:26 1350
thy *R* the Holy One of Israel Is 54:5 1350
on thee, saith the LORD thy *R* Is 54:8 1350
the *R* shall come to Zion, and unto Is 59:20 1350
the LORD am thy Saviour and thy *R* Is 60:16 1350
O LORD, art our father, our *r* Is 63:16 1350
Their *R* is strong Jer 50:34 1350

REDEEMETH
The LORD *r* the soul of his Ps 34:22 6299
Who *r* thy life from destruction Ps 103:4 1350

REDEEMING
time in Israel concerning *r* Ruth 4:7 1353
R the time, because the days are Eph 5:16 *1805*
them that are without, *r* the time Col 4:5 *1805*

REDEMPTION
ye shall grant a *r* for the land Lev 25:24 1353
give again the price of his *r* out Lev 25:51 1353
give him again the price of his *r* Lev 25:52 1353
Moses took the *r* money of them Num 3:49 6306
(For the *r* of their soul is Ps 49:8 6306
He sent *r* unto his people Ps 111:9 6304
mercy, and with him is plenteous *r* Ps 130:7 6304
for the right of *r* is thine to Jer 32:7 1353
is thine, and the *r* is thine Jer 32:8 1353
that looked for *r* in Jerusalem Lk 2:38 *3085*
for your *r* draweth nigh Lk 21:28 *629*
the *r* that is in Christ Jesus Rom 3:24 *629*
to wit, the *r* of our body Rom 8:23 *629*
and sanctification, and *r* 1Cor 1:30 *629*
In whom we have *r* through his Eph 1:7 *629*
the *r* of the purchased possession Eph 1:14 *629*
ye are sealed unto the day of *r* Eph 4:30 *629*
In whom we have *r* through his Col 1:14 *629*
having obtained eternal *r* for us Heb 9:12 *3085*
for the *r* of the transgressions Heb 9:15 *629*

REDNESS
who hath *r* of eyes Prov 23:29 2498

REDOUND
of many *r* to the glory of God 2Cor 4:15 *4052*

REED
as a *r* is shaken in the water, and 1Kin 14:15 7070
upon the staff of this bruised *r* 2Kin 18:21 7070
trees, in the covert of the *r* Job 40:21 7070
in the staff of this broken *r* Is 36:6 7070
A bruised *r* shall he not break, Is 42:3 7070
staff of *r* to the house of Israel Eze 29:6 7070
in his hand, and a measuring *r* Eze 40:3 7070
in the man's hand a measuring *r* Eze 40:5 7070
breadth of the building, one *r* Eze 40:5 7070
and the height, one *r* Eze 40:5 7070
the gate, which was one *r* broad Eze 40:6 7070
the gate, which was one *r* broad Eze 40:6 7070
was one *r* long, and one *r* broad Eze 40:7 7070
of the gate within was one *r* Eze 40:7 7070
porch of the gate within, one *r* Eze 40:8 7070
were a full *r* of six great cubits Eze 41:8 7070
east side with the measuring *r* Eze 42:16 7070
with the measuring *r* round about Eze 42:16 7070
with the measuring *r* round about Eze 42:17 7070
reeds, with the measuring *r* Eze 42:18 7070
reeds with the measuring *r* Eze 42:19 7070
A *r* shaken with the wind Mt 11:7 *2563*
A bruised *r* shall he not break, Mt 12:20 *2563*
head, and a *r* in his right hand Mt 27:29 *2563*
they spit upon him, and took the *r* Mt 27:30 *2563*
it with vinegar, and put it on a *r* Mt 27:48 *2563*
smote him on the head with a *r* Mk 15:19 *2563*
full of vinegar, and put it on a *r* Mk 15:36 *2563*
A *r* shaken with the wind Lk 7:24 *2563*
was given me a *r* like unto a rod Rev 11:1 *2563*
a golden *r* to measure the city Rev 21:15 *2563*
he measured the city with the *r* Rev 21:16 *2563*

REEDS
the *r* and flags shall wither Is 19:6 7070
The paper *r* by the brooks, by the Is 19:7
each lay, shall be grass with *r* Is 35:7 7070
the *r* they have burned with fire, Jer 51:32 98
measuring reed, five hundred *r* Eze 42:16 7070
the north side, five hundred *r* Eze 42:17 7070
the south side, five hundred *r* Eze 42:18 7070
measured five hundred *r* with the Eze 42:19 7070
round about, five hundred *r* long Eze 42:20
of five and twenty thousand *r* Eze 45:1
and twenty thousand *r* in breadth Eze 48:8

REEL
They *r* to and fro, and stagger like Ps 107:27 2287
The earth shall *r* to and fro like Is 24:20 5128

REELAIAH (*re-el-ah'-yah*) *A clan leader with Zerubbabel.*
Jeshua, Nehemiah, Seraiah, *R* Ezr 2:2 7480

REFINE
will *r* them as silver is refined, Zec 13:9 6884

REFINED
altar of incense *r* gold by weight 1Chr 28:18 2212
thousand talents of *r* silver 1Chr 29:4 2212
of wines on the lees well *r* Is 25:6 2212
Behold, I have *r* thee, but not Is 48:10 6884
will refine them as silver is *r* Zec 13:9 6884

REFINER
And he shall sit as a *r* and Mal 3:3 6884

REFINER'S
for he is like a *r* fire, and like Mal 3:2 6884

REFORMATION
on them until the time of *r* Heb 9:10 *1357*

REFORMED
if ye will not be *r* by me by Lev 26:23 3256

REFRAIN
Then Joseph could not *r* himself Gen 45:1 662
Therefore I will not *r* my mouth Job 7:11 2820
r thy foot from their path Prov 1:15 4513
a time to *r* from embracing Eccl 3:5 7368
for my praise will I *r* for thee Is 48:9 2413
Wilt thou *r* thyself for these Is 64:12 662
R thy voice from weeping, and Jer 31:16 4513
R from these men, and let them Acts 5:38 *868*
let him *r* his tongue from evil, 1Pet 3:10 *3973*

REFRAINED
r himself, and said, Set on bread Gen 43:31 662
Nevertheless Haman *r* himself Est 5:10 662
The princes *r* talking, and laid Job 29:9 6113
lo, I have not *r* my lips, O LORD, Ps 40:9 3607
I have *r* my feet from every evil Ps 119:101 3601
I have been still, and *r* myself Is 42:14 662
they have not *r* their feet Jer 14:10 2820

REFRAINETH
but he that *r* his lips is wise Prov 10:19 2820

REFRESH
r thyself, and I will give thee a 1Kin 13:7 5582
go unto his friends to *r* himself Acts 27:3
r my bowels in the Lord Philem 20 *373*

REFRESHED
and the stranger, may be *r* Ex 23:12 5314
seventh day he rested, and was *r* Ex 31:17 5314
so Saul was *r*, and was well, and 1Sa 16:23 7304
came weary, and *r* themselves there 2Sa 16:14 5314
I will speak, that I may be *r* Job 32:20 7304
will of God, and may with you be *r* Rom 15:32 *4875*
For they have *r* my spirit 1Cor 16:18 *373*
his spirit was *r* by you all 2Cor 7:13 *373*
for he oft *r* me, and was not 2Ti 1:16 *404*
of the saints are *r* by thee Philem 7 *373*

REFRESHETH
for he *r* the soul of his masters Prov 25:13 7725

REFRESHING
and this is the *r* Is 28:12 4774
when the times of *r* shall come Acts 3:19 *403*

REFUGE
there shall be six cities for *r* Num 35:6 4733
cities to be cities of *r* for you Num 35:11 4733
you cities for *r* from the avenger Num 35:12 4733
six cities shall ye have for *r* Num 35:13 4733
which shall be cities of *r* Num 35:14 4733
These six cities shall be a *r* Num 35:15 4733
restore him to the city of his *r* Num 35:25 4733
the border of the city of his *r* Num 35:26 4733
the borders of the city of his *r* Num 35:27 4733
his *r* until the death of the high Num 35:28 4733
that is fled to the city of his *r* Num 35:32 4733
The eternal God is thy *r*, and Deut 33:27 4585
Appoint out for you cities of *r* Josh 20:2 4733
they shall be your *r* from the Josh 20:3 4733
to be a city of *r* for the slayer Josh 21:13 4733
to be a city of *r* for the slayer Josh 21:21 4733
to be a city of *r* for the slayer Josh 21:27 4733
to be a city of *r* for the slayer Josh 21:32 4733
to be a city of *r* for the slayer Josh 21:38 4733
salvation, my high tower, and my *r* 2Sa 22:3 4498
namely, Hebron, the city of *r* 1Chr 6:57 4733
unto them, of the cities of *r* 1Chr 6:67 4733
will be a *r* for the oppressed Ps 9:9 4869
a *r* in times of trouble Ps 9:9 4869
poor, because the LORD is his *r* Ps 14:6 4268
God is our *r* and strength, a very Ps 46:1 4268
the God of Jacob is our *r* Ps 46:7 4869
the God of Jacob is our *r* Ps 46:11 4869
is known in her palaces for a *r* Ps 48:3 4869
of thy wings will I make my *r* Ps 57:1 2620
r in the day of my trouble Ps 59:16 4498
the rock of my strength, and my *r* Ps 62:7 4268
God is a *r* for us Ps 62:8 4268
but thou art my strong *r* Ps 71:7 4268
will say of the LORD, He is my *r* Ps 91:2 4268
hast made the LORD, which is my *r* Ps 91:9 4268
and my God is the rock of my *r* Ps 94:22 4268
hills are a *r* for the wild goats Ps 104:18 4268
r failed me Ps 142:4 4498
I said, Thou art my *r* and my Ps 142:5 4268

children shall have a place of *r* Prov 14:26 4268
the heat, and for a place of *r* Is 4:6 4268
a *r* from the storm, a shadow from Is 25:4 4268
for we have made lies our *r* Is 28:15 4268
shall sweep away the *r* of lies Is 28:17 4268
my *r* in the day of affliction, Jer 16:19 4498
who have fled for *r* to lay hold Heb 6:18 *2703*

REFUSE
if thou *r* to let him go, behold, Ex 4:23 3985
if thou *r* to let them go, behold, Ex 8:2 3986
For if thou *r* to let them go, and Ex 9:2 3986
How long wilt thou *r* to humble Ex 10:3 3985
if thou *r* to let my people go, Ex 10:4 3986
Moses, How long *r* ye to keep my Ex 16:28 3985
utterly *r* to give her unto him Ex 22:17 3985
every thing that was vile and *r* 1Sa 15:9 4549
recompense it, whether thou *r* Job 34:33 3988
and be wise, and *r* it not Prov 8:33 6544
because they *r* to do judgment Prov 21:7 3985
for his hands *r* to labour Prov 21:25 3985
But if ye *r* and rebel, ye shall be Is 1:20 3985
that he may know to *r* the evil Is 7:15 3988
child shall know to *r* the evil Is 7:16 3988
fast deceit, they *r* to return Jer 8:5 3985
through deceit they *r* to know me Jer 9:6 3985
which *r* to hear my words, which Jer 13:10 3987
if they *r* to take the cup at Jer 25:28 3985
But if thou *r* to go forth Jer 38:21 3986
r in the midst of the people Lam 3:45 3973
yea, and sell the *r* of the wheat Amos 8:6 4651
worthy of death, I *r* not to die Acts 25:11 *3868*
But *r* profane and old wives' 1Ti 4:7 *3868*
But the younger widows *r* 1Ti 5:11 *3868*
See that ye *r* not him that Heb 12:25 *3868*

REFUSED
but he *r* to be comforted Gen 37:35 3985
But he *r*, and said unto his Gen 39:8 3985
And his father *r*, and said, I know Gen 48:19 3985
Thus Edom *r* to give Israel Num 20:21 3985
Nevertheless the people *r* to obey 1Sa 8:19 3985
because I have *r* him 1Sa 16:7 3988
But he *r*, and said, I will not eat 1Sa 28:23 3985
Howbeit he *r* to turn aside 2Sa 2:23 3985
but he *r* to eat 2Sa 13:9 3985
And the man *r* to smite him 1Kin 20:35 3985
which he *r* to give thee for money 1Kin 21:15 3985
to take it; but he *r* 2Kin 5:16 3985
r to obey, neither were mindful Neh 9:17 3985
But the queen Vashti *r* to come at Est 1:12 3985
The things that my soul *r* to Job 6:7 3985
my soul *r* to be comforted Ps 77:2 3985
of God, and *r* to walk in his law Ps 78:10 3985
Moreover he *r* the tabernacle of Ps 78:67 3988
The stone which the builders *r* is Ps 118:22 3988
Because I have called, and ye *r* Prov 1:24 3985
a wife of youth, when thou wast *r* Is 54:6 3988
but they have *r* to receive Jer 5:3 3985
they have *r* to return Jer 5:3 3985
which *r* to hear my words Jer 11:10 3985
r to be comforted for her Jer 31:15 3985
they *r* to let them go Jer 50:33 3985
for they have *r* my judgments Eze 5:6 3988
king, because they *r* to return Hos 11:5 3985
But they *r* to hearken, and pulled Zec 7:11 3985
This Moses whom they *r*, saying, Acts 7:35 720
God is good, and nothing to be *r* 1Ti 4:4 579
r to be called the son of Heb 11:24 720
not who *r* him that spake on earth Heb 12:25 *3868*

REFUSEDST
forehead, thou *r* to be ashamed Jer 3:3 3985

REFUSETH
he *r* to let the people go Ex 7:14 3985
for the LORD *r* to give me leave Num 22:13 3985
and said, Balaam *r* to come with us Num 22:14 3985
My husband's brother *r* to raise Deut 25:7 3985
but he that *r* reproof erreth Prov 10:17 5800
be to him that *r* instruction Prov 13:18 6544
He that *r* instruction despiseth Prov 15:32 6544
Forasmuch as this people *r* the Is 8:6 3988
incurable, which *r* to be healed Jer 15:18 3985

REGARD
Also *r* not your stuff Gen 45:20
and let them not *r* vain words Ex 5:9 8159
R not them that have familiar Lev 19:31 6437
which shall not *r* the person of Deut 28:50 5375
not, neither did she *r* it 1Sa 4:20 3820
r this man of Belial, even Nabal 1Sa 25:25 3820
r not this thing 2Sa 13:20 3820
were it not that I *r* the presence 2Kin 3:14 5375
let not God *r* it from above, Job 3:4 1875
neither will the Almighty *r* it Job 35:13 7789
Take heed, *r* not iniquity Job 36:21 6437
Because they *r* not the works of Ps 28:5 995
hated them that *r* lying vanities Ps 31:6 8104
If I *r* iniquity in my heart, the Ps 66:18 7200
shall the God of Jacob *r* it Ps 94:7 995
He will *r* the prayer of the Ps 102:17 6437
That thou mayest *r* discretion Prov 5:2 8104
He will not *r* any ransom Prov 6:35
that in *r* of the oath of God Eccl 8:2
but they *r* not the work of the Is 5:12 5027
them, which shall not *r* silver Is 13:17 2803
he will no more *r* them Lam 4:16 5027
Neither shall he *r* the God of his Dan 11:37 995
desire of women, nor *r* any god Dan 11:37 995
neither will I *r* the peace Amos 5:22 5027
Behold ye among the heathen, and *r* Hab 1:5 5027
will he *r* your persons Mal 1:9 5375
Though I fear not God, nor *r* man Lk 18:4 *1788*
And to him they had *r*, because Acts 8:11 *4337*
day, to the Lord he doth not *r* it Rom 14:6 *5426*

REGARDED
he that *r* not the word of the Ex 9:21 3820
nor any to answer, nor any that *r* 1Kin 18:29 7182
hast *r* me according to the estate 1Chr 17:17 7200
Nevertheless he *r* their Ps 106:44 7200
out my hand, and no man *r* Prov 1:24 7181
men, O king, have not *r* thee Dan 3:12
For he hath *r* the low estate of Lk 1:48 *1914*
feared not God, neither *r* man Lk 18:2 *1788*
I *r* them not, saith the Lord Heb 8:9 *272*

REGARDEST
that thou *r* neither princes nor 2Sa 19:6
I stand up, and thou *r* me not Job 30:20 995
for thou *r* not the person of men Mt 22:16 *991*
for thou *r* not the person of men, Mk 12:14 *991*

REGARDETH
which *r* not persons, nor taketh Deut 10:17 5375
nor *r* the rich more than the poor Job 34:19 5234
neither *r* he the crying of the Job 39:7 8085
A righteous man *r* the life of his Prov 12:10 3045
but he that *r* reproof shall be Prov 13:18 8104
but he that *r* reproof is prudent Prov 15:5 8104
but the wicked *r* not to know it Prov 29:7 995
that is higher than the highest *r* Eccl 5:8 8104
he that *r* the clouds shall not Eccl 11:4 7200
despised the cities, he *r* no man Is 33:8 2803
r not thee, O king, nor the Dan 6:13
insomuch that he *r* not the Mal 2:13 6437
He that *r* the day, *r* it Rom 14:6 *5426*
he that *r* not the day, to the Rom 14:6 *5426*

REGARDING
perish for ever without any *r* it Job 4:20 7760
not *r* his life, to supply your Phil 2:30 *3851*

REGEM (*re'-ghem*) *A son of Jahdai.*
R, and Jotham, and Gesham 1Chr 2:47 7276

REGEM-MELECH (*re''-ghem-me'-lek*) *A messenger for Zechariah.*
the house of God Sherezer and *R* Zec 7:2 7278

REGENERATION
in the *r* when the Son of man Mt 19:28 *3824*
he saved us, by the washing of *r* Titus 3:5 *3824*

REGION
all the *r* of Argob, the kingdom Deut 3:4 2256
all the *r* of Argob, with all Deut 3:13 2256
of Abinadab, in all the *r* of Dor 1Kin 4:11 5299
him also pertained the *r* of Argob 1Kin 4:13 2256
all the *r* on this side the river 1Kin 4:24
all the *r* round about Jordan, Mt 3:5 *4066*
and to them which sat in the *r* Mt 4:16 *5561*
all the *r* round about Galilee Mk 1:28 *4066*
through that whole *r* round about Mk 6:55 *4066*
of the *r* of Trachonitis, and Lk 3:1 *5561*
him through all the *r* round about Lk 4:14 *4066*
throughout all the *r* round about Lk 7:17 *4066*
published throughout all the *r* Acts 13:49 *5561*
unto the *r* that lieth round about Acts 14:6 *4066*
the *r* of Galatia, and were Acts 16:6 *5561*

REGIONS
abroad throughout the *r* of Judaea Acts 8:1 *5561*
the gospel in the *r* beyond you 2Cor 10:16
this boasting in the *r* of Achaia 2Cor 11:10 *2825*
I came into the *r* of Syria Gal 1:21 *2825*

REGISTER
These sought their *r* among those Ezr 2:62 3791
I found a *r* of the genealogy of Neh 7:5 5612
These sought their *r* among those Neh 7:64 3791

REHABIAH (*re-hab-i'-ah*) *A son of Eliezer.*
sons of Eliezer were, *R* the chief 1Chr 23:17 7345
but the sons of *R* were very many 1Chr 23:17 7345
Concerning *R* 1Chr 24:21 7345
of the sons of *R*, the first was 1Chr 24:21 7345
R his son, and Jeshaiah his son, 1Chr 26:25 7345

REHEARSE
r it in the ears of Joshua Ex 17:14 7760
there shall they *r* the righteous Judg 5:11 8567

REHEARSED
he *r* them in the ears of the LORD 1Sa 8:21 1696
spake, they *r* them before Saul 1Sa 17:31 5046
But Peter *r* the matter from the Acts 11:4 *756*
they *r* all that God had done with Acts 14:27 *312*

REHOB (*re'-hob*)
1. A Levitical city in Asher.
from the wilderness of Zin unto *R* Num 13:21 7340
and *R*, and Hammon, and Josh 19:28 7340
Ummah also, and Aphek, and *R* Josh 19:30 7340
suburbs, and *R* with her suburbs Josh 21:31 7340
of Helbah, nor of Aphik, nor of *R* Judg 1:31 7340
and the Syrians of Zoba, and of *R* 2Sa 10:8 7340
suburbs, and *R* with her suburbs 1Chr 6:75 7340
2. Father of Hadadezer.
also Hadadezer, the son of *R* 2Sa 8:3 7340
the spoil of Hadadezer, son of *R* 2Sa 8:12 7340
3. A Levite.
Micha, *R*, Hashabiah, Neh 10:11 7340

REHOBOAM (*re-ho-bo'-am*) See ROBOAM. *A son of Solomon and king of Judah.*
R his son reigned in his stead 1Kin 11:43 7346
And *R* went to Shechem 1Kin 12:1 7346
of Israel came, and spake unto *R* 1Kin 12:3 7346
king *R* consulted with the old men 1Kin 12:6 7346
people came to *R* the third day 1Kin 12:12 7346
of Judah, *R* reigned over them 1Kin 12:17 7346
Then king *R* sent Adoram, who was 1Kin 12:18 7346
Therefore king *R* made speed to 1Kin 12:18 7346
when *R* was come to Jerusalem, he 1Kin 12:21 7346
again to *R* the son of Solomon 1Kin 12:21 7346
Speak unto *R*, the son of Solomon, 1Kin 12:23 7346
even unto *R* king of Judah, and 1Kin 12:27 7346
go again to *R* king of Judah 1Kin 12:27 7346
R the son of Solomon reigned in 1Kin 14:21 7346
R was forty and one years old when 1Kin 14:21 7346
pass in the fifth year of king *R* 1Kin 14:25 7346
king *R* made in their stead brasen 1Kin 14:27 7346
Now the rest of the acts of *R* 1Kin 14:29 7346
And there was war between *R* 1Kin 14:30 7346
R slept with his fathers, and was 1Kin 14:31 7346
And there was war between *R* 1Kin 15:6 7346
And Solomon's son was *R*, Abia his 1Chr 3:10 7346
R his son reigned in his stead 2Chr 9:31 7346
And *R* went to Shechem 2Chr 10:1 7346
and all Israel came and spake to *R* 2Chr 10:3 7346
king *R* took counsel with the old 2Chr 10:6 7346
people came to *R* on the third day 2Chr 10:12 7346
king *R* forsook the counsel of the 2Chr 10:13 7346
of Judah, *R* reigned over them 2Chr 10:17 7346
Then king *R* sent Hadoram that was 2Chr 10:18 7346
But king *R* made speed to get him 2Chr 10:18 7346
when *R* was come to Jerusalem, he 2Chr 11:1 7346
bring the kingdom again to *R* 2Chr 11:1 7346
Speak unto *R* the son of Solomon, 2Chr 11:3 7346
R dwelt in Jerusalem, and built 2Chr 11:5 7346
made *R* the son of Solomon strong 2Chr 11:17 7346
R took him Mahalath the daughter 2Chr 11:18 7346
R loved Maachah the daughter of 2Chr 11:21 7346
R made Abijah the son of Maachah 2Chr 11:22 7346
when *R* had established the 2Chr 12:1 7346
R Shishak king of Egypt came up 2Chr 12:2 7346
came Shemaiah the prophet to *R* 2Chr 12:5 7346
king *R* made shields of brass 2Chr 12:10 7346
So king *R* strengthened himself in 2Chr 12:13 7346
for *R* was one and forty years old 2Chr 12:13 7346
Now the acts of *R*, first and last, 2Chr 12:15 7346
And there were wars between *R* 2Chr 12:15 7346
R slept with his fathers, and was 2Chr 12:16 7346
against *R* the son of Solomon 2Chr 13:7 7346
when *R* was young and tenderhearted. 2Chr 13:7 7346

REHOBOTH (*re'-ho-both*)
1. A city in Assyria.
and builded Nineveh, and the city *R* Gen 10:11 7344
Saul of *R* by the river reigned in Gen 36:37 7344
Shaul of *R* by the river reigned 1Chr 1:48 7344
2. A well Isaac dug.
and he called the name of it *R* Gen 26:22 7344

REHOBOTH-BY-THE-WATER See REHOBOTH.

REHOBOTH-IR See REHOBOTH.

REHUM (*re'-hum*) See NEHUM.
1. A clan leader with Zerubbabel.
Bilshan, Mizpar, Bigvai, *R* Ezr 2:2 7348
Shechaniah, *R*, Meremoth, Neh 12:3 7348
2. An officer of King Artaxerxes.
R the chancellor and Shimshai the Ezr 4:8 7348
Then wrote *R* the chancellor, and Ezr 4:9 7348
an answer unto *R* the chancellor Ezr 4:17 7348
letter was read before *R*, and Ezr 4:23 7348
3. A Levite rebuilder of Jerusalem's wall.
the Levites, *R* the son of Bani Neh 3:17 7348
4. A renewer of the covenant.
R, Hashabnah, Maaseiah, Neh 10:25 7348

REI (*re'-i*) *A friend of David.*
the prophet, and Shimei, and *R* 1Kin 1:8 7472

REIGN
him, Shalt thou indeed *r* over us Gen 37:8 4427
The LORD shall *r* for ever Ex 15:18 4427
that hate you shall *r* over you Lev 26:17 7287
thou shalt *r* over many nations, Deut 15:6 4910
but they shall not *r* over thee Deut 15:6 4910
r over you, or that one *r* Judg 9:2 4910
the olive tree, *R* thou over us Judg 9:8 4427
fig tree, Come thou, and *r* over us Judg 9:10 4427
the vine, Come thou, and *r* over us Judg 9:12 4427
bramble, Come thou, and *r* over us Judg 9:14 4427
me, that I should not *r* over them 1Sa 8:7 4427
the king that shall *r* over them 1Sa 8:9 4427
of the king that shall *r* over you 1Sa 8:11 4427
this same shall *r* over my people 1Sa 9:17 6113
that said, Shall Saul *r* over us 1Sa 11:12 4427
but a king shall *r* over us 1Sa 12:12 4427
when he began to *r* over Israel 2Sa 2:10 4427
that thou mayest *r* over all that 2Sa 3:21 4427
years old when he began to *r* 2Sa 5:4 4427
the son of Haggith doth *r* 1Kin 1:11 4427
Solomon thy son shall *r* after me 1Kin 1:13 4427
why then doth Adonijah *r* 1Kin 1:13 4427
Solomon thy son shall *r* after me 1Kin 1:17 4427
said, Adonijah shall *r* after me 1Kin 1:24 4427
Solomon thy son shall *r* after me 1Kin 1:30 4427
faces on me, that I should *r* 1Kin 2:15 4427
year of Solomon's *r* over Israel 1Kin 6:1 4427
thou shalt *r* according to all 1Kin 11:37 4427
one years old when he began to *r* 1Kin 14:21 4427
the son of Jeroboam began to *r* 1Kin 15:25 4427
to *r* over all Israel in Tirzah 1Kin 15:33 4427
Baasha to *r* over Israel in Tirzah 1Kin 16:8 4427
came to pass, when he began to *r* 1Kin 16:11 4427
did Zimri *r* seven days in Tirzah 1Kin 16:15 4427
Judah began Omri to *r* over Israel 1Kin 16:23 4427
the son of Omri to *r* over Israel 1Kin 16:29 4427
the son of Asa began to *r* over 1Kin 22:41 4427
five years old when he began to *r* 1Kin 22:42 4427
the son of Ahab began to *r* over 1Kin 22:51 4427
the son of Ahab began to *r* over 2Kin 3:1 4427
king of Judah began to *r* 2Kin 8:16 4427
old was he when he began to *r* 2Kin 8:17 4427
Jehoram king of Judah begin to *r* 2Kin 8:25 4427
was Ahaziah when he began to *r* 2Kin 8:26 4427
began Ahaziah to *r* over Judah 2Kin 9:29 4427
Athaliah did *r* over the land 2Kin 11:3 4427
was Jehoash when he began to *r* 2Kin 11:21 4427

year of Jehu Jehoash began to *r* ... 2Kin 12:1 4427
began to *r* over Israel in Samaria ... 2Kin 13:1 4427
to *r* over Israel in Samaria ... 2Kin 13:10 4427
five years old when he began to *r* ... 2Kin 14:2 4427
of Israel began to *r* in Samaria ... 2Kin 14:23 4427
son of Amaziah king of Judah to *r* ... 2Kin 15:1 4427
old was he when he began to *r* ... 2Kin 15:2 4427
r over Israel in Samaria six ... 2Kin 15:8 4427
of Jabesh began to *r* in the nine ... 2Kin 15:13 4427
the son of Gadi to *r* over Israel ... 2Kin 15:17 4427
began to *r* over Israel in Samaria ... 2Kin 15:23 4427
began to *r* over Israel in Samaria ... 2Kin 15:27 4427
son of Uzziah king of Judah to *r* ... 2Kin 15:32 4427
old was he when he began to *r* ... 2Kin 15:33 4427
Jotham king of Judah began to *r* ... 2Kin 16:1 4427
old was Ahaz when he began to *r* ... 2Kin 16:2 4427
to *r* in Samaria over Israel nine ... 2Kin 17:1 4427
of Ahaz king of Judah began to *r* ... 2Kin 18:1 4427
old was he when he began to *r* ... 2Kin 18:2 4427
years old when he began to *r* ... 2Kin 21:1 4427
two years old when he began to *r* ... 2Kin 21:19 4427
years old when he began to *r* ... 2Kin 22:1 4427
years old when he began to *r* ... 2Kin 23:31 4427
that he might not *r* in Jerusalem ... 2Kin 23:33 4427
five years old when he began to *r* ... 2Kin 23:36 4427
years old when he began to *r* ... 2Kin 24:8 4427
him in the eighth year of his *r* ... 2Kin 24:12 4427
one years old when he began to *r* ... 2Kin 24:18 4427
pass in the ninth year of his *r* ... 2Kin 25:1 4427
to *r* did lift up the head of ... 2Kin 25:27 4427
their cities unto the *r* of David ... 1Chr 4:31 4427
In the fortieth year of the *r* of ... 1Chr 26:31 4438
With all his *r* and his might, and ... 1Chr 29:30 4438
and hast made me to *r* in his stead ... 2Chr 1:8 4427
in the fourth year of his *r* ... 2Chr 3:2 4438
years old when he began to *r* ... 2Chr 12:13 4427
began Abijah to *r* over Judah ... 2Chr 13:1 4427
fifteenth year of the *r* of Asa ... 2Chr 15:10 4438
and thirtieth year of the *r* of Asa ... 2Chr 15:19 4438
thirtieth year of the *r* of Asa ... 2Chr 16:1 4438
ninth year of his *r* was diseased ... 2Chr 16:12 4438
the one and fortieth year of his *r* ... 2Chr 16:13 4427
of his *r* he sent to his princes ... 2Chr 17:7 4427
five years old when he began to *r* ... 2Chr 20:31 4427
two years old when he began to *r* ... 2Chr 21:5 4427
old was he when he began to *r* ... 2Chr 21:20 4427
was Ahaziah when he began to *r* ... 2Chr 22:2 4427
Behold, the king's son shall *r* ... 2Chr 23:3 4427
years old when he began to *r* ... 2Chr 24:1 4427
five years old when he began to *r* ... 2Chr 25:1 4427
old was Uzziah when he began to *r* ... 2Chr 26:3 4427
five years old when he began to *r* ... 2Chr 27:1 4427
years old when he began to *r* ... 2Chr 27:8 4427
years old when he began to *r* ... 2Chr 28:1 4427
began to *r* when he was five ... 2Chr 29:1 4427
He in the first year of his *r* ... 2Chr 29:3 4427
in his *r* did cast away in his ... 2Chr 29:19 4438
years old when he began to *r* ... 2Chr 33:1 4427
years old when he began to *r* ... 2Chr 33:21 4427
years old when he began to *r* ... 2Chr 34:1 4427
For in the eighth year of his *r* ... 2Chr 34:3 4427
in the eighteenth year of his *r* ... 2Chr 34:8 4427
the *r* of Josiah was this passover ... 2Chr 35:19 4438
years old when he began to *r* ... 2Chr 36:2 4427
five years old when he began to *r* ... 2Chr 36:5 4427
years old when he began to *r* ... 2Chr 36:9 4427
years old when he began to *r* ... 2Chr 36:11 4427
his sons until the *r* of the ... 2Chr 36:20 4427
even until the *r* of Darius king ... Ezr 4:5 4438
in the *r* of Ahasuerus, in the ... Ezr 4:6 4438
in the beginning of his *r* ... Ezr 4:6 4438
of the *r* of Darius king of Persia ... Ezr 4:24 4437
year of the *r* of Darius the king ... Ezr 6:15 4437
in the *r* of Artaxerxes king of ... Ezr 7:1 4438
in the *r* of Artaxerxes the king ... Ezr 8:1 4438
to the *r* of Darius the Persian ... Neh 12:22 4438
In the third year of his *r* ... Est 1:3 4427
in the seventh year of his *r* ... Est 2:16 4438
That the hypocrite *r* not, lest ... Job 34:30 4427
The LORD shall *r* for ever ... Ps 146:10 4427
By me kings *r*, and princes decree ... Prov 8:15 4427
For out of prison he cometh to *r* ... Eccl 4:14 4427
of hosts shall *r* in mount Zion ... Is 24:23 4427
a king shall *r* in righteousness, ... Is 32:1 4427
in the thirteenth year of his *r* ... Jer 1:2 4427
Shalt thou *r*, because thou ... Jer 22:15 4427
Branch, and a King shall *r* ... Jer 23:5 4427
In the beginning of the *r* of ... Jer 26:1 4468
In the beginning of the *r* of ... Jer 27:1 4467
in the beginning of the *r* of ... Jer 28:1 4467
have a son to *r* upon his throne ... Jer 33:21 4427
the *r* of Zedekiah king of Judah ... Jer 49:34 4438
in the fourth year of his *r* ... Jer 51:59 4427
years old when he began to *r* ... Jer 52:1 4427
pass in the ninth year of his *r* ... Jer 52:4 4427
of his *r* lifted up the head of ... Jer 52:31 4438
In the third year of the *r* of ... Dan 1:1 4438
year of the *r* of Nebuchadnezzar ... Dan 2:1 4438
prospered in the *r* of Darius ... Dan 6:28 4437
in the *r* of Cyrus the Persian ... Dan 6:28 4437
In the third year of the *r* of ... Dan 8:1 4438
In the first year of his *r* I ... Dan 9:2 4427
the LORD shall *r* over them in ... Mic 4:7 4427
he heard that Archelaus did *r* in ... Mt 2:22 *936*
he shall *r* over the house of ... Lk 1:33 *936*
year of the *r* of Tiberius Caesar ... Lk 3:1 *2231*
not have this man to *r* over us ... Lk 19:14 *936*
not that I should *r* over them ... Lk 19:27 *936*
shall *r* in life by one, Jesus ... Rom 5:17 *936*
even so might grace *r* through ... Rom 5:21 *936*
therefore *r* in your mortal body ... Rom 6:12 *936*
shall rise to *r* over the Gentiles ... Rom 15:12 *757*
and I would to God ye did *r* ... 1Cor 4:8 *936*
that we also might *r* with you ... 1Cor 4:8 *4821*
For he must *r*, till he hath put ... 1Cor 15:25 *936*
suffer, we shall also *r* with him ... 2Ti 2:12 *4821*
and we shall *r* on the earth ... Rev 5:10 *936*
and he shall *r* for ever and ever ... Rev 11:15 *936*
shall *r* with him a thousand years ... Rev 20:6 *936*
and they shall *r* for ever and ever ... Rev 22:5 *936*

REIGNED

kings that *r* in the land of Edom ... Gen 36:31 4427
before there *r* any king over the ... Gen 36:31 4427
And Bela the son of Beor *r* in Edom ... Gen 36:32 4427
of Zerah of Bozrah *r* in his stead ... Gen 36:33 4427
the land of Temani *r* in his stead ... Gen 36:34 4427
the field of Moab, *r* in his stead ... Gen 36:35 4427
Samlah of Masrekah *r* in his stead ... Gen 36:36 4427
by the river *r* in his stead ... Gen 36:37 4427
the son of Achbor *r* in his stead ... Gen 36:38 4427
died, and Hadar *r* in his stead ... Gen 36:39 4427
r in mount Hermon, and in Salcah, ... Josh 12:5 4910
which *r* in Heshbon, unto the ... Josh 13:10 4427
which *r* in Ashtaroth and in Edrei, ... Josh 13:12 4427
which *r* in Heshbon, whom Moses ... Josh 13:21 4427
king of Canaan, that *r* in Hazor ... Judg 4:2 4427
When Abimelech had *r* three years ... Judg 9:22 7786
Saul *r* one year ... 1Sa 13:1 4427
when he had *r* two years over ... 1Sa 13:1 4427
reign over Israel, and *r* two years ... 2Sa 2:10 4427
to reign, and he *r* forty years ... 2Sa 5:4 4427
In Hebron he *r* over Judah seven ... 2Sa 5:5 4427
and in Jerusalem he *r* thirty ... 2Sa 5:5 4427
And David *r* over all Israel ... 2Sa 8:15 4427
and Hanun his son *r* in his stead ... 2Sa 10:1 4427
Saul, in whose stead thou hast *r* ... 2Sa 16:8 4427
the days that David *r* over Israel ... 1Kin 2:11 4427
seven years *r* he in Hebron, and ... 1Kin 2:11 4427
three years *r* he in Jerusalem ... 1Kin 2:11 4427
Solomon *r* over all kingdoms from ... 1Kin 4:21 4910
dwelt therein, and *r* in Damascus ... 1Kin 11:24 4427
abhorred Israel, and *r* over Syria ... 1Kin 11:25 4427
the time that Solomon *r* in ... 1Kin 11:42 4427
Rehoboam his son *r* in his stead ... 1Kin 11:43 4427
of Judah, Rehoboam *r* over them ... 1Kin 12:17 4427
how he warred, and how he *r* ... 1Kin 14:19 4427
days which Jeroboam *r* were two ... 1Kin 14:20 4427
and Nadab his son *r* in his stead ... 1Kin 14:20 4427
the son of Solomon *r* in Judah ... 1Kin 14:21 4427
he *r* seventeen years in Jerusalem ... 1Kin 14:21 4427
And Abijam his son *r* in his stead ... 1Kin 14:31 4427
son of Nebat *r* Abijam over Judah ... 1Kin 15:1 4427
Three years *r* he in Jerusalem ... 1Kin 15:2 4427
Asa his son *r* in his stead ... 1Kin 15:8 4427
king of Israel *r* Asa over Judah ... 1Kin 15:9 4427
one years *r* he in Jerusalem ... 1Kin 15:10 4427
his son *r* in his stead ... 1Kin 15:24 4427
Judah, and *r* over Israel two years ... 1Kin 15:25 4427
slay him, and *r* in his stead ... 1Kin 15:28 4427
And it came to pass, when he *r* ... 1Kin 15:29 4427
and Elah his son *r* in his stead ... 1Kin 16:6 4427
king of Judah, and *r* in his stead ... 1Kin 16:10 4427
so Tibni died, and Omri *r* ... 1Kin 16:22 4427
six years *r* he in Tirzah ... 1Kin 16:23 4427
and Ahab his son *r* in his stead ... 1Kin 16:28 4427
Ahab the son of Omri *r* over ... 1Kin 16:29 4427
and Ahaziah his son *r* in his stead ... 1Kin 22:40 4427
he *r* twenty and five years in ... 1Kin 22:42 4427
and Jehoram his son *r* in his stead ... 1Kin 22:50 4427
Judah, and *r* two years over Israel ... 1Kin 22:51 4427
Jehoram *r* in his stead in the ... 2Kin 1:17 4427
king of Judah, and *r* twelve years ... 2Kin 3:1 4427
that should have *r* in his stead ... 2Kin 3:27 4427
and Hazael *r* in his stead ... 2Kin 8:15 4427
he *r* eight years in Jerusalem ... 2Kin 8:17 4427
and Ahaziah his son *r* in his stead ... 2Kin 8:24 4427
he *r* one year in Jerusalem ... 2Kin 8:26
Jehoahaz his son *r* in his stead ... 2Kin 10:35 4427
the time that Jehu *r* over Israel ... 2Kin 10:36 4427
forty years *r* he in Jerusalem ... 2Kin 12:1 4427
and Amaziah his son *r* in his stead ... 2Kin 12:21 4427
in Samaria, and *r* seventeen years ... 2Kin 13:1
and Joash his son *r* in his stead ... 2Kin 13:9 4427
in Samaria, and *r* sixteen years ... 2Kin 13:10
Ben-hadad his son *r* in his stead ... 2Kin 13:24 4427
r Amaziah the son of Joash king ... 2Kin 14:1 4427
r twenty and nine years in ... 2Kin 14:2 4427
Jeroboam his son *r* in his stead ... 2Kin 14:16 4427
Samaria, and *r* forty and one years ... 2Kin 14:23
Zachariah his son *r* in his stead ... 2Kin 14:29 4427
he *r* two and fifty years in ... 2Kin 15:2 4427
and Jotham his son *r* in his stead ... 2Kin 15:7 4427
and slew him, and *r* in his stead ... 2Kin 15:10 4427
he *r* a full month in Samaria ... 2Kin 15:13 4427
and slew him, and *r* in his stead ... 2Kin 15:14 4427
Israel, and *r* ten years in Samaria ... 2Kin 15:17
Pekahiah his son *r* in his stead ... 2Kin 15:22 4427
Israel in Samaria, and *r* two years ... 2Kin 15:23
he killed him, and *r* in his room ... 2Kin 15:25 4427
in Samaria, and *r* twenty years ... 2Kin 15:27
r in his stead, in the twentieth ... 2Kin 15:30 4427
he *r* sixteen years in Jerusalem ... 2Kin 15:33 4427
and Ahaz his son *r* in his stead ... 2Kin 15:38 4427
r sixteen years in Jerusalem, and ... 2Kin 16:2 4427
Hezekiah his son *r* in his stead ... 2Kin 16:20 4427
he *r* twenty and nine years in ... 2Kin 18:2 4427
his son *r* in his stead ... 2Kin 19:37 4427
Manasseh his son *r* in his stead ... 2Kin 20:21 4427
and *r* fifty and five years in ... 2Kin 21:1 4427
and Amon his son *r* in his stead ... 2Kin 21:18 4427
he *r* two years in Jerusalem ... 2Kin 21:19 4427
and Josiah his son *r* in his stead ... 2Kin 21:26 4427
he *r* thirty and one years in ... 2Kin 22:1 4427
he *r* three months in Jerusalem ... 2Kin 23:31 4427
he *r* eleven years in Jerusalem ... 2Kin 23:36 4427
Jehoiachin his son *r* in his stead ... 2Kin 24:6 4427
he *r* in Jerusalem three months ... 2Kin 24:8 4427
he *r* eleven years in Jerusalem ... 2Kin 24:18 4427
Now these are the kings that *r* in ... 1Chr 1:43 4427
r over the children of Israel ... 1Chr 1:43 4427
of Zerah of Bozrah *r* in his stead ... 1Chr 1:44 4427
of the Temanites *r* in his stead ... 1Chr 1:45 4427
the field of Moab, *r* in his stead ... 1Chr 1:46 4427
Samlah of Masrekah *r* in his stead ... 1Chr 1:47 4427
by the river *r* in his stead ... 1Chr 1:48 4427
the son of Achbor *r* in his stead ... 1Chr 1:49 4427
was dead, Hadad *r* in his stead ... 1Chr 1:50 4427
there he *r* seven years and six ... 1Chr 3:4 4427
and in Jerusalem he *r* thirty ... 1Chr 3:4 4427
So David *r* over all Israel, and ... 1Chr 18:14 4427
died, and his son *r* in his stead ... 1Chr 19:1 4427
son of Jesse *r* over all Israel ... 1Chr 29:26 4427
the time that he *r* over Israel ... 1Chr 29:27 4427
seven years *r* he in Hebron, and ... 1Chr 29:27 4427
three years *r* he in Jerusalem ... 1Chr 29:27 4427
and Solomon his son *r* in his stead ... 1Chr 29:28 4427
congregation, and *r* over Israel ... 2Chr 1:13 4427
he *r* over all the kings from the ... 2Chr 9:26 4910
Solomon *r* in Jerusalem over all ... 2Chr 9:30 4427
Rehoboam his son *r* in his stead ... 2Chr 9:31 4427
of Judah, Rehoboam *r* over them ... 2Chr 10:17 4427
himself in Jerusalem, and *r* ... 2Chr 12:13 4427
he *r* seventeen years in Jerusalem ... 2Chr 12:13 4427
and Abijah his son *r* in his stead ... 2Chr 12:16 4427
He *r* three years in Jerusalem ... 2Chr 13:2 4427
Asa his son *r* in his stead ... 2Chr 14:1 4427
his son *r* in his stead, and ... 2Chr 17:1 4427
And Jehoshaphat *r* over Judah ... 2Chr 20:31 4427
he *r* twenty and five years in ... 2Chr 20:31 4427
And Jehoram his son *r* in his stead ... 2Chr 21:1 4427
he *r* eight years in Jerusalem ... 2Chr 21:5 4427
he *r* in Jerusalem eight years, and ... 2Chr 21:20 4427
son of Jehoram king of Judah *r* ... 2Chr 22:1 4427
he *r* one year in Jerusalem ... 2Chr 22:2 4427
and Athaliah *r* over the land ... 2Chr 22:12 4427
he *r* forty years in Jerusalem ... 2Chr 24:1 4427
And Amaziah his son *r* in his stead ... 2Chr 24:27 4427
he *r* twenty and nine years in ... 2Chr 25:1 4427
he *r* fifty and two years in ... 2Chr 26:3 4427
and Jotham his son *r* in his stead ... 2Chr 26:23 4427
he *r* sixteen years in Jerusalem ... 2Chr 27:1 4427
r sixteen years in Jerusalem ... 2Chr 27:8 4427
and Ahaz his son *r* in his stead ... 2Chr 27:9 4427
he *r* sixteen years in Jerusalem ... 2Chr 28:1 4427
Hezekiah his son *r* in his stead ... 2Chr 28:27 4427
he *r* nine and twenty years in ... 2Chr 29:1 4427
Manasseh his son *r* in his stead ... 2Chr 32:33 4427
he *r* fifty and five years in ... 2Chr 33:1 4427
and Amon his son *r* in his stead ... 2Chr 33:20 4427
and *r* two years in Jerusalem ... 2Chr 33:21 4427
he *r* in Jerusalem one and thirty ... 2Chr 34:1 4427
he *r* three months in Jerusalem ... 2Chr 36:2 4427
he *r* eleven years in Jerusalem ... 2Chr 36:5 4427
Jehoiachin his son *r* in his stead ... 2Chr 36:8 4427
he *r* three months and ten days in ... 2Chr 36:9 4427
r eleven years in Jerusalem ... 2Chr 36:11 4427
(this is Ahasuerus which *r* from ... Est 1:1 4427
his son *r* in his stead ... Is 37:38 4427
which *r* instead of Josiah his ... Jer 22:11 4427
r instead of Coniah the son of ... Jer 37:1 4427
he *r* eleven years in Jerusalem ... Jer 52:1 4427
death *r* from Adam to Moses ... Rom 5:14 *936*
one man's offence death *r* by one ... Rom 5:17 *936*
That as sin hath *r* unto death ... Rom 5:21 *936*
ye have *r* as kings without us ... 1Cor 4:8 *936*
thee thy great power, and hast *r* ... Rev 11:17 *936*
r with Christ a thousand years ... Rev 20:4 *936*

REIGNEST

come of thee, and thou *r* over all ... 1Chr 29:12 4910

REIGNETH

also the king that *r* over you ... 1Sa 12:14 4427
ye shall say, Absalom *r* in Hebron ... 2Sa 15:10 4427
And now, behold, Adonijah *r* ... 1Kin 1:18 4427
say among the nations, The LORD *r* ... 1Chr 16:31 4427
God *r* over the heathen ... Ps 47:8 4427
The LORD *r*, he is clothed with ... Ps 93:1 4427
among the heathen that the LORD *r* ... Ps 96:10 4427
The LORD *r* ... Ps 97:1 4427
The LORD *r* ... Ps 99:1 4427
For a servant when he *r* ... Prov 30:22 4427
that saith unto Zion, Thy God *r* ... Is 52:7 4427
which *r* over the kings of the ... Rev 17:18
for the Lord God omnipotent *r* ... Rev 19:6 *936*

REIGNING

rejected him from *r* over Israel ... 1Sa 16:1 4427

REINS

about, he cleaveth my *r* asunder ... Job 16:13 3629
though my *r* be consumed within me ... Job 19:27 3629
God trieth the hearts and *r* ... Ps 7:9 3629
my *r* also instruct me in the ... Ps 16:7 3629
try my *r* and my heart ... Ps 26:2 3629
grieved, and I was pricked in my *r* ... Ps 73:21 3629
For thou hast possessed my *r* ... Ps 139:13 3629
my *r* shall rejoice, when thy lips ... Prov 23:16 3629
faithfulness the girdle of his *r* ... Is 11:5 2504
righteously, that triest the *r* ... Jer 11:20 3629
their mouth, and far from their *r* ... Jer 12:2 3629
search the heart, I try the *r* ... Jer 17:10 3629
the righteous, and seest the *r* ... Jer 20:12 3629
of his quiver to enter into my *r* ... Lam 3:13 3629
I am he which searcheth the *r* ... Rev 2:23 *3510*

REJECT

knowledge, I will also *r* thee ... Hos 4:6 3988
sat with him, he would not *r* her ... Mk 6:26 *114*
Full well ye *r* the commandment of ... Mk 7:9 *114*
the first and second admonition *r* ... Titus 3:10 *3868*

REJECTED
r thee, but they have r me 1Sa 8:7 3988
And ye have this day r your God 1Sa 10:19 3988
Because thou hast r the word of 1Sa 15:23 3988
he hath also r thee from being 1Sa 15:23 3988
for thou hast r the word of the 1Sa 15:26 3988
the LORD hath r thee from being 1Sa 15:26 3988
seeing I have r him from reigning 1Sa 16:1 3988
they r his statutes, and his 2Kin 17:15 3988
the LORD r all the seed of Israel 2Kin 17:20 3988
He is despised and r of men Is 53:3 2310
the LORD hath r thy confidences Jer 2:37 3988
my words, nor to my law, but r it Jer 6:19 3988
because the LORD hath r them Jer 6:30 3988
for the LORD hath r and forsaken Jer 7:29 3988
they have r the word of the LORD Jer 8:9 3988
Hast thou utterly r Judah Jer 14:19 3988
But thou hast utterly r us Lam 5:22 3988
because thou hast r knowledge Hos 4:6 3988
The stone which the builders r Mt 21:42 593
be r of the elders, and of the Mk 8:31 593
r is become the head of the Mk 12:10 593
lawyers r the counsel of God Lk 7:30 114
be r of the elders and chief Lk 9:22 593
and be r of this generation Lk 17:25 593
The stone which the builders r Lk 20:17 593
my flesh ye despised not, nor r Gal 4:14 1609
beareth thorns and briers is r Heb 6:8 96
inherited the blessing, he was r Heb 12:17 593

REJECTETH
He that r me, and receiveth not my Jn 12:48 14

REJOICE
ye shall r before the LORD your Lev 23:40 8055
ye shall r in all that ye put Deut 12:7 8055
ye shall r before the LORD your Deut 12:12 8055
thou shalt r before the LORD thy Deut 12:18 8055
the LORD thy God, and thou shalt r Deut 14:26 8055
thou shalt r before the LORD thy Deut 16:11 8055
thou shalt r in thy feast, thou, Deut 16:14 8055
therefore thou shalt surely r Deut 16:15 8055
thou shalt r in every good thing Deut 26:11 8056
r before the LORD thy God Deut 27:7 8055
so the LORD will r over you to Deut 28:63 7797
will again r over thee for good Deut 30:9 7797
R, O ye nations, with his people Deut 32:43 7442
And of Zebulun he said, R, Zebulun Deut 33:18 8055
then r ye in Abimelech Judg 9:19 8055
and let him also r in you Judg 9:19 8055
unto Dagon their god, and to r Judg 16:23 8057
because I r in thy salvation 1Sa 2:1 8055
thou sawest it, and didst r 1Sa 19:5 8055
daughters of the Philistines r 2Sa 1:20 8055
of them r that seek the LORD 1Chr 16:10 8055
be glad, and let the earth r 1Chr 16:31 1523
let the fields r, and all that is 1Chr 16:32 5970
and let thy saints r in goodness 2Chr 6:41 8055
made them to r over their enemies 2Chr 20:27 8055
had made them r with great joy Neh 12:43 8055
Which r exceedingly, and are glad, Job 3:22 8055
be, and he shall not r therein Job 20:18 5965
r at the sound of the organ Job 21:12 8055
with fear, and r with trembling Ps 2:11 1523
that put their trust in thee r Ps 5:11 8055
I will be glad and r in thee Ps 9:2 5970
I will r in thy salvation Ps 9:14 1523
that trouble me r when I am moved Ps 13:4 1523
my heart shall r in thy salvation Ps 13:5 1523
of his people, Jacob shall r Ps 14:7 1523
We will r in thy salvation, and in Ps 20:5 7442
salvation how greatly shall he r Ps 21:1 1523
not made my foes to r over me Ps 30:1 8055
I will be glad and r in thy mercy Ps 31:7 8055
Be glad in the LORD, and r Ps 32:11 1524
R in the LORD, O ye righteous Ps 33:1 7442
For our heart shall r in him Ps 33:21 8055
it shall r in his salvation Ps 35:9 7797
mine enemies wrongfully r over me Ps 35:19 8055
and let them not r over me Ps 35:24 8055
together that r at mine hurt Ps 35:26 8055
otherwise they should r over me Ps 38:16 8056
Let all those that seek thee r Ps 40:16 7797
Let mount Zion r, let the Ps 48:11 8055
which thou hast broken may r Ps 51:8 1523
of his people, Jacob shall r Ps 53:6 1523
The righteous shall r when he Ps 58:10 8055
I will r, I will divide Shechem, Ps 60:6 5937
the shadow of thy wings will I r Ps 63:7 7442
But the king shall r in God Ps 63:11 8055
of the morning and evening to r Ps 65:8 7442
the little hills r on every side Ps 65:12 1524
there did we r in him Ps 66:6 8055
let them r before God Ps 68:3 5970
yea, let them exceedingly r Ps 68:3 7797
by his name JAH, and r before him Ps 68:4 5937
Let all those that seek thee r Ps 70:4 7797
greatly r when I sing unto thee Ps 71:23 7442
that thy people may r in thee Ps 85:6 8055
R the soul of thy servant Ps 86:4 8055
and Hermon shall r in thy name Ps 89:12 7442
thy name shall they r all the day Ps 89:16 1523
hast made all his enemies to r Ps 89:42 8055
that we may r and be glad all our Ps 90:14 7442
Let the heavens r, and let the Ps 96:11 8056
shall all the trees of the wood r Ps 96:12 7442
let the earth r Ps 97:1 1523
R in the LORD, ye righteous Ps 97:12 8055
make a loud noise, and r, and sing Ps 98:4 7442
the LORD shall r in his works Ps 104:31 8055
of them r that seek the LORD Ps 105:3 8055
that I may r in the gladness of Ps 106:5 8055
The righteous shall see it, and r Ps 107:42 8055
I will r, I will divide Shechem, Ps 108:7 5937
but let thy servant r Ps 109:28 8055
we will r and be glad in it Ps 118:24 1523
I r at thy word, as one that Ps 119:162 7797
Let Israel r in him that made him Ps 149:2 8055
Who r to do evil, and delight in Prov 2:14 8056
r with the wife of thy youth Prov 5:18 8055
heart be wise, my heart shall r Prov 23:15 8055
Yea, my reins shall r, when thy Prov 23:16 5937
of the righteous shall greatly r Prov 23:24 1523
and she that bare thee shall r Prov 23:25 1523
R not when thine enemy falleth, Prov 24:17 8055
Ointment and perfume r the heart Prov 27:9 8055
When righteous men do r, there is Prov 28:12 5970
are in authority, the people r Prov 29:2 8055
but the righteous doth sing and r Prov 29:6 8055
she shall r in time to come Prov 31:25 7832
good in them, but for a man to r Eccl 3:12 8055
a man should r in his own works Eccl 3:22 8055
come after shall not r in him Eccl 4:16 8055
portion, and to r in his labour Eccl 5:19 8055
live many years, and r in them all Eccl 11:8 8055
R, O young man, in thy youth Eccl 11:9 8055
r in thee, we will remember thy Song 1:4 8055
r in Rezin and Remaliah's son Is 8:6 4885
as men r when they divide the Is 9:3 1523
even them that r in my highness Is 13:3 5947
Yea, the fir trees r at thee Is 14:8 8055
R not thou, whole Palestina, Is 14:29 8055
And he said, Thou shalt no more r Is 23:12 5937
the noise of them that r endeth Is 24:8 5947
be glad and r in his salvation Is 25:9 8055
the poor among men shall r in the Is 29:19 1523
and the desert shall r, and blossom Is 35:1 1523
r even with joy and singing Is 35:2 1523
thou shalt r in the LORD, and Is 41:16 1523
they shall r in their portion Is 61:7 7442
I will greatly r in the LORD Is 61:10 7797
so shall thy God r over thee Is 62:5 7797
behold, my servants shall r Is 65:13 8055
r for ever in that which I create Is 65:18 1523
I will r in Jerusalem, and joy in Is 65:19 1523
R ye with Jerusalem, and be glad Is 66:10 8055
r for joy with her, all ye that Is 66:10 7797
ye see this, your heart shall r Is 66:14 7797
shall the virgin r in the dance Jer 31:13 8057
make them r from their sorrow Jer 31:13 8057
I will r over them to do them Jer 32:41 7797
them drunken, that they may r Jer 51:39 5937
caused thine enemy to r over thee Lam 2:17 8055
R and be glad, O daughter of Edom, Lam 4:21 7797
let not the buyer r, nor the Eze 7:12 8055
As thou didst r at the Eze 35:15 8057
R not, O Israel, for joy, as Hos 9:1 8055
be glad and r Joel 2:21 8055
Zion, and r in the LORD your God Joel 2:23 8055
Ye which r in a thing of nought, Amos 6:13 8055
R not against me, O mine enemy Mic 7:8 8056
therefore they r and are glad Hab 1:15 8055
Yet I will r in the LORD, I will Hab 3:18 5937
of thee them that r in thy pride Zeph 3:11 5947
r with all the heart, O daughter Zeph 3:14 5937
he will r over thee with joy Zeph 3:17 7797
Sing and r, O daughter of Zion Zec 2:10 8055
for they shall r, and shall see Zec 4:10 8055
R greatly, O daughter of Zion Zec 9:9 1523
heart shall r as through wine Zec 10:7 8055
their heart shall r in the LORD Zec 10:7 1523
R, and be exceeding glad Mt 5:12 5463
many shall r at his birth Lk 1:14 5463
R ye in that day, and leap for joy Lk 6:23 5463
Notwithstanding in this r not Lk 10:20 5463
but rather r, because your names Lk 10:20 5463
saying unto them, R with me Lk 15:6 4796
together, saying, R with me Lk 15:9 4796
of the disciples began to r Lk 19:37 5463
and he that reapeth may r together Jn 4:36 5463
for a season to r in his light Jn 5:35 21
If ye loved me, ye would r Jn 14:28 5463
and lament, but the world shall r Jn 16:20 5463
you again, and your heart shall r Jn 16:22 5463
Therefore did my heart r, and my Acts 2:26 2165
r in hope of the glory of God Rom 5:2 2744
R with them that do r Rom 12:15 5463
And again he saith, R, ye Gentiles Rom 15:10 2165
and they that r, as though they 1Cor 7:30 5463
all the members r with it 1Cor 12:26 4796
from them of whom I ought to r 2Cor 2:3 5463
Now I r, not that ye were made 2Cor 7:9 5463
I r therefore that I have 2Cor 7:16 5463
For it is written, R, thou barren Gal 4:27 2165
do r, yea, and will r Phil 1:18 5463
that I may r in the day of Christ Phil 2:16 2745
faith, I joy, and r with you all Phil 2:17 4796
also do ye joy, and r with me Phil 2:18 4796
when ye see him again, ye may r Phil 2:28 5463
my brethren, r in the Lord Phil 3:1 5463
r in Christ Jesus, and have no Phil 3:3 2744
R in the Lord alway Phil 4:4 5463
and again I say, R Phil 4:4 5463
Who now r in my sufferings for Col 1:24 5463
R evermore 1Th 5:16 5463
degree r in that he is exalted Jas 1:9 2744
But now ye r in your boastings Jas 4:16 2744
Wherein ye greatly r, though now 1Pet 1:6 21
ye r with joy unspeakable and full 1Pet 1:8 21
But r, inasmuch as ye are 1Pet 4:13 5463
upon the earth shall r over them Rev 11:10 5463
Therefore r, ye heavens, and ye Rev 12:12 2165
R over her, thou heaven, and ye Rev 18:20 2165
Let us be glad and r, and give Rev 19:7 21

REJOICED
Jethro r for all the goodness Ex 18:9 2302
that as the LORD r over you to do Deut 28:63 7797
good, as he r over thy fathers Deut 30:9 7797
damsel saw him, he r to meet him Judg 19:3 8055
and saw the ark, and r to see it 1Sa 6:13 8055
all the men of Israel r greatly 1Sa 11:15 8055
r with great joy, so that the 1Kin 1:40 8056
of Solomon, that he r greatly 1Kin 5:7 8055
and all the people of the land r 2Kin 11:14 8056
And all the people of the land r 2Kin 11:20 8055
Then the people r, for that they 1Chr 29:9 8055
the king also r with great joy 1Chr 29:9 8055
And all Judah r at the oath 2Chr 15:15 8055
and all the people of the land r 2Chr 23:13 8056
And all the people of the land r 2Chr 23:21 8055
the princes and all the people r 2Chr 24:10 8055
And Hezekiah r, and all the people, 2Chr 29:36 8055
Israel, and that dwelt in Judah, r 2Chr 30:25 8055
offered great sacrifices, and r Neh 12:43 8055
the wives also and the children r Neh 12:43 8055
for Judah r for the priests and Neh 12:44 8057
and the city of Shushan r and was Est 8:15 6670
If I r because my wealth was Job 31:25 8055
If I r at the destruction of him Job 31:29 8055
But in mine adversity they r Ps 35:15 8055
the daughters of Judah r because Ps 97:8 1523
I have r in the way of thy Ps 119:14 7797
for my heart r in all my labour Eccl 2:10 8055
assembly of the mockers, nor r Jer 15:17 5937
ye were glad, because ye r Jer 50:11 5937
r in heart with all thy despite Eze 25:6 8055
the priests thereof that r on it Hos 10:5 1523
neither shouldest thou have r Obad 12 8055
they r with exceeding great joy Mt 2:10 5463
my spirit hath r in God my Lk 1:47 21
and they r with her Lk 1:58 4796
In that hour Jesus r in spirit Lk 10:21 21
all the people r for all the Lk 13:17 5463
father Abraham r to see my day Jn 8:56 21
r in the works of their own hands Acts 7:41 2165
they r for the consolation Acts 15:31 5463
he set meat before them, and r Acts 16:34 21
rejoice, as though they r not 1Cor 7:30 5463
so that I r the more 2Cor 7:7 5463
But I r in the Lord greatly, that Phil 4:10 5463
I r greatly that I found of thy 2Jn 4 5463
For I r greatly, when the 3Jn 3 5463

REJOICEST
when thou doest evil, then thou r Jer 11:15 5937

REJOICETH
My heart r in the LORD, mine horn 1Sa 2:1 5970
the valley, and r in his strength Job 39:21 7797
my heart is glad, and my glory r Ps 16:9 1523
r as a strong man to run a race Ps 19:5 7797
therefore my heart greatly r Ps 28:7 5937
with the righteous, the city r Prov 11:10 5970
The light of the righteous r Prov 13:9 8055
The light of the eyes r the heart Prov 15:30 8055
Whoso loveth wisdom r his father Prov 29:3 8055
and their pomp, and he that r Is 5:14 5938
the bridegroom r over the bride Is 62:5 4885
Thou meetest him that r and Is 64:5 7797
When the whole earth r, I will Eze 35:14 8055
he r more of that sheep, than of Mt 18:13 5463
him, r greatly because of the Jn 3:29 5463
R not in iniquity 1Cor 13:6 5463
but r in the truth 1Cor 13:6 4796
and mercy r against judgment Jas 2:13 2620

REJOICING
and they are come up from thence r 1Kin 1:45 8056
in the law of Moses, with r 2Chr 23:18 8057
with laughing, and thy lips with r Job 8:21 8643
the LORD are right, r the heart Ps 19:8 8055
and r shall they be brought Ps 45:15 1524
and declare his works with r Ps 107:22 7440
The voice of r and salvation is in Ps 118:15 7440
for they are the r of my heart Ps 119:111 8342
shall doubtless come again with r Ps 126:6 7440
his delight, r always before him Prov 8:30 7832
R in the habitable part of his Prov 8:31 7832
behold, I create Jerusalem a r Is 65:18 1525
me the joy and r of mine heart Jer 15:16 8057
their r was as to devour the poor Hab 3:14 5951
This is the r city that dwelt Zeph 2:15 5947
he layeth it on his shoulders, r Lk 15:5 5463
r that they were counted worthy Acts 5:41 5463
and he went on his way r Acts 8:39 5463
R in hope Rom 12:12 5463
I protest by your r which I have 1Cor 15:31 2746
For our r is this, the testimony 2Cor 1:12 2746
us in part, that we are your r 2Cor 1:14 2745
As sorrowful, yet alway r 2Cor 6:10 5463
shall he have r in himself alone Gal 6:4 2745
That your r may be more abundant Phil 1:26 2745
our hope, or joy, or crown of r 1Th 2:19 2746
the r of the hope firm unto the Heb 3:6 2745
all such r is evil Jas 4:16 2746

REKEM (re'-kem)
1. A prince of Midian.
namely, Evi, and R, and Zur, and Hur Num 31:8 7552
the princes of Midian, Evi, and R Josh 13:21 7552
2. A son of Hebron.
Korah, and Tappuah, and R 1Chr 2:43 7552
and R begat Shammai 1Chr 2:44 7552
3. A city in Benjamin.
And R, and Irpeel, and Taralah, Josh 18:27 7552

RELEASE
seven years thou shalt make a r Deut 15:1 8059
And this is the manner of the r Deut 15:2 8059
unto his neighbour shall r it Deut 15:2 8058
because it is called the LORD's r Deut 15:2 8059
thy brother thine hand shall r Deut 15:3 8058
The seventh year, the year of r Deut 15:9 8059
in the solemnity of the year of r Deut 31:10 8059

R

he made a *r* to the provinces, and... Est 2:18 2010
to *r* unto the people a prisoner... Mt 27:15 *630*
Whom will ye that I *r* unto you... Mt 27:17 *630*
twain will ye that I *r* unto you... Mt 27:21 *630*
Will ye that I *r* unto you the... Mk 15:9 *630*
rather *r* Barabbas unto them... Mk 15:11 *630*
therefore chastise him, and *r* him... Lk 23:16 *630*
(For of necessity he must *r* one... Lk 23:17 *630*
this man, and *r* unto us Barabbas... Lk 23:18 *630*
therefore, willing to *r* Jesus... Lk 23:20 *630*
that I should *r* unto you one at... Jn 18:39 *630*
will ye therefore that I *r* unto... Jn 18:39 *630*
thee, and have power to *r* thee... Jn 19:10 *630*
Pilate sought to *r* him... Jn 19:12 *630*

RELEASED
Then *r* he Barabbas unto them... Mt 27:26 *630*
Now at that feast he *r* unto them... Mk 15:6 *630*
people, *r* Barabbas unto them, and... Mk 15:15 *630*
he *r* unto them him that for... Lk 23:25 *630*

RELIED
because they *r* upon the LORD God... 2Chr 13:18 8172
Because thou hast *r* on the king... 2Chr 16:7 8172
not *r* on the LORD thy God,... 2Chr 16:7 8172

RELIEF
determined to send *r* unto the... Acts 11:29 *1248*

RELIEVE
then thou shalt *r* him... Lev 25:35 2388
r the oppressed, judge the... Is 1:17 833
things for meat to *r* the soul... Lam 1:11 7725
should *r* my soul is far from me... Lam 1:16 7725
their meat to *r* their souls... Lam 1:19 7725
have widows, let them *r* them... 1Ti 5:16 *1884*
that it may *r* them that are... 1Ti 5:16 *1884*

RELIEVED
if she have *r* the afflicted, if... 1Ti 5:10 *1884*

RELIEVETH
he *r* the fatherless and widow... Ps 146:9 5749

RELIGION
sect of our *r* I lived a Pharisee... Acts 26:5 *2356*
in time past in the Jews' *r*... Gal 1:13 *2454*
profited in the Jews' *r* above... Gal 1:14 *2454*
own heart, this man's *r* is vain... Jas 1:26 *2356*
Pure *r* and undefiled before God and... Jas 1:27 *2356*

RELIGIOUS
r proselytes followed Paul and... Acts 13:43 *4576*
If any man among you seem to be *r*... Jas 1:26 *2357*

RELY
because thou didst *r* on the LORD... 2Chr 16:8 8172

REMAIN
R a widow at thy father's house,... Gen 38:11 3427
that they may *r* in the river only... Ex 8:9 7604
they shall *r* in the river only... Ex 8:11 7604
nothing of it *r* until the morning... Ex 12:10 3498
my sacrifice *r* until the morning... Ex 23:18 3885
r unto the morning, then thou... Ex 29:34 3498
if ought *r* until the third day,... Lev 19:6 3498
r in the hand of him that hath... Lev 25:28 1961
if there *r* but few years unto the... Lev 25:52 7604
according to the years that *r*... Lev 27:18 3498
that those which ye let *r* of them... Num 33:55 3498
of every city, we left none to *r*... Deut 2:34 8300
r all night until the morning... Deut 16:4 3885
And those which *r* shall hear... Deut 19:20 7604
shall *r* in thine house, and bewail... Deut 21:13 3427
His body shall not *r* all night... Deut 21:23 3885
shall *r* in the land which Moses... Josh 1:14 3427
neither did there *r* any more... Josh 2:11 6965
they let none of them *r* or escape... Josh 8:22 8300
which *r* until this very day... Josh 10:27
he let none *r*... Josh 10:28 8300
he let none *r* in it... Josh 10:30 8300
you by lot these nations that *r*... Josh 23:4 7604
nations, these that *r* among you... Josh 23:7 7604
even these that *r* among you... Josh 23:12 7604
and why did Dan *r* in ships... Judg 5:17 1481
we do for wives for them that *r*... Judg 21:7 3498
we do for wives for them that *r*... Judg 21:16 3498
shalt *r* by the stone Ezel... 1Sa 20:19 3427
did Joab *r* there with all Israel... 1Kin 11:16 3427
I only, *r* a prophet of the LORD... 1Kin 18:22 3498
thee, five of the horses that *r*... 2Kin 7:13 7604
for we *r* yet escaped, as it is... Ezr 9:15 7604
the grave, and shall *r* in the tomb... Job 21:32 8245
Those that *r* of him shall be... Job 27:15 8300
into dens, and *r* in their places... Job 37:8 7931
far off, and *r* in the wilderness... Ps 55:7 3885
and the perfect shall *r* in it... Prov 2:21 3498
the way of understanding shall *r*... Prov 21:16 5117
As yet shall he *r* at Nob that day... Is 10:32 5975
righteousness *r* in the fruitful... Is 32:16 3427
that it may *r* in the house... Is 44:13 3427
Which *r* among the graves, and... Is 65:4 3427
shall *r* before me, saith the LORD... Is 66:22 5975
so shall your seed and your name *r*... Is 66:22 5975
them that *r* of this evil family... Jer 8:3 7604
which *r* in all the places whither... Jer 8:3 7604
and this city shall *r* for ever... Jer 17:25 3427
that *r* in this land, and them that... Jer 24:8 7604
those will I let *r* still in their... Jer 27:11 3241
the vessels that *r* in this city... Jer 27:19 3498
that *r* in the house of the LORD... Jer 27:21 3498
the palace shall *r* after the... Jer 30:18 3427
men of war that *r* in this city... Jer 38:4 7604
none of them shall *r* or escape... Jer 42:17 8300
of Judah, to leave you none to *r*... Jer 44:7 7611
sojourn there, shall escape or *r*... Jer 44:14 8300
it off, that none shall *r* in it... Jer 51:62 3427
none of them shall *r*, nor of... Eze 7:11
they that *r* shall be scattered... Eze 17:21 7604
all the fowls of the heaven *r*... Eze 31:13 7931
of the heaven to *r* upon thee... Eze 32:4 7931
that *r* upon the face of the earth... Eze 39:14 3498
if there *r* ten men in one house,... Amos 6:9 3498
that did *r* in the day of distress... Obad 14 8300
it shall *r* in the midst of his... Zec 5:4 3885
All the families that *r*, every... Zec 12:14 7604
And in the same house *r*, eating and... Lk 10:7 *3306*
Gather up the fragments that *r*... Jn 6:12 *4052*
you, that my joy might *r* in you... Jn 15:11 *3306*
and that your fruit should *r*... Jn 15:16 *3306*
that the bodies should not *r* upon... Jn 19:31 *3306*
let her *r* unmarried, or be... 1Cor 7:11 *3306*
greater part *r* unto this present... 1Cor 15:6 *3306*
r unto the coming of the Lord... 1Th 4:15 *4035*
r shall be caught up together... 1Th 4:17 *4035*
which cannot be shaken may *r*... Heb 12:27 *3306*
from the beginning shall *r* in you... 1Jn 2:24 *3306*
and strengthen the things which *r*... Rev 3:2 *3062*

REMAINDER
thou shalt burn the *r* with fire... Ex 29:34 3498
the *r* thereof shall Aaron and his... Lev 6:16 3498
also the *r* of it shall be eaten... Lev 7:16 3498
But the *r* of the flesh of the... Lev 7:17 3498
neither name nor *r* upon the earth... 2Sa 14:7 7611
the *r* of wrath shalt thou... Ps 76:10 7611

REMAINED
and Noah only *r* alive, and they... Gen 7:23 7604
they that *r* fled to the mountain... Gen 14:10 7604
there *r* not one... Ex 8:31 7604
there *r* not any green thing in... Ex 10:15 3498
there *r* not one locust in all the... Ex 10:19 7604
there *r* not so much as one of... Ex 14:28 7604
But there *r* two of the men in the... Num 11:26 7604
Because he should have *r* in the... Num 35:28 3427
their inheritance *r* in the tribe... Num 36:12 1961
Bashan *r* of the remnant of giants... Deut 3:11 7604
ye shall have *r* long in the land,... Deut 4:25 3462
that the rest which *r* of them... Josh 10:20 8277
in Gath, and in Ashdod, there *r*... Josh 11:22 7604
who *r* of the remnant of the... Josh 13:12 7604
there *r* among the children of... Josh 18:2 3498
the Levites which *r* of the... Josh 21:20 3498
of the children of Kohath that *r*... Josh 21:26 3498
and there *r* ten thousand... Judg 7:3 7604
that they which *r* were scattered... 1Sa 11:11 7604
r in a mountain in the wilderness... 1Sa 23:14 3427
his men *r* in the sides of the... 1Sa 24:3 3427
So Tamar *r* desolate in her... 2Sa 13:20 3427
which *r* in the days of his father... 1Kin 22:46 7604
So Jehu slew all that *r* of the... 2Kin 10:11 7604
he slew all that *r* unto Ahab in... 2Kin 10:17 7604
there *r* the grove also in Samaria... 2Kin 13:6 5975
none *r*, save the poorest sort of... 2Kin 24:14 7604
that *r* in the land of Judah... 2Kin 25:22 7604
the ark of God *r* with the family... 1Chr 13:14 3427
also my wisdom *r* with me... Eccl 2:9 5975
cities *r* of the cities of Judah... Jer 34:7 7604
there *r* but wounded men among... Jer 37:10 7604
Jeremiah had *r* there many days... Jer 37:16 3427
Thus Jeremiah *r* in the court of... Jer 37:21 3427
Jeremiah *r* in the court of the... Jer 38:13 3427
of the people that *r* in the city... Jer 39:9 7604
the rest of the people that *r*... Jer 39:9 7604
all the people that *r* in Mizpah... Jer 41:10 7604
therefore his taste *r* in him... Jer 48:11 5975
they have *r* in their holds... Jer 51:30 3427
of the people that *r* in the city... Jer 52:15 7604
LORD's anger none escaped nor *r*... Lam 2:22 8300
r there astonished among them... Eze 3:15 3427
there *r* no strength in me... Dan 10:8 7604
I *r* there with the kings of... Dan 10:13 3498
there *r* no strength in me... Dan 10:17 5975
it would have *r* until this day... Mt 11:23 *3306*
that *r* twelve baskets full... Mt 14:20 *4052*
unto them, and *r* speechless... Lk 1:22 *1265*
that *r* to them twelve baskets... Lk 9:17 *4052*
five barley loaves, which *r* over... Jn 6:13 *4052*
Whiles it *r*, was it not thine own... Acts 5:4 *3306*
r unmoveable, but the hinder part... Acts 27:41 *3306*

REMAINEST
Thou, O LORD, *r* for ever... Lam 5:19 3427
but thou *r*... Heb 1:11 *1265*

REMAINETH
While the earth *r*, seedtime and... Gen 8:22 3117
which *r* unto you from the hail,... Ex 10:5 7604
that which *r* of it until the... Ex 12:10 3498
that which *r* over lay up for you... Ex 16:23 5736
the remnant that *r* of the... Ex 26:12 5736
the tent, the half curtain that *r*... Ex 26:12 5736
r in the length of the curtains... Ex 26:13 5736
that which *r* of the flesh and of... Lev 8:32 3498
Take the meat offering that *r* of... Lev 10:12 3498
that *r* among them in the midst of... Lev 16:16 7931
destroy him that *r* of the city... Num 24:19 8300
of stones, that *r* unto this day... Josh 8:29
there *r* yet very much land to be... Josh 13:1 7604
This is the land that yet *r*... Josh 13:2 7604
Then he made him that *r* have... Judg 5:13 8300
which stone *r* unto this day in... 1Sa 6:18
There *r* yet the youngest, and,... 1Sa 16:11 7604
of the LORD *r* under curtains... 1Chr 17:1
whosoever *r* in any place where he... Ezr 1:4 7604
erred, mine error *r* with myself... Job 19:4 3885
in your answers there *r* falsehood... Job 21:34 7604
In his neck *r* strength, and sorrow... Job 41:22 3885
he that *r* in Jerusalem, shall be... Is 4:3 3498
He that *r* in this city shall die... Jer 38:2 3427
and Zidon every helper that *r*... Jer 47:4 8300
and he that *r* and is besieged shall... Eze 6:12 7604
Egypt, so my spirit *r* among you... Hag 2:5 5975
but he that *r*, even he, shall be... Zec 9:7 7604
therefore your sin *r*... Jn 9:41 *3306*
it *r*, that both they that have... 1Cor 7:29
more that which *r* is glorious... 2Cor 3:11 *3306*
for until this day *r* the same... 2Cor 3:14 *3306*
his righteousness *r* for ever... 2Cor 9:9 *3306*
Seeing therefore it *r* that some... Heb 4:6 *620*
There *r* therefore a rest to the... Heb 4:9 *620*
there *r* no more sacrifice for... Heb 10:26 *620*
for his seed *r* in him... 1Jn 3:9 *3306*

REMAINING
r thereon, the children of Israel... Num 9:22 7931
him until none was left to him *r*... Deut 3:3 8300
until he had left him none *r*... Josh 10:33 8300
he left none *r*, according to all... Josh 10:37 8300
he left none *r*... Josh 10:39 8300
he left none *r*, but utterly... Josh 10:40 8300
them, until they left them none *r*... Josh 11:8 8300
which were *r* of the families of... Josh 21:40 3498
we should be destroyed from *r* in... 2Sa 21:5 3320
priests, until he left him none *r*... 2Kin 10:11 8300
who *r* in the chambers were free... 1Chr 9:33
nor any *r* in his dwellings... Job 18:19 8300
not be any *r* of the house of Esau... Obad 18 8300
r on him, the same is he which... Jn 1:33 *3306*

REMALIAH (*rem-a-li'-ah*) See REMALIAH'S. *Father of Pekah.*
But Pekah the son of *R*, a captain... 2Kin 15:25 7425
R began to reign over Israel in... 2Kin 15:27 7425
against Pekah the son of *R*... 2Kin 15:30 7425
R king of Israel began Jotham the... 2Kin 15:32 7425
of Syria, and Pekah the son of *R*... 2Kin 15:37 7425
year of Pekah the son of *R* Ahaz... 2Kin 16:1 7425
Pekah son of *R* king of Israel... 2Kin 16:5 7425
For Pekah the son of *R* slew in... 2Chr 28:6 7425
of Syria, and Pekah the son of *R*... Is 7:1 7425
with Syria, and of the son of *R*... Is 7:4 7425
Syria, Ephraim, and the son of *R*... Is 7:5 7425

REMALIAH'S (*rem-a-li'-ahs*)
and the head of Samaria is *R* son... Is 7:9 7425
and rejoice in Rezin and *R* son... Is 8:6 7425

REMEDY
his people, till there was no *r*... 2Chr 36:16 4832
shall he be broken without *r*... Prov 6:15 4832
be destroyed, and that without *r*... Prov 29:1 4832

REMEMBER
I will *r* my covenant, which is... Gen 9:15 2142
that I may *r* the everlasting... Gen 9:16 2142
did not the chief butler *r* Joseph... Gen 40:23 2142
I do *r* my faults this day... Gen 41:9 2142
R this day, in which ye came out... Ex 13:3 2142
R the sabbath day, to keep it... Ex 20:8 2142
R Abraham, Isaac, and Israel, thy... Ex 32:13 2142
Then will I *r* my covenant with... Lev 26:42 2142
my covenant with Abraham will I *r*... Lev 26:42 2142
and I will *r* the land... Lev 26:42 2142
But I will for their sakes *r* the... Lev 26:45 2142
We *r* the fish, which we did eat... Num 11:5 2142
r all the commandments of the... Num 15:39 2142
That ye may *r*, and do all my... Num 15:40 2142
r that thou wast a servant in the... Deut 5:15 2142
but shalt well *r* what the LORD... Deut 7:18 2142
thou shalt *r* all the way which... Deut 8:2 2142
But thou shalt *r* the LORD thy God... Deut 8:18 2142
R, and forget not, how thou... Deut 9:7 2142
R thy servants, Abraham, Isaac,... Deut 9:27 2142
thou shalt *r* that thou wast a... Deut 15:15 2142
that thou mayest *r* the day when... Deut 16:3 2142
thou shalt *r* that thou wast a... Deut 16:12 2142
R what the LORD thy God did unto... Deut 24:9 2142
But thou shalt *r* that thou wast a... Deut 24:18 2142
thou shalt *r* that thou wast a... Deut 24:22 2142
R what Amalek did unto thee by... Deut 25:17 2142
R the days of old, consider the... Deut 32:7 2142
R the word which Moses the... Josh 1:13 2142
r also that I am your bone and... Judg 9:2 2142
r me, I pray thee, and strengthen... Judg 16:28 2142
r me, and not forget thine... 1Sa 1:11 2142
I *r* that which Amalek did to... 1Sa 15:2 6485
my lord, then *r* thine handmaid... 1Sa 25:31 2142
let the king *r* the LORD thy God,... 2Sa 14:11 2142
neither do thou *r* that which thy... 2Sa 19:19 2142
for *r* how that, when I and thou... 2Kin 9:25 2142
r now how I have walked before... 2Kin 20:3 2142
R his marvellous works that he... 1Chr 16:12 2142
r the mercies of David thy... 2Chr 6:42 2142
R, I beseech thee, the word that... Neh 1:8 2142
r the LORD, which is great and... Neh 4:14 2142
R me, O my God, concerning this,... Neh 13:14 2142
R me, O my God, concerning this... Neh 13:22 2142
R them, O my God, because they... Neh 13:29 2142
R me, O my God, for good... Neh 13:31 2142
R, I pray thee, who ever perished... Job 4:7 2142
O *r* that my life is wind... Job 7:7 2142
R, I beseech thee, that thou hast... Job 10:9 2142
r it as waters that pass away... Job 11:16 2142
appoint me a set time, and *r* me... Job 14:13 2142
Even when I *r* I am afraid... Job 21:6 2142
R that thou magnify his work,... Job 36:24 2142
him, *r* the battle, do no more... Job 41:8 2142
R all thy offerings, and accept... Ps 20:3 2142
but we will *r* the name of the... Ps 20:7 2142
All the ends of the world shall *r*... Ps 22:27 2142
R, O LORD, thy tender mercies and... Ps 25:6 2142
R not the sins of my youth, nor... Ps 25:7 2142
according to thy mercy *r* thou me... Ps 25:7 2142
When I *r* these things, I pour out... Ps 42:4 2142
therefore will I *r* thee from the... Ps 42:6 2142
When I *r* thee upon my bed, and... Ps 63:6 2142
R thy congregation, which thou... Ps 74:2 2142
R this, that the enemy hath... Ps 74:18 2142
r how the foolish man reproacheth... Ps 74:22 2142

but I will r the years of the... Ps 77:10 2142
I will r the works of the LORD... Ps 77:11 2142
surely I will r thy wonders of... Ps 77:11 2142
O r not against us former... Ps 79:8 2142
R how short my time is... Ps 89:47 2142
R, Lord, the reproach of thy... Ps 89:50 2142
to those that r his commandments... Ps 103:18 2142
R his marvellous works that he... Ps 105:5 2142
R me, O LORD, with the favour... Ps 106:4 2142
R the word unto thy servant, upon... Ps 119:49 2142
r David, and all his afflictions... Ps 132:1 2142
If I do not r thee, let my tongue... Ps 137:6 2142
R, O LORD, the children of Edom... Ps 137:7 2142
I r the days of old... Ps 143:5 2142
poverty, and r his misery no more... Prov 31:7 2142
not much r the days of his life... Eccl 5:20 2142
yet let him r the days of... Eccl 11:8 2142
R now thy Creator in the days of... Eccl 12:1 2142
we will r thy love more than wine... Song 1:4 2142
R now, O LORD, I beseech thee,... Is 38:3 2142
R ye not the former things,... Is 43:18 2142
own sake, and will not r thy sins... Is 43:25 2142
R these, O Jacob and Israel... Is 44:21 2142
R this, and shew yourselves men... Is 46:8 2142
R the former things of old... Is 46:9 2142
neither didst r the latter end of... Is 47:7 2142
shalt not r the reproach of thy... Is 54:4 2142
those that r thee in thy ways... Is 64:5 2142
neither r iniquity for ever... Is 64:9 2142
I r thee, the kindness of thy... Jer 2:2 2142
neither shall they r it... Jer 3:16 2142
he will now r their iniquity, and... Jer 14:10 2142
r, break not thy covenant with us... Jer 14:21 2142
r me, and visit me, and revenge me... Jer 15:15 2142
their children r their altars... Jer 17:2 2142
R that I stood before thee to... Jer 18:20 2142
him, I do earnestly r him still... Jer 31:20 2142
I will r their sin no more... Jer 31:34 2142
the land, did not the LORD r them... Jer 44:21 2142
r the LORD afar off, and let... Jer 51:50 2142
R, O LORD, what is come upon us... Lam 5:1 2142
r me among the nations whither... Eze 6:9 2142
Nevertheless I will r my covenant... Eze 16:60 2142
Then thou shalt r thy ways... Eze 16:61 2142
That thou mayest r, and be... Eze 16:63 2142
And there shall ye r your ways... Eze 20:43 2142
unto them, nor r Egypt any more... Eze 23:27 2142
Then shall ye r your own evil... Eze 36:31 2142
that I r all their wickedness... Hos 7:2 2142
now will he r their iniquity, and... Hos 8:13 2142
he will r their iniquity, he will... Hos 9:9 2142
r now what Balak king of Moab... Mic 6:5 2142
in wrath r mercy... Hab 3:2 2142
they shall r me in far countries... Zec 10:9 2142
R ye the law of Moses my servant,... Mal 4:4 2142
neither r the five loaves of the... Mt 16:9 3421
we r that that deceiver said,... Mt 27:63 3415
and do ye not r... Mk 8:18 3421
and to r his holy covenant... Lk 1:72 3415
r that thou in thy lifetime... Lk 16:25 3415
R Lot's wife... Lk 17:32 3421
r me when thou comest into thy... Lk 23:42 3415
r how he spake unto you when he... Lk 24:6 3415
R the word that I said unto you,... Jn 15:20 3421
ye may r that I told you of them... Jn 16:4 3421
Therefore watch, and r, that by... Acts 20:31 3421
to r the words of the Lord Jesus,... Acts 20:35 3421
that ye r me in all things, and... 1Cor 11:2 3415
would that we should r the poor... Gal 2:10 3421
Wherefore r, that ye being in... Eph 2:11 3421
R my bonds... Col 4:18 3421
For ye r, brethren, our labour and... 1Th 2:9 3421
R ye not, that, when I was yet... 2Th 2:5 3421
R that Jesus Christ of the seed... 2Ti 2:8 3421
their iniquities will I r no more... Heb 8:12 3415
and iniquities will I r no more... Heb 10:17 3415
R them that are in bonds, as... Heb 13:3 3403
R them which have the rule over... Heb 13:7 3421
I will r his deeds which he doeth... 3Jn 10 5279
r ye the words which were spoken... Jude 17 3415
R therefore from whence thou art... Rev 2:5 3421
R therefore how thou hast... Rev 3:3 3421

REMEMBERED

God r Noah, and every living thing... Gen 8:1 2142
of the plain, that God r Abraham... Gen 19:29 2142
God r Rachel, and God hearkened to... Gen 30:22 2142
Joseph r the dreams which he... Gen 42:9 2142
God r his covenant with Abraham,... Ex 2:24 2142
and I have r my covenant... Ex 6:5 2142
ye shall be r before the LORD... Num 10:9 2142
Israel r not the LORD their God... Judg 8:34 2142
and the LORD r her... 1Sa 1:19 2142
Thus Joash the king r not the... 2Chr 24:22 2142
he r Vashti, and what she had done... Est 2:1 2142
And that these days should be r... Est 9:28 2142
he shall be no more r... Job 24:20 2142
name to be r in all generations... Ps 45:17 2142
I r God, and was troubled... Ps 77:3 2142
they r that God was their rock,... Ps 78:35 2142
For he r that they were but flesh... Ps 78:39 2142
They r not his hand, nor the day... Ps 78:42 2142
He hath r his mercy and his truth... Ps 98:3 2142
He hath r his covenant for ever,... Ps 105:8 2142
For he r his holy promise, and... Ps 105:42 2142
they r not the multitude of thy... Ps 106:7 2142
he r for them his covenant, and... Ps 106:45 2142
of his fathers be r with the LORD... Ps 109:14 2142
Because that he r not to shew... Ps 109:16 2142
made his wonderful works to be r... Ps 111:4 2143
I r thy judgments of old, O LORD... Ps 119:52 2142
I have r thy name, O LORD, in the... Ps 119:55 2142
Who r us in our low estate... Ps 136:23 2142
yea, we wept, when we r Zion... Ps 137:1 2142
yet no man r that same poor man... Eccl 9:15 2142
many songs, that thou mayest be r... Is 23:16 2142
thou hast lied, and hast not r me... Is 57:11 2142
Then he r the days of old, Moses,... Is 63:11 2142
and the former shall not be r,... Is 65:17 2142
that his name may be no more r... Jer 11:19 2142
Jerusalem r in the days of her... Lam 1:7 2142
r not his footstool in the day of... Lam 2:1 2142
which he hath done shall not be r... Eze 3:20 2142
hast not r the days of thy youth... Eze 16:22 2142
hast not r the days of thy youth... Eze 16:43 2142
have made your iniquity to be r... Eze 21:24 2142
thou shalt be no more r... Eze 21:32 2142
may not be r among the nations... Eze 25:10 2142
righteousnesses shall not be r... Eze 33:13 2142
shall no more be r by their name... Hos 2:17 2142
r not the brotherly covenant... Amos 1:9 2142
fainted within me I r the LORD... Jonah 2:7 2142
land, and they shall no more be r... Zec 13:2 2142
Peter r the word of Jesus, which... Mt 26:75 3415
Peter r the word of the Lord, how... Lk 22:61 5279
And they r his words,... Lk 24:8 3415
his disciples r that it was... Jn 2:17 3415
his disciples r that he had said... Jn 2:22 3415
then r they that these things... Jn 12:16 3415
Then r I the word of the Lord,... Acts 11:16 3415
God hath r her iniquities... Rev 18:5 3421

REMEMBEREST

in the grave, whom thou r no more... Ps 88:5 2142
there r that thy brother hath... Mt 5:23 3415

REMEMBERETH

inquisition for blood, he r them... Ps 9:12 2142
he r that we are dust... Ps 103:14 2142
she r not her last end... Lam 1:9 2142
she r no more the anguish, for... Jn 16:21 3421
whilst he r the obedience of you... 2Cor 7:15 363

REMEMBERING

R mine affliction and my misery,... Lam 3:19 2142
R without ceasing your work of... 1Th 1:3 3421

REMEMBRANCE

the r of Amalek from under heaven... Ex 17:14 2143
memorial, bringing iniquity to r... Num 5:15 2142
the r of Amalek from under heaven... Deut 25:19 2143
I would make the r of them to... Deut 32:26 2143
have no son to keep my name in r... 2Sa 18:18 2142
come unto me to call my sin to r... 1Kin 17:18 2142
His r shall perish from the earth... Job 18:17 2143
in death there is no r of thee... Ps 6:5 2143
thanks at the r of his holiness... Ps 30:4 2143
to cut off the r of them from the... Ps 34:16 2143
A Psalm of David, to bring to r... Ps 38:t 2142
A Psalm of David, to bring to r... Ps 70:t 2142
I call to r my song in the night... Ps 77:6 2142
of Israel may be no more in r... Ps 83:4 2142
thanks at the r of his holiness... Ps 97:12 2143
thy r unto all generations... Ps 102:12 2143
shall be in everlasting r... Ps 112:6 2143
There is no r of former things... Eccl 1:11 2146
neither shall there be any r of... Eccl 1:11 2146
For there is no r of the wise... Eccl 2:16 2146
to thy name, and to the r of thee... Is 26:8 2143
Put me in r... Is 43:26 2142
the posts hast thou set up thy r... Is 57:8 2146
My soul hath them still in r... Lam 3:20 2142
he will call to r the iniquity... Eze 21:23 2142
I say, that ye are come to r... Eze 21:24 2142
in calling to r the days of her... Eze 23:19 2142
Thus thou calledst to r the... Eze 23:21 6485
bringeth their iniquity to r... Eze 29:16 2142
a book of r was written before... Mal 3:16 2146
Peter calling to r saith unto him... Mk 11:21 364
servant Israel, in r of his mercy... Lk 1:54 3415
this do in r of me... Lk 22:19 364
and bring all things to your r... Jn 14:26 5279
are had in r in the sight of God... Acts 10:31 3415
who shall bring you into r of my... 1Cor 4:17 363
this do in r of me... 1Cor 11:24 364
as oft as ye drink it, in r of me... 1Cor 11:25 364
thank my God upon every r of you... Phil 1:3 3417
that ye have good r of us always... 1Th 3:6 3417
the brethren in r of these things... 1Ti 4:6 5294
r of thee in my prayers night... 2Ti 1:3 3417
When I call to r the unfeigned... 2Ti 1:5 5280
Wherefore I put thee in r that... 2Ti 1:6 363
Of these things put them in r... 2Ti 2:14 5279
a r again made of sins every year... Heb 10:3 364
But call to r the former days, in... Heb 10:32 363
you always in r of these things... 2Pet 1:12 5179
stir you up by putting you in r... 2Pet 1:13 5280
to have these things always in r... 2Pet 1:15 3418
up your pure minds by way of r... 2Pet 3:1 5280
I will therefore put you in r... Jude 5 5179
Babylon came in r before God... Rev 16:19 3415

REMEMBRANCES

Your r are like unto ashes, your... Job 13:12 2146

REMETH (*re'-meth*) See RAMOTH, JARMUTH. *A Levitical city in Issachar.*

And R, and En-gannim... Josh 19:21 7432

REMISSION

shed for many for the r of sins... Mt 26:28 859
of repentance for the r of sins... Mk 1:4 859
his people by the r of their sins... Lk 1:77 859
of repentance for the r of sins... Lk 3:3 859
r of sins should be preached in... Lk 24:47 859
of Jesus Christ for the r of sins... Acts 2:38 859
in him shall receive r of sins... Acts 10:43 859
for the r of sins that are past... Rom 3:25 3929
without shedding of blood is no r... Heb 9:22 859
Now where r of these is, there is... Heb 10:18 859

REMIT

Whose soever sins ye r, they are... Jn 20:23 863

REMITTED

ye remit, they are r unto them... Jn 20:23 863

REMMON (*rem'-mon*) See RIMMON. *A city in Judah.*

Ain, R, and Ether, and Ashan... Josh 19:7 7417

REMMON-METHOAR (*rem''-mon-meth'-o-ar*) *A city in Zebulun.*

and goeth out to R to Neah... Josh 19:13 7417

REMNANT

the r that remaineth of the... Ex 26:12 5629
the r of the meat offerings shall... Lev 2:3 3498
the r shall be the priest's, as a... Lev 5:13
the r of the oil that is in the... Lev 14:18 3498
remained of the r of giants... Deut 3:11 3499
toward the r of his children... Deut 28:54 3499
which was of the r of the giants... Josh 12:4 3499
remained of the r of the giants... Josh 13:12 3499
cleave unto the r of these... Josh 23:12 3499
but of the r of the Amorites... 2Sa 21:2 3499
to the r of the people, saying,... 1Kin 12:23 3499
will take away the r of the house... 1Kin 14:10 310
the r of the sodomites, which... 1Kin 22:46 3499
prayer for the r that are left... 2Kin 19:4 7611
the r that is escaped of the... 2Kin 19:30 7604
of Jerusalem shall go forth a r... 2Kin 19:31 7611
I will forsake the r of mine... 2Kin 21:14 7611
with the r of the multitude, did... 2Kin 25:11 3499
of the r of the sons of Kohath... 1Chr 6:70 3498
and he will return to the r of you... 2Chr 30:6 7604
and of all the r of Israel... 2Chr 34:9 7611
the r of their brethren the... Ezr 3:8 7605
God, to leave us a r to escape... Ezr 9:8
there should be no r nor escaping... Ezr 9:14 7611
The r that are left of the... Neh 1:3 7604
but the r of them the fire... Job 22:20 3499
had left unto us a very small r... Is 1:9 8300
that the r of Israel, and such as... Is 10:20 7605
The r shall return, even the... Is 10:21 7605
shall return, even the r of Jacob... Is 10:21 7605
yet a r of them shall return... Is 10:22 7605
to recover the r of his people... Is 11:11 7605
highway for the r of his people... Is 11:16 7605
off from Babylon the name, and r... Is 14:22 7605
famine, and he shall slay thy r... Is 14:30 7611
Moab, and upon the r of the land... Is 15:9 7611
the r shall be very small and... Is 16:14 7605
from Damascus, and the r of Syria... Is 17:3 7605
thy prayer for the r that is left... Is 37:4 7611
the r that is escaped of the... Is 37:31 7604
of Jerusalem shall go forth a r... Is 37:32 7611
all the r of the house of Israel,... Is 46:3 7611
glean the r of Israel as a vine... Jer 6:9 7611
And there shall be no r of them... Jer 11:23 7611
it shall be well with thy r... Jer 15:11 8293
I will gather the r of my flock... Jer 23:3 7611
and Ekron, and the r of Ashdod,... Jer 25:20 7611
save thy people, the r of Israel... Jer 31:7 7611
away captive into Babylon the r... Jer 39:9 3499
of Babylon had left a r of Judah... Jer 40:11 7611
and the r in Judah perish... Jer 40:15 7611
all the r of the people whom he... Jer 41:16 7611
LORD thy God, even for all this r... Jer 42:2 7611
word of the LORD, ye r of Judah... Jer 42:15 7611
concerning you, O ye r of Judah... Jer 42:19 7611
forces, took all the r of Judah... Jer 43:5 7611
And I will take the r of Judah... Jer 44:12 7611
So that none of the r of Judah... Jer 44:14 7611
all the r of Judah, that are gone... Jer 44:28 7611
the r of the country of Caphtor... Jer 47:4 7611
off with the r of their valley... Jer 47:5 7611
the whole r of thee will I... Eze 5:10 7611
Yet will I leave a r, that ye may... Eze 6:8 3498
a full end of the r of Israel... Eze 11:13 7611
therein shall be left a r that... Eze 14:22 6413
thy r shall fall by the sword... Eze 23:25 319
destroy the r of the sea coast... Eze 25:16 7611
in the r whom the LORD shall call... Joel 2:32 8300
the r of the Philistines shall... Amos 1:8 7611
be gracious unto the r of Joseph... Amos 5:15 7611
they may possess the r of Edom... Amos 9:12 7611
surely gather the r of Israel... Mic 2:12 7611
I will make her that halted a r... Mic 4:7 7611
then the r of his brethren shall... Mic 5:3 3499
the r of Jacob shall be in the... Mic 5:7 7611
the r of Jacob shall be among the... Mic 5:8 7611
of the r of his heritage... Mic 7:18 7611
all the r of the people shall... Hab 2:8 3499
I will cut off the r of Baal from... Zeph 1:4 7605
for the r of the house of Judah... Zeph 2:7 7611
the r of my people shall possess... Zeph 2:9 3499
The r of Israel shall not do... Zeph 3:13 7611
with all the r of the people,... Hag 1:12 7611
spirit of all the r of the people... Hag 1:14 7611
r of this people in these days... Zec 8:6 7611
I will cause the r of this people... Zec 8:12 7611
the r took his servants, and... Mt 22:6 3062
of the sea, a r shall be saved... Rom 9:27 2640
a r according to the election of... Rom 11:5 3005
the r were affrighted, and gave... Rev 11:13 3062
make war with the r of her seed... Rev 12:17 3062
the r were slain with the sword... Rev 19:21 3062

REMOVE

to r it from Ephraim's head unto... Gen 48:17 5493
of Israel r from tribe to tribe... Num 36:7 5437
Neither shall the inheritance r... Num 36:9 5437
Thou shalt not r thy neighbour's... Deut 19:14 5253
then ye shall r from your place,... Josh 3:3 5265
then would I r Abimelech... Judg 9:29 5493
So David would not r the ark of... 2Sa 6:10 5493

R

I will r Judah also out of my 2Kin 23:27 5493
to r them out of his sight, for 2Kin 24:3 5493
Neither will I any more r the 2Chr 33:8 5493
Some r the landmarks Job 24:2 5472
till I die I will not r mine Job 27:5 5493
not the hand of the wicked r me Ps 36:11 5110
R thy stroke away from me Ps 39:10 5493
R from me reproach and contempt Ps 119:22 1556
R from me the way of lying Ps 119:29 5493
r thy foot from evil Prov 4:27 5493
R thy way far from her, and come Prov 5:8 7368
R not the ancient landmark, which Prov 22:28 5253
R not the old landmark Prov 23:10 5253
R far from me vanity and lies Prov 30:8 7368
Therefore r sorrow from thy heart Eccl 11:10 5493
the earth shall r out of her Is 13:13 7493
from his place shall he not r Is 46:7 4185
my sight, then shalt thou not r Jer 4:1 5110
to r you far from your land Jer 27:10 7368
that I should r it from before my Jer 32:31 5493
they shall r, they shall depart, Jer 50:3 5110
R out of the midst of Babylon, and Jer 50:8 5110
and r by day in their sight Eze 12:3 1540
thou shalt r from thy place to Eze 12:3 1540
they shall r and go into captivity Eze 12:11 5493
R the diadem, and take off the Eze 21:26 5493
r violence and spoil, and execute Eze 45:9 5493
were like them that r the bound Hos 5:10 5253
But I will r far off from you the Joel 2:20 7368
that ye might r them far from Joel 3:6 7368
which ye shall not r your necks Mic 2:3 4185
I will r the iniquity of that Zec 3:9 4185
mountain shall r toward the north Zec 14:4 4185
mountain, R hence to yonder place Mt 17:20 3327
and it shall r Mt 17:20 3327
be willing, r this cup from me Lk 22:42 3911
so that I could r mountains 1Cor 13:2 3179
will r thy candlestick out of his Rev 2:5 2795

REMOVED
Noah r the covering of the ark, Gen 8:13 5493
he r from thence unto a mountain Gen 12:8 6275
Then Abram r his tent, and came and Gen 13:18 167
he r from thence, and digged Gen 26:22 6275
he r that day the he goats that Gen 30:35 5493
he r them to cities from one end Gen 47:21 5674
he r the swarms of flies from Ex 8:31 5493
went before the camp of Israel, r Ex 14:19 5265
and when the people saw it, they r Ex 20:18 5128
the people r from Hazeroth Num 12:16 5265
From thence they r, and pitched in Num 21:12 5265
From thence they r, and pitched on Num 21:13 5265
children of Israel r from Rameses Num 33:5 5265
they r from Etham, and turned Num 33:7 5265
they r from Marah, and came unto Num 33:9 5265
they r from Elim, and encamped by Num 33:10 5265
they r from the Red sea, and Num 33:11 5265
they r from Alush, and encamped at Num 33:14 5265
they r from the desert of Sinai, Num 33:16 5265
they r from Libnah, and pitched at Num 33:21 5265
they r from mount Shapher, and Num 33:24 5265
they r from Haradah, and pitched Num 33:25 5265
they r from Makheloth, and Num 33:26 5265
they r from Tarah, and pitched in Num 33:28 5265
they r from Bene-jaakan, and Num 33:32 5265
they r from Jotbathah, and Num 33:34 5265
they r from Ezion-gaber, and Num 33:36 5265
they r from Kadesh, and pitched in Num 33:37 5265
they r from Dibon-gad, and Num 33:46 5265
they r from Almon-diblathaim, and Num 33:47 5265
shalt be r into all the kingdoms Deut 28:25 2189
they r from Shittim, and came to Josh 3:1 5265
when the people r from their Josh 3:14 5265
why his hand is not r from you 1Sa 6:3 5493
Therefore Saul r him from him 1Sa 18:13 5493
he r Amasa out of the highway 2Sa 20:12 5437
When he was r out of the highway, 2Sa 20:13 3014
r all the idols that his fathers 1Kin 15:12 5493
even her he r from being queen, 1Kin 15:13 5493
But the high places were not r 1Kin 15:14 5493
that the high places were not r 2Kin 15:4 5493
the high places were not r 2Kin 15:35 5493
r the laver from off them 2Kin 16:17 5493
and r them out of his sight 2Kin 17:18 5493
Until the LORD r Israel out of 2Kin 17:23 5493
The nations which thou hast r 2Kin 17:26 1540
He r the high places, and brake 2Kin 18:4 5493
of my sight, as I have r Israel 2Kin 23:27 5493
Geba, and they r them to Manahath 1Chr 8:6 1540
he r them, and begat Uzza, and 1Chr 8:7 1540
he r her from being queen, 2Chr 15:16 5493
they r the burnt offerings, that 2Chr 35:12 5493
the rock is r out of his place Job 14:18 6275
the rock be r out of his place Job 18:4 6275
mine hope hath he r like a tree Job 19:10 5265
Even so would he have r thee out Job 36:16 5493
we fear, though the earth be r Ps 46:2 4171
I r his shoulder from the burden Ps 81:6 5493
the west, so far hath he r our Ps 103:12 7368
that it should not be r for ever Ps 104:5 4131
as mount Zion, which cannot be r Ps 125:1 4131
The righteous shall never be r Prov 10:30 4131
And the LORD have r men far away Is 6:12 7368
I have r the bounds of the people Is 10:13 5493
Madmenah is r Is 10:31 5074
fastened in the sure place be r Is 22:25 4185
shall be r like a cottage Is 24:20 5110
thou hadst r it far unto all the Is 26:15 7368
but have r their heart far from Is 29:13 7368
be r into a corner any more Is 30:20 3670
stakes thereof shall ever be r Is 33:20 5265
is r from me as a shepherd's tent Is 38:12 1556
shall depart, and the hills be r Is 54:10 4131
the covenant of my peace be r Is 54:10 4131

I will cause them to be r into Jer 15:4 2189
I will deliver them to be r into Jer 24:9 2189
will deliver them to be r to all Jer 29:18 2189
I will make you to be r into all Jer 34:17 2189
therefore she is r Lam 1:8 5206
thou hast r my soul far off from Lam 3:17 2186
streets, and their gold shall be r Eze 7:19 5079
them, and will give them to be r Eze 23:46 2189
as the uncleanness of a r woman Eze 36:17 5079
stretched themselves shall be r Amos 6:7 5493
how hath he r it from me Mic 2:4 4185
day shall the decree be far r Mic 7:11
say unto this mountain, Be thou r Mt 21:21 142
say unto this mountain, Be thou r Mk 11:23 142
he r him into this land, wherein Acts 7:4 3351
And when he had r him, he raised Acts 13:22 3179
I marvel that ye are so soon r Gal 1:6 3346

REMOVETH
Cursed be he that r his Deut 27:17 5253
Which r the mountains, and they Job 9:5 6275
He r away the speech of the Job 12:20 5493
Whoso r stones shall be hurt Eccl 10:9 5265
he r kings, and setteth up kings Dan 2:21 5709

REMOVING
r from thence all the speckled and Gen 30:32 5493
a captive, and r to and fro Is 49:21 5493
of man, prepare thee stuff for r Eze 12:3 1473
in their sight, as stuff for r Eze 12:4 1473
signifieth the r of those things Heb 12:27 3331

REMPHAN *(rem'-fan) An idol worshipped by Israel.*
Moloch, and the star of your god R Acts 7:43 4481

REND
the hole, that it should not r Ex 39:23
heads, neither r your clothes Lev 10:6 6533
then he shall r it out of the Lev 13:56 7167
his head, nor r his clothes Lev 21:10 6533
R your clothes, and gird you with 2Sa 3:31 7167
I will surely r the kingdom from 1Kin 11:11 7167
but I will r it out of the hand 1Kin 11:12 7167
Howbeit I will not r away all the 1Kin 11:13 7167
I will r the kingdom out of the 1Kin 11:31 7167
didst r thy clothes, and weep 2Chr 34:27 7167
A time to r, and a time to sew Eccl 3:7 7167
that thou wouldest r the heavens Is 64:1 7167
and a stormy wind shall r it Eze 13:11 1234
I will even r it with a stormy Eze 13:13 1234
break, and r all their shoulder Eze 29:7 1234
will r the caul of their heart, Hos 13:8 7167
r your heart, and not your Joel 2:13 7167
feet, and turn again and r you Mt 7:6 4486
among themselves, Let us not r it Jn 19:24 4977

RENDER
which they shall r unto me Num 18:9 7725
I will r vengeance to mine Deut 32:41 7725
and will r vengeance to his Deut 32:43 7725
did God r upon their heads Judg 9:57 7725
The LORD r to every man his 1Sa 26:23 7725
r unto every man according unto 2Chr 6:30 5415
for he will r unto man his Job 33:26 7725
work of a man shall he r unto him Job 34:11 7999
r to them their desert Ps 28:4 7725
They also that r evil for good Ps 38:20 7999
I will r praises unto thee Ps 56:12 7999
r unto our neighbours sevenfold Ps 79:12 7725
r a reward to the proud Ps 94:2 7725
What shall I r unto the LORD for Ps 116:12 7725
shall not he r to every man Prov 24:12 7725
I will r to the man according to Prov 24:29 7725
seven men that can r a reason Prov 26:16 7725
to r his anger with fury, and his Is 66:15 7725
he will r unto her a recompence Jer 51:6 7999
I will r unto Babylon and to all Jer 51:24 7999
R unto them a recompence, O LORD, Lam 3:64 7725
so will we r the calves of our Hos 14:2 7999
will ye r me a recompence Joel 3:4 7999
that I will r double unto thee Zec 9:12 7725
which shall r him the fruits in Mt 21:41 591
R therefore unto Caesar the Mt 22:21 591
R to Caesar the things that are Mk 12:17 591
R therefore unto Caesar the Lk 20:25 591
Who will r to every man according Rom 2:6 591
R therefore to all their dues Rom 13:7 591
Let the husband r unto the wife 1Cor 7:3 591
can we r to God again for you 1Th 3:9 467
See that none r evil for evil 1Th 5:15 591

RENDERED
Thus God r the wickedness of Judg 9:56 7725
r unto the king of Israel an 2Kin 3:4 7725
But Hezekiah r not again 2Chr 32:25 7725
a man's hands shall be r unto him Prov 12:14 7725

RENDEREST
for thou r to every man according Ps 62:12 7999

RENDERETH
a voice of the LORD that r Is 66:6 7999

RENDERING
Not r evil for evil, or railing 1Pet 3:9 591

RENDING
r it in pieces, while there is Ps 7:2 6561

RENEW
to Gilgal, and r the kingdom there 1Sa 11:14 2318
r a right spirit within me Ps 51:10 2318
the LORD shall r their strength Is 40:31 2498
let the people r their strength Is 41:1 2498
r our days as of old Lam 5:21 2318
to r them again unto repentance Heb 6:6 340

RENEWED
r the altar of the LORD, that was 2Chr 15:8 2318
in me, and my bow was r in my hand Job 29:20 2498
thy youth is r like the eagle's Ps 103:5 2318
the inward man is r day by day 2Cor 4:16 341
be r in the spirit of your mind Eph 4:23 365
which is r in knowledge after the Col 3:10 341

RENEWEST
Thou r thy witnesses against me, Job 10:17 2318
thou r the face of the earth Ps 104:30 2318

RENEWING
transformed by the r of your mind Rom 12:2 342
and r of the Holy Ghost Titus 3:5 342

RENOUNCED
But have r the hidden things of 2Cor 4:2 550

RENOWN
men which were of old, men of r Gen 6:4 8034
in the congregation, men of r Num 16:2 8034
thy r went forth among the Eze 16:14 8034
the harlot because of thy r Eze 16:15 8034
raise up for them a plant of r Eze 34:29 8034
it shall be to them a r the day Eze 39:13 8034
hand, and hast gotten thee r Dan 9:15 8034

RENOWNED
These were the r of the Num 1:16 7121
of evildoers shall never be r Is 14:20 7121
and rulers, great lords and r Eze 23:23 7121
the r city, which wast strong in Eze 26:17 1984

RENT
and he r his clothes Gen 37:29 7167
is without doubt r in pieces Gen 37:33 2963
Jacob r his clothes, and put Gen 37:34 7167
Then they r their clothes, and Gen 44:13 7167
of an habergeon, that it be not r Ex 28:32 7167
plague is, his clothes shall be r Lev 13:45 6533
the land, r their clothes Num 14:6 7167
Joshua r his clothes, and fell to Josh 7:6 7167
asses, and wine bottles, old, and r Josh 9:4 1234
and, behold, they be r Josh 9:13 1234
that he r his clothes, and said, Judg 11:35 7167
he r him as he would have r a Judg 14:6 8156
r him as he would have r a kid Judg 14:6 8156
the same day with his clothes r 1Sa 4:12 7167
the skirt of his mantle, and it r 1Sa 15:27 7167
The LORD hath r the kingdom of 1Sa 15:28 7167
for the LORD hath r the kingdom 1Sa 28:17 7167
camp from Saul with his clothes r 2Sa 1:2 7167
hold on his clothes, and r them 2Sa 1:11 7167
r her garment of divers colours 2Sa 13:19 7167
stood by with their clothes r 2Sa 13:31 7167
came to meet him with his coat r 2Sa 15:32 7167
so that the earth r with the 1Kin 1:40 1234
on him, and r it in twelve pieces 1Kin 11:30 7167
Behold, the altar shall be r 1Kin 13:3 7167
The altar also was r, and the 1Kin 13:5 7167
r the kingdom away from the house 1Kin 14:8 7167
strong wind r the mountains, and 1Kin 19:11 6561
that he r his clothes, and put 1Kin 21:27 7167
clothes, and r them in two pieces 2Kin 2:12 7167
that he r his clothes, and said, 2Kin 5:7 7167
king of Israel had r his clothes 2Kin 5:8 7167
Wherefore hast thou r thy clothes 2Kin 5:8 7167
the woman, that he r his clothes 2Kin 6:30 7167
Athaliah r her clothes, and cried, 2Kin 11:14 7167
For he r Israel from the house of 2Kin 17:21 7167
to Hezekiah with their clothes r 2Kin 18:37 7167
that he r his clothes, and covered 2Kin 19:1 7167
of the law, that he r his clothes 2Kin 22:11 7167
hast r thy clothes, and wept 2Kin 22:19 7167
Then Athaliah r her clothes 2Chr 23:13 7167
of the law, that he r his clothes 2Chr 34:19 7167
I r my garment and my mantle, and Ezr 9:3 7167
having r my garment and my mantle, Ezr 9:5 7167
Mordecai r his clothes, and put on Est 4:1 7167
r his mantle, and shaved his head, Job 1:20 7167
they r every one his mantle, and Job 2:12 7167
and the cloud is not r under them Job 26:8 1234
and instead of a girdle a r Is 3:24 5364
to Hezekiah with their clothes r Is 36:22 7167
that he r his clothes, and covered Is 37:1 7167
nor r their garments, neither the Jer 36:24 7167
beards shaven, and their clothes r Jer 41:5 7167
pain, and No shall be r asunder Eze 30:16 1234
garment, and the r is made worse Mt 9:16 4978
the high priest r his clothes Mt 26:65 1284
the veil of the temple was r in Mt 27:51 4977
earth did quake, and the rocks r Mt 27:51 4977
the old, and the r is made worse Mk 2:21 4978
r him sore, and came out of him Mk 9:26 4682
the high priest r his clothes Mk 14:63 1284
the veil of the temple was r in Mk 15:38 4977
then both the new maketh a r Lk 5:36 4977
of the temple was r in the midst Lk 23:45 4977
they r their clothes, and ran in Acts 14:14 1284
the magistrates r off their Acts 16:22 4048

RENTEST
though thou r thy face with Jer 4:30 7167

REPAID
to the righteous good shall be r Prov 13:21 7999

REPAIR
let them r the breaches of the 2Kin 12:5 2388
Why r ye not the breaches of the 2Kin 12:7 2388
neither to r the breaches of the 2Kin 12:8 2388
hewed stone to r the breaches of 2Kin 12:12 2388
laid out for the house to r it 2Kin 12:12 2393
to r the breaches of the house, 2Kin 22:5 2388
and hewn stone to r the house 2Kin 22:6 2388
minded to r the house of the LORD 2Chr 24:4 2318
gather of all Israel money to r 2Chr 24:5 2388

carpenters to r the house of the ... 2Chr 24:12 2318
to r the house of the LORD his ... 2Chr 34:8 2388
in the house of the LORD, to r ... 2Chr 34:10 918
to r the desolations thereof, and ... Ezr 9:9 5975
they shall r the waste cities, ... Is 61:4 2318

REPAIRED
r the cities, and dwelt in them ... Judg 21:23 1129
r the breaches of the city of ... 1Kin 11:27 5462
he r the altar of the LORD that ... 1Kin 18:30 7495
not r the breaches of the house ... 2Kin 12:6 2388
r therewith the house of the LORD ... 2Kin 12:14 2388
Joab r the rest of the city ... 1Chr 11:8 2421
the house of the LORD, and r them ... 2Chr 29:3 2388
r Millo in the city of David, and ... 2Chr 32:5 2388
he r the altar of the LORD, and ... 2Chr 33:16 1129
next unto them r Meremoth the son ... Neh 3:4 2388
next unto them r Meshullam the ... Neh 3:4 2388
next unto them r Zadok the son of ... Neh 3:4 2388
And next unto them the Tekoites r ... Neh 3:5 2388
Moreover the old gate r Jehoiada ... Neh 3:6 2388
next unto them r Melatiah the ... Neh 3:7 2388
Next unto him r Uzziel the son of ... Neh 3:8 2388
Next unto him also r Hananiah the ... Neh 3:8 2388
next unto them r Rephaiah the son ... Neh 3:9 2388
next unto them r Jedaiah the son ... Neh 3:10 2388
next unto him r Hattush the son ... Neh 3:10 2388
r the other piece, and the tower ... Neh 3:11 2388
next unto him r Shallum the son ... Neh 3:12 2388
The valley gate r Hanun, and the ... Neh 3:13 2388
But the dung gate r Malchiah the ... Neh 3:14 2388
r Shallun the son of Colhozeh ... Neh 3:15 2388
After him r Nehemiah the son of ... Neh 3:16 2388
After him r the Levites, Rehum ... Neh 3:17 2388
Next unto him r Hashabiah ... Neh 3:17 2388
After him r their brethren, Bavai ... Neh 3:18 2388
next to him r Ezer the son of ... Neh 3:19 2388
earnestly r the other piece ... Neh 3:20 2388
After him r Meremoth the son of ... Neh 3:21 2388
after him r the priests, the men ... Neh 3:22 2388
After him r Benjamin and Hashub ... Neh 3:23 2388
After him r Azariah the son of ... Neh 3:23 2388
After him r Binnui the son of ... Neh 3:24 2388
them the Tekoites r another piece ... Neh 3:27 2388
the horse gate r the priests ... Neh 3:28 2388
After them r Zadok the son of ... Neh 3:29 2388
After him r also Shemaiah the son ... Neh 3:29 2388
After him r Hananiah the son of ... Neh 3:30 2388
After him r Meshullam the son of ... Neh 3:30 2388
After him r Malchiah the ... Neh 3:31 2388
the sheep gate r the goldsmiths ... Neh 3:32 2388

REPAIRER
The r of the breach, The restorer ... Is 58:12 1443

REPAIRING
the r of the house of God, behold ... 2Chr 24:27 3247

REPAY
he will r him to his face ... Deut 7:10 7999
who shall r him what he hath done ... Job 21:31 7999
prevented me, that I should r him ... Job 41:11 7999
deeds, accordingly he will r ... Is 59:18 7999
the islands he will r recompence ... Is 59:18 7999
when I come again, I will r thee ... Lk 10:35 591
I will r, saith the Lord ... Rom 12:19 457
with mine own hand, I will r it ... Philem 19 661

REPAYETH
r them that hate him to their ... Deut 7:10 7999

REPEATETH
but he that r a matter separateth ... Prov 17:9 8138

REPENT
the people r when they see war ... Ex 13:17 5162
r of this evil against thy people ... Ex 32:12 5162
the son of man, that he should r ... Num 23:19 5162
r himself for his servants, when ... Deut 32:36 5162
of Israel will not lie nor r ... 1Sa 15:29 5162
he is not a man, that he should r ... 1Sa 15:29 5162
they were carried captives, and r ... 1Kin 8:47 7725
myself, and r in dust and ashes ... Job 42:6 5162
let it r thee concerning thy ... Ps 90:13 5162
LORD hath sworn, and will not r ... Ps 110:4 5162
he will r himself concerning his ... Ps 135:14 5162
I have purposed it, and will not r ... Jer 4:28 5162
I will r of the evil that I ... Jer 18:8 5162
voice, then I will r of the good ... Jer 18:10 5162
that I may r me of the evil, ... Jer 26:3 5162
the LORD will r him of the evil ... Jer 26:13 5162
for I r me of the evil that I ... Jer 42:10 5162
R, and turn yourselves from your ... Eze 14:6 7725
R, and turn yourselves from all ... Eze 18:30 7725
will I spare, neither will I r ... Eze 24:14 5162
knoweth if he will return and r ... Joel 2:14 5162
can tell if God will turn and r ... Jonah 3:9 5162
And saying, R ye ... Mt 3:2 3340
began to preach, and to say, R ... Mt 4:17 3340
r ye, and believe the gospel ... Mk 1:15 3340
and preached that men should r ... Mk 6:12 3340
but, except ye r, ye shall all ... Lk 13:3 3340
but, except ye r, ye shall all ... Lk 13:5 3340
them from the dead, they will r ... Lk 16:30 3340
and if he r, forgive him ... Lk 17:3 3340
turn again to thee, saying, I r ... Lk 17:4 3340
Then Peter said unto them, R ... Acts 2:38 3340
R ye therefore, and be converted, ... Acts 3:19 3340
R therefore of this thy ... Acts 8:22 3340
all men every where to r ... Acts 17:30 3340
the Gentiles, that they should r ... Acts 26:20 3340
I do not r, though I did r ... 2Cor 7:8 3338
him, The Lord sware and will not r ... Heb 7:21 3338
from whence thou art fallen, and r ... Rev 2:5 3340
out of his place, except thou r ... Rev 2:5 3340
R; or else I will ... Rev 2:16 3340
her space to r of her fornication ... Rev 2:21 3340
except they r of their deeds ... Rev 2:22 3340
and heard, and hold fast, and r ... Rev 3:3 3340
be zealous therefore, and r ... Rev 3:19 3340

REPENTANCE
r shall be hid from mine eyes ... Hos 13:14 5164
forth therefore fruits meet for r ... Mt 3:8 3341
baptize you with water unto r ... Mt 3:11 3341
the righteous, but sinners to r ... Mt 9:13 3341
preach the baptism of r for the ... Mk 1:4 3341
the righteous, but sinners to r ... Mk 2:17 3341
preaching the baptism of r for ... Lk 3:3 3341
therefore fruits worthy of r ... Lk 3:8 3341
the righteous, but sinners to r ... Lk 5:32 3341
just persons, which need no r ... Lk 15:7 3341
And that r and remission of sins ... Lk 24:47 3341
Saviour, for to give r to Israel ... Acts 5:31 3341
the Gentiles granted r unto life ... Acts 11:18 3341
his coming the baptism of r to ... Acts 13:24 3341
baptized with the baptism of r ... Acts 19:4 3341
r toward God, and faith toward our ... Acts 20:21 3341
to God, and do works meet for r ... Acts 26:20 3341
goodness of God leadeth thee to r ... Rom 2:4 3341
and calling of God are without r ... Rom 11:29 278
sorry, but that ye sorrowed to r ... 2Cor 7:9 3341
For godly sorrow worketh r to ... 2Cor 7:10 3341
r to the acknowledging of the ... 2Ti 2:25 3341
foundation of r from dead works ... Heb 6:1 3341
away, to renew them again unto r ... Heb 6:6 3341
for he found no place of r ... Heb 12:17 3341
but that all should come to r ... 2Pet 3:9 3341

REPENTED
it r the LORD that he had made ... Gen 6:6 5162
the LORD r of the evil which he ... Ex 32:14 5162
for it r the LORD because of ... Judg 2:18 5162
the children of Israel r them for ... Judg 21:6 5162
the people r them for Benjamin, ... Judg 21:15 5162
the LORD r that he had made Saul ... 1Sa 15:35 5162
the LORD r him of the evil, and ... 2Sa 24:16 5162
he r him of the evil, and said to ... 1Chr 21:15 5162
r according to the multitude of ... Ps 106:45 5162
no man r him of his wickedness, ... Jer 8:6 5162
the LORD overthrew, and r not ... Jer 20:16 5162
the LORD r him of the evil which ... Jer 26:19 5162
after that I was turned, I r ... Jer 31:19 5162
The LORD r for this ... Amos 7:3 5162
The LORD r for this ... Amos 7:6 5162
God r of the evil, that he had ... Jonah 3:10 5162
the LORD of hosts, and I r not ... Zec 8:14 5162
were done, because they r not ... Mt 11:20 3340
they would have r long ago in ... Mt 11:21 3340
because they r at the preaching ... Mt 12:41 3340
but afterward he r, and went ... Mt 21:29 3338
r not afterward, that ye might ... Mt 21:32 3338
r himself, and brought again the ... Mt 27:3 3338
you, they had a great while ago r ... Lk 10:13 3340
for they r at the preaching of ... Lk 11:32 3340
to salvation not to be r of ... 2Cor 7:10 278
have not r of the uncleanness and ... 2Cor 12:21 3340
and she r not ... Rev 2:21 3340
r not of the works of their hands ... Rev 9:20 3340
Neither r they of their murders, ... Rev 9:21 3340
they r not to give him glory ... Rev 16:9 3340
sores, and r not of their deeds ... Rev 16:11 3340

REPENTEST
kindness, and r thee of the evil ... Jonah 4:2 5162

REPENTETH
for it r me that I have made them ... Gen 6:7 5162
It r me that I have set up Saul ... 1Sa 15:11 5162
kindness, and r him of the evil ... Joel 2:13 5162
in heaven over one sinner that r ... Lk 15:7 3340
of God over one sinner that r ... Lk 15:10 3340

REPENTING
I am weary with r ... Jer 15:6 5162

REPENTINGS
my r are kindled together ... Hos 11:8 5150

REPETITIONS
But when ye pray, use not vain r ... Mt 6:7 945

REPHAEL *(re'-fa-el) A sanctuary servant.*
Othni, and R, and Obed, Elzabad, ... 1Chr 26:7 7501

REPHAH *(re'-fah) A grandson of Ephraim.*
R was his son, also Resheph, and ... 1Chr 7:25 7506

REPHAIAH *(ref-a-i'-ah)* See RAPHA, RHESA.
1. Head of a family.
the sons of R, the sons of Arnan, ... 1Chr 3:21 7509
2. A captain of Simeon.
Pelatiah, and Neariah, and R ... 1Chr 4:42 7509
3. A son of Tola.
Uzzi, and R, and Jeriel, and Jahmai, ... 1Chr 7:2 7509
4. Son of Binea.
R his son, Eleasah his son, Azel ... 1Chr 9:43 7509
5. A repairer of Jerusalem's wall.
them repaired R the son of Hur ... Neh 3:9 7509

REPHAIM *(re-fa'-im)* See REPHAIMS. *A valley near Jerusalem.*
themselves in the valley of R ... 2Sa 5:18 7497
themselves in the valley of R ... 2Sa 5:22 7497
pitched in the valley of R ... 2Sa 23:13 7497
encamped in the valley of R ... 1Chr 11:15 7497
themselves in the valley of R ... 1Chr 14:9 7497
gathereth ears in the valley of R ... Is 17:5 7497

REPHAIMS *(re-fa'-ims)* See REPHAIM. *A tribe of Canaanites.*
smote the R in Ashteroth Karnaim, ... Gen 14:5 7497
and the Perizzites, and the R ... Gen 15:20 7497

REPHAN See REMPHAN.

REPHIDIM *(ref'-i-dim) An Israelite encampment in the wilderness.*
of the LORD, and pitched in R ... Ex 17:1 7508
and fought with Israel in R ... Ex 17:8 7508
For they were departed from R ... Ex 19:2 7508
from Alush, and encamped at R ... Num 33:14 7508
And they departed from R, and ... Num 33:15 7508

REPLENISH
r the earth, and subdue it ... Gen 1:28 4390
and multiply, and r the earth ... Gen 9:1 4390

REPLENISHED
because they be r from the east ... Is 2:6 4390
that pass over the sea, have r ... Is 23:2 4390
I have r every sorrowful soul ... Jer 31:25 4390
I shall be r, now she is laid ... Eze 26:2 4390
and thou wast r, and made very ... Eze 27:25 4390

REPLIEST
who art thou that r against God ... Rom 9:20 470

REPORT
unto his father their evil r ... Gen 37:2 1681
Thou shalt not raise a false r ... Ex 23:1 8088
they brought up an evil r of the ... Num 13:32 1681
bring up the evil r upon the land ... Num 14:37 1681
heaven, who shall hear r of thee ... Deut 2:25 8088
for it is no good r that I hear ... 1Sa 2:24 8052
It was a true r that I heard in ... 1Kin 10:6 1697
It was a true r which I heard in ... 2Chr 9:5 1697
might have matter for an evil r ... Neh 6:13 8034
a good r maketh the bones fat ... Prov 15:30 8052
As at the r concerning Egypt, so ... Is 23:5 8088
be sorely pained at the r of Tyre ... Is 23:5 8088
vexation only to understand the r ... Is 28:19 8052
Who hath believed our r ... Is 53:1 8052
R, say they, and we will r it ... Jer 20:10 5046
Babylon hath heard the r of them ... Jer 50:43 8088
Lord, who hath believed our r ... Jn 12:38 189
among you seven men of honest r ... Acts 6:3 3140
of good r among all the nation of ... Acts 10:22 3140
having a good r of all the Jews ... Acts 22:12 3140
Lord, who hath believed our r ... Rom 10:16 189
r that God is in you of a truth ... 1Cor 14:25 518
By honour and dishonour, by evil r ... 2Cor 6:8 1426
and good r: as deceivers ... 2Cor 6:8 2162
whatsoever things are of good r ... Phil 4:8 2163
good r of them which are without ... 1Ti 3:7 3141
it the elders obtained a good r ... Heb 11:2 3140
obtained a good r through faith ... Heb 11:39 3140
Demetrius hath good r of all men ... 3Jn 12 3140

REPORTED
It is r among the heathen, and ... Neh 6:6 8085
now shall it be r to the king ... Neh 6:7 8085
Also they r his good deeds before ... Neh 6:19 559
in their eyes, when it shall be r ... Est 1:17 559
r the matter, saying, I have done ... Eze 9:11 7725
this saying is commonly r among ... Mt 28:15 1310
r all that the chief priests and ... Acts 4:23 518
Which was well r of by the ... Acts 16:2 3140
rather, (as we be slanderously r ... Rom 3:8 987
It is r commonly that there is ... 1Cor 5:1 191
Well r of for good works ... 1Ti 5:10 3140
which are now r unto you by them ... 1Pet 1:12 312

REPROACH
and said, God hath taken away my r ... Gen 30:23 2781
for that were a r unto us ... Gen 34:14 2781
away the r of Egypt from off you ... Josh 5:9 2781
among the sheaves, and r her not ... Ruth 2:15 3637
lay it for a r upon all Israel ... 1Sa 11:2 2781
and taketh away the r from Israel ... 1Sa 17:26 2781
of my r from the hand of Nabal ... 1Sa 25:39 2781
hath sent to r the living God ... 2Kin 19:4 2778
hath sent him to r the living God ... 2Kin 19:16 2778
are in great affliction and r ... Neh 1:3 2781
Jerusalem, that we be no more a r ... Neh 2:17 2781
turn their r upon their own head, ... Neh 4:4 2781
the r of the heathen our enemies ... Neh 5:9 2781
evil report, that they might r me ... Neh 6:13 2778
me, and plead against me my r ... Job 19:5 2781
I have heard the check of my r ... Job 20:3 3639
my heart shall not r me so long ... Job 27:6 2778
nor taketh up a r against his ... Ps 15:3 2781
a r of men, and despised of the ... Ps 22:6 2781
I was a r among all mine enemies, ... Ps 31:11 2781
make me not the r of the foolish ... Ps 39:8 2781
in my bones, mine enemies r me ... Ps 42:10 2778
Thou makest us a r to our ... Ps 44:13 2781
save me from the r of him that ... Ps 57:3 2778
for thy sake I have borne r ... Ps 69:7 2781
with fasting, that was to my r ... Ps 69:10 2781
Thou hast known my r ... Ps 69:19 2781
R hath broken my heart ... Ps 69:20 2781
let them be covered with r ... Ps 71:13 2781
how long shall the adversary r ... Ps 74:10 2778
he put them to a perpetual r ... Ps 78:66 2781
We are become a r to our ... Ps 79:4 2781
into their bosom their r, ... Ps 79:12 2781
he is a r to his neighbours ... Ps 89:41 2781
Lord, the r of thy servants ... Ps 89:50 2781
the r of all the mighty people ... Ps 89:50
Mine enemies r me all the day ... Ps 102:8 2778
I became also a r unto them ... Ps 109:25 2781
Remove from me r and contempt ... Ps 119:22 2781
Turn away my r which I fear ... Ps 119:39 2781
his r shall not be wiped away ... Prov 6:33 2781
but sin is a r to any people ... Prov 14:34 2617
also contempt, and with ignominy r ... Prov 18:3 2781
that causeth shame, and bringeth r ... Prov 19:26 2659
yea, strife and r shall cease ... Prov 22:10 7036
by thy name, to take away our r ... Is 4:1 2781
profit, but a shame, and also a r ... Is 30:5 2781

hath sent to *r* the living God ... Is 37:4 2778
hath sent to *r* the living God ... Is 37:17 2778
fear ye not the *r* of men, neither ... Is 51:7 2781
shalt not remember the *r* of thy ... Is 54:4 2781
word of the LORD is unto them a *r* ... Jer 6:10 2781
of the LORD was made a *r* unto me ... Jer 20:8 2781
bring an everlasting *r* upon you ... Jer 23:40 2781
earth for their hurt, to be a *r* ... Jer 24:9 2781
and an hissing, and a *r*, among all ... Jer 29:18 2781
I did bear the *r* of my youth ... Jer 31:19 2781
astonishment, and a curse, and a *r* ... Jer 42:18 2781
a *r* among all the nations of the ... Jer 44:8 2781
astonishment, and a curse, and a *r* ... Jer 44:12 2781
shall become a desolation, a *r* ... Jer 49:13 2781
because we have heard *r* ... Jer 51:51 2781
he is filled full with *r* ... Lam 3:30 2781
Thou hast heard their *r*, O LORD, ... Lam 3:61 2781
consider, and behold our *r* ... Lam 5:1 2781
a *r* among the nations that are ... Eze 5:14 2781
So it shall be a *r* and a taunt, an ... Eze 5:15 2781
as at the time of thy *r* of the ... Eze 16:57 2781
Ammonites, and concerning their *r* ... Eze 21:28 2781
I made thee a *r* unto the heathen ... Eze 22:4 2781
bear the *r* of the people any more ... Eze 36:15 2781
r of famine among the heathen ... Eze 36:30 2781
thy people are become a *r* to all ... Dan 9:16 2781
the *r* offered by him to cease ... Dan 11:18 2781
without his own *r* he shall cause ... Dan 11:18 2781
his *r* shall his Lord return unto ... Hos 12:14 2781
and give not thine heritage to *r* ... Joel 2:17 2781
make you a *r* among the heathen ... Joel 2:19 2781
ye shall bear the *r* of my people ... Mic 6:16 2781
I have heard the *r* of Moab ... Zeph 2:8 2781
to whom the *r* of it was a burden ... Zeph 3:18 2781
me, to take away my *r* among men ... Lk 1:25 *3681*
their company, and shall *r* you ... Lk 6:22 *3679*
I speak as concerning *r*, as ... 2Cor 11:21 *819*
lest he fall into *r* and the snare ... 1Ti 3:7 *3680*
we both labour and suffer *r* ... 1Ti 4:10 *3679*
Esteeming the *r* of Christ greater ... Heb 11:26 *3680*
without the camp, bearing his *r* ... Heb 13:13 *3680*

REPROACHED

Whom hast thou *r* and blasphemed ... 2Kin 19:22 2778
messengers thou hast *r* the Lord ... 2Kin 19:23 2778
These ten times have ye *r* me ... Job 19:3 3637
For it was not an enemy that *r* me ... Ps 55:12 2778
that *r* thee are fallen upon me ... Ps 69:9 2778
this, that the enemy hath *r* ... Ps 74:18 2778
wherewith they have *r* thee ... Ps 79:12 2778
Wherewith thine enemies have *r* ... Ps 89:51 2778
wherewith they have *r* the ... Ps 89:51 2778
Whom hast thou *r* and blasphemed ... Is 37:23 2778
thy servants hast thou *r* the Lord ... Is 37:24 2778
whereby they have *r* my people ... Zeph 2:8 2778
their pride, because they have *r* ... Zeph 2:10 2778
of them that *r* thee fell on me ... Rom 15:3 *3679*
If ye be *r* for the name of Christ ... 1Pet 4:14 *3679*

REPROACHES

the *r* of them that reproached ... Ps 69:9 2781
to the curse, and Israel to *r* ... Is 43:28 1421
The *r* of them that reproached ... Rom 15:3 *3679*
pleasure in infirmities, in *r* ... 2Cor 12:10 *5196*
were made a gazingstock both by *r* ... Heb 10:33 *3680*

REPROACHEST

thus saying thou *r* us also ... Lk 11:45 *5195*

REPROACHETH

a stranger, the same *r* the LORD ... Num 15:30 1442
For the voice of him that *r* ... Ps 44:16 2778
how the foolish man *r* thee daily ... Ps 74:22 2781
wherewith to answer him that *r* me ... Ps 119:42 2778
oppresseth the poor *r* his Maker ... Prov 14:31 2778
mocketh the poor *r* his Maker ... Prov 17:5 2778
that I may answer him that *r* me ... Prov 27:11 2778

REPROACHFULLY

have smitten me upon the cheek *r* ... Job 16:10 2781
to the adversary to speak *r* ... 1Ti 5:14

REPROBATE

R silver shall men call them, ... Jer 6:30 3988
God gave them over to a *r* mind ... Rom 1:28 *96*
minds, *r* concerning the faith ... 2Ti 3:8 *96*
and unto every good work *r* ... Titus 1:16 *96*

REPROBATES

Christ is in you, except ye be *r* ... 2Cor 13:5 *96*
ye shall know that we are not *r* ... 2Cor 13:6 *96*
is honest, though we be as *r* ... 2Cor 13:7 *96*

REPROOF

and are astonished at his *r* ... Job 26:11 1606
Turn you at my *r* ... Prov 1:23 8433
my counsel, and would none of my *r* ... Prov 1:25 8433
they despised all my *r* ... Prov 1:30 8433
and my heart despised *r* ... Prov 5:12 8433
but he that refuseth *r* erreth ... Prov 10:17 8433
but he that hateth *r* is brutish ... Prov 12:1 8433
regardeth *r* shall be honoured ... Prov 13:18 8433
he that regardeth *r* is prudent ... Prov 15:5 8433
and he that hateth *r* shall die ... Prov 15:10 8433
The ear that heareth the *r* of ... Prov 15:31 8433
but he that heareth *r* getteth ... Prov 15:32 8433
A *r* entereth more into a wise man ... Prov 17:10 1606
The rod and *r* give wisdom ... Prov 29:15 8433
is profitable for doctrine, for *r* ... 2Ti 3:16 *1650*

REPROOFS

not, and in whose mouth are no *r* ... Ps 38:14 8433
r of instruction are the way of ... Prov 6:23 8433

REPROVE

will *r* the words which the LORD ... 2Kin 19:4 3198
but what doth your arguing *r* ... Job 6:25 3198
Do ye imagine to *r* words, and the ... Job 6:26 3198
He will surely *r* you, if ye do ... Job 13:10 3198
Will he *r* thee for fear of thee ... Job 22:4 3198
I will not *r* thee for thy ... Ps 50:8 3198
but I will *r* thee, and set them in ... Ps 50:21 3198
and let him *r* me ... Ps 141:5 3198
R not a scorner, lest he hate ... Prov 9:8 3198
r one that hath understanding, and ... Prov 19:25 3198
unto his words, lest he *r* thee ... Prov 30:6 3198
neither *r* after the hearing of ... Is 11:3 3198
r with equity for the meek of the ... Is 11:4 3198
will *r* the words which the LORD ... Is 37:4 3198
and thy backslidings shall *r* thee ... Jer 2:19 3198
let no man strive, nor *r* another ... Hos 4:4 3198
he will *r* the world of sin, and of ... Jn 16:8 *1651*
of darkness, but rather *r* them ... Eph 5:11 *1651*
r, rebuke, exhort with all ... 2Ti 4:2 *1651*

REPROVED

thus she was *r* ... Gen 20:16 3198
Abraham *r* Abimelech because of a ... Gen 21:25 3198
he *r* kings for their sakes, ... 1Chr 16:21 3198
he *r* kings for their sakes ... Ps 105:14 3198
that being often *r* hardeneth his ... Prov 29:1 8433
thou not *r* Jeremiah of Anathoth ... Jer 29:27 1605
what I shall answer when I am *r* ... Hab 2:1 8433
being *r* by him for Herodias his ... Lk 3:19 *1651*
light, lest his deeds should be *r* ... Jn 3:20 *1651*
But all things that are *r* are ... Eph 5:13 *1651*

REPROVER

so is a wise *r* upon an obedient ... Prov 25:12 3198
dumb, and shalt not be to them a *r* ... Eze 3:26 3198

REPROVETH

he that *r* God, let him answer it ... Job 40:2 3198
He that *r* a scorner getteth to ... Prov 9:7 3256
scorner loveth not one that *r* him ... Prov 15:12 3198
snare for him that *r* in the gate ... Is 29:21 3198

REPUTATION

folly him that is in *r* for wisdom ... Eccl 10:1 3368
had in *r* among all the people, and ... Acts 5:34 *5093*
privately to them which were of *r* ... Gal 2:2 *1380*
But made himself of no *r*, and took ... Phil 2:7 *2758*
and hold such in *r* ... Phil 2:29 *1784*

REPUTED

beasts, and *r* vile in your sight ... Job 18:3 2804
of the earth are *r* as nothing ... Dan 4:35 2804

REQUEST

them, I would desire a *r* of you ... Judg 8:24 7596
perform the *r* of his handmaid ... 2Sa 14:15 1697
fulfilled the *r* of his servant ... 2Sa 14:22 1697
and the king granted him all his *r* ... Ezr 7:6 1246
me, For what dost thou make *r* ... Neh 2:4 1245
to make *r* before him for her ... Est 4:8 1245
and what is thy *r* ... Est 5:3 1246
and what is thy *r* ... Est 5:6 1246
and said, My petition and my *r* is ... Est 5:7 1246
my petition, and to perform my *r* ... Est 5:8 1246
and what is thy *r* ... Est 7:2 1246
my petition, and my people at my *r* ... Est 7:3 1246
Haman stood up to make *r* for his ... Est 7:7 1245
or what is thy *r* further ... Est 9:12 1246
Oh that I might have my *r* ... Job 6:8 7596
not withholden the *r* of his lips ... Ps 21:2 782
And he gave them their *r* ... Ps 106:15 7596
Making *r*, if by any means now at ... Rom 1:10 *1189*
for you all making *r* with joy ... Phil 1:4 *1162*

REQUESTED

earrings that he *r* was a thousand ... Judg 8:26 7592
he *r* for himself that he might ... 1Kin 19:4 7592
God granted him that which he *r* ... 1Chr 4:10 7592
therefore he *r* of the prince of ... Dan 1:8 1245
Then Daniel *r* of the king ... Dan 2:49 1156

REQUESTS

let your *r* be made known unto God ... Phil 4:6 *155*

REQUIRE

your blood of your lives will I *r* ... Gen 9:5 1875
hand of every beast will I *r* it ... Gen 9:5 1875
brother will I *r* the life of man ... Gen 9:5 1875
of my hand didst thou *r* it ... Gen 31:39 1245
of my hand shalt thou *r* him ... Gen 43:9 1245
doth the LORD thy God *r* of thee ... Deut 10:12 7592
in my name, I will *r* it of him ... Deut 18:19 1875
thy God will surely *r* it of thee ... Deut 23:21 1875
let the LORD himself *r* it ... Josh 22:23 1245
Let the LORD even *r* it at the ... 1Sa 20:16 1245
but one thing I *r* of thee ... 2Sa 3:13 7592
now *r* his blood of your hand ... 2Sa 4:11 1245
and whatsoever thou shalt *r* of me ... 2Sa 19:38 977
all times, as the matter shall *r* ... 1Kin 8:59 3117
then doth my lord *r* this thing ... 1Chr 21:3 1245
The LORD look upon it, and *r* it ... 2Chr 24:22 1875
shall *r* of you, it be done ... Ezr 7:21 7593
For I was ashamed to *r* of the ... Ezr 8:22 7592
them, and will *r* nothing of them ... Neh 5:12 1245
in his heart, Thou wilt not *r* it ... Ps 10:13 1875
his blood will I *r* at thine hand ... Eze 3:18 1245
his blood will I *r* at thine hand ... Eze 3:20 1245
there will I *r* your offerings, and ... Eze 20:40 1875
but his blood will I *r* at the ... Eze 33:6 1875
his blood will I *r* at thine hand ... Eze 33:8 1245
I will *r* my flock at their hand ... Eze 34:10 1875
and what doth the LORD *r* of thee ... Mic 6:8 1875
For the Jews *r* a sign, and the ... 1Cor 1:22 *154*
flower of her age, and need so *r* ... 1Cor 7:36 *1096*

REQUIRED

behold, also his blood is *r* ... Gen 42:22 1875
unto them such things as they *r* ... Ex 12:36
the king's business *r* haste ... 1Sa 21:8 1961
and when he *r*, they set bread ... 2Sa 12:20 7592
as every day's work *r* ... 1Chr 16:37 3117
as the duty of every day *r* ... 2Chr 8:14 3117
Why hast thou not *r* of the ... 2Chr 24:6 1875
as the duty of every day *r* ... Ezr 3:4 3117
yet for all this *r* not I the ... Neh 5:18 1245
she *r* nothing but what Hegai the ... Est 2:15 1245
and sin offering hast thou not *r* ... Ps 40:6 7592
us away captive *r* of us a song ... Ps 137:3 7592
they that wasted us *r* of us mirth ... Ps 137:3
Two things have I *r* of thee ... Prov 30:7 7592
who hath *r* this at your hand, to ... Is 1:12 1245
may be *r* of this generation ... Lk 11:50 *1567*
It shall be *r* of this generation ... Lk 11:51 *1567*
night thy soul shall be *r* of thee ... Lk 12:20 *523*
is given, of him shall be much *r* ... Lk 12:48 *2212*
might have *r* mine own with usury ... Lk 19:23 *4238*
that it should be as they *r* ... Lk 23:24 *155*
Moreover it is *r* in stewards ... 1Cor 4:2 *2212*

REQUIREST

I will do to thee all that thou *r* ... Ruth 3:11 559

REQUIRETH

and God *r* that which is past ... Eccl 3:15 1245
is a rare thing that the king *r* ... Dan 2:11 7593

REQUIRING

r that he might be crucified ... Lk 23:23 *154*

REQUITE

will certainly *r* us all the evil ... Gen 50:15 7725
Do ye thus *r* the LORD, O foolish ... Deut 32:6 1580
I also will *r* you this kindness, ... 2Sa 2:6 6213
that the LORD will *r* me good for ... 2Sa 16:12 7725
I will *r* thee in this plat, saith ... 2Kin 9:26 7999
and spite, to *r* it with thy hand ... Ps 10:14 5414
and raise me up, that I may *r* them ... Ps 41:10 7999
God of recompences shall surely *r* ... Jer 51:56 7999
at home, and to *r* their parents ... 1Ti 5:4

REQUITED

as I have done, so God hath *r* me ... Judg 1:7 7999
he hath *r* me evil for good ... 1Sa 25:21 7725

REQUITING

by *r* the wicked, by recompensing ... 2Chr 6:23 7725

REREWARD

which was the *r* of all the camps ... Num 10:25 622
the *r* came after the ark, the ... Josh 6:9 622
but the *r* came after the ark of ... Josh 6:13 622
passed on in the *r* with Achish ... 1Sa 29:2 314
the God of Israel will be your *r* ... Is 52:12 622
glory of the LORD shall be thy *r* ... Is 58:8 622

RESCUE

and thou shalt have none to *r* them ... Deut 28:31 3467
r my soul from their destructions ... Ps 35:17 7725
take away, and none shall *r* him ... Hos 5:14 5337

RESCUED

So the people *r* Jonathan, that he ... 1Sa 14:45 6299
and David *r* his two wives ... 1Sa 30:18 5337
r him, having understood that he ... Acts 23:27 *1807*

RESCUETH

He delivereth and *r*, and he worketh ... Dan 6:27 5338

RESEMBLANCE

This is their *r* through all the ... Zec 5:6 5869

RESEMBLE

and whereunto shall I *r* it ... Lk 13:18 *3666*

RESEMBLED

each one *r* the children of a king ... Judg 8:18 8389

RESEN (*re'-zen*) *A city between Nineveh and Calah.*

R between Nineveh and Calah ... Gen 10:12 7449

RESERVE

Will he *r* his anger for ever ... Jer 3:5 5201
for I will pardon them whom I *r* ... Jer 50:20 7604
to *r* the unjust unto the day of ... 2Pet 2:9 5083

RESERVED

Hast thou not *r* a blessing for me ... Gen 27:36 680
most holy things, *r* from the fire ... Num 18:9
because we *r* not to each man his ... Judg 21:22 3947
she had *r* after she was sufficed ... Ruth 2:18 3498
but *r* of them for an hundred ... 2Sa 8:4 3498
but *r* of them an hundred chariots ... 1Chr 18:4 3498
That the wicked is *r* to the day ... Job 21:30 2820
Which I have *r* against the time ... Job 38:23 2820
be *r* unto the hearing of Augustus ... Acts 25:21 *5083*
I have *r* to myself seven thousand ... Rom 11:4 *2641*
not away, *r* in heaven for you, ... 1Pet 1:4 *5083*
darkness, to be *r* unto judgment ... 2Pet 2:4 *5083*
mist of darkness is *r* for ever ... 2Pet 2:17 *5083*
r unto fire against the day of ... 2Pet 3:7 *5083*
he hath *r* in everlasting chains ... Jude 6 *5083*
to whom is *r* the blackness of ... Jude 13 *5083*

RESERVETH

he *r* unto us the appointed weeks ... Jer 5:24 8104
he *r* wrath for his enemies ... Nah 1:2 5201

RESHEPH (*re'-shef*) *A son of Rephah.*

And Rephah was his son, also *R* ... 1Chr 7:25 7566

RESIDUE

they shall eat the *r* of that ... Ex 10:5 3499
the *r* of the families of the sons ... 1Chr 6:66
the *r* of Israel, of the priests, ... Neh 11:20 7605
the *r* of the number of archers ... Is 21:17 7605
unto the *r* of his people, ... Is 28:5 7605
am deprived of the *r* of my years ... Is 38:10 3499
the *r* thereof he maketh a god, ... Is 44:17 7611
shall I make the *r* thereof an ... Is 44:19 3499
the *r* of them that remain of this ... Jer 8:3 7611
the *r* of them will I deliver to ... Jer 15:9 7611
the *r* of Jerusalem, that remain ... Jer 24:8 7611
concerning the *r* of the vessels ... Jer 27:19 3499
the *r* of the elders which were ... Jer 29:1 3499
with all the *r* of the princes of ... Jer 39:3 7611

the *r* of the people that were in Jer 41:10 7611
the *r* of the people that remained Jer 52:15 3499
wilt thou destroy all the *r* of Eze 9:8 7611
thy *r* shall be devoured by the Eze 23:25 319
your feet the *r* of your pastures Eze 34:18 3499
ye must foul the *r* with your feet Eze 34:18 3498
unto the *r* of the heathen Eze 36:3 7611
derision to the *r* of the heathen Eze 36:4 7611
against the *r* of the heathen Eze 36:5 7611
the *r* in length over against the Eze 48:18 3498
the *r* shall be for the prince, on Eze 48:21 3498
stamped the *r* with the feet of it Dan 7:7 7606
stamped the *r* with his feet Dan 7:19 7606
the *r* of my people shall spoil Zeph 2:9 7611
to the *r* of the people, saying, Hag 2:2 7611
But now I will not be unto the *r* Zec 8:11 7611
the *r* of the people shall not be Zec 14:2 3499
Yet had he the *r* of the spirit Mal 2:15 7605
they went and told it unto the *r* Mk 16:13 *3062*
That the *r* of men might seek Acts 15:17 *2645*

RESIST
at his right hand to *r* him Zec 3:1 7853
say unto you, That ye *r* not evil Mt 5:39 *436*
not be able to gainsay nor *r* Lk 21:15 *436*
were not able to *r* the wisdom Acts 6:10 *436*
ye do always *r* the Holy Ghost Acts 7:51 *496*
they that *r* shall receive to Rom 13:2 *436*
so do these also *r* the truth 2Ti 3:8 *436*
R the devil, and he will flee from Jas 4:7 *436*
and he doth not *r* you Jas 5:6 *498*
Whom *r* stedfast in the faith, 1Pet 5:9 *436*

RESISTED
For who hath *r* his will Rom 9:19 *436*
Ye have not yet *r* unto blood Heb 12:4 *478*

RESISTETH
Whosoever therefore *r* the power Rom 13:2 *498*
the power, *r* the ordinance of God Rom 13:2 *436*
God *r* the proud, but giveth grace Jas 4:6 *498*
for God *r* the proud, and giveth 1Pet 5:5 *498*

RESOLVED
I am *r* what to do, that, when I Lk 16:4 *1097*

RESORT
the trumpet, *r* ye thither unto us Neh 4:20 6908
whereunto I may continually *r* Ps 71:3 935
the people *r* unto him again Mk 10:1 *4848*
temple, whither the Jews always *r* Jn 18:20 *4905*

RESORTED
r to him out of all their coasts 2Chr 11:13 3320
and all the multitude *r* unto him Mk 2:13 *2064*
many *r* unto him, and said, John Jn 10:41 *2064*
for Jesus ofttimes *r* thither with Jn 18:2 *4863*
unto the women which *r* thither Acts 16:13 *4905*

RESPECT
And the LORD had *r* unto Abel Gen 4:4 8159
and to his offering he had not *r* Gen 4:5 8159
of Israel, and God had *r* unto them Ex 2:25 3045
thou shalt not *r* the person of Lev 19:15 5375
For I will have *r* unto you Lev 26:9 6437
R not thou their offering Num 16:15 6437
Ye shall not *r* persons in Deut 1:17 5234
thou shalt not *r* persons, neither Deut 16:19 6437
neither doth God *r* any person 2Sa 14:14 5375
Yet have thou *r* unto the prayer 1Kin 8:28 6437
had *r* unto them, because of his 2Kin 13:23 6437
Have *r* therefore to the prayer of 2Chr 6:19 6437
nor *r* of persons, nor taking of 2Chr 19:7 4856
Have *r* unto the covenant Ps 74:20 5027
when I have *r* unto all thy Ps 119:6 5027
precepts, and have *r* unto thy ways Ps 119:15 5027
I will have *r* unto thy statutes Ps 119:117 8159
yet hath he *r* unto the lowly Ps 138:6 7200
to have *r* of persons in judgment Prov 24:23 5234
To have *r* of persons is not good Prov 28:21 5234
his eyes shall have *r* to the Holy Is 17:7 7200
neither shall *r* that which his Is 17:8 7200
neither had *r* unto him that Is 22:11 7200
For there is no *r* of persons with Rom 2:11 *4382*
glorious had no glory in this *r* 2Cor 3:10 *3313*
neither is there *r* of persons Eph 6:9 *4382*
Not that I speak in *r* of want Phil 4:11 *2596*
or in *r* of an holyday, or of the Col 2:16 *3313*
and there is no *r* of persons Col 3:25 *4382*
for he had *r* unto the recompence Heb 11:26 *578*
Lord of glory, with *r* of persons Jas 2:1 *4382*
ye have *r* to him that weareth the Jas 2:3 *1914*
But if ye have *r* to persons Jas 2:9 *4380*
who without *r* of persons judgeth 1Pet 1:17 *678*

RESPECTED
they *r* not the persons of the Lam 4:16 5375

RESPECTER
that God is no *r* of persons Acts 10:34 *4381*

RESPECTETH
he *r* not any that are wise of Job 37:24 7200
r not the proud, nor such as turn Ps 40:4 6437

RESPITE
when Pharaoh saw that there was *r* Ex 8:15 7309
unto him, Give us seven days' *r* 1Sa 11:3 7503

REST
But the dove found no *r* for the Gen 8:9 4494
r yourselves under the tree Gen 18:4 8172
Jacob fed the *r* of Laban's flocks Gen 30:36 3498
And he saw that *r* was good Gen 49:15 4496
ye make them *r* from their burdens Ex 5:5 7673
To morrow is the *r* of the holy Ex 16:23 7677
seventh year thou shalt let it *r* Ex 23:11 8058
on the seventh day thou shalt *r* Ex 23:12 7673
that thine ox and thine ass may *r* Ex 23:12 5117
names of the *r* on the other stone Ex 28:10 3498
the seventh is the sabbath of *r* Ex 31:15 7677
with thee, and I will give thee *r* Ex 33:14 5117
on the seventh day thou shalt *r* Ex 34:21 7673
time and in harvest thou shalt *r* Ex 34:21 7673
day, a sabbath of *r* to the LORD Ex 35:2 7677
the *r* of the blood shall be wrung Lev 5:9 7604
of the *r* of the oil that is in Lev 14:17 3499
the *r* of the oil that is in the Lev 14:29 3498
shall be a sabbath of *r* unto you Lev 16:31 7677
seventh day is the sabbath of *r* Lev 23:3 7677
shall be unto you a sabbath of *r* Lev 23:32 7677
be a sabbath of *r* unto the land Lev 25:4 7677
it is a year of *r* unto the land Lev 25:5 7677
even then shall the land *r* Lev 26:34 7673
as it lieth desolate it shall *r* Lev 26:35 7673
it did not *r* in your sabbaths Lev 26:35 7673
beside the *r* of them that were Num 31:8
being the *r* of the prey which the Num 31:32 3499
the *r* of Gilead, and all Bashan, Deut 3:13 3499
have given *r* unto your brethren Deut 3:20 5117
maidservant may *r* as well as thou Deut 5:14 5117
ye are not as yet come to the *r* Deut 12:9 4496
when he giveth you *r* from all Deut 12:10 5117
r from all thine enemies round Deut 25:19 5117
shall the sole of thy foot have *r* Deut 28:65 4494
LORD your God hath given you *r* Josh 1:13 5117
LORD have given your brethren *r* Josh 1:15 5117
shall *r* in the waters of Jordan, Josh 3:13 5117
that the *r* which remained of them Josh 10:20 8300
the *r* of the kingdom of Sihon Josh 13:27 3499
And the land had *r* from war Josh 14:15 8252
There was also a lot for the *r* of Josh 17:2 3498
the *r* of Manasseh's sons had the Josh 17:6 3498
the *r* of the children of Kohath Josh 21:5 3498
the *r* of the Levites, out of the Josh 21:34 3498
the LORD gave them *r* round about Josh 21:44 5117
hath given *r* unto your brethren Josh 22:4 5117
r unto Israel from all their Josh 23:1 5117
And the land had *r* forty years Judg 3:11 8252
the land had *r* fourscore years Judg 3:30 8252
And the land had *r* forty years Judg 5:31 8252
but all the *r* of the people bowed Judg 7:6 3499
he sent all the *r* of Israel every Judg 7:8
LORD grant you that ye may find *r* Ruth 1:9 4496
shall I not seek *r* for thee Ruth 3:1 4494
for the man will not be in *r* Ruth 3:18 8252
the *r* of the people he sent every 1Sa 13:2 3499
the *r* we have utterly destroyed 1Sa 15:15 3498
Let it *r* on the head of Joab, and 2Sa 3:29 2342
the LORD had given him *r* round 2Sa 7:1 5117
have caused thee to *r* from all 2Sa 7:11 5117
the *r* of the people he delivered 2Sa 10:10 3499
the *r* of the people together 2Sa 12:28 3499
of the air to *r* on them by day 2Sa 21:10 5117
God hath given me *r* on every side 1Kin 5:4 5117
that hath given *r* unto his people 1Kin 8:56 4496
the *r* of the acts of Solomon, and 1Kin 11:41 3499
the *r* of the acts of Jeroboam, 1Kin 14:19 3499
Now the *r* of the acts of Rehoboam 1Kin 14:29 3499
Now the *r* of the acts of Abijam, 1Kin 15:7 3499
The *r* of all the acts of Asa, and 1Kin 15:23 3499
Now the *r* of the acts of Nadab, 1Kin 15:31 3499
Now the *r* of the acts of Baasha, 1Kin 16:5 3499
Now the *r* of the acts of Elah, and 1Kin 16:14 3499
Now the *r* of the acts of Zimri, 1Kin 16:20 3499
Now the *r* of the acts of Omri 1Kin 16:27 3499
But the *r* fled to Aphek, into the 1Kin 20:30 3498
Now the *r* of the acts of Ahab, and 1Kin 22:39 3499
Now the *r* of the acts of 1Kin 22:45 3499
Now the *r* of the acts of Ahaziah 2Kin 1:18 3499
spirit of Elijah doth *r* on Elisha 2Kin 2:15 5117
thou and thy children of the *r* 2Kin 4:7 3498
the *r* of the acts of Joram, and 2Kin 8:23 3499
Now the *r* of the acts of Jehu, and 2Kin 10:34 3499
the *r* of the acts of Joash, and 2Kin 12:19 3499
Now the *r* of the acts of Jehoahaz 2Kin 13:8 3499
the *r* of the acts of Joash, and 2Kin 13:12 3499
Now the *r* of the acts of Jehoash 2Kin 14:15 3499
the *r* of the acts of Amaziah, are 2Kin 14:18 3499
Now the *r* of the acts of Jeroboam 2Kin 14:28 3499
the *r* of the acts of Azariah, and 2Kin 15:6 3499
the *r* of the acts of Zachariah, 2Kin 15:11 3499
the *r* of the acts of Shallum, and 2Kin 15:15 3499
the *r* of the acts of Menahem, and 2Kin 15:21 3499
the *r* of the acts of Pekahiah, and 2Kin 15:26 3499
the *r* of the acts of Pekah, and 2Kin 15:31 3499
Now the *r* of the acts of Jotham, 2Kin 15:36 3499
Now the *r* of the acts of Ahaz 2Kin 16:19 3499
the *r* of the acts of Hezekiah, and 2Kin 20:20 3499
Now the *r* of the acts of Manasseh 2Kin 21:17 3499
Now the *r* of the acts of Amon 2Kin 21:25 3499
Now the *r* of the acts of Josiah, 2Kin 23:28 3499
Now the *r* of the acts of 2Kin 24:5 3499
Now the *r* of the people that were 2Kin 25:11 3499
And they smote the *r* of the 1Chr 4:43 7611
LORD, after that the ark had *r* 1Chr 6:31 4494
Unto the *r* of the children of 1Chr 6:77 3498
Joab repaired the *r* of the city 1Chr 11:8 7605
all the *r* also of Israel were of 1Chr 12:38 7611
the *r* that were chosen, who were 1Chr 16:41 7605
the *r* of the people he delivered 1Chr 19:11 3499
to thee, who shall be a man of *r* 1Chr 22:9 4496
I will give him *r* from all his 1Chr 22:9 5117
he not given you *r* on every side 1Chr 22:18 3499
hath given *r* unto his people 1Chr 23:25 3499
the *r* of the sons of Levi were 1Chr 24:20 3498
r for the ark of the covenant of 1Chr 28:2 4496
Now the *r* of the acts of Solomon, 2Chr 9:29 7605
the *r* of the acts of Abijah, and 2Chr 13:22 3499
for the land had *r*, and he had no 2Chr 14:6 8252
because the LORD had given him *r* 2Chr 14:6 5117
he hath given us *r* on every side 2Chr 14:7 5117
for we *r* on thee, and in thy name 2Chr 14:11 8172
the LORD gave them *r* round about 2Chr 15:15 5117
his God gave him *r* round about 2Chr 20:30 5117
Now the *r* of the acts of 2Chr 20:34 3499
they brought the *r* of the money 2Chr 24:14 7605
Now the *r* of the acts of Amaziah, 2Chr 25:26 3499
Now the *r* of the acts of Uzziah, 2Chr 26:22 3499
Now the *r* of the acts of Jotham, 2Chr 27:7 3499
Now the *r* of his acts and of all 2Chr 28:26 3499
Now the *r* of the acts of Hezekiah 2Chr 32:32 3499
Now the *r* of the acts of Manasseh 2Chr 33:18 3499
Now the *r* of the acts of Josiah, 2Chr 35:26 3499
Now the *r* of the acts of 2Chr 36:8 3499
the *r* of the chief of the fathers Ezr 4:3 7605
the *r* of their companions, unto Ezr 4:7 7605
the *r* of their companions Ezr 4:9 7606
the *r* of the nations whom the Ezr 4:10 7606
the *r* that are on this side the Ezr 4:10 7606
to the *r* of their companions that Ezr 4:17 7606
unto the *r* beyond the river, Ezr 4:17 7606
the *r* of the children of the Ezr 6:16 7606
to do with the *r* of the silver Ezr 7:18 7606
nor to the *r* that did the work Neh 2:16 3499
to the *r* of the people, Be not ye Neh 4:14 3499
to the *r* of the people, The work Neh 4:19 3499
the *r* of our enemies, heard that Neh 6:1 3499
the *r* of the prophets, that would Neh 6:14 3499
that which the *r* of the people Neh 7:72 7611
But after they had *r*, they did Neh 9:28 5117
the *r* of the people, the priests, Neh 10:28 7605
the *r* of the people also cast Neh 11:1 7605
in the *r* of the king's provinces Est 9:12 7605
had *r* from their enemies, and slew Est 9:16 5118
then had I been at *r*, Job 3:13 5117
and there the weary be at *r* Job 3:17 5117
There the prisoners *r* together Job 3:18 7599
not in safety, neither had I *r*, Job 3:26 8252
thou shalt take thy *r* in safety Job 11:18 7901
Turn from him, that he may *r* Job 14:6 2308
when our *r* together is in the Job 17:16 5183
and my sinews take no *r* Job 30:17 7901
my flesh also shall *r* in hope Ps 16:9 7931
leave the *r* of their substance to Ps 17:14 3499
R in the LORD, and wait patiently Ps 37:7 1826
neither is there any *r* in my Ps 38:3 7965
then would I fly away, and be at *r* Ps 55:6 7931
That thou mayest give him *r* from Ps 94:13 8252
they should not enter into my *r* Ps 95:11 4496
Return unto thy *r*, O my soul Ps 116:7 4496
r upon the lot of the righteous Ps 125:3 5117
Arise, O LORD, into thy *r* Ps 132:8 4496
This is my *r* for ever Ps 132:14 4496
neither will he *r* content Prov 6:35
he rage or laugh, there is no *r* Prov 29:9 5183
thy son, and he shall give thee *r* Prov 29:17 5117
heart taketh not *r* in the night Eccl 2:23
this hath more *r* than the other Eccl 6:5 5183
makest thy flock to *r* at noon Song 1:7 7257
shall *r* all of them in the Is 7:19 5117
the *r* of the trees of his forest Is 10:19 7605
of the LORD shall *r* upon him Is 11:2 5117
and his *r* shall be glorious Is 11:10 4496
shall give thee *r* from thy sorrow Is 14:3 5117
The whole earth is at *r*, and is Is 14:7 5117
said unto me, I will take my *r* Is 18:4 8252
there also shalt thou have no *r* Is 23:12 5117
shall the hand of the LORD *r* Is 25:10 5117
This is the *r* wherewith ye may Is 28:12 4496
ye may cause the weary to *r* Is 28:12 5117
returning and *r* shall ye be saved Is 30:15 5183
screech owl also shall *r* there Is 34:14 7280
and find for herself a place of *r* Is 34:14 4494
to *r* for a light of the people Is 51:4 7280
they shall *r* in their beds, each Is 57:2 5117
troubled sea, when it cannot *r* Is 57:20 8252
for Jerusalem's sake I will not *r* Is 62:1 8252
And give him no *r*, till he Is 62:7 1824
of the LORD caused him to *r* Is 63:14 5117
and where is the place of my *r* Is 66:1 4496
ye shall find *r* for your souls Jer 6:16 4771
shall return, and shall be in *r* Jer 30:10 8252
when I went to cause him to *r* Jer 31:2 7280
with the *r* of the people that Jer 39:9 3499
in my sighing, and I find no *r* Jer 45:3 4496
and Jacob shall return, and be in *r* Jer 46:27 8252
up thyself into thy scabbard, *r* Jer 47:6 7280
that he may give *r* to the land Jer 50:34 7280
and the *r* of the multitude Jer 52:15 3499
the heathen, she findeth no *r* Lam 1:3 4494
give thyself no *r* Lam 2:18 6314
we labour, and have no *r* Lam 5:5 5117
will cause my fury to *r* upon them Eze 5:13 5117
I make my fury toward thee to *r* Eze 16:42 5117
and I will cause my fury to *r* Eze 21:17 5117
caused my fury to *r* upon thee Eze 24:13 5117
I will go to them that are at *r* Eze 38:11 8252
the blessing to *r* in thine house Eze 44:30 5117
the *r* of the land shall they give Eze 45:8
As for the *r* of the tribes, from Eze 48:23 3499
the *r* of the wise men of Babylon Dan 2:18 7606
was at *r* in mine house, and Dan 4:4 7954
As concerning the *r* of the beasts Dan 7:12 7606
for thou shalt *r*, and stand in thy Dan 12:13 5117
for this is not your *r* Mic 2:10 4496
that I might *r* in the day of Hab 3:16 5117
he will *r* in his love, he will Zeph 3:17 2790
earth sitteth still, and is at *r* Zec 1:11 8252
Damascus shall be the *r* thereof Zec 9:1 4496
let the *r* eat every one the flesh Zec 11:9 7604
heavy laden, and I will give you *r* Mt 11:28 *373*
ye shall find *r* unto your souls Mt 11:29 *372*
through dry places, seeking *r* Mt 12:43 *372*
Sleep on now, and take your *r* Mt 26:45 *373*
The *r* said, Let be, let us see Mt 27:49 *3062*
into a desert place, and *r* a while Mk 6:31 *373*
Sleep on now, and take your *r* Mk 14:41 *373*

there, your peace shall r upon it Lk 10:6 1879
through dry places, seeking r Lk 11:24 372
why take ye thought for the r Lk 12:26 3062
unto the eleven, and to all the r Lk 24:9 3062
spoken of taking of r in sleep Jn 11:13 2681
also my flesh shall r in hope Acts 2:26 3062
to the r of the apostles, Men and Acts 2:37 3062
of the r durst no man join Acts 5:13 2663
or what is the place of my r Acts 7:49 1515
churches r throughout all Judaea Acts 9:31 3062
And the r, some on boards, and some Acts 27:44 3062
it, and the r were blinded Rom 11:7 3062
But to the r speak I, not the 1Cor 7:12 3062
the r will I set in order when I 1Cor 11:34 3062
I had no r in my spirit, because 2Cor 2:13 425
Macedonia, our flesh had no r 2Cor 7:5 425
the power of Christ may r upon me 2Cor 12:9 1981
to you who are troubled r with us 2Th 1:7 425
They shall not enter into my r Heb 3:11 2663
they should not enter into his r Heb 3:18 2663
left us of entering into his r Heb 4:1 2663
have believed do enter into r Heb 4:3 2663
if they shall enter into my r Heb 4:3 2663
God did r the seventh day from Heb 4:4 2664
If they shall enter into my r Heb 4:5 2663
For if Jesus had given them r Heb 4:8 2664
a r to the people of God Heb 4:9 4520
For he that is entered into his r Heb 4:10 2663
therefore to enter into that r Heb 4:11 2663
he no longer should live the r of 1Pet 4:2 1954
unto the r in Thyatira, as many Rev 2:24 3062
they r not day and night, saying Rev 4:8
that they should r yet for a Rev 6:11 373
the r of the men which were not Rev 9:20 3062
they have no r day nor night, who Rev 14:11 372
that they may r from their Rev 14:13 373
But the r of the dead lived not Rev 20:5 3062

RESTED

he r on the seventh day from all Gen 2:2 7673
because that in it he had r from Gen 2:3 7673
the ark r in the seventh month, Gen 8:4 5117
r in all the coasts of Egypt Ex 10:14 5117
So the people r on the seventh Ex 16:30 7673
in them is, and r the seventh day Ex 20:11 5117
earth, and on the seventh day he r Ex 31:17 7673
tabernacle they r in their tents Num 9:18 2583
of the LORD they r in the tents Num 9:23 2583
the cloud r in the wilderness of Num 10:12 7931
And when it r, he said, Return, O Num 10:36 5117
that, when the spirit r upon them Num 11:25 5117
and the spirit r upon them Num 11:26 5117
And the land r from war Josh 11:23 8252
they r on the house with timber 1Kin 6:10 270
the people r themselves upon the 2Chr 32:8 5564
fourteenth day of the same r they Est 9:17 5118
fifteenth day of the same they r Est 9:18 5118
the Jews r from their enemies Est 9:22 5117
My bowels boiled, and r not Job 30:27 1826
r the sabbath day according to Lk 23:56 2270

RESTEST

r in the law, and makest thy boast Rom 2:17 1879

RESTETH

him to be in safety, whereon he r Job 24:23 8172
Wisdom r in the heart of him that Prov 14:33 5117
for anger r in the bosom of fools Eccl 7:9 5117
of glory and of God r upon you 1Pet 4:14 373

RESTING

to search out a r place for them Num 10:33 4496
O LORD God, into thy r place 2Chr 6:41 5118
spoil not his r place Prov 24:15 7258
dwellings, and in quiet r places Is 32:18 4496

RESTINGPLACE

hill, they have forgotten their r Jer 50:6 7258

RESTITUTION

for he should make full r Ex 22:3 7999
his own vineyard, shall he make r Ex 22:5 7999
the fire shall surely make r Ex 22:6 7999
he shall make r unto the owner Ex 22:12 7999
to his substance shall the r be Job 20:18 8545
the times of r of all things Acts 3:21 605

RESTORE

Now therefore r the man his wife Gen 20:7 7725
and if thou r her not, know thou Gen 20:7 7725
head, and r thee unto thy place Gen 40:13 7725
to r every man's money into his Gen 42:25 7725
he shall r five oxen for an ox, Ex 22:1 7999
he shall r double Ex 22:4 7999
that he shall r that which he Lev 6:4 7725
he shall even r it in the Lev 6:5 7999
killeth a beast, he shall r it Lev 24:21 7999
r the overplus unto the man to Lev 25:27 7725
if he be not able to r it to him Lev 25:28 7725
the congregation shall r him to Num 35:25 7725
thou shalt r it to him again Deut 22:2 7725
now therefore r those lands again Judg 11:13 7725
therefore I will r it unto thee Judg 17:3 7725
and I will r it you 1Sa 12:3 7725
will r thee all the land of Saul 2Sa 9:7 7725
he shall r the lamb fourfold 2Sa 12:6 7999
r me the kingdom of my father 2Sa 16:3 7725
took from thy father, I will r 1Kin 20:34 7725
R all that was hers, and all the 2Kin 8:6 7725
R, I pray you, to them, even this Neh 5:11 7725
Then said they, We will r them Neh 5:12 7725
and his hands shall r their goods Job 20:10 7725
which he laboured for shall he r Job 20:18 7725
R unto me the joy of thy Ps 51:12 7725
he be found, he shall r sevenfold Prov 6:31 7999
I will r thy judges as at the Is 1:26 7725
for a spoil, and none saith, R Is 42:22 7725
to r the preserved of Israel Is 49:6 7725
r comforts unto him and to his Is 57:18 7999
them up, and r them to this place Jer 27:22 7725
For I will r health unto thee, and Jer 30:17 5927
If the wicked r the pledge Eze 33:15 7725
forth of the commandment to r Dan 9:25 7725
I will r to you the years that Joel 2:25 7999
shall first come, and r all things Mt 17:11 600
accusation, I r him fourfold Lk 19:8 591
wilt thou at this time r again Acts 1:6 600
r such an one in the spirit of Gal 6:1 2675

RESTORED

Abraham, and r him Sarah his wife Gen 20:14 7725
he r the chief butler unto his Gen 40:21 7725
me he r unto mine office, and him Gen 41:13 7725
unto his brethren, My money is r Gen 42:28 7725
face, and shall not be r to thee Deut 28:31 7725
when he had r the eleven hundred Judg 17:3 7725
Yet he r the money unto his Judg 17:4 7725
from Israel were r to Israel 1Sa 7:14 7725
that my hand may be r me again 1Kin 13:6 7725
the king's hand was r him again 1Kin 13:6 7725
woman, whose son he had r to life 2Kin 8:1 2421
how he had r a dead body to life 2Kin 8:5 2421
woman, whose son he had r to life 2Kin 8:5 2421
is her son, whom Elisha r to life 2Kin 8:5 2421
r it to Judah, after that the 2Kin 14:22 7725
He r the coast of Israel from the 2Kin 14:25 7725
which Huram had r to Solomon 2Chr 8:2 5414
r it to Judah, after that the 2Chr 26:2 7725
and brought unto Babylon, be r Ezr 6:5 8421
then I r that which I took not Ps 69:4 7725
but hath r to the debtor his Eze 18:7 7725
hath not r the pledge, and hath Eze 18:12 7725
and it was r whole, like as the Mt 12:13 600
his hand was r whole as the other Mk 3:5 600
and he was r, and saw every man Mk 8:25 600
his hand was r whole as the other Lk 6:10 600
that I may be r to you the sooner Heb 13:19 600

RESTORER

be unto thee a r of thy life Ruth 4:15 7725
The r of paths to dwell in Is 58:12 7725

RESTORETH

He r my soul Ps 23:3 7725
cometh first, and r all things Mk 9:12 600

RESTRAIN

dost thou r wisdom to thyself Job 15:8 1639
remainder of wrath shalt thou r Ps 76:10 2296

RESTRAINED

and the rain from heaven was r Gen 8:2 3607
now nothing will be r from them Gen 11:6 1219
the LORD hath r me from bearing Gen 16:2 6113
the people were r from bringing Ex 36:6 3607
themselves vile, and he r them not 1Sa 3:13 3543
are they r Is 63:15 662
I r the floods thereof, and the Eze 31:15 4513
sayings scarce r they the people Acts 14:18 2664

RESTRAINEST

off fear, and r prayer before God Job 15:4 1639

RESTRAINT

for there is no r to the LORD to 1Sa 14:6 4622

RESTS

he made narrowed r round about 1Kin 6:6

RESURRECTION

which say that there is no r Mt 22:23 386
Therefore in the r whose wife Mt 22:28 386
For in the r they neither marry Mt 22:30 386
But as touching the r of the dead Mt 22:31 386
out of the graves after his r Mt 27:53 1454
which say there is no r Mk 12:18 386
In the r therefore, when they Mk 12:23 386
recompensed at the r of the just Lk 14:14 386
which deny that there is any r Lk 20:27 386
Therefore in the r whose wife of Lk 20:33 386
the r from the dead, neither Lk 20:35 386
God, being the children of the r Lk 20:36 386
done good, unto the r of life Jn 5:29 386
evil, unto the r of damnation Jn 5:29 386
again in the r at the last day Jn 11:24 386
Jesus said unto her, I am the r Jn 11:25 386
to be a witness with us of his r Acts 1:22 386
before spake of the r of Christ Acts 2:31 386
through Jesus the r from the dead Acts 4:2 386
of the r of the Lord Jesus Acts 4:33 386
unto them Jesus, and the r Acts 17:18 386
they heard of the r of the dead Acts 17:32 386
r of the dead I am called in Acts 23:6 386
Sadducees say that there is no r Acts 23:8 386
there shall be a r of the dead Acts 24:15 386
Touching the r of the dead I am Acts 24:21 386
holiness, by the r from the dead Rom 1:4 386
be also in the likeness of his r Rom 6:5 386
that there is no r of the dead 1Cor 15:12 386
But if there be no r of the dead 1Cor 15:13 386
man came also the r of the dead 1Cor 15:21 386
So also is the r of the dead 1Cor 15:42 386
know him, and the power of his r Phil 3:10 386
attain unto the r of the dead Phil 3:11 1815
saying that the r is past already 2Ti 2:18 386
of r of the dead, and of eternal Heb 6:2 386
that they might obtain a better r Heb 11:35 386
r of Jesus Christ from the dead 1Pet 1:3 386
by the r of Jesus Christ 1Pet 3:21 386
This is the first r Rev 20:5 386
he that hath part in the first r Rev 20:6 386

RETAIN

Dost thou still r thine integrity Job 2:9 2388
me, Let thine heart r my words Prov 4:4 8551
and strong men r riches Prov 11:16 8551
over the spirit to r the spirit Eccl 8:8 3607
but she shall not r the power of Dan 11:6 6113
and whose soever sins ye r Jn 20:23 2902
like to r God in their knowledge Rom 1:28 2192

RETAINED

r those three hundred men Judg 7:8 2388
law, the damsel's father, r him Judg 19:4 2388
corruption, and I r no strength Dan 10:8 6113
upon me, and I have r no strength Dan 10:16 6113
soever sins ye retain, they are r Jn 20:23 2902
Whom I would have r with me Philem 13 2722

RETAINETH

and happy is every one that r her Prov 3:18 8551
A gracious woman r honour Prov 11:16 8551
he r not his anger for ever, Mic 7:18 2388

RETIRE

r ye from him, that he may be 2Sa 11:15 7725
r, stay not Jer 4:6 5756

RETIRED

the men of Israel r in the battle Judg 20:39 2015
they r from the city, every man 2Sa 20:22 6327

RETURN

till thou r unto the ground Gen 3:19 7725
art, and unto dust shalt thou r Gen 3:19 7725
after his r from the slaughter of Gen 14:17 7725
R to thy mistress, and submit Gen 16:9 7725
I will certainly r unto thee Gen 18:10 7725
time appointed I will r unto thee Gen 18:14 7725
R unto the land of thy fathers, Gen 31:3 7725
r unto the land of thy kindred Gen 31:13 7725
R unto thy country, and to thy Gen 32:9 7725
r unto my brethren which are in Ex 4:18 7725
Moses in Midian, Go, r into Egypt Ex 4:19 7725
When thou goest to r into Egypt Ex 4:21 7725
they see war, and they r to Egypt Ex 13:17 7725
ye shall r every man unto his Lev 25:10 7725
ye shall r every man unto his Lev 25:10 7725
year of this jubile ye shall r Lev 25:13 7725
that he may r unto his possession Lev 25:27 7725
he shall r unto his possession Lev 25:28 7725
shall r unto his own family, and Lev 25:41 7725
of his fathers shall he r Lev 25:41 7725
of the jubile the field shall r Lev 27:24 7725
And when it rested, he said, R Num 10:36 7725
not better for us to r into Egypt Num 14:3 7725
a captain, and let us r into Egypt Num 14:4 7725
R unto Balak, and thus thou shalt Num 23:5 7725
We will not r unto our houses, Num 32:18 7725
then afterward ye shall r Num 32:22 7725
high priest the slayer shall r Num 35:28 7725
then shall ye r every man unto Deut 3:20 7725
cause the people to r to Egypt Deut 17:16 7725
henceforth r no more that way Deut 17:16 7725
r to his house, lest he die in Deut 20:5 7725
r unto his house, lest he die in Deut 20:6 7725
r unto his house, lest he die in Deut 20:7 7725
r unto his house, lest his Deut 20:8 7725
shalt r unto the LORD thy God, and Deut 30:2 7725
compassion upon thee, and will r Deut 30:3 7725
And thou shalt r and obey the voice Deut 30:8 7725
then ye shall r unto the land of Josh 1:15 7725
then shall the slayer r, and come Josh 20:6 7725
therefore now r ye, and get you Josh 22:4 6437
R with much riches unto your Josh 22:8 7725
is fearful and afraid, let him r Judg 7:3 7725
when I r in peace from the Judg 11:31 7725
that she might r from the country Ruth 1:6 7725
way to r unto the land of Judah Ruth 1:7 7725
r each to her mother's house Ruth 1:8 7725
Surely we will r with thee unto Ruth 1:10 7725
r thou after thy sister in law Ruth 1:15 7725
or to r from following after thee Ruth 1:16 7725
but in any wise r him a trespass 1Sa 6:3 7725
offering which we shall r to him 1Sa 6:4 7725
which ye r him for a trespass 1Sa 6:8 7725
If ye do r unto the LORD with all 1Sa 7:3 7725
And his r was to Ramah 1Sa 7:17 8666
was with him, Come, and let us r 1Sa 9:5 7725
unto Saul, I will not r with thee 1Sa 15:26 7725
r, my son David 1Sa 26:21 7725
said unto him, Make this fellow r 1Sa 29:4 7725
Wherefore now r, and go in peace, 1Sa 29:7 7725
to r into the land of the 1Sa 29:11 7725
ere thou bid the people r from 2Sa 2:26 7725
Then said Abner unto him, Go, r 2Sa 3:16 7725
your beards be grown, and then r 2Sa 10:5 7725
to him, but he shall not r to me 2Sa 12:23 7725
r to thy place, and abide with the 2Sa 15:19 7725
r thou, and take back thy brethren 2Sa 15:20 7725
r into the city in peace, and your 2Sa 15:27 7725
But if thou r to the city 2Sa 15:34 7725
R thou, and all thy servants 2Sa 19:14 7725
I shall r to him that sent me 2Sa 24:13 7725
the LORD shall r his blood upon 1Kin 2:32 7725
therefore r upon the head of Joab 1Kin 2:33 7725
therefore the LORD shall r thy 1Kin 2:44 7725
so r unto thee with all their 1Kin 8:48 7725
r every man to his house 1Kin 12:24 7725
kingdom r to the house of David 1Kin 12:26 7725
And he said, I may not r with thee 1Kin 13:16 7725
r on thy way to the wilderness of 1Kin 19:15 7725
for at the r of the year the king 1Kin 20:22 8666
came to pass at the r of the year 1Kin 20:26 8666
let them r every man to his house 1Kin 22:17 7725
If thou r at all in peace, the 1Kin 22:28 7725
r from me 2Kin 18:14 7725
and shall r to his own land 2Kin 19:7 7725
he came, by the same shall he r 2Kin 19:33 7725
but let the shadow r backward ten 2Kin 20:10 7725
your beards be grown, and then r 1Chr 19:5 7725
and shall r and confess thy name, 2Chr 6:24 7725

If they *r* to thee with all their	2Chr 6:38	7725
ye me to *r* answer to this people	2Chr 10:6	7725
we may *r* answer to this people	2Chr 10:9	7725
r every man to his house	2Chr 11:4	7725
let them *r* therefore every man to	2Chr 18:16	7725
of affliction, until I *r* in peace	2Chr 18:26	7725
If thou certainly *r* in peace	2Chr 18:27	7725
he will *r* to the remnant of you,	2Chr 30:6	7725
face from you, if ye *r* unto him	2Chr 30:9	7725
and when wilt thou *r*	Neh 2:6	7725
r unto us they will be upon you	Neh 4:12	7725
a captain to *r* to their bondage	Neh 9:17	7725
bade them *r* Mordecai this answer	Est 4:15	7725
should *r* upon his own head, and	Est 9:25	7725
womb, and naked shall I *r* thither	Job 1:21	7725
R, I pray you, let it not be	Job 6:29	7725
r again, my righteousness is in	Job 6:29	7725
He shall *r* no more to his house,	Job 7:10	7725
Before I go whence I shall not *r*	Job 10:21	7725
that he shall *r* out of darkness	Job 15:22	7725
go the way whence I shall not *r*	Job 16:22	7725
But as for you all, do ye *r*	Job 17:10	7725
If thou *r* to the Almighty, thou	Job 22:23	7725
he shall *r* to the days of his	Job 33:25	7725
that they *r* from iniquity	Job 36:10	7725
they go forth, and *r* not unto them	Job 39:4	7725
R, O LORD, deliver my soul	Ps 6:4	7725
let them *r* and be ashamed suddenly	Ps 6:10	7725
sakes therefore *r* thou on high	Ps 7:7	7725
shall *r* upon his own head	Ps 7:16	7725
They *r* at evening	Ps 59:6	7725
And at evening let them *r*	Ps 59:14	7725
Therefore his people *r* hither	Ps 73:10	7725
O let not the oppressed *r* ashamed	Ps 74:21	7725
R, we beseech thee, O God of	Ps 80:14	7725
and sayest, *R*, ye children of men	Ps 90:3	7725
R, O LORD, how long	Ps 90:13	7725
shall *r* unto righteousness	Ps 94:15	7725
they die, and *r* to their dust	Ps 104:29	7725
R unto thy rest, O my soul	Ps 116:7	7725
None that go unto her *r* again	Prov 2:19	7725
a stone, it will *r* upon him	Prov 26:27	7725
rivers come, thither they *r* again	Eccl 1:7	7725
naked shall he *r* to go as he came	Eccl 5:15	7725
nor the clouds *r* after the rain	Eccl 12:2	7725
Then shall the dust *r* to the	Eccl 12:7	7725
the spirit shall *r* unto God who	Eccl 12:7	7725
R, *r*, O Shulamite	Song 6:13	7725
r, *r*, that we may look upon	Song 6:13	7725
shall be a tenth, and it shall *r*	Is 6:13	7725
The remnant shall *r*, even the	Is 10:21	7725
yet a remnant of them shall *r*	Is 10:22	7725
they shall *r* even to the LORD, and	Is 19:22	7725
enquire ye: *r*, come	Is 21:12	7725
the ransomed of the LORD shall *r*	Is 35:10	7725
a rumour, and *r* to his own land	Is 37:7	7725
he came, by the same shall he *r*	Is 37:34	7725
r unto me	Is 44:22	7725
in righteousness, and shall not *r*	Is 45:23	7725
the redeemed of the LORD shall *r*	Is 51:11	7725
let him *r* unto the LORD, and he	Is 55:7	7725
it shall not *r* unto me void	Is 55:11	7725
R for thy servants' sake, the	Is 63:17	7725
shall he *r* unto her again	Jer 3:1	7725
yet *r* again to me, saith the LORD	Jer 3:1	7725
words toward the north, and say, *R*	Jer 3:12	7725
R, ye backsliding children, and I	Jer 3:22	7725
If thou wilt *r*, O Israel, saith	Jer 4:1	7725
Israel, saith the LORD, *r* unto me	Jer 4:1	7725
they have refused to *r*	Jer 5:3	7725
shall he turn away, and not *r*	Jer 8:4	7725
fast deceit, they refuse to *r*	Jer 8:5	7725
I have plucked them out I will *r*	Jer 12:15	7725
since they *r* not from their ways	Jer 15:7	7725
thus saith the LORD, If thou *r*	Jer 15:19	7725
let them *r* unto thee	Jer 15:19	7725
but *r* not thou unto them	Jer 15:19	7725
r ye now every one from his evil	Jer 18:11	7725
for he shall *r* no more, nor see	Jer 22:10	7725
He shall not *r* thither any more	Jer 22:11	7725
land whereunto they desire to *r*	Jer 22:27	7725
thither shall they not *r*	Jer 22:27	7725
that none doth *r* from his	Jer 23:14	7725
The anger of the LORD shall not *r*	Jer 23:20	7725
for they shall *r* unto me with	Jer 24:7	7725
in causing you to *r* to this place	Jer 29:10	7725
I will cause them to *r* to the	Jer 30:3	7725
and Jacob shall *r*, and shall be in	Jer 30:10	7725
anger of the LORD shall not *r*	Jer 30:24	7725
a great company shall *r* thither	Jer 31:8	7725
I will cause their captivity to *r*	Jer 32:44	7725
and the captivity of Israel to *r*	Jer 33:7	7725
For I will cause to *r* the	Jer 33:11	7725
I will cause their captivity to *r*	Jer 33:26	7725
whom they had let go free, to *r*	Jer 34:11	7725
liberty at their pleasure, to *r*	Jer 34:16	7725
and cause them to *r* to this city	Jer 34:22	7725
R ye now every man from his evil	Jer 35:15	7725
that they may *r* every man from	Jer 36:3	7725
will *r* every one from his evil	Jer 36:7	7725
shall *r* to Egypt into their own	Jer 37:7	7725
that thou cause me not to *r* to	Jer 37:20	7725
cause me to *r* to Jonathan's house	Jer 38:26	7725
cause you to *r* to your own land	Jer 42:12	7725
that they should *r* into the land	Jer 44:14	7725
have a desire to *r* to dwell there	Jer 44:14	7725
for none shall *r* but such as	Jer 44:14	7725
that escape the sword shall *r* out	Jer 44:28	7725
and Jacob shall *r*, and be in rest	Jer 46:27	7725
none shall *r* in vain	Jer 50:9	7725
shall not *r* to that which is sold	Eze 7:13	7725
thereof, which shall not *r*	Eze 7:13	7725
that he should not *r* from his	Eze 13:22	7725
shall *r* to their former estate,	Eze 16:55	7725
her daughters shall *r* to their	Eze 16:55	7725
thy daughters shall *r* to your	Eze 16:55	7725
that he should *r* from his ways	Eze 18:23	7725
it shall not *r* any more	Eze 21:5	7725
I cause it to *r* into his sheath	Eze 21:30	7725
will cause them to *r* into the	Eze 29:14	7725
and thy cities shall not *r*	Eze 35:9	3427
he shall not *r* by the way of the	Eze 46:9	7725
after, it shall *r* to the prince	Eze 46:17	7725
caused me to *r* to the brink of	Eze 47:6	7725
now will I *r* to fight with the	Dan 10:20	7725
shall *r* into his own land	Dan 11:9	7725
then shall he *r*, and be stirred up	Dan 11:10	7725
For the king of the north shall *r*	Dan 11:13	7725
Then shall he *r* into his land	Dan 11:28	7725
do exploits, and *r* to his own land	Dan 11:28	7725
At the time appointed he shall *r*	Dan 11:29	7725
he shall be grieved, and *r*	Dan 11:30	7725
he shall even *r*, and have	Dan 11:30	7725
will go and *r* to my first husband	Hos 2:7	7725
Therefore will I *r*, and take away	Hos 2:9	7725
shall the children of Israel *r*	Hos 3:5	7725
go and *r* to my place, till they	Hos 5:15	7725
Come, and let us *r* unto the LORD	Hos 6:1	7725
they do not *r* to the LORD their	Hos 7:10	7725
They *r*, but not to the most High	Hos 7:16	7725
they shall *r* to Egypt	Hos 8:13	7725
but Ephraim shall *r* to Egypt	Hos 9:3	7725
He shall not *r* into the land of	Hos 11:5	7725
king, because they refused to *r*	Hos 11:5	7725
I will not *r* to destroy Ephraim	Hos 11:9	7725
shall his Lord *r* unto him	Hos 12:14	7725
O Israel, *r* unto the LORD thy God	Hos 14:1	7725
dwell under his shadow shall *r*	Hos 14:7	7725
Who knoweth if he will *r* and	Joel 2:14	7725
speedily will I *r* your recompence	Joel 3:4	7725
will *r* your recompence upon your	Joel 3:7	7725
thy reward shall *r* upon thine own	Obad 15	7725
they shall *r* to the hire of an	Mic 1:7	7725
r unto the children of Israel	Mic 5:3	7725
are impoverished, but we will *r*	Mal 1:4	7725
R unto me, and I will *r* unto	Mal 3:7	7725
But ye said, Wherein shall we *r*	Mal 3:7	7725
Then shall ye *r*, and discern	Mal 3:18	7725
that they should not *r* to Herod	Mt 2:12	844
worthy, let your peace *r* to you	Mt 10:13	1994
I will *r* into my house from	Mt 12:44	1994
field *r* back to take his clothes	Mt 24:18	1994
R to thine own house, and shew how	Lk 8:39	5290
I will *r* unto my house whence I	Lk 11:24	5290
when he will *r* from the wedding	Lk 12:36	360
let him likewise not *r* back	Lk 17:31	1994
for himself a kingdom, and to *r*	Lk 19:12	5290
now no more to *r* to corruption	Acts 13:34	5290
After this I will *r*, and will	Acts 15:16	390
but I will *r* again unto you, if	Acts 18:21	344
Syria, he purposed to *r* through	Acts 20:3	5290

RETURNED

the waters *r* from off the earth	Gen 8:3	7725
she *r* unto him into the ark, for	Gen 8:9	7725
which *r* not again unto him any	Gen 8:12	7725
And they *r*, and came to En-mishpat,	Gen 14:7	7725
and Abraham *r* unto his place	Gen 18:33	7725
they *r* into the land of the	Gen 21:32	7725
So Abraham *r* unto his young men,	Gen 22:19	7725
departed, and *r* unto his place	Gen 31:55	7725
And the messengers *r* to Jacob	Gen 32:6	7725
So Esau *r* that day on his way	Gen 33:16	7725
And Reuben *r* unto the pit	Gen 37:29	7725
he *r* unto his brethren, and said,	Gen 37:30	7725
he *r* to Judah, and said, I cannot	Gen 38:22	7725
r to them again, and communed with	Gen 42:24	7725
now we had *r* this second time	Gen 43:10	7725
Because of the money that was *r*	Gen 43:18	7725
man his ass, and *r* to the city	Gen 44:13	7725
Joseph *r* into Egypt, he, and his	Gen 50:14	7725
r to Jethro his father in law, and	Ex 4:18	7725
he *r* to the land of Egypt	Ex 4:20	7725
Moses *r* unto the LORD, and said,	Ex 5:22	7725
the sea *r* to his strength when	Ex 14:27	7725
And the waters *r*, and covered the	Ex 14:28	7725
Moses *r* the words of the people	Ex 19:8	7725
Moses *r* unto the LORD, and said,	Ex 32:31	7725
of the congregation *r* unto him	Ex 34:31	7725
is *r* unto her father's house, as	Lev 22:13	7725
they *r* from searching of the land	Num 13:25	7725
sent to search the land, who *r*	Num 14:36	7725
Aaron *r* unto Moses unto the door	Num 16:50	7725
he *r* unto him and, lo, he stood by	Num 23:6	7725
up, and went and *r* to his place	Num 24:25	7725
And ye *r* and wept before the LORD	Deut 1:45	7725
days, until the pursuers be *r*	Josh 2:16	7725
days, until the pursuers were *r*	Josh 2:22	7725
So the two men *r*, and descended	Josh 2:23	7725
of Jordan *r* unto their place	Josh 4:18	7725
the city once, and *r* into the camp	Josh 6:14	7725
they *r* to Joshua, and said unto	Josh 7:3	7725
that all the Israelites *r* unto Ai	Josh 8:24	7725
And Joshua *r*, and all Israel with	Josh 10:15	7725
all the people *r* to the camp to	Josh 10:21	7725
And Joshua *r*, and all Israel with	Josh 10:38	7725
And Joshua *r*, and all Israel with	Josh 10:43	7725
and the half tribe of Manasseh *r*	Josh 22:9	7725
r from the children of Reuben, and	Josh 22:32	7725
the judge was dead, that they *r*	Judg 2:19	7725
yea, she *r* answer to herself,	Judg 5:29	7725
there *r* of the people twenty and	Judg 7:3	7725
r into the host of Israel, and	Judg 7:15	7725
Gideon the son of Joash *r* from	Judg 8:13	7725
that she *r* unto her father, who	Judg 11:39	7725
And after a time he *r* to take her	Judg 14:8	7725
r unto their inheritance, and	Judg 21:23	7725
So Naomi *r*, and Ruth the Moabitess	Ruth 1:22	7725
which *r* out of the country of	Ruth 1:22	7725
worshipped before the LORD, and *r*	1Sa 1:19	7725
they *r* to Ekron the same day	1Sa 6:16	7725
r for a trespass offering unto	1Sa 6:17	7725
r from Saul to feed his father's	1Sa 17:15	7725
Israel *r* from chasing after the	1Sa 17:53	7725
as David *r* from the slaughter of	1Sa 17:57	7725
when David was *r* from the	1Sa 18:6	7725
Wherefore Saul *r* from pursuing	1Sa 23:28	7725
when Saul was *r* from following	1Sa 24:1	7725
for the LORD hath *r* the	1Sa 25:39	7725
his way, and Saul *r* to his place	1Sa 26:25	7725
the camels, and the apparel, and *r*	1Sa 27:9	7725
when David was *r* from the	2Sa 1:1	7725
and the sword of Saul *r* not empty	2Sa 1:22	7725
Joab *r* from following Abner	2Sa 2:30	7725
Go, return. And he *r*	2Sa 3:16	7725
And when Abner was *r* to Hebron	2Sa 3:27	7725
Then David *r* to bless his	2Sa 6:20	7725
David gat him a name when he *r*	2Sa 8:13	7725
So Joab *r* from the children of	2Sa 10:14	7725
and she *r* unto her house	2Sa 11:4	7725
all the people *r* unto Jerusalem	2Sa 12:31	7725
So Absalom *r* to his own house, and	2Sa 14:24	5437
The LORD hath *r* upon thee all the	2Sa 16:8	7725
whom thou seekest is as if all *r*	2Sa 17:3	7725
find them, they *r* to Jerusalem	2Sa 17:20	7725
the people *r* from pursuing after	2Sa 18:16	7725
So the king *r*, and came to Jordan	2Sa 19:15	7725
and he *r* unto his own place	2Sa 19:39	7725
Joab *r* to Jerusalem unto the king	2Sa 20:22	7725
the people *r* after him only to	2Sa 23:10	7725
r to depart, according to the	1Kin 12:24	7725
r not by the way that he came to	1Kin 13:10	7725
Jeroboam *r* not from his evil way	1Kin 13:33	7725
he *r* back from him, and took a	1Kin 19:21	7725
and from thence he *r* to Samaria	2Kin 2:25	7725
from him, and *r* to their own land	2Kin 3:27	7725
Then he *r*, and walked in the house	2Kin 4:35	7725
he *r* to the man of God, he and all	2Kin 5:15	7725
And the messengers *r*, and told the	2Kin 7:15	7725
that the woman *r* out of the land	2Kin 8:3	7725
But king Joram was *r* to be healed	2Kin 9:15	7725
and hostages, and *r* to Samaria	2Kin 14:14	7725
So Rab-shakeh *r*, and found the	2Kin 19:8	7725
of Assyria departed, and went and *r*	2Kin 19:36	7725
upon them, and *r* to Jerusalem	2Kin 23:20	7725
David *r* to bless his house	1Chr 16:43	5437
and all the people *r* to Jerusalem	1Chr 20:3	7725
it, that Jeroboam *r* out of Egypt	2Chr 10:2	7725
r from going against Jeroboam	2Chr 11:4	7725
in abundance, and *r* to Jerusalem	2Chr 14:15	7725
Judah *r* to his house in peace to	2Chr 19:1	7725
when they *r* to Jerusalem	2Chr 19:8	7725
Then they *r*, every man of Judah	2Chr 20:27	7725
he *r* to be healed in Jezreel	2Chr 22:6	7725
they *r* home in great anger	2Chr 25:10	7725
hostages also, and *r* to Samaria	2Chr 25:24	7725
then they *r* to Samaria	2Chr 28:15	7725
Then all the children of Israel *r*	2Chr 31:1	7725
So he *r* with shame of face to his	2Chr 32:21	7725
land of Israel, he *r* to Jerusalem	2Chr 34:7	7725
and they *r* to Jerusalem	2Chr 34:9	7725
then they *r* answer by letter	Ezr 5:5	8421
And thus they *r* us answer, saying,	Ezr 5:11	8421
the gate of the valley, and so *r*	Neh 2:15	7725
that we *r* all of us to the wall,	Neh 4:15	7725
yet when they *r*, and cried unto	Neh 9:28	7725
on the morrow she *r* into the	Est 2:14	7725
Then the king *r* out of the palace	Est 7:8	7725
my prayer *r* into mine own bosom	Ps 35:13	7725
and with Aram-zobah, when Joab *r*	Ps 60:t	7725
and they *r* and enquired early after	Ps 78:34	7725
So I *r*, and considered all the	Eccl 4:1	7725
Then I *r*, and I saw vanity under	Eccl 4:7	7725
I *r*, and saw under the sun, that	Eccl 9:11	7725
So Rabshakeh *r*, and found the king	Is 37:8	7725
of Assyria departed, and went and *r*	Is 37:37	7725
So the sun *r* ten degrees, by	Is 38:8	7725
But she *r* not	Jer 3:7	7725
they *r* with their vessels empty	Jer 14:3	7725
Even all the Jews *r* out of all	Jer 40:12	7725
from Mizpah cast about and *r*	Jer 41:14	7725
that were *r* from all nations,	Jer 43:5	7725
r as the appearance of a flash of	Eze 1:14	7725
have *r* to provoke me to anger	Eze 8:17	7725
Now when I had *r*, behold, at the	Eze 47:7	7725
and mine understanding *r* unto me	Dan 4:34	7725
the same time my reason *r* unto me	Dan 4:36	7725
honour and brightness *r* unto me	Dan 4:36	7725
when I *r* the captivity of my	Hos 6:11	7725
yet have ye not *r* unto me	Amos 4:6	7725
yet have ye not *r* unto me	Amos 4:8	7725
yet have ye not *r* unto me	Amos 4:9	7725
yet have ye not *r* unto me	Amos 4:10	7725
yet have ye not *r* unto me	Amos 4:11	7725
and they *r* and said, Like as the	Zec 1:6	7725
I am *r* to Jerusalem with mercies	Zec 1:16	7725
that no man passed through nor *r*	Zec 7:14	7725
I am *r* unto Zion, and will dwell	Zec 8:3	7725
the morning as he *r* into the city	Mt 21:18	1877
And when he *r*, he found them	Mk 14:40	5290
months, and *r* to her own house	Lk 1:56	5290
And the shepherds *r*, glorifying and	Lk 2:20	1994
they *r* into Galilee, to their own	Lk 2:39	5290
had fulfilled the days, as they *r*	Lk 2:43	5290
of the Holy Ghost *r* from Jordan	Lk 4:1	5290
Jesus *r* in the power of the	Lk 4:14	5290
up into the ship, and *r* back again	Lk 8:37	5290
to pass, that, when Jesus was *r*	Lk 8:40	5290
And the apostles, when they were *r*	Lk 9:10	5290
the seventy *r* again with joy,	Lk 10:17	5290
found that *r* to give glory to God	Lk 17:18	5290
came to pass, that when he was *r*	Lk 19:15	1880

R

done, smote their breasts, and r Lk 23:48 *5290*
And they r, and prepared spices and Lk 23:56 *5290*
r from the sepulchre, and told all Lk 24:9 *5290*
r to Jerusalem, and found the Lk 24:33 *5290*
r to Jerusalem with great joy Lk 24:52 *5290*
Then r they unto Jerusalem from Acts 1:12 *5290*
them not in the prison, they r Acts 5:22 *390*
r to Jerusalem, and preached the Acts 8:25 *5290*
Saul r from Jerusalem, when they Acts 12:25 *5290*
from them r to Jerusalem Acts 13:13 *5290*
they r again to Lystra, and to Acts 14:21 *5290*
and they r home again Acts 21:6 *5290*
go with him, and r to the castle Acts 23:32 *5290*
Arabia, and r again unto Damascus Gal 1:17 *5290*
have had opportunity to have r Heb 11:15 *344*
but are now r unto the Shepherd 1Pet 2:25 *1994*

RETURNETH
goeth forth, he r to his earth Ps 146:4 7725
As a dog r to his vomit Prov 26:11 7725
so a fool r to his folly Prov 26:11 8138
the wind r again according to his Eccl 1:6 7725
r not thither, but watereth the Is 55:10 7725
that passeth out and him that r Eze 35:7 7725
by, and because of him that r Zec 9:8 7725

RETURNING
In r and rest shall ye be saved Is 30:15 7729
r to the house, found the servant Lk 7:10 *5290*
Was r, and sitting in his chariot Acts 8:28 *5290*
who met Abraham r from the Heb 7:1 *5290*

REU (*re'-u*) See RAGAU. *Son of Peleg.*
lived thirty years, and begat R Gen 11:18 7466
after he begat R two hundred Gen 11:19 7466
R lived two and thirty years, and Gen 11:20 7466
R lived after he begat Serug two Gen 11:21 7466
Eber, Peleg, R, 1Chr 1:25 7466

REUBEN (*ru'-ben*) See REUBENITE.
1. A son of Jacob and Leah.
a son, and she called his name R Gen 29:32 7205
R went in the days of wheat Gen 30:14 7205
dwelt in that land, that R went Gen 35:22 7205
R, Jacob's firstborn, and Simeon, Gen 35:23 7205
R heard it, and he delivered him Gen 37:21 7205
R said unto them, Shed no blood, Gen 37:22 7205
And R returned unto the pit Gen 37:29 7205
R answered them, saying, Spake I Gen 42:22 7205
R spake unto his father, saying, Gen 42:37 7205
R, Jacob's firstborn Gen 46:8 7205
And the sons of R Gen 46:9 7205
as R and Simeon, they shall be Gen 48:5 7205
R, thou art my firstborn, my Gen 49:3 7205
R, Simeon, Levi, and Judah, Ex 1:2 7205
The sons of R the firstborn of Ex 6:14 7205
these be the families of R Ex 6:14 7205
And the children of R, Israel's Num 1:20 7205
On, the son of Peleth, sons of R Num 16:1 7205
R, the eldest son of Israel Num 26:5 7205
the children of R Num 26:5 7205
the sons of Eliab, the son of R Deut 11:6 7205
the stone of Bohan the son of R Josh 15:6 7205
the stone of Bohan the son of R Josh 18:17 7205
R, Simeon, Levi, and Judah, 1Chr 2:1 7205
Now the sons of R the firstborn 1Chr 5:1 7205
of R the firstborn of Israel were 1Chr 5:3 7205
2. Descendants of Reuben 1.
of the tribe of R Num 1:5 7205
of them, even of the tribe of R Num 1:21 7205
of R according to their armies Num 2:10 7205
of R shall be Elizur the son of Num 2:10 7205
of R were an hundred thousand Num 2:16 7205
prince of the children of R Num 7:30 7205
the standard of the camp of R set Num 10:18 7205
of the tribe of R, Shammua the Num 13:4 7205
Now the children of R and the Num 32:1 7205
of Gad and the children of R came Num 32:2 7205
of Gad and to the children of R Num 32:6 7205
the children of R spake unto Num 32:25 7205
the children of R will pass with Num 32:29 7205
Gad and the children of R answered Num 32:31 7205
of Gad, and to the children of R Num 32:33 7205
the children of R built Heshbon Num 32:37 7205
the tribe of the children of R Num 34:14 7206
R, Gad, and Asher, and Zebulun, Dan Deut 27:13 7205
Let R live, and not die Deut 33:6 7205
And the children of R, and the Josh 4:12 7205
the tribe of the children of R Josh 13:15 7205
of the children of R was Jordan Josh 13:23 7205
of R after their families Josh 13:23 7205
and Gad, and R, and half the tribe Josh 18:7 7205
the plain out of the tribe of R Josh 20:8 7205
had out of the tribe of R Josh 21:7 7205
And out of the tribe of R, Bezer Josh 21:36 7205
And the children of R and the Josh 22:9 7205
land of Canaan, the children of R Josh 22:10 7205
say, Behold, the children of R Josh 22:11 7205
sent unto the children of R Josh 22:13 7205
they came unto the children of R Josh 22:15 7205
Then the children of R and the Josh 22:21 7205
us and you, ye children of R Josh 22:25 7205
the words that the children of R Josh 22:30 7205
said unto the children of R Josh 22:31 7205
returned from the children of R Josh 22:32 7205
land wherein the children of R Josh 22:33 7205
And the children of R and the Josh 22:34 7205
For the divisions of R there were Judg 5:15 7205
For the divisions of R there were Judg 5:16 7205
The sons of R, and the Gadites, and 1Chr 5:18 7205
families, out of the tribe of R 1Chr 6:63 7205
given them out of the tribe of R 1Chr 6:78 7205
the west side, a portion for R Eze 48:6 7205
And by the border of R, from the Eze 48:7 7205
one gate of R, one gate of Judah, Eze 48:31 7205
Of the tribe of R were sealed Rev 7:5 *4502*

REUBENITE (*ru'-ben-ite*) See REUBENITES. *A descendant of Reuben.*
Adina the son of Shiza the R 1Chr 11:42 7206

REUBENITES (*ru'-ben-ites*)
These are the families of the R Num 26:7 7206
cities thereof, gave I unto the R Deut 3:12 7206
And unto the R and unto the Gadites Deut 3:16 7206
in the plain country, of the R Deut 4:43 7206
it for an inheritance unto the R Deut 29:8 7206
And to the R, and to the Gadites, Josh 1:12 7206
it for a possession unto the R Josh 12:6 7206
With whom the R and the Gadites Josh 13:8 7206
Then Joshua called the R, and the Josh 22:1 7206
of Gilead, the Gadites, and the R 2Kin 10:33 7206
he was prince of the R 1Chr 5:6 7206
he carried them away, even the R 1Chr 5:26 7206
the Reubenite, a captain of the R 1Chr 11:42 7206
other side of Jordan, of the R 1Chr 12:37 7206
king David made rulers over the R 1Chr 26:32 7206
the ruler of the R was Eliezer 1Chr 27:16 7206

REUEL (*re-u'-el*) See DEUEL, JETHRO, RAGUEL.
1. A son of Esau.
and Bashemath bare R Gen 36:4 7467
R the son of Bashemath the wife Gen 36:10 7467
And these are the sons of R Gen 36:13 7467
are the sons of R Esau's son Gen 36:17 7467
came of R in the land of Edom Gen 36:17 7467
Eliphaz, R, and Jeush, and Jaalam, 1Chr 1:35 7467
The sons of R 1Chr 1:37 7467
2. Same as Jethro.
when they came to R their father Ex 2:18 7467
3. Father of Eliasaph.
shall be Eliasaph the son of R Num 2:14 7467
4. A Benjamite.
son of Shephatiah, the son of R 1Chr 9:8 7467

REUMAH (*re-u'-mah*) *Concubine of Nahor.*
his concubine, whose name was R Gen 22:24 7208

REVEAL
The heaven shall r his iniquity Job 20:27 1540
will r unto them the abundance of Jer 33:6 1540
seeing thou couldst r this secret Dan 2:47 1541
to whomsoever the Son will r him Mt 11:27 *601*
and he to whom the Son will r him Lk 10:22 *601*
To r his Son in me, that I might Gal 1:16 *601*
God shall r even this unto you Phil 3:15 *601*

REVEALED
things which are r belong unto us Deut 29:29 1540
word of the LORD yet r unto him 1Sa 3:7 1540
for the LORD r himself to Samuel 1Sa 3:21 1540
hast r to thy servant, saying, I 2Sa 7:27 1540
it was r in mine ears by the LORD Is 22:14 1540
land of Chittim it is r to them Is 23:1 1540
the glory of the LORD shall be r Is 40:5 1540
to whom is the arm of the LORD r Is 53:1 1540
come, and my righteousness to be r Is 56:1 1540
for unto thee have I r my cause Jer 11:20 1540
Then was the secret r unto Daniel Dan 2:19 1541
this secret is not r to me for Dan 2:30 1541
Persia a thing was r unto Daniel Dan 10:1 1540
covered, that shall not be r Mt 10:26 *601*
and hast r them unto babes Mt 11:25 *601*
and blood hath not r it unto thee Mt 16:17 *601*
it was r unto him by the Holy Lk 2:26 *5537*
thoughts of many hearts may be r Lk 2:35 *601*
and hast r them unto babes Lk 10:21 *601*
covered, that shall not be r Lk 12:2 *601*
the day when the Son of man is r Lk 17:30 *601*
hath the arm of the Lord been r Jn 12:38 *601*
of God r from faith to faith Rom 1:17 *601*
God is r from heaven against all Rom 1:18 *601*
the glory which shall be r in us Rom 8:18 *601*
But God hath r them unto us by 1Cor 2:10 *601*
it, because it shall be r by fire 1Cor 3:13 *601*
If any thing be r to another that 1Cor 14:30 *601*
which should afterwards be r Gal 3:23 *601*
as it is now r unto his holy Eph 3:5 *601*
be r from heaven with his mighty 2Th 1:7 *602*
first, and that man of sin be r 2Th 2:3 *601*
that he might be r in his time 2Th 2:6 *601*
And then shall that Wicked be r 2Th 2:8 *601*
ready to be r in the last time 1Pet 1:5 *601*
Unto whom it was r, that not unto 1Pet 1:12 *601*
that, when his glory shall be r 1Pet 4:13 *602*
of the glory that shall be r 1Pet 5:1 *601*

REVEALER
a r of secrets, seeing thou Dan 2:47 1541

REVEALETH
A talebearer r secrets Prov 11:13 1540
about as a talebearer r secrets Prov 20:19 1540
He r the deep and secret things Dan 2:22 1541
is a God in heaven that r secrets Dan 2:28 1541
he that r secrets maketh known to Dan 2:29 1541
but he r his secret unto his Amos 3:7 1540

REVELATION
r of the righteous judgment of Rom 2:5 *602*
according to the r of the mystery Rom 16:25 *602*
I shall speak to you either by r 1Cor 14:6 *602*
doctrine, hath a tongue, hath a r 1Cor 14:26 *602*
but by the r of Jesus Christ Gal 1:12 *602*
And I went up by r, and Gal 2:2 *602*
r in the knowledge of him Eph 1:17 *602*
How that by r he made known unto Eph 3:3 *602*
unto you at the r of Jesus Christ 1Pet 1:13 *602*
The R of Jesus Christ, which God Rev 1:1 *602*

REVELATIONS
come to visions and r of the Lord 2Cor 12:1 *602*
through the abundance of the r 2Cor 12:7 *602*

REVELLINGS
Envyings, murders, drunkenness, r Gal 5:21 *2970*
lusts, excess of wine, r 1Pet 4:3 *2970*

REVENGE
me, and r me of my persecutors Jer 15:15 5358
and we shall take our r on him Jer 20:10 5360
the Philistines have dealt by r Eze 25:15 5360
yea, what zeal, yea, what r 2Cor 7:11 *1557*
a readiness to r all disobedience 2Cor 10:6 *1556*

REVENGED
offended, and r himself upon them Eze 25:12 5358

REVENGER
The r of blood himself shall slay Num 35:19 1350
the r of blood shall slay the Num 35:21 1350
the r of blood according to these Num 35:24 1350
out of the hand of the r of blood Num 35:25 1350
the r of blood find him without Num 35:27 1350
the r of blood kill the slayer Num 35:27 1350
a r to execute wrath upon him Rom 13:4 *1558*

REVENGERS
r of blood to destroy any more 2Sa 14:11 1350

REVENGES
the beginning of r upon the enemy Deut 32:42 6546

REVENGETH
God is jealous, and the LORD r Nah 1:2 5358
the LORD r, and is furious Nah 1:2 5358

REVENGING
r of the blood of thy servants Ps 79:10 5360

REVENUE
shalt endamage the r of the kings Ezr 4:13 674
and my r than choice silver Prov 8:19 8393
harvest of the river, is her r Is 23:3 8393

REVENUES
but in the r of the wicked is Prov 15:6 8393
than great r without right Prov 16:8 8393
they shall be ashamed of your r Jer 12:13 8393

REVERENCE
my sabbaths, and r my sanctuary Lev 19:30 3372
my sabbaths, and r my sanctuary Lev 26:2 7812
he fell on his face, and did r 2Sa 9:6 7812
did r to the king, and said, Let 1Kin 1:31 7812
Mordecai bowed not, nor did him r Est 3:2 7812
Mordecai bowed not, nor did him r Est 3:5 7812
to be had in r of all them that Ps 89:7 3372
son, saying, They will r my son Mt 21:37 *1788*
them, saying, They will r my son Mk 12:6 *1788*
it may be they will r him when Lk 20:13 *1788*
wife see that she r her husband Eph 5:33 *5399*
corrected us, and we gave them r Heb 12:9 *1788*
may serve God acceptably with r Heb 12:28 *127*

REVERENCED
king's gate, bowed, and r Haman Est 3:2 7812

REVEREND
holy and r is his name Ps 111:9 3372

REVERSE
and I cannot r it Num 23:20 7725
let it be written to r the Est 8:5 7725
the king's ring, may no man r Est 8:8 7725

REVILE
Thou shalt not r the gods Ex 22:28 7043
are ye, when men shall r you Mt 5:11 *3679*

REVILED
And they that passed by r him Mt 27:39 *937*
were crucified with him r him Mk 15:32 *3679*
Then they r him, and said, Thou Jn 9:28 *3058*
being r, we bless 1Cor 4:12 *3058*
when he was r, r not again 1Pet 2:23 *486*

REVILERS
covetous, nor drunkards, nor r 1Cor 6:10 *3060*

REVILEST
by said, R thou God's high priest Acts 23:4 *3058*

REVILINGS
neither be ye afraid of their r Is 51:7 1421
the r of the children of Ammon, Zeph 2:8 1421

REVIVE
will they r the stones out of the Neh 4:2 2421
Wilt thou not r us again Ps 85:6 2421
midst of trouble, thou wilt r me Ps 138:7 2421
to r the spirit of the humble, and Is 57:15 2421
to r the heart of the contrite Is 57:15 2421
After two days will he r us Hos 6:2 2421
they shall r as the corn, and grow Hos 14:7 2421
r thy work in the midst of the Hab 3:2 2421

REVIVED
spirit of Jacob their father r Gen 45:27 2421
his spirit came again, and he r Judg 15:19 2421
came into him again, and he r 1Kin 17:22 2421
touched the bones of Elisha, he r 2Kin 13:21 2421
when the commandment came, sin r Rom 7:9 *326*
Christ both died, and rose, and r Rom 14:9 *326*

REVIVING
give us a little r in our bondage Ezr 9:8 4241
kings of Persia, to give us a r Ezr 9:9 4241

REVOLT
did Libnah r from under his hand 2Chr 21:10 6586
ye will r more and more Is 1:5 5627
our God, speaking oppression and r Is 59:13 5627

REVOLTED
In his days Edom r from under the 2Kin 8:20 6586
Yet Edom r from under the hand of 2Kin 8:22 6586
Then Libnah r at the same time 2Kin 8:22 6586
In his days the Edomites r from 2Chr 21:8 6586

So the Edomites r from under the 2Chr 21:10 6586
children of Israel have deeply r Is 31:6 5627
they are r and gone Jer 5:23 5498

REVOLTERS
They are all grievous r, walking Jer 6:28 5637
the r are profound to make Hos 5:2 7846
all their princes are r Hos 9:15 5637

REVOLTING
But this people hath a r and a Jer 5:23 5637

REWARD
shield, and thy exceeding great r Gen 15:1 7939
for it is your r for your service Num 18:31 7939
not persons, nor taketh r Deut 10:17 7810
Cursed be he that taketh r to Deut 27:25 7810
and will r them that hate me Deut 32:41 7999
a full r be given thee of the Ruth 2:12 4909
wherefore the LORD r thee good 1Sa 24:19 7999
the LORD shall r the doer of evil 2Sa 3:39 7999
given him a r for his tidings 2Sa 4:10 1309
recompense it me with such a r 2Sa 19:36 1578
thyself, and I will give thee a r 1Kin 13:7 4991
Behold, I say, how they r us 2Chr 20:11 1580
Give a r for me of your substance Job 6:22 7809
looketh for the r of his work Job 7:2
nor taketh r against the innocent Ps 15:5 7810
keeping of them there is great r Ps 19:11 6118
Let them be desolate for a r of Ps 40:15 6118
He shall r evil unto mine enemies Ps 54:5 7725
there is a r for the righteous Ps 58:11 6529
for a r of their shame that say Ps 70:3 6118
behold and see the r of the wicked Ps 91:8 8011
render a r to the proud Ps 94:2 1576
Let this be the r of mine Ps 109:20 6468
and the fruit of the womb is his r Ps 127:3 7939
righteousness shall be a sure r Prov 11:18 7938
a r in the bosom strong wrath Prov 21:14 7810
found it, then there shall be a r Prov 24:14 319
shall be no r to the evil man Prov 24:20 319
head, and the LORD shall r thee Prov 25:22 7999
have a good r for their labour Eccl 4:9 7999
neither have they any more a r Eccl 9:5 7999
for the r of his hands shall be Is 3:11 1576
Which justify the wicked for r Is 5:23 7810
his r is with him, and his work Is 40:10 7939
my captives, not for price nor r Is 45:13 7810
his r is with him, and his work Is 62:11 7939
guard gave him victuals and a r Jer 40:5 4864
and in that thou givest a r Eze 16:34 868
and no r is given unto thee, Eze 16:34 868
ways, and r them their doings Hos 4:9 7725
thou hast loved a r upon every Hos 9:1 868
thy r shall return upon thine own Obad 15 1576
The heads thereof judge for r Mic 3:11 7810
and the judge asketh for a r Mic 7:3 7966
for great is your r in heaven Mt 5:12 3408
which love you, what r have ye Mt 5:46 3408
otherwise ye have no r of your Mt 6:1 3408
I say unto you, They have their r Mt 6:2 3408
himself shall r thee openly Mt 6:4 591
I say unto you, They have their r Mt 6:5 3408
in secret shall r thee openly Mt 6:6 591
I say unto you, They have their r Mt 6:16 3408
in secret, shall r thee openly Mt 6:18 591
shall receive a prophet's r Mt 10:41 3408
shall receive a righteous man's r Mt 10:41 3408
he shall in no wise lose his r Mt 10:42 3408
then he shall r every man Mt 16:27 591
unto you, he shall not lose his r Mk 9:41 3408
your r is great in heaven Lk 6:23 3408
your r shall be great, and ye Lk 6:35 3408
we receive the due r of our deeds Lk 23:41 514
a field with the r of iniquity Acts 1:18 3408
is the r not reckoned of grace Rom 4:4 3408
own r according to his own labour 1Cor 3:8 3408
thereupon, he shall receive a r 1Cor 3:14 3408
this thing willingly, I have a r 1Cor 9:17 3408
What is my r then 1Cor 9:18 3408
of your r in a voluntary humility Col 2:18 2603
receive the r of the inheritance Col 3:24 469
The labourer is worthy of his r 1Ti 5:18 3408
the Lord r him according to his 2Ti 4:14 591
received a just recompence of r Heb 2:2 3405
which hath great recompence of r Heb 10:35 3405
unto the recompence of the r Heb 11:26 3405
And shall receive the r of 2Pet 2:13 3408
but that we receive a full r 2Jn 8 3408
after the error of Balaam for r Jude 11 3408
that thou shouldest give r unto Rev 11:18 3408
R her even as she rewarded you, Rev 18:6 591
my r is with me, to give every Rev 22:12 3408

REWARDED
Wherefore have ye r evil for good Gen 44:4 7999
for thou hast r me good, whereas 1Sa 24:17 1580
good, whereas I have r thee evil 1Sa 24:17 1580
The LORD r me according to my 2Sa 22:21 1580
for your work shall be r 2Chr 15:7 7939
If I have r evil unto him that Ps 7:4 1580
The LORD r me according to my Ps 18:20 1580
They r me evil for good to the Ps 35:12 7999
nor r us according to our Ps 103:10 1580
they have r me evil for good, and Ps 109:5 7760
the commandment shall be r Prov 13:13 7999
for they have r evil unto Is 3:9 1580
for thy work shall be r, saith Jer 31:16 7939
Reward her even as she r you Rev 18:6 591

REWARDER
that he is a r of them that Heb 11:6 3406

REWARDETH
he r him, and he shall know it Job 21:19 7999
plentifully r the proud doer Ps 31:23 7999
that r thee as thou hast served Ps 137:8 7999

Whoso r evil for good, evil shall Prov 17:13 7725
formed all things both r the fool Prov 26:10 7936
and r transgressors Prov 26:10 7936

REWARDS
the r of divination in their hand Num 22:7
gifts, and followeth after r Is 1:23 8021
ye shall receive of me gifts and r Dan 2:6 5023
thyself, and give thy r to another Dan 5:17 5023
These are my r that my lovers Hos 2:12 866

REZEPH (re'-zef) *A fortress near Haran.*
as Gozan, and Haran, and R, and the 2Kin 19:12 7530
as Gozan, and Haran, and R Is 37:12 7530

REZIA (re-zi'-ah) *Son of Ulla.*
Arah, and Haniel, and R 1Chr 7:39 7525

REZIN (re'-zin)
1. A king of Syria.
against Judah R the king of Syria 2Kin 15:37 7526
Then R king of Syria and Pekah son 2Kin 16:5 7526
At that time R king of Syria 2Kin 16:6 7526
of it captive to Kir, and slew R 2Kin 16:9 7526
the fierce anger of R with Syria Is 7:4 7526
and the head of Damascus is R Is 7:8 7526
that go softly, and rejoice in R Is 8:6 7526
the adversaries of R against him Is 9:11 7526
2. A family of exiles.
The children of R, the children Ezr 2:48 7526
of Reaiah, the children of R Neh 7:50 7526

REZON (re'-zon) *An enemy of Solomon.*
R the son of Eliadah, which fled 1Kin 11:23 7331

RHEGIUM (re'-je-um) *A port of southern Italy.*
fetched a compass, and came to R Acts 28:13 4484

RHESA (re'-sah) *Son of Zorobabel; an ancestor of Jesus.*
of Joanna, which was the son of R Lk 3:27 4488

RHODA (ro'-dah) *A maiden in Mary's house.*
a damsel came to hearken, named R Acts 12:13 4498

RHODES (rodes) *A Mediterranean island.*
Coos, and the day following unto R Acts 21:1

RIB
And the r, which the LORD God had Gen 2:22 6763
spear smote him under the fifth r 2Sa 2:23
smote him there under the fifth r 2Sa 3:27
they smote him under the fifth r 2Sa 4:6
him therewith in the fifth r 2Sa 20:10

RIBAI (rib'-ahee) *Father of Ittai.*
Ittai the son of R out of Gibeah 2Sa 23:29 7380
Ithai the son of R of Gibeah 1Chr 11:31 7380

RIBBAND
fringe of the borders a r of blue Num 15:38 6616

RIBLAH (rib'-lah) *A city on the Orontes River.*
shall go down from Shepham to R Num 34:11 7247
put him in bands at R in the land 2Kin 23:33 7247
up to the king of Babylon to R 2Kin 25:6 7247
them to the king of Babylon to R 2Kin 25:20 7247
slew them at R in the land of 2Kin 25:21 7247
king of Babylon to R in the land Jer 39:5 7247
of Zedekiah in R before his eyes Jer 39:6 7247
to R in the land of Hamath Jer 52:9 7247
all the princes of Judah in R Jer 52:10 7247
them to the king of Babylon to R Jer 52:26 7247
put them to death in R in the Jer 52:27 7247

RIBS
and he took one of his r, and Gen 2:21 6763
it had three r in the mouth of it Dan 7:5 6763

RICH
And Abram was very r in cattle Gen 13:2 3513
say, I have made Abram r Gen 14:23 6238
The r shall not give more, and the Ex 30:15 6223
or stranger wax r by thee Lev 25:47 5381
not young men, whether poor or r Ruth 3:10 6223
The LORD maketh poor, and maketh r 1Sa 2:7 6238
the one r, and the other poor 2Sa 12:1 6223
The r man had exceeding many 2Sa 12:2 6223
came a traveller unto the r man 2Sa 12:4 6223
He shall not be r, neither shall Job 15:29 6238
The r man shall lie down, but he Job 27:19 6223
nor regardeth the r more than the Job 34:19 7771
even the r among the people shall Ps 45:12 6223
Both low and high, r and poor, Ps 49:2 6223
thou afraid when one is made r Ps 49:16 6238
the hand of the diligent maketh r Prov 10:4 6238
The r man's wealth is his strong Prov 10:15 6223
blessing of the LORD, it maketh r Prov 10:22 6238
There is that maketh himself r Prov 13:7 6238
but the r hath many friends Prov 14:20 6223
The r man's wealth is his strong Prov 18:11 6223
but the r answereth roughly Prov 18:23 6223
loveth wine and oil shall not be r Prov 21:17 6238
The r and poor meet together Prov 22:2 6223
The r ruleth over the poor, and Prov 22:7 6223
and he that giveth to the r Prov 22:16 6223
Labour not to be r Prov 23:4 6238
in his ways, though he be r Prov 28:6 6223
The r man is wise in his own Prov 28:11 6223
to be r shall not be innocent Prov 28:20 6238
hasteth to be r hath an evil eye Prov 28:22 1952
but the abundance of the r will Eccl 5:12 6223
and the r sit in low place Eccl 10:6 6223
curse not the r in thy bedchamber Eccl 10:20 6223
and with the r in his death Is 53:9 6223
they are become great, and waxen r Jer 5:27 6238
let not the r man glory in his Jer 9:23 6223
work, and in chests of r apparel Eze 27:24
Ephraim said, Yet I am become r Hos 12:8 6238
For the r men thereof are full of Mic 6:12 6223
for I am r Zec 11:5 6238

That a r man shall hardly enter Mt 19:23 4145
than for a r man to enter into Mt 19:24 4145
there came a r man of Arimathaea, Mt 27:57 4145
than for a r man to enter into Mk 10:25 4145
and many that were r cast in much Mk 12:41 4145
the r he hath sent empty away Lk 1:53 4147
But woe unto you that are r Lk 6:24 4145
The ground of a certain r man Lk 12:16 4145
himself, and is not r toward God Lk 12:21 4147
thy kinsmen, nor thy r neighbours Lk 14:12 4145
There was a certain r man Lk 16:1 4145
There was a certain r man Lk 16:19 4145
which fell from the r man's table Lk 16:21 4145
the r man also died, and was Lk 16:22 4145
for he was very r Lk 18:23 4145
than for a r man to enter into Lk 18:25 4145
among the publicans, and he was r Lk 19:2 4145
saw the r men casting their gifts Lk 21:1 4145
is r unto all that call upon him Rom 10:12 4147
Now ye are full, now ye are r 1Cor 4:8 4147
as poor, yet making many r 2Cor 6:10 4148
Christ, that, though he was r 2Cor 8:9 4145
ye through his poverty might be r 2Cor 8:9 4147
who is r in mercy, for his great Eph 2:4 4145
will be r fall into temptation 1Ti 6:9 4147
them that are r in this world 1Ti 6:17 4145
that they be r in good works, 1Ti 6:18 4147
But the r, in that he is made low Jas 1:10 4145
so also shall the r man fade away Jas 1:11 4145
the poor of this world r in faith Jas 2:5 4145
Do not r men oppress you, and draw Jas 2:6 4145
ye r men, weep and howl for your Jas 5:1 4145
and poverty, (but thou art r) Rev 2:9 4145
Because thou sayest, I am r Rev 3:17 4145
the fire, that thou mayest be r Rev 3:18 4147
and the great men, and the r men Rev 6:15 4145
all, both small and great, r Rev 13:16 4145
of the earth are waxed r through Rev 18:3 4147
things, which were made r by her Rev 18:15 4147
wherein were made r all that had Rev 18:19 4147

RICHER
shall be far r than they all Dan 11:2 6238

RICHES
For all the r which God hath Gen 31:16 6239
For their r were more than that Gen 36:7 7399
with much r unto your tents Josh 22:8 5233
king will enrich him with great r 1Sa 17:25 6239
neither hast asked r for thyself 1Kin 3:11 6239
which thou hast not asked, both r 1Kin 3:13 6239
all the kings of the earth for r 1Kin 10:23 6239
Both r and honour come of thee, and 1Chr 29:12 6239
a good old age, full of days, r 1Chr 29:28 6239
heart, and thou hast not asked r 2Chr 1:11 6239
and I will give thee r, and wealth, 2Chr 1:12 6239
all the kings of the earth in r 2Chr 9:22 6239
and he had r and honour in 2Chr 17:5 6239
Now Jehoshaphat had r and honour 2Chr 18:1 6239
both r with the dead bodies 2Chr 20:25 7399
And Hezekiah had exceeding much r 2Chr 32:27 6239
When he shewed the r of his Est 1:4 6239
told them of the glory of his r Est 5:11 6239
He hath swallowed down r, and he Job 20:15 2428
Will he esteem thy r Job 36:19 7769
better than the r of many wicked Ps 37:16 1995
he heapeth up r, and knoweth not Ps 39:6
in the multitude of their r Ps 49:6 6239
trusted in the abundance of his r Ps 52:7 6239
if r increase, set not your heart Ps 62:10 2428
they increase in r Ps 73:12 2428
the earth is full of thy r Ps 104:24 7075
Wealth and r shall be in his house Ps 112:3 6239
testimonies, as much as in all r Ps 119:14 1952
and in her left hand r and honour Prov 3:16 6239
R and honour are with me Prov 8:18 6239
yea, durable r and righteousness Prov 8:18 1952
R profit not in the day of wrath Prov 11:4 1952
and strong men retain r Prov 11:16 6239
that trusteth in his r shall fall Prov 11:28 6239
himself poor, yet hath great r Prov 13:7 1952
ransom of a man's life are his r Prov 13:8 6239
The crown of the wise is their r Prov 14:24 6239
r are the inheritance of fathers Prov 19:14 1952
rather to be chosen than great r Prov 22:1 6239
and the fear of the LORD are r Prov 22:4 6239
the poor to increase his r Prov 22:16
for r certainly make themselves Prov 23:5
with all precious and pleasant r Prov 24:4 1952
For r are not for ever Prov 27:24 2633
give me neither poverty nor r Prov 30:8 6239
is his eye satisfied with r Eccl 4:8 6239
r kept for the owners thereof to Eccl 5:13 6239
But those r perish by evil Eccl 5:14 6239
man also to whom God hath given r Eccl 5:19 6239
A man to whom God hath given r Eccl 6:2 6239
nor yet r to men of understanding Eccl 9:11 6239
the r of Damascus and the spoil of Is 8:4 2428
as a nest the r of the people Is 10:14 2428
they will carry their r upon the Is 30:6 2428
hidden r of secret places, that Is 45:3 4301
shall eat the r of the Gentiles Is 61:6 2428
not the rich man glory in his r Jer 9:23 6239
so he that getteth r, and not by Jer 17:11 6239
because the r that he hath gotten Jer 48:36 3502
they shall make a spoil of thy r Eze 26:12 2428
of the multitude of all kind of r Eze 27:12 1952
for the multitude of all r Eze 27:18 1952
Thy r, and thy fairs, thy Eze 27:27 1952
earth with the multitude of thy r Eze 27:33 6239
thou hast gotten thee r, and hast Eze 28:4 2428
hast thou increased thy r Eze 28:5 2428
is lifted up because of thy r Eze 28:5 2428
by his strength through his r he Dan 11:2 6239
with a great army and with much r Dan 11:13 7399

R

them the prey, and spoil, and *r* Dan 11:24 7399
return into his land with great *r* Dan 11:28 7399
world, and the deceitfulness of *r* Mt 13:22 *4149*
world, and the deceitfulness of *r* Mk 4:19 *4149*
r enter into the kingdom of God Mk 10:23 *5536*
in *r* to enter into the kingdom of Mk 10:24 *5536*
and are choked with cares and *r* Lk 8:14 *4149*
commit to your trust the true *r* Lk 16:11
r enter into the kingdom of God Lk 18:24 *5536*
thou the *r* of his goodness Rom 2:4 *4149*
that he might make known the *r* of Rom 9:23 *4149*
of them be the *r* of the world Rom 11:12 *4149*
of them the *r* of the Gentiles Rom 11:12 *4149*
depth of the *r* both of the wisdom Rom 11:33 *4149*
unto the *r* of their liberality 2Cor 8:2 *4149*
according to the *r* of his grace Eph 1:7 *4149*
what the *r* of the glory of his Eph 1:18 *4149*
he might shew the exceeding *r* of Eph 2:7 *4149*
the unsearchable *r* of Christ Eph 3:8 *4149*
according to the *r* of his glory Eph 3:16 *4149*
to his *r* in glory by Christ Jesus Phil 4:19 *4149*
r of the glory of this mystery Col 1:27 *4149*
unto all *r* of the full assurance Col 2:2 *4149*
nor trust in uncertain *r* 1Ti 6:17 *4149*
r than the treasures in Egypt Heb 11:26 *4149*
Your *r* are corrupted, and your Jas 5:2 *4149*
was slain to receive power, and *r* Rev 5:12 *4149*
hour so great *r* is come to nought Rev 18:17 *4149*

RICHLY
dwell in you *r* in all wisdom Col 3:16 *4146*
who giveth us *r* all things to 1Ti 6:17 *4146*

RID
that he might *r* him out of their Gen 37:22 5337
I will *r* you out of their bondage Ex 6:6 5337
I will *r* evil beasts out of the Lev 26:6 7673
r them out of the hand of the Ps 82:4 5337
r me, and deliver me out of great Ps 144:7 6475
R me, and deliver me from the hand Ps 144:11 6475

RIDDANCE
thou shalt not make clean *r* of Lev 23:22 3615
r of all them that dwell in the Zeph 1:18 3617

RIDDEN
upon which thou hast *r* ever since Num 22:30 7392

RIDDLE
I will now put forth a *r* unto you Judg 14:12 2420
said unto him, Put forth thy *r* Judg 14:13 2420
not in three days expound the *r* Judg 14:14 2420
that he may declare unto us the *r* Judg 14:15 2420
thou hast put forth a *r* unto the Judg 14:16 2420
she told the *r* to the children of Judg 14:17 2420
heifer, ye had not found out my *r* Judg 14:18 2420
unto them which expounded the *r* Judg 14:19 2420
Son of man, put forth a *r* Eze 17:2 2420

RIDE
he made him to *r* in the second Gen 41:43 7392
He made him *r* on the high places Deut 32:13 7392
ye that *r* on white asses, ye that Judg 5:10 7392
for the king's household to *r* on 2Sa 16:2 7392
me an ass, that I may *r* thereon 2Sa 19:26 7392
my son to *r* upon mine own mule 1Kin 1:33 7392
caused Solomon to *r* upon king 1Kin 1:38 7392
him to *r* upon the king's mule 1Kin 1:44 7392
So they made him *r* in his chariot 2Kin 10:16 7392
thou causest me to *r* upon it Job 30:22 7392
in thy majesty *r* prosperously Ps 45:4 7392
caused men to *r* over our heads Ps 66:12 7392
and, We will *r* upon the swift Is 30:16 7392
I will cause thee to *r* upon the Is 58:14 7392
they *r* upon horses, set in array Jer 6:23 7392
they shall *r* upon horses, every Jer 50:42 7392
I will make Ephraim to *r* Hos 10:11 7392
we will not *r* upon horses Hos 14:3 7392
that thou didst *r* upon thine Hab 3:8 7392
chariots, and those that *r* in them Hag 2:22 7392

RIDER
so that his *r* shall fall backward Gen 49:17 7392
his *r* hath he thrown into the sea Ex 15:1 7392
his *r* hath he thrown into the sea Ex 15:21 7392
she scorneth the horse and his *r* Job 39:18 7392
in pieces the horse and his *r* Jer 51:21 7392
in pieces the chariot and his *r* Jer 51:21 7392
and his *r* with madness Zec 12:4 7392

RIDERS
on thy part to set *r* upon them 2Kin 18:23 7392
r on mules, camels, and young Est 8:10 7392
on thy part to set *r* upon them Is 36:8 7392
their *r* shall come down, every Hag 2:22 7392
them, and the *r* on horses shall be Zec 10:5 7392

RIDETH
what saddle soever he *r* upon that Lev 15:9 7392
who *r* upon the heaven in thy help Deut 33:26 7392
and the horse that the king *r* upon Est 6:8 7392
extol him that *r* upon the heavens Ps 68:4 7392
To him that *r* upon the heavens of Ps 68:33 7392
the LORD *r* upon a swift cloud, and Is 19:1 7392
neither shall he that *r* the horse Amos 2:15 7392

RIDGES
Thou waterest the *r* thereof Ps 65:10 8525

RIDING
Now he was *r* upon his ass, and his Num 22:22 7392
slack not thy *r* for me, except I 2Kin 4:24 7392
r in chariots and on horses, they, Jer 17:25 7392
r in chariots and on horses, he, Jer 22:4 7392
young men, horsemen *r* upon horses Eze 23:6 7392
horsemen *r* upon horses, all of Eze 23:12 7392
all of them *r* upon horses Eze 23:23 7392
thee, all of them *r* upon horses Eze 38:15 7392
behold a man *r* upon a red horse, Zec 1:8 7392
r upon an ass, and upon a colt the Zec 9:9 7392

RIE
wheat and the *r* were not smitten Ex 9:32 3698
barley and the *r* in their place Is 28:25 3698

RIFLED
shall be taken, and the houses *r* Zec 14:2 8155

RIGHT
hand, then I will go to the *r* Gen 13:9 3231
or if thou depart to the *r* hand Gen 13:9 3225
the Judge of all the earth do *r* Gen 18:25 4941
in the *r* way to take my master's Gen 24:48 571
that I may turn to the *r* hand Gen 24:49 3225
Ephraim in his *r* hand toward Gen 48:13 3225
left hand toward Israel's *r* hand Gen 48:13 3225
Israel stretched out his *r* hand Gen 48:14 3225
saw that his father laid his *r* Gen 48:17 3225
put thy *r* hand upon his head Gen 48:18 3225
a wall unto them on their *r* hand Ex 14:22 3225
a wall unto them on their *r* hand Ex 14:29 3225
Thy *r* hand, O LORD, is become Ex 15:6 3225
thy *r* hand, O LORD, hath dashed Ex 15:6 3225
Thou stretchedst out thy *r* hand Ex 15:12 3225
do that which is *r* in his sight Ex 15:26 3477
the tip of the *r* ear of Aaron Ex 29:20
the tip of the *r* ear of his sons Ex 29:20 3233
and upon the thumb of their *r* hand Ex 29:20 3233
the great toe of their *r* foot Ex 29:20 3233
is upon them, and the *r* shoulder Ex 29:22 3225
the *r* shoulder shall ye give unto Lev 7:32 3225
shall have the *r* shoulder for his Lev 7:33 3225
it upon the tip of Aaron's *r* ear Lev 8:23 3233
and upon the thumb of his *r* hand Lev 8:23 3233
upon the great toe of his *r* foot Lev 8:23 3233
blood upon the tip of their *r* ear Lev 8:24 3233
upon the thumbs of their *r* hands Lev 8:24 3233
the great toes of their *r* feet Lev 8:24 3233
and their fat, and the *r* shoulder Lev 8:25 3225
the fat, and upon the *r* shoulder Lev 8:26 3225
the *r* shoulder Aaron waved for a Lev 9:21 3225
of the *r* ear of him that is to be Lev 14:14 3233
and upon the thumb of his *r* hand Lev 14:14 3233
upon the great toe of his *r* foot Lev 14:14 3233
the priest shall dip his *r* finger Lev 14:16 3233
of the *r* ear of him that is to be Lev 14:17 3233
and upon the thumb of his *r* hand Lev 14:17 3233
upon the great toe of his *r* foot Lev 14:17 3233
of the *r* ear of him that is to be Lev 14:25 3233
and upon the thumb of his *r* hand Lev 14:25 3233
upon the great toe of his *r* foot Lev 14:25 3233
r finger some of the oil that is Lev 14:27 3233
of the *r* ear of him that is to be Lev 14:28 3233
and upon the thumb of his *r* hand Lev 14:28 3233
upon the great toe of his *r* foot Lev 14:28 3233
as the *r* shoulder are thine Num 18:18 3225
to the *r* hand nor to the left Num 20:17 3225
to the *r* hand or to the left Num 22:26 3225
daughters of Zelophehad speak *r* Num 27:7 3651
unto the *r* hand nor to the left Deut 2:27 3225
to the *r* hand or to the left Deut 5:32 3225
And thou shalt do that which is *r* Deut 6:18 3477
whatsoever is *r* in his own eyes Deut 12:8 3477
is *r* in the sight of the LORD Deut 12:25 3477
r in the sight of the LORD thy Deut 12:28 3477
to do that which is *r* in the eyes Deut 13:18 3477
shall shew thee, to the *r* hand Deut 17:11 3225
the commandment, to the *r* hand Deut 17:20 3225
is *r* in the sight of the LORD Deut 21:9 3477
the *r* of the firstborn is his Deut 21:17 4941
thee this day, to the *r* hand Deut 28:14 3225
without iniquity, just and *r* is he Deut 32:4 3477
from his *r* hand went a fiery law Deut 33:2 3225
it to the *r* hand or to the left Josh 1:7 3225
passed over *r* against Jericho Josh 3:16
r unto thee to do unto us, do Josh 9:25 3477
r hand unto the inhabitants of Josh 17:7 3225
to the *r* hand or to the left Josh 23:6 3225
his raiment upon his *r* thigh Judg 3:16 3225
took the dagger from his *r* thigh Judg 3:21 3225
her *r* hand to the workmen's Judg 5:26 3225
in their *r* hands to blow withal Judg 7:20 3225
could not frame to pronounce it *r* Judg 12:6 3651
up, of the one with his *r* hand Judg 16:29 3225
that which was *r* in his own eyes Judg 17:6 3477
that which was *r* in his own eyes Judg 21:25 3477
redeem thou my *r* to thyself Ruth 4:6 1353
to the *r* hand or to the left 1Sa 6:12 3225
I may thrust out all your *r* eyes 1Sa 11:2 3225
teach you the good and the *r* way 1Sa 12:23 3477
the *r* hand nor to the left from 2Sa 2:19 3225
to thy *r* hand or to thy left 2Sa 2:21 3225
none can turn to the *r* hand or to 2Sa 14:19 3231
See, thy matters are good and *r* 2Sa 15:3 5228
the mighty men were on his *r* hand 2Sa 16:6 3225
What *r* therefore have I yet to 2Sa 19:28 6666
have also more *r* in David than ye 2Sa 19:43 3225
beard with the *r* hand to kiss him 2Sa 20:9 3225
on the *r* side of the city that 2Sa 24:5 3225
and she sat on his *r* hand 1Kin 2:19 3225
was in the *r* side of the house 1Kin 6:8 3233
and he set up the *r* pillar 1Kin 7:21 3225
bases on the *r* side of the house 1Kin 7:39 3225
he set the sea on the *r* side of 1Kin 7:39 3233
of pure gold, five on the *r* side 1Kin 7:49 3225
do that which is *r* in mine eyes 1Kin 11:33 3477
do that is *r* in my sight, to keep 1Kin 11:38 3477
only which was *r* in mine eyes 1Kin 14:8 3477
was *r* in the eyes of the LORD 1Kin 15:5 3477
Asa did that which was *r* in the 1Kin 15:11 3477
standing by him on his *r* hand 1Kin 22:19 3225
doing that which was *r* in the 1Kin 22:43 3477
and said to him, Is thine heart *r* 2Kin 10:15 3225
that which is *r* in mine eyes 2Kin 10:30 3225
from the *r* corner of the temple 2Kin 11:11 3233
Jehoash did that which was *r* in 2Kin 12:2 3477
on the *r* side as one cometh into 2Kin 12:9 3225
he did that which was *r* in the 2Kin 14:3 3477
he did that which was *r* in the 2Kin 15:3 3477
he did that which was *r* in the 2Kin 15:34 3477
did not that which was *r* in the 2Kin 16:2 3477
not *r* against the LORD their God 2Kin 17:9 3651
he did that which was *r* in the 2Kin 18:3 3477
he did that which was *r* in the 2Kin 22:2 3477
to the *r* hand or to the left 2Kin 22:2 3225
which were on the *r* hand of the 2Kin 23:13 3225
Asaph, who stood on his *r* hand 1Chr 6:39 3225
and could use both the *r* hand 1Chr 12:2 3231
for the thing was *r* in the eyes 1Chr 13:4 3477
the temple, one on the *r* hand 2Chr 3:17 3225
name of that on the *r* hand Jachin 2Chr 3:17 3227
lavers, and put five on the *r* hand 2Chr 4:6 3225
in the temple, five on the *r* hand 2Chr 4:7 3225
in the temple, five on the *r* side 2Chr 4:8 3225
sea on the *r* side of the east end 2Chr 4:10 3233
r in the eyes of the LORD his God 2Chr 14:2 3477
of heaven standing on his *r* hand 2Chr 18:18 3225
doing that which was *r* in the 2Chr 20:32 3477
from the *r* side of the temple to 2Chr 23:10 3233
Joash did that which was *r* in the 2Chr 24:2 3477
he did that which was *r* in the 2Chr 25:2 3477
he did that which was *r* in the 2Chr 26:4 3477
he did that which was *r* in the 2Chr 27:2 3477
was *r* in the sight of the LORD 2Chr 28:1 3477
he did that which was *r* in the 2Chr 29:2 3477
wrought that which was good and *r* 2Chr 31:20 3477
he did that which was *r* in the 2Chr 34:2 3477
and declined neither to the *r* hand 2Chr 34:2 3225
to seek of him a *r* way for us Ezr 8:21 3477
but ye have no portion, nor *r* Neh 2:20 6666
and Maaseiah, on his *r* hand Neh 8:4 3225
and gavest them *r* judgments Neh 9:13 3477
for thou hast done *r*, but we have Neh 9:33 571
whereof one went on the *r* hand Neh 12:31 3225
the thing seem *r* before the king, Est 8:5 3787
How forcible are *r* words Job 6:25 3476
he hideth himself on the *r* hand Job 23:9 3225
Upon my *r* hand rise the youth Job 30:12 3225
and perverted that which was *r* Job 33:27 3477
Should I lie against my *r* Job 34:6 4941
even he that hateth *r* govern Job 34:17 4941
will not lay upon man more than *r* Job 34:23 4941
Thinkest thou this to be *r* Job 35:2 4941
but giveth *r* to the poor Job 36:6 4941
thine own *r* hand can save thee Job 40:14 3225
spoken of me the thing that is *r* Job 42:7 3559
spoken of me the thing which is *r* Job 42:8 3559
For thou hast maintained my *r* Ps 9:4 4941
satest in the throne judging *r* Ps 9:4 6664
because he is at my *r* hand Ps 16:8 3225
at thy *r* hand there are pleasures Ps 16:11 3225
Hear the *r*, O LORD, attend unto Ps 17:1 6664
O thou that savest by thy *r* hand Ps 17:7 3225
thy *r* hand hath holden me up, and Ps 18:35 3225
The statutes of the LORD are *r* Ps 19:8 3477
the saving strength of his *r* hand Ps 20:6 3225
thy *r* hand shall find out those Ps 21:8 3225
their *r* hand is full of bribes Ps 26:10 3225
For the word of the LORD is *r* Ps 33:4 3477
but thy *r* hand, and thine arm, and Ps 44:3 3225
thy *r* hand shall teach thee Ps 45:4 3225
of thy kingdom is a *r* sceptre Ps 45:6 4334
upon thy *r* hand did stand the Ps 45:9 3225
shall help her, and that *r* early Ps 46:5 6437
thy *r* hand is full of Ps 48:10 3225
renew a *r* spirit within me Ps 51:10 3559
save with thy *r* hand, and hear me Ps 60:5 3225
thy *r* hand upholdeth me Ps 63:8 3225
thou hast holden me by my *r* hand Ps 73:23 3225
thou thy hand, even thy *r* hand Ps 74:11 3225
of the *r* hand of the most High Ps 77:10 3225
their heart was not *r* with him Ps 78:37 3559
which his *r* hand had purchased Ps 78:54 3225
which thy *r* hand hath planted Ps 80:15 3225
be upon the man of thy *r* hand Ps 80:17 3225
thy hand, and high is thy *r* hand Ps 89:13 3225
sea, and his *r* hand in the rivers Ps 89:25 3225
Thou hast set up the *r* hand of Ps 89:42 3225
and ten thousand at thy *r* hand Ps 91:7 3225
his *r* hand, and his holy arm, hath Ps 98:1 3225
And he led them forth by the *r* way Ps 107:7 3477
save with thy *r* hand, and answer Ps 108:6 3225
and let Satan stand at his *r* hand Ps 109:6 3225
stand at the *r* hand of the poor Ps 109:31 3225
my Lord, Sit thou at my *r* hand Ps 110:1 3225
The LORD at thy *r* hand shall Ps 110:5 3225
the *r* hand of the LORD doeth Ps 118:15 3225
The *r* hand of the LORD is exalted Ps 118:16 3225
the *r* hand of the LORD doeth Ps 118:16 3225
O LORD, that thy judgments are *r* Ps 119:75 6664
concerning all things to be *r* Ps 119:128 3474
LORD is thy shade upon thy *r* hand Ps 121:5 3225
let my *r* hand forget her cunning Ps 137:5 3225
and thy *r* hand shall save me Ps 138:7 3225
me, and thy *r* hand shall hold me Ps 139:10 3225
and that my soul knoweth *r* well Ps 139:14
afflicted, and the *r* of the poor Ps 140:12 4941
I looked on my *r* hand, and beheld, Ps 142:4 3225
their *r* hand is a *r* hand of Ps 144:8 3225
their *r* hand is a *r* hand of Ps 144:11 3225
Length of days is in her *r* hand Prov 3:16 3225
I have led thee in *r* paths Prov 4:11 3476
Let thine eyes look *r* on, and let Prov 4:25 5227
Turn not to the *r* hand nor to the Prov 4:27 3225
of my lips shall be *r* things Prov 8:6 4339
r to them that find knowledge Prov 8:9 3477
passengers who go *r* on their ways Prov 9:15 3474
thoughts of the righteous are *r* Prov 12:5 4941

of a fool is r in his own eyes ... Prov 12:15 3477
a way which seemeth r unto a man ... Prov 14:12 3477
than great revenues without r ... Prov 16:8 4941
and they love him that speaketh r ... Prov 16:13 3477
a way that seemeth r unto a man ... Prov 16:25 3477
work be pure, and whether it be r ... Prov 20:11 3477
way of a man is r in his own eyes ... Prov 21:2 3477
as for the pure, his work is r ... Prov 21:8 3477
when thy lips speak r things ... Prov 23:16 4339
his lips that giveth a r answer ... Prov 24:26 5228
and the ointment of his r hand ... Prov 27:16 3225
all travail, and every r work ... Eccl 4:4 3788
wise man's heart is at his r hand ... Eccl 10:2 3225
his r hand doth embrace me ... Song 2:6 3225
his r hand should embrace me ... Song 8:3 3225
And he shall snatch on the r hand ... Is 9:20 3225
to take away the r from the poor ... Is 10:2 4941
Prophesy not unto us r things ... Is 30:10 5229
in it, when ye turn to the r hand ... Is 30:21 541
even when the needy speaketh r ... Is 32:7 4941
the r hand of my righteousness ... Is 41:10 3225
LORD thy God will hold thy r hand ... Is 41:13 3225
Is there not a lie in my r hand ... Is 44:20 3225
whose r hand I have holden, to ... Is 45:1 3225
I declare things that are r ... Is 45:19 4339
my r hand hath spanned the ... Is 48:13 3225
shalt break forth on the r hand ... Is 54:3 3225
The LORD hath sworn by his r hand ... Is 62:8 3225
That led them by the r hand of ... Is 63:12 3225
a noble vine, wholly a r seed ... Jer 2:21 571
the r of the needy do they not ... Jer 5:28 4941
that getteth riches, and not by r ... Jer 17:11 4941
out of my lips was r before thee ... Jer 17:16 5227
were the signet upon my r hand ... Jer 22:24 3225
is evil, and their force is not r ... Jer 23:10
for the r of redemption is thine ... Jer 32:7 4941
for the r of inheritance is thine ... Jer 32:8 4941
had done r in my sight, in ... Jer 34:15 3477
be driven out every man r forth ... Jer 49:5 6440
he hath drawn back his r hand ... Lam 2:3 3225
he stood with his r hand as an ... Lam 2:4 3225
To turn aside the r of a man ... Lam 3:35 4941
the face of a lion, on the r side ... Eze 1:10 3225
them, lie again on thy r side ... Eze 4:6 6227
stood on the r side of the house ... Eze 10:3 3225
that dwelleth at thy r hand ... Eze 16:46 3225
and do that which is lawful and r ... Eze 18:5 6666
done that which is lawful and r ... Eze 18:19 6666
and do that which is lawful and r ... Eze 18:21 6666
doeth that which is lawful and r ... Eze 18:27 6666
or other, either on the r hand ... Eze 21:16 3231
At his r hand was the divination ... Eze 21:22 3225
more, until he come whose r it is ... Eze 21:27 4941
and do that which is lawful and r ... Eze 33:14 6666
done that which is lawful and r ... Eze 33:16 6666
and do that which is lawful and r ... Eze 33:19 6666
arrows to fall out of thy r hand ... Eze 39:3 3225
from the r side of the house ... Eze 47:1 3233
ran out waters on the r side ... Eze 47:2 3233
river, when he held up his r hand ... Dan 12:7 3225
for the ways of the LORD are r ... Hos 14:9 3477
For they know not to do r ... Amos 3:10 5229
the poor in the gate from their r ... Amos 5:12
discern between their r hand ... Jonah 4:11 3225
the cup of the LORD's r hand ... Hab 2:16 3225
at his r hand to resist him ... Zec 3:1 3225
one upon the r side of the bowl, ... Zec 4:3 3225
the r side of the candlestick ... Zec 4:11 3225
upon his arm, and upon his r eye ... Zec 11:17 3225
his r eye shall be utterly ... Zec 11:17 3225
people round about, on the r hand ... Zec 12:6 3225
aside the stranger from his r ... Mal 3:5 3225
if thy r eye offend thee, pluck ... Mt 5:29 *1188*
if thy r hand offend thee, cut it ... Mt 5:30 *1188*
shall smite thee on thy r cheek ... Mt 5:39 *1188*
hand know what thy r hand doeth ... Mt 6:3 *1188*
whatsoever is r I will give you ... Mt 20:4 *1342*
and whatsoever is r, that shall ye ... Mt 20:7 *1342*
may sit, the one on thy r hand ... Mt 20:21 *1188*
but to sit on my r hand, and on my ... Mt 20:23 *1188*
my Lord, Sit thou on my r hand ... Mt 22:44 *1188*
shall set the sheep on his r hand ... Mt 25:33 *1188*
King say unto them on his r hand ... Mt 25:34 *1188*
sitting on the r hand of power ... Mt 26:64 *1188*
his head, and a reed in his r hand ... Mt 27:29 *1188*
with him, one on the r hand ... Mt 27:38 *1188*
and clothed, and in his r mind ... Mk 5:15 *4993*
we may sit, one on thy r hand ... Mk 10:37 *1188*
But to sit on my r hand and on my ... Mk 10:40 *1188*
to my Lord, Sit thou on my r hand ... Mk 12:36 *1188*
sitting on the r hand of power ... Mk 14:62 *1188*
the one on his r hand, and the ... Mk 15:27 *1188*
a young man sitting on the r side ... Mk 16:5 *1188*
and sat on the r hand of God ... Mk 16:19 *1188*
of the Lord standing on the r ... Lk 1:11 *1188*
a man whose r hand was withered ... Lk 6:6 *1188*
Jesus, clothed, and in his r mind ... Lk 8:35 *4993*
unto him, Thou hast answered r ... Lk 10:28 *3723*
yourselves judge ye not what is r ... Lk 12:57 *1342*
my Lord, Sit thou on my r hand ... Lk 20:42 *1188*
high priest, and cut off his r ear ... Lk 22:50 *1188*
on the r hand of the power of God ... Lk 22:69 *1188*
malefactors, one on the r hand ... Lk 23:33 *1188*
servant, and cut off his r ear ... Jn 18:10 *1188*
the net on the r side of the ship ... Jn 21:6 *1188*
my face, for he is on my r hand ... Acts 2:25 *1188*
by the r hand of God exalted ... Acts 2:33 *1188*
my Lord, Sit thou on my r hand ... Acts 2:34 *1188*
And he took him by the r hand ... Acts 3:7 *1188*
Whether it be r in the sight of ... Acts 4:19 *1342*
with his r hand to be a Prince ... Acts 5:31 *1188*
standing on the r hand of God ... Acts 7:55 *1188*
man standing on the r hand of God ... Acts 7:56 *1188*
is not r in the sight of God ... Acts 8:21 *2117*
to pervert the r ways of the Lord ... Acts 13:10 *2117*
who is even at the r hand of God ... Rom 8:34 *1188*
of righteousness on the r hand ... 2Cor 6:7 *1188*
to me and Barnabas the r hands of ... Gal 2:9 *1188*
set him at his own r hand in the ... Eph 1:20 *1188*
for this is r ... Eph 6:1 *1342*
sitteth on the r hand of God ... Col 3:1 *1188*
sat down on the r hand of the ... Heb 1:3 *1188*
he at any times, Sit on my r hand ... Heb 1:13 *1188*
who is set on the r hand of the ... Heb 8:1 *1188*
sat down on the r hand of God ... Heb 10:12 *1188*
is set down at the r hand of the ... Heb 12:2 *1188*
whereof they have no r to eat ... Heb 13:10 *1849*
and is on the r hand of God ... 1Pet 3:22 *1188*
Which have forsaken the r way ... 2Pet 2:15 *2117*
he had in his r hand seven stars ... Rev 1:16 *1188*
he laid his r hand upon me, ... Rev 1:17 *1188*
which thou sawest in my r hand ... Rev 1:20 *1188*
the seven stars in his r hand ... Rev 2:1 *1188*
I saw in the r hand of him that ... Rev 5:1 *1188*
took the book out of the r hand ... Rev 5:7 *1188*
he set his r foot upon the sea, ... Rev 10:2 *1188*
to receive a mark in their r hand ... Rev 13:16 *1188*
that they may have r to the tree ... Rev 22:14 *1849*

RIGHTEOUS

for thee have I seen r before me ... Gen 7:1 6662
destroy the r with the wicked ... Gen 18:23 6662
there be fifty r within the city ... Gen 18:24 6662
for the fifty r that are therein ... Gen 18:24 6662
to slay the r with the wicked ... Gen 18:25 6662
that the r should be as the ... Gen 18:25 6662
in Sodom fifty r within the city ... Gen 18:26 6662
shall lack five of the fifty r ... Gen 18:28 6662
wilt thou slay also a r nation ... Gen 20:4 6662
said, She hath been more r than I ... Gen 38:26 6663
the LORD is r, and I and my people ... Ex 9:27 6662
the innocent and r slay thou not ... Ex 23:7 6662
and perverteth the words of the r ... Ex 23:8 6662
Let me die the death of the r ... Num 23:10 3477
judgments so r as all this law, ... Deut 4:8 6662
and pervert the words of the r ... Deut 16:19 6662
then they shall justify the r ... Deut 25:1 6662
rehearse the r acts of the LORD ... Judg 5:11 6666
even the r acts toward the ... Judg 5:11 6666
of all the r acts of the LORD ... 1Sa 12:7 6666
to David, Thou art more r than I ... 1Sa 24:17 6662
a r person in his own house upon ... 2Sa 4:11 6662
who fell upon two men more r ... 1Kin 2:32 6662
and justifying the r, to give him ... 1Kin 8:32 6662
said to all the people, Ye be r ... 2Kin 10:9 6662
and by justifying the r, by giving ... 2Chr 6:23 6662
and they said, The LORD is r ... 2Chr 12:6 6662
O LORD God of Israel, thou art r ... Ezr 9:15 6662
for thou art r ... Neh 9:8 6662
or where were the r cut off ... Job 4:7 6662
Whom, though I were r, yet would ... Job 9:15 6663
and if I be r, yet will I not lift ... Job 10:15 6662
of a woman, that he should be r ... Job 15:14 6662
The r also shall hold on his way, ... Job 17:9 6662
to the Almighty, that thou art r ... Job 22:3 6663
The r see it, and are glad ... Job 22:19 6662
There the r might dispute with ... Job 23:7 3477
because he was r in his own eyes ... Job 32:1 6662
For Job hath said, I am r ... Job 34:5 6663
If thou be r, what givest thou ... Job 35:7 6663
not his eyes from the r ... Job 36:7 6662
condemn me, that thou mayest be r ... Job 40:8 6663
in the congregation of the r ... Ps 1:5 6662
the LORD knoweth the way of the r ... Ps 1:6 6662
For thou, LORD, wilt bless the r ... Ps 5:12 6662
for the r God trieth the hearts ... Ps 7:9 6662
God judgeth the r, and God is ... Ps 7:11 6662
be destroyed, what can the r do ... Ps 11:3 6662
The LORD trieth the r ... Ps 11:5 6662
For the r LORD loveth ... Ps 11:7 6662
God is in the generation of the r ... Ps 14:5 6662
the LORD are true and r altogether ... Ps 19:9 6663
and contemptuously against the r ... Ps 31:18 6662
in the LORD, and rejoice, ye r ... Ps 32:11 6662
Rejoice in the LORD, O ye r ... Ps 33:1 6662
eyes of the LORD are upon the r ... Ps 34:15 6662
The r cry, and the LORD heareth, ... Ps 34:17
Many are the afflictions of the r ... Ps 34:19 6662
that hate the r shall be desolate ... Ps 34:21 6662
be glad, that favour my r cause ... Ps 35:27 6664
A little that a r man hath is ... Ps 37:16 6662
but the LORD upholdeth the r ... Ps 37:17 6662
but the r sheweth mercy, and ... Ps 37:21 6662
have I not seen the r forsaken ... Ps 37:25 6662
The r shall inherit the land, and ... Ps 37:29 6662
mouth of the r speaketh wisdom ... Ps 37:30 6662
The wicked watcheth the r ... Ps 37:32 6662
salvation of the r is of the LORD ... Ps 37:39 6662
The r also shall see, and fear, and ... Ps 52:6 6662
never suffer the r to be moved ... Ps 55:22 6662
The r shall rejoice when he seeth ... Ps 58:10 6662
there is a reward for the r ... Ps 58:11 6662
The r shall be glad in the LORD, ... Ps 64:10 6662
But let the r be glad ... Ps 68:3 6662
and not be written with the r ... Ps 69:28 6662
In his days shall the r flourish ... Ps 72:7 6662
horns of the r shall be exalted ... Ps 75:10 6662
The r shall flourish like the ... Ps 92:12 6662
against the soul of the r ... Ps 94:21 6662
Light is sown for the r, and ... Ps 97:11 6662
Rejoice in the LORD, ye r ... Ps 97:12 6662
The r shall see it, and rejoice ... Ps 107:42 3477
and full of compassion, and r ... Ps 112:4 6662
the r shall be in everlasting ... Ps 112:6 6662
Gracious is the LORD, and r ... Ps 116:5 6662
is in the tabernacles of the r ... Ps 118:15 6662
into which the r shall enter ... Ps 118:20 6662
have learned thy r judgments ... Ps 119:7 6664
thee because of thy r judgments ... Ps 119:62 6664
that I will keep thy r judgments ... Ps 119:106 6664
R art thou, O LORD, and upright ... Ps 119:137 6662
that thou hast commanded are r ... Ps 119:138 6664
every one of thy r judgments ... Ps 119:160 6664
thee because of thy r judgments ... Ps 119:164 6664
not rest upon the lot of the r ... Ps 125:3 6662
lest the r put forth their hands ... Ps 125:3 6662
The LORD is r ... Ps 129:4 6662
Surely the r shall give thanks ... Ps 140:13 6662
Let the r smite me ... Ps 141:5 6662
the r shall compass me about ... Ps 142:7 6662
The LORD is r in all his ways, and ... Ps 145:17 6662
the LORD loveth the r ... Ps 146:8 6662
layeth up sound wisdom for the r ... Prov 2:7 3477
men, and keep the paths of the r ... Prov 2:20 6662
but his secret is with the r ... Prov 3:32 3477
the soul of the r to famish ... Prov 10:3 6662
The mouth of a r man is a well of ... Prov 10:11 6662
labour of the r tendeth to life ... Prov 10:16 6662
The lips of the r feed many ... Prov 10:21 6662
desire of the r shall be granted ... Prov 10:24 6662
but the r is an everlasting ... Prov 10:25 6662
The hope of the r shall be ... Prov 10:28 6662
The r shall never be removed ... Prov 10:30 6662
The lips of the r know what is ... Prov 10:32 6662
The r is delivered out of trouble ... Prov 11:8 6662
When it goeth well with the r ... Prov 11:10 6662
seed of the r shall be delivered ... Prov 11:21 6662
The desire of the r is only good ... Prov 11:23 6662
but the r shall flourish as a ... Prov 11:28 6662
The fruit of the r is a tree of ... Prov 11:30 6662
the r shall be recompensed in the ... Prov 11:31 6662
root of the r shall not be moved ... Prov 12:3 6662
The thoughts of the r are right ... Prov 12:5 6662
the house of the r shall stand ... Prov 12:7 6662
A r man regardeth the life of his ... Prov 12:10 6662
the root of the r yieldeth fruit ... Prov 12:12 6662
The r is more excellent than his ... Prov 12:26 6662
A r man hateth lying ... Prov 13:5 6662
The light of the r rejoiceth ... Prov 13:9 6662
but to the r good shall be repaid ... Prov 13:21 6662
The r eateth to the satisfying of ... Prov 13:25 6662
but among the r there is favour ... Prov 14:9 3477
the wicked at the gates of the r ... Prov 14:19 6662
but the r hath hope in his death ... Prov 14:32 6662
house of the r is much treasure ... Prov 15:6 6662
the way of the r is made plain ... Prov 15:19 3477
The heart of the r studieth to ... Prov 15:28 6662
he heareth the prayer of the r ... Prov 15:29 6662
R lips are the delight of kings ... Prov 16:13 6664
to overthrow the r in judgment ... Prov 18:5 6662
the r runneth into it, and is safe ... Prov 18:10 6662
The r man wisely considereth the ... Prov 21:12 6662
shall be a ransom for the r ... Prov 21:18 6662
but the r giveth and spareth not ... Prov 21:26 6662
The father of the r shall greatly ... Prov 23:24 6662
against the dwelling of the r ... Prov 24:15 6662
saith unto the wicked, Thou art r ... Prov 24:24 6662
A r man falling down before the ... Prov 25:26 6662
but the r are bold as a lion ... Prov 28:1 6662
Whoso causeth the r to go astray ... Prov 28:10 3477
When r men do rejoice, there is ... Prov 28:12 6662
when they perish, the r increase ... Prov 28:28 6662
When the r are in authority, the ... Prov 29:2 6662
but the r doth sing and rejoice ... Prov 29:6 6662
The r considereth the cause of ... Prov 29:7 6662
but the r shall see their fall ... Prov 29:16 6662
mine heart, God shall judge the r ... Eccl 3:17 6662
Be not r over much ... Eccl 7:16 6662
according to the work of the r ... Eccl 8:14 6662
to declare all this, that the r ... Eccl 9:1 6662
there is one event to the r ... Eccl 9:2 6662
Say ye to the r, that it shall be ... Is 3:10 6662
righteousness of the r from him ... Is 5:23 6662
heard songs, even glory to the r ... Is 24:16 6662
that the r nation which keepeth ... Is 26:2 6662
raised up the r man from the east ... Is 41:2 6664
that we may say, He is r ... Is 41:26 6662
shall my r servant justify many ... Is 53:11 6662
The r perisheth, and no man layeth ... Is 57:1 6662
none considering that the r is ... Is 57:1 6662
Thy people also shall be all r ... Is 60:21 6662
R art thou, O LORD, when I plead ... Jer 12:1 6662
LORD of hosts, that triest the r ... Jer 20:12 6662
will raise unto David a r Branch ... Jer 23:5 6662
The LORD is r ... Lam 1:18 6662
When a r man doth turn from his ... Eze 3:20 6662
if thou warn the r man ... Eze 3:21 6662
that the r sin not ... Eze 3:21 6662
have made the heart of the r sad ... Eze 13:22 6662
they are more r than thou ... Eze 16:52 6663
of the r shall be upon him ... Eze 18:20 6662
But when the r turneth away from ... Eze 18:24 6662
When a r man turneth away from ... Eze 18:26 6662
and will cut off from thee the r ... Eze 21:3 6662
I will cut off from thee the r ... Eze 21:4 6662
And the r men, they shall judge ... Eze 23:45 6662
The righteousness of the r shall ... Eze 33:12 6662
neither shall the r be able to ... Eze 33:12 6662
When I shall say to the r ... Eze 33:13 6662
When the r turneth from his ... Eze 33:18 6662
for the LORD our God is r in all ... Dan 9:14 6662
they sold the r for silver ... Amos 2:6 6662
wicked doth compass about the r ... Hab 1:4 6662
the man that is more r than he ... Hab 1:13 6662
return, and discern between the r ... Mal 3:18 6662
for I am not come to call the r ... Mt 9:13 *1342*
he that receiveth a r man in the ... Mt 10:41 *1342*
a r man shall receive a r ... Mt 10:41 *1342*
r men have desired to see those ... Mt 13:17 *1342*
Then shall the r shine forth as ... Mt 13:43 *1342*
also outwardly appear r unto men ... Mt 23:28 *1342*
garnish the sepulchres of the r ... Mt 23:29 *1342*

the *r* blood shed upon the earth	Mt 23:35	*1342*
from the blood of *r* Abel unto the	Mt 23:35	*1342*
Then shall the *r* answer him	Mt 25:37	*1342*
but the *r* into life eternal	Mt 25:46	*1342*
I came not to call the *r*, but	Mk 2:17	*1342*
And they were both *r* before God	Lk 1:6	*1342*
I came not to call the *r*, but	Lk 5:32	*1342*
in themselves that they were *r*	Lk 18:9	*1342*
Certainly this was a *r* man	Lk 23:47	*1342*
appearance, but judge *r* judgment	Jn 7:24	*1342*
O *r* Father, the world hath not	Jn 17:25	*1342*
of the *r* judgment of God	Rom 2:5	*1341*
As it is written, There is none *r*	Rom 3:10	*1342*
scarcely for a *r* man will one die	Rom 5:7	*1342*
of one shall many be made *r*	Rom 5:19	*1342*
token of the *r* judgment of God	2Th 1:5	*1342*
Seeing it is a *r* thing with God	2Th 1:6	*1342*
the law is not made for a *r* man	1Ti 1:9	*1342*
the *r* judge, shall give me at	2Ti 4:8	*1342*
he obtained witness that he was *r*	Heb 11:4	*1342*
prayer of a *r* man availeth much	Jas 5:16	*1342*
eyes of the Lord are over the *r*	1Pet 3:12	*1342*
if the *r* scarcely be saved, where	1Pet 4:18	*1342*
(For that *r* man dwelling among	2Pet 2:8	*1342*
vexed his *r* soul from day to day	2Pet 2:8	*1342*
the Father, Jesus Christ the *r*	1Jn 2:1	*1342*
If ye know that he is *r*, ye know	1Jn 2:29	*1342*
he that doeth righteousness is *r*	1Jn 3:7	*1342*
even as he is *r*	1Jn 3:7	*1342*
were evil, and his brother's *r*	1Jn 3:12	*1342*
of the waters say, Thou art *r*	Rev 16:5	*1342*
true and *r* are thy judgments	Rev 16:7	*1342*
For true and *r* are his judgments	Rev 19:2	*1342*
is *r*, let him be *r* still	Rev 22:11	*1343*

RIGHTEOUSLY

judge *r* between every man and his	Deut 1:16	6664
for thou shalt judge the people *r*	Ps 67:4	4334
he shall judge the people *r*	Ps 96:10	4339
Open thy mouth, judge *r*, and plead	Prov 31:9	6664
He that walketh *r*, and speaketh	Is 33:15	6666
O LORD of hosts, that judgest *r*	Jer 11:20	6664
lusts, we should live soberly, *r*	Titus 2:12	*1346*
himself to him that judgeth *r*	1Pet 2:23	*1346*

RIGHTEOUSNESS

and he counted it to him for *r*	Gen 15:6	6666
So shall my *r* answer for me in	Gen 30:33	6666
but in *r* shalt thou judge thy	Lev 19:15	6664
And it shall be our *r*, if we	Deut 6:25	6666
For my *r* the LORD hath brought me	Deut 9:4	6666
Not for thy *r*, or for the	Deut 9:5	6666
good land to possess it for thy *r*	Deut 9:6	6666
it shall be *r* unto thee before	Deut 24:13	6666
they shall offer sacrifices of *r*	Deut 33:19	6664
LORD render to every man his *r*	1Sa 26:23	6666
rewarded me according to my *r*	2Sa 22:21	6666
recompensed me according to my *r*	2Sa 22:25	6666
before thee in truth, and in *r*	1Kin 3:6	6666
to give him according to his *r*	1Kin 8:32	6666
by giving him according to his *r*	2Chr 6:23	6666
yea, return again, my *r* is in it	Job 6:29	6664
habitation of thy *r* prosperous	Job 8:6	6664
My *r* I hold fast, and will not let	Job 27:6	6666
I put on *r*, and it clothed me	Job 29:14	6664
for he will render unto man his *r*	Job 33:26	6666
saidst, My *r* is more than God's	Job 35:2	6664
thy *r* may profit the son of man	Job 35:8	6666
and will ascribe *r* to my Maker	Job 36:3	6664
me when I call, O God of my *r*	Ps 4:1	6664
Offer the sacrifices of *r*	Ps 4:5	6664
in thy *r* because of mine enemies	Ps 5:8	6666
me, O LORD, according to my *r*	Ps 7:8	6664
the LORD according to his *r*	Ps 7:17	6664
And he shall judge the world in *r*	Ps 9:8	6664
For the righteous LORD loveth *r*	Ps 11:7	6666
walketh uprightly, and worketh *r*	Ps 15:2	6664
me, I will behold thy face in *r*	Ps 17:15	6664
rewarded me according to my *r*	Ps 18:20	6664
recompensed me according to my *r*	Ps 18:24	6664
shall declare his *r* unto a people	Ps 22:31	6666
paths of *r* for his name's sake	Ps 23:3	6664
r from the God of his salvation	Ps 24:5	6666
deliver me in thy *r*	Ps 31:1	6666
He loveth *r* and judgment	Ps 33:5	6666
O LORD my God, according to thy *r*	Ps 35:24	6664
And my tongue shall speak of thy *r*	Ps 35:28	6664
Thy *r* is like the great mountains	Ps 36:6	6666
thy *r* to the upright in heart	Ps 36:10	6666
bring forth thy *r* as the light	Ps 37:6	6664
I have preached *r* in the great	Ps 40:9	6664
not hid thy *r* within my heart	Ps 40:10	6666
because of truth and meekness and *r*	Ps 45:4	6664
Thou lovest *r*, and hatest	Ps 45:7	6664
thy right hand is full of *r*	Ps 48:10	6664
the heavens shall declare his *r*	Ps 50:6	6664
tongue shall sing aloud of thy *r*	Ps 51:14	6666
pleased with the sacrifices of *r*	Ps 51:19	6664
and lying rather than to speak *r*	Ps 52:3	6664
Do ye indeed speak *r*, O	Ps 58:1	6664
things in *r* wilt thou answer us	Ps 65:5	6664
and let them not come into thy *r*	Ps 69:27	6666
Deliver me in thy *r*, and cause me	Ps 71:2	6666
My mouth shall shew forth thy *r*	Ps 71:15	6666
I will make mention of thy *r*	Ps 71:16	6666
Thy *r* also, O God, is very high,	Ps 71:19	6666
talk of thy *r* all the day long	Ps 71:24	6666
thy *r* unto the king's son	Ps 72:1	6666
He shall judge thy people with *r*	Ps 72:2	6664
people, and the little hills, by *r*	Ps 72:3	6666
r and peace have kissed each other	Ps 85:10	6664
r shall look down from heaven	Ps 85:11	6664
R shall go before him	Ps 85:13	6664
and thy *r* in the land of	Ps 88:12	6666
in thy *r* shall they be exalted	Ps 89:16	6666
But judgment shall return unto *r*	Ps 94:15	6664
he shall judge the world with *r*	Ps 96:13	6664
r and judgment are the habitation	Ps 97:2	6664
The heavens declare his *r*	Ps 97:6	6664
his *r* hath he openly shewed in	Ps 98:2	6666
with *r* shall he judge the world,	Ps 98:9	6664
executest judgment and *r* in Jacob	Ps 99:4	6666
The LORD executeth *r* and judgment	Ps 103:6	6666
his *r* unto children's children	Ps 103:17	6666
and he that doeth *r* at all times	Ps 106:3	6666
for *r* unto all generations for	Ps 106:31	6666
and his *r* endureth for ever	Ps 111:3	6666
and his *r* endureth for ever	Ps 112:3	6666
his *r* endureth for ever	Ps 112:9	6666
Open to me the gates of *r*	Ps 118:19	6664
quicken me in thy *r*	Ps 119:40	6666
and for the word of thy *r*	Ps 119:123	6664
Thy *r* is an everlasting	Ps 119:142	6666
r is an everlasting *r*	Ps 119:142	6664
The *r* of thy testimonies is	Ps 119:144	6664
for all thy commandments are *r*	Ps 119:172	6664
Let thy priests be clothed with *r*	Ps 132:9	6664
answer me, and in thy *r*	Ps 143:1	6666
goodness, and shall sing of thy *r*	Ps 145:7	6666
Then shalt thou understand *r*	Prov 2:9	6664
the words of my mouth are in *r*	Prov 8:8	6664
yea, durable riches and *r*	Prov 8:18	6666
I lead in the way of *r*, in the	Prov 8:20	6666
but *r* delivereth from death	Prov 10:2	6666
but *r* delivereth from death	Prov 11:4	6666
The *r* of the perfect shall direct	Prov 11:5	6666
The *r* of the upright shall	Prov 11:6	6666
soweth *r* shall be a sure reward	Prov 11:18	6666
As *r* tendeth to life	Prov 11:19	6666
speaketh truth sheweth forth *r*	Prov 12:17	6664
In the way of *r* is life	Prov 12:28	6666
R keepeth him that is upright in	Prov 13:6	6666
R exalteth a nation	Prov 14:34	6666
loveth him that followeth after *r*	Prov 15:9	6666
Better is a little with *r* than	Prov 16:8	6666
the throne is established by *r*	Prov 16:12	6666
if it be found in the way of *r*	Prov 16:31	6666
He that followeth after *r*	Prov 21:21	6666
and mercy findeth life, *r*, and	Prov 21:21	6666
throne shall be established in *r*	Prov 25:5	6664
and the place of *r*, that iniquity	Eccl 3:16	6664
just man that perisheth in his *r*	Eccl 7:15	6664
r lodged in it	Is 1:21	6664
shalt be called, The city of *r*	Is 1:26	6664
judgment, and her converts with *r*	Is 1:27	6666
for *r*, but behold a cry	Is 5:7	6666
is holy shall be sanctified in *r*	Is 5:16	6666
take away the *r* of the righteous	Is 5:23	6666
decreed shall overflow with *r*	Is 10:22	6666
But with *r* shall he judge the	Is 11:4	6664
r shall be the girdle of his	Is 11:5	6664
and seeking judgment, and hasting *r*	Is 16:5	6664
of the world will learn *r*	Is 26:9	6664
wicked, yet will he not learn *r*	Is 26:10	6664
to the line, and *r* to the plummet	Is 28:17	6666
Behold, a king shall reign in *r*	Is 32:1	6664
r remain in the fruitful field	Is 32:16	6666
the work of *r* shall be peace	Is 32:17	6666
and the effect of *r* quietness	Is 32:17	6666
filled Zion with judgment and *r*	Is 33:5	6666
thee with the right hand of my *r*	Is 41:10	6664
I the LORD have called thee in *r*	Is 42:6	6664
and let the skies pour down *r*	Is 45:8	6664
and let *r* spring up together	Is 45:8	6666
I have raised him up in *r*	Is 45:13	6664
I the LORD speak *r*, I declare	Is 45:19	6664
word is gone out of my mouth in *r*	Is 45:23	6666
one say, in the LORD have I *r*	Is 45:24	6666
stouthearted, that are far from *r*	Is 46:12	6666
I bring near my *r*	Is 46:13	6666
but not in truth, nor in *r*	Is 48:1	6666
thy *r* as the waves of the sea	Is 48:18	6666
to me, ye that follow after *r*	Is 51:1	6664
My *r* is near	Is 51:5	6664
my *r* shall not be abolished	Is 51:6	6666
Hearken unto me, ye that know *r*	Is 51:7	6664
but my *r* shall be for ever, and my	Is 51:8	6666
In *r* shalt thou be established	Is 54:14	6666
their *r* is of me, saith the LORD	Is 54:17	6666
to come, and my *r* to be revealed	Is 56:1	6666
I will declare thy *r*, and thy	Is 57:12	6666
my ways, as a nation that did *r*	Is 58:2	6666
thy *r* shall go before thee	Is 58:8	6664
and his *r*, it sustained him	Is 59:16	6666
For he put on *r* as a breastplate,	Is 59:17	6666
peace, and thine exactors *r*	Is 60:17	6666
they might be called trees of *r*	Is 61:3	6664
covered me with the robe of *r*	Is 61:10	6666
so the Lord GOD will cause *r*	Is 61:11	6666
until the *r* thereof go forth as	Is 62:1	6664
And the Gentiles shall see thy *r*	Is 62:2	6664
I that speak in *r*, mighty to save	Is 63:1	6666
him that rejoiceth and worketh *r*	Is 64:5	6664
in truth, in judgment, and in *r*	Jer 4:2	6666
lovingkindness, judgment, and *r*	Jer 9:24	6666
Execute ye judgment and *r*, and	Jer 22:3	6666
shall be called, THE LORD OUR *R*	Jer 23:6	6664
Branch of *r* to grow up unto David	Jer 33:15	6666
execute judgment and *r* in the land	Jer 33:15	6666
shall be called, The LORD our *r*	Jer 33:16	6664
The LORD hath brought forth our *r*	Jer 51:10	6666
man doth turn from his *r*, and	Eze 3:20	6664
his *r* which he hath done shall	Eze 3:20	6666
but their own souls by their *r*	Eze 14:14	6666
their own souls by their *r*	Eze 14:20	6666
the *r* of the righteous shall be	Eze 18:20	6666
in his *r* that he hath done he	Eze 18:22	6666
righteous turneth away from his *r*	Eze 18:24	6666
All his *r* that he hath done shall	Eze 18:24	6666
man turneth away from his *r*	Eze 18:26	6666
The *r* of the righteous shall not	Eze 33:12	6666
be able to live for his *r* in the	Eze 33:12	
if he trust to his own *r*, and	Eze 33:13	6666
the righteous turneth from his *r*	Eze 33:18	6666
thee, and break off thy sins by *r*	Dan 4:27	6665
r belongeth unto thee, but unto	Dan 9:7	6666
O Lord, according to all thy *r*	Dan 9:16	6666
and to bring in everlasting *r*	Dan 9:24	6664
many to *r* as the stars for ever	Dan 12:3	6663
I will betroth thee unto me in *r*	Hos 2:19	6664
Sow to yourselves in *r*, reap in	Hos 10:12	6666
till he come and rain *r* upon you	Hos 10:12	6664
leave off *r* in the earth,	Amos 5:7	6666
waters, and *r* as a mighty stream	Amos 5:24	6666
and the fruit of *r* into hemlock	Amos 6:12	6666
ye may know the *r* of the LORD	Mic 6:5	6666
light, and I shall behold his *r*	Mic 7:9	6666
seek *r*, seek meekness	Zeph 2:3	6664
be their God, in truth and in *r*	Zec 8:8	6666
unto the LORD an offering in *r*	Mal 3:3	6666
fear my name shall the Sun of *r*	Mal 4:2	6666
it becometh us to fulfil all *r*	Mt 3:15	*1343*
which do hunger and thirst after *r*	Mt 5:6	*1343*
That except your *r* shall exceed	Mt 5:20	*1343*
shall exceed the *r* of the scribes	Mt 5:20	*1343*
the kingdom of God, and his *r*	Mt 6:33	*1343*
came unto you in the way of *r*	Mt 21:32	*1343*
r before him, all the days of our	Lk 1:75	*1343*
reprove the world of sin, and of *r*	Jn 16:8	*1343*
Of *r*, because I go to my Father,	Jn 16:10	*1343*
he that feareth him, and worketh *r*	Acts 10:35	*1343*
of the devil, thou enemy of all *r*	Acts 13:10	*1343*
in *r* by that man whom he hath	Acts 17:31	*1343*
And as he reasoned of *r*,	Acts 24:25	*1343*
For therein is the *r* of God	Rom 1:17	*1343*
keep the *r* of the law, shall not	Rom 2:26	*1345*
commend the *r* of God, what shall	Rom 3:5	*1343*
But now the *r* of God without the	Rom 3:21	*1343*
Even the *r* of God which is by	Rom 3:22	*1343*
blood, to declare his *r* for the	Rom 3:25	*1343*
I say, at this time his *r*	Rom 3:26	*1343*
and it was counted unto him for *r*	Rom 4:3	*1343*
his faith is counted for *r*	Rom 4:5	*1343*
whom God imputeth *r* without works	Rom 4:6	*1343*
was reckoned to Abraham for *r*	Rom 4:9	*1343*
a seal of the *r* of the faith	Rom 4:11	*1343*
that *r* might be imputed unto them	Rom 4:11	*1343*
law, but through the *r* of faith	Rom 4:13	*1343*
it was imputed to him for *r*	Rom 4:22	*1343*
of the gift of *r* shall reign in	Rom 5:17	*1343*
even so by the *r* of one the free	Rom 5:18	*1345*
r unto eternal life by Jesus	Rom 5:21	*1343*
as instruments of *r* unto God	Rom 6:13	*1343*
death, or of obedience unto *r*	Rom 6:16	*1343*
sin, ye became the servants of *r*	Rom 6:18	*1343*
servants to *r* unto holiness	Rom 6:19	*1343*
of sin, ye were free from *r*	Rom 6:20	*1343*
That the *r* of the law might be	Rom 8:4	*1345*
the Spirit is life because of *r*	Rom 8:10	*1343*
the work, and cut it short in *r*	Rom 9:28	*1343*
which followed not after *r*	Rom 9:30	*1343*
have attained to *r*	Rom 9:30	*1343*
even the *r* which is of faith	Rom 9:30	*1343*
which followed after the law of *r*	Rom 9:31	*1343*
hath not attained to the law of *r*	Rom 9:31	*1343*
they being ignorant of God's *r*	Rom 10:3	*1343*
about to establish their own *r*	Rom 10:3	*1343*
themselves unto the *r* of God	Rom 10:3	*1343*
is the end of the law for *r* to	Rom 10:4	*1343*
the *r* which is of the law	Rom 10:5	*1343*
But the *r* which is of faith	Rom 10:6	*1343*
the heart man believeth unto *r*	Rom 10:10	*1343*
but *r*, and peace, and joy in the	Rom 14:17	*1343*
God is made unto us wisdom, and *r*	1Cor 1:30	*1343*
Awake to *r*, and sin not	1Cor 15:34	*1346*
ministration of *r* exceed in glory	2Cor 3:9	*1343*
might be made the *r* of God in him	2Cor 5:21	*1343*
by the armour of *r* on the right	2Cor 6:7	*1343*
hath *r* with unrighteousness	2Cor 6:14	*1343*
his *r* remaineth for ever	2Cor 9:9	*1343*
and increase the fruits of your *r*	2Cor 9:10	*1343*
transformed as the ministers of *r*	2Cor 11:15	*1343*
for if *r* come by the law, then	Gal 2:21	*1343*
and it was accounted to him for *r*	Gal 3:6	*1343*
verily *r* should have been by the	Gal 3:21	*1343*
wait for the hope of *r* by faith	Gal 5:5	*1343*
which after God is created in *r*	Eph 4:24	*1343*
Spirit is in all goodness and *r*	Eph 5:9	*1343*
and having on the breastplate of *r*	Eph 6:14	*1343*
Being filled with the fruits of *r*	Phil 1:11	*1343*
touching the *r* which is in the	Phil 3:6	*1343*
in him, not having mine own *r*	Phil 3:9	*1343*
the *r* which is of God by faith	Phil 3:9	*1343*
and follow after *r*, godliness,	1Ti 6:11	*1343*
but follow *r*, faith, charity,	2Ti 2:22	*1343*
correction, for instruction in *r*	2Ti 3:16	*1343*
is laid up for me a crown of *r*	2Ti 4:8	*1343*
Not by works of *r* which we have	Titus 3:5	*1343*
a sceptre of *r* is the sceptre of	Heb 1:8	*2118*
Thou hast loved *r*, and hated	Heb 1:9	*1343*
is unskilful in the word of *r*	Heb 5:13	*1343*
being by interpretation King of *r*	Heb 7:2	*1343*
heir of the *r* which is by faith	Heb 11:7	*1343*
faith subdued kingdoms, wrought *r*	Heb 11:33	*1343*
r unto them which are exercised	Heb 12:11	*1343*
of man worketh not the *r* of God	Jas 1:20	*1343*
and it was imputed unto him for *r*	Jas 2:23	*1343*
the fruit of *r* is sown in peace	Jas 3:18	*1343*
dead to sins, should live unto *r*	1Pet 2:24	*1343*
with us through the *r* of God	2Pet 1:1	*1343*
eighth person, a preacher of *r*	2Pet 2:5	*1343*
not to have known the way of *r*	2Pet 2:21	*1343*
a new earth, wherein dwelleth *r*	2Pet 3:13	*1343*

one that doeth *r* is born of him 1Jn 2:29 *1343*
he that doeth *r* is righteous 1Jn 3:7 *1343*
doeth not *r* is not of God 1Jn 3:10 *1343*
the fine linen is the *r* of saints Rev 19:8 *1345*
in *r* he doth judge and make war Rev 19:11 *1343*

RIGHTEOUSNESS'
for thy *r* sake bring my soul out Ps 143:11 6666
is well pleased for his *r* sake Is 42:21 6664
which are persecuted for *r* sake Mt 5:10 *1343*
But and if ye suffer for *r* sake 1Pet 3:14 *1343*

RIGHTEOUSNESSES
all our *r* are as filthy rags Is 64:6 6666
all his *r* shall not be remembered Eze 33:13 6666
before thee for our *r*, but for Dan 9:18 6666

RIGHTLY
he said, Is not he *r* named Jacob Gen 27:36 3588
said unto him, Thou hast *r* judged Lk 7:43 *3723*
that thou sayest and teachest *r* Lk 20:21 *3723*
r dividing the word of truth 2Ti 2:15 *3723*

RIGOUR
of Israel to serve with *r* Ex 1:13 6531
they made them serve, was with *r* Ex 1:14 6531
shalt not rule over him with *r* Lev 25:43 6531
not rule one over another with *r* Lev 25:46 6531
rule with *r* over him in thy sight Lev 25:53 6531

RIMMON (*rim'-mon*)
1. A city in Zebulun.
Lebaoth, and Shilhim, and Ain, and *R* Josh 15:32 7417
R with her suburbs, Tabor with 1Chr 6:77 7417
from Geba to *R* south of Jerusalem Zec 14:10 7417
2. A rock near Gibeah.
the wilderness unto the rock of *R* Judg 20:45 7417
to the wilderness unto the rock *R* Judg 20:47 7417
abode in the rock *R* four months Judg 20:47 7417
Benjamin that were in the rock *R* Judg 21:13 7417
3. Father of Baanah and Rechab.
the sons of *R* a Beerothite, of 2Sa 4:2 7417
the sons of *R* the Beerothite, 2Sa 4:5 7417
the sons of *R* the Beerothite, and 2Sa 4:9 7417
4. A Syrian god.
the house of *R* to worship there 2Kin 5:18 7417
and I bow myself in the house of *R* 2Kin 5:18 7417
bow down myself in the house of *R* 2Kin 5:18 7417
5. A city in Simeon.
villages were, Etam, and Ain, *R* 1Chr 4:32 7417

RIMMONO See RIMMON.

RIMMON-PAREZ (*rim''-mon-pa'-rez*) *An Israelite encampment in the wilderness.*
from Rithmah, and pitched at *R* Num 33:19 7428
And they departed from *R*, and Num 33:20 7428

RING
took off his *r* from his hand Gen 41:42 2885
above the head of it unto one *r* Ex 26:24 2885
at the head thereof, to one *r* Ex 36:29 2885
the king took his *r* from his hand Est 3:10 2885
and sealed with the king's *r* Est 3:12 2885
And the king took off his *r* Est 8:2 2885
and seal it with the king's *r* Est 8:8 2885
name, and sealed with the king's *r* Est 8:8 2885
and sealed it with the king's *r* Est 8:10 2885
put a *r* on his hand, and shoes on Lk 15:22 *1146*
your assembly a man with a gold *r* Jas 2:2 *5554*

RINGLEADER
a *r* of the sect of the Nazarenes Acts 24:5 *4414*

RINGS
shalt cast four *r* of gold for it Ex 25:12 2885
two *r* shall be in the one side of Ex 25:12 2885
two *r* in the other side of it Ex 25:12 2885
the *r* by the sides of the ark Ex 25:14 2885
shall be in the *r* of the ark Ex 25:15 2885
shalt make for it four *r* of gold Ex 25:26 2885
put the *r* in the four corners Ex 25:26 2885
against the border shall the *r* be Ex 25:27 2885
make their *r* of gold for places Ex 26:29 2885
r in the four corners thereof Ex 27:4 2885
staves shall be put into the *r* Ex 27:7 2885
the breastplate two *r* of gold Ex 28:23 2885
shalt put the two *r* on the two Ex 28:23 2885
chains of gold in the two *r* which Ex 28:24 2885
And thou shalt make two *r* of gold Ex 28:26 2885
two other *r* of gold thou shalt Ex 28:27 2885
bind the breastplate by the *r* Ex 28:28 2885
the *r* of the ephod with a lace of Ex 28:28 2885
two golden *r* shalt thou make to Ex 30:4 2885
bracelets, and earrings, and *r* Ex 35:22 2885
made their *r* of gold to be places Ex 36:34 2885
And he cast for it four *r* of gold Ex 37:3 2885
even two *r* upon the one side of Ex 37:3 2885
two *r* upon the other side of it Ex 37:3 2885
the *r* by the sides of the ark Ex 37:5 2885
And he cast for it four *r* of gold Ex 37:13 2885
put the *r* upon the four corners Ex 37:13 2885
against the border were the *r* Ex 37:14 2885
he made two *r* of gold for it Ex 37:27 2885
he cast four *r* for the four ends Ex 38:5 2885
the *r* on the sides of the altar Ex 38:7 2885
two ouches of gold, and two gold *r* Ex 39:16 2885
put the two *r* in the two ends of Ex 39:16 2885
chains of gold in the two *r* on Ex 39:17 2885
And they made two *r* of gold Ex 39:19 2885
And they made two other golden *r* Ex 39:20 2885
his *r* unto the *r* of the ephod Ex 39:21 2885
of gold, chains, and bracelets, *r* Num 31:50 2885
fine linen and purple to silver *r* Est 1:6 1550
are as gold *r* set with the beryl Song 5:14 1550
The *r*, and nose jewels, Is 3:21 2885
As for their *r*, they were so high Eze 1:18 1354
their *r* were full of eyes round Eze 1:18 1354

RINGSTRAKED
that day the he goats that were *r* Gen 30:35 6124
rods, and brought forth cattle *r* Gen 30:39 6124
faces of the flocks toward the *r* Gen 30:40 6124
thus, The *r* shall be thy hire Gen 31:8 6124
then bare all the cattle *r* Gen 31:8 6124
leaped upon the cattle were *r* Gen 31:10 6124
which leap upon the cattle are *r* Gen 31:12 6124

RINNAH (*rin'-nah*) *A descendant of Caleb.*
sons of Shimon were, Amnon, and *R* 1Chr 4:20 7441

RINSED
be both scoured, and *r* in water Lev 6:28 7857
hath not *r* his hands in water, he Lev 15:11 7857
of wood shall be *r* in water Lev 15:12 7857

RIOT
not accused of *r* or unruly Titus 1:6 *810*
with them to the same excess of *r* 1Pet 4:4 *810*
it pleasure to *r* in the daytime 2Pet 2:13 *5172*

RIOTING
not in *r* and drunkenness, not in Rom 13:13 *2970*

RIOTOUS
among *r* eaters of flesh Prov 23:20 2151
of *r* men shameth his father Prov 28:7 2151
his substance with *r* living Lk 15:13 *811*

RIP
r up their women with child 2Kin 8:12 1234

RIPE
thereof brought forth *r* grapes Gen 40:10 1310
offer the first of thy *r* fruits Ex 22:29
whatsoever is first *r* in the land Num 18:13
like the figs that are first *r* Jer 24:2
the sickle, for the harvest is *r* Joel 3:13 1310
for the harvest of the earth is *r* Rev 14:15 *3583*
for her grapes are fully *r* Rev 14:18 *187*

RIPENING
the sour grape is *r* in the flower Is 18:5 1580

RIPHATH (*ri'-fath*) *A son of Gomer.*
Ashkenaz, and *R*, and Togarmah Gen 10:3 7384
Ashchenaz, and *R*, and Togarmah 1Chr 1:6 7384

RIPPED
that were with child he *r* up 2Kin 15:16 1234
women with child shall be *r* up Hos 13:16 1234
because they have *r* up the women Amos 1:13 1234

RISE
your feet, and ye shall *r* up early Gen 19:2 7925
that I cannot *r* up before thee Gen 31:35 6965
R up early in the morning, and Ex 8:20 7925
R up early in the morning, and Ex 9:13 6965
R up, and get you forth from among Ex 12:31 6965
If he *r* again, and walk abroad Ex 21:19 6965
Thou shalt *r* up before the hoary Lev 19:32 6965
R up, LORD, and let thine enemies Num 10:35 6965
call thee, *r* up, and go with them Num 22:20 6965
and said, *R* up, Balak, and hear Num 23:18 6965
the people shall *r* up as a great Num 23:24 6965
a Sceptre shall *r* out of Israel Num 24:17 6965
Now *r* up, said I, and get you over Deut 2:13 6965
R ye up, take your journey, and Deut 2:24 6965
r up against him, and smite him Deut 19:11 6965
One witness shall not *r* up Deut 19:15 6965
If a false witness *r* up against Deut 19:16 6965
r up against thee to be smitten Deut 28:7 6965
that shall *r* up after you Deut 29:22 6965
and this people will *r* up, and go a Deut 31:16 6965
Let them *r* up and help you, and be Deut 32:38 6965
loins of them that *r* against him Deut 33:11 6965
hate him, that they *r* not again Deut 33:11 6965
Then ye shall *r* up from the Josh 8:7 6965
I will send them, and they shall *r* Josh 18:4 6965
said, *R* thou, and fall upon us Judg 8:21 6965
the sun is up, thou shalt *r* early Judg 9:33 7925
with smoke *r* up out of the city Judg 20:38 5927
him, that he should *r* against me 1Sa 22:13 6965
them not to *r* against Saul 1Sa 24:7 6965
Wherefore now *r* up early in the 1Sa 29:10 7925
the child was dead, thou didst *r* 2Sa 12:21 6965
all that *r* against thee to do 2Sa 18:32 6965
of Israel, which *r* up against me 2Kin 16:7 6965
And they said, Let us *r* up Neh 2:18 6965
the earth shall *r* up against him Job 20:27 6965
Upon my right hand *r* the youth Job 30:12 6965
are they that *r* up against me Ps 3:1 6965
from those that *r* up against them Ps 17:7 6965
them that they were not able to *r* Ps 18:38 6965
above those that *r* up against me Ps 18:48 6965
though war should *r* against me Ps 27:3 6965
False witnesses did *r* up Ps 35:11 6965
down, and shall not be able to *r* Ps 36:12 6965
he lieth he shall *r* up no more Ps 41:8 6965
them under that *r* up against us Ps 44:5 6965
me from them that *r* up against me Ps 59:1 6965
the tumult of those that *r* up Ps 74:23 6965
the wicked that *r* up against me Ps 92:11 6965
Who will *r* up for me against the Ps 94:16 6965
At midnight I will *r* to give Ps 119:62 6965
It is vain for you to *r* up early Ps 127:2 6965
with those that *r* up against thee Ps 139:21 8618
pits, that they *r* not up again Ps 140:10 6965
their calamity shall *r* suddenly Prov 24:22 6965
but when the wicked *r*, a man is Prov 28:12 6965
When the wicked *r*, men hide Prov 28:28 6965
of the ruler *r* up against thee Eccl 10:4 5927
he shall *r* up at the voice of the Eccl 12:4 6965
R up, my love, my fair one, and Song 2:10 6965
I will *r* now, and go about the Song 3:2 6965
Woe unto them that *r* up early in Is 5:11 7925
that they do not *r*, nor possess Is 14:21 6965
For I will *r* up against them, Is 14:22 6965
and it shall fall, and not *r* again Is 24:20 6965
are deceased, they shall not *r* Is 26:14 6965
For the LORD shall *r* up as in Is 28:21 6965
R up, ye women that are at ease Is 32:9 6965
Now will I *r*, saith the LORD Is 33:10 6965
down together, they shall not *r* Is 43:17 6965
every tongue that shall *r* against Is 54:17 6965
shall thy light *r* in obscurity Is 58:10 2224
r no more, because of the sword Jer 25:27 6965
yet should they *r* up every man in Jer 37:10 6965
waters *r* up out of the north, and Jer 47:2 5927
her, and *r* up to the battle Jer 49:14 6965
of them that *r* up against me Jer 51:1 6965
shall not *r* from the evil that I Jer 51:64 6965
from whom I am not able to *r* up Lam 1:14 6965
and another shall *r* after them Dan 7:24 6966
she shall no more *r* Amos 5:2 6965
I will *r* against the house of Amos 7:9 6965
it shall *r* up wholly as a flood Amos 8:8 5927
shall fall, and never *r* up again Amos 8:14 6965
it shall *r* up wholly like a flood Amos 9:5 5927
let us *r* up against her in battle Obad 1 6965
shall not *r* up the second time Nah 1:9 6965
Shall they not *r* up suddenly that Hab 2:7 6965
the day that I *r* up to the prey Zeph 3:8 6965
his hand shall *r* up against the Zec 14:13 5927
maketh his sun to *r* on the evil Mt 5:45 *393*
the children shall *r* up against Mt 10:21 *1881*
shall *r* in judgment with this Mt 12:41 *450*
r up in the judgment with this Mt 12:42 *1453*
and the third day he shall *r* again Mt 20:19 *450*
For nation shall *r* against nation Mt 24:7 *1453*
And many false prophets shall *r* Mt 24:11 *1453*
R, let us be going Mt 26:46 *1453*
After three days I will *r* again Mt 27:63 *1453*
if Satan *r* up against himself, and Mk 3:26 *450*
r night and day, and the seed Mk 4:27 *1453*
and after three days *r* again Mk 8:31 *450*
killed, he shall *r* the third day Mk 9:31 *450*
and the third day he shall *r* again Mk 10:34 *450*
unto him, Be of good comfort, *r* Mk 10:49 *1453*
therefore, when they shall *r* Mk 12:23 *450*
when they shall *r* from the dead Mk 12:25 *450*
as touching the dead, that they *r* Mk 12:26 *1453*
For nation shall *r* against nation Mk 13:8 *1453*
children shall *r* up against their Mk 13:12 *1881*
Christs and false prophets shall *r* Mk 13:22 *1453*
R up, let us go Mk 14:42 *1453*
or to say, *R* up and walk Lk 5:23 *1453*
R up, and stand forth in the midst Lk 6:8 *1453*
I cannot *r* and give thee Lk 11:7 *450*
unto you, Though he will not *r* Lk 11:8 *1453*
of his importunity he will *r* Lk 11:8 *450*
The queen of the south shall *r* up Lk 11:31 *1453*
The men of Nineve shall *r* up in Lk 11:32 *450*
ye see a cloud *r* out of the west Lk 12:54 *393*
and the third day he shall *r* again Lk 18:33 *450*
Nation shall *r* against nation, and Lk 21:10 *1453*
r and pray, lest ye enter into Lk 22:46 *450*
and the third day *r* again Lk 24:7 *450*
to *r* from the dead the third day Lk 24:46 *450*
Jesus saith unto him, *R*, take up Jn 5:8 *1453*
her, Thy brother shall *r* again Jn 11:23 *450*
I know that he shall *r* again in Jn 11:24 *450*
that he must *r* again from the Jn 20:9 *450*
of Jesus Christ of Nazareth *r* up Acts 3:6 *1453*
And there came a voice to him, *R* Acts 10:13 *450*
But *r*, and stand upon thy feet Acts 26:16 *450*
first that should *r* from the dead Acts 26:23 *386*
he that shall *r* to reign over the Rom 15:12 *450*
up, if so be that the dead *r* not 1Cor 15:15 *1453*
For if the dead *r* not, then is 1Cor 15:16 *1453*
dead, if the dead *r* not at all 1Cor 15:29 *1453*
it me, if the dead *r* not 1Cor 15:32 *1453*
the dead in Christ shall *r* first 1Th 4:16 *450*
that another priest should *r* Heb 7:11 *450*
and the angel stood, saying, *R* Rev 11:1 *1453*
saw a beast *r* up out of the sea, Rev 13:1 *305*

RISEN
The sun was *r* upon the earth when Gen 19:23 3318
If the sun be *r* upon him, there Ex 22:3 2224
ye are *r* up in your fathers' Num 32:14 6965
ye are *r* up against my father's Judg 9:18 6965
And when she was *r* up to glean Ruth 2:15 6965
Yet a man is *r* to pursue thee, and 1Sa 25:29 6965
the whole family is *r* against 2Sa 14:7 6965
I am *r* up in the room of David my 1Kin 8:20 6965
of the man of God was *r* early 2Kin 6:15 6965
for I am *r* up in the room of 2Chr 6:10 6965
Solomon the son of David, is *r* up 2Chr 13:6 6965
Now when Jehoram was *r* up to the 2Chr 21:4 6965
but we are *r*, and stand upright Ps 20:8 6965
witnesses are *r* up against me Ps 27:12 6965
For strangers are *r* up against me Ps 54:3 6965
O God, the proud are *r* against me Ps 86:14 6965
glory of the LORD is *r* upon thee Is 60:1 2224
Violence is *r* up into a rod of Eze 7:11 6965
for the waters were *r*, waters to Eze 47:5 1342
my people is *r* up as an enemy Mic 2:8 6965
born of women there hath not *r* a Mt 11:11 *1453*
he is *r* from the dead Mt 14:2 *1453*
of man be *r* again from the dead Mt 17:9 *450*
But after I am *r* again, I will go Mt 26:32 *1453*
the people, He is *r* from the dead Mt 27:64 *1453*
for he is *r*, as he said Mt 28:6 *1453*
that he is *r* from the dead Mt 28:7 *1453*
the Baptist was *r* from the dead Mk 6:14 *1453*
he is *r* from the dead Mk 6:16 *1453*
Son of man were *r* from the dead Mk 9:9 *450*
But after that I am *r*, I will go Mk 14:28 *1453*
he is *r* Mk 16:6 *1453*
Now when Jesus was *r* early the Mk 16:9 *450*
which had seen him after he was *r* Mk 16:14 *1453*

R

a great prophet is *r* up among us — Lk 7:16 — *1453*
that John was *r* from the dead — Lk 9:7 — *1453*
of the old prophets was *r* again — Lk 9:8 — *450*
of the old prophets is *r* again — Lk 9:19 — *450*
the master of the house is *r* up — Lk 13:25 — *1453*
He is not here, but is *r* — Lk 24:6 — *1453*
Saying, The Lord is *r* indeed — Lk 24:34 — *1453*
therefore he was *r* from the dead — Jn 2:22 — *1453*
after that he was *r* from the dead — Jn 21:14 — *1453*
and *r* again from the dead — Acts 17:3 — *450*
died, yea rather, that is *r* again — Rom 8:34 — *1453*
of the dead, then is Christ not *r* — 1Cor 15:13 — *1453*
And if Christ be not *r*, then is — 1Cor 15:14 — *1453*
But now is Christ *r* from the dead — 1Cor 15:20 — *1453*
wherein also ye are *r* with him — Col 2:12 — *4891*
If ye then be *r* with Christ — Col 3:1 — *4891*
no sooner *r* with a burning heat — Jas 1:11 — *393*

RISEST
liest down, and when thou *r* up — Deut 6:7 — 6965
liest down, and when thou *r* up — Deut 11:19 — 6965

RISETH
for as when a man *r* against his — Deut 22:26 — 6965
man before the LORD, that *r* up — Josh 6:26 — 6965
of the morning, when the sun *r* — 2Sa 23:4 — 2224
commandeth the sun, and it *r* not — Job 9:7 — 2224
So man lieth down, and *r* not — Job 14:12 — 6965
he *r* up, and no man is sure of — Job 24:22 — 6965
he that *r* up against me as the — Job 27:7 — 6965
then shall I do when God *r* up — Job 31:14 — 6965
seven times, and *r* up again — Prov 24:16 — 6965
She *r* also while it is yet night — Prov 31:15 — 6965
shalt not know from whence it *r* — Is 47:11 — 7837
Egypt *r* up like a flood, and his — Jer 46:8 — 5927
the daughter *r* up against her — Mic 7:6 — 6965
He *r* from supper, and laid aside — Jn 13:4 — *1453*

RISING
have in the skin of his flesh a *r* — Lev 13:2 — 7613
if the *r* be white in the skin, and — Lev 13:10 — 7613
there be quick raw flesh in the *r* — Lev 13:10 — 7613
of the boil there be a white *r* — Lev 13:19 — 7613
it is a *r* of the burning, and the — Lev 13:28 — 7613
if the *r* of the sore be white — Lev 13:43 — 7613
And for a *r*, and for a scab, and for — Lev 14:56 — 7613
on the east side toward the *r* of — Num 2:3 — 4217
Jordan toward the *r* of the sun — Josh 12:1 — 4217
r up betimes, and sending — 2Chr 36:15 — 7925
r of the morning till the stars — Neh 4:21 — 5927
my leanness *r* up in me beareth — Job 16:8 — 6965
r betimes for a prey — Job 24:5 — 7836
The murderer *r* with the light — Job 24:14 — 7925
called the earth from the *r* of — Ps 50:1 — 4217
From the *r* of the sun unto the — Ps 113:3 — 4217
r early in the morning, it shall — Prov 27:14 — 7925
against whom there is no *r* up — Prov 30:31 — 510
from the *r* of the sun shall he — Is 41:25 — 4217
may know from the *r* of the sun — Is 45:6 — 4217
his glory from the *r* of the sun — Is 59:19 — 4217
kings to the brightness of thy *r* — Is 60:3 — 2225
r up early and speaking, but ye — Jer 7:13 — 7925
daily *r* up early and sending them — Jer 7:25 — 7925
r early and protesting, saying — Jer 11:7 — 7925
unto you, *r* early and speaking — Jer 25:3 — 7925
prophets, *r* early and sending them — Jer 25:4 — 7925
both *r* up early, and sending them — Jer 26:5 — 7925
r up early and sending them — Jer 29:19 — 7925
r up early and teaching them, yet — Jer 32:33 — 7925
unto you, *r* early and speaking — Jer 35:14 — 7925
r up early and sending them — Jer 35:15 — 7925
r early and sending them, saying — Jer 44:4 — 7925
their sitting down, and their *r* up — Lam 3:63 — 7012
For from the *r* of the sun even — Mal 1:11 — 4217
r up a great while before day, he — Mk 1:35 — *450*
the *r* from the dead should mean — Mk 9:10 — *305*
the sepulchre at the *r* of the sun — Mk 16:2 — *393*
r again of many in Israel — Lk 2:34 — *386*

RISSAH
(*ris'-sah*) *An Israelite encampment in the wilderness.*
from Libnah, and pitched at *R* — Num 33:21 — 7446
And they journeyed from *R*, and — Num 33:22 — 7446

RITES
according to all the *r* of it — Num 9:3 — 2708

RITHMAH
(*rith'-mah*) *An Israelite encampment in the wilderness.*
from Hazeroth, and pitched in *R* — Num 33:18 — 7575
And they departed from *R*, and — Num 33:19 — 7575

RIVER
a *r* went out of Eden to water the — Gen 2:10 — 5104
the name of the second *r* is Gihon — Gen 2:13 — 5104
name of the third *r* is Hiddekel — Gen 2:14 — 5104
the fourth *r* is Euphrates — Gen 2:14 — 5104
from the *r* of Egypt unto the — Gen 15:18 — 5104
the great *r*, the *r* Euphrates — Gen 15:18 — 5104
he rose up, and passed over the *r* — Gen 31:21 — 5104
by the *r* reigned in his stead — Gen 36:37 — 5104
and, behold, he stood by the *r* — Gen 41:1 — 2975
of the *r* seven well favoured kine — Gen 41:2 — 2975
came up after them out of the *r* — Gen 41:3 — 2975
kine upon the brink of the *r* — Gen 41:3 — 2975
I stood upon the bank of the *r* — Gen 41:17 — 2975
came up out of the *r* seven kine — Gen 41:18 — 2975
is born ye shall cast into the *r* — Ex 1:22 — 2975
down to wash herself at the *r* — Ex 2:5 — 2975
shalt take of the water of the *r* — Ex 4:9 — 2975
which thou takest out of the *r* — Ex 4:9 — 2975
the waters which are in the *r* — Ex 7:17 — 2975
fish that is in the *r* shall die — Ex 7:18 — 2975
and the *r* shall stink — Ex 7:18 — 2975
to drink of the water of the *r* — Ex 7:18 — 2975
the waters that were in the *r* — Ex 7:20 — 2975
in the *r* were turned to blood — Ex 7:20 — 2975
the fish that was in the *r* died — Ex 7:21 — 2975
the *r* stank, and the Egyptians — Ex 7:21 — 2975
not drink of the water of the *r* — Ex 7:21 — 2975
about the *r* for water to drink — Ex 7:24 — 2975
not drink of the water of the *r* — Ex 7:24 — 2975
that the LORD had smitten the *r* — Ex 7:25 — 2975
the *r* shall bring forth frogs — Ex 8:3 — 2975
they may remain in the *r* only — Ex 8:9 — 2975
they shall remain in the *r* only — Ex 8:11 — 2975
rod, wherewith thou smotest the *r* — Ex 17:5 — 2975
and from the desert unto the *r* — Ex 23:31 — 5104
which is by the *r* of the land of — Num 22:5 — 5104
from Azmon unto the *r* of Egypt — Num 34:5 — 5158
and unto Lebanon, unto the great *r* — Deut 1:7 — 5104
the great *r*, the *r* Euphrates — Deut 1:7 — 5104
journey, and pass over the *r* Arnon — Deut 2:24 — 5158
is by the brink of the *r* of Arnon — Deut 2:36 — 5158
and from the city that is by the *r* — Deut 2:36 — 5158
unto any place of the *r* Jabbok — Deut 2:37 — 5158
from the *r* of Arnon unto mount — Deut 3:8 — 5158
Aroer, which is by the *r* Arnon — Deut 3:12 — 5158
unto the *r* Arnon half the valley — Deut 3:16 — 5158
the border even unto the *r* Jabbok — Deut 3:16 — 5158
is by the bank of the *r* Arnon — Deut 4:48 — 5158
wilderness and Lebanon, from the *r* — Deut 11:24 — 5104
the *r* Euphrates, even unto the — Deut 11:24 — 5104
Lebanon even unto the great *r* — Josh 1:4 — 5104
the *r* Euphrates, all the land of — Josh 1:4 — 5104
from the *r* Arnon unto mount — Josh 12:1 — 5158
is upon the bank of the *r* Arnon — Josh 12:2 — 5158
and from the middle of the *r* — Josh 12:2 — 5158
Gilead, even unto the *r* Jabbok — Josh 12:2 — 5158
is upon the bank of the *r* Arnon — Josh 13:9 — 5158
that is in the midst of the *r* — Josh 13:9 — 5158
is on the bank of the *r* Arnon — Josh 13:16 — 5158
that is in the midst of the *r* — Josh 13:16 — 5158
and went out unto the *r* of Egypt — Josh 15:4 — 5158
is on the south side of the *r* — Josh 15:7 — 5158
her villages, unto the *r* of Egypt — Josh 15:47 — 5158
Tappuah westward unto the *r* Kanah — Josh 16:8 — 5158
r Kanah, southward of the *r* — Josh 17:9 — 5158
was on the north side of the *r* — Josh 17:9 — 5158
reached to the *r* that is before — Josh 19:11 — 5158
draw unto thee to the *r* Kishon — Judg 4:7 — 5158
the Gentiles unto the *r* of Kishon — Judg 4:13 — 5158
The *r* of Kishon swept them away — Judg 5:21 — 5158
that ancient *r*, the *r* Kishon — Judg 5:21 — 5158
his border at the *r* Euphrates — 2Sa 8:3 — 5104
Syrians that were beyond the *r* — 2Sa 10:16 — 5104
and we will draw it into the *r* — 2Sa 17:13 — 5158
in the midst of the *r* of Gad — 2Sa 24:5 — 5158
from the *r* unto the land of the — 1Kin 4:21 — 5104
all the region on this side the *r* — 1Kin 4:24 — 5104
all the kings on this side the *r* — 1Kin 4:24 — 5104
in of Hamath unto the *r* of Egypt — 1Kin 8:65 — 5158
shall scatter them beyond the *r* — 1Kin 14:15 — 5104
Aroer, which is by the *r* Arnon — 2Kin 10:33 — 5158
and in Habor by the *r* of Gozan — 2Kin 17:6 — 5104
and in Habor by the *r* of Gozan — 2Kin 18:11 — 5104
of Assyria to the *r* Euphrates — 2Kin 23:29 — 5104
the *r* of Egypt unto the *r* — 2Kin 24:7 — 5158
by the *r* reigned in his stead — 1Chr 1:48 — 5104
wilderness from the *r* Euphrates — 1Chr 5:9 — 5104
Habor, and Hara, and to the *r* Gozan — 1Chr 5:26 — 5104
his dominion by the *r* Euphrates — 1Chr 18:3 — 5104
Syrians that were beyond the *r* — 1Chr 19:16 — 5104
in of Hamath unto the *r* of Egypt — 2Chr 7:8 — 5158
the *r* even unto the land of the — 2Chr 9:26 — 5104
rest that are on this side the *r* — Ezr 4:10 — 5103
the men on this side the *r* — Ezr 4:11 — 5103
no portion on this side the *r* — Ezr 4:16 — 5103
and unto the rest beyond the *r* — Ezr 4:17 — 5103
over all countries beyond the *r* — Ezr 4:20 — 5103
governor on this side the *r* — Ezr 5:3 — 5103
governor on this side the *r* — Ezr 5:6 — 5103
which were on this side the *r* — Ezr 5:6 — 5103
Tatnai, governor beyond the *r* — Ezr 6:6 — 5103
which are beyond the *r*, be ye — Ezr 6:6 — 5103
even of the tribute beyond the *r* — Ezr 6:8 — 5103
governor on this side the *r* — Ezr 6:13 — 5103
treasurers which are beyond the *r* — Ezr 7:21 — 5103
the people that are beyond the *r* — Ezr 7:25 — 5103
to the *r* that runneth to Ahava — Ezr 8:15 — 5104
at the *r* of Ahava, that we might — Ezr 8:21 — 5104
Then we departed from the *r* of — Ezr 8:31 — 5104
the governors on this side the *r* — Ezr 8:36 — 5104
me to the governors beyond the *r* — Neh 2:7 — 5104
to the governors beyond the *r* — Neh 2:9 — 5104
the governor on this side the *r* — Neh 3:7 — 5104
Behold, he drinketh up a *r* — Job 40:23 — 5104
drink of the *r* of thy pleasures — Ps 36:8 — 5158
There is a *r*, the streams whereof — Ps 46:4 — 5104
enrichest it with the *r* of God — Ps 65:9 — 6388
from the *r* unto the ends of the — Ps 72:8 — 5104
sea, and her branches unto the *r* — Ps 80:11 — 5104
ran in the dry places like a *r* — Ps 105:41 — 5104
namely, by them beyond the *r* — Is 7:20 — 5104
up upon them the waters of the *r* — Is 8:7 — 5104
he shake his hand over the *r* — Is 11:15 — 5104
the *r* shall be wasted and dried up — Is 19:5 — 5104
of Sihor, the harvest of the *r* — Is 23:3 — 2975
Pass through thy land as a *r* — Is 23:10 — 2975
of the *r* unto the stream of Egypt — Is 27:12 — 5104
then had thy peace been as a *r* — Is 48:18 — 5104
will extend peace to her like a *r* — Is 66:12 — 5104
to drink the waters of the *r* — Jer 2:18 — 5104
spreadeth out her roots by the *r* — Jer 17:8 — 3105
which was by the *r* Euphrates in — Jer 46:2 — 5104
the north by the *r* Euphrates — Jer 46:6 — 5104
north country by the *r* Euphrates — Jer 46:10 — 5104
let tears run down like a *r* day — Lam 2:18 — 5158
the captives by the *r* of Chebar — Eze 1:1 — 5104
of the Chaldeans by the *r* Chebar — Eze 1:3 — 5104
that dwelt by the *r* of Chebar — Eze 3:15 — 5104
which I saw by the *r* of Chebar — Eze 3:23 — 5104
that I saw by the *r* of Chebar — Eze 10:15 — 5104
God of Israel by the *r* of Chebar — Eze 10:20 — 5104
which I saw by the *r* of Chebar — Eze 10:22 — 5104
My *r* is mine own, and I have made — Eze 29:3 — 2975
The *r* is mine, and I have made it — Eze 29:9 — 2975
vision that I saw by the *r* Chebar — Eze 43:3 — 5104
it was a *r* that I could not pass — Eze 47:5 — 5158
a *r* that could not be passed over — Eze 47:5 — 5158
to return to the brink of the *r* — Eze 47:6 — 5158
at the bank of the *r* were very — Eze 47:7 — 5158
shall live whither the *r* cometh — Eze 47:9 — 5158
by the *r* upon the bank thereof — Eze 47:12 — 5158
in Kadesh, the *r* to the great sea — Eze 47:19 — 5158
to the *r* toward the great sea — Eze 48:28 — 5158
vision, and I was by the *r* of Ulai — Dan 8:2 — 180
there stood before the *r* a ram — Dan 8:3 — 180
I had seen standing before the *r* — Dan 8:6 — 180
I was by the side of the great *r* — Dan 10:4 — 5104
on this side of the bank of the *r* — Dan 12:5 — 2975
on that side of the bank of the *r* — Dan 12:5 — 2975
was upon the waters of the *r* — Dan 12:6 — 2975
was upon the waters of the *r* — Dan 12:7 — 2975
unto the *r* of the wilderness — Amos 6:14 — 5158
from the fortress even to the *r* — Mic 7:12 — 5104
from the *r* even to the ends of — Zec 9:10 — 5104
the deeps of the *r* shall dry up — Zec 10:11 — 2975
of him in the *r* of Jordan — Mk 1:5 — *4215*
went out of the city by a *r* side — Acts 16:13 — *4215*
bound in the great *r* Euphrates — Rev 9:14 — *4215*
vial upon the great *r* Euphrates — Rev 16:12 — *4215*
me a pure *r* of water of life — Rev 22:1 — *4215*
of it, and on either side of the *r* — Rev 22:2 — *4215*

RIVER'S
it in the flags by the *r* brink — Ex 2:3 — 2975
walked along by the *r* side — Ex 2:5 — 2975
by the *r* brink against he come — Ex 7:15 — 2975
forth, as gardens by the *r* side — Num 24:6 — 5104

RIVERS
upon their streams, upon their *r* — Ex 7:19 — 2975
rod over the streams, over the *r* — Ex 8:5 — 2975
waters, in the seas, and in the *r* — Lev 11:9 — 5158
scales in the seas, and in the *r* — Lev 11:10 — 5158
to Jotbath, a land of *r* of waters — Deut 10:7 — 5158
r of Damascus, better than all — 2Kin 5:12 — 5104
up all the *r* of besieged places — 2Kin 19:24 — 2975
He shall not see the *r*, the — Job 20:17 — 6390
He cutteth out *r* among the rocks — Job 28:10 — 2975
the rock poured me out *r* of oil — Job 29:6 — 6388
a tree planted by the *r* of water — Ps 1:3 — 6388
thou driedst up mighty *r* — Ps 74:15 — 5104
caused waters to run down like *r* — Ps 78:16 — 5104
And had turned their *r* into blood — Ps 78:44 — 2975
sea, and his right hand in the *r* — Ps 89:25 — 5104
He turneth *r* into a wilderness — Ps 107:33 — 5104
R of waters run down mine eyes — Ps 119:136 — 6388
By the *r* of Babylon, there we sat — Ps 137:1 — 5104
r of waters in the streets — Prov 5:16 — 6388
of the LORD, as the *r* of water — Prov 21:1 — 6388
All the *r* run into the sea — Eccl 1:7 — 5158
the place from whence the *r* come — Eccl 1:7 — 5158
eyes of doves by the *r* of waters — Song 5:12 — 650
uttermost part of the *r* of Egypt — Is 7:18 — 2975
which is beyond the *r* of Ethiopia — Is 18:1 — 5104
whose land the *r* have spoiled — Is 18:2 — 5104
whose land the *r* have spoiled — Is 18:7 — 5104
And they shall turn the *r* far away — Is 19:6 — 5104
and upon every high hill, *r* — Is 30:25 — 6388
as *r* of water in a dry place, as — Is 32:2 — 6388
be unto us a place of broad *r* — Is 33:21 — 5103
all the *r* of the besieged places — Is 37:25 — 2975
I will open *r* in high places, and — Is 41:18 — 5103
and I will make the *r* islands — Is 42:15 — 5103
and through the *r*, they shall not — Is 43:2 — 5103
wilderness, and *r* in the desert — Is 43:19 — 5103
r in the desert, to give drink to — Is 43:20 — 5103
Be dry, and I will dry up thy *r* — Is 44:27 — 5103
the thigh, pass over the *r* — Is 47:2 — 5103
I make the *r* a wilderness — Is 50:2 — 5103
the *r* of waters in a straight way — Jer 31:9 — 5158
whose waters are moved as the *r* — Jer 46:7 — 5104
his waters are moved like the *r* — Jer 46:8 — 5104
Mine eye runneth down with *r* of — Lam 3:48 — 6388
and to the hills, to the *r* — Eze 6:3 — 650
that lieth in the midst of his *r* — Eze 29:3 — 2975
of thy *r* to stick unto thy scales — Eze 29:4 — 2975
thee up out of the midst of thy *r* — Eze 29:4 — 2975
all the fish of thy *r* shall stick — Eze 29:4 — 2975
thee and all the fish of thy *r* — Eze 29:5 — 2975
am against thee, and against thy *r* — Eze 29:10 — 2975
And I will make the *r* dry, and sell — Eze 30:12 — 2975
set him up on high with her *r* — Eze 31:4 — 5104
sent out her little *r* unto all — Eze 31:4 — 8585
broken by all the *r* of the land — Eze 31:12 — 650
and thou camest forth with thy *r* — Eze 32:2 — 5104
thy feet, and fouledst their *r* — Eze 32:2 — 5104
the *r* shall be full of thee — Eze 32:6 — 650
cause their *r* to run like oil — Eze 32:14 — 5104
the mountains of Israel by the *r* — Eze 34:13 — 650
in thy valleys, and in all thy *r* — Eze 35:8 — 650
and to the hills, to the *r* — Eze 36:4 — 650
and to the hills, to the *r* — Eze 36:6 — 650
whithersoever the *r* shall come — Eze 47:9 — 5158
for the *r* of waters are dried up — Joel 1:20 — 650
all the *r* of Judah shall flow — Joel 3:18 — 650
or with ten thousands of *r* of oil — Mic 6:7 — 5158
it dry, and drieth up all the *r* — Nah 1:4 — 5104
gates of the *r* shall be opened — Nah 2:6 — 5104
No, that was situate among the *r* — Nah 3:8 — 2975
the LORD displeased against the *r* — Hab 3:8 — 5104
was thine anger against the *r* — Hab 3:8 — 5104
didst cleave the earth with *r* — Hab 3:9 — 5104
From beyond the *r* of Ethiopia my — Zeph 3:10 — 5104

shall flow *r* of living water — Jn 7:38 — *4215*
fell upon the third part of the *r* — Rev 8:10 — *4215*
poured out his vial upon the *r* — Rev 16:4 — *4215*

RIZIA See REZIA.

RIZPAH (*riz'-pah*) *A concubine of Saul.*
had a concubine, whose name was *R* — 2Sa 3:7 — 7532
sons of *R* the daughter of Aiah — 2Sa 21:8 — 7532
R the daughter of Aiah took — 2Sa 21:10 — 7532
David what *R* the daughter of Aiah — 2Sa 21:11 — 7532

ROAD
Whither have ye made a *r* to day — 1Sa 27:10 — 6584

ROAR
Let the sea *r*, and the fulness — 1Chr 16:32 — 7481
Though the waters thereof *r* — Ps 46:3 — 1993
Thine enemies *r* in the midst of — Ps 74:4 — 7580
let the sea *r*, and the fulness — Ps 96:11 — 7580
Let the sea *r*, and the fulness — Ps 98:7 — 7481
The young lions *r* after their — Ps 104:21 — 7580
they shall *r* like young lions — Is 5:29 — 7580
yea, they shall *r*, and lay hold of — Is 5:29 — 5098
in that day they shall *r* against — Is 5:30 — 5098
he shall cry, yea, *r* — Is 42:13 — 6873
We *r* all like bears, and mourn — Is 59:11 — 1993
though they *r*, yet can they not — Jer 5:22 — 1993
The LORD shall *r* from on high — Jer 25:30 — 7580
he shall mightily *r* upon his — Jer 25:30 — 7580
the sea when the waves thereof *r* — Jer 31:35 — 1993
their voice shall *r* like the sea — Jer 50:42 — 1993
They shall *r* together like lions — Jer 51:38 — 7580
her waves do *r* like great waters — Jer 51:55 — 1993
he shall *r* like a lion — Hos 11:10 — 7580
when he shall *r*, then the — Hos 11:10 — 7580
The LORD also shall *r* out of Zion — Joel 3:16 — 7580
said, The LORD will *r* from Zion — Amos 1:2 — 7580
Will a lion *r* in the forest, when — Amos 3:4 — 7580

ROARED
a young lion *r* against him — Judg 14:5 — 7580
I have *r* by reason of the — Ps 38:8 — 7580
divided the sea, whose waves *r* — Is 51:15 — 1993
The young lions *r* upon him — Jer 2:15 — 7580
The lion hath *r*, who will not — Amos 3:8 — 7580

ROARETH
After it a voice *r* — Job 37:4 — 7580
their voice *r* like the sea — Jer 6:23 — 1993
a loud voice, as when a lion *r* — Rev 10:3 — *3455*

ROARING
The *r* of the lion, and the voice — Job 4:10 — 7581
me, and from the words of my *r* — Ps 22:1 — 7581
mouths, as a ravening and a *r* lion — Ps 22:13 — 7580
old through my *r* all the day long — Ps 32:3 — 7581
wrath is as the *r* of a lion — Prov 19:12 — 5099
of a king is as the *r* of a lion — Prov 20:2 — 5099
As a *r* lion, and a ranging bear — Prov 28:15 — 5098
Their *r* shall be like a lion — Is 5:29 — 7581
them like the *r* of the sea — Is 5:30 — 5100
and the young lion *r* on his prey — Is 31:4 — 1897
thereof, by the noise of his *r* — Eze 19:7 — 7581
like a *r* lion ravening the prey — Eze 22:25 — 7580
princes within her are *r* lions — Zeph 3:3
a voice of the *r* of young lions — Zec 11:3 — 7581
the sea and the waves *r* — Lk 21:25 — *2278*
adversary the devil, as a *r* lion — 1Pet 5:8 — *5612*

ROARINGS
my *r* are poured out like the — Job 3:24 — 7581

ROAST
r with fire, and unleavened bread — Ex 12:8 — 6748
all with water, but *r* with fire — Ex 12:9 — 6748
And thou shalt *r* and eat it in the — Deut 16:7 — 1310
Give flesh to *r* for the priest — 1Sa 2:15 — 6740
he roasteth *r*, and is satisfied — Is 44:16 — 6748

ROASTED
they *r* the passover with fire — 2Chr 35:13 — 1310
I have *r* flesh, and eaten it — Is 44:19 — 6740
the king of Babylon *r* in the fire — Jer 29:22 — 7033

ROASTETH
The slothful man *r* not that which — Prov 12:27 — 2760
he *r* roast, and is satisfied — Is 44:16 — 740

ROB
thy neighbour, neither *r* him — Lev 19:13 — 1497
which shall *r* you of your — Lev 26:22 — 7921
they *r* the threshingfloors — 1Sa 23:1 — 8154
R not the poor, because he is — Prov 22:22 — 1497
that they may *r* the fatherless — Is 10:2 — 962
us, and the lot of them that *r* us — Is 17:14 — 962
r those that robbed them, saith — Eze 39:10 — 962
Will a man *r* God — Mal 3:8 — 6906

ROBBED
they *r* all that came along that — Judg 9:25 — 1497
as a bear *r* of her whelps in the — 2Sa 17:8 — 7909
The bands of the wicked have *r* me — Ps 119:61 — 5749
Let a bear *r* of her whelps meet a — Prov 17:12 — 7909
have *r* their treasures, and I have — Is 10:13 — 8154
But this is a people *r* and spoiled — Is 42:22 — 962
and they shall be *r* — Jer 50:37 — 962
pledge, give again that he had *r* — Eze 33:15 — 5100
them, and rob those that *r* them — Eze 39:10 — 962
Yet ye have *r* me — Mal 3:8 — 6906
ye say, Wherein have we *r* thee — Mal 3:8 — 962
for ye have *r* me, even this whole — Mal 3:9 — 6906
I *r* other churches, taking wages — 2Cor 11:8 — *4813*

ROBBER
the *r* swalloweth up their — Job 5:5 — 6782
the *r* shall prevail against him — Job 18:9 — 6782
If he beget a son that is a *r* — Eze 18:10 — 6530
way, the same is a thief and a *r* — Jn 10:1 — *3027*
Now Barabbas was a *r* — Jn 18:40 — *3027*

ROBBERS
The tabernacles of *r* prosper — Job 12:6 — 7703
for a spoil, and Israel to the *r* — Is 42:24 — 962
become a den of *r* in your eyes — Jer 7:11 — 6530
for the *r* shall enter into it, and — Eze 7:22 — 6530
also the *r* of thy people shall — Dan 11:14 — 6530
as troops of *r* wait for a man, so — Hos 6:9
the troop of *r* spoileth without — Hos 7:1
if *r* by night, (how art thou cut — Obad 5 — 7703
came before me are thieves and *r* — Jn 10:8 — *3027*
which are neither *r* of churches — Acts 19:37 — *2417*
perils of waters, in perils of *r* — 2Cor 11:26 — *3027*

ROBBERY
and become not vain in *r* — Ps 62:10 — 1498
The *r* of the wicked shall destroy — Prov 21:7 — 7701
I hate *r* for burnt offering — Is 61:8 — 1498
used oppression, and exercised *r* — Eze 22:29 — 1498
up violence and *r* in their palaces — Amos 3:10 — 7701
it is all full of lies and *r* — Nah 3:1 — 6503
thought it not *r* to be equal with — Phil 2:6 — *725*

ROBBETH
Whoso *r* his father or his mother — Prov 28:24 — 1497

ROBE
breastplate, and an ephod, and a *r* — Ex 28:4 — 4598
thou shalt make the *r* of the — Ex 28:31 — 4598
upon the hem of the *r* round about — Ex 28:34 — 4598
the *r* of the ephod, and the ephod — Ex 29:5 — 4598
he made the *r* of the ephod of — Ex 39:22 — 4598
was an hole in the midst of the *r* — Ex 39:23 — 4598
of the *r* pomegranates of blue — Ex 39:24 — 4598
upon the hem of the *r*, round — Ex 39:25 — 4598
the hem of the *r* to minister in — Ex 39:26 — 4598
girdle, and clothed him with the *r* — Lev 8:7 — 4598
of the *r* that was upon him — 1Sa 18:4 — 4598
off the skirt of Saul's *r* privily — 1Sa 24:4 — 4598
see the skirt of thy *r* in my hand — 1Sa 24:11 — 4598
that I cut off the skirt of thy *r* — 1Sa 24:11 — 4598
clothed with a *r* of fine linen — 1Chr 15:27 — 4598
my judgment was as a *r* and a — Job 29:14 — 4598
And I will clothe him with thy *r* — Is 22:21 — 3301
me with the *r* of righteousness — Is 61:10 — 4598
throne, and he laid his *r* from him — Jonah 3:6 — 155
ye pull off the *r* with the — Mic 2:8 — 145
him, and put on him a scarlet *r* — Mt 27:28 — *5511*
him, they took the *r* off from him — Mt 27:31 — *5511*
servants, Bring forth the best *r* — Lk 15:22 — *4749*
and arrayed him in a gorgeous *r* — Lk 23:11 — *2066*
and they put on him a purple *r* — Jn 19:2 — *2440*
crown of thorns, and the purple *r* — Jn 19:5 — *2440*

ROBES
for with such *r* were the king's — 2Sa 13:18 — 4598
his throne, having put on their *r* — 1Kin 22:10 — 899
but put thou on thy *r* — 1Kin 22:30 — 899
on his throne, clothed in their *r* — 2Chr 18:9 — 899
but put thou on thy *r* — 2Chr 18:29 — 899
thrones, and lay away their *r* — Eze 26:16 — 4598
which desire to walk in long *r* — Lk 20:46 — *4749*
white *r* were given unto every one — Rev 6:11 — *4749*
the Lamb, clothed with white *r* — Rev 7:9 — *4749*
which are arrayed in white *r* — Rev 7:13 — *4749*
and have washed their *r*, and made — Rev 7:14 — *4749*

ROBOAM (*ro-bo'-am*) See REHOBOAM. *Same as Rehoboam; an ancestor of Jesus.*
And Solomon begat *R* — Mt 1:7 — 4497
and *R* begat Abia — Mt 1:7 — *4497*

ROCK
thee there upon the *r* in Horeb — Ex 17:6 — 6697
and thou shalt smite the *r* — Ex 17:6 — 6697
me, and thou shalt stand upon a *r* — Ex 33:21 — 6697
will put thee in a clift of the *r* — Ex 33:22 — 6697
ye unto the *r* before their eyes — Num 20:8 — 5553
forth to them water out of the *r* — Num 20:8 — 5553
together before the *r*, and he said — Num 20:10 — 5553
we fetch you water out of this *r* — Num 20:10 — 5553
with his rod he smote the *r* twice — Num 20:11 — 5553
and thou puttest thy nest in a *r* — Num 24:21 — 5553
forth water out of the *r* of flint — Deut 8:15 — 6697
He is the *R*, his work is perfect — Deut 32:4 — 6697
him to suck honey out of the *r* — Deut 32:13 — 5553
and oil out of the flinty *r* — Deut 32:13 — 6697
esteemed the *R* of his salvation — Deut 32:15 — 6697
Of the *R* that begat thee thou art — Deut 32:18 — 6697
except their *R* had sold them, and — Deut 32:30 — 6697
For their *r* is not as our *R* — Deut 32:31 — 6697
their *r* in whom they trusted — Deut 32:37 — 6697
going up to Akrabbim, from the *r* — Judg 1:36 — 5553
cakes, and lay them upon this *r* — Judg 6:20 — 5553
there rose up fire out of the *r* — Judg 6:21 — 6697
thy God upon the top of this *r* — Judg 6:26 — 4581
and they slew Oreb upon the *r* Oreb — Judg 7:25 — 6697
offered it upon a *r* unto the LORD — Judg 13:19 — 6697
and dwelt in the top of the *r* Etam — Judg 15:8 — 5553
went to the top of the *r* Etam — Judg 15:11 — 5553
and brought him up from the *r* — Judg 15:13 — 5553
wilderness unto the *r* of Rimmon — Judg 20:45 — 5553
the wilderness unto the *r* Rimmon — Judg 20:47 — 5553
abode in the *r* Rimmon four months — Judg 20:47 — 5553
that were in the *r* Rimmon — Judg 21:13 — 5553
is there any *r* like our God — 1Sa 2:2 — 6697
was a sharp *r* on the one side — 1Sa 14:4 — 5553
a sharp *r* on the other side — 1Sa 14:4 — 5553
wherefore he came down into a *r* — 1Sa 23:25 — 5553
and spread it for her upon the *r* — 2Sa 21:10 — 6697
And he said, The LORD is my *r* — 2Sa 22:2 — 5553
The God of my *r* — 2Sa 22:3 — 6697
and who is a *r*, save our God — 2Sa 22:32 — 6697
and blessed be my *r* — 2Sa 22:47 — 6697
and the God of the *r* of my salvation — 2Sa 22:47 — 6697
the *R* of Israel spake to me, He — 2Sa 23:3 — 6697
went down to the *r* to David — 1Chr 11:15 — 6697
them unto the top of the *r* — 2Chr 25:12 — 5553
them down from the top of the *r* — 2Chr 25:12 — 5553
out of the *r* for their thirst — Neh 9:15 — 5553
the *r* is removed out of his place — Job 14:18 — 6697
shall the *r* be removed out of his — Job 18:4 — 6697
pen and lead in the *r* for ever — Job 19:24 — 6697
embrace the *r* for want of a — Job 24:8 — 6697
putteth forth his hand upon the *r* — Job 28:9 — 2496
the *r* poured me out rivers of oil — Job 29:6 — 6697
wild goats of the *r* bring forth — Job 39:1 — 5553
She dwelleth and abideth on the *r* — Job 39:28 — 5553
upon the crag of the *r* — Job 39:28 — 5553
The LORD is my *r*, and my fortress — Ps 18:2 — 5553
or who is a *r* save our God — Ps 18:31 — 6697
and blessed be my *r* — Ps 18:46 — 6697
he shall set me up upon a *r* — Ps 27:5 — 6697
Unto thee will I cry, O LORD my *r* — Ps 28:1 — 6697
be thou my strong *r*, for an house — Ps 31:2 — 6697
For thou art my *r* and my fortress — Ps 31:3 — 5553
clay, and set my feet upon a *r* — Ps 40:2 — 5553
I will say unto God my *r*, Why — Ps 42:9 — 5553
lead me to the *r* that is higher — Ps 61:2 — 6697
He only is my *r* and my salvation — Ps 62:2 — 6697
He only is my *r* and my salvation — Ps 62:6 — 6697
the *r* of my strength, and my — Ps 62:7 — 6697
to save me, for thou art my *r* — Ps 71:3 — 5553
brought streams also out of the *r* — Ps 78:16 — 5553
Behold, he smote the *r*, that the — Ps 78:20 — 6697
remembered that God was their *r* — Ps 78:35 — 6697
with honey out of the *r* should I — Ps 81:16 — 6697
my God, and the *r* of my salvation — Ps 89:26 — 6697
he is my *r*, and there is no — Ps 92:15 — 6697
and my God is the *r* of my refuge — Ps 94:22 — 6697
noise to the *r* of our salvation — Ps 95:1 — 6697
He opened the *r*, and the waters — Ps 105:41 — 6697
Which turned the *r* into a — Ps 114:8 — 6697
the way of a serpent upon a *r* — Prov 30:19 — 6697
that art in the clefts of the *r* — Song 2:14 — 5553
Enter into the *r*, and hide thee in — Is 2:10 — 6697
for a *r* of offence to both the — Is 8:14 — 6697
of Midian at the *r* of Oreb — Is 10:26 — 6697
mindful of the *r* of thy strength — Is 17:10 — 6697
an habitation for himself in a *r* — Is 22:16 — 5553
of a great *r* in a weary land — Is 32:2 — 5553
let the inhabitants of the *r* sing — Is 42:11 — 5553
to flow out of the *r* for them — Is 48:21 — 6697
he clave the *r* also, and the — Is 48:21 — 6697
look unto the *r* whence ye are — Is 51:1 — 6697
made their faces harder than a *r* — Jer 5:3 — 5553
hide it there in a hole of the *r* — Jer 13:4
cometh from the *r* of the field — Jer 18:14 — 6697
r of the plain, saith the LORD — Jer 21:13 — 6697
that breaketh the *r* in pieces — Jer 23:29 — 5553
the cities, and dwell in the *r* — Jer 48:28 — 5553
dwellest in the clefts of the *r* — Jer 49:16 — 5553
she set it upon the top of a *r* — Eze 24:7 — 5553
set her blood upon the top of a *r* — Eze 24:8 — 5553
and make her like the top of a *r* — Eze 26:4 — 5553
make thee like the top of a *r* — Eze 26:14 — 5553
Shall horses run upon the *r* — Amos 6:12 — 5558
dwellest in the clefts of the *r* — Obad 3 — 5553
which built his house upon a *r* — Mt 7:24 — *4073*
for it was founded upon a *r* — Mt 7:25 — *4073*
upon this *r* I will build my — Mt 16:18 — *4073*
which he had hewn out in the *r* — Mt 27:60 — *4073*
which was hewn out of a *r* — Mk 15:46 — *4073*
and laid the foundation on a *r* — Lk 6:48 — *4073*
for it was founded upon a *r* — Lk 6:48 — *4073*
And some fell upon a *r* — Lk 8:6 — *4073*
They on the *r* are they, which — Lk 8:13 — *4073*
a stumblingstone and *r* of offence — Rom 9:33 — *4073*
spiritual *R* that followed them — 1Cor 10:4 — *4073*
and that *R* was Christ — 1Cor 10:4 — *4073*
a *r* of offence, even to them — 1Pet 2:8 — *4073*

ROCKS
from the top of the *r* I see him — Num 23:9 — 6697
in caves, and in thickets, and in *r* — 1Sa 13:6 — 5553
his men upon the *r* of the wild — 1Sa 24:2 — 6697
in pieces the *r* before the LORD — 1Kin 19:11 — 5553
He cutteth out rivers among the *r* — Job 28:10 — 6697
caves of the earth, and in the *r* — Job 30:6 — 3710
He clave the *r* in the wilderness — Ps 78:15 — 6697
and the *r* for the conies — Ps 104:18 — 5553
make they their houses in the *r* — Prov 30:26 — 5553
shall go into the holes of the *r* — Is 2:19 — 6697
To go into the clefts of the *r* — Is 2:21 — 6697
and into the tops of the ragged *r* — Is 2:21 — 5553
valleys, and in the holes of the *r* — Is 7:19 — 5553
shall be the munitions of *r* — Is 33:16 — 5553
valleys under the clifts of the *r* — Is 57:5 — 5553
thickets, and climb up upon the *r* — Jer 4:29 — 3710
and out of the holes of the *r* — Jer 16:16 — 5553
and roll thee down from the *r* — Jer 51:25 — 5553
the *r* are thrown down by him — Nah 1:6 — 6697
earth did quake, and the *r* rent — Mt 27:51 — *4073*
lest we should have fallen upon *r* — Acts 27:29
in the *r* of the mountains — Rev 6:15 — *4073*
And said to the mountains and *r* — Rev 6:16 — *4073*

ROD
And he said, A *r* — Ex 4:2 — 4294
it, and it became a *r* in his hand — Ex 4:4 — 4294
shalt take this *r* in thine hand — Ex 4:17 — 4294
Moses took the *r* of God in his — Ex 4:20 — 4294
shalt say unto Aaron, Take thy *r* — Ex 7:9 — 4294
cast down his *r* before Pharaoh — Ex 7:10 — 4294
they cast down every man his *r* — Ex 7:12 — 4294
but Aaron's *r* swallowed up their — Ex 7:12 — 4294
the *r* which was turned to a — Ex 7:15 — 4294
I will smite with the *r* that is — Ex 7:17 — 4294
Moses, Say unto Aaron, Take thy *r* — Ex 7:19 — 4294
and he lifted up the *r*, and smote — Ex 7:20 — 4294
hand with thy *r* over the streams — Ex 8:5 — 4294
Say unto Aaron, Stretch out thy *r* — Ex 8:16 — 4294
stretched out his hand with his *r* — Ex 8:17 — 4294

R

forth his *r* toward heaven Ex 9:23 4294
his *r* over the land of Egypt Ex 10:13 4294
But lift thou up thy *r*, and Ex 14:16 4294
and thy *r*, wherewith thou smotest Ex 17:5 4294
with the *r* of God in mine hand Ex 17:9 4294
servant, or his maid, with a *r* Ex 21:20 7626
of whatsoever passeth under the *r* Lev 27:32 7626
take of every one of them a *r* Num 17:2 4294
thou every man's name upon his *r* Num 17:2 4294
Aaron's name upon the *r* of Levi Num 17:3 4294
for one *r* shall be for the head Num 17:3 4294
come to pass, that the man's *r* Num 17:5 4294
their princes gave him a *r* apiece Num 17:6 4294
the *r* of Aaron was among their Num 17:6 4294
the *r* of Aaron for the house of Num 17:8 4294
looked, and took every man his *r* Num 17:9 4294
Bring Aaron's *r* again before the Num 17:10 4294
Take the *r*, and gather thou the Num 20:8 4294
Moses took the *r* from before the Num 20:9 4294
with his *r* he smote the rock Num 20:11 4294
end of the *r* that was in his hand 1Sa 14:27 4294
of the *r* that was in mine hand 1Sa 14:43 4294
chasten him with the *r* of men 2Sa 7:14 7626
Let him take his *r* away from me Job 9:34 7626
neither is the *r* of God upon them Job 21:9 7626
shalt break them with a *r* of iron Ps 2:9 7626
thy *r* and thy staff they comfort Ps 23:4 7626
the *r* of thine inheritance, which Ps 74:2 7626
their transgression with the *r* Ps 89:32 7626
The LORD shall send the *r* of thy Ps 110:2 4294
For the *r* of the wicked shall not Ps 125:3 7626
but a *r* is for the back of him Prov 10:13 7626
that spareth his *r* hateth his son Prov 13:24 7626
of the foolish is a *r* of pride Prov 14:3 2415
the *r* of his anger shall fail Prov 22:8 7626
but the *r* of correction shall Prov 22:15 7626
if thou beatest him with the *r* Prov 23:13 7626
Thou shalt beat him with the *r* Prov 23:14 7626
ass, and a *r* for the fool's back Prov 26:3 7626
The *r* and reproof give wisdom Prov 29:15 7626
the *r* of his oppressor, as in the Is 9:4 7626
the *r* of mine anger, and the staff Is 10:5 7626
as if the *r* should shake itself Is 10:15 7626
he shall smite thee with a *r* Is 10:24 7626
as his *r* was upon the sea, so Is 10:26 4294
a *r* out of the stem of Jesse Is 11:1 2415
the earth with the *r* of his mouth Is 11:4 7626
because the *r* of him that smote Is 14:29 7626
a staff, and the cummin with a *r* Is 28:27 7626
beaten down, which smote with a *r* Is 30:31 7626
I see a *r* of an almond tree Jer 1:11 4731
and Israel is the *r* of his Jer 10:16 7626
staff broken, and the beautiful *r* Jer 48:17 4731
and Israel is the *r* of his Jer 51:19 7626
affliction by the *r* of his wrath Lam 3:1 7626
the *r* hath blossomed, pride hath Eze 7:10 4294
risen up into a *r* of wickedness Eze 7:11 4294
gone out of a *r* of her branches Eze 19:14 4294
strong *r* to be a sceptre to rule Eze 19:14 4294
cause you to pass under the *r* Eze 20:37 7626
it contemneth the *r* of my son Eze 21:10 7626
if the sword contemn even the *r* Eze 21:13 7626
of Israel with a *r* upon the cheek Mic 5:1 7626
hear ye the *r*, and who hath Mic 6:9 4294
Feed thy people with thy *r* Mic 7:14 7626
shall I come unto you with a *r* 1Cor 4:21 *4464*
Aaron's *r* that budded, and the Heb 9:4 *4464*
shall rule them with a *r* of iron Rev 2:27 *4464*
was given me a reed like unto a *r* Rev 11:1 *4464*
rule all nations with a *r* of iron Rev 12:5 *4464*
shall rule them with a *r* of iron Rev 19:15 *4464*

RODANIM See DODANIM.

RODE
they *r* upon the camels, and Gen 24:61 7392
sons that *r* on thirty ass colts Judg 10:4 7392
that *r* on threescore and ten ass Judg 12:14 7392
as she *r* on the ass, that she 1Sa 25:20 7392
r upon an ass, with five damsels 1Sa 25:42 7392
which *r* upon camels, and fled 1Sa 30:17 7392
Absalom *r* upon a mule, and the 2Sa 18:9 7392
he *r* upon a cherub, and did fly 2Sa 22:11 7392
and he *r* thereon, 1Kin 13:13 7392
And Ahab *r*, and went to Jezreel 1Kin 18:45 7392
So Jehu *r* in a chariot, and went 2Kin 9:16 7392
thou *r* together after Ahab his 2Kin 9:25 7392
me, save the beast that I *r* upon Neh 2:12 7392
So the posts that *r* upon mules Est 8:14 7392
he *r* upon a cherub, and did fly Ps 18:10 7392

RODS
Jacob took him *r* of green poplar, Gen 30:37 4731
white appear which was in the *r* Gen 30:37 4731
he set the *r* which he had pilled Gen 30:38 4731
the flocks conceived before the *r* Gen 30:39 4731
that Jacob laid the *r* before the Gen 30:41 4731
they might conceive among the *r* Gen 30:41 4731
Aaron's rod swallowed up their *r* Ex 7:12 4294
house of their fathers twelve *r* Num 17:2 4294
fathers' houses, even twelve *r* Num 17:6 4294
rod of Aaron was among their *r* Num 17:6 4294
Moses laid up the *r* before the Num 17:7 4294
Moses brought out all the *r* from Num 17:9 4294
she had strong *r* for the sceptres Eze 19:11 4294
her strong *r* were broken and Eze 19:12 4294
Thrice was I beaten with *r* 2Cor 11:25 *4463*

ROE
was as light of foot as a wild *r* 2Sa 2:18 6643
as the loving hind and pleasant *r* Prov 5:19 3280
Deliver thyself as a *r* from the Prov 6:5 6643
is like a *r* or a young hart Song 2:9 6643
be thou like a *r* or a young hart Song 2:17 6643
be thou like to a *r* or to a young Song 8:14 6643
And it shall be as the chased *r* Is 13:14 6643

ROEBUCK
may eat thereof, as of the *r* Deut 12:15 6643
Even as the *r* and the hart is Deut 12:22 6643
The hart, and the *r*, and the fallow Deut 14:5 6643
shall eat it alike, as the *r* Deut 15:22 6643

ROEBUCKS
hundred sheep, beside harts, and *r* 1Kin 4:23 6643

ROES
swift as the *r* upon the mountains 1Chr 12:8 6643
daughters of Jerusalem, by the *r* Song 2:7 6643
daughters of Jerusalem, by the *r* Song 3:5 6643
like two young *r* that are twins Song 4:5 6646
like two young *r* that are twins Song 7:3 6646

ROGELIM (*ro'-ghel-im*) *A city in Gilead.*
and Barzillai the Gileadite of *R* 2Sa 17:27 7274
the Gileadite came down from *R* 2Sa 19:31 7274

ROHGAH (*ro'-gah*) *A son of Shamer.*
Ahi, and *R*, Jehubbah, and Aram 1Chr 7:34 7303

ROLL
till they *r* the stone from the Gen 29:8 1556
R great stones upon the mouth of Josh 10:18 1556
r a great stone unto me this day 1Sa 14:33 1556
in the province of the Medes, a *r* Ezr 6:2 4040
said unto me, Take thee a great *r* Is 8:1 1549
Take thee a *r* of a book, and write Jer 36:2 4039
unto him, upon a *r* of a book Jer 36:4 4039
go thou, and read in the *r* Jer 36:6 4039
Take in thine hand the *r* wherein Jer 36:14 4039
of Neriah took the *r* in his hand Jer 36:14 4039
but they laid up the *r* in the Jer 36:20 4039
king sent Jehudi to fetch the *r* Jer 36:21 4039
until all the *r* was consumed in Jer 36:23 4039
king that he would not burn the *r* Jer 36:25 4039
that the king had burned the *r* Jer 36:27 4039
Take thee again another *r* Jer 36:28 4039
words that were in the first *r* Jer 36:28 4039
Thou hast burned this *r*, saying, Jer 36:29 4039
Then took Jeremiah another *r* Jer 36:32 4039
r thee down from the rocks, and Jer 51:25 1556
a *r* of a book was therein Eze 2:9 4040
eat this *r*, and go speak unto the Eze 3:1 4040
and he caused me to eat that *r* Eze 3:2 4040
with this *r* that I give thee Eze 3:3 4040
of Aphrah *r* thyself in the dust Mic 1:10 6428
and looked, and behold a flying *r* Zec 5:1 4040
And I answered, I see a flying *r* Zec 5:2 4040
Who shall *r* us away the stone Mk 16:3 *617*

ROLLED
they *r* the stone from the well's Gen 29:3 1556
r the stone from the well's mouth Gen 29:10 1556
This day have I *r* away the Josh 5:9 1556
they *r* themselves upon me Job 30:14 1556
noise, and garments *r* in blood Is 9:5 1556
shall be *r* together as a scroll Is 34:4 1556
he *r* a great stone to the door of Mt 27:60 *4351*
r back the stone from the door, Mt 28:2 *617*
r a stone unto the door of the Mk 15:46 *4351*
saw that the stone was *r* away Mk 16:4 *617*
they found the stone *r* away from Lk 24:2 *617*
as a scroll when it is *r* together Rev 6:14 *1507*

ROLLER
to put a *r* to bind it, to make it Eze 30:21 2848

ROLLETH
and he that *r* a stone, it will Prov 26:27 1556

ROLLING
like a *r* thing before the Is 17:13 1534

ROLLS
was made in the house of the *r* Ezr 6:1 5609

ROMAMTI-EZER (*romam''-ti-e'-zur*) *A sanctuary servant.*
Hanani, Eliathah, Giddalti, and *R* 1Chr 25:4 7320
The four and twentieth to *R* 1Chr 25:31 7320

ROMAN (*ro'-mun*) See ROMANS. *A citizen of Rome.*
you to scourge a man that is a *R* Acts 22:25 *4514*
for this man is a *R* Acts 22:26 *4514*
unto him, Tell me, art thou a *R* Acts 22:27 *4514*
after he knew that he was a *R* Acts 22:29 *4514*
having understood that he was a *R* Acts 23:27 *4514*

ROMANS (*ro'-muns*)
the *R* shall come and take away Jn 11:48 *4514*
neither to observe, being *R* Acts 16:21 *4514*
us openly uncondemned, being *R* Acts 16:37 *4514*
when they heard that they were *R* Acts 16:38 *4514*
the *R* to deliver any man to die Acts 25:16 *4514*
Jerusalem into the hands of the *R* Acts 28:17 *4514*
Written to the *R* from Corinthus Rom *s* *4514*

ROME (*rome*) See ROMAN. *Administrative center of the Roman Empire.*
about Cyrene, and strangers of *R* Acts 2:10 *4516*
all Jews to depart from *R* Acts 18:2 *4516*
been there, I must also see *R* Acts 19:21 *4516*
must thou bear witness also at *R* Acts 23:11 *4516*
and so we went toward *R* Acts 28:14 *4516*
And when we came to *R*, the Acts 28:16 *4516*
To all that be in *R*, beloved of Rom 1:7 *4516*
gospel to you that are at *R* also Rom 1:15 *4516*
Unto the Galatians written from *R* Gal *s* *4516*
Written from *R* unto the Ephesians Eph *s* *4516*
from *R* by Epaphroditus Phil *s* *4516*
Written from *R* to the Colossians Col *s* *4516*
But, when he was in *R*, he sought 2Ti 1:17 *4516*
the Ephesians, was written from *R* 2Ti *s* *4516*
Written from *R* to Philemon Philem *s* *4516*

ROMPHA See REMPHAN.

ROOF
they under the shadow of my *r* Gen 19:8 6982
shalt make a battlement for thy *r* Deut 22:8 1406
them up to the *r* of the house Josh 2:6 1406
she had laid in order upon the *r* Josh 2:6 1406
she came up unto them upon the *r* Josh 2:8 1406
there were upon the *r* about three Judg 16:27 1406
walked upon the *r* of the king's 2Sa 11:2 1406
from the *r* he saw a woman washing 2Sa 11:2 1406
the *r* over the gate unto the wall 2Sa 18:24 1406
every one upon the *r* of his house Neh 8:16 1406
cleaved to the *r* of their mouth Job 29:10 2441
cleave to the *r* of my mouth Ps 137:6 2441
the *r* of thy mouth like the best Song 7:9 2441
to the *r* of his mouth for thirst Lam 4:4 2441
cleave to the *r* of thy mouth Eze 3:26 2441
r of one little chamber to the Eze 40:13 1406
chamber to the *r* of another Eze 40:13 1406
thou shouldest come under my *r* Mt 8:8 *4721*
they uncovered the *r* where he was Mk 2:4 *4721*
thou shouldest enter under my *r* Lk 7:6 *4721*

ROOFS
of all the houses upon whose *r* Jer 19:13 1406
upon whose *r* they have offered Jer 32:29 1406

ROOM
is there *r* in thy father's house Gen 24:23 4725
enough, and *r* to lodge in Gen 24:25 4725
the house, and *r* for the camels Gen 24:31 4725
now the LORD hath made *r* for us Gen 26:22 7337
me continually in the *r* of Joab 2Sa 19:13 8478
Jehoiada in his *r* over the host 1Kin 2:35 8478
the king put in the *r* of Abiathar 1Kin 2:35 8478
him king in the *r* of his father 1Kin 5:1 8478
will set upon thy throne in thy *r* 1Kin 5:5 8478
up in the *r* of David my father 1Kin 8:20 8478
anoint to be prophet in thy *r* 1Kin 19:16 8478
killed him, and reigned in his *r* 2Kin 15:25 8478
in the *r* of Josiah his father 2Kin 23:34 8478
up in the *r* of David my father 2Chr 6:10 8478
made him king in the *r* of his 2Chr 26:1 8478
hast set my feet in a large *r* Ps 31:8 4800
Thou preparedst *r* before it Ps 80:9
A man's gift maketh *r* for him Prov 18:16 7337
not be *r* enough to receive it Mal 3:10
in the *r* of his father Herod Mt 2:22 *473*
there was no *r* to receive them Mk 2:2 *5562*
you a large upper *r* furnished Mk 14:15 *508*
was no *r* for them in the inn Lk 2:7 *5117*
because I have no *r* where to Lk 12:17
sit not down in the highest *r* Lk 14:8 *4411*
with shame to take the lowest *r* Lk 14:9 *5117*
go and sit down in the lowest *r* Lk 14:10 *5117*
hast commanded, and yet there is *r* Lk 14:22 *5117*
you a large upper *r* furnished Lk 22:12
in, they went up into an upper *r* Acts 1:13 *5253*
Porcius Festus came into Felix' *r* Acts 24:27 *1240*
r of the unlearned say Amen at 1Cor 14:16 *5117*

ROOMS
r shalt thou make in the ark, and Gen 6:14 7064
place, and put captains in their *r* 1Kin 20:24 8478
this day, and dwelt in their *r* 1Chr 4:41 8478
And love the uppermost *r* at feasts Mt 23:6 *4411*
and the uppermost *r* at feasts Mk 12:39 *4411*
how they chose out the chief *r* Lk 14:7 *4411*
and the chief *r* at feasts Lk 20:46 *4411*

ROOT
among you a *r* that beareth gall Deut 29:18 8328
there a *r* of them against Amalek Judg 5:14 8328
he shall *r* up Israel out of this 1Kin 14:15 5428
shall yet again take *r* downward 2Kin 19:30 8328
I have seen the foolish taking *r* Job 5:3 8327
Though the *r* thereof wax old in Job 14:8 8328
seeing the *r* of the matter is Job 19:28 8328
My *r* was spread out by the waters Job 29:19 8328
would *r* out all mine increase Job 31:12 8327
r thee out of the land of the Ps 52:5 8327
and didst cause it to take deep *r* Ps 80:9 8327
but the *r* of the righteous shall Prov 12:3 8328
but the *r* of the righteous Prov 12:12 8328
so their *r* shall be as rottenness Is 5:24 8328
day there shall be a *r* of Jesse Is 11:10 8328
for out of the serpent's *r* shall Is 14:29 8328
and I will kill thy *r* with famine Is 14:30 8328
them that come of Jacob to take *r* Is 27:6 8327
Judah shall again take *r* downward Is 37:31 8328
shall not take *r* in the earth Is 40:24 8327
as a *r* out of a dry ground Is 53:2 8328
to *r* out, and to pull down, and to Jer 1:10 5428
them, yea, they have taken *r* Jer 12:2 8327
for his *r* was by great waters Eze 31:7 8328
their *r* is dried up, they shall Hos 9:16 8328
leave them neither *r* nor branch Mal 4:1 8328
is laid unto the *r* of the trees Mt 3:10 *4491*
and because they had no *r*, they Mt 13:6 *4491*
Yet hath he not *r* in himself Mt 13:21 *4491*
ye *r* up also the wheat with them Mt 13:29 *1610*
and because it had no *r*, it Mk 4:6 *4491*
have no *r* in themselves, and so Mk 4:17 *4491*
is laid unto the *r* of the trees Lk 3:9 *4491*
and these have no *r*, which for a Lk 8:13 *4491*
tree, Be thou plucked up by the *r* Lk 17:6 *1610*
if the *r* be holy, so are the Rom 11:16 *4491*
and with them partakest of the *r* Rom 11:17 *4491*
not the *r*, but the *r* thee Rom 11:18 *4491*
There shall be a *r* of Jesse Rom 15:12 *4491*
of money is the *r* of all evil 1Ti 6:10 *4491*
lest any *r* of bitterness Heb 12:15 *4491*
the *R* of David, hath prevailed to Rev 5:5 *4491*
I am the *r* and the offspring of Rev 22:16 *4491*

ROOTED
the LORD r them out of their land......... Deut 29:28 5428
shall be r out of his tabernacle.............. Job 18:14 5423
yea, let my offspring be r out.............. Job 31:8 8327
shall be r out of it............................... Prov 2:22 5255
noonday, and Ekron shall be r up.......... Zeph 2:4 6131
hath not planted, shall be r up.............. Mt 15:13 1610
that ye, being r and grounded in........... Eph 3:17 4492
R and built up in him, and.................... Col 2:7 4492

ROOTS
the r out of my land which I have......... 2Chr 7:20 5428
His r are wrapped about the heap,.......... Job 8:17 8328
His r shall be dried up beneath,............. Job 18:16 8328
the mountains by the r........................... Job 28:9 8328
and juniper r for their meat................... Job 30:4 8328
a Branch shall grow out of his r............. Is 11:1 8328
spreadeth out her r by the river.............. Jer 17:8 8328
the r thereof were under him.................. Eze 17:6 8328
vine did bend her r toward him.............. Eze 17:7 8328
he not pull up the r thereof.................... Eze 17:9 8328
to pluck it up by the r thereof............... Eze 17:9 8328
the stump of his r in the earth.............. Dan 4:15 8330
of the r thereof in the earth.................. Dan 4:23 8330
to leave the stump of the tree r............. Dan 4:26 8330
first horns plucked up by the r.............. Dan 7:8 6132
her r shall one stand up in his............... Dan 11:7 8328
and cast forth his r as Lebanon.............. Hos 14:5 8328
from above, and his r from beneath........ Amos 2:9 8328
the fig tree dried up from the r............. Mk 11:20 4491
twice dead, plucked up by the r............. Jude 12 1610

ROPE
and sin as it were with a cart r.............. Is 5:18 5688

ROPES
new r that never were occupied............ Judg 16:11 5688
Delilah therefore took new r.................. Judg 16:12 5688
all Israel bring r to that city................. 2Sa 17:13 2256
r upon our heads, and go out to............ 1Kin 20:31 2256
put r on their heads, and came to......... 1Kin 20:32 2256
cut off the r of the boat........................ Acts 27:32 4979

ROSE
that Cain r up against Abel his............... Gen 4:8 6965
the men r up from thence, and.............. Gen 18:16 6965
Lot seeing them r up to meet them....... Gen 19:1 6965
Therefore Abimelech r early in.............. Gen 20:8 7925
Abraham r up early in the morning....... Gen 21:14 7925
then Abimelech r up, and Phichol......... Gen 21:32 6965
Abraham r up early in the morning....... Gen 22:3 7925
r up, and went unto the place of........... Gen 22:3 6965
unto his young men, and they r up....... Gen 22:19 6965
they r up in the morning, and he.......... Gen 24:54 6965
drink, and r up, and went his way......... Gen 25:34 6965
they r up betimes in the morning,......... Gen 26:31 7925
Jacob r up early in the morning,............ Gen 28:18 7925
Then Jacob r up, and set his sons......... Gen 31:17 6965
and he r up, and passed over the.......... Gen 31:21 6965
early in the morning Laban r up............ Gen 31:55 7925
he r up that night, and took his............ Gen 32:22 6965
over Penuel the sun r upon him............. Gen 32:31 2224
his daughters r up to comfort him......... Gen 37:35 6965
r up, and went down to Egypt, and........ Gen 43:15 6965
Jacob r up from Beer-sheba.................... Gen 46:5 6965
neither r any from his place for............. Ex 10:23 6965
Pharaoh r up in the night, he, and......... Ex 12:30 6965
them that r up against thee.................. Ex 15:7 6965
r up early in the morning, and.............. Ex 24:4 7925
And Moses r up, and his minister........... Ex 24:13 6965
they r up early on the morrow, and........ Ex 32:6 7925
eat and to drink, and r up to play......... Ex 32:6 6965
that all the people r up......................... Ex 33:8 6965
and all the people r up and.................. Ex 33:10 6965
Moses r up early in the morning,........... Ex 34:4 7925
they r up early in the morning,............. Num 14:40 7925
they r up before Moses, with................ Num 16:2 6965
And Moses r up and went..................... Num 16:25 6965
Balaam r up in the morning, and........... Num 22:13 6965
And the princes of Moab r up............... Num 22:14 6965
Balaam r up in the morning, and........... Num 22:21 6965
And Balaam r up, and went and............ Num 24:25 6965
saw it, he r up from among the............. Num 25:7 6965
and r up from Seir unto them............... Deut 33:2 2224
Joshua r early in the morning................ Josh 3:1 7925
r up upon an heap very far from........... Josh 3:16 6965
Joshua r early in the morning, and........ Josh 6:12 7925
that they r early about the.................... Josh 6:15 7925
So Joshua r up early in the.................... Josh 7:16 7925
Joshua r up early in the morning,.......... Josh 8:10 7925
r up early, and the men of the.............. Josh 8:14 7925
there r up fire out of the rock,............... Judg 6:21 5927
for he r up early on the morrow,........... Judg 6:38 7925
r up early, and pitched beside the......... Judg 7:1 7925
And Abimelech r up, and all the............ Judg 9:34 6965
and Abimelech r up, and the people...... Judg 9:35 6965
he r up against them, and smote.......... Judg 9:43 6965
morning, that he r up to depart............ Judg 19:5 6965
And when the man r up to depart......... Judg 19:7 6965
And when the man r up to depart......... Judg 19:9 6965
not tarry that night, but he r up........... Judg 19:10 6965
her lord r up in the morning, and.......... Judg 19:27 6965
up upon an ass, and the man r up......... Judg 19:28 6965
And the men of Gibeah r against me...... Judg 20:5 6965
of Israel r up in the morning................. Judg 20:19 6965
of Israel r up out of their place............. Judg 20:33 6965
morrow, that the people r early............. Judg 21:4 7925
she r up before one could know............. Ruth 3:14 6965
So Hannah r up after they had.............. 1Sa 1:9 6965
they r up in the morning early,.............. 1Sa 1:19 7925
when Samuel r early to meet Saul.......... 1Sa 15:12 7925
So Samuel r up, and went to Ramah....... 1Sa 16:13 6965
David r up early in the morning,............ 1Sa 17:20 7925
But Saul r up out of the cave, and......... 1Sa 24:7 6965
Then they r up, and went away that...... 1Sa 28:25 6965
his men r up early to depart in.............. 1Sa 29:11 7925
Absalom r up early, and stood............... 2Sa 15:2 7925
all them that r up against thee.............. 2Sa 18:31 6965
them that r up against me hast.............. 2Sa 22:40 6965
above them that r up against me........... 2Sa 22:49 6965
r up, and went every man his way......... 1Kin 1:49 6965
the king r up to meet her, and.............. 1Kin 2:19 6965
when I r in the morning to give............. 1Kin 3:21 6965
that Ahab r up to go down to the.......... 1Kin 21:16 6965
they r up early in the morning,.............. 2Kin 3:22 7925
of Israel, the Israelites r up.................. 2Kin 3:24 6965
they r up in the twilight, to go.............. 2Kin 7:5 6965
he r by night, and smote the................ 2Kin 8:21 6965
they r early in the morning, and............ 2Chr 20:20 7925
he r up by night, and smote the........... 2Chr 21:9 6965
the leprosy even r up in his.................. 2Chr 26:19 2224
which were expressed by name r up...... 2Chr 28:15 6965
Then Hezekiah the king r early............. 2Chr 29:20 7925
Then r up the chief of the.................... Ezr 1:5 6965
Then r up Zerubbabel the son of........... Ezr 5:2 6965
Then Ezra r up from before the............ Ezr 10:6 6965
priest r up with his brethren the.......... Neh 3:1 6965
r up, and said unto the nobles, and...... Neh 4:14 6965
r up early in the morning, and.............. Job 1:5 7925
me those that r up against me.............. Ps 18:39 6965
side, when men r up against us............ Ps 124:2 6965
I am the r of Sharon, and the lily.......... Song 2:1 2261
I r up to open to my beloved............... Song 5:5 6965
rejoice, and blossom as the r............... Is 35:1 2261
Then r up certain of the elders............. Jer 26:17 6965
of those that r up against me............... Lam 3:62 6965
r up in haste, and spake, and said........ Dan 3:24 6965
afterward I r up, and did the................ Dan 8:27 6965
But Jonah r up to flee unto................. Jonah 1:3 6965
when the morning r the next day.......... Jonah 4:7 5927
but they r early, and corrupted............. Zeph 3:7 7925
he, casting away his garment, r............ Mk 10:50 450
r up, and thrust him out of the............. Lk 4:29 450
immediately he r up before them.......... Lk 5:25 450
left all, r up, and followed him............. Lk 5:28 450
though one r from the dead.................. Lk 16:31 450
when he r up from prayer, and was...... Lk 22:45 450
they r up the same hour, and............... Lk 24:33 450
that she r up hastily and went out........ Jn 11:31 450
Then the high priest r up..................... Acts 5:17 450
before these days r up Theudas............. Acts 5:36 450
After this man r up Judas of................. Acts 5:37 450
with him after he r from the dead......... Acts 10:41 450
stood round about him, he r up............. Acts 14:20 450
But there r up certain of the............... Acts 15:5 1817
been much disputing, Peter r up........... Acts 15:7 450
the multitude r up together................. Acts 16:22 4911
he had thus spoken, the king r up........ Acts 26:30 450
this end Christ both died, and r........... Rom 14:9 450
to eat and drink, and r up to play........ 1Cor 10:7 450
that he r again the third day............... 1Cor 15:4 1453
preached that he r from the dead......... 1Cor 15:12 1453
which died for them, and r again.......... 2Cor 5:15 1453
r again, even so them also which.......... 1Th 4:14 450
her smoke r up for ever and ever......... Rev 19:3 305

ROSH (*rosh*) *A son of Benjamin.*
Gera, and Naaman, Ehi, and R................ Gen 46:21 7220

ROT
the LORD doth make thy thigh to r......... Num 5:21 5307
belly to swell, and thy thigh to r........... Num 5:22 5307
shall swell, and her thigh shall r........... Num 5:27 5307
the name of the wicked shall r............... Prov 10:7 7537
chooseth a tree that will not r............... Is 40:20 7537

ROTTEN
as a r thing, consumeth, as a................. Job 13:28 7538
iron as straw, and brass as r wood......... Job 41:27 7539
old r rags, and let them down by.......... Jer 38:11 4418
r rags under thine armholes under......... Jer 38:12 4418
The seed is r under their clods,............. Joel 1:17 5685

ROTTENNESS
ashamed is as r in his bones................. Prov 12:4 7538
but envy the r of the bones.................. Prov 14:30 7538
so their root shall be as r..................... Is 5:24 4716
and to the house of Judah as r.............. Hos 5:12 7538
r entered into my bones, and I.............. Hab 3:16 7538

ROUGH
down the heifer unto a r valley............. Deut 21:4 386
he stayeth his r wind in the day............ Is 27:8 7186
straight, and the r places plain............. Is 40:4 7406
to come up as the r caterpillers............ Jer 51:27 5569
the r goat is the king of Grecia............. Dan 8:21 8163
they wear a r garment to deceive.......... Zec 13:4 8181
the r ways shall be made smooth.......... Lk 3:5 5138

ROUGHLY
unto them, and spake r unto them........ Gen 42:7 7186
lord of the land, spake r to us............... Gen 42:30 7186
what if thy father answer thee r............ 1Sa 20:10 7186
And the king answered the people r...... 1Kin 12:13 7186
And the king answered them r............... 2Chr 10:13 7186
but the rich answereth r....................... Prov 18:23 5794

ROUND
of Sodom, compassed the house r.......... Gen 19:4 5921
were in all the borders r about.............. Gen 23:17 5439
the cities that were r about them.......... Gen 35:5 5439
your sheaves stood r about................... Gen 37:7 5437
which was r about every city,................ Gen 41:48 5439
all the Egyptians digged r about............ Ex 7:24 5439
the dew lay r about the host................. Ex 16:13 5439
there lay a small r thing....................... Ex 16:14 2636
bounds unto the people r about............. Ex 19:12 5439
upon it a crown of gold r about............. Ex 25:11 5439
thereto a crown of gold r about............. Ex 25:24 5439
border of an hand breadth r about......... Ex 25:25 5439
to the border thereof r about................ Ex 25:25 5439
All the pillars r about the court............. Ex 27:17 5439
woven work r about the hole of it.......... Ex 28:32 5439
scarlet, r about the hem thereof............ Ex 28:33 5439
of gold between them r about................ Ex 28:33 5439
upon the hem of the robe r about.......... Ex 28:34 5439
sprinkle it r about upon the................... Ex 29:16 5439
the blood upon the altar r about............ Ex 29:20 5439
and the sides thereof r about................ Ex 30:3 5439
unto it a crown of gold r about............. Ex 30:3 5439
a crown of gold to it r about................. Ex 37:2 5439
thereunto a crown of gold r about......... Ex 37:11 5439
border of an handbreadth r about......... Ex 37:12 5439
for the border thereof r about.............. Ex 37:12 5439
it, and the sides thereof r about........... Ex 37:26 5439
unto it a crown of gold r about............. Ex 37:26 5439
All the hangings of the court r.............. Ex 38:16 5439
and of the court r about, were of.......... Ex 38:20 5439
the sockets of the court r about............ Ex 38:31 5439
all the pins of the court r about........... Ex 38:31 5439
with a band r about the hole,................. Ex 39:23 5439
r about between the pomegranates....... Ex 39:25 5439
r about the hem of the robe to............. Ex 39:26 5439
shalt set up the court r about............... Ex 40:8 5439
the court r about the tabernacle........... Ex 40:33 5439
sprinkle the blood r about upon........... Lev 1:5 5439
his blood r about upon the altar............ Lev 1:11 5439
the blood upon the altar r about........... Lev 3:2 5439
thereof r about upon the altar.............. Lev 3:8 5439
thereof upon the altar r about............... Lev 3:13 5439
sprinkle r about upon the altar.............. Lev 7:2 5439
the altar r about with his finger............ Lev 8:15 5439
the blood upon the altar r about........... Lev 8:19 5439
the blood upon the altar r about........... Lev 8:24 5439
which he sprinkled r about upon............ Lev 9:12 5439
sprinkled upon the altar r about........... Lev 9:18 5439
to be scraped within r about................ Lev 14:41 5439
the horns of the altar r about.............. Lev 16:18 5439
Ye shall not r the corners of.................. Lev 19:27 5362
r about them shall be counted as.......... Lev 25:31 5439
the heathen that are r about you.......... Lev 25:44 5439
it, and shall encamp r about the............ Num 1:50 5439
pitch r about the tabernacle of............. Num 1:53 5439
and by the altar r about, and the.......... Num 3:26 5439
the pillars of the court r about............. Num 3:37 5439
and by the altar r about, and their........ Num 4:26 5439
the pillars of the court r about............. Num 4:32 5439
set them r about the tabernacle............ Num 11:24 5439
r about the camp, and as it were........... Num 11:31 5439
for themselves r about the camp........... Num 11:32 5439
all Israel that were r about them.......... Num 16:34 5439
lick up all that are r about us............... Num 22:4 5439
the cities of the country r about........... Num 32:33 5439
with the coasts thereof r about............. Num 34:12 5439
for the cities r about them................... Num 35:2 5439
outward a thousand cubits r about........ Num 35:4 5439
the people which are r about you.......... Deut 6:14 5439
from all your enemies r about............... Deut 12:10 5439
the people which are r about you.......... Deut 13:7 5439
are r about him that is slain................. Deut 21:2 5439
from all thine enemies r about............. Deut 25:19 5439
war, and go r about the city once.......... Josh 6:3 5362
hear of it, and shall environ us r.......... Josh 7:9 5921
Judah r about according to their............ Josh 15:12 5439
by the coasts thereof r about................ Josh 18:20 5439
that were r about these cities to........... Josh 19:8 5439
the suburbs thereof r about.................. Josh 21:11 5439
with their suburbs r about them............ Josh 21:42 5439
the LORD gave them rest r about............ Josh 21:44 5439
from all their enemies r about.............. Josh 23:1 5439
the people that were r about them........ Judg 2:12 5439
hands of their enemies r about............. Judg 2:14 5439
man in his place r about the camp......... Judg 7:21 5439
Belial, beset the house r about............ Judg 19:22 5437
beset the house r about upon me.......... Judg 20:5 5437
set liers in wait r about Gibeah............ Judg 20:29 5439
inclosed the Benjamites r about............ Judg 20:43 3803
the camp from the country r about........ 1Sa 14:21 5439
his men r about to take them................ 1Sa 23:26
and the people pitched r about him....... 1Sa 26:5 5439
and the people lay r about him............. 1Sa 26:7 5439
land of the Philistines r about.............. 1Sa 31:9 5439
David built r about from Millo and......... 2Sa 5:9 5439
rest r about from all his enemies.......... 2Sa 7:1 5439
darkness pavilions r about him.............. 2Sa 22:12 5439
and the wall of Jerusalem r about.......... 1Kin 3:1 5439
peace on all sides r about him.............. 1Kin 4:24 5439
fame was in all nations r about............. 1Kin 4:31 5439
house he built chambers r about........... 1Kin 6:5 5439
the walls of the house r about.............. 1Kin 6:5 5439
and he made chambers r about.............. 1Kin 6:5 5439
he made narrowed rests r about............ 1Kin 6:6 5439
all the walls of the house r.................... 1Kin 6:29 4524
the great court r about was with........... 1Kin 7:12 5439
two rows r about upon the one.............. 1Kin 7:18 5439
were two hundred in rows r about......... 1Kin 7:20 5439
it was r all about, and his height.......... 1Kin 7:23 5696
cubits did compass it r about................ 1Kin 7:23 5439
under the brim of it r about................. 1Kin 7:24 5439
cubit, compassing the sea r about......... 1Kin 7:24 5439
but the mouth thereof was r after......... 1Kin 7:31 5696
their borders, foursquare, not r............ 1Kin 7:31 5696
a r compass of half a cubit high............ 1Kin 7:35 5696
every one, and additions r about........... 1Kin 7:36 5439
top of the throne was r behind............. 1Kin 10:19 5696
the water ran r about the altar............. 1Kin 18:35 5439
chariots of fire r about Elisha............... 2Kin 6:17 5439
ye shall compass the king r about......... 2Kin 11:8 5439
r about the king, from the right............ 2Kin 11:11 5439
heathen that were r about them............ 2Kin 17:15 5439
in the places r about Jerusalem............ 2Kin 23:5 4524
built forts against it r about................. 2Kin 25:1 5439
were against the city r about................ 2Kin 25:4 5439
the walls of Jerusalem r about.............. 2Kin 25:10 5439
upon the chapiter r about..................... 2Kin 25:17 5439
that were r about the same cities.......... 1Chr 4:33 5439
and the suburbs thereof r about it........ 1Chr 6:55 5439

R

they lodged *r* about the house of 1Chr 9:27 5439
land of the Philistines *r* about 1Chr 10:9 5439
And he built the city *r* about 1Chr 11:8 5439
about, even from Millo *r* about 1Chr 11:8 5439
rest from all his enemies *r* about 1Chr 22:9 5439
and of all the chambers *r* about 1Chr 28:12 5439
r in compass, and five cubits the 2Chr 4:2 5696
cubits did compass it *r* about 2Chr 4:2 5439
which did compass it *r* about 2Chr 4:3 5439
cubit, compassing the sea *r* about 2Chr 4:3 5439
all the cities *r* about Gerar 2Chr 14:14 5439
the LORD gave them rest *r* about 2Chr 15:15 5439
the lands that were *r* about Judah 2Chr 17:10 5439
for his God gave him rest *r* about 2Chr 20:30 5439
shall compass the king *r* about 2Chr 23:7 5439
the temple, by the king *r* about 2Chr 23:10 5439
with their mattocks *r* about 2Chr 34:6 5439
plain country *r* about Jerusalem Neh 12:28 5439
them villages *r* about Jerusalem Neh 12:29 5439
and fashioned me together *r* about Job 10:8 5439
His archers compass me *r* about Job 16:13 5437
encamp *r* about my tabernacle Job 19:12 5439
Therefore snares are *r* about thee Job 22:10 5439
it is turned *r* about by his Job 37:12 4524
his teeth are terrible *r* about Job 41:14 5439
set themselves against me *r* about Ps 3:6 5439
his pavilion *r* about him were Ps 18:11 5439
bulls of Bashan have beset me *r* Ps 22:12 3803
up above mine enemies *r* about me Ps 27:6 5439
r about them that fear him Ps 34:7 5439
to them that are *r* about us Ps 44:13 5439
about Zion, and go *r* about her Ps 48:12 5362
be very tempestuous *r* about him Ps 50:3 5439
a dog, and go *r* about the city Ps 59:6 5437
a dog, and go *r* about the city Ps 59:14 5437
let all that be *r* about him bring Ps 76:11 5439
r about their habitations Ps 78:28 5439
shed like water *r* about Jerusalem Ps 79:3 5439
to them that are *r* about us Ps 79:4 5439
They came *r* about me daily like Ps 88:17 5437
to thy faithfulness *r* about thee Ps 89:8 5439
and darkness are *r* about him Ps 97:2 5439
and burneth up his enemies *r* about Ps 97:3 5439
mountains are *r* about Jerusalem Ps 125:2 5439
so the LORD is *r* about his people Ps 125:2 5439
olive plants *r* about thy table Ps 128:3 5439
Thy navel is like a *r* goblet Song 7:2 5469
their *r* tires like the moon, Is 3:18 7720
For the cry is gone *r* about the Is 15:8 5362
I will camp against thee *r* about Is 29:3 1754
it hath set him on fire *r* about Is 42:25 5439
Lift up thine eyes *r* about Is 49:18 5439
Lift up thine eyes *r* about Is 60:4 5439
all the walls thereof *r* about Jer 1:15 5439
are they against her *r* about Jer 4:17 5439
their tents against her *r* about Jer 6:3 5439
the birds *r* about are against her Jer 12:9 5439
devour all things *r* about it Jer 21:14 5439
against all these nations *r* about Jer 25:9 5439
for fear was *r* about, saith the Jer 46:5 5439
sword shall devour *r* about thee Jer 46:14 5439
in array against Babylon *r* about Jer 50:14 5439
Shout against her *r* about Jer 50:15 5439
the bow, camp against it *r* about Jer 50:29 5439
it shall devour all *r* about him Jer 50:32 5439
they shall be against her *r* about Jer 51:2 5439
and built forts against it *r* about Jer 52:4 5439
were by the city *r* about Jer 52:7 5439
the walls of Jerusalem *r* about Jer 52:14 5439
upon the chapiters *r* about Jer 52:22 5439
network were an hundred *r* about Jer 52:23 5439
adversaries should be *r* about him Lam 1:17 5439
fire, which devoureth *r* about Lam 2:3 5439
a solemn day my terrors *r* about Lam 2:22 5439
full of eyes *r* about them four Eze 1:18 5439
of fire *r* about within it Eze 1:27 5439
and it had brightness *r* about Eze 1:27 5439
of the brightness *r* about Eze 1:28 5439
battering rams against it *r* about Eze 4:2 5439
and countries that are *r* about her Eze 5:5 5439
countries that are *r* about her Eze 5:6 5439
the nations that are *r* about you Eze 5:7 5439
the nations that are *r* about you Eze 5:7 5439
fall by the sword *r* about thee Eze 5:12 5439
the nations that are *r* about thee Eze 5:14 5439
the nations that are *r* about thee Eze 5:15 5439
your bones *r* about your altars Eze 6:5 5439
their idols *r* about their altars Eze 6:13 5439
pourtrayed upon the wall *r* about Eze 8:10 5439
wheels, were full of eyes *r* about Eze 10:12 5439
the heathen that are *r* about you Eze 11:12 5439
gather them *r* about against thee Eze 16:37 5439
and all that are *r* about her Eze 16:57 5439
which despise thee *r* about Eze 16:57 5439
and shield and helmet *r* about Eze 23:24 5439
army were upon thy walls *r* about Eze 27:11 5439
shields upon thy walls *r* about Eze 27:11 5439
of all that are *r* about them Eze 28:24 5439
that despise them *r* about them Eze 28:26 5439
rivers running *r* about his plants Eze 31:4 5439
her company is *r* about her grave Eze 32:23 5439
her multitude *r* about her grave Eze 32:24 5439
her graves are *r* about him Eze 32:25 5439
her graves are *r* about him Eze 32:26 5439
the places *r* about my hill a Eze 34:26 5439
of the heathen that are *r* about Eze 36:4 5439
Then the heathen that are left *r* Eze 36:36 5439
caused me to pass by them *r* about Eze 37:2 5439
the outside of the house *r* about Eze 40:5 5439
of the court *r* about the gate Eze 40:14 5439
posts within the gate *r* about Eze 40:16 5439
and windows were *r* about inward Eze 40:16 5439
made for the court *r* about Eze 40:17 5439
and in the arches thereof *r* about Eze 40:25 5439
and in the arches thereof *r* about Eze 40:29 5439
the arches *r* about were five and Eze 40:30 5439
and in the arches thereof *r* about Eze 40:33 5439
and the windows to it *r* about Eze 40:36 5439
an hand broad, fastened *r* about Eze 40:43 5439
r about the house on every side Eze 41:5 5439
for the side chambers *r* about Eze 41:6 5439
still upward *r* about the house Eze 41:7 5439
the height of the house *r* about Eze 41:8 5439
r about the house on every side Eze 41:10 5439
was left was five cubits *r* about Eze 41:11 5439
was five cubits thick *r* about Eze 41:12 5439
the galleries *r* about on their Eze 41:16 5439
door, cieled with wood *r* about Eze 41:16 5439
and by all the wall *r* about within Eze 41:17 5439
through all the house *r* about Eze 41:19 5439
the east, and measured it *r* about Eze 42:15 5439
with the measuring reed *r* about Eze 42:16 5439
with the measuring reed *r* about Eze 42:17 5439
it had a wall *r* about, five Eze 42:20 5439
the whole limit thereof *r* about Eze 43:12 5439
thereof *r* about shall be a span Eze 43:13 5439
and upon the border *r* about Eze 43:20 5439
all the borders thereof *r* about Eze 45:1 5439
in breadth, square *r* about Eze 45:2 5439
fifty cubits *r* about for the Eze 45:2 5439
a row of building *r* about in them Eze 46:23 5439
r about them four, and it was made Eze 46:23 5439
places under the rows *r* about Eze 46:23 5439
It was *r* about eighteen thousand Eze 48:35 5439
yourselves together *r* about Joel 3:11 5439
to judge all the heathen *r* about Joel 3:12 5439
shall be even *r* about the land Amos 3:11 5439
the depth closed me *r* about Jonah 2:5 5437
that had the waters *r* about it Nah 3:8 5439
unto her a wall of fire *r* about Zec 2:5 5439
and the cities thereof *r* about her Zec 7:7 5439
unto all the people *r* about Zec 12:2 5439
devour all the people *r* about Zec 12:6 5439
heathen *r* about shall be gathered Zec 14:14 5439
and all the region *r* about Jordan Mt 3:5 *4066*
out into all that country *r* about Mt 14:35 *4066*
a vineyard, and hedged it *r* about Mt 21:33
all the region *r* about Galilee Mk 1:28 *4066*
when he had looked *r* about on Mk 3:5 *4017*
he looked *r* about on them which Mk 3:34 *2943*
he looked *r* about to see her that Mk 5:32 *4017*
he went *r* about the villages, Mk 6:6 *2943*
may go into the country *r* about Mk 6:36 *2943*
through that whole region *r* about Mk 6:55 *4066*
when they had looked *r* about Mk 9:8 *4017*
And Jesus looked *r* about, and saith Mk 10:23 *4017*
when he had looked *r* about upon Mk 11:11 *4017*
on all that dwelt *r* about them Lk 1:65 *4039*
of the Lord shone *r* about them Lk 2:9 *4034*
through all the region *r* about Lk 4:14 *4066*
place of the country *r* about Lk 4:37 *4066*
looking *r* about upon them all, he Lk 6:10
throughout all the region *r* about Lk 7:17 *4066*
r about besought him to depart Lk 8:37 *4066*
into the towns and country *r* about Lk 9:12 *2943*
about thee, and compass thee *r* Lk 19:43 *4033*
Then came the Jews *r* about him Jn 10:24 *2944*
the cities *r* about unto Jerusalem Acts 5:16 *4038*
suddenly there shined *r* about him Acts 9:3 *4015*
the region that lieth *r* about Acts 14:6 *4066*
the disciples stood *r* about him Acts 14:20 *2944*
heaven a great light *r* about me Acts 22:6 *4015*
down from Jerusalem stood *r* about Acts 25:7 *4026*
shining *r* about me and them which Acts 26:13 *4034*
r about unto Illyricum, I have Rom 15:19 *2943*
overlaid *r* about with gold Heb 9:4 *3840*
was a rainbow *r* about the throne Rev 4:3 *2943*
r about the throne were four and Rev 4:4 *2943*
r about the throne, were four Rev 4:6 *2943*
of many angels *r* about the throne Rev 5:11 *2943*
angels stood *r* about the throne Rev 7:11 *2943*

ROUSE
who shall *r* him up Gen 49:9 6965

ROVERS
David against the band of the *r* 1Chr 12:21

ROW
the first *r* shall be a sardius, a Ex 28:17 2905
this shall be the first *r* Ex 28:17 2905
the second *r* shall be an emerald, Ex 28:18 2905
And the third *r* a ligure, an agate Ex 28:19 2905
And the fourth *r* a beryl, and an Ex 28:20 2905
the first *r* was a sardius, a Ex 39:10 2905
this was the first *r* Ex 39:10 2905
And the second *r*, an emerald, a Ex 39:11 2905
And the third *r*, a ligure, an Ex 39:12 2905
And the fourth *r*, a beryl, an onyx Ex 39:13 2905
set them in two rows, six on a *r* Lev 24:6 4635
put pure frankincense upon each *r* Lev 24:7 4635
stone, and a *r* of cedar beams 1Kin 6:36 2905
five pillars, fifteen in a *r* 1Kin 7:3 2905
a *r* of cedar beams, both for the 1Kin 7:12 2905
stones, and a *r* of new timber Ezr 6:4 5073
there was a *r* of building round Eze 46:23 2905

ROWED
Nevertheless the men *r* hard to Jonah 1:13 2864
So when they had *r* about five Jn 6:19 *1643*

ROWERS
Thy *r* have brought thee into Eze 27:26 7751

ROWING
And he saw them toiling in *r* Mk 6:48 *1643*

ROWS
of stones, even four *r* of stones Ex 28:17 2905
they set in it four *r* of stones Ex 39:10 2905
And thou shalt set them in two *r* Lev 24:6 4634
court with three *r* of hewed stone 1Kin 6:36 2905
upon four *r* of cedar pillars, 1Kin 7:2 2905
And there were windows in three *r* 1Kin 7:4 2905
was with three *r* of hewed stones 1Kin 7:12 2905
two *r* round about upon the one 1Kin 7:18 2905
were two hundred in *r* round about 1Kin 7:20 2905
the knops were cast in two *r* 1Kin 7:24 2905
even two *r* of pomegranates for 1Kin 7:42 2905
Two *r* of oxen were cast, when it 2Chr 4:3 2905
two *r* of pomegranates on each 2Chr 4:13 2905
With three *r* of great stones, and Ezr 6:4 5073
are comely with *r* of jewels Song 1:10 8447
places under the *r* round about Eze 46:23 2918

ROYAL
fat, and he shall yield *r* dainties Gen 49:20 4428
city, as one of the *r* cities Josh 10:2 4467
dwell in the *r* city with thee 1Sa 27:5 4467
of Ammon, and took the *r* city 2Sa 12:26 4410
Solomon gave her of his *r* bounty 1Kin 10:13 4428
arose and destroyed all the seed *r* 2Kin 11:1 4467
son of Elishama, of the seed *r* 2Kin 25:25 4410
bestowed upon him such *r* majesty 1Chr 29:25 4438
the seed *r* of the house of Judah 2Chr 22:10 4467
r wine in abundance, according to Est 1:7 4438
r house which belonged to king Est 1:9 4438
before the king with the crown *r* Est 1:11 4438
let there go a *r* commandment from Est 1:19 4438
let the king give her *r* estate Est 1:19 4438
his house *r* in the tenth month Est 2:16 4438
so that he set the *r* crown upon Est 2:17 4438
that Esther put on her *r* apparel Est 5:1 4438
his *r* throne in the *r* house Est 5:1 4438
Let the *r* apparel be brought Est 6:8 4438
the crown *r* which is set upon his Est 6:8 4438
of the king in *r* apparel of blue Est 8:15 4438
a *r* diadem in the hand of thy God Is 62:3 4410
son of Elishama, of the seed *r* Jer 41:1 4410
spread his *r* pavilion over them Jer 43:10 8237
together to establish a *r* statute Dan 6:7 4430
day Herod, arrayed in *r* apparel Acts 12:21 *937*
If ye fulfil the *r* law according Jas 2:8 *937*
a *r* priesthood, an holy nation, a 1Pet 2:9 *934*

RUBBING
and did eat, *r* them in their hands Lk 6:1 *5597*

RUBBISH
heaps of the *r* which are burned Neh 4:2 6083
is decayed, and there is much *r* Neh 4:10 6083

RUBIES
the price of wisdom is above *r* Job 28:18 6443
She is more precious than *r* Prov 3:15 6443
For wisdom is better than *r* Prov 8:11 6443
is gold, and a multitude of *r* Prov 20:15 6443
for her price is far above *r* Prov 31:10 6443
were more ruddy in body than *r* Lam 4:7 6443

RUDDER
the sea, and loosed the *r* bands Acts 27:40 *4079*

RUDDY
Now he was *r*, and withal of a 1Sa 16:12 132
for he was but a youth, and *r* 1Sa 17:42 132
My beloved is white and *r*, the Song 5:10 132
they were more *r* in body than Lam 4:7 119

RUDE
But though I be *r* in speech 2Cor 11:6 *2399*

RUDIMENTS
after the *r* of the world, and not Col 2:8 4747
Christ from the *r* of the world Col 2:20 4747

RUE
for ye tithe mint and *r* and all Lk 11:42 *4076*

RUFUS (*ru'-fus*)
1. Son of Simon the Cyrenian.
the father of Alexander and *R* Mk 15:21 *4504*
2. A Christian in Rome.
Salute *R* chosen in the Lord, and Rom 16:13 *4504*

RUHAMAH (*ru-ha'-mah*) *A symbolic name of Israel.*
and to your sisters, *R* Hos 2:1 7355

RUIN
But they were the *r* of him 2Chr 28:23
brought his strong holds to *r* Ps 89:40 4288
and who knoweth the *r* of them both Prov 24:22 6365
and a flattering mouth worketh *r* Prov 26:28 4072
let this *r* be under thy hand Is 3:6 4384
and he brought it to *r* Is 23:13 4654
of a defenced city a *r* Is 25:2 4654
so iniquity shall not be your *r* Eze 18:30 4383
of the seas in the day of thy *r* Eze 27:27 4658
Upon his *r* shall all the fowls of Eze 31:13 4658
the *r* of that house was great Lk 6:49 *4485*

RUINED
For Jerusalem is *r*, and Judah is Is 3:8 3782
r cities are become fenced, and Eze 36:35 2040
I the LORD build the *r* places Eze 36:36 2040

RUINOUS
waste fenced cities into *r* heaps 2Kin 19:25 5327
a city, and it shall be a *r* heap Is 17:1 4654
defenced cities into *r* heaps Is 37:26 5327

RUINS
faint, and their *r* be multiplied Eze 21:15 4383
and I will raise up his *r*, and I Amos 9:11 2034
I will build again the *r* thereof Acts 15:16 *2679*

RULE
the greater light to *r* the day Gen 1:16 4475
the lesser light to *r* the night Gen 1:16 4475
to *r* over the day and over the Gen 1:18 4910
husband, and he shall *r* over thee Gen 3:16 4910
desire, and thou shalt *r* over him Gen 4:7 4910

Thou shalt not r over him with ... Lev 25:43 7287
ye shall not r one over another... Lev 25:46 7287
the other shall not r with rigour... Lev 25:53 7287
R thou over us, both thou, and thy ... Judg 8:22 4910
unto them, I will not r over you... Judg 8:23 4910
neither shall my son r over you... Judg 8:23 4910
the LORD shall r over you... Judg 8:23 4910
which bare r over the people that... 1Kin 9:23 7287
that had r over his chariots ... 1Kin 22:31
that bare r over the people ... 2Chr 8:10 7287
servants bare r over the people... Neh 5:15 7980
should bear r in his own house... Est 1:22 8323
that the Jews had r over them... Est 9:1 7980
r thou in the midst of thine... Ps 110:2 7287
The sun to r by day ... Ps 136:8 4475
The moon and stars to r by night ... Ps 136:9 4475
By me princes r, and nobles, even... Prov 8:16 8323
hand of the diligent shall bear r... Prov 12:24 4910
A wise servant shall have r over ... Prov 17:2 4910
a servant to have r over princes... Prov 19:10 4910
He that hath no r over his own ... Prov 25:28 4623
but when the wicked beareth r... Prov 29:2 4910
yet shall he have r over all my... Eccl 2:19 7980
and babes shall r over them... Is 3:4 4910
oppressors, and women r over them... Is 3:12 4910
and they shall r over their... Is 14:2 7287
a fierce king shall r over them ... Is 19:4 4910
that r this people which is in... Is 28:14 4910
and princes shall r in judgment ... Is 32:1 8323
hand, and his arm shall r for him... Is 40:10 4910
him, and made him r over kings... Is 41:2 7287
carpenter stretcheth out his r... Is 44:13 4910
they that r over them make them... Is 52:5 4910
thou never barest r over them ... Is 63:19 4910
the priests bear r by their means... Jer 5:31 7287
the sceptres of them that bare r... Eze 19:11 4910
strong rod to be a sceptre to r... Eze 19:14 4910
poured out, will I r over you ... Eze 20:33 4427
shall no more r over the nations ... Eze 29:15 7287
which shall bear r over all the ... Dan 2:39 7981
have known that the heavens do r... Dan 4:26 7990
that shall r with great dominion,... Dan 11:3 4910
shall cause them to r over many ... Dan 11:39 4910
the heathen should r over them ... Joel 2:17 4910
and shall sit and r upon his throne... Zec 6:13 4910
that shall r my people Israel... Mt 2:6 4165
to r over the Gentiles exercise ... Mk 10:42 757
when he shall have put down all r... 1Cor 15:24 746
r which God hath distributed to ... 2Cor 10:13 2583
you according to our r abundantly ... 2Cor 10:15 2583
many as walk according to this r... Gal 6:16 2583
let us walk by the same r... Phil 3:16 2583
the peace of God r in your hearts ... Col 3:15 1018
know not how to r his own house ... 1Ti 3:5 4291
Let the elders that r well be... 1Ti 5:17 4291
them which have the r over you ... Heb 13:7 2233
them that have the r over you... Heb 13:17 2233
all them that have the r over you ... Heb 13:24 2233
he shall r them with a rod of... Rev 2:27 4165
who was to r all nations with a... Rev 12:5 4165
he shall r them with a rod of... Rev 19:15 4165

RULED

that r over all that he had, Put,... Gen 24:2 4910
thy word shall all my people be r... Gen 41:40 5401
r from Aroer, which is upon the... Josh 12:2 4910
in the days when the judges r... Ruth 1:1 8199
which r over the people that ... 1Kin 5:16 7287
that r throughout the house of... 1Chr 26:6 4474
which have r over all countries ... Ezr 4:20 7990
they that hated them r over them... Ps 106:41 4910
he that r the nations in anger,... Is 14:6 7287
Servants have r over us... Lam 5:8 4910
and with cruelty have ye r them... Eze 34:4 7287
high God r in the kingdom of men ... Dan 5:21 7990
to his dominion which he r... Dan 11:4 4910

RULER

he made him r over all the land... Gen 41:43
he said to the r of his house... Gen 43:16
a r throughout all the land of... Gen 45:8 4910
nor curse the r of thy people... Ex 22:28 5387
When a r hath sinned, and done ... Lev 4:22 5387
a man, every one a r among them ... Num 13:2 5387
when Zebul the r of the city... Judg 9:30 8269
have appointed thee r over Israel... 1Sa 25:30 5057
to appoint me r over the people... 2Sa 6:21 5057
to be r over my people, over... 2Sa 7:8 5057
Jairite was a chief r about David... 2Sa 20:26
appointed him to be r over Israel... 1Kin 1:35 5057
he made him r over all the charge ... 1Kin 11:28 6485
of Ahikam, the son of Shaphan, r... 2Kin 25:22 6485
and of him came the chief r... 1Chr 5:2 5057
the r of the house of God... 1Chr 9:11 5057
was the r over them in time past ... 1Chr 9:20 5057
thou shalt be r over my people ... 1Chr 11:2 5057
be r over my people Israel... 1Chr 17:7 5057
of Moses, was r of the treasures... 1Chr 26:24 5057
his course was Mikloth also the r... 1Chr 27:4 5057
the r of the Reubenites was... 1Chr 27:16 5057
he hath chosen Judah to be the r... 1Chr 28:4 5057
to be a r over my people Israel... 2Chr 6:5 5057
fail thee a man to be r in Israel... 2Chr 7:18 4910
to be r among his brethren ... 2Chr 11:22 5057
the r of the house of Judah, for... 2Chr 19:11 5057
the scribe and Maaseiah the r... 2Chr 26:11 7860
which Cononiah the Levite was r... 2Chr 31:12 5057
Azariah the r of the house of God ... 2Chr 31:13 5057
the r of the half part of... Neh 3:9 8269
the r of the half part of... Neh 3:12 8269
the r of part of Beth-haccerem... Neh 3:14 8269
Colhozeh, the r of part of Mizpah... Neh 3:15 8269
the r of the half part of... Neh 3:16 8269
the r of the half part of Keilah,... Neh 3:17 8269
the r of the half part of Keilah... Neh 3:18 8269
the r of Mizpah, another piece... Neh 3:19 8269
Hananiah the r of the palace,... Neh 7:2 8269
was the r of the house of God... Neh 11:11 5057
is little Benjamin with their r... Ps 68:27 7287
even the r of the people, and let... Ps 105:20 4910
house, and r of all his substance... Ps 105:21 4910
having no guide, overseer, or r... Prov 6:7 4910
When thou sittest to eat with a r... Prov 23:1 4910
so is a wicked r over the poor... Prov 28:15 4910
If a r hearken to lies, all his... Prov 29:12 4910
of the r rise up against thee... Eccl 10:4 4910
error which proceedeth from the r... Eccl 10:5 7989
Thou hast clothing, be thou our r... Is 3:6 7101
make me not a r of the people... Is 3:7 7101
Send ye the lamb to the r of the ... Is 16:1 4910
in the land, r against r... Jer 51:46 4910
there is no king, lord, nor r... Dan 2:10 7990
and hath made thee r over them all ... Dan 2:38 7981
made him r over the whole... Dan 2:48 7981
be the third r in the kingdom... Dan 5:7 7981
be the third r in the kingdom... Dan 5:16 7981
be the third r in the kingdom... Dan 5:29 7990
unto me that is to be r in Israel... Mic 5:2 4910
things, that have no r over them... Hab 1:14 4910
behold, there came a certain r ... Mt 9:18 758
hath made r over his household ... Mt 24:45 2525
make him r over all his goods... Mt 24:47 2525
will make thee r over many things... Mt 25:21 2525
will make thee r over many things... Mt 25:23 2525
there came from the r of the... Mk 5:35 752
saith unto the r of the synagogue... Mk 5:36 752
house of the r of the synagogue... Mk 5:38 752
he was a r of the synagogue... Lk 8:41 758
the r of the synagogue's house... Lk 8:49 752
shall make r over his household... Lk 12:42 2525
make him r over all that he hath ... Lk 12:44 2525
the r of the synagogue answered ... Lk 13:14 752
And a certain r asked him, saying,... Lk 18:18 758
When the r of the feast had... Jn 2:9 755
named Nicodemus, a r of the Jews ... Jn 3:1 758
away, saying, Who made thee a r... Acts 7:27 758
saying, Who made thee a r... Acts 7:35 758
the same did God send to be a r... Acts 7:35 758
the chief r of the synagogue,... Acts 18:8 752
the chief r of the synagogue, and... Acts 18:17 752
speak evil of the r of thy people ... Acts 23:5 758

RULER'S

Many seek the r favour... Prov 29:26 4910
when Jesus came into the r house... Mt 9:23 758

RULERS

then make them r over my cattle... Gen 47:6 8269
all the r of the congregation... Ex 16:22 5387
to be r of thousands... Ex 18:21 8269
r of hundreds, r of fifties,... Ex 18:21 8269
r of fifties, and r of tens... Ex 18:21 8269
r of thousands... Ex 18:25 8269
r of hundreds, r of fifties,... Ex 18:25 8269
r of fifties, and r of tens... Ex 18:25 8269
all the r of the congregation... Ex 34:31 5387
the r brought onyx stones, and... Ex 35:27 5387
and I will make them r over you... Deut 1:13 7218
the Philistines are r over us... Judg 15:11 4910
and David's sons were chief r... 2Sa 8:18
r of his chariots, and his... 1Kin 9:22 8269
unto the r of Jezreel, to the... 2Kin 10:1 8269
fetched the r over hundreds, with... 2Kin 11:4 8269
he took the r over hundreds, and... 2Kin 11:19 8269
to the r of the people, Go,... 1Chr 21:2 8269
David made r over the Reubenites... 1Chr 26:32 6485
All these were the r of the... 1Chr 27:31 8269
with the r of the king's work,... 1Chr 29:6 8269
and gathered the r of the city ... 2Chr 29:20 8269
r of the house of God, gave unto ... 2Chr 35:8 5057
r hath been chief in this ... Ezr 9:2 5461
Let now our r of all the ... Ezr 10:14 8269
the r knew not whither I went, or... Neh 2:16 5461
nor to the nobles, nor to the r... Neh 2:16 5461
said unto the nobles, and to the r... Neh 4:14 5461
the r were behind all the house ... Neh 4:16 8269
said unto the nobles, and to the r... Neh 4:19 5461
and I rebuked the nobles, and the r... Neh 5:7 5461
hundred and fifty of the Jews and r... Neh 5:17 5461
together the nobles, and the r... Neh 7:5 5461
the r of the people dwelt at ... Neh 11:1 8269
I, and the half of the r with me... Neh 12:40 5461
Then contended I with the r ... Neh 13:11 5461
to the r of every people of every... Est 3:12 8269
r of the provinces which are from... Est 8:9 8269
all the r of the provinces, and ... Est 9:3 8269
the r take counsel together,... Ps 2:2 7336
word of the LORD, ye r of Sodom ... Is 1:10 7101
wicked, and the sceptre of the r... Is 14:5 4910
All thy r are fled together, they... Is 22:3 7101
the prophets and your r, the seers ... Is 29:10 7218
abhorreth, to a servant of r... Is 49:7 4910
to be r over the seed of Abraham... Jer 33:26 4910
I break in pieces captains and r... Jer 51:23 5461
thereof, and all the r thereof ... Jer 51:28 5461
wise men, her captains, and her r ... Jer 51:57 5461
clothed with blue, captains and r... Eze 23:6 5461
r clothed most gorgeously,... Eze 23:12 5461
young men, captains and r, great... Eze 23:23 5461
all the r of the provinces, to ... Dan 3:2 7984
all the r of the provinces, were... Dan 3:3 7984
her r with shame do love, Give ye ... Hos 4:18 4043
one of the r of the synagogue ... Mk 5:22 752
and ye shall be brought before r... Mk 13:9 2232
kings and r for my name's sake... Lk 21:12 2232
the chief priests and the r... Lk 23:13 758
the r also with them derided him,... Lk 23:35 758
our r delivered him to be... Lk 24:20 758
Do the r know indeed that this is ... Jn 7:26 758
Have any of the r or of the... Jn 7:48 758
chief r also many believed on him ... Jn 12:42 758
ye did it, as did also your r... Acts 3:17 758
pass on the morrow, that their r ... Acts 4:5 758
Ye r of the people, and elders of... Acts 4:8 758
the r were gathered together... Acts 4:26 758
the prophets the r of the ... Acts 13:15 752
dwell at Jerusalem, and their r... Acts 13:27 758
and also of the Jews with their r... Acts 14:5 758
into the marketplace unto the r... Acts 16:19 758
brethren unto the r of the city... Acts 17:6 4178
the r of the city, when they... Acts 17:8 4178
For r are not a terror to good ... Rom 13:3 758
against the r of the darkness of... Eph 6:12 2888

RULEST

r not thou over all the kingdoms... 2Chr 20:6 4910
Thou r the raging of the sea... Ps 89:9 4910

RULETH

He that r over men must be just,... 2Sa 23:3 4910
let them know that God r in Jacob... Ps 59:13 4910
He r by his power for ever... Ps 66:7 4910
and his kingdom r over all ... Ps 103:19 4910
he that r his spirit than he that ... Prov 16:32 4910
The rich r over the poor, and the... Prov 22:7 4910
r over another to his own hurt ... Eccl 8:9 7980
the cry of him that r among fools... Eccl 9:17 4910
most High r in the kingdom of men ... Dan 4:17 7980
most High r in the kingdom of men ... Dan 4:25 7980
most High r in the kingdom of men ... Dan 4:32 7980
but Judah yet r with God, and is... Hos 11:12 7300
he that r, with diligence... Rom 12:8 4291
One that r well his own house,... 1Ti 3:4 4291

RULING

be just, r in the fear of God... 2Sa 23:3 4910
of David, and r any more in Judah ... Jer 22:30 4910
r their children and their own... 1Ti 3:12 4291

RUMAH (*ru'-mah*) See ARUMAH. *Home of Jehoiakim's mother.*
the daughter of Pedaiah of R ... 2Kin 23:36 7316

RUMBLING

at the r of his wheels, the... Jer 47:3 1995

RUMOUR

upon him, and he shall hear a r... 2Kin 19:7 8052
upon him, and he shall hear a r... Is 37:7 8052
I have heard a r from the LORD... Jer 49:14 8052
ye fear for the r that shall be ... Jer 51:46 8052
a r shall both come one year, and... Jer 51:46 8052
in another year shall come a r... Jer 51:46 8052
and r shall be upon r ... Eze 7:26 8052
We have heard a r from the LORD... Obad 1 8052
And this r of him went forth... Lk 7:17 3056

RUMOURS

shall hear of wars and r of wars... Mt 24:6 189
r of wars, be ye not troubled... Mk 13:7 189

RUMP

take of the ram the fat and the r... Ex 29:22 451
the fat thereof, and the whole r... Lev 3:9 451
the r, and the fat that covereth ... Lev 7:3 451
And he took the fat, and the r... Lev 8:25 451
the bullock and of the ram, the r ... Lev 9:19 451

RUN

whose branches r over the wall... Gen 49:22 6805
his flesh r with his issue ... Lev 15:3 7325
or if it r beyond the time of her... Lev 15:25 2100
lest angry fellows r upon thee... Judg 18:25 6293
some shall r before his chariots ... 1Sa 8:11 7323
r to the camp to thy brethren ... 1Sa 17:17 7323
he might r to Beth-lehem his city ... 1Sa 20:6 7323
And he said unto his lad, R... 1Sa 20:36 7323
and fifty men to r before him... 2Sa 15:1 7323
the son of Zadok, Let me now r... 2Sa 18:19 7323
I pray thee, also r after Cushi ... 2Sa 18:22 7323
Joab said, Wherefore wilt thou r... 2Sa 18:22 7323
But howsoever, said he, let me r ... 2Sa 18:23 7323
And he said unto him, R... 2Sa 18:23 7323
by thee I have r through a troop... 2Sa 22:30 7323
and fifty men to r before him... 1Kin 1:5 7323
that I may r to the man of God,... 2Kin 4:22 7323
R now, I pray thee, to meet her,... 2Kin 4:26 7323
I will r after him, and take... 2Kin 5:20 7323
For the eyes of the LORD r to... 2Chr 16:9 7751
by thee I have r through a troop... Ps 18:29 7323
as a strong man to r a race... Ps 19:5 7323
as waters which r continually ... Ps 58:7 1980
They r and prepare themselves... Ps 59:4 7323
waters to r down like rivers... Ps 78:16 3381
valleys, which r among the hills ... Ps 104:10 1980
I will r the way of thy... Ps 119:32 7323
Rivers of waters r down mine eyes... Ps 119:136 3381
For their feet r to evil, and make... Prov 1:16 7323
All the rivers r into the sea... Eccl 1:7 1980
Draw me, we will r after thee ... Song 1:4 7323
of locusts shall he r upon them... Is 33:4 8264
they shall r, and not be weary ... Is 40:31 7323
that knew not thee shall r unto... Is 55:5 7323
Their feet r to evil, and they... Is 59:7 7323
R ye to and fro through the ... Jer 5:1 7751
our eyes may r down with tears... Jer 9:18 3381
If thou hast r with the footmen,... Jer 12:5 7323
r down with tears, because the ... Jer 13:17 3381
Let mine eyes r down with tears... Jer 14:17 3381
r to and fro by the hedges... Jer 49:3 7751
suddenly make him r away from her... Jer 49:19 7323
them suddenly r away from her... Jer 50:44 7323
One post shall r to meet another,... Jer 51:31 7323
let tears r down like a river day ... Lam 2:18 3381
neither shall thy tears r down ... Eze 24:16 935
cause their rivers to r like oil ... Eze 32:14 3212
many shall r to and fro, and... Dan 12:4 7751
and as horsemen, so shall they r... Joel 2:4 7323

They shall *r* like mighty men ... Joel 2:7 7323
They shall *r* to and fro in the ... Joel 2:9 8264
they shall *r* upon the wall, they ... Joel 2:9 7323
But let judgment *r* down as waters ... Amos 5:24 1556
Shall horses *r* upon the rock ... Amos 6:12 7323
even to the east, they shall *r* to ... Amos 8:12 7751
they shall *r* like the lightnings ... Nah 2:4 7323
that he may *r* that readeth it ... Hab 2:2 7323
ye *r* every man unto his own house ... Hag 1:9 7323
And said unto him, *R*, speak to ... Zec 2:4 7323
the eyes of the LORD, which *r* to ... Zec 4:10 7751
did *r* to bring his disciples word ... Mt 28:8 *5143*
they which *r* in a race *r* all ... 1Cor 9:24 *5143*
So *r*, that ye may obtain ... 1Cor 9:24 *5143*
I therefore so *r*, not as ... 1Cor 9:26 *5143*
any means I should *r*, or had *r* ... Gal 2:2 *5143*
Ye did *r* well ... Gal 5:7 *5143*
Christ, that I have not *r* in vain ... Phil 2:16 *5143*
let us *r* with patience the race ... Heb 12:1 *5143*
ye *r* not with them to the same ... 1Pet 4:4 *4936*

RUNNEST
and when thou *r*, thou shalt not ... Prov 4:12 7323

RUNNETH
to the river than *r* to Ahava ... Ezr 8:15 935
He *r* upon him, even on his neck, ... Job 15:26 7323
he *r* upon me like a giant ... Job 16:14 7323
my cup *r* over ... Ps 23:5 7310
his word *r* very swiftly ... Ps 147:15 7323
the righteous *r* into it, and is ... Prov 18:10 7323
mine eye *r* down with water, ... Lam 1:16 3381
Mine eye *r* down with rivers of ... Lam 3:48 3381
bottles break, and the wine *r* out ... Mt 9:17 *1632*
Then she *r*, and cometh to Simon ... Jn 20:2 *5143*
that willeth, nor of him that *r* ... Rom 9:16 *5143*

RUNNING
in an earthen vessel over *r* water ... Lev 14:5 2416
that was killed over the *r* water ... Lev 14:6 2416
in an earthen vessel over *r* water ... Lev 14:50 2416
the slain bird, and in the *r* water ... Lev 14:51 2416
of the bird, and with the *r* water ... Lev 14:52 2416
When any man hath a *r* issue out ... Lev 15:2 2100
and bathe his flesh in *r* water ... Lev 15:13 2416
is a leper, or hath a *r* issue ... Lev 22:4 2100
r water shall be put thereto in a ... Num 19:17 2416
looked, and behold a man *r* alone ... 2Sa 18:24 7323
watchman saw another man *r* ... 2Sa 18:26 7323
said, Behold another man *r* alone ... 2Sa 18:26 7323
Me thinketh the *r* of the foremost ... 2Sa 18:27 4794
the *r* of Ahimaaz the son of Zadok ... 2Sa 18:27 4794
when Naaman saw him *r* after him ... 2Kin 5:21 7323
heard the noise of the people *r* ... 2Chr 23:12 7323
r waters out of thine own well ... Prov 5:15 5140
that be swift in *r* to mischief ... Prov 6:18 7323
as the *r* to and fro of locusts ... Is 33:4 4944
rivers *r* round about his plants ... Eze 31:4 1980
amazed, and *r* to him saluted him ... Mk 9:15 *4370*
that the people came *r* together ... Mk 9:25 *1998*
into the way, there came one *r* ... Mk 10:17 *4370*
r over, shall men give into your ... Lk 6:38 *5240*
r under a certain island which is ... Acts 27:16 *5295*
of many horses *r* to battle ... Rev 9:9 *5143*

RUSH
Can the *r* grow up without mire ... Job 8:11 1573
Israel head and tail, branch and *r* ... Is 9:14 100
The nations shall *r* like the ... Is 17:13 7582
the head or tail, branch or *r* ... Is 19:15 100

RUSHED
r forward, and stood in the ... Judg 9:44 6584
in wait hasted, and *r* upon Gibeah ... Judg 20:37 6584
they *r* with one accord into the ... Acts 19:29 *3729*

RUSHES
shall be grass with reeds and *r* ... Is 35:7 1573

RUSHETH
as the horse *r* into the battle ... Jer 8:6 7857

RUSHING
to the *r* of nations ... Is 17:12 7588
that make a *r* like the *r* of ... Is 17:12 7582
rush like the *r* of many waters ... Is 17:13 7588
at the *r* of his chariots, and at ... Jer 47:3 7494
behind me a voice of a great *r* ... Eze 3:12 7494
them, and a noise of a great *r* ... Eze 3:13 7494
from heaven as of a *r* mighty wind ... Acts 2:2 *5342*

RUST
r doth corrupt, and where thieves ... Mt 6:19 *1035*
neither moth nor *r* doth corrupt ... Mt 6:20 *1035*
the *r* of them shall be a witness ... Jas 5:3 *2447*

RUTH (*rooth*) *Wife of Boaz; an ancestor of Jesus.*
Orpah, and the name of the other *R* ... Ruth 1:4 7327
but *R* clave unto her ... Ruth 1:14 7327
R said, Intreat me not to leave ... Ruth 1:16 7327
R the Moabitess, her daughter in ... Ruth 1:22 7327
R the Moabitess said unto Naomi, ... Ruth 2:2 7327
Then said Boaz unto *R*, Hearest ... Ruth 2:8 7327
R the Moabitess said, He said ... Ruth 2:21 7327
Naomi said unto *R* her daughter in ... Ruth 2:22 7327
answered, I am *R* thine handmaid ... Ruth 3:9 7327
buy it also of *R* the Moabitess ... Ruth 4:5 7327
Moreover *R* the Moabitess, the ... Ruth 4:10 7327
So Boaz took *R*, and she was his ... Ruth 4:13 7327
and Booz begat Obed of *R* ... Mt 1:5 *4503*

S

SABACHTHANI
voice, saying, Eli, Eli, lama *s* ... Mt 27:46 *4518*
voice, saying, Eloi, Eloi, lama *s* ... Mk 15:34 *4518*

SABAOTH (*sab'-a-oth*) *Title meaning "Lord of Hosts."*
the Lord of *S* had left us a seed ... Rom 9:29 *4519*
into the ears of the Lord of *S* ... Jas 5:4 *4519*

SABBATH
rest of the holy *s* unto the LORD ... Ex 16:23 7676
for to day is a *s* unto the LORD ... Ex 16:25 7676
the seventh day, which is the *s* ... Ex 16:26 7676
the LORD hath given you the *s* ... Ex 16:29 7676
Remember the *s* day, to keep it ... Ex 20:8 7676
day is the *s* of the LORD thy God ... Ex 20:10 7676
the LORD blessed the *s* day ... Ex 20:11 7676
Ye shall keep the *s* therefore ... Ex 31:14 7676
in the seventh is the *s* of rest ... Ex 31:15 7676
doeth any work in the *s* day ... Ex 31:15 7676
of Israel shall keep the *s* ... Ex 31:16 7676
to observe the *s* throughout their ... Ex 31:16 7676
holy day, a *s* of rest to the LORD ... Ex 35:2 7676
your habitations upon the *s* day ... Ex 35:3 7676
It shall be a *s* of rest unto you, ... Lev 16:31 7676
the seventh day is the *s* of rest ... Lev 23:3 7676
it is the *s* of the LORD in all ... Lev 23:3 7676
on the morrow after the *s* the ... Lev 23:11 7676
you from the morrow after the *s* ... Lev 23:15 7676
s shall ye number fifty days ... Lev 23:16 7676
of the month, shall ye have a *s* ... Lev 23:24 7677
It shall be unto you a *s* of rest ... Lev 23:32 7676
even, shall ye celebrate your *s* ... Lev 23:32 7676
on the first day shall be a *s* ... Lev 23:39 7677
and on the eighth day shall be a *s* ... Lev 23:39 7677
Every *s* he shall set it in order ... Lev 24:8 7676
the land keep a *s* unto the LORD ... Lev 25:2 7676
be a *s* of rest unto the land ... Lev 25:4 7676
unto the land, a *s* for the LORD ... Lev 25:4 7676
the *s* of the land shall be meat ... Lev 25:6 7676
gathered sticks upon the *s* day ... Num 15:32 7676
on the *s* day two lambs of the ... Num 28:9 7676
is the burnt offering of every *s* ... Num 28:10 7676
Keep the *s* day to sanctify it, as ... Deut 5:12 7676
day is the *s* of the LORD thy God ... Deut 5:14 7676
commanded thee to keep the *s* day ... Deut 5:15 7676
it is neither new moon, nor *s* ... 2Kin 4:23 7676
of you that enter in on the *s* ... 2Kin 11:5 7676
of all you that go forth on the *s* ... 2Kin 11:7 7676
men that were to come in on the *s* ... 2Kin 11:9 7676
them that should go out on the *s* ... 2Kin 11:9 7676
the covert for the *s* that they ... 2Kin 16:18 7676
shewbread, to prepare it every *s* ... 1Chr 9:32 7676
part of you entering on the *s* ... 2Chr 23:4 7676
men that were to come in on the *s* ... 2Chr 23:8 7676
them that were to go out on the *s* ... 2Chr 23:8 7676
as she lay desolate she kept *s* ... 2Chr 36:21 7673
madest known unto them thy holy *s* ... Neh 9:14 7676
any victuals on the *s* day to sell ... Neh 10:31 7676
would not buy it of them on the *s* ... Neh 10:31 7676
treading winepresses on the *s* ... Neh 13:15 7676
into Jerusalem on the *s* day ... Neh 13:15 7676
sold on the *s* unto the children ... Neh 13:16 7676
that ye do, and profane the *s* day ... Neh 13:17 7676
upon Israel by profaning the *s* ... Neh 13:18 7676
began to be dark before the *s* ... Neh 13:19 7676
not be opened till after the *s* ... Neh 13:19 7676
burden be brought in on the *s* day ... Neh 13:19 7676
forth came they no more on the *s* ... Neh 13:21 7676
the gates, to sanctify the *s* day ... Neh 13:22 7676
A Psalm or Song for the *s* day ... Ps 92:*t* 7676
that keepeth the *s* from polluting ... Is 56:2 7676
keepeth the *s* from polluting it ... Is 56:6 7676
turn away thy foot from the *s* ... Is 58:13 7676
call the *s* a delight, the holy of ... Is 58:13 7676
from one *s* to another, shall all ... Is 66:23 7676
and bear no burden on the *s* day ... Jer 17:21 7676
out of your houses on the *s* day ... Jer 17:22 7676
any work, but hallow ye the *s* day ... Jer 17:22 7676
gates of this city on the *s* day ... Jer 17:24 7676
but hallow the *s* day ... Jer 17:24 7676
unto me to hallow the *s* day ... Jer 17:27 7676
gates of Jerusalem on the *s* day ... Jer 17:27 7676
but on the *s* it shall be opened, ... Eze 46:1 7676
offer unto the LORD in the *s* day ... Eze 46:4 7676
offerings, as he did on the *s* day ... Eze 46:12 7676
and the *s*, that we may set forth ... Amos 8:5 7676
on the *s* day through the corn ... Mt 12:1 *4521*
not lawful to do upon the *s* day ... Mt 12:2 *4521*
how that on the *s* days the ... Mt 12:5 *4521*
in the temple profane the *s* ... Mt 12:5 *4521*
of man is Lord even of the *s* day ... Mt 12:8 *4521*
it lawful to heal on the *s* days ... Mt 12:10 *4521*
it fall into a pit on the *s* day ... Mt 12:11 *4521*
lawful to do well on the *s* days ... Mt 12:12 *4521*
the winter, neither on the *s* day ... Mt 24:20 *4521*
In the end of the *s*, as it began ... Mt 28:1 *4521*
straightway on the *s* day he ... Mk 1:21 *4521*
the corn fields on the *s* day ... Mk 2:23 *4521*
why do they on the *s* day that ... Mk 2:24 *4521*
The *s* was made for man ... Mk 2:27 *4521*
and not man for the *s* ... Mk 2:27 *4521*
Son of man is Lord also of the *s* ... Mk 2:28 *4521*
he would heal him on the *s* day ... Mk 3:2 *4521*
lawful to do good on the *s* days ... Mk 3:4 *4521*
when the *s* day was come, he began ... Mk 6:2 *4521*
that is, the day before the *s* ... Mk 15:42 *4315*
And when the *s* was past, Mary ... Mk 16:1 *4521*
into the synagogue on the *s* day ... Lk 4:16 *4521*
and taught them on the *s* days ... Lk 4:31 *4521*
on the second *s* after the first ... Lk 6:1 *4521*
is not lawful to do on the *s* days ... Lk 6:2 *4521*
Son of man is Lord also of the *s* ... Lk 6:5 *4521*
it came to pass also on another *s* ... Lk 6:6 *4521*
he would heal on the *s* day ... Lk 6:7 *4521*
lawful on the *s* days to do good ... Lk 6:9 *4521*
in one of the synagogues on the *s* ... Lk 13:10 *4521*
Jesus had healed on the *s* day ... Lk 13:14 *4521*
and be healed, and not on the *s* day ... Lk 13:14 *4521*
s loose his ox or his ass from ... Lk 13:15 *4521*
from this bond on the *s* day ... Lk 13:16 *4521*
to eat bread on the *s* day ... Lk 14:1 *4521*
Is it lawful to heal on the *s* day ... Lk 14:3 *4521*
pull him out on the *s* day ... Lk 14:5 *4521*
the preparation, and the *s* drew on ... Lk 23:54 *4521*
rested the *s* day according to the ... Lk 23:56 *4521*
and on the same day was the *s* ... Jn 5:9 *4521*
that was cured, It is the *s* day ... Jn 5:10 *4521*
done these things on the *s* day ... Jn 5:16 *4521*
he not only had broken the *s* ... Jn 5:18 *4521*
ye on the *s* day circumcise a man ... Jn 7:22 *4521*
If a man on the *s* day receive ... Jn 7:23 *4521*
man every whit whole on the *s* day ... Jn 7:23 *4521*
it was the *s* day when Jesus made ... Jn 9:14 *4521*
because he keepeth not the *s* day ... Jn 9:16 *4521*
upon the cross on the *s* day ... Jn 19:31 *4521*
(for that *s* day was an high day,) ... Jn 19:31 *4521*
from Jerusalem a *s* day's journey ... Acts 1:12 *4521*
into the synagogue on the *s* day ... Acts 13:14 *4521*
which are read every *s* day ... Acts 13:27 *4521*
be preached to them the next *s* ... Acts 13:42 *4521*
the next *s* day came almost the ... Acts 13:44 *4521*
in the synagogues every *s* day ... Acts 15:21 *4521*
on the *s* we went out of the city ... Acts 16:13 *4521*
three *s* days reasoned with them ... Acts 17:2 *4521*
reasoned in the synagogue every *s* ... Acts 18:4 *4521*
of the new moon, or of the *s* days ... Col 2:16 *4521*

SABBATHS
Verily my *s* ye shall keep ... Ex 31:13 7676
and his father, and keep my *s* ... Lev 19:3 7676
Ye shall keep my *s*, and reverence ... Lev 19:30 7676
seven *s* shall be complete ... Lev 23:15 7676
Beside the *s* of the LORD, and ... Lev 23:38 7676
number seven *s* of years unto thee ... Lev 25:8 7676
the space of the seven *s* of years ... Lev 25:8 7676
Ye shall keep my *s*, and reverence ... Lev 26:2 7676
Then shall the land enjoy her *s* ... Lev 26:34 7676
the land rest, and enjoy her *s* ... Lev 26:34 7676
because it did not rest in your *s* ... Lev 26:35 7676
of them, and shall enjoy her *s* ... Lev 26:43 7676
sacrifices unto the LORD in the *s* ... 1Chr 23:31 7676
morning and evening, on the *s* ... 2Chr 2:4 7676
commandment of Moses, on the *s* ... 2Chr 8:13 7676
and the burnt offerings for the *s* ... 2Chr 31:3 7676
until the land had enjoyed her *s* ... 2Chr 36:21 7676
burnt offering, of the *s*, of the ... Neh 10:33 7676
the new moons and *s*, the calling ... Is 1:13 7676
unto the eunuchs that keep my *s* ... Is 56:4 7676
saw her, and did mock at her *s* ... Lam 1:7 4868
s to be forgotten in Zion, and ... Lam 2:6 7676
Moreover also I gave them my *s* ... Eze 20:12 7676
my *s* they greatly polluted ... Eze 20:13 7676
in my statutes, but polluted my *s* ... Eze 20:16 7676
And hallow my *s* ... Eze 20:20 7676
they polluted my *s* ... Eze 20:21 7676
my statutes, and had polluted my *s* ... Eze 20:24 7676
things, and hast profaned my *s* ... Eze 22:8 7676
and have hid their eyes from my *s* ... Eze 22:26 7676
same day, and have profaned my *s* ... Eze 23:38 7676
and they shall hallow my *s* ... Eze 44:24 7676
and in the new moons, and in the *s* ... Eze 45:17 7676
gate before the LORD in the *s* ... Eze 46:3 7676
days, her new moons, and her *s* ... Hos 2:11 7676

SABEANS (*sab-e'-uns*)
1. Descendants of Sheba.
the *S* fell upon them, and took ... Job 1:15 7614
and they shall sell them to the *S* ... Joel 3:8 7615
2. Descendants of Seba.
of Ethiopia and of the *S*, men of ... Is 45:14 5436
brought *S* from the wilderness ... Eze 23:42 5433

SABTA (*sab'-tah*) See SABTAH. *A son of Cush.*
Seba, and Havilah, and *S* ... 1Chr 1:9 5454

SABTAH (*sab'-tah*) See SABTA. *Same as Sabta.*
Seba, and Havilah, and *S* ... Gen 10:7 5454

SABTECA See SABTECHAH.

SABTECHA (*sab'-te-kah*) See SABTECHAH. *A son of Cush.*
and Sabta, and Raamah, and *S* ... 1Chr 1:9 5455

SABTECHAH (*sab'-te-kah*) See SABTECHA.
Same as Sabtecha.
and Sabtah, and Raamah, and *S* Gen 10:7 5455

SACAR (*sa'-kar*) See SHARAR.
1. Father of Ahiham.
Ahiam the son of *S* the Hararite 1Chr 11:35 7940
2. A sanctuary servant.
S the fourth, and Nethaneel the 1Chr 26:4 7940

SACHIA See SHACHIA.

SACK
every man's money into his *s* Gen 42:25 8242
as one of them opened his *s* to Gen 42:27 8242
and, lo, it is even in my *s* Gen 42:28 572
bundle of money was in his *s* Gen 42:35 8242
money was in the mouth of his *s* Gen 43:21 572
every man his *s* to the ground Gen 44:11 572
and opened every man his *s* Gen 44:11 572
the cup was found in Benjamin's *s* Gen 44:12 572
wood, or raiment, or skin, or *s* Lev 11:32 8242

SACKBUT
of the cornet, flute, harp, *s* Dan 3:5 5443
of the cornet, flute, harp, *s* Dan 3:7 5443
of the cornet, flute, harp, *s* Dan 3:10 5443
of the cornet, flute, harp, *s* Dan 3:15 5443

SACKCLOTH
put *s* upon his loins, and mourned Gen 37:34 8242
your clothes, and gird you with *s* 2Sa 3:31 8242
the daughter of Aiah took *s* 2Sa 21:10 8242
put *s* on our loins, and ropes upon 1Kin 20:31 8242
So they girded *s* on their loins 1Kin 20:32 8242
put *s* upon his flesh, and fasted, 1Kin 21:27 8242
his flesh, and fasted, and lay in *s* 1Kin 21:27 8242
he had *s* within upon his flesh 2Kin 6:30 8242
and covered himself with *s* 2Kin 19:1 8242
of the priests, covered with *s* 2Kin 19:2 8242
of Israel, who were clothed in *s* 1Chr 21:16 8242
put on *s* with ashes, and went out Est 4:1 8242
the king's gate clothed with *s* Est 4:2 8242
and many lay in *s* and ashes Est 4:3 8242
and to take away his *s* from him Est 4:4 8242
I have sewed *s* upon my skin Job 16:15 8242
thou hast put off my *s*, and girded Ps 30:11 8242
they were sick, my clothing was *s* Ps 35:13 8242
I made *s* also my garment Ps 69:11 8242
of a stomacher a girding of *s* Is 3:24 8242
they shall gird themselves with *s* Is 15:3 8242
loose the *s* from off thy loins, Is 20:2 8242
to baldness, and to girding with *s* Is 22:12 8242
bare, and gird *s* upon your loins Is 32:11
and covered himself with *s* Is 37:1 8242
of the priests covered with *s* Is 37:2 8242
and I make *s* their covering Is 50:3 8242
head as a bulrush, and to spread *s* Is 58:5 8242
For this gird you with *s*, lament Jer 4:8 8242
of my people, gird thee with *s* Jer 6:26 8242
be cuttings, and upon the loins *s* Jer 48:37 8242
of Rabbah, gird you with *s* Jer 49:3 8242
have girded themselves with *s* Lam 2:10 8242
shall also gird themselves with *s* Eze 7:18 8242
for thee, and gird them with *s* Eze 27:31 8242
supplications, with fasting, and *s* Dan 9:3 8242
like a virgin girded with *s* for Joel 1:8 8242
come, lie all night in *s*, ye Joel 1:13 8242
I will bring up *s* upon all loins Amos 8:10 8242
and proclaimed a fast, and put on *s* Jonah 3:5 8242
from him, and covered him with *s* Jonah 3:6 8242
man and beast be covered with *s* Jonah 3:8 8242
would have repented long ago in *s* Mt 11:21 4526
while ago repented, sitting in *s* Lk 10:13 4526
the sun became black as *s* of hair Rev 6:12 4526
and threescore days, clothed in *s* Rev 11:3 4526

SACKCLOTHES
assembled with fasting, and with *s* Neh 9:1 8242

SACK'S
behold, it was in his *s* mouth Gen 42:27 572
every man's money in his *s* mouth Gen 44:1 572
in the *s* mouth of the youngest, Gen 44:2 572

SACKS
to fill their *s* with corn Gen 42:25 3672
to pass as they emptied their *s* Gen 42:35 8242
again in the mouth of your *s* Gen 43:12 572
in our *s* at the first time are we Gen 43:18 572
to the inn, that we opened our *s* Gen 43:21 572
tell who put our money in our *s* Gen 43:22 572
hath given you treasure in your *s* Gen 43:23 572
Fill the men's *s* with food Gen 44:1 572
took old *s* upon their asses, and Josh 9:4 8242

SACKS'
which we found in our *s* mouths Gen 44:8 572

SACRIFICE
Jacob offered *s* upon the mount Gen 31:54 2077
that we may *s* to the LORD our God Ex 3:18 2076
and *s* unto the LORD our God Ex 5:3 2076
saying, Let us go and *s* to our God Ex 5:8 2076
Let us go and do *s* to the LORD Ex 5:17 2076
that they may do *s* unto the LORD Ex 8:8 2076
s to your God in the land Ex 8:25 2076
for we shall *s* the abomination of Ex 8:26 2076
shall we *s* the abomination of the Ex 8:26 2076
s to the LORD our God, as he Ex 8:27 2076
that ye may *s* to the LORD your Ex 8:28 2076
the people go to *s* to the LORD Ex 8:29 2076
that we may *s* unto the LORD our Ex 10:25 2077
It is the *s* of the LORD's Ex 12:27 2077
therefore I *s* to the LORD all Ex 13:15 2076
shalt *s* thereon thy burnt Ex 20:24 2076
blood of my *s* with leavened bread Ex 23:18 2077
of my *s* remain until the morning Ex 23:18 2282
of the *s* of their peace offerings Ex 29:28 2077
incense thereon, nor burnt *s* Ex 30:9
do *s* unto their gods, and one call Ex 34:15 2076
call thee, and thou eat of his *s* Ex 34:15 2077
the blood of my *s* with leaven Ex 34:25 2077
neither shall the *s* of the feast Ex 34:25 2077
offering be a burnt *s* of the herd Lev 1:3
all on the altar, to be a burnt *s* Lev 1:9
or of the goats, for a burnt *s* Lev 1:10
it is a burnt *s*, an offering made Lev 1:13
if the burnt *s* for his offering Lev 1:14
it is a burnt *s*, an offering made Lev 1:17
oblation be a *s* of peace offering Lev 3:1 2077
he shall offer of the *s* of the Lev 3:3 2077
it on the altar upon the burnt *s* Lev 3:5
if his offering for a *s* of peace Lev 3:6 2077
he shall offer of the *s* of the Lev 3:9 2077
of the *s* of peace offerings Lev 4:10 2077
as the fat of the *s* of peace Lev 4:26 2077
from off the *s* of peace offerings Lev 4:31 2077
from the *s* of the peace offerings Lev 4:35 2077
law of the *s* of peace offerings Lev 7:11 2077
the *s* of thanksgiving unleavened Lev 7:12 2077
leavened bread with the *s* of Lev 7:13 2077
the flesh of the *s* of his peace Lev 7:15 2077
But if the *s* of his offering be a Lev 7:16 2077
same day that he offereth his *s* Lev 7:16 2077
remainder of the flesh of the *s* Lev 7:17 2077
if any of the flesh of the *s* of Lev 7:18 2077
flesh of the *s* of peace offerings Lev 7:20 2077
flesh of the *s* of peace offerings Lev 7:21 2077
He that offereth the *s* of his Lev 7:29 2077
of the *s* of his peace offerings Lev 7:29 2077
of the *s* of the peace offerings Lev 7:37 2077
it was a burnt *s* for a sweet Lev 8:21
offerings, to *s* before the LORD Lev 9:4 2076
beside the burnt *s* of the morning Lev 9:17
and the ram for a *s* of peace Lev 9:18 2077
offereth a burnt offering or *s* Lev 17:8 2077
And if ye offer a *s* of peace Lev 19:5 2077
whosoever offereth a *s* of peace Lev 22:21 2077
when ye will offer a *s* of Lev 22:29 2077
Then ye shall *s* one kid of the Lev 23:19 6213
year for a *s* of peace offerings Lev 23:19 2077
offering, and a meat offering, a *s* Lev 23:37 2077
do not offer a *s* unto the LORD Lev 27:11 7133
a *s* of peace offerings unto the Num 6:17 2077
the *s* of the peace offerings Num 6:18 2077
for a *s* of peace offerings, two Num 7:17 2077
for a *s* of peace offerings, two Num 7:23 2077
for a *s* of peace offerings, two Num 7:29 2077
for a *s* of peace offerings, two Num 7:35 2077
for a *s* of peace offerings, two Num 7:41 2077
for a *s* of peace offerings, two Num 7:47 2077
for a *s* of peace offerings, two Num 7:53 2077
for a *s* of peace offerings, two Num 7:59 2077
for a *s* of peace offerings, two Num 7:65 2077
for a *s* of peace offerings, two Num 7:71 2077
for a *s* of peace offerings, two Num 7:77 2077
for a *s* of peace offerings, two Num 7:83 2077
all the oxen for the *s* of the Num 7:88 2077
or a *s* in performing a vow, or in Num 15:3 2077
with the burnt offering or *s* Num 15:5 2077
or for a *s* in performing a vow, Num 15:8 2077
a *s* made by fire unto the LORD, Num 15:25
and, lo, he stood by his burnt *s* Num 23:6
a *s* made by fire unto the LORD Num 28:6
a *s* made by fire, of a sweet Num 28:8
a *s* made by fire unto the LORD Num 28:13
But ye shall offer a *s* made by Num 28:19
the meat of the *s* made by fire Num 28:24
a *s* made by fire unto the LORD Num 29:6
a *s* made by fire, of a sweet Num 29:13
a *s* made by fire, of a sweet Num 29:36
thou shalt not *s* it unto the LORD Deut 15:21 2076
Thou shalt therefore *s* the Deut 16:2 2076
Thou mayest not *s* the passover Deut 16:5 2076
there thou shalt *s* the passover Deut 16:6 2076
Thou shalt not *s* unto the LORD Deut 17:1 2076
people, from them that offer a *s* Deut 18:3 2077
whole burnt *s* upon thine altar Deut 33:10
not for burnt offering, nor for *s* Josh 22:26 2077
offer a burnt *s* with the wood of Judg 6:26
a great *s* unto Dagon their god Judg 16:23 2077
to *s* unto the LORD of hosts in 1Sa 1:3 2076
offer unto the LORD the yearly *s* 1Sa 1:21 2077
was, that, when any man offered *s* 1Sa 2:13 2077
her husband to offer the yearly *s* 1Sa 2:19 2077
Wherefore kick ye at my *s* 1Sa 2:29 2077
with *s* nor offering for ever 1Sa 3:14 2077
for there is a *s* of the people to 1Sa 9:12 2077
come, because he doth bless the *s* 1Sa 9:13 2077
and to *s* sacrifices of peace 1Sa 10:8 2076
to *s* unto the LORD thy God 1Sa 15:15 2076
to *s* unto the LORD thy God in 1Sa 15:21 2076
Behold, to obey is better than *s* 1Sa 15:22 2077
say, I am come to *s* to the LORD 1Sa 16:2 2076
And call Jesse to the *s*, and I will 1Sa 16:3 2077
I am come to *s* unto the LORD 1Sa 16:5 2076
and come with me to the *s* 1Sa 16:5 2077
his sons, and called them to the *s* 1Sa 16:5 2077
for there is a yearly *s* there for 1Sa 20:6 2077
our family hath a *s* in the city 1Sa 20:29 2077
behold, here be oxen for burnt *s* 2Sa 24:22
king went to Gibeon to *s* there 1Kin 3:4 2076
offered *s* before the LORD 1Kin 8:62 2077
Solomon offered a *s* of peace 1Kin 8:63 2077
If this people go up to do *s* in 1Kin 12:27 2077
of the offering of the evening *s* 1Kin 18:29 4503
water, and pour it on the burnt *s* 1Kin 18:33
of the offering of the evening *s* 1Kin 18:36 4503
fell, and consumed the burnt *s* 1Kin 18:38
offering nor *s* unto other gods 2Kin 5:17 2077
I have a great *s* to do to Baal 2Kin 10:19 2077
as yet the people did *s* and burnt 2Kin 14:4 2076
offering, and the king's burnt *s* 2Kin 16:15
and all the blood of the *s* 2Kin 16:15 2077
nor serve them, nor *s* to them 2Kin 17:35 2076
worship, and to him shall ye do *s* 2Kin 17:36 2076
save only to burn *s* before him 2Chr 2:6
Solomon offered a *s* of twenty 2Chr 7:5 2077
place to myself for an house of *s* 2Chr 7:12 2077
to *s* unto the LORD God of their 2Chr 11:16 2076
them, therefore will I *s* to them 2Chr 28:23 2076
did *s* still in the high places 2Chr 33:17 2076
we do *s* unto him since the days Ezr 4:2 2076
sat astonied until the evening *s* Ezr 9:4 4503
at the evening *s* I arose up from Ezr 9:5 4503
will they *s* Neh 4:2 2076
offerings, and accept thy burnt *s* Ps 20:3
S and offering thou didst not Ps 40:6 2077
have made a covenant with me by *s* Ps 50:5 2077
For thou desirest not *s* Ps 51:16 2077
I will freely *s* unto thee Ps 54:6 2076
let them *s* the sacrifices of Ps 107:22 2076
to thee the *s* of thanksgiving Ps 116:17 2077
bind the *s* with cords, even unto Ps 118:27 2282
up of my hands as the evening *s* Ps 141:2 4503
The *s* of the wicked is an Prov 15:8 2077
acceptable to the LORD than *s* Prov 21:3 2077
The *s* of the wicked is Prov 21:27 2077
hear, than to give the *s* of fools Eccl 5:1 2077
LORD in that day, and shall do *s* Is 19:21 2077
for the LORD hath a *s* in Bozrah Is 34:6 2077
wentest thou up to offer *s* Is 57:7 2077
of them that shall bring the *s* of Jer 33:11
offerings, and to do *s* continually Jer 33:18 2077
a *s* in the north country by the Jer 46:10 2077
every side to my *s* Eze 39:17 2077
that I do *s* for you Eze 39:17 2076
even a great *s* upon the mountains Eze 39:17 2077
of my *s* which I have sacrificed Eze 39:19 2076
slew the burnt offering and the *s* Eze 40:42 2077
the *s* for the people, and they Eze 44:11 2077
shall boil the *s* of the people Eze 46:24 2077
by him the daily *s* was taken away Dan 8:11
s by reason of transgression Dan 8:12
the vision concerning the daily *s* Dan 8:13
of the week he shall cause the *s* Dan 9:27 2077
and shall take away the daily *s* Dan 11:31
the daily *s* shall be taken away Dan 12:11
without a prince, and without a *s* Hos 3:4 2077
They *s* upon the tops of the Hos 4:13 2076
whores, and they *s* with harlots Hos 4:14 2076
For I desired mercy, and not *s* Hos 6:6 2077
They *s* flesh for the sacrifices Hos 8:13 2076
they *s* bullocks in Gilgal Hos 12:11 2076
the men that *s* kiss the calves Hos 13:2 2076
offer a *s* of thanksgiving with Amos 4:5
offered a *s* unto the LORD, and Jonah 1:16 2077
But I will *s* unto thee with the Jonah 2:9 2076
Therefore they *s* unto their net Hab 1:16 2076
for the LORD hath prepared a *s* Zeph 1:7 2077
pass in the day of the LORD's *s* Zeph 1:8 2077
and all they that *s* shall come Zec 14:21 2076
And if ye offer the blind for *s* Mal 1:8 2076
I will have mercy, and not *s* Mt 9:13 2378
I will have mercy, and not *s* Mt 12:7 2378
every *s* shall be salted with salt Mk 9:49 2378
to offer a *s* according to that Lk 2:24 2378
offered *s* unto the idol, and Acts 7:41 2378
would have done *s* with the people Acts 14:13 2380
they had not done *s* unto them Acts 14:18 2380
ye present your bodies a living *s* Rom 12:1 2378
that are offered in *s* unto idols 1Cor 8:4 1494
in *s* to idols is any thing 1Cor 10:19 1494
the things which the Gentiles *s* 1Cor 10:20 2380
they *s* to devils, and not to God 1Cor 10:20 2380
This is offered in *s* unto idols 1Cor 10:28 1494
a *s* to God for a sweetsmelling Eph 5:2 2378
and if I be offered upon the *s* Phil 2:17 2378
a *s* acceptable, wellpleasing to Phil 4:18 2378
those high priests, to offer up *s* Heb 7:27 2378
put away sin by the *s* of himself Heb 9:26 2378
into the world, he saith, *S* Heb 10:5 2378
Above when he said, *S* and offering Heb 10:8 2378
offered one *s* for sins for ever Heb 10:12 2378
remaineth no more *s* for sins Heb 10:26 2378
God a more excellent *s* than Cain Heb 11:4 2378
s of praise to God continually Heb 13:15 2378

SACRIFICED
s peace offerings of oxen unto Ex 24:5 2076
have *s* thereunto, and said, These Ex 32:8 2076
They *s* unto devils, not to God Deut 32:17 2076
the LORD, and *s* peace offerings Josh 8:31 2076
they *s* there unto the LORD Judg 2:5 2076
came, and said to the man that *s* 1Sa 2:15 2076
s sacrifices the same day unto 1Sa 6:15 2076
there they *s* sacrifices of peace 1Sa 11:15 2076
six paces, he *s* oxen and fatlings 2Sa 6:13 2076
Only the people *s* in high places 1Kin 3:2 2076
only he *s* and burnt incense in 1Kin 3:3 2076
incense and *s* unto their gods 1Kin 11:8 2076
the people still *s* and burnt 2Kin 12:3 2076
the people *s* and burnt incense 2Kin 15:4 2076
the people *s* and burned incense 2Kin 15:35 2076
And he *s* and burnt incense in the 2Kin 16:4 2076
which *s* for them in the houses of 2Kin 17:32 6213
the Jebusite, then he *s* there 1Chr 21:28 2076
they *s* sacrifices unto the LORD, 1Chr 29:21 2076
s sheep and oxen, which could not 2Chr 5:6 2076
He *s* also and burnt incense in the 2Chr 28:4 2076
For he *s* unto the gods of 2Chr 28:23 2076
s thereon peace offerings and 2Chr 33:16 2076
for Amon *s* unto all the carved 2Chr 33:22 2076
of them that had *s* unto them 2Chr 34:4 2076
they *s* their sons and their Ps 106:37 2076
whom they *s* unto the idols of Ps 106:38 2076

S

these hast thou s unto them to be ... Eze 16:20 2076
sacrifice which I have s for you ... Eze 39:19 2076
they s unto Baalim, and burned ... Hos 11:2 2076
Christ our passover is s for us ... 1Cor 5:7 2380
to eat things s unto idols ... Rev 2:14 1494
and to eat things s unto idols ... Rev 2:20 1494

SACRIFICEDST
which thou s the first day at ... Deut 16:4 2076

SACRIFICES
offered s unto the God of his ... Gen 46:1 2077
said, Thou must give us also s ... Ex 10:25 2077
a burnt offering and s for God ... Ex 18:12 2077
of the s of your peace offerings ... Lev 7:32 2077
the s of their peace offerings ... Lev 7:34 2077
of the s of the LORD made by fire ... Lev 10:13
the s of peace offerings of the ... Lev 10:14 2077
of Israel may bring their s ... Lev 17:5 2077
no more offer their s unto devils ... Lev 17:7 2077
and over the s of your peace ... Num 10:10 2077
people unto the s of their gods ... Num 25:2 2077
and my bread for my s made by fire ... Num 28:2
your burnt offerings, and your s ... Deut 12:6 2077
your burnt offerings, and your s ... Deut 12:11 2077
the blood of thy s shall be ... Deut 12:27 2077
Which did eat the fat of their s ... Deut 32:38 2077
shall offer s of righteousness ... Deut 33:19 2077
the s of the LORD God of Israel ... Josh 13:14
burnt offerings, and with our s ... Josh 22:27 2077
for burnt offerings, nor for s ... Josh 22:28 2077
for meat offerings, or for s ... Josh 22:29 2077
sacrificed s the same day unto ... 1Sa 6:15 2077
to sacrifice s of peace offerings ... 1Sa 10:8 2077
there they sacrificed s of peace ... 1Sa 11:15 2077
delight in burnt offerings and s ... 1Sa 15:22 2077
from Giloh, while he offered s ... 2Sa 15:12 2077
And when they went in to offer s ... 2Kin 10:24 2077
and they offered burnt s and peace ... 1Chr 16:1
to offer all burnt s unto the ... 1Chr 23:31
they sacrificed s unto the LORD ... 1Chr 29:21 2077
s in abundance for all Israel ... 1Chr 29:21 2077
the burnt offering and the s ... 2Chr 7:1 2077
people offered s before the LORD ... 2Chr 7:4 2077
morning and every evening burnt s ... 2Chr 13:11
the LORD, come near and bring s ... 2Chr 29:31 2077
And the congregation brought in s ... 2Chr 29:31 2077
the place where they offered s ... Ezr 6:3 1685
That they may offer s of sweet ... Ezr 6:10
that day they offered great s ... Neh 12:43 2077
Offer the s of righteousness, and ... Ps 4:5 2077
offer in his tabernacle s of joy ... Ps 27:6 2077
for thy s or thy burnt offerings ... Ps 50:8 2077
The s of God are a broken spirit ... Ps 51:17 2077
with the s of righteousness ... Ps 51:19 2077
unto thee burnt s of fatlings ... Ps 66:15
and ate the s of the dead ... Ps 106:28 2077
sacrifice the s of thanksgiving ... Ps 107:22 2077
an house full of s with strife ... Prov 17:1 2077
the multitude of your s unto me ... Is 1:11 2077
let them kill s ... Is 29:1 2282
hast thou honoured me with thy s ... Is 43:23 2077
filled me with the fat of thy s ... Is 43:24 2077
their s shall be accepted upon ... Is 56:7 2077
nor your s sweet unto me ... Jer 6:20 2077
your burnt offerings unto your s ... Jer 7:21 2077
concerning burnt offerings or s ... Jer 7:22 2077
bringing burnt offerings, and s ... Jer 17:26 2077
bringing s of praise, unto the ... Jer 17:26
and they offered there their s ... Eze 20:28 2077
whereupon they slew their s ... Eze 40:41
be ashamed because of their s ... Hos 4:19 2077
flesh for the s of mine offerings ... Hos 8:13 2077
their s shall be unto them as the ... Hos 9:4 2077
bring your s every morning, and ... Amos 4:4 2077
Have ye offered unto me s ... Amos 5:25 2077
all whole burnt offerings and s ... Mk 12:33 2378
Pilate had mingled with their s ... Lk 13:1 2378
s by the space of forty years in ... Acts 7:42 2378
of the s partakers of the altar ... 1Cor 10:18 2378
offer both gifts and s for sins ... Heb 5:1 2378
is ordained to offer gifts and s ... Heb 8:3 2378
were offered both gifts and s ... Heb 9:9 2378
with better s than these ... Heb 9:23 2378
can never with those s which they ... Heb 10:1 2378
But in those s there is a ... Heb 10:3
s for sin thou hast had no ... Heb 10:6
and offering oftentimes the same s ... Heb 10:11 2378
for with such s God is well ... Heb 13:16 2378
to offer up spiritual s, ... 1Pet 2:5 2378

SACRIFICETH
He that s unto any god, save unto ... Ex 22:20 2076
to him that s, and to him that ... Eccl 9:2 2076
s, and to him that s not ... Eccl 9:2 2076
that s in gardens, and burneth ... Is 65:3 2076
he that s a lamb, as if he cut ... Is 66:3 2076
s unto the Lord a corrupt thing ... Mal 1:14 2076

SACRIFICING
s sheep and oxen, that could not ... 1Kin 8:5 2076
s unto the calves that he had ... 1Kin 12:32 2076

SACRILEGE
idols, dost thou commit s ... Rom 2:22 2416

SAD
them, and, behold, they were s ... Gen 40:6 2196
and her countenance was no more s ... 1Sa 1:18
unto him, Why is thy spirit so s ... 1Kin 21:5 5620
been beforetime s in his presence ... Neh 2:1 7451
unto me, Why is thy countenance s ... Neh 2:2 7451
should not my countenance be s ... Neh 2:3 7489
made the heart of the righteous s ... Eze 13:22 3512
s, whom I have not made s ... Eze 13:22 3510
hypocrites, of a s countenance ... Mt 6:16 4659
he was s at that saying, and went ... Mk 10:22 4768
to another, as ye walk, and are s ... Lk 24:17 4659

SADDLE
what s soever he rideth upon that ... Lev 15:9 4817
I will s me an ass, that I may ... 2Sa 19:26 2280
said unto his sons, S me the ass ... 1Kin 13:13 2280
to his sons, saying, S me the ass ... 1Kin 13:27 2280

SADDLED
s his ass, and took two of his ... Gen 22:3 2280
s his ass, and went with the ... Num 22:21 2280
there were with him two asses s ... Judg 19:10 2280
met him, with a couple of asses s ... 2Sa 16:1 2280
he s his ass, and arose, and gat ... 2Sa 17:23 2280
s his ass, and went to Gath to ... 1Kin 2:40 2280
So they s him the ass ... 1Kin 13:13 2280
that he s for him the ass, to wit ... 1Kin 13:23 2280
And they s him ... 1Kin 13:27 2280
Then she s an ass, and said to her ... 2Kin 4:24 2280

SADDUCEES (*sad'-du-sees*) *Members of a Jewish sect.*
S come to his baptism, he said ... Mt 3:7 4523
Pharisees also with the S came ... Mt 16:1 4523
of the Pharisees and of the S ... Mt 16:6 4523
of the Pharisees and of the S ... Mt 16:11 4523
of the Pharisees and of the S ... Mt 16:12 4523
The same day came to him the S ... Mt 22:23 4523
that he had put the S to silence ... Mt 22:34 4523
Then come unto him the S, which ... Mk 12:18 4523
Then came to him certain of the S ... Lk 20:27 4523
captain of the temple, and the S ... Acts 4:1 4523
him, (which is the sect of the S ... Acts 5:17 4523
that the one part were S, and the ... Acts 23:6 4523
between the Pharisees and the S ... Acts 23:7 4523
For the S say that there is no ... Acts 23:8 4523

SADLY
Wherefore look ye so s to day ... Gen 40:7 7451

SADNESS
for by the s of the countenance ... Eccl 7:3 7455

SADOC (*sa'-dok*) *Father of Achim; an ancestor of Jesus.*
And Azor begat S ... Mt 1:14 4524
and S begat Achim ... Mt 1:14

SAFE
on every side, and ye dwelled s ... 1Sa 12:11 983
said, Is the young man Absalom s ... 2Sa 18:29 7965
Cushi, Is the young man Absalom s ... 2Sa 18:32 7965
Their houses are s from fear ... Job 21:9 7965
Hold thou me up, and I shall be s ... Ps 119:117 3467
runneth into it, and is s ... Prov 18:10 7682
his trust in the LORD shall be s ... Prov 29:25 7682
prey, and shall carry it away s ... Is 5:29 6403
and they shall be s in their land ... Eze 34:27 983
because he hath received him s ... Lk 15:27 5198
bring him s unto Felix the ... Acts 23:24 1295
that they escaped all s to land ... Acts 27:44 1295
not grievous, but for you it is s ... Phil 3:1 809

SAFEGUARD
but with me thou shalt be in s ... 1Sa 22:23 4931

SAFELY
the full, and dwell in your land s ... Lev 26:5 983
And Judah and Israel dwelt s ... 1Kin 4:25 983
And he led them on s, so that they ... Ps 78:53 983
hearkeneth unto me shall dwell s ... Prov 1:33 983
Then shalt thou walk in thy way s ... Prov 3:23 983
her husband doth s trust in her ... Prov 31:11 983
He pursued them, and passed s ... Is 41:3 7965
be saved, and Israel shall dwell s ... Jer 23:6 983
and I will cause them to dwell s ... Jer 32:37 983
saved, and Jerusalem shall dwell s ... Jer 33:16 983
And they shall dwell s therein ... Eze 28:26 983
they shall dwell s in the ... Eze 34:25 983
but they shall dwell s, and none ... Eze 34:28 983
and they shall dwell s all of them ... Eze 38:8 983
that are at rest, that dwell s ... Eze 38:11 983
my people of Israel dwelleth s ... Eze 38:14 983
when they dwelt s in their land ... Eze 39:26 983
and will make them to lie down s ... Hos 2:18 983
Jerusalem shall be s inhabited ... Zec 14:11 983
take him, and lead him away s ... Mk 14:44 806
the jailer to keep them s ... Acts 16:23 806

SAFETY
ye shall dwell in the land in s ... Lev 25:18 983
your fill, and dwell therein in s ... Lev 25:19 983
about, so that ye dwell in s ... Deut 12:10 983
the LORD shall dwell in s by him ... Deut 33:12 983
then shall dwell in s alone ... Deut 33:28 983
I was not in s, neither had I ... Job 3:26 7951
His children are far from s ... Job 5:4 3468
which mourn may be exalted to s ... Job 5:11 3468
and thou shalt take thy rest in s ... Job 11:18 983
Though it be given him to be in s ... Job 24:23 983
LORD, only makest me dwell in s ... Ps 4:8 983
I will set him in s from him that ... Ps 12:5 3468
An horse is a vain thing for s ... Ps 33:17 8668
of counsellors there is s ... Prov 11:14 8668
but s is of the LORD ... Prov 21:31 8668
of counsellors there is s ... Prov 24:6 8668
and the needy shall lie down in s ... Is 14:30 983
truly found we shut with all s ... Acts 5:23 803
when they shall say, Peace and s ... 1Th 5:3 803

SAFFRON
Spikenard and s ... Song 4:14 3750

SAID
And God s, Let there be light ... Gen 1:3 559
And God s, Let there be a ... Gen 1:6 559
And God s, Let the waters under ... Gen 1:9 559
And God s, Let the earth bring ... Gen 1:11 559
And God s, Let there be lights in ... Gen 1:14 559
And God s, Let the waters bring ... Gen 1:20 559
And God s, Let the earth bring ... Gen 1:24 559
And God s, Let us make man in our ... Gen 1:26 559
God s unto them, Be fruitful, and ... Gen 1:28 559
And God s, Behold, I have given ... Gen 1:29 559
And the LORD God s, It is not good ... Gen 2:18 559
And Adam s, This is now bone of my ... Gen 2:23 559
he s unto the woman, Yea, hath ... Gen 3:1 559
unto the woman, Yea, hath God s ... Gen 3:1 559
the woman s unto the serpent, We ... Gen 3:2 559
midst of the garden, God hath s ... Gen 3:3 559
the serpent s unto the woman, Ye ... Gen 3:4 559
s unto him, Where art thou ... Gen 3:9 559
And he s, I heard thy voice in the ... Gen 3:10 559
And he s, Who told thee that thou ... Gen 3:11 559
And the man s, The woman ... Gen 3:12 559
the LORD God s unto the woman, ... Gen 3:13 559
And the woman s, The serpent ... Gen 3:13 559
the LORD God s unto the serpent, ... Gen 3:14 559
Unto the woman he s, I will ... Gen 3:16 559
And unto Adam he s, Because thou ... Gen 3:17 559
And the LORD God s, Behold, the ... Gen 3:22 559
she conceived, and bare Cain, and s ... Gen 4:1 559
the LORD s unto Cain, Why art ... Gen 4:6 559
the LORD s unto Cain, Where is ... Gen 4:9 559
And he s, I know not ... Gen 4:9 559
And he s, What hast thou done ... Gen 4:10 559
And Cain s unto the LORD, My ... Gen 4:13 559
And the LORD s unto him, Therefore ... Gen 4:15 559
Lamech s unto his wives, Adah and ... Gen 4:23 559
s she, hath appointed me another ... Gen 4:25
And the LORD s, My spirit shall ... Gen 6:3 559
And the LORD s, I will destroy man ... Gen 6:7 559
God s unto Noah, The end of all ... Gen 6:13 559
the LORD s unto Noah, Come thou ... Gen 7:1 559
the LORD s in his heart, I will ... Gen 8:21 559
s unto them, Be fruitful, and ... Gen 9:1 559
And God s, This is the token of ... Gen 9:12 559
God s unto Noah, This is the ... Gen 9:17 559
And he s, Cursed be Canaan ... Gen 9:25 559
And he s, Blessed be the LORD God ... Gen 9:26 559
wherefore it is s, Even as Nimrod ... Gen 10:9 559
they s one to another, Go to, let ... Gen 11:3 559
And they s, Go to, let us build us ... Gen 11:4 559
And the LORD s, Behold, the people ... Gen 11:6 559
Now the LORD had s unto Abram ... Gen 12:1 559
LORD appeared unto Abram, and s ... Gen 12:7 559
that he s unto Sarai his wife, ... Gen 12:11 559
And Pharaoh called Abram, and s ... Gen 12:18 559
Abram s unto Lot, Let there be no ... Gen 13:8 559
the LORD s unto Abram, after that ... Gen 13:14 559
And he blessed him, and s, Blessed ... Gen 14:19 559
And the king of Sodom s unto Abram ... Gen 14:21 559
Abram s to the king of Sodom, I ... Gen 14:22 559
And Abram s, Lord GOD, what wilt ... Gen 15:2 559
And Abram s, Behold, to me thou ... Gen 15:3 559
he brought him forth abroad, and s ... Gen 15:5 559
he s unto him, So shall thy seed ... Gen 15:5 559
he s unto him, I am the LORD that ... Gen 15:7 559
And he s, Lord GOD, whereby shall ... Gen 15:8 559
he s unto him, Take me an heifer ... Gen 15:9 559
he s unto Abram, Know of a surety ... Gen 15:13 559
Sarai s unto Abram, Behold now, ... Gen 16:2 559
Sarai s unto Abram, My wrong be ... Gen 16:5 559
But Abram s unto Sarai, Behold, ... Gen 16:6 559
And he s, Hagar, Sarai's maid, ... Gen 16:8 559
And she s, I flee from the face of ... Gen 16:8 559
the angel of the LORD s unto her ... Gen 16:9 559
the angel of the LORD s unto her ... Gen 16:10 559
the angel of the LORD s unto her ... Gen 16:11 559
for she s, Have I also here ... Gen 16:13 559
s unto him, I am the Almighty God ... Gen 17:1 559
God s unto Abraham, Thou shalt ... Gen 17:9 559
God s unto Abraham, As for Sarai ... Gen 17:15 559
s in his heart, Shall a child be ... Gen 17:17 559
Abraham s unto God, O that ... Gen 17:18 559
And God s, Sarah thy wife shall ... Gen 17:19 559
day, as God had s unto him ... Gen 17:23 1696
And s, My Lord, if now I have ... Gen 18:3 559
And they s, So do, as thou hast ... Gen 18:5 1696
So do, as thou hast s ... Gen 18:5 559
into the tent unto Sarah, and s ... Gen 18:6 559
they s unto him, Where is Sarah ... Gen 18:9 559
And he s, Behold, in the tent ... Gen 18:9 559
And he s, I will certainly return ... Gen 18:10 559
And the LORD s unto Abraham, ... Gen 18:13 559
And he s, Nay ... Gen 18:15 559
And the LORD s, Shall I hide from ... Gen 18:17 559
And the LORD s, Because the cry of ... Gen 18:20 559
And Abraham drew near, and s ... Gen 18:23 559
And the LORD s, If I find in Sodom ... Gen 18:26 559
And Abraham answered and s, Behold ... Gen 18:27 559
And he s, If I find there forty and ... Gen 18:28 559
he spake unto him yet again, and s ... Gen 18:29 559
And he s, I will not do it for ... Gen 18:29 559
he s unto him, Oh let not the ... Gen 18:30 559
And he s, I will not do it, if I ... Gen 18:30 559
And he s, Behold now, I have taken ... Gen 18:31 559
And he s, I will not destroy it ... Gen 18:31 559
And he s, Oh let not the Lord be ... Gen 18:32 559
And he s, I will not destroy it ... Gen 18:32 559
And he s, Behold now, my lords, ... Gen 19:2 559
And they s, Nay ... Gen 19:2 559
s unto him, Where are the men ... Gen 19:5 559
And s, I pray you, brethren, do ... Gen 19:7 559
And they s, Stand back ... Gen 19:9 559
they s again, This one fellow ... Gen 19:9 559
the men s unto Lot, Hast thou ... Gen 19:12 559
which married his daughters, and s ... Gen 19:14 559
them forth abroad, that he s ... Gen 19:17 559
Lot s unto them, Oh, not so, my ... Gen 19:18 559
he s unto him, See, I have ... Gen 19:21 559
the firstborn s unto the younger, ... Gen 19:31 559
the firstborn s unto the younger ... Gen 19:34 559
Abraham s of Sarah his wife, She ... Gen 20:2 559

s to him, Behold, thou art but a ... Gen 20:3 559
and he *s*, Lord, wilt thou slay ... Gen 20:4 559
S he not unto me, She is my ... Gen 20:5 559
and she, even she herself *s* ... Gen 20:5 559
God *s* unto him in a dream, Yea, I ... Gen 20:6 559
s unto him, What hast thou done ... Gen 20:9 559
Abimelech *s* unto Abraham, What ... Gen 20:10 559
And Abraham *s*, Because I thought, ... Gen 20:11 559
that I *s* unto her, This is thy ... Gen 20:13 559
And Abimelech *s*, Behold, my land ... Gen 20:15 559
And unto Sarah he *s*, Behold, I ... Gen 20:16 559
LORD visited Sarah as he had *s* ... Gen 21:1 559
And Sarah *s*, God hath made me to ... Gen 21:6 559
And she *s*, Who would have ... Gen 21:7 559
Who would have *s* unto Abraham ... Gen 21:7 4448
Wherefore she *s* unto Abraham ... Gen 21:10 559
God *s* unto Abraham, Let it not be ... Gen 21:12 559
all that Sarah hath *s* unto thee ... Gen 21:12 559
for she *s*, Let me not see the ... Gen 21:16 559
s unto her, What aileth thee, ... Gen 21:17 559
And Abraham *s*, I will swear ... Gen 21:24 559
And Abimelech *s*, I wot not who ... Gen 21:26 559
Abimelech *s* unto Abraham, What ... Gen 21:29 559
And he *s*, For these seven ewe ... Gen 21:30 559
Abraham, and *s* unto him, Abraham ... Gen 22:1 559
and he *s*, Behold, here I am ... Gen 22:1 559
And he *s*, Take now thy son, thine ... Gen 22:2 559
Abraham *s* unto his young men, ... Gen 22:5 559
unto Abraham his father, and *s* ... Gen 22:7 559
and he *s*, Here am I, my son ... Gen 22:7 559
And he *s*, Behold the fire and the ... Gen 22:7 559
And Abraham *s*, My son, God will ... Gen 22:8 559
unto him out of heaven, and *s* ... Gen 22:11 559
and he *s*, Here am I ... Gen 22:11 559
And he *s*, Lay not thine hand upon ... Gen 22:12 559
as it is *s* to this day, In the ... Gen 22:14 559
And *s*, By myself have I sworn, ... Gen 22:16 559
Abraham *s* unto his eldest servant ... Gen 24:2 559
And the servant *s* unto him ... Gen 24:5 559
Abraham *s* unto him, Beware thou ... Gen 24:6 559
And he *s*, O LORD God of my master ... Gen 24:12 559
the servant ran to meet her, and *s* ... Gen 24:17 559
And she *s*, Drink, my lord ... Gen 24:18 559
had done giving him drink, she *s* ... Gen 24:19 559
And *s*, Whose daughter art thou ... Gen 24:23 559
she *s* unto him, I am the daughter ... Gen 24:24 559
She *s* moreover unto him, We have ... Gen 24:25 559
And he *s*, Blessed be the LORD God ... Gen 24:27 559
And he *s*, Come in, thou blessed of ... Gen 24:31 559
but he *s*, I will not eat, until I ... Gen 24:33 559
And he *s*, Speak on ... Gen 24:33 559
And he *s*, I am Abraham's servant ... Gen 24:34 559
I *s* unto my master, Peradventure ... Gen 24:39 559
he *s* unto me, The LORD, before ... Gen 24:40 559
came this day unto the well, and *s* ... Gen 24:42 559
I *s* unto her, Let me drink, I ... Gen 24:45 559
pitcher from her shoulder, and *s* ... Gen 24:46 559
And I asked her, and *s*, Whose ... Gen 24:47 559
And she *s*, The daughter of Bethuel ... Gen 24:47 559
Laban and Bethuel answered and *s* ... Gen 24:50 559
rose up in the morning, and he *s* ... Gen 24:54 559
And her brother and her mother *s* ... Gen 24:55 559
he *s* unto them, Hinder me not, ... Gen 24:56 559
And they *s*, We will call the ... Gen 24:57 559
s unto her, Wilt thou go with ... Gen 24:58 559
And she *s*, I will go ... Gen 24:58 559
s unto her, Thou art our sister, ... Gen 24:60 559
For she had *s* unto the servant, ... Gen 24:65 559
And the servant had *s*, It is my ... Gen 24:65 559
and she *s*, If it be so, why am I ... Gen 25:22 559
And the LORD *s* unto her, Two ... Gen 25:23 559
Esau *s* to Jacob, Feed me, I pray ... Gen 25:30 559
And Jacob *s*, Sell me this day thy ... Gen 25:31 559
And Esau *s*, Behold, I am at the ... Gen 25:32 559
And Jacob *s*, Swear to me this day ... Gen 25:33 559
the LORD appeared unto him, and *s* ... Gen 26:2 559
and he *s*, She is my sister ... Gen 26:7 559
s he, the men of the place should ... Gen 26:7 559
And Abimelech called Isaac, and *s* ... Gen 26:9 559
Isaac *s* unto him, Because I *s*, ... Gen 26:9 559
And Abimelech *s*, What is this thou ... Gen 26:10 559
Abimelech *s* unto Isaac, Go from ... Gen 26:16 559
and he *s*, For now the LORD hath ... Gen 26:22 559
unto him the same night, and *s* ... Gen 26:24 559
Isaac *s* unto them, Wherefore come ... Gen 26:27 559
And they *s*, We saw certainly that ... Gen 26:28 559
and we *s*, Let there be now an oath ... Gen 26:28 559
s unto him, We have found water ... Gen 26:32 559
eldest son, and *s* unto him, My son ... Gen 27:1 559
he *s* unto him, Behold, here am I ... Gen 27:1 559
And he *s*, Behold now, I am old, I ... Gen 27:2 559
Jacob *s* to Rebekah his mother, ... Gen 27:11 559
And his mother *s* unto him, Upon me ... Gen 27:13 559
And he came unto his father, and *s* ... Gen 27:18 559
and he *s*, Here am I ... Gen 27:18 559
Jacob *s* unto his father, I am ... Gen 27:19 559
Isaac *s* unto his son, How is it ... Gen 27:20 559
And he *s*, Because the LORD thy God ... Gen 27:20 559
Isaac *s* unto Jacob, Come near, I ... Gen 27:21 559
and he felt him, and *s*, The voice ... Gen 27:22 559
And he *s*, Art thou my very son ... Gen 27:24 559
And he *s*, I am ... Gen 27:24 559
And he *s*, Bring it near to me, and ... Gen 27:25 559
And his father Isaac *s* unto him ... Gen 27:26 559
his raiment, and blessed him, and *s* ... Gen 27:27 559
s unto his father, Let my father ... Gen 27:31 559
And Isaac his father *s* unto him ... Gen 27:32 559
And he *s*, I am thy son, thy ... Gen 27:32 559
trembled very exceedingly, and *s* ... Gen 27:33 559
s unto his father, Bless me, even ... Gen 27:34 559
And he *s*, Thy brother came with ... Gen 27:35 559
And he *s*, Is not he rightly named ... Gen 27:36 559
And he *s*, Hast thou not reserved a ... Gen 27:36 559
s unto Esau, Behold, I have made ... Gen 27:37 559
Esau *s* unto his father, Hast thou ... Gen 27:38 559
s unto him, Behold, thy dwelling ... Gen 27:39 559
Esau *s* in his heart, The days of ... Gen 27:41 559
s unto him, Behold, thy brother ... Gen 27:42 559
Rebekah *s* to Isaac, I am weary of ... Gen 27:46 559
s unto him, Thou shalt not take a ... Gen 28:1 559
the LORD stood above it, and *s* ... Gen 28:13 559
awaked out of his sleep, and he *s* ... Gen 28:16 559
And he was afraid, and *s*, How ... Gen 28:17 559
Jacob *s* unto them, My brethren, ... Gen 29:4 559
And they *s*, Of Haran are we ... Gen 29:4 559
he *s* unto them, Know ye Laban the ... Gen 29:5 559
And they *s*, We know him ... Gen 29:5 559
he *s* unto them, Is he well ... Gen 29:6 559
And they *s*, He is well ... Gen 29:6 559
And he *s*, Lo, it is yet high day, ... Gen 29:7 559
And they *s*, We cannot, until all ... Gen 29:8 559
Laban *s* to him, Surely thou art ... Gen 29:14 559
Laban *s* unto Jacob, Because thou ... Gen 29:15 559
and *s*, I will serve thee seven ... Gen 29:18 559
And Laban *s*, It is better that I ... Gen 29:19 559
Jacob *s* unto Laban, Give me my ... Gen 29:21 559
he *s* to Laban, What is this thou ... Gen 29:25 559
And Laban *s*, It must not be so ... Gen 29:26 559
for she *s*, Surely the LORD hath ... Gen 29:32 559
and *s*, Because the LORD hath heard ... Gen 29:33 559
and *s*, Now this time will my ... Gen 29:34 559
and she *s*, Now will I praise the ... Gen 29:35 559
s unto Jacob, Give me children, ... Gen 30:1 559
and he *s*, Am I in God's stead, who ... Gen 30:2 559
And she *s*, Behold my maid Bilhah, ... Gen 30:3 559
And Rachel *s*, God hath judged me, ... Gen 30:6 559
And Rachel *s*, With great ... Gen 30:8 559
And Leah *s*, A troop cometh ... Gen 30:11 559
And Leah *s*, Happy am I, for the ... Gen 30:13 559
Then Rachel *s* to Leah, Give me, I ... Gen 30:14 559
she *s* unto her, Is it a small ... Gen 30:15 559
And Rachel *s*, Therefore he shall ... Gen 30:15 559
Leah went out to meet him, and *s* ... Gen 30:16 559
And Leah *s*, God hath given me my ... Gen 30:18 559
And Leah *s*, God hath endued me ... Gen 30:20 559
and *s*, God hath taken away my ... Gen 30:23 559
and *s*, The LORD shall add to me ... Gen 30:24 559
Joseph, that Jacob *s* unto Laban ... Gen 30:25 559
Laban *s* unto him, I pray thee, if ... Gen 30:27 559
And he *s*, Appoint me thy wages, and ... Gen 30:28 559
he *s* unto him, Thou knowest how I ... Gen 30:29 559
And he *s*, What shall I give thee ... Gen 30:31 559
And Jacob *s*, Thou shalt not give ... Gen 30:31 559
And Laban *s*, Behold, I would it ... Gen 30:34 559
the LORD *s* unto Jacob, Return ... Gen 31:3 559
s unto them, I see your father's ... Gen 31:5 559
If he *s* thus, The speckled shall ... Gen 31:8 559
and if he *s* thus, The ringstraked ... Gen 31:8 559
And I *s*, Here am I ... Gen 31:11 559
And he *s*, Lift up now thine eyes, ... Gen 31:12 559
s unto him, Is there yet any ... Gen 31:14 559
whatsoever God hath *s* unto thee ... Gen 31:16 559
s unto him, Take heed that thou ... Gen 31:24 559
Laban *s* to Jacob, What hast thou ... Gen 31:26 559
s to Laban, Because I was afraid ... Gen 31:31 559
for I *s*, Peradventure thou ... Gen 31:31 559
she *s* to her father, Let it not ... Gen 31:35 559
s to Laban, What is my trespass ... Gen 31:36 559
s unto Jacob, These daughters are ... Gen 31:43 559
Jacob *s* unto his brethren, Gather ... Gen 31:46 559
And Laban *s*, This heap is a ... Gen 31:48 559
for he *s*, The LORD watch between ... Gen 31:49 559
Laban *s* to Jacob, Behold this ... Gen 31:51 559
And when Jacob saw them, he *s* ... Gen 32:2 559
And *s*, If Esau come to the one ... Gen 32:8 559
And Jacob *s*, O God of my father ... Gen 32:9 559
s unto his servants, Pass over ... Gen 32:16 559
For he *s*, I will appease him with ... Gen 32:20 559
And he *s*, Let me go, for the day ... Gen 32:26 559
And he *s*, I will not let thee go, ... Gen 32:26 559
he *s* unto him, What is thy name ... Gen 32:27 559
And he *s*, Jacob ... Gen 32:27 559
And he *s*, Thy name shall be called ... Gen 32:28 559
And Jacob asked him, and *s*, Tell me ... Gen 32:29 559
And he *s*, Wherefore is it that ... Gen 32:29 559
and *s*, Who are those with thee ... Gen 33:5 559
And he *s*, The children which God ... Gen 33:5 559
And he *s*, What meanest thou by all ... Gen 33:8 559
And he *s*, These are to find grace ... Gen 33:8 559
And Esau *s*, I have enough, my ... Gen 33:9 559
And Jacob *s*, Nay, I pray thee, if ... Gen 33:10 559
And he *s*, Let us take our journey, ... Gen 33:12 559
he *s* unto him, My lord knoweth ... Gen 33:13 559
And Esau *s*, Let me now leave with ... Gen 33:15 559
And he *s*, What needeth it ... Gen 33:15 559
Shechem *s* unto her father and unto ... Gen 34:11 559
his father deceitfully, and *s* ... Gen 34:13 1696
they *s* unto them, We cannot do ... Gen 34:14 559
Jacob *s* to Simeon and Levi, Ye ... Gen 34:30 559
And they *s*, Should he deal with ... Gen 34:31 559
God *s* unto Jacob, Arise, go up to ... Gen 35:1 559
Then Jacob *s* unto his household, ... Gen 35:2 559
God *s* unto him, Thy name is Jacob ... Gen 35:10 559
God *s* unto him, I am God Almighty ... Gen 35:11 559
that the midwife *s* unto her ... Gen 35:17 559
he *s* unto them, Hear, I pray you, ... Gen 37:6 559
And his brethren *s* to him, Shalt ... Gen 37:8 559
and told it his brethren, and *s* ... Gen 37:9 559
s unto him, What is this dream ... Gen 37:10 559
Israel *s* unto Joseph, Do not thy ... Gen 37:13 559
And he *s* to him, Here am I ... Gen 37:13 559
he *s* to him, Go, I pray thee, see ... Gen 37:14 559
And he *s*, I seek my brethren ... Gen 37:16 559
And the man *s*, They are departed ... Gen 37:17 559
they *s* one to another, Behold, ... Gen 37:19 559
and *s*, Let us not kill him ... Gen 37:21 559
Reuben *s* unto them, Shed no blood ... Gen 37:22 559
Judah *s* unto his brethren, What ... Gen 37:26 559
returned unto his brethren, and *s* ... Gen 37:30 559
and *s*, This have we found ... Gen 37:32 559
And he knew it, and *s*, It is my ... Gen 37:33 559
and he *s*, For I will go down into ... Gen 37:35 559
Judah *s* unto Onan, Go in unto thy ... Gen 38:8 559
Then *s* Judah to Tamar his ... Gen 38:11 559
for he *s*, Lest peradventure he ... Gen 38:11 559
turned unto her by the way, and *s* ... Gen 38:16 559
And she *s*, What wilt thou give me ... Gen 38:16 559
And he *s*, I will send thee a kid ... Gen 38:17 559
And she *s*, Wilt thou give me a ... Gen 38:17 559
And he *s*, What pledge shall I give ... Gen 38:18 559
And she *s*, Thy signet, and thy ... Gen 38:18 559
And they *s*, There was no harlot in ... Gen 38:21 559
And he returned to Judah, and *s* ... Gen 38:22 559
and also the men of the place *s* ... Gen 38:22 559
And Judah *s*, Let her take it to ... Gen 38:23 559
And Judah *s*, Bring her forth, and ... Gen 38:24 559
and she *s*, Discern, I pray thee, ... Gen 38:25 559
And Judah acknowledged them, and *s*. Gen 38:26 559
and she *s*, How hast thou broken ... Gen 38:29 559
and she *s*, Lie with me ... Gen 39:7 559
s unto his master's wife, Behold, ... Gen 39:8 559
they *s* unto him, We have dreamed ... Gen 40:8 559
Joseph *s* unto them, Do not ... Gen 40:8 559
s to him, In my dream, behold, a ... Gen 40:9 559
Joseph *s* unto him, This is the ... Gen 40:12 559
he *s* unto Joseph, I also was in ... Gen 40:16 559
And Joseph answered and *s*, This is ... Gen 40:18 559
Pharaoh *s* unto Joseph, I have ... Gen 41:15 559
Pharaoh *s* unto Joseph, In my ... Gen 41:17 1696
Joseph *s* unto Pharaoh, The dream ... Gen 41:25 559
Pharaoh *s* unto his servants, Can ... Gen 41:38 559
Pharaoh *s* unto Joseph, Forasmuch ... Gen 41:39 559
Pharaoh *s* unto Joseph, See, I ... Gen 41:41 559
Pharaoh *s* unto Joseph, I am ... Gen 41:44 559
s he, hath made me forget all my ... Gen 41:51
come, according as Joseph had *s* ... Gen 41:54 559
Pharaoh *s* unto all the Egyptians, ... Gen 41:55 559
Jacob *s* unto his sons, Why do ye ... Gen 42:1 559
And he *s*, Behold, I have heard ... Gen 42:2 559
for he *s*, Lest peradventure ... Gen 42:4 559
he *s* unto them, Whence come ye ... Gen 42:7 559
And they *s*, From the land of ... Gen 42:7 559
s unto them, Ye are spies ... Gen 42:9 559
they *s* unto him, Nay, my lord, ... Gen 42:10 559
he *s* unto them, Nay, but to see ... Gen 42:12 559
And they *s*, Thy servants are ... Gen 42:13 559
Joseph *s* unto them, That is it ... Gen 42:14 559
Joseph *s* unto them the third day, ... Gen 42:18 559
they *s* one to another, We are ... Gen 42:21 559
he *s* unto his brethren, My money ... Gen 42:28 559
we *s* unto him, We are true men ... Gen 42:31 559
s unto us, Hereby shall I know ... Gen 42:33 559
And Jacob their father *s* unto them ... Gen 42:36 559
And he *s*, My son shall not go down ... Gen 42:38 559
Egypt, their father *s* unto them ... Gen 43:2 559
for the man *s* unto us, Ye shall ... Gen 43:5 559
And Israel *s*, Wherefore dealt ye ... Gen 43:6 559
And they *s*, The man asked us ... Gen 43:7 559
Judah *s* unto Israel his father, ... Gen 43:8 559
their father Israel *s* unto them ... Gen 43:11 559
he *s* to the ruler of his house, ... Gen 43:16 559
and they *s*, Because of the money ... Gen 43:18 559
And *s*, O sir, we came indeed down ... Gen 43:20 559
And he *s*, Peace be to you, fear ... Gen 43:23 559
asked them of their welfare, and *s* ... Gen 43:27 559
Benjamin, his mother's son, and *s* ... Gen 43:29 559
And he *s*, God be gracious unto ... Gen 43:29 559
out, and refrained himself, and *s* ... Gen 43:31 559
Joseph *s* unto his steward, Up, ... Gen 44:4 559
they *s* unto him, Wherefore saith ... Gen 44:7 559
And he *s*, Now also let it be ... Gen 44:10 559
Joseph *s* unto them, What deed is ... Gen 44:15 559
And Judah *s*, What shall we say ... Gen 44:16 559
And he *s*, God forbid that I should ... Gen 44:17 559
Judah came near unto him, and *s* ... Gen 44:18 559
we *s* unto my lord, We have a ... Gen 44:20 559
we *s* unto my lord, The lad cannot ... Gen 44:22 559
And our father *s*, Go again, and buy ... Gen 44:25 559
And we *s*, We cannot go down ... Gen 44:26 559
thy servant my father *s* unto us ... Gen 44:27 559
the one went out from me, and I *s* ... Gen 44:28 559
Joseph *s* unto his brethren, I am ... Gen 45:3 559
Joseph *s* unto his brethren, Come ... Gen 45:4 559
And he *s*, I am Joseph your brother ... Gen 45:4 559
Pharaoh *s* unto Joseph, Say unto ... Gen 45:17 559
he *s* unto them, See that ye fall ... Gen 45:24 559
Joseph, which he had *s* unto them ... Gen 45:27 1697
And Israel *s*, It is enough ... Gen 45:28 559
in the visions of the night, and *s* ... Gen 46:2 559
And he *s*, Here am I ... Gen 46:2 559
And he *s*, I am God, the God of thy ... Gen 46:3 559
Israel *s* unto Joseph, Now let me ... Gen 46:30 559
Joseph *s* unto his brethren, and ... Gen 46:31 559
Joseph came and told Pharaoh, and *s* ... Gen 47:1 559
Pharaoh *s* unto his brethren, What ... Gen 47:3 559
they *s* unto Pharaoh, Thy servants ... Gen 47:3 559
They *s* moreover unto Pharaoh, For ... Gen 47:4 559
Pharaoh *s* unto Jacob, How old art ... Gen 47:8 559
Jacob *s* unto Pharaoh, The days of ... Gen 47:9 559
Egyptians came unto Joseph, and *s* ... Gen 47:15 559
And Joseph *s*, Give your cattle ... Gen 47:16 559
s unto him, We will not hide it ... Gen 47:18 559
Then Joseph *s* unto the people, ... Gen 47:23 559
And they *s*, Thou hast saved our ... Gen 47:25 559
s unto him, If now I have found ... Gen 47:29 559
And he *s*, I will do as thou hast ... Gen 47:30 559
I will do as thou hast *s* ... Gen 47:30 1697
And he *s*, Swear unto me ... Gen 47:31 559
And one told Jacob, and *s*, Behold, ... Gen 48:2 559
Jacob *s* unto Joseph, God Almighty ... Gen 48:3 559
s unto me, Behold, I will make ... Gen 48:4 559
Israel beheld Joseph's sons, and *s* ... Gen 48:8 559

Joseph s unto his father, They	Gen 48:9	559
And he s, Bring them, I pray thee,	Gen 48:9	559
Israel s unto Joseph, I had not	Gen 48:11	559
And he blessed Joseph, and s	Gen 48:15	559
Joseph s unto his father, Not so,	Gen 48:18	559
And his father refused, and s	Gen 48:19	559
Israel s unto Joseph, Behold, I	Gen 48:21	559
Jacob called unto his sons, and s	Gen 49:1	559
s unto them, I am to be gathered	Gen 49:29	559
And Pharaoh s, Go up, and bury thy	Gen 50:6	559
in the floor of Atad, they s	Gen 50:11	559
their father was dead, they s	Gen 50:15	559
and they s, Behold, we be thy	Gen 50:18	559
Joseph s unto them, Fear not	Gen 50:19	559
Joseph s unto his brethren, I die	Gen 50:24	559
he s unto his people, Behold, the	Ex 1:9	559
And he s, When ye do the office of	Ex 1:16	559
s unto them, Why have ye done	Ex 1:18	559
And the midwives s unto Pharaoh	Ex 1:19	559
she had compassion on him, and s	Ex 2:6	559
Then s his sister to Pharaoh's	Ex 2:7	559
And Pharaoh's daughter s to her	Ex 2:8	559
And Pharaoh's daughter s unto her	Ex 2:9	559
and she s, Because I drew him out	Ex 2:10	559
he s to him that did the wrong,	Ex 2:13	559
And he s, Who made thee a prince	Ex 2:14	559
And Moses feared, and s, Surely	Ex 2:14	559
came to Reuel their father, he s	Ex 2:18	559
And they s, An Egyptian delivered	Ex 2:19	559
he s unto his daughters, And where	Ex 2:20	559
for he s, I have been a stranger	Ex 2:22	559
And Moses s, I will now turn aside	Ex 3:3	559
of the midst of the bush, and s	Ex 3:4	559
And he s, Here am I	Ex 3:4	559
And he s, Draw not nigh hither	Ex 3:5	559
Moreover he s, I am the God of	Ex 3:6	559
And the LORD s, I have surely seen	Ex 3:7	559
Moses s unto God, Who am I, that	Ex 3:11	559
And he s, Certainly I will be with	Ex 3:12	559
Moses s unto God, Behold, when I	Ex 3:13	559
God s unto Moses, I AM THAT I AM	Ex 3:14	559
and he s, Thus shalt thou say unto	Ex 3:14	559
God s moreover unto Moses, Thus	Ex 3:15	559
And I have s, I will bring you up	Ex 3:17	559
And Moses answered and s, But,	Ex 4:1	559
And the LORD s unto him, What is	Ex 4:2	559
And he s, A rod	Ex 4:2	559
And he s, Cast it on the ground	Ex 4:3	559
the LORD s unto Moses, Put forth	Ex 4:4	559
the LORD s furthermore unto him,	Ex 4:6	559
And he s, Put thine hand into thy	Ex 4:7	559
Moses s unto the LORD, O my Lord,	Ex 4:10	559
And the LORD s unto him, Who hath	Ex 4:11	559
And he s, O my Lord, send, I pray	Ex 4:13	559
kindled against Moses, and he s	Ex 4:14	559
s unto him, Let me go, I pray	Ex 4:18	559
Jethro s to Moses, Go in peace	Ex 4:18	559
the LORD s unto Moses in Midian,	Ex 4:19	559
the LORD s unto Moses, When thou	Ex 4:21	559
son, and cast it at his feet, and s	Ex 4:25	559
then she s, A bloody husband thou	Ex 4:26	559
And the LORD s to Aaron, Go into	Ex 4:27	559
And Pharaoh s, Who is the LORD,	Ex 5:2	559
And they s, The God of the Hebrews	Ex 5:3	559
And the king of Egypt s unto them	Ex 5:4	559
And Pharaoh s, Behold, the people	Ex 5:5	559
But he s, Ye are idle, ye are	Ex 5:17	559
were in evil case, after it was s	Ex 5:19	559
they s unto them, The LORD look	Ex 5:21	559
returned unto the LORD, and s	Ex 5:22	559
Then the LORD s unto Moses	Ex 6:1	559
s unto him, I am the LORD	Ex 6:2	559
and Moses, to whom the LORD s	Ex 6:26	559
Moses s before the LORD, Behold,	Ex 6:30	559
the LORD s unto Moses, See, I	Ex 7:1	559
as the LORD had s	Ex 7:13	1696
the LORD s unto Moses, Pharaoh's	Ex 7:14	559
as the LORD had s	Ex 7:22	1696
called for Moses and Aaron, and s	Ex 8:8	559
Moses s unto Pharaoh, Glory over	Ex 8:9	559
And he s, To morrow	Ex 8:10	559
And he s, Be it according to thy	Ex 8:10	559
as the LORD had s	Ex 8:15	1696
the LORD s unto Moses, Say unto	Ex 8:16	559
Then the magicians s unto Pharaoh	Ex 8:19	559
as the LORD had s	Ex 8:19	1696
the LORD s unto Moses, Rise up	Ex 8:20	559
for Moses and for Aaron, and s	Ex 8:25	559
And Moses s, It is not meet so to	Ex 8:26	559
And Pharaoh s, I will let you go,	Ex 8:28	559
And Moses s, Behold, I go out from	Ex 8:29	559
Then the LORD s unto Moses	Ex 9:1	559
the LORD s unto Moses and unto	Ex 9:8	559
the LORD s unto Moses, Rise up	Ex 9:13	559
the LORD s unto Moses, Stretch	Ex 9:22	559
s unto them, I have sinned this	Ex 9:27	559
Moses s unto him, As soon as I am	Ex 9:29	559
the LORD s unto Moses, Go in unto	Ex 10:1	559
s unto him, Thus saith the LORD	Ex 10:3	559
And Pharaoh's servants s unto him	Ex 10:7	559
he s unto them, Go, serve the	Ex 10:8	559
And Moses s, We will go with our	Ex 10:9	559
he s unto them, Let the LORD be	Ex 10:10	559
the LORD s unto Moses, Stretch	Ex 10:12	559
and he s, I have sinned against	Ex 10:16	559
the LORD s unto Moses, Stretch	Ex 10:21	559
Pharaoh called unto Moses, and s	Ex 10:24	559
And Moses s, Thou must give us	Ex 10:25	559
Pharaoh s unto him, Get thee from	Ex 10:28	559
And Moses s, Thou hast spoken well	Ex 10:29	559
the LORD s unto Moses, Yet will I	Ex 11:1	559
And Moses s, Thus saith the LORD,	Ex 11:4	559
the LORD s unto Moses, Pharaoh	Ex 11:9	559
s unto them, Draw out and take you	Ex 12:21	559
for Moses and Aaron by night, and s	Ex 12:31	559
go, serve the LORD, as ye have s	Ex 12:31	1696
and your herds, as ye have s	Ex 12:32	1696
for they s, We be all dead men	Ex 12:33	559
the LORD s unto Moses and Aaron,	Ex 12:43	559
Moses s unto the people, Remember	Ex 13:3	559
for God s, Lest peradventure the	Ex 13:17	559
against the people, and they s	Ex 14:5	559
they s unto Moses, Because there	Ex 14:11	559
Moses s unto the people, Fear ye	Ex 14:13	559
the LORD s unto Moses, Wherefore	Ex 14:15	559
so that the Egyptians s, Let us	Ex 14:25	559
the LORD s unto Moses, Stretch	Ex 14:26	559
The enemy s, I will pursue, I	Ex 15:9	559
And s, If thou wilt diligently	Ex 15:26	559
children of Israel s unto them	Ex 16:3	559
Then s the LORD unto Moses,	Ex 16:4	559
Aaron s unto all the children of	Ex 16:6	559
And Moses s, This shall be, when	Ex 16:8	559
they s one to another, It is	Ex 16:15	559
Moses s unto them, This is the	Ex 16:15	559
And Moses s, Let no man leave of	Ex 16:19	559
he s unto them, This is that	Ex 16:23	559
is that which the LORD hath s	Ex 16:23	1696
And Moses s, Eat that to day	Ex 16:25	559
the LORD s unto Moses, How long	Ex 16:28	559
And Moses s, This is the thing	Ex 16:32	559
Moses s unto Aaron, Take a pot,	Ex 16:33	559
people did chide with Moses, and s	Ex 17:2	559
Moses s unto them, Why chide ye	Ex 17:2	559
murmured against Moses, and s	Ex 17:3	559
the LORD s unto Moses, Go on	Ex 17:5	559
Moses s unto Joshua, Choose us	Ex 17:9	559
Joshua did as Moses had s to him	Ex 17:10	559
the LORD s unto Moses, Write this	Ex 17:14	559
For he s, Because the LORD hath	Ex 17:16	559
for he s, I have been an alien in	Ex 18:3	559
s he, was mine help, and delivered	Ex 18:4	
he s unto Moses, I thy father in	Ex 18:6	559
And Jethro s, Blessed be the LORD,	Ex 18:10	559
that he did to the people, he s	Ex 18:14	559
Moses s unto his father in law,	Ex 18:15	559
Moses' father in law s unto him	Ex 18:17	559
in law, and did all that he had s	Ex 18:24	559
people answered together, and s	Ex 19:8	559
the LORD s unto Moses, Lo, I come	Ex 19:9	559
the LORD s unto Moses, Go unto	Ex 19:10	559
he s unto the people, Be ready	Ex 19:15	559
the LORD s unto Moses, Go down,	Ex 19:21	559
Moses s unto the LORD, The people	Ex 19:23	559
And the LORD s unto him, Away, get	Ex 19:24	559
they s unto Moses, Speak thou	Ex 20:19	559
Moses s unto the people, Fear not	Ex 20:20	559
the LORD s unto Moses, Thus thou	Ex 20:22	559
I have s unto you be circumspect	Ex 23:13	559
he s unto Moses, Come up unto the	Ex 24:1	559
answered with one voice, and s	Ex 24:3	559
which the LORD hath s will we do	Ex 24:3	1696
and they s, All that the LORD hath	Ex 24:7	559
that the LORD hath s will we do	Ex 24:7	1696
sprinkled it on the people, and s	Ex 24:8	559
the LORD s unto Moses, Come up to	Ex 24:12	559
he s unto the elders, Tarry ye	Ex 24:14	559
the LORD s unto Moses, Take unto	Ex 30:34	559
s unto him, Up, make us gods,	Ex 32:1	559
Aaron s unto them, Break off the	Ex 32:2	559
and they s, These be thy gods, O	Ex 32:4	559
and Aaron made proclamation, and s	Ex 32:5	559
the LORD s unto Moses, Go, get	Ex 32:7	1696
have sacrificed thereunto, and s	Ex 32:8	559
the LORD s unto Moses, I have	Ex 32:9	559
besought the LORD his God, and s	Ex 32:11	559
he s unto Moses, There is a noise	Ex 32:17	559
And he s, It is not the voice of	Ex 32:18	559
Moses s unto Aaron, What did this	Ex 32:21	559
And Aaron s, Let not the anger of	Ex 32:22	559
For they s unto me, Make us gods,	Ex 32:23	559
I s unto them, Whosoever hath any	Ex 32:24	559
in the gate of the camp, and s	Ex 32:26	559
he s unto them, Thus saith the	Ex 32:27	559
For Moses had s, Consecrate	Ex 32:29	559
that Moses s unto the people, Ye	Ex 32:30	559
returned unto the LORD, and s	Ex 32:31	559
the LORD s unto Moses, Whosoever	Ex 32:33	559
the LORD s unto Moses, Depart, and	Ex 33:1	1696
For the LORD had s unto Moses	Ex 33:5	559
Moses s unto the LORD, See, thou	Ex 33:12	559
Yet thou hast s, I know thee by	Ex 33:12	559
And he s, My presence shall go	Ex 33:14	559
he s unto him, If thy presence go	Ex 33:15	559
the LORD s unto Moses, I will do	Ex 33:17	559
And he s, I beseech thee, shew me	Ex 33:18	559
And he s, I will make all my	Ex 33:19	559
And he s, Thou canst not see my	Ex 33:20	559
And the LORD s, Behold, there is a	Ex 33:21	559
the LORD s unto Moses, Hew thee	Ex 34:1	559
And he s, If now I have found	Ex 34:9	559
And he s, Behold, I make a	Ex 34:10	559
the LORD s unto Moses, Write thou	Ex 34:27	559
s unto them, These are the words	Ex 35:1	559
Moses s unto the children of	Ex 35:30	559
Moses s unto the congregation,	Lev 8:5	559
Moses s unto Aaron and to his sons	Lev 8:31	559
he s unto Aaron, Take thee a	Lev 9:2	559
And Moses s, This is the thing	Lev 9:6	559
Moses s unto Aaron, Go unto the	Lev 9:7	559
Then Moses s unto Aaron, This is	Lev 10:3	559
s unto them, Come near, carry	Lev 10:4	559
as Moses had s	Lev 10:5	1696
Moses s unto Aaron, and unto	Lev 10:6	559
Aaron s unto Moses, Behold, this	Lev 10:19	1696
the LORD s unto Moses, Speak unto	Lev 16:2	559
Therefore I s unto the children	Lev 17:12	559
therefore I s unto the children	Lev 17:14	559
But I have s unto you, Ye shall	Lev 20:24	559
the LORD s unto Moses, Speak unto	Lev 21:1	559
the LORD s unto Moses, Number all	Num 3:40	559
the LORD s unto Moses, They shall	Num 7:11	559
And those men s unto him, We are	Num 9:7	559
Moses s unto them, Stand still,	Num 9:8	559
Moses s unto Hobab, the son of	Num 10:29	559
the place of which the LORD s	Num 10:29	559
he s unto him, I will not go	Num 10:30	559
And he s, Leave us not, I pray	Num 10:31	559
the ark set forward, that Moses s	Num 10:35	559
And when it rested, he s, Return,	Num 10:36	559
of Israel also wept again, and s	Num 11:4	559
Moses s unto the LORD, Wherefore	Num 11:11	559
the LORD s unto Moses, Gather	Num 11:16	559
And Moses s, The people, among	Num 11:21	559
and thou hast s, I will give them	Num 11:21	559
the LORD s unto Moses, Is the	Num 11:23	559
a young man, and told Moses, and s	Num 11:27	559
of his young men, answered and s	Num 11:28	559
Moses s unto him, Enviest thou	Num 11:29	559
And they s, Hath the LORD indeed	Num 12:2	559
And he s, Hear now my words	Num 12:6	559
Aaron s unto Moses, Alas, my lord	Num 12:11	559
the LORD s unto Moses, If her	Num 12:14	559
s unto them, Get you up this way	Num 13:17	559
And they told him, and s, We came	Num 13:27	559
the people before Moses, and s	Num 13:30	559
the men that went up with him s	Num 13:31	559
whole congregation s unto them	Num 14:2	559
they s one to another, Let us	Num 14:4	559
the LORD s unto Moses, How long	Num 14:11	559
Moses s unto the LORD, Then the	Num 14:13	559
And the LORD s, I have pardoned	Num 14:20	559
which ye s should be a prey, them	Num 14:31	559
I the LORD have s, I will surely	Num 14:35	1696
And Moses s, Wherefore now do ye	Num 14:41	559
the LORD s unto Moses, The man	Num 15:35	559
s unto them, Ye take too much	Num 16:3	559
Moses s unto Korah, Hear, I pray	Num 16:8	559
which s, We will not come up	Num 16:12	559
s unto the LORD, Respect not thou	Num 16:15	559
Moses s unto Korah, Be thou and	Num 16:16	559
they fell upon their faces, and s	Num 16:22	559
And Moses s, Hereby ye shall know	Num 16:28	559
for they s, Lest the earth	Num 16:34	559
as the LORD s to him by the hand	Num 16:40	1696
Moses s unto Aaron, Take a censer	Num 16:46	559
the LORD s unto Moses, Bring	Num 17:10	559
the LORD s unto Aaron, Thou and	Num 18:1	559
therefore I have s unto them	Num 18:24	559
he s unto them, Hear now, ye	Num 20:10	559
Edom s unto him, Thou shalt not	Num 20:18	559
the children of Israel s unto him	Num 20:19	559
And he s, Thou shalt not go	Num 20:20	559
vowed a vow unto the LORD, and s	Num 21:2	559
the people came to Moses, and s	Num 21:7	559
the LORD s unto Moses, Make thee	Num 21:8	559
Wherefore it is s in the book of	Num 21:14	559
the LORD s unto Moses, Fear him	Num 21:34	559
Moab s unto the elders of Midian,	Num 22:4	559
he s unto them, Lodge here this	Num 22:8	559
And God came unto Balaam, and s	Num 22:9	559
Balaam s unto God, Balak the son	Num 22:10	559
God s unto Balaam, Thou shalt not	Num 22:12	559
s unto the princes of Balak, Get	Num 22:13	559
up, and they went unto Balak, and s	Num 22:14	559
s to him, Thus saith Balak the	Num 22:16	559
s unto the servants of Balak, If	Num 22:18	559
s unto him, If the men come to	Num 22:20	559
she s unto Balaam, What have I	Num 22:28	559
Balaam s unto the ass, Because	Num 22:29	559
the ass s unto Balaam, Am not I	Num 22:30	559
And he s, Nay	Num 22:30	559
the angel of the LORD s unto him	Num 22:32	559
Balaam s unto the angel of the	Num 22:34	559
angel of the LORD s unto Balaam	Num 22:35	559
Balak s unto Balaam, Did I not	Num 22:37	559
Balaam s unto Balak, Lo, I am	Num 22:38	559
Balaam s unto Balak, Build me	Num 23:1	559
Balaam s unto Balak, Stand by thy	Num 23:3	559
he s unto him, I have prepared	Num 23:4	559
a word in Balaam's mouth, and s	Num 23:5	559
And he took up his parable, and s	Num 23:7	559
Balak s unto Balaam, What hast	Num 23:11	559
And he answered and s, Must I not	Num 23:12	559
Balak s unto him, Come, I pray	Num 23:13	559
he s unto Balak, Stand here by	Num 23:15	559
and put a word in his mouth, and s	Num 23:16	559
Balak s unto him, What hath the	Num 23:17	559
And he took up his parable, and s	Num 23:18	559
hath he s, and shall he not do it	Num 23:19	559
this time it shall be s of Jacob	Num 23:23	559
Balak s unto Balaam, Neither	Num 23:25	559
s unto Balak, Told not I thee,	Num 23:26	559
Balak s unto Balaam, Come, I pray	Num 23:27	559
Balaam s unto Balak, Build me	Num 23:29	559
And Balak did as Balaam had s	Num 23:30	559
And he took up his parable, and s	Num 24:3	559
Balaam the son of Beor hath s	Num 24:3	5002
man whose eyes are open hath s	Num 24:3	5002
He hath s, which heard the words	Num 24:4	5002
Balak s unto Balaam, I called	Num 24:10	559
Balaam s unto Balak, Spake I not	Num 24:12	559
And he took up his parable, and s	Num 24:15	559
Balaam the son of Beor hath s	Num 24:15	5002
man whose eyes are open hath s	Num 24:15	5002
He hath s, which heard the words	Num 24:16	5002
he took up his parable, and s	Num 24:20	559
and took up his parable, and s	Num 24:21	559
And he took up his parable, and s	Num 24:23	559
the LORD s unto Moses, Take all	Num 25:4	559
Moses s unto the judges of Israel	Num 25:5	559
For the LORD had s of them	Num 26:65	559

the LORD s unto Moses, Get thee	Num 27:12	559
the LORD s unto Moses, Take thee	Num 27:18	559
Moses s unto them, Have ye saved	Num 31:15	559
Eleazar the priest s unto the men	Num 31:21	559
they s unto Moses, Thy servants	Num 31:49	559
s they, if we have found grace in	Num 32:5	559
Moses s unto the children of Gad	Num 32:6	559
And they came near unto him, and s	Num 32:16	559
Moses s unto them, If ye will do	Num 32:20	559
Moses s unto them, If the	Num 32:29	559
As the LORD hath s unto thy	Num 32:31	1696
And they s, The LORD commanded my	Num 36:2	559
of the sons of Joseph hath s well	Num 36:5	1696
And ye answered me, and s, The	Deut 1:14	559
I s unto you, Ye are come unto	Deut 1:20	559
of thy fathers hath s unto thee	Deut 1:21	1696
unto me every one of you, and s	Deut 1:22	559
and brought us word again, and s	Deut 1:25	559
ye murmured in your tents, and s	Deut 1:27	559
Then I s unto you, Dread not,	Deut 1:29	559
which ye s should be a prey, and	Deut 1:39	559
s unto me, We have sinned against	Deut 1:41	559
And the LORD s unto me, Say unto	Deut 1:42	559
And the LORD s unto me, Distress	Deut 2:9	559
s I, and get you over the brook	Deut 2:13	
And the LORD s unto me, Behold, I	Deut 2:31	559
And the LORD s unto me, Fear him	Deut 3:2	559
and the LORD s unto me, Let it	Deut 3:26	559
in Horeb, when the LORD s unto me	Deut 4:10	559
s unto them, Hear, O Israel, the	Deut 5:1	559
And ye s, Behold, the LORD our God	Deut 5:24	559
and the LORD s unto me, I have	Deut 5:28	559
they have well s all that they	Deut 5:28	
as the LORD hath s unto thee	Deut 9:3	1696
And the LORD s unto me, Arise, get	Deut 9:12	559
LORD had s he would destroy you	Deut 9:25	559
therefore unto the LORD, and s	Deut 9:26	559
At that time the LORD s unto me	Deut 10:1	559
And the LORD s unto me, Arise,	Deut 10:11	559
tread upon, as he hath s unto you	Deut 11:25	1696
as the LORD hath s unto you	Deut 17:16	559
as he hath s unto them	Deut 18:2	1696
And the LORD s unto me, They have	Deut 18:17	559
s unto them, Ye have seen all	Deut 29:2	559
a God, as he hath s unto thee	Deut 29:13	1696
he s unto them, I am an hundred	Deut 31:2	559
also the LORD hath s unto me	Deut 31:2	559
before thee, as the LORD hath s	Deut 31:3	1696
s unto him in the sight of all	Deut 31:7	559
the LORD s unto Moses, Behold,	Deut 31:14	559
the LORD s unto Moses, Behold,	Deut 31:16	559
the son of Nun a charge, and s	Deut 31:23	559
And he s, I will hide my face from	Deut 32:20	559
I s, I would scatter them into	Deut 32:26	559
he s unto them, Set your hearts	Deut 32:46	559
And he s, The LORD came from Sinai	Deut 33:2	559
and he s, Hear, LORD, the voice of	Deut 33:7	559
And of Levi he s, Let thy Thummim	Deut 33:8	559
Who s unto his father and to his	Deut 33:9	559
And of Benjamin he s, The beloved	Deut 33:12	559
And of Joseph he s, Blessed of the	Deut 33:13	559
And of Zebulun he s, Rejoice,	Deut 33:18	559
And of Gad he s, Blessed be he	Deut 33:20	559
And of Dan he s, Dan is a lion's	Deut 33:22	559
And of Naphtali he s, O Naphtali,	Deut 33:23	559
And of Asher he s, Let Asher be	Deut 33:24	559
And the LORD s unto him, This is	Deut 34:4	559
given unto you, as I s unto Moses	Josh 1:3	1696
s thus, There came men unto me,	Josh 2:4	559
she s unto the men, I know that	Josh 2:9	559
she s unto them, Get you to the	Josh 2:16	559
the men s unto her, We will be	Josh 2:17	559
And she s, According unto your	Josh 2:21	559
they s unto Joshua, Truly the	Josh 2:24	559
Joshua s unto the people,	Josh 3:5	559
the LORD s unto Joshua, This day	Josh 3:7	559
Joshua s unto the children of	Josh 3:9	559
And Joshua s, Hereby ye shall know	Josh 3:10	559
Joshua s unto them, Pass over	Josh 4:5	559
that time the LORD s unto Joshua	Josh 5:2	559
the LORD s unto Joshua, This day	Josh 5:9	559
s unto him, Art thou for us, or	Josh 5:13	559
And he s, Nay	Josh 5:14	559
s unto him, What saith my lord	Josh 5:14	559
of the LORD's host s unto Joshua	Josh 5:15	559
the LORD s unto Joshua, See, I	Josh 6:2	559
s unto them, Take up the ark of	Josh 6:6	559
he s unto the people, Pass on, and	Josh 6:7	559
Joshua s unto the people, Shout	Josh 6:16	559
But Joshua had s unto the two men	Josh 6:22	559
s unto him, Let not all the	Josh 7:3	559
And Joshua s, Alas, O Lord GOD,	Josh 7:7	559
the LORD s unto Joshua, Get thee	Josh 7:10	559
Joshua s unto Achan, My son, give	Josh 7:19	559
And Achan answered Joshua, and s	Josh 7:20	559
And Joshua s, Why hast thou	Josh 7:25	559
the LORD s unto Joshua, Fear not,	Josh 8:1	559
the LORD s unto Joshua, Stretch	Josh 8:18	559
s unto him, and to the men of	Josh 9:6	559
men of Israel s unto the Hivites	Josh 9:7	559
they s unto Joshua, We are thy	Josh 9:8	559
Joshua s unto them, Who are ye	Josh 9:8	559
they s unto him, From a very far	Josh 9:9	559
But all the princes s unto all	Josh 9:19	559
And the princes s unto them	Josh 9:21	559
And they answered Joshua, and s	Josh 9:24	559
the LORD s unto Joshua, Fear them	Josh 10:8	559
he s in the sight of Israel, Sun,	Josh 10:12	559
And Joshua s, Roll great stones	Josh 10:18	559
Then s Joshua, Open the mouth of	Josh 10:22	559
s unto the captains of the men of	Josh 10:24	559
Joshua s unto them, Fear not, nor	Josh 10:25	559
the LORD s unto Joshua, Be not	Josh 11:6	559
to all that the LORD s unto Moses	Josh 11:23	1696
and the LORD s unto him, Thou art	Josh 13:1	559
inheritance, as he s unto them	Josh 13:14	1696
inheritance, as he s unto them	Josh 13:33	1696
Jephunneh the Kenezite s unto him	Josh 14:6	559
LORD s unto Moses the man of God	Josh 14:6	1696
LORD hath kept me alive, as he s	Josh 14:10	1696
to drive them out, as the LORD s	Josh 14:12	1696
And Caleb s, He that smiteth	Josh 15:16	559
Caleb s unto her, What wouldest	Josh 15:18	559
And the children of Joseph s	Josh 17:16	559
Joshua s unto the children of	Josh 18:3	559
s unto them, Ye have kept all	Josh 22:2	559
s unto the heads of the thousands	Josh 22:21	1696
Therefore we s, Let us now	Josh 22:26	559
Therefore s we, that it shall be,	Josh 22:28	559
s unto the children of Reuben	Josh 22:31	559
s unto them, I am old and stricken	Josh 23:2	559
Joshua s unto all the people,	Josh 24:2	559
And the people answered and s	Josh 24:16	559
Joshua s unto the people, Ye	Josh 24:19	559
the people s unto Joshua, Nay	Josh 24:21	559
Joshua s unto the people, Ye are	Josh 24:22	559
And they s, We are witnesses	Josh 24:22	559
s he, the strange gods which are	Josh 24:23	
the people s unto Joshua, The	Josh 24:24	559
Joshua s unto all the people,	Josh 24:27	559
And the LORD s, Judah shall go up	Judg 1:2	559
Judah s unto Simeon his brother,	Judg 1:3	559
And Adoni-bezek s, Threescore and	Judg 1:7	559
And Caleb s, He that smiteth	Judg 1:12	559
Caleb s unto her, What wilt thou	Judg 1:14	559
she s unto him, Give me a	Judg 1:15	559
Hebron unto Caleb, as Moses s	Judg 1:20	1696
they s unto him, Shew us, we pray	Judg 1:24	559
up from Gilgal to Bochim, and s	Judg 2:1	559
and I s, I will never break my	Judg 2:1	559
Wherefore I also s, I will not	Judg 2:3	559
them for evil, as the LORD had s	Judg 2:15	1696
and he s, Because that this people	Judg 2:20	559
that were by Gilgal, and s	Judg 3:19	559
who s, Keep silence	Judg 3:19	559
And Ehud s, I have a message from	Judg 3:20	559
the parlour were locked, they s	Judg 3:24	559
he s unto them, Follow after me	Judg 3:28	559
s unto him, Hath not the LORD God	Judg 4:6	559
Barak s unto her, If thou wilt go	Judg 4:8	559
And she s, I will surely go with	Judg 4:9	559
And Deborah s unto Barak, Up	Judg 4:14	559
s unto him, Turn in, my lord,	Judg 4:18	559
he s unto her, Give me, I pray	Judg 4:19	559
Again he s unto her, Stand in the	Judg 4:20	559
s unto him, Come, and I will shew	Judg 4:22	559
s the angel of the LORD, curse ye	Judg 5:23	559
which s unto them, Thus saith the	Judg 6:8	559
I s unto you, I am the LORD your	Judg 6:10	559
s unto him, The LORD is with thee	Judg 6:12	559
Gideon s unto him, Oh my Lord, if	Judg 6:13	559
And the LORD looked upon him, and s.	Judg 6:14	559
he s unto him, Oh my Lord,	Judg 6:15	559
And the LORD s unto him, Surely I	Judg 6:16	559
he s unto him, If now I have	Judg 6:17	559
And he s, I will tarry until thou	Judg 6:18	559
And the angel of God s unto him	Judg 6:20	559
an angel of the LORD, Gideon s	Judg 6:22	559
And the LORD s unto him, Peace be	Judg 6:23	559
night, that the LORD s unto him	Judg 6:25	559
and did as the LORD had s unto him	Judg 6:27	1696
they s one to another, Who hath	Judg 6:29	559
they enquired and asked, they s	Judg 6:29	559
the men of the city s unto Joash	Judg 6:30	559
Joash s unto all that stood	Judg 6:31	559
Gideon s unto God, If thou wilt	Judg 6:36	559
by mine hand, as thou hast s	Judg 6:36	1696
by mine hand, as thou hast s	Judg 6:37	1696
Gideon s unto God, Let not thine	Judg 6:39	559
the LORD s unto Gideon, The	Judg 7:2	559
the LORD s unto Gideon, The	Judg 7:4	559
the LORD s unto Gideon, Every one	Judg 7:5	559
the LORD s unto Gideon, By the	Judg 7:7	559
night, that the LORD s unto him	Judg 7:9	559
a dream unto his fellow, and s	Judg 7:13	559
And his fellow answered and s	Judg 7:14	559
into the host of Israel, and s	Judg 7:15	559
he s unto them, Look on me, and do	Judg 7:17	559
And the men of Ephraim s unto him	Judg 8:1	559
he s unto them, What have I done	Judg 8:2	559
toward him, when he had s that	Judg 8:3	1696
he s unto the men of Succoth,	Judg 8:5	559
And the princes of Succoth s	Judg 8:6	559
And Gideon s, Therefore when the	Judg 8:7	559
unto the men of Succoth, and s	Judg 8:15	559
Then s he unto Zebah and Zalmunna,	Judg 8:18	559
And he s, They were my brethren,	Judg 8:19	559
he s unto Jether his firstborn,	Judg 8:20	559
Then Zebah and Zalmunna s, Rise	Judg 8:21	559
the men of Israel s unto Gideon	Judg 8:22	559
Gideon s unto them, I will not	Judg 8:23	559
Gideon s unto them, I would	Judg 8:24	559
for they s, He is our brother	Judg 9:3	559
s unto them, Hearken unto me, ye	Judg 9:7	559
they s unto the olive tree, Reign	Judg 9:8	559
But the olive tree s unto them	Judg 9:9	559
the trees s to the fig tree, Come	Judg 9:10	559
But the fig tree s unto them	Judg 9:11	559
Then s the trees unto the vine,	Judg 9:12	559
the vine s unto them, Should I	Judg 9:13	559
Then s all the trees unto the	Judg 9:14	559
the bramble s unto the trees, If	Judg 9:15	559
And Gaal the son of Ebed s	Judg 9:28	559
he s to Abimelech, Increase thine	Judg 9:29	559
he s to Zebul, Behold, there come	Judg 9:36	559
Zebul s unto him, Thou seest the	Judg 9:36	559
And Gaal spake again and s, See	Judg 9:37	559
Then s Zebul unto him, Where is	Judg 9:38	559
s unto the people that were with	Judg 9:48	559
s unto him, Draw thy sword, and	Judg 9:54	559
the LORD s unto the children of	Judg 10:11	559
of Israel s unto the LORD	Judg 10:15	559
of Gilead s one to another	Judg 10:18	559
s unto him, Thou shalt not	Judg 11:2	559
they s unto Jephthah, Come, and be	Judg 11:6	559
Jephthah s unto the elders of	Judg 11:7	559
elders of Gilead s unto Jephthah	Judg 11:8	559
Jephthah s unto the elders of	Judg 11:9	559
elders of Gilead s unto Jephthah	Judg 11:10	559
s unto him, Thus saith Jephthah,	Judg 11:15	559
Israel s unto him, Let us pass,	Judg 11:19	559
vowed a vow unto the LORD, and s	Judg 11:30	559
that he rent his clothes, and s	Judg 11:35	559
she s unto him, My father, if	Judg 11:36	559
she s unto her father, Let this	Judg 11:37	559
And he s, Go	Judg 11:38	559
s unto Jephthah, Wherefore	Judg 12:1	559
Jephthah s unto them, I and my	Judg 12:2	559
smote Ephraim, because they s	Judg 12:4	559
Ephraimites which were escaped s	Judg 12:5	559
that the men of Gilead s unto him	Judg 12:5	559
If he s, Nay	Judg 12:5	559
Then s they unto him, Say now	Judg 12:6	559
and he s Sibboleth	Judg 12:6	559
s unto her, Behold now, thou art	Judg 13:3	559
But he s unto me, Behold, thou	Judg 13:7	559
Manoah intreated the LORD, and s	Judg 13:8	559
s unto him, Behold, the man hath	Judg 13:10	559
s unto him, Art thou the man that	Judg 13:11	559
And he s, I am	Judg 13:11	559
And Manoah s, Now let thy words	Judg 13:12	559
angel of the LORD s unto Manoah	Judg 13:13	559
Of all that I s unto the woman	Judg 13:13	559
Manoah s unto the angel of the	Judg 13:15	559
angel of the LORD s unto Manoah	Judg 13:16	559
Manoah s unto the angel of the	Judg 13:17	559
the angel of the LORD s unto him	Judg 13:18	559
Manoah s unto his wife, We shall	Judg 13:22	559
But his wife s unto him, If the	Judg 13:23	559
his father and his mother, and s	Judg 14:2	559
father and his mother s unto him	Judg 14:3	559
Samson s unto his father, Get her	Judg 14:3	559
Samson s unto them, I will now	Judg 14:12	559
they s unto him, Put forth thy	Judg 14:13	559
he s unto them, Out of the eater	Judg 14:14	559
that they s unto Samson's wife,	Judg 14:15	559
wife wept before him, and s	Judg 14:16	559
he s unto her, Behold, I have not	Judg 14:16	559
the men of the city s unto him on	Judg 14:18	559
he s unto them, If ye had not	Judg 14:18	559
and he s, I will go in to my wife	Judg 15:1	559
And her father s, I verily thought	Judg 15:2	559
Samson s concerning them, Now	Judg 15:3	559
Then the Philistines s, Who hath	Judg 15:6	559
Samson s unto them, Though ye	Judg 15:7	559
And the men of Judah s, Why are ye	Judg 15:10	559
s to Samson, Knowest thou not	Judg 15:11	559
he s unto them, As they did unto	Judg 15:11	559
they s unto him, We are come down	Judg 15:12	559
Samson s unto them, Swear unto me	Judg 15:12	559
And Samson s, With the jawbone of	Judg 15:16	559
and called on the LORD, and s	Judg 15:18	559
s unto her, Entice him, and see	Judg 16:5	559
Delilah s to Samson, Tell me, I	Judg 16:6	559
Samson s unto her, If they bind	Judg 16:7	559
she s unto him, The Philistines	Judg 16:9	559
Delilah s unto Samson, Behold,	Judg 16:10	559
he s unto her, If they bind me	Judg 16:11	559
s unto him, The Philistines be	Judg 16:12	559
Delilah s unto Samson, Hitherto	Judg 16:13	559
he s unto her, If thou weavest	Judg 16:13	559
s unto him, The Philistines be	Judg 16:14	559
she s unto him, How canst thou	Judg 16:15	559
s unto her, There hath not come a	Judg 16:17	559
And she s, The Philistines be upon	Judg 16:20	559
he awoke out of his sleep, and s	Judg 16:20	559
for they s, Our god hath	Judg 16:23	559
for they s, Our god hath	Judg 16:24	559
hearts were merry, that they s	Judg 16:25	559
Samson s unto the lad that held	Judg 16:26	559
Samson called unto the LORD, and s	Judg 16:28	559
And Samson s, Let me die with the	Judg 16:30	559
he s unto his mother, The eleven	Judg 17:2	559
And his mother s, Blessed be thou	Judg 17:2	559
to his mother, his mother s	Judg 17:3	559
Micah s unto him, Whence comest	Judg 17:9	559
he s unto him, I am a Levite of	Judg 17:9	559
Micah s unto him, Dwell with me,	Judg 17:10	559
Then s Micah, Now know I that the	Judg 17:13	559
they s unto them, Go, search the	Judg 18:2	559
s unto him, Who brought thee	Judg 18:3	559
he s unto them, Thus and thus	Judg 18:4	559
they s unto him, Ask counsel, we	Judg 18:5	559
And the priest s unto them	Judg 18:6	559
and their brethren s unto them	Judg 18:8	559
And they s, Arise, that we may go	Judg 18:9	559
s unto their brethren, Do ye know	Judg 18:14	559
Then s the priest unto them, What	Judg 18:18	559
they s unto him, Hold thy peace,	Judg 18:19	559
s unto Micah, What aileth thee,	Judg 18:23	559
And he s, Ye have taken away my	Judg 18:24	559
And the children of Dan s unto him	Judg 18:25	559
father s unto his son in law	Judg 19:5	559
father had s unto the man	Judg 19:6	559
and the damsel's father s, Comfort	Judg 19:8	559
s unto him, Behold, now the day	Judg 19:9	559
the servant s unto his master,	Judg 19:11	559
And his master s unto him, We will	Judg 19:12	559
he s unto his servant, Come, and	Judg 19:13	559
and the old man s, Whither goest	Judg 19:17	559
he s unto him, We are passing	Judg 19:18	559
And the old man s, Peace be with	Judg 19:20	559

s unto them, Nay, my brethren, Judg 19:23 559
he s unto her, Up, and let us be Judg 19:28 559
it was so, that all that saw it s Judg 19:30 559
Then s the children of Israel Judg 20:3 559
that was slain, answered and s Judg 20:4 559
and asked counsel of God, and s Judg 20:18 559
And the LORD s, Judah shall go up Judg 20:18 559
And the LORD s, Go up against him Judg 20:23 559
And the LORD s, Go up Judg 20:28 559
And the children of Benjamin s Judg 20:32 559
But the children of Israel s Judg 20:32 559
for they s, Surely they are Judg 20:39 559
And s, O LORD God of Israel, why Judg 21:3 559
And the children of Israel s Judg 21:5 559
for Benjamin their brother, and s Judg 21:6 559
And they s, What one is there of Judg 21:8 559
the elders of the congregation s Judg 21:16 559
And they s, There must be an Judg 21:17 559
Then they s, Behold, there is a Judg 21:19 559
Naomi s unto her two daughters in Ruth 1:8 559
they s unto her, Surely we will Ruth 1:10 559
And Naomi s, Turn again, my Ruth 1:11 559
And she s, Behold, thy sister in Ruth 1:15 559
And Ruth s, Intreat me not to Ruth 1:16 559
was moved about them, and they s Ruth 1:19 559
she s unto them, Call me not Ruth 1:20 559
Ruth the Moabitess s unto Naomi Ruth 2:2 559
she s unto her, Go, my daughter Ruth 2:2 559
s unto the reapers, The LORD be Ruth 2:4 559
Then s Boaz unto his servant that Ruth 2:5 559
over the reapers answered and s Ruth 2:6 559
And she s, I pray you, let me Ruth 2:7 559
Then s Boaz unto Ruth, Hearest Ruth 2:8 559
s unto him, Why have I found Ruth 2:10 559
s unto her, It hath fully been Ruth 2:11 559
Then she s, Let me find favour in Ruth 2:13 559
Boaz s unto her, At mealtime come Ruth 2:14 559
And her mother in law s unto her Ruth 2:19 559
with whom she had wrought, and s Ruth 2:19 559
Naomi s unto her daughter in law, Ruth 2:20 559
Naomi s unto her, The man is near Ruth 2:20 559
And Ruth the Moabitess s, He s Ruth 2:21 559
Naomi s unto Ruth her daughter in Ruth 2:22 559
her mother in law s unto her Ruth 3:1 559
she s unto her, All that thou Ruth 3:5 559
And he s, Who art thou Ruth 3:9 559
And he s, Blessed be thou of the Ruth 3:10 559
And he s, Let it not be known that Ruth 3:14 559
Also he s, Bring the vail that Ruth 3:15 559
came to her mother in law, she s Ruth 3:16 559
And she s, These six measures of Ruth 3:17 559
for he s to me, Go not empty unto Ruth 3:17 559
Then s she, Sit still, my Ruth 3:18 559
unto whom he s, Ho, such a one Ruth 4:1 559
of the elders of the city, and s Ruth 4:2 559
he s unto the kinsman, Naomi, Ruth 4:3 559
And he s, I will redeem it Ruth 4:4 559
Then s Boaz, What day thou buyest Ruth 4:5 559
And the kinsman s, I cannot redeem Ruth 4:6 559
Therefore the kinsman s unto Boaz Ruth 4:8 559
Boaz s unto the elders, and unto Ruth 4:9 559
in the gate, and the elders, s Ruth 4:11 559
the women s unto Naomi, Blessed Ruth 4:14 559
Then s Elkanah her husband to her 1Sa 1:8 559
And she vowed a vow, and s, O LORD 1Sa 1:11 559
Eli s unto her, How long wilt 1Sa 1:14 559
And Hannah answered and s, No, my 1Sa 1:15 559
Then Eli answered and s, Go in 1Sa 1:17 559
And she s, Let thine handmaid find 1Sa 1:18 559
for she s unto her husband, I 1Sa 1:22 559
And Elkanah her husband s unto her 1Sa 1:23 559
And she s, Oh my lord, as thy soul 1Sa 1:26 559
And Hannah prayed, and s, My heart 1Sa 2:1 559
s to the man that sacrificed, 1Sa 2:15 559
And if any man s unto him, Let 1Sa 2:16 559
blessed Elkanah and his wife, and s 1Sa 2:20 559
he s unto them, Why do ye such 1Sa 2:23 559
s unto him, Thus saith the LORD, 1Sa 2:27 559
I s indeed that thy house, and the 1Sa 2:30 559
And he ran unto Eli, and s, Here am 1Sa 3:5 559
And he s, I called not 1Sa 3:5 559
Samuel arose and went to Eli, and s 1Sa 3:6 559
And he arose and went to Eli, and s 1Sa 3:8 559
Therefore Eli s unto Samuel 1Sa 3:9 559
the LORD s to Samuel, Behold, I 1Sa 3:11 559
Then Eli called Samuel, and s 1Sa 3:16 559
And he s, What is the thing that 1Sa 3:17 559
that the LORD hath s unto thee 1Sa 3:17 1696
the things that he s unto thee 1Sa 3:17 1696
And he s, It is the LORD 1Sa 3:18 559
the camp, the elders of Israel s 1Sa 4:3 559
the noise of the shout, they s 1Sa 4:6 559
were afraid, for they s, God is 1Sa 4:7 559
And they s, Woe unto us 1Sa 4:7 559
the noise of the crying, he s 1Sa 4:14 559
the man s unto Eli, I am he that 1Sa 4:16 559
And he s, What is there done, my 1Sa 4:16 559
And the messenger answered and s 1Sa 4:17 559
that stood by her s unto her 1Sa 4:20 1696
And she s, The glory is departed 1Sa 4:22 559
Ashdod saw that it was so, they s 1Sa 5:7 559
the Philistines unto them, and s 1Sa 5:8 559
lords of the Philistines, and s 1Sa 5:11 559
And they s, If ye send away the 1Sa 6:3 559
Then s they, What shall be the 1Sa 6:4 559
And the men of Beth-shemesh s 1Sa 6:20 559
And Samuel s, Gather all Israel to 1Sa 7:5 559
s there, We have sinned against 1Sa 7:6 559
children of Israel s to Samuel 1Sa 7:8 559
s unto him, Behold, thou art old, 1Sa 8:5 559
displeased Samuel, when they s 1Sa 8:6 559
the LORD s unto Samuel, Hearken 1Sa 8:7 559
And he s, This will be the manner 1Sa 8:11 559
and they s, Nay 1Sa 8:19 559
the LORD s to Samuel, Hearken 1Sa 8:22 559
Samuel s unto the men of Israel, 1Sa 8:22 559
Kish s to Saul his son, Take now 1Sa 9:3 559
Saul s to his servant that was 1Sa 9:5 559
he s unto him, Behold now, there 1Sa 9:6 559
Then s Saul to his servant, But, 1Sa 9:7 559
servant answered Saul again, and s 1Sa 9:8 559
Then s Saul to his servant, Well 1Sa 9:10 1697
Saul to his servant, Well s 1Sa 9:10 559
s unto them, Is the seer here 1Sa 9:11 559
And they answered them, and s 1Sa 9:12 559
saw Saul, the LORD s unto him 1Sa 9:17 6030
near to Samuel in the gate, and s 1Sa 9:18 559
And Samuel answered Saul, and s 1Sa 9:19 559
And Saul answered and s, Am not I a 1Sa 9:21 559
Samuel s unto the cook, Bring the 1Sa 9:23 559
gave thee, of which I s unto thee 1Sa 9:23 559
And Samuel s, Behold that which is 1Sa 9:24 559
it been kept for thee since I s 1Sa 9:24 559
Samuel s to Saul, Bid the servant 1Sa 9:27 559
his head, and kissed him, and s 1Sa 10:1 559
then the people s one to another 1Sa 10:11 559
of the same place answered and s 1Sa 10:12 559
And Saul's uncle s unto him 1Sa 10:14 559
And he s, To seek the asses 1Sa 10:14 559
And Saul's uncle s, Tell me, I 1Sa 10:15 559
pray thee, what Samuel s unto you 1Sa 10:15 559
Saul s unto his uncle, He told us 1Sa 10:16 559
s unto the children of Israel, 1Sa 10:18 559
ye have s unto him, Nay, but set 1Sa 10:19 559
Samuel s to all the people, See 1Sa 10:24 559
And all the people shouted, and s 1Sa 10:24 559
But the children of Belial s 1Sa 10:27 559
the men of Jabesh s unto Nahash 1Sa 11:1 559
the elders of Jabesh s unto him 1Sa 11:3 559
and Saul s, What aileth the people 1Sa 11:5 559
they s unto the messengers that 1Sa 11:9 559
Therefore the men of Jabesh s 1Sa 11:10 559
the people s unto Samuel, Who is 1Sa 11:12 559
unto Samuel, Who is he that s 1Sa 11:12 559
And Saul s, There shall not a man 1Sa 11:13 559
Then s Samuel to the people, Come 1Sa 11:14 559
Samuel s unto all Israel, Behold, 1Sa 12:1 559
voice in all that ye s unto me 1Sa 12:1 559
And they s, Thou hast not 1Sa 12:4 559
he s unto them, The LORD is 1Sa 12:5 559
Samuel s unto the people, It is 1Sa 12:6 559
And they cried unto the LORD, and s 1Sa 12:10 559
against you, ye s unto me, Nay 1Sa 12:12 559
And all the people s unto Samuel 1Sa 12:19 559
Samuel s unto the people, Fear 1Sa 12:20 559
And Saul s, Bring hither a burnt 1Sa 13:9 559
And Samuel s, What hast thou done 1Sa 13:11 559
And Saul s, Because I saw that the 1Sa 13:11 559
Therefore s I, The Philistines 1Sa 13:12 559
Samuel s to Saul, Thou hast done 1Sa 13:13 559
for the Philistines s, Lest the 1Sa 13:19 559
s unto the young man that bare 1Sa 14:1 559
Jonathan s to the young man that 1Sa 14:6 559
And his armourbearer s unto him 1Sa 14:7 559
Then s Jonathan, Behold, we will 1Sa 14:8 559
and the Philistines s, Behold, the 1Sa 14:11 559
and his armourbearer, and s 1Sa 14:12 559
Jonathan s unto his armourbearer, 1Sa 14:12 559
Then s Saul unto the people that 1Sa 14:17 559
Saul s unto Ahiah, Bring hither 1Sa 14:18 559
Saul s unto the priest, Withdraw 1Sa 14:19 559
answered one of the people, and s 1Sa 14:28 559
Then s Jonathan, My father hath 1Sa 14:29 559
And he s, Ye have transgressed 1Sa 14:33 559
And Saul s, Disperse yourselves 1Sa 14:34 559
And Saul s, Let us go down after 1Sa 14:36 559
And they s, Do whatsoever seemeth 1Sa 14:36 559
Then s the priest, Let us draw 1Sa 14:36 559
And Saul s, Draw ye near hither, 1Sa 14:38 559
Then s he unto all Israel, Be ye 1Sa 14:40 559
And the people s unto Saul 1Sa 14:40 559
Therefore Saul s unto the LORD 1Sa 14:41 559
And Saul s, Cast lots between me 1Sa 14:42 559
Then Saul s to Jonathan, Tell me 1Sa 14:43 559
And Jonathan told him, and s 1Sa 14:43 559
And the people s unto Saul 1Sa 14:45 559
Samuel also s unto Saul, The LORD 1Sa 15:1 559
Saul s unto the Kenites, Go, 1Sa 15:6 559
Saul s unto him, Blessed be thou 1Sa 15:13 559
And Samuel s, What meaneth then 1Sa 15:14 559
And Saul s, They have brought them 1Sa 15:15 559
Then Samuel s unto Saul, Stay, and 1Sa 15:16 559
the LORD hath s to me this night 1Sa 15:16 1696
And he s unto him, Say on 1Sa 15:16 559
And Samuel s, When thou wast 1Sa 15:17 559
LORD sent thee on a journey, and s 1Sa 15:18 559
Saul s unto Samuel, Yea, I have 1Sa 15:20 559
And Samuel s, Hath the LORD as 1Sa 15:22 559
Saul s unto Samuel, I have sinned 1Sa 15:24 559
Samuel s unto Saul, I will not 1Sa 15:26 559
Samuel s unto him, The LORD hath 1Sa 15:28 559
Then he s, I have sinned 1Sa 15:30 559
Then s Samuel, Bring ye hither to 1Sa 15:32 559
And Agag s, Surely the bitterness 1Sa 15:32 559
And Samuel s, As thy sword hath 1Sa 15:33 559
the LORD s unto Samuel, How long 1Sa 16:1 559
And Samuel s, How can I go 1Sa 16:2 559
And the LORD s, Take an heifer 1Sa 16:2 559
town trembled at his coming, and s 1Sa 16:4 559
And he s, Peaceably 1Sa 16:5 559
that he looked on Eliab, and s 1Sa 16:6 559
But the LORD s unto Samuel 1Sa 16:7 559
And he s, Neither hath the LORD 1Sa 16:8 559
And he s, Neither hath the LORD 1Sa 16:9 559
Samuel s unto Jesse, The LORD 1Sa 16:10 559
Samuel s unto Jesse, Are here all 1Sa 16:11 559
And he s, There remaineth yet the 1Sa 16:11 559
Samuel s unto Jesse, Send and 1Sa 16:11 559
And the LORD s, Arise, anoint him 1Sa 16:12 559
And Saul's servants s unto him 1Sa 16:15 559
Saul s unto his servants, Provide 1Sa 16:17 559
one of the servants, and s 1Sa 16:18 559
sent messengers unto Jesse, and s 1Sa 16:19 559
s unto them, Why are ye come out 1Sa 17:8 559
And the Philistine s, I defy the 1Sa 17:10 559
Jesse s unto David his son, Take 1Sa 17:17 559
And the men of Israel s, Have ye 1Sa 17:25 559
kindled against David, and he s 1Sa 17:28 559
And David s, What have I now done 1Sa 17:29 559
David s to Saul, Let no man's 1Sa 17:32 559
Saul s to David, Thou art not 1Sa 17:33 559
David s unto Saul, Thy servant 1Sa 17:34 559
David s moreover, The LORD that 1Sa 17:37 559
Saul s unto David, Go, and the 1Sa 17:37 559
David s unto Saul, I cannot go 1Sa 17:39 559
And the Philistine s unto David 1Sa 17:43 559
And the Philistine s to David 1Sa 17:44 559
Then s David to the Philistine, 1Sa 17:45 559
he s unto Abner, the captain of 1Sa 17:55 559
And Abner s, As thy soul liveth, O 1Sa 17:55 559
And the king s, Enquire thou whose 1Sa 17:56 559
Saul s to him, Whose son art thou 1Sa 17:58 559
one another as they played, and s 1Sa 18:7 559
and he s, They have ascribed unto 1Sa 18:8 559
for he s, I will smite David even 1Sa 18:11 559
Saul s to David, Behold my elder 1Sa 18:17 559
For Saul s, Let not mine hand be 1Sa 18:17 559
David s unto Saul, Who am I 1Sa 18:18 559
And Saul s, I will give him her, 1Sa 18:21 559
Wherefore Saul s to David 1Sa 18:21 559
And David s, Seemeth it to you a 1Sa 18:23 559
And Saul s, Thus shall ye say to 1Sa 18:25 559
s unto him, Let not the king sin 1Sa 19:4 559
messengers to take David, she s 1Sa 19:14 559
Saul s unto Michal, Why hast thou 1Sa 19:17 559
Saul, He s unto me, Let me go 1Sa 19:17 559
and he asked and s, Where are 1Sa 19:22 559
And one s, Behold, they be at 1Sa 19:22 559
s before Jonathan, What have I 1Sa 20:1 559
he s unto him, God forbid 1Sa 20:2 559
And David sware moreover, and s 1Sa 20:3 559
Then s Jonathan unto David, 1Sa 20:4 559
David s unto Jonathan, Behold, to 1Sa 20:5 559
And Jonathan s, Far be it from 1Sa 20:9 559
Then s David to Jonathan, Who 1Sa 20:10 559
Jonathan s unto David, Come, and 1Sa 20:11 559
Jonathan s unto David, O LORD God 1Sa 20:12 559
Then Jonathan s to David, To 1Sa 20:18 559
Saul s unto Jonathan his son, 1Sa 20:27 559
And he s, Let me go, I pray thee 1Sa 20:29 559
he s unto him, Thou son of the 1Sa 20:30 559
s unto him, Wherefore shall he be 1Sa 20:32 559
he s unto his lad, Run, find out 1Sa 20:36 559
cried after the lad, and s 1Sa 20:37 559
s unto him, Go, carry them to the 1Sa 20:40 559
And Jonathan s to David, Go in 1Sa 20:42 559
s unto him, Why art thou alone, 1Sa 21:1 559
David s unto Ahimelech the priest 1Sa 21:2 559
hath s unto me, Let no man know 1Sa 21:2 559
the priest answered David, and s 1Sa 21:4 559
s unto him, Of a truth women have 1Sa 21:5 559
David s unto Ahimelech, And is 1Sa 21:8 559
And the priest s, The sword of 1Sa 21:9 559
And David s, There is none like 1Sa 21:9 559
the servants of Achish s unto him 1Sa 21:11 559
Then s Achish unto his servants, 1Sa 21:14 559
he s unto the king of Moab, Let 1Sa 22:3 559
And the prophet Gad s unto David 1Sa 22:5 559
Then Saul s unto his servants 1Sa 22:7 559
over the servants of Saul, and s 1Sa 22:9 559
And Saul s, Hear now, thou son of 1Sa 22:12 559
Saul s unto him, Why have ye 1Sa 22:13 559
Ahimelech answered the king, and s 1Sa 22:14 559
And the king s, Thou shalt surely 1Sa 22:16 559
the king s unto the footmen that 1Sa 22:17 559
And the king s to Doeg, Turn thou, 1Sa 22:18 559
David s unto Abiathar, I knew it 1Sa 22:22 559
the LORD s unto David, Go, and 1Sa 23:2 559
And David's men s unto him 1Sa 23:3 559
And the LORD answered him and s 1Sa 23:4 559
And Saul s, God hath delivered him 1Sa 23:7 559
he s to Abiathar the priest, 1Sa 23:9 559
Then s David, O LORD God of 1Sa 23:10 559
And the LORD s, He will come down 1Sa 23:11 559
Then s David, Will the men of 1Sa 23:12 559
And the LORD s, They will deliver 1Sa 23:12 559
And he s unto him, Fear not 1Sa 23:17 559
And Saul s, Blessed be ye of the 1Sa 23:21 559
And the men of David s unto him 1Sa 24:4 559
day of which the LORD s unto thee 1Sa 24:4 559
he s unto his men, The LORD 1Sa 24:6 559
David s to Saul, Wherefore 1Sa 24:9 559
and I s, I will not put forth mine 1Sa 24:10 559
words unto Saul, that Saul s 1Sa 24:16 559
he s to David, Thou art more 1Sa 24:17 559
David s unto the young men, Get 1Sa 25:5 559
answered David's servants, and s 1Sa 25:10 559
David s unto his men, Gird ye on 1Sa 25:13 559
she s unto her servants, Go on 1Sa 25:19 559
Now David had s, Surely in vain 1Sa 25:21 559
And fell at his feet, and s 1Sa 25:24 559
David s to Abigail, Blessed be 1Sa 25:32 559
s unto her, Go up in peace to 1Sa 25:35 559
heard that Nabal was dead, he s 1Sa 25:39 559
on her face to the earth, and s 1Sa 25:41 559
s to Ahimelech the Hittite, and to 1Sa 26:6 559
And Abishai s, I will go down with 1Sa 26:6 559
Then s Abishai to David, God hath 1Sa 26:8 559
David s to Abishai, Destroy him 1Sa 26:9 559
David s furthermore, As the LORD 1Sa 26:10 559
Then Abner answered and s, Who art 1Sa 26:14 559
David s to Abner, Art not thou a 1Sa 26:15 559

And Saul knew David's voice, and *s* 1Sa 26:17 559
And David *s*, It is my voice, my 1Sa 26:17 559
And he *s*, Wherefore doth my lord 1Sa 26:18 559
Then *s* Saul, I have sinned 1Sa 26:21 559
And David answered and *s*, Behold 1Sa 26:22 559
Then Saul *s* to David, Blessed be 1Sa 26:25 559
David *s* in his heart, I shall now 1Sa 27:1 559
David *s* unto Achish, If I have 1Sa 27:5 559
And Achish *s*, Whither have ye made 1Sa 27:10 559
And David *s*, Against the south of 1Sa 27:10 559
Achish *s* unto David, Know thou 1Sa 28:1 559
David *s* to Achish, Surely thou 1Sa 28:2 559
Achish *s* to David, Therefore will 1Sa 28:2 559
Then *s* Saul unto his servants, 1Sa 28:7 559
And his servants *s* to him, Behold, 1Sa 28:7 559
and he *s*, I pray thee, divine unto 1Sa 28:8 559
And the woman *s* unto him, Behold, 1Sa 28:9 559
Then *s* the woman, Whom shall I 1Sa 28:11 559
And he *s*, Bring me up Samuel 1Sa 28:11 559
And the king *s* unto her, Be not 1Sa 28:13 559
And the woman *s* unto Saul, I saw 1Sa 28:13 559
he *s* unto her, What form is he of 1Sa 28:14 559
And she *s*, An old man cometh up 1Sa 28:14 559
Samuel *s* to Saul, Why hast thou 1Sa 28:15 559
Then *s* Samuel, Wherefore then 1Sa 28:16 559
s unto him, Behold, thine 1Sa 28:21 559
But he refused, and *s*, I will not 1Sa 28:23 559
Then *s* the princes of the 1Sa 29:3 559
Achish *s* unto the princes of the 1Sa 29:3 559
of the Philistines *s* unto him 1Sa 29:4 559
s unto him, Surely, as the LORD 1Sa 29:6 559
David *s* unto Achish, But what 1Sa 29:8 559
s to David, I know that thou art 1Sa 29:9 559
princes of the Philistines have *s* 1Sa 29:9 559
David *s* to Abiathar the priest, 1Sa 30:7 559
David *s* unto him, To whom 1Sa 30:13 559
And he *s*, I am a young man of 1Sa 30:13 559
David *s* to him, Canst thou bring 1Sa 30:15 559
And he *s*, Swear unto me by God, 1Sa 30:15 559
before those other cattle, and *s* 1Sa 30:20 559
those that went with David, and *s* 1Sa 30:22 559
Then *s* David, Ye shall not do so, 1Sa 30:23 559
Then *s* Saul unto his armourbearer 1Sa 31:4 559
David *s* unto him, From whence 2Sa 1:3 559
he *s* unto him, Out of the camp of 2Sa 1:3 559
David *s* unto him, How went the 2Sa 1:4 559
David *s* unto the young man that 2Sa 1:5 559
And the young man that told him *s* 2Sa 1:6 559
he *s* unto me, Who art thou 2Sa 1:8 559
He *s* unto me again, Stand, I pray 2Sa 1:9 559
David *s* unto the young man that 2Sa 1:13 559
David *s* unto him, How wast thou 2Sa 1:14 559
called one of the young men, and *s* 2Sa 1:15 559
David *s* unto him, Thy blood be 2Sa 1:16 559
And the LORD *s* unto him, Go up 2Sa 2:1 559
And David *s*, Whither shall I go up 2Sa 2:1 559
And he *s*, Unto Hebron 2Sa 2:1 559
s unto them, Blessed be ye of the 2Sa 2:5 559
Abner *s* to Joab, Let the young 2Sa 2:14 559
And Joab *s*, Let them arise 2Sa 2:14 559
Abner looked behind him, and *s* 2Sa 2:20 559
Abner *s* to him, Turn thee aside 2Sa 2:21 559
Abner *s* again to Asahel, Turn 2Sa 2:22 559
Then Abner called to Joab, and *s* 2Sa 2:26 559
And Joab *s*, As God liveth, unless 2Sa 2:27 559
and Ish-bosheth *s* to Abner 2Sa 3:7 559
the words of Ish-bosheth, and *s* 2Sa 3:8 559
And he *s*, Well 2Sa 3:13 559
Then *s* Abner unto him, Go, return 2Sa 3:16 559
Abner *s* unto David, I will arise 2Sa 3:21 559
Then Joab came to the king, and *s* 2Sa 3:24 559
when David heard it, he *s* 2Sa 3:28 559
David *s* to Joab, and to all the 2Sa 3:31 559
king lamented over Abner, and *s* 2Sa 3:33 559
the king *s* unto his servants, 2Sa 3:38 559
s to the king, Behold the head of 2Sa 4:8 559
s unto them, As the LORD liveth, 2Sa 4:9 559
and the LORD *s* to thee, Thou shalt 2Sa 5:2 559
David *s* on that day, Whosoever 2Sa 5:8 559
Wherefore they *s*, The blind and 2Sa 5:8 559
the LORD *s* unto David, Go up 2Sa 5:19 559
and David smote them there, and *s* 2Sa 5:20 559
David enquired of the LORD, he *s* 2Sa 5:23 559
afraid of the LORD that day, and *s* 2Sa 6:9 559
Saul came out to meet David, and *s* 2Sa 6:20 559
David *s* unto Michal, It was 2Sa 6:21 559
That the king *s* unto Nathan the 2Sa 7:2 559
Nathan *s* to the king, Go, do all 2Sa 7:3 559
and sat before the LORD, and he *s* 2Sa 7:18 559
it for ever, and do as thou hast *s* 2Sa 7:25 1696
And David *s*, Is there yet any that 2Sa 9:1 559
unto David, the king *s* unto him 2Sa 9:2 559
And he *s*, Thy servant is he 2Sa 9:2 559
And the king *s*, is there not yet 2Sa 9:3 559
Ziba *s* unto the king, Jonathan 2Sa 9:3 559
And the king *s* unto him, Where is 2Sa 9:4 559
Ziba *s* unto the king, Behold, he 2Sa 9:4 559
And David *s*, Mephibosheth 2Sa 9:6 559
David *s* unto him, Fear not 2Sa 9:7 559
And he bowed himself, and *s* 2Sa 9:8 559
s unto him, I have given unto thy 2Sa 9:9 559
Then *s* Ziba unto the king, 2Sa 9:11 559
s the king, he shall eat at my 2Sa 9:11
Then *s* David, I will shew 2Sa 10:2 559
of Ammon *s* unto Hanun their lord 2Sa 10:3 559
and the king *s*, Tarry at Jericho 2Sa 10:5 559
And he *s*, If the Syrians be too 2Sa 10:11 559
And one *s*, Is not this Bath-sheba, 2Sa 11:3 559
and sent and told David, and *s* 2Sa 11:5 559
David *s* to Uriah, Go down to thy 2Sa 11:8 559
David *s* unto Uriah, Camest thou 2Sa 11:10 559
Uriah *s* unto David, The ark, and 2Sa 11:11 559
David *s* to Uriah, Tarry here to 2Sa 11:12 559
And the messenger *s* unto David 2Sa 11:23 559

Then David *s* unto the messenger, 2Sa 11:25 559
s unto him, There were two men in 2Sa 12:1 559
he *s* to Nathan, As the LORD 2Sa 12:5 559
Nathan *s* to David, Thou art the 2Sa 12:7 559
David *s* unto Nathan, I have 2Sa 12:13 559
Nathan *s* unto David, The LORD 2Sa 12:13 559
for they *s*, Behold, while the 2Sa 12:18 559
therefore David *s* unto his 2Sa 12:19 559
And they *s*, He is dead 2Sa 12:19 559
Then *s* his servants unto him, 2Sa 12:21 559
And he *s*, While the child was yet 2Sa 12:22 559
for I *s*, Who can tell whether GOD 2Sa 12:22 559
sent messengers to David, and *s* 2Sa 12:27 559
he *s* unto him, Why art thou, 2Sa 13:4 559
Amnon *s* unto him, I love Tamar, 2Sa 13:4 559
Jonadab *s* unto him, Lay thee down 2Sa 13:5 559
Amnon *s* unto the king, I pray 2Sa 13:6 559
And Amnon *s*, Have out all men from 2Sa 13:9 559
Amnon *s* unto Tamar, Bring the 2Sa 13:10 559
s unto her, Come lie with me, my 2Sa 13:11 559
Amnon *s* unto her, Arise, be gone 2Sa 13:15 559
she *s* unto him, There is no cause 2Sa 13:16 559
that ministered unto him, and *s* 2Sa 13:17 559
And Absalom her brother *s* unto her 2Sa 13:20 559
And Absalom came to the king, and *s* 2Sa 13:24 559
the king *s* to Absalom, Nay, my 2Sa 13:25 559
Then *s* Absalom, If not, I pray 2Sa 13:26 559
And the king *s* unto him, Why 2Sa 13:26 559
David's brother, answered and *s* 2Sa 13:32 559
Jonadab *s* unto the king, Behold, 2Sa 13:35 559
as thy servant *s*, so it is 2Sa 13:35 1697
s unto her, I pray thee, feign 2Sa 14:2 559
ground, and did obeisance, and *s* 2Sa 14:4 559
And the king *s* unto her, What 2Sa 14:5 559
against thine handmaid, and they *s* 2Sa 14:7 559
the king *s* unto the woman, Go to 2Sa 14:8 559
woman of Tekoah *s* unto the king 2Sa 14:9 559
And the king *s*, Whosoever saith 2Sa 14:10 559
Then *s* she, I pray thee, let the 2Sa 14:11 559
And he *s*, As the LORD liveth, 2Sa 14:11 559
Then the woman *s*, Let thine 2Sa 14:12 559
And he *s*, Say on 2Sa 14:12 559
And the woman *s*, Wherefore then 2Sa 14:13 559
and thy handmaid *s*, I will now 2Sa 14:15 559
Then thine handmaid *s*, The word 2Sa 14:17 559
s unto the woman, Hide not from 2Sa 14:18 559
And the woman *s*, Let my lord the 2Sa 14:18 559
And the king *s*, Is not the hand of 2Sa 14:19 559
And the woman answered and *s* 2Sa 14:19 559
the king *s* unto Joab, Behold now, 2Sa 14:21 559
and Joab *s*, Today thy servant 2Sa 14:22 559
And the king *s*, Let him turn to 2Sa 14:24 559
Therefore he *s* unto his servants, 2Sa 14:30 559
s unto him, Wherefore have thy 2Sa 14:31 559
Absalom called unto him, and *s* 2Sa 15:2 559
And he *s*, Thy servant is of one of 2Sa 15:2 559
Absalom *s* unto him, See, thy 2Sa 15:3 559
Absalom *s* moreover, Oh that I 2Sa 15:4 559
that Absalom *s* unto the king, I 2Sa 15:7 559
And the king *s* unto him, Go in 2Sa 15:9 559
David *s* unto all his servants 2Sa 15:14 559
king's servants *s* unto the king 2Sa 15:15 559
Then *s* the king to Ittai the 2Sa 15:19 559
And Ittai answered the king, and *s* 2Sa 15:21 559
David *s* to Ittai, Go and pass over 2Sa 15:22 559
the king *s* unto Zadok, Carry back 2Sa 15:25 559
The king *s* also unto Zadok the 2Sa 15:27 559
And David *s*, O LORD, I pray thee, 2Sa 15:31 559
Unto whom David *s*, If thou 2Sa 15:33 559
the king *s* unto Ziba, What 2Sa 16:2 559
And Ziba *s*, The asses be for the 2Sa 16:2 559
And the king *s*, And where is thy 2Sa 16:3 559
Ziba *s* unto the king, Behold, he 2Sa 16:3 559
for he *s*, Today shall the house 2Sa 16:3 559
Then *s* the king to Ziba, Behold, 2Sa 16:4 559
And Ziba *s*, I humbly beseech thee 2Sa 16:4 559
thus *s* Shimei when he cursed, 2Sa 16:7 559
Then *s* Abishai the son of Zeruiah 2Sa 16:9 559
And the king *s*, What have I to do 2Sa 16:10 559
because the LORD hath *s* unto him 2Sa 16:10 559
David *s* to Abishai, and to all his 2Sa 16:11 559
that Hushai *s* unto Absalom, God 2Sa 16:16 559
Absalom *s* to Hushai, Is this thy 2Sa 16:17 559
Hushai *s* unto Absalom, Nay 2Sa 16:18 559
Then *s* Absalom to Ahithophel, 2Sa 16:20 559
Ahithophel *s* unto Absalom, Go in 2Sa 16:21 559
Ahithophel *s* unto Absalom 2Sa 17:1 559
Then *s* Absalom, Call now Hushai 2Sa 17:5 559
Hushai *s* unto Absalom, The 2Sa 17:7 559
s Hushai, thou knowest thy father 2Sa 17:8 559
and all the men of Israel *s* 2Sa 17:14 559
Then *s* Hushai unto Zadok and to 2Sa 17:15 559
to the woman to the house, they *s* 2Sa 17:20 559
And the woman *s* unto them, They be 2Sa 17:20 559
s unto David, Arise, and pass 2Sa 17:21 559
for they *s*, The people is hungry, 2Sa 17:29 559
the king *s* unto the people, I 2Sa 18:2 559
the king *s* unto them, What 2Sa 18:4 559
man saw it, and told Joab, and *s* 2Sa 18:10 559
Joab *s* unto the man that told him 2Sa 18:11 559
the man *s* unto Joab, Though I 2Sa 18:12 559
Then *s* Joab, I may not tarry thus 2Sa 18:14 559
for he *s*, I have no son to keep 2Sa 18:18 559
Then *s* Ahimaaz the son of Zadok, 2Sa 18:19 559
Joab *s* unto him, Thou shalt not 2Sa 18:20 559
Then *s* Joab to Cushi, Go tell the 2Sa 18:21 559
Then *s* Ahimaaz the son of Zadok 2Sa 18:22 559
And Joab *s*, Wherefore wilt thou 2Sa 18:22 559
But howsoever, *s* he, let me run 2Sa 18:23
And he *s* unto him, Run 2Sa 18:23 559
And the king *s*, If he be alone, 2Sa 18:25 559
called unto the porter, and *s* 2Sa 18:26 559
And the king *s*, He also bringeth 2Sa 18:26 559
And the watchman *s*, Me thinketh 2Sa 18:27 559

And the king *s*, He is a good man, 2Sa 18:27 559
s unto the king, All is well 2Sa 18:28 559
his face before the king, and *s* 2Sa 18:28 559
And the king *s*, Is the young man 2Sa 18:29 559
And the king *s* unto him, Turn 2Sa 18:30 559
and Cushi *s*, Tidings, my lord the 2Sa 18:31 559
the king *s* unto Cushi, Is the 2Sa 18:32 559
and as he went, thus he *s*, O my 2Sa 18:33 559
s Thou hast shamed this day the 2Sa 19:5 559
s unto the king, Let not my lord 2Sa 19:19 559
the son of Zeruiah answered and *s* 2Sa 19:21 559
And David *s*, What have I to do 2Sa 19:22 559
Therefore the king *s* unto Shimei 2Sa 19:23 559
king, that the king *s* unto him 2Sa 19:25 559
for thy servant *s*, I will saddle 2Sa 19:26 559
And the king *s* unto him, Why 2Sa 19:29 559
I have *s*, Thou and Ziba divide the 2Sa 19:29 559
Mephibosheth *s* unto the king, Yea 2Sa 19:30 559
the king *s* unto Barzillai, Come 2Sa 19:33 559
Barzillai *s* unto the king, How 2Sa 19:34 559
s unto the king, Why have our 2Sa 19:41 559
answered the men of Judah, and *s* 2Sa 19:43 559
and he blew a trumpet, and *s* 2Sa 20:1 559
Then *s* the king to Amasa, 2Sa 20:4 559
David *s* to Abishai, Now shall 2Sa 20:6 559
Joab *s* to Amasa, Art thou in 2Sa 20:9 559
of Joab's men stood by him, and *s* 2Sa 20:11 559
come near unto her, the woman *s* 2Sa 20:17 559
Then she *s* unto him, Hear the 2Sa 20:17 559
And Joab answered and *s*, Far be it, 2Sa 20:20 559
And the woman *s* unto Joab, Behold, 2Sa 20:21 559
the Gibeonites, and *s* unto them 2Sa 21:2 559
Wherefore David *s* unto the 2Sa 21:3 559
And the Gibeonites *s* unto him 2Sa 21:4 559
And he *s*, What ye shall say, that 2Sa 21:4 559
And the king *s*, I will give them 2Sa 21:6 559
And he *s*, The LORD is my rock, and 2Sa 22:2 559
David the son of Jesse *s*, and the 2Sa 23:1 5002
the sweet psalmist of Israel, *s* 2Sa 23:1 5002
The God of Israel *s*, the Rock of 2Sa 23:3 559
And David longed, and *s*, Oh that 2Sa 23:15 559
And he *s*, Be it far from me, O 2Sa 23:17 559
For the king *s* to Joab the 2Sa 24:2 559
Joab *s* unto the king, Now the 2Sa 24:3 559
David *s* unto the LORD, I have 2Sa 24:10 559
s unto him, Shall seven years of 2Sa 24:13 559
David *s* unto Gad, I am in a great 2Sa 24:14 559
s to the angel that destroyed the 2Sa 24:16 559
angel that smote the people, and *s* 2Sa 24:17 559
s unto him, Go up, rear an altar 2Sa 24:18 559
And Araunah *s*, Wherefore is my 2Sa 24:21 559
And David *s*, To buy the 2Sa 24:21 559
Araunah *s* unto David, Let my lord 2Sa 24:22 559
Araunah *s* unto the king, The LORD 2Sa 24:23 559
the king *s* unto Araunah, Nay 2Sa 24:24 559
Wherefore his servants *s* unto him 1Kin 1:2 559
And the king *s*, What wouldest thou 1Kin 1:16 559
she *s* unto him, My lord, thou 1Kin 1:17 559
And Nathan *s*, My lord, O king, 1Kin 1:24 559
My lord, O king, hast thou *s* 1Kin 1:24 559
Then king David answered and *s* 1Kin 1:28 559
And the king sware, and *s*, As the 1Kin 1:29 559
did reverence to the king, and *s* 1Kin 1:31 559
And king David *s*, Call me Zadok 1Kin 1:32 559
The king also *s* unto them 1Kin 1:33 559
Jehoiada answered the king, and *s* 1Kin 1:36 559
and all the people *s*, God save 1Kin 1:39 559
the sound of the trumpet, he *s* 1Kin 1:41 559
and Adonijah *s* unto him, Come in 1Kin 1:42 559
s to Adonijah, Verily our lord 1Kin 1:43 559
And also thus *s* the king, Blessed 1Kin 1:48 559
And Solomon *s*, If he will shew 1Kin 1:52 559
Solomon *s* unto him, Go to thine 1Kin 1:53 559
(*s* he) a man on the throne of 1Kin 2:4 559
And she *s*, Comest thou peaceably 1Kin 2:13 559
And he *s*, Peaceably 1Kin 2:13 559
He *s* moreover, I have somewhat to 1Kin 2:14 559
And she *s*, Say on 1Kin 2:14 559
And he *s*, Thou knowest that the 1Kin 2:15 559
And she *s* unto him, Say on 1Kin 2:16 559
And he *s*, Speak, I pray thee, unto 1Kin 2:17 559
And Bath-sheba *s*, Well 1Kin 2:18 559
Then she *s*, I desire one small 1Kin 2:20 559
And the king *s* unto her, Ask on, 1Kin 2:20 559
And she *s*, Let Abishag the 1Kin 2:21 559
s unto his mother, And why dost 1Kin 2:22 559
Abiathar the priest *s* the king 1Kin 2:26 559
s unto him, Thus saith the king, 1Kin 2:30 559
And he *s*, Nay 1Kin 2:30 559
word again, saying, Thus *s* Joab 1Kin 2:30 1696
And the king *s* unto him, Do as he 1Kin 2:31 559
Do as he hath *s* 1Kin 2:31 1696
s unto him, Build thee an house 1Kin 2:36 559
Shimei *s* unto the king, The 1Kin 2:38 559
as my lord the king hath *s* 1Kin 2:38 1696
s unto him, Did I not make thee 1Kin 2:42 559
The king *s* moreover to Shimei, 1Kin 2:44 559
and God *s*, Ask what I shall give 1Kin 3:5 559
And Solomon *s*, Thou hast shewed 1Kin 3:6 559
God *s* unto him, Because thou hast 1Kin 3:11 559
And the one woman *s*, O my lord, I 1Kin 3:17 559
And the other woman *s*, Nay 1Kin 3:22 559
And this *s*, No 1Kin 3:22 559
Then *s* the king, The one saith, 1Kin 3:23 559
And the king *s*, Bring me a sword 1Kin 3:24 559
And the king *s*, Divide the living 1Kin 3:25 559
yearned upon her son, and she *s* 1Kin 3:26 559
But the other *s*, Let it be 1Kin 3:26 559
Then the king answered and *s* 1Kin 3:27 559
that he rejoiced greatly, and *s* 1Kin 5:7 559
The LORD *s* that he would dwell in 1Kin 8:12 559
And he *s*, Blessed be the LORD God 1Kin 8:15 559
the LORD *s* unto David my father, 1Kin 8:18 559
And he *s*, LORD God of Israel, 1Kin 8:23 559

the place of which thou hast *s*	1Kin 8:29	559
And the LORD *s* unto him, I have	1Kin 9:3	559
And he *s*, What cities are these	1Kin 9:13	559
she *s* to the king, It was a true	1Kin 10:6	559
concerning which the LORD *s* unto	1Kin 11:2	559
Wherefore the LORD *s* unto Solomon	1Kin 11:11	559
Hadad *s* to Pharaoh, Let me depart	1Kin 11:21	559
Then Pharaoh *s* unto him, But what	1Kin 11:22	559
he *s* to Jeroboam, Take thee ten	1Kin 11:31	559
he *s* unto them, Depart yet for	1Kin 12:5	559
father while he yet lived, and *s*	1Kin 12:6	559
he *s* unto them, What counsel give	1Kin 12:9	559
Jeroboam *s* in his heart, Now	1Kin 12:26	559
s unto them, It is too much for	1Kin 12:28	559
in the word of the LORD, and *s*	1Kin 13:2	559
s unto the man of God, Intreat	1Kin 13:6	559
the king *s* unto the man of God,	1Kin 13:7	1696
And the man of God *s* unto the king	1Kin 13:8	559
And their father *s* unto them	1Kin 13:12	1696
he *s* unto his sons, Saddle me the	1Kin 13:13	559
he *s* unto him, Art thou the man	1Kin 13:14	559
And he *s*, I am	1Kin 13:14	559
Then he *s* unto him, Come home	1Kin 13:15	559
And he *s*, I may not return with	1Kin 13:16	559
For it was *s* to me by the word of	1Kin 13:17	1697
He *s* unto him, I am a prophet	1Kin 13:18	559
from the way heard thereof, he *s*	1Kin 13:26	559
Jeroboam *s* to his wife, Arise, I	1Kin 14:2	559
the LORD *s* unto Ahijah, Behold,	1Kin 14:5	559
came in at the door, that he *s*	1Kin 14:6	559
s unto Ahab, As the LORD God of	1Kin 17:1	559
and he called to her, and *s*	1Kin 17:10	559
fetch it, he called to her, and *s*	1Kin 17:11	559
And she *s*, As the LORD thy God	1Kin 17:12	559
Elijah *s* unto her, Fear not	1Kin 17:13	559
go and do as thou hast *s*	1Kin 17:13	559
she *s* unto Elijah, What have I to	1Kin 17:18	559
he *s* unto her, Give me thy son	1Kin 17:19	559
And he cried unto the LORD, and *s*	1Kin 17:20	559
and cried unto the LORD, and *s*	1Kin 17:21	559
and Elijah *s*, See, thy son liveth	1Kin 17:23	559
And the woman *s* to Elijah, Now by	1Kin 17:24	559
Ahab *s* unto Obadiah, Go into the	1Kin 18:5	559
him, and fell on his face, and *s*	1Kin 18:7	559
And he *s*, What have I sinned, that	1Kin 18:9	559
and when they *s*, He is not there	1Kin 18:10	559
And Elijah *s*, As the LORD of hosts	1Kin 18:15	559
saw Elijah, that Ahab *s* unto him	1Kin 18:17	559
came unto all the people, and *s*	1Kin 18:21	559
Then *s* Elijah unto the people, I,	1Kin 18:22	559
And all the people answered and *s*	1Kin 18:24	559
Elijah *s* unto the prophets of	1Kin 18:25	559
that Elijah mocked them, and *s*	1Kin 18:27	559
Elijah *s* unto all the people,	1Kin 18:30	559
and laid him on the wood, and *s*	1Kin 18:33	559
And he *s*, Do it the second time	1Kin 18:34	559
And he *s*, Do it the third time	1Kin 18:34	559
the prophet came near, and *s*	1Kin 18:36	559
and they *s*, The LORD, he is the	1Kin 18:39	559
Elijah *s* unto them, Take the	1Kin 18:40	559
Elijah *s* unto Ahab, Get thee up,	1Kin 18:41	559
s to his servant, Go up now, look	1Kin 18:43	559
And he went up, and looked, and *s*	1Kin 18:43	559
And he *s*, Go again seven times	1Kin 18:43	559
at the seventh time, that he *s*	1Kin 18:44	559
And he *s*, Go up, say unto Ahab,	1Kin 18:44	559
and *s*, It is enough	1Kin 19:4	559
him, and *s* unto him, Arise and eat	1Kin 19:5	559
second time, and touched him, and *s*	1Kin 19:7	559
he *s* unto him, What doest thou	1Kin 19:9	559
And he *s*, I have been very jealous	1Kin 19:10	559
And he *s*, Go forth, and stand upon	1Kin 19:11	559
there came a voice unto him, and *s*	1Kin 19:13	559
And he *s*, I have been very jealous	1Kin 19:14	559
And the LORD *s* unto him, Go,	1Kin 19:15	559
oxen, and ran after Elijah, and *s*	1Kin 19:20	559
he *s* unto him, Go back again	1Kin 19:20	559
s unto him, Thus saith Ben-hadad,	1Kin 20:2	559
the king of Israel answered and *s*	1Kin 20:4	559
the messengers came again, and *s*	1Kin 20:5	559
all the elders of the land, and *s*	1Kin 20:7	559
and all the people *s* unto him	1Kin 20:8	559
Wherefore he *s* unto the	1Kin 20:9	559
And Ben-hadad sent unto him, and *s*	1Kin 20:10	559
the king of Israel answered and *s*	1Kin 20:11	559
that he *s* unto his servants, Set	1Kin 20:12	559
And Ahab *s*, By whom	1Kin 20:14	559
And he *s*, Thus saith the LORD,	1Kin 20:14	559
Then he *s*, Who shall order the	1Kin 20:14	559
And he *s*, Whether they be come out	1Kin 20:18	559
s unto him, Go, strengthen	1Kin 20:22	559
of the king of Syria *s* unto him	1Kin 20:23	559
unto the king of Israel, and *s*	1Kin 20:28	
LORD, Because the Syrians have *s*	1Kin 20:28	559
And his servants *s* unto him	1Kin 20:31	559
came to the king of Israel, and *s*	1Kin 20:32	559
And he *s*, Is he yet alive	1Kin 20:32	559
and they *s*, Thy brother Ben-hadad	1Kin 20:33	559
Then he *s*, Go ye, bring him	1Kin 20:33	559
And Ben-hadad *s* unto him, The	1Kin 20:34	559
Then *s* Ahab, I will send thee	1Kin 20:34	
s unto his neighbour in the word	1Kin 20:35	559
Then *s* he unto him, Because thou	1Kin 20:36	559
Then he found another man, and *s*	1Kin 20:37	559
and he *s*, Thy servant went out	1Kin 20:39	559
and brought a man unto me, and *s*	1Kin 20:39	559
And the king of Israel *s* unto him	1Kin 20:40	559
he *s* unto him, Thus saith the	1Kin 20:42	559
Naboth *s* to Ahab, The LORD forbid	1Kin 21:3	559
for he had *s*, I will not give	1Kin 21:4	559
s unto him, Why is thy spirit so	1Kin 21:5	1696
he *s* unto her, Because I spake	1Kin 21:6	1696
s unto him, Give me thy vineyard	1Kin 21:6	559
And Jezebel his wife *s* unto him	1Kin 21:7	559
was dead, that Jezebel *s* to Ahab	1Kin 21:15	559
Ahab *s* to Elijah, Hast thou found	1Kin 21:20	559
of Israel *s* unto his servants	1Kin 22:3	559
he *s* unto Jehoshaphat, Wilt thou	1Kin 22:4	559
Jehoshaphat *s* to the king of	1Kin 22:4	559
Jehoshaphat *s* unto the king of	1Kin 22:5	559
s unto them, Shall I go against	1Kin 22:6	559
And they *s*, Go up	1Kin 22:6	559
And Jehoshaphat *s*, Is there not	1Kin 22:7	559
king of Israel *s* unto Jehoshaphat	1Kin 22:8	559
And Jehoshaphat *s*, Let not the	1Kin 22:8	559
of Israel called an officer, and *s*	1Kin 22:9	559
and he *s*, Thus saith the LORD,	1Kin 22:11	559
And Micaiah *s*, As the LORD liveth,	1Kin 22:14	559
And the king *s* unto him, Micaiah,	1Kin 22:15	559
And the king *s* unto him, How many	1Kin 22:16	559
And he *s*, I saw all Israel	1Kin 22:17	559
and the LORD *s*, These have no	1Kin 22:17	559
king of Israel *s* unto Jehoshaphat	1Kin 22:18	559
And he *s*, Hear thou therefore the	1Kin 22:19	559
And the LORD *s*, Who shall persuade	1Kin 22:20	559
one *s* on this manner, and another	1Kin 22:20	559
and another *s* on that manner	1Kin 22:20	559
and stood before the LORD, and *s*	1Kin 22:21	559
And the LORD *s* unto him, Wherewith	1Kin 22:22	559
And he *s*, I will go forth, and I	1Kin 22:22	559
And he *s*, Thou shalt persuade him,	1Kin 22:22	559
smote Micaiah on the cheek, and *s*	1Kin 22:24	559
And Micaiah *s*, Behold, thou shalt	1Kin 22:25	559
And the king of Israel *s*, Take	1Kin 22:26	559
And Micaiah *s*, If thou return at	1Kin 22:28	559
And he *s*, Hearken, O people, every	1Kin 22:28	559
king of Israel *s* unto Jehoshaphat	1Kin 22:30	559
saw Jehoshaphat, that they *s*	1Kin 22:32	559
wherefore he *s* unto the driver of	1Kin 22:34	559
Then *s* Ahaziah the son of Ahab	1Kin 22:49	559
s unto them, Go, enquire of	2Kin 1:2	559
the LORD *s* to Elijah the Tishbite	2Kin 1:3	1696
he *s* unto them, Why are ye now	2Kin 1:5	559
they *s* unto him, There came a man	2Kin 1:6	559
s unto us, Go, turn again unto	2Kin 1:6	559
he *s* unto them, What manner of	2Kin 1:7	1696
And he *s*, It is Elijah the	2Kin 1:8	559
Thou man of God, the king hath *s*	2Kin 1:9	1696
s to the captain of fifty, If I	2Kin 1:10	1696
s unto him, O man of God, thus	2Kin 1:11	1696
man of God, thus hath the king *s*	2Kin 1:11	559
s unto them, If I be a man of God	2Kin 1:12	1696
s unto him, O man of God, I pray	2Kin 1:13	1696
angel of the LORD *s* unto Elijah	2Kin 1:15	1696
he *s* unto him, Thus saith the	2Kin 1:16	1696
Elijah *s* unto Elisha, Tarry here,	2Kin 2:2	559
Elisha *s* unto him, As the LORD	2Kin 2:2	559
s unto him, Knowest thou that the	2Kin 2:3	559
And he *s*, Yea, I know it	2Kin 2:3	559
Elijah *s* unto him, Elisha, tarry	2Kin 2:4	559
And he *s*, As the LORD liveth, and	2Kin 2:4	559
s unto him, Knowest thou that the	2Kin 2:5	559
Elijah *s* unto him, Tarry, I pray	2Kin 2:6	559
And he *s*, As the LORD liveth, and	2Kin 2:6	559
over, that Elijah *s* unto Elisha	2Kin 2:9	559
And Elisha *s*, I pray thee, let a	2Kin 2:9	559
And he *s*, Thou hast asked a hard	2Kin 2:10	559
him, and smote the waters, and *s*	2Kin 2:14	559
view at Jericho saw him, they *s*	2Kin 2:15	559
they *s* unto him, Behold now,	2Kin 2:16	559
And he *s*, Ye shall not send	2Kin 2:16	559
him till he was ashamed, he *s*	2Kin 2:17	559
he *s* unto them, Did I not say	2Kin 2:18	559
the men of the city *s* unto Elisha	2Kin 2:19	559
And he *s*, Bring me a new cruse, and	2Kin 2:20	559
and cast the salt in there, and *s*	2Kin 2:21	559
s unto him, Go up, thou bald head	2Kin 2:23	559
And he *s*, I will go up	2Kin 3:7	559
And he *s*, Which way shall we go up	2Kin 3:8	559
And the king of Israel *s*, Alas	2Kin 3:10	559
But Jehoshaphat *s*, Is there not	2Kin 3:11	559
Israel's servants answered and *s*	2Kin 3:11	559
And Jehoshaphat *s*, The word of the	2Kin 3:12	559
Elisha *s* unto the king of Israel,	2Kin 3:13	559
And the king of Israel *s* unto him	2Kin 3:13	559
And Elisha *s*, As the LORD of hosts	2Kin 3:14	559
And he *s*, Thus saith the LORD,	2Kin 3:16	559
And they *s*, This is blood	2Kin 3:23	559
Elisha *s* unto her, What shall I	2Kin 4:2	559
And she *s*, Thine handmaid hath not	2Kin 4:2	559
Then he *s*, Go, borrow thee	2Kin 4:3	559
that she *s* unto her son, Bring me	2Kin 4:6	559
he *s* unto her, There is not a	2Kin 4:6	559
And he *s*, Go, sell the oil, and pay	2Kin 4:7	559
she *s* unto her husband, Behold	2Kin 4:9	559
he *s* to Gehazi his servant, Call	2Kin 4:12	559
he *s* unto him, Say now unto her,	2Kin 4:13	559
And he *s*, What then is to be done	2Kin 4:14	559
And he *s*, Call her	2Kin 4:15	559
And he *s*, About this season,	2Kin 4:16	559
And she *s*, Nay, my lord, thou man	2Kin 4:16	559
season that Elisha had *s* unto her	2Kin 4:17	1696
he *s* unto his father, My head, my	2Kin 4:19	559
he *s* to a lad, Carry him to his	2Kin 4:19	559
she called unto her husband, and *s*	2Kin 4:22	559
And he *s*, Wherefore wilt thou go	2Kin 4:23	559
And she *s*, It shall be well	2Kin 4:23	559
s to her servant, Drive, and go	2Kin 4:24	559
that he *s* to Gehazi his servant,	2Kin 4:25	559
And the man of God *s*, Let her	2Kin 4:27	559
Then she *s*, Did I desire a son of	2Kin 4:28	559
Then he *s* to Gehazi, Gird up thy	2Kin 4:29	559
And the mother of the child *s*	2Kin 4:30	559
And he called Gehazi, and *s*	2Kin 4:36	559
she was come in unto him, he *s*	2Kin 4:36	559
he *s* unto his servant, Set on the	2Kin 4:38	559
that they cried out, and *s*	2Kin 4:40	559
But he *s*, Then bring meal	2Kin 4:41	559
and he *s*, Pour out for the people,	2Kin 4:41	559
And he *s*, Give unto the people,	2Kin 4:42	559
And his servitor *s*, What, should I	2Kin 4:43	559
He *s* again, Give the people, that	2Kin 4:43	559
she *s* unto her mistress, Would	2Kin 5:3	559
thus *s* the maid that is of the	2Kin 5:4	1696
And the king of Syria *s*, Go to, go	2Kin 5:5	559
that he rent his clothes, and *s*	2Kin 5:7	559
was wroth, and went away, and *s*	2Kin 5:11	559
near, and spake unto him, and *s*	2Kin 5:13	559
and he *s*, Behold, now I know that	2Kin 5:15	559
But he *s*, As the LORD liveth,	2Kin 5:16	559
And Naaman *s*, Shall there not then	2Kin 5:17	559
he *s* unto him, Go in peace	2Kin 5:19	559
of Elisha the man of God, *s*	2Kin 5:20	559
the chariot to meet him, and *s*	2Kin 5:21	559
And he *s*, All is well	2Kin 5:22	559
And Naaman *s*, Be content, take two	2Kin 5:23	559
Elisha *s* unto him, Whence comest	2Kin 5:25	559
And he *s*, Thy servant went no	2Kin 5:25	559
he *s* unto him, Went not mine	2Kin 5:26	559
of the prophets *s* unto Elisha	2Kin 6:1	559
And one *s*, Be content, I pray thee	2Kin 6:3	559
and he cried, and *s*, Alas, master	2Kin 6:5	559
And the man of God *s*, Where fell	2Kin 6:6	559
Therefore *s* he, Take it up to	2Kin 6:7	559
s unto them, Will ye not shew me	2Kin 6:11	559
And one of his servants *s*, None,	2Kin 6:12	559
And he *s*, Go and spy where he is,	2Kin 6:13	559
And his servant *s* unto him	2Kin 6:15	559
And Elisha prayed, and *s*, LORD, I	2Kin 6:17	559
Elisha prayed unto the LORD, and *s*	2Kin 6:18	559
Elisha *s* unto them, This is not	2Kin 6:19	559
come into Samaria, that Elisha *s*	2Kin 6:20	559
the king of Israel *s* unto Elisha	2Kin 6:21	559
And he *s*, If the LORD do not help	2Kin 6:27	559
And the king *s* unto her, What	2Kin 6:28	559
answered, This woman *s* unto me	2Kin 6:28	559
I *s* unto her on the next day,	2Kin 6:29	559
Then he *s*, God do so and more also	2Kin 6:31	559
he *s* to the elders, See ye how	2Kin 6:32	559
and he *s*, Behold, this evil is of	2Kin 6:33	559
Then Elisha *s*, Hear ye the word	2Kin 7:1	559
answered the man of God, and *s*	2Kin 7:2	559
And he *s*, Behold, thou shalt see	2Kin 7:2	559
they *s* one to another, Why sit we	2Kin 7:3	559
they *s* one to another, Lo, the	2Kin 7:6	559
Then they *s* one to another, We do	2Kin 7:9	559
s unto his servants, I will now	2Kin 7:12	559
one of his servants answered and *s*	2Kin 7:13	559
he died, as the man of God had *s*	2Kin 7:17	1696
answered the man of God, and *s*	2Kin 7:19	559
And he *s*, Behold, thou shalt see	2Kin 7:19	559
And Gehazi *s*, My lord, O king,	2Kin 8:5	559
the king *s* unto Hazael, Take a	2Kin 8:8	559
and came and stood before him, and *s*.	2Kin 8:9	559
Elisha *s* unto him, Go, say unto	2Kin 8:10	559
And Hazael *s*, Why weepeth my lord	2Kin 8:12	559
And Hazael *s*, But what, is thy	2Kin 8:13	559
who *s* to him, What *s* Elisha to	2Kin 8:14	559
s unto him, Gird up thy loins, and	2Kin 9:1	559
and he *s*, I have an errand to thee	2Kin 9:5	559
And Jehu *s*, Unto which of all us	2Kin 9:5	559
And he *s*, To thee, O captain	2Kin 9:5	559
s unto him, Thus saith the LORD	2Kin 9:6	559
one *s* unto him, Is all well	2Kin 9:11	559
he *s* unto them, Ye know the man,	2Kin 9:11	559
And they *s*, It is false	2Kin 9:12	559
And he *s*, Thus and thus spake he to	2Kin 9:12	559
And Jehu *s*, If it be your minds	2Kin 9:15	559
company of Jehu as he came, and *s*	2Kin 9:17	559
And Joram *s*, Take an horseman, and	2Kin 9:17	559
on horseback to meet him, and *s*	2Kin 9:18	559
And Jehu *s*, What hast thou to do	2Kin 9:18	559
which came to them, and *s*	2Kin 9:19	559
And Joram *s*, Make ready	2Kin 9:21	559
when Joram saw Jehu, that he *s*	2Kin 9:22	559
s to Ahaziah, There is treachery,	2Kin 9:23	559
Then *s* Jehu to Bidkar his captain	2Kin 9:25	559
And Jehu followed after him, and *s*	2Kin 9:27	559
entered in at the gate, she *s*	2Kin 9:31	559
up his face to the window, and *s*	2Kin 9:32	559
And he *s*, Throw her down	2Kin 9:33	559
in, he did eat and drink, and *s*	2Kin 9:34	559
And he *s*, This is the word of the	2Kin 9:36	559
were exceedingly afraid, and *s*	2Kin 10:4	559
And he *s*, Lay ye them in two heaps	2Kin 10:8	559
s to all the people, Ye be	2Kin 10:9	559
of Ahaziah king of Judah, and *s*	2Kin 10:13	559
And he *s*, Take them alive	2Kin 10:14	559
s to him, Is thine heart right,	2Kin 10:15	559
And he *s*, Come with me, and see my	2Kin 10:16	559
s unto them, Ahab served Baal a	2Kin 10:18	559
And Jehu *s*, Proclaim a solemn	2Kin 10:20	559
he *s* unto him that was over the	2Kin 10:22	559
s unto the worshippers of Baal,	2Kin 10:23	559
fourscore men without, and *s*	2Kin 10:24	559
that Jehu *s* to the guard and to	2Kin 10:25	559
the LORD *s* unto Jehu, Because	2Kin 10:30	559
and they clapped their hands, and *s*	2Kin 11:12	559
s unto them, Have her forth	2Kin 11:15	559
For the priest had *s*, Let her not	2Kin 11:15	559
Jehoash *s* to the priests, All the	2Kin 12:4	559
s unto them, Why repair ye not	2Kin 12:7	559
him, and wept over his face, and *s*	2Kin 13:14	559
Elisha *s* unto him, Take bow and	2Kin 13:15	559
he *s* to the king of Israel, Put	2Kin 13:16	559
And he *s*, Open the window eastward	2Kin 13:17	559
Then Elisha *s*, Shoot	2Kin 13:17	559
And he *s*, The arrow of the LORD's	2Kin 13:17	559
And he *s*, Take the arrows	2Kin 13:18	559
he *s* unto the king of Israel,	2Kin 13:18	559
of God was wroth with him, and *s*	2Kin 13:19	559
the LORD *s* not that he would blot	2Kin 14:27	1696

whereof the LORD had s unto them	2Kin 17:12	559
as he had s by all his servants	2Kin 17:23	1696
And Rab-shakeh s unto them	2Kin 18:19	559
hath s to Judah and Jerusalem, Ye	2Kin 18:22	559
The LORD s to me, Go up against	2Kin 18:25	559
Then s Eliakim the son of Hilkiah	2Kin 18:26	559
But Rab-shakeh s unto them	2Kin 18:27	559
they s unto him, Thus saith	2Kin 19:3	559
Isaiah s unto them, Thus shall ye	2Kin 19:6	559
prayed before the LORD, and s	2Kin 19:15	559
reproached the Lord, and hast s	2Kin 19:23	559
s unto him, Thus saith the LORD,	2Kin 20:1	559
And Isaiah s, Take a lump of figs	2Kin 20:7	559
Hezekiah s unto Isaiah, What	2Kin 20:8	559
And Isaiah s, This sign shalt thou	2Kin 20:9	559
s unto him, What s these men	2Kin 20:14	559
And Hezekiah s, They are come from	2Kin 20:14	559
And he s, What have they seen in	2Kin 20:15	559
Isaiah s unto Hezekiah, Hear the	2Kin 20:16	559
Then s Hezekiah unto Isaiah, Good	2Kin 20:19	559
And he s, Is it not good, if peace	2Kin 20:19	559
of the LORD, of which the LORD s	2Kin 21:4	559
of which the LORD s to David	2Kin 21:7	559
priest s unto Shaphan the scribe	2Kin 22:8	559
brought the king word again, and s	2Kin 22:9	559
she s unto them, Thus saith the	2Kin 22:15	559
Then he s, What title is that	2Kin 23:17	559
And he s, Let him alone	2Kin 23:18	559
And the LORD s, I will remove	2Kin 23:27	559
chosen, and the house of which I s	2Kin 23:27	559
of the LORD, as the LORD had s	2Kin 24:13	1696
s unto them, Fear not to be the	2Kin 25:24	559
Then s Saul to his armourbearer,	1Chr 10:4	559
and the LORD thy God s unto thee	1Chr 11:2	559
inhabitants of Jebus s to David	1Chr 11:5	559
And David s, Whosoever smiteth the	1Chr 11:6	559
And David longed, and s, Oh that	1Chr 11:17	559
And s, My God forbid it me, that I	1Chr 11:19	559
s unto them, If ye be come	1Chr 12:17	559
chief of the captains, and he s	1Chr 12:18	
David s unto all the congregation	1Chr 13:2	559
all the congregation s that they	1Chr 13:4	559
And the LORD s unto him, Go up	1Chr 14:10	559
Then David s, God hath broken in	1Chr 14:11	559
God s unto him, Go not up after	1Chr 14:14	559
Then David s, None ought to carry	1Chr 15:2	559
s unto them, Ye are the chief of	1Chr 15:12	559
And all the people s, Amen, and	1Chr 16:36	559
that David s to Nathan the	1Chr 17:1	559
Then Nathan s unto David, Do all	1Chr 17:2	559
came and sat before the LORD, and s	1Chr 17:16	559
for ever, and do as thou hast s	1Chr 17:23	1696
And David s, I will shew kindness	1Chr 19:2	559
the children of Ammon s to Hanun	1Chr 19:3	559
And the king s, Tarry at Jericho	1Chr 19:5	559
And he s, If the Syrians be too	1Chr 19:12	559
David s to Joab and to the rulers	1Chr 21:2	559
David s unto God, I have sinned	1Chr 21:8	559
s unto him, Thus saith the LORD,	1Chr 21:11	559
David s unto Gad, I am in a great	1Chr 21:13	559
s to the angel that destroyed, It	1Chr 21:15	559
David s unto God, Is it not I	1Chr 21:17	559
Then David s to Ornan, Grant me	1Chr 21:22	559
Ornan s unto David, Take it to	1Chr 21:23	559
And king David s to Ornan, Nay	1Chr 21:24	559
Then David s, This is the house	1Chr 22:1	559
And David s, Solomon my son is	1Chr 22:5	559
David s to Solomon, My son, as	1Chr 22:7	559
thy God, as he hath s of thee	1Chr 22:11	1696
s David, to praise therewith	1Chr 23:5	
For David s, The LORD God of	1Chr 23:25	559
because the LORD had s he would	1Chr 27:23	559
king stood up upon his feet, and s	1Chr 28:2	559
But God s unto me, Thou shalt not	1Chr 28:3	559
he s unto me, Solomon thy son, he	1Chr 28:6	559
s David, the LORD made me	1Chr 28:19	
David s to Solomon his son, Be	1Chr 28:20	559
king s unto all the congregation	1Chr 29:1	559
and David s, Blessed be thou, LORD	1Chr 29:10	559
David s to all the congregation,	1Chr 29:20	559
s unto him, Ask what I shall give	2Chr 1:7	559
Solomon s unto God, Thou hast	2Chr 1:8	559
God s to Solomon, Because this	2Chr 1:11	559
Huram s moreover, Blessed be the	2Chr 2:12	559
Then s Solomon, The LORD hath	2Chr 6:1	559
The LORD hath s that he would	2Chr 6:1	559
And he s, Blessed be the LORD God	2Chr 6:4	559
But the LORD s to David my father	2Chr 6:8	559
And s, O LORD God of Israel, there	2Chr 6:14	559
the place whereof thou hast s	2Chr 6:20	559
s unto him, I have heard thy	2Chr 7:12	559
for he s, My wife shall not dwell	2Chr 8:11	559
she s to the king, It was a true	2Chr 9:5	559
he s unto them, Come again unto	2Chr 10:5	559
he s unto them, What advice give	2Chr 10:9	559
s unto them, Thus saith the LORD,	2Chr 12:5	559
and they s, The LORD is righteous	2Chr 12:6	559
which is in mount Ephraim, and s	2Chr 13:4	559
Therefore he s unto Judah	2Chr 14:7	559
cried unto the LORD his God, and s	2Chr 14:11	559
s unto him, Hear ye me, Asa, and	2Chr 15:2	559
s unto him, Because thou hast	2Chr 16:7	559
Ahab king of Israel s unto	2Chr 18:3	559
Jehoshaphat s unto the king of	2Chr 18:4	559
s unto them, Shall we go to	2Chr 18:5	559
And they s, Go up	2Chr 18:5	559
But Jehoshaphat s, Is there not	2Chr 18:6	559
king of Israel s unto Jehoshaphat	2Chr 18:7	559
And Jehoshaphat s, Let not the	2Chr 18:7	559
for one of his officers, and s	2Chr 18:8	559
had made him horns of iron, and s	2Chr 18:10	559
And Micaiah s, As the LORD liveth,	2Chr 18:13	559
to the king, the king s unto him	2Chr 18:14	559
And he s, Go ye up, and prosper, and	2Chr 18:14	559
And the king s to him, How many	2Chr 18:15	559
Then he s, I did see all Israel	2Chr 18:16	559
and the LORD s, These have no	2Chr 18:16	559
king of Israel s to Jehoshaphat	2Chr 18:17	559
Again he s, Therefore hear the	2Chr 18:18	559
And the LORD s, Who shall entice	2Chr 18:19	559
and stood before the LORD, and s	2Chr 18:20	559
And the LORD s unto him, Wherewith	2Chr 18:20	559
And he s, I will go out, and be a	2Chr 18:21	559
And the LORD s, Thou shalt entice	2Chr 18:21	559
Micaiah upon the cheek, and s	2Chr 18:23	559
And Micaiah s, Behold, thou shalt	2Chr 18:24	559
Then the king of Israel s	2Chr 18:25	559
And Micaiah s, If thou certainly	2Chr 18:27	559
And he s, Hearken, all ye people	2Chr 18:27	559
king of Israel s unto Jehoshaphat	2Chr 18:29	559
saw Jehoshaphat, that they s	2Chr 18:31	559
therefore he s to his chariot man	2Chr 18:33	559
s to king Jehoshaphat, Shouldest	2Chr 19:2	559
s to the judges, Take heed what	2Chr 19:6	559
And s, O LORD God of our fathers,	2Chr 20:6	559
And he s, Hearken ye, all Judah,	2Chr 20:15	559
forth, Jehoshaphat stood and s	2Chr 20:20	559
Because, s they, he is the son of	2Chr 22:9	559
he s unto them, Behold, the	2Chr 23:3	559
as the LORD hath s of the sons of	2Chr 23:3	1696
and his sons anointed him, and s	2Chr 23:11	559
Athaliah rent her clothes, and s	2Chr 23:13	559
s unto them, Have her forth of	2Chr 23:14	559
For the priest s, Slay her not in	2Chr 23:14	559
s to them, Go out unto the cities	2Chr 24:5	559
s unto him, Why hast thou not	2Chr 24:6	559
s unto them, Thus saith God, Why	2Chr 24:20	559
And when he died, he s, The LORD	2Chr 24:22	559
Amaziah s to the man of God, But	2Chr 25:9	559
which s unto him, Why hast thou	2Chr 25:15	559
him, that the king s unto him	2Chr 25:16	559
Then the prophet forbare, and s	2Chr 25:16	559
s unto him, It appertaineth not	2Chr 26:18	559
for they s, He is a leper	2Chr 26:23	559
s unto them, Behold, because the	2Chr 28:9	559
s unto them, Ye shall not bring	2Chr 28:13	559
and he s, Because the gods of the	2Chr 28:23	559
s unto them, Hear me, ye Levites,	2Chr 29:5	559
in to Hezekiah the king, and s	2Chr 29:18	559
Then Hezekiah answered and s	2Chr 29:31	559
house of Zadok answered him, and s	2Chr 31:10	559
the LORD, whereof the LORD had s	2Chr 33:4	559
God, of which God had s to David	2Chr 33:7	559
s to Shaphan the scribe, I have	2Chr 34:15	559
s unto the Levites that taught	2Chr 35:3	559
the king s to his servants, Have	2Chr 35:23	559
And the Tirshatha s unto them	Ezr 2:63	559
s unto them, Let us build with	Ezr 4:2	559
s unto them, Ye have nothing to	Ezr 4:3	559
s thus unto them, Who hath	Ezr 5:3	560
Then s we unto them after this	Ezr 5:4	560
s unto them thus, Who commanded	Ezr 5:9	560
s unto him, Take these vessels,	Ezr 5:15	560
I s unto them, Ye are holy unto	Ezr 8:28	559
And s, O my God, I am ashamed and	Ezr 9:6	559
s unto Ezra, We have trespassed	Ezr 10:2	559
s unto them, Ye have transgressed	Ezr 10:10	559
s with a loud voice, As thou hast	Ezr 10:12	559
with a loud voice, As thou hast s	Ezr 10:12	1697
they s unto me, The remnant that	Neh 1:3	559
And s, I beseech thee, O LORD God	Neh 1:5	559
Wherefore the king s unto me	Neh 2:2	559
s unto the king, Let the king	Neh 2:3	559
Then the king s unto me, For what	Neh 2:4	559
I s unto the king, If it please	Neh 2:5	559
And the king s unto me, (the queen	Neh 2:6	559
Moreover I s unto the king, If it	Neh 2:7	559
Then s I unto them, Ye see the	Neh 2:17	559
And they s, Let us rise up and	Neh 2:18	559
us to scorn, and despised us, and s	Neh 2:19	559
s unto them, The God of heaven,	Neh 2:20	559
and the army of Samaria, and s	Neh 4:2	559
the Ammonite was by him, and he s	Neh 4:3	559
And Judah s, The strength of the	Neh 4:10	559
And our adversaries s, They shall	Neh 4:11	559
they s unto us ten times, From	Neh 4:12	559
s unto the nobles, and to the	Neh 4:14	559
I s unto the nobles, and to the	Neh 4:19	559
the same time s I unto the people	Neh 4:22	559
For there were that s, We, our	Neh 5:2	559
Some also there were that s	Neh 5:3	559
There were also that s, We have	Neh 5:4	559
s unto them, Ye exact usury,	Neh 5:7	559
I s unto them, We after our	Neh 5:8	559
Also I s, It is not good that ye	Neh 5:9	559
Then s they, We will restore them	Neh 5:12	559
Also I shook my lap, and s	Neh 5:13	559
And all the congregation s	Neh 5:13	559
and he s, Let us meet together in	Neh 6:10	559
And I s, Should such a man as I	Neh 6:11	559
I s unto them, Let not the gates	Neh 7:3	559
And the Tirshatha s unto them	Neh 7:65	559
s unto all the people, This day	Neh 8:9	559
Then he s unto them, Go your way,	Neh 8:10	559
Shebaniah, and Pethahiah, s	Neh 9:5	559
had made them a molten calf, and s	Neh 9:18	559
contended I with the rulers, and s	Neh 13:11	559
s unto them, What evil thing is	Neh 13:17	559
s unto them, Why lodge ye about	Neh 13:21	559
Then the king s to the wise men,	Est 1:13	559
Then s the king's servants that	Est 2:2	559
king's gate, s unto Mordecai, Why	Est 3:3	559
Haman s unto king Ahasuerus,	Est 3:8	559
the king s unto Haman, The silver	Est 3:11	559
Then s the king unto her, What	Est 5:3	559
Then the king s, Cause Haman to	Est 5:5	559
that he may do as Esther hath s	Est 5:5	1697
the king s unto Esther at the	Est 5:6	559
Then answered Esther, and s	Est 5:7	559
do to morrow as the king hath s	Est 5:8	1697
Haman s moreover, Yea, Esther the	Est 5:12	559
Then s Zeresh his wife and all his	Est 5:14	559
And the king s, What honour and	Est 6:3	559
Then s the king's servants that	Est 6:3	559
And the king s, Who is in the	Est 6:4	559
And the king's servants s unto him	Est 6:5	559
And the king s, Let him come in	Est 6:5	559
And the king s unto him, What	Est 6:6	559
Then the king s to Haman, Make	Est 6:10	559
and the horse, as thou hast s	Est 6:10	1696
Then s his wise men and Zeresh his	Est 6:13	559
the king s again unto Esther on	Est 7:2	559
Esther the queen answered and s	Est 7:3	559
s unto Esther the queen, Who is	Est 7:5	559
And Esther s, The adversary and	Est 7:6	559
Then s the king, Will he force	Est 7:8	559
s before the king, Behold also,	Est 7:9	559
Then the king s, Hang him thereon	Est 7:9	559
And s, If it please the king, and	Est 8:5	559
Ahasuerus s unto Esther the queen	Est 8:7	559
the king s unto Esther the queen,	Est 9:12	559
Then s Esther, If it please the	Est 9:13	559
for Job s, It may be that my sons	Job 1:5	559
the LORD s unto Satan, Whence	Job 1:7	559
Satan answered the LORD, and s	Job 1:7	559
the LORD s unto Satan, Hast thou	Job 1:8	559
Satan answered the LORD, and s	Job 1:9	559
the LORD s unto Satan, Behold,	Job 1:12	559
came a messenger unto Job, and s	Job 1:14	559
there came also another, and s	Job 1:16	559
there came also another, and s	Job 1:17	559
there came also another, and s	Job 1:18	559
And s, Naked came I out of my	Job 1:21	559
the LORD s unto Satan, From	Job 2:2	559
And Satan answered the LORD, and s	Job 2:2	559
the LORD s unto Satan, Hast thou	Job 2:3	559
And Satan answered the LORD, and s	Job 2:4	559
the LORD s unto Satan, Behold, he	Job 2:6	559
Then s his wife unto him, Dost	Job 2:9	559
But he s unto her, Thou speakest	Job 2:10	559
And Job spake, and s,	Job 3:2	559
and the night in which it was s	Job 3:3	559
the Temanite answered and s	Job 4:1	559
But Job answered and s,	Job 6:1	559
answered Bildad the Shuhite, and s	Job 8:1	559
Then Job answered and s,	Job 9:1	559
is one thing, therefore I s it	Job 9:22	559
Zophar the Naamathite, and s	Job 11:1	559
For thou hast s, My doctrine is	Job 11:4	559
And Job answered and s,	Job 12:1	559
Eliphaz the Temanite, and s	Job 15:1	559
Then Job answered and s,	Job 16:1	559
I have s to corruption, Thou art	Job 17:14	7121
answered Bildad the Shuhite, and s	Job 18:1	559
Then Job answered and s,	Job 19:1	559
Zophar the Naamathite, and s	Job 20:1	559
But Job answered and s,	Job 21:1	559
the Temanite answered and s	Job 22:1	559
Which s unto God, Depart from us	Job 22:17	559
Then Job answered and s,	Job 23:1	559
answered Bildad the Shuhite, and s	Job 25:1	559
But Job answered and s,	Job 26:1	559
Job continued his parable, and s	Job 27:1	559
And unto man he s, Behold, the	Job 28:28	559
Job continued his parable, and s	Job 29:1	559
Then I s, I shall die in my nest,	Job 29:18	559
or have s to the fine gold, Thou	Job 31:24	559
If the men of my tabernacle s not	Job 31:31	559
Barachel the Buzite answered and s	Job 32:6	559
I s, Days should speak, and	Job 32:7	559
Therefore I s, Hearken to me	Job 32:10	559
I s, I will answer also my part,	Job 32:17	
Furthermore Elihu answered and s	Job 34:1	559
For Job hath s, I am righteous	Job 34:5	559
For he hath s, It profiteth a man	Job 34:9	559
it is meet to be s unto God	Job 34:31	559
Elihu spake moreover, and s	Job 35:1	559
Elihu also proceeded, and s	Job 36:1	559
Job out of the whirlwind, and s	Job 38:1	559
And s, Hitherto shalt thou come,	Job 38:11	559
the LORD answered Job, and s	Job 40:1	559
Then Job answered the LORD, and s	Job 40:3	559
Job out of the whirlwind, and s	Job 40:6	559
Then Job answered the LORD, and s	Job 42:1	559
the LORD s to Eliphaz the	Job 42:7	559
The LORD hath s unto me, Thou art	Ps 2:7	559
He hath s in his heart, I shall	Ps 10:6	559
He hath s in his heart, God hath	Ps 10:11	559
he hath s in his heart, Thou wilt	Ps 10:13	559
Who have s, With our tongue will	Ps 12:4	559
The fool hath s in his heart	Ps 14:1	559
thou hast s unto the LORD, Thou	Ps 16:2	559
hand of Saul: And he s	Ps 18:t	559
my heart s unto thee, Thy face,	Ps 27:8	559
And in my prosperity I s, I shall	Ps 30:6	559
I s, Thou art my God	Ps 31:14	559
For I s in my haste, I am cut off	Ps 31:22	559
I s, I will confess my	Ps 32:5	559
their mouth wide against me, and s	Ps 35:21	559
For I s, Hear me, lest otherwise	Ps 38:16	559
I s, I will take heed to my ways,	Ps 39:1	559
Then s I, Lo, I come	Ps 40:7	559
I s, LORD, be merciful unto me	Ps 41:4	559
s unto him, David is come to the	Ps 52:t	559
The fool hath s in his heart	Ps 53:1	559
s to Saul, Doth not David hide	Ps 54:t	559
And I s, Oh that I had wings like	Ps 55:6	559
The Lord s, I will bring again	Ps 68:22	559
They s in their hearts, Let us	Ps 74:8	559
I s unto the fools, Deal not	Ps 75:4	559
And I s, This is my infirmity	Ps 77:10	559
they s, Can God furnish a table	Ps 78:19	559

I have *s*, Ye are gods Ps 82:6 559
They have *s*, Come, and let us cut Ps 83:4 559
Who *s*, Let us take to ourselves Ps 83:12 559
And of Zion it shall be *s*, This and Ps 87:5 559
For I have *s*, Mercy shall be Ps 89:2 559
When I *s*, My foot slippeth Ps 94:18 559
with this generation, and *s* Ps 95:10 559
I *s*, O my God, take me not away Ps 102:24 559
Therefore he *s* that he would Ps 106:23 559
The LORD *s* unto my Lord, Sit thou Ps 110:1 5002
I *s* in my haste, All men are Ps 116:11 559
I have *s* that I would keep thy Ps 119:57 559
I was glad when they *s* unto me Ps 122:1 559
then *s* they among the heathen, Ps 126:2 559
who *s*, Rase it, rase it, even to Ps 137:7 559
I *s* unto the LORD, Thou art my Ps 140:6 559
I *s*, Thou art my refuge and my Ps 142:5 559
s unto me, Let thine heart retain Prov 4:4 559
with an impudent face *s* unto him Prov 7:13 559
it is that it be *s* unto thee Prov 25:7 559
any thing whereof it may be *s* Eccl 1:10 559
I *s* in mine heart, Go to now, I Eccl 2:1 559
I *s* of laughter, It is mad Eccl 2:2 559
Then *s* I in my heart, As it Eccl 2:15 559
Then I *s* in my heart, that this Eccl 2:15 1696
I *s* in mine heart, God shall Eccl 3:17 559
I *s* in mine heart concerning the Eccl 3:18 559
I *s*, I will be wise Eccl 7:23 559
I *s* that this also is vanity Eccl 8:14 559
Then *s* I, Wisdom is better than Eccl 9:16 559
s unto me, Rise up, my love, my Song 2:10 559
to whom I *s*, Saw ye him whom my Song 3:3
I *s*, I will go up to the palm Song 7:8 559
In mine ears *s* the LORD of hosts, Is 5:9
And one cried unto another, and *s* Is 6:3 559
Then *s* I, Woe is me Is 6:5 559
And he laid it upon my mouth, and *s* Is 6:7 559
Then *s* I, Here am I Is 6:8 559
And he *s*, Go, and tell this people, Is 6:9 559
Then *s* I, Lord, how long Is 6:11 559
Then *s* the LORD unto Isaiah, Go Is 7:3 559
But Ahaz *s*, I will not ask, Is 7:12 559
And he *s*, Hear ye now, O house of Is 7:13 559
Moreover the LORD *s* unto me Is 8:1 559
Then *s* the LORD to me, Call his Is 8:3 559
For thou hast *s* in thine heart, I Is 14:13 559
For so the LORD *s* unto me Is 18:4 559
And the LORD *s*, Like as my servant Is 20:3 559
For thus hath the Lord *s* unto me Is 21:6 559
And he answered and *s*, Babylon is Is 21:9 559
The watchman *s*, The morning Is 21:12 559
For thus hath the Lord *s* unto me Is 21:16 559
Therefore *s* I, Look away from me Is 22:4 559
And he *s*, Thou shalt no more Is 23:12 559
But I *s*, My leanness, my leanness Is 24:16 559
And it shall be *s* in that day Is 25:9 559
To whom he *s*, This is the rest Is 28:12 559
Because ye have *s*, We have made a Is 28:15 559
Wherefore the Lord *s*, Forasmuch Is 29:13 559
But ye *s*, No Is 30:16 559
nor the churl *s* to be bountiful Is 32:5 559
And Rabshakeh *s* unto them, Say ye Is 36:4 559
s to Judah and to Jerusalem, Ye Is 36:7 559
the LORD *s* unto me, Go up against Is 36:10 559
Then *s* Eliakim and Shebna and Joah Is 36:11 559
But Rabshakeh *s*, Hath my master Is 36:12 559
voice in the Jews' language, and *s* Is 36:13 559
they *s* unto him, Thus saith Is 37:3 559
Isaiah *s* unto them, Thus shall ye Is 37:6 559
reproached the Lord, and hast *s* Is 37:24 559
s unto him, Thus saith the LORD, Is 38:1 559
And *s*, Remember now, O LORD, I Is 38:3 559
I *s* in the cutting off of my days Is 38:10 559
I *s*, I shall not see the LORD, Is 38:11 559
For Isaiah had *s*, Let them take a Is 38:21 559
Hezekiah also had *s*, What is the Is 38:22 559
s unto him, What *s* these men Is 39:3 559
And Hezekiah *s*, They are come from Is 39:3 559
Then *s* he, What have they seen in Is 39:4 559
Then *s* Isaiah to Hezekiah, Hear Is 39:5 559
Then *s* Hezekiah to Isaiah, Good Is 39:8 559
He *s* moreover, For there shall be Is 39:8 559
The voice *s*, Cry Is 40:6 559
And he *s*, What shall I cry Is 40:6 559
every one *s* to his brother, Be of Is 41:6 559
s unto thee, Thou art my servant Is 41:9 559
I *s* not unto the seed of Jacob, Is 45:19 559
thou hast *s*, None seeth me Is 47:10 559
thou hast *s* in thine heart, I am, Is 47:10 559
s unto me, Thou art my servant, O Is 49:3 559
Then I *s*, I have laboured in vain Is 49:4 559
And he *s*, It is a light thing that Is 49:6 559
But Zion *s*, The LORD hath Is 49:14 559
which have *s* to thy soul, Bow Is 51:23 559
For he *s*, Surely they are my Is 63:8 559
I *s*, Behold me, behold me, unto a Is 65:1 559
you out for my name's sake, *s* Is 66:5 559
Then *s* I, Ah, Lord GOD Jer 1:6 559
But the LORD *s* unto me, Say not, Jer 1:7 559
And the LORD *s* unto me, Behold, I Jer 1:9 559
And I *s*, I see a rod of an almond Jer 1:11 559
Then *s* the LORD unto me, Thou Jer 1:12 559
and I *s*, I see a seething pot Jer 1:13 559
Then the LORD *s* unto me, Out of Jer 1:14 559
Neither *s* they, Where is the LORD Jer 2:6 559
The priests *s* not, Where is the Jer 2:8 559
The LORD *s* also unto me in the Jer 3:6 559
I *s* after she had done all these Jer 3:7 559
And the LORD *s* unto me, The Jer 3:11 559
But I *s*, How shall I put thee Jer 3:19 559
and I *s*, Thou shalt call me, My Jer 3:19 559
Then *s* I, Ah, Lord GOD Jer 4:10 559
time shall it be *s* to this people Jer 4:11 559
For thus hath the LORD *s*, The Jer 4:27 559

Therefore I *s*, Surely these are Jer 5:4 559
They have belied the LORD, and *s* Jer 5:12 559
For thus hath the LORD of hosts *s* Jer 6:6 559
But they *s*, We will not walk Jer 6:16 559
But they *s*, We will not hearken Jer 6:17 559
but I *s*, Truly this is a grief, Jer 10:19 559
Then answered I, and *s*, So be it, Jer 11:5 559
Then the LORD *s* unto me, Proclaim Jer 11:6 559
And the LORD *s* unto me, A Jer 11:9 559
because they *s*, He shall not see Jer 12:4 559
days, that the LORD *s* unto me Jer 13:6 559
Then *s* the LORD unto me, Pray not Jer 14:11 559
Then *s* I, Ah, Lord GOD Jer 14:13 559
Then the LORD *s* unto me, The Jer 14:14 559
Then *s* the LORD unto me, Though Jer 15:1 559
The LORD *s*, Verily it shall be Jer 15:11 559
LORD, that it shall no more be *s* Jer 16:14 559
Thus *s* the LORD unto me Jer 17:19 559
wherewith I *s* I would benefit Jer 18:10 559
And they *s*, There is no hope Jer 18:12 559
Then *s* they, Come, and let us Jer 18:18 559
and *s* to all the people, Jer 19:14 559
Then *s* Jeremiah unto him, The Jer 20:3 559
Then I *s*, I will not make mention Jer 20:9 559
Then *s* Jeremiah unto them, Thus Jer 21:3 559
that despise me, The LORD hath *s* Jer 23:17 1696
I have heard what the prophets *s* Jer 23:25 559
Then *s* the LORD unto me, What Jer 24:3 559
And I *s*, Figs Jer 24:3 559
They *s*, Turn ye again now every Jer 25:5 559
Then *s* the princes and all the Jer 26:16 559
Then the prophet Jeremiah *s* unto Jer 28:5 559
Even the prophet Jeremiah *s* Jer 28:6 559
Then *s* the prophet Jeremiah unto Jer 28:15 559
Because ye have *s*, The LORD hath Jer 29:15 559
And Jeremiah *s*, The word of the Jer 32:6 559
s unto me, Buy my field, I pray Jer 32:8 559
And thou hast *s* unto me, O Lord Jer 32:25 559
I *s* unto them, Drink ye wine Jer 35:5 559
But they *s*, We will drink no wine Jer 35:6 559
came up into the land, that we *s* Jer 35:11 559
Jeremiah *s* unto the house of the Jer 35:18 559
they *s* unto him, Sit down now, and Jer 36:15 559
s unto Baruch, We will surely Jer 36:16 559
Then *s* the princes unto Baruch, Jer 36:19 559
Then *s* Jeremiah, It is false Jer 37:14 559
him secretly in his house, and *s* Jer 37:17 559
And Jeremiah *s*, There is Jer 37:17 559
s he, thou shalt be delivered Jer 37:17 559
Moreover Jeremiah *s* unto king Jer 37:18 559
the princes *s* unto the king Jer 38:4 559
Then Zedekiah the king *s*, Behold, Jer 38:5 559
the Ethiopian *s* unto Jeremiah Jer 38:12 559
the king *s* unto Jeremiah, I will Jer 38:14 559
Then Jeremiah *s* unto Zedekiah Jer 38:15 559
Then *s* Jeremiah unto Zedekiah, Jer 38:17 559
Zedekiah the king *s* unto Jeremiah Jer 38:19 559
But Jeremiah *s*, They shall not Jer 38:20 559
Then *s* Zedekiah unto Jeremiah, Jer 38:24 559
what thou hast *s* unto the king Jer 38:25 1696
also what the king *s* unto thee Jer 38:25 1696
s unto him, The LORD thy God hath Jer 40:2 1696
and done according as he hath *s* Jer 40:3 1696
he was not yet gone back, he *s* Jer 40:5
s unto him, Dost thou certainly Jer 40:14 559
s unto Johanan the son of Kareah Jer 40:16 559
he *s* unto them, Come to Gedaliah Jer 41:6 559
among them that *s* unto Ishmael Jer 41:8 559
s unto Jeremiah the prophet, Let, Jer 42:2 559
Jeremiah the prophet *s* unto them Jer 42:4 559
Then they *s* to Jeremiah, The LORD Jer 42:5 559
s unto them, Thus saith the LORD, Jer 42:9 559
The LORD hath *s* concerning you, O Jer 42:19 1696
Then Jeremiah *s* unto all the Jer 44:20 559
Moreover Jeremiah *s* unto all the Jer 44:24 559
and they *s*, Arise, and let us go Jer 46:16 559
and their adversaries *s*, We offend Jer 50:7 559
Jeremiah *s* to Seraiah, When thou Jer 51:61 559
And I *s*, My strength and my hope is Lam 3:18 559
then I *s*, I am cut off Lam 3:54 559
they *s* among the heathen, They Lam 4:15 559
taken in their pits, of whom we *s* Lam 4:20 559
he *s* unto me, Son of man, stand Eze 2:1 559
he *s* unto me, Son of man, I send Eze 2:3 559
Moreover he *s* unto me, Son of man Eze 3:1 559
he *s* unto me, Son of man, cause Eze 3:3 559
he *s* unto me, Son of man, go, get Eze 3:4 559
Moreover he *s* unto me, Son of man Eze 3:10 559
he *s* unto me, Arise, go forth Eze 3:22 559
s unto me, Go, shut thyself Eze 3:24 559
And the LORD *s*, Even thus shall Eze 4:13 559
Then *s* I, Ah Lord GOD Eze 4:14 559
Then he *s* unto me, Lo, I have Eze 4:15 559
Moreover he *s* unto me, Son of man Eze 4:16 559
that I have not *s* in vain that I Eze 6:10 1696
Then *s* he unto me, Son of man, Eze 8:5 559
He *s* furthermore unto me, Son of Eze 8:6 559
Then *s* he unto me, Son of man, Eze 8:8 559
he *s* unto me, Go in, and behold Eze 8:9 559
Then *s* he unto me, Son of man, Eze 8:12 559
He *s* also unto me, Turn thee yet Eze 8:13 559
Then *s* he unto me, Hast thou seen Eze 8:15 559
Then he *s* unto me, Hast thou seen Eze 8:17 559
And the LORD *s* unto him, Go Eze 9:4 559
the others he *s* in mine hearing Eze 9:5 559
he *s* unto them, Defile the house, Eze 9:7 559
fell upon my face, and cried, and *s* Eze 9:8 559
Then *s* he unto me, The iniquity Eze 9:9 559
the man clothed with linen, and *s* Eze 10:2 559
Then *s* he unto me, Son of man, Eze 11:2 559
fell upon me, and *s* unto me, Speak Eze 11:5 559
Thus have ye *s*, O house of Israel Eze 11:5 559
and cried with a loud voice, and *s* Eze 11:13 559
inhabitants of Jerusalem have *s* Eze 11:15 559

s unto thee, What dost thou Eze 12:9 559
shall it not be *s* unto you Eze 13:12 559
I *s* unto thee when thou wast in Eze 16:6 559
I *s* unto thee when thou wast in Eze 16:6 559
Then *s* I unto them, Cast ye away Eze 20:7 559
then I *s*, I will pour out my fury Eze 20:8 559
then I *s*, I would pour out my Eze 20:13 559
But I *s* unto their children in Eze 20:18 559
then I *s*, I would pour out my Eze 20:21 559
Then I *s* unto them, What is the Eze 20:29 559
Then *s* I, Ah Lord GOD Eze 20:49 559
I the LORD have *s* it Eze 21:17 1696
The LORD *s* moreover unto me Eze 23:36 559
Then *s* I unto her that was old in Eze 23:43 559
And the people *s* unto me, Wilt Eze 24:19 559
Tyrus hath *s* against Jerusalem Eze 26:2 559
O Tyrus, thou hast *s*, I am of Eze 27:3 559
is lifted up, and thou hast *s* Eze 28:2 559
midst of his rivers, which hath *s* Eze 29:3 559
because he hath *s*, The river is Eze 29:9 559
Because thou hast *s*, These two Eze 35:10 559
the enemy hath *s* against you Eze 36:2 559
my holy name, when they *s* to them Eze 36:20 559
he *s* unto me, Son of man, can Eze 37:3 559
Again he *s* unto me, Prophesy upon Eze 37:4 559
Then *s* he unto me, Prophesy unto Eze 37:9 559
Then he *s* unto me, Son of man, Eze 37:11 559
And the man *s* unto me, Son of man, Eze 40:4 1696
he *s* unto me, This chamber, whose Eze 40:45 1696
he *s* unto me, This is the most Eze 41:4 559
he *s* unto me, This is the table Eze 41:22 1696
Then *s* he unto me, The north Eze 42:13 559
he *s* unto me, Son of man, the Eze 43:7 559
he *s* unto me, Son of man, thus Eze 43:18 559
Then *s* the LORD unto me Eze 44:2 559
And the LORD *s* unto me, Son of man Eze 44:5 559
Then *s* he unto me, This is the Eze 46:20 559
Then *s* he unto me, These are the Eze 46:24 559
he *s* unto me, Son of man, hast Eze 47:6 559
Then *s* he unto me, These waters Eze 47:8 559
of the eunuchs *s* unto Daniel Dan 1:10 559
Then *s* Daniel to Melzar, whom the Dan 1:11 559
had *s* he should bring them in Dan 1:18 559
the king *s* unto them, I have Dan 2:3 559
s to the Chaldeans, The thing is Dan 2:5 560
They answered again and *s*, Let the Dan 2:7 560
The king answered and *s*, I know of Dan 2:8 560
answered before the king, and *s* Dan 2:10 560
s to Arioch the king's captain, Dan 2:15 560
Daniel answered and *s*, Blessed be Dan 2:20 560
he went and *s* thus unto him Dan 2:24 560
s thus unto him, I have found a Dan 2:25 560
s to Daniel, whose name was Dan 2:26 560
in the presence of the king, and *s* Dan 2:27 560
king answered unto Daniel, and *s* Dan 2:47 560
s to the king Nebuchadnezzar, O Dan 3:9 560
s unto them, Is it true, O Dan 3:14 560
s to the king, O Nebuchadnezzar, Dan 3:16 560
s unto his counsellors, Did not Dan 3:24 560
s unto the king, True, O king Dan 3:24 560
He answered and *s*, Lo, I see four Dan 3:25 560
fiery furnace, and spake, and *s* Dan 3:26 560
Then Nebuchadnezzar spake, and *s* Dan 3:28 560
s thus, Hew down the tree, and cut Dan 4:14 560
The king spake, and *s*, Dan 4:19 560
Belteshazzar answered and *s* Dan 4:19 560
The king spake, and *s*, Is not this Dan 4:30 560
s to the wise men of Babylon, Dan 5:7 560
and the queen spake and *s*, O king, Dan 5:10 560
s unto Daniel, Art thou that Dan 5:13 560
s before the king, Let thy gifts Dan 5:17 560
Then *s* these men, We shall not Dan 6:5 560
s thus unto him, King Darius, Dan 6:6 560
The king answered and *s*, The thing Dan 6:12 560
s before the king, That Daniel, Dan 6:13 560
s unto the king, Know, O king, Dan 6:15 560
s unto Daniel, Thy God whom thou Dan 6:16 560
s to Daniel, O Daniel, servant of Dan 6:20 560
Then *s* Daniel unto the king, O Dan 6:21 4449
Daniel spake and *s*, I saw in my Dan 7:2 560
they *s* thus unto it, Arise, Dan 7:5 560
Thus he *s*, The fourth beast shall Dan 7:23 560
another saint *s* unto that certain Dan 8:13 559
he *s* unto me, Unto two thousand Dan 8:14 559
banks of Ulai, which called, and *s* Dan 8:16 559
but he *s* unto me, Understand, O Dan 8:17 559
And he *s*, Behold, I will make thee Dan 8:19 559
God, and made my confession, and *s* Dan 9:4 559
me, and talked with me, and *s* Dan 9:22 559
he *s* unto me, O Daniel, a man Dan 10:11 559
Then *s* he unto me, Fear not, Dan 10:12 559
s unto him that stood before me, Dan 10:16 559
And *s*, O man greatly beloved, fear Dan 10:19 559
unto me, I was strengthened, and *s* Dan 10:19 559
Then *s* he, Knowest thou wherefore Dan 10:20 559
one *s* to the man clothed in linen Dan 12:6 559
then *s* I, O my Lord, what shall Dan 12:8 559
And he *s*, Go thy way, Daniel Dan 12:9 559
And the LORD *s* to Hosea, Go, take Hos 1:2 559
And the LORD *s* unto him, Call his Hos 1:4 559
God *s* unto him, Call her name Hos 1:6 559
Then *s* God, Call his name Lo-ammi Hos 1:9 559
place where it was *s* unto them Hos 1:10 559
there it shall be *s* unto them Hos 1:10 559
for she *s*, I will go after my Hos 2:5 559
her fig trees, whereof she hath *s* Hos 2:12 559
Then *s* the LORD unto me, Go yet, Hos 3:1 559
I *s* unto her, Thou shalt abide Hos 3:3 559
And Ephraim *s*, Yet I am become Hos 12:8 559
deliverance, as the LORD hath *s* Joel 2:32 559
And he *s*, The LORD will roar from Amos 1:2 559
the grass of the land, then I *s* Amos 7:2 559
Then *s* I, O Lord GOD, cease, I Amos 7:5 559
And the LORD *s* unto me, Amos, what Amos 7:8 559

And I s, A plumbline Amos 7:8 559
Then s the Lord, Behold, I will Amos 7:8 559
Also Amaziah s unto Amos, O thou Amos 7:12 559
s to Amaziah, I was no prophet, Amos 7:14 559
the flock, and the LORD s unto me Amos 7:15 559
And he s, Amos, what seest thou Amos 8:2 559
And I s, A basket of summer fruit Amos 8:2 559
Then s the LORD unto me, The end Amos 8:2 559
and he s, Smite the lintel of the Amos 9:1 559
s unto him, What meanest thou, O Jonah 1:6 559
they s every one to his fellow, Jonah 1:7 559
Then s they unto him, Tell us, we Jonah 1:8 559
he s unto them, I am an Hebrew Jonah 1:9 559
s unto him, Why hast thou done Jonah 1:10 559
Then s they unto him, What shall Jonah 1:11 559
he s unto them, Take me up, and Jonah 1:12 559
they cried unto the LORD, and s Jonah 1:14 559
And s, I cried by reason of mine Jonah 2:2 559
Then I s, I am cast out of thy Jonah 2:4 559
day's journey, and he cried, and s Jonah 3:4 559
that he had s that he would do Jonah 3:10 1696
And he prayed unto the LORD, and s Jonah 4:2 559
Then s the LORD, Doest thou well Jonah 4:4 559
and wished in himself to die, and s Jonah 4:8 559
God s to Jonah, Doest thou well Jonah 4:9 559
And he s, I do well to be angry, Jonah 4:9 559
Then s the LORD, Thou hast had Jonah 4:10 559
And I s, Hear, I pray you, O heads Mic 3:1 559
shall cover her which s unto me Mic 7:10 559
And the LORD answered me, and s Hab 2:2 559
that s in her heart, I am, and Zeph 2:15 559
I s, Surely thou wilt fear me, Zeph 3:7 559
day it shall be s to Jerusalem Zeph 3:16 559
And the priests answered and s Hag 2:12 559
Then s Haggai, If one that is Hag 2:13 559
And the priests answered and s Hag 2:13 559
Then answered Haggai, and s Hag 2:14 559
and they returned and s, Like as Zec 1:6 559
Then s I, O my lord, what are Zec 1:9 559
that talked with me s unto me Zec 1:9 559
the myrtle trees answered and s Zec 1:10 559
among the myrtle trees, and s Zec 1:11 559
angel of the LORD answered and s Zec 1:12 559
that communed with me s unto me Zec 1:14 559
I s unto the angel that talked Zec 1:19 559
Then s I, What come these to do Zec 1:21 559
Then s I, Whither goest thou Zec 2:2 559
And he s unto me, To measure Zec 2:2 559
s unto him, Run, speak to this Zec 2:4 559
the LORD s unto Satan, The LORD Zec 3:2 559
And unto him he s, Behold, I have Zec 3:4 559
And I s, Let them set a fair mitre Zec 3:5 559
s unto me, What seest thou Zec 4:2 559
And I s, I have looked, and behold Zec 4:2 559
s unto me, Knowest thou not what Zec 4:5 559
And I s, No, my lord Zec 4:5 559
s unto him, What are these two Zec 4:11 559
s unto him, What be these two Zec 4:12 559
And he answered me and s, Knowest Zec 4:13 559
And I s, No, my lord Zec 4:13 559
Then s he, These are the two Zec 4:14 559
he s unto me, What seest thou Zec 5:2 559
Then s he unto me, This is the Zec 5:3 559
s unto me, Lift up now thine eyes Zec 5:5 559
And I s, What is it Zec 5:6 559
And he s, This is an ephah that Zec 5:6 559
He s moreover, This is their Zec 5:6 559
And he s, This is wickedness Zec 5:8 559
Then s I to the angel that talked Zec 5:10 559
he s unto me, To build it an Zec 5:11 559
s unto the angel that talked with Zec 6:4 559
s unto me, These are the four Zec 6:5 559
and he s, Get you hence, walk to Zec 6:7 559
Then s I, I will not feed you Zec 11:9 559
I s unto them, If ye think good, Zec 11:12 559
And the LORD s unto me, Cast it Zec 11:13 559
And the LORD s unto me, Take unto Zec 11:15 559
Ye s also, Behold, what a Mal 1:13 559
But ye s, Wherein shall we return Mal 3:7 559
Ye have s, It is vain to serve Mal 3:14 559
they s unto him, In Bethlehem of Mt 2:5 2036
he sent them to Bethlehem, and s Mt 2:8 2036
he s unto them, O generation of Mt 3:7 2036
And Jesus answering s unto him Mt 3:15 2036
the tempter came to him, he s Mt 4:3 2036
But he answered and s, It is Mt 4:4 2036
Jesus s unto him, It is written Mt 4:7 5346
that it was s by them of old time Mt 5:21 2046
that it was s by them of old time Mt 5:27 2046
It hath been s, Whosoever shall Mt 5:31 2046
hath been s by them of old time Mt 5:33 2046
Ye have heard that it hath been s Mt 5:38 2046
Ye have heard that it hath been s Mt 5:43 2046
The centurion answered and s Mt 8:8 5346
s to them that followed, Verily I Mt 8:10 4483
Jesus s unto the centurion, Go Mt 8:13 4483
s unto him, Master, I will follow Mt 8:19 4483
of his disciples s unto him Mt 8:21 4483
But Jesus s unto him, Follow me Mt 8:22 4483
And he s unto them, Go Mt 8:32 4483
Jesus seeing their faith s unto Mt 9:2 4483
the scribes s within themselves Mt 9:3 4483
And Jesus knowing their thoughts s Mt 9:4 4483
they s unto his disciples, Why Mt 9:11 4483
he s unto them, They that be Mt 9:12 4483
Jesus s unto them, Can the Mt 9:15 4483
For she s within herself, If I Mt 9:21 3004
about, and when he saw her, he s Mt 9:22 2036
He s unto them, Give place Mt 9:24 3004
They s unto him, Yea, Lord Mt 9:28 3004
But the Pharisees s, He casteth Mt 9:34 3004
s unto him, Art thou he that Mt 11:3 2036
s unto them, Go and shew John Mt 11:4 2036
At that time Jesus answered and s Mt 11:25 2036
they s unto him, Behold, thy Mt 12:2 2036
But he s unto them, Have ye not Mt 12:3 2036
he s unto them, What man shall Mt 12:11 2036
all the people were amazed, and s Mt 12:23 3004
the Pharisees heard it, they s Mt 12:24 2036
s unto them, Every kingdom Mt 12:25 2036
and s unto them, An evil and Mt 12:39 2036
Then one s unto him, Behold, thy Mt 12:47 2036
s unto him that told him, Who is Mt 12:48 2036
hand toward his disciples, and s Mt 12:49 2036
s unto him, Why speakest thou Mt 13:10 2036
s unto them, Because it is given Mt 13:11 2063
s unto him, Sir, didst not thou Mt 13:27 2063
He s unto them, An enemy hath Mt 13:28 2063
The servants s unto him, Wilt Mt 13:28 5346
But he s, Nay Mt 13:29 5346
s unto them, He that soweth the Mt 13:37 2036
Then s he unto them, Therefore Mt 13:52 2036
that they were astonished, and s Mt 13:54 3004
But Jesus s unto them, A prophet Mt 13:57 2036
s unto his servants, This is John Mt 14:2 2036
For John s unto him, It is not Mt 14:4 3004
instructed of her mother, s Mt 14:8 5346
But Jesus s unto them, They need Mt 14:16 2036
He s, Bring them hither to me Mt 14:18 2036
And Peter answered him and s Mt 14:28 2036
And he s, Come Mt 14:29 2036
s unto him, O thou of little Mt 14:31 3004
s unto them, Why do ye also Mt 15:3 2036
s unto them, Hear, and understand Mt 15:10 2036
s unto him, Knowest thou that the Mt 15:12 2036
But he answered and s, Every plant Mt 15:13 2036
s unto him, Declare unto us this Mt 15:15 2036
And Jesus s, Are ye also yet Mt 15:16 2036
But he answered and s, I am not Mt 15:24 2036
But he answered and s, It is not Mt 15:26 2036
And she s, Truth, Lord Mt 15:27 2036
s unto her, O woman, great is thy Mt 15:28 2036
his disciples unto him, and s Mt 15:32 2036
And they s, Seven, and a few little Mt 15:34 2036
s unto them, When it is evening, Mt 16:2 2036
Then Jesus s unto them, Take heed Mt 16:6 2036
he s unto them, O ye of little Mt 16:8 2036
And they s, Some say that thou art Mt 16:14 2036
And Simon Peter answered and s Mt 16:16 2036
s unto him, Blessed art thou, Mt 16:17 2036
s unto Peter, Get thee behind me, Mt 16:23 2036
Then s Jesus unto his disciples, Mt 16:24 2036
s unto Jesus, Lord, it is good Mt 17:4 2036
a voice out of the cloud, which s Mt 17:5 3004
Jesus came and touched them, and s Mt 17:7 2036
s unto them, Elias truly shall Mt 17:11 2036
Then Jesus answered and s, O Mt 17:17 2036
disciples to Jesus apart, and s Mt 17:19 2036
Jesus s unto them, Because of Mt 17:20 2036
Jesus s unto them, The Son of man Mt 17:22 2036
tribute money came to Peter, and s Mt 17:24 2036
And s, Verily I say unto you, Mt 18:3 2036
Then came Peter to him, and s Mt 18:21 2036
s unto him, O thou wicked servant Mt 18:32 3004
s unto them, Have ye not read, Mt 19:4 2036
And s, For this cause shall a man Mt 19:5 2036
But he s unto them, All men Mt 19:11 2036
But Jesus s, Suffer little Mt 19:14 2036
s unto him, Good Master, what Mt 19:16 2036
he s unto him, Why callest thou Mt 19:17 2036
Jesus s, Thou shalt do no murder, Mt 19:18 2036
Jesus s unto him, If thou wilt be Mt 19:21 5346
Then s Jesus unto his disciples, Mt 19:23 2036
s unto them, With men this is Mt 19:26 2036
s unto him, Behold, we have Mt 19:27 2036
Jesus s unto them, Verily I say Mt 19:28 2036
s unto them; Go ye also Mt 20:4 2036
But he answered one of them, and s Mt 20:13 2036
apart in the way, and s unto them, Mt 20:17 2036
he s unto her, What wilt thou Mt 20:21 2036
But Jesus answered and s, Ye know Mt 20:22 2036
Jesus called them unto him, and s Mt 20:25 2036
stood still, and called them, and s Mt 20:32 2036
And the multitude s, This is Jesus Mt 21:11 3004
s unto them, It is written, My Mt 21:13 3004
s unto him, Hearest thou what Mt 21:16 2036
s unto it, Let no fruit grow on Mt 21:19 3004
s unto them, Verily I say unto Mt 21:21 2036
unto him as he was teaching, and s Mt 21:23 3004
s unto them, I also will ask you Mt 21:24 2036
And they answered Jesus, and s Mt 21:27 2036
he s unto them, Neither tell I Mt 21:27 5346
and he came to the first, and s Mt 21:28 2036
He answered and s, I will not Mt 21:29 2036
came to the second, and s likewise Mt 21:30 2036
And he answered and s, I go sir Mt 21:30 2036
they s among themselves, This is Mt 21:38 2036
unto them again by parables, and s Mt 22:1 3004
Then s the king to the servants, Mt 22:13 2036
perceived their wickedness, and s Mt 22:18 2036
Saying, Master, Moses s, If a man Mt 22:24 2036
s unto them, Ye do err, not Mt 22:29 2036
Jesus s unto him, Thou shalt love Mt 22:37 2036
The LORD s unto my Lord, Sit thou Mt 22:44 2036
Jesus s unto them, See ye not all Mt 24:2 2036
s unto them, Take heed that no Mt 24:4 2036
the foolish s unto the wise, Give Mt 25:8 2036
But he answered and s, Verily I Mt 25:12 2036
His lord s unto him, Well done, Mt 25:21 5346
received two talents came and s Mt 25:22 2036
His lord s unto him, Well done, Mt 25:23 5346
received the one talent came and s Mt 25:24 2036
s unto him, Thou wicked and Mt 25:26 2036
sayings, he s unto his disciples, Mt 26:1 2036
But they s, Not on the feast day, Mt 26:5 3004
he s unto them, Why trouble ye Mt 26:10 2036
s unto them, What will ye give me Mt 26:15 2036
And he s, Go into the city to such Mt 26:18 2036
And as they did eat, he s, Verily Mt 26:21 2036
And he answered and s, He that Mt 26:23 2036
which betrayed him, answered and s Mt 26:25 2036
He s unto him, Thou hast Mt 26:25 3004
unto him, Thou hast s Mt 26:25 2036
and gave it to the disciples, and s Mt 26:26 2036
s unto him, Though all men shall Mt 26:33 2036
Jesus s unto him, Verily I say Mt 26:34 5346
Peter s unto him, Though I should Mt 26:35 3004
Likewise also s all the disciples Mt 26:35 2036
forthwith he came to Jesus, and s Mt 26:49 2036
Jesus s unto him, Friend, Mt 26:50 2036
Then s Jesus unto him, Put up Mt 26:52 3004
In that same hour s Jesus to the Mt 26:55 2036
And s, This fellow Mt 26:61 2036
This fellow s, I am Mt 26:61 5346
s unto him, Answerest thou Mt 26:62 2036
s unto him, I adjure thee by the Mt 26:63 2036
Jesus saith unto him, Thou hast s Mt 26:64 2036
They answered and s, He is guilty Mt 26:66 2036
s unto them that were there, This Mt 26:71 3004
s to Peter, Surely thou also art Mt 26:73 2036
which s unto him, Before the cock Mt 26:75 2046
And they s, What is that to us Mt 27:4 2036
took the silver pieces, and s Mt 27:6 2036
Jesus s unto him, Thou sayest Mt 27:11 5346
Then s Pilate unto him, Hearest Mt 27:13 3004
Pilate s unto them, Whom will ye Mt 27:17 2036
s unto them, Whether of the twain Mt 27:21 2036
They s, Barabbas Mt 27:21 2036
And the governor s, Why, what evil Mt 27:23 5346
answered all the people, and s Mt 27:25 2036
with the scribes and elders, s Mt 27:41 3004
for he s, I am the Son of God Mt 27:43 2036
there, when they heard that, s Mt 27:47 3004
The rest s, Let be, let us see Mt 27:49 3004
we remember that that deceiver s Mt 27:63 2036
Pilate s unto them, Ye have a Mt 27:65 5346
s unto the women, Fear not ye Mt 28:5 2036
for he is risen, as he s Mt 28:6 2036
Then s Jesus unto them, Be not Mt 28:10 3004
Jesus s unto them, Come ye after Mk 1:17 2036
they s unto him, All men seek for Mk 1:37 3004
he s unto them, Let us go into Mk 1:38 3004
he s unto the sick of the palsy, Mk 2:5 3004
he s unto them, Why reason ye Mk 2:8 2036
custom, and s unto him, Follow me Mk 2:14 3004
they s unto his disciples, How is Mk 2:16 3004
Jesus s unto them, Can the Mk 2:19 2036
And the Pharisees s unto him Mk 2:24 3004
he s unto them, Have ye never Mk 2:25 3004
he s unto them, The sabbath was Mk 2:27 3004
for they s, He is beside himself Mk 3:21 3004
which came down from Jerusalem s Mk 3:22 3004
s unto them in parables, How can Mk 3:23 3004
Because they s, He hath an Mk 3:30 3004
they s unto him, Behold, thy Mk 3:32 2036
on them which sat about him, and s Mk 3:34 3004
s unto them in his doctrine, Mk 4:2 3004
he s unto them, He that hath ears Mk 4:9 3004
he s unto them, Unto you it is Mk 4:11 3004
he s unto them, Know ye not this Mk 4:13 3004
he s unto them, Is a candle Mk 4:21 3004
he s unto them, Take heed what ye Mk 4:24 3004
And he s, So is the kingdom of God Mk 4:26 3004
And he s, Whereunto shall we liken Mk 4:30 3004
s unto the sea, Peace, be still Mk 4:39 2036
he s unto them, Why are ye so Mk 4:40 2036
s one to another, What manner of Mk 4:41 3004
And cried with a loud voice, and s Mk 5:7 2036
For he s unto him, Come out of Mk 5:8 3004
For she s, If I may touch but his Mk 5:28 3004
him about in the press, and s Mk 5:30 3004
And his disciples s unto him Mk 5:31 3004
he s unto her, Daughter, thy Mk 5:34 2036
synagogue's house certain which s Mk 5:35 3004
hand, and s unto her, Talitha cumi Mk 5:41 3004
But Jesus s unto them, A prophet Mk 6:4 3004
he s unto them, In what place Mk 6:10 3004
and he s, That John the Baptist Mk 6:14 3004
Others s, That it is Elias Mk 6:15 3004
And others s, That it is a prophet Mk 6:15 3004
when Herod heard thereof, he s Mk 6:16 2036
For John had s unto Herod Mk 6:18 3004
of the s Herodias came in Mk 6:22 846
the king s unto the damsel, Ask Mk 6:22 2036
s unto her mother, What shall I Mk 6:24 2036
And she s, The head of John the Mk 6:24 2036
And he s unto them, Come ye Mk 6:31 2036
his disciples came unto him, and s Mk 6:35 3004
s unto them, Give ye them to eat Mk 6:37 2036
s unto them, Well hath Esaias Mk 7:6 2036
he s unto them, Full well ye Mk 7:9 3004
For Moses s, Honour thy father and Mk 7:10 2036
he s unto them, Hearken unto me Mk 7:14 3004
And he s, That which cometh out of Mk 7:20 3004
But Jesus s unto her, Let the Mk 7:27 2036
answered and s unto him, Yes, Lord Mk 7:28 3004
he s unto her, For this saying go Mk 7:29 2036
And they s, Seven Mk 8:5 2036
And they s, Seven Mk 8:20 2036
he s unto them, How is it that ye Mk 8:21 3004
And he looked up, and s, I see men Mk 8:24 3004
he s unto them, Whosoever will Mk 8:34 2036
he s unto them, Verily I say unto Mk 9:1 3004
s to Jesus, Master, it is good Mk 9:5 3004
of the multitude answered and s Mk 9:17 2036
And he s, Of a child Mk 9:21 2036
Jesus s unto him, If thou canst Mk 9:23 2036
s with tears, Lord, I believe Mk 9:24 3004
insomuch that many s, He is dead Mk 9:26 3004
he s unto them, This kind can Mk 9:29 2036
s unto them, The Son of man is Mk 9:31 3004
him in his arms, he s unto them, Mk 9:36 2036

But Jesus *s*, Forbid him not	Mk 9:39	2036
s unto them, What did Moses	Mk 10:3	2036
And they *s*, Moses suffered to	Mk 10:4	2036
s unto them, For the hardness of	Mk 10:5	2036
s unto them, Suffer the little	Mk 10:14	2036
Jesus *s* unto him, Why callest	Mk 10:18	2036
s unto him, Master, all these	Mk 10:20	2036
s unto him, One thing thou	Mk 10:21	2036
And Jesus answered and *s*, Verily I	Mk 10:29	2036
he *s* unto them, What would ye	Mk 10:36	2036
They *s* unto him, Grant unto us	Mk 10:37	2036
But Jesus *s* unto them, Ye know	Mk 10:38	2036
And they *s* unto him, We can	Mk 10:39	2036
Jesus *s* unto them, Ye shall	Mk 10:39	2036
s unto him, What wilt thou that I	Mk 10:51	3004
The blind man *s* unto him, Lord,	Mk 10:51	2036
Jesus *s* unto him, Go thy way	Mk 10:52	2036
them that stood there *s* unto them	Mk 11:5	3004
they *s* unto them even as Jesus	Mk 11:6	2036
s unto it, No man eat fruit of	Mk 11:14	2036
s unto them, I will also ask of	Mk 11:29	2036
s unto Jesus, We cannot tell	Mk 11:33	3004
husbandmen *s* among themselves	Mk 12:7	2036
s unto them, Why tempt ye me	Mk 12:15	2036
they *s* unto him, Caesar's	Mk 12:16	2036
And Jesus answering *s* unto them	Mk 12:17	2036
And Jesus answering *s* unto them	Mk 12:24	2036
And the scribe *s* unto him, Well,	Mk 12:32	2036
Master, thou hast *s* the truth	Mk 12:32	2036
he *s* unto him, Thou art not far	Mk 12:34	2036
And Jesus answered and *s*, while he	Mk 12:35	3004
David himself *s* by the Holy Ghost	Mk 12:36	2036
The Lord *s* to my Lord, Sit thou	Mk 12:36	2036
he *s* unto them in his doctrine,	Mk 12:38	3004
And Jesus answering *s* unto them	Mk 13:2	2036
But they *s*, Not on the feast day,	Mk 14:2	3004
within themselves, and *s*, Why was	Mk 14:4	3004
And Jesus *s*, Let her alone	Mk 14:6	2036
his disciples *s* unto him	Mk 14:12	3004
and found as he had *s* unto them	Mk 14:16	2036
as they sat and did eat, Jesus *s*	Mk 14:18	2036
and another *s*, Is it I	Mk 14:19	
s unto them, It is one of the	Mk 14:20	2036
and brake it and gave to them, and *s*	Mk 14:22	2036
he *s* unto them, This is my blood	Mk 14:24	2036
But Peter *s* unto him, Although	Mk 14:29	5346
Likewise also *s* they all	Mk 14:31	3004
And he *s*, Abba, Father, all things	Mk 14:36	3004
s unto them, Are ye come out, as	Mk 14:48	2036
s unto him, Art thou the Christ,	Mk 14:61	3004
And Jesus *s*, I am	Mk 14:62	2036
she looked upon him, and *s*	Mk 14:67	3004
that stood by *s* again to Peter	Mk 14:70	3004
the word that Jesus *s* unto him	Mk 14:72	2036
And he answering *s* unto him	Mk 15:2	3004
s again unto them, What will ye	Mk 15:12	2036
Then Pilate *s* unto them, Why,	Mk 15:14	3004
s among themselves with the	Mk 15:31	3004
stood by, when they heard it *s*	Mk 15:35	3004
out, and gave up the ghost, he *s*	Mk 15:39	2036
they *s* among themselves, Who	Mk 16:3	3004
ye see him, as he *s* unto you	Mk 16:7	2036
neither *s* they any thing to any	Mk 16:8	2036
he *s* unto them, Go ye into all	Mk 16:15	2036
But the angel *s* unto him, Fear	Lk 1:13	2036
Zacharias *s* unto the angel,	Lk 1:18	2036
And the angel answering *s* unto him	Lk 1:19	2036
the angel came in unto her, and *s*	Lk 1:28	2036
And the angel *s* unto her, Fear not	Lk 1:30	2036
Then *s* Mary unto the angel, How	Lk 1:34	2036
s unto her, The Holy Ghost shall	Lk 1:35	2036
And Mary *s*, Behold the handmaid of	Lk 1:38	2036
spake out with a loud voice, and *s*	Lk 1:42	2036
And Mary *s*, My soul doth magnify	Lk 1:46	2036
And his mother answered and *s*	Lk 1:60	2036
they *s* unto her, There is none of	Lk 1:61	2036
And the angel *s* unto them, Fear	Lk 2:10	2036
the shepherds *s* one to another,	Lk 2:15	2036
which is *s* in the law of the Lord	Lk 2:24	2046
in his arms, and blessed God, and *s*	Lk 2:28	2036
s unto Mary his mother, Behold,	Lk 2:34	2036
and his mother *s* unto him, Son,	Lk 2:48	2036
he *s* unto them, How is it that ye	Lk 2:49	2036
Then *s* he to the multitude that	Lk 3:7	3004
s unto him, Master, what shall we	Lk 3:12	2036
he *s* unto them, Exact no more	Lk 3:13	2036
he *s* unto them, Do violence to no	Lk 3:14	2036
a voice came from heaven, which *s*	Lk 3:22	3004
And the devil *s* unto him, If thou	Lk 4:3	2036
And the devil *s* unto him, All this	Lk 4:6	2036
s unto him, Get thee behind me,	Lk 4:8	2036
s unto him, If thou be the Son of	Lk 4:9	2036
And Jesus answering *s* unto him	Lk 4:12	2036
unto him, It is *s*	Lk 4:12	2046
And they *s*, Is not this Joseph's	Lk 4:22	3004
he *s* unto them, Ye will surely	Lk 4:23	2036
And he *s*, Verily I say unto you,	Lk 4:24	2036
he *s* unto them, I must preach the	Lk 4:43	2036
he *s* unto Simon, Launch out into	Lk 5:4	2036
And Simon answering *s* unto him	Lk 5:5	2036
Jesus *s* unto Simon, Fear not	Lk 5:10	2036
he *s* unto him, Man, thy sins are	Lk 5:20	2036
he answering *s* unto them	Lk 5:22	2036
(he *s* unto the sick of the palsy,	Lk 5:24	2036
and he *s* unto him, Follow me	Lk 5:27	2036
And Jesus answering *s* unto them	Lk 5:31	2036
they *s* unto him, Why do the	Lk 5:33	2036
he *s* unto them, Can ye make the	Lk 5:34	2036
of the Pharisees *s* unto them	Lk 6:2	2036
And Jesus answering them *s*	Lk 6:3	2036
he *s* unto them, That the Son of	Lk 6:5	3004
s to the man which had the	Lk 6:8	2036
Then *s* Jesus unto them, I will	Lk 6:9	2036
he *s* unto the man, Stretch forth	Lk 6:10	2036
his eyes on his disciples, and *s*	Lk 6:20	3004
s unto the people that followed	Lk 7:9	2036
on her, and *s* unto her, Weep not	Lk 7:13	2036
And he *s*, Young man, I say unto	Lk 7:14	2036
men were come unto him, they *s*	Lk 7:20	2036
Then Jesus answering *s* unto them	Lk 7:22	2036
And the Lord *s*, Whereunto then	Lk 7:31	2036
And Jesus answering *s* unto him	Lk 7:40	2036
Simon answered and *s*, I suppose	Lk 7:43	2036
he *s* unto him, Thou hast rightly	Lk 7:43	2036
s unto Simon, Seest thou this	Lk 7:44	5346
he *s* unto her, Thy sins are	Lk 7:48	2036
he *s* to the woman, Thy faith hath	Lk 7:50	2036
when he had *s* these things, he	Lk 8:8	3004
And he *s*, Unto you it is given to	Lk 8:10	2036
was told him by certain which *s*	Lk 8:20	3004
s unto them, My mother and my	Lk 8:21	2036
he *s* unto them, Let us go over	Lk 8:22	2036
he *s* unto them, Where is your	Lk 8:25	2036
him, and with a loud voice *s*	Lk 8:28	2036
And he *s*, Legion	Lk 8:30	2036
And Jesus *s*, Who touched me	Lk 8:45	2036
and they that were with him *s*	Lk 8:45	2036
And Jesus *s*, Somebody hath touched	Lk 8:46	2036
he *s* unto her, Daughter, be of	Lk 8:48	2036
but he *s*, Weep not	Lk 8:52	2036
he *s* unto them, Take nothing for	Lk 9:3	2036
because that it was *s* of some	Lk 9:7	3004
And Herod *s*, John have I beheaded	Lk 9:9	2036
s unto him, Send the multitude	Lk 9:12	2036
But he *s* unto them, Give ye them	Lk 9:13	2036
And they *s*, We have no more but	Lk 9:13	2036
he *s* to his disciples, Make them	Lk 9:14	2036
They answering *s*, John the	Lk 9:19	2036
He *s* unto them, But whom say ye	Lk 9:20	2036
Peter answering *s*, The Christ of	Lk 9:20	2036
he *s* to them all, If any man will	Lk 9:23	3004
Peter *s* unto Jesus, Master, it is	Lk 9:33	2036
not knowing what he *s*	Lk 9:33	3004
And Jesus answering *s*, O faithless	Lk 9:41	2036
did, he *s* unto his disciples,	Lk 9:43	2036
s unto them, Whosoever shall	Lk 9:48	2036
And John answered and *s*, Master, we	Lk 9:49	2036
Jesus *s* unto him, Forbid him not	Lk 9:50	2036
James and John saw this, they *s*	Lk 9:54	2036
he turned, and rebuked them, and *s*	Lk 9:55	2036
the way, a certain man *s* unto him	Lk 9:57	2036
Jesus *s* unto him, Foxes have	Lk 9:58	2036
he *s* unto another, Follow me	Lk 9:59	2036
But he *s*, Lord, suffer me first	Lk 9:59	2036
Jesus *s* unto him, Let the dead	Lk 9:60	2036
And another also *s*, Lord, I will	Lk 9:61	2036
Jesus *s* unto him, No man, having	Lk 9:62	2036
Therefore *s* he unto them, The	Lk 10:2	3004
he *s* unto them, I beheld Satan as	Lk 10:18	2036
Jesus rejoiced in spirit, and *s*	Lk 10:21	2036
s privately, Blessed are the eyes	Lk 10:23	2036
He *s* unto him, What is written in	Lk 10:26	2036
And he answering *s*, Thou shalt	Lk 10:27	2036
he *s* unto him, Thou hast answered	Lk 10:28	2036
s unto Jesus, And who is my	Lk 10:29	2036
And Jesus answering *s*, A certain	Lk 10:30	2036
s unto him, Take care of him	Lk 10:35	2036
And he *s*, He that shewed mercy on	Lk 10:37	2036
Then *s* Jesus unto him, Go, and do	Lk 10:37	2036
serving, and came to him, and *s*	Lk 10:40	2036
s unto her, Martha, Martha, thou	Lk 10:41	2036
one of his disciples *s* unto him	Lk 11:1	2036
he *s* unto them, When ye pray, say	Lk 11:2	2036
he *s* unto them, Which of you	Lk 11:5	2036
But some of them *s*, He casteth	Lk 11:15	2036
s unto them, Every kingdom	Lk 11:17	2036
s unto him, Blessed is the womb	Lk 11:27	2036
But he *s*, Yea rather, blessed are	Lk 11:28	2036
And the Lord *s* unto him, Now do ye	Lk 11:39	2036
s unto him, Master, thus saying	Lk 11:45	3004
And he *s*, Woe unto you also, ye	Lk 11:46	2036
Therefore also *s* the wisdom of	Lk 11:49	2036
as he *s* these things unto them,	Lk 11:53	3004
And one of the company *s* unto him	Lk 12:13	2036
he *s* unto him, Man, who made me a	Lk 12:14	2036
he *s* unto them, Take heed, and	Lk 12:15	2036
And he *s*, This will I do.	Lk 12:18	2036
But God *s* unto him, Thou fool,	Lk 12:20	2036
And he *s* unto his disciples,	Lk 12:22	2036
Then Peter *s* unto him, Lord,	Lk 12:41	2036
And the Lord *s*, Who then is that	Lk 12:42	2036
he *s* also to the people, When ye	Lk 12:54	3004
And Jesus answering *s* unto them	Lk 13:2	2036
Then *s* he unto the dresser of his	Lk 13:7	2036
And he answering *s* unto him	Lk 13:8	3004
s unto her, Woman, thou art	Lk 13:12	2036
s unto the people, There are six	Lk 13:14	3004
The Lord then answered him, and *s*	Lk 13:15	2036
when he had *s* these things, all	Lk 13:17	3004
Then *s* he, Unto what is the	Lk 13:18	3004
And again he *s*, Whereunto shall I	Lk 13:20	2036
Then *s* one unto him, Lord, are	Lk 13:23	2036
And he *s* unto them,	Lk 13:23	2036
he *s* unto them, Go ye, and tell	Lk 13:32	2036
Then *s* he also to him that bade	Lk 14:12	3004
he *s* unto him, Blessed is he that	Lk 14:15	2036
Then *s* he unto him, A certain man	Lk 14:16	2036
The first *s* unto him, I have	Lk 14:18	2036
And another *s*, I have bought five	Lk 14:19	2036
And another *s*, I have married a	Lk 14:20	2036
being angry *s* to his servant	Lk 14:21	2036
And the servant *s*, Lord, it is	Lk 14:22	2036
the lord *s* unto the servant, Go	Lk 14:23	2036
and he turned, and *s* unto them,	Lk 14:25	2036
And he *s*, A certain man had two	Lk 15:11	2036
younger of them *s* to his father	Lk 15:12	2036
And when he came to himself, he *s*	Lk 15:17	2036
the son *s* unto him, Father, I	Lk 15:21	2036
But the father *s* to his servants,	Lk 15:22	2036
he *s* unto him, Thy brother is	Lk 15:27	2036
he answering *s* to his father, Lo,	Lk 15:29	2036
he *s* unto him, Son, thou art ever	Lk 15:31	2036
he *s* also unto his disciples,	Lk 16:1	3004
s unto him, How is it that I hear	Lk 16:2	2036
Then the steward *s* within himself	Lk 16:3	2036
s unto the first, How much owest	Lk 16:5	3004
And he *s*, An hundred measures of	Lk 16:6	2036
he *s* unto him, Take thy bill, and	Lk 16:6	2036
Then *s* he to another, And how much	Lk 16:7	2036
And he *s*, An hundred measures of	Lk 16:7	2036
he *s* unto him, Take thy bill, and	Lk 16:7	3004
he *s* unto them, Ye are they which	Lk 16:15	2036
And he cried and *s*, Father Abraham,	Lk 16:24	2036
But Abraham *s*, Son, remember that	Lk 16:25	2036
Then he *s*, I pray thee therefore,	Lk 16:27	2036
And he *s*, Nay, father Abraham	Lk 16:30	2036
he *s* unto him, If they hear not	Lk 16:31	2036
Then *s* he unto the disciples, It	Lk 17:1	2036
the apostles *s* unto the Lord,	Lk 17:5	2036
And the Lord *s*, If ye had faith as	Lk 17:6	2036
they lifted up their voices, and *s*	Lk 17:13	3004
saw them, he *s* unto them, Go shew	Lk 17:14	2036
And Jesus answering *s*, Were there	Lk 17:17	2036
he *s* unto him, Arise, go thy way	Lk 17:19	2036
come, he answered them and *s*	Lk 17:20	2036
he *s* unto the disciples, The days	Lk 17:22	2036
and *s* unto him, Where, Lord	Lk 17:37	3004
he *s* unto them, Wheresoever the	Lk 17:37	2036
but afterward he *s* within himself	Lk 18:4	2036
And the Lord *s*, Hear what the	Lk 18:6	2036
Jesus called them unto him, and *s*	Lk 18:16	2036
Jesus *s* unto him, Why callest	Lk 18:19	2036
And he *s*, All these have I kept	Lk 18:21	2036
he *s* unto him, Yet lackest thou	Lk 18:22	2036
that he was very sorrowful, he *s*	Lk 18:24	2036
And they that heard it *s*, Who then	Lk 18:26	2036
And he *s*, The things which are	Lk 18:27	2036
Then Peter *s*, Lo, we have left	Lk 18:28	2036
he *s* unto them, Verily I say unto	Lk 18:29	2036
s unto them, Behold, we go up to	Lk 18:31	2036
And he *s*, Lord, that I may receive	Lk 18:41	2036
Jesus *s* unto him, Receive thy	Lk 18:42	2036
s unto him, Zacchaeus, make haste	Lk 19:5	2036
stood, and *s* unto the Lord	Lk 19:8	2036
Jesus *s* unto him, This day is	Lk 19:9	2036
He *s* therefore, A certain	Lk 19:12	2036
s unto them, Occupy till I come	Lk 19:13	2036
he *s* unto him, Well, thou good	Lk 19:17	2036
he *s* likewise to him, Be thou	Lk 19:19	2036
he *s* unto them that stood by,	Lk 19:24	2036
they *s* unto him, Lord, he hath	Lk 19:25	2036
found even as he had *s* unto them	Lk 19:32	2036
the owners thereof *s* unto them	Lk 19:33	2036
And they *s*, The Lord hath need of	Lk 19:34	2036
among the multitude *s* unto him	Lk 19:39	2036
s unto them, I tell you that, if	Lk 19:40	2036
s unto them, I will also ask you	Lk 20:3	2036
Jesus *s* unto them, Neither tell I	Lk 20:8	2036
Then *s* the lord of the vineyard,	Lk 20:13	2036
And when they heard it, they *s*	Lk 20:16	2036
And he beheld them, and *s*, What is	Lk 20:17	2036
s unto them, Why tempt ye me	Lk 20:23	2036
They answered and *s*, Caesar's	Lk 20:24	2036
he *s* unto them, Render therefore	Lk 20:25	2036
And Jesus answering *s* unto them	Lk 20:34	2036
of the scribes answering *s*	Lk 20:39	2036
Master, thou hast well *s*	Lk 20:39	2036
he *s* unto them, How say they that	Lk 20:41	2036
The Lord *s* unto my Lord, Sit thou	Lk 20:42	2036
people he *s* unto his disciples	Lk 20:45	2036
And he *s*, Of a truth I say unto	Lk 21:3	2036
with goodly stones and gifts, he *s*	Lk 21:5	2036
And he *s*, Take heed that ye be not	Lk 21:8	2036
Then *s* he unto them, Nation shall	Lk 21:10	3004
they *s* unto him, Where wilt thou	Lk 22:9	2036
he *s* unto them, Behold, when ye	Lk 22:10	2036
and found as he had *s* unto them	Lk 22:13	2046
he *s* unto them, With desire I	Lk 22:15	2036
the cup, and gave thanks, and *s*	Lk 22:17	2036
he *s* unto them, The kings of the	Lk 22:25	2036
And the Lord *s*, Simon, Simon,	Lk 22:31	2036
he *s* unto him, Lord, I am ready	Lk 22:33	2036
And he *s*, I tell thee, Peter, the	Lk 22:34	3004
he *s* unto them, When I sent you	Lk 22:35	2036
And they *s*, Nothing	Lk 22:35	2036
Then *s* he unto them, But now, he	Lk 22:36	2036
And they *s*, Lord, behold, here are	Lk 22:38	2036
he *s* unto them, It is enough	Lk 22:38	2036
he *s* unto them, Pray that ye	Lk 22:40	2036
s unto them, Why sleep ye	Lk 22:46	2036
But Jesus *s* unto him, Judas,	Lk 22:48	2036
they *s* unto him, Lord, shall we	Lk 22:49	2036
And Jesus answered and *s*, Suffer ye	Lk 22:51	2036
Then Jesus *s* unto the chief	Lk 22:52	2036
earnestly looked upon him, and *s*	Lk 22:56	2036
while another saw him, and *s*	Lk 22:58	5346
And Peter *s*, Man, I am not	Lk 22:58	2036
And Peter *s*, Man, I know not what	Lk 22:60	2036
the Lord, how he had *s* unto him	Lk 22:61	2036
he *s* unto them, If I tell you, ye	Lk 22:67	2036
Then *s* they all, Art thou then	Lk 22:70	5346
he *s* unto them, Ye say that I am	Lk 22:70	2036
And they *s*, What need we any	Lk 22:71	2036
And he answered him and *s*, Thou	Lk 23:3	5346
Then *s* Pilate to the chief	Lk 23:4	2036
S unto them, Ye have brought this	Lk 23:14	2036
he *s* unto them the third time,	Lk 23:22	2036
But Jesus turning unto them *s*	Lk 23:28	2036
Then *s* Jesus, Father, forgive	Lk 23:34	3004
he *s* unto Jesus, Lord, remember	Lk 23:42	3004
Jesus *s* unto him, Verily I say	Lk 23:43	2036
had cried with a loud voice, he *s*	Lk 23:46	2036

and having s thus, he gave up the	Lk 23:46	2036
they s unto them, Why seek ye the	Lk 24:5	2036
he s unto them, What manner of	Lk 24:17	2036
was Cleopas, answering s unto him	Lk 24:18	2036
he s unto them, What things	Lk 24:19	2036
they s unto him, Concerning Jesus	Lk 24:19	2036
which s that he was alive	Lk 24:23	3004
it even so as the women had s	Lk 24:24	2036
Then he s unto them, O fools, and	Lk 24:25	2036
they s one to another, Did not	Lk 24:32	2036
he s unto them, Why are ye	Lk 24:38	2036
he s unto them, Have ye here any	Lk 24:41	2036
he s unto them, These are the	Lk 24:44	2036
s unto them, Thus it is written,	Lk 24:46	2036
Then s they unto him, Who art	Jn 1:22	2036
He s, I am the voice of one	Jn 1:23	5346
the Lord, as s the prophet Esaias	Jn 1:23	2036
s unto him, Why baptizest thou	Jn 1:25	2036
This is he of whom I s, After me	Jn 1:30	2036
with water, the same s unto me	Jn 1:33	2036
They s unto him, Rabbi, (which is	Jn 1:38	2036
And when Jesus beheld him, he s	Jn 1:42	2036
And Nathanael s unto him, Can	Jn 1:46	2036
s unto him, Before that Philip	Jn 1:48	2036
s unto him, Because I s unto	Jn 1:50	2036
s unto them that sold doves, Take	Jn 2:16	2036
s unto him, What sign shewest	Jn 2:18	2036
s unto them, Destroy this temple,	Jn 2:19	2036
Then s the Jews, Forty and six	Jn 2:20	2036
that he had s this unto them	Jn 2:22	3004
and the word which Jesus had s	Jn 2:22	2036
s unto him, Rabbi, we know that	Jn 3:2	2036
s unto him, Verily, verily, I say	Jn 3:3	2036
Marvel not that I s unto thee	Jn 3:7	2036
s unto him, How can these things	Jn 3:9	2036
s unto him, Art thou a master of	Jn 3:10	2036
s unto him, Rabbi, he that was	Jn 3:26	2036
John answered and s, A man can	Jn 3:27	2036
bear me witness, that I s	Jn 3:28	2036
s unto her, If thou knewest the	Jn 4:10	2036
s unto her, Whosoever drinketh of	Jn 4:13	2036
The woman answered and s, I have	Jn 4:17	2036
Jesus s unto her, Thou hast well	Jn 4:17	3004
unto her, Thou hast well s	Jn 4:17	2036
yet no man s, What seekest thou	Jn 4:27	2036
But he s unto them, I have meat	Jn 4:32	2036
Therefore s the disciples one to	Jn 4:33	3004
s unto the woman, Now we believe,	Jn 4:42	3004
Then s Jesus unto him, Except ye	Jn 4:48	2036
they s unto him, Yesterday at the	Jn 4:52	2036
in the which Jesus s unto him	Jn 4:53	2036
The Jews therefore s unto him	Jn 5:10	3004
made me whole, the same s unto me	Jn 5:11	2036
man is that which s unto thee	Jn 5:12	2036
s unto him, Behold, thou art made	Jn 5:14	2036
but s also that God was his	Jn 5:18	3004
s unto them, Verily, verily, I	Jn 5:19	2036
And this he s to prove him	Jn 6:6	3004
And Jesus s, Make the men sit down	Jn 6:10	2036
he s unto his disciples, Gather	Jn 6:12	3004
the miracle that Jesus did, s	Jn 6:14	3004
they s unto him, Rabbi, when	Jn 6:25	2036
Jesus answered them and s, Verily,	Jn 6:26	2036
Then s they unto him, What shall	Jn 6:28	2036
s unto them, This is the work of	Jn 6:29	2036
They s therefore unto him, What	Jn 6:30	2036
Then Jesus s unto them, Verily,	Jn 6:32	2036
Then s they unto him, Lord,	Jn 6:34	2036
Jesus s unto them, I am the bread	Jn 6:35	2036
But I s unto you, That ye also	Jn 6:36	2036
murmured at him, because he s	Jn 6:41	2036
And they s, Is not this Jesus, the	Jn 6:42	3004
s unto them, Murmur not among	Jn 6:43	2036
Then Jesus s unto them, Verily,	Jn 6:53	2036
These things s he in the	Jn 6:59	2036
when they had heard this, s	Jn 6:60	2036
he s unto them, Doth this offend	Jn 6:61	2036
And he s, Therefore s I unto	Jn 6:65	3004
Therefore s I unto you, that no	Jn 6:65	2046
Then s Jesus unto the twelve,	Jn 6:67	2036
His brethren therefore s unto him	Jn 7:3	2036
Then Jesus s unto them, My time	Jn 7:6	3004
When he had s these words unto	Jn 7:9	2036
sought him at the feast, and s	Jn 7:11	3004
for some s, He is a good man	Jn 7:12	3004
others s, Nay	Jn 7:12	3004
Jesus answered them, and s	Jn 7:16	2036
The people answered and s, Thou	Jn 7:20	2036
s unto them, I have done one work	Jn 7:21	2036
Then s some of them of Jerusalem,	Jn 7:25	3004
the people believed on him, and s	Jn 7:31	3004
Then s Jesus unto them, Yet a	Jn 7:33	2036
Then s the Jews among themselves,	Jn 7:35	2036
of saying is this that he s	Jn 7:36	2036
on me, as the scripture hath s	Jn 7:38	2036
when they heard this saying, s	Jn 7:40	3004
Others s, This is the Christ	Jn 7:41	3004
But some s, Shall Christ come out	Jn 7:41	3004
Hath not the scripture s, That	Jn 7:42	2036
they s unto them, Why have ye not	Jn 7:45	2036
s unto him, Art thou also of	Jn 7:52	2036
This they s, tempting him, that	Jn 8:6	3004
s unto them, He that is without	Jn 8:7	2036
he s unto her, Woman, where are	Jn 8:10	2036
She s, No man, Lord	Jn 8:11	2036
Jesus s unto her, Neither do I	Jn 8:11	2036
Pharisees therefore s unto him	Jn 8:13	2036
s unto them, Though I bear record	Jn 8:14	2036
Then s they unto him, Where is	Jn 8:19	3004
Then s Jesus again unto them, I	Jn 8:21	2036
Then s the Jews, Will he kill	Jn 8:22	3004
he s unto them, Ye are from	Jn 8:23	2036
I s therefore unto you, that ye	Jn 8:24	2036
Then s they unto him, Who art	Jn 8:25	3004
Even the same that I s unto you	Jn 8:25	2980
Then s Jesus unto them, When ye	Jn 8:28	2036
Then s Jesus to those Jews which	Jn 8:31	3004
s unto him, Abraham is our father	Jn 8:39	2036
Then s they to him, We be not	Jn 8:41	2036
Jesus s unto them, If God were	Jn 8:42	2036
s unto him, Say we not well that	Jn 8:48	2036
Then s the Jews unto him, Now we	Jn 8:52	2036
Then s the Jews unto him, Thou	Jn 8:57	2036
Jesus s unto them, Verily, verily	Jn 8:58	2036
s unto him, Go, wash in the pool	Jn 9:7	2036
had seen him that he was blind, s	Jn 9:8	3004
Some s, This is he	Jn 9:9	3004
others s, He is like him	Jn 9:9	
but he s, I am he	Jn 9:9	3004
Therefore s they unto him, How	Jn 9:10	3004
He answered and s, A man that is	Jn 9:11	2036
s unto me, Go to the pool of	Jn 9:11	2036
Then s they unto him, Where is he	Jn 9:12	2036
He s, I know not	Jn 9:12	3004
He s unto them, He put clay upon	Jn 9:15	2036
Therefore s some of the Pharisees	Jn 9:16	3004
Others s, How can a man that is a	Jn 9:16	3004
He s, He is a prophet	Jn 9:17	2036
His parents answered them and s	Jn 9:20	2036
Therefore s his parents, He is of	Jn 9:23	2036
s unto him, Give God the praise	Jn 9:24	2036
He answered and s, Whether he be a	Jn 9:25	2036
Then s they to him again, What	Jn 9:26	2036
Then they reviled him, and s	Jn 9:28	2036
s unto them, Why herein is a	Jn 9:30	2036
s unto him, Thou wast altogether	Jn 9:34	2036
he s unto him, Dost thou believe	Jn 9:35	2036
He answered and s, Who is he, Lord	Jn 9:36	2036
Jesus s unto him, Thou hast both	Jn 9:37	2036
And he s, Lord, I believe	Jn 9:38	5346
And Jesus s, For judgment I am	Jn 9:39	2036
s unto him, Are we blind also	Jn 9:40	2036
Jesus s unto them, If ye were	Jn 9:41	2036
Then s Jesus unto them again,	Jn 10:7	2036
And many of them s, He hath a	Jn 10:20	3004
Others s, These are not the words	Jn 10:21	3004
s unto him, How long dost thou	Jn 10:24	3004
not of my sheep, as I s unto you	Jn 10:26	2036
it not written in your law, I s	Jn 10:34	2036
because I s, I am the Son of God	Jn 10:36	2036
And many resorted unto him, and s	Jn 10:41	3004
When Jesus heard that, he s	Jn 11:4	2036
These things s he	Jn 11:11	2036
Then s his disciples, Lord, if he	Jn 11:12	2036
Then s Jesus unto them plainly,	Jn 11:14	2036
Then s Thomas, which is called	Jn 11:16	2036
Then s Martha unto Jesus, Lord,	Jn 11:21	2036
Jesus s unto her, I am the	Jn 11:25	2036
And when she had so s, she went	Jn 11:28	2036
And s, Where have ye laid him	Jn 11:34	2036
They s unto him, Lord, come and	Jn 11:34	3004
Then s the Jews, Behold how he	Jn 11:36	3004
And some of them s, Could not this	Jn 11:37	2036
Jesus s, Take ye away the stone	Jn 11:39	3004
S I not unto thee, that, if thou	Jn 11:40	2036
And Jesus lifted up his eyes, and s	Jn 11:41	2036
the people which stand by I s it	Jn 11:42	2036
and the Pharisees a council, and s	Jn 11:47	3004
s unto them, Ye know nothing at	Jn 11:49	2036
This he s, not that he cared for	Jn 12:6	2036
Then s Jesus, Let her alone	Jn 12:7	2036
therefore s among themselves	Jn 12:19	2036
and heard it, s that it thundered	Jn 12:29	3004
others s, An angel spake to him	Jn 12:29	3004
Jesus answered and s, This voice	Jn 12:30	2036
This he s, signifying what death	Jn 12:33	3004
Then Jesus s unto them, Yet a	Jn 12:35	2036
because that Esaias s again	Jn 12:39	2036
These things s Esaias, when he	Jn 12:41	2036
Jesus cried and s, He that	Jn 12:44	2036
even as the Father s unto me	Jn 12:50	2046
s unto him, What I do thou	Jn 13:7	2036
therefore s he, Ye are not all	Jn 13:11	2036
he s unto them, Know ye what I	Jn 13:12	2036
When Jesus had thus s, he was	Jn 13:21	2036
in spirit, and testified, and s	Jn 13:21	2036
Then s Jesus unto him, That thou	Jn 13:27	3004
bag, that Jesus had s unto him	Jn 13:29	3004
when he was gone out, Jesus s	Jn 13:31	3004
as I s unto the Jews, Whither I	Jn 13:33	2036
Simon Peter s unto him, Lord,	Jn 13:36	3004
Peter s unto him, Lord, why	Jn 13:37	3004
s unto him, If a man love me, he	Jn 14:23	2036
whatsoever I have s unto you	Jn 14:26	2036
Ye have heard how I s unto you	Jn 14:28	2036
me, ye would rejoice, because I s	Jn 14:28	2036
the word that I s unto you	Jn 15:20	2036
these things I s not unto you at	Jn 16:4	2036
But because I have s these things	Jn 16:6	2980
therefore s I, that he shall take	Jn 16:15	2036
Then s some of his disciples	Jn 16:17	2036
They s therefore, What is this	Jn 16:18	3004
s unto them, Do ye enquire among	Jn 16:19	2036
among yourselves of that I s	Jn 16:19	2036
His disciples s unto him, Lo, now	Jn 16:29	3004
up his eyes to heaven, and s	Jn 17:1	2036
s unto them, Whom seek ye	Jn 18:4	2036
soon then as he had s unto them	Jn 18:6	2036
And they s, Jesus of Nazareth	Jn 18:7	2036
Then s Jesus unto Peter, Put up	Jn 18:11	2036
and in secret have I s nothing	Jn 18:20	2980
heard me, what I have s unto them	Jn 18:21	2980
behold, they know what I s	Jn 18:21	2036
They s therefore unto him, Art	Jn 18:25	2036
He denied it, and s, I am not	Jn 18:25	2036
then went out unto them, and s	Jn 18:29	2036
s unto him, If he were not a	Jn 18:30	2036
Then s Pilate unto them, Take ye	Jn 18:31	2036
The Jews therefore s unto him	Jn 18:31	2036
s unto him, Art thou the King of	Jn 18:33	2036
Pilate therefore s unto him	Jn 18:37	2036
And when he had s this, he went	Jn 18:38	2036
And s, Hail, King of the Jews	Jn 19:3	3004
Then s the chief priests of the	Jn 19:21	3004
but that he s, I am King of the	Jn 19:21	2036
They s therefore among themselves	Jn 19:24	2036
had received the vinegar, he s	Jn 19:30	2036
And when she had thus s, she	Jn 20:14	2036
And when he had so s, he shewed	Jn 20:20	2036
Then s Jesus to them again, Peace	Jn 20:21	2036
And when he had s this, he	Jn 20:22	2036
disciples therefore s unto him	Jn 20:25	3004
But he s unto them, Except I	Jn 20:25	2036
shut, and stood in the midst, and s	Jn 20:26	2036
s unto him, My Lord and my God	Jn 20:28	2036
he s unto them, Cast the net on	Jn 21:6	2036
he s unto him the third time	Jn 21:17	2036
he s unto him, Lord, thou knowest	Jn 21:17	2036
on his breast at supper, and s	Jn 21:20	2036
yet Jesus s not unto him, He	Jn 21:23	2036
he s unto them, It is not for you	Acts 1:7	2036
Which also s, Ye men of Galilee,	Acts 1:11	2036
the midst of the disciples, and s	Acts 1:15	2036
And they prayed, and s, Thou, Lord,	Acts 1:24	2036
Others mocking s, These men are	Acts 2:13	3004
s unto them, Ye men of Judaea, and	Acts 2:14	669
The Lord s unto my Lord, Sit thou	Acts 2:34	2036
s unto Peter and to the rest of	Acts 2:37	2036
Then Peter s unto them, Repent,	Acts 2:38	5346
his eyes upon him with John, s	Acts 3:4	2036
Then Peter s, Silver and gold have	Acts 3:6	2036
For Moses truly s unto the	Acts 3:22	2036
s unto them, Ye rulers of the	Acts 4:8	2036
s unto them, Whether it be right	Acts 4:19	2036
priests and elders had s unto them	Acts 4:23	2036
to God with one accord, and s	Acts 4:24	2036
mouth of thy servant David hast s	Acts 4:25	2036
neither s any of them that ought	Acts 4:32	3004
But Peter s, Ananias, why hath	Acts 5:3	2036
And she s, Yea, for so much	Acts 5:8	2036
Then Peter s unto her, How is it	Acts 5:9	2036
and brought them forth, and s	Acts 5:19	2036
the other apostles answered and s	Acts 5:29	2036
s unto them, Ye men of Israel,	Acts 5:35	2036
of the disciples unto them, and s	Acts 6:2	2036
Then they suborned men, which s	Acts 6:11	3004
set up false witnesses, which s	Acts 6:13	3004
Then s the high priest, Are these	Acts 7:1	2036
And he s, Men, brethren, and	Acts 7:2	5346
s unto him, Get thee out of thy	Acts 7:3	2036
be in bondage will I judge, s God	Acts 7:7	2036
Then s the Lord to him, Put off	Acts 7:33	2036
which s unto the children of	Acts 7:37	2036
And s, Behold, I see the heavens	Acts 7:56	2036
And when he had s this, he fell	Acts 7:60	2036
But Peter s unto him, Thy money	Acts 8:20	2036
Then answered Simon, and s	Acts 8:24	2036
Then the Spirit s unto Philip	Acts 8:29	2036
him read the prophet Esaias, and s	Acts 8:30	2036
And he s, How can I, except some	Acts 8:31	2036
the eunuch answered Philip, and s	Acts 8:34	2036
and the eunuch s, See, here is	Acts 8:36	5346
And Philip s, If thou believest	Acts 8:37	2036
And he answered and s, I believe	Acts 8:37	2036
And he s, Who art thou, Lord	Acts 9:5	2036
And the Lord s, I am Jesus whom	Acts 9:5	
And he trembling and astonished s	Acts 9:6	2036
And the Lord s unto him, Arise, and	Acts 9:6	
to him s the Lord in a vision,	Acts 9:10	2036
And he s, Behold, I am here, Lord	Acts 9:10	2036
And the Lord s unto him, Arise, and	Acts 9:11	
But the Lord s unto him, Go thy	Acts 9:15	2036
and putting his hands on him s	Acts 9:17	2036
that heard him were amazed, and s	Acts 9:21	3004
Peter s unto him, Aeneas, Jesus	Acts 9:34	2036
and turning him to the body s	Acts 9:40	2036
on him, he was afraid, and s	Acts 10:4	2036
he s unto him, Thy prayers and	Acts 10:4	2036
But Peter s, Not so, Lord	Acts 10:14	2036
the vision, the Spirit s unto him	Acts 10:19	2036
and s, Behold, I am he whom ye	Acts 10:21	2036
And they s, Cornelius the	Acts 10:22	2036
he s unto them, Ye know how that	Acts 10:28	5346
And Cornelius s, Four days ago I	Acts 10:30	5346
And s, Cornelius, thy prayer is	Acts 10:31	5346
Then Peter opened his mouth, and s	Acts 10:34	2036
But I s, Not so, Lord	Acts 11:8	2036
s unto him, Send men to Joppa, and	Acts 11:13	2036
word of the Lord, how that he s	Acts 11:16	3004
And the angel s unto him, Gird	Acts 12:8	2036
Peter was come to himself, he s	Acts 12:11	2036
they s unto her, Thou art mad	Acts 12:15	2036
Then s they, It is his angel	Acts 12:15	3004
And he s, Go shew these things	Acts 12:17	2036
Lord, and fasted, the Holy Ghost s	Acts 13:2	2036
And s, O full of all subtilty and	Acts 13:10	2036
up, and beckoning with his hand s	Acts 13:16	2036
whom also he gave testimony, and s	Acts 13:22	2036
John fulfilled his course, he s	Acts 13:25	3004
he s on this wise, I will give	Acts 13:34	5346
Paul and Barnabas waxed bold, and s	Acts 13:46	2036
S with a loud voice, Stand	Acts 14:10	2036
Judaea taught the brethren, and s	Acts 15:1	
s unto them, Men and brethren, ye	Acts 15:7	2036
days after Paul s unto Barnabas	Acts 15:36	2036
s to the spirit, I command thee	Acts 16:18	2036
And brought them out, and s	Acts 16:30	5346
And they s, Believe on the Lord	Acts 16:31	2036
But Paul s unto them, They have	Acts 16:37	5346
And some s, What will this babbler	Acts 17:18	3004
in the midst of Mars' hill, and s	Acts 17:22	5346
also of your own poets have s	Acts 17:28	2046

S

and others *s*, We will hear thee	Acts 17:32	2036
s unto them, Your blood be upon	Acts 18:6	2036
Gallio *s* unto the Jews, If it	Acts 18:14	2036
He *s* unto them, Have ye received	Acts 19:2	2036
they *s* unto him, We have not so	Acts 19:2	2036
he *s* unto them, Unto what then	Acts 19:3	2036
And they *s*, Unto John's baptism	Acts 19:3	2036
Then *s* Paul, John verily baptized	Acts 19:4	2036
And the evil spirit answered and *s*	Acts 19:15	2036
workmen of like occupation, and *s*	Acts 19:25	2036
had appeased the people, he *s*	Acts 19:35	5346
fell on him, and embracing him *s*	Acts 20:10	2036
he *s* unto them, Ye know, from the	Acts 20:18	2036
words of the Lord Jesus, how he *s*	Acts 20:35	2036
who *s* to Paul through the Spirit,	Acts 21:4	3004
bound his own hands and feet, and *s*	Acts 21:11	2036
s unto him, Thou seest, brother,	Acts 21:20	2036
he *s* unto the chief captain, May	Acts 21:37	3004
Who *s*, Canst thou speak Greek	Acts 21:37	5346
But Paul *s*, I am a man which am a	Acts 21:39	2036
he *s* unto me, I am Jesus of	Acts 22:8	2036
And I *s*, What shall I do, Lord	Acts 22:10	2036
And the Lord *s* unto me, Arise, and	Acts 22:10	2036
s unto me, Brother Saul, receive	Acts 22:13	2036
And he *s*, The God of our fathers	Acts 22:14	2036
And I *s*, Lord, they know that I	Acts 22:19	2036
And he *s* unto me, Depart	Acts 22:21	2036
then lifted up their voices, and *s*	Acts 22:22	3004
Paul *s* unto the centurion that	Acts 22:25	2036
s unto him, Tell me, art thou a	Acts 22:27	2036
He *s*, Yea	Acts 22:27	5346
And Paul *s*, But I was free born	Acts 22:28	5346
beholding the council, *s*, Men and	Acts 23:1	2036
Then *s* Paul unto him, God shall	Acts 23:3	2036
And they that stood by *s*, Revilest	Acts 23:4	2036
Then *s* Paul, I wist not, brethren	Acts 23:5	5346
And when he had so *s*, there arose	Acts 23:7	2980
the Lord stood by him, and *s*	Acts 23:11	2036
the chief priests and elders, and *s*	Acts 23:14	2036
of the centurions unto him, and *s*	Acts 23:17	5346
him to the chief captain, and *s*	Acts 23:18	5346
And he *s*, The Jews have agreed to	Acts 23:20	2036
s he, when thine accusers are	Acts 23:35	5346
that way, he deferred them, and *s*	Acts 24:22	2036
s he, which among you are able,	Acts 25:5	5346
a pleasure, answered Paul, and *s*	Acts 25:9	2036
Then *s* Paul, I stand at Caesar's	Acts 25:10	2036
Then Agrippa *s* unto Festus	Acts 25:22	5346
s he, thou shalt hear him	Acts 25:22	5346
And Festus *s*, King Agrippa, and all	Acts 25:24	5346
Then Agrippa *s* unto Paul, Thou	Acts 26:1	5346
And I *s*, Who art thou, Lord	Acts 26:15	2036
And he *s*, I am Jesus whom thou	Acts 26:15	2036
Festus *s* with a loud voice, Paul,	Acts 26:24	5346
But he *s*, I am not mad, most	Acts 26:25	5346
Then Agrippa *s* unto Paul, Almost	Acts 26:28	5346
And Paul *s*, I would to God, that	Acts 26:29	2036
Then *s* Agrippa unto Festus, This	Acts 26:32	5346
s unto them, Sirs, I perceive	Acts 27:10	3004
forth in the midst of them, and *s*	Acts 27:21	2036
Paul *s* to the centurion and to the	Acts 27:31	2036
they *s* among themselves, No doubt	Acts 28:4	3004
minds, and *s* that he was a god	Acts 28:6	3004
he *s* unto them, Men and brethren,	Acts 28:17	3004
they *s* unto him, We neither	Acts 28:21	2036
And when he had *s* these words	Acts 28:29	2036
known lust, except the law had *s*	Rom 7:7	3004
It was *s* unto her, The elder	Rom 9:12	4483
place where it was *s* unto them	Rom 9:26	4483
And as Esaias *s* before, Except the	Rom 9:29	4280
given thanks, he brake it, and *s*	1Cor 11:24	2036
as God hath *s*, I will dwell in	2Cor 6:16	2036
for I have *s* before, that ye are	2Cor 7:3	4280
that, as I *s*, ye may be ready	2Cor 9:3	3004
he *s* unto me, My grace is	2Cor 12:9	2046
As we *s* before, so say I now	Gal 1:9	4280
I *s* unto Peter before them all,	Gal 2:14	2036
even a prophet of their own, *s*	Titus 1:12	2036
of the angels *s* he at any time	Heb 1:5	2036
of the angels *s* he at any times	Heb 1:13	2046
with that generation, and *s*	Heb 3:10	2036
While it is *s*, To day if ye will	Heb 3:15	3004
do enter into rest, as he *s*	Heb 4:3	2046
as it is *s*, To day if ye will	Heb 4:7	2046
but he that *s* unto him, Thou art	Heb 5:5	2980
an oath by him that *s* unto him	Heb 7:21	3004
Then *s* I, Lo, I come (in the	Heb 10:7	2036
Above when he *s*, Sacrifice and	Heb 10:8	3004
Then *s* he, Lo, I come to do thy	Heb 10:9	2046
for after that he had *s* before	Heb 10:15	4280
For we know him that hath *s*	Heb 10:30	2036
Of whom it was *s*, That in Isaac	Heb 11:18	2980
was the sight, that Moses *s*	Heb 12:21	2036
for he hath *s*, I will never leave	Heb 13:5	2046
For he that *s*, Do not commit	Jas 2:11	2036
adultery, *s* also, Do not kill	Jas 2:11	2036
him a railing accusation, but *s*	Jude 9	2036
which *s*, Come up hither, and I	Rev 4:1	3004
And the four beasts *s*, Amen	Rev 5:14	3004
it was *s* unto them, that they	Rev 6:11	4483
s to the mountains and rocks, Fall	Rev 6:16	3004
I *s* unto him, Sir, thou knowest	Rev 7:14	2046
he *s* to me, These are they which	Rev 7:14	2036
heaven spake unto me again, and *s*	Rev 10:8	3004
s unto him, Give me the little	Rev 10:9	3004
he *s* unto me, Take it, and eat it	Rev 10:9	3004
he *s* unto me, Thou must prophesy	Rev 10:11	3004
And the angel *s* unto me, Wherefore	Rev 17:7	2036
And again they *s*, Alleluia	Rev 19:3	2046
he *s* unto me, See thou do it not	Rev 19:10	3004
And he that sat upon the throne *s*	Rev 21:5	2036
And he *s* unto me, Write	Rev 21:5	3004
And he *s* unto me, It is done	Rev 21:6	2036
he *s* unto me, These sayings are	Rev 22:6	2036

SAIDST

Why *s* thou, She is my sister	Gen 12:19	559
how *s* thou, She is my sister	Gen 26:9	559
Isaac, the LORD which *s* unto me	Gen 32:9	559
And thou *s*, I will surely do thee	Gen 32:12	559
thou *s* unto thy servants, Bring	Gen 44:21	559
thou *s* unto thy servants, Except	Gen 44:23	559
s unto them, I will multiply your	Ex 32:13	1696
now thy mouth, wherewith thou *s*	Judg 9:38	559
thou *s* unto me, The word that I	1Kin 2:42	559
this to be right, that thou *s*	Job 35:2	559
For thou *s*, What advantage will	Job 35:3	559
When thou *s*, Seek ye my face	Ps 27:8	559
in vision to thy holy one, and *s*	Ps 89:19	559
And thou *s*, I shall be a lady for	Is 47:7	559
yet *s* thou not, There is no hope	Is 57:10	559
and thou *s*, I will not transgress	Jer 2:20	559
but thou *s*, There is no hope	Jer 2:25	559
but thou *s*, I will not hear	Jer 22:21	559
thou *s*, Fear not	Lam 3:57	559
Because thou *s*, Aha, against my	Eze 25:3	559
and thy judges of whom thou *s*	Hos 13:10	559
in that *s* thou truly	Jn 4:18	2046

SAIL

mast, they could not spread the *s*	Is 33:23	5251
thou spreadest forth to be thy *s*	Eze 27:7	5251
as he was about to *s* into Syria	Acts 20:3	321
had determined to *s* by Ephesus	Acts 20:16	3896
that we should *s* into Italy	Acts 27:1	636
meaning to *s* by the coasts of	Acts 27:2	4126
into the quicksands, strake *s*	Acts 27:17	4632
thee all them that *s* with thee	Acts 27:24	4126

SAILED

But as they *s* he fell asleep	Lk 8:23	4126
and from thence they *s* to Cyprus	Acts 13:4	636
thence *s* to Antioch, from whence	Acts 14:26	636
took Mark, and *s* unto Cyprus	Acts 15:39	1602
s thence into Syria, and with him	Acts 18:18	1602
And he *s* from Ephesus	Acts 18:21	321
we *s* away from Philippi after the	Acts 20:6	1602
s unto Assos, there intending to	Acts 20:13	321
we *s* thence, and came the next day	Acts 20:15	636
s into Syria, and landed at Tyre	Acts 21:3	4126
we *s* under Cyprus, because the	Acts 27:4	5284
when we had *s* over the sea of	Acts 27:5	1277
when we had *s* slowly many days,	Acts 27:7	1020
we *s* under Crete, over against	Acts 27:7	5284
thence, they *s* close by Crete	Acts 27:13	3881

SAILING

finding a ship *s* over unto	Acts 21:2	1276
a ship of Alexandria *s* into Italy	Acts 27:6	4126
when *s* was now dangerous, because	Acts 27:9	4144

SAILORS

and all the company in ships, and *s*	Rev 18:17	3492

SAINT

camp, and Aaron the *s* of the LORD	Ps 106:16	6918
Then I heard one *s* speaking	Dan 8:13	6918
another *s* said unto that certain	Dan 8:13	6918
unto that certain *s* which spake	Dan 8:13	
Salute every *s* in Christ Jesus	Phil 4:21	40

SAINTS

he came with ten thousands of *s*	Deut 33:2	6944
all his *s* are in thy hand	Deut 33:3	6918
He will keep the feet of his *s*	1Sa 2:9	2623
let thy *s* rejoice in goodness	2Chr 6:41	2623
to which of the *s* wilt thou turn	Job 5:1	6918
he putteth no trust in his *s*	Job 15:15	6918
But to the *s* that are in the	Ps 16:3	6918
O ye *s* of his, and give thanks at	Ps 30:4	2623
O love the LORD, all ye his *s*	Ps 31:23	2623
O fear the LORD, ye his *s*	Ps 34:9	6918
judgment, and forsaketh not his *s*	Ps 37:28	2623
Gather my *s* together unto me	Ps 50:5	2623
for it is good before thy *s*	Ps 52:9	2623
the flesh of thy *s* unto the	Ps 79:2	2623
unto his people, and to his *s*	Ps 85:8	2623
also in the congregation of the *s*	Ps 89:5	6918
feared in the assembly of the *s*	Ps 89:7	6918
he preserveth the souls of his *s*	Ps 97:10	2623
of the LORD is the death of his *s*	Ps 116:15	2623
and let thy *s* shout for joy	Ps 132:9	2623
her *s* shall shout aloud for joy	Ps 132:16	2623
and thy *s* shall bless thee	Ps 145:10	2623
people, the praise of all his *s*	Ps 148:14	2623
praise in the congregation of *s*	Ps 149:1	2623
Let the *s* be joyful in glory	Ps 149:5	2623
this honour have all his *s*	Ps 149:9	2623
and preserveth the way of his *s*	Prov 2:8	2623
But the *s* of the most High shall	Dan 7:18	6922
the same horn made war with the *s*	Dan 7:21	6922
given to the *s* of the most High	Dan 7:22	6922
that the *s* possessed the kingdom	Dan 7:22	6922
wear out the *s* of the most High	Dan 7:25	6922
people of the *s* of the most High	Dan 7:27	6922
God, and is faithful with the *s*	Hos 11:12	6918
come, and all the *s* with thee	Zec 14:5	6918
bodies of the *s* which slept arose	Mt 27:52	40
hath done to thy *s* at Jerusalem	Acts 9:13	40
to the *s* which dwelt at Lydda	Acts 9:32	40
up, and when he had called the *s*	Acts 9:41	40
many of the *s* did I shut up in	Acts 26:10	40
beloved of God, called to be *s*	Rom 1:7	40
s according to the will of God	Rom 8:27	40
to the necessity of *s*	Rom 12:13	40
Jerusalem to minister unto the *s*	Rom 15:25	40
the poor *s* which are at Jerusalem	Rom 15:26	40
may be accepted of the *s*	Rom 15:31	40
her in the Lord, as becometh *s*	Rom 16:2	40
all the *s* which are with them	Rom 16:15	40
in Christ Jesus, called to be *s*	1Cor 1:2	40
the unjust, and not before the *s*	1Cor 6:1	40
that the *s* shall judge the world	1Cor 6:2	40
as in all churches of the *s*	1Cor 14:33	40
the collection for the *s*, as I	1Cor 16:1	40
to the ministry of the *s*,)	1Cor 16:15	40
with all the *s* which are in all	2Cor 1:1	40
of the ministering to the *s*	2Cor 8:4	40
touching the ministering to the *s*	2Cor 9:1	40
only supplieth the want of the *s*	2Cor 9:12	40
All the *s* salute you	2Cor 13:13	40
to the *s* which are at Ephesus, and	Eph 1:1	40
Jesus, and love unto all the *s*	Eph 1:15	40
glory of his inheritance in the *s*	Eph 1:18	40
but fellowcitizens with the *s*	Eph 2:19	40
am less than the least of all *s*	Eph 3:8	40
with all *s* what is the breadth	Eph 3:18	40
For the perfecting of the *s*	Eph 4:12	40
named among you, as becometh *s*	Eph 5:3	40
and supplication for all *s*	Eph 6:18	40
to all the *s* in Christ Jesus	Phil 1:1	40
All the *s* salute you, chiefly	Phil 4:22	40
To the *s* and faithful brethren in	Col 1:2	40
love which ye have to all the *s*	Col 1:4	40
the inheritance of the *s* in light	Col 1:12	40
but now is made manifest to his *s*	Col 1:26	40
Lord Jesus Christ with all his *s*	1Th 3:13	40
come to be glorified in his *s*	2Th 1:10	40
the Lord Jesus, and toward all *s*	Philem 5	40
of the *s* are refreshed by thee	Philem 7	40
that ye have ministered to the *s*	Heb 6:10	40
the rule over you, and all the *s*	Heb 13:24	40
was once delivered unto the *s*	Jude 3	40
with ten thousands of his *s*	Jude 14	40
which are the prayers of *s*	Rev 5:8	40
it with the prayers of all *s* upon	Rev 8:3	40
came with the prayers of the *s*	Rev 8:4	40
the prophets, and to the *s*	Rev 11:18	40
unto him to make war with the *s*	Rev 13:7	40
patience and the faith of the *s*	Rev 13:10	40
Here is the patience of the *s*	Rev 14:12	40
true are thy ways, thou King of *s*	Rev 15:3	40
For they have shed the blood of *s*	Rev 16:6	40
drunken with the blood of the *s*	Rev 17:6	40
the blood of prophets, and of *s*	Rev 18:24	40
linen is the righteousness of *s*	Rev 19:8	40
compassed the camp of the *s* about	Rev 20:9	40

SAINTS'

if she have washed the *s* feet	1Ti 5:10	40

SAITH

s the LORD, for because thou hast	Gen 22:16	5002
Thy servant Jacob *s* thus, I have	Gen 32:4	559
what he *s* to you, do	Gen 41:55	559
Wherefore *s* my lord these words	Gen 44:7	1696
Thus *s* thy son Joseph, God hath	Gen 45:9	559
Thus *s* the LORD, Israel is my son	Ex 4:22	559
Thus *s* the LORD God of Israel,	Ex 5:1	559
Thus *s* Pharaoh, I will not give	Ex 5:10	559
Thus *s* the LORD, In this thou	Ex 7:17	559
Thus *s* the LORD, Let my people go	Ex 8:1	559
Thus *s* the LORD, Let my people go	Ex 8:20	559
Thus *s* the LORD God of the	Ex 9:1	559
Thus *s* the LORD God of the	Ex 9:13	559
Thus *s* the LORD God of the	Ex 10:3	559
Thus *s* the LORD, About midnight	Ex 11:4	559
Thus *s* the LORD God of Israel,	Ex 32:27	559
s the LORD, as ye have spoken in	Num 14:28	5002
Thus *s* thy brother Israel, Thou	Num 20:14	559
Thus *s* Balak the son of Zippor,	Num 22:16	559
but what the LORD *s*, that will I	Num 24:13	1696
the LORD to battle, as my lord *s*	Num 32:27	1696
What *s* my lord unto his servant	Josh 5:14	1696
for thus *s* the LORD God of Israel	Josh 7:13	559
Thus *s* the whole congregation of	Josh 22:16	559
Thus *s* the LORD God of Israel,	Josh 24:2	559
Thus *s* the LORD God of Israel, I	Judg 6:8	559
Thus *s* Jephthah, Israel took not	Judg 11:15	559
Thus *s* the LORD, Did I plainly	1Sa 2:27	559
the LORD God of Israel *s*, I said	1Sa 2:30	5002
but now the LORD *s*, Be it far	1Sa 2:30	5002
all that he *s* cometh surely to	1Sa 9:6	1696
Thus *s* the LORD God of Israel, I	1Sa 10:18	559
Thus *s* the LORD of hosts, I	1Sa 15:2	559
and he *s*, Let not Jonathan know	1Sa 20:3	559
As *s* the proverb of the ancients	1Sa 24:13	559
Thus *s* the LORD, Shalt thou build	2Sa 7:5	559
Thus *s* the LORD of hosts, I took	2Sa 7:8	559
Thus *s* the LORD God of Israel, I	2Sa 12:7	559
Thus *s* the LORD, Behold, I will	2Sa 12:11	559
Whosoever *s* ought unto thee,	2Sa 14:10	1696
and let us hear likewise what he *s*	2Sa 17:5	6310
Thus *s* the LORD, I offer thee	2Sa 24:12	1696
Thus *s* the king, Come forth	1Kin 2:30	559
Then said the king, The one *s*	1Kin 3:23	559
and the other *s*, Nay	1Kin 3:23	559
for thus *s* the LORD, the God of	1Kin 11:31	559
Thus *s* the LORD, Ye shall not go	1Kin 12:24	559
O altar, altar, thus *s* the LORD	1Kin 13:2	559
Thus *s* the LORD, Forasmuch as	1Kin 13:21	559
Thus *s* the LORD God of Israel,	1Kin 14:7	559
For thus *s* the LORD God of Israel	1Kin 17:14	559
said unto him, Thus *s* Ben-hadad,	1Kin 20:2	559
Thus *s* the LORD, Hast thou seen	1Kin 20:13	559
Thus *s* the LORD, Even by the	1Kin 20:14	559
Thus *s* the LORD, Because the	1Kin 20:28	559
and said, Thy servant Ben-hadad *s*	1Kin 20:32	559
Thus *s* the LORD, Because thou	1Kin 20:42	559
Thus *s* the LORD, Hast thou killed	1Kin 21:19	559
Thus *s* the LORD, In the place	1Kin 21:19	559
Thus *s* the LORD, With these shalt	1Kin 22:11	559
liveth, what the LORD *s* unto me	1Kin 22:14	559
Thus *s* the king, Put this fellow	1Kin 22:27	559
Now therefore thus *s* the LORD	2Kin 1:4	559
Thus *s* the LORD, Is it not	2Kin 1:6	559
Thus *s* the LORD, Forasmuch as	2Kin 1:16	559

Thus s the LORD, I have healed 2Kin 2:21 559
Thus s the LORD, Make this valley 2Kin 3:16 559
For thus s the LORD, Ye shall not 2Kin 3:17 559
for thus s the LORD, They shall 2Kin 4:43 559
rather then, when he s to thee 2Kin 5:13 559
Thus s the LORD, To morrow about 2Kin 7:1 559
Thus s the LORD, I have anointed 2Kin 9:3 559
Thus s the LORD God of Israel, I 2Kin 9:6 559
Thus s the LORD, I have anointed 2Kin 9:12 559
Thus s the king, Is it peace 2Kin 9:18 559
Thus s the king, Is it peace 2Kin 9:19 559
the blood of his sons, s the LORD 2Kin 9:26 559
thee in this plat, s the LORD 2Kin 9:26 5002
Thus s the great king, the king 2Kin 18:19 559
Thus s the king, Let not Hezekiah 2Kin 18:29 559
for thus s the king of Assyria, 2Kin 18:31 559
Thus s Hezekiah, This day is a 2Kin 19:3 559
Thus s the LORD, Be not afraid of 2Kin 19:6 559
Thus s the LORD God of Israel, 2Kin 19:20 559
Therefore thus s the LORD 2Kin 19:32 559
come into this city, s the LORD 2Kin 19:33 5002
Thus s the LORD, Set thine house 2Kin 20:1 559
Thus s the LORD, the God of David 2Kin 20:5 559
nothing shall be left, s the LORD 2Kin 20:17 559
Therefore thus s the LORD God of 2Kin 21:12 559
Thus s the LORD God of Israel, 2Kin 22:15 559
Thus s the LORD, Behold, I will 2Kin 22:16 559
Thus s the LORD God of Israel, As 2Kin 22:18 559
also have heard thee, s the LORD 2Kin 22:19 5002
Thus s the LORD, Thou shalt not 1Chr 17:4 559
Thus s the LORD of hosts, I took 1Chr 17:7 559
Thus s the LORD, I offer thee 1Chr 21:10 559
Thus s the LORD, Choose thee 1Chr 21:11 559
Thus s the LORD, Ye shall not go 2Chr 11:4 559
Thus s the LORD, Ye have forsaken 2Chr 12:5 559
Thus s the LORD, With these thou 2Chr 18:10 559
LORD liveth, even what my God s 2Chr 18:13 559
Thus s the king, Put this fellow 2Chr 18:26 559
Thus s the LORD unto you, Be not 2Chr 20:15 559
Thus s the LORD God of David thy 2Chr 21:12 559
and said unto them, Thus s God 2Chr 24:20 559
Thus s Sennacherib king of 2Chr 32:10 559
Thus s the LORD God of Israel, 2Chr 34:23 559
Thus s the LORD, Behold, I will 2Chr 34:24 559
Thus s the LORD God of Israel 2Chr 34:26 559
even heard thee also, s the LORD 2Chr 34:27 5002
Thus s Cyrus king of Persia, All 2Chr 36:23 559
Thus s Cyrus king of Persia, The Ezr 1:2 559
among the heathen, and Gashmu s it Neh 6:6 559
The depth s, It is not in me Job 28:14 559
and the sea s, It is not with me Job 28:14 559
he is gracious unto him, and s Job 33:24 559
But none s, Where is God my maker Job 35:10 559
For he s to the snow, Be thou on Job 37:6 559
He s among the trumpets, Ha, ha Job 39:25 559
now will I arise, s the LORD Ps 12:5 559
of the wicked s within my heart Ps 36:1 5002
But unto the wicked God s Ps 50:16 559
understanding, she s to him, Prov 9:4 559
understanding, she s to him, Prov 9:16 559
naught, it is naught, s the buyer Prov 20:14 559
The slothful man s, There is a Prov 22:13 559
Eat and drink, s he to thee Prov 23:7 559
He that s unto the wicked, Thou Prov 24:24 559
The slothful man s, There is a Prov 26:13 559
deceiveth his neighbour, and s Prov 26:19 559
his father or his mother, and s Prov 28:24 559
and the fire that s not, It is Prov 30:16 559
eateth, and wipeth her mouth, and s Prov 30:20 559
s the Preacher, vanity of Eccl 1:2 559
neither s he, For whom do I Eccl 4:8
s the preacher, counting one by Eccl 7:27 559
he s to every one that he is a Eccl 10:3 559
of vanities, s the preacher Eccl 12:8 559
s the LORD Is 1:11 559
us reason together, s the LORD Is 1:18 559
Therefore s the Lord, the LORD of Is 1:24 5002
s the Lord GOD of hosts Is 3:15 5002
Moreover the LORD s, Because the Is 3:16 559
Thus s the Lord GOD, It shall not Is 7:7 559
For he s, Are not my princes Is 10:8 559
For he s, By the strength of my Is 10:13 559
Therefore thus s the Lord GOD of Is 10:24 559
s the LORD of hosts, and cut off Is 14:22 5002
and son, and nephew, s the LORD Is 14:22 5002
destruction, s the LORD of hosts Is 14:23 5002
of Israel, s the LORD of hosts Is 17:3 5002
thereof, s the LORD God of Israel Is 17:6 5002
s the Lord, the LORD of hosts Is 19:4 5002
ye die, s the Lord GOD of hosts Is 22:14 559
Thus s the Lord GOD of hosts, Go, Is 22:15 559
s the LORD of hosts, shall the Is 22:25 5002
Therefore thus s the Lord GOD Is 28:16 559
and he s, I cannot Is 29:11 559
and he s, I am not learned Is 29:12 559
Therefore thus s the LORD Is 29:22 559
s the LORD, that take counsel, Is 30:1 5002
Wherefore thus s the Holy One of Is 30:12 559
For thus s the Lord GOD, the Holy Is 30:15 559
s the LORD, whose fire is in Zion Is 31:9 5002
Now will I rise, s the LORD Is 33:10 559
Thus s the great king, the king Is 36:4 559
Thus s the king, Let not Hezekiah Is 36:14 559
for thus s the king of Assyria, Is 36:16 559
Thus s Hezekiah, This day is a Is 37:3 559
Thus s the LORD, Be not afraid of Is 37:6 559
Thus s the LORD God of Israel, Is 37:21 559
Therefore thus s the LORD Is 37:33 559
come into this city, s the LORD Is 37:34 5002
Thus s the LORD, Set thine house Is 38:1 559
Thus s the LORD, the God of David Is 38:5 559
nothing shall be left, s the LORD Is 39:6 559
comfort ye my people, s your God Is 40:1 559
s the Holy One Is 40:25 559
s the LORD, and thy redeemer, the Is 41:14 5002
Produce your cause, s the LORD Is 41:21 559
reasons, s the King of Jacob Is 41:21 559
Thus s God the LORD, he that Is 42:5 559
for a spoil, and none s, Restore Is 42:22 559
But now thus s the LORD that Is 43:1 559
s the LORD, and my servant whom I Is 43:10 5002
s the LORD, that I am God Is 43:12 5002
Thus s the LORD, your redeemer, Is 43:14 559
Thus s the LORD, which maketh a Is 43:16 559
Thus s the LORD that made thee, Is 44:2 559
Thus s the LORD the King of Is 44:6 559
yea, he warmeth himself, and s Is 44:16 559
it, and prayeth unto it, and s Is 44:17 559
Thus s the LORD, thy redeemer, and Is 44:24 559
that s to Jerusalem, Thou shalt Is 44:26 559
That s to the deep, Be dry, and I Is 44:27 559
That s of Cyrus, He is my Is 44:28 559
Thus s the LORD to his anointed, Is 45:1 559
unto him that s unto his father Is 45:10 559
Thus s the LORD, the Holy One of Is 45:11 559
nor reward, s the LORD of hosts Is 45:13 559
Thus s the LORD, The labour of Is 45:14 559
For thus s the LORD that created Is 45:18 559
Thus s the LORD, thy Redeemer, Is 48:17 559
s the LORD, unto the wicked Is 48:22 559
s the LORD that formed me from Is 49:5 559
Thus s the LORD, the Redeemer of Is 49:7 559
Thus s the LORD, In an acceptable Is 49:8 559
s the LORD, thou shalt surely Is 49:18 5002
Thus s the Lord GOD, Behold, I Is 49:22 559
But thus s the LORD, Even the Is 49:25 559
Thus s the LORD, Where is the Is 50:1 559
Thus s thy Lord the LORD, and thy Is 51:22 559
For thus s the LORD, Ye have sold Is 52:3 559
For thus s the Lord GOD, My Is 52:4 559
s the LORD, that my people is Is 52:5 5002
make them to howl, s the LORD Is 52:5 5002
that s unto Zion, Thy God Is 52:7 559
of the married wife, s the LORD Is 54:1 559
when thou wast refused, s thy God Is 54:6 559
on thee, s the LORD thy Redeemer Is 54:8 559
s the LORD that hath mercy on Is 54:10 559
is of me, s the LORD Is 54:17 5002
are your ways my ways, s the LORD Is 55:8 5002
Thus s the LORD, Keep ye judgment Is 56:1 559
For thus s the LORD unto the Is 56:4 559
the outcasts of Israel s, Yet Is 56:8 5002
For thus s the high and lofty One Is 57:15 559
to him that is near, s the LORD Is 57:19 559
no peace, s my God, to the wicked Is 57:21 559
in Jacob, s the LORD Is 59:20 5002
my covenant with them, s the LORD Is 59:21 559
s the LORD, from henceforth and Is 59:21 559
s the LORD, which have burned Is 65:7 559
Thus s the LORD, As the new wine Is 65:8 559
is found in the cluster, and one s Is 65:8 559
Therefore thus s the Lord GOD Is 65:13 559
all my holy mountain, s the LORD Is 65:25 559
Thus s the LORD, The heaven is my Is 66:1 559
things have been, s the LORD Is 66:2 5002
s the LORD Is 66:9 559
s thy God Is 66:9 559
For thus s the LORD, Behold, I Is 66:12 559
be consumed together, s the LORD Is 66:17 5002
s the LORD, as the children of Is 66:20 559
and for Levites, s the LORD Is 66:21 559
s the LORD, so shall your seed and Is 66:22 5002
to worship before me, s the LORD Is 66:23 559
thee to deliver thee, s the LORD Jer 1:8 5002
kingdoms of the north, s the LORD Jer 1:15 5002
s the LORD, to deliver thee Jer 1:19 5002
saying, Thus s the LORD Jer 2:2 559
shall come upon them, s the LORD Jer 2:3 5002
Thus s the LORD, What iniquity Jer 2:5 559
you, s the LORD, and with your Jer 2:9 5002
be ye very desolate, s the LORD Jer 2:12 5002
in thee, s the Lord GOD of hosts Jer 2:19 5002
marked before me, s the Lord GOD Jer 2:22 5002
against me, s the LORD Jer 2:29 5002
return again to me, s the LORD Jer 3:1 5002
heart, but feignedly, s the LORD Jer 3:10 5002
backsliding Israel, s the LORD Jer 3:12 5002
s the LORD, and I will not keep Jer 3:12 5002
not obeyed my voice, s the LORD Jer 3:13 5002
backsliding children, s the LORD Jer 3:14 5002
s the LORD, they shall say no Jer 3:16 5002
me, O house of Israel, s the LORD Jer 3:20 5002
s the LORD, return unto me Jer 4:1 5002
For thus s the LORD to the men of Jer 4:3 559
s the LORD, that the heart of the Jer 4:9 5002
rebellious against me, s the LORD Jer 4:17 5002
s the LORD Jer 5:9 5002
against me, s the LORD Jer 5:11 5002
Wherefore thus s the LORD God of Jer 5:14 559
O house of Israel, s the LORD Jer 5:15 5002
s the LORD, I will not make a Jer 5:18 5002
s the LORD Jer 5:22 5002
s the LORD Jer 5:29 5002
Thus s the LORD of hosts, They Jer 6:9 559
of the land, s the LORD Jer 6:12 5002
shall be cast down, s the LORD Jer 6:15 559
Thus s the LORD, Stand ye in the Jer 6:16 559
Therefore thus s the LORD Jer 6:21 559
Thus s the LORD, Behold, a people Jer 6:22 559
Thus s the LORD of hosts, the God Jer 7:3 559
even I have seen it, s the LORD Jer 7:11 5002
s the LORD, and I spake unto you, Jer 7:13 5002
s the LORD Jer 7:19 5002
Therefore thus s the Lord GOD Jer 7:20 559
Thus s the LORD of hosts, the God Jer 7:21 559
done evil in my sight, s the LORD Jer 7:30 5002
s the LORD, that it shall no more Jer 7:32 5002
s the LORD, they shall bring out Jer 8:1 5002
driven them, s the LORD of hosts Jer 8:3 5002
say unto them, Thus s the LORD Jer 8:4 559
shall be cast down, s the LORD Jer 8:12 559
surely consume them, s the LORD Jer 8:13 5002
they shall bite you, s the LORD Jer 8:17 5002
and they know not me, s the LORD Jer 9:3 5002
refuse to know me, s the LORD Jer 9:6 5002
Therefore thus s the LORD of Jer 9:7 559
s the LORD Jer 9:9 5002
And the LORD s, Because they have Jer 9:13 559
Therefore thus s the LORD of Jer 9:15 559
Thus s the LORD of hosts, Jer 9:17 559
Thus s the LORD, Even the Jer 9:22 5002
Thus s the LORD, Let not the wise Jer 9:23 559
things I delight, s the LORD Jer 9:24 5002
s the LORD, that I will punish Jer 9:25 5002
Thus s the LORD, Learn not the Jer 10:2 559
For thus s the LORD, Behold, I Jer 10:18 559
Thus s the LORD God of Israel Jer 11:3 559
Therefore thus s the LORD Jer 11:11 559
Therefore thus s the LORD of the Jer 11:21 559
Therefore thus s the LORD of Jer 11:22 559
Thus s the LORD against all mine Jer 12:14 559
destroy that nation, s the LORD Jer 12:17 5002
Thus s the LORD unto me, Go and Jer 13:1 559
Thus s the LORD, After this Jer 13:9 559
whole house of Judah, s the LORD Jer 13:11 5002
Thus s the LORD God of Israel, Jer 13:12 559
Thus s the LORD, Behold, I will Jer 13:13 559
and the sons together, s the LORD Jer 13:14 5002
thy measures from me, s the LORD Jer 13:25 5002
Thus s the LORD unto this people, Jer 14:10 559
Therefore thus s the LORD Jer 14:15 559
shalt tell them, Thus s the LORD Jer 15:2 559
over them four kinds, s the LORD Jer 15:3 5002
s the LORD, thou art gone Jer 15:6 5002
before their enemies, s the LORD Jer 15:9 5002
Therefore thus s the LORD Jer 15:19 559
and to deliver thee, s the LORD Jer 15:20 5002
For thus s the LORD concerning Jer 16:3 559
For thus s the LORD, Enter not Jer 16:5 559
s the LORD, even lovingkindness Jer 16:5 5002
For thus s the LORD of hosts, the Jer 16:9 559
s the LORD, and have walked after Jer 16:11 5002
s the LORD, that it shall no more Jer 16:14 5002
s the LORD, and they shall fish Jer 16:16 5002
Thus s the LORD Jer 17:5 559
Thus s the LORD Jer 17:21 559
s the LORD, to bring in no burden Jer 17:24 5002
s the LORD Jer 18:6 5002
saying, Thus s the LORD Jer 18:11 559
Therefore thus s the LORD Jer 18:13 559
Thus s the LORD, Go and get a Jer 19:1 559
Thus s the LORD of hosts, the God Jer 19:3 559
s the LORD, that this place shall Jer 19:6 5002
them, Thus s the LORD of hosts Jer 19:11 559
s the LORD, and to the inhabitants Jer 19:12 5002
Thus s the LORD of hosts, the God Jer 19:15 559
For thus s the LORD, Behold, I Jer 20:4 559
Thus s the LORD God of Israel Jer 21:4 559
s the LORD, I will deliver Jer 21:7 5002
thou shalt say, Thus s the LORD Jer 21:8 559
evil, and not for good, s the LORD Jer 21:10 5002
O house of David, thus s the LORD Jer 21:12 559
and rock of the plain, s the LORD Jer 21:13 5002
fruit of your doings, s the LORD Jer 21:14 5002
Thus s the LORD Jer 22:1 559
Thus s the LORD Jer 22:3 559
s the LORD, that this house shall Jer 22:5 5002
For thus s the LORD unto the Jer 22:6 559
For thus s the LORD touching Jer 22:11 559
That s, I will build me a wide Jer 22:14 559
s the LORD Jer 22:16 5002
Therefore thus s the LORD Jer 22:18 559
s the LORD, though Coniah the son Jer 22:24 5002
Thus s the LORD, Write ye this Jer 22:30 559
s the LORD Jer 23:1 5002
Therefore thus s the LORD God of Jer 23:2 559
evil of your doings, s the LORD Jer 23:2 5002
shall they be lacking, s the LORD Jer 23:4 5002
s the LORD, that I will raise Jer 23:5 5002
s the LORD, that they shall no Jer 23:7 5002
their wickedness, s the LORD Jer 23:11 5002
of their visitation, s the LORD Jer 23:12 5002
Therefore thus s the LORD of Jer 23:15 559
Thus s the LORD of hosts, Hearken Jer 23:16 559
s the LORD, and not a God afar off Jer 23:23 5002
s the LORD Jer 23:24 5002
s the LORD Jer 23:24 5002
s the LORD Jer 23:28 5002
s the LORD Jer 23:29 5002
s the LORD, that steal my words Jer 23:30 5002
s the LORD, that use their Jer 23:31 5002
use their tongues, and say, He s Jer 23:31 5002
s the LORD, and do tell them, and Jer 23:32 5002
this people at all, s the LORD Jer 23:32 5002
will even forsake you, s the LORD Jer 23:33 5002
therefore thus s the LORD Jer 23:38 559
Thus s the LORD, the God of Jer 24:5 559
surely thus s the LORD, So will I Jer 24:8 559
not hearkened unto me, s the LORD Jer 25:7 5002
Therefore thus s the LORD of hosts, Jer 25:8 559
s the LORD, and Nebuchadrezzar the Jer 25:9 5002
s the LORD, for their iniquity, Jer 25:12 5002
For thus s the LORD God of Israel Jer 25:15 559
Thus s the LORD of hosts, the God Jer 25:27 559
them, Thus s the LORD of hosts Jer 25:28 559
of the earth, s the LORD of hosts Jer 25:29 5002
wicked to the sword, s the LORD Jer 25:31 5002
Thus s the LORD of hosts, Behold, Jer 25:32 559
Thus s the LORD Jer 26:2 559
say unto them, Thus s the LORD Jer 26:4 559
saying, Thus s the LORD of hosts Jer 26:18 559
Thus s the LORD to me Jer 27:2 559

Thus *s* the LORD of hosts, the God Jer 27:4 559
s the LORD, with the sword, and Jer 27:8 5002
in their own land, *s* the LORD Jer 27:11 5002
s the LORD, yet they prophesy a Jer 27:15 5002
people, saying, Thus *s* the LORD Jer 27:16 559
For thus *s* the LORD of hosts Jer 27:19 559
thus *s* the LORD of hosts, the God Jer 27:21 559
day that I visit them, *s* the LORD Jer 27:22 5002
went into Babylon, *s* the LORD Jer 28:4 5002
people, saying, Thus *s* the LORD Jer 28:11 559
Hananiah, saying, Thus *s* the LORD Jer 28:13 559
For thus *s* the LORD of hosts, the Jer 28:14 559
Therefore thus *s* the LORD Jer 28:16 559
Thus *s* the LORD of hosts, the God Jer 29:4 559
For thus *s* the LORD of hosts, the Jer 29:8 559
I have not sent them, *s* the LORD Jer 29:9 5002
For thus *s* the LORD, That after Jer 29:10 559
s the LORD, thoughts of peace, and Jer 29:11 5002
will be found of you, *s* the LORD Jer 29:14 5002
I have driven you, *s* the LORD Jer 29:14 5002
Know that thus *s* the LORD of the Jer 29:16 559
Thus *s* the LORD of hosts Jer 29:17 559
s the LORD, which I sent unto Jer 29:19 5002
but ye would not hear, *s* the LORD Jer 29:19 5002
Thus *s* the LORD of hosts, the God Jer 29:21 559
know, and am a witness, *s* the LORD Jer 29:23 5002
Thus *s* the LORD concerning Jer 29:31 559
Therefore thus *s* the LORD Jer 29:32 559
will do for my people, *s* the LORD Jer 29:32 5002
s the LORD, that I will bring Jer 30:3 5002
Israel and Judah, *s* the LORD Jer 30:3 559
For thus *s* the LORD Jer 30:5 559
s the LORD of hosts, that I will Jer 30:8 5002
O my servant Jacob, *s* the LORD Jer 30:10 5002
thee, *s* the LORD, to save thee Jer 30:11 5002
For thus *s* the LORD, Thy bruise Jer 30:12 5002
thee of thy wounds, *s* the LORD Jer 30:17
Thus *s* the LORD Jer 30:18 559
s the LORD Jer 30:21 5002
s the LORD, will I be the God of Jer 31:1 5002
Thus *s* the LORD, The people which Jer 31:2 559
For thus *s* the LORD Jer 31:7 559
with my goodness, *s* the LORD Jer 31:14 5002
Thus *s* the LORD Jer 31:15 559
Thus *s* the LORD Jer 31:16 559
shall be rewarded, *s* the LORD Jer 31:16 5002
s the LORD, that thy children Jer 31:17 5002
have mercy upon him, *s* the LORD Jer 31:20 5002
Thus *s* the LORD of hosts, the God Jer 31:23 559
s the LORD, that I will sow the Jer 31:27 5002
to build, and to plant, *s* the LORD Jer 31:28 5002
s the LORD, that I will make a Jer 31:31 5002
an husband unto them, *s* the LORD Jer 31:32 5002
s the LORD, I will put my law in Jer 31:33 5002
the greatest of them, *s* the LORD Jer 31:34 5002
Thus *s* the LORD, which giveth the Jer 31:35 559
s the LORD, then the seed of Jer 31:36 5002
Thus *s* the LORD Jer 31:37 559
that they have done, *s* the LORD Jer 31:37 5002
s the LORD, that the city shall Jer 31:38 5002
Thus *s* the LORD, Behold, I will Jer 32:3 559
be until I visit him, *s* the LORD Jer 32:5 5002
Thus *s* the LORD of hosts, the God Jer 32:14 559
For thus *s* the LORD of hosts, the Jer 32:15 559
Therefore thus *s* the LORD Jer 32:28 559
work of their hands, *s* the LORD Jer 32:30 5002
And now therefore thus *s* the LORD Jer 32:36 559
For thus *s* the LORD Jer 32:42 559
captivity to return, *s* the LORD Jer 32:44 5002
Thus *s* the LORD the maker thereof Jer 33:2 559
For thus *s* the LORD, the God of Jer 33:4 559
Thus *s* the LORD Jer 33:10 559
land, as at the first, *s* the LORD Jer 33:11 559
Thus *s* the LORD of hosts Jer 33:12 559
him that telleth them, *s* the LORD Jer 33:13 559
s the LORD, that I will perform Jer 33:14 5002
For thus *s* the LORD Jer 33:17 559
Thus *s* the LORD Jer 33:20 559
Thus *s* the LORD Jer 33:25 559
Thus *s* the LORD, the God of Jer 34:2 559
and tell him, Thus *s* the LORD Jer 34:2 559
Thus *s* the LORD of thee, Thou Jer 34:4 559
pronounced the word, *s* the LORD Jer 34:5 5002
Thus *s* the LORD, the God of Jer 34:13 559
Therefore thus *s* the LORD Jer 34:17 559
s the LORD, to the sword, to the Jer 34:17 5002
s the LORD, and cause them to Jer 34:22 5002
Thus *s* the LORD of hosts, the God Jer 35:13 559
s the LORD Jer 35:13 5002
Therefore thus *s* the LORD God of Jer 35:17 559
Thus *s* the LORD of hosts, the God Jer 35:18 559
Therefore thus *s* the LORD of Jer 35:19 559
king of Judah, Thus *s* the LORD Jer 36:29 559
Therefore thus *s* the LORD of Jer 36:30 559
Thus *s* the LORD, the God of Jer 37:7 559
Thus *s* the LORD Jer 37:9 559
Thus *s* the LORD, He that Jer 38:2 559
Thus *s* the LORD, This city shall Jer 38:3 559
Thus *s* the LORD, the God of hosts Jer 38:17 559
Thus *s* the LORD of hosts, the God Jer 39:16 559
thee in that day, *s* the LORD Jer 39:17 5002
put thy trust in me, *s* the LORD Jer 39:18 5002
Thus *s* the LORD, the God of Jer 42:9 559
be not afraid of him, *s* the LORD Jer 42:11 5002
Thus *s* the LORD of hosts, the God Jer 42:15 559
For thus *s* the LORD of hosts, the Jer 42:18 559
Thus *s* the LORD of hosts, the God Jer 43:10 559
Thus *s* the LORD of hosts, the God Jer 44:2 559
Therefore now thus *s* the LORD Jer 44:7 559
Therefore thus *s* the LORD of Jer 44:11 559
Thus *s* the LORD of hosts, the God Jer 44:25 559
s the LORD, that my name shall no Jer 44:26 559
s the LORD, that I will punish Jer 44:29 5002
Thus *s* the LORD Jer 44:30 559

Thus *s* the LORD, the God of Jer 45:2 559
say unto him, The LORD *s* thus Jer 45:4 559
evil upon all flesh, *s* the LORD Jer 45:5 5002
fear was round about, *s* the LORD Jer 46:5 5002
and he *s*, I will go up, and will Jer 46:8 559
s the King, whose name is the Jer 46:18 5002
s the LORD, though it cannot be Jer 46:23 5002
of hosts, the God of Israel, *s* Jer 46:25 559
as in the days of old, *s* the LORD Jer 46:26 5002
O Jacob my servant, *s* the LORD Jer 46:28 5002
Thus *s* the LORD Jer 47:2 559
Moab thus *s* the LORD of hosts Jer 48:1 559
s the LORD, that I will send unto Jer 48:12 5002
s the King, whose name is the Jer 48:15 5002
and his arm is broken, *s* the LORD Jer 48:25 5002
I know his wrath, *s* the LORD Jer 48:30 5002
s the LORD, him that offereth in Jer 48:35 5002
is no pleasure, *s* the LORD Jer 48:38 5002
For thus *s* the LORD Jer 48:40 559
O inhabitant of Moab, *s* the LORD Jer 48:43 5002
of their visitation, *s* the LORD Jer 48:44 5002
in the latter days, *s* the LORD Jer 48:47 5002
The Ammonites, thus *s* the LORD Jer 49:1 559
s the LORD, that I will cause an Jer 49:2 559
that were his heirs, *s* the LORD Jer 49:2 5002
s the Lord GOD of hosts, from all Jer 49:5 5002
the children of Ammon, *s* the LORD Jer 49:6 5002
Edom, thus *s* the LORD of hosts Jer 49:7 559
For thus *s* the LORD Jer 49:12 559
s the LORD, that Bozrah shall Jer 49:13 5002
thee down from thence, *s* the LORD Jer 49:16 5002
s the LORD, no man shall abide Jer 49:18 559
in that day, *s* the LORD of hosts Jer 49:26 5002
shall smite, thus *s* the LORD Jer 49:28 559
inhabitants of Hazor, *s* the LORD Jer 49:30 5002
s the LORD, which have neither Jer 49:31 5002
all sides thereof, *s* the LORD Jer 49:32 5002
Thus *s* the LORD of hosts Jer 49:35 559
even my fierce anger, *s* the LORD Jer 49:37 5002
king and the princes, *s* the LORD Jer 49:38 5002
the captivity of Elam, *s* the LORD Jer 49:39 5002
s the LORD, the children of Jer 50:4 5002
shall be satisfied, *s* the LORD Jer 50:10 5002
Therefore thus *s* the LORD of Jer 50:18 559
s the LORD, the iniquity of Jer 50:20 5002
s the LORD, and do according to Jer 50:21 5002
cut off in that day, *s* the LORD Jer 50:30 5002
proud, *s* the Lord GOD of hosts Jer 50:31 5002
Thus *s* the LORD of hosts Jer 50:33 559
s the LORD, and upon the Jer 50:35 5002
cities thereof, *s* the LORD Jer 50:40 5002
Thus *s* the LORD Jer 51:1 559
in Zion in your sight, *s* the LORD Jer 51:24 5002
s the LORD, which destroyest all Jer 51:25 5002
be desolate for ever, *s* the LORD Jer 51:26 5002
For thus *s* the LORD of hosts, the Jer 51:33 559
Therefore thus *s* the LORD Jer 51:36 559
sleep, and not wake, *s* the LORD Jer 51:39 5002
her from the north, *s* the LORD Jer 51:48 5002
s the LORD, that I will do Jer 51:52 5002
come unto her, *s* the LORD Jer 51:53 5002
s the King, whose name is the Jer 51:57 5002
Thus *s* the LORD of hosts Jer 51:58 559
The LORD is my portion, *s* my soul Lam 3:24 559
Who is he that *s*, and it cometh to Lam 3:37 559
unto them, Thus *s* the Lord GOD Eze 2:4 559
and tell them, Thus *s* the Lord GOD Eze 3:11 559
unto them, Thus *s* the Lord GOD Eze 3:27 559
Thus *s* the Lord GOD Eze 5:5 559
Therefore thus *s* the Lord GOD Eze 5:7 559
Therefore thus *s* the Lord GOD Eze 5:8 559
as I live, *s* the Lord GOD Eze 5:11 5002
Thus *s* the Lord GOD to the Eze 6:3 559
Thus *s* the Lord GOD Eze 6:11 559
thus *s* the Lord GOD unto the land Eze 7:2 559
Thus *s* the Lord GOD Eze 7:5 559
Thus *s* the LORD Eze 11:5 559
Therefore thus *s* the Lord GOD Eze 11:7 559
a sword upon you, *s* the Lord GOD Eze 11:8 5002
say, Thus *s* the Lord GOD Eze 11:16 559
say, Thus *s* the Lord GOD Eze 11:17 559
their own heads, *s* the Lord GOD Eze 11:21 5002
unto them, Thus *s* the Lord GOD Eze 12:10 559
Thus *s* the Lord GOD of the Eze 12:19 559
therefore, Thus *s* the Lord GOD Eze 12:23 559
will perform it, *s* the Lord GOD Eze 12:25 5002
unto them, Thus *s* the Lord GOD Eze 12:28 559
shall be done, *s* the Lord GOD Eze 12:28 5002
Thus *s* the Lord GOD Eze 13:3 559
divination, saying, The LORD *s* Eze 13:6 5002
whereas ye say, The LORD *s* it Eze 13:7 5002
Therefore thus *s* the Lord GOD Eze 13:8 559
I am against you, *s* the Lord GOD Eze 13:8 5002
Therefore thus *s* the Lord GOD Eze 13:13 559
there is no peace, *s* the Lord GOD Eze 13:16 5002
And say, Thus *s* the Lord GOD Eze 13:18 559
Wherefore thus *s* the Lord GOD Eze 13:20 559
unto them, Thus *s* the Lord GOD Eze 14:4 559
of Israel, Thus *s* the Lord GOD Eze 14:6 559
may be their God, *s* the Lord GOD Eze 14:11 5002
righteousness, *s* the Lord GOD Eze 14:14 5002
s the Lord GOD, they shall Eze 14:16 5002
s the Lord GOD, they shall Eze 14:18 5002
s the Lord GOD, they shall Eze 14:20 5002
For thus *s* the Lord GOD Eze 14:21 559
I have done in it, *s* the Lord GOD Eze 14:23 5002
Therefore thus *s* the Lord GOD Eze 15:6 559
a trespass, *s* the Lord GOD Eze 15:8 5002
And say, Thus *s* the Lord GOD unto Eze 16:3 559
s the Lord GOD, and thou becamest Eze 16:8 5002
had put upon thee, *s* the Lord GOD Eze 16:14 5002
and thus it was, *s* the Lord GOD Eze 16:19 5002
s the Lord GOD Eze 16:23 5002
s the Lord GOD, seeing thou doest Eze 16:30 5002

Thus *s* the Lord GOD Eze 16:36 559
upon thine head, *s* the Lord GOD Eze 16:43 5002
s the Lord GOD, Sodom thy sister Eze 16:48 5002
and thine abominations, *s* the LORD Eze 16:58 5002
For thus *s* the Lord GOD Eze 16:59 559
thou hast done, *s* the Lord GOD Eze 16:63 5002
And say, Thus *s* the Lord GOD Eze 17:3 559
Say thou, Thus *s* the Lord GOD Eze 17:9 559
s the Lord GOD, surely in the Eze 17:16 5002
Therefore thus *s* the Lord GOD Eze 17:19 559
Thus *s* the Lord GOD Eze 17:22 559
s the Lord GOD, ye shall not have Eze 18:3 5002
shall surely live, *s* the Lord GOD Eze 18:9 5002
s the Lord GOD Eze 18:23 5002
Yet *s* the house of Israel, The Eze 18:29 559
to his ways, *s* the Lord GOD Eze 18:30 5002
of him that dieth, *s* the Lord GOD Eze 18:32 5002
unto them, Thus *s* the Lord GOD Eze 20:3 559
s the Lord GOD, I will not be Eze 20:3 5002
unto them, Thus *s* the Lord GOD Eze 20:5 559
unto them, Thus *s* the Lord GOD Eze 20:27 559
of Israel, Thus *s* the Lord GOD Eze 20:30 559
s the Lord GOD, I will not be Eze 20:31 5002
s the Lord GOD, surely with a Eze 20:33 5002
I plead with you, *s* the Lord GOD Eze 20:36 5002
of Israel, thus *s* the Lord GOD Eze 20:39 559
s the Lord GOD, there shall all Eze 20:40 5002
house of Israel, *s* the Lord GOD Eze 20:44 5002
Thus *s* the Lord GOD Eze 20:47 559
land of Israel, Thus *s* the LORD Eze 21:3 559
brought to pass, *s* the Lord GOD Eze 21:7 5002
prophesy, and say, Thus *s* the LORD Eze 21:9 559
shall be no more, *s* the Lord GOD Eze 21:13 5002
Therefore thus *s* the Lord GOD Eze 21:24 559
Thus *s* the Lord GOD Eze 21:26 559
Thus *s* the Lord GOD concerning Eze 21:28 559
Thus *s* the Lord GOD, The city Eze 22:3 559
hast forgotten me, *s* the Lord GOD Eze 22:12 5002
Therefore thus *s* the Lord GOD Eze 22:19 559
Thus *s* the Lord GOD, when the Eze 22:28 559
upon their heads, *s* the Lord GOD Eze 22:31 5002
O Aholibah, thus *s* the Lord GOD Eze 23:22 559
For thus *s* the Lord GOD Eze 23:28 559
Thus *s* the Lord GOD Eze 23:32 559
I have spoken it, *s* the Lord GOD Eze 23:34 559
Therefore thus *s* the Lord GOD Eze 23:35 559
For thus *s* the Lord GOD Eze 23:46 559
unto them, Thus *s* the Lord GOD Eze 24:3 559
Wherefore thus *s* the Lord GOD Eze 24:6 559
Therefore thus *s* the Lord GOD Eze 24:9 559
they judge thee, *s* the Lord GOD Eze 24:14 5002
of Israel, Thus *s* the Lord GOD Eze 24:21 559
Thus *s* the Lord GOD Eze 25:3 559
For thus *s* the Lord GOD Eze 25:6 559
Thus *s* the Lord GOD Eze 25:8 559
Thus *s* the Lord GOD Eze 25:12 559
Therefore thus *s* the Lord GOD Eze 25:13 559
know my vengeance, *s* the Lord GOD Eze 25:14 5002
Thus *s* the Lord GOD Eze 25:15 559
Therefore thus *s* the Lord GOD Eze 25:16 559
Therefore thus *s* the Lord GOD Eze 26:3 559
I have spoken it, *s* the Lord GOD Eze 26:5 5002
For thus *s* the Lord GOD Eze 26:7 559
have spoken it, *s* the Lord GOD Eze 26:14 5002
Thus *s* the Lord GOD to Tyrus Eze 26:15 559
For thus *s* the Lord GOD Eze 26:19 559
be found again, *s* the Lord GOD Eze 26:21 5001
many isles, Thus *s* the Lord GOD Eze 27:3 559
of Tyrus, Thus *s* the Lord GOD Eze 28:2 559
Therefore thus *s* the Lord GOD Eze 28:6 559
I have spoken it, *s* the Lord GOD Eze 28:10 5002
say unto him, Thus *s* the Lord GOD Eze 28:12 559
And say, Thus *s* the Lord GOD Eze 28:22 559
Thus *s* the Lord GOD Eze 28:25 559
and say, Thus *s* the Lord GOD Eze 29:3 559
Therefore thus *s* the Lord GOD Eze 29:8 559
Yet thus *s* the Lord GOD Eze 29:13 559
Therefore thus *s* the Lord GOD Eze 29:19 559
wrought for me, *s* the Lord GOD Eze 29:20 5002
and say, Thus *s* the Lord GOD Eze 30:2 559
Thus *s* the LORD Eze 30:6 559
it by the sword, *s* the Lord GOD Eze 30:6 5002
Thus *s* the Lord GOD Eze 30:10 559
Thus *s* the Lord GOD Eze 30:13 559
Therefore thus *s* the Lord GOD Eze 30:22 559
Therefore thus *s* the Lord GOD Eze 31:10 559
Thus *s* the Lord GOD Eze 31:15 559
all his multitude, *s* the Lord GOD Eze 31:18 5002
Thus *s* the Lord GOD Eze 32:3 559
upon thy land, *s* the Lord GOD Eze 32:8 5002
For thus *s* the Lord GOD Eze 32:11 559
to run like oil, *s* the Lord GOD Eze 32:14 5002
all her multitude, *s* the Lord GOD Eze 32:16 5002
by the sword, *s* the Lord GOD Eze 32:31 5002
all his multitude, *s* the Lord GOD Eze 32:32 5002
s the Lord GOD, I have no Eze 33:11 5002
unto them, Thus *s* the Lord GOD Eze 33:25 559
unto them, Thus *s* the Lord GOD Eze 33:27 559
Thus *s* the Lord GOD unto the Eze 34:2 559
As I live *s* the Lord GOD, surely Eze 34:8 5002
Thus *s* the Lord GOD Eze 34:10 559
For thus *s* the Lord GOD Eze 34:11 559
them to lie down, *s* the Lord GOD Eze 34:15 5002
O my flock, thus *s* the Lord GOD Eze 34:17 559
Therefore thus *s* the Lord GOD Eze 34:20 559
are my people, *s* the Lord GOD Eze 34:30 5002
and I am your God, *s* the Lord GOD Eze 34:31 5002
say unto it, Thus *s* the Lord GOD Eze 35:3 559
s the Lord GOD, I will prepare Eze 35:6 5002
s the Lord GOD, I will even do Eze 35:11 5002
Thus *s* the Lord GOD Eze 35:14 559
Thus *s* the Lord GOD Eze 36:2 559
and say, Thus *s* the Lord GOD Eze 36:3 559
Thus *s* the Lord GOD to the Eze 36:4 559

Therefore thus s the Lord GOD	Eze 36:5	559
the valleys, Thus s the Lord GOD	Eze 36:6	559
Therefore thus s the Lord GOD	Eze 36:7	559
Thus s the Lord GOD	Eze 36:13	559
nations any more, s the Lord GOD	Eze 36:14	5002
to fall any more, s the Lord GOD	Eze 36:15	5002
of Israel, Thus s the Lord GOD	Eze 36:22	559
s the Lord GOD, when I shall be	Eze 36:23	5002
s the Lord GOD, be it known unto	Eze 36:32	5002
Thus s the Lord GOD	Eze 36:33	559
Thus s the Lord GOD	Eze 36:37	559
Thus s the Lord GOD unto these	Eze 37:5	559
to the wind, Thus s the Lord GOD	Eze 37:9	559
unto them, Thus s the Lord GOD	Eze 37:12	559
it, and performed it, s the LORD	Eze 37:14	5002
unto them, Thus s the Lord GOD	Eze 37:19	559
unto them, Thus s the Lord GOD	Eze 37:21	559
And say, Thus s the Lord GOD	Eze 38:3	559
Thus s the Lord GOD	Eze 38:10	559
say unto Gog, Thus s the Lord GOD	Eze 38:14	559
Thus s the Lord GOD	Eze 38:17	559
s the Lord GOD, that my fury	Eze 38:18	5002
all my mountains, s the Lord GOD	Eze 38:21	5002
Gog, and say, Thus s the Lord GOD	Eze 39:1	559
I have spoken it, s the Lord GOD	Eze 39:5	5002
and it is done, s the Lord GOD	Eze 39:8	5002
that robbed them, s the Lord GOD	Eze 39:10	5002
be glorified, s the Lord GOD	Eze 39:13	5002
son of man, thus s the Lord GOD	Eze 39:17	559
all men of war, s the Lord GOD	Eze 39:20	5002
Therefore thus s the Lord GOD	Eze 39:25	559
house of Israel, s the Lord GOD	Eze 39:29	5002
Son of man, thus s the Lord GOD	Eze 43:18	559
s the Lord GOD, a young bullock	Eze 43:19	5002
I will accept you, s the Lord GOD	Eze 43:27	5002
of Israel, Thus s the Lord GOD	Eze 44:6	559
Thus s the Lord GOD	Eze 44:9	559
s the Lord GOD, and they shall	Eze 44:12	5002
fat and the blood, s the Lord GOD	Eze 44:15	5002
his sin offering, s the Lord GOD	Eze 44:27	5002
Thus s the Lord GOD	Eze 45:9	559
from my people, s the Lord GOD	Eze 45:9	5002
for them, s the Lord GOD	Eze 45:15	5002
Thus s the Lord GOD	Eze 45:18	559
Thus s the Lord GOD	Eze 46:1	559
Thus s the Lord GOD	Eze 46:16	559
Thus s the Lord GOD	Eze 47:13	559
his inheritance, s the Lord GOD	Eze 47:23	5002
their portions, s the Lord GOD	Eze 48:29	5002
lovers, and forgat me, s the LORD	Hos 2:13	5002
s the LORD, that thou shalt call	Hos 2:16	5002
s the LORD, I will hear the	Hos 2:21	5002
them in their houses, s the LORD	Hos 11:11	5002
s the LORD, turn ye even to me	Joel 2:12	5002
Thus s the LORD	Amos 1:3	559
captivity unto Kir, s the LORD	Amos 1:5	559
Thus s the LORD	Amos 1:6	559
shall perish, s the Lord GOD	Amos 1:8	559
Thus s the LORD	Amos 1:9	559
Thus s the LORD	Amos 1:11	559
Thus s the LORD	Amos 1:13	559
his princes together, s the LORD	Amos 1:15	559
Thus s the LORD	Amos 2:1	559
thereof with him, s the LORD	Amos 2:3	559
Thus s the LORD	Amos 2:4	559
Thus s the LORD	Amos 2:6	559
s the LORD	Amos 2:11	5002
naked in that day, s the LORD	Amos 2:16	5002
s the LORD, who store up violence	Amos 3:10	5002
Therefore thus s the Lord GOD	Amos 3:11	559
Thus s the LORD	Amos 3:12	559
s the Lord GOD, the God of hosts,	Amos 3:13	5001
shall have an end, s the LORD	Amos 3:15	5001
them into the palace, s the LORD	Amos 4:3	5001
of Israel, s the Lord GOD	Amos 4:5	5001
not returned unto me, s the LORD	Amos 4:6	5001
not returned unto me, s the LORD	Amos 4:8	5001
not returned unto me, s the LORD	Amos 4:9	5001
not returned unto me, s the LORD	Amos 4:10	5001
not returned unto me, s the LORD	Amos 4:11	5001
For thus s the Lord GOD	Amos 5:3	559
For thus s the LORD unto the	Amos 5:4	559
God of hosts, the Lord, s thus	Amos 5:16	559
pass through thee, s the LORD	Amos 5:17	559
s the LORD, whose name is The God	Amos 5:27	559
s the LORD the God of hosts, I	Amos 6:8	5002
s the LORD the God of hosts	Amos 6:14	5002
It shall not be, s the LORD	Amos 7:3	559
also shall not be, s the Lord GOD	Amos 7:6	559
For thus Amos s, Jeroboam shall	Amos 7:11	559
Therefore thus s the LORD	Amos 7:17	559
in that day, s the Lord GOD	Amos 8:3	5002
s the Lord GOD, that I will cause	Amos 8:9	5002
s the Lord GOD, that I will send	Amos 8:11	5002
s the LORD	Amos 9:7	5002
the house of Jacob, s the LORD	Amos 9:8	5002
s the LORD that doeth this	Amos 9:12	5002
s the LORD, that the plowman	Amos 9:13	5002
given them, s the LORD thy God	Amos 9:15	559
Thus s the Lord GOD concerning	Obad 1	559
that s in his heart, Who shall	Obad 3	559
I bring thee down, s the LORD	Obad 4	5002
s the LORD, even destroy the wise	Obad 8	5002
Therefore thus s the LORD	Mic 2:3	559
Thus s the LORD concerning the	Mic 3:5	559
s the LORD, will I assemble her	Mic 4:6	5002
s the LORD, that I will cut off	Mic 5:10	5002
Hear ye now what the LORD s	Mic 6:1	559
Thus s the LORD	Nah 1:12	559
s the LORD of hosts, and I will	Nah 2:13	5002
against thee, s the LORD of hosts	Nah 3:5	5002
Woe unto him that s to the wood	Hab 2:19	559
from off the land, s the LORD	Zeph 1:2	5002
man from off the land, s the LORD	Zeph 1:3	5002
s the LORD, that there shall be	Zeph 1:10	5002
s the LORD of hosts, the God of	Zeph 2:9	5002
s the LORD, until the day that I	Zeph 3:8	5002
before your eyes, s the LORD	Zeph 3:20	559
thus s the LORD of hosts	Hag 1:5	559
Thus s the LORD of hosts	Hag 1:7	559
I will be glorified, s the LORD	Hag 1:8	559
s the LORD of hosts	Hag 1:9	5002
saying, I am with you, s the LORD	Hag 1:13	5002
strong, O Zerubbabel, s the LORD	Hag 2:4	5002
of the land, s the LORD, and work	Hag 2:4	5002
am with you, s the LORD of hosts	Hag 2:4	5002
For thus s the LORD of hosts	Hag 2:6	559
with glory, s the LORD of hosts	Hag 2:7	559
gold is mine, s the LORD of hosts	Hag 2:8	5002
the former, s the LORD of hosts	Hag 2:9	5002
I give peace, s the LORD of hosts	Hag 2:9	559
Thus s the LORD of hosts	Hag 2:11	559
this nation before me, s the LORD	Hag 2:14	5002
ye turned not to me, s the LORD	Hag 2:17	5002
s the LORD of hosts, will I take	Hag 2:23	5002
s the LORD, and will make thee as	Hag 2:23	5002
chosen thee, s the LORD of hosts	Hag 2:23	5002
them, Thus s the LORD of hosts	Zec 1:3	559
s the LORD of hosts, and I will	Zec 1:3	5002
unto you, s the LORD of hosts	Zec 1:3	559
saying, Thus s the LORD of hosts	Zec 1:4	559
nor hearken unto me, s the LORD	Zec 1:4	5002
saying, Thus s the LORD of hosts	Zec 1:14	559
Therefore thus s the LORD	Zec 1:16	559
s the LORD of hosts, and a line	Zec 1:16	5002
saying, Thus s the LORD of hosts	Zec 1:17	559
s the LORD, will be unto her a	Zec 2:5	5002
the land of the north, s the LORD	Zec 2:6	5002
winds of the heaven, s the LORD	Zec 2:6	5002
For thus s the LORD of hosts	Zec 2:8	559
in the midst of thee, s the LORD	Zec 2:10	5002
Thus s the LORD of hosts	Zec 3:7	559
s the LORD of hosts, and I will	Zec 3:9	5002
s the LORD of hosts, shall ye	Zec 3:10	5002
by my spirit, s the LORD of hosts	Zec 4:6	559
s the LORD of hosts, and it shall	Zec 5:4	5002
not hear, s the LORD of hosts	Zec 7:13	559
Thus s the LORD of hosts	Zec 8:2	559
Thus s the LORD	Zec 8:3	559
Thus s the LORD of hosts	Zec 8:4	559
Thus s the LORD of hosts	Zec 8:6	559
s the LORD of hosts	Zec 8:6	5002
Thus s the LORD of hosts	Zec 8:7	559
Thus s the LORD of hosts	Zec 8:9	559
former days, s the LORD of hosts	Zec 8:11	5002
For thus s the LORD of hosts	Zec 8:14	559
s the LORD of hosts, and I	Zec 8:14	559
things that I hate, s the LORD	Zec 8:17	5002
Thus s the LORD of hosts	Zec 8:19	559
Thus s the LORD of hosts	Zec 8:20	559
Thus s the LORD of hosts	Zec 8:23	559
and down in his name, s the LORD	Zec 10:12	5002
Thus s the LORD my God	Zec 11:4	559
of the land, s the LORD	Zec 11:6	5002
s the LORD, which stretcheth	Zec 12:1	5002
s the LORD, I will smite every	Zec 12:4	5002
s the LORD of hosts, that I will	Zec 13:2	5002
is my fellow, s the LORD of hosts	Zec 13:7	5002
s the LORD, two parts therein	Zec 13:8	5002
I have loved you, s the LORD	Mal 1:2	5002
s the LORD	Mal 1:2	559
Whereas Edom s, We are	Mal 1:4	559
thus s the LORD of hosts, They	Mal 1:4	559
s the LORD of hosts unto you, O	Mal 1:6	559
s the LORD of hosts	Mal 1:8	559
s the LORD of hosts	Mal 1:9	559
s the LORD of hosts, neither will	Mal 1:10	559
the heathen, s the LORD of hosts	Mal 1:11	559
at it, s the LORD of hosts	Mal 1:13	559
s the LORD	Mal 1:13	559
s the LORD of hosts, and my name	Mal 1:14	559
s the LORD of hosts, I will even	Mal 2:2	559
be with Levi, s the LORD of hosts	Mal 2:4	559
of Levi, s the LORD of hosts	Mal 2:8	559
s that he hateth putting away	Mal 2:16	559
his garment, s the LORD of hosts	Mal 2:16	559
shall come, s the LORD of hosts	Mal 3:1	559
fear not me, s the LORD of hosts	Mal 3:5	559
unto you, s the LORD of hosts	Mal 3:7	559
s the LORD of hosts, if I will	Mal 3:10	559
in the field, s the LORD of hosts	Mal 3:11	559
land, s the LORD of hosts	Mal 3:12	559
been stout against me, s the LORD	Mal 3:13	559
s the LORD of hosts, in that day	Mal 3:17	559
s the LORD of hosts, that it	Mal 4:1	559
do this, s the LORD of hosts	Mal 4:3	559
s unto him, If thou be the Son of	Mt 4:6	*3004*
s unto him, All these things will	Mt 4:9	*3004*
Then s Jesus unto him, Get thee	Mt 4:10	*3004*
he s unto them, Follow me, and I	Mt 4:19	*3004*
Not every one that s unto me	Mt 7:21	*3004*
Jesus s unto him, See thou tell	Mt 8:4	*3004*
Jesus s unto him, I will come and	Mt 8:7	*3004*
Jesus s unto him, The foxes have	Mt 8:20	*3004*
he s unto them, Why are ye	Mt 8:26	*3004*
(then s he to the sick of the	Mt 9:6	*3004*
and he s unto him, Follow me	Mt 9:9	*3004*
Jesus s unto them, Believe ye	Mt 9:28	*3004*
Then s he unto his disciples, The	Mt 9:37	*3004*
Then s he to the man, Stretch	Mt 12:13	*3004*
Then he s, I will return into my	Mt 12:44	*3004*
the prophecy of Esaias, which s	Mt 13:14	*3004*
Jesus s unto them, Have ye	Mt 13:51	*3004*
Jesus s unto them, How many	Mt 15:34	*3004*
He s unto them, But whom say ye	Mt 16:15	*3004*
He s, Yes	Mt 17:25	*3004*
Peter s unto him, Of strangers	Mt 17:26	*3004*
Jesus s unto him, Then are the	Mt 17:26	*5346*
Jesus s unto him, I say not unto	Mt 18:22	*3004*
He s unto them, Moses because of	Mt 19:8	*3004*
He s unto him, Which	Mt 19:18	*3004*
The young man s unto him, All	Mt 19:20	*3004*
s unto them, Why stand ye here	Mt 20:6	*3004*
He s unto them, Go ye also into	Mt 20:7	*3004*
the vineyard s unto his steward	Mt 20:8	*3004*
She s unto him, Grant that these	Mt 20:21	*3004*
he s unto them, Ye shall drink	Mt 20:23	*3004*
And Jesus s unto them, Yea	Mt 21:16	*3004*
Jesus s unto them, Verily I say	Mt 21:31	*3004*
Jesus s unto them, Did ye never	Mt 21:42	*3004*
Then s he to his servants, The	Mt 22:8	*3004*
he s unto him, Friend, how camest	Mt 22:12	*3004*
he s unto them, Whose is this	Mt 22:20	*3004*
Then s he unto them, Render	Mt 22:21	*3004*
He s unto them, How then doth	Mt 22:43	*3004*
and say unto him, The Master s	Mt 26:18	*3004*
Then s Jesus unto them, All ye	Mt 26:31	*3004*
s unto the disciples, Sit ye here	Mt 26:36	*3004*
Then s he unto them, My soul is	Mt 26:38	*3004*
s unto Peter, What, could ye not	Mt 26:40	*3004*
s unto them, Sleep on now, and	Mt 26:45	*3004*
Jesus s unto him, Thou hast said	Mt 26:64	*3004*
Pilate s unto them, What shall I	Mt 27:22	*3004*
him, and s unto him, I will	Mk 1:41	*3004*
s unto him, See thou say nothing	Mk 1:44	*3004*
(he s to the sick of the palsy,)	Mk 2:10	*3004*
he s unto them, They that are	Mk 2:17	*3004*
he s unto the man which had the	Mk 3:3	*3004*
he s unto them, Is it lawful to	Mk 3:4	*3004*
he s unto the man, Stretch forth	Mk 3:5	*3004*
he s unto them, Let us pass over	Mk 4:35	*3004*
but s unto him, Go home to thy	Mk 5:19	*3004*
he s unto the ruler of the	Mk 5:36	*3004*
he s unto them, Why make ye this	Mk 5:39	*3004*
He s unto them, How many loaves	Mk 6:38	*3004*
s unto them, Be of good cheer	Mk 6:50	*3004*
he s unto them, Are ye so without	Mk 7:18	*3004*
s unto him, Ephphatha, that is,	Mk 7:34	*3004*
unto him, and s unto them,	Mk 8:1	*3004*
sighed deeply in his spirit, and s	Mk 8:12	*3004*
he s unto them, Why reason ye,	Mk 8:17	*3004*
he s unto them, But whom say ye	Mk 8:29	*3004*
s unto him, Thou art the Christ	Mk 8:29	*3004*
He answereth him, and s, O	Mk 9:19	*3004*
s unto them, If any man desire to	Mk 9:35	*3004*
he s unto them, Whosoever shall	Mk 10:11	*3004*
s unto his disciples, How hardly	Mk 10:23	*3004*
s unto them, Children, how hard	Mk 10:24	*3004*
And Jesus looking upon them s	Mk 10:27	*3004*
s unto them, Ye know that they	Mk 10:42	*3004*
s unto them, Go your way into the	Mk 11:2	*3004*
calling to remembrance s unto him	Mk 11:21	*3004*
And Jesus answering s unto them	Mk 11:22	*3004*
which he s shall come to pass	Mk 11:23	*3004*
he shall have whatsoever he s	Mk 11:23	*3004*
And Jesus answering s unto them	Mk 11:33	*3004*
he s unto them, Whose is this	Mk 12:16	*3004*
s unto them, Verily I say unto	Mk 12:43	*3004*
one of his disciples s unto him	Mk 13:1	*3004*
s unto them, Go ye into the city,	Mk 14:13	*3004*
of the house, The Master s	Mk 14:14	*3004*
Jesus s unto them, All ye shall	Mk 14:27	*3004*
Jesus s unto him, Verily I say	Mk 14:30	*3004*
he s to his disciples, Sit ye	Mk 14:32	*3004*
s unto them, My soul is exceeding	Mk 14:34	*3004*
s unto Peter, Simon, sleepest	Mk 14:37	*3004*
s unto them, Sleep on now, and	Mk 14:41	*3004*
he goeth straightway to him, and s	Mk 14:45	*3004*
priest rent his clothes, and s	Mk 14:63	*3004*
scripture was fulfilled, which s	Mk 15:28	*3004*
he s unto them, Be not affrighted	Mk 16:6	*3004*
s unto them, He that hath two	Lk 3:11	*3004*
for he s, The old is better	Lk 5:39	*3004*
And he s, Master, say on	Lk 7:40	*5346*
and finding none, he s, I will	Lk 11:24	*3004*
Abraham s unto him, They have	Lk 16:29	*3004*
Hear what the unjust judge s	Lk 18:6	*3004*
he s unto him, Out of thine own	Lk 19:22	*3004*
David himself s in the book of	Lk 20:42	*3004*
the house, The Master s unto thee	Lk 22:11	*3004*
s unto them, Peace be unto you	Lk 24:36	*3004*
And he s, I am not	Jn 1:21	*3004*
seeth Jesus coming unto him, and s	Jn 1:29	*3004*
upon Jesus as he walked, he s	Jn 1:36	*3004*
s unto them, What seek ye	Jn 1:38	*3004*
He s unto them, Come and see	Jn 1:39	*3004*
s unto him, We have found the	Jn 1:41	*3004*
Philip, and s unto him, Follow me	Jn 1:43	*3004*
s unto him, We have found him, of	Jn 1:45	*3004*
Philip s unto him, Come and see	Jn 1:46	*3004*
s of him, Behold an Israelite	Jn 1:47	*3004*
Nathanael s unto him, Whence	Jn 1:48	*3004*
s unto him, Rabbi, thou art the	Jn 1:49	*3004*
he s unto him, Verily, verily, I	Jn 1:51	*3004*
the mother of Jesus s unto him	Jn 2:3	*3004*
Jesus s unto her, Woman, what	Jn 2:4	*3004*
His mother s unto the servants,	Jn 2:5	*3004*
Whatsoever he s unto you	Jn 2:5	*3004*
Jesus s unto them, Fill the	Jn 2:7	*3004*
he s unto them, Draw out now, and	Jn 2:8	*3004*
s unto him, Every man at the	Jn 2:10	*3004*
Nicodemus s unto him, How can a	Jn 3:4	*3004*
Jesus s unto her, Give me to	Jn 4:7	*3004*
Then s the woman of Samaria unto	Jn 4:9	*3004*
God, and who it is that s to thee	Jn 4:10	*3004*
The woman s unto him, Sir, thou	Jn 4:11	*3004*
The woman s unto him, Sir, give	Jn 4:15	*3004*
Jesus s unto her, Go, call thy	Jn 4:16	*3004*
The woman s unto him, Sir, I	Jn 4:19	*3004*
Jesus s unto her, Woman, believe	Jn 4:21	*3004*
The woman s unto him, I know that	Jn 4:25	*3004*
Jesus s unto her, I that speak	Jn 4:26	*3004*

into the city, and s to the men, Jn 4:28 3004
Jesus s unto them, My meat is to Jn 4:34 3004
The nobleman s unto him, Sir, Jn 4:49 3004
Jesus s unto him, Go thy way Jn 4:50 3004
he s unto him, Wilt thou be made Jn 5:6 3004
Jesus s unto him, Rise, take up Jn 5:8 3004
he s unto Philip, Whence shall we Jn 6:5 3004
Peter's brother, s unto him, Jn 6:8 3004
But he s unto them, It is I Jn 6:20 3004
how is it then that he s, I came Jn 6:42 3004
Nicodemus s unto them, (he that Jn 7:50 3004
because he s, Whither I go, ye Jn 8:22 3004
Jesus s unto them, Even the same Jn 8:25 3004
Jesus s unto them, If ye were Jn 8:39 3004
Then after that s he to his Jn 11:7 3004
and after that he s unto them Jn 11:11 3004
Jesus s unto her, Thy brother Jn 11:23 3004
Martha s unto him, I know that he Jn 11:24 3004
She s unto him, Yea, Lord Jn 11:27 3004
s unto him, Lord, by this time he Jn 11:39 3004
Jesus s unto her, Said I not unto Jn 11:40 3004
Jesus s unto them, Loose him, and Jn 11:44 3004
Then s one of his disciples, Jn 12:4 3004
Peter s unto him, Lord, dost thou Jn 13:6 3004
Peter s unto him, Thou shalt Jn 13:8 3004
Simon Peter s unto him, Lord, not Jn 13:9 3004
Jesus s to him, He that is washed Jn 13:10 3004
lying on Jesus' breast s unto him Jn 13:25 3004
Thomas s unto him, Lord, we know Jn 14:5 3004
Jesus s unto him, I am the way, Jn 14:6 3004
Philip s unto him, Lord, shew us Jn 14:8 3004
Jesus s unto him, Have I been so Jn 14:9 3004
Judas s unto him, not Iscariot, Jn 14:22 3004
What is this that he s unto us Jn 16:17 3004
therefore, What is this that he s Jn 16:18 3004
we cannot tell what he s Jn 16:18 2980
Jesus s unto them, I am he Jn 18:5 3004
Then s the damsel that kept the Jn 18:17 3004
He s, I am not Jn 18:17 3004
whose ear Peter cut off, s Jn 18:26 3004
Pilate s unto him, What is truth Jn 18:38 3004
s unto them, I find in him no Jn 18:38 3004
s unto them, Behold, I bring him Jn 19:4 3004
Pilate s unto them, Behold the Jn 19:5 3004
Pilate s unto them, Take ye him, Jn 19:6 3004
s unto Jesus, Whence art thou Jn 19:9 3004
Then s Pilate unto him, Speakest Jn 19:10 3004
he s unto the Jews, Behold your Jn 19:14 3004
Pilate s unto them, Shall I Jn 19:15 3004
might be fulfilled, which s Jn 19:24 3004
he s unto his mother, Woman, Jn 19:26 3004
Then s he to the disciple, Behold Jn 19:27 3004
scripture might be fulfilled, s Jn 19:28 3004
and he knoweth that he s true Jn 19:35 3004
And again another scripture s Jn 19:37 3004
s unto them, They have taken away Jn 20:2 3004
She s unto them, Because they Jn 20:13 3004
Jesus s unto her, Woman, why Jn 20:15 3004
s unto him, Sir, if thou have Jn 20:15 3004
Jesus s unto her, Mary Jn 20:16 3004
herself, and s unto him, Rabboni Jn 20:16 3004
Jesus s unto her, Touch me not Jn 20:17 3004
s unto them, Peace be unto you Jn 20:19 3004
s unto them, Receive ye the Holy Jn 20:22 3004
Then s he to Thomas, Reach hither Jn 20:27 3004
Jesus s unto him, Thomas, because Jn 20:29 3004
Simon Peter s unto them, I go a Jn 21:3 3004
Then Jesus s unto them, Children, Jn 21:5 3004
whom Jesus loved s unto Peter Jn 21:7 3004
Jesus s unto them, Bring of the Jn 21:10 3004
Jesus s unto them, Come and dine Jn 21:12 3004
Jesus s to Simon Peter, Simon, Jn 21:15 3004
He s unto him, Yea, Lord Jn 21:15 3004
He s unto him, Feed my lambs Jn 21:15 3004
He s to him again the second time Jn 21:16 3004
He s unto him, Yea, Lord Jn 21:16 3004
He s unto him, Feed my sheep Jn 21:16 3004
He s unto him the third time, Jn 21:17 3004
Jesus s unto him, Feed my sheep Jn 21:17 3004
this, he s unto him, Follow me Jn 21:19 3004
Peter seeing him s to Jesus Jn 21:21 3004
Jesus s unto him, If I will that Jn 21:22 3004
s he, ye have heard of me Acts 1:4
s God, I will pour out of my Acts 2:17 3004
but he s himself, The Lord said Acts 2:34 3004
as s the prophet, Acts 7:48 3004
s the Lord Acts 7:49 3004
he s unto him, Cast thy garment Acts 12:8 3004
Wherefore he s also in another Acts 13:35 3004
s the Lord, who doeth all these Acts 15:17 3004
Thus s the Holy Ghost, So shall Acts 21:11 3004
and he s,) Acts 22:2 5346
that what things soever the law s Rom 3:19 3004
it s to them who are under the Rom 3:19 2980
For what s the scripture Rom 4:3 3004
For he s to Moses, I will have Rom 9:15 3004
For the scripture s unto Pharaoh Rom 9:17 3004
As he s also in Osee, I will call Rom 9:25 3004
But what s it Rom 10:8 3004
For the scripture s, Whosoever Rom 10:11 3004
For Esaias s, Lord, who hath Rom 10:16 3004
First Moses s, I will provoke you Rom 10:19 3004
But Esaias is very bold, and s Rom 10:20 3004
But to Israel he s, All day long Rom 10:21 3004
not what the scripture s of Elias Rom 11:2 3004
But what s the answer of God unto Rom 11:4 3004
And David s, Let their table be Rom 11:9 3004
I will repay, s the Lord Rom 12:19 3004
s the Lord, every knee shall bow Rom 14:11 3004
And again he s, Rejoice, ye Rom 15:10 3004
And again, Esaias s, There shall Rom 15:12 3004
I say, that every one of you s 1Cor 1:12 3004
For while one s, I am of Paul 1Cor 3:4 3004
for two, s he, shall be one flesh 1Cor 6:16 5346
or s not the law the same also 1Cor 9:8 3004
Or s he it altogether for our 1Cor 9:10 3004
will they not hear me, s the Lord 1Cor 14:21 3004
obedience, as also s the law 1Cor 14:34 3004
But when he s all things are put 1Cor 15:27 2036
(For he s, I have heard thee in a 2Cor 6:2 3004
s the Lord, and touch not the 2Cor 6:17 3004
and daughters, s the Lord Almighty 2Cor 6:18 3004
He s not, And to seeds, as of many Gal 3:16 3004
Nevertheless what s the scripture Gal 4:30 3004
Wherefore he s, When he ascended Eph 4:8 3004
Wherefore he s, Awake thou that Eph 5:14 3004
For the scripture s, Thou shalt 1Ti 5:18 3004
into the world, he s, And let all Heb 1:6 3004
And of the angels he s, Who maketh Heb 1:7 3004
But unto the Son he s, Thy throne Heb 1:8
Wherefore (as the Holy Ghost s Heb 3:7 3004
As he s also in another place, Heb 5:6 3004
s he, that thou make all things Heb 8:5 5346
For finding fault with them, he s Heb 8:8 3004
s the Lord, when I will make a Heb 8:8 3004
I regarded them not, s the Lord Heb 8:9 3004
after those days, s the Lord Heb 8:10 3004
In that he s, A new covenant, he Heb 8:13 3004
he cometh into the world, he s Heb 10:5 3004
s the Lord, I will put my laws Heb 10:16 3004
me, I will recompense, s the Lord Heb 10:30 3004
scripture was fulfilled which s Jas 2:23 3004
that the scripture s in vain Jas 4:5 3004
Wherefore he s, God resisteth the Jas 4:6 3004
He that s, I know him, and keepeth 1Jn 2:4 3004
He that s he abideth in him ought 1Jn 2:6 3004
He that s he is in the light, and 1Jn 2:9 3004
s the Lord, which is, and which Rev 1:8 3004
These things s he that holdeth Rev 2:1 3004
the Spirit s unto the churches Rev 2:7 3004
These things s the first and the Rev 2:8 3004
the Spirit s unto the churches Rev 2:11 3004
These things s he which hath the Rev 2:12 3004
the Spirit s unto the churches Rev 2:17 3004
These things s the Son of God, Rev 2:18 3004
the Spirit s unto the churches Rev 2:29 3004
These things s he that hath the Rev 3:1 3004
the Spirit s unto the churches Rev 3:6 3004
These things s he that is holy, Rev 3:7 3004
the Spirit s unto the churches Rev 3:13 3004
These things s the Amen, the Rev 3:14 3004
the Spirit s unto the churches Rev 3:22 3004
And one of the elders s unto me Rev 5:5 3004
s the Spirit, that they may rest Rev 14:13 3004
he s unto me, The waters which Rev 17:15 3004
for she s in her heart, I sit a Rev 18:7 3004
he s unto me, Write, Blessed are Rev 19:9 3004
he s unto me, These are the true Rev 19:9 3004
Then s he unto me, See thou do it Rev 22:9 3004
he s unto me, Seal not the Rev 22:10 3004
which testifieth these things s Rev 22:20 3004

SAKE

cursed is the ground for thy s Gen 3:17 5668
the ground any more for man's s Gen 8:21 5668
it may be well with me for thy s Gen 12:13 5668
he entreated Abram well for her s Gen 12:16 5668
I will not do it for forty's s Gen 18:29 5668
not destroy it for twenty's s Gen 18:31 5668
I will not destroy it for ten's s Gen 18:32 5668
they will slay me for my wife's s Gen 20:11 1697
seed for my servant Abraham's s Gen 26:24 5668
LORD hath blessed me for thy s Gen 30:27 1558
Egyptian's house for Joseph's s Gen 39:5 1558
to the Egyptians for Israel's s Ex 18:8 182
let him go free for his eye's s Ex 21:26 8478
let him go free for his tooth's s Ex 21:27 8478
unto him, Enviest thou for my s Num 11:29
was zealous for my s among them Num 25:11 7068
day of the plague for Peor's s Num 25:18 1697
his people for his great name's s 1Sa 12:22 5668
to destroy the city for my s 1Sa 23:10 5668
kingdom for his people Israel's s 2Sa 5:12 5668
For thy word's s, and according to 2Sa 7:21 5668
him kindness for Jonathan's s 2Sa 9:1 5668
for Jonathan thy father's s 2Sa 9:7 5668
for my s with the young man 2Sa 18:5
of a far country for thy name's s 1Kin 8:41 4616
do it for David thy father's s 1Kin 11:12 4616
thy son for David my servant's s 1Kin 11:13 4616
for Jerusalem's s which I have 1Kin 11:13 4616
tribe for my servant David's s 1Kin 11:32 4616
and for Jerusalem's s 1Kin 11:32 4616
his life for David my servant's s 1Kin 11:34 4616
Nevertheless for David's s did 1Kin 15:4 4616
Judah for David his servant's s 2Kin 8:19 4616
city, to save it, for mine own s 2Kin 19:34 4616
s, and for my servant David's s 2Kin 19:34 4616
defend this city for mine own s 2Kin 20:6 4616
and for my servant David's s 2Kin 20:6 4616
O LORD, for thy servant's s 1Chr 17:19 4616
country for thy great name's s 2Chr 6:32 4616
for thy great mercies' s thou Neh 9:31
the children's s of mine own body Job 19:17
oh save me for thy mercies' s Ps 6:4 4616
of righteousness for his name's s Ps 23:3 4616
thou me for thy goodness' s Ps 25:7 4616
For thy name's s, O LORD, pardon Ps 25:11 4616
for thy name's s lead me, and Ps 31:3 4616
save me for thy mercies' s Ps 31:16
for thy s are we killed all the Ps 44:22
and redeem us for thy mercies' s Ps 44:26 4616
GOD of hosts, be ashamed for my s Ps 69:6
seek thee be confounded for my s Ps 69:6
Because for thy s I have borne Ps 69:7 4616
away our sins, for thy name's s Ps 79:9 4616
he saved them for his name's s Ps 106:8 4616
O GOD the Lord, for thy name's s Ps 109:21 4616
thy mercy, and for thy truth's s Ps 115:1
For thy servant David's s turn Ps 132:10 5668
me, O LORD, for thy name's s Ps 143:11
for thy righteousness' s bring my Ps 143:11
city to save it for mine own s Is 37:35
and for my servant David's s Is 37:35 4616
pleased for his righteousness' s Is 42:21 4616
For your s I have sent to Babylon Is 43:14 4616
thy transgressions for mine own s Is 43:25 4616
For Jacob my servant's s, and Is 45:4 4616
For my name's s will I defer mine Is 48:9 4616
own s, even for mine own s Is 48:11 4616
against thee shall fall for thy s Is 54:15 4616
For Zion's s will I not hold my Is 62:1 4616
for Jerusalem's s I will not rest Is 62:1 4616
Return for thy servants' s Is 63:17 4616
that cast you out for my name's s Is 66:5 4616
us, do thou it for thy name's s Jer 14:7 4616
Do not abhor us, for thy name's s Jer 14:21 4616
know that for thy s I have Jer 15:15
But I wrought for my name's s Eze 20:9 4616
But I wrought for my name's s Eze 20:14 4616
hand, and wrought for my name's s Eze 20:22 4616
wrought with you for my name's s Eze 20:44 4616
but for mine holy name's s Eze 36:22
is desolate, for the Lord's s Dan 9:17 4616
defer not, for thine own s Dan 9:19 4616
for I know that for my s this Jonah 1:12 7945
for your s be plowed as a field Mic 3:12 1558
persecuted for righteousness' s Mt 5:10 1752
against you falsely, for my s Mt 5:11 1752
governors and kings for my s Mt 10:18 1752
hated of all men for my name's s Mt 10:22
his life for my s shall find it Mt 10:39 1752
put him in prison for Herodias' s Mt 14:3
nevertheless for the oath's s Mt 14:9
his life for my s shall find it Mt 16:25 1752
for the kingdom of heaven's s Mt 19:12
or lands, for my name's s Mt 19:29 1752
of all nations for my name's s Mt 24:9
but for the elect's s those days Mt 24:22
ariseth for the word's s Mk 4:17
him in prison for Herodias' s Mk 6:17
yet for his oath's s, and for Mk 6:26
shall lose his life for my s Mk 8:35 1752
or children, or lands, for my s Mk 10:29 1752
before rulers and kings for my s Mk 13:9 1752
hated of all men for my name's s Mk 13:13
but for the elect's s, whom he Mk 13:20
as evil, for the Son of man's s Lk 6:22 1752
will lose his life for my s Lk 9:24 1752
for the kingdom of God's s Lk 18:29 1752
kings and rulers for my name's s Lk 21:12 1752
hated of all men for my name's s Lk 21:17
they came not for Jesus' s only Jn 12:9
I will lay down my life for thy s Jn 13:37
thou lay down thy life for my s Jn 13:38
believe me for the very works' s Jn 14:11
they do unto you for my name's s Jn 15:21
he must suffer for my name's s Acts 9:16
For which hope's s, king Agrippa, Acts 26:7
was not written for his s alone Rom 4:23
For thy s we are killed all the Rom 8:36 1752
wrath, but also for conscience s Rom 13:5
for the Lord Jesus Christ's s Rom 15:30
We are fools for Christ's s 1Cor 4:10
And this I do for the gospel's s 1Cor 9:23
no question for conscience s 1Cor 10:25
no question for conscience s 1Cor 10:27
eat not for his s that shewed it 1Cor 10:28
shewed it, and for conscience s 1Cor 10:28
your servants for Jesus' s 2Cor 4:5
delivered unto death for Jesus' s 2Cor 4:11
in distresses for Christ's s 2Cor 12:10
for Christ's s hath forgiven you Eph 4:32 1722
him, but also to suffer for his s Phil 1:29
in my flesh for his body's s Col 1:24
For which things' s the wrath of Col 3:6
men we were among you for your s 1Th 1:5
highly in love for their work's s 1Th 5:13
a little wine for thy stomach's s 1Ti 5:23
ought not, for filthy lucre's s Titus 1:11
Yet for love's s I rather beseech Philem 9
ordinance of man for the Lord's s 1Pet 2:13
if ye suffer for righteousness' s 1Pet 3:14
are forgiven you for his name's s 1Jn 2:12
For the truth's s, which dwelleth 2Jn 2
for his name's s they went forth 3Jn 7
and for my name's s hast laboured Rev 2:3

SAKES

spare all the place for their s Gen 18:26 5668
But I will for their s remember Lev 26:45
LORD was angry with me for your s Deut 1:37 1558
LORD was wroth with me for your s Deut 3:26 6616
LORD was angry with me for your s Deut 4:21 1697
Be favourable unto them for our s Judg 21:22
s that the hand of the LORD is Ruth 1:13
he reproved kings for their s 1Chr 16:21 5921
for their s therefore return thou Ps 7:7 5921
he reproved kings for their s Ps 105:14 5921
went ill with Moses for their s Ps 106:32 6616
For my brethren and companions' s Ps 122:8 6616
so will I do for my servants' s Is 65:8 6616
I do not this for your s, O house Eze 36:22 6616
Not for your s do I this, saith Eze 36:32 6616
but for their s that shall make Dan 2:30 1701
rebuke the devourer for your s Mal 3:11
for their s which sat with him, Mk 6:26
I am glad for your s that I was Jn 11:15
not because of me, but for your s Jn 12:30
for their s I sanctify myself, Jn 17:19
they are enemies for your s Rom 11:28
are beloved for the fathers' s Rom 11:28

myself and to Apollos for your s ... 1Cor 4:6
saith he it altogether for our s ... 1Cor 9:10
For our s, no doubt, this is ... 1Cor 9:10
for your s forgave I it in the ... 2Cor 2:10
For all things are for your s ... 2Cor 4:15
yet for your s he became poor, ... 2Cor 8:9
we joy for your s before our God ... 1Th 3:9
all things for the elect's s ... 2Ti 2:10

SAKIA See SHACHIA.

SALA (sa'-lah) See SALAH. *Father of Heber; an ancestor of Jesus.*
of Heber, which was the son of S ... Lk 3:35 4527

SALAH (sa'-lah) See SALA. *Son of Arphaxad.*
And Arphaxad begat S ... Gen 10:24 7974
and S begat Eber ... Gen 10:24 7974
five and thirty years, and begat S ... Gen 11:12 7974
after he begat S four hundred ... Gen 11:13 7974
S lived thirty years, and begat ... Gen 11:14 7974
S lived after he begat Eber four ... Gen 11:15 7974

SALAMIS (sal'-a-mis) *A city on Cyprus.*
And when they were at S, they ... Acts 13:5 4529

SALATHIEL (sa-la'-the-el) See SHEALTIEL. *Descendant of Jehoiakim; an ancestor of Jesus.*
Assir, S his son, ... 1Chr 3:17 7597
to Babylon, Jechonias begat S ... Mt 1:12 4528
and S begat Zorobabel ... Mt 1:12 4528
Zorobabel, which was the son of S ... Lk 3:27 4528

SALCAH (sal'-kah) See SALCHAH. *A city in Gad.*
reigned in mount Hermon, and in S ... Josh 12:5 5548
Hermon, and all Bashan unto S ... Josh 13:11 5548

SALCHAH (sal'-kah) See SALCAH. *Same as Salcah.*
all Gilead, and all Bashan, unto S ... Deut 3:10 5548
in the land of Bashan unto S ... 1Chr 5:11 5548

SALE
count the years of the s thereof ... Lev 25:27 4465
the price of his s shall be ... Lev 25:50 4465
cometh of the s of his patrimony ... Deut 18:8 4465

SALECAH See SALCHAH.

SALEM (sa'-lem) See JERUSALEM. *The city of Melchizedek.*
king of S brought forth bread ... Gen 14:18 8004
In S also is his tabernacle, and ... Ps 76:2 8004
For this Melchisedec, king of S ... Heb 7:1 4532
and after that also King of S ... Heb 7:2 4532

SALIM (sa'-lim) *A city near Aenon.*
was baptizing in Aenon near to S ... Jn 3:23 4530

SALLAI (sal'-lahee) See SALLU.
1. An exile.
And after him Gabbai, S, nine ... Neh 11:8 5543
2. A priest with Zerubbabel.
Of S, Kallai ... Neh 12:20 5543

SALLU (sal'-lu) See SALLAI. *A priest with Zerubbabel.*
S, Amok, Hilkiah, Jedaiah ... Neh 12:7 5543
S the son of Meshullam, the son ... 1Chr 9:7 5543
S the son of Meshullam, the son ... Neh 11:7 5543

SALMA (sal'-mah) See SALMON, ZALMA.
1. Father of Boaz.
And Nahshon begat S, and S ... 1Chr 2:11 8007
2. A son of Caleb.
begat Salma, and S begat Boaz, ... 1Chr 2:11 8007
S the father of Beth-lehem, ... 1Chr 2:51 8007
The sons of S ... 1Chr 2:54 8007

SALMI See SALMA.

SALMON (sal'-mon) See SALMA.
1. Father of Boaz.
begat Nahshon, and Nahshon begat S. Ruth 4:20 8009
S begat Boaz, and Boaz begat Obed, ... Ruth 4:21 8012
and Naasson begat S ... Mt 1:4 4533
And S begat Booz of Rachab ... Mt 1:5 4533
of Booz, which was the son of S ... Lk 3:32 4533
2. A mountain near Shechem.
in it, it was white as snow in S ... Ps 68:14 6756

SALMONE (sal-mo'-ne) *A promontory on Crete.*
under Crete, over against S ... Acts 27:7 4534

SALOME (sa-lo'-me) *A woman follower of Jesus.*
James the less and of Joses, and S ... Mk 15:40 4539
and Mary the mother of James, and S. Mk 16:1 4539

SALT
of Siddim, which is the S Sea ... Gen 14:3 4417
him, and she became a pillar of s ... Gen 19:26 4417
offering shalt thou season with s ... Lev 2:13 4417
s of the covenant of thy God to ... Lev 2:13 4417
offerings thou shalt offer s ... Lev 2:13 4417
it is a covenant of s for ever ... Num 18:19 4417
coast of the s sea eastward ... Num 34:3 4417
out of it shall be at the s sea ... Num 34:12 4417
sea of the plain, even the s sea ... Deut 3:17 4417
land thereof is brimstone, and s ... Deut 29:23 4417
sea of the plain, even the s sea ... Josh 3:16 4417
even the s sea on the east, the ... Josh 12:3 4417
was from the shore of the s sea ... Josh 15:2 4417
And the east border was the s sea ... Josh 15:5 4417
And Nibshan, and the city of S ... Josh 15:62 5898
were at the north bay of the s sea ... Josh 18:19 4417
down the city, and sowed it with s ... Judg 9:45 4417
of the Syrians in the valley of s ... 2Sa 8:13 4417
me a new cruse, and put s therein ... 2Kin 2:20 4417
waters, and cast the s in there ... 2Kin 2:21 4417
in the valley of s ten thousand ... 2Kin 14:7 4417
the valley of s eighteen thousand ... 1Chr 18:12 4417
and to his sons by a covenant of s ... 2Chr 13:5 4417
and went to the valley of s ... 2Chr 25:11 4417
of the God of heaven, wheat, s ... Ezr 6:9 4416
s without prescribing how much ... Ezr 7:22 4416
is unsavoury be eaten without s ... Job 6:6 4417
the valley of s twelve thousand ... Ps 60:t 4417
in the wilderness, in a s land ... Jer 17:6 4420
priests shall cast s upon them ... Eze 43:24 4417
they shall be given to s ... Eze 47:11 4417
Ye are the s of the earth ... Mt 5:13 217
but if the s have lost his savour ... Mt 5:13 217
sacrifice shall be salted with s ... Mk 9:49 251
S is good ... Mk 9:50 217
but if the s have lost his saltness ... Mk 9:50 217
Have s in yourselves, and have ... Mk 9:50 217
S is good ... Lk 14:34 217
but if the s have lost his savour ... Lk 14:34 217
alway with grace, seasoned with s ... Col 4:6 217
no fountain both yield s water ... Jas 3:12 252

SALTED
thou wast not s at all, nor ... Eze 16:4 4414
savour, wherewith shall it be s ... Mt 5:13 233
every one shall be s with fire ... Mk 9:49 233
sacrifice shall be s with salt ... Mk 9:49 233

SALTNESS
but if the salt have lost his s ... Mk 9:50

SALTPITS
the breeding of nettles, and s ... Zeph 2:9 4417

SALU (sa'-lu) *Father of Zimri.*
woman, was Zimri, the son of S ... Num 25:14 5543

SALUTATION
what manner of s this should be ... Lk 1:29 783
Elisabeth heard the s of Mary ... Lk 1:41 783
of thy s sounded in mine ears ... Lk 1:44 783
The s of me Paul with mine own ... 1Cor 16:21 783
The s by the hand of me Paul ... Col 4:18 783
The s of Paul with mine own hand, ... 2Th 3:17 783

SALUTATIONS
love s in the marketplaces, ... Mk 12:38 783

SALUTE
And they will s thee, and give thee ... 1Sa 10:4 7965
to meet him, that he might s him ... 1Sa 13:10 1288
of the wilderness to s our master ... 1Sa 25:14 1288
to s him, and to bless him, ... 2Sa 8:10
if thou meet any man, s him not ... 2Kin 4:29 1288
and if any s thee, answer him not ... 2Kin 4:29 1288
we go down to s the children of ... 2Kin 10:13 7965
if ye s your brethren only, what ... Mt 5:47 782
when ye come into an house, s it ... Mt 10:12 782
And began to s him, Hail, King of ... Mk 15:18 782
and s no man by the way ... Lk 10:4 782
came unto Caesarea to s Festus ... Acts 25:13 782
S my wellbeloved Epaenetus, who ... Rom 16:5 782
S Andronicus and Junia, my kinsmen ... Rom 16:7 782
S Urbane, our helper in Christ, ... Rom 16:9 782
S Apelles approved in Christ ... Rom 16:10 782
S them which are of Aristobulus' ... Rom 16:10 782
S Herodion my kinsman ... Rom 16:11 782
S Tryphena and Tryphosa, who ... Rom 16:12 782
S the beloved Persis, which ... Rom 16:12 782
S Rufus chosen in the Lord, and ... Rom 16:13 782
S Asyncritus, Phlegon, Hermas, ... Rom 16:14 782
S Philologus, and Julia, Nereus, ... Rom 16:15 782
S one another with an holy kiss ... Rom 16:16 782
The churches of Christ s you ... Rom 16:16 782
and Sosipater, my kinsmen, s you ... Rom 16:21 782
this epistle, s you in the Lord ... Rom 16:22 782
The churches of Asia s you ... 1Cor 16:19 782
Priscilla s you much in the Lord, ... 1Cor 16:19 782
All the saints s you ... 2Cor 13:13 782
S every saint in Christ Jesus ... Phil 4:21 782
All the saints s you, chiefly ... Phil 4:22 782
S the brethren which are in ... Col 4:15 782
S Prisca and Aquila, and the ... 2Ti 4:19 782
All that are with me s thee ... Titus 3:15 782
There s thee Epaphras, my ... Philem 23 782
S all them that have the rule ... Heb 13:24 782
They of Italy s you ... Heb 13:24 782
Our friends s thee ... 3Jn 14 782

SALUTED
unto the house of Micah, and s him ... Judg 18:15
army, and came and s his brethren ... 1Sa 17:22
near to the people, he s them ... 1Sa 30:21
he s him, and said to him, Is ... 2Kin 10:15 1288
amazed, and running to him s him ... Mk 9:15 782
of Zacharias, and s Elisabeth ... Lk 1:40 782
s the church, he went down to ... Acts 18:22 782
s the brethren, and abode with ... Acts 21:7 782
And when he had s them, he ... Acts 21:19 782

SALUTETH
and of the whole church, s you ... Rom 16:23 782
the chamberlain of the city s you ... Rom 16:23 782
my fellowprisoner s you, and ... Col 4:10 782
s you, always labouring fervently ... Col 4:12 782
elected together with you, s you ... 1Pet 5:13 782

SALVATION
I have waited for thy s, O LORD ... Gen 49:18 3444
see the s of the LORD, which he ... Ex 14:13 3444
and song, and he is become my s ... Ex 15:2 3444
esteemed the Rock of his s ... Deut 32:15 3444
because I rejoice in thy s ... 1Sa 2:1 3444
the LORD hath wrought s in Israel ... 1Sa 11:13 8668
wrought this great s in Israel ... 1Sa 14:45 3444
wrought a great s for all Israel ... 1Sa 19:5 8668
is my shield, and the horn of my s ... 2Sa 22:3 3468
also given me the shield of thy s ... 2Sa 22:36 3468
be the God of the rock of my s ... 2Sa 22:47 3468
He is the tower of s for his king ... 2Sa 22:51 3444
for this is all my s, and all my ... 2Sa 23:5 3468
shew forth from day to day his s ... 1Chr 16:23 3444
say ye, Save us, O God of our s ... 1Chr 16:35 3468
O LORD God, be clothed with s ... 2Chr 6:41 8668
see the s of the LORD with you, O ... 2Chr 20:17 3444
He also shall be my s ... Job 13:16 3444
S belongeth unto the LORD ... Ps 3:8 3444
I will rejoice in thy s ... Ps 9:14 3444
my heart shall rejoice in thy s ... Ps 13:5 3444
Oh that the s of Israel were come ... Ps 14:7 3444
my buckler, and the horn of my s ... Ps 18:2 3468
also given me the shield of thy s ... Ps 18:35 3468
and let the God of my s be exalted ... Ps 18:46 3468
We will rejoice in thy s, and in ... Ps 20:5 3444
in thy s how greatly shall he ... Ps 21:1 3444
His glory is great in thy s ... Ps 21:5 3444
from the God of his s ... Ps 24:5 3468
for thou art the God of my s ... Ps 25:5 3468
The LORD is my light and my s ... Ps 27:1 3468
neither forsake me, O God of my s ... Ps 27:9 3468
say unto my soul, I am thy s ... Ps 35:3 3444
it shall rejoice in his s ... Ps 35:9 3444
But the s of the righteous is of ... Ps 37:39 8668
haste to help me, O Lord my s ... Ps 38:22 8668
thy faithfulness and thy s ... Ps 40:10 8668
as love thy s say continually ... Ps 40:16 8668
aright will I shew the s of God ... Ps 50:23 3468
Restore unto me the joy of thy s ... Ps 51:12 3468
O God, thou God of my s ... Ps 51:14 8668
Oh that the s of Israel were come ... Ps 53:6 3444
from him cometh my s ... Ps 62:1 3444
He only is my rock and my s ... Ps 62:2 3444
He only is my rock and my s ... Ps 62:6 3444
In God is my s and my glory ... Ps 62:7 3468
thou answer us, O God of our s ... Ps 65:5 3468
benefits, even the God of our s ... Ps 68:19 3444
that is our God is the God of s ... Ps 68:20 4190
hear me, in the truth of thy s ... Ps 69:13 3468
let thy s, O God, set me up on ... Ps 69:29 3444
as love thy s say continually ... Ps 70:4 3444
and thy s all the day ... Ps 71:15 8668
working s in the midst of the ... Ps 74:12 3444
in God, and trusted not in his s ... Ps 78:22 3444
Help us, O God of our s, for the ... Ps 79:9 3468
Turn us, O God of our s, and cause ... Ps 85:4 3468
mercy, O LORD, and grant us thy s ... Ps 85:7 3468
Surely his s is nigh them that ... Ps 85:9 3468
O lord God of my s, I have cried ... Ps 88:1 3444
my God, and the rock of my s ... Ps 89:26 3444
I satisfy him, and shew him my s ... Ps 91:16 3444
joyful noise to the rock of our s ... Ps 95:1 3468
shew forth his s from day to day ... Ps 96:2 3444
The LORD hath made known his s ... Ps 98:2 3444
earth have seen the s of our God ... Ps 98:3 3444
O visit me with thy s ... Ps 106:4 3444
I will take the cup of s, and call ... Ps 116:13 3444
and song, and is become my s ... Ps 118:14 3444
s is in the tabernacles of the ... Ps 118:15 3444
hast heard me, and art become my s ... Ps 118:21 3444
also unto me, O LORD, even thy s ... Ps 119:41 8668
My soul fainteth for thy s ... Ps 119:81 8668
Mine eyes fail for thy s, and for ... Ps 119:123 3444
S is far from the wicked ... Ps 119:155 3444
LORD, I have hoped for thy s ... Ps 119:166 3444
I have longed for thy s, O LORD ... Ps 119:174 3444
also clothe her priests with s ... Ps 132:16 3468
the Lord, the strength of my s ... Ps 140:7 3444
It is he that giveth s unto kings ... Ps 144:10 8668
he will beautify the meek with s ... Ps 149:4 3444
Behold, God is my s ... Is 12:2 3444
he also is become my s ... Is 12:2 3444
draw water out of the wells of s ... Is 12:3 3444
hast forgotten the God of thy s ... Is 17:10 3468
will be glad and rejoice in his s ... Is 25:9 3444
s will God appoint for walls and ... Is 26:1 3444
our s also in the time of trouble ... Is 33:2 3444
of thy times, and strength of s ... Is 33:6 3444
open, and let them bring forth s ... Is 45:8 3468
in the LORD with an everlasting s ... Is 45:17 8668
far off, and my s shall not tarry ... Is 46:13 8668
I will place s in Zion for Israel ... Is 46:13 8668
that thou mayest be my s unto the ... Is 49:6 3444
in a day of s have I helped thee ... Is 49:8 3444
my s is gone forth, and mine arms ... Is 51:5 3468
but my s shall be for ever, and my ... Is 51:6 3444
ever, and my s from generation to ... Is 51:8 3444
of good, that publisheth s ... Is 52:7 3444
earth shall see the s of our God ... Is 52:10 3444
for my s is near to come, and my ... Is 56:1 3444
for s, but it is far off from us ... Is 59:11 3444
his arm brought s unto him ... Is 59:16 3467
an helmet of s upon his head ... Is 59:17 3444
but thou shalt call thy walls S ... Is 60:18 3444
clothed me with the garments of s ... Is 61:10 3468
the s thereof as a lamp that ... Is 62:1 3444
of Zion, Behold, thy s cometh ... Is 62:11 3468
mine own arm brought s unto me ... Is 63:5 3467
Truly in vain is s hoped for from ... Jer 3:23
LORD our God is the s of Israel ... Jer 3:23 8668
wait for the s of the LORD ... Lam 3:26 8668
S is of the LORD ... Jonah 2:9 3444
I will wait for the God of my s ... Mic 7:7 3468
thine horses and thy chariots of s ... Hab 3:8 3444
forth for the s of thy people ... Hab 3:13 3468
even for s with thine anointed ... Hab 3:13 3468
I will joy in the God of my s ... Hab 3:18 3468
he is just, and having s ... Zec 9:9 3467
hath raised up an horn of s for ... Lk 1:69 4991
To give knowledge of s unto his ... Lk 1:77 4991
For mine eyes have seen thy s ... Lk 2:30 4992
all flesh shall see the s of God ... Lk 3:6 4992
This day is s come to this house, ... Lk 19:9 4991
for s is of the Jews ... Jn 4:22 4991
Neither is there s in any other ... Acts 4:12 4991
to you is the word of this s sent ... Acts 13:26 4991

for s unto the ends of the earth Acts 13:47 4991
which shew unto us the way of s Acts 16:17 4991
that the s of God is sent unto Acts 28:28 4992
s to every one that believeth Rom 1:16 4991
mouth confession is made unto s Rom 10:10 4991
fall s is come unto the Gentiles Rom 11:11 4991
for now is our s nearer than when Rom 13:11 4991
it is for your consolation and s 2Cor 1:6 4991
it is for your consolation and s 2Cor 1:6 4991
in the day of s have I succoured 2Cor 6:2 4991
behold, now is the day of s 2Cor 6:2 4991
to s not to be repented of 2Cor 7:10 4991
of truth, the gospel of your s Eph 1:13 4991
And take the helmet of s, and the Eph 6:17 4992
turn to my s through your prayer Phil 1:19 4991
of perdition, but to you of s Phil 1:28 4991
work out your own s with fear Phil 2:12 4991
and for an helmet, the hope of s 1Th 5:8 4991
but to obtain s by our Lord Jesus 1Th 5:9 4991
the beginning chosen you to s 2Th 2:13 4991
s which is in Christ Jesus with 2Ti 2:10 4991
unto s through faith which is in 2Ti 3:15 4991
s hath appeared to all men Titus 2:11 4992
for them who shall be heirs of s Heb 1:14 4991
escape, if we neglect so great s Heb 2:3 4991
s perfect through sufferings Heb 2:10 4991
s unto all them that obey him Heb 5:9 4991
you, and things that accompany s Heb 6:9 4991
second time without sin unto s Heb 9:28 4991
s ready to be revealed in the 1Pet 1:5 4991
faith, even the s of your souls 1Pet 1:9 4991
Of which s the prophets have 1Pet 1:10 4991
longsuffering of our Lord is s 2Pet 3:15 4991
to write unto you of the common s Jude 3 4991
S to our God which sitteth upon Rev 7:10 4991
saying in heaven, Now is come s Rev 12:10 4991
S, and glory, and honour, and power, Rev 19:1 4991

SAMARIA (*sa-ma'-re-ah*) See SAMARITAN.
1. A city in Ephraim.
he bought the hill S of Shemer 1Kin 16:24 8111
of Shemer, owner of the hill, S 1Kin 16:24 8111
his fathers, and was buried in S 1Kin 16:28 8111
reigned over Israel in S twenty 1Kin 16:29 8111
of Baal, which he had built in S 1Kin 16:32 8111
And there was a sore famine in S 1Kin 18:2 8111
and he went up and besieged S 1Kin 20:1 8111
if the dust of S shall suffice 1Kin 20:10 8111
There are men come out of S 1Kin 20:17 8111
Damascus, as my father made in S 1Kin 20:34 8111
heavy and displeased, and came to S 1Kin 20:43 8111
king of Israel, which is in S 1Kin 21:18 8111
in the entrance of the gate of S 1Kin 22:10 8111
king died, and was brought to S 1Kin 22:37 8111
and they buried the king in S 1Kin 22:37 8111
the chariot in the pool of S 1Kin 22:38 8111
in S the seventeenth year of 1Kin 22:51 8111
his upper chamber that was in S 2Kin 1:2 8111
and from thence he returned to S 2Kin 2:25 8111
in S the eighteenth year of 2Kin 3:1 8111
went out of S the same time 2Kin 3:6 8111
with the prophet that is in S 2Kin 5:3 8111
But he led them to S 2Kin 6:19 8111
pass, when they were come into S 2Kin 6:20 8111
they were in the midst of S 2Kin 6:20 8111
host, and went up, and besieged S 2Kin 6:24 8111
And there was a great famine in S 2Kin 6:25 8111
for a shekel, in the gate of S 2Kin 7:1 8111
about this time in the gate of S 2Kin 7:18 8111
And Ahab had seventy sons in S 2Kin 10:1 8111
Jehu wrote letters, and sent to S 2Kin 10:1 8111
arose and departed, and came to S 2Kin 10:12 8111
And when he came to S, he slew all 2Kin 10:17 8111
all that remained unto Ahab in S 2Kin 10:17 8111
and they buried him in S 2Kin 10:35 8111
over Israel in S was twenty 2Kin 10:36 8111
began to reign over Israel in S 2Kin 13:1 8111
remained the grove also in S 2Kin 13:6 8111
and they buried him in S 2Kin 13:9 8111
to reign over Israel in S 2Kin 13:10 8111
Joash was buried in S with the 2Kin 13:13 8111
and hostages, and returned to S 2Kin 14:14 8111
was buried in S with the kings of 2Kin 14:16 8111
of Israel began to reign in S 2Kin 14:23 8111
reign over Israel in S six months 2Kin 15:8 8111
and he reigned a full month in S 2Kin 15:13 8111
went up from Tirzah, and came to S 2Kin 15:14 8111
Shallum the son of Jabesh in S 2Kin 15:14 8111
Israel, and reigned ten years in S 2Kin 15:17 8111
began to reign over Israel in S 2Kin 15:23 8111
against him, and smote him in S 2Kin 15:25 8111
began to reign over Israel in S 2Kin 15:27 8111
reign in S over Israel nine years 2Kin 17:1 8111
all the land, and went up to S 2Kin 17:5 8111
Hoshea the king of Assyria took S 2Kin 17:6 8111
king of Assyria came up against S 2Kin 18:9 8111
king of Israel, S was taken 2Kin 18:10 8111
they delivered S out of mine hand 2Kin 18:34 8111
over Jerusalem the line of S 2Kin 21:13 8111
the entering in of the gate of S 2Chr 18:9 8111
caught him, (for he was hid in S 2Chr 22:9 8111
from S even unto Beth-horon, and 2Chr 25:13 8111
hostages also, and returned to S 2Chr 25:24 8111
them, and brought the spoil to S 2Chr 28:8 8111
before the host that came to S 2Chr 28:9 8111
then they returned to S 2Chr 28:15 8111
And the head of Ephraim is S Is 7:9 8111
the head of S is Remaliah's son Is 7:9 8111
the spoil of S shall be taken Is 8:4 8111
Ephraim and the inhabitant of S Is 9:9 8111
is not S as Damascus Is 10:9 8111
excel them of Jerusalem and of S Is 10:10 8111
I not, as I have done unto S Is 10:11 8111
And thine elder sister is S Eze 16:46 8111
Neither hath S committed half of Eze 16:51 8111
daughters, and the captivity of S Eze 16:53 8111
to their former estate, and S Eze 16:55 8111
S is Aholah, and Jerusalem Eze 23:4 8111
with the cup of thy sister S Eze 23:33 8111
S shall become desolate Hos 13:16 8111
dwell in S in the corner of a bed Amos 3:12 8111
Judah, which he saw concerning S Mic 1:1 8111
is it not S Mic 1:5 8111
Therefore I will make S as an Mic 1:6 8111
Philip went down to the city of S Acts 8:5 4540
and bewitched the people of S Acts 8:9 4540
S had received the word of God Acts 8:14 4540
2. Territory of the northern tribes.
which are in the cities of S 1Kin 13:32 8111
by the palace of Ahab king of S 1Kin 21:1 8111
the messengers of the king of S 2Kin 1:3 8111
of S instead of the children of 2Kin 17:24 8111
and they possessed S, and dwelt in 2Kin 17:24 8111
and placed in the cities of S 2Kin 17:26 8111
they had carried away from S came 2Kin 17:28 8111
of the prophet that came out of S 2Kin 23:18 8111
that were in the cities of S 2Kin 23:19 8111
years he went down to Ahab to S 2Chr 18:2 8111
over, and set in the cities of S Ezr 4:10 8115
their companions that dwell in S Ezr 4:17 8115
his brethren and the army of S Neh 4:2 8111
they delivered S out of my hand Is 36:19 8111
seen folly in the prophets of S Jer 23:13 8111
vines upon the mountains of S Jer 31:5 8111
Shechem, from Shiloh, and from S Jer 41:5 8111
and the wickedness of S Hos 7:1 8111
Thy calf, O S, hath cast thee off Hos 8:5 8111
but the calf of S shall be broken Hos 8:6 8111
The inhabitants of S shall fear Hos 10:5 8111
As for S, her king is cut off as Hos 10:7 8111
upon the mountains of S, and Amos 3:9 8111
that are in the mountain of S Amos 4:1 8111
and trust in the mountain of S Amos 6:1 8111
They that swear by the sin of S Amos 8:14 8111
of Ephraim, and the fields of S Obad 19 8111
3. District north of Judah.
he passed through the midst of S Lk 17:11 4540
And he must needs go through S Jn 4:4 4540
Then cometh he to a city of S Jn 4:5 4540
cometh a woman of S to draw water Jn 4:7 4540
saith the woman of S unto him Jn 4:9 4540
of me, which am a woman of S Jn 4:9 4540
and in all Judaea, and in S Acts 1:8 4540
the regions of Judaea and of S Acts 8:1 4540
all Judaea and Galilee and S Acts 9:31 4540
they passed through Phenice and S Acts 15:3 4540

SAMARITAN (*sa-mar'-i-tun*) See SAMARITANS.
An inhabitant of Samaria.
But a certain S, as he journeyed, Lk 10:33 4541
and he was a S Lk 17:16 4541
Say we not well that thou art a S Jn 8:48 4541

SAMARITANS (*sa-mar'-i-tuns*)
high places which the S had made 2Kin 17:29 8118
any city of the S enter ye not Mt 10:5 4541
entered into a village of the S Lk 9:52 4541
Jews have no dealings with the S Jn 4:9 4541
many of the S of that city Jn 4:39 4541
So when the S were come unto him, Jn 4:40 4541
gospel in many villages of the S Acts 8:25 4541

SAME
the s is it that compasseth the Gen 2:13 1931
saying, This s shall comfort us Gen 5:29
the s became mighty men which Gen 6:4 1992
the s day were all the fountains Gen 7:11 2088
the s is a great city Gen 10:12 1931
the king of Bela (the s is Zoar Gen 14:8 1931
In the s day the LORD made a Gen 15:18 1931
the s is the father of the Gen 19:37 1931
the s is the father of the Gen 19:38 1931
the s day that Isaac was weaned Gen 21:8
the s is Hebron in the land of Gen 23:2 1931
the s is Hebron in the land of Gen 23:19 1931
let the s be she that thou hast Gen 24:14 1931
let the s be the woman whom the Gen 24:44 1931
thee, with that s red pottage Gen 25:30 2088
received in the s year an Gen 26:12 1931
appeared unto him the s night Gen 26:24 1931
And it came to pass the s day Gen 26:32 1931
And he lodged there that s night Gen 32:13 1931
every city, laid he up in the s Gen 41:48
he spake unto them these s words Gen 44:6
the s is Beth-lehem Gen 48:7 1931
Pharaoh commanded the s day the Ex 5:6 1931
the fourteenth day of the s month Ex 12:6 2088
the s day came they into the Ex 19:1 1931
and his flowers, shall be of the s Ex 25:31
knop under two branches of the s Ex 25:35
knop under two branches of the s Ex 25:35
knop under two branches of the s Ex 25:35
their branches shall be of the s Ex 25:36
his horns shall be of the s Ex 27:2 1931
is upon it, shall be of the s Ex 28:8
horns thereof shall be of the s Ex 30:2
and his flowers, were of the s Ex 37:17
knop under two branches of the s Ex 37:21
knop under two branches of the s Ex 37:21
knop under two branches of the s Ex 37:21
and their branches were of the s Ex 37:22
the horns thereof were of the s Ex 37:25
the horns thereof were of the s Ex 38:2
that was upon it, was of the s Ex 39:5
the s day that it is offered Lev 7:15
it shall be eaten the s day that Lev 7:16
be eaten the s day ye offer it Lev 19:6
On the s day it shall be eaten up Lev 22:30 1931
of the s month is the feast of Lev 23:6 2088
ye shall do no work in that s day Lev 23:28 6106
not be afflicted in that s day Lev 23:29 6106
that doeth any work in that s day Lev 23:30 6106
the s soul will I destroy from Lev 23:30 6106
cover the s with a covering of Num 4:8 1931
shall hallow his head that s day Num 6:11 1931
even the s soul shall be cut off Num 9:13 1931
the s will we do unto thee Num 10:32
the s reproacheth the LORD Num 15:30 1931
anger was kindled the s time Num 32:10 1931
prayed for Aaron also the s time Deut 9:20 1931
of thine increase the s year Deut 14:28 1931
charged the people the s day Deut 27:11 1931
wrote this song the s day Deut 31:22 1931
after the s manner seven times Josh 6:15 2088
of Israel, and the valley of the s Josh 11:16
the s is Jerusalem Josh 15:8 1931
And it came to pass the s night Judg 6:25 1931
thee, the s shall go with thee Judg 7:4 1931
go with thee, the s shall not go Judg 7:4 1931
And it came to pass the s night Judg 7:9 1931
came to Shiloh the s day with his 1Sa 4:12 1931
the s day unto the LORD 1Sa 6:15 1931
they returned to Ekron the s day 1Sa 6:16 1931
this s shall reign over my people 1Sa 9:17 2088
one of the s place answered and 1Sa 10:12
the s was the first altar that he 1Sa 14:35
and spake according to the s words 1Sa 17:23 428
and spake after the s manner 1Sa 17:30 2088
all his men, that s day together 1Sa 31:6 1931
there, and died in the s place 2Sa 2:23 8478
the s is the city of David 2Sa 5:7 1931
burned with fire in the s place 2Sa 23:7
the s was Adino the Eznite 2Sa 23:8 1931
the borders thereof were of the s 1Kin 7:35
The s day did the king hallow the 1Kin 8:64 1931
And he gave a sign the s day 1Kin 13:3 1931
by the s way that thou camest 1Kin 13:9
went out of Samaria the s time 2Kin 3:6 1931
Libnah revolted at the s time 2Kin 8:22 1931
that which springeth of the s 2Kin 19:29
by the s shall he return, and 2Kin 19:33
the s is Abraham 1Chr 1:27 1931
were round about the s cities 1Chr 4:33
the s to Jacob for a law, and to 1Chr 16:17
And it came to pass the s night 1Chr 17:3 1931
Also at the s time Solomon kept 2Chr 7:8 1931
the s may be a priest of them 2Chr 13:9
offered unto the LORD the s time 2Chr 15:11 1931
some of the people the s time 2Chr 16:10 1931
the s is Micaiah the son of Imla 2Chr 18:7 1931
name of the s place was called 2Chr 20:26 1931
The s time also did Libnah revolt 2Chr 21:10 1931
the s year an hundred talents of 2Chr 27:5 1931
Hath not the s Hezekiah taken 2Chr 32:12 1931
This s Hezekiah also stopped the 2Chr 32:30 1931
and upon the inhabitants of the s 2Chr 34:28
the LORD was prepared the s day 2Chr 35:16 1931
sedition within the s of old time Ezr 4:15 1459
At the s time came to them Tatnai Ezr 5:3
the s king Cyrus made a decree to Ezr 5:13
Then came the s Sheshbazzar Ezr 5:16 1791
year of Cyrus the king the s Ezr 6:3
(the s is Kelita,) Pethahiah, Ezr 10:23 1933
Likewise at the s time said I Neh 4:22 1931
answered them after the s manner Neh 6:4 2088
that the s Levites might have the Neh 10:37 1992
on the thirteenth day of the s Est 9:1
day of the s rested they, and made Est 9:17
day of the s they rested, and made Est 9:18
and the fifteenth day of the s Est 9:21
and sow wickedness, reap the s Job 4:8
ye know, the s do I know also Job 13:2
the tongue of thy dogs in the s Ps 68:23
and he poureth out of the s Ps 75:8 2088
But thou art the s, and thy years Ps 102:27 1931
confirmed the s unto Jacob for a Ps 105:10
of the s the LORD's name is to be Ps 113:3
the s is the companion of a Prov 28:24 1931
no man remembered that s poor man Eccl 9:15 1931
In the s day shall the Lord shave Is 7:20 1931
At the s time spake the LORD by Is 20:2 1931
that which springeth of the s Is 37:30
by the s shall he return, and Is 37:34
which will not serve the s Jer 27:8
And it came to pass the s year Jer 28:1 1931
the s year in the seventh month Jer 28:17 1931
At the s time, saith the LORD, Jer 31:1 1931
vineyards and fields at the s time Jer 39:10 1931
the s wicked man shall die in his Eze 3:18 1931
the s wheels also turned not from Eze 10:16 1992
s faces which I saw by the river Eze 10:22 1992
this shall not be the s Eze 21:26 2063
defiled my sanctuary in the s day Eze 23:38 1931
then they came the s day into my Eze 23:39 1931
of the day, even of this s day Eze 24:2 6106
against Jerusalem this s day Eze 24:2 6106
that at the s time shall things Eze 38:10 1931
at the s time when Gog shall come Eze 38:18 1931
shall go out by the way of the s Eze 44:3
worshippeth shall the s hour be Dan 3:6
ye shall be cast the s hour into Dan 3:15
The s hour was the thing Dan 4:33
At the s time my reason returned Dan 4:36
In the s hour came forth fingers Dan 5:5
were found in the s Daniel Dan 5:12
the s horn made war with the Dan 7:21 1797
was a nation even to that s time Dan 12:1 1931
father will go in unto the s maid Amos 2:7
In the s day also will I punish Zeph 1:9 1931
Babylon, and come thou the s day Zec 6:10 1931
s my name shall be great among Mal 1:11
the s John had his raiment of Mt 3:4 846
the s shall be called great in Mt 5:19 3778

do not even the publicans the s Mt 5:46 846
that s hour what ye shall speak Mt 10:19 1565
the s is my brother, and sister, Mt 12:50 846
The s day went Jesus out of the Mt 13:1 1565
the s is he that heareth the word Mt 13:20 3778
Canaan came out of the s coasts Mt 15:22 1565
At the s time came the disciples Mt 18:1 1565
the s is greatest in the kingdom Mt 18:4 3778
But the s servant went out, and Mt 18:28 1565
the s is become the head of the Mt 21:42 3778
The s day came to him the Mt 22:23 1565
the end, the s shall be saved Mt 24:13 3778
talents went and traded with the s Mt 25:16 846
the dish, the s shall betray me Mt 26:23 3778
third time, saying the s words Mt 26:44 846
I shall kiss, that s is he Mt 26:48 846
In that s hour said Jesus to the Mt 26:55 1565
with him, cast the s in his teeth Mt 27:44 846
the s is my brother, and my sister Mk 3:35 3778
And the s day, when the even was Mk 4:35 1565
the gospel's, the s shall save it Mk 8:35 3778
the s shall be last of all, and Mk 9:35
asked him again of the s matter Mk 10:10 846
the end, the s shall be saved Mk 13:13 3778
and prayed, and spake the s words Mk 14:39 846
I shall kiss, that s is he Mk 14:44 846
there were in the s country Lk 2:8 846
the s man was just and devout, Lk 2:25 3778
for sinners also do even the s Lk 6:33 846
For with the s measure that ye Lk 6:38 846
in that s hour he cured many of Lk 7:21 846
is forgiven, the s loveth little Lk 7:47
for my sake, the s shall save it Lk 9:24 3778
you all, the s shall be great Lk 9:48 3778
in the s house remain, eating and Lk 10:7 846
out into the streets of the s Lk 10:10 846
the s hour what ye ought to say Lk 12:12 846
The s day there came certain of Lk 13:31 846
the s was accused unto him that Lk 16:1 3778
But the s day that Lot went out Lk 17:29
the s is become the head of the Lk 20:17 3778
the scribes the s hour sought to Lk 20:19 846
the s shall receive greater Lk 20:47 3778
the s day Pilate and Herod were Lk 23:12 846
thou art in the s condemnation Lk 23:40 846
(The s had not consented to the Lk 23:51 3778
two of them went that s day to a Lk 24:13 846
And they rose up the s hour Lk 24:33 846
The s was in the beginning with Jn 1:2 3778
The s came for a witness, to bear Jn 1:7 3778
the s said unto me, Upon whom Jn 1:33 1565
the s is he which baptizeth with Jn 1:33 3778
The s came to Jesus by night, and Jn 3:2 3778
the s baptizeth, and all men come Jn 3:26 3778
knew that it was at the s hour Jn 4:53 1565
on the s day was the sabbath Jn 5:9 1565
the s said unto me, Take up thy Jn 5:11 1565
the s works that I do, bear Jn 5:36 846
sent him, the s is true, and no Jn 7:18 3778
Even the s that I said unto you Jn 8:25 3748
the s is a thief and a robber Jn 10:1 1565
still in the s place where he was Jn 11:6
being the high priest that s year Jn 11:49 1565
The s came therefore to Philip, Jn 12:21 3778
the s shall judge him in the last Jn 12:48 1565
the s bringeth forth much fruit Jn 15:5 3778
was the high priest that s year Jn 18:13 1565
Then the s day at evening, being Jn 20:19 1565
this s Jesus, which is taken up Acts 1:11 3778
unto that s day that he was taken Acts 1:22
that God hath made that s Jesus Acts 2:36 5126
the s day there were added unto Acts 2:41 1565
The s dealt subtilly with our Acts 7:19 3778
the s did God send to be a ruler Acts 7:35 5126
in the s city used sorcery Acts 8:9
and began at the s scripture Acts 8:35 5026
the s night Peter was sleeping Acts 12:6 1565
the s unto us their children Acts 13:33 5026
The s heard Paul speak Acts 14:9 3778
tell you the s things by mouth Acts 15:27 846
The s followed Paul and us, and Acts 16:17 3778
And he came out the s hour Acts 16:18 846
he took them the s hour of the Acts 16:33 1565
And because he was of the s craft Acts 18:3 3673
the s time there arose no small Acts 19:23 1565
the s man had four daughters, Acts 21:9 5129
the s hour I looked up upon him Acts 22:13 846
Or else let these s here say Acts 24:20 3778
In the s quarters were Acts 28:7 1565
of death, not only do the s Rom 1:32 846
that judgest doest the s things Rom 2:1 846
do such things, and doest the s Rom 2:3 846
who hath subjected the s in hope Rom 8:20
Even for this s purpose have I Rom 9:17 846
of the s lump to make one vessel Rom 9:21 846
for the s Lord over all is rich Rom 10:12 846
all members have not the s office Rom 12:4 846
Be of the s mind one toward Rom 12:16 846
thou shalt have praise of the s Rom 13:3 846
that ye all speak the s thing 1Cor 1:10 846
joined together in the s mind 1Cor 1:10 846
s mind and in the s judgment 1Cor 1:10 846
Let every man abide in the s 1Cor 7:20 5026
love God, the s is known of him 1Cor 8:3 3778
or saith not the law the s also 1Cor 9:8 5023
did all eat the s spiritual meat 1Cor 10:3 846
all drink the s spiritual drink 1Cor 10:4 846
That the Lord Jesus the s night 1Cor 11:23 846
After the s manner also he took 1Cor 11:25 5615
of gifts, but the s Spirit 1Cor 12:4 846
administrations, but the s Lord 1Cor 12:5 846
but it is the s God which worketh 1Cor 12:6 846
word of knowledge by the s Spirit 1Cor 12:8 846
To another faith by the s Spirit 1Cor 12:9 846
gifts of healing by the s Spirit 1Cor 12:9 846
have the s care one for another 1Cor 12:25 846
All flesh is not the s flesh 1Cor 15:39 846
in the enduring of the s 2Cor 1:6 846
but the s which is made sorry by 2Cor 2:2
And I wrote this s unto you 2Cor 2:3 846
the s vail untaken away in the 2Cor 3:14 846
are changed into the s image from 2Cor 3:18 846
We having the s spirit of faith, 2Cor 4:13 846
Now for a recompence in the s 2Cor 6:13 846
for I perceive that the s epistle 2Cor 7:8 1565
finish in you the s grace also 2Cor 8:6 846
which put the s earnest care into 2Cor 8:16 846
by us to the glory of the s Lord 2Cor 8:19 3778
in this s confident boasting 2Cor 9:4 5026
that the s might be ready, as a 2Cor 9:5 5026
walked we not in the s spirit 2Cor 12:18 846
walked we not in the s steps 2Cor 12:18 846
the s was mighty in me toward the Gal 2:8 2532
the s which I also was forward to Gal 2:10
the s are the children of Abraham Gal 3:7 3778
be fellowheirs, and of the s body Eph 3:6 4954
He that descended is the s also Eph 4:10 846
the s shall he receive of the Eph 6:8 3778
do the s things unto them, Eph 6:9 846
sent unto you for the s purpose Eph 6:22 846
Having the s conflict which ye Phil 1:30 846
be likeminded, having the s love Phil 2:2 846
For the s cause also do ye joy, Phil 2:18 846
To write the s things to you, to Phil 3:1 846
let us walk by the s rule Phil 3:16 846
let us mind the s thing Phil 3:16 846
they be of the s mind in the Lord Phil 4:2 846
watch in the s with thanksgiving Col 4:2 846
sent unto you for the s purpose Col 4:8 846
the s commit thou to faithful men 2Ti 2:2 5023
but thou art the s, and thy years Heb 1:12 846
likewise took part of the s Heb 2:14 846
after the s example of unbelief Heb 4:11 846
every one of you do shew the s Heb 6:11 846
oftentimes the s sacrifices Heb 10:11 846
heirs with him of the s promise Heb 11:9
Jesus Christ the s yesterday Heb 13:8 846
the s is a perfect man, and able Jas 3:2 3778
Out of the s mouth proceedeth Jas 3:10 846
forth at the s place sweet water Jas 3:11 846
the s is made the head of the 1Pet 2:7 3778
likewise with the s mind 1Pet 4:1 846
with them to the s excess of riot 1Pet 4:4 846
so minister the s one to another 1Pet 4:10 846
knowing that the s afflictions 1Pet 5:9 846
of the s is he brought in bondage 2Pet 2:19 3778
by the s word are kept in store, 2Pet 3:7 846
the s hath not the Father 1Jn 2:23 3761
but as the s anointing teacheth 1Jn 2:27 846
the s shall be clothed in white Rev 3:5 3778
the s hour was there a great Rev 11:13 1565
The s shall drink of the wine of Rev 14:10 846

SAMGAR-NEBO (sam''-gar-ne'-bo) *A prince of Babylon.*
gate, even Nergal-sharezer, S Jer 39:3 5562

SAMLAH (sam'-lah) *A king of Edom.*
S of Masrekah reigned in his Gen 36:36 8072
S died, and Saul of Rehoboth by Gen 36:37 8072
S of Masrekah reigned in his 1Chr 1:47 8072
when S was dead, Shaul of 1Chr 1:48 8072

SAMOS (sa'-mos) *An island in the Aegean Sea.*
and the next day we arrived at S Acts 20:15 4544

SAMOTHRACE See SAMOTHRACIA.

SAMOTHRACIA (sam-o-thra'-she-ah) *An island in the Aegean Sea.*
came with a straight course to S Acts 16:11 4543

SAMSON (sam'-sun) See SAMSON'S. *A judge of Israel.*
bare a son, and called his name S Judg 13:24 8123
S went down to Timnath, and saw a Judg 14:1 8123
S said unto his father, Get her Judg 14:3 8123
Then went S down, and his father Judg 14:5 8123
and she pleased S well Judg 14:7 8123
and S made there a feast Judg 14:10 8123
S said unto them, I will now put Judg 14:12 8123
that S visited his wife with a Judg 15:1 8123
S said concerning them, Now shall Judg 15:3 8123
S went and caught three hundred Judg 15:4 8123
And they answered, S, the son in Judg 15:6 8123
S said unto them, Though ye have Judg 15:7 8123
To bind S are we come up, to do Judg 15:10 8123
of the rock Etam, and said to S Judg 15:11 8123
S said unto them, Swear unto me, Judg 15:12 8123
S said, With the jawbone of an Judg 15:16 8123
Then went S to Gaza, and saw there Judg 16:1 8123
Gazites, saying, S is come hither Judg 16:2 8123
S lay till midnight, and arose at Judg 16:3 8123
And Delilah said to S, Tell me, I Judg 16:6 8123
S said unto her, If they bind me Judg 16:7 8123
The Philistines be upon thee, S Judg 16:9 8123
And Delilah said unto S, Behold, Judg 16:10 8123
The Philistines be upon thee, S Judg 16:12 8123
And Delilah said unto S, Hitherto Judg 16:13 8123
The Philistines be upon thee, S Judg 16:14 8123
The Philistines be upon thee, S Judg 16:20 8123
Our god hath delivered S our Judg 16:23 8123
merry, that they said, Call for S Judg 16:25 8123
they called for S out of the Judg 16:25 8123
S said unto the lad that held him Judg 16:26 8123
that beheld while S made sport Judg 16:27 8123
S called unto the LORD, and said, Judg 16:28 8123
S took hold of the two middle Judg 16:29 8123
S said, Let me die with the Judg 16:30 8123
of Gedeon, and of Barak, and of S Heb 11:32 4546

SAMSON'S (sam'-suns)
day, that they said unto S wife Judg 14:15 8123
S wife wept before him, and said, Judg 14:16 8123
But S wife was given to his Judg 14:20 8123

SAMUEL (sam'-u-el) See SHEMUEL. *A priest and judge of Israel.*
bare a son, and called his name S 1Sa 1:20 8050
But S ministered before the LORD, 1Sa 2:18 8050
the child S grew before the LORD 1Sa 2:21 8050
And the child S grew on, and was in 1Sa 2:26 8050
the child S ministered unto the 1Sa 3:1 8050
was, and S was laid down to sleep 1Sa 3:3 8050
That the LORD called S 1Sa 3:4 8050
And the LORD called yet again, S 1Sa 3:6 8050
S arose and went to Eli, and said, 1Sa 3:6 8050
Now S did not yet know the LORD, 1Sa 3:7 8050
the LORD called S again the third 1Sa 3:8 8050
Therefore Eli said unto S 1Sa 3:9 8050
So S went and lay down in his 1Sa 3:9 8050
as at other times, S, S 1Sa 3:10 8050
Then S answered, Speak 1Sa 3:10 8050
And the LORD said to S, Behold, I 1Sa 3:11 8050
S lay until the morning, and 1Sa 3:15 8050
S feared to shew Eli the vision 1Sa 3:15 8050
Eli called S, and said, S 1Sa 3:16 8050
S told him every whit, and hid 1Sa 3:18 8050
S grew, and the LORD was with him, 1Sa 3:19 8050
even to Beer-sheba knew that S 1Sa 3:20 8050
to S in Shiloh by the word of the 1Sa 3:21 8050
the word of S came to all Israel 1Sa 4:1 8050
S spake unto all the house of 1Sa 7:3 8050
S said, Gather all Israel to 1Sa 7:5 8050
S judged the children of Israel 1Sa 7:6 8050
the children of Israel said to S 1Sa 7:8 8050
S took a sucking lamb, and offered 1Sa 7:9 8050
S cried unto the LORD for Israel 1Sa 7:9 8050
as S was offering up the burnt 1Sa 7:10 8050
Then S took a stone, and set it 1Sa 7:12 8050
the Philistines all the days of S 1Sa 7:13 8050
S judged Israel all the days of 1Sa 7:15 8050
when S was old, that he made his 1Sa 8:1 8050
and came to S unto Ramah, 1Sa 8:4 8050
But the thing displeased S 1Sa 8:6 8050
And S prayed unto the LORD 1Sa 8:6 8050
And the LORD said unto S, Hearken 1Sa 8:7 8050
S told all the words of the LORD 1Sa 8:10 8050
refused to obey the voice of S 1Sa 8:19 8050
S heard all the words of the 1Sa 8:21 8050
And the LORD said to S, Hearken 1Sa 8:22 8050
S said unto the men of Israel, Go 1Sa 8:22 8050
S came out against them, for to 1Sa 9:14 8050
Now the LORD had told S in his 1Sa 9:15 8050
when S saw Saul, the LORD said 1Sa 9:17 8050
Saul drew near to S in the gate 1Sa 9:18 8050
S answered Saul, and said, I am 1Sa 9:19 8050
S took Saul and his servant, and 1Sa 9:22 8050
S said unto the cook, Bring the 1Sa 9:23 8050
S said, Behold that which is left 1Sa 9:24
So Saul did eat with S that day 1Sa 9:24 8050
S communed with Saul upon the top 1Sa 9:25
that S called Saul to the top of 1Sa 9:26 8050
went out both of them, he and S 1Sa 9:26 8050
S said to Saul, Bid the servant 1Sa 9:27 8050
Then S took a vial of oil, and 1Sa 10:1 8050
had turned his back to go from S 1Sa 10:9 8050
they were no where, we came to S 1Sa 10:14 8050
I pray thee, what S said unto you 1Sa 10:15 8050
of the kingdom, whereof S spake 1Sa 10:16 8050
S called the people together unto 1Sa 10:17 8050
when S had caused all the tribes 1Sa 10:20 8050
S said to all the people, See ye 1Sa 10:24 8050
Then S told the people the manner 1Sa 10:25 8050
S sent all the people away, every 1Sa 10:25 8050
not forth after Saul and after S 1Sa 11:7 8050
And the people said unto S 1Sa 11:12 8050
Then said S to the people, Come, 1Sa 11:14 8050
S said unto all Israel, Behold, I 1Sa 12:1 8050
S said unto the people, It is the 1Sa 12:6 8050
and Bedan, and Jephthah, and S 1Sa 12:11 8050
So S called unto the LORD 1Sa 12:18 8050
greatly feared the LORD and S 1Sa 12:18 8050
And all the people said unto S 1Sa 12:19 8050
S said unto the people, Fear not 1Sa 12:20 8050
the set time that S had appointed 1Sa 13:8 8050
but S came not to Gilgal 1Sa 13:8 8050
burnt offering, behold, S came 1Sa 13:10 8050
S said, What hast thou done 1Sa 13:11 8050
S said to Saul, Thou hast done 1Sa 13:13 8050
S arose, and gat him up from 1Sa 13:15 8050
S also said unto Saul, The LORD 1Sa 15:1 8050
came the word of the LORD unto S 1Sa 15:10 8050
And it grieved S 1Sa 15:11 8050
when S rose early to meet Saul in 1Sa 15:12 8050
in the morning, it was told S 1Sa 15:12 8050
And S came to Saul 1Sa 15:13 8050
S said, What meaneth then this 1Sa 15:14 8050
Then S said unto Saul, Stay, and I 1Sa 15:16 8050
S said, When thou wast little in 1Sa 15:17 8050
And Saul said unto S, Yea, I have 1Sa 15:20 8050
S said, Hath the LORD as great 1Sa 15:22 8050
And Saul said unto S, I have 1Sa 15:24 8050
S said unto Saul, I will not 1Sa 15:26 8050
as S turned about to go away, he 1Sa 15:27 8050
S said unto him, The LORD hath 1Sa 15:28 8050
So S turned again after Saul 1Sa 15:31 8050
Then said S, Bring ye hither to 1Sa 15:32 8050
S said, As thy sword hath made 1Sa 15:33 8050
S hewed Agag in pieces before the 1Sa 15:33 8050
Then S went to Ramah 1Sa 15:34 8050
S came no more to see Saul until 1Sa 15:35 8050
nevertheless S mourned for Saul 1Sa 15:35 8050
And the LORD said unto S, How long 1Sa 16:1 8050
And S said, How can I go 1Sa 16:2 8050

S did that which the LORD spake, 1Sa 16:4 8050
But the LORD said unto *S*, Look 1Sa 16:7 8050
and made him pass before *S* 1Sa 16:8 8050
of his sons to pass before *S* 1Sa 16:10 8050
S said unto Jesse, The LORD hath 1Sa 16:10 8050
S said unto Jesse, Are here all 1Sa 16:11 8050
S said unto Jesse, Send and fetch 1Sa 16:11 8050
Then *S* took the horn of oil, and 1Sa 16:13 8050
So *S* rose up, and went to Ramah 1Sa 16:13 8050
came to *S* to Ramah, and told him 1Sa 19:18 8050
S went and dwelt in Naioth 1Sa 19:18 8050
S standing as appointed over them 1Sa 19:20 8050
and he asked and said, Where are *S* 1Sa 19:22 8050
before *S* in like manner, and lay 1Sa 19:24 8050
And *S* died 1Sa 25:1 8050
Now *S* was dead, and all Israel had 1Sa 28:3 8050
And he said, Bring me up *S* 1Sa 28:11 8050
And when the woman saw *S*, she 1Sa 28:12 8050
And Saul perceived that it was *S* 1Sa 28:14 8050
S said to Saul, Why hast thou 1Sa 28:15 8050
Then said *S*, Wherefore then dost 1Sa 28:16 8050
afraid, because of the words of *S* 1Sa 28:20 8050
And the sons of *S* 1Chr 6:28 8050
S the seer did ordain in their 1Chr 9:22 8050
to the word of the LORD by *S* 1Chr 11:3 8050
And all that *S* the seer, and Saul 1Chr 26:28 8050
written in the book of *S* the seer 1Chr 29:29 8050
from the days of *S* the prophet 2Chr 35:18 8050
S among them that call upon his Ps 99:6 8050
S stood before me, yet my mind Jer 15:1 8050
Yea, and all the prophets from *S* Acts 3:24 *4545*
fifty years, until *S* the prophet Acts 13:20 *4545*
of David also, and *S*, and of the Heb 11:32 *4545*

SANBALLAT (*san-bal'-lat*) *An opponent of Nehemiah.*
When *S* the Horonite, and Tobiah Neh 2:10 5571
But when *S* the Horonite, and Neh 2:19 5571
that when *S* heard that we builded Neh 4:1 5571
But it came to pass, that when *S* Neh 4:7 5571
Now it came to pass, when *S* Neh 6:1 5571
That *S* and Geshem sent unto me, Neh 6:2 5571
Then sent *S* his servant unto me Neh 6:5 5571
for Tobiah and *S* had hired him Neh 6:12 5571
S according to these their works, Neh 6:14 5571
was son in law to *S* the Horonite Neh 13:28 5571

SANCTIFICATION
us wisdom, and righteousness, and *s* 1Cor 1:30 *38*
is the will of God, even your *s* 1Th 4:3 *38*
how to possess his vessel in *s* 1Th 4:4 *38*
salvation through *s* of the Spirit 2Th 2:13 *38*
through *s* of the Spirit, unto 1Pet 1:2 *38*

SANCTIFIED
blessed the seventh day, and *s* it Gen 2:3 6942
unto the people, and *s* the people Ex 19:14 6942
tabernacle shall be *s* by my glory Ex 29:43 6942
all that was therein, and *s* them Lev 8:10 6942
s it, to make reconciliation upon Lev 8:15 6942
s Aaron, and his garments, and his Lev 8:30 6942
I will be *s* in them that come Lev 10:3 6942
if he that *s* it will redeem his Lev 27:15 6942
if he that *s* the field will in Lev 27:19 6942
s it, and all the instruments Num 7:1 6942
and had anointed them, and *s* them Num 7:1 6942
land of Egypt I *s* them for myself Num 8:17 6942
the LORD, and he was *s* in them Num 20:13 6942
because ye *s* me not in the midst Deut 32:51 6942
s Eleazar his son to keep the ark 1Sa 7:1 6942
he *s* Jesse and his sons, and called 1Sa 16:5 6942
though it were *s* this day in the 1Sa 21:5 6942
the Levites *s* themselves to bring 1Chr 15:14 6942
priests that were present were *s* 2Chr 5:11 6942
s this house, that my name may be 2Chr 7:16 6942
house, which I have *s* for my name 2Chr 7:20 6942
s themselves, and came, according 2Chr 29:15 6942
so they *s* the house of the LORD 2Chr 29:17 6942
have we prepared and *s*, and, 2Chr 29:19 6942
other priests had *s* themselves 2Chr 29:34 6942
had not *s* themselves sufficiently 2Chr 30:3 6942
which he hath *s* for ever 2Chr 30:8 6942
s themselves, and brought in the 2Chr 30:15 6942
the congregation that were not *s* 2Chr 30:17 6942
number of priests *s* themselves 2Chr 30:24 6942
they *s* themselves in holiness 2Chr 31:18 6942
they *s* it, and set up the doors of Neh 3:1 6942
unto the tower of Meah they *s* it Neh 3:1 6942
they *s* holy things unto the Neh 12:47 6942
the Levites *s* them unto the Neh 12:47 6942
s them, and rose up early in the Job 1:5 6942
holy shall be *s* in righteousness Is 5:16 6942
I have commanded my *s* ones Is 13:3 6942
forth out of the womb I *s* thee Jer 1:5 6942
I will be *s* in you before the Eze 20:41 6942
in her, and shall be *s* in her Eze 28:22 6942
shall be *s* in them in the sight Eze 28:25 6942
when I shall be *s* in you before Eze 36:23 6942
me, when I shall be *s* in thee Eze 38:16 6942
am *s* in them in the sight of many Eze 39:27 6942
that are *s* of the sons of Zadok Eze 48:11 6942
ye of him, whom the Father hath *s* Jn 10:36 *37*
also might be *s* through the truth Jn 17:19 *37*
among all them which are *s* Acts 20:32 *37*
among them which are *s* by faith Acts 26:18 *37*
being *s* by the Holy Ghost Rom 15:16 *37*
them that are *s* in Christ Jesus 1Cor 1:2 *37*
but ye are washed, but ye are *s* 1Cor 6:11 *37*
husband is *s* by the wife, and the 1Cor 7:14 *37*
wife is *s* by the husband 1Cor 7:14 *37*
For it is *s* by the word of God and 1Ti 4:5 *37*
shall be a vessel unto honour, *s* 2Ti 2:21 *37*
they who are *s* are all of one Heb 2:11 *37*
By the which will we are *s* Heb 10:10 *37*
for ever them that are *s* Heb 10:14 *37*
the covenant, wherewith he was *s* Heb 10:29 *37*
to them that are *s* by God the Jude 1 *37*

SANCTIFIETH
or the temple that *s* the gold Mt 23:17 *37*
or the altar that *s* the gift Mt 23:19 *37*
For both he that *s* and they who Heb 2:11 *37*
s to the purifying of the flesh Heb 9:13 *37*

SANCTIFY
S unto me all the firstborn, Ex 13:2 6942
s them to day and to morrow, and Ex 19:10 6942
s themselves, lest the LORD break Ex 19:22 6942
bounds about the mount, and *s* it Ex 19:23 6942
s them, that they may minister Ex 28:41 6942
thou shalt *s* the breast of the Ex 29:27 6942
made, to consecrate and to *s* them Ex 29:33 6942
and thou shalt anoint it, to *s* it Ex 29:36 6942
atonement for the altar, and *s* it Ex 29:37 6942
I will *s* the tabernacle of the Ex 29:44 6942
I will *s* also both Aaron and his Ex 29:44 6942
And thou shalt *s* them, that they Ex 30:29 6942
I am the LORD that doth *s* you Ex 31:13 6942
all his vessels, and *s* the altar Ex 40:10 6942
the laver and his foot, and *s* it Ex 40:11 6942
garments, and anoint him, and *s* him Ex 40:13 6942
the laver and his foot, to *s* them Lev 8:11 6942
head, and anointed him, to *s* him Lev 8:12 6942
ye shall therefore *s* yourselves Lev 11:44 6942
S yourselves therefore, and be ye Lev 20:7 6942
I am the LORD which *s* you Lev 20:8 6942
Thou shalt *s* him therefore Lev 21:8 6942
for I the LORD, which *s* you Lev 21:8 6942
for I the LORD do *s* him Lev 21:15 6942
for I the LORD do *s* them Lev 21:23 6942
I the LORD do *s* them Lev 22:9 6942
for I the LORD do *s* them Lev 22:16 6942
when a man shall *s* his house to Lev 27:14 6942
if a man shall *s* unto the LORD Lev 27:16 6942
If he *s* his field from the year Lev 27:17 6942
But if he *s* his field after the Lev 27:18 6942
if a man *s* unto the LORD a field Lev 27:22 6942
firstling, no man shall *s* it Lev 27:26 6942
S yourselves against to morrow, Num 11:18 6942
to *s* me in the eyes of the Num 20:12 6942
to *s* me at the water before their Num 27:14 6942
Keep the sabbath day to *s* it Deut 5:12 6942
shalt *s* unto the LORD thy God Deut 15:19 6942
unto the people, *S* yourselves Josh 3:5 6942
s the people, and say, *S* Josh 7:13 6942
s yourselves, and come with me to 1Sa 16:5 6942
s yourselves, both ye and your 1Chr 15:12 6942
that he should *s* the most holy 1Chr 23:13 6942
s now yourselves 2Chr 29:5 6942
s the house of the LORD God of 2Chr 29:5 6942
first day of the first month to *s* 2Chr 29:17 6942
to *s* themselves than the priests 2Chr 29:34 6942
clean, to *s* them unto the LORD 2Chr 30:17 6942
s yourselves, and prepare your 2Chr 35:6 6942
the gates, to *s* the sabbath day Neh 13:22 6942
S the LORD of hosts himself Is 8:13 6942
of him, they shall *s* my name Is 29:23 6942
s the Holy One of Jacob, and shall Is 29:23 6942
They that *s* themselves, and purify Is 66:17 6942
that I am the LORD that *s* them Eze 20:12 6942
I will *s* my great name, which was Eze 36:23 6942
know that I the LORD do *s* Israel Eze 37:28 6942
I magnify myself, and *s* myself Eze 38:23 6942
they shall not *s* the people with Eze 44:19 6942
the utter court, to *s* the people Eze 46:20 6942
S ye a fast, call a solemn Joel 1:14 6942
s a fast, call a solemn assembly Joel 2:15 6942
s the congregation, assemble the Joel 2:16 6942
S them through thy truth Jn 17:17 *37*
And for their sakes I *s* myself Jn 17:19 *37*
That he might *s* and cleanse it Eph 5:26 *37*
very God of peace *s* you wholly 1Th 5:23 *37*
that he might *s* the people with Heb 13:12 *37*
But *s* the Lord God in your hearts 1Pet 3:15 *37*

SANCTUARIES
that he profane not my *s* Lev 21:23 4720
bring your *s* unto desolation, and Lev 26:31 4720
into the *s* of the LORD's house Jer 51:51 4720
Thou hast defiled thy *s* by the Eze 28:18 4720
the *s* of Israel shall be laid Amos 7:9 4720

SANCTUARY
for thee to dwell in, in the *S* Ex 15:17 4720
And let them make me a *s* Ex 25:8 4720
shekel after the shekel of the *s* Ex 30:13 6944
after the shekel of the *s* Ex 30:24 6944
of work for the service of the *s* Ex 36:1 6944
the work of the service of the *s* Ex 36:3 6944
wrought all the work of the *s* Ex 36:4 6944
work for the offering of the *s* Ex 36:6 6944
after the shekel of the *s* Ex 38:24 6944
after the shekel of the *s* Ex 38:25 6944
shekel, after the shekel of the *s* Ex 38:26 6944
were cast the sockets of the *s* Ex 38:27 6944
LORD, before the vail of the *s* Lev 4:6 6944
silver, after the shekel of the *s* Lev 5:15 6944
from before the *s* out of the camp Lev 10:4 6944
thing, nor come into the *s* Lev 12:4 4720
make an atonement for the holy *s* Lev 16:33 4720
my sabbaths, and reverence my *s* Lev 19:30 4720
seed unto Molech, to defile my *s* Lev 20:3 4720
Neither shall he go out of the *s* Lev 21:12 4720
nor profane the *s* of his God Lev 21:12 4720
my sabbaths, and reverence my *s* Lev 26:2 4720
silver, after the shekel of the *s* Lev 27:3 6944
according to the shekel of the *s* Lev 27:25 6944
keeping the charge of the *s* Num 3:28 6944
the vessels of the *s* wherewith Num 3:31 6944
that keep the charge of the *s* Num 3:32 6944
keeping the charge of the *s* for Num 3:38 4720
of the *s* shalt thou take them Num 3:47 6944
after the shekel of the *s* Num 3:50 6944
wherewith they minister in the *s* Num 4:12 6944
made an end of covering the *s* Num 4:15 6944
and all the vessels of the *s* Num 4:15 6944
of all that therein is, in the *s* Num 4:16 6944
because the service of the *s* Num 7:9 6944
after the shekel of the *s* Num 7:13 6944
after the shekel of the *s* Num 7:19 6944
after the shekel of the *s* Num 7:25 6944
after the shekel of the *s* Num 7:31 6944
after the shekel of the *s* Num 7:37 6944
after the shekel of the *s* Num 7:43 6944
after the shekel of the *s* Num 7:49 6944
after the shekel of the *s* Num 7:55 6944
after the shekel of the *s* Num 7:61 6944
after the shekel of the *s* Num 7:67 6944
after the shekel of the *s* Num 7:73 6944
after the shekel of the *s* Num 7:79 6944
after the shekel of the *s* Num 7:85 6944
apiece, after the shekel of the *s* Num 7:86 6944
of Israel come nigh unto the *s* Num 8:19 6944
set forward, bearing the *s* Num 10:21 4720
shall bear the iniquity of the *s* Num 18:1 4720
come nigh the vessels of the *s* Num 18:3 6944
ye shall keep the charge of the *s* Num 18:5 6944
after the shekel of the *s* Num 18:16 6944
he hath defiled the *s* of the LORD Num 19:20 4720
that was by the *s* of the LORD Josh 24:26 4720
and all the instruments of the *s* 1Chr 9:29 6944
build ye the *s* of the LORD God, 1Chr 22:19 4720
for the governors of the *s* 1Chr 24:5 6944
thee to build an house for the *s* 1Chr 28:10 4720
have built thee a *s* therein for 2Chr 20:8 4720
go out of the *s* 2Chr 26:18 4720
for the kingdom, and for the *s* 2Chr 29:21 4720
the LORD, and enter into his *s* 2Chr 30:8 4720
to the purification of the *s* 2Chr 30:19 6944
the sword in the house of their *s* 2Chr 36:17 4720
where are the vessels of the *s* Neh 10:39 4720
Send thee help from the *s* Ps 20:2 6944
so as I have seen thee in the *s* Ps 63:2 6944
of my God, my King, in the *s* Ps 68:24 6944
Until I went into the *s* of God Ps 73:17 4720
enemy hath done wickedly in the *s* Ps 74:3 6944
They have cast fire into thy *s* Ps 74:7 4720
Thy way, O God, is in the *s* Ps 77:13 6944
them to the border of his *s* Ps 78:54 6944
he built his *s* like high palaces, Ps 78:69 4720
strength and beauty are in his *s* Ps 96:6 4720
down from the height of his *s* Ps 102:19 6944
Judah was his *s*, and Israel his Ps 114:2 6944
Lift up your hands in the *s* Ps 134:2 6944
Praise God in his *s* Ps 150:1 6944
And he shall be for a *s* Is 8:14 4720
he shall come to his *s* to pray Is 16:12 4720
profaned the princes of the *s* Is 43:28 6944
to beautify the place of my *s* Is 60:13 4720
have trodden down thy *s* Is 63:18 4720
beginning is the place of our *s* Jer 17:12 4720
the heathen entered into her *s* Lam 1:10 4720
his altar, he hath abhorred his *s* Lam 2:7 4720
be slain in the *s* of the Lord Lam 2:20 4720
the stones of the *s* are poured Lam 4:1 6944
because thou hast defiled my *s* Eze 5:11 4720
I should go far off from my *s* Eze 8:6 4720
and begin at my *s* Eze 9:6 4720
s in the countries where they Eze 11:16 4720
have defiled my *s* in the same day Eze 23:38 4720
same day into my *s* to profane it Eze 23:39 4720
Behold, I will profane my *s* Eze 24:21 4720
thou saidst, Aha, against my *s* Eze 25:3 4720
will set my *s* in the midst of Eze 37:26 4720
when my *s* shall be in the midst Eze 37:28 4720
squared, and the face of the *s* Eze 41:21 6944
the temple and the *s* had two doors Eze 41:23 6944
make a separation between the *s* Eze 42:20 6944
place of the house, without the *s* Eze 43:21 4720
s which looketh toward the east Eze 44:1 4720
with every going forth of the *s* Eze 44:5 4720
have brought into my *s* strangers Eze 44:7
in flesh, to be in my *s*, to Eze 44:7 4720
my charge in my *s* for yourselves Eze 44:8 4720
in flesh, shall enter into my *s* Eze 44:9 4720
they shall be ministers in my *s* Eze 44:11 4720
that kept the charge of my *s* when Eze 44:15 4720
They shall enter into my *s* Eze 44:16 4720
the day that he goeth into the *s* Eze 44:27 6944
inner court, to minister in the *s* Eze 44:27 6944
for the *s* five hundred in length Eze 45:2 6944
and in it shall be the *s* and the Eze 45:3 4720
priests the ministers of the *s* Eze 45:4 4720
and an holy place for the *s* Eze 45:4 4720
without blemish, and cleanse the *s* Eze 45:18 4720
they they issued out of the *s* Eze 47:12 4720
the *s* shall be in the midst of it Eze 48:8 4720
the *s* of the LORD shall be in the Eze 48:10 4720
the *s* of the house shall be in Eze 48:21 4720
the place of his *s* was cast down Dan 8:11 4720
of desolation, to give both the *s* Dan 8:13 6944
then shall the *s* be cleansed Dan 8:14 6944
shine upon thy *s* that is desolate Dan 9:17 4720
shall destroy the city and the *s* Dan 9:26 6944
shall pollute the *s* of strength Dan 11:31 4720
her priests have polluted the *s* Zeph 3:4 6944
A minister of the *s*, and of the Heb 8:2 *39*
of divine service, and a worldly *s* Heb 9:1 *39*
which is called the *s* Heb 9:2 *39*
the *s* by the high priest for sin Heb 13:11 *39*

SAND
as the *s* which is upon the sea Gen 22:17 2344
make thy seed as the *s* of the sea Gen 32:12 2344
gathered corn as the *s* of the sea Gen 41:49 2344

the Egyptian, and hid him in the *s* Ex 2:12 2344
and of treasures hid in the *s* Deut 33:19 2344
even as the *s* that is upon the Josh 11:4 2344
as the *s* by the sea side for Judg 7:12 2344
people as the *s* which is on the 1Sa 13:5 2344
as the *s* that is by the sea for 2Sa 17:11 2344
as the *s* which is by the sea in 1Kin 4:20 2344
even as the *s* that is on the sea 1Kin 4:29 2344
be heavier than the *s* of the sea Job 6:3 2344
I shall multiply my days as the *s* Job 29:18 2344
fowls like as the *s* of the sea Ps 78:27 2344
are more in number than the *s* Ps 139:18 2344
stone is heavy, and the *s* weighty Prov 27:3 2344
Israel be as the *s* of the sea Is 10:22 2344
Thy seed also had been as the *s* Is 48:19 2344
which have placed the *s* for the Jer 5:22 2344
to me above the *s* of the seas Jer 15:8 2344
neither the *s* of the sea measured Jer 33:22 2344
shall be as the *s* of the sea Hos 1:10 2344
gather the captivity as the *s* Hab 1:9 2344
which built his house upon the *s* Mt 7:26 *285*
of Israel be as the *s* of the sea Rom 9:27 *285*
as the *s* which is by the sea Heb 11:12 *285*
And I stood upon the *s* of the sea Rev 13:1 *285*
of whom is as the *s* of the sea Rev 20:8 *285*

SANDALS
But be shod with *s* Mk 6:9 *4547*
Gird thyself, and bind on thy *s* Acts 12:8 *4547*

SANG
Then *s* Moses and the children of Ex 15:1 7891
Then Israel *s* this song, Spring Num 21:17 7891
Then *s* Deborah and Barak the son Judg 5:1 7891
of whom they *s* one to another in 1Sa 29:5 6030
worshipped, and the singers *s* 2Chr 29:28 7891
they *s* praises with gladness, and 2Chr 29:30
they *s* together by course in Ezr 3:11 6030
And the singers *s* loud, with Neh 12:42 7891
When the morning stars *s* together Job 38:7 7442
which he *s* unto the LORD, Ps 7:*t* 7891
they *s* his praise Ps 106:12 7891
prayed, and *s* praises unto God Acts 16:25 *5214*

SANK
they *s* into the bottom as a stone Ex 15:5 3381
they *s* as lead in the mighty Ex 15:10 6749

SANSANNAH (*san-san'-nah*) *A city in Judah.*
And Ziklag, and Madmannah, and *S* Josh 15:31 5578

SAP
trees of the LORD are full of *s* Ps 104:16

SAPH (*saf*) See SIPHAI. *A descendant of Rapha.*
Sibbechai the Hushathite slew *S* 2Sa 21:18 5593

SAPHIR (*sa'-fur*) *A city in Ephraim.*
ye away, thou inhabitant of *S* Mic 1:11 8208

SAPPHIRA (*saf-fi'-rah*) *Wife of Ananias.*
Ananias, with *S* his wife, sold a Acts 5:1 *4551*

SAPPHIRE
it were a paved work of a *s* stone Ex 24:10 5601
row shall be an emerald, a *s* Ex 28:18 5601
the second row, an emerald, a *s* Ex 39:11 5601
with the precious onyx, or the *s* Job 28:16 5601
rubies, their polishing was of *s* Lam 4:7 5601
as the appearance of a *s* stone Eze 1:26 5601
over them as it were a *s* stone Eze 10:1 5601
the onyx, and the jasper, the *s* Eze 28:13 5601
the second, *s* Rev 21:19 *4552*

SAPPHIRES
stones of it are the place of *s* Job 28:6 5601
as bright ivory overlaid with *s* Song 5:14 5601
and lay thy foundations with *s* Is 54:11 5601

SARA (*sa'-rah*) See SARAH. *Greek form of Sarah.*
Through faith also *S* herself Heb 11:11 *4564*

SARAH (*sa'-rah*) See SARA, SARAH'S, SARAI, SE-RAH.
1. Wife of Abraham.
Sarai, but *S* shall her name be Gen 17:15 8283
and shall *S*, that is ninety years Gen 17:17 8283
S thy wife shall bear thee a son Gen 17:19 8283
which *S* shall bear unto thee at Gen 17:21 8283
hastened into the tent unto *S* Gen 18:6 8283
unto him, Where is *S* thy wife Gen 18:9 8283
S thy wife shall have a son Gen 18:10 8283
S heard it in the tent door, Gen 18:10 8283
S were old and well stricken in Gen 18:11 8283
it ceased to be with *S* after the Gen 18:11 8283
Therefore *S* laughed within Gen 18:12 8283
Abraham, Wherefore did *S* laugh Gen 18:13 8283
of life, and *S* shall have a son Gen 18:14 8283
Then *S* denied, saying, I laughed Gen 18:15 8283
And Abraham said of *S* his wife Gen 20:2 8283
king of Gerar sent, and took *S* Gen 20:2 8283
and restored him *S* his wife Gen 20:14 8283
unto *S* he said, Behold, I have Gen 20:16 8283
because of *S* Abraham's wife Gen 20:18 8283
the LORD visited *S* as he had said Gen 21:1 8283
LORD did unto *S* as he had spoken Gen 21:1 8283
For *S* conceived, and bare Abraham Gen 21:2 8283
whom *S* bare to him, Isaac Gen 21:3 8283
S said, God hath made me to laugh Gen 21:6 8283
that *S* should have given children Gen 21:7 8283
S saw the son of Hagar the Gen 21:9 8283
in all that *S* hath said unto thee Gen 21:12 8283
S was an hundred and seven and Gen 23:1 8283
were the years of the life of *S* Gen 23:1 8283
And *S* died in Kirjath-arba Gen 23:2 8283
and Abraham came to mourn for *S* Gen 23:2 8283
Abraham buried *S* his wife in the Gen 23:19 8283
S my master's wife bare a son to Gen 24:36 8283
was Abraham buried, and *S* his wife Gen 25:10 8283
they buried Abraham and *S* his wife Gen 49:31 8283
father, and unto *S* that bare you Is 51:2 8283
I come, and *S* shall have a son Rom 9:9 *4564*
Even as *S* obeyed Abraham, calling 1Pet 3:6 *4564*
2. A daughter of Asher.
of the daughter of Asher was *S* Num 26:46 8294

SARAH'S (*sa'-rahs*)
her into his mother *S* tent Gen 24:67 8283
S handmaid, bare unto Abraham Gen 25:12 8283
yet the deadness of *S* womb Rom 4:19 *4564*

SARAI (*sa'-rahee*) See SARAH, SARAI'S. *The original name of Sarah.*
the name of Abram's wife was *S* Gen 11:29 8297
But *S* was barren Gen 11:30 8297
S his daughter in law, his son Gen 11:31 8297
And Abram took *S* his wife, and Lot Gen 12:5 8297
that he said unto *S* his wife Gen 12:11 8297
plagues because of *S* Abram's wife Gen 12:17 8297
Now *S* Abram's wife bare him no Gen 16:1 8297
S said unto Abram, Behold now, Gen 16:2 8297
Abram hearkened to the voice of *S* Gen 16:2 8297
S Abram's wife took Hagar her Gen 16:3 8297
S said unto Abram, My wrong be Gen 16:5 8297
But Abram said unto *S*, Behold, Gen 16:6 8297
when *S* dealt hardly with her, she Gen 16:6 8297
from the face of my mistress *S* Gen 16:8 8297
As for *S* thy wife, thou shalt not Gen 17:15 8297
thou shalt not call her name *S* Gen 17:15 8297

SARAI'S (*sa'-rahees*)
S maid, whence camest thou Gen 16:8 8297

SARAPH (*sa'-raf*) *A descendant of Shelah.*
men of Chozeba, and Joash, and *S* 1Chr 4:22 8315

SARDINE
upon like a jasper and a *s* stone Rev 4:3 *4555*

SARDIS (*sar'-dis*) *A city in Lydia in Asia Minor.*
and unto Thyatira, and unto *S* Rev 1:11 *4554*
angel of the church in *S* write Rev 3:1 *4554*
in *S* which have not defiled their Rev 3:4 *4554*

SARDITES (*sar'-dites*) *Descendants of Sered.*
of Sered, the family of the *S* Num 26:26 5625

SARDIUS
the first row shall be a *s* Ex 28:17 124
the first row was a *s*, a topaz, Ex 39:10 124
stone was thy covering, the *s* Eze 28:13 124
the sixth, *s* Rev 21:20 *4556*

SARDONYX
The fifth, *s* Rev 21:20 *4557*

SAREPTA (*sa-rep'-tah*) See ZAREPHATH. *A city near Sidon.*
them was Elias sent, save unto *S* Lk 4:26 *4558*

SARGON (*sar'-gon*) *An Assyrian king.*
(when *S* the king of Assyria sent Is 20:1 5623

SARID (*sa'-rid*) *A city in Zebulun.*
of their inheritance was unto *S* Josh 19:10 8301
turned from *S* eastward toward the Josh 19:12 8301

SARON (*sa'-ron*) See SHARON. *The area between Joppa and Caesarea.*
S saw him, and turned to the Lord Acts 9:35 *4565*

SARSECHIM (*sar'-se-kim*) *A prince of Babylon.*
Nergal-sharezer, Samgar-nebo, *S* Jer 39:3 8310

SAR-SEKIM See SARSECHIM.

SARUCH (*sa'-ruk*) See SERUG. *Father of Nahor; an ancestor of Jesus.*
Which was the son of *S*, which was Lk 3:35 *4562*

SAT
he *s* in the tent door in the heat Gen 18:1 3427
Lot *s* in the gate of Sodom Gen 19:1 3427
s her down over against him a Gen 21:16 3427
she *s* over against him, and lift Gen 21:16 3427
camel's furniture, and *s* upon them Gen 31:34 3427
And they *s* down to eat bread Gen 37:25 3427
s in an open place, which is by Gen 38:14 3427
they *s* before him, the firstborn Gen 43:33 3427
himself, and *s* upon the bed Gen 48:2 3427
and he *s* down by a well Ex 2:15 3427
that *s* on his throne unto the Ex 12:29 3427
when we *s* by the flesh pots, and Ex 16:3 3427
put it under him, and he *s* thereon Ex 17:12 3427
that Moses *s* to judge the people Ex 18:13 3427
the people *s* down to eat and to Ex 32:6 3427
s that hath the issue shall wash Lev 15:6 3427
she *s* upon shall wash his clothes Lev 15:22 3427
and they *s* down at thy feet Deut 33:3 8497
s under an oak which was in Judg 6:11 3427
the woman as she *s* in the field Judg 13:9 3427
and they *s* down, and did eat and Judg 19:6 3427
he *s* him down in a street of the Judg 19:15 3427
s there before the LORD, and Judg 20:26 3427
And she *s* beside the reapers Ruth 2:14 3427
to the gate, and *s* him down there Ruth 4:1 3427
And he turned aside, and *s* down Ruth 4:1 3427
And they *s* down Ruth 4:2 3427
Now Eli the priest *s* upon a seat 1Sa 1:9 3427
Eli *s* upon a seat by the wayside 1Sa 4:13 3427
as he *s* in his house with his 1Sa 19:9 3427
the king *s* him down to eat meat 1Sa 20:24 3427
the king *s* upon his seat, as at 1Sa 20:25 3427
Abner *s* by Saul's side, and 1Sa 20:25 3427
from the earth, and *s* upon the bed 1Sa 28:23 3427
and they *s* down, the one on the 2Sa 2:13 3427
when the king *s* in his house 2Sa 7:1 3427
s before the LORD, and he said, 2Sa 7:18 3427
David *s* between the two gates 2Sa 18:24 3427
the king arose, and *s* in the gate 2Sa 19:8 3427
The Tachmonite that *s* in the seat 2Sa 23:8 3427
Then *s* Solomon upon the throne of 1Kin 2:12 3427
s down on his throne, and caused a 1Kin 2:19 3427
and she *s* on his right hand 1Kin 2:19 3427
as they *s* at the table, that the 1Kin 13:20 3427
as soon as he *s* on his throne 1Kin 16:11 3427
s down under a juniper tree 1Kin 19:4 3427
of Belial, and *s* before him 1Kin 21:13 3427
of Judah *s* each on his throne 1Kin 22:10 3427
he *s* on the top of an hill 2Kin 1:9 3427
he *s* on her knees till noon, and 2Kin 4:20 3427
But Elisha *s* in his house, and the 2Kin 6:32 3427
house, and the elders *s* with him 2Kin 6:32 3427
he *s* on the throne of the kings 2Kin 11:19 3427
Jeroboam *s* upon his throne 2Kin 13:13 3427
as David *s* in his house, that 1Chr 17:1 3427
s before the LORD, and said, Who 1Chr 17:16 3427
Then Solomon *s* on the throne of 1Chr 29:23 3427
Jehoshaphat king of Judah *s* 2Chr 18:9 3427
they *s* in a void place at the 2Chr 18:9 3427
of my beard, and *s* down astonied Ezr 9:3 3427
I *s* astonied until the evening Ezr 9:4 3427
all the people *s* in the street of Ezr 10:9 3427
s down in the first day of the Ezr 10:16 3427
heard these words, that I *s* down Neh 1:4 3427
booths, and *s* under the booths Neh 8:17 3427
when the king Ahasuerus *s* on the Est 1:2 3427
which *s* the first in the kingdom Est 1:14 3427
then Mordecai *s* in the king's Est 2:19 3427
while Mordecai *s* in the king's Est 2:21 3427
the king and Haman *s* down to drink Est 3:15 3427
the king *s* upon his royal throne Est 5:1 3427
he *s* down among the ashes Job 2:8 3427
So they *s* down with him upon the Job 2:13 3427
s chief, and dwelt as a king in Job 29:25 3427
I have not *s* with vain persons, Ps 26:4 3427
of Babylon, there we *s* down Ps 137:1 3427
I *s* down under his shadow with Song 2:3 3427
In the ways hast thou *s* for them Jer 3:2 3427
I *s* not in the assembly of the Jer 15:17 3427
I *s* alone because of thy hand Jer 15:17 3427
s down in the entry of the new Jer 26:10 3427
before all the Jews that *s* in the Jer 32:12 3427
and, lo, all the princes *s* there Jer 36:12 3427
Now the king *s* in the winterhouse Jer 36:22 3427
s in the middle gate, even Jer 39:3 3427
I *s* where they *s*, and remained Eze 3:15 3427
of Chebar, and I *s* where they *s* Eze 3:15 3427
as I *s* in mine house, and the Eze 8:1 3427
the elders of Judah *s* before me Eze 8:1 3427
there *s* women weeping for Tammuz Eze 8:14 3427
of Israel unto me, and *s* before me Eze 14:1 3427
of the LORD, and *s* before me Eze 20:1 3427
but Daniel *s* in the gate of the Dan 2:49
him with sackcloth, and *s* in ashes Jonah 3:6 3427
s on the east side of the city, Jonah 4:5 3427
s under it in the shadow, till he Jonah 4:5 3427
The people which *s* in darkness Mt 4:16 *2521*
and to them which *s* in the region Mt 4:16 *2521*
as Jesus *s* at meat in the house, Mt 9:10 *345*
s down with him and his disciples Mt 9:10 *4873*
the house, and *s* by the sea side Mt 13:1 *2521*
so that he went into a ship, and *s* Mt 13:2 *2521*
s down, and gathered the good into Mt 13:48 *2523*
them which *s* with him at meat, he Mt 14:9 *4873*
into a mountain, and *s* down there Mt 15:29 *2521*
as he *s* upon the mount of Olives, Mt 24:3 *2521*
it on his head, as he *s* at meat Mt 26:7 *345*
he *s* down with the twelve Mt 26:20 *345*
I *s* daily with you teaching in Mt 26:55 *2516*
s with the servants, to see the Mt 26:58 *2521*
Now Peter *s* without in the palace Mt 26:69 *2521*
stone from the door, and *s* upon it Mt 28:2 *2521*
as Jesus *s* at meat in his house, Mk 2:15 *2621*
sinners *s* also together with Mk 2:15 *4873*
And the multitude *s* about him Mk 3:32 *2521*
about on them which *s* about him Mk 3:34 *2521*
into a ship, and *s* in the sea Mk 4:1 *2521*
Herod and them that *s* with him Mk 6:22 *4873*
for their sakes which *s* with him Mk 6:26 *4873*
they *s* down in ranks, by hundreds Mk 6:40 *377*
he *s* down, and called the twelve, Mk 9:35 *2523*
s by the highway side begging Mk 10:46 *2521*
a colt tied, whereon never man *s* Mk 11:2 *2523*
and he *s* upon him Mk 11:7 *2523*
Jesus *s* over against the treasury Mk 12:41 *2523*
as he *s* upon the mount of Olives Mk 13:3 *2521*
as he *s* at meat, there came a Mk 14:3 *2621*
And as they *s* and did eat, Jesus Mk 14:18 *345*
he *s* with the servants, and warmed Mk 14:54 *4775*
unto the eleven as they *s* at meat Mk 16:14 *345*
s on the right hand of God Mk 16:19 *2523*
again to the minister, and *s* down Lk 4:20 *2523*
he *s* down, and taught the people Lk 5:3 *2523*
of others that *s* down with them Lk 5:29 *2621*
And he that was dead *s* up, and Lk 7:15 *339*
house, and *s* down to meat Lk 7:36 *347*
when she knew that Jesus *s* at Lk 7:37 *345*
they that *s* at meat with him Lk 7:49 *4873*
which also *s* at Jesus' feet, and Lk 10:39 *3869*
and he went in, and *s* down to meat Lk 11:37 *377*
when one of them that *s* at meat Lk 14:15 *4873*
a certain blind man *s* by the way Lk 18:35 *2521*
tied, whereon yet never man *s* Lk 19:30 *2523*
he *s* down, and the twelve apostles Lk 22:14 *377*
together, Peter *s* down among them Lk 22:55 *2521*
beheld him as he *s* by the fire Lk 22:56 *2521*
as he *s* at meat with them, he Lk 24:30 *2625*
his journey, *s* thus on the well Jn 4:6 *2516*
there he *s* with his disciples Jn 6:3 *2521*
So the men *s* down, in number Jn 6:10 *377*
he *s* down, and taught them Jn 8:2 *2523*
said, Is not this he that *s* Jn 9:8 *2521*
but Mary *s* still in the house Jn 11:20 *2516*

them that s at the table with him Jn 12:2 4873
had found a young ass, s thereon Jn 12:14 2523
s down in the judgment seat in a Jn 19:13 2523
fire, and it s upon each of them Acts 2:3 2523
s for alms at the Beautiful gate Acts 3:10 2521
all that s in the council, Acts 6:15 2516
and when she saw Peter, she s up Acts 9:40 339
s upon his throne, and made an Acts 12:21 2523
on the sabbath day, and s down Acts 13:14 2523
there s a certain man at Lystra, Acts 14:8 2521
we s down, and spake unto the Acts 16:13 2523
there s in a window a certain Acts 20:9 2521
morrow I s on the judgment seat Acts 25:17 2523
Bernice, and they that s with them Acts 26:30 4775
The people s down to eat and drink 1Cor 10:7 2523
s down on the right hand of the Heb 1:3 2523
s down on the right hand of God Heb 10:12 2523
in heaven, and one s on the throne Rev 4:2 2521
he that s was to look upon like a Rev 4:3 2521
to him that s on the throne Rev 4:9 2521
before him that s on the throne Rev 4:10 2521
s on the throne a book written Rev 5:1 2521
of him that s upon the throne Rev 5:7 2521
he that s on him had a bow Rev 6:2 2521
power was given to him that s Rev 6:4 2521
he that s on him had a pair of Rev 6:5 2521
his name that s on him was Death, Rev 6:8 2521
vision, and them that s on them Rev 9:17 2521
which s before God on their seats Rev 11:16 2521
upon the cloud one s like unto Rev 14:14 2521
voice to him that s on the cloud Rev 14:15 2521
he that s on the cloud thrust in Rev 14:16 2521
God that s on the throne, saying, Rev 19:4 2521
he that s upon him was called Rev 19:11 2521
against him that s on the horse Rev 19:19 2521
of him that s upon the horse Rev 19:21 2521
they s upon them, and judgment was Rev 20:4 2523
white throne, and him that s on it Rev 20:11 2521
he that s upon the throne said, Rev 21:5 2521

SATAN (*sa'-tun*) *The adversary.*
S stood up against Israel, and 1Chr 21:1 7854
LORD, and S came also among them Job 1:6 7854
And the LORD said unto S, Whence Job 1:7 7854
Then S answered the LORD, and said Job 1:7 7854
And the LORD said unto S, Hast Job 1:8 7854
Then S answered the LORD, and said Job 1:9 7854
And the LORD said unto S, Behold, Job 1:12 7854
So S went forth from the presence Job 1:12 7854
S came also among them to present Job 2:1 7854
And the LORD said unto S, From Job 2:2 7854
S answered the LORD, and said, Job 2:2 7854
And the LORD said unto S, Hast Job 2:3 7854
S answered the LORD, and said, Job 2:4 7854
And the LORD said unto S, Behold, Job 2:6 7854
So went S forth from the presence Job 2:7 7854
let S stand at his right hand Ps 109:6 7854
S standing at his right hand to Zec 3:1 7854
S, The LORD rebuke thee, O S Zec 3:2 7854
Jesus unto him, Get thee hence, S Mt 4:10 4567
And if S cast out S, he is Mt 12:26 4567
unto Peter, Get thee behind me, S Mt 16:23 4567
forty days, tempted of S Mk 1:13 4567
How can S cast out S Mk 3:23 4567
if S rise up against himself, and Mk 3:26 4567
S cometh immediately, and taketh Mk 4:15 4567
saying, Get thee behind me, S Mk 8:33 4567
unto him, Get thee behind me, S Lk 4:8 4567
I beheld S as lightning fall from Lk 10:18 4567
If S also be divided against Lk 11:18 4567
whom S hath bound, lo, these Lk 13:16 4567
Then entered S into Judas Lk 22:3 4567
S hath desired to have you, that Lk 22:31 4567
after the sop S entered into him Jn 13:27 4567
why hath S filled thine heart to Acts 5:3 4567
and from the power of S unto God Acts 26:18 4567
bruise S under your feet shortly Rom 16:20 4567
unto S for the destruction of the 1Cor 5:5 4567
that S tempt you not for your 1Cor 7:5 4567
Lest S should get an advantage of 2Cor 2:11 4567
for S himself is transformed into 2Cor 11:14 4567
the messenger of S to buffet me 2Cor 12:7 4567
but S hindered us 1Th 2:18 4567
the working of S with all power 2Th 2:9 4567
whom I have delivered unto S 1Ti 1:20 4567
are already turned aside after S 1Ti 5:15 4567
not, but are the synagogue of S Rev 2:9 4567
slain among you, where S dwelleth Rev 2:13 4567
have not known the depths of S Rev 2:24 4567
make them of the synagogue of S Rev 3:9 4567
serpent, called the Devil, and S Rev 12:9 4567
serpent, which is the Devil, and S Rev 20:2 4567
S shall be loosed out of his Rev 20:7 4567

SATAN'S (*sa'-tuns*)
dwellest, even where S seat is Rev 2:13 4567

SATEST
thou s in the throne judging Ps 9:4 3427
s upon a stately bed, and a table Eze 23:41 3427

SATIATE
I will s the soul of the priests Jer 31:14 7301
shall devour, and it shall be s Jer 46:10 7646

SATIATED
For I have s the weary soul, and I Jer 31:25 7301

SATISFACTION
Moreover ye shall take no s for Num 35:31 3724
ye shall take no s for him that Num 35:32 3724

SATISFIED
my lust shall be s upon them Ex 15:9 4390
and ye shall eat, and not be s Lev 26:26 7646
shall come, and shall eat and be s Deut 14:29 7646
s with favour, and full with the Deut 33:23 7649
God, and are not s with my flesh Job 19:22 7646
shall not be s with bread Job 27:14 7646
we cannot be s Job 31:31 7646
I shall be s, when I awake, with Ps 17:15 7646
The meek shall eat and be s Ps 22:26 7646
They shall be abundantly s with Ps 36:8 7301
days of famine they shall be s Ps 37:19 7646
meat, and grudge if they be not s Ps 59:15 7646
My soul shall be s as with marrow Ps 63:5 7646
we shall be s with the goodness Ps 65:4 7646
of the rock should I have s thee Ps 81:16 7649
the earth is s with the fruit of Ps 104:13 7646
his land shall be s with bread Prov 12:11 7646
A man shall be s with good by the Prov 12:14 7646
good man shall be s from himself Prov 14:14
A man's belly shall be s with the Prov 18:20 7646
and he that hath it shall abide s Prov 19:23 7649
and thou shalt be s with bread Prov 20:13 7646
so the eyes of man are never s Prov 27:20 7646
are three things that are never s Prov 30:15 7646
the eye is not s with seeing Eccl 1:8 7646
neither is his eye s with riches Eccl 4:8 7646
silver shall not be s with silver Eccl 5:10 7646
left hand, and they shall not be s Is 9:20 7646
he roasteth roast, and is s Is 44:16 7646
of his soul, and shall be s Is 53:11 7646
be s with the breasts of her Is 66:11 7646
shall be s with my goodness Jer 31:14 7646
all that spoil her shall be s Jer 50:10 7646
his soul shall be s upon mount Jer 50:19 7646
the Assyrians, to be s with bread Lam 5:6 7646
them, and yet couldest not be s Eze 16:28 7646
and yet thou wast not s herewith Eze 16:29 7646
oil, and ye shall be s therewith Joel 2:19 7646
ye shall eat in plenty, and be s Joel 2:26 7646
but they were not s Amos 4:8 7646
Thou shalt eat, but not be s Mic 6:14 7646
and is as death, and cannot be s Hab 2:5 7646

SATISFIEST
s the desire of every living Ps 145:16 7646

SATISFIETH
Who s thy mouth with good things Ps 103:5 7646
For he s the longing soul, and Ps 107:9 7646
your labour for that which s not Is 55:2 7654

SATISFY
To s the desolate and waste ground Job 38:27 7646
O s us early with thy mercy Ps 90:14 7646
With long life will I s him Ps 91:16 7646
I will s her poor with bread Ps 132:15 7646
let her breasts s thee at all Prov 5:19 7301
if he steal to s his soul when he Prov 6:30 4390
hungry, and s the afflicted soul Is 58:10 7646
s thy soul in drought, and make Is 58:11 7646
they shall not s their souls Eze 7:19 7646
From whence can a man s these men Mk 8:4 5526

SATISFYING
eateth to the s of his soul Prov 13:25 7648
any honour to the s of the flesh Col 2:23 4140

SATISIFED
s them with the bread of heaven Ps 105:40 7649

SATYR
the s shall cry to his fellow Is 34:14 8163

SATYRS
there, and s shall dance there Is 13:21 8163

SAUL (*sawl*) See PAUL, SAUL'S, SHAUL.
I. The first king of Israel.
And he had a son, whose name was S 1Sa 9:2 7586
And Kish said to S his son 1Sa 9:3 7586
S said to his servant that was 1Sa 9:5 7586
Then said S to his servant, But, 1Sa 9:7 7586
And the servant answered S again 1Sa 9:8 7586
Then said S to his servant, Well 1Sa 9:10 7586
in his ear a day before S came 1Sa 9:15 7586
And when Samuel saw S, the LORD 1Sa 9:17 7586
Then S drew near to Samuel in the 1Sa 9:18 7586
And Samuel answered S, and said, I 1Sa 9:19 7586
S answered and said, Am not I a 1Sa 9:21 7586
And Samuel took S and his servant, 1Sa 9:22 7586
was upon it, and set it before S 1Sa 9:24 7586
So S did eat with Samuel that day 1Sa 9:24 7586
Samuel communed with S upon the 1Sa 9:25 7586
that Samuel called S to the top 1Sa 9:26 7586
S arose, and they went out both of 1Sa 9:26 7586
end of the city, Samuel said to S 1Sa 9:27 7586
Is S also among the prophets 1Sa 10:11 7586
Is S also among the prophets 1Sa 10:12 7586
S said unto his uncle, He told us 1Sa 10:16 7586
S the son of Kish was taken 1Sa 10:21 7586
S also went home to Gibeah 1Sa 10:26 7586
the messengers to Gibeah of S 1Sa 11:4 7586
S came after the herd out of the 1Sa 11:5 7586
S said, What aileth the people 1Sa 11:5 7586
S when he heard those tidings 1Sa 11:6 7586
cometh not forth after S and after 1Sa 11:7 7586
that S put the people in three 1Sa 11:11 7586
that said, Shall S reign over us 1Sa 11:12 7586
S said, There shall not a man be 1Sa 11:13 7586
there they made S king before the 1Sa 11:15 7586
and there S and all the men of 1Sa 11:15 7586
S reigned one year 1Sa 13:1 7586
S chose him three thousand men of 1Sa 13:2 7586
thousand were with S in Michmash 1Sa 13:2 7586
S blew the trumpet throughout all 1Sa 13:3 7586
all Israel heard say that S had 1Sa 13:4 7586
called together after S to Gilgal 1Sa 13:4 7586
As for S, he was yet in Gilgal, 1Sa 13:7 7586
S said, Bring hither a burnt 1Sa 13:9 7586
S went out to meet him, that he 1Sa 13:10 7586
S said, Because I saw that the 1Sa 13:11 7586
And Samuel said to S, Thou hast 1Sa 13:13 7586
S numbered the people that were 1Sa 13:15 7586
And S, and Jonathan his son, and the 1Sa 13:16 7586
of the people that were with S 1Sa 13:22 7586
but with S and with Jonathan his 1Sa 13:22 7586
that Jonathan the son of S said 1Sa 14:1 7586
S tarried in the uttermost part 1Sa 14:2 7586
the watchmen of S in Gibeah of 1Sa 14:16 7586
Then said S unto the people that 1Sa 14:17 7586
S said unto Ahiah, Bring hither 1Sa 14:18 7586
while S talked unto the priest, 1Sa 14:19 7586
S said unto the priest, Withdraw 1Sa 14:19 7586
And S and all the people that were 1Sa 14:20 7586
the Israelites that were with S 1Sa 14:21 7586
for S had adjured the people, 1Sa 14:24 7586
Then they told S, saying, Behold, 1Sa 14:33 7586
S said, Disperse yourselves among 1Sa 14:34 7586
S built an altar unto the LORD 1Sa 14:35 7586
S said, Let us go down after the 1Sa 14:36 7586
S asked counsel of God, Shall I 1Sa 14:37 7586
S said, Draw ye near hither, all 1Sa 14:38 7586
And the people said unto S 1Sa 14:40 7586
Therefore S said unto the LORD 1Sa 14:41 7586
And S and Jonathan were taken 1Sa 14:41 7586
S said, Cast lots between me and 1Sa 14:42 7586
Then S said to Jonathan, Tell me 1Sa 14:43 7586
S answered, God do so and more 1Sa 14:44 7586
And the people said unto S 1Sa 14:45 7586
Then S went up from following the 1Sa 14:46 7586
So S took the kingdom over Israel 1Sa 14:47 7586
Now the sons of S were Jonathan 1Sa 14:49 7586
And Kish was the father of S 1Sa 14:51 7586
the Philistines all the days of S 1Sa 14:52 7586
when S saw any strong man, or any 1Sa 14:52 7586
Samuel also said unto S, The LORD 1Sa 15:1 7586
S gathered the people together, 1Sa 15:4 7586
S came to a city of Amalek, and 1Sa 15:5 7586
S said unto the Kenites, Go, 1Sa 15:6 7586
S smote the Amalekites from 1Sa 15:7 7586
But S and the people spared Agag, 1Sa 15:9 7586
that I have set up S to be king 1Sa 15:11 7586
early to meet S in the morning 1Sa 15:12 7586
S came to Carmel, and, behold, he 1Sa 15:12 7586
And Samuel came to S 1Sa 15:13 7586
S said unto him, Blessed be thou 1Sa 15:13 7586
S said, They have brought them 1Sa 15:15 7586
Then Samuel said unto S, Stay, and 1Sa 15:16 7586
S said unto Samuel, Yea, I have 1Sa 15:20 7586
S said unto Samuel, I have sinned 1Sa 15:24 7586
And Samuel said unto S, I will not 1Sa 15:26 7586
So Samuel turned again after S 1Sa 15:31 7586
and S worshipped the LORD 1Sa 15:31 7586
S went up to his house to Gibeah 1Sa 15:34 7586
up to his house to Gibeah of S 1Sa 15:34 7586
see S until the day of his death 1Sa 15:35 7586
nevertheless Samuel mourned for S 1Sa 15:35 7586
he had made S king over Israel 1Sa 15:35 7586
How long wilt thou mourn for S 1Sa 16:1 7586
if S hear it, he will kill me 1Sa 16:2 7586
of the LORD departed from S 1Sa 16:14 7586
S said unto his servants, Provide 1Sa 16:17 7586
Wherefore S sent messengers unto 1Sa 16:19 7586
sent them by David his son unto S 1Sa 16:20 7586
And David came to S, and stood 1Sa 16:21 7586
S sent to Jesse, saying, Let 1Sa 16:22 7586
evil spirit from God was upon S 1Sa 16:23 7586
so S was refreshed, and was well, 1Sa 16:23 7586
And S and the men of Israel were 1Sa 17:2 7586
a Philistine, and ye servants to S 1Sa 17:8 7586
When S and all Israel heard those 1Sa 17:11 7586
for an old man in the days of S 1Sa 17:12 7586
went and followed S to the battle 1Sa 17:13 7586
and the three eldest followed S 1Sa 17:14 7586
returned from S to feed his 1Sa 17:15 7586
Now S, and they, and all the men of 1Sa 17:19 7586
they rehearsed them before S 1Sa 17:31 7586
And David said to S, Let no man's 1Sa 17:32 7586
S said to David, Thou art not 1Sa 17:33 7586
And David said unto S, Thy servant 1Sa 17:34 7586
S said unto David, Go, and the 1Sa 17:37 7586
S armed David with his armour, and 1Sa 17:38 7586
And David said unto S, I cannot go 1Sa 17:39 7586
when S saw David go forth against 1Sa 17:55 7586
brought him before S with the 1Sa 17:57 7586
S said to him, Whose son art thou 1Sa 17:58 7586
made an end of speaking unto S 1Sa 18:1 7586
S took him that day, and would let 1Sa 18:2 7586
went out whithersoever S sent him 1Sa 18:5 7586
S set him over the men of war, and 1Sa 18:5 7586
and dancing, to meet king S 1Sa 18:6 7586
S hath slain his thousands, and 1Sa 18:7 7586
S was very wroth, and the saying 1Sa 18:8 7586
S eyed David from that day and 1Sa 18:9 7586
evil spirit from God came upon S 1Sa 18:10 7586
And S cast the javelin 1Sa 18:11 7586
S was afraid of David, because 1Sa 18:12 7586
with him, and was departed from S 1Sa 18:12 7586
Therefore S removed him from him, 1Sa 18:13 7586
Wherefore when S saw that he 1Sa 18:15 7586
S said to David, Behold my elder 1Sa 18:17 7586
For S said, Let not mine hand be 1Sa 18:17 7586
And David said unto S, Who am I 1Sa 18:18 7586
and they told S, and the thing 1Sa 18:20 7586
S said, I will give him her, that 1Sa 18:21 7586
Wherefore S said to David, Thou 1Sa 18:21 7586
S commanded his servants, saying, 1Sa 18:22 7586
And the servants of S told him 1Sa 18:24 7586
S said, Thus shall ye say to 1Sa 18:25 7586
But S thought to make David fall 1Sa 18:25 7586
S gave him Michal his daughter to 1Sa 18:27 7586
S saw and knew that the LORD was 1Sa 18:28 7586
S was yet the more afraid of 1Sa 18:29 7586
and S became David's enemy 1Sa 18:29 7586
wisely than all the servants of S 1Sa 18:30 7586
S spake to Jonathan his son, and 1Sa 19:1 7586

S my father seeketh to kill thee	1Sa 19:2	7586
good of David unto *S* his father	1Sa 19:4	7586
S hearkened unto the voice of	1Sa 19:6	7586
S sware, As the LORD liveth, he	1Sa 19:6	7586
And Jonathan brought David to *S*	1Sa 19:7	7586
spirit from the LORD was upon *S*	1Sa 19:9	7586
S sought to smite David even to	1Sa 19:10	7586
S also sent messengers unto	1Sa 19:11	7586
when *S* sent messengers to take	1Sa 19:14	7586
S sent the messengers again to	1Sa 19:15	7586
S said unto Michal, Why hast thou	1Sa 19:17	7586
And Michal answered *S*, He said	1Sa 19:17	7586
him all that *S* had done to him	1Sa 19:18	7586
And it was told *S*, saying, Behold,	1Sa 19:19	7586
S sent messengers to take David	1Sa 19:20	7586
God was upon the messengers of *S*	1Sa 19:20	7586
And when it was told *S*, he sent	1Sa 19:21	7586
S sent messengers again the third	1Sa 19:21	7586
Is *S* also among the prophets	1Sa 19:24	7586
Nevertheless *S* spake not any	1Sa 20:26	7586
S said unto Jonathan his son,	1Sa 20:27	7586
And Jonathan answered *S*, David	1Sa 20:28	7586
And Jonathan answered *S* his father	1Sa 20:32	7586
S cast a javelin at him to smite	1Sa 20:33	7586
servants of *S* was there that day	1Sa 21:7	7586
of the herdmen that belonged to *S*	1Sa 21:7	7586
and fled that day for fear of *S*	1Sa 21:10	7586
S hath slain his thousands, and	1Sa 21:11	7586
When *S* heard that David was	1Sa 22:6	7586
(now *S* abode in Gibeah under a	1Sa 22:6	7586
Then *S* said unto his servants	1Sa 22:7	7586
was set over the servants of *S*	1Sa 22:9	7586
S said, Hear now, thou son of	1Sa 22:12	7586
S said unto him, Why have ye	1Sa 22:13	7586
Abiathar shewed David that *S* had	1Sa 22:21	7586
that he would surely tell *S*	1Sa 22:22	7586
it was told *S* that David was come	1Sa 23:7	7586
S said, God hath delivered him	1Sa 23:7	7586
S called all the people together	1Sa 23:8	7586
David knew that *S* secretly	1Sa 23:9	7586
that *S* seeketh to come to Keilah	1Sa 23:10	7586
will *S* come down, as thy servant	1Sa 23:11	7586
me and my men into the hand of *S*	1Sa 23:12	7586
it was told *S* that David was	1Sa 23:13	7586
S sought him every day, but God	1Sa 23:14	7586
David saw that *S* was come out to	1Sa 23:15	7586
for the hand of *S* my father shall	1Sa 23:17	7586
that also *S* my father knoweth	1Sa 23:17	7586
up the Ziphites to *S* to Gibeah	1Sa 23:19	7586
S said, Blessed be ye of the LORD	1Sa 23:21	7586
arose, and went to Ziph before *S*	1Sa 23:24	7586
S also and his men went to seek	1Sa 23:25	7586
when *S* heard that, he pursued	1Sa 23:25	7586
S went on this side of the	1Sa 23:26	7586
haste to get away for fear of *S*	1Sa 23:26	7586
for *S* and his men compassed David	1Sa 23:26	7586
But there came a messenger unto *S*	1Sa 23:27	7586
Wherefore *S* returned from	1Sa 23:28	7586
to pass, when *S* was returned from	1Sa 24:1	7586
Then *S* took three thousand chosen	1Sa 24:2	7586
S went in to cover his feet	1Sa 24:3	7586
them not to rise against *S*	1Sa 24:7	7586
But *S* rose up out of the cave, and	1Sa 24:7	7586
out of the cave, and cried after *S*	1Sa 24:8	7586
when *S* looked behind him, David	1Sa 24:8	7586
And David said to *S*, Wherefore	1Sa 24:9	7586
words unto *S*, that *S* said	1Sa 24:16	7586
S lifted up his voice, and wept	1Sa 24:16	7586
And David sware unto *S*	1Sa 24:22	7586
And *S* went home	1Sa 24:22	7586
But *S* had given Michal his	1Sa 25:44	7586
Ziphites came unto *S* to Gibeah	1Sa 26:1	7586
Then *S* arose, and went down to the	1Sa 26:2	7586
S pitched in the hill of Hachilah	1Sa 26:3	7586
he saw that *S* came after him into	1Sa 26:3	7586
understood that *S* was come in	1Sa 26:4	7586
to the place where *S* had pitched	1Sa 26:5	7586
beheld the place where *S* lay	1Sa 26:5	7586
S lay in the trench, and the	1Sa 26:5	7586
go down with me to *S* to the camp	1Sa 26:6	7586
S lay sleeping within the trench,	1Sa 26:7	7586
S knew David's voice, and said, Is	1Sa 26:17	7586
Then said *S*, I have sinned	1Sa 26:21	7586
Then *S* said to David, Blessed be	1Sa 26:25	7586
way, and *S* returned to his place	1Sa 26:25	7586
perish one day by the hand of *S*	1Sa 27:1	7586
S shall despair of me, to seek me	1Sa 27:1	7586
it was told *S* that David was fled	1Sa 27:4	7586
S had put away those that had	1Sa 28:3	7586
S gathered all Israel together,	1Sa 28:4	7586
when *S* saw the host of the	1Sa 28:5	7586
when *S* enquired of the LORD, the	1Sa 28:6	7586
Then said *S* unto his servants,	1Sa 28:7	7586
S disguised himself, and put on	1Sa 28:8	7586
thou knowest what *S* hath done	1Sa 28:9	7586
S sware to her by the LORD,	1Sa 28:10	7586
and the woman spake to *S*, saying,	1Sa 28:12	7586
for thou art *S*	1Sa 28:12	7586
And the woman said unto *S*, I saw	1Sa 28:13	7586
S perceived that it was Samuel,	1Sa 28:14	7586
And Samuel said to *S*, Why hast	1Sa 28:15	7586
S answered, I am sore distressed	1Sa 28:15	7586
Then *S* fell straightway all along	1Sa 28:20	7586
And the woman came unto *S*	1Sa 28:21	7586
And she brought it before *S*	1Sa 28:25	7586
the servant of *S* the king of	1Sa 29:3	7586
S slew his thousands, and David	1Sa 29:5	7586
Philistines followed hard upon *S*	1Sa 31:2	7586
And the battle went sore against *S*	1Sa 31:3	7586
Then said *S* unto his armourbearer	1Sa 31:4	7586
Therefore *S* took a sword, and fell	1Sa 31:4	7586
armourbearer saw that *S* was dead	1Sa 31:5	7586
So *S* died, and his three sons, and	1Sa 31:6	7586
the men of Israel fled, and that *S*	1Sa 31:7	7586
the slain, that they found *S*	1Sa 31:8	7586
the Philistines had done to *S*	1Sa 31:11	7586
all night, and took the body of *S*	1Sa 31:12	7586
came to pass after the death of *S*	2Sa 1:1	7586
camp from *S* with his clothes rent	2Sa 1:2	7586
and *S* and Jonathan his son are dead	2Sa 1:4	7586
told him, How knowest thou that *S*	2Sa 1:5	7586
behold, *S* leaned upon his spear	2Sa 1:6	7586
wept, and fasted until even, for *S*	2Sa 1:12	7586
with this lamentation over *S*	2Sa 1:17	7586
vilely cast away, the shield of *S*	2Sa 1:21	7586
the sword of *S* returned not empty	2Sa 1:22	7586
S and Jonathan were lovely and	2Sa 1:23	7586
daughters of Israel, weep over *S*	2Sa 1:24	7586
were they that buried *S*	2Sa 2:4	7586
unto your lord, even unto *S*	2Sa 2:5	7586
for your master *S* is dead	2Sa 2:7	7586
took Ish-bosheth the son of *S*	2Sa 2:8	7586
of Ish-bosheth the son of *S*	2Sa 2:12	7586
to Ish-bosheth the son of *S*	2Sa 2:15	7586
long war between the house of *S*	2Sa 3:1	7586
and the house of *S* waxed weaker	2Sa 3:1	7586
was war between the house of *S*	2Sa 3:6	7586
himself strong for the house of *S*	2Sa 3:6	7586
S had a concubine, whose name was	2Sa 3:7	7586
unto the house of *S* thy father	2Sa 3:8	7586
the kingdom from the house of *S*	2Sa 3:10	7586
old when the tidings came of *S*	2Sa 4:4	7586
the son of *S* thine enemy, which	2Sa 4:8	7586
my lord the king this day of *S*	2Sa 4:8	7586
S is dead, thinking to have	2Sa 4:10	7586
when *S* was king over us, thou	2Sa 5:2	7586
of *S* came out to meet David	2Sa 6:20	7586
Michal the daughter of *S* had no	2Sa 6:23	7586
from him, as I took it from *S*	2Sa 7:15	7586
that is left of the house of *S*	2Sa 9:1	7586
there was of the house of *S* a	2Sa 9:2	7586
not yet any of the house of *S*	2Sa 9:3	7586
the son of Jonathan, the son of *S*	2Sa 9:6	7586
thee all the land of *S* thy father	2Sa 9:7	7586
son all that pertained to *S*	2Sa 9:9	7586
thee out of the hand of *S*	2Sa 12:7	7586
of the family of the house of *S*	2Sa 16:5	7586
all the blood of the house of *S*	2Sa 16:8	7586
the servant of the house of *S*	2Sa 19:17	7586
Mephibosheth the son of *S* came	2Sa 19:24	7586
And the LORD answered, It is for *S*	2Sa 21:1	7586
S sought to slay them in his zeal	2Sa 21:2	7586
will have no silver nor gold of *S*	2Sa 21:4	7586
up unto the LORD in Gibeah of *S*	2Sa 21:6	7586
the son of Jonathan the son of *S*	2Sa 21:7	7586
David and Jonathan the son of *S*	2Sa 21:7	7586
of Aiah, whom she bare unto *S*	2Sa 21:8	7586
sons of Michal the daughter of *S*	2Sa 21:8	7586
of Aiah, the concubine of *S*	2Sa 21:11	7586
David went and took the bones of *S*	2Sa 21:12	7586
Philistines had slain *S* in Gilboa	2Sa 21:12	7586
up from thence the bones of *S*	2Sa 21:13	7586
And the bones of *S* and Jonathan his	2Sa 21:14	7586
enemies, and out of the hand of *S*	2Sa 22:1	7586
in the days of *S* they made war	1Chr 5:10	7586
Ner begat Kish, and Kish begat *S*	1Chr 8:33	7586
S begat Jonathan, and Malchi-shua,	1Chr 8:33	7586
and Kish begat *S*	1Chr 9:39	7586
S begat Jonathan, and Malchi-shua,	1Chr 9:39	7586
Philistines followed hard after *S*	1Chr 10:2	7586
and Malchi-shua, the sons of *S*	1Chr 10:2	7586
And the battle went sore against *S*	1Chr 10:3	7586
Then said *S* to his armourbearer,	1Chr 10:4	7586
So *S* took a sword, and fell upon	1Chr 10:4	7586
armourbearer saw that *S* was dead	1Chr 10:5	7586
So *S* died, and his three sons, and	1Chr 10:6	7586
saw that they fled, and that *S*	1Chr 10:7	7586
the slain, that they found *S*	1Chr 10:8	7586
the Philistines had done to *S*	1Chr 10:11	7586
men, and took away the body of *S*	1Chr 10:12	7586
So *S* died for his transgression	1Chr 10:13	7586
time past, even when *S* was king	1Chr 11:2	7586
because of *S* the son of Kish	1Chr 12:1	7586
Philistines against *S* to battle	1Chr 12:19	7586
He will fall to his master *S* to	1Chr 12:19	7586
to turn the kingdom of *S* to him	1Chr 12:23	7586
of Benjamin, the kindred of *S*	1Chr 12:29	7586
kept the ward of the house of *S*	1Chr 12:29	7586
not at it in the days of *S*	1Chr 13:3	7586
of *S* looking out at a window saw	1Chr 15:29	7586
S the son of Kish, and Abner the	1Chr 26:28	7586
enemies, and from the hand of *S*	Ps 18:*t*	7586
Doeg the Edomite came and told *S*	Ps 52:*t*	7586
the Ziphims came and said to *S*	Ps 54:*t*	7586
when he fled from *S* in the cave	Ps 57:*t*	7586
when *S* sent, and they watched the	Ps 59:*t*	7586
Gibeah of *S* is fled	Is 10:29	7586
gave unto them *S* the son of Cis	Acts 13:21	4569
2. An Edomite king.		
S of Rehoboth by the river	Gen 36:37	7586
S died, and Baal-hanan the son of	Gen 36:38	7586
3. Original name of Paul.		
man's feet, whose name was *S*	Acts 7:58	4569
S was consenting unto his death	Acts 8:1	4569
As for *S*, he made havock of the	Acts 8:3	4569
And *S*, yet breathing out	Acts 9:1	4569
a voice saying unto him, Saul, *S*	Acts 9:4	4569
And *S* arose from the earth	Acts 9:8	4569
house of Judas for one called *S*	Acts 9:11	4569
his hands on him said, Brother *S*	Acts 9:17	4569
Then was *S* certain days with the	Acts 9:19	4569
But *S* increased the more in	Acts 9:22	4569
their laying await was known of *S*	Acts 9:24	4569
when *S* was come to Jerusalem, he	Acts 9:26	4569
Barnabas to Tarsus, for to seek *S*	Acts 11:25	4569
by the hands of Barnabas and *S*	Acts 11:30	4569
S returned from Jerusalem, when	Acts 12:25	4569
up with Herod the tetrarch, and *S*	Acts 13:1	4569
S for the work whereunto I have	Acts 13:2	4569
who called for Barnabas and *S*	Acts 13:7	4569
Then *S*, (who also is called Paul,	Acts 13:9	4569
a voice saying unto me, Saul, *S*	Acts 22:7	4569
stood, and said unto me, Brother *S*	Acts 22:13	4569
in the Hebrew tongue, Saul, *S*	Acts 26:14	4569

SAUL'S *Refers to Saul 1.*

asses of Kish *S* father were lost	1Sa 9:3	7586
S uncle said unto him and to his	1Sa 10:14	7586
S uncle said, Tell me, I pray	1Sa 10:15	7586
the name of *S* wife was Ahinoam,	1Sa 14:50	7586
Abner, the son of Ner, *S* uncle	1Sa 14:50	7586
S servants said unto him, Behold	1Sa 16:15	7586
also in the sight of *S* servants	1Sa 18:5	7586
and there was a javelin in *S* hand	1Sa 18:10	7586
to pass at the time when Merab *S*	1Sa 18:19	7586
Michal *S* daughter loved David	1Sa 18:20	7586
S servants spake those words in	1Sa 18:23	7586
that Michal *S* daughter loved him	1Sa 18:28	7586
But Jonathan *S* son delighted much	1Sa 19:2	7586
he slipped away out of *S* presence	1Sa 19:10	7586
arose, and Abner sat by *S* side	1Sa 20:25	7586
Then *S* anger was kindled against	1Sa 20:30	7586
Jonathan *S* son arose, and went to	1Sa 23:16	7586
off the skirt of *S* robe privily	1Sa 24:4	7586
because he had cut off *S* skirt	1Sa 24:5	7586
the cruse of water from *S* bolster	1Sa 26:12	7586
Abinadab, and Melchi-shua, *S* sons	1Sa 31:2	7586
the son of Ner, captain of *S* host	2Sa 2:8	7586
Ish-bosheth *S* son was forty years	2Sa 2:10	7586
first bring Michal *S* daughter	2Sa 3:13	7586
messengers to Ish-bosheth *S* son	2Sa 3:14	7586
when *S* son heard that Abner was	2Sa 4:1	7586
S son had two men that were	2Sa 4:2	7586
S son, had a son that was lame of	2Sa 4:4	7586
Michal *S* daughter looked through	2Sa 6:16	7586
S servant, and said unto him, I	2Sa 9:9	7586
even of *S* brethren of Benjamin	1Chr 12:2	7586

SAVE

me, but they will *s* thee alive	Gen 12:12	2421
S only that which the young men	Gen 14:24	1107
s the bread which he did eat	Gen 39:6	
to *s* your lives by a great	Gen 45:7	2421
this day, to *s* much people alive	Gen 50:20	2421
every daughter ye shall *s* alive	Ex 1:22	2421
s that which every man must eat,	Ex 12:16	389
s unto the LORD only, he shall be	Ex 22:20	1115
s Caleb the son of Jephunneh, and	Num 14:30	
s Caleb the son of Jephunneh, and	Num 26:65	
S Caleb the son of Jephunneh the	Num 32:12	
S Caleb the son of Jephunneh	Deut 1:36	2108
S when there shall be no poor	Deut 15:4	657
against your enemies, to *s* you	Deut 20:4	3467
thou shalt *s* alive nothing that	Deut 20:16	2421
cried, and there was none to *s* her	Deut 22:27	3467
evermore, and no man shall *s* thee	Deut 28:29	3467
that ye will *s* alive my father,	Josh 2:13	2421
us quickly, and *s* us, and help us	Josh 10:6	3467
burned none of them, *s* Hazor only	Josh 11:13	2108
s the Hivites the inhabitants of	Josh 11:19	1115
s cities to dwell in, with their	Josh 14:4	
the LORD, (*s* us not this day,)	Josh 22:22	3467
thou shalt *s* Israel from the hand	Judg 6:14	3467
Lord, wherewith shall I *s* Israel	Judg 6:15	3467
will ye *s* him	Judg 6:31	3467
If thou wilt *s* Israel by mine	Judg 6:36	3467
thou wilt *s* Israel by mine hand	Judg 6:37	3467
men that lapped will I *s* you	Judg 7:7	3467
This is nothing else *s* the sword	Judg 7:14	
it may *s* us out of the hand of	1Sa 4:3	3467
that he will *s* us out of the hand	1Sa 7:8	3467
that he may *s* my people out of	1Sa 9:16	3467
shouted, and said, God *s* the king	1Sa 10:24	2421
said, How shall this man *s* us	1Sa 10:27	3467
then, if there be no man to *s* us	1Sa 11:3	3467
the LORD to *s* by many or by few	1Sa 14:6	3467
If thou *s* not thy to night, to	1Sa 19:11	4422
for there is no other *s* that here	1Sa 21:9	2108
the Philistines, and *s* Keilah	1Sa 23:2	3467
s four hundred young men, which	1Sa 30:17	
s to every man his wife and his	1Sa 30:22	
s my people Israel out of the	2Sa 3:18	3467
s one little ewe lamb, which he	2Sa 12:3	
God *s* the king, God *s* the king	2Sa 16:16	2421
God *s* the king, God *s* the king	2Sa 16:16	2421
the afflicted people thou wilt *s*	2Sa 22:28	3467
For who is God, *s* the LORD	2Sa 22:32	1107
and who is a rock, *s* our God	2Sa 22:32	1107
looked, but there was none to *s*	2Sa 22:42	3467
that thou mayest *s* thine own life	1Kin 1:12	4422
him, and say, God *s* king Adonijah	1Kin 1:25	2421
and say, God *s* king Solomon	1Kin 1:34	2421
people said, God *s* king Solomon	1Kin 1:39	2421
the house, *s* we two in the house	1Kin 3:18	2108
the ark *s* the two tables of stone	1Kin 8:9	7535
s only in the matter of Uriah the	1Kin 15:5	
we may find grass to *s* the horses	1Kin 18:5	2421
peradventure he will *s* thy life	1Kin 20:31	2421
s only with the king of Israel	1Kin 22:31	
in the house, *s* a pot of oil	2Kin 4:2	3467
if they *s* us alive, we shall live	2Kin 7:4	2421
hands, and said, God *s* the king	2Kin 11:12	2421
S that the high places were not	2Kin 15:4	7535
s me out of the hand of the king	2Kin 16:7	3467
s thou us out of his hand, that	2Kin 19:19	3467
I will defend this city, to *s* it	2Kin 19:34	3467
s the poorest sort of the people	2Kin 24:14	2108
S us, O God of our salvation, and	1Chr 16:35	3467
s only to burn sacrifice before	2Chr 2:6	518
There was nothing in the ark *s*	2Chr 5:10	7535
s only with the king of Israel	2Chr 18:30	
s Jehoahaz, the youngest of his	2Chr 21:17	3467
s the priests, and they that	2Chr 23:6	

S

him, and said, God *s* the king 2Chr 23:11 2421
s the beast that I rode upon Neh 2:12
go into the temple to *s* his life Neh 6:11 2425
but *s* his life Job 2:6 8104
he shall not *s* of that which he Job 20:20 4422
he shall *s* the humble person Job 22:29 3467
thine own right hand can *s* thee Job 40:14 3467
s me, O my God Ps 3:7 3467
oh *s* me for thy mercies' sake Ps 6:4 3467
s me from all them that persecute Ps 7:1 3467
For thou wilt *s* the afflicted Ps 18:27 3467
For who is God *s* the LORD Ps 18:31 1107
or who is a rock *s* our God Ps 18:31 2108
but there was none to *s* them Ps 18:41 3467
S, LORD Ps 20:9 3467
S me from the lion's mouth Ps 22:21 3467
S thy people, and bless thine Ps 28:9 3467
for an house of defence to *s* me Ps 31:2 3467
s me for thy mercies' sake Ps 31:16 3467
s them, because they trust in him Ps 37:40 3467
neither did their own arm *s* them Ps 44:3 3467
bow, neither shall my sword *s* me Ps 44:6 3467
S me, O God, by thy name, and Ps 54:1 3467
and the LORD shall *s* me Ps 55:16 3467
s me from the reproach of him Ps 57:3 3467
iniquity, and *s* me from bloody men Ps 59:2 3467
s with thy right hand, and hear me Ps 60:5 3467
S me, O God Ps 69:1 3467
For God will *s* Zion, and will Ps 69:35 3467
thine ear unto me, and *s* me Ps 71:2 3467
hast given commandment to *s* me Ps 71:3 3467
he shall *s* the children of the Ps 72:4 3467
shall *s* the souls of the needy Ps 72:13 3467
to *s* all the meek of the earth Ps 76:9 3467
up thy strength, and come and *s* us Ps 80:2 3444
s thy servant that trusteth in Ps 86:2 3467
s the son of thine handmaid Ps 86:16 3467
S us, O LORD our God, and gather Ps 106:47 3467
s with thy right hand, and answer Ps 108:6 3467
O *s* me according to thy mercy Ps 109:26 3467
to *s* him from those that condemn Ps 109:31 3467
S now, I beseech thee, O LORD Ps 118:25 3467
I am thine, *s* me Ps 119:94 3467
s me, and I shall keep thy Ps 119:146 3467
and thy right hand shall *s* me Ps 138:7 3467
hear their cry, and will *s* them Ps 145:19 3467
on the LORD, and he shall *s* thee Prov 20:22 3467
waited for him, and he will *s* us Is 25:9 3467
he will *s* us Is 33:22 3467
he will come and *s* you Is 35:4 3467
s us from his hand, that all the Is 37:20 3467
city to *s* it for mine own sake Is 37:35 3467
The LORD was ready to *s* me Is 38:20 3467
and pray unto a god that cannot *s* Is 45:20 3467
nor *s* him out of his trouble Is 46:7 3467
s thee from these things that Is 47:13 3467
none shall *s* thee Is 47:15 3467
thee, and I will *s* thy children Is 49:25 3467
not shortened, that it cannot *s* Is 59:1 3467
in righteousness, mighty to *s* Is 63:1 3467
they will say, Arise, and *s* us Jer 2:27 3467
if they can *s* thee in the time of Jer 2:28 3467
but they shall not *s* them at all Jer 11:12 3467
as a mighty man that cannot *s* Jer 14:9 3467
for I am with thee to *s* thee Jer 15:20 3467
s me, and I shall be saved Jer 17:14 3467
I will *s* thee from afar, and thy Jer 30:10 3467
thee, saith the LORD, to *s* thee Jer 30:11 3467
s thy people, the remnant of Jer 31:7 3467
for I am with you to *s* you Jer 42:11 3467
I will *s* thee from afar off, and Jer 46:27 3467
s your lives, and be like the Jer 48:6 4422
for a nation that could not *s* us Lam 4:17 3467
his wicked way, to *s* his life Eze 3:18 2421
will ye *s* the souls alive that Eze 13:18 2421
to *s* the souls alive that should Eze 13:19 2421
he shall *s* his soul alive Eze 18:27 2421
Therefore will I *s* my flock Eze 34:22 3467
I will also *s* you from all your Eze 36:29 3467
but I will *s* them out of all Eze 37:23 3467
s of thee, O king, he shall be Dan 6:7 3861
s of thee, O king, shall be cast Dan 6:12 3861
will *s* them by the LORD their God Hos 1:7 3467
will not *s* them by bow, nor by Hos 1:7 3467
that may *s* thee in all thy cities Hos 13:10 3467
Asshur shall not *s* us Hos 14:3 3467
of violence, and thou wilt not *s* Hab 1:2 3467
he will *s*, he will rejoice over Zeph 3:17 3467
I will *s* her that halteth, and Zeph 3:19 3467
I will *s* my people from the east Zec 8:7 3467
so will I *s* you, and ye shall be a Zec 8:13 3467
the LORD their God shall *s* them Zec 9:16 3467
I will *s* the house of Joseph, and Zec 10:6 3467
The LORD also shall *s* the tents Zec 12:7 3467
for he shall *s* his people from Mt 1:21 4982
and awoke him, saying, Lord, *s* us Mt 8:25 4982
s the Son, and he to whomsoever Mt 11:27 1508
s in his own country, and in his Mt 13:57 1508
he cried, saying, Lord, *s* me Mt 14:30 4982
For whosoever will *s* his life Mt 16:25 4982
they saw no man, *s* Jesus only Mt 17:8 1508
is come to *s* that which was lost Mt 18:11 4982
s they to whom it is given Mt 19:11 235
it in three days, *s* thyself Mt 27:40 4982
himself he cannot *s* Mt 27:42 4982
whether Elias will come to *s* him Mt 27:49 4982
to *s* life, or to kill Mk 3:4 4982
s Peter, and James, and John the Mk 5:37 1508
s that he laid his hands upon a Mk 6:5 1508
for their journey, *s* a staff only Mk 6:8 1508
For whosoever will *s* his life Mk 8:35 4982
the gospel's, the same shall *s* it Mk 8:35 4982
s Jesus only with themselves Mk 9:8 235
S thyself, and come down from the Mk 15:30 4982

himself he cannot *s* Mk 15:31 4982
s unto Sarepta, a city of Sidon, Lk 4:26 1508
to *s* life, or to destroy it Lk 6:9 4982
s Peter, and James, and John, and Lk 8:51 1508
For whosoever will *s* his life Lk 9:24 4982
for my sake, the same shall *s* it Lk 9:24 4982
men's lives, but to *s* them Lk 9:56 4982
glory to God, *s* this stranger Lk 17:18 1508
seek to *s* his life shall lose it Lk 17:33 4982
none is good, *s* one, that is, God Lk 18:19 1508
seek and to *s* that which was lost Lk 19:10 4982
let him *s* himself, if he be Lk 23:35 4982
the king of the Jews, *s* thyself Lk 23:37 4982
thou be Christ, *s* thyself and us Lk 23:39 4982
there, *s* that one whereinto his Jn 6:22 1508
s he which is of God, he hath Jn 6:46 1508
Father, *s* me from this hour Jn 12:27 4982
the world, but to *s* the world Jn 12:47 4982
needeth not *s* to wash his feet Jn 13:10 2228
S yourselves from this untoward Acts 2:40 4982
S that the Holy Ghost witnesseth Acts 20:23 4133
s only that they keep themselves Acts 21:25 1508
the centurion, willing to *s* Paul Acts 27:43 1295
my flesh, and might *s* some of them Rom 11:14 4982
preaching to *s* them that believe 1Cor 1:21 4982
s Jesus Christ, and him crucified 1Cor 2:2 1508
s the spirit of man which is in 1Cor 2:11 1508
whether thou shalt *s* thy husband 1Cor 7:16 4982
whether thou shalt *s* thy wife 1Cor 7:16 4982
that I might by all means *s* some 1Cor 9:22 4982
received I forty stripes *s* one 2Cor 11:24 3844
s James the Lord's brother Gal 1:19 1508
s in the cross of our Lord Jesus Gal 6:14 1508
came into the world to *s* sinners 1Ti 1:15 4982
this thou shalt both *s* thyself 1Ti 4:16 4982
that was able to *s* him from death Heb 5:7 4982
Wherefore he is able also to *s* Heb 7:25 4982
which is able to *s* your souls Jas 1:21 4982
can faith *s* him Jas 2:14 4982
is one lawgiver, who is able to *s* Jas 4:12 4982
prayer of faith shall *s* the sick Jas 5:15 4982
his way shall *s* a soul from death Jas 5:20 4982
even baptism doth also now *s* us 1Pet 3:21 4982
others *s* with fear, pulling them Jude 23 4982
s he that had the mark, or the Rev 13:17 1508

SAVED

they said, Thou hast *s* our lives Gen 47:25
but *s* the men children alive Ex 1:17 2421
have *s* the men children alive Ex 1:18 2421
Thus the LORD *s* Israel that day Ex 14:30 3467
ye shall be *s* from your enemies Num 10:9 3467
I had slain thee, and *s* her alive Num 22:33 2421
Have ye *s* all the women alive Num 31:15 2421
O people *s* by the LORD, the Deut 33:29 3467
Joshua *s* Rahab the harlot alive, Josh 6:25 2421
saying, Mine own hand hath *s* me Judg 7:2 3467
if ye had *s* them alive, I would Judg 8:19 2421
they had *s* alive of the women of Judg 21:14 2421
who himself *s* you out of all your 1Sa 10:19 3467
So the LORD *s* Israel that day 1Sa 14:23 3467
So David *s* the inhabitants of 1Sa 23:5 3467
David *s* neither man nor woman 1Sa 27:11 2421
which this day have *s* thy life 2Sa 19:5 4422
The king *s* us out of the hand of 2Sa 19:9 5337
so shall I be *s* from mine enemies 2Sa 22:4 3467
s himself there, not once nor 2Kin 6:10 8104
but he *s* them by the hand of 2Kin 14:27 3467
the LORD *s* them by a great 1Chr 11:14 3467
Thus the LORD *s* Hezekiah and the 2Chr 32:22 3467
who *s* them out of the hand of Neh 9:27 3467
so shall I be *s* from mine enemies Ps 18:3 3467
There is no king *s* by the Ps 33:16 3467
s him out of all his troubles Ps 34:6 3467
But thou hast *s* us from our Ps 44:7 3467
and we shall be *s* Ps 80:3 3467
and we shall be *s* Ps 80:7 3467
and we shall be *s* Ps 80:19 3467
Nevertheless he *s* them for his Ps 106:8 3467
he *s* them from the hand of him Ps 106:10 3467
he *s* them out of their distresses Ps 107:13 3467
walketh uprightly shall be *s* Prov 28:18 3467
returning and rest shall ye be *s* Is 30:15 3467
I have declared, and have *s* Is 43:12 3467
But Israel shall be *s* in the LORD Is 45:17 3467
Look unto me, and be ye *s*, all the Is 45:22 3467
the angel of his presence *s* them Is 63:9 3467
is continuance, and we shall be *s* Is 64:5 3467
wickedness, that thou mayest be *s* Jer 4:14 3467
summer is ended, and we are not *s* Jer 8:20 3467
save me, and I shall be *s* Jer 17:14 3467
In his days Judah shall be *s* Jer 23:6 3467
but he shall be *s* out of it Jer 30:7 3467
In those days shall Judah be *s* Jer 33:16 3467
endureth to the end shall be *s* Mt 10:22 4982
amazed, saying, Who then can be *s* Mt 19:25 4982
unto the end, the same shall be *s* Mt 24:13 4982
there should no flesh be *s* Mt 24:22 4982
He *s* others; himself he Mt 27:42 4982
themselves, Who then can be *s* Mk 10:26 4982
unto the end, the same shall be *s* Mk 13:13 4982
those days, no flesh should be *s* Mk 13:20 4982
with the scribes, He *s* others Mk 15:31 4982
and is baptized shall be *s* Mk 16:16 4982
we should be *s* from our enemies Lk 1:71 4991
the woman, Thy faith hath *s* thee Lk 7:50 4982
lest they should believe and be *s* Lk 8:12 4982
Lord, are there few that be *s* Lk 13:23 4982
heard it said, Who then can be *s* Lk 18:26 4982
thy faith hath *s* thee Lk 18:42 4982
derided him, saying, He *s* others Lk 23:35 4982
the world through him might be *s* Jn 3:17 4982
things I say, that ye might be *s* Jn 5:34 4982
any man enter in, he shall be *s* Jn 10:9 4982

the name of the Lord shall be *s* Acts 2:21 4982
church daily such as should be *s* Acts 2:47 4982
among men, whereby we must be *s* Acts 4:12 4982
thou and all thy house shall be *s* Acts 11:14 4982
manner of Moses, ye cannot be *s* Acts 15:1 4982
Lord Jesus Christ we shall be *s* Acts 15:11 4982
Sirs, what must I do to be *s* Acts 16:30 4982
Jesus Christ, and thou shalt be *s* Acts 16:31 4982
should be *s* was then taken away Acts 27:20 4982
abide in the ship, ye cannot be *s* Acts 27:31 4982
we shall be *s* from wrath through Rom 5:9 4982
we shall be *s* by his life Rom 5:10 4982
For we are *s* by hope Rom 8:24 4982
of the sea, a remnant shall be *s* Rom 9:27 4982
Israel is, that they might be *s* Rom 10:1 4991
from the dead, thou shalt be *s* Rom 10:9 4982
the name of the Lord shall be *s* Rom 10:13 4982
And so all Israel shall be *s* Rom 11:26 4982
but unto us which are *s* it is the 1Cor 1:18 4982
but he himself shall be *s* 1Cor 3:15 4982
that the spirit may be *s* in the 1Cor 5:5 4982
of many, that they may be *s* 1Cor 10:33 4982
By which also ye are *s*, if ye 1Cor 15:2 4982
of Christ, in them that are *s* 2Cor 2:15 4982
with Christ, (by grace ye are *s* Eph 2:5 4982
by grace are ye *s* through faith Eph 2:8 4982
the Gentiles that they might be *s* 1Th 2:16 4982
the truth, that they might be *s* 2Th 2:10 4982
Who will have all men to be *s* 1Ti 2:4 4982
she shall be *s* in childbearing 1Ti 2:15 4982
Who hath *s* us, and called us with 2Ti 1:9 4982
according to his mercy he *s* us Titus 3:5 4982
is, eight souls were *s* by water 1Pet 3:20 1295
And if the righteous scarcely be *s* 1Pet 4:18 4982
but *s* Noah the eighth person, a 2Pet 2:5 5442
having *s* the people out of the Jude 5 4982
s shall walk in the light of it Rev 21:24 4982

SAVEST

thou *s* me from violence 2Sa 22:3 3467
how *s* thou the arm that hath no Job 26:2 3467
O thou that *s* by thy right hand Ps 17:7 3467

SAVETH

which *s* Israel, though it be in 1Sa 14:39 3467
that the LORD *s* not with sword 1Sa 17:47 3467
But he *s* the poor from the sword, Job 5:15 3467
which *s* the upright in heart Ps 7:10 3467
I that the LORD *s* his anointed Ps 20:6 3467
s such as be of a contrite spirit Ps 34:18 3467
he *s* them out of their distresses Ps 107:19 3467

SAVING

hast shewed unto me in *s* my life Gen 19:19 2421
s that every one put them off for Neh 4:23
the *s* strength of his right hand Ps 20:6 3468
he is the *s* strength of his Ps 28:8 3444
thy *s* health among all nations Ps 67:2 3444
s the beholding of them with Eccl 5:11 518
s that I will not utterly destroy Amos 9:8 657
s for the cause of fornication, Mt 5:32 3924
was cleansed, *s* Naaman the Syrian Lk 4:27 1508
that believe to the *s* of the soul Heb 10:39 4047
an ark to the *s* of his house Heb 11:7 4991
knoweth *s* he that receiveth it Rev 2:17 1508

SAVIOUR

my high tower, and my refuge, my *s* 2Sa 22:3 3467
(And the LORD gave Israel a *s* 2Kin 13:5 3467
They forgat God their *s*, which Ps 106:21 3467
and he shall send them a *s* Is 19:20 3467
the Holy One of Israel, thy *S* Is 43:3 3467
and beside me there is no *s* Is 43:11 3467
thyself, O God of Israel, the *S* Is 45:15 3467
a just God and a *S* Is 45:21 3467
know that I the LORD am thy *S* Is 49:26 3467
know that I the LORD am thy *S* Is 60:16 3467
so he was their *S* Is 63:8 3467
the *s* thereof in time of trouble, Jer 14:8 3467
for there is no *s* beside me Hos 13:4 3467
spirit hath rejoiced in God my *S* Lk 1:47 4990
this day in the city of David a *S* Lk 2:11 4990
the Christ, the *S* of the world Jn 4:42 4990
right hand to be a Prince and a *S* Acts 5:31 4990
promise raised unto Israel a *S* Acts 13:23 4990
and he is the *s* of the body Eph 5:23 4990
whence also we look for the *S* Phil 3:20 4990
by the commandment of God our *S* 1Ti 1:1 4990
in the sight of God our *S* 1Ti 2:3 4990
God, who is the *S* of all men 1Ti 4:10 4990
appearing of our *S* Jesus Christ 2Ti 1:10 4990
to the commandment of God our *S* Titus 1:3 4990
and the Lord Jesus Christ our *S* Titus 1:4 4990
of God our *S* in all things Titus 2:10 4990
great God and our *S* Jesus Christ Titus 2:13 4990
love of God our *S* toward man Titus 3:4 4990
through Jesus Christ our *S* Titus 3:6 4990
of God and our *S* Jesus Christ 2Pet 1:1 4990
of our Lord and *S* Jesus Christ 2Pet 1:11 4990
S Jesus Christ, they are again 2Pet 2:20 4990
us the apostles of the Lord and *S* 2Pet 3:2 4990
of our Lord and *S* Jesus Christ 2Pet 3:18 4990
the Son to be the *S* of the world 1Jn 4:14 4990
To the only wise God our *S* Jude 25 4990

SAVIOURS

mercies thou gavest them *s* Neh 9:27 3467
s shall come up on mount Zion to Obad 21 3467

SAVOUR

And the LORD smelled a sweet *s* Gen 8:21 7381
because ye have made our *s* to be Ex 5:21 7381
it is a sweet *s*, an offering made Ex 29:18 7381
for a sweet *s* before the LORD Ex 29:25 7381
offering thereof, for a sweet *s* Ex 29:41 7381
of a sweet *s* unto the LORD Lev 1:9 7381
of a sweet *s* unto the LORD Lev 1:13 7381

of a sweet s unto the LORD	Lev 1:17	7381
of a sweet s unto the LORD	Lev 2:2	7381
of a sweet s unto the LORD	Lev 2:9	7381
burnt on the altar for a sweet s	Lev 2:12	7381
of a sweet s unto the LORD	Lev 3:5	7381
made by fire for a sweet s	Lev 3:16	7381
altar for a sweet s unto the LORD	Lev 4:31	7381
it upon the altar for a sweet s	Lev 6:15	7381
offer for a sweet s unto the LORD	Lev 6:21	7381
a burnt sacrifice for a sweet s	Lev 8:21	7381
were consecrations for a sweet s	Lev 8:28	7381
fat for a sweet s unto the LORD	Lev 17:6	7381
fire unto the LORD for a sweet s	Lev 23:13	7381
by fire, of sweet s unto the LORD	Lev 23:18	7381
smell the s of your sweet odours	Lev 26:31	7381
to make a sweet s unto the LORD	Num 15:3	7381
for a sweet s unto the LORD	Num 15:7	7381
of a sweet s unto the LORD	Num 15:10	7381
of a sweet s unto the LORD	Num 15:13	7381
of a sweet s unto the LORD	Num 15:14	7381
for a sweet s unto the LORD, with	Num 15:24	7381
for a sweet s unto the LORD	Num 18:17	7381
by fire, for a sweet s unto me	Num 28:2	7381
in mount Sinai for a sweet s	Num 28:6	7381
of a sweet s unto the LORD	Num 28:8	7381
for a burnt offering of a sweet s	Num 28:13	7381
of a sweet s unto the LORD	Num 28:24	7381
for a sweet s unto the LORD	Num 28:27	7381
for a sweet s unto the LORD	Num 29:2	7381
unto their manner, for a sweet s	Num 29:6	7381
unto the LORD for a sweet s	Num 29:8	7381
of a sweet s unto the LORD	Num 29:13	7381
of a sweet s unto the LORD	Num 29:36	7381
to send forth a stinking s	Eccl 10:1	7381
Because of the s of thy good	Song 1:3	7381
offer sweet s to all their idols	Eze 6:13	7381
set it before them for a sweet s	Eze 16:19	7381
also they made their sweet s	Eze 20:28	7381
will accept you with your sweet s	Eze 20:41	7381
his ill s shall come up, because	Joel 2:20	6709
but if the salt have lost his s	Mt 5:13	*3471*
but if the salt have lost his s	Lk 14:34	*3471*
maketh manifest the s of his	2Cor 2:14	*3744*
are unto God a sweet s of Christ	2Cor 2:15	*2175*
we are the s of death unto death	2Cor 2:16	*3744*
to the other the s of life unto	2Cor 2:16	*3744*
to God for a sweetsmelling s	Eph 5:2	*3744*

SAVOUREST

for thou s not the things that be	Mt 16:23	*5426*
for thou s not the things that be	Mk 8:33	*5426*

SAVOURS

of sweet s unto the God of heaven	Ezr 6:10	5208

SAVOURY

And make me s meat, such as I love	Gen 27:4	4303
me venison, and make me s meat	Gen 27:7	4303
I will make them s meat for thy	Gen 27:9	4303
and his mother made s meat	Gen 27:14	4303
And she gave the s meat and the	Gen 27:17	4303
And he also had made s meat	Gen 27:31	4303

SAW

God s the light, that it was good	Gen 1:4	7200
and God s that it was good	Gen 1:10	7200
and God s that it was good	Gen 1:12	7200
and God s that it was good	Gen 1:18	7200
and God s that it was good	Gen 1:21	7200
and God s that it was good	Gen 1:25	7200
God s every thing that he had	Gen 1:31	7200
when the woman s that the tree	Gen 3:6	7200
That the sons of God s the	Gen 6:2	7200
God s that the wickedness of man	Gen 6:5	7200
s the nakedness of his father, and	Gen 9:22	7200
they s not their father's	Gen 9:23	7200
The princes also of Pharaoh s her	Gen 12:15	7200
when she s that she had conceived	Gen 16:4	7200
when she s that she had conceived	Gen 16:5	7200
and when he s them, he ran to meet	Gen 18:2	7200
Sarah s the son of Hagar the	Gen 21:9	7200
eyes, and she s a well of water	Gen 21:19	7200
his eyes, and s the place afar off	Gen 22:4	7200
to pass, when he s the earring and	Gen 24:30	7200
and he lifted up his eyes, and s	Gen 24:63	7200
up her eyes, and when she s Isaac	Gen 24:64	7200
looked out at a window, and s	Gen 26:8	7200
We s certainly that the LORD was	Gen 26:28	7200
When Esau s that Isaac had	Gen 28:6	7200
when Jacob s Rachel the daughter	Gen 29:10	7200
when the LORD s that Leah was	Gen 29:31	7200
when Rachel s that she bare Jacob	Gen 30:1	7200
When Leah s that she had left	Gen 30:9	7200
s in a dream, and, behold, the	Gen 31:10	7200
And when Jacob s them, he said,	Gen 32:2	7200
when he s that he prevailed not	Gen 32:25	7200
s the women and the children	Gen 33:5	7200
s her, he took her, and lay with	Gen 34:2	7200
when his brethren s that their	Gen 37:4	7200
when they s him afar off, even	Gen 37:18	7200
Judah s there a daughter of a	Gen 38:2	7200
for she s that Shelah was grown,	Gen 38:14	7200
When Judah s her, he thought her	Gen 38:15	7200
his master s that the LORD was	Gen 39:3	7200
when she s that he had left his	Gen 39:13	7200
When the chief baker s that the	Gen 40:16	7200
such as I never s in all the land	Gen 41:19	7200
I s in my dream, and, behold,	Gen 41:22	7200
Now when Jacob s that there was	Gen 42:1	7200
Joseph s his brethren, and he knew	Gen 42:7	7200
in that we s the anguish of his	Gen 42:21	7200
their father s the bundles of	Gen 42:35	7200
when Joseph s Benjamin with them,	Gen 43:16	7200
s his brother Benjamin, his	Gen 43:29	7200
and I s him not since	Gen 44:28	7200
when he s the wagons which Joseph	Gen 45:27	7200
when Joseph s that his father	Gen 48:17	7200
he s that rest was good, and the	Gen 49:15	7200
s the mourning in the floor of	Gen 50:11	7200
when Joseph's brethren s that	Gen 50:15	7200
Joseph s Ephraim's children of	Gen 50:23	7200
when she s him that he was a	Ex 2:2	7200
when she s the ark among the	Ex 2:5	7200
had opened it, she s the child	Ex 2:6	7200
when he s that there was no man,	Ex 2:12	7200
when the LORD s that he turned	Ex 3:4	7200
But when Pharaoh s that there was	Ex 8:15	7200
when Pharaoh s that the rain and	Ex 9:34	7200
They s not one another, neither	Ex 10:23	7200
Israel s the Egyptians dead upon	Ex 14:30	7200
Israel s that great work which	Ex 14:31	7200
when the children of Israel s it	Ex 16:15	7200
when Moses' father in law s all	Ex 18:14	7200
all the people s the thunderings,	Ex 20:18	7200
and when the people s it, they	Ex 20:18	7200
And they s the God of Israel	Ex 24:10	7200
also they s God, and did eat and	Ex 24:11	2372
when the people s that Moses	Ex 32:1	7200
And when Aaron s it, he built an	Ex 32:5	7200
that he s the calf, and the	Ex 32:19	7200
when Moses s that the people were	Ex 32:25	7200
all the people s the cloudy	Ex 33:10	7200
the children of Israel s Moses	Ex 34:30	7200
of Israel s the face of Moses	Ex 34:35	7200
which when all the people s	Lev 9:24	7200
moreover we s the children of	Num 13:28	7200
all the people that we s in it	Num 13:32	7200
there we s the giants, the sons	Num 13:33	7200
s that Aaron was dead, they	Num 20:29	7200
Balak the son of Zippor s all	Num 22:2	7200
the ass s the angel of the LORD	Num 22:23	7200
when the ass s the angel of the	Num 22:25	7200
when the ass s the angel of the	Num 22:27	7200
he s the angel of the LORD	Num 22:31	7200
And the ass s me, and turned from	Num 22:33	7200
when Balaam s that it pleased the	Num 24:1	7200
he s Israel abiding in his tents	Num 24:2	7200
which s the vision of the	Num 24:4	2372
which s the vision of the	Num 24:16	2372
s it, he rose up from among the	Num 25:7	7200
when they s the land of Jazer, and	Num 32:1	7200
s the land, they discouraged the	Num 32:9	7200
which ye s by the way of the	Deut 1:19	7200
of the words, but s no similitude	Deut 4:12	7200
for ye s no manner of similitude	Deut 4:15	7200
temptations which thine eyes s	Deut 7:19	7200
And when the LORD s it, he	Deut 32:19	7200
When I s among the spoils a	Josh 7:21	7200
to pass, when the king of Ai s it	Josh 8:14	7200
of Ai looked behind them, they s	Josh 8:20	7200
all Israel s that the ambush had	Josh 8:21	7200
the spies s a man come forth out	Judg 1:24	7200
and when they s that, behold, the	Judg 3:24	7200
when Gaal s the people, he said	Judg 9:36	7200
when the men of Israel s that	Judg 9:55	7200
And it came to pass, when he s her	Judg 11:35	7200
when I s that ye delivered me not	Judg 12:3	7200
s a woman in Timnath of the	Judg 14:1	7200
it came to pass, when they s him	Judg 14:11	7200
s there an harlot, and went in	Judg 16:1	7200
when Delilah s that he had told	Judg 16:18	7200
And when the people s him, they	Judg 16:24	7200
s the people that were therein,	Judg 18:7	7200
when Micah s that they were too	Judg 18:26	7200
the father of the damsel s him	Judg 19:3	7200
he s a wayfaring man in the	Judg 19:17	7200
was so, that all that s it said	Judg 19:30	7200
Benjamin s that they were smitten	Judg 20:36	7200
for they s that evil was come	Judg 20:41	7200
When she s that she was	Ruth 1:18	7200
her mother in law s what she had	Ruth 2:18	7200
men of Ashdod s that it was so	1Sa 5:7	7200
s the ark, and rejoiced to see it	1Sa 6:13	7200
And when Samuel s Saul, the LORD	1Sa 9:17	7200
that knew him beforetime s that	1Sa 10:11	7200
when we s that they were no where	1Sa 10:14	7200
when ye s that Nahash the king of	1Sa 12:12	7200
When the men of Israel s that	1Sa 13:6	7200
Because I s that the people were	1Sa 13:11	7200
when Saul s any strong man, or	1Sa 14:52	7200
of Israel, when they s the man	1Sa 17:24	7200
s David, he disdained him	1Sa 17:42	7200
when the Philistines s their	1Sa 17:51	7200
when Saul s David go forth	1Sa 17:55	7200
Wherefore when Saul s that he	1Sa 18:15	7200
And Saul s and knew that the LORD	1Sa 18:28	7200
when they s the company of the	1Sa 19:20	7200
I s the son of Jesse coming to	1Sa 22:9	7200
David s that Saul was come out to	1Sa 23:15	7200
And when Abigail s David, she	1Sa 25:23	7200
but I thine handmaid s not the	1Sa 25:25	7200
he s that Saul came after him	1Sa 26:3	7200
gat them away, and no man s it	1Sa 26:12	7200
when Saul s the host of the	1Sa 28:5	7200
And when the woman s Samuel	1Sa 28:12	7200
I s gods ascending out of the	1Sa 28:13	7200
s that he was sore troubled, and	1Sa 28:21	7200
armourbearer s that Saul was dead	1Sa 31:5	7200
s that the men of Israel fled, and	1Sa 31:7	7200
he looked behind him, he s me	2Sa 1:7	7200
s king David leaping and dancing	2Sa 6:16	7200
when the children of Ammon s that	2Sa 10:6	7200
When Joab s that the front of the	2Sa 10:9	7200
s that the Syrians were fled	2Sa 10:14	7200
when the Syrians s that they were	2Sa 10:15	7200
s that they were smitten before	2Sa 10:19	7200
from the roof he s a woman	2Sa 11:2	7200
But when David s that his	2Sa 12:19	7200
house, and s not the king's face	2Sa 14:24	7200
and s not the king's face	2Sa 14:28	7200
Nevertheless a lad s them	2Sa 17:18	7200
when Ahithophel s that his	2Sa 17:23	7200
And a certain man s it, and told	2Sa 18:10	7200
I s Absalom hanged in an oak	2Sa 18:10	7200
the watchman s another man	2Sa 18:26	7200
I s a great tumult, but I knew	2Sa 18:29	7200
when the man s that all the	2Sa 20:12	7200
when he s that every one that	2Sa 20:12	7200
spake unto the LORD when he s the	2Sa 24:17	7200
s the king and his servants coming	2Sa 24:20	7200
for they s that the wisdom of God	1Kin 3:28	7200
So when all Israel s that the	1Kin 12:16	7200
s the carcase cast in the way, and	1Kin 13:25	7200
when Zimri s that the city was	1Kin 16:18	7200
came to pass, when Ahab s Elijah	1Kin 18:17	7200
And when all the people s it	1Kin 18:39	7200
And when he s that, he arose, and	1Kin 19:3	7200
I s all Israel scattered upon the	1Kin 22:17	7200
I s the LORD sitting on his	1Kin 22:19	7200
of the chariots s Jehoshaphat	1Kin 22:32	7200
And Elisha s it, and he cried, My	2Kin 2:12	7200
And he s him no more	2Kin 2:12	7200
were to view at Jericho s him	2Kin 2:15	7200
the Moabites s the water on the	2Kin 3:22	7200
when the king of Moab s that the	2Kin 3:26	7200
the man of God s her afar off	2Kin 4:25	7200
when Naaman s him running after	2Kin 5:21	7200
and he s: and	2Kin 6:17	7200
LORD opened their eyes, and they s	2Kin 6:20	7200
said unto Elisha, when he s them	2Kin 6:21	7200
came to pass, when Joram s Jehu	2Kin 9:22	7200
Ahaziah the king of Judah s this	2Kin 9:27	7200
Athaliah s that her son was dead	2Kin 11:1	7200
when they s that there was much	2Kin 12:10	7200
for he s the oppression of Israel	2Kin 13:4	7200
For the LORD s the affliction of	2Kin 14:26	7200
s an altar that was at Damascus	2Kin 16:10	7200
Damascus, the king s the altar	2Kin 16:12	7200
armourbearer s that Saul was dead	1Chr 10:5	7200
in the valley s that they fled	1Chr 10:7	7200
at a window s king David dancing	1Chr 15:29	7200
when the children of Ammon s that	1Chr 19:6	7200
Now when Joab s that the battle	1Chr 19:10	7200
s that the Syrians were fled	1Chr 19:15	7200
when the Syrians s that they were	1Chr 19:16	7200
when the servants of Hadarezer s	1Chr 19:19	7200
s the angel of the LORD stand	1Chr 21:16	7200
Ornan turned back, and s the angel	1Chr 21:20	7200
s David, and went out of the	1Chr 21:21	7200
At that time when David s that	1Chr 21:28	7200
Israel s how the fire came down	2Chr 7:3	7200
when all Israel s that the king	2Chr 10:16	7200
when the LORD s that they humbled	2Chr 12:7	7200
when they s that the LORD his God	2Chr 15:9	7200
I s the LORD sitting upon his	2Chr 18:18	7200
of the chariots s Jehoshaphat	2Chr 18:31	7200
Athaliah s that her son was dead	2Chr 22:10	7200
when they s that there was much	2Chr 24:11	7200
they s one another in the face,	2Chr 25:21	7200
s the heaps, they blessed the	2Chr 31:8	7200
when Hezekiah s that Sennacherib	2Chr 32:2	7200
that were about us s these things	Neh 6:16	7200
In those days s I in Judah some	Neh 13:15	7200
In those days also s I Jews that	Neh 13:23	7200
which s the king's face, and which	Est 1:14	7200
when Haman s that Mordecai bowed	Est 3:5	7200
when the king s Esther the queen	Est 5:2	7200
but when Haman s Mordecai in the	Est 5:9	7200
for he s that there was evil	Est 7:7	7200
for they s that his grief was	Job 2:13	7200
as infants which never s light	Job 3:16	7200
The eye also which s him shall	Job 20:9	7805
The young men s me, and hid	Job 29:8	7200
and when the eye s me, it gave	Job 29:11	7200
when I s my help in the gate	Job 31:21	7200
When Elihu s that there was no	Job 32:5	7200
s his sons, and his sons' sons,	Job 42:16	7200
They s it, and so they marvelled	Ps 48:5	7200
when I s the prosperity of the	Ps 73:3	7200
The waters s thee, O God, the	Ps 77:16	7200
thee, O God, the waters s thee	Ps 77:16	7200
me, proved me, and s my work	Ps 95:9	7200
the earth s, and trembled	Ps 97:4	7200
The sea s it, and fled	Ps 114:3	7200
Then I s, and considered it well	Prov 24:32	2372
Then I s that wisdom excelleth	Eccl 2:13	7200
This also I s, that it was from	Eccl 2:24	7200
moreover I s under the sun the	Eccl 3:16	7200
and I s vanity under the sun	Eccl 4:7	7200
so I s the wicked buried, who had	Eccl 8:10	7200
s under the sun, that the race is	Eccl 9:11	7200
S ye him whom my soul loveth	Song 3:3	7200
The daughters s her, and blessed	Song 6:9	7200
which he s concerning Judah and	Is 1:1	2372
son of Amoz s concerning Judah	Is 2:1	2372
I s also the Lord sitting upon a	Is 6:1	7200
or shall the s magnify itself	Is 10:15	4883
he s a chariot with a couple of	Is 21:7	7200
The isles s it, and feared	Is 41:5	7200
and the LORD s it, and it	Is 59:15	7200
he s that there was no man, and	Is 59:16	7200
her treacherous sister Judah s it	Jer 3:7	7200
And I s, when for all the causes	Jer 3:8	7200
Zedekiah the king of Judah s them	Jer 39:4	7200
s Johanan the son of Kareah	Jer 41:13	7200
and were well, and s no evil	Jer 44:17	7200
the adversaries s her, and did	Lam 1:7	7200
opened, and I s visions of God	Eze 1:1	7200
I s as the colour of amber, as	Eze 1:27	7200
I s as it were the appearance of	Eze 1:27	7200
And when I s it, I fell upon my	Eze 1:28	7200
as the glory which I s by the	Eze 3:23	7200
the vision that I s in the plain	Eze 8:4	7200
So I went in and s	Eze 8:10	7200

that I *s* by the river of Chebar Eze 10:15 7200
is the living creature that I *s* Eze 10:20 7200
which I *s* by the river of Chebar Eze 10:22 7200
among whom I *s* Jaazaniah the son Eze 11:1 7200
s thee polluted in thine own Eze 16:6 7200
I took them away as I *s* good Eze 16:50 7200
Now when she *s* that she had Eze 19:5 7200
then they *s* every high hill, and Eze 20:28 7200
when her sister Aholibah *s* this Eze 23:11 7200
Then I *s* that she was defiled, Eze 23:13 7200
for when she *s* men pourtrayed Eze 23:14 7200
as soon as she *s* them with her Eze 23:16
I *s* also the height of the house Eze 41:8 7200
of the vision which I *s*, even Eze 43:3 7200
according to the vision that I *s* Eze 43:3 7200
that I *s* by the river Chebar Eze 43:3 7200
s these men, upon whose bodies Dan 3:27 2370
I *s* a dream which made me afraid, Dan 4:5 2370
I *s*, and behold a tree in the Dan 4:10 2370
I *s* in the visions of my head Dan 4:13 2370
And whereas the king *s* a watcher Dan 4:23 2370
the king *s* the part of the hand Dan 5:5 2370
I *s* in my vision by night, and, Dan 7:2 2370
After this I *s* in the night Dan 7:7 2370
I *s* in the night visions, and, Dan 7:13 2370
And I *s* in a vision Dan 8:2 7200
and it came to pass, when I *s* Dan 8:2 7200
I *s* in a vision, and I was by the Dan 8:2 7200
Then I lifted up mine eyes, and *s* Dan 8:3 7200
I *s* the ram pushing westward, and Dan 8:4 7200
I *s* him come close unto the ram, Dan 8:7 7200
And I Daniel alone *s* the vision Dan 10:7 7200
were with me *s* not the vision Dan 10:7 7200
s this great vision, and there Dan 10:8 7200
When Ephraim *s* his sickness Hos 5:13 7200
Judah *s* his wound, then went Hos 5:13
I *s* your fathers as the firstripe Hos 9:10 7200
as I *s* Tyrus, is planted in a Hos 9:13 7200
which he *s* concerning Israel in Amos 1:1 2372
I *s* the Lord standing upon the Amos 9:1 7200
God *s* their works, that they Jonah 3:10 7200
which he *s* concerning Samaria and Mic 1:1 2372
I *s* the tents of Cushan in Hab 3:7 7200
The mountains *s* thee, and they Hab 3:10 7200
Who is left among you that *s* this Hag 2:3 7200
I *s* by night, and behold a man Zec 1:8 7200
Then lifted I up mine eyes, and *s* Zec 1:18 7200
which they *s* in the east, went Mt 2:9 1492
When they *s* the star, they Mt 2:10 1492
they *s* the young child with Mary Mt 2:11 2147
when he *s* that he was mocked of Mt 2:16 1492
But when he *s* many of the Mt 3:7 1492
he *s* the Spirit of God descending Mt 3:16 1492
sat in darkness *s* great light Mt 4:16 1492
s two brethren, Simon called Mt 4:18 1492
he *s* other two brethren, James Mt 4:21 1492
he *s* his wife's mother laid, and Mt 8:14 1492
Now when Jesus *s* great multitudes Mt 8:18 1492
and when they *s* him, they besought Mt 8:34 1492
But when the multitudes *s* it Mt 9:8 1492
he *s* a man, named Matthew, Mt 9:9 1492
And when the Pharisees *s* it Mt 9:11 1492
him about, and when he *s* her Mt 9:22 1492
s the minstrels and the people Mt 9:23 1492
But when he *s* the multitudes, he Mt 9:36 1492
But when the Pharisees *s* it Mt 12:2 1492
the blind and dumb both spake and *s* Mt 12:22 991
s a great multitude, and was moved Mt 14:14 1492
when the disciples *s* him walking Mt 14:26 1492
But when he *s* the wind boisterous Mt 14:30 991
when they *s* the dumb to speak, Mt 15:31 991
they *s* no man, save Jesus only Mt 17:8 1492
fellowservants *s* what was done Mt 18:31 1492
s others standing idle in the Mt 20:3 1492
scribes *s* the wonderful things Mt 21:15 1492
when he *s* a fig tree in the way, Mt 21:19 1492
And when the disciples *s* it Mt 21:20 1492
But when the husbandmen *s* the son Mt 21:38 1492
he *s* there a man which had not on Mt 22:11 1492
when *s* we thee an hungred, and fed Mt 25:37 1492
When *s* we thee a stranger, and Mt 25:38 1492
Or when *s* we thee sick, or in Mt 25:39 1492
when *s* we thee an hungred, or Mt 25:44 1492
But when his disciples *s* it Mt 26:8 1492
the porch, another maid *s* him Mt 26:71 1492
when he *s* that he was condemned, Mt 27:3 1492
When Pilate *s* that he could Mt 27:24 1492
s the earthquake, and those things Mt 27:54 1492
And when they *s* him, they Mt 28:17 1492
he *s* the heavens opened, and the Mk 1:10 1492
he *s* Simon and Andrew his brother Mk 1:16 1492
he *s* James the son of Zebedee, and Mk 1:19 1492
When Jesus *s* their faith, he said Mk 2:5 1492
We never *s* it on this fashion Mk 2:12 1492
he *s* Levi the son of Alphaeus Mk 2:14 1492
and Pharisees *s* him eat with Mk 2:16 1492
unclean spirits, when they *s* him Mk 3:11 2334
But when he *s* Jesus afar off, he Mk 5:6 1492
they that *s* it told them how it Mk 5:16 1492
and when he *s* him, he fell at his Mk 5:22 1492
the people *s* them departing, and Mk 6:33 1492
s much people, and was moved with Mk 6:34 1492
he *s* them toiling in rowing Mk 6:48 1492
But when they *s* him walking upon Mk 6:49 1492
For they all *s* him, and were Mk 6:50 1492
when they *s* some of his disciples Mk 7:2 1492
him, he asked him if he *s* ought Mk 8:23 991
restored, and *s* every man clearly Mk 8:25 1689
they *s* no man any more, save Mk 9:8 1492
he *s* a great multitude about them Mk 9:14 1492
and when he *s* him, straightway the Mk 9:20 1492
When Jesus *s* that the people came Mk 9:25 1492
we *s* one casting out devils in Mk 9:38 1492
But when Jesus *s* it, he was much Mk 10:14 1492
they *s* the fig tree dried up from Mk 11:20 1492
when Jesus *s* that he answered Mk 12:34 1492
when she *s* Peter warming himself, Mk 14:67 1492
a maid *s* him again, and began to Mk 14:69 1492
s that he so cried out, and gave Mk 15:39 1492
they *s* that the stone was rolled Mk 16:4 2334
they *s* a young man sitting on the Mk 16:5 1492
And when Zacharias *s* him, he was Lk 1:12 1492
And when she *s* him, she was Lk 1:29 1492
And when they *s* him, they were Lk 2:48 1492
s two ships standing by the lake Lk 5:2 1492
When Simon Peter *s* it, he fell Lk 5:8 1492
when he *s* their faith, he said Lk 5:20 1492
s a publican, named Levi, sitting Lk 5:27 2300
And when the Lord *s* her, he had Lk 7:13 1492
which had bidden him *s* it Lk 7:39 1492
When he *s* Jesus, he cried out, and Lk 8:28 1492
that fed them *s* what was done Lk 8:34 1492
They also which *s* it told them by Lk 8:36 1492
when the woman *s* that she was not Lk 8:47 1492
they *s* his glory, and the two men Lk 9:32 1492
we *s* one casting out devils in Lk 9:49 1492
disciples James and John *s* this Lk 9:54 1492
and when he *s* him, he passed by on Lk 10:31 1492
and when he *s* him, he had Lk 10:33 1492
And when the Pharisee *s* it Lk 11:38 1492
And when Jesus *s* her, he called Lk 13:12 1492
a great way off, his father *s* him Lk 15:20 1492
And when he *s* them, he said unto Lk 17:14 1492
when he *s* that he was healed, Lk 17:15 1492
but when his disciples *s* it Lk 18:15 1492
when Jesus *s* that he was very Lk 18:24 1492
and all the people, when they *s* it Lk 18:43 1492
up, and *s* him, and said unto him, Lk 19:5 1492
And when they *s* it, they all Lk 19:7 1492
But when the husbandmen *s* him Lk 20:14 1492
s the rich men casting their Lk 21:1 1492
he *s* also a certain poor widow Lk 21:2 1492
about him *s* what would follow Lk 22:49 1492
a little while another *s* him Lk 22:58 1492
And when Herod *s* Jesus, he was Lk 23:8 1492
the centurion *s* what was done Lk 23:47 1492
but him they *s* not Lk 24:24 1492
I *s* the Spirit descending from Jn 1:32 2300
And I *s*, and bare record that this Jn 1:34 3708
s them following, and saith unto Jn 1:38 2300
s where he dwelt, and abode with Jn 1:39 1492
Jesus *s* Nathanael coming to him, Jn 1:47 1492
wast under the fig tree, I *s* thee Jn 1:48 1492
I *s* thee under the fig tree, Jn 1:50 1492
when they *s* the miracles which he Jn 2:23 2334
When Jesus *s* him lie, and knew Jn 5:6 1492
because they *s* his miracles which Jn 6:2 3708
s a great company come unto him, Jn 6:5 2300
on the other side of the sea *s* Jn 6:22 1492
s that Jesus was not there Jn 6:24 1492
me, not because ye *s* the miracles Jn 6:26 1492
s none but the woman, he said Jn 8:10 2300
and he *s* it, and was glad Jn 8:56 1492
he *s* a man which was blind from Jn 9:1 1492
comforted her, when they *s* Mary Jn 11:31 1492
s him, she fell down at his feet, Jn 11:32 1492
Jesus therefore *s* her weeping Jn 11:33 1492
when he *s* his glory, and spake of Jn 12:41 1492
therefore and officers *s* him Jn 19:6 1492
When Jesus therefore *s* his mother Jn 19:26 1492
s that he was dead already, they Jn 19:33 1492
he that *s* it bare record, and his Jn 19:35 3708
s the linen clothes lying Jn 20:5 991
first to the sepulchre, and he *s* Jn 20:8 1492
s Jesus standing, and knew not Jn 20:14 2334
glad, when they *s* the Lord Jn 20:20 1492
they *s* a fire of coals there, and Jn 21:9 991
And all the people *s* him walking Acts 3:9 1492
And when Peter *s* it, he answered Acts 3:12 1492
Now when they *s* the boldness of Acts 4:13 2334
s his face as it had been the Acts 6:15 1492
When Moses *s* it, he wondered at Acts 7:31 1492
s the glory of God, and Jesus Acts 7:55 1492
when Simon *s* that through laying Acts 8:18 2300
that the eunuch *s* him no more Acts 8:39 1492
his eyes were opened, he *s* no man Acts 9:8 991
dwelt at Lydda and Saron *s* him Acts 9:35 1492
and when she *s* Peter, she sat up Acts 9:40 1492
He *s* in a vision evidently about Acts 10:3 1492
s heaven opened, and a certain Acts 10:11 2334
and in a trance I *s* a vision Acts 11:5 1492
s fourfooted beasts of the earth, Acts 11:6 1492
because he *s* it pleased the Jews, Acts 12:3 1492
but thought he *s* a vision Acts 12:9 991
s him, they were astonished Acts 12:16 1492
when he *s* what was done, believed Acts 13:12 1492
unto his fathers, and *s* corruption Acts 13:36 1492
God raised again, *s* no corruption Acts 13:37 1492
when the Jews *s* the multitudes Acts 13:45 1492
when the people *s* what Paul had Acts 14:11 1492
when her masters *s* that the hope Acts 16:19 1492
when he *s* the city wholly given Acts 17:16 2334
when they *s* him in the temple, Acts 21:27 2300
when they *s* the chief captain and Acts 21:32 1492
were with me *s* indeed the light Acts 22:9 2300
s him saying unto me, Make haste, Acts 22:18 1492
I *s* in the way a light from Acts 26:13 1492
when the barbarians *s* the Acts 28:4 1492
s no harm come to him, they Acts 28:6 2334
whom when Paul *s*, he thanked God, Acts 28:15 1492
other of the apostles *s* I none Gal 1:19 1492
when they *s* that the gospel of Gal 2:7 1492
But when I *s* that they walked not Gal 2:14 1492
same conflict which ye *s* in me Phil 1:30 1492
me, and *s* my works forty years Heb 3:9 1492
because they *s* he was a proper Heb 11:23 1492
and of all things that he *s* Rev 1:2 1492
I *s* seven golden candlesticks Rev 1:12 1492
And when I *s* him, I fell at his Rev 1:17 1492
and upon the seats I *s* four Rev 4:4 1492
I *s* in the right hand of him that Rev 5:1 1492
I *s* a strong angel proclaiming Rev 5:2 1492
I *s* when the Lamb opened one of Rev 6:1 1492
And I *s*, and behold a white horse Rev 6:2 1492
I *s* under the altar the souls of Rev 6:9 1492
after these things I *s* four Rev 7:1 1492
I *s* another angel ascending from Rev 7:2 1492
I *s* the seven angels which stood Rev 8:2 1492
I *s* a star fall from heaven unto Rev 9:1 1492
thus I *s* the horses in the vision Rev 9:17 1492
I *s* another mighty angel come Rev 10:1 1492
the angel which I *s* stand upon Rev 10:5 1492
fear fell upon them which *s* them Rev 11:11 2334
when the dragon *s* that he was Rev 12:13 1492
s a beast rise up out of the sea, Rev 13:1 1492
the beast which I *s* was like unto Rev 13:2 1492
I *s* one of his heads as it were Rev 13:3 1492
I *s* another angel fly in the Rev 14:6 1492
I *s* another sign in heaven, great Rev 15:1 1492
I *s* as it were a sea of glass Rev 15:2 1492
I *s* three unclean spirits like Rev 16:13 1492
I *s* a woman sit upon a scarlet Rev 17:3 1492
I *s* the woman drunken with the Rev 17:6 1492
and when I *s* her, I wondered with Rev 17:6 1492
after these things I *s* another Rev 18:1 1492
cried when they *s* the smoke of Rev 18:18 3708
I *s* heaven opened, and behold a Rev 19:11 1492
I *s* an angel standing in the sun Rev 19:17 1492
I *s* the beast, and the kings of Rev 19:19 1492
I *s* an angel come down from Rev 20:1 1492
I *s* thrones, and they sat upon Rev 20:4 1492
I *s* the souls of them that were Rev 20:4
I *s* a great white throne, and him Rev 20:11 1492
I *s* the dead, small and great, Rev 20:12 1492
I *s* a new heaven and a new earth Rev 21:1 1492
I John *s* the holy city, new Rev 21:2 1492
And I *s* no temple therein Rev 21:22 1492
I John *s* these things, and heard Rev 22:8 991

SAWED

s with saws, within and without, 1Kin 7:9 1641

SAWEST

said unto Abraham, What *s* thou Gen 20:10 7200
thou *s* it, and didst rejoice 1Sa 19:5 7200
for what *s* thou 1Sa 28:13 7200
told him, And, behold, thou *s* him 2Sa 18:11 7200
When thou *s* a thief, then thou Ps 50:18 7200
lovedst their bed where thou *s* it Is 57:8 2372
Thou, O king, *s*, and behold a Dan 2:31 2370
Thou *s* till that a stone was cut Dan 2:34 2370
And whereas thou *s* the feet Dan 2:41 2370
forasmuch as thou *s* the iron Dan 2:41 2370
whereas thou *s* iron mixed with Dan 2:43 2370
Forasmuch as thou *s* that the Dan 2:45 2370
The tree that thou *s*, which grew, Dan 4:20 2370
The ram which thou *s* having two Dan 8:20 7200
which thou *s* in my right hand Rev 1:20 1492
thou *s* are the seven churches Rev 1:20 1492
The beast that thou *s* was Rev 17:8 1492
horns which thou *s* are ten kings Rev 17:12 1492
unto me, The waters which thou *s* Rev 17:15 1492
horns which thou *s* upon the beast Rev 17:16 1492
which thou *s* is that great city Rev 17:18 1492

SAWN

were stoned, they were *s* asunder Heb 11:37 4249

SAWS

were therein, and put them under *s* 2Sa 12:31 4050
of hewed stones, sawed with *s* 1Kin 7:9 4050
were in it, and cut them with *s* 1Chr 20:3 4050

SAY

shall see thee, that they shall *s* Gen 12:12 559
S, I pray thee, thou art my Gen 12:13 559
is thine, lest thou shouldest *s* Gen 14:23 559
s of me, He is my brother Gen 20:13 559
that the damsel to whom I shall *s* Gen 24:14 559
and she shall *s*, Drink, and I will Gen 24:14 559
I *s* to her, Give me, I pray thee, Gen 24:43 559
she *s* to me, Both drink thou, and Gen 24:44 559
for he feared to *s*, She is my Gen 26:7 559
Then thou shalt *s*, They be thy Gen 32:18 559
s ye moreover, Behold, thy Gen 32:20 559
what ye shall *s* unto me I will Gen 34:11 559
according as ye shall *s* unto me Gen 34:12 559
for I heard them *s*, Let us go to Gen 37:17 559
him into some pit, and we will *s* Gen 37:20 559
and I have heard *s* of thee Gen 41:15 559
we certainly know that he would *s* Gen 43:7 559
s unto them, Wherefore have ye Gen 44:4 559
What shall we *s* unto my lord Gen 44:16 559
s unto him, Thus saith thy son Gen 45:9 559
S unto thy brethren, This do ye Gen 45:17 559
s unto him, My brethren, and my Gen 46:31 559
shall call you, and shall *s* Gen 46:33 559
That ye shall *s*, Thy servants' Gen 46:34 559
So shall ye *s* unto Joseph Gen 50:17 559
shall *s* unto them, The God of Ex 3:13 559
and they shall *s* to me, What is Ex 3:13 559
what shall I *s* unto them Ex 3:13 559
Thus shalt thou *s* unto the Ex 3:14 559
Thus shalt thou *s* unto the Ex 3:15 559
s unto them, The LORD God of your Ex 3:16 559
of Egypt, and ye shall *s* unto him Ex 3:18 559
for they will *s*, The LORD hath Ex 4:1 559
and teach thee what thou shalt *s* Ex 4:12 1696
thou shalt *s* unto Pharaoh, Thus Ex 4:22 559
I *s* unto thee, Let my son go, Ex 4:23 559
and they *s* to us, Make brick Ex 5:16 559
therefore ye *s*, Let us go and do Ex 5:17 559
Wherefore *s* unto the children of Ex 6:6 559
of Egypt all that I *s* unto thee Ex 6:29 1696

then thou shalt *s* unto Aaron	Ex 7:9	559
And thou shalt *s* unto him, The	Ex 7:16	559
S unto Aaron, Take thy rod, and	Ex 7:19	559
s unto him, Thus saith the LORD,	Ex 8:1	559
S unto Aaron, Stretch forth thine	Ex 8:5	559
S unto Aaron, Stretch out thy rod	Ex 8:16	559
s unto him, Thus saith the LORD,	Ex 8:20	559
s unto him, Thus saith the LORD	Ex 9:13	559
your children shall *s* unto you	Ex 12:26	559
That ye shall *s*, It is the	Ex 12:27	559
that thou shalt *s* unto him	Ex 13:14	559
For Pharaoh will *s* of the	Ex 14:3	559
S unto all the congregation of	Ex 16:9	559
Thus shalt thou *s* to the house of	Ex 19:3	559
Thus thou shalt *s* unto the	Ex 20:22	559
And if the servant shall plainly *s*	Ex 21:5	559
should the Egyptians speak, and *s*	Ex 32:12	559
S unto the children of Israel, Ye	Ex 33:5	559
s unto them, If any man of you	Lev 1:2	559
s unto them, When any man hath a	Lev 15:2	559
of Israel, and *s* unto them	Lev 17:2	559
And thou shalt *s* unto them	Lev 17:8	559
s unto them, I am the LORD your	Lev 18:2	559
s unto them, Ye shall be holy	Lev 19:2	559
thou shalt *s* to the children of	Lev 20:2	559
s unto them, There shall none be	Lev 21:1	559
S unto them, Whosoever he be of	Lev 22:3	559
s unto them, Whatsoever he be of	Lev 22:18	559
s unto them, Concerning the	Lev 23:2	559
s unto them, When ye be come into	Lev 23:10	559
s unto them, When ye come into	Lev 25:2	559
And if ye shall *s*, What shall we	Lev 25:20	559
s unto them, When a man shall	Lev 27:2	559
s unto them, If any man's wife go	Num 5:12	559
s unto the woman, If no man have	Num 5:19	559
the priest shall *s* unto the woman	Num 5:21	559
And the woman shall *s*, Amen, amen	Num 5:22	559
s unto them, When either man or	Num 6:2	559
s unto him, When thou lightest	Num 8:2	559
that thou shouldest *s* unto me	Num 11:12	559
s thou unto the people, Sanctify	Num 11:18	559
S unto them, As truly as I live,	Num 14:28	559
s unto them, When ye be come into	Num 15:2	559
s unto them, When ye come into	Num 15:18	559
s unto them, When ye take of the	Num 18:26	559
Therefore thou shalt *s* unto them	Num 18:30	559
they that speak in proverbs *s*	Num 21:27	559
what the LORD will *s* unto me more	Num 22:19	1696
word which I shall *s* unto thee	Num 22:20	1696
any power at all to *s* any thing	Num 22:38	1696
Go again unto Balak, and *s* thus	Num 23:16	1696
Wherefore *s*, Behold, I give unto	Num 25:12	559
s unto them, My offering, and my	Num 28:2	559
And thou shalt *s* unto them	Num 28:3	559
s unto them, When ye are passed	Num 33:51	559
s unto them, When ye come into	Num 34:2	559
s unto them, When ye be come over	Num 35:10	559
S unto them, Go not up, neither	Deut 1:42	559
hear all these statutes, and *s*	Deut 4:6	559
all that the LORD our God shall *s*	Deut 5:27	559
Go *s* to them, Get you into your	Deut 5:30	559
Then thou shalt *s* unto thy son	Deut 6:21	559
If thou shalt *s* in thine heart,	Deut 7:17	559
thou *s* in thine heart, My power	Deut 8:17	559
and of whom thou hast heard *s*	Deut 9:2	
whence thou broughtest us out *s*	Deut 9:28	559
promised thee, and thou shalt *s*	Deut 12:20	559
If thou shalt hear *s* in one of	Deut 13:12	
if he *s* unto thee, I will not go	Deut 15:16	559
shalt dwell therein, and shalt *s*	Deut 17:14	559
if thou *s* in thine heart, How	Deut 18:21	559
shall *s* unto them, Hear, O Israel	Deut 20:3	559
unto the people, and they shall *s*	Deut 20:8	559
And they shall answer and *s*	Deut 21:7	559
they shall *s* unto the elders of	Deut 21:20	559
up an evil name upon her, and *s*	Deut 22:14	559
father shall *s* unto the elders	Deut 22:16	559
to the gate unto the elders, and *s*	Deut 25:7	559
and if he stand to it, and *s*	Deut 25:8	559
in his face, and shall answer and *s*	Deut 25:9	559
s unto him, I profess this day	Deut 26:3	559
s before the LORD thy God, A	Deut 26:5	559
Then thou shalt *s* before the LORD	Deut 26:13	559
s unto all the men of Israel with	Deut 27:14	559
all the people shall answer and *s*	Deut 27:15	559
and all the people shall *s*	Deut 27:16	559
And all the people shall *s*	Deut 27:17	559
And all the people shall *s*	Deut 27:18	559
And all the people shall *s*	Deut 27:19	559
And all the people shall *s*	Deut 27:20	559
And all the people shall *s*	Deut 27:21	559
And all the people shall *s*	Deut 27:22	559
And all the people shall *s*	Deut 27:23	559
And all the people shall *s*	Deut 27:24	559
And all the people shall *s*	Deut 27:25	559
And all the people shall *s*	Deut 27:26	559
In the morning thou shalt *s*	Deut 28:67	559
and at even thou shalt *s*, Would	Deut 28:67	559
come from a far land, shall *s*	Deut 29:22	559
Even all nations shall *s*,	Deut 29:24	559
Then men shall *s*, Because they	Deut 29:25	559
in heaven, that thou shouldest *s*	Deut 30:12	559
the sea, that thou shouldest *s*	Deut 30:13	559
so that they will *s* in that day	Deut 31:17	559
strangely, and lest they should *s*	Deut 32:27	559
And he shall *s*, Where are their	Deut 32:37	559
I lift up my hand to heaven, and *s*	Deut 32:40	559
and shall *s*, Destroy them	Deut 33:27	559
O Lord, what shall I *s*, when	Josh 7:8	559
Up, sanctify the people, and *s*	Josh 7:13	559
for they will *s*, They flee before	Josh 8:6	559
s unto them, We are your servants	Josh 9:11	559
And the children of Israel heard *s*	Josh 22:11	559
that your children may not *s* to	Josh 22:27	559
when they should so *s* to us or to	Josh 22:28	559
time to come, that we may *s* again	Josh 22:28	559
come and enquire of thee, and *s*	Judg 4:20	559
that thou shalt *s*, No	Judg 4:20	559
be, that of whom I *s* unto thee	Judg 7:4	559
and of whomsoever I *s* unto thee	Judg 7:4	559
And thou shalt hear what they *s*	Judg 7:11	1696
every side of all the camp, and *s*	Judg 7:18	559
that men *s* not of me, A woman	Judg 9:54	559
they unto him, *S* now Shibboleth	Judg 12:6	559
said unto him, How canst thou *s*	Judg 16:15	559
said unto them, What *s* ye	Judg 18:8	559
and what is this that ye *s* unto me	Judg 18:24	559
that we will *s* unto them	Judg 21:22	559
If I should *s*, I have hope, if I	Ruth 1:12	559
and a morsel of bread, and shall *s*	1Sa 2:36	559
he call thee, that thou shalt *s*	1Sa 3:9	559
in all that they *s* unto thee	1Sa 8:7	559
and they will *s* unto thee, The	1Sa 10:2	559
Thus shall ye *s* unto the men of	1Sa 11:9	559
all Israel heard *s* that Saul had	1Sa 13:4	559
If they *s* thus unto us, Tarry	1Sa 14:9	559
But if they *s* thus, Come up unto	1Sa 14:10	559
s unto them, Bring me hither	1Sa 14:34	559
And he said unto him, *S* on	1Sa 15:16	1696
Take an heifer with thee, and *s*	1Sa 16:2	559
Commune with David secretly, and *s*	1Sa 18:22	559
said, Thus shall ye *s* to David	1Sa 18:25	559
Wherefore they *s*, Is Saul also	1Sa 19:24	559
thy father at all miss me, then *s*	1Sa 20:6	559
If he *s* thus, It is well	1Sa 20:7	559
If I expressly *s* unto the lad	1Sa 20:21	559
But if I *s* thus unto the young	1Sa 20:22	559
thus shall ye *s* to him that	1Sa 25:6	559
thou *s* unto my servant David	2Sa 7:8	559
what can David *s* more unto thee	2Sa 7:20	1696
he *s* unto thee, Wherefore	2Sa 11:20	559
then *s* thou, Thy servant Uriah	2Sa 11:21	559
Thus shalt thou *s* unto Joab	2Sa 11:25	559
s unto him, I pray thee, let my	2Sa 13:5	559
when I *s* unto you, Smite Amnon	2Sa 13:28	559
And he said, *S* on	2Sa 14:12	1696
I may send thee to the king, to *s*	2Sa 14:32	559
of the trumpet, then ye shall *s*	2Sa 15:10	559
But if he thus *s*, I have no	2Sa 15:26	559
s unto Absalom, I will be thy	2Sa 15:34	559
Who shall then *s*, Wherefore hast	2Sa 16:10	559
that whosoever heareth it will *s*	2Sa 17:9	559
for the people heard *s* that day	2Sa 19:2	559
s ye to Amasa, Art thou not of my	2Sa 19:13	559
s, I pray you, unto Joab, Come	2Sa 20:16	559
And he said, What ye shall *s*	2Sa 21:4	559
he moved David against them to *s*	2Sa 24:1	559
s unto David, Thus saith the LORD	2Sa 24:12	559
s unto him, Didst not thou, my	1Kin 1:13	559
eat and drink before him, and *s*	1Kin 1:25	559
and blow ye with the trumpet, and *s*	1Kin 1:34	559
God of my lord the king *s* so too	1Kin 1:36	559
I have somewhat to *s* unto thee	1Kin 2:14	1697
And she said, *S* on	1Kin 2:14	1696
And she said unto him, *S* on	1Kin 2:16	1696
king, (for he will not *s* thee nay	1Kin 2:17	559
I pray thee, *s* me not nay	1Kin 2:20	559
for I will not *s* thee nay	1Kin 2:20	559
and they shall *s*, Why hath the	1Kin 9:8	559
thus shalt thou *s* unto them	1Kin 12:10	559
the which the LORD did *s* to thee	1Kin 13:22	1696
and thus shalt thou *s* unto her	1Kin 14:5	1696
people that were encamped heard *s*	1Kin 16:16	559
s unto Ahab, Prepare thy chariot,	1Kin 18:44	559
said, Let not the king *s* so	1Kin 22:8	559
And *s*, Thus saith the king, Put	1Kin 22:27	559
s unto them, Is it not because	2Kin 1:3	1696
s unto him, Thus saith the LORD,	2Kin 1:6	1696
unto them, Did I not *s* unto you	2Kin 2:18	559
S now unto her, Behold, thou hast	2Kin 4:13	559
s unto her, Is it well with thee	2Kin 4:26	559
did I not *s*, Do not deceive me	2Kin 4:28	559
If we *s*, We will enter into the	2Kin 7:4	559
behold, I *s*, they are even as all	2Kin 7:13	
s unto him, Thou mayest certainly	2Kin 8:10	559
oil, and pour it on his head, and *s*	2Kin 9:3	559
send to meet them, and let him *s*	2Kin 9:17	559
so that they shall not *s*, This is	2Kin 9:37	559
But if ye *s* unto me, We trust in	2Kin 18:22	559
Thus shall ye *s* to your master,	2Kin 19:6	559
when he heard *s* of Tirhakah king	2Kin 19:9	559
the LORD, thus shall ye *s* to him	2Kin 22:18	559
The sons, I *s*, of Reuben the	1Chr 5:3	
let men *s* among the nations, The	1Chr 16:31	559
s ye, Save us, O God of our	1Chr 16:35	559
thou *s* unto my servant David	1Chr 17:7	559
LORD commanded Gad to *s* to David	1Chr 21:18	559
so that he shall *s*, Why hath the	2Chr 7:21	559
thus shalt thou *s* unto them	2Chr 10:10	559
said, Let not the king *s* so	2Chr 18:7	559
shall I adjure thee that thou *s*	2Chr 18:15	559
And *s*, Thus saith the king, Put	2Chr 18:26	559
Behold, I *s*, how they reward us,	2Chr 20:11	
went out before the army, and to *s*	2Chr 20:21	559
the LORD, so shall ye *s* unto him	2Chr 34:26	559
them what they should *s* unto Iddo	Ezr 8:17	1696
God, what shall we *s* after this	Ezr 9:10	559
The number, I *s*, of the men of	Neh 7:7	
the Girgashites, to give it, I *s*	Neh 9:8	
Media *s* this day unto all the	Est 1:18	559
Did I *s*, Bring unto me	Job 6:22	559
When I lie down, I *s*, When shall	Job 7:4	559
When I *s*, My bed shall comfort me	Job 7:13	559
who will *s* unto him, What doest	Job 9:12	559
if I *s*, I am perfect, it shall	Job 9:20	
If I *s*, I will forget my	Job 9:27	559
I will *s* unto God, Do not condemn	Job 10:2	559
But ye should *s*, Why persecute we	Job 19:28	559
they which have seen him shall *s*	Job 20:7	559
Therefore they *s* unto God	Job 21:14	559
For ye *s*, Where is the house of	Job 21:28	559
are cast down, then thou shalt *s*	Job 22:29	559
what he would *s* unto me	Job 23:5	559
Destruction and death *s*, We have	Job 28:22	559
whilst ye searched out what to *s*	Job 32:11	4405
Lest ye should *s*, We have found	Job 32:13	559
He looketh upon men, and if any *s*	Job 33:27	559
If thou hast any thing to *s*	Job 33:32	4405
Is it fit to *s* to a king, Thou	Job 34:18	559
or who can *s*, Thou hast wrought	Job 36:23	559
Teach us what we shall *s* unto him	Job 37:19	559
go, and *s* unto thee, Here we are	Job 38:35	559
Many there be which *s* of my soul	Ps 3:2	559
There be many that *s*, Who will	Ps 4:6	559
how *s* ye to my soul, Flee as a	Ps 11:1	559
Lest mine enemy *s*, I have	Ps 13:4	559
wait, I *s*, on the LORD	Ps 27:14	
s unto my soul, I am thy	Ps 35:3	559
All my bones shall *s*, LORD, who	Ps 35:10	559
Let them not *s* in their hearts,	Ps 35:25	559
let them not *s*, We have swallowed	Ps 35:25	559
let them *s* continually, Let the	Ps 35:27	559
of their shame that *s* unto me	Ps 40:15	559
love thy salvation *s* continually	Ps 40:16	559
s they, cleaveth fast unto him	Ps 41:8	
while they continually *s* unto me	Ps 42:3	559
I will *s* unto God my rock, Why	Ps 42:9	559
while they *s* daily unto me, Where	Ps 42:10	559
So that a man shall *s*, Verily	Ps 58:11	559
for who, *s* they, doth hear	Ps 59:7	
they *s*, Who shall see them	Ps 64:5	559
S unto God, How terrible art thou	Ps 66:3	559
a reward of their shame that *s*	Ps 70:3	559
love thy salvation *s* continually	Ps 70:4	559
And they *s*, How doth God know	Ps 73:11	559
If I *s*, I will speak thus	Ps 73:15	559
Wherefore should the heathen *s*	Ps 79:10	559
I will *s* of the LORD, He is my	Ps 91:2	559
Yet they *s*, The LORD shall not	Ps 94:7	559
S among the heathen that the LORD	Ps 96:10	559
and let all the people *s*, Amen	Ps 106:48	559
Let the redeemed of the LORD *s* so	Ps 107:2	559
Wherefore should the heathen *s*	Ps 115:2	559
Let Israel now *s*, that his mercy	Ps 118:2	559
Let the house of Aaron now *s*	Ps 118:3	559
Let them now that fear the LORD *s*	Ps 118:4	559
companions' sakes, I will now *s*	Ps 122:8	1696
was on our side, now may Israel *s*	Ps 124:1	559
from my youth, may Israel now *s*	Ps 129:1	559
Neither do they which go by *s*	Ps 129:8	559
I *s*, more than they that watch	Ps 130:6	
If I *s*, Surely the darkness shall	Ps 139:11	559
If they *s*, Come with us, let us	Prov 1:11	559
S not unto thy neighbour, Go, and	Prov 3:28	559
And *s*, How have I hated	Prov 5:12	559
S unto wisdom, Thou art my sister	Prov 7:4	559
Who can *s*, I have made my heart	Prov 20:9	559
S not thou, I will recompense	Prov 20:22	559
have stricken me, shalt thou *s*	Prov 23:35	559
S not, I will do so to him as he	Prov 24:29	559
I be full, and deny thee, and *s*	Prov 30:9	559
satisfied, yea, four things *s* not	Prov 30:15	559
neither *s* thou before the angel,	Eccl 5:6	559
I *s*, that an untimely birth is	Eccl 6:3	559
S not thou, What is the cause	Eccl 7:10	559
who may *s* unto him, What doest	Eccl 8:4	559
draw nigh, when thou shalt *s*	Eccl 12:1	559
And many people shall go and *s*	Is 2:3	559
S ye to the righteous, that it	Is 3:10	559
That *s*, Let him make speed, and	Is 5:19	559
s unto him, Take heed, and be	Is 7:4	559
S ye not, A confederacy, to all	Is 8:12	559
them to whom this people shall *s*	Is 8:12	559
And when they shall *s* unto you	Is 8:19	559
that *s* in the pride and stoutness	Is 9:9	559
And in that day thou shalt *s*	Is 12:1	559
And in that day shall ye *s*	Is 12:4	559
against the king of Babylon, and *s*	Is 14:4	559
s unto thee, Art thou also become	Is 14:10	559
how *s* ye unto Pharaoh, I am the	Is 19:11	559
of this isle shall *s* in that day	Is 20:6	559
which is over the house, and *s*	Is 22:15	559
works are in the dark, and they *s*	Is 29:15	559
for shall the work *s* of him that	Is 29:16	559
framed *s* of him that framed it	Is 29:16	559
Which *s* to the seers, See not	Is 30:10	559
thou shalt *s* unto it, Get thee	Is 30:22	559
And the inhabitant shall not *s*	Is 33:24	559
S to them that are of a fearful	Is 35:4	559
S ye now to Hezekiah, Thus saith	Is 36:4	559
I *s*, sayest thou, (but they are	Is 36:5	559
But if thou *s* to me, We trust in	Is 36:7	559
Thus shall ye *s* unto your master,	Is 37:6	559
he heard *s* concerning Tirhakah	Is 37:9	559
s to Hezekiah, Thus saith the	Is 38:5	559
What shall I *s*	Is 38:15	1696
s unto the cities of Judah,	Is 40:9	559
and beforetime, that we may *s*	Is 41:26	559
The first shall *s* to Zion	Is 41:27	
that *s* to the molten images, Ye	Is 42:17	559
I will *s* to the north, Give up	Is 43:6	559
or let them hear, and *s*, It is	Is 43:9	559
One shall *s*, I am the LORD's	Is 44:5	559
knowledge nor understanding to *s*	Is 44:19	559
he cannot deliver his soul, nor *s*	Is 44:20	559
Shall the clay *s* to him that	Is 45:9	559
Surely, shall one *s*, in the LORD	Is 45:24	559
lest thou shouldest *s*, Mine idol	Is 48:5	559
lest thou shouldest *s*, Behold, I	Is 48:7	559
s ye, The LORD hath redeemed his	Is 48:20	559
thou mayest *s* to the prisoners	Is 49:9	559
shall *s* again in thine ears, The	Is 49:20	559

Then shalt thou *s* in thine heart	Is 49:21	559
s unto Zion, Thou art my people	Is 51:16	559
neither let the eunuch *s*, Behold,	Is 56:3	559
s they, I will fetch wine, and we	Is 56:12	
And shall *s*, Cast ye up, cast ye	Is 57:14	559
s they, and thou seest not	Is 58:3	
thou shalt cry, and he shall *s*	Is 58:9	559
S ye to the daughter of Zion,	Is 62:11	559
Which *s*, Stand by thyself, come	Is 65:5	559
said unto me, *S* not, I am a child	Jer 1:7	559
How canst thou *s*, I am not	Jer 2:23	559
time of their trouble they will *s*	Jer 2:27	559
wherefore *s* my people, We are	Jer 2:31	559
They *s*, If a man put away his	Jer 3:1	559
words toward the north, and *s*	Jer 3:12	559
the LORD, they shall *s* no more	Jer 3:16	559
and *s*, Blow ye the trumpet in the	Jer 4:5	559
cry, gather together, and *s*	Jer 4:5	559
And though they *s*, The LORD liveth	Jer 5:2	559
neither understandest what they *s*	Jer 5:15	1696
come to pass, when ye shall *s*	Jer 5:19	559
Neither *s* they in their heart,	Jer 5:24	559
and proclaim there this word, and *s*	Jer 7:2	559
which is called by my name, and *s*	Jer 7:10	559
But thou shalt *s* unto them	Jer 7:28	559
Moreover thou shalt *s* unto them	Jer 8:4	559
How do ye *s*, We are wise, and the	Jer 8:8	559
Thus shall ye *s* unto them	Jer 10:11	560
s thou unto them, Thus saith the	Jer 11:3	559
and they shall *s* to thee	Jer 13:12	559
Then shalt thou *s* unto them	Jer 13:13	559
S unto the king and to the queen,	Jer 13:18	559
What wilt thou *s* when he shall	Jer 13:21	559
if thou *s* in thine heart,	Jer 13:22	559
behold, the prophets *s* unto them	Jer 14:13	559
and I sent them not, yet they *s*	Jer 14:15	559
thou shalt *s* this word unto them	Jer 14:17	559
if they *s* unto thee, Whither	Jer 15:2	559
words, and they shall *s* unto thee	Jer 16:10	559
Then shalt thou *s* unto them	Jer 16:11	559
the ends of the earth, and shall *s*	Jer 16:19	559
they *s* unto me, Where is the word	Jer 17:15	559
s unto them, Hear ye the word of	Jer 17:20	559
And *s*, Hear ye the word of the	Jer 19:3	559
shalt *s* unto them, Thus saith the	Jer 19:11	559
s they, and we will report it	Jer 20:10	
them, Thus shall ye *s* to Zedekiah	Jer 21:3	559
And unto this people thou shalt *s*	Jer 21:8	559
the house of the king of Judah, *s*	Jer 21:11	
which *s*, Who shall come down	Jer 21:13	559
And *s*, Hear the word of the LORD,	Jer 22:2	559
they shall *s* every man to his	Jer 22:8	559
LORD, that they shall no more *s*	Jer 23:7	559
They *s* still unto them that	Jer 23:17	559
they *s* unto every one that	Jer 23:17	559
that use their tongues, and *s*	Jer 23:31	
thou shalt then *s* unto them	Jer 23:33	559
and the people, that shall *s*	Jer 23:34	559
Thus shall ye *s* every one to his	Jer 23:35	559
Thus shalt thou *s* to the prophet	Jer 23:37	559
But since ye *s*, The burden of the	Jer 23:38	559
Because ye *s* this word, The	Jer 23:38	559
unto you, saying, Ye shall not *s*	Jer 23:38	559
Therefore thou shalt *s* unto them	Jer 25:27	559
then shalt thou *s* unto them	Jer 25:28	559
s unto them, The LORD shall roar	Jer 25:30	559
And thou shalt *s* unto them	Jer 26:4	559
command them to *s* unto their	Jer 27:4	559
Thus shall ye *s* unto your masters	Jer 27:4	559
publish ye, praise ye, and *s*	Jer 31:7	559
it in the isles afar off, and *s*	Jer 31:10	559
those days they shall *s* no more	Jer 31:29	559
dost thou prophesy, and *s*, Thus	Jer 32:3	559
this city, whereof ye *s*, It shall	Jer 32:36	559
bought in this land, whereof ye *s*	Jer 32:43	559
which ye *s* shall be desolate	Jer 33:10	559
the voice of them that shall *s*	Jer 33:11	559
thou shalt *s* to Jehoiakim king of	Jer 36:29	559
Thus shall ye *s* to the king of	Jer 37:7	559
princes, and those women shall *s*	Jer 38:22	559
s unto thee, Declare unto us now	Jer 38:25	559
Then thou shalt *s* unto them	Jer 38:26	559
him even as he shall *s* unto thee	Jer 39:12	1696
But if ye *s*, We will not dwell in	Jer 42:13	559
all that the LORD our God shall *s*	Jer 42:20	559
our God hath not sent thee to *s*	Jer 43:2	559
s unto them, Thus saith the LORD	Jer 43:10	559
Thou didst *s*, Woe is me now	Jer 45:3	559
Thus shalt thou *s* unto him	Jer 45:4	559
s ye, Stand fast, and prepare thee	Jer 46:14	559
How *s* ye, We are mighty and strong	Jer 48:14	559
and all ye that know his name, *s*	Jer 48:17	559
and her that escapeth, and *s*	Jer 48:19	559
s, Babylon is taken, Bel is	Jer 50:2	559
shall the inhabitant of Zion *s*	Jer 51:35	559
of Chaldea, shall Jerusalem *s*	Jer 51:35	559
Then shalt thou *s*, O LORD, thou	Jer 51:62	559
And thou shalt *s*, Thus shall	Jer 51:64	559
They *s* to their mothers, Where is	Lam 2:12	559
they *s*, We have swallowed her up	Lam 2:16	559
and thou shalt *s* unto them	Eze 2:4	559
of man, hear what I *s* unto thee	Eze 2:8	1696
When I *s* unto the wicked, Thou	Eze 3:18	559
mouth, and thou shalt *s* unto them	Eze 3:27	559
And *s*, Ye mountains of Israel,	Eze 6:3	559
and stamp with thy foot, and *s*	Eze 6:11	559
for they *s*, The LORD seeth us not	Eze 8:12	559
for they *s*, The LORD hath	Eze 9:9	559
Which *s*, It is not near	Eze 11:3	559
Therefore *s*, Thus saith the Lord	Eze 11:16	559
Therefore *s*, Thus saith the Lord	Eze 11:17	559
S thou unto them, Thus saith the	Eze 12:10	559
S, I am your sign	Eze 12:11	559
s unto the people of the land,	Eze 12:19	559
but *s* unto them, The days are at	Eze 12:23	1696
will I *s* the word, and will	Eze 12:25	1696
they of the house of Israel *s*	Eze 12:27	559
Therefore *s* unto them, Thus saith	Eze 12:28	559
s thou unto them that prophesy	Eze 13:2	559
a lying divination, whereas ye *s*	Eze 13:7	559
S unto them which daub it with	Eze 13:11	559
will *s* unto you, The wall is no	Eze 13:15	559
And *s*, Thus saith the Lord GOD	Eze 13:18	559
s unto them, Thus saith the Lord	Eze 14:4	559
Therefore *s* unto the house of	Eze 14:6	559
a sword upon that land, and *s*	Eze 14:17	559
And *s*, Thus saith the Lord GOD	Eze 16:3	559
And *s*, Thus saith the Lord GOD	Eze 17:3	559
S thou, Thus saith the Lord GOD	Eze 17:9	559
S now to the rebellious house,	Eze 17:12	559
Yet *s* ye, Why	Eze 18:19	559
Yet ye *s*, The way of the Lord is	Eze 18:25	559
And *s*, What is thy mother	Eze 19:2	559
s unto them, Thus saith the Lord	Eze 20:3	559
s unto them, Thus saith the Lord	Eze 20:5	559
s unto them, Thus saith the Lord	Eze 20:27	559
Wherefore *s* unto the house of	Eze 20:30	559
shall not be at all, that ye *s*	Eze 20:32	559
s to the forest of the south,	Eze 20:47	559
they *s* of me, Doth he not speak	Eze 20:49	559
s to the land of Israel, Thus	Eze 21:3	559
shall be, when they *s* unto thee	Eze 21:7	559
Son of man, prophesy, and *s*	Eze 21:9	559
S, A sword, a sword is sharpened,	Eze 21:9	559
because, I *s*, that ye are come to	Eze 21:24	
thou, son of man, prophesy and *s*	Eze 21:28	559
even *s* thou, The sword, the sword	Eze 21:28	559
Then *s* thou, Thus saith the Lord	Eze 22:3	559
s unto her, Thou art the land	Eze 22:24	559
s unto them, Thus saith the Lord	Eze 24:3	559
s unto the Ammonites, Hear the	Eze 25:3	559
Because that Moab and Seir do *s*	Eze 25:8	559
s to thee, How art thou destroyed	Eze 26:17	559
s unto Tyrus, O thou that art	Eze 27:3	559
s unto the prince of Tyrus, Thus	Eze 28:2	559
Wilt thou yet *s* before him that	Eze 28:9	559
s unto him, Thus saith the Lord	Eze 28:12	559
And *s*, Thus saith the Lord GOD	Eze 28:22	559
Speak, and *s*, Thus saith the Lord	Eze 29:3	559
Son of man, prophesy and *s*	Eze 30:2	559
s unto him, Thou art like a young	Eze 32:2	559
s unto them, When I bring the	Eze 33:2	559
When I *s* unto the wicked, O	Eze 33:8	559
S unto them, As I live, saith the	Eze 33:11	559
s unto the children of thy people	Eze 33:12	559
When I shall *s* to the righteous,	Eze 33:13	559
when I *s* unto the wicked, Thou	Eze 33:14	559
Yet the children of thy people *s*	Eze 33:17	559
Yet ye *s*, The way of the Lord is	Eze 33:20	559
Wherefore *s* unto them, Thus saith	Eze 33:25	559
S thou thus unto them, Thus saith	Eze 33:27	559
s unto them, Thus saith the Lord	Eze 34:2	559
s unto it, Thus saith the Lord	Eze 35:3	559
the mountains of Israel, and *s*	Eze 36:1	559
Therefore prophesy and *s*, Thus	Eze 36:3	559
s unto the mountains, and to the	Eze 36:6	559
Because they *s* unto you, Thou	Eze 36:13	559
Therefore *s* unto the house of	Eze 36:22	559
And they shall *s*, This land that	Eze 36:35	559
s unto them, O ye dry bones, hear	Eze 37:4	559
s to the wind, Thus saith the	Eze 37:9	559
behold, they *s*, Our bones are	Eze 37:11	559
s unto them, Thus saith the Lord	Eze 37:12	559
S unto them, Thus saith the Lord	Eze 37:19	1696
s unto them, Thus saith the Lord	Eze 37:21	1696
And *s*, Thus saith the Lord GOD	Eze 38:3	559
And thou shalt *s*, I will go up to	Eze 38:11	559
shall *s* unto thee, Art thou come	Eze 38:13	559
s unto Gog, Thus saith the Lord	Eze 38:14	559
man, prophesy against Gog, and *s*	Eze 39:1	559
I *s* unto thee concerning all the	Eze 44:5	1696
thou shalt *s* to the rebellious,	Eze 44:6	559
or *s* unto him, What doest thou	Dan 4:35	560
thy father, the king, I *s*	Dan 5:11	
S ye unto your brethren, Ammi	Hos 2:1	559
then shall she *s*, I will go and	Hos 2:7	559
I will *s* to them which were not	Hos 2:23	559
and they shall *s*, Thou art my God	Hos 2:23	559
For now they shall *s*, We have no	Hos 10:3	559
they shall *s* to the mountains,	Hos 10:8	559
they *s* of them, Let the men that	Hos 13:2	559
s unto him, Take away all	Hos 14:2	559
neither will we *s* any more to the	Hos 14:3	559
Ephraim shall *s*, What have I to	Hos 14:8	559
porch and the altar, and let them *s*	Joel 2:17	559
should they *s* among the people	Joel 2:17	559
s unto his people, Behold, I will	Joel 2:19	559
let the weak *s*, I am strong	Joel 3:10	559
in the land of Egypt, and *s*	Amos 3:9	559
which *s* to their masters, Bring,	Amos 4:1	559
they shall *s* in all the highways,	Amos 5:16	559
shall *s* unto him that is by the	Amos 6:10	559
and he shall *s*, No	Amos 6:10	559
Then shall he *s*, Hold thy tongue	Amos 6:10	559
in a thing of nought, which *s*	Amos 6:13	559
swear by the sin of Samaria, and *s*	Amos 8:14	559
shall die by the sword, which *s*	Amos 9:10	559
with a doleful lamentation, and *s*	Mic 2:4	559
s they to them that prophesy	Mic 2:6	559
they lean upon the LORD, and *s*	Mic 3:11	559
And many nations shall come, and *s*	Mic 4:2	559
are gathered against thee, that *s*	Mic 4:11	559
thee shall flee from thee, and *s*	Nah 3:7	559
to see what he will *s* unto me	Hab 2:1	1696
proverb against him, and *s*	Hab 2:6	559
that *s* in their heart, The LORD	Zeph 1:12	559
of hosts, saying, This people *s*	Hag 1:2	559
Therefore *s* thou unto them, Thus	Zec 1:3	559
and they that sell them *s*, Blessed	Zec 11:5	559
of Judah shall *s* in their heart	Zec 12:5	559
that begat him shall *s* unto him	Zec 13:3	559
But he shall *s*, I am no prophet,	Zec 13:5	559
And one shall *s* unto him, What are	Zec 13:6	559
I will *s*, It is my people	Zec 13:9	559
and they shall *s*, The LORD is my	Zec 13:9	559
Yet ye *s*, Wherein hast thou loved	Mal 1:2	559
eyes shall see, and ye shall *s*	Mal 1:5	559
And ye *s*, Wherein have we despised	Mal 1:6	559
and ye *s*, Wherein have we polluted	Mal 1:7	559
In that ye *s*, The table of the	Mal 1:7	559
ye have profaned it, in that ye *s*	Mal 1:12	559
Yet ye *s*, Wherefore	Mal 2:14	559
Yet ye *s*, Wherein have we wearied	Mal 2:17	559
When ye *s*, Every one that doeth	Mal 2:17	559
But ye *s*, Wherein have we robbed	Mal 3:8	559
Yet ye *s*, What have we spoken so	Mal 3:13	559
think not to *s* within yourselves,	Mt 3:9	3004
for I *s* unto you, that God is	Mt 3:9	3004
Jesus began to preach, and to *s*	Mt 4:17	3004
shall *s* all manner of evil	Mt 5:11	2036
For verily I *s* unto you, Till	Mt 5:18	3004
For I *s* unto you, That except	Mt 5:20	3004
But I *s* unto you, That whosoever	Mt 5:22	3004
whosoever shall *s* to his brother	Mt 5:22	2036
but whosoever shall *s*, Thou fool,	Mt 5:22	2036
Verily I *s* unto thee, Thou shalt	Mt 5:26	3004
But I *s* unto you, That whosoever	Mt 5:28	3004
But I *s* unto you, That whosoever	Mt 5:32	3004
But I *s* unto you, Swear not at	Mt 5:34	3004
But I *s* unto you, That ye resist	Mt 5:39	3004
But I *s* unto you, Love your	Mt 5:44	3004
Verily I *s* unto you, They have	Mt 6:2	3004
Verily I *s* unto you, They have	Mt 6:5	3004
Verily I *s* unto you, They have	Mt 6:16	3004
Therefore I *s* unto you, Take no	Mt 6:25	3004
yet I *s* unto you, That even	Mt 6:29	3004
Or how wilt thou *s* to thy brother	Mt 7:4	3004
Many will *s* to me in that day,	Mt 7:22	3004
I *s* to this man, Go, and he goeth	Mt 8:9	3004
followed, Verily I *s* unto you	Mt 8:10	3004
I *s* unto you, That many shall	Mt 8:11	3004
For whether is easier, to *s*	Mt 9:5	3004
or to *s*, Arise, and walk	Mt 9:5	3004
Verily I *s* unto you, It shall be	Mt 10:15	3004
for verily I *s* unto you, Ye shall	Mt 10:23	3004
a disciple, verily I *s* unto you	Mt 10:42	3004
Jesus began to *s* unto the	Mt 11:7	3004
I *s* unto you, and more than a	Mt 11:9	3004
Verily I *s* unto you, Among them	Mt 11:11	3004
eating nor drinking, and they *s*	Mt 11:18	3004
eating and drinking, and they *s*	Mt 11:19	3004
But I *s* unto you, It shall be	Mt 11:22	3004
But I *s* unto you, That it shall	Mt 11:24	3004
But I *s* unto you, That in this	Mt 12:6	3004
Wherefore I *s* unto you, All	Mt 12:31	3004
But I *s* unto you, That every idle	Mt 12:36	3004
For verily I *s* unto you, That	Mt 13:17	3004
harvest I will *s* to the reapers	Mt 13:30	2046
They *s* unto him, Yea, Lord	Mt 13:51	3004
they *s* unto him, We have here but	Mt 14:17	3004
But ye *s*, Whosoever shall	Mt 15:5	3004
Whosoever shall *s* to his father	Mt 15:5	2036
And his disciples *s* unto him	Mt 15:33	3004
them, When it is evening, ye *s*	Mt 16:2	3004
Whom do men *s* that I the Son of	Mt 16:13	3004
Some *s* that thou art John the	Mt 16:14	3004
them, But whom *s* ye that I am	Mt 16:15	3004
I *s* also unto thee, That thou art	Mt 16:18	3004
Verily I *s* unto you, There be	Mt 16:28	3004
Why then *s* the scribes that Elias	Mt 17:10	3004
But I *s* unto you, That Elias is	Mt 17:12	3004
for verily I *s* unto you, If ye	Mt 17:20	3004
ye shall *s* unto this mountain,	Mt 17:20	2046
And said, Verily I *s* unto you	Mt 18:3	3004
for I *s* unto you, That in heaven	Mt 18:10	3004
he find it, verily I *s* unto you	Mt 18:13	3004
Verily I *s* unto you, Whatsoever	Mt 18:18	3004
Again I *s* unto you, That if two	Mt 18:19	3004
I *s* not unto thee, Until seven	Mt 18:22	3004
They *s* unto him, Why did Moses	Mt 19:7	3004
I *s* unto you, Whosoever shall put	Mt 19:9	3004
His disciples *s* unto him, If the	Mt 19:10	3004
disciples, Verily I *s* unto you	Mt 19:23	3004
again I *s* unto you, It is easier	Mt 19:24	3004
unto them, Verily I *s* unto you	Mt 19:28	3004
They *s* unto him, Because no man	Mt 20:7	3004
They *s* unto him, We are able	Mt 20:22	3004
They *s* unto him, Lord, that our	Mt 20:33	3004
if any man *s* ought unto you, ye	Mt 21:3	2036
ought unto you, ye shall *s*	Mt 21:3	2046
him, Hearest thou what these *s*	Mt 21:16	3004
unto them, Verily I *s* unto you	Mt 21:21	3004
if ye shall *s* unto this mountain	Mt 21:21	2036
themselves, saying, If we shall *s*	Mt 21:25	2036
he will *s* unto us, Why did ye not	Mt 21:25	2046
But if we shall *s*, Of men	Mt 21:26	2036
They *s* unto him, The first	Mt 21:31	3004
unto them, Verily I *s* unto you	Mt 21:31	3004
They *s* unto him, He will	Mt 21:41	3004
Therefore *s* I unto you, The	Mt 21:43	3004
They *s* unto him, Caesar's	Mt 22:21	3004
which *s* that there is no	Mt 22:23	3004
They *s* unto him, The son of David	Mt 22:42	3004
for they *s*, and do not	Mt 23:3	3004
you, ye blind guides, which *s*	Mt 23:16	3004
And *s*, If we had been in the days	Mt 23:30	3004
Verily I *s* unto you, All these	Mt 23:36	3004
For I *s* unto you, Ye shall not	Mt 23:39	3004
me henceforth, till ye shall *s*	Mt 23:39	2036
verily I *s* unto you, There shall	Mt 24:2	3004
Then if any man shall *s* unto you	Mt 24:23	2036
if they shall *s* unto you, Behold,	Mt 24:26	2036

Verily I s unto you, This Mt 24:34 3004
Verily I s unto you, That he Mt 24:47 3004
evil servant shall s in his heart Mt 24:48 2036
and said, Verily I s unto you Mt 25:12 3004
Then shall the King s unto them Mt 25:34 2046
s unto them, Verily I Mt 25:40 2046
unto them, Verily I s unto you Mt 25:40 3004
Then shall he s also unto them on Mt 25:41 2046
them, saying, Verily I s unto you Mt 25:45 3004
Verily I s unto you, Wheresoever Mt 26:13 3004
s unto him, The Master saith, My Mt 26:18 2036
eat, he said, Verily I s unto you Mt 26:21 3004
every one of them to s unto him Mt 26:22 3004
But I s unto you, I will not Mt 26:29 3004
Verily I s unto thee, That this Mt 26:34 5346
nevertheless I s unto you Mt 26:64 3004
They all s unto him, Let him be Mt 27:22 3004
called Golgotha, that is to s Mt 27:33 3004
that is to s, My God, my God, why Mt 27:46
s unto the people, He is risen Mt 27:64 2036
S ye, His disciples came by night Mt 28:13 2036
See thou s nothing to any man Mk 1:44 2036
Whether is it easier to s to the Mk 2:9 2036
or to s, Arise, and take up thy Mk 2:9 2036
I s unto thee, Arise, and take up Mk 2:11 3004
s unto him, Why do the disciples Mk 2:18 3004
Verily I s unto you, All sins Mk 3:28 3004
s unto him, Master, carest thou Mk 4:38 3004
Damsel, I s unto thee, arise Mk 5:41 3004
Verily I s unto you, It shall be Mk 6:11 3004
they s unto him, Shall we go and Mk 6:37 3004
And when they knew, they s Mk 6:38 3004
bread with defiled, that is to s Mk 7:2 3004
But ye s, If a man shall Mk 7:11 3004
If a man shall s to his father or Mk 7:11 2036
It is Corban, that is to s Mk 7:11
verily I s unto you, There shall Mk 8:12 3004
They s unto him, Twelve Mk 8:19 3004
them, Whom do men s that I am Mk 8:27 3004
but some s, Elias Mk 8:28
them, But whom s ye that I am Mk 8:29 3004
unto them, Verily I s unto you Mk 9:1 3004
For he wist not what to s Mk 9:6 2980
Why s the scribes that Elias must Mk 9:11 3004
But I s unto you, That Elias is Mk 9:13 3004
to Christ, verily I s unto you Mk 9:41 3004
Verily I s unto you, Whosoever Mk 10:15 3004
Then Peter began to s unto him Mk 10:28 3004
and said, Verily I s unto you Mk 10:29 3004
he began to cry out, and s Mk 10:47 3004
And if any man s unto you, Why do Mk 11:3 2036
s ye that the Lord hath need of Mk 11:3 2036
For verily I s unto you, That Mk 11:23 3004
shall s unto this mountain Mk 11:23 2036
Therefore I s unto you, What Mk 11:24 3004
s unto him, By what authority Mk 11:28 3004
themselves, saying, If we shall s Mk 11:31 2036
he will s, Why then did ye not Mk 11:31 2046
But if we shall s, Of men Mk 11:32 2036
they s unto him, Master, we know Mk 12:14 3004
which s there is no resurrection Mk 12:18 3004
How s the scribes that Christ is Mk 12:35 3004
unto them, Verily I s unto you Mk 12:43 3004
Jesus answering them began to s Mk 13:5 3004
And then if any man shall s to you Mk 13:21 2036
Verily I s unto you, that this Mk 13:30 3004
what I s unto you I s unto all Mk 13:37 3004
Verily I s unto you, Wheresoever Mk 14:9 3004
s ye to the goodman of the house, Mk 14:14 2036
Jesus said, Verily I s unto you Mk 14:18 3004
to s unto him one by one, Is it I Mk 14:19 3004
Verily I s unto you, I will drink Mk 14:25 3004
Verily I s unto thee, That this Mk 14:30 3004
We heard him s, I will destroy Mk 14:58 3004
him, and to s unto him, Prophesy Mk 14:65 3004
began to s to them that stood by, Mk 14:69 3004
begin not to s within yourselves, Lk 3:8 3004
for I s unto you, That God is Lk 3:8 3004
And he began to s unto them Lk 4:21 3004
Ye will surely s unto me this Lk 4:23 2046
And he said, Verily I s unto you Lk 4:24 3004
Whether is easier, to s, Thy sins Lk 5:23 2036
or to s, Rise up and walk Lk 5:23 2036
I s unto thee, Arise, and take up Lk 5:24 3004
But I s unto you which hear, Love Lk 6:27 3004
how canst thou s to thy brother Lk 6:42 3004
and do not the things which I s Lk 6:46 3004
but s in a word, and my servant Lk 7:7 2036
I s unto one, Go, and he goeth Lk 7:8 3004
I s unto you, I have not found so Lk 7:9 3004
Young man, I s unto thee, Arise Lk 7:14 3004
I s unto you, and much more than a Lk 7:26 3004
For I s unto you, Among those Lk 7:28 3004
and ye s, He hath a devil Lk 7:33 3004
and ye s, Behold a gluttonous man, Lk 7:34 3004
I have somewhat to s unto thee Lk 7:40 2036
And he saith, Master, s on Lk 7:40 2036
Wherefore I s unto thee, Her sins Lk 7:47 3004
him began to s within themselves Lk 7:49 3004
Whom s the people that I am Lk 9:18 3004
but some s Elias Lk 9:19 2036
and others s, that one of the old Lk 9:19
them, But whom s ye that I am Lk 9:20 3004
house ye enter, first s, Peace be Lk 10:5 3004
s unto them, The kingdom of God Lk 10:9 3004
the streets of the same, and s Lk 10:10 2036
But I s unto you, that it shall Lk 10:12 3004
said unto them, When ye pray, s Lk 11:2 3004
s unto him, Friend, lend me three Lk 11:5 2036
he from within shall answer and s Lk 11:7 2036
I s unto you, Though he will not Lk 11:8 3004
I s unto you, Ask, and it shall be Lk 11:9 3004
because ye s that I cast out Lk 11:18 3004
thick together, he began to s Lk 11:29 3004
verily I s unto you, It shall be Lk 11:51 3004
he began to s unto his disciples Lk 12:1 3004
I s unto you my friends, Be not Lk 12:4 3004
yea, I s unto you, Fear him Lk 12:5 3004
Also I s unto you, Whosoever Lk 12:8 3004
shall answer, or what ye shall s Lk 12:11 2036
the same hour what ye ought to s Lk 12:12 2036
I will s to my soul, Soul, thou Lk 12:19 2046
disciples, Therefore I s unto you Lk 12:22 3004
yet I s unto you, that Solomon in Lk 12:27 3004
verily I s unto you, that he Lk 12:37 3004
Of a truth I s unto you, that he Lk 12:44 3004
and if that servant s in his heart Lk 12:45 2036
out of the west, straightway ye s Lk 12:54 3004
ye see the south wind blow, ye s Lk 12:55 3004
I s unto you, will seek to enter Lk 13:24 3004
s unto you, I know you not whence Lk 13:25 2046
Then shall ye begin to s, We have Lk 13:26 3004
But he shall s, I tell you, I Lk 13:27 2046
and verily I s unto you, Ye shall Lk 13:35 3004
the time come when ye shall s Lk 13:35 2036
s to thee, Give this man place Lk 14:9 2046
he may s unto thee, Friend, go up Lk 14:10 2036
to s to them that were bidden Lk 14:17 2036
For I s unto you, That none of Lk 14:24 3004
I s unto you, that likewise joy Lk 15:7 3004
I s unto you, there is joy in the Lk 15:10 3004
will s unto him, Father, I have Lk 15:18 2046
I s unto you, Make to yourselves Lk 16:9 3004
ye might s unto this sycamine Lk 17:6 3004
will s unto him by and by, when he Lk 17:7 2046
And will not rather s unto him Lk 17:8 2046
things which are commanded you, s Lk 17:10 3004
Neither shall they s, Lo here Lk 17:21 2046
And they shall s to you, See here Lk 17:23 2046
Verily I s unto you, Whosoever Lk 18:17 3004
unto them, Verily I s unto you Lk 18:29 3004
For I s unto you, That unto every Lk 19:26 3004
thus shall ye s unto him, Because Lk 19:31 2046
themselves, saying, If we shall s Lk 20:5 2036
he will s, Why then believed ye Lk 20:5 2046
But and if we s, Of men Lk 20:6 2036
How s they that Christ is David's Lk 20:41 2036
he said, Of a truth I s unto you Lk 21:3 3004
Verily I s unto you, This Lk 21:32 3004
ye shall s unto the goodman of Lk 22:11 2046
For I s unto you, I will not any Lk 22:16 3004
For I s unto you, I will not Lk 22:18 3004
For I s unto you, that this that Lk 22:37 3004
he said unto them, Ye s that I am Lk 22:70 3004
coming, in the which they shall s Lk 23:29 2046
they begin to s to the mountains Lk 23:30 3004
Verily I s unto thee, To day Lk 23:43 3004
unto him, Rabbi, (which is to s Jn 1:38 3004
I s unto you, Hereafter ye shall Jn 1:51 3004
I s unto thee, Except a man be Jn 3:3 3004
I s unto thee, Except a man be Jn 3:5 3004
I s unto thee, We speak that we Jn 3:11 3004
and ye s, that in Jerusalem is the Jn 4:20 3004
S not ye, There are yet four Jn 4:35 3004
I s unto you, Lift up your eyes, Jn 4:35 3004
I s unto you, The Son can do Jn 5:19 3004
I s unto you, He that heareth my Jn 5:24 3004
I s unto you, The hour is coming, Jn 5:25 3004
but these things I s, that ye Jn 5:34 3004
I s unto you, Ye seek me, not Jn 6:26 3004
I s unto you, Moses gave you not Jn 6:32 3004
I s unto you, He that believeth Jn 6:47 3004
I s unto you, Except ye eat the Jn 6:53 3004
and they s nothing unto him Jn 7:26 3004
They s unto him, Master, this Jn 8:4 3004
I have many things to s and to Jn 8:26 2980
verily, I s unto you, Whosoever Jn 8:34 3004
if I s the truth, why do ye not Jn 8:46 3004
S we not well that thou art a Jn 8:48 3004
I s unto you, If a man keep my Jn 8:51 3004
of whom ye s, that he is your God Jn 8:54 3004
and if I should s, I know him not, Jn 8:55 3004
I s unto you, Before Abraham was, Jn 8:58 3004
They s unto the blind man again, Jn 9:17 3004
your son, who ye s was born blind Jn 9:19 3004
but now ye s, We see Jn 9:41 3004
I s unto you, He that entereth Jn 10:1 3004
I s unto you, I am the door of Jn 10:7 3004
S ye of him, whom the Father hath Jn 10:36 3004
His disciples s unto him, Master, Jn 11:8 3004
I s unto you, Except a corn of Jn 12:24 3004
and what shall I s Jn 12:27 2036
me a commandment, what I should s Jn 12:49 2036
and ye s well Jn 13:13 3004
I s unto you, The servant is not Jn 13:16 3004
I s unto you, He that receiveth Jn 13:20 3004
I s unto you, that one of you Jn 13:21 3004
so now I s to you Jn 13:33 3004
I s unto thee, The cock shall not Jn 13:38 3004
I s unto you, He that believeth Jn 14:12 3004
yet many things to s unto you Jn 16:12 3004
I s unto you, That ye shall weep Jn 16:20 3004
I s unto you, Whatsoever ye shall Jn 16:23 3004
I s not unto you, that I will Jn 16:26 3004
they s unto her, Woman, why Jn 20:13 3004
which is to s, Master Jn 20:16 3004
s unto them, I ascend unto my Jn 20:17 2036
They s unto him, We also go with Jn 21:3 3004
I s unto thee, When thou wast Jn 21:18 3004
tongue, Aceldama, that is to s Acts 1:19
whatsoever he shall s unto you Acts 3:22 2980
they could s nothing against it Acts 4:14 471
now I s unto you, Refrain from Acts 5:38 3004
For we have heard him s, that Acts 6:14 3004
That word, I s, ye know, which Acts 10:37 3004
exhortation for the people, s on Acts 13:15 3004
said, What will this babbler s Acts 17:18 3004
therefore this that we s to thee Acts 21:23 3004
For the Sadducees s that there is Acts 23:8 3004
who hath something to s unto thee Acts 23:18 2980
to his accusers also to s before Acts 23:30 3004
Or else let these same here s Acts 24:20 2036
and Moses did s should come Acts 26:22 2980
Saying, Go unto this people, and s Acts 28:26 2036
of God, what shall we s Rom 3:5 2046
and as some affirm that we s Rom 3:8 3004
To declare, I s, at this time his Rom 3:26
What shall we s then that Abraham Rom 4:1 2046
for we s that faith was reckoned Rom 4:9 3004
What shall we s then Rom 6:1 3004
What shall we s then Rom 7:7 2046
shall we then s to these things Rom 8:31 2046
I s the truth in Christ, I lie Rom 9:1 3004
What shall we s then Rom 9:14 2046
Thou wilt s then unto me, Why Rom 9:19 2046
formed s to him that formed it Rom 9:20 2046
What shall we s then Rom 9:30 2046
S not in thine heart, Who shall Rom 10:6 2036
But I s, Have they not heard Rom 10:18 3004
But I s, Did not Israel know Rom 10:19 3004
I s then, Hath God cast away his Rom 11:1 2046
I s then, Have they stumbled that Rom 11:11 2046
Thou wilt s then, The branches Rom 11:19 2046
For I s, through the grace given Rom 12:3 3004
Now I s that Jesus Christ was a Rom 15:8 3004
Now this I s, that every one of 1Cor 1:12 3004
Lest any should s that I had 1Cor 1:15 2036
I s therefore to the unmarried and 1Cor 7:8 3004
for the present distress, I s 1Cor 7:26
But this I s, brethren, the time 1Cor 7:29 5346
S I these things as a man 1Cor 9:8 2980
judge ye what I s 1Cor 10:15 5346
What s I then 1Cor 10:19 5346
But I s, that the things which 1Cor 10:20
But if any man s unto you 1Cor 10:28 2036
Conscience, I s, not thine own, 1Cor 10:29 3004
What shall I s to you 1Cor 11:22 2036
that no man can s that Jesus is 1Cor 12:3 2036
If the foot shall s, Because I am 1Cor 12:15 2036
And if the ear shall s, Because I 1Cor 12:16 2036
And the eye cannot s unto the hand 1Cor 12:21 2036
the room of the unlearned s Amen 1Cor 14:16 2046
will they not s that ye are mad 1Cor 14:23 2046
how s some among you that there 1Cor 15:12 3004
But some man will s, How are the 1Cor 15:35 2046
Now this I s, brethren, that 1Cor 15:50 5346
We are confident, I s, and willing 2Cor 5:8
you unprepared, we (that we s not 2Cor 9:4 3004
But this I s, He which soweth 2Cor 9:6
s they, are weighty and powerful 2Cor 10:10 5346
I s again, Let no man think me a 2Cor 11:16 3004
for I will s the truth 2Cor 12:6 2046
so s I now again, If any man Gal 1:9 3004
And this I s, that the covenant, Gal 3:17 3004
Now I s, That the heir, as long Gal 4:1 3004
I Paul s unto you, that if ye be Gal 5:2 3004
This I s then, Walk in the Spirit Gal 5:16 3004
This I s therefore, and testify in Eph 4:17 3004
and again I s, Rejoice Phil 4:4 2046
by him, I s, whether they be Col 1:20
And this I s, lest any man should Col 2:4 3004
s to Archippus, Take heed to the Col 4:17 2036
For this we s unto you by the 1Th 4:15 3004
For when they shall s, Peace and 1Th 5:3 3004
understanding neither what they s 1Ti 1:7 3004
Consider what I s 2Ti 2:7 3004
having no evil thing to s of you Titus 2:8 3004
albeit I do not s to thee how Philem 19 3004
thou wilt also do more than I s Philem 21 3004
Of whom we have many things to s Heb 5:11 3056
And as I may so s, Levi also, who Heb 7:9
not made with hands, that is to s Heb 9:11
through the veil, that is to s Heb 10:20
For they that s such things Heb 11:14 3004
And what shall I more s Heb 11:32 3004
So that we may boldly s, The Lord Heb 13:6 3004
Let no man s when he is tempted, Jas 1:13 3004
s unto him, Sit thou here in a Jas 2:3 2036
s to the poor, Stand thou there, Jas 2:3 2036
though a man s he hath faith, and Jas 2:14 3004
And one of you s unto them Jas 2:16 2036
Yea, a man may s, Thou hast faith Jas 2:18 2046
Go to now, ye that s, To day or Jas 4:13 3004
For that ye ought to s, If the Jas 4:15 3004
If we s that we have fellowship 1Jn 1:6 2036
If we s that we have no sin, we 1Jn 1:8 2036
If we s that we have not sinned, 1Jn 1:10 2036
If a man s, I love God, and hateth 1Jn 4:20 2036
I do not s that he shall pray for 1Jn 5:16 3004
them which s they are apostles Rev 2:2 5335
of them which s they are Jews Rev 2:9 3004
But unto you I s, and unto the Rev 2:24 3004
which s they are Jews, and are not Rev 3:9 3004
seal, I heard the second beast s Rev 6:3 3004
seal, I heard the third beast s Rev 6:5 3004
in the midst of the four beasts s Rev 6:6 3004
the voice of the fourth beast s Rev 6:7 3004
I heard the angel of the waters s Rev 16:5 3004
heard another out of the altar s Rev 16:7 3004
And the Spirit and the bride s Rev 22:17 3004
And let him that heareth s Rev 22:17 2036

SAYEST

thou s unto me, Bring up this Ex 33:12 559
will do whatsoever thou s unto me Num 22:17 559
All that thou s unto me I will do Ruth 3:5 559
And now thou s, Go, tell thy lord, 1Kin 18:11 559
And now thou s, Go, tell thy lord, 1Kin 18:14 559
Thou s, (but they are but vain 2Kin 18:20 559
Thou s, Lo, thou hast smitten the 2Chr 25:19 559
so will we do as thou s Neh 5:12 559
are no such things done as thou s Neh 6:8 559

Context	Reference	Strong's
And thou s, How doth God know	Job 22:13	559
Although thou s thou shalt not	Job 35:14	559
and s, Return, ye children of men	Ps 90:3	559
If thou s, Behold, we knew it not	Prov 24:12	559
s thou, (but they are but vain	Is 36:5	
Why s thou, O Jacob, and speakest,	Is 40:27	559
that s in thine heart, I am, and	Is 47:8	559
Yet thou s, Because I am innocent	Jer 2:35	559
plead with thee, because thou s	Jer 2:35	559
Thou s, Prophesy not against	Amos 7:16	559
saying, I know not what thou s	Mt 26:70	3004
And Jesus said unto him, Thou s	Mt 27:11	3004
thee, and s thou, Who touched me	Mk 5:31	3004
neither understand I what thou s	Mk 14:68	3004
said unto him, Thou s it	Mk 15:2	3004
thee, and s thou, Who touched me	Lk 8:45	2036
Master, we know that thou s	Lk 20:21	3004
said, Man, I know not what thou s	Lk 22:60	3004
answered him and said, Thou s it	Lk 23:3	3004
What s thou of thyself	Jn 1:22	3004
but what s thou	Jn 8:5	3004
how s thou, Ye shall be made free	Jn 8:33	3004
and thou s, If a man keep my	Jn 8:52	3004
What s thou of him, that he hath	Jn 9:17	3004
how s thou, The Son of man must	Jn 12:34	3004
how s thou then, Shew us the	Jn 14:9	3004
S thou this thing of thyself, or	Jn 18:34	3004
answered, Thou s that I am a king	Jn 18:37	3004
Thou that s a man should not	Rom 2:22	3004
he understandeth not what thou s	1Cor 14:16	3004
Because thou s, I am rich, and	Rev 3:17	3004

SAYING

Context	Reference	Strong's
And God blessed them, s, Be	Gen 1:22	559
the LORD God commanded the man, s	Gen 2:16	559
of which I commanded thee, s	Gen 3:17	559
And he called his name Noah, s	Gen 5:29	559
And God spake unto Noah, s	Gen 8:15	559
Noah, and to his sons with him, s	Gen 9:8	559
came unto Abram in a vision, s	Gen 15:1	559
word of the LORD came unto him, s	Gen 15:4	559
made a covenant with Abram, s	Gen 15:18	559
and God talked with him, s	Gen 17:3	559
Sarah laughed within herself, s	Gen 18:12	559
Wherefore did Sarah laugh, s	Gen 18:13	559
Then Sarah denied, s, I laughed	Gen 18:15	559
then the angels hastened Lot, s	Gen 19:15	559
of his host spake unto Abraham, s	Gen 21:22	559
that it was told Abraham, s	Gen 22:20	559
and spake unto the sons of Heth, s	Gen 23:3	559
answered Abraham, s unto him,	Gen 23:5	559
And he communed with them, s	Gen 23:8	559
in at the gate of his city, s	Gen 23:10	559
of the people of the land, s	Gen 23:13	559
answered Abraham, s unto him,	Gen 23:14	559
unto me, and that sware unto me, s	Gen 24:7	559
words of Rebekah his sister, s	Gen 24:30	559
And my master made me swear, s	Gen 24:37	559
charged all his people, s	Gen 26:11	559
strive with Isaac's herdmen, s	Gen 26:20	559
spake unto Jacob her son, s	Gen 27:6	559
speak unto Esau thy brother, s	Gen 27:6	559
him he gave him a charge, s	Gen 28:6	559
And Jacob vowed a vow, s, If God	Gen 28:20	559
the words of Laban's sons, s	Gen 31:1	559
God spake unto me in a dream, s	Gen 31:11	
spake unto me yesternight, s	Gen 31:29	559
And he commanded them, s, Thus	Gen 32:4	559
messengers returned to Jacob, s	Gen 32:6	559
And he commanded the foremost, s	Gen 32:17	559
meeteth thee, and asketh thee, s	Gen 32:17	559
all that followed the droves, s	Gen 32:19	559
spake unto his father Hamor, s	Gen 34:4	559
And Hamor communed with them, s	Gen 34:8	559
with the men of their city, s	Gen 34:20	559
but his father observed the s	Gen 37:11	1697
and the man asked him, s, What	Gen 37:15	559
And it was told Tamar, s, Behold	Gen 38:13	559
he asked the men of that place, s	Gen 38:21	559
after, that it was told Judah, s	Gen 38:24	559
she sent to her father in law, s	Gen 38:25	559
upon his hand a scarlet thread, s	Gen 38:28	559
she caught him by his garment, s	Gen 39:12	559
her house, and spake unto them, s	Gen 39:14	559
him according to these words, s	Gen 39:17	559
wife, which she spake unto him, s	Gen 39:19	559
the ward of his lord's house, s	Gen 40:7	559
the chief butler unto Pharaoh, s	Gen 41:9	559
And Joseph answered Pharaoh, s	Gen 41:16	559
is it that I spake unto you, s	Gen 42:14	559
And Reuben answered them, s	Gen 42:22	559
s, Spake I not unto you, s	Gen 42:22	559
s one to another, What is this	Gen 42:28	559
that befell unto them; s	Gen 42:29	559
Reuben spake unto his father, s	Gen 42:37	559
And Judah spake unto him, s	Gen 43:3	559
did solemnly protest unto us, s	Gen 43:3	559
our state, and of our kindred, s	Gen 43:7	559
the steward of his house, s	Gen 44:1	559
My lord asked his servants, s	Gen 44:19	559
for the lad unto my father, s	Gen 44:32	559
was heard in Pharaoh's house, s	Gen 45:16	559
And told him, s, Joseph is yet	Gen 45:26	559
And Pharaoh spake unto Joseph, s	Gen 47:5	559
And he blessed them that day, s	Gen 48:20	559
In thee shall Israel bless, s	Gen 48:20	559
unto the house of Pharaoh, s	Gen 50:4	559
you, in the ears of Pharaoh, s	Gen 50:4	559
My father made me swear, s	Gen 50:5	559
sent a messenger unto Joseph, s	Gen 50:16	559
did command before he died, s	Gen 50:16	559
oath of the children of Israel, s	Gen 50:25	559
Pharaoh charged all his people, s	Ex 1:22	559
and of Jacob, appeared unto me, s	Ex 3:16	559
the people, and their officers, s	Ex 5:6	559
therefore they cry, s, Let us go	Ex 5:8	559
and they spake to the people, s	Ex 5:10	559
And the taskmasters hasted them, s	Ex 5:13	559
came and cried unto Pharaoh, s	Ex 5:15	559
And the LORD spake unto Moses, s	Ex 6:10	559
And Moses spake before the LORD, s	Ex 6:12	559
That the LORD spake unto Moses, s	Ex 6:29	559
spake unto Moses and unto Aaron, s	Ex 7:8	559
Pharaoh shall speak unto you, s	Ex 7:9	559
Hebrews hath sent me unto thee, s	Ex 7:16	559
the LORD appointed a set time, s	Ex 9:5	559
and bow down themselves unto me, s	Ex 11:8	559
and Aaron in the land of Egypt, s	Ex 12:1	559
all the congregation of Israel, s	Ex 12:3	559
And the LORD spake unto Moses, s	Ex 13:1	559
shalt shew thy son in that day, s	Ex 13:8	559
asketh thee in time to come, s	Ex 13:14	559
sworn the children of Israel, s	Ex 13:19	559
And the LORD spake unto Moses, s	Ex 14:1	559
that we did tell thee in Egypt, s	Ex 14:12	559
song unto the LORD, and spake, s	Ex 15:1	559
people murmured against Moses, s	Ex 15:24	559
And the LORD spake unto Moses, s	Ex 16:11	559
speak unto them, s, At even ye	Ex 16:12	559
And Moses cried unto the LORD, s	Ex 17:4	559
because they tempted the LORD, s	Ex 17:7	559
unto him out of the mountain, s	Ex 19:3	559
unto the people round about, s	Ex 19:12	559
for thou chargedst us, s, Set	Ex 19:23	559
And God spake all these words, s	Ex 20:1	559
And the LORD spake unto Moses, s	Ex 25:1	559
And the LORD spake unto Moses, s	Ex 30:11	559
And the LORD spake unto Moses, s	Ex 30:17	559
the LORD spake unto Moses, s	Ex 30:22	559
unto the children of Israel, s	Ex 30:31	559
And the LORD spake unto Moses, s	Ex 31:1	559
And the LORD spake unto Moses, s	Ex 31:12	559
unto the children of Israel, s	Ex 31:13	559
Abraham, to Isaac, and to Jacob, s	Ex 33:1	559
of the children of Israel, s	Ex 35:4	559
thing which the LORD commanded, s	Ex 35:4	559
And they spake unto Moses, s	Ex 36:5	559
proclaimed throughout the camp, s	Ex 36:6	559
And the LORD spake unto Moses, s	Ex 40:1	559
tabernacle of the congregation, s	Lev 1:1	559
And the LORD spake unto Moses, s	Lev 4:1	559
unto the children of Israel, s	Lev 4:2	559
And the LORD spake unto Moses, s	Lev 5:14	559
And the LORD spake unto Moses, s	Lev 6:1	559
And the LORD spake unto Moses, s	Lev 6:8	559
Command Aaron and his sons, s	Lev 6:9	559
And the LORD spake unto Moses, s	Lev 6:19	559
And the LORD spake unto Moses, s	Lev 6:24	559
unto Aaron and to his sons, s	Lev 6:25	559
And the LORD spake unto Moses, s	Lev 7:22	559
unto the children of Israel, s	Lev 7:23	559
And the LORD spake unto Moses, s	Lev 7:28	559
unto the children of Israel, s	Lev 7:29	559
And the LORD spake unto Moses, s	Lev 8:1	559
consecrations, as I commanded, s	Lev 8:31	559
of Israel thou shalt speak, s	Lev 9:3	559
This is it that the LORD spake, s	Lev 10:3	559
And the LORD spake unto Aaron, s	Lev 10:8	559
of Aaron which were left alive, s	Lev 10:16	559
Moses and to Aaron, s unto them,	Lev 11:1	559
unto the children of Israel, s	Lev 11:2	559
And the LORD spake unto Moses, s	Lev 12:1	559
unto the children of Israel, s	Lev 12:2	559
LORD spake unto Moses and Aaron, s	Lev 13:1	559
And the LORD spake unto Moses, s	Lev 14:1	559
spake unto Moses and unto Aaron, s	Lev 14:33	559
shall come and tell the priest, s	Lev 14:35	559
spake unto Moses and to Aaron, s	Lev 15:1	559
And the LORD spake unto Moses, s	Lev 17:1	559
which the LORD hath commanded, s	Lev 17:2	559
And the LORD spake unto Moses, s	Lev 18:1	559
And the LORD spake unto Moses, s	Lev 19:1	559
And the LORD spake unto Moses, s	Lev 20:1	559
And the LORD spake unto Moses, s	Lev 21:16	559
Speak unto Aaron, s, Whosoever he	Lev 21:17	559
And the LORD spake unto Moses, s	Lev 22:1	559
And the LORD spake unto Moses, s	Lev 22:17	559
And the LORD spake unto Moses, s	Lev 22:26	559
And the LORD spake unto Moses, s	Lev 23:1	559
And the LORD spake unto Moses, s	Lev 23:9	559
And the LORD spake unto Moses, s	Lev 23:23	559
unto the children of Israel, s	Lev 23:24	559
And the LORD spake unto Moses, s	Lev 23:26	559
And the LORD spake unto Moses, s	Lev 23:33	559
unto the children of Israel, s	Lev 23:34	559
And the LORD spake unto Moses, s	Lev 24:1	559
And the LORD spake unto Moses, s	Lev 24:13	559
unto the children of Israel, s	Lev 24:15	559
unto Moses in mount Sinai, s	Lev 25:1	559
And the LORD spake unto Moses, s	Lev 27:1	559
come out of the land of Egypt, s	Num 1:1	559
the LORD had spoken unto Moses, s	Num 1:48	559
spake unto Moses and unto Aaron, s	Num 2:1	559
And the LORD spake unto Moses, s	Num 3:5	559
And the LORD spake unto Moses, s	Num 3:11	559
in the wilderness of Sinai, s	Num 3:14	559
And the LORD spake unto Moses, s	Num 3:44	559
spake unto Moses and unto Aaron, s	Num 4:1	559
spake unto Moses and unto Aaron, s	Num 4:17	559
And the LORD spake unto Moses, s	Num 4:21	559
And the LORD spake unto Moses, s	Num 5:1	559
And the LORD spake unto Moses, s	Num 5:5	559
And the LORD spake unto Moses, s	Num 5:11	559
And the LORD spake unto Moses, s	Num 6:1	559
And the LORD spake unto Moses, s	Num 6:22	559
unto Aaron and unto his sons, s	Num 6:23	559
children of Israel, s unto them,	Num 6:23	559
And the LORD spake unto Moses, s	Num 7:4	559
And the LORD spake unto Moses, s	Num 8:1	559
And the LORD spake unto Moses, s	Num 8:5	559
And the LORD spake unto Moses, s	Num 8:23	559
come out of the land of Egypt, s	Num 9:1	559
And the LORD spake unto Moses, s	Num 9:9	559
unto the children of Israel, s	Num 9:10	559
And the LORD spake unto Moses, s	Num 10:1	559
for they weep unto me, s, Give us	Num 11:13	559
wept in the ears of the LORD, s	Num 11:18	559
you, and have wept before him, s	Num 11:20	559
And Moses cried unto the LORD, s	Num 12:13	559
And the LORD spake unto Moses, s	Num 13:1	559
unto the children of Israel, s	Num 13:32	559
of the children of Israel, s	Num 14:7	559
the fame of thee will speak, s	Num 14:15	559
according as thou hast spoken, s	Num 14:17	559
spake unto Moses and unto Aaron, s	Num 14:26	559
into the top of the mountain, s	Num 14:40	559
And the LORD spake unto Moses, s	Num 15:1	559
And the LORD spake unto Moses, s	Num 15:17	559
And the LORD spake unto Moses, s	Num 15:37	559
Korah and unto all his company, s	Num 16:5	559
spake unto Moses and unto Aaron, s	Num 16:20	559
And the LORD spake unto Moses, s	Num 16:23	559
Speak unto the congregation, s	Num 16:24	559
he spake unto the congregation, s	Num 16:26	559
And the LORD spake unto Moses, s	Num 16:36	559
against Moses and against Aaron, s	Num 16:41	559
And the LORD spake unto Moses, s	Num 16:44	559
And the LORD spake unto Moses, s	Num 17:1	559
of Israel spake unto Moses, s	Num 17:12	559
And the LORD spake unto Moses, s	Num 18:25	559
spake unto Moses and unto Aaron, s	Num 19:1	559
which the LORD hath commanded, s	Num 19:2	559
chode with Moses, and spake, s	Num 20:3	559
And the LORD spake unto Moses, s	Num 20:7	559
the coast of the land of Edom, s	Num 20:23	559
Sihon king of the Amorites, s	Num 21:21	559
of his people, to call him, s	Num 22:5	559
of Moab, hath sent unto me, s	Num 22:10	
of the mountains of the east, s	Num 23:7	
unto Balak, Told not I thee, s	Num 23:26	559
which thou sentest unto me, s	Num 24:12	559
And the LORD spake unto Moses, s	Num 25:10	559
And the LORD spake unto Moses, s	Num 25:16	559
the son of Aaron the priest, s	Num 26:1	559
of Moab by Jordan near Jericho, s	Num 26:3	559
And the LORD spake unto Moses, s	Num 26:52	559
tabernacle of the congregation, s	Num 27:2	559
And the LORD spake unto Moses, s	Num 27:6	559
unto the children of Israel, s	Num 27:8	559
And Moses spake unto the LORD, s	Num 27:15	559
And the LORD spake unto Moses, s	Num 28:1	559
the children of Israel, s	Num 30:1	559
And the LORD spake unto Moses, s	Num 31:1	559
And Moses spake unto the people, s	Num 31:3	559
And the LORD spake unto Moses, s	Num 31:25	559
princes of the congregation, s	Num 32:2	559
the same time, and he sware, s	Num 32:10	559
of Reuben spake unto Moses, s	Num 32:25	559
children of Reuben answered, s	Num 32:31	559
Moab by Jordan, near Jericho, s	Num 33:50	559
And the LORD spake unto Moses, s	Num 34:1	559
the children of Israel, s	Num 34:13	559
And the LORD spake unto Moses, s	Num 34:16	559
of Moab by Jordan near Jericho, s	Num 35:1	559
And the LORD spake unto Moses, s	Num 35:9	559
to the word of the LORD, s	Num 36:5	559
the daughters of Zelophehad, s	Num 36:6	559
Moses to declare this law, s	Deut 1:5	559
our God spake unto us in Horeb, s	Deut 1:6	559
I spake unto you at that time, s	Deut 1:9	559
your judges at that time, s	Deut 1:16	559
And the s pleased me well	Deut 1:23	1697
have discouraged our heart, s	Deut 1:28	559
words, and was wroth, and sware, s	Deut 1:34	559
angry with me for your sakes, s	Deut 1:37	559
And the LORD spake unto me, s	Deut 2:2	559
And command thou the people, s	Deut 2:4	559
That the LORD spake unto me, s	Deut 2:17	559
of Heshbon with words of peace, s	Deut 2:26	559
I commanded you at that time, s	Deut 3:18	559
commanded Joshua at that time, s	Deut 3:21	559
besought the LORD at that time, s	Deut 3:23	559
up into the mount;) s	Deut 5:5	559
asketh thee in time to come, s	Deut 6:20	559
cast them out from before thee, s	Deut 9:4	559
the LORD spake unto me, s	Deut 9:13	559
sent you from Kadesh-barnea, s	Deut 9:23	559
enquire not after their gods, s	Deut 12:30	559
whereof he spake unto thee, s	Deut 13:2	559
own soul, entice thee secretly, s	Deut 13:6	559
hath given thee to dwell there, s	Deut 13:12	559
the inhabitants of their city, s	Deut 13:13	559
a thought in thy wicked heart, s	Deut 15:9	559
therefore I command thee, s	Deut 15:11	559
in the day of the assembly, s	Deut 18:16	559
Wherefore I command thee, s	Deut 19:7	559
shall speak unto the people, s	Deut 20:5	559
of speech against her, s, I found	Deut 22:17	559
of Israel commanded the people, s	Deut 27:1	559
Levites spake unto all Israel, s	Deut 27:9	559
the people the same day, s	Deut 27:11	559
he bless himself in his heart, s	Deut 29:19	559
And Moses commanded them, s	Deut 31:10	559
of the covenant of the LORD, s	Deut 31:25	559
unto Moses that selfsame day, s	Deut 32:48	559
unto Isaac, and unto Jacob, s	Deut 34:4	559
son of Nun, Moses' minister, s	Josh 1:1	559
the officers of the people, s	Josh 1:10	559
host, and command the people, s	Josh 1:11	559
of Manasseh, spake Joshua, s	Josh 1:12	559
of the LORD commanded you, s	Josh 1:13	559
And they answered Joshua, s	Josh 1:16	559

two men to spy secretly, s	Josh 2:1	559
was told the king of Jericho, s	Josh 2:2	559
of Jericho sent unto Rahab, s	Josh 2:3	559
And they commanded the people, s	Josh 3:3	559
Joshua spake unto the priests, s	Josh 3:6	559
bear the ark of the covenant, s	Josh 3:8	559
the LORD spake unto Joshua, s	Josh 4:1	559
And command ye them, s, Take you	Josh 4:3	559
their fathers in time to come, s	Josh 4:6	559
And the LORD spake unto Joshua, s	Josh 4:15	559
commanded the priests, s, Come ye	Josh 4:17	559
unto the children of Israel, s	Josh 4:21	559
their fathers in time to come, s	Josh 4:21	559
shall let your children know, s	Josh 4:22	559
had commanded the people, s	Josh 6:10	559
adjured them at that time, s	Josh 6:26	559
of Beth-el, and spake unto them, s	Josh 7:2	559
And he commanded them, s, Behold,	Josh 8:4	559
of our country spake to us, s	Josh 9:11	559
them, and he spake unto them, s	Josh 9:22	559
Wherefore have ye beguiled us, s	Josh 9:22	559
and unto Debir king of Eglon, s	Josh 10:3	559
Joshua to the camp to Gilgal, s	Josh 10:6	559
And it was told Joshua, s, The	Josh 10:17	559
And Moses sware on that day, s	Josh 14:9	559
of Nun, and before the princes, s	Josh 17:4	559
of Joseph spake unto Joshua, s	Josh 17:14	559
even to Ephraim and to Manasseh, s	Josh 17:17	559
that went to describe the land, s	Josh 18:8	559
LORD also spake unto Joshua, s	Josh 20:1	559
to the children of Israel, s	Josh 20:2	559
Shiloh in the land of Canaan, s	Josh 21:2	559
And he spake unto them, s, Return	Josh 22:8	559
and they spake with them, s	Josh 22:15	559
done it for fear of this thing, s	Josh 22:24	559
might speak unto our children, s	Josh 22:24	559
of Israel asked the LORD, s	Judg 1:1	559
LORD God of Israel commanded, s	Judg 4:6	
the son of Abinoam on that day, s	Judg 5:1	559
which our fathers told us of, s	Judg 6:13	559
day he called him Jerubbaal, s	Judg 6:32	559
vaunt themselves against me, s	Judg 7:2	559
in the ears of the people, s	Judg 7:3	559
throughout all mount Ephraim, s	Judg 7:24	559
also unto the men of Penuel, s	Judg 8:9	559
with whom ye did upbraid me, s	Judg 8:15	559
house of his mother's father, s	Judg 9:1	559
unto Abimelech privily, s	Judg 9:31	559
of Israel cried unto the LORD, s	Judg 10:10	559
king of the children of Ammon, s	Judg 11:12	559
unto the king of Edom, s, Let me,	Judg 11:17	559
woman came and told her husband, s	Judg 13:6	559
And they spake unto him, s	Judg 15:13	559
And it was told the Gazites, s	Judg 16:2	559
and were quiet all the night, s	Judg 16:2	559
the lords of the Philistines, s	Judg 16:18	559
of the house, the old man, s	Judg 19:22	559
the people arose as one man, s	Judg 20:8	559
all the tribe of Benjamin, s	Judg 20:12	559
and asked counsel of the LORD, s	Judg 20:23	559
stood before it in those days,) s	Judg 20:28	559
of Israel had sworn in Mizpeh, s	Judg 21:1	559
not up to the LORD to Mizpeh, s	Judg 21:5	559
valiantest, and commanded them, s	Judg 21:10	559
children of Israel have sworn, s	Judg 21:18	559
the children of Benjamin, s	Judg 21:20	559
Boaz commanded his young men, s	Ruth 2:15	559
And I thought to advertise thee, s	Ruth 4:4	559
her neighbours gave it a name, s	Ruth 4:17	559
son, and called his name Samuel, s	1Sa 1:20	
she named the child I-chabod, s	1Sa 4:21	559
that the Ekronites cried out, s	1Sa 5:10	559
the priests and the diviners, s	1Sa 6:2	559
inhabitants of Kirjath-jearim, s	1Sa 6:21	559
unto all the house of Israel, s	1Sa 7:3	559
the name of it Eben-ezer, s	1Sa 7:12	559
his ear a day before Saul came, s	1Sa 9:15	559
Saul to the top of the house, s	1Sa 9:26	559
asses, and sorroweth for you, s	1Sa 10:2	559
by the hands of messengers, s	1Sa 11:7	559
throughout all the land, s	1Sa 13:3	559
Saul had adjured the people, s	1Sa 14:24	559
the people with an oath, s	1Sa 14:28	559
Then they told Saul, s, Behold,	1Sa 14:33	559
word of the LORD unto Samuel, s	1Sa 15:10	559
morning, it was told Samuel, s	1Sa 15:12	559
And Saul sent to Jesse, s, Let	1Sa 16:22	559
to the men that stood by him, s	1Sa 17:26	559
answered him after this manner, s	1Sa 17:27	559
wroth, and the s displeased him	1Sa 18:8	1697
And Saul commanded his servants, s	1Sa 18:22	
the servants of Saul told him, s	1Sa 18:24	559
and Jonathan told David, s	1Sa 19:2	559
Michal David's wife told him, s	1Sa 19:11	559
messengers again to see David, s	1Sa 19:15	559
And it was told Saul, s, Behold,	1Sa 19:19	559
with the house of David, s	1Sa 20:16	
And, behold, I will send a lad, s	1Sa 20:21	
of us in the name of the LORD, s	1Sa 20:42	559
to another of him in dances, s	1Sa 21:11	559
Then they told David, s, Behold,	1Sa 23:1	559
David enquired of the LORD, s	1Sa 23:2	559
the Ziphites to Saul to Gibeah, s	1Sa 23:19	559
came a messenger unto Saul, s	1Sa 23:27	559
that it was told him, s, Behold,	1Sa 24:1	559
the cave, and cried after Saul, s	1Sa 24:8	559
hearest thou men's words, s	1Sa 24:9	559
men told Abigail, Nabal's wife, s	1Sa 25:14	559
to Carmel, they spake unto her, s	1Sa 25:40	559
came unto Saul to Gibeah, s	1Sa 26:1	559
of Zeruiah, brother to Joab, s	1Sa 26:6	559
and to Abner the son of Ner, s	1Sa 26:14	559
in the inheritance of the LORD, s	1Sa 26:19	559
to bring tidings to Gath, s	1Sa 27:11	559
Lest they should tell on us, s	1Sa 27:11	559
And Achish believed David, s	1Sa 27:12	559
Saul sware to her by the LORD, s	1Sa 28:10	559
and the woman spake to Saul, s	1Sa 28:12	559
sang one to another in dances, s	1Sa 29:5	559
And David enquired at the LORD, s	1Sa 30:8	559
of Judah, even to his friends, s	1Sa 30:26	559
hath testified against thee, s	2Sa 1:16	559
David enquired of the LORD, s	2Sa 2:1	559
And they told David, s, That the	2Sa 2:4	559
to David on his behalf, s	2Sa 3:12	559
s also, Make thy league with me,	2Sa 3:12	559
to Ish-bosheth Saul's son, s	2Sa 3:14	559
with the elders of Israel, s	2Sa 3:17	559
the LORD hath spoken of David, s	2Sa 3:18	559
him were come, they told Joab, s	2Sa 3:23	559
it was yet day, David sware, s	2Sa 3:35	559
When one told me, s, Behold, Saul	2Sa 4:10	559
to David unto Hebron, and spake, s	2Sa 5:1	559
which spake unto David, s	2Sa 5:6	559
And David enquired of the LORD, s	2Sa 5:19	559
And it was told king David, s	2Sa 6:12	559
of the LORD came unto Nathan, s	2Sa 7:4	559
to feed my people Israel, s	2Sa 7:7	559
thy name be magnified for ever, s	2Sa 7:26	559
hast revealed to thy servant, s	2Sa 7:27	559
And David sent to Joab, s, Send me	2Sa 11:6	559
And when they had told David, s	2Sa 11:10	559
And he wrote in the letter, s	2Sa 11:15	559
And charged the messenger, s	2Sa 11:19	559
Then David sent home to Tamar, s	2Sa 13:7	559
had commanded his servants, s	2Sa 13:28	559
that tidings came to David, s	2Sa 13:30	559
Joab, Behold, I sent unto thee, s	2Sa 14:32	559
I abode at Geshur in Syria, s	2Sa 15:8	559
all the tribes of Israel, s	2Sa 15:10	559
came a messenger to David, s	2Sa 15:13	559
And one told David, s, Ahithophel	2Sa 15:31	559
the s pleased Absalom well, and	2Sa 17:4	1697
Absalom spake unto him, s	2Sa 17:6	559
shall we do after his s	2Sa 17:6	1697
send quickly, and tell David, s	2Sa 17:16	559
Joab and Abishai and Ittai, s	2Sa 18:5	559
thee and Abishai and Ittai, s	2Sa 18:12	559
they told unto all the people, s	2Sa 19:8	559
all the tribes of Israel, s	2Sa 19:9	559
and to Abiathar the priests, s	2Sa 19:11	559
Speak unto the elders of Judah, s	2Sa 19:11	559
Then she spake, s, They were wont	2Sa 20:18	559
were wont to speak in old time, s	2Sa 20:18	559
men of David sware unto him, s	2Sa 21:17	559
the prophet Gad, David's seer, s	2Sa 24:11	559
David, according to the s of Gad	2Sa 24:19	1697
son of Haggith exalted himself, s	1Kin 1:5	559
displeased him at any time in s	1Kin 1:6	559
the mother of Solomon, s, Hast	1Kin 1:11	559
swear unto thine handmaid, s	1Kin 1:13	559
thy God unto thine handmaid, s	1Kin 1:17	
And they told the king, s, Behold	1Kin 1:23	559
thee by the LORD God of Israel, s	1Kin 1:30	559
to bless our lord king David, s	1Kin 1:47	559
And it was told Solomon, s	1Kin 1:51	559
hold on the horns of the altar, s	1Kin 1:51	559
and he charged Solomon his son, s	1Kin 2:1	559
which he spake concerning me, s	1Kin 2:4	559
and I sware to him by the LORD, s	1Kin 2:8	559
king Solomon sware by the LORD, s	1Kin 2:23	559
Benaiah the son of Jehoiada, s	1Kin 2:29	559
brought the king word again, s	1Kin 2:30	559
said unto the king, The s is good	1Kin 2:38	1697
And they told Shimei, s, Behold,	1Kin 2:39	559
LORD, and protested unto thee, s	1Kin 2:42	559
And Solomon sent to Hiram, s	1Kin 5:2	559
spake unto David my father, s	1Kin 5:5	559
And Hiram sent to Solomon, s	1Kin 5:8	559
of the LORD came to Solomon, s	1Kin 6:11	559
with his hand fulfilled it, s	1Kin 8:15	559
that thou promisedst him, s	1Kin 8:25	559
that carried them captives, s	1Kin 8:47	559
of Israel with a loud voice, s	1Kin 8:55	559
I promised to David thy father, s	1Kin 9:5	559
came, and spake unto Rehoboam, s	1Kin 12:3	559
And they spake unto him, s	1Kin 12:7	559
people, who have spoken to me, s	1Kin 12:9	559
up with him spake unto him, s	1Kin 12:10	559
people that spake unto thee, s	1Kin 12:10	559
day, as the king had appointed, s	1Kin 12:12	559
the counsel of the young men, s	1Kin 12:14	559
LORD, that he might perform his s	1Kin 12:15	1697
the people answered the king, s	1Kin 12:16	559
unto Shemaiah the man of God, s	1Kin 12:22	559
to the remnant of the people, s	1Kin 12:23	559
And he gave a sign the same day, s	1Kin 13:3	559
heard the s of the man of God	1Kin 13:4	1697
forth his hand from the altar, s	1Kin 13:4	559
me by the word of the LORD, s	1Kin 13:9	559
me by the word of the LORD, s	1Kin 13:18	559
of God that came from Judah, s	1Kin 13:21	559
And he spake to his sons, s	1Kin 13:27	559
and they mourned over him, s	1Kin 13:30	
him, that he spake to his sons, s	1Kin 13:31	559
For the s which he cried by the	1Kin 13:32	1697
Syria, that dwelt at Damascus, s	1Kin 15:18	559
according unto the s of the LORD	1Kin 15:29	1697
son of Hanani against Baasha, s	1Kin 16:1	559
word of the LORD came unto him, s	1Kin 17:2	559
word of the LORD came unto him, s	1Kin 17:8	559
did according to the s of Elijah	1Kin 17:15	1697
to Elijah in the third year, s	1Kin 18:1	559
from morning even until noon, s	1Kin 18:26	559
whom the word of the LORD came, s	1Kin 18:31	559
sent a messenger unto Elijah, s	1Kin 19:2	559
lord, O king, according to thy s	1Kin 20:4	1697
said, Thus speaketh Ben-hadad, s	1Kin 20:5	559
Although I have sent unto thee, s	1Kin 20:5	559
unto Ahab king of Israel, s	1Kin 20:13	559
sent out, and they told him, s	1Kin 20:17	559
And Ahab spake unto Naboth, s	1Kin 21:2	559
And she wrote in the letters, s	1Kin 21:9	559
to bear witness against him, s	1Kin 21:10	559
in the presence of the people, s	1Kin 21:13	559
Then they sent to Jezebel, s	1Kin 21:14	559
came to Elijah the Tishbite, s	1Kin 21:17	559
And thou shalt speak unto him, s	1Kin 21:19	559
And thou shalt speak unto him, s	1Kin 21:19	559
of Jezebel also spake the LORD, s	1Kin 21:23	559
came to Elijah the Tishbite, s	1Kin 21:28	559
all the prophets prophesied so, s	1Kin 22:12	559
to call Micaiah spake unto him, s	1Kin 22:13	559
had rule over his chariots, s	1Kin 22:31	559
the going down of the sun, s	1Kin 22:36	559
according to the s of Elisha	2Kin 2:22	1697
Jehoshaphat the king of Judah, s	2Kin 3:7	559
of the prophets unto Elisha, s	2Kin 4:1	559
again to meet him, and told him, s	2Kin 4:31	559
one went in, and told his lord, s	2Kin 5:4	559
letter to the king of Israel, s	2Kin 5:6	559
that he sent to the king, s	2Kin 5:8	559
sent a messenger unto him, s	2Kin 5:10	559
according to the s of the man of	2Kin 5:14	1697
My master hath sent me, s	2Kin 5:22	559
took counsel with his servants, s	2Kin 6:8	559
sent unto the king of Israel, s	2Kin 6:9	559
And it was told him, s, Behold, he	2Kin 6:13	559
there cried a woman unto him, s	2Kin 6:26	559
and they told them, s, We came to	2Kin 7:10	559
hide themselves in the field, s	2Kin 7:12	559
after the host of the Syrians, s	2Kin 7:14	559
of God had spoken to the king, s	2Kin 7:18	559
son he had restored to life, s	2Kin 8:1	559
did after the s of the man of God	2Kin 8:2	1697
the servant of the man of God, s	2Kin 8:4	559
unto her a certain officer, s	2Kin 8:6	559
and it was told him, s, The man of	2Kin 8:7	559
and enquire of the LORD by him, s	2Kin 8:8	559
of Syria hath sent me to thee, s	2Kin 8:9	559
Thus and thus spake he to me, s	2Kin 9:12	559
stairs, and blew with trumpets, s	2Kin 9:13	559
And the watchman told, s, The	2Kin 9:18	559
And the watchman told, s, He came	2Kin 9:20	559
servant Elijah the Tishbite, s	2Kin 9:36	559
brought up Ahab's children, s	2Kin 10:1	559
of the children, sent to Jehu, s	2Kin 10:5	559
letter the second time to them, s	2Kin 10:6	559
came a messenger, and told him, s	2Kin 10:8	559
according to the s of the LORD	2Kin 10:17	1697
And he commanded them, s, This is	2Kin 11:5	559
wherein the LORD commanded, s	2Kin 14:6	559
son of Jehu, king of Israel, s	2Kin 14:8	559
sent to Amaziah king of Judah, s	2Kin 14:9	559
the cedar that was in Lebanon, s	2Kin 14:9	559
LORD which he spake unto Jehu, s	2Kin 15:12	559
king of Assyria, s, I am thy	2Kin 16:7	559
commanded Urijah the priest, s	2Kin 16:15	559
prophets, and by all the seers, s	2Kin 17:13	559
spake to the king of Assyria, s	2Kin 17:26	559
the king of Assyria commanded, s	2Kin 17:27	559
a covenant, and charged them, s	2Kin 17:35	559
the king of Assyria to Lachish, s	2Kin 18:14	559
the Jews' language, and spake, s	2Kin 18:28	559
make you trust in the LORD, s	2Kin 18:30	559
when he persuadeth you, s	2Kin 18:32	559
for the king's commandment was, s	2Kin 18:36	559
messengers again unto Hezekiah, s	2Kin 19:9	559
to Hezekiah king of Judah, s	2Kin 19:10	559
thou trustest deceive thee, s	2Kin 19:10	559
son of Amoz sent to Hezekiah, s	2Kin 19:20	559
wall, and prayed unto the LORD, s	2Kin 20:2	559
word of the LORD came to him, s	2Kin 20:4	559
by his servants the prophets, s	2Kin 21:10	559
to the house of the LORD, s	2Kin 22:3	559
the scribe shewed the king, s	2Kin 22:10	559
a servant of the king's, s	2Kin 22:12	559
king commanded all the people, s	2Kin 23:21	559
mother called his name Jabez, s	1Chr 4:9	559
called on the God of Israel, s	1Chr 4:10	559
to David unto Hebron, s, Behold,	1Chr 11:1	559
upon advisement sent him away, s	1Chr 12:19	559
was afraid of God that day, s	1Chr 13:12	559
And David enquired of God, s	1Chr 14:10	559
S, Unto thee will I give the land	1Chr 16:18	559
S, Touch not mine anointed, and do	1Chr 16:22	
the word of God came to Nathan, s	1Chr 17:3	559
I commanded to feed my people, s	1Chr 17:6	559
name may be magnified for ever, s	1Chr 17:24	559
spake unto Gad, David's seer, s	1Chr 21:9	559
Go and tell David, s, Thus saith	1Chr 21:10	559
And David went up at the s of Gad	1Chr 21:19	1697
word of the LORD came to me, s	1Chr 22:8	559
Israel to help Solomon his son, s	1Chr 22:17	
sent to Huram the king of Tyre, s	2Chr 2:3	559
of musick, and praised the LORD, s	2Chr 5:13	
his mouth to my father David, s	2Chr 6:4	559
which thou hast promised him, s	2Chr 6:16	559
in the land of their captivity, s	2Chr 6:37	559
and praised the LORD, s, For he	2Chr 7:3	
with David thy father, s, There	2Chr 7:18	559
came and spake to Rehoboam, s	2Chr 10:3	559
his father while he yet lived, s	2Chr 10:6	559
And they spake unto him, s	2Chr 10:7	559
which have spoken to me, s	2Chr 10:9	559
up with him spake unto him, s	2Chr 10:10	559
people that spake unto thee, s	2Chr 10:10	559
third day, as the king bade, s	2Chr 10:12	559
the advice of the young men, s	2Chr 10:14	559
the people answered the king, s	2Chr 10:16	559
to Shemaiah the man of God, s	2Chr 11:2	559
Israel in Judah and Benjamin, s	2Chr 11:3	559

of the LORD came to Shemaiah, *s*	2Chr 12:7	559
Syria, that dwelt at Damascus, *s*	2Chr 16:2	559
all the prophets prophesied so, *s*	2Chr 18:11	559
to call Micaiah spake to him, *s*	2Chr 18:12	559
one spake *s* after this manner, and	2Chr 18:19	559
another *s* after that manner	2Chr 18:19	559
chariots that were with him, *s*	2Chr 18:30	559
And he charged them, *s*, Thus shall	2Chr 19:9	559
some that told Jehoshaphat, *s*	2Chr 20:2	559
sanctuary therein for thy name, *s*	2Chr 20:8	559
prophesied against Jehoshaphat, *s*	2Chr 20:37	559
to him from Elijah the prophet, *s*	2Chr 21:12	559
where the LORD commanded, *s*	2Chr 25:4	559
there came a man of God to him, *s*	2Chr 25:7	559
son of Jehu, king of Israel, *s*	2Chr 25:17	559
sent to Amaziah king of Judah, *s*	2Chr 25:18	559
the cedar that was in Lebanon, *s*	2Chr 25:18	559
to the commandment of the king, *s*	2Chr 30:6	559
But Hezekiah prayed for them, *s*	2Chr 30:18	559
through the midst of the land, *s*	2Chr 32:4	559
and spake comfortably to them, *s*	2Chr 32:6	559
Judah that were at Jerusalem, *s*	2Chr 32:9	559
to die by famine and by thirst, *s*	2Chr 32:11	559
commanded Judah and Jerusalem, *s*	2Chr 32:12	559
and to speak against him, *s*	2Chr 32:17	559
the king word back again, *s*	2Chr 34:16	559
the scribe told the king, *s*	2Chr 34:18	559
Asaiah a servant of the king's, *s*	2Chr 34:20	559
But he sent ambassadors to him, *s*	2Chr 35:21	559
and put it also in writing, *s*	2Chr 36:22	559
and put it also in writing, *s*	Ezr 1:1	559
thus they returned us answer, *s*	Ezr 5:11	560
we had spoken unto the king, *s*	Ezr 8:22	559
done, the princes came to me, *s*	Ezr 9:1	559
by thy servants the prophets, *s*	Ezr 9:11	559
commandedst thy servant Moses, *s*	Neh 1:8	559
and Geshem sent unto me, *s*	Neh 6:2	559
And I sent messengers unto them, *s*	Neh 6:3	559
to preach of thee at Jerusalem, *s*	Neh 6:7	559
Then I sent unto him, *s*, There	Neh 6:8	559
For they all made us afraid, *s*	Neh 6:9	559
Levites stilled all the people, *s*	Neh 8:11	559
their cities, and in Jerusalem, *s*	Neh 8:15	559
and made them swear by God, *s*	Neh 13:25	
the *s* pleased the king and the	Est 1:21	1697
silence, and I heard a voice, *s*	Job 4:16	
place, then it shall deny him, *s*	Job 8:18	
He wandereth abroad for bread, *s*	Job 15:23	
waiteth for the twilight, *s*	Job 24:15	559
heard the voice of thy words, *s*	Job 33:8	
LORD, and against his anointed, *s*	Ps 2:2	
the lip, they shake the head, *s*	Ps 22:7	
will open my dark *s* upon the harp	Ps 49:4	2420
S, God hath forsaken him	Ps 71:11	559
S, Unto thee will I give the land	Ps 105:11	559
S, Touch not mine anointed, and do	Ps 105:15	
Mine eyes fail for thy word, *s*	Ps 119:82	559
wasted us required of us mirth, *s*	Ps 137:3	
city she uttereth her words, *s*	Prov 1:21	
I communed with mine own heart, *s*	Eccl 1:16	559
of my beloved that knocketh, *s*	Song 5:2	
of the house of his father, *s*	Is 3:6	
In that day shall he swear, *s*	Is 3:7	559
shall take hold of one man, *s*	Is 4:1	559
I heard the voice of the Lord, *s*	Is 6:8	559
it was told the house of David, *s*	Is 7:2	559
evil counsel against thee, *s*	Is 7:5	559
the LORD spake again unto Ahaz, *s*	Is 7:10	559
LORD spake also unto me again, *s*	Is 8:5	559
walk in the way of this people, *s*	Is 8:11	559
thee, and the cedars of Lebanon, *s*	Is 14:8	
upon thee, and consider thee, *s*	Is 14:16	559
The LORD of hosts hath sworn, *s*	Is 14:24	559
But now the LORD hath spoken, *s*	Is 16:14	559
of bulrushes upon the waters, *s*	Is 18:2	
the LORD of hosts shall bless, *s*	Is 19:25	559
LORD by Isaiah the son of Amoz, *s*	Is 20:2	559
even the strength of the sea, *s*	Is 23:4	559
deliver to one that is learned, *s*	Is 29:11	559
to him that is not learned, *s*	Is 29:12	559
shall hear a word behind thee, *s*	Is 30:21	559
make you trust in the LORD, *s*	Is 36:15	559
lest Hezekiah persuade you, *s*	Is 36:18	559
for the king's commandment was, *s*	Is 36:21	559
he sent messengers to Hezekiah, *s*	Is 37:9	559
to Hezekiah king of Judah, *s*	Is 37:10	559
thou trustest, deceive thee, *s*	Is 37:10	559
Hezekiah prayed unto the LORD, *s*	Is 37:15	559
son of Amoz sent unto Hezekiah, *s*	Is 37:21	559
the word of the LORD to Isaiah, *s*	Is 38:4	559
him that smote the anvil, *s*	Is 41:7	559
right hand, *s* unto thee, Fear not	Is 41:13	559
even *s* to Jerusalem, Thou shalt	Is 44:28	559
make supplication unto thee, *s*	Is 45:14	
things that are not yet done, *s*	Is 46:10	559
himself to the LORD, speak, *s*	Is 56:3	559
of old, Moses, and his people, *s*	Is 63:11	
word of the LORD came unto me, *s*	Jer 1:4	559
word of the LORD came unto me, *s*	Jer 1:11	559
came unto me the second time, *s*	Jer 1:13	559
word of the LORD came to me, *s*	Jer 2:1	559
cry in the ears of Jerusalem, *s*	Jer 2:2	559
S to a stock, Thou art my father	Jer 2:27	559
this people and Jerusalem, *s*	Jer 4:10	559
that spreadeth her hands, *s*	Jer 4:31	
Jacob, and publish it in Judah, *s*	Jer 5:20	559
daughter of my people slightly, *s*	Jer 6:14	559
Also I set watchmen over you, *s*	Jer 6:17	
came to Jeremiah from the LORD, *s*	Jer 7:1	559
Trust ye not in lying words, *s*	Jer 7:4	559
this thing commanded I them, *s*	Jer 7:23	559
repented him of his wickedness, *s*	Jer 8:6	559
daughter of my people slightly, *s*	Jer 8:11	559
came to Jeremiah from the LORD, *s*	Jer 11:1	559
Egypt, from the iron furnace, *s*	Jer 11:4	559
and in the streets of Jerusalem, *s*	Jer 11:6	559
rising early and protesting, *s*	Jer 11:7	559
had devised devices against me, *s*	Jer 11:19	
Anathoth, that seek thy life, *s*	Jer 11:21	559
came unto me the second time, *s*	Jer 13:3	559
word of the LORD came unto me, *s*	Jer 13:8	559
of the LORD came also unto me, *s*	Jer 16:1	559
came to Jeremiah from the LORD, *s*	Jer 18:1	559
word of the LORD came to me, *s*	Jer 18:5	559
the inhabitants of Jerusalem, *s*	Jer 18:11	559
watched for my halting, *s*	Jer 20:10	
brought tidings to my father, *s*	Jer 20:15	559
the son of Maaseiah the priest, *s*	Jer 21:1	559
They shall not lament for him, *s*	Jer 22:18	
they shall not lament for him, *s*	Jer 22:18	
that prophesy lies in my name, *s*	Jer 23:25	559
or a priest, shall ask thee, *s*	Jer 23:33	559
LORD, and I have sent unto you, *s*	Jer 23:38	559
word of the LORD came unto me, *s*	Jer 24:4	559
the inhabitants of Jerusalem, *s*	Jer 25:2	559
came this word from the LORD, *s*	Jer 26:1	559
and all the people took him, *s*	Jer 26:8	559
in the name of the LORD, *s*	Jer 26:9	559
princes and to all the people, *s*	Jer 26:11	559
princes and to all the people, *s*	Jer 26:12	559
all the assembly of the people, *s*	Jer 26:17	559
to all the people of Judah, *s*	Jer 26:18	559
unto Jeremiah from the LORD, *s*	Jer 27:1	559
which speak unto you, *s*, Ye	Jer 27:9	559
according to all these words, *s*	Jer 27:12	559
prophets that speak unto you, *s*	Jer 27:14	559
priests and to all this people, *s*	Jer 27:16	559
that prophesy unto you, *s*	Jer 27:16	559
priests and of all the people, *s*	Jer 28:1	559
of hosts, the God of Israel, *s*	Jer 28:2	559
the presence of all the people, *s*	Jer 28:11	559
neck of the prophet Jeremiah, *s*	Jer 28:12	559
Go and tell Hananiah, *s*, Thus	Jer 28:13	559
Nebuchadnezzar king of Babylon) *s*	Jer 29:3	559
of Judah which are in Babylon, *s*	Jer 29:22	559
to Shemaiah the Nehelamite, *s*	Jer 29:24	559
of hosts, the God of Israel, *s*	Jer 29:25	559
priest, and to all the priests, *s*	Jer 29:25	559
he sent unto us in Babylon, *s*	Jer 29:28	559
word of the LORD unto Jeremiah, *s*	Jer 29:30	559
to all them of the captivity, *s*	Jer 29:31	559
came to Jeremiah from the LORD, *s*	Jer 30:1	559
the LORD God of Israel, *s*	Jer 30:2	559
they called thee an Outcast, *s*	Jer 30:17	
hath appeared of old unto me, *s*	Jer 31:3	
and every man his brother, *s*	Jer 31:34	559
king of Judah had shut him up, *s*	Jer 32:3	559
word of the LORD came unto me, *s*	Jer 32:6	559
uncle shall come unto thee, *s*	Jer 32:7	559
I charged Baruch before them, *s*	Jer 32:13	559
Neriah, I prayed unto the LORD, *s*	Jer 32:16	559
word of the LORD unto Jeremiah, *s*	Jer 32:26	559
up in the court of the prison, *s*	Jer 33:1	559
of the LORD came unto Jeremiah, *s*	Jer 33:19	559
of the LORD came to Jeremiah, *s*	Jer 33:23	559
what this people have spoken, *s*	Jer 33:24	559
against all the cities thereof, *s*	Jer 34:1	559
and they will lament thee, *s*	Jer 34:5	
came to Jeremiah from the LORD, *s*	Jer 34:12	559
out of the house of bondmen, *s*	Jer 34:13	559
son of Josiah king of Judah, *s*	Jer 35:1	559
Rechab our father commanded us, *s*	Jer 35:6	559
word of the LORD unto Jeremiah, *s*	Jer 35:12	559
up early and sending them, *s*	Jer 35:15	559
unto Jeremiah from the LORD, *s*	Jer 36:1	559
And Jeremiah commanded Baruch, *s*	Jer 36:5	559
the son of Cushi, unto Baruch, *s*	Jer 36:14	559
And they asked Baruch, *s*, Tell us	Jer 36:17	559
wrote at the mouth of Jeremiah, *s*	Jer 36:27	559
Thou hast burned this roll, *s*	Jer 36:29	559
Why hast thou written therein, *s*	Jer 36:29	559
priest to the prophet Jeremiah, *s*	Jer 37:3	559
LORD unto the prophet Jeremiah, *s*	Jer 37:6	559
Deceive not yourselves, *s*	Jer 37:9	559
he took Jeremiah the prophet, *s*	Jer 37:13	559
which prophesied unto you, *s*	Jer 37:19	559
had spoken unto all the people, *s*	Jer 38:1	559
house, and spake to the king, *s*	Jer 38:8	559
Ebed-melech the Ethiopian, *s*	Jer 38:10	559
sware secretly unto Jeremiah, *s*	Jer 38:16	559
the captain of the guard, *s*	Jer 39:11	559
up in the court of the prison, *s*	Jer 39:15	559
to Ebed-melech the Ethiopian, *s*	Jer 39:16	559
unto them and to their men, *s*	Jer 40:9	559
to Gedaliah in Mizpah secretly, *s*	Jer 40:15	559
S, No; but we will	Jer 42:14	559
sent me unto the LORD your God, *s*	Jer 42:20	559
s unto Jeremiah, Thou speakest	Jer 43:2	559
unto Jeremiah in Tahpanhes, *s*	Jer 43:8	559
and in the country of Pathros, *s*	Jer 44:1	559
rising early and sending them, *s*	Jer 44:4	559
in Pathros, answered Jeremiah, *s*	Jer 44:15	559
had given him that answer, *s*	Jer 44:20	559
of hosts, the God of Israel, *s*	Jer 44:25	559
and fulfilled with your hand, *s*	Jer 44:25	559
Judah in all the land of Egypt, *s*	Jer 44:26	559
son of Josiah king of Judah, *s*	Jer 45:1	559
They shall howl, *s*, How is it	Jer 48:39	
that trusted in her treasures, *s*	Jer 49:4	
is sent unto the heathen, *s*	Jer 49:14	
of Zedekiah king of Judah, *s*	Jer 49:34	559
with their faces thitherward, *s*	Jer 50:5	
of hosts hath sworn by himself, *s*	Jer 51:14	
at the daughter of Jerusalem, *s*	Lam 2:15	
me a voice of a great rushing, *s*	Eze 3:12	
word of the LORD came unto me, *s*	Eze 3:16	559
word of the LORD came unto me, *s*	Eze 6:1	559
word of the LORD came unto me, *s*	Eze 7:1	559
in mine ears with a loud voice, *s*	Eze 9:1	559
his side, reported the matter, *s*	Eze 9:11	559
the man clothed with linen, *s*	Eze 10:6	559
word of the LORD came unto me, *s*	Eze 11:14	559
of the LORD also came unto me, *s*	Eze 12:1	559
the word of the LORD unto me, *s*	Eze 12:8	559
word of the LORD came to me, *s*	Eze 12:17	559
word of the LORD came unto me, *s*	Eze 12:21	559
ye have in the land of Israel, *s*	Eze 12:22	559
word of the LORD came to me, *s*	Eze 12:26	559
word of the LORD came unto me, *s*	Eze 13:1	559
vanity and lying divination, *s*	Eze 13:6	559
they have seduced my people, *s*	Eze 13:10	559
word of the LORD came unto me, *s*	Eze 14:2	559
of the LORD came again to me, *s*	Eze 14:12	559
word of the LORD came unto me, *s*	Eze 15:1	559
word of the LORD came unto me, *s*	Eze 16:1	559
use this proverb against thee, *s*	Eze 16:44	559
word of the LORD came unto me, *s*	Eze 17:1	559
word of the LORD came unto me, *s*	Eze 17:11	559
of the LORD came unto me again, *s*	Eze 18:1	559
concerning the land of Israel, *s*	Eze 18:2	559
the word of the LORD unto me, *s*	Eze 20:2	559
lifted up mine hand unto them, *s*	Eze 20:5	559
word of the LORD came unto me, *s*	Eze 20:45	559
word of the LORD came unto me, *s*	Eze 21:1	559
word of the LORD came unto me, *s*	Eze 21:8	559
of the LORD came unto me again, *s*	Eze 21:18	559
word of the LORD came unto me, *s*	Eze 22:1	559
word of the LORD came unto me, *s*	Eze 22:17	559
word of the LORD came unto me, *s*	Eze 22:23	559
and divining lies unto them, *s*	Eze 22:28	559
of the LORD came again unto me, *s*	Eze 23:1	559
word of the LORD came unto me, *s*	Eze 24:1	559
word of the LORD came unto me, *s*	Eze 24:15	559
word of the LORD came unto me, *s*	Eze 24:20	559
of the LORD came again unto me, *s*	Eze 25:1	559
word of the LORD came unto me, *s*	Eze 26:1	559
of the LORD came again unto me, *s*	Eze 27:1	559
for thee, and lament over thee, *s*	Eze 27:32	
of the LORD came again unto me, *s*	Eze 28:1	559
word of the LORD came unto me, *s*	Eze 28:11	559
word of the LORD came unto me, *s*	Eze 28:20	559
word of the LORD came unto me, *s*	Eze 29:1	559
word of the LORD came unto me, *s*	Eze 29:17	559
of the LORD came again unto me, *s*	Eze 30:1	559
word of the LORD came unto me, *s*	Eze 30:20	559
word of the LORD came unto me, *s*	Eze 31:1	559
word of the LORD came unto me, *s*	Eze 32:1	559
word of the LORD came unto me, *s*	Eze 32:17	559
word of the LORD came unto me, *s*	Eze 33:1	559
Thus ye speak, *s*, If our	Eze 33:10	559
out of Jerusalem came unto me, *s*	Eze 33:21	559
word of the LORD came unto me, *s*	Eze 33:23	559
of the land of Israel speak, *s*	Eze 33:24	559
every one to his brother, *s*	Eze 33:30	559
word of the Lord came unto me, *s*	Eze 34:1	559
word of the LORD came unto me, *s*	Eze 35:1	559
the mountains of Israel, *s*	Eze 35:12	559
word of the LORD came unto me, *s*	Eze 36:16	559
of the LORD came again unto me, *s*	Eze 37:15	559
people shall speak unto thee, *s*	Eze 37:18	559
word of the LORD came unto me, *s*	Eze 38:1	559
and before him I told the dream, *s*	Dan 4:8	
one coming down from heaven, and *s*	Dan 4:23	560
there fell a voice from heaven, *s*	Dan 4:31	
and commanded the prophets, *s*	Amos 2:12	559
up from the land of Egypt, *s*	Amos 3:1	559
to Jeroboam king of Israel, *s*	Amos 7:10	559
S, When will the new moon be gone	Amos 8:5	559
unto Jonah the son of Amittai, *s*	Jonah 1:1	559
unto Jonah the second time, *s*	Jonah 3:1	559
of the king and his nobles, *s*	Jonah 3:7	559
thee, O LORD, was not this my *s*	Jonah 4:2	1697
the spirit and falsehood do lie, *s*	Mic 2:11	
of Josedech, the high priest, *s*	Hag 1:1	559
speaketh the LORD of hosts, *s*	Hag 1:2	559
the LORD by Haggai the prophet, *s*	Hag 1:3	559
LORD's message unto the people, *s*	Hag 1:13	559
the LORD by the prophet Haggai, *s*	Hag 2:1	559
to the residue of the people, *s*	Hag 2:2	559
the LORD by Haggai the prophet, *s*	Hag 2:10	559
the priests concerning the law, *s*	Hag 2:11	559
and twentieth day of the month, *s*	Hag 2:20	559
Zerubbabel, governor of Judah, *s*	Hag 2:21	559
the son of Iddo the prophet, *s*	Zec 1:1	559
the former prophets have cried, *s*	Zec 1:4	559
the son of Iddo the prophet, *s*	Zec 1:7	559
with me said unto me, Cry thou, *s*	Zec 1:14	559
Cry yet, *s*, Thus saith the LORD	Zec 1:17	559
And he spake, *s*, These are the	Zec 1:21	559
Run, speak to this young man, *s*	Zec 2:4	559
those that stood before him, *s*	Zec 3:4	559
the LORD protested unto Joshua, *s*	Zec 3:6	559
the angel that talked with me, *s*	Zec 4:4	559
he answered and spake unto me, *s*	Zec 4:6	559
of the LORD unto Zerubbabel, *s*	Zec 4:6	559
word of the LORD came unto me, *s*	Zec 4:8	559
he upon me, and spake unto me, *s*	Zec 6:8	559
word of the LORD came unto me, *s*	Zec 6:9	559
And speak unto him, *s*, Thus	Zec 6:12	559
speaketh the LORD of hosts, *s*	Zec 6:12	559
of hosts, and to the prophets, *s*	Zec 7:3	559
of the LORD of hosts unto me, *s*	Zec 7:4	559
of the land, and to the priests, *s*	Zec 7:5	559
the LORD came unto Zechariah, *s*	Zec 7:8	559
speaketh the LORD of hosts, *s*	Zec 7:9	559
the LORD of hosts came to me, *s*	Zec 8:1	559
the LORD of hosts came unto me, *s*	Zec 8:18	559
one city shall go to another, *s*	Zec 8:21	559
the skirt of him that is a Jew, *s*	Zec 8:23	559
appeared unto him in a dream, *s*	Mt 1:20	*3004*
of the Lord by the prophet, *s*	Mt 1:22	*3004*
S, Where is he that is born King	Mt 2:2	*3004*

appeareth to Joseph in a dream, *s*	Mt 2:13	*3004*
of the Lord by the prophet, *s*	Mt 2:15	*3004*
spoken by Jeremy the prophet, *s*	Mt 2:17	*3004*
S, Arise, and take the young child	Mt 2:20	*3004*
And *s*, Repent ye	Mt 3:2	*3004*
of by the prophet Esaias, *s*	Mt 3:3	*3004*
But John forbad him, *s*, I have	Mt 3:14	*3004*
And lo a voice from heaven, *s*	Mt 3:17	*3004*
spoken by Esaias the prophet, *s*	Mt 4:14	*3004*
his mouth, and taught them, *s*	Mt 5:2	*3004*
Therefore take no thought, *s*	Mt 6:31	*3004*
came a leper and worshipped him, *s*	Mt 8:2	*3004*
forth his hand, and touched him, *s*	Mt 8:3	*3004*
And *s*, Lord, my servant lieth at	Mt 8:6	*3004*
spoken by Esaias the prophet, *s*	Mt 8:17	*3004*
came to him, and awoke him, *s*	Mt 8:25	*3004*
But the men marvelled, *s*, What	Mt 8:27	*3004*
And, behold, they cried out, *s*	Mt 8:29	*3004*
So the devils besought him, *s*	Mt 8:31	*3004*
to him the disciples of John, *s*	Mt 9:14	*3004*
ruler, and worshipped him, *s*	Mt 9:18	*3004*
men followed him, crying, and *s*	Mt 9:27	*3004*
Then touched he their eyes, *s*	Mt 9:29	*3004*
and Jesus straitly charged them, *s*	Mt 9:30	*3004*
and the multitudes marvelled, *s*	Mt 9:33	*3004*
sent forth, and commanded them, *s*	Mt 10:5	*3004*
And as ye go, preach, *s*, The	Mt 10:7	*3004*
And *s*, We have piped unto you, and	Mt 11:17	*3004*
And they asked him, *s*, Is it	Mt 12:10	*3004*
spoken by Esaias the prophet, *s*	Mt 12:17	*3004*
and of the Pharisees answered, *s*	Mt 12:38	*3004*
things unto them in parables, *s*	Mt 13:3	*3004*
parable put he forth unto them, *s*	Mt 13:24	*3004*
parable put he forth unto them, *s*	Mt 13:31	*3004*
was spoken by the prophet, *s*	Mt 13:35	*3004*
and his disciples came unto him, *s*	Mt 13:36	*3004*
his disciples came to him, *s*	Mt 14:15	*3004*
on the sea, they were troubled, *s*	Mt 14:26	*3004*
Jesus spake unto them, *s*, Be of	Mt 14:27	*3004*
and beginning to sink, he cried, *s*	Mt 14:30	*3004*
ship came and worshipped him, *s*	Mt 14:33	*3004*
which were of Jerusalem, *s*	Mt 15:1	*3004*
For God commanded, *s*, Honour thy	Mt 15:4	*3004*
did Esaias prophesy of you, *s*	Mt 15:7	*3004*
offended, after they heard this *s*	Mt 15:12	*3058*
same coasts, and cried unto him, *s*	Mt 15:22	*3004*
disciples came and besought him, *s*	Mt 15:23	*3004*
came she and worshipped him, *s*	Mt 15:25	*3004*
they reasoned among themselves, *s*	Mt 16:7	*3004*
he asked his disciples, *s*	Mt 16:13	*3004*
him, and began to rebuke him, *s*	Mt 16:22	*3004*
mountain, Jesus charged them, *s*	Mt 17:9	*3004*
And his disciples asked him, *s*	Mt 17:10	*3004*
man, kneeling down to him, and *s*	Mt 17:14	*3004*
the house, Jesus prevented him, *s*	Mt 17:25	*3004*
came the disciples unto Jesus, *s*	Mt 18:1	*3004*
fell down, and worshipped him, *s*	Mt 18:26	*3004*
him, and took him by the throat, *s*	Mt 18:28	*3004*
at his feet, and besought him, *s*	Mt 18:29	*3004*
s unto him, Is it lawful for a	Mt 19:3	*3004*
All men cannot receive this *s*	Mt 19:11	*3056*
when the young man heard that *s*	Mt 19:22	*3056*
they were exceedingly amazed, *s*	Mt 19:25	*3004*
S, These last have wrought but	Mt 20:12	*3004*
Jesus passed by, cried out, *s*	Mt 20:30	*3004*
but they cried the more, *s*	Mt 20:31	*3004*
S unto them, Go into the village	Mt 21:2	*3004*
was spoken by the prophet, *s*	Mt 21:4	*3004*
and that followed, cried, *s*	Mt 21:9	*3004*
all the city was moved, *s*	Mt 21:10	*3004*
crying in the temple, and *s*	Mt 21:15	*3004*
saw it, they marvelled, *s*	Mt 21:20	*3004*
they reasoned with themselves, *s*	Mt 21:25	*3004*
all he sent unto them his son, *s*	Mt 21:37	*3004*
he sent forth other servants, *s*	Mt 22:4	*3004*
disciples with the Herodians, *s*	Mt 22:16	*3004*
S, Master, Moses said, If a man	Mt 22:24	*3004*
was spoken unto you by God, *s*	Mt 22:31	*3004*
a question, tempting him, and *s*	Mt 22:35	*3004*
S, What think ye of Christ	Mt 22:42	*3004*
David in spirit call him Lord, *s*	Mt 22:43	*3004*
S, The scribes and the Pharisees	Mt 23:2	*3004*
came unto him privately, *s*	Mt 24:3	*3004*
For many shall come in my name, *s*	Mt 24:5	*3004*
But the wise answered, *s*, Not so	Mt 25:9	*3004*
came also the other virgins, *s*	Mt 25:11	*3004*
and brought other five talents, *s*	Mt 25:20	*3004*
shall the righteous answer him, *s*	Mt 25:37	*3004*
shall they also answer him, *s*	Mt 25:44	*3004*
Then shall he answer them, *s*	Mt 25:45	*3004*
saw it, they had indignation, *s*	Mt 26:8	*3004*
s unto him, Where wilt thou that	Mt 26:17	*3004*
thanks, and gave it to them, *s*	Mt 26:27	*3004*
and fell on his face, and prayed, *s*	Mt 26:39	*3004*
the second time, and prayed, *s*	Mt 26:42	*3004*
the third time, *s* the same words	Mt 26:44	*2036*
betrayed him gave them a sign, *s*	Mt 26:48	*3004*
high priest rent his clothes, *s*	Mt 26:65	*3004*
S, Prophesy unto us, thou Christ,	Mt 26:68	*3004*
and a damsel came unto him, *s*	Mt 26:69	*3004*
But he denied before them all, *s*	Mt 26:70	*3004*
began he to curse and to swear, *s*	Mt 26:74	
S, I have sinned in that I have	Mt 27:4	*3004*
spoken by Jeremy the prophet, *s*	Mt 27:9	*3004*
and the governor asked him, *s*	Mt 27:11	*3004*
seat, his wife sent unto him, *s*	Mt 27:19	*3004*
But they cried out the more, *s*	Mt 27:23	*3004*
his hands before the multitude, *s*	Mt 27:24	*3004*
knee before him, and mocked him, *s*	Mt 27:29	*3004*
And *s*, Thou that destroyest the	Mt 27:40	*3004*
Jesus cried with a loud voice, *s*	Mt 27:46	*3004*
were done, they feared greatly, *s*	Mt 27:54	*3004*
S, Sir, we remember that that	Mt 27:63	*3004*
behold, Jesus met them, *s*	Mt 28:9	*3004*

S, Say ye, His disciples came by	Mt 28:13	*3004*
this *s* is commonly reported among	Mt 28:15	*3056*
Jesus came and spake unto them, *s*	Mt 28:18	*3004*
And preached, *s*, There cometh one	Mk 1:7	*3004*
there came a voice from heaven, *s*	Mk 1:11	
And *s*, The time is fulfilled, and	Mk 1:15	*3004*
S, Let us alone	Mk 1:24	*3004*
And Jesus rebuked him, *s*, Hold thy	Mk 1:25	*3004*
questioned among themselves, *s*	Mk 1:27	*3004*
s unto him, If thou wilt, thou	Mk 1:40	*3004*
all amazed, and glorified God, *s*	Mk 2:12	*3004*
fell down before him, and cried, *s*	Mk 3:11	*3004*
And he answered them, *s*, Who is my	Mk 3:33	*3004*
And he answered, *s*, My name is	Mk 5:9	*3004*
And all the devils besought him, *s*	Mk 5:12	*3004*
And besought him greatly, *s*	Mk 5:23	*3004*
hearing him were astonished, *s*	Mk 6:2	*3004*
haste unto the king, and asked, *s*	Mk 6:25	*3004*
unto her, For this *s* go thy way	Mk 7:29	*3056*
were beyond measure astonished, *s*	Mk 7:37	*3004*
And he charged them, *s*, Take heed,	Mk 8:15	*3004*
they reasoned among themselves, *s*	Mk 8:16	*3004*
he sent him away to his house, *s*	Mk 8:26	*3004*
s unto them, Whom do men say that	Mk 8:27	*3004*
And he spake that *s* openly	Mk 8:32	*3056*
disciples, he rebuked Peter, *s*	Mk 8:33	*3004*
a voice came out of the cloud, *s*	Mk 9:7	*3004*
they kept that *s* with themselves,	Mk 9:10	*3056*
And they asked him, *s*, Why say the	Mk 9:11	*3004*
s unto him, Thou dumb and deaf	Mk 9:25	*3004*
But they understood not that *s*	Mk 9:32	*4487*
And John answered him, *s*, Master,	Mk 9:38	*3004*
And he was sad at that *s*, and went	Mk 10:22	*3056*
s among themselves, Who then can	Mk 10:26	*3004*
S, Behold, we go up to Jerusalem	Mk 10:33	
sons of Zebedee, come unto him, *s*	Mk 10:35	*3004*
s unto him, Be of good comfort,	Mk 10:49	*3004*
and they that followed, cried, *s*	Mk 11:9	*3004*
s unto them, Is it not written,	Mk 11:17	*3004*
they reasoned with themselves, *s*	Mk 11:31	*3004*
sent him also last unto them, *s*	Mk 12:6	*3004*
and they asked him, *s*,	Mk 12:18	*3004*
in the bush God spake unto him, *s*	Mk 12:26	*3004*
For many shall come in my name, *s*	Mk 13:6	*3004*
him had given them a token, *s*	Mk 14:44	*3004*
bare false witness against him, *s*	Mk 14:57	*3004*
in the midst, and asked Jesus, *s*	Mk 14:60	*3004*
But he denied, *s*, I know not,	Mk 14:68	*3004*
he began to curse and to swear, *s*	Mk 14:71	
And Pilate asked him again, *s*	Mk 15:4	*3004*
But Pilate answered them, *s*	Mk 15:9	*3004*
on him, wagging their heads, and *s*	Mk 15:29	*3004*
Jesus cried with a loud voice, *s*	Mk 15:34	*3004*
a reed, and gave him to drink, *s*	Mk 15:36	*3004*
and hid herself five months, *s*	Lk 1:24	*3004*
him, she was troubled at his *s*	Lk 1:29	*3056*
for a writing table, and wrote, *s*	Lk 1:63	*3004*
laid them up in their hearts, *s*	Lk 1:66	*3004*
the Holy Ghost, and prophesied, *s*	Lk 1:67	*3004*
heavenly host praising God, and *s*	Lk 2:13	*3004*
they made known abroad the *s*	Lk 2:17	*4487*
they understood not the *s* which	Lk 2:50	*4487*
words of Esaias the prophet, *s*	Lk 3:4	*3004*
And the people asked him, *s*	Lk 3:10	*3004*
likewise demanded of him, *s*	Lk 3:14	*3004*
s unto them all, I indeed baptize	Lk 3:16	*3004*
And Jesus answered him, *s*, It is	Lk 4:4	*3004*
S, Let us alone	Lk 4:34	*3004*
And Jesus rebuked him, *s*, Hold thy	Lk 4:35	*3004*
and spake among themselves, *s*	Lk 4:36	*3004*
out of many, crying out, and *s*	Lk 4:41	*3004*
he fell down at Jesus' knees, *s*	Lk 5:8	*3004*
on his face, and besought him, *s*	Lk 5:12	*3004*
forth his hand, and touched him, *s*	Lk 5:13	*2036*
the Pharisees began to reason, *s*	Lk 5:21	*3004*
God, and were filled with fear, *s*	Lk 5:26	*3004*
murmured against his disciples, *s*	Lk 5:30	*3004*
they besought him instantly, *s*	Lk 7:4	*3004*
s unto him, Lord, trouble not	Lk 7:6	*3004*
and they glorified God, *s*, That a	Lk 7:16	*3004*
disciples sent them to Jesus, *s*	Lk 7:19	*3004*
Baptist hath sent us unto thee, *s*	Lk 7:20	*3004*
and calling one to another, and *s*	Lk 7:32	*3004*
it, he spake within himself, *s*	Lk 7:39	*3004*
And his disciples asked him, *s*	Lk 8:9	*3004*
they came to him, and awoke him, *s*	Lk 8:24	*3004*
s one to another, What manner of	Lk 8:25	*3004*
And Jesus asked him, *s*, What is	Lk 8:30	*3004*
but Jesus sent him away, *s*	Lk 8:38	*3004*
s to him, Thy daughter is dead	Lk 8:49	*3004*
heard it, he answered him, *s*	Lk 8:50	*3004*
her by the hand, and called, *s*	Lk 8:54	*3004*
and he asked them, *s*, Whom say the	Lk 9:18	*3004*
S, The Son of man must suffer	Lk 9:22	*2036*
came a voice out of the cloud, *s*	Lk 9:35	*3004*
a man of the company cried out, *s*	Lk 9:38	*3004*
But they understood not this *s*	Lk 9:45	*4487*
they feared to ask him of that *s*	Lk 9:45	*4487*
returned again with joy, *s*	Lk 10:17	*3004*
stood up, and tempted him, *s*	Lk 10:25	*3004*
thus *s* thou reproachest us also	Lk 11:45	*3004*
he spake a parable unto them, *s*	Lk 12:16	*3004*
And he thought within himself, *s*	Lk 12:17	*3004*
and to knock at the door, *s*	Lk 13:25	*3004*
s unto him, Get thee out, and	Lk 13:31	*3004*
unto the lawyers and Pharisees, *s*	Lk 14:3	*3004*
And answered them, *s*, Which of you	Lk 14:5	*2036*
chief rooms; *s* unto them	Lk 14:7	*3004*
S, This man began to build, and	Lk 14:30	*3004*
Pharisees and scribes murmured, *s*	Lk 15:2	*3004*
spake this parable unto them, *s*	Lk 15:3	*3004*
s unto them, Rejoice with me	Lk 15:6	*3004*
and her neighbours together, *s*	Lk 15:9	*3004*
in a day turn again to thee, *s*	Lk 17:4	*3004*

S, There was in a city a judge,	Lk 18:2	*3004*
and she came unto him, *s*, Avenge	Lk 18:3	*3004*
but smote upon his breast, *s*	Lk 18:13	*3004*
And a certain ruler asked him, *s*	Lk 18:18	*3004*
this *s* was hid from them, neither	Lk 18:34	*4487*
And he cried, *s*, Jesus, thou son	Lk 18:38	*3004*
S, What wilt thou that I shall do	Lk 18:41	*3004*
they saw it, they all murmured, *s*	Lk 19:7	*3004*
and sent a message after him, *s*	Lk 19:14	*3004*
Then came the first, *s*, Lord, thy	Lk 19:16	*3004*
And the second came, *s*, Lord, thy	Lk 19:18	*3004*
And another came, *s*, Lord, behold,	Lk 19:20	*3004*
S, Go ye into the village over	Lk 19:30	*2036*
S, Blessed be the King that	Lk 19:38	*3004*
S, If thou hadst known, even thou	Lk 19:42	*3004*
S unto them, It is written, My	Lk 19:46	*3004*
And spake unto him, *s*, Tell us, by	Lk 20:2	*3004*
they reasoned with themselves, *s*	Lk 20:5	*3004*
they reasoned among themselves, *s*	Lk 20:14	*3004*
And they asked him, *s*, Master, we	Lk 20:21	*3004*
S, Master, Moses wrote unto us,	Lk 20:28	*3004*
And they asked him, *s*, Master, but	Lk 21:7	*3004*
for many shall come in my name, *s*	Lk 21:8	*3004*
And he sent Peter and John, *s*	Lk 22:8	*2036*
and brake it, and gave unto them, *s*	Lk 22:19	*3004*
also the cup after supper, *s*	Lk 22:20	*3004*
S, Father, if thou be willing,	Lk 22:42	*3004*
And he denied him, *s*, Woman, I	Lk 22:57	*3004*
another confidently affirmed, *s*	Lk 22:59	*3004*
him on the face, and asked him, *s*	Lk 22:64	*3004*
and led him into their council, *s*	Lk 22:66	*3004*
And they began to accuse him, *s*	Lk 23:2	*3004*
s that he himself is Christ a	Lk 23:2	*3004*
And Pilate asked him, *s*, Art thou	Lk 23:3	*3004*
And they were the more fierce, *s*	Lk 23:5	*3004*
And they cried out all at once, *s*	Lk 23:18	*3004*
But they cried, *s*, Crucify him,	Lk 23:21	*3004*
also with them derided him, *s*	Lk 23:35	*3004*
And *s*, If thou be the king of the	Lk 23:37	*3004*
were hanged railed on him, *s*	Lk 23:39	*3004*
other answering rebuked him, *s*	Lk 23:40	*3004*
was done, he glorified God, *s*	Lk 23:47	*3004*
S, The Son of man must be	Lk 24:7	*3004*
found not his body, they came, *s*	Lk 24:23	*3004*
But they constrained him, *s*	Lk 24:29	*3004*
S, The Lord is risen indeed, and	Lk 24:34	*3004*
bare witness of him, and cried, *s*	Jn 1:15	*3004*
John answered them, *s*, I baptize	Jn 1:26	*3004*
And John bare record, *s*, I saw the	Jn 1:32	*3004*
while his disciples prayed him, *s*	Jn 4:31	*3004*
And herein is that *s* true, One	Jn 4:37	*3056*
on him for the *s* of the woman	Jn 4:39	*3056*
we believe, not because of thy *s*	Jn 4:42	*2981*
servants met him, and told him, *s*	Jn 4:51	*3004*
strove among themselves, *s*	Jn 6:52	*3004*
this, said, This is an hard *s*	Jn 6:60	*3056*
And the Jews marvelled, *s*, How	Jn 7:15	*3004*
in the temple as he taught, *s*	Jn 7:28	*3004*
What manner of *s* is this that he	Jn 7:36	*3056*
feast, Jesus stood and cried, *s*	Jn 7:37	*3004*
therefore, when they heard this *s*	Jn 7:40	*3056*
spake Jesus again unto them, *s*	Jn 8:12	*3004*
say unto you, If a man keep my *s*	Jn 8:51	*3056*
thou sayest, If a man keep my *s*	Jn 8:52	*3056*
but I know him, and keep his *s*	Jn 8:55	*3056*
And his disciples asked him, *s*	Jn 9:2	*3004*
And they asked them, *s*, Is this	Jn 9:19	*3004*
The Jews answered him, *s*, For a	Jn 10:33	*3004*
his sisters sent unto him, *s*	Jn 11:3	*3004*
Mary her sister secretly, *s*	Jn 11:28	*2036*
and went out, followed her, *s*	Jn 11:31	*3004*
s unto him, Lord, if thou hadst	Jn 11:32	*3004*
of Galilee, and desired him, *s*	Jn 12:21	*3004*
And Jesus answered them, *s*	Jn 12:23	*3004*
came there a voice from heaven, *s*	Jn 12:28	
That the *s* of Esaias the prophet	Jn 12:38	*3056*
if they have kept my *s*, they will	Jn 15:20	*3056*
That the *s* might be fulfilled,	Jn 18:9	*3056*
with the palm of his hand, *s*	Jn 18:22	*2036*
That the *s* of Jesus might be	Jn 18:32	*3056*
Then cried they all again, *s*	Jn 18:40	*3004*
saw him, they cried out, *s*	Jn 19:6	*3004*
Pilate therefore heard that *s*	Jn 19:8	*3056*
but the Jews cried out, *s*	Jn 19:12	*3004*
Pilate therefore heard that *s*	Jn 19:13	*3056*
Then went this *s* abroad among the	Jn 21:23	*3056*
together, they asked of him, *s*	Acts 1:6	*3004*
s one to another, Behold, are not	Acts 2:7	*3004*
s one to another, What meaneth	Acts 2:12	*3004*
words did he testify and exhort, *s*	Acts 2:40	*3004*
s unto Abraham, And in thy seed	Acts 3:25	*3004*
S, What shall we do to these men	Acts 4:16	*3004*
S, The prison truly found we shut	Acts 5:23	*3004*
Then came one and told them, *s*	Acts 5:25	*3004*
S, Did not we straitly command	Acts 5:28	*3004*
the *s* pleased the whole multitude	Acts 6:5	*3056*
have set them at one again, *s*	Acts 7:26	*2036*
wrong thrust him away, *s*, Who	Acts 7:27	*2036*
Then fled Moses at this *s*	Acts 7:29	*3056*
S, I am the God of thy fathers,	Acts 7:32	
This Moses whom they refused, *s*	Acts 7:35	*2036*
S unto Aaron, Make us gods to go	Acts 7:40	*2036*
Stephen, calling upon God, and *s*	Acts 7:59	*3007*
from the least to the greatest, *s*	Acts 8:10	*3007*
S, Give me also this power, that	Acts 8:19	*3007*
of the Lord spake unto Philip, *s*	Acts 8:26	*3007*
and heard a voice *s* unto him	Acts 9:4	*3007*
to him, and *s* unto him, Cornelius	Acts 10:3	*2036*
But Peter took him up, *s*, Stand	Acts 10:26	*3004*
S, Thou wentest in to men	Acts 11:3	*3004*
it by order unto them, *s*,	Acts 11:4	*3004*
And I heard a voice *s* unto me	Acts 11:7	*3004*
their peace, and glorified God, *s*	Acts 11:18	*3004*
on the side, and raised him up, *s*	Acts 12:7	*3004*

And the people gave a shout, s ... Acts 12:22
the synagogue sent unto them, s ... Acts 13:15 3004
so hath the Lord commanded us, s ... Acts 13:47
s in the speech of Lycaonia, The ... Acts 14:11 3004
And s, Sirs, why do ye these ... Acts 14:15 3004
the Pharisees which believed, s ... Acts 15:5 3004
their peace, James answered, s ... Acts 15:13 3004
words, subverting your souls, s ... Acts 15:24 3004
of Macedonia, and prayed him, s ... Acts 16:9 3004
her household, she besought us, s ... Acts 16:15 3004
followed Paul and us, and cried, s ... Acts 16:17 3004
them to the magistrates, s ... Acts 16:20 2036
Paul cried with a loud voice, s ... Acts 16:28 3004
magistrates sent the serjeants, s ... Acts 16:35 3004
of the prison told this s to Paul ... Acts 16:36 3056
s that there is another king, one ... Acts 17:7 3004
and brought him unto Areopagus, s ... Acts 17:19 3004
S, This fellow persuadeth men to ... Acts 18:13 3004
But bade them farewell, s ... Acts 18:21 2036
s unto the people, that they ... Acts 19:4 3004
the name of the Lord Jesus, s ... Acts 19:13 3004
and Achaia, to go to Jerusalem, s ... Acts 19:21 2036
s that they be no gods, which are ... Acts 19:26 3004
full of wrath, and cried out, s ... Acts 19:28 3004
s that bonds and afflictions abide ... Acts 20:23 3004
not be persuaded, we ceased, s ... Acts 21:14 2036
Moses, s that they ought not to ... Acts 21:21 3004
unto them in the Hebrew tongue, s ... Acts 21:40 3004
and heard a voice s unto me ... Acts 22:7 3004
And saw him s unto me, Make haste, ... Acts 22:18 3004
went and told the chief captain, s ... Acts 22:26 3004
part arose, and strove, s, We find ... Acts 23:9 3004
s that they would neither eat nor ... Acts 23:12 3004
called unto him two centurions, s ... Acts 23:23 2036
Tertullus began to accuse him, s ... Acts 24:2 3004
s that these things were so ... Acts 24:9 5335
Paul's cause unto the king, s ... Acts 25:14 3004
s in the Hebrew tongue, Saul, ... Acts 26:14 3004
s none other things than those ... Acts 26:22 3004
they talked between themselves, s ... Acts 26:31 3004
S, Fear not, Paul ... Acts 27:24 3004
besought them all to take meat, s ... Acts 27:33 3004
S, Go unto this people, and say, ... Acts 28:26 3004
S, Blessed are they whose ... Rom 4:7
to God against Israel, s ... Rom 11:2 3004
is briefly comprehended in this s ... Rom 13:9 3056
the cup, when he had supped, s ... 1Cor 11:25 3004
to pass the s that is written ... 1Cor 15:54 3056
before the gospel unto Abraham, s ... Gal 3:8
This is a faithful s, and worthy ... 1Ti 1:15 3056
This is a true s, If a man desire ... 1Ti 3:1 3056
This is a faithful s and worthy of ... 1Ti 4:9 3056
It is a faithful s ... 2Ti 2:11 3056
s that the resurrection is past ... 2Ti 2:18 3004
This is a faithful s, and these ... Titus 3:8 3056
in a certain place testified, s ... Heb 2:6 3004
S, I will declare thy name unto ... Heb 2:12 3004
s in David, To day, after so long ... Heb 4:7 3004
S, Surely blessing I will bless ... Heb 6:14 3004
and every man his brother, s ... Heb 8:11 3004
S, This is the blood of the ... Heb 9:20 3004
but now he hath promised, s ... Heb 12:26 3004
And s, Where is the promise of his ... 2Pet 3:4 3004
from Adam, prophesied of these, s ... Jude 14 3004
S, I am Alpha and Omega, the first ... Rev 1:11 3004
hand upon me, s unto me, Fear not ... Rev 1:17 3004
and they rest not day and night, s ... Rev 4:8 3004
their crowns before the throne, s ... Rev 4:10 3004
And they sung a new song, s ... Rev 5:9 3004
S with a loud voice, Worthy is ... Rev 5:12 3004
all that are in them, heard I s ... Rev 5:13 3004
thunder, one of the four beasts s ... Rev 6:1 3004
they cried with a loud voice, s ... Rev 6:10 3004
S, Hurt not the earth, neither ... Rev 7:3 3004
And cried with a loud voice, s ... Rev 7:10 3004
S, Amen ... Rev 7:12 3004
s unto me, What are these which ... Rev 7:13 3004
s with a loud voice, Woe, woe, ... Rev 8:13 3004
S to the sixth angel which had ... Rev 9:14 3004
a voice from heaven s unto me ... Rev 10:4 3004
and the angel stood, s, Rise, and ... Rev 11:1 3004
voice from heaven s unto them ... Rev 11:12 3004
were great voices in heaven, s ... Rev 11:15 3004
S, We give thee thanks, O Lord ... Rev 11:17 3004
I heard a loud voice s in heaven ... Rev 12:10 3004
and they worshipped the beast, s ... Rev 13:4 3004
s to them that dwell on the earth ... Rev 13:14 3004
S with a loud voice, Fear God, and ... Rev 14:7 3004
there followed another angel, s ... Rev 14:8 3004
s with a loud voice, If any man ... Rev 14:9 3004
a voice from heaven s unto me ... Rev 14:13 3004
him that had the sharp sickle, s ... Rev 14:18 3004
God, and the song of the Lamb, s ... Rev 15:3 3004
the temple s to the seven angels ... Rev 16:1 3004
of heaven, from the throne, s ... Rev 16:17 3004
with me, s unto me, Come hither ... Rev 17:1 3004
mightily with a strong voice, s ... Rev 18:2 3004
another voice from heaven, s ... Rev 18:4 3004
for the fear of her torment, s ... Rev 18:10 3004
And s, Alas, alas that great city, ... Rev 18:16 3004
saw the smoke of her burning, s ... Rev 18:18 3004
and cried, weeping and wailing, s ... Rev 18:19 3004
and cast it into the sea, s ... Rev 18:21 3004
voice of much people in heaven, s ... Rev 19:1 3004
God that sat on the throne, s ... Rev 19:4 3004
a voice came out of the throne, s ... Rev 19:5 3004
voice of mighty thunderings, s ... Rev 19:6 3004
s to all the fowls that fly in ... Rev 19:17 3004
a great voice out of heaven s ... Rev 21:3 3004
plagues, and talked with me, s ... Rev 21:9 3004

SAYINGS

Moses told these s unto all the ... Num 14:39 1697
that when thy s come to pass we ... Judg 13:17 1697
and came and told him all those s ... 1Sa 25:12 1697
of Abijah, and his ways, and his s ... 2Chr 13:22 1697
written among the s of the seers ... 2Chr 33:19 1697
their posterity approve their s ... Ps 49:13 6310
I will utter dark s of old ... Ps 78:2 2420
of the wise, and their dark s ... Prov 1:6 2420
Hear, O my son, and receive my s ... Prov 4:10 561
incline thine ear unto my s ... Prov 4:20 561
whosoever heareth these s of mine ... Mt 7:24 3056
one that heareth these s of mine ... Mt 7:26 3056
when Jesus had ended these s ... Mt 7:28 3056
when Jesus had finished these s ... Mt 19:1 3056
Jesus had finished all these s ... Mt 26:1 3056
all these s were noised abroad ... Lk 1:65 4487
kept all these s in her heart ... Lk 2:51 4487
cometh to me, and heareth my s ... Lk 6:47 3056
s in the audience of the people ... Lk 7:1 4487
about an eight days after these s ... Lk 9:28 3056
Let these s sink down into your ... Lk 9:44 3056
again among the Jews for these s ... Jn 10:19 3056
loveth me not keepeth not my s ... Jn 14:24 3056
with these s scarce restrained ... Acts 14:18 3004
And when they heard these s ... Acts 19:28
mightest be justified in thy s ... Rom 3:4 3056
me, These are the true s of God ... Rev 19:9 3056
These s are faithful and true ... Rev 22:6 3056
s of the prophecy of this book ... Rev 22:7 3056
which keep the s of this book ... Rev 22:9 3056
Seal not the s of the prophecy of ... Rev 22:10 3056

SCAB

skin of his flesh a rising, a s ... Lev 13:2 5597
it is but a s ... Lev 13:6 4556
But if the s spread much abroad ... Lev 13:7 4556
the s spreadeth in the skin, then ... Lev 13:8 4556
And for a rising, and for a s ... Lev 14:56 5597
with the emerods, and with the s ... Deut 28:27 1618
the Lord will smite with a s the ... Is 3:17 5597

SCABBARD

put up thyself into thy s ... Jer 47:6 8593

SCABBED

in his eye, or be scurvy, or s ... Lev 21:20 3217
or having a wen, or scurvy, or s ... Lev 22:22 3217

SCAFFOLD

For Solomon had made a brasen s ... 2Chr 6:13 3595

SCALES

s in the waters, in the seas, and ... Lev 11:9 7193
s in the seas, and in the rivers, ... Lev 11:10 7193
hath no fins nor s in the waters ... Lev 11:12 7193
that have fins and s shall ye eat ... Deut 14:9 7193
hath not fins and s ye may not eat ... Deut 14:10 7193
His s are his pride, shut up ... Job 41:15
and weighed the mountains in s ... Is 40:12 6425
of thy rivers to stick unto thy s ... Eze 29:4 7193
thy rivers shall stick unto thy s ... Eze 29:4 7193
from his eyes as it had been s ... Acts 9:18 3013

SCALETH

A wise man s the city of the ... Prov 21:22 5927

SCALL

it is a dry s, even a leprosy ... Lev 13:30 5424
look on the plague of the s ... Lev 13:31 5424
the plague of the s seven days ... Lev 13:31 5424
if the s spread not, and there be ... Lev 13:32 5424
the s be not in sight deeper than ... Lev 13:32 5424
but the s shall he not shave ... Lev 13:33 5424
that hath the s seven days more ... Lev 13:33 5424
the priest shall look on the s ... Lev 13:34 5424
if the s be not spread in the ... Lev 13:34 5424
But if the s spread much in the ... Lev 13:35 5424
if the s be spread in the skin, ... Lev 13:36 5424
But if the s be in his sight at a ... Lev 13:37 5424
the s is healed, he is clean ... Lev 13:37 5424
manner of plague of leprosy, and s ... Lev 14:54 5424

SCALP

the hairy s of such an one as ... Ps 68:21 6936

SCANT

the s measure that is abominable ... Mic 6:10 7332

SCAPEGOAT

LORD, and the other lot for the s ... Lev 16:8 5799
on which the lot fell to be the s ... Lev 16:10 5799
go for a s into the wilderness ... Lev 16:10 5799
for the s shall wash his clothes ... Lev 16:26 5799

SCARCE

Jacob was yet s gone out from the ... Gen 27:30
with these sayings s restrained ... Acts 14:18 3433
s were come over against Cnidus, ... Acts 27:7 3433

SCARCELY

For s for a righteous man will ... Rom 5:7 3433
And if the righteous s be saved ... 1Pet 4:18 3433

SCARCENESS

thou shalt eat bread without s ... Deut 8:9 4544

SCAREST

Then thou s me with dreams, and ... Job 7:14 2865

SCARLET

and bound upon his hand a s thread ... Gen 38:28 8144
that had the s thread upon his ... Gen 38:30 8144
And blue, and purple, and s, and fine ... Ex 25:4 8144
linen, and blue, and purple, and s ... Ex 26:1
a vail of blue, and purple, and s ... Ex 26:31
tent, of blue, and purple, and s ... Ex 26:36
cubits, of blue, and purple, and s ... Ex 27:16
gold, and blue, and purple, and s ... Ex 28:5
gold, of blue, and of purple, of s ... Ex 28:6
of gold, of blue, and purple, and s ... Ex 28:8
of blue, and of purple, and of s ... Ex 28:15
of blue, and of purple, and of s ... Ex 28:33
And blue, and purple, and s, and fine ... Ex 35:6
was found blue, and purple, and s ... Ex 35:23
of blue, and of purple, and of s ... Ex 35:25
in blue, and in purple, in s ... Ex 35:35
linen, and blue, and purple, and s ... Ex 36:8
a vail of blue, and purple, and s ... Ex 36:35
door of blue, and purple, and s ... Ex 36:37
of blue, and purple, and s ... Ex 38:18
in blue, and in purple, and in s ... Ex 38:23
And of the blue, and purple, and s ... Ex 39:1
of gold, blue, and purple, and s ... Ex 39:2
and in the purple, and in the s ... Ex 39:3
of gold, blue, and purple, and s ... Ex 39:5
of gold, blue, and purple, and s ... Ex 39:8
of blue, and purple, and s, and ... Ex 39:24
linen, and blue, and purple, and s ... Ex 39:29
and clean, and cedar wood, and s ... Lev 14:4
it, and the cedar wood, and the s ... Lev 14:6
two birds, and cedar wood, and s ... Lev 14:49
wood, and the hyssop, and the s ... Lev 14:51
and with the hyssop, and with the s ... Lev 14:52
spread upon them a cloth of s ... Num 4:8
take cedar wood, and hyssop, and s ... Num 19:6
thou shalt bind this line of s ... Josh 2:18 8144
she bound the s line in the ... Josh 2:21 8144
over Saul, who clothed you in s ... 2Sa 1:24 8144
her household are clothed with s ... Prov 31:21 8144
Thy lips are like a thread of s ... Song 4:3 8144
though your sins be as s, they ... Is 1:18 8144
brought up in s embrace dunghills ... Lam 4:5 8144
thereof, shall be clothed with s ... Dan 5:7 711
thou shalt be clothed with s ... Dan 5:16 711
and they clothed Daniel with s ... Dan 5:29 711
red, the valiant men are in s ... Nah 2:3 8529
him, and put on him a s robe ... Mt 27:28 2847
s wool, and hyssop, and sprinkled ... Heb 9:19 2847
woman sit upon a s coloured beast ... Rev 17:3 2847
s colour, and decked with gold and ... Rev 17:4 2847
linen, and purple, and silk, and s ... Rev 18:12 2847
in fine linen, and purple, and s ... Rev 18:16 2847

SCATTER

from thence did the LORD s them ... Gen 11:9 6327
in Jacob, and s them in Israel ... Gen 49:7 6327
I will s you among the heathen, ... Lev 26:33 2210
and s thou the fire yonder ... Num 16:37 2219
the LORD shall s you among the ... Deut 4:27 6327
the LORD shall s thee among all ... Deut 28:64 6327
I would s them into corners, I ... Deut 32:26 6284
shall s them beyond the river, ... 1Kin 14:15 2219
I will s you abroad among the ... Neh 1:8 6327
s them by thy power ... Ps 59:11 5128
s thou the people that delight in ... Ps 68:30 967
and to s them in the lands ... Ps 106:27 2219
Cast forth lightning, and s them ... Ps 144:6 6327
s the cummin, and cast in the ... Is 28:25 2236
and the whirlwind shall s them ... Is 41:16 6327
I will s them also among the ... Jer 9:16 6327
Therefore will I s them as the ... Jer 13:24 6327
I will s them as with an east ... Jer 18:17 6327
s the sheep of my pasture ... Jer 23:1 6327
I will s into all winds them that ... Jer 49:32 2219
will s them toward all those ... Jer 49:36 2219
part thou shalt s in the wind ... Eze 5:2 2219
thee will I s into all the winds ... Eze 5:10 2219
I will s a third part into all ... Eze 5:12 2219
I will s your bones round about ... Eze 6:5 2219
and s them over the city ... Eze 10:2 2236
I will s toward every wind all ... Eze 12:14 2219
when I shall s them among the ... Eze 12:15 6327
that I would s them among the ... Eze 20:23 6327
I will s thee among the heathen, ... Eze 22:15 6327
I will s the Egyptians among the ... Eze 29:12 6327
I will s the Egyptians among the ... Eze 30:23 6327
I will s the Egyptians among the ... Eze 30:26 6327
off his leaves, and s his fruit ... Dan 4:14 921
he shall s among them the prey, ... Dan 11:24 967
to s the power of the holy people ... Dan 12:7 5310
came out as a whirlwind to s me ... Hab 3:14 6327
over the land of Judah to s it ... Zec 1:21 2219

SCATTERED

lest we be s abroad upon the face ... Gen 11:4 6327
So the LORD s them abroad from ... Gen 11:8 6327
So the people were s abroad ... Ex 5:12 6327
LORD, and let thine enemies be s ... Num 10:35 6327
the LORD thy God hath s thee ... Deut 30:3 6327
that they which remained were s ... 1Sa 11:11 6327
and the people were s from him ... 1Sa 13:8 6327
that the people were s from me ... 1Sa 13:11 5310
there s over the face of all the ... 2Sa 18:8 6327
And he sent out arrows, and s them ... 2Sa 22:15 6327
I saw all Israel s upon the hills ... 1Kin 22:17 6327
and all his army were s from him ... 2Kin 25:5 6327
all Israel s upon the mountains ... 2Chr 18:16 6327
is a certain people s abroad ... Est 3:8 6340
stout lion's whelps are s abroad ... Job 4:11 6504
brimstone shall be s upon his ... Job 18:15 2219
he sent out his arrows, and s them ... Ps 18:14 6327
hast s us among the heathen ... Ps 44:11 2219
for God hath s the bones of him ... Ps 53:5 6340
hast cast us off, thou hast s us ... Ps 60:1 6555
God arise, let his enemies be s ... Ps 68:1 6327
When the Almighty s kings in it ... Ps 68:14 6566
thou hast s thine enemies with ... Ps 89:10 6340
workers of iniquity shall be s ... Ps 92:9 6504
Our bones are s at the grave's ... Ps 141:7 6340
swift messengers, to a nation s ... Is 18:2 4900
the LORD of hosts of a people s ... Is 18:7 4900
up of thyself the nations were s ... Is 33:3 5310
hast s thy ways to the strangers ... Jer 3:13 6340
and all their flocks shall be s ... Jer 10:21 6327
Ye have s my flock, and driven ... Jer 23:2 6327
all nations whither I have s thee ... Jer 30:11 6327
He that s Israel will gather him, ... Jer 31:10 2219
gathered unto thee should be s ... Jer 40:15 6327

Israel is a s sheep	Jer 50:17	6340
and all his army was s from him	Jer 52:8	6327
when ye shall be s through the	Eze 6:8	2219
although I have s them among the	Eze 11:16	6327
countries where ye have been s	Eze 11:17	6327
shall be s toward all winds	Eze 17:21	6566
of the countries wherein ye are s	Eze 20:34	6327
countries wherein ye have been s	Eze 20:41	6327
the people among whom they are s	Eze 28:25	6327
the people whither they were s	Eze 29:13	6327
And they were s, because there is	Eze 34:5	6327
of the field, when they were s	Eze 34:5	6327
my flock was s upon all the face	Eze 34:6	6327
he is among his sheep that are s	Eze 34:12	6566
they have been s in the cloudy	Eze 34:12	6327
horns, till ye have s them abroad	Eze 34:21	6327
I s them among the heathen, and	Eze 36:19	6327
that my people be not s every man	Eze 46:18	
whom they have s among the	Joel 3:2	6327
thy people is s upon the	Nah 3:18	6340
the everlasting mountains were s	Hab 3:6	6327
are the horns which have s Judah	Zec 1:19	2219
are the horns which have s Judah	Zec 1:21	2219
But I s them with a whirlwind	Zec 7:14	
shepherd, and the sheep shall be s	Zec 13:7	6327
were s abroad, as sheep having no	Mt 9:36	4496
of the flock shall be s abroad	Mt 26:31	1287
shepherd, and the sheep shall be s	Mk 14:27	1287
he hath s the proud in the	Lk 1:51	1287
of God that were s abroad	Jn 11:52	1287
is now come, that ye shall be s	Jn 16:32	4650
as many as obeyed him, were s	Acts 5:36	1262
they were all s abroad throughout	Acts 8:1	1289
were s abroad went every where	Acts 8:4	1289
Now they which were s abroad upon	Acts 11:19	1289
twelve tribes which are s abroad	Jas 1:1	1290
to the strangers s throughout	1Pet 1:1	1290

SCATTERETH

he s his bright cloud	Job 37:11	6327
which s the east wind upon the	Job 38:24	6327
he s the hoar frost like ashes	Ps 147:16	6340
There is that s, and yet	Prov 11:24	6340
in the throne of judgment s away	Prov 20:8	2219
A wise king s the wicked, and	Prov 20:26	2219
s abroad the inhabitants thereof	Is 24:1	6327
gathereth not with me s abroad	Mt 12:30	4650
he that gathereth not with me s	Lk 11:23	4650
catcheth them, and s the sheep	Jn 10:12	4650

SCATTERING

flame of a devouring fire, with s	Is 30:30	5311

SCENT

Yet through the s of water it	Job 14:9	7381
in him, and his s is not changed	Jer 48:11	7381
the s thereof shall be as the	Hos 14:7	2143

SCEPTRE

The s shall not depart from Judah	Gen 49:10	7626
a S shall rise out of Israel, and	Num 24:17	7626
king shall hold out the golden s	Est 4:11	8275
the golden s that was in his hand	Est 5:2	8275
near, and touched the top of the s	Est 5:2	8275
out the golden s toward Esther	Est 8:4	8275
the s of thy kingdom is a right	Ps 45:6	7626
of thy kingdom is a right s	Ps 45:6	7626
wicked, and the s of the rulers	Is 14:5	7626
no strong rod to be a s to rule	Eze 19:14	7626
him that holdeth the s from the	Amos 1:5	7626
that holdeth the s from Ashkelon	Amos 1:8	7626
the s of Egypt shall depart away	Zec 10:11	7626
a s of righteousness is the	Heb 1:8	4464
is the s of thy kingdom	Heb 1:8	4464

SCEPTRES

for the s of them that bare rule	Eze 19:11	7626

SCEVA (see'-vah) *A Jewish priest at Ephesus.*

And there were seven sons of one S	Acts 19:14	4630

SCHISM

there should be no s in the body	1Cor 12:25	4978

SCHOLAR

the great, the teacher as the s	1Chr 25:8	8527
doeth this, the master and the s	Mal 2:12	6030

SCHOOL

daily in the s of one Tyrannus	Acts 19:9	4981

SCHOOLMASTER

was our s to bring us unto Christ	Gal 3:24	3807
come, we are no longer under a s	Gal 3:25	3807

SCIENCE

in knowledge, and understanding s	Dan 1:4	4093
oppositions of s falsely so	1Ti 6:20	1108

SCOFF

they shall s at the kings, and the	Hab 1:10	7046

SCOFFERS

shall come in the last days s	2Pet 3:3	1703

SCORCH

given unto him to s men with fire	Rev 16:8	2739

SCORCHED

when the sun was up, they were s	Mt 13:6	2739
But when the sun was up, it was s	Mk 4:6	2739
men were s with great heat, and	Rev 16:9	2739

SCORN

thee, and laughed thee to s	2Kin 19:21	
but they laughed them to s	2Chr 30:10	
heard it, they laughed us to s	Neh 2:19	
he thought s to lay hands on	Est 3:6	959
just upright man is laughed to s	Job 12:4	
My friends s me	Job 16:20	3887
and the innocent laugh them to s	Job 22:19	
they that see me laugh me to s	Ps 22:7	
a reproach to our neighbours, a s	Ps 44:13	3933
a reproach to our neighbours, a s	Ps 79:4	3933
thee, and laughed thee to s	Is 37:22	
thou shalt be laughed to s	Eze 23:32	
princes shall be a s unto them	Hab 1:10	4890
And they laughed him to s	Mt 9:24	2606
And they laughed him to s	Mk 5:40	2606
And they laughed him to s, knowing	Lk 8:53	2606

SCORNER

He that reproveth a s getteth to	Prov 9:7	3887
Reprove not a s, lest he hate	Prov 9:8	3887
but a s heareth not rebuke	Prov 13:1	3887
A s seeketh wisdom, and findeth it	Prov 14:6	3887
A s loveth not one that reproveth	Prov 15:12	3887
Smite a s, and the simple will	Prov 19:25	3887
When the s is punished, the	Prov 21:11	3887
haughty s is his name, who	Prov 21:24	3887
Cast out the s, and contention	Prov 22:10	3887
the s is an abomination to men	Prov 24:9	3887
the s is consumed, and all that	Is 29:20	3887

SCORNERS

the s delight in their scorning	Prov 1:22	3887
Surely he scorneth the s	Prov 3:34	3887
Judgments are prepared for s	Prov 19:29	3887
he stretched out his hand with s	Hos 7:5	3945

SCORNEST

but if thou s, thou alone shalt	Prov 9:12	3887
as an harlot, in that thou s hire	Eze 16:31	7046

SCORNETH

He s the multitude of the city	Job 39:7	7832
she s the horse and his rider	Job 39:18	7832
Surely he s the scorners	Prov 3:34	3887
An ungodly witness s judgment	Prov 19:28	3887

SCORNFUL

nor sitteth in the seat of the s	Ps 1:1	3887
S men bring a city into a snare	Prov 29:8	3944
ye s men, that rule this people	Is 28:14	3944

SCORNING

Job, who drinketh up s like water	Job 34:7	3933
the s of those that are at ease	Ps 123:4	3933
the scorners delight in their s	Prov 1:22	3944

SCORPION

ask an egg, will he offer him a s	Lk 11:12	4651
torment was as the torment of a s	Rev 9:5	4651

SCORPION PASS See MAALEH-ACRABBIM.

SCORPIONS

wherein were fiery serpents, and s	Deut 8:15	6137
but I will chastise you with s	1Kin 12:11	6137
but I will chastise you with s	1Kin 12:14	6137
but I will chastise you with s	2Chr 10:11	6137
but I will chastise you with s	2Chr 10:14	6137
thee, and thou dost dwell among s	Eze 2:6	6137
power to tread on serpents and s	Lk 10:19	4651
as the s of the earth have power	Rev 9:3	4651
And they had tails like unto s	Rev 9:10	4651

SCOURED

a brasen pot, it shall be both s	Lev 6:28	4838

SCOURGE

be hid from the s of the tongue	Job 5:21	7752
If the s slay suddenly, he will	Job 9:23	7752
up a s for him according to the	Is 10:26	7752
overflowing s shall pass through	Is 28:15	7885
overflowing s shall pass through	Is 28:18	7752
and they will s you in their	Mt 10:17	3164
to the Gentiles to mock, and to s	Mt 20:19	3164
shall ye s in your synagogues	Mt 23:34	3164
shall mock him, and shall s him	Mk 10:34	3164
And they shall s him, and put him	Lk 18:33	3164
he had made a s of small cords	Jn 2:15	5416
you to s a man that is a Roman	Acts 22:25	3147

SCOURGED

she shall be s	Lev 19:20	1244
and when he had s Jesus, he	Mt 27:26	5417
Jesus, when he had s him, to be	Mk 15:15	5417
therefore took Jesus, and s him	Jn 19:1	3146

SCOURGES

s in your sides, and thorns in	Josh 23:13	7850

SCOURGETH

s every son whom he receiveth	Heb 12:6	3146

SCOURGING

that he should be examined by s	Acts 22:24	3148

SCOURGINGS

had trial of cruel mockings and s	Heb 11:36	3148

SCRABBLED

s on the doors of the gate, and	1Sa 21:13	8427

SCRAPE

pour out the dust that they s off	Lev 14:41	7096
a potsherd to s himself withal	Job 2:8	1623
I will also s her dust from her	Eze 26:4	5500

SCRAPED

house to be s within round about	Lev 14:41	7106
and after he hath s the house	Lev 14:43	7096

SCREECH

the s owl also shall rest there	Is 34:14	3917

SCRIBE

and Seraiah was the s	2Sa 8:17	5608
And Sheva was s	2Sa 20:25	5608
in the chest, that the king's s	2Kin 12:10	5608
the household, and Shebna the s	2Kin 18:18	5608
the household, and Shebna the s	2Kin 18:37	5608
the household, and Shebna the s	2Kin 19:2	5608
the son of Meshullam, the s	2Kin 22:3	5608
priest said unto Shaphan the s	2Kin 22:8	5608
Shaphan the s came to the king	2Kin 22:9	5608
Shaphan the s shewed the king	2Kin 22:10	5608
son of Michaiah, and Shaphan the s	2Kin 22:12	5608
and the principal s of the host	2Kin 25:19	5608
and Shavsha was s	1Chr 18:16	5608
the son of Nethaneel the s	1Chr 24:6	5608
a counsellor, a wise man, and a s	1Chr 27:32	5608
was much money, the king's s	2Chr 24:11	5608
by the hand of Jeiel the s	2Chr 26:11	5608
answered and said to Shaphan the s	2Chr 34:15	5608
Then Shaphan the s told the king	2Chr 34:18	5608
son of Micah, and Shaphan the s	2Chr 34:20	5608
Shimshai the s wrote a letter	Ezr 4:8	5613
the chancellor, and Shimshai the s	Ezr 4:9	5613
chancellor, and to Shimshai the s	Ezr 4:17	5613
before Rehum, and Shimshai the s	Ezr 4:23	5613
he was a ready s in the law of	Ezr 7:6	5608
gave unto Ezra the priest, the s	Ezr 7:11	5608
even a s of the words of the	Ezr 7:11	5608
a s of the law of the God of	Ezr 7:12	5613
the s of the law of the God of	Ezr 7:21	5613
they spake unto Ezra the s to	Neh 8:1	5608
Ezra the s stood upon a pulpit of	Neh 8:4	5608
and Ezra the priest the s	Neh 8:9	5608
and the Levites, unto Ezra the s	Neh 8:13	5608
and of Ezra the priest, the s	Neh 12:26	5608
of God, and Ezra the s before them	Neh 12:36	5608
the priest, and Zadok the s	Neh 13:13	5608
Where is the s	Is 33:18	5608
over the house, and Shebna the s	Is 36:3	5608
the household, and Shebna the s	Is 36:22	5608
the household, and Shebna the s	Is 37:2	5608
Gemariah the son of Shaphan the s	Jer 36:10	5608
sat there, even Elishama the s	Jer 36:12	5608
in the chamber of Elishama the s	Jer 36:20	5608
of Abdeel, to take Baruch the s	Jer 36:26	5608
roll, and gave it to Baruch the s	Jer 36:32	5608
in the house of Jonathan the s	Jer 37:15	5608
to the house of Jonathan the s	Jer 37:20	5608
and the principal s of the host	Jer 52:25	5608
And a certain s came, and said unto	Mt 8:19	1122
Therefore every s which is	Mt 13:52	1122
the s said unto him, Well, Master	Mk 12:32	1122
where is the s	1Cor 1:20	1122

SCRIBE'S

king's house, into the s chamber	Jer 36:12	5608
it out of Elishama the s chamber	Jer 36:21	5608

SCRIBES

and Ahiah, the sons of Shisha, s	1Kin 4:3	5608
the families of the s which dwelt	1Chr 2:55	5608
and of the Levites there were s	2Chr 34:13	5608
Then were the king's s called on	Est 3:12	5608
Then were the king's s called at	Est 8:9	5608
the pen of the s is in vain	Jer 8:8	5608
s of the people together, he	Mt 2:4	1122
exceed the righteousness of the s	Mt 5:20	1122
having authority, and not as the s	Mt 7:29	1122
certain of the s said within	Mt 9:3	1122
Then certain of the s and of the	Mt 12:38	1122
Then came to Jesus s and Pharisees	Mt 15:1	1122
the elders and chief priests and s	Mt 16:21	1122
Why then say the s that Elias	Mt 17:10	1122
the chief priests and unto the s	Mt 20:18	1122
s saw the wonderful things that	Mt 21:15	1122
Saying, The s and the Pharisees	Mt 23:2	1122
But woe unto you, s and Pharisees	Mt 23:13	1122
Woe unto you, s and Pharisees	Mt 23:14	1122
Woe unto you, s and Pharisees	Mt 23:15	1122
Woe unto you, s and Pharisees	Mt 23:23	1122
Woe unto you, s and Pharisees	Mt 23:25	1122
Woe unto you, s and Pharisees	Mt 23:27	1122
Woe unto you, s and Pharisees	Mt 23:29	1122
you prophets, and wise men, and s	Mt 23:34	1122
the chief priests, and the s	Mt 26:3	1122
the high priest, where the s	Mt 26:57	1122
priests mocking him, with the s	Mt 27:41	1122
had authority, and not as the s	Mk 1:22	1122
certain of the s sitting there	Mk 2:6	1122
And when the s and Pharisees saw	Mk 2:16	1122
the s which came down from	Mk 3:22	1122
Pharisees, and certain of the s	Mk 7:1	1122
s asked him, Why walk not thy	Mk 7:5	1122
and of the chief priests, and s	Mk 8:31	1122
Why say the s that Elias must	Mk 9:11	1122
the s questioning with them	Mk 9:14	1122
And he asked the s, What question	Mk 9:16	1122
the chief priests, and unto the s	Mk 10:33	1122
And the s and chief priests heard	Mk 11:18	1122
him the chief priests, and the s	Mk 11:27	1122
And one of the s came, and having	Mk 12:28	1122
How say the s that Christ is the	Mk 12:35	1122
in his doctrine, Beware of the s	Mk 12:38	1122
the s sought how they might take	Mk 14:1	1122
from the chief priest and the s	Mk 14:43	1122
priests and the elders and the s	Mk 14:53	1122
consultation with the elders and s	Mk 15:1	1122
said among themselves with the s	Mk 15:31	1122
And the s and the Pharisees began	Lk 5:21	1122
But their s and Pharisees murmured	Lk 5:30	1122
And the s and Pharisees watched him	Lk 6:7	1122
the elders and chief priests and s	Lk 9:22	1122
Woe unto you, s and Pharisees	Lk 11:44	1122
these things unto them, the s	Lk 11:53	1122
s murmured, saying, This man	Lk 15:2	1122
But the chief priests and the s	Lk 19:47	1122
the s came upon him with the	Lk 20:1	1122
the s the same hour sought to lay	Lk 20:19	1122
certain of the s answering said	Lk 20:39	1122
Beware of the s, which desire to	Lk 20:46	1122
s sought how they might kill him	Lk 22:2	1122
the s came together, and led him	Lk 22:66	1122
s stood and vehemently accused him	Lk 23:10	1122
And the s and Pharisees brought	Jn 8:3	1122

S

their rulers, and elders, and *s* .... Acts 4:5 *1122*
people, and the elders, and the *s* .... Acts 6:12 *1122*
the *s* that were of the Pharisees' .... Acts 23:9 *1122*

SCRIP
bag which he had, even in a *s* 1Sa 17:40 3219
Nor *s* for your journey, neither .... Mt 10:10 *4082*
no *s*, no bread, no money in their .... Mk 6:8 *4082*
journey, neither staves, nor *s* .... Lk 9:3 *4082*
Carry neither purse, nor *s* .... Lk 10:4 *4082*
I sent you without purse, and *s* .... Lk 22:35 *4082*
him take it, and likewise his *s* .... Lk 22:36 *4082*

SCRIPTURE
which is noted in the *s* of truth .... Dan 10:21 3791
And have ye not read this *s* .... Mk 12:10 *1124*
the *s* was fulfilled, which saith, ... Mk 15:28 *1124*
This day is this *s* fulfilled in .... Lk 4:21 *1124*
and they believed the *s*, and the .... Jn 2:22 *1124*
as the *s* hath said, out of his .... Jn 7:38 *1124*
Hath not the *s* said, That Christ .... Jn 7:42 *1124*
came, and the *s* cannot be broken .... Jn 10:35 *1124*
but that the *s* may be fulfilled, ... Jn 13:18 *1124*
that the *s* might be fulfilled .... Jn 17:12 *1124*
that the *s* might be fulfilled, ... Jn 19:24 *1124*
that the *s* might be fulfilled, ... Jn 19:28 *1124*
that the *s* should be fulfilled, A .... Jn 19:36 *1124*
And again another *s* saith, They .... Jn 19:37 *1124*
For as yet they knew not the *s* .... Jn 20:9 *1124*
this *s* must needs have been .... Acts 1:16 *1124*
The place of the *s* which he read .... Acts 8:32 *1124*
his mouth, and began at the same *s* .... Acts 8:35 *1124*
For what saith the *s* .... Rom 4:3 *1124*
For the *s* saith unto Pharaoh, ... Rom 9:17 *1124*
For the *s* saith, Whosoever .... Rom 10:11 *1124*
ye not what the *s* saith of Elias .... Rom 11:2 *1124*
And the *s*, foreseeing that God .... Gal 3:8 *1124*
But the *s* hath concluded all .... Gal 3:22 *1124*
Nevertheless what saith the *s* .... Gal 4:30 *1124*
For the *s* saith, Thou shalt not 1Ti 5:18 *1124*
All *s* is given by inspiration of 2Ti 3:16 *1124*
the royal law according to the *s* .... Jas 2:8 *1124*
the *s* was fulfilled which saith, ... Jas 2:23 *1124*
ye think that the *s* saith in vain .... Jas 4:5 *1124*
also it is contained in the *s* 1Pet 2:6 *1124*
of the *s* is of any private 2Pet 1:20 *1124*

SCRIPTURES
them, Did ye never read in the *s* .... Mt 21:42 *1124*
Ye do err, not knowing the *s* .... Mt 22:29 *1124*
how then shall the *s* be fulfilled .... Mt 26:54 *1124*
that the *s* of the prophets might .... Mt 26:56 *1124*
err, because ye know not the *s* .... Mk 12:24 *1124*
but the *s* must be fulfilled .... Mk 14:49 *1124*
s the things concerning himself .... Lk 24:27 *1124*
and while he opened to us the *s* .... Lk 24:32 *1124*
that they might understand the *s* .... Lk 24:45 *1124*
Search the *s* .... Jn 5:39 *1124*
reasoned with them out of the *s* .... Acts 17:2 *1124*
of mind, and searched the *s* daily .... Acts 17:11 *1124*
eloquent man, and mighty in the *s* .... Acts 18:24 *1124*
shewing by the *s* that Jesus was .... Acts 18:28 *1124*
by his prophets in the holy *s* .... Rom 1:2 *1124*
comfort of the *s* might have hope .... Rom 15:4 *1124*
by the *s* of the prophets, ... Rom 16:26 *1124*
for our sins according to the *s* 1Cor 15:3 *1124*
the third day according to the *s* 1Cor 15:4 *1124*
child thou hast known the holy *s* 2Ti 3:15 *1121*
as they do also the other *s* 2Pet 3:16 *1124*

SCROLL
shall be rolled together as a *s* .... Is 34:4 5612
the heaven departed as a *s* when .... Rev 6:14 *975*

SCUM
to the pot whose *s* is therein .... Eze 24:6 2457
whose *s* is not gone out of it .... Eze 24:6 2457
that the *s* of it may be consumed .... Eze 24:11 2457
her great *s* went not forth out of .... Eze 24:12 2457
her *s* shall be in the fire .... Eze 24:12 2457

SCURVY
a blemish in his eye, or be *s* .... Lev 21:20 1618
or maimed, or having a wen, or *s* .... Lev 22:22 1618

SCYTHIAN (*sith'-e-un*) *A barbarous people north of the Black Sea.*
nor uncircumcision, Barbarian, *S* .... Col 3:11 *4658*

SEA
dominion over the fish of the *s* .... Gen 1:26 3220
dominion over the fish of the *s* .... Gen 1:28 3220
and upon all the fishes of the *s* .... Gen 9:2 3220
of Siddim, which is the Salt *S* .... Gen 14:3 3220
sand which is upon the *s* shore .... Gen 22:17 3220
thy seed as the sand of the *s* .... Gen 32:12 3220
corn as the sand of the *s* .... Gen 41:49 3220
shall dwell at the haven of the *s* .... Gen 49:13 3220
and cast them into the Red *s* .... Ex 10:19 3220
of the wilderness of the Red *s* .... Ex 13:18 3220
between Migdol and the *s*, over .... Ex 14:2 3220
it shall ye encamp by the *s* .... Ex 14:2 3220
overtook them encamping by the *s* .... Ex 14:9 3220
stretch out thine hand over the *s* .... Ex 14:16 3220
ground through the midst of the *s* .... Ex 14:16 3220
stretched out his hand over the *s* .... Ex 14:21 3220
the LORD caused the *s* to go back .... Ex 14:21 3220
night, and made the *s* dry land .... Ex 14:21 3220
of the *s* upon the dry ground .... Ex 14:22 3220
after them to the midst of the *s* .... Ex 14:23 3220
Stretch out thine hand over the *s* .... Ex 14:26 3220
forth his hand over the *s* .... Ex 14:27 3220
the *s* returned to his strength .... Ex 14:27 3220
Egyptians in the midst of the *s* .... Ex 14:27 3220
that came into the *s* after them .... Ex 14:28 3220
dry land in the midst of the *s* .... Ex 14:29 3220
Egyptians dead upon the *s* shore .... Ex 14:30 3220
rider hath he thrown into the *s* .... Ex 15:1 3220
his host hath he cast into the *s* .... Ex 15:4 3220
also are drowned in the Red *s* .... Ex 15:4 3220
congealed in the heart of the *s* .... Ex 15:8 3220
with thy wind, the *s* covered them .... Ex 15:10 3220
and with his horsemen into the *s* .... Ex 15:19 3220
the waters of the *s* upon them .... Ex 15:19 3220
on dry land in the midst of the *s* .... Ex 15:19 3220
rider hath he thrown into the *s* .... Ex 15:21 3220
brought Israel from the Red *s* .... Ex 15:22 3220
LORD made heaven and earth, the *s* .... Ex 20:11 3220
Red *s* even unto the *s* of the .... Ex 23:31 3220
or shall all the fish of the *s* be .... Num 11:22 3220
and brought quails from the *s* .... Num 11:31 3220
and the Canaanites dwell by the *s* .... Num 13:29 3220
by the way of the Red *s* .... Num 14:25 3220
mount Hor by the way of the Red *s* .... Num 21:4 3220
LORD, What he did in the Red *s* .... Num 21:14 3220
of the *s* into the wilderness .... Num 33:8 3220
Elim, and encamped by the Red *s* .... Num 33:10 3220
And they removed from the Red *s* .... Num 33:11 3220
coast of the salt *s* eastward .... Num 34:3 3220
out of it shall be at the *s* .... Num 34:5 3220
have the great *s* for a border .... Num 34:6 3220
from the great *s* ye shall point .... Num 34:7 3220
of the *s* of Chinnereth eastward .... Num 34:11 3220
out of it shall be at the salt *s* .... Num 34:12 3220
the plain over against the Red *s* .... Deut 1:1 3220
and in the south, and by the *s* side .... Deut 1:7 3220
by the way of the Red *s* .... Deut 1:40 3220
by the way of the Red *s*, as the .... Deut 2:1 3220
s of the plain, even the salt *s* .... Deut 3:17 3220
even unto the *s* of the plain .... Deut 4:49 3220
Red *s* to overflow them as they .... Deut 11:4 3220
uttermost *s* shall your coast be .... Deut 11:24 3220
Neither is it beyond the *s* .... Deut 30:13 3220
Who shall go over the *s* for us .... Deut 30:13 3220
land of Judah, unto the utmost *s* .... Deut 34:2 3220
unto the great *s* toward the going .... Josh 1:4 3220
up the water of the Red *s* for you .... Josh 2:10 3220
s of the plain, even the salt *s* .... Josh 3:16 3220
LORD your God did to the Red *s* .... Josh 4:23 3220
Canaanites, which were by the *s* .... Josh 5:1 3220
the great *s* over against Lebanon .... Josh 9:1 3220
is upon the *s* shore in multitude .... Josh 11:4 3220
from the plain to the *s* of .... Josh 12:3 3220
unto the *s* of the plain .... Josh 12:3 3220
even the salt *s* on the east .... Josh 12:3 3220
even unto the edge of the *s* of .... Josh 13:27 3220
was from the shore of the salt *s* .... Josh 15:2 3220
out of that coast were at the *s* .... Josh 15:4 3220
And the east border was the salt *s* .... Josh 15:5 3220
s at the uttermost part of Jordan .... Josh 15:5 3220
out of the border were at the *s* .... Josh 15:11 3220
west border was to the great *s* .... Josh 15:12 3220
From Ekron even unto the *s* .... Josh 15:46 3220
river of Egypt, and the great *s* .... Josh 15:47 3220
goings out thereof are at the *s* .... Josh 16:3 3220
the border went out toward the *s* .... Josh 16:6 3220
goings out thereof were at the *s* .... Josh 16:8 3220
the outgoings of it were at the *s* .... Josh 17:9 3220
and the *s* is his border .... Josh 17:10 3220
the corner of the *s* southward .... Josh 18:14 3220
salt *s* at the south end of Jordan .... Josh 18:19 3220
their border went up toward the *s* .... Josh 19:11 3220
at the *s* from the coast to Achzib .... Josh 19:29 3220
even unto the great *s* westward .... Josh 23:4 3220
and ye came unto the *s* .... Josh 24:6 3220
and horsemen unto the Red *s* .... Josh 24:6 3220
and brought the *s* upon them .... Josh 24:7 3220
Asher continued on the *s* shore .... Judg 5:17 3220
sand by the *s* side for multitude .... Judg 7:12 3220
the wilderness unto the Red *s* .... Judg 11:16 3220
is on the *s* shore in multitude 1Sa 13:5 3220
that is by the *s* for multitude 2Sa 17:11 3220
And the channels of the *s* appeared 2Sa 22:16 3220
which is by the *s* in multitude 1Kin 4:20 3220
the sand that is on the *s* shore 1Kin 4:29 3220
them down from Lebanon unto the *s* 1Kin 5:9 3220
I will convey them by *s* in floats 1Kin 5:9 3220
And he made a molten *s*, ten cubits 1Kin 7:23 3220
compassing the *s* round about 1Kin 7:24 3220
the *s* was set above upon them, and 1Kin 7:25 3220
he set the *s* on the right side of 1Kin 7:39 3220
And one *s*, and twelve oxen under 1Kin 7:44 3220
s, and twelve oxen under the *s* 1Kin 7:44 3220
Eloth, on the shore of the Red *s* 1Kin 9:26 3220
that had knowledge of the *s* 1Kin 9:27 3220
For the king had at *s* a navy of 1Kin 10:22 3220
Go up now, look toward the *s* 1Kin 18:43 3220
a little cloud out of the *s* 1Kin 18:44 3220
of Hamath unto the *s* of the plain 2Kin 14:25 3220
took down the *s* from off the 2Kin 16:17 3220
the brasen *s* that was in the 2Kin 25:13 3220
The two pillars, one *s*, and the 2Kin 25:16 3220
Let the *s* roar, and the fulness 1Chr 16:32 3220
Solomon made the brasen *s* 1Chr 18:8 3220
to thee in flotes by *s* to Joppa 2Chr 2:16 3220
Also he made a molten *s* of ten 2Chr 4:2 3220
compassing the *s* round about 2Chr 4:3 3220
the *s* was set above upon them, and 2Chr 4:4 3220
but the *s* was for the priests to 2Chr 4:6 3220
he set the *s* on the right side of 2Chr 4:10 3220
One *s*, and twelve oxen under it 2Chr 4:15 3220
at the *s* side in the land of Edom 2Chr 8:17 3220
that had knowledge of the *s* 2Chr 8:18 3220
beyond the *s* on this side Syria 2Chr 20:2 3220
from Lebanon to the *s* of Joppa .... Ezr 3:7 3220
heardest their cry by the Red *s* .... Neh 9:9 3220
didst divide the *s* before them .... Neh 9:11 3220
midst of the *s* on the dry land .... Neh 9:11 3220
land, and upon the isles of the *s* .... Est 10:1 3220
be heavier than the sand of the *s* .... Job 6:3 3220
Am I a *s*, or a whale, that thou .... Job 7:12 3220
treadeth upon the waves of the *s* .... Job 9:8 3220
the earth, and broader than the *s* .... Job 11:9 3220
the fishes of the *s* shall declare .... Job 12:8 3220
As the waters fail from the *s* .... Job 14:11 3220
He divideth the *s* with his power .... Job 26:12 3220
the *s* saith, It is not with me .... Job 28:14 3220
and covereth the bottom of the *s* .... Job 36:30 3220
Or who shut up the *s* with doors .... Job 38:8 3220
entered into the springs of the *s* .... Job 38:16 3220
he maketh the *s* like a pot of .... Job 41:31 3220
of the air, and the fish of the *s* .... Ps 8:8 3220
of the *s* together as an heap .... Ps 33:7 3220
carried into the midst of the *s* .... Ps 46:2 3220
them that are afar off upon the *s* .... Ps 65:5 3220
He turned the *s* into dry land .... Ps 66:6 3220
again from the depths of the *s* .... Ps 68:22 3220
have dominion also from *s* to *s* .... Ps 72:8 3220
divide the *s* by thy strength .... Ps 74:13 3220
Thy way is in the *s*, and thy path .... Ps 77:19 3220
He divided the *s*, and caused them .... Ps 78:13 3220
fowls like as the sand of the *s* .... Ps 78:27 3220
but the *s* overwhelmed their .... Ps 78:53 3220
sent out her boughs unto the *s* .... Ps 80:11 3220
Thou rulest the raging of the *s* .... Ps 89:9 3220
I will set his hand also in the *s* .... Ps 89:25 3220
than the mighty waves of the *s* .... Ps 93:4 3220
The *s* is his, and he made it .... Ps 95:5 3220
let the *s* roar, and the fulness .... Ps 96:11 3220
Let the *s* roar, and the fulness .... Ps 98:7 3220
So is this great and wide *s* .... Ps 104:25 3220
him at the *s*, even at the Red *s* .... Ps 106:7 3220
He rebuked the Red *s* also .... Ps 106:9 3220
and terrible things by the Red *s* .... Ps 106:22 3220
that go down to the *s* in ships .... Ps 107:23 3220
The *s* saw it, and fled .... Ps 114:3 3220
What ailed thee, O thou *s* .... Ps 114:5 3220
divided the Red *s* into parts .... Ps 136:13 3220
Pharaoh and his host in the Red *s* .... Ps 136:15 3220
in the uttermost parts of the *s* .... Ps 139:9 3220
made heaven, and earth, the *s* .... Ps 146:6 3220
When he gave to the *s* his decree .... Prov 8:29 3220
lieth down in the midst of the *s* .... Prov 23:34 3220
of a ship in the midst of the *s* .... Prov 30:19 3220
All the rivers run into the *s* .... Eccl 1:7 3220
yet the *s* is not full .... Eccl 1:7 3220
them like the roaring of the *s* .... Is 5:30 3220
afflict her by the way of the *s* .... Is 9:1 3220
Israel be as the sand of the *s* .... Is 10:22 3220
and as his rod was upon the *s* .... Is 10:26 3220
LORD, as the waters cover the *s* .... Is 11:9 3220
and from the islands of the *s* .... Is 11:11 3220
the tongue of the Egyptian *s* .... Is 11:15 3220
out, they are gone over the *s* .... Is 16:8 3220
That sendeth ambassadors by the *s* .... Is 18:2 3220
the waters shall fail from the *s* .... Is 19:5 3220
The burden of the desert of the *s* .... Is 21:1 3220
of Zidon, that pass over the *s* .... Is 23:2 3220
for the *s* hath spoken, even the .... Is 23:4 3220
even the strength of the *s* .... Is 23:4 3220
stretched out his hand over the *s* .... Is 23:11 3220
they shall cry aloud from the *s* .... Is 24:14 3220
of Israel in the isles of the *s* .... Is 24:15 3220
slay the dragon that is in the *s* .... Is 27:1 3220
earth, ye that go down to the *s* .... Is 42:10 3220
LORD, which maketh a way in the *s* .... Is 43:16 3220
as the waves of the *s* .... Is 48:18 3220
at my rebuke I dry up the *s* .... Is 50:2 3220
not it which hath dried the *s* .... Is 51:10 3220
hath made the depths of the *s* a .... Is 51:10 3220
LORD thy God, that divided the *s* .... Is 51:15 3220
wicked are like the troubled *s* .... Is 57:20 3220
s shall be converted unto thee .... Is 60:5 3220
s with the shepherd of his flock .... Is 63:11 3220
of the *s* by a perpetual decree .... Jer 5:22 3220
their voice roareth like the *s* .... Jer 6:23 3220
the isles which are beyond the *s* .... Jer 25:22 3220
the pillars, and concerning the *s* .... Jer 27:19 3220
which divideth the *s* when the .... Jer 31:35 3220
the sand of the *s* measured .... Jer 33:22 3220
mountains, and as Carmel by the *s* .... Jer 46:18 3220
Ashkelon, and against the *s* shore .... Jer 47:7 3220
thy plants are gone over the *s* .... Jer 48:32 3220
they reach even to the *s* of Jazer .... Jer 48:32 3220
thereof was heard in the Red *s* .... Jer 49:21 3220
there is sorrow on the *s* .... Jer 49:23 3220
their voice shall roar like the *s* .... Jer 50:42 3220
and I will dry up her *s*, and make .... Jer 51:36 3220
The *s* is come up upon Babylon .... Jer 51:42 3220
the brasen *s* that was in the .... Jer 52:17 3220
The two pillars, one *s*, and twelve .... Jer 52:20 3220
thy breach is great like the *s* .... Lam 2:13 3220
Even the *s* monsters draw out the .... Lam 4:3
the remnant of the *s* coast .... Eze 25:16 3220
as the *s* causeth his waves to .... Eze 26:3 3220
of nets in the midst of the *s* .... Eze 26:5 3220
the *s* shall come down from their .... Eze 26:16 3220
city, which wast strong in the *s* .... Eze 26:17 3220
in the *s* shall be troubled at thy .... Eze 26:18 3220
art situate at the entry of the *s* .... Eze 27:3 3220
all the ships of the *s* with their .... Eze 27:9 3220
and all the pilots of the *s* .... Eze 27:29 3220
destroyed in the midst of the *s* .... Eze 27:32 3220
So that the fishes of the *s* .... Eze 38:20 3220
passengers on the east of the *s* .... Eze 39:11 3220
into the desert, and go into the *s* .... Eze 47:8 3220
being brought forth into the *s* .... Eze 47:8 3220
kinds, as the fish of the great *s* .... Eze 47:10 3220
the north side, from the great *s* .... Eze 47:15 3220
from the *s* shall be Hazar-enan .... Eze 47:17 3220
from the border unto the east *s* .... Eze 47:18 3220
Kadesh, the river to the great *s* .... Eze 47:19 3220
be the great *s* from the border .... Eze 47:20 3220
to the river toward the great *s* .... Eze 48:28 3220

heaven strove upon the great *s*	Dan 7:2	3221
great beasts came up from the *s*	Dan 7:3	3221
shall be as the sand of the *s*	Hos 1:10	3220
the fishes of the *s* also shall be	Hos 4:3	3220
with his face toward the east *s*	Joel 2:20	3220
hinder part toward the utmost *s*	Joel 2:20	3220
calleth for the waters of the *s*	Amos 5:8	3220
they shall wander from *s* to *s*	Amos 8:12	3220
my sight in the bottom of the *s*	Amos 9:3	3220
calleth for the waters of the *s*	Amos 9:6	3220
sent out a great wind into the *s*	Jonah 1:4	3220
was a mighty tempest in the *s*	Jonah 1:4	3220
that were in the ship into the *s*	Jonah 1:5	3220
of heaven, which hath made the *s*	Jonah 1:9	3220
that the *s* may be calm unto us	Jonah 1:11	3220
for the *s* wrought, and was	Jonah 1:11	3220
up, and cast me forth into the *s*	Jonah 1:12	3220
so shall the *s* be calm unto you	Jonah 1:12	3220
for the *s* wrought, and was	Jonah 1:13	3220
and cast him forth into the *s*	Jonah 1:15	3220
the *s* ceased from her raging	Jonah 1:15	3220
from *s* to *s*, and from mountain	Mic 7:12	3220
sins into the depths of the *s*	Mic 7:19	3220
He rebuketh the *s*, and maketh it	Nah 1:4	3220
about it, whose rampart was the *s*	Nah 3:8	3220
and her wall was from the *s*	Nah 3:8	3220
makest men as the fishes of the *s*	Hab 1:14	3220
LORD, as the waters cover the *s*	Hab 2:14	3220
was thy wrath against the *s*	Hab 3:8	3220
through the *s* with thine horses	Hab 3:15	3220
heaven, and the fishes of the *s*	Zeph 1:3	3220
the inhabitants of the *s* coast	Zeph 2:5	3220
the *s* coast shall be dwellings and	Zeph 2:6	3220
heavens, and the earth, and the *s*	Hag 2:6	3220
he will smite her power in the *s*	Zec 9:4	3220
shall be from *s* even to *s*	Zec 9:10	3220
through the *s* with affliction	Zec 10:11	3220
and shall smite the waves in the *s*	Zec 10:11	3220
half of them toward the former *s*	Zec 14:8	3220
half of them toward the hinder *s*	Zec 14:8	3220
which is upon the *s* coast	Mt 4:13	3864
Nephthalim, by the way of the *s*	Mt 4:15	2281
walking by the *s* of Galilee	Mt 4:18	2281
brother, casting a net into the *s*	Mt 4:18	2281
arose a great tempest in the *s*	Mt 8:24	2281
and rebuked the winds and the *s*	Mt 8:26	2281
even the winds and the *s* obey him	Mt 8:27	2281
down a steep place into the *s*	Mt 8:32	2281
the house, and sat by the *s* side	Mt 13:1	2281
a net, that was cast into the *s*	Mt 13:47	2281
was now in the midst of the *s*	Mt 14:24	2281
went unto them, walking on the *s*	Mt 14:25	2281
saw him walking on the *s*, they	Mt 14:26	2281
came nigh unto the *s* of Galilee	Mt 15:29	2281
offend them, go thou to the *s*	Mt 17:27	2281
drowned in the depth of the *s*	Mt 18:6	2281
and be thou cast into the *s*	Mt 21:21	2281
for ye compass *s* and land to make	Mt 23:15	2281
as he walked by the *s* of Galilee	Mk 1:16	2281
brother casting a net into the *s*	Mk 1:16	2281
he went forth again by the *s* side	Mk 2:13	2281
with his disciples to the *s*	Mk 3:7	2281
again to teach by the *s* side	Mk 4:1	2281
into a ship, and sat in the *s*	Mk 4:1	2281
was by the *s* on the land	Mk 4:1	2281
the wind, and said unto the *s*	Mk 4:39	2281
even the wind and the *s* obey him	Mk 4:41	2281
over unto the other side of the *s*	Mk 5:1	2281
down a steep place into the *s*	Mk 5:13	2281
and were choked in the *s*	Mk 5:13	2281
and he was nigh unto the *s*	Mk 5:21	2281
ship was in the midst of the *s*	Mk 6:47	2281
unto them, walking upon the *s*	Mk 6:48	2281
they saw him walking upon the *s*	Mk 6:49	2281
he came unto the *s* of Galilee	Mk 7:31	2281
neck, and he were cast into the *s*	Mk 9:42	2281
and be thou cast into the *s*	Mk 11:23	2281
from the *s* coast of Tyre and Sidon	Lk 6:17	3882
his neck, and he cast into the *s*	Lk 17:2	2281
root, and be thou planted in the *s*	Lk 17:6	2281
the *s* and the waves roaring	Lk 21:25	2281
Jesus went over the *s* of Galilee	Jn 6:1	2281
which is the *s* of Tiberias	Jn 6:1	2281
disciples went down unto the *s*	Jn 6:16	2281
went over the *s* toward Capernaum	Jn 6:17	2281
the *s* arose by reason of a great	Jn 6:18	2281
they see Jesus walking on the *s*	Jn 6:19	2281
s saw that there was none other	Jn 6:22	2281
him on the other side of the *s*	Jn 6:25	2281
disciples at the *s* of Tiberias	Jn 21:1	2281
and did cast himself into the *s*	Jn 21:7	2281
made heaven, and earth, and the *s*	Acts 4:24	2281
land of Egypt, and in the Red *s*	Acts 7:36	2281
whose house is by the *s* side	Acts 10:6	2281
one Simon a tanner by the *s* side	Acts 10:32	2281
made heaven, and earth, and the *s*	Acts 14:15	2281
Paul to go as it were to the *s*	Acts 17:14	2281
had sailed over the *s* of Cilicia	Acts 27:5	3989
had let down the boat into the *s*	Acts 27:30	2281
and cast out the wheat into the *s*	Acts 27:38	2281
committed themselves unto the *s*	Acts 27:40	2281
cast themselves first into the *s*	Acts 27:43	
though he hath escaped the *s*	Acts 28:4	2281
of Israel be as the sand of the *s*	Rom 9:27	2281
and all passed through the *s*	1Cor 10:1	2281
Moses in the cloud and in the *s*	1Cor 10:2	2281
wilderness, in perils in the *s*	2Cor 11:26	2281
is by the *s* shore innumerable	Heb 11:12	2281
through the Red *s* as by dry land	Heb 11:29	2281
of the *s* driven with the wind	Jas 1:6	2281
serpents, and of things in the *s*	Jas 3:7	1724
Raging waves of the *s*, foaming	Jude 13	2281
a *s* of glass like unto crystal	Rev 4:6	2281
earth, and such as are in the *s*	Rev 5:13	2281
blow on the earth, nor on the *s*	Rev 7:1	2281
given to hurt the earth and the *s*	Rev 7:2	2281
Hurt not the earth, neither the *s*	Rev 7:3	2281
with fire was cast into the *s*	Rev 8:8	2281
third part of the *s* became blood	Rev 8:8	2281
the creatures which were in the *s*	Rev 8:9	2281
he set his right foot upon the *s*	Rev 10:2	2281
which I saw stand upon the *s*	Rev 10:5	2281
things that therein are, and the *s*	Rev 10:6	2281
angel which standeth upon the *s*	Rev 10:8	2281
of the earth and of the *s*	Rev 12:12	2281
And I stood upon the sand of the *s*	Rev 13:1	2281
saw a beast rise up out of the *s*	Rev 13:1	2281
made heaven, and earth, and the *s*	Rev 14:7	2281
I saw as it were a *s* of glass	Rev 15:2	2281
his name, stand on the *s* of glass	Rev 15:2	2281
poured out his vial upon the *s*	Rev 16:3	2281
every living soul died in the *s*	Rev 16:3	2281
sailors, and as many as trade by *s*	Rev 18:17	2281
the *s* by reason of her costliness	Rev 18:19	2281
millstone, and cast it into the *s*	Rev 18:21	2281
of whom is as the sand of the *s*	Rev 20:8	2281
the *s* gave up the dead which were	Rev 20:13	2281
and there was no more *s*	Rev 21:1	2281

SEAFARING

that wast inhabited of *s* men	Eze 26:17	3220

SEAL

name, and sealed them with his *s*	1Kin 21:8	2368
Levites, and priests, *s* unto it	Neh 9:38	2856
s it with the king's ring	Est 8:8	2856
It is turned as clay to the *s*	Job 38:14	2368
up together as with a close *s*	Job 41:15	2368
Set me as a *s* upon thine heart,	Song 8:6	2368
heart, as a *s* upon thine arm	Song 8:6	2368
s the law among my disciples	Is 8:16	2856
s them, and take witnesses in the	Jer 32:44	2856
to *s* up the vision and prophecy,	Dan 9:24	2856
s the book, even to the time of	Dan 12:4	2856
set to his *s* that God is true	Jn 3:33	4972
a *s* of the righteousness of the	Rom 4:11	4973
for the *s* of mine apostleship are	1Cor 9:2	4973
God standeth sure, having this *s*	2Ti 2:19	4973
when he had opened the second *s*	Rev 6:3	4973
And when he had opened the third *s*	Rev 6:5	4973
when he had opened the fourth *s*	Rev 6:7	4973
And when he had opened the fifth *s*	Rev 6:9	4973
when he had opened the sixth *s*	Rev 6:12	4973
having the *s* of the living God	Rev 7:2	4973
when he had opened the seventh *s*	Rev 8:1	4973
the *s* of God in their foreheads	Rev 9:4	4973
S up those things which the seven	Rev 10:4	4972
set a *s* upon him, that he should	Rev 20:3	4972
S not the sayings of the prophecy	Rev 22:10	4972

SEALED

me, and *s* up among my treasures	Deut 32:34	2856
s them with his seal, and sent the	1Kin 21:8	2856
Now those that *s* were, Nehemiah,	Neh 10:1	2856
and *s* with the king's ring	Est 3:12	2856
s with the king's ring, may no	Est 8:8	2856
s it with the king's ring, and	Est 8:10	2856
My transgression is *s* up in a bag	Job 14:17	2856
a spring shut up, a fountain *s*	Song 4:12	2856
as the words of a book that is *s*	Is 29:11	2856
for it is *s*	Is 29:11	2856
s it, and took witnesses, and	Jer 32:10	2856
both that which was *s* according	Jer 32:11	2856
of the purchase, both which is *s*	Jer 32:14	2856
the king *s* it with his own signet	Dan 6:17	2857
s till the time of the end	Dan 12:9	2856
for him hath God the Father *s*	Jn 6:27	4972
have *s* to them this fruit, I will	Rom 15:28	4972
Who hath also *s* us, and given the	2Cor 1:22	4972
ye were *s* with that holy Spirit	Eph 1:13	4972
whereby ye are *s* unto the day of	Eph 4:30	4972
the backside, *s* with seven seals	Rev 5:1	2696
till we have *s* the servants of	Rev 7:3	4972
the number of them which were *s*	Rev 7:4	4972
and there were *s* an hundred	Rev 7:4	4972
of Juda were *s* twelve thousand	Rev 7:5	4972
of Reuben were *s* twelve thousand	Rev 7:5	4972
of Gad were *s* twelve thousand	Rev 7:5	4972
of Aser were *s* twelve thousand	Rev 7:6	4972
Nepthalim were *s* twelve thousand	Rev 7:6	4972
Manasses were *s* twelve thousand	Rev 7:6	4972
of Simeon were *s* twelve thousand	Rev 7:7	4972
of Levi were *s* twelve thousand	Rev 7:7	4972
Issachar were *s* twelve thousand	Rev 7:7	4972
of Zabulon were *s* twelve thousand	Rev 7:8	4972
of Joseph were *s* twelve thousand	Rev 7:8	4972
Benjamin were *s* twelve thousand	Rev 7:8	4972

SEALEST

Thou *s* up the sum, full of wisdom	Eze 28:12	2856

SEALETH

and *s* up the stars	Job 9:7	2856
of men, and *s* their instruction,	Job 33:16	2856
He *s* up the hand of every man	Job 37:7	2856

SEALING

s the stone, and setting a watch	Mt 27:66	4972

SEALS

the backside, sealed with seven *s*	Rev 5:1	4973
book, and to loose the *s* thereof	Rev 5:2	4973
and to loose the seven *s* thereof	Rev 5:5	4973
book, and to open the *s* thereof	Rev 5:9	4973
when the Lamb opened one of the *s*	Rev 6:1	4973

SEAM

now the coat was without *s*	Jn 19:23	729

SEARCH

He shall not *s* whether it be good	Lev 27:33	1239
to *s* out a resting place for them	Num 10:33	8446
that they may *s* the land of	Num 13:2	8446
which we have gone to *s* it	Num 13:32	8446
which we passed through to *s* it	Num 14:7	8446
which Moses sent to *s* the land	Num 14:36	8446
the men that went to *s* the land	Num 14:38	8446
they shall *s* us out the land, and	Deut 1:22	2658
to *s* you out a place to pitch	Deut 1:33	8446
shalt thou enquire, and make *s*	Deut 13:14	2713
of Israel to *s* out the country	Josh 2:2	2658
be come to *s* out all the country	Josh 2:3	2658
to spy out the land, and to *s* it	Judg 18:2	2713
said unto them, Go, *s* the land	Judg 18:2	2713
that I will *s* him out throughout	1Sa 23:23	2664
to *s* the city, and to spy it out,	2Sa 10:3	2713
they shall *s* thine house, and the	1Kin 20:6	2664
unto the worshippers of Baal, *S*	2Kin 10:23	2664
servants come unto thee for to *s*	1Chr 19:3	2713
That *s* may be made in the book of	Ezr 4:15	1240
s hath been made, and it is found	Ezr 4:19	1240
let there be *s* made in the king's	Ezr 5:17	1240
s was made in the house of the	Ezr 6:1	1240
thyself to the *s* of their fathers	Job 8:8	2714
it good that he should *s* you out	Job 13:9	2713
thou walked in the *s* of the depth	Job 38:16	2714
Shall not God *s* this out	Ps 44:21	2713
They *s* out iniquities	Ps 64:6	2664
they accomplish a diligent *s*	Ps 64:6	2665
and my spirit made diligent *s*	Ps 77:6	2664
S me, O God, and know my heart	Ps 139:23	2713
of kings is to *s* out a matter	Prov 25:2	2713
so for men to *s* their own glory	Prov 25:27	2714
s out by wisdom concerning all	Eccl 1:13	8446
mine heart to know, and to *s*	Eccl 7:25	8446
I have not found it by secret *s*	Jer 2:34	4290
I the LORD *s* the heart, I try the	Jer 17:10	2713
when ye shall *s* for me with all	Jer 29:13	1875
Let us *s* and try our ways, and turn	Lam 3:40	2664
none did *s* or seek after them	Eze 34:6	1875
did my shepherds *s* for my flock	Eze 34:8	1875
I, even I, will both *s* my sheep	Eze 34:11	1875
end of seven months shall they *s*	Eze 39:14	2713
in the top of Carmel, I will *s*	Amos 9:3	2664
that I will *s* Jerusalem with	Zeph 1:12	2664
s diligently for the young child	Mt 2:8	1833
S the scriptures	Jn 5:39	2045
S, and look	Jn 7:52	2045

SEARCHED

Laban *s* all the tent, but found	Gen 31:34	4959
And he *s*, but found not the images	Gen 31:35	2664
Whereas thou hast *s* all my stuff	Gen 31:37	4959
And he *s*, and began at the eldest,	Gen 44:12	2664
s the land from the wilderness of	Num 13:21	8446
of the land which they had *s* unto	Num 13:32	8446
were of them that *s* the land	Num 14:6	8446
the days in which ye *s* the land	Num 14:34	8446
the valley of Eshcol, and *s* it out	Deut 1:24	7270
Lo this, we have *s* it, so it is	Job 5:27	2713
he prepared it, yea, and *s* it out	Job 28:27	2713
cause which I knew not I *s* out	Job 29:16	2713
whilst ye *s* out what to say	Job 32:11	2713
the number of his years be *s* out	Job 36:26	2714
O lord, thou hast *s* me, and known	Ps 139:1	2713
of the earth *s* out beneath	Jer 31:37	2713
the LORD, though it cannot be *s*	Jer 46:23	2713
How are the things of Esau *s* out	Obad 6	2664
s the scriptures daily, whether	Acts 17:11	350
s diligently, who prophesied of	1Pet 1:10	1830

SEARCHEST

mine iniquity, and *s* after my sin	Job 10:6	1875
s for her as for hid treasures	Prov 2:4	2664

SEARCHETH

for the LORD *s* all hearts	1Chr 28:9	1875
darkness, and *s* out all perfection	Job 28:3	2713
he *s* after every green thing	Job 39:8	1875
but his neighbour cometh and *s* him	Prov 18:17	2713
that hath understanding *s* him out	Prov 28:11	2713
he that *s* the hearts knoweth what	Rom 8:27	2045
for the Spirit *s* all things	1Cor 2:10	2045
that I am he which *s* the reins	Rev 2:23	2045

SEARCHING

they returned from *s* of the land	Num 13:25	8446
Canst thou by *s* find out God	Job 11:7	2714
s all the inward parts of the	Prov 20:27	2664
there is no *s* of his	Is 40:28	2714
S what, or what manner of time	1Pet 1:11	2045

SEARCHINGS

there were great *s* of heart	Judg 5:16	2714

SEARED

conscience *s* with a hot iron	1Ti 4:2	2743

SEAS

of the waters called he *S*	Gen 1:10	3220
and fill the waters in the *s*	Gen 1:22	3220
and scales in the waters, in the *s*	Lev 11:9	3220
have not fins and scales in the *s*	Lev 11:10	3220
suck of the abundance of the *s*	Deut 33:19	3220
things that are therein, the *s*	Neh 9:6	3220
through the paths of the *s*	Ps 8:8	3220
For he hath founded it upon the *s*	Ps 24:2	3220
Which stilleth the noise of the *s*	Ps 65:7	3220
heaven and earth praise him, the *s*	Ps 69:34	3220
in heaven, and in earth, in the *s*	Ps 135:6	3220
a noise like the noise of the *s*	Is 17:12	3220
to me above the sand of the *s*	Jer 15:8	3220
borders are in the midst of the *s*	Eze 27:4	3220
glorious in the midst of the *s*	Eze 27:25	3220
broken thee in the midst of the *s*	Eze 27:26	3220
of the *s* in the day of thy ruin	Eze 27:27	3220
thy wares went forth out of the *s*	Eze 27:33	3220
thou shalt be broken by the *s* in	Eze 27:34	3220
of God, in the midst of the *s*	Eze 28:2	3220

S

are slain in the midst of the *s* ... Eze 28:8 3220
and thou art as a whale in the *s* ... Eze 32:2 3220
of his palace between the *s* in ... Dan 11:45 3220
the deep, in the midst of the *s* ... Jonah 2:3 3220
into a place where two *s* met ... Acts 27:41 1337

SEASON
and they continued a *s* in ward ... Gen 40:4 3117
in his *s* from year to year ... Ex 13:10 4150
offering shalt thou *s* with salt ... Lev 2:13 4414
I will give you rain in due *s* ... Lev 26:4 6256
the passover at his appointed *s* ... Num 9:2 4150
shall keep it in his appointed *s* ... Num 9:3 4150
s among the children of Israel ... Num 9:7 4150
of the LORD in his appointed *s* ... Num 9:13 4150
to offer unto me in their due *s* ... Num 28:2 4150
rain of your land in his due *s* ... Deut 11:14 6256
at the *s* that thou camest forth ... Deut 16:6 4150
the rain unto thy land in his *s* ... Deut 28:12 6256
dwelt in the wilderness a long *s* ... Josh 24:7 3117
And he said, About this *s*, ... 2Kin 4:16 4150
bare a son at that *s* that Elisha ... 2Kin 4:17 4150
were at that *s* in the high place ... 1Chr 21:29 6256
Now for a long *s* Israel hath been ... 2Chr 15:3 3117
shock of corn cometh in in his *s* ... Job 5:26 6256
are pierced in me in the night *s* ... Job 30:17
bring forth Mazzaroth in his *s* ... Job 38:32 6256
bringeth forth his fruit in his *s* ... Ps 1:3 6256
and in the night *s*, and am not ... Ps 22:2
give them their meat in due *s* ... Ps 104:27 6256
givest them their meat in due *s* ... Ps 145:15 6256
and a word spoken in due *s* ... Prov 15:23 6256
To every thing there is a *s* ... Eccl 3:1 2165
and thy princes eat in due *s* ... Eccl 10:17 6256
a word in *s* to him that is weary ... Is 50:4
former and the latter, in his *s* ... Jer 5:24 6256
not be day and night in their *s* ... Jer 33:20 6256
the shower to come down in his *s* ... Eze 34:26 6256
lives were prolonged for a *s* ... Dan 7:12 2166
and my wine in the *s* thereof ... Hos 2:9 4150
to give them meat in due *s* ... Mt 24:45 2540
saltness, wherewith will ye *s* it ... Mk 9:50 741
And at the *s* he sent to the ... Mk 12:2 2540
shall be fulfilled in their *s* ... Lk 1:20 2540
he departed from him for a *s* ... Lk 4:13 2540
their portion of meat in due *s* ... Lk 12:42 2540
that *s* some that told him of the ... Lk 13:1 2540
at the *s* he sent a servant to the ... Lk 20:10 2540
desirous to see him of a long *s* ... Lk 23:8
down at a certain *s* into the pool ... Jn 5:4 2540
ye were willing for a *s* to ... Jn 5:35 5610
blind, not seeing the sun for a *s* ... Acts 13:11 2540
he himself stayed in Asia for a *s* ... Acts 19:22 5550
when I have a convenient *s* ... Acts 24:25 2540
sorry, though it were but for a *s* ... 2Cor 7:8 5610
for in due *s* we shall reap, if we ... Gal 6:9 2540
be instant in *s* ... 2Ti 4:2 2121
out of *s*; reprove ... 2Ti 4:2 171
he therefore departed for a *s* ... Philem 15 5610
the pleasures of sin for a *s* ... Heb 11:25 4340
rejoice, though now for a *s* ... 1Pet 1:6 3641
should rest yet for a little *s* ... Rev 6:11 5550
that he must be loosed a little *s* ... Rev 20:3 5550

SEASONED
savour, wherewith shall it be *s* ... Lk 14:34 741
s with salt, that ye may know how ... Col 4:6 741

SEASONS
let them be for signs, and for *s* ... Gen 1:14 4150
them judge the people at all *s* ... Ex 18:22 6256
they judged the people at all *s* ... Ex 18:26 6256
ye shall proclaim in their *s* ... Lev 23:4 4150
also instruct me in the night *s* ... Ps 16:7
He appointed the moon for *s* ... Ps 104:19 4150
And he changeth the times and the *s* .. Dan 2:21 2166
render him the fruits in their *s* ... Mt 21:41 2540
you to know the times or the *s* ... Acts 1:7 2540
rain from heaven, and fruitful *s* ... Acts 14:17 2540
I have been with you at all *s* ... Acts 20:18 5550
But of the times and the *s* ... 1Th 5:1 2540

SEAT
shalt make a mercy *s* of pure gold ... Ex 25:17
in the two ends of the mercy *s* ... Ex 25:18
even of the mercy *s* shall ye make ... Ex 25:19
the mercy *s* with their wings ... Ex 25:20
toward the mercy *s* shall the ... Ex 25:20
the mercy *s* above upon the ark ... Ex 25:21
with thee from above the mercy *s* ... Ex 25:22
thou shalt put the mercy *s* upon ... Ex 26:34
before the mercy *s* that is over ... Ex 30:6
the mercy *s* that is thereupon, and ... Ex 31:7
staves thereof, with the mercy *s* ... Ex 35:12
he made the mercy *s* of pure gold ... Ex 37:6
on the two ends of the mercy *s* ... Ex 37:7
out of the mercy *s* made he the ... Ex 37:8
with their wings over the mercy *s* ... Ex 37:9
staves thereof, and the mercy *s* ... Ex 39:35
put the mercy *s* above upon the ... Ex 40:20
the vail before the mercy *s* ... Lev 16:2
in the cloud upon the mercy *s* ... Lev 16:2
s that is upon the testimony ... Lev 16:13
finger upon the mercy *s* eastward ... Lev 16:14
before the mercy *s* shall he ... Lev 16:14
and sprinkle it upon the mercy *s* ... Lev 16:15
and before the mercy *s* ... Lev 16:15
mercy *s* that was upon the ark of ... Num 7:89
And he arose out of his *s* ... Judg 3:20 3678
Now Eli the priest sat upon a *s* ... 1Sa 1:9 3678
Eli sat upon a *s* by the wayside ... 1Sa 4:13 3678
that he fell from off the *s* ... 1Sa 4:18 3678
because thy *s* will be empty ... 1Sa 20:18 4186
And the king sat upon his *s* ... 1Sa 20:25 4186
times, even upon a *s* by the wall ... 1Sa 20:25 4186
The Tachmonite that sat in the *s* ... 2Sa 23:8 7674
caused a *s* to be set for the ... 1Kin 2:19 3678
either side on the place of the *s* ... 1Kin 10:19 7675
and of the place of the mercy *s* ... 1Chr 28:11
set his *s* above all the princes ... Est 3:1 3678
that I might come even to his *s* ... Job 23:3 8499
I prepared my *s* in the street ... Job 29:7 4186
sitteth in the *s* of the scornful ... Ps 1:1 4186
on a *s* in the high places of the ... Prov 9:14 3678
where was the *s* of the image of ... Eze 8:3 4186
I am a God, I sit in the *s* of God ... Eze 28:2 4186
cause the *s* of violence to come ... Amos 6:3 7675
and the Pharisees sit in Moses' *s* ... Mt 23:2 2515
he was set down on the judgment *s* ... Mt 27:19 968
sat down in the judgment *s* in a ... Jn 19:13 968
and brought him to the judgment *s* ... Acts 18:12 968
he drave them from the judgment *s* ... Acts 18:16 968
and beat him before the judgment *s* ... Acts 18:17 968
day sitting on the judgment *s* ... Acts 25:6 968
I stand at Caesar's judgment *s* ... Acts 25:10 968
morrow I sat on the judgment *s* ... Acts 25:17 968
before the judgment *s* of Christ ... Rom 14:10 968
before the judgment *s* of Christ ... 2Cor 5:10 968
dwellest, even where Satan's *s* is ... Rev 2:13 2362
gave him his power, and his *s* ... Rev 13:2 2362
his vial upon the *s* of the beast ... Rev 16:10 2362

SEATED
portion of the lawgiver, was he *s* ... Deut 33:21 5603

SEATS
the *s* of them that sold doves, ... Mt 21:12 2515
the chief *s* in the synagogues, ... Mt 23:6 4410
the *s* of them that sold doves ... Mk 11:15 2515
the chief *s* in the synagogues, and ... Mk 12:39 4410
put down the mighty from their *s* ... Lk 1:52 2362
the uppermost *s* in the synagogues ... Lk 11:43 4410
the highest *s* in the synagogues, ... Lk 20:46 4410
and draw you before the judgment *s* ... Jas 2:6
the throne were four and twenty *s* ... Rev 4:4 2362
upon the *s* I saw four and twenty ... Rev 4:4 2362
which sat before God on their *s* ... Rev 11:16 2362

SEATWARD
even to the mercy *s* were the ... Ex 37:9

SEBA (*se'-bah*) See SABEANS, SHEBA.
1. A son of Cush.
S, and Havilah, and Sabtah, and ... Gen 10:7 5434
S, and Havilah, and Sabta, and ... 1Chr 1:9 5434
2. The land.
of Sheba and *S* shall offer gifts ... Ps 72:10 5434
ransom, Ethiopia and *S* for thee ... Is 43:3 5434

SEBAM See SHEBAM.

SEBAT (*se'-bat*) *The eleventh month of the Hebrew year.*
month, which is the month *S* ... Zec 1:7 7627

SECACAH (*se-ca'-cah*) *A village in Judah.*
Beth-arabah, Middin, and *S* ... Josh 15:61 5527

SECHU (*se'-ku*) *A city in Benjamin.*
came to a great well that is in *S* ... 1Sa 19:22 7906

SECOND
and the morning were the *s* day ... Gen 1:8 8145
the name of the *s* river is Gihon ... Gen 2:13 8145
with lower, *s*, and third stories ... Gen 6:16 8145
of Noah's life, in the *s* month ... Gen 7:11 8145
And in the *s* month, on the seven ... Gen 8:14 8145
Abraham out of heaven the *s* time ... Gen 22:15 8145
again, and bare Jacob a *s* son ... Gen 30:7 8145
Leah's maid bare Jacob a *s* son ... Gen 30:12 8145
And so commanded he the *s*, and the .. Gen 32:19 8145
And he slept and dreamed the *s* time ... Gen 41:5 8145
in the *s* chariot which he had ... Gen 41:43 4932
the name of the *s* called he ... Gen 41:52 8145
now we had returned this *s* time ... Gen 43:10
they came unto him the *s* year ... Gen 47:18 8145
And when he went out the *s* day ... Ex 2:13 8145
on the fifteenth day of the *s* ... Ex 16:1 8145
curtain, in the coupling of the *s* ... Ex 26:4 8145
that is in the coupling of the *s* ... Ex 26:5 8145
the curtain which coupleth the *s* ... Ex 26:10 8145
for the *s* side of the tabernacle ... Ex 26:20 8145
the *s* row shall be an emerald, a ... Ex 28:18 8145
curtain, in the coupling of the *s* ... Ex 36:11 8145
was in the coupling of the *s* ... Ex 36:12 8145
the curtain which coupleth the *s* ... Ex 36:17 8145
And the *s* row, an emerald, a ... Ex 39:11 8145
in the first month in the *s* year ... Ex 40:17 8145
he shall offer the *s* for a burnt ... Lev 5:10 8145
it shall be washed the *s* time ... Lev 13:58 8145
on the first day of the *s* month ... Num 1:1 8145
in the *s* year after they were ... Num 1:1 8145
on the first day of the *s* month ... Num 1:18 8145
shall set forth in the *s* rank ... Num 2:16 8145
On the *s* day Nethaneel the son of ... Num 7:18 8145
in the first month of the *s* year ... Num 9:1 8145
The fourteenth day of the *s* month ... Num 9:11 8145
When ye blow an alarm the *s* time ... Num 10:6 8145
the *s* month, in the *s* year ... Num 10:11 8145
on the *s* day ye shall offer ... Num 29:17 8145
the children of Israel the *s* time ... Josh 5:2 8145
the *s* day they compassed the city ... Josh 6:14 8145
which took it on the *s* day ... Josh 10:32 8145
the *s* lot came forth to Simeon, ... Josh 19:1 8145
even the *s* bullock of seven years ... Judg 6:25 8145
place, and take the *s* bullock ... Judg 6:26 8145
the *s* bullock was offered upon ... Judg 6:28 8145
children of Benjamin the *s* day ... Judg 20:24 8145
them out of Gibeah the *s* day ... Judg 20:25 8145
and the name of his *s*, Abiah ... 1Sa 8:2 4932
which was the *s* day of the month, ... 1Sa 20:27 8145
no meat the *s* day of the month ... 1Sa 20:34 8145
I will not smite him the *s* time ... 1Sa 26:8 8138
And his *s*, Chileab, of Abigail the ... 2Sa 3:3 4932
and when he sent again the *s* time ... 2Sa 14:29 8145
month Zif, which is the *s* month ... 1Kin 6:1 8145
appeared to Solomon the *s* time ... 1Kin 9:2 8145
the *s* year of Asa king of Judah ... 1Kin 15:25 8147
And he said, Do it the *s* time ... 1Kin 18:34 8138
And they did it the *s* time ... 1Kin 18:34 8138
of the LORD came again the *s* time ... 1Kin 19:7 8145
the *s* year of Jehoram the son of ... 2Kin 1:17 8147
Then he sent out a *s* on horseback ... 2Kin 9:19 8145
wrote a letter the *s* time to them ... 2Kin 10:6 8145
In the *s* year of Joash son of ... 2Kin 14:1 8147
In the *s* year of Pekah the son of ... 2Kin 15:32 8147
and in the *s* year that which ... 2Kin 19:29 8145
and the priests of the *s* order ... 2Kin 23:4 4932
like unto these had the *s* pillar ... 2Kin 25:17 8145
priest, and Zephaniah the *s* priest ... 2Kin 25:18 4932
Eliab, and Abinadab the *s*, and ... 1Chr 2:13 8145
the *s* Daniel, of Abigail the ... 1Chr 3:1 8145
the *s* Jehoiakim, the third ... 1Chr 3:15 8145
the name of the *s* was Zelophehad ... 1Chr 7:15 8145
Bela his firstborn, Ashbel the *s* ... 1Chr 8:1 8145
Ulam his firstborn, Jehush the *s* ... 1Chr 8:39 8145
Ezer the first, Obadiah the *s* ... 1Chr 12:9 8145
their brethren of the *s* degree ... 1Chr 15:18 4932
was the chief, and Zizah the *s* ... 1Chr 23:11 8145
Jeriah the first, Amariah the *s* ... 1Chr 23:19 8145
Micah the first, and Jesiah the *s* ... 1Chr 23:20 8145
to Jehoiarib, the *s* to Jedaiah, ... 1Chr 24:7 8145
Jeriah the first, Amariah the *s* ... 1Chr 24:23 8145
the *s* to Gedaliah, who with his ... 1Chr 25:9 8145
the firstborn, Jediael the *s* ... 1Chr 26:2 8145
the firstborn, Jehozabad the *s* ... 1Chr 26:4 8145
Hilkiah the *s*, Tebaliah the third ... 1Chr 26:11 8145
over the course of the *s* month ... 1Chr 27:4 8145
the son of David king the *s* time ... 1Chr 29:22 8145
in the *s* day of the *s* month ... 2Chr 3:2 8145
pay unto him, both the *s* year ... 2Chr 27:5 8145
keep the passover in the *s* month ... 2Chr 30:2 8145
unleavened bread in the *s* month ... 2Chr 30:13 8145
the fourteenth day of the *s* month ... 2Chr 30:15 8145
put him in the *s* chariot that he ... 2Chr 35:24 4932
basons of a *s* sort four hundred ... Ezr 1:10 4932
Now in the *s* year of their coming ... Ezr 3:8 8145
God at Jerusalem, in the *s* month ... Ezr 3:8 8145
So it ceased unto the *s* year of ... Ezr 4:24 8648
on the *s* day were gathered ... Neh 8:13 8145
son of Senuah was *s* over the city ... Neh 11:9 4932
Bakbukiah the *s* among his ... Neh 11:17 4932
into the *s* house of the women ... Est 2:14 8145
were gathered together the *s* time ... Est 2:19 8145
the *s* day at the banquet of wine ... Est 7:2 8145
to confirm this *s* letter of Purim ... Est 9:29 8145
and the name of the *s*, Kezia ... Job 42:14 8145
is one alone, and there is not a *s* ... Eccl 4:8 8145
with the *s* child that shall stand ... Eccl 4:15 8145
shall set his hand again the *s* ... Is 11:11 8145
the *s* year that which springeth ... Is 37:30 8145
the LORD came unto me the *s* time ... Jer 1:13 8145
the LORD came unto me the *s* time ... Jer 13:3 8145
came unto Jeremiah the *s* time ... Jer 33:1 8145
it came to pass the *s* day after ... Jer 41:4 8145
The *s* pillar also and the ... Jer 52:22 8145
priest, and Zephaniah the *s* priest ... Jer 52:24 4932
the *s* face was the face of a man, ... Eze 10:14 8145
on the *s* day thou shalt offer a ... Eze 43:22 8145
in the *s* year of the reign of ... Dan 2:1 8147
And behold another beast, a *s* ... Dan 7:5 8578
LORD came unto Jonah the *s* time ... Jonah 3:1 8145
shall not rise up the *s* time ... Nah 1:9
gate, and an howling from the *s* ... Zeph 1:10 4932
In the *s* year of Darius the king, ... Hag 1:1 8147
in the *s* year of Darius the king ... Hag 1:15 8147
in the *s* year of Darius, came the ... Hag 2:10 8147
in the *s* year of Darius, came the ... Zec 1:1 8147
in the *s* year of Darius, came the ... Zec 1:7 8147
in the *s* chariot black horses ... Zec 6:2 8145
And he came to the *s*, and said ... Mt 21:30 1208
Likewise the *s* also, and the third ... Mt 22:26 1208
the *s* is like unto it, Thou shalt ... Mt 22:39 1208
He went away again the *s* time ... Mt 26:42 1208
the *s* took her, and died, neither ... Mk 12:21 1208
the *s* is like, namely this, Thou ... Mk 12:31 1208
And the *s* time the cock crew ... Mk 14:72 1208
it came to pass on the *s* sabbath ... Lk 6:1 1207
if he shall come in the *s* watch ... Lk 12:38 1208
the *s* came, saying, Lord, thy ... Lk 19:18 1208
the *s* took her to wife, and he ... Lk 20:30 1208
can he enter the *s* time into his ... Jn 3:4 1208
This is again the *s* miracle that ... Jn 4:54 1208
He saith to him again the *s* time ... Jn 21:16 1208
at the *s* time Joseph was made ... Acts 7:13 1208
spake unto him again the *s* time ... Acts 10:15 1208
the *s* ward, they came unto the ... Acts 12:10 1208
it is also written in the *s* psalm ... Acts 13:33 1208
the *s* man is the Lord from heaven ... 1Cor 15:47 1208
that ye might have a *s* benefit ... 2Cor 1:15 1208
as if I were present, the *s* time ... 2Cor 13:2 1208
The *s* epistle to the Corinthians ... 2Cor *s* 1208
The *s* epistle to the ... 2Th *s* 1208
The *s* epistle unto Timotheus, ... 2Ti *s* 1208
brought before Nero the *s* time ... 2Ti *s* 1208
the first and *s* admonition reject ... Titus 3:10 1208
place have been sought for the *s* ... Heb 8:7 1208
And after the *s* veil, the ... Heb 9:3 1208
But into the *s* went the high ... Heb 9:7 1208
for him shall he appear the *s* ... Heb 9:28 1208
that he may establish the *s* ... Heb 10:9 1208
This *s* epistle, beloved, I now ... 2Pet 3:1 1208
shall not be hurt of the *s* death ... Rev 2:11 1208
the *s* beast like a calf, and the ... Rev 4:7 1208
And when he had opened the *s* seal ... Rev 6:3 1208
I heard the *s* beast say ... Rev 6:3 1208
the *s* angel sounded, and as it ... Rev 8:8 1208
The *s* woe is past ... Rev 11:14 1208

the *s* angel poured out his vial Rev 16:3 *1208*
on such the *s* death hath no power Rev 20:6 *1208*
This is the *s* death Rev 20:14 *1208*
which is the *s* death Rev 21:8 *1208*
the *s*, sapphire Rev 21:19 *1208*

SECONDARILY
s prophets, thirdly teachers, 1Cor 12:28 *1208*

SECRET
soul, come not thou into their *s* Gen 49:6 5475
and putteth it in a *s* place Deut 27:15 5643
The *s* things belong unto the LORD Deut 29:29 5641
I have a *s* errand unto thee, O Judg 3:19 5643
after my name, seeing it is *s* Judg 13:18 6383
they had emerods in their *s* parts 1Sa 5:9 8368
morning, and abide in a *s* place 1Sa 19:2 5643
that thou wouldest keep me *s* Job 14:13 5641
Hast thou heard the *s* of God Job 15:8 5475
is there any *s* thing with thee Job 15:11 328
shall be hid in his *s* places Job 20:26 6845
when the *s* of God was upon my Job 29:4 5475
and bind their faces in *s* Job 40:13 2934
in the *s* places doth he murder Ps 10:8 4565
a young lion lurking in *s* places Ps 17:12 4565
He made darkness his *s* place Ps 18:11 5643
cleanse thou me from *s* faults Ps 19:12 5641
The *s* of the LORD is with them Ps 25:14 5475
in the *s* of his tabernacle shall Ps 27:5 5643
Thou shalt hide them in the *s* of Ps 31:20 5643
Hide me from the *s* counsel of the Ps 64:2 5475
may shoot in *s* at the perfect Ps 64:4 4565
thee in the *s* place of thunder Ps 81:7 5643
our *s* sins in the light of thy Ps 90:8 5956
He that dwelleth in the *s* place Ps 91:1 5643
from thee, when I was made in *s* Ps 139:15 5643
but his *s* is with the righteous Prov 3:32 5475
and bread eaten in *s* is pleasant Prov 9:17 5643
A gift in *s* pacifieth anger Prov 21:14 5643
and discover not a *s* to another Prov 25:9 5475
Open rebuke is better than *s* love Prov 27:5 5641
into judgment, with every *s* thing Eccl 12:14 5956
in the *s* places of the stairs, Song 2:14 5643
LORD will discover their *s* parts Is 3:17 6596
and hidden riches of *s* places Is 45:3 4565
I have not spoken in *s*, in a dark Is 45:19 5643
spoken in *s* from the beginning Is 48:16 5643
I have not found it by *s* search Jer 2:34 5643
weep in *s* places for your pride Jer 13:17 4565
Can any hide himself in *s* places Jer 23:24 4565
I have uncovered his *s* places Jer 49:10 4565
in wait, and as a lion in *s* places Lam 3:10 4565
and they shall pollute my *s* place Eze 7:22 6845
there is no *s* that they can hide Eze 28:3 5640
God of heaven concerning this *s* Dan 2:18 7328
Then was the *s* revealed unto Dan 2:19 7328
He revealeth the deep and *s* things Dan 2:22 5642
The *s* which the king hath Dan 2:27 7328
this *s* is not revealed to me for Dan 2:30 7328
seeing thou couldst reveal this *s* Dan 2:47 7328
no *s* troubleth thee, tell me the Dan 4:9 7328
but he revealeth his *s* unto his Amos 3:7 5475
That thine alms may be in *s* Mt 6:4 *2927*
in *s* himself shall reward thee Mt 6:4 *2927*
pray to thy Father which is in *s* Mt 6:6 *2927*
in *s* shall reward thee openly Mt 6:6 *2927*
but unto thy Father which is in *s* Mt 6:18 *2927*
and thy Father, which seeth in *s* Mt 6:18 *2927*
kept *s* from the foundation of the Mt 13:35 *2928*
behold, he is in the *s* chambers Mt 24:26 *5009*
neither was any thing kept *s* Mk 4:22 *614*
For nothing is *s*, that shall not Lk 8:17 *2927*
a candle, putteth it in a *s* place Lk 11:33 *2926*
no man that doeth any thing in *s* Jn 7:4 *2927*
not openly, but as it were in *s* Jn 7:10 *2927*
and in *s* have I said nothing Jn 18:20 *2927*
which was kept *s* since the world Rom 16:25 *4601*
which are done of them in *s* Eph 5:12 *2931*

SECRETLY
Wherefore didst thou flee away *s* Gen 31:27 2244
as thine own soul, entice thee *s* Deut 13:6 5643
he that smiteth his neighbour *s* Deut 27:24 5643
want of all things *s* in the siege Deut 28:57 5643
out of Shittim two men to spy *s* Josh 2:1 2791
saying, Commune with David *s* 1Sa 18:22 3909
David knew that Saul *s* practised 1Sa 23:9 2790
For thou didst it *s* 2Sa 12:12 5643
did *s* those things that were not 2Kin 17:9 2644
Now a thing was *s* brought to me Job 4:12 1589
if ye do *s* accept persons Job 13:10 5643
And my heart hath been *s* enticed Job 31:27 5643
He lieth in wait *s* as a lion in Ps 10:9 4565
thou shalt keep them *s* in a Ps 31:20 6845
the king asked him *s* in his house Jer 37:17 5643
the king sware *s* unto Jeremiah Jer 38:16 5643
spake to Gedaliah in Mizpah *s* Jer 40:15 5643
was as to devour the poor *s* Hab 3:14 4565
way, and called Mary her sister *s* Jn 11:28 *2977*
but *s* for fear of the Jews, Jn 19:38 *2928*

SECRETS
her hand, and taketh him by the *s* Deut 25:11 4016
would shew thee the *s* of wisdom Job 11:6 8587
for he knoweth the *s* of the heart Ps 44:21 8587
A talebearer revealeth *s* Prov 11:13 5475
about as a talebearer revealeth *s* Prov 20:19 5475
a God in heaven that revealeth *s* Dan 2:28 7328
he that revealeth *s* maketh known Dan 2:29 7328
LORD of kings, and a revealer of *s* Dan 2:47 7328
the *s* of men by Jesus Christ Rom 2:16 *2927*
thus are the *s* of his heart made 1Cor 14:25 *2927*

SECT
(which is the *s* of the Sadducees, Acts 5:17 *139*
there rose up certain of the *s* of Acts 15:5 *139*
of the *s* of the Nazarenes Acts 24:5 *139*
s of our religion I lived a Acts 26:5 *139*
for as concerning this *s*, we know Acts 28:22 *139*

SECU See SECHU.

SECUNDUS (*se-cun'-dus*) *A Christian in Thessalonica.*
Thessalonians, Aristarchus and *S* Acts 20:4 *4580*

SECURE
for the host was *s* Judg 8:11 983
of the Zidonians, quiet and *s* Judg 18:7 982
go, ye shall come unto a people *s* Judg 18:10 982
a people that were at quiet and *s* Judg 18:27 982
And thou shalt be *s*, because there Job 11:18 982
and they that provoke God are *s* Job 12:6 987
we will persuade him, and *s* you Mt 28:14

SECURELY
seeing he dwelleth *s* by thee Prov 3:29 983
pass by *s* as men averse from war Mic 2:8 983

SECURITY
And when they had taken *s* of Jason Acts 17:9 *2425*

SEDITION
that they have moved *s* within the Ezr 4:15 849
and *s* have been made therein Ezr 4:19 849
for a certain *s* made in the city Lk 23:19 *4714*
released unto them him that for *s* Lk 23:25 *4714*
a mover of *s* among all the Jews Acts 24:5 *4714*

SEDITIONS
emulations, wrath, strife, *s* Gal 5:20 *1370*

SEDUCE
shall shew signs and wonders, to *s* Mk 13:22 *635*
you concerning them that *s* you 1Jn 2:26 *4105*
to *s* my servants to commit Rev 2:20 *4105*

SEDUCED
Manasseh *s* them to do more evil 2Kin 21:9 8582
they have also *s* Egypt, even they Is 19:13 8582
because they have *s* my people Eze 13:10 2937

SEDUCERS
s shall wax worse and worse, 2Ti 3:13 *1114*

SEDUCETH
but the way of the wicked *s* them Prov 12:26 8582

SEDUCING
faith, giving heed to *s* spirits 1Ti 4:1 *4108*

SEE
Adam to *s* what he would call them Gen 2:19 7200
to *s* if the waters were abated Gen 8:8 7200
the LORD came down to *s* the city Gen 11:5 7200
when the Egyptians shall *s* thee Gen 12:12 7200
now, and *s* whether they have done Gen 18:21 7200
And he said unto him, *S*, I have Gen 19:21 2009
Let me not *s* the death of the Gen 21:16 7200
were dim, so that he could not *s* Gen 27:1 7200
and blessed him, and said, *S* Gen 27:27 7200
I *s* your father's countenance, Gen 31:5 7200
Lift up now thine eyes, and *s* Gen 31:12 7200
s, God is witness betwixt me and Gen 31:50 7200
and afterward I will *s* his face Gen 32:20 7200
went out to *s* the daughters of Gen 34:1 7200
s whether it be well with thy Gen 37:14 7200
we shall *s* what will become of Gen 37:20 7200
and spake unto them, saying, *S* Gen 39:14 7200
And Pharaoh said unto Joseph, *S* Gen 41:41 7200
to *s* the nakedness of the land ye Gen 42:9 7200
but to *s* the nakedness of the Gen 42:12 7200
saying, Ye shall not *s* my face Gen 43:3 7200
unto us, Ye shall not *s* my face Gen 43:5 7200
ye shall *s* my face no more Gen 44:23 7200
for we may not *s* the man's face Gen 44:26 7200
lest peradventure I *s* the evil Gen 44:34 7200
And, behold, your eyes *s*, and the Gen 45:12 7200
S that ye fall not out by the way Gen 45:24
I will go and *s* him before I die Gen 45:28 7200
for age, so that he could not *s* Gen 48:10 7200
I had not thought to *s* thy face Gen 48:11 7200
women, and *s* them upon the stools Ex 1:16 7200
s this great sight, why the bush Ex 3:3 7200
saw that he turned aside to *s* Ex 3:4 7200
s whether they be yet alive Ex 4:18 7200
s that thou do all those wonders Ex 4:21 7200
did *s* that they were in evil case Ex 5:19 7200
Now shalt thou *s* what I will do Ex 6:1 7200
And the LORD said unto Moses, *S* Ex 7:1 7200
one cannot be able to *s* the earth Ex 10:5 7200
to thyself, *s* my face no more Ex 10:28 7200
I will *s* thy face again no more Ex 10:29 7200
when I *s* the blood, I will pass Ex 12:13 7200
the people repent when they *s* war Ex 13:17 7200
s the salvation of the LORD, Ex 14:13 7200
ye shall *s* them again no more for Ex 14:13 7200
then ye shall *s* the glory of the Ex 16:7 7200
S, for that the LORD hath given Ex 16:29 7200
that they may *s* the bread Ex 16:32 7200
to *s* whether he have put his hand Ex 22:8
If thou *s* the ass of him that Ex 23:5 7200
S, I have called by name Bezaleel Ex 31:2 7200
And Moses said unto the LORD, *S* Ex 33:12 7200
he said, Thou canst not *s* my face Ex 33:20 7200
for there shall no man *s* me Ex 33:20 7200
thou shalt *s* my back parts Ex 33:23 7200
art shall *s* the work of the LORD Ex 34:10 7200
unto the children of Israel, *S* Ex 35:30 7200
And if the priest *s* that, behold, Lev 13:8 7200
And the priest shall *s* him Lev 13:10 7200
the priest shall *s* the raw flesh Lev 13:15 7200
And the priest shall *s* him Lev 13:17 7200
the priest shall *s* the plague Lev 13:30 7200
priest go into it to *s* the plague Lev 14:36 7200
priest shall go in to *s* the house Lev 14:36 7200
s her nakedness, and she *s* his Lev 20:17 7200
in to *s* when the holy things are Num 4:20 7200
let me not *s* my wretchedness Num 11:15 7200
thou shalt *s* now whether my word Num 11:23 7200
And *s* the land, what it is Num 13:18 7200
Surely they shall not *s* the land Num 14:23 7200
any of them that provoked me *s* it Num 14:23 7200
that thence he might *s* the utmost Num 22:41 7200
from the top of the rocks I *s* him Num 23:9 7200
from whence thou mayest *s* them Num 23:13 7200
thou shalt *s* but the utmost part Num 23:13 7200
of them, and shalt not *s* them all Num 23:13 7200
I shall *s* him, but not now Num 24:17 7200
s the land which I have given Num 27:12 7200
from Kadesh-barnea to *s* the land Num 32:8 7200
shall *s* the land which I sware Num 32:11 7200
evil generation *s* that good land Deut 1:35 7200
he shall *s* it, and to him will I Deut 1:36 7200
s the good land that is beyond Deut 3:25 7200
the land which thou shalt *s* Deut 3:28 7200
wood and stone, which neither *s* Deut 4:28 7200
neither let me *s* this great fire Deut 18:16 7200
Thou shalt not *s* thy brother's ox Deut 22:1 7200
Thou shalt not *s* thy brother's Deut 22:4 7200
that he *s* no unclean thing in Deut 23:14 7200
s that thou art called by the Deut 28:10 7200
of thine eyes which thou shalt *s* Deut 28:34 7200
of thine eyes which thou shalt *s* Deut 28:67 7200
Thou shalt *s* it no more again Deut 28:68 7200
heart to perceive, and eyes to *s* Deut 29:4 7200
when they *s* the plagues of that Deut 29:22 7200
S, I have set before thee this Deut 30:15 7200
I will *s* what their end shall be Deut 32:20 7200
S now that I, even I, am he, and Deut 32:39 7200
Yet thou shalt *s* the land before Deut 32:52 7200
thee to *s* it with thine eyes Deut 34:4 7200
When ye *s* the ark of the covenant Josh 3:3 7200
And the LORD said unto Joshua, *S* Josh 6:2 7200
s, I have given into thy hand the Josh 8:1 7200
S, I have commanded you Josh 8:8 7200
by Jordan, a great altar to *s* to Josh 22:10 4758
S there come people down by the Judg 9:37 2009
he turned aside to *s* the carcase Judg 14:8 7200
s wherein his great strength Judg 16:5 7200
And *s*, and, behold, if the Judg 21:21 7200
thou shalt *s* an enemy in my 1Sa 2:32 5027
to wax dim, that he could not *s* 1Sa 3:2 7200
were dim, that he could not *s* 1Sa 4:15 7200
And *s*, if it goeth up by the way 1Sa 6:9 7200
saw the ark, and rejoiced to *s* it 1Sa 6:13 7200
S ye him whom the LORD hath 1Sa 10:24 7200
s this great thing, which the 1Sa 12:16 7200
s that your wickedness is great, 1Sa 12:17 7200
now, and *s* who is gone from us 1Sa 14:17 7200
s, I pray you, how mine eyes have 1Sa 14:29 7200
s wherein this sin hath been this 1Sa 14:38 7200
Samuel came no more to *s* Saul 1Sa 15:35 7200
that thou mightest *s* the battle 1Sa 17:28 7200
and what I *s*, that I will tell 1Sa 19:3 7200
the messengers again to *s* David 1Sa 19:15 7200
I pray thee, and *s* my brethren 1Sa 20:29 7200
servants, Lo, ye *s* the man is mad 1Sa 21:14 7200
s his place where his haunt is, 1Sa 23:22 7200
S therefore, and take knowledge of 1Sa 23:23 7200
Moreover, my father, *s*, yea, *s* 1Sa 24:11 7200
s that there is neither evil nor 1Sa 24:11 7200
and judge between me and thee, and *s* 1Sa 24:15 7200
s, I have hearkened to thy voice, 1Sa 25:35 7200
now *s* where the king's spear is, 1Sa 26:16 7200
that is, Thou shalt not *s* my face 2Sa 3:13 7200
when thou comest to *s* my face 2Sa 3:13 7200
S now, I dwell in an house of 2Sa 7:2 7200
when thy father cometh to *s* thee 2Sa 13:5 7200
meat in my sight, that I may *s* it 2Sa 13:5 7200
when the king was come to *s* him 2Sa 13:6 7200
house, and let him not *s* my face 2Sa 14:24 7200
he said unto his servants, *S* 2Sa 14:30 7200
let me *s* the king's face 2Sa 14:32 7200
And Absalom said unto him, *S* 2Sa 15:3 7200
S, I will tarry in the plain of 2Sa 15:28 7200
eyes of my lord the king may *s* it 2Sa 24:3 7200
s what answer I shall return to 2Sa 24:13 7200
Hiram came out from Tyre to *s* the 1Kin 9:12 7200
now *s* to thine own house, David 1Kin 12:16 7200
But Ahijah could not *s* 1Kin 14:4 7200
and Elijah said, *S*, thy son liveth 1Kin 17:23 7200
s how this man seeketh mischief 1Kin 20:7 7200
and mark, and *s* what thou doest 1Kin 20:22 7200
thou shalt *s* in that day, when 1Kin 22:25 7200
if thou *s* me when I am taken from 2Kin 2:10 7200
not look toward thee, nor *s* thee 2Kin 3:14 7200
s wind, neither shall ye *s* rain 2Kin 3:17 7200
s how he seeketh a quarrel 2Kin 5:7 7200
open his eyes, that he may *s* 2Kin 6:17 7200
of these men, that they may *s* 2Kin 6:20 7200
S ye how this son of a murderer 2Kin 6:32 7200
thou shalt *s* it with thine eyes, 2Kin 7:2 7200
and let us send and *s* 2Kin 7:13 7200
of the Syrians, saying, Go and *s* 2Kin 7:14 7200
thou shalt *s* it with thine eyes, 2Kin 7:19 7200
to *s* Joram the son of Ahab in 2Kin 8:29 7200
of Judah was come down to *s* Joram 2Kin 9:16 7200
he came, and said, I *s* a company 2Kin 9:17 7200
s now this cursed woman, and bury 2Kin 9:34
me, and *s* my zeal for the LORD 2Kin 10:16 7200
open, LORD, thine eyes, and *s* 2Kin 19:16 7200
thine eyes shall not *s* all the 2Kin 22:20 7200
said, What title is that that I *s* 2Kin 23:17 7200
now, David, *s* to thine own house 2Chr 10:16 7200
I did *s* all Israel scattered upon 2Chr 18:16 7200
thou shalt *s* on that day when 2Chr 18:24 7200
s the salvation of the LORD with 2Chr 20:17 7200
to *s* Jehoram the son of Ahab at 2Chr 22:6 7200
s that ye hasten the matter 2Chr 24:5

let us s one another in the face 2Chr 25:17 7200
hissing, as ye s with your eyes 2Chr 29:8 7200
them up to desolation, as ye s 2Chr 30:7 7200
neither shall thine eyes s all 2Chr 34:28 7200
for us to s the king's dishonour Ezr 4:14 2370
Ye s the distress that we are in, Neh 2:17 7200
They shall not know, neither s Neh 4:11 7200
didst s the affliction of our Neh 9:9 7200
to s whether Mordecai's matters Est 3:4 7200
so long as I s Mordecai the Jew Est 5:13 7200
For how can I endure to s the Est 8:6 7200
or how can I endure to s the Est 8:6 7200
neither let it s the dawning of Job 3:9 7200
ye s my casting down, and are Job 6:21 7200
mine eye shall no more s good Job 7:7 7200
hath seen me shall s me no more Job 7:8 7789
he goeth by me, and I s him not Job 9:11 7200
they flee away, they s no good Job 9:25 7200
therefore s thou mine affliction Job 10:15 7200
as for my hope, who shall s it Job 17:15 7789
yet in my flesh shall I s God Job 19:26 2372
Whom I shall s for myself Job 19:27 2372
which saw him shall s him no more Job 20:9
He shall not s the rivers Job 20:17 7200
His eyes shall s his destruction, Job 21:20 7200
darkness, that thou canst not s Job 22:11 7200
The righteous s it, and are glad Job 22:19 7200
right hand, that I cannot s him Job 23:9 7200
they that know him not s his days Job 24:1 2372
saying, No eye shall s me Job 24:15 7789
Then did he s it, and declare it Job 28:27 7200
Doth not he s my ways, and count Job 31:4 7200
he shall s his face with joy Job 33:26 7200
and his life shall s the light Job 33:28 7200
That which I s not teach thou me Job 34:32 2372
Look unto the heavens, and s Job 35:5 7200
thou sayest thou shalt not s him Job 35:14 7789
Every man may s it Job 36:25 2372
now men s not the bright light Job 37:21 7200
he will never s it Ps 10:11 7200
to s if there were any that did Ps 14:2 7200
thine Holy One to s corruption Ps 16:10 7200
All they that s me laugh me to Ps 22:7 7200
unless I had believed to s the Ps 27:13 7200
they that did s me without fled Ps 31:11 7200
taste and s that the LORD is good Ps 34:8 7200
many days, that he may s good Ps 34:12 7200
in thy light shall we s light Ps 36:9 7200
are cut off, thou shalt s it Ps 37:34 7200
many shall s it, and fear, and Ps 40:3 7200
And if he come to s me, he Ps 41:6 7200
for ever, and not s corruption Ps 49:9 7200
they shall never s light Ps 49:19 7200
The righteous also shall s Ps 52:6 7200
to s if there were any that did Ps 53:2 7200
that they may not s the sun Ps 58:8 2372
God shall let me s my desire upon Ps 59:10 7200
To s thy power and thy glory, so Ps 63:2 7200
they say, Who shall s them Ps 64:5 7200
all that s them shall flee away Ps 64:8 7200
Come and s the works of God Ps 66:5 7200
eyes be darkened, that they s not Ps 69:23 7200
The humble shall s this, and be Ps 69:32 7200
We s not our signs Ps 74:9 7200
that they which hate me may s it Ps 86:17 7200
that liveth, and shall not s death Ps 89:48 7200
s the reward of the wicked Ps 91:8 7200
Mine eye also shall s my desire Ps 92:11 5027
they say, The LORD shall not s Ps 94:7 7200
formed the eye, shall he not s Ps 94:9 5027
and all the people s his glory Ps 97:6 7200
That I may s the good of thy Ps 106:5 7200
These s the works of the LORD, and Ps 107:24 7200
The righteous shall s it, and Ps 107:42 7200
until he s his desire upon his Ps 112:8 7200
The wicked shall s it, and be Ps 112:10 7200
eyes have they, but they s not Ps 115:5 7200
therefore shall I s my desire Ps 118:7 7200
thee will be glad when they s me Ps 119:74 7200
and thou shalt s the good of Ps 128:5 7200
thou shalt s thy children's Ps 128:6 7200
eyes have they, but they s not Ps 135:16 7200
Thine eyes did s my substance Ps 139:16 7200
s if there be any wicked way in Ps 139:24 7200
Lest the LORD s it, and it Prov 24:18 7200
the righteous shall s their fall Prov 29:16 7200
thing whereof it may be said, S Eccl 1:10 7200
till I might s what was that good Eccl 2:3 7200
that they might s that they Eccl 3:18 7200
him to s what shall be after him Eccl 3:22 7200
is profit to them that s the sun Eccl 7:11 7200
to s the business that is done Eccl 8:16 7200
let me s thy countenance, let me Song 2:14 7200
to s the fruits of the valley Song 6:11 7200
to s whether the vine flourished, Song 6:11 7200
What will ye s in the Shulamite Song 6:13 2372
let us s if the vine flourish, Song 7:12 7200
hasten his work, that we may s it Is 5:19 7200
s ye indeed, but perceive not Is 6:9 7200
lest they s with their eyes, and Is 6:10 7200
Isaiah the son of Amoz did s Is 13:1 2372
They that s thee shall narrowly Is 14:16 7200
s ye, when he lifteth up an Is 18:3 7200
is lifted up, they will not s Is 26:11 2372
but they shall s, and be ashamed Is 26:11 2372
blind shall s out of obscurity Is 29:18 7200
Which say to the seers, S not Is 30:10 7200
thine eyes shall s thy teachers Is 30:20 7200
of them that s shall not be dim Is 32:3 7200
Thine eyes shall s the king in Is 33:17 2372
Thou shalt not s a fierce people, Is 33:19 7200
thine eyes shall s Jerusalem a Is 33:20 7200
they shall s the glory of the Is 35:2 7200
open thine eyes, O LORD, and s Is 37:17 7200
I said, I shall not s the LORD Is 38:11 7200
and all flesh shall s it together Is 40:5 7200
That they may s, and know, and Is 41:20 7200
and look, ye blind, that ye may s Is 42:18 7200
they s not, nor know Is 44:9 7200
their eyes, that they cannot s Is 44:18 7200
Thou hast heard, s all this Is 48:6 2372
servant of rulers, Kings shall s Is 49:7 7200
for they shall s eye to eye Is 52:8 7200
shall s the salvation of our God Is 52:10 7200
not been told them shall they s Is 52:15 7200
and when we shall s him, there is Is 53:2 7200
for sin, he shall s his seed Is 53:10 7200
He shall s of the travail of his Is 53:11 7200
up thine eyes round about, and s Is 60:4 7200
Then thou shalt s, and flow Is 60:5
all that s them shall acknowledge Is 61:9 7200
shall s thy righteousness Is 62:2 7200
behold, s, we beseech thee, we Is 64:9 5027
And when ye s this, your heart Is 66:14 7200
and they shall come, and s my glory Is 66:18 7200
S, I have this day set thee over Jer 1:10 7200
I s a rod of an almond tree Jer 1:11 7200
and I said, I s a seething pot Jer 1:13 7200
over the isles of Chittim, and s Jer 2:10 7200
s if there be such a thing Jer 2:10 7200
s that it is an evil thing and Jer 2:19 7200
s thy way in the valley, know Jer 2:23 7200
s ye the word of the LORD Jer 2:31 7200
s where thou hast not been lien Jer 3:2 7200
How long shall I s the standard Jer 4:21 7200
s now, and know, and seek in the Jer 5:1 7200
shall we s sword nor famine Jer 5:12 7200
which have eyes, and s not Jer 5:21 7200
LORD, Stand ye in the ways, and s Jer 6:16 7200
s what I did to it for the Jer 7:12 7200
let me s thy vengeance on them Jer 11:20 7200
said, He shall not s our last end Jer 12:4 7200
them, Ye shall not s the sword Jer 14:13 7200
shall not s when good cometh Jer 17:6 7200
shall not s when heat cometh, but Jer 17:8 7200
let me s thy vengeance on them Jer 20:12 7200
forth out of the womb to s labour Jer 20:18 7200
no more, nor s his native country Jer 22:10 7200
shall s this land no more Jer 22:12 7200
places that I shall not s him Jer 23:24 7200
s whether a man doth travail with Jer 30:6 7200
wherefore do I s every man with Jer 30:6 7200
of Egypt, where we shall s no war Jer 42:14 7200
ye shall s this place no more Jer 42:18 7200
comest to Babylon, and shalt s Jer 51:61 7200
s, O LORD, and consider Lam 1:11 7200
s if there be any sorrow like Lam 1:12 7200
thou shalt s greater abominations Eze 8:6 7200
thou shalt s greater abominations Eze 8:13 7200
thou shalt s greater abominations Eze 8:15 7200
which have eyes to s, and s not Eze 12:2 7200
that thou s not the ground Eze 12:6 7200
that he s not the ground with his Eze 12:12 7200
yet shall he not s it, though he Eze 12:13 7200
upon the prophets that s vanity Eze 13:9 2374
which s visions of peace for her, Eze 13:16 2374
ye shall s no more vanity Eze 13:23 2372
ye shall s their way and their Eze 14:22 7200
when ye s their ways and their Eze 14:23 7200
that they may s all thy nakedness Eze 16:37 7200
all flesh shall s that I the LORD Eze 20:48 7200
Whiles they s vanity unto thee, Eze 21:29 2372
Pharaoh shall s them, and shall be Eze 32:31 7200
if the watchman s the sword come Eze 33:6 7200
all the heathen shall s my Eze 39:21 7200
for why should he s your faces Dan 1:10 7200
because ye s the thing is gone Dan 2:8 2370
I s four men loose, walking in Dan 3:25 2370
iron, wood, and stone, which s not Dan 5:23 2370
your young men shall s visions Joel 2:28 7200
Pass ye unto Calneh, and s Amos 6:2 7200
till he might s what would become Jonah 4:5 7200
man of wisdom shall s thy name Mic 6:9 7200
she that is mine enemy shall s it Mic 7:10 7200
The nations shall s and be Mic 7:16 7200
which Habakkuk the prophet did s Hab 1:1 2372
will watch to s what he will say Hab 2:1 7200
thou shalt not s evil any more Zeph 3:15 7200
and how do ye s it now Hag 2:3 7200
to s what is the breadth thereof, Zec 2:2 7200
shall s the plummet in the hand Zec 4:10 7200
And I answered, I s a flying roll Zec 5:2 7200
s what is this that goeth forth Zec 5:5 7200
Ashkelon shall s it, and fear Zec 9:5 7200
Gaza also shall s it, and be very Zec 9:5
yea, their children shall s it Zec 10:7 7200
And your eyes shall s, and ye shall Mal 1:5 7200
for they shall s God Mt 5:8 3700
that they may s your good works, Mt 5:16 1492
then shalt thou s clearly to cast Mt 7:5 1227
unto him, S thou tell no man Mt 8:4 3708
saying, S that no man know it Mt 9:30 3708
things which ye do hear and s Mt 11:4 991
ye out into the wilderness to s Mt 11:7 2300
But what went ye out for to s Mt 11:8 1492
But what went ye out for to s Mt 11:9 1492
we would s a sign from thee Mt 12:38 1492
because they seeing s not Mt 13:13 991
and seeing ye shall s, and shall Mt 13:14 991
they should s with their eyes Mt 13:15 1492
blessed are your eyes, for they s Mt 13:16 991
to s those things which ye Mt 13:17 1492
those things which ye s Mt 13:17 991
lame to walk, and the blind to s Mt 15:31 991
till they s the Son of man coming Mt 16:28 1492
the king came in to s the guests Mt 22:11 2300
Ye shall not s me henceforth, Mt 23:39 1492
S ye not all these things Mt 24:2 991
s that ye be not troubled Mt 24:6 3708
When ye therefore shall s the Mt 24:15 1492
they shall s the Son of man Mt 24:30 3700
when ye shall s all these things, Mt 24:33 1492
with the servants, to s the end Mt 26:58 1492
Hereafter shall ye s the Son of Mt 26:64 3700
s thou to that Mt 27:4 3700
s ye to it Mt 27:24 3700
let us s whether Elias will come Mt 27:49 1492
the other Mary to s the sepulchre Mt 28:1 2334
s the place where the Lord lay Mt 28:6 1492
there shall ye s him Mt 28:7 3700
Galilee, and there shall they s me Mt 28:10 3700
S thou say nothing to any man Mk 1:44 3708
That seeing they may s, and not Mk 4:12 991
they went out to s what it was Mk 5:14 1492
s him that was possessed with the Mk 5:15 2334
he looked round about to s her Mk 5:32 1492
go and s Mk 6:38 1492
Having eyes, s ye not Mk 8:18 991
I s men as trees, walking Mk 8:24 991
bring me a penny, that I may s it Mk 12:15 1492
s what manner of stones and what Mk 13:1 2396
But when ye shall s the Mk 13:14 1492
then shall they s the Son of man Mk 13:26 3700
when ye shall s these things come Mk 13:29 1492
ye shall s the Son of man sitting Mk 14:62 3700
now from the cross, that we may s Mk 15:32 1492
let us s whether Elias will come Mk 15:36 1492
there shall ye s him, as he said Mk 16:7 3700
s this thing which is come to Lk 2:15 1492
Ghost, that he should not s death Lk 2:26 1492
all flesh shall s the salvation Lk 3:6 3700
then shalt thou s clearly to pull Lk 6:42 1227
how that the blind s, the lame Lk 7:22 308
out into the wilderness for to s Lk 7:24 2300
But what went ye out for to s Lk 7:25 1492
But what went ye out for to s Lk 7:26 1492
that seeing they might not s Lk 8:10 991
which enter in may s the light Lk 8:16 991
stand without, desiring to s thee Lk 8:20 1492
they went out to s what was done Lk 8:35 1492
And he desired to s him Lk 9:9 1492
till they s the kingdom of God Lk 9:27 1492
which s the things that ye s Lk 10:23 991
kings have desired to s those Lk 10:24 1492
those things which ye s Lk 10:24 991
which come in may s the light Lk 11:33 991
When ye s a cloud rise out of the Lk 12:54 1492
when ye s the south wind blow, ye Lk 12:55
of teeth, when ye shall s Abraham Lk 13:28 3700
I say unto you, Ye shall not s me Lk 13:35 1492
and I must needs go and s it Lk 14:18 1492
when ye shall desire to s one of Lk 17:22 1492
Son of man, and ye shall not s it Lk 17:22 3700
And they shall say to you, S here Lk 17:23 2400
or, s there Lk 17:23 2400
he sought to s Jesus who he was Lk 19:3 1492
up into a sycomore tree to s him Lk 19:4 1492
reverence him when they s him Lk 20:13 1492
when ye shall s Jerusalem Lk 21:20 1492
then shall they s the Son of man Lk 21:27 3700
When they now shoot forth, ye s Lk 21:30 991
when ye s these things come to Lk 21:31 1492
to s him of a long season Lk 23:8 1492
handle me, and s Lk 24:39 1492
flesh and bones, as ye s me have Lk 24:39 2334
Upon whom thou shalt s the Spirit Jn 1:33 1492
He saith unto them, Come and s Jn 1:39 1492
Philip saith unto him, Come and s Jn 1:46 1492
thou shalt s greater things than Jn 1:50 3700
Hereafter ye shall s heaven open Jn 1:51 3700
he cannot s the kingdom of God Jn 3:3 1492
not the Son shall not s life Jn 3:36 3700
s a man, which told me all things Jn 4:29 1492
Jesus unto him, Except ye s signs Jn 4:48 1492
they s Jesus walking on the sea, Jn 6:19 2334
shewest thou then, that we may s Jn 6:30 1492
if ye shall s the Son of man Jn 6:62 2334
may s the works that thou doest Jn 7:3 2334
my saying, he shall never s death Jn 8:51 2334
Abraham rejoiced to s my day Jn 8:56 1492
mine eyes, and I washed, and do s Jn 9:15 991
how then doth he now s Jn 9:19 991
whereas I was blind, now I s Jn 9:25 991
that they which s not might s Jn 9:39 991
that they which s might be made Jn 9:39 991
but now ye say, We s Jn 9:41 991
said unto him, Lord, come and s Jn 11:34 1492
thou shouldest s the glory of God Jn 11:40 3700
that they might s Lazarus also Jn 12:9 1492
saying, Sir, we would s Jesus Jn 12:21 1492
they should not s with their eyes Jn 12:40 1492
but ye s me Jn 14:19 2334
to my Father, and ye s me no more Jn 16:10 2334
while, and ye shall not s me Jn 16:16 2334
a little while, and ye shall s me Jn 16:16 3700
while, and ye shall not s me Jn 16:17 2334
a little while, and ye shall s me Jn 16:17 3700
while, and ye shall not s me Jn 16:19 2334
a little while, and ye shall s me Jn 16:19 3700
but I will s you again, and your Jn 16:22 3700
Did not I s thee in the garden Jn 18:26 1492
Except I shall s in his hands the Jn 20:25 1492
and your young men shall s visions Acts 2:17 3070
thine Holy One to s corruption Acts 2:27 1492
his flesh did s corruption Acts 2:31 1492
shed forth this, which ye now s Acts 2:33 991
made this man strong, whom ye s Acts 3:16 2334
I s the heavens opened, and the Acts 7:56 2334
and the eunuch said, S, here is Acts 8:36 2400
thine Holy One to s corruption Acts 13:35 1492
of the Lord, and s how they do Acts 15:36
been there, I must also s Rome Acts 19:21 1492

Moreover ye s and hear, that not ... Acts 19:26 2334
of God, shall s my face no more ... Acts 20:25 3700
they should s his face no more ... Acts 20:38 2334
when I could not s for the glory ... Acts 22:11 1689
s that Just One, and shouldest ... Acts 22:14 1492
S thou tell no man that thou hast ... Acts 23:22
ye s this man, about whom all the ... Acts 25:24 2334
to s you, and to speak with you ... Acts 28:20 1492
and seeing ye shall s, and not ... Acts 28:26 991
they should s with their eyes ... Acts 28:27 1492
For I long to s you, that I may ... Rom 1:11 1492
But I s another law in my members ... Rom 7:23 991
But if we hope for that we s not ... Rom 8:25 991
eyes that they should not s ... Rom 11:8 991
be darkened, that they may not s ... Rom 11:10 991
was not spoken of, they shall s ... Rom 15:21 3700
for I trust to s you in my ... Rom 15:24 2300
For ye s your calling, brethren, ... 1Cor 1:26 991
For if any man s thee which hast ... 1Cor 8:10 1492
For now we s through a glass, ... 1Cor 13:12 991
For I will not s you now by the ... 1Cor 16:7 1492
s that he may be with you without ... 1Cor 16:10 991
s that ye abound in this grace ... 2Cor 8:7
I went up to Jerusalem to s Peter ... Gal 1:18 2477
Ye s how large a letter I have ... Gal 6:11 1492
to make all men s what is the ... Eph 3:9 5461
S then that ye walk circumspectly ... Eph 5:15 991
the wife s that she reverence her ... Eph 5:33 1492
s you, or else be absent, I may ... Phil 1:27 1492
so soon as I shall s how it will ... Phil 2:23 542
when ye s him again, ye may ... Phil 2:28 1492
the more abundantly to s your ... 1Th 2:17 1492
always, desiring greatly to s us ... 1Th 3:6 1492
as we also to s you ... 1Th 3:6
that we might s your face ... 1Th 3:10 1492
S that none render evil for evil ... 1Th 5:15 3708
whom no man hath seen, nor can s ... 1Ti 6:16 1492
Greatly desiring to s thee ... 2Ti 1:4 1492
But now we s not yet all things ... Heb 2:8 3708
But we s Jesus, who was made a ... Heb 2:9 991
So we s that they could not enter ... Heb 3:19 991
for, S, saith he, that thou make ... Heb 8:5 3708
as ye s the day approaching ... Heb 10:25 991
that he should not s death ... Heb 11:5 1492
which no man shall s the Lord ... Heb 12:14 3700
S that ye refuse not him that ... Heb 12:25 991
if he come shortly, I will s you ... Heb 13:23 3700
Ye s then how that by works a man ... Jas 2:24 3708
in whom, though now ye s him not ... 1Pet 1:8 3708
s that ye love one another with a ... 1Pet 1:22
s good days, let him refrain his ... 1Pet 3:10 1492
cannot s afar off, and hath ... 2Pet 1:9 3467
for we shall s him as he is ... 1Jn 3:2 3700
If any man s his brother sin a ... 1Jn 5:16 1492
I trust I shall shortly s thee ... 3Jn 14 1492
and every eye shall s him, and they ... Rev 1:7 3700
I turned to s the voice that ... Rev 1:12 991
with eyesalve, that thou mayest s ... Rev 3:18 991
the four beasts saying, Come and s ... Rev 6:1 991
the second beast say, Come and s ... Rev 6:3 991
the third beast say, Come and s ... Rev 6:5 991
s thou hurt not the oil and the ... Rev 6:6
the fourth beast say, Come and s ... Rev 6:7 991
which neither can s, nor hear, ... Rev 9:20 991
nations shall s their dead bodies ... Rev 11:9 991
walk naked, and they s his shame ... Rev 16:15 991
am no widow, and shall s no sorrow ... Rev 18:7 1492
when they shall s the smoke of ... Rev 18:9 991
he said unto me, S thou do it not ... Rev 19:10 3700
And they shall s his face ... Rev 22:4 3708
he unto me, S thou do it not ... Rev 22:9 3708

SEED

forth grass, the herb yielding s ... Gen 1:11 2233
whose s is in itself, upon the ... Gen 1:11 2233
herb yielding s after his kind, ... Gen 1:12 2233
whose s was in itself, after his ... Gen 1:12 2233
given you every herb bearing s ... Gen 1:29 2233
is the fruit of a tree yielding s ... Gen 1:29 2233
and between thy s and her s ... Gen 3:15 2233
me another s instead of Abel ... Gen 4:25 2233
to keep s alive upon the face of ... Gen 7:3 2233
you, and with your s after you ... Gen 9:9 2233
Unto thy s will I give this land ... Gen 12:7 2233
I give it, and to thy s for ever ... Gen 13:15 2233
I will make thy s as the dust of ... Gen 13:16 2233
then shall thy s also be numbered ... Gen 13:16 2233
to me thou hast given no s ... Gen 15:3 2233
said unto him, So shall thy s be ... Gen 15:5 2233
Know of a surety that thy s shall ... Gen 15:13 2233
Unto thy s have I given this land ... Gen 15:18 2233
I will multiply thy s exceedingly ... Gen 16:10 2233
thy s after thee in their ... Gen 17:7 2233
unto thee, and to thy s after thee ... Gen 17:7 2233
to thy s after thee, the land ... Gen 17:8 2233
thy s after thee in their ... Gen 17:9 2233
me and you and thy s after thee ... Gen 17:10 2233
stranger, which is not of thy s ... Gen 17:12 2233
covenant, and with his s after him ... Gen 17:19 2233
we may preserve s of our father ... Gen 19:32 2233
we may preserve s of our father ... Gen 19:34 2233
in Isaac shall thy s be called ... Gen 21:12 2233
a nation, because he is thy s ... Gen 21:13 2233
thy s as the stars of the heaven ... Gen 22:17 2233
thy s shall possess the gate of ... Gen 22:17 2233
in thy s shall all the nations of ... Gen 22:18 2233
Unto thy s will I give this land ... Gen 24:7 2233
let thy s possess the gate of ... Gen 24:60 2233
for unto thee, and unto thy s ... Gen 26:3 2233
I will make thy s to multiply as ... Gen 26:4 2233
will give unto thy s all these ... Gen 26:4 2233
in thy s shall all the nations of ... Gen 26:4 2233
multiply thy s for my servant ... Gen 26:24 2233
to thee, and to thy s with thee ... Gen 28:4 2233
thee will I give it, and to thy s ... Gen 28:13 2233
thy s shall be as the dust of the ... Gen 28:14 2233
in thy s shall all the families ... Gen 28:14 2233
make thy s as the sand of the sea ... Gen 32:12 2233
to thy s after thee will I give ... Gen 35:12 2233
raise up s to thy brother ... Gen 38:8 2233
knew that the s should not be his ... Gen 38:9 2233
he should give s to his brother ... Gen 38:9 2233
Jacob, and all his s with him ... Gen 46:6 2233
all his s brought he with him ... Gen 46:7 2233
and give us s, that we may live, ... Gen 47:19 2233
lo, here is s for you, and ye ... Gen 47:23 2233
for s of the field, and for your ... Gen 47:24 2233
will give this land to thy s ... Gen 48:4 2233
lo, God hath shewed me also thy s ... Gen 48:11 2233
his s shall become a multitude of ... Gen 48:19 2233
and it was like coriander s ... Ex 16:31 2233
ever unto him and his s after him ... Ex 28:43 2233
to his s throughout their ... Ex 30:21 2233
I will multiply your s as the ... Ex 32:13 2233
spoken of will I give unto your s ... Ex 32:13 2233
Unto thy s will I give it ... Ex 33:1 2233
any sowing s which is to be sown ... Lev 11:37 2233
if any water be put upon the s ... Lev 11:38 2233
If a woman have conceived s ... Lev 12:2 2233
if any man's s of copulation go ... Lev 15:16 2233
whereon is the s of copulation ... Lev 15:17 2233
shall lie with s of copulation ... Lev 15:18 2233
of him whose s goeth from him, and ... Lev 15:32 2233
thou shalt not let any of thy s ... Lev 18:21 2233
not sow thy field with mingled s ... Lev 19:19
giveth any of his s unto Molech ... Lev 20:2 2233
hath given of his s unto Molech ... Lev 20:3 2233
he giveth of his s unto Molech ... Lev 20:4 2233
he profane his s among his people ... Lev 21:15 2233
Whosoever he be of thy s in their ... Lev 21:17 2233
s of Aaron the priest shall come ... Lev 21:21 2233
all your s among your generations ... Lev 22:3 2233
of the s of Aaron is a leper ... Lev 22:4 2233
or a man whose s goeth from him ... Lev 22:4
and ye shall sow your s in vain ... Lev 26:16 2233
be according to the s thereof ... Lev 27:16 2233
a homer of barley s shall be ... Lev 27:16 2233
whether of the s of the land ... Lev 27:30 2233
be free, and shall conceive s ... Num 5:28 2233
And the manna was as coriander s ... Num 11:7 2233
and his s shall possess it ... Num 14:24 2233
which is not of the s of Aaron ... Num 16:40 2233
unto thee and to thy s with thee ... Num 18:19 2233
it is no place of s, or of figs, ... Num 20:5 2233
his s shall be in many waters, and ... Num 24:7 2233
his s after him, even the ... Num 25:13 2233
them and to their s after them ... Deut 1:8 2233
he chose their s after them ... Deut 4:37 2233
and he chose their s after them ... Deut 10:15 2233
to give unto them and to their s ... Deut 11:9 2233
out, where thou sowedst thy s ... Deut 11:10 2233
tithe all the increase of thy s ... Deut 14:22 2233
of thy s which thou hast sown ... Deut 22:9 2233
carry much s out into the field ... Deut 28:38 2233
a wonder, and upon thy s for ever ... Deut 28:46 2233
and the plagues of thy s, even ... Deut 28:59 2233
heart, and the heart of thy s ... Deut 30:6 2233
that both thou and thy s may live ... Deut 30:19 2233
out of the mouths of their s ... Deut 31:21 2233
saying, I will give it unto thy s ... Deut 34:4 2233
of Canaan, and multiplied his s ... Josh 24:3 2233
of the s which the LORD shall ... Ruth 4:12 2233
The LORD give thee s of this ... 1Sa 2:20 2233
he will take the tenth of your s ... 1Sa 8:15 2233
between my s and thy s for ever ... 1Sa 20:42 2233
wilt not cut off my s after me ... 1Sa 24:21 2233
this day of Saul, and of his s ... 2Sa 4:8 2233
I will set up thy s after thee ... 2Sa 7:12 2233
David, and to his s for evermore ... 2Sa 22:51 2233
upon the head of his s for ever ... 1Kin 2:33 2233
but upon David, and upon his s ... 1Kin 2:33 2233
he was of the king's s in Edom ... 1Kin 11:14 2233
for this afflict the s of David ... 1Kin 11:39 2233
would contain two measures of s ... 1Kin 18:32 2233
unto thee, and unto thy s for ever ... 2Kin 5:27 2233
and destroyed all the s royal ... 2Kin 11:1 2233
LORD rejected all the s of Israel ... 2Kin 17:20 2233
son of Elishama, of the s royal ... 2Kin 25:25 2233
O ye s of Israel his servant, ye ... 1Chr 16:13 2233
I will raise up thy s after thee ... 1Chr 17:11 2233
gavest it to the s of Abraham thy ... 2Chr 20:7 2233
destroyed all the s royal of the ... 2Chr 22:10 2233
their father's house, and their s ... Ezr 2:59 2233
so that the holy s have mingled ... Ezr 9:2 2233
their father's house, nor their s ... Neh 7:61 2233
the s of Israel separated ... Neh 9:2 2233
to give it, I say, to his s ... Neh 9:8 2233
Mordecai be of the s of the Jews ... Est 6:13 2233
took upon them, and upon their s ... Est 9:27 2233
of them perish from their s ... Est 9:28 2233
for themselves and for their s ... Est 9:31 2233
and speaking peace to all his s ... Est 10:3 2233
also that thy s shall be great ... Job 5:25 2233
Their s is established in their ... Job 21:8 2233
that he will bring home thy s ... Job 39:12 2233
David, and to his s for evermore ... Ps 18:50 2233
their s from among the children ... Ps 21:10 2233
all ye the s of Jacob, glorify ... Ps 22:23 2233
fear him, all ye the s of Israel ... Ps 22:23 2233
A s shall serve him ... Ps 22:30 2233
his s shall inherit the earth ... Ps 25:13 2233
forsaken, nor his s begging bread ... Ps 37:25 2233
and his s is blessed ... Ps 37:26 2233
but the s of the wicked shall be ... Ps 37:28 2233
The s also of his servants shall ... Ps 69:36 2233
Thy s will I establish for ever, ... Ps 89:4 2233
His s also will I make to endure ... Ps 89:29 2233
His s shall endure for ever, and ... Ps 89:36 2233
their s shall be established ... Ps 102:28 2233
O ye s of Abraham his servant, ye ... Ps 105:6 2233
To overthrow their s also among ... Ps 106:27 2233
His s shall be mighty upon earth ... Ps 112:2 2233
and weepeth, bearing precious s ... Ps 126:6 2233
but the s of the righteous shall ... Prov 11:21 2233
In the morning sow thy s, and in ... Eccl 11:6 2233
a s of evildoers, children that ... Is 1:4 2233
the s of an homer shall yield an ... Is 5:10 2233
so the holy s shall be the ... Is 6:13 2233
the s of evildoers shall never be ... Is 14:20 2233
shalt thou make thy s to flourish ... Is 17:11 2233
And by great waters the s of Sihor ... Is 23:3 2233
shall he give the rain of thy s ... Is 30:23 2233
the s of Abraham my friend ... Is 41:8 2233
I will bring thy s from the east ... Is 43:5 2233
I will pour my spirit upon thy s ... Is 44:3 2233
I said not unto the s of Jacob ... Is 45:19 2233
all the s of Israel be justified ... Is 45:25 2233
Thy s also had been as the sand, ... Is 48:19 2233
for sin, he shall see his s ... Is 53:10 2233
thy s shall inherit the Gentiles, ... Is 54:3 2233
that it may give s to the sower ... Is 55:10 2233
the s of the adulterer and the ... Is 57:3 2233
transgression, a s of falsehood, ... Is 57:4 2233
nor out of the mouth of thy s ... Is 59:21 2233
out of the mouth of thy seed's s ... Is 59:21 2233
their s shall be known among the ... Is 61:9 2233
that they are the s which the ... Is 61:9 2233
will bring forth a s out of Jacob ... Is 65:9 2233
for they are the s of the blessed ... Is 65:23 2233
saith the LORD, so shall your s ... Is 66:22 2233
a noble vine, wholly a right s ... Jer 2:21 2233
even the whole s of Ephraim ... Jer 7:15 2233
are they cast out, he and his s ... Jer 22:28 2233
for no man of his s shall prosper ... Jer 22:30 2233
which led the s of the house of ... Jer 23:8 2233
Shemaiah the Nehelamite, and his s ... Jer 29:32 2233
thy s from the land of their ... Jer 30:10 2233
house of Judah with the s of man ... Jer 31:27 2233
of man, and with the s of beast ... Jer 31:27 2233
then the s of Israel also shall ... Jer 31:36 2233
the s of Israel for all that they ... Jer 31:37 2233
the s of David my servant ... Jer 33:22 2233
will I cast away the s of Jacob ... Jer 33:26 2233
s to be rulers over the s of ... Jer 33:26 2233
be rulers over the s of Abraham ... Jer 33:26 2233
shall ye build house, nor sow s ... Jer 35:7 2233
we vineyard, nor field, nor s ... Jer 35:9 2233
And I will punish him and his s ... Jer 36:31 2233
son of Elishama, of the s royal ... Jer 41:1 2233
thy s from the land of their ... Jer 46:27 2233
his s is spoiled, and his brethren ... Jer 49:10 2233
He took also of the s of the land ... Eze 17:5 2233
And hath taken of the king's s ... Eze 17:13 2233
unto the s of the house of Jacob ... Eze 20:5 2233
Levites that be of the s of Zadok ... Eze 43:19 2233
of the s of the house of Israel ... Eze 44:22 2233
of Israel, and of the king's s ... Dan 1:3 2233
themselves with the s of men ... Dan 2:43 2234
of the s of the Medes, which was ... Dan 9:1 2233
The s is rotten under their clods ... Joel 1:17 6507
of grapes him that soweth s ... Amos 9:13 2233
Is the s yet in the barn ... Hag 2:19 2233
For the s shall be prosperous ... Zec 8:12 2233
Behold, I will corrupt your s ... Mal 2:3 2233
That he might seek a godly s ... Mal 2:15 2233
which received s by the way side ... Mt 13:19 4687
received the s into stony places ... Mt 13:20 4687
He also that received s among the ... Mt 13:22 4687
But he that received s into the ... Mt 13:23 4687
which sowed good s in his field ... Mt 13:24 4690
not thou sow good s in thy field ... Mt 13:27 4690
is like to a grain of mustard s ... Mt 13:31
the good s is the Son of man ... Mt 13:37 4690
the good s are the children of ... Mt 13:38 4690
faith as a grain of mustard s ... Mt 17:20
raise up s unto his brother ... Mt 22:24 4690
man should cast s into the ground ... Mk 4:26 4703
the s should spring and grow up, ... Mk 4:27 4703
It is like a grain of mustard s ... Mk 4:31 4690
raise up s unto his brother ... Mk 12:19 4690
took a wife, and dying left no s ... Mk 12:20 4690
and died, neither left he any s ... Mk 12:21 4690
the seven had her, and left no s ... Mk 12:22 4690
to Abraham, and to his s for ever ... Lk 1:55 4690
A sower went out to sow his s ... Lk 8:5 4703
The s is the word of God ... Lk 8:11 4703
It is like a grain of mustard s ... Lk 13:19 4690
had faith as a grain of mustard s ... Lk 17:6
raise up s unto his brother ... Lk 20:28 4690
Christ cometh of the s of David ... Jn 7:42 4690
answered him, We be Abraham's s ... Jn 8:33 4690
I know that ye are Abraham's s ... Jn 8:37 4690
in thy s shall all the kindreds ... Acts 3:25 4690
to his s after him, when as yet ... Acts 7:5 4690
That his s should sojourn in a ... Acts 7:6 4690
Of this man's s hath God ... Acts 13:23 4690
which was made of the s of David ... Rom 1:3 4690
was not to Abraham, or to his s ... Rom 4:13 4690
might be sure to all the s ... Rom 4:16 4690
was spoken, So shall thy s be ... Rom 4:18 4690
because they are the s of Abraham ... Rom 9:7 4690
In Isaac shall thy s be called ... Rom 9:7 4690
the promise are counted for the s ... Rom 9:8 4690
Lord of Sabaoth had left us a s ... Rom 9:29 4690
of the s of Abraham, of the tribe ... Rom 11:1 4690
him, and to every s his own body ... 1Cor 15:38 4690
Now he that ministereth s to the ... 2Cor 9:10 4690
food, and multiply your s sown ... 2Cor 9:10 4703
Are they the s of Abraham ... 2Cor 11:22 4690
his s were the promises made ... Gal 3:16 4690
but as of one, And to thy s ... Gal 3:16 4690
till the s should come to whom ... Gal 3:19 4690

Christ's, then are ye Abraham's *s*	Gal 3:29	4690
that Jesus Christ of the *s* of	2Ti 2:8	4690
he took on him the *s* of Abraham	Heb 2:16	4690
received strength to conceive *s*	Heb 11:11	4690
in Isaac shall thy *s* be called	Heb 11:18	4690
born again, not of corruptible *s*	1Pet 1:23	4701
for his *s* remaineth in him	1Jn 3:9	4690
war with the remnant of her *s*	Rev 12:17	4690

SEED'S

out of the mouth of thy *s* seed	Is 59:21	2233

SEEDS

sow thy vineyard with divers *s*	Deut 22:9	
some *s* fell by the way side, and	Mt 13:4	
indeed is the least of all *s*	Mt 13:32	4690
all the *s* that be in the earth	Mk 4:31	4690
He saith not, And to *s*, as of many	Gal 3:16	4690

SEEDTIME

While the earth remaineth, *s*	Gen 8:22	2233

SEEING

s I go childless, and the steward	Gen 15:2	
S that Abraham shall surely	Gen 18:18	
Lot *s* them rose up to meet them	Gen 19:1	7200
s thou hast not withheld thy son,	Gen 22:12	7200
s the LORD hath prospered my way	Gen 24:56	
s ye hate me, and have sent me	Gen 26:27	7200
Esau *s* that the daughters of	Gen 28:8	7200
s that his life is bound up in	Gen 44:30	
the dumb, or deaf, or the *s*	Ex 4:11	6493
s he hath dealt deceitfully with	Ex 21:8	
hurt, or driven away, no man *s* it	Ex 22:10	7200
s ye were strangers in the land	Ex 23:9	3588
s it is most holy, and God hath	Lev 10:17	3588
s all the people were in	Num 15:26	3588
s all the congregation are holy,	Num 16:3	3588
s him not, and cast it upon him,	Num 35:23	7200
s I am a great people, forasmuch	Josh 17:14	
s ye rebel to day against the	Josh 22:18	
after my name, *s* it is secret	Judg 13:18	
s I have a Levite to my priest	Judg 17:13	3588
s that this man is come into mine	Judg 19:23	310
s we have sworn by the LORD that	Judg 21:7	7200
s the women are destroyed out of	Judg 21:16	3588
s the LORD hath testified against	Ruth 1:21	
of me, *s* I am a stranger	Ruth 2:10	
s I have rejected him from	1Sa 16:1	
s he hath defied the armies of	1Sa 17:36	3588
s that I am a poor man, and	1Sa 18:23	
s he is the anointed of the LORD	1Sa 24:6	
s the LORD hath withholden thee	1Sa 25:26	
s the LORD is departed from thee,	1Sa 28:16	
concerning Amnon, *s* he was dead	2Sa 13:39	
s I go whither I may, return thou	2Sa 15:20	
s that thou hast no tidings ready	2Sa 18:22	
s the speech of all Israel is	2Sa 19:11	
this day, mine eyes even *s* it	1Kin 1:48	7200
Solomon *s* the young man that he	1Kin 11:28	7200
s your master's sons are with you	2Kin 10:2	
s there is no wrong in mine hands	1Chr 12:17	
s the heaven and heaven of heavens	2Chr 2:6	
s that thou our God hast punished	Ezr 9:13	3588
sad, *s* thou art not sick	Neh 2:2	
S his days are determined, the	Job 14:5	518
s the root of the matter is found	Job 19:28	
s he judgeth those that are high	Job 21:22	
s in your answers there remaineth	Job 21:34	
s times are not hidden from the	Job 24:1	7200
S it is hid from the eyes of all	Job 28:21	
him, *s* he delighted in him	Ps 22:8	
S thou hatest instruction, and	Ps 50:17	
s he dwelleth securely by thee	Prov 3:29	[illegible]
wisdom, *s* he hath no heart to it	Prov 17:16	
The hearing ear, and the *s* eye	Prov 20:12	7200
the eye is not satisfied with *s*	Eccl 1:8	7200
s that which now is in the days	Eccl 2:16	
S there be many things that	Eccl 6:11	3588
I was dismayed at the *s* of it	Is 21:3	7200
and shutteth his eyes from *s* evil	Is 33:15	7200
S many things, but thou observest	Is 42:20	7200
s I have lost my children, and am	Is 49:21	
s she hath wrought lewdness with	Jer 11:15	
s the LORD hath given it a charge	Jer 47:7	
s thou doest all these things,	Eze 16:30	
S he despised the oath by	Eze 17:18	
S then that I will cut off from	Eze 21:4	3282
s vanity, and divining lies unto	Eze 22:28	
s thou couldest reveal this secret	Dan 2:47	1768
s thou hast forgotten the law of	Hos 4:6	
s the multitudes, he went up into	Mt 5:1	1492
Jesus *s* their faith said unto the	Mt 9:2	1492
because they *s* see not	Mt 13:13	991
s ye shall see, and shall not	Mt 13:14	991
That *s* they may see, and not	Mk 4:12	991
s a fig tree afar off having	Mk 11:13	1492
shall this be, *s* I know not a man	Lk 1:34	1893
who *s* Jesus fell on his face, and	Lk 5:12	1492
that *s* they might not see, and	Lk 8:10	991
fear God, *s* thou art in the same	Lk 23:40	3754
s that thou doest these things	Jn 2:18	
therefore, and washed, and came *s*	Jn 9:7	991
Peter *s* him saith to Jesus, Lord,	Jn 21:21	1492
s it is but the third hour of the	Acts 2:15	1063
He *s* this before spake of the	Acts 2:31	4275
Who *s* Peter and John about to go	Acts 3:3	1492
s one of them suffer wrong, he	Acts 7:24	1492
s the miracles which he did	Acts 8:6	991
hearing a voice, but *s* no man	Acts 9:7	2334
not *s* the sun for a season	Acts 13:11	991
but *s* ye put it from you, and	Acts 13:46	1894
s the prison doors open, he drew	Acts 16:27	1492
s that he is Lord of heaven and	Acts 17:24	
s he giveth to all life, and	Acts 17:25	
S then that these things cannot	Acts 19:36	
S that by thee we enjoy great	Acts 24:2	
s ye shall see, and not perceive	Acts 28:26	991
S it is one God, which shall	Rom 3:30	1897
s he understandeth not what thou	1Cor 14:16	1894
S then that we have such hope, we	2Cor 3:12	
s we have this ministry, as we	2Cor 4:1	
S that many glory after the flesh	2Cor 11:18	1893
gladly, *s* ye yourselves are wise	2Cor 11:19	
s that ye have put off the old	Col 3:9	
S it is a righteous thing with	2Th 1:6	1512
S therefore it remaineth that	Heb 4:6	1893
S then that we have a great high	Heb 4:14	
uttered, *s* ye are dull of hearing	Heb 5:11	1893
s they crucify to themselves the	Heb 6:6	
by him, *s* he ever liveth to make	Heb 7:25	
s that there are priests that	Heb 8:4	
as *s* him who is invisible	Heb 11:27	3708
Wherefore *s* we also are compassed	Heb 12:1	
S ye have purified your souls in	1Pet 1:22	
man dwelling among them, in *s*	2Pet 2:8	990
S then that all these things	2Pet 3:11	
s that ye look for such things,	2Pet 3:14	
s ye know these things before,	2Pet 3:17	

SEEK

And he said, I *s* my brethren	Gen 37:16	1245
that he may *s* occasion against us	Gen 43:18	1556
shall not *s* for yellow hair	Lev 13:36	1239
neither *s* after wizards, to be	Lev 19:31	1245
that ye *s* not after your own	Num 15:39	8446
and *s* ye the priesthood also	Num 16:10	1245
to *s* for enchantments, but he set	Num 24:1	7125
thou shalt *s* the LORD thy God	Deut 4:29	1245
if thou *s* him with all thy heart	Deut 4:29	1875
unto his habitation shall ye *s*	Deut 12:5	1875
thee until thy brother *s* after it	Deut 22:2	1875
Thou shalt not *s* their peace nor	Deut 23:6	1875
shall I not *s* rest for thee, that	Ruth 3:1	1245
thee, and arise, go *s* the asses	1Sa 9:3	1245
which thou wentest to *s* are found	1Sa 10:2	1245
And he said, To *s* the asses	1Sa 10:14	1245
to *s* out a man, who is a cunning	1Sa 16:16	1245
Saul was come out to *s* his life	1Sa 23:15	1245
also and his men went to *s* him	1Sa 23:25	1245
of all Israel, and went to *s* David	1Sa 24:2	1245
they that *s* evil to my lord, be	1Sa 25:26	1245
to pursue thee, and to *s* thy soul	1Sa 25:29	1245
to *s* David in the wilderness of	1Sa 26:2	1245
of Israel is come out to *s* a flea	1Sa 26:20	1245
to *s* me any more in any coast of	1Sa 27:1	1245
S me a woman that hath a familiar	1Sa 28:7	1245
Philistines came up to *s* David	2Sa 5:17	1245
Gath to Achish to *s* his servants	1Kin 2:40	1245
my lord hath not sent to *s* thee	1Kin 18:10	1245
they *s* my life, to take it away	1Kin 19:10	1245
they *s* my life, to take it away	1Kin 19:14	1245
go, we pray thee, and *s* thy master	2Kin 2:16	1245
bring you to the man whom ye *s*	2Kin 6:19	1245
to *s* pasture for their flocks	1Chr 4:39	1245
Philistines went up to *s* David	1Chr 14:8	1245
of them rejoice that *s* the LORD	1Chr 16:10	1245
S the LORD and his strength	1Chr 16:11	1875
s his face continually	1Chr 16:11	1245
your soul to *s* the LORD your God	1Chr 22:19	1875
s for all the commandments of the	1Chr 28:8	1875
if thou *s* him, he will be found	1Chr 28:9	1875
s my face, and turn from their	2Chr 7:14	1245
such as set their hearts to *s* the	2Chr 11:16	1245
not his heart to *s* the LORD	2Chr 12:14	1875
commanded Judah to *s* the LORD God	2Chr 14:4	1875
and if ye *s* him, he will be found	2Chr 15:2	1875
s the LORD God of their fathers	2Chr 15:12	1875
That whosoever would not *s* the	2Chr 15:13	1875
prepared thine heart to *s* God	2Chr 19:3	1875
and set himself to *s* the LORD	2Chr 20:3	1875
of Judah they came to *s* the LORD	2Chr 20:4	1245
That prepareth his heart to *s* God	2Chr 30:19	1875
to *s* his God, he did it with all	2Chr 31:21	1875
he began to *s* after the God of	2Chr 34:3	1875
for we *s* your God, as ye do	Ezr 4:2	1875
to *s* the LORD God of Israel, did	Ezr 6:21	1875
heart to *s* the law of the LORD	Ezr 7:10	1875
to *s* of him a right way for us,	Ezr 8:21	1245
upon all them for good that *s* him	Ezr 8:22	1245
nor *s* their peace or their wealth	Ezr 9:12	1875
that there was come a man to *s*	Neh 2:10	1245
I would *s* unto God, and unto God	Job 5:8	1875
thou shalt *s* me in the morning,	Job 7:21	7836
thou wouldest *s* unto God betimes	Job 8:5	7836
shall *s* to please the poor	Job 20:10	1245
love vanity, and *s* after leasing	Ps 4:2	1245
not forsaken them that *s* thee	Ps 9:10	1875
countenance, will not *s* after God	Ps 10:4	1875
s out his wickedness till thou	Ps 10:15	1875
any that did understand, and *s* God	Ps 14:2	1875
shall praise the LORD that *s* him	Ps 22:26	1875
the generation of them that *s* him	Ps 24:6	1875
him, that *s* thy face, O Jacob	Ps 24:6	1245
of the LORD, that will I *s* after	Ps 27:4	1245
When thou saidst, *S* ye my face	Ps 27:8	1245
thee, Thy face, LORD, will I *s*	Ps 27:8	1245
but they that *s* the LORD shall	Ps 34:10	1875
s peace, and pursue it	Ps 34:14	1245
put to shame that *s* after my soul	Ps 35:4	1245
They also that *s* after my life	Ps 38:12	1245
they that *s* my hurt speak	Ps 38:12	1875
confounded together that *s* after	Ps 40:14	1245
Let all those that *s* thee rejoice	Ps 40:16	1245
did understand, that did *s* God	Ps 53:2	1875
oppressors *s* after my soul	Ps 54:3	1245
early will I *s* thee	Ps 63:1	7836
But those that *s* my soul, to	Ps 63:9	1245
let not those that *s* thee be	Ps 69:6	1245
your heart shall live that *s* God	Ps 69:32	1875
confounded that *s* after my soul	Ps 70:2	1245
Let all those that *s* thee rejoice	Ps 70:4	1245
and dishonour that *s* my hurt	Ps 71:13	1245
unto shame, that *s* my hurt	Ps 71:24	1245
that they may *s* thy name, O LORD	Ps 83:16	1245
prey, and *s* their meat from God	Ps 104:21	1245
of them rejoice that *s* the LORD	Ps 105:3	1245
S the LORD, and his strength	Ps 105:4	1875
s his face evermore	Ps 105:4	1245
let them *s* their bread also out	Ps 109:10	1875
that *s* him with the whole heart	Ps 119:2	1875
for I *s* thy precepts	Ps 119:45	1875
for they *s* not thy statutes	Ps 119:155	1875
s thy servant	Ps 119:176	1245
LORD our God I will *s* thy good	Ps 122:9	1245
they shall *s* me early, but they	Prov 1:28	7836
thee, diligently to *s* thy face	Prov 7:15	7836
those that *s* me early shall find	Prov 8:17	7836
to and fro of them that *s* death	Prov 21:6	1245
they that go to *s* mixed wine	Prov 23:30	2713
I will *s* it yet again	Prov 23:35	1245
but they that *s* the LORD	Prov 28:5	1245
but the just *s* his soul	Prov 29:10	1245
Many *s* the ruler's favour	Prov 29:26	1245
And I gave my heart to *s* and search	Eccl 1:13	1875
to *s* out wisdom, and the reason of	Eccl 7:25	1245
though a man labour to *s* it out	Eccl 8:17	1245
I will *s* him whom my soul loveth	Song 3:2	1245
that we may *s* him with thee	Song 6:1	1245
s judgment, relieve the oppressed	Is 1:17	1875
S unto them that have familiar	Is 8:19	1875
not a people *s* unto their God	Is 8:19	1875
neither do they *s* the LORD of	Is 9:13	1875
to it shall the Gentiles *s*	Is 11:10	1875
they shall *s* to the idols, and to	Is 19:3	1875
within me will I *s* thee early	Is 26:9	7836
Woe unto them that *s* deep to hide	Is 29:15	
One of Israel, neither *s* the LORD	Is 31:1	1875
S ye out of the book of the LORD,	Is 34:16	1875
Thou shalt *s* them, and shalt not	Is 41:12	1245
When the poor and needy *s* water	Is 41:17	1245
seed of Jacob, *S* ye me in vain	Is 45:19	1245
righteousness, ye that *s* the LORD	Is 51:1	1245
S ye the LORD while he may be	Is 55:6	1875
Yet they *s* me daily, and delight	Is 58:2	1875
all they that *s* her will not	Jer 2:24	1245
trimmest thou thy way to *s* love	Jer 2:33	1245
thee, they will *s* thy life	Jer 4:30	1245
s in the broad places thereof, if	Jer 5:1	1245
that *s* thy life, saying, Prophesy	Jer 11:21	1245
hands of them that *s* their lives	Jer 19:7	1245
they that *s* their lives, shall	Jer 19:9	1245
hand of those that *s* their life	Jer 21:7	1245
the hand of them that *s* thy life	Jer 22:25	1245
s the peace of the city whither I	Jer 29:7	1875
And ye shall *s* me, and find me,	Jer 29:13	1245
they *s* thee not	Jer 30:14	1875
hand of them that *s* their life	Jer 34:20	1245
hand of them that *s* their life	Jer 34:21	1245
hand of these men that *s* thy life	Jer 38:16	1245
the hand of them that *s* his life	Jer 44:30	1245
s them not	Jer 45:5	1245
hand of those that *s* their lives	Jer 46:26	1245
and before them that *s* their life	Jer 49:37	1245
shall go, and *s* the LORD their God	Jer 50:4	1245
All her people sigh, they *s* bread	Lam 1:11	1245
and they shall *s* peace, and there	Eze 7:25	1245
then shall they *s* a vision of the	Eze 7:26	1245
none did search or *s* after them	Eze 34:6	1245
search my sheep, and *s* them out	Eze 34:11	1239
so will I *s* out my sheep, and will	Eze 34:12	1239
I will *s* that which was lost, and	Eze 34:16	1245
to *s* by prayer and supplications,	Dan 9:3	1245
and she shall *s* them, but shall	Hos 2:7	1245
s the LORD their God, and David	Hos 3:5	1245
and with their herds to *s* the LORD	Hos 5:6	1245
their offence, and *s* my face	Hos 5:15	1245
affliction they will *s* me early	Hos 5:15	7836
their God, nor *s* him for all this	Hos 7:10	1245
for it is time to *s* the LORD	Hos 10:12	1875
S ye me, and ye shall live	Amos 5:4	1875
But *s* not Beth-el, nor enter into	Amos 5:5	1875
S the LORD, and ye shall live	Amos 5:6	1875
S him that maketh the seven stars	Amos 5:8	
S good, and not evil, that ye may	Amos 5:14	1875
fro to *s* the word of the LORD, and	Amos 8:12	1245
whence shall I *s* comforters for	Nah 3:7	1245
thou also shalt *s* strength	Nah 3:11	1245
S ye the LORD, all ye meek of the	Zeph 2:3	1245
s righteousness, *s* meekness	Zeph 2:3	1245
LORD, and to *s* the LORD of hosts	Zec 8:21	1245
strong nations shall come to *s*	Zec 8:22	1245
neither shall *s* the young one	Zec 11:16	1245
that I will *s* to destroy all the	Zec 12:9	1245
they should *s* the law at his	Mal 2:7	1245
That he might *s* a godly seed	Mal 2:15	1245
and the Lord, whom ye *s*, shall	Mal 3:1	1245
for Herod will *s* the young child	Mt 2:13	2212
these things do the Gentiles *s*	Mt 6:32	1934
But *s* ye first the kingdom of God	Mt 6:33	2212
s, and ye shall find	Mt 7:7	2212
for I know that ye *s* Jesus	Mt 28:5	2212
said unto him, All men *s* for thee	Mk 1:37	2212
thy brethren without *s* for thee	Mk 3:32	2212
this generation *s* after a sign	Mk 8:12	1934
Ye *s* Jesus of Nazareth, which was	Mk 16:6	2212
s, and ye shall find	Lk 11:9	2212
they *s* a sign	Lk 11:29	1934
s not ye what ye shall eat, or	Lk 12:29	2212
the nations of the world *s* after	Lk 12:30	1934
But rather *s* ye the kingdom of	Lk 12:31	2212
will *s* to enter in, and shall not	Lk 13:24	2212
s diligently till she find it	Lk 15:8	2212
Whosoever shall *s* to save his	Lk 17:33	2212

For the Son of man is come to s ... Lk 19:10 2212
Why s ye the living among the ... Lk 24:5 2212
and saith unto them, What s ye ... Jn 1:38 2212
because I s not mine own will, ... Jn 5:30 2212
s not the honour that cometh from ... Jn 5:44 2212
verily, I say unto you, Ye s me ... Jn 6:26 2212
not this he, whom they s to kill ... Jn 7:25 2212
Ye shall s me, and shall not find ... Jn 7:34 2212
this that he said, Ye shall s me ... Jn 7:36 2212
I go my way, and ye shall s me ... Jn 8:21 2212
but ye s to kill me, because my ... Jn 8:37 2212
But now ye s to kill me, a man ... Jn 8:40 2212
And I s not mine own glory ... Jn 8:50 2212
Ye shall s me ... Jn 13:33 2212
and said unto them, Whom s ye ... Jn 18:4 2212
asked he them again, Whom s ye ... Jn 18:7 2212
if therefore ye s me, let these ... Jn 18:8 2212
him, Behold, three men s thee ... Acts 10:19 2212
said, Behold, I am he whom ye s ... Acts 10:21 2212
Barnabas to Tarsus, for to s Saul ... Acts 11:25 327
of men might s after the Lord ... Acts 15:17 1567
That they should s the Lord ... Acts 17:27 2212
in well doing s for glory ... Rom 2:7 2212
am left alone, and they s my life ... Rom 11:3 2212
the Greeks s after wisdom ... 1Cor 1:22 2212
s not to be loosed ... 1Cor 7:27 2212
s not a wife ... 1Cor 7:27 2212
Let no man s his own, but every ... 1Cor 10:24 2212
s that ye may excel to the ... 1Cor 14:12 2212
for I s not yours, but you ... 2Cor 12:14 2212
Since ye s a proof of Christ ... 2Cor 13:3 2212
or do I s to please men ... Gal 1:10 2212
while we s to be justified by ... Gal 2:17 2212
For all s their own, not the ... Phil 2:21 2212
s those things which are above, ... Col 3:1 2212
of them that diligently s him ... Heb 11:6 1567
plainly that they s a country ... Heb 11:14 1934
city, but we s one to come ... Heb 13:14 1934
let him s peace, and ensue it ... 1Pet 3:11 2212
in those days shall men s death ... Rev 9:6 2212

SEEKEST

asked him, saying, What s thou ... Gen 37:15 1245
shew thee the man whom thou s ... Judg 4:22 1245
the man whom thou s is as if all ... 2Sa 17:3 1245
thou s to destroy a city and a ... 2Sa 20:19 1245
thou s to go to thine own country ... 1Kin 11:22 1245
If thou s her as silver, and ... Prov 2:4 1245
s thou great things for thyself ... Jer 45:5 1245
yet no man said, What s thou ... Jn 4:27 2212
whom s thou ... Jn 20:15 2212

SEEKETH

Saul my father s to kill thee ... 1Sa 19:2 1245
thy father, that he s my life ... 1Sa 20:1 1245
for he that s my life s thy ... 1Sa 22:23 1245
that s my life s thy life ... 1Sa 22:23 1245
that Saul s to come to Keilah ... 1Sa 23:10 1245
saying, Behold, David s thy hurt ... 1Sa 24:9 1245
forth of my bowels, s my life ... 2Sa 16:11 1245
and see how this man s mischief ... 1Kin 20:7 1245
see how he s a quarrel against me ... 2Kin 5:7 579
From thence she s the prey ... Job 39:29 2658
the righteous, and s to slay him ... Ps 37:32 1245
He that diligently s good ... Prov 11:27 7836
but he that s mischief, it shall ... Prov 11:27 1875
A scorner s wisdom, and findeth it ... Prov 14:6 1245
hath understanding s knowledge ... Prov 15:14 1245
covereth a transgression s love ... Prov 17:9 1245
An evil man s only rebellion ... Prov 17:11 1245
exalteth his gate s destruction ... Prov 17:19 1245
man, having separated himself, s ... Prov 18:1 1245
the ear of the wise s knowledge ... Prov 18:15 1245
She s wool, and flax, and worketh ... Prov 31:13 1875
Which yet my soul s, but I find ... Eccl 7:28 1245
he s unto him a cunning workman ... Is 40:20 1245
judgment, that s the truth ... Jer 5:1 1245
This is Zion, whom no man s after ... Jer 30:17 1875
for this man s not the welfare of ... Jer 38:4 1875
for him, to the soul that s him ... Lam 3:25 1875
punishment of him that s unto him ... Eze 14:10 1875
As a shepherd s out his flock in ... Eze 34:12 1243
and he that s findeth ... Mt 7:8 2212
generation s after a sign ... Mt 12:39 1934
generation s after a sign ... Mt 16:4 1934
s that which is gone astray ... Mt 18:12 2212
and he that s findeth ... Lk 11:10 2212
for the Father s such to worship ... Jn 4:23 2212
he himself s to be known openly ... Jn 7:4 2212
of himself s his own glory ... Jn 7:18 2212
but he that s his glory that sent ... Jn 7:18 2212
there is one that s and judgeth ... Jn 8:50 2212
there is none that s after God ... Rom 3:11 1567
not obtained that which he s for ... Rom 11:7 1934
s not her own, is not easily ... 1Cor 13:5 2212

SEEKING

s the wealth of his people, and ... Est 10:3 1875
and s judgment, and hasting ... Is 16:5 1875
places, s rest, and findeth none ... Mt 12:43 2212
a merchant man, s goodly pearls ... Mt 13:45 2212
s of him a sign from heaven, ... Mk 8:11 2212
back again to Jerusalem, s him ... Lk 2:45 2212
through dry places, s rest ... Lk 11:24 2212
s to catch something out of his ... Lk 11:54 2212
I come s fruit on this fig tree ... Lk 13:7 2212
and came to Capernaum, s for Jesus ... Jn 6:24 2212
s to turn away the deputy from ... Acts 13:8 2212
he went about s some to lead him ... Acts 13:11 2212
not s mine own profit, but the ... 1Cor 10:33 2212
about, s whom he may devour ... 1Pet 5:8 2212

SEEM

I shall s to him as a deceiver ... Gen 27:12
It shall not s hard unto thee, ... Deut 15:18 7185
brother should s vile unto thee ... Deut 25:3 7034
if it s evil unto you to serve ... Josh 24:15
him as it shall s good unto thee ... 1Sa 24:4
him what shall s good unto thee ... 2Sa 19:37
that which shall s good unto thee ... 2Sa 19:38
if it s good to thee, I will give ... 1Kin 21:2
If it s good unto you, and that it ... 1Chr 13:2
if it s good to the king, let ... Ezr 5:17
whatsoever shall s good to thee ... Ezr 7:18 3191
the trouble s little before thee ... Neh 9:32 4591
If it s good unto the king, let ... Est 5:4
the thing s right before the king ... Est 8:5
If it s good unto thee to come ... Jer 40:4 5869
but if it s ill unto thee to come ... Jer 40:4 5869
they shall s like torches, they ... Nah 2:4 4758
But if any man s to be ... 1Cor 11:16 1380
which s to be more feeble, are ... 1Cor 12:22 1380
That I may not s as if I would ... 2Cor 10:9 1380
any of you should s to come short ... Heb 4:1 1380
man among you s to be religious ... Jas 1:26 1380

SEEMED

But he s as one that mocked unto ... Gen 19:14
they s unto him but a few days, ... Gen 29:20
Hebron all that s good to Israel ... 2Sa 3:19 5869
that s good to the whole house of ... 2Sa 3:19 5869
the sun, and it s great unto me ... Eccl 9:13
as s good to the potter to make ... Jer 18:4 5869
it unto whom it s meet unto me ... Jer 27:5 5869
for so it s good in thy sight ... Mt 11:26
It s good to me also, having had ... Lk 1:3 1380
for so it s good in thy sight ... Lk 10:21
their words s to them as idle ... Lk 24:11 5316
It s good unto us, being ... Acts 15:25 1380
For it s good to the Holy Ghost, ... Acts 15:28 1380
But of these who s to be somewhat ... Gal 2:6 1380
for they who s to be somewhat in ... Gal 2:6 1380
who s to be pillars, perceived ... Gal 2:9 1380

SEEMETH

It s to me there is as it were a ... Lev 14:35 7200
S it but a small thing unto you, ... Num 16:9
as it s good and right unto thee ... Josh 9:25 5869
us whatsoever s good unto thee ... Judg 10:15 5869
do with them what s good unto you ... Judg 19:24 5869
unto her, Do what s thee good ... 1Sa 1:23 5869
let him do what s him good ... 1Sa 3:18 5869
with us all that s good unto you ... 1Sa 11:10 5869
Do whatsoever s good unto thee ... 1Sa 14:36 5869
Saul, Do what s good unto thee ... 1Sa 14:40 5869
S it to you a light thing to be ... 1Sa 18:23 5869
the LORD do that which s him good ... 2Sa 10:12 5869
him do to me as s good unto him ... 2Sa 15:26 5869
What s you best I will do ... 2Sa 18:4 5869
and offer up what s good unto him ... 2Sa 24:22 5869
do with them as it s good to thee ... Est 3:11 5869
is a way which s right unto a man ... Prov 14:12 6440
is a way that s right unto a man ... Prov 16:25 6440
is first in his own cause s just ... Prov 18:17
do with me as s good and meet unto ... Jer 26:14 5869
whither it s good and convenient ... Jer 40:4 5869
or go wheresoever it s convenient ... Jer 40:5 5869
S it a small thing unto you to ... Eze 34:18 5869
even that which he s to have ... Lk 8:18 1380
He s to be a setter forth of ... Acts 17:18 1380
For it s to me unreasonable to ... Acts 25:27 1380
If any man among you s to be wise ... 1Cor 3:18 1380
for the present s to be joyous ... Heb 12:11 1380

SEEMLY

Delight is not s for a fool ... Prov 19:10 5000
so honour is not s for a fool ... Prov 26:1 5000

SEEN

for thee have I s righteous ... Gen 7:1 7200
were the tops of the mountains s ... Gen 8:5 7200
the bow shall be s in the cloud ... Gen 9:14 7200
mount of the LORD it shall be s ... Gen 22:14 7200
for I have s all that Laban doeth ... Gen 31:12 7200
God hath s mine affliction and the ... Gen 31:42 7200
for I have s God face to face, and ... Gen 32:30 7200
for therefore I have s thy face ... Gen 33:10 7200
as though I had s the face of God ... Gen 33:10 7200
Egypt, and of all that ye have s ... Gen 45:13 7200
me die, since I have s thy face ... Gen 46:30 7200
I have surely s the affliction of ... Ex 3:7 7200
I have also s the oppression ... Ex 3:9 7200
s that which is done to you in ... Ex 3:16
nor thy fathers' fathers have s ... Ex 10:6 7200
no leavened bread be s with thee ... Ex 13:7 7200
s with thee in all thy quarters ... Ex 13:7 7200
Egyptians whom ye have s to day ... Ex 14:13 7200
Ye have s what I did unto the ... Ex 19:4 7200
Ye have s that I have talked with ... Ex 20:22 7200
I have s this people, and, behold, ... Ex 32:9 7200
but my face shall not be s ... Ex 33:23 7200
thee, neither let any man be s ... Ex 34:3 7200
whether he hath s or known of it ... Lev 5:1 7200
after that he hath been s of the ... Lev 13:7 7200
he shall be s of the priest again ... Lev 13:7 7200
that thou LORD art s face to face ... Num 14:14 7200
those men which have s my glory ... Num 14:22 7200
neither hath he s perverseness in ... Num 23:21 7200
And when thou hast s it, thou also ... Num 27:13 7200
moreover we have s the sons of ... Deut 1:28 7200
where thou hast s how that the ... Deut 1:31 7200
Thine eyes have s all that the ... Deut 3:21 7200
Your eyes have s what the LORD ... Deut 4:3 7200
things which thine eyes have s ... Deut 4:9 7200
we have s this day that God doth ... Deut 5:24 7200
I have s this people, and, behold, ... Deut 9:13 7200
things, which thine eyes have s ... Deut 10:21 7200
which have not s the chastisement ... Deut 11:2 7200
But your eyes have s all the ... Deut 11:7 7200
s with thee in all thy coast ... Deut 16:4 7200
blood, neither have our eyes s it ... Deut 21:7 7200
Ye have s all that the LORD did ... Deut 29:2 7200
which thine eyes have s, the ... Deut 29:3 7200
ye have s their abominations, and ... Deut 29:17 7200
to his mother, I have not s him ... Deut 33:9 7200
ye have s all that the LORD your ... Josh 23:3 7200
your eyes have s what I have done ... Josh 24:7 7200
who had s all the great works of ... Judg 2:7 7200
was there a shield or spear s ... Judg 5:8 7200
for because I have s an angel of ... Judg 6:22 7200
with him, What ye have s me do ... Judg 9:48 7200
surely die, because we have s God ... Judg 13:22 7200
I have s a woman in Timnath of ... Judg 14:2 7200
for we have s the land, and, ... Judg 18:9 7200
s from the day that the children ... Judg 19:30 7200
lords of the Philistines had s it ... 1Sa 6:16 7200
I have s a son of Jesse the ... 1Sa 16:18 7200
Have ye s this man that is come ... 1Sa 17:25 7200
haunt is, and who hath s him there ... 1Sa 23:22 7200
this day thine eyes have s how ... 1Sa 24:10 7200
not be s to come into the city ... 2Sa 17:17 7200
Go tell the king what thou hast s ... 2Sa 18:21 7200
he was s upon the wings of the ... 2Sa 22:11 7200
there was no stone s ... 1Kin 6:18 7200
the ends of the staves were s out ... 1Kin 8:8 7200
and they were not s without ... 1Kin 8:8 7200
Sheba had s all Solomon's wisdom ... 1Kin 10:4 7200
I came, and mine eyes had s it ... 1Kin 10:7 7200
trees, nor were s unto this day ... 1Kin 10:12 7200
For his sons had s what way the ... 1Kin 13:12 7200
Hast thou s all this great ... 1Kin 20:13 7200
Surely I have s yesterday the ... 2Kin 9:26 7200
thy prayer, I have s thy tears ... 2Kin 20:5 7200
What have they s in thine house ... 2Kin 20:15 7200
are in mine house have they s ... 2Kin 20:15 7200
him at Megiddo, when he had s him ... 2Kin 23:29 7200
now have I s with joy thy people, ... 1Chr 29:17 7200
the ends of the staves were s ... 2Chr 5:9 7200
but they were not s without ... 2Chr 5:9 7200
Sheba had s the wisdom of Solomon ... 2Chr 9:3 7200
I came, and mine eyes had s it ... 2Chr 9:6 7200
there were none such s before in ... 2Chr 9:11 7200
that had s the first house, when ... Ezr 3:12 7200
they had s concerning this matter ... Est 9:26 7200
Even as I have s, they that plow ... Job 4:8 7200
I have s the foolish taking root ... Job 5:3 7200
hath s me shall see me no more ... Job 7:8 7210
him, saying, I have not s thee ... Job 8:18 7200
up the ghost, and no eye had s me ... Job 10:18 7200
Lo, mine eye hath s all this ... Job 13:1 7200
which I have s I will declare ... Job 15:17 2372
they which have s him shall say ... Job 20:7 7200
all ye yourselves have s it ... Job 27:12 2372
the vulture's eye hath not s ... Job 28:7 7805
If I have s any perish for want ... Job 31:19 7200
away, that it cannot be s ... Job 33:21 7210
bones that were not s stick out ... Job 33:21 7200
or hast thou s the doors of the ... Job 38:17 7200
or hast thou s the treasures of ... Job 38:22 7200
Thou hast s it ... Ps 10:14 7200
the channels of waters were s ... Ps 18:15 7200
said, Aha, aha, our eye hath s it ... Ps 35:21 7200
This thou hast s, O LORD ... Ps 35:22 7200
yet have I not s the righteous ... Ps 37:25 7200
I have s the wicked in great ... Ps 37:35 7200
so have we s in the city of the ... Ps 48:8 7200
mine eye hath s his desire upon ... Ps 54:7 7200
for I have s violence and strife ... Ps 55:9 7200
so as I have s thee in the ... Ps 63:2 2372
They have s thy goings, O God ... Ps 68:24 7200
the years wherein we have s evil ... Ps 90:15 7200
have s the salvation of our God ... Ps 98:3 7200
I have s an end of all perfection ... Ps 119:96 7200
the prince whom thine eyes have s ... Prov 25:7 7200
I have s all the works that are ... Eccl 1:14 7200
I have s the travail, which God ... Eccl 3:10 7200
who hath not s the evil work that ... Eccl 4:3 7200
evil which I have s under the sun ... Eccl 5:13 7200
Behold that which I have s ... Eccl 5:18 7200
evil which I have s under the sun ... Eccl 6:1 7200
Moreover he hath not s the sun ... Eccl 6:5 7200
twice told, yet hath he s no good ... Eccl 6:6 7200
All things have I s in the days ... Eccl 7:15 7200
All this have I s, and applied my ... Eccl 8:9 7200
have I s also under the sun ... Eccl 9:13 7200
evil which I have s under the sun ... Eccl 10:5 7200
I have s servants upon horses, and ... Eccl 10:7 7200
for mine eyes have s the King ... Is 6:5 7200
in darkness have s a great light ... Is 9:2 7200
when it is s that Moab is weary ... Is 16:12 7200
Ye have s also the breaches of ... Is 22:9 7200
thy prayer, I have s thy tears ... Is 38:5 7200
What have they s in thine house ... Is 39:4 7200
that is in mine house have they s ... Is 39:4 7200
Aha, I am warm, I have s the fire ... Is 44:16 7200
yea, thy shame shall be s ... Is 47:3 7200
I have s his ways, and will heal ... Is 57:18 7200
and his glory shall be s upon thee ... Is 60:2 7200
the ear, neither hath the eye s ... Is 64:4 7200
who hath s such things ... Is 66:8 7200
my fame, neither have s my glory ... Is 66:19 7200
LORD unto me, Thou hast well s ... Jer 1:12 7200
the king, Hast thou s that which ... Jer 3:6 7200
Behold, even I have s it, saith ... Jer 7:11 7200
thou hast s me, and tried mine ... Jer 12:3 7200
I have s thine adulteries, and thy ... Jer 13:27 7200
I have s folly in the prophets of ... Jer 23:13 7200
I have s also in the prophets of ... Jer 23:14 7200
Ye have s all the evil that I ... Jer 44:2 7200
Wherefore have I s them dismayed ... Jer 46:5 7200
because they have s her nakedness ... Lam 1:8 7200
for she hath s that the heathen ... Lam 1:10 7200
Thy prophets have s vain and ... Lam 2:14 2372
but have s for thee false burdens ... Lam 2:14 2372
we have found, we have s it ... Lam 2:16 7200
I am the man that hath s ... Lam 3:1 7200

O LORD, thou hast s my wrong Lam 3:59 7200
Thou hast s all their vengeance Lam 3:60 7200
hast thou s what the ancients of Eze 8:12 7200
said he unto me, Hast thou s this Eze 8:15 7200
he said unto me, Hast thou s this Eze 8:17 7200
that I had s went up from me Eze 11:24 7200
own spirit, and have s nothing Eze 13:3 7200
They have s vanity and lying Eze 13:6 2372
Have ye not s a vain vision, and Eze 13:7 2372
s lies, therefore, behold, I am Eze 13:8 2372
me, Son of man, hast thou s this Eze 47:6 7200
unto me the dream which I have s Dan 2:26 2370
visions of my dream that I have s Dan 4:9 2370
I king Nebuchadnezzar have s Dan 4:18 2370
which I had s standing before the Dan 8:6 7200
had s the vision, and sought for Dan 8:15 7200
whom I had s in the vision at the Dan 9:21 7200
I have s an horrible thing in the Hos 6:10 7200
for now have I s with mine eyes Zec 9:8 7200
And the LORD shall be s over them Zec 9:14 7200
and the diviners have s a lie Zec 10:2 2372
for we have s his star in the Mt 2:2 *1492*
alms before men, to be s of them Mt 6:1 *2300*
that they may be s of men Mt 6:5 *5316*
It was never so s in Israel Mt 9:33 *5316*
which ye see, and have not s them Mt 13:17 *1492*
and ye, when ye had s it, repented Mt 21:32 *1492*
works they do for to be s of men Mt 23:5 *2300*
till they have s the kingdom of Mk 9:1 *1492*
no man what things they had s Mk 9:9 *1492*
was alive, and had been s of her Mk 16:11 *2300*
had s him after he was risen Mk 16:14 *2300*
he had s a vision in the temple Lk 1:22 *3708*
And when they had s it, they made Lk 2:17 *1492*
things that they had heard and s Lk 2:20 *1492*
before he had s the Lord's Christ Lk 2:26 *1492*
mine eyes have s thy salvation Lk 2:30 *1492*
We have s strange things to day Lk 5:26 *1492*
tell John what things ye have s Lk 7:22 *1492*
of those things which they had s Lk 9:36 *3708*
which ye see, and have not s them Lk 10:24 *1492*
the mighty works that they had s Lk 19:37 *1492*
he hoped to have s some miracle Lk 23:8 *1492*
had also s a vision of angels Lk 24:23 *3708*
supposed that they had s a spirit Lk 24:37 *2334*
No man hath s God at any time Jn 1:18 *3708*
know, and testify that we have s Jn 3:11 *3708*
And what he hath s and heard, that Jn 3:32 *3708*
having s all the things that he Jn 4:45 *3708*
at any time, nor s his shape Jn 5:37 *3708*
when they had s the miracle that Jn 6:14 *1492*
unto you, That ye also have s me Jn 6:36 *3708*
that any man hath s the Father Jn 6:46 *3708*
is of God, he hath s the Father Jn 6:46 *3708*
which I have s with my Father Jn 8:38 *3708*
which ye have s with your father Jn 8:38 *3708*
years old, and hast thou s Abraham Jn 8:57 *3708*
had s him that he was blind Jn 9:8 *2334*
unto him, Thou hast both s him Jn 9:37 *3708*
had s the things which Jesus did, Jn 11:45 *2300*
ye know him, and have s him Jn 14:7 *3708*
hath s me hath s the Father Jn 14:9 *3708*
but now have they both s and hated Jn 15:24 *3708*
disciples that she had s the Lord Jn 20:18 *3708*
said unto him, We have s the Lord Jn 20:25 *3708*
Thomas, because thou hast s me Jn 20:29 *3708*
blessed are they that have not s Jn 20:29 *1492*
being s of them forty days, and Acts 1:3 *3700*
as ye have s him go into heaven Acts 1:11 *2300*
speak the things which we have s Acts 4:20 *1492*
I have s, I have s the Acts 7:34 *1492*
to the fashion that he had s Acts 7:44 *3708*
hath s in a vision a man named Acts 9:12 *1492*
how he had s the Lord in the way Acts 9:27 *1492*
vision which he had s should mean Acts 10:17 *1492*
he had s an angel in his house Acts 11:13 *1492*
had s the grace of God, was glad, Acts 11:23 *1492*
he was s many days of them which Acts 13:31 *3700*
And after he had s the vision Acts 16:10 *1492*
and when they had s the brethren Acts 16:40 *1492*
(For they had s before with him Acts 21:29 *4308*
unto all men of what thou hast s Acts 22:15 *3708*
of these things which thou hast s Acts 26:16 *1492*
of the world are clearly s Rom 1:20 *2529*
but hope that is s is not hope Rom 8:24 *991*
as it is written, Eye hath not s 1Cor 2:9 *1492*
have I not s Jesus Christ our 1Cor 9:1 *3708*
And that he was s of Cephas 1Cor 15:5 *3700*
he was s of above five hundred 1Cor 15:6 *3700*
After that, he was s of James 1Cor 15:7 *3700*
last of all he was s of me also 1Cor 15:8 *3700*
not at the things which are s 2Cor 4:18 *991*
but at the things which are not s 2Cor 4:18 *991*
things which are s are temporal 2Cor 4:18 *991*
which are not s are eternal 2Cor 4:18 *991*
and heard, and s in me, do Phil 4:9 *1492*
have not s my face in the flesh Col 2:1 *3708*
those things which he hath not s Col 2:18 *3708*
s of angels, preached unto the 1Ti 3:16 *3700*
whom no man hath s, nor can see 1Ti 6:16 *1492*
for, the evidence of things not s Heb 11:1 *991*
so that things which are s were Heb 11:3 *991*
of God of things not s as yet Heb 11:7 *991*
but having s them afar off, and Heb 11:13 *1492*
have s the end of the Lord Jas 5:11 *1492*
Whom having not s, ye love 1Pet 1:8 *1492*
which we have s with our eyes 1Jn 1:1 *3708*
was manifested, and we have s it 1Jn 1:2 *3708*
That which we have s and heard 1Jn 1:3 *3708*
whosoever sinneth hath not s him 1Jn 3:6 *3708*
No man hath s God at any time 1Jn 4:12 *2300*
And we have s and do testify that 1Jn 4:14 *2300*
not his brother whom he hath s 1Jn 4:20 *3708*
he love God whom he hath not s 1Jn 4:20 *3708*
he that doeth evil hath not s God 3Jn 11 *3780*
the things which thou hast s Rev 1:19 *1492*
there was s in his temple the ark Rev 11:19 *3700*
And when I had heard and s, I fell Rev 22:8 *991*

SEER

Come, and let us go to the s 1Sa 9:9 7200
Prophet was beforetime called a S 1Sa 9:9 7200
and said unto them, Is the s here 1Sa 9:11 7200
Saul, and said, I am the s 1Sa 9:19 7200
the priest, Art not thou a s 2Sa 15:27 7200
unto the prophet Gad, David's s 2Sa 24:11 2374
Samuel the s did ordain in their 1Chr 9:22 7200
LORD spake unto Gad, David's s 1Chr 21:9 2374
the king's s in the words of God 1Chr 25:5 2374
And all that Samuel the s, and Saul 1Chr 26:28 7200
in the book of Samuel the s 1Chr 29:29 7200
and in the book of Gad the s 1Chr 29:29 2374
in the visions of Iddo the s 2Chr 9:29 2374
and of Iddo the s concerning 2Chr 12:15 2374
at that time Hanani the s came to 2Chr 16:7 7200
Then Asa was wroth with the s 2Chr 16:10 7200
Hanani the s went out to meet him 2Chr 19:2 2374
of David, and of Gad the king's s 2Chr 29:25 2374
words of David, and of Asaph the s 2Chr 29:30 2374
Heman, and Jeduthun the king's s 2Chr 35:15 2374
Amaziah said unto Amos, O thou s Amos 7:12 2374

SEER'S

I pray thee, where the s house is 1Sa 9:18 7200

SEERS

all the prophets, and by all the s 2Kin 17:13 2374
the words of the s that spake to 2Chr 33:18 2374
among the sayings of the s 2Chr 33:19 2374
rulers, the s hath he covered Is 29:10 2374
Which say to the s, See not Is 30:10 7200
Then shall the s be ashamed Mic 3:7 2374

SEEST

For all the land which thou s Gen 13:15 7200
spake unto her, Thou God s me Gen 16:13 7210
and all that thou s is mine Gen 31:43 7200
for in that day thou s my face Ex 10:28 7200
heaven, and when thou s the sun Deut 4:19 7200
in every place that thou s Deut 12:13 7200
s horses, and chariots, and a Deut 20:1 7200
s among the captives a beautiful Deut 21:11 7200
him, Thou s the shadow of the Judg 9:36 7200
S thou how Ahab humbleth himself 1Kin 21:29 7200
or s thou as man seeth Job 10:4 7200
S thou a man diligent in his Prov 22:29 2372
S thou a man wise in his own Prov 26:12 7200
S thou a man that is hasty in his Prov 29:20 2372
If thou s the oppression of the Eccl 5:8 7200
fasted, say they, and thou s not Is 58:3 7200
when thou s the naked, that thou Is 58:7 7200
me, saying, Jeremiah, what s thou Jer 1:11 7200
second time, saying, What s thou Jer 1:13 7200
S thou not what they do in the Jer 7:17 7200
s the reins and the heart, let me Jer 20:12 7200
the LORD unto me, What s thou Jer 24:3 7200
and, behold, thou s it Jer 32:24 7200
Son of man, s thou what they do Eze 8:6 7200
declare all that thou s to the Eze 40:4 7200
and as thou s, deal with thy Dan 1:13 7200
said unto me, Amos, what s thou Amos 7:8 7200
And he said, Amos, what s thou Amos 8:2 7200
And said unto me, What s thou Zec 4:2 7200
And he said unto me, What s thou Zec 5:2 7200
Thou s the multitude thronging Mk 5:31 *991*
S thou these great buildings Mk 13:2 *991*
unto Simon, S thou this woman Lk 7:44 *991*
Lord, and said unto him, Thou s Acts 21:20 *2334*
S thou how faith wrought with his Jas 2:22 *991*
and, What thou s, write in a book, Rev 1:11 *991*

SEETH

here looked after him that s me Gen 16:13 7210
when he s that the lad is not Gen 44:31 7200
and when he s thee, he will be Ex 4:14 7200
when he s the blood upon the Ex 12:23 7200
And if, when the priest s it Lev 13:20 7200
when he s that their power is Deut 32:36 7200
for the LORD s not as man s 1Sa 16:7 7200
city is pleasant, as my lord s 2Kin 2:19 7200
heap, and s the place of stones Job 8:17 2372
or seest thou as man s Job 10:4 7200
he s wickedness also Job 11:11 7200
a covering to him, that he s not Job 22:14 7200
his eye s every precious thing Job 28:10 7200
and s under the whole heaven Job 28:24 7200
of man, and he s all his goings Job 34:21 7200
but now mine eye s thee Job 42:5 7200
for he s that his day is coming Ps 37:13 7200
For he s that wise men die, Ps 49:10 7200
rejoice when he s the vengeance Ps 58:10 2372
nor night s sleep with his eyes Eccl 8:16 7200
let him declare what he s Is 21:6 7200
when he that looketh upon it s Is 28:4 7200
the dark, and they say, Who s us Is 29:15 7200
But when he s his children, the Is 29:23 7200
thou hast said, None s me Is 47:10 7200
for they say, The LORD s us not Eze 8:12 7200
the earth, and the LORD s not Eze 9:9 7200
The vision that he s is for many Eze 12:27 2372
that s all his father's sins Eze 18:14 7200
If when he s the sword come upon Eze 33:3 7200
when any s a man's bone, then Eze 39:15 7200
thy Father which s in secret Mt 6:4 *991*
thy Father which s in secret Mt 6:6 *991*
which s in secret, shall reward Mt 6:18 *991*
s the tumult, and them that wept Mk 5:38 *2334*
s Abraham afar off, and Lazarus in Lk 16:23 *3708*
The next day John s Jesus coming Jn 1:29 *991*
but what he s the Father do Jn 5:19 *991*
that every one which s the Son Jn 6:40 *2334*
But by what means he now s Jn 9:21 *991*
s the wolf coming, and leaveth the Jn 10:12 *2334*
because he s the light of this Jn 11:9 *991*
that s me s him that sent me Jn 12:45 *2334*
receive, because it s him not Jn 14:17 *2334*
while, and the world s me no more Jn 14:19 *2334*
s the stone taken away from the Jn 20:1 *991*
and s the linen clothes lie, Jn 20:6 *2334*
s two angels in white sitting, Jn 20:12 *2334*
s the disciple whom Jesus loved Jn 21:20 *991*
for what a man s, why doth he yet Rom 8:24 *991*
me above that which he s me to be 2Cor 12:6 *991*
s his brother have need, and 1Jn 3:17 *2334*

SEETHE

to day, and s that ye will s Ex 16:23 1310
Thou shalt not s a kid in his Ex 23:19 1310
s his flesh in the holy place Ex 29:31 1310
Thou shalt not s a kid in his Ex 34:26 1310
Thou shalt not s a kid in his Deut 14:21 1310
s pottage for the sons of the 2Kin 4:38 1310
let them s the bones of it Eze 24:5 1310
and take of them, and s therein Zec 14:21 1310

SEETHING

came, while the flesh was in s 1Sa 2:13 1310
as out of a s pot or caldron Job 41:20 5301
and I said, I see a s pot Jer 1:13 5301

SEGUB (*se'-gub*)
1. A son of Hiel.
thereof in his youngest son S 1Kin 16:34 7687
2. A son of Hezron.
and she bare him S 1Chr 2:21 7687
S begat Jair, who had three and 1Chr 2:22 7687

SEIR (*se'-ur*)
1. A region south of the Dead Sea.
And the Horites in their mount S Gen 14:6 8165
his brother unto the land of S Gen 32:3 8165
until I come unto my lord unto S Gen 33:14 8165
that day on his way unto S Gen 33:16 8165
Thus dwelt Esau in mount S Gen 36:8 8165
father of the Edomites in mount S Gen 36:9 8165
the children of S in the land of Gen 36:21 8165
their dukes in the land of S Gen 36:30 8165
S also shall be a possession for Num 24:18 8165
way of mount S unto Kadesh-barnea Deut 1:2 8165
as bees do, and destroyed you in S Deut 1:44 8165
and we compassed mount S Deut 2:1 8165
of Esau, which dwell in S Deut 2:4 8165
S unto Esau for a possession Deut 2:5 8165
of Esau, which dwelt in S Deut 2:8 8165
Horims also dwelt in S beforetime Deut 2:12 8165
of Esau, which dwelt in S Deut 2:22 8165
children of Esau which dwell in S Deut 2:29 8165
and rose up from S unto them Deut 33:2 8165
mount Halak, that goeth up to S Josh 11:17 8165
mount Halak, that goeth up to S Josh 12:7 8165
from Baalah westward unto mount S Josh 15:10 8165
and I gave unto Esau mount S Josh 24:4 8165
LORD, when thou wentest out of S Judg 5:4 8165
five hundred men, went to mount S 1Chr 4:42 8165
of Ammon and Moab and mount S 2Chr 20:10 8165
of Ammon, Moab, and mount S 2Chr 20:22 8165
the inhabitants of mount S 2Chr 20:23 8165
an end of the inhabitants of S 2Chr 20:23 8165
of the children of S ten thousand 2Chr 25:11 8165
the gods of the children of S 2Chr 25:14 8165
He calleth to me out of S Is 21:11 8165
S do say, Behold, the house of Eze 25:8 8165
man, set thy face against mount S Eze 35:2 8165
Behold, O mount S, I am against Eze 35:3 8165
will I make mount S most desolate Eze 35:7 8165
thou shalt be desolate, O mount S Eze 35:15 8165
2. Grandfather of Hori.
are the sons of S the Horite Gen 36:20 8165
And the sons of S 1Chr 1:38 8165

SEIRAH See SEIRATH.

SEIRATH (*se'-ur-ath*) *A city in Ephraim.*
the quarries, and escaped unto S Judg 3:26 8167

SEIZE

the ambush, and s upon the city Josh 8:7 3423
night, let darkness s upon it Job 3:6 3947
Let death s upon them, and let Ps 55:15 3451
let us s on his inheritance Mt 21:38 *2722*

SEIZED

to flee, and fear hath s on her Jer 49:24 2388

SELA (*se'-lah*) See SELAH. *Same as Selah 1.*
the land from S to the wilderness Is 16:1 5554

SELAH (*se'-lah*) See JOKTHEEL, SELA.
1. Capital of Edom.
took S by war, and called the name 2Kin 14:7 5554
2. A musical notation.
no help for him in God. S Ps 3:2 5542
me out of his holy hill. S Ps 3:4 5542
blessing is upon thy people. S Ps 3:8 5542
vanity, and seek after leasing? S Ps 4:2 5542
your bed, and be still. S Ps 4:4 5542
mine honour in the dust. S Ps 7:5 5542
his own hands. Higgaion. S Ps 9:16 5542
themselves to be but men. S Ps 9:20 5542
accept thy burnt sacrifice; S Ps 20:3 5542
the request of his lips. S Ps 21:2 5542
thy face, O Jacob. S Ps 24:6 5542
he is the King of glory. S Ps 24:10 5542
the drought of summer. S Ps 32:4 5542
the iniquity of my sin. S Ps 32:5 5542
songs of deliverance. S Ps 32:7 5542
state is altogether vanity. S Ps 39:5 5542
every man is vanity. S Ps 39:11 5542
thy name for ever. S Ps 44:8 5542

with the swelling thereof. S Ps 46:3 5542
Jacob is our refuge. S Ps 46:7 5542
Jacob is our refuge. S Ps 46:11 5542
Jacob whom he loved. S Ps 47:4 5542
establish it for ever. S Ps 48:8 5542
approve their sayings. S Ps 49:13 5542
he shall receive me. S Ps 49:15 5542
God is judge himself. S Ps 50:6 5542
to speak righteousness. S Ps 52:3 5542
land of the living. S Ps 52:5 5542
set God before them. S Ps 54:3 5542
remain in the wilderness. S Ps 55:7 5542
that abideth of old. S Ps 55:19 5542
swallow me up. S Ps 57:3 5542
are fallen themselves. S Ps 57:6 5542
wicked transgressors. S Ps 59:5 5542
ends of the earth. S Ps 59:13 5542
because of the truth. S Ps 60:4 5542
the covert of thy wings. S Ps 61:4 5542
but they curse inwardly. S Ps 62:4 5542
is a refuge for us. S Ps 62:8 5542
sing to thy name. S Ps 66:4 5542
exalt themselves. S Ps 66:7 5542
offer bullocks with goats. S Ps 66:15 5542
face to shine upon us; S Ps 67:1 5542
the nations upon earth. S Ps 67:4 5542
through the wilderness; S Ps 68:7 5542
the God of our salvation. S Ps 68:19 5542
praises unto the Lord. S Ps 68:32 5542
up the pillars of it. S Ps 75:3 5542
sword, and the battle. S Ps 76:3 5542
the meek of the earth. S Ps 76:9 5542
was overwhelmed. S Ps 77:3 5542
up his tender mercies? S Ps 77:9 5542
of Jacob and Joseph. S Ps 77:15 5542
the waters of Meribah. S Ps 81:7 5542
persons of the wicked? S Ps 82:2 5542
the children of Lot. S Ps 83:8 5542
be still praising thee. S Ps 84:4 5542
O God of Jacob. S Ps 84:8 5542
covered all their sin. S Ps 85:2 5542
O city of God. S Ps 87:3 5542
man was born there. S Ps 87:6 5542
me with all thy waves. S Ps 88:7 5542
dead arise and praise thee? S Ps 88:10 5542
throne to all generations. S Ps 89:4 5542
witness in heaven. S Ps 89:37 5542
him with shame. S Ps 89:45 5542
hand of the grave? S Ps 89:48 5542
is under their lips. S Ps 140:3 5542
have set gins for me. S Ps 140:5 5542
they exalt themselves. S Ps 140:8 5542
as a thirsty land. S Ps 143:6 5542
from mount Paran. S Hab 3:3 5542
even thy word. S Hab 3:9 5542
foundation unto the neck. S Hab 3:13 5542

SELA-HAMMAHLEKOTH *(se''-lah-ham-mah'-le-koth) A hill in the wilderness of Maon.*
they called that place S 1Sa 23:28 5555

SELED *(se'-led) A descendant of Jerahmeel.*
S, and Appaim: but S died 1Chr 2:30 5540

SELEUCIA *(sel-u-si'-ah) A city in Syria.*
the Holy Ghost, departed unto S Acts 13:4 *4581*

SELF
whom thou swarest by thine own s Ex 32:13
I can of mine own s do nothing Jn 5:30 *1683*
glorify thou me with thine own s Jn 17:5 *4572*
yea, I judge not mine own s 1Cor 4:3 *1683*
unto me even thine own s besides Philem 19 *4572*
Who his own s bare our sins in 1Pet 2:24 *846*

SELFSAME
In the s day entered Noah, and Gen 7:13
of their foreskin in the s day Gen 17:23
In the s day was Abraham Gen 17:26
for in this s day have I brought Ex 12:17
even the s day it came to pass, Ex 12:41
And it came to pass the s day Ex 12:51
until the s day that ye have Lev 23:14
And ye shall proclaim on the s day Lev 23:21
LORD spake unto Moses that s day Deut 32:48
and parched corn in the s day Josh 5:11
in the s day the hand of the LORD Eze 40:1
servant was healed in the s hour Mt 8:13 *1565*
the s Spirit, dividing to every 1Cor 12:11 *846*
wrought us for the s thing is God 2Cor 5:5
For behold this s thing, that ye 2Cor 7:11 *846*

SELFWILL
in their s they digged down a Gen 49:6 7522

SELFWILLED
not s, not soon angry, not given Titus 1:7 *829*
Presumptuous are they, s, they 2Pet 2:10 *829*

SELL
S me this day thy birthright Gen 25:31 4376
let us s him to the Ishmeelites, Gen 37:27 4376
if a man s his daughter to be a Ex 21:7 4376
to s her unto a strange nation he Ex 21:8 4376
then they shall s the live ox Ex 21:35 4376
or a sheep, and kill it, or s it Ex 22:1 4376
And if thou s ought unto thy Lev 25:14 4376
the fruits he shall s unto thee Lev 25:15 4376
of the fruits doth he s unto thee Lev 25:16 4376
if a man s a dwelling house in a Lev 25:29 4376
s himself unto the stranger or Lev 25:47 4376
Thou shalt s me meat for money, Deut 2:28 7666
or thou mayest s it unto an alien Deut 14:21 4376
but thou shalt not s her at all Deut 21:14 4376
for the LORD shall s Sisera into Judg 4:9 4376
which did s himself to work 1Kin 21:25 4376
s the oil, and pay thy debt, and 2Kin 4:7 4376
will ye even s your brethren Neh 5:8 4376
victuals on the sabbath day to s Neh 10:31 4376
Buy the truth, and s it not Prov 23:23 4376
s the land into the hand of the Eze 30:12 4376
And they shall not s of it Eze 48:14 4376
I will s your sons and your Joel 3:8 4376
they shall s them to the Sabeans, Joel 3:8 4376
moon be gone, that we may s corn Amos 8:5 7666
s the refuse of the wheat Amos 8:6 7666
and they that s them say, Blessed Zec 11:5 4376
s that thou hast, and give to the Mt 19:21 *4453*
but go ye rather to them that s Mt 25:9 *4453*
s whatsoever thou hast, and give Mk 10:21 *4453*
S that ye have, and give alms Lk 12:33 *4453*
s all that thou hast, and Lk 18:22 *4453*
let him s his garment, and buy one Lk 22:36 *4453*
there a year, and buy and s Jas 4:13 *1710*
And that no man might buy or s Rev 13:17 *4453*

SELLER
as with the buyer, so with the s Is 24:2 4376
buyer rejoice, nor the s mourn Eze 7:12 4376
For the s shall not return to Eze 7:13 4376
a s of purple, of the city of Acts 16:14 *4211*

SELLERS
s of all kind of ware lodged Neh 13:20 4376

SELLEST
Thou s thy people for nought, and Ps 44:12 4376

SELLETH
s him, or if he be found in his Ex 21:16 4376
merchandise of him, or s him Deut 24:7 4376
s a parcel of land, which was our Ruth 4:3 4376
be upon the head of him that s it Prov 11:26 7666
She maketh fine linen, and s it Prov 31:24 4376
that s nations through her Nah 3:4 4376
s all that he hath, and buyeth Mt 13:44 *4453*

SELVEDGE
from the s in the coupling Ex 26:4 7098
from the s in the coupling Ex 36:11 7098

SELVES
know of your own s that summer is Lk 21:30 *1438*
of your own s shall men arise Acts 20:30 *846*
gave their own s to the Lord 2Cor 8:5 *1438*
prove your own s 2Cor 13:5 *1438*
Know ye not your own s, how that 2Cor 13:5 *1438*
shall be lovers of their own s 2Ti 3:2 *5367*
only, deceiving your own s Jas 1:22 *846*

SEM *(sem)* See SHEM. *Greek form of Shem.*
Arphaxad, which was the son of S Lk 3:36 *4590*

SEMACHIAH *(sem-a-ki'-ah) A sanctuary servant.*
were strong men, Elihu, and S 1Chr 26:7 5565

SEMEI *(sem'-e-i)* See SHEMAIAH. *A son of Joseph; an ancestor of Jesus.*
which was the son of S, which Lk 3:26 *4584*

SEMEIN See SEMEI.

SENAAH *(sen'-a-ah)* See HASSENAAH. *A city in Judah.*
The children of S, three thousand Ezr 2:35 5570
The children of S, three thousand Neh 7:38 5570

SENATE
all the s of the children of Acts 5:21 *1087*

SENATORS
and teach his s wisdom Ps 105:22 2205

SEND
he shall s his angel before thee, Gen 24:7 7971
s me good speed this day, and shew Gen 24:12 7136
will s his angel with thee, and Gen 24:40 7971
he said, S me away unto my master Gen 24:54 7971
s me away that I may go to my Gen 24:56 7971
then I will s, and fetch thee from Gen 27:45 7971
S me away, that I may go unto Gen 30:25 7971
come, and I will s thee unto them Gen 37:13 7971
I will s thee a kid from the Gen 38:17 7971
give me a pledge, till thou s it Gen 38:17 7971
S one of you, and let him fetch Gen 42:16 7971
If thou wilt s our brother with Gen 43:4 7971
But if thou wilt not s him Gen 43:5 7971
S the lad with me, and we will Gen 43:8 7971
that he may s away your other Gen 43:14 7971
for God did s me before you to Gen 45:5 7971
I will s thee unto Pharaoh, that Ex 3:10 7971
And he said, O my Lord, s, I pray Ex 4:13 7971
the hand of him whom thou wilt s Ex 4:13 7971
that he s the children of Israel Ex 7:2 7971
I will s swarms of flies upon Ex 8:21 7971
For I will at this time s all my Ex 9:14 7971
S therefore now, and gather thy Ex 9:19 7971
that they might s them out of the Ex 12:33 7971
I s an Angel before thee, to keep Ex 23:20 7971
I will s my fear before thee, and Ex 23:27 7971
I will s hornets before thee, Ex 23:28 7971
I will s an angel before thee Ex 33:2 7971
me know whom thou wilt s with me Ex 33:12 7971
shall s him away by the hand of a Lev 16:21 7971
I will also s wild beasts among Lev 26:22 7971
I will s the pestilence among you Lev 26:25 7971
are left alive of you I will s a Lev 26:36 935
S thou men, that they may search Num 13:2 7971
of their fathers shall ye s a man Num 13:2 7971
Did I not earnestly s unto thee Num 22:37 7971
of Israel, shall ye s to the war Num 31:4 7971
We will s men before us, and they Deut 1:22 7971
God will s the hornet among them Deut 7:20 7971
I will s grass in thy fields for Deut 11:15 5414
the elders of his city shall s Deut 19:12 7971
hand, and s her out of his house Deut 24:1 7971
The LORD shall s upon thee Deut 28:20 7971
the LORD shall s against thee Deut 28:48 7971
I will also s the teeth of beasts Deut 32:24 7971
and I will s them, and they shall Josh 18:4 7971
thou didst s come again unto us Judg 13:8 7971
S away the ark of the God of 1Sa 5:11 7971
we shall s it to his place 1Sa 6:2 7971
If ye s away the ark of the God 1Sa 6:3 7971
the God of Israel, s it not empty 1Sa 6:3 7971
s it away, that it may go 1Sa 6:8 7971
s thee a man out of the land of 1Sa 9:16 7971
Up, that I may s thee away 1Sa 9:26 7971
that we may s messengers unto all 1Sa 11:3 7971
the LORD, and he shall s thunder 1Sa 12:17 5414
I will s thee to Jesse the 1Sa 16:1 7971
And Samuel said unto Jesse, S 1Sa 16:11 7971
S me David thy son, which is with 1Sa 16:19 7971
I then s not unto thee, and shew 1Sa 20:12 7971
s thee away, that thou mayest go 1Sa 20:13 7971
And, behold, I will s a lad 1Sa 20:21 7971
Wherefore now s and fetch him unto 1Sa 20:31 7971
the business whereabout I s thee 1Sa 21:2 7971
men of my lord, whom thou didst s 1Sa 25:25 7971
saying, S me Uriah the Hittite 2Sa 11:6 7971
that I may s thee to the king, to 2Sa 14:32 7971
by them ye shall s unto me every 2Sa 15:36 7971
Now therefore s quickly, and tell 2Sa 17:16 7971
whithersoever thou shalt s them 1Kin 8:44 7971
I will s rain upon the earth 1Kin 18:1 5414
Now therefore s, and gather to me 1Kin 18:19 7971
Yet I will s my servants unto 1Kin 20:6 7971
All that thou didst s for to thy 1Kin 20:9 7971
I will s thee away with this 1Kin 20:34 7971
And he said, Ye shall not s 2Kin 2:16 7971
till he was ashamed, he said, S 2Kin 2:17 7971
S me, I pray thee, one of the 2Kin 4:22 7971
I will s a letter unto the king 2Kin 5:5 7971
that this man doth s unto me to 2Kin 5:7 7971
and spy where he is, that I may s 2Kin 6:13 7971
and let us s and see 2Kin 7:13 7971
s to meet them, and let him say, 2Kin 9:17 7971
s against Judah Rezin the king of 2Kin 15:37 7971
I will s a blast upon him, and he 2Kin 19:7 5414
let us s abroad unto our brethren 1Chr 13:2 7971
didst s him cedars to build him 2Chr 2:3 7971
S me now therefore a man cunning 2Chr 2:7 7971
S me also cedar trees, fir trees, 2Chr 2:8 7971
let him s unto his servants 2Chr 2:15 7971
s rain upon thy land, which thou 2Chr 6:27 5414
by the way that thou shalt s them 2Chr 6:34 7971
or if I s pestilence among my 2Chr 7:13 7971
At that time did king Ahaz s unto 2Chr 28:16 7971
s his servants to Jerusalem 2Chr 32:9 7971
let the king s his pleasure to us Ezr 5:17 7972
thou wouldest s me unto Judah Neh 2:5 7971
So it pleased the king to s me Neh 2:6 7971
s portions unto them for whom Neh 8:10 7971
to s portions, and to make great Neh 8:12 7971
They s forth their little ones Job 21:11 7971
Canst thou s lightnings, that Job 38:35 7971
S thee help from the sanctuary, Ps 20:2 7971
O s out thy light and thy truth Ps 43:3 7971
He shall s from heaven, and save Ps 57:3 7971
God shall s forth his mercy and Ps 57:3 7971
didst s a plentiful rain, whereby Ps 68:9 5130
he doth s out his voice, and that Ps 68:33 5414
The LORD shall s the rod of thy Ps 110:2 7971
I beseech thee, s now prosperity Ps 118:25
S thine hand from above Ps 144:7 7971
the sluggard to them that s him Prov 10:26 7971
of truth to them that s unto thee Prov 22:21 7971
messenger to them that s him Prov 25:13 7971
to s forth a stinking savour Eccl 10:1 5042
the Lord, saying, Whom shall I s Is 6:8 7971
Here am I; s me Is 6:8 7971
I will s him against an Is 10:6 7971
s among his fat ones leanness Is 10:16 7971
S ye the lamb to the ruler of the Is 16:1 7971
he shall s them a saviour, and a Is 19:20 7971
that s forth thither the feet of Is 32:20 7971
I will s a blast upon him, and he Is 37:7 7971
didst s thy messengers far off, Is 57:9 7971
I will s those that escape of Is 66:19 7971
go to all that I shall s thee Jer 1:7 7971
s unto Kedar, and consider Jer 2:10 7971
I will s serpents, cockatrices, Jer 8:17 7971
I will s a sword after them, till Jer 9:16 7971
s for cunning women, that they Jer 9:17 7971
I will s for many fishers, saith Jer 16:16 7971
after will I s for many hunters, Jer 16:16 7971
I will s the sword, the famine, Jer 24:10 7971
Behold, I will s and take all the Jer 25:9 7971
all the nations, to whom I s thee Jer 25:15 7971
sword that I will s among them Jer 25:16 7971
sword which I will s among you Jer 25:27 7971
s them to the king of Edom, and to Jer 27:3 7971
I will s upon them the sword, the Jer 29:17 7971
S to all them of the captivity, Jer 29:31 7971
LORD thy God shall s thee to us Jer 42:5 7971
LORD our God, to whom we s thee Jer 42:6 7971
Behold, I will s and take Jer 43:10 7971
that I will s unto him wanderers, Jer 48:12 7971
I will s the sword after them, Jer 49:37 7971
will s unto Babylon fanners, that Jer 51:2 7971
I s thee to the children of Eze 2:3 7971
I do s thee unto them Eze 2:4 7971
When I shall s upon them the evil Eze 5:16 7971
which I will s to destroy you Eze 5:16 7971
So will I s upon you famine and Eze 5:17 7971
I will s mine anger upon thee, and Eze 7:3 7971
will s famine upon it, and will Eze 14:13 7971
Or if I s a pestilence into that Eze 14:19 7971
How much more when I s my four Eze 14:21 7971
For I will s into her pestilence, Eze 28:23 7971
I will s a fire on Magog, and Eze 39:6 7971

S

but I will *s* a fire upon his Hos 8:14 7971
I will *s* you corn, and wine, and Joel 2:19 7971
But I will *s* a fire into the Amos 1:4 7971
But I will *s* a fire on the wall Amos 1:7 7971
But I will *s* a fire on the wall Amos 1:10 7971
But I will *s* a fire upon Teman, Amos 1:12 7971
But I will *s* a fire upon Moab, and Amos 2:2 7971
But I will *s* a fire upon Judah, Amos 2:5 7971
that I will *s* a famine in the Amos 8:11 7971
I will even *s* a curse upon you, Mal 2:2 7971
I will *s* my messenger, and he Mal 3:1 7971
I will *s* you Elijah the prophet Mal 4:5 7971
that he will *s* forth labourers Mt 9:38 *1544*
I *s* you forth as sheep in the Mt 10:16 *649*
I am come to *s* peace on earth Mt 10:34 *906*
I came not to *s* peace, but a Mt 10:34 *906*
I *s* my messenger before thy face, Mt 11:10 *649*
till he *s* forth judgment unto Mt 12:20 *1544*
of man shall *s* forth his angels Mt 13:41 *649*
s the multitude away, that they Mt 14:15 *630*
besought him, saying, *S* her away Mt 15:23 *630*
I will not *s* them away fasting, Mt 15:32 *630*
and straightway he will *s* them Mt 21:3 *649*
I *s* unto you prophets, and wise Mt 23:34 *649*
he shall *s* his angels with a Mt 24:31 *649*
I *s* my messenger before thy face, Mk 1:2 *649*
that he might *s* them forth to Mk 3:14 *649*
him much that he would not *s* them Mk 5:10 *649*
S us into the swine, that we may Mk 5:12 *3992*
began to *s* them forth by two and Mk 6:7 *649*
S them away, that they may go Mk 6:36 *630*
if I *s* them away fasting to their Mk 8:3 *630*
straightway he will *s* him hither Mk 11:3 *649*
they *s* unto him certain of the Mk 12:13 *649*
And then shall he *s* his angels Mk 13:27 *649*
I *s* my messenger before thy face, Lk 7:27 *649*
S the multitude away, that they Lk 9:12 *630*
that he would *s* forth labourers Lk 10:2 *1544*
I *s* you forth as lambs among Lk 10:3 *649*
I will *s* them prophets and Lk 11:49 *649*
I am come to *s* fire on the earth Lk 12:49 *906*
s Lazarus, that he may dip the Lk 16:24 *3992*
that thou wouldest *s* him to my Lk 16:27 *3992*
I will *s* my beloved son Lk 20:13 *3992*
I *s* the promise of my Father upon Lk 24:49 *649*
whomsoever I *s* receiveth me Jn 13:20 *3992*
whom the Father will *s* in my name Jn 14:26 *3992*
whom I will *s* unto you from the Jn 15:26 *3992*
I depart, I will *s* him unto you Jn 16:7 *3992*
believed that thou didst *s* me Jn 17:8 *649*
hath sent me, even so *s* I you Jn 20:21 *3992*
he shall *s* Jesus Christ, which Acts 3:20 *649*
come, I will *s* thee into Egypt Acts 7:34 *649*
the same did God *s* to be a ruler Acts 7:35 *649*
now *s* men to Joppa, and call for Acts 10:5 *3992*
to *s* for thee into his house Acts 10:22 *3343*
S therefore to Joppa, and call Acts 10:32 *3992*
S men to Joppa, and call for Simon Acts 11:13 *649*
determined to *s* relief unto the Acts 11:29 *3992*
to *s* chosen men of their own Acts 15:22 *3992*
brethren *s* greeting unto the Acts 15:23
to *s* chosen men unto you with our Acts 15:25 *3992*
for I will *s* thee far hence unto Acts 22:21 *1821*
that he would *s* for him to Acts 25:3 *3343*
kept till I might *s* him to Caesar Acts 25:21 *3992*
I have determined to *s* him Acts 25:25 *3992*
me unreasonable to *s* a prisoner Acts 25:27 *3992*
Gentiles, unto whom now I *s* thee Acts 26:17 *649*
them will I *s* to bring your 1Cor 16:3 *3992*
to *s* Timotheus shortly unto you Phil 2:19 *3992*
therefore I hope to *s* presently Phil 2:23 *3992*
to *s* to you Epaphroditus, my Phil 2:25 *3992*
God shall *s* them strong delusion 2Th 2:11 *3992*
When I shall *s* Artemas unto thee, Titus 3:12 *3992*
Doth a fountain *s* forth at the Jas 3:11 *1032*
s it unto the seven churches Rev 1:11 *3992*
shall *s* gifts one to another Rev 11:10 *3992*

SENDEST
when thou *s* him out free from Deut 15:13 7971
when thou *s* him away free from Deut 15:18 7971
do, and whithersoever thou *s* us Josh 1:16 7971
that thou *s* to enquire of 2Kin 1:6 7971
his countenance, and *s* him away Job 14:20 7971
Thou *s* forth thy spirit, they are Ps 104:30 7971

SENDETH
hand, and *s* her out of his house Deut 24:3 7971
the LORD *s* rain upon the earth 1Kin 17:14 5414
and *s* waters upon the fields Job 5:10 7971
also he *s* them out, and they Job 12:15 7971
He *s* the springs into the valleys Ps 104:10 7971
He *s* forth his commandment upon Ps 147:15 7971
He *s* out his word, and melteth Ps 147:18 7971
He that *s* a message by the hand Prov 26:6 7971
my spikenard *s* forth the smell Song 1:12 5414
That *s* ambassadors by the sea, Is 18:2 7971
s rain on the just and on the Mt 5:45 *1026*
he *s* forth two of his disciples, Mk 11:1 *649*
he *s* forth two of his disciples, Mk 14:13 *649*
he *s* an ambassage, and desireth Lk 14:32 *649*
governor Felix *s* greeting Acts 23:26 *649*

SENDING
this evil in *s* me away is greater 2Sa 13:16 7971
rising up betimes, and *s* 2Chr 36:15 7971
of *s* portions one to another Est 9:19 4916
of *s* portions one to another, and Est 9:22 4916
by *s* evil angels among them Ps 78:49 4917
shall be for the *s* forth of oxen Is 7:25 4916
daily rising up early and *s* them Jer 7:25 7971
prophets, rising early and *s* them Jer 25:4 7971
s them, but ye have not hearkened Jer 26:5 7971
rising up early and *s* them Jer 29:19 7971
s them, saying, Return ye now Jer 35:15 7971
s them, saying, Oh, do not this Jer 44:4 7971
in *s* his ambassadors into Egypt Eze 17:15 7971
God *s* his own Son in the likeness Rom 8:3 *3992*

SENEH *(se'-neh) A rock in Benjamin.*
Bozez, and the name of the other *S* 1Sa 14:4 5573

SENIR *(se'-nur)* See SHENIR. *A mountain between Amana and Hermon.*
from Bashan unto Baal-hermon and *S*. 1Chr 5:23 8149
thy ship boards of fir trees of *S* Eze 27:5 8149

SENNACHERIB *(sen-nak'-er-ib) An Assyrian king.*
year of king Hezekiah did *S* king 2Kin 18:13 5576
and hear the words of *S*, which 2Kin 19:16 5576
S king of Assyria I have heard 2Kin 19:20 5576
So *S* king of Assyria departed, and 2Kin 19:36 5576
S king of Assyria came, and 2Chr 32:1 5576
when Hezekiah saw that *S* was come 2Chr 32:2 5576
After this did *S* king of Assyria 2Chr 32:9 5576
Thus saith *S* king of Assyria, 2Chr 32:10 5576
the hand of *S* the king of Assyria 2Chr 32:22 5576
that *S* king of Assyria came up Is 36:1 5576
and hear all the words of *S* Is 37:17 5576
to me against *S* king of Assyria Is 37:21 5576
So *S* king of Assyria departed, and Is 37:37 5576

SENSE
of God distinctly, and gave the *s* Neh 8:8 7922

SENSES
s exercised to discern both good Heb 5:14 *145*

SENSUAL
not from above, but is earthly, *s* Jas 3:15 *5591*
they who separate themselves, *s* Jude 19 *5591*

SENT
Therefore the LORD God *s* him Gen 3:23 7971
he *s* forth a raven, which went Gen 8:7 7971
Also he *s* forth a dove from him, Gen 8:8 7971
again he *s* forth the dove out of Gen 8:10 7971
and *s* forth the dove Gen 8:12 7971
they *s* him away, and his wife, and Gen 12:20 7971
the LORD hath *s* us to destroy it Gen 19:13 7971
s Lot out of the midst of the Gen 19:29 7971
and Abimelech king of Gerar *s* Gen 20:2 7971
and the child, and *s* her away Gen 21:14 7971
they *s* away Rebekah their sister, Gen 24:59 7971
s them away from Isaac his son, Gen 25:6 7971
me, and have *s* me away from you Gen 26:27 7971
have *s* thee away in peace Gen 26:29 7971
Isaac *s* them away, and they Gen 26:31 7971
and she *s* and called Jacob her Gen 27:42 7971
And Isaac *s* away Jacob Gen 28:5 7971
s him away to Padan-aram, to take Gen 28:6 7971
And Jacob *s* and called Rachel and Gen 31:4 7971
that I might have *s* thee away Gen 31:27 7971
thou hadst *s* me away now empty Gen 31:42 7971
Jacob *s* messengers before him to Gen 32:3 7971
I have *s* to tell my lord, that I Gen 32:5 7971
it is a present *s* unto my lord Gen 32:18 7971
s them over the brook Gen 32:23 5674
and *s* over that he had Gen 32:23 5674
So he *s* him out of the vale of Gen 37:14 7971
they *s* the coat of many colours, Gen 37:32 7971
Judah *s* the kid by the hand of Gen 38:20 7971
I *s* this kid, and thou hast not Gen 38:23 7971
she *s* to her father in law, Gen 38:25 7971
and he *s* and called for all the Gen 41:8 7971
Then Pharaoh *s* and called Joseph, Gen 41:14 7971
Jacob *s* not with his brethren Gen 42:4 7971
s messes unto them from before Gen 43:34 7971
was light, the men were *s* away Gen 44:3 7971
God *s* me before you to preserve Gen 45:7 7971
it was not you that *s* me hither Gen 45:8 7971
to his father he *s* after this Gen 45:23 7971
So he *s* his brethren away, and Gen 45:24 7971
which Joseph had *s* to carry him Gen 45:27 7971
which Pharaoh had *s* to carry him Gen 46:5 7971
he *s* Judah before him unto Joseph Gen 46:28 7971
they *s* a messenger unto Joseph, Gen 50:16
she *s* her maid to fetch it Ex 2:5 7971
unto thee, that I have *s* thee Ex 3:12 7971
your fathers hath *s* me unto you Ex 3:13 7971
Israel, I AM hath *s* me unto you Ex 3:14 7971
God of Jacob, hath *s* me unto you Ex 3:15 7971
words of the LORD who had *s* him Ex 4:28 7971
why is it that thou hast *s* me Ex 5:22 7971
the Hebrews hath *s* me unto thee Ex 7:16 7971
And Pharaoh *s*, and, behold, there Ex 9:7 7971
and the LORD *s* thunder and hail, and Ex 9:23 5414
And Pharaoh *s*, and called for Moses Ex 9:27 7971
wife, after he had *s* her back Ex 18:2 7964
he *s* young men of the children of Ex 24:5 7971
s them from the wilderness of Num 13:3 7971
which Moses *s* to spy out the land Num 13:16 7971
Moses *s* them to spy out the land Num 13:17 7971
which Moses *s* to search the land, Num 14:36 7971
Moses *s* to call Dathan and Abiram, Num 16:12 7971
hath *s* me to do all these works Num 16:28 7971
then the LORD hath not *s* me Num 16:29 7971
Moses *s* messengers from Kadesh Num 20:14 7971
s an angel, and hath brought us Num 20:16 7971
the LORD *s* fiery serpents among Num 21:6 7971
Israel *s* messengers unto Sihon Num 21:21 7971
Moses *s* to spy out Jaazer, and Num 21:32 7971
He *s* messengers therefore unto Num 22:5 7971
of Moab, hath *s* unto me, saying, Num 22:10 7971
Balak *s* yet again princes, more, Num 22:15 7971
s to Balaam, and to the princes Num 22:40 7971
Moses *s* them to the war, a Num 31:6 7971
when I *s* them from Kadesh-barnea Num 32:8 7971
I *s* messengers out of the Deut 2:26 7971
the LORD *s* you from Kadesh-barnea Deut 9:23 7971
which *s* her away, may not take Deut 24:4 7971
which the LORD *s* him to do in the Deut 34:11 7971
Joshua the son of Nun *s* out of Josh 2:1 7971
the king of Jericho *s* unto Rahab Josh 2:3 7971
she *s* them away, and they departed Josh 2:21 7971
she hid the messengers that we *s* Josh 6:17 7971
which Joshua *s* to spy out Jericho Josh 6:25 7971
Joshua *s* men from Jericho to Ai, Josh 7:2 7971
So Joshua *s* messengers, and they Josh 7:22 7971
valour, and *s* them away by night Josh 8:3 7971
Joshua therefore *s* them forth Josh 8:9 7971
s unto Hoham king of Hebron Josh 10:3 7971
the men of Gibeon *s* unto Joshua Josh 10:6 7971
that he *s* to Jobab king of Madon, Josh 11:1 7971
s me from Kadesh-barnea to espy Josh 14:7 7971
I was in the day that Moses *s* me Josh 14:11 7971
blessed them, and *s* them away Josh 22:6 7971
when Joshua *s* them away also unto Josh 22:7 7971
the children of Israel *s* unto the Josh 22:13 7971
I *s* Moses also and Aaron, and I Josh 24:5 7971
and warred against Israel, and *s* Josh 24:9 7971
I *s* the hornet before you, which Josh 24:12 7971
of Joseph *s* to descry Beth-el Judg 1:23
s a present unto Eglon the king Judg 3:15 7971
he *s* away the people that bare Judg 3:18 7971
And she *s* and called Barak the son Judg 4:6 7971
he was *s* on foot into the valley Judg 5:15 7971
That the LORD *s* a prophet unto Judg 6:8 7971
have not I *s* thee Judg 6:14 7971
he *s* messengers throughout all Judg 6:35 7971
he *s* messengers unto Asher, and Judg 6:35 7971
he *s* all the rest of Israel every Judg 7:8 7971
Gideon *s* messengers throughout Judg 7:24 7971
Then God *s* an evil spirit between Judg 9:23 7971
he *s* messengers unto Abimelech Judg 9:31 7971
Jephthah *s* messengers unto the Judg 11:12 7971
Jephthah *s* messengers again unto Judg 11:14 7971
Then Israel *s* messengers unto the Judg 11:17 7971
in like manner they *s* unto the Judg 11:17 7971
Israel *s* messengers unto Sihon Judg 11:19 7971
words of Jephthah which he *s* him Judg 11:28 7971
he *s* her away for two months Judg 11:38 7971
daughters, whom he *s* abroad Judg 12:9 7971
had told her all his heart, she *s* Judg 16:18 7971
the children of Dan *s* of their Judg 18:2 7971
s her into all the coasts of Judg 19:29 7971
s her throughout all the country Judg 20:6 7971
the tribes of Israel *s* men Judg 20:12 7971
the congregation *s* thither twelve Judg 21:10 7971
the whole congregation *s* some to Judg 21:13 7971
So the people *s* to Shiloh 1Sa 4:4 7971
They *s* therefore and gathered all 1Sa 5:8 7971
Therefore they *s* the ark of God 1Sa 5:10 7971
So they *s* and gathered together 1Sa 5:11 7971
And they *s* messengers to the 1Sa 6:21 7971
Samuel *s* all the people away, 1Sa 10:25 7971
s them throughout all the coasts 1Sa 11:7 7971
the LORD, then the LORD *s* Moses 1Sa 12:8 7971
the LORD *s* Jerubbaal, and Bedan, 1Sa 12:11 7971
and the LORD *s* thunder and rain 1Sa 12:18 5414
people he *s* every man to his tent 1Sa 13:2 7971
The LORD *s* me to anoint thee to 1Sa 15:1 7971
the LORD *s* thee on a journey, and 1Sa 15:18 7971
gone the way which the LORD *s* me 1Sa 15:20 7971
And he *s*, and brought him in 1Sa 16:12 7971
Wherefore Saul *s* messengers unto 1Sa 16:19 7971
s them by David his son unto Saul 1Sa 16:20 7971
Saul *s* to Jesse, saying, Let 1Sa 16:22 7971
and he *s* for him 1Sa 17:31 3947
went out whithersoever Saul *s* him 1Sa 18:5 7971
Saul also *s* messengers unto 1Sa 19:11 7971
when Saul *s* messengers to take 1Sa 19:14 7971
Saul *s* the messengers again to 1Sa 19:15 7971
s away mine enemy, that he is 1Sa 19:17 7971
Saul *s* messengers to take David 1Sa 19:20 7971
he *s* other messengers, and they 1Sa 19:21 7971
Saul *s* messengers again the third 1Sa 19:21 7971
for the LORD hath *s* thee away 1Sa 20:22 7971
Then the king *s* to call Ahimelech 1Sa 22:11 7971
David *s* out ten young men, and 1Sa 25:5 7971
David *s* messengers out of the 1Sa 25:14 7971
which *s* thee this day to meet me 1Sa 25:32 7971
And David *s* and communed with 1Sa 25:39 7971
David *s* us unto thee, to take 1Sa 25:40 7971
David therefore *s* out spies 1Sa 26:4 7971
he *s* of the spoil unto the elders 1Sa 30:26 7971
armour, and *s* into the land of the 1Sa 31:9 7971
David *s* messengers unto the men 2Sa 2:5 7971
Abner *s* messengers to David on 2Sa 3:12 7971
David *s* messengers to Ish-bosheth 2Sa 3:14 7971
And Ish-bosheth *s*, and took her 2Sa 3:15 7971
And David *s* Abner away 2Sa 3:21 7971
for he had *s* him away, and he was 2Sa 3:22 7971
he hath *s* him away, and he is gone 2Sa 3:23 7971
is it that thou hast *s* him away 2Sa 3:24 7971
he *s* messengers after Abner, 2Sa 3:26 7971
Hiram king of Tyre *s* messengers 2Sa 5:11 7971
Then Toi *s* Joram his son unto 2Sa 8:10 7971
Then king David *s*, and fetched him 2Sa 9:5 7971
David *s* to comfort him by the 2Sa 10:2 7971
that he hath *s* comforters unto 2Sa 10:3 7971
hath not David rather *s* his 2Sa 10:3 7971
to their buttocks, and *s* them away 2Sa 10:4 7971
he *s* to meet them, because the 2Sa 10:5 7971
David, the children of Ammon *s* 2Sa 10:6 7971
he *s* Joab, and all the host of the 2Sa 10:7 7971
And Hadarezer *s*, and brought out 2Sa 10:16 7971
to battle, that David *s* Joab 2Sa 11:1 7971
And David *s* and enquired after the 2Sa 11:3 7971
David *s* messengers, and took her 2Sa 11:4 7971
And the woman conceived, and *s* 2Sa 11:5 7971
David *s* to Joab, saying, Send me 2Sa 11:6 7971
And Joab *s* Uriah to David 2Sa 11:6 7971
s it by the hand of Uriah 2Sa 11:14 7971
Then Joab *s* and told David all the 2Sa 11:18 7971

David all that Joab had s him for	2Sa 11:22	7971
the mourning was past, David s	2Sa 11:27	7971
the LORD s Nathan unto David	2Sa 12:1	7971
he s by the hand of Nathan the	2Sa 12:25	7971
Joab s messengers to David, and	2Sa 12:27	7971
Then David s home to Tamar,	2Sa 13:7	7971
Joab s to Tekoah, and fetched	2Sa 14:2	7971
Therefore Absalom s for Joab	2Sa 14:29	7971
to have s him to the king	2Sa 14:29	
when he s again the second time,	2Sa 14:29	7971
I s unto thee, saying, Come	2Sa 14:32	7971
But Absalom s spies throughout	2Sa 15:10	7971
Absalom s for Ahithophel the	2Sa 15:12	7971
David s forth a third part of the	2Sa 18:2	7971
When Joab s the king's servant,	2Sa 18:29	7971
And king David s to Zadok and to	2Sa 19:11	7971
so that they s this word unto the	2Sa 19:14	7971
he s out arrows, and scattered	2Sa 22:15	7971
He s from above, he took me	2Sa 22:17	7971
I shall return to him that s me	2Sa 24:13	7971
So the LORD s a pestilence upon	2Sa 24:15	5414
the king hath s with him Zadok	1Kin 1:44	7971
So king Solomon s, and they	1Kin 1:53	7971
king Solomon s by the hand of	1Kin 2:25	7971
Then Solomon s Benaiah the son of	1Kin 2:29	7971
And the king s and called for	1Kin 2:36	7971
And the king s and called for	1Kin 2:42	7971
Hiram king of Tyre s his servants	1Kin 5:1	7971
Solomon s to Hiram, saying,	1Kin 5:2	7971
Hiram s to Solomon, saying, I	1Kin 5:8	7971
he s them to Lebanon, ten	1Kin 5:14	7971
And king Solomon s and fetched	1Kin 7:13	7971
eighth day he s the people away	1Kin 8:66	7971
Hiram s to the king sixscore	1Kin 9:14	7971
Hiram s in the navy his servants,	1Kin 9:27	7971
That they s and called him	1Kin 12:3	7971
Then king Rehoboam s Adoram	1Kin 12:18	7971
was come again, that they s	1Kin 12:20	7971
for I am s to thee with heavy	1Kin 14:6	7971
king Asa s them to Ben-hadad, the	1Kin 15:18	7971
I have s unto thee a present of	1Kin 15:19	7971
s the captains of the hosts which	1Kin 15:20	7971
my lord hath not s to seek thee	1Kin 18:10	7971
So Ahab s unto all the children	1Kin 18:20	7971
Then Jezebel s a messenger unto	1Kin 19:2	7971
he s messengers to Ahab king of	1Kin 20:2	7971
Although I have s unto thee	1Kin 20:5	7971
for he s unto me for my wives, and	1Kin 20:7	7971
And Ben-hadad s unto him, and said,	1Kin 20:10	7971
and Ben-hadad s out, and they told	1Kin 20:17	7971
covenant with him, and s him away	1Kin 20:34	7971
s the letters unto the elders and	1Kin 21:8	7971
did as Jezebel had s unto them	1Kin 21:11	7971
letters which she had s unto them	1Kin 21:11	7971
Then they s to Jezebel, saying,	1Kin 21:14	7971
he s messengers, and said unto	2Kin 1:2	7971
again unto the king that s you	2Kin 1:6	7971
Then the king s unto him a	2Kin 1:9	7971
Again also he s unto him another	2Kin 1:11	7971
he s again a captain of the third	2Kin 1:13	7971
LORD, Forasmuch as thou hast s	2Kin 1:16	7971
for the LORD hath s me to Beth-el	2Kin 2:2	7971
for the LORD hath s me to Jericho	2Kin 2:4	7971
for the LORD hath s me to Jordan	2Kin 2:6	7971
They s therefore fifty men	2Kin 2:17	7971
s to Jehoshaphat the king of	2Kin 3:7	7971
I have therewith s Naaman my	2Kin 5:6	7971
that he s to the king, saying,	2Kin 5:8	7971
Elisha s a messenger unto him,	2Kin 5:10	7971
My master hath s me, saying,	2Kin 5:22	7971
the man of God s unto the king of	2Kin 6:9	7971
the king of Israel s to the place	2Kin 6:10	7971
Therefore s he thither horses, and	2Kin 6:14	7971
he s them away, and they went to	2Kin 6:23	7971
the king s a man from before him	2Kin 6:32	7971
hath s to take away mine head	2Kin 6:32	7971
the king s after the host of the	2Kin 7:14	7971
king of Syria hath s me to thee	2Kin 8:9	7971
Then he s out a second on	2Kin 9:19	7971
s to Samaria, unto the rulers of	2Kin 10:1	7971
s to Jehu, saying, We are thy	2Kin 10:5	7971
baskets, and s him them to Jezreel	2Kin 10:7	7971
Jehu s through all Israel	2Kin 10:21	7971
And the seventh year Jehoiada s	2Kin 11:4	7971
s it to Hazael king of Syria	2Kin 12:18	7971
Then Amaziah s messengers to	2Kin 14:8	7971
Israel s to Amaziah king of Judah	2Kin 14:9	7971
s to the cedar that was in	2Kin 14:9	7971
but they s after him to Lachish,	2Kin 14:19	7971
So Ahaz s messengers to	2Kin 16:7	7971
s it for a present to the king of	2Kin 16:8	7971
king Ahaz s to Urijah the priest	2Kin 16:10	7971
king Ahaz had s from Damascus	2Kin 16:11	7971
for he had s messengers to So	2Kin 17:4	7971
which I s to you by my servants	2Kin 17:13	7971
the LORD s lions among them	2Kin 17:25	7971
he hath s lions among them	2Kin 17:26	7971
Hezekiah king of Judah s to the	2Kin 18:14	7971
And the king of Assyria s Tartan	2Kin 18:17	7971
Hath my master s me to thy master	2Kin 18:27	7971
hath he not s me to the men which	2Kin 18:27	
he s Eliakim, which was over the	2Kin 19:2	7971
hath s to reproach the living God	2Kin 19:4	7971
he s messengers again unto	2Kin 19:9	7971
which hath s him to reproach the	2Kin 19:16	7971
the son of Amoz s to Hezekiah	2Kin 19:20	7971
s letters and a present unto	2Kin 20:12	7971
that the king s Shaphan the son	2Kin 22:3	7971
Tell the man that s you to me	2Kin 22:15	7971
s you to enquire of the LORD	2Kin 22:18	7971
And the king s, and they gathered	2Kin 23:1	7971
were there in the mount, and s	2Kin 23:16	7971
the LORD s against him bands of	2Kin 24:2	7971
s them against Judah to destroy	2Kin 24:2	7971
of Moab, after he had s them away	1Chr 8:8	7971
armour, and s into the land of the	1Chr 10:9	7971
upon advisement s him away	1Chr 12:19	7971
of Tyre s messengers to David	1Chr 14:1	7971
He s Hadoram his son to king	1Chr 18:10	7971
David s messengers to comfort him	1Chr 19:2	7971
that he hath s comforters unto	1Chr 19:3	7971
by their buttocks, and s them away	1Chr 19:4	7971
And he s to meet them	1Chr 19:5	7971
the children of Ammon s a	1Chr 19:6	7971
he s Joab, and all the host of the	1Chr 19:8	7971
they s messengers, and drew forth	1Chr 19:16	7971
bring again to him that s me	1Chr 21:12	7971
So the LORD s pestilence upon	1Chr 21:14	5414
God s an angel unto Jerusalem to	1Chr 21:15	7971
Solomon s to Huram the king of	2Chr 2:3	7971
which he s to Solomon, Because	2Chr 2:11	7971
now I have s a cunning man,	2Chr 2:13	7971
he s the people away into their	2Chr 7:10	7971
Huram s him by the hands of his	2Chr 8:18	7971
And they s and called him	2Chr 10:3	7971
Then king Rehoboam s Hadoram that	2Chr 10:18	7971
s to Ben-hadad king of Syria,	2Chr 16:2	7971
I have s thee silver and gold	2Chr 16:3	7971
s the captains of his armies	2Chr 16:4	7971
of his reign he s to his princes	2Chr 17:7	7971
And with them he s Levites	2Chr 17:8	
Yet he s prophets to them, to	2Chr 24:19	7971
s all the spoil of them unto the	2Chr 24:23	7971
of the army which Amaziah s back	2Chr 25:13	7725
he s unto him a prophet, which	2Chr 25:15	7971
s to Joash, the son of Jehoahaz,	2Chr 25:17	7971
Joash king of Israel s to Amaziah	2Chr 25:18	7971
s to the cedar that was in	2Chr 25:18	7971
but they s to Lachish after him,	2Chr 25:27	7971
Hezekiah s to all Israel and Judah	2Chr 30:1	7971
And the LORD s an angel, which cut	2Chr 32:21	7971
who s unto him to enquire of the	2Chr 32:31	7971
he s Shaphan the son of Azaliah,	2Chr 34:8	7971
Tell ye the man that s you to me	2Chr 34:23	7971
who s you to enquire of the LORD,	2Chr 34:26	7971
Then the king s and gathered	2Chr 34:29	7971
But he s ambassadors to him,	2Chr 35:21	7971
expired, king Nebuchadnezzar s	2Chr 36:10	7971
s to them by his messengers	2Chr 36:15	7971
the letter that they s unto him	Ezr 4:11	7972
dishonour, therefore have we s	Ezr 4:14	7972
Then s the king an answer unto	Ezr 4:17	7972
The letter which ye s unto us	Ezr 4:18	7972
the river, s unto Darius the king	Ezr 5:6	7972
They s a letter unto him, wherein	Ezr 5:7	7972
that which Darius the king had s	Ezr 6:13	7972
as thou art s of the king	Ezr 7:14	7972
Then s I for Eliezer, for Ariel,	Ezr 8:16	7971
I s them with commandment unto	Ezr 8:17	6680
Now the king had s captains of	Neh 2:9	7971
Geshem s unto me, saying, Come,	Neh 6:2	7971
I s messengers unto them, saying,	Neh 6:3	7971
Yet they s unto me four times	Neh 6:4	7971
Then s Sanballat his servant unto	Neh 6:5	7971
Then I s unto him, saying, There	Neh 6:8	7971
perceived that God had not s him	Neh 6:12	7971
Judah s many letters unto Tobiah	Neh 6:17	1980
Tobiah s letters to put me in	Neh 6:19	7971
For he s letters into all the	Est 1:22	7971
the letters were s by posts into	Est 3:13	7971
she s raiment to clothe Mordecai,	Est 4:4	7971
and when he came home, he s	Est 5:10	7971
s letters by posts on horseback,	Est 8:10	7971
s letters unto all the Jews that	Est 9:20	7971
he s the letters unto all the	Est 9:30	7971
and s and called for their three	Job 1:4	7971
were gone about, that Job s	Job 1:5	7971
Thou hast s widows away empty, and	Job 22:9	7971
Who hath s out the wild ass free	Job 39:5	7971
he s out his arrows, and scattered	Ps 18:14	7971
He s from above, he took me, he	Ps 18:16	7971
when Saul s, and they watched the	Ps 59:t	7971
the skies s out a sound	Ps 77:17	5414
he s them meat to the full	Ps 78:25	7971
He s divers sorts of flies among	Ps 78:45	7971
She s out her boughs unto the sea	Ps 80:11	7971
He s a man before them, even	Ps 105:17	7971
The king s and loosed him	Ps 105:20	7971
He s Moses his servant	Ps 105:26	7971
He s darkness, and made it dark	Ps 105:28	7971
but s leanness into their soul	Ps 106:15	7971
He s his word, and healed them, and	Ps 107:20	7971
He s redemption unto his people	Ps 111:9	7971
Who s tokens and wonders into the	Ps 135:9	7971
She hath s forth her maidens	Prov 9:3	7971
messenger shall be s against him	Prov 17:11	7971
The Lord s a word into Jacob, and	Is 9:8	7971
Sargon the king of Assyria s him	Is 20:1	7971
the king of Assyria s Rabshakeh	Is 36:2	7971
Hath my master s me to thy master	Is 36:12	7971
hath he not s me to the men that	Is 36:12	
he s Eliakim, who was over the	Is 37:2	7971
hath s to reproach the living God	Is 37:4	7971
he s messengers to Hezekiah,	Is 37:9	7971
which hath s to reproach the	Is 37:17	7971
the son of Amoz s unto Hezekiah	Is 37:21	7971
s letters and a present to	Is 39:1	7971
or deaf, as my messenger that I s	Is 42:19	7971
For your sake I have s to Babylon	Is 43:14	7971
GOD, and his Spirit, hath s me	Is 48:16	7971
in the thing whereto I s it	Is 55:11	7971
he hath s me to bind up the	Is 61:1	7971
s unto you all my servants the	Jer 7:25	7971
their nobles have s their little	Jer 14:3	7971
I s them not, neither have I	Jer 14:14	7971
I s them not, yet they say, Sword	Jer 14:15	7971
the LORD had s him to prophesy	Jer 19:14	7971
when king Zedekiah s unto him	Jer 21:1	7971
I have not s these prophets, yet	Jer 23:21	7971
yet I s them not, nor commanded	Jer 23:32	7971
I have s unto you, saying, Ye	Jer 23:38	7971
whom I have s out of this place	Jer 24:5	7971
the LORD hath s unto you all his	Jer 25:4	7971
unto whom the LORD had s me	Jer 25:17	7971
whom I s unto you, both rising up	Jer 26:5	7971
The LORD s me to prophesy against	Jer 26:12	7971
for of a truth the LORD hath s me	Jer 26:15	7971
the king s men into Egypt	Jer 26:22	7971
For I have not s them, saith the	Jer 27:15	7971
that the LORD hath truly s him	Jer 28:9	7971
The LORD hath not s thee	Jer 28:15	7971
that Jeremiah the prophet s from	Jer 29:1	7971
(whom Zedekiah king of Judah s	Jer 29:3	7971
I have not s them, saith the LORD	Jer 29:9	7971
which I s unto them by my	Jer 29:19	7971
whom I have s from Jerusalem to	Jer 29:20	7971
Because thou hast s letters in	Jer 29:25	7971
For therefore he s unto us in	Jer 29:28	7971
I s him not, and he caused you to	Jer 29:31	7971
I have s also unto you all my	Jer 35:15	7971
Therefore all the princes s	Jer 36:14	7971
So the king s Jehudi to fetch the	Jer 36:21	7971
Zedekiah the king s Jehucal the	Jer 37:3	7971
that s you unto me to enquire of	Jer 37:7	7971
Then Zedekiah the king s, and took	Jer 37:17	7971
Then Zedekiah the king s, and took	Jer 38:14	7971
the captain of the guard s	Jer 39:13	7971
Even they s, and took Jeremiah out	Jer 39:14	7971
the king of the Ammonites hath s	Jer 40:14	7971
unto whom ye s me to present your	Jer 42:9	7971
when ye s me unto the LORD your	Jer 42:20	7971
the which he hath s me unto you	Jer 42:21	7971
LORD their God had s him to them	Jer 43:1	7971
our God hath not s thee to say	Jer 43:2	7971
Howbeit I s unto you all my	Jer 44:4	7971
ambassador is s unto the heathen	Jer 49:14	7971
hath he s fire into my bones	Lam 1:13	7971
behold, an hand was s unto me	Eze 2:9	7971
For thou art not s to a people of	Eze 3:5	7971
had I s thee to them, they would	Eze 3:6	7971
and the LORD hath not s them	Eze 13:6	7971
s messengers unto them into	Eze 23:16	7971
that ye have s for men to come	Eze 23:40	7971
far, unto whom a messenger was s	Eze 23:40	7971
s out her little rivers unto all	Eze 31:4	7971
Then Nebuchadnezzar the king s to	Dan 3:2	7972
who hath s his angel, and	Dan 3:28	7972
the part of the hand s from him	Dan 5:24	7972
My God hath s his angel, and hath	Dan 6:22	7972
for unto thee am I now s	Dan 10:11	7971
the Assyrian, and s to king Jareb	Hos 5:13	7971
my great army which I s among you	Joel 2:25	7971
I have s among you the pestilence	Amos 4:10	7971
s to Jeroboam king of Israel	Amos 7:10	7971
an ambassador is s among the	Obad 1	7971
But the LORD s out a great wind	Jonah 1:4	2904
I s before thee Moses, Aaron, and	Mic 6:4	7971
as the LORD their God had s him	Hag 1:12	7971
whom the LORD hath s to walk to	Zec 1:10	7971
After the glory hath he s me unto	Zec 2:8	7971
that the LORD of hosts hath s me	Zec 2:9	7971
LORD of hosts hath s me unto thee	Zec 2:11	7971
LORD of hosts hath s me unto you	Zec 4:9	7971
LORD of hosts hath s me unto you	Zec 6:15	7971
When they had s unto the house of	Zec 7:2	7971
s in his spirit by the former	Zec 7:12	7971
blood of thy covenant I have s	Zec 9:11	7971
have s this commandment unto you	Mal 2:4	7971
he s them to Bethlehem, and said,	Mt 2:8	3992
s forth, and slew all the children	Mt 2:16	649
These twelve Jesus s forth	Mt 10:5	649
me receiveth him that s me	Mt 10:40	649
he s two of his disciples,	Mt 11:2	3992
Then Jesus s the multitude away,	Mt 13:36	863
And he s, and beheaded John in the	Mt 14:10	3992
while he s the multitudes away	Mt 14:22	630
when he had s the multitudes away	Mt 14:23	630
they s out into all that country	Mt 14:35	649
I am not s but unto the lost	Mt 15:24	649
he s away the multitude, and took	Mt 15:39	630
he s them into his vineyard	Mt 20:2	649
then s Jesus two disciples,	Mt 21:1	649
near, he s his servants to the	Mt 21:34	649
he s other servants more than the	Mt 21:36	649
of all he s unto them his son	Mt 21:37	649
s forth his servants to call them	Mt 22:3	649
he s forth other servants, saying	Mt 22:4	649
he s forth his armies, and	Mt 22:7	3992
they s out unto him their	Mt 22:16	649
them which are s unto thee	Mt 23:37	649
seat, his wife s unto him	Mt 27:19	649
him, and forthwith s him away	Mk 1:43	1544
without, s unto him, calling him	Mk 3:31	649
And when they had s away the	Mk 4:36	863
For Herod himself had s forth	Mk 6:17	649
the king s an executioner	Mk 6:27	649
while he s away the people	Mk 6:45	628
And when he had s them away	Mk 6:46	657
and he s them away	Mk 8:9	630
he s him away to his house,	Mk 8:26	649
not me, but him that s me	Mk 9:37	649
at the season he s to the	Mk 12:2	649
and beat him, and s him away empty	Mk 12:3	649
again he s unto them another	Mk 12:4	649
s him away shamefully handled	Mk 12:4	649
And again he s another	Mk 12:5	649
he s him also last unto them,	Mk 12:6	649
am s to speak unto thee, and to	Lk 1:19	649
month the angel Gabriel was s	Lk 1:26	649
and the rich he hath s empty away	Lk 1:53	1821
he hath s me to heal the	Lk 4:18	649
But unto none of them was Elias s	Lk 4:26	3992

for therefore am I s. Lk 4:43 649
he s unto him the elders of the Lk 7:3 649
the centurion s friends to him, Lk 7:6 3992
And they that were s, returning to Lk 7:10 3992
of his disciples s them to Jesus Lk 7:19
John Baptist hath s us unto thee Lk 7:20 649
but Jesus s him away, saying, Lk 8:38 630
he s them to preach the kingdom Lk 9:2 649
me receiveth him that s me Lk 9:48 649
s messengers before his face Lk 9:52 649
s them two and two before his face Lk 10:1 649
me despiseth him that s me Lk 10:16 649
stonest them that are s unto thee Lk 13:34 649
s his servant at supper time to Lk 14:17 649
he s him into his fields to feed Lk 15:15 3992
s a message after him, saying, We Lk 19:14 649
he s two of his disciples, Lk 19:29 649
they that were s went their way Lk 19:32 649
at the season he s a servant to Lk 20:10 640
beat him, and s him away empty Lk 20:10 1821
again he s another servant Lk 20:11 3992
shamefully, and s him away empty Lk 20:11 1821
And again he s a third Lk 20:12 3992
s forth spies, which should feign Lk 20:20 649
he s Peter and John, saying, Go and Lk 22:8 649
When I s you without purse, and Lk 22:35 649
he s him to Herod, who himself Lk 23:7 375
robe, and s him again to Pilate Lk 23:11 375
for I s you to him Lk 23:15 375
There was a man s from God Jn 1:6 649
but was s to bear witness of that Jn 1:8
of John, when the Jews s priests Jn 1:19 649
give an answer to them that s us Jn 1:22 3992
they which were s were of the Jn 1:24 649
but he that s me to baptize with Jn 1:33 3992
For God s not his Son into the Jn 3:17 649
but that I am s before him Jn 3:28 649
For he whom God hath s speaketh Jn 3:34 649
to do the will of him that s me Jn 4:34 3992
I s you to reap that whereon ye Jn 4:38 649
not the Father which hath s him Jn 5:23 3992
and believeth on him that s me Jn 5:24 3992
of the Father which hath s me Jn 5:30 3992
Ye s unto John, and he bare Jn 5:33 649
of me, that the Father hath s me Jn 5:36 649
Father himself, which hath s me Jn 5:37 3992
for whom he hath s, him ye Jn 5:38 649
ye believe on him whom he hath s Jn 6:29 649
but the will of him that s me Jn 6:38 3992
the Father's will which hath s me Jn 6:39 3992
this is the will of him that s me Jn 6:40 3992
Father which hath s me draw him Jn 6:44 3992
As the living Father hath s me Jn 6:57 649
is not mine, but his that s me Jn 7:16 3992
that seeketh his glory that s him Jn 7:18 3992
myself, but he that s me is true Jn 7:28 3992
I am from him, and he hath s me Jn 7:29 649
the chief priests s officers to Jn 7:32 649
and then I go unto him that s me Jn 7:33 3992
but I and the Father that s me Jn 8:16 3992
the Father that s me beareth Jn 8:18 3992
but he that s me is true Jn 8:26 3992
And he that s me is with me Jn 8:29 3992
came I of myself, but he s me Jn 8:42 649
work the works of him that s me Jn 9:4 3992
(which is by interpretation, S Jn 9:7 649
and s into the world, Thou Jn 10:36 649
Therefore his sisters s unto him Jn 11:3 649
may believe that thou hast s me Jn 11:42 649
not on me, but on him that s me Jn 12:44 3992
that seeth me seeth him that s me Jn 12:45 3992
but the Father which s me Jn 12:49 3992
neither he that is s is greater than Jn 13:16 652
greater than he that s him Jn 13:16 652
me receiveth him that s me Jn 13:20 3992
mine, but the Father's which s me Jn 14:24 3992
they know not him that s me Jn 15:21 3992
now I go my way to him that s me Jn 16:5 3992
and Jesus Christ, whom thou hast s Jn 17:3 649
As thou hast s me into the world, Jn 17:18 649
have I also s them into the world Jn 17:18 649
may believe that thou hast s me Jn 17:21 649
may know that thou hast s me Jn 17:23 649
have known that thou hast s me Jn 17:25 649
Now Annas had s him bound unto Jn 18:24 649
as my Father hath s me, even so Jn 20:21 649
s him to bless you, in turning Acts 3:26 649
s to the prison to have them Acts 5:21 649
he s out our fathers first Acts 7:12 1821
Then s Joseph, and called his Acts 7:14 649
they s unto them Peter and John Acts 8:14 649
the way as thou camest, hath s me Acts 9:17 649
and s him forth to Tarsus Acts 9:30 1821
they s unto him two men, desiring Acts 9:38 649
unto them, he s them to Joppa Acts 10:8 649
the men which were s from Acts 10:17 649
for I have s them Acts 10:20 649
were s unto him from Cornelius Acts 10:21 649
as soon as I was s for Acts 10:29 3343
for what intent ye have s for me Acts 10:29 3343
Immediately therefore I s to thee Acts 10:33 3992
The word which God s unto the Acts 10:36 649
I was, s from Caesarea unto me Acts 11:11 649
they s forth Barnabas, that he Acts 11:22 1821
s it to the elders by the hands Acts 11:30 649
that the Lord hath s his angel Acts 12:11 1821
hands on them, they s them away Acts 13:3 630
being s forth by the Holy Ghost, Acts 13:4 1599
of the synagogue s unto them Acts 13:15 649
is the word of this salvation s Acts 13:26 649
We have s therefore Judas and Acts 15:27 649
the magistrates s the serjeants Acts 16:35 649
magistrates have s to let you go Acts 16:36 649
brethren immediately s away Paul Acts 17:10 1599
s away Paul to go as it were to Acts 17:14 1821
So he s into Macedonia two of Acts 19:22 649
s unto him, desiring him that he Acts 19:31 3992
And from Miletus he s to Ephesus Acts 20:17 3992
I s straightway to thee, and gave Acts 23:30 3992
he s for Paul, and heard him Acts 24:24 3343
wherefore he s for him the Acts 24:26 3343
of God is s unto the Gentiles Acts 28:28 649
they preach, except they be s Rom 10:15 649
s by Phebe servant of the church Rom s
For Christ s me not to baptize, 1Cor 1:17 649
cause have I s unto you Timotheus 1Cor 4:17
we have s with him the brother, 2Cor 8:18 4842
we have s with them our brother, 2Cor 8:22 4842
Yet have I s the brethren, lest 2Cor 9:3 3992
by any of them whom I s unto you 2Cor 12:17 649
Titus, and with him I s a brother 2Cor 12:18 4882
God s forth his Son, made of a Gal 4:4 1821
God hath s forth the Spirit of Gal 4:6 1821
Whom I have s unto you for the Eph 6:22 3992
I s him therefore the more Phil 2:28 3992
even in Thessalonica ye s once Phil 4:16 3992
the things which were s from you Phil 4:18
Whom I have s unto you for the Col 4:8 3992
s Timotheus, our brother, and 1Th 3:2 3992
I s to know your faith, lest by 1Th 3:5 375
And Tychicus have I s to Ephesus 2Ti 4:12 649
Whom I have s again Philem 12 628
s forth to minister for them who Heb 1:14 649
had s them out another way Jas 2:25 1524
the Holy Ghost s down from heaven 1Pet 1:12 649
as unto them that are s by him 1Pet 2:14 3992
because that God s his only 1Jn 4:9 649
s his Son to be the propitiation 1Jn 4:10 649
do testify that the Father s the 1Jn 4:14 649
and he s and signified it by his Rev 1:1 649
of God s forth into all the earth Rev 5:6 649
s his angel to shew unto his Rev 22:6 649
I Jesus have s mine angel to Rev 22:16 3992

SENTENCE
shall shew thee the s of judgment Deut 17:9 1697
thou shalt do according to the s Deut 17:10 1697
According to the s of the law Deut 17:11 6310
the s which they shall shew thee Deut 17:11 1697
Let my s come forth from thy Ps 17:2 4941
A divine s is in the lips of the Prov 16:10 7081
Because s against an evil work is Eccl 8:11 6599
also will I give s against them Jer 4:12 4941
Pilate gave s that it should be Lk 23:24 1948
Wherefore my s is, that we Acts 15:19 2919
But we had the s of death in 2Cor 1:9 610

SENTENCES
of dreams, and shewing of hard s Dan 5:12 280
and understanding dark s, shall Dan 8:23 2420

SENTEST
thou s forth thy wrath, which Ex 15:7 7971
unto the land whither thou s us Num 13:27 7971
messengers which thou s unto me Num 24:12 7971
the things which thou s to me for 1Kin 5:8 7971

SENUAH (*sen'-u-ah*) See HASSENUAH. *Father of Judah.*
Judah the son of S was second Neh 11:9 5574

SEORIM (*se-o'-rim*) *A sanctuary servant.*
third to Harim, the fourth to S 1Chr 24:8 8188

SEPARATE
s thyself, I pray thee, from me Gen 13:9 6504
And Jacob did s the lambs, and set Gen 30:40 6504
him that was s from his brethren Gen 49:26 5139
Thus shall ye s the children of Lev 15:31 5144
that they s themselves from the Lev 22:2 5144
s themselves to vow a vow of a Num 6:2 6381
to s themselves unto the LORD Num 6:2 5144
He shall s himself from wine and Num 6:3 5144
Thus shalt thou s the Levites Num 8:14 914
S yourselves from among this Num 16:21 914
Thou shalt s three cities for Deut 19:2 914
Thou shalt s three cities for Deut 19:7 914
the LORD shall s him unto evil Deut 29:21 914
the s cities for the children of Josh 16:9 3995
For thou didst s them from among 1Kin 8:53 914
s yourselves from the people of Ezr 10:11 914
to s himself thence in the midst Jer 37:12 2505
the s place at the end toward the Eze 41:12 1508
the s place, and the building, Eze 41:13 1508
of the s place toward the east, Eze 41:14 1508
the s place which was behind it Eze 41:15 1508
that was over against the s place Eze 42:1 1508
east, over against the s place Eze 42:10 1508
which are before the s place Eze 42:13 1508
he shall s them one from another, Mt 25:32 873
when they shall s you from their Lk 6:22 873
S me Barnabas and Saul for the Acts 13:2 873
Who shall s us from the love of Rom 8:35 5562
shall be able to s us from the Rom 8:39 5562
out from among them, and be ye s 2Cor 6:17 873
s from sinners, and made higher Heb 7:26 5562
These be they who s themselves Jude 19 873

SEPARATED
they s themselves the one from Gen 13:11 6504
after that Lot was s from him Gen 13:14 6504
people shall be s from thy bowels Gen 25:23 6504
so shall we be s, I and thy people Ex 33:16 6395
which have s you from other Lev 20:24 914
which I have s from you as Lev 20:25 914
that the God of Israel hath s you Num 16:9 914
time the LORD s the tribe of Levi Deut 10:8 914
when he s the sons of Adam, he Deut 32:8 6504
him that was s from his brethren Deut 33:16 5139
of the Gadites there s themselves 1Chr 12:8 914
and Aaron was s, that he should 1Chr 23:13 914
the captains of the host s to the 1Chr 25:1 914
Then Amaziah s them, to wit, the 2Chr 25:10 914
all such as had s themselves unto Ezr 6:21 6395
Then I s twelve of the chief of Ezr 8:24 914
have not s themselves from the Ezr 9:1 914
himself s from the congregation Ezr 10:8 914
of them by their names, were s Ezr 10:16 914
we are s upon the wall, one far Neh 4:19 6504
the seed of Israel s themselves Neh 9:2 914
all they that had s themselves Neh 10:28 914
that they s from Israel all the Neh 13:3 914
having s himself, seeketh and Prov 18:1 6504
but the poor is s from his Prov 19:4 6504
hath utterly s me from his people Is 56:3 914
iniquities have s between you Is 59:2 914
for themselves are s with whores Hos 4:14 6504
s themselves unto that shame Hos 9:10 5144
s the disciples, disputing daily Acts 19:9 873
s unto the gospel of God, Rom 1:1 873
who s me from my mother's womb, Gal 1:15 873
s himself, fearing them which Gal 2:12 873

SEPARATETH
in the which he s himself unto Num 6:5 5144
All the days that he s himself Num 6:6 5144
a whisperer s chief friends Prov 16:28 6504
repeateth a matter s very friends Prov 17:9 6504
which s himself from me, and Eze 14:7 5144

SEPARATING
s myself, as I have done these so Zec 7:3 5144

SEPARATION
according to the days of the s Lev 12:2 5079
be unclean two weeks, as in her s Lev 12:5 5079
upon in her s shall be unclean Lev 15:20 5079
days out of the time of her s Lev 15:25 5079
it run beyond the time of her s Lev 15:25 5079
shall be as the days of her s Lev 15:25 5079
be unto her as the bed of her s Lev 15:26 5079
as the uncleanness of her s Lev 15:26 5079
All the days of his s shall he Num 6:4 5145
s there shall no razor come upon Num 6:5 5145
All the days of his s he is holy Num 6:8 5145
unto the LORD the days of his s Num 6:12 5145
lost, because his s was defiled Num 6:12 5145
the days of his s are fulfilled Num 6:13 5145
shall shave the head of his s at Num 6:18 5145
the hair of the head of his s Num 6:18 5145
after the hair of his s is shaven Num 6:19 5145
offering unto the LORD for his s Num 6:21 5145
he must do after the law of his s Num 6:21 5145
of Israel for a water of s Num 19:9 5079
because the water of s was not Num 19:13 5079
the water of s hath not been Num 19:20 5079
water of s shall wash his clothes Num 19:21 5079
of s shall be unclean until even Num 19:21 5079
be purified with the water of s Num 31:23 5079
to make a s between the sanctuary Eze 42:20 914

SEPHAR (*se'-far*) *A mountain in Arabia.*
as thou goest unto S a mount of Gen 10:30 5611

SEPHARAD (*sef'-a-rad*) *A city in Media.*
of Jerusalem, which is in S Obad 20 5614

SEPHARVAIM (*sef-ar-va'-im*) See SEPHARVITES. *A city in Mesopotamia.*
Ava, and from Hamath, and from S 2Kin 17:24 5617
and Anammelech, the gods of S 2Kin 17:31 5617
where are the gods of S, Hena, and 2Kin 18:34 5617
and the king of the city of S 2Kin 19:13 5617
where are the gods of S Is 36:19 5617
and the king of the city of S Is 37:13 5617

SEPHARVITES (*sef'-ar-vites*) *Inhabitants of Sepharvaim.*
the S burnt their children in 2Kin 17:31 5616

SEPULCHRE
us shall withhold from thee his s Gen 23:6 6913
knoweth of his s unto this day Deut 34:6 6900
was buried in the s of Joash his Judg 8:32 6913
s in the border of Benjamin at 1Sa 10:2 6900
buried him in the s of his father 2Sa 2:32 6913
buried it in the s of Abner in 2Sa 4:12 6913
was buried in the s of his father 2Sa 17:23 6913
in the s of Kish his father 2Sa 21:14 6913
come unto the s of thy fathers 1Kin 13:22 6913
then bury me in the s wherein the 1Kin 13:31 6913
buried him in his s with his 2Kin 9:28 6900
cast the man into the s of Elisha 2Kin 13:21 6913
he was buried in his s in the 2Kin 21:26 6900
It is the s of the man of God, 2Kin 23:17 6913
and buried him in his own s 2Kin 23:30 6900
their throat is an open s Ps 5:9 6913
thou hast hewed thee out a s here Is 22:16 6913
that heweth him out an s on high Is 22:16 6913
Their quiver is as an open s Jer 5:16 6913
great stone to the door of the s Mt 27:60 3419
Mary, sitting over against the s Mt 27:61 5028
Command therefore that the s be Mt 27:64 5028
So they went, and made the s sure Mt 27:66 5028
and the other Mary to see the s Mt 28:1 5028
quickly from the s with fear Mt 28:8 3419
laid him in a s which was hewn Mk 15:46 3419
a stone unto the door of the s Mk 15:46 3419
they came unto the s at the Mk 16:2 3419
the stone from the door of the s Mk 16:3 3419
And entering into the s, they saw Mk 16:5 3419
out quickly, and fled from the s Mk 16:8 3419
laid it in a s that was hewn in Lk 23:53 3418
followed after, and beheld the s Lk 23:55 3419
the morning, they came unto the s Lk 24:1 3418
the stone rolled away from the s Lk 24:2 3419
And returned from the s, and told Lk 24:9 3419
arose Peter, and ran unto the s Lk 24:12 3419
which were early at the s Lk 24:22 3419

which were with us went to the *s* Lk 24:24 *3419*
and in the garden a new *s*, wherein Jn 19:41 *3419*
for the *s* was nigh at hand Jn 19:42 *3419*
when it was yet dark, unto the *s* Jn 20:1 *3419*
the stone taken away from the *s* Jn 20:1 *3419*
taken away the Lord out of the *s* Jn 20:2 *3419*
other disciple, and came to the *s* Jn 20:3 *3419*
Peter, and came first to the *s* Jn 20:4 *3419*
following him, and went into the *s* Jn 20:6 *3419*
which came first to the *s* Jn 20:8 *3419*
stood without at the *s* weeping Jn 20:11 *3419*
down, and looked into the *s* Jn 20:11 *3419*
his *s* is with us unto this day Acts 2:29 *3418*
laid in the *s* that Abraham bought Acts 7:16 *3418*
from the tree, and laid him in a *s* Acts 13:29 *3419*
Their throat is an open *s* Rom 3:13 *5028*

SEPULCHRES
the choice of our *s* bury thy dead Gen 23:6 6913
he spied the *s* that were there in 2Kin 23:16 6913
and took the bones out of the *s* 2Kin 23:16 6913
And they buried him in his own *s* 2Chr 16:14 6913
but not in the *s* of the kings 2Chr 21:20 6913
him not in the *s* of the kings 2Chr 24:25 6913
into the *s* of the kings of Israel 2Chr 28:27 6913
of the *s* of the sons of David 2Chr 32:33 6913
in one of the *s* of his fathers 2Chr 35:24 6913
city, the place of my fathers' *s* Neh 2:3 6913
unto the city of my fathers' *s* Neh 2:5 6913
place over against the *s* of David Neh 3:16 6913
for ye are like unto whited *s* Mt 23:27 *5028*
garnish the *s* of the righteous Mt 23:29 *3419*
ye build the *s* of the prophets Lk 11:47 *3419*
killed them, and ye build their *s* Lk 11:48 *3419*

SERAH (*se'-rah*) See SARAH. *A daughter of Asher.*
and Beriah, and *S* their sister Gen 46:17 8294
and Beriah, and *S* their sister 1Chr 7:30 8294

SERAIAH (*se-ra-i'-ah*) See SHAVSHA.
1. David's scribe.
and *S* was the scribe 2Sa 8:17 8304
2. High priest in Zedekiah's time.
the guard took *S* the chief priest 2Kin 25:18 8304
And Azariah begat *S*, and Seraiah 1Chr 6:14 8304
Seraiah, and *S* begat Jehozadak 1Chr 6:14 8304
king of Persia, Ezra the son of *S* Ezr 7:1 8304
the guard took *S* the chief priest Jer 52:24 8304
3. Son of Tanhumeth.
S the son of Tanhumeth the 2Kin 25:23 8304
S the son of Tanhumeth, and the Jer 40:8 8304
4. A son of Kenaz.
Othniel, and *S* 1Chr 4:13 8304
S begat Joab, the father of the 1Chr 4:14 8304
5. Son of Asiel.
the son of Josibiah, the son of *S* 1Chr 4:35 8304
6. A priest with Zerubbabel.
Jeshua, Nehemiah, *S*, Reelaiah Ezr 2:2 8304
S, Azariah, Jeremiah Neh 10:2 8304
S, Jeremiah, Ezra Neh 12:1 8304
of *S*, Meraiah Neh 12:12 8304
7. An exile.
S the son of Hilkiah, the son of Neh 11:11 8304
8. Son of Azriel.
S the son of Azriel, and Shelemiah Jer 36:26 8304
9. Son of Neriah.
commanded *S* the son of Neriah Jer 51:59 8304
this *S* was a quiet prince Jer 51:59 8304
And Jeremiah said to *S*, When thou Jer 51:61 8304

SERAPHIMS
Above it stood the *s* Is 6:2 8314
Then flew one of the *s* unto me Is 6:6 8314

SERED (*se'-red*) See SARDITES. *A son of Zebulun.*
S, and Elon, and Jahleel Gen 46:14 5624
of *S*, the family of the Sardites Num 26:26 5624

SEREDITES See SARDITES.

SERGIUS (*sur'-je-us*) *Roman governor of Cyprus.*
country, *S* Paulus, a prudent man Acts 13:7 4588

SERJEANTS
day, the magistrates sent the *s* Acts 16:35 *4465*
the *s* told these words unto the Acts 16:38 *4465*

SERPENT
Now the *s* was more subtil than Gen 3:1 5175
And the woman said unto the *s* Gen 3:2 5175
the *s* said unto the woman, Ye Gen 3:4 5175
The *s* beguiled me, and I did eat Gen 3:13 5175
And the LORD God said unto the *s* Gen 3:14 5175
Dan shall be a *s* by the way Gen 49:17 5175
on the ground, and it became a *s* Ex 4:3 5175
Pharaoh, and it shall become a *s* Ex 7:9 8577
his servants, and it became a *s* Ex 7:10 8577
a *s* shalt thou take in thine hand Ex 7:15 5175
unto Moses, Make thee a fiery *s* Num 21:8 8314
And Moses made a *s* of brass Num 21:9 5175
that if a *s* had bitten any man Num 21:9 5175
when he beheld the *s* of brass Num 21:9 5175
the brasen *s* that Moses had made 2Kin 18:4 5175
hand hath formed the crooked *s* Job 26:13 5175
poison is like the poison of a *s* Ps 58:4 5175
sharpened their tongues like a *s* Ps 140:3 5175
At the last it biteth like a *s* Prov 23:32 5175
the way of a *s* upon a rock Prov 30:19 5175
an hedge, a *s* shall bite him Eccl 10:8 5175
Surely the *s* will bite without Eccl 10:11 5175
fruit shall be a fiery flying *s* Is 14:29 8314
punish leviathan the piercing *s* Is 27:1 5175
even leviathan that crooked *s* Is 27:1 5175
lion, the viper and fiery flying *s* Is 30:6 8314
voice thereof shall go like a *s* Jer 46:22 5175
hand on the wall, and a *s* bit him Amos 5:19 5175
sea, thence will I command the *s* Amos 9:3 5175
They shall lick the dust like a *s* Mic 7:17 5175
ask a fish, will he give him a *s* Mt 7:10 3789
will he for a fish give him a *s* Lk 11:11 3789
lifted up the *s* in the wilderness Jn 3:14 3789
as the *s* beguiled Eve through his 2Cor 11:3 3789
dragon was cast out, that old *s* Rev 12:9 3789
a time, from the face of the *s* Rev 12:14 3789
the *s* cast out of his mouth water Rev 12:15 3789
hold on the dragon, that old *s* Rev 20:2 3789

SERPENT'S
for out of the *s* root shall come Is 14:29 5175
and dust shall be the *s* meat Is 65:25 5175

SERPENTS
man his rod, and they became *s* Ex 7:12 8577
sent fiery *s* among the people Num 21:6 5175
that he take away the *s* from us Num 21:7 5175
wilderness, wherein were fiery *s* Deut 8:15 5175
with the poison of *s* of the dust Deut 32:24 2119
For, behold, I will send *s* Jer 8:17 5175
be ye therefore wise as *s* Mt 10:16 3789
Ye *s*, ye generation of vipers Mt 23:33 3789
They shall take up *s* Mk 16:18 3789
give unto you power to tread on *s* Lk 10:19 3789
tempted, and were destroyed of *s* 1Cor 10:9 3789
of beasts, and of birds, and of *s* Jas 3:7 *2062*
for their tails were like unto *s* Rev 9:19 3789

SERUG (*se'-rug*) See SARUCH. *Father of Nahor.*
two and thirty years, and begat *S* Gen 11:20 8286
after he begat *S* two hundred Gen 11:21 8286
S lived thirty years, and begat Gen 11:22 8286
S lived after he begat Nahor two Gen 11:23 8286
S, Nahor, Terah 1Chr 1:26 8286

SERVANT
a *s* of servants shall he be unto Gen 9:25 5650
and Canaan shall be his *s* Gen 9:26 5650
and Canaan shall be his *s* Gen 9:27 5650
not away, I pray thee, from thy *s* Gen 18:3 5650
therefore are ye come to your *s* Gen 18:5 5650
thy *s* hath found grace in thy Gen 19:19 5650
unto his eldest *s* of his house Gen 24:2 5650
the *s* said unto him, Peradventure Gen 24:5 5650
the *s* put his hand under the Gen 24:9 5650
the *s* took ten camels of the Gen 24:10 5650
hast appointed for thy *s* Isaac Gen 24:14 5650
the *s* ran to meet her, and said Gen 24:17 5650
And he said, I am Abraham's *s* Gen 24:34 5650
when Abraham's *s* heard their Gen 24:52 5650
the *s* brought forth jewels of Gen 24:53 5650
and her nurse, and Abraham's *s* Gen 24:59 5650
the *s* took Rebekah, and went his Gen 24:61 5650
For she had said unto the *s* Gen 24:65 5650
the *s* had said, It is my master Gen 24:65 5650
the *s* told Isaac all things that Gen 24:66 5650
thy seed for my *s* Abraham's sake Gen 26:24 5650
Thy *s* Jacob saith thus, I have Gen 32:4 5650
which thou hast shewed unto thy *s* Gen 32:10 5650
shalt say, They be thy *s* Jacob's Gen 32:18 5650
Behold, thy *s* Jacob is behind us Gen 32:20 5650
God hath graciously given thy *s* Gen 33:5 5650
pray thee, pass over before his *s* Gen 33:14 5650
these words, saying, The Hebrew *s* Gen 39:17 5650
After this manner did thy *s* to me Gen 39:19 5650
s to the captain of the guard Gen 41:12 5650
Thy *s* our father is in good Gen 43:28 5650
whom it is found shall be my *s* Gen 44:10 5650
cup is found, he shall be my *s* Gen 44:17 5650
and said, Oh my lord, let thy *s* Gen 44:18 5650
thine anger burn against thy *s* Gen 44:18 5650
we came up unto thy *s* my father Gen 44:24 5650
thy *s* my father said unto us, Ye Gen 44:27 5650
when I come to thy *s* my father Gen 44:30 5650
down the gray hairs of thy *s* our Gen 44:31 5650
For thy *s* became surety for the Gen 44:32 5650
let thy servants abide instead of the Gen 44:33 5650
bear, and became a *s* unto tribute Gen 49:15 5647
since thou hast spoken unto thy *s* Ex 4:10 5650
But every man's *s* that is bought Ex 12:44 5650
an hired *s* shall not eat thereof Ex 12:45 7916
believed the LORD, and his *s* Moses Ex 14:31 5650
If thou buy an Hebrew *s*, six Ex 21:2 5650
if the *s* shall plainly say, I Ex 21:5 5650
And if a man smite his *s*, or his Ex 21:20 5650
if a man smite the eye of his *s* Ex 21:26 5650
but his *s* Joshua, the son of Nun Ex 33:11 8334
of the priest, or an hired *s* Lev 22:10 7916
for thee, and for thy *s*, and for Lev 25:6 5650
for thy maid, and for thy hired *s* Lev 25:6 7916
But as an hired *s*, and as a Lev 25:40 7916
an hired *s* shall it be with him Lev 25:50 7916
as a yearly hired *s* shall he be Lev 25:53 7916
hast thou afflicted thy *s* Num 11:11 5650
the *s* of Moses, one of his young Num 11:28 8334
My *s* Moses is not so, who is Num 12:7 5650
to speak against my *s* Moses Num 12:8 5650
But my *s* Caleb, because he had Num 14:24 5650
begun to shew thy *s* thy greatness Deut 3:24 5650
wast a *s* in the land of Egypt Deut 5:15 5650
and he shall be thy *s* for ever Deut 15:17 5650
worth a double hired *s* to thee Deut 15:18 7916
the *s* which is escaped from his Deut 23:15 5650
oppress an hired *s* that is poor Deut 24:14 7916
So Moses the *s* of the LORD died Deut 34:5 5650
the *s* of the LORD it came to pass Josh 1:1 5650
Moses my *s* is dead Josh 1:2 5650
which Moses my *s* commanded thee Josh 1:7 5650
the word which Moses the *s* of the Josh 1:13 5650
which Moses the LORD'S *s* gave you Josh 1:15 5650
What saith my lord unto his *s* Josh 5:14 5650
As Moses the *s* of the LORD Josh 8:31 5650
as Moses the *s* of the LORD had Josh 8:33 5650
s Moses to give you all the land Josh 9:24 5650
as Moses the *s* of the LORD Josh 11:12 5650
As the LORD commanded Moses his *s* Josh 11:15 5650
Them did Moses the *s* of the LORD Josh 12:6 5650
Moses the *s* of the LORD gave it Josh 12:6 5650
even as Moses the *s* of the LORD Josh 13:8 5650
the *s* of the LORD sent me from Josh 14:7 5650
which Moses the *s* of the LORD Josh 18:7 5650
the *s* of the LORD commanded you Josh 22:2 5650
which Moses the *s* of the LORD Josh 22:4 5650
which Moses the *s* of the LORD Josh 22:5 5650
the *s* of the LORD, died, being an Josh 24:29 5650
the *s* of the LORD, died, being an Judg 2:8 5650
Phurah thy *s* down to the host Judg 7:10 5288
went he down with Phurah his *s* Judg 7:11 5288
into the hand of thy *s* Judg 15:18 5650
her again, having his *s* with him Judg 19:3 5288
he, and his concubine, and his *s* Judg 19:9 5288
the *s* said unto his master, Come Judg 19:11 5288
And he said unto his *s*, Come, and Judg 19:13 5288
Then said Boaz unto his *s* that Ruth 2:5 5288
the *s* that was set over the Ruth 2:6 5288
sacrifice, the priest's *s* came 1Sa 2:13 5288
the fat, the priest's *s* came 1Sa 2:15 5288
for thy *s* heareth 1Sa 3:9 5650
for thy *s* heareth 1Sa 3:10 5650
Saul said to his *s* that was with 1Sa 9:5 5288
Then said Saul to his *s*, But 1Sa 9:7 5288
the *s* answered Saul again, and 1Sa 9:8 5288
Then said Saul to his *s*, Well 1Sa 9:10 5288
And Samuel took Saul and his *s* 1Sa 9:22 5288
Bid the *s* pass on before us, (and 1Sa 9:27 5288
uncle said unto him and to his *s* 1Sa 10:14 5288
thy *s* will go and fight with this 1Sa 17:32 5650
Thy *s* kept his father's sheep, and 1Sa 17:34 5650
Thy *s* slew both the lion and the 1Sa 17:36 5650
I am the son of thy *s* Jesse the 1Sa 17:58 5650
not the king sin against his *s* 1Sa 19:4 5650
thy *s* shall have peace 1Sa 20:7 5650
thou shalt deal kindly with thy *s* 1Sa 20:8 5650
for thou hast brought thy *s* into 1Sa 20:8 5650
hath stirred up my *s* against me 1Sa 22:8 5650
king impute any thing unto his *s* 1Sa 22:15 5650
for thy *s* knew nothing of all 1Sa 22:15 5650
thy *s* hath certainly heard that 1Sa 23:10 5650
come down, as thy *s* hath heard 1Sa 23:11 5650
I beseech thee, tell thy *s* 1Sa 23:11 5650
and hath kept his *s* from evil 1Sa 25:39 5650
be a *s* to wash the feet of the 1Sa 25:41 5650
my lord thus pursue after his *s* 1Sa 26:18 5650
the king hear the words of his *s* 1Sa 26:19 5650
for why should thy *s* dwell in the 1Sa 27:5 5650
he shall be my *s* for ever 1Sa 27:12 5650
thou shalt know what thy *s* can do 1Sa 28:2 5650
the *s* of Saul the king of Israel 1Sa 29:3 5650
thy *s* so long as I have been with 1Sa 29:8 5650
man of Egypt, *s* to an Amalekite 1Sa 30:13 5650
By the hand of my *s* David I will 2Sa 3:18 5650
Go and tell my *s* David, Thus saith 2Sa 7:5 5650
so shalt thou say unto my *s* David 2Sa 7:8 5650
for thou, Lord GOD, knowest thy *s* 2Sa 7:20 5650
things, to make thy *s* know them 2Sa 7:21 5650
thou hast spoken concerning thy *s* 2Sa 7:25 5650
let the house of thy *s* David be 2Sa 7:26 5650
of Israel, hast revealed to thy *s* 2Sa 7:27 5650
therefore hath thy *s* found in his 2Sa 7:27 5650
promised this goodness unto thy *s* 2Sa 7:28 5650
thee to bless the house of thy *s* 2Sa 7:29 5650
of thy *s* be blessed for ever 2Sa 7:29 5650
of Saul a *s* whose name was Ziba 2Sa 9:2 5650
And he said, Thy *s* is he 2Sa 9:2 5650
And he answered, Behold thy *s* 2Sa 9:6 5650
himself, and said, What is thy *s* 2Sa 9:8 5650
the king called to Ziba, Saul's *s* 2Sa 9:9 5288
his *s*, so shall thy *s* do 2Sa 9:11 5650
Thy *s* Uriah the Hittite is dead 2Sa 11:21 5650
thy *s* Uriah the Hittite is dead 2Sa 11:24 5650
Then he called his *s* that 2Sa 13:17 5288
Then his *s* brought her out, and 2Sa 13:18 8334
now, thy *s* hath sheepshearers 2Sa 13:24 5650
and his servants go with thy *s* 2Sa 13:24 5650
as thy *s* said, so it is 2Sa 13:35 5650
for thy *s* Joab, he bade me, and he 2Sa 14:19 5650
hath thy *s* Joab done this thing 2Sa 14:20 5650
Today thy *s* knoweth that I have 2Sa 14:22 5650
fulfilled the request of his *s* 2Sa 14:22 5650
Thy *s* is of one of the tribes of 2Sa 15:2 5650
For thy *s* vowed a vow while I 2Sa 15:8 5650
even there also will thy *s* be 2Sa 15:21 5650
say unto Absalom, I will be thy *s* 2Sa 15:34 5650
have been thy father's *s* hitherto 2Sa 15:34 5650
so will I now also be thy *s* 2Sa 15:34 5650
Ziba the *s* of Mephibosheth met 2Sa 16:1 5288
the king's *s*, and me thy *s* 2Sa 18:29 5650
Ziba the *s* of the house of Saul 2Sa 19:17 5288
s did perversely the day that my 2Sa 19:19 5650
For thy *s* doth know that I have 2Sa 19:20 5650
My lord, O king, my *s* deceived me 2Sa 19:26 5650
for thy *s* said, I will saddle me 2Sa 19:26 5650
because thy *s* is lame 2Sa 19:26 5650
thy *s* unto my lord the king 2Sa 19:27 5650
yet didst thou set thy *s* among 2Sa 19:28 5650
can thy *s* taste what I eat or 2Sa 19:35 5650
wherefore then should thy *s* be 2Sa 19:35 5650
Thy *s* will go a little way over 2Sa 19:36 5650
Let thy *s*, I pray thee, turn back 2Sa 19:37 5650
But behold thy *s* Chimham 2Sa 19:37 5650
take away the iniquity of thy *s* 2Sa 24:10 5650
is my lord the king come to his *s* 2Sa 24:21 5650
but Solomon thy *s* hath he not 1Kin 1:19 5650
But me, even me thy *s*, and Zadok 1Kin 1:26 5650
thy *s* Solomon, hath he not called 1Kin 1:26 5650
hast not shewed it unto thy *s* 1Kin 1:27 5650
not slay his *s* with the sword 1Kin 1:51 5650

S

king hath said, so will thy s do 1Kin 2:38 5650
Thou hast shewed unto thy s David 1Kin 3:6 5650
thou hast made thy s king instead 1Kin 3:7 5650
thy s is in the midst of thy 1Kin 3:8 5650
Give therefore thy s an 1Kin 3:9 5650
Who hast kept with thy s David my 1Kin 8:24 5650
keep with thy s David my father 1Kin 8:25 5650
unto thy s David my father 1Kin 8:26 5650
respect unto the prayer of thy s 1Kin 8:28 5650
which thy s prayeth before thee 1Kin 8:28 5650
unto the prayer which thy s shall 1Kin 8:29 5650
thou to the supplication of thy s 1Kin 8:30 5650
unto the supplication of thy s 1Kin 8:52 5650
by the hand of Moses thy s 1Kin 8:53 5650
by the hand of Moses his s 1Kin 8:56 5650
he maintain the cause of his s 1Kin 8:59 5650
the LORD had done for David his s 1Kin 8:66 5650
thee, and will give it to thy s 1Kin 11:11 5650
Ephrathite of Zereda, Solomon's s 1Kin 11:26 5650
one tribe for my s David's sake 1Kin 11:32 5650
that David my s may have a light 1Kin 11:36 5650
commandments, as David my s did 1Kin 11:38 5650
If thou wilt be a s unto this 1Kin 12:7 5650
thou hast not been as my s David 1Kin 14:8 5650
hand of his s Ahijah the prophet 1Kin 14:18 5650
by his s Ahijah the Shilonite 1Kin 15:29 5650
his s Zimri, captain of half his 1Kin 16:9 5650
thy s into the hand of Ahab 1Kin 18:9 5650
but I thy s fear the LORD from my 1Kin 18:12 5650
God in Israel, and that I am thy s 1Kin 18:36 5650
And said to his s, Go up now, look 1Kin 18:43 5288
to Judah, and left his s there 1Kin 19:3 5288
to thy s at the first I will do 1Kin 20:9 5650
Thy s Ben-hadad saith, I pray 1Kin 20:32 5650
Thy s went out into the midst of 1Kin 20:39 5650
as thy s was busy here and there 1Kin 20:40 5650
saying, Thy s my husband is dead 2Kin 4:1 5650
that thy s did fear the LORD 2Kin 4:1 5650
And he said to Gehazi his s 2Kin 4:12 5288
saddled an ass, and said to her s 2Kin 4:24 5288
off, that he said to Gehazi his s 2Kin 4:25 5288
and he said unto his s, Set on the 2Kin 4:38 5288
sent Naaman my s to thee, that 2Kin 5:6 5650
thee, take a blessing of thy s 2Kin 5:15 5650
be given to thy s two mules' 2Kin 5:17 5650
for thy s will henceforth offer 2Kin 5:17 5650
this thing the LORD pardon thy s 2Kin 5:18 5650
LORD pardon thy s in this thing 2Kin 5:18 5650
the s of Elisha the man of God 2Kin 5:20 5288
And he said, Thy s went no whither 2Kin 5:25 5650
when the s of the man of God was 2Kin 6:15 8334
his s said unto him, Alas, my 2Kin 6:15 5288
Gehazi the s of the man of God 2Kin 8:4 5288
said, But what, is thy s a dog 2Kin 8:13 5650
by his s Elijah the Tishbite 2Kin 9:36 5650
which he spake by his s Elijah 2Kin 10:10 5650
spake by the hand of his s Jonah 2Kin 14:25 5650
of Assyria, saying, I am thy s 2Kin 16:7 5650
and Hoshea became his s, and gave 2Kin 17:3 5650
all that Moses the s of the LORD 2Kin 18:12 5650
sake, and for my s David's sake 2Kin 19:34 5650
sake, and for my s David's sake 2Kin 20:6 5650
that my s Moses commanded them 2Kin 21:8 5650
Asahiah a s of the king's, saying 2Kin 22:12 5650
became his s three years 2Kin 24:1 5650
a s of the king of Babylon, unto 2Kin 25:8 5650
And Sheshan had a s, an Egyptian 1Chr 2:34 5650
daughter to Jarha his s to wife 1Chr 2:35 5650
Moses the s of God had commanded 1Chr 6:49 5650
O ye seed of Israel his s 1Chr 16:13 5650
Go and tell David my s, Thus saith 1Chr 17:4 5650
shalt thou say unto my s David 1Chr 17:7 5650
to thee for the honour of thy s 1Chr 17:18 5650
for thou knowest thy s 1Chr 17:18 5650
thou hast spoken concerning thy s 1Chr 17:23 5650
thy s be established before thee 1Chr 17:24 5650
hast told thy s that thou wilt 1Chr 17:25 5650
therefore thy s hath found in his 1Chr 17:25 5650
promised this goodness unto thy s 1Chr 17:26 5650
thee to bless the house of thy s 1Chr 17:27 5650
do away the iniquity of thy s 1Chr 21:8 5650
which Moses the s of the LORD had 2Chr 1:3 5650
Thou which hast kept with thy s 2Chr 6:15 5650
keep with thy s David my father 2Chr 6:16 5650
thou hast spoken unto thy s David 2Chr 6:17 5650
therefore to the prayer of thy s 2Chr 6:19 5650
which thy s prayeth before thee 2Chr 6:19 5650
thy s prayeth toward this place 2Chr 6:20 5650
unto the supplications of thy s 2Chr 6:21 5650
the mercies of David thy s 2Chr 6:42 5650
the s of Solomon the son of David 2Chr 13:6 5650
of Moses the s of the LORD 2Chr 24:6 5650
the collection that Moses the s 2Chr 24:9 5650
God, and against his s Hezekiah 2Chr 32:16 5650
Asaiah a s of the king's, saying 2Chr 34:20 5650
mayest hear the prayer of thy s Neh 1:6 5650
thou commandedst thy s Moses Neh 1:7 5650
that thou commandedst thy s Moses Neh 1:8 5650
attentive to the prayer of thy s Neh 1:11 5650
thy s this day, and grant him Neh 1:11 5650
if thy s have found favour in thy Neh 2:5 5650
the Horonite, and Tobiah the s Neh 2:10 5650
the Horonite, and Tobiah the s Neh 2:19 5650
with his s lodge within Jerusalem Neh 4:22 5650
Then sent Sanballat his s unto me Neh 6:5 5650
laws, by the hand of Moses thy s Neh 9:14 5650
was given by Moses the s of God Neh 10:29 5650
Hast thou considered my s Job Job 1:8 5650
Hast thou considered my s Job Job 2:3 5650
the s is free from his master Job 3:19 5650
As a s earnestly desireth the Job 7:2 5650
I called my s, and he gave me no Job 19:16 5650
thou take him for a s for ever Job 41:4 5650
that is right, as my s Job hath Job 42:7 5650
and seven rams, and go to my s Job Job 42:8 5650
my s Job shall pray for you Job 42:8 5650
which is right, like my s Job Job 42:8 5650
the s of the LORD, who spake unto Ps 18:*t* 5650
Moreover by them is thy s warned Ps 19:11 5650
Keep back thy s also from Ps 19:13 5650
put not thy s away in anger Ps 27:9 5650
Make thy face to shine upon thy s Ps 31:16 5650
in the prosperity of his s Ps 35:27 5650
Psalm of David, the s of the LORD Ps 36:*t* 5650
And hide not thy face from thy s Ps 69:17 5650
He chose David also his s Ps 78:70 5650
save thy s that trusteth in thee Ps 86:2 5650
Rejoice the soul of thy s Ps 86:4 5650
give thy strength unto thy s Ps 86:16 5650
I have sworn unto David my s Ps 89:3 5650
I have found David my s Ps 89:20 5650
made void the covenant of thy s Ps 89:39 5650
O ye seed of Abraham his s Ps 105:6 5650
even Joseph, who was sold for a s Ps 105:17 5650
He sent Moses his s Ps 105:26 5650
holy promise, and Abraham his s Ps 105:42 5650
but let thy s rejoice Ps 109:28 5650
O LORD, truly I am thy s Ps 116:16 5650
I am thy s, and the son of thine Ps 116:16 5650
Deal bountifully with thy s Ps 119:17 5650
but thy s did meditate in thy Ps 119:23 5650
Stablish thy word unto thy s Ps 119:38 5650
Remember the word unto thy s Ps 119:49 5650
Thou hast dealt well with thy s Ps 119:65 5650
according to thy word unto thy s Ps 119:76 5650
How many are the days of thy s Ps 119:84 5650
Be surety for thy s for good Ps 119:122 5650
Deal with thy s according unto Ps 119:124 5650
I am thy s Ps 119:125 5650
Make thy face to shine upon thy s Ps 119:135 5650
therefore thy s loveth it Ps 119:140 5650
seek thy s Ps 119:176 5650
For thy s David's sake turn not Ps 132:10 5650
an heritage unto Israel his s Ps 136:22 5650
not into judgment with thy s Ps 143:2 5650
for I am thy s Ps 143:12 5650
his s from the hurtful sword Ps 144:10 5650
the fool shall be s to the wise Prov 11:29 5650
He that is despised, and hath a s Prov 12:9 5650
king's favour is toward a wise s Prov 14:35 5650
A wise s shall have rule over a Prov 17:2 5650
much less for a s to have rule Prov 19:10 5650
the borrower is s to the lender Prov 22:7 5650
A s will not be corrected by Prov 29:19 5650
his s from a child shall have him Prov 29:21 5650
Accuse not a s unto his master Prov 30:10 5650
For a s when he reigneth Prov 30:22 5650
lest thou hear thy s curse thee Eccl 7:21 5650
Like as my s Isaiah hath walked Is 20:3 5650
that I will call my s Eliakim the Is 22:20 5650
as with the s, so with his master Is 24:2 5650
sake, and for my s David's sake Is 37:35 5650
But thou, Israel, art my s Is 41:8 5650
and said unto thee, Thou art my s Is 41:9 5650
Behold my s, whom I uphold Is 42:1 5650
Who is blind, but my s Is 42:19 5650
perfect, and blind as the LORD's s Is 42:19 5650
LORD, and my s whom I have chosen Is 43:10 5650
Yet now hear, O Jacob my s Is 44:1 5650
Fear not, O Jacob, my s Is 44:2 5650
for thou art my s Is 44:21 5650
thou art my s Is 44:21 5650
That confirmeth the word of his s Is 44:26 5650
LORD hath redeemed his s Jacob Is 48:20 5650
And said unto me, Thou art my s Is 49:3 5650
me from the womb to be his s Is 49:5 5650
s to raise up the tribes of Jacob Is 49:6 5650
to a s of rulers, Kings shall see Is 49:7 5650
that obeyeth the voice of his s Is 50:10 5650
my s shall deal prudently, he Is 52:13 5650
shall my righteous s justify many Is 53:11 5650
Is Israel a s Jer 2:14 5650
the king of Babylon, my s Jer 25:9 5650
the king of Babylon, my s Jer 27:6 5650
O my s Jacob, saith the LORD Jer 30:10 5650
be broken with David my s Jer 33:21 5650
I multiply the seed of David my s Jer 33:22 5650
the seed of Jacob, and David my s Jer 33:26 5650
name, and caused every man his s Jer 34:16 5650
the king of Babylon, my s Jer 43:10 5650
O my s Jacob, and be not dismayed Jer 46:27 5650
Fear thou not, O Jacob my s Jer 46:28 5650
that I have given to my s Jacob Eze 28:25 5650
shall feed them, even my s David Eze 34:23 5650
my s David a prince among them Eze 34:24 5650
David my s shall be king over Eze 37:24 5650
that I have given unto Jacob my s Eze 37:25 5650
my s David shall be their prince Eze 37:25 5650
s of the living God, is thy God Dan 6:20 5649
in the law of Moses the s of God Dan 9:11 5650
our God, hear the prayer of thy s Dan 9:17 5650
For how can the s of this my lord Dan 10:17 5650
I take thee, O Zerubbabel, my s Hag 2:23 5650
will bring forth my s the BRANCH Zec 3:8 5650
his father, and a s his master Mal 1:6 5650
Remember ye the law of Moses my s Mal 4:4 5650
my s lieth at home sick of the Mt 8:6 *3816*
only, and my s shall be healed Mt 8:8 *3816*
and to my s, Do this, and he doeth Mt 8:9 *1401*
his s was healed in the selfsame Mt 8:13 *3816*
master, nor the s above his lord Mt 10:24 *1401*
his master, and the s as his lord Mt 10:25 *1401*
Behold my s, whom I have chosen Mt 12:18 *3816*
The s therefore fell down, and Mt 18:26 *1401*
Then the lord of that s was moved Mt 18:27 *1401*
But the same s went out, and found Mt 18:28 *1401*
said unto him, O thou wicked s Mt 18:32 *1401*
among you, let him be your s Mt 20:27 *1401*
among you shall be your s Mt 23:11 *1249*
Who then is a faithful and wise s Mt 24:45 *1401*
Blessed is that s, whom his lord Mt 24:46 *1401*
if that evil s shall say in his Mt 24:48 *1401*
The lord of that s shall come in Mt 24:50 *1401*
done, thou good and faithful s Mt 25:21 *1401*
Well done, good and faithful s Mt 25:23 *1401*
him, Thou wicked and slothful s Mt 25:26 *1401*
s into outer darkness Mt 25:30 *1401*
struck a s of the high priest's Mt 26:51 *1401*
shall be last of all, and s of all Mk 9:35 *1249*
the chiefest, shall be s of all Mk 10:44 *1401*
he sent to the husbandmen a s Mk 12:2 *1401*
again he sent unto them another s Mk 12:4 *1401*
smote a s of the high priest, and Mk 14:47 *1401*
He hath holpen his s Israel Lk 1:54 *3816*
us in the house of his s David Lk 1:69 *3816*
thou thy s depart in peace Lk 2:29 *1401*
And a certain centurion's s Lk 7:2 *1401*
that he would come and heal his s Lk 7:3 *1401*
a word, and my s shall be healed Lk 7:7 *3816*
and to my s, Do this, and he doeth Lk 7:8 *1401*
found the s whole that had been Lk 7:10 *1401*
Blessed is that s, whom his lord Lk 12:43 *1401*
if that s say in his heart, My Lk 12:45 *1401*
The lord of that s will come in a Lk 12:46 *1401*
And that s, which knew his lord's Lk 12:47 *1401*
sent his s at supper time to say Lk 14:17 *1401*
So that s came, and shewed his Lk 14:21 *1401*
house being angry said to his s Lk 14:21 *1401*
the s said, Lord, it is done as Lk 14:22 *1401*
And the lord said unto the s Lk 14:23 *1401*
No s can serve two masters Lk 16:13 *3610*
having a s plowing or feeding Lk 17:7 *1401*
Doth he thank that s because he Lk 17:9 *1401*
said unto him, Well, thou good s Lk 19:17 *1401*
will I judge thee, thou wicked s Lk 19:22 *1401*
he sent a s to the husbandmen Lk 20:10 *1401*
And again he sent another s Lk 20:11 *1401*
smote the s of the high priest Lk 22:50 *1401*
committeth sin is the s of sin Jn 8:34 *1401*
the s abideth not in the house Jn 8:35 *1401*
I am, there shall also my s be Jn 12:26 *1249*
The s is not greater than his Jn 13:16 *1401*
for the s knoweth not what his Jn 15:15 *1401*
The s is not greater than his Jn 15:20 *1401*
it, and smote the high priest's s Jn 18:10 *1401*
mouth of thy s David hast said Acts 4:25 *3816*
a s of Jesus Christ, called to be Rom 1:1 *1401*
thou that judgest another man's s Rom 14:4 *3610*
which is a s of the church which Rom 16:1 *1248*
sent by Phebe s of the church at Rom *s* *1248*
Art thou called being a s 1Cor 7:21 *1401*
is called in the Lord, being a s 1Cor 7:22 *1401*
called, being free, is Christ's s 1Cor 7:22 *1401*
yet have I made myself s unto all 1Cor 9:19 *1402*
I should not be the s of Christ Gal 1:10 *1401*
child, differeth nothing from a s Gal 4:1 *1401*
Wherefore thou art no more a s Gal 4:7 *1401*
and took upon him the form of a s Phil 2:7 *1401*
a s of Christ, saluteth you Col 4:12 *1401*
the s of the Lord must not strive 2Ti 2:24 *1401*
a s of God, and an apostle of Titus 1:1 *1401*
Not now as a s, but above a Philem 16 *1401*
now as a s, but above a s Philem 16 *1401*
to Philemon, by Onesimus, a s Philem *s* *3610*
faithful in all his house, as a s Heb 3:5 *2324*
a s of God and of the Lord Jesus Jas 1:1 *1401*
Simon Peter, a s and an apostle of 2Pet 1:1 *1401*
the s of Jesus Christ, and brother Jude 1 *1401*
it by his angel unto his s John Rev 1:1 *1401*
the song of Moses the s of God Rev 15:3 *1401*

SERVANT'S

in, I pray you, into your s house Gen 19:2 5650
thou hast spoken also of thy s 2Sa 7:19 5650
to thy son for David my s sake 1Kin 11:13 5650
of his life for David my s sake 1Kin 11:34 5650
Judah for David his s sake 2Kin 8:19 5650
thou hast also spoken of thy s 1Chr 17:17 5650
O LORD, for thy s sake, and 1Chr 17:19 5650
For Jacob my s sake, and Israel Is 45:4 5650
The s name was Malchus Jn 18:10 *1401*

SERVANTS

a servant of s shall he be unto Gen 9:25 5650
captive, he armed his trained s Gen 14:14
himself against them, he and his s Gen 14:15 5650
the morning, and called all his s Gen 20:8 5650
which Abimelech's s had violently Gen 21:25 5650
of herds, and great store of s Gen 26:14 5657
s had digged in the days of Gen 26:15 5650
Isaac's s digged in the valley Gen 26:19 5650
and there Isaac's s digged a well Gen 26:25 5650
the same day, that Isaac's s came Gen 26:32 5650
have I given to him for s Gen 27:37 5650
them into the hand of his s Gen 32:16 5650
and said unto his s, Pass over Gen 32:16 5650
he made a feast unto all his s Gen 40:20 5650
and of the chief baker among his s Gen 40:20 5650
Pharaoh was wroth with his s Gen 41:10 5650
and in the eyes of all his s Gen 41:37 5650
And Pharaoh said unto his s Gen 41:38 5650
but to buy food are thy s come Gen 42:10 5650
are true men, thy s are no spies Gen 42:11 5650
Thy s are twelve brethren, the Gen 42:13 5650
God forbid that thy s should do Gen 44:7 5650
whomsoever of thy s it be found Gen 44:9 5650
found out the iniquity of thy s Gen 44:16 5650
behold, we are my lord's s Gen 44:16 5650
My lord asked his s, saying, Have Gen 44:19 5650
And thou saidst unto thy s Gen 44:21 5650
And thou saidst unto thy s Gen 44:23 5650
thy s shall bring down the gray Gen 44:31 5650
it pleased Pharaoh well, and his s Gen 45:16 5650

Thy s are shepherds, both we, and Gen 47:3 5650
for thy s have no pasture for Gen 47:4 5650
let thy s dwell in the land of Gen 47:4 5650
our land will be s unto Pharaoh Gen 47:19 5650
lord, and we will be Pharaoh's s Gen 47:25 5650
Joseph commanded his s the Gen 50:2 5650
him went up all the s of Pharaoh Gen 50:7 5650
of the s of the God of thy father Gen 50:17 5650
and they said, Behold, we be thy s Gen 50:18 5650
dealest thou thus with thy s Ex 5:15 5650
is no straw given unto thy s Ex 5:16 5650
and, behold, thy s are beaten Ex 5:16 5650
Pharaoh, and in the eyes of his s Ex 5:21 5650
before Pharaoh, and before his s Ex 7:10 5650
Pharaoh, and in the sight of his s Ex 7:20 5650
bed, and into the house of thy s Ex 8:3 5650
thy people, and upon all thy s Ex 8:4 5650
I intreat for thee, and for thy s Ex 8:9 5650
and from thy houses, and from thy s Ex 8:11 5650
of flies upon thee, and upon thy s Ex 8:21 5650
depart from Pharaoh, from his s Ex 8:29 5650
of flies from Pharaoh, from his s Ex 8:31 5650
upon thine heart, and upon thy s Ex 9:14 5650
s of Pharaoh made his s Ex 9:20 5650
the word of the LORD left his s Ex 9:21 5650
But as for thee and thy s, I know Ex 9:30 5650
hardened his heart, he and his s Ex 9:34 5650
his heart, and the heart of his s Ex 10:1 5650
and the houses of all thy s Ex 10:6 5650
Pharaoh's s said unto him, How Ex 10:7 5650
in the sight of Pharaoh's s Ex 11:3 5650
all these thy s shall come down Ex 11:8 5650
up in the night, he, and all his s Ex 12:30 5650
of his s was turned against the Ex 14:5 5650
Abraham, Isaac, and Israel, thy s Ex 32:13 5650
For they are my s, which I Lev 25:42 5650
me the children of Israel are s Lev 25:55 5650
they are my s whom I brought Lev 25:55 5650
and said unto the s of Balak Num 22:18 5650
ass, and his two s were with him Num 22:22 5288
Thy s have taken the sum of the Num 31:49 5650
for cattle, and thy s have cattle Num 32:4 5650
given unto thy s for a possession Num 32:5 5650
saying, Thy s will do as my lord Num 32:25 5650
But thy s will pass over, every Num 32:27 5650
As the LORD hath said unto thy s Num 32:31 5650
Remember thy s, Abraham, Isaac, Deut 9:27 5650
unto Pharaoh, and unto all his s Deut 29:2 5650
and repent himself for his s Deut 32:36 5650
he will avenge the blood of his s Deut 32:43 5650
Egypt to Pharaoh, and to all his s Deut 34:11 5650
said unto Joshua, We are thy s Josh 9:8 5650
From a very far country thy s are Josh 9:9 5650
and say unto them, We are your s Josh 9:11 5650
it was certainly told thy s Josh 9:24 5650
Slack not thy hand from thy s Josh 10:6 5650
When he was gone out, his s came Judg 3:24 5650
Then Gideon took ten men of his s Judg 6:27 5650
the young man which is with thy s Judg 19:19 5650
that ye be not s unto the Hebrews 1Sa 4:9 5647
of them, and give them to his s 1Sa 8:14 5650
give to his officers, and to his s 1Sa 8:15 5650
and ye shall be his s 1Sa 8:17 5650
Take now one of the s with thee 1Sa 9:3 5650
Pray for thy s unto the LORD thy 1Sa 12:19 5650
Saul's s said unto him, Behold 1Sa 16:15 5650
Let our lord now command thy s 1Sa 16:16 5650
And Saul said unto his s, Provide 1Sa 16:17 5650
Then answered one of the s 1Sa 16:18 5288
I a Philistine, and ye s to Saul 1Sa 17:8 5650
kill me, then will we be your s 1Sa 17:9 5650
kill him, then shall ye be our s 1Sa 17:9 5650
and also in the sight of Saul's s 1Sa 18:5 5650
And Saul commanded his s, saying, 1Sa 18:22 5650
in thee, and all his s love thee 1Sa 18:22 5650
Saul's s spake those words in the 1Sa 18:23 5650
the s of Saul told him, saying, 1Sa 18:24 5650
when his s told David these words 1Sa 18:26 5650
wisely than all the s of Saul 1Sa 18:30 5650
Jonathan his son, and to all his s 1Sa 19:1 5650
and I have appointed my s to such 1Sa 21:2 5288
Now a certain man of the s of 1Sa 21:7 5650
the s of Achish said unto him, Is 1Sa 21:11 5650
Then said Achish unto his s 1Sa 21:14 5650
all his s were standing about him 1Sa 22:6 5650
unto his s that stood about him 1Sa 22:7 5650
which was set over the s of Saul 1Sa 22:9 5650
faithful among all thy s as David 1Sa 22:14 5650
But the s of the king would not 1Sa 22:17 5650
stayed his s with these words 1Sa 24:7 582
cometh to thine hand unto thy s 1Sa 25:8 5650
And Nabal answered David's s 1Sa 25:10 5650
there be many s now a days that 1Sa 25:10 5650
And she said unto her s, Go on 1Sa 25:19 5288
when the s of David were come to 1Sa 25:40 5650
wash the feet of the s of my lord 1Sa 25:41 5650
Then said Saul unto his s 1Sa 28:7 5650
his s said to him, Behold, there 1Sa 28:7 5650
But his s, together with the 1Sa 28:23 5650
it before Saul, and before his s 1Sa 28:25 5650
s that are come with thee 1Sa 29:10 5650
the s of Ish-bosheth the son of 2Sa 2:12 5650
the s of David, went out, and met 2Sa 2:13 5650
Saul, and twelve of the s of David 2Sa 2:15 5650
of Israel, before the s of David 2Sa 2:17 5650
lacked of David's s nineteen men 2Sa 2:30 5650
But the s of David had smitten of 2Sa 2:31 5650
the s of David and Joab came from 2Sa 3:22 5650
And the king said unto his s 2Sa 3:38 5650
eyes of the handmaids of his s 2Sa 6:20 5650
so the Moabites became David's s 2Sa 8:2 5650
and the Syrians became s to David 2Sa 8:6 5650
that were on the s of Hadadezer 2Sa 8:7 5650
all they of Edom became David's s 2Sa 8:14 5650

therefore, and thy sons, and thy s 2Sa 9:10 5650
Ziba had fifteen sons and twenty s 2Sa 9:10 5650
of Ziba were s unto Mephibosheth 2Sa 9:12 5650
the hand of his s for his father 2Sa 10:2 5650
David's s came into the land of 2Sa 10:2 5650
David rather sent his s unto thee 2Sa 10:3 5650
Wherefore Hanun took David's s 2Sa 10:4 5650
when all the kings that were s to 2Sa 10:19 5650
his s with him, and all Israel 2Sa 11:1 5650
house with all the s of his lord 2Sa 11:9 5650
the s of my lord, are encamped in 2Sa 11:11 5650
on his bed with the s of his lord 2Sa 11:13 5650
of the people of the s of David 2Sa 11:17 5650
shot from off the wall upon thy s 2Sa 11:24 5650
and some of the king's s be dead 2Sa 11:24 5650
the s of David feared to tell him 2Sa 12:18 5650
David saw that his s whispered 2Sa 12:19 5650
therefore David said unto his s 2Sa 12:19 5650
Then said his s unto him, What 2Sa 12:21 5650
his s go with thy servant 2Sa 13:24 5650
Now Absalom had commanded his s 2Sa 13:28 5288
the s of Absalom did unto Amnon 2Sa 13:29 5288
all his s stood by with their 2Sa 13:31 5650
also and all his s wept very sore 2Sa 13:36 5650
Therefore he said unto his s 2Sa 14:30 5650
Absalom's s set the field on fire 2Sa 14:30 5650
Wherefore have thy s set my field 2Sa 14:31 5650
David said unto all his s that 2Sa 15:14 5650
the king's s said unto the king, 2Sa 15:15 5650
thy s are ready to do whatsoever 2Sa 15:15 5650
all his s passed on beside him 2Sa 15:18 5650
at all the s of king David 2Sa 16:6 5650
said to Abishai, and to all his s 2Sa 16:11 5650
when Absalom's s came to the 2Sa 17:20 5650
were slain before the s of David 2Sa 18:7 5650
And Absalom met the s of David 2Sa 18:9 5650
this day the faces of all thy s 2Sa 19:5 5650
regardest neither princes nor s 2Sa 19:6 5650
and speak comfortably unto thy s 2Sa 19:7 5650
king, Return thou, and all thy s 2Sa 19:14 5650
sons and his twenty s with him 2Sa 19:17 5650
take thou thy lord's s, and pursue 2Sa 20:6 5650
his s with him, and fought against 2Sa 21:15 5650
of David, and by the hand of his s 2Sa 21:22 5650
his s coming on toward him 2Sa 24:20 5650
Wherefore his s said unto him 1Kin 1:2 5650
all the men of Judah the king's s 1Kin 1:9 5650
Take with you the s of your lord 1Kin 1:33 5650
moreover the king's s came to 1Kin 1:47 5650
that two of the s of Shimei ran 1Kin 2:39 5650
saying, Behold, thy s be in Gath 1Kin 2:39 5650
to Gath to Achish to seek his s 1Kin 2:40 5650
went, and brought his s from Gath 1Kin 2:40 5650
and made a feast to all his s 1Kin 3:15 5650
of Tyre sent his s unto Solomon 1Kin 5:1 5650
my s shall be with thy s 1Kin 5:6 5650
thy s according to all that thou 1Kin 5:6 5650
My s shall bring them down from 1Kin 5:9 5650
mercy with thy s that walk before 1Kin 8:23 5650
in heaven, and do, and judge thy s 1Kin 8:32 5650
and forgive the sin of thy s 1Kin 8:36 5650
they were men of war, and his s 1Kin 9:22 5650
And Hiram sent in the navy his s 1Kin 9:27 5650
of the sea, with the s of Solomon 1Kin 9:27 5650
table, and the sitting of his s 1Kin 10:5 5650
thy men, happy are these thy s 1Kin 10:8 5650
to her own country, she and her s 1Kin 10:13 5650
of his father's s with him 1Kin 11:17 5650
then they will be thy s for ever 1Kin 12:7 5650
them into the hand of his s 1Kin 15:18 5650
Yet I will send my s unto thee to 1Kin 20:6 5650
house, and the houses of thy s 1Kin 20:6 5650
that he said unto his s, Set 1Kin 20:12 5650
the s of the king of Syria said 1Kin 20:23 5650
his s said unto him, Behold now, 1Kin 20:31 5650
king of Israel said unto his s 1Kin 22:3 5650
Let my s go with thy s in 1Kin 22:49 5650
and the life of these fifty thy s 2Kin 1:13 5650
be with thy s fifty strong men 2Kin 2:16 5650
the king of Israel's s answered 2Kin 3:11 5650
his s came near, and spake unto 2Kin 5:13 5650
and laid them upon two of his s 2Kin 5:23 5288
I pray thee, and go with thy s 2Kin 6:3 5650
and took counsel with his s 2Kin 6:8 5650
and he called his s, and said unto 2Kin 6:11 5650
And one of his s said, None, my 2Kin 6:12 5650
in the night, and said unto his s 2Kin 7:12 5650
And one of his s answered and said, 2Kin 7:13 5650
the blood of my s the prophets 2Kin 9:7 5650
blood of all the s of the LORD 2Kin 9:7 5650
came forth to the s of his lord 2Kin 9:11 5650
his s carried him in a chariot to 2Kin 9:28 5650
to Jehu, saying, We are thy s 2Kin 10:5 5650
the prophets of Baal, all his s 2Kin 10:19 5647
you none of the s of the LORD 2Kin 10:23 5650
his s arose, and made a conspiracy 2Kin 12:20 5650
the son of Shomer, his s, smote 2Kin 12:21 5650
that he slew his s which had 2Kin 14:5 5650
sent to you by my s the prophets 2Kin 17:13 5650
said by all his s the prophets 2Kin 17:23 5650
of the least of my master's s 2Kin 18:24 5650
to thy s in the Syrian language 2Kin 18:26 5650
So the s of king Hezekiah came to 2Kin 19:5 5650
with which the s of the king of 2Kin 19:6 5288
LORD spake by his s the prophets 2Kin 21:10 5650
the s of Amon conspired against 2Kin 21:23 5650
Thy s have gathered the money 2Kin 22:9 5650
his s carried him in a chariot 2Kin 23:30 5650
he spake by his s the prophets 2Kin 24:2 5650
At that time the s of 2Kin 24:10 5650
the city, and his s did besiege it 2Kin 24:11 5650
he, and his mother, and his s 2Kin 24:12 5650
not to be the s of the Chaldees 2Kin 25:24 5650
and the Moabites became David's s 1Chr 18:2 5650

and the Syrians became David's s 1Chr 18:6 5650
that were on the s of Hadarezer 1Chr 18:7 5650
all the Edomites became David's s 1Chr 18:13 5650
So the s of David came into the 1Chr 19:2 5650
are not his s come unto thee for 1Chr 19:3 5650
Wherefore Hanun took David's s 1Chr 19:4 5650
when the s of Hadarezer saw that 1Chr 19:19 5650
peace with David, and became his s 1Chr 19:19 5647
of David, and by the hand of his s 1Chr 20:8 5650
are they not all my lord's s 1Chr 21:3 5650
for I know that thy s can skill 2Chr 2:8 5650
my s shall be with thy s, 2Chr 2:8 5650
And, behold, I will give to thy s 2Chr 2:10 5650
of, let him send unto his s 2Chr 2:15 5650
and shewest mercy unto thy s 2Chr 6:14 5650
heaven, and do, and judge thy s 2Chr 6:23 5650
and forgive the sin of thy s 2Chr 6:27 5650
Solomon make no s for his work 2Chr 8:9 5650
him by the hands of his s ships 2Chr 8:18 5650
s that had knowledge of the sea 2Chr 8:18 5650
they went with the s of Solomon 2Chr 8:18 5650
table, and the sitting of his s 2Chr 9:4 5650
thy men, and happy are these thy s 2Chr 9:7 5650
the s also of Huram, and the 2Chr 9:10 5650
the s of Solomon, which brought 2Chr 9:10 5650
to her own land, she and her s 2Chr 9:12 5650
to Tarshish with the s of Huram 2Chr 9:21 5650
them, they will be thy s for ever 2Chr 10:7 5650
Nevertheless they shall be his s 2Chr 12:8 5650
his own s conspired against him 2Chr 24:25 5650
that he slew his s that had 2Chr 25:3 5650
Assyria send his s to Jerusalem 2Chr 32:9 5650
his s spake yet more against the 2Chr 32:16 5650
his s conspired against him, and 2Chr 33:24 5650
All that was committed to thy s 2Chr 34:16 5650
and the king said to his s 2Chr 35:23 5650
His s therefore took him out of 2Chr 35:24 5650
where they were s to him and his 2Chr 36:20 5650
The children of Solomon's s Ezr 2:55 5650
and the children of Solomon's s Ezr 2:58 5650
Beside their s and their maids, of Ezr 2:65 5650
Thy s the men on this side the Ezr 4:11 5649
We are the s of the God of heaven Ezr 5:11 5649
commanded by thy s the prophets Ezr 9:11 5650
for the children of Israel thy s Neh 1:6 5650
Now these are thy s and thy people Neh 1:10 5650
and to the prayer of thy s Neh 1:11 5650
therefore we his s will arise Neh 2:20 5650
half of my s wrought in the work Neh 4:16 5288
I, nor my brethren, nor my s Neh 4:23 5288
our sons and our daughters to be s Neh 5:5 5650
likewise, and my brethren, and my s Neh 5:10 5288
even their s bare rule over the Neh 5:15 5288
all my s were gathered thither Neh 5:16 5288
The children of Solomon's s Neh 7:57 5650
and the children of Solomon's s Neh 7:60 5650
upon Pharaoh, and on all his s Neh 9:10 5650
we are s this day, and for the Neh 9:36 5650
thereof, behold, we are s in it Neh 9:36 5650
and the children of Solomon's s Neh 11:3 5650
some of my s set I at the gates, Neh 13:19 5288
unto all his princes and his s Est 1:3 5650
Then said the king's s that Est 2:2 5288
unto all his princes and his s Est 2:18 5650
And all the king's s, that were in Est 3:2 5650
Then the king's s, which were in Est 3:3 5650
All the king's s, and the people Est 4:11 5650
the princes and s of the king Est 5:11 5650
Then said the king's s that Est 6:3 5288
the king's s said unto him, Est 6:5 5288
they have slain the s with the Job 1:15 5288
burned up the sheep, and the s Job 1:16 5288
slain the s with the edge of the Job 1:17 5288
Behold, he put no trust in his s Job 4:18 5650
LORD redeemeth the soul of his s Ps 34:22 5650
also of his s shall inherit it Ps 69:36 5650
The dead bodies of thy s have Ps 79:2 5650
the blood of thy s which is shed Ps 79:10 5650
Lord, the reproach of thy s Ps 89:50 5650
it repent thee concerning thy s Ps 90:13 5650
Let thy work appear unto thy s Ps 90:16 5650
For thy s take pleasure in her Ps 102:14 5650
children of thy s shall continue Ps 102:28 5650
to deal subtilly with his s Ps 105:25 5650
O ye s of the LORD, praise the Ps 113:1 5650
for all are thy s Ps 119:91 5650
as the eyes of s look unto the Ps 123:2 5650
all ye s of the LORD, which by Ps 134:1 5650
praise him, O ye s of the LORD Ps 135:1 5650
upon Pharaoh, and upon all his s Ps 135:9 5650
repent himself concerning his s Ps 135:14 5650
to lies, all his s are wicked Prov 29:12 8334
I got me s and maidens, and had Eccl 2:7 5650
and had s born in my house Eccl 2:7
I have seen s upon horses Eccl 10:7 5650
walking as s upon the earth Eccl 10:7 5650
in the land of the LORD for s Is 14:2 5650
of the least of my master's s Is 36:9 5650
unto thy s in the Syrian language Is 36:11 5650
So the s of king Hezekiah came to Is 37:5 5650
wherewith the s of the king of Is 37:6 5288
By thy s hast thou reproached the Is 37:24 5650
the heritage of the s of the LORD Is 54:17 5650
the name of the LORD, to be his s Is 56:6 5650
it, and my s shall dwell there Is 65:9 5650
my s shall eat, but ye shall be Is 65:13 5650
my s shall drink, but ye shall be Is 65:13 5650
my s shall rejoice, but ye shall Is 65:13 5650
my s shall sing for joy of heart, Is 65:14 5650
call his s by another name Is 65:15 5650
LORD shall be known toward his s Is 66:14 5650
unto you all my s the prophets Jer 7:25 5650
Zedekiah king of Judah, and his s Jer 21:7 5650
throne of David, thou, and thy s Jer 22:2 5650

S

and on horses, he, and his *s*	Jer 22:4	5650
unto you all his *s* the prophets	Jer 25:4	5650
Pharaoh king of Egypt, and his *s*	Jer 25:19	5650
to the words of my *s* the prophets	Jer 26:5	5650
unto them by my *s* the prophets	Jer 29:19	5650
they turned, and caused the *s*	Jer 34:11	5650
them into subjection for *s*	Jer 34:11	5650
subjection, to be unto you for *s*	Jer 34:16	5650
unto you all my *s* the prophets	Jer 35:15	5650
nor any of his *s* that heard all	Jer 36:24	5650
seed and his *s* for their iniquity	Jer 36:31	5650
But neither he, nor his *s*	Jer 37:2	5650
against thee, or against thy *s*	Jer 37:18	5650
unto you all my *s* the prophets	Jer 44:4	5650
and into the hand of his *s*	Jer 46:26	5650
S have ruled over us	Lam 5:8	5650
by my *s* the prophets of Israel	Eze 38:17	5650
his inheritance to one of his *s*	Eze 46:17	5650
Prove thy *s*, I beseech thee, ten	Dan 1:12	5650
and as thou seest, deal with thy *s*	Dan 1:13	5650
tell thy *s* the dream, and we will	Dan 2:4	5649
Let the king tell his *s* the dream	Dan 2:7	5649
ye *s* of the most high God, come	Dan 3:26	5649
delivered his *s* that trusted in	Dan 3:28	5649
hearkened unto thy *s* the prophets	Dan 9:6	5650
before us by his *s* the prophets	Dan 9:10	5650
And also upon the *s* and upon the	Joel 2:29	5650
secret unto his *s* the prophets	Amos 3:7	5650
thee out of the house of *s*	Mic 6:4	5650
I commanded my *s* the prophets	Zec 1:6	5650
they shall be a spoil to their *s*	Zec 2:9	5647
So the *s* of the householder came	Mt 13:27	*1401*
The *s* said unto him, Wilt thou	Mt 13:28	*1401*
And said unto his *s*, This is John	Mt 14:2	*1401*
which would take account of his *s*	Mt 18:23	*1401*
he sent his *s* to the husbandmen,	Mt 21:34	*1401*
And the husbandmen took his *s*	Mt 21:35	*1401*
he sent other *s* more than the	Mt 21:36	*1401*
sent forth his *s* to call them	Mt 22:3	*1401*
Again, he sent forth other *s*	Mt 22:4	*1401*
And the remnant took his *s*	Mt 22:6	*1401*
Then saith he to his *s*, The	Mt 22:8	*1401*
So those *s* went out into the	Mt 22:10	*1401*
Then said the king to the *s*	Mt 22:13	*1401*
far country, who called his own *s*	Mt 25:14	*1401*
time the lord of those *s* cometh	Mt 25:19	*1401*
and went in, and sat with the *s*	Mt 26:58	*5257*
in the ship with the hired *s*	Mk 1:20	*341*
house, and gave authority to his *s*	Mk 13:34	*1401*
and he sat with the *s*, and warmed	Mk 14:54	*5257*
the *s* did strike him with the	Mk 14:65	*5257*
Blessed are those *s*, whom the	Lk 12:37	*1401*
find them so, blessed are those *s*	Lk 12:38	*1401*
How many hired *s* of my father's	Lk 15:17	*3407*
make me as one of thy hired *s*	Lk 15:19	*3407*
But the father said to his *s*	Lk 15:22	*1401*
And he called one of the *s*	Lk 15:26	*3816*
you, say, We are unprofitable *s*	Lk 17:10	*1401*
And he called his ten *s*, and	Lk 19:13	*1401*
these *s* to be called unto him	Lk 19:15	*1401*
His mother saith unto the *s*	Jn 2:5	*1249*
(but the *s* which drew the water	Jn 2:9	*1249*
his *s* met him, and told him,	Jn 4:51	*1401*
Henceforth I call you not *s*	Jn 15:15	*1401*
And the *s* and officers stood there,	Jn 18:18	*1401*
One of the *s* of the high priest,	Jn 18:26	*1401*
this world, then would my *s* fight	Jn 18:36	*5257*
And on my *s* and on my	Acts 2:18	*1401*
and grant unto thy *s*, that with	Acts 4:29	*1401*
he called two of his household *s*	Acts 10:7	
These men are the *s* of the most	Acts 16:17	*1401*
ye yield yourselves *s* to obey	Rom 6:16	*1401*
his *s* ye are to whom ye obey	Rom 6:16	*1401*
that ye were the *s* of sin	Rom 6:17	*1401*
ye became the *s* of righteousness	Rom 6:18	*1402*
your members *s* to uncleanness	Rom 6:19	*1401*
s to righteousness unto holiness	Rom 6:19	*1401*
For when ye were the *s* of sin	Rom 6:20	*1401*
free from sin, and become *s* to God	Rom 6:22	*1402*
be not ye the *s* of men	1Cor 7:23	*1401*
ourselves your *s* for Jesus' sake	2Cor 4:5	*1401*
S, be obedient to them that are	Eph 6:5	*1401*
but as the *s* of Christ, doing the	Eph 6:6	*1401*
the *s* of Jesus Christ, to all the	Phil 1:1	*1401*
S, obey in all things your	Col 3:22	*1401*
give unto your *s* that which is	Col 4:1	*1401*
Let as many *s* as are under the	1Ti 6:1	*1401*
Exhort *s* to be obedient unto	Titus 2:9	*1401*
but as the *s* of God	1Pet 2:16	*1401*
S, be subject to your masters	1Pet 2:18	*3610*
are the *s* of corruption	2Pet 2:19	*1401*
to shew unto his *s* things which	Rev 1:1	*1401*
teach and to seduce my *s* to commit	Rev 2:20	*1401*
till we have sealed the *s* of our	Rev 7:3	*1401*
declared to his *s* the prophets	Rev 10:7	*1401*
reward unto thy *s* the prophets	Rev 11:18	*1401*
the blood of his *s* at her hand	Rev 19:2	*1401*
Praise our God, all ye his *s*	Rev 19:5	*1401*
and his *s* shall serve him	Rev 22:3	*1401*
s the things which must shortly	Rev 22:6	*1401*

SERVANTS'

Thy *s* trade hath been about	Gen 46:34	5650
of Pharaoh, and into his *s* houses	Ex 8:24	5650
Return for thy *s* sake, the tribes	Is 63:17	5650
so will I do for my *s* sakes	Is 65:8	5650

SERVE

is not theirs, and shall *s* them	Gen 15:13	5647
that nation, whom they shall *s*	Gen 15:14	5647
and the elder shall *s* the younger	Gen 25:23	5647
Let people *s* thee, and nations bow	Gen 27:29	5647
thou live, and shalt *s* thy brother	Gen 27:40	5647
thou therefore *s* me for nought	Gen 29:15	5647
I will *s* thee seven years for	Gen 29:18	5647
did not I *s* with thee for Rachel	Gen 29:25	5647
the service which thou shalt *s*	Gen 29:27	5647
of Israel to *s* with rigour	Ex 1:13	5647
service, wherein they made them *s*	Ex 1:14	5647
ye shall *s* God upon this mountain	Ex 3:12	5647
Let my son go, that he may *s* me	Ex 4:23	5647
that they may *s* me in the	Ex 7:16	5647
my people go, that they may *s* me	Ex 8:1	5647
my people go, that they may *s* me	Ex 8:20	5647
my people go, that they may *s* me	Ex 9:1	5647
my people go, that they may *s* me	Ex 9:13	5647
my people go, that they may *s* me	Ex 10:3	5647
that they may *s* the LORD their	Ex 10:7	5647
them, Go, *s* the LORD your God	Ex 10:8	5647
ye that are men, and *s* the LORD	Ex 10:11	5647
Moses, and said, Go ye, *s* the LORD	Ex 10:24	5647
we take to *s* the LORD our God	Ex 10:26	5647
not with what we must *s* the LORD	Ex 10:26	5647
s the LORD, as ye have said	Ex 12:31	5647
that we may *s* the Egyptians	Ex 14:12	5647
better for us to *s* the Egyptians	Ex 14:12	5647
down thyself to them, nor *s* them	Ex 20:5	5647
servant, six years he shall *s*	Ex 21:2	5647
and he shall *s* him for ever	Ex 21:6	5647
nor *s* them, nor do after their	Ex 23:24	5647
ye shall *s* the LORD your God, and	Ex 23:25	5647
for if thou *s* their gods, it will	Ex 23:33	5647
compel him to *s* as a bondservant	Lev 25:39	5656
shall *s* thee unto the year of	Lev 25:40	5647
families of the Gershonites, to *s*	Num 4:24	5647
so shall they *s*	Num 4:26	5647
thereof, and shall *s* no more	Num 8:25	5647
and ye shall *s*	Num 18:7	5647
for their service which they *s*	Num 18:21	5647
s them, which the LORD thy God	Deut 4:19	5647
And there ye shall *s* gods, the	Deut 4:28	5647
thyself unto them, nor *s* them	Deut 5:9	5647
s him, and shalt swear by his name	Deut 6:13	5647
me, that they may *s* other gods	Deut 7:4	5647
neither shalt thou *s* their gods	Deut 7:16	5647
s them, and worship them, I	Deut 8:19	5647
to *s* the LORD thy God with all	Deut 10:12	5647
him shalt thou *s*, and to him shalt	Deut 10:20	5647
to *s* him with all your heart and	Deut 11:13	5647
s other gods, and worship them	Deut 11:16	5647
did these nations *s* their gods	Deut 12:30	5647
hast not known, and let us *s* them	Deut 13:2	5647
obey his voice, and ye shall *s* him	Deut 13:4	5647
s other gods, which thou hast not	Deut 13:6	5647
s other gods, which ye have not	Deut 13:13	5647
unto thee, and *s* thee six years	Deut 15:12	5647
unto thee, and they shall *s* thee	Deut 20:11	5647
to go after other gods to *s* them	Deut 28:14	5647
and there shalt thou *s* other gods	Deut 28:36	5647
Therefore shalt thou *s* thine	Deut 28:48	5647
and there thou shalt *s* other gods	Deut 28:64	5647
s the gods of these nations	Deut 29:18	5647
and worship other gods, and *s* them	Deut 30:17	5647
s them, and provoke me, and break	Deut 31:20	5647
unto this day, and *s* under tribute	Josh 16:10	5647
to *s* him with all your heart and	Josh 22:5	5647
to swear by them, neither *s* them	Josh 23:7	5647
s him in sincerity and in truth	Josh 24:14	5647
and *s* ye the LORD	Josh 24:14	5647
seem evil unto you to *s* the LORD	Josh 24:15	5647
you this day whom ye will *s*	Josh 24:15	5647
and my house, we will *s* the LORD	Josh 24:15	5647
forsake the LORD, to *s* other gods	Josh 24:16	5647
therefore will we also *s* the LORD	Josh 24:18	5647
the people, Ye cannot *s* the LORD	Josh 24:19	5647
s strange gods, then he will turn	Josh 24:20	5647
but we will *s* the LORD	Josh 24:21	5647
chosen you the LORD, to *s* him	Josh 24:22	5647
The LORD our God will we *s*	Josh 24:24	5647
in following other gods to *s* them	Judg 2:19	5647
is Shechem, that we should *s* him	Judg 9:28	5647
s the men of Hamor the father of	Judg 9:28	5647
for why should we *s* him	Judg 9:28	5647
Abimelech, that we should *s* him	Judg 9:38	5647
unto the LORD, and *s* him only	1Sa 7:3	5647
that thou do as occasion *s* thee	1Sa 10:7	5647
with us, and we will *s* thee	1Sa 11:1	5647
of our enemies, and we will *s* thee	1Sa 12:10	5647
s him, and obey his voice, and not	1Sa 12:14	5647
but *s* the LORD with all your	1Sa 12:20	5647
s him in truth with all your	1Sa 12:24	5647
shall ye be our servants, and *s* us	1Sa 17:9	5647
LORD, saying, Go, *s* other gods	1Sa 26:19	5647
Jerusalem, then I will *s* the LORD	2Sa 15:8	5647
And again, whom should I *s*	2Sa 16:19	5647
should I not *s* in the presence of	2Sa 16:19	5647
which I knew not shall *s* me	2Sa 22:44	5647
s other gods, and worship them	1Kin 9:6	5647
us, lighter, and we will *s* thee	1Kin 12:4	5647
people this day, and wilt *s* them	1Kin 12:7	5647
but Jehu shall *s* him much	2Kin 10:18	5647
nor *s* them, nor sacrifice to them	2Kin 17:35	5647
land, and *s* the king of Babylon	2Kin 25:24	5647
s him with a perfect heart and	1Chr 28:9	5647
s other gods, and worship them	2Chr 7:19	5647
he put upon us, and we will *s* thee	2Chr 10:4	5647
to *s* him, and that ye should	2Chr 29:11	8334
s the LORD your God, that the	2Chr 30:8	5647
commanded Judah to *s* the LORD God	2Chr 33:16	5647
that were present in Israel to *s*	2Chr 34:33	5647
even to *s* the LORD their God	2Chr 34:33	5647
s now the LORD your God, and his	2Chr 35:3	5647
Almighty, that we should *s* him	Job 21:15	5647
s him, they shall spend their	Job 36:11	5647
the unicorn be willing to *s* thee	Job 39:9	5647
S the LORD with fear, and rejoice	Ps 2:11	5647
whom I have not known shall *s* me	Ps 18:43	5647
A seed shall *s* him	Ps 22:30	5647
all nations shall *s* him	Ps 72:11	5647
be all they that *s* graven images	Ps 97:7	5647
S the LORD with gladness	Ps 100:2	5647
in a perfect way, he shall *s* me	Ps 101:6	8334
and the kingdoms, to *s* the LORD	Ps 102:22	5647
wherein thou wast made to *s*	Is 14:3	5647
shall *s* with the Assyrians	Is 19:23	5647
caused thee to *s* with an offering	Is 43:23	5647
hast made me to *s* with thy sins	Is 43:24	5647
to *s* him, and to love the name of	Is 56:6	8334
that will not *s* thee shall perish	Is 60:12	5647
so shall ye *s* strangers in a land	Jer 5:19	5647
went after other gods to *s* them	Jer 11:10	5647
to *s* them, and to worship them,	Jer 13:10	5647
there shall ye *s* other gods day	Jer 16:13	5647
I will cause thee to *s* thine	Jer 17:4	5647
go not after other gods to *s* them	Jer 25:6	5647
these nations shall *s* the king of	Jer 25:11	5647
great kings shall *s* themselves of	Jer 25:14	5647
field have I given also to *s* him	Jer 27:6	5647
And all nations shall *s* him	Jer 27:7	5647
kings shall *s* themselves of him	Jer 27:7	5647
kingdom which will not *s* the same	Jer 27:8	5647
Ye shall not *s* the king of	Jer 27:9	5647
s him, those will I let remain	Jer 27:11	5647
s him and his people, and live	Jer 27:12	5647
will not *s* the king of Babylon	Jer 27:13	5647
Ye shall not *s* the king of	Jer 27:14	5647
s the king of Babylon, and live	Jer 27:17	5647
that they may *s* Nebuchadnezzar	Jer 28:14	5647
and they shall *s* him	Jer 28:14	5647
shall no more *s* themselves of him	Jer 30:8	5647
But they shall *s* the LORD their	Jer 30:9	5647
none should *s* himself of them	Jer 34:9	5647
that none should *s* themselves of	Jer 34:10	5647
go not after other gods to *s* them	Jer 35:15	5647
Fear not to *s* the Chaldeans	Jer 40:9	5647
s the king of Babylon, and it	Jer 40:9	5647
at Mizpah to *s* the Chaldeans	Jer 40:10	5975
to *s* other gods, whom they knew	Jer 44:3	5647
the countries, to *s* wood and stone	Eze 20:32	8334
s ye every one his idols, and	Eze 20:39	5647
all of them in the land, *s* me	Eze 20:40	5647
s a great service against Tyrus	Eze 29:18	5647
food unto them that *s* the city	Eze 48:18	5647
they that *s* the city shall *s*	Eze 48:19	5647
they *s* not thy gods, nor worship	Dan 3:12	6399
and Abed-nego, do not ye *s* my gods	Dan 3:14	6399
our God whom we *s* is able to	Dan 3:17	6399
king, that we will not *s* thy gods	Dan 3:18	6399
might not *s* nor worship any god	Dan 3:28	6399
and languages, should *s* him	Dan 7:14	6399
kingdom, and all dominions shall *s*	Dan 7:27	6399
to *s* him with one consent	Zeph 3:9	5647
Ye have said, It is vain to *s* God	Mal 3:14	5647
thy God, and him only shalt thou *s*	Mt 4:10	*3000*
No man can *s* two masters	Mt 6:24	*1398*
Ye cannot *s* God and mammon	Mt 6:24	*1398*
enemies might *s* him without fear	Lk 1:74	*3000*
thy God, and him only shalt thou *s*	Lk 4:8	*3000*
my sister hath left me to *s* alone	Lk 10:40	*1247*
and will come forth and *s* them	Lk 12:37	*1247*
Lo, these many years do I *s* thee	Lk 15:29	*1398*
No servant can *s* two masters	Lk 16:13	*1398*
Ye cannot *s* God and mammon	Lk 16:13	*1398*
s me, till I have eaten and	Lk 17:8	*1247*
that is chief, as he that doth *s*	Lk 22:26	*1247*
If any man *s* me, let him follow	Jn 12:26	*1247*
if any man *s* me, him will my	Jn 12:26	*1247*
the word of God, and *s* tables	Acts 6:2	*1247*
come forth, and *s* me in this place	Acts 7:7	*3000*
of God, whose I am, and whom I *s*	Acts 27:23	*3000*
whom I *s* with my spirit in the	Rom 1:9	*3000*
henceforth we should not *s* sin	Rom 6:6	*1398*
that we should *s* in newness of	Rom 7:6	*1398*
mind I myself *s* the law of God	Rom 7:25	*1398*
The elder shall *s* the younger	Rom 9:12	*1398*
For they that are such *s* not our	Rom 16:18	*1398*
flesh, but by love *s* one another	Gal 5:13	*1398*
for ye *s* the Lord Christ	Col 3:24	*1398*
to God from idols to *s* the living	1Th 1:9	*1398*
whom I *s* from my forefathers with	2Ti 1:3	*3000*
Who *s* unto the example and shadow	Heb 8:5	*3000*
dead works to *s* the living God	Heb 9:14	*3000*
whereby we may *s* God acceptably	Heb 12:28	*3000*
to eat which *s* the tabernacle	Heb 13:10	*3000*
s him day and night in his temple	Rev 7:15	*3000*
and his servants shall *s* him	Rev 22:3	*3000*

SERVED

Twelve years they *s* Chedorlaomer	Gen 14:4	5647
Jacob *s* seven years for Rachel	Gen 29:20	5647
s with him yet seven other years	Gen 29:30	5647
children, for whom I have *s* thee	Gen 30:26	5647
Thou knowest how I have *s* thee	Gen 30:29	5647
all my power I have *s* your father	Gen 31:6	5647
I *s* thee fourteen years for thy	Gen 31:41	5647
grace in his sight, and he *s* him	Gen 39:4	8334
Joseph with them, and he *s* them	Gen 40:4	8334
ye shall possess *s* their gods	Deut 12:2	5647
s other gods, and worshipped them,	Deut 17:3	5647
s other gods, and worshipped them,	Deut 29:26	5647
s other gods, and bowed yourselves	Josh 23:16	5647
and they *s* other gods	Josh 24:2	5647
the gods which your fathers *s* on	Josh 24:14	5647
the gods which your fathers *s*	Josh 24:15	5647
Israel *s* the LORD all the days of	Josh 24:31	5647
the people *s* the LORD all the	Judg 2:7	5647
sight of the LORD, and *s* Baalim	Judg 2:11	5647
the LORD, and *s* Baal and Ashtaroth	Judg 2:13	5647
to their sons, and *s* their gods	Judg 3:6	5647
God, and *s* Baalim and the groves	Judg 3:7	5647
and the children of Israel *s*	Judg 3:8	5647
So the children of Israel *s* Eglon	Judg 3:14	5647
unto him, Why hast thou *s* us thus	Judg 8:1	6213

s Baalim, and Ashtaroth, and the Judg 10:6 5647
and forsook the LORD, and *s* not him Judg 10:6 5647
our God, and also *s* Baalim Judg 10:10 5647
have forsaken me, and *s* other gods Judg 10:13 5647
from among them, and *s* the LORD Judg 10:16 5647
and Ashtaroth, and *s* the LORD only 1Sa 7:4 5647
s other gods, so do they also 1Sa 8:8 5647
have *s* Baalim and Ashtaroth 1Sa 12:10 5647
made peace with Israel, and *s* them 2Sa 10:19 5647
as I have *s* in thy father's 2Sa 16:19 5647
s Solomon all the days of his 1Kin 4:21 5647
have worshipped them, and *s* them 1Kin 9:9 5647
s Baal, and worshipped him 1Kin 16:31 5647
For he *s* Baal, and worshipped him, 1Kin 22:53 5647
unto them, Ahab *s* Baal a little 2Kin 10:18 5647
For they *s* idols, whereof the 2Kin 17:12 5647
all the host of heaven, and *s* Baal 2Kin 17:16 5647
s their own gods, after the 2Kin 17:33 5647
s their graven images, both their 2Kin 17:41 5647
the king of Assyria, and *s* him not 2Kin 18:7 5647
all the host of heaven, and *s* them 2Kin 21:3 5647
s the idols that his father 2Kin 21:21 5647
the idols that his father *s* 2Kin 21:21 5647
and told David how the men were *s* 1Chr 19:5
their officers that *s* the king in 1Chr 27:1 8334
and worshipped them, and *s* them 2Chr 7:22 5647
fathers, and *s* groves and idols 2Chr 24:18 5647
all the host of heaven, and *s* them 2Chr 33:3 5647
his father had made, and *s* them 2Chr 33:22 5647
For they have not *s* thee in their Neh 9:35 5647
the seven chamberlains that *s* in Est 1:10 8334
And they *s* their idols Ps 106:36 5647
rewardeth thee as thou hast *s* us Ps 137:8 1580
king himself is *s* by the field Eccl 5:9 5647
s strange gods in your land, so Jer 5:19 5647
have loved, and whom they have *s* Jer 8:2 5647
after other gods, and have *s* them Jer 16:11 5647
worshipped other gods, and *s* them Jer 22:9 5647
when he hath *s* thee six years, Jer 34:14 5647
which *s* the king of Babylon, into Jer 52:12 5975
service that he had *s* against it Eze 29:18 5647
labour wherewith he *s* against it Eze 29:20 5647
those that *s* themselves of them Eze 34:27 5647
Israel *s* for a wife, and for a Hos 12:12 5647
but *s* God with fastings and Lk 2:37 *3000*
and Martha *s* Jn 12:2 *1247*
after he had *s* his own generation Acts 13:36 *5256*
s the creature more than the Rom 1:25 *3000*
he hath *s* with me in the gospel Phil 2:22 *1398*

SERVEDST
Because thou *s* not the LORD thy Deut 28:47 5647

SERVEST
Thy God whom thou *s* continually Dan 6:16 6399
whom thou *s* continually, able to Dan 6:20 6399

SERVETH
thereof, and all that *s* thereto Num 3:36 5656
spareth his own son that *s* him Mal 3:17 5647
s God and him that *s* him not Mal 3:18 5647
sitteth at meat, or he that *s* Lk 22:27 *1247*
but I am among you as he that *s* Lk 22:27 *1247*
s Christ is acceptable to God Rom 14:18 *1398*
but prophesying *s* not for them 1Cor 14:22
Wherefore then *s* the law Gal 3:19

SERVICE
give thee this also for the *s* Gen 29:27 5656
for thou knowest my *s* which I Gen 30:26 5656
in all manner of *s* in the field Ex 1:14 5656
all their *s*, wherein they made Ex 1:14 5656
that ye shall keep this *s* Ex 12:25 5656
unto you, What mean ye by this *s* Ex 12:26 5656
shalt keep this *s* in this month Ex 13:5 5656
tabernacle in all the *s* thereof Ex 27:19 5656
the *s* of the tabernacle of the Ex 30:16 5656
And the cloths of *s*, and the holy Ex 31:10 8278
The cloths of *s*, to do *s* in Ex 35:19 8278
to do *s* in the holy place, the Ex 35:19 8334
congregation, and for all his *s* Ex 35:21 5656
wood for any work of the *s* Ex 35:24 5656
work for the *s* of the sanctuary Ex 36:1 5656
work of the *s* of the sanctuary Ex 36:3 5656
than enough for the *s* of the work Ex 36:5 5656
for the *s* of the Levites, by the Ex 38:21 5656
and scarlet, they made cloths of *s* Ex 39:1 8278
to do *s* in the holy place, and Ex 39:1 8334
of the *s* of the tabernacle Ex 39:40 5656
The cloths of *s* to do Ex 39:41 8278
to do *s* in the holy place Ex 39:41 8334
to do the *s* of the tabernacle Num 3:7 5656
to do the *s* of the tabernacle Num 3:8 5656
cords of it for all the *s* thereof Num 3:26 5656
the hanging, and all the *s* thereof Num 3:31 5656
This shall be the *s* of the sons Num 4:4 5656
appoint them every one to his *s* Num 4:19 5656
that enter in to perform the *s* Num 4:23 5656
This is the *s* of the families of Num 4:24 5656
and all the instruments of their *s* Num 4:26 5656
his sons shall be all the *s* of Num 4:27 5656
their burdens, and in all their *s* Num 4:27 5656
This is the *s* of the families of Num 4:28 5656
one that entereth into the *s* Num 4:30 6635
according to all their *s* in the Num 4:31 5656
instruments, and with all their *s* Num 4:32 5656
This is the *s* of the families of Num 4:33 5656
Merari, according to all their *s* Num 4:33 5656
one that entereth into the *s* Num 4:35 6635
all that might do *s* in the Num 4:37 5647
one that entereth into the *s* Num 4:39 6635
of all that might do *s* in the Num 4:41 5647
one that entereth into the *s* Num 4:43 6635
came to do the *s* of the ministry Num 4:47 5656
the *s* of the burden in the Num 4:47 5656
every one according to his *s* Num 4:49 5656
do the *s* of the tabernacle of the Num 7:5 5656
to every man according to his *s* Num 7:5 5656
of Gershon, according to their *s* Num 7:7 5656
of Merari, according unto their *s* Num 7:8 5656
because the *s* of the sanctuary Num 7:9 5656
may execute the *s* of the LORD Num 8:11 5656
do the *s* of the tabernacle of the Num 8:15 5647
to do the *s* of the children of Num 8:19 5656
their *s* in the tabernacle of the Num 8:22 5656
the *s* of the tabernacle of the Num 8:24 5656
cease waiting upon the *s* thereof Num 8:25 5656
keep the charge, and shall do no *s* Num 8:26 5656
s of the tabernacle of the LORD Num 16:9 5656
for all the *s* of the tabernacle Num 18:4 5656
to do the *s* of the tabernacle of Num 18:6 5656
office unto you as a *s* of gift Num 18:7 5656
for their *s* which they serve, Num 18:21 5656
even the *s* of the tabernacle of Num 18:21 5656
do the *s* of the tabernacle of the Num 18:23 5656
your *s* in the tabernacle of the Num 18:31 5656
that we might do the *s* of the Josh 22:27 5656
thou the grievous *s* of thy father 1Kin 12:4 5656
the *s* of song in the house of the 1Chr 6:31 3027
appointed unto all manner of *s* of 1Chr 6:48 5656
work of the *s* of the house of God 1Chr 9:13 5656
were over the work of the *s* 1Chr 9:19 5656
the *s* of the house of the LORD 1Chr 23:24 5656
vessels of it for the *s* thereof 1Chr 23:26 5656
the *s* of the house of the LORD 1Chr 23:28 5656
the work of the *s* of the house of 1Chr 23:28 5656
in the *s* of the house of the LORD 1Chr 23:32 5656
to their offices in their *s* 1Chr 24:3 5656
s to come into the house of the 1Chr 24:19 5656
to the *s* of the sons of Asaph 1Chr 25:1 5656
workmen according to their *s* was 1Chr 25:1 5656
for the *s* of the house of God, 1Chr 25:6 5656
able men for strength for the *s* 1Chr 26:8 5656
the LORD, and in the *s* of the king 1Chr 26:30 5656
for all the work of the *s* of the 1Chr 28:13 5656
for all the vessels of *s* in the 1Chr 28:13 5656
instruments of all manner of *s* 1Chr 28:14 5656
instruments of every kind of *s* 1Chr 28:14 5656
the *s* of the house of the LORD 1Chr 28:20 5656
for all the *s* of the house of God 1Chr 28:21 5656
skilful man, for any manner of *s* 1Chr 28:21 5656
his *s* this day unto the LORD 1Chr 29:5 3027
gave for the *s* of the house of 1Chr 29:7 5656
courses of the priests to their *s* 2Chr 8:14 5656
that they may know my *s*, and the 2Chr 12:8 5656
the *s* of the kingdoms of the 2Chr 12:8 5656
of the *s* of the house of the LORD 2Chr 24:12 5656
So the *s* of the house of the LORD 2Chr 29:35 5656
every man according to his *s* 2Chr 31:2 5656
his daily portion for their *s* in 2Chr 31:16 5656
in the *s* of the house of God 2Chr 31:21 5656
the work in any manner of *s* 2Chr 34:13 5656
encouraged them to the *s* of the 2Chr 35:2 5656
So the *s* was prepared, and the 2Chr 35:10 5656
might not depart from their *s* 2Chr 35:15 5656
So all the *s* of the LORD was 2Chr 35:16 5656
their courses, for the *s* of God Ezr 6:18 5673
for the *s* of the house of thy God Ezr 7:19 6402
for the *s* of the Levites, two Ezr 8:20 5656
for the *s* of the house of our God Neh 10:32 5656
cattle, and herb for the *s* of man Ps 104:14 5656
his neighbour's *s* without wages Jer 22:13 5647
to serve a great *s* against Tyrus Eze 29:18 5656
for the *s* that he had served Eze 29:18 5656
the house, for all the *s* thereof Eze 44:14 5656
will think that he doeth God *s* Jn 16:2 *2999*
the *s* of God, and the promises Rom 9:4 *2999*
God, which is your reasonable *s* Rom 12:1 *2999*
that my *s* which I have for Rom 15:31 *1248*
s not only supplieth the want of 2Cor 9:12 *3009*
taking wages of them, to do you *s* 2Cor 11:8 *1248*
ye did *s* unto them which by Gal 4:8 *1398*
With good will doing *s*, as to the Eph 6:7 *1398*
s of your faith, I joy, and Phil 2:17 *3009*
supply your lack of *s* toward me Phil 2:30 *3009*
but rather do them *s*, because 1Ti 6:2 *1398*
had also ordinances of divine *s* Heb 9:1 *2999*
accomplishing the *s* of God Heb 9:6 *2999*
make him that did the *s* perfect Heb 9:9 *3000*
know thy works, and charity, and *s* Rev 2:19 *1248*

SERVILE
ye shall do no *s* work therein Lev 23:7 5656
ye shall do no *s* work therein Lev 23:8 5656
ye shall do no *s* work therein Lev 23:21 5656
Ye shall do no *s* work therein Lev 23:25 5656
ye shall do no *s* work therein Lev 23:35 5656
and ye shall do no *s* work therein Lev 23:36 5656
do no manner of *s* work therein Num 28:18 5656
ye shall do no *s* work Num 28:25 5656
ye shall do no *s* work Num 28:26 5656
ye shall do no *s* work Num 29:1 5656
ye shall do no *s* work, and ye Num 29:12 5656
ye shall do no *s* work therein Num 29:35 5656

SERVING
we have let Israel go from *s* us Ex 14:5 5647
to thee, in *s* thee six years Deut 15:18 5647
Martha was cumbered about much *s* Lk 10:40 *1248*
S the Lord with all humility of Acts 20:19 *1398*
tribes, instantly *s* God day Acts 26:7 *3000*
fervent in spirit; *s* the Lord Rom 12:11 *1398*
s divers lusts and pleasures, Titus 3:3 *1398*

SERVITOR
his *s* said, What, should I set 2Kin 4:43 8334

SERVITUDE
the grievous *s* of thy father 2Chr 10:4 5656
affliction, and because of great *s* Lam 1:3 5656

SET
God *s* them in the firmament of Gen 1:17 5414
the LORD *s* a mark upon Cain, lest Gen 4:15 7760
shalt thou *s* in the side thereof Gen 6:16 7760
I do *s* my bow in the cloud, and it Gen 9:13 5414
at this *s* time in the next year Gen 17:21 4150
had dressed, and *s* it before them Gen 18:8 5414
forth, and *s* him without the city Gen 19:16 3240
at the *s* time of which God had Gen 21:2 4150
Abraham *s* seven ewe lambs of the Gen 21:28 5324
which thou hast *s* by themselves Gen 21:29 5324
there was *s* meat before him to Gen 24:33 7760
all night, because the sun was *s* Gen 28:11 935
behold a ladder *s* up on the earth Gen 28:12 5324
s it up for a pillar, and poured Gen 28:18 7760
which I have *s* for a pillar Gen 28:22 7760
he *s* three days' journey betwixt Gen 30:36 7760
he *s* the rods which he had pilled Gen 30:38 3322
s the faces of the flocks toward Gen 30:40 5414
s his sons and his wives upon Gen 31:17 5375
s his face toward the mount Gen 31:21 7760
s it here before my brethren and Gen 31:37 7760
a stone, and *s* it up for a pillar Gen 31:45 7311
Jacob *s* up a pillar in the place Gen 35:14 5324
Jacob *s* a pillar upon her grave Gen 35:20 5324
s him over the land of Egypt Gen 41:33 7896
I have *s* thee over all the land Gen 41:41 5414
s him before thee, then let me Gen 43:9 3322
himself, and said, *S* on bread Gen 43:31 7760
they *s* on for him by himself, and Gen 43:32 7760
that I may *s* mine eyes upon him Gen 44:21 7760
father, and *s* him before Pharaoh Gen 47:7 5975
he *s* Ephraim before Manasseh Gen 48:20 7760
Therefore they did *s* over them Ex 1:11 7760
s them upon an ass, and he Ex 4:20 7392
taskmasters had *s* over them Ex 5:14 7760
neither did he *s* his heart to Ex 7:23 7896
And the LORD appointed a *s* time Ex 9:5 4150
That thou shalt *s* apart unto the Ex 13:12
thou shalt *s* bounds unto the Ex 19:12
S bounds about the mount, and Ex 19:23
which thou shalt *s* before them Ex 21:1 7760
I will *s* thy bounds from the Red Ex 23:31 7896
and stones to be *s* in the ephod Ex 25:7 4394
thou shalt *s* upon the table Ex 25:30 5414
s in order one against another Ex 26:17 7947
thou shalt *s* the table without Ex 26:35 7760
them to be *s* in ouches of gold Ex 28:11 4142
thou shalt *s* in it settings of Ex 28:17 4390
they shall be *s* in gold in their Ex 28:20 7660
to *s* them, and in carving of Ex 31:5 4390
that they are *s* on mischief Ex 32:22
stones to be *s* for the ephod, and Ex 35:9 4394
onyx stones, and stones to be *s* Ex 35:27 4394
to *s* them, and in carving of wood, Ex 35:33 4390
to be *s* by the four corners of it Ex 37:3
they *s* in it four rows of stones Ex 39:10 4390
with the lamps to be *s* in order Ex 39:37
s up the tabernacle of the tent Ex 40:2 6965
s in order the things that are to Ex 40:4
that are to be *s* in order upon it Ex 40:4
thou shalt *s* the altar of gold Ex 40:5 5414
thou shalt *s* the altar of the Ex 40:6 5414
thou shalt *s* the laver between Ex 40:7 5414
thou shalt *s* up the court round Ex 40:8 7760
s up the boards thereof, and put Ex 40:18 7760
s the staves on the ark, and put Ex 40:20 7760
s up the vail of the covering, and Ex 40:21 7760
he *s* the bread in order upon it Ex 40:23 6186
he *s* up the hanging at the door Ex 40:28 7760
he *s* the laver between the tent Ex 40:30 7760
s up the hanging of the court Ex 40:33 5414
I will even *s* my face against Lev 17:10 5414
I will *s* my face against that man Lev 20:3 5414
Then I will *s* my face against Lev 20:5 7760
I will even *s* my face against Lev 20:6 5414
thou shalt *s* them in two rows, Lev 24:6 7760
Every sabbath he shall *s* it in Lev 24:8
neither shall ye *s* up any image Lev 26:1 5414
I will *s* my tabernacle among you Lev 26:11 5414
I will *s* my face against you, and Lev 26:17 5414
the Levites shall *s* it up Num 1:51 6965
These shall first *s* forth Num 2:9 5265
they shall *s* forth in the second Num 2:16 5265
of the congregation shall *s* Num 2:17 5265
encamp, so shall they *s* forward Num 2:17 5265
standards, and so they *s* forward Num 2:34 5265
as the camp is to *s* forward Num 4:15 5265
near, and *s* her before the LORD Num 5:16 5975
the priest shall *s* the woman Num 5:18 5975
shall *s* the woman before the LORD Num 5:30 5975
had fully *s* up the tabernacle Num 7:1 6965
thou shalt *s* the Levites before Num 8:13 5975
and the sons of Merari *s* forward Num 10:17 5265
s forward according to their Num 10:18 5265
And the Kohathites *s* forward Num 10:21 5265
the other did *s* up the tabernacle Num 10:21 6965
s forward according to their Num 10:22 5265
of the children of Dan *s* forward Num 10:25 5265
their armies, when they *s* forward Num 10:28 5265
to pass, when the ark *s* forward Num 10:35 5265
s them round about the tabernacle Num 11:24 5975
serpent, and *s* it upon a pole Num 21:8 7760
the children of Israel *s* forward Num 21:10 5265
the children of Israel *s* forward Num 22:1 5265
but he *s* his face toward the Num 24:1 7896
s a man over the congregation, Num 27:16 6485
s him before Eleazar the priest, Num 27:19 5975
s him before Eleazar the priest, Num 27:22 5975
do unto the LORD in your *s* feasts Num 29:39 4150
I have *s* the land before you Deut 1:8 5414
God hath *s* the land before thee Deut 1:21 5414
which I *s* before you this day Deut 4:8 5414
this is the law which Moses *s* Deut 4:44 7760

S

The LORD did not *s* his love upon	Deut 7:7	
I *s* before you this day a	Deut 11:26	5414
judgments which I *s* before you	Deut 11:32	5414
shall choose to *s* his name there	Deut 14:24	7760
shalt thou *s* thee up any image	Deut 16:22	6965
I will *s* a king over me, like as	Deut 17:14	7760
in any wise *s* him king over thee	Deut 17:15	7760
shalt thou *s* king over thee	Deut 17:15	7760
thou mayest not *s* a stranger over	Deut 17:15	5414
time have *s* in thine inheritance	Deut 19:14	1379
s it down before the altar of the	Deut 26:4	3240
thou shalt *s* it before the LORD	Deut 26:10	3240
that thou shalt *s* thee up great	Deut 27:2	6965
that ye shall *s* up these stones,	Deut 27:4	6965
that the LORD thy God will *s* thee	Deut 28:1	5414
king which thou shalt *s* over thee	Deut 28:36	6965
which would not adventure to *s*	Deut 28:56	3322
curse, which I have *s* before thee	Deut 30:1	5414
I have *s* before thee this day	Deut 30:15	5414
that I have *s* before you life and	Deut 30:19	5414
he *s* the bounds of the people	Deut 32:8	5324
s on fire the foundations of the	Deut 32:22	
S your hearts unto all the words	Deut 32:46	7760
Joshua *s* up twelve stones in the	Josh 4:9	6965
son shall he *s* up the gates of it	Josh 6:26	5324
that ye shall *s* the city on fire	Josh 8:8	3341
s them to lie in ambush between	Josh 8:12	7760
And when they had *s* the people	Josh 8:13	7760
and hasted and *s* the city on fire	Josh 8:19	
s men by it for to keep them	Josh 10:18	6485
s up the tabernacle of the	Josh 18:1	7931
s them a statute and an ordinance	Josh 24:25	7760
s it up there under an oak, that	Josh 24:26	6965
the sword, and *s* the city on fire	Judg 1:8	7971
my present, and *s* it before thee	Judg 6:18	3240
him shalt thou *s* by himself	Judg 7:5	3322
and they had but newly *s* the watch	Judg 7:19	6965
the LORD *s* every man's sword	Judg 7:22	7760
the men of Shechem *s* liers in	Judg 9:25	7760
rise early, and *s* upon the city	Judg 9:33	6584
s the hold on fire upon them	Judg 9:49	
when he had *s* the brands on fire,	Judg 15:5	
they *s* him between the pillars	Judg 16:25	5975
of Dan *s* up the graven image	Judg 18:30	6965
they *s* them up Micah's graven	Judg 18:31	7760
s their battle again in array in	Judg 20:22	
Israel *s* liers in wait round	Judg 20:29	7760
which they had *s* beside Gibeah	Judg 20:36	7760
also they *s* on fire all the	Judg 20:48	7971
that was *s* over the reapers	Ruth 2:5	5324
the servant that was *s* over the	Ruth 2:6	5324
to *s* them among princes, and to	1Sa 2:8	3427
he hath *s* the world upon them	1Sa 2:8	7896
house of Dagon, and *s* it by Dagon	1Sa 5:2	3322
and *s* him in his place again	1Sa 5:3	7725
whereon they *s* down the ark of	1Sa 6:18	3240
s it between Mizpeh and Shen, and	1Sa 7:12	7760
will *s* them to ear his ground, and	1Sa 8:12	
days ago, *s* not thy mind on them	1Sa 9:20	7760
I said unto thee, *S* it by thee	1Sa 9:23	7760
was upon it, and *s* it before Saul	1Sa 9:24	7760
s it before thee, and eat	1Sa 9:24	7760
him, Nay, but *s* a king over us	1Sa 10:19	7760
the LORD hath *s* a king over you	1Sa 12:13	5414
according to the *s* time that	1Sa 13:8	4150
that I have *s* up Saul to be king	1Sa 15:11	4427
he *s* him up a place, and is gone	1Sa 15:12	5324
s the battle in array against the	1Sa 17:2	
out to *s* your battle in array	1Sa 17:8	
Saul *s* him over the men of war,	1Sa 18:5	7760
so that his name was much *s* by	1Sa 18:30	3335
which was *s* over the servants of	1Sa 22:9	5324
as thy life was much *s* by this	1Sa 26:24	1431
so let my life be much *s* by in	1Sa 26:24	1431
let me *s* a morsel of bread before	1Sa 28:22	7760
to *s* up the throne of David over	2Sa 3:10	6965
they *s* the ark of God upon a new	2Sa 6:3	7392
s it in his place, in the midst	2Sa 6:17	3322
I will *s* up thy seed after thee,	2Sa 7:12	6965
the Syrians *s* themselves in array	2Sa 10:17	
S ye Uriah in the forefront of	2Sa 11:15	3051
they *s* bread before him, and he	2Sa 12:20	7760
and it was *s* on David's head	2Sa 12:30	
go and *s* it on fire	2Sa 14:30	
servants *s* the field on fire	2Sa 14:30	
thy servants *s* my field on fire	2Sa 14:31	
they *s* down the ark of God	2Sa 15:24	3332
s captains of thousands and	2Sa 18:1	7760
have *s* thyself against me	2Sa 18:13	3320
yet didst thou *s* thy servant	2Sa 19:28	7896
but he tarried longer than the *s*	2Sa 20:5	4150
David *s* him over his guard	2Sa 23:23	7760
that all Israel *s* their faces on	1Kin 2:15	7760
caused a seat to be *s* for the	1Kin 2:19	7760
s me on the throne of David my	1Kin 2:24	3427
whom I will *s* upon thy throne in	1Kin 5:5	5414
to *s* there the ark of the	1Kin 6:19	5414
he *s* the cherubims within the	1Kin 6:27	5414
to *s* upon the tops of the pillars	1Kin 7:16	5414
he *s* up the pillars in the porch	1Kin 7:21	6965
he *s* up the right pillar, and	1Kin 7:21	6965
he *s* up the left pillar, and	1Kin 7:21	6965
the sea was *s* above upon them, and	1Kin 7:25	
he *s* the sea on the right side of	1Kin 7:39	5414
I have *s* there a place for the	1Kin 8:21	7760
which I have *s* before you	1Kin 9:6	5414
to *s* thee on the throne of Israel	1Kin 10:9	5414
he *s* the one in Beth-el, and the	1Kin 12:29	7760
for his eyes were *s* by reason of	1Kin 14:4	6965
to *s* up his son after him, and to	1Kin 15:4	6965
s up the gates thereof in his	1Kin 16:34	5324
servants, *S* yourselves in array	1Kin 20:12	7760
they *s* themselves in array	1Kin 20:12	7760
s Naboth on high among the people	1Kin 21:9	3427
s two men, sons of Belial, before	1Kin 21:10	3427
s Naboth on high among the people	1Kin 21:12	3427
thou shalt *s* aside that which is	2Kin 4:4	5265
let us *s* for him there a bed, and	2Kin 4:10	7760
S on the great pot, and seethe	2Kin 4:38	8239
should I *s* this before an hundred	2Kin 4:43	5414
So he *s* it before them, and they	2Kin 4:44	5414
s bread and water before them,	2Kin 6:22	7760
strong holds wilt thou *s* on fire	2Kin 8:12	7971
s him on his father's throne, and	2Kin 10:3	7760
the money that every man is *s* at	2Kin 12:4	6187
s it beside the altar, on the	2Kin 12:9	5414
Hazael *s* his face to go up to	2Kin 12:17	7760
they *s* them up images and groves	2Kin 17:10	5324
on thy part to *s* riders upon them	2Kin 18:23	5414
the LORD, *S* thine house in order	2Kin 20:1	
he *s* a graven image of the grove	2Kin 21:7	7760
that was *s* over the men of war	2Kin 25:19	6496
s his throne above the throne of	2Kin 25:28	5414
these are they whom David *s* over	1Chr 6:31	5975
seer did ordain in their *s* office	1Chr 9:22	530
porters, were in their *s* office	1Chr 9:26	530
had the *s* office over the things	1Chr 9:31	530
they *s* themselves in the midst of	1Chr 11:14	3320
David *s* him over his guard	1Chr 11:25	7760
s it in the midst of the tent	1Chr 16:1	3322
battle was *s* against him before	1Chr 19:10	
they *s* themselves in array	1Chr 19:11	
s the battle in array against	1Chr 19:17	
it was *s* upon David's head	1Chr 20:2	
s up an altar unto the LORD in	1Chr 21:18	6965
he *s* masons to hew wrought stones	1Chr 22:2	5975
Now *s* your heart and your soul to	1Chr 22:19	5414
four thousand were to *s* forward	1Chr 23:4	5329
the new moons, and on the *s* feasts	1Chr 23:31	4150
onyx stones, and stones to be *s*	1Chr 29:2	4394
because I have *s* my affection to	1Chr 29:3	
he *s* threescore and ten thousand	2Chr 2:18	6213
overseers to *s* the people a work	2Chr 2:18	
s thereon palm trees and chains	2Chr 3:5	5927
the sea was *s* above upon them, and	2Chr 4:4	
s them in the temple, five on the	2Chr 4:7	5414
he *s* the sea on the right side of	2Chr 4:10	5414
whereon the shewbread was *s*	2Chr 4:19	
am *s* on the throne of Israel, as	2Chr 6:10	3427
had *s* it in the midst of the	2Chr 6:13	5414
which I have *s* before you	2Chr 7:19	5414
in thee to *s* thee on his throne	2Chr 9:8	5414
the tribes of Israel such as *s*	2Chr 11:16	5414
Abijah *s* the battle in array with	2Chr 13:3	631
Jeroboam also *s* the battle in	2Chr 13:3	
the shewbread also *s* they in	2Chr 13:11	
they *s* the battle in array in the	2Chr 14:10	
s garrisons in the land of Judah,	2Chr 17:2	5414
And he *s* judges in the land	2Chr 19:5	5975
did Jehoshaphat *s* of the Levites	2Chr 19:8	5975
s himself to seek the LORD, and	2Chr 20:3	5414
s yourselves, stand ye still, and	2Chr 20:17	3320
the LORD *s* ambushments against	2Chr 20:22	5414
he *s* all the people, every man	2Chr 23:10	5975
that were *s* over the host	2Chr 23:14	6485
he *s* the porters at the gates of	2Chr 23:19	5975
s the king upon the throne of the	2Chr 23:20	3427
s it without at the gate of the	2Chr 24:8	5414
they *s* the house of God in his	2Chr 24:13	5975
s them up to be his gods, and	2Chr 25:14	5975
he *s* the Levites in the house of	2Chr 29:25	5975
house of the LORD was *s* in order	2Chr 29:35	3559
new moons, and for the *s* feasts	2Chr 31:3	4150
of the priests, in their *s* office	2Chr 31:15	530
for in their *s* office they	2Chr 31:18	530
he *s* captains of war over the	2Chr 32:6	5414
he *s* a carved image, the idol	2Chr 33:7	7760
s up groves and graven images,	2Chr 33:19	5975
the Kohathites, to *s* it forward	2Chr 34:12	5329
he *s* the priests in their charges	2Chr 35:2	5975
of God to *s* it up in his place	Ezr 2:68	5975
they *s* the altar upon his bases	Ezr 3:3	3559
of all the *s* feasts of the LORD	Ezr 3:5	4150
to *s* forward the work of the	Ezr 3:8	5329
to *s* forward the workmen in the	Ezr 3:9	5329
they *s* the priests in their	Ezr 3:10	5975
s in the cities of Samaria, and	Ezr 4:10	3488
have *s* up the walls thereof, and	Ezr 4:12	3635
builded, and the walls *s* up again	Ezr 4:13	3635
again, and the walls thereof *s* up	Ezr 4:16	3635
king of Israel builded and *s* up	Ezr 5:11	3635
from his house, and being *s* up	Ezr 6:11	2211
they *s* the priests in their	Ezr 6:18	6966
s magistrates and judges, which	Ezr 7:25	4483
to *s* up the house of our God, and	Ezr 9:9	7311
I have chosen to *s* my name there	Neh 1:9	7931
and I *s* him a time	Neh 2:6	5414
it, and *s* up the doors of it	Neh 3:1	5975
s up the doors thereof, the locks	Neh 3:3	5975
s up the doors thereof, and the	Neh 3:6	5975
s up the doors thereof, the locks	Neh 3:13	5975
s up the doors thereof, the locks	Neh 3:14	5975
s up the doors thereof, the locks	Neh 3:15	5975
s a watch against them day and	Neh 4:9	5975
Therefore *s* I in the lower places	Neh 4:13	5975
I even *s* the people after their	Neh 4:13	5975
I *s* a great assembly against them	Neh 5:7	5414
not *s* up the doors upon the gates	Neh 6:1	5975
I had *s* up the doors, and the	Neh 7:1	5975
s over us because of our sins	Neh 9:37	5414
the new moons, for the *s* feasts	Neh 10:33	4150
and *s* them in their place	Neh 13:11	5975
of my servants *s* I at the gates	Neh 13:19	5975
so that he *s* the royal crown upon	Est 2:17	7760
s his seat above all the princes	Est 3:1	7760
royal which is *s* upon his head	Est 6:8	5414
Esther *s* Mordecai over the house	Est 8:2	7760
To *s* up on high those that be low	Job 5:11	7760
the terrors of God do *s*	Job 6:4	
that thou shouldest *s* thine heart	Job 7:17	7896
why hast thou *s* me as a mark	Job 7:20	7760
who shall *s* me a time to plead	Job 9:19	3259
thou wouldest appoint me a *s* time	Job 14:13	2706
pieces, and *s* me up for his mark	Job 16:12	6965
he hath *s* darkness in my paths	Job 19:8	7760
have *s* with the dogs of my flock	Job 30:1	7896
they *s* forward my calamity, they	Job 30:13	
s thy words in order before me,	Job 33:5	
If he *s* his heart upon man, if he	Job 34:14	7760
and *s* others in their stead	Job 34:24	5975
that which should be *s* on thy	Job 36:16	5183
place, and *s* bars and doors,	Job 38:10	7760
canst thou *s* the dominion thereof	Job 38:33	7760
kings of the earth *s* themselves	Ps 2:2	3320
Yet have I *s* my king upon my holy	Ps 2:6	5258
that have *s* themselves against me	Ps 3:6	7896
s apart him that is godly for	Ps 4:3	6395
who hast *s* thy glory above the	Ps 8:1	5414
are privily *s* against the poor	Ps 10:8	6845
I will *s* him in safety from him	Ps 12:5	7896
I have *s* the LORD always before	Ps 16:8	7737
they have *s* their eyes bowing	Ps 17:11	7896
In them hath he *s* a tabernacle	Ps 19:4	7760
our God we will *s* up our banners	Ps 20:5	
he shall *s* me up upon a rock	Ps 27:5	7311
thou hast *s* my feet in a large	Ps 31:8	5975
s my feet upon a rock, and	Ps 40:2	6965
s them in order before thine eyes	Ps 50:21	
they have not *s* God before them	Ps 54:3	7760
among them that are *s* on fire	Ps 57:4	
s not your heart upon them	Ps 62:10	7896
salvation, O God, *s* me up on high	Ps 69:29	
They *s* their mouth against the	Ps 73:9	8371
Surely thou didst *s* them in	Ps 73:18	7896
they *s* up their ensigns for signs	Ps 74:4	7760
Thou hast *s* all the borders of	Ps 74:17	5324
That they might *s* their hope in	Ps 78:7	7760
a generation that *s* not their	Ps 78:8	3559
shall *s* us in the way of his	Ps 85:13	7760
have not *s* thee before them	Ps 86:14	7760
I will *s* his hand also in the sea	Ps 89:25	7760
Thou hast *s* up the right hand of	Ps 89:42	7311
Thou hast *s* our iniquities before	Ps 90:8	7896
Because he hath *s* his love upon	Ps 91:14	
I will *s* him on high, because he	Ps 91:14	
I will *s* no wicked thing before	Ps 101:3	7896
her, yea, the *s* time, is come	Ps 102:13	
Thou hast *s* a bound that they may	Ps 104:9	7760
S thou a wicked man over him	Ps 109:6	6485
That he may *s* him with princes,	Ps 113:8	3427
me, and *s* me in a large place	Ps 118:5	
For there are *s* thrones of	Ps 122:5	3427
thy body will I *s* upon thy throne	Ps 132:11	7896
they have *s* gins for me	Ps 140:5	7896
Let my prayer be *s* forth before	Ps 141:2	3559
S a watch, O LORD, before my	Ps 141:3	7896
But ye have *s* at nought all my	Prov 1:25	
I was *s* up from everlasting, from	Prov 8:23	5258
when he *s* a compass upon the face	Prov 8:27	2710
which thy fathers have *s*	Prov 22:28	6213
Wilt thou *s* thine eyes upon that	Prov 23:5	5774
also he hath *s* the world in their	Eccl 3:11	5414
God also hath *s* the one over	Eccl 7:14	6213
men is fully *s* in them to do evil	Eccl 8:11	
Folly is *s* in great dignity, and	Eccl 10:6	5414
out, and *s* in order many proverbs	Eccl 12:9	
washed with milk, and fitly *s*	Song 5:12	3427
as gold rings *s* with the beryl	Song 5:14	4390
s upon sockets of fine gold	Song 5:15	3245
heap of wheat *s* about with lilies	Song 7:2	5473
S me as a seal upon thine heart,	Song 8:6	7760
instead of well *s* hair baldness	Is 3:24	
s a king in the midst of it, even	Is 7:6	
Therefore the LORD shall *s* up the	Is 9:11	7682
that the Lord shall *s* his hand	Is 11:11	
he shall *s* up an ensign for the	Is 11:12	5375
and *s* them in their own land	Is 14:1	3240
shalt *s* it with strange slips	Is 17:10	2232
I will *s* the Egyptians against	Is 19:2	5526
s a watchman, let him declare	Is 21:6	5975
I am *s* in my ward whole nights	Is 21:8	5324
the horsemen shall *s* themselves	Is 22:7	7896
they *s* up the towers thereof,	Is 23:13	6965
who would *s* the briers and thorns	Is 27:4	5414
the women come, and *s* them on fire	Is 27:11	
on thy part to *s* riders upon them	Is 36:8	5414
the LORD, *S* thine house in order	Is 38:1	
I will *s* in the desert the fir	Is 41:19	7760
till he have *s* judgment in the	Is 42:4	7760
it hath *s* him on fire round about	Is 42:25	7760
s it in order for me, since I	Is 44:7	
s up the wood of their graven	Is 45:20	5375
s him in his place, and he	Is 46:7	3240
s up my standard to the people	Is 49:22	7311
therefore have I *s* my face like a	Is 50:7	7760
high mountain hast thou *s* thy bed	Is 57:7	7760
hast thou *s* up thy remembrance	Is 57:8	7760
I have *s* watchmen upon thy walls,	Is 62:6	6485
I will *s* a sign among them, and I	Is 66:19	7760
I have this day *s* thee over the	Jer 1:10	6485
they shall *s* every one his throne	Jer 1:15	5414
S up the standard toward Zion	Jer 4:6	5375
they *s* a trap, they catch men	Jer 5:26	5324
Tekoa, and *s* up a sign of fire in	Jer 6:1	5375
Also I *s* watchmen over you,	Jer 6:17	6965
s in array as men for war against	Jer 6:23	
I have *s* thee for a tower and a	Jer 6:27	5414
where I *s* my name at the first,	Jer 7:12	7931
they have *s* their abominations in	Jer 7:30	7760
my law which I *s* before them	Jer 9:13	5414
any more, and to *s* up my curtains	Jer 10:20	6965
ye *s* up altars to that shameful	Jer 11:13	7760

I *s* before you the way of life, Jer 21:8 5414
For I have *s* my face against this Jer 21:10 7760
I will *s* up shepherds over them Jer 23:4 6965
two baskets of figs were *s* before Jer 24:1 3259
For I will *s* mine eyes upon them Jer 24:6 7760
my law, which I have *s* before you Jer 26:4 5414
S thee up waymarks, make thee Jer 31:21 5324
s thine heart toward the highway, Jer 31:21 7896
children's teeth are *s* on edge Jer 31:29
his teeth shall be *s* on edge Jer 31:30
Which hast *s* signs and wonders in Jer 32:20 7760
s fire on this city, and burn it Jer 32:29
But they *s* their abominations in Jer 32:34 7760
whom he had *s* at liberty at their Jer 34:16 7971
I *s* before the sons of the house Jer 35:5 5414
say, Thy friends have *s* thee on Jer 38:22 5496
that he had *s* over them Gedaliah Jer 40:11 6485
If ye wholly *s* your faces to Jer 42:15 7760
it be with all the men that *s* Jer 42:17 7760
will *s* his throne upon these Jer 43:10 7760
that I *s* before you and before Jer 44:10 5414
I will *s* my face against you for Jer 44:11 7760
that have *s* their faces to go Jer 44:12 7760
I will *s* my throne in Elam, and Jer 49:38 7760
and publish, and *s* up a standard Jer 50:2 5375
they shall *s* themselves in array Jer 50:9
S up the standard upon the walls Jer 51:12 5375
s up the watchmen, prepare the Jer 51:12 6965
S ye up a standard in the land, Jer 51:27 5375
s his throne above the throne of Jer 52:32 5414
he hath *s* up the horn of thine Lam 2:17 7311
He hath *s* me in dark places, as Lam 3:6 3427
s me as a mark for the arrow Lam 3:12 5324
s me upon my feet, that I heard Eze 2:2 5975
s me upon my feet, and spake with Eze 3:24 5975
s the camp also against it, and Eze 4:2 5414
s battering rams against it round Eze 4:2 7760
s it for a wall of iron between Eze 4:3 5414
s thy face against it, and it Eze 4:3 3559
Therefore thou shalt *s* thy face Eze 4:7 3559
I have *s* it in the midst of the Eze 5:5 7760
s thy face toward the mountains Eze 6:2 7760
his ornament, he *s* it in majesty Eze 7:20 7760
have I *s* it far from them Eze 7:20 5414
s a mark upon the foreheads of Eze 9:4 8427
for I have *s* thee for a sign unto Eze 12:6 5414
s thy face against the daughters Eze 13:17 7760
these men have *s* up their idols Eze 14:3 5927
I will *s* my face against that man Eze 14:8 5414
I will *s* my face against them Eze 15:7 5414
when I *s* my face against them Eze 15:7 7760
and thou hast *s* mine oil and mine Eze 16:18 5414
thou hast even *s* it before them Eze 16:19 5414
he *s* it in a city of merchants Eze 17:4 7760
waters, and *s* it as a willow tree Eze 17:5 7760
of the high cedar, and will *s* it Eze 17:22 5414
children's teeth are *s* on edge Eze 18:2
Then the nations *s* against him on Eze 19:8 5414
s thy face toward the south, and Eze 20:46 7760
s thy face toward Jerusalem, and Eze 21:2 7760
I have *s* the point of the sword Eze 21:15 5414
left, whithersoever thy face is *s* Eze 21:16 3259
thee have they *s* light by father Eze 22:7
that was *s* apart for pollution Eze 22:10 5079
which shall *s* against thee Eze 23:24 7760
I will *s* judgment before them, and Eze 23:24 5414
I will *s* my jealousy against thee Eze 23:25 5414
thou hast *s* mine incense and mine Eze 23:41 7760
the king of Babylon *s* himself Eze 24:2 5564
S on a pot, *s* it on, and also Eze 24:3 8239
she *s* it upon the top of a rock Eze 24:7 7760
I have *s* her blood upon the top Eze 24:8 5414
Then *s* it empty upon the coals Eze 24:11 5975
that whereupon they *s* their minds Eze 24:25 4853
s thy face against the Ammonites, Eze 25:2 7760
they shall *s* their palaces in Eze 25:4 3427
he shall *s* engines of war against Eze 26:9 5414
shall *s* thee in the low parts of Eze 26:20 3427
I shall *s* glory in the land of Eze 26:20 5414
they *s* forth thy comeliness Eze 27:10 5414
though thou *s* thine heart as the Eze 28:2 5414
Because thou hast *s* thine heart Eze 28:6 5414
and I have *s* thee so Eze 28:14 5414
s thy face against Zidon, and Eze 28:21 7760
s thy face against Pharaoh king Eze 29:2 7760
when I have *s* a fire in Egypt, and Eze 30:8 5414
will *s* fire in Zoan, and will Eze 30:14 5414
And I will *s* fire in Egypt Eze 30:16 5414
the deep *s* him up on high with Eze 31:4 7311
s darkness upon thy land, saith Eze 32:8 5414
Whose graves are *s* in the sides Eze 32:23 5414
They have *s* her a bed in the Eze 32:25 5414
and *s* him for their watchman Eze 33:2 5414
I have *s* thee a watchman unto the Eze 33:7 5414
I will *s* up one shepherd over Eze 34:23 6965
s thy face against mount Seir, and Eze 35:2 7760
s me down in the midst of the Eze 37:1 5117
will *s* my sanctuary in the midst Eze 37:26 5414
s thy face against Gog, the land Eze 38:2 7760
shall *s* on fire and burn the Eze 39:9 1197
then shall he *s* up a sign by it, Eze 39:15 1129
I will *s* my glory among the Eze 39:21 5414
s me upon a very high mountain, Eze 40:2 5117
s thine heart upon all that I Eze 40:4 7760
but ye have *s* keepers of my Eze 44:8 7760
of the eunuchs had *s* over Daniel Dan 1:11 4487
the God of heaven *s* up a kingdom Dan 2:44 6966
he *s* Shadrach, Meshach, and Dan 2:49 4483
he *s* it up in the plain of Dura, Dan 3:1 6966
Nebuchadnezzar the king had *s* up Dan 3:2 6966
Nebuchadnezzar the king had *s* up Dan 3:3 6966
that Nebuchadnezzar had *s* up Dan 3:3 6966
Nebuchadnezzar the king hath *s* up Dan 3:5 6966
Nebuchadnezzar the king had *s* up Dan 3:7 6966
hast *s* over the affairs of the Dan 3:12 4483
golden image which thou hast *s* up Dan 3:12 6966
golden image which I have *s* up Dan 3:14 6966
golden image which thou hast *s* up Dan 3:18 6966
and whom he would he *s* up Dan 5:19 7313
It pleased Darius to *s* over the Dan 6:1 6966
the king thought to *s* him over Dan 6:3 6966
s his heart on Daniel to deliver Dan 6:14 7761
the judgment was *s*, and the books Dan 7:10 3488
he touched me, and *s* me upright Dan 8:18 5975
I *s* my face unto the Lord God, to Dan 9:3 5414
which he *s* before us by his Dan 9:10 5414
which *s* me upon my knees and upon Dan 10:10 5128
didst *s* thine heart to understand Dan 10:12 5414
I *s* my face toward the ground, and Dan 10:15 5414
and he shall *s* forth a great Dan 11:11 5975
shall *s* forth a multitude greater Dan 11:13 5975
He shall also *s* his face to enter Dan 11:17 7760
that maketh desolate *s* up Dan 12:11 5414
s her as in the day that she was Hos 2:3 3322
s her like a dry land, and slay Hos 2:3 7896
they *s* their heart on their Hos 4:8 5375
he hath *s* an harvest for thee, Hos 6:11 7896
S the trumpet to thy mouth Hos 8:1
They have *s* up kings, but not by Hos 8:4
how shall I *s* thee as Zeboim Hos 11:8 7761
a strong people *s* in battle array Joel 2:5
I will *s* a plumbline in the midst Amos 7:8 7760
that we may *s* forth wheat Amos 8:5 6605
I will *s* mine eyes upon them for Amos 9:4 7760
though thou *s* thy nest among the Obad 4 7760
will *s* thee as a gazingstock Nah 3:6 7760
be *s* wide open unto thine enemies Nah 3:13
s me upon the tower, and will Hab 2:1 3320
that he may *s* his nest on high, Hab 2:9 7760
Let them *s* a fair mitre upon his Zec 3:5 7760
So they *s* a fair mitre upon his Zec 3:5 7760
s there upon her own base Zec 5:11 3240
s them upon the head of Joshua Zec 6:11 7760
for I *s* all men every one against Zec 8:10 7971
that work wickedness are *s* up Mal 3:15 1129
and when he was *s*, his disciples Mt 5:1 *2523*
A city that is *s* on an hill Mt 5:14 *2749*
For I am come to *s* a man at Mt 10:35 *1369*
s him in the midst of them, Mt 18:2 *2476*
clothes, and they *s* him thereon Mt 21:7 *1940*
he shall *s* the sheep on his right Mt 25:33 *2476*
When he was *s* down on the Mt 27:19 *2521*
s up over his head his accusation Mt 27:37 *2007*
And at even, when the sun did *s* Mk 1:32 *1416*
not to be *s* on a candlestick Mk 4:21 *2007*
to his disciples to *s* before them Mk 6:41 *3908*
to his disciples to *s* before them Mk 8:6 *3908*
they did *s* them before the people Mk 8:6 *3908*
commanded to *s* them also before Mk 8:7 *3908*
many things, and be *s* at nought Mk 9:12 *1847*
s him in the midst of them Mk 9:36 *2476*
s an hedge about it, and digged a Mk 12:1 *4060*
as many have taken in hand to *s* Lk 1:1 *392*
this child is *s* for the fall Lk 2:34 *2749*
s him on a pinnacle of the temple Lk 4:9 *2476*
to *s* at liberty them that are Lk 4:18 *649*
I also am a man *s* under authority Lk 7:8 *5021*
to *s* before the multitude Lk 9:16 *3908*
took a child, and *s* him by him, Lk 9:47 *2476*
he stedfastly *s* his face to go to Lk 9:51 *4741*
such things as are *s* before you Lk 10:8 *3908*
s him on his own beast, and Lk 10:34 *1913*
and I have nothing to *s* before him Lk 11:6 *3908*
the colt, and they *s* Jesus thereon Lk 19:35 *1913*
were *s* down together, Peter sat Lk 22:55 *4776*
his men of war *s* him at nought Lk 23:11 *1848*
there were *s* there six waterpots Jn 2:6 *2749*
beginning doth *s* forth good wine Jn 2:10 *5087*
received his testimony hath *s* to Jn 3:33 *4972*
to them that were *s* down Jn 6:11 *345*
when they had *s* her in the midst, Jn 8:3 *2476*
was *s* down again, he said unto Jn 13:12 *377*
Now there was *s* a vessel full of Jn 19:29 *2749*
when they had *s* them in the midst Acts 4:7 *2476*
was *s* at nought of you builders Acts 4:11 *1848*
they *s* them before the council Acts 5:27 *2476*
Whom they *s* before the apostles Acts 6:6 *2476*
s up false witnesses, which said, Acts 6:13 *2476*
not so much as to *s* his foot on Acts 7:5 *968*
would have *s* them at one again, Acts 7:26 *4900*
upon a *s* day Herod, arrayed in Acts 12:21 *5002*
Holy Ghost, *s* his eyes on him, Acts 13:9 *816*
I have *s* thee to be a light of Acts 13:47 *5087*
ruins thereof, and I will *s* it up Acts 15:16 *461*
he *s* meat before them, and Acts 16:34 *3908*
s all the city on an uproar, and Acts 17:5 *2350*
no man shall *s* on thee to hurt Acts 18:10 *2007*
is in danger to be *s* at nought Acts 19:27 *2064*
we went aboard, and *s* forth Acts 21:2 *321*
Paul down, and *s* him before them Acts 22:30 *2476*
beasts, that they may *s* Paul on Acts 23:24 *1913*
man might have been *s* at liberty Acts 26:32 *630*
Whom God hath *s* forth to be a Rom 3:25 4388
or why dost thou *s* at nought thy Rom 14:10 *1848*
For I think that God hath *s* forth 1Cor 4:9 *584*
s them to judge who are least 1Cor 6:4 *2523*
whatsoever is *s* before you 1Cor 10:27 *3908*
the rest will I *s* in order when I 1Cor 11:34 *1299*
But now hath God *s* the members 1Cor 12:18 *5087*
God hath *s* some in the church, 1Cor 12:28 *5087*
hath been evidently *s* forth Gal 3:1 *4270*
s him at his own right hand in Eph 1:20 *2523*
knowing that I am *s* for the Phil 1:17 *2749*
S your affection on things above, Col 3:2 *5426*
that thou shouldest *s* in order Titus 1:5 *1930*
didst *s* him over the works of thy Heb 2:7 *2525*
hold upon the hope *s* before us Heb 6:18 *4295*
who is *s* on the right hand of the Heb 8:1 *2523*
the race that is *s* before us Heb 12:1 *4295*
who for the joy that was *s* before Heb 12:2 *4295*
is *s* down at the right hand of Heb 12:2 *2523*
brother Timothy is *s* at liberty Heb 13:23 *630*
and it is *s* on fire of hell Jas 3:6 *5394*
are *s* forth for an example, Jude 7 *4295*
I have *s* before thee an open door Rev 3:8 *1325*
am *s* down with my Father in his Rev 3:21 *2523*
behold, a throne was *s* in heaven Rev 4:2 *2749*
he *s* his right foot upon the sea, Rev 10:2 *5087*
s a seal upon him, that he should Rev 20:3 *4972*

SETH (*seth*) See SHETH. *A son of Adam and Eve.*
bare a son, and called his name *S* Gen 4:25 8352
And to *S*, to him also there was Gen 4:26 8352
and called his name *S* Gen 5:3 8352
S were eight hundred years Gen 5:4 8352
S lived an hundred and five years, Gen 5:6 8352
S lived after he begat Enos eight Gen 5:7 8352
all the days of *S* were nine Gen 5:8 8352
of Enos, which was the son of *S* Lk 3:38 *4589*

SETHUR (*se'-thur*) *A spy sent to the Promised Land.*
of Asher, *S* the son of Michael Num 13:13 5639

SETTER
He seemeth to be a *s* forth of Acts 17:18 *2604*

SETTEST
thou *s* thine hand to in the land Deut 23:20 4916
all that thou *s* thine hand unto Deut 28:8 4916
in all that thou *s* thine hand Deut 28:20 4916
that thou *s* a watch over me Job 7:12 7760
thou *s* a print upon the heels of Job 13:27
thou *s* a crown of pure gold on Ps 21:3 7896
s me before thy face for ever Ps 41:12 5324

SETTETH
And when the tabernacle *s* forward Num 1:51 5265
And when the camp *s* forward Num 4:5 5265
is poor, and *s* his heart upon it Deut 24:15 5375
Cursed be he that *s* light by his Deut 27:16 7034
and *s* me upon my high places 2Sa 22:34 5975
He *s* an end to darkness, and Job 28:3 7760
feet, and *s* me upon my high places Ps 18:33 5975
he *s* himself in a way that is not Ps 36:4 3320
his strength *s* fast the mountains Ps 65:6 3559
God *s* the solitary in families Ps 68:6 3427
putteth down one, and *s* up another Ps 75:7 7311
as the flame *s* the mountains on Ps 83:14 3857
Yet *s* he the poor on high from Ps 107:41
lay wait, as he that *s* snares Jer 5:26 7918
of Neriah *s* thee on against us Jer 43:3 5496
that *s* up his idols in his heart Eze 14:4 5927
s up his idols in his heart, and Eze 14:7 5927
he removeth kings, and *s* up kings Dan 2:21 6966
s up over it the basest of men Dan 4:17 6966
s him on a pinnacle of the temple Mt 4:5 *2476*
but *s* it on a candlestick, that Lk 8:16 *2007*
s on fire the course of nature Jas 3:6 *5394*

SETTING
In their *s* of their threshold by Eze 43:8 5414
sealing the stone, and *s* a watch Mt 27:66 *3326*
Now when the sun was *s*, all they Lk 4:40 *1416*

SETTINGS
thou shalt set in it *s* of stones Ex 28:17 4396

SETTLE
But I will *s* him in mine house and 1Chr 17:14 5975
I will *s* you after your old Eze 36:11 3427
the lower *s* shall be two cubits Eze 43:14 5835
from the lesser *s* even to the Eze 43:14 5835
greater *s* shall be four cubits Eze 43:14 5835
the *s* shall be fourteen cubits Eze 43:17 5835
and on the four corners of the *s* Eze 43:20 5835
corners of the *s* of the altar Eze 45:19 5835
S it therefore in your hearts, Lk 21:14 *5087*
stablish, strengthen, *s* you 1Pet 5:10 *2311*

SETTLED
a *s* place for thee to abide in 1Kin 8:13 4349
he *s* his countenance stedfastly, 2Kin 8:11 5975
O LORD, thy word is *s* in heaven Ps 119:89 5324
Before the mountains were *s* Prov 8:25 2883
he hath *s* on his lees, and hath Jer 48:11 8252
the men that are *s* on their lees Zeph 1:12 7087
in the faith grounded and *s* Col 1:23 *1476*

SETTLEST
thou *s* the furrows thereof Ps 65:10 5181

SEVEN
s years, and begat sons and Gen 5:7 7651
and *s* years, and begat Lamech Gen 5:25 7651
he begat Lamech *s* hundred eighty Gen 5:26 7651
s hundred seventy and *s* years Gen 5:31 7651
For yet *s* days, and I will cause Gen 7:4 7651
And it came to pass after *s* days Gen 7:10 7651
And he stayed yet other *s* days Gen 8:10 7651
And he stayed yet other *s* days Gen 8:12 7651
And in the second month, on the *s* Gen 8:14 7651
s years, and begat sons and Gen 11:21 7651
Abraham set *s* ewe lambs of the Gen 21:28 7651
What mean these *s* ewe lambs which Gen 21:29 7651
For these *s* ewe lambs shalt thou Gen 21:30 7651
And Sarah was an hundred and *s* Gen 23:1 7651
an hundred and thirty and *s* years Gen 25:17 7651
I will serve thee *s* years for Gen 29:18 7651
Jacob served *s* years for Rachel Gen 29:20 7651
serve with me yet *s* other years Gen 29:27 7651
served with him yet *s* other years Gen 29:30 7651
pursued after him *s* days' journey Gen 31:23 7651
himself to the ground *s* times Gen 33:3 7651
of the river *s* well favoured kine Gen 41:2 7651
s other kine came up after them Gen 41:3 7651

S

did eat up the *s* well favoured ... Gen 41:4 7651
s ears of corn came up upon one ... Gen 41:5 7651
s thin ears and blasted with the ... Gen 41:6 7651
the *s* thin ears devoured the ... Gen 41:7
thin ears devoured the *s* rank ... Gen 41:7 7651
came up out of the river *s* kine ... Gen 41:18 7651
s other kine came up after them, ... Gen 41:19 7651
did eat up the first *s* fat kine ... Gen 41:20 7651
s ears came up in one stalk, full ... Gen 41:22 7651
s ears, withered, thin, and ... Gen 41:23 7651
ears devoured the *s* good ears ... Gen 41:24 7651
The *s* good kine are *s* years ... Gen 41:26 7651
the *s* good ears are *s* years ... Gen 41:26 7651
the *s* thin and ill favoured kine ... Gen 41:27 7651
came up after them are *s* years ... Gen 41:27 7651
the *s* empty ears blasted with the ... Gen 41:27 7651
wind shall be *s* years of famine ... Gen 41:27 7651
there come *s* years of great ... Gen 41:29 7651
after them *s* years of famine ... Gen 41:30 7651
of Egypt in the *s* plenteous years ... Gen 41:34 7651
against the *s* years of famine ... Gen 41:36 7651
in the *s* plenteous years the ... Gen 41:47 7651
up all the food of the *s* years ... Gen 41:48 7651
the *s* years of plenteousness, ... Gen 41:53 7651
the *s* years of dearth began to ... Gen 41:54 7651
all the souls were *s* ... Gen 46:25 7651
was an hundred forty and *s* years ... Gen 47:28 7651
a mourning for his father *s* days ... Gen 50:10 7651
priest of Midian had *s* daughters ... Ex 2:16 7651
were an hundred thirty and *s* years ... Ex 6:16 7651
an hundred and thirty and *s* years ... Ex 6:20 7651
s days were fulfilled, after that ... Ex 7:25 7651
S days shall ye eat unleavened ... Ex 12:15 7651
S days shall there be no leaven ... Ex 12:19 7651
S days thou shalt eat unleavened ... Ex 13:6 7651
bread shall be eaten *s* days ... Ex 13:7 7651
s days it shall be with his dam ... Ex 22:30 7651
shalt eat unleavened bread *s* days ... Ex 23:15 7651
shalt make the *s* lamps thereof ... Ex 25:37 7651
stead shall put them on *s* days ... Ex 29:30 7651
s days shalt thou consecrate them ... Ex 29:35 7651
S days thou shalt make an ... Ex 29:37 7651
S days thou shalt eat unleavened ... Ex 34:18 7651
And he made his *s* lamps, and his ... Ex 37:23 7651
s hundred and thirty shekels, ... Ex 38:24 7651
talents, and a thousand *s* hundred ... Ex 38:25 7651
of the thousand *s* hundred seventy ... Ex 38:28 7651
the blood *s* times before the LORD ... Lev 4:6 7651
sprinkle it *s* times before the ... Lev 4:17 7651
thereof upon the altar *s* times ... Lev 8:11 7651
of the congregation in *s* days ... Lev 8:33 7651
for *s* days shall he consecrate ... Lev 8:33 7651
congregation day and night *s* days ... Lev 8:35 7651
then she shall be unclean *s* days ... Lev 12:2 7651
him that hath the plague *s* days ... Lev 13:4 7651
shall shut him up *s* days more ... Lev 13:5 7651
priest shall shut him up *s* days ... Lev 13:21 7651
priest shall shut him up *s* days ... Lev 13:26 7651
the plague of the scall *s* days ... Lev 13:31 7651
that hath the scall *s* days more ... Lev 13:33 7651
up it that hath the plague *s* days ... Lev 13:50 7651
he shall shut it up *s* days more ... Lev 13:54 7651
cleansed from the leprosy *s* times ... Lev 14:7 7651
abroad out of his tent *s* days ... Lev 14:8 7651
finger *s* times before the LORD ... Lev 14:16 7651
left hand *s* times before the LORD ... Lev 14:27 7651
and shut up the house *s* days ... Lev 14:38 7651
and sprinkle the house *s* times ... Lev 14:51 7651
himself *s* days for his cleansing ... Lev 15:13 7651
she shall be put apart *s* days ... Lev 15:19 7651
him, he shall be unclean *s* days ... Lev 15:24 7651
shall number to herself *s* days ... Lev 15:28 7651
the blood with his finger *s* times ... Lev 16:14 7651
upon it with his finger *s* times ... Lev 16:19 7651
then it shall be *s* days under the ... Lev 22:27 7651
s days ye must eat unleavened ... Lev 23:6 7651
made by fire unto the LORD *s* days ... Lev 23:8 7651
s sabbaths shall be complete ... Lev 23:15 7651
s lambs without blemish of the ... Lev 23:18 7651
for *s* days unto the LORD ... Lev 23:34 7651
S days ye shall offer an offering ... Lev 23:36 7651
keep a feast unto the LORD *s* days ... Lev 23:39 7651
before the LORD your God *s* days ... Lev 23:40 7651
unto the LORD *s* days in the year ... Lev 23:41 7651
Ye shall dwell in booths *s* days ... Lev 23:42 7651
thou shalt number *s* sabbaths of ... Lev 25:8 7651
unto thee, *s* times *s* years ... Lev 25:8 7651
the space of the *s* sabbaths of ... Lev 25:8 7651
then I will punish you *s* times ... Lev 26:18 7651
I will bring *s* times more plagues ... Lev 26:21 7651
you yet *s* times for your sins ... Lev 26:24 7651
will chastise you *s* times for ... Lev 26:28 7651
s thousand and four hundred ... Num 1:31 7651
and two thousand and *s* hundred ... Num 1:39 7651
s thousand and four hundred ... Num 2:8 7651
and two thousand and *s* hundred ... Num 2:26 7651
s thousand and six hundred ... Num 2:31 7651
numbered of them were *s* thousand ... Num 3:22 7651
were two thousand *s* hundred ... Num 4:36 7651
the *s* lamps shall give light over ... Num 8:2 7651
should she not be ashamed *s* days ... Num 12:14 7651
be shut out from the camp *s* days ... Num 12:14 7651
was shut out from the camp *s* days ... Num 12:15 7651
(Now Hebron was built *s* years ... Num 13:22 7651
s hundred, beside them that died ... Num 16:49 7651
of the congregation *s* times ... Num 19:4 7651
any man shall be unclean *s* days ... Num 19:11 7651
the tent, shall be unclean *s* days ... Num 19:14 7651
a grave, shall be unclean *s* days ... Num 19:16 7651
Balak, Build me here *s* altars ... Num 23:1 7651
me here *s* oxen and *s* rams ... Num 23:1 7651
him, I have prepared *s* altars ... Num 23:4 7651
built *s* altars, and offered a ... Num 23:14 7651
Balak, Build me here *s* altars ... Num 23:29 7651

me here *s* bullocks and *s* rams ... Num 23:29 7651
thousand and *s* hundred and thirty ... Num 26:7 7651
and two thousand and *s* hundred ... Num 26:34 7651
thousand and a thousand *s* hundred ... Num 26:51 7651
s lambs of the first year without ... Num 28:11 7651
s days shall unleavened bread be ... Num 28:17 7651
s lambs of the first year ... Num 28:19 7651
lamb, throughout the *s* lambs ... Num 28:21 7651
daily, throughout the *s* days ... Num 28:24 7651
s lambs of the first year ... Num 28:27 7651
one lamb, throughout the *s* lambs ... Num 28:29 7651
s lambs of the first year without ... Num 29:2 7651
one lamb, throughout the *s* lambs ... Num 29:4 7651
s lambs of the first year ... Num 29:8 7651
one lamb, throughout the *s* lambs ... Num 29:10 7651
keep a feast unto the LORD *s* days ... Num 29:12 7651
And on the seventh day *s* bullocks ... Num 29:32 7651
s lambs of the first year without ... Num 29:36 7651
ye abide without the camp *s* days ... Num 31:19 7651
three hundred thousand and *s* ... Num 31:36 7651
s thousand and five hundred sheep, ... Num 31:43 7651
was sixteen thousand *s* hundred ... Num 31:52 7651
s nations greater and mightier ... Deut 7:1 7651
At the end of every *s* years thou ... Deut 15:1 7651
s days shalt thou eat unleavened ... Deut 16:3 7651
with thee in all thy coast *s* days ... Deut 16:4 7651
S weeks shalt thou number unto ... Deut 16:9 7651
begin to number the *s* weeks from ... Deut 16:9 7651
the feast of tabernacles *s* days ... Deut 16:13 7651
S days shalt thou keep a solemn ... Deut 16:15 7651
way, and flee before thee *s* ways ... Deut 28:7 7651
them, and flee *s* ways before them ... Deut 28:25 7651
At the end of every *s* years ... Deut 31:10 7651
s priests shall bear before the ... Josh 6:4 7651
the ark *s* trumpets of rams' horns ... Josh 6:4 7651
ye shall compass the city *s* times ... Josh 6:4 7651
let *s* priests bear *s* trumpets ... Josh 6:6 7651
the *s* priests bearing the *s* ... Josh 6:8 7651
s priests bearing *s* trumpets ... Josh 6:13 7651
after the same manner *s* times ... Josh 6:15 7651
they compassed the city *s* times ... Josh 6:15 7651
the children of Israel *s* tribes ... Josh 18:2 7651
they shall divide it into *s* parts ... Josh 18:5 7651
describe the land into *s* parts ... Josh 18:6 7651
by cities into *s* parts in a book ... Josh 18:9 7651
into the hand of Midian *s* years ... Judg 6:1 7651
the second bullock of *s* years old ... Judg 6:25 7651
s hundred shekels of gold ... Judg 8:26 7651
And he judged Israel *s* years ... Judg 12:9 7651
me within the *s* days of the feast ... Judg 14:12 7651
And she wept before him the *s* days ... Judg 14:17 7651
If they bind me with *s* green ... Judg 16:7 7651
Philistines brought up to her *s* ... Judg 16:8 7651
If thou weavest the *s* locks of my ... Judg 16:13 7651
shave off the *s* locks of his head ... Judg 16:19 7651
numbered *s* hundred chosen men ... Judg 20:15 7651
all this people there were *s* ... Judg 20:16 7651
is better to thee than *s* sons ... Ruth 4:15 7651
so that the barren hath born *s* ... 1Sa 2:5 7651
of the Philistines *s* months ... 1Sa 6:1 7651
s days shalt thou tarry, till I ... 1Sa 10:8 7651
Give us *s* days' respite, that we ... 1Sa 11:3 7651
And he tarried *s* days, according ... 1Sa 13:8 7651
Jesse made *s* of his sons to pass ... 1Sa 16:10 7651
tree at Jabesh, and fasted *s* days ... 1Sa 31:13 7651
the house of Judah was *s* years ... 2Sa 2:11 7651
he reigned over Judah *s* years ... 2Sa 5:5 7651
s hundred horsemen, and twenty ... 2Sa 8:4 7651
David slew the men of *s* hundred ... 2Sa 10:18 7651
Let *s* men of his sons be ... 2Sa 21:6 7651
and they fell all *s* together ... 2Sa 21:9 7651
thirty and *s* in all ... 2Sa 23:39 7651
Shall *s* years of famine come unto ... 2Sa 24:13 7651
s years reigned he in Hebron, and ... 1Kin 2:11 7651
and the third was *s* cubits broad ... 1Kin 6:6 7651
So was he *s* years in building it ... 1Kin 6:38 7651
s for the one chapiter ... 1Kin 7:17 7651
and *s* for the other chapiter ... 1Kin 7:17 7651
s days and *s* days, even ... 1Kin 8:65 7651
And he had *s* hundred wives, ... 1Kin 11:3 7651
did Zimri reign *s* days in Tirzah ... 1Kin 16:15 7651
And he said, Go again *s* times ... 1Kin 18:43 7651
have left me *s* thousand in Israel ... 1Kin 19:18 7651
of Israel, being *s* thousand ... 1Kin 20:15 7651
one over against the other *s* days ... 1Kin 20:29 7651
s thousand of the men that were ... 1Kin 20:30 7651
a compass of *s* days' journey ... 2Kin 3:9 7651
he took with him *s* hundred men ... 2Kin 3:26 7651
and the child sneezed *s* times ... 2Kin 4:35 7651
Go and wash in Jordan *s* times ... 2Kin 5:10 7651
dipped himself *s* times in Jordan, ... 2Kin 5:14 7651
also come upon the land *s* years ... 2Kin 8:1 7651
land of the Philistines *s* years ... 2Kin 8:2 7651
came to pass at the *s* years' end ... 2Kin 8:3 7651
S years old was Jehoash when he ... 2Kin 11:21 7651
even *s* thousand, and craftsmen and ... 2Kin 24:16 7651
And it came to pass in the *s* ... 2Kin 25:27 7651
in the twelfth month, on the *s* ... 2Kin 25:27 7651
and there he reigned *s* years ... 1Chr 3:4 7651
Johanan, and Dalaiah, and Anani, *s* ... 1Chr 3:24 7651
and Jachan, and Zia, and Heber, *s* ... 1Chr 5:13 7651
four and forty thousand *s* hundred ... 1Chr 5:18 7651
fourscore and *s* thousand ... 1Chr 7:5 7651
and *s* hundred and threescore ... 1Chr 9:13 7651
were to come after *s* days from ... 1Chr 9:25 7651
oak in Jabesh, and fasted *s* days ... 1Chr 10:12 7651
s thousand and one hundred ... 1Chr 12:25 7651
were three thousand and *s* hundred ... 1Chr 12:27 7651
and spear thirty and *s* thousand ... 1Chr 12:34 7651
offered *s* bullocks and *s* rams ... 1Chr 15:26 7651
s thousand horsemen, and twenty ... 1Chr 18:4 7651
David slew of the Syrians *s* ... 1Chr 19:18 7651
s hundred, were officers among ... 1Chr 26:30 7651
s hundred chief fathers, whom ... 1Chr 26:32 7651

s thousand talents of refined ... 1Chr 29:4 7651
s years reigned he in Hebron, and ... 1Chr 29:27 7651
Solomon kept the feast *s* days ... 2Chr 7:8 7651
dedication of the altar *s* days ... 2Chr 7:9 7651
s days, and the feast *s* days ... 2Chr 7:9 7651
s rams, the same may be a priest ... 2Chr 13:9 7651
s hundred oxen and *s* thousand ... 2Chr 15:11 7651
s thousand and *s* hundred rams, ... 2Chr 17:11 7651
s thousand and *s* hundred he ... 2Chr 17:11 7651
Joash was *s* years old when he ... 2Chr 24:1 7651
s thousand and five hundred, that ... 2Chr 26:13 7651
And they brought *s* bullocks ... 2Chr 29:21 7651
s rams, and *s* lambs ... 2Chr 29:21 7651
s he goats, for a sin offering ... 2Chr 29:21 7651
bread *s* days with great gladness ... 2Chr 30:21 7651
eat throughout the feast *s* days ... 2Chr 30:22 7651
took counsel to keep other *s* days ... 2Chr 30:23 7651
they kept other *s* days with ... 2Chr 30:23 7651
bullocks and *s* thousand sheep ... 2Chr 30:24 7651
feast of unleavened bread *s* days ... 2Chr 35:17 7651
s hundred seventy and five ... Ezr 2:5 7651
Zaccai, *s* hundred and threescore ... Ezr 2:9 7651
s hundred and forty and three ... Ezr 2:25 7651
and Ono, *s* hundred twenty and five ... Ezr 2:33 7651
a thousand two hundred forty and *s* ... Ezr 2:38 7651
of whom there were *s* thousand ... Ezr 2:65 7651
three hundred thirty and *s* ... Ezr 2:65 7651
horses were *s* hundred thirty ... Ezr 2:66 7651
asses, six thousand *s* hundred ... Ezr 2:67 7651
unleavened bread *s* days with joy ... Ezr 6:22 7651
of his *s* counsellors, to enquire ... Ezr 7:14 7655
s lambs, twelve he goats for a ... Ezr 8:35 7651
Zaccai, *s* hundred and threescore ... Neh 7:14 7651
six hundred threescore and *s* ... Neh 7:18 7651
two thousand threescore and *s* ... Neh 7:19 7651
Beeroth, *s* hundred forty and three ... Neh 7:29 7651
and Ono, *s* hundred twenty and one ... Neh 7:37 7651
a thousand two hundred forty and *s* ... Neh 7:41 7651
of whom there were *s* thousand ... Neh 7:67 7651
three hundred thirty and *s* ... Neh 7:67 7651
horses, *s* hundred thirty and six ... Neh 7:68 7651
six thousand *s* hundred and twenty ... Neh 7:69 7651
threescore and *s* priests' garments ... Neh 7:72 7651
And they kept the feast *s* days ... Neh 8:18 7651
Ethiopia, over an hundred and *s* ... Est 1:1 7651
s days, in the court of the ... Est 1:5 7651
the *s* chamberlains that served in ... Est 1:10 7651
the *s* princes of Persia and Media, ... Est 1:14 7651
s maidens, which were meet to be ... Est 2:9 7651
s provinces, unto every province ... Est 8:9 7651
s provinces of the kingdom of ... Est 9:30 7651
there were born unto him *s* sons ... Job 1:2 7651
also was *s* thousand sheep ... Job 1:3 7651
with him upon the ground *s* days ... Job 2:13 7651
s nights, and none spake a word ... Job 2:13 7651
in *s* there shall no evil touch ... Job 5:19 7651
take unto you now *s* bullocks ... Job 42:8 7651
s rams, and go to my servant Job, ... Job 42:8 7651
He had also *s* sons and three ... Job 42:13 7658
of earth, purified *s* times ... Ps 12:6 7659
S times a day do I praise thee ... Ps 119:164 7651
s are an abomination unto him ... Prov 6:16 7651
she hath hewn out her *s* pillars ... Prov 9:1 7651
For a just man falleth *s* times ... Prov 24:16 7651
s men that can render a reason ... Prov 26:16 7651
for there are *s* abominations in ... Prov 26:25 7651
Give a portion to *s*, and also to ... Eccl 11:2 7651
in that day *s* women shall take ... Is 4:1 7651
shall smite it in the *s* streams ... Is 11:15 7651
sevenfold, as the light of *s* days ... Is 30:26 7651
She that hath borne *s* languisheth ... Jer 15:9 7651
At the end of *s* years let ye go ... Jer 34:14 7651
s men of them that were near the ... Jer 52:25 7651
of the Jews *s* hundred forty ... Jer 52:30 7651
And it came to pass in the *s* ... Jer 52:31 7651
astonished among them *s* days ... Eze 3:15 7651
came to pass at the end of *s* days ... Eze 3:16 7651
And it came to pass in the *s* ... Eze 29:17 7651
shall burn them with fire *s* years ... Eze 39:9 7651
s months shall the house of ... Eze 39:12 7651
after the end of *s* months shall ... Eze 39:14 7651
they went up unto it by *s* steps ... Eze 40:22 7651
there were *s* steps to go up to it ... Eze 40:26 7651
the breadth of the door, *s* cubits ... Eze 41:3 7651
S days shalt thou prepare every ... Eze 43:25 7651
S days shall they purge the altar ... Eze 43:26 7651
they shall reckon unto him *s* days ... Eze 44:26 7651
the passover, a feast of *s* days ... Eze 45:21 7651
s days of the feast he shall ... Eze 45:23 7651
s bullocks and *s* rams without ... Eze 45:23 7651
s rams without blemish daily the ... Eze 45:23 7651
without blemish daily the *s* days ... Eze 45:23 7651
like in the feast of the *s* days ... Eze 45:25 7651
should heat the furnace one *s* ... Dan 3:19 7655
let *s* times pass over him ... Dan 4:16 7655
till *s* times pass over him ... Dan 4:23 7655
s times shall pass over thee, ... Dan 4:25 7655
s times shall pass over thee, ... Dan 4:32 7655
the Prince shall be *s* weeks ... Dan 9:25 7651
Seek him that maketh the *s* stars ... Amos 5:8 3598
we raise against him *s* shepherds ... Mic 5:5 7651
upon one stone shall be *s* eyes ... Zec 3:9 7651
his *s* lamps thereon ... Zec 4:2 7651
and *s* pipes to the *s* lamps ... Zec 4:2 7651
hand of Zerubbabel with those *s* ... Zec 4:10 7651
taketh with himself *s* other ... Mt 12:45 *2033*
And they said, *S*, and a few little ... Mt 15:34 *2033*
And he took the *s* loaves and the ... Mt 15:36 *2033*
meat that was left *s* baskets full ... Mt 15:37 *2033*
Neither the *s* loaves of the four ... Mt 16:10 *2033*
till *s* times ... Mt 18:21 *2034*
say not unto thee, Until *s* times ... Mt 18:22 *2034*
but, Until seventy times *s* ... Mt 18:22 *2033*
Now there were with us *s* brethren ... Mt 22:25 *2033*

whose wife shall she be of the s — Mt 22:28 2033
And they said, S — Mk 8:5 2033
and he took the s loaves, and gave — Mk 8:6 2033
meat that was left s baskets — Mk 8:8 2033
when the s among four thousand, — Mk 8:20 2033
And they said, S — Mk 8:20 2033
Now there were s brethren — Mk 12:20 2033
the s had her, and left no seed — Mk 12:22 2033
for the s had her to wife — Mk 12:23 2033
out of whom he had cast s devils — Mk 16:9 2033
s years from her virginity — Lk 2:36 2033
out of whom went s devils — Lk 8:2 2033
taketh to him s other spirits — Lk 11:26 2033
against thee s times in a day — Lk 17:4 2034
s times in a day turn again to — Lk 17:4 2034
There were therefore s brethren — Lk 20:29 2033
and in like manner the s also — Lk 20:31 2033
for s had her to wife — Lk 20:33 2033
among you s men of honest report — Acts 6:3 2033
when he had destroyed s nations — Acts 13:19 2033
there were s sons of one Sceva, a — Acts 19:14 2033
where we abode s days — Acts 20:6 2033
we tarried there s days — Acts 21:4 2033
which was one of the s — Acts 21:8 2033
when the s days were almost ended — Acts 21:27 2033
desired to tarry with them s days — Acts 28:14 2033
reserved to myself s thousand men — Rom 11:4 2035
they were compassed about s days — Heb 11:30 2033
John to the s churches which are — Rev 1:4 2033
from the s Spirits which are — Rev 1:4 2033
send it unto the s churches which — Rev 1:11 2033
I saw s golden candlesticks — Rev 1:12 2033
And in the midst of the s — Rev 1:13 2033
he had in his right hand s stars — Rev 1:16 2033
The mystery of the s stars which — Rev 1:20 2033
the s golden candlesticks — Rev 1:20 2033
The s stars are the angels of the — Rev 1:20 2033
are the angels of the s churches — Rev 1:20 2033
the s candlesticks which thou — Rev 1:20 2033
thou sawest are the s churches — Rev 1:20 2033
the s stars in his right hand — Rev 2:1 2033
of the s golden candlesticks — Rev 2:1 2033
he that hath the s Spirits of God — Rev 3:1 2033
Spirits of God, and the s stars — Rev 3:1 2033
there were s lamps of fire — Rev 4:5 2033
which are the s Spirits of God — Rev 4:5 2033
the backside, sealed with s seals — Rev 5:1 2033
to loose the s seals thereof — Rev 5:5 2033
it had been slain, having s horns — Rev 5:6 2033
horns and s eyes, which are — Rev 5:6 2033
which are the s Spirits of God — Rev 5:6 2033
I saw the s angels which stood — Rev 8:2 2033
and to them were given s trumpets — Rev 8:2 2033
the s angels which had the s — Rev 8:6 2033
s thunders uttered their voices — Rev 10:3 2033
when the s thunders had uttered — Rev 10:4 2033
which the s thunders uttered — Rev 10:4 2033
were slain of men s thousand — Rev 11:13 2033
great red dragon, having s heads — Rev 12:3 2033
horns, and s crowns upon his heads — Rev 12:3 2033
up out of the sea, having s heads — Rev 13:1 2033
s angels having the s last — Rev 15:1 2033
the s angels came out of the — Rev 15:6 2033
the temple, having the s plagues — Rev 15:6 2033
gave unto the s angels s — Rev 15:7 2033
till the s plagues of the s — Rev 15:8 2033
the temple saying to the s angels — Rev 16:1 2033
there came one of the s angels — Rev 17:1 2033
angels which had the s vials — Rev 17:1 2033
of blasphemy, having s heads — Rev 17:3 2033
her, which hath the s heads — Rev 17:7 2033
The s heads are s mountains, — Rev 17:9 2033
And there are s kings — Rev 17:10 2033
he is the eighth, and is of the s — Rev 17:11 2033
the s angels which had the — Rev 21:9 2033
s vials full of the s last — Rev 21:9 2033

SEVENFOLD
vengeance shall be taken on him s — Gen 4:15 7659
If Cain shall be avenged s — Gen 4:24 7659
truly Lamech seventy and s — Gen 4:24 7659
render unto our neighbours s into — Ps 79:12 7659
he be found, he shall restore s — Prov 6:31 7659
the light of the sun shall be s — Is 30:26 7659

SEVENS
thou shalt take to thee by s — Gen 7:2 7651
Of fowls also of the air by s — Gen 7:3 7651

SEVENTEEN
being s years old, was feeding — Gen 37:2 7651
in the land of Egypt s years — Gen 47:28 7651
thereof, even threescore and s men — Judg 8:14 7657
he reigned s years in Jerusalem, — 1Kin 14:21 7651
in Samaria, and reigned s years — 2Kin 13:1 7651
were s thousand and two hundred — 1Chr 7:11 7651
he reigned s years in Jerusalem, — 2Chr 12:13 7651
of Harim, a thousand and s — Ezr 2:39 7651
of Harim, a thousand and s — Neh 7:42 7651
money, even s shekels of silver — Jer 32:9 7651

SEVENTEENTH
the s day of the month, the same — Gen 7:11 7651
on the s day of the month, upon — Gen 8:4 7651
over Israel in Samaria the s year — 1Kin 22:51 7651
In the s year of Pekah the son of — 2Kin 16:1 7651
The s to Hezir, the eighteenth to — 1Chr 24:15 7651
The s to Joshbekashah, he, his — 1Chr 25:24 7651

SEVENTH
on the s day God ended his work — Gen 2:2 7637
he rested on the s day from all — Gen 2:2 7637
And God blessed the s day, and — Gen 2:3 7637
And the ark rested in the s month — Gen 8:4 7637
the first day until the s day — Ex 12:15 7637
in the s day there shall be an — Ex 12:16 7637
in the s day shall be a feast to — Ex 13:6 7637
but on the s day, which is the — Ex 16:26 7637
people on the s day for to gather — Ex 16:27 7637
go out of his place on the s day — Ex 16:29 7637
So the people rested on the s day — Ex 16:30 7637
But the s day is the sabbath of — Ex 20:10 7637
in them is, and rested the s day — Ex 20:11 7637
in the s he shall go out free for — Ex 21:2 7637
But the s year thou shalt let it — Ex 23:11 7637
on the s day thou shalt rest — Ex 23:12 7637
the s day he called unto Moses — Ex 24:16 7637
but in the s is the sabbath of — Ex 31:15 7637
on the s day he rested, and was — Ex 31:17 7637
but on the s day thou shalt rest — Ex 34:21 7637
but on the s day there shall be — Ex 35:2 7637
shall look on him the s day — Lev 13:5 7637
shall look on him again the s day — Lev 13:6 7637
shall look upon him the s day — Lev 13:27 7637
in the s day the priest shall — Lev 13:32 7637
in the s day the priest shall — Lev 13:34 7637
look on the plague on the s day — Lev 13:51 7637
But it shall be on the s day — Lev 14:9 7637
priest shall come again the s day — Lev 14:39 7637
that in the s month, on the tenth — Lev 16:29 7637
but the s day is the sabbath of — Lev 23:3 7637
in the s day is an holy — Lev 23:8 7637
s sabbath shall ye number fifty — Lev 23:16 7637
of Israel, saying, In the s month — Lev 23:24 7637
s month there shall be a day of — Lev 23:27 7637
The fifteenth day of this s month — Lev 23:34 7637
the fifteenth day of the s month — Lev 23:39 7637
shall celebrate it in the s month — Lev 23:41 7637
But in the s year shall be a — Lev 25:4 7637
on the tenth day of the s month — Lev 25:9 7637
say, What shall we eat the s year — Lev 25:20 7637
on the s day shall he shave it — Num 6:9 7637
On the s day Elishama the son of — Num 7:48 7637
on the s day he shall be clean — Num 19:12 7637
then the s day he shall not be — Num 19:12 7637
on the third day, and on the s day — Num 19:19 7637
on the s day he shall purify — Num 19:19 7637
on the s day ye shall have an — Num 28:25 7637
And in the s month, on the first — Num 29:1 7637
this s month an holy convocation — Num 29:7 7637
the s month ye shall have an holy — Num 29:12 7637
on the s day seven bullocks, two — Num 29:32 7637
on the third day, and on the s day — Num 31:19 7637
wash your clothes on the s day — Num 31:24 7637
But the s day is the sabbath of — Deut 5:14 7637
The s year, the year of release, — Deut 15:9 7637
then in the s year thou shalt let — Deut 15:12 7637
on the s day shall be a solemn — Deut 16:8 7637
the s day ye shall compass the — Josh 6:4 7637
And it came to pass on the s day — Josh 6:15 7637
And it came to pass at the s time — Josh 6:16 7637
the s lot came out for the tribe — Josh 19:40 7637
And it came to pass on the s day — Judg 14:15 7637
and it came to pass on the s day — Judg 14:17 7637
s day before the sun went down — Judg 14:18 7637
And it came to pass on the s day — 2Sa 12:18 7637
Ethanim, which is the s month — 1Kin 8:2 7637
s year of Asa king of Judah, and — 1Kin 16:10 7651
s year of Asa king of Judah did — 1Kin 16:15 7651
And it came to pass at the s time — 1Kin 18:44 7637
that in the s day the battle was — 1Kin 20:29 7637
the s year Jehoiada sent and — 2Kin 11:4 7637
In the s year of Jehu Jehoash — 2Kin 12:1 7651
s year of Joash king of Judah — 2Kin 13:10 7651
s year of Jeroboam king of Israel — 2Kin 15:1 7651
which was the s year of Hoshea — 2Kin 18:9 7651
on the s day of the month, which — 2Kin 25:8 7651
it came to pass in the s month — 2Kin 25:25 7637
Ozem the sixth, David the s — 1Chr 2:15 7637
Attai the sixth, Eliel the s — 1Chr 12:11 7637
The s to Hakkoz, the eighth to — 1Chr 24:10 7637
The s to Jesharelah, he, his sons — 1Chr 25:14 7637
the sixth, Elioenai the s — 1Chr 26:3 7637
Ammiel the sixth, Issachar the s — 1Chr 26:5 7637
The s captain for the s — 1Chr 27:10 7637
feast which was in the s month — 2Chr 5:3 7637
twentieth day of the s month he — 2Chr 7:10 7637
And in the s year Jehoiada — 2Chr 23:1 7637
and finished them in the s month — 2Chr 31:7 7637
when the s month was come, and the — Ezr 3:1 7637
From the first day of the s month — Ezr 3:6 7637
in the s year of Artaxerxes the — Ezr 7:7 7651
was in the s year of the king — Ezr 7:8 7637
when the s month came, the — Neh 7:73 7637
upon the first day of the s month — Neh 8:2 7637
in the feast of the s month — Neh 8:14 7637
and that we would leave the s year — Neh 10:31 7637
On the s day, when the heart of — Est 1:10 7637
in the s year of his reign — Est 2:16 7651
died the same year in the s month — Jer 28:17 7637
it came to pass in the s month — Jer 41:1 7637
in the s year three thousand Jews — Jer 52:28 7651
And it came to pass in the s year — Eze 20:1 7637
in the s day of the month, that — Eze 30:20 7651
so thou shalt do the s day of the — Eze 45:20 7651
In the s month, in the fifteenth — Eze 45:25 7651
In the s month, in the one and — Hag 2:1 7637
s month, even those seventy years — Zec 7:5 7637
the fifth, and the fast of the s — Zec 8:19 7637
also, and the third, unto the s — Mt 22:26 2035
Yesterday at the s hour the fever — Jn 4:52 1442
place of the s day on this wise — Heb 4:4 1442
God did rest the s day from all — Heb 4:4 1442
the s from Adam, prophesied of — Jude 14 1442
And when he had opened the s seal — Rev 8:1 1442
days of the voice of the s angel — Rev 10:7 1442
And the s angel sounded — Rev 11:15 1442
the s angel poured out his vial — Rev 16:17 1442
the s, chrysolite — Rev 21:20 1442

SEVENTY
avenged sevenfold, truly Lamech s — Gen 4:24 7657
And Cainan lived s years, and begat — Gen 5:12 7657
of Lamech were seven hundred s — Gen 5:31 7657
And Terah lived s years, and begat — Gen 11:26 7657
and Abram was s and five years old — Gen 12:4 7657
the loins of Jacob were s souls — Ex 1:5 7657
s of the elders of Israel — Ex 24:1 7657
s of the elders of Israel — Ex 24:9 7657
of the thousand seven hundred s — Ex 38:28 7657
of the offering was s talents — Ex 38:29 7657
one silver bowl of s shekels — Num 7:13 7657
one silver bowl of s shekels — Num 7:19 7657
one silver bowl of s shekels — Num 7:25 7657
one silver bowl of s shekels — Num 7:31 7657
one silver bowl of s shekels — Num 7:37 7657
a silver bowl of s shekels — Num 7:43 7657
one silver bowl of s shekels — Num 7:49 7657
one silver bowl of s shekels — Num 7:55 7657
one silver bowl of s shekels — Num 7:61 7657
one silver bowl of s shekels — Num 7:67 7657
one silver bowl of s shekels — Num 7:73 7657
one silver bowl of s shekels — Num 7:79 7657
and thirty shekels, each bowl s — Num 7:85 7657
Gather unto me s men of the — Num 11:16 7657
gathered the s men of the elders — Num 11:24 7657
him, and gave it unto the s elders — Num 11:25 7657
s thousand and five thousand sheep — Num 31:32 7657
father, in slaying his s brethren — Judg 9:56 7657
even to Beer-sheba s thousand men — 2Sa 24:15 7657
Ahab had s sons in Samaria — 2Kin 10:1 7657
being s persons, were with the — 2Kin 10:6 7657
slew s persons, and put their — 2Kin 10:7 7657
fell of Israel s thousand men — 1Chr 21:14 7657
Parosh, two thousand an hundred s — Ezr 2:3 7657
of Shephatiah, three hundred s — Ezr 2:4 7657
children of Arah, seven hundred s — Ezr 2:5 7657
house of Jeshua, nine hundred s — Ezr 2:36 7657
of the children of Hodaviah, s — Ezr 2:40 7657
of Athaliah, and with him s males — Ezr 8:7 7657
and Zabbud, and with them s males — Ezr 8:14 7657
all Israel, ninety and six rams, s — Ezr 8:35 7657
Parosh, two thousand an hundred s — Neh 7:8 7657
of Shephatiah, three hundred s — Neh 7:9 7657
house of Jeshua, nine hundred s — Neh 7:39 7657
and of the children of Hodevah, s — Neh 7:43 7657
kept the gates, were an hundred s — Neh 11:19 7657
enemies, and slew of their foes s — Est 9:16 7657
Tyre shall be forgotten s years — Is 23:15 7657
after the end of s years shall — Is 23:15 7657
to pass after the end of s years — Is 23:17 7657
serve the king of Babylon s years — Jer 25:11 7657
when s years are accomplished, — Jer 25:12 7657
the LORD, That after s years be — Jer 29:10 7657
there stood before them s men of — Eze 8:11 7657
the west was s cubits broad — Eze 41:12 7657
that he would accomplish s years — Dan 9:2 7657
S weeks are determined upon thy — Dan 9:24 7657
seventh month, even those s years — Zec 7:5 7657
but, Until s times seven — Mt 18:22 1441
the Lord appointed other s also — Lk 10:1 1440
the s returned again with joy, — Lk 10:17 1440

SEVER
I will s in that day the land of — Ex 8:22 6395
the LORD shall s between the — Ex 9:4 6395
they shall s out men of continual — Eze 39:14 914
s the wicked from among the just, — Mt 13:49 873

SEVERAL
a s tenth deal of flour mingled — Num 28:13
A s tenth deal shalt thou offer — Num 28:21
A s tenth deal unto one lamb, — Num 28:29
A s tenth deal for one lamb, — Num 29:10
a s tenth deal to each lamb of — Num 29:15
his death, and dwelt in a s house — 2Kin 15:5 2669
in every s city he put shields and — 2Chr 11:12
his death, and dwelt in a s house — 2Chr 26:21 2669
in every s city of Judah he made — 2Chr 28:25
of their cities, in every s city — 2Chr 31:19
man according to his s ability — Mt 25:15 2398
every s gate was of one pearl — Rev 21:21

SEVERALLY
to every man s as he will — 1Cor 12:11 2398

SEVERED
have s you from other people, — Lev 20:26 914
Then Moses s three cities on this — Deut 4:41 914
had s himself from the Kenites, — Judg 4:11 6504

SEVERITY
the goodness and s of God — Rom 11:22 663
on them which fell, s — Rom 11:22 663

SEW
A time to rend, and a time to s — Eccl 3:7 8609
Woe to the women that s pillows — Eze 13:18 8609

SEWED
they s fig leaves together, and — Gen 3:7 8609
I have s sackcloth upon my skin, — Job 16:15 8609

SEWEST
a bag, and thou s up mine iniquity — Job 14:17 2950

SEWETH
No man also s a piece of new — Mk 2:21 1976

SHAALABBIN (*sha-al-ab'-bin*) See SHAALBIM.
A city in Dan.
And S, and Ajalon, and Jethlah, — Josh 19:42 8169

SHAALBIM (*sha-al'-bim*) See SHAALABBIN, SHAALBONITE. *Same as Shaalabbin.*
mount Heres in Aijalon, and in S — Judg 1:35 8169
son of Dekar, in Makaz, and in S — 1Kin 4:9 8169

S

SHAALBON See SHAALBONITE.

SHAALBONITE (*sha-al'-bo-nite*) *A native of Shaalabbin.*
Eliahba the S, of the sons of 2Sa 23:32 8170
the Baharumite, Eliahba the S 1Chr 11:33 8170

SHAALIM See SHALIM.

SHAAPH (*sha'-af*) *A son of Jahdai.*
Gesham, and Pelet, and Ephah, and S.. 1Chr 2:47 8174
She bare also S the father of 1Chr 2:49 8174

SHAARAIM (*sha-a-ra'-im*) See SHARAIM, SHARUHEN. *A city in Judah.*
fell down by the way to S 1Sa 17:52 8189
and at Beth-birei, and at S 1Chr 4:31 8189

SHAASHGAZ (*sha-ash'-gaz*) *A servant of King Ahasuerus.*
of the women, to the custody of S Est 2:14 8190

SHABBETHAI (*shab'-be-thahee*)
1. A Levite who dealt with the foreign wife problem.
and S the Levite helped them Ezr 10:15 7678
2. A Levite who aided Ezra.
and Sherebiah, Jamin, Akkub, S Neh 8:7 7678
3. A family of exiles.
And S and Jozabad, of the chief of Neh 11:16 7678

SHACHIA (*sha-ki'-ah*) *A son of Shaharaim.*
And Jeuz, and S, and Mirma 1Chr 8:10 7634

SHADE
the LORD is thy s upon thy right Ps 121:5 6783

SHADOW
came they under the s of my roof Gen 19:8 6738
come and put your trust in my s Judg 9:15 6738
Thou seest the s of the mountains Judg 9:36 6738
shall the s go forward ten 2Kin 20:9 6738
for the s to go down ten degrees 2Kin 20:10 6738
but let the s return backward ten 2Kin 20:10 6738
he brought the s ten degrees 2Kin 20:11 6738
our days on the earth are as a s 1Chr 29:15 6738
and the s of death stain it Job 3:5 6757
servant earnestly desireth the s Job 7:2 6738
our days upon earth are a s Job 8:9 6738
of darkness and the s of death Job 10:21 6757
of the s of death, without any Job 10:22 6738
out to light the s of death Job 12:22 6757
he fleeth also as a s, and Job 14:2 6738
on my eyelids is the s of death Job 16:16 6757
and all my members are as a s Job 17:7 6738
is to them even as the s of death Job 24:17 6757
in the terrors of the s of death Job 24:17 6757
of darkness, and the s of death Job 28:3 6757
nor s of death, where the workers Job 34:22 6757
seen the doors of the s of death Job 38:17 6757
trees cover him with their s Job 40:22 6752
hide me under the s of thy wings Ps 17:8 6738
the valley of the s of death Ps 23:4 6757
trust under the s of thy wings Ps 36:7 6738
and covered us with the s of death Ps 44:19 6757
in the s of thy wings will I make Ps 57:1 6738
therefore in the s of thy wings Ps 63:7 6738
were covered with the s of it Ps 80:10 6738
abide under the s of the Almighty Ps 91:1 6738
days are like a s that declineth Ps 102:11 6738
in the s of death, being bound in Ps 107:10 6757
the s of death, and brake their Ps 107:14 6738
gone like the s when it declineth Ps 109:23 6738
days are as a s that passeth away Ps 144:4 6738
life which he spendeth as a s Eccl 6:12 6738
his days, which are as a s Eccl 8:13 6738
under his s with great delight Song 2:3 6738
shall be a tabernacle for a s in Is 4:6 6738
in the land of the s of death Is 9:2 6757
make thy s as the night in the Is 16:3 6738
a s from the heat, when the blast Is 25:4 6738
the heat with the s of a cloud Is 25:5 6738
and to trust in the s of Egypt Is 30:2 6738
the trust in the s of Egypt your Is 30:3 6738
as the s of a great rock in a Is 32:2 6738
and hatch, and gather under her s Is 34:15 6738
bring again the s of the degrees Is 38:8 6738
in the s of his hand hath he hid Is 49:2 6738
thee in the s of mine hand Is 51:16 6738
of the s of death, through a land Jer 2:6 6757
he turn it into the s of death Jer 13:16 6757
They that fled stood under the s Jer 48:45 6738
Under his s we shall live among Lam 4:20 6738
in the s of the branches thereof Eze 17:23 6738
under his s dwelt all great Eze 31:6 6738
earth are gone down from his s Eze 31:12 6738
that dwelt under his s in the Eze 31:17 6738
of the field had s under it Dan 4:12 2927
because the s thereof is good Hos 4:13 6738
dwell under his s shall return Hos 14:7 6738
turneth the s of death into the Amos 5:8 6757
a booth, and sat under it in the s Jonah 4:5 6738
it might be a s over his head Jonah 4:6 6738
s of death light is sprung up Mt 4:16 *4639*
air may lodge under the s of it Mk 4:32 *4639*
in the s of death, to guide our Lk 1:79 *4639*
that at the least the s of Peter Acts 5:15 *4639*
Which are a s of things to come Col 2:17 *4639*
s of heavenly things, as Moses Heb 8:5 *4639*
For the law having a s of good Heb 10:1 *4639*
neither s of turning Jas 1:17 *644*

SHADOWING
Woe to the land s with wings Is 18:1 6767
fair branches, and with a s shroud Eze 31:3 6751
of glory s the mercyseat Heb 9:5 *2683*

SHADOWS
the s flee away, turn, my beloved Song 2:17 6752
the s flee away, I will get me to Song 4:6 6752
for the s of the evening are Jer 6:4 6752

SHADRACH (*sha'-drak*) See HANANIAH. *A companion of Daniel.*
and to Hananiah, of S Dan 1:7 7714
of the king, and he set S, Meshach Dan 2:49 7715
of the province of Babylon, S Dan 3:12 7715
rage and fury commanded to bring S Dan 3:13 7715
said unto them, Is it true, O S Dan 3:14 7715
S, Meshach, and Abed-nego, Dan 3:16 7715
his visage was changed against S Dan 3:19 7715
that were in his army to bind S Dan 3:20 7715
slew those men that took up S Dan 3:22 7715
And these three men, S, Meshach, Dan 3:23 7715
furnace, and spake, and said, S Dan 3:26 7715
Then S, Meshach, and Abed-nego, Dan 3:26 7715
and said, Blessed be the God of S Dan 3:28 7715
thing amiss against the God of S Dan 3:29 7715
Then the king promoted S, Meshach Dan 3:30 7715

SHADY
He lieth under the s trees Job 40:21 6628
The s trees cover him with their Job 40:22 6628

SHAFT
his s, and his branches, his bowls Ex 25:31 3409
his s, and his branch, his bowls, Ex 37:17 3409
beaten gold, unto the s thereof Num 8:4 3409
hid me, and made me a polished s Is 49:2 2671

SHAGE (*sha'-ghe*) *A "mighty man" of David.*
the son of S the Hararite 1Chr 11:34 7681

SHAGEE See SHAGE.

SHAGEH See SHAGE.

SHAHAR (*sha'-har*) *A musical notation.*
chief Musician upon Aijeleth S Ps 22:t 7837

SHAHARAIM (*sha-ha-ra'-im*) *A Benjamite from Moab.*
S begat children in the country 1Chr 8:8 7842

SHAHAZIMAH (*sha-haz'-i-mah*) *A city in Issachar.*
the coast reacheth to Tabor, and S Josh 19:22 7831

SHAHAZUMAH See SHAHAZIMAH.

SHAKE
other times before, and s myself Judg 16:20 5287
So God s out every man from his Neh 5:13 5287
which made all my bones to s Job 4:14 6342
He shall s off his unripe grape Job 15:33 2554
you, and s mine head at you Job 16:4 5128
the lip, they s the head, saying, Ps 22:7 5128
though the mountains s with the Ps 46:3 7493
make their loins continually to s Ps 69:23 4571
thereof shall s like Lebanon Ps 72:16 7493
ariseth to s terribly the earth Is 2:19 6206
ariseth to s terribly the earth Is 2:21 6206
as if the rod should s itself Is 10:15 5130
he shall s his hand against the Is 10:32 5130
he s his hand over the river Is 11:15 5130
s the hand, that they may go into Is 13:2 5130
Therefore I will s the heavens Is 13:13 7264
to tremble, that did s kingdoms Is 14:16 7493
the foundations of the earth do s Is 24:18 7493
Carmel s off their fruits Is 33:9 5287
S thyself from the dust Is 52:2 5287
all my bones s Jer 23:9 7363
thy walls shall s at the noise of Eze 26:10 7493
Shall not the isles s at the Eze 26:15 7493
The suburbs shall s at the sound Eze 27:28 7493
I made the nations to s at the Eze 31:16 7493
shall s at my presence, and the Eze 38:20 7493
s off his leaves, and scatter his Dan 4:14 5426
the heavens and the earth shall s Joel 3:16 7493
of the door, that the posts may s Amos 9:1 7493
I will s the heavens, and the Hag 2:6 7493
I will s all nations, and the Hag 2:7 7493
I will s the heavens and the earth Hag 2:21 7493
I will s mine hand upon them, and Zec 2:9 5130
s off the dust of your feet Mt 10:14 *1621*
for fear of him the keepers did s Mt 28:4 *4579*
s off the dust under your feet Mk 6:11 *1621*
that house, and could not s it Lk 6:48 *4531*
s off the very dust from your Lk 9:5 *660*
Yet once more I s not the earth Heb 12:26 *4579*

SHAKED
looked upon me they s their heads Ps 109:25 5128

SHAKEN
the sound of a s leaf shall chase Lev 26:36 5086
as a reed is s in the water 1Kin 14:15 5110
Jerusalem hath s her head at thee 2Kin 19:21 5128
promise, even thus be he s out Neh 5:13 5287
s me to pieces, and set me up for Job 16:12 6327
the wicked might be s out of it Job 38:13 5287
also of the hills moved and were s Ps 18:7 1607
Jerusalem hath s her head at thee Is 37:22 5128
the fir trees shall be terribly s Nah 2:3 7477
if they be s, they shall even Nah 3:12 5128
A reed s with the wind Mt 11:7 *4531*
powers of the heavens shall be s Mt 24:29 *4531*
that are in heaven shall be s Mk 13:25 *4531*
s together, and running over, Lk 6:38 *4531*
A reed s with the wind Lk 7:24 *4531*
the powers of heaven shall be s Lk 21:26 *4531*
the place was s where they were Acts 4:31 *4531*
foundations of the prison were s Acts 16:26 *4531*
That ye be not soon s in mind 2Th 2:2 *4531*
of those things that are s Heb 12:27 *4531*
which cannot be s may remain Heb 12:27 *4531*
when she is s of a mighty wind Rev 6:13 *4579*

SHAKETH
Which s the earth out of her Job 9:6 7264
of the LORD s the wilderness Ps 29:8 2342
the LORD s the wilderness of Ps 29:8 2342
thereof; for it s Ps 60:2 4131
itself against him that s it Is 10:15 5130
LORD of hosts, which he s over it Is 19:16 5130
that s his hands from holding of Is 33:15 5287

SHAKING
he laugheth at the s of a spear Job 41:29 7494
a s of the head among the people Ps 44:14 4493
as the s of an olive tree, two or Is 17:6 5363
fear because of the s of the hand Is 19:16 8573
be as the s of an olive tree Is 24:13 5363
in battles of s will he fight Is 30:32 8573
there was a noise, and behold a s Eze 37:7 7494
a great s in the land of Israel Eze 38:19 7494

SHALEM (*sha'-lem*) *A city in Ephraim.*
And Jacob came to S, a city of Gen 33:18 8003

SHALIM (*sha'-lim*) *A district in Dan.*
they passed through the land of S 1Sa 9:4 8171

SHALISHA (*shal'-i-shah*) *A district in Ephraim.*
and passed through the land of S 1Sa 9:4 8031

SHALISHAH See SHALISHA.

SHALL See PREFACE.

SHALLECHETH (*shal'-le-keth*) *A gate of the First Temple.*
forth westward, with the gate S 1Chr 26:16 7996

SHALLIM See SHALIM.

SHALLUM (*shal'-lum*) See JEHOAHAZ, MESHELEMIAH, SHILLEM.
1. A king of Israel.
S the son of Jabesh conspired 2Kin 15:10 7967
S the son of Jabesh began to 2Kin 15:13 7967
smote S the son of Jabesh in 2Kin 15:14 7967
And the rest of the acts of S 2Kin 15:15 7967
2. Husband of Huldah.
the wife of S the son of Tikvah, 2Kin 22:14 7967
the wife of S the son of Tikvath, 2Chr 34:22 7967
3. A descendant of Jerahmeel.
begat Sisamai, and Sisamai begat S 1Chr 2:40 7967
S begat Jekamiah, and Jekamiah 1Chr 2:41 7967
4. A son of King Josiah.
the third Zedekiah, the fourth S 1Chr 3:15 7967
thus saith the LORD touching S Jer 22:11 7967
5. Grandson of Simeon.
S his son, Mibsam his son, Mishma 1Chr 4:25 7967
6. Father of Hilkiah.
begat Zadok, and Zadok begat S 1Chr 6:12 7967
S begat Hilkiah, and Hilkiah begat 1Chr 6:13 7967
The son of S, the son of Zadok, Ezr 7:2 7967
7. Son of Naphtali.
Jahziel, and Guni, and Jezer, and S 1Chr 7:13 7967
8. A family of exiles.
And the porters were, S, and Akkub, 1Chr 9:17 7967
S was the chief 1Chr 9:17 7967
S the son of Kore, the son of 1Chr 9:19 7967
the firstborn of S the Korahite 1Chr 9:31 7967
the children of S, the children Ezr 2:42 7967
the children of S, the children Neh 7:45 7967
9. Father of Jehizkiah.
and Jehizkiah the son of S 2Chr 28:12 7967
10. A gatekeeper who married a foreigner.
S, and Telem, and Uri Ezr 10:24 7967
11. A son of Bani who married a foreigner.
S, Amariah, and Joseph Ezr 10:42 7967
12. A rebuilder of Jerusalem's wall.
repaired S the son of Halohesh Neh 3:12 7967
13. Father of Hanameel.
Hanameel the son of S thine uncle Jer 32:7 7967
14. Father of Maaseiah.
chamber of Maaseiah the son of S Jer 35:4 7967

SHALLUN (*shal'-lun*) *A rebuilder of Jerusalem's wall.*
repaired S the son of Colhozeh Neh 3:15 7968

SHALMAI (*shal'-mahee*) *A family of exiles.*
of Hagab, the children of S Ezr 2:46 8073
of Hagaba, the children of S Neh 7:48 8014

SHALMAN (*shal'-man*) See SHALMANESER. *A king of Assyria.*
as S spoiled Beth-arbel in the Hos 10:14 8020

SHALMANESER (*shal-man-e'-zer*) See SHALMAN. *A king of Assyria.*
him came up S king of Assyria 2Kin 17:3 8022
that S king of Assyria came up 2Kin 18:9 8022

SHALT See PREFACE.

SHAMA (*sha'-mah*) *A "mighty man" of David.*
Uzzia the Ashterathite, S 1Chr 11:44 8091

SHAMARIAH *Son of Rehoboam.*
Jeush, and S, and Zaham 2Chr 11:19

SHAMBLES
Whatsoever is sold in the s 1Cor 10:25 *3111*

SHAME
unto their s among their enemies Ex 32:25 8103
might put them to s in any thing Judg 18:7 3637
because his father had done him s 1Sa 20:34 3637
whither shall I cause my s to go 2Sa 13:13 2781
So he returned with s of face to 2Chr 32:21 1322
hate thee shall be clothed with s Job 8:22 1322
long will ye turn my glory into s Ps 4:2 3639
put to s that seek after my soul Ps 35:4 3637
let them be clothed with s Ps 35:26 1322
put to s that wish me evil Ps 40:14 3637
of their s that say unto me Ps 40:15 1322
hast put them to s that hated us Ps 44:7 954

hast cast off, and put us to s .... Ps 44:9 3637
the s of my face hath covered me, ... Ps 44:15 1322
thou hast put them to s, because .... Ps 53:5 954
s hath covered my face .... Ps 69:7 3639
hast known my reproach, and my s .... Ps 69:19 1322
for a reward of their s that say .... Ps 70:3 1322
for they are brought unto s .... Ps 71:24 2659
Fill their faces with s .... Ps 83:16 7036
yea, let them be put to s .... Ps 83:17 2659
thou hast covered him with s .... Ps 89:45 955
adversaries be clothed with s .... Ps 109:29 3639
O LORD, put me not to s .... Ps 119:31 954
His enemies will I clothe with s .... Ps 132:18 1322
but s shall be the promotion of .... Prov 3:35 7036
a scorner getteth to himself s .... Prov 9:7 7036
harvest is a son that causeth s .... Prov 10:5 954
When pride cometh, then cometh s .... Prov 11:2 7036
but a prudent man covereth s .... Prov 12:16 7036
man is loathsome, and cometh to s .... Prov 13:5 2659
s shall be to him that refuseth .... Prov 13:18 7036
is against him that causeth s .... Prov 14:35 954
rule over a son that causeth s .... Prov 17:2 954
it, it is folly and s unto him .... Prov 18:13 3639
mother, is a son that causeth s .... Prov 19:26 954
thy neighbour hath put thee to s .... Prov 25:8 3637
he that heareth it put thee to s .... Prov 25:10 2616
himself bringeth his mother to s .... Prov 29:15 954
uncovered, to the s of Egypt .... Is 20:4 6172
be the s of thy lord's house .... Is 22:18 7036
the strength of Pharaoh be your s .... Is 30:3 1322
be an help nor profit, but a s .... Is 30:5 1322
yea, thy s shall be seen .... Is 47:3 2781
I hid not my face from s and .... Is 50:6 3639
for thou shalt not be put to s .... Is 54:4 2659
shalt forget the s of thy youth .... Is 54:4 1322
For your s ye shall have double .... Is 61:7 1322
For s hath devoured the labour of .... Jer 3:24 1322
We lie down in our s, and our .... Jer 3:25 1322
thy face, that thy s may appear .... Jer 13:26 7036
my days should be consumed with s .... Jer 20:18 1322
upon you, and a perpetual s .... Jer 23:40 3640
The nations have heard of thy s .... Jer 46:12 7036
hath Moab turned the back with s .... Jer 48:39 954
s hath covered our faces .... Jer 51:51 3639
s shall be upon all faces, and .... Eze 7:18 955
bear thine own s for thy sins .... Eze 16:52 3639
confounded also, and bear thy s .... Eze 16:52 3639
That thou mayest bear thine own s .... Eze 16:54 3639
mouth any more because of thy s .... Eze 16:63 3639
yet have they borne their s with .... Eze 32:24 3639
yet have they borne their s with .... Eze 32:25 3639
bear their s with them that go .... Eze 32:30 3639
neither bear the s of the heathen .... Eze 34:29 3639
have borne the s of the heathen .... Eze 36:6 3639
you, they shall bear their s .... Eze 36:7 3639
the s of the heathen any more .... Eze 36:15 3639
that they have borne their s .... Eze 39:26 3639
but they shall bear their s .... Eze 44:13 3639
to everlasting life, and some to s .... Dan 12:2 2781
will I change their glory into s .... Hos 4:7 7036
her rulers with s do love .... Hos 4:18 7036
separated themselves unto that s .... Hos 9:10 1322
Ephraim shall receive s, and .... Hos 10:6 1317
brother Jacob s shall cover thee .... Obad 10 955
of Saphir, having thy s naked .... Mic 1:11 1322
them, that they shall not take s .... Mic 2:6 3639
s shall cover her which said unto .... Mic 7:10 955
nakedness, and the kingdoms thy s .... Nah 3:5 7036
Thou hast consulted s to thy .... Hab 2:10 1322
Thou art filled with s for glory .... Hab 2:16 7036
but the unjust knoweth no s .... Zeph 3:5 1322
where they have been put to s .... Zeph 3:19 1322
thou begin with s to take the .... Lk 14:9 *152*
worthy to suffer s for his name .... Acts 5:41 818
I write not these things to s you 1Cor 4:14 *1788*
I speak to your s 1Cor 6:5 *1791*
but if it be a s for a woman to 1Cor 11:6 149
long hair, it is a s unto him 1Cor 11:14 *819*
of God, and s them that have not 1Cor 11:22 *2617*
for it is a s for women to speak 1Cor 14:35 *149*
I speak this to your s 1Cor 15:34 *1791*
For it is a s even to speak of .... Eph 5:12 *149*
and whose glory is in their s .... Phil 3:19 *152*
afresh, and put him to an open s .... Heb 6:6 *3856*
the cross, despising the s .... Heb 12:2 *152*
the sea, foaming out their own s .... Jude 13 *152*
that the s of thy nakedness do .... Rev 3:18 *152*
he walk naked, and they see his s .... Rev 16:15 808

SHAMED (sha'-med) *A son of Elpaal.*
her take it to her, lest we be s .... Gen 38:23 937
said Thou hast s this day the 2Sa 19:5 3001
Eber, and Misham, and S, who built 1Chr 8:12 8106
Ye have s the counsel of the poor .... Ps 14:6 954

SHAMEFACEDNESS
in modest apparel, with s 1Ti 2:9 *127*

SHAMEFUL
ye set up altars to that s thing .... Jer 11:13 1322
s spewing shall be on thy glory .... Hab 2:16 7022

SHAMEFULLY
that conceived them hath done s .... Hos 2:5 3001
head, and sent him away s handled .... Mk 12:4 *821*
beat him also, and entreated him s .... Lk 20:11 *818*
were s entreated, as ye know, at 1Th 2:2 *5195*

SHAMELESSLY
vain fellows s uncovereth himself 2Sa 6:20 1540

SHAMER (sha'-mur) See SHOMER.
1. Son of Mahli.
the son of Bani, the son of S 1Chr 6:46 8106
2. Son of Heber.
And the sons of S 1Chr 7:34 8106

SHAMETH
of riotous men s his father .... Prov 28:7 3637

SHAMGAR (sham'-gar) *A judge of Israel.*
after him was S the son of Anath .... Judg 3:31 8044
In the days of S the son of Anath .... Judg 5:6 8044

SHAMHUTH (sham'-huth) See SHAMMOTH. *A captain in David's army.*
fifth month was S the Izrahite 1Chr 27:8 8049

SHAMIR (sha'-mur)
1. A city in Judah.
And in the mountains, S, and Jattir .... Josh 15:48 8069
2. A city near Mt. Ephraim.
he dwelt in S in mount Ephraim .... Judg 10:1 8069
and died, and was buried in S .... Judg 10:2 8069
3. Son of Micah the Levite.
the sons of Michah; S 1Chr 24:24 8069

SHAMLAI See SAMLAH.

SHAMMA (sham'-mah) See SHAMMAH. *A son of Zophah.*
Bezer, and Hod, and S, and Shilshah, ... 1Chr 7:37 8037

SHAMMAH (sham'-mah) See SHAMMA, SHAMMOTH, SHIMEA, SHIMMA.
1. A son of Reuel.
Nahath, and Zerah, S, and Mizzah .... Gen 36:13 8048
duke Nahath, duke Zerah, duke S .... Gen 36:17 8048
Nahath, Zerah, S, and Mizzah 1Chr 1:37 8048
2. A son of Jesse.
Then Jesse made S to pass by 1Sa 16:9 8048
unto him Abinadab, and the third S 1Sa 17:13 8048
3. A "mighty man" of David.
after him was S the son of Agee 2Sa 23:11 8048
4. A Hararite "mighty man" of David.
S the Hararite, Ahiam the son of 2Sa 23:33 8048
5. A Harodite "mighty man" of David.
S the Harodite, Elika the 2Sa 23:25 8048

SHAMMAI (sham'-mahee)
1. A son of Onan.
And the sons of Onam were, S 1Chr 2:28 8060
And the sons of S 1Chr 2:28 8060
the sons of Jada the brother of S 1Chr 2:32 8060
2. Father of Maon.
and Rekem begat S 1Chr 2:44 8060
And the son of S was Maon 1Chr 2:45 8060
3. A descendant of Caleb.
and she bare Miriam, and S, and 1Chr 4:17 8060

SHAMMOTH (sham'-moth) See SHAMMAH, SHAMHUTH. *A "mighty man" of David.*
S the Harorite, Helez the 1Chr 11:27 8054

SHAMMUA (sham-mu'-ah) See SHAMMUAH, SHEMAIH, SHIMEA.
1. A spy sent to the Promised Land.
of Reuben, S the son of Zaccur .... Num 13:4 8051
2. A son of David.
S, and Shobab, Nathan, and Solomon, ... 1Chr 14:4 8051
3. A family of exiles.
brethren, and Abda the son of S .... Neh 11:17 8051
4. A priest with Zerubbabel.
Of Bilgah, S .... Neh 12:18 8051

SHAMMUAH (sham-mu'-ah) See SHAMMUA. *Same as Shammua 2.*
S, and Shobab, and Nathan, and 2Sa 5:14 8051

SHAMSHERAI (sham'-she-rahee) *A son of Jeroham.*
And S, and Shehariah, and Athaliah, ... 1Chr 8:26 8125

SHAPE
a bodily s like a dove upon him .... Lk 3:22 *1491*
voice at any time, nor seen his s .... Jn 5:37 *1491*

SHAPEN
Behold, I was s in iniquity .... Ps 51:5 2342

SHAPES
the s of the locusts were like .... Rev 9:7 *3667*

SHAPHAM (sha'-fam) *A Gadite chief.*
S the next, and Jaanai, and Shaphat 1Chr 5:12 8223

SHAPHAN (sha'-fan)
1. A scribe in Josiah's time.
king sent S the son of Azaliah 2Kin 22:3 8227
priest said unto S the scribe 2Kin 22:8 8227
And Hilkiah gave the book to S 2Kin 22:8 8227
S the scribe came to the king, and 2Kin 22:9 8227
S the scribe shewed the king, ... 2Kin 22:10 8227
S read it before the king 2Kin 22:10 8227
S the scribe, and Asahiah a 2Kin 22:12 8227
and Ahikam, and Achbor, and S 2Kin 22:14 8227
he sent S the son of Azaliah, and 2Chr 34:8 8227
said to S the scribe, I have 2Chr 34:15 8227
Hilkiah delivered the book to S 2Chr 34:15 8227
S carried the book to the king, ... 2Chr 34:16 8227
Then S the scribe told the king, ... 2Chr 34:18 8227
S read it before the king 2Chr 34:18 8227
S the scribe, and Asaiah a servant 2Chr 34:20 8227
Gemariah the son of S the scribe .... Jer 36:10 8227
the son of Gemariah, the son of S .... Jer 36:11 8227
Achbor, and Gemariah the son of S .... Jer 36:12 8227
2. Father of Ahikam.
priest, and Ahikam the son of S 2Kin 22:12 8227
the son of Ahikam, the son of S 2Kin 25:22 8227
Hilkiah, and Ahikam the son of S 2Chr 34:20 8227
the son of S was with Jeremiah .... Jer 26:24 8227
the son of Ahikam the son of S .... Jer 39:14 8227
the son of Ahikam the son of S .... Jer 40:5 8227
the son of S sware unto them .... Jer 40:9 8227
the son of Ahikam the son of S .... Jer 40:11 8227
the son of S with the sword .... Jer 41:2 8227
the son of Ahikam the son of S .... Jer 43:6 8227
3. Messenger for Jeremiah.
the hand of Elasah the son of S .... Jer 29:3 8227
4. Father of Jaazaniah.
them stood Jaazaniah the son of S .... Eze 8:11 8227

SHAPHAT (sha'-fat)
1. A spy sent to the Promised Land.
of Simeon, S the son of Hori .... Num 13:5 8202
2. Father of Elisha the prophet.
and Elisha the son of S of 1Kin 19:16 8202
and found Elisha the son of S 1Kin 19:19 8202
said, Here is Elisha the son of S 2Kin 3:11 8202
of S shall stand on him this day 2Kin 6:31 8202
3. A grandson of Shechaniah.
and Bariah, and Neariah, and S 1Chr 3:22 8202
4. A chief Gadite.
next, and Jaanai, and S in Bashan 1Chr 5:12 8202
5. A shepherd of David's herds.
valleys was S the son of Adlai 1Chr 27:29 8202

SHAPHER (sha'-fur) *An Israelite encampment in the wilderness.*
Kehelathah, and pitched in mount S .... Num 33:23 8234
And they removed from mount S .... Num 33:24 8234

SHAPHIR See SHAPHER.

SHARAI (sha'-rahee) *Married a foreigner in exile.*
Machnadebai, Shashai, S, ... Ezr 10:40 8298

SHARAIM (sha-ra'-im) See SHAARAIM. *Same as Shaaraim.*
And S, and Adithaim, and .... Josh 15:36 8189

SHARAR (sha'-rar) See SARAR. *A "mighty man" of David.*
Ahiam the son of S the Hararite 2Sa 23:33 8325

SHARE
to sharpen every man his s 1Sa 13:20 4282

SHAREZER (sha-re'-zur) See SHEREZER. *Son of Sennacherib.*
S his sons smote him with the 2Kin 19:37 8272
S his sons smote him with the .... Is 37:38 8272

SHARON (sha'-run) See SARON, SHARONITE.
1. A plain of Ephraim.
in S was Shitrai the Sharonite 1Chr 27:29 8289
I am the rose of S, and the lily .... Song 2:1 8289
S is like a wilderness .... Is 33:9 8289
it, the excellency of Carmel and S .... Is 35:2 8289
S shall be a fold of flocks, and .... Is 65:10 8289
2. A plain or city in Gad.
towns, and in all the suburbs of S 1Chr 5:16 8289

SHARONITE (sha'-run-ite) *An inhabitant of Sharon 1.*
fed in Sharon was Shitrai the S 1Chr 27:29 8290

SHARP
Then Zipporah took a s stone .... Ex 4:25 6864
unto Joshua, Make thee s knives .... Josh 5:2 6697
And Joshua made him s knives .... Josh 5:3 6697
there was a s rock on the one 1Sa 14:4 8127
a s rock on the other side 1Sa 14:4 8127
S stones are under him .... Job 41:30 2303
he spreadeth s pointed things .... Job 41:30 2742
Thine arrows are s in the heart .... Ps 45:5 8150
like a s rasor, working .... Ps 52:2 3913
arrows, and their tongue a s sword .... Ps 57:4 2299
S arrows of the mighty, with .... Ps 120:4 8150
wormwood, s as a twoedged sword .... Prov 5:4 2299
a maul, and a sword, and a s arrow .... Prov 25:18 8150
Whose arrows are s, and all their .... Is 5:28 8150
Behold, I will make thee a new s .... Is 41:15 2742
hath made my mouth like a s sword .... Is 49:2 2299
son of man, take thee a s knife .... Eze 5:1 2299
contention was so s between them .... Acts 15:39
his mouth went a s twoedged sword .... Rev 1:16 *3691*
hath the s sword with two edges .... Rev 2:12 *3691*
crown, and in his hand a s sickle .... Rev 14:14 *3691*
heaven, he also having a s sickle .... Rev 14:17 *3691*
cry to him that had the s sickle .... Rev 14:18 *3691*
saying, Thrust in thy s sickle .... Rev 14:18 *3691*
out of his mouth goeth a s sword .... Rev 19:15 *3691*

SHARPEN
to s every man his share, and his 1Sa 13:20 3913
for the axes, and to s the goads 1Sa 13:21 5324

SHARPENED
They have s their tongues like a .... Ps 140:3 8150
Say, A sword, a sword is s .... Eze 21:9 2300
It is s to make a sore slaughter .... Eze 21:10 2300
this sword is s, and it is .... Eze 21:11 2300

SHARPENETH
mine enemy s his eyes upon me .... Job 16:9 3913
Iron s iron .... Prov 27:17 2300
so a man s the countenance of his .... Prov 27:17 2300

SHARPER
upright is s than a thorn hedge .... Mic 7:4
s than any twoedged sword, ... Heb 4:12 *5114*

SHARPLY
And they did chide with him s .... Judg 8:1 2394
Wherefore rebuke them s, that .... Titus 1:13 *664*

SHARPNESS
lest being present I should use s 2Cor 13:10 *664*

SHARUHEN (sha-ru'-hen) See SHAARAIM, SHILHIM. *A city in Simeon.*
And Beth-lebaoth, and S .... Josh 19:6 8287

SHASHAI (sha'-shahee) *Married a foreigner in exile.*
Machnadebai, S, Sharai, ... Ezr 10:40 8343

SHASHAK (sha'-shak) *A son of Elpaal.*
And Ahio, S, and Jeremoth, ... 1Chr 8:14 8349
and Penuel, the sons of S 1Chr 8:25 8349

SHAUL (*sha'-ul*) See SAUL, SHAULITES.
1. A son of Simeon.
S the son of a Canaanitish woman Gen 46:10 7586
S the son of a Canaanitish woman Ex 6:15 7586
of *S*, the family of the Shaulites Num 26:13 7586
and Jamin, Jarib, Zerah, and *S* 1Chr 4:24 7586
2. A king of Edom.
S of Rehoboth by the river 1Chr 1:48 7586
when *S* was dead, Baal-hanan the 1Chr 1:49 7586
3. Son of Kohath.
son, Uzziah his son, and *S* his son 1Chr 6:24 7586

SHAULITES (*sha'-ul-ites*) *Decendants of Shaul 1.*
of Shaul, the family of the *S* Num 26:13 7587

SHAVE
but the scall shall he not *s* Lev 13:33 1548
s off all his hair, and wash Lev 14:8 1548
that he shall *s* all his hair off Lev 14:9 1548
even all his hair he shall *s* off Lev 14:9 1548
neither shall they *s* off the Lev 21:5 1548
then he shall *s* his head in the Num 6:9 1548
on the seventh day shall he *s* it Num 6:9 1548
the Nazarite shall *s* the head of Num 6:18 1548
let them *s* all their flesh, and Num 8:7 5674
and she shall *s* her head, and pare Deut 21:12 1548
she caused him to *s* off the seven Judg 16:19 1548
Lord *s* with a razor that is hired Is 7:20 1548
Neither shall they *s* their heads Eze 44:20 1548
them, that they may *s* their heads Acts 21:24 3587

SHAVED
he *s* himself, and changed his Gen 41:14 1548
s off the one half of their 2Sa 10:4 1548
s them, and cut off their garments 1Chr 19:4 1548
s his head, and fell down upon the Job 1:20 1494

SHAVEH (*sha'-veh*) *A valley near Aenon.*
Ham, and the Emims in *S* Kiriathaim Gen 14:5 7741
were with him, at the valley of *S* Gen 14:17 7740

SHAVEN
He shall be *s*, but the scall Lev 13:33 1548
the hair of his separation is *s* Num 6:19 1548
if I be *s*, then my strength will Judg 16:17 1548
to grow again after he was *s* Judg 16:22 1548
men, having their beards *s* Jer 41:5 1548
is even all one as if she were *s* 1Cor 11:5 3587
for a woman to be shorn or *s* 1Cor 11:6 3587

SHAVSHA (*shav'-shah*) See SERAIAH, SHEVA, SHISHA. *David's scribe.*
and *S* was scribe 1Chr 18:16 7798

SHE See PREFACE.

SHEAF
my *s* arose, and also stood upright Gen 37:7 485
about, and made obeisance to my *s* Gen 37:7 485
then ye shall bring a *s* of the Lev 23:10 6016
shall wave the *s* before the LORD Lev 23:11 6016
s an he lamb without blemish of Lev 23:12 6016
the *s* of the wave offering Lev 23:15 6016
and hast forgot a *s* in the field Deut 24:19 6016
take away the *s* from the hungry Job 24:10 6016
and like a torch of fire in a *s* Zec 12:6 5995

SHEAL (*she'-al*) *Married a foreigner in exile.*
Malluch, and Adaiah, Jashub, and *S* Ezr 10:29 7594

SHEALTIEL (*she-al'-te-el*) See SALATHIEL. *Father of Zerubbabel.*
and Zerubbabel the son of *S* Ezr 3:2 7597
began Zerubbabel the son of *S* Ezr 3:8 7597
rose up Zerubbabel the son of *S* Ezr 5:2 7597
up with Zerubbabel the son of *S* Neh 12:1 7597
unto Zerubbabel the son of *S* Hag 1:1 7597
Then Zerubbabel the son of *S* Hag 1:12 7597
spirit of Zerubbabel the son of *S* Hag 1:14 7597
now to Zerubbabel the son of *S* Hag 2:2 7597
my servant, the son of *S* Hag 2:23 7597

SHEAR
And Laban went to *s* his sheep Gen 31:19 1494
up to Timnath to *s* his sheep Gen 38:13 1494
nor *s* the firstling of thy sheep Deut 15:19 1494
that Nabal did *s* his sheep 1Sa 25:4 1494

SHEARER
and like a lamb dumb before his *s* Acts 8:32 *2751*

SHEARERS
now I have heard that thou hast *s* 1Sa 25:7 1494
flesh that I have killed for my *s* 1Sa 25:11 1494
as a sheep before her *s* is dumb Is 53:7 1494

SHEARIAH (*she-a-ri'-ah*) *Son of Azel.*
Bocheru, and Ishmael, and *S* 1Chr 8:38 8187
Bocheru, and Ishmael, and *S* 1Chr 9:44 8187

SHEARING
he was *s* his sheep in Carmel 1Sa 25:2 1494
he was at the *s* house in the way 2Kin 10:12
them at the pit of the *s* house 2Kin 10:14 1044

SHEAR-JASHUB (*she'-ar-ja'-shub*) *Symbolic name of a son of Isaiah.*
S thy son, at the end of the Is 7:3 7610

SHEATH
and drew it out of the *s* thereof 1Sa 17:51 8593
upon his loins in the *s* thereof 2Sa 20:8 8593
sword again into the *s* thereof 1Chr 21:27 5084
draw forth my sword out of his *s* Eze 21:3 8593
his *s* against all flesh from the Eze 21:4 8593
drawn forth my sword out of his *s* Eze 21:5 8593
I cause it to return into his *s* Eze 21:30 8593
Put up thy sword into the *s* Jn 18:11 2336

SHEAVES
we were binding *s* in the field Gen 37:7 485
your *s* stood round about, and made Gen 37:7 485
after the reapers among the *s* Ruth 2:7 6016
Let her glean even among the *s* Ruth 2:15 6016
on the sabbath, and bringing in *s* Neh 13:15 6194
bringing his *s* with him Ps 126:6 485
nor he that bindeth *s* his bosom Ps 129:7
cart is pressed that is full of *s* Amos 2:13 5995
them as the *s* into the floor Mic 4:12 5995

SHEBA (*she'-bah*) See BATH-SHEBA, BEERSHEBA, SHEBAH.
1. Son of Raamah.
Raamah; *S*, and Dedan Gen 10:7 7614
Raamah; *S*, and Dedan 1Chr 1:9 7614
2. Son of Yoktan.
And Obal, and Abimael, and *S* Gen 10:28 7614
And Ebal, and Abimael, and *S* 1Chr 1:22 7614
3. Son of Yokshan.
And Jokshan begat *S*, and Dedan Gen 25:3 7614
Jokshan; *S*, and Dedan 1Chr 1:32 7614
4. A region in southwestern Arabia.
when the queen of *S* heard of the 1Kin 10:1 7614
when the queen of *S* had seen all 1Kin 10:4 7614
queen of *S* gave to king Solomon 1Kin 10:10 7614
the queen of *S* all her desire 1Kin 10:13 7614
when the queen of *S* heard of the 2Chr 9:1 7614
when the queen of *S* had seen the 2Chr 9:3 7614
the queen of *S* gave king Solomon 2Chr 9:9 7614
to the queen of *S* all her desire 2Chr 9:12 7614
companies of *S* waited for them Job 6:19 7614
the kings of *S* and Seba shall Ps 72:10 7614
shall be given of the gold of *S* Ps 72:15 7614
all they from *S* shall come Is 60:6 7614
cometh there to me incense from *S* Jer 6:20 7614
The merchants of *S* and Raamah Eze 27:22 7614
and Eden, the merchants of *S* Eze 27:23 7614
S, and Dedan, and the merchants of Eze 38:13 7614
5. A city in Simeon.
inheritance Beer-sheba, or *S* Josh 19:2 7652
6. A son of Bichri.
a man of Belial, whose name was *S* 2Sa 20:1 7652
followed *S* the son of Bichri 2Sa 20:2 7652
Now shall *S* the son of Bichri do 2Sa 20:6 7652
to pursue after *S* the son of 2Sa 20:7 7652
pursued after *S* the son of Bichri 2Sa 20:10 7652
to pursue after *S* the son of 2Sa 20:13 7652
S the son of Bichri by name, hath 2Sa 20:21 7652
the head of *S* the son of Bichri 2Sa 20:22 7652
7. A chief Gadite.
were, Michael, and Meshullam, and *S* 1Chr 5:13 7652

SHEBAH (*she'-bah*) See SHEBA. *A well at Beersheba.*
And he called it *S* Gen 26:33 7656

SHEBAM (*she'-bam*) See SHIBMAH. *A city in Reuben.*
and Heshbon, and Elealeh, and *S* Num 32:3 7643

SHEBANIAH (*sheb-a-ni'-ah*) See SHECHANIAH.
1. A priest who moved the Ark.
And *S*, and Jehoshaphat, and 1Chr 15:24 7645
2. A Levite who aided Ezra.
Jeshua, and Bani, Kadmiel, *S* Neh 9:4 7645
Hashabniah, Sherebiah, Hodijah, *S* Neh 9:5 7645
And their brethren, *S*, Hodijah Neh 10:10 7645
3. A priest who renewed the covenant.
Hattush, *S*, Malluch Neh 10:4 7645
of *S*, Joseph Neh 12:14 7645
4. A Levite who renewed the covenant.
Zaccur, Sherebiah, *S* Neh 10:12 7645

SHEBARIM (*sheb'-a-rim*) *A place near Jericho.*
from before the gate even unto *S* Josh 7:5 7671

SHEBAT See SEBAT.

SHEBER (*she'-bur*) *A son of Caleb.*
Caleb's concubine, bare *S* 1Chr 2:48 7669

SHEBNA (*sheb'-nah*)
1. King Hezekiah's scribe.
S the scribe, and Joah the son of 2Kin 18:18 7644
Eliakim the son of Hilkiah, and *S* 2Kin 18:26 7644
S the scribe, and Joah the son of 2Kin 18:37 7644
S the scribe, and the elders of 2Kin 19:2 7644
S the scribe, and Joah, Asaph's Is 36:3 7644
Then said Eliakim and *S* and Joah Is 36:11 7644
S the scribe, and Joah, the son of Is 36:22 7644
S the scribe, and the elders of Is 37:2 7644
2. An unspecified treasurer.
unto this treasurer, even unto *S* Is 22:15 7644

SHEBNAH See SHEBNA.

SHEBUEL (*she-bu'-el*) See SHUBAEL.
1. A son of Gershom.
sons of Gershom, *S* was the chief 1Chr 23:16 7619
S the son of Gershom, the son of 1Chr 26:24 7619
2. A son of Haman.
Bukkiah, Mattaniah, Uzziel, *S* 1Chr 25:4 7619

SHECANIAH (*shek-a-ni'-ah*) See SHEBANIAH, SHECHANIAH.
1. A priest in David's time.
ninth to Jeshua, the tenth to *S* 1Chr 24:11 7935
2. A priest in Hezekiah's time.
and Shemaiah, Amariah, and *S* 2Chr 31:15 7935

SHECHANIAH (*shek-a-ni'-ah*) See SHEBANIAH, SHECANIAH.
1. Head of a Davidic family.
sons of Obadiah, the sons of *S* 1Chr 3:21 7935
And the sons of *S* 1Chr 3:22 7935
2. A family of exiles.
Of the sons of *S*, of the sons of Ezr 8:3 7935
3. Another family of exiles.
Of the sons of *S* Ezr 8:5 7935
4. Married a foreigner in exile.
S the son of Jehiel, one of the Ezr 10:2 7935
5. Father of Shemaiah.
also Shemaiah the son of *S* Neh 3:29 7935
6. Son of Arah.
son in law of *S* the son of Arah Neh 6:18 7935
7. A priest with Zerubbabel.
S, Rehum, Meremoth Neh 12:3 7935

SHECHEM (*she'-kem*) See SHECHEMITES, SHECHEM'S, SICHEM, SYCHEM.
1. A Levitical city near Mt. Ephraim.
Jacob came to Shalem, a city of *S* Gen 33:18 7927
them under the oak which was by *S* Gen 35:4 7927
to feed their father's flock in *S* Gen 37:12 7927
thy brethren feed the flock in *S* Gen 37:13 7927
vale of Hebron, and he came to *S* Gen 37:14 7927
Michmethah, that lieth before *S* Josh 17:7 7927
and *S* in mount Ephraim, and Josh 20:7 7927
For they gave them *S* with her Josh 21:21 7927
all the tribes of Israel to *S* Josh 24:1 7927
a statute and an ordinance in *S* Josh 24:25 7927
And his concubine that was in *S* Judg 8:31 7927
to *S* unto his mother's brethren Judg 9:1 7927
in the ears of all the men of *S* Judg 9:2 7927
all the men of *S* all these words Judg 9:3 7927
all the men of *S* gathered Judg 9:6 7927
plain of the pillar that was in *S* Judg 9:6 7927
Hearken unto me, ye men of *S* Judg 9:7 7927
king over the men of *S*, because Judg 9:18 7927
Abimelech, and devour the men of *S* Judg 9:20 7927
fire come out from the men of *S* Judg 9:20 7927
between Abimelech and the men of *S* Judg 9:23 7927
the men of *S* dealt treacherously Judg 9:23 7927
and upon the men of *S*, which aided Judg 9:24 7927
the men of *S* set liers in wait Judg 9:25 7927
his brethren, and went over to *S* Judg 9:26 7927
the men of *S* put their confidence Judg 9:26 7927
Ebed and his brethren be come to *S* Judg 9:31 7927
wait against *S* in four companies Judg 9:34 7927
Gaal went out before the men of *S* Judg 9:39 7927
that they should not dwell in *S* Judg 9:41 7927
men of the tower of *S* heard that Judg 9:46 7927
tower of *S* were gathered together Judg 9:47 7927
men of the tower of *S* died also Judg 9:49 7927
all the evil of the men of *S* did Judg 9:57 7927
that goeth up from Beth-el to *S* Judg 21:19 7927
And Rehoboam went to *S* 1Kin 12:1 7927
were come to *S* to make him king 1Kin 12:1 7927
Jeroboam built *S* in mount Ephraim 1Kin 12:25 7927
S in mount Ephraim with her 1Chr 6:67 7927
S also and the towns thereof, unto 1Chr 7:28 7927
And Rehoboam went to *S* 2Chr 10:1 7927
for to *S* were all Israel come to 2Chr 10:1 7927
I will rejoice, I will divide *S* Ps 60:6 7927
I will rejoice, I will divide *S* Ps 108:7 7927
That there came certain from *S* Jer 41:5 7927
2. Son of Hamor.
when *S* the son of Hamor the Gen 34:2 7927
S spake unto his father Hamor Gen 34:4 7927
Hamor the father of *S* went out Gen 34:6 7927
The soul of my son *S* longeth for Gen 34:8 7927
S said unto her father and unto Gen 34:11 7927
And the sons of Jacob answered *S* Gen 34:13 7927
pleased Hamor, and *S* Hamor's son Gen 34:18 7927
S his son came unto the gate of Gen 34:20 7927
unto *S* his son hearkened all that Gen 34:24 7927
S his son with the edge of the Gen 34:26 7927
up out of Egypt, buried they in *S* Josh 24:32 7927
S for an hundred pieces of silver Josh 24:32 7927
Who is Abimelech, and who is *S* Judg 9:28 7927
the men of Hamor the father of *S* Judg 9:28 7927
3. Son of Gilead.
and of *S*, the family of the Num 26:31 7928
Asriel, and for the children of *S* Josh 17:2 7928
4. A son of Shemidah.
of Shemidah were, Ahian, and *S* 1Chr 7:19 7928

SHECHEMITES (*she'-kem-ites*) *Descendants of Shechem.*
of Shechem, the family of the *S* Num 26:31 7930

SHECHEM'S (*she'-kems*) *Refers to Shechem 2.*
S father, for an hundred pieces Gen 33:19 7927
and took Dinah out of *S* house Gen 34:26 7927

SHED
by man shall his blood be *s* Gen 9:6 8210
S no blood, but cast him into Gen 37:22 8210
there shall no blood be *s* for him Ex 22:2
there shall be blood *s* for him Ex 22:3
he hath *s* blood Lev 17:4 8210
of the blood that is *s* therein Num 35:33 8210
but by the blood of him that *s* it Num 35:33 8210
blood be not *s* in thy land Deut 19:10 8210
Our hands have not *s* this blood Deut 21:7 8210
thee from coming to *s* blood 1Sa 25:26
that thou hast *s* blood causeless 1Sa 25:31 8210
this day from coming to *s* blood 1Sa 25:33
s out his bowels to the ground 2Sa 20:10 8210
s the blood of war in peace, and 1Kin 2:5 7760
the innocent blood, which Joab *s* 1Kin 2:31 8210
Moreover Manasseh *s* innocent 2Kin 21:16 8210
for the innocent blood that he *s* 2Kin 24:4 8210
Thou hast *s* blood abundantly, and 1Chr 22:8 8210
because thou hast *s* much blood 1Chr 22:8 8210
a man of war, and hast *s* blood 1Chr 28:3 8210
Their blood have they *s* like Ps 79:3 8210
blood of thy servants which is *s* Ps 79:10 8210
s innocent blood, even the blood Ps 106:38 8210
to evil, and make haste to *s* blood Prov 1:16 8210
hands that *s* innocent blood Prov 6:17 8210
make haste to *s* innocent blood Is 59:7 8210
s not innocent blood in this Jer 7:6 8210
neither *s* innocent blood in this Jer 22:3 8210
for to *s* innocent blood, and for Jer 22:17 8210
that have *s* the blood of the just Lam 4:13 8210
wedlock and *s* blood are judged Eze 16:38 8210
in thy blood that thou hast *s* Eze 22:4 8210

in thee to their power to s blood Eze 22:6 8210
men that carry tales to s blood Eze 22:9 8210
have they taken gifts to s blood Eze 22:12 8210
to s blood, and to destroy souls, Eze 22:27 8210
the manner of women that s blood Eze 23:45 8210
toward your idols, and s blood Eze 33:25 8210
hast s the blood of the children Eze 35:5 5064
that they had s upon the land Eze 36:18 8210
because they have s innocent Joel 3:19 8210
righteous blood s upon the earth Mt 23:35 1632
which is s for many for the Mt 26:28 1632
testament, which is s for many Mk 14:24 1632
which was s from the foundation Lk 11:50 1632
in my blood, which is s for you Lk 22:20 1632
he hath s forth this, which ye Acts 2:33 1632
blood of thy martyr Stephen was s Acts 22:20 1632
Their feet are swift to s blood Rom 3:15 1632
because the love of God is s Rom 5:5 1632
Which he s on us abundantly Titus 3:6 1632
For they have s the blood of Rev 16:6 1632

SHEDDER
a s of blood, and that doeth the Eze 18:10 8210

SHEDDETH
Whoso s man's blood, by man shall Gen 9:6 8210
The city s blood in the midst of Eze 22:3 8210

SHEDDING
and without s of blood is no Heb 9:22 130

SHEDEUR (*shed'-e-ur*) *A Reubenite who counted the people.*
Elizur the son of S Num 1:5 7707
shall be Elizur the son of S Num 2:10 7707
fourth day Elizur the son of S Num 7:30 7707
offering of Elizur the son of S Num 7:35 7707
his host was Elizur the son of S Num 10:18 7707

SHEEP
And Abel was a keeper of s Gen 4:2 6629
and he had s, and oxen, and he asses Gen 12:16 6629
And Abimelech took s, and oxen, and Gen 20:14 6629
And Abraham took s and oxen, and Gen 21:27 6629
three flocks of s lying by it Gen 29:2 6629
well's mouth, and watered the s Gen 29:3 6629
his daughter cometh with the s Gen 29:6 6629
water ye the s, and go and feed Gen 29:7 6629
then we water the s Gen 29:8 6629
Rachel came with her father's s Gen 29:9 6629
the s of Laban his mother's Gen 29:10 6629
all the brown cattle among the s Gen 30:32 3775
the goats, and brown among the s Gen 30:33 3775
it, and all the brown among the s Gen 30:35 3775
And Laban went to shear his s Gen 31:19 6629
They took their s, and their oxen, Gen 34:28 6629
up to Timnath to shear his s Gen 38:13 6629
upon the oxen, and upon the s Ex 9:3 6629
ye shall take it out from the s Ex 12:5 3532
and thy peace offerings, thy s Ex 20:24 6629
a man shall steal an ox, or a s Ex 22:1 7716
for an ox, and four s for a s Ex 22:1 6629
whether it be ox, or ass, or s Ex 22:4 7716
it be for ox, for ass, for s Ex 22:9 7716
an ass, or an ox, or a s, or any Ex 22:10 7716
do with thine oxen, and with thy s Ex 22:30 6629
among thy cattle, whether ox or s Ex 34:19 7716
of the flocks, namely, of the s Lev 1:10 3775
no manner of fat, of ox, or of s Lev 7:23 3775
blemish, of the beeves, of the s Lev 22:19 3775
freewill offering in beeves or s Lev 22:21 6629
When a bullock, or a s, or a goat Lev 22:27 3775
whether it be ox, or s Lev 27:26 7716
of a cow, or the firstling of a s Num 18:17 3775
And Balak offered oxen and s Num 22:40 6629
of the LORD be not as s which Num 27:17 6629
and of the asses, and of the s Num 31:28 6629
thousand and five thousand s Num 31:32 6629
thirty thousand and five hundred s Num 31:36 6629
tribute of the s was six hundred Num 31:37 6629
seven thousand and five hundred s Num 31:43 6629
little ones, and folds for your s Num 32:24 6792
and folds of s Num 32:36 6629
thy kine, and the flocks of thy s Deut 7:13 6629
the ox, the s, and the goat, Deut 14:4 3775
lusteth after, for oxen, or for s Deut 14:26 6629
nor shear the firstling of thy s Deut 15:19 6629
LORD thy God any bullock, or s Deut 17:1 7716
sacrifice, whether it be ox or s Deut 18:3 7716
the first of the fleece of thy s Deut 18:4 6629
brother's ox or his s go astray Deut 22:1 7716
thy kine, and the flocks of thy s Deut 28:4 6629
thy kine, and the flocks of thy s Deut 28:18 6629
thy s shall be given unto thine Deut 28:31 6629
of thy kine, or flocks of thy s Deut 28:51 6629
Butter of kine, and milk of s Deut 32:14 6629
woman, young and old, and ox, and s Josh 6:21 7716
his oxen, and his asses, and his s Josh 7:24 6629
sustenance for Israel, neither s Judg 6:4 7716
He will take the tenth of your s 1Sa 8:17 6629
flew upon the spoil, and took s 1Sa 14:32 6629
man his ox, and every man his s 1Sa 14:34 7716
infant and suckling, ox and s 1Sa 15:3 7716
spared Agag, and the best of the s 1Sa 15:9 6629
bleating of the s in mine ears 1Sa 15:14 6629
people spared the best of the s 1Sa 15:15 6629
the people took of the spoil, s 1Sa 15:21 6629
and, behold, he keepeth the s 1Sa 16:11 6629
thy son, which is with the s 1Sa 16:19 6629
feed his father's s at Beth-lehem 1Sa 17:15 6629
left the s with a keeper, and took 1Sa 17:20 6629
those few s in the wilderness 1Sa 17:28 6629
Thy servant kept his father's s 1Sa 17:34 6629
and oxen, and asses, and s, with 1Sa 22:19 7716
great, and he had three thousand s 1Sa 25:2 6629
he was shearing his s in Carmel 1Sa 25:2 6629
that Nabal did shear his s 1Sa 25:4 6629
we were with them keeping the s 1Sa 25:16 6629
five s ready dressed, and five 1Sa 25:18 6629
woman alive, and took away the s 1Sa 27:9 6629
sheepcote, from following the s 2Sa 7:8 6629
And honey, and butter, and s 2Sa 17:29 6629
but these s, what have they done 2Sa 24:17 6629
And Adonijah slew s and oxen and fat 1Kin 1:9 6629
s in abundance, and hath called 1Kin 1:19 6629
s in abundance, and hath called 1Kin 1:25 6629
of the pastures, and an hundred s 1Kin 4:23 6629
him before the ark, sacrificing s 1Kin 8:5 6629
an hundred and twenty thousand s 1Kin 8:63 6629
as s that have not a shepherd 1Kin 22:17 6629
and oliveyards, and vineyards, and s 2Kin 5:26 6629
of s two hundred and fifty 1Chr 5:21 6629
and oil, and oxen, and s abundantly 1Chr 12:40 6629
even from following the s 1Chr 17:7 6629
but as for these s, what have 1Chr 21:17 6629
him before the ark, sacrificed s 2Chr 5:6 6629
an hundred and twenty thousand s 2Chr 7:5 6629
of cattle, and carried away s 2Chr 14:15 6629
hundred oxen and seven thousand s 2Chr 15:11 6629
And Ahab killed s and oxen for him 2Chr 18:2 6629
as s that have no shepherd 2Chr 18:16 6629
hundred oxen and three thousand s 2Chr 29:33 6629
bullocks and seven thousand s 2Chr 30:24 6629
bullocks and ten thousand s 2Chr 30:24 6629
brought in the tithe of oxen and s 2Chr 31:6 6629
and they builded the s gate Neh 3:1 6629
s gate repaired the goldsmiths Neh 3:32 6629
daily was one ox and six choice s Neh 5:18 6629
of Meah, even unto the s gate Neh 12:39 6629
also was seven thousand s Job 1:3 6629
heaven, and hath burned up the s Job 1:16 6629
warmed with the fleece of my s Job 31:20 3532
for he had fourteen thousand s Job 42:12 6629
All s and oxen, yea, and the beasts Ps 8:7 6792
us like s appointed for meat Ps 44:11 6629
counted as s for the slaughter Ps 44:22 6629
Like s they are laid in the grave Ps 49:14 6629
against the s of thy pasture Ps 74:1 6629
his own people to go forth like s Ps 78:52 6629
s of thy pasture will give thee Ps 79:13 6629
his pasture, and the s of his hand Ps 95:7 6629
people, and the s of his pasture Ps 100:3 6629
I have gone astray like a lost s Ps 119:176 7716
that our s may bring forth Ps 144:13 6629
a flock of s that are even shorn Song 4:2
Thy teeth are as a flock of s Song 6:6 7353
nourish a young cow, and two s Is 7:21 6629
as a s that no man taketh up Is 13:14 6629
slaying oxen, and killing s Is 22:13 6629
All we like s have gone astray Is 53:6 6629
as a s before her shearers is Is 53:7 7353
them out like s for the slaughter Jer 12:3 6629
scatter the s of my pasture Jer 23:1 6629
My people hath been lost s Jer 50:6 6629
Israel is a scattered s Jer 50:17 7716
My s wandered through all the Eze 34:6 6629
I, even I, will both search my s Eze 34:11 6629
is among his s that are scattered Eze 34:12 6629
so will I seek out my s, and will Eze 34:12 6629
a wife, and for a wife he kept s Hos 12:12
the flocks of s are made desolate Joel 1:18 6629
them together as the s of Bozrah Mic 2:12 6629
young lion among the flocks of s Mic 5:8 6629
and the s shall be scattered Zec 13:7 6629
abroad, as s having no shepherd Mt 9:36 4263
the lost s of the house of Israel Mt 10:6 4263
I send you forth as s in the Mt 10:16 4263
among you, that shall have one s Mt 12:11 4263
then is a man better than a s Mt 12:12 4263
the lost s of the house of Israel Mt 15:24 4263
if a man have an hundred s Mt 18:12 4263
you, he rejoiceth more of that s Mt 18:13 4263
divideth his s from the goats Mt 25:32 4263
he shall set the s on his right Mt 25:33 4263
the s of the flock shall be Mt 26:31 4263
because they were as s not having Mk 6:34 4263
and the s shall be scattered Mk 14:27 4263
man of you, having an hundred s Lk 15:4 4263
I have found my s which was lost Lk 15:6 4263
temple those that sold oxen and s Jn 2:14 4263
all out of the temple, and the s Jn 2:15 4263
Jerusalem by the s market a pool Jn 5:2 4262
the door is the shepherd of the s Jn 10:2 4263
and the s hear his voice Jn 10:3 4263
and he calleth his own s by name Jn 10:3 4263
when he putteth forth his own s Jn 10:4 4263
before them, and the s follow him Jn 10:4 4263
unto you, I am the door of the s Jn 10:7 4263
but the s did not hear them Jn 10:8 4263
giveth his life for the s Jn 10:11 4263
shepherd, whose own the s are not Jn 10:12 4263
the wolf coming, and leaveth the s Jn 10:12 4263
them, and scattereth the s Jn 10:12 4263
hireling, and careth not for the s Jn 10:13 4263
the good shepherd, and know my s Jn 10:14
and I lay down my life for the s Jn 10:15 4263
other s I have, which are not of Jn 10:16 4263
not, because ye are not of my s Jn 10:26 4263
My s hear my voice, and I know Jn 10:27 4263
He saith unto him, Feed my s Jn 21:16 4263
Jesus saith unto him, Feed my s Jn 21:17 4263
this, He was led as a s to the Acts 8:32 4263
accounted as s for the slaughter Rom 8:36 4263
that great shepherd of the s Heb 13:20 4263
For ye were as s going astray 1Pet 2:25 4263
flour, and wheat, and beasts, and s Rev 18:13 4263

SHEEPCOTE
of hosts, I took thee from the s 2Sa 7:8 5116
of hosts, I took thee from the s 1Chr 17:7 5116

SHEEPCOTES
And he came to the s by the way 1Sa 24:3 6629

SHEEPFOLD
not by the door into the s Jn 10:1 833

SHEEPFOLDS
We will build s here for our Num 32:16
Why abodest thou among the s Judg 5:16 4942
servant, and took him from the s Ps 78:70

SHEEPMASTER
And Mesha king of Moab was a s 2Kin 3:4 5349

SHEEP'S
which come to you in s clothing Mt 7:15 4263

SHEEPSHEARERS
and went up unto his s to Timnath Gen 38:12
that Absalom had s in Baal-hazor 2Sa 13:23 1494
Behold now, thy servant hath s 2Sa 13:24 1494

SHEEPSKINS
they wandered about in s and Heb 11:37 3374

SHEERAH See SHERAH.

SHEET
as it had been a great s knit at Acts 10:11 3607
descend, as it had been a great s Acts 11:5 3607

SHEETS
then I will give you thirty s Judg 14:12 5466
then shall ye give me thirty s Judg 14:13 5466

SHEHARIAH (*she-ha-ri'-ah*) *A son of Jeroham.*
And Shamsherai, and S, and Athaliah, 1Chr 8:26 7841

SHEKEL
golden earring of half a s weight Gen 24:22 1235
half a s after the s of the Ex 30:13 8255
(a s is twenty gerahs Ex 30:13 8255
an half s shall be the offering Ex 30:13 8255
shall not give less than half a s Ex 30:15 8255
after the s of the sanctuary, and Ex 30:24 8255
after the s of the sanctuary Ex 38:24 8255
after the s of the sanctuary Ex 38:25 8255
for every man, that is, half a s Ex 38:26 8255
after the s of the sanctuary, for Ex 38:26 8255
after the s of the sanctuary, for Lev 5:15 8255
after the s of the sanctuary Lev 27:3 8255
to the s of the sanctuary Lev 27:25 8255
twenty gerahs shall be the s Lev 27:25 8255
after the s of the sanctuary Num 3:47 8255
(the s is twenty gerahs Num 3:47 8255
after the s of the sanctuary Num 3:50 8255
after the s of the sanctuary Num 7:13 8255
after the s of the sanctuary Num 7:19 8255
after the s of the sanctuary Num 7:25 8255
after the s of the sanctuary Num 7:31 8255
after the s of the sanctuary Num 7:37 8255
after the s of the sanctuary Num 7:43 8255
after the s of the sanctuary Num 7:49 8255
after the s of the sanctuary Num 7:55 8255
after the s of the sanctuary Num 7:61 8255
after the s of the sanctuary Num 7:67 8255
after the s of the sanctuary Num 7:73 8255
after the s of the sanctuary Num 7:79 8255
after the s of the sanctuary Num 7:85 8255
after the s of the sanctuary Num 7:86 8255
after the s of the sanctuary, Num 18:16 8255
the fourth part of a s of silver 1Sa 9:8 8255
of fine flour be sold for a s 2Kin 7:1 8255
and two measures of barley for a s 2Kin 7:1 8255
of fine flour was sold for a s 2Kin 7:16 8255
and two measures of barley for a s 2Kin 7:16 8255
Two measures of barley for a s 2Kin 7:18 8255
a measure of fine flour for a s 2Kin 7:18 8255
s for the service of the house of Neh 10:32 8255
the s shall be twenty gerahs Eze 45:12 8255
the s great, and falsifying the Amos 8:5 8255

SHEKELS
is worth four hundred s of silver Gen 23:15 8255
of Heth, four hundred s of silver Gen 23:16 8255
her hands of ten s weight of gold Gen 24:22 8255
their master thirty s of silver Ex 21:32 8255
of pure myrrh five hundred s Ex 30:23
much, even two hundred and fifty s Ex 30:23
calamus two hundred and fifty s Ex 30:23
And of cassia five hundred s Ex 30:24
and seven hundred and thirty s Ex 38:24 8255
and threescore and fifteen s Ex 38:25 8255
five s he made hooks for the Ex 38:28
and two thousand and four hundred s. Ex 38:29 8255
thy estimation by s of silver Lev 5:15 8255
shall be fifty s of silver Lev 27:3 8255
thy estimation shall be thirty s Lev 27:4 8255
shall be of the male twenty s Lev 27:5 8255
and for the female ten s Lev 27:5 8255
be of the male five s of silver Lev 27:6 8255
shall be three s of silver Lev 27:6 8255
thy estimation shall be fifteen s Lev 27:7 8255
and for the female ten s Lev 27:7 8255
be valued at fifty s of silver Lev 27:16 8255
take five s apiece by the poll Num 3:47 8255
hundred and threescore and five s Num 3:50
was an hundred and thirty s Num 7:13
one silver bowl of seventy s Num 7:13
One spoon of ten s of gold Num 7:14
was an hundred and thirty s Num 7:19
one silver bowl of seventy s Num 7:19 8255
One spoon of gold of ten s Num 7:20
was an hundred and thirty s Num 7:25
one silver bowl of seventy s Num 7:25 8255
One golden spoon of ten s Num 7:26
weight of an hundred and thirty s Num 7:31
one silver bowl of seventy s Num 7:31 8255
One golden spoon of ten s Num 7:32
was an hundred and thirty s Num 7:37

S

one silver bowl of seventy *s*.................... Num 7:37 8255
One golden spoon of ten *s*...................... Num 7:38
weight of an hundred and thirty *s* .... Num 7:43
a silver bowl of seventy *s*..................... Num 7:43 8255
One golden spoon of ten *s*...................... Num 7:44
was an hundred and thirty *s*................. Num 7:49
one silver bowl of seventy *s*.................. Num 7:49 8255
One golden spoon of ten *s*...................... Num 7:50
weight of an hundred and thirty *s* .... Num 7:55
one silver bowl of seventy *s*.................. Num 7:55 8255
One golden spoon of ten *s*...................... Num 7:56
was an hundred and thirty *s*................. Num 7:61
one silver bowl of seventy *s*.................. Num 7:61 8255
One golden spoon of ten *s*...................... Num 7:62
was an hundred and thirty *s*................. Num 7:67
one silver bowl of seventy *s*.................. Num 7:67 8255
One golden spoon of ten *s*...................... Num 7:68
was an hundred and thirty *s*................. Num 7:73
one silver bowl of seventy *s*.................. Num 7:73 8255
One golden spoon of ten *s*...................... Num 7:74
was an hundred and thirty *s*................. Num 7:79
one silver bowl of seventy *s*.................. Num 7:79 8255
One golden spoon of ten *s*...................... Num 7:80
weighing an hundred and thirty *s*........ Num 7:85
two thousand and four hundred *s*......... Num 7:85
of incense, weighing ten *s* apiece .... Num 7:86
spoons was an hundred and twenty *s* .. Num 7:86
for the money of five *s*, after................ Num 18:16 8255
thousand seven hundred and fifty *s*...... Num 31:52 8255
him in an hundred *s* of silver .... Deut 22:19
damsel's father fifty *s* of silver............. Deut 22:29
and two hundred *s* of silver................... Josh 7:21 8255
a wedge of gold of fifty *s* weight........... Josh 7:21 8255
and seven hundred *s* of gold.................. Judg 8:26
The eleven hundred *s* of silver.............. Judg 17:2
hundred *s* of silver to his mother .... Judg 17:3
took two hundred *s* of silver.................. Judg 17:4
I will give thee ten *s* of silver............... Judg 17:10
coat was five thousand *s* of brass.......... 1Sa 17:5 8255
weighed six hundred *s* of iron................. 1Sa 17:7 8255
hundred *s* after the king's weight 2Sa 14:26 8255
have given thee ten *s* of silver............... 2Sa 18:11
thousand *s* of silver in mine hand.......... 2Sa 18:12
hundred *s* of brass in weight.................. 2Sa 21:16
and the oxen for fifty *s* of silver........... 2Sa 24:24 8255
six hundred *s* of gold went to one.......... 1Kin 10:16
Egypt for six hundred *s* of silver 1Kin 10:29
of each man fifty *s* of silver.................. 2Kin 15:20 8255
six hundred *s* of gold by weight............. 1Chr 21:25 8255
for six hundred *s* of silver..................... 2Chr 1:17
of the nails was fifty *s* of gold............. 2Chr 3:9 8255
six hundred *s* of beaten gold went 2Chr 9:15
three hundred *s* of gold went to............ 2Chr 9:16
and wine, beside forty *s* of silver.......... Neh 5:15 8255
money, even seventeen *s* of silver.......... Jer 32:9 8255
be by weight, twenty *s* a day .... Eze 4:10 8255
twenty *s*, five and twenty...................... Eze 45:12 8255
five and twenty *s*, fifteen *s*................... Eze 45:12 8255

SHELAH (*she'-lah*) See SHELAH, SHELANITES.
1. Son of Judah.
and called his name *S*........................... Gen 38:5 7956
house, till *S* my son be grown................ Gen 38:11 7956
for she saw that *S* was grown................ Gen 38:14 7956
that I gave her not to *S* my son............. Gen 38:26 7956
Er, and Onan, and *S*, and Pharez, and . Gen 46:12 7956
of *S*, the family of the........................... Num 26:20 7956
Er, and Onan, and *S* 1Chr 2:3 7956
The sons of *S* the son of Judah............. 1Chr 4:21 7956
2. Son of Arphaxad.
And Arphaxad begat *S*, and Shelah...... 1Chr 1:18 7974
begat Shelah, and *S* begat Eber............ 1Chr 1:18 7956
Shem, Arphaxad, *S*,................................ 1Chr 1:24 7956

SHELANITE See SHELANITES.

SHELANITES (*she'-lan-ites*) *Descendants of Shelah.*
of Shelah, the family of the *S*................ Num 26:20 8024

SHELEMIAH (*shel-e-mi'-ah*) See MESHELEMIAH, SHALLUM.
1. A sanctuary servant.
And the lot eastward fell to *S*............... 1Chr 26:14 8018
2. A son of Bani who married a foreigner.
And *S*, and Nathan, and Adaiah, ... Ezr 10:39 8018
3. Another son of Bani.
Azareel, and *S*, Shemariah, ... Ezr 10:41 8018
4. Father of Hananiah.
repaired Hananiah the son of *S* .... Neh 3:30 8018
5. A treasury servant.
S the priest, and Zadok the scribe .... Neh 13:13 8018
6. Son of Cushi.
son of Nethaniah, the son of *S* .... Jer 36:14 8018
7. Son of Abdeel.
S the son of Abdeel, to take .... Jer 36:26 8018
8. Father of Jehucal.
king sent Jehucal the son of *S*.............. Jer 37:3 8018
of Pashur, and Jucal the son of *S*.......... Jer 38:1 8018
9. Father of Irijah.
name was Irijah, the son of *S* .... Jer 37:13 8018

SHELEPH (*she'-lef*) *A son of Joktan.*
And Joktan begat Almodad, and *S* .... Gen 10:26 8026
And Joktan begat Almodad, and *S* 1Chr 1:20 8026

SHELESH (*she'-lesh*) *A son of Helem.*
Zophah, and Imna, and *S*, and Amal.... 1Chr 7:35 8028

SHELOMI (*shel'-o-mi*) *Father of Ahihud.*
of Asher, Ahihud the son of *S*............... Num 34:27 8015

SHELOMITH (*shel'-o-mith*)
1. Daughter of Debri.
(and his mother's name was *S* .... Lev 24:11 8019
2. Daughter of Zerubbabel.
and Hananiah, and *S* their sister 1Chr 3:19 8019
3. A son of Shimei.
S, and Haziel, and Haran, three............ 1Chr 23:9 8013
4. A son of Izhar.
S the chief... 1Chr 23:18 8013
5. A descendant of Eliezer.
and Zichri his son, and *S* his son........... 1Chr 26:25 8013
Which *S* and his brethren were over...... 1Chr 26:26 8013
thing, it was under the hand of *S*.......... 1Chr 26:28 8019
6. A child of King Rehoboam.
Abijah, and Attai, and Ziza, and *S*......... 2Chr 11:20 8019
7. A family of exiles.
And of the sons of *S*.............................. Ezr 8:10 8019

SHELOMOTH (*shel'-o-moth*) See SHELOMITH.
A descendant of Izhar.
S: of the sons of *S*................................ 1Chr 24:22 8013

SHELTER
embrace the rock for want of a *s* .... Job 24:8 4268
For thou hast been a *s* for me.............. Ps 61:3 4268

SHELUMIEL
S the son of Zurishaddai .... Num 1:6 8017
shall be *S* the son of Zurishaddai .... Num 2:12 8017
On the fifth day *S* the son of................ Num 7:36 8017
of *S* the son of Zurishaddai.................... Num 7:41 8017
was *S* the son of Zurishaddai .... Num 10:19 8017

SHEM (*shem*) See SEM. *A son of Noah.*
and Noah begat *S*, Ham, and Japheth.. Gen 5:32 8035
And Noah begat three sons, *S*.............. Gen 6:10 8035
selfsame day entered Noah, and *S* .... Gen 7:13 8035
went forth of the ark, were *S*................ Gen 9:18 8035
And *S* and Japheth took a garment,..... Gen 9:23 8035
Blessed be the LORD God of *S* .... Gen 9:26 8035
he shall dwell in the tents of *S* .... Gen 9:27 8035
of the sons of Noah, *S*, Ham, and.......... Gen 10:1 8035
Unto *S* also, the father of all .... Gen 10:21 8035
The children of *S*.................................. Gen 10:22 8035
These are the sons of *S*, after.............. Gen 10:31 8035
These are the generations of *S* .... Gen 11:10 8035
S was an hundred years old, and.......... Gen 11:10 8035
S lived after he begat Arphaxad .... Gen 11:11 8035
Noah, *S*, Ham, and Japheth 1Chr 1:4 8035
The sons of *S*... 1Chr 1:17 8035
S, Arphaxad, Shelah, ... 1Chr 1:24 8035

SHEMA (*she'-mah*) See SHEMAIAH, SHIMHI.
1. A city in Judah.
Amam, and *S*, and Moladah,................. Josh 15:26 8087
2. A son of Hebron.
Tappuah, and Rekem, and *S*.................. 1Chr 2:43 8087
S begat Raham, the father of 1Chr 2:44 8087
3. Father of Azaz.
the son of Azaz, the son of *S* 1Chr 5:8 8087
4. A Benjamite chief.
Beriah also, and *S*, who were heads...... 1Chr 8:13 8087
5. A priest who aided Ezra.
beside him stood Mattithiah, and *S* ...... Neh 8:4 8087

SHEMAAH (*shem'-a-ah*) *Father of two warriors in David's army.*
the sons of *S* the Gibeathite 1Chr 12:3 8093

SHEMAIAH (*shem-a-i'-ah*) See SHAMMUA, SHEMA, SHIMEI, SEMEI.
1. A prophet in King Rehoboam's time.
of God came unto *S* the man of God ... 1Kin 12:22 8098
the LORD came to *S* the man of God.... 2Chr 11:2 8098
Then came *S* the prophet to.................. 2Chr 12:5 8098
the word of the LORD came to *S*........... 2Chr 12:7 8098
in the book of *S* the prophet 2Chr 12:15 8098
2. Son of Shechaniah.
S: and the sons of Shemaiah 1Chr 3:22 8098
3. Father of Shimri.
the son of Shimri, the son of *S* 1Chr 4:37 8098
4. Son of Joel.
S his son, Gog his son, Shimei 1Chr 5:4 8098
5. Son of Hasshub.
S the son of Hasshub, the son of.......... 1Chr 9:14 8098
S the son of Hashub, the son of .... Neh 11:15 8098
6. Father of Obadiah.
And Obadiah the son of *S*, the son 1Chr 9:16 8098
7. A priest who moved the Ark.
S the chief, and his brethren two.......... 1Chr 15:8 8098
for Uriel, Asaiah, and Joel, *S* 1Chr 15:11 8098
8. Son of Nathaneel.
S the son of Nethaneel the scribe 1Chr 24:6 8098
9. A sanctuary servant.
S the firstborn, Jehozabad the 1Chr 26:4 8098
Also unto *S* his son were sons 1Chr 26:6 8098
The sons of *S*... 1Chr 26:7 8098
10. A Levite teacher of the people.
with them he sent Levites, even *S*.......... 2Chr 17:8 8098
11. A Levite who cleansed the Temple.
S, and Uzziel... 2Chr 29:14 8098
12. A Levite in Hezekiah's time.
and Miniamin, and Jeshua, and *S*.......... 2Chr 31:15 8098
13. A Levite in Josiah's time.
Conaniah also, and *S* and Nethaneel,... 2Chr 35:9 8098
14. A family of exiles.
are these, Eliphelet, Jeiel, and *S* .... Ezr 8:13 8098
15. A messenger of Ezra.
I for Eliezer, for Ariel, for *S*................. Ezr 8:16 8098
16. A priest who married a foreigner.
Maaseiah, and Elijah, and *S*.................. Ezr 10:21 8098
17. A son of Harim.
Eliezer, Ishijah, Malchiah, *S* .... Ezr 10:31 8098
18. A rebuilder of Jerusalem's wall.
also *S* the son of Shechaniah .... Neh 3:29 8098
19. Son of Delaiah.
I came unto the house of *S* the............ Neh 6:10 8098
20. A priest who renewed the covenant.
Maaziah, Bilgai, *S*................................. Neh 10:8 8098
S, and Joiarib, Jedaiah,......................... Neh 12:6 8098
of *S*, Jehonathan................................... Neh 12:18 8098
Judah, and Benjamin, and *S*, and.......... Neh 12:34 8098
the son of Jonathan, the son of *S* .... Neh 12:35 8098
21. A priest who dedicated the wall.
And his brethren, *S*, and Azarael, ... Neh 12:36 8098
22. A priest who gave thanks at the wall.
And Maaseiah, and *S*............................. Neh 12:42 8098
23. Father of Urijah.
the son of *S* of Kirjath-jearim................ Jer 26:20 8098
24. A false prophet.
also speak to *S* the Nehelamite............. Jer 29:24 8098
LORD concerning *S* the Nehelamite .... Jer 29:31 8098
Because that *S* hath prophesied............ Jer 29:31 8098
I will punish *S* the Nehelamite,............. Jer 29:32 8098
25. Father of Delaiah.
scribe, and Delaiah the son of *S* .... Jer 36:12 8098

SHEMARIAH (*shem-a-ri'-ah*)
1. A warrior in David's army.
and Jerimoth, and Bealiah, and *S*......... 1Chr 12:5 8114
3. Married a foreigner in exile.
Benjamin, Malluch, and *S*...................... Ezr 10:32 8114
4. Married a foreigner in exile.
Azareel, and Shelemiah, *S*,.................... Ezr 10:41 8114

SHEMEBER (*shem-e'-ber*) *King of Zeboim.*
S king of Zeboiim, and the king of....... Gen 14:2 8038

SHEMED See SHAMED.

SHEMER (*she'-mur*) *Owner of a hill, later the site of Samaria.*
of *S* for two talents of silver................. 1Kin 16:24 8106
he built, after the name of *S*................. 1Kin 16:24 8106

SHEMIDA (*shem-i'-dah*) See SHEMIDAH. *Son of Gilead.*
And of *S*, the family of the .... Num 26:32 8061
Hepher, and for the children of *S*.......... Josh 17:2 8061

SHEMIDAH (*shem-i'-dah*) See SHEMIDA, SHEMIDAITES. *Same as Shemida.*
And the sons of *S* were, Ahian, and..... 1Chr 7:19 8061

SHEMIDAITES (*shem'-i-dah-ites*) *Descendants of Shemida.*
of Shemida, the family of the *S* .... Num 26:32 8062

SHEMINITH (*shem'-i-nith*) *A musical notation.*
with harps on the *S* to excel.................. 1Chr 15:21 8067
chief Musician on Neginoth upon *S* .... Ps 6:*t* 8067
To the chief Musician upon *S* .... Ps 12:*t* 8067

SHEMIRAMOTH (*she-mir'-a-moth*)
1. A priest who moved the Ark.
Zechariah, Ben, and Jaaziel, and *S* 1Chr 15:18 8070
And Zechariah, and Aziel, and *S* 1Chr 15:20 8070
to him Zechariah, Jeiel, and *S*............... 1Chr 16:5 8070
2. A Levite in Jehoshaphat's time.
and Zebadiah, and Asahel, and *S*.......... 2Chr 17:8 8070

SHEMUEL (*shem-u-'el*) See SAMUEL.
1. A Simeonite prince.
of Simeon, *S* the son of Ammihud .... Num 34:20 8050
2. Another name for Samuel the prophet.
the son of Joel, the son of *S*.................. 1Chr 6:33 8050
3. Head of a family in Issachar.
and Jahmai, and Jibsam, and *S*............. 1Chr 7:2 8050

SHEN (*shen*) *A place in Benjamin.*
and set it between Mizpeh and *S* 1Sa 7:12 8129

SHENAZAR (*she-na'-zar*) *Descendant of King Jehoiakim.*
Malchiram also, and Pedaiah, and *S*..... 1Chr 3:18 8137

SHENAZZAR See SHENAZAR.

SHENIR (*she'-nur*) See SENIR, SION. *A mountain between Amana and Hermon.*
and the Amorites call it *S* .... Deut 3:9 8140
top of Amana, from the top of *S*........... Song 4:8 8149

SHEOL See HELL.

SHEPHAM (*she'-fam*) See SHIPMITE. *A place east of the Sea of Cinneroth.*
east border from Hazar-enan to *S*......... Num 34:10 8221
shall go down from *S* to Riblah .... Num 34:11 8221

SHEPHATIAH (*shef-a-ti'-ah*)
1. A son of David.
and the fifth, *S* the son of Abital.......... 2Sa 3:4 8203
The fifth, *S* of Abital.............................. 1Chr 3:3 8203
Michri, and Meshullam the son of *S*...... 1Chr 9:8 8203
3. A warrior in David's army.
and Shemariah, and *S* the Haruphite, .. 1Chr 12:5 8203
4. A Simeonite prince.
Simeonites, *S* the son of Maachah 1Chr 27:16 8203
5. A son of King Jehoshaphat.
and Azariah, and Michael, and *S*.......... 2Chr 21:2 8203
6. A family of exiles with Zerubbabel.
The children of *S*, three hundred.......... Ezr 2:4 8203
The children of *S*, three hundred.......... Neh 7:9 8203
7. Descendants of a servant of Solomon.
The children of *S*, the children.............. Ezr 2:57 8203
The children of *S*, the children.............. Neh 7:59 8203
8. A family of exiles with Ezra.
And of the sons of *S*.............................. Ezr 8:8 8203
9. A family of exiles who resettled in Jerusalem.
the son of Amariah, the son of *S*.......... Neh 11:4 8203
10. A prince of Judah.
Then *S* the son of Mattan, and............ Jer 38:1 8203

SHEPHELAH See PLAIN.

SHEPHER See SHAPHER.

SHEPHERD
for every *s* is an abomination................ Gen 46:34
(from thence is the *s*, the stone .... Gen 49:24 7462
be not as sheep which have no *s*........... Num 27:17 7462
hills, as sheep that have not a *s*........... 1Kin 22:17 7462
as sheep that have no *s* 2Chr 18:16 7462
The LORD is my *s*.................................. Ps 23:1 7462
O *S* of Israel, thou that leadest............ Ps 80:1 7462

which are given from one s ... Eccl 12:11 7462
He shall feed his flock like a s ... Is 40:11 7462
That saith of Cyrus, He is my s ... Is 44:28 7462
the sea with the s of his flock ... Is 63:11 7462
keep him, as a s doth his flock ... Jer 31:10 7462
as a s putteth on his garment ... Jer 43:12 7462
who is that s that will stand ... Jer 49:19 7462
who is that s that will stand ... Jer 50:44 7462
break in pieces with thee the s ... Jer 51:23 7462
scattered, because there is no s ... Eze 34:5 7462
the field, because there was no s ... Eze 34:8 7462
As a s seeketh out his flock in ... Eze 34:12 7462
And I will set up one s over them ... Eze 34:23 7462
feed them, and he shall be their s ... Eze 34:23 7462
and they all shall have one s ... Eze 37:24 7462
As the s taketh out of the mouth ... Amos 3:12 7462
troubled, because there was no s ... Zec 10:2 7462
the instruments of a foolish s ... Zec 11:15 7462
I will raise up a s in the land ... Zec 11:16 7462
Woe to the idol s that leaveth ... Zec 11:17 7473
Awake, O sword, against my s ... Zec 13:7 7462
smite the s, and the sheep shall ... Zec 13:7 7462
abroad, as sheep having no s ... Mt 9:36 *4166*
as a s divideth his sheep from ... Mt 25:32 *4166*
it is written, I will smite the s ... Mt 26:31 *4166*
they were as sheep not having a s ... Mk 6:34 *4166*
it is written, I will smite the s ... Mk 14:27 *4166*
by the door is the s of the sheep ... Jn 10:2 *4166*
I am the good s ... Jn 10:11 *4166*
the good s giveth his life for ... Jn 10:11 *4166*
that is an hireling, and not the s ... Jn 10:12 *4166*
I am the good s, and know my sheep .. Jn 10:14 *4166*
there shall be one fold, and one s ... Jn 10:16 *4166*
that great s of the sheep, ... Heb 13:20 *4166*
but are now returned unto the S ... 1Pet 2:25 *4166*
And when the chief S shall appear ... 1Pet 5:4 *750*

SHEPHERD'S
put them in a s bag which he had, ... 1Sa 17:40 7462
and is removed from me as a s tent ... Is 38:12 7473

SHEPHERDS
And the men are s, for their trade ... Gen 46:32
unto Pharaoh, Thy servants are s ... Gen 47:3
the s came and drove them away ... Ex 2:17 7462
us out of the hand of the s ... Ex 2:19 7462
now thy s which were with us, we ... 1Sa 25:7 7462
neither shall the s make their ... Is 13:20 7462
when a multitude of s is called ... Is 31:4 7462
they are s that cannot understand ... Is 56:11 7462
The s with their flocks shall ... Jer 6:3 7462
I will set up s over them which ... Jer 23:4 7462
Howl, ye s, and cry ... Jer 25:34 7462
the s shall have no way to flee, ... Jer 25:35 7462
A voice of the cry of the s ... Jer 25:36 7462
shall be an habitation of s ... Jer 33:12 7462
their s have caused them to go ... Jer 50:6 7462
prophesy against the s of Israel ... Eze 34:2 7462
saith the Lord GOD unto the s ... Eze 34:2 7462
Woe be to the s of Israel that do ... Eze 34:2 7462
should not the s feed the flocks ... Eze 34:2 7462
Therefore, ye s, hear the word of ... Eze 34:7 7462
neither did my s search for my ... Eze 34:8 7462
but the s fed themselves, and fed ... Eze 34:8 7462
Therefore, O ye s, hear the word ... Eze 34:9 7462
Behold, I am against the s ... Eze 34:10 7462
neither shall the s feed ... Eze 34:10 7462
habitations of the s shall mourn ... Amos 1:2 7462
we raise against him seven s ... Mic 5:5 7462
Thy s slumber, O king of Assyria ... Nah 3:18 7462
be dwellings and cottages for s ... Zeph 2:6 7462
anger was kindled against the s ... Zec 10:3 7462
a voice of the howling of the s ... Zec 11:3 7462
their own s pity them not ... Zec 11:5 7462
Three s also I cut off in one ... Zec 11:8 7462
country s abiding in the field ... Lk 2:8 *4166*
the s said one to another, Let us ... Lk 2:15 *4166*
which were told them by the s ... Lk 2:18 *4166*
the s returned, glorifying and ... Lk 2:20 *4166*

SHEPHERDS'
feed thy kids beside the s tents ... Song 1:8 7462

SHEPHI (*she'-fi*) See SHEPHO. *A son of Shobal.*
Alian, and Manahath, and Ebal, S ... 1Chr 1:40 8195

SHEPHO (*she'-fo*) See SHEPHI. *Same as Shephi.*
Alvan, and Manahath, and Ebal, S ... Gen 36:23 8195

SHEPHUPHAM See SHUPHAM.

SHEPHUPHAN (*shef'-u-fan*) See SHUPHAM, SHUPPIM. *A son of Bela.*
And Gera, and S, and Huram ... 1Chr 8:5 8197

SHERAH (*she'-rah*) *Daughter of Beriah.*
(And his daughter was S, who built ... 1Chr 7:24 7609

SHERD
a s to take fire from the hearth ... Is 30:14 2789

SHERDS
and thou shalt break the s thereof ... Eze 23:34 2789

SHEREBIAH (*sher-e-bi'-ah*)
1. A family of exiles.
and S, with his sons and his ... Ezr 8:18 8274
of the chief of the priests, S ... Ezr 8:24 8274
Also Jeshua, and Bani, and S ... Neh 8:7 8274
Kadmiel, Shebaniah, Bunni, S ... Neh 9:4 8274
and Kadmiel, Bani, Hashabniah, S ... Neh 9:5 8274
2. A Levite who renewed the covenant.
Zaccur, S, Shebaniah, ... Neh 10:12 8274
Jeshua, Binnui, Kadmiel, S ... Neh 12:8 8274
Hashabiah, S, and Jeshua the son ... Neh 12:24 8274

SHERESH (*she'-resh*) *Son of Machir.*
and the name of his brother was S ... 1Chr 7:16 8329

SHEREZER (*she-re'-zur*) See SHAREZER. *A messenger in Zechariah's time.*
had sent unto the house of God S ... Zec 7:2 8272

SHERIFFS
the counsellors, the s, and all ... Dan 3:2 8614
the counsellors, the s, and all ... Dan 3:3 8614

SHESHACH (*she'-shak*) See BABYLON. *Another name for Babylon.*
the king of S shall drink after ... Jer 25:26 8347
How is S taken ... Jer 51:41 8347

SHESHAI (*she'-shahee*) *A son of Anak.*
where Ahiman, S, and Talmai, the ... Num 13:22 8344
thence the three sons of Anak, S ... Josh 15:14 8344
and they slew S, and Ahiman, and ... Judg 1:10 8344

SHESHAK See SHESHACH.

SHESHAN (*she'-shan*) *A descendant of Jerahmeel.*
S. And the children of S ... 1Chr 2:31 8348
Now S had no sons, but daughters ... 1Chr 2:34 8348
S had a servant, an Egyptian, ... 1Chr 2:34 8348
S gave his daughter to Jarha his ... 1Chr 2:35 8348

SHESHBAZZAR (*shesh-baz'-zur*) See ZERUBBABEL. *Same as Zerubbabel.*
and numbered them unto S, the ... Ezr 1:8 8339
All these did S bring up with ... Ezr 1:11 8339
unto one, whose name was S ... Ezr 5:14 8339
Then came the same S, and laid the ... Ezr 5:16 8339

SHETH (*sheth*) See SETH.
1. A Moabite chief.
and destroy all the children of S ... Num 24:17 8352
2. Same as Seth.
Adam, S, Enosh, ... 1Chr 1:1 8352

SHETHAR (*she'-thar*) *A prince of Media and Persia.*
the next unto him was Carshena, S ... Est 1:14 8369

SHETHAR-BOZENAI See SHETHAR-BOZNAI.

SHETHAR-BOZNAI (*she''-thar-boz'-nahee*) *A Persian official.*
on this side the river, and S ... Ezr 5:3 8370
on this side the river, and S ... Ezr 5:6 8370
governor beyond the river, S ... Ezr 6:6 8370
on this side the river, S ... Ezr 6:13 8370

SHETHER BAZNAI See SHETHAR BOZNAI.

SHEVA (*she'-vah*) See SHAVSHA.
1. David's scribe.
And S was scribe ... 2Sa 20:25 7724
2. Son of Maachah.
S the father of Machbenah, and the ... 1Chr 2:49 7724

SHEW
unto a land that I will s thee ... Gen 12:1 7200
which thou shalt s unto me ... Gen 20:13 6213
s kindness unto my master Abraham ... Gen 24:12 6213
s kindness, I pray thee, unto me, ... Gen 40:14 6213
s Pharaoh, and say unto him, My ... Gen 46:31 5046
you, saying, S a miracle for you ... Ex 7:9 5414
for to s in thee my power ... Ex 9:16 7200
that I might s these my signs ... Ex 10:1 7896
thou shalt s thy son in that day, ... Ex 13:8 5046
which he will s to you to day ... Ex 14:13 6213
shalt s them the way wherein they ... Ex 18:20 3045
According to all that I s thee ... Ex 25:9 7200
s me now thy way, that I may know ... Ex 33:13 3045
I beseech thee, s me thy glory ... Ex 33:18 7200
s mercy on whom I will s mercy ... Ex 33:19
the LORD will s who are his ... Num 16:5 3045
to s you by what way ye should go ... Deut 1:33 7200
thou hast begun to s thy servant ... Deut 3:24 7200
to s you the word of the LORD ... Deut 5:5 5046
with them, nor s mercy unto them ... Deut 7:2
s thee mercy, and have compassion ... Deut 13:17 5414
they shall s thee the sentence of ... Deut 17:9 5046
LORD shall choose shall s thee ... Deut 17:10 5046
sentence which they shall s thee ... Deut 17:11 5046
nor s favour to the young ... Deut 28:50
ask thy father, and he will s thee ... Deut 32:7 5046
that ye will also s kindness unto ... Josh 2:12 6213
that he would not s them the land ... Josh 5:6 7200
S us, we pray thee, the entrance ... Judg 1:24 7200
the city, and we will s thee mercy ... Judg 1:24 6213
I will s thee the man whom thou ... Judg 4:22 7200
then s me a sign that thou ... Judg 6:17 6213
Samuel feared to s Eli the vision ... 1Sa 3:15 5046
s them the manner of the king ... 1Sa 8:9 5046
peradventure he can s us our way ... 1Sa 9:6 5046
that I may s thee the word of God ... 1Sa 9:27 8085
s thee what thou shalt do ... 1Sa 10:8 3045
to us, and we will s you a thing ... 1Sa 14:12 3045
I will s thee what thou shalt do ... 1Sa 16:3 3045
small, but that he will s it me ... 1Sa 20:2 1540
send not unto thee, and s it thee ... 1Sa 20:12 1540
thee evil, then I will s it thee ... 1Sa 20:13 1540
s me the kindness of the LORD ... 1Sa 20:14 6213
he fled, and did not s it to me ... 1Sa 22:17 1540
young men, and they will s thee ... 1Sa 25:8 5046
And now the LORD s kindness ... 2Sa 2:6 6213
which against Judah do s kindness ... 2Sa 3:8 6213
that I may s him kindness for ... 2Sa 9:1 6213
that I may s the kindness of God ... 2Sa 9:3 6213
for I will surely s thee kindness ... 2Sa 9:7 6213
I will s kindness unto Hanun the ... 2Sa 10:2 6213
s me both it, and his habitation ... 2Sa 15:25 7200
thou wilt s thyself merciful ... 2Sa 22:26
man thou wilt s thyself upright ... 2Sa 22:26
the pure thou wilt s thyself pure ... 2Sa 22:27
thou wilt s thyself unsavoury ... 2Sa 22:27
If he will s himself a worthy man ... 1Kin 1:52
therefore, and s thyself a man ... 1Kin 2:2
But s kindness unto the sons of ... 1Kin 2:7 6213
saying, Go, s thyself unto Ahab ... 1Kin 18:1 7200
Elijah went to s himself unto ... 1Kin 18:2 7200
I will surely s myself unto him ... 1Kin 18:15 7200
Will ye not s me which of us is ... 2Kin 6:11 5046
I will now s you what the Syrians ... 2Kin 7:12 5046
s forth from day to day his ... 1Chr 16:23 1319
I will s kindness unto Hanun the ... 1Chr 19:2 6213
to s himself strong in the behalf ... 2Chr 16:9
but they could not s their ... Ezr 2:59 5046
but they could not s their ... Neh 7:61 5046
to s them light, and the way ... Neh 9:19
to s the people and the princes ... Est 1:11 7200
her that she should not s it ... Est 2:10 5046
to s it unto Esther, and to ... Est 4:8 7200
s me wherefore thou contendest ... Job 10:2 3045
that he would s thee the secrets ... Job 11:6 5046
I will s thee, hear me ... Job 15:17 2331
durst not s you mine opinion ... Job 32:6 2331
I also will s mine opinion ... Job 32:10 2331
I also will s mine opinion ... Job 32:17 2331
to s unto man his uprightness ... Job 33:23 5046
I will s thee that I have yet to ... Job 36:2 2331
that say, Who will s us any good ... Ps 4:6 7200
I will s forth all thy marvellous ... Ps 9:1 5608
That I may s forth all thy praise ... Ps 9:14 5608
Thou wilt s me the path of life ... Ps 16:11 3045
S thy marvellous lovingkindness, ... Ps 17:7
thou wilt s thyself merciful ... Ps 18:25
man thou wilt s thyself upright ... Ps 18:25
the pure thou wilt s thyself pure ... Ps 18:26
thou wilt s thyself froward ... Ps 18:26
S me thy ways, O LORD ... Ps 25:4 3045
he will s them his covenant ... Ps 25:14 3045
every man walketh in a vain s ... Ps 39:6 6754
will I s the salvation of God ... Ps 50:23 7200
my mouth shall s forth thy praise ... Ps 51:15 5046
My mouth shall s forth thy ... Ps 71:15 5608
we will s forth thy praise to all ... Ps 79:13 5608
S us thy mercy, O LORD, and grant ... Ps 85:7 7200
S me a token for good ... Ps 86:17 6213
Wilt thou s wonders to the dead ... Ps 88:10 6213
him, and s him my salvation ... Ps 91:16 7200
To s forth thy lovingkindness in ... Ps 92:2 5046
To s that the LORD is upright ... Ps 92:15 5046
vengeance belongeth, s thyself ... Ps 94:1 3313
s forth his salvation from day to ... Ps 96:2 1319
who can s forth all his praise ... Ps 106:2 8085
that he remembered not to s mercy ... Ps 109:16 6213
friends must s himself friendly ... Prov 18:24
The s of their countenance doth ... Is 3:9 1971
formed them will s them no favour ... Is 27:11
shall s the lighting down of his ... Is 30:30 7200
forth, and s us what shall happen ... Is 41:22 5046
let them s the former things, ... Is 41:22 5046
S the things that are to come ... Is 41:23 5046
this, and s us former things ... Is 43:9 8085
they shall s forth my praise ... Is 43:21 5608
shall come, let them s unto them ... Is 44:7 5046
this, and s yourselves men ... Is 46:8
thou didst s them no mercy ... Is 47:6 7760
are in darkness, S yourselves ... Is 49:9 1540
s my people their transgression, ... Is 58:1 5046
they shall s forth the praises of ... Is 60:6 1319
when thou shalt s this people all ... Jer 16:10 5046
where I will not s you favour ... Jer 16:13 5414
I will s them the back, and not ... Jer 18:17 7200
s thee great and mighty things, ... Jer 33:3 5046
That the LORD thy God may s us ... Jer 42:3 5046
I will s mercies unto you, that ... Jer 42:12 5414
are cruel, and will not s mercy ... Jer 50:42
to s the king of Babylon that his ... Jer 51:31 5046
yea, thou shalt s her all her ... Eze 22:2 3045
with their mouth they s much love ... Eze 33:31 6213
Wilt thou not s us what thou ... Eze 37:18 5046
upon all that I shall s thee ... Eze 40:4 7200
for to the intent that I might s ... Eze 40:4 7200
s the house to the house of ... Eze 43:10 5046
s them the form of the house, and ... Eze 43:11 3045
for to s the king his dreams ... Dan 2:2 5046
we will s the interpretation ... Dan 2:4 2324
But if ye s the dream, and the ... Dan 2:6 2324
therefore s me the dream, and the ... Dan 2:6 2324
we will s the interpretation of ... Dan 2:7 2324
I shall know that ye can s me the ... Dan 2:9 2324
that can s the king's matter ... Dan 2:10 2324
that can s it before the king ... Dan 2:11 2324
that he would s the king the ... Dan 2:16 2324
I will s unto the king the ... Dan 2:24 2324
the soothsayers, s unto the king ... Dan 2:27 2324
I thought it good to s the signs ... Dan 4:2 2324
s me the interpretation thereof, ... Dan 5:7 2324
he will s the interpretation ... Dan 5:12 2324
but they could not s the ... Dan 5:15 2324
forth, and I am come to s thee ... Dan 9:23 5046
But I will s thee that which is ... Dan 10:21 5046
now will I s thee the truth ... Dan 11:2 5046
I will s wonders in the heavens ... Joel 2:30 5414
I s unto him marvellous things ... Mic 7:15 7200
face, and I will s the nations thy ... Nah 3:5 7200
Why dost thou s me iniquity ... Hab 1:3 7200
I will s thee what these be ... Zec 1:9 7200
s mercy and compassions every man ... Zec 7:9 6213
s thyself to the priest, and offer ... Mt 8:4 *1166*
s John again those things which ... Mt 11:4 *518*
he shall s judgment to the ... Mt 12:18 *518*
do s forth themselves in him ... Mt 14:2 *1754*
would s them a sign from heaven ... Mt 16:1 *1925*
Jesus to s unto his disciples ... Mt 16:21 *1166*
S me the tribute money ... Mt 22:19 *1925*
disciples came to him for to s ... Mt 24:1 *1925*
shall s great signs and wonders ... Mt 24:24 *1325*

s thyself to the priest, and offer Mk 1:44 1166
do s forth themselves in him Mk 6:14 1754
shall rise, and shall s signs Mk 13:22 1325
he will s you a large upper room Mk 14:15 1166
to s thee these glad tidings Lk 1:19 2097
s thyself to the priest, and offer Lk 5:14 1166
I will s you to whom he is like Lk 6:47 5263
s how great things God hath done Lk 8:39 1334
Go s yourselves unto the priests Lk 17:14 1925
S me a penny Lk 20:24 1925
for a s make long prayers Lk 20:47 4392
he shall s you a large upper room Lk 22:12 1166
he will s him greater works than Jn 5:20 1166
things, s thyself to the world Jn 7:4 5319
where he were, he should s it Jn 11:57 3377
s us the Father, and it sufficeth Jn 14:8 1166
sayest thou then, S us the Father Jn 14:9 1166
he will s you things to come Jn 16:13 312
of mine, and shall s it unto you Jn 16:14 312
of mine, and shall s it unto you Jn 16:15 312
but I shall s you plainly of the Jn 16:25 312
s whether of these two thou hast Acts 1:24 322
I will s wonders in heaven above Acts 2:19 1325
the land which I shall s thee Acts 7:3 1166
For I will s him how great things Acts 9:16 5263
Go s these things unto James, and Acts 12:17 518
which s unto us the way of Acts 16:17 2605
willing to s the Jews a pleasure, Acts 24:27 2698
should s light unto the people, Acts 26:23 2605
Which s the work of the law Rom 2:15 1731
that I might s my power in thee, Rom 9:17 1731
if God, willing to s his wrath Rom 9:22 1731
ye do s the Lord's death till he 1Cor 11:26 2605
yet s I unto you a more excellent 1Cor 12:31 1166
Behold, I s you a mystery 1Cor 15:51 3004
Wherefore s ye to them, and before 2Cor 8:24 1731
to make a fair s in the flesh Gal 6:12 2146
s the exceeding riches of his Eph 2:7 1731
he made a s of them openly, Col 2:15 1165
a s of wisdom in will worship Col 2:23 3056
For they themselves s of us what 1Th 1:9 518
might s forth all longsuffering 1Ti 1:16 1731
learn first to s piety at home 1Ti 5:4 2151
Which in his times he shall s 1Ti 6:15 1166
Study to s thyself approved unto 2Ti 2:15 3936
s the same diligence to the full Heb 6:11 1731
willing more abundantly to s unto Heb 6:17 1925
s me thy faith without thy works, Jas 2:18 1166
I will s thee my faith by my Jas 2:18 1166
let him s out of a good Jas 3:13 1166
that ye should s forth the 1Pet 2:9 1804
s unto you that eternal life, 1Jn 1:2 518
to s unto his servants things Rev 1:1 1166
I will s thee things which must Rev 4:1 1166
I will s unto thee the judgment Rev 17:1 1166
I will s thee the bride, the Rev 21:9 1166
to s unto his servants the things Rev 22:6 1166

SHEWBREAD

upon the table s before me alway Ex 25:30
and all his vessels, and the s Ex 35:13
all the vessels thereof, and the s Ex 39:36
upon the table of s they shall Num 4:7 6440
was no bread there but the s 1Sa 21:6
of gold, whereupon the s was 1Kin 7:48
the Kohathites, were over the s 1Chr 9:32
Both for the s, and for the fine 1Chr 23:29
he gave gold for the tables of s 1Chr 28:16 4635
incense, and for the continual s 2Chr 2:4 4635
the tables whereon the s was set 2Chr 4:19
the s also set they in order upon 2Chr 13:11
the s table, with all the vessels 2Chr 29:18 4635
For the s, and for the continual Neh 10:33
house of God, and did eat the s Mt 12:4
the high priest, and did eat the s Mk 2:26
of God, and did take and eat the s Lk 6:4
and the table, and the s Heb 9:2

SHEWED

which thou hast s unto me in Gen 19:19 6213
hast s kindness unto my master Gen 24:14 6213
which thou hast s unto thy Gen 32:10 6213
s him mercy, and gave him favour Gen 39:21 5186
God hath s Pharaoh what he is Gen 41:25 5046
as God hath s thee all this Gen 41:39 3045
God hath s me also thy seed Gen 48:11 7200
the LORD s him a tree, which when Ex 15:25 3384
which was s thee in the mount Ex 25:40 7200
which was s thee in the mount Ex 26:30 7200
as it was s thee in the mount, so Ex 27:8 7200
reddish, and it be s to the priest Lev 13:19 7200
shall be s unto the priest Lev 13:49 7200
mind of the LORD might be s them Lev 24:12 6567
which the LORD had s Moses Num 8:4 7200
s them the fruit of the land Num 13:26 7200
signs which I have s among them Num 14:11 6213
Unto thee it was s, that thou Deut 4:35 7200
upon earth he s thee his great Deut 4:36 7200
LORD our God hath s us his glory Deut 5:24 7200
And the LORD s signs and wonders, Deut 6:22 5414
the LORD s him all the land of Deut 34:1 7200
s in the sight of all Israel Deut 34:12 6213
LORD, since I have s you kindness Josh 2:12 6213
when he s them the entrance into Judg 1:25 7200
they s Sisera that Barak the son Judg 4:12 5046
Neither s they kindness to the Judg 8:35 6213
which he had s unto Israel Judg 8:35 6213
s her husband, and said unto him, Judg 13:10 5046
he have s us all these things Judg 13:23 7200
for he hath s me all his heart Judg 16:18 5046
unto her, It hath fully been s me Ruth 2:11 5046
she s her mother in law with whom Ruth 2:19 5046
for thou hast s more kindness in Ruth 3:10 3190
s it to the men of Jabesh 1Sa 11:9 5046
for ye s kindness to all the 1Sa 15:6 6213
Jonathan s him all those things 1Sa 19:7 5046
Abiathar s David that Saul had 1Sa 22:21 5046
thou hast s this day how that 1Sa 24:18 5046
that ye have s this kindness unto 2Sa 2:5 6213
as his father s kindness unto me 2Sa 10:2 6213
s David all that Joab had sent 2Sa 11:22 5046
thou hast not s it unto thy 1Kin 1:27 3045
Thou hast s unto thy servant 1Kin 3:6 6213
he did, and his might that he s 1Kin 16:27 6213
and his might that he s, and how 1Kin 22:45 6213
And he s him the place 2Kin 6:6 7200
howbeit the LORD hath s me that 2Kin 8:10 7200
The LORD hath s me that thou 2Kin 8:13 7200
LORD, and s them the king's son 2Kin 11:4 7200
s them all the house of his 2Kin 20:13 7200
that Hezekiah s them not 2Kin 20:13 7200
treasures that I have not s them 2Kin 20:15 7200
And Shaphan the scribe s the king 2Kin 22:10 7200
his father s kindness to me 1Chr 19:2 6213
Thou hast s great mercy unto 2Chr 1:8 6213
that the LORD had s unto David 2Chr 7:10 6213
hath been s from the LORD our God Ezr 9:8
When he s the riches of his Est 1:4 7200
Esther had not s her people nor Est 2:10 5046
Esther had not yet s her kindred Est 2:20 5046
for they had s him the people of Est 3:6 5046
pity should be s from his friend Job 6:14
for he hath s me his marvellous Ps 31:21
Thou hast s thy people hard Ps 60:3
until I have s thy strength unto Ps 71:18 5046
Thou, which hast s me great Ps 71:20 7200
and his wonders that he had s them Ps 78:11 7200
s in the sight of the heathen Ps 98:2 1540
They s his signs among them, and Ps 105:27 7760
He hath s his people the power of Ps 111:6 5046
the LORD, which hath s us light Ps 118:27
I s before him my trouble Ps 142:2 5046
his wickedness shall be s before Prov 26:26 1540
wherein I have s myself wise Eccl 2:19
Let favour be s to the wicked Is 26:10
s them the house of his precious Is 39:2 7200
that Hezekiah s them not Is 39:2 7200
treasures that I have not s them Is 39:4 7200
s to him the way of understanding Is 40:14 3045
and have saved, and I have s Is 43:12 8085
out of my mouth, and I s them Is 48:3 8085
it came to pass I s it thee Is 48:5 8085
I have s thee new things from Is 48:6 8085
The LORD s me, and, behold, two Jer 24:1 7200
the word that the LORD hath s me Jer 38:21 7200
the things that the LORD had s me Eze 11:25 7200
s them my judgments, which if a Eze 20:11 3045
neither have they s difference Eze 22:26 3045
Thus hath the Lord GOD s unto me Amos 7:1 7200
Thus hath the Lord GOD s unto me Amos 7:4 7200
Thus he s me Amos 7:7 7200
Thus hath the Lord GOD s unto me Amos 8:1 7200
He hath s thee, O man, what is Mic 6:8 5046
the LORD s me four carpenters Zec 1:20 7200
he s me Joshua the high priest Zec 3:1 7200
s unto the chief priests all the Mt 28:11 518
He hath s strength with his arm Lk 1:51 4160
Lord had s great mercy upon her Lk 1:58 3170
s unto him all the kingdoms of Lk 4:5 1166
the disciples of John s him of Lk 7:18 518
he said, He that s mercy on him Lk 10:37 4160
came, and s his lord these things Lk 14:21 518
even Moses s at the bush, when he Lk 20:37 3377
he s them his hands and his feet Lk 24:40 1925
works have I s you from my Father Jn 10:32 1166
he s unto them his hands and his Jn 20:20 1166
After these things Jesus s Jn 21:1 5319
and on this wise s he himself Jn 21:1 5319
Jesus s himself to his disciples Jn 21:14 5319
To whom also he s himself alive Acts 1:3 3936
which God before had s by the Acts 3:18 4293
this miracle of healing was s Acts 4:22 1096
the next day he s himself unto Acts 7:26 3700
out, after that he had s wonders Acts 7:36 4160
they have slain them which s Acts 7:52 4293
but God hath s me that I should Acts 10:28 1166
up the third day, and s him openly Acts 10:40
he s us how he had seen an angel Acts 11:13 518
and confessed, and s their deeds Acts 19:18 312
unto you, but have s you, and have Acts 20:20 312
I have s you all things, how that Acts 20:35 5268
thou hast s these things to me Acts 23:22 1718
But s first unto them of Damascus Acts 26:20 518
the barbarous people s us no Acts 28:2 3930
came s or spake any harm of thee Acts 28:21 518
for God hath s it unto them Rom 1:19 5319
eat not for his sake that s it 1Cor 10:28 3377
which ye have s toward his name, Heb 6:10 1731
pattern s to thee in the mount Heb 8:5 1166
mercy, that hath s no mercy Jas 2:13 4160
our Lord Jesus Christ hath s me 2Pet 1:14 1213
s me that great city, the holy Rev 21:10 1166
he s me a pure river of water of Rev 22:1 1166
the angel which s me these things Rev 22:8 1166

SHEWEDST

s signs and wonders upon Pharaoh, Neh 9:10 5414
then thou s me their doings Jer 11:18 7200

SHEWEST

s mercy unto thy servants, that 2Chr 6:14
again thou s thyself marvellous Job 10:16
Thou s lovingkindness unto Jer 32:18 6213
What sign s thou unto us, seeing Jn 2:18 1166
unto him, What sign s thou then Jn 6:30 4160

SHEWETH

is about to do he s unto Pharaoh Gen 41:28 7200
whatsoever he s me I will tell Num 23:3 7200
there is none that s me that my 1Sa 22:8
or s unto me that my son hath 1Sa 22:8
s mercy to his anointed, unto 2Sa 22:51 6213
Then he s them their work, and Job 36:9 5046
The noise thereof s concerning it Job 36:33 5046
s mercy to his anointed, to David Ps 18:50 6213
and the firmament s his handywork Ps 19:1 5046
and night unto night s knowledge Ps 19:2 2331
but the righteous s mercy Ps 37:21
A good man s favour, and lendeth Ps 112:5
He s his word unto Jacob, his Ps 147:19 5046
truth s forth righteousness Prov 12:17 5046
and the tender grass s itself Prov 27:25 7200
yea, there is none that s Is 41:26 5046
s him all the kingdoms of the Mt 4:8 1166
s him all things that himself Jn 5:20 1166
runneth, but of God that s mercy Rom 9:16 1658
he that s mercy, with Rom 12:8 1658

SHEWING

s mercy unto thousands of them Ex 20:6 6213
s mercy unto thousands of them Deut 5:10 6213
s to the generation to come the Ps 78:4 5608
s himself through the lattice Song 2:9 6692
iniquities by s mercy to the poor Dan 4:27
and s of hard sentences, and Dan 5:12 263
till the day of his s unto Israel Lk 1:80 323
s the glad tidings of the kingdom Lk 8:1
s the coats and garments which Acts 9:39 1925
s by the scriptures that Jesus Acts 18:28 1925
of God, s himself that he is God 2Th 2:4 584
In all things s thyself a pattern Titus 2:7 3930
in doctrine s uncorruptness, Titus 2:7
but s all good fidelity Titus 2:10 1731
s all meekness unto all men Titus 3:2 1731

SHIBAH See SHEBAH.

SHIBBOLETH (*shib'-bo-leth*) See SIBBOLETH. *Password that distinguished Gileadites from Ephraimites.*

said they unto him, Say now S Judg 12:6 7641

SHIBMAH (*shib'-mah*) See SHEBAM, SIBMAH. *A city in Reuben.*

(their names being changed,) and S Num 32:38 7643

SHICRON (*shi'-cron*) *A city in Judah.*

and the border was drawn to S Josh 15:11 7942

SHIELD

I am thy s, and thy exceeding Gen 15:1 4043
the s of thy help, and who is the Deut 33:29 4043
was there a s or spear seen among Judg 5:8 4043
one bearing a s went before him 1Sa 17:7 6793
that bare the s went before him 1Sa 17:41 6793
and with a spear, and with a s 1Sa 17:45 3591
for there the s of the mighty is 2Sa 1:21 4043
the s of Saul, as though he had 2Sa 1:21 4043
he is my s, and the horn of my 2Sa 22:3 4043
given me the s of thy salvation 2Sa 22:36 4043
three pound of gold went to one s 1Kin 10:17 4043
there, nor come before it with s 2Kin 19:32 4043
the battle, that could handle s 1Chr 12:8 6793
The children of Judah that bare s 1Chr 12:24 6793
captains, and with them with s 1Chr 12:34 6793
shekels of gold went to one s 2Chr 9:16 4043
bow and s two hundred thousand 2Chr 17:17 4043
war, that could handle spear and s 2Chr 25:5 6793
the glittering spear and the s Job 39:23 3591
But thou, O LORD, art a s for me Ps 3:3 4043
wilt thou compass him as with a s Ps 5:12 6793
given me the s of thy salvation Ps 18:35 4043
The LORD is my strength and my s Ps 28:7 4043
he is our help and our s Ps 33:20 4043
Take hold of s and buckler, and Ps 35:2 4043
and bring them down, O Lord our s Ps 59:11 4043
he the arrows of the bow, the s Ps 76:3 4043
Behold, O God our s, and look upon Ps 84:9 4043
For the LORD God is a sun and s Ps 84:11 4043
his truth shall be thy s and Ps 91:4 6793
he is their help and their s Ps 115:9 4043
he is their help and their s Ps 115:10 4043
he is their help and their s Ps 115:11 4043
Thou art my hiding place and my s Ps 119:114 4043
my s, and he in whom I trust Ps 144:2 4043
he is a s unto them that put Prov 30:5 4043
ye princes, and anoint the s Is 21:5 4043
horsemen, and Kir uncovered the s Is 22:6 4043
Order ye the buckler and s Jer 46:3 6793
and the Libyans, that handle the s Jer 46:9 4043
set against thee buckler and s Eze 23:24 4043
they hanged the s and helmet in Eze 27:10 4043
all of them with s and helmet Eze 38:5 4043
The s of his mighty men is made Nah 2:3 4043
Above all, taking the s of faith Eph 6:16 2375

SHIELDS

David took the s of gold that 2Sa 8:7 7982
three hundred s of beaten gold 1Kin 10:17 4043
he took away all the s of gold 1Kin 14:26 4043
made in their stead brasen s 1Kin 14:27 4043
give king David's spears and s 2Kin 11:10 7982
David took the s of gold that 1Chr 18:7 7982
three hundred s made he of beaten 2Chr 9:16 4043
And in every several city he put s 2Chr 11:12 6793
he carried away also the s of 2Chr 12:9 4043
king Rehoboam made s of brass 2Chr 12:10 4043
and out of Benjamin, that bare s 2Chr 14:8 4043
spears, and bucklers, and s 2Chr 23:9 7982
them throughout all the host s 2Chr 26:14 4043
and made darts and s in abundance 2Chr 32:5 4043
stones, and for spices, and for s 2Chr 32:27 4043
them held both the spears, the s Neh 4:16 4043
for the s of the earth belong Ps 47:9 4043
bucklers, all s of mighty men Song 4:4 7982
there, nor come before it with s Is 37:33 4043
gather the s Jer 51:11 7982

they hanged their *s* upon thy Eze 27:11 7982
great company with bucklers and *s* Eze 38:4 4043
and burn the weapons, both the *s* Eze 39:9 4043

SHIGGAION (*shig-gah'-yon*) See SHIGIONOTH.
A musical notation.
S of David, which he sang unto Ps 7:t 7692

SHIGIONOTH (*shig-i'-o-noth*) See SHIGGAION.
A musical notation.
of Habakkuk the prophet upon *S* Hab 3:1 7692

SHIHON (*shi'-hon*) *A city in Issachar.*
And Haphraim, and *S*, and Anaharath, Josh 19:19 7866

SHIHOR (*shi'-hor*) See SHIHOR-LIBNATH. *Same as Sihor.*
from *S* of Egypt even unto the 1Chr 13:5 7883

SHIHOR-LIBNATH (*shi''-hor-lib'-nath*) *A small river in Asher.*
to Carmel westward, and to *S* Josh 19:26 7884

SHIKKERON See SHICRON.

SHILHI (*shil'-hi*) *Father of Azubah.*
name was Azubah the daughter of *S* 1Kin 22:42 7977
name was Azubah the daughter of *S* 2Chr 20:31 7977

SHILHIM (*shil'-him*) See SHAARAIM, SHARUHEN.
A city in Judah.
And Lebaoth, and *S*, and Ain, and Josh 15:32 7978

SHILLEM (*shil'-lem*) See SHALLUM, SHILLEMITES. *A son of Naphtali.*
Jahzeel, and Guni, and Jezer, and *S* Gen 46:24 8006
of *S*, the family of the Num 26:49 8006

SHILLEMITES (*shil'-lem-ites*) *Descendants of Shillem.*
of Shillem, the family of the *S* Num 26:49 8016

SHILOAH (*shi-lo'-ah*) See SILOAH, SILOAM. *A fountain in Jerusalem.*
the waters of *S* that go softly Is 8:6 7975

SHILOH (*shi'-loh*) See SHILONITE.
1. Symbolic name for the Ruler from Judah.
between his feet, until *S* come Gen 49:10 7886
2. A city in Ephraim.
of Israel assembled together at *S* Josh 18:1 7887
lots for you before the LORD in *S* Josh 18:8 7887
again to Joshua to the host at *S* Josh 18:9 7887
for them in *S* before the LORD Josh 18:10 7887
by lot in *S* before the LORD Josh 19:51 7887
them at *S* in the land of Canaan Josh 21:2 7887
the children of Israel out of *S* Josh 22:9 7887
gathered themselves together at *S* Josh 22:12 7887
that the house of God was in *S* Judg 18:31 7887
brought them unto the camp to *S* Judg 21:12 7887
S yearly in a place which is on Judg 21:19 7887
if the daughters of *S* come out to Judg 21:21 7887
his wife of the daughters of *S* Judg 21:21 7887
unto the LORD of hosts in *S* 1Sa 1:3 7887
rose up after they had eaten in *S* 1Sa 1:9 7887
unto the house of the LORD in *S* 1Sa 1:24 7887
So they did in *S* unto all the 1Sa 2:14 7887
And the LORD appeared again in *S* 1Sa 3:21 7887
in *S* by the word of the LORD 1Sa 3:21 7887
of the LORD out of *S* unto us 1Sa 4:3 7887
So the people sent to *S*, that 1Sa 4:4 7887
came to *S* the same day with his 1Sa 4:12 7887
of Eli, the LORD's priest in *S* 1Sa 14:3 7887
concerning the house of Eli in *S* 1Kin 2:27 7887
and get thee to *S* 1Kin 14:2 7887
did so, and arose, and went to *S* 1Kin 14:4 7887
he forsook the tabernacle of *S* Ps 78:60 7887
now unto my place which was in *S* Jer 7:12 7887
your fathers, as I have done to *S* Jer 7:14 7887
will I make this house like *S* Jer 26:6 7887
This house shall be like *S* Jer 26:9 7887
came certain from Shechem, from *S* Jer 41:5 7887

SHILONI (*shi-lo'-ni*) See SHILONITE. *Father of Zechariah.*
son of Zechariah, the son of *S* Neh 11:5 8023

SHILONITE (*shi'-lon-ite*) See SHILONI, SHILONITES. *An inhabitant of Shiloh.*
Ahijah the *S* found him in the way 1Kin 11:29 7888
the LORD spake by Ahijah the *S* 1Kin 12:15 7888
spake by his servant Ahijah the *S* 1Kin 15:29 7888
in the prophecy of Ahijah the *S* 2Chr 9:29 7888
S to Jeroboam the son of Nebat 2Chr 10:15 7888

SHILONITES (*shi'-lon-ites*)
And of the *S* 1Chr 9:5 7888

SHILSHAH (*shil'-shah*) *Son of Zophah.*
Bezer, and Hod, and Shamma, and *S* 1Chr 7:37 8030

SHIMEA (*shim'-e-ah*) See SHAMMAH, SHAMMUA, SHAMMUAH, SHIMEAH, SHIMEATHITES, SHIMMA.
1. David's brother.
Jonathan the son of *S* David's 1Chr 20:7 8092
2. A son of David.
S, and Shobab, and Nathan, and 1Chr 3:5 8092
3. Father of Haggiah.
S his son, Haggiah his son, 1Chr 6:30 8092
4. Father of Berachiah.
son of Berachiah, the son of *S* 1Chr 6:39 8092

SHIMEAH (*shim'-e-ah*) See SHIMEA, SHIMEAM.
1. Same as Shimea 1.
the son of *S* David's brother 2Sa 13:3 8093
the son of *S* David's brother, 2Sa 13:32 8093
Jonathan the son of *S* the brother 2Sa 21:21 8096
2. A relative of King Saul.
And Mikloth begat *S* 1Chr 8:32 8039

SHIMEAM (*shim'-e-am*) See SHIMEA. *Son of Mikloth.*
And Mikloth begat *S* 1Chr 9:38 8043

SHIMEATH (*shim'-e-ath*) *Mother of Jozachar.*
For Jozachar the son of *S* 2Kin 12:21 8100
Zabad the son of *S* an Ammonitess 2Chr 24:26 8100

SHIMEATHITES (*shim'-e-ath-ites*) *A family of scribes.*
the Tirathites, the *S*, and 1Chr 2:55 8101

SHIMEI (*shim'-e-i*) See SHEMAIAH, SHIMHI, SHIMI, SHIMITES.
1. A son of Gershon.
families; Libni, and *S* Num 3:18 8096
Gershom; Libni, and *S* 1Chr 6:17 8096
the son of Zimmah, the son of *S* 1Chr 6:42 8096
Gershonites were, Laadan, and *S* 1Chr 23:7 8096
And the sons of *S* were, Jahath, 1Chr 23:10 8096
These four were the sons of *S* 1Chr 23:10 8096
2. A son of Gera.
house of Saul, whose name was *S* 2Sa 16:5 8096
thus said *S* when he cursed, Come 2Sa 16:7 8096
S went along on the hill's side 2Sa 16:13 8096
S the son of Gera, a Benjamite, 2Sa 19:16 8096
S the son of Gera fell down 2Sa 19:18 8096
Shall not *S* be put to death for 2Sa 19:21 8096
Therefore the king said unto *S* 2Sa 19:23 8096
hast with thee *S* the son of Gera 1Kin 2:8 8096
And the king sent and called for *S* 1Kin 2:36 8096
S said unto the king, The saying 1Kin 2:38 8096
S dwelt in Jerusalem many days 1Kin 2:38 8096
of *S* ran away unto Achish son of 1Kin 2:39 8096
And they told *S*, saying, Behold, 1Kin 2:39 8096
S arose, and saddled his ass, and 1Kin 2:40 8096
S went, and brought his servants 1Kin 2:40 8096
it was told Solomon that *S* had 1Kin 2:41 8096
And the king sent and called for *S* 1Kin 2:42 8096
The king said moreover to *S* 1Kin 2:44 8096
3. An officer of David.
and Nathan the prophet, and *S* 1Kin 1:8 8096
4. An officer of Solomon.
S the son of Elah, in Benjamin 1Kin 4:18 8096
5. A descendant of King Jehoiakim.
of Pedaiah were, Zerubbabel, and *S* 1Chr 3:19 8096
6. Son of Zacchur.
son, Zacchur his son, *S* his son 1Chr 4:26 8096
S had sixteen sons and six 1Chr 4:27 8096
7. Son of Gog.
his son, Gog his son, *S* his son, 1Chr 5:4 8096
8. Son of Libni.
his son, *S* his son, Uzza his son, 1Chr 6:29 8096
9. A Levite of the Laadan family.
The sons of *S* 1Chr 23:9 8096
10. A sanctuary servant.
The tenth to *S*, he, his sons, and 1Chr 25:17 8096
11. A vineyard keeper.
the vineyards was *S* the Ramathite 1Chr 27:27 8096
12. A Levite who cleansed the Temple.
Jehiel, and *S* 2Chr 29:14 8096
13. A Temple servant in Hezekiah's time.
S his brother was the next 2Chr 31:12 8096
S his brother, at the commandment 2Chr 31:13 8096
14. A Levite who married a foreigner.
Jozabad, and *S*, and Kelaiah, (the Ezr 10:23 8096
15. A Hashumite who married a foreigner.
Jeremai, Manasseh, and *S* Ezr 10:33 8096
16. A Banite who married a foreigner.
And Bani, and Binnui, *S*, Ezr 10:38 8096
17. Grandfather of Mordecai.
the son of Jair, the son of *S* Est 2:5 8096
18. A representative of the Gershonites.
the family of *S* apart, and their Zec 12:13 8097

SHIMEITES See SHIMITES.

SHIMEON (*shim'-e-on*) See SIMEON. *A member of the Harim family.*
Ishijah, Malchiah, Shemaiah, *S* Ezr 10:31 8095

SHIMHI (*shim'-hi*) See SHEMA, SHIMEI. *Father of a chief family in Judah.*
and Shimrath, the sons of *S* 1Chr 8:21 8096

SHIMI (*shi'-mi*) See SHIMEI, SHIMITES. *Same as Shimei 1.*
Libni, and *S*, according to their Ex 6:17 8096

SHIMITES (*shi'-mites*) *Descendants of Shimei 1.*
Libnites, and the family of the *S* Num 3:21 8097

SHIMMA (*shim'-mah*) See SHAMMAH. *Same as Shamma.*
the second, and *S* the third, 1Chr 2:13 8092

SHIMON (*shi'-mon*) *A descendant of Caleb.*
And the sons of *S* were, Amnon, and 1Chr 4:20 7889

SHIMRATH (*shim'-rath*) *A son of Shimri.*
And Adaiah, and Beraiah, and *S* 1Chr 8:21 8119

SHIMRI (*shim'-ri*) See SIMRI.
1. Head of a family in Simeon.
the son of Jedaiah, the son of *S* 1Chr 4:37 8113
2. Father of Jedaiah.
Jediael the son of *S*, and Joha his 1Chr 11:45 8113
3. A Levite who cleansed the Temple.
S, and Jeiel 2Chr 29:13 8113

SHIMRITH (*shim'-rith*) See SHOMER. *Mother of Jehozabad.*
the son of *S* a Moabitess 2Chr 24:26 8116

SHIMROM (*shim'-rom*) See SHIMRON. *A son of Issachar.*
were, Tola, and Puah, Jashub, and *S* 1Chr 7:1 8110

SHIMRON (*shim'-ron*) See SHIMROM, SHIMRONITES. *Same as Shimrom.*
Tola, and Phuvah, and Job, and *S* Gen 46:13 8110
of *S*, the family of the Num 26:24 8110
of Madon, and to the king of *S* Josh 11:1 8110
And Kattath, and Nahallal, and *S* Josh 19:15 8110

SHIMRONITE See SHIMRONITES.

SHIMRONITES (*shim'-ron-ites*) *Descendants of Shimrom.*
of Shimron, the family of the *S* Num 26:24 8117

SHIMRON-MERON (*shim''-ron-me'-ron*) *A city in Galilee.*
The king of *S*, one Josh 12:20 8112

SHIMSHAI (*shim'-shahee*) *An opponent of Nehemiah.*
S the scribe wrote a letter Ezr 4:8 8124
S the scribe, and the rest of Ezr 4:9 8124
to *S* the scribe, and to the rest Ezr 4:17 8124
S the scribe, and their companions Ezr 4:23 8124

SHINAB (*shi'-nab*) *King of Admah.*
S king of Admah, and Shemeber king Gen 14:2 8134

SHINAR (*shi'-nar*) *A nation in Babylonia.*
and Calneh, in the land of *S* Gen 10:10 8152
found a plain in the land of *S* Gen 11:2 8152
in the days of Amraphel king of *S* Gen 14:1 8152
of nations, and Amraphel king of *S* Gen 14:9 8152
Cush, and from Elam, and from *S* Is 11:11 8152
land of *S* to the house of his god Dan 1:2 8152
it an house in the land of *S* Zec 5:11 8152

SHINE
LORD make his face *s* upon thee Num 6:25 215
neither let the light *s* upon it Job 3:4 3313
s upon the counsel of the wicked Job 10:3 3313
thou shalt *s* forth, thou shalt be Job 11:17 5774
the spark of his fire shall not *s* Job 18:5 5050
the light shall *s* upon thy ways Job 22:28 5050
commandeth it not to *s* by the Job 36:32
the light of his cloud to *s* Job 37:15 3313
By his neesings a light doth *s* Job 41:18 1984
He maketh a path to *s* after him Job 41:32 215
thy face to *s* upon thy servant Ps 31:16 215
and cause his face to *s* upon us Ps 67:1 215
between the cherubims, *s* forth Ps 80:1 3313
O God, and cause thy face to *s* Ps 80:3 215
of hosts, and cause thy face to *s* Ps 80:7 215
God of hosts, cause thy face to *s* Ps 80:19 215
man, and oil to make his face to *s* Ps 104:15 6670
thy face to *s* upon thy servant Ps 119:135 215
man's wisdom maketh his face to *s* Eccl 8:1 215
shall not cause her light to *s* Is 13:10 5050
Arise, *s*; for thy light Is 60:1 215
They are waxen fat, they *s* Jer 5:28 6245
cause thy face to *s* upon thy Dan 9:17 215
they that be wise shall *s* as the Dan 12:3 2094
Let your light so *s* before men Mt 5:16 *2989*
Then shall the righteous *s* forth Mt 13:43 *1584*
and his face did *s* as the sun Mt 17:2 *2989*
image of God, should *s* unto them 2Cor 4:4 *826*
the light to *s* out of darkness 2Cor 4:6 *2989*
among whom ye *s* as lights in the Phil 2:15 *5316*
shall *s* no more at all in thee Rev 18:23 *5316*
neither of the moon, to *s* in it Rev 21:23 *5316*

SHINED
he *s* forth from mount Paran, and Deut 33:2 3313
When his candle *s* upon my head Job 29:3 1984
If I beheld the sun when it *s* Job 31:26 1984
perfection of beauty, God hath *s* Ps 50:2 3313
death, upon them hath the light *s* Is 9:2 5050
the earth *s* with his glory Eze 43:2 215
suddenly there *s* round about him Acts 9:3 *4015*
him, and a light *s* in the prison Acts 12:7 *2989*
hath *s* in our hearts, to give the 2Cor 4:6 *2989*

SHINETH
even to the moon, and it *s* not Job 25:5 166
but the night *s* as the day Ps 139:12 215
as the shining light, that *s* more Prov 4:18 215
the east, and *s* even unto the west Mt 24:27 *5316*
s unto the other part under Lk 17:24 *2989*
And the light *s* in darkness Jn 1:5 *5316*
a light that *s* in a dark place 2Pet 1:19 *5316*
is past, and the true light now *s* 1Jn 2:8 *5316*
was as the sun *s* in his strength Rev 1:16 *5316*

SHINING
the earth by clear *s* after rain 2Sa 23:4 5051
of the just is as the *s* light Prov 4:18 5051
the *s* of a flaming fire by night Is 4:5 5051
the stars shall withdraw their *s* Joel 2:10 5051
the stars shall withdraw their *s* Joel 3:15 5051
at the *s* of thy glittering spear Hab 3:11 5051
And his raiment became *s*, Mk 9:3 *4744*
as when the bright *s* of a candle Lk 11:36 *796*
men stood by them in *s* garments Lk 24:4 *797*
He was a burning and a *s* light Jn 5:35 *5316*
s round about me and them which Acts 26:13 *4034*

SHION See SHIHON.

SHIP
the way of a *s* in the midst of Prov 30:19 591
shall gallant *s* pass thereby Is 33:21 6716
They have made all thy *s* boards Eze 27:5
he found a *s* going to Tarshish Jonah 1:3 591
so that the *s* was like to be Jonah 1:4 591
that were in the *s* into the sea Jonah 1:5 591
gone down into the sides of the *s* Jonah 1:5 5600
in a *s* with Zebedee their father, Mt 4:21 *4143*
And they immediately left the *s* Mt 4:22 *4143*
And when he was entered into a *s* Mt 8:23 *4143*
insomuch that the *s* was covered Mt 8:24 *4143*
And he entered into a *s*, and passed Mt 9:1 *4143*
him, so that he went into a *s* Mt 13:2 *4143*
he departed thence by *s* into a Mt 14:13 *4143*
his disciples to get into a *s* Mt 14:22 *4143*
But the *s* was now in the midst of Mt 14:24 *4143*
Peter was come down out of the *s* Mt 14:29 *4143*
And when they were come into the *s* Mt 14:32 *4143*

Then they that were in the s came Mt 14:33 4143
away the multitude, and took s Mt 15:39 4143
were in the s mending their nets Mk 1:19 4143
in the s with the hired servants Mk 1:20 4143
that a small s should wait on him Mk 3:9 4142
so that he entered into a s Mk 4:1 4143
took him even as he was in the s Mk 4:36 4143
and the waves beat into the s Mk 4:37 4143
was in the hinder part of the s Mk 4:38
And when he was come out of the s Mk 5:2 4143
And when he was come into the s Mk 5:18 4143
again by s unto the other side Mk 5:21 4143
a desert place by s privately Mk 6:32 4143
his disciples to get into the s Mk 6:45 4143
the s was in the midst of the sea Mk 6:47 4143
he went up unto them into the s Mk 6:51 4143
when they were come out of the s Mk 6:54 4143
into a s with his disciples Mk 8:10 4143
entering into the s again Mk 8:13 4143
neither had they in the s with Mk 8:14 4143
and taught the people out of the s Lk 5:3 4143
which were in the other s Lk 5:7 4143
went into a s with his disciples Lk 8:22 4143
and he went up into the s, and Lk 8:37 4143
And entered into a s, and went over Jn 6:17 4143
sea, and drawing nigh unto the s Jn 6:19 4143
willingly received him into the s Jn 6:21 4143
immediately the s was at the land Jn 6:21 4143
and entered into a s immediately Jn 21:3 4143
net on the right side of the s Jn 21:6 4143
disciples came in a little s Jn 21:8 4142
And we went before to s, and sailed Acts 20:13 4143
they accompanied him unto the s Acts 20:38 4143
finding a s sailing over unto Acts 21:2 4143
for there the s was to unlade her Acts 21:3 4143
leave one of another, we took s Acts 21:6 4143
entering into a s of Adramyttium Acts 27:2 4143
a s of Alexandria sailing into Acts 27:6 4143
not only of the lading and s Acts 27:10 4143
the master and the owner of the s Acts 27:11 3490
when the s was caught, and could Acts 27:15 4143
used helps, undergirding the s Acts 27:17 4143
the next day they lightened the s Acts 27:18
own hands the tackling of the s Acts 27:19 4143
life among you, but of the s Acts 27:22 4143
were about to flee out of the s Acts 27:30 4143
Except these abide in the s Acts 27:31 4143
we were in all in the s two Acts 27:37 4143
enough, they lightened the s Acts 27:38 4143
were possible, to thrust in the s Acts 27:39 4143
seas met, they ran the s aground Acts 27:41 3491
and some on broken pieces of the s Acts 27:44 4143
we departed in a s of Alexandria Acts 28:11 4143

SHIPHI (shi'-fi) *Father of Ziza.*
And Ziza the son of S, the son of 1Chr 4:37 8230

SHIPHMITE (shif'-mite) *Family name of Zabdi.*
the wine cellars was Zabdi the S 1Chr 27:27 8225

SHIPHRAH (shif'-rah) *A Hebrew midwife in Egypt.*
which the name of the one was S Ex 1:15 8236

SHIPHTAN (shif'-tan) *Father of Kemuel.*
of Ephraim, Kemuel the son of S Num 34:24 8204

SHIPMASTER
So the s came to him, and said Jonah 1:6
And every s, and all the company in Rev 18:17 2942

SHIPMEN
s that had knowledge of the sea, 1Kin 9:27
about midnight the s deemed that Acts 27:27 3492
as the s were about to flee out Acts 27:30 3492

SHIPPING
his disciples, they also took s Jn 6:24 4143

SHIPS
and he shall be for an haven of s Gen 49:13 591
s shall come come from the coast Num 24:24 6716
thee into Egypt again with s Deut 28:68 591
and why did Dan remain in s Judg 5:17 591
made a navy of s in Ezion-geber 1Kin 9:26
Jehoshaphat made s of Tharshish 1Kin 22:48 591
for the s were broken at 1Kin 22:48 591
go with thy servants in the s 1Kin 22:49 591
by the hands of his servants s 2Chr 8:18 591
For the king's s went to Tarshish 2Chr 9:21 591
the s of Tarshish bringing gold 2Chr 9:21 591
him to make s to go to Tarshish 2Chr 20:36 591
they made the s in Ezion-gaber 2Chr 20:36 591
the s were broken, that they were 2Chr 20:37 591
are passed away as the swift s Job 9:26 591
Thou breakest the s of Tarshish Ps 48:7 591
There go the s Ps 104:26 591
They that go down to the sea in s Ps 107:23 591
She is like the merchants' s Prov 31:14 591
And upon all the s of Tarshish Is 2:16 591
Howl, ye s of Tarshish Is 23:1 591
Howl, ye s of Tarshish Is 23:14 591
Chaldeans, whose cry is in the s Is 43:14 591
the s of Tarshish first, to bring Is 60:9 591
all the s of the sea with their Eze 27:9 591
The s of Tarshish did sing of Eze 27:25 591
sea, shall come down from their s Eze 27:29 591
messengers go forth from me in s Eze 30:9 6716
For the s of Chittim shall come Dan 11:30 6716
and with horsemen, and with many s Dan 11:40 591
were also with him other little s Mk 4:36 4142
saw two s standing by the lake Lk 5:2 4143
And he entered into one of the s Lk 5:3 4143
they came, and filled both the s Lk 5:7 4143
they had brought their s to land Lk 5:11 4143
Behold also the s, which though Jas 3:4 4143
part of the s were destroyed Rev 8:9 4143
and all the company in s, and Rev 18:17 4143
had s in the sea by reason of her Rev 18:19 4143

SHIPWRECK
was I stoned, thrice I suffered s 2Cor 11:25 3489
away concerning faith have made s 1Ti 1:19 3489

SHISHA (shi'-shah) See SHAVSHA. *Father of Elihoreph and Ahiah.*
Elihoreph and Ahiah, the sons of S 1Kin 4:3 7894

SHISHAK (shi'-shak) *A king of Egypt.*
unto S king of Egypt, and was in 1Kin 11:40 7895
that S king of Egypt came up 1Kin 14:25 7895
S king of Egypt came up against 2Chr 12:2 7895
to Jerusalem because of S 2Chr 12:5 7895
I also left you in the hand of S 2Chr 12:5 7895
upon Jerusalem by the hand of S 2Chr 12:7 7895
So S king of Egypt came up 2Chr 12:9 7895

SHITRAI (shit'-ra-i) *A herdsman in David's court.*
fed in Sharon was S the Sharonite 1Chr 27:29 7861

SHITTAH
the s tree, and the myrtle, and the Is 41:19 7848

SHITTIM (shit'-tim) *A place in Moab.*
and badgers' skins, and s wood, Ex 25:5 7848
they shall make an ark of s wood Ex 25:10 7848
thou shalt make staves of s wood Ex 25:13 7848
shalt also make a table of s wood Ex 25:23 7848
shalt make the staves of s wood Ex 25:28 7848
tabernacle of s wood standing up Ex 26:15 7848
And thou shalt make bars of s wood Ex 26:26 7848
of s wood overlaid with gold Ex 26:32 7848
hanging five pillars of s wood Ex 26:37 7848
shalt make an altar of s wood Ex 27:1 7848
for the altar, staves of s wood Ex 27:6 7848
of s wood shalt thou make it Ex 30:1 7848
shalt make the staves of s wood Ex 30:5 7848
and badgers' skins, and s wood, Ex 35:7 7848
with whom was found s wood for Ex 35:24 7848
for the tabernacle of s wood Ex 36:20 7848
And he made bars of s wood Ex 36:31 7848
thereunto four pillars of s wood Ex 36:36 7848
Bezaleel made the ark of s wood Ex 37:1 7848
And he made staves of s wood Ex 37:4 7848
And he made the table of s wood Ex 37:10 7848
And he made the staves of s wood Ex 37:15 7848
made the incense altar of s wood Ex 37:25 7848
And he made the staves of s wood Ex 37:28 7848
altar of burnt offering of s wood Ex 38:1 7848
And he made the staves of s wood Ex 38:6 7848
And Israel abode in S, and the Num 25:1 7851
And I made an ark of s wood Deut 10:3 7848
out of S two men to spy secretly Josh 2:1 7851
and they removed from S, and came Josh 3:1 7851
and shall water the valley of S Joel 3:18 7851
answered him from S unto Gilgal Mic 6:5 7851

SHIVERS
potter shall they be broken to s Rev 2:27 4937

SHIZA (shi'-zah) *A "mighty man" of David.*
Adina the son of S the Reubenite 1Chr 11:42 7877

SHOA (sho'-ah) *A tribal enemy of Israel.*
and all the Chaldeans, Pekod, and S Eze 23:23 7772

SHOBAB (sho'-bab)
1. A son of David.
Shammuah, and S, and Nathan, and 2Sa 5:14 7727
Shimea, and S, and Nathan, and 1Chr 3:5 7727
and S, Nathan, and Solomon 1Chr 14:4 7727
2. A son of Caleb.
Jesher, and S, and Ardon 1Chr 2:18 7727

SHOBACH (sho'-bak) See SHOPHACH. *A Syrian defeated by David.*
S the captain of the host of 2Sa 10:16 7731
smote S the captain of their host 2Sa 10:18 7731

SHOBAI (sho'-bahee) *A family of exiles.*
of Hatita, the children of S Ezr 2:42 7630
of Hatita, the children of S Neh 7:45 7630

SHOBAL (sho'-bal)
1. A son of Seir.
Lotan, and S, and Zibeon, and Anah, Gen 36:20 7732
And the children of S were these Gen 36:23 7732
duke Lotan, duke S, duke Zibeon, Gen 36:29 7732
Lotan, and S, and Zibeon, and Anah, 1Chr 1:38 7732
The sons of S 1Chr 1:40 7732
2. A son of Caleb.
S the father of Kirjath-jearim, 1Chr 2:50 7732
S the father of Kirjath-jearim 1Chr 2:52 7732
3. A son of Judah.
Hezron, and Carmi, and Hur, and S 1Chr 4:1 7732
Reaiah the son of S begat Jahath 1Chr 4:2 7732

SHOBEK (sho'-bek) *A clan leader who renewed the covenant.*
Hallohesh, Pileha, S, Neh 10:24 7733

SHOBI (sho'-bi) *A son of Nahash.*
that S the son of Nahash of 2Sa 17:27 7629

SHOCHO (sho'-ko) See CHOCHO. *A city in Judah.*
S with the villages thereof, and 2Chr 28:18 7755

SHOCHOH (sho'-ko) See SHOCHO, SHOCO, SOCHOH, SOCO, SOCOH. *Same as Shocho.*
and were gathered together at S 1Sa 17:1 7755
to Judah, and pitched between S 1Sa 17:1 7755

SHOCK
like as a s of corn cometh in in Job 5:26 1430

SHOCKS
and burnt up both the s, and also Judg 15:5 1430

SHOCO (sho'-ko) See SHOCHOH. *Same as Shocho.*
And Beth-zur, and S, and Adullam, 2Chr 11:7 7755

SHOD
s them, and gave them to eat and to 2Chr 28:15 5274
s thee with badgers' skin, and I Eze 16:10 5274
But be s with sandals Mk 6:9 5265
your feet s with the preparation Eph 6:15 5265

SHOE
loose his s from off his foot, and Deut 25:9 5275
of him that hath his s loosed Deut 25:10 5275
thy s is not waxen old upon thy Deut 29:5 5275
Loose thy s from off thy foot Josh 5:15 5275
a man plucked off his s, and gave Ruth 4:7 5275
So he drew off his s Ruth 4:8 5275
over Edom will I cast out my s Ps 60:8 5275
over Edom will I cast out my s Ps 108:9 5275
put off thy s from thy foot Is 20:2 5275

SHOELATCHET
take from a thread even to a s Gen 14:23

SHOE'S
whose s latchet I am not worthy Jn 1:27 5266

SHOES
put off thy s from off thy feet, Ex 3:5 5275
your s on your feet, and your Ex 12:11 5275
Thy s shall be iron and brass Deut 33:25 4515
And old s and clouted upon their Josh 9:5 5275
our s are become old by reason of Josh 9:13 5275
in his s that were on his feet 1Kin 2:5 5275
How beautiful are thy feet with s Song 7:1 5275
the latchet of their s be broken Is 5:27 5275
put on thy s upon thy feet, and Eze 24:17 5275
heads, and your s upon your feet Eze 24:23 5275
and the poor for a pair of s Amos 2:6 5275
and the needy for a pair of s Amos 8:6 5275
whose s I am not worthy to bear Mt 3:11 5266
neither two coats, neither s Mt 10:10 5266
the latchet of whose s I am not Mk 1:7 5266
the latchet of whose s I am not Lk 3:16 5266
neither purse, nor scrip, nor s Lk 10:4 5266
on his hand, and s on his feet Lk 15:22 5266
you without purse, and scrip, and s Lk 22:35 5266
Put off thy s from thy feet Acts 7:33 5266
whose s of his feet I am not Acts 13:25 5266

SHOHAM (sho'-ham) *A Merarite.*
Beno, and S, and Zaccur, and Ibri 1Chr 24:27 7719

SHOMER (sho'-mur) See SHAMER, SHIMRITH.
1. Same as Shimrith.
and Jehozabad the son of S 2Kin 12:21 7763
2. Son of Heber.
And Heber begat Japhlet, and S 1Chr 7:32 7763

SHONE
face s while he talked with him Ex 34:29 7160
behold, the skin of his face s Ex 34:30 7160
that the skin of Moses' face s Ex 34:35 7160
the sun s upon the water, and the 2Kin 3:22 2224
of the Lord s round about them Lk 2:9 4034
suddenly there s from heaven a Acts 22:6 4015
the day s not for a third part of Rev 8:12 5316

SHOOK
for the oxen s it 2Sa 6:6 8058
Then the earth s and trembled 2Sa 22:8 1607
foundations of heaven moved and s 2Sa 22:8 1607
Also I s my lap, and said, So God Neh 5:13 5287
Then the earth s and trembled Ps 18:7 1607
The earth s, the heavens also Ps 68:8 7493
the earth trembled and s Ps 77:18 7493
over the sea, he s the kingdoms Is 23:11 7264
But they s off the dust of their Acts 13:51 1621
he s his raiment, and said unto Acts 18:6 1621
he s off the beast into the fire, Acts 28:5 660
Whose voice then s the earth Heb 12:26 4531

SHOOT
he made the middle bar to s Ex 36:33 1272
I will s three arrows on the side 1Sa 20:20 3384
find out now the arrows which I s 1Sa 20:36 3384
that they would s from the wall 2Sa 11:20 3384
Then Elisha said, S 2Kin 13:17 3384
nor s an arrow there, nor come 2Kin 19:32 3384
to s with bow, and skilful in war, 1Chr 5:18 1869
to s arrows and great stones 2Chr 26:15 3384
that they may privily s at the Ps 11:2 3384
they s out the lip, they shake Ps 22:7 6362
bendeth his bow to s his arrows Ps 58:7
bend their bows to s their arrows Ps 64:3
That they may s in secret at the Ps 64:4 3384
suddenly do they s at him Ps 64:4 3384
But God shall s at them with an Ps 64:7 3384
s out thine arrows, and destroy Ps 144:6 7971
nor s an arrow there, nor come Is 37:33
s at her, spare no arrows Jer 50:14 3034
neither s up their top among the Eze 31:14 5414
ye shall s forth your branches, Eze 36:8 5414
When they now s forth, ye see and Lk 21:30 4261

SHOOTERS
the s shot from off the wall upon 2Sa 11:24 3384

SHOOTETH
his branch s forth in his garden Job 8:16 3318
In measure, when it s forth Is 27:8 7971
herbs, and s out great branches Mk 4:32 4160

SHOOTING
s arrows out of a bow, even of 1Chr 12:2
of the *s* up of the latter growth Amos 7:1 5927

SHOPHACH (*sho'-fak*) See SHOBACH. *Same as Shoback.*
S the captain of the host of 1Chr 19:16 7780
killed *S* the captain of the host 1Chr 19:18 7780

SHOPHAN (*sho'-fan*) See ZAPHON. *A city in Gad.*
And Atroth, *S*, and Jaazer, and Num 32:35 5855

SHORE
the sand which is upon the sea *s* Gen 22:17 8193
the Egyptians dead upon the sea *s* Ex 14:30 8193
is upon the sea *s* in multitude Josh 11:4 8193
was from the *s* of the salt sea Josh 15:2 7097
Asher continued on the sea *s* Judg 5:17 2348
is on the sea *s* in multitude 1Sa 13:5 8193
as the sand that is on the sea *s* 1Kin 4:29 8193
on the *s* of the Red sea, in the 1Kin 9:26 8193
Ashkelon, and against the sea *s* Jer 47:7 2348
whole multitude stood on the *s* Mt 13:2 123
when it was full, they drew to *s* Mt 13:48 123
of Gennesaret, and drew to the *s* Mk 6:53 4358
now come, Jesus stood on the *s* Jn 21:4 123
and we kneeled down on the *s* Acts 21:5 123
a certain creek with a *s*, into Acts 27:39 123
to the wind, and made toward *s* Acts 27:40 123
which is by the sea *s* innumerable Heb 11:12 5491

SHORN
a flock of sheep that are even *s* Song 4:2 7094
having *s* his head in Cenchrea Acts 18:18 2751
be not covered, let her also be *s* 1Cor 11:6 2751
for a woman to be *s* or shaven 1Cor 11:6 2751

SHORT
Moses, Is the LORD's hand waxed *s* Num 11:23 7114
the LORD began to cut Israel *s* 2Kin 10:32
the light is *s* because of Job 17:12 7138
the triumphing of the wicked is *s* Job 20:5 7138
Remember how *s* my time is Ps 89:47 2465
come *s* of the glory of God Rom 3:23 5302
cut it *s* in righteousness Rom 9:28 4932
because a *s* work will the Lord Rom 9:28 4932
I say, brethren, the time is *s* 1Cor 7:29 4958
from you for a *s* time in presence 1Th 2:17 5610
you should seem to come *s* of it Heb 4:1 5302
knoweth that he hath but a *s* time Rev 12:12 3641
he must continue a *s* space Rev 17:10 3641

SHORTENED
The days of his youth hast thou *s* Ps 89:45 7114
he *s* my days Ps 102:23 7114
years of the wicked shall be *s* Prov 10:27 7114
Is my hand *s* at all, that it Is 50:2 7114
Behold, the LORD's hand is not *s* Is 59:1 7114
And except those days should be *s* Mt 24:22 2856
sake those days shall be *s* Mt 24:22 2856
that the Lord had *s* those days Mk 13:20 2856
hath chosen, he hath *s* the days Mk 13:20 2856

SHORTER
For the bed is *s* than that a man Is 28:20 7114
Now the upper chambers were *s* Eze 42:5 7114

SHORTLY
God will *s* bring it to pass Gen 41:32 4116
s be brought again from Babylon Jer 27:16 4120
Now will I *s* pour out my fury Eze 7:8 7138
he himself would depart *s* thither Acts 25:4
bruise Satan under your feet *s* Rom 16:20
But I will come to you *s*, if the 1Cor 4:19 5030
to send Timotheus *s* unto you Phil 2:19 5030
that I also myself shall come *s* Phil 2:24 5030
thee, hoping to come unto thee *s* 1Ti 3:14 5032
thy diligence to come *s* unto me 2Ti 4:9 5030
with whom, if he come *s*, I will Heb 13:23 5032
Knowing that *s* I must put off 2Pet 1:14 5031
But I trust I shall *s* see thee 3Jn 14 2112
things which must *s* come to pass Rev 1:1
the things which must *s* be done Rev 22:6

SHOSHANNIM (*sho-shan'-nim*) *A musical notation.*
To the chief Musician upon *S* Ps 45:t 7799
To the chief Musician upon *S* Ps 69:t 7799

SHOSHANNIM-EDUTH (*sho-shan''-nim-e'-duth*) *A musical notation.*
To the chief Musician upon *S* Ps 80:t 7802

SHOT
budded, and her blossoms *s* forth Gen 40:10 5927
him, and *s* at him, and hated him Gen 49:23 7232
surely be stoned, or *s* through Ex 19:13 3384
We have *s* at them Num 21:30 3384
thereof, as though I *s* at a mark 1Sa 20:20 7971
lad ran, he *s* an arrow beyond him 1Sa 20:36 3384
of the arrow which Jonathan had *s* 1Sa 20:37 3384
the shooters *s* from off the wall 2Sa 11:24 3384
said, Shoot. And he *s* 2Kin 13:17 3384
the archers *s* at king Josiah 2Chr 35:23 3384
and he *s* out lightnings, and Ps 18:14 7232
Their tongue is as an arrow *s* out Jer 9:8 7819
forth branches, and *s* forth sprigs Eze 17:6 7971
s forth her branches toward him, Eze 17:7 7971
of waters, when he *s* forth Eze 31:5 7971
he hath *s* up his top among the Eze 31:10 7971

SHOULD
not good that the man *s* be alone Gen 2:18
lest any finding him *s* kill him Gen 4:15
the righteous *s* be as the wicked Gen 18:25
that Sarah *s* have given children Gen 21:7
If it be your mind that I *s* bury Gen 23:8
the place *s* kill me for Rebekah Gen 26:7
why *s* I be deprived also of you Gen 27:45
the cattle *s* be gathered together Gen 29:7
than that I *s* give her to another Gen 29:19
that they *s* conceive when they Gen 30:38
if men *s* overdrive them one day, Gen 33:13
S he deal with our sister as with Gen 34:31
knew that the seed *s* not be his Gen 38:9
lest that he *s* give seed to his Gen 38:9
they *s* put me into the dungeon Gen 40:15
heard that they *s* eat bread there Gen 43:25
s do according to this thing Gen 44:7
how then *s* we steal out of thy Gen 44:8
said, God forbid that I *s* do so Gen 44:17
for if he *s* leave his father, his Gen 44:22
for why *s* we die in thy presence Gen 47:15
that Pharaoh *s* have the fifth Gen 47:26
that I *s* go unto Pharaoh Ex 3:11
that I *s* bring forth the children Ex 3:11
that I *s* obey his voice to let Ex 5:2
than that we *s* die in the Ex 14:12
for he *s* make full restitution Ex 22:3
Wherefore *s* the Egyptians speak, Ex 32:12
hath commanded, that ye *s* do them Ex 35:1
that they *s* be stones for a Ex 39:7
the hole, that it *s* not rend Ex 39:23
things which *s* not be done Lev 4:13
things which *s* not be done Lev 4:22
the LORD commanded that ye *s* do Lev 9:6
ye *s* indeed have eaten it in the Lev 10:18
s it have been accepted in the Lev 10:19
that ye *s* be defiled thereby Lev 11:43
other people, that ye *s* be mine Lev 20:26
that they *s* bring forth him that Lev 24:23
that ye *s* not be their bondmen Lev 26:13
which *s* be the LORD's firstling, Lev 27:26
unto them was that they *s* bear Num 7:9
that they *s* keep the passover Num 9:4
Whence *s* I have flesh to give Num 11:13
s she not be ashamed seven days Num 12:14
wives and our children *s* be a prey Num 14:3
ones, which ye said *s* be a prey Num 14:31
declared what *s* be done to him Num 15:34
that we and our cattle *s* die there Num 20:4
God is not a man, that he *s* lie Num 23:19
the son of man, that he *s* repent Num 23:19
Why *s* the name of our father be Num 27:4
that they *s* not go into the land Num 32:9
Because he *s* have remained in the Num 35:28
that he *s* come again to dwell in Num 35:32
time all the things which ye *s* do Deut 1:18
to shew you by what way ye *s* go Deut 1:33
ones, which ye said *s* be a prey Deut 1:39
that ye *s* do so in the land Deut 4:5
sware that I *s* not go over Jordan Deut 4:21
that I *s* not go in unto that good Deut 4:21
which *s* kill his neighbour Deut 4:42
Now therefore why *s* we die Deut 5:25
the end that he *s* multiply horses Deut 17:16
so *s* ye sin against the LORD your Deut 20:18
if he *s* exceed, and beat him above Deut 25:3
then thy brother *s* seem vile unto Deut 25:3
Lest there *s* be among you man, or Deut 29:18
lest there *s* be among you a root Deut 29:18
lest their adversaries *s* behave Deut 32:27
strangely, and lest they *s* say Deut 32:27
How *s* one chase a thousand, and Deut 32:30
Joshua commanded that they *s* take Josh 8:29
that they *s* bless the people of Josh 8:33
in the place which he *s* choose Josh 9:27
that they *s* come against Israel Josh 11:20
when they *s* so say to us or to Josh 22:28
God forbid that we *s* rebel Josh 22:29
forbid that we *s* forsake the LORD Josh 24:16
that we *s* give bread unto thine Judg 8:6
that we *s* give bread unto thy men Judg 8:15
S I leave my fatness, wherewith Judg 9:9
S I forsake my sweetness, and my Judg 9:11
S I leave my wine, which cheereth Judg 9:13
is Shechem, that we *s* serve him Judg 9:28
for why *s* we serve him Judg 9:28
is Abimelech, that we *s* serve him Judg 9:38
that they *s* not dwell in Shechem Judg 9:41
that they *s* make a great flame Judg 20:38
that there *s* be to day one tribe Judg 21:3
at this time, that ye *s* be guilty Judg 21:22
If I *s* say, I have hope Ruth 1:12
if I *s* have an husband also to Ruth 1:12
to night, and *s* also bear sons Ruth 1:12
s walk before me for ever 1Sa 2:30
that I *s* not reign over them 1Sa 8:7
can shew us our way that we *s* go 1Sa 9:6
if the man *s* yet come thither 1Sa 10:22
for then *s* ye go after vain 1Sa 12:21
God forbid that I *s* sin against 1Sa 12:23
s have been utterly destroyed 1Sa 15:21
he is not a man, that he *s* repent 1Sa 15:29
that he *s* defy the armies of the 1Sa 17:26
that I *s* be son in law to the 1Sa 18:18
s have been given to David 1Sa 18:19
servants, that they *s* kill David 1Sa 19:1
why *s* I kill thee 1Sa 19:17
why *s* my father hide this thing 1Sa 20:2
I *s* not fail to sit with the king 1Sa 20:5
that he *s* rise against me, to lie 1Sa 22:13
The LORD forbid that I *s* do this 1Sa 24:6
The LORD forbid that I *s* stretch 1Sa 26:11
better for me than that I *s* 1Sa 27:1
for why *s* thy servant dwell in 1Sa 27:5
Lest they *s* tell on us, saying, 1Sa 27:11
for wherewith *s* he reconcile 1Sa 29:4
s it not be with the heads of 1Sa 29:4
wherefore *s* I smite thee to the 2Sa 2:22
how then *s* I hold up my face to 2Sa 2:22
he is dead, wherefore *s* I fast 2Sa 12:23
unto him, Why *s* he go with thee 2Sa 13:26
s I this day make thee go up and 2Sa 15:20
Why *s* this dead dog curse my lord 2Sa 16:9
And again, whom *s* I serve 2Sa 16:19
s I not serve in the presence of 2Sa 16:19
Though I *s* receive a thousand 2Sa 18:12
Otherwise I *s* have wrought 2Sa 18:13
that the king *s* take it to his 2Sa 19:19
that ye *s* this day be adversaries 2Sa 19:22
that I *s* go up with the king unto 2Sa 19:34
wherefore then *s* thy servant be 2Sa 19:35
why *s* the king recompense it me 2Sa 19:36
that our advice *s* not be first 2Sa 19:43
that I *s* swallow up or destroy 2Sa 20:20
s be destroyed from remaining in 2Sa 21:5
from me, O LORD, that I *s* do this 2Sa 23:17
who *s* sit on the throne of my 1Kin 1:27
of David drew nigh that he *s* die 1Kin 2:1
their faces on me, that I *s* reign 1Kin 2:15
that the beams *s* not be fastened 1Kin 6:6
the good way wherein they *s* walk 1Kin 8:36
that he *s* not go after other gods 1Kin 11:10
which told me that I *s* be king 1Kin 14:2
that I *s* give the inheritance of 1Kin 21:3
that *s* have reigned in his stead 2Kin 3:27
s I set this before an hundred 2Kin 4:43
what *s* I wait for the LORD any 2Kin 6:33
if the LORD *s* make windows in 2Kin 7:19
that he *s* do this great thing 2Kin 8:13
with them that *s* go out on the 2Kin 11:9
that they *s* be the LORD's people 2Kin 11:17
that they *s* not do like them 2Kin 17:15
them how they *s* fear the LORD 2Kin 17:28
that the LORD *s* deliver Jerusalem 2Kin 18:35
that they *s* become a desolation 2Kin 22:19
that they *s* bring them in and out 1Chr 9:28
it me, that I *s* do this thing 1Chr 11:19
for those that *s* make a sound 1Chr 16:42
people, that they *s* be plagued 1Chr 21:17
say to David, that David *s* go up 1Chr 21:18
that he *s* sanctify the most holy 1Chr 23:13
that they *s* keep the charge of 1Chr 23:32
who *s* prophesy with harps, with 1Chr 25:1
that we *s* be able to offer so 1Chr 29:14
that I *s* build him an house, save 2Chr 2:6
that they *s* burn after the manner 2Chr 4:20
the good way, wherein they *s* walk 2Chr 6:27
God of Israel *s* be put to death 2Chr 15:13
that *s* praise the beauty of 2Chr 20:21
that they *s* be the LORD's people 2Chr 23:16
unclean in any thing *s* enter in 2Chr 23:19
that they *s* not go with him to 2Chr 25:13
that ye *s* minister unto him, and 2Chr 29:11
the sin offering *s* be made for 2Chr 29:24
that they *s* come to the house of 2Chr 30:1
that they *s* come to keep the 2Chr 30:5
Why *s* the kings of Assyria come, 2Chr 32:4
that your God *s* be able to 2Chr 32:14
that they *s* not eat of the most Ezr 2:63
why *s* damage grow to the hurt of Ezr 4:22
for why *s* there be wrath against Ezr 7:23
them what they *s* say unto Iddo Ezr 8:17
that they *s* bring unto us Ezr 8:17
S we again break thy commandments Ezr 9:14
so that there *s* be no remnant nor Ezr 9:14
to swear that they *s* do according Ezr 10:5
that they *s* gather themselves Ezr 10:7
all his substance *s* be forfeited Ezr 10:8
why *s* not my countenance be sad, Neh 2:3
that they *s* do according to this Neh 5:12
why *s* the work cease, whilst I Neh 6:3
And I said, *S* such a man as I flee Neh 6:11
that I *s* be afraid, and do so, and Neh 6:13
that they *s* not eat of the most Neh 7:65
that the children of Israel *s* Neh 8:14
And that they *s* publish and Neh 8:15
in the way wherein they *s* go Neh 9:12
promisedst them that they *s* go in Neh 9:15
and the way wherein they *s* go Neh 9:19
that they *s* go in to possess it Neh 9:23
that we *s* bring the firstfruits Neh 10:37
portion *s* be for the singers Neh 11:23
the Moabite *s* not come into the Neh 13:1
them, that he *s* curse them Neh 13:2
that the gates *s* be shut, and Neh 13:19
charged that they *s* not be opened Neh 13:19
that there *s* no burden be brought Neh 13:19
that they *s* cleanse themselves Neh 13:22
and that they *s* come Neh 13:22
that they *s* do according to every Est 1:8
that every man *s* bear rule in his Est 1:22
that it *s* be published according Est 1:22
her that she *s* not shew it Est 2:10
did, and what *s* become of her Est 2:11
that they *s* be ready against that Est 3:14
that she *s* go in unto the king Est 4:8
that the Jews *s* be ready against Est 8:13
that they *s* keep the fourteenth Est 9:21
that they *s* make them days of Est 9:22
s return upon his own head, and Est 9:25
his sons *s* be hanged on the Est 9:25
unto them, so as it *s* not fail Est 9:27
that these days *s* be remembered Est 9:28
that these days of Purim *s* not Est 9:28
or why the breasts that I *s* suck Job 3:12
For now *s* I have lain still and Job 3:13
and been quiet, I *s* have slept Job 3:13
Then *s* I yet have comfort Job 6:10
is my strength, that I *s* hope Job 6:11
end, that I *s* prolong my life Job 6:11
pity *s* be shewed from his friend Job 6:14
thy latter end *s* greatly increase Job 8:7
but how *s* man be just with God Job 9:2
that I *s* answer him Job 9:32
we *s* come together in judgment Job 9:32

I *s* have been as though I had not Job 10:19
I *s* have been carried from the Job 10:19
S not the multitude of words be Job 11:2
s a man full of talk be justified Job 11:2
S thy lies make men hold their Job 11:3
and it *s* be your wisdom Job 13:5
it good that he *s* search you out Job 13:9
S a wise man utter vain knowledge Job 15:2
S he reason with unprofitable Job 15:3
What is man, that he *s* be clean Job 15:14
a woman, that he *s* be righteous Job 15:14
of my lips *s* asswage your grief Job 16:5
But ye *s* say, Why persecute we Job 19:28
why *s* not my spirit be troubled Job 21:4
the Almighty, that we *s* serve him Job 21:15
and what profit *s* we have, if we Job 21:15
so *s* I be delivered for ever from Job 23:7
God forbid that I *s* justify you Job 27:5
why then *s* I think upon a maid Job 31:1
for I *s* have denied the God that Job 31:28
Days *s* speak, and multitude of Job 32:7
multitude of years *s* teach wisdom Job 32:7
Lest ye *s* say, We have found out Job 32:13
S I lie against my right Job 34:6
he *s* delight himself with God Job 34:9
from God, that he *s* do wickedness Job 34:10
that he *s* commit iniquity Job 34:10
that he *s* enter into judgment Job 34:23
S it be according to thy mind Job 34:33
that which *s* be set on thy table Job 36:16
on thy table *s* be full of fatness Job 36:16
prevented me, that I *s* repay him Job 41:11
Though an host *s* encamp against Ps 27:3
though war *s* rise against me, in Ps 27:3
that I *s* not go down to the pit Ps 30:3
otherwise they *s* rejoice over me Ps 38:16
Wherefore *s* I fear in the days of Ps 49:5
That he *s* still live for ever, and Ps 49:9
that which *s* have been for their Ps 69:22
I *s* offend against the generation Ps 73:15
that they *s* make them known to Ps 78:5
even the children which *s* be born Ps 78:6
who *s* arise and declare them to Ps 78:6
Wherefore *s* the heathen say, Ps 79:10
I *s* soon have subdued their Ps 81:14
The haters of the LORD *s* have Ps 81:15
but their time *s* have endured for Ps 81:15
He *s* have fed them also with the Ps 81:16
the rock *s* I have satisfied thee Ps 81:16
they *s* not enter into my rest Ps 95:11
that it *s* not be removed for ever Ps 104:5
his wrath, lest he *s* destroy them Ps 106:23
Wherefore *s* the heathen say, Ps 115:2
I *s* then have perished in mine Ps 119:92
If I *s* count them, they are more Ps 139:18
to know the way wherein I *s* walk Ps 143:8
that the waters *s* not pass his Prov 8:29
up a child in the way he *s* go Prov 22:6
why *s* he take away thy bed from Prov 22:27
which they *s* do under the heaven Eccl 2:3
because I *s* leave it unto the man Eccl 2:18
for a man, than that he *s* eat Eccl 2:24
that he *s* make his soul enjoy Eccl 2:24
And also that every man *s* eat Eccl 3:13
that men *s* fear before him Eccl 3:14
than that a man *s* rejoice in his Eccl 3:22
wherefore *s* God be angry at thy Eccl 5:6
to the end that man *s* find Eccl 7:14
for why *s* I be as one that Song 1:7
when I *s* find thee without, I Song 8:1
yea, I *s* not be despised Song 8:1
His left hand *s* be under my head, Song 8:3
and his right hand *s* embrace me Song 8:3
Why *s* ye be stricken any more Is 1:5
we *s* have been as Sodom Is 1:9
we *s* have been like unto Gomorrah Is 1:9
he looked that it *s* bring forth Is 5:2
that it *s* bring forth grapes Is 5:4
instructed me that I *s* not walk Is 8:11
s not a people seek unto their Is 8:19
as if the rod *s* shake itself Is 10:15
as if the staff *s* lift up itself Is 10:15
that the LORD *s* deliver Jerusalem Is 36:20
nails, that it *s* not be moved Is 41:7
for how *s* my name be polluted Is 48:11
his name *s* not have been cut off Is 48:19
that she *s* not have compassion on Is 49:15
that I *s* know how to speak a word Is 50:4
that he *s* not die in the pit Is 51:14
nor that his bread *s* fail Is 51:14
is no beauty that we *s* desire him Is 53:2
Noah *s* no more go over the earth Is 54:9
S I receive comfort in these Is 57:6
for the spirit *s* fail before me Is 57:16
that they *s* not stumble Is 63:13
thy sons and thy daughters *s* eat Jer 5:17
that my days *s* be consumed with Jer 20:18
then they *s* have turned them from Jer 23:22
s ye be utterly unpunished Jer 25:29
that they *s* not give him into the Jer 26:24
that I *s* drive you out Jer 27:10
drive you out, and ye *s* perish Jer 27:10
wherefore *s* this city be laid Jer 27:17
that ye *s* be officers in the Jer 29:26
that I *s* remove it from before my Jer 32:31
that they *s* do this abomination, Jer 32:35
night, and that there *s* not be day Jer 33:20
that he *s* not have a son to reign Jer 33:21
that they *s* be no more a nation Jer 33:24
That every man *s* let his Jer 34:9
that none *s* serve himself of them Jer 34:9
every one *s* let his manservant Jer 34:10
that none *s* serve themselves of Jer 34:10
yet *s* they rise up every man in Jer 37:10

the king commanded that they *s* Jer 37:21
that they *s* give him daily a Jer 37:21
Shaphan, that he *s* carry him home Jer 39:14
wherefore *s* he slay thee, that Jer 40:15
gathered unto thee *s* be scattered Jer 40:15
that they *s* return into the land Jer 44:14
king of Babylon *s* come and smite Jer 46:13
Though Babylon *s* mount up to Jer 51:53
though she *s* fortify the height Jer 51:53
the evil that *s* come upon Babylon Jer 51:60
thou didst command that they *s* Lam 1:10
because the comforter that *s* Lam 1:16
adversaries *s* be round about him Lam 1:17
It is good that a man *s* both hope Lam 3:26
that our prayer *s* not pass Lam 3:44
the enemy *s* have entered into the Lam 4:12
that I *s* go far off from my Eze 8:6
to slay the souls that *s* not die Eze 13:19
the souls alive that *s* not live Eze 13:19
that he *s* not return from his Eze 13:22
s I be enquired of at all by them Eze 14:3
they *s* deliver but their own Eze 14:14
at all that the wicked *s* die Eze 18:23
not that he *s* return from his Eze 18:23
that his voice *s* no more be heard Eze 19:9
that it *s* not be polluted before Eze 20:9
that it *s* not be polluted before Eze 20:14
that it *s* not be polluted in the Eze 20:22
judgments whereby they *s* not live Eze 20:25
s we then make mirth Eze 21:10
that *s* make up the hedge, and Eze 22:30
the land, that I *s* not destroy it Eze 22:30
a rock, that it *s* not be covered Eze 24:8
away in them, how *s* we then live Eze 33:10
s not the shepherds feed the Eze 34:2
that he *s* bring certain of the Dan 1:3
for why *s* he see your faces worse Dan 1:10
and the wine that they *s* drink Dan 1:16
king had said he *s* bring them in Dan 1:18
that the wise men *s* be slain Dan 2:13
his fellows *s* not perish with the Dan 2:18
what *s* come to pass hereafter Dan 2:29
that they *s* offer an oblation Dan 2:46
that he *s* be cast into the midst Dan 3:11
commanded that they *s* heat the Dan 3:19
that they *s* read this writing, and Dan 5:15
that he *s* be the third ruler in Dan 5:29
which *s* be over the whole kingdom Dan 6:1
the king *s* have no damage Dan 6:2
commanded that they *s* take Daniel Dan 6:23
and languages, *s* serve him Dan 7:14
what then *s* a king do to us Hos 10:3
my desire that I *s* chastise them Hos 10:10
for he *s* not stay long in the Hos 13:13
that the heathen *s* rule over them Joel 2:17
wherefore *s* they say among the Joel 2:17
s not I spare Nineveh, that great Jonah 4:11
that I *s* make thee a desolation, Mic 6:16
their dwelling *s* not be cut off Zeph 3:7
that the LORD's house *s* be built Hag 1:2
S I weep in the fifth month, Zec 7:3
S ye not hear the words which the Zec 7:7
their ears, that they *s* not hear Zec 7:11
lest they *s* hear the law, and the Zec 7:12
s it also be marvellous in mine Zec 8:6
s I accept this of your hand Mal 1:13
priest's lips *s* keep knowledge Mal 2:7
they *s* seek the law at his mouth Mal 2:7
of them where Christ *s* be born Mt 2:4
that they *s* not return to Herod Mt 2:12
that one of thy members *s* perish Mt 5:29
whole body *s* be cast into hell Mt 5:29
that one of thy members *s* perish Mt 5:30
whole body *s* be cast into hell Mt 5:30
ye would that men *s* do to you Mt 7:12
unto him, Art thou he that *s* come Mt 11:3
that they *s* not make him known Mt 12:16
time they *s* see with their eyes Mt 13:15
s understand with their heart, and Mt 13:15
s be converted, and I *s* heal Mt 13:15
Whence *s* we have so much bread in Mt 15:33
that ye *s* beware of the leaven of Mt 16:11
he his disciples that they *s* tell Mt 16:20
lest we *s* offend them, go thou to Mt 17:27
one of these little ones *s* perish Mt 18:14
prison, till he *s* pay the debt Mt 18:30
till he *s* pay all that was due Mt 18:34
that he *s* put his hands on them, Mt 19:13
that they *s* have received more Mt 20:10
because they *s* hold their peace Mt 20:31
except those days *s* be shortened Mt 24:22
there *s* no flesh be saved Mt 24:22
then at my coming I *s* have Mt 25:27
Though I *s* die with thee, yet Mt 26:35 1163
that they *s* ask Barabbas, and Mt 27:20
that a small ship *s* wait on him Mk 3:9
multitude, lest they *s* throng him Mk 3:9
that they *s* not make him known Mk 3:12
that they *s* be with him, and that Mk 3:14
at any time they *s* be converted Mk 4:12
their sins *s* be forgiven them Mk 4:12
secret, but that it *s* come abroad Mk 4:22
as if a man *s* cast seed into the Mk 4:26
s sleep, and rise night and day Mk 4:27
and the seed *s* spring Mk 4:27
straitly that no man *s* know it Mk 5:43
something *s* be given her to eat Mk 5:43
commanded them that they *s* take Mk 6:8
and preached that men *s* repent Mk 6:12
them that they *s* tell no man Mk 7:36
that they *s* tell no man of him Mk 8:30
he charged them that they *s* tell Mk 9:9
the rising from the dead *s* mean Mk 9:10
that they *s* cast him out Mk 9:18

would not that any man *s* know it Mk 9:30
themselves, who *s* be the greatest Mk 9:34
to him, that he *s* touch them Mk 10:13
what things *s* happen unto him Mk 10:32 3195
What would ye that I *s* do for you Mk 10:36
him that he *s* hold his peace Mk 10:48
wilt thou that I *s* do unto thee Mk 10:51
s carry any vessel through the Mk 11:16
that his brother *s* take his wife Mk 12:19
those days, no flesh *s* be saved Mk 13:20
If I *s* die with thee, I will not Mk 14:31 1163
that he *s* rather release Barabbas Mk 15:11
upon them, what every man *s* take Mk 15:24
manner of salutation this *s* be Lk 1:29
mother of my Lord *s* come to me Lk 1:43
time came that she *s* be delivered Lk 1:57
That we *s* be saved from our Lk 1:71
that all the world *s* be taxed Lk 2:1
that she *s* be delivered Lk 2:6
that he *s* not see death, before Lk 2:26
that he *s* not depart from them Lk 4:42
the other ship, that they *s* come Lk 5:7
as ye would that men *s* do to you Lk 6:31
was worthy for whom he *s* do this Lk 7:4
saying, Art thou he that *s* come Lk 7:19
saying, Art thou he that *s* come Lk 7:20
their hearts, lest they *s* believe Lk 8:12
they *s* tell no man what was done Lk 8:56
except we *s* go and buy meat for Lk 9:13
he *s* accomplish at Jerusalem Lk 9:31 3195
them, which of them *s* be greatest Lk 9:46
was come that he *s* be received up Lk 9:51
It was meet that we *s* make merry Lk 15:32
than that he *s* offend one of Lk 17:2
and it *s* obey you Lk 17:6
when the kingdom of God *s* come Lk 17:20
him, that he *s* hold his peace Lk 18:39
of God *s* immediately appear Lk 19:11 3195
not that I *s* reign over them Lk 19:27
if these *s* hold their peace, the Lk 19:40
that they *s* give him of the fruit Lk 20:10
which *s* feign themselves just men Lk 20:20
that his brother *s* take his wife Lk 20:28
them it was that *s* do this thing Lk 22:23 3195
which of them *s* be accounted the Lk 22:24
that it *s* be as they required Lk 23:24
holden that they *s* not know him Lk 24:16
he which *s* have redeemed Israel Lk 24:21 3195
remission of sins *s* be preached Lk 24:47
but that he *s* be made manifest to Jn 1:31
not that any *s* testify of man Jn 2:25
believeth in him *s* not perish Jn 3:15
believeth in him *s* not perish Jn 3:16
lest his deeds *s* be reproved Jn 3:20
That all men *s* honour the Son, Jn 5:23
that *s* come into the world Jn 6:14
he hath given me I *s* lose nothing Jn 6:39
but *s* raise it up again at the Jn 6:39
believed not, and who *s* betray him Jn 6:64
for he it was that *s* betray him Jn 6:71 3195
the law of Moses *s* not be broken Jn 7:23
that believe on him *s* receive Jn 7:39 3195
us, that such *s* be stoned Jn 8:5
ye *s* have known my Father also Jn 8:19
and if I *s* say, I know him not, I Jn 8:55
of God *s* be made manifest in him Jn 9:3
he *s* be put out of the synagogue Jn 9:22
ye were blind, ye *s* have no sin Jn 9:41
which *s* come into the world Jn 11:27
even this man *s* not have died Jn 11:37
that one man *s* die for the people Jn 11:50
that Jesus *s* die for that nation Jn 11:51 3195
but that also he *s* gather Jn 11:52
he *s* shew it, that they might Jn 11:57
Simon's son, which *s* betray him, Jn 12:4 3195
the Son of man *s* be glorified Jn 12:23
signifying what death he *s* die Jn 12:33 3195
that they *s* not see with their Jn 12:40
and be converted, and I *s* heal them Jn 12:40
lest they *s* be put out of the Jn 12:42
on me *s* not abide in darkness Jn 12:46
I *s* say, and what I *s* speak Jn 12:49
s depart out of this world unto Jn 13:1
For he knew who *s* betray him Jn 13:11
that ye *s* do as I have done to Jn 13:15
that he *s* ask who it *s* be of Jn 13:24
that he *s* give something to the Jn 13:29
ye *s* have known my Father also Jn 14:7
and ordained you, that ye *s* go Jn 15:16
and that your fruit *s* remain Jn 15:16
that ye *s* not be offended Jn 16:1
not that any man *s* ask thee Jn 16:30
that he *s* give eternal life to as Jn 17:2
all things that *s* come upon him Jn 18:4
that one man *s* die for the people Jn 18:14
hall, lest they *s* be defiled Jn 18:28
signifying what death he *s* die Jn 18:32 3195
that I *s* not be delivered to the Jn 18:36
that I *s* bear witness unto the Jn 18:37
that I *s* release unto you one at Jn 18:39
that the bodies *s* not remain upon Jn 19:31
that the scripture *s* be fulfilled Jn 19:36
by what death he *s* glorify God Jn 21:19
that that disciple *s* not die Jn 21:23
if they *s* be written every one, I Jn 21:25
the books that *s* be written Jn 21:25
commanded them that they *s* not Acts 1:4
that he *s* be holden of it Acts 2:24
right hand, that I *s* not be moved Acts 2:25
church daily such as *s* be saved Acts 2:47
prophets, that Christ *s* suffer Acts 3:18
lest they *s* have been stoned Acts 5:26
that ye *s* not teach in this name Acts 5:28
they commanded that they *s* not Acts 5:40

that we s leave the word of God ... Acts 6:2
That his seed s sojourn in a ... Acts 7:6
that they s bring them into ... Acts 7:6
that he s make it according to ... Acts 7:44
can I, except some man s guide me ... Acts 8:31
vision which he had seen s mean ... Acts 10:17
I s not call any man common or ... Acts 10:28
that these s not be baptized, ... Acts 10:47
that he s go as far as Antioch ... Acts 11:22
by the Spirit that there s be ... Acts 11:28 3195
that they s be put to death ... Acts 12:19
they Pilate that he s be slain ... Acts 13:28
s first have been spoken to you ... Acts 13:46
preach unto you that ye s turn ... Acts 14:15
s go up to Jerusalem unto the ... Acts 15:2
s hear the word of the gospel ... Acts 15:7
That they s seek the Lord, if ... Acts 17:27
would that I s bear with you ... Acts 18:14
that they s believe on him which ... Acts 19:4
on him which s come after him ... Acts 19:4
great goddess Diana s be despised ... Acts 19:27
her magnificence s be destroyed ... Acts 19:27 3195
that they s see his face no more ... Acts 20:38 3195
that he s not go up to Jerusalem ... Acts 21:4
disciple, with whom we s lodge ... Acts 21:16
until that an offering s be ... Acts 21:26
for it is not fit that he s live ... Acts 22:22
bade that he s be examined by ... Acts 22:24
him which s have examined him ... Acts 22:29 3195
fearing lest Paul s have been ... Acts 23:10
s have been killed of them ... Acts 23:27 3195
that he s forbid none of his ... Acts 24:23
He hoped also that money s have ... Acts 24:26
that Paul s be kept at Caesarea, ... Acts 25:4
Why s it be thought a thing ... Acts 26:8
that God s raise the dead ... Acts 26:8
the Gentiles, that they s repent ... Acts 26:20
prophets and Moses did say s come ... Acts 26:22 3195
That Christ s suffer, and that he ... Acts 26:23
that he s be the first that ... Acts 26:23
first that s rise from the dead ... Acts 26:23
s shew light unto the people, and ... Acts 26:23 3195
that we s sail into Italy ... Acts 27:1
fearing lest they s fall into the ... Acts 27:17
all hope that we s be saved was ... Acts 27:20
ye s have hearkened unto me, and ... Acts 27:21 1163
Then fearing lest we s have ... Acts 27:29
lest any of them s swim out ... Acts 27:42
that they which could swim s cast ... Acts 27:43
looked when he s have swollen ... Acts 28:6 3195
lest they s see with their eyes, ... Acts 28:27
s be converted, and I s heal ... Acts 28:27
that preachest a man s not steal ... Rom 2:21
a man s not commit adultery ... Rom 2:22
that he s be the heir of the ... Rom 4:13
even so we also s walk in newness ... Rom 6:4
henceforth we s not serve sin ... Rom 6:6
that ye s obey it in the lusts ... Rom 6:12
that ye s be married to another, ... Rom 7:4
that we s bring forth fruit unto ... Rom 7:4
that we s serve in newness of ... Rom 7:6
what we s pray for as we ought ... Rom 8:26
slumber, eyes that they s not see ... Rom 11:8
and ears that they s not hear ... Rom 11:8
they stumbled that they s fall ... Rom 11:11
that ye s be ignorant of this ... Rom 11:25
lest ye s be wise in your own ... Rom 11:25
That I s be the minister of Jesus ... Rom 15:16
lest I s build upon another man's ... Rom 15:20
Lest any s say that I had ... 1Cor 1:15
Christ s be made of none effect ... 1Cor 1:17
That no flesh s glory in his ... 1Cor 1:29
That your faith s not stand in ... 1Cor 2:5
thing that I s be judged of you ... 1Cor 4:3
that one s have his father's wife ... 1Cor 5:1
he that ploweth s plow in hope ... 1Cor 9:10 3784
in hope s be partaker of his hope ... 1Cor 9:10
lest we s hinder the gospel of ... 1Cor 9:12
the gospel s live of the gospel ... 1Cor 9:14
that it s be so done unto me ... 1Cor 9:15
than that any man s make my ... 1Cor 9:15
others, I myself s be a castaway ... 1Cor 9:27
I would not that ye s be ignorant ... 1Cor 10:1
to the intent we s not lust after ... 1Cor 10:6
I would not that ye s have ... 1Cor 10:20
ourselves, we s not be judged ... 1Cor 11:31
that we s not be condemned with ... 1Cor 11:32
That there s be no schism in the ... 1Cor 12:25
but that the members s have the ... 1Cor 12:25
that we s not trust in ourselves, ... 2Cor 1:9
that with me there s be yea yea ... 2Cor 1:17
I s have sorrow from them of whom ... 2Cor 2:3
not that ye s be grieved, but ... 2Cor 2:4
lest perhaps such a one s be ... 2Cor 2:7
Lest Satan s get an advantage of ... 2Cor 2:11
image of God, s shine unto them ... 2Cor 4:4
that they which live s not ... 2Cor 5:15
that no man s blame us in this ... 2Cor 8:20
lest our boasting of you s be in ... 2Cor 9:3
ye) s be ashamed in this same ... 2Cor 9:4
For though I s boast somewhat ... 2Cor 10:8
destruction, I s not be ashamed ... 2Cor 10:8
so your minds s be corrupted from ... 2Cor 11:3
lest any man s think of me above ... 2Cor 12:6
lest I s be exalted above measure ... 2Cor 12:7
lest I s be exalted above measure ... 2Cor 12:7
not that we s appear approved, ... 2Cor 13:7
but that ye s do that which is ... 2Cor 13:7
being present I s use sharpness ... 2Cor 13:10
I s not be the servant of Christ ... Gal 1:10
lest by any means I s run ... Gal 2:2
that we s go unto the heathen, and ... Gal 2:9
would that we s remember the poor ... Gal 2:10
that ye s not obey the truth, ... Gal 3:1
that it s make the promise of ... Gal 3:17
till the seed s come to whom the ... Gal 3:19
s have been by the law ... Gal 3:21
which s afterwards be revealed ... Gal 3:23 3195
you that ye s not obey the truth ... Gal 5:7
only lest they s suffer ... Gal 6:12
But God forbid that I s glory ... Gal 6:14
of the world, that we s be holy ... Eph 1:4
That we s be to the praise of his ... Eph 1:12
of works, lest any man s boast ... Eph 2:9
ordained that we s walk in them ... Eph 2:10
the Gentiles s be fellowheirs ... Eph 3:6
that I s preach among the ... Eph 3:8
but that it s be holy and without ... Eph 5:27
But I would ye s understand ... Phil 1:12
name of Jesus every knee s bow ... Phil 2:10
that every tongue s confess that ... Phil 2:11
lest I s have sorrow upon sorrow ... Phil 2:27
that in him s all fulness dwell ... Col 1:19
lest any man s beguile you with ... Col 2:4
That no man s be moved by these ... 1Th 3:3
that we s suffer tribulation ... 1Th 3:4 3195
that ye s abstain from ... 1Th 4:3
That every one of you s know how ... 1Th 4:4
that that day s overtake you as a ... 1Th 5:4
we s live together with him ... 1Th 5:10
that they s believe a lie ... 2Th 2:11
would not work, neither s he eat ... 2Th 3:10
s hereafter believe on him to ... 1Ti 1:16 3195
we s live soberly, righteously, ... Titus 2:12
we s be made heirs according to ... Titus 3:7
that thy benefit s not be as it ... Philem 14
at any time we s let them slip ... Heb 2:1
God s taste death for every man ... Heb 2:9
they s not enter into his rest ... Heb 3:18
any of you s seem to come short ... Heb 4:1
priest s rise after the order of ... Heb 7:11
he s not be a priest, seeing that ... Heb 8:4
then s no place have been sought ... Heb 8:7
heavens s be purified with these ... Heb 9:23
Nor yet that he s offer himself ... Heb 9:25
the worshippers once purged s ... Heb 10:2
of goats s take away sins ... Heb 10:4
that he s not see death ... Heb 11:5
which he s after receive for an ... Heb 11:8 3195
the firstborn s touch them ... Heb 11:28
without us s not be made perfect ... Heb 11:40
heard intreated that the word s ... Heb 12:19
of truth, that we s be a kind of ... Jas 1:18
of the grace that s come unto you ... 1Pet 1:10
and the glory that s follow ... 1Pet 1:11
that ye s shew forth the praises ... 1Pet 2:9
that ye s follow his steps ... 1Pet 2:21
s live unto righteousness ... 1Pet 2:24
that ye s inherit a blessing ... 1Pet 3:9
That he no longer s live the rest ... 1Pet 4:2
those that after s live ungodly ... 2Pet 2:6 3195
not willing that any s perish ... 2Pet 3:9
but that all s come to repentance ... 2Pet 3:9
that we s be called the sons of ... 1Jn 3:1
that we s love one another ... 1Jn 3:11
That we s believe on the name of ... 1Jn 3:23
ye have heard that it s come ... 1Jn 4:3
the beginning, ye s walk in it ... 2Jn 6
exhort you that ye s earnestly ... Jude 3
s be mockers in the last time ... Jude 18
who s walk after their own ... Jude 18
that they s kill one another ... Rev 6:4
that they s rest yet for a little ... Rev 6:11
that s be killed as they were, ... Rev 6:11 3195
as they were, s be fulfilled ... Rev 6:11
that the wind s not blow on the ... Rev 7:1
that he s offer it with the ... Rev 8:3
s not hurt the grass of the earth ... Rev 9:4
given that they s not kill them ... Rev 9:5
but that they s be tormented five ... Rev 9:5
that they s not worship devils, ... Rev 9:20
that there s be time no longer ... Rev 10:6
the mystery of God s be finished ... Rev 10:7
the dead, that they s be judged ... Rev 11:18
that they s feed her there a ... Rev 12:6
that they s make an image to the ... Rev 13:14
image of the beast s both speak ... Rev 13:15
image of the beast s be killed ... Rev 13:15
she s be arrayed in fine linen ... Rev 19:8
that with it he s smite the ... Rev 19:15
that he s deceive the nations no ... Rev 20:3
the thousand years s be fulfilled ... Rev 20:3

SHOULDER

unto Hagar, putting it on her s ... Gen 21:14 7926
with her pitcher upon her s ... Gen 24:15 7926
forth with her pitcher on her s ... Gen 24:45 7926
let down her pitcher from her s ... Gen 24:46
and bowed his s to bear, and became ... Gen 49:15 7926
that is upon them, and the right s ... Ex 29:22 7785
the s of the heave offering, ... Ex 29:27 7785
the right s shall ye give unto ... Lev 7:32 7785
have the right s for his part ... Lev 7:33 7785
the heave s have I taken of the ... Lev 7:34 7785
and their fat, and the right s ... Lev 8:25 7785
on the fat, and upon the right s ... Lev 8:26 7785
the right s Aaron waved for a ... Lev 9:21 7785
heave s shall ye eat in a clean ... Lev 10:14 7785
The heave s and the wave breast ... Lev 10:15 7785
take the sodden s of the ram ... Num 6:19 2220
with the wave breast and heave s ... Num 6:20 7785
and as the right s are thine ... Num 18:18 7785
shall give unto the priest the s ... Deut 18:3 2220
man of you a stone upon his s ... Josh 4:5 7926
and took it, and laid it on his s ... Judg 9:48 7926
And the cook took up the s ... 1Sa 9:24 7785
and withdrew the s, and hardened ... Neh 9:29 3802
let mine arm fall from my s blade ... Job 31:22 7929
Surely I would take it upon my s ... Job 31:36 7926
I removed his s from the burden ... Ps 81:6 7926
his burden, and the staff of his s ... Is 9:4 7926
government shall be upon his s ... Is 9:6 7926
be taken away from off thy s ... Is 10:27 7926
of David will I lay upon his s ... Is 22:22 7926
They bear him upon the s, they ... Is 46:7 3802
bare it upon my s in their sight ... Eze 12:7 3802
bear upon his s in the twilight ... Eze 12:12 3802
good piece, the thigh, and the s ... Eze 24:4 3802
didst break, and rend all their s ... Eze 29:7 3802
made bald, and every s was peeled ... Eze 29:18 3802
have thrust with side and with s ... Eze 34:21 3802
to hearken, and pulled away the s ... Zec 7:11 3802

SHOULDERPIECES

It shall have the two s thereof ... Ex 28:7 3802
put them on the s of the ephod ... Ex 28:25 3802
They made s for it, to couple it ... Ex 39:4 3802
and put them on the s of the ephod ... Ex 39:18 3802

SHOULDERS

and laid it upon both their s ... Gen 9:23 7926
up in their clothes upon their s ... Ex 12:34 7926
the s of the ephod for stones of ... Ex 28:12 3802
upon his two s for a memorial ... Ex 28:12 3802
he put them on the s of the ephod ... Ex 39:7 3802
they should bear upon their s ... Num 7:9 3802
and he shall dwell between his s ... Deut 33:12 3802
and all, and put them upon his s ... Judg 16:3 3802
from his s and upward he was ... 1Sa 9:2 7926
than any of the people from his s ... 1Sa 10:23 7926
a target of brass between his s ... 1Sa 17:6 3802
their s with the staves thereon ... 1Chr 15:15 3802
shall not be a burden upon your s ... 2Chr 35:3 3802
But they shall fly upon the s of ... Is 11:14 3802
burden depart from off their s ... Is 14:25 7926
riches upon the s of young asses ... Is 30:6 3802
shall be carried upon their s ... Is 49:22 3802
shalt thou bear it upon thy s ... Eze 12:6 3802
be borne, and lay them on men's s ... Mt 23:4 5606
found it, he layeth it on his s ... Lk 15:5 5606

SHOULDEST

thee that thou s not eat ... Gen 3:11
that is thine, lest thou s say ... Gen 14:23
thou s have brought guiltiness ... Gen 26:10
s thou therefore serve me for ... Gen 29:15
that thou s say unto me, Carry ... Num 11:12
s be driven to worship them, and ... Deut 4:19
thee, and that thou s keep all his ... Deut 26:18
That thou s enter into covenant ... Deut 29:12
is not in heaven, that thou s say ... Deut 30:12
beyond the sea, that thou s say ... Deut 30:13
Israel, and s thou possess it ... Judg 11:23
that thou s take knowledge of me, ... Ruth 2:10
for why s thou bring me to thy ... 1Sa 20:8
that thou s look upon such a dead ... 2Sa 9:8
that thou s tell them who shall ... 1Kin 1:20
me that thou s surely recover ... 2Kin 8:14
Thou s have smitten five or six ... 2Kin 13:19
for why s thou meddle to thy hurt ... 2Kin 14:10
to thy hurt, that thou s fall ... 2Kin 14:10
that thou s be to lay waste ... 2Kin 19:25
that thou s be ruler over my ... 1Chr 17:7
S thou help the ungodly, and love ... 2Chr 19:2
why s thou be smitten ... 2Chr 25:16
why s thou meddle to thine hurt, ... 2Chr 25:19
to thine hurt, that thou s fall ... 2Chr 25:19
is man, that thou s magnify him ... Job 7:17
that thou s set thine heart upon ... Job 7:17
that thou s visit him every ... Job 7:18
unto thee that thou s oppress ... Job 10:3
that thou s despise the work of ... Job 10:3
That thou s take it to the bound ... Job 38:20
that thou s know the paths to the ... Job 38:20
or that thou s take my covenant ... Ps 50:16
s mark iniquities, O Lord, who ... Ps 130:3
Lest thou s ponder the path of ... Prov 5:6
than that thou s be put lower in ... Prov 25:7
Though thou s bray a fool in a ... Prov 27:22
Better is it that thou s not vow ... Eccl 5:5
than that thou s vow ... Eccl 5:5
why s thou destroy thyself ... Eccl 7:16
why s thou die before thy time ... Eccl 7:17
that thou s take hold of this ... Eccl 7:18
that thou s be to lay waste ... Is 37:26
lest thou s say, Mine idol hath ... Is 48:5
lest thou s say, Behold, I knew ... Is 48:7
thee by the way that thou s go ... Is 48:17
s be my servant to raise up the ... Is 49:6
that thou s be afraid of a man ... Is 51:12
why s thou be as a stranger in ... Jer 14:8
Why s thou be as a man astonied, ... Jer 14:9
that thou s put him in prison, and ... Jer 29:26
though thou s make thy nest as ... Jer 49:16
But thou s not have looked on the ... Obad 12
neither s thou have rejoiced over ... Obad 12
neither s thou have spoken ... Obad 12
Thou s not have entered into the ... Obad 13
thou s not have looked on their ... Obad 13
Neither s thou have stood in the ... Obad 14
neither s thou have delivered up ... Obad 14
that thou s come under my roof ... Mt 8:8
S not thou also have had ... Mt 18:33
we would that thou s do for us ... Mk 10:35
that thou s enter under my roof ... Lk 7:6
thou s see the glory of God ... Jn 11:40
I pray not that thou s take them ... Jn 17:15
but that thou s keep them from ... Jn 17:15
that thou s be for salvation unto ... Acts 13:47
that thou s know his will, and see ... Acts 22:14
s hear the voice of his mouth ... Acts 22:14
that thou s set in order the ... Titus 1:5
that thou s receive him for ever ... Philem 15

that thou *s* give reward unto thy ... Rev 11:18
s destroy them which destroy the ... Rev 11:18

SHOUT
voice of them that *s* for mastery ... Ex 32:18 6030
the *s* of a king is among them ... Num 23:21 8643
people shall *s* with a great *s* ... Josh 6:5 7321
people shall *s* with a great *s* ... Josh 6:5 8643
people, saying, Ye shall not *s* ... Josh 6:10 7321
mouth, until the day I bid you *s* ... Josh 6:10 7321
then shall ye *s* ... Josh 6:10 7321
Joshua said unto the people, *S* ... Josh 6:16 7321
the people shouted with a great *s* ... Josh 6:20 8643
all Israel shouted with a great *s* ... 1Sa 4:5 8643
heard the noise of the *s*, they ... 1Sa 4:6 8643
s in the camp of the Hebrews ... 1Sa 4:6
Then the men of Judah gave a *s* ... 2Chr 13:15 7321
the people shouted with a great *s* ... Ezr 3:11 8643
s of joy from the noise of the ... Ezr 3:13 8643
the people shouted with a loud *s* ... Ezr 3:13 8643
let them ever *s* for joy, because ... Ps 5:11 7442
s for joy, all ye that are ... Ps 32:11 7442
Let them *s* for joy, and be glad, ... Ps 35:27 7442
s unto God with the voice of ... Ps 47:1 7321
God is gone up with a *s*, the LORD ... Ps 47:5 8643
they *s* for joy, they also sing ... Ps 65:13 7321
and let thy saints *s* for joy ... Ps 132:9 7442
her saints shall *s* aloud for joy ... Ps 132:16 7442
Cry out and *s*, thou inhabitant of ... Is 12:6 7442
let them *s* from the top of the ... Is 42:11 6681
s, ye lower parts of the earth ... Is 44:23 7321
he shall give a *s*, as they that ... Jer 25:30
s among the chief of the nations ... Jer 31:7 6670
S against her round about ... Jer 50:15 7321
shall lift up a *s* against thee ... Jer 51:14 1959
Also when I cry and *s*, he shutteth ... Lam 3:8 7768
s, O Israel ... Zeph 3:14 7321
s, O daughter of Jerusalem ... Zec 9:9 7321
And the people gave a *s*, saying, ... Acts 12:22 *2019*
descend from heaven with a *s* ... 1Th 4:16 *2752*

SHOUTED
the noise of the people as they *s* ... Ex 32:17 7452
when all the people saw, they *s* ... Lev 9:24 7442
So the people *s* when the priests ... Josh 6:20 7321
the people *s* with a great shout, ... Josh 6:20 7321
the Philistines *s* against him ... Judg 15:14 7321
all Israel *s* with a great shout, ... 1Sa 4:5 7321
And all the people *s*, and said, God ... 1Sa 10:24 7321
to the fight, and *s* for the battle ... 1Sa 17:20 7321
of Israel and of Judah arose, and *s* ... 1Sa 17:52 7321
and as the men of Judah *s*, it came ... 2Chr 13:15 7321
all the people *s* with a great ... Ezr 3:11 7321
and many *s* aloud for joy ... Ezr 3:12 8643
for the people *s* with a loud ... Ezr 3:13 7321
and all the sons of God *s* for joy ... Job 38:7 7321

SHOUTETH
man that *s* by reason of wine ... Ps 78:65 7442

SHOUTING
up the ark of the LORD with *s* ... 2Sa 6:15 8643
the covenant of the LORD with *s* ... 1Chr 15:28 8643
LORD with a loud voice, and with *s* ... 2Chr 15:14 8643
thunder of the captains, and the *s* ... Job 39:25 8643
the wicked perish, there is *s* ... Prov 11:10 7440
for the *s* for thy summer fruits ... Is 16:9 1959
singing, neither shall there be *s* ... Is 16:10 7321
made their vintage *s* to cease ... Is 16:10 1959
the morning, and the *s* at noontide ... Jer 20:16 8643
none shall tread with *s* ... Jer 48:33 1959
their *s* shall be no *s* ... Jer 48:33 1959
to lift up the voice with *s* ... Eze 21:22 8643
with *s* in the day of battle, with ... Amos 1:14 8643
shall die with tumult, with *s* ... Amos 2:2 8643

SHOUTINGS
the headstone thereof with *s* ... Zec 4:7 8663

SHOVEL
hath been winnowed with the *s* ... Is 30:24 7371

SHOVELS
to receive his ashes, and his *s* ... Ex 27:3 3257
of the altar, the pots, and the *s* ... Ex 38:3 3257
censers, the fleshhooks, and the *s* ... Num 4:14 3257
Hiram made the lavers, and the *s* ... 1Kin 7:40 3257
And the pots, and the *s*, and the ... 1Kin 7:45 3257
And the pots, and the *s*, and the ... 2Kin 25:14 3257
And Huram made the pots, and the *s* ... 2Chr 4:11 3257
The pots also, and the *s*, and the ... 2Chr 4:16 3257
The caldrons also, and the *s* ... Jer 52:18 3257

SHOWER
there shall be an overflowing *s* ... Eze 13:11 1653
be an overflowing *s* in mine anger ... Eze 13:13 1653
I will cause the *s* to come down ... Eze 34:26 1653
ye say, There cometh a *s* ... Lk 12:54 *3655*

SHOWERS
herb, and as the *s* upon the grass ... Deut 32:2 7241
wet with the *s* of the mountains ... Job 24:8 2230
thou makest it soft with *s* ... Ps 65:10 7241
as *s* that water the earth ... Ps 72:6 7241
Therefore the *s* have been ... Jer 3:3 7241
or can the heavens give *s* ... Jer 14:22 7241
there shall be *s* of blessing ... Eze 34:26 1653
as the *s* upon the grass, that ... Mic 5:7 7241
clouds, and give them *s* of rain ... Zec 10:1 1653

SHRANK
eat not of the sinew which *s* ... Gen 32:32 5384
Jacob's thigh in the sinew that *s* ... Gen 32:32 5384

SHRED
s them into the pot of pottage ... 2Kin 4:39 6398

SHRINES
which made silver *s* for Diana ... Acts 19:24 *3485*

SHROUD
branches, and with a shadowing *s* ... Eze 31:3 2793

SHRUBS
cast the child under one of the *s* ... Gen 21:15 7880

SHUA (*shu'-ah*) See SHUAH.
1. Daughter of Judah.
the daughter of *S* the Canaanitess ... 1Chr 2:3 7770
2. Daughter of Heber.
and Hotham, and *S* their sister ... 1Chr 7:32 7774

SHUAH (*shu'-ah*)
1. A son of Abraham.
Medan, and Midian, and Ishbak, and *S* Gen 25:2 7744
Medan, and Midian, and Ishbak, and *S* 1Chr 1:32 7744
2. Same as Shua 1.
Canaanite, whose name was *S* ... Gen 38:2 7770
daughter of *S* Judah's wife died ... Gen 38:12 7770
3. A descendant of Caleb.
the brother of *S* begat Mehir ... 1Chr 4:11 7746

SHUAL (*shu'-al*)
1. A district in Benjamin.
to Ophrah, unto the land of *S* ... 1Sa 13:17 7777
2. Son of Zophah.
Suah, and Harnepher, and *S*, and Beri. 1Chr 7:36 7777

SHUBAEL (*shu'-ba-el*) See SHEBUEL.
1. Son of Amram.
sons of Amram; *S* ... 1Chr 24:20 2619
of the sons of *S* ... 1Chr 24:20 2619
2. A sanctuary servant.
The thirteenth to *S*, he, his sons ... 1Chr 25:20 2619

SHUHAH See SHUAH.

SHUHAM (*shu'-ham*) See HUSHIM, SHUHAMITES.
A son of Dan.
of *S*, the family of the ... Num 26:42 7748

SHUHAMITES (*shu'-ham-ites*) *Descendants of Shuham.*
of Shuham, the family of the *S* ... Num 26:42 7749
All the families of the *S* ... Num 26:43 7749

SHUHITE (*shu'-hite*) *A descendant of Shuah.*
the Temanite, and Bildad the *S* ... Job 2:11 7747
Then answered Bildad the *S* ... Job 8:1 7747
Then answered Bildad the *S* ... Job 18:1 7747
Then answered Bildad the *S* ... Job 25:1 7747
the Temanite and Bildad the *S* ... Job 42:9 7747

SHULAMITE (*shu'-lam-ite*) *An inhabitant of Shulam.*
Return, return, O *S* ... Song 6:13 7759
What will ye see in the *S* ... Song 6:13 7759

SHULAMMITE See SHULAMITE.

SHUMATHITES (*shu'-math-ites*) *Descendants of Shobal.*
and the Puhites, and the *S* ... 1Chr 2:53 8126

SHUN
But *s* profane and vain babblings ... 2Ti 2:16 *4026*

SHUNAMMITE (*shu'-nam-mite*) *An inhabitant of Shunem.*
of Israel, and found Abishag a *S* ... 1Kin 1:3 7767
Abishag the *S* ministered unto the ... 1Kin 1:15 7767
he give me Abishag the *S* to wife ... 1Kin 2:17 7767
Let Abishag the *S* be given to ... 1Kin 2:21 7767
ask Abishag the *S* for Adonijah ... 1Kin 2:22 7767
Gehazi his servant, Call this *S* ... 2Kin 4:12 7767
servant, Behold, yonder is that *S* ... 2Kin 4:25 7767
Gehazi, and said, Call this *S* ... 2Kin 4:36 7767

SHUNEM (*shu'-nem*) See SHUNAMMITE. *A city in Issachar.*
Jezreel, and Chesulloth, and *S* ... Josh 19:18 7766
together, and came and pitched in *S* ... 1Sa 28:4 7766
on a day, that Elisha passed to *S* ... 2Kin 4:8 7766

SHUNI (*shu'-ni*) See SHUNITES. *A son of Gad.*
Ziphion, and Haggi, *S*, and Ezbon, ... Gen 46:16 7764
of *S*, the family of the Shunites ... Num 26:15 7764

SHUNITES (*shu'-nites*) *Descendants of Shuni.*
of Shuni, the family of the *S* ... Num 26:15 7765

SHUNNED
For I have not *s* to declare unto ... Acts 20:27 *5288*

SHUPHAM (*shu'-fam*) See SHEPHUPHAN, SHUPHAMITES. *A son of Benjamin.*
Of *S*, the family of the ... Num 26:39 8197

SHUPHAMITES (*shu'-fam-ites*) *Descendants of Shupham.*
Of Shupham, the family of the *S* ... Num 26:39 7781

SHUPPIM (*shup'-pim*) See MUPPIM, SHEPHUPHAN.
1. A Benjamite.
S also, and Huppim, the children ... 1Chr 7:12 8206
to wife the sister of Huppim and *S* ... 1Chr 7:15 8206
2. A Levite gatekeeper.
To *S* and Hosah the lot came forth ... 1Chr 26:16 8206

SHUR (*shur*) *A wilderness east of Egypt.*
by the fountain in the way to *S* ... Gen 16:7 7793
and dwelled between Kadesh and *S* ... Gen 20:1 7793
And they dwelt from Havilah unto *S* ... Gen 25:18 7793
went out into the wilderness of *S* ... Ex 15:22 7793
Havilah until thou comest to *S* ... 1Sa 15:7 7793
of the land, as thou goest to *S* ... 1Sa 27:8 7793

SHUSHAN (*shu'-shan*) See SHOSHANNIM. *Capital of Persia.*
year, as I was in *S* the palace ... Neh 1:1 7800
which was in *S* the palace ... Est 1:2 7800
that were present in *S* the palace ... Est 1:5 7800
young virgins unto *S* the palace ... Est 2:3 7800
Now in *S* the palace there was a ... Est 2:5 7800
together unto *S* the palace ... Est 2:8 7800
decree was given in *S* the palace ... Est 3:15 7800
but the city *S* was perplexed ... Est 3:15 7800
was given at *S* to destroy them ... Est 4:8 7800
the Jews that are present in *S* ... Est 4:16 7800
decree was given at *S* the palace ... Est 8:14 7800
and the city of *S* rejoiced ... Est 8:15 7800
in *S* the palace the Jews slew and ... Est 9:6 7800
of those that were slain in *S* the ... Est 9:11 7800
five hundred men in *S* the palace ... Est 9:12 7800
to the Jews which are in *S* to do ... Est 9:13 7800
and the decree was given at *S* ... Est 9:14 7800
For the Jews that were in *S* ... Est 9:15 7800
and slew three hundred men at *S* ... Est 9:15 7800
at *S* assembled together on the ... Est 9:18 7800
that I was at *S* in the palace ... Dan 8:2 7800

SHUSHAN-EDUTH (*shu'-shan-e'-duth*)
To the chief Musician upon *S* ... Ps 60:*t* 7802

SHUT
and the LORD *s* him in ... Gen 7:16 5462
them, and *s* the door after him, ... Gen 19:6 5462
house to them, and *s* to the door ... Gen 19:10 5462
the wilderness hath *s* them in ... Ex 14:3 5462
then the priest shall *s* up him ... Lev 13:4 5462
then the priest shall *s* him up ... Lev 13:5 5462
unclean, and shall not *s* him up ... Lev 13:11 5462
priest shall *s* him up seven days ... Lev 13:21 5462
priest shall *s* him up seven days ... Lev 13:26 5462
then the priest shall *s* up him ... Lev 13:31 5462
the priest shall *s* up him that ... Lev 13:33 5462
s up it that hath the plague ... Lev 13:50 5462
he shall *s* it up seven days more ... Lev 13:54 5462
s up the house seven days ... Lev 14:38 5462
s up shall be unclean until the ... Lev 14:46 5462
let her be *s* out from the camp ... Num 12:14 5462
Miriam was *s* out from the camp ... Num 12:15 5462
he *s* up the heaven, that there be ... Deut 11:17 6113
nor *s* thine hand from thy poor ... Deut 15:7 7092
them, and the LORD had *s* them up ... Deut 32:30 5462
is gone, and there is none *s* up ... Deut 32:36 6113
were gone out, they *s* the gate ... Josh 2:7 5462
Now Jericho was straitly *s* up ... Josh 6:1 5462
s the doors of the parlour upon ... Judg 3:23 5462
s it to them, and gat them up to ... Judg 9:51 5462
but the LORD had *s* up her womb ... 1Sa 1:5 5462
the LORD had *s* up her womb ... 1Sa 1:6 5462
s up their calves at home ... 1Sa 6:10 3607
for he is *s* in, by entering into ... 1Sa 23:7 5462
So they were *s* up unto the day of ... 2Sa 20:3 6887
When heaven is *s* up, and there is ... 1Kin 8:35 6113
the wall, and him that is *s* up ... 1Kin 14:10 6113
the wall, and him that is *s* up ... 1Kin 21:21 6113
thou shalt *s* the door upon thee ... 2Kin 4:4 5462
s the door upon her and upon her ... 2Kin 4:5 5462
s the door upon him, and went out ... 2Kin 4:21 5462
s the door upon them twain, and ... 2Kin 4:33 5462
s the door, and hold him fast at ... 2Kin 6:32 5462
the wall, and him that is *s* up ... 2Kin 9:8 6113
for there was not any *s* up ... 2Kin 14:26 6113
the king of Assyria *s* him up ... 2Kin 17:4 6113
When the heaven is *s* up, and there ... 2Chr 6:26 6113
If I *s* up heaven that there be no ... 2Chr 7:13 6113
s up the doors of the house of ... 2Chr 28:24 5462
Also they have *s* up the doors of ... 2Chr 29:7 5462
son of Mehetabeel, who was *s* up ... Neh 6:10 6113
let us *s* the doors of the temple ... Neh 6:10 5462
let them *s* the doors, and bar them ... Neh 7:3 1479
that the gates should be *s* ... Neh 13:19 5462
Because it *s* not up the doors of ... Job 3:10 5462
s up, or gather together, then ... Job 11:10 5462
Or who *s* up the sea with doors, ... Job 38:8 5526
s up together as with a close ... Job 41:15 5462
hast not *s* me up into the hand of ... Ps 31:8 5462
let not the pit *s* her mouth upon ... Ps 69:15 332
hath he in anger *s* up his tender ... Ps 77:9 7092
I am *s* up, and I cannot come forth ... Ps 88:8 3607
doors shall be *s* in the streets ... Eccl 12:4 5462
a spring *s* up, a fountain sealed ... Song 4:12 5274
their ears heavy, and *s* their eyes ... Is 6:10 8173
so he shall open, and none shall *s* ... Is 22:22 5462
and he shall *s*, and none shall open ... Is 22:22 5462
every house is *s* up, that no man ... Is 24:10 5462
shall be *s* up in the prison, and ... Is 24:22 5462
and *s* thy doors about thee ... Is 26:20 5462
for he hath *s* their eyes, that ... Is 44:18 2902
and the gates shall not be *s* ... Is 45:1 5462
the kings shall *s* their mouths at ... Is 52:15 7092
they shall not be *s* day nor night ... Is 60:11 5462
to bring forth, and *s* the womb ... Is 66:9 6113
cities of the south shall be *s* up ... Jer 13:19 5462
a burning fire *s* up in my bones ... Jer 20:9 6113
Jeremiah the prophet was *s* up in ... Jer 32:2 3607
king of Judah had *s* him up ... Jer 32:3 3607
while he was yet *s* up in the ... Jer 33:1 6113
Baruch, saying, I am *s* up ... Jer 36:5 6113
while he was *s* up in the court of ... Jer 39:15 6113
s thyself within thine house ... Eze 3:24 5462
and it was *s* ... Eze 44:1 5462
This gate shall be *s*, it shall ... Eze 44:2 5462
in by it, therefore it shall be *s* ... Eze 44:2 5462
shall be *s* the six working days ... Eze 46:1 5462
shall not be *s* until the evening ... Eze 46:2 5462
going forth one shall *s* the gate ... Eze 46:12 5462
hath *s* the lions' mouths, that ... Dan 6:22 5463
wherefore *s* thou up the vision ... Dan 8:26 5640

s up the words, and seal the book, Dan 12:4 5640
that would s the doors for nought Mal 1:10 5462
and when thou hast s thy door Mt 6:6 2808
for ye s up the kingdom of heaven Mt 23:13 2808
and the door was s Mt 25:10 2808
that he s up John in prison Lk 3:20 2623
the heaven was s up three years Lk 4:25 2808
the door is now s, and my children Lk 11:7 2808
hath s to the door, and ye begin Lk 13:25 608
when the doors were s where the Jn 20:19 2808
came Jesus, the doors being s Jn 20:26 2808
truly found we s with all safety Acts 5:23 2808
and forthwith the doors were s Acts 21:30 2808
the saints did I s up in prison Acts 26:10 2623
s up unto the faith which should Gal 3:23 4788
an open door, and no man can s it Rev 3:8 2808
These have power to s heaven Rev 11:6 2808
s him up, and set a seal upon him, Rev 20:3 2808
it shall not be s at all by day Rev 21:25 2808

SHUTHALHITES (*shu'-thal-hites*) *Descendants of Shuthelah.*
of Shuthelah, the family of the S Num 26:35 8364

SHUTHELAH (*shu'-the-lah*) See SHUTHALHITES.
1. A son of Ephraim.
of S, the family of the Num 26:35 7803
And these are the sons of S Num 26:36 7803
S, and Bered his son, and Tahath 1Chr 7:20 7803
2. Son of Zabad.
S his son, and Ezer, and Elead, 1Chr 7:21 7803

SHUTHELAHITES See SHUTHALHITES.

SHUTTETH
he s up a man, and there can be no Job 12:14 5462
He s his eyes to devise froward Prov 16:30 6095
he that s his lips is esteemed a Prov 17:28 331
s his eyes from seeing evil Is 33:15 6105
cry and shout, he s out my prayer Lam 3:8 5640
s up his bowels of compassion 1Jn 3:17 2808
he that openeth, and no man s Rev 3:7 2808
and s, and no man openeth Rev 3:7 2808

SHUTTING
about the time of s of the gate Josh 2:5 5462

SHUTTLE
are swifter than a weaver's s Job 7:6 708

SIA (*si'-ah*) See SIAHA. *A family of exiles.*
of Keros, the children of S Neh 7:47 5517

SIAHA (*si'-a-hah*) See SIA. *Same as Sia.*
of Keros, the children of S Ezr 2:44 5517

SIBBECAI (*sib'-be-cahee*) See SIBBECHAI. *A "mighty man" of David.*
S the Hushathite, Ilai the 1Chr 11:29 5444
eighth month was S the Hushathite 1Chr 27:11 5444

SIBBECHAI (*sib'-be-kahee*) See SIBBECAI. *Same as Sibbecai.*
then S the Hushathite slew Saph, 2Sa 21:18 5444
at which time S the Hushathite 1Chr 20:4 5444

SIBBOLETH (*sib'-bo-leth*) See SHIBBOLETH. *The Ephraimite pronunciation of Shibboleth.*
and he said S Judg 12:6 5451

SIBMAH (*sib'-mah*) *A city in Reuben.*
And Kirjathaim, and S, and Josh 13:19 7643
languish, and the vine of S Is 16:8 7643
weeping of Jazer the vine of S Is 16:9 7643
O vine of S, I will weep for thee Jer 48:32 7643

SIBRAIM (*sib'-ra-im*) *A city in Syria between Damascus and Hamath.*
Hamath, Berothah, S, which is Eze 47:16 5453

SICHEM (*si'-kem*) See SHECHEM, SYCHEM. *A place on the plain of Moreh.*
the land unto the place of S Gen 12:6 7927

SICK
Joseph, Behold, thy father is s Gen 48:1 2470
of her that is s of her flowers Lev 15:33 1739
to take David, she said, He is s 1Sa 19:14 2470
because three days agone I fell s 1Sa 30:13 2470
bare unto David, and it was very s 2Sa 12:15 605
that he fell s for his sister 2Sa 13:2 2470
on thy bed, and make thyself s 2Sa 13:5 2470
Amnon lay down, and made himself s 2Sa 13:6 2470
Abijah the son of Jeroboam fell s 1Kin 14:1 2470
for he is s 1Kin 14:5 2470
the mistress of the house, fell s 1Kin 17:17 2470
that was in Samaria, and was s 2Kin 1:2 2470
Ben-hadad the king of Syria was s 2Kin 8:7 2470
Ahab in Jezreel, because he was s 2Kin 8:29 2470
Now Elisha was fallen s of his 2Kin 13:14 2470
days was Hezekiah s unto death 2Kin 20:1 2470
heard that Hezekiah had been s 2Kin 20:12 2470
Ahab at Jezreel, because he was s 2Chr 22:6 2470
days Hezekiah was s to the death 2Chr 32:24 2470
sad, seeing thou art not s Neh 2:2 2470
But as for me, when they were s Ps 35:13 2470
Hope deferred maketh the heart s Prov 13:12 2470
shalt thou say, and I was not s Prov 23:35 2470
for I am s of love Song 2:5 2470
ye tell him, that I am s of love Song 5:8 2470
the whole head is s, and the whole Is 1:5 2483
inhabitant shall not say, I am s Is 33:24 2470
days was Hezekiah s unto death Is 38:1 2470
king of Judah, when he had been s Is 38:9 2470
he had heard that he had been s Is 39:1 2470
them that are s with famine Jer 14:18 8463
have ye healed that which was s Eze 34:4 2470
will strengthen that which was s Eze 34:16 2470
fainted, and was s certain days Dan 8:27 2470
made him s with bottles of wine Hos 7:5 2470
I make thee s in smiting thee Mic 6:13 2470
and if ye offer the lame and s Mal 1:8 2470
was torn, and the lame, and the s Mal 1:13 2470
they brought unto him all s Mt 4:24
lieth at home s of the palsy Mt 8:6 3885
mother laid, and s of a fever Mt 8:14 4445
word, and healed all that were s Mt 8:16 2192
to him a man s of the palsy Mt 9:2 3885
said unto the s of the palsy Mt 9:2 3885
saith he to the s of the palsy Mt 9:6 3885
a physician, but they that are s Mt 9:12 2192
Heal the s, cleanse the lepers, Mt 10:8 770
toward them, and he healed their s Mt 14:14 732
I was s, and ye visited me Mt 25:36 770
Or when saw we thee s, or in Mt 25:39 772
s, and in prison, and ye visited me Mt 25:43 772
or a stranger, or naked, or s Mt 25:44 772
wife's mother lay s of a fever Mk 1:30 4445
that were s of divers diseases Mk 1:34
him, bringing one s of the palsy Mk 2:3 3885
wherein the s of the palsy lay Mk 2:4 3885
he said unto the s of the palsy Mk 2:5 3885
to say to the s of the palsy Mk 2:9 3885
(he saith to the s of the palsy Mk 2:10 3885
physician, but they that are s Mk 2:17
laid his hands upon a few s folk Mk 6:5 732
with oil many that were s Mk 6:13 732
about in beds those that were s Mk 6:55
they laid the s in the streets, Mk 6:56 770
they shall lay hands on the s Mk 16:18 732
all they that had any s with Lk 4:40 770
(he said unto the s of the palsy Lk 5:24 3885
but they that are s Lk 5:31
who was dear unto him, was s Lk 7:2
the servant whole that had been s Lk 7:10 770
kingdom of God, and to heal the s Lk 9:2 770
heal the s that are therein, and Lk 10:9 772
whose son was s at Capernaum Jn 4:46 770
Now a certain man was s, named Jn 11:1 770
hair, whose brother Lazarus was s Jn 11:2 770
behold, he whom thou lovest is s Jn 11:3 770
had heard therefore that he was s Jn 11:6 770
forth the s into the streets Acts 5:15 772
unto Jerusalem, bringing s folks Acts 5:16 772
years, and was s of the palsy Acts 9:33 3885
in those days, that she was s Acts 9:37 770
the s handkerchiefs or aprons Acts 19:12 770
of Publius lay s of a fever Acts 28:8
ye had heard that he had been s Phil 2:26 770
indeed he was s nigh unto death Phil 2:27 770
have I left at Miletum s 2Ti 4:20 770
Is any s among you Jas 5:14 770
prayer of faith shall save the s Jas 5:15 2577

SICKLE
to put the s to the corn Deut 16:9 2770
but thou shalt not move a s unto Deut 23:25 2770
him that handleth the s in the Jer 50:16 4038
Put ye in the s, for the harvest Joel 3:13 4038
immediately he putteth in the s Mk 4:29 1407
crown, and in his hand a sharp s Rev 14:14 1407
sat on the cloud, Thrust in thy s Rev 14:15 1407
thrust in his s on the earth Rev 14:16 1407
heaven, he also having a sharp s Rev 14:17 1407
cry to him that had the sharp s Rev 14:18 1407
saying, Thrust in thy sharp s Rev 14:18 1407
thrust in his s into the earth Rev 14:19 1407

SICKLY
s among you, and many sleep 1Cor 11:30 732

SICKNESS
I will take s away from the midst Ex 23:25 4245
lie with a woman having her s Lev 20:18 1739
will take away from thee all s Deut 7:15 2483
Also every s, and every plague, Deut 28:61 2483
plague, whatsoever s there be 1Kin 8:37 4245
his s was so sore, that there was 1Kin 17:17 2483
sick of his s whereof he died 2Kin 13:14 2483
sore or whatsoever s there be 2Chr 6:28 4245
thou shalt have great s by 2Chr 21:15 2483
out by reason of the s day by day 2Chr 21:15 2483
fell out by reason of his s 2Chr 21:19 2483
wilt make all his bed in his s Ps 41:3 2483
much sorrow and wrath with his s Eccl 5:17 2483
sick, and was recovered of his s Is 38:9 2483
he will cut me off with pining s Is 38:12
When Ephraim saw his s, and Judah Hos 5:13 2483
and healing all manner of s Mt 4:23 3554
the kingdom, and healing every s Mt 9:35 3554
out, and to heal all manner of s Mt 10:1 3554
This s is not unto death, but for Jn 11:4 769

SICKNESSES
and of long continuance, and sore s Deut 28:59 2483
the s which the LORD hath laid Deut 29:22 8463
our infirmities, and bare our s Mt 8:17 3554
And to have power to heal s Mk 3:15 3554

SIDDIM (*sid'-dim*) *Area of Sodom and Gomorrah.*
joined together in the vale of S Gen 14:3 7708
battle with them in the vale of S Gen 14:8 7708
the vale of S was full of Gen 14:10 7708

SIDE
shalt thou set in the s thereof Gen 6:16 6654
that was openly by the way s Gen 38:21
walked along by the river's s Ex 2:5 3027
and strike it on the two s posts Ex 12:7
the two s posts with the blood Ex 12:22
the lintel, and on the two s posts Ex 12:23
his hands, the one on the one s Ex 17:12
and the other on the other s Ex 17:12
rings shall be in the one s of it Ex 25:12 6753
and two rings in the other s of it Ex 25:12 6753
the candlestick out of the one s Ex 25:32 6654
candlestick out of the other s Ex 25:32 6654
And a cubit on the one s Ex 26:13
a cubit on the other s of that Ex 26:13
on this s and on that s Ex 26:13
boards on the south s southward Ex 26:18 6285
And for the second s of the Ex 26:20 6763
s there shall be twenty boards Ex 26:20 6285
of the one s of the tabernacle Ex 26:26 6763
of the other s of the tabernacle Ex 26:27 6763
boards of the s of the tabernacle Ex 26:27 6763
s of the tabernacle toward the Ex 26:35 6763
put the table on the north s Ex 26:35 6763
for the south s southward there Ex 27:9 6285
an hundred cubits long for one s Ex 27:9
likewise for the north s in Ex 27:11 6285
of the court on the west s shall Ex 27:12 6285
of the court on the east s Ex 27:13 6285
The hangings of one s of the gate Ex 27:14 3802
on the other s shall be hangings Ex 27:15 3802
which is in the s of the ephod Ex 28:26 5676
on the one s and on the other were Ex 32:15
and said, Who is on the LORD's s Ex 32:26
Put every man his sword by his s Ex 32:27 3409
uttermost s of another curtain Ex 36:11 8193
boards for the south s southward Ex 36:23 6285
for the other s of the tabernacle Ex 36:25 6763
of the one s of the tabernacle Ex 36:31 6763
of the other s of the tabernacle Ex 36:32 6763
two rings upon the one s of it Ex 37:3 6763
two rings upon the other s of it Ex 37:3 6763
One cherub on the end on this s Ex 37:8
cherub on the other end on that s Ex 37:8
out of the one s thereof, and Ex 37:18 6654
out of the other s thereof Ex 37:18 6654
on the south s southward the Ex 38:9 6285
for the north s the hangings were Ex 38:11 6285
for the west s were hangings of Ex 38:12 6285
for the east s eastward fifty Ex 38:13 6285
The hangings of the one s of the Ex 38:14 3802
for the other s of the court gate Ex 38:15 3802
which was on the s of the ephod Ex 39:19 5676
upon the s of the tabernacle Ex 40:22 3409
on the s of the tabernacle Ex 40:24 3409
he shall kill it on the s of the Lev 1:11 3409
wrung out at the s of the altar Lev 1:15 7023
offering upon the s of the altar Lev 5:9 7023
on the east s toward the rising Num 2:3 6924
On the south s shall be the Num 2:10
On the west s shall be the Num 2:18
be on the north s by their armies Num 2:25
the s of the tabernacle southward Num 3:29 3409
these shall pitch on the s of the Num 3:35 3409
south s shall take their journey Num 10:6
it were a day's journey on this s Num 11:31 3541
a day's journey on the other s Num 11:31 3541
Dathan, and Abiram, on every s Num 16:27 5439
pitched on the other s of Arnon Num 21:13 5676
Moab on this s Jordan by Jericho Num 22:1 5676
on this s, and a wall on that s Num 22:24
as gardens by the river's s Num 24:6
with them on yonder s Jordan Num 32:19 5676
to us on this s Jordan eastward Num 32:19 5676
on this s Jordan may be ours Num 32:32 5676
to Riblah, on the east s of Ain Num 34:11 6924
shall reach unto the s of the sea Num 34:11 3802
their inheritance on this s Num 34:15 5676
on the east s two thousand cubits Num 35:5 6285
on the south s two thousand Num 35:5 6285
on the west s two thousand cubits Num 35:5 6285
on the north s two thousand Num 35:5 6285
three cities on this s Jordan Num 35:14 5676
this s Jordan in the wilderness Deut 1:1 5676
On this s Jordan, in the land of Deut 1:5 5676
and in the south, and by the sea s Deut 1:7 2348
land that was on this s Jordan Deut 3:8 5676
ask from the one s of heaven unto Deut 4:32 7097
s Jordan toward the sunrising Deut 4:41 5676
On this s Jordan, in the valley Deut 4:46 5676
which were on this s Jordan Deut 4:47 5676
plain on this s Jordan eastward Deut 4:49 5676
they not on the other s Jordan Deut 11:30 5676
put it in the s of the ark of the Deut 31:26 6654
Moses gave you on this s Jordan Josh 1:14 5676
s Jordan toward the sunrising Josh 1:15 5676
that were on the other s Jordan Josh 2:10 5676
which were on the s of Jordan Josh 5:1 5676
on the east s of Beth-el Josh 7:2
and dwelt on the other s Jordan Josh 7:7 5676
and Ai, on the west s of Ai Josh 8:9
and pitched on the north s of Ai Josh 8:11
and Ai, on the west s of the city Josh 8:12
on this s, and some on that s Josh 8:22
judges, stood on this s the ark Josh 8:33
on that s before the priests the Josh 8:33
kings which were on this s Jordan Josh 9:1 5676
their land on the other s Jordan Josh 12:1 5676
on this s Jordan on the west Josh 12:7 5676
on the other s Jordan eastward Josh 13:27 5676
of Moab, on the other s Jordan Josh 13:32 5676
half tribe on the other s Jordan Josh 14:3 5676
to the south s to Maaleh-acrabbim Josh 15:3
on the south s unto Kadesh-barnea Josh 15:3
is on the south s of the river Josh 15:7
unto the south s of the Jebusite Josh 15:8 3802
along unto the s of mount Jearim Josh 15:10 3802
which is Chesalon, on the north s Josh 15:10
out unto the s of Ekron northward Josh 15:11 3802
on the east s was Ataroth-addar Josh 16:5
sea to Michmethah on the north s Josh 16:6
which were on the other s Jordan Josh 17:5 5676
was on the north s of the river Josh 17:9
on the north s was from Jordan Josh 18:12 6285
the border went up to the s of Josh 18:12 3802
of Jericho on the north s Josh 18:12
toward Luz, to the s of Luz Josh 18:13 3802

south *s* of the nether Beth-horon ... Josh 18:13
to the *s* of Jebusi on the south, ... Josh 18:16 3802
passed along toward the *s* over ... Josh 18:18 3802
to the *s* of Beth-hoglah northward ... Josh 18:19 3802
the border of it on the east *s* ... Josh 18:20 6285
it on the north *s* to Hannathon ... Josh 19:14
toward the north *s* of Beth-emek ... Josh 19:27
to Zebulun on the south *s* ... Josh 19:34
reacheth to Asher on the west *s* ... Josh 19:34
on the other *s* Jordan by Jericho ... Josh 20:8 5676
gave you on the other *s* Jordan ... Josh 22:4 5676
on this *s* Jordan westward ... Josh 22:7 5676
other *s* of the flood in old time ... Josh 24:2 5676
from the other *s* of the flood ... Josh 24:3 5676
which dwelt on the other *s* Jordan ... Josh 24:8 5676
on the other *s* of the flood ... Josh 24:14 5676
were on the other *s* of the flood ... Josh 24:15 5676
on the north *s* of the hill of ... Josh 24:30
on the north *s* of the hill Gaash ... Judg 2:9
were on the north *s* of them ... Judg 7:1
sand by the sea *s* for multitude ... Judg 7:12 8193
also on every *s* of all the camp ... Judg 7:18 5439
to Gideon on the other *s* Jordan ... Judg 7:25 5676
of all their enemies on every *s* ... Judg 8:34 5439
other *s* Jordan in the land of the ... Judg 10:8 5676
came by the east *s* of the land of ... Judg 11:18
pitched on the other *s* of Arnon ... Judg 11:18 5676
on the *s* of mount Ephraim ... Judg 19:1 3411
toward the *s* of mount Ephraim ... Judg 19:18 3411
is on the north *s* of Beth-el ... Judg 21:19
on the east *s* of the highway that ... Judg 21:19
backward by the *s* of the gate ... 1Sa 4:18 3027
in a coffer by the *s* thereof ... 1Sa 6:8 6654
hand of your enemies on every *s* ... 1Sa 12:11 5439
garrison, that is on the other *s* ... 1Sa 14:1 5676
was a sharp rock on the one *s* ... 1Sa 14:4 5676
and a sharp rock on the other *s* ... 1Sa 14:4 5676
unto all Israel, Be ye on one *s* ... 1Sa 14:40 5676
my son will be on the other *s* ... 1Sa 14:40 5676
all his enemies on every *s* ... 1Sa 14:47 5439
stood on a mountain on the one *s* ... 1Sa 17:3
on a mountain on the other *s* ... 1Sa 17:3
three arrows on the *s* thereof ... 1Sa 20:20 6654
the arrows are on this *s* of thee ... 1Sa 20:21
arose, and Abner sat by Saul's *s* ... 1Sa 20:25 6654
went on this *s* of the mountain ... 1Sa 23:26 6654
his men on that *s* of the mountain ... 1Sa 23:26 6654
David went over to the other *s* ... 1Sa 26:13 5676
were on the other *s* of the valley ... 1Sa 31:7 5676
that were on the other *s* Jordan ... 1Sa 31:7 5676
the one on the one *s* of the pool ... 2Sa 2:13
other on the other *s* of the pool ... 2Sa 2:13
his sword in his fellow's *s* ... 2Sa 2:16 6654
the way of the hill *s* behind him ... 2Sa 13:34 6654
on the hill's *s* over against him ... 2Sa 16:13 6763
And the king stood by the gate *s* ... 2Sa 18:4 3027
on the right *s* of the city that ... 2Sa 24:5 3225
the region on this *s* the river ... 1Kin 4:24 5676
all the kings on this *s* the river ... 1Kin 4:24 5676
which were about him on every *s* ... 1Kin 5:3
God hath given me rest on every *s* ... 1Kin 5:4 5439
was in the right *s* of the house ... 1Kin 6:8 3802
s posts were a fifth part of the ... 1Kin 6:31
one *s* of the floor to the other ... 1Kin 7:7
at the *s* of every addition ... 1Kin 7:30 5676
bases on the right *s* of the house ... 1Kin 7:39 3802
five on the left *s* of the house ... 1Kin 7:39 3802
s of the house eastward over ... 1Kin 7:39 3802
of pure gold, five on the right *s* ... 1Kin 7:49
either *s* on the place of the seat ... 1Kin 10:19
lions stood there on the one *s* ... 1Kin 10:20
on the other *s* as red as blood ... 2Kin 3:22 5048
window, and said, Who is on my *s* ... 2Kin 9:32
on the right *s* as one cometh into ... 2Kin 12:9 3225
it on the north *s* of the altar ... 2Kin 16:14 3409
unto the east *s* of the valley ... 1Chr 4:39 4217
on the other *s* Jordan by Jericho, ... 1Chr 6:78 5676
on the east *s* of Jordan ... 1Chr 6:78 4217
Thine are we, David, and on thy *s* ... 1Chr 12:18
And on the other *s* of Jordan ... 1Chr 12:37 5676
he not given you rest on every *s* ... 1Chr 22:18 5439
this *s* Jordan westward in all the ... 1Chr 26:30 5676
the temple, five on the right *s* ... 2Chr 4:8
on the right *s* of the east end ... 2Chr 4:10 3802
at the sea *s* in the land of Edom ... 2Chr 8:17 8193
stays on each *s* of the sitting ... 2Chr 9:18
lions stood there on the one *s* ... 2Chr 9:19
having Judah and Benjamin on his *s* ... 2Chr 11:12
he hath given us rest on every *s* ... 2Chr 14:7 5439
beyond the sea on this *s* Syria ... 2Chr 20:2
from the right *s* of the temple to ... 2Chr 23:10 3802
to the left *s* of the temple ... 2Chr 23:10 3802
other, and guided them on every *s* ... 2Chr 32:22 5439
the west *s* of the city of David ... 2Chr 32:30
of David, on the west *s* of Gihon ... 2Chr 33:14
rest that are on this *s* the river ... Ezr 4:10 5675
the men on this *s* the river ... Ezr 4:11 5675
no portion on this *s* the river ... Ezr 4:16 5675
governor on this *s* the river ... Ezr 5:3 5675
governor on this *s* the river ... Ezr 5:6 5675
which were on this *s* the river ... Ezr 5:6 5675
governor on this *s* the river ... Ezr 6:13 5675
the governors on this *s* the river ... Ezr 8:36 5676
the governor on this *s* the river ... Neh 3:7 5676
one had his sword girded by his *s* ... Neh 4:18 4975
about all that he hath on every *s* ... Job 1:10 5439
shall make him afraid on every *s* ... Job 18:11 5439
shall be ready at his *s* ... Job 18:12 6763
He hath destroyed me on every *s* ... Job 19:10 5439
The wicked walk on every *s* ... Ps 12:8 5439
fear was on every *s* ... Ps 31:13 5439
little hills rejoice on every *s* ... Ps 65:12 2296
and comfort me on every *s* ... Ps 71:21 5437
A thousand shall fall at thy *s* ... Ps 91:7 6654
The LORD is on my *s* ... Ps 118:6
been the LORD who was on our *s* ... Ps 124:1
been the LORD who was on our *s* ... Ps 124:2
on the *s* of their oppressors ... Eccl 4:1 3027
shall be nursed at thy *s* ... Is 60:4 6654
the enemy and fear is on every *s* ... Jer 6:25 5439
defaming of many, fear on every *s* ... Jer 20:10 5439
cry unto them, Fear is on every *s* ... Jer 49:29 5439
ninety and six pomegranates on a *s* ... Jer 52:23 7307
face of a lion, on the right *s* ... Eze 1:10 3225
the face of an ox on the left *s* ... Eze 1:10 8040
had two, which covered on this *s* ... Eze 1:23
had two, which covered on that *s* ... Eze 1:23
Lie thou also upon thy left *s* ... Eze 4:4 6654
them, lie again on thy right *s* ... Eze 4:6 6654
turn thee from one *s* to another ... Eze 4:8 6654
that thou shalt lie upon thy *s* ... Eze 4:9 6654
with a writer's inkhorn by his *s* ... Eze 9:2 4975
had the writer's inkhorn by his *s* ... Eze 9:3 4975
which had the inkhorn by his *s* ... Eze 9:11 4975
stood on the right *s* of the house ... Eze 10:3 3225
is on the east *s* of the city ... Eze 11:23 6954
thee on every *s* for thy whoredom ... Eze 16:33 5439
him on every *s* from the provinces ... Eze 19:8 5439
them against thee on every *s* ... Eze 23:22 5439
I will open the *s* of Moab from ... Eze 25:9 3802
by the sword upon her on every *s* ... Eze 28:23 5439
Because ye have thrust with *s* ... Eze 34:21 6654
and swallowed you up on every *s* ... Eze 36:3 5439
and will gather them on every *s* ... Eze 37:21 5439
every *s* to my sacrifice that I do ... Eze 39:17 5439
on this *s*, and three on that *s* ... Eze 40:10 6311
measure on this *s* and on that *s* ... Eze 40:10
chambers was one cubit on this *s* ... Eze 40:12
the space was one cubit on that *s* ... Eze 40:12
were six cubits on this *s* ... Eze 40:12
and six cubits on that *s* ... Eze 40:12
the pavement by the *s* of the ... Eze 40:18 3802
on this *s* and three on that *s* ... Eze 40:21
this *s*, and another on that *s* ... Eze 40:26
on this *s*, and on that *s* ... Eze 40:34
on this *s*, and on that *s* ... Eze 40:37
gate were two tables on this *s* ... Eze 40:39
and two tables on that *s* ... Eze 40:39
at the *s* without, as one goeth up ... Eze 40:40 3802
and on the other *s*, which was at ... Eze 40:40 3802
Four tables were on this *s* ... Eze 40:41 3802
that *s*, by the *s* of the gate ... Eze 40:41 3802
which was at the *s* of the north ... Eze 40:44 3802
one at the *s* of the east gate ... Eze 40:44 3802
the porch, five cubits on this *s* ... Eze 40:48
and five cubits on that *s* ... Eze 40:48
gate was three cubits on this *s* ... Eze 40:48
and three cubits on that *s* ... Eze 40:48
this *s*, and another on that *s* ... Eze 40:49
six cubits broad on the one *s* ... Eze 41:1 6311
six cubits broad on the other *s* ... Eze 41:1
were five cubits on the one *s* ... Eze 41:2
and five cubits on the other *s* ... Eze 41:2
and the breadth of every *s* chamber ... Eze 41:5 6763
round about the house on every *s* ... Eze 41:5 5439
the *s* chambers were three, one ... Eze 41:6 6763
for the *s* chambers round about ... Eze 41:6 6763
still upward to the *s* chambers ... Eze 41:7 6763
the foundations of the *s* chambers ... Eze 41:8 6763
was for the *s* chamber without ... Eze 41:9 6763
the *s* chambers that were within ... Eze 41:9 6763
round about the house on every *s* ... Eze 41:10 5439
the doors of the *s* chambers were ... Eze 41:11 6763
on the one *s* and on the other *s* ... Eze 41:15
toward the palm tree on the one *s* ... Eze 41:19
the palm tree on the other *s* ... Eze 41:19
on the one *s* and on the other *s* ... Eze 41:26
upon the *s* chambers of the house, ... Eze 41:26 6763
was the entry on the east *s* ... Eze 42:9 6921
He measured the east *s* with the ... Eze 42:16 7307
He measured the north *s*, five ... Eze 42:17 7307
He measured the south *s*, five ... Eze 42:18 7307
He turned about to the west *s* ... Eze 42:19 7307
be for the prince on the one *s* ... Eze 45:7
on the other *s* of the oblation of ... Eze 45:7
city, from the west *s* westward ... Eze 45:7 6285
and from the east *s* eastward ... Eze 45:7 6285
which was at the *s* of the gate ... Eze 46:19
from the right *s* of the house ... Eze 47:1
at the south *s* of the altar ... Eze 47:1
ran out waters on the right *s* ... Eze 47:2 3802
were very many trees on the one *s* ... Eze 47:7
on this *s* and on that *s* ... Eze 47:12
of the land toward the north *s* ... Eze 47:15 6285
And this is the north *s* ... Eze 47:17 6285
the east *s* ye shall measure from ... Eze 47:18 6285
And this is the east *s* ... Eze 47:18 6285
And the south *s* southward, from ... Eze 47:19 6285
And this is the south *s* southward ... Eze 47:19 6285
The west *s* also shall be the ... Eze 47:20 6285
This is the west *s* ... Eze 47:20 6285
the east *s* unto the west *s* ... Eze 48:2 6285
east *s* even unto the west *s* ... Eze 48:3 6285
the east *s* unto the west *s* ... Eze 48:4 6285
the east *s* unto the west *s* ... Eze 48:5 6285
east *s* even unto the west *s* ... Eze 48:6 6285
the east *s* unto the west *s* ... Eze 48:7 6285
the east *s* unto the west *s* ... Eze 48:8 6285
the east *s* unto the west *s* ... Eze 48:8 6285
the north *s* four thousand and five ... Eze 48:16 6285
the south *s* four thousand and five ... Eze 48:16 6285
on the east *s* four thousand and ... Eze 48:16 6285
the west *s* four thousand and five ... Eze 48:16 6285
be for the prince, on the one *s* ... Eze 48:21 6285
the east *s* unto the west *s* ... Eze 48:23 6285
the east *s* unto the west *s* ... Eze 48:24 6285
the east *s* unto the west *s* ... Eze 48:25 6285
the east *s* unto the west *s* ... Eze 48:26 6285
the east *s* unto the west *s* ... Eze 48:27 6285
of Gad, at the south *s* southward ... Eze 48:28 6285
out of the city on the north *s* ... Eze 48:30 6285
at the east *s* four thousand and ... Eze 48:32 6285
at the south *s* four thousand and ... Eze 48:33 6285
At the west *s* four thousand and ... Eze 48:34 6285
and it raised up itself on one *s* ... Dan 7:5 7859
as I was by the *s* of the great ... Dan 10:4 3027
but she shall not stand on his *s* ... Dan 11:17
the one on this *s* of the bank of ... Dan 12:5
the other on that *s* of the bank ... Dan 12:5
that thou stoodest on the other *s* ... Obad 11 5048
and sat on the east *s* of the city ... Jonah 4:5 6924
one upon the right *s* of the bowl ... Zec 4:3
the other upon the left *s* thereof ... Zec 4:3
the right *s* of the candlestick ... Zec 4:11
and upon the left *s* thereof ... Zec 4:11
off as on this *s* according to it ... Zec 5:3
off as on that *s* according to it ... Zec 5:3
to depart unto the other *s* ... Mt 8:18 4008
other *s* into the country of the ... Mt 8:28 4008
of the house, and sat by the sea *s* ... Mt 13:1 3844
some seeds fell by the way *s* ... Mt 13:4 3844
which received seed by the way *s* ... Mt 13:19 3844
to go before him unto the other *s* ... Mt 14:22 4008
were come to the other *s*, they ... Mt 16:5 4008
blind men sitting by the way *s* ... Mt 20:30 3844
he went forth again by the sea *s* ... Mk 2:13 3844
began again to teach by the sea *s* ... Mk 4:1 3844
he sowed, some fell by the way *s* ... Mk 4:4 3844
And these are they by the way *s* ... Mk 4:15 3844
Let us pass over unto the other *s* ... Mk 4:35 4008
over unto the other *s* of the sea ... Mk 5:1 4008
again by ship unto the other *s* ... Mk 5:21 4008
to go to the other *s* before unto ... Mk 6:45 4008
again departed to the other *s* ... Mk 8:13 4008
Judaea by the farther *s* of Jordan ... Mk 10:1 4008
sat by the highway *s* begging ... Mk 10:46 3844
young man sitting on the right *s* ... Mk 16:5 1188
right *s* of the altar of incense ... Lk 1:11 1188
he sowed, some fell by the way *s* ... Lk 8:5 3844
Those by the way *s* are they that ... Lk 8:12 3844
over unto the other *s* of the lake ... Lk 8:22 4008
him, he passed by on the other *s* ... Lk 10:31 492
him, and passed by on the other *s* ... Lk 10:32 492
man sat by the way *s* begging ... Lk 18:35 3844
round, and keep thee in on every *s* ... Lk 19:43 3840
s of the sea saw that there was ... Jn 6:22 4008
him on the other *s* of the sea ... Jn 6:25 4008
others with him, on either *s* one ... Jn 19:18 1782
with a spear pierced his *s* ... Jn 19:34 4125
unto them his hands and his *s* ... Jn 20:20 4125
and thrust my hand into his *s* ... Jn 20:25 4125
thy hand, and thrust it into my *s* ... Jn 20:27 4125
net on the right *s* of the ship ... Jn 21:6 3313
whose house is by the sea *s* ... Acts 10:6 3844
one Simon a tanner by the sea *s* ... Acts 10:32 3844
and he smote Peter on the *s* ... Acts 12:7 4125
went out of the city by a river *s* ... Acts 16:13 3844
We are troubled on every *s* ... 2Cor 4:8
but we were troubled on every *s* ... 2Cor 7:5
on either *s* of the river, was ... Rev 22:2 1782

SIDES

the rings by the *s* of the ark ... Ex 25:14 6763
shall come out of the *s* of it ... Ex 25:32 6654
it shall hang over the *s* of the ... Ex 26:13 6654
for the *s* of the tabernacle ... Ex 26:22 3411
of the tabernacle in the two *s* ... Ex 26:23 3411
for the two *s* westward ... Ex 26:27 3411
be upon the two *s* of the altar ... Ex 27:7 6763
the two *s* of the ephod underneath ... Ex 28:27 3802
the *s* thereof round about, and the ... Ex 30:3 7023
upon the two *s* of it shalt thou ... Ex 30:4 6654
were written on both their *s* ... Ex 32:15 5676
for the *s* of the tabernacle ... Ex 36:27 3411
of the tabernacle in the two *s* ... Ex 36:28 3411
the tabernacle for the *s* westward ... Ex 36:32 3411
the rings by the *s* of the ark ... Ex 37:5 6763
going out of the *s* thereof ... Ex 37:18 6654
the *s* thereof round about, and the ... Ex 37:26 7023
of it, upon the two *s* thereof ... Ex 37:27 6654
the rings on the *s* of the altar ... Ex 38:7 6763
put them on the two *s* of the ... Ex 39:20 3802
in your eyes, and thorns in your *s* ... Num 33:55 6654
unto you, and scourges in your *s* ... Josh 23:13 6654
they shall be as thorns in your *s* ... Judg 2:3 6654
colours of needlework on both *s* ... Judg 5:30
men remained in the *s* of the cave ... 1Sa 24:3 3411
peace on all *s* round about him ... 1Kin 4:24 5676
cubits on the *s* of the house ... 1Kin 6:16 3411
to the *s* of Lebanon, and will cut ... 2Kin 19:23 3411
on the *s* of the north, the city ... Ps 48:2 3411
vine by the *s* of thine house ... Ps 128:3 3411
in the *s* of the north ... Is 14:13 3411
down to hell, to the *s* of the pit ... Is 14:15 3411
mountains, to the *s* of Lebanon ... Is 37:24 3411
ye shall be borne upon her *s* ... Is 66:12 6654
be raised from the *s* of the earth ... Jer 6:22 3411
nest in the *s* of the hole's mouth ... Jer 48:28 5676
their calamity from all *s* thereof ... Jer 49:32 5676
under their wings on their four *s* ... Eze 1:8 7253
went, they went upon their four *s* ... Eze 1:17 7253
went, they went upon their four *s* ... Eze 10:11 7253
are set in the *s* of the pit ... Eze 32:23 3411
the *s* of the door were five ... Eze 41:2 3802
on the *s* of the porch, and upon ... Eze 41:26 3802
He measured it by the four *s* ... Eze 42:20 7307
was a place on the two *s* westward ... Eze 46:19 3411
for these are his *s* east and west ... Eze 48:1 6285
him that is by the *s* of the house ... Amos 6:10 3411
gone down into the *s* of the ship ... Jonah 1:5 3411

SIDON (*si'-don*) See SIDONIANS, ZIDON.
1. Son of Canaan.
Canaan begat *S* his firstborn, and Gen 10:15 6721
2. Phoenician city north of Tyre.
of the Canaanites was from *S* Gen 10:19 6721
you, had been done in Tyre and *S* Mt 11:21 *4605*
S at the day of judgment, than Mt 11:22 *4605*
into the coasts of Tyre and *S* Mt 15:21 *4605*
and they about Tyre and *S*, a great Mk 3:8 *4605*
into the borders of Tyre and *S* Mk 7:24 *4605*
from the coasts of Tyre and *S* Mk 7:31 *4605*
save unto Sarepta, a city of *S* Lk 4:26 *4605*
from the sea coast of Tyre and *S* Lk 6:17 *4605*
works had been done in Tyre and *S* Lk 10:13 *4605*
S at the judgment, than for you Lk 10:14 *4605*
displeased with them of Tyre and *S* Acts 12:20 *4605*
And the next day we touched at *S* Acts 27:3 *4605*

SIDONIANS (*si-do'-ne-uns*) See ZIDONIANS. *Inhabitants of Sidon.*
(Which Hermon the *S* call Sirion Deut 3:9 6722
and Mearah that is beside the *S* Josh 13:4 6722
Misrephoth-maim, and all the *S* Josh 13:6 6722
and all the Canaanites, and the *S* Judg 3:3 6722
to hew timber like unto the *S* 1Kin 5:6 6722

SIEGE
life) to employ them in the *s* Deut 20:19 4692
thy God hath given thee, in the *s* Deut 28:53 4692
he hath nothing left him in the *s* Deut 28:55 4692
of all things secretly in the *s* Deut 28:57 4692
and all Israel laid *s* to Gibbethon 1Kin 15:27 6696
he himself laid *s* against Lachish 2Chr 32:9
ye abide in the *s* in Jerusalem 2Chr 32:10 4692
will lay *s* against thee with a Is 29:3 6696
the flesh of his friend in the *s* Jer 19:9 4692
lay *s* against it, and build a fort Eze 4:2 4692
and thou shalt lay *s* against it Eze 4:3 6696
face toward the *s* of Jerusalem Eze 4:7 4692
thou hast ended the days of thy *s* Eze 4:8 4692
the days of the *s* are fulfilled Eze 5:2 4692
he hath laid *s* against us Mic 5:1 4692
Draw thee waters for the *s* Nah 3:14 4692
be in the *s* both against Judah Zec 12:2 4692

SIEVE
the nations with the *s* of vanity Is 30:28 5299
like as corn is sifted in a *s* Amos 9:9 3531

SIFT
to *s* the nations with the sieve Is 30:28 5130
I will *s* the house of Israel Amos 9:9 5128
that he may *s* you as wheat Lk 22:31 *4617*

SIFTED
like as corn is *s* in a sieve Amos 9:9 5128

SIGH
all the merryhearted do *s* Is 24:7 584
her priests *s*, her virgins are Lam 1:4 584
All her people *s*, they seek bread Lam 1:11 584
They have heard that I *s* Lam 1:21 584
the foreheads of the men that *s* Eze 9:4 584
S therefore, thou son of man, Eze 21:6 584
with bitterness *s* before their Eze 21:6 584

SIGHED
the children of Israel *s* by Ex 2:23 584
And looking up to heaven, he *s* Mk 7:34 *4727*
he *s* deeply in his spirit, and Mk 8:12 *389*

SIGHEST
say unto thee, Wherefore *s* thou Eze 21:7 584

SIGHETH
yea, she *s*, and turneth backward Lam 1:8 584

SIGHING
For my *s* cometh before I eat, and Job 3:24 585
for the *s* of the needy, now will Ps 12:5 603
with grief, and my years with *s* Ps 31:10 585
Let the *s* of the prisoner come Ps 79:11 603
all the *s* thereof have I made to Is 21:2 585
and sorrow and *s* shall flee away Is 35:10 585
I fainted in my *s*, and I find no Jer 45:3 585

SIGHS
for my *s* are many, and my heart is Lam 1:22 585

SIGHT
tree that is pleasant to the *s* Gen 2:9 4758
now I have found favour in thy *s* Gen 18:3 5869
servant hath found grace in thy *s* Gen 19:19 5869
in Abraham's *s* because of his son Gen 21:11 5869
in thy *s* because of the lad Gen 21:12 5869
I may bury my dead out of my *s* Gen 23:4 6440
I should bury my dead out of my *s* Gen 23:8 6440
that I may find grace in thy *s* Gen 32:5 5869
to find grace in the *s* of my lord Gen 33:8 5869
now I have found grace in thy *s* Gen 33:10 5869
me find grace in the *s* of my lord Gen 33:15 5869
was wicked in the *s* of the LORD Gen 38:7 5869
And Joseph found grace in his *s* Gen 39:4 5869
gave him favour in the *s* of the Gen 39:21 5869
ought left in the *s* of my lord Gen 47:18 6440
us find grace in the *s* of my lord Gen 47:25 5869
now I have found grace in thy *s* Gen 47:29 5869
turn aside, and see this great *s* Ex 3:3 4758
favour in the *s* of the Egyptians Ex 3:21 5869
the signs in the *s* of the people Ex 4:30 5869
in the *s* of Pharaoh, and in the Ex 7:20 5869
and in the *s* of his servants Ex 7:20 5869
the heaven in the *s* of Pharaoh Ex 9:8 5869
favour in the *s* of the Egyptians Ex 11:3 5869
in the *s* of Pharaoh's servants, Ex 11:3 5869
and in the *s* of the people Ex 11:3 5869
favour in the *s* of the Egyptians Ex 12:36 5869
do that which is right in his *s* Ex 15:26 5869
Moses did so in the *s* of the Ex 17:6 5869
s of all the people upon mount Ex 19:11 5869
the *s* of the glory of the LORD Ex 24:17 4758
hast also found grace in my *s* Ex 33:12 5869
if I have found grace in thy *s* Ex 33:13 5869
that I may find grace in thy *s* Ex 33:13 5869
people have found grace in thy *s* Ex 33:16 5869
for thou hast found grace in my *s* Ex 33:17 5869
now I have found grace in thy *s* Ex 34:9 5869
in the *s* of all the house of Ex 40:38 5869
accepted in the *s* of the LORD Lev 10:19 5869
the plague in *s* be deeper than Lev 13:3 4758
in *s* be not deeper than the skin, Lev 13:4 4758
the plague in his *s* be at a stay Lev 13:5 5869
it be in *s* lower than the skin, Lev 13:20 4758
it be in *s* deeper than the skin Lev 13:25 4758
if it be in *s* deeper than the Lev 13:30 4758
it be not in *s* deeper than the Lev 13:31 4758
the scall be not in *s* deeper than Lev 13:32 4758
nor be in *s* deeper than the skin Lev 13:34 4758
the scall be in his *s* at a stay Lev 13:37 5869
which in *s* are lower than the Lev 14:37 4758
cut off in the *s* of their people Lev 20:17 5869
with rigour over him in thy *s* Lev 25:53 5869
of Egypt in the *s* of the heathen Lev 26:45 5869
in the *s* of Aaron their father Num 3:4 6440
have I not found favour in thy *s* Num 11:11 5869
if I have found favour in thy *s* Num 11:15 5869
were in our own *s* as grasshoppers Num 13:33 5869
and so we were in their *s* Num 13:33 5869
shall burn the heifer in his *s* Num 19:5 5869
in the *s* of all the congregation Num 20:27 5869
woman in the *s* of Moses, and in Num 25:6 5869
in the *s* of all the congregation Num 25:6 5869
and give him a charge in their *s* Num 27:19 5869
if we have found grace in thy *s* Num 32:5 5869
done evil in the *s* of the LORD Num 32:13 5869
in the *s* of all the Egyptians Num 33:3 5869
in the *s* of the nations, which Deut 4:6 5869
evil in the *s* of the LORD thy God Deut 4:25 5869
brought thee out in his *s* with Deut 4:37 6440
and good in the *s* of the LORD Deut 6:18 5869
wickedly in the *s* of the LORD Deut 9:18 5869
is right in the *s* of the LORD Deut 12:25 5869
right in the *s* of the LORD thy Deut 12:28 5869
in the *s* of the LORD thy God Deut 17:2 5869
is right in the *s* of the LORD Deut 21:9 5869
s of thine eyes which thou shalt Deut 28:34 4758
for the *s* of thine eyes which Deut 28:67 4758
unto him in the *s* of all Israel Deut 31:7 5869
will do evil in the *s* of the LORD Deut 31:29 5869
shewed in the *s* of all Israel Deut 34:12 5869
thee in the *s* of all Israel Josh 3:7 5869
Joshua in the *s* of all Israel Josh 4:14 5869
and he said in the *s* of Israel Josh 10:12 5869
and drive them from out of your *s* Josh 23:5 6440
did those great signs in our *s* Josh 24:17 5869
did evil in the *s* of the LORD Judg 2:11 5869
did evil in the *s* of the LORD Judg 3:7 5869
evil again in the *s* of the LORD Judg 3:12 5869
done evil in the *s* of the LORD Judg 3:12 5869
did evil in the *s* of the LORD Judg 4:1 5869
did evil in the *s* of the LORD Judg 6:1 5869
now I have found grace in thy *s* Judg 6:17 5869
of the LORD departed out of his *s* Judg 6:21 5869
evil again in the *s* of the LORD Judg 10:6 5869
evil again in the *s* of the LORD Judg 13:1 5869
him in whose *s* I shall find grace Ruth 2:2 5869
said, Let me find favour in thy *s* Ruth 2:13 5869
handmaid find grace in thy *s* 1Sa 1:18 5869
ye have done in the *s* of the LORD 1Sa 12:17 5869
thou wast little in thine own *s* 1Sa 15:17 5869
didst evil in the *s* of the LORD 1Sa 15:19 5869
for he hath found favour in my *s* 1Sa 16:22 5869
in the *s* of all the people 1Sa 18:5 5869
also in the *s* of Saul's servants 1Sa 18:5 5869
me in the host is good in my *s* 1Sa 29:6 5869
I know that thou art good in my *s* 1Sa 29:9 5869
and will be base in mine own *s* 2Sa 6:22 5869
all thine enemies out of thy *s* 2Sa 7:9 6440
was yet a small thing in thy *s* 2Sa 7:19 5869
of the LORD, to do evil in his *s* 2Sa 12:9 5869
thy wives in the *s* of this sun 2Sa 12:11 5869
meat, and dress the meat in my *s* 2Sa 13:5 5869
make me a couple of cakes in my *s* 2Sa 13:6 5869
it, and made cakes in his *s* 2Sa 13:8 5869
that I have found grace in thy *s* 2Sa 14:22 5869
that I may find grace in thy *s* 2Sa 16:4 5869
concubines in the *s* of all Israel 2Sa 16:22 5869
to my cleanness in his eye *s* 2Sa 22:25 5869
s to sit on the throne of Israel 1Kin 8:25 6440
my name, will I cast out of my *s* 1Kin 9:7 6440
did evil in the *s* of the LORD 1Kin 11:6 5869
great favour in the *s* of Pharaoh 1Kin 11:19 5869
ways, and do that is right in my *s* 1Kin 11:38 5869
did evil in the *s* of the LORD 1Kin 14:22 5869
he did evil in the *s* of the LORD 1Kin 15:26 5869
he did evil in the *s* of the LORD 1Kin 15:34 5869
that he did in the *s* of the LORD 1Kin 16:7 5869
doing evil in the *s* of the LORD 1Kin 16:19 5869
s of the LORD above all that were 1Kin 16:30 5869
to work evil in the *s* of the LORD 1Kin 21:20 5869
wickedness in the *s* of the LORD 1Kin 21:25 5869
he did evil in the *s* of the LORD 1Kin 22:52 5869
servants, be precious in thy *s* 2Kin 1:13 5869
my life now be precious in thy *s* 2Kin 1:14 5869
wrought evil in the *s* of the LORD 2Kin 3:2 5869
light thing in the *s* of the LORD 2Kin 3:18 5869
he did evil in the *s* of the LORD 2Kin 8:18 5869
and did evil in the *s* of the LORD 2Kin 8:27 5869
in the *s* of the LORD all his days 2Kin 12:2 5869
was evil in the *s* of the LORD 2Kin 13:2 5869
was evil in the *s* of the LORD 2Kin 13:11 5869
was right in the *s* of the LORD 2Kin 14:3 5869
was evil in the *s* of the LORD 2Kin 14:24 5869
was right in the *s* of the LORD 2Kin 15:3 5869
was evil in the *s* of the LORD 2Kin 15:9 5869
was evil in the *s* of the LORD 2Kin 15:18 5869
was evil in the *s* of the LORD 2Kin 15:24 5869
was evil in the *s* of the LORD 2Kin 15:28 5869
was right in the *s* of the LORD 2Kin 15:34 5869
in the *s* of the LORD his God 2Kin 16:2 5869
was evil in the *s* of the LORD 2Kin 17:2 5869
to do evil in the *s* of the LORD 2Kin 17:17 5869
and removed them out of his *s* 2Kin 17:18 6440
he had cast them out of his *s* 2Kin 17:20 6440
LORD removed Israel out of his *s* 2Kin 17:23 6440
was right in the *s* of the LORD 2Kin 18:3 5869
done that which is good in thy *s* 2Kin 20:3 5869
was evil in the *s* of the LORD 2Kin 21:2 5869
wickedness in the *s* of the LORD 2Kin 21:6 5869
done that which was evil in my *s* 2Kin 21:15 5869
was evil in the *s* of the LORD 2Kin 21:16 5869
was evil in the *s* of the LORD 2Kin 21:20 5869
was right in the *s* of the LORD 2Kin 22:2 5869
remove Judah also out of my *s* 2Kin 23:27 6440
was evil in the *s* of the LORD 2Kin 23:32 5869
was evil in the *s* of the LORD 2Kin 23:37 5869
to remove them out of his *s* 2Kin 24:3 6440
was evil in the *s* of the LORD 2Kin 24:9 5869
was evil in the *s* of the LORD 2Kin 24:19 5869
was evil in the *s* of the LORD 1Chr 2:3 5869
do that which is good in his *s* 1Chr 19:13 5869
much blood upon the earth in my *s* 1Chr 22:8 6440
in the *s* of all Israel the 1Chr 28:8 5869
in the *s* of all Israel, and 1Chr 29:25 5869
in my *s* to sit upon the throne of 2Chr 6:16 6440
my name, will I cast out of my *s* 2Chr 7:20 6440
was right in the *s* of the LORD 2Chr 20:32 5869
Wherefore he did evil in the *s* of 2Chr 22:4 5869
the *s* of the LORD all the days of 2Chr 24:2 5869
was right in the *s* of the LORD 2Chr 25:2 5869
was right in the *s* of the LORD 2Chr 26:4 5869
was right in the *s* of the LORD 2Chr 27:2 5869
was right in the *s* of the LORD 2Chr 28:1 5869
was right in the *s* of the LORD 2Chr 29:2 5869
s of all nations from thenceforth 2Chr 32:23 5869
was evil in the *s* of the LORD 2Chr 33:2 5869
much evil in the *s* of the LORD 2Chr 33:6 5869
was evil in the *s* of the LORD 2Chr 33:22 5869
was right in the *s* of the LORD 2Chr 34:2 5869
evil in the *s* of the LORD his God 2Chr 36:5 5869
was evil in the *s* of the LORD 2Chr 36:9 5869
evil in the *s* of the LORD his God 2Chr 36:12 5869
in the *s* of the kings of Persia Ezr 9:9 6440
him mercy in the *s* of this man Neh 1:11 6440
have found favour in thy *s* Neh 2:5 6440
the book in the *s* of all people Neh 8:5 5869
s of all them that looked upon Est 2:15 5869
favour in his *s* more than all the Est 2:17 6440
that she obtained favour in his *s* Est 5:2 5869
found favour in the *s* of the king Est 5:8 5869
If I have found favour in thy *s* Est 7:3 5869
if I have found favour in his *s* Est 8:5 5869
heavens are not clean in his *s* Job 15:15 5869
beasts, and reputed vile in your *s* Job 18:3 5869
I am an alien in their *s* Job 19:15 5869
established in their *s* with them Job 21:8 6440
the stars are not pure in his *s* Job 25:5 5869
men in the open *s* of others Job 34:26 7200
be cast down even at the *s* of him Job 41:9 4758
foolish shall not stand in thy *s* Ps 5:5 5869
the heathen be judged in thy *s* Ps 9:19 6440
are far above out of his *s* Ps 10:5 5048
my heart, be acceptable in thy *s* Ps 19:14 6440
and done this evil in thy *s* Ps 51:4 5869
shall their blood be in his *s* Ps 72:14 5869
who may stand in thy *s* when once Ps 76:7 6440
did he in the *s* of their fathers Ps 78:12 5048
s by the revenging of the blood Ps 79:10 5869
For a thousand years in thy *s* are Ps 90:4 5869
shewed in the *s* of the heathen Ps 98:2 5869
lies shall not tarry in my *s* Ps 101:7 5869
Precious in the *s* of the LORD is Ps 116:15 5869
for in thy *s* shall no man living Ps 143:2 6440
is spread in the *s* of any bird Prov 1:17 5869
understanding in the *s* of God Prov 3:4 5869
beloved in the *s* of my mother Prov 4:3 6440
man that is good in his *s* wisdom Eccl 2:26 6440
Better is the *s* of the eyes than Eccl 6:9 4758
Be not hasty to go out of his *s* Eccl 8:3 6440
heart, and in the *s* of thine eyes Eccl 11:9 4758
eyes, and prudent in their own *s* Is 5:21 6440
not judge after the *s* of his eyes Is 11:3 4758
so have we been in thy *s*, O LORD Is 26:17 6440
done that which is good in thy *s* Is 38:3 5869
Since thou wast precious in my *s* Is 43:4 5869
thine abominations out of my *s* Jer 4:1 6440
And I will cast you out of my *s* Jer 7:15 6440
of Judah have done evil in my *s* Jer 7:30 5869
cast them out of my *s*, and let Jer 15:1 6440
If it do evil in my *s*, that it Jer 18:10 5869
blot out their sin from thy *s* Jer 18:23 6440
s of the men that go with thee Jer 19:10 5869
in the *s* of Hanameel mine uncle's Jer 32:12 5869
turned, and had done right in my *s* Jer 34:15 5869
in the *s* of the men of Judah Jer 43:9 5869
they have done in Zion in your *s* Jer 51:24 5869
cometh out of man, in their *s* Eze 4:12 5869
of thee in the *s* of the nations Eze 5:8 5869
in the *s* of all that pass by Eze 5:14 5869
And he went in in my *s* Eze 10:2 5869
mounted up from the earth in my *s* Eze 10:19 5869
and remove by day in their *s* Eze 12:3 5869
place to another place in their *s* Eze 12:3 5869
forth thy stuff by day in their *s* Eze 12:4 5869
shalt go forth at even in their *s* Eze 12:4 5869
thou through the wall in their *s* Eze 12:5 5869
In their *s* shalt thou bear it Eze 12:6 5869
it upon my shoulder in their *s* Eze 12:7 5869

upon thee in the *s* of many women ... Eze 16:41 5869
in whose *s* I made myself known ... Eze 20:9 5869
in whose *s* I brought them out ... Eze 20:14 5869
polluted in the *s* of the heathen ... Eze 20:22 5869
in whose *s* I brought them forth ... Eze 20:22 5869
lothe yourselves in your own *s* ... Eze 20:43 6440
as a false divination in their *s* ... Eze 21:23 5869
thyself in the *s* of the heathen ... Eze 22:16 5869
s of all them that behold thee ... Eze 28:18 5869
in them in the *s* of the heathen ... Eze 28:25 5869
in your own *s* for your iniquities ... Eze 36:31 6440
in the *s* of all that passed by ... Eze 36:34 5869
in them in the *s* of many nations ... Eze 39:27 5869
and write it in their *s*, that they ... Eze 43:11 5869
the *s* thereof to the end of all ... Dan 4:11 2379
the *s* thereof to all the earth ... Dan 4:20 2379
away her whoredoms out of her *s* ... Hos 2:2 6440
lewdness in the *s* of her lovers ... Hos 2:10 5869
us up, and we shall live in his *s* ... Hos 6:2 6440
my *s* in the bottom of the sea ... Amos 9:3 5869
I said, I am cast out of thy *s* ... Jonah 2:4 5869
evil is good in the *s* of the LORD ... Mal 2:17 5869
The blind receive their *s* ... Mt 11:5 308
for so it seemed good in thy *s* ... Mt 11:26 1715
immediately their eyes received *s* ... Mt 20:34 308
Lord, that I might receive my *s* ... Mk 10:51 308
And immediately he received his *s* ... Mk 10:52 308
be great in the *s* of the Lord ... Lk 1:15 1799
and recovering of *s* to the blind ... Lk 4:18 309
many that were blind he gave *s* ... Lk 7:21 991
for so it seemed good in thy *s* ... Lk 10:21 1715
against heaven, and in thy *s* ... Lk 15:21 1799
is abomination in the *s* of God ... Lk 16:15 1799
Lord, that I may receive my *s* ... Lk 18:41 308
said unto him, Receive thy *s* ... Lk 18:42 308
And immediately he received his *s* ... Lk 18:43 308
that came together to that *s* ... Lk 23:48 2335
and he vanished out of their *s* ... Lk 24:31
I went and washed, and I received *s* ... Jn 9:11 308
him how he had received his *s* ... Jn 9:15 308
had been blind, and received his *s* ... Jn 9:18 308
of him that had received his *s* ... Jn 9:18 308
cloud received him out of their *s* ... Acts 1:9 3788
Whether it be right in the *s* of ... Acts 4:19 1799
wisdom in the *s* of Pharaoh king ... Acts 7:10 1726
saw it, he wondered at the *s* ... Acts 7:31 3705
is not right in the *s* of God ... Acts 8:21 1799
And he was three days without *s* ... Acts 9:9 991
him, that he might receive his *s* ... Acts 9:12 308
that thou mightest receive thy *s* ... Acts 9:17 308
and he received *s* forthwith ... Acts 9:18 308
in remembrance in the *s* of God ... Acts 10:31 1799
me, Brother Saul, receive thy *s* ... Acts 22:13 308
no flesh be justified in his *s* ... Rom 3:20 1799
things honest in the *s* of all men ... Rom 12:17 1799
in the *s* of God speak we in ... 2Cor 2:17 2714
man's conscience in the *s* of God ... 2Cor 4:2 1799
(For we walk by faith, not by *s* ... 2Cor 5:7 1491
s of God might appear unto you ... 2Cor 7:12 1799
not only in the *s* of the Lord ... 2Cor 8:21 1799
but also in the *s* of men ... 2Cor 8:21 1799
by the law in the *s* of God ... Gal 3:11 3844
and unreproveable in his *s* ... Col 1:22 2714
Jesus Christ, in the *s* of God ... 1Th 1:3 1715
acceptable in the *s* of God our ... 1Ti 2:3 1799
give thee charge in the *s* of God ... 1Ti 6:13 1799
that is not manifest in his *s* ... Heb 4:13 1799
And so terrible was the *s*, that ... Heb 12:21 5324
which is wellpleasing in his *s* ... Heb 13:21 1799
yourselves in the *s* of the Lord ... Jas 4:10 1799
which is in the *s* of God of great ... 1Pet 3:4 1799
things that are pleasing in his *s* ... 1Jn 3:22 1799
in *s* like unto an emerald ... Rev 4:3 3706
on the earth in the *s* of men ... Rev 13:13 1799
power to do in the *s* of the beast ... Rev 13:14 1799

SIGHTS

and fearful *s* and great signs shall ... Lk 21:11 5400

SIGN

to the voice of the first *s* ... Ex 4:8 226
believe the voice of the latter *s* ... Ex 4:8 226
to morrow shall this *s* be ... Ex 8:23 226
it shall be for a *s* unto thee ... Ex 13:9 226
for it is a *s* between me and you ... Ex 31:13 226
It is a *s* between me and the ... Ex 31:17 226
they shall be a *s* unto the ... Num 16:38 226
and they became a *s* ... Num 26:10 5251
bind them for a *s* upon thine hand ... Deut 6:8 226
bind them for a *s* upon your hand ... Deut 11:18 226
and giveth thee a *s* or a wonder ... Deut 13:1 226
the *s* or the wonder come to pass, ... Deut 13:2 226
they shall be upon thee for a *s* ... Deut 28:46 226
That this may be a *s* among you ... Josh 4:6 226
then shew me a *s* that thou ... Judg 6:17 226
s between the men of Israel ... Judg 20:38
And this shall be a *s* unto thee ... 1Sa 2:34 226
and this shall be a *s* unto us ... 1Sa 14:10 226
he gave a *s* the same day, saying, ... 1Kin 13:3 4159
This is the *s* which the LORD hath ... 1Kin 13:3 4159
according to the *s* which the man ... 1Kin 13:5 4159
And this shall be a *s* unto thee ... 2Kin 19:29 226
What shall be the *s* that the LORD ... 2Kin 20:8 226
This *s* shalt thou have of the ... 2Kin 20:9 226
unto him, and he gave him a *s* ... 2Chr 32:24 4159
Ask thee a *s* of the LORD thy God ... Is 7:11 226
Lord himself shall give you a *s* ... Is 7:14 226
And it shall be for a *s* and for a ... Is 19:20 226
and barefoot three years for a *s* ... Is 20:3 226
And this shall be a *s* unto thee ... Is 37:30 226
this shall be a *s* unto thee from ... Is 38:7 226
What is the *s* that I shall go up ... Is 38:22 226
for an everlasting *s* that shall ... Is 55:13 226
And I will set a *s* among them ... Is 66:19 226
Tekoa, and set up a *s* of fire in ... Jer 6:1 4864
And this shall be a *s* unto you ... Jer 44:29 226
This shall be a *s* to the house of ... Eze 4:3 226
for a *s* unto the house of Israel ... Eze 12:6 4159
Say, I am your *s* ... Eze 12:11 4159
that man, and will make him a *s* ... Eze 14:8 226
to be a *s* between me and them, ... Eze 20:12 226
and they shall be a *s* between me ... Eze 20:20 226
Thus Ezekiel is unto you a *s* ... Eze 24:24 4159
and thou shalt be a *s* unto them ... Eze 24:27 4159
then shall he set up a *s* by it ... Eze 39:15 6725
s the writing, that it be not ... Dan 6:8 7560
we would see a *s* from thee ... Mt 12:38 4592
generation seeketh after a *s* ... Mt 12:39 4592
there shall no *s* be given to it ... Mt 12:39 4592
but the *s* of the prophet Jonas ... Mt 12:39 4592
would shew them a *s* from heaven ... Mt 16:1 4592
generation seeketh after a *s* ... Mt 16:4 4592
there shall no *s* be given unto it ... Mt 16:4 4592
but the *s* of the prophet Jonas ... Mt 16:4 4592
what shall be the *s* of thy coming ... Mt 24:3 4592
then shall appear the *s* of the ... Mt 24:30 4592
that betrayed him gave them a *s* ... Mt 26:48 4592
seeking of him a *s* from heaven ... Mk 8:11 4592
this generation seek after a *s* ... Mk 8:12 4592
There shall no *s* be given unto ... Mk 8:12 4592
what shall be the *s* when all ... Mk 13:4 4592
And this shall be a *s* unto you ... Lk 2:12 4592
for a *s* which shall be spoken ... Lk 2:34 4592
sought of him a *s* from heaven ... Lk 11:16 4592
they seek a *s* ... Lk 11:29 4592
and there shall no *s* be given it ... Lk 11:29 4592
but the *s* of Jonas the prophet ... Lk 11:29 4592
Jonas was a *s* unto the Ninevites ... Lk 11:30 4592
what *s* will there be when these ... Lk 21:7 4592
What *s* shewest thou unto us, ... Jn 2:18 4592
What *s* shewest thou then, that we ... Jn 6:30 4592
whose *s* was Castor and Pollux ... Acts 28:11 3902
he received the *s* of circumcision ... Rom 4:11 4592
For the Jews require a *s*, and the ... 1Cor 1:22 4592
Wherefore tongues are for a *s* ... 1Cor 14:22 4592
And I saw another *s* in heaven ... Rev 15:1 4592

SIGNED

king Darius *s* the writing ... Dan 6:9 7560
knew that the writing was *s* ... Dan 6:10 7560
Hast thou not *s* a decree, that ... Dan 6:12 7560
nor the decree that thou hast *s* ... Dan 6:13 7560

SIGNET

And she said, Thy *s*, and thy ... Gen 38:18 2368
pray thee, whose are these, the *s* ... Gen 38:25 2858
stone, like the engravings of a *s* ... Ex 28:11 2368
names, like the engravings of a *s* ... Ex 28:21 2368
it, like the engravings of a *s* ... Ex 28:36 2368
names, like the engravings of a *s* ... Ex 39:14 2368
like to the engravings of a *s* ... Ex 39:30 2368
were the *s* upon my right hand ... Jer 22:24 2368
the king sealed it with his own *s* ... Dan 6:17 5824
and with the *s* of his lords ... Dan 6:17 5824
LORD, and will make thee as a *s* ... Hag 2:23 2368

SIGNETS

as *s* are graven, with the names ... Ex 39:6 2368

SIGNIFICATION

and none of them is without *s* ... 1Cor 14:10 880

SIGNIFIED

s by the Spirit that there should ... Acts 11:28 4591
s it by his angel unto his ... Rev 1:1 4591

SIGNIFIETH

s the removing of those things ... Heb 12:27 1213

SIGNIFY

to *s* the accomplishment of the ... Acts 21:26 1229
s to the chief captain that he ... Acts 23:15 1718
not withal to *s* the crimes laid ... Acts 25:27 4591
of Christ which was in them did *s* ... 1Pet 1:11 1213

SIGNIFYING

s what death he should die ... Jn 12:33 4591
s what death he should die ... Jn 18:32 4591
s by what death he should glorify ... Jn 21:19 4591
The Holy Ghost this *s*, that the ... Heb 9:8 1213

SIGNS

and let them be for *s*, and for ... Gen 1:14 226
will not believe also these two *s* ... Ex 4:9 226
hand, wherewith thou shalt do *s* ... Ex 4:17 226
all the *s* which he had commanded ... Ex 4:28 226
did the *s* in the sight of the ... Ex 4:30 226
Pharaoh's heart, and multiply my *s* ... Ex 7:3 226
might shew these my *s* before him ... Ex 10:1 226
my *s* which I have done among them ... Ex 10:2 226
for all the *s* which I have shewed ... Num 14:11 226
nation, by temptations, by *s* ... Deut 4:34 226
And the LORD shewed *s* and wonders, ... Deut 6:22 226
which thine eyes saw, and the *s* ... Deut 7:19 226
great terribleness, and with *s* ... Deut 26:8 226
which thine eyes have seen, the *s* ... Deut 29:3 226
In all the *s* and the wonders, ... Deut 34:11 226
did those great *s* in our sight ... Josh 24:17 226
when these *s* are come unto thee, ... 1Sa 10:7 226
all those *s* came to pass that day ... 1Sa 10:9 226
And shewedst *s* and wonders upon ... Neh 9:10 226
they set up their ensigns for *s* ... Ps 74:4 226
We see not our *s* ... Ps 74:9 226
How he had wrought his *s* in Egypt ... Ps 78:43 226
They shewed his *s* among them ... Ps 105:27 226
the LORD hath given me are for *s* ... Is 8:18 226
not dismayed at the *s* of heaven ... Jer 10:2 226
Which hast set *s* and wonders in ... Jer 32:20 226
out of the land of Egypt with *s* ... Jer 32:21 226
I thought it good to shew the *s* ... Dan 4:2 852
How great are his *s* ... Dan 4:3 852
and rescueth, and he worketh *s* ... Dan 6:27 852
ye not discern the *s* of the times ... Mt 16:3 4592
prophets, and shall shew great *s* ... Mt 24:24 4592
shall rise, and shall shew *s* ... Mk 13:22 4592
these *s* shall follow them that ... Mk 16:17 4592
the word with *s* following ... Mk 16:20 4592
they made *s* to his father, how he ... Lk 1:62 1770
great *s* shall there be from ... Lk 21:11 4591
And there shall be *s* in the sun ... Lk 21:25 4591
Jesus unto him, Except ye see *s* ... Jn 4:48 4591
many other *s* truly did Jesus in ... Jn 20:30 4591
above, and *s* in the earth beneath ... Acts 2:19 4591
you by miracles and wonders and *s* ... Acts 2:22 4591
s were done by the apostles ... Acts 2:43 4591
and that *s* and wonders may be done ... Acts 4:30 4591
hands of the apostles were many *s* ... Acts 5:12 4591
s in the land of Egypt, and in the ... Acts 7:36 4591
the miracles and *s* which were done ... Acts 8:13 4591
word of his grace, and granted *s* ... Acts 14:3 4591
Through mighty *s* and wonders, by ... Rom 15:19 4591
Truly the *s* of an apostle were ... 2Cor 12:12 4591
among you in all patience, in *s* ... 2Cor 12:12 4591
of Satan with all power and *s* ... 2Th 2:9 4591
bearing them witness, both with *s* ... Heb 2:4 4591

SIHON (*si'-hon*) *An Amorite king.*

unto *S* king of the Amorites ... Num 21:21 5511
S would not suffer Israel to pass ... Num 21:23 5511
but *S* gathered all his people ... Num 21:23 5511
of *S* the king of the Amorites ... Num 21:26 5511
let the city of *S* be built ... Num 21:27 5511
a flame from the city of *S* ... Num 21:28 5511
into captivity unto *S* king of the ... Num 21:29 5511
didst unto *S* king of the Amorites ... Num 21:34 5511
the kingdom of *S* king of the ... Num 32:33 5511
After he had slain *S* the king of ... Deut 1:4 5511
into thine hand *S* the Amorite ... Deut 2:24 5511
S king of Heshbon with words of ... Deut 2:26 5511
But *S* king of Heshbon would not ... Deut 2:30 5511
Behold, I have begun to give *S* ... Deut 2:31 5511
Then *S* came out against us, he and ... Deut 2:32 5511
didst unto *S* king of the Amorites ... Deut 3:2 5511
as we did unto *S* king of Heshbon, ... Deut 3:6 5511
in the land of *S* king of the ... Deut 4:46 5511
S the king of Heshbon, and Og the ... Deut 29:7 5511
shall do unto them as he did to *S* ... Deut 31:4 5511
were on the other side Jordan, *S* ... Josh 2:10 5511
to *S* king of Heshbon, and to Og ... Josh 9:10 5511
S king of the Amorites, who dwelt ... Josh 12:2 5511
the border of *S* king of Heshbon ... Josh 12:5 5511
all the cities of *S* king of the ... Josh 13:10 5511
all the kingdom of *S* king of the ... Josh 13:21 5511
and Reba, which were dukes of *S* ... Josh 13:21 5511
the kingdom of *S* king of Heshbon ... Josh 13:27 5511
unto *S* king of the Amorites ... Judg 11:19 5511
But *S* trusted not Israel to pass ... Judg 11:20 5511
but *S* gathered all his people ... Judg 11:20 5511
LORD God of Israel delivered *S* ... Judg 11:21 5511
in the country of *S* king of the ... 1Kin 4:19 5511
so they possessed the land of *S* ... Neh 9:22 5511
S king of the Amorites, and Og ... Ps 135:11 5511
S king of the Amorites ... Ps 136:19 5511
and a flame from the midst of *S* ... Jer 48:45 5511

SIHOR (*si'-hor*) See SHIHOR. *A river in southern Canaan.*

From *S*, which is before Egypt, ... Josh 13:3 7883
And by great waters the seed of *S* ... Is 23:3 7883
Egypt, to drink the waters of *S* ... Jer 2:18 7883

SIKKUTH See MOLOCH.

SILAS (*si'-las*) See SILVANUS. *A co-worker with Paul.*

Judas surnamed Barsabas, and *S* ... Acts 15:22 4609
We have sent therefore Judas and *S* ... Acts 15:27 4609
And Judas and *S*, being prophets ... Acts 15:32 4609
it pleased *S* to abide there still ... Acts 15:34 4609
And Paul chose *S*, and departed, ... Acts 15:40 4609
was gone, they caught Paul and *S* ... Acts 16:19 4609
S prayed, and sang praises unto ... Acts 16:25 4609
and fell down before Paul and *S* ... Acts 16:29 4609
and consorted with Paul and *S* ... Acts 17:4 4609
Paul and *S* by night unto Berea ... Acts 17:10 4609
but *S* and Timotheus abode there ... Acts 17:14 4609
and receiving a commandment unto *S* ... Acts 17:15 4609
And when *S* and Timotheus ... Acts 18:5 4609

SILENCE

who said, Keep *s* ... Judg 3:19 2013
was before mine eyes, there was *s* ... Job 4:16 1827
waited, and kept *s* at my counsel ... Job 29:21 1826
terrify me, that I kept *s* ... Job 31:34 1826
Let the lying lips be put to *s* ... Ps 31:18 481
When I kept *s*, my bones waxed old ... Ps 32:3 2790
keep not *s* ... Ps 35:22 2790
I was dumb with *s*, I held my ... Ps 39:2 1747
shall come, and shall not keep *s* ... Ps 50:3 2790
hast thou done, and I kept *s* ... Ps 50:21 2790
Keep not thou *s*, O God ... Ps 83:1 1824
my soul had almost dwelt in *s* ... Ps 94:17 1745
neither any that go down into *s* ... Ps 115:17 1745
a time to keep *s*, and a time to ... Eccl 3:7 2814
is laid waste, and brought to *s* ... Is 15:1 1820
is laid waste, and brought to *s* ... Is 15:1
Keep *s* before me, O islands ... Is 41:1 2790
mention of the LORD, keep not *s* ... Is 62:6 1824
I will not keep *s*, but will ... Is 65:6 2814
the LORD our God hath put us to *s* ... Jer 8:14 1826
sit upon the ground, and keep *s* ... Lam 2:10 1826
He sitteth alone and keepeth *s* ... Lam 3:28 1826
prudent shall keep *s* in that time ... Amos 5:13 1826
they shall cast them forth with *s* ... Amos 8:3 2013
all the earth keep *s* before him ... Hab 2:20 2013
he had put the Sadducees to *s* ... Mt 22:34 5392
Then all the multitude kept *s* ... Acts 15:12 4601
And when there was made a great *s* ... Acts 21:40 4602
to them, they kept the more *s* ... Acts 22:2 2271

let him keep s in the church 1Cor 14:28 *4601*
your women keep s in the churches 1Cor 14:34 *4601*
learn in s with all subjection 1Ti 2:11 *2271*
over the man, but to be in s 1Ti 2:12 *2271*
to s the ignorance of foolish men 1Pet 2:15 *5392*
there was s in heaven about the Rev 8:1 *4602*

SILENT
the wicked shall be s in darkness 1Sa 2:9 1826
in the night season, and am not s Ps 22:2 1947
be not s to me Ps 28:1 2790
lest, if thou be s to me, I Ps 28:1 2790
sing praise to thee, and not be s Ps 30:12 1826
let them be s in the grave Ps 31:17 1826
Sit thou s, and get thee into Is 47:5 1748
cities, and let us be s there Jer 8:14 1826
Be s, O all flesh, before the Zec 2:13 2013

SILK
her clothing is s and purple Prov 31:22 8336
linen, and I covered thee with s Eze 16:10 4897
raiment was of fine linen, and s Eze 16:13 4897
and fine linen, and purple, and s Rev 18:12 *2596*

SILLA (*sil'-lah*) *A place near Jerusalem.*
of Millo, which goeth down to S 2Kin 12:20 5538

SILLY
man, and envy slayeth the s one Job 5:2 6601
is like a s dove without heart Hos 7:11 6601
lead captive s women laden with 2Ti 3:6 *1133*

SILOAH (*si-lo'-ah*) See SHILOAH, SILOAM. *Same as Siloam.*
pool of S by the king's garden Neh 3:15 7975

SILOAM (*si'-lo-am*) See SILOAH. *A pool south of Jerusalem.*
upon whom the tower in S fell Lk 13:4 *4611*
him, Go, wash in the pool of S Jn 9:7 *4611*
said unto me, Go to the pool of S Jn 9:11 *4611*

SILVANUS (*sil-va'-nus*) See SILAS.
1. A co-worker with Paul.
among you by us, even by me and S 2Cor 1:19 *4610*
Paul, and S, and Timotheus, unto 1Th 1:1 *4610*
Paul, and S, and Timotheus, unto 2Th 1:1 *4610*
2. A messenger for Peter.
By S, a faithful brother unto you 1Pet 5:12 *4610*

SILVER
was very rich in cattle, in s Gen 13:2 3701
brother a thousand pieces of s Gen 20:16 3701
worth four hundred shekels of s Gen 23:15 3701
Abraham weighed to Ephron the s Gen 23:16 3701
Heth, four hundred shekels of s Gen 23:16 3701
given him flocks, and herds, and s Gen 24:35 3701
servant brought forth jewels of s Gen 24:53 3701
for twenty pieces of s Gen 37:28 3701
And put my cup, the s cup, in the Gen 44:2 3701
out of thy lord's house s or gold Gen 44:8 3701
he gave three hundred pieces of s Gen 45:22 3701
in her house, jewels of s Ex 3:22 3701
of her neighbour, jewels of s Ex 11:2 3701
of the Egyptians jewels of s Ex 12:35 3701
shall not make with me gods of s Ex 20:23 3701
their master thirty shekels of s Ex 21:32 3701
gold, and s, and brass, Ex 25:3 3701
of s under the twenty boards Ex 26:19 3701
And their forty sockets of s Ex 26:21 3701
boards, and their sockets of s Ex 26:25 3701
gold, upon the four sockets of s Ex 26:32 3701
and their fillets shall be of s Ex 27:10 3701
the pillars and their fillets of s Ex 27:11 3701
court shall be filleted with s Ex 27:17 3701
their hooks shall be of s Ex 27:17 3701
works, to work in gold, and in s Ex 31:4 3701
gold, and s, and brass, Ex 35:5 3701
that did offer an offering of s Ex 35:24 3701
works, to work in gold, and in s Ex 35:32 3701
forty sockets of s he made under Ex 36:24 3701
And their forty sockets of s Ex 36:26 3701
sockets were sixteen sockets of s Ex 36:30 3701
cast for them four sockets of s Ex 36:36 3701
and their fillets were of s Ex 38:10 3701
the pillars and their fillets of s Ex 38:11 3701
the pillars and their fillets of s Ex 38:12 3701
the pillars and their fillets of s Ex 38:17 3701
of their chapiters of s Ex 38:17 3701
of the court were filleted with s Ex 38:17 3701
their hooks of s, and the Ex 38:19 3701
chapiters and their fillets of s Ex 38:19 3701
the s of them that were numbered Ex 38:25 3701
of the hundred talents of s were Ex 38:27 3701
thy estimation by shekels of s Lev 5:15 3701
shall be fifty shekels of s Lev 27:3 3701
be of the male five shekels of s Lev 27:6 3701
shall be three shekels of s Lev 27:6 3701
be valued at fifty shekels of s Lev 27:16 3701
And his offering was one s charger Num 7:13 3701
one s bowl of seventy shekels, Num 7:13 3701
for his offering one s charger Num 7:19 3701
one s bowl of seventy shekels, Num 7:19 3701
His offering was one s charger Num 7:25 3701
one s bowl of seventy shekels, Num 7:25 3701
His offering was one s charger of Num 7:31 3701
one s bowl of seventy shekels, Num 7:31 3701
His offering was one s charger Num 7:37 3701
one s bowl of seventy shekels, Num 7:37 3701
His offering was one s charger of Num 7:43 3701
a s bowl of seventy shekels, Num 7:43 3701
His offering was one s charger Num 7:49 3701
one s bowl of seventy shekels, Num 7:49 3701
His offering was one s charger of Num 7:55 3701
one s bowl of seventy shekels, Num 7:55 3701
His offering was one s charger Num 7:61 3701
one s bowl of seventy shekels, Num 7:61 3701
His offering was one s charger Num 7:67 3701
one s bowl of seventy shekels, Num 7:67 3701
His offering was one s charger Num 7:73 3701
one s bowl of seventy shekels, Num 7:73 3701
His offering was one s charger Num 7:79 3701
one s bowl of seventy shekels, Num 7:79 3701
of s, twelve s bowls Num 7:84 3701
Each charger of s weighing an Num 7:85 3701
all the s vessels weighed two Num 7:85 3701
Make thee two trumpets of s Num 10:2 3701
would give me his house full of s Num 22:18 3701
would give me his house full of s Num 24:13 3701
Only the gold, and the s, the Num 31:22 3701
the s or gold that is on them Deut 7:25 3701
and thy flocks multiply, and thy s Deut 8:13 3701
he greatly multiply to himself s Deut 17:17 3701
him in an hundred shekels of s Deut 22:19 3701
father fifty shekels of s Deut 22:29 3701
and their idols, wood and stone, s Deut 29:17 3701
But all the s, and gold, and Josh 6:19 3701
only the s, and the gold, and the Josh 6:24 3701
and two hundred shekels of s Josh 7:21 3701
of my tent, and the s under it Josh 7:21 3701
in his tent, and the s under it Josh 7:22 3701
Achan the son of Zerah, and the s Josh 7:24 3701
and with very much cattle, with s Josh 22:8 3701
for an hundred pieces of s Josh 24:32 7192
ten pieces of s out of the house Judg 9:4 3701
of us eleven hundred pieces of s Judg 16:5 3701
of s that were taken from thee Judg 17:2 3701
ears, behold, the s is with me Judg 17:2 3701
shekels of s to his mother Judg 17:3 3701
I had wholly dedicated the s unto Judg 17:3 3701
took two hundred shekels of s Judg 17:4 3701
thee ten shekels of s by the year Judg 17:10 3701
and crouch to him for a piece of s 1Sa 2:36 3701
the fourth part of a shekel of s 1Sa 9:8 3701
brought with him vessels of s 2Sa 8:10 3701
unto the LORD, with the s 2Sa 8:11 3701
have given thee ten shekels of s 2Sa 18:11 3701
shekels of s in mine hand 2Sa 18:12 3701
We will have no s nor gold of 2Sa 21:4 3701
the oxen for fifty shekels of s 2Sa 24:24 3701
even the s, and the gold, and the 1Kin 7:51 3701
none were of s 1Kin 10:21 3701
of Tharshish, bringing gold, and s 1Kin 10:22 3701
man his present, vessels of s 1Kin 10:25 3701
And the king made s to be in 1Kin 10:27 3701
for six hundred shekels of s 1Kin 10:29 3701
into the house of the LORD, s 1Kin 15:15 3701
Then Asa took all the s and the 1Kin 15:18 3701
sent unto thee a present of s 1Kin 15:19 3701
of Shemer for two talents of s 1Kin 16:24 3701
Thy s and thy gold is mine 1Kin 20:3 3701
Thou shalt deliver me thy s 1Kin 20:5 3701
and for my children, and for my s 1Kin 20:7 3701
else thou shalt pay a talent of s 1Kin 20:39 3701
and took with him ten talents of s 2Kin 5:5 3701
them, I pray thee, a talent of s 2Kin 5:22 3701
two talents of s in two bags 2Kin 5:23 3701
sold for fourscore pieces of s 2Kin 6:25 3701
dove's dung for five pieces of s 2Kin 6:25 3701
eat and drink, and carried thence s 2Kin 7:8 3701
the house of the LORD bowls of s 2Kin 12:13 3701
vessels of gold, or vessels of s 2Kin 12:13 3701
And he took all the gold and s 2Kin 14:14 3701
gave Pul a thousand talents of s 2Kin 15:19 3701
of each man fifty shekels of s 2Kin 15:20 3701
And Ahaz took the s and gold that 2Kin 16:8 3701
Judah three hundred talents of s 2Kin 18:14 3701
Hezekiah gave him all the s that 2Kin 18:15 3701
of his precious things, the s 2Kin 20:13 3701
that he may sum the s which is 2Kin 22:4 3701
of an hundred talents of s 2Kin 23:33 3701
And Jehoiakim gave the s and the 2Kin 23:35 3701
he exacted the s and the gold of 2Kin 23:35 3701
gold, in gold, and of s, in s 2Kin 25:15 3701
manner of vessels of gold and s 1Chr 18:10 3701
unto the LORD, with the s 1Chr 18:11 3701
of s to hire them chariots 1Chr 19:6 3701
a thousand thousand talents of s 1Chr 22:14 3701
Of the gold, the s, and the brass, 1Chr 22:16 3701
s also for all instruments of 1Chr 28:14
all instruments of s by weight 1Chr 28:14 3701
the candlesticks of s by weight 1Chr 28:15 3701
s for the tables of s 1Chr 28:16 3701
likewise s by weight for every 1Chr 28:17
by weight for every bason of s 1Chr 28:17 3701
the s for things of s, and 1Chr 29:2 3701
own proper good, of gold and s 1Chr 29:3 3701
thousand talents of refined s 1Chr 29:4 3701
and the s for things of s 1Chr 29:5 3701
of s ten thousand talents, and of 1Chr 29:7 3701
And the king made s and gold at 2Chr 1:15 3701
for six hundred shekels of s 2Chr 1:17 3701
cunning to work in gold, and in s 2Chr 2:7 3701
skilful to work in gold, and in s 2Chr 2:14 3701
and the s, and the gold, and all the 2Chr 5:1 3701
brought gold and s to Solomon 2Chr 9:14 3701
none were of s 2Chr 9:20 3701
of Tarshish bringing gold, and s 2Chr 9:21 3701
man his present, vessels of s 2Chr 9:24 3701
the king made s in Jerusalem as 2Chr 9:27 3701
that he himself had dedicated, s 2Chr 15:18 3701
Then Asa brought out s and gold 2Chr 16:2 3701
behold, I have sent thee s 2Chr 16:3 3701
presents, and tribute s 2Chr 17:11 3701
father gave them great gifts of s 2Chr 21:3 3701
spoons, and vessels of gold and s 2Chr 24:14 3701
for an hundred talents of s 2Chr 25:6 3701
same year an hundred talents of s 2Chr 27:5 3701
he made himself treasuries for s 2Chr 32:27 3701
land in an hundred talents of s 2Chr 36:3 3701
men of his place help him with s Ezr 1:4 3701
their hands with vessels of s Ezr 1:6 3701
of gold, a thousand chargers of s Ezr 1:9 3701
s basons of a second sort four Ezr 1:10 3701
of s were five thousand and four Ezr 1:11 3701
gold, and five thousand pound of s Ezr 2:69 3701
s of the house of God, which Ezr 5:14 3702
s vessels of the house of God, Ezr 6:5 3702
And to carry the s and gold, which Ezr 7:15 3702
And all the s and gold that thou Ezr 7:16 3702
to do with the rest of the s Ezr 7:18 3702
Unto an hundred talents of s Ezr 7:22 3702
And weighed unto them the s Ezr 8:25 3701
six hundred and fifty talents of s Ezr 8:26 3701
s vessels an hundred talents, and Ezr 8:26 3701
and the s and the gold are a Ezr 8:28 3701
the Levites the weight of the s Ezr 8:30 3701
Now on the fourth day was the s Ezr 8:33 3701
wine, beside forty shekels of s Neh 5:15 3701
and two hundred pounds of s Neh 7:71 3701
gold, and two thousand pounds of s Neh 7:72 3701
fine linen and purple to s rings Est 1:6 3701
the beds were of gold and s Est 1:6 3701
pay ten thousand talents of s to Est 3:9 3701
The s is given to thee, the Est 3:11 3701
who filled their houses with s Job 3:15 3701
and thou shalt have plenty of s Job 22:25 3701
Though he heap up s as the dust Job 27:16 3701
the innocent shall divide the s Job 27:17 3701
Surely there is a vein for the s Job 28:1 3701
neither shall s be weighed for Job 28:15 3701
as s tried in a furnace of earth, Ps 12:6 3701
thou hast tried us, as s is tried Ps 66:10 3701
wings of a dove covered with s Ps 68:13 3701
submit himself with pieces of s Ps 68:30 3701
He brought them forth also with s Ps 105:37 3701
Their idols are s and gold, the Ps 115:4 3701
me than thousands of gold and s Ps 119:72 3701
The idols of the heathen are s Ps 135:15 3701
If thou seekest her as s, and Prov 2:4 3701
better than the merchandise of s Prov 3:14 3701
Receive my instruction, and not s Prov 8:10 3701
and my revenue than choice s Prov 8:19 3701
tongue of the just is as choice s Prov 10:20 3701
rather to be chosen than s Prov 16:16 3701
The fining pot is for s, and the Prov 17:3 3701
and loving favour rather than s Prov 22:1 3701
Take away the dross from the s Prov 25:4 3701
apples of gold in pictures of s Prov 25:11 3701
a potsherd covered with s dross Prov 26:23 3701
As the fining pot for s, and the Prov 27:21 3701
I gathered me also s and gold, and Eccl 2:8 3701
He that loveth s shall not be Eccl 5:10 3701
shall not be satisfied with s Eccl 5:10 3701
Or ever the s cord be loosed, or Eccl 12:6 3701
borders of gold with studs of s Song 1:11 3701
He made the pillars thereof of s Song 3:10 3701
will build upon her a palace of s Song 8:9 3701
to bring a thousand pieces of s Song 8:11 3701
Thy s is become dross, thy wine Is 1:22 3701
Their land also is full of s Is 2:7 3701
a man shall cast his idols of s Is 2:20 3701
them, which shall not regard s Is 13:17 3701
of thy graven images of s Is 30:22 3701
shall cast away his idols of s Is 31:7 3701
of his precious things, the s Is 39:2 3701
with gold, and casteth s chains Is 40:19 3701
weigh s in the balance, and hire a Is 46:6 3701
have refined thee, but not with s Is 48:10 3701
bring thy sons from far, their s Is 60:9 3701
gold, and for iron I will bring s Is 60:17 3701
Reprobate s shall men call them Jer 6:30 3701
They deck it with s and with gold Jer 10:4 3701
S spread into plates is brought Jer 10:9 3701
even seventeen shekels of s Jer 32:9 3701
and that which was of s in s Jer 52:19 3701
shall cast their s in the streets Eze 7:19 3701
their s and their gold shall not Eze 7:19 3701
wast thou decked with gold and s Eze 16:13 3701
fair jewels of my gold and of my s Eze 16:17 3701
they are even the dross of s Eze 22:18 3701
As they gather s, and brass, and Eze 22:20 3701
As s is melted in the midst of Eze 22:22 3701
with s, iron, tin, and lead, they Eze 27:12 3701
gold and s into thy treasures Eze 28:4 3701
to carry away s and gold, to take Eze 38:13 3701
gold, his breast and his arms of s Dan 2:32 3702
iron, the clay, the brass, the s Dan 2:35 3702
iron, the brass, the clay, the s Dan 2:45 3702
s vessels which his father Dan 5:2 3702
praised the gods of gold, and of s Dan 5:4 3702
thou hast praised the gods of s Dan 5:23 3702
with their precious vessels of s Dan 11:8 3701
shall he honour with gold, and s Dan 11:38 3701
the treasures of gold and of s Dan 11:43 3701
wine, and oil, and multiplied her s Hos 2:8 3701
her to me for fifteen pieces of s Hos 3:2 3701
of their s and their gold have Hos 8:4 3701
the pleasant places for their s Hos 9:6 3701
them molten images of their s Hos 13:2 3701
Because ye have taken my s Joel 3:5 3701
they sold the righteous for s Amos 2:6 3701
That we may buy the poor for s Amos 8:6 3701
Take ye the spoil of s, take the Nah 2:9 3701
it is laid over with gold and s Hab 2:19 3701
all they that bear s are cut off Zeph 1:11 3701
Neither their s nor their gold Zeph 1:18 3701
The s is mine, and the gold is Hag 2:8 3701
Then take s and gold, and make Zec 6:11 3701
heaped up s as the dust, and fine Zec 9:3 3701
for my price thirty pieces of s Zec 11:12 3701
And I took the thirty pieces of s Zec 11:13 3701
will refine them as s is refined Zec 13:9 3701
be gathered together, gold, and s Zec 14:14 3701
sit as a refiner and purifier of s Mal 3:3 3701
Levi, and purge them as gold and s Mal 3:3 3701

S

Provide neither gold, nor s ... Mt 10:9 696
with him for thirty pieces of s ... Mt 26:15 694
pieces of s to the chief priests ... Mt 27:3 694
the pieces of s in the temple ... Mt 27:5 694
chief priests took the s pieces ... Mt 27:6 694
they took the thirty pieces of s ... Mt 27:9 694
what woman having ten pieces of s ... Lk 15:8 1406
Then Peter said, S and gold have I ... Acts 3:6 694
Godhead is like unto gold, or s ... Acts 17:29 696
it fifty thousand pieces of s ... Acts 19:19 694
which made s shrines for Diana, ... Acts 19:24 693
I have coveted no man's s ... Acts 20:33 694
upon this foundation gold, s ... 1Cor 3:12 696
not only vessels of gold and of s ... 2Ti 2:20 693
Your gold and s is cankered ... Jas 5:3 696
with corruptible things, as s ... 1Pet 1:18 694
devils, and idols of gold, and s ... Rev 9:20 693
The merchandise of gold, and s ... Rev 18:12 696

SILVERLINGS
a thousand vines at a thousand s ... Is 7:23 3701

SILVERSMITH
certain man named Demetrius, a s ... Acts 19:24 695

SIMEON (*sim'-e-un*) See SHIMEON, SIMEONITES, SIMON.
1. A son of Jacob.
and she called his name S ... Gen 29:33 8095
that two of the sons of Jacob, S ... Gen 34:25 8095
And Jacob said to S and Levi, Ye ... Gen 34:30 8095
Reuben, Jacob's firstborn, and S ... Gen 35:23 8095
with them, and took from them S ... Gen 42:24 8095
S is not, and ye will take ... Gen 42:36 8095
he brought S out unto them ... Gen 43:23 8095
And the sons of S ... Gen 46:10 8095
as Reuben and S, they shall be ... Gen 48:5 8095
S and Levi are brethren ... Gen 49:5 8095
Reuben, S, Levi, and Judah, ... Ex 1:2 8095
And the sons of S ... Ex 6:15 8095
these are the families of S ... Ex 6:15 8095
2. Descendents of Simeon 1 and their land.
Of S ... Num 1:6 8095
Of the children of S, by their ... Num 1:22 8095
of them, even of the tribe of S ... Num 1:23 8095
by him shall be the tribe of S ... Num 2:12 8095
S shall be Shelumiel the son of ... Num 2:12 8095
prince of the children of S ... Num 7:36 8095
of S was Shelumiel the son of ... Num 10:19 8095
Of the tribe of S, Shaphat the ... Num 13:5 8095
The sons of S after their ... Num 26:12 8095
of the tribe of the children of S ... Num 34:20 8095
S, and Levi, and Judah, and Issachar ... Deut 27:12 8095
And the second lot came forth to S ... Josh 19:1 8095
of S according to their families ... Josh 19:1 8095
of S according to their families ... Josh 19:8 8095
inheritance of the children of S ... Josh 19:9 8095
therefore the children of S had ... Josh 19:9 8095
Judah, and out of the tribe of S ... Josh 21:4 8099
of the tribe of the children of S ... Josh 21:9 8095
And Judah said unto S his brother ... Judg 1:3 8095
So S went with him ... Judg 1:3 8095
And Judah went with S his brother ... Judg 1:17 8095
Reuben, S, Levi, and Judah, ... 1Chr 2:1 8095
The sons of S were, Nemuel, and ... 1Chr 4:24 8095
of them, even of the sons of S ... 1Chr 4:42 8095
of the tribe of the children of S ... 1Chr 6:65 8095
Of the children of S, mighty men ... 1Chr 12:25 8095
Ephraim and Manasseh, and out of S ... 2Chr 15:9 8095
of Manasseh, and Ephraim, and S ... 2Chr 34:6 8095
west side, S shall have a portion ... Eze 48:24 8095
And by the border of S, from the ... Eze 48:25 8095
one gate of S, one gate of ... Eze 48:33 8095
Of the tribe of S were sealed ... Rev 7:7 4826
3. A devout man who blessed Jesus.
in Jerusalem, whose name was S ... Lk 2:25 4826
S blessed them, and said unto Mary ... Lk 2:34 4826
4. Father of Levi; an ancestor of Jesus.
Which was the son of S, which was ... Lk 3:30 4826
5. A prophet of Antioch.
S that was called Niger, and ... Acts 13:1 4826
6. Same as Simon Peter.
S hath declared how God at the ... Acts 15:14 4826

SIMEONITES (*sim'-e-un-ites*) *Descendants of Simeon 1.*
of a chief house among the S ... Num 25:14 8099
These are the families of the S ... Num 26:14 8099
of the S, Shephatiah the son of ... 1Chr 27:16 8099

SIMILITUDE
the s of the LORD shall he behold ... Num 12:8 8544
voice of the words, but saw no s ... Deut 4:12 8544
for ye saw no manner of s on the ... Deut 4:15 8544
the s of any figure, the likeness ... Deut 4:16 8544
And under it was the s of oxen ... 2Chr 4:3 1823
the s of an ox that eateth grass ... Ps 106:20 8403
polished after the s of a palace ... Ps 144:12 8403
one like the s of the sons of men ... Dan 10:16 1823
the s of Adam's transgression ... Rom 5:14 3667
for that after the s of ... Heb 7:15 3665
which are made after the s of God ... Jas 3:9 3669

SIMILITUDES
multiplied visions, and used s ... Hos 12:10 1819

SIMON (*si'mun*) See BAR-JONA, NIGER, PETER, SIMEON, SIMON'S, ZELOTES.
1. Same as Peter.
S called Peter, and Andrew his ... Mt 4:18 4613
The first, S, who is called Peter ... Mt 10:2 4613
S Peter answered and said, Thou ... Mt 16:16 4613
him, Blessed art thou, S Bar-jona ... Mt 16:17 4613
saying, What thinkest thou, S ... Mt 17:25 4613
by the sea of Galilee, he saw S ... Mk 1:16 4613
they entered into the house of S ... Mk 1:29 4613
And S and they that were with him ... Mk 1:36 4613
And S he surnamed Peter ... Mk 3:16 4613
sleeping, and saith unto Peter, S ... Mk 14:37 4613
had left speaking, he said unto S ... Lk 5:4 4613
S answering said unto him, Master ... Lk 5:5 4613
When S Peter saw it, he fell down ... Lk 5:8 4613
which were partners with S ... Lk 5:10 4613
And Jesus said unto S, Fear not ... Lk 5:10 4613
S, (whom he also named Peter,) and ... Lk 6:14 4613
And the Lord said, S, S, ... Lk 22:31 4613
indeed, and hath appeared to S ... Lk 24:34 4613
was Andrew, S Peter's brother ... Jn 1:40 4613
first findeth his own brother S ... Jn 1:41 4613
Thou art S the son of Jona ... Jn 1:42 4613
S Peter's brother, saith unto him ... Jn 6:8 4613
Then S Peter answered him, Lord, ... Jn 6:68 4613
Then cometh he to S Peter ... Jn 13:6 4613
S Peter saith unto him, Lord, not ... Jn 13:9 4613
S Peter therefore beckoned to him ... Jn 13:24 4613
S Peter said unto him, Lord, ... Jn 13:36 4613
Then S Peter having a sword drew ... Jn 18:10 4613
S Peter followed Jesus, and so did ... Jn 18:15 4613
S Peter stood and warmed himself ... Jn 18:25 4613
she runneth, and cometh to S Peter ... Jn 20:2 4613
Then cometh S Peter following him ... Jn 20:6 4613
There were together S Peter ... Jn 21:2 4613
S Peter saith unto them, I go a ... Jn 21:3 4613
Now when S Peter heard that it ... Jn 21:7 4613
S Peter went up, and drew the net ... Jn 21:11 4613
Jesus saith to S Peter, S ... Jn 21:15 4613
to him again the second time, S ... Jn 21:16 4613
saith unto him the third time, S ... Jn 21:17 4613
men to Joppa, and call for one S ... Acts 10:5 4613
And called, and asked whether S ... Acts 10:18 4613
to Joppa, and call hither S ... Acts 10:32 4613
Send men to Joppa, and call for S ... Acts 11:13 4613
S Peter, a servant and an apostle ... 2Pet 1:1 4613
2. A Canaanite disciple of Jesus.
S the Canaanite, and Judas ... Mt 10:4 4613
and Thaddaeus, and S the Canaanite, ... Mk 3:18 4613
of Alphaeus, and S called Zelotes, ... Lk 6:15 4613
S Zelotes, and Judas the brother ... Acts 1:13 4613
3. A brother of Jesus.
brethren, James, and Joses, and S ... Mt 13:55 4613
James, and Joses, and of Juda, and S ... Mk 6:3 4613
4. A leper in Bethany.
in the house of S the leper ... Mt 26:6 4613
in the house of S the leper ... Mk 14:3 4613
5. A Cyrenian who bore Jesus' cross.
found a man of Cyrene, S by name ... Mt 27:32 4613
And they compel one S a Cyrenian ... Mk 15:21 4613
away, they laid hold upon one S ... Lk 23:26 4613
6. A Pharisee.
Jesus answering said unto him, S ... Lk 7:40 4613
S answered and said, I suppose ... Lk 7:43 4613
to the woman, and said unto S ... Lk 7:44 4613
7. Father of Judas Iscariot.
of Judas Iscariot the son of S ... Jn 6:71 4613
to Judas Iscariot, the son of S ... Jn 13:26 4613
8. A Samaritan sorcerer.
there was a certain man, called S ... Acts 8:9 4613
Then S himself believed also ... Acts 8:13 4613
when S saw that through laying on ... Acts 8:18 4613
Then answered S, and said, Pray ye ... Acts 8:24 4613
9. A tanner at Joppa.
days in Joppa with one S a tanner ... Acts 9:43 4613
He lodgeth with one S a tanner ... Acts 10:6 4613
of one S a tanner by the sea side ... Acts 10:32 4613

SIMON'S (*si'-muns*)
1. Refers to Simon 1.
But S wife's mother lay sick of a ... Mk 1:30 4613
and entered into S house ... Lk 4:38 4613
S wife's mother was taken with a ... Lk 4:38 4613
one of the ships, which was S ... Lk 5:3 4613
2. Refers to Simon 7.
S son, which should betray him, ... Jn 12:4 4613
Iscariot, S son, to betray him ... Jn 13:2 4613
3. Refers to Simon 9.
had made enquiry for S house ... Acts 10:17 4613

SIMPLE
LORD is sure, making wise the s ... Ps 19:7 6612
The LORD preserveth the s ... Ps 116:6 6612
giveth understanding unto the s ... Ps 119:130 6612
To give subtilty to the s ... Prov 1:4 6612
How long, ye s ones, will ye love ... Prov 1:22 6612
away of the s shall slay them ... Prov 1:32 6612
And beheld among the s ones ... Prov 7:7 6612
O ye s, understand wisdom ... Prov 8:5 6612
Whoso is s, let him turn in ... Prov 9:4 6612
she is s, and knoweth nothing ... Prov 9:13 6615
Whoso is s, let him turn in ... Prov 9:16 6612
The s believeth every word ... Prov 14:15 6612
The s inherit folly ... Prov 14:18 6612
a scorner, and the s will beware ... Prov 19:25 6612
is punished, the s is made wise ... Prov 21:11 6612
but the s pass on, and are ... Prov 22:3 6612
but the s pass on, and are ... Prov 27:12 6612
that erreth, and for him that is s ... Eze 45:20 6612
deceive the hearts of the s ... Rom 16:18 172
is good, and s concerning evil ... Rom 16:19 185

SIMPLICITY
and they went in their s, and they ... 2Sa 15:11 8537
ye simple ones, will ye love s ... Prov 1:22 6612
that giveth, let him do it with s ... Rom 12:8 572
of our conscience, that in s ... 2Cor 1:12 572
from the s that is in Christ ... 2Cor 11:3 572

SIMRI (*sim'-ri*) See SHIMRI. *A sanctuary servant.*
S the chief, (for though he was ... 1Chr 26:10 8113

SIN (*sin*)
1. A transgression.
not well, s lieth at the door ... Gen 4:7 2403
because their s is very grievous ... Gen 18:20 2403
on me and on my kingdom a great s ... Gen 20:9 2401
what is my s, that thou hast so ... Gen 31:36 2403
wickedness, and s against God ... Gen 39:9 2398
Do not s against the child ... Gen 42:22 2398
of thy brethren, and their s ... Gen 50:17 2403
my s only this once, and intreat ... Ex 10:17 2403
before your faces, that ye s not ... Ex 20:20 2398
lest they make thee s against me ... Ex 23:33 2398
it is a s offering ... Ex 29:14 2403
for a s offering for atonement ... Ex 29:36 2403
of the s offering of atonements ... Ex 30:10 2403
brought so great a s upon them ... Ex 32:21 2401
people, Ye have sinned a great s ... Ex 32:30 2401
make an atonement for your s ... Ex 32:30 2403
this people have sinned a great s ... Ex 32:31 2401
now, if thou wilt forgive their s ... Ex 32:32 2403
I will visit their s upon them ... Ex 32:34 2403
iniquity and transgression and s ... Ex 34:7 2402
and pardon our iniquity and our s ... Ex 34:9 2403
If a soul shall s through ... Lev 4:2 2398
do s according to the ... Lev 4:3 2398
according to the s of the people ... Lev 4:3 819
then let him bring for his s ... Lev 4:3 2403
unto the LORD for a s offering ... Lev 4:3 2403
of the bullock for the s offering ... Lev 4:8 2403
of Israel s through ignorance ... Lev 4:13 7686
When the s, which they have ... Lev 4:14 2403
offer a young bullock for the s ... Lev 4:14 2403
with the bullock for a s offering ... Lev 4:20 2403
it is a s offering for the ... Lev 4:21 2403
Or if his s, wherein he hath ... Lev 4:23 2403
it is a s offering ... Lev 4:24 2403
of the s offering with his finger ... Lev 4:25 2403
for him as concerning his s ... Lev 4:26 2403
common people s through ignorance ... Lev 4:27 2398
Or if his s, which he hath sinned ... Lev 4:28 2403
for his s which he hath sinned ... Lev 4:28 2403
upon the head of the s offering ... Lev 4:29 2403
slay the s offering in the place ... Lev 4:29 2403
he bring a lamb for a s offering ... Lev 4:32 2403
upon the head of the s offering ... Lev 4:33 2403
slay it for a s offering in the ... Lev 4:33 2403
of the s offering with his finger ... Lev 4:34 2403
for his s that he hath committed ... Lev 4:35 2403
And if a soul s, and hear the voice ... Lev 5:1 2398
for his s which he hath sinned ... Lev 5:6 2403
of the goats, for a s offering ... Lev 5:6 2403
for him concerning his s ... Lev 5:6 2403
one for a s offering, and the ... Lev 5:7 2403
which is for the s offering first ... Lev 5:8 2403
sprinkle of the blood of the s ... Lev 5:9 2403
it is a s offering ... Lev 5:9 2403
for his s which he hath sinned ... Lev 5:10 2403
of fine flour for a s offering ... Lev 5:11 2403
for it is a s offering ... Lev 5:11 2403
it is a s offering ... Lev 5:12 2403
for him as touching his s that he ... Lev 5:13 2403
s through ignorance, in the holy ... Lev 5:15 2398
And if a soul s, and commit any of ... Lev 5:17 2398
If a soul s, and commit a trespass ... Lev 6:2 2398
most holy, as is the s offering ... Lev 6:17 2403
This is the law of the s offering ... Lev 6:25 2403
offering is killed shall the s ... Lev 6:25 2403
offereth it for s shall eat it ... Lev 6:26 2398
no s offering, whereof any of the ... Lev 6:30 2403
As the s offering is, so is the ... Lev 7:7 2403
of the s offering, and of the ... Lev 7:37 2403
and a bullock for the s offering ... Lev 8:2 2403
the bullock for the s offering ... Lev 8:14 2403
of the bullock for the s offering ... Lev 8:14 2403
a young calf for a s offering ... Lev 9:2 2403
kid of the goats for a s offering ... Lev 9:3 2403
altar, and offer thy s offering ... Lev 9:7 2403
slew the calf of the s offering ... Lev 9:8 2403
above the liver of the s offering ... Lev 9:10 2403
which was the s offering for the ... Lev 9:15 2403
and slew it, and offered it for s ... Lev 9:15 2403
from offering of the s offering ... Lev 9:22 2403
sought the goat of the s offering ... Lev 10:16 2403
the s offering in the holy place ... Lev 10:17 2403
they offered their s offering ... Lev 10:19 2403
I had eaten the s offering to day ... Lev 10:19 2403
for a s offering, unto the door ... Lev 12:6 2403
and the other for a s offering ... Lev 12:8 2403
he shall kill the s offering ... Lev 14:13 2403
for as the s offering is the ... Lev 14:13 2403
priest shall offer the s offering ... Lev 14:19 2403
and the one shall be a s offering ... Lev 14:22 2403
to get, the one for a s offering ... Lev 14:31 2403
them, the one for a s offering ... Lev 15:15 2403
offer the one for a s offering ... Lev 15:30 2403
a young bullock for a s offering ... Lev 16:3 2403
of the goats for a s offering ... Lev 16:5 2403
his bullock of the s offering ... Lev 16:6 2403
and offer him for a s offering ... Lev 16:9 2403
the bullock of the s offering ... Lev 16:11 2403
s offering which is for himself ... Lev 16:11 2403
kill the goat of the s offering ... Lev 16:15 2403
the fat of the s offering shall ... Lev 16:25 2403
And the bullock for the s offering ... Lev 16:27 2403
and the goat for the s offering ... Lev 16:27 2403
and not suffer s upon him ... Lev 19:17 2399
LORD for his s which he hath done ... Lev 19:22 2403
the s which he hath done shall be ... Lev 19:22 2403
they shall bear their s ... Lev 20:20 2399
lest they bear s for it, and die ... Lev 22:9 2399
kid of the goats for a s offering ... Lev 23:19 2403
curseth his God shall bear his s ... Lev 24:15 2399
commit any s that men commit ... Num 5:6 2403
their s which they have done ... Num 5:7 2403
offer the one for a s offering ... Num 6:11 2403
without blemish for a s offering ... Num 6:14 2403
and shall offer his s offering ... Num 6:16 2403

kid of the goats for a s offering Num 7:16 2403
kid of the goats for a s offering Num 7:22 2403
kid of the goats for a s offering Num 7:28 2403
kid of the goats for a s offering Num 7:34 2403
kid of the goats for a s offering Num 7:40 2403
kid of the goats for a s offering Num 7:46 2403
kid of the goats for a s offering Num 7:52 2403
kid of the goats for a s offering Num 7:58 2403
kid of the goats for a s offering Num 7:64 2403
kid of the goats for a s offering Num 7:70 2403
kid of the goats for a s offering Num 7:76 2403
kid of the goats for a s offering Num 7:82 2403
the goats for s offering twelve Num 7:87 2403
shalt thou take for a s offering Num 8:8 2403
offer the one for a s offering Num 8:12 2403
season, that man shall bear his s Num 9:13 2399
thee, lay not the s upon us Num 12:11 2403
kid of the goats for a s offering Num 15:24 2403
their s offering before the LORD, Num 15:25 2403
if any soul s through ignorance, Num 15:27 2398
the first year for a s offering Num 15:27 2403
of all flesh, shall one man s Num 16:22 2398
every s offering of theirs, and Num 18:9 2403
congregation, lest they bear s Num 18:22 2399
shall bear no s by reason of it Num 18:32 2399
it is a purification for s Num 19:9 2403
heifer of purification for s Num 19:17 2403
but died in his own s, and had no Num 27:3 2399
one kid of the goats for a s Num 28:15 2403
And one goat for a s offering Num 28:22 2403
kid of the goats for a s offering Num 29:5 2403
kid of the goats for a s offering Num 29:11 2403
beside the s offering of Num 29:11 2403
kid of the goats for a s offering Num 29:16 2403
kid of the goats for a s offering Num 29:19 2403
And one goat for a s offering Num 29:22 2403
kid of the goats for a s offering Num 29:25 2403
And one goat for a s offering Num 29:28 2403
And one goat for a s offering Num 29:31 2403
And one goat for a s offering Num 29:34 2403
And one goat for a s offering Num 29:38 2403
be sure your s will find you out Num 32:23 2403
And I took your s, the calf which Deut 9:21 2403
their wickedness, nor to their s Deut 9:27 2403
thee, and it be s unto thee Deut 15:9 2399
for any iniquity, or for any s Deut 19:15 2403
in any s that he sinneth Deut 19:15 2399
so should ye s against the LORD Deut 20:18 2398
committed a s worthy of death Deut 21:22 2399
the damsel no s worthy of death Deut 22:26 2399
and it would be s in thee Deut 23:21 2399
to vow, it shall be no s in thee Deut 23:22 2399
shalt not cause the land to s Deut 24:4 2398
the LORD, and it be s unto thee Deut 24:15 2399
be put to death for his own s Deut 24:16 2399
Wherefore the s of the young men 1Sa 2:17 2403
If one man s against another, the 1Sa 2:25 2398
but if a man s against the LORD, 1Sa 2:25 2398
God forbid that I should s 1Sa 12:23 2398
the people s against the LORD, in 1Sa 14:33 2398
s not against the LORD in eating 1Sa 14:34 2398
see wherein this s hath been this 1Sa 14:38 2403
is as the s of witchcraft 1Sa 15:23 2403
I pray thee, pardon my s 1Sa 15:25 2403
Let not the king s against his 1Sa 19:4 2398
thou s against innocent blood 1Sa 19:5 2398
what is my s before thy father, 1Sa 20:1 2403
The LORD also hath put away thy s 2Sa 12:13 2403
forgive the s of thy people 1Kin 8:34 2403
thy name, and turn from their s 1Kin 8:35 2403
forgive the s of thy servants, and 1Kin 8:36 2403
If they s against thee, (for 1Kin 8:46 2398
And this thing became a s 1Kin 12:30 2403
this thing became s unto the 1Kin 13:34 2403
the sins of Jeroboam, who did s 1Kin 14:16 2398
and who made Israel to s 1Kin 14:16 2398
in his s wherewith he made Israel 1Kin 15:26 2403
wherewith he made Israel to s 1Kin 15:26 2398
sinned, and which he made Israel s 1Kin 15:30 2398
in his s wherewith he made Israel 1Kin 15:34 2403
wherewith he made Israel to s 1Kin 15:34 2398
hast made my people Israel to s 1Kin 16:2 2398
and by which they made Israel to s 1Kin 16:13 2398
in his s which he did, to make 1Kin 16:19 2403
which he did, to make Israel to s 1Kin 16:19 2398
in his s wherewith he made Israel 1Kin 16:26 2403
wherewith he made Israel to s 1Kin 16:26 2398
me to call my s to remembrance 1Kin 17:18 5771
me to anger, and made Israel to s 1Kin 21:22 2398
of Nebat, who made Israel to s 1Kin 22:52 2398
of Nebat, which made Israel to s 2Kin 3:3 2398
of Nebat, who made Israel to s 2Kin 10:29 2398
Jeroboam, which made Israel to s 2Kin 10:31 2398
s money was not brought into the 2Kin 12:16
of Nebat, which made Israel to s 2Kin 13:2 2398
of Jeroboam, who made Israel s 2Kin 13:6 2398
son of Nebat, who made Israel s 2Kin 13:11 2398
be put to death for his own s 2Kin 14:6 2399
of Nebat, who made Israel to s 2Kin 14:24 2398
of Nebat, who made Israel to s 2Kin 15:9 2398
of Nebat, who made Israel to s 2Kin 15:18 2398
of Nebat, who made Israel to s 2Kin 15:24 2398
of Nebat, who made Israel to s 2Kin 15:28 2398
LORD, and made them s 2Kin 17:21 2398
a great s 2Kin 17:21 2401
Judah also to s with his idols 2Kin 21:11 2398
beside his s wherewith he made 2Kin 21:16 2403
wherewith he made Judah to s 2Kin 21:16 2398
his s that he sinned, are they 2Kin 21:17 2403
of Nebat, who made Israel to s 2Kin 23:15 2398
If a man s against his neighbour, 2Chr 6:22 2398
forgive the s of thy people 2Chr 6:25 2403
thy name, and turn from their s 2Chr 6:26 2403
forgive the s of thy servants, and 2Chr 6:27 2403
If they s against thee, (for 2Chr 6:36 2398
heaven, and will forgive their s 2Chr 7:14 2403
every man shall die for his own s 2Chr 25:4 2399
for a s offering for the kingdom, 2Chr 29:21 2403
the s offering before the king 2Chr 29:23 2403
the s offering should be made for 2Chr 29:24 2403
intreated of him, and all his s 2Chr 33:19
for a s offering for all Israel, Ezr 6:17 2409
twelve he goats for a s offering Ezr 8:35 2403
let not their s be blotted out Neh 4:5 2403
should be afraid, and do so, and s Neh 6:13 2398
for the s offerings to make an Neh 10:33 2403
king of Israel s by these things Neh 13:26 2398
did outlandish women cause to s Neh 13:26 2398
this did not Job s with his lips Job 2:10 2398
thy habitation, and shalt not s Job 5:24 2398
iniquity, and searchest after my s Job 10:6 2403
If I s, then thou markest me, and Job 10:14 2398
to know my transgression and my s Job 13:23 2403
dost thou not watch over my s Job 14:16 2403
are full of the s of his youth Job 20:11
have I suffered my mouth to s by Job 31:30 2398
he addeth rebellion unto his s Job 34:37 2403
have, if I be cleansed from my s Job 35:3 2403
Stand in awe, and s not Ps 4:4 2398
is forgiven, whose s is covered Ps 32:1 2401
I acknowledged my s unto thee Ps 32:5 2403
forgavest the iniquity of my s Ps 32:5 2403
rest in my bones because of my s Ps 38:3 2403
I will be sorry for my s Ps 38:18 2403
that I s not with my tongue Ps 39:1 2398
s offering hast thou not required Ps 40:6 2401
iniquity, and cleanse me from my s Ps 51:2 2403
and my s is ever before me Ps 51:3 2403
in s did my mother conceive me Ps 51:5 2399
my transgression, nor for my s Ps 59:3 2403
For the s of their mouth and the Ps 59:12 2403
thou hast covered all their s Ps 85:2 2403
and let his prayer become s Ps 109:7 2401
let not the s of his mother be Ps 109:14 2403
that I might not s against thee Ps 119:11 2398
the fruit of the wicked to s Prov 10:16 2403
of words there wanteth not s Prov 10:19 6588
Fools make a mock at s Prov 14:9 817
but s is a reproach to any people Prov 14:34 2403
heart clean, I am pure from my s Prov 20:9 2403
the plowing of the wicked, is s Prov 21:4 2403
The thought of foolishness is s Prov 24:9 2403
thy mouth to cause thy flesh to s Eccl 5:6 2398
and they declare their s as Sodom Is 3:9 2403
s as it were with a cart rope Is 5:18 2402
is taken away, and thy s purged Is 6:7 2403
all the fruit to take away his s Is 27:9 2403
that they may add s to s Is 30:1 2403
hands have made unto you for a s Is 31:7 2399
make his soul an offering for s Is 53:10 817
and he bare the s of many, and made Is 53:12 2399
or what is our s that we have Jer 16:10 2403
their iniquity and their s double Jer 16:18 2403
The s of Judah is written with a Jer 17:1 2403
spoil, and thy high places for s Jer 17:3 2403
blot out their s from thy sight Jer 18:23 2403
I will remember their s no more Jer 31:34 2403
abomination, to cause Judah to s Jer 32:35 2398
forgive their iniquity and their s Jer 36:3 2403
their land was filled with s Jer 51:5 817
the punishment of the s of Sodom Lam 4:6
warning, he shall die in his s Eze 3:20 2403
s not, and he doth not s Eze 3:21 2398
in his s that he hath sinned, in Eze 18:24 2403
if he turn from his s, and do that Eze 33:14 2403
the s offering and the trespass Eze 40:39 2403
the s offering, and the trespass Eze 42:13 2403
a young bullock for a s offering Eze 43:19 2403
bullock also of the s offering Eze 43:21 2403
without blemish for a s offering Eze 43:22 2403
every day a goat for a s offering Eze 43:25 2403
he shall offer his s offering Eze 44:27 2403
the s offering, and the trespass Eze 44:29 2403
he shall prepare the s offering Eze 45:17 2403
of the blood of the s offering Eze 45:19 2403
land a bullock for a s offering Eze 45:22 2403
the goats daily for a s offering Eze 45:23 2403
days, according to the s offering Eze 45:25 2403
the s offering, where they shall Eze 46:20 2403
and praying, and confessing my s Dan 9:20 2403
the s of my people Israel, and Dan 9:20 2403
They eat up the s of my people Hos 4:8 2403
hath made many altars to s Hos 8:11 2398
altars shall be unto him to s Hos 8:11 2398
the s of Israel, shall be Hos 10:8 2403
none iniquity in me that were s Hos 12:8 2399
And now they s more and more, and Hos 13:2 2398
his s is hid Hos 13:12 2403
that swear by the s of Samaria Amos 8:14 819
of the s to the daughter of Zion Mic 1:13 2403
transgression, and to Israel his s Mic 3:8 2403
of my body for the s of my soul Mic 6:7 2403
inhabitants of Jerusalem for s Zec 13:1 2403
I say unto you, All manner of s Mt 12:31 *266*
oft shall my brother s against me Mt 18:21 *264*
taketh away the s of the world Jn 1:29 *266*
s no more, lest a worse thing Jn 5:14 *264*
He that is without s among you Jn 8:7 *361*
go, and s no more Jn 8:11 *264*
Whosoever committeth s is the Jn 8:34 *266*
is the servant of s Jn 8:34 *266*
Which of you convinceth me of s Jn 8:46 *266*
him, saying, Master, who did s Jn 9:2 *264*
were blind, ye should have no s Jn 9:41 *266*
therefore your s remaineth Jn 9:41 *266*
unto them, they had not had s Jn 15:22 *266*
they have no cloke for their s Jn 15:22 *266*
other man did, they had not had s Jn 15:24 *266*
he will reprove the world of s Jn 16:8 *266*
Of s, because they believe not on Jn 16:9 *266*
me unto thee hath the greater s Jn 19:11 *266*
lay not this s to their charge Acts 7:60 *266*
that they are all under s Rom 3:9 *266*
by the law is the knowledge of s Rom 3:20 *266*
whom the Lord will not impute s Rom 4:8 *266*
as by one man s entered into the Rom 5:12 *266*
into the world, and death by s Rom 5:12 *266*
until the law s was in the world Rom 5:13 *266*
but s is not imputed when there Rom 5:13 *266*
But where s abounded, grace did Rom 5:20 *266*
That as s hath reigned unto death Rom 5:21 *266*
Shall we continue in s, that Rom 6:1 *266*
How shall we, that are dead to s Rom 6:2 *266*
that the body of s might be Rom 6:6 *266*
henceforth we should not serve s Rom 6:6 *266*
he that is dead is freed from s Rom 6:7 *266*
that he died, he died unto s once Rom 6:10 *266*
to be dead indeed unto s, but Rom 6:11 *266*
Let not s therefore reign in your Rom 6:12 *266*
of unrighteousness unto s Rom 6:13 *266*
For s shall not have dominion Rom 6:14 *266*
shall we s, because we are not Rom 6:15 *264*
whether of s unto death, or of Rom 6:16 *266*
that ye were the servants of s Rom 6:17 *266*
Being then made free from s Rom 6:18 *266*
when ye were the servants of s Rom 6:20 *266*
But now being made free from s Rom 6:22 *266*
For the wages of s is death Rom 6:23 *266*
Is the law s Rom 7:7 *266*
Nay, I had not known s, but by Rom 7:7 *266*
But s, taking occasion by the Rom 7:8 *266*
For without the law s was dead Rom 7:8 *266*
came, s revived, and I died Rom 7:9 *266*
For s, taking occasion by the Rom 7:11 *266*
But s, that it might appear s, Rom 7:13 *266*
that s by the commandment might Rom 7:13 *266*
but I am carnal, sold under s Rom 7:14 *266*
but s that dwelleth in me Rom 7:17 *266*
but s that dwelleth in me Rom 7:20 *266*
law of s which is in my members Rom 7:23 *266*
but with the flesh the law of s Rom 7:25 *266*
made me free from the law of s Rom 8:2 *266*
for s, condemned s in the flesh Rom 8:3 *266*
the body is dead because of s Rom 8:10 *266*
whatsoever is not of faith is s Rom 14:23 *266*
Every s that a man doeth is 1Cor 6:18 *265*
But when ye s so against the 1Cor 8:12 *264*
conscience, ye s against Christ 1Cor 8:12 *264*
Awake to righteousness, and s not 1Cor 15:34 *264*
The sting of death is s 1Cor 15:56 *266*
and the strength of s is the law 1Cor 15:56 *266*
to be s for us, who knew no s 2Cor 5:21 *266*
Christ the minister of s Gal 2:17 *266*
hath concluded all under s Gal 3:22 *266*
Be ye angry, and s not Eph 4:26 *264*
and that man of s be revealed 2Th 2:3 *266*
Them that s rebuke before all, 1Ti 5:20 *264*
through the deceitfulness of s Heb 3:13 *266*
like as we are, yet without s Heb 4:15 *266*
s by the sacrifice of himself Heb 9:26 *266*
time without s unto salvation Heb 9:28 *266*
sacrifices for s thou hast had no Heb 10:6 *266*
offering for s thou wouldest not, Heb 10:8 *266*
there is no more offering for s Heb 10:18 *266*
For if we s wilfully after that Heb 10:26 *264*
the pleasures of s for a season Heb 11:25 *266*
the s which doth so easily beset Heb 12:1 *266*
unto blood, striving against s Heb 12:4 *266*
by the high priest for s, are Heb 13:11 *266*
conceived, it bringeth forth s Jas 1:15 *266*
and s, when it is finished, Jas 1:15 *266*
respect to persons, ye commit s Jas 2:9 *266*
and doeth it not, to him it is s Jas 4:17 *266*
Who did no s, neither was guile 1Pet 2:22 *266*
in the flesh hath ceased from s 1Pet 4:1 *266*
and that cannot cease from s 2Pet 2:14 *266*
his Son cleanseth us from all s 1Jn 1:7 *266*
If we say that we have no s 1Jn 1:8 *266*
write I unto you, that ye s not 1Jn 2:1 *264*
And if any man s, we have an 1Jn 2:1 *264*
Whosoever committeth s 1Jn 3:4 *266*
for s is the transgression of the 1Jn 3:4 *266*
and in him is no s 1Jn 3:5 *266*
that committeth s is of the devil 1Jn 3:8 *266*
is born of God doth not commit s 1Jn 3:9 *266*
and he cannot s, because he is 1Jn 3:9 *264*
s a s which is not unto death 1Jn 5:16 *266*
for them that s not unto death 1Jn 5:16 *264*
There is a s unto death 1Jn 5:16 *266*
All unrighteousness is s 1Jn 5:17 *266*
there is a s not unto death 1Jn 5:17 *266*

2. Eastern border of Egypt.
And I will pour my fury upon S Eze 30:15 5512
S shall have great pain, and No Eze 30:16 5512

3. Desert between Elim and Sinai.
came unto the wilderness of S Ex 16:1 5512
from the wilderness of S, after Ex 17:1 5512
encamped in the wilderness of S Num 33:11 5512
out of the wilderness of S Num 33:12 5512

SINA (*si'-nah*) See SINAI. *Greek form of Sinai.*
him in the wilderness of mount S Acts 7:30 *4614*
which spake to him in the mount S Acts 7:38 *4614*

SINAI (*si'-nahee*) See HOREB, SINA. *Mountainous district in the southern Sinai peninsula.*
Sin, which is between Elim and S Ex 16:1 5514
they into the wilderness of S Ex 19:1 5514
and were come to the desert of S Ex 19:2 5514
of all the people upon mount S Ex 19:11 5514
mount S was altogether on a smoke Ex 19:18 5514
the LORD came down upon mount S Ex 19:20 5514
people cannot come up to mount S Ex 19:23 5514

S

of the LORD abode upon mount *S* ... Ex 24:16 5514
communing with him upon mount *S* ... Ex 31:18 5514
up in the morning unto mount *S* ... Ex 34:2 5514
morning, and went up unto mount *S* ... Ex 34:4 5514
mount *S* with the two tables of ... Ex 34:29 5514
had spoken with him in mount *S* ... Ex 34:32 5514
LORD commanded Moses in mount *S* ... Lev 7:38 5514
the LORD, in the wilderness of *S* ... Lev 7:38 5514
LORD spake unto Moses in mount *S* ... Lev 25:1 5514
in mount *S* by the hand of Moses ... Lev 26:46 5514
the children of Israel in mount *S* ... Lev 27:34 5514
unto Moses in the wilderness of *S* ... Num 1:1 5514
them in the wilderness of *S* ... Num 1:19 5514
LORD spake with Moses in mount *S* ... Num 3:1 5514
the LORD, in the wilderness of *S* ... Num 3:4 5514
unto Moses in the wilderness of *S* ... Num 3:14 5514
unto Moses in the wilderness of *S* ... Num 9:1 5514
at even in the wilderness of *S* ... Num 9:5 5514
out of the wilderness of *S* ... Num 10:12 5514
of Israel in the wilderness of *S* ... Num 26:64 5514
in mount *S* for a sweet savour ... Num 28:6 5514
and pitched in the wilderness of *S* ... Num 33:15 5514
they removed from the desert of *S* ... Num 33:16 5514
And he said, The LORD came from *S* ... Deut 33:2 5514
even that *S* from before the LORD ... Judg 5:5 5514
camest down also upon mount *S* ... Neh 9:13 5514
even *S* itself was moved at the ... Ps 68:8 5514
the Lord is among them, as in *S* ... Ps 68:17 5514
the one from the mount *S*, which ... Gal 4:24 *4614*
this Agar is mount *S* in Arabia ... Gal 4:25 *4614*

SINCE

hath blessed thee *s* my coming ... Gen 30:30
and I saw him not *s* ... Gen 44:28 2008
s I have seen thy face, because ... Gen 46:30 310
nor *s* thou hast spoken unto thy ... Ex 4:10 227
For *s* I came to Pharaoh to speak ... Ex 5:23 4480
s the foundation thereof even ... Ex 9:18 4480
of Egypt *s* it became a nation ... Ex 9:24 4480
s the day that they were upon the ... Ex 10:6 4480
ever *s* I was thine unto this day ... Num 22:30 5750
s the day that God created man ... Deut 4:32 4480
s in Israel like unto Moses ... Deut 34:10 5750
s I have shewed you kindness, ... Josh 2:12 3588
even *s* the LORD spake this word ... Josh 14:10 227
law *s* the death of thine husband ... Ruth 2:11 310
s the day that I brought them up ... 1Sa 8:8
it been kept for thee *s* I said ... 1Sa 9:24
s I came out, and the vessels of ... 1Sa 21:5
I have found no fault in him *s* he ... 1Sa 29:3
s the day of thy coming unto me ... 1Sa 29:6
I have not dwelt in any house *s* ... 2Sa 7:6
as *s* the time that I commanded ... 2Sa 7:11 4480
S the day that I brought forth my ... 1Kin 8:16 4480
all the fruits of the field *s* the ... 2Kin 8:6
s the day their fathers came ... 2Kin 21:15 4480
house *s* the day that I brought up ... 1Chr 17:5 4480
s the time that I commanded ... 1Chr 17:10
S the day that I brought forth my ... 2Chr 6:5 4480
for *s* the time of Solomon the son ... 2Chr 30:26
S the people began to bring the ... 2Chr 31:10
we do sacrifice unto him *s* the ... Ezr 4:2
s that time even until now hath ... Ezr 5:16 4481
S the days of our fathers have we ... Ezr 9:7
for *s* the days of Jeshua the son ... Neh 8:17
s the time of the kings of ... Neh 9:32
s man was placed upon earth, ... Job 20:4 4480
commanded the morning *s* thy days ... Job 38:12
S thou art laid down, no feller ... Is 14:8 227
concerning Moab *s* that time ... Is 16:13
S thou wast precious in my sight, ... Is 43:4
s I appointed the ancient people ... Is 44:7
For *s* the beginning of the world ... Is 64:4
S the day that your fathers came ... Jer 7:25 4480
s they return not from their ways ... Jer 15:7
For *s* I spake, I cried out, I ... Jer 20:8 1767
But *s* ye say, The burden of the ... Jer 23:38 518
for *s* I spake against him, I do ... Jer 31:20 1767
But *s* we left off to burn incense ... Jer 44:18
for *s* thou spakest of him, thou ... Jer 48:27 1767
such as never was *s* there was a ... Dan 12:1
S those days were, when one came ... Hag 2:16
such as was not *s* the beginning ... Mt 24:21 *575*
is it ago *s* this came unto him ... Mk 9:21 *5613*
which have been *s* the world began ... Lk 1:70 *575*
but this woman *s* the time I came ... Lk 7:45 *575*
s that time the kingdom of God is ... Lk 16:16 *575*
day *s* these things were done ... Lk 24:21 *575*
S the world began was it not ... Jn 9:32 *1537*
holy prophets *s* the world began ... Acts 3:21 *575*
the Holy Ghost *s* ye believed ... Acts 19:2
s I went up to Jerusalem for to ... Acts 24:11
was kept secret *s* the world began ... Rom 16:25
For *s* by man came death, by man ... 1Cor 15:21 *1894*
S ye seek a proof of Christ ... 2Cor 13:3 *1893*
S we heard of your faith in ... Col 1:4
s the day ye heard of it, and knew ... Col 1:6 *575*
s the day we heard it, do not ... Col 1:9 *575*
of the oath, which was *s* the law ... Heb 7:28 *3326*
s the foundation of the world ... Heb 9:26 *575*
for *s* the fathers fell asleep, ... 2Pet 3:4
such as was not *s* men were upon ... Rev 16:18

SINCERE

that ye may be *s* and without ... Phil 1:10 *1506*
desire the *s* milk of the word, ... 1Pet 2:2 *97*

SINCERELY

if ye have done truly and *s* ... Judg 9:16 8549
s with Jerubbaal and with his ... Judg 9:19 8549
Christ of contention, not *s* ... Phil 1:16 *55*

SINCERITY

fear the LORD, and serve him in *s* ... Josh 24:14 8549
with the unleavened bread of *s* ... 1Cor 5:8 *1505*
that in simplicity and godly *s* ... 2Cor 1:12 *1505*
but as of *s*, but as of God, in ... 2Cor 2:17 *1505*
and to prove the *s* of your love ... 2Cor 8:8 *1103*
love our Lord Jesus Christ in *s* ... Eph 6:24 *861*
shewing uncorruptness, gravity, *s* ... Titus 2:7 *861*

SINEW

eat not of the *s* which shrank ... Gen 32:32 1517
thigh in the *s* that shrank ... Gen 32:32 1517
and thy neck is an iron *s* ... Is 48:4 1517

SINEWS

and hast fenced me with bones and *s* ... Job 10:11 1517
and my *s* take no rest ... Job 30:17 6207
the *s* of his stones are wrapped ... Job 40:17 1517
And I will lay *s* upon you, and will ... Eze 37:6 1517
And when I beheld, lo, the *s* ... Eze 37:8 1517

SINFUL

stead, an increase of *s* men ... Num 32:14 2400
Ah *s* nation, a people laden with ... Is 1:4 2398
Lord GOD are upon the *s* kingdom ... Amos 9:8 2401
this adulterous and *s* generation ... Mk 8:38 *268*
for I am a *s* man, O Lord ... Lk 5:8 *268*
delivered into the hands of *s* men ... Lk 24:7 *268*
might become exceeding *s* ... Rom 7:13 *268*
Son in the likeness of *s* flesh ... Rom 8:3 *266*

SING

I will *s* unto the LORD, for he ... Ex 15:1 7891
S ye to the LORD, for he hath ... Ex 15:21 7891
noise of them that *s* do I hear ... Ex 32:18 6031
s ye unto it ... Num 21:17 6030
I, even I, will *s* unto the LORD ... Judg 5:3 7891
I will *s* praise to the LORD God ... Judg 5:3 2167
did they not *s* one to another of ... 1Sa 21:11 6030
S unto him, *s* psalms unto him, ... 1Chr 16:9 7891
S unto the LORD, all the earth ... 1Chr 16:23 7891
shall the trees of the wood *s* out ... 1Chr 16:33 7442
And when they began to *s* and to ... 2Chr 20:22 7440
and such as taught to *s* praise ... 2Chr 23:13 1984
commanded the Levites to *s* praise ... 2Chr 29:30 1984
the widow's heart to *s* for joy ... Job 29:13 7442
will *s* praise to the name of the ... Ps 7:17
I will *s* praise to thy name, O ... Ps 9:2
S praises to the LORD, which ... Ps 9:11
I will *s* unto the LORD, because ... Ps 13:6 7891
and *s* praises unto thy name ... Ps 18:49
so will we *s* and praise thy power ... Ps 21:13 7891
I will *s*, yea ... Ps 27:6 7891
I will *s* praises unto the LORD ... Ps 27:6 2167
S unto the LORD, O ye saints of ... Ps 30:4 2167
my glory may *s* praise to thee ... Ps 30:12 2167
s unto him with the psaltery and ... Ps 33:2 2167
S unto him a new song ... Ps 33:3 7891
S praises to God, *s* praises ... Ps 47:6 2167
s praises unto our King, *s* ... Ps 47:6 2167
s ye praises with understanding ... Ps 47:7 2167
my tongue shall *s* aloud of thy ... Ps 51:14 7442
I will *s* and give praise ... Ps 57:7 7891
I will *s* unto thee among the ... Ps 57:9 2167
But I will *s* of thy power ... Ps 59:16 7891
I will *s* aloud of thy mercy in ... Ps 59:16 7442
thee, O my strength, will I *s* ... Ps 59:17 2167
So will I *s* praise unto thy name ... Ps 61:8 2167
they shout for joy, they also *s* ... Ps 65:13 7891
S forth the honour of his name ... Ps 66:2 2167
thee, and shall *s* unto thee ... Ps 66:4 2167
they shall *s* to thy name ... Ps 66:4 2167
the nations be glad and *s* for joy ... Ps 67:4 7442
S unto God ... Ps 68:4 7891
s praises to his name ... Ps 68:4 2167
S unto God, ye kingdoms of the ... Ps 68:32 7891
O *s* praises unto the Lord ... Ps 68:32 2167
unto thee will I *s* with the harp ... Ps 71:22 2167
rejoice when I *s* unto thee ... Ps 71:23 2167
I will *s* praises to the God of ... Ps 75:9
S aloud unto God our strength ... Ps 81:1 7442
I will *s* of the mercies of the ... Ps 89:1 7891
to *s* praises unto thy name, O ... Ps 92:1 2167
O come, let us *s* unto the LORD ... Ps 95:1 7442
O *s* unto the LORD a new song ... Ps 96:1 7891
s unto the LORD, all the earth ... Ps 96:1 7891
S unto the LORD, bless his name ... Ps 96:2 7891
O *s* unto the LORD a new song ... Ps 98:1 7891
noise, and rejoice, and *s* praise ... Ps 98:4 2167
S unto the LORD with the harp ... Ps 98:5 2167
I will *s* of mercy and judgment ... Ps 101:1 7891
unto thee, O LORD, will I *s* ... Ps 101:1 2167
which *s* among the branches ... Ps 104:12
I will *s* unto the LORD as long as ... Ps 104:33 7891
I will *s* praise to my God while I ... Ps 104:33 2167
S unto him ... Ps 105:2 7891
s psalms unto him ... Ps 105:2 2167
I will *s* and give praise, even ... Ps 108:1 7891
I will *s* praises unto thee among ... Ps 108:3 2167
s praises unto his name ... Ps 135:3 2167
S us one of the songs of Zion ... Ps 137:3 7891
How shall we *s* the LORD's song in ... Ps 137:4 7891
gods will I *s* praise unto thee ... Ps 138:1 2167
they shall *s* in the ways of the ... Ps 138:5 7891
I will *s* a new song unto thee, O ... Ps 144:9 7891
will I *s* praises unto thee ... Ps 144:9 2167
shall *s* of thy righteousness ... Ps 145:7 7442
I will *s* praises unto my God ... Ps 146:2 2167
for it is good to *s* praises unto ... Ps 147:1 2167
S unto the LORD with thanksgiving ... Ps 147:7 6030
s praise upon the harp unto our ... Ps 147:7 2167
S unto the LORD a new song, and ... Ps 149:1 7891
let them *s* praises unto him with ... Ps 149:3 2167
let them *s* aloud upon their beds ... Ps 149:5 7442
but the righteous doth *s* and ... Prov 29:6 7442
Now will I *s* to my wellbeloved a ... Is 5:1 7891
S unto the LORD ... Is 12:5 2167
years shall Tyre *s* as an harlot ... Is 23:15 7892
s many songs, that thou mayest be ... Is 23:16
they shall *s* for the majesty of ... Is 24:14 7442
Awake and *s*, ye that dwell in dust ... Is 26:19 7442
In that day *s* ye unto her ... Is 27:2 6031
hart, and the tongue of the dumb *s* ... Is 35:6 7442
therefore we will *s* my songs to ... Is 38:20
S unto the LORD a new song, and ... Is 42:10 7891
let the inhabitants of the rock *s* ... Is 42:11 7442
S, O ye heavens ... Is 44:23 7442
S, O heavens ... Is 49:13 7442
the voice together shall they *s* ... Is 52:8 7442
s together, ye waste places of ... Is 52:9 7442
S, O barren, thou that didst not ... Is 54:1 7442
servants shall *s* for joy of heart ... Is 65:14 7442
S unto the LORD, praise ye the ... Jer 20:13 7891
S with gladness for Jacob, and ... Jer 31:7 7442
s in the height of Zion, and shall ... Jer 31:12 7442
is therein, shall *s* for Babylon ... Jer 51:48 7442
did *s* of thee in thy market ... Eze 27:25 7788
and she shall *s* there, as in the ... Hos 2:15 6030
voice shall *s* in the windows ... Zeph 2:14 7891
S, O daughter of Zion ... Zeph 3:14 7442
S and rejoice, O daughter of Zion ... Zec 2:10 7442
the Gentiles, and *s* unto thy name ... Rom 15:9 *5567*
I will *s* with the spirit ... 1Cor 14:15 *5567*
I will *s* with the understanding ... 1Cor 14:15 *5567*
church will I *s* praise unto thee ... Heb 2:12 *5214*
let him *s* psalms ... Jas 5:13 *5567*
they *s* the song of Moses the ... Rev 15:3 *103*

SINGED

nor was an hair of their head *s* ... Dan 3:27 2761

SINGER

Heman a *s*, the son of Joel, the ... 1Chr 6:33 7891
To the chief *s* on my stringed ... Hab 3:19 5329

SINGERS

harps also and psalteries for *s* ... 1Kin 10:12 7891
And these are the *s*, chief of the ... 1Chr 9:33 7891
their brethren to be the *s* with ... 1Chr 15:16 7891
So the *s*, Heman, Asaph, and Ethan, ... 1Chr 15:19 7891
that bare the ark, and the *s* ... 1Chr 15:27 7891
the master of the song with the *s* ... 1Chr 15:27 7891
Also the Levites which were the *s* ... 2Chr 5:12 7891
s were as one, to make one sound ... 2Chr 5:13 7891
and harps and psalteries for *s* ... 2Chr 9:11 7891
he appointed *s* unto the LORD, and ... 2Chr 20:21 7891
also the *s* with instruments of ... 2Chr 23:13 7891
the *s* sang, and the trumpeters ... 2Chr 29:28 7892
the *s* the sons of Asaph were in ... 2Chr 35:15 7891
The *s*: the children of Asaph ... Ezr 2:41 7891
and some of the people, and the *s* ... Ezr 2:70 7891
priests, and the Levites, and the *s* ... Ezr 7:7 7891
any of the priests and Levites, *s* ... Ezr 7:24 2171
Of the *s* also ... Ezr 10:24 7891
doors, and the porters and the *s* ... Neh 7:1 7891
The *s*: the children of Asaph ... Neh 7:44 7891
Levites, and the porters, and the *s* ... Neh 7:73 7891
the Levites, the porters, the *s* ... Neh 10:28 7891
and the porters, and the *s* ... Neh 10:39 7891
the *s* were over the business of ... Neh 11:22 7891
portion should be for the *s* ... Neh 11:23 7891
the sons of the *s* gathered ... Neh 12:28 7891
for the *s* had builded them ... Neh 12:29 7891
the *s* sang loud, with Jezrahiah ... Neh 12:42 7891
And both the *s* and the porters kept ... Neh 12:45 7891
of old there were chief of the *s* ... Neh 12:46 7891
gave the portions of the *s* ... Neh 12:47 7891
be given to the Levites, and the *s* ... Neh 13:5 7891
for the Levites and the *s*, that ... Neh 13:10 7891
The *s* went before, the players on ... Ps 68:25 7891
As well the *s* as the players on ... Ps 87:7 7891
I gat me men *s* and women *s* ... Eccl 2:8 7891
of the *s* in the inner court ... Eze 40:44 7891

SINGETH

so is he that *s* songs to an heavy ... Prov 25:20 7891

SINGING

out of all cities of Israel, *s* ... 1Sa 18:6 7891
voice of *s* men and *s* women ... 2Sa 19:35 7891
of the congregation with *s* ... 1Chr 6:32 7892
with all their might, and with *s* ... 1Chr 13:8 7892
Moses, with rejoicing and with *s* ... 2Chr 23:18 7892
s with loud instruments unto the ... 2Chr 30:21
and all the *s* men and the *s* ... 2Chr 35:25 7891
hundred *s* men and *s* women ... Ezr 2:65 7891
and five *s* men and *s* women ... Neh 7:67 7891
with thanksgivings, and with *s* ... Neh 12:27 7892
come before his presence with *s* ... Ps 100:2 7445
laughter, and our tongue with *s* ... Ps 126:2 7440
the time of the *s* of birds is ... Song 2:12 2158
they break forth into *s* ... Is 14:7 7440
the vineyards there shall be no *s* ... Is 16:10 7442
and rejoice even with joy and *s* ... Is 35:2 7442
break forth into *s*, ye mountains, ... Is 44:23 7440
with a voice of *s* declare ye ... Is 48:20 7440
and break forth into *s*, O ... Is 49:13 7440
return, and come with *s* unto Zion ... Is 51:11 7440
break forth into *s*, and cry aloud, ... Is 54:1 7440
break forth before you into *s* ... Is 55:12 7440
he will joy over thee with *s* ... Zeph 3:17 7440
and hymns and spiritual songs, *s* ... Eph 5:19 *103*
s with grace in your hearts to ... Col 3:16 *103*

SINGLE

if therefore thine eye be *s* ... Mt 6:22 *573*
therefore when thine eye is *s* ... Lk 11:34 *573*

SINGLENESS

meat with gladness and *s* of heart, ... Acts 2:46 *858*
in *s* of your heart, as unto ... Eph 6:5 *572*
but in *s* of heart, fearing God ... Col 3:22 *572*

SINGULAR
When a man shall make a *s* vow Lev 27:2 6381

SINIM (*si'-nim*) *An unspecified people.*
and these from the land of *S* Is 49:12 5515

SINITE (*si'-nite*) *A tribe of Canaanites.*
Hivite, and the Arkite, and the *S* Gen 10:17 5513
Hivite, and the Arkite, and the *S* 1Chr 1:15 5513

SINK
I *s* in deep mire, where there is Ps 69:2 2883
out of the mire, and let me not *s* Ps 69:14 2883
shalt say, Thus shall Babylon *s* Jer 51:64 8257
and beginning to *s*, he cried, Mt 14:30 2670
ships, so that they began to *s* Lk 5:7 1036
Let these sayings *s* down into Lk 9:44 5087

SINNED
unto them, I have *s* this time Ex 9:27 2398
he *s* yet more, and hardened his Ex 9:34 2398
I have *s* against the LORD your Ex 10:16 2398
the people, Ye have *s* a great sin Ex 32:30 2398
this people have *s* a great sin Ex 32:31 2398
Whosoever hath *s* against me Ex 32:33 2398
for his sin, which he hath *s* Lev 4:3 2398
sin, which they have *s* against it Lev 4:14 2398
When a ruler hath *s*, and done Lev 4:22 2398
Or if his sin, wherein he hath *s* Lev 4:23 2398
Or if his sin, which he hath *s* Lev 4:28 2398
for his sin which he hath *s* Lev 4:28 2398
that he hath *s* in that thing Lev 5:5 2398
LORD for his sin which he hath *s* Lev 5:6 2398
him for his sin which he hath *s* Lev 5:10 2398
then he that *s* shall bring for Lev 5:11 2398
that he hath *s* in one of these Lev 5:13 2398
it shall be, because he hath *s* Lev 6:4 2398
him, for that he *s* by the dead Num 6:11 2398
foolishly, and wherein we have *s* Num 12:11 2398
for we have *s* Num 14:40 2398
came to Moses, and said, We have *s* Num 21:7 2398
the angel of the LORD, I have *s* Num 22:34 2398
ye have *s* against the LORD Num 32:23 2398
We have *s* against the LORD, we Deut 1:41 2398
ye had *s* against the LORD your Deut 9:16 2398
of all your sins which ye *s* Deut 9:18 2398
Israel hath *s*, and they have also Josh 7:11 2398
Indeed I have *s* against the LORD Josh 7:20 2398
We have *s* against thee, both Judg 10:10 2398
said unto the LORD, We have *s* Judg 10:15 2398
I have not *s* against thee Judg 11:27 2398
We have *s* against the LORD 1Sa 7:6 2398
unto the LORD, and said, We have *s* 1Sa 12:10 2398
Saul said unto Samuel, I have *s* 1Sa 15:24 2398
Then he said, I have *s* 1Sa 15:30 2398
he hath not *s* against thee 1Sa 19:4 2398
I have not *s* against thee 1Sa 24:11 2398
Then said Saul, I have *s* 1Sa 26:21 2398
I have *s* against the LORD 2Sa 12:13 2398
servant doth know that I have *s* 2Sa 19:20 2398
I have *s* greatly in that I have 2Sa 24:10 2398
the people, and said, Lo, I have *s* 2Sa 24:17 2398
because they have *s* against thee 1Kin 8:33 2398
because they have *s* against thee 1Kin 8:35 2398
them captives, saying, We have *s* 1Kin 8:47 2398
people that have *s* against thee 1Kin 8:50 2398
the sins of Jeroboam which he *s* 1Kin 15:30 2398
of Elah his son, by which they *s* 1Kin 16:13 2398
For his sins which he *s* in doing 1Kin 16:19 2398
And he said, What have I *s* 1Kin 18:9 2398
had *s* against the LORD their God 2Kin 17:7 2398
that he did, and his sin that he *s* 2Kin 21:17 2398
I have *s* greatly, because I have 1Chr 21:8 2398
even I it is that have *s* and done 1Chr 21:17 2398
because they have *s* against thee 2Chr 6:24 2398
because they have *s* against thee 2Chr 6:26 2398
captivity, saying, We have *s* 2Chr 6:37 2398
people which have *s* against thee 2Chr 6:39 2398
which we have *s* against thee Neh 1:6 2398
I and my father's house have *s* Neh 1:6 2398
but *s* against thy judgments, (Neh 9:29 2398
It may be that my sons have *s* Job 1:5 2398
In all this Job *s* not, nor Job 1:22 2398
I have *s* Job 7:20 2398
thy children have *s* against him Job 8:4 2398
doth the grave those which have *s* Job 24:19 2398
upon men, and if any say, I have *s* Job 33:27 2398
for I have *s* against thee Ps 41:4 2398
Against thee, thee only, have I *s* Ps 51:4 2398
they *s* yet more against him by Ps 78:17 2398
For all this they *s* still Ps 78:32 2398
We have *s* with our fathers, we Ps 106:6 2398
LORD, he against whom we have *s* Is 42:24 2398
Thy first father hath *s*, and thy Is 43:27 2398
for we have *s* Is 64:5 2398
because thou sayest, I have not *s* Jer 2:35 2398
for we have *s* against the LORD Jer 3:25 2398
because we have *s* against the Jer 8:14 2398
we have *s* against thee Jer 14:7 2398
for we have *s* against thee Jer 14:20 2398
whereby they have *s* against me Jer 33:8 2398
iniquities, whereby they have *s* Jer 33:8 2398
because ye have *s* against the Jer 40:3 2398
because ye have *s* against the Jer 44:23 2398
they have *s* against the LORD Jer 50:7 2398
for she hath *s* against the LORD Jer 50:14 2398
Jerusalem hath grievously *s* Lam 1:8 2398
Our fathers have *s*, and are not Lam 5:7 2398
woe unto us, that we have *s* Lam 5:16 2398
and in his sin that he hath *s* Eze 18:24 2398
with violence, and thou hast *s* Eze 28:16 2398
wherein they have *s*, and will Eze 37:23 2398
We have *s*, and have committed Dan 9:5 2398
because we have *s* against thee Dan 9:8 2398
because we have *s* against him Dan 9:11 2398
we have *s*, we have done wickedly Dan 9:15 2398
increased, so they *s* against me Hos 4:7 2398
thou hast *s* from the days of Hos 10:9 2398
because I have *s* against him Mic 7:9 2398
and hast *s* against thy soul Hab 2:10 2398
they have *s* against the LORD Zeph 1:17 2398
I have *s* in that I have betrayed Mt 27:4 264
I have *s* against heaven, and Lk 15:18 264
I have *s* against heaven, and in Lk 15:21 264
answered, Neither hath this man *s* Jn 9:3 264
For as many as have *s* without law Rom 2:12 264
as many as have *s* in the law Rom 2:12 264
For all have *s*, and come short of Rom 3:23 264
upon all men, for that all have *s* Rom 5:12 264
even over them that had not *s* Rom 5:14 264
And not as it was by one that *s* Rom 5:16 264
and if thou marry, thou hast not *s* 1Cor 7:28 264
if a virgin marry, she hath not *s* 1Cor 7:28 264
bewail many which have *s* already 2Cor 12:21 4258
to them which heretofore have *s* 2Cor 13:2 4258
was it not with them that had *s* Heb 3:17 264
God spared not the angels that *s* 2Pet 2:4 264
If we say that we have not *s* 1Jn 1:10 264

SINNER
much more the wicked and the *s* Prov 11:31 2398
but wickedness overthroweth the *s* Prov 13:6 2403
the wealth of the *s* is laid up Prov 13:22 2398
but to the *s* he giveth travail, Eccl 2:26 2398
but the *s* shall be taken by her Eccl 7:26 2398
Though a *s* do evil an hundred Eccl 8:12 2398
as is the good, so is the *s* Eccl 9:2 2398
but one *s* destroyeth much good Eccl 9:18 2398
but the *s* being an hundred years Is 65:20 2398
woman in the city, which was a *s* Lk 7:37 268
for she is a *s* Lk 7:39 268
heaven over one *s* that repenteth Lk 15:7 268
of God over one *s* that repenteth Lk 15:10 268
saying, God be merciful to me a *s* Lk 18:13 268
be guest with a man that is a *s* Lk 19:7 268
man that is a *s* do such miracles Jn 9:16 268
we know that this man is a *s* Jn 9:24 268
and said, Whether he be a *s* or no Jn 9:25 268
why yet am I also judged as a *s* Rom 3:7 268
that he which converteth the *s* Jas 5:20 268
shall the ungodly and the *s* appear 1Pet 4:18 268

SINNERS
s before the LORD exceedingly Gen 13:13 2400
The censers of these *s* against Num 16:38 2400
destroy the *s* the Amalekites 1Sa 15:18 2400
nor standeth in the way of *s* Ps 1:1 2400
nor *s* in the congregation of the Ps 1:5 2400
will he teach *s* in the way Ps 25:8 2400
Gather not my soul with *s* Ps 26:9 2400
s shall be converted unto thee Ps 51:13 2400
Let the *s* be consumed out of the Ps 104:35 2400
if *s* entice thee, consent thou Prov 1:10 2400
Evil pursueth *s* Prov 13:21 2400
Let not thine heart envy *s* Prov 23:17 2400
of the *s* shall be together, and Is 1:28 2400
destroy the *s* thereof out of it Is 13:9 2400
The *s* in Zion are afraid Is 33:14 2400
All the *s* of my people shall die Amos 9:10 2400
s came and sat down with him and Mt 9:10 268
your Master with publicans and *s* Mt 9:11 268
righteous, but *s* to repentance Mt 9:13 268
a friend of publicans and *s* Mt 11:19 268
is betrayed into the hands of *s* Mt 26:45 268
s sat also together with Jesus and Mk 2:15 268
saw him eat with publicans and *s* Mk 2:16 268
and drinketh with publicans and *s* Mk 2:16 268
righteous, but *s* to repentance Mk 2:17 268
is betrayed into the hands of *s* Mk 14:41 268
eat and drink with publicans and *s* Lk 5:30 268
righteous, but *s* to repentance Lk 5:32 268
for *s* also love those that love Lk 6:32 268
for *s* also do even the same Lk 6:33 268
for *s* also lend to *s* Lk 6:34 268
a friend of publicans and *s* Lk 7:34 268
were *s* above all the Galilaeans Lk 13:2 268
think ye that they were *s* above Lk 13:4 3781
publicans and *s* for to hear him Lk 15:1 268
saying, This man receiveth *s* Lk 15:2 268
we know that God heareth not *s* Jn 9:31 268
us, in that, while we were yet *s* Rom 5:8 268
disobedience many were made *s* Rom 5:19 268
nature, and not *s* of the Gentiles, Gal 2:15 268
we ourselves also are found *s* Gal 2:17 268
for the ungodly and for *s* 1Ti 1:9 268
came into the world to save *s* 1Ti 1:15 268
undefiled, separate from *s* Heb 7:26 268
of *s* against himself, lest ye be Heb 12:3 268
Cleanse your hands, ye *s* Jas 4:8 268
ungodly *s* have spoken against him Jude 15 268

SINNEST
If thou *s*, what doest thou Job 35:6 2398

SINNETH
for the soul that *s* ignorantly Num 15:28 7683
when he *s* by ignorance before the Num 15:28 2398
for him that *s* through ignorance Num 15:29 6213
for any sin, in any sin that he *s* Deut 19:15 2398
(for there is no man that *s* not 1Kin 8:46 2398
(for there is no man which *s* not 2Chr 6:36 2398
But he that *s* against me wrongeth Prov 8:36 2398
He that despiseth his neighbour *s* Prov 14:21 2398
he that hasteth with his feet *s* Prov 19:2 2398
to anger *s* against his own soul Prov 20:2 2398
earth, that doeth good, and *s* not Eccl 7:20 2398
when the land *s* against me by Eze 14:13 2398
the soul that *s*, it shall die Eze 18:4 2398
The soul that *s*, it shall die Eze 18:20 2398
in the day that he *s* Eze 33:12 2398
s against his own body 1Cor 6:18 264
let him do what he will, he *s* not 1Cor 7:36 264
that is such is subverted, and *s* Titus 3:11 264
Whosoever abideth in him *s* not 1Jn 3:6 264
whosoever *s* hath not seen him, 1Jn 3:6 264
for the devil *s* from the 1Jn 3:8 264
whosoever is born of God *s* not 1Jn 5:18 264

SINNING
withheld thee from *s* against me Gen 20:6 2398
these that a man doeth, *s* therein Lev 6:3 2398

SINS
transgressions in all their *s* Lev 16:16 2403
transgressions in all their *s* Lev 16:21 2403
from all your *s* before the LORD Lev 16:30 2403
for all their *s* once a year Lev 16:34 2403
you seven times more for your *s* Lev 26:18 2403
upon you according to your *s* Lev 26:21 2403
you yet seven times for your *s* Lev 26:24 2403
you seven times for your *s* Lev 26:28 2403
ye be consumed in all their *s* Num 16:26 2403
of all your *s* which ye sinned Deut 9:18 2403
your transgressions nor your *s* Josh 24:19 2403
added unto all our *s* this evil 1Sa 12:19 2403
up because of the *s* of Jeroboam 1Kin 14:16 2403
their *s* which they had committed 1Kin 14:22 2403
walked in all the *s* of his father 1Kin 15:3 2403
Because of the *s* of Jeroboam 1Kin 15:30 2403
provoke me to anger with their *s* 1Kin 16:2 2403
For all the *s* of Baasha, and the 1Kin 16:13 2403
the *s* of Elah his son, by which 1Kin 16:13 2403
For his *s* which he sinned in 1Kin 16:19 2403
s of Jeroboam the son of Nebat 1Kin 16:31 2403
he cleaved unto the *s* of Jeroboam 2Kin 3:3 2403
Howbeit from the *s* of Jeroboam 2Kin 10:29 2399
not from the *s* of Jeroboam 2Kin 10:31 2403
followed the *s* of Jeroboam the 2Kin 13:2 2403
the *s* of the house of Jeroboam 2Kin 13:6 2403
s of Jeroboam the son of Nebat 2Kin 13:11 2403
s of Jeroboam the son of Nebat 2Kin 14:24 2403
he departed not from the *s* of 2Kin 15:9 2403
not all his days from the *s* of 2Kin 15:18 2403
he departed not from the *s* of 2Kin 15:24 2403
he departed not from the *s* of 2Kin 15:28 2403
the *s* of Jeroboam which he did 2Kin 17:22 2403
for the *s* of Manasseh, according 2Kin 24:3 2403
s against the LORD your God 2Chr 28:10 819
ye intend to add more to our *s* 2Chr 28:13 2403
confess the *s* of the children of Neh 1:6 2403
and stood and confessed their *s* Neh 9:2 2403
hast set over us because of our *s* Neh 9:37 2403
How many are mine iniquities and *s* Job 13:23 2403
servant also from presumptuous *s* Ps 19:13
Remember not the *s* of my youth Ps 25:7 2403
and forgive all my *s* Ps 25:18 2403
Hide thy face from my *s*, and blot Ps 51:9 2399
my *s* are not hid from thee Ps 69:5 819
deliver us, and purge away our *s* Ps 79:9 2403
our secret *s* in the light of thy Ps 90:8
not dealt with us after our *s* Ps 103:10 2399
be holden with the cords of his *s* Prov 5:22 2403
but love covereth all *s* Prov 10:12 6588
covereth his *s* shall not prosper Prov 28:13 6588
though your *s* be as scarlet, they Is 1:18 2399
cast all my *s* behind thy back Is 38:17 2399
LORD's hand double for all her *s* Is 40:2 2403
hast made me to serve with thy *s* Is 43:24 2403
sake, and will not remember thy *s* Is 43:25 2403
and, as a cloud, thy *s* Is 44:22 2403
and the house of Jacob their *s* Is 58:1 2403
your *s* have hid his face from you Is 59:2 2403
thee, and our *s* testify against us Is 59:12 2403
your *s* have withholden good Jer 5:25 2403
their iniquity, and visit their *s* Jer 14:10 2403
price, and that for all thy *s* Jer 15:13 2403
because thy *s* were increased Jer 30:14 2403
because thy *s* were increased, I Jer 30:15 2403
the *s* of Judah, and they shall not Jer 50:20 2403
a man for the punishment of his *s* Lam 3:39 2399
For the *s* of her prophets, and the Lam 4:13 2403
he will discover thy *s* Lam 4:22 2403
Samaria committed half of thy *s* Eze 16:51 2403
bear thine own shame for thy *s* Eze 16:52 2403
his father's *s* which he hath done Eze 18:14 2403
all his *s* that he hath committed Eze 18:21 2403
all your doings your *s* do appear Eze 21:24 2403
ye shall bear the *s* of your idols Eze 23:49 2399
our *s* be upon us, and we pine away Eze 33:10 2403
None of his *s* that he hath Eze 33:16 2403
break off thy *s* by righteousness, Dan 4:27 2408
because for our *s*, and for the Dan 9:16 2399
and to make an end of *s*, and to Dan 9:24 2403
their iniquity, and visit their *s* Hos 8:13 2403
iniquity, he will visit their *s* Hos 9:9 2403
transgressions and your mighty *s* Amos 5:12 2403
for the *s* of the house of Israel Mic 1:5 2403
thee desolate because of thy *s* Mic 6:13 2403
thou wilt cast all their *s* into Mic 7:19 2403
save his people from their *s* Mt 1:21 266
him in Jordan, confessing their *s* Mt 3:6 266
thy *s* be forgiven thee Mt 9:2 266
to say, Thy *s* be forgiven thee Mt 9:5 266
hath power on earth to forgive *s* Mt 9:6 266
for many for the remission of *s* Mt 26:28 266
repentance for the remission of *s* Mk 1:4 266
of Jordan, confessing their *s* Mk 1:5 266
Son, thy *s* be forgiven thee Mk 2:5 266
who can forgive *s* but God only Mk 2:7 266
the palsy, Thy *s* be forgiven thee Mk 2:9 266
hath power on earth to forgive *s* Mk 2:10 266
All *s* shall be forgiven unto the Mk 3:28 265
their *s* should be forgiven them Mk 4:12 265
by the remission of their *s* Lk 1:77 266
repentance for the remission of *s* Lk 3:3 266
him, Man, thy *s* are forgiven thee Lk 5:20 266
Who can forgive *s*, but God alone Lk 5:21 266

S

to say, Thy s be forgiven thee ... Lk 5:23 266
power upon earth to forgive s ... Lk 5:24 266
Wherefore I say unto thee, Her s ... Lk 7:47 266
said unto her, Thy s are forgiven ... Lk 7:48 266
Who is this that forgiveth s also ... Lk 7:49 266
And forgive us our s ... Lk 11:4 266
remission of s should be preached ... Lk 24:47 266
seek me, and shall die in your s ... Jn 8:21 266
you, that ye shall die in your s ... Jn 8:24 266
I am he, ye shall die in your s ... Jn 8:24 266
Thou wast altogether born in s ... Jn 9:34 266
Whose soever s ye remit, they are ... Jn 20:23 266
and whose soever s ye retain ... Jn 20:23
Christ for the remission of s ... Acts 2:38 266
that your s may be blotted out, ... Acts 3:19 266
to Israel, and forgiveness of s ... Acts 5:31 266
him shall receive remission of s ... Acts 10:43 266
unto you the forgiveness of s ... Acts 13:38 266
be baptized, and wash away thy s ... Acts 22:16 266
they may receive forgiveness of s ... Acts 26:18 266
the remission of s that are past ... Rom 3:25 265
forgiven, and whose s are covered ... Rom 4:7 266
in the flesh, the motions of s ... Rom 7:5 266
when I shall take away their s ... Rom 11:27 266
our s according to the scriptures ... 1Cor 15:3 266
ye are yet in your s ... 1Cor 15:17 266
Who gave himself for our s ... Gal 1:4 266
his blood, the forgiveness of s ... Eph 1:7 3900
who were dead in trespasses and s ... Eph 2:1 266
Even when we were dead in s ... Eph 2:5 3900
blood, even the forgiveness of s ... Col 1:14 266
body of the s of the flesh by the ... Col 2:11 266
And you, being dead in your s ... Col 2:13 3900
saved, to fill up their s alway ... 1Th 2:16 266
be partaker of other men's s ... 1Ti 5:22 266
Some men's s are open beforehand, ... 1Ti 5:24 266
captive silly women laden with s ... 2Ti 3:6 266
he had by himself purged our s ... Heb 1:3 266
for the s of the people ... Heb 2:17 266
both gifts and sacrifices for s ... Heb 5:1 266
also for himself, to offer for s ... Heb 5:3 266
up sacrifice, first for his own s ... Heb 7:27 266
their unrighteousness, and their s ... Heb 8:12 266
offered to bear the s of many ... Heb 9:28 266
have had no more conscience of s ... Heb 10:2 266
again made of s every year ... Heb 10:3 266
and of goats should take away s ... Heb 10:4 266
which can never take away s ... Heb 10:11 266
one sacrifice for s for ever ... Heb 10:12 266
And their s and iniquities will I ... Heb 10:17 266
remaineth no more sacrifice for s ... Heb 10:26 266
and if he have committed s ... Jas 5:15 266
and shall hide a multitude of s ... Jas 5:20 266
Who his own self bare our s in ... 1Pet 2:24 266
tree, that we, being dead to s ... 1Pet 2:24 266
also hath once suffered for s ... 1Pet 3:18 266
shall cover the multitude of s ... 1Pet 4:8 266
that he was purged from his old s ... 2Pet 1:9 266
If we confess our s, he is ... 1Jn 1:9 266
and just to forgive us our s ... 1Jn 1:9 266
he is the propitiation for our s ... 1Jn 2:2 266
but also for the s of the whole ... 1Jn 2:2
because your s are forgiven you ... 1Jn 2:12 266
was manifested to take away our s ... 1Jn 3:5 266
to be the propitiation for our s ... 1Jn 4:10 266
us from our s in his own blood ... Rev 1:5 266
that ye be not partakers of her s ... Rev 18:4 266
For her s have reached unto ... Rev 18:5 266

SION (*si'-on*) See SHENIR, SIRION, ZION.
1. The peak of Mount Hermon.
even unto mount S which is Hermon ... Deut 4:48 7865
2. A district of Jerusalem.
waiteth for thee, O God in S ... Ps 65:1 6726
Tell ye the daughter of S ... Mt 21:5 4622
Fear not, daughter of S ... Jn 12:15 4622
I lay in S a stumblingstone and ... Rom 9:33 4622
shall come out of S the Deliverer ... Rom 11:26 4622
But ye are come unto mount S ... Heb 12:22 4622
I lay in S a chief corner stone, ... 1Pet 2:6 4622
lo, a Lamb stood on the mount S ... Rev 14:1 4622

SIPHMOTH (*sif'-moth*) *A city in Judah.*
Aroer, and to them which were in S ... 1Sa 30:28 8224

SIPPAI (*sip'-pahee*) See SAPH. *Son of Rapha.*
Sibbechai the Hushathite slew S ... 1Chr 20:4 5598

SIR
And said, O s, we came indeed down ... Gen 43:20 113
came and said unto him, S, didst ... Mt 13:27 2962
And he answered and said, I go s ... Mt 21:30 2962
Saying, S, we remember that that ... Mt 27:63 2962
The woman saith unto him, S ... Jn 4:11 2962
The woman saith unto him, S ... Jn 4:15 2962
The woman saith unto him, S ... Jn 4:19 2962
The nobleman saith unto him, S ... Jn 4:49 2962
The impotent man answered him, S ... Jn 5:7 2962
and desired him, saying, S ... Jn 12:21 2962
the gardener, saith unto him, S ... Jn 20:15 2962
And I said unto him, S, thou ... Rev 7:14 2962

SIRAH (*si'-rah*) *A well near Hebron.*
him again from the well of S ... 2Sa 3:26 5626

SIRION (*sir'-e-on*) See HERMON. *A Sidonian name for Mount Hermon.*
Which Hermon the Sidonians call S ... Deut 3:9 8304
Lebanon and S like a young unicorn ... Ps 29:6 8304

SIRS
set them at one again, saying, S ... Acts 7:26 435
And saying, S, why do ye these ... Acts 14:15 435
And brought them out, and said, S ... Acts 16:30 2962
of like occupation, and said, S ... Acts 19:25 435
And said unto them, S, I perceive ... Acts 27:10 435
in the midst of them, and said, S ... Acts 27:21 435
Wherefore, s, be of good cheer ... Acts 27:25 435

SISAMAI (*sis'-a-mahee*) *Son of Eleasah.*
And Eleasah begat S ... 1Chr 2:40 5581
and S begat Shallum ... 1Chr 2:40 5581

SISERA (*sis'-e-rah*)
1. A captain in the Canaanite army.
the captain of whose host was S ... Judg 4:2 5516
unto thee to the river Kishon, S ... Judg 4:7 5516
for the LORD shall sell S into ... Judg 4:9 5516
they shewed S that Barak the son ... Judg 4:12 5516
S gathered together all his ... Judg 4:13 5516
hath delivered S into thine hand ... Judg 4:14 5516
And the LORD discomfited S ... Judg 4:15 5516
so that S lighted down off his ... Judg 4:15 5516
all the host of S fell upon the ... Judg 4:16 5516
Howbeit S fled away on his feet ... Judg 4:17 5516
And Jael went out to meet S ... Judg 4:18 5516
And, behold, as Barak pursued S ... Judg 4:22 5516
S lay dead, and the nail was in ... Judg 4:22 5516
in their courses fought against S ... Judg 5:20 5516
and with the hammer she smote S ... Judg 5:26 5516
The mother of S looked out at a ... Judg 5:28 5516
to S a prey of divers colours, a ... Judg 5:30 5516
he sold them into the hand of S ... 1Sa 12:9 5516
as to S, as to Jabin, at the ... Ps 83:9 5516
2. A family of exiles.
of Barkos, the children of S ... Ezr 2:53 5516
of Barkos, the children of S ... Neh 7:55 5516

SISMAI See SISAMAI.

SISTER
the s of Tubal-cain was Naamah ... Gen 4:22 269
Say, I pray thee, thou art my s ... Gen 12:13 269
Why saidst thou, She is my s ... Gen 12:19 269
of Sarah his wife, She is my s ... Gen 20:2 269
Said he not unto me, She is my s ... Gen 20:5 269
And yet indeed she is my s ... Gen 20:12 269
heard the words of Rebekah his s ... Gen 24:30 269
And they sent away Rebekah their s ... Gen 24:59 269
and said unto her, Thou art our s ... Gen 24:60 269
the s to Laban the Syrian ... Gen 25:20 269
and he said, She is my s ... Gen 26:7 269
and how saidst thou, She is my s ... Gen 26:9 269
the s of Nebajoth, to be his wife ... Gen 28:9 269
no children, Rachel envied her s ... Gen 30:1 269
have I wrestled with my s ... Gen 30:8 269
he had defiled Dinah their s ... Gen 34:13 269
to give our s to one that is ... Gen 34:14 269
because they had defiled their s ... Gen 34:27 269
deal with our s as with an harlot ... Gen 34:31 269
Ishmael's daughter, s of Nebajoth ... Gen 36:3 269
and Lotan's s was Timna ... Gen 36:22 269
Isui, and Beriah, and Serah their s ... Gen 46:17 269
his s stood afar off, to wit what ... Ex 2:4 269
Then said his s to Pharaoh's ... Ex 2:7 269
Jochebed his father's s to wife ... Ex 6:20 1733
Amminadab, s of Naashon, to wife ... Ex 6:23 269
the s of Aaron, took a timbrel in ... Ex 15:20 269
The nakedness of thy s, the ... Lev 18:9 269
of thy father, she is thy s ... Lev 18:11 269
the nakedness of thy father's s ... Lev 18:12 269
the nakedness of thy mother's s ... Lev 18:13 269
shalt thou take a wife to her s ... Lev 18:18 269
And if a man shall take his s ... Lev 20:17 269
the nakedness of thy mother's s ... Lev 20:19 269
nor of thy father's s ... Lev 20:19 269
for his s a virgin, that is nigh ... Lev 21:3 269
for his brother, or for his s ... Num 6:7 269
of a prince of Midian, their s ... Num 25:18 269
Aaron and Moses, and Miriam their s ... Num 26:59 269
be he that lieth with his s ... Deut 27:22 269
not her younger s fairer than she ... Judg 15:2 269
thy s in law is gone back unto ... Ruth 1:15 2994
return thou after thy s in law ... Ruth 1:15 2994
the son of David had a fair s ... 2Sa 13:1 269
that he fell sick for his s Tamar ... 2Sa 13:2 269
Tamar, my brother Absalom's s ... 2Sa 13:4 269
let my s Tamar come, and give me ... 2Sa 13:5 269
I pray thee, let Tamar my s come ... 2Sa 13:6 269
unto her, Come lie with me, my s ... 2Sa 13:11 269
but hold now thy peace, my s ... 2Sa 13:20 269
because he had forced his s Tamar ... 2Sa 13:22 269
day that he forced his s Tamar ... 2Sa 13:32 269
s to Zeruiah Joab's mother ... 2Sa 17:25 269
him to wife the s of his own wife ... 1Kin 11:19 269
the s of Tahpenes the queen ... 1Kin 11:19 269
the s of Tahpenes bare him ... 1Kin 11:20 269
s of Ahaziah, took Joash the son ... 2Kin 11:2 269
and Timna was Lotan's s ... 1Chr 1:39 269
the concubines, and Tamar their s ... 1Chr 3:9 269
and Hananiah, and Shelomith their s ... 1Chr 3:19 269
name of their s was Hazelelponi ... 1Chr 4:3 269
of his wife Hodiah the s of Naham ... 1Chr 4:19 269
took to wife the s of Huppim ... 1Chr 7:15 269
his s Hammoleketh bare Ishod, and ... 1Chr 7:18 269
and Beriah, and Serah their s ... 1Chr 7:30 269
and Hotham, and Shua their s ... 1Chr 7:32 269
(for she was the s of Ahaziah ... 2Chr 22:11 269
worm, Thou art my mother, and my s ... Job 17:14 269
Say unto wisdom, Thou art my s ... Prov 7:4 269
Thou hast ravished my heart, my s ... Song 4:9 269
How fair is thy love, my s ... Song 4:10 269
A garden inclosed is my s ... Song 4:12 269
I am come into my garden, my s ... Song 5:1 269
saying, Open to me, my s ... Song 5:2 269
We have a little s, and she hath ... Song 8:8 269
what shall we do for our s in the ... Song 8:8 269
And her treacherous s Judah saw it ... Jer 3:7 269
treacherous s Judah feared not ... Jer 3:8 269
for all this her treacherous s ... Jer 3:10 269
my brother! or, Ah s! ... Jer 22:18 269
thou art the s of thy sisters, ... Eze 16:45 269
And thine elder s is Samaria ... Eze 16:46 269
and thy younger s, that dwelleth ... Eze 16:46 269
Sodom thy s hath not done, she ... Eze 16:48 269
was the iniquity of thy s Sodom ... Eze 16:49 269
For thy s Sodom was not mentioned ... Eze 16:56 269
in thee hath humbled his s ... Eze 22:11 269
the elder, and Aholibah her s ... Eze 23:4 269
when her s Aholibah saw this, she ... Eze 23:11 269
more than her s in her whoredoms ... Eze 23:11 269
my mind was alienated from her s ... Eze 23:18 269
hast walked in the way of thy s ... Eze 23:31 269
with the cup of thy s Samaria ... Eze 23:33 269
or for s that hath had no husband ... Eze 44:25 269
the same is my brother, and s ... Mt 12:50 79
the same is my brother, and my s ... Mk 3:35 79
she had a s called Mary, which ... Lk 10:39 79
dost thou not care that my s hath ... Lk 10:40 79
the town of Mary and her s Martha ... Jn 11:1 79
Now Jesus loved Martha, and her s ... Jn 11:5 79
and called Mary her s secretly ... Jn 11:28 79
the s of him that was dead, saith ... Jn 11:39 79
his mother, and his mother's s ... Jn 19:25 79
I commend unto you Phebe our s ... Rom 16:1 79
and Julia, Nereus, and his s ... Rom 16:15 79
A brother or a s is not under ... 1Cor 7:15 79
we not power to lead about a s ... 1Cor 9:5 79
If a brother or s be naked ... Jas 2:15 79
of thy elect s greet thee ... 2Jn 13 79

SISTER'S
and bracelets upon his s hands ... Gen 24:30 269
the tidings of Jacob his s son ... Gen 29:13 269
he hath uncovered his s nakedness ... Lev 20:17 269
Shuppim, whose s name was Maachah ... 1Chr 7:15 269
shalt drink of thy s cup deep ... Eze 23:32 269
when Paul's s son heard of their ... Acts 23:16 79
s son to Barnabas, (touching whom ... Col 4:10 431

SISTERS
mother, and my brethren, and my s ... Josh 2:13 269
Whose s were Zeruiah, and Abigail ... 1Chr 2:16 269
called for their three s to eat ... Job 1:4 269
all his brethren, and all his s ... Job 42:11 269
and thou art the sister of thy s ... Eze 16:45 269
hast justified thy s in all thine ... Eze 16:51 269
also, which hast judged thy s ... Eze 16:52 269
in that thou hast justified thy s ... Eze 16:52 269
When thy s, Sodom and her ... Eze 16:55 269
when thou shalt receive thy s ... Eze 16:61 269
and to your s, Ruhamah ... Hos 2:1 269
And his s, are they not all with ... Mt 13:56 79
houses, or brethren, or s ... Mt 19:29 79
are not his s here with us ... Mk 6:3 79
left house, or brethren, or s ... Mk 10:29 79
time, houses, and brethren, and s ... Mk 10:30 79
and children, and brethren, and s ... Lk 14:26 79
Therefore his s sent unto him ... Jn 11:3 79
the younger as s, with all purity ... 1Ti 5:2 79

SIT
arise, I pray thee, s and eat of ... Gen 27:19 3427
go to war, and shall ye s here ... Num 32:6 3427
ye that s in judgment, and walk by ... Judg 5:10 3427
S still, my daughter, until thou ... Ruth 3:18 3427
turn aside, s down here ... Ruth 4:1 3427
the city, and said, S ye down here ... Ruth 4:2 3427
made them s in the chiefest place ... 1Sa 9:22 5414
for we will not s down till he ... 1Sa 16:11 5437
I should not fail to s with the ... 1Sa 20:5 3427
the king doth s in the gate ... 2Sa 19:8 3427
he shall s upon my throne ... 1Kin 1:13 3427
he shall s upon my throne ... 1Kin 1:17 3427
s on the throne of my lord the ... 1Kin 1:20 3427
he shall s upon my throne ... 1Kin 1:24 3427
who should s on the throne of my ... 1Kin 1:27 3427
he shall s upon my throne in my ... 1Kin 1:30 3427
he may come and s upon my throne ... 1Kin 1:35 3427
one to s on my throne this day ... 1Kin 1:48 3427
him a son to s on his throne ... 1Kin 3:6 3427
s on the throne of Israel, as the ... 1Kin 8:20 3427
to s on the throne of Israel ... 1Kin 8:25 3427
Why s we here until we die ... 2Kin 7:3 3427
if we s still here, we die also ... 2Kin 7:4 3427
shall s on the throne of Israel ... 2Kin 10:30 3427
Thy sons shall s on the throne of ... 2Kin 15:12 3427
me to the men which s on the wall ... 2Kin 18:27 3427
hath chosen Solomon my son to s ... 1Chr 28:5 3427
to s upon the throne of Israel ... 2Chr 6:16 3427
will not s with the wicked ... Ps 26:5 3427
They that s in the gate speak ... Ps 69:12 3427
Such as s in darkness and in the ... Ps 107:10 3427
S thou at my right hand, until I ... Ps 110:1 3427
Princes also did s and speak ... Ps 119:23 3427
to s up late, to eat the bread of ... Ps 127:2 3427
their children shall also s upon ... Ps 132:12 3427
and the rich s in low place ... Eccl 10:6 3427
desolate shall s upon the ground ... Is 3:26 3427
I will s also upon the mount of ... Is 14:13 3427
he shall s upon it in truth in ... Is 16:5 3427
Their strength is to s still ... Is 30:7 7674
to the men that s upon the wall ... Is 36:12 3427
them that s in darkness out of ... Is 42:7 3427
s in the dust, O virgin daughter ... Is 47:1 3427
of Babylon, s on the ground ... Is 47:1 3427
S thou silent, and get thee into ... Is 47:5 3427
I shall not s as a widow, neither ... Is 47:8 3427
warm at, nor fire to s before it ... Is 47:14 3427
arise, and s down, O Jerusalem ... Is 52:2 3427
Why do we s still ... Jer 8:14 3427
kings that s upon David's throne ... Jer 13:13 3427
queen, Humble yourselves, s down ... Jer 13:18 3427
to s with them to eat and to drink ... Jer 16:8 3427
s upon the throne of the house of ... Jer 33:17 3427
S down now, and read it in our ... Jer 36:15 3427
He shall have none to s upon the ... Jer 36:30 3427
from thy glory, and s in thirst ... Jer 48:18 3427

How doth the city *s* solitary Lam 1:1 3427
of Zion *s* upon the ground Lam 2:10 3427
they shall *s* upon the ground, and Eze 26:16 3427
I *s* in the seat of God, in the Eze 28:2 3427
they *s* before thee as my people, Eze 33:31 3427
he shall *s* in it to eat bread Eze 44:3 3427
and the Ancient of days did *s* Dan 7:9 3488
But the judgment shall *s*, and they Dan 7:26 3488
for there will I *s* to judge all Joel 3:12 3427
But they shall *s* every man under Mic 4:4 3427
when I *s* in darkness, the LORD Mic 7:8 3427
and thy fellows that *s* before thee Zec 3:8 3427
shall bear the glory, and shall *s* Zec 6:13 3427
he shall *s* as a refiner and Mal 3:3 3427
shall *s* down with Abraham, and Mt 8:11 *347*
multitude to *s* down on the grass Mt 14:19 *347*
multitude to *s* down on the ground Mt 15:35 *377*
when the Son of man shall *s* in Mt 19:28 *2523*
ye also shall *s* upon twelve Mt 19:28 *2523*
that these my two sons may *s* Mt 20:21 *2523*
but to *s* on my right hand, and on Mt 20:23 *2523*
S thou on my right hand, till I Mt 22:44 *2521*
the Pharisees *s* in Moses' seat Mt 23:2 *2523*
then shall he *s* upon the throne Mt 25:31 *2523*
S ye here, while I go and pray Mt 26:36 *2523*
all *s* down by companies upon the Mk 6:39 *347*
people to *s* down on the ground Mk 8:6 *377*
him, Grant unto us that we may *s* Mk 10:37 *2523*
But to *s* on my right hand and on Mk 10:40 *2523*
S thou on my right hand, till I Mk 12:36 *2521*
S ye here, while I shall pray Mk 14:32 *2523*
light to them that *s* in darkness Lk 1:79 *2521*
Make them *s* down by fifties in a Lk 9:14 *2625*
did so, and made them all *s* down Lk 9:15 *347*
and make them to *s* down to meat Lk 12:37 *347*
shall *s* down in the kingdom of Lk 13:29 *347*
s not down in the highest room Lk 14:8 *2625*
s down in the lowest room Lk 14:10 *377*
of them that *s* at meat with thee Lk 14:10 *4873*
s down quickly, and write fifty Lk 16:6 *2523*
the field, Go and *s* down to meat Lk 17:7 *377*
my Lord, *S* thou on my right hand, Lk 20:42 *2521*
s on thrones judging the twelve Lk 22:30 *2523*
s on the right hand of the power Lk 22:69 *2521*
Jesus said, Make the men *s* down Jn 6:10 *377*
up Christ to *s* on his throne Acts 2:30 *2523*
my Lord, *S* thou on my right hand, Acts 2:34 *2521*
he would come up and *s* with him Acts 8:31 *2523*
s at meat in the idol's temple 1Cor 8:10 *2621*
made us *s* together in heavenly Eph 2:6 *4776*
S on my right hand, until I make Heb 1:13 *2521*
S thou here in a good place Jas 2:3 *2521*
or *s* here under my footstool Jas 2:3 *2521*
I grant to *s* with me in my throne Rev 3:21 *2523*
I saw a woman *s* upon a scarlet Rev 17:3 *2521*
I *s* a queen, and am no widow, and Rev 18:7 *2521*
horses, and of them that *s* on them Rev 19:18 *2521*

SITH
s thou hast not hated blood, even Eze 35:6 518

SITHRI See ZITHRI.

SITNAH (*sit'-nah*) *A well near Gerar.*
and he called the name of it *S* Gen 26:21 7856

SITTEST
why *s* thou thyself alone, and all Ex 18:14 3427
them when thou *s* in thine house Deut 6:7 3427
them when thou *s* in thine house Deut 11:19 3427
Thou *s* and speakest against thy Ps 50:20 3427
When thou *s* to eat with a ruler, Prov 23:1 3427
that *s* upon the throne of David, Jer 22:2 3427
for *s* thou to judge me after the Acts 23:3 *2521*

SITTETH
of Pharaoh that *s* upon his throne Ex 11:5 3427
and every thing, whereon he *s* Lev 15:4 3427
he that *s* on any thing whereon he Lev 15:6 3427
that she *s* upon shall be unclean Lev 15:20 3427
or on any thing whereon she *s* Lev 15:23 3427
whatsoever she *s* upon shall be Lev 15:26 3427
when he *s* upon the throne of his Deut 17:18 3427
also Solomon *s* on the throne of 1Kin 1:46 3427
that *s* at the king's gate Est 6:10 3427
nor *s* in the seat of the scornful Ps 1:1 3427
He that *s* in the heavens shall Ps 2:4 3427
He *s* in the lurking places of the Ps 10:8 3427
The LORD *s* upon the flood Ps 29:10 3427
yea, the LORD *s* King for ever Ps 29:10 3427
God *s* upon the throne of his Ps 47:8 3427
he *s* between the cherubims Ps 99:1 3427
For she *s* at the door of her Prov 9:14 3427
A king that *s* in the throne of Prov 20:8 3427
when he *s* among the elders of the Prov 31:23 3427
While the king *s* at his table Song 1:12
to him that *s* in judgment Is 28:6 3427
It is he that *s* upon the circle Is 40:22 3427
As the partridge *s* on eggs Jer 17:11 1716
that *s* upon the throne of David Jer 29:16 3427
He *s* alone and keepeth silence, Lam 3:28 3427
and, behold, all the earth *s* still Zec 1:11 3427
this is a woman that *s* in the Zec 5:7 3427
of God, and by him that *s* thereon Mt 23:22 *2521*
s not down first, and counteth the Lk 14:28 *2523*
s not down first, and consulteth Lk 14:31 *2523*
is greater, he that *s* at meat Lk 22:27 *345*
is not he that *s* at meat Lk 22:27 *345*
be revealed to another that *s* by 1Cor 14:30 *2521*
where Christ *s* on the right hand Col 3:1 *2521*
so that he as God *s* in the temple 2Th 2:4 *2523*
unto him that *s* upon the throne Rev 5:13 *2521*
face of him that *s* on the throne Rev 6:16 *2521*
our God which *s* upon the throne Rev 7:10 *2521*
he that *s* on the throne shall Rev 7:15 *2521*
whore that *s* upon many waters Rev 17:1 *2521*
mountains, on which the woman *s* Rev 17:9 *2521*
thou sawest, where the whore *s* Rev 17:15 *2521*

SITTING
the dam *s* upon the young, or upon Deut 22:6 7257
he was *s* in a summer parlour, Judg 3:20 3427
the *s* of his servants, and the 1Kin 10:5 4186
God, and found him *s* under an oak 1Kin 13:14 3427
I saw the LORD *s* on his throne 1Kin 22:19 3427
of the prophets were *s* before him 2Kin 4:38 3427
the captains of the host were *s* 2Kin 9:5 3427
the *s* of his servants, and the 2Chr 9:4 4186
stays on each side of the *s* place 2Chr 9:18 3427
I saw the LORD *s* upon his throne, 2Chr 18:18 3427
unto me, (the queen also *s* by him Neh 2:6 3427
the Jew *s* at the king's gate Est 5:13 3427
saw also the Lord *s* upon a throne Is 6:1 3427
princes *s* upon the throne of Jer 17:25 3427
kings *s* upon the throne of David Jer 22:4 3427
s upon the throne of David, and Jer 22:30 3427
the king then *s* in the gate of Jer 38:7 3427
Behold their *s* down, and their Lam 3:63 3427
s at the receipt of custom Mt 9:9 *2521*
unto children *s* in the markets Mt 11:16 *2521*
two blind men *s* by the way side, Mt 20:30 *2521*
s upon an ass, and a colt the foal Mt 21:5 *1910*
man *s* on the right hand of power Mt 26:64 *2521*
s down they watched him there Mt 27:36 *2521*
s over against the sepulchre Mt 27:61 *2521*
certain of the scribes *s* there Mk 2:6 *2521*
s at the receipt of custom Mk 2:14 *2521*
the devil, and had the legion, *s* Mk 5:15 *2521*
man *s* on the right hand of power Mk 14:62 *2521*
a young man *s* on the right side Mk 16:5 *2521*
s in the midst of the doctors, Lk 2:46 *2516*
and doctors of the law *s* by Lk 5:17 *2521*
s at the receipt of custom Lk 5:27 *2521*
children *s* in the marketplace Lk 7:32 *2521*
s at the feet of Jesus, clothed, Lk 8:35 *2521*
repented, *s* in sackcloth and ashes Lk 10:13 *2521*
doves, and the changers of money *s* Jn 2:14 *2521*
King cometh, *s* on an ass's colt Jn 12:15 *2521*
And seeth two angels in white *s* Jn 20:12 *2516*
all the house where they were *s* Acts 2:2 *2521*
s in his chariot read Esaias the Acts 8:28 *2521*
the next day *s* on the judgment Acts 25:6 *2523*
I saw four and twenty elders *s* Rev 4:4 *2521*

SITUATE
The forefront of the one was *s* 1Sa 14:5 4690
O thou that art *s* at the entry of Eze 27:3 3427
that was *s* among the rivers, that Nah 3:8 3427

SITUATION
the *s* of this city is pleasant, 2Kin 2:19 4186
Beautiful for *s*, the joy of the Ps 48:2 5131

SIVAN (*si'-van*) *Third month of the Hebrew year.*
third month, that is, the month *S* Est 8:9 5510

SIX
Noah was *s* hundred years old when Gen 7:6 8337
In the *s* hundredth year of Noah's Gen 7:11 8337
came to pass in the *s* hundredth Gen 8:13 8337
s years old, when Hagar bare Gen 16:16 8337
because I have born him *s* sons Gen 30:20 8337
and *s* years for thy cattle Gen 31:41 8337
the souls were threescore and *s* Gen 46:26 8337
about *s* hundred thousand on foot Ex 12:37 8337
he took *s* hundred chosen chariots Ex 14:7 8337
S days ye shall gather it Ex 16:26 8337
S days shalt thou labour, and do Ex 20:9 8337
For in *s* days the LORD made Ex 20:11 8337
servant, *s* years he shall serve Ex 21:2 8337
s years thou shalt sow thy land, Ex 23:10 8337
S days thou shalt do thy work, and Ex 23:12 8337
and the cloud covered it *s* days Ex 24:16 8337
s branches shall come out of the Ex 25:32 8337
so in the *s* branches that come Ex 25:33 8337
according to the *s* branches that Ex 25:35 8337
s curtains by themselves, and Ex 26:9 8337
westward thou shalt make *s* boards Ex 26:22 8337
S of their names on one stone, and Ex 28:10 8337
the other *s* names of the rest on Ex 28:10 8337
S days may work be done Ex 31:15 8337
for in *s* days the LORD made Ex 31:17 8337
S days thou shalt work, but on Ex 34:21 8337
S days shall work be done, but on Ex 35:2 8337
and *s* curtains by themselves Ex 36:16 8337
westward he made *s* boards Ex 36:27 8337
s branches going out of the sides Ex 37:18 8337
so throughout the *s* branches Ex 37:19 8337
according to the *s* branches going Ex 37:21 8337
for *s* hundred thousand and three Ex 38:26 8337
purifying threescore and *s* days Lev 12:5 8337
S days shall work be done Lev 23:3 8337
s on a row, upon the pure table Lev 24:6 8337
S years thou shalt sow thy field, Lev 25:3 8337
s years thou shalt prune thy Lev 25:3 8337
s thousand and five hundred Num 1:21 8337
forty and five thousand *s* hundred Num 1:25 8337
and fourteen thousand and *s* hundred Num 1:27 8337
numbered were *s* hundred thousand Num 1:46 8337
and fourteen thousand and *s* hundred Num 2:4 8337
s thousand and four hundred, Num 2:9 8337
s thousand and five hundred Num 2:11 8337
thousand and *s* hundred and fifty Num 2:15 8337
and seven thousand and *s* hundred Num 2:31 8337
hosts were *s* hundred thousand Num 2:32 8337
s hundred, keeping the charge of Num 3:28 8337
were *s* thousand and two hundred Num 3:34 8337
thousand and *s* hundred and thirty Num 4:40 8337
s covered wagons, and twelve oxen Num 7:3 8337
are *s* hundred thousand footmen Num 11:21 8337
and five thousand and *s* hundred Num 26:41 8337
s hundred thousand and a thousand Num 26:51 8337
was *s* hundred thousand and seventy Num 31:32 8337
of the sheep was *s* hundred Num 31:37 8337
beeves were thirty and *s* thousand Num 31:38 8337
And thirty and *s* thousand beeves, Num 31:44 8337
shall be *s* cities for refuge Num 35:6 8337
cities which ye shall give *s* Num 35:13 8337
These *s* cities shall be a refuge, Num 35:15 8337
S days thou shalt labour, and do Deut 5:13 8337
unto thee, and serve thee *s* years Deut 15:12 8337
to thee, in serving thee *s* years Deut 15:18 8337
S days thou shalt eat unleavened Deut 16:8 8337
Thus shalt thou do *s* days Josh 6:3 8337
so they did *s* days Josh 6:14 8337
of them about thirty and *s* men Josh 7:5 8337
s cities with their villages Josh 15:59 8337
s cities with their villages Josh 15:62 8337
s hundred men with an ox goad Judg 3:31 8337
And Jephthah judged Israel *s* years Judg 12:7 8337
s hundred men appointed with Judg 18:11 8337
the *s* hundred men appointed with Judg 18:16 8337
entering of the gate with the *s* Judg 18:17 8337
s thousand men that drew sword, Judg 20:15 8337
But *s* hundred men turned and fled Judg 20:47 8337
he measured *s* measures of barley, Ruth 3:15 8337
These *s* measures of barley gave Ruth 3:17 8337
s thousand horsemen, and people as 1Sa 13:5 8337
with him, about *s* hundred men 1Sa 13:15 8337
with him were about *s* hundred men 1Sa 14:2 8337
Gath, whose height was *s* cubits 1Sa 17:4 8337
weighed *s* hundred shekels of iron 1Sa 17:7 8337
men, which were about *s* hundred 1Sa 23:13 8337
he passed over with the *s* hundred 1Sa 27:2 8337
the *s* hundred men that were with 1Sa 30:9 8337
Judah was seven years and *s* months 2Sa 2:11 8337
Judah seven years and *s* months 2Sa 5:5 8337
ark of the LORD had gone *s* paces 2Sa 6:13 8337
s hundred men which came after 2Sa 15:18 8337
that had on every hand *s* fingers 2Sa 21:20 8337
fingers, and on every foot *s* toes 2Sa 21:20 8337
and the middle was *s* cubits broad 1Kin 6:6 8337
one year was *s* hundred threescore 1Kin 10:14 8337
threescore and *s* talents of gold, 1Kin 10:14 8337
s hundred shekels of gold went to 1Kin 10:16 8337
The throne had *s* steps, and the 1Kin 10:19 8337
and on the other upon the *s* steps 1Kin 10:20 8337
went out of Egypt for *s* hundred 1Kin 10:29 8337
(For *s* months did Joab remain 1Kin 11:16 8337
s years reigned he in Tirzah 1Kin 16:23 8337
s thousand pieces of gold, and ten 2Kin 5:5 8337
in the house of the LORD *s* years 2Kin 11:3 8337
have smitten five or *s* times 2Kin 13:19 8337
over Israel in Samaria *s* months 2Kin 15:8 8337
These *s* were born unto him in 1Chr 3:4 8337
reigned seven years and *s* months 1Chr 3:4 8337
Bariah, and Neariah, and Shaphat, *s* 1Chr 3:22 8337
had sixteen sons and *s* daughters 1Chr 4:27 8337
and twenty thousand and *s* hundred 1Chr 7:2 8337
were bands of soldiers for war, *s* 1Chr 7:4 8337
was twenty and *s* thousand men 1Chr 7:40 8337
And Azel had *s* sons, whose names 1Chr 8:38 8337
brethren, *s* hundred and ninety 1Chr 9:6 8337
nine hundred and fifty and *s* 1Chr 9:9 8337
And Azel had *s* sons, whose names 1Chr 9:44 8337
shield and spear were *s* thousand 1Chr 12:24 8337
Levi four thousand and *s* hundred 1Chr 12:26 8337
and eight thousand and *s* hundred 1Chr 12:35 8337
s on each hand, and *s* on each 1Chr 20:6 8337
s hundred shekels of gold by 1Chr 21:25 8337
s thousand were officers and 1Chr 23:4 8337
Hashabiah, and Mattithiah, *s* 1Chr 25:3 8337
Eastward were *s* Levites, 1Chr 26:17 8337
for *s* hundred shekels of silver 2Chr 1:17 8337
s hundred to oversee them 2Chr 2:2 8337
and three thousand and *s* hundred 2Chr 2:17 8337
s hundred overseers to set the 2Chr 2:18 8337
amounting to *s* hundred talents 2Chr 3:8 8337
Solomon in one year was *s* hundred 2Chr 9:13 8337
threescore and *s* talents of gold 2Chr 9:13 8337
s hundred shekels of beaten gold 2Chr 9:15 8337
there were *s* steps to the throne, 2Chr 9:18 8337
and on the other upon the *s* steps 2Chr 9:19 8337
In the *s* and thirtieth year of the 2Chr 16:1 8337
hid in the house of God *s* years 2Chr 22:12 8337
were two thousand and *s* hundred 2Chr 26:12 8337
things were *s* hundred oxen 2Chr 29:33 8337
s hundred small cattle, and three 2Chr 35:8 8337
of Bani, *s* hundred forty and two Ezr 2:10 8337
s hundred twenty and three Ezr 2:11 8337
Adonikam, *s* hundred sixty and *s* Ezr 2:13 8337
Bigvai, two thousand fifty and *s* Ezr 2:14 8337
The men of Netophah, fifty and *s* Ezr 2:22 8337
and Gaba, *s* hundred twenty and one Ezr 2:26 8337
of Magbish, an hundred fifty and *s* Ezr 2:30 8337
thousand and *s* hundred and thirty Ezr 2:35 8337
of Nekoda, *s* hundred fifty and two Ezr 2:60 8337
were seven hundred thirty and *s* Ezr 2:66 8337
s thousand seven hundred and Ezr 2:67 8337
weighed unto their hand *s* hundred Ezr 8:26 8337
s rams, seventy and seven lambs, Ezr 8:35 8337
was one ox and *s* choice sheep Neh 5:18 8337
of Arah, *s* hundred fifty and two Neh 7:10 8337
Binnui, *s* hundred forty and eight Neh 7:15 8337
s hundred twenty and eight Neh 7:16 8337
s hundred threescore and seven Neh 7:18 8337
of Adin, *s* hundred fifty and five Neh 7:20 8337
and Gaba, *s* hundred twenty and one Neh 7:30 8337
of Nekoda, *s* hundred forty and two Neh 7:62 8337
horses, seven hundred thirty and *s* Neh 7:68 8337
s thousand seven hundred and Neh 7:69 8337
s months with oil of myrrh, and Est 2:12 8337
s months with sweet odours, and Est 2:12 8337
shall deliver thee in *s* troubles Job 5:19 8337
s thousand camels, and a thousand Job 42:12 8337

These *s* things doth the LORD hate Prov 6:16 8337
each one had *s* wings Is 6:2 8337
when he hath served thee *s* years Jer 34:14 8337
and *s* pomegranates on a side Jer 52:23 8337
were four thousand and *s* hundred Jer 52:30 8337
s men came from the way of the Eze 9:2 8337
of *s* cubits long by the cubit Eze 40:5 8337
were *s* cubits on this side Eze 40:12 8337
and *s* cubits on that side Eze 40:12 8337
s cubits broad on the one side, Eze 41:1 8337
s cubits broad on the other side, Eze 41:1 8337
and the door, *s* cubits Eze 41:3 8337
the wall of the house, *s* cubits Eze 41:5 8337
a full reed of *s* great cubits Eze 41:8 8337
shall be shut the *s* working days Eze 46:1 8337
shall be *s* lambs without blemish Eze 46:4 8337
blemish, and *s* lambs, and a ram Eze 46:6 8337
and the breadth thereof *s* cubits Dan 3:1 8353
after *s* days Jesus taketh Peter, Mt 17:1 *1803*
after *s* days Jesus taketh with Mk 9:2 *1803*
s months, when great famine was Lk 4:25 *1803*
There are *s* days in which men Lk 13:14 *1803*
set there *s* waterpots of stone Jn 2:6 *1803*
s years was this temple in Jn 2:20 *1803*
Then Jesus *s* days before the Jn 12:1 *1803*
Moreover these *s* brethren Acts 11:12 *1803*
s months, teaching the word of Acts 18:11 *1803*
space of three years and *s* months Jas 5:17 *1803*
each of them *s* wings about him Rev 4:8 *1803*
is *s* hundred threescore and *s* Rev 13:18 *5516*
a thousand and *s* hundred furlongs Rev 14:20 *1812*

SIXSCORE
to the king *s* talents of gold 1Kin 9:14
wherein are more than *s* thousand Jonah 4:11

SIXTEEN
she bare unto Jacob, even *s* souls Gen 46:18
sockets of silver, *s* sockets Ex 26:25
sockets were *s* sockets of silver Ex 36:30
s thousand and five hundred Num 26:22
And the persons were *s* thousand Num 31:40
And *s* thousand persons Num 31:46
was *s* thousand seven hundred and Num 31:52
s cities with their villages Josh 15:41
s cities with their villages Josh 19:22
in Samaria, and reigned *s* years 2Kin 13:10
Azariah, which was *s* years old 2Kin 14:21
S years old was he when he began 2Kin 15:2
he reigned *s* years in Jerusalem 2Kin 15:33
reigned *s* years in Jerusalem, and 2Kin 16:2
And Shimei had *s* sons and six 1Chr 4:27
the sons of Eleazar there were *s* 1Chr 24:4
and two sons, and *s* daughters 2Chr 13:21
who was *s* years old, and made him 2Chr 26:1
S years old was Uzziah when he 2Chr 26:3
he reigned *s* years in Jerusalem 2Chr 27:1
reigned *s* years in Jerusalem 2Chr 27:8
he reigned *s* years in Jerusalem 2Chr 28:1
two hundred threescore and *s* souls Acts 27:37

SIXTEENTH
to Bilgah, the *s* to Immer, 1Chr 24:14
The *s* to Hananiah, he, his sons, 1Chr 25:23
in the *s* day of the first month 2Chr 29:17

SIXTH
and the morning were the *s* day Gen 1:31 8345
again, and bare Jacob the *s* son Gen 30:19 8345
that on the *s* day they shall Ex 16:5 8345
that on the *s* day they gathered Ex 16:22 8345
the *s* day the bread of two days Ex 16:29 8345
shalt double the *s* curtain in the Ex 26:9 8345
blessing upon you in the *s* year Lev 25:21 8345
On the *s* day Eliasaph the son of Num 7:42 8345
on the *s* day eight bullocks, two Num 29:29 8345
The *s* lot came out to the Josh 19:32 8345
And the *s*, Ithream, by Eglah 2Sa 3:5 8345
s year of Asa king of Judah began 1Kin 16:8 8337
even in the *s* year of Hezekiah, 2Kin 18:10 8337
Ozem the *s*, David the seventh 1Chr 2:15 8345
the *s*, Ithream by Eglah his wife 1Chr 3:3 8345
Attai the *s*, Eliel the seventh, 1Chr 12:11 8345
to Malchijah, the *s* to Mijamin, 1Chr 24:9 8345
The *s* to Bukkiah, he, his sons, 1Chr 25:13 8345
Elam the fifth, Jehohanan the *s* 1Chr 26:3 8345
Ammiel the *s*, Issachar the 1Chr 26:5 8345
The *s* captain for the *s* month 1Chr 27:9 8345
which was in the *s* year of the Ezr 6:15 8353
Hanun the *s* son of Zalaph, Neh 3:30 8345
by measure, the *s* part of an hin Eze 4:11 8345
in the *s* year, in the *s* month Eze 8:1 8345
and leave but the *s* part of thee Eze 39:2 8338
the *s* part of an ephah of an Eze 45:13 8345
ye shall give the *s* part of an Eze 45:13 8341
the *s* part of an ephah, and the Eze 46:14 8345
Darius the king, in the *s* month Hag 1:1 8345
and twentieth day of the *s* month Hag 1:15 8345
Again he went out about the *s* Mt 20:5 *1623*
Now from the *s* hour there was Mt 27:45 *1623*
when the *s* hour was come, there Mk 15:33 *1623*
in the *s* month the angel Gabriel Lk 1:26 *1623*
this is the *s* month with her, who Lk 1:36 *1623*
And it was about the *s* hour Lk 23:44 *1623*
and it was about the *s* hour Jn 4:6 *1623*
the passover, and about the *s* hour Jn 19:14 *1623*
housetop to pray about the *s* hour Acts 10:9 *1623*
when he had opened the *s* seal Rev 6:12 *1623*
the *s* angel sounded, and I heard a Rev 9:13 *1623*
Saying to the *s* angel which had Rev 9:14 *1623*
the *s* angel poured out his vial Rev 16:12 *1623*
the *s*, sardius Rev 21:20 *1623*

SIXTY
And Mahalaleel lived *s* and five Gen 5:15 8346
And Jared lived an hundred *s* Gen 5:18 8346
days of Jared were nine hundred *s* Gen 5:20 8346
And Enoch lived *s* and five years, Gen 5:21 8346
of Enoch were three hundred *s* Gen 5:23 8346
of Methuselah were nine hundred *s* Gen 5:27 8346
years old even unto *s* years old Lev 27:3 8346
And if it be from *s* years old Lev 27:7 8346
the rams *s*, the he goats *s* Num 7:88 8346
the lambs of the first year *s* Num 7:88 8346
of Adonikam, six hundred *s* Ezr 2:13 8346
some an hundredfold, some *s* Mt 13:23 *1835*
forth, some thirty, and some *s* Mk 4:8 *1835*
fruit, some thirtyfold, some *s* Mk 4:20 *1835*

SIXTYFOLD
some an hundredfold, some *s* Mt 13:8 *1835*

SIYON See SION.

SIZE
the curtains were all of one *s* Ex 36:9 4060
the eleven curtains were of one *s* Ex 36:15 4060
were of one measure and one *s* 1Kin 6:25 7095
casting, one measure, and one *s* 1Kin 7:37 7095
and for all manner of measure and *s* 1Chr 23:29 4060

SKIES
waters, and thick clouds of the *s* 2Sa 22:12 7834
waters and thick clouds of the *s* Ps 18:11 7834
the *s* sent out a sound Ps 77:17 7834
let the *s* pour down righteousness Is 45:8 7834
and is lifted up even to the *s* Jer 51:9 7834

SKILFUL
s in war, were four and forty 1Chr 5:18 3925
about the song, because he was *s* 1Chr 15:22 995
workmanship every willing *s* man 1Chr 28:21 2451
s to work in gold, and in silver, 2Chr 2:14 3045
of brutish men, and *s* to destroy Eze 21:31 2796
s in all wisdom, and cunning in Dan 1:4 7919
such as are *s* of lamentation to Amos 5:16 3045

SKILFULLY
play *s* with a loud noise Ps 33:3 3190

SKILFULNESS
guided them by the *s* of his hands Ps 78:72 8394

SKILL
can *s* to hew timber like unto the 1Kin 5:6 3045
that can *s* to grave with the 2Chr 2:7 3045
can *s* to cut timber in Lebanon 2Chr 2:8 3045
all that could *s* of instruments 2Chr 34:12 995
nor yet favour to men of *s* Eccl 9:11 3045
s in all learning and wisdom Dan 1:17 7919
am now come forth to give thee *s* Dan 9:22 7919

SKIN
only, it is his raiment for his *s* Ex 22:27 5785
flesh of the bullock, and his *s* Ex 29:14 5785
the *s* of his face shone while he Ex 34:29 5785
behold, the *s* of his face shone Ex 34:30 5785
that the *s* of Moses' face shone Ex 34:35 5785
the *s* of the bullock, and all his Lev 4:11 5785
shall have to himself the *s* of Lev 7:8 5785
vessel of wood, or raiment, or *s* Lev 11:32 5785
in the *s* of his flesh a rising Lev 13:2 5785
it be in the *s* of his flesh like Lev 13:2 5785
the plague in the *s* of the flesh Lev 13:3 5785
be deeper than the *s* of his flesh Lev 13:3 5785
be white in the *s* of his flesh Lev 13:4 5785
in sight be not deeper than the *s* Lev 13:4 5785
and the plague spread not in the *s* Lev 13:5 5785
and the plague spread not abroad in the *s* Lev 13:6 5785
scab spread much abroad in the *s* Lev 13:7 5785
the scab spreadeth in the *s* Lev 13:8 5785
if the rising be white in the *s* Lev 13:10 5785
old leprosy in the *s* of his flesh Lev 13:11 5785
leprosy break out abroad in the *s* Lev 13:12 5785
the leprosy cover all the *s* of Lev 13:12 5785
in which, even in the *s* thereof Lev 13:18 5785
it be in sight lower than the *s* Lev 13:20 5785
and if it be not lower than the *s* Lev 13:21 5785
if it spread much abroad in the *s* Lev 13:22 5785
in the *s* whereof there is a hot Lev 13:24 5785
it be in sight deeper than the *s* Lev 13:25 5785
it be no lower than the other *s* Lev 13:26 5785
it be spread much abroad in the *s* Lev 13:27 5785
his place, and spread not in the *s* Lev 13:28 5785
it be in sight deeper than the *s* Lev 13:30 5785
be not in sight deeper than the *s* Lev 13:31 5785
be not in sight deeper than the *s* Lev 13:32 5785
the scall be not spread in the *s* Lev 13:34 5785
nor be in sight deeper than the *s* Lev 13:34 5785
much in the *s* after his cleansing Lev 13:35 5785
if the scall be spread in the *s* Lev 13:36 5785
the *s* of their flesh bright spots Lev 13:38 5785
if the bright spots in the *s* of Lev 13:39 5785
spot that groweth in the *s* Lev 13:39 5785
appeareth in the *s* of the flesh Lev 13:43 5785
a *s*, or in any thing made of *s* Lev 13:48 5785
in the garment, or in the *s* Lev 13:49 5785
in the woof, or in any thing of *s* Lev 13:49 5785
warp, or in the woof, or in a *s* Lev 13:51 5785
or in any work that is made of *s* Lev 13:51 5785
or in linen, or any thing of *s* Lev 13:52 5785
in the woof, or in any thing of *s* Lev 13:53 5785
of the garment, or out of the *s* Lev 13:56 5785
in the woof, or in any thing of *s* Lev 13:57 5785
or whatsoever thing of *s* it be Lev 13:58 5785
And every garment, and every *s* Lev 15:17 5785
her *s*, and her flesh, and her blood Num 19:5 5785
S for *s*, yea, all that a man Job 2:4 5785
my *s* is broken, and become Job 7:5 5785
Thou hast clothed me with *s* Job 10:11 5785
I have sewed sackcloth upon my *s* Job 16:15 1539
devour the strength of his *s* Job 18:13 5785
My bone cleaveth to my *s* and to my Job 19:20 5785
am escaped with the *s* of my teeth Job 19:20 5785
though after my *s* worms destroy Job 19:26 5785
My *s* is black upon me, and my Job 30:30 5785
thou fill his *s* with barbed irons Job 41:7 5785
groaning my bones cleave to my *s* Ps 102:5 1320
Can the Ethiopian change his *s* Jer 13:23 5785
My flesh and my *s* hath he made old Lam 3:4 5785
their *s* cleaveth to their bones Lam 4:8 5785
Our *s* was black like an oven Lam 5:10 5785
and shod thee with badgers' *s* Eze 16:10
upon you, and cover you with *s* Eze 37:6 5785
them, and the *s* covered them above Eze 37:8 5785
pluck off their *s* from off them Mic 3:2 5785
flay their *s* from off them Mic 3:3 5785
a girdle of a *s* about his loins Mk 1:6 *1193*

SKINS
did the LORD God make coats of *s* Gen 3:21 5785
she put the *s* of the kids of the Gen 27:16 5785
s dyed red, and badgers' *s* Ex 25:5 5785
for the tent of rams' *s* dyed red Ex 26:14 5785
and a covering above of badgers' *s* Ex 26:14 5785
s dyed red, and badgers' *s* Ex 35:7 5785
red *s* of rams, and badgers' *s* Ex 35:23 5785
for the tent of rams' *s* dyed red Ex 36:19 5785
covering of badgers' *s* above that Ex 36:19 5785
the covering of rams' *s* dyed red Ex 39:34 5785
and the covering of badgers' *s* Ex 39:34 5785
warp, or woof, or any thing of *s* Lev 13:59 5785
shall burn in the fire their *s* Lev 16:27 5785
the covering of badgers' *s* Num 4:6 5785
with a covering of badgers' *s* Num 4:8 5785
within a covering of badgers' *s* Num 4:10 5785
it with a covering of badgers' *s* Num 4:11 5785
with a covering of badgers' *s* Num 4:12 5785
upon it a covering of badgers' *s* Num 4:14 5785
badgers' *s* that is above upon it Num 4:25
raiment, and all that is made of *s* Num 31:20 5785

SKIP
maketh them also to *s* like a calf Ps 29:6 7540

SKIPPED
The mountains *s* like rams Ps 114:4 7540
Ye mountains, that ye *s* like rams Ps 114:6 7540

SKIPPEDST
spakest of him, thou *s* for joy Jer 48:27 5110

SKIPPING
the mountains, *s* upon the hills Song 2:8 7092

SKIRT
wife, nor discover his father's *s* Deut 22:30 3671
he uncovereth his father's *s* Deut 27:20 3671
thy *s* over thine handmaid Ruth 3:9 3671
hold upon the *s* of his mantle 1Sa 15:27 3671
cut off the *s* of Saul's robe 1Sa 24:4 3671
because he had cut off Saul's *s* 1Sa 24:5 3671
see the *s* of thy robe in my hand 1Sa 24:11 3671
that I cut off the *s* of thy robe 1Sa 24:11 3671
and I spread my *s* over thee Eze 16:8 3671
flesh in the *s* of his garment Hag 2:12 3671
with his *s* do touch bread, or Hag 2:12 3671
of the *s* of him that is a Jew Zec 8:23 3671

SKIRTS
down to the *s* of his garments Ps 133:2 6310
Also in thy *s* is found the blood Jer 2:34 3671
iniquity are thy *s* discovered Jer 13:22 7757
I discover thy *s* upon thy face Jer 13:26 7757
Her filthiness is in her *s* Lam 1:9 7757
in number, and bind them in thy *s* Eze 5:3 3671
will discover thy *s* upon thy face Nah 3:5 7757

SKULL
head, and all to brake his *s* Judg 9:53 1538
found no more of her than the *s* 2Kin 9:35 1538
that is to say, a place of a *s* Mt 27:33 *2898*
interpreted, The place of a *s* Mk 15:22 *2898*
a place called the place of a *s* Jn 19:17 *2898*

SKY
and in his excellency on the *s* Deut 33:26 7834
thou with him spread out the *s* Job 37:18 7834
for the *s* is red Mt 16:2 *3772*
for the *s* is red and lowring Mt 16:3 *3772*
ye can discern the face of the *s* Mt 16:3 *3772*
ye can discern the face of the *s* Lk 12:56 *3772*
the stars of the *s* in multitude Heb 11:12 *3772*

SLACK
he will not be *s* to him that Deut 7:10 309
God, thou shalt not *s* to pay it Deut 23:21 309
S not thy hand from thy servants Josh 10:6 7503
How long are ye *s* to go to Josh 18:3 7503
s not thy riding for me, except I 2Kin 4:24 6113
poor that dealeth with a *s* hand Prov 10:4 7423
to Zion, Let not thine hands be *s* Zeph 3:16 7503
The Lord is not *s* concerning his 2Pet 3:9 *1019*

SLACKED
Therefore the law is *s*, and Hab 1:4 6313

SLACKNESS
his promise, as some men count *s* 2Pet 3:9 *1022*

SLAIN
for I have *s* a man to my wounding Gen 4:23 2026
The sons of Jacob came upon the *s* Gen 34:27 2491
them in the blood of the *s* bird Lev 14:51 7819
ye shall be *s* before your enemies Lev 26:17 5062
flocks and the herds be *s* for them Num 11:22 7819
therefore he hath *s* them in the Num 14:16 7819
whosoever toucheth one that is *s* Num 19:16 2491
him that touched a bone, or one *s* Num 19:18 2491
me, surely now also I had *s* thee Num 22:33 2026
prey, and drink the blood of the *s* Num 23:24 2491
name of the Israelite that was *s* Num 25:14 5221
even that was *s* with the Num 25:14 5221
woman that was *s* was Cozbi Num 25:15 5221

which was s in the day of the Num 25:18 5221
the rest of them that were s Num 31:8 2491
and whosoever hath touched any s Num 31:19 2491
After he had s Sihon the king of Deut 1:4 5221
If one be found s in the land Deut 21:1 2491
and it be not known who hath s him Deut 21:1 2491
are round about him that is s Deut 21:2 2491
city which is next unto the s man Deut 21:3 2491
that are next unto the s man Deut 21:6 2491
ox shall be s before thine eyes Deut 28:31 2873
and that with the blood of the s Deut 32:42 2491
them up all s before Israel Josh 11:6 2491
among them that were s by them Josh 13:22 2491
have s his sons, threescore and Judg 9:18 2026
of an ass have I s a thousand men Judg 15:16 5221
husband of the woman that was s Judg 20:4 7523
by night, and thought to have s me Judg 20:5 2026
Eli, Hophni and Phinehas, were s 1Sa 4:11 4191
Saul hath s his thousands, and 1Sa 18:7 5221
LORD liveth, he shall not be s 1Sa 19:6 4191
night, to morrow thou shalt be s 1Sa 19:11 4191
unto him, Wherefore shall he be s 1Sa 20:32 4191
Saul hath s his thousands, and 1Sa 21:11 5221
Saul had s the LORD's priests 1Sa 22:21 2026
fell down s in mount Gilboa 1Sa 31:1 2491
Philistines came to strip the s 1Sa 31:8 2491
I have s the LORD's anointed 2Sa 1:16 4191
Israel is s upon thy high places 2Sa 1:19 2491
From the blood of the s, from the 2Sa 1:22 2491
thou wast s in thine high places 2Sa 1:25 2491
because he had s their brother 2Sa 3:30 4191
more, when wicked men have s a 2Sa 4:11 2026
hast s him with the sword of the 2Sa 12:9 2026
Absalom hath s all the king's 2Sa 13:30 5221
s all the young men the king's 2Sa 13:32 4191
s before the servants of David 2Sa 18:7 5062
Philistines had s Saul in Gilboa 2Sa 21:12 5221
sword, thought to have s David 2Sa 21:16 5221
And he hath s oxen and fat cattle 1Kin 1:19 2076
down this day, and hath s oxen 1Kin 1:25 2076
s the Canaanites that dwelt in 1Kin 9:16 2026
host was gone up to bury the s 1Kin 11:15 2491
s him, according to the word of 1Kin 13:26 4191
and hath also s the king 1Kin 16:16 5221
withal how he had s all the 1Kin 19:1 2026
s thy prophets with the sword 1Kin 19:10 2026
s thy prophets with the sword 1Kin 19:14 2026
the kings are surely s, and they 2Kin 3:23 2717
the king's sons which were s 2Kin 11:2 4191
Athaliah, so that he was not s 2Kin 11:2 4191
within the ranges, let him be s 2Kin 11:8 4191
Let her not be s in the house of 2Kin 11:15 4191
and there was she s 2Kin 11:16 4191
which had s the king his father 2Kin 14:5 5221
For there fell down many s 1Chr 5:22 2491
fell down s in mount Gilboa 1Chr 10:1 2491
Philistines came to strip the s 1Chr 10:8 2491
hundred s by him at one time 1Chr 11:11 2491
so there fell down s of Israel 2Chr 13:17 2491
also hast s thy brethren of thy 2Chr 21:13 2026
to the camp had s all the eldest 2Chr 22:1 2026
and when they had s him, they 2Chr 22:9 4191
among the king's sons that were s 2Chr 22:11 4191
let him be s with the sword 2Chr 23:14 4191
after that they had s Athaliah 2Chr 23:21 4191
ye have s them in a rage that 2Chr 28:9 2026
people, to be destroyed, to be s Est 7:4 2026
were s in Shushan the palace was Est 9:11 2026
Esther the queen, The Jews have s Est 9:12 2026
they have s the servants with the Job 1:15 5221
s the servants with the edge of Job 1:17 5221
and where the s are, there is she Job 39:30 2491
ye shall be s all of you Ps 62:3 7523
like the s that lie in the grave, Ps 88:5 2491
Rahab in pieces, as one that is s Ps 89:10 2491
strong men have been s by her Prov 7:26 2026
I shall be s in the streets Prov 22:13 7523
and those that are ready to be s Prov 24:11 2027
and they shall fall under the s Is 10:4 2026
the raiment of those that are s Is 14:19 2026
thy land, and s thy people Is 14:20 2026
thy s men are not s with the Is 22:2 2491
and shall no more cover her s Is 26:21 2026
or is he s according to the Is 27:7 2026
of them that are s by him Is 27:7 2026
Their s also shall be cast out, Is 34:3 2491
the s of the LORD shall be many Is 66:16 2491
night for the s of the daughter Jer 9:1 2491
then behold the s with the sword Jer 14:18 2491
men be s by the sword in battle Jer 18:21 5221
the s of the LORD shall be at Jer 25:33 2491
whom I have s in mine anger and in Jer 33:5 5221
day after he had s Gedaliah Jer 41:4 4191
whom he had s because of Gedaliah Jer 41:9 5221
filled it with them that were s Jer 41:9 2491
after that he had s Gedaliah the Jer 41:16 5221
the son of Nethaniah had s Jer 41:18 5221
Thus the s shall fall in the land Jer 51:4 2491
all her s shall fall in the midst Jer 51:47 2491
caused the s of Israel to fall Jer 51:49 2491
shall fall the s of all the earth Jer 51:49 2491
the prophet be s in the sanctuary Lam 2:20 2026
thou hast s them in the day of Lam 2:21 2026
thou hast s, thou hast not pitied Lam 3:43 2026
They that be s with the sword are Lam 4:9 2491
than they that be s with hunger Lam 4:9 2491
down your s men before your idols Eze 6:4 2491
the s shall fall in the midst of Eze 6:7 2491
when their s men shall be among Eze 6:13 2491
and fill the courts with the s Eze 9:7 2491
multiplied your s in this city Eze 11:6 2491
the streets thereof with the s Eze 11:6 2491
Your s whom ye have laid in the Eze 11:7 2491
That thou hast s my children Eze 16:21 7819
third time, the sword of the s Eze 21:14 2491
sword of the great men that are s Eze 21:14 2491
upon the necks of them that are s Eze 21:29 2491
For when they had s their Eze 23:39 7819
the field shall be s by the sword Eze 26:6 2026
are s in the midst of the seas Eze 28:8 2491
when the s shall fall in Egypt, Eze 30:4 2491
and fill the land with the s Eze 30:11 2491
them that be s with the sword Eze 31:17 2491
with them that be s by the sword Eze 31:18 2491
of them that are s by the sword Eze 32:20 2491
lie uncircumcised, s by the sword Eze 32:21 2491
all of them s, fallen by the Eze 32:22 2491
all of them s, fallen by the Eze 32:23 2491
about her grave, all of them s Eze 32:24 2491
of the s with all her multitude Eze 32:25 2491
uncircumcised, s by the sword Eze 32:25 2491
in the midst of them that be s Eze 32:25 2491
s by the sword, though they Eze 32:26 2490
them that are s with the sword Eze 32:28 2491
by them that were s by the sword Eze 32:29 2491
which are gone down with the s Eze 32:30 2491
with them that be s by the sword Eze 32:30 2491
and all his army s by the sword Eze 32:31 2491
them that are s with the sword Eze 32:32 2491
fill his mountains with his s men Eze 35:8 2491
fall that are s with the sword Eze 35:8 2491
O breath, and breathe upon these s Eze 37:9 2026
that the wise men should be s Dan 2:13 6992
Daniel and his fellows to be s Dan 2:13 6992
the king of the Chaldeans s Dan 5:30 6992
beheld even till the beast was s Dan 7:11 6992
and many shall fall down s Dan 11:26 2491
I have s them by the words of my Hos 6:5 2026
young men have I s with the sword Amos 4:10 2026
and there is a multitude of s Nah 3:3 2491
also, ye shall be s by my sword Zeph 2:12 2491
chief priests and scribes, and be s Lk 9:22 615
wicked hands have crucified and s Acts 2:23 337
who was s; and all Acts 5:36 337
have ye offered to me s beasts Acts 7:42 4968
they have s them which shewed Acts 7:52 615
they Pilate that he should be s Acts 13:28 337
eat nothing until we have s Paul Acts 23:14 615
having s the enmity thereby Eph 2:16 615
tempted, were s with the sword Heb 11:37 615
who was s among you, where Satan Rev 2:13 615
stood a Lamb as it had been s Rev 5:6 4969
for thou wast s, and hast redeemed Rev 5:9 4969
Lamb that was s to receive power Rev 5:12 4969
that were s for the word of God Rev 6:9 4969
were s of men seven thousand Rev 11:13 615
Lamb s from the foundation of the Rev 13:8 4969
of all that were s upon the earth Rev 18:24 4969
the remnant were s with the sword Rev 19:21 615

SLANDER
by bringing up a s upon the land Num 14:36 1681
For I have heard the s of many Ps 31:13 1681
lips, and he that uttereth a s Prov 10:18 1681

SLANDERED
he hath s thy servant unto my 2Sa 19:27 7270

SLANDERERS
must their wives be grave, not s 1Ti 3:11 1228

SLANDEREST
thou s thine own mother's son Ps 50:20

SLANDERETH
Whoso privily s his neighbour Ps 101:5 3960

SLANDEROUSLY
not rather, (as we be s reported Rom 3:8 987

SLANDERS
revolters, walking with s Jer 6:28 7400
every neighbour will walk with s Jer 9:4 7400

SLANG
s it, and smote the Philistine in 1Sa 17:49 7049

SLAUGHTER
return from the s of Chedorlaomer Gen 14:17 5221
them with a great s at Gibeon Josh 10:10 4347
slaying them with a very great s Josh 10:20 4347
vineyards, with a very great s Judg 11:33 4347
them hip and thigh with a great s Judg 15:8 4347
and there was a very great s 1Sa 4:10 4347
also a great s among the people 1Sa 4:17 4046
many of the people with a great s 1Sa 6:19 4347
And that first s, which Jonathan 1Sa 14:14 4347
greater s among the Philistines 1Sa 14:30 4347
from the s of the Philistine 1Sa 17:57 5221
from the s of the Philistine 1Sa 18:6 5221
and slew them with a great s 1Sa 19:8 4347
and smote them with a great s 1Sa 23:5 4347
from the s of the Amalekites 2Sa 1:1 5221
There is a s among the people 2Sa 17:9 4046
there was there a great s that 2Sa 18:7 4046
slew the Syrians with a great s 1Kin 20:21 4347
people slew them with a great s 2Chr 13:17 4347
come from the s of the Edomites 2Chr 25:14 5221
who smote him with a great s 2Chr 28:5 4347
the stroke of the sword, and s Est 9:5 2027
we are counted as sheep for the s Ps 44:22 2878
as an ox goeth to the s, or as a Prov 7:22 2875
for him according to the s of Is 10:26 4347
Prepare s for his children for Is 14:21 4293
s of them that are slain by him Is 27:7 2027
waters in the day of the great s Is 30:25 2027
he hath delivered them to the s Is 34:2 2875
a great s in the land of Idumea Is 34:6 2875
he is brought as a lamb to the s Is 53:7 2875
and ye shall all bow down to the s Is 65:12 2875
of Hinnom, but the valley of s Jer 7:32 2028
or an ox that is brought to the s Jer 11:19 2873
them out like sheep for the s Jer 12:3 2873
and prepare them for the day of s Jer 12:3 2028
of Hinnom, but The valley of s Jer 19:6 2028
for the days of your s and of your Jer 25:34 2873
young men are gone down to the s Jer 48:15 2875
let them go down to the s Jer 50:27 2875
them down like lambs to the s Jer 51:40 2873
every man a s weapon in his hand Eze 9:2 4660
It is sharpened to make a sore s Eze 21:10 2873
it is wrapped up for the s Eze 21:15 2875
to open the mouth in the s Eze 21:22 7524
for the s it is furbished, to Eze 21:28 2875
when the s is made in the midst Eze 26:15 2027
revolters are profound to make s Hos 5:2 7819
mount of Esau may be cut off by s Obad 9 6993
Feed the flock of the s Zec 11:4 2028
And I will feed the flock of s Zec 11:7 2028
He was led as a sheep to the s Acts 8:32 4967
s against the disciples of the Acts 9:1 5408
are accounted as sheep for the s Rom 8:36 4967
returning from the s of the kings Heb 7:1 2871
your hearts, as in a day of s Jas 5:5 4967

SLAVE
is he a homeborn s Jer 2:14

SLAVES
and horses, and chariots, and s Rev 18:13 4983

SLAY
one that findeth me shall s me Gen 4:14 2026
to s the righteous with the Gen 18:25 4191
wilt thou s also a righteous Gen 20:4 2026
they will s me for my wife's sake Gen 20:11 2026
and took the knife to s his son Gen 22:10 7819
then will I s my brother Jacob Gen 27:41 2026
together against me, and s me Gen 34:30 5221
conspired against him to s him Gen 37:18 4191
now therefore, and let us s him Gen 37:20 2026
profit is it if we s our brother Gen 37:26 2026
S my two sons, if I bring him not Gen 42:37 4191
house, Bring these men home, and s Gen 43:16 2875
this thing, he sought to s Moses Ex 2:15 2026
I will s thy son, even thy Ex 4:23 2026
put a sword in their hand to s us Ex 5:21 2026
neighbour, to s him with guile Ex 21:14 2026
innocent and righteous s thou not Ex 23:7 2026
And thou shalt s the ram, and thou Ex 29:16 7819
to s them in the mountains, and to Ex 32:12 2026
s every man his brother, and every Ex 32:27 2026
s the sin offering in the place Lev 4:29 7819
s it for a sin offering in the Lev 4:33 7819
he shall s the lamb in the place Lev 14:13 7819
and ye shall s the beast Lev 20:15 2026
one shall s her before his face Num 19:3 7819
S ye every one his men that were Num 25:5 2026
himself shall s the murderer Num 35:19 4191
he meeteth him, he shall s him Num 35:19 4191
of blood shall s the murderer Num 35:21 4191
out to s them in the wilderness Deut 9:28 4191
because the way is long, and s him Deut 19:6 5221
reward to s an innocent person Deut 27:25 5221
did the children of Israel s with Josh 13:22 2026
them alive, I would not s you Judg 8:19 2026
his firstborn, Up, and s them Judg 8:20 2026
s me, that men say not of me, A Judg 9:54 4191
because the LORD would s them 1Sa 2:25 4191
the God of Israel to us, to s us 1Sa 5:10 4191
his own place, that it s us not 1Sa 5:11 4191
his sheep, and s them here, and eat 1Sa 14:34 7819
but s both man and woman, infant 1Sa 15:3 4191
to s David without a cause 1Sa 19:5 4191
him, and to s him in the morning 1Sa 19:11 4191
me in the bed, that I may s him 1Sa 19:15 4191
be in me iniquity, s me thyself 1Sa 20:8 4191
of his father to s David 1Sa 20:33 4191
s the priests of the LORD 1Sa 22:17 4191
I pray thee, upon me, and s me 2Sa 1:9 4191
king to s Abner the son of Ner 2Sa 3:37 4191
Saul sought to s them in his zeal 2Sa 21:2 5221
not s his servant with the sword 1Kin 1:51 4191
living child, and in no wise s it 1Kin 3:26 4191
living child, and in no wise s it 1Kin 3:27 4191
king of Judah did Baasha s him 1Kin 15:28 4191
to remembrance, and to s my son 1Kin 17:18 4191
into the hand of Ahab, to s me 1Kin 18:9 4191
cannot find thee, he shall s me 1Kin 18:12 2026
and he shall s me 1Kin 18:14 2026
the sword of Hazael shall Jehu s 1Kin 19:17 4191
the sword of Jehu shall Elisha s 1Kin 19:17 4191
from me, a lion shall s thee 1Kin 20:36 5221
men wilt thou s with the sword 2Kin 8:12 2026
to the captains, Go in, and s them 2Kin 10:25 5221
them, and, behold, they s them 2Kin 17:26 4191
of mount Seir, utterly to s 2Chr 20:23 2763
S her not in the house of the 2Chr 23:14 4191
s them, and cause the work to Neh 4:11 2026
for they will come to s thee Neh 6:10 2026
night will they come to s thee Neh 6:10 2026
for their life, to destroy, to s Est 8:11 2026
If the scourge s suddenly Job 9:23 4191
Though he s me, yet will I trust Job 13:15 6991
the viper's tongue shall s him Job 20:16 2026
Evil shall s the wicked Ps 34:21 4191
to s such as be of upright Ps 37:14 2873
righteous, and seeketh to s him Ps 37:32 4191
S them not, lest my people forget Ps 59:11 2026
They s the widow and the stranger, Ps 94:6 2026
that he might even s the broken Ps 109:16 4191
Surely thou wilt s the wicked Ps 139:19 6991
away of the simple shall s them Prov 1:32 2026
of his lips shall he s the wicked Is 11:4 4191
famine, and he shall s thy remnant Is 14:30 2026
he shall s the dragon that is in Is 27:1 2026
for the Lord GOD shall s thee Is 65:15 4191

out of the forest shall *s* them	Jer 5:6	5221
the sword to *s*, and the dogs to	Jer 15:3	2026
their counsel against me to *s* me	Jer 18:23	1194
shall *s* them with the sword	Jer 20:4	5221
he shall *s* them before your eyes	Jer 29:21	5221
the son of Nethaniah to *s* thee	Jer 40:14	
I will *s* Ishmael the son of	Jer 40:15	5221
wherefore should he *s* thee	Jer 40:15	5221
that said unto Ishmael, *S* us not	Jer 41:8	4191
S all her bullocks	Jer 50:27	2717
S utterly old and young, both	Eze 9:6	2026
to *s* the souls that should not	Eze 13:19	4191
they shall *s* their sons and their	Eze 23:47	4191
He shall *s* with the sword thy	Eze 26:8	4191
he shall *s* thy people by the	Eze 26:11	4191
to *s* thereon the burnt offering	Eze 40:39	7819
they shall *s* the burnt offering	Eze 44:11	7819
to *s* the wise men of Babylon	Dan 2:14	6992
a dry land, and *s* her with thirst	Hos 2:3	4191
yet will I *s* even the beloved	Hos 9:16	4191
will *s* all the princes thereof	Amos 2:3	2026
I will *s* the last of them with	Amos 9:1	2026
the sword, and it shall *s* them	Amos 9:4	2026
continually to *s* the nations	Hab 1:17	2026
Whose possessors *s* them, and hold	Zec 11:5	2026
and some of them they shall *s*	Lk 11:49	*615*
bring hither, and *s* them before me	Lk 19:27	*2695*
Jesus, and sought to *s* him	Jn 5:16	*615*
heart, and took counsel to *s* them	Acts 5:33	*337*
but they went about to *s* him	Acts 9:29	*337*
s and eat	Acts 11:7	*2380*
for to *s* the third part of men	Rev 9:15	*615*

SLAYER

that the *s* may flee thither,	Num 35:11	7523
shall judge between the *s*	Num 35:24	5221
congregation shall deliver the *s*	Num 35:25	7523
But if the *s* shall at any time	Num 35:26	7523
the revenger of blood kill the *s*	Num 35:27	7523
death of the high priest the *s*	Num 35:28	7523
That the *s* might flee thither,	Deut 4:42	7523
that every *s* may flee thither	Deut 19:3	7523
And this is the case of the *s*	Deut 19:4	7523
avenger of the blood pursue the *s*	Deut 19:6	7523
That the *s* that killeth any	Josh 20:3	7523
deliver the *s* up into his hand	Josh 20:5	7523
then shall the *s* return, and come	Josh 20:6	7523
to be a city of refuge for the *s*	Josh 21:13	7523
to be a city of refuge for the *s*	Josh 21:21	7523
to be a city of refuge for the *s*	Josh 21:27	7523
to be a city of refuge for the *s*	Josh 21:32	7523
to be a city of refuge for the *s*	Josh 21:38	7523
to give it into the hand of the *s*	Eze 21:11	2026

SLAYETH

him, Therefore whosoever *s* Cain	Gen 4:15	2026
s him, even so is this matter	Deut 22:26	
man, and envy *s* the silly one	Job 5:2	4191
yet say before him that *s* thee	Eze 28:9	2026
in the hand of him that *s* thee	Eze 28:9	2490

SLAYING

of *s* all the inhabitants of Ai in	Josh 8:24	2026
end of *s* them with a very great	Josh 10:20	5221
in *s* his seventy brethren	Judg 9:56	2026
with whom I sojourn, by *s* her son	1Kin 17:20	4191
s oxen, and killing sheep, eating	Is 22:13	2026
s the children in the valleys	Is 57:5	7819
to pass, while they were *s* them	Eze 9:8	5221

SLEEP

caused a deep *s* to fall upon Adam	Gen 2:21	3462
down, a deep *s* fell upon Abram	Gen 15:12	8639
and lay down in that place to *s*	Gen 28:11	7901
And Jacob awaked out of his *s*	Gen 28:16	8142
my *s* departed from mine eyes	Gen 31:40	8142
wherein shall he *s*	Ex 22:27	7901
thou shalt not *s* with his pledge	Deut 24:12	7901
that he may *s* in his own raiment,	Deut 24:13	7901
thou shalt *s* with thy fathers	Deut 31:16	7901
And he awaked out of his *s*	Judg 16:14	8142
she made him *s* upon her knees	Judg 16:19	3462
And he awoke out of his *s*, and said	Judg 16:20	8142
was, and Samuel was laid down to *s*	1Sa 3:3	
because a deep *s* from the LORD	1Sa 26:12	8639
thou shalt *s* with thy fathers, I	2Sa 7:12	7901
the king shall *s* with his fathers	1Kin 1:21	7901
that night could not the king *s*	Est 6:1	8142
when deep *s* falleth on men,	Job 4:13	8639
for now shall I *s* in the dust	Job 7:21	7901
nor be raised out of their *s*	Job 14:12	8142
when deep *s* falleth upon men, in	Job 33:15	
both lay me down in peace, and *s*	Ps 4:8	3462
lest I *s* the *s* of death	Ps 13:3	3462
spoiled, they have slept their *s*	Ps 76:5	8142
and horse are cast into a dead *s*	Ps 76:6	7290
the Lord awaked as one out of *s*	Ps 78:65	3463
they are as a *s*	Ps 90:5	8142
shall neither slumber nor *s*	Ps 121:4	3462
for so he giveth his beloved *s*	Ps 127:2	8142
I will not give *s* to mine eyes	Ps 132:4	8142
lie down, and thy *s* shall be sweet	Prov 3:24	8142
For they *s* not, except they have	Prov 4:16	3462
their *s* is taken away, unless	Prov 4:16	8142
Give not *s* to thine eyes, nor	Prov 6:4	8142
How long wilt thou *s*, O sluggard	Prov 6:9	7901
when wilt thou arise out of thy *s*	Prov 6:9	8142
Yet a little *s*, a little slumber,	Prov 6:10	8142
little folding of the hands to *s*	Prov 6:10	7901
casteth into a deep *s*	Prov 19:15	3462
Love not *s*, lest thou come to	Prov 20:13	8142
Yet a little *s*, a little slumber,	Prov 24:33	8142
little folding of the hands to *s*	Prov 24:33	7901
The *s* of a labouring man is sweet	Eccl 5:12	8142
the rich will not suffer him to *s*	Eccl 5:12	3462
nor night seeth *s* with his eyes	Eccl 8:16	8142
I *s*, but my heart waketh	Song 5:2	3463
none shall slumber nor *s*	Is 5:27	3463
out upon you the spirit of deep *s*	Is 29:10	8639
and my *s* was sweet unto me	Jer 31:26	8142
they may rejoice, and *s*	Jer 51:39	3462
a perpetual *s*, and not wake	Jer 51:39	8142
they shall *s* a perpetual *s*,	Jer 51:57	3462
and they shall *s* a perpetual *s*	Jer 51:57	8142
the wilderness, and *s* in the woods	Eze 34:25	3462
troubled, and his *s* brake from him	Dan 2:1	8142
and his *s* went from him	Dan 6:18	8139
I was in a deep *s* on my face	Dan 8:18	7290
then was I in a deep *s* on my face	Dan 10:9	7290
many of them that *s* in the dust	Dan 12:2	3463
man that is wakened out of his *s*	Zec 4:1	8142
s did as the angel of the Lord	Mt 1:24	*5258*
S on now, and take your rest	Mt 26:45	*2518*
And should *s*, and rise night and day	Mk 4:27	*2518*
S on now, and take your rest	Mk 14:41	*2518*
were with him were heavy with *s*	Lk 9:32	*5258*
And said unto them, Why *s* ye	Lk 22:46	*2518*
go, that I may awake him out of *s*	Jn 11:11	*1852*
said his disciples, Lord, if he *s*	Jn 11:12	*2837*
had spoken of taking of rest in *s*	Jn 11:13	*5258*
by the will of God, fell on *s*	Acts 13:36	*2837*
the prison awaking out of his *s*	Acts 16:27	*1853*
being fallen into a deep *s*	Acts 20:9	*5258*
preaching, he sunk down with *s*	Acts 20:9	*5258*
it is high time to awake out of *s*	Rom 13:11	*5258*
and sickly among you, and many *s*	1Cor 11:30	*2837*
We shall not all *s*, but we shall	1Cor 15:51	*2837*
even so them also which *s* in	1Th 4:14	*2837*
Therefore let us not *s*, as do	1Th 5:6	*2518*
they that *s* *s* in the night	1Th 5:7	*2518*
us, that, whether we wake or *s*	1Th 5:10	*2518*

SLEEPER

unto him, What meanest thou, O *s*	Jonah 1:6	7290

SLEEPEST

Awake, why *s* thou, O Lord	Ps 44:23	3462
when thou *s*, it shall keep thee	Prov 6:22	7901
saith unto Peter, Simon, *s* thou	Mk 14:37	*2518*
he saith, Awake thou that *s*	Eph 5:14	*2518*

SLEEPETH

a journey, or peradventure he *s*	1Kin 18:27	3463
but he that *s* in harvest is a son	Prov 10:5	7290
their baker *s* all the night	Hos 7:6	3463
for the maid is not dead, but *s*	Mt 9:24	*2518*
the damsel is not dead, but *s*	Mk 5:39	*2518*
she is not dead, but *s*	Lk 8:52	*2518*
unto them, Our friend Lazarus *s*	Jn 11:11	*2837*

SLEEPING

Saul lay *s* within the trench, and	1Sa 26:7	3463
s, lying down, loving to slumber	Is 56:10	1957
coming suddenly he find you *s*	Mk 13:36	*2518*
And he cometh, and findeth them *s*	Mk 14:37	*2518*
he found them *s* for sorrow	Lk 22:45	*2837*
Peter was *s* between two soldiers	Acts 12:6	*2837*

SLEIGHT

wind of doctrine, by the *s* of men	Eph 4:14	*2940*

SLEPT

sleep to fall upon Adam, and he *s*	Gen 2:21	3462
And he *s* and dreamed the second	Gen 41:5	3462
But Uriah *s* at the door of the	2Sa 11:9	7901
So David *s* with his fathers, and	1Kin 2:10	7901
beside me, while thine handmaid *s*	1Kin 3:20	3463
that David *s* with his fathers	1Kin 11:21	7901
Solomon *s* with his fathers, and	1Kin 11:43	7901
he *s* with his fathers, and Nadab	1Kin 14:20	7901
Rehoboam *s* with his fathers, and	1Kin 14:31	7901
Abijam *s* with his fathers	1Kin 15:8	7901
Asa *s* with his fathers, and was	1Kin 15:24	7901
So Baasha *s* with his fathers, and	1Kin 16:6	7901
So Omri *s* with his fathers, and	1Kin 16:28	7901
s under a juniper tree, behold,	1Kin 19:5	3462
So Ahab *s* with his fathers	1Kin 22:40	7901
Jehoshaphat *s* with his fathers,	1Kin 22:50	7901
Joram *s* with his fathers, and was	2Kin 8:24	7901
And Jehu *s* with his fathers	2Kin 10:35	7901
Jehoahaz *s* with his fathers	2Kin 13:9	7901
And Joash *s* with his fathers	2Kin 13:13	7901
Jehoash *s* with his fathers, and	2Kin 14:16	7901
that the king *s* with his fathers	2Kin 14:22	7901
Jeroboam *s* with his fathers, even	2Kin 14:29	7901
So Azariah *s* with his fathers	2Kin 15:7	7901
Menahem *s* with his fathers	2Kin 15:22	7901
Jotham *s* with his fathers, and was	2Kin 15:38	7901
Ahaz *s* with his fathers, and was	2Kin 16:20	7901
Hezekiah *s* with his fathers	2Kin 20:21	7901
Manasseh *s* with his fathers, and	2Kin 21:18	7901
So Jehoiakim *s* with his fathers	2Kin 24:6	7901
Solomon *s* with his fathers, and he	2Chr 9:31	7901
Rehoboam *s* with his fathers, and	2Chr 12:16	7901
So Abijah *s* with his fathers, and	2Chr 14:1	7901
Asa *s* with his fathers, and died	2Chr 16:13	7901
Now Jehoshaphat *s* with his	2Chr 21:1	7901
that the king *s* with his fathers	2Chr 26:2	7901
So Uzziah *s* with his fathers, and	2Chr 26:23	7901
Jotham *s* with his fathers, and	2Chr 27:9	7901
Ahaz *s* with his fathers, and they	2Chr 28:27	7901
Hezekiah *s* with his fathers, and	2Chr 32:33	7901
So Manasseh *s* with his fathers,	2Chr 33:20	7901
and been quiet, I should have *s*	Job 3:13	3462
I laid me down and *s*	Ps 3:5	3462
spoiled, they have *s* their sleep	Ps 76:5	5123
But while men *s*, his enemy came	Mt 13:25	*2518*
tarried, they all slumbered and *s*	Mt 25:5	*2518*
of the saints which *s* arose	Mt 27:52	*2837*
and stole him away while we *s*	Mt 28:13	*2837*
the firstfruits of them that *s*	1Cor 15:20	*2837*

SLEW

Abel his brother, and *s* him	Gen 4:8	2026
seed instead of Abel, whom Cain *s*	Gen 4:25	2026
city boldly, and *s* all the males	Gen 34:25	2026
they *s* Hamor and Shechem his son	Gen 34:26	2026
and the LORD *s* him	Gen 38:7	4191
wherefore he *s* him also	Gen 38:10	4191
for in their anger they *s* a man	Gen 49:6	2026
he *s* the Egyptian, and hid him in	Ex 2:12	5221
that the LORD *s* all the firstborn	Ex 13:15	2026
And he *s* it	Lev 8:15	7819
And he *s* it	Lev 8:23	7819
s the calf of the sin offering,	Lev 9:8	7819
And he *s* the burnt offering	Lev 9:12	7819
s it, and offered it for sin, as	Lev 9:15	7819
He *s* also the bullock and the ram	Lev 9:18	7819
and they *s* all the males	Num 31:7	2026
they *s* the kings of Midian,	Num 31:8	2026
son of Beor they *s* with the sword	Num 31:8	2026
turned again, and *s* the men of Ai	Josh 8:21	5221
of Israel, that they *s* them not	Josh 9:26	2026
s them with a great slaughter at	Josh 10:10	5221
of Israel *s* with the sword	Josh 10:11	2026
s them, and hanged them on five	Josh 10:26	4191
he took, and smote them, and *s* them	Josh 11:17	4191
they *s* of them in Bezek ten	Judg 1:4	5221
they *s* the Canaanites and the	Judg 1:5	5221
they *s* Sheshai, and Ahiman, and	Judg 1:10	5221
they *s* the Canaanites that	Judg 1:17	5221
they *s* of Moab at that time about	Judg 3:29	5221
which *s* of the Philistines six	Judg 3:31	5221
they *s* Oreb upon the rock Oreb,	Judg 7:25	2026
Zeeb they *s* at the winepress of	Judg 7:25	2026
Penuel, and *s* the men of the city	Judg 8:17	2026
men were they whom ye *s* at Tabor	Judg 8:18	2026
s Zebah and Zalmunna	Judg 8:21	2026
s his brethren the sons of	Judg 9:5	2026
their brother, which *s* them	Judg 9:24	2026
were in the fields, and *s* them	Judg 9:44	5221
s the people that was therein, and	Judg 9:45	2026
men say not of me, A woman *s* him	Judg 9:54	2026
s him at the passages of Jordan	Judg 12:6	7819
s thirty men of them, and took	Judg 14:19	5221
s a thousand men therewith	Judg 15:15	5221
our country, which *s* many of us	Judg 16:24	2491
So the dead which he *s* at his	Judg 16:30	4191
than they which he *s* in his life	Judg 16:30	4191
s two thousand men of them	Judg 20:45	5221
they *s* a bullock, and brought the	1Sa 1:25	7819
they *s* of the army in the field	1Sa 4:2	5221
s the Ammonites until the heat of	1Sa 11:11	5221
and his armourbearer *s* after him	1Sa 14:13	4191
calves, and *s* them on the ground	1Sa 14:32	7819
him that night, and *s* them there	1Sa 14:34	7819
his beard, and smote him, and *s* him	1Sa 17:35	4191
Thy servant *s* both the lion and	1Sa 17:36	5221
and smote the Philistine, and *s* him	1Sa 17:50	4191
s him, and cut off his head	1Sa 17:51	4191
s of the Philistines two hundred	1Sa 18:27	5221
s the Philistine, and the LORD	1Sa 19:5	5221
s them with a great slaughter	1Sa 19:8	5221
s on that day fourscore and five	1Sa 22:18	4191
Saul *s* his thousands, and David	1Sa 29:5	5221
they *s* not any, either great or	1Sa 30:2	4191
and the Philistines *s* Jonathan	1Sa 31:2	5221
s him, because I was sure that he	2Sa 1:10	4191
and Abishai his brother *s* Abner	2Sa 3:30	2026
s him, and beheaded him, and took	2Sa 4:7	4191
s him in Ziklag, who thought that	2Sa 4:10	2026
his young men, and they *s* them	2Sa 4:12	2026
David *s* of the Syrians two and	2Sa 8:5	5221
David *s* the men of seven hundred	2Sa 10:18	2126
the one smote the other, and *s* him	2Sa 14:6	4191
the life of his brother whom he *s*	2Sa 14:7	2026
about and smote Absalom, and *s* him	2Sa 18:15	4191
because he *s* the Gibeonites	2Sa 21:1	4191
Sibbechai the Hushathite *s* Saph	2Sa 21:18	5221
s the brother of Goliath the	2Sa 21:19	5221
the brother of David *s* him	2Sa 21:21	5221
hundred, whom he *s* at one time	2Sa 23:8	2491
defended it, and *s* the Philistines	2Sa 23:12	5221
s them, and had the name among	2Sa 23:18	2491
he *s* two lionlike men of Moab	2Sa 23:20	5221
s a lion in the midst of a pit in	2Sa 23:20	5221
he *s* an Egyptian, a goodly man	2Sa 23:21	2026
hand, and *s* him with his own spear	2Sa 23:21	5221
And Adonijah *s* sheep and oxen and	1Kin 1:9	2076
the son of Jether, whom he *s*	1Kin 2:5	2026
s them with the sword, my father	1Kin 2:32	2026
up, and fell upon him, and *s* him	1Kin 2:34	4191
when David *s* them of Zobah	1Kin 11:24	2026
lion met him by the way, and *s* him	1Kin 13:24	4191
that he *s* all the house of Baasha	1Kin 16:11	5221
s the prophets of the LORD	1Kin 18:13	2026
the brook Kishon, and *s* them there	1Kin 18:40	7819
s them, and boiled their flesh	1Kin 19:21	2076
And they *s* every one his man	1Kin 20:20	5221
s the Syrians with a great	1Kin 20:21	5221
the children of Israel *s* of the	1Kin 20:29	5221
him, a lion found him, and *s* him	1Kin 20:36	5221
Had Zimri peace, who *s* his master	2Kin 9:31	2026
s seventy persons, and put their	2Kin 10:7	7819
against my master, and *s* him	2Kin 10:9	2026
but who *s* all these	2Kin 10:9	5221
So Jehu *s* all that remained of	2Kin 10:11	5221
s them at the pit of the shearing	2Kin 10:14	7819
he *s* all that remained unto Ahab	2Kin 10:17	5221
s Mattan the priest of Baal	2Kin 11:18	2026
they *s* Athaliah with the sword	2Kin 11:20	4191
s Joash in the house of Millo	2Kin 12:20	5221
that he *s* his servants which had	2Kin 14:5	5221
of the murderers he *s* not	2Kin 14:6	4191
He *s* of Edom in the valley of	2Kin 14:7	5221
him to Lachish, and *s* him there	2Kin 14:19	4191

s him, and reigned in his stead 2Kin 15:10 4191
s him, and reigned in his stead 2Kin 15:14 4191
s him, and reigned in his stead 2Kin 15:30 4191
of it captive to Kir, and *s* Rezin 2Kin 16:9 4191
among them, which *s* some of them 2Kin 17:25 2026
s the king in his own house 2Kin 21:23 4191
the people of the land *s* all them 2Kin 21:24 5221
he *s* all the priests of the high 2Kin 23:20 2076
he *s* him at Megiddo, when he had 2Kin 23:29 4191
they *s* the sons of Zedekiah 2Kin 25:7 7819
s them at Riblah in the land of 2Kin 25:21 4191
and he *s* him 1Chr 2:3 4191
that were born in that land *s* 1Chr 7:21 2026
and the Philistines *s* Jonathan 1Chr 10:2 5221
therefore he *s* him, and turned the 1Chr 10:14 4191
it, and *s* the Philistines 1Chr 11:14 5221
he *s* them, and had a name among 1Chr 11:20 2490
he *s* two lionlike men of Moab 1Chr 11:22 5221
s a lion in a pit in a snowy day 1Chr 11:22 5221
he *s* an Egyptian, a man of great 1Chr 11:23 5221
hand, and *s* him with his own spear 1Chr 11:23 2026
David *s* of the Syrians two and 1Chr 18:5 5221
Abishai the son Zeruiah *s* of the 1Chr 18:12 5221
David *s* of the Syrians seven 1Chr 19:18 2026
Sibbechai the Hushathite *s* Sippai 1Chr 20:4 5221
Elhanan the son of Jair *s* Lahmi 1Chr 20:5 5221
of Shimea David's brother *s* him 1Chr 20:7 5221
his people *s* them with a great 2Chr 13:17 5221
s all his brethren with the sword 2Chr 21:4 2026
ministered to Ahaziah, he *s* them 2Chr 22:8 2026
Athaliah, so that she *s* him not 2Chr 22:11 4191
king's house, they *s* her there 2Chr 23:15 4191
s Mattan the priest of Baal 2Chr 23:17 2026
had done to him, but *s* his son 2Chr 24:22 2026
s him on his bed, and he died 2Chr 24:25 2026
that he *s* his servants that had 2Chr 25:3 2026
But he *s* not their children, but 2Chr 25:4 4191
Lachish after him, and *s* him there 2Chr 25:27 4191
of Remaliah *s* in Judah an hundred 2Chr 28:6 2026
s Maaseiah the king's son, and 2Chr 28:7 2026
bowels *s* him there with the sword 2Chr 32:21 5307
him, and *s* him in his own house 2Chr 33:24 4191
But the people of the land *s* all 2Chr 33:25 5221
who *s* their young men with the 2Chr 36:17 2026
s thy prophets which testified Neh 9:26 2026
in Shushan the palace the Jews *s* Est 9:6 2026
the enemy of the Jews, *s* they Est 9:10 2026
s three hundred men at Shushan Est 9:15 2026
s of their foes seventy and five Est 9:16 2026
s the fattest of them, and smote Ps 78:31 2026
When he *s* them, then they sought Ps 78:34 2026
into blood, and *s* their fish Ps 105:29 4191
great nations, and *s* mighty kings Ps 135:10 2026
And *s* famous kings Ps 136:18 2026
killeth an ox is as if he *s* a man Is 66:3 5221
Because he *s* me not from the womb Jer 20:17 4191
who *s* him with the sword, and cast Jer 26:23 5221
Then the king of Babylon *s* the Jer 39:6 7819
Babylon *s* all the nobles of Judah Jer 39:6 7819
s him, whom the king of Babylon Jer 41:2 4191
Ishmael also *s* all the Jews that Jer 41:3 5221
the son of Nethaniah *s* them Jer 41:7 7819
s them not among their brethren Jer 41:8 4191
the king of Babylon *s* the sons of Jer 52:10 7819
he *s* also all the princes of Jer 52:10 7819
s all that were pleasant to the Lam 2:4 2026
they went forth, and *s* in the city Eze 9:7 5221
and *s* her with the sword Eze 23:10 2026
whereupon they *s* their sacrifices Eze 40:41 7819
they *s* the burnt offering Eze 40:42 7819
the flame of the fire *s* those men Dan 3:22 6992
whom he would he *s* Dan 5:19 6992
s all the children that were in Mt 2:16 *337*
him out of the vineyard, and *s* him Mt 21:39 *615*
them spitefully, and *s* them Mt 22:6 *615*
whom ye *s* between the temple and Mt 23:35 *5407*
s them, think ye that they were Lk 13:4 *615*
raised up Jesus, whom ye *s* Acts 5:30 *1315*
whom they *s* and hanged on a tree Acts 10:39 *337*
the raiment of them that *s* him Acts 22:20 *337*
deceived me, and by it *s* me Rom 7:11 *615*
that wicked one, and *s* his brother 1Jn 3:12 *4969*
And wherefore *s* he him 1Jn 3:12 *4969*

SLEWEST
whom thou *s* in the valley of Elah 1Sa 21:9 5221

SLIDDEN
is this people of Jerusalem *s* Jer 8:5 7725

SLIDE
their foot shall *s* in due time Deut 32:35 4131
therefore I shall not *s* Ps 26:1 4571
none of his steps shall *s* Ps 37:31 4571

SLIDETH
For Israel *s* back as a Hos 4:16 5637

SLIGHTLY
of the daughter of my people *s* Jer 6:14 7043
of the daughter of my people *s* Jer 8:11 7043

SLIME
stone, and *s* had they for morter Gen 11:3 2564
of bulrushes, and daubed it with *s* Ex 2:3 2564

SLIMEPITS
the vale of Siddim was full of *s* Gen 14:10 2564

SLING
every one could *s* stones at an Judg 20:16 7049
and his *s* was in his hand 1Sa 17:40 7050
over the Philistine with a *s* 1Sa 17:50 7050
enemies, them shall he *s* out 1Sa 25:29 7049
as out of the middle of a *s* 1Sa 25:29 7050
As he that bindeth a stone in a *s* Prov 26:8 4773
I will *s* out the inhabitants of Jer 10:18 7049
devour, and subdue with *s* stones Zec 9:15 7050

SLINGERS
howbeit the *s* went about it, and 2Kin 3:25 7051

SLINGS
and bows, and *s* to cast stones 2Chr 26:14 7050

SLINGSTONES
s are turned with him into Job 41:28

SLIP
so that my feet did not *s* 2Sa 22:37 4571
He that is ready to *s* with his Job 12:5 4571
paths, that my footsteps *s* not Ps 17:5 4131
under me, that my feet did not *s* Ps 18:36 4571
at any time we should let them *s* Heb 2:1 *3901*

SLIPPED
but he *s* away out of Saul's 1Sa 19:10 6362
my steps had well nigh *s* Ps 73:2 8210

SLIPPERY
Let their way be dark and *s* Ps 35:6 2519
thou didst set them in *s* places Ps 73:18 2513
them as *s* ways in the darkness Jer 23:12 2519

SLIPPETH
the head *s* from the helve, and Deut 19:5 5394
when my foot *s*, they magnify Ps 38:16 4131
When I said, My foot *s* Ps 94:18 4131

SLIPS
and shalt set it with strange *s* Is 17:10 2156

SLIVER
And he took all the gold and the *s* 2Chr 25:24

SLOTHFUL
be not *s* to go, and to enter to Judg 18:9 6101
but the *s* shall be under tribute Prov 12:24 7423
The *s* man roasteth not that which Prov 12:27 7423
The way of the *s* man is as an Prov 15:19 6102
He also that is *s* in his work is Prov 18:9 7503
A *s* man hideth his hand in his Prov 19:24 6102
The desire of the *s* killeth him Prov 21:25 6102
The *s* man saith, There is a lion Prov 22:13 6102
I went by the field of the *s* Prov 24:30 6102
The *s* man saith, There is a lion Prov 26:13 6102
so doth the *s* upon his bed Prov 26:14 6102
The *s* hideth his hand in his Prov 26:15 6102
s servant, thou knewest that I Mt 25:26 *3636*
Not *s* in business Rom 12:11 *3636*
That ye be not *s*, but followers Heb 6:12 *3576*

SLOTHFULNESS
S casteth into a deep sleep Prov 19:15 6103
By much *s* the building decayeth Eccl 10:18 6103

SLOW
but I am *s* of speech Ex 4:10 3515
and of a *s* tongue Ex 4:10 750
s to anger, and of great kindness, Neh 9:17 750
s to anger, and plenteous in mercy Ps 103:8 750
s to anger, and of great mercy Ps 145:8 750
He that is *s* to wrath is of great Prov 14:29 750
but he that is *s* to anger Prov 15:18 750
He that is *s* to anger is better Prov 16:32 750
s to anger, and of great kindness, Joel 2:13 750
s to anger, and of great kindness, Jonah 4:2 750
The LORD is *s* to anger, and great Nah 1:3 750
s of heart to believe all that Lk 24:25 *1021*
liars, evil beasts, *s* bellies Titus 1:12 *692*
s to speak, *s* to wrath Jas 1:19 *1021*

SLOWLY
And when we had sailed *s* many days Acts 27:7 *1020*

SLUGGARD
Go to the ant, thou *s* Prov 6:6 6102
How long wilt thou sleep, O *s* Prov 6:9 6102
so is the *s* to them that send him Prov 10:26 6102
The soul of the *s* desireth Prov 13:4 6102
The *s* will not plow by reason of Prov 20:4 6102
The *s* is wiser in his own conceit Prov 26:16 6102

SLUICES
purposes thereof, all that make *s* Is 19:10 7938

SLUMBER
he that keepeth thee will not *s* Ps 121:3 5123
Israel shall neither *s* nor sleep Ps 121:4 5123
mine eyes, or *s* to mine eyelids, Ps 132:4 8572
eyes, nor *s* to thine eyelids Prov 6:4 8572
Yet a little sleep, a little *s* Prov 6:10 8572
Yet a little sleep, a little *s* Prov 24:33 8572
none shall *s* nor sleep Is 5:27 5123
sleeping, lying down, loving to *s* Is 56:10 5123
Thy shepherds *s*, O king of Nah 3:18 5123
hath given them the spirit of *s* Rom 11:8 *2659*

SLUMBERED
bridegroom tarried, they all *s* Mt 25:5 *3573*

SLUMBERETH
not, and their damnation *s* not 2Pet 2:3 *3573*

SLUMBERINGS
upon men, in *s* upon the bed Job 33:15 8572

SMALL
the house with blindness, both *s* Gen 19:11 6996
Is it a *s* matter that thou hast Gen 30:15 4592
it shall become *s* dust in all the Ex 9:9
there lay a *s* round thing Ex 16:14 1851
as *s* as the hoar frost on the Ex 16:14 1851
but every *s* matter they shall Ex 18:22 6996
but every *s* matter they judged Ex 18:26 6996
thou shalt beat some of it very *s* Ex 30:36 1854
full of sweet incense beaten *s* Lev 16:12 1851
Seemeth it but a *s* thing unto you Num 16:9 4592
Is it a *s* thing that thou hast Num 16:13 4592
took the *s* towns thereof, and Num 32:41
hear the *s* as well as the great Deut 1:17 6996
stamped it, and ground it very *s* Deut 9:21 3190
even until it was as *s* as dust Deut 9:21 1854
divers weights, a great and a *s* Deut 25:13 6996
divers measures, a great and a *s* Deut 25:14 6996
as the *s* rain upon the tender Deut 32:2
smote the men of the city, both *s* 1Sa 5:9 6996
will do nothing either great or *s* 1Sa 20:2 6996
slew not any, either great or *s* 1Sa 30:2 6996
neither *s* nor great, neither sons 1Sa 30:19 6996
this was yet a *s* thing in thy 2Sa 7:19 6994
be not one *s* stone found there 2Sa 17:13 1571
Then did I beat them as *s* as the 2Sa 22:43
I desire one *s* petition of thee 1Kin 2:20 6996
and after the fire a still *s* voice 1Kin 19:12 1851
Fight neither with *s* nor great 1Kin 22:31 6996
their inhabitants were of *s* power 2Kin 19:26 7116
and all the people, both *s* 2Kin 23:2 6996
Kidron, and stamped it *s* to powder 2Kin 23:6 1854
place, and stamped it *s* to powder 2Kin 23:15 1854
And all the people, both *s* 2Kin 25:26 6996
yet this was a *s* thing in thine 1Chr 17:17 6994
as well the *s* as the great, the 1Chr 25:8 6996
as well the *s* as the great, 1Chr 26:13 6996
whether *s* or great, whether man 2Chr 15:13 6996
Fight ye not with *s* or great 2Chr 18:30 6996
came with a *s* company of men 2Chr 24:24 4705
as well to the great as to the *s* 2Chr 31:15 6996
and all the people, great and *s* 2Chr 34:30 6996
thousand and six hundred *s* cattle 2Chr 35:8
offerings five thousand *s* cattle 2Chr 35:9
of the house of God, great and *s* 2Chr 36:18 6996
the palace, both unto great and *s* Est 1:5 6996
honour, both to great and *s* Est 1:20 6996
The *s* and great are there Job 3:19 6996
Though thy beginning was *s* Job 8:7 4705
consolations of God *s* with thee Job 15:11 4592
For he maketh *s* the drops of Job 36:27 1639
likewise to the *s* rain, and to the Job 37:6
Then did I beat them *s* as the Ps 18:42
creeping innumerable, both *s* Ps 104:25 6996
them that fear the LORD, both *s* Ps 115:13 6996
I am *s* and despised Ps 119:141 6810
of adversity, thy strength is *s* Prov 24:10 6862
s cattle above all that were in Eccl 2:7
had left unto us a very *s* remnant Is 1:9 4592
Is it a *s* thing for you to weary Is 7:13 4592
and the remnant shall be very *s* Is 16:14 4213
issue, all vessels of *s* quantity Is 22:24 6996
strangers shall be like *s* dust Is 29:5 1851
their inhabitants were of *s* power Is 37:27 7116
are counted as the *s* dust of the Is 40:15
the mountains, and beat them *s* Is 41:15 1854
Thou hast not brought me the *s* Is 43:23
For a *s* moment have I forsaken Is 54:7 6996
and a *s* one a strong nation Is 60:22 6810
the *s* shall die in this land Jer 16:6 6996
them, and they shall not be *s* Jer 30:19 6819
Yet a *s* number that escape the Jer 44:28 4962
I will make thee *s* among the Jer 49:15 6996
this of thy whoredoms a *s* matter Eze 16:20 4592
Seemeth it a *s* thing unto you to Eze 34:18 4592
become strong with a *s* people Dan 11:23 4592
for he is *s* Amos 7:2 6996
for he is *s* Amos 7:5 6996
forth wheat, making the ephah *s* Amos 8:5 6694
I have made thee *s* among the Obad 2 6996
hath despised the day of *s* things Zec 4:10 6996
that a *s* ship should wait on him Mk 3:9 *4142*
And they had a few *s* fishes Mk 8:7 *2485*
he had made a scourge of *s* cords Jn 2:15 *4979*
barley loaves, and two *s* fishes Jn 6:9 *3795*
there was no *s* stir among the Acts 12:18 *3641*
and Barnabas had no *s* dissension Acts 15:2 *3641*
arose no *s* stir about that way Acts 19:23 *3641*
brought no *s* gain unto the Acts 19:24 *3641*
this day, witnessing both to *s* Acts 26:22 *3398*
no *s* tempest lay on us, all hope Acts 27:20 *3641*
But with me it is a very *s* thing 1Cor 4:3 *1646*
turned about with a very *s* helm Jas 3:4 *1646*
and them that fear thy name, *s* Rev 11:18 *3398*
And he causeth all, both *s* Rev 13:16 *3398*
and ye that fear him, both *s* Rev 19:5 *3398*
men, both free and bond, both *s* Rev 19:18 *3398*
And I saw the dead, *s* and great, Rev 20:12 *3398*

SMALLEST
of the *s* of the tribes of Israel 1Sa 9:21 6996
unworthy to judge the *s* matters 1Cor 6:2 *1646*

SMART
for a stranger shall *s* for it Prov 11:15

SMELL
he smelled the *s* of his raiment Gen 27:27 7381
the *s* of my son is as the *s* Gen 27:27 7381
to *s* thereto, shall even be cut Ex 30:38 7306
I will not *s* the savour of your Lev 26:31 7306
see, nor hear, nor eat, nor *s* Deut 4:28 7306
All thy garments *s* of myrrh Ps 45:8
noses have they, but they *s* not Ps 115:6 7306
sendeth forth the *s* thereof Song 1:12 7381
the tender grape give a good *s* Song 2:13 7381
the *s* of thine ointments than all Song 4:10 7381
the *s* of thy garments is like the Song 4:11 7381
garments is like the *s* of Lebanon Song 4:11 7381
the *s* of thy nose like apples Song 7:8 7381
The mandrakes give a *s*, and at our Song 7:13 7381
of sweet *s* there shall be stink Is 3:24 1314
nor the *s* of fire had passed on Dan 3:27 7382
olive tree, and his *s* as Lebanon Hos 14:6 7381
I will not *s* in your solemn Amos 5:21 7306
from you, an odour of a sweet *s* Phil 4:18 *2175*

SMELLED
the LORD *s* a sweet savour Gen 8:21 7306
he *s* the smell of his raiment, and Gen 27:27 7306

SMELLETH
he *s* the battle afar off, the Job 39:25 7306

SMELLING
and my fingers with sweet *s* myrrh Song 5:5 5674
lilies, dropping sweet *s* myrrh Song 5:13 5674
were hearing, where were the *s* 1Cor 12:17 *3750*

SMITE
neither will I again *s* any more Gen 8:21 5221
s it, then the other company Gen 32:8 5221
s me, and the mother with the Gen 32:11 5221
s Egypt with all my wonders which Ex 3:20 5221
I will *s* with the rod that is in Ex 7:17 5221
I will *s* all thy borders with Ex 8:2 5062
s the dust of the land, that it Ex 8:16 5221
out my hand, that I may *s* thee Ex 9:15 5221
will *s* all the firstborn in the Ex 12:12 5221
when I *s* the land of Egypt Ex 12:13 5221
pass through to *s* the Egyptians Ex 12:23 5062
come in unto your houses to *s* you Ex 12:23 5062
and thou shalt *s* the rock, and Ex 17:6 5221
one *s* another with a stone, or Ex 21:18 5221
if a man *s* his servant, or his Ex 21:20 5221
if a man *s* the eye of his servant Ex 21:26 5221
if he *s* out his manservant's Ex 21:27 5307
I will *s* them with the pestilence Num 14:12 5221
shall prevail, that we may *s* them Num 22:6 5221
shall *s* the corners of Moab, and Num 24:17 4272
Vex the Midianites, and *s* them Num 25:17 5221
if he *s* him with an instrument of Num 35:16 5221
if he *s* him with throwing a stone Num 35:17 5221
Or if he *s* him with an hand Num 35:18 5221
Or in enmity *s* him with his hand, Num 35:21 5221
thou shalt *s* them, and utterly Deut 7:2 5221
Thou shalt surely *s* the Deut 13:15 5221
s him mortally that he die, and Deut 19:11 5221
thou shalt *s* every male thereof Deut 20:13 5221
The LORD shall *s* thee with a Deut 28:22 5221
The LORD will *s* thee with the Deut 28:27 5221
The LORD shall *s* thee with Deut 28:28 5221
The LORD shall *s* thee in the Deut 28:35 5221
s through the loins of them that Deut 33:11 4272
three thousand men go up and *s* Ai Josh 7:3 6221
and help me, that we may *s* Gibeon Josh 10:4 6221
and *s* the hindmost of them Josh 10:19
LORD and the children of Israel *s* Josh 12:6 5221
for these did Moses *s*, and cast Josh 13:12 5221
thou shalt *s* the Midianites as Judg 6:16 5221
and they began to *s* of the people Judg 20:31 5221
the battle, Benjamin began to *s* Judg 20:39 5221
Go and *s* the inhabitants of Judg 21:10 5221
s Amalek, and utterly destroy all 1Sa 15:3 5221
and I will *s* thee, and take thine 1Sa 17:46 5221
I will *s* David even to the wall 1Sa 18:11 5221
Saul sought to *s* David even to 1Sa 19:10 5221
cast a javelin at him to *s* him 1Sa 20:33 5221
Shall I go and *s* these Philistines 1Sa 23:2 5221
s the Philistines, and save Keilah 1Sa 23:2 5221
now therefore let me *s* him 1Sa 26:8 5221
I will not *s* him the second time 1Sa 26:8
LORD liveth, the LORD shall *s* him 1Sa 26:10 5062
should I *s* thee to the ground 2Sa 2:22 5221
to *s* the host of the Philistines 2Sa 5:24 5221
and when I say unto you, *S* Amnon 2Sa 13:28 5221
s the city with the edge of the 2Sa 15:14 5221
and I will *s* the king only 2Sa 17:2 5221
why didst thou not *s* him there to 2Sa 18:11 5221
For the LORD shall *s* Israel 1Kin 14:15 5221
of the LORD, *S* me, I pray thee 1Kin 20:35 5221
And the man refused to *s* him 1Kin 20:35 5221
man, and said, *S* me, I pray thee 1Kin 20:37 5221
ye shall *s* every fenced city, and 2Kin 3:19 5221
S this people, I pray thee, with 2Kin 6:18 5221
them, My father, shall I *s* them 2Kin 6:21 5221
shall I *s* them 2Kin 6:21 5221
answered, Thou shalt not *s* them 2Kin 6:22 5221
wouldest thou *s* those whom thou 2Kin 6:22 5221
thou shalt *s* the house of Ahab 2Kin 9:7 5221
S him also in the chariot 2Kin 9:27 5221
for thou shalt *s* the Syrians in 2Kin 13:17 5221
king of Israel, *S* upon the ground 2Kin 13:18 5221
now thou shalt *s* Syria but thrice 2Kin 13:19 5221
to *s* the host of the Philistines 1Chr 14:15 5221
plague will the LORD *s* thy people 2Chr 21:14 5062
The sun shall not *s* thee by day Ps 121:6 5221
Let the righteous *s* me Ps 141:5 1986
S a scorner, and the simple will Prov 19:25 5221
Therefore the Lord will *s* with a Is 3:17 5596
he shall *s* thee with a rod, and Is 10:24 5221
he shall *s* the earth with the rod Is 11:4 5221
shall *s* it in the seven streams, Is 11:15 5221
And the LORD shall *s* Egypt Is 19:22 5062
he shall *s* and heal it Is 19:22 5062
shall the heat nor sun *s* them Is 49:10 5221
to *s* with the fist of wickedness Is 58:4 5221
let us *s* him with the tongue, and Jer 18:18 5221
I will *s* the inhabitants of this Jer 21:6 5221
he shall *s* them with the edge of Jer 21:7 5221
he shall *s* the land of Egypt, and Jer 43:11 5221
come and *s* the land of Egypt Jer 46:13 5221
king of Babylon shall *s*, thus Jer 49:28 5221
part, and *s* about it with a knife Eze 5:2 5221
S with thine hand, and stamp with Eze 6:11 5221
after him through the city, and *s* Eze 9:5 5221
s therefore upon thy thigh Eze 21:12 5606
s thine hands together, and let Eze 21:14 5221
I will also *s* mine hands together Eze 21:17 5221
when I shall *s* all them that Eze 32:15 5221
I will *s* thy bow out of thy left Eze 39:3 5221
I will *s* the winter house with Amos 3:15 5221
he will *s* the great house with Amos 6:11 5221
S the lintel of the door, that Amos 9:1 5221
they shall *s* the judge of Israel Mic 5:1 5221
melteth, and the knees *s* together Nah 2:10 6375
he will *s* her power in the sea Zec 9:4 5221
shall *s* the waves in the sea, and Zec 10:11 5221
and they shall *s* the land, and out Zec 11:6 3807
I will *s* every horse with Zec 12:4 5221
will *s* every horse of the people Zec 12:4 5221
s the shepherd, and the sheep Zec 13:7 5221
plague wherewith the LORD will *s* Zec 14:12 5062
wherewith the LORD will *s* the Zec 14:18 5062
come and *s* the earth with a curse Mal 4:6 5221
but whosoever shall *s* thee on thy Mt 5:39 *4474*
And shall begin to *s* his Mt 24:49 *5180*
I will *s* the shepherd, and the Mt 26:31 *3960*
I will *s* the shepherd, and the Mk 14:27 *3960*
shall we *s* with the sword Lk 22:49 *3960*
by him to *s* him on the mouth Acts 23:2 *5180*
Paul unto him, God shall *s* thee Acts 23:3 *5180*
if a man *s* you on the face 2Cor 11:20 *1194*
to *s* the earth with all plagues, Rev 11:6 *3960*
with it he should *s* the nations Rev 19:15 *3960*

SMITERS
I gave my back to the *s*, and my Is 50:6 5221

SMITEST
Wherefore *s* thou thy fellow Ex 2:13 5221
but if well, why *s* thou me Jn 18:23 *1194*

SMITETH
He that *s* a man, so that he die, Ex 21:12 5221
he that *s* his father, or his Ex 21:15 5221
out of the hand of him that *s* him Deut 25:11 5221
Cursed be he that *s* his neighbour Deut 27:24 5221
He that *s* Kirjath-sepher, and Josh 15:16 5221
He that *s* Kirjath-sepher, and Judg 1:12 5221
s the Jebusites, and the lame and 2Sa 5:8 5221
Whosoever *s* the Jebusites first 1Chr 11:6 5221
he *s* through the proud Job 26:12 4272
turneth not unto him that *s* them Is 9:13 5221
his cheek to him that *s* him Lam 3:30 5221
know that I am the LORD that *s* Eze 7:9 5221
unto him that *s* thee on the one Lk 6:29 *5180*

SMITH
Now there was no *s* found 1Sa 13:19 2796
The *s* with the tongs both worketh Is 44:12
I have created the *s* that bloweth Is 54:16 2796

SMITHS
and all the craftsmen and *s* 2Kin 24:14 4525
s a thousand, all that were 2Kin 24:16 4525
Judah, with the carpenters and *s* Jer 24:1 4525
and the carpenters, and the *s* Jer 29:2 4525

SMITING
he spied an Egyptian *s* an Hebrew Ex 2:11 5221
a name when he returned from *s* of 2Sa 8:13 5221
so that in *s* he wounded him 1Kin 20:37 5221
they went forward *s* the Moabites 2Kin 3:24 5221
will I make thee sick in *s* thee Mic 6:13 5221

SMITTEN
that the LORD had *s* the river Ex 7:25 5221
And the flax and the barley was *s* Ex 9:31 5221
the wheat and the rie were not *s* Ex 9:32 5221
be *s* that he die, there shall no Ex 22:2 5221
that ye be not *s* before your Num 14:42 5062
that thou hast *s* me these three Num 22:28 5221
Wherefore hast thou *s* thine ass Num 22:32 5221
which the LORD had *s* among them Num 33:4 5221
lest ye be *s* before your enemies Deut 1:42 5062
thee to be *s* before thy face Deut 28:7 5062
thee to be *s* before thine enemies Deut 28:25 5062
s it with the edge of the sword, Judg 1:8 5221
They are *s* down before us, as at Judg 20:32 5062
of Benjamin saw that they were *s* Judg 20:36 5062
Surely they are *s* down before us Judg 20:39 5062
battle, Israel was *s* before the 1Sa 4:2 5062
the LORD *s* us to day before the 1Sa 4:3 5062
fought, and Israel was *s*, and they 1Sa 4:10 5062
died not were *s* with the emerods 1Sa 5:12 5221
because the LORD had *s* many of 1Sa 6:19 5221
they were *s* before Israel 1Sa 7:10 5062
s a garrison of the Philistines 1Sa 13:4 5221
s Ziklag, and burned it with fire 1Sa 30:1 5221
of David had *s* of Benjamin 2Sa 2:31 5221
had *s* all the host of Hadadezer 2Sa 8:9 5221
against Hadadezer, and *s* him 2Sa 8:10 5221
that they were *s* before Israel 2Sa 10:15 5062
that they were *s* before Israel 2Sa 10:19 5062
ye from him, that he may be *s* 2Sa 11:15 5221
Israel be *s* down before the enemy 1Kin 8:33 5062
after he had *s* every male in Edom 1Kin 11:15 5221
and when he also had *s* the waters 2Kin 2:14 5221
slain, and they have *s* one another 2Kin 3:23 5221
have *s* five or six times 2Kin 13:19 5221
then hadst thou *s* Syria till thou 2Kin 13:19 5221
Thou hast indeed *s* Edom, and thine 2Kin 14:10 5221
of Hamath heard how David had *s* 1Chr 18:9 5221
against Hadarezer, and *s* him 1Chr 18:10 5221
and they were *s* 2Chr 20:22 5062
why shouldest thou be *s* 2Chr 25:16 5221
Lo, thou hast *s* the Edomites 2Chr 25:19 5221
out, because the LORD had *s* him 2Chr 26:20 5060
s Judah, and carried away captives 2Chr 28:17 5221
they have *s* me upon the cheek Job 16:10 5221
for thou hast *s* all mine enemies Ps 3:7 5221
persecute him whom thou hast *s* Ps 69:26 5221
My heart is *s*, and withered like Ps 102:4 5221
he hath *s* my life down to the Ps 143:3 1792
hand against them, and hath *s* them Is 5:25 5221
the gate is *s* with destruction Is 24:12 3807
Hath he *s* him, as he smote those Is 27:7 5221
stricken, *s* of God, and afflicted Is 53:4 5221
In vain have I *s* your children Jer 2:30 5221
why hast thou *s* us, and there is Jer 14:19 5221
For though ye had *s* the whole Jer 37:10 5221
therefore I have *s* mine hand at Eze 22:13 5221
unto me, saying, The city is *s* Eze 33:21 5221
year after that the city was *s* Eze 40:1 5221
he hath *s*, and he will bind us up Hos 6:1 5221
Ephraim is *s*, their root is dried Hos 9:16 5221
I have *s* you with blasting and Amos 4:9 5221
me to be *s* contrary to the law Acts 23:3 *5180*
the third part of the sun was *s* Rev 8:12 *4141*

SMOKE
the *s* of the country went up as Gen 19:28 7008
went up as the *s* of a furnace Gen 19:28 7008
mount Sinai was altogether on a *s* Ex 19:18 6225
the *s* thereof ascended as the Ex 19:18 6227
ascended as the *s* of a furnace Ex 19:18 6227
jealousy shall *s* against that man Deut 29:20 6225
the *s* of the city ascended up to Josh 8:20 6227
that the *s* of the city ascended, Josh 8:21 6227
with *s* rise up out of the city Judg 20:38 6227
of the city with a pillar of *s* Judg 20:40 6227
There went up a *s* out of his 2Sa 22:9 6227
Out of his nostrils goeth *s* Job 41:20 6227
There went up a *s* out of his Ps 18:8 6227
into *s* shall they consume away Ps 37:20 6227
As *s* is driven away, so drive Ps 68:2 6227
why doth thine anger *s* against Ps 74:1 6225
For my days are consumed like *s* Ps 102:3 6227
he toucheth the hills, and they *s* Ps 104:32 6225
am become like a bottle in the *s* Ps 119:83 7008
the mountains, and they shall *s* Ps 144:5 6225
as *s* to the eyes, so is the Prov 10:26 6227
the wilderness like pillars of *s* Song 3:6 6227
s by day, and the shining of a Is 4:5 6227
and the house was filled with *s* Is 6:4 6227
mount up like the lifting up of *s* Is 9:18 6227
shall come from the north a *s* Is 14:31 6227
the *s* thereof shall go up for Is 34:10 6227
heavens shall vanish away like *s* Is 51:6 6227
These are a *s* in my nose, a fire Is 65:5 6227
as the *s* out of the chimney Hos 13:3 6227
blood, and fire, and pillars of *s* Joel 2:30 6227
I will burn her chariots in the *s* Nah 2:13 6227
blood, and fire, and vapour of *s* Acts 2:19 *2586*
the *s* of the incense, which came Rev 8:4 *2586*
there arose a *s* out of the pit, Rev 9:2 *2586*
as the *s* of a great furnace Rev 9:2 *2586*
by reason of the *s* of the pit Rev 9:2 *2586*
there came out of the *s* locusts Rev 9:3 *2586*
of their mouths issued fire and *s* Rev 9:17 *2586*
killed, by the fire, and by the *s* Rev 9:18 *2586*
the *s* of their torment ascendeth Rev 14:11 *2586*
with *s* from the glory of God Rev 15:8 *2586*
shall see the *s* of her burning Rev 18:9 *2586*
they saw the *s* of her burning Rev 18:18 *2586*
her *s* rose up for ever and ever Rev 19:3 *2586*

SMOKING
it was dark, behold a *s* furnace Gen 15:17 6227
of the trumpet, and the mountain *s* Ex 20:18 6226
two tails of these *s* firebrands Is 7:4 6226
the *s* flax shall he not quench Is 42:3 3544
s flax shall he not quench, till Mt 12:20 *5187*

SMOOTH
is a hairy man, and I am a *s* man Gen 27:11 2509
hands, and upon the *s* of his neck Gen 27:16 2513
chose him five *s* stones out of 1Sa 17:40 2512
things, speak unto us *s* things Is 30:10 2513
Among the *s* stones of the stream Is 57:6 2511
and the rough ways shall be made *s* Lk 3:5 *3006*

SMOOTHER
of his mouth were *s* than butter Ps 55:21 2505
and her mouth is *s* than oil Prov 5:3 2513

SMOOTHETH
he that *s* with the hammer him Is 41:7 2505

SMOTE
s the Rephaims in Ashteroth Gen 14:5 5221
and *s* all the country of the Gen 14:7 5221
s them, and pursued them unto Gen 14:15 5221
they *s* the men that were at the Gen 19:11 5221
who *s* Midian in the field of Moab Gen 36:35 5221
s the waters that were in the Ex 7:20 5221
s the dust of the earth, and it Ex 8:17 5221
the hail *s* throughout all the Ex 9:25 5221
the hail *s* every herb of the Ex 9:25 5221
when he *s* the Egyptians, and Ex 12:27 5062
that at midnight the LORD *s* all Ex 12:29 5221
then shall he that *s* him be quit Ex 21:19 5221
for on the day that I *s* all the Num 3:13 5221
on the day that I *s* every Num 8:17 5221
the LORD *s* the people with a very Num 11:33 5221
s them, and discomfited them, even Num 14:45 5221
with his rod he *s* the rock twice Num 20:11 5221
Israel *s* him with the edge of the Num 21:24 5221
So they *s* him, and his sons, and Num 21:35 5221
Balaam *s* the ass, to turn her Num 22:23 5221
and he *s* her again Num 22:25 5221
he *s* the ass with a staff Num 22:27 5221
and he *s* his hands together Num 24:10 5606
LORD *s* before the congregation of Num 32:4 5221
he that *s* him shall surely be put Num 35:21 5221
we *s* him, and his sons, and all his Deut 2:33 5221
we *s* him until none was left to Deut 3:3 5221
Moses and the children of Israel *s* Deut 4:46 5221
s the hindmost of thee, even all Deut 25:18
us unto battle, and we *s* them Deut 29:7 5221
the men of Ai *s* of them about Josh 7:5 5221
and *s* them in the going down Josh 7:5 5221
and they *s* them, so that they let Josh 8:22 5221
s it with the edge of the sword Josh 8:24 5221
the children of Israel *s* them not Josh 9:18 5221
s them to Azekah, and unto Josh 10:10 5221
And afterward Joshua *s* them Josh 10:26 5221
s it with the edge of the sword, Josh 10:28 5221
he *s* it with the edge of the Josh 10:30 5221

s it with the edge of the sword, Josh 10:32 5221
and Joshua s him and his people, Josh 10:33 5221
s it with the edge of the sword, Josh 10:35 5221
s it with the edge of the sword, Josh 10:37 5221
they s them with the edge of the Josh 10:39 5221
So Joshua s all the country of Josh 10:40 5221
Joshua s them from Kadesh-barnea Josh 10:41 5221
who s them, and chased them unto Josh 11:8 5221
and they s them, until they left Josh 11:8 5221
s the king thereof with the sword Josh 11:10 5221
they s all the souls that were Josh 11:11 5221
s them with the edge of the sword Josh 11:12 5221
but every man they s with the Josh 11:14 5221
he took, and s them, and slew them Josh 11:17 5221
which the children of Israel s Josh 12:1 5221
the children of Israel s on this Josh 12:7 5221
whom Moses s with the princes of Josh 13:21 5221
s it with the edge of the sword, Josh 19:47 5221
because he s his neighbour Josh 20:5 5221
they s the city with the edge of Judg 1:25 5221
s Israel, and possessed the city Judg 3:13 5221
s the nail into his temples, and Judg 4:21 8628
and with the hammer she s Sisera Judg 5:26 1986
she s off his head, when she had Judg 5:26 4277
s it that it fell, and overturned Judg 7:13 5221
Nobah and Jogbehah, and s the host Judg 8:11 5221
rose up against them, and s them Judg 9:43 5221
hand of Israel, and they s them Judg 11:21 5221
he s them from Aroer, even till Judg 11:33 5221
and the men of Gilead s Ephraim Judg 12:4 5221
he s them hip and thigh with a Judg 15:8 5221
they s them with the edge of the Judg 18:27 5221
the LORD s Benjamin before Israel Judg 20:35 5062
s all the city with the edge of Judg 20:37 5221
s them with the edge of the sword Judg 20:48 5221
these are the Gods that s the 1Sa 4:8 5221
s them with emerods, even Ashdod 1Sa 5:6 5221
he s the men of the city, both 1Sa 5:9 5221
that it is not his hand that s us 1Sa 6:9 5060
he s the men of Beth-shemesh, 1Sa 6:19 5221
even he s of the people fifty 1Sa 6:19 5221
s them, until they came under 1Sa 7:11 5221
Jonathan s the garrison of the 1Sa 13:3 5221
they s the Philistines that day 1Sa 14:31 5221
s the Amalekites, and delivered 1Sa 14:48 5221
Saul s the Amalekites from 1Sa 15:7 5221
s him, and delivered it out of his 1Sa 17:35 5221
his beard, and s him, and slew him 1Sa 17:35 5221
s the Philistine in his forehead, 1Sa 17:49 5221
s the Philistine, and slew him 1Sa 17:50 5221
he s the javelin into the wall 1Sa 19:10 5221
s he with the edge of the sword, 1Sa 22:19 5221
s them with a great slaughter 1Sa 23:5 5221
that David's heart s him 1Sa 24:5 5221
days after, that the LORD s Nabal 1Sa 25:38 5062
David s the land, and left neither 1Sa 27:9 5221
David s them from the twilight 1Sa 30:17 5221
And he s him that he died 2Sa 1:15 5221
spear s him under the fifth rib 2Sa 2:23 5221
s him there under the fifth rib, 2Sa 3:27 5221
they s him under the fifth rib 2Sa 4:6 5221
in his bedchamber, and they s him 2Sa 4:7 5221
David s them there, and said, The 2Sa 5:20 5221
s the Philistines from Geba until 2Sa 5:25 5221
God s him there for his error 2Sa 6:7 5221
that David s the Philistines, and 2Sa 8:1 5221
he s Moab, and measured them with 2Sa 8:2 5221
David s also Hadadezer, the son 2Sa 8:3 5221
s Shobach the captain of their 2Sa 10:18 5221
Who s Abimelech the son of 2Sa 11:21 5221
them, but the one s the other 2Sa 14:6 5221
Deliver him that s his brother 2Sa 14:7 5221
about and s Absalom, and slew him 2Sa 18:15 5221
so he s him therewith in the 2Sa 20:10 5221
s the Philistine, and killed him 2Sa 21:17 5221
s the Philistines until his hand 2Sa 23:10 5221
David's heart s him after that he 2Sa 24:10 5221
saw the angel that s the people 2Sa 24:17 5221
of Israel, and s Ijon, and Dan, and 1Kin 15:20 5221
Baasha s him at Gibbethon, which 1Kin 15:27 5221
that he s all the house of 1Kin 15:29 5221
s him, and killed him, in the 1Kin 16:10 5221
s the horses and chariots, and slew 1Kin 20:21 5221
And the man s him, so that in 1Kin 20:37 5221
s Micaiah on the cheek, and said, 1Kin 22:24 5221
s the king of Israel between the 1Kin 22:34 5221
s the waters, and they were 2Kin 2:8 5221
s the waters, and said, Where is 2Kin 2:14 5221
s the Moabites, so that they fled 2Kin 3:24 5221
slingers went about it, and s it 2Kin 3:25 5221
And he s them with blindness 2Kin 6:18 5221
s the Edomites which compassed 2Kin 8:21 5221
s Jehoram between his arms, and 2Kin 9:24 5221
they s them with the edge of the 2Kin 10:25 5221
Hazael s them in all the coasts 2Kin 10:32 5221
his servants, s him, and he died 2Kin 12:21 5221
And he s thrice, and stayed 2Kin 13:18 5221
And the LORD s the king, so that 2Kin 15:5 5221
s him before the people, and slew 2Kin 15:10 5221
s Shallum the son of Jabesh in 2Kin 15:14 5221
Then Menahem s Tiphsah, and all 2Kin 15:16 5221
not to him, therefore he s it 2Kin 15:16 5221
s him in Samaria, in the palace 2Kin 15:25 5221
s him, and slew him, and reigned in 2Kin 15:30 5221
He s the Philistines, even unto 2Kin 18:8 5221
s in the camp of the Assyrians an 2Kin 19:35 5221
Sharezer his sons s him with the 2Kin 19:37 5221
And the king of Babylon s them 2Kin 25:21 5221
s Gedaliah, that he died, and the 2Kin 25:25 5221
which s Midian in the field of 1Chr 1:46 5221
s their tents, and the habitations 1Chr 4:41 5221
they s the rest of the Amalekites 1Chr 4:43 5221
he s him, because he put his hand 1Chr 13:10 5221
and David s them there 1Chr 14:11 5221
and they s the host of the 1Chr 14:16 5221
that David s the Philistines, and 1Chr 18:1 5221
And he s Moab 1Chr 18:2 5221
David s Hadarezer king of Zobah 1Chr 18:3 5221
Joab s Rabbah, and destroyed it 1Chr 20:1 5221
therefore he s Israel 1Chr 21:7 5221
came to pass, that God s Jeroboam 2Chr 13:15 5062
So the LORD s the Ethiopians 2Chr 14:12 5062
they s all the cities round about 2Chr 14:14 5221
They s also the tents of cattle, 2Chr 14:15 5221
and they s Ijon, and Dan, and 2Chr 16:4 5221
s Micaiah upon the cheek, and said 2Chr 18:23 5221
s the king of Israel between the 2Chr 18:33 5221
s the Edomites which compassed 2Chr 21:9 5221
after all this the LORD s him in 2Chr 21:18 5062
and the Syrians s Joram 2Chr 22:5 5221
s of the children of Seir ten 2Chr 25:11 5221
s three thousand of them, and took 2Chr 25:13 5221
and they s him, and carried away a 2Chr 28:5 5221
who s him with a great slaughter 2Chr 28:5 5221
the gods of Damascus, which s him 2Chr 28:23 5221
s certain of them, and plucked off Neh 13:25 5221
Thus the Jews s all their enemies Est 9:5 5221
s the four corners of the house, Job 1:19 5060
s Job with sore boils from the Job 2:7 5221
s of Edom in the valley of salt Ps 60:t 5221
he s the rock, that the waters Ps 78:20 5221
s down the chosen men of Israel Ps 78:31 3766
s all the firstborn in Egypt Ps 78:51 5221
he s his enemies in the hinder Ps 78:66 5221
He s their vines also and their Ps 105:33 5221
He s also all the firstborn in Ps 105:36 5221
Who s the firstborn of Egypt, Ps 135:8 5221
Who s great nations, and slew Ps 135:10 5221
To him that s Egypt in their Ps 136:10 5221
To him which s great kings Ps 136:17 5221
the city found me, they s me Song 5:7 5221
again stay upon him that s them Is 10:20 5221
He who s the people in wrath with Is 14:6 5221
rod of him that s thee is broken Is 14:29 5221
as he s those that Is 27:7 4347
those that s him Is 27:7 5221
beaten down, which s with a rod Is 30:31 5221
s in the camp of the Assyrians an Is 37:36 5221
Sharezer his sons s him with the Is 37:38 5221
the hammer him that s the anvil Is 41:7 1986
was I wroth, and s him Is 57:17 5221
for in my wrath I s thee, but in Is 60:10 5221
Then Pashur s Jeremiah the Jer 20:2 5221
was instructed, I s upon my thigh Jer 31:19 5606
s him, and put him in prison in Jer 37:15 5221
s Gedaliah the son of Ahikam the Jer 41:2 5221
Nebuchadrezzar king of Babylon s Jer 46:2 5221
before that Pharaoh s Gaza Jer 47:1 5221
And the king of Babylon s them Jer 52:27 5221
which s the image upon his feet Dan 2:34 4223
the stone that s the image became Dan 2:35 4223
his knees s one against another Dan 5:6 5368
s the ram, and brake his two horns Dan 8:7 5221
it s the gourd that it withered Jonah 4:7 5221
I s you with blasting and with Hag 2:17 5221
high priest's, and s off his ear Mt 26:51 851
others s him with the palms of Mt 26:67 4474
Christ, Who is he that s thee Mt 26:68 3817
the reed, and s him on the head Mt 27:30 5180
s a servant of the high priest, Mk 14:47 3817
they s him on the head with a Mk 15:19 5180
but s upon his breast, saying, Lk 18:13 5180
one of them s the servant of the Lk 22:50 3960
held Jesus mocked him, and s him Lk 22:63 1194
Prophesy, who is it that s thee Lk 22:64 3817
s their breasts, and returned Lk 23:48 5180
s the high priest's servant, and Jn 18:10 3817
they s him with their hands Jn 19:3
was oppressed, and s the Egyptian Acts 7:24 3960
he s Peter on the side, and raised Acts 12:7 3960
the angel of the Lord s him Acts 12:23 3960

SMOTEST
rod, wherewith thou s the river Ex 17:5 5221

SMYRNA (*smir'-na*) *A city of Ionia in Asia Minor.*
unto Ephesus, and unto S, and unto Rev 1:11 4667
angel of the church in S write Rev 2:8 4668

SNAIL
and the lizard, and the s, and the Lev 11:30 2546
As a s which melteth, let every Ps 58:8 7642

SNARE
shall this man be a s unto us Ex 10:7 4170
it will surely be a s unto thee Ex 23:33 4170
lest it be for a s in the midst Ex 34:12 4170
for that will be a s unto thee Deut 7:16 4170
their gods shall be a s unto you Judg 2:3 4170
thing became a s unto Gideon Judg 8:27 4170
her, that she may be a s to him 1Sa 18:21 4170
then layest thou a s for my life 1Sa 28:9 5367
own feet, and he walketh upon a s Job 18:8 7639
The s is laid for him in the Job 18:10 2256
table become a s before them Ps 69:22 6341
thee from the s of the fowler Ps 91:3 6341
which were a s unto them Ps 106:36 4170
The wicked have laid a s for me Ps 119:110 6341
bird out of the s of the fowlers Ps 124:7 6341
the s is broken, and we are Ps 124:7 6341
The proud have hid a s for me Ps 140:5 6341
have they privily laid a s for me Ps 142:3 6341
as a bird hasteth to the s Prov 7:23 6341
and his lips are the s of his soul Prov 18:7 4170
It is a s to the man who Prov 20:25 4170
his ways, and get a s to thy soul Prov 22:25 4170
of an evil man there is a s Prov 29:6 4170
men bring a city into a s Prov 29:8 6315
The fear of man bringeth a s Prov 29:25 4170
birds that are caught in the s Eccl 9:12 6341
for a s to the inhabitants of Is 8:14 4170
Fear, and the pit, and the s Is 24:17 6341
the pit shall be taken in the s Is 24:18 6341
lay a s for him that reproveth in Is 29:21 6983
Fear, and the pit, and the s Jer 48:43 6341
the pit shall be taken in the s Jer 48:44 6341
I have laid a s for thee, and thou Jer 50:24 3369
a s is come upon us, desolation Lam 3:47 6354
him, and he shall be taken in my s Eze 12:13 4686
him, and he shall be taken in my s Eze 17:20 4686
ye have been a s on Mizpah Hos 5:1 6341
but the prophet is a s of a Hos 9:8 6341
a bird fall in a s upon the earth Amos 3:5 6341
one take up a s from the earth Amos 3:5 6341
For as a s shall it come on all Lk 21:35 3803
Let their table be made a s Rom 11:9 3803
not that I may cast a s upon you 1Cor 7:35 1029
reproach and the s of the devil 1Ti 3:7 3803
rich fall into temptation and a s 1Ti 6:9 3803
out of the s of the devil 2Ti 2:26 3803

SNARED
unto thee, lest thou be s therein Deut 7:25 3369
thou be not s by following them Deut 12:30 5367
the wicked is s in the work of Ps 9:16 5367
Thou art s with the words of thy Prov 6:2 3369
The wicked is s by the Prov 12:13 4170
the sons of men s in an evil time Eccl 9:12 3369
and fall, and be broken, and be s Is 8:15 3369
fall backward, and be broken, and s Is 28:13 3369
they are all of them s in holes Is 42:22 6351

SNARES
but they shall be s and traps unto Josh 23:13 6341
the s of death prevented me 2Sa 22:6 4170
Therefore s are round about thee, Job 22:10 6341
his nose pierceth through s Job 40:24 4170
Upon the wicked he shall rain s Ps 11:6 6341
the s of death prevented me Ps 18:5 4170
seek after my life lay s for me Ps 38:12 5367
they commune of laying s privily Ps 64:5 4170
Keep me from the s which they Ps 141:9 6341
to depart from the s of death Prov 13:14 4170
to depart from the s of death Prov 14:27 4170
s are in the way of the froward Prov 22:5 6341
death the woman, whose heart is s Eccl 7:26 4685
lay wait, as he that setteth s Jer 5:26 3353
to take me, and hid s for my feet Jer 18:22 6341

SNATCH
he shall s on the right hand, and Is 9:20 1504

SNEEZED
the child s seven times, and the 2Kin 4:35 2237

SNORTING
The s of his horses was heard Jer 8:16 5170

SNOUT
As a jewel of gold in a swine's s Prov 11:22 639

SNOW
behold, his hand was leprous as s Ex 4:6 7950
Miriam became leprous, white as s Num 12:10 7950
the midst of a pit in time of s 2Sa 23:20 7950
presence a leper as white as s 2Kin 5:27 7950
the ice, and wherein the s is hid Job 6:16 7950
If I wash myself with s water Job 9:30 7950
and heat consume the s waters Job 24:19 7950
For he saith to the s, Be thou on Job 37:6 7950
into the treasures of the s Job 38:22 7950
me, and I shall be whiter than s Ps 51:7 7950
it, it was white as s in Salmon Ps 68:14 7949
He giveth s like wool Ps 147:16 7950
Fire, and hail; s, and vapours Ps 148:8 7950
As the cold of s in the time of Prov 25:13 7950
As s in summer, and as rain in Prov 26:1 7950
afraid of the s for her household Prov 31:21 7950
they shall be as white as s Is 1:18 7950
the s from heaven, and returneth Is 55:10 7950
Will a man leave the s of Lebanon Jer 18:14 7950
Her Nazarites were purer than s Lam 4:7 7950
sit, whose garment was white as s Dan 7:9 8517
and his raiment white as s Mt 28:3 5510
shining, exceeding white as s Mk 9:3 5510
white like wool, as white as s Rev 1:14 5510

SNOWY
slew a lion in a pit in a s day 1Chr 11:22 7950

SNUFFDISHES
the s thereof, shall be of pure Ex 25:38 4289
lamps, and his snuffers, and his s Ex 37:23 4289
his lamps, and his tongs, and his s Num 4:9 4289

SNUFFED
they s up the wind like dragons Jer 14:6 7602
and ye have s at it, saith the Mal 1:13 5301

SNUFFERS
he made his seven lamps, and his s Ex 37:23 4457
And the bowls, and the s, and the 1Kin 7:50 4212
of the LORD bowls of silver, s 2Kin 12:13 4212
pots, and the shovels, and the s 2Kin 25:14 4212
And the s, and the basons, and the 2Chr 4:22 4212
also, and the shovels, and the s Jer 52:18 4212

SNUFFETH
that s up the wind at her Jer 2:24 7602

SO (*so*)
1. An adverb, adjective and conjunction.
firmament: and it was s Gen 1:7 3651
appear: and it was s Gen 1:9 3651
earth: and it was s Gen 1:11 3651
earth: and it was s Gen 1:15 3651
kind: and it was s Gen 1:24 3651
S God created man in his own Gen 1:27
meat: and it was s Gen 1:30 3651

S he drove out the man ... Gen 3:24
that God commanded him, *s* did he ... Gen 6:22 3651
s Noah knew that the waters were ... Gen 8:11
S the LORD scattered them abroad ... Gen 11:8
S Abram departed, as the LORD had ... Gen 12:4
s I might have taken her to me to ... Gen 12:19
s that they could not dwell ... Gen 13:6
s that if a man can number the ... Gen 13:16 834
unto him, *S* shall thy seed be ... Gen 15:5 3541
said, *S* do, as thou hast said ... Gen 18:5 3651
you, brethren, do not *s* wickedly ... Gen 19:7
s that they wearied themselves to ... Gen 19:11
And Lot said unto them, Oh, not *s* ... Gen 19:18
S Abraham prayed unto God ... Gen 20:17
s that all that hear will laugh ... Gen 21:6
s they went both of them together ... Gen 22:8
S Abraham returned unto his young ... Gen 22:19
s I drank, and she made the camels ... Gen 24:46
and she said, If it be *s*, why am I ... Gen 25:22 3651
s that he could not see, he ... Gen 27:1
that thou hast found it *s* quickly ... Gen 27:20
s he blessed him ... Gen 27:23
S that I come again to my ... Gen 28:21
It must not be *s* done in our ... Gen 29:26 3651
And Jacob did *s*, and fulfilled her ... Gen 29:28 3651
S shall my righteousness answer ... Gen 30:33
s the feebler were Laban's, and ... Gen 30:42
S he fled with all that he had ... Gen 31:21
now done foolishly in *s* doing ... Gen 31:28
that thou hast *s* hotly pursued ... Gen 31:36
s commanded he the second, and the .. Gen 32:19 1571
S went the present over before ... Gen 32:21
S Esau returned that day on his ... Gen 33:16
Ask me never *s* much dowry ... Gen 34:12
S Jacob came to Luz, which is in ... Gen 35:6
S he sent him out of the vale of ... Gen 37:14
Wherefore look ye *s* sadly to day ... Gen 40:7
S Pharaoh awoke ... Gen 41:4
as he interpreted to us, *s* it was ... Gen 41:13 3651
S I awoke ... Gen 41:21
this, there is none *s* discreet ... Gen 41:39
famine was *s* sore in all lands ... Gen 41:57
s shall your words be verified, ... Gen 42:20
And they did *s* ... Gen 42:20 3651
s will I deliver you your brother ... Gen 42:34
Wherefore dealt ye *s* ill with me ... Gen 43:6
unto them, If it must be *s* now ... Gen 43:11 3651
times *s* much as any of theirs ... Gen 43:34
ye have done evil in *s* doing ... Gen 44:5 834
God forbid that I should do *s* ... Gen 44:17 2063
S now it was not you that sent me ... Gen 45:8
And the children of Israel did *s* ... Gen 45:21 3651
S he sent his brethren away, and ... Gen 45:24
s that the land of Egypt and all ... Gen 47:13
s the land became Pharaoh's ... Gen 47:20
s the whole age of Jacob was an ... Gen 47:28
for age, *s* that he could not see ... Gen 48:10
said unto his father, Not *s* ... Gen 48:18 3651
s that his rider shall fall ... Gen 49:17
for *s* are fulfilled the days of ... Gen 50:3 3651
S shall ye say unto Joseph, ... Gen 50:17 3541
S Joseph died, being an hundred ... Gen 50:26
s get them up out of the land ... Ex 1:10
it that ye are come *s* soon to day ... Ex 2:18
S he let him go ... Ex 4:26
S the people were scattered ... Ex 5:12
wherefore hast thou *s* evil ... Ex 5:22
Moses spake *s* unto the children ... Ex 6:9 3651
LORD commanded them, *s* did they ... Ex 7:6 3651
they did *s* as the LORD had ... Ex 7:10 3651
And Moses and Aaron did *s*, as the ... Ex 7:20 3651
did *s* with their enchantments ... Ex 7:22 3651
the magicians did *s* with their ... Ex 8:7
And they did *s* ... Ex 8:17
the magicians did *s* with their ... Ex 8:18
s there were lice upon man, and ... Ex 8:18
And the LORD did *s* ... Ex 8:24 3651
said, It is not meet *s* to do ... Ex 8:26 3651
S there was hail, and fire mingled ... Ex 9:24
them, Let the LORD be *s* with you ... Ex 10:10 3651
Not *s* ... Ex 10:11 3651
s that the land was darkened ... Ex 10:15
s that he would not let the ... Ex 10:20
s that he would not let the ... Ex 11:10
Moses and Aaron, *s* did they ... Ex 12:28 3651
s that they lent unto them such ... Ex 12:36
Moses and Aaron, *s* did they ... Ex 12:50 3651
And they did *s* ... Ex 14:4 3651
s that the one came not near the ... Ex 14:20
s that the Egyptians said, Let us ... Ex 14:25
there remained not *s* much as one ... Ex 14:28 5704
S Moses brought Israel from the ... Ex 15:22
And the children of Israel did *s* ... Ex 16:17
S the people rested on the ... Ex 16:30
s Aaron laid it up before the ... Ex 16:34
Moses did *s* in the sight of the ... Ex 17:6 3651
S Joshua did as Moses had said to ... Ex 17:10
s shall it be easier for thyself, ... Ex 18:22
this thing, and God command thee *s* ... Ex 18:23
S Moses hearkened to the voice of ... Ex 18:24
s that all the people that was in ... Ex 19:16
S Moses went down unto the people ... Ex 19:25
s that he die, shall be surely ... Ex 21:12
s that her fruit depart from her, ... Ex 21:22
s that the stacks of corn, or the ... Ex 22:6
thereof, even *s* shall ye make it ... Ex 25:9 3651
s in the six branches that come ... Ex 25:33 3651
the mount, *s* shall they make it ... Ex 27:8 3651
s it shall be joined together ... Ex 28:7
S they shall wash their hands and ... Ex 30:21
and of sweet cinnamon half *s* much ... Ex 30:23
brought *s* great a sin upon them ... Ex 32:21
S they gave it me ... Ex 32:24
s shall we be separated, I and thy ... Ex 33:16
S the people were restrained from ... Ex 36:6
s it became one tabernacle ... Ex 36:13
s throughout the six branches ... Ex 37:19 3651
LORD commanded Moses, *s* did they ... Ex 39:32 3651
s the children of Israel made all ... Ex 39:42 3651
even *s* had they done it ... Ex 39:43 3651
the LORD commanded him, *s* did he ... Ex 40:16 3651
S Moses finished the work ... Ex 40:33
offering, *s* shall he do with this ... Lev 4:20 3651
s is the trespass offering ... Lev 7:7
s the LORD hath commanded to do, ... Lev 8:34
for *s* I am commanded ... Lev 8:35 3651
S Aaron and his sons did all ... Lev 8:36
S they went near, and carried them ... Lev 10:5
for *s* I am commanded ... Lev 10:13 3651
s it shall be cleansed ... Lev 11:32
s is the trespass offering ... Lev 14:13
he be poor, and cannot get *s* much ... Lev 14:21
flesh in water, and *s* put them on ... Lev 16:4
s shall he do for the tabernacle ... Lev 16:16 3651
s shall it be done to him ... Lev 24:19 3651
s shall it be done to him again ... Lev 24:20 3651
s that ye will not do all my ... Lev 26:15
who art the priest, *s* shall it be ... Lev 27:12 3651
estimate it, *s* shall it stand ... Lev 27:14 3651
s he numbered them in the ... Num 1:19
S were all those that were ... Num 1:45
LORD commanded Moses, *s* did they ... Num 1:54 3651
s shall they set forward, every ... Num 2:17 3651
s they pitched by their standards ... Num 2:34 3651
s they set forward, every one ... Num 2:34 3651
s shall they serve ... Num 4:26
And the children of Israel did *s* ... Num 5:4 3651
s did the children of Israel ... Num 5:4 3651
s he must do after the law of his ... Num 6:21 3651
And Aaron did *s* ... Num 8:3
s he made the candlestick ... Num 8:4 3651
and *s* make themselves clean ... Num 8:7
s did the children of Israel unto ... Num 8:20 3651
the Levites, *s* did they unto them ... Num 8:22 3651
s did the children of Israel ... Num 9:5 3651
the manner thereof, *s* shall he do ... Num 9:14 3651
S it was alway ... Num 9:16 3651
s it was, when the cloud was a ... Num 9:20
s it was, when the cloud abode ... Num 9:21
My servant Moses is not *s* ... Num 12:7 3651
S they went up, and searched the ... Num 13:21
and *s* we were in their sight ... Num 13:33
in mine ears, *s* will I do to you ... Num 14:28 3651
s shall ye do to every one ... Num 15:12 3602
as ye do, *s* he shall do ... Num 15:14 3651
s shall the stranger be before ... Num 15:15
s shall ye heave it ... Num 15:20 3651
S they gat up from the tabernacle ... Num 16:27
And Moses did *s* ... Num 17:11
the LORD commanded him, *s* did he ... Num 17:11 3651
s thou shalt give the ... Num 20:8
S they smote him, and his sons, and ... Num 21:35
was I ever wont to do *s* unto thee ... Num 22:30
S Balaam went with the princes of ... Num 22:35
S the plague was stayed from the ... Num 25:8
S there were delivered out of the ... Num 31:5
But if ye will not do *s*, behold, ... Num 32:23 3651
S concerning them Moses commanded Num 32:28
unto thy servants, *s* will we do ... Num 32:31 3651
S all the cities which ye shall ... Num 35:7
s that he die, he is a murderer ... Num 35:16
S these things shall be for a ... Num 35:29
S ye shall not pollute the land ... Num 35:33
s shall it be taken from the lot ... Num 36:3
s shall their inheritance be ... Num 36:4
S shall not the inheritance of ... Num 36:7
s did the daughters of Zelophehad ... Num 36:10 3651
times *s* many more as ye are ... Deut 1:11
S I took the chief of your tribes ... Deut 1:15
S I spake unto you ... Deut 1:43
S ye abode in Kadesh many days, ... Deut 1:46
not *s* much as a footbreadth ... Deut 2:5
S it came to pass, when all the ... Deut 2:16
S the LORD our God delivered into ... Deut 3:3
s shall the LORD do unto all the ... Deut 3:21 3651
S we abode in the valley over ... Deut 3:29
that ye should do *s* in the land ... Deut 4:5 3651
For what nation is there *s* great ... Deut 4:7
who hath God *s* nigh unto them, as ... Deut 4:7
And what nation is there *s* great ... Deut 4:8
judgments *s* righteous as all this ... Deut 4:8
s will the anger of the LORD be ... Deut 7:4
s shall the LORD thy God do unto ... Deut 7:19 3651
s the LORD thy God chasteneth ... Deut 8:5
your face, *s* shall ye perish ... Deut 8:20 3651
s shalt thou drive them out, and ... Deut 9:3
s that the LORD was angry with ... Deut 9:8
S I turned and came down from the ... Deut 9:15
Ye shall not do *s* unto the LORD ... Deut 12:4 3651
s that ye dwell in safety ... Deut 12:10
is eaten, *s* thou shalt eat them ... Deut 12:22 3651
even *s* will I do likewise ... Deut 12:30 3651
Thou shalt not do *s* unto the LORD ... Deut 12:31 3651
S shalt thou put the evil away ... Deut 13:5
s that thou art not able to carry ... Deut 14:24
S thou shalt put the evil away ... Deut 17:7
hath not suffered thee *s* to do ... Deut 18:14 3651
and *s* blood be upon thee ... Deut 19:10
s shalt thou put the evil away ... Deut 19:19
s should ye sin against the LORD ... Deut 20:18
S shalt thou put away the guilt ... Deut 21:9
s shalt thou put evil away from ... Deut 21:21
s shalt thou do with his raiment ... Deut 22:3 3651
for all that do *s* are abomination ... Deut 22:5 428
s shalt thou put evil away from ... Deut 22:21
s shalt thou put away evil from ... Deut 22:22
s thou shalt put away evil from ... Deut 22:24
him, even *s* is this matter ... Deut 22:26 3651
them, *s* ye shall observe to do ... Deut 24:8
S shall it be done unto that man ... Deut 25:9 3602
S that thou shalt be mad for the ... Deut 28:34
S that the man that is tender ... Deut 28:54
S that he will not give to any of ... Deut 28:55
s the LORD will rejoice over you ... Deut 28:63 3651
S that the generation to come of ... Deut 29:22
s that thou wilt not hear, but ... Deut 30:17
s that they will say in that day, ... Deut 31:17
S the LORD alone did lead him, and ... Deut 32:12 3651
thy days, *s* shall thy strength be ... Deut 33:25
S Moses the servant of the LORD ... Deut 34:5
s the days of weeping and mourning ... Deut 34:8
with Moses, *s* I will be with thee ... Josh 1:5
s will we hearken unto thee ... Josh 1:17 3651
unto your words, *s* be it ... Josh 2:21 3651
S the two men returned, and ... Josh 2:23
with Moses, *s* I will be with thee ... Josh 3:7
Israel did *s* as Joshua commanded ... Josh 4:8 3651
And Joshua did *s* ... Josh 5:15 3651
S the ark of the LORD compassed ... Josh 6:11
s they did six days ... Josh 6:14 3541
S the people shouted when the ... Josh 6:20
s that the people went up into ... Josh 6:20
S the LORD was with Joshua ... Josh 6:27
S there went up thither of the ... Josh 7:4
S Joshua rose up early in the ... Josh 7:16
S Joshua sent messengers, and they ... Josh 7:22
S the LORD turned from the ... Josh 7:26
S Joshua arose, and all the people ... Josh 8:3
s they were in the midst of ... Josh 8:22
s that they let none of them ... Josh 8:22 5704
s it was, that all that fell that ... Josh 8:25
s did he unto them, and delivered ... Josh 9:26 3651
s he had done to Ai and her king ... Josh 10:1 3651
S Joshua ascended from Gilgal, he ... Josh 10:7
S the sun stood still in the ... Josh 10:13
And they did *s*, and brought forth ... Josh 10:23 3651
s he did to Debir, and to the king ... Josh 10:39 3651
S Joshua smote all the country of ... Josh 10:40
S Joshua came, and all the people ... Josh 11:7
s did Moses command Joshua, and *s* ... Josh 11:15 3651
S Joshua took all that land, the ... Josh 11:16
S Joshua took the whole land, ... Josh 11:23
s the children of Israel did, and ... Josh 14:5 3651
even *s* is my strength now, for ... Josh 14:11
if *s* be the LORD will be with me, ... Josh 14:12
s northward, looking toward ... Josh 15:7
S the children of Joseph, ... Josh 16:4
S they made an end of dividing ... Josh 19:51
S all the cities for the children ... Josh 21:40
S Joshua blessed them, and sent ... Josh 22:6
s shall your children make our ... Josh 22:25
when they should *s* say to us or ... Josh 22:28
s shall the LORD bring upon you ... Josh 23:15 3651
s I delivered you out of his hand ... Josh 24:10
S Joshua made a covenant with the ... Josh 24:25
S Joshua let the people depart, ... Josh 24:28
S Simeon went with him ... Judg 1:3
have done, *s* God hath requited me ... Judg 1:7 3651
s that they became tributaries ... Judg 1:35
s that they could not any longer ... Judg 2:14
but they did not *s* ... Judg 2:17 3651
S the children of Israel served ... Judg 3:14
s that he could not draw the ... Judg 3:22 3588
S Moab was subdued that day under ... Judg 3:30
S Barak went down from mount ... Judg 4:14
s that Sisera lighted down off ... Judg 4:15
S he died ... Judg 4:21
S God subdued on that day Jabin ... Judg 4:23
is his chariot *s* long in coming ... Judg 5:28
S let all thine enemies perish, O ... Judg 5:31 3651
s it was, when Israel had sown, ... Judg 6:3
And he did *s* ... Judg 6:20 3651
s it was, because he feared his ... Judg 6:27
And it was *s* ... Judg 6:38 3651
And God did *s* that night ... Judg 6:40 3651
s that the host of the Midianites ... Judg 7:1
S he brought down the people unto ... Judg 7:5
S the people took victuals in ... Judg 7:8
And it was *s*, when Gideon heard ... Judg 7:15
be that, as I do, *s* shall ye do ... Judg 7:17 3651
S Gideon, and the hundred men that ... Judg 7:19
As thou art, *s* were they ... Judg 8:18 1992
as the man is, *s* is his strength ... Judg 8:21
s that they lifted up their heads ... Judg 8:28
s that all the men of the tower ... Judg 9:49
s that Israel was sore distressed ... Judg 10:9
And it was *s*, that when the ... Judg 11:5
if we do not *s* according to thy ... Judg 11:10 3651
s Israel possessed all the land ... Judg 11:21
S now the LORD God of Israel hath ... Judg 11:23
S whomsoever the LORD our God ... Judg 11:24
S Jephthah passed over unto the ... Judg 11:32
and it was *s*, that when those ... Judg 12:5
S Manoah took a kid with a meat ... Judg 13:19
S his father went down unto the ... Judg 14:10
for *s* used the young men to do ... Judg 14:10 3651
is it not *s* ... Judg 14:15
unto me, *s* have I done unto them ... Judg 15:11 3651
S his strength was not known ... Judg 16:9
s that his soul was vexed unto ... Judg 16:16
S the dead which he slew at his ... Judg 16:30
S the Levite went in ... Judg 17:10
S they turned and departed, and put ... Judg 18:21
s they did eat and drink, and ... Judg 19:4
S he brought him into his house, ... Judg 19:21
I pray you, do not *s* wickedly ... Judg 19:23
this man do not *s* vile a thing ... Judg 19:24 2063
s the man took his concubine, and ... Judg 19:25
And it was *s*, that all that saw it ... Judg 19:30
S all the men of Israel were ... Judg 20:11
S the children of Benjamin saw ... Judg 20:36
S that all which fell that day of ... Judg 20:46

Text	Reference	Strong's
yet *s* they sufficed them not	Judg 21:14	3651
And the children of Benjamin did *s*	Judg 21:23	3651
the LORD do *s* to me, and more also	Ruth 1:17	3541
S they two went until they came	Ruth 1:19	
S Naomi returned, and Ruth the	Ruth 1:22	
s she came, and hath continued	Ruth 2:7	
S she gleaned in the field until	Ruth 2:17	
S she kept fast by the maidens of	Ruth 2:23	
S he drew off his shoe	Ruth 4:8	
S Boaz took Ruth, and she was his	Ruth 4:13	
as he did *s* year by year, when	1Sa 1:7	3651
of the LORD, *s* she provoked her	1Sa 1:7	3651
S Hannah rose up after they had	1Sa 1:9	
S the woman went her way, and did	1Sa 1:18	
S the woman abode, and gave her	1Sa 1:23	
Talk no more *s* exceeding proudly	1Sa 2:3	
s that the barren hath born seven	1Sa 2:5	5704
S they did in Shiloh unto all the	1Sa 2:14	3602
s that she conceived, and bare	1Sa 2:21	
S Samuel went and lay down in his	1Sa 3:9	
God do *s* to thee, and more also,	1Sa 3:17	3541
S the people sent to Shiloh, that	1Sa 4:4	
s that the earth rang again	1Sa 4:5	
men of Ashdod saw that it was *s*	1Sa 5:7	3651
And it was *s*, that, after they had	1Sa 5:9	
S they sent and gathered together	1Sa 5:11	
And the men did *s*	1Sa 6:10	3651
S the Philistines were subdued,	1Sa 7:13	
gods, *s* do they also unto thee	1Sa 8:8	3651
S they went unto the city where	1Sa 9:10	
then speakest thou *s* to me	1Sa 9:21	1697
S Saul did eat with Samuel that	1Sa 9:24	
And it was *s*, that when he had	1Sa 10:9	
s shall it be done unto his oxen	1Sa 11:7	3541
it was *s* on the morrow, that Saul	1Sa 11:11	
s that two of them were not left	1Sa 11:11	
S Samuel called unto the LORD	1Sa 12:18	
S it came to pass in the day of	1Sa 13:22	
s it was a very great trembling	1Sa 14:15	
S the LORD saved Israel that day	1Sa 14:23	
S none of the people tasted any	1Sa 14:24	
And Saul answered, God do *s*	1Sa 14:44	3541
S the people rescued Jonathan,	1Sa 14:45	
S Saul took the kingdom over	1Sa 14:47	
S the Kenites departed from among	1Sa 15:6	
S Samuel turned again after Saul	1Sa 15:31	
s shall thy mother be childless	1Sa 15:33	3651
S Samuel rose up, and went to	1Sa 16:13	
s Saul was refreshed, and was well	1Sa 16:23	
s shall it be done to the man	1Sa 17:27	3541
S David prevailed over the	1Sa 17:50	
s that his name was much set by	1Sa 18:30	
S Michal let David down through a	1Sa 19:12	
Why hast thou deceived me *s*	1Sa 19:17	3602
S David fled, and escaped, and came	1Sa 19:18	
it is not *s*	1Sa 20:2	
The LORD do *s* and much more to	1Sa 20:13	3541
S Jonathan made a covenant with	1Sa 20:16	
S David hid himself in the field	1Sa 20:24	
S Jonathan arose from the table	1Sa 20:34	
S the priest gave him hallowed	1Sa 21:6	
who is *s* faithful among all thy	1Sa 22:14	
S David and his men went to Keilah	1Sa 23:5	
S David saved the inhabitants of	1Sa 23:5	
S David stayed his servants with	1Sa 24:7	
S David's young men turned their	1Sa 25:12	
And it was *s*, as she rode on the	1Sa 25:20	
s that nothing was missed of all	1Sa 25:21	
S and more also do God unto the	1Sa 25:22	3541
for as his name is, *s* is he	1Sa 25:25	3651
S David received of her hand that	1Sa 25:35	
S David and Abishai came to the	1Sa 26:7	
S David took the spear and the	1Sa 26:12	
s let my life be much set by in	1Sa 26:24	3651
S David went on his way, and Saul	1Sa 26:25	
s shall I escape out of his hand	1Sa 27:1	
S did David, and *s* will be his	1Sa 27:11	3541
S he arose from the earth, and sat	1Sa 28:23	
s long as I have been with thee	1Sa 29:8	
S David and his men rose up early	1Sa 29:11	
S David and his men came to the	1Sa 30:3	
S David went, he and the six	1Sa 30:9	
which were *s* faint that they	1Sa 30:10	
which were *s* faint that they	1Sa 30:21	
said David, Ye shall not do *s*	1Sa 30:23	3651
s shall his part be that tarrieth	1Sa 30:24	
it was *s* from that day forward,	1Sa 30:25	
S Saul died, and his three sons,	1Sa 31:6	
s it was, when he came to David,	2Sa 1:2	
S I stood upon him, and slew him,	2Sa 1:10	
S David went up thither, and his	2Sa 2:2	
s they fell down together	2Sa 2:16	
S Joab blew a trumpet, and all the	2Sa 2:28	
men, *s* that three hundred and	2Sa 2:31	
S do God to Abner, and more also,	2Sa 3:9	3541
to David, even *s* I do to him	2Sa 3:9	3651
S Abner came to David to Hebron,	2Sa 3:20	
S Joab and Abishai his brother	2Sa 3:30	
before wicked men, *s* fellest thou	2Sa 3:34	
S do God to me, and more also, if	2Sa 3:35	3541
S all the elders of Israel came	2Sa 5:3	
S David dwelt in the fort, and	2Sa 5:9	
And David did *s*, as the LORD had	2Sa 5:25	3651
S David would not remove the ark	2Sa 6:10	
S David went and brought up the	2Sa 6:12	
And it was *s*, that when they that	2Sa 6:13	
S David and all the house of	2Sa 6:15	
S all the people departed every	2Sa 6:19	
Now therefore *s* shalt thou say	2Sa 7:8	
s did Nathan speak unto David	2Sa 7:17	3651
s the Moabites became David's	2Sa 8:2	
servant, *s* shall thy servant do	2Sa 9:11	3651
S Mephibosheth dwelt in Jerusalem	2Sa 9:13	
S Joab returned from the children	2Sa 10:14	
S the Syrians feared to help the	2Sa 10:19	
S Uriah abode in Jerusalem that	2Sa 11:12	
if *s* be that the king's wrath	2Sa 11:20	
Wherefore approached ye *s* nigh	2Sa 11:20	
S the messenger went, and came and	2Sa 11:22	
S David and all the people	2Sa 12:31	
And Amnon was *s* vexed, that he	2Sa 13:2	
S Amnon lay down, and made himself	2Sa 13:6	
S Tamar went to her brother	2Sa 13:8	
s that the hatred wherewith he	2Sa 13:15	
S Tamar remained desolate in her	2Sa 13:20	
as thy servant said, *s* it is	2Sa 13:35	3651
S Absalom fled, and went to Geshur	2Sa 13:38	
S Joab put the words in her mouth	2Sa 14:3	
s they shall quench my coal which	2Sa 14:7	
s is my lord the king to discern	2Sa 14:17	3651
S Joab arose and went to Geshur,	2Sa 14:23	
S Absalom returned to his own	2Sa 14:24	3651
s much praised as Absalom for his	2Sa 14:25	
S Absalom dwelt two full years in	2Sa 14:28	
S Joab came to the king, and told	2Sa 14:33	
and it was *s*, that when any man	2Sa 15:2	
And it was *s*, that when any man	2Sa 15:5	
s Absalom stole the hearts of the	2Sa 15:6	
S he arose, and went to Hebron	2Sa 15:9	
s will I now also be thy servant	2Sa 15:34	
S Hushai David's friend came into	2Sa 15:37	
s let him curse, because the LORD	2Sa 16:10	3588
say, Wherefore hast thou done *s*	2Sa 16:10	3651
s will I be in thy presence	2Sa 16:19	3651
S they spread Absalom a tent upon	2Sa 16:22	
s was all the counsel of	2Sa 16:23	3651
s all the people shall be in	2Sa 17:3	
S shall we come upon him in some	2Sa 17:12	
shall not be left *s* much as one	2Sa 17:12	1571
S Israel and Absalom pitched in	2Sa 17:26	
S the people went out into the	2Sa 18:6	
God do *s* to me, and more also, if	2Sa 19:13	3541
s that they sent this word unto	2Sa 19:14	
S the king returned, and came to	2Sa 19:15	
S every man of Israel went up	2Sa 20:2	
S they were shut up unto the day	2Sa 20:3	
S Amasa went to assemble the men	2Sa 20:5	
s he smote him therewith in the	2Sa 20:10	
S Joab and Abishai his brother	2Sa 20:10	
and *s* they ended the matter	2Sa 20:18	3651
The matter is not *s*	2Sa 20:21	3651
s shall I be saved from mine	2Sa 22:4	
s that a bow of steel is broken	2Sa 22:35	
s that my feet did not slip	2Sa 22:37	
my house be not *s* with God	2Sa 23:5	3651
S when they had gone through all	2Sa 24:8	
S Gad came to David, and told him,	2Sa 24:13	
S the LORD sent a pestilence upon	2Sa 24:15	
S David bought the threshingfloor	2Sa 24:24	
S the LORD was intreated for the	2Sa 24:25	
S they sought for a fair damsel	1Kin 1:3	
in saying, Why hast thou done *s*	1Kin 1:6	3602
even *s* will I certainly do this	1Kin 1:30	3651
God of my lord the king say *s* too	1Kin 1:36	3651
even *s* be he with Solomon, and	1Kin 1:37	3651
S Zadok the priest, and Nathan the	1Kin 1:38	
s that the earth rent with the	1Kin 1:40	
s that the city rang again	1Kin 1:45	
S king Solomon sent, and they	1Kin 1:53	
for *s* they came to me when I fled	1Kin 2:7	3651
S David slept with his fathers,	1Kin 2:10	
the LORD, saying, God do *s* to me	1Kin 2:23	
S Solomon thrust out Abiathar	1Kin 2:27	
S Benaiah the son of Jehoiada	1Kin 2:34	
hath said, *s* will thy servant do	1Kin 2:38	3651
S the king commanded Benaiah the	1Kin 2:46	
judge this thy *s* great a people	1Kin 3:9	
s that there was none like thee	1Kin 3:12	
s that there shall not be any	1Kin 3:13	
S king Solomon was king over all	1Kin 4:1	
s that there is neither adversary	1Kin 5:4	
S Hiram gave Solomon cedar trees	1Kin 5:10	
s they prepared timber and stones	1Kin 5:18	
s that there was neither hammer	1Kin 6:7	
S he built the house, and finished	1Kin 6:9	
S Solomon built the house, and	1Kin 6:14	
s covered the altar which was of	1Kin 6:20	
S Solomon overlaid the house	1Kin 6:21	
s was it of the other cherub	1Kin 6:26	3651
s that the wing of the one	1Kin 6:27	
S also made he for the door of	1Kin 6:33	3651
S was he seven years in building	1Kin 6:38	
s on the outside toward the great	1Kin 7:9	
s did he for the other chapiter	1Kin 7:18	3651
s was the work of the pillars	1Kin 7:22	
S Hiram made an end of doing all	1Kin 7:40	
S was ended all the work that	1Kin 7:51	
S that the priests could not	1Kin 8:11	
s that thy children take heed to	1Kin 8:25	7535
s that they carry them away	1Kin 8:46	
s return unto thee with all their	1Kin 8:48	
And it was *s*, that when Solomon	1Kin 8:54	
S the king and all the children of	1Kin 8:63	
S he finished the house	1Kin 9:25	
S she turned and went to her own	1Kin 10:13	
S king Solomon exceeded all the	1Kin 10:23	
s for all the kings of the	1Kin 10:29	
s that he gave him to wife the	1Kin 11:19	
S Jeroboam and all the people came	1Kin 12:12	
S when all Israel saw that the	1Kin 12:16	
S Israel departed unto their	1Kin 12:16	
S Israel rebelled against the	1Kin 12:19	
S did he in Beth-el, sacrificing	1Kin 12:32	3651
S he offered upon the altar which	1Kin 12:33	
s that he could not pull it in	1Kin 13:4	
For *s* was it charged me by the	1Kin 13:9	3651
S he went another way, and	1Kin 13:10	
S they saddled him the ass	1Kin 13:13	
S he went back with him, and did	1Kin 13:19	
And Jeroboam's wife did *s*, and	1Kin 14:4	3651
And it was *s*, when Ahijah heard	1Kin 14:6	
And it was *s*, when the king went	1Kin 14:28	
S Ben-hadad hearkened unto king	1Kin 15:20	
S Baasha slept with his fathers,	1Kin 16:6	
s Tibni died, and Omri reigned	1Kin 16:22	
S Omri slept with his fathers, and	1Kin 16:28	
S he went and did according unto	1Kin 17:5	
S he arose and went to Zarephath	1Kin 17:10	
and his sickness was *s* sore	1Kin 17:17	3966
For it was *s*, when Jezebel cut	1Kin 18:4	
S they divided the land between	1Kin 18:6	
s when I come and tell Ahab, and he	1Kin 18:12	
S Obadiah went to meet Ahab, and	1Kin 18:16	
S Ahab sent unto all the children	1Kin 18:20	
S Ahab went up to eat and to drink	1Kin 18:42	
S let the gods do to me, and more	1Kin 19:2	3541
And it was *s*, when Elijah heard it	1Kin 19:13	
S he departed thence, and found	1Kin 19:19	
and said, The gods do *s* unto me	1Kin 20:10	3541
S these young men of the princes	1Kin 20:19	
unto their voice, and did *s*	1Kin 20:25	3651
s it was, that in the seventh day	1Kin 20:29	
S they girded sackcloth on their	1Kin 20:32	
S he made a covenant with him, and	1Kin 20:34	
s that in smiting he wounded him	1Kin 20:37	
S the prophet departed, and waited	1Kin 20:38	
unto him, *S* shall thy judgment be	1Kin 20:40	3651
unto him, Why is thy spirit *s* sad	1Kin 21:5	
S she wrote letters in Ahab's	1Kin 21:8	
said, Let not the king say *s*	1Kin 22:8	3651
And all the prophets prophesied *s*	1Kin 22:12	
S he came to the king	1Kin 22:15	
go forth, and do *s*	1Kin 22:22	3651
S the king of Israel and	1Kin 22:29	
S the king died, and was brought	1Kin 22:37	
S Ahab slept with his fathers	1Kin 22:40	
S he died according to the word	2Kin 1:17	
S they went down to Beth-el	2Kin 2:2	
S they came to Jericho	2Kin 2:4	
s that they two went over on dry	2Kin 2:8	
thee, it shall be *s* unto thee	2Kin 2:10	3651
but if not, it shall not be *s*	2Kin 2:10	
S the waters were healed unto	2Kin 2:22	
S the king of Israel went, and the	2Kin 3:9	
S the king of Israel and	2Kin 3:12	
s that they fled before them	2Kin 3:24	
S she went from him, and shut the	2Kin 4:5	
s it was, that as oft as he	2Kin 4:8	
S she went and came unto the man	2Kin 4:25	
S he called her	2Kin 4:36	
S they poured out for the men to	2Kin 4:40	
S he set it before them, and they	2Kin 4:44	
And it was *s*, when Elisha the man	2Kin 5:8	
S Naaman came with his horses and	2Kin 5:9	
S he turned and went away in a	2Kin 5:12	
S he departed from him a little	2Kin 5:19	
S Gehazi followed after Naaman	2Kin 5:21	
S he went with them	2Kin 6:4	
S the bands of Syria came no more	2Kin 6:23	
S we boiled my son, and did eat	2Kin 6:29	
Then he said, God do *s* and more	2Kin 6:31	3541
S they came and called unto the	2Kin 7:10	
S a measure of fine flour was	2Kin 7:16	
And *s* it fell out unto him	2Kin 7:20	3651
S the king appointed unto her a	2Kin 8:6	
S Hazael went to meet him, and	2Kin 8:9	
S he departed from Elisha, and	2Kin 8:14	
it on his face, *s* that he died	2Kin 8:15	
S Joram went over to Zair, and all	2Kin 8:21	
S the young man, even the young	2Kin 9:4	
S Jehu the son of Jehoshaphat the	2Kin 9:14	
S Jehu rode in a chariot, and went	2Kin 9:16	
S there went one on horseback to	2Kin 9:18	
s long as the whoredoms of thy	2Kin 9:22	
and her witchcrafts are *s* many	2Kin 9:22	
they did *s* at the going up to Gur	2Kin 9:27	
S they threw her down	2Kin 9:33	
s that they shall not say, This	2Kin 9:37	
S Jehu slew all that remained of	2Kin 10:11	
S they made him ride in his	2Kin 10:16	
s that there was not a man left	2Kin 10:21	
Athaliah, *s* that he was not slain	2Kin 11:2	
s shall ye keep the watch of the	2Kin 11:6	
But it was *s*, that in the three	2Kin 12:6	
And it was *s*, when they saw that	2Kin 12:10	
s that they went out from under	2Kin 13:5	
S Hazael king of Syria died	2Kin 13:24	
s that he was a leper unto the	2Kin 15:5	
S Azariah slept with his fathers	2Kin 15:7	
And *s* it came to pass	2Kin 15:12	3651
S the king of Assyria turned back	2Kin 15:20	
S Ahaz sent messengers to	2Kin 16:7	
s Urijah the priest made it	2Kin 16:11	3651
For *s* it was, that the children	2Kin 17:7	
S was Israel carried away out of	2Kin 17:23	
s it was at the beginning of	2Kin 17:25	
S they feared the LORD, and made	2Kin 17:32	
S these nations feared the LORD,	2Kin 17:41	
fathers, *s* do they unto this day	2Kin 17:41	
s that after him was none like	2Kin 18:5	
s is Pharaoh king of Egypt unto	2Kin 18:21	3651
S the servants of king Hezekiah	2Kin 19:5	
S Rab-shakeh returned, and found	2Kin 19:8	
S Sennacherib king of Assyria	2Kin 19:36	
S Hilkiah the priest, and Ahikam,	2Kin 22:14	
S they let his bones alone, with	2Kin 23:18	
S Jehoiakim slept with his	2Kin 24:6	
S they took the king, and brought	2Kin 25:6	
S Judah was carried away out of	2Kin 25:21	
S all Israel were reckoned by	1Chr 9:1	
S they and their children had the	1Chr 9:23	
S Saul took a sword, and fell upon	1Chr 10:4	

S Saul died, and his three sons, ... 1Chr 10:6
S Saul died for his transgression ... 1Chr 10:13
S Joab the son of Zeruiah went ... 1Chr 11:6
S David waxed greater and greater ... 1Chr 11:9
said that they would do *s* ... 1Chr 13:4 3651
S David gathered all Israel ... 1Chr 13:5
S David brought not the ark home ... 1Chr 13:13
S they came up to Baal-perazim ... 1Chr 14:11
S the priests and the Levites ... 1Chr 15:14
S the Levites appointed Heman the ... 1Chr 15:17
S the singers, Heman, Asaph, and ... 1Chr 15:19
S David, and the elders of Israel, ... 1Chr 15:25
S they brought the ark of God, and ... 1Chr 16:1
S he left there before the ark of ... 1Chr 16:37
s did Nathan speak unto David ... 1Chr 17:15 3651
S David reigned over all Israel, ... 1Chr 18:14
S the servants of David came into ... 1Chr 19:2
S they hired thirty and two ... 1Chr 19:7
S Joab and the people that were ... 1Chr 19:14
S when David had put the battle ... 1Chr 19:17
Even *s* dealt David with all the ... 1Chr 20:3 3651
times *s* many more as they be ... 1Chr 21:3 1992
S Gad came to David, and said unto ... 1Chr 21:11
S the LORD sent pestilence upon ... 1Chr 21:14
S David gave to Ornan for the ... 1Chr 21:25
S David prepared abundantly ... 1Chr 22:5
S when David was old and full of ... 1Chr 23:1
S the number of them, with their ... 1Chr 25:7
offer *s* willingly after this sort ... 1Chr 29:14
S Solomon, and all the ... 2Chr 1:3
this thy people, that is *s* great ... 2Chr 1:10
s brought they out horses for all ... 2Chr 1:17
therein, even *s* deal with me ... 2Chr 2:3
S that the priests could not ... 2Chr 5:14
yet *s* that thy children take heed ... 2Chr 6:16
s long as they live in the land ... 2Chr 6:31 3605
s the king and all the people ... 2Chr 7:5
s that he shall say, Why hath the ... 2Chr 7:21
for *s* had David the man of God ... 2Chr 8:14 3651
S the house of the LORD was ... 2Chr 8:16
S she turned, and went away to her ... 2Chr 9:12
S Jeroboam and all Israel came and ... 2Chr 10:3
S Jeroboam and all the people came ... 2Chr 10:12
S the king hearkened not unto the ... 2Chr 10:15
s all Israel went to their tents ... 2Chr 10:16
S they strengthened the kingdom ... 2Chr 11:17
S Shishak king of Egypt came up ... 2Chr 12:9
S king Rehoboam strengthened ... 2Chr 12:13
s that whosoever cometh to ... 2Chr 13:9
s they were before Judah, and the ... 2Chr 13:13
s there fell down slain of Israel ... 2Chr 13:17
S Abijah slept with his fathers, ... 2Chr 14:1
S they built and prospered ... 2Chr 14:7
S the LORD smote the Ethiopians ... 2Chr 14:12
S they gathered themselves ... 2Chr 15:10
s that they made no war against ... 2Chr 17:10
said, Let not the king say *s* ... 2Chr 18:7 3651
And all the prophets prophesied *s* ... 2Chr 18:11 3651
go out, and do even *s* ... 2Chr 18:21 3651
S the king of Israel and ... 2Chr 18:28
S the king of Israel disguised ... 2Chr 18:29
s wrath come upon you, and upon ... 2Chr 19:10
s that none is able to withstand ... 2Chr 20:6
s shall ye be established ... 2Chr 20:20
his prophets, *s* shall ye prosper ... 2Chr 20:20
of the spoil, it was *s* much ... 2Chr 20:25
S the realm of Jehoshaphat was ... 2Chr 20:30
S the Edomites revolted from ... 2Chr 21:10
s that there was never a son left ... 2Chr 21:17
s he died of sore diseases ... 2Chr 21:19
S Ahaziah the son of Jehoram king ... 2Chr 22:1
S the house of Ahaziah had no ... 2Chr 22:9
S Jehoshabeath, the daughter of ... 2Chr 22:11
Athaliah, *s* that she slew him not ... 2Chr 22:11
S the Levites and all Judah did ... 2Chr 23:8
S they laid hands on her ... 2Chr 23:15
S the workmen wrought, and the ... 2Chr 24:13
S they executed judgment against ... 2Chr 24:24
S Joash the king of Israel went ... 2Chr 25:21
S Uzziah slept with his fathers, ... 2Chr 26:23
S much did the children of Ammon ... 2Chr 27:5 2063
S Jotham became mighty, because ... 2Chr 27:6
S the armed men left the captives ... 2Chr 28:14
s they sanctified the house of ... 2Chr 29:17
S they killed the bullocks, and ... 2Chr 29:22
for *s* was the commandment of the ... 2Chr 29:25
s that they could not flay all ... 2Chr 29:34
S the service of the house of the ... 2Chr 29:35
S they established a decree to ... 2Chr 30:5
S the posts went with the letters ... 2Chr 30:6
s that they shall come again into ... 2Chr 30:9
S the posts passed from city to ... 2Chr 30:10
S there was great joy in ... 2Chr 30:26
S there was gathered much people ... 2Chr 32:4
s shall not the God of Hezekiah ... 2Chr 32:17 3651
S he returned with shame of face ... 2Chr 32:21
s that he was magnified in the ... 2Chr 32:23
s that the wrath of the LORD came ... 2Chr 32:26
s that they will take heed to do ... 2Chr 33:8
S Manasseh made Judah and the ... 2Chr 33:9
S Manasseh slept with his fathers ... 2Chr 33:20
s did he in the cities of ... 2Chr 34:6
s shall ye say unto him, Thus ... 2Chr 34:26
S they brought the king word ... 2Chr 34:28
S kill the passover, and sanctify ... 2Chr 35:6
S the service was prepared, and ... 2Chr 35:10
And *s* did they with the oxen ... 2Chr 35:12 3651
S all the service of the LORD was ... 2Chr 35:16
S the priests, and the Levites, and ... Ezr 2:70
S that the people could not ... Ezr 3:13
s thou shalt endamage the revenue ... Ezr 4:13
s shalt thou find in the book of ... Ezr 4:15
S it ceased unto the second year ... Ezr 4:24
there at Babylon, whether it be *s* ... Ezr 5:17
had sent, *s* they did speedily ... Ezr 6:13 3660
S we fasted and besought our God ... Ezr 8:23
S took the priests and the Levites ... Ezr 8:30
s that the holy seed have mingled ... Ezr 9:2
s that there should be no remnant ... Ezr 9:14
As thou hast said, *s* must we do ... Ezr 10:12 3651
children of the captivity did *s* ... Ezr 10:16 3651
S I prayed to the God of heaven ... Neh 2:4
S it pleased the king to send me ... Neh 2:6
S I came to Jerusalem, and was ... Neh 2:11
gate of the valley, and *s* returned ... Neh 2:15
S they strengthened their hands ... Neh 2:18
S built we the wall ... Neh 4:6
s that we are not able to build ... Neh 4:10
girded by his side, and *s* builded ... Neh 4:18
S we laboured in the work ... Neh 4:21
S neither I, nor my brethren, nor ... Neh 4:23
s will we do as thou sayest ... Neh 5:12 3651
S God shake out every man from ... Neh 5:13 3602
but *s* did not I, because of the ... Neh 5:15 3651
s that I cannot come down ... Neh 6:3
that I should be afraid, and do *s* ... Neh 6:13 3651
S the wall was finished in the ... Neh 6:15
S the priests, and the Levites, and ... Neh 7:73
S they read in the book in the ... Neh 8:8
S the Levites stilled all the ... Neh 8:11
S the people went forth, and ... Neh 8:16
not the children of Israel done *s* ... Neh 8:17 3651
S didst thou get thee a name, as ... Neh 9:10
s that they went through the ... Neh 9:11
s that they lacked nothing ... Neh 9:21
s they possessed the land of ... Neh 9:22
S the children went in and ... Neh 9:24
s they did eat, and were filled, ... Neh 9:25
s that they had the dominion over ... Neh 9:28
S stood the two companies of them ... Neh 12:40
s that the joy of Jerusalem was ... Neh 12:43
S the merchants and sellers of all ... Neh 13:20
if ye do *s* again, I will lay ... Neh 13:21
for *s* the king had appointed to ... Est 1:8 3651
(for *s* was the king's manner ... Est 1:13 3651
s that they shall despise their ... Est 1:17
and he did *s* ... Est 2:4 3651
S it came to pass, when the ... Est 2:8
(for *s* were the days of their ... Est 2:12 3651
S Esther was taken unto king ... Est 2:16
s that he set the royal crown ... Est 2:17
for the king had *s* commanded ... Est 3:2 3651
S Esther's maids and her ... Est 4:4
S Hatach went forth to Mordecai ... Est 4:6
s will I go in unto the king, ... Est 4:16 3651
S Mordecai went his way, and did ... Est 4:17
And it was *s*, when the king saw ... Est 5:2
S Esther drew near, and touched ... Est 5:2
S the king and Haman came to the ... Est 5:5
s long as I see Mordecai the Jew ... Est 5:13 6256
S Haman came in ... Est 6:6
do even *s* to Mordecai the Jew, ... Est 6:10 3651
S the king and Haman came to ... Est 7:1
presume in his heart to do *s* ... Est 7:5 3651
S they hanged Haman on the ... Est 7:10
S Esther arose, and stood before ... Est 8:4
S the posts that rode upon mules ... Est 8:14
king commanded it *s* to be done ... Est 9:14 3651
s as it should not fail, that ... Est 9:27
s that this man was the greatest ... Job 1:3
And it was *s*, when the days of ... Job 1:5
S Satan went forth from the ... Job 1:12
S went Satan forth from the ... Job 2:7
S they sat down with him upon the ... Job 2:13
s that their hands cannot perform ... Job 5:12
S the poor hath hope, and iniquity ... Job 5:16
we have searched it, *s* it is ... Job 5:27 3651
S am I made to possess months of ... Job 7:3 3651
s he that goeth down to the grave ... Job 7:9 3651
S that my soul chooseth ... Job 7:15
s that I am a burden to myself ... Job 7:20
S are the paths of all that ... Job 8:13 3651
I know it is *s* of a truth ... Job 9:2 3651
and make my hands never *s* clean ... Job 9:30
but it is not *s* with me ... Job 9:35 3651
mocketh another, do ye *s* mock him ... Job 13:9
S man lieth down, and riseth not ... Job 14:12
And if it were *s*, why should not ... Job 21:4
s should I be delivered for ever ... Job 23:7
s doth the grave those which have ... Job 24:19
And if it be not *s* now, who will ... Job 24:25
not reproach me *s* long as I live ... Job 27:6 3605
S these three men ceased to ... Job 32:1
in *s* doing my maker would soon ... Job 32:22
S that his life abhorreth bread, ... Job 33:20
s that they are destroyed ... Job 34:25
S that they cause the cry of the ... Job 34:28
But now, because it is not *s* ... Job 35:15
Even *s* would he have removed thee ... Job 36:16
None is *s* fierce that dare stir ... Job 41:10
One is *s* near to another, that no ... Job 41:16
And it was *s*, that after the LORD ... Job 42:7
S Eliphaz the Temanite and Bildad ... Job 42:9
S the LORD blessed the latter end ... Job 42:12
s fair as the daughters of Job ... Job 42:15
S Job died, being old and full of ... Job 42:17
The ungodly are not *s* ... Ps 1:4 3651
S shall the congregation of the ... Ps 7:7
s shall I be saved from mine ... Ps 18:3
s that a bow of steel is broken ... Ps 18:34
s will we sing and praise thy ... Ps 21:13
why art thou *s* far from helping ... Ps 22:1
s will I compass thine altar, O ... Ps 26:6
hearts, Ah, *s* would we have it ... Ps 35:25
s shalt thou dwell in the land, ... Ps 37:3
s that I am not able to look up ... Ps 40:12
s panteth my soul after thee, O ... Ps 42:1 3651
S shall the king greatly desire ... Ps 45:11
They saw it, and *s* they marvelled ... Ps 48:5 3651
s have we seen in the city of the ... Ps 48:8 3651
s is thy praise unto the ends of ... Ps 48:10 3651
charmers, charming never *s* wisely ... Ps 58:5
S that a man shall say, Verily ... Ps 58:11
S will I sing praise unto thy ... Ps 61:8 3651
s as I have seen thee in the ... Ps 63:2 3651
S they shall make their own ... Ps 64:8
when thou hast *s* provided for it ... Ps 65:9 3651
is driven away, *s* drive them away ... Ps 68:2
s let the wicked perish at the ... Ps 68:2
abundance of peace *s* long as the ... Ps 72:7 5704
s, O Lord, when thou awakest, ... Ps 73:20
S foolish was I, and ignorant ... Ps 73:22
I am *s* troubled that I cannot ... Ps 77:4 3651
who is *s* great a God as our God ... Ps 77:13
s a fire was kindled against ... Ps 78:21
S they did eat, and were well ... Ps 78:29
on safely, *s* that they feared not ... Ps 78:53
S that he forsook the tabernacle ... Ps 78:60
S he fed them according to the ... Ps 78:72
S we thy people and sheep of thy ... Ps 79:13
s that all they which pass by the ... Ps 80:12
S will not we go back from thee ... Ps 80:18
S I gave them up unto their own ... Ps 81:12
S persecute them with thy tempest ... Ps 83:15 3651
to thy fear, *s* is thy wrath ... Ps 90:11
S teach us to number our days, ... Ps 90:12 3651
s that I forget to eat my bread ... Ps 102:4
S the heathen shall fear the name ... Ps 102:15
s that thy youth is renewed like ... Ps 103:5
s great is his mercy toward them ... Ps 103:11
s far hath he removed our ... Ps 103:12
s the LORD pitieth them that fear ... Ps 103:13
of the field, *s* he flourisheth ... Ps 103:15
S is this great and wide sea, ... Ps 104:25
s he led them through the depths, ... Ps 106:9
and *s* the plague was stayed ... Ps 106:30
s that it went ill with Moses for ... Ps 106:32
s that he spake unadvisedly with ... Ps 106:33
the redeemed of the LORD say *s* ... Ps 107:2
s that the waves thereof are ... Ps 107:29
s he bringeth them unto their ... Ps 107:30
s that they are multiplied ... Ps 107:38
cursing, *s* let it come unto him ... Ps 109:17
s let it be far from him ... Ps 109:17
s let it come into his bowels ... Ps 109:18
s is every one that trusteth in ... Ps 115:8
s shall I talk of thy wondrous ... Ps 119:27
S shall I have wherewith to ... Ps 119:42
S shall I keep thy law ... Ps 119:44
s shall I keep the testimony of ... Ps 119:88
s will I keep thy precepts ... Ps 119:134
s our eyes wait upon the LORD our ... Ps 123:2 3651
s the LORD is round about his ... Ps 125:2
for *s* he giveth his beloved sleep ... Ps 127:2 3651
s are children of the youth ... Ps 127:4 3651
s is every one that trusteth in ... Ps 135:18
hath not dealt *s* with any nation ... Ps 147:20 3651
S are the ways of every one that ... Prov 1:19 3651
S that thou incline thine ear ... Prov 2:2
S shalt thou find favour and good ... Prov 3:4
S shall thy barns be filled with ... Prov 3:10
S shall they be life unto thy ... Prov 3:22
S shall thy poverty come as one ... Prov 6:11
S he that goeth in to his ... Prov 6:29 3651
S she caught him, and kissed him, ... Prov 7:13
passeth, *s* is the wicked no more ... Prov 10:25
s is the sluggard to them that ... Prov 10:26
s he that pursueth evil pursueth ... Prov 11:19
s is a fair woman which is ... Prov 11:22
heart of the foolish doeth not *s* ... Prov 15:7 3651
will not *s* much as bring it to ... Prov 19:24
s do stripes the inward parts of ... Prov 20:30
he thinketh in his heart, *s* is he ... Prov 23:7 3651
S shall the knowledge of wisdom ... Prov 24:14 3651
I will do *s* to him as he hath ... Prov 24:29 3651
S shall thy poverty come as one ... Prov 24:34
s is a wise reprover upon an ... Prov 25:12
s is a faithful messenger to them ... Prov 25:13
eat *s* much as is sufficient for ... Prov 25:16
be weary of thee, and *s* hate thee ... Prov 25:17
s is he that singeth songs to an ... Prov 25:20
s doth an angry countenance a ... Prov 25:23
s is good news from a far country ... Prov 25:25
s for men to search their own ... Prov 25:27
s honour is not seemly for a fool ... Prov 26:1 3651
s the curse causeless shall not ... Prov 26:2 3651
s is a parable in the mouth of ... Prov 26:7
s is he that giveth honour to a ... Prov 26:8 3651
s is a parable in the mouth of ... Prov 26:9
s a fool returneth to his folly ... Prov 26:11
s doth the slothful upon his bed ... Prov 26:14
S is the man that deceiveth his ... Prov 26:19 3651
s where there is no talebearer ... Prov 26:20
s is a contentious man to kindle ... Prov 26:21
s is a man that wandereth from ... Prov 27:8 3651
s doth the sweetness of a man's ... Prov 27:9
s a man sharpeneth the ... Prov 27:17
s he that waiteth on his master ... Prov 27:18
s the heart of man to man ... Prov 27:19 3651
s the eyes of man are never ... Prov 27:20
s is a man to his praise ... Prov 27:21
s is a wicked ruler over the poor ... Prov 28:15
s the forcing of wrath bringeth ... Prov 30:33
s that he shall have no need of ... Prov 31:11
S I was great, and increased more ... Eccl 2:9
s it happeneth even to me ... Eccl 2:15
s that no man can find out the ... Eccl 3:11
the one dieth, *s* dieth the other ... Eccl 3:19 3651
s that a man hath no preeminence ... Eccl 3:19
S I returned, and considered all ... Eccl 4:1
points as he came, *s* shall he go ... Eccl 5:16 3651
s that he wanteth nothing for his ... Eccl 6:2

s that the days of his years be Eccl 6:3
s is the laughter of the fool Eccl 7:6 3651
s I saw the wicked buried, who Eccl 8:10 3651
in the city where they had s done Eccl 8:10 3651
as is the good, s is the sinner Eccl 9:2
s are the sons of men snared in Eccl 9:12 1992
s doth a little folly him that is Eccl 10:1
even s thou knowest not the works Eccl 11:5
s is my love among the daughters Song 2:2 3651
s is my beloved among the sons Song 2:3 3651
that thou dost s charge us Song 5:9 3602
chaff, s their root shall be as Is 5:24
s the holy seed shall be the Is 6:13
Howbeit he meaneth not s, neither Is 10:7 3651
neither doth his heart think s Is 10:7 3651
s do to Jerusalem and her idols Is 10:11 3651
s shall he lift it up after the Is 10:26
thought, s shall it come to pass Is 14:24
I have purposed, s shall it stand Is 14:24 3651
s the daughters of Moab shall be Is 16:2
but his lies shall not be s Is 16:6 3651
For s the LORD said unto me, I Is 18:4 3541
And he did s, walking naked and Is 20:2 3651
S shall the king of Assyria lead Is 20:4 3651
s it cometh from the desert, from Is 21:1
s he shall open, and none shall Is 22:22
s that there is no house, no Is 23:1
s shall they be sorely pained at Is 23:5
the people, s with the priest Is 24:2
the servant, s with his master Is 24:2
the maid, s with her mistress Is 24:2
with the buyer, s with the seller Is 24:2
the lender, s with the borrower Is 24:2
s with the giver of usury to him Is 24:2
s have we been in thy sight, O Is 26:17 3651
s that there is no place clean Is 28:8
s shall the multitude of all the Is 29:8
s that there shall not be found Is 30:14
s shall the LORD of hosts come Is 31:4 3651
s will the LORD of hosts defend Is 31:5
s is Pharaoh king of Egypt to all Is 36:6 3651
S the servants of king Hezekiah Is 37:5
S Rabshakeh returned, and found Is 37:8
S Sennacherib king of Assyria Is 37:37
S the sun returned ten degrees, Is 38:8
s will he break all my bones Is 38:13 3651
or a swallow, s did I chatter Is 38:14 3651
s wilt thou recover me, and make Is 38:16
He that is s impoverished that he Is 40:20
S the carpenter encouraged the Is 41:7
s that thou didst not lay these Is 47:7 5704
if s be thou shalt be able to Is 47:12
if s be thou mayest prevail Is 47:12
his visage was s marred more than Is 52:14
S shall he sprinkle many nations Is 52:15 3651
s he openeth not his mouth Is 53:7
s have I sworn that I would not Is 54:9 3651
s are my ways higher than your Is 55:9 3651
S shall my word be that goeth Is 55:11 3651
S shall they fear the name of the Is 59:19
s that no man went through thee, Is 60:15
s the Lord GOD will cause Is 61:11 3651
s shall thy sons marry thee Is 62:5
s shall thy God rejoice over thee Is 62:5
s he was their Saviour Is 63:8
s didst thou lead thy people, to Is 63:14 3651
s will I do for my servants' Is 65:8 3651
comforteth, s will I comfort you Is 66:13 3651
s shall your seed and your name Is 66:22 3651
s is the house of Israel ashamed Jer 2:26 3651
about s much to change thy way Jer 2:36
s have ye dealt treacherously Jer 3:20 3651
s shall ye serve strangers in a Jer 5:19 3651
s are their houses full of deceit Jer 5:27 3651
and my people love to have it s Jer 5:31 3651
s she casteth out her wickedness Jer 6:7 3651
s that none can pass through them Jer 9:10
them, that they may find it s Jer 10:18
s shall ye be my people, and I Jer 11:4
I, and said, S be it, O LORD Jer 11:5 543
S I got a girdle according to the Jer 13:2
S I went, and hid it by Euphrates, Jer 13:5
s have I caused to cleave unto me Jer 13:11 3651
s he that getteth riches, and not Jer 17:11
s he made it again another vessel Jer 18:4
s are ye in mine hand, O house of Jer 18:6 3651
Even s will I break this people Jer 19:11 3602
if s be that the LORD will deal Jer 21:2
not be eaten, they were s bad Jer 24:2
cannot be eaten, they are s evil Jer 24:3
s will I acknowledge them that Jer 24:5 3651
cannot be eaten, they are s evil Jer 24:8
S will I give Zedekiah the king Jer 24:8 3651
If s be they will hearken, and Jer 26:3
S the priests and the prophets and Jer 26:7
the LORD do s Jer 28:6 3651
Even s will I break the yoke of Jer 28:11 3602
S Hananiah the prophet died the Jer 28:17
cannot be eaten, they are s evil Jer 29:17
is great, s that none is like it Jer 30:7
s will I watch over them, to Jer 31:28 3651
S Hanameel mine uncle's son came Jer 32:8
S I took the evidence of the Jer 32:11
s will I bring upon them all the Jer 32:42 3651
s will I multiply the seed of Jer 33:22 3651
s that I will not take any of his Jer 33:26
s shall they burn odours for thee Jer 34:5 3651
s we dwell at Jerusalem Jer 35:11
S Baruch the son of Neriah took Jer 36:14
S Baruch read it in their ears Jer 36:15
S the king sent Jehudi to fetch Jer 36:21
s Irijah took Jeremiah, and Jer 37:14
s Jeremiah sunk in the mire Jer 38:6
S Ebed-melech took the men with Jer 38:11
And Jeremiah did s Jer 38:12 3651
S they drew up Jeremiah with Jer 38:13
S Zedekiah the king sware Jer 38:16
s it shall be well unto thee, and Jer 38:20
S they shall bring out all thy Jer 38:23
S they left off speaking with him Jer 38:27
S Jeremiah abode in the court of Jer 38:28
S Nebuzar-adan the captain of the Jer 39:13
s he dwelt among the people Jer 39:14
S the captain of the guard gave Jer 40:5
And it was s, when they came into Jer 41:7
S he forbare, and slew them not Jer 41:8
S all the people that Ishmael had Jer 41:14
S shall it be with all the men Jer 42:17
s shall my fury be poured forth Jer 42:18 3651
s declare unto us, and we will do Jer 42:20 3651
S Johanan the son of Kareah, and Jer 43:4
S they came into the land of Jer 43:7
S that none of the remnant of Jer 44:14
S that the LORD could no longer Jer 44:22
by the sea, s shall he come Jer 46:18
but it shall not be s Jer 48:30 3651
his lies shall not s effect it Jer 48:30 3651
s shall Moab be a derision and a Jer 48:39
s shall no man abide there, Jer 50:40
if s be she may be healed Jer 51:8
s at Babylon shall fall the slain Jer 51:49
S Jeremiah wrote in a book all Jer 51:60
S the city was besieged unto the Jer 52:5
s that there was no bread for the Jer 52:6
S Nebuzar-adan the captain of the Jer 52:26
s that in the day of the LORD's Lam 2:22
if s be there may be hope Lam 3:29
s that men could not touch their Lam 4:14
ever, and forsake us s long time Lam 5:20
they were s high that they were Eze 1:18
s was the appearance of the Eze 1:28 3651
S I opened my mouth, and he caused Eze 3:2
S the spirit lifted me up, and Eze 3:14
s shalt thou bear the iniquity of Eze 4:5
S it shall be a reproach and a Eze 5:15
S will I send upon you famine and Eze 5:17
S will I stretch out my hand upon Eze 6:14
S I lifted up mine eyes the way Eze 8:5
S I went in and saw Eze 8:10
S the vision that I had seen went Eze 11:24
I did s as I was commanded Eze 12:7 3651
s shall it be done unto them Eze 12:11 3651
S will I break down the wall that Eze 13:14
s that the foundation thereof Eze 13:14
s that it be desolate, that no Eze 14:15
s that I cut off man and beast Eze 14:17
s will I give the inhabitants of Eze 15:6 3651
not come, neither shall it be s Eze 16:16
S will I make my fury toward thee Eze 16:42
is the mother, s is her daughter Eze 16:44
s it became a vine, and brought Eze 17:6
s also the soul of the son is Eze 18:4
s iniquity shall not be your ruin Eze 18:30
s that she hath no strong rod to Eze 19:14
s will I plead with you, saith Eze 20:36 3651
s that in all your doings your Eze 21:24
s will I gather you in mine anger Eze 22:20 3651
s shall ye be melted in the midst Eze 22:22 3651
S she discovered her whoredoms, Eze 23:18
s that thou shalt not lift up Eze 23:27
s went they in unto Aholah and Eze 23:44 3651
S I spake unto the people in the Eze 24:18
are to us, that thou doest s Eze 24:19
and I have set thee s Eze 28:14
s that all the trees of Eden, Eze 31:9
S thou, O son of man, I have set Eze 33:7
s will I seek out my sheep, and Eze 34:12 3651
desolate, s will I do unto thee Eze 35:15 3651
s shall the waste cities be Eze 36:38 3651
S I prophesied as I was commanded Eze 37:7
S I prophesied as he commanded me Eze 37:10
s shall they be my people, and I Eze 37:23
S that the fishes of the sea, and Eze 38:20
S will I make my holy name known Eze 39:7
S that they shall take no wood Eze 39:10
S the house of Israel shall know Eze 39:22
s fell they all by the sword Eze 39:23
s he measured the breadth of the Eze 40:5
S he measured the court, an Eze 40:47
S he measured the length thereof, Eze 41:4
s increased from the lowest Eze 41:7
S he measured the house, an Eze 41:13
s that a palm tree was between a Eze 41:18
S that the face of a man was Eze 41:19
S the spirit took me up, and Eze 43:5
S the altar shall be four cubits Eze 43:15
s forward, the priests shall make Eze 43:27
s thou shalt do the seventh day Eze 45:20 3651
s shall ye reconcile the house Eze 45:20
S shall ye divide this land unto Eze 47:21
s nourishing them three years, Dan 1:5
S he consented to them in this Dan 1:14
S they came and stood before the Dan 2:2
Why is the decree s hasty from Dan 2:15
s the kingdom shall be partly Dan 2:42
If it be s, our God whom we serve Dan 3:17
s that the joints of his loins Dan 5:6
S Daniel was taken up out of the Dan 6:23
S this Daniel prospered in the Dan 6:28
S he told me, and made me know the Dan 7:16
s that no beasts might stand Dan 8:4
S he came near where I stood Dan 8:17
them, s that they fled to hide Dan 10:7
S the king of the south shall Dan 11:9
S the king of the north shall Dan 11:15
s shall he do Dan 11:30
S he went and took Gomer the Hos 1:3
S I bought her to me for fifteen Hos 3:2
s will I also be for thee Hos 3:3 1571
s they sinned against me Hos 4:7 3651
s the company of priests murder Hos 6:9
if s be it yield, the strangers Hos 8:7
S shall Beth-el do unto you Hos 10:15 3602
them, s they went from them Hos 11:2 3602
their pasture, s were they filled Hos 13:6
s will we render the calves of Hos 14:2
and as horsemen, s shall they run Joel 2:4 3651
S shall ye know that I am the Joel 3:17
s shall the children of Israel be Amos 3:12 3651
S two or three cities wandered Amos 4:8
s that the spoiled shall come Amos 5:9
s the LORD, the God of hosts, Amos 5:14 3651
s shall all the heathen drink Obad 16
s he paid the fare thereof, and Jonah 1:3
s that the ship was like to be Jonah 1:4
S the shipmaster came to him, and Jonah 1:6
if s be that God will think upon Jonah 1:6
S they cast lots, and the lot fell Jonah 1:7
s shall the sea be calm unto you Jonah 1:12
S they took up Jonah, and cast him Jonah 1:15
S Jonah arose, and went unto Jonah 3:3
S the people of Nineveh believed Jonah 3:5
S Jonah went out of the city, and Jonah 4:5
S Jonah was exceeding glad of the Jonah 4:6
s they oppress a man and his house Mic 2:2
s will I destroy thy cities Mic 5:14
s they wrap it up Mic 7:3
s that there is no man, that Zeph 3:6
s their dwelling should not be Zeph 3:7
s my spirit remaineth among you Hag 2:5
S is this people, and s is this Hag 2:14 3651
s is every work of their hands Hag 2:14 3651
doings, s hath he dealt with us Zec 1:6 3651
S the angel that communed with me Zec 1:14
s that no man did lift up his Zec 1:21
S they set a fair mitre upon his Zec 3:5
S I answered and spake to the Zec 4:4
S they walked to and fro through Zec 6:7
as I have done these s many years Zec 7:3
s they cried, and I would not hear Zec 7:13 3651
s will I save you, and ye shall be Zec 8:13
S again have I thought in these Zec 8:15 3651
s the LORD shall make bright Zec 10:1
s the poor of the flock that Zec 11:11 3651
S they weighed for my price Zec 11:12
s shall be the plague of the Zec 14:15 3651
we spoken s much against thee Mal 3:13
S all the generations from Mt 1:17 3767
unto him, Suffer it to be s now Mt 3:15
for s persecuted they the Mt 5:12 3779
Let your light s shine before men Mt 5:16 3779
and shall teach men s, he shall Mt 5:19 3779
do not even the publicans s Mt 5:47 3779
if God s clothe the grass of the Mt 6:30 3779
do to you, do ye even s to them Mt 7:12 3779
Even s every good tree bringeth Mt 7:17 3779
I have not found s great faith Mt 8:10 5118
believed, s be it done unto thee Mt 8:13
s that no man might pass by that Mt 8:28 5620
S the devils besought him, saying Mt 8:31 1161
him, and s did his disciples Mt 9:19
It was never s seen in Israel Mt 9:33 3779
Even s, Father Mt 11:26 3779
for s it seemed good in thy sight Mt 11:26 3779
s shall the Son of man be three Mt 12:40 3779
Even s shall it be also unto this Mt 12:45 3779
s that he went into a ship, and Mt 13:2 5620
S the servants of the householder Mt 13:27 1161
s that the birds of the air come Mt 13:32 5620
s shall it be in the end of this Mt 13:40 3779
S shall it be at the end of the Mt 13:49 3779
Whence should we have s much Mt 15:33 5118
as to fill s great a multitude Mt 15:33 5118
if s be that he find it, verily I Mt 18:13 1437
Even s it is not the will of your Mt 18:14 3779
S when his fellowservants saw Mt 18:31 1161
S likewise shall my heavenly Mt 18:35 3779
from the beginning it was not s Mt 19:8 3779
of the man be s with his wife Mt 19:10 3779
which were s born from their Mt 19:12 3779
S when even was come, the lord of Mt 20:8 1161
S the last shall be first, and the Mt 20:16 3779
But it shall not be s among you Mt 20:26 3779
S Jesus had compassion on them, Mt 20:34 1161
S those servants went out into Mt 22:10 2532
Even s ye also outwardly appear Mt 23:28 3779
s shall also the coming of the Mt 24:27 3779
S likewise ye, when ye shall see Mt 24:33 3779
s shall also the coming of the Mt 24:37 3779
s shall also the coming of the Mt 24:39 3779
when he cometh shall find s doing Mt 24:46 3779
the wise answered, saying, Not s Mt 25:9
s he that had received five Mt 25:20 2532
s the last error shall be worse Mt 27:64 2532
S they went, and made the Mt 27:66
S they took the money, and did as Mt 28:15 1161
not s much as about the door Mk 2:2 3366
in his spirit that they s Mk 2:8 3779
s that they could not Mk 3:20 5620
could not s much as eat bread Mk 3:20 3383
s that he entered into a ship, and Mk 4:1 5620
and s endure but for a time Mk 4:17
S is the kingdom of God, as if a Mk 4:26 3779
s that the fowls of the air may Mk 4:32 5620
the ship, s that it was now full Mk 4:37 5620
unto them, Why are ye s fearful Mk 4:40 3779
had no leisure s much as to eat Mk 6:31 3761
Are ye s without understanding Mk 7:18 3779
s much the more a great deal they Mk 7:36
S they did eat, and were filled Mk 8:8 1161
s as no fuller on earth can white Mk 9:3 3634
s then they are no more twain, Mk 10:8 5620

S

But s shall it not be among you ... Mk 10:43 3779
S ye in like manner, when ye ... Mk 13:29 2532
But neither s did their witness ... Mk 14:59 3779
s that Pilate marvelled ... Mk 15:5 5620
s Pilate, willing to content the ... Mk 15:15
him, saw that he s cried out ... Mk 15:39 3779
S then after the Lord had spoken ... Mk 16:19 3303
he tarried s long in the temple ... Lk 1:21
mother answered and said, Not s ... Lk 1:60
s it was, that, while they were ... Lk 2:6
which was s named of the angel ... Lk 2:21
s that they began to sink ... Lk 5:7 5620
s was also James, and John, the ... Lk 5:10 3668
But s much the more went there a ... Lk 5:15
Have ye not read s much as this ... Lk 6:3 3761
And he did s ... Lk 6:10 3779
for s did their fathers to the ... Lk 6:26
I have not found s great faith ... Lk 7:9 5118
And they did s, and made them all ... Lk 9:15 3779
even s, Father ... Lk 10:21 3483
for s it seemed good in thy sight ... Lk 10:21 3779
be done, as in heaven, s in earth ... Lk 11:2 2532
s shall also the Son of man be to ... Lk 11:30 3779
S is he that layeth up treasure ... Lk 12:21 3779
If then God s clothe the grass, ... Lk 12:28 3779
the third watch, and find them s ... Lk 12:38 3779
when he cometh shall find s doing ... Lk 12:43 3779
and s it is ... Lk 12:54 3779
S that servant came, and shewed ... Lk 14:21 2532
S likewise, whosoever he be of ... Lk 14:33 3767
S he called every one of his ... Lk 16:5 2532
s that they which would pass from ... Lk 16:26 3704
S likewise ye, when ye shall have ... Lk 17:10 3779
s shall also the Son of man be in ... Lk 17:24 3779
s shall it be also in the days of ... Lk 17:26 3779
would not lift up s much as his ... Lk 18:13 3761
but he cried s much the more, ... Lk 18:39 3123
S they cast him out of the ... Lk 20:15 2532
that s they might deliver him ... Lk 20:20 1519
S likewise ye, when ye see these ... Lk 21:31 3779
s that day come upon you unawares ... Lk 21:34
But ye shall not be s ... Lk 22:26 3779
found it even s as the women had ... Lk 24:24 3779
s is every one that is born of ... Jn 3:8 3779
even s must the Son of man be ... Jn 3:14 3779
For God s loved the world, that ... Jn 3:16 3779
S when the Samaritans were come ... Jn 4:40 3767
S Jesus came again into Cana of ... Jn 4:46 3767
S the father knew that it was at ... Jn 4:53 3767
even s the Son quickeneth whom he ... Jn 5:21 3779
s hath he given to the Son to ... Jn 5:26 3779
but what are they among s many ... Jn 6:9 5118
S the men sat down, in number ... Jn 6:10 3767
S when they had rowed about five ... Jn 6:19 3767
s he that eateth me, even he ... Jn 6:57 2532
S there was a division among the ... Jn 7:43 3767
S when they continued asking him, ... Jn 8:7 1161
the midst of them, and s passed by ... Jn 8:59 3779
me, even s know I the Father ... Jn 10:15
And when she had s said, she went ... Jn 11:28 5023
But though he had done s many ... Jn 12:37 5118
Father said unto me, s I speak ... Jn 12:50 3779
S after he had washed their feet, ... Jn 13:12 3767
for s I am ... Jn 13:13
s now I say to you ... Jn 13:33 2532
if it were not s, I would have ... Jn 14:2
Have I been s long time with you, ... Jn 14:9 5118
gave me commandment, even s I do ... Jn 14:31 3779
s shall ye be my disciples ... Jn 15:8 2532
hath loved me, s have I loved you ... Jn 15:9 2504
even s have I also sent them into ... Jn 17:18
Jesus, and s did another disciple ... Jn 18:15
Answerest thou the high priest s ... Jn 18:22 3779
S they ran both together ... Jn 20:4 1161
And when he had s said, he shewed ... Jn 20:20 5124
hath sent me, even s send I you ... Jn 20:21
and for all there were s many ... Jn 21:11 5118
S when they had dined, Jesus ... Jn 21:15 3767
shall s come in like manner as ye ... Acts 1:11 3779
or why look ye s earnestly on us, ... Acts 3:12
suffer, he hath s fulfilled ... Acts 3:18 3779
S when they had further ... Acts 4:21 1161
ye sold the land for s much ... Acts 5:8 5118
And she said, Yea, for s much ... Acts 5:8 5118
s is also the Holy Ghost, whom ... Acts 5:32
high priest, Are these things s ... Acts 7:1 3779
not s much as to set his foot on ... Acts 7:5
s Abraham begat Isaac, and ... Acts 7:8 3779
S Jacob went down into Egypt, and ... Acts 7:15 1161
s that they cast out their young ... Acts 7:19
as your fathers did, s do ye ... Acts 7:51 2532
s opened he not his mouth ... Acts 8:32 3779
But Peter said, Not s, Lord ... Acts 10:14 3365
But I said, Not s, Lord ... Acts 11:8 3365
And s he did ... Acts 12:8 3779
affirmed that it was even s ... Acts 12:15 3779
S they, being sent forth by the ... Acts 13:4 3767
But Elymas the sorcerer (for s is ... Acts 13:8 3779
For s hath the Lord commanded us, ... Acts 13:47 3779
s spake, that a great multitude ... Acts 14:1 3779
S when they were dismissed, they ... Acts 15:30 3767
was s sharp between them, that ... Acts 15:39 5620
s Barnabas took Mark, and sailed ... Acts 15:39 5037
s were the churches established ... Acts 16:5 3767
s that the foundations of the ... Acts 16:26 5620
whether those things were s ... Acts 17:11 3779
S Paul departed from among them ... Acts 17:33 3779
We have not s much as heard ... Acts 19:2 3761
s that all they which dwelt in ... Acts 19:10 5620
S that from his body were brought ... Acts 19:12 5620
chief of the priests, which did s ... Acts 19:14 5124
s that they fled out of that ... Acts 19:16 5620
S mightily grew the word of God ... Acts 19:20 3779
S he sent into Macedonia two of ... Acts 19:22

S that not only this our craft is ... Acts 19:27
till break of day, s he departed ... Acts 20:11 3779
for s had he appointed, minding ... Acts 20:13 3779
s that I might finish my course ... Acts 20:24 5613
how that s labouring ye ought to ... Acts 20:35 3779
S shall the Jews at Jerusalem ... Acts 21:11 3779
s it was, that he was borne of ... Acts 21:35 4819
they cried s against him ... Acts 22:24 3779
And when he had s said, there ... Acts 23:7 5124
s must thou bear witness also at ... Acts 23:11 3779
S he took him, and brought him to ... Acts 23:18 3767
S the chief captain then let the ... Acts 23:22 3767
saying that these things were s ... Acts 24:9 3779
s worship I the God of my fathers ... Acts 24:14 3779
strake sail, and s were driven ... Acts 27:17 3779
s it came to pass, that they ... Acts 27:44 3779
S when this was done, others also ... Acts 28:9 3767
and s we went toward Rome ... Acts 28:14 3779
S, as much as in me is, I am ... Rom 1:15 3779
s that they are without excuse ... Rom 1:20 1519
was spoken, S shall thy seed be ... Rom 4:18 3779
And not only s, but we glory in ... Rom 5:3
And not only s, but we also joy in ... Rom 5:11
s death passed upon all men, for ... Rom 5:12 3779
offence, s also is the free gift ... Rom 5:15 3779
by one that sinned, s is the gift ... Rom 5:16
even s by the righteousness of ... Rom 5:18 3779
s by the obedience of one shall ... Rom 5:19 3779
even s might grace reign through ... Rom 5:21 3779
that s many of us as were ... Rom 6:3 3745
even s we also should walk in ... Rom 6:4 3779
even s now yield your members ... Rom 6:19 3779
her husband s long as he liveth ... Rom 7:2
S then if, while her husband ... Rom 7:3 686
s that she is no adulteress, ... Rom 7:3
S then with the mind I myself ... Rom 7:25 686
S then they that are in the flesh ... Rom 8:8
if s be that the Spirit of God ... Rom 8:9
if s be that we suffer with him, ... Rom 8:17
S then it is not of him that ... Rom 9:16 686
S then faith cometh by hearing, ... Rom 10:17 686
Even s then at this present time ... Rom 11:5 3779
root be holy, s are the branches ... Rom 11:16 2532
s all Israel shall be saved ... Rom 11:26 3779
Even s have these also now not ... Rom 11:31 3779
S we, being many, are one body in ... Rom 12:5 3779
for in s doing thou shalt heap ... Rom 12:20 5124
S then every one of us shall give ... Rom 14:12 686
s that from Jerusalem, and round ... Rom 15:19 5620
s have I strived to preach the ... Rom 15:20 3779
S that ye come behind in no gift ... 1Cor 1:7 5620
even s the things of God knoweth ... 1Cor 2:11 3779
S then neither is he that ... 1Cor 3:7 5620
yet s as by fire ... 1Cor 3:15 3779
Let a man s account of us, as of ... 1Cor 4:1 3779
is not s much as named among the ... 1Cor 5:1 3761
him that hath s done this deed ... 1Cor 5:3 3779
Is it s, that there is not a wise ... 1Cor 6:5 3779
called every one, s let him walk ... 1Cor 7:17 3779
s ordain I in all churches ... 1Cor 7:17 3779
that it is good for a man s to be ... 1Cor 7:26 3779
need s require, let him do what ... 1Cor 7:36 3779
hath s decreed in his heart that ... 1Cor 7:37 5124
S then he that giveth her in ... 1Cor 7:38 5620
But she is happier if she s abide ... 1Cor 7:40 3779
But when ye sin s against the ... 1Cor 8:12 3779
Even s hath the Lord ordained ... 1Cor 9:14 3779
that it should be s done unto me ... 1Cor 9:15 3779
S run, that ye may obtain ... 1Cor 9:24 3779
I therefore s run, not as ... 1Cor 9:26 3779
s fight I, not as one that ... 1Cor 9:26 3779
even s is the man also by the ... 1Cor 11:12 3779
s let him eat of that bread, and ... 1Cor 11:28 3779
s also is Christ ... 1Cor 12:12 3779
s that I could remove mountains, ... 1Cor 13:2 5620
S likewise ye, except ye utter by ... 1Cor 14:9 3779
s many kinds of voices in the ... 1Cor 14:10 5118
Even s ye, forasmuch as ye are ... 1Cor 14:12 3779
s falling down on his face he ... 1Cor 14:25 3779
s we preach, and s ye believed ... 1Cor 15:11 3779
if s be that the dead rise not ... 1Cor 15:15 686
even s in Christ shall all be ... 1Cor 15:22 3779
S also is the resurrection of the ... 1Cor 15:42 3779
s it is written, The first man ... 1Cor 15:45 3779
S when this corruptible shall ... 1Cor 15:54 1161
churches of Galatia, even s do ye ... 1Cor 16:1 3779
s our consolation also aboundeth ... 2Cor 1:5 3779
s shall ye be also of the ... 2Cor 1:7 3779
delivered us from s great a death ... 2Cor 1:10 5082
S that contrariwise ye ought ... 2Cor 2:7 5620
s that the children of Israel ... 2Cor 3:7 5620
S then death worketh in us, but ... 2Cor 4:12 5620
If s be that being clothed we ... 2Cor 5:3
s that I rejoiced the more ... 2Cor 7:7 5620
even s our boasting, which I made ... 2Cor 7:14 3779
s he would also finish in you the ... 2Cor 8:6 3779
s there may be a performance also ... 2Cor 8:11 3779
in his heart, s let him give ... 2Cor 9:7
Christ's, even s are we Christ's ... 2Cor 10:7 3779
s your minds should be corrupted ... 2Cor 11:3 3779
unto you, and s will I keep myself ... 2Cor 11:9
Hebrews? s am I ... 2Cor 11:22 2504
Israelites? s am I ... 2Cor 11:22 2504
Abraham? s am I ... 2Cor 11:22 2504
But be it s, I did not burden you ... 2Cor 12:16
I marvel that ye are s soon ... Gal 1:6 3779
s say I now again, If any man ... Gal 1:9 2532
Are ye s foolish ... Gal 3:3 3779
Have ye suffered s many things in ... Gal 3:4 5118
S then they which be of faith are ... Gal 3:9 5620
Even s we, when we were children, ... Gal 4:3 3779
the Spirit, even s it is now ... Gal 4:29 3779
S then, brethren, we are not ... Gal 4:31 686
s that ye cannot do the things ... Gal 5:17 2443

s fulfil the law of Christ ... Gal 6:2 3779
twain one new man, s making peace ... Eph 2:15
But ye have not s learned Christ ... Eph 4:20 3779
If s be that ye have heard him, ... Eph 4:21 3779
s let the wives be to their own ... Eph 5:24 3779
S ought men to love their wives ... Eph 5:28 3779
s love his wife even as himself ... Eph 5:33 3779
S that my bonds in Christ are ... Phil 1:13 5620
s now also Christ shall be ... Phil 1:20
s soon as I shall see how it will ... Phil 2:23 5613
mark them which walk s as ye have ... Phil 3:17 3779
s stand fast in the Lord, my ... Phil 4:1 3779
Jesus the Lord, s walk ye in him ... Col 2:6
Christ forgave you, s also do ye ... Col 3:13 3779
S that we were ensamples to all ... 1Th 1:7 5620
s that we need not to speak any ... 1Th 1:8 5620
with the gospel, even s we speak ... 1Th 2:4 3779
S being affectionately desirous ... 1Th 2:8 3779
s ye would abound more and more ... 1Th 4:1
even s them also which sleep in ... 1Th 4:14 3779
s shall we ever be with the Lord ... 1Th 4:17 3779
that the day of the Lord s cometh ... 1Th 5:2 3779
S that we ourselves glory in you ... 2Th 1:4 5620
s that he as God sitteth in the ... 2Th 2:4 5620
epistle: s I write ... 2Th 3:17 3779
which is in faith: s do ... 1Ti 1:4
Even s must their wives be grave, ... 1Ti 3:11 5615
of science falsely s called ... 1Ti 6:20
s do these also resist the truth ... 2Ti 3:8 3779
Being made s much better than the ... Heb 1:4 5118
if we neglect s great salvation ... Heb 2:3 5082
S I sware in my wrath, They shall ... Heb 3:11 5613
S we see that they could not ... Heb 3:19 2532
To day, after s long a time ... Heb 4:7 5118
s also for himself, to offer for ... Heb 5:3 3779
S also Christ glorified not ... Heb 5:5 3779
And s, after he had patiently ... Heb 6:15 3779
And as I may s say, Levi also, who ... Heb 7:9 5613
By s much was Jesus made a surety ... Heb 7:22 5118
S Christ was once offered to bear ... Heb 9:28 3779
s much the more, as ye see the ... Heb 10:25 5118
of them that were s used ... Heb 10:33 3779
s that things which are seen were ... Heb 11:3 1519
s many as the stars of the sky in ... Heb 11:12
with s great a cloud of witnesses ... Heb 12:1 5118
sin which doth s easily beset us ... Heb 12:1
if s much as a beast touch the ... Heb 12:20
s terrible was the sight, that ... Heb 12:21 3779
S that we may boldly say, The ... Heb 13:6 5620
s also shall the rich man fade ... Jas 1:11 3779
S speak ye, and s do, as they ... Jas 2:12 3779
Even s faith, if it hath not ... Jas 2:17 3779
s faith without works is dead ... Jas 2:26 3779
which though they be s great ... Jas 3:4 5082
Even s the tongue is a little ... Jas 3:5 3779
s is the tongue among our members ... Jas 3:6 3779
these things ought not s to be ... Jas 3:10 3779
s can no fountain both yield salt ... Jas 3:12 3779
s be ye holy in all manner of ... 1Pet 1:15 2532
If s be ye have tasted that the ... 1Pet 2:3
For s is the will of God, that ... 1Pet 2:15 3779
better, if the will of God be s ... 1Pet 3:17
even s minister the same one to ... 1Pet 4:10
and s doth Marcus my son ... 1Pet 5:13
For s an entrance shall be ... 2Pet 1:11 3779
him ought himself also s to walk ... 1Jn 2:6 3779
if God s loved us, we ought also ... 1Jn 4:11 3779
as he is, s are we in this world ... 1Jn 4:17 2532
Even s, Amen ... Rev 1:7 3483
S hast thou also them that hold ... Rev 2:15 3779
S then because thou art lukewarm, ... Rev 3:16 3779
s as the third part of them was ... Rev 8:12 2443
s that he maketh fire come down ... Rev 13:13 2443
out of the altar say, Even s ... Rev 16:7 3483
s mighty an earthquake ... Rev 16:18 5082
mighty an earthquake, and s great ... Rev 16:18 3779
S he carried me away in the ... Rev 17:3
s much torment and sorrow give her ... Rev 18:7 5118
For in one hour s great riches is ... Rev 18:17 5118
Even s, come, Lord Jesus ... Rev 22:20 3483

2. A king of Egypt.
messengers to S king of Egypt ... 2Kin 17:4 5471

SOAKED
their land shall be s with blood ... Is 34:7 7301

SOBER
or whether we be s, it is for ... 2Cor 5:13 4993
but let us watch and be s ... 1Th 5:6 3525
let us, who are of the day, be s ... 1Th 5:8 3525
husband of one wife, vigilant, s ... 1Ti 3:2 4998
wives be grave, not slanderers, s ... 1Ti 3:11 3524
a lover of good men, s, just, ... Titus 1:8 4998
That the aged men be s, grave, ... Titus 2:2 3524
may teach the young women to be s ... Titus 2:4 4994
likewise exhort to be s minded ... Titus 2:6 4993
up the loins of your mind, be s ... 1Pet 1:13 3525
be ye therefore s, and watch unto ... 1Pet 4:7 4993
Be s, be vigilant ... 1Pet 5:8 3525

SOBERLY
but to think s, according as God ... Rom 12:3
worldly lusts, we should live s ... Titus 2:12 4996

SOBERNESS
forth the words of truth and s ... Acts 26:25 4997

SOBRIETY
apparel, with shamefacedness and s ... 1Ti 2:9 4997
and charity and holiness with s ... 1Ti 2:15 4997

SOCHO (so'-ko) See SOCHOH. *A son of Heber.*
Gedor, and Heber the father of S ... 1Chr 4:18 7755

SOCHOH (so'-ko) See SHOCHOH, SOCHO, SOCOH.
A city in Judah near Adullam.
to him pertained S, and all the ... 1Kin 4:10 7755

SOCKET
hundred talents, a talent for a *s* .... Ex 38:27 134

SOCKETS
thou shalt make forty *s* of silver .... Ex 26:19 134
two *s* under one board for his two .... Ex 26:19 134
two *s* under another board for his .... Ex 26:19 134
And their forty *s* of silver .... Ex 26:21 134
two *s* under one board .... Ex 26:21 134
two *s* under another board .... Ex 26:21 134
s of silver, sixteen *s* .... Ex 26:25 134
two *s* under one board .... Ex 26:25 134
two *s* under another board .... Ex 26:25 134
gold, upon the four *s* of silver .... Ex 26:32 134
cast five *s* of brass for them .... Ex 26:37 134
their twenty *s* shall be of brass .... Ex 27:10 134
and their twenty *s* of brass .... Ex 27:11 134
their pillars ten, and their *s* ten .... Ex 27:12 134
pillars three, and their *s* three .... Ex 27:14 134
pillars three, and their *s* three .... Ex 27:15 134
shall be four, and their *s* four .... Ex 27:16 134
be of silver, and their *s* of brass .... Ex 27:17 134
twined linen, and their *s* of brass .... Ex 27:18 134
his bars, his pillars, and his *s* .... Ex 35:11 134
court, his pillars, and their *s* .... Ex 35:17 134
forty *s* of silver he made under .... Ex 36:24 134
two *s* under one board for his two .... Ex 36:24 134
two *s* under another board for his .... Ex 36:24 134
And their forty *s* of silver .... Ex 36:26 134
two *s* under one board .... Ex 36:26 134
two *s* under another board .... Ex 36:26 134
s were sixteen *s* of silver .... Ex 36:30 134
under every board two *s* .... Ex 36:30 134
he cast for them four *s* of silver .... Ex 36:36 134
but their five *s* were of brass .... Ex 36:38 134
twenty, and their brasen *s* twenty .... Ex 38:10 134
and their *s* of brass twenty .... Ex 38:11 134
their pillars ten, and their *s* ten .... Ex 38:12 134
pillars three, and their *s* three .... Ex 38:14 134
pillars three, and their *s* three .... Ex 38:15 134
the *s* for the pillars were of .... Ex 38:17 134
four, and their *s* of brass four .... Ex 38:19 134
were cast the *s* of the sanctuary .... Ex 38:27 134
and the *s* of the vail .... Ex 38:27 134
an hundred *s* of the hundred .... Ex 38:27 134
therewith he made the *s* to the .... Ex 38:30 134
the *s* of the court round about, ... Ex 38:31 134
the *s* of the court gate, and all .... Ex 38:31 134
bars, and his pillars, and his *s* .... Ex 39:33 134
the court, his pillars, and his *s* .... Ex 39:40 134
the tabernacle, and fastened his *s* .... Ex 40:18 134
the *s* thereof, and all the vessels .... Num 3:36 134
the court round about, and their *s* .... Num 3:37 134
pillars thereof, and *s* thereof, ... Num 4:31 134
the court round about, and their *s* .... Num 4:32 134
marble, set upon *s* of fine gold .... Song 5:15 134

SOCOH (*so'-ko*) See SOCHOH.
1. Same as Sochoh.
Jarmuth, and Adullam, *S*, and Azekah. Josh 15:35 7755
2. A city in the hill country of Judah.
Shamir, and Jattir, and *S*, ... Josh 15:48 7755

SOD
And Jacob *s* pottage .... Gen 25:29 2102
holy offerings *s* they in pots 2Chr 35:13 1310

SODDEN
nor *s* at all with water, but .... Ex 12:9 1310
wherein it is *s* shall be broken .... Lev 6:28 1310
if it be *s* in a brasen pot, it .... Lev 6:28 1310
take the *s* shoulder of the ram .... Num 6:19 1311
he will not have *s* flesh of thee 1Sa 2:15 1310
women have *s* their own children .... Lam 4:10 1310

SODERING
saying, It is ready for the *s* .... Is 41:7 1694

SODI (*so'-di*) *A spy sent to the Promised Land.*
of Zebulun, Gaddiel the son of *S* .... Num 13:10 5476

SODOM (*sod'-om*) See SODOMA, SODOMITE. *A city on the Salt Sea.*
as thou goest, unto *S*, and .... Gen 10:19 5467
before the LORD destroyed *S* .... Gen 13:10 5467
and pitched his tent toward *S* .... Gen 13:12 5467
But the men of *S* were wicked .... Gen 13:13 5467
made war with Bera king of *S* .... Gen 14:2 5467
And there went out the king of *S* .... Gen 14:8 5467
and the kings of *S* and Gomorrah .... Gen 14:10 5467
And they took all the goods of *S* .... Gen 14:11 5467
brother's son, who dwelt in *S* .... Gen 14:12 5467
the king of *S* went out to meet .... Gen 14:17 5467
the king of *S* said unto Abram, ... Gen 14:21 5467
And Abram said to the king of *S* .... Gen 14:22 5467
from thence, and looked toward *S* .... Gen 18:16 5467
LORD said, Because the cry of *S* .... Gen 18:20 5467
from thence, and went toward *S* .... Gen 18:22 5467
If I find in *S* fifty righteous .... Gen 18:26 5467
came two angels to *S* at even .... Gen 19:1 5467
and Lot sat in the gate of *S* .... Gen 19:1 5467
of the city, even the men of *S* .... Gen 19:4 5467
Then the LORD rained upon *S* .... Gen 19:24 5467
looked toward *S* and Gomorrah .... Gen 19:28 5467
therein, like the overthrow of *S* .... Deut 29:23 5467
their vine is of the vine of *S* .... Deut 32:32 5467
remnant, we should have been as *S* .... Is 1:9 5467
word of the LORD, ye rulers of *S* .... Is 1:10 5467
and they declare their sin as *S* .... Is 3:9 5467
shall be as when God overthrew *S* .... Is 13:19 5467
they are all of them unto me as *S* .... Jer 23:14 5467
As in the overthrow of *S* and .... Jer 49:18 5467
overthrew *S* and Gomorrah .... Jer 50:40 5467
the punishment of the sin of *S* .... Lam 4:6 5467
dwelleth at thy right hand, is *S* .... Eze 16:46 5467
S thy sister hath not done, she .... Eze 16:48 5467
was the iniquity of thy sister *S* .... Eze 16:49 5467
captivity, the captivity of *S* .... Eze 16:53 5467
When thy sisters, *S* and her .... Eze 16:55 5467
For thy sister *S* was not .... Eze 16:56 5467
some of you, as God overthrew *S* .... Amos 4:11 5467
Israel, Surely Moab shall be as *S* .... Zeph 2:9 5467
more tolerable for the land of *S* .... Mt 10:15 *4670*
done in thee, had been done in *S* .... Mt 11:23 *4670*
land of *S* in the day of judgment .... Mt 11:24 *4670*
It shall be more tolerable for *S* .... Mk 6:11 *4670*
more tolerable in that day for *S* .... Lk 10:12 *4670*
Lot went out of *S* it rained fire .... Lk 17:29 *4670*
And turning the cities of *S* 2Pet 2:6 *4670*
Even as *S* and Gomorrha, and the .... Jude 7 *4670*
which spiritually is called *S* .... Rev 11:8 *4670*

SODOMA (*sod'-o-mah*) See SODOM. *Greek form of Sodom.*
left us a seed, we had been as *S* .... Rom 9:29 *4670*

SODOMITE
nor a *s* of the sons of Israel .... Deut 23:17 6945

SODOMITES
And there were also *s* in the land 1Kin 14:24 6945
took away the *s* out of the land 1Kin 15:12 6945
And the remnant of the *s*, which 1Kin 22:46 6945

SOEVER
what saddle *s* he rideth upon that .... Lev 15:9 834
What man *s* there be of the house .... Lev 17:3
What man *s* of the seed of Aaron .... Lev 22:4
What thing *s* I command you, ... Deut 12:32 834
that what thing *s* thou shalt hear 2Sa 15:35 834
the people, how many *s* they be 2Sa 24:3
supplication *s* be made by any man 1Kin 8:38 834
s shall be made of any man 2Chr 6:29 834
what cause *s* shall come to you of 2Chr 19:10
wherewith *s* they shall blaspheme .... Mk 3:28
In what place *s* ye enter into a .... Mk 6:10 *1437*
unto you, What things *s* ye desire .... Mk 11:24
for what things *s* he doeth .... Jn 5:19 *302*
Whose *s* sins ye remit, they are .... Jn 20:23 *302*
whose *s* sins ye retain, they are .... Jn 20:23 *302*
that what things *s* the law saith .... Rom 3:19 *1437*

SOFT
For God maketh my heart *s* .... Job 23:16 7401
will he speak *s* words unto thee .... Job 41:3 7390
thou makest it *s* with showers .... Ps 65:10 4127
A *s* answer turneth away wrath .... Prov 15:1 7390
a *s* tongue breaketh the bone .... Prov 25:15 7390
A man clothed in *s* raiment .... Mt 11:8 *3120*
they that wear *s* clothing are in .... Mt 11:8 *3120*
A man clothed in *s* raiment .... Lk 7:25 *3120*

SOFTER
his words were *s* than oil .... Ps 55:21 7401

SOFTLY
and I will lead on *s*, according as .... Gen 33:14 328
went *s* unto him, and smote the .... Judg 4:21 3814
and she came *s*, and uncovered his .... Ruth 3:7 3909
and lay in sackcloth, and went *s* 1Kin 21:27 328
the waters of Shiloah that go *s* .... Is 8:6 328
I shall go *s* all my years in the .... Is 38:15
And when the south wind blew *s* .... Acts 27:13 *5285*

SOIL
in a good *s* by great waters .... Eze 17:8 7704

SOJOURN
went down into Egypt to *s* there .... Gen 12:10 1481
This one fellow came in to *s* .... Gen 19:9 1481
S in this land, and I will be with .... Gen 26:3 1481
For to *s* in the land are we come .... Gen 47:4 1481
when a stranger shall *s* with thee .... Ex 12:48 1481
the strangers which *s* among you .... Lev 17:8 1481
of the strangers that *s* among you .... Lev 17:10 1481
of the strangers that *s* among you .... Lev 17:13 1481
if a stranger *s* with thee in your .... Lev 19:33 1481
of the strangers that *s* in Israel .... Lev 20:2 1481
the strangers that do *s* among you .... Lev 25:45 1481
if a stranger shall *s* among you .... Num 9:14 1481
And if a stranger *s* with you .... Num 15:14 1481
to *s* where he could find a place .... Judg 17:8 1481
I go to *s* where I may find a .... Judg 17:9 1481
went to *s* in the country of Moab .... Ruth 1:1 1481
evil upon the widow with whom I *s* 1Kin 17:20 1481
s wheresoever thou canst *s* 2Kin 8:1 1481
that I *s* in Mesech, that I dwell .... Ps 120:5 1481
shall carry her afar off to *s* .... Is 23:7 1481
aforetime into Egypt to *s* there .... Is 52:4 1481
into Egypt, and go to *s* there .... Jer 42:15 1481
faces to go into Egypt to *s* there .... Jer 42:17 1481
whither ye desire to go and to *s* .... Jer 42:22 1481
say, Go not into Egypt to *s* there .... Jer 43:2 1481
into the land of Egypt to *s* there .... Jer 44:12 1481
into the land of Egypt to *s* there .... Jer 44:14 1481
into the land of Egypt to *s* there .... Jer 44:28 1481
They shall no more *s* there .... Lam 4:15 1481
out of the country where they *s* .... Eze 20:38 4033
to the strangers that *s* among you .... Eze 47:22 1481
seed should *s* in a strange land .... Acts 7:6

SOJOURNED
Kadesh and Shur, and *s* in Gerar .... Gen 20:1 1481
to the land wherein thou hast *s* .... Gen 21:23 1481
Abraham *s* in the Philistines' .... Gen 21:34 1481
I have *s* with Laban, and stayed .... Gen 32:4 1481
Hebron, where Abraham and Isaac *s* .... Gen 35:27 1481
out of all Israel, where he *s* .... Deut 18:6 1481
s there with a few, and became .... Deut 26:5 1481
who was a Levite, and he *s* there .... Judg 17:7 1481
and he *s* in Gibeah .... Judg 19:16 1481
s in the land of the Philistines 2Kin 8:2 1481
Jacob *s* in the land of Ham .... Ps 105:23 1481
By faith he *s* in the land of .... Heb 11:9 *3939*

SOJOURNER
I am a stranger and a *s* with you .... Gen 23:4 8453
a *s* of the priest, or an hired .... Lev 22:10 8453
though he be a stranger, or a *s* .... Lev 25:35 8453
as an hired servant, and as a *s* .... Lev 25:40 8453
if a *s* or stranger wax rich by .... Lev 25:47 1616
unto the stranger or *s* by thee .... Lev 25:47 8453
stranger, and for the *s* among them .... Num 35:15 8453
I am a stranger with thee, and a *s* .... Ps 39:12 8453

SOJOURNERS
for ye are strangers and *s* with me .... Lev 25:23 8453
were *s* there until this day 2Sa 4:3 1481
are strangers before thee, and *s* 1Chr 29:15 8453

SOJOURNETH
of her that *s* in her house, ... Ex 3:22 1481
the stranger that *s* among you .... Ex 12:49 1481
or a stranger that *s* among you .... Lev 16:29 1481
that *s* among you eat blood .... Lev 17:12 1481
nor any stranger that *s* among you .... Lev 18:26 1481
for thy stranger that *s* with thee .... Lev 25:6 1481
for the stranger that *s* with you .... Num 15:15 1481
for the stranger that *s* with you .... Num 15:16 1481
and the stranger that *s* among them .... Num 15:26 1481
the stranger that *s* among them .... Num 15:29 1481
the stranger that *s* among them .... Num 19:10 1481
the stranger that *s* among them .... Josh 20:9 1481
remaineth in any place where he *s* .... Ezr 1:4 1481
of the stranger that *s* in Israel .... Eze 14:7 1481
that in what tribe the stranger *s* .... Eze 47:23 1481

SOJOURNING
Now the *s* of the children of .... Ex 12:40 4186
s on the side of mount Ephraim .... Judg 19:1 1481
the time of your *s* here in fear 1Pet 1:17 *3940*

SOLACE
let us *s* ourselves with loves .... Prov 7:18 5965

SOLD
he *s* his birthright unto Jacob .... Gen 25:33 4376
for he hath *s* us, and hath quite .... Gen 31:15 4376
s Joseph to the Ishmeelites for .... Gen 37:28 4376
the Midianites *s* him into Egypt .... Gen 37:36 4376
and *s* unto the Egyptians .... Gen 41:56 7666
he it was that *s* to all the .... Gen 42:6 7666
brother, whom ye *s* into Egypt .... Gen 45:4 4376
yourselves, that ye *s* me hither .... Gen 45:5 4376
for the Egyptians *s* every man his .... Gen 47:20 4376
wherefore they *s* not their lands .... Gen 47:22 4376
then he shall be *s* for his theft .... Ex 22:3 4376
The land shall not be *s* for ever .... Lev 25:23 4376
poor, and hath *s* away some of his .... Lev 25:25 4376
redeem that which his brother *s* .... Lev 25:25 4465
unto the man to whom he *s* it .... Lev 25:27 4376
then that which is *s* shall remain .... Lev 25:28 4465
within a whole year after it is *s* .... Lev 25:29 4465
then the house that was *s* .... Lev 25:33 4465
of their cities may not be *s* .... Lev 25:34 4376
be waxen poor, and be *s* unto thee .... Lev 25:39 4376
they shall not be *s* as bondmen .... Lev 25:42 4376
After that he is *s* he may be .... Lev 25:48 4376
him from the year that he was *s* .... Lev 25:50 4376
or if he have *s* the field to .... Lev 27:20 4376
then it shall be *s* according to .... Lev 27:27 4376
shall be *s* or redeemed .... Lev 27:28 4376
be *s* unto thee, and serve thee six .... Deut 15:12 4376
there ye shall be *s* unto your .... Deut 28:68 4376
except their Rock had *s* them .... Deut 32:30 4376
he *s* them into the hands of their .... Judg 2:14 4376
he *s* them into the hand of .... Judg 3:8 4376
the LORD *s* them into the hand of .... Judg 4:2 4376
he *s* them into the hands of the .... Judg 10:7 4376
he *s* them into the hand of Sisera 1Sa 12:9 4376
because thou hast *s* thyself to 1Kin 21:20 4376
until an ass's head was *s* for 2Kin 6:25
of fine flour be *s* for a shekel 2Kin 7:1
of fine flour was *s* for a shekel 2Kin 7:16
s themselves to do evil in the 2Kin 17:17 4376
which were *s* unto the heathen .... Neh 5:8 4376
or shall they be *s* unto us .... Neh 5:8 4376
the day wherein they *s* victuals .... Neh 13:15 4376
s on the sabbath unto the .... Neh 13:16 4376
For we are *s*, I and my people, to .... Est 7:4 4376
But if we had been *s* for bondmen .... Est 7:4 4376
Joseph, who was *s* for a servant .... Ps 105:17 4376
is it to whom I have *s* you .... Is 50:1 4376
iniquities have ye *s* yourselves .... Is 50:1 4376
Ye have *s* yourselves for nought .... Is 52:3 4376
which hath been *s* unto thee .... Jer 34:14 4376
our wood is *s* unto us .... Lam 5:4
not return to that which is *s* .... Eze 7:13 4465
s a girl for wine, that they .... Joel 3:3 4376
have ye *s* unto the Grecians .... Joel 3:6 4376
the place whither ye have *s* them .... Joel 3:7 4376
because they *s* the righteous for .... Amos 2:6 4376
not two sparrows *s* for a farthing .... Mt 10:29 *4453*
s all that he had, and bought it .... Mt 13:46 *4097*
his lord commanded him to be *s* .... Mt 18:25 *4097*
God, and cast out all them that *s* .... Mt 21:12 *4453*
and the seats of them that *s* doves .... Mt 21:12 *4453*
might have been *s* for much .... Mt 26:9 *4097*
and began to cast out them that *s* .... Mk 11:15 *4453*
and the seats of them that *s* doves .... Mk 11:15 *4453*
For it might have been *s* for more .... Mk 14:5 *4097*
five sparrows *s* for two farthings .... Lk 12:6 *4453*
they drank, they bought, they *s* .... Lk 17:28 *4453*
to cast out them that *s* therein .... Lk 19:45 *4453*
in the temple those that *s* oxen .... Jn 2:14 *4453*
And said unto them that *s* doves .... Jn 2:16 *4453*
s for three hundred pence .... Jn 12:5 *4097*
s their possessions and goods, and .... Acts 2:45 *4097*
of lands or houses *s* them .... Acts 4:34 *4453*
prices of the things that were *s* .... Acts 4:34 *4097*
s it, and brought the money, and .... Acts 4:37 *4453*

S

his wife, *s* a possession, Acts 5:1 *4453*
and after it was *s*, was it not in Acts 5:4 *4097*
Tell me whether ye *s* the land for Acts 5:8 *591*
with envy, *s* Joseph into Egypt Acts 7:9 *591*
but I am carnal, *s* under sin Rom 7:14 *4097*
Whatsoever is *s* in the shambles, 1Cor 10:25 *4453*
morsel of meat *s* his birthright Heb 12:16 *591*

SOLDIER
four parts, to every *s* a part Jn 19:23 *4757*
a devout *s* of them that waited on Acts 10:7 *4757*
by himself with a *s* that kept him Acts 28:16 *4757*
companion in labour, and fellow *s* Phil 2:25
as a good *s* of Jesus Christ 2Ti 2:3 *4757*
him who hath chosen him to be a *s* 2Ti 2:4 *4758*

SOLDIERS
fathers, were bands of *s* for war 1Chr 7:4 6635
thousand and two hundred *s* 1Chr 7:11
But the *s* of the army which 2Chr 25:13 1121
require of the king a band of *s* Ezr 8:22 2428
therefore the armed *s* of Moab Is 15:4 2502
authority, having *s* under me Mt 8:9 *4757*
Then the *s* of the governor took Mt 27:27 *4757*
unto him the whole band of *s* Mt 27:27
they gave large money unto the *s* Mt 28:12 *4757*
the *s* led him away into the hall, Mk 15:16 *4757*
the *s* likewise demanded of him, Lk 3:14 *4754*
authority, having under me *s* Lk 7:8 *4757*
the *s* also mocked him, coming to Lk 23:36 *4757*
the *s* platted a crown of thorns, Jn 19:2 *4757*
Then the *s*, when they had Jn 19:23 *4757*
These things therefore the *s* did Jn 19:24 *4757*
Then came the *s*, and brake the Jn 19:32 *4757*
But one of the *s* with a spear Jn 19:34 *4757*
four quaternions of *s* to keep him Acts 12:4 *4757*
Peter was sleeping between two *s* Acts 12:6 *4757*
was no small stir among the *s* Acts 12:18 *4757*
Who immediately took *s* and Acts 21:32 *4757*
saw the chief captain and the *s* Acts 21:32 *4757*
that he was borne of the *s* for Acts 21:35 *4757*
them, commanded the *s* to go down Acts 23:10 *4753*
two hundred *s* to go to Caesarea Acts 23:23 *4757*
Then the *s*, as it was commanded Acts 23:31 *4757*
said to the centurion and to the *s* Acts 27:31 *4757*
Then the *s* cut off the ropes of Acts 27:32 *4757*

SOLDIERS'
the *s* counsel was to kill the Acts 27:42 *4757*

SOLE
no rest for the *s* of her foot Gen 8:9 3709
from the *s* of thy foot unto the Deut 28:35 3709
would not adventure to set the *s* Deut 28:56 3709
neither shall the *s* of thy foot Deut 28:65 3709
Every place that the *s* of your Josh 1:3 3709
from the *s* of his foot even to 2Sa 14:25 3709
with the *s* of my feet have I 2Kin 19:24 3709
the *s* of his foot unto his crown Job 2:7 3709
From the *s* of the foot even unto Is 1:6 3709
with the *s* of my feet have I Is 37:25 3709
the *s* of their feet was like the Eze 1:7 3709
was like the *s* of a calf's foot Eze 1:7 3709

SOLEMN
it is a *s* assembly Lev 23:36 6116
your gladness, and in your *s* days Num 10:10 4150
offering, or in your *s* feasts Num 15:3 4150
day ye shall have a *s* assembly Num 29:35 6116
a *s* assembly to the LORD thy God Deut 16:8 6116
Seven days shalt thou keep a *s* Deut 16:15 2287
Proclaim a *s* assembly for Baal 2Kin 10:20 6116
on the *s* feasts of the LORD our 2Chr 2:4 4150
eighth day they made a *s* assembly 2Chr 7:9 6116
the new moons, and on the *s* feasts 2Chr 8:13 4150
the eighth day was a *s* assembly Neh 8:18 6116
appointed, on our *s* feast day Ps 81:3 2282
upon the harp with a *s* sound Ps 92:3
is iniquity, even the *s* meeting Is 1:13 6116
because none come to the *s* feasts Lam 1:4 4150
the LORD hath caused the *s* feasts Lam 2:6 4150
LORD, as in the day of a *s* feast Lam 2:7 4150
Thou hast called as in a *s* day my Lam 2:22 4150
of Jerusalem in her *s* feasts Eze 36:38 4150
before the LORD in the *s* feasts Eze 46:9 4150
her sabbaths, and all her *s* feasts Hos 2:11 4150
What will ye do in the *s* day Hos 9:5 4150
as in the days of the *s* feast Hos 12:9 4150
call a *s* assembly, gather the Joel 1:14 6116
a fast, call a *s* assembly Joel 2:15 6116
not smell in your *s* assemblies Amos 5:21 6116
O Judah, keep thy *s* feasts Nah 1:15 2282
are sorrowful for the *s* assembly Zeph 3:18 4150
even the dung of your *s* feasts Mal 2:3 2282

SOLEMNITIES
Look upon Zion, the city of our *s* Is 33:20 4150
in all *s* of the house of Israel Eze 45:17 4150
in the *s* the meat offering shall Eze 46:11 4150

SOLEMNITY
in the *s* of the year of release, Deut 31:10 4150
the night when a holy *s* is kept Is 30:29 2282

SOLEMNLY
The man did *s* protest unto us, Gen 43:3 5749
howbeit yet protest *s* unto them 1Sa 8:9 5749

SOLES
Every place whereon the *s* of your Deut 11:24 3709
as soon as the *s* of the feet of Josh 3:13 3709
the *s* of the priests' feet were Josh 4:18 3709
put them under the *s* of his feet 1Kin 5:3 3709
down at the *s* of thy feet Is 60:14 3709
and the place of the *s* of my feet Eze 43:7 3709
they shall be ashes under the *s* Mal 4:3 3709

SOLITARILY
which dwell *s* in the wood Mic 7:14 910

SOLITARY
Lo, let that night be *s* Job 3:7 1565
For want and famine they were *s* Job 30:3 1565
God setteth the *s* in families Ps 68:6 3173
in the wilderness in a *s* way Ps 107:4 3452
the *s* place shall be glad for Is 35:1 6723
How doth the city sit *s*, that was Lam 1:1 910
out, and departed into a *s* place Mk 1:35 *2048*

SOLOMON (*sol'-o-mun*) See JEDIDIAH, SOLOMON'S. *Son of David; king of Israel.*
and Shobab, and Nathan, and *S* 2Sa 5:14 8010
a son, and he called his name *S* 2Sa 12:24 8010
S his brother, he called not 1Kin 1:10 8010
unto Bath-sheba the mother of *S* 1Kin 1:11 8010
life, and the life of thy son *S* 1Kin 1:12 8010
Assuredly *S* thy son shall reign 1Kin 1:13 8010
Assuredly *S* thy son shall reign 1Kin 1:17 8010
but *S* thy servant hath he not 1Kin 1:19 8010
my son *S* shall be counted 1Kin 1:21 8010
son of Jehoiada, and thy servant *S* 1Kin 1:26 8010
Assuredly *S* thy son shall reign 1Kin 1:30 8010
cause *S* my son to ride upon mine 1Kin 1:33 8010
trumpet, and say, God save king *S* 1Kin 1:34 8010
the king, even so be he with *S* 1Kin 1:37 8010
caused *S* to ride upon king 1Kin 1:38 8010
of the tabernacle, and anointed *S* 1Kin 1:39 8010
the people said, God save king *S* 1Kin 1:39 8010
lord king David hath made *S* king 1Kin 1:43 8010
also *S* sitteth on the throne of 1Kin 1:46 8010
name of *S* better than thy name 1Kin 1:47 8010
And Adonijah feared because of *S* 1Kin 1:50 8010
And it was told *S*, saying, Behold, 1Kin 1:51 8010
Behold, Adonijah feareth king *S* 1Kin 1:51 8010
Let king *S* swear unto me to day 1Kin 1:51 8010
S said, If he will shew himself a 1Kin 1:52 8010
So king *S* sent, and they brought 1Kin 1:53 8010
came and bowed himself to king *S* 1Kin 1:53 8010
S said unto him, Go to thine 1Kin 1:53 8010
and he charged *S* his son, saying, 1Kin 2:1 8010
Then sat *S* upon the throne of 1Kin 2:12 8010
to Bath-sheba the mother of *S* 1Kin 2:13 8010
unto *S* the king, (for he will not 1Kin 2:17 8010
therefore went unto king *S* 1Kin 2:19 8010
king *S* answered and said unto his 1Kin 2:22 8010
Then king *S* sware by the LORD, 1Kin 2:23 8010
king *S* sent by the hand of 1Kin 2:25 8010
So *S* thrust out Abiathar from 1Kin 2:27 8010
it was told king *S* that Joab was 1Kin 2:29 8010
Then *S* sent Benaiah the son of 1Kin 2:29 8010
it was told *S* that Shimei had 1Kin 2:41 8010
king *S* shall be blessed, and the 1Kin 2:45 8010
was established in the hand of *S* 1Kin 2:46 8010
S made affinity with Pharaoh king 1Kin 3:1 8010
S loved the LORD, walking in the 1Kin 3:3 8010
did *S* offer upon that altar 1Kin 3:4 8010
appeared to *S* in a dream by night 1Kin 3:5 8010
S said, Thou hast shewed unto thy 1Kin 3:6 8010
that *S* had asked this thing 1Kin 3:10 8010
And *S* awoke 1Kin 3:15 8010
So king *S* was king over all 1Kin 4:1 8010
S had twelve officers over all 1Kin 4:7 8010
Taphath the daughter of *S* to wife 1Kin 4:11 8010
Basmath the daughter of *S* to wife 1Kin 4:15 8010
S reigned over all kingdoms from 1Kin 4:21 8010
served *S* all the days of his life 1Kin 4:21 8010
to Beer-sheba, all the days of *S* 1Kin 4:25 8010
S had forty thousand stalls of 1Kin 4:26 8010
provided victual for king *S* 1Kin 4:27 8010
And God gave *S* wisdom and 1Kin 4:29 8010
people to hear the wisdom of *S* 1Kin 4:34 8010
of Tyre sent his servants unto *S* 1Kin 5:1 8010
And *S* sent to Hiram, saying, 1Kin 5:2 8010
when Hiram heard the words of *S* 1Kin 5:7 8010
And Hiram sent to *S*, saying, I 1Kin 5:8 8010
So Hiram gave *S* cedar trees 1Kin 5:10 8010
S gave Hiram twenty thousand 1Kin 5:11 8010
thus gave *S* to Hiram year by year 1Kin 5:11 8010
And the LORD gave *S* wisdom 1Kin 5:12 8010
was peace between Hiram and *S* 1Kin 5:12 8010
king *S* raised a levy out of all 1Kin 5:13 8010
S had threescore and ten thousand 1Kin 5:15 8010
which king *S* built for the LORD 1Kin 6:2 8010
And the word of the LORD came to *S* 1Kin 6:11 8010
So *S* built the house, and finished 1Kin 6:14 8010
So *S* overlaid the house within 1Kin 6:21 8010
But *S* was building his own house 1Kin 7:1 8010
S made also an house for 1Kin 7:8 8010
And king *S* sent and fetched Hiram 1Kin 7:13 8010
And he came to king *S*, and wrought 1Kin 7:14 8010
king *S* for the house of the LORD 1Kin 7:40 8010
which Hiram made to king *S* for 1Kin 7:45 8010
S left all the vessels unweighed, 1Kin 7:47 8010
S made all the vessels that 1Kin 7:48 8010
ended all the work that king *S* 1Kin 7:51 8010
S brought in the things which 1Kin 7:51 8010
Then *S* assembled the elders of 1Kin 8:1 8010
unto king *S* in Jerusalem, that 1Kin 8:1 8010
king *S* at the feast in the month 1Kin 8:2 8010
And king *S*, and all the 1Kin 8:5 8010
Then spake *S*, The LORD said that 1Kin 8:12 8010
S stood before the altar of the 1Kin 8:22 8010
that when *S* had made an end of 1Kin 8:54 8010
S offered a sacrifice of peace 1Kin 8:63 8010
And at that time *S* held a feast 1Kin 8:65 8010
when *S* had finished the building 1Kin 9:1 8010
appeared to *S* the second time 1Kin 9:2 8010
when *S* had built the two houses, 1Kin 9:10 8010
had furnished *S* with cedar trees 1Kin 9:11 8010
that then king *S* gave Hiram 1Kin 9:11 8010
the cities which *S* had given him 1Kin 9:12 8010
of the levy which king *S* raised 1Kin 9:15 8010
S built Gezer, and Beth-horon the 1Kin 9:17 8010
the cities of store that *S* had 1Kin 9:19 8010
that which *S* desired to build in 1Kin 9:19 8010
upon those did *S* levy a tribute 1Kin 9:21 8010
of Israel did *S* make no bondmen 1Kin 9:22 8010
house which *S* had built for her 1Kin 9:24
year did *S* offer burnt offerings 1Kin 9:25 8010
king *S* made a navy of ships in 1Kin 9:26 8010
the sea, with the servants of *S* 1Kin 9:27 8010
talents, and brought it to king *S* 1Kin 9:28 8010
of Sheba heard of the fame of *S* 1Kin 10:1 8010
and when she was come to *S* 1Kin 10:2 8010
S told her all her questions 1Kin 10:3 8010
the queen of Sheba gave to king *S* 1Kin 10:10 8010
king *S* gave unto the queen of 1Kin 10:13 8010
beside that which *S* gave her of 1Kin 10:13 8010
to *S* in one year was six hundred 1Kin 10:14 8010
king *S* made two hundred targets 1Kin 10:16 8010
accounted of in the days of *S* 1Kin 10:21 8010
So king *S* exceeded all the kings 1Kin 10:23 8010
And all the earth sought to *S* 1Kin 10:24 8010
S gathered together chariots and 1Kin 10:26 8010
S had horses brought out of Egypt 1Kin 10:28 8010
But king *S* loved many strange 1Kin 11:1 8010
S clave unto these in love 1Kin 11:2 8010
when *S* was old, that his wives 1Kin 11:4 8010
For *S* went after Ashtoreth the 1Kin 11:5 8010
S did evil in the sight of the 1Kin 11:6 8010
Then did *S* build an high place 1Kin 11:7 8010
And the LORD was angry with *S* 1Kin 11:9 8010
Wherefore the LORD said unto *S* 1Kin 11:11 8010
stirred up an adversary unto *S* 1Kin 11:14 8010
to Israel all the days of *S* 1Kin 11:25 8010
S built Millo, and repaired the 1Kin 11:27 8010
S seeing the young man that he 1Kin 11:28 8010
the kingdom out of the hand of *S* 1Kin 11:31 8010
S sought therefore to kill 1Kin 11:40 8010
was in Egypt until the death of *S* 1Kin 11:40 8010
And the rest of the acts of *S* 1Kin 11:41 8010
in the book of the acts of *S* 1Kin 11:41 8010
the time that *S* reigned in 1Kin 11:42 8010
S slept with his fathers, and was 1Kin 11:43 8010
fled from the presence of king *S* 1Kin 12:2 8010
that stood before *S* his father 1Kin 12:6 8010
again to Rehoboam the son of *S* 1Kin 12:21 8010
Speak unto Rehoboam, the son of *S* 1Kin 12:23 8010
the son of *S* reigned in Judah 1Kin 14:21 8010
shields of gold which *S* had made 1Kin 14:26 8010
to *S* his son, In this house, and 2Kin 21:7 8010
which *S* the king of Israel had 2Kin 23:13 8010
all the vessels of gold which *S* 2Kin 24:13 8010
the bases which *S* had made for 2Kin 25:16 8010
and Shobab, and Nathan, and *S* 1Chr 3:5 8010
temple that *S* built in Jerusalem 1Chr 6:10 8010
until *S* had built the house of 1Chr 6:32 8010
Shammua, and Shobab, Nathan, and *S* 1Chr 14:4 8010
wherewith *S* made the brasen sea, 1Chr 18:8 8010
S my son is young and tender, and 1Chr 22:5 8010
Then he called for *S* his son 1Chr 22:6 8010
And David said to *S*, My son, as 1Chr 22:7 8010
for his name shall be *S*, and I 1Chr 22:9 8010
of Israel to help *S* his son 1Chr 22:17 8010
he made *S* his son king over 1Chr 23:1 8010
he hath chosen *S* my son to sit 1Chr 28:5 8010
S thy son, he shall build my 1Chr 28:6 8010
S my son, know thou the God of 1Chr 28:9 8010
Then David gave to *S* his son the 1Chr 28:11 8010
And David said to *S* his son 1Chr 28:20 8010
S my son, whom alone God hath 1Chr 29:1 8010
give unto *S* my son a perfect 1Chr 29:19 8010
they made *S* the son of David king 1Chr 29:22 8010
Then *S* sat on the throne of the 1Chr 29:23 8010
themselves unto *S* the king 1Chr 29:24 8010
the LORD magnified *S* exceedingly 1Chr 29:25 8010
S his son reigned in his stead 1Chr 29:28 8010
And *S* the son of David was 2Chr 1:1 8010
Then *S* spake unto all Israel, to 2Chr 1:2 8010
So *S*, and all the congregation 2Chr 1:3 8010
and *S* and the congregation sought 2Chr 1:5 8010
S went up thither to the brasen 2Chr 1:6 8010
that night did God appear unto *S* 2Chr 1:7 8010
S said unto God, Thou hast shewed 2Chr 1:8 8010
And God said to *S*, Because this 2Chr 1:11 8010
Then *S* came from his journey to 2Chr 1:13 8010
S gathered chariots and horsemen 2Chr 1:14 8010
S had horses brought out of Egypt 2Chr 1:16 8010
S determined to build an house 2Chr 2:1 8010
S told out threescore and ten 2Chr 2:2 8010
S sent to Huram the king of Tyre, 2Chr 2:3 8010
in writing, which he sent to *S* 2Chr 2:11 8010
S numbered all the strangers that 2Chr 2:17 8010
Then *S* began to build the house 2Chr 3:1 8010
these are the things wherein *S* 2Chr 3:3 8010
for king *S* for the house of God 2Chr 4:11 8010
S for the house of the LORD of 2Chr 4:16 8010
Thus *S* made all these vessels in 2Chr 4:18 8010
S made all the vessels that were 2Chr 4:19 8010
Thus all the work that *S* made for 2Chr 5:1 8010
S brought in all the things that 2Chr 5:1 8010
Then *S* assembled the elders of 2Chr 5:2 8010
Also king *S*, and all the 2Chr 5:6 8010
Then said *S*, The LORD hath said 2Chr 6:1 8010
For *S* had made a brasen scaffold, 2Chr 6:13 8010
Now when *S* had made an end of 2Chr 7:1 8010
king *S* offered a sacrifice of 2Chr 7:5 8010
Moreover *S* hallowed the middle of 2Chr 7:7 8010
which *S* had made was not able to 2Chr 7:7 8010
Also at the same time *S* kept the 2Chr 7:8 8010
had shewed unto David, and to *S* 2Chr 7:10 8010
Thus *S* finished the house of the 2Chr 7:11 8010
the LORD appeared to *S* by night 2Chr 7:12 8010
wherein *S* had built the house of 2Chr 8:1 8010
which Huram had restored to *S* 2Chr 8:2 8010
S built them, and caused the 2Chr 8:2 8010

S went to Hamath-zobah, and 2Chr 8:3 8010
all the store cities that S had 2Chr 8:6 8010
all that S desired to build in 2Chr 8:6 8010
them did S make to pay tribute 2Chr 8:8 8010
S make no servants for his work 2Chr 8:9 8010
S brought up the daughter of 2Chr 8:11 8010
Then S offered burnt offerings 2Chr 8:12 8010
Now all the work of S was 2Chr 8:16 8010
Then went S to Ezion-geber, and to 2Chr 8:17 8010
with the servants of S to Ophir 2Chr 8:18 8010
gold, and brought them to king S 2Chr 8:18 8010
of Sheba heard of the fame of S 2Chr 9:1 8010
she came to prove S with hard 2Chr 9:1 8010
and when she was come to S 2Chr 9:1 8010
S told her all her questions 2Chr 9:2 8010
hid from S which he told her not 2Chr 9:2 8010
of Sheba had seen the wisdom of S 2Chr 9:3 8010
as the queen of Sheba gave king S 2Chr 9:9 8010
of Huram, and the servants of S 2Chr 9:10 8010
king S gave to the queen of Sheba 2Chr 9:12 8010
to S in one year was six hundred 2Chr 9:13 8010
brought gold and silver to S 2Chr 9:14 8010
king S made two hundred targets 2Chr 9:15 8010
vessels of king S were of gold 2Chr 9:20 8010
accounted of in the days of S 2Chr 9:20 8010
king S passed all the kings of 2Chr 9:22 8010
earth sought the presence of S 2Chr 9:23 8010
S had four thousand stalls for 2Chr 9:25 8010
they brought unto S horses out of 2Chr 9:28 8010
Now the rest of the acts of S 2Chr 9:29 8010
S reigned in Jerusalem over all 2Chr 9:30 8010
S slept with his fathers, and he 2Chr 9:31 8010
from the presence of S the king 2Chr 10:2 8010
S his father while he yet lived 2Chr 10:6 8010
Speak unto Rehoboam the son of S 2Chr 11:3 8010
made Rehoboam the son of S strong 2Chr 11:17 8010
walked in the way of David and S 2Chr 11:17 8010
shields of gold which S had made 2Chr 12:9 8010
the servant of S the son of David 2Chr 13:6 8010
against Rehoboam the son of S 2Chr 13:7 8010
for since the time of S the son 2Chr 30:26 8010
to S his son, In this house, and 2Chr 33:7 8010
S the son of David king of Israel 2Chr 35:3 8010
to the writing of S his son 2Chr 35:4 8010
of David, and of S his son Neh 12:45 8010
Did not S king of Israel sin by Neh 13:26 8010
A Psalm for S Ps 72:t 8010
A Song of degrees for S Ps 127:t 8010
The Proverbs of S the son of Prov 1:1 8010
The proverbs of S Prov 10:1 8010
These are also proverbs of S Prov 25:1 8010
of Kedar, as the curtains of S Song 1:5 8010
King S made himself a chariot of Song 3:9 8010
behold king S with the crown Song 3:11 8010
S had a vineyard at Baal-hamon Song 8:11 8010
thou, O S, must have a thousand, Song 8:12 8010
which king S had made in the Jer 52:20 8010
David the king begat S of her Mt 1:6 4672
And S begat Roboam Mt 1:7 4672
That even S in all his glory was Mt 6:29 4672
the earth to hear the wisdom of S Mt 12:42 4672
behold, a greater than S is here Mt 12:42 4672
the earth to hear the wisdom of S Lk 11:31 4672
behold, a greater than S is here Lk 11:31 4672
that S in all his glory was not Lk 12:27 4672
But S built him an house Acts 7:47 4672

SOLOMON'S (*sol'-o-muns*)
S provision for one day was 1Kin 4:22 8010
all that came unto king S table 1Kin 4:27 8010
S wisdom excelled the wisdom of 1Kin 4:30 8010
Beside the chief of S officers 1Kin 5:16 8010
S builders and Hiram's builders 1Kin 5:18 8010
year of S reign over Israel 1Kin 6:1 8010
all S desire which he was pleased 1Kin 9:1 8010
present unto his daughter, S wife 1Kin 9:16 8010
officers that were over S work 1Kin 9:23 8010
of Sheba had seen all S wisdom 1Kin 10:4 8010
all king S drinking vessels were 1Kin 10:21 8010
S servant, whose mother's name 1Kin 11:26 8010
S son was Rehoboam, Abia his son, 1Chr 3:10 8010
all that came into S heart to 2Chr 7:11 8010
were the chief of king S officers 2Chr 8:10 8010
The children of S servants Ezr 2:55 8010
and the children of S servants Ezr 2:58 8010
The children of S servants Neh 7:57 8010
and the children of S servants Neh 7:60 8010
and the children of S servants Neh 11:3 8010
The song of songs, which is S Song 1:1 8010
Behold his bed, which is S Song 3:7 8010
walked in the temple in S porch Jn 10:23 4672
in the porch that is called S Acts 3:11 4672
all with one accord in S porch Acts 5:12 4672

SOME
lest s evil take me, and I die Gen 19:19
the field, and take me s venison Gen 27:3
every one that had s white in it Gen 30:35
Let me now leave with thee s of Gen 33:15
slay him, and cast him into s pit Gen 37:20 259
S evil beast hath devoured him Gen 37:20
he took s of his brethren, even Gen 47:2 7097
and gathered, s more, s less Ex 16:17
but s of them left of it until Ex 16:20 582
that there went out s of the Ex 16:27
thou shalt beat s of it very Ex 30:36
the priest shall put s of the Lev 4:7
dip his finger in s of the blood Lev 4:17
he shall put s of the blood upon Lev 4:18
the priest shall take s of the Lev 14:14
shall take s of the log of oil Lev 14:15
the priest shall take s of the Lev 14:25
s of the oil that is in his left Lev 14:27
poor, and hath sold away s of his Lev 25:25
the LORD s part of a field of his Lev 27:16
s man have lain with thee beside Num 5:20
and took s of them prisoners Num 21:1
thou shalt put s of thine honour Num 27:20
Arm s of yourselves unto the war, Num 31:3 582
hath found s uncleanness in her Deut 24:1 1697
s on this side, and s on that Josh 8:22 428
s to speak to the children of Judg 21:13
let fall also s of the handfuls Ruth 2:16
s shall run before his chariots 1Sa 8:11
s of the Hebrews went over Jordan 1Sa 13:7
and s bade me kill thee 1Sa 24:10
a place in s town in the country 1Sa 27:5 259
there fell s of the people of the 2Sa 11:17
s of the king's servants be dead, 2Sa 11:24
in s pit, or in s other place 2Sa 17:9 259
when s of them be overthrown at 2Sa 17:9 259
So shall we come upon him in s 2Sa 17:12 259
because in him there is found s 1Kin 14:13
up, and cast him upon s mountain 2Kin 2:16 259
s mountain, or into s valley 2Kin 2:16 259
had bid thee do s great thing 2Kin 5:13
s mischief will come upon us 2Kin 7:9
Let s take, I pray thee, five of 2Kin 7:13
s of her blood was sprinkled on 2Kin 9:33
among them, which slew s of them 2Kin 17:25
s of them, even of the sons of 1Chr 4:42
S of them also were appointed to 1Chr 9:29
s of the sons of the priests made 1Chr 9:30
there fell s of Manasseh to David 1Chr 12:19
I will grant them s deliverance 2Chr 12:7 4592
Asa oppressed s of the people the 2Chr 16:10
Also s of the Philistines brought 2Chr 17:11
Then there came s that told 2Chr 20:2
s of the chief of the fathers, Ezr 2:68
s of the people, and the singers, Ezr 2:70
there went up s of the children Ezr 7:7
s of them had wives by whom they Ezr 10:44
the night, I and s few men with me Neh 2:12 4592
S also there were that said, We Neh 5:3
s of our daughters are brought Neh 5:5
let us meet together in s one of Neh 6:2
s of the chief of the fathers Neh 7:70 7097
s of the chief of the fathers Neh 7:71
s of the people, and the Nethinims Neh 7:73
s of the children of Judah dwelt Neh 11:25
at that time were s appointed Neh 12:44 582
s treading winepresses on the Neh 13:15
s of my servants set I at the Neh 13:19
S remove the landmarks Job 24:2
S trust in chariots, and s in Ps 20:7 428
and I looked for s to take pity Ps 69:20
away, unless they cause s to fall Prov 4:16
they not leave s gleaning grapes Jer 49:9
that ye may have s that shall Eze 6:8
and it cast down s of the host Dan 8:10
s of them of understanding shall Dan 11:35
s to everlasting life, and s to Dan 12:2 428
I have overthrown s of you Amos 4:11
would they not leave s grapes Obad 5
s seeds fell by the way side, and Mt 13:4
S fell upon stony places, where Mt 13:5
And s fell among thorns Mt 13:7
s an hundredfold, s sixtyfold, Mt 13:8
s sixtyfold, s thirtyfold Mt 13:8
s an hundredfold, s sixty, Mt 13:23
s sixty, s thirty Mt 13:23
S say that thou art John the Mt 16:14
s, Elias Mt 16:14
There be s standing here, which Mt 16:28 5100
For there are s eunuchs, which Mt 19:12
and there are s eunuchs, which Mt 19:12
s of them ye shall kill and Mt 23:34
s of them shall ye scourge in Mt 23:34
S of them that stood there, when Mt 27:47 5100
s of the watch came into the city Mt 28:11 5100
but s doubted Mt 28:17 3588
into Capernaum after s days Mk 2:1
s fell by the way side, and the Mk 4:4
s fell on stony ground, where it Mk 4:5 243
s fell among thorns, and the Mk 4:7 243
s thirty, and s sixty, and s Mk 4:8 1520
s thirtyfold, s sixty, and s Mk 4:20 1520
when they saw s of his disciples Mk 7:2 5100
but s say, Elias Mk 8:28 243
That there be s of them that Mk 9:1 5100
beating s, and killing s Mk 12:5 3588
there were s that had indignation Mk 14:4 5100
s began to spit on him, and to Mk 14:65 5100
s of them that stood by, when Mk 15:35 5100
he sowed, s fell by the way side Lk 8:5
And s fell upon a rock Lk 8:6 2087
And s fell among thorns Lk 8:7 2087
because that it was said of s Lk 9:7 5100
And of s, that Elias had appeared Lk 9:8 5100
but s say Elias Lk 9:19 243
there be s standing here, which Lk 9:27 5100
But s of them said, He casteth Lk 11:15 5100
s of them they shall slay and Lk 11:49
were present at that season s Lk 13:1 5100
s of the Pharisees from among the Lk 19:39 5100
as s spake of the temple, how it Lk 21:5 5100
s of you shall they cause to be Lk 21:16
have seen s miracle done by him Lk 23:8 5100
between s of John's disciples Jn 3:25
But there are s of you that Jn 6:64 5100
for s said, He is a good man Jn 7:12
Then said s of them of Jerusalem, Jn 7:25 5100
But s said, Shall Christ come out Jn 7:41 243
s of them would have taken him Jn 7:44 5100
S said, This is he Jn 9:9 243
Therefore said s of the Pharisees Jn 9:16 5100
s of the Pharisees which were Jn 9:40
but climbeth up s other way Jn 10:1
s of them said, Could not this Jn 11:37 5100
But s of them went their ways to Jn 11:46 5100
For s of them thought, because Jn 13:29 5100
Then said s of his disciples Jn 16:17
by might overshadow s of them Acts 5:15 5100
out that himself was s great one Acts 8:9 5100
except s man should guide me Acts 8:31 5100
of himself, or of s other man Acts 8:34 5100
s of them were men of Cyprus and Acts 11:20 5100
he went about seeking s to lead Acts 13:11
s days after Paul said unto Acts 15:36 5100
s of them believed, and consorted Acts 17:4 5100
s said, What will this babbler Acts 17:18 5100
other s, He seemeth to be a Acts 17:18 3588
to tell, or to hear s new thing Acts 17:21 5100
of the dead, s mocked Acts 17:32
after he had spent s time there Acts 18:23 5100
S therefore cried one thing, and Acts 19:32 243
cried one thing, and s another Acts 19:32 243
s cried one thing, s another, Acts 21:34 243
that they drew near to s country Acts 27:27 5100
I pray you to take s meat Acts 27:34
cheer, and they also took s meat Acts 27:36
s on boards, and s on broken Acts 27:44
s believed the things which were Acts 28:24
were spoken, and s believed not Acts 28:24 3588
impart unto you s spiritual gift Rom 1:11 5100
that I might have s fruit among Rom 1:13 5100
For what if s did not believe Rom 3:3 5100
as s affirm that we say,) Let us Rom 3:8 5100
good man s would even dare to die Rom 5:7 5100
my flesh, and might save s of them Rom 11:14 5100
if s of the branches be broken Rom 11:17 5100
more boldly unto you in s sort Rom 15:15
Now s are puffed up, as though I 1Cor 4:18 5100
And such were s of you 1Cor 6:11 5100
for s with conscience of the idol 1Cor 8:7 5100
that I might by all means save s 1Cor 9:22 5100
ye idolaters, as were s of them 1Cor 10:7 5100
as s of them committed, and fell 1Cor 10:8 5100
as s of them also tempted, and 1Cor 10:9 5100
as s of them also murmured, and 1Cor 10:10 5100
God hath set s in the church, 1Cor 12:28
present, but s are fallen asleep 1Cor 15:6 5100
how say s among you that there is 1Cor 15:12 5100
for s have not the knowledge of 1Cor 15:34 5100
But s man will say, How are the 1Cor 15:35 5100
of wheat, or of s other grain 1Cor 15:37 5100
need we, as s others, epistles of 2Cor 3:1 5100
I think to be bold against s 2Cor 10:2 5100
with s that commend themselves 2Cor 10:12 5100
but there be s that trouble you, Gal 1:7 5100
And he gave s, apostles Eph 4:11
and s, prophets Eph 4:11 3588
and s, evangelists Eph 4:11 3588
and s, pastors and teachers Eph 4:11 3588
S indeed preach Christ even of Phil 1:15 5100
and s also of good will Phil 1:15 5100
the which ye also walked s time Col 3:7 4218
lest by s means the tempter have 1Th 3:5 3381
For we hear that there are s 2Th 3:11 5100
charge s that they teach no other 1Ti 1:3 5100
From which s having swerved have 1Ti 1:6 5100
which s having put away 1Ti 1:19 5100
that in the latter times s shall 1Ti 4:1 5100
For s are already turned aside 1Ti 5:15 5100
S men's sins are open beforehand, 1Ti 5:24 5100
and s men they follow after 1Ti 5:24 5100
of s are manifest beforehand 1Ti 5:25
which while s coveted after, they 1Ti 6:10 5100
Which s professing have erred 1Ti 6:21 5100
and overthrow the faith of s 2Ti 2:18 5100
s to honour, and s to dishonour 2Ti 2:20
every house is builded by s man Heb 3:4 5100
For s, when they had heard, did Heb 3:16 5100
that s must enter therein Heb 4:6 5100
together, as the manner of s is Heb 10:25 5100
provided s better thing for us Heb 11:40 5100
for thereby s have entertained Heb 13:2 5100
as though s strange thing 1Pet 4:12
promise, as s men count slackness 2Pet 3:9 5100
in which are s things hard to be 2Pet 3:16 5100
of s have compassion, making a Jude 22
shall cast s of you into prison Rev 2:10

SOMEBODY
And Jesus said, S hath touched me Lk 8:46 5100
Theudas, boasting himself to be s Acts 5:36 5100

SOMETHING
S hath befallen him, he is not 1Sa 20:26 4745
commanded that s should be given Mk 5:43
to catch s out of his mouth Lk 11:54 5100
that he should give s to the poor Jn 13:29 5100
expecting to receive s of them Acts 3:5 5100
as though ye would enquire s more Acts 23:15
who hath s to say unto thee Acts 23:18 5100
if a man think himself to be s Gal 6:3 5100

SOMETIME
And you, that were s alienated Col 1:21 4218
Which s were disobedient, when 1Pet 3:20 4218

SOMETIMES
s were far off are made nigh by Eph 2:13 4218
For ye were s darkness, but now Eph 5:8 4218
we ourselves also were s foolish Titus 3:3 4218

SOMEWHAT
they have done s against any of Lev 4:13
done s through ignorance against Lev 4:22
while he doeth s against any of Lev 4:27
behold, if the plague be s dark Lev 13:6 3544
s reddish, and it be shewed to the Lev 13:19
than the skin, but be s dark Lev 13:21 3544
bright spot, s reddish, or white Lev 13:24
the other skin, but be s dark Lev 13:26 3544

not in the skin, but it be *s* dark	Lev 13:28	3544
the plague be *s* dark after the	Lev 13:56	3544
I have *s* to say unto thee	1Kin 2:14	
run after him, and take *s* of him	2Kin 5:20	3972
now therefore ease thou *s* the	2Chr 10:4	
Ease *s* the yoke that thy father	2Chr 10:9	
but make thou it *s* lighter for us	2Chr 10:10	
I have *s* to say unto thee	Lk 7:40	*5100*
enquire *s* of him more perfectly	Acts 23:20	*5100*
had, I might have *s* to write	Acts 25:26	*5100*
if first I be *s* filled with your	Rom 15:24	*3313*
that ye may have *s* to answer them	2Cor 5:12	
boast *s* more of our authority	2Cor 10:8	*5100*
But of these who seemed to be *s*	Gal 2:6	*5100*
for they who seemed to be *s* in	Gal 2:6	
this man have *s* also to offer	Heb 8:3	*5100*
I have *s* against thee, because	Rev 2:4	

SON

the city, after the name of his *s*	Gen 4:17	1121
and she bare a *s*, and called his	Gen 4:25	1121
to him also there was born a *s*	Gen 4:26	1121
begat a *s* in his own likeness,	Gen 5:3	
eighty and two years, and begat a *s*	Gen 5:28	1121
his younger *s* had done unto him	Gen 9:24	1121
And Terah took Abram his *s*	Gen 11:31	1121
Lot the *s* of Haran his son's *s*,	Gen 11:31	
in law, his *s* Abram's wife	Gen 11:31	
his wife, and Lot his brother's *s*	Gen 12:5	1121
took Lot, Abram's brother's *s*	Gen 14:12	1121
art with child, and shalt bear a *s*	Gen 16:11	1121
And Hagar bare Abram a *s*	Gen 16:15	1121
her, and give thee a *s* also of her	Gen 17:16	1121
wife shall bear thee a *s* indeed	Gen 17:19	1121
And Abraham took Ishmael his *s*	Gen 17:23	1121
Ishmael his *s* was thirteen years	Gen 17:25	1121
circumcised, and Ishmael his *s*	Gen 17:26	1121
lo, Sarah thy wife shall have a *s*	Gen 18:10	1121
of life, and Sarah shall have a *s*	Gen 18:14	1121
s in law, and thy sons, and thy	Gen 19:12	1121
And the firstborn bare a *s*	Gen 19:37	1121
And the younger, she also bare a *s*	Gen 19:38	1121
bare Abraham a *s* in his old age	Gen 21:2	1121
of his *s* that was born unto him	Gen 21:3	1121
Abraham circumcised his *s* Isaac	Gen 21:4	1121
when his *s* Isaac was born unto	Gen 21:5	1121
have born him a *s* in his old age	Gen 21:7	1121
Sarah saw the *s* of Hagar the	Gen 21:9	1121
Cast out this bondwoman and her *s*	Gen 21:10	1121
for the *s* of this bondwoman shall	Gen 21:10	1121
shall not be heir with my *s*	Gen 21:10	
Abraham's sight because of his *s*	Gen 21:11	1121
also of the *s* of the bondwoman	Gen 21:13	1121
with my *s*, nor with my son's *s*	Gen 21:23	5220
and he said, Take now thy *s*	Gen 22:2	1121
thine only *s* Isaac	Gen 22:2	
men with him, and Isaac his *s*	Gen 22:3	1121
and laid it upon Isaac his *s*	Gen 22:6	1121
and he said, Here am I, my *s*	Gen 22:7	1121
And Abraham said, My *s*, God will	Gen 22:8	1121
in order, and bound Isaac his *s*	Gen 22:9	1121
and took the knife to slay his *s*	Gen 22:10	1121
thou hast not withheld thy *s*	Gen 22:12	1121
thine only *s* from me	Gen 22:12	
offering in the stead of his *s*	Gen 22:13	1121
thing, and hast not withheld thy *s*	Gen 22:16	1121
thine only *s*	Gen 22:16	
for me to Ephron the *s* of Zohar	Gen 23:8	1121
unto my *s* of the daughters of the	Gen 24:3	1121
and take a wife unto my *s* Isaac	Gen 24:4	1121
must I needs bring thy *s* again	Gen 24:5	1121
thou bring not my *s* thither again	Gen 24:6	1121
take a wife unto my *s* from thence	Gen 24:7	1121
only bring not my *s* thither again	Gen 24:8	1121
s of Milcah, the wife of Nahor,	Gen 24:15	1121
of Bethuel the *s* of Milcah	Gen 24:24	1121
a *s* to my master when she was old	Gen 24:36	1121
to my *s* of the daughters of the	Gen 24:37	1121
kindred, and take a wife unto my *s*	Gen 24:38	1121
a wife for my *s* of my kindred	Gen 24:40	1121
appointed out for my master's *s*	Gen 24:44	1121
daughter of Bethuel, Nahor's *s*	Gen 24:47	1121
brother's daughter unto his *s*	Gen 24:48	1121
sent them away from Isaac his *s*	Gen 25:6	1121
Ephron the *s* of Zohar the Hittite	Gen 25:9	1121
that God blessed his *s* Isaac	Gen 25:11	1121
of Ishmael, Abraham's *s*, whom	Gen 25:12	1121
generations of Isaac, Abraham's *s*	Gen 25:19	1121
see, he called Esau his eldest *s*	Gen 27:1	1121
and said unto him, My *s*	Gen 27:1	1121
when Isaac spake to Esau his *s*	Gen 27:5	1121
And Rebekah spake unto Jacob her *s*	Gen 27:6	1121
Now therefore, my *s*, obey my	Gen 27:8	1121
him, Upon me be thy curse, my *s*	Gen 27:13	1121
raiment of her eldest *s* Esau	Gen 27:15	1121
put them upon Jacob her younger *s*	Gen 27:15	1121
into the hand of her *s* Jacob	Gen 27:17	1121
who art thou, my *s*	Gen 27:18	1121
And Isaac said unto his *s*, How is	Gen 27:20	1121
hast found it so quickly, my *s*	Gen 27:20	1121
thee, that I may feel thee, my *s*	Gen 27:21	1121
thou be my very *s* Esau or not	Gen 27:21	1121
he said, Art thou my very *s* Esau	Gen 27:24	1121
Come near now, and kiss me, my *s*	Gen 27:26	1121
the smell of my *s* is as the smell	Gen 27:27	1121
And he said, I am thy *s*, thy	Gen 27:32	1121
shall I do now unto thee, my *s*	Gen 27:37	1121
her elder *s* were told to Rebekah	Gen 27:42	1121
and called Jacob her younger *s*	Gen 27:42	1121
Now therefore, my *s*, obey my	Gen 27:43	1121
s of Bethuel the Syrian, the	Gen 28:5	1121
daughter of Ishmael Abraham's *s*	Gen 28:9	1121
Know ye Laban the *s* of Nahor	Gen 29:5	1121
and that he was Rebekah's *s*	Gen 29:12	1121
tidings of Jacob his sister's *s*	Gen 29:13	1121
And Leah conceived, and bare a *s*	Gen 29:32	1121
she conceived again, and bare a *s*	Gen 29:33	1121
therefore given me this *s* also	Gen 29:33	
she conceived again, and bare a *s*	Gen 29:34	1121
she conceived again, and bare a *s*	Gen 29:35	1121
conceived, and bare Jacob a *s*	Gen 30:5	1121
my voice, and hath given me a *s*	Gen 30:6	1121
again, and bare Jacob a second *s*	Gen 30:7	1121
Zilpah Leah's maid bare Jacob a *s*	Gen 30:10	1121
Leah's maid bare Jacob a second *s*	Gen 30:12	1121
and bare Jacob the fifth *s*	Gen 30:17	1121
again, and bare Jacob the sixth *s*	Gen 30:19	1121
And she conceived, and bare a *s*	Gen 30:23	1121
LORD shall add to me another *s*	Gen 30:24	1121
when Shechem the *s* of Hamor the	Gen 34:2	1121
The soul of my *s* Shechem longeth	Gen 34:8	1121
Hamor, and Shechem Hamor's *s*	Gen 34:18	1121
Shechem his *s* came unto the gate	Gen 34:20	1121
unto Shechem his *s* hearkened all	Gen 34:24	1121
Shechem his *s* with the edge of	Gen 34:26	1121
thou shalt have this *s* also	Gen 35:17	1121
Eliphaz the *s* of Adah the wife of	Gen 36:10	1121
Reuel the *s* of Bashemath the wife	Gen 36:10	1121
was concubine to Eliphaz Esau's *s*	Gen 36:12	1121
Eliphaz the firstborn *s* of Esau	Gen 36:15	
are the sons of Reuel Esau's *s*	Gen 36:17	1121
Bela the *s* of Beor reigned in	Gen 36:32	1121
Jobab the *s* of Zerah of Bozrah	Gen 36:33	1121
died, and Hadad the *s* of Bedad	Gen 36:35	1121
Baal-hanan the *s* of Achbor	Gen 36:38	1121
Baal-hanan the *s* of Achbor died	Gen 36:39	1121
he was the *s* of his old age	Gen 37:3	1121
and mourned for his *s* many days	Gen 37:34	1121
into the grave unto my *s* mourning	Gen 37:35	1121
And she conceived, and bare a *s*	Gen 38:3	1121
she conceived again, and bare a *s*	Gen 38:4	1121
yet again conceived, and bare a *s*	Gen 38:5	1121
house, till Shelah my *s* be grown	Gen 38:11	1121
I gave her not to Shelah my *s*	Gen 38:26	1121
My *s* shall not go down with you	Gen 42:38	1121
brother Benjamin, his mother's *s*	Gen 43:29	1121
God be gracious unto thee, my *s*	Gen 43:29	1121
unto him, Thus saith thy *s* Joseph	Gen 45:9	1121
Joseph my *s* is yet alive	Gen 45:28	1121
Shaul the *s* of a Canaanitish	Gen 46:10	1121
and he called his *s* Joseph	Gen 47:29	1121
thy *s* Joseph cometh unto thee	Gen 48:2	1121
refused, and said, I know it, my *s*	Gen 48:19	1121
from the prey, my *s*, thou art	Gen 49:9	1121
the *s* of Manasseh were brought up	Gen 50:23	1121
if it be a *s*, then ye shall kill	Ex 1:16	1121
Every *s* that is born ye shall	Ex 1:22	1121
the woman conceived, and bare a *s*	Ex 2:2	1121
daughter, and he became her *s*	Ex 2:10	1121
And she bare him a *s*, and he called	Ex 2:22	1121
saith the LORD, Israel is my *s*	Ex 4:22	1121
And I say unto thee, Let my *s* go	Ex 4:23	1121
him go, behold, I will slay thy *s*	Ex 4:23	1121
and cut off the foreskin of her *s*	Ex 4:25	1121
Shaul the *s* of a Canaanitish	Ex 6:15	1121
Eleazar Aaron's *s* took him one of	Ex 6:25	1121
of thy *s*, and of thy son's *s*	Ex 10:2	1121
thou shalt shew thy *s* in that day	Ex 13:8	1121
it shall be when thy *s* asketh	Ex 13:14	1121
not do any work, thou, nor thy *s*	Ex 20:10	1121
he have betrothed her unto his *s*	Ex 21:9	1121
Whether he have gored a *s*	Ex 21:31	1121
the *s* of thy handmaid, and the	Ex 23:12	1121
that *s* that is priest in his	Ex 29:30	1121
by name Bezaleel the *s* of Uri	Ex 31:2	1121
the *s* of Hur, of the tribe of	Ex 31:2	1121
the *s* of Ahisamach, of the tribe	Ex 31:6	1121
LORD, even every man upon his *s*	Ex 32:29	1121
s of Nun, a young man,	Ex 33:11	1121
by name Bezaleel the *s* of Uri	Ex 35:30	1121
the *s* of Hur, of the tribe of	Ex 35:30	1121
the *s* of Ahisamach, of the tribe	Ex 35:34	1121
of Ithamar, *s* to Aaron the priest	Ex 38:21	1121
And Bezaleel the *s* of Uri	Ex 38:22	1121
the *s* of Hur, of the tribe of	Ex 38:22	1121
s of Ahisamach, of the tribe of	Ex 38:23	1121
purifying are fulfilled, for a *s*	Lev 12:6	1121
and for his father, and for his *s*	Lev 21:2	1121
the *s* of an Israelitish woman,	Lev 24:10	1121
this *s* of the Israelitish woman	Lev 24:10	1121
the Israelitish woman's *s*	Lev 24:11	1121
his uncle, or his uncle's *s*	Lev 25:49	1121
Elizur the *s* of Shedeur	Num 1:5	1121
Shelumiel the *s* of Zurishaddai	Num 1:6	1121
Nahshon the *s* of Amminadab	Num 1:7	1121
Nethaneel the *s* of Zuar	Num 1:8	1121
Eliab the *s* of Helon	Num 1:9	1121
Elishama the *s* of Ammihud	Num 1:10	1121
Gamaliel the *s* of Pedahzur	Num 1:10	1121
Abidan the *s* of Gideoni	Num 1:11	1121
Ahiezer the *s* of Ammishaddai	Num 1:12	1121
Pagiel the *s* of Ocran	Num 1:13	1121
Eliasaph the *s* of Deuel	Num 1:14	1121
Ahira the *s* of Enan	Num 1:15	1121
of Reuben, Israel's eldest *s*	Num 1:20	
Nahshon the *s* of Amminadab shall	Num 2:3	1121
Nethaneel the *s* of Zuar shall be	Num 2:5	1121
Eliab the *s* of Helon shall be	Num 2:7	1121
shall be Elizur the *s* of Shedeur	Num 2:10	1121
be Shelumiel the *s* of Zurishaddai	Num 2:12	1121
shall be Eliasaph the *s* of Reuel	Num 2:14	1121
be Elishama the *s* of Ammihud	Num 2:18	1121
be Gamaliel the *s* of Pedahzur	Num 2:20	1121
shall be Abidan the *s* of Gideoni	Num 2:22	1121
be Ahiezer the *s* of Ammishaddai	Num 2:25	1121
shall be Pagiel the *s* of Ocran	Num 2:27	1121
shall be Ahira the *s* of Enan	Num 2:29	1121
shall be Eliasaph the *s* of Lael	Num 3:24	1121
be Elizaphan the *s* of Uzziel	Num 3:30	1121
Eleazar the *s* of Aaron the priest	Num 3:32	1121
was Zuriel the *s* of Abihail	Num 3:35	1121
to the office of Eleazar the *s* of	Num 4:16	1121
Ithamar the *s* of Aaron the priest	Num 4:28	1121
Ithamar the *s* of Aaron the priest	Num 4:33	1121
Ithamar the *s* of Aaron the priest	Num 7:8	1121
was Nahshon the *s* of Amminadab	Num 7:12	1121
of Nahshon the *s* of Amminadab	Num 7:17	1121
day Nethaneel the *s* of Zuar	Num 7:18	1121
of Nethaneel the *s* of Zuar	Num 7:23	1121
third day Eliab the *s* of Helon	Num 7:24	1121
offering of Eliab the *s* of Helon	Num 7:29	1121
day Elizur the *s* of Shedeur	Num 7:30	1121
of Elizur the *s* of Shedeur	Num 7:35	1121
Shelumiel the *s* of Zurishaddai	Num 7:36	1121
of Shelumiel the *s* of Zurishaddai	Num 7:41	1121
sixth day Eliasaph the *s* of Deuel	Num 7:42	1121
of Eliasaph the *s* of Deuel	Num 7:47	1121
day Elishama the *s* of Ammihud	Num 7:48	1121
of Elishama the *s* of Ammihud	Num 7:53	1121
Gamaliel the *s* of Pedahzur	Num 7:54	1121
of Gamaliel the *s* of Pedahzur	Num 7:59	1121
ninth day Abidan the *s* of Gideoni	Num 7:60	1121
of Abidan the *s* of Gideoni	Num 7:65	1121
day Ahiezer the *s* of Ammishaddai	Num 7:66	1121
of Ahiezer the *s* of Ammishaddai	Num 7:71	1121
day Pagiel the *s* of Ocran	Num 7:72	1121
offering of Pagiel the *s* of Ocran	Num 7:77	1121
twelfth day Ahira the *s* of Enan	Num 7:78	1121
offering of Ahira the *s* of Enan	Num 7:83	1121
was Nahshon the *s* of Amminadab	Num 10:14	1121
was Nethaneel the *s* of Zuar	Num 10:15	1121
Zebulun was Eliab the *s* of Helon	Num 10:16	1121
host was Elizur the *s* of Shedeur	Num 10:18	1121
Shelumiel the *s* of Zurishaddai	Num 10:19	1121
Gad was Eliasaph the *s* of Deuel	Num 10:20	1121
was Elishama the *s* of Ammihud	Num 10:22	1121
was Gamaliel the *s* of Pedahzur	Num 10:23	1121
was Abidan the *s* of Gideoni	Num 10:24	1121
was Ahiezer the *s* of Ammishaddai	Num 10:25	1121
Asher was Pagiel the *s* of Ocran	Num 10:26	1121
Naphtali was Ahira the *s* of Enan	Num 10:27	1121
the *s* of Raguel the Midianite,	Num 10:29	1121
And Joshua the *s* of Nun, the	Num 11:28	1121
Reuben, Shammua the *s* of Zaccur	Num 13:4	1121
of Simeon, Shaphat the *s* of Hori	Num 13:5	1121
Judah, Caleb the *s* of Jephunneh	Num 13:6	1121
of Issachar, Igal the *s* of Joseph	Num 13:7	1121
of Ephraim, Oshea the *s* of Nun	Num 13:8	1121
of Benjamin, Palti the *s* of Raphu	Num 13:9	1121
of Zebulun, Gaddiel the *s* of Sodi	Num 13:10	1121
of Manasseh, Gaddi the *s* of Susi	Num 13:11	1121
of Dan, Ammiel the *s* of Gemalli	Num 13:12	1121
of Asher, Sethur the *s* of Michael	Num 13:13	1121
Naphtali, Nahbi the *s* of Vophsi	Num 13:14	1121
of Gad, Geuel the *s* of Machi	Num 13:15	1121
Oshea the *s* of Nun Jehoshua	Num 13:16	1121
And Joshua the *s* of Nun, and Caleb	Num 14:6	1121
Caleb the *s* of Jephunneh, which	Num 14:6	1121
save Caleb the *s* of Jephunneh	Num 14:30	1121
Jephunneh, and Joshua the *s* of Nun	Num 14:30	1121
But Joshua the *s* of Nun, and Caleb	Num 14:38	1121
Caleb the *s* of Jephunneh, which	Num 14:38	1121
the *s* of Izhar, the *s* of Kohath	Num 16:1	1121
the *s* of Levi, and Dathan and	Num 16:1	1121
the *s* of Peleth, sons of Reuben,	Num 16:1	1121
Eleazar the *s* of Aaron the priest	Num 16:37	1121
Take Aaron and Eleazar his *s*	Num 20:25	1121
and put them upon Eleazar his *s*	Num 20:26	1121
and put them upon Eleazar his *s*	Num 20:28	1121
Balak the *s* of Zippor saw all	Num 22:2	1121
Balak the *s* of Zippor was king of	Num 22:4	1121
Balaam the *s* of Beor to Pethor	Num 22:5	1121
unto God, Balak the *s* of Zippor	Num 22:10	1121
Thus saith Balak the *s* of Zippor	Num 22:16	1121
hearken unto me, thou *s* of Zippor	Num 23:18	1121
neither the *s* of man, that he	Num 23:19	1121
Balaam the *s* of Beor hath said,	Num 24:3	1121
Balaam the *s* of Beor hath said,	Num 24:15	1121
the *s* of Eleazar	Num 25:7	1121
the *s* of Aaron the priest, saw it	Num 25:7	1121
the *s* of Eleazar	Num 25:11	1121
the *s* of Aaron the priest, hath	Num 25:11	1121
the *s* of Salu, a prince of a	Num 25:14	1121
unto Eleazar the *s* of Aaron the	Num 26:1	1121
Reuben, the eldest *s* of Israel	Num 26:5	
Zelophehad the *s* of Hepher had no	Num 26:33	1121
save Caleb the *s* of Jephunneh	Num 26:65	1121
Jephunneh, and Joshua the *s* of Nun	Num 26:65	1121
the *s* of Hepher	Num 27:1	1121
the *s* of Gilead	Num 27:1	1121
the *s* of Machir	Num 27:1	1121
the *s* of Manasseh, of the	Num 27:1	1121
of Manasseh the *s* of Joseph	Num 27:1	1121
his family, because he hath no *s*	Num 27:4	1121
If a man die, and have no *s*	Num 27:8	1121
Take thee Joshua the *s* of Nun	Num 27:18	1121
Phinehas the *s* of Eleazar the	Num 31:6	1121
Balaam also the *s* of Beor they	Num 31:8	1121
Save Caleb the *s* of Jephunneh the	Num 32:12	1121
Kenezite, and Joshua the *s* of Nun	Num 32:12	1121
priest, and Joshua the *s* of Nun	Num 32:28	1121
tribe of Manasseh the *s* of Joseph	Num 32:33	1121
the *s* of Manasseh went to Gilead	Num 32:39	1121
unto Machir the *s* of Manasseh	Num 32:40	1121
Jair the *s* of Manasseh went and	Num 32:41	1121
priest, and Joshua the *s* of Nun	Num 34:17	1121
Judah, Caleb the *s* of Jephunneh	Num 34:19	1121
Simeon, Shemuel the *s* of Ammihud	Num 34:20	1121
Benjamin, Elidad the *s* of Chislon	Num 34:21	1121
of Dan, Bukki the *s* of Jogli	Num 34:22	1121
Manasseh, Hanniel the *s* of Ephod	Num 34:23	1121
Ephraim, Kemuel the *s* of Shiphtan	Num 34:24	1121

Elizaphan the *s* of Parnach ... Num 34:25 1121
Issachar, Paltiel the *s* of Azzan ... Num 34:26 1121
of Asher, Ahihud the *s* of Shelomi ... Num 34:27 1121
Pedahel the *s* of Ammihud ... Num 34:28 1121
the *s* of Machir ... Num 36:1 1121
the *s* of Manasseh, of the ... Num 36:1 1121
sons of Manasseh the *s* of Joseph ... Num 36:12 1121
thee, as a man doth bear his *s* ... Deut 1:31 1121
Save Caleb the *s* of Jephunneh ... Deut 1:36 1121
But Joshua the *s* of Nun, which ... Deut 1:38 1121
Jair the *s* of Manasseh took all ... Deut 3:14 1121
not do any work, thou, nor thy *s* ... Deut 5:14 1121
thou, and thy *s*, and thy son's *s* ... Deut 6:2 1121
when thy *s* asketh thee in time to ... Deut 6:20 1121
Then thou shalt say unto thy *s* ... Deut 6:21 1121
thou shalt not give unto his *s* ... Deut 7:3 1121
shalt thou take unto thy *s* ... Deut 7:3 1121
turn away thy *s* from following me ... Deut 7:4 1121
that, as a man chasteneth his *s* ... Deut 8:5 1121
Eleazar his *s* ministered in the ... Deut 10:6 1121
sons of Eliab, the *s* of Reuben ... Deut 11:6 1121
God shall choose, thou, and thy *s* ... Deut 12:18 1121
the *s* of thy mother, or thy *s*, ... Deut 13:6 1121
the LORD thy God, thou, and thy *s* ... Deut 16:11 1121
in thy feast, thou, and thy *s* ... Deut 16:14 1121
you any one that maketh his *s* or ... Deut 18:10 1121
if the firstborn *s* be hers that ... Deut 21:15 1121
that he may not make the *s* of the ... Deut 21:16 1121
before the *s* of the hated ... Deut 21:16 1121
But he shall acknowledge the *s* of ... Deut 21:17 1121
have a stubborn and rebellious *s* ... Deut 21:18 1121
This our *s* is stubborn and ... Deut 21:20 1121
Balaam the *s* of Beor of Pethor of ... Deut 23:4 1121
of her bosom, and toward her *s* ... Deut 28:56 1121
gave Joshua the *s* of Nun a charge ... Deut 31:23 1121
he, and Hoshea the *s* of Nun ... Deut 32:44 1121
Joshua the *s* of Nun was full of ... Deut 34:9 1121
spake unto Joshua the *s* of Nun ... Josh 1:1 1121
Joshua the *s* of Nun sent out of ... Josh 2:1 1121
and came to Joshua the *s* of Nun ... Josh 2:23 1121
Joshua the *s* of Nun called the ... Josh 6:6 1121
in his youngest *s* shall he set up ... Josh 6:26
the *s* of Carmi, the *s* of Zabdi, ... Josh 7:1 1121
the *s* of Zerah, of the tribe of ... Josh 7:1 1121
the *s* of Carmi, the *s* of Zabdi, ... Josh 7:18 1121
the *s* of Zabdi, the *s* of Zerah, ... Josh 7:18 1121
the *s* of Zerah, of the tribe of ... Josh 7:18 1121
And Joshua said unto Achan, My *s* ... Josh 7:19 1121
him, took Achan the *s* of Zerah ... Josh 7:24 1121
Balaam also the *s* of Beor ... Josh 13:22 1121
of Machir the *s* of Manasseh ... Josh 13:31 1121
priest, and Joshua the *s* of Nun ... Josh 14:1 1121
Caleb the *s* of Jephunneh the ... Josh 14:6 1121
him, and gave unto Caleb the *s* of ... Josh 14:13 1121
the inheritance of Caleb the *s* of ... Josh 14:14 1121
stone of Bohan the *s* of Reuben ... Josh 15:6 1121
went up by the valley of the *s* of ... Josh 15:8 1121
unto Caleb the *s* of Jephunneh he ... Josh 15:13 1121
And Othniel the *s* of Kenaz ... Josh 15:17 1121
the *s* of Joseph by their families ... Josh 17:2 1121
the *s* of Hepher ... Josh 17:3 1121
the *s* of Gilead ... Josh 17:3 1121
the *s* of Machir ... Josh 17:3 1121
the *s* of Manasseh, had no sons, ... Josh 17:3 1121
and before Joshua the *s* of Nun ... Josh 17:4 1121
the valley of the *s* of Hinnom ... Josh 18:16 1121
stone of Bohan the *s* of Reuben ... Josh 18:17 1121
to Joshua the *s* of Nun among them ... Josh 19:49 1121
priest, and Joshua the *s* of Nun ... Josh 19:51 1121
and unto Joshua the *s* of Nun ... Josh 21:1 1121
gave they to Caleb the *s* of ... Josh 21:12 1121
Phinehas the *s* of Eleazar the ... Josh 22:13 1121
Did not Achan the *s* of Zerah ... Josh 22:20 1121
Phinehas the *s* of Eleazar the ... Josh 22:31 1121
Phinehas the *s* of Eleazar the ... Josh 22:32 1121
Then Balak the *s* of Zippor ... Josh 24:9 1121
called Balaam the *s* of Beor to ... Josh 24:9 1121
things, that Joshua the *s* of Nun ... Josh 24:29 1121
Eleazar the *s* of Aaron died ... Josh 24:33 1121
that pertained to Phinehas his *s* ... Josh 24:33 1121
And Othniel the *s* of Kenaz ... Judg 1:13 1121
And Joshua the *s* of Nun, the ... Judg 2:8 1121
them, even Othniel the *s* of Kenaz ... Judg 3:9 1121
Othniel the *s* of Kenaz died ... Judg 3:11 1121
a deliverer, Ehud the *s* of Gera ... Judg 3:15 1121
him was Shamgar the *s* of Anath ... Judg 3:31 1121
called Barak the *s* of Abinoam out ... Judg 4:6 1121
shewed Sisera that Barak the *s* of ... Judg 4:12 1121
Barak the *s* of Abinoam on that ... Judg 5:1 1121
days of Shamgar the *s* of Anath ... Judg 5:6 1121
captive, thou *s* of Abinoam ... Judg 5:12 1121
his *s* Gideon threshed wheat by ... Judg 6:11 1121
Gideon the *s* of Joash hath done ... Judg 6:29 1121
said unto Joash, Bring out thy *s* ... Judg 6:30 1121
sword of Gideon the *s* of Joash ... Judg 7:14 1121
Gideon the *s* of Joash returned ... Judg 8:13 1121
and thy *s*, and thy son's *s* also ... Judg 8:22 1121
neither shall my *s* rule over you ... Judg 8:23 1121
And Jerubbaal the *s* of Joash went ... Judg 8:29 1121
in Shechem, she also bare him a *s* ... Judg 8:31 1121
Gideon the *s* of Joash died in a ... Judg 8:32 1121
Abimelech the *s* of Jerubbaal went ... Judg 9:1 1121
youngest *s* of Jerubbaal was left ... Judg 9:5 1121
the *s* of his maidservant, king ... Judg 9:18 1121
Gaal the *s* of Ebed came with his ... Judg 9:26 1121
Gaal the *s* of Ebed said, Who is ... Judg 9:28 1121
is not he the *s* of Jerubbaal ... Judg 9:28 1121
the words of Gaal the *s* of Ebed ... Judg 9:30 1121
Behold, Gaal the *s* of Ebed ... Judg 9:31 1121
Gaal the *s* of Ebed went out, and ... Judg 9:35 1121
of Jotham the *s* of Jerubbaal ... Judg 9:57 1121
defend Israel Tola the *s* of Puah ... Judg 10:1 1121
the *s* of Dodo, a man of Issachar ... Judg 10:1 1121
he was the *s* of an harlot ... Judg 11:1 1121

for thou art the *s* of a strange ... Judg 11:2 1121
better than Balak the *s* of Zippor ... Judg 11:25 1121
her he had neither *s* nor daughter ... Judg 11:34 1121
after him Abdon the *s* of Hillel ... Judg 12:13 1121
Abdon the *s* of Hillel the ... Judg 12:15 1121
thou shalt conceive, and bear a *s* ... Judg 13:3 1121
thou shalt conceive, and bear a *s* ... Judg 13:5 1121
thou shalt conceive, and bear a *s* ... Judg 13:7 1121
And the woman bare a *s*, and called ... Judg 13:24 1121
the *s* in law of the Timnite, ... Judg 15:6 2860
Blessed be thou of the LORD, my *s* ... Judg 17:2 1121
the LORD from my hand for my *s* ... Judg 17:3 1121
the *s* of Gershom ... Judg 18:30 1121
the *s* of Manasseh, he and his sons ... Judg 18:30 1121
father said unto his *s* in law ... Judg 19:5 2860
the *s* of Eleazar ... Judg 20:28 1121
the *s* of Aaron, stood before it ... Judg 20:28 1121
her conception, and she bare a *s* ... Ruth 4:13 1121
There is a *s* born to Naomi ... Ruth 4:17 1121
the *s* of Jeroham ... 1Sa 1:1 1121
the *s* of Elihu, the *s* of Tohu, ... 1Sa 1:1 1121
the *s* of Zuph, an Ephrathite ... 1Sa 1:1 1121
had conceived, that she bare a *s* ... 1Sa 1:20 1121
gave her *s* suck until she weaned ... 1Sa 1:23 1121
he answered, I called not, my *s* ... 1Sa 3:6 1121
Samuel, and said, Samuel, my *s* ... 1Sa 3:16 1121
he said, What is there done, my *s* ... 1Sa 4:16 1121
for thou hast born a *s* ... 1Sa 4:20 1121
sanctified Eleazar his *s* to keep ... 1Sa 7:1 1121
the *s* of Abiel, the *s* of Zeror, ... 1Sa 9:1 1121
the *s* of Bechorath ... 1Sa 9:1 1121
the *s* of Aphiah, a Benjamite, a ... 1Sa 9:1 1121
And he had a *s*, whose name was ... 1Sa 9:2 1121
And Kish said to Saul his *s* ... 1Sa 9:3 1121
saying, What shall I do for my *s* ... 1Sa 10:2 1121
that is come unto the *s* of Kish ... 1Sa 10:11 1121
Saul the *s* of Kish was taken ... 1Sa 10:21 1121
And Saul, and Jonathan his *s* ... 1Sa 13:16 1121
Jonathan his *s* was there found ... 1Sa 13:22 1121
that Jonathan the *s* of Saul said ... 1Sa 14:1 1121
the *s* of Ahitub, I-chabod's ... 1Sa 14:3 1121
the *s* of Phinehas, the *s* of Eli ... 1Sa 14:3 1121
though it be in Jonathan my *s* ... 1Sa 14:39 1121
Jonathan my *s* will be on the ... 1Sa 14:40 1121
lots between me and Jonathan my *s* ... 1Sa 14:42 1121
the *s* of Ner, Saul's uncle ... 1Sa 14:50 1121
of Abner was the *s* of Abiel ... 1Sa 14:51 1121
I have seen a *s* of Jesse the ... 1Sa 16:18 1121
and said, Send me David thy *s* ... 1Sa 16:19 1121
them by David his *s* unto Saul ... 1Sa 16:20 1121
Now David was the *s* of that ... 1Sa 17:12 1121
And Jesse said unto David his *s* ... 1Sa 17:17 1121
Abner, whose *s* is this youth ... 1Sa 17:55 1121
thou whose *s* the stripling is ... 1Sa 17:56 1121
Whose *s* art thou, thou young man ... 1Sa 17:58 1121
I am the *s* of thy servant Jesse ... 1Sa 17:58 1121
that I should be *s* in law to the ... 1Sa 18:18 2860
Thou shalt this day be my *s* in ... 1Sa 18:21 2859
therefore be the king's *s* in law ... 1Sa 18:22 2859
thing to be a king's *s* in law ... 1Sa 18:23 2859
well to be the king's *s* in law ... 1Sa 18:26 2859
he might be the king's *s* in law ... 1Sa 18:27 2859
And Saul spake to Jonathan his *s* ... 1Sa 19:1 1121
But Jonathan Saul's *s* delighted ... 1Sa 19:2 1121
and Saul said unto Jonathan his *s* ... 1Sa 20:27 1121
cometh not the *s* of Jesse to meat ... 1Sa 20:27 1121
Thou *s* of the perverse rebellious ... 1Sa 20:30 1121
know that thou hast chosen the *s* ... 1Sa 20:30 1121
For as long as the *s* of Jesse ... 1Sa 20:31 1121
will the *s* of Jesse give every ... 1Sa 22:7 1121
s hath made a league with the *s* ... 1Sa 22:8 1121
my *s* hath stirred up my servant ... 1Sa 22:8 1121
I saw the *s* of Jesse coming to ... 1Sa 22:9 1121
Nob, to Ahimelech the *s* of Ahitub ... 1Sa 22:9 1121
the *s* of Ahitub, and all his ... 1Sa 22:11 1121
said, Hear now, thou *s* of Ahitub ... 1Sa 22:12 1121
the *s* of Jesse, in that thou hast ... 1Sa 22:13 1121
which is the king's *s* in law ... 1Sa 22:14 2860
sons of Ahimelech the *s* of Ahitub ... 1Sa 22:20 1121
when Abiathar the *s* of Ahimelech ... 1Sa 23:6 1121
And Jonathan Saul's *s* arose ... 1Sa 23:16 1121
Is this thy voice, my *s* David ... 1Sa 24:16 1121
thy servants, and to thy *s* David ... 1Sa 25:8 1121
and who is the *s* of Jesse ... 1Sa 25:10 1121
for he is such a *s* of Belial ... 1Sa 25:17 1121
wife, to Phalti the *s* of Laish ... 1Sa 25:44 1121
Saul lay, and Abner the *s* of Ner ... 1Sa 26:5 1121
and to Abishai the *s* of Zeruiah ... 1Sa 26:6 1121
people, and to Abner the *s* of Ner ... 1Sa 26:14 1121
Is this thy voice, my *s* David ... 1Sa 26:17 1121
return, my *s* David ... 1Sa 26:21 1121
Blessed be thou, my *s* David ... 1Sa 26:25 1121
the *s* of Maoch, king of Gath ... 1Sa 27:2 1121
the priest, Ahimelech's *s* ... 1Sa 30:7 1121
Jonathan his *s* are dead also ... 2Sa 1:4 1121
Saul and Jonathan his *s* be dead ... 2Sa 1:5 1121
for Saul, and for Jonathan his *s* ... 2Sa 1:12 1121
I am the *s* of a stranger, an ... 2Sa 1:13 1121
over Saul and over Jonathan his *s* ... 2Sa 1:17 1121
But Abner the *s* of Ner, captain ... 2Sa 2:8 1121
took Ish-bosheth the *s* of Saul ... 2Sa 2:8 1121
Ish-bosheth Saul's *s* was forty ... 2Sa 2:10 1121
And Abner the *s* of Ner, and the ... 2Sa 2:12 1121
of Ish-bosheth the *s* of Saul ... 2Sa 2:12 1121
Joab the *s* of Zeruiah, and the ... 2Sa 2:13 1121
to Ish-bosheth the *s* of Saul ... 2Sa 2:15 1121
Absalom the *s* of Maacah the ... 2Sa 3:3 1121
fourth, Adonijah the *s* of Haggith ... 2Sa 3:4 1121
fifth, Shephatiah the *s* of Abital ... 2Sa 3:4 1121
to Ish-bosheth Saul's *s*, saying, ... 2Sa 3:14 1121
even from Phaltiel the *s* of Laish ... 2Sa 3:15 1121
Abner the *s* of Ner came to the ... 2Sa 3:23 1121
Thou knowest Abner the *s* of Ner ... 2Sa 3:25 1121
the blood of Abner the *s* of Ner ... 2Sa 3:28 1121

king to slay Abner the *s* of Ner ... 2Sa 3:37 1121
when Saul's *s* heard that Abner ... 2Sa 4:1 1121
Saul's *s* had two men that were ... 2Sa 4:2 1121
And Jonathan, Saul's *s*, had a *s* ... 2Sa 4:4 1121
the *s* of Saul thine enemy ... 2Sa 4:8 1121
his father, and he shall be my *s* ... 2Sa 7:14 1121
the *s* of Rehob, king of Zobah, as ... 2Sa 8:3 1121
sent Joram his *s* unto king David ... 2Sa 8:10 1121
s of Rehob, king of Zobah ... 2Sa 8:12 1121
Joab the *s* of Zeruiah was over ... 2Sa 8:16 1121
Jehoshaphat the *s* of Ahilud was ... 2Sa 8:16 1121
And Zadok the *s* of Ahitub, and ... 2Sa 8:17 1121
and Ahimelech the *s* of Abiathar ... 2Sa 8:17 1121
Benaiah the *s* of Jehoiada was ... 2Sa 8:18 1121
the king, Jonathan hath yet a *s* ... 2Sa 9:3 1121
the *s* of Ammiel, in Lo-debar ... 2Sa 9:4 1121
the *s* of Ammiel, from Lo-debar ... 2Sa 9:5 1121
the *s* of Jonathan ... 2Sa 9:6 1121
the *s* of Saul, was come unto ... 2Sa 9:6 1121
s all that pertained to Saul ... 2Sa 9:9 1121
that thy master's *s* may have food ... 2Sa 9:10 1121
s shall eat bread alway at my ... 2Sa 9:10 1121
And Mephibosheth had a young *s* ... 2Sa 9:12 1121
Hanun his *s* reigned in his stead ... 2Sa 10:1 1121
unto Hanun the *s* of Nahash ... 2Sa 10:2 1121
Abimelech the *s* of Jerubbesheth ... 2Sa 11:21 1121
became his wife, and bare him a *s* ... 2Sa 11:27 1121
and she bare a *s*, and he called his ... 2Sa 12:24 1121
that Absalom the *s* of David had a ... 2Sa 13:1 1121
Amnon the *s* of David loved her ... 2Sa 13:1 1121
the *s* of Shimeah David's brother ... 2Sa 13:3 1121
Why art thou, being the king's *s* ... 2Sa 13:4 1121
king said to Absalom, Nay, my *s* ... 2Sa 13:25 1121
the *s* of Shimeah David's brother, ... 2Sa 13:32 1121
the *s* of Ammihud, king of Geshur ... 2Sa 13:37 1121
David mourned for his *s* every day ... 2Sa 13:37 1121
Now Joab the *s* of Zeruiah ... 2Sa 14:1 1121
any more, lest they destroy my *s* ... 2Sa 14:11 1121
hair of thy *s* fall to the earth ... 2Sa 14:11 1121
me and my *s* together out of the ... 2Sa 14:16 1121
two sons with you, Ahimaaz thy *s* ... 2Sa 15:27 1121
and Jonathan the *s* of Abiathar ... 2Sa 15:27 1121
their two sons, Ahimaaz Zadok's *s* ... 2Sa 15:36
and Jonathan Abiathar's *s* ... 2Sa 15:36
said, And where is thy master's *s* ... 2Sa 16:3 1121
name was Shimei, the *s* of Gera ... 2Sa 16:5 1121
into the hand of Absalom thy *s* ... 2Sa 16:8 1121
Then said Abishai the *s* of ... 2Sa 16:9 1121
to all his servants, Behold, my *s* ... 2Sa 16:11 1121
serve in the presence of his *s* ... 2Sa 16:19 1121
which Amasa was a man's *s* ... 2Sa 17:25 1121
that Shobi the *s* of Nahash of ... 2Sa 17:27 1121
Machir the *s* of Ammiel of ... 2Sa 17:27 1121
hand of Abishai the *s* of Zeruiah ... 2Sa 18:2 1121
mine hand against the king's *s* ... 2Sa 18:12 1121
I have no *s* to keep my name in ... 2Sa 18:18 1121
Then said Ahimaaz the *s* of Zadok ... 2Sa 18:19 1121
because the king's *s* is dead ... 2Sa 18:20 1121
Then said Ahimaaz the *s* of Zadok ... 2Sa 18:22 1121
Wherefore wilt thou run, my *s* ... 2Sa 18:22 1121
running of Ahimaaz the *s* of Zadok ... 2Sa 18:27 1121
O my *s* Absalom, my *s*, my *s* ... 2Sa 18:33 1121
for thee, O Absalom, my *s*, my *s* ... 2Sa 18:33 1121
the king was grieved for his *s* ... 2Sa 19:2 1121
O my *s* Absalom ... 2Sa 19:4 1121
O Absalom, my *s*, my *s* ... 2Sa 19:4 1121
And Shimei the *s* of Gera, a ... 2Sa 19:16 1121
Shimei the *s* of Gera fell down ... 2Sa 19:18 1121
But Abishai the *s* of Zeruiah ... 2Sa 19:21 1121
Mephibosheth the *s* of Saul came ... 2Sa 19:24 1121
the *s* of Bichri, a Benjamite ... 2Sa 20:1 1121
we inheritance in the *s* of Jesse ... 2Sa 20:1 1121
and followed Sheba the *s* of Bichri ... 2Sa 20:2 1121
Now shall Sheba the *s* of Bichri ... 2Sa 20:6 1121
after Sheba the *s* of Bichri ... 2Sa 20:7 1121
after Sheba the *s* of Bichri ... 2Sa 20:10 1121
after Sheba the *s* of Bichri ... 2Sa 20:13 1121
Sheba the *s* of Bichri by name, ... 2Sa 20:21 1121
the head of Sheba the *s* of Bichri ... 2Sa 20:22 1121
Benaiah the *s* of Jehoiada was ... 2Sa 20:23 1121
Jehoshaphat the *s* of Ahilud was ... 2Sa 20:24 1121
the *s* of Jonathan the *s* of Saul ... 2Sa 21:7 1121
David and Jonathan the *s* of Saul ... 2Sa 21:7 1121
s of Barzillai the Meholathite ... 2Sa 21:8 1121
the bones of Jonathan his *s* from ... 2Sa 21:12 1121
and the bones of Jonathan his *s* ... 2Sa 21:13 1121
Jonathan his *s* buried they in the ... 2Sa 21:14 1121
But Abishai the *s* of Zeruiah ... 2Sa 21:17 1121
Elhanan the *s* of Jaare-oregim ... 2Sa 21:19 1121
Jonathan the *s* of Shimeah the ... 2Sa 21:21 1121
David the *s* of Jesse said, and the ... 2Sa 23:1 1121
Eleazar the *s* of Dodo the Ahohite ... 2Sa 23:9 1121
the *s* of Agee the Hararite ... 2Sa 23:11 1121
the *s* of Zeruiah, was chief among ... 2Sa 23:18 1121
And Benaiah the *s* of Jehoiada ... 2Sa 23:20 1121
the *s* of a valiant man, of ... 2Sa 23:20 1121
did Benaiah the *s* of Jehoiada ... 2Sa 23:22 1121
Elhanan the *s* of Dodo of ... 2Sa 23:24 1121
Ira the *s* of Ikkesh the Tekoite, ... 2Sa 23:26 1121
Heleb the *s* of Baanah, a ... 2Sa 23:29 1121
Ittai the *s* of Ribai out of ... 2Sa 23:29 1121
Ahiam the *s* of Sharar the ... 2Sa 23:33 1121
Eliphelet the *s* of Ahasbai ... 2Sa 23:34 1121
the *s* of the Maachathite, Eliam ... 2Sa 23:34 1121
Eliam the *s* of Ahithophel the ... 2Sa 23:34 1121
Igal the *s* of Nathan of Zobah, ... 2Sa 23:36 1121
to Joab the *s* of Zeruiah, ... 2Sa 23:37 1121
Then Adonijah the *s* of Haggith ... 1Kin 1:5 1121
with Joab the *s* of Zeruiah ... 1Kin 1:7 1121
and Benaiah the *s* of Jehoiada ... 1Kin 1:8 1121
the *s* of Haggith doth reign ... 1Kin 1:11 1121
and the life of thy *s* Solomon ... 1Kin 1:12 1121
thy *s* shall reign after me ... 1Kin 1:13 1121
thy *s* shall reign after me ... 1Kin 1:17 1121

my s Solomon shall be counted	1Kin 1:21	1121
and Benaiah the s of Jehoiada	1Kin 1:26	1121
thy s shall reign after me	1Kin 1:30	1121
and Benaiah the s of Jehoiada	1Kin 1:32	1121
cause Solomon my s to ride upon	1Kin 1:33	1121
Benaiah the s of Jehoiada	1Kin 1:36	1121
and Benaiah the s of Jehoiada	1Kin 1:38	1121
Jonathan the s of Abiathar the	1Kin 1:42	1121
and Benaiah the s of Jehoiada	1Kin 1:44	1121
and he charged Solomon his s	1Kin 2:1	1121
Joab the s of Zeruiah did to me	1Kin 2:5	1121
Israel, unto Abner the s of Ner	1Kin 2:5	1121
and unto Amasa the s of Jether	1Kin 2:5	1121
with thee Shimei the s of Gera	1Kin 2:8	1121
Adonijah the s of Haggith came to	1Kin 2:13	1121
and for Joab the s of Zeruiah	1Kin 2:22	1121
hand of Benaiah the s of Jehoiada	1Kin 2:25	1121
sent Benaiah the s of Jehoiada	1Kin 2:29	1121
to wit, Abner the s of Ner	1Kin 2:32	1121
Israel, and Amasa the s of Jether	1Kin 2:32	1121
So Benaiah the s of Jehoiada went	1Kin 2:34	1121
the king put Benaiah the s of	1Kin 2:35	1121
Achish s of Maachah king of Gath	1Kin 2:39	1121
Benaiah the s of Jehoiada	1Kin 2:46	1121
him a s to sit on his throne	1Kin 3:6	1121
took my s from beside me, while	1Kin 3:20	1121
morning, behold, it was not my s	1Kin 3:21	1121
is my s, and the dead is thy s	1Kin 3:22	1121
is thy s, and the living is my s	1Kin 3:22	1121
This is my s that liveth, and thy	1Kin 3:23	1121
that liveth, and thy s is the dead	1Kin 3:23	1121
but thy s is the dead, and my s	1Kin 3:23	1121
for her bowels yearned upon her s	1Kin 3:26	1121
Azariah the s of Zadok the priest	1Kin 4:2	1121
Jehoshaphat the s of Ahilud	1Kin 4:3	1121
Benaiah the s of Jehoiada was	1Kin 4:4	1121
Azariah the s of Nathan was over	1Kin 4:5	1121
Zabud the s of Nathan was	1Kin 4:5	1121
Adoniram the s of Abda was over	1Kin 4:6	1121
The s of Hur, in mount Ephraim	1Kin 4:8	1133
The s of Dekar, in Makaz, and in	1Kin 4:9	1128
The s of Hesed, in Aruboth	1Kin 4:10	1136
The s of Abinadab, in all the	1Kin 4:11	1125
Baana the s of Ahilud	1Kin 4:12	1121
The s of Geber, in Ramoth-gilead	1Kin 4:13	1127
towns of Jair the s of Manasseh	1Kin 4:13	1121
Ahinadab the s of Iddo had	1Kin 4:14	1121
Baanah the s of Hushai was in	1Kin 4:16	1121
Jehoshaphat the s of Paruah	1Kin 4:17	1121
Shimei the s of Elah, in Benjamin	1Kin 4:18	1121
Geber the s of Uri was in the	1Kin 4:19	1121
David my father, saying, Thy s	1Kin 5:5	1121
a wise s over this great people	1Kin 5:7	1121
He was a widow's s of the tribe	1Kin 7:14	1121
but thy s that shall come forth	1Kin 8:19	1121
rend it out of the hand of thy s	1Kin 11:12	1121
thy s for David my servant's sake	1Kin 11:13	1121
Tahpenes bare him Genubath his s	1Kin 11:20	1121
Rezon the s of Eliadah, which	1Kin 11:23	1121
And Jeroboam the s of Nebat	1Kin 11:26	1121
unto his s will I give one tribe,	1Kin 11:36	1121
Rehoboam his s reigned in his	1Kin 11:43	1121
when Jeroboam the s of Nebat	1Kin 12:2	1121
unto Jeroboam the s of Nebat	1Kin 12:15	1121
we inheritance in the s of Jesse	1Kin 12:16	1121
to Rehoboam the s of Solomon	1Kin 12:21	1121
the s of Solomon, king of Judah,	1Kin 12:23	1121
the s of Jeroboam fell sick	1Kin 14:1	1121
to ask a thing of thee for her s	1Kin 14:5	1121
Nadab his s reigned in his stead	1Kin 14:20	1121
Rehoboam the s of Solomon reigned	1Kin 14:21	1121
Abijam his s reigned in his stead	1Kin 14:31	1121
year of king Jeroboam the s of	1Kin 15:1	1121
to set up his s after him	1Kin 15:4	1121
Asa his s reigned in his stead	1Kin 15:8	1121
the s of Tabrimon	1Kin 15:18	1121
the s of Hezion, king of Syria,	1Kin 15:18	1121
Jehoshaphat his s reigned in his	1Kin 15:24	1121
Nadab the s of Jeroboam began to	1Kin 15:25	1121
And Baasha the s of Ahijah	1Kin 15:27	1121
the s of Ahijah to reign over all	1Kin 15:33	1121
the s of Hanani against Baasha	1Kin 16:1	1121
house of Jeroboam the s of Nebat	1Kin 16:3	1121
Elah his s reigned in his stead	1Kin 16:6	1121
hand of the prophet Jehu the s of	1Kin 16:7	1121
king of Judah began Elah the s of	1Kin 16:8	1121
Baasha, and the sins of Elah his s	1Kin 16:13	1121
followed Tibni the s of Ginath	1Kin 16:21	1121
followed Tibni the s of Ginath	1Kin 16:22	1121
way of Jeroboam the s of Nebat	1Kin 16:26	1121
Ahab his s reigned in his stead	1Kin 16:28	1121
s of Omri to reign over Israel	1Kin 16:29	1121
Ahab the s of Omri reigned over	1Kin 16:29	1121
Ahab the s of Omri did evil in	1Kin 16:30	1121
sins of Jeroboam the s of Nebat	1Kin 16:31	1121
thereof in his youngest s Segub	1Kin 16:34	
he spake by Joshua the s of Nun	1Kin 16:34	1121
go in and dress it for me and my s	1Kin 17:12	1121
after make for thee and for thy s	1Kin 17:13	1121
that the s of the woman, the	1Kin 17:17	1121
to remembrance, and to slay my s	1Kin 17:18	1121
he said unto her, Give me thy s	1Kin 17:19	1121
whom I sojourn, by slaying her s	1Kin 17:20	1121
and Elijah said, See, thy s liveth	1Kin 17:23	1121
Jehu the s of Nimshi shalt thou	1Kin 19:16	1121
Elisha the s of Shaphat of	1Kin 19:16	1121
and found Elisha the s of Shaphat	1Kin 19:19	1121
house of Jeroboam the s of Nebat	1Kin 21:22	1121
house of Baasha the s of Ahijah	1Kin 21:22	1121
one man, Micaiah the s of Imlah	1Kin 22:8	1121
hither Micaiah the s of Imlah	1Kin 22:9	1121
Zedekiah the s of Chenaanah made	1Kin 22:11	1121
But Zedekiah the s of Chenaanah	1Kin 22:24	1121
city, and to Joash the king's s	1Kin 22:26	1121
Ahaziah his s reigned in his	1Kin 22:40	1121
Jehoshaphat the s of Asa began to	1Kin 22:41	1121
Then said Ahaziah the s of Ahab	1Kin 22:49	1121
Jehoram his s reigned in his	1Kin 22:50	1121
Ahaziah the s of Ahab began to	1Kin 22:51	1121
way of Jeroboam the s of Nebat	1Kin 22:52	1121
s of Jehoshaphat king of Judah	2Kin 1:17	1121
because he had no s	2Kin 1:17	1121
Now Jehoram the s of Ahab began	2Kin 3:1	1121
sins of Jeroboam the s of Nebat	2Kin 3:3	1121
Here is Elisha the s of Shaphat	2Kin 3:11	1121
Then he took his eldest s that	2Kin 3:27	1121
full, that she said unto her s	2Kin 4:6	1121
of life, thou shalt embrace a s	2Kin 4:16	1121
bare a s at that season that	2Kin 4:17	1121
said, Did I desire a s of my lord	2Kin 4:28	1121
unto him, he said, Take up thy s	2Kin 4:36	1121
to the ground, and took up her s	2Kin 4:37	1121
woman said unto me, Give thy s	2Kin 6:28	1121
and we will eat my s to morrow	2Kin 6:28	1121
So we boiled my s, and did eat him	2Kin 6:29	1121
her on the next day, Give thy s	2Kin 6:29	1121
and she hath hid her s	2Kin 6:29	1121
if the head of Elisha the s of	2Kin 6:31	1121
See ye how this s of a murderer	2Kin 6:32	1121
whose s he had restored to life,	2Kin 8:1	1121
whose s he had restored to life,	2Kin 8:5	1121
is the woman, and this is her s	2Kin 8:5	1121
Thy s Ben-hadad king of Syria	2Kin 8:9	1121
the s of Ahab king of Israel	2Kin 8:16	1121
Jehoram the s of Jehoshaphat king	2Kin 8:16	1121
Ahaziah his s reigned in his	2Kin 8:24	1121
the s of Ahab king of Israel did	2Kin 8:25	1121
s of Jehoram king of Judah begin	2Kin 8:25	1121
for he was the s in law of the	2Kin 8:27	2860
he went with Joram the s of Ahab	2Kin 8:28	1121
Ahaziah the s of Jehoram king of	2Kin 8:29	1121
Joram the s of Ahab in Jezreel	2Kin 8:29	1121
Jehu the s of Jehoshaphat	2Kin 9:2	1121
Jehoshaphat the s of Nimshi	2Kin 9:2	1121
house of Jeroboam the s of Nebat	2Kin 9:9	1121
house of Baasha the s of Ahijah	2Kin 9:9	1121
So Jehu the s of Jehoshaphat the	2Kin 9:14	1121
the s of Nimshi conspired against	2Kin 9:14	1121
driving of Jehu the s of Nimshi	2Kin 9:20	1121
s of Ahab began Ahaziah to reign	2Kin 9:29	1121
he lighted on Jehonadab the s of	2Kin 10:15	1121
and Jehonadab the s of Rechab	2Kin 10:23	1121
sins of Jeroboam the s of Nebat	2Kin 10:29	1121
Jehoahaz his s reigned in his	2Kin 10:35	1121
Ahaziah saw that her s was dead	2Kin 11:1	1121
took Joash the s of Ahaziah	2Kin 11:2	1121
LORD, and shewed them the king's s	2Kin 11:4	1121
And he brought forth the king's s	2Kin 11:12	1121
For Jozachar the s of Shimeath	2Kin 12:21	1121
and Jehozabad the s of Shomer	2Kin 12:21	1121
Amaziah his s reigned in his	2Kin 12:21	1121
the s of Ahaziah king of Judah	2Kin 13:1	1121
king of Judah Jehoahaz the s of	2Kin 13:1	1121
sins of Jeroboam the s of Nebat	2Kin 13:2	1121
hand of Ben-hadad the s of Hazael	2Kin 13:3	1121
Joash his s reigned in his stead	2Kin 13:9	1121
the s of Jehoahaz to reign over	2Kin 13:10	1121
sins of Jeroboam the s of Nebat	2Kin 13:11	1121
Ben-hadad his s reigned in his	2Kin 13:24	1121
Jehoash the s of Jehoahaz took	2Kin 13:25	1121
the s of Hazael the cities	2Kin 13:25	1121
s of Jehoahaz king of Israel	2Kin 14:1	1121
the s of Joash king of Judah	2Kin 14:1	1121
the s of Jehoahaz s of Jehu,	2Kin 14:8	1121
Give thy daughter to my s to wife	2Kin 14:9	1121
s of Jehoash the s of Ahaziah	2Kin 14:13	1121
Jeroboam his s reigned in his	2Kin 14:16	1121
Amaziah the s of Joash king of	2Kin 14:17	1121
s of Jehoahaz king of Israel	2Kin 14:17	1121
fifteenth year of Amaziah the s	2Kin 14:23	1121
king of Judah Jeroboam the s of	2Kin 14:23	1121
sins of Jeroboam the s of Nebat	2Kin 14:24	1121
the s of Amittai, the prophet,	2Kin 14:25	1121
hand of Jeroboam the s of Joash	2Kin 14:27	1121
Zachariah his s reigned in his	2Kin 14:29	1121
s of Amaziah king of Judah to	2Kin 15:1	1121
Jotham the king's s was over the	2Kin 15:5	1121
Jotham his s reigned in his stead	2Kin 15:7	1121
s of Jeroboam reign over Israel	2Kin 15:8	1121
sins of Jeroboam the s of Nebat	2Kin 15:9	1121
Shallum the s of Jabesh conspired	2Kin 15:10	1121
Shallum the s of Jabesh began to	2Kin 15:13	1121
For Menahem the s of Gadi went up	2Kin 15:14	1121
smote Shallum the s of Jabesh in	2Kin 15:14	1121
s of Gadi to reign over Israel	2Kin 15:17	1121
sins of Jeroboam the s of Nebat	2Kin 15:18	1121
Pekahiah his s reigned in his	2Kin 15:22	1121
king of Judah Pekahiah the s of	2Kin 15:23	1121
sins of Jeroboam the s of Nebat	2Kin 15:24	1121
But Pekah the s of Remaliah	2Kin 15:25	1121
s of Remaliah began to reign over	2Kin 15:27	1121
sins of Jeroboam the s of Nebat	2Kin 15:28	1121
Hoshea the s of Elah made a	2Kin 15:30	1121
against Pekah the s of Remaliah	2Kin 15:30	1121
year of Jotham the s of Uzziah	2Kin 15:30	1121
the s of Remaliah king of Israel	2Kin 15:32	1121
the s of Uzziah king of Judah to	2Kin 15:32	1121
Syria, and Pekah the s of Remaliah	2Kin 15:37	1121
Ahaz his s reigned in his stead	2Kin 15:38	1121
the s of Remaliah	2Kin 16:1	1121
Ahaz the s of Jotham	2Kin 16:1	1121
made his s to pass through the	2Kin 16:3	1121
Pekah s of Remaliah king of	2Kin 16:5	1121
saying, I am thy servant and thy s	2Kin 16:7	1121
Hezekiah his s reigned in his	2Kin 16:20	1121
the s of Elah to reign in Samaria	2Kin 17:1	1121
made Jeroboam the s of Nebat king	2Kin 17:21	1121
Hoshea s of Elah king of Israel	2Kin 18:1	1121
that Hezekiah the s of Ahaz king	2Kin 18:1	1121
Hoshea s of Elah king of Israel	2Kin 18:9	1121
to them Eliakim the s of Hilkiah	2Kin 18:18	1121
Joah the s of Asaph the recorder	2Kin 18:18	1121
said Eliakim the s of Hilkiah	2Kin 18:26	1121
came Eliakim the s of Hilkiah	2Kin 18:37	1121
Joah the s of Asaph the recorder,	2Kin 18:37	1121
Isaiah the prophet the s of Amoz	2Kin 19:2	1121
Then Isaiah the s of Amoz sent to	2Kin 19:20	1121
Esar-haddon his s reigned in his	2Kin 19:37	1121
Isaiah the s of Amoz came to him	2Kin 20:1	1121
the s of Baladan, king of Babylon	2Kin 20:12	1121
Manasseh his s reigned in his	2Kin 20:21	1121
he made his s pass through the	2Kin 21:6	1121
to David, and to Solomon his s	2Kin 21:7	1121
Amon his s reigned in his stead	2Kin 21:18	1121
Josiah his s king in his stead	2Kin 21:24	1121
Josiah his s reigned in his stead	2Kin 21:26	1121
sent Shaphan the s of Azaliah	2Kin 22:3	1121
the s of Meshullam, the scribe,	2Kin 22:3	1121
and Ahikam the s of Shaphan	2Kin 22:12	1121
Achbor the s of Michaiah, and	2Kin 22:12	1121
wife of Shallum the s of Tikvah	2Kin 22:14	1121
the s of Harhas, keeper of the	2Kin 22:14	1121
that no man might make his s or	2Kin 23:10	1121
which Jeroboam the s of Nebat	2Kin 23:15	1121
took Jehoahaz the s of Josiah	2Kin 23:30	1121
s of Josiah king in the room of	2Kin 23:34	1121
Jehoiachin his s reigned in his	2Kin 24:6	1121
he made Gedaliah the s of Ahikam	2Kin 25:22	1121
Ahikam, the s of Shaphan, ruler	2Kin 25:22	1121
even Ishmael the s of Nethaniah	2Kin 25:23	1121
and Johanan the s of Careah	2Kin 25:23	1121
Seraiah the s of Tanhumeth the	2Kin 25:23	1121
Jaazaniah the s of a Maachathite,	2Kin 25:23	1121
that Ishmael the s of Nethaniah	2Kin 25:25	1121
the s of Elishama, of the seed	2Kin 25:25	1121
Bela the s of Beor	1Chr 1:43	1121
Jobab the s of Zerah of Bozrah	1Chr 1:44	1121
was dead, Hadad the s of Bedad	1Chr 1:46	1121
Baal-hanan the s of Achbor	1Chr 1:49	1121
Caleb the s of Hezron begat	1Chr 2:18	1121
the s of Shammai was Maon	1Chr 2:45	1121
the sons of Caleb the s of Hur	1Chr 2:50	1121
Absalom the s of Maachah the	1Chr 3:2	1121
fourth, Adonijah the s of Haggith	1Chr 3:2	1121
s was Rehoboam, Abia his s	1Chr 3:10	1121
Asa his s, Jehoshaphat his s	1Chr 3:10	1121
Joram his s, Ahaziah his s	1Chr 3:11	1121
Joash his s	1Chr 3:11	1121
Amaziah his s	1Chr 3:12	1121
Azariah his s	1Chr 3:12	1121
Jotham his s	1Chr 3:12	1121
Ahaz his s	1Chr 3:13	1121
Hezekiah his s	1Chr 3:13	1121
Manasseh his s	1Chr 3:13	1121
Amon his s, Josiah his s	1Chr 3:14	1121
Jeconiah his s, Zedekiah his s	1Chr 3:16	1121
Assir, Salathiel his s,	1Chr 3:17	1121
Reaiah the s of Shobal begat	1Chr 4:2	1121
of Aharhel the s of Harum	1Chr 4:8	1121
sons of Caleb the s of Jephunneh	1Chr 4:15	1121
of Shelah the s of Judah were	1Chr 4:21	1121
Shallum his s, Mibsam his s,	1Chr 4:25	1121
Mishma his s	1Chr 4:25	1121
Hamuel his s, Zacchur his s	1Chr 4:26	1121
Shimei his s	1Chr 4:26	1121
and Joshah the s of Amaziah	1Chr 4:34	1121
Jehu the s of Josibiah	1Chr 4:35	1121
s of Seraiah, the s of Asiel,	1Chr 4:35	1121
Ziza the s of Shiphi	1Chr 4:37	1121
the s of Allon	1Chr 4:37	1121
the s of Jedaiah	1Chr 4:37	1121
s of Shimri, the s of Shemaiah	1Chr 4:37	1121
sons of Joseph the s of Israel	1Chr 5:1	1121
Shemaiah his s, Gog his s,	1Chr 5:4	1121
Shimei his s	1Chr 5:4	1121
Micah his s, Reaia his s	1Chr 5:5	1121
Baal his s	1Chr 5:5	1121
Beerah his s, whom	1Chr 5:6	1121
And Bela the s of Azaz	1Chr 5:8	1121
the s of Shema, the s of Joel,	1Chr 5:8	1121
children of Abihail the s of Huri	1Chr 5:14	1121
the s of Jaroah	1Chr 5:14	1121
the s of Gilead	1Chr 5:14	1121
the s of Michael	1Chr 5:14	1121
the s of Jeshishai	1Chr 5:14	1121
the s of Jahdo, the s of Buz	1Chr 5:14	1121
Ahi the s of Abdiel	1Chr 5:15	1121
the s of Guni, chief of the house	1Chr 5:15	1121
Libni his s, Jahath his s	1Chr 6:20	1121
Zimmah his s	1Chr 6:20	1121
Joah his s, Iddo his s, Zerah	1Chr 6:21	1121
Zerah his s, Jeaterai his s	1Chr 6:21	1121
Amminadab his s, Korah his s	1Chr 6:22	1121
Assir his s	1Chr 6:22	1121
Elkanah his s	1Chr 6:23	1121
Ebiasaph his s, and Assir his s	1Chr 6:23	1121
Tahath his s, Uriel his s	1Chr 6:24	1121
Uzziah his s, and Shaul his s	1Chr 6:24	1121
Zophai his s, and Nahath his s,	1Chr 6:26	1121
Eliab his s, Jeroham his s	1Chr 6:27	1121
Elkanah his s	1Chr 6:27	1121
Mahli, Libni his s, Shimei his	1Chr 6:29	1121
s, Shimei his s, Uzza his s	1Chr 6:29	1121
Shimea his s, Haggiah his s	1Chr 6:30	1121
Asaiah his s	1Chr 6:30	1121
the s of Joel, the s of Shemuel	1Chr 6:33	1121
The s of Elkanah	1Chr 6:34	1121
the s of Jeroham	1Chr 6:34	1121
the s of Eliel, the s of Toah,	1Chr 6:34	1121
The s of Zuph, the s of Elkanah	1Chr 6:35	1121
s of Mahath, the s of Amasai,	1Chr 6:35	1121
The s of Elkanah, the s of Joel	1Chr 6:36	1121

of Azariah, the s of Zephaniah, 1Chr 6:36 1121
The s of Tahath, the s of Assir 1Chr 6:37 1121
s of Ebiasaph, the s of Korah, 1Chr 6:37 1121
The s of Izhar, the s of Kohath 1Chr 6:38 1121
the s of Levi, the s of Israel 1Chr 6:38 1121
even Asaph the s of Berachiah 1Chr 6:39 1121
of Berachiah, the s of Shimea, 1Chr 6:39 1121
The s of Michael 1Chr 6:40 1121
the s of Baaseiah 1Chr 6:40 1121
the s of Malchiah 1Chr 6:40 1121
The s of Ethni, the s of Zerah, 1Chr 6:41 1121
the s of Adaiah 1Chr 6:41 1121
The s of Ethan, the s of Zimmah 1Chr 6:42 1121
the s of Shimei 1Chr 6:42 1121
The s of Jahath 1Chr 6:43 1121
the s of Gershom, the s of Levi 1Chr 6:43 1121
Ethan the s of Kishi 1Chr 6:44 1121
the s of Abdi, the s of Malluch 1Chr 6:44 1121
The s of Hashabiah 1Chr 6:45 1121
s of Amaziah, the s of Hilkiah, 1Chr 6:45 1121
The s of Amzi, the s of Bani, 1Chr 6:46 1121
the s of Shamer 1Chr 6:46 1121
The s of Mahli, the s of Mushi, 1Chr 6:47 1121
the s of Merari, the s of Levi 1Chr 6:47 1121
Eleazar his s, Phinehas his s 1Chr 6:50 1121
Abishua his s 1Chr 6:50 1121
Bukki his s, Uzzi his s 1Chr 6:51 1121
Zerahiah his s 1Chr 6:51 1121
Meraioth his s, Amariah his s 1Chr 6:52 1121
Ahitub his s 1Chr 6:52 1121
Zadok his s, Ahimaaz his s 1Chr 6:53 1121
gave to Caleb the s of Jephunneh 1Chr 6:56 1121
the wife of Machir bare a s 1Chr 7:16 1121
s of Machir, the s of Manasseh 1Chr 7:17 1121
and Bered his s, and Tahath his s 1Chr 7:20 1121
Eladah his s, and Tahath his s 1Chr 7:20 1121
Zabad his s, and Shuthelah his s 1Chr 7:21 1121
wife, she conceived, and bare a s 1Chr 7:23 1121
And Rephah was his s, also Resheph 1Chr 7:25 1121
and Telah his s, and Tahan his s 1Chr 7:25 1121
Laadan his s, Ammihud his s, 1Chr 7:26 1121
Laadan his s, Ammihud his s 1Chr 7:26 1121
Elishama his s 1Chr 7:26 1121
Non his s, Jehoshuah his s 1Chr 7:27 1121
of Joseph the s of Israel 1Chr 7:29 1121
And his firstborn s Abdon, and Zur, 1Chr 8:30 1121
the s of Jonathan was Merib-baal 1Chr 8:34 1121
Rapha was his s, Eleasah his s, 1Chr 8:37 1121
Azel his s 1Chr 8:37 1121
Uthai the s of Ammihud 1Chr 9:4 1121
the s of Omri, the s of Imri, 1Chr 9:4 1121
the s of Bani, of the children of 1Chr 9:4 1121
children of Pharez the s of Judah 1Chr 9:4 1121
Sallu the s of Meshullam 1Chr 9:7 1121
the s of Hodaviah 1Chr 9:7 1121
of Hodaviah, the s of Hasenuah, 1Chr 9:7 1121
And Ibneiah the s of Jeroham 1Chr 9:8 1121
of Jeroham, and Elah the s of Uzzi 1Chr 9:8 1121
the s of Michri, and Meshullam the 1Chr 9:8 1121
and Meshullam the s of Shephatiah 1Chr 9:8 1121
s of Reuel, the s of Ibnijah 1Chr 9:8 1121
And Azariah the s of Hilkiah 1Chr 9:11 1121
the s of Meshullam 1Chr 9:11 1121
the s of Zadok 1Chr 9:11 1121
the s of Meraioth 1Chr 9:11 1121
the s of Ahitub, the ruler of the 1Chr 9:11 1121
And Adaiah the s of Jeroham 1Chr 9:12 1121
the s of Pashur 1Chr 9:12 1121
the s of Malchijah 1Chr 9:12 1121
and Maasiai the s of Adiel 1Chr 9:12 1121
the s of Jahzerah 1Chr 9:12 1121
the s of Meshullam 1Chr 9:12 1121
the s of Meshillemith 1Chr 9:12 1121
of Meshillemith, the s of Immer 1Chr 9:12 1121
Shemaiah the s of Hasshub 1Chr 9:14 1121
the s of Azrikam 1Chr 9:14 1121
the s of Hashabiah, of the sons 1Chr 9:14 1121
and Mattaniah the s of Micah 1Chr 9:15 1121
the s of Zichri, the s of Asaph 1Chr 9:15 1121
And Obadiah the s of Shemaiah 1Chr 9:16 1121
the s of Galal 1Chr 9:16 1121
the s of Jeduthun, and Berechiah 1Chr 9:16 1121
and Berechiah the s of Asa 1Chr 9:16 1121
the s of Elkanah, that dwelt in 1Chr 9:16 1121
And Shallum the s of Kore 1Chr 9:19 1121
the s of Ebiasaph 1Chr 9:19 1121
the s of Korah, and his brethren, 1Chr 9:19 1121
Phinehas the s of Eleazar was the 1Chr 9:20 1121
Zechariah the s of Meshelemiah 1Chr 9:21 1121
And his firstborn s Abdon, then 1Chr 9:36 1121
the s of Jonathan was Merib-baal 1Chr 9:40 1121
Rephaiah his s, Eleasah his s 1Chr 9:43 1121
Azel his s 1Chr 9:43 1121
kingdom unto David the s of Jesse 1Chr 10:14 1121
So Joab the s of Zeruiah went 1Chr 11:6 1121
him was Eleazar the s of Dodo 1Chr 11:12 1121
Benaiah the s of Jehoiada 1Chr 11:22 1121
the s of a valiant man of Kabzeel 1Chr 11:22 1121
did Benaiah the s of Jehoiada 1Chr 11:24 1121
of Joab, Elhanan the s of Dodo of 1Chr 11:26 1121
Ira the s of Ikkesh the Tekoite, 1Chr 11:28 1121
Heled the s of Baanah the 1Chr 11:30 1121
Ithai the s of Ribai of Gibeah, 1Chr 11:31 1121
Jonathan the s of Shage the 1Chr 11:34 1121
Ahiam the s of Sacar the Hararite 1Chr 11:35 1121
the Hararite, Eliphal the s of Ur 1Chr 11:35 1121
Carmelite, Naarai the s of Ezbai 1Chr 11:37 1121
Nathan, Mibhar the s of Haggeri 1Chr 11:38 1121
of Joab the s of Zeruiah, 1Chr 11:39 1121
the Hittite, Zabad the s of Ahlai 1Chr 11:41 1121
Adina the s of Shiza the 1Chr 11:42 1121
Hanan the s of Maachah, and 1Chr 11:43 1121
Jediael the s of Shimri, and Joha 1Chr 11:45 1121
because of Saul the s of Kish 1Chr 12:1 1121

and on thy side, thou s of Jesse 1Chr 12:18 1121
appointed Heman the s of Joel 1Chr 15:17 1121
Asaph the s of Berechiah 1Chr 15:17 1121
brethren, Ethan the s of Kushaiah 1Chr 15:17 1121
Obed-edom also the s of Jeduthun 1Chr 16:38 1121
his father, and he shall be my s 1Chr 17:13 1121
sent Hadoram his s to king David 1Chr 18:10 1121
Abishai the s of Zeruiah slew of the 1Chr 18:12 1121
Joab the s of Zeruiah was over 1Chr 18:15 1121
and Jehoshaphat the s of Ahilud 1Chr 18:15 1121
And Zadok the s of Ahitub, and 1Chr 18:16 1121
and Abimelech the s of Abiathar 1Chr 18:16 1121
Benaiah the s of Jehoiada was 1Chr 18:17 1121
his s reigned in his stead 1Chr 19:1 1121
unto Hanun the s of Nahash 1Chr 19:2 1121
Elhanan the s of Jair slew Lahmi 1Chr 20:5 1121
and he also was the s of the giant 1Chr 20:6 3025
Jonathan the s of Shimea David's 1Chr 20:7 1121
David said, Solomon my s is young 1Chr 22:5 1121
Then he called for Solomon his s 1Chr 22:6 1121
And David said to Solomon, My s 1Chr 22:7 1121
a s shall be born to thee, who 1Chr 22:9 1121
and he shall be my s, and I will be 1Chr 22:10 1121
Now, my s, the LORD be with thee 1Chr 22:11 1121
of Israel to help Solomon his s 1Chr 22:17 1121
Solomon his s king over Israel 1Chr 23:1 1121
Shemaiah the s of Nethaneel the 1Chr 24:6 1121
and Ahimelech the s of Abiathar 1Chr 24:6 1121
the s of Kish was Jerahmeel 1Chr 24:29 1121
was Meshelemiah the s of Kore 1Chr 26:1 1121
Shemaiah his s were sons born 1Chr 26:6 1121
Then for Zechariah his s, a wise 1Chr 26:14 1121
And Shebuel the s of Gershom 1Chr 26:24 1121
the s of Moses, was ruler of the 1Chr 26:24 1121
Rehabiah his s 1Chr 26:25 1121
and Jeshaiah his s 1Chr 26:25 1121
and Joram his s, and Zichri his s 1Chr 26:25 1121
and Shelomith his s 1Chr 26:25 1121
the seer, and Saul the s of Kish 1Chr 26:28 1121
of Kish, and Abner the s of Ner 1Chr 26:28 1121
Joab the s of Zeruiah, had 1Chr 26:28 1121
was Jashobeam the s of Zabdiel 1Chr 27:2 1121
was Benaiah the s of Jehoiada 1Chr 27:5 1121
in his course was Ammizabad his s 1Chr 27:6 1121
Joab, and Zebadiah his s after him 1Chr 27:7 1121
Ira the s of Ikkesh the Tekoite 1Chr 27:9 1121
was Eliezer the s of Zichri 1Chr 27:16 1121
Shephatiah the s of Maachah 1Chr 27:16 1121
Hashabiah the s of Kemuel 1Chr 27:17 1121
Issachar, Omri the s of Michael 1Chr 27:18 1121
Ishmaiah the s of Obadiah 1Chr 27:19 1121
Jerimoth the s of Azriel 1Chr 27:19 1121
Ephraim, Hoshea the s of Azaziah 1Chr 27:20 1121
Manasseh, Joel the s of Pedaiah 1Chr 27:20 1121
Gilead, Iddo the s of Zechariah 1Chr 27:21 1121
Benjamin, Jaasiel the s of Abner 1Chr 27:21 1121
Of Dan, Azareel the s of Jeroham 1Chr 27:22 1121
Joab the s of Zeruiah began to 1Chr 27:24 1121
was Azmaveth the s of Adiel 1Chr 27:25 1121
was Jehonathan the s of Uzziah 1Chr 27:25 1121
ground was Ezri the s of Chelub 1Chr 27:26 1121
was Shaphat the s of Adlai 1Chr 27:29 1121
Jehiel the s of Hachmoni was with 1Chr 27:32 1121
was Jehoiada the s of Benaiah 1Chr 27:34 1121
he hath chosen Solomon my s to 1Chr 28:5 1121
And he said unto me, Solomon thy s 1Chr 28:6 1121
for I have chosen him to be my s 1Chr 28:6 1121
And thou, Solomon my s, know thou 1Chr 28:9 1121
his s the pattern of the porch 1Chr 28:11 1121
And David said to Solomon his s 1Chr 28:20 1121
the congregation, Solomon my s 1Chr 29:1 1121
unto Solomon my s a perfect heart 1Chr 29:19 1121
they made Solomon the s of David 1Chr 29:22 1121
Thus David the s of Jesse reigned 1Chr 29:26 1121
Solomon his s reigned in his 1Chr 29:28 1121
Solomon the s of David was 2Chr 1:1 1121
altar, that Bezaleel the s of Uri 2Chr 1:5 1121
the s of Hur, had made, he put 2Chr 1:5 1121
given to David the king a wise s 2Chr 2:12 1121
The s of a woman of the daughters 2Chr 2:14 1121
but thy s which shall come forth 2Chr 6:9 1121
against Jeroboam the s of Nebat 2Chr 9:29 1121
Rehoboam his s reigned in his 2Chr 9:31 1121
when Jeroboam the s of Nebat 2Chr 10:2 1121
to Jeroboam the s of Nebat 2Chr 10:15 1121
inheritance in the s of Jesse 2Chr 10:16 1121
unto Rehoboam the s of Solomon 2Chr 11:3 1121
Rehoboam the s of Solomon strong 2Chr 11:17 1121
Jerimoth the s of David to wife 2Chr 11:18 1121
daughter of Eliab the s of Jesse 2Chr 11:18 1121
Abijah the s of Maachah the chief 2Chr 11:22 1121
Abijah his s reigned in his stead 2Chr 12:16 1121
Yet Jeroboam the s of Nebat 2Chr 13:6 1121
servant of Solomon the s of David 2Chr 13:6 1121
against Rehoboam the s of Solomon 2Chr 13:7 1121
Asa his s reigned in his stead 2Chr 14:1 1121
came upon Azariah the s of Oded 2Chr 15:1 1121
Jehoshaphat his s reigned in his 2Chr 17:1 1121
him was Amasiah the s of Zichri 2Chr 17:16 1121
the same is Micaiah the s of Imla 2Chr 18:7 1121
quickly Micaiah the s of Imla 2Chr 18:8 1121
Zedekiah the s of Chenaanah had 2Chr 18:10 1121
Then Zedekiah the s of Chenaanah 2Chr 18:23 1121
city, and to Joash the king's s 2Chr 18:25 1121
Jehu the s of Hanani the seer 2Chr 19:2 1121
and Zebadiah the s of Ishmael 2Chr 19:11 1121
upon Jahaziel the s of Zechariah 2Chr 20:14 1121
the s of Benaiah 2Chr 20:14 1121
the s of Jeiel 2Chr 20:14 1121
the s of Mattaniah 2Chr 20:14 1121
the book of Jehu the s of Hanani 2Chr 20:34 1121
Then Eliezer the s of Dodavah of 2Chr 20:37 1121
Jehoram his s reigned in his 2Chr 21:1 1121
that there was never a s left him 2Chr 21:17 1121

his youngest s king in his stead 2Chr 22:1 1121
So Ahaziah the s of Jehoram king 2Chr 22:1 1121
went with Jehoram the s of Ahab 2Chr 22:5 1121
Azariah the s of Jehoram king of 2Chr 22:6 1121
Jehoram the s of Ahab at Jezreel 2Chr 22:6 1121
against Jehu the s of Nimshi 2Chr 22:7 1121
he is the s of Jehoshaphat, who 2Chr 22:9 1121
Ahaziah saw that her s was dead 2Chr 22:10 1121
king, took Joash the s of Ahaziah 2Chr 22:11 1121
Azariah the s of Jeroham 2Chr 23:1 1121
Ishmael the s of Jehohanan 2Chr 23:1 1121
and Azariah the s of Obed 2Chr 23:1 1121
Obed, and Maaseiah the s of Adaiah 2Chr 23:1 1121
and Elishaphat the s of Zichri 2Chr 23:1 1121
the king's s shall reign, as the 2Chr 23:3 1121
they brought out the king's s 2Chr 23:11 1121
the s of Jehoiada the priest 2Chr 24:20 1121
had done to him, but slew his s 2Chr 24:22 1121
Zabad the s of Shimeath an 2Chr 24:26 1121
Jehozabad the s of Shimrith a 2Chr 24:26 1121
Amaziah his s reigned in his 2Chr 24:27 1121
the s of Jehoahaz 2Chr 25:17 1121
the s of Jehu, king of Israel, 2Chr 25:17 1121
Give thy daughter to my s to wife 2Chr 25:18 1121
the s of Joash 2Chr 25:23 1121
the s of Jehoahaz 2Chr 25:23 1121
Amaziah the s of Joash king of 2Chr 25:25 1121
s of Jehoahaz king of Israel 2Chr 25:25 1121
Jotham his s was over the king's 2Chr 26:21 1121
the prophet, the s of Amoz, write 2Chr 26:22 1121
Jotham his s reigned in his stead 2Chr 26:23 1121
Ahaz his s reigned in his stead 2Chr 27:9 1121
in the valley of the s of Hinnom 2Chr 28:3 1121
For Pekah the s of Remaliah slew 2Chr 28:6 1121
slew Maaseiah the king's s 2Chr 28:7 1121
Ephraim, Azariah the s of Johanan 2Chr 28:12 1121
Berechiah the s of Meshillemoth, 2Chr 28:12 1121
and Jehizkiah the s of Shallum 2Chr 28:12 1121
Shallum, and Amasa the s of Hadlai 2Chr 28:12 1121
Hezekiah his s reigned in his 2Chr 28:27 1121
arose, Mahath the s of Amasai 2Chr 29:12 1121
Joel the s of Azariah, of the 2Chr 29:12 1121
of Merari, Kish the s of Abdi 2Chr 29:12 1121
Azariah the s of Jehalelel 2Chr 29:12 1121
Joah the s of Zimmah, and Eden the 2Chr 29:12 1121
of Zimmah, and Eden the s of Joah 2Chr 29:12 1121
s of David king of Israel there 2Chr 30:26 1121
Kore the s of Imnah the Levite, 2Chr 31:14 1121
the prophet Isaiah the s of Amoz 2Chr 32:20 1121
the s of Amoz, and in the book of 2Chr 32:32 1121
Manasseh his s reigned in his 2Chr 32:33 1121
in the valley of the s of Hinnom 2Chr 33:6 1121
said to David and to Solomon his s 2Chr 33:7 1121
Amon his s reigned in his stead 2Chr 33:20 1121
Josiah his s king in his stead 2Chr 33:25 1121
he sent Shaphan the s of Azaliah 2Chr 34:8 1121
Joah the s of Joahaz the recorder 2Chr 34:8 1121
and Ahikam the s of Shaphan 2Chr 34:20 1121
Shaphan, and Abdon the s of Micah 2Chr 34:20 1121
wife of Shallum the s of Tikvath 2Chr 34:22 1121
the s of Hasrah, keeper of the 2Chr 34:22 1121
the s of David king of Israel did 2Chr 35:3 1121
to the writing of Solomon his s 2Chr 35:4 1121
took Jehoahaz the s of Josiah 2Chr 36:1 1121
Jehoiachin his s reigned in his 2Chr 36:8 1121
stood up Jeshua the s of Jozadak Ezr 3:2 1121
and Zerubbabel the s of Shealtiel Ezr 3:2 1121
Zerubbabel the s of Shealtiel Ezr 3:8 1121
and Jeshua the s of Jozadak Ezr 3:8 1121
and Zechariah the s of Iddo Ezr 5:1 1247
up Zerubbabel the s of Shealtiel Ezr 5:2 1247
and Jeshua the s of Jozadak Ezr 5:2 1247
and Zechariah the s of Iddo Ezr 6:14 1247
Ezra the s of Seraiah Ezr 7:1 1121
s of Azariah, the s of Hilkiah, Ezr 7:1 1121
The s of Shallum Ezr 7:2 1121
the s of Zadok, the s of Ahitub Ezr 7:2 1121
The s of Amariah Ezr 7:3 1121
the s of Azariah Ezr 7:3 1121
the s of Meraioth Ezr 7:3 1121
The s of Zerahiah Ezr 7:4 1121
the s of Uzzi, the s of Bukki, Ezr 7:4 1121
The s of Abishua Ezr 7:5 1121
the s of Phinehas Ezr 7:5 1121
the s of Eleazar Ezr 7:5 1121
the s of Aaron the chief priest Ezr 7:5 1121
Elihoenai the s of Zerahiah Ezr 8:4 1121
the s of Jahaziel, and with him Ezr 8:5 1121
Ebed the s of Jonathan, and with Ezr 8:6 1121
Jeshaiah the s of Athaliah Ezr 8:7 1121
Zebadiah the s of Michael Ezr 8:8 1121
Obadiah the s of Jehiel, and with Ezr 8:9 1121
the s of Josiphiah, and with him Ezr 8:10 1121
Zechariah the s of Bebai, and with Ezr 8:11 1121
Johanan the s of Hakkatan Ezr 8:12 1121
the s of Levi, the s of Israel Ezr 8:18 1121
the s of Uriah the priest Ezr 8:33 1121
him was Eleazar the s of Phinehas Ezr 8:33 1121
them was Jozabad the s of Jeshua Ezr 8:33 1121
and Noadiah the s of Binnui Ezr 8:33 1121
And Shechaniah the s of Jehiel Ezr 10:2 1121
of Johanan the s of Eliashib Ezr 10:6 1121
Only Jonathan the s of Asahel Ezr 10:15 1121
Jahaziah the s of Tikvah were Ezr 10:15 1121
sons of Jeshua the s of Jozadak Ezr 10:18 1121
of Nehemiah the s of Hachaliah Neh 1:1 1121
them builded Zaccur the s of Imri Neh 3:2 1121
the s of Urijah, the s of Koz Neh 3:4 1121
Meshullam the s of Berechiah Neh 3:4 1121
Berechiah, the s of Meshezabeel Neh 3:4 1121
repaired Zadok the s of Baana Neh 3:4 1121
repaired Jehoiada the s of Paseah Neh 3:6 1121
and Meshullam the s of Besodeiah Neh 3:6 1121
repaired Uzziel the s of Harhaiah Neh 3:8 1121

the *s* of one of the apothecaries	Neh 3:8	1121
repaired Rephaiah the *s* of Hur	Neh 3:9	1121
Jedaiah the *s* of Harumaph	Neh 3:10	1121
Hattush the *s* of Hashabniah	Neh 3:10	1121
Malchijah the *s* of Harim, and	Neh 3:11	1121
Hashub the *s* of Pahath-moab,	Neh 3:11	1121
Shallum the *s* of Halohesh	Neh 3:12	1121
repaired Malchiah the *s* of Rechab	Neh 3:14	1121
Shallun the *s* of Colhozeh	Neh 3:15	1121
repaired Nehemiah the *s* of Azbuk	Neh 3:16	1121
the Levites, Rehum the *s* of Bani	Neh 3:17	1121
Bavai the *s* of Henadad, the ruler	Neh 3:18	1121
him repaired Ezer the *s* of Jeshua	Neh 3:19	1121
After him Baruch the *s* of Zabbai	Neh 3:20	1121
the *s* of Urijah the *s* of Koz	Neh 3:21	1121
s of Maaseiah the *s* of Ananiah	Neh 3:23	1121
the *s* of Henadad another piece	Neh 3:24	1121
Palal the *s* of Uzai, over against	Neh 3:25	1121
After him Pedaiah the *s* of Parosh	Neh 3:25	1121
After them repaired Zadok the *s*	Neh 3:29	1121
also Shemaiah the *s* of Shechaniah	Neh 3:29	1121
Hananiah the *s* of Shelemiah	Neh 3:30	1121
and Hanun the sixth *s* of Zalaph	Neh 3:30	1121
him repaired Meshullam the *s* of	Neh 3:30	1121
Malchiah the goldsmith's *s* unto	Neh 3:31	1121
the *s* of Delaiah	Neh 6:10	1121
of Delaiah the *s* of Mehetabeel	Neh 6:10	1121
because he was the *s* in law of	Neh 6:18	2860
law of Shechaniah the *s* of Arah	Neh 6:18	1121
his *s* Johanan had taken the	Neh 6:18	1121
of Meshullam the *s* of Berechiah	Neh 6:18	1121
s of Nun unto that day had not	Neh 8:17	1121
the *s* of Hachaliah, and Zidkijah,	Neh 10:1	1121
both Jeshua the *s* of Azaniah	Neh 10:9	1121
the priest the *s* of Aaron shall	Neh 10:38	1121
Athaiah the *s* of Uzziah	Neh 11:4	1121
the *s* of Zechariah	Neh 11:4	1121
the *s* of Amariah	Neh 11:4	1121
the *s* of Shephatiah	Neh 11:4	1121
the *s* of Mahalaleel, of the	Neh 11:4	1121
And Maaseiah the *s* of Baruch	Neh 11:5	1121
the *s* of Colhozeh	Neh 11:5	1121
the *s* of Hazaiah	Neh 11:5	1121
the *s* of Adaiah	Neh 11:5	1121
the *s* of Joiarib	Neh 11:5	1121
the *s* of Zechariah	Neh 11:5	1121
of Zechariah, the *s* of Shiloni	Neh 11:5	1121
Sallu the *s* of Meshullam	Neh 11:7	1121
the *s* of Joed, the *s* of Pedaiah	Neh 11:7	1121
the *s* of Pedaiah, the *s* of	Neh 11:7	1121
the *s* of Kolaiah	Neh 11:7	1121
the *s* of Maaseiah	Neh 11:7	1121
the *s* of Ithiel, the *s* of	Neh 11:7	1121
s of Ithiel, the *s* of Jesaiah	Neh 11:7	1121
Joel the *s* of Zichri was their	Neh 11:9	1121
Judah the *s* of Senuah was second	Neh 11:9	1121
Jedaiah the *s* of Joiarib, Jachin	Neh 11:10	1121
Seraiah the *s* of Hilkiah	Neh 11:11	1121
the *s* of Meshullam	Neh 11:11	1121
the *s* of Zadok	Neh 11:11	1121
the *s* of Meraioth	Neh 11:11	1121
the *s* of Ahitub, was the ruler of	Neh 11:11	1121
and Adaiah the *s* of Jeroham	Neh 11:12	1121
the *s* of Pelaliah	Neh 11:12	1121
the *s* of Amzi	Neh 11:12	1121
the *s* of Zechariah	Neh 11:12	1121
s of Pashur, the *s* of Malchiah,	Neh 11:12	1121
and Amashai the *s* of Azareel	Neh 11:13	1121
the *s* of Ahasai	Neh 11:13	1121
the *s* of Meshillemoth	Neh 11:13	1121
the *s* of Immer	Neh 11:13	1121
the *s* of one of the great men	Neh 11:14	1121
Shemaiah the *s* of Hashub	Neh 11:15	1121
the *s* of Azrikam	Neh 11:15	1121
the *s* of Hashabiah	Neh 11:15	1121
the *s* of Bunni	Neh 11:15	1121
And Mattaniah the *s* of Micha	Neh 11:17	1121
the *s* of Zabdi, the *s* of Asaph,	Neh 11:17	1121
Abda the *s* of Shammua	Neh 11:17	1121
the *s* of Galal, the *s* of	Neh 11:17	1121
s of Galal, the *s* of Jeduthun	Neh 11:17	1121
Jerusalem was Uzzi the *s* of Bani	Neh 11:22	1121
the *s* of Hashabiah	Neh 11:22	1121
s of Mattaniah, the *s* of Micha	Neh 11:22	1121
Pethahiah the *s* of Meshezabeel,	Neh 11:24	1121
children of Zerah the *s* of Judah	Neh 11:24	1121
Zerubbabel the *s* of Shealtiel	Neh 12:1	1121
days of Johanan the *s* of Eliashib	Neh 12:23	1121
and Jeshua the *s* of Kadmiel	Neh 12:24	1121
days of Joiakim the *s* of Jeshua	Neh 12:26	1121
the *s* of Jozadak, and in the days	Neh 12:26	1121
Zechariah the *s* of Jonathan	Neh 12:35	1121
the *s* of Shemaiah	Neh 12:35	1121
the *s* of Mattaniah	Neh 12:35	1121
the *s* of Michaiah	Neh 12:35	1121
the *s* of Zaccur, the *s* of Asaph	Neh 12:35	1121
of David, and of Solomon his *s*	Neh 12:45	1121
s of Zaccur, the *s* of Mattaniah	Neh 13:13	1121
the *s* of Eliashib the high priest	Neh 13:28	1121
was *s* in law to Sanballat the	Neh 13:28	2860
the *s* of Jair, the *s* of Shimei,	Est 2:5	1121
the *s* of Kish, a Benjamite	Est 2:5	1121
the *s* of Hammedatha the Agagite	Est 3:1	1121
gave it unto Haman the *s* of	Est 3:10	1121
the *s* of Hammedatha the Agagite	Est 8:5	1121
sons of Haman the *s* of Hammedatha	Est 9:10	1121
Because Haman the *s* of Hammedatha	Est 9:24	1121
He shall neither have *s* nor	Job 18:19	5209
the *s* of man, which is a worm	Job 25:6	1121
the *s* of Barachel the Buzite	Job 32:2	1121
Elihu the *s* of Barachel the	Job 32:6	1121
may profit the *s* of man	Job 35:8	1121
hath said unto me, Thou art my *S*	Ps 2:7	1121
Kiss the *S*, lest he be angry, and	Ps 2:12	1248
when he fled from Absalom his *s*	Ps 3:*t*	1121
the *s* of man, that thou visitest	Ps 8:4	1121
slanderest thine own mother's *s*	Ps 50:20	1121
righteousness unto the king's *s*	Ps 72:1	1121
of David the *s* of Jesse are ended	Ps 72:20	1121
upon the *s* of man whom thou	Ps 80:17	1121
save the *s* of thine handmaid	Ps 86:16	1121
nor the *s* of wickedness afflict	Ps 89:22	1121
and the *s* of thine handmaid	Ps 116:16	1121
or the *s* of man, that thou makest	Ps 144:3	1121
in princes, nor in the *s* of man	Ps 146:3	1121
of Solomon the *s* of David	Prov 1:1	1121
My *s*, hear the instruction of thy	Prov 1:8	1121
My *s*, if sinners entice thee,	Prov 1:10	1121
My *s*, walk not thou in the way	Prov 1:15	1121
My *s*, if thou wilt receive my	Prov 2:1	1121
My *s*, forget not my law	Prov 3:1	1121
My *s*, despise not the chastening	Prov 3:11	1121
even as a father the *s* in whom he	Prov 3:12	1121
My *s*, let not them depart from	Prov 3:21	1121
For I was my father's *s*, tender	Prov 4:3	1121
Hear, O my *s*, and receive my	Prov 4:10	1121
My *s*, attend to my words	Prov 4:20	1121
My *s*, attend unto my wisdom, and	Prov 5:1	1121
And why wilt thou, my *s*, be	Prov 5:20	1121
My *s*, if thou be surety for thy	Prov 6:1	1121
Do this now, my *s*, and deliver	Prov 6:3	1121
My *s*, keep thy father's	Prov 6:20	1121
My *s*, keep my words, and lay up my	Prov 7:1	1121
A wise *s* maketh a glad father	Prov 10:1	1121
but a foolish *s* is the heaviness	Prov 10:1	1121
gathereth in summer is a wise *s*	Prov 10:5	1121
harvest is a *s* that causeth shame	Prov 10:5	1121
A wise *s* heareth his father's	Prov 13:1	1121
that spareth his rod hateth his *s*	Prov 13:24	1121
A wise *s* maketh a glad father	Prov 15:20	1121
rule over a *s* that causeth shame	Prov 17:2	1121
A foolish *s* is a grief to his	Prov 17:25	1121
A foolish *s* is the calamity of	Prov 19:13	1121
Chasten thy *s* while there is hope	Prov 19:18	1121
is a *s* that causeth shame, and	Prov 19:26	1121
Cease, my *s*, to hear the	Prov 19:27	1121
My *s*, if thine heart be wise, my	Prov 23:15	1121
Hear thou, my *s*, and be wise, and	Prov 23:19	1121
My *s*, give me thine heart, and let	Prov 23:26	1121
My *s*, eat thou honey, because it	Prov 24:13	1121
My *s*, fear thou the LORD and the	Prov 24:21	1121
My *s*, be wise, and make my heart	Prov 27:11	1121
Whoso keepeth the law is a wise *s*	Prov 28:7	1121
Correct thy *s*, and he shall give	Prov 29:17	1121
him become his *s* at the length	Prov 29:21	4497
The words of Agur the *s* of Jakeh	Prov 30:1	1121
What, my *s*	Prov 31:2	1248
and what, the *s* of my womb	Prov 31:2	1248
and what, the *s* of my vows	Prov 31:2	1248
the *s* of David, king in Jerusalem	Eccl 1:1	1121
and he begetteth a *s*, and there is	Eccl 5:14	1121
when thy king is the *s* of nobles	Eccl 10:17	1121
And further, by these, my *s*	Eccl 12:12	1121
vision of Isaiah the *s* of Amoz	Is 1:1	1121
The word that Isaiah the *s* of	Is 2:1	1121
the days of Ahaz the *s* of Jotham	Is 7:1	1121
the *s* of Uzziah, king of Judah,	Is 7:1	1121
Pekah the *s* of Remaliah, king of	Is 7:1	1121
Ahaz, thou, and Shear-jashub thy *s*	Is 7:3	1121
Syria, and of the *s* of Remaliah	Is 7:4	1121
the *s* of Remaliah, have taken	Is 7:5	1121
midst of it, even the *s* of Tabeal	Is 7:6	1121
head of Samaria is Remaliah's *s*	Is 7:9	1121
shall conceive, and bear a *s*	Is 7:14	1121
Zechariah the *s* of Jeberechiah	Is 8:2	1121
and she conceived, and bare a *s*	Is 8:3	1121
rejoice in Rezin and Remaliah's *s*	Is 8:6	1121
is born, unto us a *s* is given	Is 9:6	1121
Isaiah the *s* of Amoz did see	Is 13:1	1121
O Lucifer, *s* of the morning	Is 14:12	1121
the name, and remnant, and *s*	Is 14:22	5209
I am the *s* of the wise	Is 19:11	1121
the wise, the *s* of ancient kings	Is 19:11	1121
the LORD by Isaiah the *s* of Amoz	Is 20:2	1121
servant Eliakim the *s* of Hilkiah	Is 22:20	1121
unto him Eliakim, Hilkiah's *s*	Is 36:3	1121
the scribe, and Joah, Asaph's *s*	Is 36:3	1121
the *s* of Hilkiah, that was over	Is 36:22	1121
the *s* of Asaph, the recorder, to	Is 36:22	1121
Isaiah the prophet the *s* of Amoz	Is 37:2	1121
Then Isaiah the *s* of Amoz sent	Is 37:21	1121
Esar-haddon his *s* reigned in his	Is 37:38	1121
the *s* of Amoz came unto him	Is 38:1	1121
the *s* of Baladan, king of Babylon	Is 39:1	1121
compassion on the *s* of her womb	Is 49:15	1121
of the *s* of man which shall be	Is 51:12	1121
the *s* of man that layeth hold on	Is 56:2	1121
Neither let the *s* of the stranger	Is 56:3	1121
of Jeremiah the *s* of Hilkiah	Jer 1:1	1121
the *s* of Amon king of Judah	Jer 1:2	1121
the *s* of Josiah king of Judah	Jer 1:3	1121
the *s* of Josiah king of Judah	Jer 1:3	1121
thee mourning, as for an only *s*	Jer 6:26	3173
in the valley of the *s* of Hinnom	Jer 7:31	1121
nor the valley of the *s* of Hinnom	Jer 7:32	1121
because of Manasseh the *s* of	Jer 15:4	1121
the valley of the *s* of Hinnom	Jer 19:2	1121
nor The valley of the *s* of Hinnom	Jer 19:6	1121
Now Pashur the *s* of Immer the	Jer 20:1	1121
unto him Pashur the *s* of Melchiah	Jer 21:1	1121
Zephaniah the *s* of Maaseiah the	Jer 21:1	1121
the *s* of Josiah king of Judah	Jer 22:11	1121
the *s* of Josiah king of Judah	Jer 22:18	1121
though Coniah the *s* of Jehoiakim	Jer 22:24	1121
away captive Jeconiah the *s* of	Jer 24:1	1121
the *s* of Josiah king of Judah	Jer 25:1	1121
the *s* of Amon king of Judah	Jer 25:3	1121
s of Josiah king of Judah came	Jer 26:1	1121
Urijah the *s* of Shemaiah of	Jer 26:20	1121
namely, Elnathan the *s* of Achbor	Jer 26:22	1121
the hand of Ahikam the *s* of	Jer 26:24	1121
s of Josiah king of Judah came	Jer 27:1	1121
him, and his *s*, and his son's *s*	Jer 27:7	1121
away captive Jeconiah the *s* of	Jer 27:20	1121
that Hananiah the *s* of Azur the	Jer 28:1	1121
the *s* of Jehoiakim king of Judah	Jer 28:4	1121
hand of Elasah the *s* of Shaphan	Jer 29:3	1121
and Gemariah the *s* of Hilkiah	Jer 29:3	1121
Israel, of Ahab the *s* of Kolaiah	Jer 29:21	1121
and of Zedekiah the *s* of Maaseiah	Jer 29:21	1121
to Zephaniah the *s* of Maaseiah	Jer 29:25	1121
Is Ephraim my dear *s*	Jer 31:20	1121
Hanameel the *s* of Shallum thine	Jer 32:7	1121
So Hanameel mine uncle's *s* came	Jer 32:8	1121
field of Hanameel my uncle's *s*	Jer 32:9	1121
unto Baruch the *s* of Neriah	Jer 32:12	1121
the *s* of Maaseiah, in the sight	Jer 32:12	1121
sight of Hanameel mine uncle's *s*	Jer 32:12	
unto Baruch the *s* of Neriah	Jer 32:16	1121
in the valley of the *s* of Hinnom	Jer 32:35	1121
have a *s* to reign upon his throne	Jer 33:21	1121
the *s* of Josiah king of Judah	Jer 35:1	1121
took Jaazaniah the *s* of Jeremiah	Jer 35:3	1121
the *s* of Habaziniah, and his	Jer 35:3	1121
the *s* of Igdaliah, a man of God,	Jer 35:4	1121
of Maaseiah the *s* of Shallum	Jer 35:4	1121
for Jonadab the *s* of Rechab our	Jer 35:6	1121
the *s* of Rechab our father in all	Jer 35:8	1121
words of Jonadab the *s* of Rechab	Jer 35:14	1121
s of Rechab have performed the	Jer 35:16	1121
Jonadab the *s* of Rechab shall not	Jer 35:19	1121
the *s* of Josiah king of Judah	Jer 36:1	1121
called Baruch the *s* of Neriah	Jer 36:4	1121
Baruch the *s* of Neriah did	Jer 36:8	1121
the *s* of Josiah king of Judah	Jer 36:9	1121
the *s* of Shaphan the scribe	Jer 36:10	1121
When Michaiah the *s* of Gemariah	Jer 36:11	1121
the *s* of Shaphan, had heard out	Jer 36:11	1121
and Delaiah the *s* of Shemaiah	Jer 36:12	1121
and Elnathan the *s* of Achbor	Jer 36:12	1121
and Gemariah the *s* of Shaphan	Jer 36:12	1121
and Zedekiah the *s* of Hananiah	Jer 36:12	1121
sent Jehudi the *s* of Nethaniah	Jer 36:14	1121
the *s* of Shelemiah	Jer 36:14	1121
the *s* of Cushi, unto Baruch,	Jer 36:14	1121
So Baruch the *s* of Neriah took	Jer 36:14	1121
Jerahmeel the *s* of Hammelech	Jer 36:26	1121
and Seraiah the *s* of Azriel	Jer 36:26	1121
and Shelemiah the *s* of Abdeel	Jer 36:26	1121
the scribe, the *s* of Neriah	Jer 36:32	1121
king Zedekiah the *s* of Josiah	Jer 37:1	1121
of Coniah the *s* of Jehoiakim	Jer 37:1	1121
sent Jehucal the *s* of Shelemiah	Jer 37:3	1121
Zephaniah the *s* of Maaseiah the	Jer 37:3	1121
the *s* of Shelemiah	Jer 37:13	1121
the *s* of Hananiah	Jer 37:13	1121
Then Shephatiah the *s* of Mattan	Jer 38:1	1121
and Gedaliah the *s* of Pashur	Jer 38:1	1121
Jucal the *s* of Shelemiah, and	Jer 38:1	1121
Pashur the *s* of Malchiah, heard	Jer 38:1	1121
of Malchiah the *s* of Hammelech	Jer 38:6	1121
s of Ahikam the *s* of Shaphan	Jer 39:14	1121
s of Ahikam the *s* of Shaphan	Jer 40:5	1121
the *s* of Ahikam to Mizpah	Jer 40:6	1121
Babylon had made Gedaliah the *s*	Jer 40:7	1121
even Ishmael the *s* of Nethaniah	Jer 40:8	1121
Seraiah the *s* of Tanhumeth, and	Jer 40:8	1121
Jezaniah the *s* of a Maachathite,	Jer 40:8	1121
Gedaliah the *s* of Ahikam	Jer 40:9	1121
the *s* of Shaphan sware unto them	Jer 40:9	1121
s of Ahikam the *s* of Shaphan	Jer 40:11	1121
Moreover Johanan the *s* of Kareah	Jer 40:13	1121
the *s* of Nethaniah to slay thee	Jer 40:14	1121
But Gedaliah the *s* of Ahikam	Jer 40:14	1121
Then Johanan the *s* of Kareah	Jer 40:15	1121
slay Ishmael the *s* of Nethaniah	Jer 40:15	1121
But Gedaliah the *s* of Ahikam said	Jer 40:16	1121
said unto Johanan the *s* of Kareah	Jer 40:16	1121
that Ishmael the *s* of Nethaniah	Jer 41:1	1121
of Nethaniah the *s* of Elishama	Jer 41:1	1121
the *s* of Ahikam to Mizpah	Jer 41:1	1121
arose Ishmael the *s* of Nethaniah	Jer 41:2	1121
smote Gedaliah the *s* of Ahikam	Jer 41:2	1121
the *s* of Shaphan with the sword	Jer 41:2	1121
Ishmael the *s* of Nethaniah went	Jer 41:6	1121
Come to Gedaliah the *s* of Ahikam	Jer 41:6	1121
that Ishmael the *s* of Nethaniah	Jer 41:7	1121
Ishmael the *s* of Nethaniah filled	Jer 41:9	1121
to Gedaliah the *s* of Ahikam	Jer 41:10	1121
Ishmael the *s* of Nethaniah	Jer 41:10	1121
But when Johanan the *s* of Kareah	Jer 41:11	1121
the *s* of Nethaniah had done	Jer 41:11	1121
with Ishmael the *s* of Nethaniah	Jer 41:12	1121
saw Johanan the *s* of Kareah	Jer 41:13	1121
went unto Johanan the *s* of Kareah	Jer 41:14	1121
But Ishmael the *s* of Nethaniah	Jer 41:15	1121
Then took Johanan the *s* of Kareah	Jer 41:16	1121
from Ishmael the *s* of Nethaniah	Jer 41:16	1121
slain Gedaliah the *s* of Ahikam	Jer 41:16	1121
of them, because Ishmael the *s* of	Jer 41:18	1121
slain Gedaliah the *s* of Ahikam	Jer 41:18	1121
and Johanan the *s* of Kareah	Jer 42:1	1121
and Jezaniah the *s* of Hoshaiah	Jer 42:1	1121
called he Johanan the *s* of Kareah	Jer 42:8	1121
spake Azariah the *s* of Hoshaiah	Jer 43:2	1121
and Johanan the *s* of Kareah	Jer 43:2	1121
But Baruch the *s* of Neriah	Jer 43:3	1121
So Johanan the *s* of Kareah	Jer 43:4	1121
But Johanan the *s* of Kareah	Jer 43:5	1121
s of Ahikam the *s* of Shaphan	Jer 43:6	1121
and Baruch the *s* of Neriah	Jer 43:6	1121
spake unto Baruch the *s* of Neriah	Jer 45:1	1121

the *s* of Josiah king of Judah	Jer 45:1	1121
the *s* of Josiah king of Judah	Jer 46:2	1121
neither shall a *s* of man dwell in	Jer 49:18	1121
nor any *s* of man dwell in it	Jer 49:33	1121
neither shall any *s* of man dwell	Jer 50:40	1121
neither doth any *s* of man pass	Jer 51:43	1121
commanded Seraiah the *s* of Neriah	Jer 51:59	1121
the *s* of Maaseiah, when he went	Jer 51:59	1121
the *s* of Buzi, in the land of the	Eze 1:3	1121
S of man, stand upon thy feet, and	Eze 2:1	1121
S of man, I send thee to the	Eze 2:3	1121
s of man, be not afraid of them,	Eze 2:6	1121
s of man, hear what I say unto	Eze 2:8	1121
S of man, eat that thou findest	Eze 3:1	1121
S of man, cause thy belly to eat,	Eze 3:3	1121
S of man, go, get thee unto the	Eze 3:4	1121
S of man, all my words that I	Eze 3:10	1121
S of man, I have made thee a	Eze 3:17	1121
O *s* of man, behold, they shall	Eze 3:25	1121
s of man, take thee a tile, and	Eze 4:1	1121
S of man, behold, I will break	Eze 4:16	1121
s of man, take thee a sharp knife	Eze 5:1	1121
S of man, set thy face toward the	Eze 6:2	1121
thou *s* of man, thus saith the	Eze 7:2	1121
S of man, lift up thine eyes now	Eze 8:5	1121
S of man, seest thou what they do	Eze 8:6	1121
S of man, dig now in the wall	Eze 8:8	1121
stood Jaazaniah the *s* of Shaphan	Eze 8:11	1121
S of man, hast thou seen what the	Eze 8:12	1121
Hast thou seen this, O *s* of man	Eze 8:15	1121
Hast thou seen this, O *s* of man	Eze 8:17	1121
I saw Jaazaniah the *s* of Azur	Eze 11:1	1121
and Pelatiah the *s* of Benaiah	Eze 11:1	1121
S of man, these are the men that	Eze 11:2	1121
them, prophesy, O *s* of man	Eze 11:4	1121
Pelatiah the *s* of Benaiah died	Eze 11:13	1121
S of man, thy brethren, even thy	Eze 11:15	1121
S of man, thou dwellest in the	Eze 12:2	1121
thou *s* of man, prepare thee stuff	Eze 12:3	1121
S of man, hath not the house of	Eze 12:9	1121
S of man, eat thy bread with	Eze 12:18	1121
S of man, what is that proverb	Eze 12:22	1121
S of man, behold, they of the	Eze 12:27	1121
S of man, prophesy against the	Eze 13:2	1121
thou *s* of man, set thy face	Eze 13:17	1121
S of man, these men have set up	Eze 14:3	1121
S of man, when the land sinneth	Eze 14:13	1121
deliver neither *s* nor daughter	Eze 14:20	1121
S of man, What is the vine tree	Eze 15:2	1121
S of man, cause Jerusalem to know	Eze 16:2	1121
S of man, put forth a riddle, and	Eze 17:2	1121
so also the soul of the *s* is mine	Eze 18:4	1121
If he beget a *s* that is a robber,	Eze 18:10	1121
Now, lo, if he beget a *s*, that	Eze 18:14	1121
doth not the *s* bear the iniquity	Eze 18:19	1121
When the *s* hath done that which	Eze 18:19	1121
The *s* shall not bear the iniquity	Eze 18:20	1121
father bear the iniquity of the *s*	Eze 18:20	1121
S of man, speak unto the elders	Eze 20:3	1121
s of man, wilt thou judge them	Eze 20:4	1121
s of man, speak unto the house of	Eze 20:27	1121
S of man, set thy face toward the	Eze 20:46	1121
S of man, set thy face toward	Eze 21:2	1121
thou *s* of man, with the breaking	Eze 21:6	1121
S of man, prophesy, and say, Thus	Eze 21:9	1121
it contemneth the rod of my *s*	Eze 21:10	1121
Cry and howl, *s* of man	Eze 21:12	1121
s of man, prophesy, and smite	Eze 21:14	1121
thou *s* of man, appoint thee two	Eze 21:19	1121
s of man, prophesy and say, Thus	Eze 21:28	1121
thou *s* of man, wilt thou judge,	Eze 22:2	1121
S of man, the house of Israel is	Eze 22:18	1121
S of man, say unto her, Thou art	Eze 22:24	1121
S of man, there were two women,	Eze 23:2	1121
S of man, wilt thou judge Aholah	Eze 23:36	1121
S of man, write thee the name of	Eze 24:2	1121
S of man, behold, I take away	Eze 24:16	1121
thou *s* of man, shall it not be in	Eze 24:25	1121
S of man, set thy face against	Eze 25:2	1121
S of man, because that Tyrus hath	Eze 26:2	1121
Now, thou *s* of man, take up a	Eze 27:2	1121
S of man, say unto the prince of	Eze 28:2	1121
S of man, take up a lamentation	Eze 28:12	1121
S of man, set thy face against	Eze 28:21	1121
S of man, set thy face against	Eze 29:2	1121
S of man, Nebuchadrezzar king of	Eze 29:18	1121
S of man, prophesy and say, Thus	Eze 30:2	1121
S of man, I have broken the arm	Eze 30:21	1121
S of man, speak unto Pharaoh king	Eze 31:2	1121
S of man, take up a lamentation	Eze 32:2	1121
S of man, wail for the multitude	Eze 32:18	1121
S of man, speak to the children	Eze 33:2	1121
O *s* of man, I have set thee a	Eze 33:7	1121
Therefore, O thou *s* of man	Eze 33:10	1121
thou *s* of man, say unto the	Eze 33:12	1121
S of man, they that inhabit those	Eze 33:24	1121
thou *s* of man, the children of	Eze 33:30	1121
S of man, prophesy against the	Eze 34:2	1121
S of man, set thy face against	Eze 35:2	1121
thou *s* of man, prophesy unto the	Eze 36:1	1121
S of man, when the house of	Eze 36:17	1121
S of man, can these bones live	Eze 37:3	1121
s of man, and say to the wind,	Eze 37:9	1121
S of man, these bones are the	Eze 37:11	1121
thou *s* of man, take thee one	Eze 37:16	1121
S of man, set thy face against	Eze 38:2	1121
s of man, prophesy and say unto	Eze 38:14	1121
thou *s* of man, prophesy against	Eze 39:1	1121
thou *s* of man, thus saith the	Eze 39:17	1121
S of man, behold with thine eyes,	Eze 40:4	1121
S of man, the place of my throne,	Eze 43:7	1121
Thou *s* of man, shew the house to	Eze 43:10	1121
S of man, thus saith the Lord GOD	Eze 43:18	1121
S of man, mark well, and behold	Eze 44:5	1121
father, or for mother, or for *s*	Eze 44:25	1121
S of man, hast thou seen this	Eze 47:6	1121
the fourth is like the *S* of God	Dan 3:25	1247
And thou his *s*, O Belshazzar, hast	Dan 5:22	1247
one like the *S* of man came with	Dan 7:13	1247
unto me, Understand, O *s* of man	Dan 8:17	1121
year of Darius the *s* of Ahasuerus	Dan 9:1	1121
the *s* of Beeri, in the days of	Hos 1:1	1121
days of Jeroboam the *s* of Joash	Hos 1:1	1121
which conceived, and bare him a *s*	Hos 1:3	1121
she conceived, and bare a *s*	Hos 1:8	1121
him, and called my *s* out of Egypt	Hos 11:1	1121
he is an unwise *s*	Hos 13:13	1121
came to Joel the *s* of Pethuel	Joel 1:1	1121
the *s* of Joash king of Israel	Amos 1:1	1121
neither was I an prophet's *s*	Amos 7:14	1121
it as the mourning of an only *s*	Amos 8:10	
came unto Jonah the *s* of Amittai	Jonah 1:1	1121
what Balaam the *s* of Beor	Mic 6:5	1121
For the *s* dishonoureth the father	Mic 7:6	1121
unto Zephaniah the *s* of Cushi	Zeph 1:1	1121
the *s* of Gedaliah	Zeph 1:1	1121
the *s* of Amariah	Zeph 1:1	1121
the *s* of Hizkiah	Zeph 1:1	1121
the days of Josiah the *s* of Amon	Zeph 1:1	1121
Zerubbabel the *s* of Shealtiel	Hag 1:1	1121
and to Joshua the *s* of Josedech	Hag 1:1	1121
Zerubbabel the *s* of Shealtiel	Hag 1:12	1121
Joshua the *s* of Josedech, the	Hag 1:12	1121
of Zerubbabel the *s* of Shealtiel	Hag 1:14	1121
of Joshua the *s* of Josedech	Hag 1:14	1121
to Zerubbabel the *s* of Shealtiel	Hag 2:2	1121
and to Joshua the *s* of Josedech	Hag 2:2	1121
s of Josedech, the high priest	Hag 2:4	1121
the *s* of Shealtiel, saith the	Hag 2:23	1121
the *s* of Berechiah	Zec 1:1	1121
the *s* of Iddo the prophet, saying	Zec 1:1	1121
the *s* of Berechiah	Zec 1:7	1121
the *s* of Iddo the prophet, saying	Zec 1:7	1121
of Josiah the *s* of Zephaniah	Zec 6:10	1121
head of Joshua the *s* of Josedech	Zec 6:11	1121
to Hen the *s* of Zephaniah, for a	Zec 6:14	1121
as one mourneth for his only *s*	Zec 12:10	
A *s* honoureth his father, and a	Mal 1:6	1121
his own *s* that serveth him	Mal 3:17	1121
s of David, the *s* of Abraham	Mt 1:1	5207
thou *s* of David, fear not to take	Mt 1:20	5207
And she shall bring forth a *s*	Mt 1:21	5207
child, and shall bring forth a *s*	Mt 1:23	5207
had brought forth her firstborn *s*	Mt 1:25	5207
Out of Egypt have I called my *s*	Mt 2:15	5207
saying, This is my beloved *S*	Mt 3:17	5207
he said, If thou be the *S* of God	Mt 4:3	5207
unto him, If thou be the *S* of God	Mt 4:6	5207
James the *s* of Zebedee, and John	Mt 4:21	
of you, whom if his *s* ask bread	Mt 7:9	5207
but the *S* of man hath not where	Mt 8:20	5207
with thee, Jesus, thou *S* of God	Mt 8:29	5207
S, be of good cheer	Mt 9:2	5048
S of man hath power on earth to	Mt 9:6	5207
Thou *s* of David, have mercy on us	Mt 9:27	5207
James the *s* of Zebedee, and John	Mt 10:2	
James the *s* of Alphaeus, and	Mt 10:3	
till the *S* of man be come	Mt 10:23	5207
he that loveth *s* or daughter more	Mt 10:37	5207
The *S* of man came eating and	Mt 11:19	5207
and no man knoweth the *S*, but the	Mt 11:27	5207
any man the Father, save the *S*	Mt 11:27	5207
whomsoever the *S* will reveal him	Mt 11:27	5207
For the *S* of man is Lord even of	Mt 12:8	5207
said, Is not this the *s* of David	Mt 12:23	5207
a word against the *S* of man	Mt 12:32	5207
so shall the *S* of man be three	Mt 12:40	5207
the good seed is the *S* of man	Mt 13:37	5207
The *S* of man shall send forth his	Mt 13:41	5207
Is not this the carpenter's *s*	Mt 13:55	5207
Of a truth thou art the *S* of God	Mt 14:33	5207
on me, O Lord, thou *s* of David	Mt 15:22	5207
do men say that I the *S* of man am	Mt 16:13	5207
Christ, the *S* of the living God	Mt 16:16	5207
For the *S* of man shall come in	Mt 16:27	5207
till they see the *S* of man coming	Mt 16:28	5207
which said, This is my beloved *S*	Mt 17:5	5207
until the *S* of man be risen again	Mt 17:9	5207
also the *S* of man suffer of them	Mt 17:12	5207
Lord, have mercy on my *s*	Mt 17:15	5207
The *S* of man shall be betrayed	Mt 17:22	5207
For the *S* of man is come to save	Mt 18:11	5207
in the regeneration when the *S* of	Mt 19:28	5207
the *S* of man shall be betrayed	Mt 20:18	5207
Even as the *S* of man came not to	Mt 20:28	5207
on us, O Lord, thou *s* of David	Mt 20:30	5207
on us, O Lord, thou *s* of David	Mt 20:31	5207
saying, Hosanna to the *s* of David	Mt 21:9	5207
saying, Hosanna to the *s* of David	Mt 21:15	5207
he came to the first, and said, *S*	Mt 21:28	5043
of all he sent unto them his *s*	Mt 21:37	5207
saying, They will reverence my *s*	Mt 21:37	5207
But when the husbandmen saw the *s*	Mt 21:38	5207
which made a marriage for his *s*	Mt 22:2	5207
whose *s* is he	Mt 22:42	5207
They say unto him, The *s* of David	Mt 22:42	
how is he his *s*	Mt 22:45	5207
blood of Zacharias *s* of Barachias	Mt 23:35	5207
the coming of the *S* of man be	Mt 24:27	5207
sign of the *S* of man in heaven	Mt 24:30	5207
they shall see the *S* of man	Mt 24:30	5207
the coming of the *S* of man be	Mt 24:37	5207
the coming of the *S* of man be	Mt 24:39	5207
ye think not the *S* of man cometh	Mt 24:44	5207
hour wherein the *S* of man cometh	Mt 25:13	5207
When the *S* of man shall come in	Mt 25:31	5207
the *S* of man is betrayed to be	Mt 26:2	5207
The *S* of man goeth as it is	Mt 26:24	5207
by whom the *S* of man is betrayed	Mt 26:24	5207
the *S* of man is betrayed into the	Mt 26:45	5207
thou be the Christ, the *S* of God	Mt 26:63	5207
Hereafter shall ye see the *S* of	Mt 26:64	5207
If thou be the *S* of God, come	Mt 27:40	5207
for he said, I am the *S* of God	Mt 27:43	5207
Truly this was the *S* of God	Mt 27:54	5207
name of the Father, and of the *S*	Mt 28:19	5207
of Jesus Christ, the *S* of God	Mk 1:1	5207
saying, Thou art my beloved *S*	Mk 1:11	5207
he saw James the *s* of Zebedee	Mk 1:19	
unto the sick of the palsy, *S*	Mk 2:5	5043
S of man hath power on earth to	Mk 2:10	5207
he saw Levi the *s* of Alphaeus	Mk 2:14	
Therefore the *S* of man is Lord	Mk 2:28	5207
saying, Thou art the *S* of God	Mk 3:11	5207
James the *s* of Zebedee, and John	Mk 3:17	
James the *s* of Alphaeus, and	Mk 3:18	
thou *S* of the most high God	Mk 5:7	5207
the *s* of Mary, the brother of	Mk 6:3	5207
that the *S* of man must suffer	Mk 8:31	5207
shall the *S* of man be ashamed	Mk 8:38	5207
saying, This is my beloved *S*	Mk 9:7	5207
till the *S* of man were risen from	Mk 9:9	5207
how it is written of the *S* of man	Mk 9:12	5207
I have brought unto thee my *s*	Mk 9:17	5207
The *S* of man is delivered into	Mk 9:31	5207
the *S* of man shall be delivered	Mk 10:33	5207
For even the *S* of man came not to	Mk 10:45	5207
the *s* of Timaeus, sat by the	Mk 10:46	5207
thou *s* of David, have mercy on me	Mk 10:47	5207
Thou *s* of David, have mercy on me	Mk 10:48	5207
Having yet therefore one *s*	Mk 12:6	5207
saying, They will reverence my *s*	Mk 12:6	5207
that Christ is the *s* of David	Mk 12:35	5207
and whence is he then his *s*	Mk 12:37	5207
to death, and the father the *s*	Mk 13:12	5043
then shall they see the *S* of man	Mk 13:26	5207
are in heaven, neither the *S*	Mk 13:32	5207
For the *S* of man is as a man	Mk 13:34	
The *S* of man indeed goeth, as it	Mk 14:21	5207
by whom the *S* of man is betrayed	Mk 14:21	5207
the *S* of man is betrayed into the	Mk 14:41	5207
the Christ, the *S* of the Blessed	Mk 14:61	5207
ye shall see the *S* of man sitting	Mk 14:62	5207
Truly this man was the *S* of God	Mk 15:39	5207
Elisabeth shall bear thee a *s*	Lk 1:13	5207
in thy womb, and bring forth a *s*	Lk 1:31	5207
be called the *S* of the Highest	Lk 1:32	5207
thee shall be called the *S* of God	Lk 1:35	5207
also conceived a *s* in her old age	Lk 1:36	5207
and she brought forth a *s*	Lk 1:57	5207
she brought forth her firstborn *s*	Lk 2:7	5207
and his mother said unto him, *S*	Lk 2:48	5043
s of Zacharias in the wilderness	Lk 3:2	5207
which said, Thou art my beloved *S*	Lk 3:22	5207
(as was supposed) the *s* of Joseph	Lk 3:23	5207
Joseph, which was the *s* of Heli	Lk 3:23	
Which was the *s* of Matthat	Lk 3:24	
Matthat, which was the *s* of Levi	Lk 3:24	
Levi, which was the *s* of Melchi	Lk 3:24	
Melchi, which was the *s* of Janna	Lk 3:24	
Janna, which was the *s* of Joseph	Lk 3:24	
Which was the *s* of Mattathias	Lk 3:25	
which was the *s* of Amos, which	Lk 3:25	
of Amos, which was the *s* of Naum	Lk 3:25	
of Naum, which was the *s* of Esli	Lk 3:25	
of Esli, which was the *s* of Nagge	Lk 3:25	
Which was the *s* of Maath, which	Lk 3:26	
which was the *s* of Mattathias	Lk 3:26	
which was the *s* of Semei	Lk 3:26	
Semei, which was the *s* of Joseph	Lk 3:26	
Joseph, which was the *s* of Juda	Lk 3:26	
Which was the *s* of Joanna	Lk 3:27	
Joanna, which was the *s* of Rhesa	Lk 3:27	
which was the *s* of Zorobabel	Lk 3:27	
which was the *s* of Salathiel,	Lk 3:27	
which was the *s* of Neri,	Lk 3:27	
Which was the *s* of Melchi	Lk 3:28	
Melchi, which was the *s* of Addi	Lk 3:28	
of Addi, which was the *s* of Cosam	Lk 3:28	
Cosam, which was the *s* of Elmodam	Lk 3:28	
of Elmodam, which was the *s* of Er	Lk 3:28	
Which was the *s* of Jose, which	Lk 3:29	
Jose, which was the *s* of Eliezer	Lk 3:29	
Eliezer, which was the *s* of Jorim	Lk 3:29	
Jorim, which was the *s* of Matthat	Lk 3:29	
Matthat, which was the *s* of Levi	Lk 3:29	
Which was the *s* of Simeon	Lk 3:30	
Simeon, which was the *s* of Juda	Lk 3:30	
Juda, which was the *s* of Joseph	Lk 3:30	
Joseph, which was the *s* of Jonan	Lk 3:30	
Jonan, which was the *s* of Eliakim	Lk 3:30	
Which was the *s* of Melea, which	Lk 3:31	
Melea, which was the *s* of Menan	Lk 3:31	
which was the *s* of Mattatha	Lk 3:31	
which was the *s* of Nathan	Lk 3:31	
Nathan, which was the *s* of David	Lk 3:31	
Which was the *s* of Jesse, which	Lk 3:32	
of Jesse, which was the *s* of Obed	Lk 3:32	
of Obed, which was the *s* of Booz	Lk 3:32	
Booz, which was the *s* of Salmon	Lk 3:32	
which was the *s* of Naasson	Lk 3:32	
Which was the *s* of Aminadab	Lk 3:33	
Aminadab, which was the *s* of Aram	Lk 3:33	
of Aram, which was the *s* of Esrom	Lk 3:33	
Esrom, which was the *s* of Phares	Lk 3:33	
Phares, which was the *s* of Juda	Lk 3:33	
Which was the *s* of Jacob, which	Lk 3:34	
Jacob, which was the *s* of Isaac	Lk 3:34	
Isaac, which was the *s* of Abraham	Lk 3:34	
Abraham, which was the *s* of Thara	Lk 3:34	
Thara, which was the *s* of Nachor	Lk 3:34	
Which was the *s* of Saruch	Lk 3:35	

Saruch, which was the *s* of Ragau	Lk 3:35	
Ragau, which was the *s* of Phalec	Lk 3:35	
Phalec, which was the *s* of Heber	Lk 3:35	
of Heber, which was the *s* of Sala	Lk 3:35	
Which was the *s* of Cainan	Lk 3:36	
which was the *s* of Arphaxad	Lk 3:36	
Arphaxad, which was the *s* of Sem	Lk 3:36	
of Sem, which was the *s* of Noe	Lk 3:36	
of Noe, which was the *s* of Lamech	Lk 3:36	
Which was the *s* of Mathusala	Lk 3:37	
which was the *s* of Enoch	Lk 3:37	
Enoch, which was the *s* of Jared	Lk 3:37	
which was the *s* of Maleleel	Lk 3:37	
which was the *s* of Cainan	Lk 3:37	
Which was the *s* of Enos, which	Lk 3:38	
of Enos, which was the *s* of Seth	Lk 3:38	
of Seth, which was the *s* of Adam	Lk 3:38	
of Adam, which was the *s* of God	Lk 3:38	
unto him, If thou be the *S* of God	Lk 4:3	5207
unto him, If thou be the *S* of God	Lk 4:9	5207
they said, Is not this Joseph's *s*	Lk 4:22	5207
Thou art Christ the *S* of God	Lk 4:41	5207
But that ye may know that the *S*	Lk 5:24	5207
That the *S* of man is Lord also of	Lk 6:5	5207
James the *s* of Alphaeus, and Simon	Lk 6:15	
as evil, for the *S* of man's sake	Lk 6:22	5207
the only *s* of his mother, and she	Lk 7:12	5207
The *S* of man is come eating and	Lk 7:34	5207
Jesus, thou *S* of God most high	Lk 8:28	5207
The *S* of man must suffer many	Lk 9:22	5207
of him shall the *S* of man be	Lk 9:26	5207
saying, This is my beloved *S*	Lk 9:35	5207
I beseech thee, look upon my *s*	Lk 9:38	5207
Bring thy *s* hither	Lk 9:41	5207
for the *S* of man shall be	Lk 9:44	5207
For the *S* of man is not come to	Lk 9:56	5207
but the *S* of man hath not where	Lk 9:58	5207
if the *s* of peace be there, your	Lk 10:6	5207
and no man knoweth who the *S* is	Lk 10:22	5207
and who the Father is, but the *S*	Lk 10:22	5207
he to whom the *S* will reveal him	Lk 10:22	5207
If a *s* shall ask bread of any of	Lk 11:11	5207
so shall also the *S* of man be to	Lk 11:30	5207
him shall the *S* of man also	Lk 12:8	5207
speak a word against the *S* of man	Lk 12:10	5207
for the *S* of man cometh at an	Lk 12:40	5207
shall be divided against the *s*	Lk 12:53	5207
and the *s* against the father	Lk 12:53	5207
younger *s* gathered all together	Lk 15:13	5207
no more worthy to be called thy *s*	Lk 15:19	5207
the *s* said unto him, Father, I	Lk 15:21	5207
no more worthy to be called thy *s*	Lk 15:21	5207
For this my *s* was dead, and is	Lk 15:24	5207
Now his elder *s* was in the field	Lk 15:25	5207
as soon as this thy *s* was come	Lk 15:30	5207
And he said unto him, *S*, thou art	Lk 15:31	5043
But Abraham said, *S*, remember	Lk 16:25	5043
one of the days of the *S* of man	Lk 17:22	5207
so shall also the *S* of man be in	Lk 17:24	5207
also in the days of the *S* of man	Lk 17:26	5207
day when the *S* of man is revealed	Lk 17:30	5207
when the *S* of man cometh, shall	Lk 18:8	5207
S of man shall be accomplished	Lk 18:31	5207
thou *s* of David, have mercy on me	Lk 18:38	5207
Thou *s* of David, have mercy on me	Lk 18:39	5207
as he also is a *s* of Abraham	Lk 19:9	5207
For the *S* of man is come to seek	Lk 19:10	5207
I will send my beloved *s*	Lk 20:13	5207
say they that Christ is David's *s*	Lk 20:41	5207
him Lord, how is he then his *s*	Lk 20:44	5207
then shall they see the *S* of man	Lk 21:27	5207
and to stand before the *S* of man	Lk 21:36	5207
truly the *S* of man goeth, as it	Lk 22:22	5207
thou the *S* of man with a kiss	Lk 22:48	5207
Hereafter shall the *S* of man sit	Lk 22:69	5207
all, Art thou then the *S* of God	Lk 22:70	5207
The *S* of man must be delivered	Lk 24:7	5207
the only begotten *S*, which is in	Jn 1:18	5207
record that this is the *S* of God	Jn 1:34	5207
Thou art Simon the *s* of Jona	Jn 1:42	5207
of Nazareth, the *s* of Joseph	Jn 1:45	5207
him, Rabbi, thou art the *S* of God	Jn 1:49	5207
and descending upon the *S* of man	Jn 1:51	5207
even the *S* of man which is in	Jn 3:13	5207
even so must the *S* of man be	Jn 3:14	5207
that he gave his only begotten *S*	Jn 3:16	5207
For God sent not his *S* into the	Jn 3:17	5207
of the only begotten *S* of God	Jn 3:18	5207
The Father loveth the *S*, and hath	Jn 3:35	5207
on the *S* hath everlasting life	Jn 3:36	5207
not the *S* shall not see life	Jn 3:36	5207
that Jacob gave to his *s* Joseph	Jn 4:5	5207
whose *s* was sick at Capernaum	Jn 4:46	5207
he would come down, and heal his *s*	Jn 4:47	5207
thy *s* liveth	Jn 4:50	5207
and told him, saying, Thy *s* liveth	Jn 4:51	3816
Jesus said unto him, Thy *s* liveth	Jn 4:53	5207
The *S* can do nothing of himself	Jn 5:19	5207
these also doeth the *S* likewise	Jn 5:19	5207
For the Father loveth the *S*	Jn 5:20	5207
even so the *S* quickeneth whom he	Jn 5:21	5207
committed all judgment unto the *S*	Jn 5:22	5207
That all men should honour the *S*	Jn 5:23	5207
He that honoureth not the *S*	Jn 5:23	5207
hear the voice of the *S* of God	Jn 5:25	5207
to the *S* to have life in himself	Jn 5:26	5207
also, because he is the *S* of man	Jn 5:27	5207
which the *S* of man shall give	Jn 6:27	5207
that every one which seeth the *S*	Jn 6:40	5207
the *s* of Joseph, whose father and	Jn 6:42	5207
ye eat the flesh of the *S* of man	Jn 6:53	5207
if ye shall see the *S* of man	Jn 6:62	5207
Christ, the *S* of the living God	Jn 6:69	5207
of Judas Iscariot the *s* of Simon	Jn 6:71	
ye have lifted up the *S* of man	Jn 8:28	5207
but the *S* abideth ever	Jn 8:35	5207
If the *S* therefore shall make you	Jn 8:36	5207
them, saying, Is this your *s*	Jn 9:19	5207
said, We know that this is our *s*	Jn 9:20	5207
Dost thou believe on the *S* of God	Jn 9:35	5207
because I said, I am the *S* of God	Jn 10:36	5207
that the *S* of God might be	Jn 11:4	5207
the *S* of God, which should come	Jn 11:27	5207
Judas Iscariot, Simon's *s*	Jn 12:4	
that the *S* of man should be	Jn 12:23	5207
The *S* of man must be lifted up	Jn 12:34	5207
who is this *S* of man	Jn 12:34	5207
of Judas Iscariot, Simon's *s*	Jn 13:2	
to Judas Iscariot, the *s* of Simon	Jn 13:26	
Now is the *S* of man glorified, and	Jn 13:31	5207
Father may be glorified in the *S*	Jn 14:13	5207
glorify thy *S*, that thy *S* also	Jn 17:1	5207
is lost, but the *s* of perdition	Jn 17:12	5207
he made himself the *S* of God	Jn 19:7	5207
his mother, Woman, behold thy *s*	Jn 19:26	5207
Jesus is the Christ, the *S* of God	Jn 20:31	5207
s of Jonas, lovest thou me more	Jn 21:15	
s of Jonas, lovest thou me	Jn 21:16	
s of Jonas, lovest thou me	Jn 21:17	
James the *s* of Alphaeus, and Simon	Acts 1:13	
hath glorified his *S* Jesus	Acts 3:13	3816
God, having raised up his *S* Jesus	Acts 3:26	3816
The *s* of consolation,) a Levite,	Acts 4:36	5207
and nourished him for her own *s*	Acts 7:21	5207
the *S* of man standing on the	Acts 7:56	5207
that Jesus Christ is the *S* of God	Acts 8:37	5207
that he is the *S* of God	Acts 9:20	5207
gave unto them Saul the *s* of Cis	Acts 13:21	5207
I have found David the *s* of Jesse	Acts 13:22	
the second psalm, Thou art my *S*	Acts 13:33	5207
the *s* of a certain woman, which	Acts 16:1	5207
a Pharisee, the *s* of a Pharisee	Acts 23:6	5207
when Paul's sister's *s* heard of	Acts 23:16	5207
Concerning his *S* Jesus Christ our	Rom 1:3	5207
to be the *S* of God with power	Rom 1:4	5207
my spirit in the gospel of his *S*	Rom 1:9	5207
to God by the death of his *S*	Rom 5:10	5207
God sending his own *S* in the	Rom 8:3	5207
conformed to the image of his *S*	Rom 8:29	5207
He that spared not his own *S*	Rom 8:32	5207
I come, and Sarah shall have a *s*	Rom 9:9	5207
of his *S* Jesus Christ our Lord	1Cor 1:9	5207
Timotheus, who is my beloved *s*	1Cor 4:17	5043
then shall the *S* also himself be	1Cor 15:28	5207
For the *S* of God, Jesus Christ,	2Cor 1:19	5207
To reveal his *S* in me, that I	Gal 1:16	5207
live by the faith of the *S* of God	Gal 2:20	5207
was come, God sent forth his *S*	Gal 4:4	5207
Spirit of his *S* into your hearts	Gal 4:6	5207
art no more a servant, but a *s*	Gal 4:7	5207
and if a *s*, then an heir of God	Gal 4:7	5207
Cast out the bondwoman and her *s*	Gal 4:30	5207
for the *s* of the bondwoman shall	Gal 4:30	5207
heir with the *s* of the free woman	Gal 4:30	5207
of the knowledge of the *S* of God	Eph 4:13	5207
as a *s* with the father, he hath	Phil 2:22	5043
us into the kingdom of his dear *S*	Col 1:13	5207
sister's *s* to Barnabas, (touching	Col 4:10	431
And to wait for his *S* from heaven	1Th 1:10	5207
be revealed, the *s* of perdition	2Th 2:3	5207
Timothy, my own *s* in the faith	1Ti 1:2	5043
s Timothy, according to the	1Ti 1:18	5043
To Timothy, my dearly beloved *s*	2Ti 1:2	5043
Thou therefore, my *s*, be strong	2Ti 2:1	5043
mine own *s* after the common faith	Titus 1:4	5043
I beseech thee for my *s* Onesimus	Philem 10	5043
last days spoken unto us by his *S*	Heb 1:2	5207
he at any time, Thou art my *S*	Heb 1:5	5207
Father, and he shall be to me a *S*	Heb 1:5	5207
But unto the *S* he saith, Thy	Heb 1:8	5207
or the *s* of man, that thou	Heb 2:6	5207
But Christ as a *s* over his own	Heb 3:6	5207
the heavens, Jesus the *S* of God	Heb 4:14	5207
that said unto him, Thou art my *S*	Heb 5:5	5207
Though he were a *S*, yet learned	Heb 5:8	5207
to themselves the *S* of God afresh	Heb 6:6	5207
but made like unto the *S* of God	Heb 7:3	5207
was since the law, maketh the *S*	Heb 7:28	5207
trodden under foot the *S* of God	Heb 10:29	5207
offered up his only begotten *s*	Heb 11:17	
the *s* of Pharaoh's daughter	Heb 11:24	5207
unto you as unto children, My *s*	Heb 12:5	5207
scourgeth every *s* whom he	Heb 12:6	5207
for what *s* is he whom the father	Heb 12:7	5207
Isaac his *s* upon the altar	Jas 2:21	5207
and so doth Marcus my *s*	1Pet 5:13	5207
glory, This is my beloved *S*	2Pet 1:17	5207
the way of Balaam the *s* of Bosor	2Pet 2:15	
and with his *S* Jesus Christ	1Jn 1:3	5207
his *S* cleanseth us from all sin	1Jn 1:7	5207
that denieth the Father and the *S*	1Jn 2:22	5207
Whosoever denieth the *S*, the same	1Jn 2:23	5207
the *S* hath the Father also	1Jn 2:23	
ye also shall continue in the *S*	1Jn 2:24	5207
For this purpose the *S* of God was	1Jn 3:8	5207
on the name of his *S* Jesus Christ	1Jn 3:23	5207
only begotten *S* into the world	1Jn 4:9	5207
sent his *S* to be the propitiation	1Jn 4:10	5207
that the Father sent the *S* to be	1Jn 4:14	5207
that Jesus is the *S* of God	1Jn 4:15	5207
that Jesus is the *S* of God	1Jn 5:5	5207
which he hath testified of his *S*	1Jn 5:9	5207
He that believeth on the *S* of God	1Jn 5:10	5207
the record that God gave of his *S*	1Jn 5:10	5207
life, and this life is in his *S*	1Jn 5:11	5207
He that hath the *S* hath life	1Jn 5:12	5207
not the *S* of God hath not life	1Jn 5:12	5207
on the name of the *S* of God	1Jn 5:13	5207
on the name of the *S* of God	1Jn 5:13	5207
we know that the *S* of God is come	1Jn 5:20	5207
even in his *S* Jesus Christ	1Jn 5:20	5207
the *S* of the Father, in truth and	2Jn 3	5207
he hath both the Father and the *S*	2Jn 9	5207
one like unto the *S* of man	Rev 1:13	5207
These things saith the *S* of God	Rev 2:18	5207
one sat like unto the *S* of man	Rev 14:14	5207
be his God, and he shall be my *s*	Rev 21:7	5207

SONG

of Israel this *s* unto the LORD	Ex 15:1	7892
The LORD is my strength and *s*	Ex 15:2	2176
Then Israel sang this *s*, Spring	Num 21:17	7892
therefore write ye this *s* for you	Deut 31:19	7892
that this *s* may be a witness for	Deut 31:19	7892
that this *s* shall testify against	Deut 31:21	7892
wrote this *s* the same day	Deut 31:22	7892
of Israel the words of this *s*	Deut 31:30	7892
this *s* in the ears of the people	Deut 32:44	7892
awake, awake, utter a *s*	Judg 5:12	7892
unto the LORD the words of this *s*	2Sa 22:1	7892
of *s* in the house of the LORD	1Chr 6:31	7892
chief of the Levites, was for *s*	1Chr 15:22	4853
he instructed about the *s*	1Chr 15:22	4853
master of the *s* with the singers	1Chr 15:27	4853
for *s* in the house of the LORD	1Chr 25:6	7892
the *s* of the LORD began also with	2Chr 29:27	7892
And now am I their *s*, yea, I am	Job 30:9	5058
this *s* in the day that the LORD	Ps 18:*t*	7892
with my *s* will I praise him	Ps 28:7	7892
S at the dedication of the house	Ps 30:*t*	7892
Sing unto him a new *s*	Ps 33:3	7892
he hath put a new *s* in my mouth	Ps 40:3	7892
the night his *s* shall be with me	Ps 42:8	7892
of Korah, A Maschil, A *S* of loves	Ps 45:*t*	7892
sons of Korah, A *S* upon Alamoth	Ps 46:*t*	7892
A *S* and Psalm for the sons of	Ps 48:*t*	7892
Musician, A Psalm and *S* of David	Ps 65:*t*	7892
the chief Musician, A *S* or Psalm	Ps 66:*t*	7892
on Neginoth, A Psalm or *S*	Ps 67:*t*	7892
Musician, A Psalm or *S* of David	Ps 68:*t*	7892
I was the *s* of the drunkards	Ps 69:12	5058
praise the name of God with a *s*	Ps 69:30	7892
Altaschith, A Psalm or *S* of Asaph	Ps 75:*t*	7892
Neginoth, A Psalm or *S* of Asaph	Ps 76:*t*	7892
to remembrance my *s* in the night	Ps 77:6	5058
A *S* or Psalm of Asaph	Ps 83:*t*	7892
A Psalm or *S* for the sons of	Ps 87:*t*	7892
A *S* or Psalm for the sons of	Ps 88:*t*	7892
A Psalm or *S* for the sabbath day	Ps 92:*t*	7892
O sing unto the LORD a new *s*	Ps 96:1	7892
O sing unto the LORD a new *s*	Ps 98:1	7892
A *S* or Psalm of David	Ps 108:*t*	7892
The LORD is my strength and *s*	Ps 118:14	2176
A *S* of degrees	Ps 120:*t*	7892
A *S* of degrees	Ps 121:*t*	7892
A *S* of degrees of David	Ps 122:*t*	7892
A *S* of degrees	Ps 123:*t*	7892
A *S* of degrees of David	Ps 124:*t*	7892
A *S* of degrees	Ps 125:*t*	7892
A *S* of degrees	Ps 126:*t*	7892
A *S* of degrees for Solomon	Ps 127:*t*	7892
A *S* of degrees	Ps 128:*t*	7892
A *S* of degrees	Ps 129:*t*	7892
A *S* of degrees	Ps 130:*t*	7892
A *S* of degrees of David	Ps 131:*t*	7892
A *S* of degrees	Ps 132:*t*	7892
A *S* of degrees of David	Ps 133:*t*	7892
A *S* of degrees	Ps 134:*t*	7892
away captive required of us a *s*	Ps 137:3	7892
the LORD's *s* in a strange land	Ps 137:4	7892
I will sing a new *s* unto thee	Ps 144:9	7892
Sing unto the LORD a new *s*	Ps 149:1	7892
for a man to hear the *s* of fools	Eccl 7:5	7892
The *s* of songs, which is	Song 1:1	7892
a *s* of my beloved touching his	Is 5:1	7892
JEHOVAH is my strength and my *s*	Is 12:2	2176
shall not drink wine with a *s*	Is 24:9	7892
In that day shall this *s* be sung	Is 26:1	7892
Ye shall have a *s*, as in the	Is 30:29	7892
Sing unto the LORD a new *s*	Is 42:10	7892
and their *s* all the day	Lam 3:14	5058
s of one that hath a pleasant	Eze 33:32	7892
And they sung a new *s*, saying,	Rev 5:9	5603
it were a new *s* before the throne	Rev 14:3	5603
learn that *s* but the hundred	Rev 14:3	5603
they sing the *s* of Moses the	Rev 15:3	5603
the *s* of the Lamb, saying, Great	Rev 15:3	5603

SONGS

thee away with mirth, and with *s*	Gen 31:27	7892
his *s* were a thousand and five	1Kin 4:32	7892
instructed in the *s* of the LORD	1Chr 25:7	7892
s of praise and thanksgiving unto	Neh 12:46	7892
who giveth *s* in the night	Job 35:10	2158
me about with *s* of deliverance	Ps 32:7	7438
Thy statutes have been my *s* in	Ps 119:54	2158
Sing us one of the *s* of Zion	Ps 137:3	7892
that singeth *s* to an heavy heart	Prov 25:20	7892
The song of *s*, which is Solomon's	Song 1:1	7892
make sweet melody, sing many *s*	Is 23:16	7892
part of the earth have we heard *s*	Is 24:16	2158
return, and come to Zion with *s*	Is 35:10	7440
therefore we will sing my *s* to	Is 38:20	5058
cause the noise of thy *s* to cease	Eze 26:13	7892
away from me the noise of thy *s*	Amos 5:23	7892
the *s* of the temple shall be	Amos 8:3	7892
all your *s* into lamentation	Amos 8:10	7892
in psalms and hymns and spiritual *s*	Eph 5:19	5603
in psalms and hymns and spiritual *s*	Col 3:16	5603

SON'S

and Lot the son of Haran his *s* son	Gen 11:31	1121
and Abram called his *s* name	Gen 16:15	1121

with my son, nor with my s son	Gen 21:23	5220
and let her be thy master's s wife	Gen 24:51	1121
me, and I will eat of my s venison	Gen 27:25	1121
arise, and eat of his s venison	Gen 27:31	1121
I pray thee, of thy s mandrakes	Gen 30:14	1121
take away my s mandrakes also	Gen 30:15	1121
thee to night for thy s mandrakes	Gen 30:15	1121
hired thee with my s mandrakes	Gen 30:16	1121
whether it be thy s coat or no	Gen 37:32	1121
knew it, and said, It is my s coat	Gen 37:33	1121
ears of thy son, and of thy s son	Ex 10:2	1121
The nakedness of thy s daughter	Lev 18:10	1121
she is thy s wife	Lev 18:15	1121
shalt thou take her s daughter	Lev 18:17	1121
thou, and thy son, and thy s son	Deut 6:2	1121
and thy son, and thy s son also	Judg 8:22	1121
the kingdom out of his s hand	1Kin 11:35	1121
but in his s days will I bring	1Kin 21:29	1121
his name, and what is his s name	Prov 30:4	1121
him, and his son, and his s son	Jer 27:7	1121

SONS

and he begat s and daughters	Gen 5:4	1121
and seven years, and begat s	Gen 5:7	1121
and fifteen years, and begat s	Gen 5:10	1121
and forty years, and begat s	Gen 5:13	1121
and thirty years, and begat s	Gen 5:16	1121
eight hundred years, and begat s	Gen 5:19	1121
three hundred years, and begat s	Gen 5:22	1121
eighty and two years, and begat s	Gen 5:26	1121
ninety and five years, and begat s	Gen 5:30	1121
That the s of God saw the	Gen 6:2	1121
when the s of God came in unto	Gen 6:4	1121
And Noah begat three s, Shem, Ham,	Gen 6:10	1121
come into the ark, thou, and thy s	Gen 6:18	1121
And Noah went in, and his s	Gen 7:7	1121
the s of Noah, and Noah's wife, and	Gen 7:13	1121
three wives of his s with them	Gen 7:13	1121
ark, thou, and thy wife, and thy s	Gen 8:16	1121
And Noah went forth, and his s	Gen 8:18	1121
And God blessed Noah and his s	Gen 9:1	1121
to his s with him, saying,	Gen 9:8	1121
the s of Noah, that went forth of	Gen 9:18	1121
These are the three s of Noah	Gen 9:19	1121
the generations of the s of Noah	Gen 10:1	1121
unto them were s born after the	Gen 10:1	1121
The s of Japheth	Gen 10:2	1121
And the s of Gomer	Gen 10:3	1121
And the s of Javan	Gen 10:4	1121
And the s of Ham	Gen 10:6	1121
And the s of Cush	Gen 10:7	1121
and the s of Raamah	Gen 10:7	1121
These are the s of Ham, after	Gen 10:20	1121
And unto Eber were born two s	Gen 10:25	1121
all these were the s of Joktan	Gen 10:29	1121
These are the s of Shem, after	Gen 10:31	1121
are the families of the s of Noah	Gen 10:32	1121
five hundred years, and begat s	Gen 11:11	1121
and three years, and begat s	Gen 11:13	1121
and three years, and begat s	Gen 11:15	1121
and thirty years, and begat s	Gen 11:17	1121
hundred and nine years, and begat s	Gen 11:19	1121
and seven years, and begat s	Gen 11:21	1121
two hundred years, and begat s	Gen 11:23	1121
and nineteen years, and begat s	Gen 11:25	1121
son in law, and thy s, and thy	Gen 19:12	1121
out, and spake unto his s in law	Gen 19:14	2860
one that mocked unto his s in law	Gen 19:14	2860
dead, and spake unto the s of Heth	Gen 23:3	1121
in the presence of the s of my	Gen 23:11	1121
in the audience of the s of Heth	Gen 23:16	1121
a buryingplace by the s of Heth	Gen 23:20	1121
the s of Dedan were Asshurim, and	Gen 25:3	1121
And the s of Midian	Gen 25:4	1121
But unto the s of the concubines,	Gen 25:6	1121
his s Isaac and Ishmael buried him	Gen 25:9	1121
purchased of the s of Heth	Gen 25:10	1121
are the names of the s of Ishmael	Gen 25:13	1121
These are the s of Ishmael	Gen 25:16	1121
thy mother's s bow down to thee	Gen 27:29	1121
because I have born him three s	Gen 29:34	1121
me, because I have born him six s	Gen 30:20	1121
gave them into the hand of his s	Gen 30:35	1121
he heard the words of Laban's s	Gen 31:1	1121
Then Jacob rose up, and set his s	Gen 31:17	1121
hast not suffered me to kiss my s	Gen 31:28	1121
Laban rose up, and kissed his s	Gen 31:55	1121
womenservants, and his eleven s	Gen 32:22	3206
now his s were with his cattle in	Gen 34:5	1121
the s of Jacob came out of the	Gen 34:7	1121
the s of Jacob answered Shechem	Gen 34:13	1121
sore, that two of the s of Jacob	Gen 34:25	1121
The s of Jacob came upon the	Gen 34:27	1121
not pursue after the s of Jacob	Gen 35:5	1121
Now the s of Jacob were twelve	Gen 35:22	1121
The s of Leah	Gen 35:23	1121
The s of Rachel	Gen 35:24	1121
the s of Bilhah, Rachel's	Gen 35:25	1121
the s of Zilpah, Leah's handmaid	Gen 35:26	1121
these are the s of Jacob, which	Gen 35:26	1121
his s Esau and Jacob buried him	Gen 35:29	1121
these are the s of Esau, which	Gen 36:5	1121
And Esau took his wives, and his s	Gen 36:6	1121
These are the names of Esau's s	Gen 36:10	1121
the s of Eliphaz were Teman, Omar	Gen 36:11	1121
these were the s of Adah Esau's	Gen 36:12	1121
And these are the s of Reuel	Gen 36:13	1121
these were the s of Bashemath	Gen 36:13	1121
And these were the s of Aholibamah	Gen 36:14	1121
These were dukes of the s of Esau	Gen 36:15	1121
the s of Eliphaz the firstborn	Gen 36:15	1121
these were the s of Adah	Gen 36:16	1121
these are the s of Reuel Esau's	Gen 36:17	1121
these are the s of Bashemath	Gen 36:17	1121
these are the s of Aholibamah	Gen 36:18	1121
These are the s of Esau, who is	Gen 36:19	1121
These are the s of Seir the	Gen 36:20	1121
the lad was with the s of Bilhah	Gen 37:2	1121
with the s of Zilpah, his	Gen 37:2	1121
And all his s and all his daughters	Gen 37:35	1121
unto Joseph were born two s	Gen 41:50	1121
in Egypt, Jacob said unto his s	Gen 42:1	1121
the s of Israel came to buy corn	Gen 42:5	1121
We are all one man's s	Gen 42:11	1121
the s of one man in the land of	Gen 42:13	1121
twelve brethren, s of our father	Gen 42:32	1121
his father, saying, Slay my two s	Gen 42:37	1121
know that my wife bare me two s	Gen 44:27	
the s of Israel carried Jacob	Gen 46:5	1121
His s, and his sons' s with him	Gen 46:7	1121
came into Egypt, Jacob and his s	Gen 46:8	1121
And the s of Reuben	Gen 46:9	1121
And the s of Simeon	Gen 46:10	1121
And the s of Levi	Gen 46:11	1121
And the s of Judah	Gen 46:12	1121
the s of Pharez were Hezron and	Gen 46:12	1121
And the s of Issachar	Gen 46:13	1121
And the s of Zebulun	Gen 46:14	1121
These be the s of Leah, which she	Gen 46:15	1121
all the souls of his s and his	Gen 46:15	1121
And the s of Gad	Gen 46:16	1121
And the s of Asher	Gen 46:17	1121
and the s of Beriah	Gen 46:17	1121
These are the s of Zilpah	Gen 46:18	1121
The s of Rachel Jacob's wife	Gen 46:19	1121
the s of Benjamin were Belah, and	Gen 46:21	1121
These are the s of Rachel	Gen 46:22	1121
And the s of Dan	Gen 46:23	1121
And the s of Naphtali	Gen 46:24	1121
These are the s of Bilhah	Gen 46:25	1121
the s of Joseph, which were born	Gen 46:27	1121
and he took with him his two s	Gen 48:1	1121
And now thy two s, Ephraim and	Gen 48:5	1121
And Israel beheld Joseph's s	Gen 48:8	1121
unto his father, They are my s	Gen 48:9	1121
And Jacob called unto his s	Gen 49:1	1121
together, and hear, ye s of Jacob	Gen 49:2	1121
made an end of commanding his s	Gen 49:33	1121
his s did unto him according as	Gen 50:12	1121
For his s carried him into the	Gen 50:13	1121
and ye shall put them upon your s	Ex 3:22	1121
And Moses took his wife and his s	Ex 4:20	1121
The s of Reuben the firstborn of	Ex 6:14	1121
And the s of Simeon	Ex 6:15	1121
the s of Levi according to their	Ex 6:16	1121
The s of Gershon	Ex 6:17	1121
And the s of Kohath	Ex 6:18	1121
And the s of Merari	Ex 6:19	1121
And the s of Izhar	Ex 6:21	1121
And the s of Uzziel	Ex 6:22	1121
And the s of Korah	Ex 6:24	1121
young and with our old, with our s	Ex 10:9	1121
to thee and to thy s for ever	Ex 12:24	1121
And her two s; of which	Ex 18:3	1121
father in law, came with his s	Ex 18:5	1121
thy wife, and her two s with her	Ex 18:6	1121
she have born him s or daughters	Ex 21:4	1121
the firstborn of thy s shalt thou	Ex 22:29	1121
his s shall order it from evening	Ex 27:21	1121
his s with him, from among the	Ex 28:1	1121
Eleazar and Ithamar, Aaron's s	Ex 28:1	1121
for Aaron thy brother, and his s	Ex 28:4	1121
for Aaron's s thou shalt make	Ex 28:40	1121
thy brother, and his s with him	Ex 28:41	1121
be upon Aaron, and upon his s	Ex 28:43	1121
his s thou shalt bring unto the	Ex 29:4	1121
And thou shalt bring his s	Ex 29:8	1121
them with girdles, Aaron and his s	Ex 29:9	1121
shalt consecrate Aaron and his s	Ex 29:9	1121
his s shall put their hands upon	Ex 29:10	1121
his s shall put their hands upon	Ex 29:15	1121
his s shall put their hands upon	Ex 29:19	1121
the tip of the right ear of his s	Ex 29:20	1121
upon his garments, and upon his s	Ex 29:21	1121
the garments of his s with him	Ex 29:21	1121
and his garments, and his s	Ex 29:21	1121
Aaron, and in the hands of his s	Ex 29:24	1121
and of that which is for his s	Ex 29:27	1121
his s shall eat the flesh of the	Ex 29:32	1121
thou do unto Aaron, and to his s	Ex 29:35	1121
sanctify also both Aaron and his s	Ex 29:44	1121
his s shall wash their hands and	Ex 30:19	1121
thou shalt anoint Aaron and his s	Ex 30:30	1121
priest, and the garments of his s	Ex 31:10	1121
the ears of your wives, of your s	Ex 32:2	1121
all the s of Levi gathered	Ex 32:26	1121
of their daughters unto thy s	Ex 34:16	1121
make thy s go a whoring after	Ex 34:16	1121
of thy s thou shalt redeem	Ex 34:20	1121
priest, and the garments of his s	Ex 35:19	1121
work for Aaron, and for his s	Ex 39:27	1121
his s unto the door of the	Ex 40:12	1121
And thou shalt bring his s	Ex 40:14	1121
his s washed their hands and their	Ex 40:31	1121
and the priests, Aaron's s	Lev 1:5	1121
the s of Aaron the priest shall	Lev 1:7	1121
And the priests, Aaron's s	Lev 1:8	1121
and the priests, Aaron's s	Lev 1:11	1121
bring it to Aaron's s the priests	Lev 2:2	1121
Aaron's s the priests shall	Lev 3:2	1121
Aaron's s shall burn it on the	Lev 3:5	1121
Aaron's s shall sprinkle the	Lev 3:8	1121
the s of Aaron shall sprinkle the	Lev 3:13	1121
Command Aaron and his s, saying,	Lev 6:9	1121
the s of Aaron shall offer it	Lev 6:14	1121
thereof shall Aaron and his s eat	Lev 6:16	1121
the offering of Aaron and of his s	Lev 6:20	1121
the priest of his s that is	Lev 6:22	1121
Speak unto Aaron and to his s	Lev 6:25	1121
shall all the s of Aaron have	Lev 7:10	1121
He among the s of Aaron, that	Lev 7:33	1121
unto his s by a statute for ever	Lev 7:34	1121
and of the anointing of his s	Lev 7:35	1121
his s with him, and the garments,	Lev 8:2	1121
And Moses brought Aaron and his s	Lev 8:6	1121
And Moses brought Aaron's s	Lev 8:13	1121
his s laid their hands upon the	Lev 8:14	1121
his s laid their hands upon the	Lev 8:18	1121
his s laid their hands upon the	Lev 8:22	1121
And he brought Aaron's s, and Moses	Lev 8:24	1121
upon his garments, and upon his s	Lev 8:30	1121
Aaron, and his garments, and his s	Lev 8:30	1121
Moses said unto Aaron and to his s	Lev 8:31	1121
Aaron and his s shall eat it	Lev 8:31	1121
his s did all things which the	Lev 8:36	1121
that Moses called Aaron and his s	Lev 9:1	1121
the s of Aaron brought the blood	Lev 9:9	1121
Aaron's s presented unto him the	Lev 9:12	1121
Aaron's s presented unto him the	Lev 9:18	1121
the s of Aaron, took either of	Lev 10:1	1121
the s of Uzziel the uncle of	Lev 10:4	1121
Eleazar and unto Ithamar, his s	Lev 10:6	1121
nor thy s with thee, when ye go	Lev 10:9	1121
his s that were left, Take the	Lev 10:12	1121
thou, and thy s, and thy daughters	Lev 10:14	1121
the s of Aaron which were left	Lev 10:16	1121
or unto one of his s the priests	Lev 13:2	1121
the death of the two s of Aaron	Lev 16:1	1121
Speak unto Aaron, and unto his s	Lev 17:2	1121
unto the priests the s of Aaron	Lev 21:1	1121
told it unto Aaron, and to his s	Lev 21:24	1121
Speak unto Aaron and to his s	Lev 22:2	1121
Speak unto Aaron, and to his s	Lev 22:18	1121
ye shall eat the flesh of your s	Lev 26:29	1121
the captain of the s of Gad shall	Num 2:14	1121
the captain of the s of Ephraim	Num 2:18	1121
the captain of the s of Benjamin	Num 2:22	1121
are the names of the s of Aaron	Num 3:2	1121
are the names of the s of Aaron	Num 3:3	1121
Levites unto Aaron and to his s	Num 3:9	1121
thou shalt appoint Aaron and his s	Num 3:10	1121
these were the s of Levi by their	Num 3:17	1121
these are the names of the s of	Num 3:18	1121
the s of Kohath by their families	Num 3:19	1121
the s of Merari by their families	Num 3:20	1121
the charge of the s of Gershon in	Num 3:25	1121
The families of the s of Kohath	Num 3:29	1121
charge of the s of Merari shall	Num 3:36	1121
shall be Moses, and Aaron and his s	Num 3:38	1121
redeemed, unto Aaron and to his s	Num 3:48	1121
redeemed unto Aaron and to his s	Num 3:51	1121
Take the sum of the s of Kohath	Num 4:2	1121
Kohath from among the s of Levi	Num 4:2	1121
shall be the service of the s of	Num 4:4	1121
Aaron shall come, and his s	Num 4:5	1121
his s have made an end of	Num 4:15	1121
the s of Kohath shall come to	Num 4:15	1121
things are the burden of the s of	Num 4:15	1121
his s shall go in, and appoint	Num 4:19	1121
also the sum of the s of Gershon	Num 4:22	1121
his s shall be all the service of	Num 4:27	1121
of the s of the Gershonites	Num 4:27	1121
service of the families of the s	Num 4:28	1121
As for the s of Merari, thou	Num 4:29	1121
the families of the s of Merari	Num 4:33	1121
s of the Kohathites after their	Num 4:34	1121
were numbered of the s of Gershon	Num 4:38	1121
the families of the s of Gershon	Num 4:41	1121
the families of the s of Merari	Num 4:42	1121
the families of the s of Merari	Num 4:45	1121
Speak unto Aaron and unto his s	Num 6:23	1121
he gave unto the s of Gershon	Num 7:7	1121
oxen he gave unto the s of Merari	Num 7:8	1121
But unto the s of Kohath he gave	Num 7:9	1121
before Aaron, and before his s	Num 8:13	1121
to his s from among the children	Num 8:19	1121
before Aaron, and before his s	Num 8:22	1121
the s of Aaron, the priests,	Num 10:8	1121
the s of Gershon and the	Num 10:17	1121
the s of Merari set forward,	Num 10:17	1121
the s of Anak, which come of the	Num 13:33	1121
the s of Eliab, and On, the son of	Num 16:1	1121
of Peleth, s of Reuben, took men	Num 16:1	1121
too much upon you, ye s of Levi	Num 16:7	1121
Hear, I pray you, ye s of Levi	Num 16:8	1121
brethren the s of Levi with thee	Num 16:10	1121
Dathan and Abiram, the s of Eliab	Num 16:12	1121
tents, and their wives, and their s	Num 16:27	1121
said unto Aaron, Thou and thy s	Num 18:1	1121
thy s with thee shall bear the	Num 18:1	1121
thy s with thee shall minister	Num 18:2	1121
thy s with thee shall keep your	Num 18:7	1121
of the anointing, and to thy s	Num 18:8	1121
most holy for thee and for thy s	Num 18:9	1121
given them unto thee, and to thy s	Num 18:11	1121
LORD, have I given thee, and thy s	Num 18:19	1121
he hath given his s that escaped	Num 21:29	1121
So they smote him, and his s	Num 21:35	1121
And the s of Pallu	Num 26:8	1121
And the s of Eliab	Num 26:9	1121
The s of Simeon after their	Num 26:12	1121
The s of Judah were Er and Onan	Num 26:19	1121
the s of Judah after their	Num 26:20	1121
And the s of Pharez were	Num 26:21	1121
Of the s of Issachar after their	Num 26:23	1121
Of the s of Zebulun after their	Num 26:26	1121
The s of Joseph after their	Num 26:28	1121
Of the s of Manasseh	Num 26:29	1121
These are the s of Gilead	Num 26:30	1121
the son of Hepher had no s	Num 26:33	1121
These are the s of Ephraim after	Num 26:35	1121
And these are the s of Shuthelah	Num 26:36	1121

S

s of Ephraim according to those Num 26:37 1121
These are the s of Joseph after Num 26:37 1121
The s of Benjamin after their Num 26:38 1121
the s of Bela were Ard and Naaman Num 26:40 1121
These are the s of Benjamin after Num 26:41 1121
These are the s of Dan after Num 26:42 1121
Of the s of Beriah Num 26:45 1121
the s of Asher according to those Num 26:47 1121
Of the s of Naphtali after their Num 26:48 1121
died in his own sin, and had no s Num 27:3 1121
the families of the s of Joseph Num 36:1 1121
the s of the other tribes of the Num 36:3 1121
The tribe of the s of Joseph hath Num 36:5 1121
unto their father's brothers' s Num 36:11 1121
into the families of the s of Num 36:12 1121
seen the s of the Anakims there Deut 1:28 1121
and we smote him, and his s Deut 2:33 1121
them thy s, and thy sons' s Deut 4:9 1121
the s of Eliab, the son of Reuben Deut 11:6 1121
the LORD your God, ye, and your s Deut 12:12 1121
for even their s and their Deut 12:31 1121
the LORD, him and his s for ever Deut 18:5 1121
the priests the s of Levi shall Deut 21:5 1121
when he maketh his s to inherit Deut 21:16 1121
nor a sodomite of the s of Israel Deut 23:17 1121
Thy s and thy daughters shall be Deut 28:32 1121
Thou shalt beget s and daughters, Deut 28:41
own body, the flesh of thy s Deut 28:53 1121
it unto the priests the s of Levi Deut 31:9 1121
when he separated the s of Adam Deut 32:8 1121
because of the provoking of his s Deut 32:19 1121
and the wedge of gold, and his s Josh 7:24 1121
drove thence the three s of Anak Josh 15:14 1121
the son of Manasseh, had no s Josh 17:3 1121
had an inheritance among his s Josh 17:6 1121
s had the land of Gilead Josh 17:6 1121
which Jacob bought of the s of Josh 24:32 1121
thence the three s of Anak Judg 1:20 1121
gave their daughters to their s Judg 3:6 1121
brethren, even the s of my mother Judg 8:19 1121
ten s of his body begotten Judg 8:30 1121
that all the s of Jerubbaal Judg 9:2 1121
his brethren the s of Jerubbaal Judg 9:5 1121
this day, and have slain his s Judg 9:18 1121
ten s of Jerubbaal might come, and Judg 9:24 1121
he had thirty s that rode on Judg 10:4 1121
And Gilead's wife bare him s Judg 11:2 1121
and his wife's s grew up, and they Judg 11:2 1121
And he had thirty s, and thirty Judg 12:9 1121
daughters from abroad for his s Judg 12:9 1121
And he had forty s and thirty Judg 12:14 1121
and consecrated one of his s Judg 17:5 1121
man was unto him as one of his s Judg 17:11 1121
his s were priests to the tribe Judg 18:30 1121
certain s of Belial, beset the Judg 19:22 1121
he, and his wife, and his two s Ruth 1:1 1121
and the name of his two s Mahlon Ruth 1:2 1121
and she was left, and her two s Ruth 1:3 1121
the woman was left of her two s Ruth 1:5 3206
there yet any more s in my womb Ruth 1:11 1121
to night, and should also bear s Ruth 1:12 1121
is better to thee than seven s Ruth 4:15 1121
And the two s of Eli, Hophni and 1Sa 1:3 1121
his wife, and to all her s 1Sa 1:4 1121
not I better to thee than ten s 1Sa 1:8 1121
the s of Eli were s of Belial 1Sa 2:12 1121
she conceived, and bare three s 1Sa 2:21 1121
heard all that his s did unto all 1Sa 2:22 1121
Nay, my s 1Sa 2:24 1121
and honourest thy s above me 1Sa 2:29 1121
that shall come upon thy two s 1Sa 2:34 1121
because his s made themselves 1Sa 3:13 1121
and the two s of Eli, Hophni and 1Sa 4:4 1121
and the two s of Eli, Hophni and 1Sa 4:11 1121
the people, and thy two s also 1Sa 4:17 1121
that he made his s judges over 1Sa 8:1 1121
his s walked not in his ways, but 1Sa 8:3 1121
thy s walk not in thy ways 1Sa 8:5 1121
He will take your s, and appoint 1Sa 8:11 1121
and, behold, my s are with you 1Sa 12:2 1121
Now the s of Saul were Jonathan, 1Sa 14:49 1121
provided me a king among his s 1Sa 16:1 1121
And he sanctified Jesse and his s 1Sa 16:5 1121
of his s to pass before Samuel 1Sa 16:10 1121
and he had eight s 1Sa 17:12 1121
the three eldest s of Jesse went 1Sa 17:13 1121
the names of his three s that 1Sa 17:13 1121
one of the s of Ahimelech the son 1Sa 22:20 1121
shalt thou and thy s be with me 1Sa 28:19 1121
and their wives, and their s 1Sa 30:3 1121
was grieved, every man for his s 1Sa 30:6 1121
neither s nor daughters, neither 1Sa 30:19 1121
hard upon Saul and upon his s 1Sa 31:2 1121
and Melchi-shua, Saul's s 1Sa 31:2 1121
So Saul died, and his three s 1Sa 31:6 1121
his s were dead, they forsook the 1Sa 31:7 1121
his three s fallen in mount 1Sa 31:8 1121
the bodies of his s from the wall 1Sa 31:12 1121
were three s of Zeruiah there 2Sa 2:18 1121
unto David were s born in Hebron 2Sa 3:2 1121
these men the s of Zeruiah be too 2Sa 3:39 1121
the s of Rimmon a Beerothite, of 2Sa 4:2 1121
the s of Rimmon the Beerothite, 2Sa 4:5 1121
the s of Rimmon the Beerothite, 2Sa 4:9
and there were yet s and daughters 2Sa 5:13 1121
the s of Abinadab, drave the new 2Sa 6:3 1121
David's s were chief rulers 2Sa 8:18 1121
Thou therefore, and thy s, and thy 2Sa 9:10 1121
Now Ziba had fifteen s and twenty 2Sa 9:10 1121
my table, as one of the king's s 2Sa 9:11 1121
Absalom invited all the king's s 2Sa 13:23 1121
and all the king's s go with him 2Sa 13:27 1121
Then all the king's s arose 2Sa 13:29 1121
hath slain all the king's s 2Sa 13:30 1121

all the young men the king's s 2Sa 13:32 1121
that all the king's s are dead 2Sa 13:33 1121
king, Behold, the king's s come 2Sa 13:35 1121
that, behold, the king's s came 2Sa 13:36 1121
And thy handmaid had two s 2Sa 14:6 1121
Absalom there were born three s 2Sa 14:27 1121
in peace, and your two s with you 2Sa 15:27 1121
have there with them their two s 2Sa 15:36 1121
I to do with you, ye s of Zeruiah 2Sa 16:10 1121
thy life, and the lives of thy s 2Sa 19:5 1121
house of Saul, and his fifteen s 2Sa 19:17 1121
ye s of Zeruiah, that ye should 2Sa 19:22 1121
men of his s be delivered unto us 2Sa 21:6 1121
But the king took the two s of 2Sa 21:8 1121
the five s of Michal the daughter 2Sa 21:8 1121
which was of the s of the giant 2Sa 21:16 3211
which was of the s of the giant 2Sa 21:18 3211
But the s of Belial shall be all 2Sa 23:6
of the s of Jashen, Jonathan, 2Sa 23:32 1121
all his brethren the king's s 1Kin 1:9 1121
hath called all the s of the king 1Kin 1:19 1121
and hath called all the king's s 1Kin 1:25 1121
the s of Barzillai the Gileadite 1Kin 2:7 1121
Ahiah, the s of Shisha, scribes 1Kin 4:3 1121
Chalcol, and Darda, the s of Mahol 1Kin 4:31 1121
household among the s of Pharaoh 1Kin 11:20 1121
which were not of the s of Levi 1Kin 12:31 1121
his s came and told him all the 1Kin 13:11 1121
For his s had seen what way the 1Kin 13:12 1121
And he said unto his s, Saddle me 1Kin 13:13 1121
And he spake to his s, saying, 1Kin 13:27 1121
him, that he spake to his s 1Kin 13:31 1121
of the tribes of the s of Jacob 1Kin 18:31 1121
a certain man of the s of the 1Kin 20:35 1121
s of Belial, before him, to bear 1Kin 21:10 1121
the s of the prophets that were 2Kin 2:3 1121
the s of the prophets that were 2Kin 2:5 1121
fifty men of the s of the 2Kin 2:7 1121
when the s of the prophets which 2Kin 2:15 1121
woman of the wives of the s of 2Kin 4:1 1121
unto him my two s to be bondmen 2Kin 4:1 3206
the door upon thee and upon thy s 2Kin 4:4 1121
the door upon her and upon her s 2Kin 4:5 1121
the s of the prophets were 2Kin 4:38 1121
pottage for the s of the prophets 2Kin 4:38 1121
men of the s of the prophets 2Kin 5:22 1121
the s of the prophets said unto 2Kin 6:1 1121
of Naboth, and the blood of his s 2Kin 9:26 1121
And Ahab had seventy s in Samaria 2Kin 10:1 1121
your master's s are with you 2Kin 10:2 1121
and meetest of your master's s 2Kin 10:3 1121
heads of the men your master's s 2Kin 10:6 1121
Now the king's s, being seventy 2Kin 10:6 1121
them, that they took the king's s 2Kin 10:7 1121
brought the heads of the king's s 2Kin 10:8 1121
the king's s which were slain 2Kin 11:2 1121
Thy s shall sit on the throne of 2Kin 15:12 1121
And they caused their s and their 2Kin 17:17 1121
Sharezer his s smote him with the 2Kin 19:37 1121
of thy s that shall issue from 2Kin 20:18 1121
they slew the s of Zedekiah 2Kin 25:7 1121
The s of Japheth 1Chr 1:5 1121
And the s of Gomer 1Chr 1:6 1121
And the s of Javan 1Chr 1:7 1121
The s of Ham 1Chr 1:8 1121
And the s of Cush 1Chr 1:9 1121
And the s of Raamah 1Chr 1:9 1121
The s of Shem 1Chr 1:17 1121
And unto Eber were born two s 1Chr 1:19 1121
All these were the s of Joktan 1Chr 1:23 1121
The s of Abraham 1Chr 1:28 1121
These are the s of Ishmael 1Chr 1:31 1121
Now the s of Keturah, Abraham's 1Chr 1:32 1121
And the s of Jokshan 1Chr 1:32 1121
And the s of Midian 1Chr 1:33 1121
All these are the s of Keturah 1Chr 1:33 1121
The s of Isaac 1Chr 1:34 1121
The s of Esau 1Chr 1:35 1121
The s of Eliphaz 1Chr 1:36 1121
The s of Reuel 1Chr 1:37 1121
And the s of Seir 1Chr 1:38 1121
And the s of Lotan 1Chr 1:39 1121
The s of Shobal 1Chr 1:40 1121
And the s of Zibeon 1Chr 1:40 1121
The s of Anah 1Chr 1:41 1121
And the s of Dishon 1Chr 1:41 1121
The s of Ezer 1Chr 1:42 1121
The s of Dishan 1Chr 1:42 1121
These are the s of Israel 1Chr 2:1 1121
The s of Judah 1Chr 2:3 1121
All the s of Judah were five 1Chr 2:4 1121
The s of Pharez 1Chr 2:5 1121
And the s of Zerah 1Chr 2:6 1121
And the s of Carmi 1Chr 2:7 1121
And the s of Ethan 1Chr 2:8 1121
The s also of Hezron, that were 1Chr 2:9 1121
And the s of Zeruiah 1Chr 2:16 1121
of Jerioth: her s are these 1Chr 2:18 1121
All these belonged to the s of 1Chr 2:23 1121
the s of Jerahmeel the firstborn 1Chr 2:25 1121
the s of Ram the firstborn of 1Chr 2:27 1121
the s of Onam were, Shammai, and 1Chr 2:28 1121
And the s of Shammai 1Chr 2:28 1121
And the s of Nadab 1Chr 2:30 1121
And the s of Appaim 1Chr 2:31 1121
And the s of Ishi 1Chr 2:31 1121
the s of Jada the brother of 1Chr 2:32 1121
And the s of Jonathan 1Chr 2:33 1121
These were the s of Jerahmeel 1Chr 2:33 1121
Now Sheshan had no s, but 1Chr 2:34 1121
Now the s of Caleb the brother of 1Chr 2:42 1121
the s of Mareshah the father of 1Chr 2:42 1121
And the s of Hebron 1Chr 2:43 1121
And the s of Jahdai 1Chr 2:47 1121

These were the s of Caleb the son 1Chr 2:50 1121
father of Kirjath-jearim had s 1Chr 2:52 1121
The s of Salma 1Chr 2:54 1121
Now these were the s of David 1Chr 3:1 1121
These were all the s of David 1Chr 3:9 1121
beside the s of the concubines, 1Chr 3:9 1121
the s of Josiah were, the 1Chr 3:15 1121
And the s of Jehoiakim 1Chr 3:16 1121
And the s of Jeconiah 1Chr 3:17 1121
the s of Pedaiah were, Zerubbabel 1Chr 3:19 1121
and the s of Zerubbabel 1Chr 3:19 1121
And the s of Hananiah 1Chr 3:21 1121
the s of Rephaiah 1Chr 3:21 1121
the s of Arnan 1Chr 3:21 1121
the s of Obadiah 1Chr 3:21 1121
the s of Shechaniah 1Chr 3:21 1121
And the s of Shechaniah 1Chr 3:22 1121
and the s of Shemaiah 1Chr 3:22 1121
And the s of Neariah 1Chr 3:23 1121
the s of Elioenai were, Hodaiah, 1Chr 3:24 1121
The s of Judah 1Chr 4:1 1121
These are the s of Hur, the 1Chr 4:4 1121
These were the s of Naarah 1Chr 4:6 1121
the s of Helah were, Zereth, and 1Chr 4:7 1121
And the s of Kenaz 1Chr 4:13 1121
and the s of Othniel 1Chr 4:13 1121
the s of Caleb the son of 1Chr 4:15 1121
the s of Elah, even Kenaz 1Chr 4:15 1121
And the s of Jehaleleel 1Chr 4:16 1121
the s of Ezra were, Jether, and 1Chr 4:17 1121
these are the s of Bithiah the 1Chr 4:18 1121
the s of his wife Hodiah the 1Chr 4:19 1121
the s of Shimon were, Amnon, and 1Chr 4:20 1121
the s of Ishi were, Zoheth, and 1Chr 4:20 1121
The s of Shelah the son of Judah 1Chr 4:21 1121
The s of Simeon were, Nemuel, and 1Chr 4:24 1121
And the s of Mishma 1Chr 4:26 1121
And Shimei had sixteen s and six 1Chr 4:27 1121
of them, even of the s of Simeon 1Chr 4:42 1121
and Uzziel, the s of Ishi 1Chr 4:42 1121
Now the s of Reuben the firstborn 1Chr 5:1 1121
the s of Joseph the son of Israel 1Chr 5:1 1121
The s, I say, of Reuben the 1Chr 5:3 1121
The s of Joel 1Chr 5:4 1121
The s of Reuben, and the Gadites, 1Chr 5:18 1121
The s of Levi 1Chr 6:1 1121
And the s of Kohath 1Chr 6:2 1121
The s also of Aaron 1Chr 6:3 1121
The s of Levi 1Chr 6:16 1121
be the names of the s of Gershom 1Chr 6:17 1121
the s of Kohath were, Amram, and 1Chr 6:18 1121
The s of Merari 1Chr 6:19 1121
The s of Kohath 1Chr 6:22 1121
And the s of Elkanah 1Chr 6:25 1121
the s of Elkanah 1Chr 6:26 1121
And the s of Samuel 1Chr 6:28 1121
The s of Merari 1Chr 6:29 1121
Of the s of the Kohathites 1Chr 6:33 1121
their brethren the s of Merari 1Chr 6:44 1121
his s offered upon the altar of 1Chr 6:49 1121
And these are the s of Aaron 1Chr 6:50 1121
of the s of Aaron, of the 1Chr 6:54 1121
to the s of Aaron they gave the 1Chr 6:57 1121
unto the s of Kohath, which were 1Chr 6:61 1121
to the s of Gershom throughout 1Chr 6:62 1121
Unto the s of Merari were given 1Chr 6:63 1121
s of Kohath had cities of their 1Chr 6:66 1121
of the remnant of the s of Kohath 1Chr 6:70 1121
Unto the s of Gershom were given 1Chr 6:71 1121
Now the s of Issachar were, Tola, 1Chr 7:1 1121
And the s of Tola 1Chr 7:2 1121
And the s of Uzzi 1Chr 7:3 1121
and the s of Izrahiah 1Chr 7:3 1121
for they had many wives and s 1Chr 7:4 1121
The s of Benjamin 1Chr 7:6
And the s of Bela 1Chr 7:7 1121
And the s of Becher 1Chr 7:8 1121
All these are the s of Becher 1Chr 7:8 1121
The s also of Jediael 1Chr 7:10 1121
and the s of Bilhan 1Chr 7:10 1121
All these the s of Jediael 1Chr 7:11 1121
of Ir, and Hushim, the s of Aher 1Chr 7:12 1121
The s of Naphtali 1Chr 7:13 1121
and Shallum, the s of Bilhah 1Chr 7:13 1121
The s of Manasseh 1Chr 7:14 1121
and his s were Ulam and Rakem 1Chr 7:16 1121
And the s of Ulam 1Chr 7:17 1121
These were the s of Gilead 1Chr 7:17 1121
the s of Shemidah were, Ahian, and 1Chr 7:19 1121
And the s of Ephraim 1Chr 7:20 1121
The s of Asher 1Chr 7:30 1121
And the s of Beriah 1Chr 7:31 1121
And the s of Japhlet 1Chr 7:33 1121
And the s of Shamer 1Chr 7:34 1121
the s of his brother Helem 1Chr 7:35 1121
The s of Zophah 1Chr 7:36 1121
And the s of Jether 1Chr 7:38 1121
And the s of Ulla 1Chr 7:39 1121
the s of Bela were, Addar, and 1Chr 8:3 1121
And these are the s of Ehud 1Chr 8:6 1121
These were his s, heads of the 1Chr 8:10 1121
The s of Elpaal 1Chr 8:12 1121
Ispah, and Joha, the s of Beriah 1Chr 8:16 1121
and Jobab, the s of Elpaal 1Chr 8:18 1121
and Shimrath, the s of Shimhi 1Chr 8:21 1121
and Penuel, the s of Shashak 1Chr 8:25 1121
and Zichri, the s of Jeroham 1Chr 8:27 1121
the s of Micah were, Pithon, and 1Chr 8:35 1121
And Azel had six s, whose names 1Chr 8:38 1121
All these were the s of Azel 1Chr 8:38 1121
the s of Eshek his brother were, 1Chr 8:39 1121
the s of Ulam were mighty men of 1Chr 8:40 1121
of valour, archers, and had many s 1Chr 8:40 1121
and had many s, and sons' s 1Chr 8:40 1121

these are of the *s* of Benjamin	1Chr 8:40	1121
Asaiah the firstborn, and his *s*	1Chr 9:5	1121
And of the *s* of Zerah	1Chr 9:6	1121
And of the *s* of Benjamin	1Chr 9:7	1121
of Hashabiah, of the *s* of Merari	1Chr 9:14	1121
some of the *s* of the priests made	1Chr 9:30	1121
of the *s* of the Kohathites, were	1Chr 9:32	1121
the *s* of Micah were, Pithon, and	1Chr 9:41	1121
And Azel had six *s*, whose names	1Chr 9:44	1121
these were the *s* of Azel	1Chr 9:44	1121
hard after Saul, and after his *s*	1Chr 10:2	1121
and Malchi-shua, the *s* of Saul	1Chr 10:2	1121
So Saul died, and his three *s*	1Chr 10:6	1121
his *s* were dead, then they	1Chr 10:7	1121
his *s* fallen in mount Gilboa	1Chr 10:8	1121
of Saul, and the bodies of his *s*	1Chr 10:12	1121
The *s* of Hashem the Gizonite,	1Chr 11:34	1121
Jehiel the *s* of Hothan the	1Chr 11:44	1121
the *s* of Elnaam, and Ithmah the	1Chr 11:46	1121
the *s* of Shemaah the Gibeathite	1Chr 12:3	1121
and Pelet, the *s* of Azmaveth	1Chr 12:3	1121
the *s* of Jeroham of Gedor	1Chr 12:7	1121
These were of the *s* of Gad	1Chr 12:14	1121
and David begat more *s* and	1Chr 14:3	1121
Of the *s* of Kohath	1Chr 15:5	1121
Of the *s* of Merari	1Chr 15:6	1121
Of the *s* of Gershom	1Chr 15:7	1121
Of the *s* of Elizaphan	1Chr 15:8	1121
Of the *s* of Hebron	1Chr 15:9	1121
Of the *s* of Uzziel	1Chr 15:10	1121
of the *s* of Merari their brethren	1Chr 15:17	1121
the *s* of Jeduthun were porters	1Chr 16:42	1121
thee, which shall be of thy *s*	1Chr 17:11	1121
the *s* of David were chief about	1Chr 18:17	1121
and his four *s* with him hid	1Chr 21:20	1121
into courses among the *s* of Levi	1Chr 23:6	1121
The *s* of Laadan	1Chr 23:8	1121
The *s* of Shimei	1Chr 23:9	1121
the *s* of Shimei were, Jahath,	1Chr 23:10	1121
These four were the *s* of Shimei	1Chr 23:10	1121
Jeush and Beriah had not many *s*	1Chr 23:11	1121
The *s* of Kohath	1Chr 23:12	1121
The *s* of Amram	1Chr 23:13	1121
his *s* for ever, to burn incense	1Chr 23:13	1121
his *s* were named of the tribe of	1Chr 23:14	1121
The *s* of Moses were, Gershom, and	1Chr 23:15	1121
Of the *s* of Gershom, Shebuel was	1Chr 23:16	1121
the *s* of Eliezer were, Rehabiah	1Chr 23:17	1121
And Eliezer had none other *s*	1Chr 23:17	1121
but the *s* of Rehabiah were very	1Chr 23:17	1121
Of the *s* of Izhar	1Chr 23:18	1121
Of the *s* of Hebron	1Chr 23:19	1121
Of the *s* of Uzziel	1Chr 23:20	1121
The *s* of Merari	1Chr 23:21	1121
The *s* of Mahli	1Chr 23:21	1121
And Eleazar died, and had no *s*	1Chr 23:22	1121
brethren the *s* of Kish took them	1Chr 23:22	1121
The *s* of Mushi	1Chr 23:23	1121
These were the *s* of Levi after	1Chr 23:24	1121
s of Aaron for the service of the	1Chr 23:28	1121
the charge of the *s* of Aaron	1Chr 23:32	1121
the divisions of the *s* of Aaron	1Chr 24:1	1121
The *s* of Aaron	1Chr 24:1	1121
both Zadok of the *s* of Eleazar	1Chr 24:3	1121
and Ahimelech of the *s* of Ithamar	1Chr 24:3	1121
more chief men found of the *s* of	1Chr 24:4	1121
Eleazar than of the *s* of Ithamar	1Chr 24:4	1121
Among the *s* of Eleazar there were	1Chr 24:4	1121
eight among the *s* of Ithamar	1Chr 24:4	1121
of God, were of the *s* of Eleazar	1Chr 24:5	1121
Eleazar, and of the *s* of Ithamar	1Chr 24:5	1121
the rest of the *s* of Levi were	1Chr 24:20	1121
Of the *s* of Amram	1Chr 24:20	1121
of the *s* of Shubael	1Chr 24:20	1121
of the *s* of Rehabiah, the first	1Chr 24:21	1121
of the *s* of Shelomoth	1Chr 24:22	1121
And the *s* of Hebron	1Chr 24:23	1121
Of the *s* of Uzziel	1Chr 24:24	1121
of the *s* of Michah	1Chr 24:24	1121
of the *s* of Isshiah	1Chr 24:25	1121
The *s* of Merari were Mahli and	1Chr 24:26	1121
the *s* of Jaaziah	1Chr 24:26	1121
The *s* of Merari by Jaaziah	1Chr 24:27	1121
Mahli came Eleazar, who had no *s*	1Chr 24:28	1121
The *s* also of Mushi	1Chr 24:30	1121
These were the *s* of the Levites	1Chr 24:30	1121
the *s* of Aaron in the presence of	1Chr 24:31	1121
to the service of the *s* of Asaph	1Chr 25:1	1121
Of the *s* of Asaph	1Chr 25:2	1121
the *s* of Asaph under the hands of	1Chr 25:2	1121
the *s* of Jeduthun	1Chr 25:3	1121
the *s* of Heman	1Chr 25:4	1121
All these were the *s* of Heman the	1Chr 25:5	1121
And God gave to Heman fourteen *s*	1Chr 25:5	1121
his brethren and *s* were twelve	1Chr 25:9	1121
The third to Zaccur, he, his *s*	1Chr 25:10	1121
The fourth to Izri, he, his *s*	1Chr 25:11	1121
The fifth to Nethaniah, he, his *s*	1Chr 25:12	1121
The sixth to Bukkiah, he, his *s*	1Chr 25:13	1121
seventh to Jesharelah, he, his *s*	1Chr 25:14	1121
The eighth to Jeshaiah, he, his *s*	1Chr 25:15	1121
The ninth to Mattaniah, he, his *s*	1Chr 25:16	1121
The tenth to Shimei, he, his *s*	1Chr 25:17	1121
eleventh to Azareel, he, his *s*	1Chr 25:18	1121
twelfth to Hashabiah, he, his *s*	1Chr 25:19	1121
thirteenth to Shubael, he, his *s*	1Chr 25:20	1121
to Mattithiah, he, his *s*, and his	1Chr 25:21	1121
fifteenth to Jeremoth, he, his *s*	1Chr 25:22	1121
sixteenth to Hananiah, he, his *s*	1Chr 25:23	1121
to Joshbekashah, he, his *s*	1Chr 25:24	1121
eighteenth to Hanani, he, his *s*	1Chr 25:25	1121
nineteenth to Mallothi, he, his *s*	1Chr 25:26	1121
twentieth to Eliathah, he, his *s*	1Chr 25:27	1121
and twentieth to Hothir, he, his *s*	1Chr 25:28	1121
twentieth to Giddalti, he, his *s*	1Chr 25:29	1121
twentieth to Mahazioth, he, his *s*	1Chr 25:30	1121
to Romamti-ezer, he, his *s*	1Chr 25:31	1121
son of Kore, of the *s* of Asaph	1Chr 26:1	1121
the *s* of Meshelemiah were,	1Chr 26:2	1121
Moreover the *s* of Obed-edom were,	1Chr 26:4	1121
unto Shemaiah his son were *s* born	1Chr 26:6	1121
The *s* of Shemaiah	1Chr 26:7	1121
All these of the *s* of Obed-edom	1Chr 26:8	1121
they and their *s* and their brethren	1Chr 26:8	1121
And Meshelemiah had *s* and brethren,	1Chr 26:9	1121
of the children of Merari, had *s*	1Chr 26:10	1121
all the *s* and brethren of Hosah	1Chr 26:11	1121
to his *s* the house of Asuppim	1Chr 26:15	1121
the porters among the *s* of Kore	1Chr 26:19	1121
of Kore, and among the *s* of Merari	1Chr 26:19	1121
As concerning the *s* of Laadan	1Chr 26:21	1121
the *s* of the Gershonite Laadan,	1Chr 26:21	1121
The *s* of Jehieli	1Chr 26:22	1121
his *s* were for the outward	1Chr 26:29	1121
of Hachmoni was with the king's *s*	1Chr 27:32	1121
of the king, and of his *s*, with	1Chr 28:1	1121
among the *s* of my father he liked	1Chr 28:4	1121
And of all my *s*, (for the LORD	1Chr 28:5	1121
for the LORD hath given me many *s*	1Chr 28:5	1121
all the *s* likewise of king David,	1Chr 29:24	1121
Heman, of Jeduthun, with their *s*	2Chr 5:12	1121
his *s* had cast them off from	2Chr 11:14	1121
and begat twenty and eight *s*	2Chr 11:21	1121
to his *s* by a covenant of salt	2Chr 13:5	1121
in the hand of the *s* of David	2Chr 13:8	1121
the *s* of Aaron, and the Levites,	2Chr 13:9	1121
are the *s* of Aaron, and the	2Chr 13:10	1121
wives, and begat twenty and two *s*	2Chr 13:21	1121
a Levite of the *s* of Asaph	2Chr 20:14	1121
had brethren the *s* of Jehoshaphat	2Chr 21:2	1121
all these were the *s* of	2Chr 21:2	1121
light to him and to his *s* for ever	2Chr 21:7	1121
and his *s* also, and his wives	2Chr 21:17	1121
Jehoahaz, the youngest of his *s*	2Chr 21:17	1121
the *s* of the brethren of Ahaziah,	2Chr 22:8	1121
the king's *s* that were slain	2Chr 22:11	1121
LORD hath said of the *s* of David	2Chr 23:3	1121
his *s* anointed him, and said, God	2Chr 23:11	1121
and he begat *s* and daughters	2Chr 24:3	1121
For the *s* of Athaliah, that	2Chr 24:7	1121
of the *s* of Jehoiada the priest	2Chr 24:25	1121
Now concerning his *s*, and the	2Chr 24:27	1121
but to the priests the *s* of Aaron	2Chr 26:18	1121
two hundred thousand, women, *s*	2Chr 28:8	1121
fallen by the sword, and our *s*	2Chr 29:9	1121
My *s*, be not now negligent	2Chr 29:11	1121
of the *s* of the Kohathites	2Chr 29:12	1121
of the *s* of Merari, Kish the son	2Chr 29:12	1121
And of the *s* of Elizaphan	2Chr 29:13	1121
and of the *s* of Asaph	2Chr 29:13	1121
And of the *s* of Heman	2Chr 29:14	1121
and of the *s* of Jeduthun	2Chr 29:14	1121
he commanded the priests the *s* of	2Chr 29:21	1121
ones, their wives, and their *s*	2Chr 31:18	1121
Also of the *s* of Aaron the	2Chr 31:19	1121
the sepulchres of the *s* of David	2Chr 32:33	1121
the Levites, of the *s* of Merari	2Chr 34:12	1121
of the *s* of the Kohathites, to	2Chr 34:12	1121
the *s* of Aaron were busied in	2Chr 35:14	1121
and for the priests the *s* of Aaron	2Chr 35:14	1121
the singers the *s* of Asaph were	2Chr 35:15	1121
his *s* until the reign of the	2Chr 36:20	1121
Then stood Jeshua with his *s*	Ezr 3:9	1121
and his brethren, Kadmiel and his *s*	Ezr 3:9	1121
the *s* of Judah, together, to set	Ezr 3:9	1121
the *s* of Henadad, with their *s*	Ezr 3:9	1121
the Levites the *s* of Asaph with	Ezr 3:10	1121
the life of the king, and of his *s*	Ezr 6:10	1123
the realm of the king and his *s*	Ezr 7:23	1123
Of the *s* of Phinehas	Ezr 8:2	1121
of the *s* of Ithamar	Ezr 8:2	1121
of the *s* of David	Ezr 8:2	1121
Of the *s* of Shechaniah, of the	Ezr 8:3	1121
Shechaniah, of the *s* of Pharosh	Ezr 8:3	1121
Of the *s* of Pahath-moab	Ezr 8:4	1121
Of the *s* of Shechaniah	Ezr 8:5	1121
Of the *s* also of Adin	Ezr 8:6	1121
And of the *s* of Elam	Ezr 8:7	1121
And of the *s* of Shephatiah	Ezr 8:8	1121
Of the *s* of Joab	Ezr 8:9	1121
And of the *s* of Shelomith	Ezr 8:10	1121
And of the *s* of Bebai	Ezr 8:11	1121
And of the *s* of Azgad	Ezr 8:12	1121
And of the last *s* of Adonikam	Ezr 8:13	1121
Of the *s* also of Bigvai	Ezr 8:14	1121
found there none of the *s* of Levi	Ezr 8:15	1121
of the *s* of Mahli, the son of	Ezr 8:18	1121
and Sherebiah, with his *s* and his	Ezr 8:18	1121
him Jeshaiah of the *s* of Merari	Ezr 8:19	1121
his brethren and their *s*	Ezr 8:19	1121
for themselves, and for their *s*	Ezr 9:2	1121
not your daughters unto their *s*	Ezr 9:12	1121
take their daughters unto your *s*	Ezr 9:12	1121
of Jehiel, one of the *s* of Elam	Ezr 10:2	1121
among the *s* of the priests there	Ezr 10:18	1121
of the *s* of Jeshua the son of	Ezr 10:18	1121
And of the *s* of Immer	Ezr 10:20	1121
And of the *s* of Harim	Ezr 10:21	1121
And of the *s* of Pashur	Ezr 10:22	1121
of the *s* of Parosh	Ezr 10:25	1121
And of the *s* of Elam	Ezr 10:26	1121
And of the *s* of Zattu	Ezr 10:27	1121
Of the *s* also of Bebai	Ezr 10:28	1121
And of the *s* of Bani	Ezr 10:29	1121
And of the *s* of Pahath-moab	Ezr 10:30	1121
And of the *s* of Harim	Ezr 10:31	1121
Of the *s* of Hashum	Ezr 10:33	1121
Of the *s* of Bani	Ezr 10:34	1121
Of the *s* of Nebo	Ezr 10:43	1121
gate did the *s* of Hassenaah build	Neh 3:3	1121
fight for your brethren, your *s*	Neh 4:14	1121
there were that said, We, our *s*	Neh 5:2	1121
lo, we bring into bondage our *s*	Neh 5:5	1121
Binnui of the *s* of Henadad	Neh 10:9	1121
law of God, their wives, their *s*	Neh 10:28	1121
take their daughters for our *s*	Neh 10:30	1121
Also the firstborn of our *s*	Neh 10:36	1121
All the *s* of Perez that dwelt at	Neh 11:6	1121
And these are the *s* of Benjamin	Neh 11:7	1121
Of the *s* of Asaph, the singers	Neh 11:22	1121
The *s* of Levi, the chief of the	Neh 12:23	1121
the *s* of the singers gathered	Neh 12:28	1121
of the priests' *s* with trumpets	Neh 12:35	1121
give your daughters unto their *s*	Neh 13:25	1121
take their daughters unto your *s*	Neh 13:25	1121
And one of the *s* of Joiada	Neh 13:28	1121
The ten *s* of Haman the son of	Est 9:10	1121
the palace, and the ten *s* of Haman	Est 9:12	1121
let Haman's ten *s* be hanged upon	Est 9:13	1121
and they hanged Haman's ten *s*	Est 9:14	1121
his *s* should be hanged on the	Est 9:25	1121
there were born unto him seven *s*	Job 1:2	1121
his *s* went and feasted in their	Job 1:4	1121
It may be that my *s* have sinned	Job 1:5	1121
when the *s* of God came to present	Job 1:6	1121
And there was a day when his *s*	Job 1:13	1121
came also another, and said, Thy *s*	Job 1:18	1121
when the *s* of God came to present	Job 2:1	1121
His *s* come to honour, and he	Job 14:21	1121
all the *s* of God shouted for joy	Job 38:7	1121
thou guide Arcturus with his *s*	Job 38:32	1121
He had also seven *s* and three	Job 42:13	1121
and saw his *s*, and his sons' *s*	Job 42:16	1121
O ye *s* of men, how long will ye	Ps 4:2	1121
trust in thee before the *s* of men	Ps 31:19	1121
he beholdeth all the *s* of men	Ps 33:13	1121
Maschil, for the *s* of Korah	Ps 42:*t*	1121
chief Musician for the *s* of Korah	Ps 44:*t*	1121
for the *s* of Korah, A Maschil, A	Ps 45:*t*	1121
chief Musician for the *s* of Korah	Ps 46:*t*	1121
A Psalm for the *s* of Korah	Ps 47:*t*	1121
Song and Psalm for the *s* of Korah	Ps 48:*t*	1121
A Psalm for the *s* of Korah	Ps 49:*t*	1121
set on fire, even the *s* of men	Ps 57:4	1121
ye judge uprightly, O ye *s* of men	Ps 58:1	1121
people, the *s* of Jacob and Joseph	Ps 77:15	1121
A Psalm for the *s* of Korah	Ps 84:*t*	1121
A Psalm for the *s* of Korah	Ps 85:*t*	1121
Psalm or Song for the *s* of Korah	Ps 87:*t*	1121
A Song or Psalm for the *s* of	Ps 88:*t*	1121
who among the *s* of the mighty can	Ps 89:6	1121
Yea, they sacrificed their *s*	Ps 106:37	1121
blood, even the blood of their *s*	Ps 106:38	1121
That our *s* may be as plants grown	Ps 144:12	1121
To make known to the *s* of men his	Ps 145:12	1121
and my voice is to the *s* of man	Prov 8:4	1121
delights were with the *s* of men	Prov 8:31	1121
to the *s* of man to be exercised	Eccl 1:13	1121
was that good for the *s* of men	Eccl 2:3	1121
and the delights of the *s* of men	Eccl 2:8	1121
which God hath given to the *s* of	Eccl 3:10	1121
the estate of the *s* of men	Eccl 3:18	1121
the *s* of men befalleth beasts	Eccl 3:19	1121
therefore the heart of the *s* of	Eccl 8:11	1121
also the heart of the *s* of men is	Eccl 9:3	1121
so are the *s* of men snared in an	Eccl 9:12	1121
so is my beloved among the *s*	Song 2:3	1121
Sharezer his *s* smote him with the	Is 37:38	1121
of thy *s* that shall issue from	Is 39:7	1121
bring my *s* from far, and my	Is 43:6	1121
of things to come concerning my *s*	Is 45:11	1121
shall bring thy *s* in their arms	Is 49:22	1121
the *s* whom she hath brought forth	Is 51:18	1121
the *s* that she hath brought up	Is 51:18	1121
Thy *s* have fainted, they lie at	Is 51:20	1121
his form more than the *s* of men	Is 52:14	1121
place and a name better than of *s*	Is 56:5	1121
Also the *s* of the stranger, that	Is 56:6	1121
ye *s* of the sorceress, the seed	Is 57:3	1121
thy *s* shall come from far, and thy	Is 60:4	1121
first, to bring thy *s* from far	Is 60:9	1121
the *s* of strangers shall build up	Is 60:10	1121
The *s* also of them that afflicted	Is 60:14	1121
the *s* of the alien shall be your	Is 61:5	1121
virgin, so shall thy *s* marry thee	Is 62:5	1121
the *s* of the stranger shall not	Is 62:8	1121
flocks and their herds, their *s*	Jer 3:24	1121
and thy bread, which thy *s*	Jer 5:17	1121
the *s* together shall fall upon	Jer 6:21	1121
son of Hinnom, to burn their *s*	Jer 7:31	1121
their *s* and their daughters shall	Jer 11:22	1121
the *s* together, saith the LORD	Jer 13:14	1121
them, their wives, nor their *s*	Jer 14:16	1121
neither shalt thou have *s* or	Jer 16:2	1121
saith the LORD concerning the *s*	Jer 16:3	1121
to burn their *s* with fire for	Jer 19:5	1121
them to eat the flesh of their *s*	Jer 19:9	1121
Take ye wives, and beget *s*	Jer 29:6	1121
and take wives for your *s*, and give	Jer 29:6	1121
to husbands, that they may bear *s*	Jer 29:6	1121
upon all the ways of the *s* of men	Jer 32:19	1121
son of Hinnom, to cause their *s*	Jer 32:35	1121
and his brethren, and all his *s*	Jer 35:3	1121
the chamber of the *s* of Hanan	Jer 35:4	1121
I set before the *s* of the house	Jer 35:5	1121
neither ye, nor your *s* for ever	Jer 35:6	1121
our days, we, our wives, our *s*	Jer 35:8	1121
commanded his *s* not to drink wine	Jer 35:14	1121
Because the *s* of Jonadab the son	Jer 35:16	1121
s of Zedekiah in Riblah before	Jer 39:6	1121
and Jonathan the *s* of Kareah	Jer 40:8	1121
the *s* of Ephai the Netophathite,	Jer 40:8	1121

S

for thy s are taken captives, and Jer 48:46 1121
Hath Israel no s Jer 49:1 1121
the s of Zedekiah before his eyes Jer 52:10 1121
The precious s of Zion, Lam 4:2 1121
eat the s in the midst of thee Eze 5:10 1121
the s shall eat their fathers Eze 5:10 1121
deliver neither s nor daughters Eze 14:16 1121
deliver neither s nor daughters Eze 14:18 1121
shall be brought forth, both s Eze 14:22 1121
Moreover thou hast taken thy s Eze 16:20 1121
when ye make your s to pass Eze 20:31 1121
and they were mine, and they bare s Eze 23:4 1121
they took her s and her daughters, Eze 23:10 1121
they shall take thy s and thy Eze 23:25 1121
and have also caused their s Eze 23:37 1121
they shall slay their s and their Eze 23:47 1121
and your s and your daughters whom Eze 24:21 1121
they set their minds, their s Eze 24:25 1121
s of Zadok among the s of Levi Eze 40:46 1121
the s of Zadok, that kept the Eze 44:15 1121
give a gift unto any of his s Eze 46:16 1121
but he shall give his s Eze 46:18 1121
are sanctified of the s of Zadok Eze 48:11 1121
he was driven from the s of men Dan 5:21 1123
of the s of men touched my lips Dan 10:16 1121
But his s shall be stirred up, and Dan 11:10 1121
Ye are the s of the living God Hos 1:10 1121
withered away from the s of men Joel 1:12 1121
and your s and your daughters shall Joel 2:28 1121
And I will sell your s and your Joel 3:8 1121
raised up of your s for prophets Amos 2:11 1121
an harlot in the city, and thy s Amos 7:17 1121
man, nor waiteth for the s of men Mic 5:7 1121
thy s, O Zion, against thy s Zec 9:13 1121
and he shall purify the s of Levi Mal 3:3 1121
therefore ye s of Jacob are not Mal 3:6 1121
of Zebedee's children with her s Mt 20:20 *5207*
Grant that these my two s may sit Mt 20:21 *5207*
A certain man had two s Mt 21:28 *5043*
the two s of Zebedee, and began to Mt 26:37 *5207*
which is, The s of thunder Mk 3:17 *5207*
be forgiven unto the s of men Mk 3:28 *5207*
the s of Zebedee, come unto him, Mk 10:35 *5207*
the s of Zebedee, which were Lk 5:10 *5207*
by whom do your s cast them out Lk 11:19 *5207*
he said, A certain man had two s Lk 15:11 *5207*
he power to become the s of God Jn 1:12 *5043*
the s of Zebedee, and two other of Jn 21:2
and your s and your daughters shall Acts 2:17 *5207*
for a sum of money of the s of Acts 7:16 *5207*
of Madian, where he begat two s Acts 7:29 *5207*
there were seven s of one Sceva Acts 19:14 *5207*
of God, they are the s of God Rom 8:14 *5207*
the manifestation of the s of God Rom 8:19 *5207*
but as my beloved s I warn you 1Cor 4:14 *5043*
unto you, and ye shall be my s 2Cor 6:18 *5207*
might receive the adoption of s Gal 4:5 *5206*
And because ye are s, God hath Gal 4:6 *5207*
written, that Abraham had two s Gal 4:22 *5207*
not made known unto the s of men Eph 3:5 *5207*
the s of God, without rebuke, in Phil 2:15 *5043*
in bringing many s unto glory Heb 2:10 *5207*
they that are of the s of Levi Heb 7:5 *5207*
blessed both the s of Joseph Heb 11:21 *5207*
God dealeth with you as with s Heb 12:7 *5207*
then are ye bastards, and not s Heb 12:8 *5207*
we should be called the s of God 1Jn 3:1 *5043*
Beloved, now are we the s of God 1Jn 3:2 *5043*

SONS'
wife, and thy s wives with thee Gen 6:18 1121
his s wives with him, into the Gen 7:7 1121
sons, and thy s wives with thee Gen 8:16 1121
his wife, and his s wives with him Gen 8:18 1121
sons, and his s sons with him, his Gen 46:7 1121
his s daughters, and all his seed Gen 46:7 1121
loins, besides Jacob's s wives Gen 46:26 1121
sons, and his s garments with him Ex 29:21 1121
his s by a statute for ever from Ex 29:28 1121
of Aaron shall be his s after him Ex 29:29 1121
his s garments, to minister in Ex 39:41 1121
shall be Aaron's and his s Lev 2:3 1121
shall be Aaron's and his s Lev 2:10 1121
breast shall be Aaron's and his s Lev 7:31 1121
hands, and upon his s hands Lev 8:27 1121
upon his s garments with him Lev 8:30 1121
sons, and his s garments with him Lev 8:30 1121
it is thy due, and thy s due Lev 10:13 1121
for they be thy due, and thy s due Lev 10:14 1121
thy s with thee, by a statute for Lev 10:15 1121
And it shall be Aaron's and his s Lev 24:9 1121
them thy sons, and thy s sons Deut 4:9 1121
s sons, an hundred and fifty 1Chr 8:40 1121
his s sons, even four generations Job 42:16 1121
thereof shall be his s Eze 46:16 1121
shall be his s for them Eze 46:17 1121

SOON
as s as he had left communing Gen 18:33 834
as s as Isaac had made an end of Gen 27:30 834
As s as the morning was light, Gen 44:3
it that ye are come so s to day Ex 2:18 4116
As s as I am gone out of the city Ex 9:29
as s as he came nigh unto the Ex 32:19 834
that ye shall s utterly perish Deut 4:26 4116
as s as they which pursued after Josh 2:7 834
as s as we had heard these things Josh 2:11
as s as the soles of the feet of Josh 3:13
they ran as s as he had stretched Josh 8:19
as s as the sun was down, Joshua Josh 8:29
as s as Gideon was dead, that the Judg 8:33 834
as s as the sun is up, thou shalt Judg 9:33
As s as ye be come into the city, 1Sa 9:13
that as s as he had made an end 1Sa 13:10
as s as the lad was gone, David 1Sa 20:41
as s as ye be up early in the 1Sa 29:10
as s as David had made an end of 2Sa 6:18
as s as he had made an end of 2Sa 13:36
As s as ye hear the sound of the 2Sa 15:10
as s as they hear, they shall be 2Sa 22:45
as s as he sat on his throne, 1Kin 16:11
as s as I am gone from thee, that 1Kin 18:12
as s as thou art departed from me 1Kin 20:36
as s as he was departed from him, 1Kin 20:36
Now as s as this letter cometh to 2Kin 10:2
as s as he had made an end of 2Kin 10:25
as s as the kingdom was confirmed 2Kin 14:5 834
as s as the commandment came 2Chr 31:5
my maker would s take me away Job 32:22 4592
As s as they hear of me, they Ps 18:44
For they shall s be cut down like Ps 37:2 4120
go astray as s as they be born Ps 58:3
Ethiopia shall s stretch out her Ps 68:31 7323
I should s have subdued their Ps 81:14 4592
for it is s cut off, and we fly Ps 90:10 2440
They s forgat his works Ps 106:13 4116
He that is s angry dealeth Prov 14:17 7116
for as s as Zion travailed, she Is 66:8 1571
as s as she saw them with her Eze 23:16 4758
How s is the fig tree withered Mt 21:20 *3916*
And as s as he had spoken, Mk 1:42
As s as Jesus heard the word that Mk 5:36 *2112*
as s as ye be entered into it, ye Mk 11:2 *2112*
as s as he was come, he goeth Mk 14:45
that, as s as the days of his Lk 1:23
For, lo, as s as the voice of thy Lk 1:44
as s as it was sprung up, it Lk 8:6
But as s as this thy son was come Lk 15:30 *3753*
as s as it was day, the elders of Lk 22:66
as s as he knew that he belonged Lk 23:7
as s as she heard that Jesus was Jn 11:20
As s as she heard that, she arose Jn 11:29
but as s as she is delivered of Jn 16:21 *3752*
As s then as he had said unto Jn 18:6
As s then as they were come to Jn 21:9
as s as I was sent for Acts 10:29
Now as s as it was day, there was Acts 12:18 *1096*
I marvel that ye are so s removed Gal 1:6 *5030*
so s as I shall see how it will Phil 2:23
That ye be not s shaken in mind 2Th 2:2 *5030*
not s angry, not given to wine, Titus 1:7 *3711*
as s as I had eaten it, my belly Rev 10:10 *3753*
her child as s as it was born Rev 12:4 *3752*

SOONER
I may be restored to you the s Heb 13:19 *5032*
For the sun is no s risen with a Jas 1:11

SOOTHSAYER
also the son of Beor, the s Josh 13:22 7080

SOOTHSAYERS
are s like the Philistines, and Is 2:6 6049
astrologers, the magicians, the s Dan 2:27 1505
the Chaldeans, and the s Dan 4:7 1505
the Chaldeans, and the s Dan 5:7 1505
astrologers, Chaldeans, and s Dan 5:11 1505
and thou shalt have no more s Mic 5:12 6049

SOOTHSAYING
her masters much gain by s Acts 16:16 *3132*

SOP
it is, to whom I shall give a s Jn 13:26 *5596*
And when he had dipped the s Jn 13:26 *5596*
after the s Satan entered into Jn 13:27 *5596*
the s went immediately out Jn 13:30 *5596*

SOPATER (*so'-pa-ter*) See SOSIPATER. *A Christian from Berea.*
him into Asia S of Berea Acts 20:4 *4986*

SOPE
with nitre, and take thee much s Jer 2:22 1287
fire, and like fullers' s Mal 3:2 1287

SOPHERETH (*so-fe'-reth*) *A family of exiles.*
of Sotai, the children of S Ezr 2:55 5618
of Sotai, the children of S Neh 7:57 5618

SORCERER
Paphos, they found a certain s Acts 13:6 *3097*
But Elymas the s (for so is his Acts 13:8 *3097*

SORCERERS
also called the wise men and the s Ex 7:11 3784
to your enchanters, nor to your s Jer 27:9 3786
and the astrologers, and the s Dan 2:2 3784
be a swift witness against the s Mal 3:5 3784
murderers, and whoremongers, and s Rev 21:8 *5332*
For without are dogs, and s Rev 22:15 *5333*

SORCERESS
near hither, ye sons of the s Is 57:3 6049

SORCERIES
for the multitude of thy s Is 47:9 3785
and with the multitude of thy s Is 47:12 3785
time he had bewitched them with s Acts 8:11 *3095*
of their murders, nor of their s Rev 9:21 *5331*
for by thy s were all nations Rev 18:23 *5331*

SORCERY
in the same city used s, and Acts 8:9 *3096*

SORE
And they pressed s upon the man Gen 19:9 3966
and the men were s afraid Gen 20:8 3966
because thou s longedst after thy Gen 31:30
the third day, when they were s Gen 34:25 3510
the famine waxed s in the land of Gen 41:56 2388
the famine was so s in all lands Gen 41:57 2388
And the famine was s in the land Gen 43:1 3515
for the famine is s in the land Gen 47:4 3515
for the famine was very s Gen 47:13 3515
a great and very s lamentation Gen 50:10 3515
and they were s afraid Ex 14:10 3966
bald forehead, a white reddish s Lev 13:42 5061
if the rising of the s be white Lev 13:43 5061
Moab was s afraid of the people, Num 22:3 3966
signs and wonders, great and s Deut 6:22 7451
with a s botch that cannot be Deut 28:35 7451
and s sicknesses, and of long Deut 28:59 7451
therefore we were s afraid of our Josh 9:24 3966
so that Israel was s distressed Judg 10:9 3966
her, because she lay s upon him Judg 14:17
he was s athirst, and called on Judg 15:18 3966
all Israel, and the battle was s Judg 20:34 3513
lifted up their voices, and wept s Judg 21:2
her adversary also provoked her s 1Sa 1:6 3708
prayed unto the LORD, and wept s 1Sa 1:10
for his hand is s upon us 1Sa 5:7 7185
there was s war against the 1Sa 14:52 2389
fled from him, and were s afraid 1Sa 17:24 3966
was s afraid of Achish the king 1Sa 21:12 3966
Saul answered, I am s distressed 1Sa 28:15 3966
was s afraid, because of the 1Sa 28:20 3966
and saw that he was s troubled 1Sa 28:21 3966
And the battle went s against Saul 1Sa 31:3 3513
he was s wounded of the archers 1Sa 31:3 3966
for he was s afraid 1Sa 31:4 3966
was a very s battle that day 2Sa 2:17 7188
and all his servants wept very s 2Sa 13:36 1419
and his sickness was so s, that 1Kin 17:17 2389
there was a s famine in Samaria 1Kin 18:2 2389
that the battle was too s for him 2Kin 3:26 2388
was s troubled for this thing 2Kin 6:11
And Hezekiah wept s 2Kin 20:3 1419
And the battle went s against Saul 1Chr 10:3 3513
for he was s afraid 1Chr 10:4 3966
whatsoever s or whatsoever 2Chr 6:28 5061
every one shall know his own s 2Chr 6:29 5061
so he died of s diseases 2Chr 21:19 7451
transgressed s against the LORD 2Chr 28:19
for I am s wounded 2Chr 35:23 3966
for the people wept very s Ezr 10:1
Then I was very s afraid, Neh 2:2 7235
And it grieved me s Neh 13:8 3966
smote Job with s boils from the Job 2:7 7451
For he maketh s, and bindeth up Job 5:18 3510
and vex them in his s displeasure Ps 2:5
My soul is also s vexed Ps 6:3 3966
enemies be ashamed and s vexed Ps 6:10 3966
in me, and thy hand presseth me s Ps 38:2
I am feeble and s broken Ps 38:8
my friends stand aloof from my s Ps 38:11 5061
Though thou hast s broken us in Ps 44:19
My heart is s pained within me Ps 55:4
s troubles, shalt quicken me Ps 71:20 7451
my s ran in the night, and ceased Ps 77:2 3027
Thou hast thrust s at me that I Ps 118:13
The LORD hath chastened me s Ps 118:18
this s travail hath God given to Eccl 1:13 7451
vanity, yea, it is a s travail Eccl 4:8 7451
There is a s evil which I have Eccl 5:13 2470
And this also is a s evil, that in Eccl 5:16 2470
In that day the LORD with his s Is 27:1 7186
And Hezekiah wept s Is 38:3 1419
like bears, and mourn s like doves Is 59:11
Be not wroth very s, O LORD, Is 64:9 3966
thy peace, and afflict us very s Is 64:12 3966
and mine eye shall weep s, and run Jer 13:17
but weep s for him that goeth Jer 22:10
Your mother shall be s confounded Jer 50:12 3966
the famine was s in the city Jer 52:6 2388
She weepeth s in the night, and Lam 1:2
Mine enemies chased me s, like a Lam 3:52
four s judgments upon Jerusalem Eze 14:21 7451
sharpened to make a s slaughter Eze 21:10
and their kings shall be s afraid Eze 27:35 8178
was s displeased with himself, and Dan 6:14 7690
you, even with a s destruction Mic 2:10 4834
The LORD hath been s displeased Zec 1:2
I am very s displeased with the Zec 1:15
on their face, and were s afraid Mt 17:6 *4970*
for he is lunatick, and s vexed Mt 17:15 *2560*
they were s displeased, Mt 21:15 *23*
they were s amazed in themselves Mk 6:51 *3029*
for they were s afraid Mk 9:6 *1630*
the spirit cried, and rent him s Mk 9:26 *4183*
and John, and began to be s amazed Mk 14:33 *1568*
and they were s afraid Lk 2:9 *3173*
And they all wept s, and fell on Acts 20:37 *2425*
grievous s upon the men which had Rev 16:2 *1668*

SOREK (*so'-rek*) *A valley between Ashkelon and Gaza.*
loved a woman in the valley of S Judg 16:4 7796

SORELY
The archers have s grieved him Gen 49:23 4843
so shall they be s pained at the Is 23:5

SORER
Of how much s punishment, suppose Heb 10:29 *5501*

SORES
and bruises, and putrifying s Is 1:6 4347
was laid at his gate, full of s Lk 16:20 *1669*
the dogs came and licked his s Lk 16:21 *1668*
because of their pains and their s Rev 16:11 *1668*

SORROW
I will greatly multiply thy s Gen 3:16 6093
in s thou shalt bring forth Gen 3:16 6089
in s shalt thou eat of it all the Gen 3:17 6093
my gray hairs with s to the grave Gen 42:38 3015
my gray hairs with s to the grave Gen 44:29 7451
our father with s to the grave Gen 44:31 3015
s shall take hold on the Ex 15:14 2427
the eyes, and cause s of heart Lev 26:16 1727
and failing of eyes, and s of mind Deut 28:65 1671

saying, Because I bare him with *s* … 1Chr 4:9 6090
is nothing else but *s* of heart … Neh 2:2 7455
turned unto them from *s* to joy … Est 9:22 3015
womb, nor hid *s* from mine eyes … Job 3:10 5999
yea, I would harden myself in *s* … Job 6:10 2427
eye also is dim by reason of *s* … Job 17:7 3708
s is turned into joy before him … Job 41:22 1670
having *s* in my heart daily … Ps 13:2 3015
my *s* is continually before me … Ps 38:17 4341
and my *s* was stirred … Ps 39:2 3511
also and *s* are in the midst of it … Ps 55:10 5999
yet is their strength labour and *s* … Ps 90:10 205
oppression, affliction, and *s* … Ps 107:39 3015
I found trouble and *s* … Ps 116:3 3015
winketh with the eye causeth *s* … Prov 10:10 6094
rich, and he addeth no *s* with it … Prov 10:22 6089
but by *s* of the heart the spirit … Prov 15:13 6094
a fool doeth it to his *s* … Prov 17:21 8424
who hath *s* … Prov 23:29 17
increaseth knowledge increaseth *s* … Eccl 1:18 4341
in darkness, and he hath much *s* … Eccl 5:17 3708
S is better than laughter … Eccl 7:3 3708
Therefore remove *s* from thy heart … Eccl 11:10 3708
the land, behold darkness and *s* … Is 5:30 6862
shall give thee rest from thy *s* … Is 14:3 6090
day of grief and of desperate *s* … Is 17:11 3511
and there shall be heaviness and *s* … Is 29:2 592
obtain joy and gladness, and *s* … Is 35:10 3015
ye shall lie down in *s* … Is 50:11 4620
and *s* and mourning shall flee away … Is 51:11 3015
but ye shall cry for *s* of heart … Is 65:14 3511
I would comfort myself against *s* … Jer 8:18 3015
of the womb to see labour and *s* … Jer 20:18 3015
thy *s* is incurable for the … Jer 30:15 4341
they shall not *s* any more at all … Jer 31:12 1669
and make them rejoice from their *s* … Jer 31:13 3015
the LORD hath added grief to my *s* … Jer 45:3 4341
there is *s* on the sea … Jer 49:23 1674
And the land shall tremble and *s* … Jer 51:29 2342
be any *s* like unto my *s* … Lam 1:12 4341
you, all people, and behold my *s* … Lam 1:18 4341
Give them *s* of heart, thy curse … Lam 3:65 4044
be filled with drunkenness and *s* … Eze 23:33 3015
they shall *s* a little for the … Hos 8:10 2490
he found them sleeping for *s* … Lk 22:45 3077
you, *s* hath filled your heart … Jn 16:6 3077
but your *s* shall be turned into … Jn 16:20 3077
when she is in travail hath *s* … Jn 16:21 3077
And ye now therefore have *s* … Jn 16:22 3077
and continual *s* in my heart … Rom 9:2 3601
I should have *s* from them of whom … 2Cor 2:3 3077
be swallowed up with overmuch *s* … 2Cor 2:7 3077
For godly *s* worketh repentance to … 2Cor 7:10 3077
but the *s* of the world worketh … 2Cor 7:10 3077
lest I should have *s* upon *s* … Phil 2:27 3077
which are asleep, that ye *s* not … 1Th 4:13 3076
so much torment and *s* give her … Rev 18:7 3997
and am no widow, and shall see no *s* … Rev 18:7 3997
shall be no more death, neither *s* … Rev 21:4 3997

SORROWED
but that ye *s* to repentance … 2Cor 7:9 3076
that ye *s* after a godly sort, … 2Cor 7:11 3076

SORROWETH
s for you, saying, What shall I … 1Sa 10:2 1672

SORROWFUL
lord, I am a woman of a *s* spirit … 1Sa 1:15 7186
refused to touch are as my *s* meat … Job 6:7 1741
But I am poor and *s* … Ps 69:29 3510
Even in laughter the heart is *s* … Prov 14:13 3510
I have replenished every *s* soul … Jer 31:25 1669
are *s* for the solemn assembly … Zeph 3:18 3013
also shall see it, and be very *s* … Zec 9:5 2342
heard that saying, he went away *s* … Mt 19:22 3076
And they were exceeding *s*, and … Mt 26:22 3076
sons of Zebedee, and began to be *s* … Mt 26:37 3076
unto them, My soul is exceeding *s* … Mt 26:38 4036
And they began to be *s*, and to say … Mk 14:19 3076
My soul is exceeding *s* unto death … Mk 14:34 4036
when he heard this, he was very *s* … Lk 18:23 4036
when Jesus saw that he was very *s* … Lk 18:24 4036
and ye shall be *s*, but your sorrow … Jn 16:20 3076
As *s*, yet alway rejoicing … 2Cor 6:10 3076
and that I may be the less *s* … Phil 2:28 253

SORROWING
father and I have sought thee *s* … Lk 2:48 3600
S most of all for the words which … Acts 20:38 3600

SORROWS
for I know their *s* … Ex 3:7 4341
The *s* of hell compassed me about … 2Sa 22:6 2256
I am afraid of all my *s*, I know … Job 9:28 6094
God distributeth *s* in his anger … Job 21:17 2256
young ones, they cast out their *s* … Job 39:3 2256
Their *s* shall be multiplied that … Ps 16:4 6094
The *s* of death compassed me, and … Ps 18:4 2256
The *s* of hell compassed me about … Ps 18:5 2256
Many *s* shall be to the wicked … Ps 32:10 4341
The *s* of death compassed me, and … Ps 116:3 2256
up late, to eat the bread of *s* … Ps 127:2 6089
For all his days are *s*, and his … Eccl 2:23 4341
s shall take hold of them … Is 13:8 2256
a man of *s*, and acquainted with … Is 53:3 4341
our griefs, and carried our *s* … Is 53:4 4341
shall not *s* take thee, as a woman … Jer 13:21 2256
s have taken her, as a woman in … Jer 49:24 2256
by the vision my *s* are turned … Dan 10:16 6735
The *s* of a travailing woman shall … Hos 13:13 2256
All these are the beginning of *s* … Mt 24:8 5604
these are the beginnings of *s* … Mk 13:8 5604
themselves through with many *s* … 1Ti 6:10 3601

SORRY
is none of you that is *s* for me … 1Sa 22:8 2470
neither be ye *s* … Neh 8:10 6087
I will be *s* for my sin … Ps 38:18 1672
who shall be *s* for thee … Is 51:19 5110
And the king was *s* … Mt 14:9 3076
And they were exceeding *s* … Mt 17:23 3076
what was done, they were very *s* … Mt 18:31 3076
And the king was exceeding *s* … Mk 6:26 4036
For if I make you *s*, who is he … 2Cor 2:2 3076
the same which is made *s* by me … 2Cor 2:2 3076
though I made you *s* with a letter … 2Cor 7:8 3076
the same epistle hath made you *s* … 2Cor 7:8 3076
rejoice, not that ye were made *s* … 2Cor 7:9 3076
for ye were made *s* after a godly … 2Cor 7:9 3076

SORT
two of every *s* shalt thou bring … Gen 6:19
two of every *s* shall come unto … Gen 6:20
his kind, every bird of every *s* … Gen 7:14 3671
save the poorest *s* of the people … 2Kin 24:14
by lot, one *s* with another … 1Chr 24:5
offer so willingly after this *s* … 1Chr 29:14
time in such *s* as it was written … 2Chr 30:5
basons of a second *s* four hundred … Ezr 1:10
to Artaxerxes the king in this *s* … Ezr 4:8 3660
unto me four times after this *s* … Neh 6:4 1697
with the men of the common *s* were … Eze 23:42
the ravenous birds of every *s* … Eze 39:4 3671
of every *s* of your oblations, … Eze 44:30
the children which are of your *s* … Dan 1:10 1524
God that can deliver after this *s* … Dan 3:29
lewd fellows of the baser *s* … Acts 17:5
more boldly unto you in some *s* … Rom 15:15 3313
every man's work of what *s* it is … 1Cor 3:13 3697
that ye sorrowed after a godly *s* … 2Cor 7:11
For of this *s* are they which … 2Ti 3:6
on their journey after a godly *s* … 3Jn 6 516

SORTS
not wear a garment of divers *s* … Deut 22:11
ten days store of all *s* of wine … Neh 5:18
He sent divers *s* of flies among … Ps 78:45
and there came divers *s* of flies … Ps 105:31
instruments, and that of all *s* … Eccl 2:8
thy merchants in all *s* of things … Eze 27:24 4360
them clothed with all *s* of armour … Eze 38:4 4358

SOSIPATER (*so-sip'-a-tur*) See SOPATER. *A relative of Paul.*
and Lucius, and Jason, and *S* … Rom 16:21 4989

SOSTHENES (*sos'-the-neze*)
1. Chief ruler of a synagogue in Corinth.
Then all the Greeks took *S* … Acts 18:17 4988
2. A co-worker with Paul.
will of God, and *S* our brother, … 1Cor 1:1 4988

SOTAI (*so'-tahee*) *A family of Temple servants.*
the children of *S*, the children … Ezr 2:55 5479
the children of *S*, the children … Neh 7:57 5479

SOTTISH
they are *s* children, and they have … Jer 4:22 5530

SOUGHT
and he *s* where to weep … Gen 43:30 1245
this thing, he *s* to slay Moses … Ex 2:15 1245
the men are dead which *s* thy life … Ex 4:19 1245
LORD met him, and *s* to kill him … Ex 4:24 1245
that every one which *s* the LORD … Ex 33:7 1245
Moses diligently *s* the goat of … Lev 10:16 1875
not his enemy, neither *s* his harm … Num 35:23 1245
because he hath *s* to thrust thee … Deut 13:10 1245
the pursuers *s* them throughout … Josh 2:22 1245
that he *s* an occasion against the … Judg 14:4 1245
days the tribe of the Danites *s* … Judg 18:1 1245
and when they *s* him, he could not … 1Sa 10:21 1245
the LORD hath *s* him a man after … 1Sa 13:14 1245
by which Jonathan *s* to go over … 1Sa 14:4 1245
Saul *s* to smite David even to the … 1Sa 19:10 1245
Saul *s* him every day, but God … 1Sa 23:14 1245
he *s* no more again for him … 1Sa 27:4 1245
Ye *s* for David in times past to … 2Sa 3:17 1245
thine enemy, which *s* thy life … 2Sa 4:8 1245
And when they had *s* and could not … 2Sa 17:20 1245
Saul *s* to slay them in his zeal … 2Sa 21:2 1245
Let there be *s* for my lord the … 1Kin 1:2 1245
So they *s* for a fair damsel … 1Kin 1:3 1245
And all the earth *s* to Solomon … 1Kin 10:24 1245
Solomon *s* therefore to kill … 1Kin 11:40 1245
they *s* three days, but found him … 2Kin 2:17 1245
for that we *s* him not after the … 1Chr 15:13 1875
reign of David they were *s* for … 1Chr 26:31 1875
and the congregation *s* unto it … 2Chr 1:5 1875
earth *s* the presence of Solomon … 2Chr 9:23 1245
because we have *s* the LORD our … 2Chr 14:7 1875
the LORD our God, we have *s* him … 2Chr 14:7 1875
s him, he was found of them … 2Chr 15:4 1245
s him with their whole desire … 2Chr 15:15 1245
his disease he *s* not to the LORD … 2Chr 16:12 1875
David, and *s* not unto Baalim … 2Chr 17:3 1875
But *s* to the LORD God of his … 2Chr 17:4 1875
And he *s* Ahaziah … 2Chr 22:9 1245
who *s* the LORD with all his heart … 2Chr 22:9 1875
Why hast thou *s* after the gods of … 2Chr 25:15 1875
because they *s* after the gods of … 2Chr 25:20 1875
he *s* God in the days of Zechariah … 2Chr 26:5 1875
and as long as he *s* the LORD … 2Chr 26:5 1875
These *s* their register among … Ezr 2:62 1245
These *s* their register among … Neh 7:64 1245
s the Levites out of all their … Neh 12:27 1245
fair young virgins *s* for the king … Est 2:2 1245
s to lay hand on the king … Est 2:21 1245
wherefore Haman *s* to destroy all … Est 3:6 1245
who *s* to lay hand on the king … Est 6:2 1245
lay hand on such as *s* their hurt … Est 9:2 1245
I *s* the LORD, and he heard me, and … Ps 34:4 1875
I *s* him, but he could not be … Ps 37:36 1245
day of my trouble I *s* the Lord … Ps 77:2 1875
he slew them, then they *s* him … Ps 78:34 1875
violent men have *s* after my soul … Ps 86:14 1245
s out of all them that have … Ps 111:2 1875
With my whole heart have I *s* thee … Ps 119:10 1875
for I have *s* thy precepts … Ps 119:94 1875
I *s* in mine heart to give myself … Eccl 2:3 8446
but they have *s* out many … Eccl 7:29 1245
s out, and set in order many … Eccl 12:9 2713
The preacher *s* to find out … Eccl 12:10 1245
By night on my bed I *s* him whom … Song 3:1 1245
I *s* him, but I found him not … Song 3:1 1245
I *s* him, but I found him not … Song 3:2
I *s* him, but I could not find him … Song 5:6 1245
S out, A city not forsaken … Is 62:12 1875
I am *s* of them that asked not for … Is 65:1 1875
I am found of them that *s* me not … Is 65:1 1245
in, for my people that have *s* me … Is 65:10 1875
have walked, and whom they have *s* … Jer 8:2 1875
brutish, and have not *s* the LORD … Jer 10:21 1875
the king *s* to put him to death … Jer 26:21 1245
his enemy, and that *s* his life … Jer 44:30 1245
iniquity of Israel shall be *s* for … Jer 50:20 1245
while they *s* their meat to … Lam 1:19 1245
I *s* for a man among them, that … Eze 22:30 1245
though thou be *s* for, yet shalt … Eze 26:21 1245
neither have ye *s* that which was … Eze 34:4 1245
they *s* Daniel and his fellows to … Dan 2:13 1158
counsellors and my lords *s* unto me … Dan 4:36 1158
princes *s* to find occasion … Dan 6:4 1158
s for the meaning, then, behold, … Dan 8:15 1245
how are his hidden things *s* up … Obad 6 1156
and those that have not *s* the LORD … Zeph 1:6 1245
s to go that they might walk to … Zec 6:7 1245
which *s* the young child's life … Mt 2:20 2212
But when they *s* to lay hands on … Mt 21:46 2212
from that time he *s* opportunity … Mt 26:16 2212
s false witness against Jesus, to … Mt 26:59 2212
s how they might destroy him … Mk 11:18 2212
they *s* to lay hold on him, but … Mk 12:12 2212
the scribes *s* how they might take … Mk 14:1 2212
he *s* how he might conveniently … Mk 14:11 2212
all the council *s* for witness … Mk 14:55 2212
they *s* him among their kinsfolk … Lk 2:44 327
father and I have *s* thee sorrowing … Lk 2:48 2212
unto them, How is it that ye *s* me … Lk 2:49 2212
and the people *s* him, and came unto … Lk 4:42 2212
they *s* means to bring him in, and … Lk 5:18 2212
whole multitude *s* to touch him … Lk 6:19 2212
s of him a sign from heaven … Lk 11:16 2212
s fruit thereon, and found none … Lk 13:6 2212
he *s* to see Jesus who he was … Lk 19:3 2212
of the people *s* to destroy him … Lk 19:47 2212
same hour *s* to lay hands on him … Lk 20:19 2212
scribes *s* how they might kill him … Lk 22:2 2212
s opportunity to betray him unto … Lk 22:6 2212
s to slay him, because he had … Jn 5:16 2212
Therefore the Jews *s* the more to … Jn 5:18 2212
because the Jews *s* to kill him … Jn 7:1 2212
Then the Jews *s* him at the feast, … Jn 7:11 2212
Then they *s* to take him … Jn 7:30 2212
Therefore they *s* again to take … Jn 10:39 2212
the Jews of late *s* to stone thee … Jn 11:8 2212
Then *s* they for Jesus, and spake … Jn 11:56 2212
Pilate *s* to release him … Jn 19:12 2212
And when Herod had *s* for him … Acts 12:19 1934
s to bring them out to the people … Acts 17:5 2212
Because they *s* it not by faith, … Rom 9:32 2212
I was found of them that *s* me not … Rom 10:20 2212
Nor of men *s* we glory, neither of … 1Th 2:6 2212
he *s* me out very diligently, and … 2Ti 1:17 2212
place have been *s* for the second … Heb 8:7 2212
though he *s* it carefully with … Heb 12:17 1567

SOUL
and man became a living *s* … Gen 2:7 5315
my *s* shall live because of thee … Gen 12:13 5315
that *s* shall be cut off from his … Gen 17:14 5315
and my *s* shall live … Gen 19:20 5315
that my *s* may bless thee before I … Gen 27:4 5315
venison, that thy *s* may bless me … Gen 27:19 5315
venison, that my *s* may bless thee … Gen 27:25 5315
venison, that thy *s* may bless me … Gen 27:31 5315
his *s* clave unto Dinah the … Gen 34:3 5315
The *s* of my son Shechem longeth … Gen 34:8 5315
as her *s* was in departing, (for … Gen 35:18 5315
that we saw the anguish of his *s* … Gen 42:21 5315
O my *s*, come not thou into their … Gen 49:6 5315
that *s* shall be cut off from … Ex 12:15 5315
even that *s* shall be cut off from … Ex 12:19 5315
a ransom for his *s* unto the LORD … Ex 30:12 5315
that *s* shall be cut off from … Ex 31:14 5315
saying, If a *s* shall sin through … Lev 4:2 5315
And if a *s* sin, and hear the voice … Lev 5:1 5315
Or if a *s* touch any unclean thing … Lev 5:2 5315
Or if a *s* swear, pronouncing with … Lev 5:4 5315
If a *s* commit a trespass, and sin … Lev 5:15 5315
And if a *s* sin, and commit any of … Lev 5:17 5315
If a *s* sin, and commit a trespass … Lev 6:2 5315
the *s* that eateth of it shall … Lev 7:18 5315
But the *s* that eateth of the … Lev 7:20 5315
even that *s* shall be cut off from … Lev 7:20 5315
Moreover the *s* that shall touch … Lev 7:21 5315
even that *s* shall be cut off from … Lev 7:21 5315
even the *s* that eateth it shall … Lev 7:25 5315
Whatsoever *s* it be that eateth … Lev 7:27 5315
even that *s* shall be cut off from … Lev 7:27 5315
against that *s* that eateth blood … Lev 17:10 5315
maketh an atonement for the *s* … Lev 17:11 5315
No *s* of you shall eat blood, … Lev 17:12 5315
every *s* that eateth that which … Lev 17:15 5315
that *s* shall be cut off from … Lev 19:8 5315

Context	Reference	Number
the *s* that turneth after such as	Lev 20:6	5315
even set my face against that *s*	Lev 20:6	5315
that *s* shall be cut off from my	Lev 22:3	5315
The *s* which hath touched any such	Lev 22:6	5315
priest buy any *s* with his money	Lev 22:11	5315
For whatsoever *s* it be that shall	Lev 23:29	5315
whatsoever *s* it be that doeth any	Lev 23:30	5315
the same *s* will I destroy from	Lev 23:30	5315
and my *s* shall not abhor you	Lev 26:11	5315
or if your *s* abhor my judgments,	Lev 26:15	5315
idols, and my *s* shall abhor you	Lev 26:30	5315
because their *s* abhorred my	Lev 26:43	5315
even the same *s* shall be cut off	Num 9:13	5315
But now our *s* is dried away	Num 11:6	5315
if any *s* sin through ignorance,	Num 15:27	5315
for the *s* that sinneth ignorantly	Num 15:28	5315
But the *s* that doeth ought	Num 15:30	5315
that *s* shall be cut off from	Num 15:30	5315
that *s* shall utterly be cut off	Num 15:31	5315
that *s* shall be cut off from	Num 19:13	5315
that *s* shall be cut off from	Num 19:20	5315
the *s* that toucheth it shall be	Num 19:22	5315
the *s* of the people was much	Num 21:4	5315
our *s* loatheth this light bread	Num 21:5	5315
an oath to bind his *s* with a bond	Num 30:2	5315
wherewith she hath bound her *s*	Num 30:4	5315
she hath bound her *s* shall stand	Num 30:4	5315
wherewith she hath bound her *s*	Num 30:5	5315
lips, wherewith she bound her *s*	Num 30:6	5315
she bound her *s* shall stand	Num 30:7	5315
lips, wherewith she bound her *s*	Num 30:8	5315
or bound her *s* by a bond with an	Num 30:10	5315
she bound her *s* shall stand	Num 30:11	5315
or concerning the bond of her *s*	Num 30:12	5315
binding oath to afflict the *s*	Num 30:13	5315
one *s* of five hundred, both of	Num 31:28	5315
keep thy *s* diligently, lest thou	Deut 4:9	5315
all thy heart and with all thy *s*	Deut 4:29	5315
thine heart, and with all thy *s*	Deut 6:5	5315
all thy heart and with all thy *s*	Deut 10:12	5315
all your heart and with all your *s*	Deut 11:13	5315
words in your heart and in your *s*	Deut 11:18	5315
whatsoever thy *s* lusteth after	Deut 12:15	5315
because thy *s* longeth to eat	Deut 12:20	5315
whatsoever thy *s* lusteth after	Deut 12:20	5315
whatsoever thy *s* lusteth after	Deut 12:21	5315
all your heart and with all your *s*	Deut 13:3	5315
friend, which is as thine own *s*	Deut 13:6	5315
whatsoever thy *s* lusteth after	Deut 14:26	5315
or for whatsoever thy *s* desireth	Deut 14:26	5315
thine heart, and with all thy *s*	Deut 26:16	5315
thine heart, and with all thy *s*	Deut 30:2	5315
thine heart, and with all thy *s*	Deut 30:6	5315
thine heart, and with all thy *s*	Deut 30:10	5315
all your heart and with all your *s*	Josh 22:5	5315
O my *s*, thou hast trodden down	Judg 5:21	5315
his *s* was grieved for the misery	Judg 10:16	5315
so that his *s* was vexed unto	Judg 16:16	5315
And she was in bitterness of *s*	1Sa 1:10	5315
poured out my *s* before the LORD	1Sa 1:15	5315
said, Oh my lord, as thy *s* liveth	1Sa 1:26	5315
take as much as thy *s* desireth	1Sa 2:16	5315
And Abner said, As thy *s* liveth	1Sa 17:55	5315
that the *s* of Jonathan was knit	1Sa 18:1	5315
was knit with the *s* of David	1Sa 18:1	5315
Jonathan loved him as his own *s*	1Sa 18:1	5315
because he loved him as his own *s*	1Sa 18:3	5315
LORD liveth, and as thy *s* liveth	1Sa 20:3	5315
David, Whatsoever thy *s* desireth	1Sa 20:4	5315
loved him as he loved his own *s*	1Sa 20:17	5315
the desire of thy *s* to come down	1Sa 23:20	5315
yet thou huntest my *s* to take it	1Sa 24:11	5315
LORD liveth, and as thy *s* liveth	1Sa 25:26	5315
to pursue thee, and to seek thy *s*	1Sa 25:29	5315
but the *s* of my lord shall be	1Sa 25:29	5315
because my *s* was precious in	1Sa 26:21	5315
because the *s* of all the people	1Sa 30:6	5315
my *s* out of all adversity	2Sa 4:9	5315
that are hated of David's *s*	2Sa 5:8	5315
thou livest, and as thy *s* liveth	2Sa 11:11	5315
the *s* of king David longed to go	2Sa 13:39	
answered and said, As thy *s* liveth	2Sa 14:19	5315
redeemed my *s* out of all distress	1Kin 1:29	5315
their heart and with all their *s*	1Kin 2:4	5315
their heart, and with all their *s*	1Kin 8:48	5315
to all that thy *s* desireth	1Kin 11:37	5315
let this child's *s* come into him	1Kin 17:21	5315
the *s* of the child came into him	1Kin 17:22	5315
LORD liveth, and as thy *s* liveth	2Kin 2:2	5315
LORD liveth, and as thy *s* liveth	2Kin 2:4	5315
LORD liveth, and as thy *s* liveth	2Kin 2:6	5315
for her *s* is vexed within her	2Kin 4:27	5315
LORD liveth, and as thy *s* liveth	2Kin 4:30	5315
all their heart and all their *s*	2Kin 23:3	5315
all his heart, and with all his *s*	2Kin 23:25	5315
your *s* to seek the LORD your God	1Chr 22:19	5315
with all their *s* in the land of	2Chr 6:38	5315
their heart and with all their *s*	2Chr 15:12	5315
all his heart, and with all his *s*	2Chr 34:31	5315
and life unto the bitter in *s*	Job 3:20	5315
The things that my *s* refused to	Job 6:7	5315
in the bitterness of my *s*	Job 7:11	5315
So that my *s* chooseth strangling,	Job 7:15	5315
yet would I not know my *s*	Job 9:21	5315
My *s* is weary of my life	Job 10:1	5315
speak in the bitterness of my *s*	Job 10:1	5315
In whose hand is the *s* of every	Job 12:10	5315
his *s* within him shall mourn	Job 14:22	5315
if your *s* were in my soul's stead	Job 16:4	5315
How long will ye vex my *s*	Job 19:2	5315
dieth in the bitterness of his *s*	Job 21:25	5315
And what his *s* desireth, even that	Job 23:13	5315
the *s* of the wounded crieth out	Job 24:12	5315
the Almighty, who hath vexed my *s*	Job 27:2	5315
when God taketh away his *s*	Job 27:8	5315
they pursue my *s* as the wind	Job 30:15	5082
now my *s* is poured out upon me	Job 30:16	5315
was not my *s* grieved for the poor	Job 30:25	5315
sin by wishing a curse to his *s*	Job 31:30	5315
keepeth back his *s* from the pit	Job 33:18	5315
bread, and his *s* dainty meat	Job 33:20	5315
his *s* draweth near unto the grave	Job 33:22	5315
He will deliver his *s* from going	Job 33:28	5315
To bring back his *s* from the pit	Job 33:30	5315
Many there be which say of my *s*	Ps 3:2	5315
My *s* is also sore vexed	Ps 6:3	5315
Return, O LORD, deliver my *s*	Ps 6:4	5315
Lest he tear my *s* like a lion	Ps 7:2	5315
Let the enemy persecute my *s*	Ps 7:5	5315
how say ye to my *s*, Flee as a	Ps 11:1	5315
that loveth violence his *s* hateth	Ps 11:5	5315
long shall I take counsel in my *s*	Ps 13:2	5315
O my *s*, thou hast said unto the	Ps 16:2	
thou wilt not leave my *s* in hell	Ps 16:10	5315
deliver my *s* from the wicked,	Ps 17:13	5315
LORD is perfect, converting the *s*	Ps 19:7	5315
Deliver my *s* from the sword	Ps 22:20	5315
and none can keep alive his own *s*	Ps 22:29	5315
He restoreth my *s*	Ps 23:3	5315
not lifted up his *s* unto vanity	Ps 24:4	5315
thee, O LORD, do I lift up my *s*	Ps 25:1	5315
His *s* shall dwell at ease	Ps 25:13	5315
O keep my *s*, and deliver me	Ps 25:20	5315
Gather not my *s* with sinners	Ps 26:9	5315
brought up my *s* from the grave	Ps 30:3	5315
hast known my *s* in adversities	Ps 31:7	5315
is consumed with grief, yea, my *s*	Ps 31:9	5315
To deliver their *s* from death	Ps 33:19	5315
Our *s* waiteth for the LORD	Ps 33:20	5315
My *s* shall make her boast in the	Ps 34:2	5315
redeemeth the *s* of his servants	Ps 34:22	5315
say unto my *s*, I am thy salvation	Ps 35:3	5315
put to shame that seek after my *s*	Ps 35:4	5315
cause they have digged for my *s*	Ps 35:7	5315
my *s* shall be joyful in the LORD	Ps 35:9	5315
for good to the spoiling of my *s*	Ps 35:12	5315
I humbled my *s* with fasting	Ps 35:13	5315
rescue my *s* from their	Ps 35:17	5315
seek after my *s* to destroy it	Ps 40:14	5315
heal my *s*	Ps 41:4	5315
so panteth my *s* after thee	Ps 42:1	5315
My *s* thirsteth for God, for the	Ps 42:2	5315
things, I pour out my *s* in me	Ps 42:4	5315
Why art thou cast down, O my *s*	Ps 42:5	5315
my *s* is cast down within me	Ps 42:6	5315
Why art thou cast down, O my *s*	Ps 42:11	5315
Why art thou cast down, O my *s*	Ps 43:5	5315
For our *s* is bowed down to the	Ps 44:25	5315
redemption of their *s* is precious	Ps 49:8	5315
But God will redeem my *s* from the	Ps 49:15	5315
while he lived he blessed his *s*	Ps 49:18	5315
me, and oppressors seek after my *s*	Ps 54:3	5315
is with them that uphold my *s*	Ps 54:4	5315
He hath delivered my *s* in peace	Ps 55:18	5315
my steps, when they wait for my *s*	Ps 56:6	5315
hast delivered my *s* from death	Ps 56:13	5315
for my *s* trusteth in thee	Ps 57:1	5315
My *s* is among lions	Ps 57:4	5315
my *s* is bowed down	Ps 57:6	5315
lo, they lie in wait for my *s*	Ps 59:3	5315
Truly my *s* waiteth upon God	Ps 62:1	5315
My *s*, wait thou only upon God	Ps 62:5	5315
my *s* thirsteth for thee, my flesh	Ps 63:1	5315
My *s* shall be satisfied as with	Ps 63:5	5315
My *s* followeth hard after thee	Ps 63:8	5315
But those that seek my *s*, to	Ps 63:9	5315
Which holdeth our *s* in life	Ps 66:9	5315
what he hath done for my *s*	Ps 66:16	5315
the waters are come in unto my *s*	Ps 69:1	5315
and chastened my *s* with fasting	Ps 69:10	5315
Draw nigh unto my *s*, and redeem it	Ps 69:18	5315
confounded that seek after my *s*	Ps 70:2	5315
for my *s* take counsel together	Ps 71:10	5315
that are adversaries to my *s*	Ps 71:13	5315
and my *s*, which thou hast redeemed	Ps 71:23	5315
shall redeem their *s* from deceit	Ps 72:14	5315
O deliver not the *s* of thy	Ps 74:19	5315
my *s* refused to be comforted	Ps 77:2	5315
he spared not their *s* from death	Ps 78:50	5315
My *s* longeth, yea, even fainteth	Ps 84:2	5315
Preserve my *s*	Ps 86:2	5315
Rejoice the *s* of thy servant	Ps 86:4	5315
thee, O Lord, do I lift up my *s*	Ps 86:4	5315
my *s* from the lowest hell	Ps 86:13	5315
men have sought after my *s*	Ps 86:14	5315
For my *s* is full of troubles	Ps 88:3	5315
LORD, why castest thou off my *s*	Ps 88:14	5315
shall he deliver his *s* from the	Ps 89:48	5315
my *s* had almost dwelt in silence	Ps 94:17	5315
me thy comforts delight my *s*	Ps 94:19	5315
against the *s* of the righteous	Ps 94:21	5315
Bless the LORD, O my *s*	Ps 103:1	5315
Bless the LORD, O my *s*, and forget	Ps 103:2	5315
bless the LORD, O my *s*	Ps 103:22	5315
Bless the LORD, O my *s*	Ps 104:1	5315
Bless thou the LORD, O my *s*	Ps 104:35	5315
but sent leanness into their *s*	Ps 106:15	5315
thirsty, their *s* fainted in them	Ps 107:5	5315
For he satisfieth the longing *s*	Ps 107:9	5315
the hungry *s* with goodness	Ps 107:9	5315
Their *s* abhorreth all manner of	Ps 107:18	5315
their *s* is melted because of	Ps 107:26	5315
them that speak evil against my *s*	Ps 109:20	5315
him from those that condemn his *s*	Ps 109:31	5315
I beseech thee, deliver my *s*	Ps 116:4	5315
Return unto thy rest, O my *s*	Ps 116:7	5315
hast delivered my *s* from death	Ps 116:8	5315
My *s* breaketh for the longing	Ps 119:20	5315
My *s* cleaveth unto the dust	Ps 119:25	5315
My *s* melteth for heaviness	Ps 119:28	5315
My *s* fainteth for thy salvation	Ps 119:81	5315
My *s* is continually in my hand	Ps 119:109	5315
therefore doth my *s* keep them	Ps 119:129	5315
My *s* hath kept thy testimonies	Ps 119:167	5315
Let my *s* live, and it shall praise	Ps 119:175	5315
Deliver my *s*, O LORD, from lying	Ps 120:2	5315
My *s* hath long dwelt with him	Ps 120:6	5315
he shall preserve thy *s*	Ps 121:7	5315
Our *s* is exceedingly filled with	Ps 123:4	5315
the stream had gone over our *s*	Ps 124:4	5315
proud waters had gone over our *s*	Ps 124:5	5315
Our *s* is escaped as a bird out of	Ps 124:7	5315
my *s* doth wait, and in his word do	Ps 130:5	5315
My *s* waiteth for the Lord more	Ps 130:6	5315
my *s* is even as a weaned child	Ps 131:2	5315
me with strength in my *s*	Ps 138:3	5315
that my *s* knoweth right well	Ps 139:14	5315
leave not my *s* destitute	Ps 141:8	5315
no man cared for my *s*	Ps 142:4	5315
Bring my *s* out of prison, that I	Ps 142:7	5315
the enemy hath persecuted my *s*	Ps 143:3	5315
my *s* thirsteth after thee, as a	Ps 143:6	5315
for I lift up my *s* unto thee	Ps 143:8	5315
sake bring my *s* out of trouble	Ps 143:11	5315
all them that afflict my *s*	Ps 143:12	5315
Praise the LORD, O my *s*	Ps 146:1	5315
knowledge is pleasant unto thy *s*	Prov 2:10	5315
So shall they be life unto thy *s*	Prov 3:22	5315
satisfy his *s* when he is hungry	Prov 6:30	5315
doeth it destroyeth his own *s*	Prov 6:32	5315
against me wrongeth his own *s*	Prov 8:36	5315
the *s* of the righteous to famish	Prov 10:3	5315
man doeth good to his own *s*	Prov 11:17	5315
The liberal *s* shall be made fat	Prov 11:25	5315
but the *s* of the transgressors	Prov 13:2	5315
The *s* of the sluggard desireth,	Prov 13:4	5315
but the *s* of the diligent shall	Prov 13:4	5315
accomplished is sweet to the *s*	Prov 13:19	5315
eateth to the satisfying of his *s*	Prov 13:25	5315
instruction despiseth his own *s*	Prov 15:32	5315
keepeth his way preserveth his *s*	Prov 16:17	5315
as an honeycomb, sweet to the *s*	Prov 16:24	5315
his lips are the snare of his *s*	Prov 18:7	5315
that the *s* be without knowledge,	Prov 19:2	5315
getteth wisdom loveth his own *s*	Prov 19:8	5315
an idle *s* shall suffer hunger	Prov 19:15	5315
the commandment keepeth his own *s*	Prov 19:16	5315
let not thy *s* spare for his	Prov 19:18	5315
anger sinneth against his own *s*	Prov 20:2	5315
The *s* of the wicked desireth evil	Prov 21:10	5315
keepeth his *s* from troubles	Prov 21:23	5315
he that doth keep his *s* shall be	Prov 22:5	5315
spoil the *s* of those that spoiled	Prov 22:23	5315
his ways, and get a snare to thy *s*	Prov 22:25	5315
and shalt deliver his *s* from hell	Prov 23:14	5315
and he that keepeth thy *s*, doth	Prov 24:12	5315
knowledge of wisdom be unto thy *s*	Prov 24:14	5315
refresheth the *s* of his masters	Prov 25:13	5315
As cold waters to a thirsty *s*	Prov 25:25	5315
The full *s* loatheth an honeycomb	Prov 27:7	5315
but to the hungry *s* every bitter	Prov 27:7	5315
but the just seek his *s*	Prov 29:10	5315
he shall give delight unto thy *s*	Prov 29:17	5315
with a thief hateth his own *s*	Prov 29:24	5315
that he should make his *s* enjoy	Eccl 2:24	5315
I labour, and bereave my *s* of good	Eccl 4:8	5315
for his *s* of all that he desireth	Eccl 6:2	5315
his *s* be not filled with good, and	Eccl 6:3	5315
Which yet my *s* seeketh, but I	Eccl 7:28	5315
Tell me, O thou whom my *s* loveth	Song 1:7	5315
bed I sought him whom my *s* loveth	Song 3:1	5315
I will seek him whom my *s* loveth	Song 3:2	5315
said, Saw ye him whom my *s* loveth	Song 3:3	5315
but I found him whom my *s* loveth	Song 3:4	5315
my *s* failed when he spake	Song 5:6	5315
my *s* made me like the chariots of	Song 6:12	5315
your appointed feasts my *s* hateth	Is 1:14	5315
Woe unto their *s*	Is 3:9	5315
and of his fruitful field, both *s*	Is 10:18	5315
desire of our *s* is to thy name	Is 26:8	5315
With my *s* have I desired thee in	Is 26:9	5315
but he awaketh, and his *s* is empty	Is 29:8	5315
is faint, and his *s* hath appetite	Is 29:8	5315
to make empty the *s* of the hungry	Is 32:6	5315
years in the bitterness of my *s*	Is 38:15	5315
but thou hast in love to my *s*	Is 38:17	5315
elect, in whom my *s* delighteth	Is 42:1	5315
that he cannot deliver his *s*	Is 44:20	5315
which have said to thy *s*, Bow	Is 51:23	5315
make his *s* an offering for sin	Is 53:10	5315
shall see of the travail of his *s*	Is 53:11	5315
hath poured out his *s* unto death	Is 53:12	5315
let your *s* delight itself in	Is 55:2	5315
hear, and your *s* shall live	Is 55:3	5315
wherefore have we afflicted our *s*	Is 58:3	5315
a day for a man to afflict his *s*	Is 58:5	5315
thou draw out thy *s* to the hungry	Is 58:10	5315
and satisfy the afflicted *s*	Is 58:10	5315
and satisfy thy *s* in drought	Is 58:11	5315
my *s* shall be joyful in my God	Is 61:10	5315
their *s* delighteth in their	Is 66:3	5315
the sword reacheth unto the *s*	Jer 4:10	5315
because thou hast heard, O my *s*	Jer 4:19	5315
for my *s* is wearied because of	Jer 4:31	5315
shall not my *s* be avenged on such	Jer 5:9	5315
shall not my *s* be avenged on such	Jer 5:29	5315
lest my *s* depart from thee	Jer 6:8	5315
shall not my *s* be avenged on such	Jer 9:9	5315
my *s* into the hand of her enemies	Jer 12:7	5315
my *s* shall weep in secret places	Jer 13:17	5315
hath thy *s* lothed Zion	Jer 14:19	5315
they have digged a pit for my *s*	Jer 18:20	5315

for he hath delivered the s of	Jer 20:13	5315
their s shall be as a watered	Jer 31:12	5315
I will satiate the s of the	Jer 31:14	5315
For I have satiated the weary s	Jer 31:25	5315
replenished every sorrowful s	Jer 31:25	5315
my whole heart and with my whole s	Jer 32:41	5315
LORD liveth, that made us this s	Jer 38:16	5315
then thy s shall live, and this	Jer 38:17	5315
unto thee, and thy s shall live	Jer 38:20	5315
his s shall be satisfied upon	Jer 50:19	5315
and deliver every man his s	Jer 51:6	5315
deliver ye every man his s from	Jer 51:45	5315
things for meat to relieve the s	Lam 1:11	5315
relieve my s is far from me	Lam 1:16	5315
when their s was poured out into	Lam 2:12	5315
removed my s far off from peace	Lam 3:17	5315
My s hath them still in	Lam 3:20	5315
LORD is my portion, saith my s	Lam 3:24	5315
to the s that seeketh him	Lam 3:25	5315
hast pleaded the causes of my s	Lam 3:58	5315
but thou hast delivered thy s	Eze 3:19	5315
also thou hast delivered thy s	Eze 3:21	5315
my s hath not been polluted	Eze 4:14	5315
as the s of the father, so also	Eze 18:4	5315
so also the s of the son is mine	Eze 18:4	5315
the s that sinneth, it shall die	Eze 18:4	5315
The s that sinneth, it shall die	Eze 18:20	5315
right, he shall save his s alive	Eze 18:27	5315
and that which your s pitieth	Eze 24:21	5315
warning shall deliver his s	Eze 33:5	5315
but thou hast delivered thy s	Eze 33:9	5315
for their bread for their s shall	Hos 9:4	5315
compassed me about, even to the s	Jonah 2:5	5315
When my s fainted within me I	Jonah 2:7	5315
of my body for the sin of my s	Mic 6:7	5315
my s desired the firstripe fruit	Mic 7:1	5315
his s which is lifted up is not	Hab 2:4	5315
and hast sinned against thy s	Hab 2:10	5315
my s lothed them	Zec 11:8	5315
and their s also abhorred me	Zec 11:8	5315
but are not able to kill the s	Mt 10:28	*5590*
which is able to destroy both s	Mt 10:28	*5590*
in whom my s is well pleased	Mt 12:18	*5590*
whole world, and lose his own s	Mt 16:26	*5590*
a man give in exchange for his s	Mt 16:26	*5590*
all thy heart, and with all thy s	Mt 22:37	*5590*
My s is exceeding sorrowful, even	Mt 26:38	*5590*
whole world, and lose his own s	Mk 8:36	*5590*
a man give in exchange for his s	Mk 8:37	*5590*
all thy heart, and with all thy s	Mk 12:30	*5590*
understanding, and with all the s	Mk 12:33	*5590*
My s is exceeding sorrowful unto	Mk 14:34	*5590*
My s doth magnify the Lord,	Lk 1:46	*5590*
pierce through thy own s also	Lk 2:35	*5590*
all thy heart, and with all thy s	Lk 10:27	*5590*
And I will say to my s, thou	Lk 12:19	*5590*
And I will say to my s, S,	Lk 12:19	*5590*
this night thy s shall be	Lk 12:20	*5590*
Now is my s troubled	Jn 12:27	*5590*
thou wilt not leave my s in hell	Acts 2:27	*5590*
that his s was not left in hell,	Acts 2:31	*5590*
And fear came upon every s	Acts 2:43	*5590*
shall come to pass, that every s	Acts 3:23	*5590*
were of one heart and of one s	Acts 4:32	*5590*
upon every s of man that doeth	Rom 2:9	*5590*
Let every s be subject unto the	Rom 13:1	*5590*
man Adam was made a living s	1Cor 15:45	*5590*
I call God for a record upon my s	2Cor 1:23	*5590*
I pray God your whole spirit and s	1Th 5:23	*5590*
even to the dividing asunder of s	Heb 4:12	*5590*
we have as an anchor of the s	Heb 6:19	*5590*
my s shall have no pleasure in	Heb 10:38	*5590*
believe to the saving of the s	Heb 10:39	*5590*
his way shall save a s from death	Jas 5:20	*5590*
lusts, which war against the s	1Pet 2:11	*5590*
vexed his righteous s from day to	2Pet 2:8	*5590*
health, even as thy s prospereth	3Jn 2	*5590*
every living s died in the sea	Rev 16:3	*5590*
the fruits that thy s lusted	Rev 18:14	*5590*

SOUL'S

if your soul were in my s stead	Job 16:4	5315

SOULS

the s that they had gotten in	Gen 12:5	5315
all the s of his sons and his	Gen 46:15	5315
bare unto Jacob, even sixteen s	Gen 46:18	5315
all the s were fourteen	Gen 46:22	5315
all the s were seven	Gen 46:25	5315
All the s that came with Jacob	Gen 46:26	5315
all the s were threescore and six	Gen 46:26	5315
born him in Egypt, were two s	Gen 46:27	5315
all the s of the house of Jacob,	Gen 46:27	5315
all the s that came out of the	Ex 1:5	5315
the loins of Jacob were seventy s	Ex 1:5	5315
according to the number of the s	Ex 12:4	5315
to make an atonement for your s	Ex 30:15	5315
to make an atonement for your s	Ex 30:16	5315
month, ye shall afflict your s	Lev 16:29	5315
you, and ye shall afflict your s	Lev 16:31	5315
to make an atonement for your s	Lev 17:11	5315
even the s that commit them shall	Lev 18:29	5315
make your s abominable by beast	Lev 20:25	5315
and ye shall afflict your s	Lev 23:27	5315
rest, and ye shall afflict your s	Lev 23:32	5315
these sinners against their own s	Num 16:38	5315
and ye shall afflict your s	Num 29:7	5315
wherewith they have bound their s	Num 30:9	5315
for our s before the LORD	Num 31:50	5315
all the s that were therein	Josh 10:28	5315
all the s that were therein,	Josh 10:30	5315
all the s that were therein,	Josh 10:32	5315
all the s that were therein he	Josh 10:35	5315
all the s that were therein	Josh 10:37	5315
all the s that were therein	Josh 10:37	5315
all the s that were therein	Josh 10:39	5315
they smote all the s that were	Josh 11:11	5315
all your hearts and in all your s	Josh 23:14	5315
the s of thine enemies, them	1Sa 25:29	5315
and shall save the s of the needy	Ps 72:13	5315
he preserveth the s of his saints	Ps 97:10	5315
and he that winneth s is wise	Prov 11:30	5315
A true witness delivereth s	Prov 14:25	5315
me, and the s which I have made	Is 57:16	5397
of the s of the poor innocents	Jer 2:34	5315
and ye shall find rest for your s	Jer 6:16	5315
procure great evil against our s	Jer 26:19	5315
ye this great evil against your s	Jer 44:7	5315
their meat to relieve their s	Lam 1:19	5315
they shall not satisfy their s	Eze 7:19	5315
head of every stature to hunt s	Eze 13:18	5315
Will ye hunt the s of my people	Eze 13:18	5315
will ye save the s alive that	Eze 13:18	5315
to slay the s that should not die	Eze 13:19	5315
to save the s alive that should	Eze 13:19	5315
there hunt the s to make them fly	Eze 13:20	5315
your arms, and will let the s go	Eze 13:20	5315
even the s that ye hunt to make	Eze 13:20	5315
own s by their righteousness	Eze 14:14	5315
own s by their righteousness	Eze 14:20	5315
Behold, all s are mine	Eze 18:4	5315
they have devoured s	Eze 22:25	5315
to shed blood, and to destroy s	Eze 22:27	5315
and ye shall find rest unto your s	Mt 11:29	*5590*
your patience possess ye your s	Lk 21:19	*5590*
unto them about three thousand s	Acts 2:41	*5590*
kindred, threescore and fifteen s	Acts 7:14	*5590*
Confirming the s of the disciples	Acts 14:22	*5590*
you with words, subverting your s	Acts 15:24	*5590*
hundred threescore and sixteen s	Acts 27:37	*5590*
of God only, but also our own s	1Th 2:8	*5590*
for they watch for your s	Heb 13:17	*5590*
which is able to save your s	Jas 1:21	*5590*
even the salvation of your s	1Pet 1:9	*5590*
s in obeying the truth through	1Pet 1:22	*5590*
the Shepherd and Bishop of your s	1Pet 2:25	*5590*
eight s were saved by water	1Pet 3:20	*5590*
of their s to him in well doing	1Pet 4:19	*5590*
beguiling unstable s	2Pet 2:14	*5590*
I saw under the altar the s of	Rev 6:9	*5590*
chariots, and slaves, and s of men	Rev 18:13	*5590*
I saw the s of them that were	Rev 20:4	*5590*

SOUND

his s shall be heard when he	Ex 28:35	6963
the trumpet of the jubile to s on	Lev 25:9	5674
s throughout all your land	Lev 25:9	5674
the s of a shaken leaf shall	Lev 26:36	6963
blow, but ye shall not s an alarm	Num 10:7	7321
when ye hear the s of the trumpet	Josh 6:5	6963
people heard the s of the trumpet	Josh 6:20	6963
when thou hearest the s of a	2Sa 5:24	6963
with the s of the trumpet	2Sa 6:15	6963
as ye hear the s of the trumpet	2Sa 15:10	6963
the earth rent with the s of them	1Kin 1:40	6963
Joab heard the s of the trumpet	1Kin 1:41	6963
Ahijah heard the s of her feet	1Kin 14:6	6963
for there is a s of abundance of	1Kin 18:41	6963
is not the s of his master's feet	2Kin 6:32	6963
when thou shalt hear a s of going	1Chr 14:15	6963
were appointed to s with cymbals	1Chr 15:19	8085
with s of the cornet, and with	1Chr 15:28	6963
but Asaph made a s with cymbals	1Chr 16:5	8085
for those that should make a s	1Chr 16:42	8085
to make one s to be heard in	2Chr 5:13	6963
ye hear the s of the trumpet	Neh 4:20	6963
A dreadful s is in his ears	Job 15:21	6963
and rejoice at the s of the organ	Job 21:12	6963
the s that goeth out of his mouth	Job 37:2	1899
that it is the s of the trumpet	Job 39:24	6963
the LORD with the s of a trumpet	Ps 47:5	6963
the skies sent out a s	Ps 77:17	6963
the people that know the joyful s	Ps 89:15	8643
upon the harp with a solemn s	Ps 92:3	1902
s of cornet make a joyful noise	Ps 98:6	6963
Let my heart be s in thy statutes	Ps 119:80	8549
him with the s of the trumpet	Ps 150:3	8629
He layeth up s wisdom for the	Prov 2:7	8454
keep s wisdom and discretion	Prov 3:21	8454
Counsel is mine, and s wisdom	Prov 8:14	8454
A s heart is the life of the	Prov 14:30	4832
when the s of the grinding is low	Eccl 12:4	6963
shall s like an harp for Moab	Is 16:11	1993
the s of the trumpet, the alarm	Jer 4:19	6963
hear the s of the trumpet	Jer 4:21	6963
Hearken to the s of the trumpet	Jer 6:17	6963
s of the neighing of his strong	Jer 8:16	6963
the s of the millstones, and the	Jer 25:10	6963
nor hear the s of the trumpet,	Jer 42:14	6963
heart shall s for Moab like pipes	Jer 48:36	1993
mine heart shall s like pipes for	Jer 48:36	1993
A s of battle is in the land, and	Jer 50:22	6963
A s of a cry cometh from Babylon,	Jer 51:54	6963
the s of the cherubims' wings was	Eze 10:5	6963
the s of thy harps shall be no	Eze 26:13	6963
isles shake at the s of thy fall	Eze 26:15	6963
at the s of the cry of thy pilots	Eze 27:28	6963
to shake at the s of his fall	Eze 31:16	6963
heareth the s of the trumpet	Eze 33:4	6963
He heard the s of the trumpet, and	Eze 33:5	6963
time ye hear the s of the cornet	Dan 3:5	7032
people heard the s of the cornet	Dan 3:7	7032
shall hear the s of the cornet	Dan 3:10	7032
time ye hear the s of the cornet	Dan 3:15	7032
s an alarm in my holy mountain	Joel 2:1	7321
with the s of the trumpet	Amos 2:2	6963
That chant to the s of the viol	Amos 6:5	6310
do not s a trumpet before thee,	Mt 6:2	*4537*
with a great s of a trumpet	Mt 24:31	*5456*
he hath received him safe and s	Lk 15:27	*5198*
and thou hearest the s thereof	Jn 3:8	*5456*
suddenly there came a s from	Acts 2:2	*2279*
their s went into all the earth,	Rom 10:18	*5353*
even things without life giving s	1Cor 14:7	*5456*
the trumpet give an uncertain s	1Cor 14:8	*5456*
for the trumpet shall s, and the	1Cor 15:52	*4537*
that is contrary to s doctrine	1Ti 1:10	*5198*
power, and of love, and of a s mind	2Ti 1:7	*4995*
Hold fast the form of s words	2Ti 1:13	*5198*
they will not endure s doctrine	2Ti 4:3	*5198*
that he may be able by s doctrine	Titus 1:9	*5198*
that they may be s in the faith	Titus 1:13	*5198*
things which become s doctrine	Titus 2:1	*5198*
s in faith, in charity, in	Titus 2:2	*5198*
S speech, that cannot be	Titus 2:8	*5199*
the s of a trumpet, and the voice	Heb 12:19	*2279*
his voice as the s of many waters	Rev 1:15	*5456*
trumpets prepared themselves to s	Rev 8:6	*4537*
three angels, which are yet to s	Rev 8:13	*4537*
the s of their wings was as the	Rev 9:9	*5456*
the s of chariots of many horses	Rev 9:9	*5456*
angel, when he shall begin to s	Rev 10:7	*4537*
the s of a millstone shall be	Rev 18:22	*5456*

SOUNDED

the voice of the trumpet s long	Ex 19:19	
when I have s my father about to	1Sa 20:12	2713
the priests s trumpets before	2Chr 7:6	2690
the priests s with the trumpets	2Chr 13:14	2690
s with trumpets, also the singers	2Chr 23:13	8628
singers sang, and the trumpeters s	2Chr 29:28	2690
he that s the trumpet was by me	Neh 4:18	8628
of thy salutation s in mine ears	Lk 1:44	*1096*
And s, and found it twenty fathoms	Acts 27:28	*1001*
they s again, and found it fifteen	Acts 27:28	*1001*
For from you s out the word of	1Th 1:8	*1837*
The first angel s, and there	Rev 8:7	*4537*
And the second angel s, and as it	Rev 8:8	*4537*
And the third angel s, and there	Rev 8:10	*4537*
And the fourth angel s, and the	Rev 8:12	*4537*
And the fifth angel s, and I saw a	Rev 9:1	*4537*
And the sixth angel s, and I heard	Rev 9:13	*4537*
And the seventh angel s	Rev 11:15	*4537*

SOUNDETH

when the trumpet s long, they	Ex 19:13	

SOUNDING

psalteries and harps and cymbals, s	1Chr 15:16	8085
and twenty priests s with trumpets	2Chr 5:12	2690
his priests with s trumpets to	2Chr 13:12	8643
him upon the high s cymbals	Ps 150:5	8643
the s of thy bowels and of thy	Is 63:15	1995
not the s again of the mountains	Eze 7:7	1906
charity, I am become as s brass	1Cor 13:1	*2278*

SOUNDNESS

There is no s in my flesh because	Ps 38:3	4974
and there is no s in my flesh	Ps 38:7	4974
unto the head there is no s in it	Is 1:6	4974
s in the presence of you all	Acts 3:16	*3647*

SOUNDS

they give a distinction in the s	1Cor 14:7	*5353*

SOUR

the s grape is ripening in the	Is 18:5	1155
The fathers have eaten a s grape	Jer 31:29	1155
every man that eateth the s grape	Jer 31:30	1155
The fathers have eaten s grapes	Eze 18:2	1155
Their drink is s	Hos 4:18	5493

SOUTH

going on still toward the s	Gen 12:9	5045
had, and Lot with him, into the s	Gen 13:1	5045
from the s even to Beth-el	Gen 13:3	5045
from thence toward the s country	Gen 20:1	5045
for he dwelt in the s country	Gen 24:62	5045
and to the north, and to the s	Gen 28:14	5045
boards on the s side southward	Ex 26:18	5045
of the tabernacle toward the s	Ex 26:35	8486
for the s side southward there	Ex 27:9	5045
boards for the s side southward	Ex 36:23	5045
on the s side southward the	Ex 38:9	5045
On the s side shall be the	Num 2:10	8486
s side shall take their journey	Num 10:6	8486
And they ascended by the s	Num 13:22	5045
dwell in the land of the s	Num 13:29	5045
Canaanite, which dwelt in the s	Num 21:1	5045
which dwelt in the s in the land	Num 33:40	5045
Then your s quarter shall be from	Num 34:3	5045
your s border shall be the	Num 34:3	5045
the s to the ascent of Akrabbim	Num 34:4	5045
be from the s to Kadesh-barnea	Num 34:4	5045
on the s side two thousand cubits	Num 35:5	5045
and in the vale, and in the s	Deut 1:7	5045
possess thou the west and the s	Deut 33:23	1864
And the s, and the plain of the	Deut 34:3	5045
country of the hills, and of the s	Josh 10:40	5045
and of the plains s of Chinneroth	Josh 11:2	5045
the hills, and all the s country	Josh 11:16	5045
and from the s, under	Josh 12:3	8486
wilderness, and in the s country	Josh 12:8	5045
From the s, all the land of the	Josh 13:4	8486
the uttermost part of the s coast	Josh 15:1	5045
their s border was from the shore	Josh 15:2	5045
it went out to the s side to	Josh 15:3	5045
ascended up on the s side unto	Josh 15:3	5045
this shall be your s coast	Josh 15:4	5045
which is on the s side of the	Josh 15:7	5045
unto the s side of the Jebusite	Josh 15:8	5045
for thou hast given me a s land	Josh 15:19	5045
abide in their coast on the s	Josh 18:5	5045
s side of the nether Beth-horon	Josh 18:13	5045
the s quarter was from the end of	Josh 18:15	5045
to the side of Jebusi on the s	Josh 18:16	5045

S

salt sea at the s end of Jordan Josh 18:19 5045
this was the s coast Josh 18:19 5045
to Baalath-beer, Ramath of the s Josh 19:8 5045
reacheth to Zebulun on the s side Josh 19:34 5045
in the mountain, and in the s Judg 1:9 5045
for thou hast given me a s land Judg 1:15 5045
which lieth in the s of Arad Judg 1:16 5045
Shechem, and on the s of Lebonah Judg 21:19 5045
arose out of a place toward the s 1Sa 20:41 5045
which is on the s of Jeshimon 1Sa 23:19 3225
in the plain on the s of Jeshimon 1Sa 23:24 3225
said, Against the s of Judah 1Sa 27:10 5045
of Judah, and against the s of the 1Sa 27:10 5045
against the s of the Kenites 1Sa 27:10 5045
the Amalekites had invaded the s 1Sa 30:1 5045
upon the s of the Cherethites 1Sa 30:14 5045
to Judah, and upon the s of Caleb 1Sa 30:14 5045
and to them which were in s Ramoth 1Sa 30:27 5045
they went out to the s of Judah 2Sa 24:7 5045
and three looking toward the s 1Kin 7:25 5045
house eastward over against the s 1Kin 7:39 5045
the east, west, north, and s 1Chr 9:24 5045
and three looking toward the s 2Chr 4:4 5045
the east end, over against the s 2Chr 4:10 5045
of the s of Judah, and had taken 2Chr 28:18 5045
and the chambers of the s Job 9:9 8486
Out of the s cometh the whirlwind Job 37:9 2315
quieteth the earth by the s wind Job 37:17 1864
and stretch her wings toward the s Job 39:26 8486
nor from the west, nor from the s Ps 75:6 4057
power he brought in the s wind Ps 78:26 8486
the s thou hast created them Ps 89:12 3225
from the north, and from the s Ps 107:3 3220
O LORD, as the streams in the s Ps 126:4 5045
The wind goeth toward the s Eccl 1:6 1864
and if the tree fall toward the s Eccl 11:3 1864
and come, thou s Song 4:16 8486
whirlwinds in the s pass through Is 21:1 5045
The burden of the beasts of the s Is 30:6 5045
and to the s, Keep not back Is 43:6 8486
cities of the s shall be shut up Jer 13:19 5045
from the mountains, and from the s Jer 17:26 5045
valley, and in the cities of the s Jer 32:44 5045
vale, and in the cities of the s Jer 33:13 5045
of man, set thy face toward the s Eze 20:46 8486
and drop thy word toward the s Eze 20:46 1864
against the forest of the s field Eze 20:46 5045
And say to the forest of the s Eze 20:47 5045
all faces from the s to the north Eze 20:47 5045
all flesh from the s to the north Eze 21:4 5045
as the frame of a city on the s Eze 40:2 5045
that he brought me toward the s Eze 40:24 1864
and behold a gate toward the s Eze 40:24 1864
in the inner court toward the s Eze 40:27 1864
toward the s an hundred cubits Eze 40:27 1864
to the inner court by the s gate Eze 40:28 1864
he measured the s gate according Eze 40:28 1864
their prospect was toward the s Eze 40:44 1864
whose prospect is toward the s Eze 40:45 1864
and another door toward the s Eze 41:11 1864
s was a door in the head of the Eze 42:12 1864
the s chambers, which are before Eze 42:13 1864
He measured the s side, five Eze 42:18 1864
go out by the way of the s gate Eze 46:9 5045
s gate shall go forth by the way Eze 46:9 5045
at the s side of the altar Eze 47:1 5045
the s side southward, from Tamar Eze 47:19 5045
this is the s side southward Eze 47:19 8486
in breadth, and toward the s five Eze 48:10 5045
the s side four thousand and five Eze 48:16 5045
toward the s two hundred and fifty Eze 48:17 5045
at the s side southward, the Eze 48:28 5045
at the s side four thousand and Eze 48:33 5045
exceeding great, toward the s Dan 8:9 5045
the king of the s shall be strong Dan 11:5 5045
s shall come to the king of the Dan 11:6 5045
So the king of the s shall come Dan 11:9 5045
the king of the s shall be moved Dan 11:11 5045
up against the king of the s Dan 11:14 5045
the arms of the s shall not Dan 11:15 5045
king of the s with a great army Dan 11:25 5045
the king of the s shall be Dan 11:25 5045
return, and come toward the s Dan 11:29 5045
the king of the s push at him Dan 11:40 5045
they of the s shall possess the Obad 19 5045
shall possess the cities of the s Obad 20 5045
go forth toward the s country Zec 6:6 8486
her, when men inhabited the s Zec 7:7 5045
shall go with whirlwinds of the s Zec 9:14 8486
north, and half of it toward the s Zec 14:4 5045
Geba to Rimmon s of Jerusalem Zec 14:10 5045
The queen of the s shall rise up Mt 12:42 3558
The queen of the s shall rise up Lk 11:31 3558
And when ye see the s wind blow Lk 12:55 3558
and from the north, and from the s Lk 13:29 3558
go toward the s unto the way that Acts 8:26 3314
Crete, and lieth toward the s west Acts 27:12 3047
when the s wind blew softly, Acts 27:13 3558
and after one day the s wind blew Acts 28:13 3558
on the s three gates Rev 21:13 3558

SOUTHWARD
where thou art northward, and s Gen 13:14 5045
twenty boards on the south side s Ex 26:18 8486
for the south side s there shall Ex 27:9 8486
boards for the south side s Ex 36:23 8486
on the south side s the hangings Ex 38:9 8486
on the side of the tabernacle s Ex 40:24 5045
on the side of the tabernacle s Num 3:29 8486
unto them, Get you up this way s Num 13:17 5045
eyes westward, and northward, and s Deut 3:27 8486
s was the uttermost part of the Josh 15:1 8486
sea, from the bay that looketh s Josh 15:2 5045
the coast of Edom s were Kabzeel Josh 15:21 5045
the river Kanah, s of the river Josh 17:9 5045
S it was Ephraim's, and northward Josh 17:10 5045
side of Luz, which is Beth-el, s Josh 18:13 5045
compassed the corner of the sea s Josh 18:14 5045
that lieth before Beth-horon s Josh 18:14 5045
the other s over against Gibeah 1Sa 14:5 5045
To Obed-edom s 1Chr 26:15 5045
s four a day, and toward Asuppim 1Chr 26:17 5045
And the south side s, from Tamar Eze 47:19 5045
And this is the south side s Eze 47:19 5045
of Gad, at the south side s Eze 48:28 5045
westward, and northward, and s Dan 8:4 5045

SOW
for you, and ye shall s the land Gen 47:23 2232
six years thou shalt s thy land Ex 23:10 2232
thou shalt not s thy field with Lev 19:19 2232
Six years thou shalt s thy field Lev 25:3 2232
thou shalt neither s thy field Lev 25:4 2232
ye shall not s, neither reap that Lev 25:11 2232
behold, we shall not s, nor Lev 25:20 2232
ye shall s the eighth year, and Lev 25:22 2232
ye shall s your seed in vain, for Lev 26:16 2232
Thou shalt not s thy vineyard Deut 22:9 2232
and in the third year s ye 2Kin 19:29 2232
s wickedness, reap the same Job 4:8 2232
Then let me s, and let another eat Job 31:8 2232
s the fields, and plant vineyards, Ps 107:37 2232
They that s in tears shall reap Ps 126:5 2232
observeth the wind shall not s Eccl 11:4 2232
In the morning s thy seed Eccl 11:6 2232
the plowman plow all day to s Is 28:24 2232
that thou shalt s the ground Is 30:23 2232
are ye that s beside all waters Is 32:20 2232
and in the third year s ye Is 37:30 2232
ground, and s not among thorns Jer 4:3 2232
that I will s the house of Israel Jer 31:27 2232
nor s seed, nor plant vineyard, Jer 35:7 2232
I will s her unto me in the earth Hos 2:23 2232
S to yourselves in righteousness, Hos 10:12 2232
Thou shalt s, but thou shalt not Mic 6:15 2232
I will s them among the people Zec 10:9 2232
for they s not, neither do they Mt 6:26 4687
Behold, a sower went forth to s Mt 13:3 4687
didst not thou s good seed in thy Mt 13:27 4687
there went out a sower to s Mk 4:3 4687
A sower went out to s his seed Lk 8:5 4687
for they neither s nor reap Lk 12:24 4687
and reapest that thou didst not s Lk 19:21 4687
down, and reaping that I did not s Lk 19:22 4687
the s that was washed to her 2Pet 2:22 5300

SOWED
Then Isaac s in that land, and Gen 26:12 2232
down the city, and s it with salt Judg 9:45 2232
And when he s, some seeds fell by Mt 13:4 4687
which s good seed in his field Mt 13:24 4687
s tares among the wheat, and went Mt 13:25 4687
a man took, and s in his field Mt 13:31 4687
The enemy that s them is the Mt 13:39 4687
knewest that I reap where I s not Mt 25:26 4687
And it came to pass, as he s Mk 4:4 4687
and as he s, some fell by the way Lk 8:5 4687

SOWEDST
came out, where thou s thy seed Deut 11:10 2232

SOWER
that it may give seed to the s Is 55:10 2232
Cut off the s from Babylon, and Jer 50:16 2232
Behold, a s went forth to sow Mt 13:3 4687
ye therefore the parable of the s Mt 13:18 4687
Behold, there went out a s to sow Mk 4:3 4687
The s soweth the word Mk 4:14 4687
A s went out to sow his seed Lk 8:5 4687
s both minister bread for your 2Cor 9:10 4687

SOWEST
fool, that which thou s is not 1Cor 15:36 4687
And that which thou s 1Cor 15:37 4687
thou s not that body that shall 1Cor 15:37 4687

SOWETH
he s discord Prov 6:14 7971
he that s discord among brethren Prov 6:19 7971
but to him that s righteousness Prov 11:18 2232
A froward man s strife Prov 16:28 7971
He that s iniquity shall reap Prov 22:8 2232
treader of grapes him that s seed Amos 9:13 4900
He that s the good seed is the Mt 13:37 4687
The sower s the word Mk 4:14 4687
that both he that s and he that Jn 4:36 4687
herein is that saying true, One s Jn 4:37 4687
He which s sparingly shall reap 2Cor 9:6 4687
he which s bountifully shall reap 2Cor 9:6 4687
for whatsoever a man s, that Gal 6:7 4687
For he that s to his flesh shall Gal 6:8 4687
but he that s to the Spirit shall Gal 6:8 4687

SOWING
any s seed which is to be sown Lev 11:37 2221
shall reach unto the s time Lev 26:5 2233

SOWN
which thou hast s in the field Ex 23:16 2232
any sowing seed which is to be s Lev 11:37 2232
which is neither eared nor s Deut 21:4 2232
of thy seed which thou hast s Deut 22:9 2232
and burning, that it is not s Deut 29:23 2232
And so it was, when Israel had s Judg 6:3 2232
Light is s for the righteous, and Ps 97:11 2232
every thing s by the brooks, Is 19:7 4218
yea, they shall not be s Is 40:24 2232
that are s in it to spring forth Is 61:11 2221
in a land that was not s Jer 2:2 2232
They have s wheat, but shall reap Jer 12:13 2232
you, and ye shall be tilled and s Eze 36:9 2232
For they have s the wind, and they Hos 8:7 2232
that no more of thy name be s Nah 1:14 2232
Ye have s much, and bring in Hag 1:6 2232
that which was s in his heart Mt 13:19 4687
reaping where thou hast not s Mt 25:24 4687
the way side, where the word is s Mk 4:15 4687
word that was s in their hearts Mk 4:15 4687
which are s on stony ground Mk 4:16 4687
are they which are s among thorns Mk 4:18 4687
they which are s on good ground Mk 4:20 4687
when it is s in the earth, is Mk 4:31 4687
But when it is s, it groweth up, Mk 4:32 4687
If we have s unto you spiritual 1Cor 9:11 4687
It is s in corruption 1Cor 15:42 4687
It is s in dishonour 1Cor 15:43 4687
it is s in weakness 1Cor 15:43 4687
It is s a natural body 1Cor 15:44 4687
food, and multiply your seed s 2Cor 9:10
is s in peace of them that make Jas 3:18 4687

SPACE
abode with him the s of a month Gen 29:14 3117
put a s betwixt drove and drove Gen 32:16 7305
the s of the seven sabbaths of Lev 25:8 3117
within the s of a full year Lev 25:30 4390
the s in which we came from Deut 2:14 3117
there shall be a s between you Josh 3:4 7350
a great s being between them 1Sa 26:13 4725
now for a little s grace hath Ezr 9:8 7281
within the s of two full years Jer 28:11 5750
The s also before the little Eze 40:12 1366
the s was one cubit on that side Eze 40:12 1366
about the s of one hour after Lk 22:59 1339
it was about the s of three hours Acts 5:7 1292
put the apostles forth a little s Acts 5:34 1024
sacrifices by the s of forty Acts 7:42
about the s of four hundred Acts 13:20
Benjamin, by the s of forty years Acts 13:21
after they had tarried there a s Acts 15:33 5550
boldly for the s of three months Acts 19:8 1909
continued by the s of two years Acts 19:10 1909
the s of two hours cried out Acts 19:34 1909
that by the s of three years I Acts 20:31 4158
the earth by the s of three years Jas 5:17
I gave her s to repent of her Rev 2:21 5550
about the s of half an hour Rev 8:1
by the s of a thousand and six Rev 14:20 575
he must continue a short s Rev 17:10

SPAIN
(spane) *Land at the western extremity of the Mediterranean Sea.*
I take my journey into S, I will Rom 15:24 4681
fruit, I will come by you into S Rom 15:28 4681

SPAKE
And God s unto Noah, saying, Gen 8:15 1696
God s unto Noah, and to his sons Gen 9:8 559
name of the LORD that s unto her Gen 16:13 1696
he s unto him yet again, and said, Gen 18:29 1696
s unto his sons in law, which Gen 19:14 1696
of his host s unto Abraham Gen 21:22 559
Isaac s unto Abraham his father, Gen 22:7 559
s unto the sons of Heth, saying, Gen 23:3 1696
he s unto Ephron in the audience Gen 23:13 1696
which s unto me, and that sware Gen 24:7 1696
saying, Thus s the man unto me Gen 24:30 1696
when Isaac s to Esau his son Gen 27:5 1696
Rebekah s unto Jacob her son, Gen 27:6 559
And while he yet s with them Gen 29:9 1696
the angel of God s unto me in a Gen 31:11 559
your father s unto me yesternight Gen 31:29 559
and s kindly unto the damsel Gen 34:3 1696
Shechem s unto his father Hamor, Gen 34:4 559
of the place where God s with him Gen 35:15 1696
as she s to Joseph day by day, Gen 39:10 1696
s unto them, saying, See, he hath Gen 39:14 559
she s unto him according to these Gen 39:17 1696
of his wife, which she s unto him Gen 39:19 1696
Then s the chief butler unto Gen 41:9 1696
unto them, and s roughly unto them Gen 42:7 1696
That is it that I s unto you Gen 42:14 1696
S I not unto you, saying, Do not Gen 42:22 559
for he s unto them by an Gen 42:23
s roughly to us, and took us for Gen 42:30 1696
Reuben s unto his father, saying, Gen 42:37 559
Judah s unto him, saying, The man Gen 43:3 559
well, the old man of whom ye s Gen 43:27 559
brother, of whom ye s unto me Gen 43:29 559
he s unto them these same words Gen 44:6 1696
God s unto Israel in the visions Gen 46:2 559
Pharaoh s unto Joseph, saying, Gen 47:5 559
it that their father s unto them Gen 49:28 1696
Joseph s unto the house of Gen 50:4 1696
Joseph wept when they s unto him Gen 50:17 1696
them, and s kindly unto them Gen 50:21 1696
the king of Egypt s to the Hebrew Ex 1:15 559
Aaron s all the words which the Ex 4:30 1696
they s to the people, saying, Ex 5:10 559
God s unto Moses, and said unto Ex 6:2 1696
Moses s so unto the children of Ex 6:9 1696
the LORD s unto Moses, saying, Ex 6:10 1696
Moses s before the LORD, saying, Ex 6:12 1696
the LORD s unto Moses and unto Ex 6:13 1696
These are they which s to Pharaoh Ex 6:27 1696
pass on the day when the LORD s Ex 6:28 1696
That the LORD s unto Moses Ex 6:29 1696
old, when they s unto Pharaoh Ex 7:7 1696
the LORD s unto Moses and unto Ex 7:8 559
the LORD s unto Moses, Say unto Ex 7:19 559
the LORD s unto Moses, Go unto Ex 8:1 559
the LORD s unto Moses, Say unto Ex 8:5 559
the LORD s unto Moses and Aaron in Ex 12:1 559
the LORD s unto Moses, saying, Ex 13:1 1696
the LORD s unto Moses, saying, Ex 14:1 1696
this song unto the LORD, and s Ex 15:1 559
Moses s unto Aaron, Say unto all Ex 16:9 559

Context	Reference	Number
as Aaron *s* unto the whole	Ex 16:10	1696
the LORD *s* unto Moses, saying,	Ex 16:11	1696
waxed louder and louder, Moses *s*	Ex 19:19	1696
unto the people, and *s* unto them	Ex 19:25	559
God *s* all these words, saying,	Ex 20:1	1696
the LORD *s* unto Moses, saying,	Ex 25:1	1696
the LORD *s* unto Moses, saying,	Ex 30:11	1696
the LORD *s* unto Moses, saying,	Ex 30:17	1696
Moreover the LORD *s* unto Moses	Ex 30:22	1696
the LORD *s* unto Moses, saying,	Ex 31:1	1696
the LORD *s* unto Moses, saying,	Ex 31:12	559
the LORD *s* unto Moses face to	Ex 33:11	1696
s unto the children of Israel	Ex 34:34	1696
Moses *s* unto all the congregation	Ex 35:4	559
they *s* unto Moses, saying, The	Ex 36:5	559
the LORD *s* unto Moses, saying,	Ex 40:1	1696
s unto him out of the tabernacle	Lev 1:1	1696
the LORD *s* unto Moses, saying,	Lev 4:1	1696
the LORD *s* unto Moses, saying,	Lev 5:14	1696
the LORD *s* unto Moses, saying,	Lev 6:1	1696
the LORD *s* unto Moses, saying,	Lev 6:8	1696
the LORD *s* unto Moses, saying,	Lev 6:19	1696
the LORD *s* unto Moses, saying,	Lev 6:24	1696
the LORD *s* unto Moses, saying,	Lev 7:22	1696
the LORD *s* unto Moses, saying,	Lev 7:28	1696
the LORD *s* unto Moses, saying,	Lev 8:1	1696
Aaron, This is it that the LORD *s*	Lev 10:3	1696
the LORD *s* unto Aaron, saying,	Lev 10:8	1696
Moses *s* unto Aaron, and unto	Lev 10:12	1696
the LORD *s* unto Moses and to Aaron	Lev 11:1	1696
the LORD *s* unto Moses, saying,	Lev 12:1	1696
the LORD *s* unto Moses and Aaron,	Lev 13:1	1696
the LORD *s* unto Moses, saying,	Lev 14:1	1696
the LORD *s* unto Moses and unto	Lev 14:33	1696
the LORD *s* unto Moses and to Aaron	Lev 15:1	1696
the LORD *s* unto Moses after the	Lev 16:1	1696
the LORD *s* unto Moses, saying,	Lev 17:1	1696
the LORD *s* unto Moses, saying,	Lev 18:1	1696
the LORD *s* unto Moses, saying,	Lev 19:1	1696
the LORD *s* unto Moses, saying,	Lev 20:1	1696
the LORD *s* unto Moses, saying,	Lev 21:16	1696
the LORD *s* unto Moses, saying,	Lev 22:1	1696
the LORD *s* unto Moses, saying,	Lev 22:17	1696
the LORD *s* unto Moses, saying,	Lev 22:26	1696
the LORD *s* unto Moses, saying,	Lev 23:1	1696
the LORD *s* unto Moses, saying,	Lev 23:9	1696
the LORD *s* unto Moses, saying,	Lev 23:23	1696
the LORD *s* unto Moses, saying,	Lev 23:26	1696
the LORD *s* unto Moses, saying,	Lev 23:33	1696
the LORD *s* unto Moses, saying,	Lev 24:1	1696
the LORD *s* unto Moses, saying,	Lev 24:13	1696
Moses *s* to the children of Israel	Lev 24:23	1696
the LORD *s* unto Moses in mount	Lev 25:1	1696
the LORD *s* unto Moses, saying,	Lev 27:1	1696
the LORD *s* unto Moses in the	Num 1:1	1696
the LORD *s* unto Moses and unto	Num 2:1	1696
LORD *s* with Moses in mount Sinai	Num 3:1	1696
the LORD *s* unto Moses, saying,	Num 3:5	1696
the LORD *s* unto Moses, saying,	Num 3:11	1696
the LORD *s* unto Moses in the	Num 3:14	1696
the LORD *s* unto Moses, saying,	Num 3:44	1696
the LORD *s* unto Moses and unto	Num 4:1	1696
the LORD *s* unto Moses and unto	Num 4:17	1696
the LORD *s* unto Moses, saying,	Num 4:21	1696
the LORD *s* unto Moses, saying,	Num 5:1	1696
as the LORD *s* unto Moses, so did	Num 5:4	1696
the LORD *s* unto Moses, saying,	Num 5:5	1696
the LORD *s* unto Moses, saying,	Num 5:11	1696
the LORD *s* unto Moses, saying,	Num 6:1	1696
the LORD *s* unto Moses, saying,	Num 6:22	1696
the LORD *s* unto Moses, saying,	Num 7:4	559
and he *s* unto him	Num 7:89	1696
the LORD *s* unto Moses, saying,	Num 8:1	1696
the LORD *s* unto Moses, saying,	Num 8:5	1696
the LORD *s* unto Moses, saying,	Num 8:23	1696
the LORD *s* unto Moses in the	Num 9:1	1696
Moses *s* unto the children of	Num 9:4	1696
the LORD *s* unto Moses, saying,	Num 9:9	1696
the LORD *s* unto Moses, saying,	Num 10:1	1696
s unto him, and took of the spirit	Num 11:25	1696
Aaron *s* against Moses because of	Num 12:1	1696
the LORD *s* suddenly unto Moses,	Num 12:4	559
the LORD *s* unto Moses, saying,	Num 13:1	1696
they *s* unto all the company of	Num 14:7	559
the LORD *s* unto Moses and unto	Num 14:26	1696
the LORD *s* unto Moses, saying,	Num 15:1	1696
the LORD *s* unto Moses, saying,	Num 15:17	1696
the LORD *s* unto Moses, saying,	Num 15:37	559
he *s* unto Korah and unto all his	Num 16:5	1696
the LORD *s* unto Moses and unto	Num 16:20	1696
the LORD *s* unto Moses, saying,	Num 16:23	1696
he *s* unto the congregation,	Num 16:26	1696
the LORD *s* unto Moses, saying,	Num 16:36	1696
the LORD *s* unto Moses, saying,	Num 16:44	1696
the LORD *s* unto Moses, saying,	Num 17:1	1696
Moses *s* unto the children of	Num 17:6	1696
children of Israel *s* unto Moses	Num 17:12	559
the LORD *s* unto Aaron, Behold, I	Num 18:8	1696
the LORD *s* unto Aaron, Thou shalt	Num 18:20	559
the LORD *s* unto Moses, saying,	Num 18:25	1696
the LORD *s* unto Moses and unto	Num 19:1	1696
the people chode with Moses, and *s*	Num 20:3	559
the LORD *s* unto Moses, saying,	Num 20:7	1696
the LORD *s* unto Moses and Aaron,	Num 20:12	559
the LORD *s* unto Moses and Aaron in	Num 20:23	559
the people *s* against God, and	Num 21:5	1696
whereof the LORD *s* unto Moses	Num 21:16	559
s unto him the words of Balak	Num 22:7	1696
S I not also to thy messengers	Num 24:12	1696
the LORD *s* unto Moses, saying,	Num 25:10	1696
the LORD *s* unto Moses, saying,	Num 25:16	1696
that the LORD *s* unto Moses	Num 26:1	559
Eleazar the priest *s* with them in	Num 26:3	1696
the LORD *s* unto Moses, saying,	Num 26:52	1696
the LORD *s* unto Moses, saying,	Num 27:6	559
Moses *s* unto the LORD, saying,	Num 27:15	1696
the LORD *s* unto Moses, saying,	Num 28:1	1696
Moses *s* unto the heads of the	Num 30:1	1696
the LORD *s* unto Moses, saying,	Num 31:1	1696
Moses *s* unto the people, saying,	Num 31:3	1696
the LORD *s* unto Moses, saying,	Num 31:25	559
s unto Moses, and to Eleazar the	Num 32:2	559
children of Reuben *s* unto Moses	Num 32:25	559
the LORD *s* unto Moses in the	Num 33:50	1696
the LORD *s* unto Moses, saying,	Num 34:1	1696
the LORD *s* unto Moses, saying,	Num 34:16	1696
the LORD *s* unto Moses in the	Num 35:1	1696
the LORD *s* unto Moses, saying,	Num 35:9	1696
s before Moses, and before the	Num 36:1	1696
s unto all Israel on this side	Deut 1:1	1696
that Moses *s* unto the children of	Deut 1:3	1696
LORD our God *s* unto us in Horeb	Deut 1:6	1696
I *s* unto you at that time, saying	Deut 1:9	559
So I *s* unto you	Deut 1:43	1696
Red sea, as the LORD *s* unto me	Deut 2:1	1696
And the LORD *s* unto me, saying,	Deut 2:2	559
That the LORD *s* unto me, saying,	Deut 2:17	1696
the LORD *s* unto you out of the	Deut 4:12	1696
on the day that the LORD *s* unto	Deut 4:15	1696
which Moses *s* unto the children	Deut 4:45	1696
These words the LORD *s* unto all	Deut 5:22	1696
of your words, when ye *s* unto me	Deut 5:28	1696
which the LORD *s* with you in the	Deut 9:10	1696
Furthermore the LORD *s* unto me	Deut 9:13	559
which the LORD *s* unto you in the	Deut 10:4	1696
to pass, whereof he *s* unto thee	Deut 13:2	1696
the Levites *s* unto all Israel	Deut 27:9	1696
by the way whereof I *s* unto thee	Deut 28:68	559
s these words unto all Israel	Deut 31:1	1696
Moses *s* in the ears of all the	Deut 31:30	1696
s all the words of this song in	Deut 32:44	1696
the LORD *s* unto Moses that	Deut 32:48	1696
that the LORD *s* unto Joshua the	Josh 1:1	559
of Manasseh, *s* Joshua, saying,	Josh 1:12	559
Joshua *s* unto the priests, saying	Josh 3:6	559
that the LORD *s* unto Joshua	Josh 4:1	559
Jordan, as the LORD *s* unto Joshua	Josh 4:8	1696
of Israel, as Moses *s* unto them	Josh 4:12	1696
the LORD *s* unto Joshua, saying,	Josh 4:15	559
he *s* unto the children of Israel,	Josh 4:21	559
s unto them, saying, Go up and	Josh 7:2	559
of our country *s* to us, saying,	Josh 9:11	559
he *s* unto them, saying, Wherefore	Josh 9:22	1696
Then *s* Joshua to the LORD in the	Josh 10:12	1696
even since the LORD *s* this word	Josh 14:10	1696
whereof the LORD *s* in that day	Josh 14:12	1696
children of Joseph *s* unto Joshua	Josh 17:14	1696
Joshua *s* unto the house of Joseph	Josh 17:17	559
The LORD also *s* unto Joshua	Josh 20:1	1696
whereof I *s* unto you by the hand	Josh 20:2	1696
they *s* unto them at Shiloh in the	Josh 21:2	1696
he *s* unto them, saying, Return	Josh 22:8	559
they *s* with them, saying,	Josh 22:15	1696
Gad and the children of Manasseh *s*	Josh 22:30	1696
LORD your God *s* concerning you	Josh 23:14	1696
of the LORD which he *s* unto us	Josh 24:27	1696
LORD *s* these words unto all the	Judg 2:4	1696
Penuel, and *s* unto them likewise	Judg 8:8	1696
he *s* also unto the men of Penuel,	Judg 8:9	559
his mother's brethren *s* of him in	Judg 9:3	1696
Gaal *s* again and said, See there	Judg 9:37	1696
they *s* unto him, saying, No	Judg 15:13	559
s to the master of the house, the	Judg 19:22	559
kinsman of whom Boaz *s* came by	Ruth 4:1	1696
Now Hannah, she *s* in her heart	1Sa 1:13	1696
Samuel *s* unto all the house of	1Sa 7:3	559
went to enquire of God, thus he *s*	1Sa 9:9	559
the man whom I *s* to thee of	1Sa 9:17	559
of the kingdom, whereof Samuel *s*	1Sa 10:16	559
Samuel did that which the LORD *s*	1Sa 16:4	1696
s according to the same words	1Sa 17:23	1696
David *s* to the men that stood by	1Sa 17:26	559
heard when he *s* unto the men	1Sa 17:28	1696
and *s* after the same manner	1Sa 17:30	559
words were heard which David *s*	1Sa 17:31	1696
Saul's servants *s* those words in	1Sa 18:23	1696
saying, On this manner *s* David	1Sa 18:24	1696
Saul *s* to Jonathan his son, and to	1Sa 19:1	1696
Jonathan *s* good of David unto	1Sa 19:4	1696
Nevertheless Saul *s* not any thing	1Sa 20:26	1696
they *s* to Nabal according to all	1Sa 25:9	1696
they *s* unto her, saying, David	1Sa 25:40	1696
and the woman *s* to Saul, saying,	1Sa 28:12	559
hath done to him, as he *s* by me	1Sa 28:17	1696
for the people *s* of stoning him	1Sa 30:6	559
Abner also *s* in the ears of	2Sa 3:19	1696
Israel to David unto Hebron, and *s*	2Sa 5:1	559
which *s* unto David, saying,	2Sa 5:6	559
s I a word with any of the tribes	2Sa 7:7	1696
we *s* unto him, and he would not	2Sa 12:18	1696
Absalom *s* unto his brother Amnon	2Sa 13:22	1696
the woman of Tekoah *s* to the king	2Sa 14:4	559
Absalom *s* unto him, saying,	2Sa 17:6	559
Then she *s*, saying, They were	2Sa 20:18	559
David *s* unto the LORD the words	2Sa 22:1	1696
The Spirit of the LORD *s* by me	2Sa 23:2	1696
said, the Rock of Israel *s* to me	2Sa 23:3	1696
David *s* unto the LORD when he saw	2Sa 24:17	559
Wherefore Nathan *s* unto	1Kin 1:11	559
And while he yet *s*, behold,	1Kin 1:42	1696
his word which he *s* concerning me	1Kin 2:4	1696
which he *s* concerning the house	1Kin 2:27	1696
Thus they *s* before the king	1Kin 3:22	1696
Then *s* the woman whose the living	1Kin 3:26	559
he *s* three thousand proverbs	1Kin 4:32	1696
he *s* of trees, from the cedar	1Kin 4:33	1696
he *s* also of beasts, and of fowl,	1Kin 4:33	1696
as the LORD *s* unto David my	1Kin 5:5	1696
which I *s* unto David thy father	1Kin 6:12	1696
Then *s* Solomon, The LORD said	1Kin 8:12	559
which *s* with his mouth unto David	1Kin 8:15	1696
hath performed his word that he *s*	1Kin 8:20	1696
came, and *s* unto Rehoboam, saying,	1Kin 12:3	1696
they *s* unto him, saying, If thou	1Kin 12:7	1696
were grown up with him *s* unto him	1Kin 12:10	1696
unto this people that *s* unto thee	1Kin 12:10	1696
s to them after the counsel of	1Kin 12:14	1696
which the LORD *s* by Ahijah the	1Kin 12:15	1696
an angel *s* unto me by the word of	1Kin 13:18	1696
of the LORD, which he *s* unto him	1Kin 13:26	1696
he *s* to his sons, saying, Saddle	1Kin 13:27	1696
that he *s* to his sons, saying,	1Kin 13:31	559
which he *s* by the hand of his	1Kin 14:18	1696
which he *s* by his servant Ahijah	1Kin 15:29	1696
which he *s* against Baasha by Jehu	1Kin 16:12	1696
which he *s* by Joshua the son of	1Kin 16:34	1696
of the LORD, which he *s* by Elijah	1Kin 17:16	1696
s unto the king of Israel, and	1Kin 20:28	559
Ahab *s* unto Naboth, saying, Give	1Kin 21:2	1696
Because I *s* unto Naboth the	1Kin 21:6	1696
And of Jezebel also *s* the LORD	1Kin 21:23	1696
gone to call Micaiah *s* unto him	1Kin 22:13	1696
the word of the LORD which he *s*	1Kin 22:38	1696
he *s* unto him, Thou man of God,	2Kin 1:9	1696
the saying of Elisha which he *s*	2Kin 2:22	1696
s unto him, and said, My father,	2Kin 5:13	1696
who *s* when the king came down to	2Kin 7:17	1696
Then *s* Elisha unto the woman,	2Kin 8:1	1696
thus *s* he to me, saying, Thus	2Kin 9:12	559
which he *s* by his servant Elijah	2Kin 9:36	1696
which the LORD *s* concerning the	2Kin 10:10	1696
which he *s* by his servant Elijah	2Kin 10:10	1696
of the LORD, which he *s* to Elijah	2Kin 10:17	1696
which he *s* by the hand of his	2Kin 14:25	1696
of the LORD which he *s* unto Jehu	2Kin 15:12	1696
Wherefore they *s* to the king of	2Kin 17:26	559
voice in the Jews' language, and *s*	2Kin 18:28	1696
the LORD *s* by his servants the	2Kin 21:10	1696
what I *s* against this place	2Kin 22:19	1696
which he *s* by his servants the	2Kin 24:2	1696
he *s* kindly to him, and set his	2Kin 25:28	1696
David *s* to the chief of the	1Chr 15:16	559
s I a word to any of the judges	1Chr 17:6	1696
And the LORD *s* unto Gad, David's	1Chr 21:9	1696
which he *s* in the name of the	1Chr 21:19	1696
Then Solomon *s* unto all Israel,	2Chr 1:2	559
he *s* with his mouth to my father	2Chr 6:4	1696
came and *s* to Rehoboam, saying,	2Chr 10:3	1696
they *s* unto him, saying, If thou	2Chr 10:7	1696
brought up with him *s* unto him	2Chr 10:10	1696
the people that *s* unto thee	2Chr 10:10	1696
which he *s* by the hand of Ahijah	2Chr 10:15	1696
went to call Micaiah *s* to him	2Chr 18:12	1696
one *s* saying after this manner,	2Chr 18:19	559
Hezekiah *s* comfortably unto all	2Chr 30:22	1696
s comfortably to them, saying,	2Chr 32:6	1696
his servants *s* yet more against	2Chr 32:16	1696
they *s* against the God of	2Chr 32:19	1696
he *s* unto him, and he gave him a	2Chr 32:24	559
the LORD *s* to Manasseh, and to his	2Chr 33:10	1696
the words of the seers that *s* to	2Chr 33:18	1696
they *s* to her to that effect	2Chr 34:22	1696
the singing women *s* of Josiah in	2Chr 35:25	559
he *s* before his brethren and the	Neh 4:2	559
they *s* unto Ezra the scribe to	Neh 8:1	559
their children *s* half in the	Neh 13:24	1696
when they *s* daily unto him, and he	Est 3:4	559
Again Esther *s* unto Hatach	Est 4:10	559
Esther *s* yet again before the	Est 8:3	1696
nights, and none *s* a word unto him	Job 2:13	1696
And Job *s*, and said,	Job 3:2	6030
I arose, and they *s* against me	Job 19:18	1696
After my words they *s* not again	Job 29:22	
I had waited, (for they *s* not	Job 32:16	1696
Elihu *s* moreover, and said,	Job 35:1	6030
who *s* unto the LORD the words of	Ps 18:*t*	1696
For he *s*, and it was done	Ps 33:9	559
then *s* I with my tongue,	Ps 39:3	1696
Yea, they *s* against God	Ps 78:19	1696
He *s* unto them in the cloudy	Ps 99:7	1696
He *s*, and there came divers sorts	Ps 105:31	559
He *s*, and the locusts came, and	Ps 105:34	559
so that he *s* unadvisedly with his	Ps 106:33	981
the man *s* unto Ithiel, even unto	Prov 30:1	5002
My beloved *s*, and said unto me,	Song 2:10	6030
my soul failed when he *s*	Song 5:6	1696
the LORD *s* again unto Ahaz	Is 7:10	1696
The LORD *s* also unto me again,	Is 8:5	1696
For the LORD *s* thus to me with a	Is 8:11	559
At the same time *s* the LORD by	Is 20:2	1696
when I *s*, ye did not hear	Is 65:12	1696
when I *s*, they did not hear	Is 66:4	1696
I *s* unto you, rising up early and	Jer 7:13	1696
For I *s* not unto your fathers,	Jer 7:22	1696
and heard, but they *s* not aright	Jer 8:6	1696
them, neither *s* unto them	Jer 14:14	1696
which I commanded not, nor *s* it	Jer 19:5	1696
For since I *s*, I cried out, I	Jer 20:8	1696
I *s* unto thee in thy prosperity	Jer 22:21	1696
s unto all the people of Judah	Jer 25:2	1696
Then *s* the priests and the	Jer 26:11	559
Then *s* Jeremiah unto all the	Jer 26:12	559
s to all the assembly of the	Jer 26:17	559
s to all the people of Judah,	Jer 26:18	559
I *s* also to Zedekiah king of	Jer 27:12	1696
Also I *s* to the priests and to all	Jer 27:16	1696
s unto me in the house of the	Jer 28:1	559
Hananiah *s* in the presence of all	Jer 28:11	559
that the LORD *s* concerning Israel	Jer 30:4	1696
for since I *s* against him	Jer 31:20	1696
Then Jeremiah the prophet *s* all	Jer 34:6	1696
from the day I *s* unto thee	Jer 36:2	1696

S

which he s by the prophet	Jer 37:2	1696
house, and s to the king, saying,	Jer 38:8	1696
s to Gedaliah in Mizpah secretly	Jer 40:15	559
Then s Azariah the son of	Jer 43:2	559
s unto Baruch the son of Neriah	Jer 45:1	1696
The word that the LORD s to	Jer 46:13	1696
that the LORD s against Babylon	Jer 50:1	1696
done that which he s against the	Jer 51:12	1696
s kindly unto him, and set his	Jer 52:32	1696
and I heard a voice of one that s	Eze 1:28	1696
entered into me when he s unto me	Eze 2:2	1696
that I heard him that s unto me	Eze 2:2	1696
s with me, and said unto me, Go,	Eze 3:24	1696
he s unto the man clothed with	Eze 10:2	559
Then I s unto them of the	Eze 11:25	1696
So I s unto the people in the	Eze 24:18	1696
the king s unto Ashpenaz the	Dan 1:3	559
Then s the Chaldeans to the king	Dan 2:4	1696
They s and said to the king	Dan 3:9	6032
Nebuchadnezzar s and said unto	Dan 3:14	6032
therefore he s, and commanded that	Dan 3:19	6032
and rose up in haste, and s	Dan 3:24	6032
the burning fiery furnace, and s	Dan 3:26	6032
Then Nebuchadnezzar s, and said,	Dan 3:28	6032
The king s, and said, Belteshazzar	Dan 4:19	6032
The king s, and said, Is not this	Dan 4:30	6032
And the king s, and said to the	Dan 5:7	6032
and the queen s and said, O king,	Dan 5:10	6032
And the king s and said unto Daniel	Dan 5:13	6032
s before the king concerning the	Dan 6:12	560
Now the king s and said unto	Dan 6:16	6032
and the king s and said to Daniel,	Dan 6:20	6032
Daniel s and said, I saw in my	Dan 7:2	6032
the great words which the horn s	Dan 7:11	4449
a mouth that s very great things,	Dan 7:20	4449
unto that certain saint which s	Dan 8:13	1696
which s in thy name to our kings,	Dan 9:6	1696
which he s against us, and against	Dan 9:12	1696
then I opened my mouth, and s	Dan 10:16	1696
in Beth-el, and there he s with us	Hos 12:4	1696
When Ephraim s trembling, he	Hos 13:1	1696
the LORD s unto the fish, and it	Jonah 2:10	559
Then s Haggai the LORD's	Hag 1:13	559
And he s, saying, These are the	Zec 1:21	559
s unto those that stood before	Zec 3:4	559
s to the angel that talked with	Zec 4:4	559
s unto me, saying, This is the	Zec 4:6	559
s unto me, saying, Behold, these	Zec 6:8	1696
the LORD s often one to another	Mal 3:16	1696
While he s these things unto them	Mt 9:18	2980
devil was cast out, the dumb s	Mt 9:33	2980
that the blind and dumb both s	Mt 12:22	2980
he s many things unto them in	Mt 13:3	2980
Another parable s he unto them	Mt 13:33	2980
All these things s Jesus unto the	Mt 13:34	2980
a parable s he not unto them	Mt 13:34	2980
But straightway Jesus s unto them	Mt 14:27	2980
ye do not understand that I s it	Mt 16:11	2036
While he yet s, behold, a bright	Mt 17:5	2980
disciples understood that he s	Mt 17:13	2036
they perceived that he s of them	Mt 21:45	3004
s unto them again by parables, and	Mt 22:1	2036
Then s Jesus to the multitude, and	Mt 23:1	2980
And while he yet s, lo, Judas, one	Mt 26:47	2980
s unto them, saying, All power is	Mt 28:18	2980
he s to his disciples, that a	Mk 3:9	2036
parables s he the word unto them	Mk 4:33	2980
a parable s he not unto them	Mk 4:34	2980
While he yet s, there came from	Mk 5:35	2980
tongue was loosed, and he s plain	Mk 7:35	2980
And he s that saying openly	Mk 8:32	2980
I s to thy disciples that they	Mk 9:18	2036
how in the bush God s unto him	Mk 12:26	2036
But he s the more vehemently, If	Mk 14:31	3004
and prayed, and s the same words	Mk 14:39	2036
And immediately, while he yet s	Mk 14:43	2980
she s out with a loud voice, and	Lk 1:42	400
As he s to our fathers, to	Lk 1:55	2980
and his tongue loosed, and he s	Lk 1:64	2980
As he s by the mouth of his holy	Lk 1:70	2980
s of him to all them that looked	Lk 2:38	2980
the saying which he s unto them	Lk 2:50	2980
s among themselves, saying, What	Lk 4:36	4814
he s also a parable unto them	Lk 5:36	3004
he s a parable unto them, Can the	Lk 6:39	2036
he s within himself, saying, This	Lk 7:39	2036
of every city, he s by a parable	Lk 8:4	2036
While he yet s, there cometh one	Lk 8:49	2980
s unto them of the kingdom of God	Lk 9:11	2980
s of his decease which he should	Lk 9:31	3004
While he thus s, there came a	Lk 9:34	3004
devil was gone out, the dumb s	Lk 11:14	2980
as he s these things, a certain	Lk 11:27	3004
And as he s, a certain Pharisee	Lk 11:37	2980
he s a parable unto them, saying,	Lk 12:16	2036
He s also this parable	Lk 13:6	3004
Jesus answering s unto the	Lk 14:3	2036
he s this parable unto them,	Lk 15:3	2036
he s a parable unto them to this	Lk 18:1	3004
he s this parable unto certain	Lk 18:9	2036
s a parable, because he was nigh	Lk 19:11	2036
s unto him, saying, Tell us, by	Lk 20:2	2036
as some s of the temple, how it	Lk 21:5	3004
And he s to them a parable	Lk 21:29	2036
And while he yet s, behold a	Lk 22:47	2980
And immediately, while he yet s	Lk 22:60	2980
blasphemously s they against him	Lk 22:65	3004
to release Jesus, s again to them	Lk 23:20	4377
remember how he s unto you when	Lk 24:6	2980
And as they thus s, Jesus himself	Lk 24:36	2980
are the words which I s unto you	Lk 24:44	2980
saying, This was he of whom I s	Jn 1:15	2036
But he s of the temple of his	Jn 2:21	3004
He s of Judas Iscariot the son of	Jn 6:71	3004
Howbeit no man s openly of him	Jn 7:13	2980
(But this s he of the Spirit,	Jn 7:39	2036
Never man s like this man	Jn 7:46	2980
Then s Jesus again unto them,	Jn 8:12	2980
These words s Jesus in the	Jn 8:20	2980
that he s to them of the Father	Jn 8:27	3004
As he s these words, many	Jn 8:30	2980
These words s his parents	Jn 9:22	2036
We know that God s unto Moses	Jn 9:29	2980
This parable s Jesus unto them	Jn 10:6	2036
they were which he s unto them	Jn 10:6	2980
that John s of this man were true	Jn 10:41	2036
Howbeit Jesus s of his death	Jn 11:13	2046
And this s he not of himself	Jn 11:51	2036
s among themselves, as they stood	Jn 11:56	3004
others said, An angel s to him	Jn 12:29	2980
These things s Jesus, and departed	Jn 12:36	2980
might be fulfilled, which he s	Jn 12:38	2036
he saw his glory, and s of him	Jn 12:41	2980
on another, doubting of whom he s	Jn 13:22	3004
ask who it should be of whom he s	Jn 13:24	3004
what intent he s this unto him	Jn 13:28	2036
These words s Jesus, and lifted up	Jn 17:1	2980
might be fulfilled, which he s	Jn 18:9	2036
s unto her that kept the door, and	Jn 18:16	2036
him, I s openly to the world	Jn 18:20	2980
might be fulfilled, which he s	Jn 18:32	2036
This s he, signifying by what	Jn 21:19	2036
David s before concerning Judas	Acts 1:16	4227
He seeing this before s of the	Acts 2:31	2980
as they s unto the people, the	Acts 4:1	2980
they s the word of God with	Acts 4:31	2980
and the spirit by which he s	Acts 6:10	2980
God s on this wise, That his seed	Acts 7:6	2980
which s to him in the mount Sina	Acts 7:38	2980
unto those things which Philip s	Acts 8:6	3004
angel of the Lord s unto Philip	Acts 8:26	2980
he s boldly in the name of the	Acts 9:29	2980
when the angel which s unto	Acts 10:7	2980
the voice s unto him again the	Acts 10:15	
While Peter yet s these words	Acts 10:44	2980
s unto the Grecians, preaching	Acts 11:20	2980
s against those things which were	Acts 13:45	483
synagogue of the Jews, and so s	Acts 14:1	2980
s unto the women which resorted	Acts 16:13	2980
they s unto him the word of the	Acts 16:32	2980
Then s the Lord to Paul in the	Acts 18:9	2036
being fervent in the spirit, he s	Acts 18:25	2980
and they s with tongues, and	Acts 19:6	2980
s boldly for the space of three	Acts 19:8	
but s evil of that way before the	Acts 19:9	2551
of all for the words which he s	Acts 20:38	2046
he s unto them in the Hebrew	Acts 21:40	4377
when they heard that he s in the	Acts 22:2	4377
not the voice of him that s to me	Acts 22:9	2980
as he thus s for himself, Festus	Acts 26:24	626
But when the Jews s against it	Acts 28:19	483
came shewed or s any harm of thee	Acts 28:21	2980
Well s the Holy Ghost by Esaias	Acts 28:25	2980
I s as a child, I understood as a	1Cor 13:11	2980
would that ye all s with tongues	1Cor 14:5	2980
but as we s all things to you in	2Cor 7:14	2980
is then the blessedness ye s of	Gal 4:15	
in divers manners s in time past	Heb 1:1	2980
For he s in a certain place of	Heb 4:4	2046
of which tribe Moses s nothing	Heb 7:14	2980
who refused him that s on earth	Heb 12:25	5537
but holy men of God s as they	2Pet 1:21	2980
to see the voice that s with me	Rev 1:12	2980
heard from heaven s unto me again	Rev 10:8	2980
like a lamb, and he s as a dragon	Rev 13:11	2980

SPAKEST

the man that s unto the woman	Judg 13:11	1696
s of also in mine ears, behold,	Judg 17:2	559
thy words which thou s unto me	1Sa 28:21	1696
thou s also with thy mouth, and	1Kin 8:24	1696
which thou s unto thy servant	1Kin 8:26	1696
as thou s by the hand of Moses	1Kin 8:53	1696
s with thy mouth, and hast	2Chr 6:15	1696
s with them from heaven, and	Neh 9:13	1696
Then thou s in vision to thy holy	Ps 89:19	1696
for since thou s of him, thou	Jer 48:27	1697

SPAN

a s shall be the length thereof,	Ex 28:16	2239
a s shall be the breadth thereof	Ex 28:16	2239
a s was the length thereof, and a	Ex 39:9	2239
a s the breadth thereof, being	Ex 39:9	2239
height was six cubits and a s	1Sa 17:4	2239
and meted out heaven with the s	Is 40:12	2239
fruit, and children of a s long	Lam 2:20	2949
thereof round about shall be a s	Eze 43:13	2239

SPANNED

my right hand hath s the heavens	Is 48:13	2946

SPARE

not s the place for the fifty	Gen 18:24	5375
then I will s all the place for	Gen 18:26	5375
pity him, neither shalt thou s	Deut 13:8	2550
The LORD will not s him, but then	Deut 29:20	5545
all that they have, and s them not	1Sa 15:3	2550
s me according to the greatness	Neh 13:22	2347
let him not s	Job 6:10	2550
my reins asunder, and doth not s	Job 16:13	2550
Though he s it, and forsake it not	Job 20:13	2550
God shall cast upon him, and not s	Job 27:22	2550
me, and s not to spit in my face	Job 30:10	2820
O s me, that I may recover	Ps 39:13	8159
He shall s the poor and needy, and	Ps 72:13	2347
therefore he will not s in the	Prov 6:34	2550
let not thy soul s for his crying	Prov 19:18	5375
no man shall s his brother	Is 9:19	2550
their eye shall not s children	Is 13:18	2347
he shall not s	Is 30:14	2550
s not, lengthen thy cords, and	Is 54:2	2820
s not, lift up thy voice like a	Is 58:1	2820
I will not pity, nor s, nor have	Jer 13:14	2347
he shall not s them, neither have	Jer 21:7	2347
bow, shoot at her, s no arrows	Jer 50:14	2550
and s ye not her young men	Jer 51:3	2550
neither shall mine eye s, neither	Eze 5:11	2347
And mine eye shall not s thee	Eze 7:4	2347
And mine eye shall not s, neither	Eze 7:9	2347
mine eye shall not s, neither	Eze 8:18	2347
let not your eye s, neither have	Eze 9:5	2347
for me also, mine eye shall not s	Eze 9:10	2347
not go back, neither will I s	Eze 24:14	2347
S thy people, O LORD, and give not	Joel 2:17	2347
And should not I s Nineveh	Jonah 4:11	2347
not s continually to slay the	Hab 1:17	2550
and I will s them, as a man	Mal 3:17	2550
have bread enough and to s	Lk 15:17	4052
take heed lest he also s not thee	Rom 11:21	5339
but I s you	1Cor 7:28	5339
that to s you I came not as yet	2Cor 1:23	5339
if I come again, I will not s	2Cor 13:2	5339

SPARED

But Saul and the people s Agag	1Sa 15:9	2550
for the people s the best of the	1Sa 15:15	2550
but mine eye s thee	1Sa 24:10	2347
he s to take of his own flock and	2Sa 12:4	2550
But the king s Mephibosheth	2Sa 21:7	2550
my master hath s Naaman this	2Kin 5:20	2820
he s not their soul from death,	Ps 78:50	2820
Nevertheless mine eye s them from	Eze 20:17	2347
He that s not his own Son, but	Rom 8:32	5339
For if God s not the natural	Rom 11:21	5339
For if God s not the angels that	2Pet 2:4	5339
s not the old world, but saved	2Pet 2:5	5339

SPARETH

He that s his rod hateth his son	Prov 13:24	2820
that hath knowledge s his words	Prov 17:27	2820
but the righteous giveth and s not	Prov 21:26	2820
as a man s his own son that	Mal 3:17	2550

SPARING

in among you, not s the flock	Acts 20:29	5339

SPARINGLY

He which soweth s shall reap also	2Cor 9:6	5340
shall reap also s	2Cor 9:6	5340

SPARK

the s of his fire shall not shine	Job 18:5	7632
as tow, and the maker of it as a s	Is 1:31	5213

SPARKLED

they s like the colour of	Eze 1:7	5340

SPARKS

unto trouble, as the s fly upward	Job 5:7	7565
lamps, and s of fire leap out	Job 41:19	3590
compass yourselves about with s	Is 50:11	2131
in the s that ye have kindled	Is 50:11	2131

SPARROW

the s hath found an house, and the	Ps 84:3	6833
am as a s alone upon the house	Ps 102:7	6833

SPARROWS

Are not two s sold for a farthing	Mt 10:29	4765
ye are of more value than many s	Mt 10:31	4765
Are not five s sold for two	Lk 12:6	4765
ye are of more value than many s	Lk 12:7	4765

SPAT

he s on the ground, and made clay	Jn 9:6	4429

SPEAK

taken upon me to s unto the Lord	Gen 18:27	1696
the LORD be angry, and I will s	Gen 18:30	1696
taken upon me to s unto the Lord	Gen 18:31	1696
I will s yet but this once	Gen 18:32	1696
And he said, S on	Gen 24:33	1696
we cannot s unto thee bad or good	Gen 24:50	1696
I heard thy father s unto Esau	Gen 27:6	1696
Take heed that thou s not to	Gen 31:24	1696
Take thou heed that thou s not to	Gen 31:29	1696
Thus shall ye s unto my lord Esau	Gen 32:4	559
this manner shall ye s unto Esau	Gen 32:19	1696
could not s peaceably unto him	Gen 37:4	1696
what shall we s	Gen 44:16	1696
s a word in my lord's ears, and	Gen 44:18	1696
have found grace in your eyes, s	Gen 50:4	1696
I know that he can s well	Ex 4:14	1696
And thou shalt s unto him, and put	Ex 4:15	1696
came to Pharaoh to s in thy name	Ex 5:23	1696
s unto Pharaoh king of Egypt,	Ex 6:11	1696
s thou unto Pharaoh king of Egypt	Ex 6:29	1696
Thou shalt s all that I command	Ex 7:2	1696
thy brother shall s unto Pharaoh	Ex 7:2	1696
When Pharaoh shall s unto you	Ex 7:9	1696
S now in the ears of the people,	Ex 11:2	1696
S ye unto all the congregation of	Ex 12:3	1696
S unto the children of Israel,	Ex 14:2	1696
s unto the children of Israel,	Ex 14:15	1696
s unto them, saying, At even ye	Ex 16:12	1696
s unto the children of Israel	Ex 19:6	1696
may hear when I s with thee	Ex 19:9	1696
S thou with us, and we will hear	Ex 20:19	1696
but let not God s with us	Ex 20:19	1696
neither shalt thou s in a cause	Ex 23:2	6030
his voice, and do all that I s	Ex 23:22	1696
S unto the children of Israel,	Ex 25:2	1696
thou shalt s unto all that are	Ex 28:3	1696
meet you, to s there unto thee	Ex 29:42	1696
thou shalt s unto the children of	Ex 30:31	1696
S thou also unto the children of	Ex 31:13	1696
Wherefore should the Egyptians s	Ex 32:12	559
in before the LORD to s with him	Ex 34:34	1696
until he went in to s with him	Ex 34:35	1696

Context	Reference	Strong's
S unto the children of Israel, and	Lev 1:2	1696
S unto the children of Israel,	Lev 4:2	1696
S unto Aaron and to his sons,	Lev 6:25	1696
S unto the children of Israel,	Lev 7:23	1696
S unto the children of Israel,	Lev 7:29	1696
children of Israel thou shalt s	Lev 9:3	1696
S unto the children of Israel,	Lev 11:2	1696
S unto the children of Israel,	Lev 12:2	1696
S unto the children of Israel, and	Lev 15:2	1696
S unto Aaron thy brother, that he	Lev 16:2	1696
S unto Aaron, and unto his sons,	Lev 17:2	1696
S unto the children of Israel, and	Lev 18:2	1696
S unto all the congregation of	Lev 19:2	1696
S unto the priests the sons of	Lev 21:1	559
S unto Aaron, saying, Whosoever	Lev 21:17	1696
S unto Aaron and to his sons, that	Lev 22:2	1696
S unto Aaron, and to his sons, and	Lev 22:18	1696
S unto the children of Israel, and	Lev 23:2	1696
S unto the children of Israel, and	Lev 23:10	1696
S unto the children of Israel,	Lev 23:24	1696
S unto the children of Israel,	Lev 23:34	1696
thou shalt s unto the children of	Lev 24:15	1696
S unto the children of Israel, and	Lev 25:2	1696
S unto the children of Israel, and	Lev 27:2	1696
S unto the children of Israel,	Num 5:6	1696
S unto the children of Israel, and	Num 5:12	1696
S unto the children of Israel, and	Num 6:2	1696
S unto Aaron and unto his sons,	Num 6:23	1696
of the congregation to s with him	Num 7:89	1696
S unto Aaron, and say unto him,	Num 8:2	1696
S unto the children of Israel,	Num 9:10	1696
will s unto him in a dream	Num 12:6	1696
With him will I s mouth to mouth	Num 12:8	1696
to s against my servant Moses	Num 12:8	1696
heard the fame of thee will s	Num 14:15	559
S unto the children of Israel, and	Num 15:2	1696
S unto the children of Israel, and	Num 15:18	1696
S unto the children of Israel, and	Num 15:38	1696
S unto the congregation, saying,	Num 16:24	1696
S unto Eleazar the son of Aaron	Num 16:37	559
S unto the children of Israel, and	Num 17:2	1696
Thus s unto the Levites, and say	Num 18:26	1696
S unto the children of Israel,	Num 19:2	1696
s ye unto the rock before their	Num 20:8	1696
they that s in proverbs say	Num 21:27	
as the LORD shall s unto me	Num 22:8	1696
the word that I shalt s unto thee	Num 22:35	1696
unto thee, that thou shall s	Num 22:35	1696
in my mouth, that shall I s	Num 22:38	1696
unto Balak, and thus shalt s	Num 23:5	1696
Must I not take heed to s that	Num 23:12	1696
the LORD saith, that will I s	Num 24:13	1696
daughters of Zelophehad s right	Num 27:7	1696
thou shalt s unto the children of	Num 27:8	1696
S unto the children of Israel, and	Num 33:51	1696
S unto the children of Israel, and	Num 35:10	1696
s no more unto me of this matter	Deut 3:26	1696
judgments which I s in your ears	Deut 5:1	1696
s thou unto us all that the LORD	Deut 5:27	1696
LORD our God shall s unto thee	Deut 5:27	1696
I will s unto thee all the	Deut 5:31	1696
S not thou in thine heart, after	Deut 9:4	559
for I s not with your children	Deut 11:2	
he shall s unto them all that I	Deut 18:18	1696
words which he shall s in my name	Deut 18:19	1696
presume to s a word in my name	Deut 18:20	1696
I have not commanded him to s	Deut 18:20	1696
or that shall s in the name of	Deut 18:20	1696
approach and s unto the people,	Deut 20:2	1696
officers shall s unto the people	Deut 20:5	1696
the officers shall s further unto	Deut 20:8	1696
shall call him, and s unto him	Deut 25:8	1696
And thou shalt s and say before the	Deut 26:5	6030
And the Levites shall s, and say	Deut 27:14	6030
that I may s these words in their	Deut 31:28	1696
ear, O ye heavens, and I will s	Deut 32:1	1696
Joshua to s unto the people	Josh 4:10	1696
S to the children of Israel,	Josh 20:2	1696
might s unto our children	Josh 22:24	559
S, ye that ride on white asses,	Judg 5:10	7878
me, and I will s but this once	Judg 6:39	1696
S, I pray you, in the ears of all	Judg 9:2	1696
to s friendly unto her, and to	Judg 19:3	1696
it, take advice, and s your minds	Judg 19:30	1696
to s to the children of Benjamin	Judg 21:13	1696
call thee, that thou shalt say, S	1Sa 3:9	1696
Then Samuel answered, S	1Sa 3:10	1696
that a man cannot s to him	1Sa 25:17	1696
s in thine audience, and hear the	1Sa 25:24	1696
Abner went also to s in the ears	2Sa 3:19	1696
in the gate to s with him quietly	2Sa 3:27	1696
so did Nathan s unto David	2Sa 7:17	1696
I pray thee, s unto the king	2Sa 13:13	1696
s on this manner unto him	2Sa 14:3	1696
s one word unto my lord the king	2Sa 14:12	1696
for the king doth s this thing as	2Sa 14:13	1696
s of this thing unto my lord the	2Sa 14:15	1696
I will now s unto the king	2Sa 14:15	1696
said, Let my lord the king now s	2Sa 14:18	1696
if not; s thou	2Sa 17:6	1696
s comfortably unto thy servants	2Sa 19:7	1696
Now therefore why s ye not a word	2Sa 19:10	2790
S unto the elders of Judah,	2Sa 19:11	1696
hither, that I may s with thee	2Sa 20:16	1696
They were wont to s in old time	2Sa 20:18	1696
And he said, S, I pray thee, unto	1Kin 2:17	559
I will s for thee unto the king	1Kin 2:18	1696
to s unto him for Adonijah	1Kin 2:19	1696
s good words to them, then they	1Kin 12:7	1696
Thus shalt thou s unto this	1Kin 12:10	559
S unto Rehoboam, the son of	1Kin 12:23	559
And thou shalt s unto him, saying,	1Kin 21:19	1696
And thou shalt s unto him, saying,	1Kin 21:19	1696
of them, and s that which is good	1Kin 22:13	1696
LORD saith unto me, that will I s	1Kin 22:14	1696
the LORD from me to s unto thee	1Kin 22:24	1696
S ye now to Hezekiah, Thus saith	2Kin 18:19	559
and Joah, unto Rab-shakeh, S	2Kin 18:26	1696
and to thee, to s these words	2Kin 18:27	1696
Thus shall ye s to Hezekiah king	2Kin 19:10	559
so did Nathan s unto David	1Chr 17:15	1696
What can David s more to thee for	1Chr 17:18	
s good words to them, they will	2Chr 10:7	1696
S unto Rehoboam the son of	2Chr 11:3	559
one of theirs, and s thou good	2Chr 18:12	1696
what my God saith, that will I s	2Chr 18:13	1696
the LORD from me to s unto thee	2Chr 18:23	1696
to s against him, saying, As the	2Chr 32:17	559
could not s in the Jews' language	Neh 13:24	1696
to morrow s thou unto the king	Est 5:14	559
to s unto the king to hang	Est 6:4	559
I will s in the anguish of my	Job 7:11	1696
How long wilt thou s these things	Job 8:2	4448
If I s of strength, lo, he is	Job 9:19	
Then would I s, and not fear him	Job 9:35	1696
I will s in the bitterness of my	Job 10:1	1696
But oh that God would s, and open	Job 11:5	1696
Or s to the earth, and it shall	Job 12:8	7878
Surely I would s to the Almighty,	Job 13:3	1696
Will ye s wickedly for God	Job 13:7	1696
peace, let me alone, that I may s	Job 13:13	1696
or let me s, and answer thou me	Job 13:22	1696
I also could s as ye do	Job 16:4	1696
Though I s, my grief is not	Job 16:6	1696
mark, and afterwards we will s	Job 18:2	1696
Suffer me that I may s	Job 21:3	1696
My lips shall not s wickedness	Job 27:4	1696
I said, Days should s, and	Job 32:7	1696
I will s, that I may be refreshed	Job 32:20	1696
hold thy peace, and I will s	Job 33:31	1696
s, for I desire to justify thee	Job 33:32	1696
therefore s what thou knowest	Job 34:33	1696
I have yet to s on God's behalf	Job 36:2	4405
Shall it be told him that I s	Job 37:20	1696
If a man s, surely he shall be	Job 37:20	559
will he s soft words unto thee	Job 41:3	1696
Hear, I beseech thee, and I will s	Job 42:4	1696
Then shall he s unto them in his	Ps 2:5	1696
shalt destroy them that s leasing	Ps 5:6	1696
They s vanity every one with his	Ps 12:2	1696
and with a double heart do they s	Ps 12:2	1696
with their mouth they s proudly	Ps 17:10	1696
which s peace to their neighbours	Ps 28:3	1696
doth every one s of his glory	Ps 29:9	559
which s grievous things proudly	Ps 31:18	1696
For they s not peace	Ps 35:20	1696
And my tongue shall s of thy	Ps 35:28	1897
seek my hurt s mischievous things	Ps 38:12	1696
s of them, they are more than can	Ps 40:5	1696
Mine enemies s evil of me	Ps 41:5	559
I s of the things which I have	Ps 45:1	559
My mouth shall s of wisdom	Ps 49:3	1696
Hear, O my people, and I will s	Ps 50:7	1696
rather than to s righteousness	Ps 52:3	1696
Do ye indeed s righteousness, O	Ps 58:1	1696
for cursing and lying which they s	Ps 59:12	5608
them that s lies shall be stopped	Ps 63:11	1696
that sit in the gate s against me	Ps 69:12	7878
For mine enemies s against me	Ps 71:10	559
s wickedly concerning oppression	Ps 73:8	1696
they s loftily	Ps 73:8	1696
If I say, I will s thus	Ps 73:15	5608
s not with a stiff neck	Ps 75:5	1696
I am so troubled that I cannot s	Ps 77:4	1696
hear what God the LORD will s	Ps 85:8	1696
for he will s peace unto his	Ps 85:8	1696
shall they utter and s hard things	Ps 94:4	1696
of them that s evil against my	Ps 109:20	1696
They have mouths, but they s not	Ps 115:5	1696
neither s they through their	Ps 115:7	1897
also did sit and s against me	Ps 119:23	1696
I will s of thy testimonies also	Ps 119:46	1696
My tongue shall s of thy word	Ps 119:172	6030
but when I s, they are for war	Ps 120:7	1696
but they shall s with the enemies	Ps 127:5	1696
They have mouths, but they s not	Ps 135:16	1696
For they s against thee wickedly,	Ps 139:20	559
I will s of the glorious honour	Ps 145:5	7878
men shall s of the might of thy	Ps 145:6	559
They shall s of the glory of thy	Ps 145:11	559
My mouth shall s the praise of	Ps 145:21	1696
for I will s of excellent things	Prov 8:6	1696
For my mouth shall s truth	Prov 8:7	1897
S not in the ears of a fool	Prov 23:9	1696
when thy lips s right things	Prov 23:16	1696
to keep silence, and a time to s	Eccl 3:7	1696
of those that are asleep to s	Song 7:9	1680
s the word, and it shall not stand	Is 8:10	1696
if they s not according to this	Is 8:20	559
All they shall s and say unto thee	Is 14:10	6030
of Egypt s the language of Canaan	Is 19:18	1696
tongue will he s to this people	Is 28:11	1696
shalt s out of the ground, and thy	Is 29:4	1696
s unto us smooth things, prophesy	Is 30:10	1696
shall be ready to s plainly	Is 32:4	1696
the vile person will s villany	Is 32:6	1696
Shebna and Joah unto Rabshakeh, S	Is 36:11	1696
s not to us in the Jews' language	Is 36:11	1696
and to thee to s these words	Is 36:12	1696
Thus shall ye s to Hezekiah king	Is 37:10	559
S ye comfortably to Jerusalem, and	Is 40:2	1696
then let them s	Is 41:1	1696
I the LORD s righteousness, I	Is 45:19	1696
that I should know how to s a	Is 50:4	5790
that day that I am he that doth s	Is 52:6	1696
joined himself to the LORD, s	Is 56:3	559
they trust in vanity, and s lies	Is 59:4	1696
I that s in righteousness, mighty	Is 63:1	1696
behold, I cannot s	Jer 1:6	1696
I command thee thou shalt s	Jer 1:7	1696
s unto them all that I command	Jer 1:17	1696
great men, and will s unto them	Jer 5:5	1696
of hosts, Because ye s this word	Jer 5:14	1696
To whom shall I s, and give	Jer 6:10	1696
Therefore thou shalt s all these	Jer 7:27	1696
and will not s the truth	Jer 9:5	1696
taught their tongue to s lies	Jer 9:5	1696
S, Thus saith the LORD, Even the	Jer 9:22	1696
as the palm tree, but s not	Jer 10:5	1696
s unto the men of Judah, and to	Jer 11:2	1696
though they s fair words unto	Jer 12:6	1696
thou shalt s unto them this word	Jer 13:12	559
I shall s concerning a nation	Jer 18:7	1696
I shall s concerning a nation	Jer 18:9	1696
s to the men of Judah, and to the	Jer 18:11	559
before thee to s good for them	Jer 18:20	1696
nor s any more in his name	Jer 20:9	1696
of Judah, and s there this word,	Jer 22:1	1696
they s a vision of their own	Jer 23:16	1696
let him s my word faithfully	Jer 23:28	1696
s unto all the cities of Judah,	Jer 26:2	1696
I command thee to s unto them	Jer 26:2	1696
him to s unto all the people	Jer 26:8	1696
to s all these words in your ears	Jer 26:15	1696
which s unto you, saying, Ye	Jer 27:9	559
of the prophets that s unto you	Jer 27:14	559
this word that I s in thine ears	Jer 28:7	1696
Thus shalt thou also s to	Jer 29:24	559
shall s with him mouth to mouth,	Jer 32:4	1696
s to Zedekiah king of Judah, and	Jer 34:2	559
he shall s with thee mouth to	Jer 34:3	1696
s unto them, and bring them into	Jer 35:2	1696
of the LORD, which I s unto thee	Jer 38:20	1696
s to Ebed-melech the Ethiopian,	Jer 39:16	559
thy feet, and I will s unto thee	Eze 2:1	1696
thou shalt s my words unto them,	Eze 2:7	1696
go s unto the house of Israel	Eze 3:1	1696
s with my words unto them	Eze 3:4	1696
all my words that I shall s unto	Eze 3:10	1696
s unto them, and tell them, Thus	Eze 3:11	1696
But when I s with thee, I will	Eze 3:27	1696
fell upon me, and said unto me, S	Eze 11:5	559
I will s, and the word that I	Eze 12:25	1696
that I shall s shall come to pass	Eze 12:25	1696
Therefore s unto them, and say	Eze 14:4	1696
s a parable unto the house of	Eze 17:2	4911
s unto the elders of Israel, and	Eze 20:3	1696
s unto the house of Israel, and	Eze 20:27	1696
say of me, Doth he not s parables	Eze 20:49	4911
S unto the house of Israel, Thus	Eze 24:21	559
which is escaped, and thou shalt s	Eze 24:27	1696
S, and say, Thus saith the Lord	Eze 29:3	1696
s unto Pharaoh king of Egypt, and	Eze 31:2	559
strong among the mighty shall s	Eze 32:21	1696
s to the children of thy people,	Eze 33:2	1696
if thou dost not s to warn the	Eze 33:8	1696
s unto the house of Israel	Eze 33:10	559
Thus ye s, saying, If our	Eze 33:10	559
wastes of the land of Israel s	Eze 33:24	559
s one to another, every one to	Eze 33:30	1696
of thy people shall s unto thee	Eze 37:18	559
S unto every feathered fowl, and	Eze 39:17	559
and corrupt words to s before me	Dan 2:9	560
which s any thing amiss against	Dan 3:29	560
he shall s great words against	Dan 7:25	4449
the words that I s unto thee	Dan 10:11	1696
and said, Let my lord s	Dan 10:19	1696
they shall s lies at one table	Dan 11:27	1696
shall s marvellous things against	Dan 11:36	1696
and s comfortably unto her	Hos 2:14	1696
time, but at the end it shall s	Hab 2:3	6315
shall not do iniquity, nor s lies	Zeph 3:13	1696
S now to Zerubbabel the son of	Hag 2:2	559
S to Zerubbabel, governor of	Hag 2:21	559
s to this young man, saying,	Zec 2:4	1696
s unto him, saying, Thus speaketh	Zec 6:12	559
to s unto the priests which were	Zec 7:3	559
S unto all the people of the land	Zec 7:5	559
S ye every man the truth to his	Zec 8:16	1696
he shall s peace unto the heathen	Zec 9:10	1696
but s the word only, and my	Mt 8:8	2036
no thought how or what ye shall s	Mt 10:19	2980
in that same hour what ye shall s	Mt 10:19	2980
For it is not ye that s, but the	Mt 10:20	2980
in darkness, that s ye in light	Mt 10:27	2036
can ye, being evil, s good things	Mt 12:34	2980
every idle word that men shall s	Mt 12:36	2980
without, desiring to s with him	Mt 12:46	2980
without, desiring to s with thee	Mt 12:47	2980
Therefore s I to them in parables	Mt 13:13	2980
when they saw the dumb to s	Mt 15:31	2980
and suffered not the devils to s	Mk 1:34	2980
doth this man thus s blasphemies	Mk 2:7	2980
deaf to hear, and the dumb to s	Mk 7:37	2980
that can lightly s evil of me	Mk 9:39	2551
he began to s unto them by	Mk 12:1	3004
beforehand what ye shall s	Mk 13:11	2980
given you in that hour, that s ye	Mk 13:11	2980
for it is not ye that s, but the	Mk 13:11	2980
I know not this man of whom ye s	Mk 14:71	3004
they shall s with new tongues	Mk 16:17	2980
and am sent to s unto thee	Lk 1:19	2980
shalt be dumb, and not able to s	Lk 1:20	2980
out, he could not s unto them	Lk 1:22	2980
them suffered them not to s	Lk 4:41	2980
when all men shall s well of you	Lk 6:26	2036
was dead sat up, and began to s	Lk 7:15	2980
he began to s unto the people	Lk 7:24	3004
provoke him to s of many things	Lk 11:53	653
whosoever shall s a word against	Lk 12:10	2046
s to my brother, that he divide	Lk 12:13	2036
Then began he to s to the people	Lk 20:9	3004

And the two disciples heard him *s*	Jn 1:37	2980
One of the two which heard John *s*	Jn 1:40	
We *s* that we do know, and testify	Jn 3:11	2980
her, I that *s* unto thee am he	Jn 4:26	2980
the words that I *s* unto you	Jn 6:63	2980
of God, or whether I *s* of myself	Jn 7:17	2980
I *s* to the world those things	Jn 8:26	3004
hath taught me, I *s* these things	Jn 8:28	2980
I *s* that which I have seen with	Jn 8:38	2980
he shall *s* for himself	Jn 9:21	2980
I should say, and what I should *s*	Jn 12:49	2980
whatsoever I *s* therefore, even as	Jn 12:50	2980
the Father said unto me, so I *s*	Jn 12:50	2980
I *s* not of you all	Jn 13:18	3004
s unto you I *s* not of myself	Jn 14:10	2980
for he shall not *s* of himself	Jn 16:13	2980
he shall hear, that shall he *s*	Jn 16:13	2980
no more *s* unto you in proverbs	Jn 16:25	2980
and these things I *s* in the world	Jn 17:13	2980
began to *s* with other tongues, as	Acts 2:4	2980
heard them *s* in his own language	Acts 2:6	2980
not all these which *s* Galilaeans	Acts 2:7	2980
we do hear them *s* in our tongues	Acts 2:11	2980
let me freely *s* unto you of the	Acts 2:29	2036
that they *s* henceforth to no man	Acts 4:17	2980
commanded them not to *s* at all	Acts 4:18	5350
For we cannot but *s* the things	Acts 4:20	2980
all boldness they may *s* thy word	Acts 4:29	2980
s in the temple to the people all	Acts 5:20	2980
should not *s* in the name of Jesus	Acts 5:40	2980
We have heard him *s* blasphemous	Acts 6:11	2980
This man ceaseth not to *s*	Acts 6:13	2980
when he cometh, shall *s* unto thee	Acts 10:32	2980
they heard them *s* with tongues	Acts 10:46	2980
And as I began to *s*, the Holy	Acts 11:15	2980
The same heard Paul *s*	Acts 14:9	2980
by a vision, Be not afraid, but *s*	Acts 18:9	2980
he began to *s* boldly in the	Acts 18:26	
chief captain, May I *s* unto thee	Acts 21:37	2036
Who said, Canst thou *s* Greek	Acts 21:37	1097
suffer me to *s* unto the people	Acts 21:39	2980
Thou shalt not *s* evil of the	Acts 23:5	2046
had beckoned unto him to *s*	Acts 24:10	3004
art permitted to *s* for thyself	Acts 26:1	3004
but *s* forth the words of truth and	Acts 26:25	669
before whom also I *s* freely	Acts 26:26	2980
you, to see you, and to *s* with you	Acts 28:20	4354
(I *s* as a man)	Rom 3:5	3004
I *s* after the manner of men	Rom 6:19	3004
(for I *s* to them that know the	Rom 7:1	2980
For I *s* to you Gentiles, inasmuch	Rom 11:13	3004
For I will not dare to *s* of any	Rom 15:18	2980
that ye all *s* the same thing, and	1Cor 1:10	3004
Howbeit we *s* wisdom among them	1Cor 2:6	2980
But we *s* the wisdom of God in a	1Cor 2:7	2980
Which things also we *s*, not in	1Cor 2:13	2980
could not *s* unto you as unto	1Cor 3:1	2980
I *s* to your shame	1Cor 6:5	3004
But I *s* this by permission, and	1Cor 7:6	3004
But to the rest *s* I, not the Lord	1Cor 7:12	3004
this I *s* for your own profit	1Cor 7:35	3004
I *s* as to wise men	1Cor 10:15	3004
do all *s* with tongues	1Cor 12:30	2980
Though I *s* with the tongues of	1Cor 13:1	2980
except I shall *s* to you either by	1Cor 14:6	2980
for ye shall *s* into the air	1Cor 14:9	2980
I *s* with tongues more than ye all	1Cor 14:18	2980
I had rather *s* five words with my	1Cor 14:19	2980
lips will I *s* unto this people	1Cor 14:21	2980
all *s* with tongues, and there come	1Cor 14:23	2980
If any man *s* in an unknown tongue	1Cor 14:27	2980
let him *s* to himself, and to God	1Cor 14:28	2980
Let the prophets *s* two or three	1Cor 14:29	2980
is not permitted unto them to *s*	1Cor 14:34	2980
for women to *s* in the church	1Cor 14:35	2980
and forbid not to *s* with tongues	1Cor 14:39	2980
I *s* this to your shame	1Cor 15:34	3004
the sight of God *s* we in Christ	2Cor 2:17	2980
we also believe, and therefore *s*	2Cor 4:13	2980
(I *s* as unto my children,) be ye	2Cor 6:13	3004
I *s* not this to condemn you	2Cor 7:3	3004
I *s* not by commandment, but by	2Cor 8:8	3004
That which I *s*, I *s* it not	2Cor 11:17	2980
I *s* as concerning reproach, as	2Cor 11:21	3004
(I *s* foolishly,) I am bold also	2Cor 11:21	3004
(I *s* as a fool) I am more	2Cor 11:23	2980
we *s* before God in Christ	2Cor 12:19	2980
I *s* after the manner of men	Gal 3:15	3004
s every man truth with his	Eph 4:25	2980
For it is a shame even to *s* of	Eph 5:12	3004
but I *s* concerning Christ and the	Eph 5:32	3004
that therein I may *s* boldly	Eph 6:20	
as I ought to *s*	Eph 6:20	2980
bold to *s* the word without fear	Phil 1:14	2980
Not that I *s* in respect of want	Phil 4:11	3004
to *s* the mystery of Christ, for	Col 4:3	2980
make it manifest, as I ought to *s*	Col 4:4	2980
that we need not to *s* any thing	1Th 1:8	2980
we were bold in our God to *s* unto	1Th 2:2	2980
with the gospel, even so we *s*	1Th 2:4	2980
Forbidding us to *s* to the	1Th 2:16	2980
(I *s* the truth in Christ, and lie	1Ti 2:7	3004
the adversary to *s* reproachfully	1Ti 5:14	
But *s* thou the things which	Titus 2:1	2980
These things *s*, and exhort, and	Titus 2:15	2980
To *s* evil of no man, to be no	Titus 3:2	987
the world to come, whereof we *s*	Heb 2:5	2980
salvation, though we thus *s*	Heb 6:9	2980
we cannot now *s* particularly	Heb 9:5	3004
man be swift to hear, slow to *s*	Jas 1:19	2980
So *s* ye, and so do, as they that	Jas 2:12	2980
S not evil one of another,	Jas 4:11	2635
whereas they *s* against you as	1Pet 2:12	2635
and his lips that they *s* no guile	1Pet 3:10	2980
that, whereas they *s* evil of you	1Pet 3:16	2635
If any man *s*, let him *s* as	1Pet 4:11	2980
not afraid to *s* evil of dignities	2Pet 2:10	987
s evil of the things that they	2Pet 2:12	987
For when they *s* great swelling	2Pet 2:18	5350
therefore *s* they of the world, and	1Jn 4:5	2980
s face to face, that our joy may	2Jn 12	2980
thee, and we shall *s* face to face	3Jn 14	2980
dominion, and *s* evil of dignities	Jude 8	987
But these *s* evil of those things	Jude 10	987
the depths of Satan, as they *s*	Rev 2:24	3004
image of the beast should both *s*	Rev 13:15	2980

SPEAKER

Let not an evil *s* be established	Ps 140:11	
because he was the chief *s*	Acts 14:12	3056

SPEAKEST

wherefore then *s* thou so to me	1Sa 9:21	1696
Why *s* thou any more of thy	2Sa 19:29	1696
that thou *s* in thy bedchamber	2Kin 6:12	1696
Thou *s* as one of the foolish	Job 2:10	1696
sittest and *s* against thy brother	Ps 50:20	1696
mightest be justified when thou *s*	Ps 51:4	1696
Why sayest thou, O Jacob, and *s*	Is 40:27	1696
for thou *s* falsely of Ishmael	Jer 40:16	1696
unto Jeremiah, Thou *s* falsely	Jer 43:2	1696
nor *s* to warn the wicked from his	Eze 3:18	1696
for thou *s* lies in the name of	Zec 13:3	1696
Why *s* thou unto them in parables	Mt 13:10	2980
s thou this parable unto us, or	Lk 12:41	3004
now *s* thou plainly	Jn 16:29	2980
thou plainly, and *s* no proverb	Jn 16:29	3004
unto him, *S* thou not unto me	Jn 19:10	2980
this new doctrine, whereof thou *s*	Acts 17:19	2980

SPEAKETH

it is my mouth that *s* unto you	Gen 45:12	1696
as a man *s* unto his friend	Ex 33:11	1696
thee, saying, All that the LORD *s*	Num 23:26	1696
When a prophet *s* in the name of	Deut 18:22	1696
Thus *s* Ben-hadad, saying,	1Kin 20:5	559
as one of the foolish women *s*	Job 2:10	1696
He that *s* flattery to his friends	Job 17:5	5046
For God *s* once, yea twice, yet	Job 33:14	1696
and the tongue that *s* proud things	Ps 12:3	1696
and *s* the truth in his heart	Ps 15:2	1696
mouth of the righteous *s* wisdom	Ps 37:30	1897
if he come to see me, he *s* vanity	Ps 41:6	1696
Whose mouth *s* vanity, and their	Ps 144:8	1696
children, whose mouth *s* vanity	Ps 144:11	1696
the man that *s* froward things	Prov 2:12	1696
he *s* with his feet, he teacheth	Prov 6:13	4448
A false witness that *s* lies	Prov 6:19	6315
mouth of the wicked *s* frowardness	Prov 10:32	
He that *s* truth sheweth forth	Prov 12:17	6315
There is that *s* like the	Prov 12:18	981
but a deceitful witness *s* lies	Prov 14:25	6315
and they love him that *s* right	Prov 16:13	1696
he that *s* lies shall not escape	Prov 19:5	6315
he that *s* lies shall perish	Prov 19:9	6315
the man that heareth *s* constantly	Prov 21:28	1696
When he *s* fair, believe him not	Prov 26:25	6963
evildoer, and every mouth *s* folly	Is 9:17	1696
even when the needy *s* right	Is 32:7	1696
righteously, and *s* uprightly	Is 33:15	1696
it *s* deceit	Jer 9:8	1696
one *s* peaceably to his neighbour	Jer 9:8	1696
word which the LORD *s* unto you	Jer 10:1	1696
Thus *s* the LORD of hosts, the God	Jer 28:2	559
Thus *s* the LORD of hosts, the God	Jer 29:25	559
Thus *s* the LORD God of Israel,	Jer 30:2	559
of the Almighty God when he *s*	Eze 10:5	1696
they abhor him that *s* uprightly	Amos 5:10	1696
Thus *s* the LORD of hosts, saying,	Hag 1:2	559
Thus *s* the LORD of hosts, saying,	Zec 6:12	559
Thus *s* the LORD of hosts, saying,	Zec 7:9	559
of your Father which *s* in you	Mt 10:20	2980
whosoever *s* a word against the	Mt 12:32	2036
but whosoever *s* against the Holy	Mt 12:32	2036
of the heart the mouth *s*	Mt 12:34	2980
Who is this which *s* blasphemies	Lk 5:21	2980
of the heart his mouth *s*	Lk 6:45	2980
is earthly, and *s* of the earth	Jn 3:31	2980
God hath sent *s* the words of God	Jn 3:34	2980
He that *s* of himself seeketh his	Jn 7:18	2980
he *s* boldly, and they say nothing	Jn 7:26	2980
s a lie, he *s* of his own	Jn 8:44	2980
himself a king *s* against Caesar	Jn 19:12	483
For David *s* concerning him, I	Acts 2:25	3004
of whom *s* the prophet this	Acts 8:34	3004
which is of faith *s* on this wise	Rom 10:6	3004
For he that *s* in an unknown	1Cor 14:2	2980
an unknown tongue *s* not unto men	1Cor 14:2	2980
in the spirit he *s* mysteries	1Cor 14:2	2980
s unto men to edification	1Cor 14:3	2980
He that *s* in an unknown tongue	1Cor 14:4	2980
than he that *s* with tongues	1Cor 14:5	2980
be unto him that *s* a barbarian	1Cor 14:11	2980
he that *s* shall be a barbarian	1Cor 14:11	2980
Wherefore let him that *s* in an	1Cor 14:13	2980
Now the Spirit *s* expressly	1Ti 4:1	3004
and by it he being dead yet *s*	Heb 11:4	2980
which *s* unto you as unto children	Heb 12:5	1256
that *s* better things than that of	Heb 12:24	2980
See that ye refuse not him that *s*	Heb 12:25	2980
away from him that *s* from heaven	Heb 12:25	
He that *s* evil of his brother, and	Jas 4:11	2635
s evil of the law, and judgeth the	Jas 4:11	2635
their mouth *s* great swelling	Jude 16	2980

SPEAKING

to pass, before he had done *s*	Gen 24:15	1696
before I had done *s* in mine heart	Gen 24:45	1696
till Moses had done *s* with them	Ex 34:33	1696
one *s* unto him from off the mercy	Num 7:89	1696
made an end of *s* all these words	Num 16:31	1696
s out of the midst of the fire	Deut 4:33	1696
the voice of the living God *s* out	Deut 5:26	1696
s of them when thou sittest in	Deut 11:19	1696
made an end of *s* unto the people	Deut 20:9	1696
Moses made an end of *s* all these	Deut 32:45	1696
when he had made an end of *s*	Judg 15:17	1696
her, then she left *s* unto her	Ruth 1:18	1696
he had made an end of *s* unto Saul	1Sa 18:1	1696
an end of *s* these words unto Saul	1Sa 24:16	1696
soon as he had made an end of *s*	2Sa 13:36	1696
s from the mouth of the LORD	2Chr 36:12	
and *s* peace to all his seed	Est 10:3	1696
While he was yet *s*, there came	Job 1:16	1696
While he was yet *s*, there came	Job 1:17	1696
While he was yet *s*, there came	Job 1:18	1696
who can withhold himself from *s*	Job 4:2	4405
they left off *s*	Job 32:15	4405
evil, and thy lips from *s* guile	Ps 34:13	1696
as soon as they be born, *s* lies	Ps 58:3	1696
forth of the finger, and *s* vanity	Is 58:9	1696
pleasure, nor *s* thine own words	Is 58:13	1696
our God, *s* oppression and revolt,	Is 59:13	1696
and while they are yet *s*, I will	Is 65:24	1696
unto you, rising up early and *s*	Jer 7:13	1696
unto you, rising early and *s*	Jer 25:3	1696
all the people heard Jeremiah *s*	Jer 26:7	1696
Jeremiah had made an end of *s* all	Jer 26:8	1696
unto you, rising early and *s*	Jer 35:14	1696
in *s* such words unto them	Jer 38:4	1696
So they left off *s* with him	Jer 38:27	2790
of *s* unto all the people all the	Jer 43:1	1696
I heard him *s* unto me out of the	Eze 43:6	1696
of man, and a mouth *s* great things	Dan 7:8	4449
Then I heard one saint *s*, and	Dan 8:13	1696
Now as he was *s* with me, I was in	Dan 8:18	1696
And whiles I was *s*, and praying, and	Dan 9:20	1696
Yea, whiles I was *s* in prayer	Dan 9:21	1696
shall be heard for their much *s*	Mt 6:7	4180
Now when he had left *s*, he said	Lk 5:4	2980
s of the things pertaining to the	Acts 1:3	3004
s unto Moses, that he should make	Acts 7:44	2980
s to them, persuaded them to	Acts 13:43	4354
abode they *s* boldly in the Lord	Acts 14:3	
s perverse things, to draw away	Acts 20:30	2980
earth, I heard a voice *s* unto me	Acts 26:14	2980
that no man *s* by the Spirit of	1Cor 12:3	2980
if I come unto you *s* with tongues	1Cor 14:6	2980
ye seek a proof of Christ *s* in me	2Cor 13:3	2980
But *s* the truth in love, may grow	Eph 4:15	226
and anger, and clamour, and evil *s*	Eph 4:31	988
S to yourselves in psalms and	Eph 5:19	2980
S lies in hypocrisy	1Ti 4:2	5573
s things which they ought not	1Ti 5:13	2980
excess of riot, *s* evil of you	1Pet 4:4	987
the dumb ass *s* with man's voice	2Pet 2:16	5350
s in them of these things	2Pet 3:16	2980
unto him a mouth *s* great things	Rev 13:5	2980

SPEAKINGS

and envies, and all evil *s*	1Pet 2:1	2636

SPEAR

Stretch out the *s* that is in thy	Josh 8:18	3591
Joshua stretched out the *s* that	Josh 8:18	3591
wherewith he stretched out the *s*	Josh 8:26	3591
was there a shield or *s* seen	Judg 5:8	7420
there was neither sword nor *s*	1Sa 13:22	2595
the staff of his *s* was like a	1Sa 17:7	2595
to me with a sword, and with a *s*	1Sa 17:45	2595
LORD saveth not with sword and *s*	1Sa 17:47	2595
here under thine hand *s* or sword	1Sa 21:8	2595
having his *s* in his hand, and all	1Sa 22:6	2595
his *s* stuck in the ground at his	1Sa 26:7	2595
with the *s* even to the earth at	1Sa 26:8	2595
take thou now the *s* that is at	1Sa 26:11	2595
So David took the *s* and the cruse	1Sa 26:12	2595
And now see where the king's *s* is	1Sa 26:16	2595
and said, Behold the king's *s*	1Sa 26:22	2595
behold, Saul leaned upon his *s*	2Sa 1:6	2595
with the hinder end of the *s*	2Sa 2:23	2595
that the *s* came out behind him	2Sa 2:23	2595
the weight of whose *s* weighed	2Sa 21:16	7013
the staff of whose *s* was like a	2Sa 21:19	2595
with iron and the staff of a *s*	2Sa 23:7	2595
he lift up his *s* against eight	2Sa 23:8	
he lifted up his *s* against three	2Sa 23:18	2595
the Egyptian had a *s* in his hand	2Sa 23:21	2595
and plucked the *s* out of the	2Sa 23:21	2595
hand, and slew him with his own *s*	2Sa 23:21	2595
he lifted up his *s* against three	1Chr 11:11	2595
for lifting up his *s* against	1Chr 11:20	2595
hand was a *s* like a weaver's beam	1Chr 11:23	2595
and plucked the *s* out of the	1Chr 11:23	2595
hand, and slew him with his own *s*	1Chr 11:23	2595
s were six thousand and eight	1Chr 12:24	7420
s thirty and seven thousand	1Chr 12:34	2595
whose *s* staff was like a weaver's	1Chr 20:5	2595
forth to war, that could handle *s*	2Chr 25:5	7420
against him, the glittering *s*	Job 39:23	2595
the *s*, the dart, nor the	Job 41:26	2595
he laugheth at the shaking of a *s*	Job 41:29	3591
Draw out also the *s*, and stop the	Ps 35:3	2595
bow, and cutteth the *s* in sunder	Ps 46:9	2595
They shall lay hold on bow and *s*	Jer 6:23	3591
bright sword and the glittering *s*	Nah 3:3	2595
the shining of thy glittering *s*	Hab 3:11	2595
with a *s* pierced his side	Jn 19:34	3057

SPEARMEN

Rebuke the company of *s*, the	Ps 68:30	7070
s two hundred, at the third hour	Acts 23:23	1187

SPEAR'S
his *s* head weighed six hundred 1Sa 17:7 2595

SPEARS
the Hebrews make them swords or *s* 1Sa 13:19 2595
the priest give king David's *s* 2Kin 11:10 2595
several city he put shields and *s* 2Chr 11:12 7420
of men that bare targets and *s* 2Chr 14:8 7420
to the captains of hundreds *s* 2Chr 23:9 2595
all the host shields, and *s* 2Chr 26:14 7420
with their swords, their *s* Neh 4:13 7420
half of them held both the *s* Neh 4:16 7420
half of them held the *s* from the Neh 4:21 7420
or his head with fish *s* Job 41:7 6767
sons of men, whose teeth are *s* Ps 57:4 2595
their *s* into pruninghooks Is 2:4 2595
furbish the *s*, and put on the Jer 46:4 7420
and the handstaves, and the *s* Eze 39:9 7420
and your pruninghooks into *s* Joel 3:10 7420
their *s* into pruninghooks Mic 4:3 2595

SPECIAL
to be a *s* people unto himself Deut 7:6 5459
God wrought *s* miracles by the Acts 19:11

SPECIALLY
S the day that thou stoodest Deut 4:10
s before thee, O king Agrippa, Acts 25:26 *3122*
all men, *s* of those that believe 1Ti 4:10 *3122*
s for those of his own house, he 1Ti 5:8 *3122*
s they of the circumcision Titus 1:10 *3122*
s to me, but how much more unto Philem 16 *3122*

SPECKLED
removing from thence all the *s* Gen 30:32 5348
the spotted and *s* among the goats Gen 30:32 5348
every one that is not *s* and Gen 30:33 5348
and all the she goats that were *s* Gen 30:35 5348
forth cattle ringstraked, *s* Gen 30:39 5348
thus, The *s* shall be thy wages Gen 31:8 5348
then all the cattle bare *s* Gen 31:8 5348
the cattle were ringstraked, *s* Gen 31:10 5348
the cattle are ringstraked, *s* Gen 31:12 5348
heritage is unto me as a *s* bird Jer 12:9 6641
him were there red horses, *s* Zec 1:8 8320

SPECTACLE
we are made a *s* unto the world 1Cor 4:9 *2302*

SPED
Have they not *s* Judg 5:30 4672

SPEECH
of Lamech, hearken unto my *s* Gen 4:23 565
was of one language, and of one *s* Gen 11:1 1697
not understand one another's *s* Gen 11:7 8193
but I am slow of *s*, and of a slow Ex 4:10 6310
give occasions of *s* against her Deut 22:14 1697
given occasions of *s* against her Deut 22:17 1697
my *s* shall distil as the dew, as Deut 32:2 565
To fetch about this form of *s* 2Sa 14:20 1697
seeing the *s* of all Israel is 2Sa 19:11 1697
the *s* pleased the Lord, that 1Kin 3:10 1697
s unto the people of Jerusalem 2Chr 32:18 3066
spake half in the *s* of Ashdod Neh 13:24 3066
removeth away the *s* of the trusty Job 12:20 8193
Hear diligently my *s*, and my Job 13:17 4405
Hear diligently my *s*, and let this Job 21:2 4405
liar, and make my *s* nothing worth Job 24:25 4405
and my *s* dropped upon them Job 29:22 4405
order our *s* by reason of darkness Job 37:19
thine ear unto me, and hear my *s* Ps 17:6 565
Day unto day uttereth *s*, and night Ps 19:2 562
There is no *s* nor language, where Ps 19:3 562
With her much fair *s* she caused Prov 7:21 3948
Excellent *s* becometh not a fool Prov 17:7 8193
of scarlet, and thy *s* is comely Song 4:3 4057
hearken, and hear my *s* Is 28:23 565
thy *s* shall be low out of the Is 29:4 565
thy *s* shall whisper out of the Is 29:4 565
give ear unto my *s* Is 32:9 565
a people of a deeper *s* than thou Is 33:19 8193
use this *s* in the land of Judah Jer 31:23 1697
of the Almighty, the voice of *s* Eze 1:24 1999
sent to a people of a strange *s* Eze 3:5 8193
Not to many people of a strange *s* Eze 3:6 8193
O LORD, I have heard thy *s* Hab 3:2 8088
for thy *s* bewrayeth thee Mt 26:73 *2981*
and had an impediment in his *s* Mk 7:32 *3424*
and thy *s* agreeth thereto Mk 14:70 *2981*
Why do ye not understand my *s* Jn 8:43 *2981*
saying in the *s* of Lycaonia Acts 14:11 *3072*
continued his *s* until midnight Acts 20:7 *3056*
with excellency of *s* or of wisdom 1Cor 2:1 *3056*
And my *s* and my preaching was not 1Cor 2:4 *3056*
not the *s* of them which are 1Cor 4:19 *3056*
hope, we use great plainness of *s* 2Cor 3:12
is my boldness of *s* toward you 2Cor 7:4
is weak, and his *s* contemptible 2Cor 10:10 *3056*
But though I be rude in *s* 2Cor 11:6 *3056*
Let your *s* be alway with grace, Col 4:6 *3056*
Sound *s*, that cannot be condemned Titus 2:8 *3056*

SPEECHES
even apparently, and not in dark *s* Num 12:8 2420
the *s* of one that is desperate, Job 6:26 561
or with *s* wherewith he can do no Job 15:3 4405
will I answer him with your *s* Job 32:14 561
Job, I pray thee, hear my *s* Job 33:1 4405
fair *s* deceive the hearts of the Rom 16:18 *2129*
of all their hard *s* which ungodly Jude 15

SPEECHLESS
And he was *s* Mt 22:12 *5392*
beckoned unto them, and remained *s* Lk 1:22 *2974*
which journeyed with him stood *s* Acts 9:7 *1769*

SPEED
thee, send me good *s* this day Gen 24:12 7136
cried after the lad, Make *s* 1Sa 20:38 4120
make *s* to depart, lest he 2Sa 15:14 4116
s to get him up to his chariot 1Kin 12:18 553
But king Rehoboam made *s* to get 2Chr 10:18 553
let it be done with *s* Ezr 6:12 629
That say, Let him make *s*, and Is 5:19 4116
they shall come with *s* swiftly Is 5:26 4120
for to come to him with all *s* Acts 17:15
your house, neither bid him God *s* 2Jn 10 *5463*
For he that biddeth him God *s* is 2Jn 11 *5463*

SPEEDILY
Then they *s* took down every man Gen 44:11 4116
for me than that I should *s* 1Sa 27:1 4422
the wilderness, but *s* pass over 2Sa 17:16 5674
divided them *s* among all the 2Chr 35:13
the king had sent, so they did *s* Ezr 6:13 629
That thou mayest buy *s* with this Ezr 7:17 629
require of you, it be done *s* Ezr 7:21 629
judgment be executed *s* upon him Ezr 7:26 629
he *s* gave her her things for Est 2:9 926
deliver me *s* Ps 31:2 4120
hear me *s* Ps 69:17 4118
thy tender mercies *s* prevent us Ps 79:8 4118
the day when I call answer me *s* Ps 102:2 4118
Hear me *s*, O LORD Ps 143:7 4118
an evil work is not executed *s* Eccl 8:11 4120
thine health shall spring forth *s* Is 58:8 4120
s will I return your recompence Joel 3:4 4120
Let us go *s* to pray before the Zec 8:21 1980
you that he will avenge them *s* Lk 18:8

SPEEDY
for he shall make even a *s* Zeph 1:18 926

SPEND
I will *s* mine arrows upon them Deut 32:23 3615
They *s* their days in wealth, and Job 21:13 3615
they shall *s* their days in Job 36:11 3615
we *s* our years as a tale that is Ps 90:9 3615
Wherefore do ye *s* money for that Is 55:2 8254
he would not *s* the time in Asia Acts 20:16 *5551*
And I will very gladly *s* and be 2Cor 12:15 *1159*

SPENDEST
and whatsoever thou *s* more Lk 10:35 *4325*

SPENDETH
but a foolish man *s* it up Prov 21:20 1104
with harlots *s* his substance Prov 29:3 6
vain life which he *s* as a shadow Eccl 6:12 6213

SPENT
And the water was *s* in the bottle Gen 21:15 3615
my lord, how that our money is *s* Gen 47:18 8552
your strength shall be *s* in vain Lev 26:20 8552
were by Jebus, the day was far *s* Judg 19:11 7286
for the bread is *s* in our vessels 1Sa 9:7 235
shuttle, and are *s* without hope Job 7:6 3615
For my life is *s* with grief Ps 31:10 3615
I have *s* my strength for nought, Is 49:4 3615
all the bread in the city were *s* Jer 37:21 8552
had *s* all that she had, and was Mk 5:26 *1159*
And when the day was now far *s* Mk 6:35
which had *s* all her living upon Lk 8:43 *4321*
And when he had *s* all, there arose Lk 15:14 *1159*
evening, and the day is far *s* Lk 24:29 *2827*
s their time in nothing else Acts 17:21 *2119*
after he had *s* some time there, Acts 18:23 *4160*
Now when much time was *s* Acts 27:9 *1230*
The night is far *s*, the day is at Rom 13:12 *4298*
very gladly spend and be *s* for you 2Cor 12:15 *1550*

SPEWING
shameful *s* shall be on thy glory Hab 2:16 7022

SPICE
And *s*, and oil for the light, and Ex 35:28 1314
the traffick of the *s* merchants 1Kin 10:15 7402
neither was there any such *s* as 2Chr 9:9 1314
have gathered my myrrh with my *s* Song 5:1 1313
s it well, and let the bones be Eze 24:10 7543

SPICED
of *s* wine of the juice of my Song 8:2 7544

SPICERY
with their camels bearing *s* Gen 37:25 5219

SPICES
little balm, and a little honey, *s* Gen 43:11 5219
s for anointing oil, and for sweet Ex 25:6 1314
s of pure myrrh five hundred Ex 30:23 1314
Moses, Take unto thee sweet *s* Ex 30:34 5561
these sweet *s* with pure Ex 30:34 5561
s for anointing oil, and for the Ex 35:8 1314
and the pure incense of sweet *s* Ex 37:29 5561
train, with camels that bare *s* 1Kin 10:2 1314
of *s* very great store, and 1Kin 10:10 1314
of *s* as these which the queen of 1Kin 10:10 1314
and garments, and armour, and *s* 1Kin 10:25 1314
the silver, and the gold, and the *s* 2Kin 20:13 1314
and the frankincense, and the *s* 1Chr 9:29 1314
made the ointment of the *s* 1Chr 9:30 1314
company, and camels that bare *s* 2Chr 9:1 1314
of *s* great abundance, and precious 2Chr 9:9 1314
gold, and raiment, harness, and *s* 2Chr 9:24 1314
divers kinds of *s* prepared by the 2Chr 16:14 1314
and for precious stones, and for *s* 2Chr 32:27 1314
of thine ointments than all *s* Song 4:10 1314
and aloes, with all the chief *s* Song 4:14 1314
that the *s* thereof may flow out Song 4:16 1314
His cheeks are as a bed of *s* Song 5:13 1314
into his garden, to the beds of *s* Song 6:2 1314
hart upon the mountains of *s* Song 8:14 1314
the silver, and the gold, and the *s* Is 39:2 1314
in thy fairs with chief of all *s* Eze 27:22 1314

and Salome, had bought sweet *s* Mk 16:1 *759*
And they returned, and prepared *s* Lk 23:56 *759*
bringing the *s* which they had Lk 24:1 *759*
it in linen clothes with the *s* Jn 19:40 *759*

SPIDER
The *s* taketh hold with her hands, Prov 30:28 8079

SPIDER'S
and whose trust shall be a *s* web Job 8:14 5908
eggs, and weave the *s* web Is 59:5 5908

SPIED
he *s* an Egyptian smiting an Ex 2:11 7200
men that had *s* out the country Josh 6:22 7270
he *s* the company of Jehu as he 2Kin 9:17 7200
behold, they *s* a band of men 2Kin 13:21 7200
he *s* the sepulchres that were 2Kin 23:16 7200
that were *s* in the land of Judah 2Kin 23:24 7200

SPIES
them, and said unto them, Ye are *s* Gen 42:9 7270
true men, thy servants are no *s* Gen 42:11 7270
spake unto you, saying, Ye are *s* Gen 42:14 7270
life of Pharaoh surely ye are *s* Gen 42:16 7270
took us for *s* of the country Gen 42:30 7270
we are no *s* Gen 42:31 7270
shall I know that ye are no *s* Gen 42:34 7270
Israel came by the way of the *s* Num 21:1 871
the young men that were *s* went in Josh 6:23 7270
the *s* saw a man come forth out of Judg 1:24 8104
David therefore sent out *s* 1Sa 26:4 7270
But Absalom sent *s* throughout all 2Sa 15:10 7270
they watched him, and sent forth *s* Lk 20:20 *1455*
she had received the *s* with peace Heb 11:31 *2685*

SPIKENARD
my *s* sendeth forth the smell Song 1:12 5373
camphire, with *s*, Song 4:13 5373
S and saffron Song 4:14 5373
of ointment of *s* very precious Mk 14:3
Mary a pound of ointment of *s* Jn 12:3

SPILLED
that he *s* it on the ground, lest Gen 38:9 7843
the bottles, and the wine is *s* Mk 2:22 *1632*
will burst the bottles, and be *s* Lk 5:37 *1632*

SPILT
are as water *s* on the ground, 2Sa 14:14 5064

SPIN
hearted did *s* with their hands Ex 35:25 2901
they toil not, neither do they *s* Mt 6:28 *3514*
they toil not, they *s* not Lk 12:27 *3514*

SPINDLE
She layeth her hands to the *s* Prov 31:19 3601

SPIRIT
the *S* of God moved upon the face Gen 1:2 7307
My *s* shall not always strive with Gen 6:3 7307
morning that his *s* was troubled Gen 41:8 7307
is, a man in whom the *S* of God is Gen 41:38 7307
the *s* of Jacob their father Gen 45:27 7307
not unto Moses for anguish of *s* Ex 6:9 7307
have filled with the *s* of wisdom Ex 28:3 7307
have filled him with the *s* of God Ex 31:3 7307
every one whom his *s* made willing Ex 35:21 7307
hath filled him with the *s* of God Ex 35:31 7307
or woman that hath a familiar *s* Lev 20:27 178
the *s* of jealousy come upon him, Num 5:14 7307
or if the *s* of jealousy come upon Num 5:14 7307
Or when the *s* of jealousy cometh Num 5:30 7307
take of the *s* which is upon thee Num 11:17 7307
took of the *s* that was upon him, Num 11:25 7307
when the *s* rested upon them, they Num 11:25 7307
and the *s* rested upon them Num 11:26 7307
LORD would put his *s* upon them Num 11:29 7307
because he had another *s* with him Num 14:24 7307
the *s* of God came upon him Num 24:2 7307
of Nun, a man in whom is the *s* Num 27:18 7307
the LORD thy God hardened his *s* Deut 2:30 7307
Nun was full of the *s* of wisdom Deut 34:9 7307
was there *s* in them any more Josh 5:1 7307
the *S* of the LORD came upon him, Judg 3:10 7307
But the *S* of the LORD came upon Judg 6:34 7307
sent an evil *s* between Abimelech Judg 9:23 7307
Then the *S* of the LORD came upon Judg 11:29 7307
the *S* of the LORD began to move Judg 13:25 7307
the *S* of the LORD came mightily Judg 14:6 7307
the *S* of the LORD came upon him, Judg 14:19 7307
the *S* of the LORD came mightily Judg 15:14 7307
his *s* came again, and he revived Judg 15:19 7307
I am a woman of a sorrowful *s* 1Sa 1:15 7307
the *S* of the LORD will come upon 1Sa 10:6 7307
the *S* of God came upon him, and he 1Sa 10:10 7307
the *S* of God came upon Saul when 1Sa 11:6 7307
the *S* of the LORD came upon David 1Sa 16:13 7307
But the *S* of the LORD departed 1Sa 16:14 7307
an evil *s* from the LORD troubled 1Sa 16:14 7307
an evil *s* from God troubleth thee 1Sa 16:15 7307
when the evil *s* from God is upon 1Sa 16:16 7307
when the evil *s* from God was upon 1Sa 16:23 7307
the evil *s* departed from him 1Sa 16:23 7307
that the evil *s* from God came 1Sa 18:10 7307
the evil *s* from the LORD was upon 1Sa 19:9 7307
the *S* of God was upon the 1Sa 19:20 7307
the *S* of God was upon him also, 1Sa 19:23 7307
me a woman that hath a familiar *s* 1Sa 28:7 178
that hath a familiar *s* at En-dor 1Sa 28:7 178
divine unto me by the familiar *s* 1Sa 28:8 178
eaten, his *s* came again to him 1Sa 30:12 7307
The *S* of the LORD spake by me, and 2Sa 23:2 7307
there was no more *s* in her 1Kin 10:5 7307
that the *S* of the LORD shall 1Kin 18:12 7307
unto him, Why is thy *s* so sad 1Kin 21:5 7307
And there came forth a *s*, and stood 1Kin 22:21 7307
I will be a lying *s* in the mouth 1Kin 22:22 7307

S

Context	Reference	Number
the LORD hath put a lying s in	1Kin 22:23	7307
Which way went the S of the LORD	1Kin 22:24	7307
portion of thy s be upon me	2Kin 2:9	7307
The s of Elijah doth rest on	2Kin 2:15	7307
lest peradventure the S of the	2Kin 2:16	7307
up the s of Pul king of Assyria	1Chr 5:26	7307
the s of Tilgath-pilneser king of	1Chr 5:26	7307
of one that had a familiar s	1Chr 10:13	178
Then the s came upon Amasai, who	1Chr 12:18	7307
of all that he had by the s	1Chr 28:12	7307
there was no more s in her	2Chr 9:4	7307
the S of God came upon Azariah	2Chr 15:1	7307
Then there came out a s, and stood	2Chr 18:20	7307
be a lying s in the mouth of all	2Chr 18:21	7307
lying s in the mouth of these thy	2Chr 18:22	7307
Which way went the S of the LORD	2Chr 18:23	7307
came the S of the LORD in the	2Chr 20:14	7307
Jehoram the s of the Philistines	2Chr 21:16	7307
the S of God came upon Zechariah	2Chr 24:20	7307
and dealt with a familiar s	2Chr 33:6	178
up the s of Cyrus king of Persia	2Chr 36:22	7307
up the s of Cyrus king of Persia	Ezr 1:1	7307
all them whose s God had raised	Ezr 1:5	7307
also thy good s to instruct them	Neh 9:20	7307
them by thy s in thy prophets	Neh 9:30	7307
Then a s passed before my face	Job 4:15	7307
poison whereof drinketh up my s	Job 6:4	7307
will speak in the anguish of my s	Job 7:11	7307
visitation hath preserved my s	Job 10:12	7307
thou turnest thy s against God	Job 15:13	7307
the s of my understanding causeth	Job 20:3	7307
why should not my s be troubled	Job 21:4	7307
and whose s came from thee	Job 26:4	5397
By his s he hath garnished the	Job 26:13	7307
the s of God is in my nostrils	Job 27:3	7307
But there is a s in man	Job 32:8	7307
the s within me constraineth me	Job 32:18	7307
The s of God hath made me, and the	Job 33:4	7307
if he gather unto himself his s	Job 34:14	7307
Into thine hand I commit my s	Ps 31:5	7307
in whose s there is no guile	Ps 32:2	7307
saveth such as be of a contrite s	Ps 34:18	7307
and renew a right s within me	Ps 51:10	7307
and take not thy holy s from me	Ps 51:11	7307
and uphold me with thy free s	Ps 51:12	7307
sacrifices of God are a broken s	Ps 51:17	7307
He shall cut off the s of princes	Ps 76:12	7307
and my s was overwhelmed	Ps 77:3	7307
my s made diligent search	Ps 77:6	7307
whose s was not stedfast with God	Ps 78:8	7307
Thou sendest forth thy s, they	Ps 104:30	7307
Because they provoked his s	Ps 106:33	7307
Whither shall I go from thy s	Ps 139:7	7307
When my s was overwhelmed within	Ps 142:3	7307
Therefore is my s overwhelmed	Ps 143:4	7307
my s faileth	Ps 143:7	7307
thy s is good	Ps 143:10	7307
I will pour out my s unto you	Prov 1:23	7307
faithful s concealeth the matter	Prov 11:13	7307
that is hasty of s exalteth folly	Prov 14:29	7307
therein is a breach in the s	Prov 15:4	7307
of the heart the s is broken	Prov 15:13	7307
an haughty s before a fall	Prov 16:18	7307
be of an humble s with the lowly	Prov 16:19	7307
he that ruleth his s than he that	Prov 16:32	7307
but a broken s drieth the bones	Prov 17:22	7307
is of an excellent s	Prov 17:27	7307
The s of a man will sustain his	Prov 18:14	7307
but a wounded s who can bear	Prov 18:14	7307
The s of man is the candle of the	Prov 20:27	5397
s is like a city that is broken	Prov 25:28	7307
shall uphold the humble in s	Prov 29:23	7307
all is vanity and vexation of s	Eccl 1:14	7307
that this also is vexation of s	Eccl 1:17	7307
all was vanity and vexation of s	Eccl 2:11	7307
all is vanity and vexation of s	Eccl 2:17	7307
also is vanity and vexation of s	Eccl 2:26	7307
Who knoweth the s of man that	Eccl 3:21	7307
the s of the beast that goeth	Eccl 3:21	7307
is also vanity and vexation of s	Eccl 4:4	7307
with travail and vexation of s	Eccl 4:6	7307
also is vanity and vexation of s	Eccl 4:16	7307
is also vanity and vexation of s	Eccl 6:9	7307
the patient in s is better than	Eccl 7:8	7307
is better than the proud in s	Eccl 7:8	7307
Be not hasty in thy s to be angry	Eccl 7:9	7307
over the s to retain the s	Eccl 8:8	7307
If the s of the ruler rise up	Eccl 10:4	7307
not what is the way of the s	Eccl 11:5	7307
the s shall return unto God who	Eccl 12:7	7307
thereof by the s of judgment	Is 4:4	7307
and by the s of burning	Is 4:4	7307
the s of the LORD shall rest upon	Is 11:2	7307
the s of wisdom and understanding,	Is 11:2	7307
the s of counsel and might	Is 11:2	7307
the s of knowledge and of the fear	Is 11:2	7307
the s of Egypt shall fail in the	Is 19:3	7307
a perverse s in the midst thereof	Is 19:14	7307
with my s within me will I seek	Is 26:9	7307
for a s of judgment to him that	Is 28:6	7307
as of one that hath a familiar s	Is 29:4	178
out upon you the s of deep sleep	Is 29:10	7307
They also that erred in s shall	Is 29:24	7307
with a covering, but not of my s	Is 30:1	7307
and their horses flesh, and not s	Is 31:3	7307
Until the s be poured upon us	Is 32:15	7307
his s it hath gathered them	Is 34:16	7307
these things is the life of my s	Is 38:16	7307
because the s of the LORD bloweth	Is 40:7	7307
hath directed the S of the LORD	Is 40:13	7307
I have put my s upon him	Is 42:1	7307
s to them that walk therein	Is 42:5	7307
I will pour my s upon thy seed	Is 44:3	7307
and now the Lord GOD, and his S	Is 48:16	7307
a woman forsaken and grieved in s	Is 54:6	7307
that is of a contrite and humble s	Is 57:15	7307
to revive the s of the humble	Is 57:15	7307
for the s should fail before me,	Is 57:16	7307
the S of the LORD shall lift up a	Is 59:19	7307
My s that is upon thee, and my	Is 59:21	7307
The S of the Lord GOD is upon me	Is 61:1	7307
of praise for the s of heaviness	Is 61:3	7307
rebelled, and vexed his holy S	Is 63:10	7307
he that put his holy S within him	Is 63:11	7307
the S of the LORD caused him to	Is 63:14	7307
and shall howl for vexation of s	Is 65:14	7307
that is poor and of a contrite s	Is 66:2	7307
the s of the kings of the Medes	Jer 51:11	7307
whither the s was to go, they	Eze 1:12	7307
Whithersoever the s was to go	Eze 1:20	7307
went, thither was their s to go	Eze 1:20	7307
for the s of the living creature	Eze 1:20	7307
for the s of the living creature	Eze 1:21	7307
the s entered into me when he	Eze 2:2	7307
Then the s took me up, and I heard	Eze 3:12	7307
So the s lifted me up, and took me	Eze 3:14	7307
bitterness, in the heat of my s	Eze 3:14	7307
Then the s entered into me, and	Eze 3:24	7307
the s lifted me up between the	Eze 8:3	7307
for the s of the living creature	Eze 10:17	7307
Moreover the s lifted me up	Eze 11:1	7307
the S of the LORD fell upon me,	Eze 11:5	7307
and I will put a new s within you	Eze 11:19	7307
Afterwards the s took me up	Eze 11:24	7307
by the S of God into Chaldea	Eze 11:24	7307
prophets, that follow their own s	Eze 13:3	7307
make you a new heart and a new s	Eze 18:31	7307
every s shall faint, and all knees	Eze 21:7	7307
a new s will I put within you	Eze 36:26	7307
And I will put my s within you	Eze 36:27	7307
me out in the s of the LORD	Eze 37:1	7307
And shall put my s in you, and ye	Eze 37:14	7307
out my s upon the house of Israel	Eze 39:29	7307
So the s took me up, and brought	Eze 43:5	7307
wherewith his s was troubled	Dan 2:1	7307
my s was troubled to know the	Dan 2:3	7307
in whom is the s of the holy gods	Dan 4:8	7308
because I know that the s of the	Dan 4:9	7308
for the s of the holy gods is in	Dan 4:18	7308
in whom is the s of the holy gods	Dan 5:11	7308
Forasmuch as an excellent s	Dan 5:12	7308
that the s of the gods is in thee	Dan 5:14	7308
because an excellent s was in him	Dan 6:3	7308
in my s in the midst of my body	Dan 7:15	7308
for the s of whoredoms hath	Hos 4:12	7307
for the s of whoredoms is in the	Hos 5:4	7307
will pour out my s upon all flesh	Joel 2:28	7307
those days will I pour out my s	Joel 2:29	7307
is the s of the LORD straitened	Mic 2:7	7307
If a man walking in the s	Mic 2:11	7307
of power by the s of the LORD	Mic 3:8	7307
the LORD stirred up the s of	Hag 1:14	7307
the s of Joshua the son of	Hag 1:14	7307
the s of all the remnant of the	Hag 1:14	7307
so my s remaineth among you	Hag 2:5	7307
might, nor by power, but by my s	Zec 4:6	7307
quieted my s in the north country	Zec 6:8	7307
in his s by the former prophets	Zec 7:12	7307
formeth the s of man within him	Zec 12:1	7307
Jerusalem, the s of grace and of	Zec 12:10	7307
the unclean s to pass out of the	Zec 13:2	7307
Yet had he the residue of the s	Mal 2:15	7307
Therefore take heed to your s	Mal 2:15	7307
therefore take heed to your s	Mal 2:16	7307
he saw the S of God descending	Mt 3:16	4151
the s into the wilderness to be	Mt 4:1	4151
Blessed are the poor in s	Mt 5:3	4151
but the S of your Father which	Mt 10:20	4151
I will put my S upon him, and he	Mt 12:18	4151
I cast out devils by the S of God	Mt 12:28	4151
When the unclean s is gone out of	Mt 12:43	4151
were troubled, saying, It is a s	Mt 14:26	5326
doth David in s call him Lord	Mt 22:43	4151
the s indeed is willing, but the	Mt 26:41	4151
the S like a dove descending upon	Mk 1:10	4151
immediately the s driveth him	Mk 1:12	4151
synagogue a man with an unclean s	Mk 1:23	4151
when the unclean s had torn him	Mk 1:26	4151
when Jesus perceived in his s	Mk 2:8	4151
they said, He hath an unclean s	Mk 3:30	4151
the tombs a man with an unclean s	Mk 5:2	4151
out of the man, thou unclean s	Mk 5:8	4151
they supposed it had been a s	Mk 6:49	5326
young daughter had an unclean s	Mk 7:25	4151
And he sighed deeply in his s	Mk 8:12	4151
thee my son, which hath a dumb s	Mk 9:17	4151
him, straightway the s tare him	Mk 9:20	4151
together, he rebuked the foul s	Mk 9:25	4151
unto him, Thou dumb and deaf s	Mk 9:25	4151
the s cried, and rent him sore, and	Mk 9:26	
The s truly is ready, but the	Mk 14:38	4151
he shall go before him in the s	Lk 1:17	4151
my s hath rejoiced in God my	Lk 1:47	4151
child grew, and waxed strong in s	Lk 1:80	4151
he came by the S into the temple	Lk 2:27	4151
child grew, and waxed strong in s	Lk 2:40	4151
was led by the S into the	Lk 4:1	4151
the power of the S into Galilee	Lk 4:14	4151
The S of the Lord is upon me,	Lk 4:18	4151
which had a s of an unclean devil	Lk 4:33	4151
unclean s to come out of the man	Lk 8:29	4151
her s came again, and she arose	Lk 8:55	4151
a s taketh him, and he suddenly	Lk 9:39	4151
And Jesus rebuked the unclean s	Lk 9:42	4151
not what manner of s ye are of	Lk 9:55	4151
In that hour Jesus rejoiced in s	Lk 10:21	4151
the Holy S to them that ask him	Lk 11:13	4151
When the unclean s is gone out of	Lk 11:24	4151
a s of infirmity eighteen years	Lk 13:11	4151
into thy hands I commend my s	Lk 23:46	4151
supposed that they had seen a s	Lk 24:37	4151
for a s hath not flesh and bones,	Lk 24:39	4151
I saw the S descending from	Jn 1:32	4151
thou shalt see the S descending	Jn 1:33	4151
man be born of water and of the S	Jn 3:5	4151
which is born of the S is s	Jn 3:6	4151
every one that is born of the S	Jn 3:8	4151
not the S by measure unto him	Jn 3:34	4151
shall worship the Father in s	Jn 4:23	4151
God is a S	Jn 4:24	4151
worship him must worship him in s	Jn 4:24	4151
It is the s that quickeneth	Jn 6:63	4151
that I speak unto you, they are s	Jn 6:63	4151
(But this spake he of the S	Jn 7:39	4151
with her, he groaned in the s	Jn 11:33	4151
thus said, he was troubled in s	Jn 13:21	4151
Even the S of truth	Jn 14:17	4151
the Father, even the S of truth	Jn 15:26	4151
the S of truth, is come, he will	Jn 16:13	4151
as the S gave them utterance	Acts 2:4	4151
pour out of my S upon all flesh	Acts 2:17	4151
pour out in those days of my S	Acts 2:18	4151
to tempt the S of the Lord	Acts 5:9	4151
wisdom and the s by which he spake	Acts 6:10	4151
saying, Lord Jesus, receive my s	Acts 7:59	4151
Then the S said unto Philip, Go	Acts 8:29	4151
the S of the Lord caught away	Acts 8:39	4151
the S said unto him, Behold,	Acts 10:19	4151
the S bade me go with them,	Acts 11:12	4151
signified by the S that there	Acts 11:28	4151
but the S suffered them not	Acts 16:7	4151
with a s of divination met us	Acts 16:16	4151
grieved, turned and said to the s	Acts 16:18	4151
his s was stirred in him, when he	Acts 17:16	4151
Paul was pressed in the s	Acts 18:5	4151
and being fervent in the s	Acts 18:25	4151
And the evil s answered and said,	Acts 19:15	4151
the evil s was leaped on them	Acts 19:16	4151
ended, Paul purposed in the s	Acts 19:21	4151
go bound in the s unto Jerusalem	Acts 20:22	4151
who said to Paul through the S	Acts 21:4	4151
neither angel, nor s	Acts 23:8	4151
but if a s or an angel hath	Acts 23:9	4151
according to the s of holiness	Rom 1:4	4151
whom I serve with my s in the	Rom 1:9	4151
is that of the heart, in the s	Rom 2:29	4151
we should serve in newness of s	Rom 7:6	4151
after the flesh, but after the S	Rom 8:1	4151
For the law of the S of life	Rom 8:2	4151
after the flesh, but after the S	Rom 8:4	4151
the S the things of the S	Rom 8:5	4151
not in the flesh, but in the S	Rom 8:9	4151
if so be that the S of God dwell	Rom 8:9	4151
any man have not the S of Christ	Rom 8:9	4151
but the S is life because of	Rom 8:10	4151
But if the S of him that raised	Rom 8:11	4151
by his S that dwelleth in you	Rom 8:11	4151
but if ye through the S do	Rom 8:13	4151
many as are led by the S of God	Rom 8:14	4151
the s of bondage again to fear	Rom 8:15	4151
have received the S of adoption	Rom 8:15	4151
The S itself beareth witness with	Rom 8:16	4151
itself beareth witness with our s	Rom 8:16	4151
have the firstfruits of the S	Rom 8:23	4151
Likewise the S also helpeth our	Rom 8:26	4151
but the S itself maketh	Rom 8:26	4151
knoweth what is the mind of the S	Rom 8:27	4151
hath given them the s of slumber	Rom 11:8	4151
fervent in s	Rom 12:11	4151
by the power of the S of God	Rom 15:19	4151
sake, and for the love of the S	Rom 15:30	4151
but in demonstration of the S	1Cor 2:4	4151
revealed them unto us by his S	1Cor 2:10	4151
for the S searcheth all things,	1Cor 2:10	4151
save the s of man which is in him	1Cor 2:11	4151
knoweth no man, but the S of God	1Cor 2:11	4151
not the s of the world	1Cor 2:12	4151
but the s which is of God	1Cor 2:12	4151
not the things of the S of God	1Cor 2:14	4151
that the S of God dwelleth in you	1Cor 3:16	4151
in love, and in the s of meekness	1Cor 4:21	4151
absent in body, but present in s	1Cor 5:3	4151
ye are gathered together, and my s	1Cor 5:4	4151
that the s may be saved in the	1Cor 5:5	4151
Jesus, and by the S of our God	1Cor 6:11	4151
is joined unto the Lord is one s	1Cor 6:17	4151
God in your body, and in your s	1Cor 6:20	4151
may be holy both in body and in s	1Cor 7:34	4151
also that I have the S of God	1Cor 7:40	4151
that no man speaking by the S of	1Cor 12:3	4151
of gifts, but the same S	1Cor 12:4	4151
But the manifestation of the S is	1Cor 12:7	4151
given by the S the word of wisdom	1Cor 12:8	4151
word of knowledge by the same S	1Cor 12:8	4151
To another faith by the same S	1Cor 12:9	4151
gifts of healing by the same S	1Cor 12:9	4151
that one and the selfsame S	1Cor 12:11	4151
For by one S are we all baptized	1Cor 12:13	4151
been all made to drink into one S	1Cor 12:13	4151
howbeit in the s he speaketh	1Cor 14:2	4151
tongue, my s prayeth, but my	1Cor 14:14	4151
I will pray with the s, and I will	1Cor 14:15	4151
I will sing with the s, and I will	1Cor 14:15	4151
when thou shalt bless with the s	1Cor 14:16	4151
last Adam was made a quickening s	1Cor 15:45	4151
For they have refreshed my s	1Cor 16:18	4151
earnest of the S in our hearts	2Cor 1:22	4151
I had no rest in my s, because I	2Cor 2:13	4151
but with the S of the living God	2Cor 3:3	4151
not of the letter, but of the s	2Cor 3:6	4151
killeth, but the s giveth life	2Cor 3:6	4151
of the s be rather glorious	2Cor 3:8	4151

Now the Lord is that S ... 2Cor 3:17 4151
where the S of the Lord is, there ... 2Cor 3:17 4151
even as by the S of the Lord ... 2Cor 3:18 4151
We having the same s of faith ... 2Cor 4:13 4151
unto us the earnest of the S ... 2Cor 5:5 4151
all filthiness of the flesh and s ... 2Cor 7:1 4151
because his s was refreshed by ... 2Cor 7:13 4151
or if ye receive another s ... 2Cor 11:4 4151
walked we not in the same s ... 2Cor 12:18 4151
Received ye the S by the works of ... Gal 3:2 4151
having begun in the S, are ye now ... Gal 3:3 4151
that ministereth to you the S ... Gal 3:5 4151
promise of the S through faith ... Gal 3:14 4151
God hath sent forth the S of his ... Gal 4:6 4151
him that was born after the S ... Gal 4:29 4151
For we through the S wait for the ... Gal 5:5 4151
This I say then, Walk in the S ... Gal 5:16 4151
the flesh lusteth against the S ... Gal 5:17 4151
and the S against the flesh ... Gal 5:17 4151
But if ye be led of the S ... Gal 5:18 4151
But the fruit of the S is love ... Gal 5:22 4151
If we live in the S, let us also ... Gal 5:25 4151
let us also walk in the S ... Gal 5:25 4151
such an one in the s of meekness ... Gal 6:1 4151
but he that soweth to the S shall ... Gal 6:8 4151
of the S reap life everlasting ... Gal 6:8 4151
Lord Jesus Christ be with your s ... Gal 6:18 4151
with that holy S of promise ... Eph 1:13 4151
may give unto you the s of wisdom ... Eph 1:17 4151
the s that now worketh in the ... Eph 2:2 4151
access by one S unto the Father ... Eph 2:18 4151
habitation of God through the S ... Eph 2:22 4151
apostles and prophets by the S ... Eph 3:5 4151
might by his S in the inner man ... Eph 3:16 4151
of the S in the bond of peace ... Eph 4:3 4151
There is one body, and one S ... Eph 4:4 4151
be renewed in the s of your mind ... Eph 4:23 4151
And grieve not the holy S of God ... Eph 4:30 4151
fruit of the S is in all goodness ... Eph 5:9 4151
but be filled with the S ... Eph 5:18 4151
salvation, and the sword of the S ... Eph 6:17 4151
prayer and supplication in the S ... Eph 6:18 4151
supply of the S of Jesus Christ ... Phil 1:19 4151
that ye stand fast in one s ... Phil 1:27 4151
love, if any fellowship of the S ... Phil 2:1 4151
which worship God in the s ... Phil 3:3 4151
unto us your love in the S ... Col 1:8 4151
flesh, yet am I with you in the s ... Col 2:5 4151
also given unto us his holy S ... 1Th 4:8 4151
Quench not the S ... 1Th 5:19 4151
and I pray God your whole s ... 1Th 5:23 4151
or be troubled, neither by s ... 2Th 2:2 4151
consume with the s of his mouth ... 2Th 2:8 4151
through sanctification of the S ... 2Th 2:13 4151
in the flesh, justified in the S ... 1Ti 3:16 4151
Now the S speaketh expressly ... 1Ti 4:1 4151
in conversation, in charity, in s ... 1Ti 4:12 4151
hath not given us the s of fear ... 2Ti 1:7 4151
Lord Jesus Christ be with thy s ... 2Ti 4:22 4151
Lord Jesus Christ be with your s ... Philem 25 4151
the dividing asunder of soul and s ... Heb 4:12 4151
who through the eternal S offered ... Heb 9:14 4151
done despite unto the S of grace ... Heb 10:29 4151
as the body without the s is dead ... Jas 2:26 4151
The s that dwelleth in us lusteth ... Jas 4:5 4151
through sanctification of the S ... 1Pet 1:2 4151
or what manner of time the S of ... 1Pet 1:11 4151
the S unto unfeigned love of the ... 1Pet 1:22 4151
the ornament of a meek and quiet s ... 1Pet 3:4 4151
the flesh, but quickened by the S ... 1Pet 3:18 4151
live according to God in the s ... 1Pet 4:6 4151
for the s of glory and of God ... 1Pet 4:14 4151
by the S which he hath given us ... 1Jn 3:24 4151
Beloved, believe not every s ... 1Jn 4:1 4151
Hereby know ye the S of God ... 1Jn 4:2 4151
Every s that confesseth that ... 1Jn 4:2 4151
every s that confesseth not that ... 1Jn 4:3 4151
this is that s of antichrist ... 1Jn 4:3
Hereby know we the s of truth ... 1Jn 4:6 4151
of truth, and the s of error ... 1Jn 4:6 4151
because he hath given us of his S ... 1Jn 4:13 4151
it is the S that beareth witness ... 1Jn 5:6 4151
witness, because the S is truth ... 1Jn 5:6 4151
that bear witness in earth, the s ... 1Jn 5:8 4151
sensual, having not the S ... Jude 19 4151
I was in the S on the Lord's day ... Rev 1:10 4151
let him hear what the S saith ... Rev 2:7 4151
let him hear what the S saith ... Rev 2:11 4151
let him hear what the S saith ... Rev 2:17 4151
let him hear what the S saith ... Rev 2:29 4151
let him hear what the S saith ... Rev 3:6 4151
let him hear what the S saith ... Rev 3:13 4151
let him hear what the S saith ... Rev 3:22 4151
And immediately I was in the s ... Rev 4:2 4151
an half the S of life from God ... Rev 11:11 4151
Yea, saith the S, that they may ... Rev 14:13 4151
away in the s into the wilderness ... Rev 17:3 4151
and the hold of every foul s ... Rev 18:2 4151
of Jesus is the s of prophecy ... Rev 19:10 4151
me away in the s to a great ... Rev 21:10 4151
And the S and the bride say, Come ... Rev 22:17 4151

SPIRITS

not them that have familiar s ... Lev 19:31 178
after such as have familiar s ... Lev 20:6 178
the God of the s of all flesh ... Num 16:22 7307
the God of the s of all flesh ... Num 27:16 7307
or a consulter with familiar s ... Deut 18:11 178
away those that had familiar s ... 1Sa 28:3 178
off those that have familiar s ... 1Sa 28:9 178
and dealt with familiar s ... 2Kin 21:6 178
the workers with familiar s ... 2Kin 23:24 178
Who maketh his angels s ... Ps 104:4 7307
but the LORD weigheth the s ... Prov 16:2 7307
unto them that have familiar s ... Is 8:19 178
and to them that have familiar s ... Is 19:3 178
are the four s of the heavens ... Zec 6:5 7307
he cast out the s with his word ... Mt 8:16 4151
gave them power against unclean s ... Mt 10:1 4151
other s more wicked than himself ... Mt 12:45 4151
commandeth he even the unclean s ... Mk 1:27 4151
And unclean s, when they saw him ... Mk 3:11 4151
And the unclean s went out ... Mk 5:13 4151
and gave them power over unclean s ... Mk 6:7 4151
power he commandeth the unclean s ... Lk 4:36 4151
that were vexed with unclean s ... Lk 6:18 4151
and plagues, and of evil s ... Lk 7:21 4151
which had been healed of evil s ... Lk 8:2 4151
that the s are subject unto you ... Lk 10:20 4151
other s more wicked than himself ... Lk 11:26 4151
which were vexed with unclean s ... Acts 5:16 4151
For unclean s, crying with loud ... Acts 8:7 4151
the evil s went out of them ... Acts 19:12 4151
evil s the name of the Lord Jesus ... Acts 19:13 4151
to another discerning of s ... 1Cor 12:10 4151
the s of the prophets are subject ... 1Cor 14:32 4151
faith, giving heed to seducing s ... 1Ti 4:1 4151
he saith, Who maketh his angels s ... Heb 1:7 4151
Are they not all ministering s ... Heb 1:14 4151
subjection unto the Father of s ... Heb 12:9 4151
to the s of just men made perfect ... Heb 12:23 4151
and preached unto the s in prison ... 1Pet 3:19 4151
but try the s whether they are of ... 1Jn 4:1 4151
from the seven S which are before ... Rev 1:4 4151
he that hath the seven S of God ... Rev 3:1 4151
which are the seven S of God ... Rev 4:5 4151
which are the seven S of God sent ... Rev 5:6 4151
I saw three unclean s like frogs ... Rev 16:13 4151
For they are the s of devils ... Rev 16:14 4151

SPIRITUAL

the s man is mad, for the ... Hos 9:7 7307
I may impart unto you some s gift ... Rom 1:11 4152
For we know that the law is s ... Rom 7:14 4152
made partakers of their s things ... Rom 15:27 4152
comparing s things with s ... 1Cor 2:13 4152
But he that is s judgeth all ... 1Cor 2:15 4152
not speak unto you as unto s ... 1Cor 3:1 4152
If we have sown unto you s things ... 1Cor 9:11 4152
And did all eat the same s meat ... 1Cor 10:3 4152
And did all drink the same s drink ... 1Cor 10:4 4152
for they drank of that s Rock ... 1Cor 10:4 4152
Now concerning s gifts, brethren ... 1Cor 12:1 4152
after charity, and desire s gifts ... 1Cor 14:1 4152
as ye are zealous of s gifts ... 1Cor 14:12 4151
himself to be a prophet, or s ... 1Cor 14:37 4152
it is raised a s body ... 1Cor 15:44 4152
body, and there is a s body ... 1Cor 15:44 4152
that was not first which is s ... 1Cor 15:46 4152
and afterward that which is s ... 1Cor 15:46 4152
in a fault, ye which are s ... Gal 6:1 4152
who hath blessed us with all s ... Eph 1:3 4152
s songs, singing and making melody ... Eph 5:19 4152
against s wickedness in high ... Eph 6:12 4152
in all wisdom and s understanding ... Col 1:9 4152
s songs, singing with grace in ... Col 3:16 4152
stones, are built up a s house ... 1Pet 2:5 4152
to offer up s sacrifices ... 1Pet 2:5 4152

SPIRITUALLY

but to be s minded is life and ... Rom 8:6
because they are s discerned ... 1Cor 2:14 4153
which s is called Sodom and Egypt ... Rev 11:8 4153

SPIT

issue s upon him that is clean ... Lev 15:8 7556
her father had but s in her face ... Num 12:14 3417
s in his face, and shall answer and ... Deut 25:9 3417
me, and spare not to s in my face ... Job 30:10 7536
Then did they s in his face ... Mt 26:67 1716
they s upon him, and took the reed ... Mt 27:30 1716
fingers into his ears, and he s ... Mk 7:33 4429
and when he had s on his eyes ... Mk 8:23 4429
shall s upon him, and shall kill ... Mk 10:34 1716
And some began to s on him ... Mk 14:65 1716
did s upon him, and bowing their ... Mk 15:19 1716

SPITE

for thou beholdest mischief and s ... Ps 10:14 3708

SPITEFULLY

his servants, and entreated them s ... Mt 22:6 5195
s entreated, and spitted on ... Lk 18:32 5195

SPITTED

and spitefully entreated, and s on ... Lk 18:32 1716

SPITTING

I hid not my face from shame and s ... Is 50:6 7536

SPITTLE

let his s fall down upon his ... 1Sa 21:13 7388
me alone till I swallow down my s ... Job 7:19 7536
the ground, and made clay of the s ... Jn 9:6 4427

SPOIL

and at night he shall divide the s ... Gen 49:27 7998
and ye shall s the Egyptians ... Ex 3:22 5337
overtake, I will divide the s ... Ex 15:9 7998
took the s of all their cattle ... Num 31:9 962
And they took all the s, and all ... Num 31:11 7998
captives, and the prey, and the s ... Num 31:12 7998
(For the men of war had taken s ... Num 31:53 962
the s of the cities which we took ... Deut 2:35 7998
the s of the cities, we took for ... Deut 3:7 7998
thou shalt gather all the s of it ... Deut 13:16 7998
all the s thereof every whit, for ... Deut 13:16 7998
the city, even all the s thereof ... Deut 20:14 7998
shalt eat the s of thine enemies ... Deut 20:14 7998
only the s thereof, and the cattle ... Josh 8:2 7998
the s of that city Israel took ... Josh 8:27 7998
all the s of these cities, and the ... Josh 11:14 7998
divide the s of your enemies with ... Josh 22:8 7998
the necks of them that take the s ... Judg 5:30 7998
men of them, and took their s ... Judg 14:19 2488
the s of their enemies which they ... 1Sa 14:30 7998
And the people flew upon the s ... 1Sa 14:32 7998
s them until the morning light ... 1Sa 14:36 962
LORD, but didst fly upon the s ... 1Sa 15:19 7998
But the people took of the s ... 1Sa 15:21 7998
because of all the great s that ... 1Sa 30:16 7998
sons nor daughters, neither s ... 1Sa 30:19 7998
and said, This is David's s ... 1Sa 30:20 7998
of the s that we have recovered ... 1Sa 30:22 7998
he sent of the s unto the elders ... 1Sa 30:26 7998
the s of the enemies of the LORD ... 1Sa 30:26 7998
and brought in a great s with them ... 2Sa 3:22 7998
of the s of Hadadezer, son of ... 2Sa 8:12 7998
he brought forth the s of the ... 2Sa 12:30 7998
returned after him only to s ... 2Sa 23:10 6584
now therefore, Moab, to the s ... 2Kin 3:23 7998
prey and a s to all their enemies ... 2Kin 21:14 4933
exceeding much s out of the city ... 1Chr 20:2 7998
and they carried away very much s ... 2Chr 14:13 7998
was exceeding much s in them ... 2Chr 14:14 961
of the s which they had brought ... 2Chr 15:11 7998
came to take away the s of them ... 2Chr 20:25 7998
three days in gathering of the s ... 2Chr 20:25 7998
sent all the s of them unto the ... 2Chr 24:23 7998
thousand of them, and took much s ... 2Chr 25:13 961
took also away much s from them ... 2Chr 28:8 7998
and brought the s to Samaria ... 2Chr 28:8 7998
the s before the princes and all ... 2Chr 28:14 961
with the s clothed all that were ... 2Chr 28:15 7998
sword, to captivity, and to a s ... Ezr 9:7 961
to take the s of them for a prey ... Est 3:13 7998
to take the s of them for a prey ... Est 8:11 7998
but on the s laid they not their ... Est 9:10 961
plucked the s out of his teeth ... Job 29:17 2964
which hate us s for themselves ... Ps 44:10 8154
tarried at home divided the s ... Ps 68:12 7998
All that pass by the way s him ... Ps 89:41 8155
and let the strangers s his labour ... Ps 109:11 962
word, as one that findeth great s ... Ps 119:162 7998
we shall fill our houses with s ... Prov 1:13 7998
to divide the s with the proud ... Prov 16:19 7998
s the soul of those that spoiled ... Prov 22:23 6906
s not his resting place ... Prov 24:15 7703
that he shall have no need of s ... Prov 31:11 7998
little foxes, that s the vines ... Song 2:15 2254
the s of the poor is in your ... Is 3:14 1500
the s of Samaria shall be taken ... Is 8:4 7998
rejoice when they divide the s ... Is 9:3 7998
give him a charge, to take the s ... Is 10:6 7998
they shall s them of the east ... Is 11:14 962
is the portion of them that s us ... Is 17:14 8154
when thou shalt cease to s ... Is 33:1 7703
your s shall be gathered like the ... Is 33:4 7998
is the prey of a great s divided ... Is 33:23 7998
for a s, and none saith, Restore ... Is 42:22 4933
Who gave Jacob for a s, and Israel ... Is 42:24 4882
divide the s with the strong ... Is 53:12 7998
wolf of the evenings shall s them ... Jer 5:6 7703
violence and s is heard in her ... Jer 6:7 7701
I give to the s without price ... Jer 15:13 957
and all thy treasures to the s ... Jer 17:3 957
their enemies, which shall s them ... Jer 20:5 962
cried out, I cried violence and s ... Jer 20:8 7701
they that s thee shall be a ... Jer 30:16 7701
thee shall be a s ... Jer 30:16 4933
cometh to s all the Philistines ... Jer 47:4 7703
the LORD will s the Philistines ... Jer 47:4 7703
Kedar, and s the men of the east ... Jer 49:28 7703
the multitude of their cattle a s ... Jer 49:32 7998
And Chaldea shall be a s ... Jer 50:10 7998
all that s her shall be satisfied ... Jer 50:10 7998
the wicked of the earth for a s ... Eze 7:21 7998
through the land, and they s it ... Eze 14:15 7921
thee for a s to the heathen ... Eze 25:7 957
shall become a s to the nations ... Eze 26:5 957
they shall make a s of thy riches ... Eze 26:12 7997
take her multitude, and take her s ... Eze 29:19 7997
they shall s the pomp of Egypt ... Eze 32:12 7703
To take a s, and to take a prey ... Eze 38:12 7998
thee, Art thou come to take a s ... Eze 38:13 7998
and goods, to take a great s ... Eze 38:13 7998
they shall s those that spoiled ... Eze 39:10 7997
remove violence and s, and execute ... Eze 45:9 7701
scatter among them the prey, and s ... Dan 11:24 7998
by flame, by captivity, and by s ... Dan 11:33 961
altars, he shall s their images ... Hos 10:2 7703
he shall s the treasure of all ... Hos 13:15 8154
Take ye the s of silver, take the ... Nah 2:9 962
of silver, take the s of gold ... Nah 2:9 7997
of the people shall s thee ... Hab 2:8 7701
the s of beasts, which made them ... Hab 2:17 962
residue of my people shall s them ... Zeph 2:9 7998
they shall be a s to their ... Zec 2:9 7998
thy s shall be divided in the ... Zec 14:1 7998
s his goods, except he first bind ... Mt 12:29 1283
and then he will s his house ... Mt 12:29 1283
s his goods, except he will first ... Mk 3:27 1283
and then he will s his house ... Mk 3:27 1283
Beware lest any man s you through ... Col 2:8 4812

SPOILED

s the city, because they had ... Gen 34:27 962
s even all that was in the house ... Gen 34:29 962
And they s the Egyptians ... Ex 12:36 5337
s evermore, and no man shall save ... Deut 28:29 1497
the hands of spoilers that s them ... Judg 2:14 8155
of the hand of those that s them ... Judg 2:16 8154
of the hands of them that s them ... 1Sa 14:48 8154
and they s their tents ... 1Sa 17:53 8155
s the tents of the Syrians ... 2Kin 7:16 962
and they s all the cities ... 2Chr 14:14 962

He leadeth counsellors away s	Job 12:17	7758
He leadeth princes away s	Job 12:19	7758
The stouthearted are s, they have	Ps 76:5	7997
the soul of those that s them	Prov 22:23	6906
their houses shall be s, and their	Is 13:16	8155
whose land the rivers have s	Is 18:2	958
whose land the rivers have s	Is 18:7	958
be utterly emptied, and utterly s	Is 24:3	962
that spoilest, and thou wast not s	Is 33:1	7703
cease to spoil, thou shalt be s	Is 33:1	7703
But this is a people robbed and s	Is 42:22	8154
why is he s	Jer 2:14	957
for we are s	Jer 4:13	7703
for the whole land is s	Jer 4:20	7703
suddenly are my tents s, and my	Jer 4:20	7703
And when thou art s, what wilt	Jer 4:30	7703
heard out of Zion, How are we s	Jer 9:19	7703
My tabernacle is s, and all my	Jer 10:20	7703
deliver him that is s out of the	Jer 21:12	1497
deliver the s out of the hand of	Jer 22:3	1497
for the LORD hath s their pasture	Jer 25:36	7703
for it is s	Jer 48:1	7703
Moab is s, and gone up out of her	Jer 48:15	7703
ye it in Arnon, that Moab is s	Jer 48:20	7703
Howl, O Heshbon, for Ai is s	Jer 49:3	7703
his seed is s, and his brethren	Jer 49:10	7703
Because the LORD hath s Babylon	Jer 51:55	7703
hath s none by violence, hath	Eze 18:7	1497
hath s by violence, hath not	Eze 18:12	1497
neither hath s by violence	Eze 18:16	1497
s his brother by violence, and did	Eze 18:18	1497
will give them to be removed and s	Eze 23:46	957
shall spoil those that s them	Eze 39:10	7997
and all thy fortresses shall be s	Hos 10:14	7703
as Shalman s Beth-arbel in the	Hos 10:14	7701
thee, and thy palaces shall be s	Amos 3:11	962
the s against the strong, so that	Amos 5:9	7701
so that the s shall come against	Amos 5:9	7701
and say, We be utterly s	Mic 2:4	7703
Because thou hast s many nations	Hab 2:8	7997
me unto the nations which s you	Zec 2:8	7997
because the mighty are s	Zec 11:2	7703
for their glory is s	Zec 11:3	7703
for the pride of Jordan is s	Zec 11:3	7703
having s principalities and powers	Col 2:15	*554*

SPOILER

to them from the face of the s	Is 16:4	7703
the s ceaseth, the oppressors are	Is 16:4	7701
treacherously, and the s spoileth	Is 21:2	7703
for the s shall suddenly come	Jer 6:26	7703
of the young men a s at noonday	Jer 15:8	7703
the s shall come upon every city,	Jer 48:8	7703
for the s of Moab shall come upon	Jer 48:18	7703
the s is fallen upon thy summer	Jer 48:32	7703
Because the s is come upon her,	Jer 51:56	7703

SPOILERS

the hands of s that spoiled them	Judg 2:14	8154
the s came out of the camp of the	1Sa 13:17	7843
the garrison, and the s, they also	1Sa 14:15	7843
delivered them into the hand of s	2Kin 17:20	8154
The s are come upon all high	Jer 12:12	7703
for the s shall come unto her	Jer 51:48	7703
yet from me shall s come unto her	Jer 51:53	7703

SPOILEST

Woe to thee that s, and thou wast	Is 33:1	7703

SPOILETH

and the needy from him that s him	Ps 35:10	1497
treacherously, and the spoiler s	Is 21:2	7703
and the troop of robbers s without	Hos 7:1	6584
the cankerworm s, and fleeth away	Nah 3:16	6584

SPOILING

evil for good to the s of my soul	Ps 35:12	7908
because of the s of the daughter	Is 22:4	7701
crying shall be from Horonaim, s	Jer 48:3	7701
for s and violence are before me	Hab 1:3	7701
took joyfully the s of your goods	Heb 10:34	*724*

SPOILS

When I saw among the s a goodly	Josh 7:21	7998
Out of the s won in battles did	1Chr 26:27	7998
with the s of their hands	Is 25:11	698
he trusted, and divideth his s	Lk 11:22	*4661*
Abraham gave the tenth of the s	Heb 7:4	*205*

SPOKEN

as the LORD had s unto him	Gen 12:4	1696
that which he hath s of him	Gen 18:19	1696
city, for the which thou hast s	Gen 19:21	1696
LORD did unto Sarah as he had s	Gen 21:1	1696
time of which God had s to him	Gen 21:2	1696
son's wife, as the LORD hath s	Gen 24:51	1696
that which I have s to thee of	Gen 28:15	1696
thing which I have s unto Pharaoh	Gen 41:28	1696
to the word that Joseph had s	Gen 44:2	1696
thou hast s unto thy servant	Ex 4:10	1696
which the LORD had s unto Moses	Ex 4:30	1696
as the LORD had s unto Moses	Ex 9:12	1696
as the LORD had s by Moses	Ex 9:35	1696
And Moses said, Thou hast s well	Ex 10:29	1696
that the LORD hath s we will do	Ex 19:8	1696
all this land that I have s of	Ex 32:13	559
place of which I have s unto thee	Ex 32:34	1696
this thing also that thou hast s	Ex 33:17	1696
all that the LORD had s with him	Ex 34:32	1696
statutes which the LORD hath s	Lev 10:11	1696
For the LORD had s unto Moses	Num 1:48	1696
for the LORD hath s good	Num 10:29	1696
the LORD indeed s only by Moses	Num 12:2	1696
hath he not s also by us	Num 12:2	1696
great, according as thou hast s	Num 14:17	1696
as ye have s in mine ears, so	Num 14:28	1696
which the LORD hath s unto Moses	Num 15:22	1696
for we have s against the LORD,	Num 21:7	1696
And Balak did as Balaam had s	Num 23:2	1696
unto him, What hath the LORD s	Num 23:17	1696
thou hast s is good for us to do	Deut 1:14	1696
which they have s unto thee	Deut 5:28	1696
well said all that they have s	Deut 5:28	1696
before thee, as the LORD hath s	Deut 6:19	1696
because he hath s to turn you	Deut 13:5	1696
They have well s that which they	Deut 18:17	1696
that which they have s	Deut 18:17	
word which the LORD hath not s	Deut 18:21	1696
thing which the LORD hath not s	Deut 18:22	1696
prophet hath s it presumptuously	Deut 18:22	1696
the LORD thy God, as he hath s	Deut 26:19	1696
when Joshua had s unto the people	Josh 6:8	559
had s unto the house of Israel	Josh 21:45	1696
for that thou hast s friendly	Ruth 2:13	1696
and grief have I s hitherto	1Sa 1:16	1696
I have s concerning his house	1Sa 3:12	1696
matter which thou and I have s of	1Sa 20:23	1696
that he hath s concerning thee	1Sa 25:30	1696
God liveth, unless thou hadst s	2Sa 2:27	1696
for the LORD hath s of David	2Sa 3:18	559
maidservants which thou hast s of	2Sa 6:22	559
but thou hast s also of thy	2Sa 7:19	1696
hast s concerning thy servant	2Sa 7:25	1696
for thou, O Lord GOD, hast s it	2Sa 7:29	1696
that my lord the king hath s	2Sa 14:19	1696
Ahithophel hath s after this	2Sa 17:6	1696
if Adonijah have not s this word	1Kin 2:23	1696
this people, who have s to me	1Kin 12:9	1696
is the sign which the LORD hath s	1Kin 13:3	1696
which he had s unto the king	1Kin 13:11	1696
for the LORD hath s it	1Kin 14:11	1696
answered and said, It is well s	1Kin 18:24	1697
the Jezreelite had s to him	1Kin 21:4	1696
the LORD hath s evil concerning	1Kin 22:23	1696
peace, the LORD hath not s by me	1Kin 22:28	1696
of the LORD which Elijah had s	2Kin 1:17	1696
thou be s for to the king	2Kin 4:13	1696
the man of God had s to the king	2Kin 7:18	1696
the LORD hath s concerning him	2Kin 19:21	1696
will do the thing that he hath s	2Kin 20:9	1696
of the LORD which thou hast s	2Kin 20:19	1696
for thou hast also s of thy	1Chr 17:17	1696
hast s concerning thy servant	1Chr 17:23	1696
the wine, which my lord hath s of	2Chr 2:15	559
performed his word that he hath s	2Chr 6:10	1696
which thou hast s unto thy	2Chr 6:17	1696
this people, which have s to me	2Chr 10:9	1696
the LORD hath s evil against thee	2Chr 18:22	1696
then hath not the LORD s by me	2Chr 18:27	1696
that the word of the LORD s by	2Chr 36:22	1696
because we had s unto the king	Ezr 8:22	559
words that he had s unto me	Neh 2:18	559
fail of all that thou hast s	Est 6:10	1696
who had s good for the king,	Est 7:9	1696
and after that I have s, mock on	Job 21:3	1696
Elihu had waited till Job had s	Job 32:4	1697
my tongue hath s in my mouth	Job 33:2	1696
thou hast s in mine hearing	Job 33:8	559
Job hath s without knowledge, and	Job 34:35	1696
Once have I s	Job 40:5	1696
LORD had s these words unto Job	Job 42:7	1696
for ye have not s of me the thing	Job 42:7	1696
in that ye have not s of me the	Job 42:8	1696
mighty God, even the LORD, hath s	Ps 50:1	1696
God hath s in his holiness	Ps 60:6	1696
God hath s once	Ps 62:11	1696
have uttered, and my mouth hath s	Ps 66:14	1696
Glorious things are s of thee	Ps 87:3	1696
God hath s in his holiness	Ps 108:7	1696
they have s against me with a	Ps 109:2	1696
I believed, therefore have I s	Ps 116:10	1696
a word s in due season, how good	Prov 15:23	
A word fitly s is like apples of	Prov 25:11	1696
no heed unto all words that are s	Eccl 7:21	1696
the day when she shall be s for	Song 8:8	1696
for the LORD hath s, I have	Is 1:2	1696
the mouth of the LORD hath s it	Is 1:20	1696
is the word that the LORD hath s	Is 16:13	1696
But now the LORD hath s, saying,	Is 16:14	1696
the LORD God of Israel hath s it	Is 21:17	1696
for the LORD hath s it	Is 22:25	1696
for the sea hath s, even the	Is 23:4	559
for the LORD hath s this word	Is 24:3	1696
for the LORD hath s it	Is 25:8	1696
For thus hath the LORD s unto me	Is 31:4	559
the LORD hath s concerning him	Is 37:22	1696
will do this thing that he hath s	Is 38:7	1696
He hath both s unto me, and	Is 38:15	559
of the LORD which thou hast s	Is 39:8	1696
the mouth of the LORD hath s it	Is 40:5	1696
I have not s in secret, in a dark	Is 45:19	1696
yea, I have s it, I will also	Is 46:11	1696
I, even I, have s	Is 48:15	1696
I have not s in secret from the	Is 48:16	1696
the mouth of the LORD hath s it	Is 58:14	1696
your lips have s lies, your	Is 59:3	1696
Behold, thou hast s and done evil	Jer 3:5	1696
because I have s it, I have	Jer 4:28	1696
whom the mouth of the LORD hath s	Jer 9:12	1696
for the LORD hath s	Jer 13:15	1696
I have not s to them, yet they	Jer 23:21	1696
and, What hath the LORD s	Jer 23:35	1696
and, What hath the LORD s	Jer 23:37	1696
I have s unto you, rising early	Jer 25:3	1696
for he hath s to us in the name	Jer 26:16	1696
as the LORD hath s against the	Jer 27:13	1696
have s lying words in my name,	Jer 29:23	1696
that I have s unto thee in a book	Jer 30:2	1696
what thou hast s is come to pass	Jer 32:24	1696
thou not what this people have s	Jer 33:24	1696
notwithstanding I have s unto you	Jer 35:14	1696
because I have s unto them	Jer 35:17	1696
I have s unto thee against Israel	Jer 36:2	1696
the LORD, which he had s unto him	Jer 36:4	1696
had s unto all the people	Jer 38:1	1696
As for the word that thou hast s	Jer 44:16	1696
have both s with your mouths	Jer 44:25	1696
be destroyed, as the LORD hath s	Jer 48:8	559
thou hast s against this place,	Jer 51:62	1696
I the LORD have s it in my zeal	Eze 5:13	1696
I the LORD have s it	Eze 5:15	1696
I the LORD have s it	Eze 5:17	1696
word which I have s shall be done	Eze 12:28	1696
have ye not s a lying divination,	Eze 13:7	1696
albeit I have not s	Eze 13:7	559
Because ye have s vanity, and seen	Eze 13:8	1696
deceived when he hath s a thing	Eze 14:9	1696
know that I the LORD have s it	Eze 17:21	1696
I the LORD have s and have done it	Eze 17:24	1696
for I the LORD have s it	Eze 21:32	1696
I the LORD have s it, and will do	Eze 22:14	1696
GOD, when the LORD hath not s	Eze 22:28	1696
for I have s it, saith the Lord	Eze 23:34	1696
I the LORD have s it	Eze 24:14	1696
for I have s it, saith the Lord	Eze 26:5	1696
for I the LORD have s it, saith	Eze 26:14	1696
for I have s it, saith the Lord	Eze 28:10	1696
I the LORD have s it	Eze 30:12	1696
I the LORD have s it	Eze 34:24	1696
s against the mountains of Israel	Eze 35:12	559
I s against the residue of the	Eze 36:5	1696
I have s in my jealousy and in my	Eze 36:6	1696
I the LORD have s it, and I will	Eze 36:36	1696
ye know that I the LORD have s it	Eze 37:14	1696
Art thou he of whom I have s in	Eze 38:17	1696
in the fire of my wrath have I s	Eze 38:19	1696
for I have s it, saith the Lord	Eze 39:5	1696
this is the day whereof I have s	Eze 39:8	1696
Nebuchadnezzar, to thee it is s	Dan 4:31	560
when he had s this word unto me,	Dan 10:11	1696
when he had s such words unto me,	Dan 10:15	1696
And when he had s unto me, I was	Dan 10:19	1696
yet they have s lies against me	Hos 7:13	1696
They have s words, swearing	Hos 10:4	1696
I have also s by the prophets, and	Hos 12:10	1696
for the LORD hath s it	Joel 3:8	1696
that the LORD hath s against you	Amos 3:1	1696
the Lord GOD hath s, who can but	Amos 3:8	1696
shall be with you, as ye have s	Amos 5:14	559
neither shouldest thou have s	Obad 12	6310
for the LORD hath s it	Obad 18	1696
of the LORD of hosts hath s it	Mic 4:4	1696
inhabitants thereof have s lies	Mic 6:12	1696
For the idols have s vanity	Zec 10:2	1696
What have we s so much against	Mal 3:13	1696
was s of the Lord by the prophet	Mt 1:22	*4483*
was s of the Lord by the prophet	Mt 2:15	*4483*
which was s by Jeremy the prophet	Mt 2:17	*4483*
which was s by the prophets	Mt 2:23	*4483*
For this is he that was s of by	Mt 3:3	*4483*
which was s by Esaias the prophet	Mt 4:14	*4483*
which was s by Esaias the prophet	Mt 8:17	*4483*
which was s by Esaias the prophet	Mt 12:17	*4483*
which was s by the prophet	Mt 13:35	*4483*
which was s by the prophet	Mt 21:4	*4483*
that which was s unto you by God	Mt 22:31	*4483*
s of by Daniel the prophet, stand	Mt 24:15	*4483*
saying, He hath s blasphemy	Mt 26:65	*987*
which was s by Jeremy the prophet	Mt 27:9	*4483*
which was s by the prophet	Mt 27:35	*4483*
And as soon as he had s,	Mk 1:42	*2036*
Jesus heard the word that was s	Mk 5:36	*2980*
he had s the parable against them	Mk 12:12	*2036*
s of by Daniel the prophet,	Mk 13:14	*4483*
be s of for a memorial of her	Mk 14:9	*2980*
after the Lord had s unto them	Mk 16:19	*2980*
those things which were s of him	Lk 2:33	*2980*
a sign which shall be s against	Lk 2:34	*483*
Therefore whatsoever ye have s in	Lk 12:3	*2036*
that which ye have s in the ear	Lk 12:3	*2980*
knew they the things which were s	Lk 18:34	*3004*
And when he had thus s, he went	Lk 19:28	*2036*
had s this parable against them	Lk 20:19	*2036*
all that the prophets have s	Lk 24:25	*2980*
And when he had thus s, he shewed	Lk 24:40	*2036*
word that Jesus had s unto him	Jn 4:50	*2036*
When he had thus s, he spat on	Jn 9:6	*2036*
had s of taking of rest in sleep	Jn 11:13	*3004*
And when he thus had s, he cried	Jn 11:43	*2036*
the word that I have s, the same	Jn 12:48	*2980*
For I have not s of myself	Jn 12:49	*2980*
These things have I s unto you	Jn 14:25	*2980*
the word which I have s unto you	Jn 15:3	*2980*
These things have I s unto you	Jn 15:11	*2980*
s unto them, they had not had sin	Jn 15:22	*2980*
These things have I s unto you	Jn 16:1	*2980*
These things have I s unto you in	Jn 16:25	*2980*
These things I have s unto you	Jn 16:33	*2980*
When Jesus had s these words	Jn 18:1	*2036*
And when he had thus s, one of the	Jn 18:22	*2036*
answered him, If I have s evil	Jn 18:23	*2980*
that he had s these things unto	Jn 20:18	*2036*
And when he had s this, he saith	Jn 21:19	*2036*
when he had s these things, while	Acts 1:9	*2036*
which was s by the prophet Joel	Acts 2:16	*2046*
which God hath s by the mouth of	Acts 3:21	*2980*
follow after, as many as have s	Acts 3:24	*2980*
which ye have s come upon me	Acts 8:24	*2046*
the way, and that he had s to him	Acts 9:27	*2980*
which is s of in the prophets	Acts 13:40	*2046*
those things which were s by Paul	Acts 13:45	*3004*
should first have been s to you	Acts 13:46	*2980*
the things which were s of Paul	Acts 16:14	*2980*
these things cannot be s against	Acts 19:36	*369*
And when he had thus s, he	Acts 19:41	*2036*

And when he had thus s, he kneeled.... Acts 20:36 *2036*
spirit or an angel hath s to him........ Acts 23:9 *2980*
And when he had thus s, the king......... Acts 26:30 *2036*
those things which were s by Paul...... Acts 27:11 *3004*
And when he had thus s, he took......... Acts 27:35 *2036*
that every where it is s against............ Acts 28:22 *483*
believed the things which were s......... Acts 28:24 *3004*
after that Paul had s one word........... Acts 28:25 *2036*
you all, that your faith is s of................ Rom 1:8 *2605*
according to that which was s.............. Rom 4:18 *2046*
not then your good be evil s of............. Rom 14:16 *987*
written, To whom he was not s of......... Rom 15:21 *312*
why am I evil s of for that for............. 1Cor 10:30 *987*
how shall it be known what is s............. 1Cor 14:9 *2980*
I believed, and therefore have I s........... 2Cor 4:13 *2980*
last days s unto us by his Son.............. Heb 1:2 *2980*
For if the word s by angels was............. Heb 2:2 *2980*
first began to be s by the Lord............... Heb 2:3 *2980*
things which were to be s after.............. Heb 3:5 *2980*
afterward have s of another day............. Heb 4:8 *2980*
are s pertaineth to another tribe............ Heb 7:13 *3004*
which we have s this is the sum............. Heb 8:1 *3004*
For when Moses had s every.................. Heb 9:19 *2980*
should not be s to them any more........... Heb 12:19 *4369*
who have s unto you the word of............ Heb 13:7 *2980*
who have s in the name of the............... Jas 5:10 *2980*
on their part he is evil s of................... 1Pet 4:14 *987*
way of truth shall be evil s of............... 2Pet 2:2 *987*
s before by the holy prophets................ 2Pet 3:2 *4280*
sinners have s against him.................... Jude 15 *2980*
ye the words which were s before........... Jude 17 *4280*

SPOKES
and their felloes, and their s.................. 1Kin 7:33 2840

SPOKESMAN
he shall be thy s unto the people............ Ex 4:16 1696

SPOON
One s of ten shekels of gold,.................. Num 7:14 3709
One s of gold of ten shekels,.................. Num 7:20 3709
One golden s of ten shekels, full............. Num 7:26 3709
One golden s of ten shekels, full............. Num 7:32 3709
One golden s of ten shekels, full............. Num 7:38 3709
One golden s of ten shekels, full............. Num 7:44 3709
One golden s of ten shekels, full............. Num 7:50 3709
One golden s of ten shekels, full............. Num 7:56 3709
One golden s of ten shekels, full............. Num 7:62 3709
One golden s of ten shekels, full............. Num 7:68 3709
One golden s of ten shekels, full............. Num 7:74 3709
One golden s of ten shekels, full............. Num 7:80 3709

SPOONS
s thereof, and covers thereof, and.......... Ex 25:29 3709
the table, his dishes, and his s............... Ex 37:16 3709
put thereon the dishes, and the s............. Num 4:7 3709
silver bowls, twelve s of gold................. Num 7:84 3709
The golden s were twelve, full of............ Num 7:86 3709
the gold of the s was an hundred............ Num 7:86 3709
snuffers, and the basons, and the s......... 1Kin 7:50 3709
and the snuffers, and the s.................... 2Kin 25:14 3709
snuffers, and the basons, and the s......... 2Chr 4:22 3709
and to offer withal, and s...................... 2Chr 24:14 3709
snuffers, and the bowls, and the s.......... Jer 52:18 3709
and the candlesticks, and the s.............. Jer 52:19 3709

SPORT
for Samson, that he may make us s......... Judg 16:25 7832
and he made them s.............................. Judg 16:25 6711
that beheld while Samson made s............ Judg 16:27 7832
It is as s to a fool to do...................... Prov 10:23 7814
and saith, Am not I in s........................ Prov 26:19 7832
Against whom do ye s yourselves............ Is 57:4 6026

SPORTING
Isaac was s with Rebekah his wife.......... Gen 26:8 6711
s themselves with their own.................. 2Pet 2:13 *1792*

SPOT
a rising, a scab, or bright s.................... Lev 13:2 934
If the bright s be white in the................ Lev 13:4 934
be a white rising, or a bright s............... Lev 13:19 934
if the bright s stay in his place.............. Lev 13:23 934
burneth have a white bright s................. Lev 13:24 934
in the bright s be turned white............... Lev 13:25 934
be no white hair in the bright s.............. Lev 13:26 934
if the bright s stay in his place.............. Lev 13:28 934
it is a freckled s that groweth................ Lev 13:39 933
and for a scab, and for a bright s........... Lev 14:56 934
bring thee a red heifer without s............ Num 19:2 8549
first year without s day by day.............. Num 28:3 8549
lambs of the first year without s............ Num 28:9 8549
lambs of the first year without s............ Num 28:11 8549
lambs of the first year without s............ Num 29:17 8549
lambs of the first year without s............ Num 29:26 8549
their s is not the s of his...................... Deut 32:5 3971
is not the s of his children................... Deut 32:5
thou lift up thy face without s................ Job 11:15 3971
there is no s in thee............................. Song 4:7 3971
a glorious church, not having s.............. Eph 5:27 *4696*
keep this commandment without s........... 1Ti 6:14 *784*
offered himself without s to God............. Heb 9:14 *299*
lamb without blemish and without s......... 1Pet 1:19 *784*
found of him in peace, without s............ 2Pet 3:14 *784*

SPOTS
bright s, even white bright s.................. Lev 13:38 934
if the bright s in the skin of.................. Lev 13:39 934
his skin, or the leopard his s................. Jer 13:23 2272
S they are and blemishes, sporting......... 2Pet 2:13 *4696*
These are s in your feasts of................. Jude 12 *4694*

SPOTTED
s cattle, and all the brown cattle........... Gen 30:32 2921
cattle among the sheep, and the s.......... Gen 30:32 2921
s among the goats, and brown among....... Gen 30:33 2921
goats that were ringstraked and s........... Gen 30:35 2921
she goats that were speckled and s......... Gen 30:35 2921
ringstraked, speckled, and s.................... Gen 30:39 2921
even the garment s by the flesh............. Jude 23 *4695*

SPOUSE
Come with me from Lebanon, my s........... Song 4:8 3618
my heart, my sister, my s....................... Song 4:9 3618
fair is thy love, my sister, my s.............. Song 4:10 3618
Thy lips, O my s, drop as the.................. Song 4:11 3618
inclosed is my sister, my s..................... Song 4:12 3618
into my garden, my sister, my s............... Song 5:1 3618

SPOUSES
your s shall commit adultery.................. Hos 4:13 3618
nor your s when they commit.................. Hos 4:14 3618

SPRANG
and immediately it s up, because............ Mk 4:5 *1816*
and did yield fruit that s up................... Mk 4:8 *305*
and the thorns s up with it.................... Lk 8:7 *4855*
ground, and s up, and bare fruit an......... Lk 8:8 *5453*
s in, and came trembling, and fell........... Acts 16:29 *1530*
that our Lord s out of Juda.................... Heb 7:14 *393*
Therefore s there even of one, and......... Heb 11:12 *1080*

SPREAD
of the Canaanites s abroad..................... Gen 10:18 6327
thou shalt s abroad to the west,............. Gen 28:14 6555
a field, where he had s his tent.............. Gen 33:19 5186
s his tent beyond the tower of................ Gen 35:21 5186
I will s abroad my hands unto the........... Ex 9:29 6566
s abroad his hands unto the LORD............ Ex 9:33 6566
the cherubims s out their wings.............. Ex 37:9 6566
he s abroad the tent over the.................. Ex 40:19 6566
the plague s not in the skin.................... Lev 13:5 6581
the plague s not in the skin, the............. Lev 13:6 6581
But if the scab s much abroad in.............. Lev 13:7 6581
if it s much abroad in the skin,............... Lev 13:22 6581
s not, it is a burning boil...................... Lev 13:23 6581
if it be much abroad in the.................... Lev 13:27 6581
s not in the skin, but it be.................... Lev 13:28 6581
and, behold, if the scall s not................. Lev 13:32 6581
if the scall be not s in the skin.............. Lev 13:34 6581
But if the scall s much in the................. Lev 13:35 6581
if the scall be s in the skin................... Lev 13:36 6581
if the plague be s in the garment........... Lev 13:51 6581
plague be not s in the garment.............. Lev 13:53 6581
colour, and the plague be not s.............. Lev 13:55 6581
if the plague be s in the walls............... Lev 14:39 6581
if the plague be s in the house.............. Lev 14:44 6581
plague hath not s in the house.............. Lev 14:48 6581
shall s over it a cloth wholly of............. Num 4:6 6566
they shall s a cloth of blue................... Num 4:7 6566
they shall s upon them a cloth of........... Num 4:8 6566
they shall s a cloth of blue.................. Num 4:11 6566
and s a purple cloth thereon.................. Num 4:13 6566
they shall s upon it a covering.............. Num 4:14 6566
they s them all abroad for.................... Num 11:32 7849
As the valleys are they s forth............... Num 24:6 5186
they shall s the cloth before the............ Deut 22:17 6566
they s a garment, and did cast............... Judg 8:25 6566
in Judah, and s themselves in Lehi......... Judg 15:9 5203
s therefore thy skirt over thine............. Ruth 3:9 6566
they were s abroad upon all the............. 1Sa 30:16 5203
s themselves in the valley of................. 2Sa 5:18 5203
s themselves in the valley of................. 2Sa 5:22 5203
So they s Absalom a tent upon the.......... 2Sa 16:22 5186
s a covering over the well's.................. 2Sa 17:19 6566
mouth, and s ground corn thereon.......... 2Sa 17:19 7849
s it for her upon the rock, from............ 2Sa 21:10 5186
the street, and did s them abroad.......... 2Sa 22:43 7554
s gold upon the cherubims, and............. 1Kin 6:32 7286
For the cherubims s forth their.............. 1Kin 8:7 6566
s forth his hands toward heaven............ 1Kin 8:22 6566
s forth his hands toward this................ 1Kin 8:38 6566
with his hands s up to heaven............... 1Kin 8:54 6566
s it on his face, so that he died............ 2Kin 8:15 6566
the LORD, and s it before the LORD......... 2Kin 19:14 6566
s themselves in the valley of................. 1Chr 14:9 6584
the Philistines yet again s..................... 1Chr 14:13 6584
that s out their wings, and................... 1Chr 28:18 6566
The wings of these cherubims s............. 2Chr 3:13 6566
For the cherubims s forth their.............. 2Chr 5:8 6566
of Israel, and s forth his hands............. 2Chr 6:12 6566
s forth his hands toward heaven,............ 2Chr 6:13 6566
shall s forth his hands in this.............. 2Chr 6:29 6566
his name s abroad even to the.............. 2Chr 26:8 3212
And his name s far abroad.................... 2Chr 26:15 3318
s out my hands unto the LORD my.......... Ezr 9:5 6566
My root was s out by the waters,............ Job 29:19 6605
Hast thou with him s out the sky........... Job 37:18 7554
He s a cloud for a covering.................. Ps 105:39 6566
they have s a net by the wayside........... Ps 140:5 6566
net is s in the sight of any bird............. Prov 1:17 2219
when ye s forth your hands, I................ Is 1:15 6566
the worm is s under thee, and the......... Is 14:11 3331
they that s nets upon the waters............ Is 19:8 6566
vail that is s over all nations................. Is 25:7 5259
he shall s forth his hands in the............ Is 25:11 6566
mast, they could not s the sail............... Is 33:23 6566
the LORD, and s it before the LORD......... Is 37:14 6566
he that s forth the earth, and............... Is 42:5 7554
to s sackcloth and ashes under him......... Is 58:5 3331
I have s out my hands all the day.......... Is 65:2 6566
they shall s them before the sun,........... Jer 8:2 7849
Silver s into plates is brought............... Jer 10:9 7554
he shall s his royal pavilion.................. Jer 43:10 5186
shall s his wings over Moab.................. Jer 48:40 6566
eagle, and s his wings over Bozrah......... Jer 49:22 6566
The adversary hath s out his hand.......... Lam 1:10 6566
he hath s a net for my feet, he............. Lam 1:13 6566
And he s it before me........................... Eze 2:10 6566
My net also will I s upon him................. Eze 12:13 6566
I s my skirt over thee, and.................... Eze 16:8 6566
I will s my net upon him, and he............ Eze 17:20 6566
and s their net over him....................... Eze 19:8 6566
shalt be a place to s nets upon............. Eze 26:14 4894
I will therefore s out my net................. Eze 32:3 6566
shall be a place to s forth nets.............. Eze 47:10 4894
on Mizpah, and a net s upon Tabor.......... Hos 5:1 6566
I will s my net upon them..................... Hos 7:12 6566
His branches shall s, and his................. Hos 14:6 3212
as the morning s upon the..................... Joel 2:2 6566
their horsemen shall s themselves........... Hab 1:8 6335
prosperity shall yet be s abroad............. Zec 1:17 6327
for I have s you abroad as the............... Zec 2:6 6566
s dung upon your faces, even the............ Mal 2:3 2219
s abroad his fame in all that................. Mt 9:31 *1310*
a very great multitude s their................ Mt 21:8 *4766*
immediately his fame s abroad.............. Mk 1:28 *1831*
(for his name was s abroad................... Mk 6:14 *4766*
many s their garments in the way.......... Mk 11:8 *4766*
they s their clothes in the way.............. Lk 19:36 *5291*
But that it s no further among............... Acts 4:17 *1268*
faith to God-ward is s abroad................ 1Th 1:8 *1831*

SPREADEST
which thou s forth to be thy sail............. Eze 27:7 4666

SPREADETH
the scab s in the skin, then the............. Lev 13:8 6581
s abroad her wings, taketh them,........... Deut 32:11 6566
Which alone s out the heavens, and........ Job 9:8 5186
throne, and s his cloud upon it.............. Job 26:9 6576
he s his light upon it, and.................... Job 36:30 6566
he s sharp pointed things upon.............. Job 41:30 7502
neighbour s a net for his feet................ Prov 29:5 6566
as he that swimmeth s forth his............. Is 25:11 6566
the goldsmith s it over with gold............ Is 40:19 7554
s them out as a tent to dwell in............. Is 40:22 4969
that s abroad the earth by myself........... Is 44:24 7554
that s her hands, saying, Woe is............ Jer 4:31 6566
that s out her roots by the river............ Jer 17:8 7971
Zion s forth her hands, and there........... Lam 1:17 6566

SPREADING
it is a s plague.................................... Lev 13:57 6524
s himself like a green bay tree.............. Ps 37:35 6168
became a s vine of low stature,............. Eze 17:6 5628
It shall be a place for the s of............... Eze 26:5 4894

SPREADINGS
understand the s of the clouds............... Job 36:29 4666

SPRIGS
cut off the s with pruninghooks............. Is 18:5 2150
forth branches, and shot forth s............. Eze 17:6 6288

SPRING
sang this song, S up, O well................. Num 21:17 5927
depths that s out of valleys and............. Deut 8:7 3318
and when the day began to s................. Judg 19:25 5927
to pass about the s of the day.............. 1Sa 9:26 5927
forth unto the s of the waters.............. 2Kin 2:21 4161
doth trouble s out of the ground............ Job 5:6 6779
bud of the tender herb to s forth........... Job 38:27 6779
Truth shall s out of the earth................ Ps 85:11 6779
When the wicked s as the grass.............. Ps 92:7 6524
troubled fountain, and a corrupt s.......... Prov 25:26 4726
a s shut up, a fountain sealed............... Song 4:12 1530
before they s forth I tell you of............. Is 42:9 6779
now it shall s forth.............................. Is 43:19 6779
they shall s up as among the................ Is 44:4 6779
let righteousness s up together.............. Is 45:8 6779
health shall s forth speedily.................. Is 58:8 6779
like a s of water, whose waters............. Is 58:11 4161
that are sown in it to s forth................ Is 61:11 6779
praise to s forth before all the.............. Is 61:11 6779
wither in all the leaves of her s............. Eze 17:9 6780
his s shall become dry, and his.............. Hos 13:15 4726
pastures of the wilderness do s.............. Joel 2:22 1876
and day, and the seed should s.............. Mk 4:27 *985*

SPRINGETH
the hyssop that s out of the wall............ 1Kin 4:33 3318
year that which s of the same................ 2Kin 19:29 7823
year that which s of the same................ Is 37:30 7823
thus judgment s up as hemlock in............ Hos 10:4 6524

SPRINGING
and found there a well of s water.......... Gen 26:19 2416
as the tender grass s out of the............. 2Sa 23:4
thou blessest the s thereof.................... Ps 65:10 6780
water s up into everlasting life............... Jn 4:14 *242*
of bitterness s up trouble you............... Heb 12:15 *5453*

SPRINGS
the plain, under the s of Pisgah............. Deut 4:49 794
and of the vale, and of the s.................. Josh 10:40 794
and in the plains, and in the s.............. Josh 12:8 794
give me also s of water........................ Josh 15:19 1543
upper s, and the nether s..................... Josh 15:19 1543
give me also s of water........................ Judg 1:15 1543
the upper s and the nether s................. Judg 1:15 1543
entered into the s of the sea................. Job 38:16 5033
all my s are in thee.............................. Ps 87:7 4599
He sendeth the s into the valleys............ Ps 104:10 4599
and the thirsty land s of water............... Is 35:7 4002
water, and the dry land s of water........... Is 41:18 4161
even by the s of water shall he.............. Is 49:10 4002
dry up her sea, and make her s dry......... Jer 51:36 4726

SPRINKLE
let Moses s it toward the heaven............ Ex 9:8 2236
s it round about upon the altar............... Ex 29:16 2236
s the blood upon the altar round............ Ex 29:20 2236
s it upon Aaron, and upon his............... Ex 29:21 5137
s the blood round about upon the........... Lev 1:5 2236
shall s his blood round about................ Lev 1:11 2236
s the blood upon the altar round............ Lev 3:2 2236
Aaron's sons shall s the blood.............. Lev 3:8 2236
the sons of Aaron shall s the................. Lev 3:13 2236
s of the blood seven times before.......... Lev 4:6 5137
s it seven times before the LORD,........... Lev 4:17 5137
he shall s of the blood of the................ Lev 5:9 5137
he s round about upon the altar............. Lev 7:2 2236

S

he shall *s* upon him that is to be.......... Lev 14:7 5137
shall *s* of the oil with his.......... Lev 14:16 5137
the priest shall *s* with his right.......... Lev 14:27 5137
water, and *s* the house seven times...... Lev 14:51 5137
s it with his finger upon the.......... Lev 16:14 5137
he *s* of the blood with his finger.......... Lev 16:14 5137
s it upon the mercy seat, and.......... Lev 16:15 5137
he shall *s* of the blood upon it.......... Lev 16:19 5137
the priest shall *s* the blood upon.......... Lev 17:6 2236
S water of purifying upon them,.......... Num 8:7 5137
thou shalt *s* their blood upon the.......... Num 18:17 2236
s of her blood directly before.......... Num 19:4 5137
s it upon the tent, and upon all.......... Num 19:18 5137
the clean person shall *s* upon the.......... Num 19:19 5137
s upon it all the blood of the.......... 2Kin 16:15 2236
So shall he *s* many nations.......... Is 52:15 5137
Then will I *s* clean water upon.......... Eze 36:25 2236
thereon, and to *s* blood thereon.......... Eze 43:18 2236

SPRINKLED
Moses *s* it up toward heaven.......... Ex 9:10 2236
of the blood he *s* on the altar.......... Ex 24:6 2236
s it on the people, and said,.......... Ex 24:8 2236
when there is *s* of the blood.......... Lev 6:27 5137
it was *s* in the holy place.......... Lev 6:27 5137
he *s* thereof upon the altar seven.......... Lev 8:11 5137
Moses *s* the blood upon the altar.......... Lev 8:19 2236
Moses *s* the blood upon the altar.......... Lev 8:24 2236
s it upon Aaron, and upon his.......... Lev 8:30 5137
which he *s* round about upon the.......... Lev 9:12 2236
which he *s* upon the altar round.......... Lev 9:18 2236
of separation was not *s* upon him.......... Num 19:13 2236
hath not been *s* upon him.......... Num 19:20 2236
of her blood was *s* on the wall.......... 2Kin 9:33 5137
and *s* the blood of his peace.......... 2Kin 16:13 2236
the blood, and *s* it on the altar,.......... 2Chr 29:22 2236
they *s* the blood upon the altar.......... 2Chr 29:22 2236
they *s* the blood upon the altar.......... 2Chr 29:22 2236
the priests *s* the blood, which.......... 2Chr 30:16 2236
the priests *s* the blood from.......... 2Chr 35:11 2236
s dust upon their heads toward.......... Job 2:12 2236
blood shall be *s* upon my garments.......... Is 63:3 5137
s both the book, and all the.......... Heb 9:19 *4472*
Moreover he *s* with blood both the.......... Heb 9:21 *4472*
having our hearts *s* from an evil.......... Heb 10:22 *4472*

SPRINKLETH
that *s* the blood of the peace.......... Lev 7:14 2236
that he that *s* the water of.......... Num 19:21 5137

SPRINKLING
ashes of an heifer *s* the unclean.......... Heb 9:13 *4472*
the *s* of blood, lest he that.......... Heb 11:28 *4378*
covenant, and to the blood of *s*.......... Heb 12:24 *4473*
s of the blood of Jesus Christ.......... 1Pet 1:2 *4473*

SPROUT
be cut down, that it will *s* again.......... Job 14:7 2498

SPRUNG
the east wind *s* up after them.......... Gen 41:6 6779
the east wind *s* up after them.......... Gen 41:23 6779
it is a leprosy *s* up in his bald.......... Lev 13:42 6524
and shadow of death light is *s* up.......... Mt 4:16 *393*
and forthwith they *s* up, because.......... Mt 13:5 *1816*
and the thorns *s* up, and choked.......... Mt 13:7 *305*
But when the blade was *s* up.......... Mt 13:26 *985*
and as soon as it was *s* up.......... Lk 8:6 *5453*

SPUE
That the land *s* not you out also,.......... Lev 18:28 6958
to dwell therein, *s* you not out.......... Lev 20:22 6958
Drink ye, and be drunken, and *s*.......... Jer 25:27 7006
I will *s* thee out of my mouth.......... Rev 3:16 *1692*

SPUED
as it *s* out the nations that were.......... Lev 18:28 6958

SPUN
and brought that which they had *s*.......... Ex 35:25 4299
them up in wisdom *s* goats' hair.......... Ex 35:26 2901

SPUNGE
one of them ran, and took a *s*.......... Mt 27:48 *4699*
filled a *s* full of vinegar, and.......... Mk 15:36 *4699*
and they filled a *s* with vinegar.......... Jn 19:29 *4699*

SPY
Moses sent to *s* out the land.......... Num 13:16 8446
Moses sent them to *s* out the land.......... Num 13:17 8446
And Moses sent to *s* out Jaazer.......... Num 21:32 7270
of Shittim two men to *s* secretly.......... Josh 2:1 7270
Joshua sent to *s* out Jericho.......... Josh 6:25 7270
to *s* out the land, and to search.......... Judg 18:2 7270
to *s* out the country of Laish.......... Judg 18:14 7270
went to *s* out the land went up.......... Judg 18:17 7270
to *s* it out, and to overthrow it.......... 2Sa 10:3 7270
s where he is, that I may send and.......... 2Kin 6:13 7200
overthrow, and to *s* out the land.......... 1Chr 19:3 7200
who came in privily to *s* out our.......... Gal 2:4 *2684*

SQUARE
And all the doors and posts were *s*.......... 1Kin 7:5 7251
s in the four squares thereof.......... Eze 43:16 7251
hundred in breadth, *s* round about.......... Eze 45:2 7251

SQUARED
The posts of the temple were *s*.......... Eze 41:21 7251

SQUARES
square in the four *s* thereof.......... Eze 43:16 7253
broad in the four *s* thereof.......... Eze 43:17 7253

STABILITY
shall be the *s* of thy times.......... Is 33:6 530

STABLE
the world also shall be *s*.......... 1Chr 16:30 3559
I will make Rabbah a *s* for camels.......... Eze 25:5 5116

STABLISH
I will *s* the throne of his.......... 2Sa 7:13 3559
I will *s* his throne for ever.......... 1Chr 17:12 3559
as he went to *s* his dominion by.......... 1Chr 18:3 5324
Then will I *s* the throne of thy.......... 2Chr 7:18 6965
To *s* this among them, that they.......... Est 9:21 6965
S thy word unto thy servant, who.......... Ps 119:38 6965
to *s* you according to my gospel.......... Rom 16:25 *4741*
To the end he may *s* your hearts.......... 1Th 3:13 *4741*
s you in every good word and work.......... 2Th 2:17 *4741*
Lord is faithful, who shall *s* you.......... 2Th 3:3 *4741*
s your hearts.......... Jas 5:8 *4741*
a while, make you perfect, *s*.......... 1Pet 5:10 *4741*

STABLISHED
Therefore the LORD *s* the kingdom.......... 2Chr 17:5 3559
the world also is *s*, that it.......... Ps 93:1 3559
He hath also *s* them for ever and.......... Ps 148:6 5975
s in the faith, as ye have been.......... Col 2:7 *950*

STABLISHETH
blood, and *s* a city by iniquity.......... Hab 2:12 3559
Now he which *s* us with you in.......... 2Cor 1:21 *950*

STACHYS (*sta'-kis*) *A Christian in Rome.*
helper in Christ, and *S* my beloved.......... Rom 16:9 *4720*

STACKS
in thorns, so that the *s* of corn.......... Ex 22:6 1430

STACTE
Take unto thee sweet spices, *s*.......... Ex 30:34 5198

STAFF
for with my *s* I passed over this.......... Gen 32:10 4731
thy *s* that is in thine hand.......... Gen 38:18 4294
the signet, and bracelets, and *s*.......... Gen 38:25 4294
your feet, and your *s* in your hand.......... Ex 12:11 4731
again, and walk abroad upon his *s*.......... Ex 21:19 4938
I have broken the *s* of your bread.......... Lev 26:26 4294
they bare it between two upon a *s*.......... Num 13:23 4132
and he smote the ass with a *s*.......... Num 22:27 4731
end of the *s* that was in his hand.......... Judg 6:21 4938
the *s* of his spear was like a.......... 1Sa 17:7 2671
And he took his *s* in his hand.......... 1Sa 17:40 4731
a leper, or that leaneth on a *s*.......... 2Sa 3:29 6418
the *s* of whose spear was like a.......... 2Sa 21:19 6086
with iron and the *s* of a spear.......... 2Sa 23:7 6086
but he went down to him with a *s*.......... 2Sa 23:21 7626
take my *s* in thine hand, and go.......... 2Kin 4:29 4938
lay my *s* upon the face of the.......... 2Kin 4:29 4938
laid the *s* upon the face of the.......... 2Kin 4:31 4938
upon the *s* of this bruised reed.......... 2Kin 18:21 4938
and he went down to him with a *s*.......... 1Chr 11:23 7626
whose spear *s* was like a weaver's.......... 1Chr 20:5 6086
thy rod and thy *s* they comfort me.......... Ps 23:4 4938
he brake the whole *s* of bread.......... Ps 105:16 4294
and from Judah the stay and the *s*.......... Is 3:1 4938
the *s* of his shoulder, the rod of.......... Is 9:4 4294
the *s* in their hand is mine.......... Is 10:5 4294
or as if the *s* should lift up.......... Is 10:15 4294
shall lift up his *s* against thee.......... Is 10:24 4294
hath broken the *s* of the wicked.......... Is 14:5 4294
fitches are beaten out with a *s*.......... Is 28:27 4294
where the grounded *s* shall pass.......... Is 30:32 4294
in the *s* of this broken reed.......... Is 36:6 4938
say, How is the strong *s* broken.......... Jer 48:17 4294
I will break the *s* of bread in.......... Eze 4:16 4294
and will break your *s* of bread.......... Eze 5:16 4294
will break the *s* of the bread.......... Eze 14:13 4294
because they have been a *s* of.......... Eze 29:6 4938
their *s* declareth unto them.......... Hos 4:12 4731
every man with his *s* in his hand.......... Zec 8:4 4938
And I took my *s*, even Beauty, and.......... Zec 11:10 4731
Then I cut asunder mine other *s*.......... Zec 11:14 4731
for their journey, save a *s* only.......... Mk 6:8 *4464*
leaning upon the top of his *s*.......... Heb 11:21 *4464*

STAGGER
he maketh them to *s* like a.......... Job 12:25 8582
s like a drunken man, and are at.......... Ps 107:27 5128
they *s*, but not with strong drink.......... Is 29:9 5128

STAGGERED
He *s* not at the promise of God.......... Rom 4:20 *1252*

STAGGERETH
as a drunken man *s* in his vomit.......... Is 19:14 8582

STAIN
and the shadow of death *s* it.......... Job 3:5 1350
to *s* the pride of all glory, and.......... Is 23:9 2490
and I will *s* all my raiment.......... Is 63:3 1351

STAIRS
winding *s* into the middle chamber.......... 1Kin 6:8 3883
it under him on the top of the *s*.......... 2Kin 9:13 4609
unto the *s* that go down from the.......... Neh 3:15 4609
Then stood up upon the *s*, of the.......... Neh 9:4 4608
they went up by the *s* of the city.......... Neh 12:37 4609
in the secret places of the *s*.......... Song 2:14 4095
east, and went up the *s* thereof.......... Eze 40:6 4609
his *s* shall look toward the east.......... Eze 43:17 4609
And when he came upon the *s*.......... Acts 21:35 *304*
him licence, Paul stood on the *s*.......... Acts 21:40 *304*

STAKES
not one of the *s* thereof shall.......... Is 33:20 3489
thy cords, and strengthen thy *s*.......... Is 54:2 3489

STALK
ears of corn came up upon one *s*.......... Gen 41:5 7070
seven ears came up in one *s*.......... Gen 41:22 7070
it hath no *s*.......... Hos 8:7 7054

STALKS
and hid them with the *s* of flax.......... Josh 2:6 6086

STALL
calves out of the midst of the *s*.......... Amos 6:4 4770
and grow up as calves of the *s*.......... Mal 4:2 4770

his ox or his ass from the *s*.......... Lk 13:15 *5336*

STALLED
herbs where love is, than a *s* ox.......... Prov 15:17 75

STALLS
s of horses for his chariots.......... 1Kin 4:26 723
had four thousand *s* for horses.......... 2Chr 9:25 723
s for all manner of beasts, and.......... 2Chr 32:28 723
there shall be no herd in the *s*.......... Hab 3:17 7517

STAMMERERS
the tongue of the *s* shall be.......... Is 32:4 5926

STAMMERING
For with *s* lips and another tongue.......... Is 28:11 3934
of a *s* tongue, that thou canst.......... Is 33:19 3932

STAMP
I did *s* them as the mire of the.......... 2Sa 22:43 1854
s with thy foot, and say, Alas for.......... Eze 6:11 7554

STAMPED
s it, and ground it very small,.......... Deut 9:21 3807
s it small to powder, and cast the.......... 2Kin 23:6 1854
s it small to powder, and burned.......... 2Kin 23:15 1854
s it, and burnt it at the brook.......... 2Chr 15:16 1854
s with the feet, and rejoiced in.......... Eze 25:6 7554
s the residue with the feet of it.......... Dan 7:7 7512
s the residue with his feet.......... Dan 7:19 7512
down to the ground, and *s* upon him.......... Dan 8:7 7429
to the ground, and *s* upon them.......... Dan 8:10 7429

STAMPING
At the noise of the *s* of the.......... Jer 47:3 8161

STANCHED
immediately her issue of blood *s*.......... Lk 8:44 *2476*

STAND
And they said, *S* back.......... Gen 19:9 5066
I *s* here by the well of water.......... Gen 24:13 5324
Behold, I *s* by the well of water.......... Gen 24:43 5324
thou shalt *s* by the river's brink.......... Ex 7:15 5324
the morning, and *s* before Pharaoh.......... Ex 8:20 3320
the magicians could not *s* before.......... Ex 9:11 5975
s before Pharaoh, and say unto him.......... Ex 9:13 3320
s still, and see the salvation of.......... Ex 14:13 3320
I will *s* before thee there upon.......... Ex 17:6 5975
to morrow I will *s* on the top of.......... Ex 17:9 5324
all the people *s* by thee from.......... Ex 18:14 5324
pillar *s* at the tabernacle door.......... Ex 33:10 5975
me, and thou shalt *s* upon a rock.......... Ex 33:21 5324
neither shall any woman *s* before.......... Lev 18:23 5975
neither shalt thou *s* against the.......... Lev 19:16 5975
no power to *s* before your enemies.......... Lev 26:37 8617
shall estimate it, so shall it *s*.......... Lev 27:14 6965
to thy estimation it shall *s*.......... Lev 27:17 6965
of the men that shall *s* with you.......... Num 1:5 5975
S still, and I will hear what the.......... Num 9:8 5975
that they may *s* there with thee.......... Num 11:16 3320
to *s* before the congregation to.......... Num 16:9 5975
S by thy burnt offering, and I.......... Num 23:3 3320
S here by thy burnt offering,.......... Num 23:15 3320
he shall *s* before Eleazar the.......... Num 27:21 5975
then all her vows shall *s*.......... Num 30:4 6965
she hath bound her soul shall *s*.......... Num 30:4 6965
she hath bound her soul, shall *s*.......... Num 30:5 6965
then her vows shall *s*, and her.......... Num 30:7 6965
she bound her soul shall *s*.......... Num 30:7 6965
their souls, shall *s* against her.......... Num 30:9 6965
then all her vows shall *s*.......... Num 30:11 6965
she bound her soul shall *s*.......... Num 30:11 6965
the bond of her soul, shall not *s*.......... Num 30:12 6965
die not, until he *s* before the.......... Num 35:12 5975
s thou here by me, and I will.......... Deut 5:31 5975
no man be able to *s* before thee.......... Deut 7:24 3320
Who can *s* before the children of.......... Deut 9:2 3320
to *s* before the LORD to minister.......... Deut 10:8 5975
no man be able to *s* before you.......... Deut 11:25 3320
to *s* to minister in the name of.......... Deut 18:5 5975
which *s* there before the LORD.......... Deut 18:7 5975
shall *s* before the LORD, before.......... Deut 19:17 5975
Thou shalt *s* abroad, and the man.......... Deut 24:11 5975
and if he *s* to it, and say, I like.......... Deut 25:8 5975
These shall *s* upon mount Gerizim.......... Deut 27:12 5975
these shall *s* upon mount Ebal to.......... Deut 27:13 5975
Ye *s* this day all of you before.......... Deut 29:10 5324
shall not any man be able to *s*.......... Josh 1:5 3320
ye shall *s* still in Jordan.......... Josh 3:8 5975
they shall *s* upon an heap.......... Josh 3:13 5975
could not *s* before their enemies.......... Josh 7:12 6965
thou canst not *s* before thine.......... Josh 7:13 6965
not a man of them *s* before thee.......... Josh 10:8 5975
Sun, *s* thou still upon Gibeon.......... Josh 10:12 1826
s at the entering of the gate of.......... Josh 20:4 5975
that city, until he *s* before the.......... Josh 20:6 5975
to *s* before you unto this day.......... Josh 23:9 5975
any longer *s* before their enemies.......... Judg 2:14 5975
S in the door of the tent, and it.......... Judg 4:20 5975
Who is able to *s* before this holy.......... 1Sa 6:20 5975
but *s* thou still a while, that I.......... 1Sa 9:27 5975
Now therefore *s* still, that I may.......... 1Sa 12:7 3320
Now therefore *s* and see this great.......... 1Sa 12:16 3320
then we will *s* still in our place.......... 1Sa 14:9 5975
David, I pray thee, *s* before me.......... 1Sa 16:22 5975
s beside my father in the field.......... 1Sa 19:3 5975
He said unto me again, *S*, I pray.......... 2Sa 1:9 5975
unto him, Turn aside, and *s* here.......... 2Sa 18:30 3320
let her *s* before the king, and let.......... 1Kin 1:2 5975
not *s* to minister because of the.......... 1Kin 8:11 5975
which *s* continually before thee,.......... 1Kin 10:8 5975
of Israel liveth, before whom I *s*.......... 1Kin 17:1 5975
of hosts liveth, before whom I *s*.......... 1Kin 18:15 5975
s upon the mount before the LORD.......... 1Kin 19:11 5975
of hosts liveth, before whom I *s*.......... 2Kin 3:14 5975
will surely come out to me, and *s*.......... 2Kin 5:11 5975
the LORD liveth, before whom I *s*.......... 2Kin 5:16 5975

Shaphat shall s on him this day 2Kin 6:31 5975
how then shall we s 2Kin 10:4 5975
of the LORD s between the earth 1Chr 21:16 5975
to s every morning to thank and 1Chr 23:30 5975
s to minister by reason of the 2Chr 5:14 5975
which s continually before thee, 2Chr 9:7 5975
we s before this house, and in thy 2Chr 20:9 5975
s ye still, and see the salvation 2Chr 20:17 5975
hath chosen you to s before him 2Chr 29:11 5975
Jerusalem and Benjamin to s to it 2Chr 34:32 5975
s in the holy place according to 2Chr 35:5 5975
for we cannot s before thee Ezr 9:15 5975
and we are not able to s without Ezr 10:13 5975
rulers of all the congregation s Ezr 10:14 5975
and while they s by, let them shut Neh 7:3 5975
S up and bless the LORD your God Neh 9:5 6965
Mordecai's matters would s Est 3:4 5975
to s for their life, to destroy, Est 8:11 5975
his house, but it shall not s Job 8:15 5975
that he shall s at the latter day Job 19:25 6965
I s up, and thou regardest me not Job 30:20 5975
words in order before me, s up Job 33:5 3320
s still, and consider the wondrous Job 37:14 5975
and they s as a garment Job 38:14 3320
who then is able to s before me Job 41:10 3320
shall not s in the judgment Ps 1:5 6965
S in awe, and sin not Ps 4:4
foolish shall not s in thy sight Ps 5:5 3320
but we are risen, and s upright Ps 20:8 5749
or who shall s in his holy place Ps 24:3 6965
hast made my mountain to s strong Ps 30:7 5975
of the world s in awe of him Ps 33:8 1481
and buckler, and s up for mine help Ps 35:2 6965
my friends s aloof from my sore Ps 38:11 5975
and my kinsmen s afar off Ps 38:11 5975
upon thy right hand did s the Ps 45:9 5324
Their eyes s out with fatness Ps 73:7 3318
who may s in thy sight when once Ps 76:7 5975
made the waters to s as an heap Ps 78:13 5324
my covenant shall s fast with him Ps 89:28 539
not made him to s in the battle Ps 89:43 6965
or who will s up for me against Ps 94:16 3320
let Satan s at his right hand Ps 109:6 5975
For he shall s at the right hand Ps 109:31 5975
They s fast for ever and ever, and Ps 111:8 5564
Our feet shall s within thy gates Ps 122:2 5975
iniquities, O Lord, who shall s Ps 130:3 5975
which by night s in the house of Ps 134:1 5975
Ye that s in the house of the Ps 135:2 5975
who can s before his cold Ps 147:17 5975
house of the righteous shall s Prov 12:7 5975
counsel of the LORD, that shall s Prov 19:21 6965
he shall s before kings Prov 22:29 3320
he shall not s before mean men Prov 22:29 3320
s not in the place of great men Prov 25:6 5975
but who is able to s before envy Prov 27:4 5975
that shall s up in his stead Eccl 4:15 5975
s not in an evil thing Eccl 8:3 5975
the Lord GOD, It shall not s Is 7:7 6965
speak the word, and it shall not s Is 8:10 6965
which shall s for an ensign of Is 11:10 5975
as I have purposed, so shall it s Is 14:24 6965
My lord, I s continually upon the Is 21:8 5975
groves and images shall not s up Is 27:9 6965
agreement with hell shall not s Is 28:18 6965
and by liberal things shall he s Is 32:8 6965
word of our God shall s for ever Is 40:8 6965
gathered together, let them s up Is 44:11 5975
done, saying, My counsel shall s Is 46:10 6965
S now with thine enchantments, and Is 47:12 5975
s up, and save thee from these Is 47:13 5975
unto them, they s up together Is 48:13 5975
let us s together Is 50:8 5975
s up, O Jerusalem, which hast Is 51:17 6965
And strangers shall s and feed your Is 61:5 5975
S by thyself, come not near to me Is 65:5 7126
S ye in the ways, and see, and ask Jer 6:16 5975
S in the gate of the LORD's house Jer 7:2 5975
s before me in this house, which Jer 7:10 5975
asses did s in the high places Jer 14:6 5975
again, and thou shalt s before me Jer 15:19 5975
s in the gate of the children of Jer 17:19 5975
S in the court of the LORD's Jer 26:2 5975
a man to s before me for ever Jer 35:19 5975
shall know whose words shall s Jer 44:28 6965
surely s against you for evil Jer 44:29 6965
s forth with your helmets Jer 46:4 3320
say ye, S fast, and prepare thee Jer 46:14 3320
they did not s, because the day Jer 46:21 5975
of Aroer, s by the way, and espy Jer 48:19 5975
shepherd that will s before me Jer 49:19 5975
shepherd that will s before me Jer 50:44 5975
the sword, go away, s not still Jer 51:50 5975
s upon thy feet, and I will speak Eze 2:1 5975
for the house of Israel to s in Eze 13:5 5975
of his covenant it might s Eze 17:14 5975
s in the gap before me for the Eze 22:30 5975
they shall s upon the land Eze 27:29 5975
all their loins to be at a s Eze 29:7 5976
their trees s up in their height Eze 31:14 5975
Ye s upon your sword, ye work Eze 33:26 5975
they shall s before them to Eze 44:11 5975
they shall s before me to offer Eze 44:15 5975
they shall s in judgment Eze 44:24 5975
shall s by the post of the gate, Eze 46:2 5975
that the fishers shall s upon it Eze 47:10 5975
in them to s in the king's palace Dan 1:4 5975
they might s before the king Dan 1:5 5975
kingdoms, and it shall s for ever Dan 2:44 6966
made s upon the feet as a man, and Dan 7:4 6966
that no beasts might s before him Dan 8:4 5975
power in the ram to s before him Dan 8:7 5975
four kingdoms shall s up out of Dan 8:22 5975
dark sentences, shall s up Dan 8:23 5975
he shall also s up against the Dan 8:25 5975
I speak unto thee, and s upright Dan 10:11 5975
there shall s up yet three kings Dan 11:2 5975
And a mighty king shall s up Dan 11:3 5975
And when he shall s up, his Dan 11:4 5975
neither shall he s, nor his arm Dan 11:6 5975
shall one s up in his estate Dan 11:7 5975
many s up against the king of the Dan 11:14 5975
will, and none shall s before him Dan 11:16 5975
he shall s in the glorious land, Dan 11:16 5975
but she shall not s on his side Dan 11:17 5975
Then shall s up in his estate a Dan 11:20 5975
estate shall s up a vile person Dan 11:21 5975
but he shall not s Dan 11:25 5975
arms shall s on his part, and they Dan 11:31 5975
at that time shall Michael s up Dan 12:1 5975
s in thy lot at the end of the Dan 12:13 5975
Neither shall he s that handleth Amos 2:15 5975
And he shall s and feed in the Mic 5:4 5975
Who can s before his indignation Nah 1:6 5975
S, s, shall they cry Nah 2:8 5975
I will s upon my watch, and set me Hab 2:1 5975
to walk among these that s by Zec 3:7 5975
that s by the Lord of the whole Zec 4:14 5975
his feet shall s in that day upon Zec 14:4 5975
away while they s upon their feet Zec 14:12 5975
who shall s when he appeareth Mal 3:2 5975
against itself shall not s Mt 12:25 2476
how shall then his kingdom s Mt 12:26 2476
mother and thy brethren s without Mt 12:47 2476
Why s ye here all the day idle Mt 20:6 2476
s in the holy place, (whoso Mt 24:15 2476
had the withered hand, S forth Mk 3:3 1453
itself, that kingdom cannot s Mk 3:24 2476
itself, that house cannot s Mk 3:25 2476
and be divided, he cannot s Mk 3:26 2476
there be some of them that s here Mk 9:1 2476
And when ye s praying, forgive, if Mk 11:25 4739
that s in the presence of God Lk 1:19 3936
Rise up, and s forth in the midst Lk 6:8 2476
mother and thy brethren s without Lk 8:20 2476
himself, how shall his kingdom s Lk 11:18 2476
door, and ye begin to s without Lk 13:25 2476
to s before the Son of man Lk 21:36 2476
the people which s by I said it Jn 11:42 4026
why s ye gazing up into heaven Acts 1:11 2476
this man s here before you whole Acts 4:10 3936
Go, s and speak in the temple to Acts 5:20 2476
commanded the chariot to s still Acts 8:38 2476
Peter took him up, saying, S up Acts 10:26 450
loud voice, S upright on thy feet Acts 14:10 450
I s at Caesar's judgment seat, Acts 25:10 2476
And now I s and am judged for the Acts 26:6 2476
But rise, and s upon thy feet Acts 26:16 2476
into this grace wherein we s Rom 5:2 2476
God according to election might s Rom 9:11 3306
for God is able to make him s Rom 14:4 2476
for we shall all s before the Rom 14:10 3936
should not s in the wisdom of men 1Cor 2:5 1510
ye have received, and wherein ye s 1Cor 15:1 2476
why s we in jeopardy every hour 1Cor 15:30
s fast in the faith, quit you 1Cor 16:13 4739
for by faith ye s 2Cor 1:24 2476
for I s in doubt of you Gal 4:20 639
S fast therefore in the liberty Gal 5:1 4739
that ye may be able to s against Eph 6:11 2476
day, and having done all, to s Eph 6:13 2476
S therefore, having your loins Eph 6:14 2476
that ye s fast in one spirit, Phil 1:27 4739
so s fast in the Lord, my dearly Phil 4:1 4739
in prayers, that ye may s perfect Col 4:12 2476
we live, if ye s fast in the Lord 1Th 3:8 4739
s fast, and hold the traditions 2Th 2:15 4739
S thou there, or sit here under Jas 2:3 2476
true grace of God wherein ye s 1Pet 5:12 2476
I s at the door, and knock Rev 3:20 2476
and who shall be able to s Rev 6:17 2476
angel which I saw s upon the sea Rev 10:5 2476
s on the sea of glass, having the Rev 15:2 2476
shall s afar off for the fear of Rev 18:15 2476
small and great, s before God Rev 20:12 2476

STANDARD

camp, and every man by his own s Num 1:52 1714
Israel shall pitch by his own s Num 2:2 1714
the s of the camp of Judah pitch Num 2:3 1714
On the south side shall be the s Num 2:10 1714
be the s of the camp of Ephraim Num 2:18 1714
The s of the camp of Dan shall be Num 2:25 1714
In the first place went the s of Num 10:14 1714
the s of the camp of Reuben set Num 10:18 1714
the s of the camp of the children Num 10:22 1714
the s of the camp of the children Num 10:25 1714
set up my s to the people Is 49:22 5251
shall lift up a s against him Is 59:19 5127
lift up a s for the people Is 62:10 5251
Set up the s toward Zion Jer 4:6 5251
How long shall I see the s Jer 4:21 5251
and publish, and set up a s Jer 50:2 5251
Set up the s upon the walls of Jer 51:12 5251
Set ye up a s in the land Jer 51:27 5251

STANDARD-BEARER

shall be as when a s fainteth Is 10:18 5264

STANDARDS

every man in his place by their s Num 2:17 1714
shall go hindmost with their s Num 2:31 1714
so they pitched by their s Num 2:34 1714

STANDEST

wherefore s thou without Gen 24:31 5975
whereon thou s is holy ground Ex 3:5 5975
the place whereon thou s is holy Josh 5:15 5975
Why s thou afar off, O LORD Ps 10:1 5975
place where thou s is holy ground Acts 7:33 2476
broken off, and thou s by faith Rom 11:20 2476

STANDETH

and that thy cloud s over them Num 14:14 5975
which s before thee, he shall go Deut 1:38 5975
s to minister there before the Deut 17:12 5975
But with him that s here with us Deut 29:15 5975
the pillars whereupon the house s Judg 16:26 3559
him, Behold, Haman s in the court Est 6:5 5975
the king, s in the house of Haman Est 7:9 5975
nor s in the way of sinners, nor Ps 1:1 5975
My foot s in an even place Ps 26:12 5975
counsel of the LORD s for ever Ps 33:11 5975
God s in the congregation of the Ps 82:1 5324
but my heart s in awe of thy word Ps 119:161
She s in the top of high places, Prov 8:2 5324
he s behind our wall, he looketh Song 2:9 5975
The LORD s up to plead Is 3:13 5324
and s to judge the people Is 3:13 5975
and set him in his place, and he s Is 46:7 5975
backward, and justice s afar off Is 59:14 5975
the great prince which s for the Dan 12:1 5975
nor feed that that s still Zec 11:16 5324
but there s one among you, whom Jn 1:26 2476
friend of the bridegroom, which s Jn 3:29 2476
to his own master he s or falleth Rom 14:4 4739
Nevertheless he that s stedfast 1Cor 7:37 2476
eat no flesh while the world s 1Cor 8:13
he s take heed lest he fall 1Cor 10:12 2476
the foundation of God s sure 2Ti 2:19 2476
every priest s daily ministering Heb 10:11 2476
the judge s before the door Jas 5:9 2476
of the angel which s upon the sea Rev 10:8 2476

STANDING

the stacks of corn, or the s corn Ex 22:6 7054
tabernacle of shittim wood s up Ex 26:15 5975
tabernacle of shittim wood, s up Ex 36:20 5975
neither rear you up a s image Lev 26:1 4676
angel of the LORD s in the way Num 22:23 5324
angel of the LORD s in the way Num 22:31 5324
into the s corn of thy neighbour Deut 23:25 7054
unto thy neighbour's s corn Deut 23:25 7054
the s corn of the Philistines Judg 15:5 7054
the shocks, and also the s corn Judg 15:5 7054
Samuel s as appointed over them, 1Sa 19:20 5975
all his servants were s about him 1Sa 22:6 5324
the lion s by the carcase 1Kin 13:25 5975
the lion s by the carcase 1Kin 13:28 5975
all the host of heaven s by him 1Kin 22:19 5975
and two lions s by the stays 2Chr 9:18 5975
of heaven s on his right hand 2Chr 18:18 5975
Esther the queen s in the court Est 5:2 5975
in deep mire, where there is no s Ps 69:2 4613
the wilderness into a s water Ps 107:35 98
turned the rock into a s water Ps 114:8 98
I had seen s before the river Dan 8:6 5975
I saw the Lord s upon the altar Amos 9:1 5324
he shall receive of you his s Mic 1:11 5979
thy s images out of the midst of Mic 5:13 4676
me Joshua the high priest s Zec 3:1 5975
Satan s at his right hand to Zec 3:1 5975
which go forth from s before the Zec 6:5 3320
love to pray s in the synagogues Mt 6:5 2476
unto you, There be some s here Mt 16:28 2476
hour, and saw others s idle in the Mt 20:3 2476
went out, and found others s idle Mt 20:6 2476
s without, sent unto him, calling Mk 3:31 2476
s where it ought not, (let him Mk 13:14 2476
unto him an angel of the Lord s Lk 1:11 2476
And saw two ships s by the lake Lk 5:2 2476
of a truth, there be some s here Lk 9:27 2476
s afar off, would not lift up so Lk 18:13 2476
and the woman s in the midst Jn 8:9 2476
his mother, and the disciple s by Jn 19:26 3936
herself back, and saw Jesus s Jn 20:14 2476
s up with the eleven, lifted up Acts 2:14 2476
man which was healed s with them Acts 4:14 2476
the keepers s without before the Acts 5:23 2476
put in prison are s in the temple Acts 5:25 2476
Jesus s on the right hand of God, Acts 7:55 2476
the Son of man s on the right Acts 7:56 2476
Stephen was shed, I also was s by Acts 22:20 2186
voice, that I cried s among them Acts 24:21 2476
as the first tabernacle was yet s Heb 9:8
the earth s out of the water and 2Pet 3:5 4921
s on the four corners of the Rev 7:1 2476
the two candlesticks s before the Rev 11:4 2476
S afar off for the fear of her Rev 18:10 2476
And I saw an angel s in the sun Rev 19:17 2476

STANK

and the river s, and the Egyptians Ex 7:21 887
and the land s Ex 8:14 887
morning, and it bred worms, and s Ex 16:20 887
saw that they s before David 2Sa 10:6 887

STAR

there shall come a S out of Jacob Num 24:17 3556
the s of your god, which ye made Amos 5:26 3556
we have seen his s in the east Mt 2:2 792
what time the s appeared Mt 2:7 792
and, lo, the s, which they saw in Mt 2:9 792
When they saw the s, they Mt 2:10 792
the s of your god Remphan, Acts 7:43 798
for one s differeth from another 1Cor 15:41 792
differeth from another s in glory 1Cor 15:41 792
the day s arise in your hearts 2Pet 1:19 5459
And I will give him the morning s Rev 2:28 792
there fell a great s from heaven Rev 8:10 792
the name of the s is called Rev 8:11 792
I saw a s fall from heaven unto Rev 9:1 792
David, and the bright and morning s Rev 22:16 792

S

STARE
they look and *s* upon me ... Ps 22:17 7200

STARGAZERS
Let now the astrologers, the *s* ... Is 47:13

STARS
he made the *s* also ... Gen 1:16 3556
now toward heaven, and tell the *s* ... Gen 15:5 3556
thy seed as the *s* of the heaven ... Gen 22:17 3556
to multiply as the *s* of heaven ... Gen 26:4 3556
the eleven *s* made obeisance to me ... Gen 37:9 3556
your seed as the *s* of heaven ... Ex 32:13 3556
ye are this day as the *s* of ... Deut 1:10 3556
the sun, and the moon, and the *s* ... Deut 4:19 3556
as the *s* of heaven for multitude ... Deut 10:22 3556
whereas ye were as the *s* of ... Deut 28:62 3556
the *s* in their courses fought ... Judg 5:20 3556
like to the *s* of the heavens ... 1Chr 27:23 3556
the morning till the *s* appeared ... Neh 4:21 3556
thou as the *s* of heaven, and ... Neh 9:23 3556
Let the *s* of the twilight thereof ... Job 3:9 3556
and sealeth up the *s* ... Job 9:7 3556
and behold the height of the *s* ... Job 22:12 3556
the *s* are not pure in his sight ... Job 25:5 3556
When the morning *s* sang together ... Job 38:7 3556
of thy fingers, the moon and the *s* ... Ps 8:3 3556
The moon and *s* to rule by night ... Ps 136:9 3556
He telleth the number of the *s* ... Ps 147:4 3556
praise him, all ye *s* of light ... Ps 148:3 3556
the light, or the moon, or the *s* ... Eccl 12:2 3556
For the *s* of heaven and the ... Is 13:10 3556
my throne above the *s* of God ... Is 14:13 3556
of the *s* for a light by night ... Jer 31:35 3556
and make the *s* thereof dark ... Eze 32:7 3556
of the *s* to the ground, and ... Dan 8:10 3556
righteousness as the *s* for ever ... Dan 12:3 3556
the *s* shall withdraw their ... Joel 2:10 3556
the *s* shall withdraw their ... Joel 3:15 3556
Seek him that maketh the seven *s* ... Amos 5:8 3598
thou set thy nest among the *s* ... Obad 4 3556
merchants above the *s* of heaven ... Nah 3:16 3556
the *s* shall fall from heaven, and ... Mt 24:29 *792*
the *s* of heaven shall fall, and ... Mk 13:25 *792*
sun, and in the moon, and in the *s* ... Lk 21:25 *798*
when neither sun nor *s* in many ... Acts 27:20 *798*
moon, and another glory of the *s* ... 1Cor 15:41 *792*
so many as the *s* of the sky in ... Heb 11:12 *798*
wandering *s*, to whom is reserved ... Jude 13 *792*
he had in his right hand seven *s* ... Rev 1:16 *792*
The mystery of the seven *s* which ... Rev 1:20 *792*
The seven *s* are the angels of the ... Rev 1:20 *792*
the seven *s* in his right hand ... Rev 2:1 *792*
Spirits of God, and the seven *s* ... Rev 3:1 *792*
the *s* of heaven fell unto the ... Rev 6:13 *792*
moon, and the third part of the *s* ... Rev 8:12 *792*
upon her head a crown of twelve *s* ... Rev 12:1 *792*
the third part of the *s* of heaven ... Rev 12:4 *792*

STATE
man asked us straitly of our *s* ... Gen 43:7
set the house of God in his *s* ... 2Chr 24:13 4971
according to the *s* of the king ... Est 1:7 3027
according to the *s* of the king ... Est 2:18 3027
his best *s* is altogether vanity ... Ps 39:5 5324
to know the *s* of thy flocks ... Prov 27:23 6440
knowledge the *s* thereof shall be ... Prov 28:2 3651
from thy *s* shall he pull thee ... Is 22:19 4612
the last *s* of that man is worse ... Mt 12:45
the last *s* of that man is worse ... Lk 11:26
good comfort, when I know your *s* ... Phil 2:19
will naturally care for your *s* ... Phil 2:20
learned, in whatsoever *s* I am ... Phil 4:11
All my *s* shall Tychicus declare ... Col 4:7

STATELY
And satest upon a *s* bed, and a ... Eze 23:41 3520

STATION
And I will drive thee from thy *s* ... Is 22:19 4673

STATURE
we saw in it are men of a great *s* ... Num 13:32 4060
or on the height of his *s* ... 1Sa 16:7 6967
Gath, where was a man of great *s* ... 2Sa 21:20 4055
an Egyptian, a man of great *s* ... 1Chr 11:23 4060
Gath, where was a man of great *s* ... 1Chr 20:6 4060
This thy *s* is like to a palm tree ... Song 7:7 6967
the high ones of *s* shall be hewn ... Is 10:33 6967
and of the Sabeans, men of *s* ... Is 45:14 4060
the head of every *s* to hunt souls ... Eze 13:18 6967
became a spreading vine of low *s* ... Eze 17:6 6967
her *s* was exalted among the thick ... Eze 19:11 6967
shadowing shroud, and of an high *s* ... Eze 31:3 6967
can add one cubit unto his *s* ... Mt 6:27 *2244*
And Jesus increased in wisdom and *s* ... Lk 2:52 *2244*
can add to his *s* one cubit ... Lk 12:25 *2244*
press, because he was little of *s* ... Lk 19:3 *2244*
unto the measure of the *s* of the ... Eph 4:13 *2244*

STATUTE
there he made for them a *s* ... Ex 15:25 2706
it shall be a *s* for ever unto ... Ex 27:21 2708
it shall be a *s* for ever unto him ... Ex 28:43 2708
shall be theirs for a perpetual *s* ... Ex 29:9 2708
his sons' by a *s* for ever from ... Ex 29:28 2706
it shall be a *s* for ever to them, ... Ex 30:21 2706
It shall be a perpetual *s* for ... Lev 3:17 2708
It shall be a *s* for ever in your ... Lev 6:18 2706
it is a *s* for ever unto the LORD ... Lev 6:22 2706
unto his sons by a *s* for ever ... Lev 7:34 2706
by a *s* for ever throughout their ... Lev 7:36 2708
it shall be a *s* for ever ... Lev 10:9 2708
sons' with thee, by a *s* for ever ... Lev 10:15 2706
this shall be a *s* for ever unto ... Lev 16:29 2708
your souls, by a *s* for ever ... Lev 16:31 2708
be an everlasting *s* unto you ... Lev 16:34 2708
This shall be a *s* for ever unto ... Lev 17:7 2708
it shall be a *s* for ever ... Lev 23:14 2708
it shall be a *s* for ever in all ... Lev 23:21 2708
it shall be a *s* for ever ... Lev 23:31 2708
It shall be a *s* for ever in your ... Lev 23:41 2708
it shall be a *s* for ever in your ... Lev 24:3 2708
made by fire by a perpetual *s* ... Lev 24:9 2706
with thee, by a *s* for ever ... Num 18:11 2706
with thee, by a *s* for ever ... Num 18:19 2706
it shall be a *s* for ever ... Num 18:23 2708
among them, for a *s* for ever ... Num 19:10 2708
shall be a perpetual *s* unto them ... Num 19:21 2708
of Israel a *s* of judgment ... Num 27:11 2708
So these things shall be for a *s* ... Num 35:29 2708
people that day, and set them a *s* ... Josh 24:25 2706
day forward, that he made it a *s* ... 1Sa 30:25 2706
For this was a *s* for Israel ... Ps 81:4 2706
together to establish a royal *s* ... Dan 6:7 7010
That no decree nor *s* which the ... Dan 6:15 7010

STATUTES
my charge, my commandments, my *s* .. Gen 26:5 2708
commandments, and keep all his *s* ... Ex 15:26 2706
I do make them know the *s* of God ... Ex 18:16 2706
the children of Israel all the *s* ... Lev 10:11 2706
Ye shall therefore keep my *s* ... Lev 18:5 2708
Ye shall therefore keep my *s* ... Lev 18:26 2708
Ye shall keep my *s* ... Lev 19:19 2708
shall ye observe all my *s* ... Lev 19:37 2708
And ye shall keep my *s*, and do them .. Lev 20:8 2708
Ye shall therefore keep all my *s* ... Lev 20:22 2708
Wherefore ye shall do my *s* ... Lev 25:18 2708
If ye walk in my *s*, and keep my ... Lev 26:3 2708
And if ye shall despise my *s* ... Lev 26:15 2708
because their soul abhorred my *s* ... Lev 26:43 2708
These are the *s* and judgments and ... Lev 26:46 2706
These are the *s*, which the LORD ... Num 30:16 2706
hearken, O Israel, unto the *s* ... Deut 4:1 2706
Behold, I have taught you *s* ... Deut 4:5 2706
which shall hear all these *s* ... Deut 4:6 2706
is there so great, that hath *s* ... Deut 4:8 2706
me at that time to teach you *s* ... Deut 4:14 2706
Thou shalt keep therefore his *s* ... Deut 4:40 2706
are the testimonies, and the *s* ... Deut 4:45 2706
unto them, Hear, O Israel, the *s* ... Deut 5:1 2706
all the commandments, and the *s* ... Deut 5:31 2706
these are the commandments, the *s* ... Deut 6:1 2706
LORD thy God, to keep all his *s* ... Deut 6:2 2708
God, and his testimonies, and his *s* ... Deut 6:17 2706
mean the testimonies, and the *s* ... Deut 6:20 2706
commanded us to do all these *s* ... Deut 6:24 2706
keep the commandments, and the *s* ... Deut 7:11 2706
and his judgments, and his *s* ... Deut 8:11 2708
of the LORD, and his *s*, which I ... Deut 10:13 2708
God, and keep his charge, and his *s* ... Deut 11:1 2708
ye shall observe to do all the *s* ... Deut 11:32 2706
These are the *s* and judgments, ... Deut 12:1 2706
thou shalt observe and do these *s* ... Deut 16:12 2706
the words of this law and these *s* ... Deut 17:19 2706
hath commanded thee to do these *s* ... Deut 26:16 2706
in his ways, and to keep his *s* ... Deut 26:17 2706
and do his commandments and his *s* ... Deut 27:10 2706
his *s* which I command thee this ... Deut 28:15 2708
his *s* which he commanded thee ... Deut 28:45 2708
his *s* which are written in this ... Deut 30:10 2708
to keep his commandments and his *s* ... Deut 30:16 2708
and as for his *s*, I did not depart ... 2Sa 22:23 2708
walk in his ways, to keep his *s* ... 1Kin 2:3 2708
walking in the *s* of David his ... 1Kin 3:3 2708
walk in my ways, to keep my *s* ... 1Kin 3:14 2706
if thou wilt walk in my *s* ... 1Kin 6:12 2708
keep his commandments, and his *s* ... 1Kin 8:58 2706
LORD our God, to walk in his *s* ... 1Kin 8:61 2706
commanded thee, and wilt keep my *s* .. 1Kin 9:4 2706
my *s* which I have set before you ... 1Kin 9:6 2708
hast not kept my covenant and my *s* ... 1Kin 11:11 2708
in mine eyes, and to keep my *s* ... 1Kin 11:33 2708
he kept my commandments and my *s* . 1Kin 11:34 2708
right in my sight, to keep my *s* ... 1Kin 11:38 2708
walked in the *s* of the heathen, ... 2Kin 17:8 2708
my commandments and my *s* ... 2Kin 17:13 2708
And they rejected his *s*, and his ... 2Kin 17:15 2706
but walked in the *s* of Israel ... 2Kin 17:19 2708
neither do they after their *s* ... 2Kin 17:34 2708
And the *s*, and the ordinances, and ... 2Kin 17:37 2706
his *s* with all their heart and all ... 2Kin 23:3 2708
thou takest heed to fulfil the *s* ... 1Chr 22:13 2706
thy testimonies, and thy *s* ... 1Chr 29:19 2706
thee, and shalt observe my *s* ... 2Chr 7:17 2706
if ye turn away, and forsake my *s* ... 2Chr 7:19 2708
between law and commandment, *s* ... 2Chr 19:10 2706
to the whole law and the *s* ... 2Chr 33:8 2706
and his testimonies, and his *s* ... 2Chr 34:31 2706
to do it, and to teach in Israel *s* ... Ezr 7:10 2706
the LORD, and of his *s* to Israel ... Ezr 7:11 2706
kept the commandments, nor the *s* ... Neh 1:7 2706
judgments, and true laws, good *s* ... Neh 9:13 2706
and commandedst them precepts, *s* ... Neh 9:14 2706
Lord, and his judgments and his *s* ... Neh 10:29 2706
I did not put away his *s* from me ... Ps 18:22 2708
The *s* of the LORD are right, ... Ps 19:8 6490
hast thou to do to declare my *s* ... Ps 50:16 2706
If they break my *s*, and keep not ... Ps 89:31 2708
That they might observe his *s* ... Ps 105:45 2706
ways were directed to keep thy *s* ... Ps 119:5 2706
I will keep thy *s* ... Ps 119:8 2706
teach me thy *s* ... Ps 119:12 2706
I will delight myself in thy *s* ... Ps 119:16 2708
thy servant did meditate in thy *s* ... Ps 119:23 2706
teach me thy *s* ... Ps 119:26 2706
me, O LORD, the way of thy *s* ... Ps 119:33 2706
and I will meditate in thy *s* ... Ps 119:48 2706
Thy *s* have been my songs in the ... Ps 119:54 2706
teach me thy *s* ... Ps 119:64 2706
teach me thy *s* ... Ps 119:68 2706
that I might learn thy *s* ... Ps 119:71 2706
Let my heart be sound in thy *s* ... Ps 119:80 2706
yet do I not forget thy *s* ... Ps 119:83 2706
mine heart to perform thy *s* alway ... Ps 119:112 2706
respect unto thy *s* continually ... Ps 119:117 2706
down all them that err from thy *s* ... Ps 119:118 2706
unto thy mercy, and teach me thy *s* ... Ps 119:124 2706
and teach me thy *s* ... Ps 119:135 2706
I will keep thy *s* ... Ps 119:145 2706
for they seek not thy *s* ... Ps 119:155 2706
when thou hast taught me thy *s* ... Ps 119:171 2706
his word unto Jacob, his *s* ... Ps 147:19 2706
nor walked in my law, nor in my *s* ... Jer 44:10 2708
walked in his law, nor in his *s* ... Jer 44:23 2708
my *s* more than the countries that ... Eze 5:6 2708
have refused my judgments and my *s* .. Eze 5:6 2708
you, and have not walked in my *s* ... Eze 5:7 2708
for ye have not walked in my *s* ... Eze 11:12 2706
That they may walk in my *s* ... Eze 11:20 2708
Hath walked in my *s*, and hath kept ... Eze 18:9 2708
my judgments, hath walked in my *s* ... Eze 18:17 2708
and right, and hath kept all my *s* ... Eze 18:19 2708
hath committed, and keep all my *s* ... Eze 18:21 2708
And I gave them my *s*, and shewed ... Eze 20:11 2708
they walked not in my *s*, and they ... Eze 20:13 2708
judgments, and walked not in my *s* ... Eze 20:16 2708
ye not in the *s* of your fathers ... Eze 20:18 2706
walk in my *s*, and keep my ... Eze 20:19 2708
they walked not in my *s*, neither ... Eze 20:21 2708
judgments, but had despised my *s* ... Eze 20:24 2708
them also *s* that were not good ... Eze 20:25 2706
had robbed, walk in the *s* of life ... Eze 33:15 2708
you, and cause you to walk in my *s* ... Eze 36:27 2706
in my judgments, and observe my *s* ... Eze 37:24 2708
my *s* in all mine assemblies ... Eze 44:24 2708
For the *s* of Omri are kept, and ... Mic 6:16 2708
But my words and my *s*, which I ... Zec 1:6 2706
Horeb for all Israel, with the *s* ... Mal 4:4 2706

STAVES
thou shalt make *s* of shittim wood ... Ex 25:13 905
thou shalt put the *s* into the ... Ex 25:14 905
The *s* shall be in the rings of ... Ex 25:15 905
places of the *s* to bear the table ... Ex 25:27 905
shalt make the *s* of shittim wood ... Ex 25:28 905
thou shalt make *s* for the altar ... Ex 27:6 905
s of shittim wood, and overlay ... Ex 27:6 905
the *s* shall be put into the rings ... Ex 27:7 905
the *s* shall be upon the two sides ... Ex 27:7 905
for the *s* to bear it withal ... Ex 30:4 905
shalt make the *s* of shittim wood ... Ex 30:5 905
the *s* thereof, with the mercy ... Ex 35:12 905
The table, and his *s*, and all his ... Ex 35:13 905
And the incense altar, and his *s* ... Ex 35:15 905
with his brasen grate, his *s* ... Ex 35:16 905
he made *s* of shittim wood, and ... Ex 37:4 905
he put the *s* into the rings by ... Ex 37:5 905
for the *s* to bear the table ... Ex 37:14 905
he made the *s* of shittim wood, and ... Ex 37:15 905
for the *s* to bear it withal ... Ex 37:27 905
he made the *s* of shittim wood, and ... Ex 37:28 905
of brass, to be places for the *s* ... Ex 38:5 905
he made the *s* of shittim wood, and ... Ex 38:6 905
he put the *s* into the rings on ... Ex 38:7 905
the *s* thereof, and the mercy seat, ... Ex 39:35 905
and his grate of brass, his *s* ... Ex 39:39 905
set the *s* on the ark, and put the ... Ex 40:20 905
and shall put in the *s* thereof ... Num 4:6 905
and shall put in the *s* thereof ... Num 4:8 905
and shall put to the *s* thereof ... Num 4:11 905
skins, and put to the *s* of it ... Num 4:14 905
of the lawgiver, with their *s* ... Num 21:18 4938
that thou comest to me with *s* ... 1Sa 17:43 4731
the ark and the *s* thereof above ... 1Kin 8:7 905
And they drew out the *s*, that the ... 1Kin 8:8 905
that the ends of the *s* were seen ... 1Kin 8:8 905
shoulders with the *s* thereon ... 1Chr 15:15 4133
the ark and the *s* thereof above ... 2Chr 5:8 905
And they drew out the *s* of the ark ... 2Chr 5:9 905
that the ends of the *s* were seen ... 2Chr 5:9 905
his *s* the head of his villages ... Hab 3:14 4294
And I took unto me two *s* ... Zec 11:7 4731
coats, neither shoes, nor yet *s* ... Mt 10:10 *4464*
great multitude with swords and *s* ... Mt 26:47 *3586*
with swords and *s* for to take me ... Mt 26:55 *3586*
great multitude with swords and *s* ... Mk 14:43 *3586*
with swords and with *s* to take me ... Mk 14:48 *3586*
for your journey, neither *s* ... Lk 9:3 *4464*
against a thief, with swords and *s* ... Lk 22:52 *3586*

STAY
neither *s* thou in all the plain ... Gen 19:17 5975
you go, and ye shall *s* no longer ... Ex 9:28 5975
the plague in his sight be at a *s* ... Lev 13:5 5975
if the bright spot *s* in his place ... Lev 13:23 5975
if the bright spot *s* in his place ... Lev 13:28 5975
the scall be in his sight at a *s* ... Lev 13:37 5975
s ye not, but pursue after your ... Josh 10:19 5975
would ye *s* for them from having ... Ruth 1:13 5702
Then Samuel said unto Saul, *S* ... 1Sa 15:16 7503
the lad, Make speed, haste, *s* not ... 1Sa 20:38 5975
but the LORD was my *s* ... 2Sa 22:19 4937
s now thine hand ... 2Sa 24:16 7503
It is enough, *s* now thine hand ... 1Chr 21:15 7503
he will not *s* them when his voice ... Job 37:4 6117
or who can *s* the bottles of ... Job 38:37 7901
but the LORD was my *s* ... Ps 18:18 4937
let no man *s* him ... Prov 28:17 8551
S me with flagons, comfort me ... Song 2:5 5564
Jerusalem and from Judah the *s* ... Is 3:1 4937
the staff, the whole *s* of bread ... Is 3:1 8172
of bread, and the whole *s* of water ... Is 3:1 4937
shall no more again *s* upon him ... Is 10:20 4937
but shall *s* upon the LORD, the ... Is 10:20 8172

- are the s of the tribes thereof ... Is 19:13 6438
- S yourselves, and wonder ... Is 29:9 4102
- and perverseness, and s thereon ... Is 30:12 8172
- s on horses, and trust in chariots ... Is 31:1 8172
- s themselves upon the God of ... Is 48:2 5564
- of the LORD, and s upon his God ... Is 50:10 8172
- retire, s not ... Jer 4:6 5975
- with forbearing, and I could not s ... Jer 20:9
- and none can s his hand, or say ... Dan 4:35 4223
- for he should not s long in the ... Hos 13:13 5975

STAYED

- he s yet other seven days ... Gen 8:10 2342
- he s yet other seven days ... Gen 8:12 3176
- with Laban, and s there until now ... Gen 32:4 309
- your flocks and your herds be s ... Ex 10:24 3322
- Hur s up his hands, the one on ... Ex 17:12 8551
- and the plague was s ... Num 16:48 6113
- and the plague was s ... Num 16:50 6113
- So the plague was s from the ... Num 25:8 6113
- I s in the mount, according to ... Deut 10:10 5975
- sun stood still, and the moon s ... Josh 10:13 5975
- And when thou hast s three days ... 1Sa 20:19
- So David s his servants with ... 1Sa 24:7 8156
- those that were left behind s ... 1Sa 30:9 5975
- Jonathan and Ahimaaz s by En-rogel .. 2Sa 17:17 5975
- plague may be s from the people ... 2Sa 24:21 6113
- and the plague was s from Israel ... 2Sa 24:25 6113
- the king was s up in his chariot ... 1Kin 22:35 5975
- And the oil s ... 2Kin 4:6 5975
- And he smote thrice, and s ... 2Kin 13:18 5975
- back, and s not there in the land ... 2Kin 15:20 5975
- plague may be s from the people ... 1Chr 21:22 6113
- s himself up in his chariot ... 2Chr 18:34 5975
- here shall thy proud waves be s ... Job 38:11 7896
- and so the plague was s ... Ps 106:30 6113
- peace, whose mind is s on thee ... Is 26:3 5564
- in a moment, and no hands s on her ... Lam 4:6 2342
- and the great waters were s ... Eze 31:15 3607
- the heaven over you is s from dew ... Hag 1:10 3607
- the earth is s from her fruit ... Hag 1:10 3607
- s him, that he should not depart ... Lk 4:42 2722
- but he himself s in Asia for a ... Acts 19:22 1907

STAYETH

- he s his rough wind in the day of ... Is 27:8 1898

STAYS

- there were s on either side on ... 1Kin 10:19 3027
- and two lions stood beside the s ... 1Kin 10:19 3027
- s on each side of the sitting ... 2Chr 9:18 3027
- and two lions standing by the s ... 2Chr 9:18 3027

STEAD

- offering in the s of his son ... Gen 22:13 8478
- and he said, Am I in God's s ... Gen 30:2 8478
- Zerah of Bozrah reigned in his s ... Gen 36:33 8478
- land of Temani reigned in his s ... Gen 36:34 8478
- field of Moab, reigned in his s ... Gen 36:35 8478
- of Masrekah reigned in his s ... Gen 36:36 8478
- by the river reigned in his s ... Gen 36:37 8478
- son of Achbor reigned in his s ... Gen 36:38 8478
- died, and Hadar reigned in his s ... Gen 36:39 8478
- s shall put them on seven days ... Ex 29:30 8478
- anointed in his s shall offer it ... Lev 6:22 8478
- priest's office in his father's s ... Lev 16:32 8478
- are risen up in your fathers' s ... Num 32:14 8478
- before them, and dwelt in their s ... Deut 2:12 8478
- them, and dwelt in their s ... Deut 2:21 8478
- dwelt in their s even unto this ... Deut 2:22 8478
- them, and dwelt in their s ... Deut 2:23 8478
- in the priest's office in his s ... Deut 10:6 8478
- whom he raised up in their s ... Josh 5:7 8478
- and Hanun his son reigned in his s ... 2Sa 10:1 8478
- in whose s thou hast reigned ... 2Sa 16:8 8478
- shall sit upon my throne in my s ... 1Kin 1:30 8478
- for he shall be king in my s ... 1Kin 1:35 8478
- Rehoboam his son reigned in his s ... 1Kin 11:43 8478
- and Nadab his son reigned in his s ... 1Kin 14:20 8478
- made in their s brasen shields ... 1Kin 14:27 8478
- Abijam his son reigned in his s ... 1Kin 14:31 8478
- and Asa his son reigned in his s ... 1Kin 15:8 8478
- his son reigned in his s ... 1Kin 15:24 8478
- slay him, and reigned in his s ... 1Kin 15:28 8478
- and Elah his son reigned in his s ... 1Kin 16:6 8478
- of Judah, and reigned in his s ... 1Kin 16:10 8478
- and Ahab his son reigned in his s ... 1Kin 16:28 8478
- Ahaziah his son reigned in his s ... 1Kin 22:40 8478
- Jehoram his son reigned in his s ... 1Kin 22:50 8478
- Jehoram reigned in his s in the ... 2Kin 1:17 8478
- that should have reigned in his s ... 2Kin 3:27 8478
- and Hazael reigned in his s ... 2Kin 8:15 8478
- Ahaziah his son reigned in his s ... 2Kin 8:24 8478
- Jehoahaz his son reigned in his s ... 2Kin 10:35 8478
- Amaziah his son reigned in his s ... 2Kin 12:21 8478
- and Joash his son reigned in his s ... 2Kin 13:9 8478
- his son reigned in his s ... 2Kin 13:24 8478
- Jeroboam his son reigned in his s ... 2Kin 14:16 8478
- his son reigned in his s ... 2Kin 14:29 8478
- Jotham his son reigned in his s ... 2Kin 15:7 8478
- and slew him, and reigned in his s ... 2Kin 15:10 8478
- and slew him, and reigned in his s ... 2Kin 15:14 8478
- Pekahiah his son reigned in his s ... 2Kin 15:22 8478
- and slew him, and reigned in his s ... 2Kin 15:30 8478
- and Ahaz his son reigned in his s ... 2Kin 15:38 8478
- Hezekiah his son reigned in his s ... 2Kin 16:20 8478
- his son reigned in his s ... 2Kin 19:37 8478
- Manasseh his son reigned in his s ... 2Kin 20:21 8478
- and Amon his son reigned in his s ... 2Kin 21:18 8478
- made Josiah his son king in his s ... 2Kin 21:24 8478
- Josiah his son reigned in his s ... 2Kin 21:26 8478
- made him king in his father's s ... 2Kin 23:30 8478
- his son reigned in his s ... 2Kin 24:6 8478
- father's brother king in his s ... 2Kin 24:17 8478
- Zerah of Bozrah reigned in his s ... 1Chr 1:44 8478
- of the Temanites reigned in his s ... 1Chr 1:45 8478
- field of Moab, reigned in his s ... 1Chr 1:46 8478
- of Masrekah reigned in his s ... 1Chr 1:47 8478
- by the river reigned in his s ... 1Chr 1:48 8478
- son of Achbor reigned in his s ... 1Chr 1:49 8478
- was dead, Hadad reigned in his s ... 1Chr 1:50 8478
- died, and his son reigned in his s ... 1Chr 19:1 8478
- Solomon his son reigned in his s ... 1Chr 29:28 8478
- and hast made me to reign in his s ... 2Chr 1:8 8478
- Rehoboam his son reigned in his s ... 2Chr 9:31 8478
- Abijah his son reigned in his s ... 2Chr 12:16 8478
- and Asa his son reigned in his s ... 2Chr 14:1 8478
- his son reigned in his s, and ... 2Chr 17:1 8478
- Jehoram his son reigned in his s ... 2Chr 21:1 8478
- his youngest son king in his s ... 2Chr 22:1 8478
- Amaziah his son reigned in his s ... 2Chr 24:27 8478
- Jotham his son reigned in his s ... 2Chr 26:23 8478
- and Ahaz his son reigned in his s ... 2Chr 27:9 8478
- Hezekiah his son reigned in his s ... 2Chr 28:27 8478
- Manasseh his son reigned in his s ... 2Chr 32:33 8478
- and Amon his son reigned in his s ... 2Chr 33:20 8478
- made Josiah his son king in his s ... 2Chr 33:25 8478
- in his father's s in Jerusalem ... 2Chr 36:1 8478
- his son reigned in his s ... 2Chr 36:8 8478
- if your soul were in my soul's s ... Job 16:4 8478
- according to thy wish in God's s ... Job 33:6
- number, and set others in their s ... Job 34:24 8478
- and the wicked cometh in his s ... Prov 11:8 8478
- that shall stand up in his s ... Eccl 4:15 8478
- his son reigned in his s ... Is 37:38 8478
- in the s of Jehoiada the priest ... Jer 29:26 8478
- we pray you in Christ's s ... 2Cor 5:20 5228
- that in thy s he might have ... Philem 13 5228

STEADS

- in their s until the captivity ... 1Chr 5:22 8478

STEADY

- his hands were s until the going ... Ex 17:12 530

STEAL

- away secretly, and s away from me ... Gen 31:27 1589
- how then should we s out of thy ... Gen 44:8 1589
- Thou shalt not s ... Ex 20:15 1589
- If a man shall s an ox, or a ... Ex 22:1 1589
- Ye shall not s, neither deal ... Lev 19:11 1589
- Neither shalt thou s ... Deut 5:19 1589
- as people being ashamed s away ... 2Sa 19:3 1589
- if he s to satisfy his soul when ... Prov 6:30 1589
- or lest I be poor, and s, and take ... Prov 30:9 1589
- Will ye s, murder, and commit ... Jer 7:9 1589
- that s my words every one from ... Jer 23:30 1589
- where thieves break through and s ... Mt 6:19 2813
- do not break through nor s ... Mt 6:20 2813
- commit adultery, Thou shalt not s ... Mt 19:18 2813
- s him away, and say unto the ... Mt 27:64 2813
- adultery, Do not kill, Do not s ... Mk 10:19 2813
- adultery, Do not kill, Do not s ... Lk 18:20 2813
- thief cometh not, but for to s ... Jn 10:10 2813
- man should not s, dost thou s ... Rom 2:21 2813
- shalt not kill, Thou shalt not s ... Rom 13:9 2813
- Let him that stole s no more ... Eph 4:28 2813

STEALETH

- And he that s a man, and selleth ... Ex 21:16 1589
- a tempest s him away in the night ... Job 27:20 1589
- for every one that s shall be cut ... Zec 5:3 1589

STEALING

- If a man be found s any of his ... Deut 24:7 1589
- and lying, and killing, and s ... Hos 4:2 1589

STEALTH

- them by s that day into the city ... 2Sa 19:3 1589

STEDFAST

- yea, thou shalt be s, and shalt ... Job 11:15 3332
- whose spirit was not s with God ... Ps 78:8 539
- were they s in his covenant ... Ps 78:37 539
- s for ever, and his kingdom that ... Dan 6:26 7011
- he that standeth s in his heart ... 1Cor 7:37 1476
- my beloved brethren, be ye s ... 1Cor 15:58 1476
- And our hope of you is s, knowing ... 2Cor 1:7 949
- the word spoken by angels was s ... Heb 2:2 949
- of our confidence s unto the end ... Heb 3:14 949
- of the soul, both sure and s ... Heb 6:19 949
- Whom resist s in the faith ... 1Pet 5:9 4731

STEDFASTLY

- she was s minded to go with her ... Ruth 1:18 553
- And he settled his countenance s ... 2Kin 8:11 7760
- he s set his face to go to ... Lk 9:51 4741
- while they looked s toward heaven ... Acts 1:10 816
- they continued s in the apostles' ... Acts 2:42 4342
- in the council, looking s on him ... Acts 6:15 816
- looked up s into heaven, and saw ... Acts 7:55 816
- who s beholding him, and ... Acts 14:9 816
- s behold the face of Moses for ... 2Cor 3:7 816
- children of Israel could not s ... 2Cor 3:13 816

STEDFASTNESS

- the s of your faith in Christ ... Col 2:5 4733
- the wicked, fall from your own s ... 2Pet 3:17 4740

STEEL

- so that a bow of s is broken by ... 2Sa 22:35 5154
- the bow of s shall strike him ... Job 20:24 5154
- so that a bow of s is broken by ... Ps 18:34 5154
- break the northern iron and the s ... Jer 15:12 5178

STEEP

- the s places shall fall, and every ... Eze 38:20 4095
- that are poured down a s place ... Mic 1:4 4174
- down a s place into the sea ... Mt 8:32 2911
- down a s place into the sea ... Mk 5:13 2911
- down a s place into the lake ... Lk 8:33 2911

STEM

- forth a rod out of the s of Jesse ... Is 11:1 1503

STEP

- there is but a s between me ... 1Sa 20:3 6587
- If my s hath turned out of the ... Job 31:7 838

STEPHANAS (stef'-a-nas) *A convert of Paul from Achaia.*

- baptized also the household of S ... 1Cor 1:16 4734
- brethren, (ye know the house of S ... 1Cor 16:15 4734
- I am glad of the coming of S ... 1Cor 16:17 4734

STEPHANUS

- was written from Philippi by S ... 1Cor s 4734

STEPHEN (ste'-ven) *A leader of the Jerusalem church.*

- and they chose S, a man full of ... Acts 6:5 4736
- And S, full of faith and power, did ... Acts 6:8 4736
- and of Asia, disputing with S ... Acts 6:9 4736
- And they stoned S, calling upon ... Acts 7:59 4736
- men carried S to his burial ... Acts 8:2 4736
- S travelled as far as Phenice ... Acts 11:19 4736
- blood of thy martyr S was shed ... Acts 22:20 4736

STEPPED

- the troubling of the water s in ... Jn 5:4 1684

STEPPETH

- coming, another s down before me ... Jn 5:7 2597

STEPS

- thou go up by s unto mine altar ... Ex 20:26 4609
- Thou hast enlarged my s under me ... 2Sa 22:37 6806
- The throne had six s, and the top ... 1Kin 10:19 4609
- and on the other upon the six s ... 1Kin 10:20 4609
- And there were six s to the throne ... 2Chr 9:18 4609
- and on the other upon the six s ... 2Chr 9:19 4609
- For now thou numberest my s ... Job 14:16 6806
- The s of his strength shall be ... Job 18:7 6806
- My foot hath held his s, his way ... Job 23:11 838
- When I washed my s with butter ... Job 29:6 1978
- he see my ways, and count all my s ... Job 31:4 6806
- unto him the number of my s ... Job 31:37 6806
- have now compassed us in our s ... Ps 17:11 838
- Thou hast enlarged my s under me ... Ps 18:36 6806
- The s of a good man are ordered ... Ps 37:23 4703
- none of his s shall slide ... Ps 37:31 838
- neither have our s declined from ... Ps 44:18 838
- hide themselves, they mark my s ... Ps 56:6 6119
- They have prepared a net for my s ... Ps 57:6 6471
- my s had well nigh slipped ... Ps 73:2 838
- shall set us in the way of his s ... Ps 85:13 6471
- Order my s in thy word ... Ps 119:133 6471
- thy s shall not be straitened ... Prov 4:12 6806
- her s take hold on hell ... Prov 5:5 6806
- but the LORD directeth his s ... Prov 16:9 6806
- the poor, and the s of the needy ... Is 26:6 6471
- man that walketh to direct his s ... Jer 10:23 6806
- They hunt our s, that we cannot ... Lam 4:18 6806
- they went up unto it by seven s ... Eze 40:22 4609
- there were seven s to go up to it ... Eze 40:26 4609
- and the going up to it had eight s ... Eze 40:31 4609
- and the going up to it had eight s ... Eze 40:34 4609
- and the going up to it had eight s ... Eze 40:37 4609
- he brought me by the s whereby ... Eze 40:49 4609
- the Ethiopians shall be at his s ... Dan 11:43 4703
- but who also walk in the s of ... Rom 4:12 2487
- walked we not in the same s ... 2Cor 12:18 2487
- that ye should follow his s ... 1Pet 2:21 2487

STERN

- cast four anchors out of the s ... Acts 27:29 4403

STEWARD

- the s of my house is this Eliezer ... Gen 15:2
- near to the s of Joseph's house ... Gen 43:19
- he commanded the s of his house ... Gen 44:1 5921
- far off, Joseph said unto his s ... Gen 44:4 5921
- of Arza s of his house in Tirzah ... 1Kin 16:9 5921
- of the vineyard saith unto his s ... Mt 20:8 2012
- the wife of Chuza Herod's s ... Lk 8:3 2012
- then is that faithful and wise s ... Lk 12:42 3623
- a certain rich man, which had a s ... Lk 16:1 3623
- for thou mayest be no longer s ... Lk 16:2 3621
- Then the s said within himself ... Lk 16:3 3622
- the lord commended the unjust s ... Lk 16:8 3622
- be blameless, as the s of God ... Titus 1:7 3622

STEWARDS

- the s over all the substance and ... 1Chr 28:1 8269
- s of the mysteries of God ... 1Cor 4:1 3623
- Moreover it is required in s ... 1Cor 4:2 3623
- as good s of the manifold grace ... 1Pet 4:10 3623

STEWARDSHIP

- give an account of thy s ... Lk 16:2 3622
- my lord taketh away from me the s ... Lk 16:3 3622
- that, when I am put out of the s ... Lk 16:4 3622

STICK

- And he cut down a s, and cast it in ... 2Kin 6:6 6086
- bones that were not seen s out ... Job 33:21 8205
- they s together, that they cannot ... Job 41:17 3920
- For thine arrows s fast in me ... Ps 38:2 5181
- withered, it is become like a s ... Lam 4:8 6086
- thy rivers to s unto thy scales ... Eze 29:4 1692
- rivers shall s unto thy scales ... Eze 29:4 1692
- thou son of man, take thee one s ... Eze 37:16 6086
- then take another s, and write ... Eze 37:16 6086
- the s of Ephraim, and for all the ... Eze 37:16 6086
- them one to another into one s ... Eze 37:17 6086
- I will take the s of Joseph ... Eze 37:19 6086
- him, even with the s of Judah ... Eze 37:19 6086
- of Judah, and make them one s ... Eze 37:19 6086

STICKETH
that *s* closer than a brother ... Prov 18:24 1695

STICKS
gathered *s* upon the sabbath day ... Num 15:32 6086
s brought him unto Moses and Aaron.. Num 15:33 6086
woman was there gathering of *s* ... 1Kin 17:10 6086
and, behold, I am gathering two *s* ... 1Kin 17:12 6086
the *s* whereon thou writest shall ... Eze 37:20 6086
Paul had gathered a bundle of *s* ... Acts 28:3 *5484*

STIFF
know thy rebellion, and thy *s* neck ... Deut 31:27 7186
speak not with a *s* neck ... Ps 75:5 6277
their ear, but made their neck *s* ... Jer 17:23 7185

STIFFENED
but he *s* his neck, and hardened ... 2Chr 36:13 7185

STIFFHEARTED
they are impudent children and *s* ... Eze 2:4

STIFFNECKED
and, behold, it is a *s* people ... Ex 32:9
for thou art a *s* people ... Ex 33:3
of Israel, Ye are a *s* people ... Ex 33:5
for it is a *s* people ... Ex 34:9
for thou art a *s* people ... Deut 9:6
and, behold, it is a *s* people ... Deut 9:13
of your heart, and be no more *s* ... Deut 10:16
Now be ye not *s*, as your fathers ... 2Chr 30:8
Ye *s* and uncircumcised in heart and ... Acts 7:51 *4644*

STILL
going on *s* toward the south ... Gen 12:9 5265
but they were *s* ill favoured ... Gen 41:21
let them go, and wilt hold them *s* ... Ex 9:2
the people, Fear ye not, stand *s* ... Ex 14:13
arm they shall be as *s* as a stone ... Ex 15:16 1826
thou shalt let it rest and lie *s* ... Ex 23:11
if it appear *s* in the garment, ... Lev 13:57 5750
And Moses said unto them, Stand *s* ... Num 9:8
went to search the land, lived *s* ... Num 14:38
ye shall stand *s* in Jordan ... Josh 3:8
Sun, stand thou *s* upon Gibeon ... Josh 10:12 1826
And the sun stood *s*, and the moon ... Josh 10:13 1826
So the sun stood *s* in the midst ... Josh 10:13
that stood *s* in their strength ... Josh 11:13
therefore he blessed you *s* ... Josh 24:10
and are ye *s* ... Judg 18:9 2814
Then said she, Sit *s*, my daughter ... Ruth 3:18
on,) but stand thou *s* a while ... 1Sa 9:27
Now therefore stand *s*, that I may ... 1Sa 12:7
But if ye shall *s* do wickedly ... 1Sa 12:25
then we will stand *s* in our place ... 1Sa 14:9
things, and also shalt *s* prevail ... 1Sa 26:25
Asahel fell down and died stood *s* ... 2Sa 2:23
and all the people stood *s* ... 2Sa 2:28
But David tarried *s* at Jerusalem ... 2Sa 11:1
good for me to have been there *s* ... 2Sa 14:32
forth, and cursed *s* as he came ... 2Sa 16:5
And he turned aside, and stood *s* ... 2Sa 18:30
saw that all the people stood *s* ... 2Sa 20:12
one that came by him stood *s* ... 2Sa 20:12
and after the fire a *s* small voice ... 1Kin 19:12 1827
in Gilead is ours, and we be *s* ... 1Kin 22:3
came to pass, as they *s* went on ... 2Kin 2:11
and if we sit *s* here, we die also ... 2Kin 7:4
the people *s* sacrificed and burnt ... 2Kin 12:3 5750
burnt incense *s* on the high ... 2Kin 15:4 5750
burned incense *s* in the high ... 2Kin 15:35 5750
set yourselves, stand ye *s* ... 2Chr 20:17
no power to keep *s* the kingdom ... 2Chr 22:9
sacrifice *s* in the high places ... 2Chr 33:17 5750
they stood *s* in the prison gate ... Neh 12:39
s he holdeth fast his integrity, ... Job 2:3 5750
him, Dost thou *s* retain thine ... Job 2:9 5750
For now should I have lain *s* ... Job 3:13
It stood *s*, but I could not ... Job 4:16
but keep it *s* within his mouth ... Job 20:13
(for they spake not, but stood *s* ... Job 32:16 5975
stand *s*, and consider the wondrous ... Job 37:14 5975
own heart upon your bed, and be *s* ... Ps 4:4 1826
that thou mightest *s* the enemy ... Ps 8:2 7673
he leadeth me beside the *s* waters ... Ps 23:2 4496
Be *s*, and know that I am God ... Ps 46:10 7503
That he should *s* live for ever ... Ps 49:9 5750
as goeth on *s* in his trespasses ... Ps 68:21
the earth feared, and was *s* ... Ps 76:8 8252
For all this they sinned *s* ... Ps 78:32 5750
hold not thy peace, and be not *s* ... Ps 83:1 8252
they will be *s* praising thee ... Ps 84:4 5750
They shall *s* bring forth fruit in ... Ps 92:14 5750
so that the waves thereof are *s* ... Ps 107:29 2814
when I awake, I am *s* with thee ... Ps 139:18 5750
he *s* taught the people knowledge ... Eccl 12:9 5750
but his hand is stretched out *s* ... Is 5:25 5750
but his hand is stretched out *s* ... Is 9:12 5750
but his hand is stretched out *s* ... Is 9:17 5750
but his hand is stretched out *s* ... Is 9:21 5750
but his hand is stretched out *s* ... Is 10:4 5750
Be *s*, ye inhabitants of the isle ... Is 23:2 1826
this, Their strength is to sit *s* ... Is 30:7 7673
I have been *s*, and refrained ... Is 42:14 2790
Why do we sit *s* ... Jer 8:14
They say *s* unto them that despise ... Jer 23:17
I let remain *s* in their own land ... Jer 27:11
I do earnestly remember him *s* ... Jer 31:20 5750
If ye will *s* abide in this land, ... Jer 42:10
into thy scabbard, rest, and be *s* ... Jer 47:6 1826
the sword, go away, stand not *s* ... Jer 51:50 5975
soul hath them *s* in remembrance ... Lam 3:20
the children of thy people *s* are ... Eze 33:30
a winding about *s* upward to the ... Eze 41:7
s upward round about the house ... Eze 41:7
breadth of the house was *s* upward ... Eze 41:7
moon stood *s* in their habitation ... Hab 3:11
behold, all the earth sitteth *s* ... Zec 1:11
nor feed that that standeth *s* ... Zec 11:16
And Jesus stood *s*, and called them, ... Mt 20:32 *2476*
and said unto the sea, Peace, be *s* ... Mk 4:39 *5392*
And Jesus stood *s*, and commanded ... Mk 10:49 *2476*
and they that bare him stood *s* ... Lk 7:14 *2476*
unto them, he abode *s* in Galilee ... Jn 7:9
he abode two days *s* in the same ... Jn 11:6
but Mary sat *s* in the house ... Jn 11:20
commanded the chariot to stand *s* ... Acts 8:38 *2476*
it pleased Silas to abide there *s* ... Acts 15:34
Silas and Timotheus abode there *s* ... Acts 17:14
if they abide not *s* in unbelief ... Rom 11:23
thee to abide *s* at Ephesus ... 1Ti 1:3 *4357*
is unjust, let him be unjust *s* ... Rev 22:11 *2089*
is filthy, let him be filthy *s* ... Rev 22:11 *2089*
righteous, let him be righteous *s* ... Rev 22:11 *2089*
that is holy, let him be holy *s* ... Rev 22:11 *2089*

STILLED
Caleb *s* the people before Moses, ... Num 13:30 2013
So the Levites *s* all the people ... Neh 8:11 2814

STILLEST
waves thereof arise, thou *s* them ... Ps 89:9 7623

STILLETH
Which *s* the noise of the seas, ... Ps 65:7 7623

STING
O death, where is thy *s* ... 1Cor 15:55 *2759*
The *s* of death is sin ... 1Cor 15:56 *2759*

STINGETH
a serpent, and *s* like an adder ... Prov 23:32 6567

STINGS
there were *s* in their tails ... Rev 9:10 *2759*

STINK
to *s* among the inhabitants of the ... Gen 34:30 887
shall die, and the river shall *s* ... Ex 7:18 887
and it did not *s*, neither was ... Ex 16:24 887
My wounds *s* and are corrupt ... Ps 38:5 887
of sweet smell there shall be *s* ... Is 3:24 4716
their *s* shall come up out of ... Is 34:3 889
his *s* shall come up, and his ill ... Joel 2:20 889
I have made the *s* of your camps ... Amos 4:10 889

STINKETH
their fish *s*, because there is no ... Is 50:2 887
unto him, Lord, by this time he *s* ... Jn 11:39 *3605*

STINKING
to send forth a *s* savour ... Eccl 10:1 887

STIR
who shall *s* him up ... Num 24:9 6965
the innocent shall *s* up himself ... Job 17:8 5782
is so fierce that dare *s* him up ... Job 41:10 5782
S up thyself, and awake to my ... Ps 35:23 5782
did not *s* up all his wrath ... Ps 78:38 5782
Manasseh *s* up thy strength, and ... Ps 80:2 5782
but grievous words *s* up anger ... Prov 15:1 5927
of the field, that ye *s* not up ... Song 2:7 5782
of the field, that ye *s* not up ... Song 3:5 5782
of Jerusalem, that ye *s* not up ... Song 8:4 5782
the LORD of hosts shall *s* up a ... Is 10:26 5782
I will *s* up the Medes against ... Is 13:17 5782
he shall *s* up jealousy like a man ... Is 42:13 5782
s up all against the realm of ... Dan 11:2 5782
he shall *s* up his power and his ... Dan 11:25 5782
was no small *s* among the soldiers ... Acts 12:18 *5017*
arose no small *s* about that way ... Acts 19:23 *5017*
that thou *s* up the gift of God ... 2Ti 1:6 [illegible]
to *s* you up by putting you in ... 2Pet 1:13 *1326*
in both which I *s* up your pure ... 2Pet 3:1 *1326*

STIRRED
every one whose heart *s* him up ... Ex 35:21 5375
all the women whose heart *s* them ... Ex 35:26 5375
even every one whose heart *s* him ... Ex 36:2 5375
hath *s* up my servant against me ... 1Sa 22:8 6965
If the LORD have *s* thee up ... 1Sa 26:19 5496
the LORD *s* up an adversary unto ... 1Kin 11:14 6965
God *s* him up another adversary, ... 1Kin 11:23 6965
LORD, whom Jezebel his wife *s* up ... 1Kin 21:25 5496
the God of Israel *s* up the spirit ... 1Chr 5:26 5782
Moreover the LORD *s* up against ... 2Chr 21:16 5782
the LORD *s* up the spirit of Cyrus ... 2Chr 36:22 5782
the LORD *s* up the spirit of Cyrus ... Ezr 1:1 5782
and my sorrow was *s* ... Ps 39:2 5916
But his sons shall be *s* up ... Dan 11:10 1624
then shall he return, and be *s* up ... Dan 11:10 1624
s up to battle with a very great ... Dan 11:25 1624
the LORD *s* up the spirit of ... Hag 1:14 5782
they *s* up the people, and the ... Acts 6:12 *4787*
But the Jews *s* up the devout and ... Acts 13:50 *3951*
Jews *s* up the Gentiles, and made ... Acts 14:2 *1892*
thither also, and *s* up the people ... Acts 17:13 *4531*
Athens, his spirit was *s* in him ... Acts 17:16 *3947*
s up all the people, and laid ... Acts 21:27 *4797*

STIRRETH
As an eagle *s* up her nest ... Deut 32:11 5782
Hatred *s* up strifes ... Prov 10:12 5782
A wrathful man *s* up strife ... Prov 15:18 1624
is of a proud heart *s* up strife ... Prov 28:25 1624
An angry man *s* up strife, and a ... Prov 29:22 1624
it *s* up the dead for thee, even ... Is 14:9 5782
that *s* up himself to take hold of ... Is 64:7 5782
He *s* up the people, teaching ... Lk 23:5 *383*

STIRS
Thou that art full of *s*, a ... Is 22:2 8663

STOCK
or to the *s* of the stranger's ... Lev 25:47 6133
the *s* thereof die in the ground ... Job 14:8 1503
their *s* shall not take root in ... Is 40:24 1503
I fall down to the *s* of a tree ... Is 44:19 944
Saying to a *s*, Thou art my father ... Jer 2:27 6086
the *s* is a doctrine of vanities ... Jer 10:8 6086
children of the *s* of Abraham ... Acts 13:26 *1085*
of the *s* of Israel, of the tribe ... Phil 3:5 *1085*

STOCKS
puttest my feet also in the *s* ... Job 13:27 5465
He putteth my feet in the *s* ... Job 33:11 5465
a fool to the correction of the *s* ... Prov 7:22 5914
adultery with stones and with *s* ... Jer 3:9 6086
put him in the *s* that were in the ... Jer 20:2 4115
forth Jeremiah out of the *s* ... Jer 20:3 4115
put him in prison, and in the *s* ... Jer 29:26 6729
My people ask counsel at their *s* ... Hos 4:12 6086
and made their feet fast in the *s* ... Acts 16:24 *3586*

STOIC See STOICKS.

STOICKS (*sto'-ics*) *A sect of Greek philosophers.*
of the Epicureans, and of the *S* ... Acts 17:18 *4770*

STOLE
Jacob *s* away unawares to Laban ... Gen 31:20 1589
so Absalom *s* the hearts of the ... 2Sa 15:6 1589
s him from among the king's sons ... 2Kin 11:2 1589
s him from among the king's sons ... 2Chr 22:11 1589
s him away while we slept ... Mt 28:13 *2813*
Let him that *s* steal no more ... Eph 4:28 *2813*

STOLEN
that shall be counted *s* with me ... Gen 30:33 1589
Rachel had *s* the images that were ... Gen 31:19 1589
that thou hast *s* away unawares to ... Gen 31:26 1589
yet wherefore hast thou *s* my gods ... Gen 31:30 1589
knew not that Rachel had *s* them ... Gen 31:32 1589
s by day, or *s* by night ... Gen 31:39 1589
For indeed I was *s* away out of ... Gen 40:15 1589
it be *s* out of the man's house ... Ex 22:7 1589
And if it be *s* from him, he shall ... Ex 22:12 1589
accursed thing, and have also *s* ... Josh 7:11 1589
the men of Judah *s* thee away ... 2Sa 19:41 1589
which had *s* them from the street ... 2Sa 21:12 1589
S waters are sweet, and bread ... Prov 9:17 1589
not have *s* till they had enough ... Obad 5 1589

STOMACHER
instead of a *s* a girding of ... Is 3:24 6614

STOMACH'S
use a little wine for thy *s* sake ... 1Ti 5:23 *4751*

STONE
there is bdellium and the onyx *s* ... Gen 2:12 68
And they had brick for *s*, and slime ... Gen 11:3 68
took the *s* that he had put for ... Gen 28:18 68
And this *s*, which I have set for a ... Gen 28:22 68
a great *s* was upon the well's ... Gen 29:2 68
they rolled the *s* from the well's ... Gen 29:3 68
put the *s* again upon the well's ... Gen 29:3 68
till they roll the *s* from the ... Gen 29:8 68
rolled the *s* from the well's ... Gen 29:10 68
And Jacob took a *s*, and set it up ... Gen 31:45 68
with him, even a pillar of *s* ... Gen 35:14 68
is the shepherd, the *s* of Israel ... Gen 49:24 68
Then Zipporah took a sharp *s* ... Ex 4:25 6697
of wood, and in vessels of *s* ... Ex 7:19 68
their eyes, and will they not *s* us ... Ex 8:26 5619
they sank into the bottom as a *s* ... Ex 15:5 68
arm they shall be as still as a *s* ... Ex 15:16 68
they be almost ready to *s* me ... Ex 17:4 5619
and they took a *s*, and put it under ... Ex 17:12 68
thou wilt make me an altar of *s* ... Ex 20:25 [illegible]
thou shalt not build it of hewn *s* ... Ex 20:25
and one smite another with a *s* ... Ex 21:18 68
were a paved work of a sapphire *s* ... Ex 24:10
and I will give thee tables of *s* ... Ex 24:12 68
Six of their names on one *s* ... Ex 28:10 68
names of the rest on the other *s* ... Ex 28:10 68
With the work of an engraver in *s* ... Ex 28:11 68
tables of testimony, tables of *s* ... Ex 31:18 68
tables of *s* like unto the first ... Ex 34:1 68
tables of *s* like unto the first ... Ex 34:4 68
in his hand the two tables of *s* ... Ex 34:4 68
the land shall *s* him with stones ... Lev 20:2 7275
they shall *s* them with stones ... Lev 20:27 7275
and let all the congregation *s* him ... Lev 24:14 7275
shall certainly *s* him ... Lev 24:16 7275
of the camp, and *s* him with stones ... Lev 24:23 7275
up any image of *s* in your land ... Lev 26:1 68
bade *s* them with stones ... Num 14:10 7275
all the congregation shall *s* him ... Num 15:35 7275
if he smite him with throwing a *s* ... Num 35:17 68
Or with any *s*, wherewith a man ... Num 35:23 68
wrote them upon two tables of *s* ... Deut 4:13 68
work of men's hands, wood and *s* ... Deut 4:28 68
he wrote them in two tables of *s* ... Deut 5:22 68
mount to receive the tables of *s* ... Deut 9:9 68
s written with the finger of God ... Deut 9:10 68
LORD gave me the two tables of *s* ... Deut 9:11 68
tables of *s* like unto the first ... Deut 10:1 68
tables of *s* like unto the first ... Deut 10:3 68
thou shalt *s* him with stones, ... Deut 13:10 5619
shalt *s* them with stones, till ... Deut 17:5 5619
his city shall *s* him with stones ... Deut 21:21 7275
the men of her city shall *s* her ... Deut 22:21 5619
ye shall *s* them with stones that ... Deut 22:24 5619
thou serve other gods, wood and *s* ... Deut 28:36 68
have known, even wood and *s* ... Deut 28:64 68
and their idols, wood and *s* ... Deut 29:17 68
man of you a *s* upon his shoulder ... Josh 4:5 68
the border went up to the *s* of ... Josh 15:6 68
descended to the *s* of Bohan the ... Josh 18:17 68
the law of God, and took a great *s* ... Josh 24:26 68
this *s* shall be a witness unto us ... Josh 24:27 68
and ten persons, upon one *s* ... Judg 9:5 68
and ten persons, upon one *s* ... Judg 9:18 68
there, where there was a great *s* ... 1Sa 6:14 68

were, and put them on the great s	1Sa 6:15	68
even unto the great s of Abel	1Sa 6:18	
which s remaineth unto this day	1Sa 6:18	
Then Samuel took a s, and set it	1Sa 7:12	68
roll a great s unto me this day	1Sa 14:33	68
in his bag, and took thence a s	1Sa 17:49	68
that the s sunk into his forehead	1Sa 17:49	68
with a sling and with a s, and	1Sa 17:50	68
and shalt remain by the s Ezel	1Sa 20:19	68
within him, and he became as a s	1Sa 25:37	68
be not one small s found there	2Sa 17:13	6872
at the great s which is in Gibeon	2Sa 20:8	68
fat cattle by the s of Zoheleth	1Kin 1:9	68
was built of s made ready before	1Kin 6:7	68
there was no s seen	1Kin 6:18	68
court with three rows of hewed s	1Kin 6:36	1496
the ark save the two tables of s	1Kin 8:9	68
out, and s him, that he may die	1Kin 21:10	5619
of land cast every man his s	2Kin 3:25	68
And to masons, and hewers of s	2Kin 12:12	68
hewed s to repair the breaches of	2Kin 12:12	68
work of men's hands, wood and s	2Kin 19:18	68
hewn s to repair the house	2Kin 22:6	68
timber also and s have I prepared	1Chr 22:14	68
abundance, hewers and workers of s	1Chr 22:15	68
silver, in brass, in iron, in s	2Chr 2:14	68
gave they it, to buy hewn s	2Chr 34:11	68
even break down their s wall	Neh 4:3	68
as a s into the mighty waters	Neh 9:11	68
and brass is molten out of the s	Job 28:2	68
or who laid the corner s thereof	Job 38:6	68
The waters are hid as with a s	Job 38:30	68
His heart is as firm as a s	Job 41:24	68
thou dash thy foot against a s	Ps 91:12	68
The s which the builders refused	Ps 118:22	68
become the head s of the corner	Ps 118:22	
A gift is as a precious s in the	Prov 17:8	68
the s wall thereof was broken	Prov 24:31	68
As he that bindeth a s in a sling	Prov 26:8	68
and he that rolleth a s, it will	Prov 26:27	68
A s is heavy, and the sand weighty	Prov 27:3	68
but for a s of stumbling and for a	Is 8:14	68
a foundation a s, a tried s	Is 28:16	68
a precious corner s	Is 28:16	
work of men's hands, wood and s	Is 37:19	68
and to a s, Thou hast brought me	Jer 2:27	68
not take of thee a s for a corner	Jer 51:26	68
a corner, nor a s for foundations	Jer 51:26	68
that thou shalt bind a s to it	Jer 51:63	68
hath inclosed my ways with hewn s	Lam 3:9	1496
the dungeon, and cast a s upon me	Lam 3:53	68
as the appearance of a sapphire s	Eze 1:26	68
over them as it were a sapphire s	Eze 10:1	68
was as the colour of a beryl s	Eze 10:9	68
they shall s thee with stones, and	Eze 16:40	7275
the countries, to serve wood and s	Eze 20:32	68
company shall s them with stones	Eze 23:47	7275
every precious s was thy covering	Eze 28:13	68
of hewn s for the burnt offering	Eze 40:42	68
Thou sawest till that a s was cut	Dan 2:34	69
the s that smote the image became	Dan 2:35	69
as thou sawest that the s was cut	Dan 2:45	69
brass, of iron, of wood, and of s	Dan 5:4	69
gold, of brass, iron, wood, and s	Dan 5:23	69
a s was brought, and laid upon the	Dan 6:17	69
ye have built houses of hewn s	Amos 5:11	1496
For the s shall cry out of the	Hab 2:11	68
to the dumb s, Arise, it shall	Hab 2:19	68
from before a s was laid upon a	Hag 2:15	68
a s in the temple of the LORD	Hag 2:15	68
For behold the s that I have laid	Zec 3:9	68
upon one s shall be seven eyes	Zec 3:9	68
made their hearts as an adamant s	Zec 7:12	8068
a burdensome s for all people	Zec 12:3	68
thou dash thy foot against a s	Mt 4:6	3037
ask bread, will he give him a s	Mt 7:9	3037
The s which the builders rejected	Mt 21:42	3037
fall on this s shall be broken	Mt 21:44	3037
be left here one s upon another	Mt 24:2	3037
he rolled a great s to the door	Mt 27:60	3037
the sepulchre sure, sealing the s	Mt 27:66	3037
rolled back the s from the door	Mt 28:2	3037
The s which the builders rejected	Mk 12:10	3037
not be left one s upon another	Mk 13:2	3037
rolled a s unto the door of the	Mk 15:46	3037
Who shall roll us away the s from	Mk 16:3	3037
saw that the s was rolled away	Mk 16:4	3037
command this s that it be made	Lk 4:3	3037
thou dash thy foot against a s	Lk 4:11	3037
is a father, will he give him a s	Lk 11:11	3037
leave in thee one s upon another	Lk 19:44	3037
all the people will s us	Lk 20:6	2642
The s which the builders rejected	Lk 20:17	3037
fall upon that s shall be broken	Lk 20:18	3037
not be left one s upon another	Lk 21:6	3037
in a sepulchre that was hewn in s	Lk 23:53	2991
they found the s rolled away from	Lk 24:2	3037
which is by interpretation, A s	Jn 1:42	4074
were set there six waterpots of s	Jn 2:6	3035
let him first cast a s at her	Jn 8:7	3037
took up stones again to s him	Jn 10:31	3034
which of those works do ye s me	Jn 10:32	3034
For a good work we s thee not	Jn 10:33	3034
the Jews of late sought to s thee	Jn 11:8	3034
It was a cave, and a s lay upon it	Jn 11:38	3037
Jesus said, Take ye away the s	Jn 11:39	3037
Then they took away the s from	Jn 11:41	3037
seeth the s taken away from the	Jn 20:1	3037
This is the s which was set at	Acts 4:11	3037
them despitefully, and to s them	Acts 14:5	3036
like unto gold, or silver, or s	Acts 17:29	3037
not in tables of s, but in	2Cor 3:3	3035
himself being the chief corner s	Eph 2:20	
whom coming, as unto a living s	1Pet 2:4	3037
I lay in Sion a chief corner s	1Pet 2:6	3037
the s which the builders	1Pet 2:7	3037
a s of stumbling, and a rock of	1Pet 2:8	3037
manna, and will give him a white s	Rev 2:17	5586
in the s a new name written	Rev 2:17	5586
upon like a jasper and a sardine s	Rev 4:3	3037
gold, and silver, and brass, and s	Rev 9:20	3035
every s about the weight of a	Rev 16:21	
up a s like a great millstone	Rev 18:21	3037
was like unto a s most precious	Rev 21:11	3037
precious, even like a jasper s	Rev 21:11	3037

STONED

it, but he shall surely be s	Ex 19:13	5619
then the ox shall be surely s	Ex 21:28	5619
the ox shall be s, and his owner	Ex 21:29	5619
of silver, and the ox shall be s	Ex 21:32	5619
s him with stones, and he died	Num 15:36	7275
all Israel s him with stones, and	Josh 7:25	5619
after they had s them with stones	Josh 7:25	7275
all Israel s him with stones,	1Kin 12:18	7275
s him with stones, that he died	1Kin 21:13	5619
to Jezebel, saying, Naboth is s	1Kin 21:14	5619
Jezebel heard that Naboth was s	1Kin 21:15	5619
of Israel s him with stones	2Chr 10:18	7275
him, and s him with stones at the	2Chr 24:21	7275
and killed another, and s another	Mt 21:35	3036
us, that such should be s	Jn 8:5	3036
lest they should have been s	Acts 5:26	3034
him out of the city, and s him	Acts 7:58	3036
they s Stephen, calling upon God,	Acts 7:59	3036
the people, and, having s Paul	Acts 14:19	3034
I beaten with rods, once was I s	2Cor 11:25	3034
They were s, they were sawn	Heb 11:37	3034
touch the mountain, it shall be s	Heb 12:20	3036

STONE'S

from them about a s cast, and	Lk 22:41	3037

STONES

and he took of the s of that place	Gen 28:11	68
said unto his brethren, Gather s	Gen 31:46	68
and they took s, and made an heap	Gen 31:46	68
Onyx s, and s to be set in	Ex 25:7	68
And thou shalt take two onyx s	Ex 28:9	68
shalt thou engrave the two s with	Ex 28:11	68
thou shalt put the two s upon the	Ex 28:12	68
s of memorial unto the children	Ex 28:12	68
shalt set in it settings of s	Ex 28:17	68
even four rows of s	Ex 28:17	68
the s shall be with the names of	Ex 28:21	68
And in cutting of s, to set them,	Ex 31:5	68
And onyx s, and s to be set	Ex 35:9	68
And the rulers brought onyx s	Ex 35:27	68
s to be set, for the ephod, and	Ex 35:27	68
And in the cutting of s, to set	Ex 35:33	68
they wrought onyx s inclosed in	Ex 39:6	68
that they should be s for a	Ex 39:7	68
And they set in it four rows of s	Ex 39:10	68
the s were according to the names	Ex 39:14	68
away the s in which the plague is	Lev 14:40	68
And they shall take other s	Lev 14:42	68
put them in the place of those s	Lev 14:42	68
that he hath taken away the s	Lev 14:43	68
the s of it, and the timber	Lev 14:45	68
the land shall stone him with s	Lev 20:2	68
they shall stone them with s	Lev 20:27	68
or scabbed, or hath his s broken	Lev 21:20	810
of the camp, and stone him with s	Lev 24:23	68
bade stone them with s	Num 14:10	68
stone him with s without the camp	Num 15:35	68
the camp, and stoned him with s	Num 15:36	68
a land whose s are iron, and out	Deut 8:9	68
And thou shalt stone him with s	Deut 13:10	68
woman, and shalt stone them with s	Deut 17:5	68
his city shall stone him with s	Deut 21:21	68
stone her with s that she die	Deut 22:21	68
stone them with s that they die	Deut 22:24	68
He that is wounded in the s	Deut 23:1	
thou shalt set thee up great s	Deut 27:2	68
that ye shall set up these s	Deut 27:4	68
the LORD thy God, an altar of s	Deut 27:5	68
of the LORD thy God of whole s	Deut 27:6	68
thou shalt write upon the s all	Deut 27:8	68
feet stood firm, twelve s	Josh 4:3	68
saying, What mean ye by these s	Josh 4:6	68
these s shall be for a memorial	Josh 4:7	68
took up twelve s out of the midst	Josh 4:8	68
Joshua set up twelve s in the	Josh 4:9	68
And those twelve s, which they	Josh 4:20	68
come, saying, What mean these s	Josh 4:21	68
And all Israel stoned him with s	Josh 7:25	68
after they had stoned them with s	Josh 7:25	68
a great heap of s unto this day	Josh 7:26	68
raise thereon a great heap of s	Josh 8:29	68
law of Moses, an altar of whole s	Josh 8:31	68
he wrote there upon the s a copy	Josh 8:32	68
s from heaven upon them unto	Josh 10:11	68
Roll great s upon the mouth of	Josh 10:18	68
laid great s in the cave's mouth	Josh 10:27	68
could sling s at an hair breadth	Judg 20:16	68
five smooth s out of the brook	1Sa 17:40	68
of gold with the precious s	2Sa 12:30	68
he cast s at David, and at all the	2Sa 16:6	68
threw s at him, and cast dust	2Sa 16:13	68
a very great heap of s upon him	2Sa 18:17	68
s, costly s, and hewed s	1Kin 5:17	68
timber and s to build the house	1Kin 5:18	68
All these were of costly s	1Kin 7:9	68
to the measures of hewed s	1Kin 7:9	1496
of costly s, even great s	1Kin 7:10	68
s of ten cubits, and s of	1Kin 7:10	68
And above were costly s, after the	1Kin 7:11	68
after the measures of hewed s	1Kin 7:11	1496
was with three rows of hewed s	1Kin 7:12	1496
and very much gold, and precious s	1Kin 10:2	68
very great store, and precious s	1Kin 10:10	68
of almug trees, and precious s	1Kin 10:11	68
silver to be in Jerusalem as s	1Kin 10:27	68
and all Israel stoned him with s	1Kin 12:18	68
and they took away the s of Ramah	1Kin 15:22	68
And Elijah took twelve s,	1Kin 18:31	68
with the s he built an altar in	1Kin 18:32	68
sacrifice, and the wood, and the s	1Kin 18:38	68
of the city, and stoned him with s	1Kin 21:13	68
every good piece of land with s	2Kin 3:19	68
left they the s thereof	2Kin 3:25	68
and put it upon a pavement of s	2Kin 16:17	68
hand and the left in hurling s	1Chr 12:2	68
and there were precious s in it	1Chr 20:2	68
s to build the house of God	1Chr 22:2	68
onyx s, and s to be set,	1Chr 29:2	68
to be set, glistering s	1Chr 29:2	68
and all manner of precious s	1Chr 29:2	68
s, and marble s in abundance	1Chr 29:2	68
they with whom precious s were	1Chr 29:8	68
at Jerusalem as plenteous as s	2Chr 1:15	68
house with precious s for beauty	2Chr 3:6	68
gold in abundance, and precious s	2Chr 9:1	68
great abundance, and precious s	2Chr 9:9	68
brought algum trees and precious s	2Chr 9:10	68
made silver in Jerusalem as s	2Chr 9:27	68
of Israel stoned him with s	2Chr 10:18	68
they carried away the s of Ramah	2Chr 16:6	68
him, and stoned him with s at the	2Chr 24:21	68
and bows, and slings to cast s	2Chr 26:14	68
to shoot arrows and great s withal	2Chr 26:15	68
and for gold, and for precious s	2Chr 32:27	68
which is builded with great s	Ezr 5:8	69
With three rows of great s	Ezr 6:4	69
will they revive the s out of the	Neh 4:2	68
in league with the s of the field	Job 5:23	68
Is my strength the strength of s	Job 6:12	68
the heap, and seeth the place of s	Job 8:17	68
The waters wear the s	Job 14:19	68
of Ophir as the s of the brooks	Job 22:24	6697
the s of darkness, and the shadow	Job 28:3	68
The s of it are the place of	Job 28:6	68
the sinews of his s are wrapped	Job 40:17	6344
Sharp s are under him	Job 41:30	2789
his thick clouds passed, hail s	Ps 18:12	
hail s and coals of fire	Ps 18:13	
servants take pleasure in her s	Ps 102:14	68
thy little ones against the s	Ps 137:9	5553
our daughters may be as corner s	Ps 144:12	2106
A time to cast away s, and a time	Eccl 3:5	68
and a time to gather s together	Eccl 3:5	68
Whoso removeth s shall be hurt	Eccl 10:9	68
it, and gathered out the s thereof	Is 5:2	5619
but we will build with hewn s	Is 9:10	1496
that go down to the s of the pit	Is 14:19	68
when he maketh all the s of the	Is 27:9	68
confusion, and the s of emptiness	Is 34:11	68
I will lay thy s with fair colors	Is 54:11	68
and all thy borders of pleasant s	Is 54:12	68
Among the smooth s of the stream	Is 57:6	
and for wood brass, and for s iron	Is 60:17	68
gather out the s	Is 62:10	68
and committed adultery with s	Jer 3:9	68
Take great s in thine hand, and	Jer 43:9	68
upon these s that I have hid	Jer 43:10	68
broken my teeth with gravel s	Lam 3:16	2687
the s of the sanctuary are poured	Lam 4:1	68
and they shall stone thee with s	Eze 16:40	68
company shall stone them with s	Eze 23:47	68
and they shall lay thy s and thy	Eze 26:12	68
spices, and with all precious s	Eze 27:22	68
in the midst of the s of fire	Eze 28:14	68
from the midst of the s of fire	Eze 28:16	68
and silver, and with precious s	Dan 11:38	68
I will pour down the s thereof	Mic 1:6	68
timber thereof and the s thereof	Zec 5:4	68
devour, and subdue with sling s	Zec 9:15	68
they shall be as the s of a crown	Zec 9:16	68
these s to raise up children unto	Mt 3:9	3037
that these s be made bread	Mt 4:3	3037
crying, and cutting himself with s	Mk 5:5	3037
and at him they cast s, and wounded	Mk 12:4	3036
him, Master, see what manner of s	Mk 13:1	3037
these s to raise up children unto	Lk 3:8	3037
the s would immediately cry out	Lk 19:40	3037
how it was adorned with goodly s	Lk 21:5	3037
took they up s to cast at him	Jn 8:59	3037
Jews took up s again to stone him	Jn 10:31	3037
gold, silver, precious s, wood,	1Cor 3:12	3037
death, written and engraven in s	2Cor 3:7	3037
Ye also, as lively s, are built	1Pet 2:5	3037
and decked with gold and precious s	Rev 17:4	3037
of gold, and silver, and precious s	Rev 18:12	3037
decked with gold, and precious s	Rev 18:16	3037
with all manner of precious s	Rev 21:19	3037

STONESQUARERS

builders did hew them, and the s	1Kin 5:18	1382

STONEST

s them which are sent unto thee,	Mt 23:37	3036
s them that are sent unto thee	Lk 13:34	3036

STONING

for the people spake of s him	1Sa 30:6	5619

STONY

judges are overthrown in s places	Ps 141:6	5553
I will take the s heart out of	Eze 11:19	68
I will take away the s heart out	Eze 36:26	68
Some fell upon s places, where	Mt 13:5	4075
received the seed into s places	Mt 13:20	4075
And some fell on s ground, where	Mk 4:5	4075
which are sown on s ground	Mk 4:16	4075

STOOD

Context	Reference	Number
and, lo, three men s by him	Gen 18:2	5324
he s by them under the tree, and	Gen 18:8	5975
but Abraham s yet before the LORD	Gen 18:22	5975
place where he s before the LORD	Gen 19:27	5975
Abraham s up from before his dead	Gen 23:3	6965
And Abraham s up, and bowed	Gen 23:7	6965
he s by the camels at the well	Gen 24:30	5975
And, behold, the LORD s above it	Gen 28:13	5324
my sheaf arose, and also s upright	Gen 37:7	5324
your sheaves s round about	Gen 37:7	
and, behold, he s by the river	Gen 41:1	5975
s by the other kine upon the	Gen 41:3	5975
I s upon the bank of the river	Gen 41:17	5975
he s before Pharaoh king of Egypt	Gen 41:46	5975
down to Egypt, and s before Joseph	Gen 43:15	5975
before all them that s by him	Gen 45:1	5324
there s no man with him, while	Gen 45:1	5975
And his sister s afar off, to wit	Ex 2:4	3320
but Moses s up and helped them, and	Ex 2:17	6965
who s in the way, as they came	Ex 5:20	5324
the furnace, and s before Pharaoh	Ex 9:10	5975
their face, and s behind them	Ex 14:19	5975
the floods s upright as an heap,	Ex 15:8	5324
the people s by Moses from the	Ex 18:13	5975
they s at the nether part of the	Ex 19:17	3320
it, they removed, and s afar off	Ex 20:18	5975
And the people s afar off, and	Ex 20:21	5975
Then Moses s in the gate of the	Ex 32:26	5975
s every man at his tent door, and	Ex 33:8	5324
s at the door of the tabernacle,	Ex 33:9	5975
s with him there, and proclaimed	Ex 34:5	3320
drew near and s before the LORD	Lev 9:5	5975
the people s up all that day, and	Num 11:32	6965
s in the door of the tabernacle,	Num 12:5	5975
s in the door of the tabernacle	Num 16:18	5975
s in the door of their tents, and	Num 16:27	5324
he s between the dead and the	Num 16:48	5975
the angel of the LORD s in the	Num 22:22	3320
But the angel of the LORD s in a	Num 22:24	5975
s in a narrow place, where was no	Num 22:26	5975
he s by his burnt sacrifice, he,	Num 23:6	5324
he s by his burnt offering, and	Num 23:17	5324
they s before Moses, and before	Num 27:2	5975
came near and s under the mountain	Deut 4:11	5975
(I s between the LORD and you at	Deut 5:5	5975
the pillar of the cloud s over	Deut 31:15	5975
which came down from above s	Josh 3:16	5975
s firm on dry ground in the midst	Josh 3:17	5975
where the priests' feet s firm	Josh 4:3	4673
bare the ark of the covenant s	Josh 4:9	4673
the ark s in the midst of Jordan	Josh 4:10	5975
there s a man over against him	Josh 5:13	5975
s on this side the ark and on that	Josh 8:33	5975
And the sun s still, and the moon	Josh 10:13	1826
So the sun s still in the midst	Josh 10:13	5975
that s still in their strength	Josh 11:13	5975
of blood, until he s before the	Josh 20:9	5975
there s not a man of all their	Josh 21:44	5975
all that s by him went out from	Judg 3:19	5975
said unto all that s against him	Judg 6:31	5975
they s every man in his place	Judg 7:21	5975
s in the top of mount Gerizim, and	Judg 9:7	5975
s in the entering of the gate of	Judg 9:35	5975
s in the entering of the gate of	Judg 9:44	5975
pillars upon which the house s	Judg 16:29	3559
s by the entering of the gate	Judg 18:16	5324
the priest s in the entering of	Judg 18:17	5324
s before it in those days,)	Judg 20:28	5975
am the woman that s by thee here	1Sa 1:26	5324
And the LORD came, and s, and called	1Sa 3:10	3320
women that s by her said unto her	1Sa 4:20	5324
s there, where there was a great	1Sa 6:14	5975
when he s among the people, he	1Sa 10:23	3320
came to Saul, and s before him	1Sa 16:21	5975
the Philistines s on a mountain	1Sa 17:3	5975
Israel s on a mountain on the	1Sa 17:3	5975
And he s and cried unto the armies	1Sa 17:8	5975
spake to the men that s by him	1Sa 17:26	5975
s upon the Philistine, and took	1Sa 17:51	5975
his servants that s about him	1Sa 22:7	5324
unto the footmen that s about him	1Sa 22:17	5324
s on the top of an hill afar off	1Sa 26:13	5975
So I s upon him, and slew him,	2Sa 1:10	5975
Asahel fell down and died s still	2Sa 2:23	5975
troop, and s on the top of an hill	2Sa 2:25	5975
and all the people s still	2Sa 2:28	5975
all his servants s by with their	2Sa 13:31	5324
s beside the way of the gate	2Sa 15:2	
the king s by the gate side, and	2Sa 18:4	5975
And he turned aside, and s still	2Sa 18:30	5975
And one of Joab's men s by him	2Sa 20:11	5975
saw that all the people s still	2Sa 20:12	5975
one that came by him s still	2Sa 20:12	5975
the city, and it s in the trench	2Sa 20:15	5975
But he s in the midst of the	2Sa 23:12	3320
presence, and s before the king	1Kin 1:28	5975
s before the ark of the covenant	1Kin 3:15	5975
unto the king, and s before him	1Kin 3:16	5975
It s upon twelve oxen, three	1Kin 7:25	5975
all the congregation of Israel s	1Kin 8:14	5975
Solomon s before the altar of the	1Kin 8:22	5975
And he s, and blessed all the	1Kin 8:55	5975
two lions s beside the stays	1Kin 10:19	5975
twelve lions s there on the one	1Kin 10:20	5975
that s before Solomon his father	1Kin 12:6	5975
with him, and which s before him	1Kin 12:8	5975
Jeroboam s by the altar to burn	1Kin 13:1	5975
in the way, and the ass s by it	1Kin 13:24	5975
the lion also s by the carcase	1Kin 13:24	5975
s in the entering in of the cave	1Kin 19:13	5975
s before the LORD, and said, I	1Kin 22:21	5975
went, and s to view afar off	2Kin 2:7	5975
and they two s by Jordan	2Kin 2:7	5975
back, and s by the bank of Jordan	2Kin 2:13	5975
and upward, and s in the border	2Kin 3:21	5975
had called her, she s before him	2Kin 4:12	5975
had called her, she s in the door	2Kin 4:15	5975
s at the door of the house of	2Kin 5:9	5975
company, and came, and s before him	2Kin 5:15	5975
went in, and s before his master	2Kin 5:25	5975
s before him, and said, Thy son	2Kin 8:9	5975
there s a watchman on the tower	2Kin 9:17	5975
two kings s not before him	2Kin 10:4	5975
morning, that he went out, and s	2Kin 10:9	5975
And the guard s, every man with	2Kin 11:11	5975
the king s by a pillar, as the	2Kin 11:14	5975
he revived, and s up on his feet	2Kin 13:21	6965
s by the conduit of the upper	2Kin 18:17	5975
Then Rab-shakeh s and cried with a	2Kin 18:28	5975
the king s by a pillar, and made a	2Kin 23:3	5975
all the people s to the covenant	2Kin 23:3	5975
who s on his right hand, even	1Chr 6:39	5975
sons of Merari s on the left hand	1Chr 6:44	
Satan s up against Israel, and	1Chr 21:1	5975
the angel of the LORD s by the	1Chr 21:15	5975
David the king s up upon his feet	1Chr 28:2	6965
they s on their feet, and their	2Chr 3:13	5975
It s upon twelve oxen, three	2Chr 4:4	5975
s at the east end of the altar,	2Chr 5:12	5975
all the congregation of Israel s	2Chr 6:3	5975
he s before the altar of the LORD	2Chr 6:12	5975
and upon it he s, and kneeled down	2Chr 6:13	5975
before them, and all Israel s	2Chr 7:6	5975
twelve lions s there on the one	2Chr 9:19	5975
with the old men that had s	2Chr 10:6	5975
up with him, that s before him	2Chr 10:8	5975
Abijah s up upon mount Zemaraim,	2Chr 13:4	6965
s before the LORD, and said, I	2Chr 18:20	5975
Jehoshaphat s in the congregation	2Chr 20:5	5975
all Judah s before the LORD, with	2Chr 20:13	5975
s up to praise the LORD God of	2Chr 20:19	6965
as they went forth, Jehoshaphat s	2Chr 20:20	5975
Moab s up against the inhabitants	2Chr 20:23	5975
the king s at his pillar at the	2Chr 23:13	5975
which s above the people, and said	2Chr 24:20	5975
s up against them that came from	2Chr 28:12	6965
And the Levites s with the	2Chr 29:26	5975
they s in their place after their	2Chr 30:16	5975
the king s in his place, and made	2Chr 34:31	5975
the priests s in their place, and	2Chr 35:10	5975
till there s up a priest with	Ezr 2:63	5975
Then s up Jeshua the son of	Ezr 3:2	6965
Then s Jeshua with his sons and	Ezr 3:9	5975
And Ezra the priest s up, and said	Ezr 10:10	6965
till there s up a priest with	Neh 7:65	5975
Ezra the scribe s upon a pulpit	Neh 8:4	5975
and beside him s Mattithiah	Neh 8:4	5975
he opened it, all the people s up	Neh 8:5	5975
the people s in their place	Neh 8:7	
from all strangers, and s and	Neh 9:2	5975
they s up in their place, and read	Neh 9:3	6965
Then s up upon the stairs, of the	Neh 9:4	6965
they s still in the prison gate	Neh 12:39	5975
So s the two companies of them	Neh 12:40	5975
s in the inner court of the	Est 5:1	5975
the king's gate, that he s not up	Est 5:9	6965
Haman s up to make request for	Est 7:7	5975
arose, and s before the king,	Est 8:4	5975
s for their lives, and had rest	Est 9:16	5975
the hair of my flesh s up	Job 4:15	5568
It s still, but I could not	Job 4:16	5975
and the aged arose, and s up	Job 29:8	5975
I s up, and I cried in the	Job 30:28	6965
but s still, and answered no more	Job 32:16	5975
he commanded, and it s fast	Ps 33:9	5975
the waters s above the mountains	Ps 104:6	5975
chosen s before him in the breach	Ps 106:23	5975
Then s up Phinehas, and executed	Ps 106:30	5975
Above it s the seraphims	Is 6:2	5975
he s by the conduit of the upper	Is 36:2	5975
Then Rabshakeh s, and cried with a	Is 36:13	5975
Samuel s before me, yet my mind	Jer 15:1	5975
Remember that I s before thee to	Jer 18:20	5975
he s in the court of the LORD's	Jer 19:14	5975
For who hath s in the counsel of	Jer 23:18	5975
But if they had s in my counsel	Jer 23:22	5975
that s in the house of the LORD	Jer 28:5	5975
princes which s beside the king	Jer 36:21	5975
gods, and all the women that s by	Jer 44:15	5975
they s not, because the LORD did	Jer 46:15	5975
They that fled s under the shadow	Jer 48:45	5975
he s with his right hand as an	Lam 2:4	5324
and when those s, these s	Eze 1:21	5975
when they s, they let down their	Eze 1:24	5975
was over their heads, when they s	Eze 1:25	5975
the glory of the LORD s there	Eze 3:23	5975
there s before them seventy men	Eze 8:11	5975
in the midst of them s Jaazaniah	Eze 8:11	5975
s beside the brasen altar	Eze 9:2	5975
Now the cherubims s on the right	Eze 10:3	5975
s over the threshold of the house	Eze 10:4	
went in, and s beside the wheels	Eze 10:6	5975
When they s, these s	Eze 10:17	5975
house, and s over the cherubims	Eze 10:18	5975
every one s at the door of the	Eze 10:19	5975
s upon the mountain which is on	Eze 11:23	5975
For the king of Babylon s at the	Eze 21:21	5975
and s up upon their feet, an	Eze 37:10	5975
and he s in the gate	Eze 40:3	5975
and the man s by me	Eze 43:6	5975
of the house s toward the east	Eze 47:1	
therefore s they before the king	Dan 1:19	5975
So they came and s before the king	Dan 2:2	5975
was excellent, s before thee	Dan 2:31	6966
they s before the image that	Dan 3:3	6966
times ten thousand s before him	Dan 7:10	6966
near unto one of them that s by	Dan 7:16	6966
there s before the river a ram	Dan 8:3	5975
behold, there s before me as the	Dan 8:15	5975
So he came near where I s	Dan 8:17	5977
broken, whereas four s up for it	Dan 8:22	5975
this word unto me, I s trembling	Dan 10:11	5975
and said unto him that s before me	Dan 10:16	5975
s to confirm and to strengthen him	Dan 11:1	5975
there s other two, the one on	Dan 12:5	5975
there they s	Hos 10:9	5975
the Lord s upon a wall made by a	Amos 7:7	5324
thou have s in the crossway	Obad 14	5975
He s, and measured the earth	Hab 3:6	5975
moon s still in their habitation	Hab 3:11	5975
he s among the myrtle trees that	Zec 1:8	5975
the man that s among the myrtle	Zec 1:10	5975
that s among the myrtle trees	Zec 1:11	5975
garments, and s before the angel	Zec 3:3	5975
unto those that s before him	Zec 3:4	5975
And the angel of the LORD s by	Zec 3:5	5975
s over where the young child was	Mt 2:9	*2476*
mother and his brethren s without	Mt 12:46	*2476*
whole multitude s on the shore	Mt 13:2	*2476*
And Jesus s still, and called them,	Mt 20:32	*2476*
came unto him they that s by	Mt 26:73	*2476*
Jesus s before the governor	Mt 27:11	*2476*
Some of them that s there	Mt 27:47	*2476*
And Jesus s still, and commanded	Mk 10:49	*2476*
them that s there said unto them	Mk 11:5	*2476*
of them that s by drew a sword	Mk 14:47	*3936*
the high priest s up in the midst	Mk 14:60	*450*
and began to say to them that s by	Mk 14:69	*3936*
they that s by said again to	Mk 14:70	*3936*
And some of them that s by	Mk 15:35	*3936*
which s over against him, saw	Mk 15:39	*3936*
sabbath day, and s up for to read	Lk 4:16	*450*
he s over her, and rebuked the	Lk 4:39	*2186*
he s by the lake of Gennesaret,	Lk 5:1	*2476*
And he arose and s forth	Lk 6:8	*2476*
s in the plain, and the company of	Lk 6:17	*2476*
and they that bare him s still	Lk 7:14	*2476*
s at his feet behind him weeping,	Lk 7:38	*2476*
and the two men that s with him	Lk 9:32	*4921*
And, behold, a certain lawyer s up	Lk 10:25	*450*
were lepers, which s afar off	Lk 17:12	*2476*
The Pharisee s and prayed thus	Lk 18:11	*2476*
And Jesus s, and commanded him to	Lk 18:40	*2476*
And Zacchaeus s, and said unto the	Lk 19:8	*2476*
And he said unto them that s by	Lk 19:24	*3936*
And the chief priests and scribes s	Lk 23:10	*2476*
And the people s beholding	Lk 23:35	*2476*
s afar off, beholding these	Lk 23:49	*2476*
two men s by them in shining	Lk 24:4	*2186*
Jesus himself s in the midst of	Lk 24:36	*2476*
Again the next day after John s	Jn 1:35	*2476*
when the people which s on the	Jn 6:22	*2476*
great day of the feast, Jesus s	Jn 7:37	*2476*
as they s in the temple, What	Jn 11:56	*2476*
The people therefore, that s by	Jn 12:29	*2476*
which betrayed him, s with them	Jn 18:5	*2476*
But Peter s at the door without	Jn 18:16	*2476*
the servants and officers s there	Jn 18:18	*2476*
Peter s with them, and warmed	Jn 18:18	*2476*
one of the officers which s by	Jn 18:22	*3936*
And Simon Peter s and warmed	Jn 18:25	*2476*
Now there s by the cross of Jesus	Jn 19:25	*2476*
But Mary s without at the	Jn 20:11	*2476*
s in the midst, and saith unto	Jn 20:19	*2476*
s in the midst, and said, Peace be	Jn 20:26	*2476*
now come, Jesus s on the shore	Jn 21:4	*2476*
two men s by them in white	Acts 1:10	*3936*
in those days Peter s up in the	Acts 1:15	*450*
And he leaping up s, and walked, and	Acts 3:8	*2476*
The kings of the earth s up	Acts 4:26	*3936*
Then s there up one in the	Acts 5:34	*450*
journeyed with him s speechless	Acts 9:7	*2476*
all the widows s by him weeping	Acts 9:39	*3936*
house, and s before the gate,	Acts 10:17	*2186*
a man s before me in bright	Acts 10:30	*2476*
an angel in his house, which s	Acts 11:13	*2476*
there s up one of them named	Acts 11:28	*450*
told how Peter s before the gate	Acts 12:14	*2476*
Then Paul s up, and beckoning with	Acts 13:16	*450*
the disciples s round about him	Acts 14:20	*2944*
There s a man of Macedonia, and	Acts 16:9	*2476*
Then Paul s in the midst of Mars'	Acts 17:22	*2476*
Paul s on the stairs, and beckoned	Acts 21:40	*2476*
Came unto me, and s, and said unto	Acts 22:13	*2186*
said unto the centurion that s by	Acts 22:25	*2476*
that s by him to smite him on the	Acts 23:2	*3936*
And they that s by said, Revilest	Acts 23:4	*3936*
night following the Lord s by him	Acts 23:11	*2186*
while I s before the council,	Acts 24:20	*2476*
down from Jerusalem s round about	Acts 25:7	*4026*
whom when the accusers s up	Acts 25:18	*2476*
Paul s forth in the midst of them	Acts 27:21	*2476*
For there s by me this night the	Acts 27:23	*3936*
my first answer no man s with me	2Ti 4:16	*4836*
the Lord s with me, and	2Ti 4:17	*3936*
Which s only in meats and drinks,	Heb 9:10	
s a Lamb as it had been slain,	Rev 5:6	*2476*
s before the throne, and before	Rev 7:9	*2476*
all the angels s round about the	Rev 7:11	*2476*
seven angels which s before God	Rev 8:2	*2476*
s at the altar, having a golden	Rev 8:3	*2476*
and the angel s, saying, Rise, and	Rev 11:1	*2476*
them, and they s upon their feet	Rev 11:11	*2476*
the dragon s before the woman	Rev 12:4	*2476*
I s upon the sand of the sea, and	Rev 13:1	*2476*
a Lamb s on the mount Sion, and	Rev 14:1	*2476*
many as trade by sea, s afar off,	Rev 18:17	*2476*

STOODEST

Context	Reference	Number
that thou s in the way against me	Num 22:34	5324
thou s before the LORD thy God in	Deut 4:10	5975

day that thou s on the other side — Obad 11 — 5975

STOOL
there a bed, and a table, and a s — 2Kin 4:10 — 3678

STOOLS
women, and see them upon the s — Ex 1:16 — 70

STOOP
the proud helpers do s under him — Job 9:13 — 7817
in the heart of man maketh it s — Prov 12:25 — 7812
They s, they bow down together — Is 46:2 — 7164
shoes I am not worthy to s down — Mk 1:7 — 2955

STOOPED
he s down, he couched as a lion, — Gen 49:9 — 3766
David s with his face to the — 1Sa 24:8 — 6915
he s with his face to the ground, — 1Sa 28:14 — 6915
old man, or him that s for age — 2Chr 36:17 — 3486
But Jesus s down, and with his — Jn 8:6 — 2955
And again he s down, and wrote on — Jn 8:8 — 2955
she s down, and looked into the — Jn 20:11 — 3879

STOOPETH
Bel boweth down, Nebo s, their — Is 46:1 — 7164

STOOPING
s down, he beheld the linen — Lk 24:12 — 3879
he s down, and looking in, saw the — Jn 20:5 — 3879

STOP
down, that the rain s thee not — 1Kin 18:44 — 6113
s all wells of water, and mar — 2Kin 3:19 — 5640
his mighty men to s the waters of — 2Chr 32:3 — 5640
s the way against them that — Ps 35:3 — 5462
and all iniquity shall s her mouth — Ps 107:42 — 7092
it shall s the noses of the — Eze 39:11 — 2629
no man shall s me of this — 2Cor 11:10 — 5420

STOPPED
and the windows of heaven were s — Gen 8:2 — 5534
the Philistines had s them — Gen 26:15 — 5640
for the Philistines had s them — Gen 26:18 — 5640
or his flesh be s from his issue — Lev 15:3 — 2856
they s all the wells of water, and — 2Kin 3:25 — 5640
who s all the fountains, and the — 2Chr 32:4 — 5640
This same Hezekiah also s the — 2Chr 32:30 — 5640
that the breaches began to be s — Neh 4:7 — 5640
them that speak lies shall be s — Ps 63:11 — 5534
And that the passages are s — Jer 51:32 — 8610
s their ears, that they should — Zec 7:11 — 3513
s their ears, and ran upon him — Acts 7:57 — 4912
that every mouth may be s — Rom 3:19 — 5420
Whose mouths must be s, who — Titus 1:11 — 1998
promises, s the mouths of lions, — Heb 11:33 — 5420

STOPPETH
hope, and iniquity s her mouth — Job 5:16 — 7092
the deaf adder that s her ear — Ps 58:4 — 331
Whoso s his ears at the cry of — Prov 21:13 — 331
that s his ears from hearing of — Is 33:15 — 331

STORE
of herds, and great s of servants — Gen 26:14
that food shall be for s to the — Gen 41:36 — 6487
come in ye shall eat of the old s — Lev 25:22
And ye shall eat old s, and bring — Lev 26:10 — 3462
shall be thy basket and thy s — Deut 28:5 — 4863
shall be thy basket and thy s — Deut 28:17 — 4863
Is not this laid up in s with me — Deut 32:34
the cities of s that Solomon had — 1Kin 9:19 — 4543
gold, and of spices very great s — 1Kin 10:10
have laid up in s unto this day — 2Kin 20:17 — 686
all this s that we have prepared — 1Chr 29:16 — 1995
wilderness, and all the s cities — 2Chr 8:4 — 4543
all the s cities that Solomon had — 2Chr 8:6 — 4543
s of victual, and of oil and wine — 2Chr 11:11 — 214
all the s cities of Naphtali — 2Chr 16:4 — 4543
in Judah castles, and cities of s — 2Chr 17:12 — 4543
which is left is this great s — 2Chr 31:10 — 1995
once in ten days s of all sorts — Neh 5:18 — 7235
full, affording all manner of s — Ps 144:13
have laid up in s until this day — Is 39:6 — 686
who s up violence and robbery in — Amos 3:10 — 686
for there is none end of the s — Nah 2:9 — 8498
every one of you lay by him in s — 1Cor 16:2 — 2343
Laying up in s for themselves a — 1Ti 6:19 — 597
by the same word are kept in s — 2Pet 3:7 — 2343

STOREHOUSE
ye all the tithes into the s — Mal 3:10 — 214
which neither have s nor barn — Lk 12:24 — 5009

STOREHOUSES
And Joseph opened all the s — Gen 41:56 — 834
the blessing upon thee in thy s — Deut 28:8 — 618
over the s in the fields, in the — 1Chr 27:25 — 214
S also for the increase of corn, — 2Chr 32:28 — 4543
he layeth up the depth in s — Ps 33:7 — 214
the utmost border, open her s — Jer 50:26 — 3965

STORIES
third s shalt thou make it — Gen 6:16
round about on their three s — Eze 41:16
against gallery in three s — Eze 42:3
For they were in three s, but had — Eze 42:6
that buildeth his s in the heaven — Amos 9:6 — 4609

STORK
And the s, the heron after her — Lev 11:19 — 2624
And the s, and the heron after her — Deut 14:18 — 2624
as for the s, the fir trees are — Ps 104:17 — 2624
the s in the heaven knoweth her — Jer 8:7 — 2624
had wings like the wings of a s — Zec 5:9 — 2624

STORM
as chaff that the s carrieth away — Job 21:18 — 5492
as a s hurleth him out of his — Job 27:21
hasten my escape from the windy s — Ps 55:8 — 5584
and make them afraid with thy s — Ps 83:15 — 5492
He maketh the s a calm, so that — Ps 107:29 — 5591
of refuge, and for a covert from s — Is 4:6 — 2230
his distress, a refuge from the s — Is 25:4 — 2230
ones is as a s against the wall — Is 25:4 — 2230
tempest of hail and a destroying s — Is 28:2 — 8178
and great noise, with s and — Is 29:6 — 5492
shalt ascend and come like a s — Eze 38:9 — 7722
way in the whirlwind and in the s — Nah 1:3 — 8183
And there arose a great s of wind — Mk 4:37 — 2978
there came down a s of wind on — Lk 8:23 — 2978

STORMY
commandeth, and raiseth the s wind — Ps 107:25 — 5591
s wind fulfilling his word — Ps 148:8 — 5591
and a s wind shall rend it — Eze 13:11 — 5591
rend it with a s wind in my fury — Eze 13:13 — 5591

STORY
are written in the s of the — 2Chr 13:22 — 4097
they are written in the s of the — 2Chr 24:27 — 4097

STOUT
the s lion's whelps are scattered — Job 4:11
s heart of the king of Assyria — Is 10:12 — 1433
look was more s than his fellows — Dan 7:20 — 7229
Your words have been s against me — Mal 3:13 — 2388

STOUTHEARTED
The s are spoiled, they have — Ps 76:5
Hearken unto me, ye s, that are — Is 46:12

STOUTNESS
say in the pride and s of heart, — Is 9:9 — 1433

STRAIGHT
ascend up every man s before him — Josh 6:5
every man s before him, and they — Josh 6:20
the kine took the s way to the — 1Sa 6:12 — 3474
brought it s down to the west — 2Chr 32:30 — 3474
make thy way s before my face — Ps 5:8 — 3474
thine eyelids look s before thee — Prov 4:25 — 3474
which is crooked cannot be made s — Eccl 1:15 — 8626
for who can make that s, which he — Eccl 7:13 — 8626
make s in the desert a highway — Is 40:3 — 3474
and the crooked shall be made s — Is 40:4 — 4334
before them, and crooked things s — Is 42:16 — 4334
and make the crooked places s — Is 45:2 — 3474
the rivers of waters in a s way — Jer 31:9 — 3474
And their feet were s feet — Eze 1:7 — 3474
they went every one s forward — Eze 1:9 — 5676
And they went every one s forward — Eze 1:12 — 5676
the firmament were their wings s — Eze 1:23 — 3474
they went every one s forward — Eze 10:22 — 5676
way of the Lord, make his paths s — Mt 3:3 — 2117
way of the Lord, make his paths s — Mk 1:3 — 2117
way of the Lord, make his paths s — Lk 3:4 — 2117
and the crooked shall be made s — Lk 3:5 — 2117
and immediately she was made s — Lk 13:13 — 461
Make s the way of the Lord, as — Jn 1:23 — 2116
into the street which is called S — Acts 9:11 — 2117
we came with a s course to — Acts 16:11 — 2113
we came with a s course unto Coos — Acts 21:1 — 2113
make s paths for your feet, lest — Heb 12:13 — 3717

STRAIGHTWAY
the city, ye shall s find him — 1Sa 9:13 — 3651
Then Saul fell s all along on the — 1Sa 28:20 — 4116
He goeth after her s, as an ox — Prov 7:22 — 6597
s there remained no strength in — Dan 10:17 — 6258
went up s out of the water — Mt 3:16 — 2117
they s left their nets, and — Mt 4:20 — 2112
And s Jesus constrained his — Mt 14:22 — 2112
But s Jesus spake unto them, — Mt 14:27 — 2112
s ye shall find an ass tied, and a — Mt 21:2 — 2112
and s he will send them — Mt 21:3 — 2112
and s took his journey — Mt 25:15 — 2112
s one of them ran, and took a — Mt 27:48 — 2112
s coming up out of the water, he — Mk 1:10 — 2112
s they forsook their nets, and — Mk 1:18 — 2112
And s he called them — Mk 1:20 — 2112
s on the sabbath day he entered — Mk 1:21 — 2112
s many were gathered together, — Mk 2:2 — 2112
s took counsel with the Herodians — Mk 3:6 — 2112
s the fountain of her blood was — Mk 5:29 — 2112
s the damsel arose, and walked — Mk 5:42 — 2112
she came in s with haste unto the — Mk 6:25 — 2112
s he constrained his disciples to — Mk 6:45 — 2112
out of the ship, s they knew him, — Mk 6:54 — 2112
s his ears were opened, and the — Mk 7:35 — 2112
s he entered into a ship with his — Mk 8:10 — 2112
s all the people, when they — Mk 9:15 — 2112
he saw him, s the spirit tare him — Mk 9:20 — 2112
s the father of the child cried — Mk 9:24 — 2112
s he will send him hither — Mk 11:3 — 2112
as he was come, he goeth s to him — Mk 14:45 — 2112
s in the morning the chief — Mk 15:1 — 2112
drunk old wine s desireth new — Lk 5:39 — 2112
spirit came again, and she arose s — Lk 8:55 — 3916
s ye say, There cometh a shower — Lk 12:54 — 2112
will not s pull him out on the — Lk 14:5 — 2112
himself, and shall s glorify him — Jn 13:32 — 2117
Then fell she down s at his feet — Acts 5:10 — 3916
s he preached Christ in the — Acts 9:20 — 2112
and was baptized, he and all his, s — Acts 16:33 — 3916
Then s they departed from him — Acts 22:29 — 2112
I sent s to thee, and gave — Acts 23:30 — 1824
s forgetteth what manner of man — Jas 1:24 — 2112

STRAIN
which s at a gnat, and swallow a — Mt 23:24 — 1368

STRAIT
Israel saw that they were in a s — 1Sa 13:6 — 6887
said unto Gad, I am in a great s — 2Sa 24:14 — 6887
dwell with thee is too s for us — 2Kin 6:1 — 6862
said unto Gad, I am in a great s — 1Chr 21:13 — 6887
out of the s into a broad place — Job 36:16 — 6862
ears, The place is too s for me — Is 49:20 — 6862
Enter ye in at the s gate — Mt 7:13 — 4728
Because s is the gate, and narrow — Mt 7:14 — 4728
Strive to enter in at the s gate — Lk 13:24 — 4728
For I am in a s betwixt two — Phil 1:23 — 4912

STRAITEN
seek their lives, shall s them — Jer 19:9 — 6693

STRAITENED
steps of his strength shall be s — Job 18:7 — 3334
and the breadth of the waters is s — Job 37:10 — 4164
goest, thy steps shall not be s — Prov 4:12 — 3334
was s more than the lowest — Eze 42:6 — 680
is the spirit of the LORD s — Mic 2:7 — 7114
and how am I s till it be — Lk 12:50 — 4912
Ye are not s in us, but ye are — 2Cor 6:12 — 4729
but ye are s in your own bowels — 2Cor 6:12 — 4729

STRAITENETH
the nations, and s them again — Job 12:23 — 5148

STRAITEST
that after the most s sect of our — Acts 26:5 — 196

STRAITLY
The man asked us s of our state — Gen 43:7
for he had s sworn the children — Ex 13:19
Now Jericho was s shut up because — Josh 6:1
Thy father s charged the people — 1Sa 14:28
Jesus s charged them, saying, See — Mt 9:30
he s charged him, and forthwith — Mk 1:43
he s charged them that they — Mk 3:12 — 4183
he charged them s that no man — Mk 5:43 — 4183
he s charged them, and commanded — Lk 9:21
let us s threaten them, that they — Acts 4:17 — 547
Did not we s command you that ye — Acts 5:28

STRAITNESS
thee, in the siege, and in the s — Deut 28:53 — 4689
him in the siege, and in the s — Deut 28:55 — 4689
things secretly in the siege and s — Deut 28:57 — 4689
broad place, where there is no s — Job 36:16 — 4164
of his friend in the siege and s — Jer 19:9 — 4689

STRAITS
his sufficiency he shall be in s — Job 20:22 — 3334
overtook her between the s — Lam 1:3 — 4712

STRAKE
s sail, and so were driven — Acts 27:17 — 5465

STRAKES
and pilled white s in them — Gen 30:37 — 6479
walls of the house with hollow s — Lev 14:37 — 8258

STRANGE
Put away the s gods that are — Gen 35:2 — 5236
they gave unto Jacob all the s — Gen 35:4 — 5236
but made himself s unto them — Gen 42:7 — 5234
have been a stranger in a s land — Ex 2:22 — 5237
I have been an alien in a s land — Ex 18:3 — 5237
to sell her unto a s nation he — Ex 21:8 — 5237
shall offer no s incense thereon — Ex 30:9 — 2114
offered s fire before the LORD, — Lev 10:1 — 2114
when they offered s fire before — Num 3:4 — 2114
when they offered s fire before — Num 26:61 — 2114
and there was no s god with him — Deut 32:12 — 5236
him to jealousy with s gods — Deut 32:16 — 2114
forsake the LORD, and serve s gods — Josh 24:20 — 5236
the s gods which are among you, — Josh 24:23 — 5236
they put away the s gods from — Judg 10:16 — 5236
for thou art the son of a s woman — Judg 11:2 — 312
hearts, then put away the s gods — 1Sa 7:3 — 5236
king Solomon loved many s women — 1Kin 11:1 — 5237
did he for all his s wives — 1Kin 11:8 — 5237
drunk s waters, and with the sole — 2Kin 19:24 — 2114
away the altars of the s gods — 2Chr 14:3 — 5236
And he took away the s gods — 2Chr 33:15 — 5236
have taken s wives of the people — Ezr 10:2 — 5237
and have taken s wives, to — Ezr 10:10 — 5237
of the land, and from the s wives — Ezr 10:11 — 5237
s wives in our cities come at — Ezr 10:14 — 5237
s wives by the first day of the — Ezr 10:17 — 5237
were found that had taken s wives — Ezr 10:18 — 5237
All these had taken s wives — Ezr 10:44 — 5237
our God in marrying s wives — Neh 13:27 — 5237
that ye make yourselves s to me — Job 19:3 — 1970
My breath is s to my wife — Job 19:17 — 2114
a s punishment to the workers of — Job 31:3 — 5235
out our hands to a s god — Ps 44:20 — 2114
There shall no s god be in thee — Ps 81:9 — 2114
shalt thou worship any s god — Ps 81:9 — 5236
Jacob from a people of s language — Ps 114:1 — 3937
sing the LORD's song in a s land — Ps 137:4 — 5236
from the hand of s children — Ps 144:7 — 5236
me from the hand of s children — Ps 144:11 — 2114
To deliver thee from the s woman — Prov 2:16 — 2114
For the lips of a s woman drop as — Prov 5:3 — 2114
son, be ravished with a s woman — Prov 5:20 — 2114
of the tongue of a s woman — Prov 6:24 — 5237
may keep thee from the s woman — Prov 7:5 — 2114
a pledge of him for a s woman — Prov 20:16 — 5237
The way of man is froward and s — Prov 21:8 — 2114
The mouth of s women is a deep — Prov 22:14 — 2114
a s woman is a narrow pit — Prov 23:27 — 5237
Thine eyes shall behold s women — Prov 23:33 — 2114
a pledge of him for a s woman — Prov 27:13 — 5237
and shalt set it with s slips — Is 17:10 — 2114
he may do his work, his s work — Is 28:21 — 2114
bring to pass his act, his s act — Is 28:21 — 5237
when there was no s god among you — Is 43:12 — 2114
plant of a s vine unto me — Jer 2:21 — 5237
served s gods in your land, so — Jer 5:19 — 5236
graven images, and with s vanities — Jer 8:19 — 5236
sent to a people of a s speech — Eze 3:5 — 6012
Not to many people of a s speech — Eze 3:6 — 6012
most strong holds with a s god — Dan 11:39 — 5236
for they have begotten s children — Hos 5:7 — 2114
they were counted as a s thing — Hos 8:12 — 2114
as are clothed with s apparel — Zeph 1:8 — 5237

S

married the daughter of a *s* god Mal 2:11 5236
We have seen *s* things to day Lk 5:26 *3861*
seed should sojourn in a *s* land Acts 7:6 *245*
to be a setter forth of *s* gods Acts 17:18 *3581*
certain *s* things to our ears Acts 17:20 *3579*
them even unto *s* cities Acts 26:11 *1854*
of promise, as in a *s* country Heb 11:9 *245*
about with divers and *s* doctrines Heb 13:9 *3581*
Wherein they think it *s* that ye 1Pet 4:4 *3579*
think it not *s* concerning the 1Pet 4:12 *3579*
as though some *s* thing happened 1Pet 4:12 *3581*
and going after *s* flesh, are set Jude 7 *2087*

STRANGELY
should behave themselves *s* Deut 32:27 5234

STRANGER
a *s* in a land that is not theirs Gen 15:13 1616
the land wherein thou art a *s* Gen 17:8 4033
or bought with money of any *s* Gen 17:12
and bought with money of the *s* Gen 17:27
I am a *s* and a sojourner with you Gen 23:4 1616
the land wherein thou art a *s* Gen 28:4 4033
land wherein his father was a *s* Gen 37:1 4033
I have been a *s* in a strange land Ex 2:22 1616
of Israel, whether he be a *s* Ex 12:19 1616
There shall no *s* eat thereof Ex 12:43
when a *s* shall sojourn with thee, Ex 12:48 1616
unto the *s* that sojourneth among Ex 12:49 1616
nor thy *s* that is within thy Ex 20:10 1616
Thou shalt neither vex a *s* Ex 22:21 1616
Also thou shalt not oppress a *s* Ex 23:9 1616
for ye know the heart of a *s* Ex 23:9 1616
the son of thy handmaid, and the *s* Ex 23:12 1616
but a *s* shall not eat thereof, Ex 29:33 2114
putteth any of it upon a *s* Ex 30:33 2114
or a *s* that sojourneth among you Lev 16:29 1616
blood, neither shall any *s* that Lev 17:12 1616
one of your own country, or a *s* Lev 17:15 1616
nor any *s* that sojourneth among Lev 18:26 1616
leave them for the poor and *s* Lev 19:10 1616
if a *s* sojourn with thee in your Lev 19:33 1616
But the *s* that dwelleth with you Lev 19:34 1616
There shall no *s* eat of the holy Lev 22:10 2114
daughter also be married unto a *s* Lev 22:12
but there shall no *s* eat thereof Lev 22:13 2114
them unto the poor, and to the *s* Lev 23:22 1616
as well the *s*, as he that is born Lev 24:16 1616
manner of law, as well for the *s* Lev 24:22 1616
for thy *s* that sojourneth with Lev 25:6 8453
yea, though he be a *s*, or a Lev 25:35 1616
a sojourner or *s* wax rich by thee Lev 25:47 8453
unto the *s* or sojourner by thee Lev 25:47 1616
the *s* that cometh nigh shall be Num 1:51 2114
the *s* that cometh nigh shall be Num 3:10 2114
the *s* that cometh nigh shall be Num 3:38 2114
if a *s* shall sojourn among you, Num 9:14 1616
one ordinance, both for the *s* Num 9:14 1616
if a *s* sojourn with you, or Num 15:14 1616
also for the *s* that sojourneth Num 15:15 1616
so shall the *s* be before the LORD Num 15:15 1616
for the *s* that sojourneth with Num 15:16 1616
the *s* that sojourneth among them Num 15:26 1616
for the *s* that sojourneth among Num 15:29 1616
he be born in the land, or a *s* Num 15:30 1616
the children of Israel, that no *s* Num 16:40
a *s* shall not come nigh unto you Num 18:4 2114
the *s* that cometh nigh shall be Num 18:7 2114
unto the *s* that sojourneth among Num 19:10 1616
children of Israel, and for the *s* Num 35:15 1616
and the *s* that is with him Deut 1:16 1616
nor thy *s* that is within thy Deut 5:14 1616
and widow, and loveth the *s* Deut 10:18 1616
Love ye therefore the *s* Deut 10:19 1616
unto the *s* that is in thy gates Deut 14:21 1616
inheritance with thee,) and the *s* Deut 14:29 1616
is within thy gates, and the *s* Deut 16:11 1616
maidservant, and the Levite, the *s* Deut 16:14 1616
thou mayest not set a *s* over thee Deut 17:15
because thou wast a *s* in his land Deut 23:7 1616
Unto a *s* thou mayest lend upon Deut 23:20 5237
not pervert the judgment of the *s* Deut 24:17 1616
it shall be for the *s*, for the Deut 24:19 1616
it shall be for the *s*, for the Deut 24:20 1616
it shall be for the *s*, for the Deut 24:21 1616
shall not marry without unto a *s* Deut 25:5
and the *s* that is among you Deut 26:11 1616
given it unto the Levite, the *s* Deut 26:12 1616
unto the Levite, and unto the *s* Deut 26:13 1616
perverteth the judgment of the *s* Deut 27:19 1616
The *s* that is within thee shall Deut 28:43 1616
thy *s* that is in thy camp, from Deut 29:11 1616
the *s* that shall come from a far Deut 29:22 5237
thy *s* that is within thy gates, Deut 31:12 1616
of the LORD, as well the *s* Josh 8:33 1616
for the *s* that sojourneth among Josh 20:9 1616
aside hither into the city of a *s* Judg 19:12 5237
knowledge of me, seeing I am a *s* Ruth 2:10 5237
he answered, I am the son of a *s* 2Sa 1:13
for thou art a *s*, and also an 2Sa 15:19 5237
there was no *s* with us in the 1Kin 3:18 2114
Moreover concerning a *s*, that is 1Kin 8:41 5237
that the *s* calleth to thee for 1Kin 8:43 5237
Moreover concerning the *s* 2Chr 6:32 5237
that the *s* calleth to thee for 2Chr 6:33 5237
given, and no *s* passed among them Job 15:19 2114
and my maids, count me for a *s* Job 19:15 2114
The *s* did not lodge in the street Job 31:32 1616
for I am a *s* with thee, and a Ps 39:12 1616
I am become a *s* unto my brethren, Ps 69:8 2114
They slay the widow and the *s* Ps 94:6 1616
I am a *s* in the earth Ps 119:19 1616
even from the *s* which flattereth Prov 2:16 5237
labours be in the house of a *s* Prov 5:10 5237
and embrace the bosom of a *s* Prov 5:20 5237
hast stricken thy hand with a *s* Prov 6:1 2114
from the *s* which flattereth with Prov 7:5 5237
surety for a *s* shall smart for it Prov 11:15 2114
a *s* doth not intermeddle with his Prov 14:10 2114
garment that is surety for a *s* Prov 20:16 2114
a *s*, and not thine own lips Prov 27:2 5237
garment that is surety for a *s* Prov 27:13 2114
to eat thereof, but a *s* eateth it Eccl 6:2
Neither let the son of the *s* Is 56:3 5236
Also the sons of the *s*, that join Is 56:6 5236
the sons of the *s* shall not drink Is 62:8 5236
If ye oppress not the *s*, the Jer 7:6 1616
thou be as a *s* in the land Jer 14:8 1616
no wrong, do no violence to the *s* Jer 22:3 1616
or of the *s* that sojourneth in Eze 14:7 1616
dealt by oppression with the *s* Eze 22:7 1616
have oppressed the *s* wrongfully Eze 22:29 1616
No *s*, uncircumcised in heart, nor Eze 44:9
of any *s* that is among the Eze 44:9
in what tribe the *s* sojourneth Eze 47:23 1616
in the day that he became a *s* Obad 12 5235
widow, nor the fatherless, the *s* Zec 7:10 1616
turn aside the *s* from his right Mal 3:5 1616
I was a *s*, and ye took me in Mt 25:35 *3581*
When saw we thee a *s*, and took Mt 25:38 *3581*
I was a *s*, and ye took me not in Mt 25:43 *3581*
an hungred, or athirst, or a *s* Mt 25:44 *3581*
to give glory to God, save this *s* Lk 17:18 *241*
Art thou only a *s* in Jerusalem Lk 24:18 *3939*
a *s* will they not follow, but Jn 10:5 *245*
was a *s* in the land of Madian, Acts 7:29 *3941*

STRANGER'S
Neither from a *s* hand shall ye Lev 22:25
or to the stock of the *s* family Lev 25:47 1616

STRANGERS
Are we not counted of him *s* Gen 31:15 5237
the land wherein they were *s* Gen 36:7 4033
pilgrimage, wherein they were *s* Ex 6:4 1481
for ye were *s* in the land of Ex 22:21 1616
seeing ye were *s* in the land of Ex 23:9 1616
or of the *s* which sojourn among Lev 17:8 1616
or of the *s* that sojourn among Lev 17:10 1616
or of the *s* that sojourn among Lev 17:13 1616
for ye were *s* in the land of Lev 19:34 1616
or of the *s* that sojourn in Lev 20:2 1616
of Israel, or of the *s* in Israel Lev 22:18 1616
for ye are *s* and sojourners with Lev 25:23 1616
the *s* that do sojourn among you Lev 25:45 8453
for ye were *s* in the land of Deut 10:19 1616
or of thy *s* that are in thy land Deut 24:14 1616
the gods of the *s* of the land Deut 31:16 5236
the *s* that were conversant among Josh 8:35 1616
S shall submit themselves unto me 2Sa 22:45
S shall fade away, and they shall 2Sa 22:46
but few, even a few, and *s* in it 1Chr 16:19 1481
to gather together the *s* that 1Chr 22:2 1616
For we are *s* before thee, and 1Chr 29:15 1616
Solomon numbered all the *s* that 2Chr 2:17
the *s* with them out of Ephraim and 2Chr 15:9 1481
the *s* that came out of the land 2Chr 30:25 1616
separated themselves from all *s* Neh 9:2
Thus cleansed I them from all *s* Neh 13:30 5236
the *s* shall submit themselves Ps 18:44
The *s* shall fade away, and be Ps 18:45
For *s* are risen up against me, and Ps 54:3 2114
yea, very few, and *s* in it Ps 105:12 1481
let the *s* spoil his labour Ps 109:11 2114
The LORD preserveth the *s* Ps 146:9 1616
Lest *s* be filled with thy wealth Prov 5:10 2114
s devour it in your presence, and Is 1:7 2114
is desolate, as overthrown by *s* Is 1:7 2114
themselves in the children of *s* Is 2:6 5237
of the fat ones shall *s* eat Is 5:17 1481
the *s* shall be joined with them, Is 14:1 1616
a palace of *s* to be no city Is 25:2 2114
shalt bring down the noise of *s* Is 25:5 2114
of thy *s* shall be like small dust Is 29:5 2114
the sons of *s* shall build up thy Is 60:10 5236
s shall stand and feed your flocks Is 61:5 2114
for I have loved *s*, and after them Jer 2:25 2114
to the *s* under every green tree Jer 3:13 2114
so shall ye serve *s* in a land Jer 5:19 2114
s shall no more serve themselves Jer 30:8 2114
days in the land where ye be *s* Jer 35:7 1481
for *s* are come into the Jer 51:51 2114
Our inheritance is turned to *s* Lam 5:2 2114
the hands of the *s* for a prey Eze 7:21 2114
deliver you into the hands of *s* Eze 11:9 2114
which taketh *s* instead of her Eze 16:32 2114
I will bring *s* upon thee, the Eze 28:7 2114
uncircumcised by the hand of *s* Eze 28:10 2114
that is therein, by the hand of *s* Eze 30:12 2114
And *s*, the terrible of the nations Eze 31:12 2114
have brought into my sanctuary *s* Eze 44:7
to the *s* that sojourn among you, Eze 47:22 1616
S have devoured his strength, and Hos 7:9 2114
the *s* shall swallow it up Hos 8:7 2114
there shall no *s* pass through her Joel 3:17 2114
in the day that the *s* carried Obad 11 2114
of their own children, or of *s* Mt 17:25 *245*
Peter saith unto him, Of *s* Mt 17:26 *245*
the potter's field, to bury *s* in Mt 27:7 *3581*
for they know not the voice of *s* Jn 10:5 *245*
s of Rome, Jews and proselytes, Acts 2:10 *1927*
dwelt as *s* in the land of Egypt Acts 13:17
s which were there spent their Acts 17:21 *3581*
s from the covenants of promise, Eph 2:12 *3581*
Now therefore ye are no more *s* Eph 2:19 *3581*
up children, if she have lodged *s* 1Ti 5:10 *3580*
and confessed that they were *s* Heb 11:13 *3581*
Be not forgetful to entertain *s* Heb 13:2 *5381*
to the *s* scattered throughout 1Pet 1:1 *3927*
beloved, I beseech you as *s* 1Pet 2:11 *3941*
doest to the brethren, and to *s* 3Jn 5 *3581*

STRANGERS'
thine own, and not *s* with thee Prov 5:17 2114

STRANGLED
s for his lionesses, and filled Nah 2:12 2614
fornication, and from things *s* Acts 15:20 *4156*
and from blood, and from things *s* Acts 15:29 *4156*
idols, and from blood, and from *s* Acts 21:25 *4156*

STRANGLING
So that my soul chooseth *s* Job 7:15 4267

STRAW
moreover unto him, We have both *s* Gen 24:25 8401
he ungirded his camels, and gave *s* Gen 24:32 8401
give the people *s* to make brick Ex 5:7 8401
go and gather *s* for themselves Ex 5:7 8401
Pharaoh, I will not give you *s* Ex 5:10 8401
get you *s* where ye can find it Ex 5:11 8401
to gather stubble instead of *s* Ex 5:12 8401
daily tasks, as when there was *s* Ex 5:13 8401
There is no *s* given unto thy Ex 5:16 8401
for there shall no *s* be given you Ex 5:18 8401
Yet there is both *s* and provender Judg 19:19 8401
s for the horses and dromedaries 1Kin 4:28 8401
He esteemeth iron as *s*, and brass Job 41:27 8401
the lion shall eat *s* like the ox Is 11:7 8401
even as *s* is trodden down for the Is 25:10 4963
lion shall eat *s* like the bullock Is 65:25 8401

STRAWED
s it upon the water, and made the Ex 32:20 2219
the trees, and *s* them in the way Mt 21:8 *4766*
gathering where thou hast not *s* Mt 25:24 *1287*
not, and gather where I have not *s* Mt 25:26 *1287*
the trees, and *s* them in the way Mk 11:8 *4766*

STREAM
at the *s* of the brooks that goeth Num 21:15 793
as the *s* of brooks they pass away Job 6:15 650
the *s* had gone over our soul Ps 124:4 5158
of the river unto the *s* of Egypt Is 27:12 5158
his breath, as an overflowing *s* Is 30:28 5158
like a *s* of brimstone, doth Is 30:33 5158
stones of the *s* is thy portion Is 57:6 5158
of the Gentiles like a flowing *s* Is 66:12 5158
A fiery *s* issued and came forth Dan 7:10 5103
and righteousness as a mighty *s* Amos 5:24 5158
the *s* beat vehemently upon that Lk 6:48 *4215*
against which the *s* did beat Lk 6:49 *4215*

STREAMS
the waters of Egypt, upon their *s* Ex 7:19 5104
hand with thy rod over the *s* Ex 8:5 5104
the *s* whereof shall make glad the Ps 46:4 6388
He brought *s* also out of the rock Ps 78:16 5140
gushed out, and the *s* overflowed Ps 78:20 5158
O LORD, as the *s* in the south Ps 126:4 650
living waters, and *s* from Lebanon Song 4:15 5140
and shall smite it in the seven *s* Is 11:15 5158
s of waters in the day of the Is 30:25 2988
us a place of broad rivers and *s* Is 33:21 2975
the *s* thereof shall be turned Is 34:9 5158
break out, and *s* in the desert Is 35:6 5158

STREET
we will abide in the *s* all night Gen 19:2 7339
into the midst of the *s* thereof Deut 13:16 7339
the doors of thy house into the *s* Josh 2:19 2351
sat him down in a *s* of the city Judg 19:15 7339
man in the *s* of the city Judg 19:17 7339
only lodge not in the *s* Judg 19:20 7339
them from the *s* of Beth-shan 2Sa 21:12 7339
stamp them as the mire of the *s* 2Sa 22:43 2351
them together into the east *s* 2Chr 29:4 7339
in the *s* of the gate of the city 2Chr 32:6 7339
sat in the *s* of the house of God Ezr 10:9 7339
together as one man into the *s* Neh 8:1 7339
he read therein before the *s* that Neh 8:3 7339
in the *s* of the water gate, and in Neh 8:16 7339
in the *s* of the gate of Ephraim Neh 8:16 7339
Mordecai unto the *s* of the city Est 4:6 7339
through the *s* of the city Est 6:9 7339
through the *s* of the city Est 6:11 7339
and he shall have no name in the *s* Job 18:17
when I prepared my seat in the *s* Job 29:7 7339
stranger did not lodge in the *s* Job 31:32 2351
through the *s* near her corner Prov 7:8 7784
his voice to be heard in the *s* Is 42:2 2351
body as the ground, and as the *s* Is 51:23 2351
for truth is fallen in the *s* Is 59:14 7339
of bread out of the bakers' *s* Jer 37:21 2351
for hunger in the top of every *s* Lam 2:19 2351
poured out in the top of every *s* Lam 4:1 2351
thee an high place in every *s* Eze 16:24 7339
thine high place in every *s* Eze 16:31 7339
pestilence, and blood into her *s* Eze 28:23 7339
the *s* shall be built again, and Dan 9:25 7339
go into the *s* which is called Acts 9:11 *4505*
out, and passed on through one *s* Acts 12:10 *4505*
lie in the *s* of the great city Rev 11:8 *4113*
the *s* of the city was pure gold, Rev 21:21 *4113*
In the midst of the *s* of it Rev 22:2 *4113*

STREETS
it not in the *s* of Askelon 2Sa 1:20 2351
thou shalt make *s* for thee in 1Kin 20:34 2351
them out as the dirt in the *s* Ps 18:42 2351
and guile depart not from her *s* Ps 55:11 7339
and ten thousands in our *s* Ps 144:13 2351
there be no complaining in our *s* Ps 144:14 7339
she uttereth her voice in the *s* Prov 1:20 7339
and rivers of waters in the *s* Prov 5:16 7339
Now is she without, now in the *s* Prov 7:12 7339
I shall be slain in the *s* Prov 22:13 7339
a lion is in the *s* Prov 26:13 7339

the doors shall be shut in the s	Eccl 12:4	7784
and the mourners go about the s	Eccl 12:5	7784
and go about the city in the s	Song 3:2	7784
were torn in the midst of the s	Is 5:25	2351
them down like the mire of the s	Is 10:6	2351
In their s they shall gird	Is 15:3	2351
of their houses, and in their s	Is 15:3	7339
is a crying for wine in the s	Is 24:11	2351
they lie at the head of all the s	Is 51:20	2351
and fro through the s of Jerusalem	Jer 5:1	2351
of Judah and in the s of Jerusalem	Jer 7:17	2351
from the s of Jerusalem, the	Jer 7:34	2351
and the young men from the s	Jer 9:21	7339
in the s of Jerusalem, saying,	Jer 11:6	2351
the s of Jerusalem have ye set up	Jer 11:13	2351
shall be cast out in the s of	Jer 14:16	2351
in the s of Jerusalem, that are	Jer 33:10	2351
of Judah and in the s of Jerusalem	Jer 44:6	2351
Judah, and in the s of Jerusalem	Jer 44:9	2351
Judah, and in the s of Jerusalem	Jer 44:17	2351
in the s of Jerusalem, ye, and	Jer 44:21	2351
of Moab, and in the s thereof	Jer 48:38	7339
her young men shall fall in her s	Jer 49:26	7339
shall her young men fall in the s	Jer 50:30	7339
that are thrust through in her s	Jer 51:4	2351
swoon in the s of the city	Lam 2:11	7339
the wounded in the s of the city	Lam 2:12	7339
old lie on the ground in the s	Lam 2:21	2351
delicately are desolate in the s	Lam 4:5	2351
they are not known in the s	Lam 4:8	2351
wandered as blind men in the s	Lam 4:14	2351
steps, that we cannot go in our s	Lam 4:18	7339
shall cast their silver in the s	Eze 7:19	2351
ye have filled the s thereof with	Eze 11:6	2351
shall he tread down all thy s	Eze 26:11	2351
Wailing shall be in all s	Amos 5:16	7339
trodden down as the mire of the s	Mic 7:10	2351
The chariots shall rage in the s	Nah 2:4	2351
in pieces at the top of all the s	Nah 3:10	2351
I made their s waste, that none	Zeph 3:6	2351
women dwell in the s of Jerusalem	Zec 8:4	7339
the s of the city shall be full	Zec 8:5	7339
and girls playing in the s thereof	Zec 8:5	7339
and fine gold as the mire of the s	Zec 9:3	2351
the mire of the s in the battle	Zec 10:5	2351
do in the synagogues and in the s	Mt 6:2	*4505*
and in the corners of the s	Mt 6:5	*4113*
any man hear his voice in the s	Mt 12:19	*4113*
they laid the sick in the s	Mk 6:56	*58*
ways out into the s of the same	Lk 10:10	*4113*
and thou hast taught in our s	Lk 13:26	*4113*
Go out quickly into the s	Lk 14:21	*4113*
brought forth the sick into the s	Acts 5:15	*4113*

STRENGTH

henceforth yield unto thee her s	Gen 4:12	3581
might, and the beginning of my s	Gen 49:3	202
But his bow abode in s, and the	Gen 49:24	386
for by s of hand the LORD brought	Ex 13:3	2392
By s of hand the LORD brought us	Ex 13:14	2392
for by s of hand the LORD brought	Ex 13:16	2392
the sea returned to his s when	Ex 14:27	386
The LORD is my s and song, and he	Ex 15:2	5797
in thy s unto thy holy habitation	Ex 15:13	5797
your s shall be spent in vain	Lev 26:20	3581
as it were the s of a unicorn	Num 23:22	8443
as it were the s of a unicorn	Num 24:8	8443
for he is the beginning of his s	Deut 21:17	202
and as thy days, so shall thy s be	Deut 33:25	1679
that stood still in their s	Josh 11:13	8510
as my s was then, even so is my	Josh 14:11	3581
was then, even so is my s now	Josh 14:11	3581
my soul, thou hast trodden down s	Judg 5:21	5797
for as the man is, so is his s	Judg 8:21	1369
and see wherein his great s lieth	Judg 16:5	3581
thee, wherein thy great s lieth	Judg 16:6	3581
So his s was not known	Judg 16:9	3581
told me wherein thy great s lieth	Judg 16:15	3581
then my s will go from me, and I	Judg 16:17	3581
him, and his s went from him	Judg 16:19	3581
that stumbled are girded with s	1Sa 2:4	2428
for by s shall no man prevail	1Sa 2:9	3581
and he shall give s unto his king	1Sa 2:10	5797
also the S of Israel will not lie	1Sa 15:29	5331
and there was no s in him	1Sa 28:20	3581
and eat, that thou mayest have s	1Sa 28:22	3581
God is my s and power	2Sa 22:33	4581
hast girded me with s to battle	2Sa 22:40	2428
went in the s of that meat forty	1Kin 19:8	3581
Jehu drew a bow with his full s	2Kin 9:24	3027
I have counsel and s for the war	2Kin 18:20	1369
there is not s to bring forth	2Kin 19:3	3581
Seek the LORD and his s, seek his	1Chr 16:11	5797
s and gladness are in his place	1Chr 16:27	5797
give unto the LORD glory and s	1Chr 16:28	5797
able men for s for the service	1Chr 26:8	3581
make great, and to give s unto all	1Chr 29:12	2388
place, thou, and the ark of thy s	2Chr 6:41	5797
s again in the days of Abijah	2Chr 13:20	3581
The s of the bearers of burdens	Neh 4:10	3581
for the joy of the LORD is your s	Neh 8:10	4581
What is my s, that I should hope	Job 6:11	3581
Is my s the s of stones	Job 6:12	3581
is wise in heart, and mighty in s	Job 9:4	3581
If I speak of s, lo, he is strong	Job 9:19	3581
With him is wisdom and s, he hath	Job 12:13	1369
With him is s and wisdom	Job 12:16	5797
and weakeneth the s of the mighty	Job 12:21	4206
The steps of his s shall be	Job 18:7	202
His s shall be hungerbitten, and	Job 18:12	202
It shall devour the s of his skin	Job 18:13	905
of death shall devour his s	Job 18:13	905
One dieth in his full s, being	Job 21:23	6106
but he would put s in me	Job 23:6	
thou the arm that hath no s	Job 26:2	5797
whereto might the s of their	Job 30:2	3581
he is mighty in s and wisdom	Job 36:5	3581
not gold, nor all the forces of s	Job 36:19	3581
and to the great rain of his s	Job 37:6	5797
trust him, because his s is great	Job 39:11	3581
Hath thou given the horse s	Job 39:19	1369
the valley, and rejoiceth in his s	Job 39:21	3581
his s is in his loins, and his	Job 40:16	3581
In his neck remaineth s, and	Job 41:22	5797
s because of thine enemies	Ps 8:2	5797
I will love thee, O LORD, my s	Ps 18:1	2391
my God, my s, in whom I will	Ps 18:2	6697
It is God that girdeth me with s	Ps 18:32	2428
girded me with s unto the battle	Ps 18:39	2428
in thy sight, O LORD, my s	Ps 19:14	6697
the saving s of his right hand	Ps 20:6	1369
The king shall joy in thy s	Ps 21:1	5797
exalted, LORD, in thine own s	Ps 21:13	5797
My s is dried up like a potsherd	Ps 22:15	3581
O my s, haste thee to help me	Ps 22:19	360
the LORD is the s of my life	Ps 27:1	4581
The LORD is my s and my shield	Ps 28:7	5797
The LORD is their s, and he is the	Ps 28:8	5797
is the saving s of his anointed	Ps 28:8	4581
give unto the LORD glory and s	Ps 29:1	5797
LORD will give s unto his people	Ps 29:11	5797
for thou art my s	Ps 31:4	4581
my s faileth because of mine	Ps 31:10	3581
man is not delivered by much s	Ps 33:16	3581
he deliver any by his great s	Ps 33:17	2428
he is their s in the time of	Ps 37:39	4581
My heart panteth, my s faileth me	Ps 38:10	3581
O spare me, that I may recover s	Ps 39:13	1082
For thou art the God of my s	Ps 43:2	4581
God is our refuge and s, a very	Ps 46:1	5797
the man that made not God his s	Ps 52:7	4581
by thy name, and judge me by thy s	Ps 54:1	1369
Because of his s will I wait upon	Ps 59:9	5797
Unto thee, O my s, will I sing	Ps 59:17	5797
also is the s of mine head	Ps 60:7	4581
the rock of my s, and my refuge	Ps 62:7	5797
Which by his s setteth fast the	Ps 65:6	3581
Thy God hath commanded thy s	Ps 68:28	5797
Ascribe ye s unto God	Ps 68:34	5797
Israel, and his s is in the clouds	Ps 68:34	5797
God of Israel is he that giveth s	Ps 68:35	5797
forsake me not when my s faileth	Ps 71:9	3581
will go in the s of the Lord GOD	Ps 71:16	1369
shewed thy s unto this generation	Ps 71:18	2220
but their s is firm	Ps 73:4	193
but God is the s of my heart	Ps 73:26	6697
didst divide the sea by thy s	Ps 74:13	5797
declared thy s among the people	Ps 77:14	5797
the praises of the LORD, and his s	Ps 78:4	5807
the chief of their s in the	Ps 78:51	202
delivered his s into captivity	Ps 78:61	5797
and Manasseh stir up thy s	Ps 80:2	1369
Sing aloud unto God our s	Ps 81:1	5797
is the man whose s is in thee	Ps 84:5	5797
They go from s to s	Ps 84:7	2428
give thy s unto thy servant, and	Ps 86:16	5797
I am as a man that hath no s	Ps 88:4	353
For thou art the glory of their s	Ps 89:17	5797
if by reason of s they be	Ps 90:10	1369
years, yet is their s labour	Ps 90:10	7296
the LORD is clothed with s	Ps 93:1	5797
the s of the hills is his also	Ps 95:4	8443
s and beauty are in his sanctuary	Ps 96:6	5797
give unto the LORD glory and s	Ps 96:7	5797
The king's s also loveth judgment	Ps 99:4	5797
He weakened my s in the way	Ps 102:23	3581
ye his angels, that excel in s	Ps 103:20	3581
Seek the LORD, and his s	Ps 105:4	5797
land, the chief of all their s	Ps 105:36	202
also is the s of mine head	Ps 108:8	4581
send the rod of thy s out of Zion	Ps 110:2	5797
The LORD is my s and song, and is	Ps 118:14	5797
thou, and the ark of thy s	Ps 132:8	5797
me with s in my soul	Ps 138:3	5797
the s of my salvation, thou hast	Ps 140:7	5797
Blessed be the LORD my s, which	Ps 144:1	6697
not in the s of the horse	Ps 147:10	1369
I have s	Prov 8:14	1369
of the LORD is s to the upright	Prov 10:29	4581
increase is by the s of the ox	Prov 14:4	3581
The glory of young men is their s	Prov 20:29	3581
casteth down the s of the	Prov 21:22	5797
a man of knowledge increaseth s	Prov 24:5	3581
day of adversity, thy s is small	Prov 24:10	3581
Give not thy s unto women	Prov 31:3	2428
She girdeth her loins with s	Prov 31:17	5797
S and honour are her clothing	Prov 31:25	5797
said I, Wisdom is better than s	Eccl 9:16	1369
edge, then must he put to more s	Eccl 10:10	2428
princes eat in due season, for s	Eccl 10:17	1369
men of s to mingle strong drink	Is 5:22	2428
By the s of my hand I have done	Is 10:13	3581
for the LORD JEHOVAH is my s	Is 12:2	5797
been mindful of the rock of thy s	Is 17:10	4581
even the s of the sea, saying, I	Is 23:4	4581
there is no more s	Is 23:10	4206
for your s is laid waste	Is 23:14	4581
thou hast been a s to the poor	Is 25:4	4581
a s to the needy in his distress	Is 25:4	4581
the LORD JEHOVAH is everlasting s	Is 26:4	6697
Or let him take hold of my s	Is 27:5	4581
for s to them that turn the	Is 28:6	1369
themselves in the s of Pharaoh	Is 30:2	4581
Therefore shall the s of Pharaoh	Is 30:3	4581
this, Their s is to sit still	Is 30:7	7293
and in confidence shall be your s	Is 30:15	1369
of thy times, and s of salvation	Is 33:6	2633
I have counsel and s for war	Is 36:5	1369
there is not s to bring forth	Is 37:3	3581
tidings, lift up thy voice with s	Is 40:9	3581
have no might he increaseth s	Is 40:29	6109
upon the LORD shall renew their s	Is 40:31	3581
and let the people renew their s	Is 41:1	3581
of his anger, and the s of battle	Is 42:25	5807
worketh it with the s of his arms	Is 44:12	3581
he is hungry, and his s faileth	Is 44:12	3581
LORD have I righteousness and s	Is 45:24	5797
I have spent my s for nought	Is 49:4	3581
the LORD, and my God shall be my s	Is 49:5	5797
Awake, awake, put on s, O arm of	Is 51:9	5797
put on thy s, O Zion	Is 52:1	5797
hand, and by the arm of his s	Is 62:8	5797
in the greatness of his s	Is 63:1	3581
bring down their s to the earth	Is 63:6	5332
where is thy zeal and thy s	Is 63:15	1369
O LORD, my s, and my fortress, and	Jer 16:19	5797
deliver all the s of this city	Jer 20:5	2633
fortify the height of her s	Jer 51:53	5797
gone without s before the pursuer	Lam 1:6	3581
he hath made my s to fall	Lam 1:14	3581
And I said, My s and my hope is	Lam 3:18	5331
the excellency of your s	Eze 24:21	5797
day when I take from them their s	Eze 24:25	4581
my fury upon Sin, the s of Egypt	Eze 30:15	4581
the pomp of her s shall cease in	Eze 30:18	5797
and the pomp of her s shall cease	Eze 33:28	5797
given thee a kingdom, power, and s	Dan 2:37	8632
be in it of the s of the iron	Dan 2:41	5326
and there remained no s in me	Dan 10:8	3581
corruption, and I retained no s	Dan 10:8	3581
upon me, and I have retained no s	Dan 10:16	3581
there remained no s in me	Dan 10:17	3581
by his s through his riches he	Dan 11:2	2394
shall there be any s to withstand	Dan 11:15	3581
with the s of his whole kingdom	Dan 11:17	8633
shall pollute the sanctuary of s	Dan 11:31	4581
Strangers have devoured his s	Hos 7:9	3581
by his s he had power with God	Hos 12:3	202
tree and the vine do yield their s	Joel 2:22	2428
the s of the children of Israel	Joel 3:16	4581
shall bring down thy s from thee	Amos 3:11	5797
taken to us horns by our own s	Amos 6:13	2392
and feed in the s of the LORD	Mic 5:4	5797
Ethiopia and Egypt were her s	Nah 3:9	6109
shalt seek s because of the enemy	Nah 3:11	4581
The LORD God is my s, and he will	Hab 3:19	2428
I will destroy the s of the	Hag 2:22	2392
of Jerusalem shall be my s in the	Zec 12:5	556
all thy mind, and with all thy s	Mk 12:30	*2479*
all the soul, and with all the s	Mk 12:33	*2479*
He hath shewed s with his arm	Lk 1:51	*2904*
all thy soul, and with all thy s	Lk 10:27	*2479*
feet and ancle bones received s	Acts 3:7	*4732*
But Saul increased the more in s	Acts 9:22	*1743*
For when we were yet without s	Rom 5:6	*772*
and the s of sin is the law	1Cor 15:56	*1411*
pressed out of measure, above s	2Cor 1:8	*1411*
for my s is made perfect in	2Cor 12:9	*1411*
otherwise it is of no s at all	Heb 9:17	*2480*
received s to conceive seed	Heb 11:11	*1411*
was as the sun shineth in his s	Rev 1:16	*1411*
for thou hast a little s, and hast	Rev 3:8	*1411*
power, and riches, and wisdom, and s	Rev 5:12	*2479*
Now is come salvation, and s	Rev 12:10	*1411*
their power and s unto the beast	Rev 17:13	*1849*

STRENGTHEN

and encourage him, and s him	Deut 3:28	553
s me, I pray thee, only this once	Judg 16:28	2388
s thyself, and mark, and see what	1Kin 20:22	2388
to s their hands in the work of	Ezr 6:22	2388
Now therefore, O God, s my hands	Neh 6:9	2388
But I would s you with my mouth	Job 16:5	553
sanctuary, and s thee out of Zion	Ps 20:2	5582
and he shall s thine heart	Ps 27:14	553
he shall s your heart, all ye	Ps 31:24	553
The LORD will s him upon the bed	Ps 41:3	5582
s, O God, that which thou hast	Ps 68:28	5810
mine arm also shall s him	Ps 89:21	553
s thou me according unto thy word	Ps 119:28	6965
s him with thy girdle, and I will	Is 22:21	2388
to s themselves in the strength	Is 30:2	5810
they could not well s their mast	Is 33:23	2388
S ye the weak hands, and confirm	Is 35:3	2388
I will s thee	Is 41:10	553
thy cords, and s thy stakes	Is 54:2	2388
they s also the hands of	Jer 23:14	2388
neither shall any s himself in	Eze 7:13	2388
neither did she s the hand of the	Eze 16:49	2388
I will s the arms of the king of	Eze 30:24	2388
But I will s the arms of the king	Eze 30:25	2388
will s that which was sick	Eze 34:16	2388
I, stood to confirm and to s him	Dan 11:1	4581
the strong shall not s his force	Amos 2:14	553
I will s the house of Judah, and I	Zec 10:6	1396
I will s them in the LORD	Zec 10:12	1396
art converted, s thy brethren	Lk 22:32	*4741*
make you perfect, stablish, s	1Pet 5:10	*4599*
s the things which remain, that	Rev 3:2	*4741*

STRENGTHENED

Israel s himself, and sat upon the	Gen 48:2	2388
the LORD s Eglon the king of Moab	Judg 3:12	2388
be s to go down unto the host	Judg 7:11	2388
the wood, and s his hand in God	1Sa 23:16	2388
Therefore now let your hands be s	2Sa 2:7	2388
who s themselves with him in his	1Chr 11:10	2388
son of David was s in his kingdom	2Chr 1:1	2388
So they s the kingdom of Judah	2Chr 11:17	2388
had s himself, he forsook the law	2Chr 12:1	2394
So king Rehoboam s himself in	2Chr 12:13	2388
have s themselves against	2Chr 13:7	553
and s himself against Israel	2Chr 17:1	2388

S

he *s* himself, and slew all his 2Chr 21:4 2388
seventh year Jehoiada *s* himself 2Chr 23:1 2388
of God in his state, and *s* it 2Chr 24:13 553
And Amaziah *s* himself, and led 2Chr 25:11 2388
for he *s* himself exceedingly 2Chr 26:8 2388
and distressed him, but *s* him not 2Chr 28:20 2388
Also he *s* himself, and built up 2Chr 32:5 2388
s their hands with vessels of Ezr 1:6 2388
I was *s* as the hand of the LORD Ezr 7:28 2388
So they *s* their hands for this Neh 2:18 2388
thou hast *s* the weak hands Job 4:3 2388
thou hast *s* the feeble knees Job 4:4 553
s himself in his wickedness Ps 52:7 5810
For he hath *s* the bars of thy Ps 147:13 2388
when he *s* the fountains of the Prov 8:28 5810
s the hands of the wicked, that Eze 13:22 2388
The diseased have ye not *s* Eze 34:4 2388
appearance of a man, and he *s* me Dan 10:18 2388
he had spoken unto me, I was *s* Dan 10:19 2388
for thou hast *s* me Dan 10:19 2388
he that *s* her in these times Dan 11:6 2388
but he shall not be *s* by it Dan 11:12 5810
s their arms, yet do they imagine Hos 7:15 2388
he had received meat, he was *s* Acts 9:19 *1765*
to be *s* with might by his Spirit Eph 3:16 *2901*
S with all might, according to Col 1:11 *1412*
the Lord stood with me, and *s* me 2Ti 4:17 *1743*

STRENGTHENEDST
s me with strength in my soul Ps 138:3 7292

STRENGTHENETH
s himself against the Almighty Job 15:25 1396
and bread which *s* man's heart Ps 104:15 5582
with strength, and *s* her arms Prov 31:17 553
Wisdom *s* the wise more than ten Eccl 7:19 5810
which he *s* for himself among the Is 44:14 553
That *s* the spoiled against the Amos 5:9 1082
things through Christ which *s* me Phil 4:13 *1743*

STRENGTHENING
angel unto him from heaven, *s* him Lk 22:43 *1765*
in order, *s* all the disciples Acts 18:23 *1991*

STRETCH
I will *s* out my hand, and smite Ex 3:20 7971
when I *s* forth mine hand upon Ex 7:5 5186
s out thine hand upon the waters Ex 7:19 5186
S forth thine hand with thy rod Ex 8:5 5186
S out thy rod, and smite the dust Ex 8:16 5186
For now I will *s* out my hand Ex 9:15 7971
S forth thine hand toward heaven, Ex 9:22 5186
S out thine hand over the land of Ex 10:12 5186
S out thine hand toward heaven, Ex 10:21 5186
s out thine hand over the sea, and Ex 14:16 5186
S out thine hand over the sea, Ex 14:26 5186
the cherubim shall *s* forth their Ex 25:20 6566
S out the spear that is in thy Josh 8:18 5186
to *s* forth mine hand against him, 1Sa 24:6 7971
for who can *s* forth his hand 1Sa 26:9 7971
s forth mine hand against the 1Sa 26:11 7971
but I would not *s* forth mine hand 1Sa 26:23 7971
How wast thou not afraid to *s* 2Sa 1:14 7971
I will *s* over Jerusalem the line 2Kin 21:13 5186
s out thine hands toward him Job 11:13 6566
Howbeit he will not *s* out his Job 30:24 7971
s her wings toward the south Job 39:26 6566
Ethiopia shall soon *s* out her Ps 68:31 7323
thou shalt *s* forth thine hand Ps 138:7 7971
I *s* forth my hands unto thee Ps 143:6 6566
that a man can *s* himself on it Is 28:20 8311
the LORD shall *s* out his hand Is 31:3 5186
he shall *s* out upon it the line Is 34:11 5186
let them *s* forth the curtains of Is 54:2 5186
for I will *s* out my hand upon the Jer 6:12 5186
there is none to *s* forth my tent Jer 10:20 5186
therefore will I *s* out my hand Jer 15:6 5186
I will *s* out mine hand upon thee, Jer 51:25 5186
So will I *s* out my hand upon them Eze 6:14 5186
I will *s* out my hand upon him, and Eze 14:9 5186
then will I *s* out mine hand upon Eze 14:13 5186
therefore I will *s* out mine hand Eze 25:7 5186
I will also *s* out mine hand upon Eze 25:13 5186
I will *s* out mine hand upon the Eze 25:16 5186
he shall *s* it out upon the land Eze 30:25 5186
I will *s* out mine hand against Eze 35:3 5186
He shall *s* forth his hand also Dan 11:42 7971
s themselves upon their couches, Amos 6:4 5628
I will also *s* out mine hand upon Zeph 1:4 5186
he will *s* out his hand against Zeph 2:13 5186
he to the man, *S* forth thine hand Mt 12:13 *1614*
unto the man, *S* forth thine hand Mk 3:5 *1614*
unto the man, *S* forth thy hand Lk 6:10 *1614*
thou shalt *s* forth thy hands, and Jn 21:18 *1614*
For we *s* not ourselves beyond our 2Cor 10:14 *5239*

STRETCHED
Abraham *s* forth his hand, and took Gen 22:10 7971
Israel *s* out his right hand, and Gen 48:14 7971
will redeem you with a *s* out arm Ex 6:6 5186
Aaron *s* out his hand over the Ex 8:6 5186
for Aaron *s* out his hand with his Ex 8:17 5186
Moses *s* forth his rod toward Ex 9:23 5186
Moses *s* forth his rod over the Ex 10:13 5186
Moses *s* forth his hand toward Ex 10:22 5186
Moses *s* out his hand over the sea Ex 14:21 5186
Moses *s* forth his hand over the Ex 14:27 5186
by a *s* out arm, and by great Deut 4:34 5186
a mighty hand and by a *s* out arm Deut 5:15 5186
the *s* out arm, whereby the LORD Deut 7:19 5186
mighty power and by thy *s* out arm Deut 9:29 5186
mighty hand, and his *s* out arm, Deut 11:2 5186
Joshua *s* out the spear that he Josh 8:18 5186
as soon as he had *s* out his hand Josh 8:19 5186
wherewith he *s* out the spear, Josh 8:26 5186
when the angel *s* out his hand 2Sa 24:16 7971
they *s* forth the wings of the 1Kin 6:27 6566
strong hand, and of thy *s* out arm 1Kin 8:42 5186
he *s* himself upon the child three 1Kin 17:21 4058
he *s* himself upon the child 2Kin 4:34 1457
and went up, and *s* himself upon him 2Kin 4:35 1457
a *s* out arm, him shall ye fear, 2Kin 17:36 5186
in his hand *s* out over Jerusalem 1Chr 21:16 5186
thy mighty hand, and thy *s* out arm 2Chr 6:32 5186
or who hath *s* the line upon it Job 38:5 5186
or *s* out our hands to a strange Ps 44:20 6566
I have *s* out my hands unto thee Ps 88:9 7849
To him that *s* out the earth above Ps 136:6 7554
strong hand, and with a *s* out arm Ps 136:12 5186
I have *s* out my hand, and no man Prov 1:24 5186
walk with *s* forth necks and wanton Is 3:16 5186
he hath *s* forth his hand against Is 5:25 5186
away, but his hand is *s* out still Is 5:25 5186
away, but his hand is *s* out still Is 9:12 5186
away, but his hand is *s* out still Is 9:17 5186
away, but his hand is *s* out still Is 9:21 5186
away, but his hand is *s* out still Is 10:4 5186
is *s* out upon all the nations Is 14:26 5186
and his hand is *s* out, and who Is 14:27 5186
her branches are *s* out, they are Is 16:8 5203
He *s* out his hand over the sea, Is 23:11 5186
the heavens, and *s* them out Is 42:5 5186
have *s* out the heavens, and all Is 45:12 5186
that hath *s* forth the heavens, and Is 51:13 5186
shadows of the evening are *s* out Jer 6:4 5186
hath *s* out the heavens by his Jer 10:12 5186
s out arm, and there is nothing Jer 32:17 5186
with a *s* out arm, and with great Jer 32:21 5186
hath *s* out the heaven by his Jer 51:15 5186
he hath *s* out a line, he hath not Lam 2:8 5186
and their wings were *s* upward Eze 1:11 6504
s forth over their heads above Eze 1:22 5186
one cherub *s* forth his hand from Eze 10:7 7971
therefore I have *s* out my hand Eze 16:27 5186
with a *s* out arm, and with fury Eze 20:33 5186
with a *s* out arm, and with fury Eze 20:34 5186
he *s* out his hand with scorners Hos 7:5 4900
the banquet of them that *s* Amos 6:7 5628
a line shall be *s* forth upon Zec 1:16 5186
And he *s* it forth Mt 12:13 *1614*
he *s* forth his hand toward his Mt 12:49 *1614*
Jesus *s* forth his hand, and caught Mt 14:31 *1614*
were with Jesus *s* out his hand Mt 26:51 *1614*
And he *s* it out Mk 3:5 *1614*
ye *s* forth no hands against me Lk 22:53 *1614*
s forth his hands to vex certain Acts 12:1 *1911*
Then Paul *s* forth the hand, and Acts 26:1 *1614*
All day long I have *s* forth my Rom 10:21 *1600*

STRETCHEDST
Thou *s* out thy right hand, the Ex 15:12 5186

STRETCHEST
who *s* out the heavens like a Ps 104:2 5186

STRETCHETH
For he *s* out his hand against God Job 15:25 5186
He *s* out the north over the empty Job 26:7 5186
She *s* out her hand to the poor Prov 31:20 6566
that *s* out the heavens as a Is 40:22 5186
The carpenter *s* out his rule Is 44:13 5186
that *s* forth the heavens alone Is 44:24 5186
which *s* forth the heavens, and Zec 12:1 5186

STRETCHING
the *s* out of his wings shall fill Is 8:8 4298
By *s* forth thine hand to heal Acts 4:30 *1614*

STRICKEN
Sarah were old and well *s* in age Gen 18:11 935
Abraham was old, and well *s* in age Gen 24:1 935
Now Joshua was old and *s* in years Josh 13:1 935
s in years, and there remaineth Josh 13:1 935
that Joshua waxed old and *s* in age Josh 23:1 935
unto them, I am old and *s* in age Josh 23:2 935
pierced and *s* through his temples Judg 5:26 2498
king David was old and *s* in years 1Kin 1:1 935
if thou hast *s* thy hand with a Prov 6:1 8628
They have *s* me, shalt thou say, Prov 23:35 5221
Why should ye be *s* any more Is 1:5 5221
surely they are *s* Is 16:7 5218
yet we did esteem him *s*, smitten Is 53:4 5060
of my people was he *s* Is 53:8 5061
thou hast *s* them, but they have Jer 5:3 5221
s through for want of the fruits Lam 4:9 1856
both were now well *s* in years Lk 1:7 *4260*
man, and my wife well *s* in years Lk 1:18 *4260*

STRIFE
there was a *s* between the herdmen Gen 13:7 7379
said unto Lot, Let there be no *s* Gen 13:8 4808
in the *s* of the congregation, to Num 27:14 4808
and your burden, and your *s* Deut 1:12 7379
my people were at great *s* with Judg 12:2 7379
And all the people were at *s* 2Sa 19:9 1777
a pavilion from the *s* of tongues Ps 31:20 7379
seen violence and *s* in the city Ps 55:9 7379
Thou makest us a *s* unto our Ps 80:6 4066
him also at the waters of *s* Ps 106:32 4808
A wrathful man stirreth up *s* Prov 15:18 4066
that is slow to anger appeaseth *s* Prov 15:18 7379
A froward man soweth *s* Prov 16:28 4066
house full of sacrifices with *s* Prov 17:1 7379
The beginning of *s* is as when one Prov 17:14 4066
transgression that loveth *s* Prov 17:19 4683
honour for a man to cease from *s* Prov 20:3 7379
yea, *s* and reproach shall cease Prov 22:10 1779
meddleth with *s* belonging not to Prov 26:17 7379
is no talebearer, the *s* ceaseth Prov 26:20 4066
is a contentious man to kindle *s* Prov 26:21 7379
is of a proud heart stirreth up *s* Prov 28:25 4066
An angry man stirreth up *s* Prov 29:22 4066
forcing of wrath bringeth forth *s* Prov 30:33 7379
Behold, ye fast for *s* and debate, Is 58:4 7379
thou hast borne me a man of *s* Jer 15:10 7379
even to the waters of *s* in Kadesh Eze 47:19 4808
unto the waters of *s* in Kadesh Eze 48:28 4808
and there are that raise up *s* Hab 1:3 7379
And there was also a *s* among them Lk 22:24 *5379*
and wantonness, not in *s* and Rom 13:13 *2054*
there is among you envying, and *s* 1Cor 3:3 *2054*
variance, emulations, wrath, *s* Gal 5:20 *2052*
preach Christ even of envy and *s* Phil 1:15 *2054*
be done through *s* or vainglory Phil 2:3 *2052*
of words, whereof cometh envy, *s* 1Ti 6:4 *2054*
is to them an end of all *s* Heb 6:16 *485*
s in your hearts, glory not, and Jas 3:14 *2052*
s is, there is confusion and every Jas 3:16 *2052*

STRIFES
Hatred stirreth up *s* Prov 10:12 4090
be debates, envyings, wraths, *s* 2Cor 12:20 *2052*
s of words, whereof cometh envy, 1Ti 6:4 *3055*
knowing that they do gender *s* 2Ti 2:23 *3163*

STRIKE
s it on the two side posts and on Ex 12:7 5414
s the lintel and the two side Ex 12:22 5060
shall *s* off the heifer's neck Deut 21:4
s his hand over the place, and 2Kin 5:11 5130
is he that will *s* hands with me Job 17:3 8628
bow of steel shall *s* him through Job 20:24 2498
LORD at thy right hand shall *s* Ps 110:5 4272
Till a dart *s* through his liver Prov 7:23 6398
nor to *s* princes for equity Prov 17:26 5221
not thou one of them that *s* hands Prov 22:26 8628
Thou didst *s* through with his Hab 3:14 5344
the servants did *s* him with the Mk 14:65 *906*

STRIKER
Not given to wine, no *s*, not 1Ti 3:3 *4131*
angry, not given to wine, no *s* Titus 1:7 *4131*

STRIKETH
He *s* them as wicked men in the Job 34:26 5606
man void of understanding *s* hands Prov 17:18 8628
of a scorpion, when he *s* a man Rev 9:5 *3817*

STRING
make ready their arrow upon the *s* Ps 11:2 3499
the *s* of his tongue was loosed, Mk 7:35 *1199*

STRINGED
praise him with *s* instruments Ps 150:4 4482
we will sing my songs to the *s* Is 38:20 5058
chief singer on my *s* instruments Hab 3:19 5058

STRINGS
thy *s* against the face of them Ps 21:12 4340
and an instrument of ten *s* Ps 33:2
Upon an instrument of ten *s* Ps 92:3
an instrument of ten *s* will I Ps 144:9

STRIP
s Aaron of his garments, and put Num 20:26 6584
Philistines came to *s* the slain 1Sa 31:8 6584
Philistines came to *s* the slain 1Chr 10:8 6584
s you, and make you bare, and gird Is 32:11 6584
they shall *s* thee also of thy Eze 16:39 6584
They shall also *s* thee out of thy Eze 23:26 6584
Lest I *s* her naked, and set her as Hos 2:3 6584

STRIPE
wound for wound, *s* for *s* Ex 21:25 2250

STRIPES
Forty *s* he may give him, and not Deut 25:3 5221
beat him above these with many *s* Deut 25:3 4347
with the *s* of the children of men 2Sa 7:14 5061
the rod, and their iniquity with *s* Ps 89:32 5061
than an hundred *s* into a fool Prov 17:10 5221
and *s* for the back of fools Prov 19:29 4112
so do *s* the inward parts of the Prov 20:30 4347
and with his *s* we are healed Is 53:5 2250
will, shall be beaten with many *s* Lk 12:47
and did commit things worthy of *s* Lk 12:48 *4127*
shall be beaten with few *s* Lk 12:48 *4127*
they had laid many *s* upon them Acts 16:23 *4127*
of the night, and washed their *s* Acts 16:33 *4127*
In *s*, in imprisonments, in 2Cor 6:5 *4127*
in *s* above measure, in prisons 2Cor 11:23 *4127*
times received I forty *s* save one 2Cor 11:24 *4127*
by whose *s* ye were healed 1Pet 2:24 *3468*

STRIPLING
Enquire thou whose son the *s* is 1Sa 17:56 5958

STRIPPED
And the children of Israel *s* Ex 33:6 5337
Moses *s* Aaron of his garments, and Num 20:28 6584
Jonathan *s* himself of the robe 1Sa 18:4 6584
s off his armour, and sent into 1Sa 31:9 6584
And when they had *s* him, they took 1Chr 10:9 6584
which they *s* off for themselves, 2Chr 20:25 5337
He hath *s* me of my glory, and Job 19:9 6584
s the naked of their clothing Job 22:6 6584
I will wail and howl, I will go *s* Mic 1:8 7758
And they *s* him, and put on him a Mt 27:28 *1562*
which *s* him of his raiment, and Lk 10:30 *1562*

STRIPT
that they *s* Joseph out of his Gen 37:23 6584
he *s* off his clothes also, and 1Sa 19:24

STRIVE
shall not always *s* with man Gen 6:3 1777
Gerar did *s* with Isaac's herdmen Gen 26:20 7378
if men *s* together, and one smite Ex 21:18 7378
If men *s*, and hurt a woman with Ex 21:22 5327
When men *s* together one with Deut 25:11 5327
with whom thou didst *s* at the Deut 33:8 7378
did he ever *s* against Israel, or Judg 11:25 7378
Why dost thou *s* against him Job 33:13 7378
O LORD, with them that *s* with me Ps 35:1 3401

S not with a man without cause, Prov 3:30 7378
Go not forth hastily to *s* Prov 25:8 7378
they that *s* with thee shall Is 41:11 7379
Let the potsherd *s* with the Is 45:9
Yet let no man *s*, nor reprove Hos 4:4 7378
as they that *s* with the priest Hos 4:4 7378
He shall not *s*, nor cry Mt 12:19 *2051*
S to enter in at the strait gate Lk 13:24 *75*
that ye *s* together with me in Rom 15:30 *4865*
And if a man also *s* for masteries 2Ti 2:5 *118*
not crowned, except he *s* lawfully 2Ti 2:5 *118*
s not about words to no profit 2Ti 2:14 *3054*
servant of the Lord must not *s* 2Ti 2:24 *3164*

STRIVED
so have I *s* to preach the gospel, Rom 15:20 *5389*

STRIVEN
thou hast *s* against the LORD Jer 50:24 1624

STRIVETH
unto him that *s* with his Maker Is 45:9 7378
every man that *s* for the mastery 1Cor 9:25 *75*

STRIVING
with one mind *s* together for the Phil 1:27 *4866*
s according to his working, which Col 1:29 *75*
unto blood, *s* against sin Heb 12:4 *464*

STRIVINGS
me from the *s* of my people 2Sa 22:44 7379
me from the *s* of the people Ps 18:43 7379
contentions, and *s* about the law Titus 3:9 *3163*

STROKE
and plea, and between *s* and *s* Deut 17:8 5061
his hand fetcheth a *s* with the Deut 19:5
controversy and every *s* be tried Deut 21:5 5061
enemies with the *s* of the sword Est 9:5 4347
my *s* is heavier than my groaning Job 23:2 3027
lest he take thee away with his *s* Job 36:18 5607
Remove thy *s* away from me Ps 39:10 5061
in wrath with a continual *s* Is 14:6 4347
healeth the *s* of their wound Is 30:26 4273
the desire of thine eyes with a *s* Eze 24:16 4046

STROKES
and his mouth calleth for *s* Prov 18:6 4112

STRONG
Issachar is a *s* ass couching down Gen 49:14 1634
s by the hands of the mighty God Gen 49:24 6339
for with a *s* hand shall he let Ex 6:1 2389
with a *s* hand shall he drive them Ex 6:1 2389
LORD turned a mighty *s* west wind Ex 10:19 2389
for with a *s* hand hath the LORD Ex 13:9 2389
by a *s* east wind all that night Ex 14:21 5794
Do not drink wine nor *s* drink Lev 10:9
s drink, and shall drink no Num 6:3
of wine, or vinegar of *s* drink Num 6:3
whether they be *s* or weak Num 13:18 2389
whether in tents, or in *s* holds Num 13:19 4013
be *s* that dwell in the land Num 13:28 5794
much people, and with a *s* hand Num 20:20 2389
of the children of Ammon was *s* Num 21:24 5794
S is thy dwellingplace, and thou Num 24:21 386
s wine to be poured unto the LORD Num 28:7
was not one city too *s* for us Deut 2:36 7682
you this day, that ye may be *s* Deut 11:8 2388
or for wine, or for *s* drink Deut 14:26
have ye drunk wine or *s* drink Deut 29:6
Be *s* and of a good courage, fear Deut 31:6 2388
in the sight of all Israel, Be *s* Deut 31:7 2388
of Nun a charge, and said, Be *s* Deut 31:23 2388
Be *s* and of a good courage Josh 1:6 2388
Only be thou *s* and very courageous Josh 1:7 2388
Be *s* and of a good courage Josh 1:9 2388
only be *s* and of a good courage Josh 1:18 2388
Fear not, nor be dismayed, be *s* Josh 10:25 2388
As yet I am as *s* this day as I Josh 14:11 2389
children of Israel were waxen *s* Josh 17:13 2388
chariots, and though they be *s* Josh 17:18 2389
to Ramah, and to the *s* city Tyre Josh 19:29 4013
before you great nations and *s* Josh 23:9 6099
came to pass, when Israel was *s* Judg 1:28 2388
mountains, and caves, and *s* holds Judg 6:2 4679
But there was a *s* tower within Judg 9:51 5797
and drink not wine nor *s* drink Judg 13:4
and now drink no wine nor *s* drink Judg 13:7
let her drink wine or *s* drink Judg 13:14
out of the *s* came forth sweetness Judg 14:14 5794
saw that they were too *s* for him Judg 18:26 2389
drunken neither wine nor *s* drink 1Sa 1:15
Be *s*, and quit yourselves like men 1Sa 4:9 2388
and when Saul saw any *s* man 1Sa 14:52 1368
in the wilderness in *s* holds 1Sa 23:14 4679
with us in *s* holds in the wood 1Sa 23:19 4679
dwelt in *s* holds at En-gedi 1Sa 23:29 4679
himself *s* for the house of Saul 2Sa 3:6 2388
David took the *s* hold of Zion 2Sa 5:7 4686
If the Syrians be too *s* for me 2Sa 10:11 2388
of Ammon be too *s* for thee 2Sa 10:11 2388
battle more *s* against the city 2Sa 11:25 2388
And the conspiracy was *s* 2Sa 15:12 533
of all that are with thee be *s* 2Sa 16:21 2388
He delivered me from my *s* enemy 2Sa 22:18 5794
for they were too *s* for me 2Sa 22:18 553
came to the *s* hold of Tyre, and to 2Sa 24:7 4013
be thou *s* therefore, and shew 1Kin 2:2 2388
thy great name, and of thy *s* hand 1Kin 8:42 2389
s wind rent the mountains, and 1Kin 19:11 2389
be with thy servants fifty *s* men 2Kin 2:16 2428
their *s* holds wilt thou set on 2Kin 8:12 4013
a thousand, all that were *s* 2Kin 24:16 1368
If the Syrians be too *s* for me 1Chr 19:12 2388
of Ammon be too *s* for thee 1Chr 19:12 2388
be *s*, and of good courage 1Chr 22:13 2388
whose brethren were *s* men 1Chr 26:7 2428
sons and brethren, *s* men, eighteen 1Chr 26:9 2428
be *s*, and do it 1Chr 28:10 2388
said to Solomon his son, Be *s* 1Chr 28:20 2388
And he fortified the *s* holds 2Chr 11:11 4694
spears, and made them exceeding *s* 2Chr 11:12 2388
Rehoboam the son of Solomon *s* 2Chr 11:17 559
Be ye *s* therefore, and let not 2Chr 15:7 2388
to shew himself *s* in the behalf 2Chr 16:9 2388
go, do it, be *s* for the battle 2Chr 25:8 2388
helped, till he was *s* 2Chr 26:15 2388
But when he was *s*, his heart was 2Chr 26:16 2394
Be *s* and courageous, be not afraid 2Chr 32:7 2388
that ye may be *s*, and eat the good Ezr 9:12 2388
thy great power, and by thy *s* hand Neh 1:10 2389
And they took *s* cities, and a fat Neh 9:25 1219
of thy mouth be like a *s* wind Job 8:2 3524
I speak of strength, lo, he is *s* Job 9:19 533
with thy *s* hand thou opposest Job 30:21 6108
of his bones with *s* pain Job 33:19 386
spread out the sky, which is *s* Job 37:18 2389
crag of the rock, and the *s* place Job 39:28 4686
bones are as *s* pieces of brass Job 40:18 650
the poor may fall by his *s* ones Ps 10:10 6099
He delivered me from my *s* enemy Ps 18:17 5794
for they were too *s* for me Ps 18:17 553
rejoiceth as a *s* man to run a Ps 19:5 1368
s bulls of Bashan have beset me Ps 22:12 47
The LORD *s* and mighty, the LORD Ps 24:8 5808
hast made my mountain to stand *s* Ps 30:7 5797
be thou my *s* rock, for an house Ps 31:2 4581
marvellous kindness in a *s* city Ps 31:21 4692
from him that is too *s* for him Ps 35:10 2389
enemies are lively, and they are *s* Ps 38:19 6105
Who will bring me into the *s* city Ps 60:9 4692
me, and a *s* tower from the enemy Ps 61:3 5797
Be thou my *s* habitation, Ps 71:3 6697
but thou art my *s* refuge Ps 71:7 5797
that thou madest *s* for thyself Ps 80:15 553
whom thou madest *s* for thyself Ps 80:17 553
who is a *s* LORD like unto thee Ps 89:8 2626
thine enemies with thy *s* arm Ps 89:10 5797
s is thy hand, and high is thy Ps 89:13 5810
hast brought his *s* holds to ruin Ps 89:40 4013
Who will bring me into the *s* city Ps 108:10 4013
With a *s* hand, and with a Ps 136:12 2389
That our oxen may be *s* to labour Ps 144:14
many *s* men have been slain by her Prov 7:26 6099
rich man's wealth is his *s* city Prov 10:15 5797
and *s* men retain riches Prov 11:16 6184
fear of the LORD is *s* confidence Prov 14:26 5797
The name of the LORD is a *s* tower Prov 18:10 5797
rich man's wealth is his *s* city Prov 18:11 5797
is harder to be won than a *s* city Prov 18:19 5797
is a mocker, *s* drink is raging Prov 20:1
and a reward in the bosom *s* wrath Prov 21:14 5794
A wise man is *s* Prov 24:5 5797
The ants are a people not *s* Prov 30:25 5794
nor for princes *s* drink Prov 31:4
Give *s* drink unto him that is Prov 31:6
swift, nor the battle to the *s* Eccl 9:11 1368
the *s* men shall bow themselves, Eccl 12:3 2428
for love is *s* as death Song 8:6 5794
the *s* shall be as tow, and the Is 1:31 2634
that they may follow *s* drink Is 5:11
men of strength to mingle *s* drink Is 5:22
them the waters of the river, *s* Is 8:7 6099
spake thus to me with a *s* hand Is 8:11 2393
In that day shall his *s* cities be Is 17:9 4581
to destroy the *s* holds thereof Is 23:11 4581
s drink shall be bitter to them Is 24:9
shall the *s* people glorify thee Is 25:3 5794
We have a *s* city Is 26:1 5797
s sword shall punish leviathan Is 27:1 2389
s one, which as a tempest of hail Is 28:2 533
through *s* drink are out of the Is 28:7
have erred through *s* drink Is 28:7
out of the way through *s* drink Is 28:7
lest your bands be made *s* Is 28:22 2388
stagger, but not with *s* drink Is 29:9
horsemen, because they are very *s* Is 31:1 6105
pass over to his *s* hold for fear Is 31:9 5553
that are of a fearful heart, Be *s* Is 35:4 2388
Lord GOD will come with *s* hand Is 40:10 2389
might, for that he is *s* in power Is 40:26 533
bring forth your *s* reasons Is 41:21 6110
shall divide the spoil with the *s* Is 53:12 6099
will fill ourselves with *s* drink Is 56:12
and a small one a *s* nation Is 60:22 6099
of the neighing of his *s* ones Jer 8:16 47
outstretched hand and with a *s* arm Jer 21:5 2389
and with wonders, and with a *s* hand Jer 32:21 2389
of the hoofs of his *s* horses Jer 47:3 47
are mighty and *s* men for the war Jer 48:14 2428
How is the *s* staff broken, and the Jer 48:17 5797
and he shall destroy thy *s* holds Jer 48:18 4013
the *s* holds are surprised, and the Jer 48:41 4679
against the habitation of the *s* Jer 49:19 386
Their Redeemer is *s* Jer 50:34 2389
unto the habitation of the *s* Jer 50:44 386
of Babylon, make the watch *s* Jer 51:12 2388
thrown down in his wrath the *s* Lam 2:2 4013
he hath destroyed his *s* holds Lam 2:5 4013
thy face *s* against their faces Eze 3:8 2389
thy forehead *s* against their Eze 3:8 2389
hand of the LORD was *s* upon me Eze 3:14 2388
make the pomp of the *s* to cease Eze 7:24 5794
she had *s* rods for the sceptres Eze 19:11 5797
her *s* rods were broken and Eze 19:12 5797
so that she hath no *s* rod to be a Eze 19:14 5797
endure, or can thine hands be *s* Eze 22:14 2388
thy *s* garrisons shall go down to Eze 26:11 5797
city, which wast *s* in the sea Eze 26:17 2389
to make it *s* to hold the sword Eze 30:21 2388
and will break his arms, the *s* Eze 30:22 2389
The *s* among the mighty shall Eze 32:21 410
I will destroy the fat and the *s* Eze 34:16 2389
fourth kingdom shall be *s* as iron Dan 2:40 8624
so the kingdom shall be partly *s* Dan 2:42 8624
The tree grew, and was *s*, and the Dan 4:11 8631
thou sawest, which grew, and was *s* Dan 4:20 8631
king, that art grown and become *s* Dan 4:22 8631
and terrible, and *s* exceedingly Dan 7:7 8624
and when he was *s*, the great horn Dan 8:8 6105
unto thee, be *s*, yea, be *s* Dan 10:19 2388
the king of the south shall be *s* Dan 11:5 2388
and he shall be *s* above him Dan 11:5 2388
shall become *s* with a small Dan 11:23 6105
his devices against the *s* holds Dan 11:24 4013
that do know their God shall be *s* Dan 11:32 2388
most *s* holds with a strange god Dan 11:39 4581
nation is come up upon my land, *s* Joel 1:6 6099
a great people and a *s* Joel 2:2 6099
as a *s* people set in battle array Joel 2:5 6099
for he is *s* that executeth his Joel 2:11 6099
let the weak say, I am *s* Joel 3:10 1368
cedars, and he was *s* as the oaks Amos 2:9 2364
the *s* shall not strengthen his Amos 2:14 2389
the spoiled against the *s* Amos 5:9 5794
unto thee of wine and of *s* drink Mic 2:11 7941
rebuke *s* nations afar off Mic 4:3 6099
that was cast far off a *s* nation Mic 4:7 6099
the *s* hold of the daughter of Mic 4:8 6076
and throw down all thy *s* holds Mic 5:11 4013
ye *s* foundations of the earth Mic 6:2 386
a *s* hold in the day of trouble Nah 1:7 4581
watch the way, make thy loins *s* Nah 2:1 2388
All thy *s* holds shall be like fig Nah 3:12 4013
the siege, fortify thy *s* holds Nah 3:14 4013
the morter, make *s* the brickkiln Nah 3:14 2388
they shall deride every *s* hold Hab 1:10 4013
Yet now be *s*, O Zerubbabel, saith Hag 2:4 2388
and be *s*, O Joshua, son of Hag 2:4 2388
and be *s*, all ye people of the Hag 2:4 2388
Let your hands be *s*, ye that hear Zec 8:9 2388
fear not, but let your hands be *s* Zec 8:13 2388
s nations shall come to seek the Zec 8:22 6099
Tyrus did build herself a *s* hold Zec 9:3 4692
Turn you to the *s* hold, ye Zec 9:12 1225
one enter into a *s* man's house Mt 12:29 *2478*
except he first bind the *s* man Mt 12:29 *2478*
can enter into a *s* man's house Mk 3:27 *2478*
he will first bind the *s* man Mk 3:27 *2478*
drink neither wine nor *s* drink Lk 1:15 *4608*
waxed *s* in spirit, and was in the Lk 1:80 *2901*
waxed *s* in spirit, filled with Lk 2:40 *2901*
When a *s* man armed keepeth his Lk 11:21 *2478*
in his name hath made this man *s* Acts 3:16 *4732*
but was *s* in faith, giving glory Rom 4:20 *1743*
We then that are *s* ought to bear Rom 15:1 *1415*
we are weak, but ye are *s* 1Cor 4:10 *2478*
faith, quit you like men, be *s* 1Cor 16:13 *2901*
to the pulling down of *s* holds 2Cor 10:4 *3794*
for when I am weak, then am I *s* 2Cor 12:10 *1415*
when we are weak, and ye are *s* 2Cor 13:9 *1415*
be *s* in the Lord, and in the power Eph 6:10 *1743*
God shall send them *s* delusion 2Th 2:11 *1753*
be *s* in the grace that is in 2Ti 2:1 *1743*
and supplications with *s* crying Heb 5:7 *2478*
need of milk, and not of *s* meat Heb 5:12 *4731*
But *s* meat belongeth to them that Heb 5:14 *4731*
we might have a *s* consolation Heb 6:18 *2478*
out of weakness were made *s* Heb 11:34 *1743*
you, young men, because ye are *s* 1Jn 2:14 *2478*
I saw a *s* angel proclaiming with Rev 5:2 *2478*
he cried mightily with a *s* voice Rev 18:2 *3173*
for *s* is the Lord God who judgeth Rev 18:8 *2478*

STRONGER
shall be *s* than the other people Gen 25:23 553
whensoever the *s* cattle did Gen 30:41 7194
were Laban's, and the *s* Jacob's Gen 30:42 7194
for they are *s* than we Num 13:31 2389
And what is *s* than a lion Judg 14:18 5794
eagles, they were *s* than lions 2Sa 1:23 1396
but David waxed *s* and *s*, and 2Sa 3:1 2390
being *s* than she, forced her, and 2Sa 13:14 2388
therefore they were *s* than we 1Kin 20:23 2388
and surely we shall be *s* than they 1Kin 20:23 2388
and surely we shall be *s* than they 1Kin 20:25 2388
hands shall be *s* and *s* Job 17:9 555
made them *s* than their enemies Ps 105:24 6105
for they are *s* than I Ps 142:6 553
thou art *s* than I, and hast Jer 20:7 2388
hand of him that was *s* than he Jer 31:11 2388
But when a *s* than he shall come Lk 11:22 *2478*
the weakness of God is *s* than men 1Cor 1:25 *2478*
are we *s* than he 1Cor 10:22 *2478*

STRONGEST
A lion which is *s* among beasts Prov 30:30 1368

STRONGLY
the foundations thereof be *s* laid Ezr 6:3

STROVE
because they *s* with him Gen 26:20 6229
another well, and *s* for that also Gen 26:21 7378
and for that they *s* not Gen 26:22 7378
two men of the Hebrews *s* together Ex 2:13 5327
a man of Israel *s* together in the Lev 24:10 5327
of Israel *s* with the LORD Num 20:13 7378
who *s* against Moses and against Num 26:9 5327
when they *s* against the LORD Num 26:9 5327
they two *s* together in the field, 2Sa 14:6 5327
when he *s* with Aram-naharaim and Ps 60:t 5327
the heaven *s* upon the great sea Dan 7:2 1519
Jews therefore *s* among themselves Jn 6:52 *3164*
himself unto them as they *s* Acts 7:26 *3164*
the Pharisees' part arose, and *s* Acts 23:9 *1264*

S

STROWED
s it upon the graves of them that ... 2Chr 34:4 2236

STRUCK
he s it into the pan, or kettle, ... 1Sa 2:14 5221
the LORD s the child that Uriah's ... 2Sa 12:15 5062
to the ground, and s him not again ... 2Sa 20:10 8138
and the LORD s him, and he died ... 2Chr 13:20 5062
s a servant of the high priest's, ... Mt 26:51 *3960*
they s him on the face, and asked ... Lk 22:64 *5180*
of the officers which stood by s ... Jn 18:22 *3960*

STRUGGLED
the children s together within ... Gen 25:22 7533

STUBBLE
to gather s instead of straw ... Ex 5:12 7179
wrath, which consumed them as s ... Ex 15:7 7179
and wilt thou pursue the dry s ... Job 13:25 7179
They are as s before the wind, and ... Job 21:18 8401
are turned with him into s ... Job 41:28 7179
Darts are counted as s ... Job 41:29 7179
as the s before the wind ... Ps 83:13 7179
as the fire devoureth the s ... Is 5:24 7179
chaff, ye shall bring forth s ... Is 33:11 7179
shall take them away as s ... Is 40:24 7179
sword, and as driven s to his bow ... Is 41:2 7179
Behold, they shall be as s ... Is 47:14 7179
will I scatter them as the s that ... Jer 13:24 7179
of fire that devoureth the s ... Joel 2:5 7179
flame, and the house of Esau for s ... Obad 18 7179
shall be devoured as s fully dry ... Nah 1:10 7179
all that do wickedly, shall be s ... Mal 4:1 7179
precious stones, wood, hay, s ... 1Cor 3:12 *2562*

STUBBORN
If a man have a s and rebellious ... Deut 21:18 5637
of his city, This our son is s ... Deut 21:20 5637
own doings, nor from their s way ... Judg 2:19 7186
not be as their fathers, a s ... Ps 78:8 5637
(She is loud and s ... Prov 7:11 5637

STUBBORNNESS
not unto the s of this people ... Deut 9:27 7190
s is as iniquity and idolatry ... 1Sa 15:23 6484

STUCK
his spear s in the ground at his ... 1Sa 26:7 4600
I have s unto thy testimonies ... Ps 119:31 1692
and the forepart s fast, and ... Acts 27:41 *2043*

STUDIETH
of the righteous s to answer ... Prov 15:28 1897
For their heart s destruction ... Prov 24:2 1897

STUDS
borders of gold with s of silver ... Song 1:11 5351

STUDY
much s is a weariness of the ... Eccl 12:12 3854
that ye s to be quiet, and to do ... 1Th 4:11 *5389*
S to shew thyself approved unto ... 2Ti 2:15 *4704*

STUFF
thou hast searched all my s ... Gen 31:37 3627
thou found of all thy household s ... Gen 31:37 3627
Also regard not your s ... Gen 45:20 3627
his neighbour money or s to keep ... Ex 22:7 3627
For the s they had was sufficient ... Ex 36:7 4399
put it even among their own s ... Josh 7:11 3627
he hath hid himself among the s ... 1Sa 10:22 3627
and two hundred abode by the s ... 1Sa 25:13 3627
part be that tarrieth by the s ... 1Sa 30:24 3627
s of Tobiah out of the chamber ... Neh 13:8 3627
man, prepare thee s for removing ... Eze 12:3 3627
forth thy s by day in their sight ... Eze 12:4 3627
in their sight, as s for removing ... Eze 12:4 3627
I brought forth my s by day ... Eze 12:7 3627
as s for captivity, and in the ... Eze 12:7 3627
his s in the house, let him not ... Lk 17:31 *4632*

STUMBLE
safely, and thy foot shall not s ... Prov 3:23 5062
thou runnest, thou shalt not s ... Prov 4:12 3782
they know not at what they s ... Prov 4:19 3782
shall be weary nor s among them ... Is 5:27 3782
And many among them shall s ... Is 8:15 3782
err in vision, they s in judgment ... Is 28:7 6328
we s at noonday as in the night ... Is 59:10 3782
that they should not s ... Is 63:13 3782
before your feet s upon the dark ... Jer 13:16 5062
they have caused them to s in ... Jer 18:15 3782
therefore my persecutors shall s ... Jer 20:11 3782
way, wherein they shall not s ... Jer 31:9 3782
they shall s, and fall toward the ... Jer 46:6 3782
And the most proud shall s ... Jer 50:32 3782
but he shall s and fall, and not be ... Dan 11:19 3782
they shall s in their walk ... Nah 2:5 3782
they s upon their corpses ... Nah 3:3 3782
have caused many to s at the law ... Mal 2:8 3782
even to them which s at the word ... 1Pet 2:8 *4350*

STUMBLED
they that s are girded with ... 1Sa 2:4 3782
for the oxen s ... 1Chr 13:9 8058
me to eat up my flesh, they s ... Ps 27:2 3782
man hath s against the mighty ... Jer 46:12 3782
For they s at that stumblingstone ... Rom 9:32 *4350*
Have they s that they should fall ... Rom 11:11 *4417*

STUMBLETH
not thine heart be glad when he s ... Prov 24:17 3782
he s not, because he seeth the ... Jn 11:9 *4350*
if a man walk in the night, he s ... Jn 11:10 *4350*
any thing whereby thy brother s ... Rom 14:21 *4350*

STUMBLING
but for a stone of s and for a ... Is 8:14 5063
And a stone of s, and a rock of ... 1Pet 2:8
is none occasion of s in him ... 1Jn 2:10 *4625*

STUMBLINGBLOCK
nor put a s before the blind, but ... Lev 19:14 4383
take up the s out of the way of ... Is 57:14 4383
I lay a s before him, he shall ... Eze 3:20 4383
it is the s of their iniquity ... Eze 7:19 4383
put the s of their iniquity ... Eze 14:3 4383
putteth the s of his iniquity ... Eze 14:4 4383
putteth the s of his iniquity ... Eze 14:7 4383
made a snare, and a trap, and a s ... Rom 11:9 *4625*
that no man put a s or an ... Rom 14:13 *4348*
crucified, unto the Jews a s ... 1Cor 1:23 *4625*
become a s to them that are weak ... 1Cor 8:9 *4348*
who taught Balac to cast a s ... Rev 2:14 *4625*

STUMBLINGBLOCKS
I will lay s before this people, ... Jer 6:21 4383
the sea, and the s with the wicked ... Zeph 1:3 4384

STUMBLINGSTONE
For they stumbled at that s ... Rom 9:32
Behold, I lay in Sion a s ... Rom 9:33

STUMP
only the s of Dagon was left to ... 1Sa 5:4
Nevertheless leave the s of his ... Dan 4:15 6136
yet leave the s of the roots ... Dan 4:23 6136
to leave the s of the tree roots ... Dan 4:26 6136

SUAH (*su'-ah*) *Son of Zophah.*
S, and Harnepher, and Shual, and ... 1Chr 7:36 5477

SUBDUE
and replenish the earth, and s it ... Gen 1:28 3533
Moreover I will s all thine ... 1Chr 17:10 3665
He shall s the people under us, ... Ps 47:3 1696
holden, to s nations before him ... Is 45:1 7286
first, and he shall s three kings ... Dan 7:24 8214
he will s our iniquities ... Mic 7:19 3533
devour, and s with sling stones ... Zec 9:15 3533
even to s all things unto himself ... Phil 3:21 *5293*

SUBDUED
the land be s before the LORD ... Num 32:22 3533
and the land shall be s before you ... Num 32:29 3533
war with thee, until it be s ... Deut 20:20 3381
And the land was s before them ... Josh 18:1 3533
So Moab was s that day under the ... Judg 3:30 3665
So God s on that day Jabin the ... Judg 4:23 3665
Thus was Midian s before the ... Judg 8:28 3665
s before the children of Israel ... Judg 11:33 3665
So the Philistines were s ... 1Sa 7:13 3665
smote the Philistines, and s them ... 2Sa 8:1 3665
of all nations which he s ... 2Sa 8:11 3533
against me hast thou s under me ... 2Sa 22:40 3766
s them, and took Gath and her towns ... 1Chr 18:1 3665
and they were s ... 1Chr 20:4 3665
the land is s before the LORD, and ... 1Chr 22:18 3533
thou hast s under me those that ... Ps 18:39 3766
should soon have s their enemies ... Ps 81:14 3665
all things shall be s unto him ... 1Cor 15:28 *5293*
Who through faith s kingdoms ... Heb 11:33 *2610*

SUBDUEDST
land, and thou s before them the ... Neh 9:24 3665

SUBDUETH
me, and s the people under me ... Ps 18:47 1696
who s my people under me ... Ps 144:2 7286
in pieces and s all things ... Dan 2:40 2827

SUBJECT
to Nazareth, and was s unto them ... Lk 2:51 *5293*
even the devils are s unto us ... Lk 10:17 *5293*
that the spirits are s unto you ... Lk 10:20 *5293*
for it is not s to the law of God ... Rom 8:7 *5293*
the creature was made s to vanity ... Rom 8:20 *5293*
Let every soul be s unto the ... Rom 13:1 *5293*
Wherefore ye must needs be s ... Rom 13:5 *5293*
prophets are s to the prophets ... 1Cor 14:32 *5293*
be s unto him that put all things ... 1Cor 15:28 *5293*
as the church is s unto Christ ... Eph 5:24 *5293*
world, are ye s to ordinances, ... Col 2:20 *1379*
in mind to be s to principalities ... Titus 3:1 *5293*
all their lifetime s to bondage ... Heb 2:15 *1777*
Elias was a man s to like ... Jas 5:17 *3663*
be s to your masters with all ... 1Pet 2:18 *5293*
and powers being made s unto him ... 1Pet 3:22 *5293*
all of you be s one to another, ... 1Pet 5:5 *5293*

SUBJECTED
him who hath s the same in hope ... Rom 8:20 *5293*

SUBJECTION
brought into s under their hand ... Ps 106:42 3665
brought them into s for servants ... Jer 34:11 3533
to return, and brought them into s ... Jer 34:16 3533
under my body, and bring it into s ... 1Cor 9:27 *1396*
s into the gospel of Christ ... 2Cor 9:13 *5292*
To whom we gave place by s ... Gal 2:5 *5292*
woman learn in silence with all s ... 1Ti 2:11 *5292*
children in s with all gravity ... 1Ti 3:4 *5292*
he not put in s the world to come ... Heb 2:5 *5293*
all things in s under his feet ... Heb 2:8 *5293*
in that he put all in s under him ... Heb 2:8 *5293*
in s unto the Father of spirits ... Heb 12:9 *5293*
be in s to your own husbands ... 1Pet 3:1 *5293*
being in s unto their own ... 1Pet 3:5 *5293*

SUBMIT
s thyself under her hands ... Gen 16:9 6031
Strangers shall s themselves unto ... 2Sa 22:45 3584
shall s themselves unto me ... Ps 18:44 3584
enemies s themselves unto thee ... Ps 66:3 3584
till every one s himself with ... Ps 68:30 7511
That ye s yourselves unto such, ... 1Cor 16:16 *5293*
s yourselves unto your own ... Eph 5:22 *5293*
s yourselves unto your own ... Col 3:18 *5293*
rule over you, and s yourselves ... Heb 13:17 *5226*
S yourselves therefore to God ... Jas 4:7 *5293*
S yourselves to every ordinance ... 1Pet 2:13 *5293*
s yourselves unto the elder ... 1Pet 5:5 *5293*

SUBMITTED
s themselves unto Solomon the ... 1Chr 29:24
should have s themselves unto him ... Ps 81:15 3584
have not s themselves unto the ... Rom 10:3 *5293*

SUBMITTING
S yourselves one to another in ... Eph 5:21 *5293*

SUBORNED
Then they s men, which said, We ... Acts 6:11 *5260*

SUBSCRIBE
another shall s with his hand ... Is 44:5 3789
s evidences, and seal them, and ... Jer 32:44 3789

SUBSCRIBED
I s the evidence, and sealed it, ... Jer 32:10 3789
that s the book of the purchase ... Jer 32:12 3789

SUBSTANCE
every living s that I have made ... Gen 7:4 3351
every living s was destroyed ... Gen 7:23 3351
all their s that they had ... Gen 12:5 7399
for their s was great, so that ... Gen 13:6 7399
shall they come out with great s ... Gen 15:14 7399
Shall not their cattle and their s ... Gen 34:23 7075
and all his beasts, and all his s ... Gen 36:6 7075
all the s that was in their ... Deut 11:6 3351
Bless, LORD, his s, and accept the ... Deut 33:11 3428
for their cattle and for their s ... Josh 14:4 7075
of the s which was king David's ... 1Chr 27:31 7399
and the stewards over all the s ... 1Chr 28:1 7399
carried away all the s that was ... 2Chr 21:17 7399
of his s for the burnt offerings ... 2Chr 31:3 7399
for God had given him s very much ... 2Chr 32:29 7399
these were of the king's s ... 2Chr 35:7 7399
our little ones, and for all our s ... Ezr 8:21 7399
all his s should be forfeited, and ... Ezr 10:8 7399
His s also was seven thousand ... Job 1:3 4735
his s is increased in the land ... Job 1:10 4735
the robber swalloweth up their s ... Job 5:5 2428
Give a reward for me of your s ... Job 6:22 3581
neither shall his s continue ... Job 15:29 2428
according to his s shall the ... Job 20:18 2428
Whereas our s is not cut down, ... Job 22:20 7009
ride upon it, and dissolvest my s ... Job 30:22 7738
rest of their s to their babes ... Ps 17:14
his house, and ruler of all his s ... Ps 105:21 7075
My s was not hid from thee, when ... Ps 139:15 6108
Thine eyes did see my s, yet ... Ps 139:16 1564
We shall find all precious s ... Prov 1:13 1952
Honour the LORD with thy s ... Prov 3:9 1952
shall give all the s of his house ... Prov 6:31 1952
those that love me to inherit s ... Prov 8:21 3426
casteth away the s of the wicked ... Prov 10:3 1942
but the s of a diligent man is ... Prov 12:27 1952
and unjust gain increaseth his s ... Prov 28:8 1952
with harlots spendeth his s ... Prov 29:3 1952
all the s of his house for love ... Song 8:7 1952
whose s is in them, when they ... Is 6:13 4678
holy seed shall be the s thereof ... Is 6:13 4678
Thy s and thy treasures will I ... Jer 15:13 2428
in the field, I will give thy s ... Jer 17:3 2428
rich, I have found me out s ... Hos 12:8 202
s in the day of their calamity ... Obad 13 2428
their s unto the Lord of the ... Mic 4:13 2428
ministered unto him of their s ... Lk 8:3 *5224*
there wasted his s with riotous ... Lk 15:13 *3776*
heaven a better and an enduring s ... Heb 10:34 *5223*
Now faith is the s of things ... Heb 11:1 *5287*

SUBTIL
Now the serpent was more s than ... Gen 3:1 6175
and Jonadab was a very s man ... 2Sa 13:3 2450
of an harlot, and s of heart ... Prov 7:10 5341

SUBTILLY
is told me that he dealeth very s ... 1Sa 23:22 6191
to deal s with his servants ... Ps 105:25 5230
The same dealt s with our kindred ... Acts 7:19 *2686*

SUBTILTY
he said, Thy brother came with s ... Gen 27:35 4820
But Jehu did it in s, to the ... 2Kin 10:19 6122
To give s to the simple, to the ... Prov 1:4 6195
that they might take Jesus by s ... Mt 26:4 *1388*
And said, O full of all s and all ... Acts 13:10 *1388*
beguiled Eve through his s ... 2Cor 11:3 *3834*

SUBURBS
But the field of the s of their ... Lev 25:34 4054
give also unto the Levites s for ... Num 35:2 4054
the s of them shall be for their ... Num 35:3 4054
the s of the cities, which ye ... Num 35:4 4054
be to them the s of the cities ... Num 35:5 4054
them shall ye give with their s ... Num 35:7 4054
with their s for their cattle and ... Josh 14:4 4054
with the s thereof for our cattle ... Josh 21:2 4054
the LORD, these cities and their s ... Josh 21:3 4054
Levites these cities with their s ... Josh 21:8 4054
with the s thereof round about it ... Josh 21:11 4054
the priest Hebron with her s ... Josh 21:13 4054
and Libnah with her s, ... Josh 21:13 4054
And Jattir with her s, and Eshtemoa ... Josh 21:14 4054
and Eshtemoa with her s ... Josh 21:14 4054
And Holon with her s, and Debir ... Josh 21:15 4054
and Debir with her s ... Josh 21:15 4054
And Ain with her s, and Juttah with ... Josh 21:16 4054
and Juttah with her s ... Josh 21:16 4054
and Beth-shemesh with her s ... Josh 21:16 4054
of Benjamin, Gibeon with her s ... Josh 21:17 4054
Geba with her s ... Josh 21:17 4054
Anathoth with her s, and Almon ... Josh 21:18 4054
and Almon with her s ... Josh 21:18 4054
were thirteen cities with their s ... Josh 21:19 4054
with her s in mount Ephraim ... Josh 21:21 4054
and Gezer with her s, ... Josh 21:21 4054

And Kibzaim with her s, and ... Josh 21:22 4054
and Beth-horon with her s ... Josh 21:22 4054
tribe of Dan, Eltekeh with her s ... Josh 21:23 4054
Gibbethon with her s ... Josh 21:23 4054
Aijalon with her s, Gath-rimmon ... Josh 21:24 4054
Gath-rimmon with her s ... Josh 21:24 4054
of Manasseh, Tanach with her s ... Josh 21:25 4054
and Gath-rimmon with her s ... Josh 21:25 4054
their s for the families of the ... Josh 21:26 4054
gave Golan in Bashan with her s ... Josh 21:27 4054
and Beesh-terah with her s ... Josh 21:27 4054
of Issachar, Kishon with her s ... Josh 21:28 4054
Dabareh with her s ... Josh 21:28 4054
Jarmuth with her s, En-gannim ... Josh 21:29 4054
En-gannim with her s ... Josh 21:29 4054
tribe of Asher, Mishal with her s ... Josh 21:30 4054
Abdon with her s ... Josh 21:30 4054
Helkath with her s, and Rehob with ... Josh 21:31 4054
Rehob with her s ... Josh 21:31 4054
Kedesh in Galilee with her s ... Josh 21:32 4054
and Hammoth-dor with her s ... Josh 21:32 4054
and Kartan with her s ... Josh 21:32 4054
were thirteen cities with their s ... Josh 21:33 4054
of Zebulun, Jokneam with her s ... Josh 21:34 4054
and Kartah with her s ... Josh 21:34 4054
Dimnah with her s, Nahalal with ... Josh 21:35 4054
her s, Nahalal with her s ... Josh 21:35 4054
tribe of Reuben, Bezer with her s ... Josh 21:36
and Jahazah with her s ... Josh 21:36
Kedemoth with her s, and Mephaath ... Josh 21:37
and Mephaath with her s ... Josh 21:37
Gad, Ramoth in Gilead with her s ... Josh 21:38 4054
and Mahanaim with her s ... Josh 21:38 4054
Heshbon with her s, Jazer with ... Josh 21:39 4054
Jazer with her s ... Josh 21:39 4054
and eight cities with their s ... Josh 21:41 4054
one with their s round about them ... Josh 21:42 4054
chamberlain, which was in the s ... 2Kin 23:11 6503
towns, and in all the s of Sharon ... 1Chr 5:16 4054
the s thereof round about it ... 1Chr 6:55 4054
of refuge, and Libnah with her s ... 1Chr 6:57 4054
Jattir, and Eshtemoa, with their s ... 1Chr 6:57 4054
And Hilen with her s, Debir with ... 1Chr 6:58 4054
Debir with her s ... 1Chr 6:58 4054
And Ashan with her s, and ... 1Chr 6:59 4054
and Beth-shemesh with her s ... 1Chr 6:59 4054
Geba with her s ... 1Chr 6:60 4054
and Alemeth with her s ... 1Chr 6:60 4054
and Anathoth with her s ... 1Chr 6:60 4054
Levites these cities with their s ... 1Chr 6:64 4054
in mount Ephraim with her s ... 1Chr 6:67 4054
they gave also Gezer with her s ... 1Chr 6:67 4054
And Jokmeam with her s, and ... 1Chr 6:68 4054
and Beth-horon with her s ... 1Chr 6:68 4054
And Aijalon with her s, and ... 1Chr 6:69 4054
and Gath-rimmon with her s ... 1Chr 6:69 4054
Aner with her s, and Bileam with ... 1Chr 6:70 4054
and Bileam with her s ... 1Chr 6:70 4054
Golan in Bashan with her s ... 1Chr 6:71 4054
and Ashtaroth with her s ... 1Chr 6:71 4054
Kedesh with her s ... 1Chr 6:72 4054
Daberath with her s ... 1Chr 6:72 4054
And Ramoth with her s ... 1Chr 6:73 4054
and Anem with her s ... 1Chr 6:73 4054
Mashal with her s ... 1Chr 6:74 4054
and Abdon with her s ... 1Chr 6:74 4054
And Hukok with her s ... 1Chr 6:75 4054
and Rehob with her s ... 1Chr 6:75 4054
Kedesh in Galilee with her s ... 1Chr 6:76 4054
and Hammon with her s ... 1Chr 6:76 4054
and Kirjathaim with her s ... 1Chr 6:76 4054
of Zebulun, Rimmon with her s ... 1Chr 6:77 4054
Tabor with her s ... 1Chr 6:77 4054
in the wilderness with her s ... 1Chr 6:78 4054
and Jahzah with her s ... 1Chr 6:78 4054
Kedemoth also with her s, and ... 1Chr 6:79 4054
and Mephaath with her s ... 1Chr 6:79 4054
Ramoth in Gilead with her s ... 1Chr 6:80 4054
and Mahanaim with her s ... 1Chr 6:80 4054
And Heshbon with her s, and Jazer ... 1Chr 6:81 4054
and Jazer with her s ... 1Chr 6:81 4054
which are in their cities and s ... 1Chr 13:2 4054
For the Levites left their s ... 2Chr 11:14 4054
fields of the s of their cities ... 2Chr 31:19 4054
The s shall shake at the sound of ... Eze 27:28 4054
round about for the s thereof ... Eze 45:2 4054
the city, for dwelling, and for s ... Eze 48:15 4054
the s of the city shall be toward ... Eze 48:17 4054

SUBVERT
To s a man in his cause, the Lord ... Lam 3:36 5791
who s whole houses, teaching ... Titus 1:11 *396*

SUBVERTED
Knowing that he that is such is s ... Titus 3:11 *1612*

SUBVERTING
s your souls, saying, Ye must be ... Acts 15:24 *384*
but to the s of the hearers ... 2Ti 2:14 *2692*

SUCATHITES See SUCHATHITES.

SUCCEED
which she beareth shall s in the ... Deut 25:6 6965

SUCCEEDED
but the children of Esau s them ... Deut 2:12 3423
and they s them, and dwelt in their ... Deut 2:21 3423
and they s them, and dwelt in their ... Deut 2:22 3423

SUCCEEDEST
to possess them, and thou s them ... Deut 12:29 3423
God giveth thee, and thou s them ... Deut 19:1 3423

SUCCESS
and then thou shalt have good s ... Josh 1:8 7919

SUCCOTH (*suc'-coth*)
1. A place east of the Jordan.
And Jacob journeyed to S, and built ... Gen 33:17 5523
the name of the place is called S ... Gen 33:17 5523
2. An Israelite encampment in the wilderness.
journeyed from Rameses to S ... Ex 12:37 5523
And they took their journey from S ... Ex 13:20 5523
from Rameses, and pitched in S ... Num 33:5 5523
And they departed from S, and ... Num 33:6 5523
3. A place in Gad.
Beth-aram, and Beth-nimrah, and S ... Josh 13:27 5523
And he said unto the men of S ... Judg 8:5 5523
And the princes of S said, Are the ... Judg 8:6 5523
as the men of S had answered him ... Judg 8:8 5523
a young man of the men of S ... Judg 8:14 5523
unto him the princes of S ... Judg 8:14 5523
And he came unto the men of S ... Judg 8:15 5523
with them he taught the men of S ... Judg 8:16 5523
4. A city in Ephraim.
in the clay ground between S ... 1Kin 7:46 5523
in the clay ground between S ... 2Chr 4:17 5523
and mete out the valley of S ... Ps 60:6 5523
and mete out the valley of S ... Ps 108:7 5523

SUCCOTH-BENOTH (*suc''-coth-be'-noth*) *A Babylonian god.*
And the men of Babylon made S ... 2Kin 17:30 5524

SUCCOUR
came to s Hadadezer king of Zobah ... 2Sa 8:5 5826
that thou s us out of the city ... 2Sa 18:3 5826
he is able to s them that are ... Heb 2:18 *997*

SUCCOURED
Abishai the son of Zeruiah s him ... 2Sa 21:17 5826
day of salvation have I s thee ... 2Cor 6:2 *997*

SUCCOURER
for she hath been a s of many ... Rom 16:2 *4368*

SUCH
the father of s as dwell in tents ... Gen 4:20
in tents, and of s as have cattle ... Gen 4:20
of all s as handle the harp ... Gen 4:21
s as I love, and bring it to me, ... Gen 27:4
for thy father, s as he loveth ... Gen 27:9
meat, s as his father loved ... Gen 27:14
s as these which are of the ... Gen 27:46
and of s shall be my hire ... Gen 30:32
s as I never saw in all the land ... Gen 41:19 2007
Can we find s a one as this is, a ... Gen 41:38
wot ye not that s a man as I can ... Gen 44:15
s as hath not been in Egypt since ... Ex 9:18
s as there was none like it in ... Ex 9:24
there were no s locusts as they ... Ex 10:14 3651
neither after them shall be s ... Ex 10:14
s as there was none like it, nor ... Ex 11:6
them s things as they required ... Ex 12:36
s as fear God, men of truth, ... Ex 18:21
place s over them, to be rulers ... Ex 18:21
s as have not been done in all ... Ex 34:10
s things have befallen me ... Lev 10:19 428
that on which s water cometh ... Lev 11:34
every s vessel shall be unclean ... Lev 11:34
pigeons, s as he is able to get ... Lev 14:22
young pigeons, s as he can get ... Lev 14:30
Even s as he is able to get, the ... Lev 14:31
after s as have familiar spirits ... Lev 20:6
any s shall be unclean until even ... Lev 22:6
all that any man giveth of s unto ... Lev 27:9
instead of s as open every womb, ... Num 8:16
whether there hath been any s ... Deut 4:32
there were s an heart in them ... Deut 5:29 2888
shall do no more any s wickedness ... Deut 13:11
that s abomination is wrought ... Deut 13:14 2063
s time as thou beginnest to put ... Deut 16:9
that s abomination is wrought in ... Deut 17:4 2063
no more any s evil among you ... Deut 19:20
For all that do s things, and all ... Deut 25:16 428
at the least s as before knew ... Judg 3:2
have told us s things as these ... Judg 13:23
that thou comest with s a company ... Judg 18:23
There was no s deed done nor seen ... Judg 19:30 2063
unto whom he said, Ho, s a one ... Ruth 4:1 6423
unto them, Why do ye s things ... 1Sa 2:23 428
not been s a thing heretofore ... 1Sa 4:7 2063
I have appointed my servants to s ... 1Sa 21:2 6423
and s a place ... 1Sa 21:2 492
for he is s a son of Belial, that ... 1Sa 25:17
look upon s a dead dog as I am ... 2Sa 9:8
given unto thee s and s things ... 2Sa 12:8 2007
for no s thing ought to be done ... 2Sa 13:12 3651
for with s robes were the king's ... 2Sa 13:18 3651
then hast thou thought s a thing ... 2Sa 14:13 2063
that s as be faint in the ... 2Sa 16:2
recompense it me with s a reward ... 2Sa 19:36 2063
there came no more s abundance of ... 1Kin 10:10 1931
there came no s almug trees ... 1Kin 10:12 3651
with his servants, saying, In s ... 2Kin 6:8 6423
s a place shall be my camp ... 2Kin 6:8 492
that thou pass not s a place ... 2Kin 6:9 2088
in heaven, might s a thing be ... 2Kin 7:19 2088
Ye shall eat this year s things ... 2Kin 19:29
I am bringing s evil upon ... 2Kin 21:12
Surely there was not holden s a ... 2Kin 23:22 2088
s things as were of gold, in gold ... 2Kin 25:15
s as went forth to battle, expert ... 1Chr 12:33
s as went forth to battle, expert ... 1Chr 12:36
bestowed upon him s royal majesty ... 1Chr 29:25
s as none of the kings have had ... 2Chr 1:12 834
s things as they offered for the ... 2Chr 4:6
neither was there any s spice as ... 2Chr 9:9 1932
there were none s seen before in ... 2Chr 9:11 1992
s as set their hearts to seek the ... 2Chr 11:16
s as taught to sing praise ... 2Chr 23:13
Jehoiada gave it to s as did the ... 2Chr 24:12
also s as wrought iron and brass ... 2Chr 24:12
time in s sort as it was written ... 2Chr 30:5
keep s a passover as Josiah kept ... 2Chr 35:18
side the river, and at s a time ... Ezr 4:10 3706
side the river, and at s a time ... Ezr 4:11 3706
the river, Peace, and at s a time ... Ezr 4:17 3706
all s as had separated themselves ... Ezr 6:21
perfect peace, and at s a time ... Ezr 7:12 3706
all s as know the laws of thy God ... Ezr 7:25
which hath put s a thing as this ... Ezr 7:27
of s as lay in wait by the way ... Ezr 8:31
hast given us s deliverance as ... Ezr 9:13
s as are born of them, according ... Ezr 10:3
There are no s things done as ... Neh 6:8 428
I said, Should s a man as I flee ... Neh 6:11 3644
with s things as belonged to her, ... Est 2:9
except s to whom the king shall ... Est 4:11 834
the kingdom for s a time as this ... Est 4:14
to lay hand on s as sought their ... Est 9:2
upon all s as joined themselves ... Est 9:27
who knoweth not s things as these ... Job 12:3 3644
open thine eyes upon s an one ... Job 14:3 2088
lettest s words go out of thy ... Job 15:13
I have heard many s things ... Job 16:2 428
Surely s are the dwellings of the ... Job 18:21 428
many s things are with him ... Job 23:14 2007
truth unto s as keep his covenant ... Ps 25:10
me, and s as breathe out cruelty ... Ps 27:12
saveth s as be of a contrite ... Ps 34:18
to slay s as be of upright ... Ps 37:14
For s as be blessed of him shall ... Ps 37:22
nor s as turn aside to lies ... Ps 40:4
let s as love thy salvation say ... Ps 40:16
altogether s an one as thyself ... Ps 50:21
against s as be at peace with him ... Ps 55:20
the hairy scalp of s an one as ... Ps 68:21
let s as love thy salvation say ... Ps 70:4
even to s as are of a clean heart ... Ps 73:1
To s as keep his covenant, and to ... Ps 103:18
S as sit in darkness and in the ... Ps 107:10
As for s as turn aside unto their ... Ps 125:5
S knowledge is too wonderful for ... Ps 139:6
that people, that is in s a case ... Ps 144:15 3602
but s as are upright in their way ... Prov 11:20
but s as keep the law contend ... Prov 28:4
S is the way of an adulterous ... Prov 30:20 3651
the dumb in the cause of all s as ... Prov 31:8
the tears of s as were oppressed ... Eccl 4:1
not be s as was in her vexation ... Is 9:1
s as are escaped of the house of ... Is 10:20
s is our expectation, whither we ... Is 20:6 3541
this year s as groweth of itself ... Is 37:30
Is it s a fast that I have chosen ... Is 58:5 2088
Who hath heard s a thing ... Is 66:8 2063
who hath seen s things ... Is 66:8 428
and see if there be s a thing ... Jer 2:10 2063
be avenged on s a nation as this ... Jer 5:9 834
be avenged on s a nation as this ... Jer 5:29 834
be avenged on s a nation as this ... Jer 9:9 834
S as are for death, to death ... Jer 15:2
s as are for the sword, to the ... Jer 15:2
s as are for the famine, to the ... Jer 15:2
s as are for the captivity, to ... Jer 15:2
heathen, who hath heard s things ... Jer 18:13 428
s as are left in this city from ... Jer 21:7
in speaking s words unto them ... Jer 38:4 428
deliver s as are for death to ... Jer 43:11
s as are for captivity to ... Jer 43:11
s as are for the sword to the ... Jer 43:11
return but s as shall escape ... Jer 44:14
he escape that doeth s things ... Eze 17:15 428
considereth, and doeth not s like ... Eze 18:14 2007
s as had ability in them to stand ... Dan 1:4
that asked s things at any ... Dan 2:10 1836
he had spoken s words unto me ... Dan 10:15 428
s as do wickedly against the ... Dan 11:32
s as never was since there was a ... Dan 12:1 834
s as are skilful of lamentation ... Amos 5:16
heathen, s as they have not heard ... Mic 5:15
all s as are clothed with strange ... Zeph 1:8
which had given s power unto men ... Mt 9:8 *5108*
one s little child in my name ... Mt 18:5 *5108*
for of s is the kingdom of heaven ... Mt 19:14 *5108*
s as was not since the beginning ... Mt 24:21 *3634*
for in s an hour as ye think not ... Mt 24:44
said, Go into the city to s a man ... Mt 26:18 *1170*
s as hear the word, ... Mk 4:18 *3778*
s as hear the word, and receive it ... Mk 4:20 *3748*
with many s parables spake he the ... Mk 4:33 *5108*
that even s mighty works are ... Mk 6:2 *5108*
many other s like things ye do ... Mk 7:8 *5108*
and many s like things do ye ... Mk 7:13 *5108*
one of s children in my name ... Mk 9:37 *5108*
for of s is the kingdom of God ... Mk 10:14 *5108*
for s things must needs be ... Mk 13:7
s as was not from the beginning ... Mk 13:19 *3634*
is this, of whom I hear s things ... Lk 9:9 *3634*
drinking s things as they give ... Lk 10:7
eat s things as are set before ... Lk 10:8
give alms of s things as ye have ... Lk 11:41
because they suffered s things ... Lk 13:2 *5108*
for of s is the kingdom of God ... Lk 18:16 *5108*
Father seeketh s to worship him ... Jn 4:23 *5108*
murmured s things concerning him ... Jn 7:32 *5023*
us, that s should be stoned ... Jn 8:5 *5108*
that is a sinner do s miracles ... Jn 9:16 *5108*
church daily s as should be saved ... Acts 2:47
but s as I have give I thee ... Acts 3:6
to whom we gave no s commandment ... Acts 15:24
Who, having received s a charge ... Acts 16:24 *5108*
I will be no judge of s matters ... Acts 18:15 *5130*
that they observe no s thing ... Acts 21:25 *5108*

Away with *s* a fellow from the Acts 22:22 *5108*
of *s* things as I supposed Acts 25:18
doubted of *s* manner of questions Acts 25:20
almost, and altogether *s* as I am Acts 26:29 *5108*
they laded us with *s* things as Acts 28:10
that they which commit *s* things Rom 1:32 *5108*
them which commit *s* things Rom 2:2 *5108*
judgest them which do *s* things Rom 2:3 *5108*
For they that are *s* serve not our Rom 16:18 *5108*
s fornication as is not so much 1Cor 5:1 *5108*
To deliver *s* a one unto Satan for 1Cor 5:5 *5108*
with *s* an one, no not to eat 1Cor 5:11 *5108*
And *s* were some of you 1Cor 6:11 *5023*
is not under bondage in *s* cases 1Cor 7:15 *5108*
Nevertheless *s* shall have trouble 1Cor 7:28 *5108*
you but *s* as is common to man 1Cor 10:13
contentious, we have no *s* custom 1Cor 11:16 *5108*
s are they also that are earthy 1Cor 15:48 *5108*
s are they also that are heavenly 1Cor 15:48 *5108*
That ye submit yourselves unto *s* 1Cor 16:16 *5108*
acknowledge ye them that are *s* 1Cor 16:18 *5108*
Sufficient to *s* a man is this 2Cor 2:6 *5108*
lest perhaps *s* a one should be 2Cor 2:7 *5108*
s trust have we through Christ to 2Cor 3:4 *5108*
Seeing then that we have *s* hope 2Cor 3:12 *5108*
Let *s* an one think this, that, 2Cor 10:11 *3634*
s as we are in word by letters 2Cor 10:11 *5108*
s will we be also in deed when we 2Cor 10:11 *5108*
For *s* are false apostles, 2Cor 11:13 *5108*
s an one caught up to the third 2Cor 12:2 *5108*
And I knew *s* a man, (whether in 2Cor 12:3 *5108*
Of *s* an one will I glory 2Cor 12:5 *5108*
I shall not find you *s* as I would 2Cor 12:20 *3634*
found unto you *s* as ye would not 2Cor 12:20 *3634*
revellings, and *s* like Gal 5:21 *5125*
that they which do *s* things shall Gal 5:21 *5108*
against *s* there is no law Gal 5:23 *5108*
restore *s* an one in the spirit of Gal 6:1 *5108*
spot, or wrinkle, or any *s* thing Eph 5:27 *5108*
and hold *s* in reputation Phil 2:29 *5108*
the Lord is the avenger of all *s* 1Th 4:6 *5130*
Now them that are *s* we command 2Th 3:12 *5108*
from *s* withdraw thyself 1Ti 6:5 *5108*
from *s* turn away 2Ti 3:5 *5128*
that he that is *s* is subverted Titus 3:11 *5108*
being *s* an one as Paul the aged, Philem 9 *5108*
are become *s* as have need of milk Heb 5:12
For *s* an high priest became us, Heb 7:26 *5108*
We have *s* an high priest, who is Heb 8:1 *5108*
For they that say *s* things Heb 11:14 *5108*
s contradiction of sinners Heb 12:3 *5108*
be content with *s* things as ye Heb 13:5 *3588*
for with *s* sacrifices God is well Heb 13:16 *5108*
morrow we will go into *s* a city Jas 4:13 *3592*
all *s* rejoicing is evil Jas 4:16 *5108*
when there came *s* a voice to him 2Pet 1:17 *5107*
seeing that ye look for *s* things 2Pet 3:14 *5023*
We therefore ought to receive *s* 3Jn 8 *5108*
s as are in the sea, and all that Rev 5:13
s as was not since men were upon Rev 16:18 *3634*
on *s* the second death hath no Rev 20:6 *5130*

SUCHATHITES (*soo'-kath-ites*) *A family of scribes.*
the Shimeathites, and *S* 1Chr 2:55 7756

SUCK
should have given children *s* Gen 21:7 3243
he made him to *s* honey out of the Deut 32:13 3243
for they shall *s* of the abundance Deut 33:19 3243
gave her son *s* until she weaned 1Sa 1:23 3243
in the morning to give my child *s* 1Kin 3:21 3243
why the breasts that I should *s* Job 3:12 3243
He shall *s* the poison of asps Job 20:16 3243
Her young ones also *s* up blood Job 39:30 5966
Thou shalt also *s* the milk of the Is 60:16 3243
shalt *s* the breast of kings Is 60:16 3243
That ye may *s*, and be satisfied Is 66:11 3243
then shall ye *s*, ye shall be Is 66:12 3243
they give *s* to their young ones Lam 4:3 3243
s it out, and thou shalt break the Eze 23:34 4680
and those that *s* the breasts Joel 2:16 3243
to them that give *s* in those days Mt 24:19 *2337*
to them that give *s* in those days Mk 13:17 *2337*
child, and to them that give *s* Lk 21:23 *2337*
and the paps which never gave *s* Lk 23:29 *2337*

SUCKED
that *s* the breasts of my mother Song 8:1 3243
and the paps which thou hast *s* Lk 11:27 *2337*

SUCKING
father beareth the *s* child Num 11:12 3243
And Samuel took a *s* lamb, and 1Sa 7:9 2461
the *s* child shall play on the Is 11:8 3243
Can a woman forget her *s* child Is 49:15 5764
The tongue of the *s* child Lam 4:4 3243

SUCKLING
the *s* also with the man of gray Deut 32:25 3243
both man and woman, infant and *s* 1Sa 15:3 3243
man and woman, child and *s* Jer 44:7 3243

SUCKLINGS
both men and women, children and *s* 1Sa 22:19 3243
s hast thou ordained strength Ps 8:2 3243
the *s* swoon in the streets of the Lam 2:11 3243
s thou hast perfected praise Mt 21:16 *2337*

SUDDEN
thee, and *s* fear troubleth thee Job 22:10 6597
Be not afraid of *s* fear, neither Prov 3:25 6597
then *s* destruction cometh upon 1Th 5:3 *160*

SUDDENLY
And if any man die very *s* by him Num 6:9 6597
And the LORD spake *s* unto Moses Num 12:4 6597
if he thrust him *s* without enmity Num 35:22 6621
against you, and destroy thee *s* Deut 7:4 4118
Joshua therefore came unto them *s* Josh 10:9 6597
them by the waters of Merom *s* Josh 11:7 6597
to depart, lest he overtake us *s* 2Sa 15:14 4116
for the thing was done *s* 2Chr 29:36 6597
but *s* I cursed his habitation Job 5:3 6597
If the scourge slay *s*, he will Job 9:23 6597
let them return and be ashamed *s* Ps 6:10 7281
s do they shoot at him, and fear Ps 64:4 6597
s shall they be wounded Ps 64:7 6597
shall his calamity come *s* Prov 6:15 6597
s shall he be broken without Prov 6:15 6621
For their calamity shall rise *s* Prov 24:22 6597
shall *s* be destroyed, and that Prov 29:1 6621
time, when it falleth *s* upon them Eccl 9:12 6597
yea, it shall be at an instant *s* Is 29:5 6597
breaking cometh *s* at an instant Is 30:13 6597
desolation shall come upon thee *s* Is 47:11 6597
I did them *s*, and they came to Is 48:3 6597
s are my tents spoiled, and my Jer 4:20 6597
the spoiler shall *s* come upon us Jer 6:26 6597
have caused him to fall upon it *s* Jer 15:8 6597
shalt bring a troop *s* upon them Jer 18:22 6597
but I will *s* make him run away Jer 49:19 7280
make them *s* run away from her Jer 50:44 7280
Babylon is *s* fallen and destroyed Jer 51:8 6597
rise up *s* that shall bite thee Hab 2:7 6621
shall *s* come to his temple, even Mal 3:1 6597
And *s*, when they had looked round Mk 9:8 *1819*
Lest coming *s* he find you Mk 13:36 *1810*
s there was with the angel a Lk 2:13 *1810*
taketh him, and he *s* crieth out Lk 9:39 *1810*
s there came a sound from heaven Acts 2:2 *869*
s there shined round about him a Acts 9:3 *1810*
s there was a great earthquake, Acts 16:26 *869*
s there shone from heaven a great Acts 22:6 *1810*
swollen, or fallen down dead *s* Acts 28:6 *869*
Lay hands *s* on no man, neither be 1Ti 5:22 *5030*

SUE
if any man will *s* thee at the law Mt 5:40 *2919*

SUFFER
will not *s* the destroyer to come Ex 12:23 5414
Thou shalt not *s* a witch to live Ex 22:18
neither shalt thou *s* the salt of Lev 2:13
neighbour, and not *s* sin upon him Lev 19:17 5375
Or *s* them to bear the iniquity of Lev 22:16 5375
Sihon would not *s* Israel to pass Num 21:23 5414
s them not to enter into their Josh 10:19 5414
for they would not *s* them to come Judg 1:34 5414
father would not *s* him to go in Judg 15:1 5414
S me that I may feel the pillars Judg 16:26 3240
that thou wouldest not *s* the 2Sa 14:11
that he might not *s* any to go out 1Kin 15:17 5414
for the king's profit to *s* them Est 3:8 3240
He will not *s* me to take my Job 9:18 5414
S me that I may speak Job 21:3 5375
their winepresses, and *s* thirst Job 24:11
S me a little, and I will shew Job 36:2 3803
which I *s* of them that hate me Ps 9:13
neither wilt thou *s* thine Holy Ps 16:10 5414
young lions do lack, and *s* hunger Ps 34:10
he shall never *s* the righteous to Ps 55:22 5414
while I *s* thy terrors I am Ps 88:15 5375
nor *s* my faithfulness to fail Ps 89:33
and a proud heart will not I *s* Ps 101:5 3201
He will not *s* thy foot to be Ps 121:3 5414
The LORD will not *s* the soul of Prov 10:3
and an idle soul shall *s* hunger Prov 19:15
of great wrath shall *s* punishment Prov 19:19 5375
S not thy mouth to cause thy Eccl 5:6 5414
the rich will not *s* him to sleep Eccl 5:12 3240
nor *s* their locks to grow long Eze 44:20
said unto him, *S* it to be so now Mt 3:15 *863*
s me first to go and bury my Mt 8:21 *2010*
s us to go away into the herd of Mt 8:31 *2010*
s many things of the elders and Mt 16:21 *3958*
also the Son of man *s* of them Mt 17:12 *3958*
how long shall I *s* you Mt 17:17 *430*
S little children, and forbid them Mt 19:14 *863*
neither *s* ye them that are Mt 23:13 *863*
ye *s* him no more to do ought for Mk 7:12 *863*
the Son of man must *s* many things Mk 8:31 *3958*
man, that he must *s* many things Mk 9:12 *3958*
how long shall I *s* you Mk 9:19 *430*
S the little children to come Mk 10:14 *863*
would not *s* that any man should Mk 11:16 *863*
would *s* them to enter into them Lk 8:32 *2010*
The Son of man must *s* many things Lk 9:22 *3958*
shall I be with you, and *s* you Lk 9:41 *430*
s me first to go and bury my Lk 9:59 *2010*
But first must he *s* many things Lk 17:25 *3958*
S little children to come unto me Lk 18:16 *863*
this passover with you before I *s* Lk 22:15 *3958*
answered and said, *S* ye thus far Lk 22:51 *1439*
and thus it behoved Christ to *s* Lk 24:46 *3958*
neither wilt thou *s* thine Holy Acts 2:27 *1325*
prophets, that Christ should *s* Acts 3:18 *3958*
worthy to *s* shame for his name Acts 5:41 *818*
And seeing one of them *s* wrong Acts 7:24
he must *s* for my name's sake Acts 9:16 *3958*
Thou shalt not *s* thine Holy One Acts 13:35 *1325*
s me to speak unto the people Acts 21:39 *2010*
That Christ should *s*, and that he Acts 26:23 *3805*
if so be that we *s* with him Rom 8:17 *4841*
shall be burned, he shall *s* loss 1Cor 3:15 *2210*
being persecuted, we *s* it 1Cor 4:12 *430*
why do ye not rather *s* yourselves 1Cor 6:7
but *s* all things, lest we should 1Cor 9:12 *4722*
who will not *s* you to be tempted 1Cor 10:13 *1439*
And whether one member *s*, all the 1Cor 12:26 *3958*
s, all the members *s* with it 1Cor 12:26 *4841*
same sufferings which we also *s* 2Cor 1:6 *3958*
For ye *s* fools gladly, seeing ye 2Cor 11:19 *430*
For ye *s*, if a man bring you into 2Cor 11:20 *430*
why do I yet *s* persecution Gal 5:11 *1377*
only lest they should *s* Gal 6:12 *1377*
but also to *s* for his sake Phil 1:29 *3958*
both to abound and to *s* need Phil 4:12 *5302*
that we should *s* tribulation 1Th 3:4
of God, for which ye also *s* 2Th 1:5
But I *s* not a woman to teach, nor 1Ti 2:12 *2010*
s reproach, because we trust in 1Ti 4:10
which cause I also *s* these things 2Ti 1:12 *3958*
Wherein I *s* trouble, as an evil 2Ti 2:9 *2553*
If we *s*, we shall also reign with 2Ti 2:12 *5278*
Christ Jesus shall *s* persecution 2Ti 3:12 *1377*
Choosing rather to *s* affliction Heb 11:25 *4778*
and them which *s* adversity Heb 13:3 *2558*
s the word of exhortation Heb 13:22 *430*
s for it, ye take it patiently, 1Pet 2:20 *3958*
if ye *s* for righteousness' sake, 1Pet 3:14 *3958*
that ye *s* for well doing, than 1Pet 3:17 *3958*
let none of you *s* as a murderer 1Pet 4:15 *3958*
Yet if any man *s* as a Christian 1Pet 4:16
Wherefore let them that *s* 1Pet 4:19 *3958*
those things which thou shalt *s* Rev 2:10 *3958*
shall not *s* their dead bodies to Rev 11:9 *863*

SUFFERED
therefore *s* I thee not to touch Gen 20:6 5414
but God *s* him not to hurt me Gen 31:7 5414
hast not *s* me to kiss my sons and Gen 31:28 5203
s thee to hunger, and fed thee Deut 8:3
thy God hath not *s* thee so to do Deut 18:14 5414
Moab, and *s* not a man to pass over Judg 3:28 5414
s them not to rise against Saul 1Sa 24:7 5414
s neither the birds of the air to 2Sa 21:10 5414
He *s* no man to do them wrong 1Chr 16:21 3240
(Neither have I *s* my mouth to sin Job 31:30 5414
He *s* no man to do them wrong Ps 105:14 3240
that for thy sake I have *s* rebuke Jer 15:15 5375
Then he *s* him Mt 3:15 *863*
s you to put away your wives Mt 19:8 *2010*
would not have *s* his house to be Mt 24:43 *1439*
for I have *s* many things this day Mt 27:19 *3958*
s not the devils to speak, Mk 1:34 *863*
Howbeit Jesus *s* him not, but Mk 5:19 *863*
had *s* many things of many Mk 5:26 *3958*
he *s* no man to follow him, save Mk 5:37 *863*
Moses *s* to write a bill of Mk 10:4 *2010*
he rebuking them *s* them not to Lk 4:41 *1439*
And he *s* them Lk 8:32 *2010*
he *s* no man to go in, save Peter, Lk 8:51 *863*
not have *s* his house to be broken Lk 12:39 *863*
because they *s* such things Lk 13:2 *3958*
not Christ to have *s* these things Lk 24:26 *3958*
years *s* he their manners in the Acts 13:18 *5159*
Who in times past *s* all nations Acts 14:16 *1439*
but the Spirit *s* them not Acts 16:7 *1439*
that Christ must needs have *s* Acts 17:3 *3958*
people, the disciples *s* him not Acts 19:30 *1439*
but Paul was *s* to dwell by Acts 28:16 *2010*
nor for his cause that *s* wrong 2Cor 7:12
thrice I *s* shipwreck, a night and 2Cor 11:25
Have ye *s* so many things in vain Gal 3:4 *3958*
for whom I have *s* the loss of all Phil 3:8 *2210*
even after that we had *s* before 1Th 2:2 *4310*
for ye also have *s* like things of 1Th 2:14 *3958*
he himself hath *s* being tempted Heb 2:18 *3958*
by the things which he *s* Heb 5:8 *3958*
because they were not *s* to Heb 7:23 *2967*
s since the foundation of the Heb 9:26 *3958*
his own blood, *s* without the gate Heb 13:12 *3958*
because Christ also *s* for us 1Pet 2:21 *3958*
when he *s*, he threatened not 1Pet 2:23 *3958*
Christ also hath once *s* for sins 1Pet 3:18 *3958*
Christ hath *s* for us in the flesh 1Pet 4:1 *3958*
for he that hath *s* in the flesh 1Pet 4:1 *3958*
after that ye have *s* a while 1Pet 5:10 *3958*

SUFFEREST
because thou *s* that woman Jezebel Rev 2:20 *1439*

SUFFERETH
s not our feet to be moved Ps 66:9 5414
s not their cattle to decrease Ps 107:38
the kingdom of heaven *s* violence Mt 11:12 *971*
sea, yet vengeance *s* not to live Acts 28:4 *1439*
Charity *s* long, and is kind 1Cor 13:4 *3114*

SUFFERING
against Cnidus, the wind not *s* us Acts 27:7 *4330*
the angels for the *s* of death Heb 2:9 *3804*
for an example of *s* affliction Jas 5:10 *2552*
God endure grief, *s* wrongfully 1Pet 2:19 *3958*
s the vengeance of eternal fire Jude 7 *5254*

SUFFERINGS
For I reckon that the *s* of this Rom 8:18 *3804*
For as the *s* of Christ abound in 2Cor 1:5 *3804*
the same *s* which we also suffer 2Cor 1:6 *3804*
that as ye are partakers of the *s* 2Cor 1:7 *3804*
and the fellowship of his *s* Phil 3:10 *3804*
Who now rejoice in my *s* for you Col 1:24 *3804*
their salvation perfect through *s* Heb 2:10 *3804*
beforehand the *s* of Christ 1Pet 1:11 *3804*
as ye are partakers of Christ's *s* 1Pet 4:13 *3804*
and a witness of the *s* of Christ 1Pet 5:1 *3804*

SUFFICE
be slain for them, to *s* them Num 11:22 4672
together for them, to *s* them Num 11:22 4672
LORD said unto me, Let it *s* thee Deut 3:26 7227
if the dust of Samaria shall *s* 1Kin 20:10 5606
Israel, let it *s* you of all your Eze 44:6 7227
Let it *s* you, O princes of Israel Eze 45:9 7227
the time past of our life may *s* 1Pet 4:3 *713*

SUFFICED
and yet so they *s* them not Judg 21:14 4672
corn, and she did eat, and was *s* Ruth 2:14 7646
she had reserved after she was *s* Ruth 2:18 7648

SUFFICETH
shew us the Father, and it *s* us Jn 14:8 *714*

SUFFICIENCY
In the fulness of his *s* he shall Job 20:22 5607
but our *s* is of God 2Cor 3:5 *2426*
always having all *s* in all things 2Cor 9:8 *841*

SUFFICIENT
For the stuff they had was *s* for Ex 36:7 1767
surely lend him *s* for his need Deut 15:8 1767
let his hands be *s* for him Deut 33:7 7227
eat so much as is *s* for thee Prov 25:16 1767
And Lebanon is not *s* to burn Is 40:16 1767
thereof *s* for a burnt offering Is 40:16 1767
S unto the day is the evil Mt 6:34 *713*
whether he have *s* to finish it Lk 14:28
of bread is not *s* for them Jn 6:7 *714*
S to such a man is this 2Cor 2:6 *2425*
who is *s* for these things 2Cor 2:16 *2425*
Not that we are *s* of ourselves to 2Cor 3:5 *2425*
unto me, My grace is *s* for thee 2Cor 12:9 *714*

SUFFICIENTLY
had not sanctified themselves *s* 2Chr 30:3 4078
dwell before the LORD, to eat *s* Is 23:18 7654

SUIT
a *s* of apparel, and thy victuals Judg 17:10 6187
any *s* or cause might come unto me 2Sa 15:4 7379
yea, many shall make *s* unto thee Job 11:19 2470

SUITS
The changeable *s* of apparel Is 3:22

SUKKIIMS *(suk'-ke-ims) An Egyptian tribe.*
the Lubim, the *S*, and the 2Chr 12:3 5525

SUM
there be laid on him a *s* of money Ex 21:30 3724
When thou takest the *s* of the Ex 30:12 7218
This is the *s* of the tabernacle, Ex 38:21 6485
Take ye the *s* of all the Num 1:2 7218
neither take the *s* of them among Num 1:49 7218
Take the *s* of the sons of Kohath Num 4:2 7218
Take also the *s* of the sons of Num 4:22 7218
Take the *s* of all the Num 26:2 7218
Take the *s* of the people, from Num 26:4
Take the *s* of the prey that was Num 31:26 7218
the *s* of the men of war which are Num 31:49 7218
Joab gave up the *s* of the number 2Sa 24:9 4557
that he may *s* the silver which is 2Kin 22:4 8552
Joab gave the *s* of the number of 1Chr 21:5 4557
of the *s* of the money that Haman Est 4:7 6575
How great is the *s* of them Ps 139:17 7218
Thou sealest up the *s*, full of Eze 28:12 8508
told the *s* of the matters Dan 7:1 7217
that Abraham bought for a *s* of Acts 7:16 *5092*
With a great *s* obtained I this Acts 22:28 *2774*
we have spoken this is the *s* Heb 8:1 *2774*

SUMMER
and harvest, and cold and heat, and *s* Gen 8:22 7019
and he was sitting in a *s* parlour Judg 3:20 4747
his feet in his *s* chamber Judg 3:24 4747
and an hundred of *s* fruits 2Sa 16:1 7019
s fruit for the young men to eat 2Sa 16:2 7019
is turned into the drought of *s* Ps 32:4 7019
thou hast made *s* and winter Ps 74:17 7019
Provideth her meat in the *s* Prov 6:8 7019
that gathereth in *s* is a wise son Prov 10:5 7019
As snow in *s*, and as rain in Prov 26:1 7019
they prepare their meat in the *s* Prov 30:25 7019
for the shouting for thy *s* fruits Is 16:9 7019
and the fowls shall *s* upon them Is 18:6 6972
as the hasty fruit before the *s* Is 28:4 7019
the *s* is ended, and we are not Jer 8:20 7019
s fruits, and oil, and put them in Jer 40:10 7019
wine and *s* fruits very much Jer 40:12 7019
is fallen upon thy *s* fruits Jer 48:32 7019
chaff of the *s* threshingfloors Dan 2:35 7007
the winter house with the *s* house Amos 3:15 7019
and behold a basket of *s* fruit Amos 8:1 7019
And I said, A basket of *s* fruit Amos 8:2 7019
they have gathered the *s* fruits Mic 7:1 7019
in *s* and in winter shall it be Zec 14:8 7019
leaves, ye know that *s* is nigh Mt 24:32 *2330*
leaves, ye know that *s* is near Mk 13:28 *2330*
selves that *s* is now nigh at hand Lk 21:30 *2330*

SUMPTUOUSLY
fine linen, and fared *s* every day Lk 16:19 *2983*

SUN
when the *s* was going down, a deep Gen 15:12 8121
when the *s* went down, and it was Gen 15:17 8121
The *s* was risen upon the earth Gen 19:23 8121
all night, because the *s* was set Gen 28:11 8121
over Penuel the *s* rose upon him Gen 32:31 8121
and, behold, the *s* and the moon and Gen 37:9 8121
when the *s* waxed hot, it melted Ex 16:21 8121
until the going down of the *s* Ex 17:12 8121
If the *s* be risen upon him, there Ex 22:3 8121
unto him by that the *s* goeth down Ex 22:26 8121
And when the *s* is down, he shall Lev 22:7 8121
s shall they of the standard of Num 2:3
up before the LORD against the *s* Num 25:4 8121
heaven, and when thou seest the *s* Deut 4:19 8121
by the way where the *s* goeth down Deut 11:30 8121
even, at the going down of the *s* Deut 16:6 8121
and worshipped them, either the *s* Deut 17:3 8121
and when the *s* is down, he shall Deut 23:11 8121
again when the *s* goeth down Deut 24:13 8121
shall the *s* go down upon it Deut 24:15 8121
fruits brought forth by the *s* Deut 33:14 8121
toward the going down of the *s* Josh 1:4 8121
and as soon as the *s* was down Josh 8:29 8121
he said in the sight of Israel, *S* Josh 10:12 8121
the *s* stood still, and the moon Josh 10:13 8121
So the *s* stood still in the midst Josh 10:13 8121
time of the going down of the *s* Josh 10:27 8121
Jordan toward the rising of the *s* Josh 12:1 8121
the *s* when he goeth forth in his Judg 5:31 8121
from battle before the *s* was up Judg 8:13 2775
morning, as soon as the *s* is up Judg 9:33 8121
day before the *s* went down Judg 14:18 2775
the *s* went down upon them when Judg 19:14 8121
morrow, by that time the *s* be hot 1Sa 11:9 8121
the *s* went down when they were 2Sa 2:24 8121
or ought else, till the *s* be down 2Sa 3:35 8121
thy wives in the sight of this *s* 2Sa 12:11 8121
all Israel, and before the *s* 2Sa 12:12 8121
of the morning, when the *s* riseth 2Sa 23:4 8121
about the going down of the *s* 1Kin 22:36 8121
the *s* shone upon the water, and 2Kin 3:22 8121
incense unto Baal, to the *s* 2Kin 23:5 8121
kings of Judah had given to the *s* 2Kin 23:11 8121
the chariots of the *s* with fire 2Kin 23:11 8121
time of the *s* going down he died 2Chr 18:34 8121
be opened until the *s* be hot Neh 7:3 8121
He is green before the *s*, and his Job 8:16 8121
Which commandeth the *s*, and it Job 9:7 2775
I went mourning without the *s* Job 30:28 2535
If I beheld the *s* when it shined Job 31:26 216
he set a tabernacle for the *s* Ps 19:4 8121
the *s* unto the going down thereof Ps 50:1 8121
that they may not see the *s* Ps 58:8 8121
shall fear thee as long as the *s* Ps 72:5 8121
be continued as long as the *s* Ps 72:17 8121
hast prepared the light and the *s* Ps 74:16 8121
For the LORD God is a *s* and shield Ps 84:11 8121
and his throne as the *s* before me Ps 89:36 8121
the *s* knoweth his going down Ps 104:19 8121
The *s* ariseth, they gather Ps 104:22 8121
From the rising of the *s* unto the Ps 113:3 8121
The *s* shall not smite thee by day Ps 121:6 8121
The *s* to rule by day Ps 136:8 8121
Praise ye him, *s* and moon Ps 148:3 8121
which he taketh under the *s* Eccl 1:3 8121
The *s* also ariseth Eccl 1:5 8121
the *s* goeth down, and hasteth to Eccl 1:5 8121
there is no new thing under the *s* Eccl 1:9 8121
works that are done under the *s* Eccl 1:14 8121
there was no profit under the *s* Eccl 2:11 8121
under the *s* is grievous unto me Eccl 2:17 8121
which I had taken under the *s* Eccl 2:18 8121
shewed myself wise under the *s* Eccl 2:19 8121
labour which I took under the *s* Eccl 2:20 8121
he hath laboured under the *s* Eccl 2:22 8121
under the *s* the place of judgment Eccl 3:16 8121
that are done under the *s* Eccl 4:1 8121
work that is done under the *s* Eccl 4:3 8121
and I saw vanity under the *s* Eccl 4:7 8121
the living which walk under the *s* Eccl 4:15 8121
which I have seen under the *s* Eccl 5:13 8121
the *s* all the days of his life Eccl 5:18 8121
which I have seen under the *s* Eccl 6:1 8121
Moreover he hath not seen the *s* Eccl 6:5 8121
shall be after him under the *s* Eccl 6:12 8121
is profit to them that see the *s* Eccl 7:11 8121
work that is done under the *s* Eccl 8:9 8121
hath no better thing under the *s* Eccl 8:15 8121
which God giveth him under the *s* Eccl 8:15 8121
the work that is done under the *s* Eccl 8:17 8121
things that are done under the *s* Eccl 9:3 8121
thing that is done under the *s* Eccl 9:6 8121
he hath given thee under the *s* Eccl 9:9 8121
which thou takest under the *s* Eccl 9:9 8121
I returned, and saw under the *s* Eccl 9:11 8121
have I seen also under the *s* Eccl 9:13 8121
which I have seen under the *s* Eccl 10:5 8121
is for the eyes to behold the *s* Eccl 11:7 8121
While the *s*, or the light, or the Eccl 12:2 8121
because the *s* hath looked upon me Song 1:6 8121
fair as the moon, clear as the *s* Song 6:10 2535
the *s* shall be darkened in his Is 13:10 8121
the *s* ashamed, when the LORD of Is 24:23 2535
shall be as the light of the *s* Is 30:26 2535
the light of the *s* shall be Is 30:26 8121
gone down in the *s* dial of Ahaz Is 38:8 8121
So the *s* returned ten degrees, by Is 38:8 8121
from the rising of the *s* shall he Is 41:25 8121
may know from the rising of the *s* Is 45:6 8121
shall the heat nor *s* smite them Is 49:10 8121
glory from the rising of the *s* Is 59:19 8121
The *s* shall be no more thy light Is 60:19 8121
Thy *s* shall no more go down Is 60:20 8121
shall spread them before the *s* Jer 8:2 8121
her *s* is gone down while it was Jer 15:9 8121
which giveth the *s* for a light by Jer 31:35 8121
worshipped the *s* toward the east Eze 8:16 8121
I will cover the *s* with a cloud Eze 32:7 8121
down of the *s* to deliver him Dan 6:14 8122
the *s* and the moon shall be dark, Joel 2:10 8121
The *s* shall be turned into Joel 2:31 8121
The *s* and the moon shall be Joel 3:15 8121
cause the *s* to go down at noon Amos 8:9 8121
when the *s* did arise, that God Jonah 4:8 8121
the *s* beat upon the head of Jonah Jonah 4:8 8121
the *s* shall go down over the Mic 3:6 8121
but when the *s* ariseth they flee Nah 3:17 8121
The *s* and moon stood still in Hab 3:11 8121
For from the rising of the *s* even Mal 1:11 8121
the *S* of righteousness arise with Mal 4:2 8121
for he maketh his *s* to rise on Mt 5:45 *2246*
And when the *s* was up, they were Mt 13:6 *2246*
righteous shine forth as the *s* in Mt 13:43 *2246*
and his face did shine as the *s* Mt 17:2 *2246*
days shall the *s* be darkened Mt 24:29 *2246*
And at even, when the *s* did set Mk 1:32 *2246*
But when the *s* was up, it was Mk 4:6 *2246*
the *s* shall be darkened, and the Mk 13:24 *2246*
sepulchre at the rising of the *s* Mk 16:2 *2246*
Now when the *s* was setting Lk 4:40 *2246*
And there shall be signs in the *s* Lk 21:25 *2246*
the *s* was darkened, and the veil Lk 23:45 *2246*
The *s* shall be turned into Acts 2:20 *2246*
not seeing the *s* for a season Acts 13:11 *2246*
above the brightness of the *s* Acts 26:13 *2246*
when neither *s* nor stars in many Acts 27:20 *2246*
There is one glory of the *s* 1Cor 15:41 *2246*
let not the *s* go down upon your Eph 4:26 *2246*
For the *s* is no sooner risen with Jas 1:11 *2246*
as the *s* shineth in his strength Rev 1:16 *2246*
the *s* became black as sackcloth Rev 6:12 *2246*
neither shall the *s* light on them Rev 7:16 *2246*
third part of the *s* was smitten Rev 8:12 *2246*
and the *s* and the air were darkened Rev 9:2 *2246*
and his face was as it were the *s* Rev 10:1 *2246*
a woman clothed with the *s* Rev 12:1 *2246*
poured out his vial upon the *s* Rev 16:8 *2246*
I saw an angel standing in the *s* Rev 19:17 *2246*
And the city had no need of the *s* Rev 21:23 *2246*
no candle, neither light of the *s* Rev 22:5 *2246*

SUNDER
bow, and cutteth the spear in *s* Ps 46:9
death, and brake their bands in *s* Ps 107:14
and cut the bars of iron in *s* Ps 107:16
chalkstones that are beaten in *s* Is 27:9
cut in *s* the bars of iron Is 45:2
and will burst thy bonds in *s* Nah 1:13
not aware, and will cut him in *s* Lk 12:46

SUNDERED
together, that they cannot be *s* Job 41:17 6504

SUNDRY
God, who at *s* times and in divers Heb 1:1 *4181*

SUNG
song be *s* in the land of Judah Is 26:1 7891
And when they had *s* an hymn Mt 26:30 *5214*
And when they had *s* an hymn Mk 14:26 *5214*
they *s* a new song, saying, Thou Rev 5:9 *103*
they *s* as it were a new song Rev 14:3 *103*

SUNK
that the stone *s* into his 1Sa 17:49 2883
and he *s* down in his chariot 2Kin 9:24 3766
The heathen are *s* down in the pit Ps 9:15 2883
so Jeremiah *s* in the mire Jer 38:6 2883
thy feet are *s* in the mire Jer 38:22 2883
Her gates are *s* into the ground Lam 2:9 2883
he *s* down with sleep, and fell Acts 20:9 *2702*

SUNRISING
is before Moab, toward the *s* Num 21:11
Jericho eastward, toward the *s* Num 34:15 4217
on this side Jordan toward the *s* Deut 4:41
on this side Jordan toward the *s* Deut 4:47
on this side Jordan toward the *s* Josh 1:15
and all Lebanon, toward the *s* Josh 13:5
toward the *s* unto the border of Josh 19:12
toward the *s* to Beth-dagon Josh 19:27
to Judah upon Jordan toward the *s* Josh 19:34
over against Gibeah toward the *s* Judg 20:43

SUP
their faces shall *s* up as the Hab 1:9 4041
him, Make ready wherewith I may *s* Lk 17:8 *1172*
will *s* with him, and he with me Rev 3:20 *1172*

SUPERFLUITY
s of naughtiness, and receive with Jas 1:21 *4050*

SUPERFLUOUS
hath a flat nose, or any thing *s* Lev 21:18 8311
thing *s* or lacking in his parts Lev 22:23 8311
it is *s* for me to write to you 2Cor 9:1 *4053*

SUPERSCRIPTION
them, Whose is this image and *s* Mt 22:20 *1923*
them, Whose is this image and *s* Mk 12:16 *1923*
the *s* of his accusation was Mk 15:26 *1923*
Whose image and *s* hath it Lk 20:24 *1923*
a *s* also was written over him in Lk 23:38 *1923*

SUPERSTITION
against him of their own *s* Acts 25:19 *1175*

SUPERSTITIOUS
that in all things ye are too *s* Acts 17:22 *1174*

SUPPED
he took the cup, when he had *s* 1Cor 11:25 *1172*

SUPPER
birthday made a *s* to his lords Mk 6:21 *1173*
When thou makest a dinner or a *s* Lk 14:12 *1173*
him, A certain man made a great *s* Lk 14:16 *1173*
sent his servant at *s* time to say Lk 14:17 *1173*
were bidden shall taste of my *s* Lk 14:24 *1173*
Likewise also the cup after *s* Lk 22:20 *1172*
There they made him a *s* Jn 12:2 *1173*
s being ended, the devil having Jn 13:2 *1173*
He riseth from *s*, and laid aside Jn 13:4 *1173*
also leaned on his breast at *s* Jn 21:20 *1173*
this is not to eat the Lord's *s* 1Cor 11:20 *1173*
one taketh before other his own *s* 1Cor 11:21 *1173*
unto the marriage *s* of the Lamb Rev 19:9 *1173*
unto the *s* of the great God Rev 19:17 *1173*

SUPPLANT
for every brother will utterly *s* Jer 9:4 6117

SUPPLANTED
for he hath *s* me these two times Gen 27:36 6117

SUPPLE
thou washed in water to *s* thee Eze 16:4 4935

SUPPLIANTS
the rivers of Ethiopia my *s* Zeph 3:10 6282

SUPPLICATION
I have not made *s* unto the LORD 1Sa 13:12 2420
of thy servant, and to his *s* 1Kin 8:28 8467
thou to the *s* of thy servant 1Kin 8:30 8467
make *s* unto thee in this house 1Kin 8:33 2603
s soever be made by any man, or 1Kin 8:38 8467
in heaven their prayer and their *s* 1Kin 8:45 8467
make *s* unto thee in the land of 1Kin 8:47 2603
their *s* in heaven thy dwelling 1Kin 8:49 8467
be open unto the *s* of thy servant 1Kin 8:52 8467
unto the *s* of thy people Israel, 1Kin 8:52 8467
s unto the LORD, he arose from 1Kin 8:54 8467
I have made *s* before the LORD 1Kin 8:59 2603
I have heard thy prayer and thy *s* 1Kin 9:3 8467
of thy servant, and to his *s* 2Chr 6:19 8467
make *s* before thee in this house 2Chr 6:24 2603
Then what prayer or what *s* soever 2Chr 6:29 8467
heavens their prayer and their *s* 2Chr 6:35 8467
intreated of him, and heard his *s* 2Chr 33:13 8467
to make *s* unto him, and to make Est 4:8 2603
make thy *s* to the Almighty Job 8:5 2603
but I would make *s* to my judge Job 9:15 2603
The LORD hath heard my *s* Ps 6:9 8467
and unto the LORD I made *s* Ps 30:8 2603
and hide not thyself from my *s* Ps 55:1 8467
Let my *s* come before thee Ps 119:170 8467
unto the LORD did I make my *s* Ps 142:1 2603
thee, they shall make *s* unto thee Is 45:14 6419
present their *s* before the LORD Jer 36:7 8467
let my *s*, I pray thee, be Jer 37:20 8467
I presented my *s* before the king, Jer 38:26 8467
our *s* be accepted before thee, and Jer 42:2 8467
me to present your *s* before him Jer 42:9 8467
and making *s* before his God Dan 6:11 2604
presenting my *s* before the LORD Dan 9:20 8467
he wept, and made *s* unto him Hos 12:4 2603
with one accord in prayer and *s* Acts 1:14 *1162*
s in the Spirit, and watching Eph 6:18 *1162*
perseverance and *s* for all saints Eph 6:18 *1162*
s with thanksgiving let your Phil 4:6 *1162*

SUPPLICATIONS
unto the *s* of thy servant 2Chr 6:21 8469
place, their prayer and their *s* 2Chr 6:39 8467
Will he make many *s* unto thee Job 41:3 8469
Hear the voice of my *s*, when I Ps 28:2 8469
he hath heard the voice of my *s* Ps 28:6 8469
of my *s* when I cried unto thee Ps 31:22 8469
and attend to the voice of my *s* Ps 86:6 8469
he hath heard my voice and my *s* Ps 116:1 8469
be attentive to the voice of my *s* Ps 130:2 8469
hear the voice of my *s*, O LORD Ps 140:6 8469
prayer, O LORD, give ear to my *s* Ps 143:1 8469
s of the children of Israel Jer 3:21 8469
and with *s* will I lead them Jer 31:9 8469
Lord God, to seek by prayer and *s* Dan 9:3 8469
prayer of thy servant, and his *s* Dan 9:17 8469
present our *s* before thee for our Dan 9:18 8469
At the beginning of thy *s* the Dan 9:23 8469
the spirit of grace and of *s* Zec 12:10 8469
therefore, that, first of all, *s* 1Ti 2:1 *1162*
in God, and continueth in *s* 1Ti 5:5 *1162*
s with strong crying and tears Heb 5:7 *2428*

SUPPLIED
lacking on your part they have *s* 1Cor 16:17 *378*
which came from Macedonia *s* 2Cor 11:9 *4322*

SUPPLIETH
not only *s* the want of the saints 2Cor 9:12 *4322*
by that which every joint *s* Eph 4:16 *2024*

SUPPLY
may be a *s* for their want 2Cor 8:14
also may be a *s* for your want 2Cor 8:14
the *s* of the Spirit of Jesus Phil 1:19 *2024*
to *s* your lack of service toward Phil 2:30 *378*
But my God shall *s* all your need Phil 4:19 *4137*

SUPPORT
labouring ye ought to *s* the weak Acts 20:35 *482*
s the weak, be patient toward all 1Th 5:14 *472*

SUPPOSE
Let not my lord *s* that they have 2Sa 13:32 559
I *s* that he, to whom he forgave Lk 7:43 *5274*
S ye that I am come to give peace Lk 12:51 *1380*
S ye that these Galilaeans were Lk 13:2 *1380*
I *s* that even the world itself Jn 21:25 *3633*
these are not drunken, as ye *s* Acts 2:15 *5274*
I *s* therefore that this is good 1Cor 7:26 *3543*
For I *s* I was not a whit behind 2Cor 11:5 *3049*
s ye, shall he be thought worthy, Heb 10:29 *1380*
faithful brother unto you, as I *s* 1Pet 5:12 *3049*

SUPPOSED
they *s* that they should have Mt 20:10 *3543*
they *s* it had been a spirit, and Mk 6:49 *1380*
being (as was *s*) the son of Lk 3:23 *3543*
s that they had seen a spirit Lk 24:37 *1380*
For he *s* his brethren would have Acts 7:25 *3543*
whom they *s* that Paul had brought Acts 21:29 *3543*
accusation of such things as I *s* Acts 25:18 *5282*
Yet I *s* it necessary to send to Phil 2:25 *2233*

SUPPOSING
s him to have been in the company Lk 2:44 *3543*
s him to be the gardener, saith Jn 20:15 *1380*
of the city, *s* he had been dead Acts 14:19 *3543*
s that the prisoners had been Acts 16:27 *3543*
s that they had obtained their Acts 27:13 *1380*
s to add affliction to my bonds Phil 1:16 *3633*
truth, *s* that gain is godliness 1Ti 6:5 *3543*

SUPREME
whether it be to the king, as *s* 1Pet 2:13 *5242*

SUR (*sur*) *A gate of the Temple.*
part shall be at the gate of *S* 2Kin 11:6 5495

SURE
borders round about, were made *s* Gen 23:17 6965
were made *s* unto Abraham for a Gen 23:20 6965
I am *s* that the king of Egypt Ex 3:19 3045
be *s* your sin will find you out Num 32:23 3045
Only be *s* that thou eat not the Deut 12:23 2388
and I will build him a *s* house 1Sa 2:35 539
then be *s* that evil is determined 1Sa 20:7 3045
certainly make my lord a *s* house 1Sa 25:28 539
because I was *s* that he could not 2Sa 1:10 3045
ordered in all things, and *s* 2Sa 23:5 8104
thee, and build thee a *s* house 1Kin 11:38 539
of all this we make a *s* covenant Neh 9:38 548
riseth up, and no man is *s* of life Job 24:22 539
the testimony of the LORD is *s* Ps 19:7 539
Thy testimonies are very *s* Ps 93:5 539
all his commandments are *s* Ps 111:7 539
thyself, and make *s* thy friend Prov 6:3 7292
and he that hateth suretiship is *s* Prov 11:15 982
righteousness shall be a *s* reward Prov 11:18 571
fasten him as a nail in a *s* place Is 22:23 539
in the *s* place be removed Is 22:25 539
corner stone, a *s* foundation Is 28:16 3245
in *s* dwellings, and in quiet Is 32:18 4009
his waters shall be *s* Is 33:16 539
even the *s* mercies of David Is 55:3 539
and the interpretation thereof *s* Dan 2:45 546
thy kingdom shall be *s* unto thee Dan 4:26 7011
be made *s* until the third day Mt 27:64 *805*
your way, make it as *s* as ye can Mt 27:65 *805*
went, and made the sepulchre *s* Mt 27:66 *805*
notwithstanding be ye *s* of this Lk 10:11 *1097*
are *s* that thou art that Christ, Jn 6:69 *1097*
Now are we *s* that thou knowest Jn 16:30 *1492*
give you the *s* mercies of David Acts 13:34 *4103*
But we are *s* that the judgment of Rom 2:2 *1492*
might be *s* to all the seed Rom 4:16 *949*
And I am *s* that, when I come unto Rom 15:29 *1492*
the foundation of God standeth *s* 2Ti 2:19 *4731*
as an anchor of the soul, both *s* Heb 6:19 *804*
make your calling and election *s* 2Pet 1:10 *949*
also a more *s* word of prophecy 2Pet 1:19 *949*

SURELY
eatest thereof thou shalt *s* die Gen 2:17
the woman, Ye shall not *s* die Gen 3:4
s your blood of your lives will I Gen 9:5 389
Abraham shall *s* become a great Gen 18:18
know thou that thou shalt *s* die Gen 20:7 3588
S the fear of God is not in this Gen 20:11 7535
his wife shall *s* be put to death Gen 26:11
S the LORD is in this place Gen 28:16 403
I will *s* give the tenth unto thee Gen 28:22
S thou art my bone and my flesh Gen 29:14 389
S the LORD hath looked upon my Gen 29:32 3588
for *s* I have hired thee with my Gen 30:16
s thou hadst sent me away now Gen 31:42 3588
I will *s* do thee good, and make Gen 32:12
life of Pharaoh *s* ye are spies Gen 42:16
s now we had returned this second Gen 43:10 3588
and I said, *S* he is torn in pieces Gen 44:28 389
I will also *s* bring thee up again Gen 46:4
God will *s* visit you, and bring Gen 50:24
God will *s* visit you, and ye shall Gen 50:25
and said, *S* this thing is known Ex 2:14 403
I have *s* seen the affliction of Ex 3:7
I have *s* visited you, and seen Ex 3:16
S a bloody husband art thou to me Ex 4:25 3588
he shall *s* thrust you out hence Ex 11:1
saying, God will *s* visit you Ex 13:19
Thou wilt *s* wear away, both thou, Ex 18:18
the mount shall be *s* put to death Ex 19:12
it, but he shall *s* be stoned Ex 19:13 3588
he die, shall be *s* put to death Ex 21:12
mother, shall be *s* put to death Ex 21:15
he shall *s* be put to death Ex 21:16
mother, shall *s* be put to death Ex 21:17
he shall be *s* punished Ex 21:20
he shall be *s* punished, according Ex 21:22
then the ox shall be *s* stoned Ex 21:28
he shall *s* pay ox for ox Ex 21:36
the fire shall *s* make restitution Ex 22:6
with it, he shall *s* make it good Ex 22:14
he shall *s* endow her to be his Ex 22:16
a beast shall *s* be put to death Ex 22:19
unto me, I will *s* hear their cry Ex 22:23
thou shalt *s* bring it back to him Ex 23:4
thou shalt *s* help with him Ex 23:5
it will *s* be a snare unto thee Ex 23:33 3588
it shall *s* be put to death Ex 31:14
he shall *s* be put to death Ex 31:15
for their anointing shall *s* be an Ex 40:15
he shall *s* be put to death Lev 20:2
mother shall be *s* put to death Lev 20:9
shall *s* be put to death Lev 20:10
of them shall *s* be put to death Lev 20:11
of them shall *s* be put to death Lev 20:12
they shall *s* be put to death Lev 20:13
he shall *s* be put to death Lev 20:15
they shall *s* be put to death Lev 20:16
a wizard, shall *s* be put to death Lev 20:27
he shall *s* be put to death, and Lev 24:16
any man shall *s* be put to death Lev 24:17
but shall *s* be put to death Lev 27:29
s it floweth with milk and honey Num 13:27
S they shall not see the land Num 14:23 518
I will *s* do it unto all this evil Num 14:35 518
The man shall be *s* put to death Num 15:35
of man shalt thou *s* redeem Num 18:15
s now also I had slain thee, and Num 22:33 3588
S there is no enchantment against Num 23:23
of them, They shall *s* die in the Num 26:65
thou shalt *s* give them a Num 27:7
S none of the men that came up Num 32:11 518
murderer shall *s* be put to death Num 35:16
murderer shall *s* be put to death Num 35:17
murderer shall *s* be put to death Num 35:18
smote him shall *s* be put to death Num 35:21
but he shall be *s* put to death Num 35:31
S there shall not one of these Deut 1:35 518
S this great nation is a wise and Deut 4:6
this day that ye shall *s* perish Deut 8:19 3588
But thou shalt *s* kill him Deut 13:9 3588
Thou shalt *s* smite the Deut 13:15
shalt *s* lend him sufficient for Deut 15:8
Thou shalt *s* give him, and thine Deut 15:10
therefore thou shalt *s* rejoice Deut 16:15 389
thou shalt *s* help him to lift Deut 22:4
thy God will *s* require it of thee Deut 23:21
this day, that ye shall *s* perish Deut 30:18 3588
I will *s* hide my face in that day Deut 31:18
S the land whereon thy feet have Josh 14:9 518
S he covereth his feet in his Judg 3:24 389
she said, I will *s* go with thee Judg 4:9
S I will be with thee, and thou Judg 6:16 3588
shall *s* be the LORD's, and I will Judg 11:31
unto his wife, We shall *s* die Judg 13:22
but *s* we will not kill thee Judg 15:13
S they are smitten down before us Judg 20:39 389
He shall *s* be put to death Judg 21:5
S we will return with thee unto Ruth 1:10 3588
that he saith cometh *s* to pass 1Sa 9:6
Jonathan my son, he shall *s* die 1Sa 14:39 3588
for thou shalt *s* die, Jonathan 1Sa 14:44
S the bitterness of death is past 1Sa 15:32 403
S the LORD's anointed is before 1Sa 16:6 389
s to defy Israel is he come up 1Sa 17:25 3588
s he is not clean 1Sa 20:26 3588
him unto me, for he shall *s* die 1Sa 20:31
the king said, Thou shalt *s* die 1Sa 22:16
there, that he would *s* tell Saul 1Sa 22:22
well that thou shalt *s* be king 1Sa 24:20
S in vain have I kept all that 1Sa 25:21 389
s there had not been left unto 1Sa 25:34
S thou shalt know what thy 1Sa 28:2 3651
called David, and said unto him, *S* 1Sa 29:6
for thou shalt *s* overtake them 1Sa 30:8
s then in the morning the people 2Sa 2:27 3588
for I will *s* shew thee kindness 2Sa 9:7 3588
S the men prevailed against us, 2Sa 11:23 3588
hath done this thing shall *s* die 2Sa 12:5
is born unto thee shall *s* die 2Sa 12:14
s in what place my lord the king 2Sa 15:21 3588
I will *s* go forth with you myself 2Sa 18:2
They shall *s* ask counsel at Abel 2Sa 20:18
but I will *s* buy it of thee at a 2Sa 24:24
for certain that thou shalt *s* die 1Kin 2:37
whither, that thou shalt *s* die 1Kin 2:42
I have *s* built thee an house to 1Kin 8:13 403
for *s* they will turn away your 1Kin 11:2 403
I will *s* rend the kingdom from 1Kin 11:11
of Samaria, shall *s* come to pass 1Kin 13:32 3588
I will *s* shew myself unto him to 1Kin 18:15 3588
s we shall be stronger than they 1Kin 20:23 518
s we shall be stronger than they 1Kin 20:25 518
S it is the king of Israel 1Kin 22:32 389
thou art gone up, but shalt *s* die 2Kin 1:4 3588
thou art gone up, but shalt *s* die 2Kin 1:6 3588
thou art gone up, but shalt *s* die 2Kin 1:16 3588
liveth, before whom I stand, *s* 2Kin 3:14 3588
the kings are *s* slain, and they 2Kin 3:23
He will *s* come out to me, and 2Kin 5:11
shewed me that he shall *s* die 2Kin 8:10
me that thou shouldest *s* recover 2Kin 8:14
S I have seen yesterday the blood 2Kin 9:26
The LORD will *s* deliver us 2Kin 18:30
S there was not holden such a 2Kin 23:22 3588
S at the commandment of the LORD 2Kin 24:3 389
but shalt *s* fall before him Est 6:13 3588
s now he would awake for thee, and Job 8:6 3588
S I would speak to the Almighty, Job 13:3 199
He will *s* reprove you, if ye do Job 13:10
s the mountain falling cometh to Job 14:18 199
S such are the dwellings of the Job 18:21 389
S he shall not feel quietness in Job 20:20 3588
S there is a vein for the silver, Job 28:1 3588
S I would take it upon my Job 31:36
S thou hast spoken in mine Job 33:8 389
s God will not do wickedly, Job 34:12 551
S it is meet to be said unto God, Job 34:31 3588
S God will not hear vanity, Job 35:13 389
s he shall be swallowed up Job 37:20 3588
S the mountains bring him forth Job 40:20 3588
S goodness and mercy shall follow Ps 23:6 389
s in the floods of great waters Ps 32:6 7535
S every man walketh in a vain Ps 39:6 389
s they are disquieted in vain Ps 39:6 389
s every man is vanity Ps 39:11 389
S men of low degree are vanity, Ps 62:9 389
S thou didst set them in slippery Ps 73:18 389
S the wrath of man shall praise Ps 76:10 3588
s I will remember thy wonders of Ps 77:11
S his salvation is nigh them that Ps 85:9 389
S he shall deliver thee from the Ps 91:3 3588
S he shall not be moved for ever Ps 112:6 3588
S I have behaved and quieted Ps 131:2
S I will not come into the Ps 132:3 518
S the darkness shall cover me Ps 139:11 389

S thou wilt slay the wicked, O Ps 139:19 518
S the righteous shall give thanks Ps 140:13
S in vain the net is spread in Prov 1:17 3588
S he scorneth the scorners Prov 3:34 518
that walketh uprightly walketh *s* Prov 10:9 983
to the rich, shall *s* come to want Prov 22:16 389
For *s* there is an end Prov 23:18
S I am more brutish than any man, Prov 30:2 3588
S the churning of milk bringeth Prov 30:33 3588
S this also is vanity and vexation Eccl 4:16 3588
S oppression maketh a wise man Eccl 7:7 3588
yet *s* I know that it shall be Eccl 8:12 3588
S the serpent will bite without Eccl 10:11 518
s ye shall not be established Is 7:9 3588
S as I have thought, so shall it Is 14:24
s they are stricken Is 16:7 389
S the princes of Zoan are fools, Is 19:11 389
S this iniquity shall not be Is 22:14 518
captivity, and will *s* cover thee Is 22:17
He will *s* violently turn and toss Is 22:18
S your turning of things upside Is 29:16 518
The LORD will *s* deliver us Is 36:15
s the people is grass Is 40:7 403
thee, saying, *S* God is in thee Is 45:14 389
S, shall one say, in the LORD Is 45:24
yet *s* my judgment is with the Is 49:4 403
thou shalt *s* clothe thee with Is 49:18 3588
S he hath borne our griefs, and Is 53:4 403
they shall *s* gather together, but Is 54:15
S the isles shall wait for me, and Is 60:9 3588
S I will no more give thy corn to Is 62:8 518
S they are my people, children Is 63:8 389
s his anger shall turn from me Jer 2:35 389
S as a wife treacherously Jer 3:20 403
s thou hast greatly deceived this Jer 4:10 403
s they swear falsely Jer 5:2 403
I said, *S* these are poor Jer 5:4 389
I will *s* consume them, saith the Jer 8:13
S our fathers have inherited lies Jer 16:19 389
yet *s* I will make thee a Jer 22:6
s then shalt thou be ashamed and Jer 22:22 3588
s thus saith the LORD, So will I Jer 24:8 3588
him, saying, Thou shalt *s* die Jer 26:8
ye shall *s* bring innocent blood Jer 26:15 3588
I have *s* heard Ephraim bemoaning Jer 31:18
S after that I was turned, I Jer 31:19 3588
I will *s* have mercy upon him, Jer 31:20
but shall *s* be delivered into the Jer 32:4
of his hand, but shalt *s* be taken Jer 34:3 3588
We will *s* tell the king of all Jer 36:16
Chaldeans shall *s* depart from us Jer 37:9
This city shall *s* be given into Jer 38:3
wilt thou not *s* put me to death Jer 38:15
For I will *s* deliver thee, and Jer 39:18
We will *s* perform our vows that Jer 44:25
ye will *s* accomplish your vows, Jer 44:25
your vows, and *s* perform your vows Jer 44:25
s stand against you for evil Jer 44:29
S as Tabor is among the mountains Jer 46:18 3588
but thou shalt *s* drink of it Jer 49:12 3588
S the least of the flock shall Jer 49:20
s he shall make their habitations Jer 49:20
S the least of the flock shall Jer 50:45
s he shall make their habitation Jer 50:45
S I will fill thee with men, as Jer 51:14
of recompences shall *s* requite Jer 51:56
S against me is he turned Lam 3:3 389
S, had I sent thee to them, they Eze 3:6
unto the wicked, Thou shalt *s* die Eze 3:18
he doth not sin, he shall *s* live Eze 3:21
S, because thou hast defiled my Eze 5:11
s in the place where the king Eze 17:16
s mine oath that he hath despised Eze 17:19
he is just, he shall *s* live Eze 18:9
he shall *s* die Eze 18:13
of his father, he shall *s* live Eze 18:17
hath done them, he shall *s* live Eze 18:19
lawful and right, he shall *s* live Eze 18:21
hath committed, he shall *s* live Eze 18:28
s with a mighty hand, and with a Eze 20:33
he shall *s* deal with him Eze 31:11
O wicked man, thou shalt *s* die Eze 33:8
righteous, that he shall *s* live Eze 33:13
unto the wicked, Thou shalt *s* die Eze 33:14
he shall *s* live, he shall not die Eze 33:15
he shall *s* live Eze 33:16
s they that are in the wastes Eze 33:27
s because my flock became a prey, Eze 34:8
S in the fire of my jealousy have Eze 36:5
S the heathen that are about you, Eze 36:7
S in that day there shall be a Eze 38:19
made known that which shall *s* be Hos 5:9 539
s they are vanity Hos 12:11 389
S the Lord GOD will do nothing, Amos 3:7 3588
for Gilgal shall *s* go into Amos 5:5
Israel shall *s* be led away Amos 7:11
Israel shall *s* go into captivity Amos 7:17
S I will never forget any of Amos 8:7
I will *s* assemble, O Jacob, all Mic 2:12
I will *s* gather the remnant of Mic 2:12
because it will *s* come, it will Hab 2:3
S Moab shall be as Sodom, and the Zeph 2:9 3588
S thou wilt fear me, thou wilt Zeph 3:7
S thou also art one of them Mt 26:73 *230*
to Peter, *S* thou art one of them Mk 14:70 *230*
are most *s* believed among us Lk 1:1 *4135*
Ye will *s* say unto me this Lk 4:23 *3843*
have known *s* that I came out from Jn 17:8 *230*
S blessing I will bless thee, and Heb 6:14 *2229*
things saith, *S* I come quickly Rev 22:20 *3483*

SURETIES
or of them that are *s* for debts Prov 22:26 6148

SURETISHIP
and he that hateth *s* is sure Prov 11:15 8628

SURETY
Know of a *s* that thy seed shall Gen 15:13 3045
Shall I of a *s* bear a child Gen 18:13 552
Behold, of a *s* she is thy wife Gen 26:9 389
I will be *s* for him Gen 43:9 6148
For thy servant became *s* for the Gen 44:32 6148
down now, put me in a *s* with thee Job 17:3 6148
Be *s* for thy servant for good Ps 119:122 6148
if thou be *s* for thy friend, if Prov 6:1 6148
He that is *s* for a stranger shall Prov 11:15 6148
becometh *s* in the presence of his Prov 17:18 6161
garment that is *s* for a stranger Prov 20:16 6148
garment that is *s* for a stranger Prov 27:13 6148
he said, Now I know of a *s* Acts 12:11 *230*
made a *s* of a better testament Heb 7:22 *1450*

SURFEITING
your hearts be overcharged with *s* Lk 21:34 *2897*

SURMISINGS
envy, strife, railings, evil *s* 1Ti 6:4 *5283*

SURNAME
s himself by the name of Israel Is 44:5 3655
Lebbaeus, whose *s* was Thaddaeus Mt 10:3 *1941*
for one Simon, whose *s* is Peter Acts 10:5 *1941*
hither Simon, whose *s* is Peter Acts 10:32 *1941*
call for Simon, whose *s* is Peter Acts 11:13 *1941*
mother of John, whose *s* was Mark Acts 12:12 *1941*
with them John, whose *s* was Mark Acts 12:25 *1941*
with them John, whose *s* was Mark Acts 15:37 *2564*

SURNAMED
I have *s* thee, though thou hast Is 45:4 3655
And Simon he *s* Peter Mk 3:16
he *s* them Boanerges, which is, Mk 3:17
Satan into Judas *s* Iscariot Lk 22:3 *1941*
called Barsabas, who was *s* Justus Acts 1:23 *1941*
by the apostles was *s* Barnabas Acts 4:36 *1941*
whether Simon, which was *s* Peter Acts 10:18 *1941*
Judas *s* Barsabas, and Silas, chief Acts 15:22 *1941*

SURPRISED
fearfulness hath *s* the hypocrites Is 33:14 270
taken, and the strong holds are *s* Jer 48:41 8610
the praise of the whole earth *s* Jer 51:41 8610

SUSA See SHUSHAN, SUSANCHITES.

SUSANCHITES (*su'-san-kites*) *Resettled foreigners in Israel.*
the Babylonians, the *S*, the Ezr 4:9 7801

SUSANNA (*su'-zan'-nah*) *A woman follower of Jesus.*
of Chuza Herod's steward, and *S* Lk 8:3 *4677*

SUSI (*su'-si*) *Father of Gaddi.*
of Manasseh, Gaddi the son of *S* Num 13:11 5485

SUSTAIN
a widow woman there to *s* thee 1Kin 17:9 3557
thou *s* them in the wilderness Neh 9:21 3557
upon the LORD, and he shall *s* thee Ps 55:22 3557
of a man will *s* his infirmity Prov 18:14 3557

SUSTAINED
and with corn and wine have I *s* him Gen 27:37 5564
for the LORD *s* me Ps 3:5 5564
and his righteousness, it *s* him Is 59:16 5564

SUSTENANCE
left no *s* for Israel, neither Judg 6:4 4241
of *s* while he lay at Mahanaim 2Sa 19:32 3557
and our fathers found no *s* Acts 7:11 *5527*

SWADDLED
those that I have *s* and brought up Lam 2:22 2946
not salted at all, nor *s* at all Eze 16:4 2853

SWADDLING
son, and wrapped him in *s* clothes Lk 2:7 *4683*
the babe wrapped in *s* clothes Lk 2:12 *4683*

SWADDLINGBAND
and thick darkness a *s* for it Job 38:9 2854

SWALLOW
and *s* them up, with all that Num 16:30 1104
said, Lest the earth *s* us up also Num 16:34 1104
why wilt thou *s* up the 2Sa 20:19 1104
me, that I should *s* up or destroy 2Sa 20:20 1104
me alone till I *s* down my spittle Job 7:19 1104
restore, and shall not *s* it down Job 20:18 1104
the LORD shall *s* them up in his Ps 21:9 1104
for man would *s* me up Ps 56:1 7602
Mine enemies would daily *s* me up Ps 56:2 7602
of him that would *s* me up Ps 57:3 7602
me, neither let the deep *s* me up Ps 69:15 1104
the *s* a nest for herself, where Ps 84:3 1866
Let us *s* them up alive as the Prov 1:12 1104
as the *s* by flying, so the curse Prov 26:2 1866
lips of a fool will *s* up himself Eccl 10:12 1104
He will *s* up death in victory Is 25:8 1104
Like a crane or a *s*, so did I Is 38:14 5693
the *s* observe the time of their Jer 8:7 5693
the strangers shall *s* it up Hos 8:7 1104
O ye that *s* up the needy, even to Amos 8:4 7602
shall drink, and they shall *s* down Obad 16 3886
a great fish to *s* up Jonah Jonah 1:17 1104
strain at a gnat, and *s* a camel Mt 23:24 *2666*

SWALLOWED
but Aaron's rod *s* up their rods Ex 7:12 1104
thy right hand, the earth *s* them Ex 15:12 1104
s them up, and their houses, and Num 16:32 1104
s them up together with Korah, Num 26:10 1104
s them up, and their households, Deut 11:6 1104
lest the king be *s* up, and all the 2Sa 17:16 1104
therefore my words are *s* up Job 6:3 3886
He hath *s* down riches, and he Job 20:15 1104
speak, surely he shall be *s* up Job 37:20 1104
them not say, We have *s* him up Ps 35:25 1104
s up Dathan, and covered the Ps 106:17 1104
Then they had *s* us up quick Ps 124:3 1104
they are *s* up of wine, they are Is 28:7 1104
they that *s* thee up shall be far Is 49:19 1104
he hath *s* me up like a dragon, he Jer 51:34 1104
his mouth that which he hath *s* up Jer 51:44 1105
The Lord hath *s* up all the Lam 2:2 1104
he hath *s* up Israel, he hath Lam 2:5 1104
he hath *s* up all her palaces Lam 2:5 1104
they say, We have *s* her up Lam 2:16 1104
s you up on every side, that ye Eze 36:3 7602
Israel is *s* up Hos 8:8 1104
written, Death is *s* up in victory 1Cor 15:54 *2666*
be *s* up with overmuch sorrow 2Cor 2:7 *2666*
mortality might be *s* up of life 2Cor 5:4 *2666*
s up the flood which the dragon Rev 12:16 *2666*

SWALLOWETH
the robber *s* up their substance Job 5:5 7602
He *s* the ground with fierceness Job 39:24 1572

SWAN
And the *s*, and the pelican, and the Lev 11:18 8580
owl, and the great owl, and the *s* Deut 14:16 8580

SWARE
because there they *s* both of them Gen 21:31 7650
that *s* unto me, saying, Unto thy Gen 24:7 7650
s to him concerning that matter Gen 24:9 7650
and he *s* unto him Gen 25:33 7650
which I *s* unto Abraham thy father Gen 26:3 7650
the morning, and *s* one to another Gen 26:31 7650
Jacob *s* by the fear of his father Gen 31:53 7650
And he *s* unto him Gen 47:31 7650
the land which he *s* to Abraham Gen 50:24 7650
which he *s* unto thy fathers to Ex 13:5 7650
as he *s* unto thee and to thy Ex 13:11 7650
the land which I *s* unto Abraham Ex 33:1 7650
the land which he *s* unto them Num 14:16 7650
land which I *s* unto their fathers Num 14:23 7650
concerning which I *s* to make you Num 14:30 5375
kindled the same time, and he *s* Num 32:10 7650
the land which I *s* unto Abraham Num 32:11 7650
the LORD *s* unto your fathers Deut 1:8 7650
of your words, and was wroth, and *s* Deut 1:34 7650
which I *s* to give unto your Deut 1:35 7650
the host, as the LORD *s* unto them Deut 2:14 7650
s that I should not go over Deut 4:21 7650
thy fathers which he *s* unto them Deut 4:31 7650
land which he *s* unto thy fathers Deut 6:10 7650
which the LORD *s* unto thy fathers Deut 6:18 7650
land which he *s* unto our fathers Deut 6:23 7650
mercy which he *s* unto thy fathers Deut 7:12 7650
in the land which he *s* unto thy Deut 7:13 7650
the LORD *s* unto your fathers Deut 8:1 7650
which he *s* unto thy fathers Deut 8:18 7650
which the LORD *s* unto thy fathers Deut 9:5 7650
which I *s* unto their fathers to Deut 10:11 7650
which the LORD *s* unto your Deut 11:9 7650
in the land which the LORD *s* unto Deut 11:21 7650
s unto our fathers for to give us Deut 26:3 7650
in the land which the LORD *s* unto Deut 28:11 7650
which the LORD *s* unto thy fathers Deut 30:20 7650
land which I *s* unto their fathers Deut 31:20 7650
them into the land which I *s* Deut 31:21 7650
into the land which I *s* unto them Deut 31:23 7650
the land which I *s* unto Abraham Deut 34:4 7650
which I *s* unto their fathers to Josh 1:6 7650
unto whom the LORD *s* that he Josh 5:6 7650
which the LORD *s* unto their Josh 5:6 7650
that she hath, as ye *s* unto her Josh 6:22 7650
of the congregation *s* unto them Josh 9:15 7650
of the oath which we *s* unto them Josh 9:20 7650
Moses *s* on that day, saying, Josh 14:9 7650
he *s* to give unto their fathers Josh 21:43 7650
all that he *s* unto their fathers Josh 21:44 7650
land which I *s* unto your fathers Judg 2:1 7650
and Saul *s*, As the LORD liveth, he 1Sa 19:6 7650
David *s* moreover, and said, Thy 1Sa 20:3 7650
And David *s* unto Saul 1Sa 24:22 7650
Saul *s* to her by the LORD, saying 1Sa 28:10 7650
while it was yet day, David *s* 2Sa 3:35 7650
And the king *s* unto him 2Sa 19:23 7650
Then the men of David *s* unto him 2Sa 21:17 7650
And the king *s*, and said, As the 1Kin 1:29 7650
Even as I *s* unto thee by the LORD 1Kin 1:30 7650
I *s* to him by the LORD, saying, I 1Kin 2:8 7650
Then king Solomon *s* by the LORD 1Kin 2:23 7650
And Gedaliah *s* to them, and to 2Kin 25:24 7650
they *s* unto the LORD with a loud 2Chr 15:14 7650
And they *s* Ezr 10:5 7650
Unto whom I *s* in my wrath that Ps 95:11 7650
How he *s* unto the LORD, and vowed Ps 132:2 7650
So Zedekiah the king *s* secretly Jer 38:16 7650
the son of Shaphan *s* unto them Jer 40:9 7650
I *s* unto thee, and entered into a Eze 16:8 7650
s by him that liveth for ever Dan 12:7 7650
he *s* unto her, Whatsoever thou Mk 6:23 *3660*
The oath which he *s* to our father Lk 1:73 *3660*
So I *s* in my wrath, They shall Heb 3:11 *3660*
to whom *s* he that they should not Heb 3:18 *3660*
by no greater, he *s* by himself, Heb 6:13 *3660*
that said unto him, The Lord *s* Heb 7:21 *3660*
s by him that liveth for ever and Rev 10:6 *3660*

SWAREST
to whom thou *s* by thine own self, Ex 32:13 7650
which thou *s* unto their fathers Num 11:12 7650
as thou *s* unto our fathers, a Deut 26:15 7650
thou *s* by the LORD thy God unto 1Kin 1:17 7650

which thou *s* unto David in thy Ps 89:49 7650

SWARM
there came a grievous *s* of flies Ex 8:24 6157
by reason of the *s* of flies Ex 8:24 6157
and, behold, there was a *s* of bees Judg 14:8 5712

SWARMS
I will send *s* of flies upon thee, Ex 8:21 6157
shall be full of *s* of flies Ex 8:21 6157
that no *s* of flies shall be there Ex 8:22 6157
the *s* of flies may depart from Ex 8:29 6157
he removed the *s* of flies from Ex 8:31 6157

SWEAR
Now therefore *s* unto me here by Gen 21:23 7650
And Abraham said, I will *s* Gen 21:24 7650
And I will make thee *s* by the LORD Gen 24:3 7650
And my master made me *s*, saying, Gen 24:37 7650
And Jacob said, *S* to me this day Gen 25:33 7650
And he said, *S* unto me Gen 47:31 7650
My father made me *s*, saying, Lo, Gen 50:5 7650
according as he made thee *s* Gen 50:6 7650
I did *s* to give it to Abraham Ex 6:8 5375
Or if a soul *s*, pronouncing with Lev 5:4 7650
ye shall not *s* by my name falsely Lev 19:12 7650
or *s* an oath to bind his soul Num 30:2 7650
serve him, and shalt *s* by his name Deut 6:13 7650
thou cleave, and *s* by his name Deut 10:20 7650
s unto me by the LORD, since I Josh 2:12 7650
oath which thou hast made us *s* Josh 2:17 7650
oath which thou hast made us to *s* Josh 2:20 7650
gods, nor cause to *s* by them Josh 23:7 7650
S unto me, that ye will not fall Judg 15:12 7650
Jonathan caused David to *s* again 1Sa 20:17 7650
S now therefore unto me by the 1Sa 24:21 7650
S unto me by God, that thou wilt 1Sa 30:15 7650
for I *s* by the LORD, if thou go 2Sa 19:7 7650
s unto thine handmaid, saying, 1Kin 1:13 7650
Let king Solomon *s* unto me to day 1Kin 1:51 7650
I not make thee to *s* by the LORD 1Kin 2:42 7650
laid upon him to cause him to *s* 1Kin 8:31 422
be laid upon him to make him *s* 2Chr 6:22 422
who had made him *s* by God 2Chr 36:13 7650
Israel, to *s* that they should do Ezr 10:5 7650
their hair, and made them *s* by God Neh 13:25 7650
In that day shall he *s*, saying, I Is 3:7 5375
Canaan, and *s* to the LORD of hosts Is 19:18 7650
shall bow, every tongue shall *s* Is 45:23 7650
which *s* by the name of the LORD, Is 48:1 7650
earth shall *s* by the God of truth Is 65:16 7650
And thou shalt *s*, The LORD liveth, Jer 4:2 7650
surely they *s* falsely Jer 5:2 7650
s falsely, and burn incense unto Jer 7:9 7650
to *s* by my name, The LORD liveth Jer 12:16 7650
taught my people to *s* by Baal Jer 12:16 7650
I *s* by myself, saith the LORD, Jer 22:5 7650
which thou didst *s* to their Jer 32:22 7650
go ye up to Beth-aven, nor *s* Hos 4:15 7650
They that *s* by the sin of Samaria Amos 8:14 7650
that *s* by the LORD Zeph 1:5 7650
and that *s* by Malcham Zeph 1:5 7650
But I say unto you, *S* not at all Mt 5:34 *3660*
Neither shalt thou *s* by thy head Mt 5:36 *3660*
Whosoever shall *s* by the temple Mt 23:16 *3660*
but whosoever shall *s* by the gold Mt 23:16 *3660*
Whosoever shall *s* by the altar Mt 23:18 *3660*
therefore shall *s* by the altar Mt 23:20 *3660*
whoso shall *s* by the temple, Mt 23:21 *3660*
And he that shall *s* by heaven Mt 23:22 *3660*
Then began he to curse and to *s* Mt 26:74 *3660*
But he began to curse and to *s* Mk 14:71 *3660*
because he could *s* by no greater Heb 6:13 *3660*
For men verily *s* by the greater Heb 6:16 *3660*
s not, neither by heaven, neither Jas 5:12 *3660*

SWEARERS
adulterers, and against false *s* Mal 3:5 7650

SWEARETH
lieth concerning it, and *s* falsely Lev 6:3 7650
He that *s* to his own hurt, and Ps 15:4 7650
every one that *s* by him shall Ps 63:11 7650
and he that *s*, as he that feareth Eccl 9:2 7650
he that *s* in the earth shall Is 65:16 7650
every one that *s* shall be cut off Zec 5:3 7650
of him that *s* falsely by my name Zec 5:4 7650
but whosoever *s* by the gift that Mt 23:18 *3660*
s by it, and by all things thereon Mt 23:20 *3660*
s by it, and by him that dwelleth Mt 23:21 *3660*
s by the throne of God, and by him Mt 23:22 *3660*

SWEARING
soul sin, and hear the voice of *s* Lev 5:1 423
for because of *s* the land Jer 23:10 423
By *s*, and lying, and killing, and Hos 4:2 422
s falsely in making a covenant Hos 10:4 422

SWEAT
In the *s* of thy face shalt thou Gen 3:19 2188
with any thing that causeth *s* Eze 44:18 3154
his *s* was as it were great drops Lk 22:44 *2402*

SWEEP
I will *s* it with the besom of Is 14:23 2894
the hail shall *s* away the refuge Is 28:17 3261
s the house, and seek diligently Lk 15:8 *4563*

SWEEPING
a *s* rain which leaveth no food Prov 28:3 5502

SWEET
And the LORD smelled a *s* savour Gen 8:21 5207
waters, the waters were made *s* Ex 15:25 4985
anointing oil, and for *s* incense, Ex 25:6 5561
it is a *s* savour, an offering Ex 29:18 5207
for a *s* savour before the LORD Ex 29:25 5207
for a *s* savour, an offering made Ex 29:41 5207
thereon *s* incense every morning Ex 30:7 5561
of *s* cinnamon half so much, even Ex 30:23 1314
of *s* calamus two hundred and fifty Ex 30:23 1314
Moses, Take unto thee *s* spices Ex 30:34 5561
these *s* spices with pure Ex 30:34 5561
s incense for the holy place Ex 31:11 5561
oil, and for the *s* incense Ex 35:8 5561
the *s* incense, and the hanging for Ex 35:15 5561
oil, and for the *s* incense Ex 35:28 5561
and the pure incense of *s* spices Ex 37:29 5561
the *s* incense, and the hanging for Ex 39:38 5561
he burnt *s* incense thereon Ex 40:27 5561
of a *s* savour unto the LORD Lev 1:9 5207
of a *s* savour unto the LORD Lev 1:13 5207
of a *s* savour unto the LORD Lev 1:17 5207
of a *s* savour unto the LORD Lev 2:2 5207
of a *s* savour unto the LORD Lev 2:9 5207
burnt on the altar for a *s* savour Lev 2:12 5207
of a *s* savour unto the LORD Lev 3:5 5207
made by fire for a *s* savour Lev 3:16 5207
of *s* incense before the LORD Lev 4:7 5561
for a *s* savour unto the LORD Lev 4:31 5207
it upon the altar for a *s* savour Lev 6:15 5207
for a *s* savour unto the LORD Lev 6:21 5207
a burnt sacrifice for a *s* savour Lev 8:21 5207
were consecrations for a *s* savour Lev 8:28 5207
his hands full of *s* incense Lev 16:12 5561
burn the fat for a *s* savour unto Lev 17:6 5207
fire unto the LORD for a *s* savour Lev 23:13 5207
of *s* savour unto the LORD Lev 23:18 5207
smell the savour of your *s* odours Lev 26:31 5207
the *s* incense, and the daily meat Num 4:16 5561
to make a *s* savour unto the LORD, Num 15:3 5207
for a *s* savour unto the LORD Num 15:7 5207
of a *s* savour unto the LORD Num 15:10 5207
of a *s* savour unto the LORD Num 15:13 5207
of a *s* savour unto the LORD Num 15:14 5207
for a *s* savour unto the LORD, Num 15:24 5207
for a *s* savour unto the LORD Num 18:17 5207
for a *s* savour unto me, shall ye Num 28:2 5207
in mount Sinai for a *s* savour Num 28:6 5207
of a *s* savour unto the LORD Num 28:8 5207
a burnt offering of a *s* savour Num 28:13 5207
of a *s* savour unto the LORD Num 28:24 5207
for a *s* savour unto the LORD Num 28:27 5207
for a *s* savour unto the LORD Num 29:2 5207
for a *s* savour, a sacrifice made Num 29:6 5207
unto the LORD for a *s* savour Num 29:8 5207
of a *s* savour unto the LORD Num 29:13 5207
of a *s* savour unto the LORD Num 29:36 5207
the *s* psalmist of Israel, said, 2Sa 23:1 5273
and to burn before him *s* incense 2Chr 2:4 5561
burnt sacrifices and *s* incense 2Chr 13:11 5561
which was filled with *s* odours 2Chr 16:14 1314
they may offer sacrifices of *s* Ezr 6:10 5208
way, eat the fat, and drink the *s* Neh 8:10 4477
and six months with *s* odours Est 2:12 1314
wickedness be *s* in his mouth Job 20:12 4985
of the valley shall be *s* unto him Job 21:33 4985
Canst thou bind the *s* influences Job 38:31 4575
We took *s* counsel together, and Ps 55:14 4985
My meditation of him shall be *s* Ps 104:34 6148
How *s* are thy words unto my taste Ps 119:103 4452
for they are *s* Ps 141:6 5276
lie down, and thy sleep shall be *s* Prov 3:24 6148
Stolen waters are *s*, and bread Prov 9:17 4985
accomplished is *s* to the soul Prov 13:19 6148
s to the soul, and health to the Prov 16:24 4966
Bread of deceit is *s* to a man Prov 20:17 6149
vomit up, and lose thy *s* words Prov 23:8 5273
which is *s* to thy taste Prov 24:13 4966
soul every bitter thing is *s* Prov 27:7 4966
The sleep of a labouring man is *s* Eccl 5:12 4966
Truly the light is *s*, and a Eccl 11:7 4966
and his fruit was *s* to my taste Song 2:3 4966
for *s* is thy voice, and thy Song 2:14 6149
my fingers with *s* smelling myrrh Song 5:5 5674
as a bed of spices, as *s* flowers Song 5:13 4840
dropping *s* smelling myrrh Song 5:13 5674
His mouth is most *s* Song 5:16 4477
that instead of *s* smell there Is 3:24 1314
bitter for *s*, and *s* for bitter Is 5:20 4966
make *s* melody, sing many songs, Is 23:16 3190
bought me no *s* cane with money Is 43:24
their own blood, as with *s* wine Is 49:26 6071
the *s* cane from a far country Jer 6:20 2896
nor your sacrifices *s* unto me Jer 6:20 6148
and my sleep was *s* unto me Jer 31:26 6148
offer *s* savour to all their idols Eze 6:13 5207
set it before them for a *s* savour Eze 16:19 5207
also they made their *s* savour Eze 20:28 5207
accept you with your *s* savour Eze 20:41 5207
an oblation and *s* odours unto him Dan 2:46 5208
the mountains shall drop *s* wine Amos 9:13 6071
s wine, but shalt not drink wine Mic 6:15 8492
and Salome, had bought *s* spices Mk 16:1
are unto God a *s* savour of Christ 2Cor 2:15 *2175*
from you, an odour of a *s* smell Phil 4:18 *2175*
forth at the same place *s* water Jas 3:11 *1099*
shall be in thy mouth *s* as honey Rev 10:9 *1099*
and it was in my mouth *s* as honey Rev 10:10 *1099*

SWEETER
went down, What is *s* than honey Judg 14:18 4966
s also than honey and the Ps 19:10 4966
yea, *s* than honey to my mouth Ps 119:103

SWEETLY
the worm shall feed *s* on him Job 24:20 4988
for my beloved, that goeth down *s* Song 7:9 4339

SWEETNESS
unto them, Should I forsake my *s* Judg 9:11 4987
and out of the strong came forth *s* Judg 14:14 4966
the *s* of the lips increaseth Prov 16:21 4986
so doth the *s* of a man's friend Prov 27:9 4986
it was in my mouth as honey for *s* Eze 3:3 4966

SWEETSMELLING
a sacrifice to God for a *s* savour Eph 5:2 *2175*

SWELL
thigh to rot, and thy belly to *s* Num 5:21 6639
bowels, to make thy belly to *s* Num 5:22 6638
bitter, and her belly shall *s* Num 5:27 6638
upon thee, neither did thy foot *s* Deut 8:4 1216

SWELLED
not old, and their feet *s* not Neh 9:21 1216

SWELLING
shake with the *s* thereof Ps 46:3 1346
s out in a high wall, whose Is 30:13 1158
wilt thou do in the *s* of Jordan Jer 12:5 1347
from the *s* of Jordan against the Jer 49:19 1347
come up like a lion from the *s* of Jer 50:44 1347
speak great *s* words of vanity 2Pet 2:18 *5246*
mouth speaketh great *s* words Jude 16 *5246*

SWELLINGS
backbitings, whisperings, *s* 2Cor 12:20 *5450*

SWEPT
The river of Kishon *s* them away Judg 5:21 1640
Why are thy valiant men *s* away Jer 46:15 5502
is come, he findeth it empty, *s* Mt 12:44 *4563*
when he cometh, he findeth it *s* Lk 11:25 *4563*

SWERVED
From which some having *s* have 1Ti 1:6 *795*

SWIFT
earth, as *s* as the eagle flieth Deut 28:49
were as *s* as the roes upon the 1Chr 12:8 4116
are passed away as the *s* ships Job 9:26 16
He is *s* as the waters Job 24:18 7031
feet that be *s* in running to Prov 6:18 4116
that the race is not to the *s* Eccl 9:11 7031
ye *s* messengers, to a nation Is 18:2 7031
the LORD rideth upon a *s* cloud Is 19:1 7031
and, We will ride upon the *s* Is 30:16 7031
shall they that pursue you be *s* Is 30:16 7043
upon *s* beasts, to my holy Is 66:20 3753
thou art a *s* dromedary traversing Jer 2:23 7031
Let not the *s* flee away, nor the Jer 46:6 7031
flight shall perish from the *s* Amos 2:14 7031
he that is *s* of foot shall not Amos 2:15 7031
bind the chariot to the *s* beast Mic 1:13 7409
I will be a *s* witness against the Mal 3:5 4116
Their feet are *s* to shed blood Rom 3:15 *3691*
let every man be *s* to hear Jas 1:19 *5036*
upon themselves *s* destruction 2Pet 2:1 *5031*

SWIFTER
they were *s* than eagles, they 2Sa 1:23 7043
My days are *s* than a weaver's Job 7:6 7043
Now my days are *s* than a post Job 9:25 7043
his horses are *s* than eagles Jer 4:13 7043
Our persecutors are *s* than the Lam 4:19 7031
also are *s* than the leopards Hab 1:8 7043

SWIFTLY
his word runneth very *s* Ps 147:15 4120
they shall come with speed *s* Is 5:26 7031
beginning, being caused to fly *s* Dan 9:21 3288
and if ye recompense me, *s* Joel 3:4 7031

SWIM
and the iron did *s* 2Kin 6:6 6687
all the night make I my bed to *s* Ps 6:6 7811
spreadeth forth his hands to *s* Is 25:11 7811
waters were risen, waters to *s* in Eze 47:5 7813
lest any of them should *s* out Acts 27:42 *1579*
s should cast themselves first Acts 27:43 *2860*

SWIMMEST
thy blood the land wherein thou *s* Eze 32:6 6824

SWIMMETH
as he that *s* spreadeth forth his Is 25:11 7811

SWINE
And the *s*, though he divide the Lev 11:7 2386
And the *s*, because it divideth the Deut 14:8 2386
cast ye your pearls before *s* Mt 7:6 *5519*
them an herd of many *s* feeding Mt 8:30 *5519*
us to go away into the herd of *s* Mt 8:31 *5519*
out, they went into the herd of *s* Mt 8:32 *5519*
the whole herd of *s* ran violently Mt 8:32 *5519*
a great herd of *s* feeding Mk 5:11 *5519*
him, saying, Send us into the *s* Mk 5:12 *5519*
went out, and entered into the *s* Mk 5:13 *5519*
And they that fed the *s* fled Mk 5:14 *5519*
devil, and also concerning the *s* Mk 5:16 *5519*
of many *s* feeding on the mountain Lk 8:32 *5519*
of the man, and entered into the *s* Lk 8:33 *5519*
him into his fields to feed *s* Lk 15:15 *5519*
with the husks that the *s* did eat Lk 15:16 *5519*

SWINE'S
As a jewel of gold in a *s* snout Prov 11:22 2386
the monuments, which eat *s* flesh Is 65:4 2386
as if he offered *s* blood Is 66:3 2386
tree in the midst, eating *s* flesh Is 66:17 2386

SWOLLEN
they looked when he should have *s* Acts 28:6 *4092*

SWOON
the sucklings *s* in the streets of Lam 2:11 5848

SWOONED
when they *s* as the wounded in the Lam 2:12 5848

SWORD
a flaming *s* which turned every Gen 3:24 2719
by thy *s* shalt thou live, and Gen 27:40 2719
as captives taken with the *s* Gen 31:26 2719
brethren, took each man his *s* Gen 34:25 2719

his son with the edge of the *s*	Gen 34:26	2719
the hand of the Amorite with my *s*	Gen 48:22	2719
us with pestilence, or with the *s*	Ex 5:3	2719
to put a *s* in their hand to slay	Ex 5:21	2719
I will draw my *s*, my hand shall	Ex 15:9	2719
his people with the edge of the *s*	Ex 17:13	2719
me from the *s* of Pharaoh	Ex 18:4	2719
and I will kill you with the *s*	Ex 22:24	2719
Put every man his *s* by his side	Ex 32:27	2719
neither shall the *s* go through	Lev 26:6	2719
shall fall before you by the *s*	Lev 26:7	2719
shall fall before you by the *s*	Lev 26:8	2719
And I will bring a *s* upon you	Lev 26:25	2719
and will draw out a *s* after you	Lev 26:33	2719
shall flee, as fleeing from a *s*	Lev 26:36	2719
another, as it were before a *s*	Lev 26:37	2719
unto this land, to fall by the *s*	Num 14:3	2719
you, and ye shall fall by the *s*	Num 14:43	2719
slain with a *s* in the open fields	Num 19:16	2719
come out against thee with the *s*	Num 20:18	2719
smote him with the edge of the *s*	Num 21:24	2719
way, and his *s* drawn in his hand	Num 22:23	2719
would there were a *s* in mine hand	Num 22:29	2719
way, and his *s* drawn in his hand	Num 22:31	2719
son of Beor they slew with the *s*	Num 31:8	2719
that city with the edge of the *s*	Deut 13:15	2719
thereof, with the edge of the *s*	Deut 13:15	2719
thereof with the edge of the *s*	Deut 20:13	2719
an extreme burning, and with the *s*	Deut 28:22	2719
The *s* without, and terror within,	Deut 32:25	2719
If I whet my glittering *s*	Deut 32:41	2719
blood, and my *s* shall devour flesh	Deut 32:42	2719
who is the *s* of thy excellency	Deut 33:29	2719
him with his *s* drawn in his hand	Josh 5:13	2719
and ass, with the edge of the *s*	Josh 6:21	2719
all fallen on the edge of the *s*	Josh 8:24	2719
smote it with the edge of the *s*	Josh 8:24	2719
of Israel slew with the *s*	Josh 10:11	2719
smote it with the edge of the *s*	Josh 10:28	2719
smote it with the edge of the *s*	Josh 10:30	2719
smote it with the edge of the *s*	Josh 10:32	2719
smote it with the edge of the *s*	Josh 10:35	2719
smote it with the edge of the *s*	Josh 10:37	2719
slain them with the edge of the *s*	Josh 10:39	2719
smote the king thereof with the *s*	Josh 11:10	2719
therein with the edge of the *s*	Josh 11:11	2719
smote them with the edge of the *s*	Josh 11:12	2719
they smote with the edge of the *s*	Josh 11:14	2719
of Israel slay with the *s* among	Josh 13:22	2719
smote it with the edge of the *s*	Josh 19:47	2719
but not with thy *s*, nor with thy	Josh 24:12	2719
smitten it with the edge of the *s*	Judg 1:8	2719
the city with the edge of the *s*	Judg 1:25	2719
the edge of the *s* before Barak	Judg 4:15	2719
fell upon the edge of the *s*	Judg 4:16	2719
the *s* of Gideon the son of Joash	Judg 7:14	2719
The *s* of the LORD, and of Gideon	Judg 7:18	
The *s* of the LORD, and of Gideon	Judg 7:20	2719
every man's *s* against his fellow	Judg 7:22	2719
twenty thousand men that drew *s*	Judg 8:10	2719
But the youth drew not his *s*	Judg 8:20	2719
and said unto him, Draw thy *s*	Judg 9:54	2719
smote them with the edge of the *s*	Judg 18:27	2719
thousand footmen that drew *s*	Judg 20:2	2719
and six thousand men that drew *s*	Judg 20:15	2719
hundred thousand men that drew *s*	Judg 20:17	2719
all these drew the *s*	Judg 20:25	2719
all these drew the *s*	Judg 20:35	2719
the city with the edge of the *s*	Judg 20:37	2719
five thousand men that drew the *s*	Judg 20:46	2719
smote them with the edge of the *s*	Judg 20:48	2719
with the edge of the *s*, with the	Judg 21:10	2719
that there was neither *s* nor	1Sa 13:22	2719
every man's *s* was against his	1Sa 14:20	2719
the people with the edge of the *s*	1Sa 15:8	2719
said, As thy *s* hath made women	1Sa 15:33	2719
girded his *s* upon his armour	1Sa 17:39	2719
Thou comest to me with a *s*	1Sa 17:45	2719
that the LORD saveth not with *s*	1Sa 17:47	2719
but there was no *s* in the hand of	1Sa 17:50	2719
the Philistine, and took his *s*	1Sa 17:51	2719
and his garments, even to his *s*	1Sa 18:4	2719
here under thine hand spear or *s*	1Sa 21:8	2719
my *s* nor my weapons with me	1Sa 21:8	2719
The *s* of Goliath the Philistine,	1Sa 21:9	2719
gave him the *s* of Goliath the	1Sa 22:10	2719
thou hast given him bread, and a *s*	1Sa 22:13	2719
smote he with the edge of the *s*	1Sa 22:19	2719
and sheep, with the edge of the *s*	1Sa 22:19	2719
men, Gird ye on every man his *s*	1Sa 25:13	2719
And they girded on every man his *s*	1Sa 25:13	2719
and David also girded on his *s*	1Sa 25:13	2719
unto his armourbearer, Draw thy *s*	1Sa 31:4	2719
Therefore Saul took a *s*, and fell	1Sa 31:4	2719
dead, he fell likewise upon his *s*	1Sa 31:5	2719
because they were fallen by the *s*	2Sa 1:12	2719
the *s* of Saul returned not empty	2Sa 1:22	2719
thrust his *s* in his fellow's side	2Sa 2:16	2719
Shall the *s* devour for ever	2Sa 2:26	2719
a staff, or that falleth on the *s*	2Sa 3:29	2719
for the *s* devoureth one as well	2Sa 11:25	2719
Uriah the Hittite with the *s*	2Sa 12:9	2719
hast slain him with the *s* of the	2Sa 12:9	2719
Now therefore the *s* shall never	2Sa 12:10	2719
the city with the edge of the *s*	2Sa 15:14	2719
that day than the *s* devoured	2Sa 18:8	2719
upon it a girdle with a *s*	2Sa 20:8	2719
to the *s* that was in Joab's hand	2Sa 20:10	2719
he being girded with a new *s*	2Sa 21:16	
and his hand clave unto the *s*	2Sa 23:10	2719
valiant men that drew the *s*	2Sa 24:9	2719
not slay his servant with the *s*	1Kin 1:51	2719
not put thee to death with the *s*	1Kin 2:8	2719
than he, and slew them with the *s*	1Kin 2:32	2719
And the king said, Bring me a *s*	1Kin 3:24	2719
they brought a *s* before the king	1Kin 3:24	2719
slain all the prophets with the *s*	1Kin 19:1	2719
and slain thy prophets with the *s*	1Kin 19:10	2719
and slain thy prophets with the *s*	1Kin 19:14	2719
the *s* of Hazael shall Jehu slay	1Kin 19:17	2719
the *s* of Jehu shall Elisha slay	1Kin 19:17	2719
hast taken captive with thy *s*	2Kin 6:22	2719
men wilt thou slay with the *s*	2Kin 8:12	2719
smote them with the edge of the *s*	2Kin 10:25	2719
followeth her kill with the *s*	2Kin 11:15	2719
the *s* beside the king's house	2Kin 11:20	2719
to fall by the *s* in his own land	2Kin 19:7	2719
his sons smote him with the *s*	2Kin 19:37	2719
men able to bear buckler and *s*	1Chr 5:18	2719
to his armourbearer, Draw thy *s*	1Chr 10:4	2719
So Saul took a *s*, and fell upon it	1Chr 10:4	2719
dead, he fell likewise on the *s*	1Chr 10:5	2719
hundred thousand men that drew *s*	1Chr 21:5	2719
and ten thousand men that drew *s*	1Chr 21:5	2719
while that the *s* of thine enemies	1Chr 21:12	2719
else three days the *s* of the LORD	1Chr 21:12	2719
having a drawn *s* in his hand	1Chr 21:16	2719
he put up his *s* again into the	1Chr 21:27	2719
of the *s* of the angel of the LORD	1Chr 21:30	2719
evil cometh upon us, as the *s*	2Chr 20:9	2719
slew all his brethren with the *s*	2Chr 21:4	2719
her, let him be slain with the *s*	2Chr 23:14	2719
had slain Athaliah with the *s*	2Chr 23:21	2719
our fathers have fallen by the *s*	2Chr 29:9	2719
bowels slew him there with the *s*	2Chr 32:21	2719
slew their young men with the *s*	2Chr 36:17	2719
the *s* carried he away to Babylon	2Chr 36:20	2719
the kings of the lands, to the *s*	Ezr 9:7	2719
every one had his *s* girded by his	Neh 4:18	2719
enemies with the stroke of the *s*	Est 9:5	2719
servants with the edge of the *s*	Job 1:15	2719
servants with the edge of the *s*	Job 1:17	2719
But he saveth the poor from the *s*	Job 5:15	2719
and in war from the power of the *s*	Job 5:20	2719
and he is waited for of the *s*	Job 15:22	2719
Be ye afraid of the *s*	Job 19:29	2719
bringeth the punishments of the *s*	Job 19:29	2719
the glittering *s* cometh out of	Job 20:25	1300
be multiplied, it is for the *s*	Job 27:14	2719
his life from perishing by the *s*	Job 33:18	7973
not, they shall perish by the *s*	Job 36:12	7973
turneth he back from the *s*	Job 39:22	2719
make his *s* to approach unto him	Job 40:19	2719
The *s* of him that layeth at him	Job 41:26	2719
he turn not, he will whet his *s*	Ps 7:12	2719
from the wicked, which is thy *s*	Ps 17:13	2719
Deliver my soul from the *s*	Ps 22:20	2719
The wicked have drawn out the *s*	Ps 37:14	2719
Their *s* shall enter into their	Ps 37:15	2719
As with a *s* in my bones, mine	Ps 42:10	7524
land in possession by their own *s*	Ps 44:3	2719
bow, neither shall my *s* save me	Ps 44:6	2719
Gird thy *s* upon thy thigh, O most	Ps 45:3	2719
arrows, and their tongue a sharp *s*	Ps 57:4	2719
They shall fall by the *s*	Ps 63:10	2719
Who whet their tongue like a *s*	Ps 64:3	2719
of the bow, the shield, and the *s*	Ps 76:3	2719
his people over also unto the *s*	Ps 78:62	2719
Their priests fell by the *s*	Ps 78:64	2719
also turned the edge of his *s*	Ps 89:43	2719
his servant from the hurtful *s*	Ps 144:10	2719
a twoedged *s* in their hand	Ps 149:6	2719
wormwood, sharp as a twoedged *s*	Prov 5:4	2719
like the piercings of a *s*	Prov 12:18	2719
his neighbour is a maul, and a *s*	Prov 25:18	2719
every man hath his *s* upon his	Song 3:8	2719
ye shall be devoured with the *s*	Is 1:20	2719
not lift up *s* against nation	Is 2:4	2719
Thy men shall fall by the *s*	Is 3:25	2719
unto them shall fall by the *s*	Is 13:15	2719
slain, thrust through with a *s*	Is 14:19	2719
from the swords, from the drawn *s*	Is 21:15	2719
men are not slain with the *s*	Is 22:2	2719
strong *s* shall punish leviathan	Is 27:1	2719
the Assyrian fall with the *s*	Is 31:8	2719
and the *s*, not of a mean man,	Is 31:8	2719
but he shall flee from the *s*	Is 31:8	2719
For my *s* shall be bathed in	Is 34:5	2719
The *s* of the LORD is filled with	Is 34:6	2719
to fall by the *s* in his own land	Is 37:7	2719
his sons smote him with the *s*	Is 37:38	2719
he gave them as the dust to his *s*	Is 41:2	2719
hath made my mouth like a sharp *s*	Is 49:2	2719
and the famine, and the *s*	Is 51:19	2719
will I number you to the *s*	Is 65:12	2719
by his *s* will the LORD plead with	Is 66:16	2719
your own *s* hath devoured your	Jer 2:30	2719
whereas the *s* reacheth unto the	Jer 4:10	2719
neither shall we see *s* nor famine	Jer 5:12	2719
thou trustedst, with the *s*	Jer 5:17	2719
for the *s* of the enemy and fear is	Jer 6:25	2719
and I will send a *s* after them	Jer 9:16	2719
the young men shall die by the *s*	Jer 11:22	2719
for the *s* of the LORD shall	Jer 12:12	2719
but I will consume them by the *s*	Jer 14:12	2719
unto them, Ye shall not see the *s*	Jer 14:13	2719
I sent them not, yet they say, *S*	Jer 14:15	2719
By *s* and famine shall those	Jer 14:15	2719
because of the famine and the *s*	Jer 14:16	2719
then behold the slain with the *s*	Jer 14:18	2719
as are for the *s*, to the *s*	Jer 15:2	2719
the *s* to slay, and the dogs to	Jer 15:3	2719
to the *s* before their enemies	Jer 15:9	2719
they shall be consumed by the *s*	Jer 16:4	2719
their blood by the force of the *s*	Jer 18:21	2719
men be slain by the *s* in battle	Jer 18:21	2719
by the *s* before their enemies	Jer 19:7	2719
fall by the *s* of their enemies	Jer 20:4	2719
and shall slay them with the *s*	Jer 20:4	2719
from the pestilence, from the *s*	Jer 21:7	2719
smite them with the edge of the *s*	Jer 21:7	2719
in this city shall die by the *s*	Jer 21:9	2719
And I will send the *s*, the famine,	Jer 24:10	2719
because of the *s* that I will send	Jer 25:16	2719
because of the *s* which I will	Jer 25:27	2719
for I will call for a *s* upon all	Jer 25:29	2719
them that are wicked to the *s*	Jer 25:31	2719
who slew him with the *s*, and cast	Jer 26:23	2719
saith the LORD, with the *s*	Jer 27:8	2719
die, thou and thy people, by the *s*	Jer 27:13	2719
I will send upon them the *s*	Jer 29:17	2719
I will persecute them with the *s*	Jer 29:18	2719
s found grace in the wilderness	Jer 31:2	2719
against it, because of the *s*	Jer 32:24	2719
of the king of Babylon by the *s*	Jer 32:36	2719
down by the mounts, and by the *s*	Jer 33:4	2719
thee, Thou shalt not die by the *s*	Jer 34:4	2719
for you, saith the LORD, to the *s*	Jer 34:17	2719
in this city shall die by the *s*	Jer 38:2	2719
and thou shalt not fall by the *s*	Jer 39:18	2719
the son of Shaphan with the *s*	Jer 41:2	2719
it shall come to pass, that the *s*	Jer 42:16	2719
they shall die by the *s*, by the	Jer 42:17	2719
that ye shall die by the *s*	Jer 42:22	2719
as are for the *s* to the *s*	Jer 43:11	2719
shall even be consumed by the *s*	Jer 44:12	2719
even unto the greatest, by the *s*	Jer 44:12	2719
have punished Jerusalem, by the *s*	Jer 44:13	2719
and have been consumed by the *s*	Jer 44:18	2719
Egypt shall be consumed by the *s*	Jer 44:27	2719
a small number that escape the *s*	Jer 44:28	2719
the *s* shall devour, and it shall	Jer 46:10	2719
for the *s* shall devour round	Jer 46:14	2719
nativity, from the oppressing *s*	Jer 46:16	2719
O thou *s* of the LORD, how long	Jer 47:6	2719
the *s* shall pursue thee	Jer 48:2	2719
keepeth back his *s* from blood	Jer 48:10	2719
and I will send the *s* after them	Jer 49:37	2719
for fear of the oppressing *s* they	Jer 50:16	2719
A *s* is upon the Chaldeans, saith	Jer 50:35	2719
A *s* is upon the liars	Jer 50:36	2719
a *s* is upon her mighty men	Jer 50:36	2719
A *s* is upon their horses, and upon	Jer 50:37	2719
a *s* is upon her treasures	Jer 50:37	2719
Ye that have escaped the *s*	Jer 51:50	2719
abroad the *s* bereaveth, at home	Lam 1:20	2719
my young men are fallen by the *s*	Lam 2:21	2719
They that be slain with the *s* are	Lam 4:9	2719
of the *s* of the wilderness	Lam 5:9	2719
and I will draw out a *s* after them	Eze 5:2	2719
fall by the *s* round about thee	Eze 5:12	2719
and I will draw out a *s* after them	Eze 5:12	2719
and I will bring the *s* upon thee	Eze 5:17	2719
even I, will bring a *s* upon you	Eze 6:3	2719
escape the *s* among the nations	Eze 6:8	2719
for they shall fall by the *s*	Eze 6:11	2719
that is near shall fall by the *s*	Eze 6:12	2719
The *s* is without, and the	Eze 7:15	2719
in the field shall die with the *s*	Eze 7:15	2719
Ye have feared the *s*	Eze 11:8	2719
and I will bring a *s* upon you	Eze 11:8	2719
Ye shall fall by the *s*	Eze 11:10	2719
I will draw out the *s* after them	Eze 12:14	2719
a few men of them from the *s*	Eze 12:16	2719
a *s* upon that land, and say, *S*	Eze 14:17	2719
judgments upon Jerusalem, the *s*	Eze 14:21	2719
all his bands shall fall by the *s*	Eze 17:21	2719
draw forth my *s* out of his sheath	Eze 21:3	2719
therefore shall my *s* go forth out	Eze 21:4	2719
forth my *s* out of his sheath	Eze 21:5	2719
Say, A *s*, a *s* is sharpened,	Eze 21:9	2719
this *s* is sharpened, and it is	Eze 21:11	2719
of the *s* shall be upon my people	Eze 21:12	2719
what if the *s* contemn even the	Eze 21:13	
let the *s* be doubled the third	Eze 21:14	2719
third time, the *s* of the slain	Eze 21:14	2719
it is the *s* of the great men that	Eze 21:14	2719
of the *s* against all their gates	Eze 21:15	2719
that the *s* of the king of Babylon	Eze 21:19	2719
that the *s* may come to Rabbath of	Eze 21:20	2719
thou, The *s*, the *s* is drawn	Eze 21:28	2719
daughters, and slew her with the *s*	Eze 23:10	2719
thy remnant shall fall by the *s*	Eze 23:25	2719
ye have left shall fall by the *s*	Eze 24:21	2719
they of Dedan shall fall by the *s*	Eze 25:13	2719
the field shall be slain by the *s*	Eze 26:6	2719
He shall slay with the *s* thy	Eze 26:8	2719
he shall slay thy people by the *s*	Eze 26:11	2719
by the *s* upon her on every side	Eze 28:23	2719
I will bring a *s* upon thee	Eze 29:8	2719
the *s* shall come upon Egypt, and	Eze 30:4	2719
shall fall with them by the *s*	Eze 30:5	2719
shall they fall in it by the *s*	Eze 30:6	2719
of Pi-beseth shall fall by the *s*	Eze 30:17	2719
to make it strong to hold the *s*	Eze 30:21	2719
I will cause the *s* to fall out of	Eze 30:22	2719
Babylon, and put my *s* in his hand	Eze 30:24	2719
when I shall put my *s* into the	Eze 30:25	2719
them that be slain with the *s*	Eze 31:17	2719
with them that be slain by the *s*	Eze 31:18	2719
I shall brandish my *s* before them	Eze 32:10	2719
The *s* of the king of Babylon	Eze 32:11	2719
of them that are slain by the *s*	Eze 32:20	2719
she is delivered to the *s*	Eze 32:20	2719
lie uncircumcised, slain by the *s*	Eze 32:21	2719
of them slain, fallen by the *s*	Eze 32:22	2719
of them slain, fallen by the *s*	Eze 32:23	2719
of them slain, fallen by the *s*	Eze 32:24	2719
uncircumcised, slain by the *s*	Eze 32:25	2719
uncircumcised, slain by the *s*	Eze 32:26	2719
them that are slain with the *s*	Eze 32:28	2719
by them that were slain by the *s*	Eze 32:29	2719

with them that be slain by the s ... Eze 32:30 2719
and all his army slain by the s ... Eze 32:31 2719
them that are slain with the s ... Eze 32:32 2719
When I bring the s upon a land ... Eze 33:2 2719
he seeth the s come upon the land ... Eze 33:3 2719
if the s come, and take him away, ... Eze 33:4 2719
if the watchman see the s come ... Eze 33:6 2719
if the s come, and take any person ... Eze 33:6 2719
Ye stand upon your s, ye work ... Eze 33:26 2719
in the wastes shall fall by the s ... Eze 33:27 2719
s in the time of their calamity ... Eze 35:5 2719
fall that are slain with the s ... Eze 35:8 2719
that is brought back from the s ... Eze 38:8 2719
I will call for a s against him ... Eze 38:21 2719
every man's s shall be against ... Eze 38:21 2719
so fell they all by the s ... Eze 39:23 2719
yet they shall fall by the s ... Dan 11:33 2719
not save them by bow, nor by s ... Hos 1:7 2719
and I will break the bow and the s ... Hos 2:18 2719
s for the rage of their tongue ... Hos 7:16 2719
the s shall abide on his cities, ... Hos 11:6 2719
they shall fall by the s ... Hos 13:16 2719
and when they fall upon the s ... Joel 2:8 7973
did pursue his brother with the s ... Amos 1:11 2719
young men have I slain with the s ... Amos 4:10 2719
the house of Jeroboam with the s ... Amos 7:9 2719
Jeroboam shall die by the s ... Amos 7:11 2719
thy daughters shall fall by the s ... Amos 7:17 2719
slay the last of them with the s ... Amos 9:1 2719
thence will I command the s ... Amos 9:4 2719
of my people shall die by the s ... Amos 9:10 2719
not lift up a s against nation ... Mic 4:3 2719
the land of Assyria with the s ... Mic 5:6 2719
will I give up to the s ... Mic 6:14 2719
the s shall devour thy young ... Nah 2:13 2719
lifteth up both the bright s ... Nah 3:3 2719
the s shall cut thee off, it ... Nah 3:15 2719
also, ye shall be slain by my s ... Zeph 2:12 2719
every one by the s of his brother ... Hag 2:22 2719
thee as the s of a mighty man ... Zec 9:13 2719
the s shall be upon his arm, and ... Zec 11:17 2719
Awake, O s, against my shepherd, ... Zec 13:7 2719
I came not to send peace, but a s ... Mt 10:34 *3162*
out his hand, and drew his s ... Mt 26:51 *3162*
Put up again thy s into his place ... Mt 26:52 *3162*
the s shall perish with the s ... Mt 26:52 *3162*
of them that stood by drew a s ... Mk 14:47 *3162*
a s shall pierce through thy own ... Lk 2:35 *4501*
shall fall by the edge of the s ... Lk 21:24 *3162*
and he that hath no s, let him ... Lk 22:36 *3162*
Lord, shall we smite with the s ... Lk 22:49 *3162*
Simon Peter having a s drew it ... Jn 18:10 *3162*
Put up thy s into the sheath ... Jn 18:11 *3162*
the brother of John with the s ... Acts 12:2 *3162*
doors open, he drew out his s ... Acts 16:27 *3162*
or nakedness, or peril, or s ... Rom 8:35 *3162*
for he beareth not the s in vain ... Rom 13:4 *3162*
the s of the Spirit, which is the ... Eph 6:17 *3162*
and sharper than any twoedged s ... Heb 4:12 *3162*
fire, escaped the edge of the s ... Heb 11:34 *3162*
tempted, were slain with the s ... Heb 11:37 *3162*
his mouth went a sharp twoedged s ... Rev 1:16 *4501*
hath the sharp s with two edges ... Rev 2:12 *4501*
them with the s of my mouth ... Rev 2:16 *4501*
was given unto him a great s ... Rev 6:4 *3162*
part of the earth, to kill with s ... Rev 6:8 *4501*
he that killeth with the s must ... Rev 13:10 *3162*
must be killed with the s ... Rev 13:10 *3162*
beast, which had the wound by a s ... Rev 13:14 *3162*
out of his mouth goeth a sharp s ... Rev 19:15 *4501*
s of him that sat upon the horse ... Rev 19:21 *4501*
which s proceeded out of his ... Rev 19:21

SWORDS
the Hebrews make them s or spears ... 1Sa 13:19 2719
him seven hundred men that drew s ... 2Kin 3:26 2719
after their families with their s ... Neh 4:13 2719
than oil, yet were they drawn s ... Ps 55:21 6609
s are in their lips ... Ps 59:7 2719
generation, whose teeth are as s ... Prov 30:14 2719
They all hold s, being expert in ... Song 3:8 2719
beat their s into plowshares ... Is 2:4 2719
For they fled from the s, from ... Is 21:15 2719
thrust thee through with their s ... Eze 16:40 2719
and dispatch them with their s ... Eze 23:47 2719
they shall draw their s against ... Eze 28:7 2719
shall draw their s against Egypt ... Eze 30:11 2719
By the s of the mighty will I ... Eze 32:12 2719
laid their s under their heads ... Eze 32:27 2719
shields, all of them handling s ... Eze 38:4 2719
Beat your plowshares into s ... Joel 3:10 2719
beat their s into plowshares ... Mic 4:3 2719
with him a great multitude with s ... Mt 26:47 *3162*
out as against a thief with s ... Mt 26:55 *3162*
with him a great multitude with s ... Mk 14:43 *3162*
out, as against a thief, with s ... Mk 14:48 *3162*
Lord, behold, here are two s ... Lk 22:38 *3162*
out, as against a thief, with s ... Lk 22:52 *3162*

SWORN
And said, By myself have I s ... Gen 22:16 7650
for he had straitly s the ... Ex 13:19 7650
Because the LORD hath s that the ... Ex 17:16
about which he hath s falsely ... Lev 6:5 7650
which he had s unto your fathers ... Deut 7:8 7650
as he hath s unto thy fathers ... Deut 13:17 7650
as he hath s unto thy fathers, and ... Deut 19:8 7650
himself, as he hath s unto thee ... Deut 28:9 7650
as he hath s unto thy fathers, to ... Deut 29:13 7650
the land which the LORD hath s ... Deut 31:7 7650
s unto them by the LORD God of ... Josh 9:18 7650
We have s unto them by the LORD ... Josh 9:19 7650
and as the LORD had s unto them ... Judg 2:15 7650
the men of Israel had s in Mizpeh ... Judg 21:1 7650
seeing we have s by the LORD that ... Judg 21:7 7650
for the children of Israel have s ... Judg 21:18 7650
therefore I have s unto the house ... 1Sa 3:14 7650
forasmuch as we have s both of us ... 1Sa 20:42 7650
as the LORD hath s to David ... 2Sa 3:9 7650
of Israel had s unto them ... 2Sa 21:2 7650
for they had s with all their ... 2Chr 15:15 7650
were many in Judah s unto him ... Neh 6:18
which thou hadst s to give them ... Neh 9:15 5375
unto vanity, nor s deceitfully ... Ps 24:4 7650
I have s unto David my servant, ... Ps 89:3 7650
Once have I s by my holiness that ... Ps 89:35 7650
mad against me are s against me ... Ps 102:8 7650
The LORD hath s, and will not ... Ps 110:4 7650
I have s, and I will perform it, ... Ps 119:106 7650
The LORD hath s in truth unto ... Ps 132:11 7650
The LORD of hosts hath s, saying, ... Is 14:24 7650
I have s by myself, the word is ... Is 45:23 7650
for as I have s that the waters ... Is 54:9 7650
so have I s that I would not be ... Is 54:9 7650
The LORD hath s by his right hand ... Is 62:8 7650
s by them that are no gods ... Jer 5:7 7650
which I have s unto your fathers ... Jer 11:5 7650
I have s by my great name, saith ... Jer 44:26 7650
For I have s by myself, saith the ... Jer 49:13 7650
LORD of hosts hath s by himself ... Jer 51:14 7650
sight, to them that have s oaths ... Eze 21:23 7650
Lord GOD hath s by his holiness ... Amos 4:2 7650
The Lord GOD hath s by himself ... Amos 6:8 7650
The LORD hath s by the excellency ... Amos 8:7 7650
which thou hast s unto our ... Mic 7:20 7650
God had s with an oath to him ... Acts 2:30 *3660*
nigh, which God had s to Abraham ... Acts 7:17 *3660*
As I have s in my wrath, if they ... Heb 4:3 *3660*

SYCAMINE
ye might say unto this s tree ... Lk 17:6 *4807*

SYCHAR (*si'-kar*) See SHECHEM. *A city in Samaria.*
of Samaria, which is called S ... Jn 4:5 *4965*

SYCHEM (*si'-kem*) See SHECHEM. *Same as Shechem.*
And were carried over into S ... Acts 7:16 *4966*
the sons of Emmor the father of S ... Acts 7:16 *4966*

SYCOMORE
the s trees that are in the vale ... 1Kin 10:27 8256
the s trees that were in the low ... 1Chr 27:28 8256
cedar trees made he as the s ... 2Chr 1:15 8256
the s trees that are in the low ... 2Chr 9:27 8256
hail, and their s trees with frost ... Ps 78:47 8256
herdman, and a gatherer of s fruit ... Amos 7:14 8256
up into a s tree to see him ... Lk 19:4 *4809*

SYCOMORES
the s are cut down, but we will ... Is 9:10 8256

SYENE (*si-e'-ne*) *An Egyptian city.*
from the tower of S even unto the ... Eze 29:10 5482
from the tower of S shall they ... Eze 30:6 5482

SYNAGOGUE
thence, he went into their s ... Mt 12:9 *4864*
he taught them in their s ... Mt 13:54 *4864*
sabbath day he entered into the s ... Mk 1:21 *4864*
there was in their s a man with ... Mk 1:23 *4864*
when they were come out of the s ... Mk 1:29 *4864*
And he entered again into the s ... Mk 3:1 *4864*
cometh one of the rulers of the s ... Mk 5:22 *752*
he saith unto the ruler of the s ... Mk 5:36 *752*
the house of the ruler of the s ... Mk 5:38 *752*
come, he began to teach in the s ... Mk 6:2 *4864*
he went into the s on the sabbath ... Lk 4:16 *4864*
in the s were fastened on him ... Lk 4:20 *4864*
And all they in the s, when they ... Lk 4:28 *4864*
in the s there was a man, which ... Lk 4:33 *4864*
And he arose out of the s, and ... Lk 4:38 *4864*
that he entered into the s ... Lk 6:6 *4864*
nation, and he hath built us a s ... Lk 7:5 *4864*
and he was a ruler of the s ... Lk 8:41 *4864*
the ruler of the s answered with ... Lk 13:14 *752*
These things said he in the s ... Jn 6:59 *4864*
he should be put out of the s ... Jn 9:22 *656*
they should be put out of the s ... Jn 12:42 *656*
I ever taught in the s, and in the ... Jn 18:20 *4864*
Then there arose certain of the s ... Acts 6:9 *4864*
is called the s of the Libertines ... Acts 6:9 *4864*
went into the s on the sabbath ... Acts 13:14 *4864*
rulers of the s sent unto them ... Acts 13:15 *752*
the Jews were gone out of the s ... Acts 13:42 *4864*
together into the s of the Jews ... Acts 14:1 *4864*
where was a s of the Jews ... Acts 17:1 *4864*
went into the s of the Jews ... Acts 17:10 *4864*
he in the s with the Jews ... Acts 17:17 *4864*
reasoned in the s every sabbath ... Acts 18:4 *4864*
whose house joined hard to the s ... Acts 18:7 *4864*
Crispus, the chief ruler of the s ... Acts 18:8 *752*
the chief ruler of the s ... Acts 18:17 *752*
but he himself entered into the s ... Acts 18:19 *4864*
he began to speak boldly in the s ... Acts 18:26 *4864*
And he went into the s, and spake ... Acts 19:8 *4864*
beat in every s them that ... Acts 22:19 *4864*
And I punished them oft in every s ... Acts 26:11 *4864*
are not, but are the s of Satan ... Rev 2:9 *4864*
will make them of the s of Satan ... Rev 3:9 *4864*

SYNAGOGUE'S
of the s house certain which said ... Mk 5:35 *752*
one from the ruler of the s house ... Lk 8:49 *752*

SYNAGOGUES
up all the s of God in the land ... Ps 74:8 4150
all Galilee, teaching in their s ... Mt 4:23 *4864*
as the hypocrites do in the s ... Mt 6:2 *4864*
love to pray standing in the s ... Mt 6:5 *4864*
and villages, teaching in their s ... Mt 9:35 *4864*
they will scourge you in their s ... Mt 10:17 *4864*
and the chief seats in the s ... Mt 23:6 *4864*
them shall ye scourge in your s ... Mt 23:34 *4864*
he preached in their s throughout ... Mk 1:39 *4864*
And the chief seats in the s ... Mk 12:39 *4864*
in the s ye shall be beaten ... Mk 13:9 *4864*
And he taught in their s, being ... Lk 4:15 *4864*
he preached in the s of Galilee ... Lk 4:44 *4864*
love the uppermost seats in the s ... Lk 11:43 *4864*
And when they bring you unto the s ... Lk 12:11 *4864*
in one of the s on the sabbath ... Lk 13:10 *4864*
and the highest seats in the s ... Lk 20:46 *4864*
you, delivering you up to the s ... Lk 21:12 *4864*
They shall put you out of the s ... Jn 16:2 *656*
him letters to Damascus to the s ... Acts 9:2 *4864*
he preached Christ in the s ... Acts 9:20 *4864*
word of God in the s of the Jews ... Acts 13:5 *4864*
read in the s every sabbath day ... Acts 15:21 *4864*
up the people, neither in the s ... Acts 24:12 *4864*

SYNTYCHE (*sin'-ti-ke*) *A Christian at Philippi.*
I beseech Euodias, and beseech S ... Phil 4:2 *4941*

SYRACUSE (*sir'-a-cuse*) *A city on Sicily.*
And landing at S, we tarried there ... Acts 28:12 *4946*

SYRIA (*sir'-e-ah*) See ARAM, SYRIA-DAMASCUS, SYRIA-MAACHAH, SYRIAN. *Nation north of Israel.*
and Ashtaroth, and the gods of S ... Judg 10:6 758
put garrisons in S of Damascus ... 2Sa 8:6 758
Of S, and of Moab, and of the ... 2Sa 8:12 758
vow while I abode at Geshur in S ... 2Sa 15:8 758
Hittites, and for the kings of S ... 1Kin 10:29 758
Israel, and reigned over S ... 1Kin 11:25 758
the son of Hezion, king of S ... 1Kin 15:18 758
anoint Hazael to be king over S ... 1Kin 19:15 758
Ben-hadad the king of S gathered ... 1Kin 20:1 758
Ben-hadad the king of S escaped ... 1Kin 20:20 758
of S will come up against thee ... 1Kin 20:22 758
of the king of S said unto him ... 1Kin 20:23 758
three years without war between S ... 1Kin 22:1 758
out of the hand of the king of S ... 1Kin 22:3 758
But the king of S commanded his ... 1Kin 22:31 758
of the host of the king of S ... 2Kin 5:1 758
LORD had given deliverance unto S ... 2Kin 5:1 758
And the king of S said, Go to, go ... 2Kin 5:5 758
Then the king of S warred against ... 2Kin 6:8 758
the heart of the king of S was ... 2Kin 6:11 758
So the bands of S came no more ... 2Kin 6:23 758
king of S gathered all his host ... 2Kin 6:24 758
uttermost part of the camp of S ... 2Kin 7:5 758
Ben-hadad the king of S was sick ... 2Kin 8:7 758
king of S hath sent me to thee ... 2Kin 8:9 758
me that thou shalt be king over S ... 2Kin 8:13 758
Hazael king of S in Ramoth-gilead ... 2Kin 8:28 758
fought against Hazael king of S ... 2Kin 8:29 758
because of Hazael king of S ... 2Kin 9:14 758
he fought with Hazael king of S ... 2Kin 9:15 758
Then Hazael king of S went up ... 2Kin 12:17 758
and sent it to Hazael king of S ... 2Kin 12:18 758
into the hand of Hazael king of S ... 2Kin 13:3 758
the king of S oppressed them ... 2Kin 13:4 758
for the king of S had destroyed ... 2Kin 13:7 758
the arrow of deliverance from S ... 2Kin 13:17 758
then hadst thou smitten S till ... 2Kin 13:19 758
now thou shalt smite S but thrice ... 2Kin 13:19 758
But Hazael king of S oppressed ... 2Kin 13:22 758
So Hazael king of S died ... 2Kin 13:24 758
against Judah Rezin the king of S ... 2Kin 15:37 758
Then Rezin king of S and Pekah son ... 2Kin 16:5 758
of S recovered Elath to S ... 2Kin 16:6 758
out of the hand of the king of S ... 2Kin 16:7 758
Hittites, and for the kings of S ... 2Chr 1:17 758
and sent to Ben-hadad king of S ... 2Chr 16:2 758
thou hast relied on the king of S ... 2Chr 16:7 758
of S escaped out of thine hand ... 2Chr 16:7 758
push S until they be consumed ... 2Chr 18:10 758
Now the king of S had commanded ... 2Chr 18:30 758
beyond the sea on this side S ... 2Chr 20:2 758
Hazael king of S at Ramoth-gilead ... 2Chr 22:5 758
he fought with Hazael king of S ... 2Chr 22:6 758
that the host of S came up ... 2Chr 24:23 758
into the hand of the king of S ... 2Chr 28:5 758
gods of the kings of S help them ... 2Chr 28:23 758
Judah, that Rezin the king of S ... Is 7:1 758
S is confederate with Ephraim ... Is 7:2 758
the fierce anger of Rezin with S ... Is 7:4 758
Because S, Ephraim, and the son of ... Is 7:5 758
For the head of S is Damascus ... Is 7:8 758
Damascus, and the remnant of S ... Is 17:3 758
reproach of the daughters of S ... Eze 16:57 758
S was thy merchant by reason of ... Eze 27:16 758
Jacob fled into the country of S ... Hos 12:12 758
the people of S shall go into ... Amos 1:5 758
And his fame went throughout all S ... Mt 4:24 *4947*
when Cyrenius was governor of S ... Lk 2:2 *4947*
of the Gentiles in Antioch and S ... Acts 15:23 *4947*
And he went through S and Cilicia, ... Acts 15:41 *4947*
brethren, and sailed thence into S ... Acts 18:18 *4947*
as he was about to sail into S ... Acts 20:3 *4947*
the left hand, and sailed into S ... Acts 21:3 *4947*
I came into the regions of S ... Gal 1:21 *4947*

SYRIACK (*sir'-e-ak*) See SYRIAN. *Language of the Syrians.*
the Chaldeans to the king in S ... Dan 2:4 762

SYRIA-DAMASCUS (*sir''-e-ah-da-mas'-cus*) See SYRIA, DAMASCUS. *Same as Damascus.*
Then David put garrisons in S ... 1Chr 18:6

SYRIA-MAACHAH (*sir''-e-ah-ma-a-kah*) *A Syrian city-state.*
out of Mesopotamia, and out of S ... 1Chr 19:6 758

SYRIAN (*sir'-e-un*) See ARAMITES, SYRIANS, SYROPHENICIAN.
1. An inhabitant of Syria.
of Bethuel the *S* of Padan-aram ... Gen 25:20 761
the sister to Laban the *S* ... Gen 25:20 761
unto Laban, son of Bethuel the *S* ... Gen 28:5 761
away unawares to Laban the *S* ... Gen 31:20 761
Laban the *S* in a dream by night ... Gen 31:24 761
A *S* ready to perish was my father ... Deut 26:5 761
master hath spared Naaman this *S* ... 2Kin 5:20 761
was cleansed, saving Naaman the *S* ... Lk 4:27 *4948*
2. The language of Syria.
to thy servants in the *S* language ... 2Kin 18:26 762
was written in the *S* tongue ... Ezr 4:7 762
and interpreted in the *S* tongue ... Ezr 4:7 762
thy servants in the *S* language ... Is 36:11 762

SYRIANS
when the *S* of Damascus came to ... 2Sa 8:5 758
of Zobah, David slew of the *S* two ... 2Sa 8:5 758
the *S* became servants to David, ... 2Sa 8:6 758
of the *S* in the valley of salt ... 2Sa 8:13 758
hired the *S* of Beth-rehob, and the ... 2Sa 10:6 758
the *S* of Zoba, twenty thousand ... 2Sa 10:6 758
the *S* of Zoba, and of Rehob, and ... 2Sa 10:8 758
put them in array against the *S* ... 2Sa 10:9 758
If the *S* be too strong for me, ... 2Sa 10:11 758
unto the battle against the *S* ... 2Sa 10:13 758
of Ammon saw that the *S* were fled ... 2Sa 10:14 758
when the *S* saw that they were ... 2Sa 10:15 758
brought out the *S* that were ... 2Sa 10:16 758
the *S* set themselves in array ... 2Sa 10:17 758
And the *S* fled before Israel ... 2Sa 10:18 758
seven hundred chariots of the *S* ... 2Sa 10:18 758
So the *S* feared to help the ... 2Sa 10:19 758
and the *S* fled ... 1Kin 20:20 758
slew the *S* with a great slaughter ... 1Kin 20:21 758
that Ben-hadad numbered the *S* ... 1Kin 20:26 758
but the *S* filled the country ... 1Kin 20:27 758
the LORD, Because the *S* have said ... 1Kin 20:28 758
S an hundred thousand footmen in ... 1Kin 20:29 758
With these shalt thou push the *S* ... 1Kin 22:11 758
up in his chariot against the *S* ... 1Kin 22:35 758
the *S* had gone out by companies, ... 2Kin 5:2 758
for thither the *S* are come down ... 2Kin 6:9 758
us fall unto the host of the *S* ... 2Kin 7:4 758
to go unto the camp of the *S* ... 2Kin 7:5 758
the *S* to hear a noise of chariots ... 2Kin 7:6 758
We came to the camp of the *S* ... 2Kin 7:10 758
you what the *S* have done to us ... 2Kin 7:12 758
king sent after the host of the *S* ... 2Kin 7:14 758
which the *S* had cast away in ... 2Kin 7:15 758
and spoiled the tents of the *S* ... 2Kin 7:16 758
and the *S* wounded Joram ... 2Kin 8:28 761
the *S* had given him at Ramah ... 2Kin 8:29 761
wounds which the *S* had given him ... 2Kin 9:15 761
out from under the hand of the *S* ... 2Kin 13:5 758
thou shalt smite the *S* in Aphek ... 2Kin 13:17 758
the *S* came to Elath, and dwelt ... 2Kin 16:6 758
the Chaldees, and bands of the *S* ... 2Kin 24:2 758
when the *S* of Damascus came to ... 1Chr 18:5 758
of Zobah, David slew of the *S* two ... 1Chr 18:5 758
the *S* became David's servants, and ... 1Chr 18:6 758
put them in array against the *S* ... 1Chr 19:10 758
If the *S* be too strong for me, ... 1Chr 19:12 758
nigh before the *S* unto the battle ... 1Chr 19:14 758
of Ammon saw that the *S* were fled ... 1Chr 19:15 758
when the *S* saw that they were put ... 1Chr 19:16 758
drew forth the *S* that were beyond ... 1Chr 19:16 758
the battle in array against the *S* ... 1Chr 19:17 758
But the *S* fled before Israel ... 1Chr 19:18 758
David slew of the *S* seven ... 1Chr 19:18 758
neither would the *S* help the ... 1Chr 19:19 758
against the *S* until the even ... 2Chr 18:34 758
and the *S* smote Joram ... 2Chr 22:5 761
For the army of the *S* came with a ... 2Chr 24:24 758
The *S* before, and the Philistines ... Is 9:12 758
and for fear of the army of the *S* ... Jer 35:11 758
from Caphtor, and the *S* from Kir ... Amos 9:7 758

SYROPHENICIAN (*sy''-ro-fe-ne'-she-un*) *A citizen of Phenicia in Syria.*
woman was a Greek, a *S* by nation ... Mk 7:26 *4949*

SYRTIS See QUICKSANDS.

T

TAANACH (*ta'-a-nak*) See TANACH. *A Levitical city in Manasseh.*
The king of *T*, one ... Josh 12:21 8590
towns, and the inhabitants of *T* ... Josh 17:11 8590
of Beth-shean and her towns, nor *T* ... Judg 1:27 8590
in *T* by the waters of Megiddo ... Judg 5:19 8590
to him pertained *T* and Megiddo, and ... 1Kin 4:12 8590
Beth-shean and her towns, *T* ... 1Chr 7:29 8590

TAANATH-SHILOH (*ta''-a-nath-shi'-lo*) *A city on the border of Benjamin.*
border went about eastward unto *T* ... Josh 16:6 8387

TABALIAH See TEBALIAH.

TABBAOTH (*tab'-ba-oth*) *A family of exiles.*
of Hasupha, the children of *T* ... Ezr 2:43 2884
of Hashupha, the children of *T* ... Neh 7:46 2884

TABBATH (*tab'-bath*) *A city in Issachar.*
border of Abel-meholah, unto *T* ... Judg 7:22 2888

TABEAL (*tab'-e-al*) See TABEEL. *Father of a would-be king of Israel.*
midst of it, even the son of *T* ... Is 7:6 2870

TABEEL (*tab'-e-el*) See TABEAL. *A Persian official in Samaria.*
wrote Bishlam, Mithredath, *T* ... Ezr 4:7 2870

TABERAH (*tab'-e-rah*) *A place in the wilderness of Paran.*
he called the name of the place *T* ... Num 11:3 8404
And at *T*, and at Massah, and at ... Deut 9:22 8404

TABERING
of doves, *t* upon their breasts ... Nah 2:7 8608

TABERNACLE
thee, after the pattern of the *t* ... Ex 25:9 4908
the *t* with ten curtains of fine ... Ex 26:1 4908
and it shall be one *t* ... Ex 26:6 4908
hair to be a covering upon the *t* ... Ex 26:7 4908
curtain in the forefront of the *t* ... Ex 26:9 168
hang over the backside of the *t* ... Ex 26:12 4908
the sides of the *t* on this side ... Ex 26:13 4908
the *t* of shittim wood standing up ... Ex 26:15 4908
make for all the boards of the *t* ... Ex 26:17 4908
shalt make the boards for the *t* ... Ex 26:18 4908
for the second side of the *t* on ... Ex 26:20 4908
for the sides of the *t* westward ... Ex 26:22 4908
corners of the *t* in the two sides ... Ex 26:23 4908
boards of the one side of the *t* ... Ex 26:26 4908
boards of the other side of the *t* ... Ex 26:27 4908
the boards of the side of the *t* ... Ex 26:27 4908
And thou shalt rear up the *t* ... Ex 26:30 4908
side of the *t* toward the south ... Ex 26:35 4908
shalt make the court of the *t* ... Ex 27:9 4908
All the vessels of the *t* in all ... Ex 27:19 4908
In the *t* of the congregation ... Ex 27:21 168
in unto the *t* of the congregation ... Ex 28:43 168
door of the *t* of the congregation ... Ex 29:4 168
before the *t* of the congregation ... Ex 29:10 168
by the door of the *t* of the ... Ex 29:11 168
when he cometh into the *t* of the ... Ex 29:30 168
by the door of the *t* of the ... Ex 29:32 168
t of the congregation before the ... Ex 29:42 168
the *t* shall be sanctified by my ... Ex 29:43
the *t* of the congregation ... Ex 29:44 168
of the *t* of the congregation ... Ex 30:16 168
between the *t* of the congregation ... Ex 30:18 168
go into the *t* of the congregation ... Ex 30:20 168
thou shalt anoint the *t* of the ... Ex 30:26 168
in the *t* of the congregation ... Ex 30:36 168
The *t* of the congregation, and the ... Ex 31:7 168
and all the furniture of the *t* ... Ex 31:7 168
And Moses took the *t*, and pitched ... Ex 33:7 168
camp, and called it the *T* of the ... Ex 33:7 168
unto the *t* of the congregation ... Ex 33:7 168
when Moses went out unto the *t* ... Ex 33:8 168
until he was gone into the *t* ... Ex 33:8 168
pass, as Moses entered into the *t* ... Ex 33:9 168
and stood at the door of the *t* ... Ex 33:9 168
cloudy pillar stand at the *t* door ... Ex 33:10 168
man, departed not out of the *t* ... Ex 33:11 168
The *t*, his tent, and his covering, ... Ex 35:11 4908
door at the entering in of the *t* ... Ex 35:15 4908
The pins of the *t*, and the pins of ... Ex 35:18 4908
work of the *t* of the congregation ... Ex 35:21 168
the *t* made ten curtains of fine ... Ex 36:8 4908
so it became one *t* ... Ex 36:13 4908
hair for the tent over the *t* ... Ex 36:14 4908
boards for the *t* of shittim wood ... Ex 36:20 4908
make for all the boards of the *t* ... Ex 36:22 4908
And he made boards for the *t* ... Ex 36:23 4908
And for the other side of the *t* ... Ex 36:25 4908
for the sides of the *t* westward ... Ex 36:27 4908
corners of the *t* in the two sides ... Ex 36:28 4908
boards of the one side of the *t* ... Ex 36:31 4908
boards of the other side of the *t* ... Ex 36:32 4908
of the *t* for the sides westward ... Ex 36:32 4908
an hanging for the *t* door of blue ... Ex 36:37 168
door of the *t* of the congregation ... Ex 38:8 168
And all the pins of the *t*, and of ... Ex 38:20 4908
This is the sum of the *t*, even of ... Ex 38:21 4908
even of the *t* of testimony, as it ... Ex 38:21 4908
door of the *t* of the congregation ... Ex 38:30 168
gate, and all the pins of the *t* ... Ex 38:31 4908
Thus was all the work of the *t* of ... Ex 39:32 4908
And they brought the *t* unto Moses ... Ex 39:33 4908
and the hanging for the *t* door ... Ex 39:38 168
vessels of the service of the *t* ... Ex 39:40 4908
month shalt thou set up the *t* of ... Ex 40:2 4908
the hanging of the door to the *t* ... Ex 40:5 4908
t of the tent of the congregation ... Ex 40:6 4908
anointing oil, and anoint the *t* ... Ex 40:9 4908
door of the *t* of the congregation ... Ex 40:12 168
month, that the *t* was reared up ... Ex 40:17 4908
And Moses reared up the *t*, and ... Ex 40:18 4908
spread abroad the tent over the *t* ... Ex 40:19 4908
And he brought the ark into the *t* ... Ex 40:21 4908
upon the side of the *t* northward ... Ex 40:22 4908
on the side of the *t* southward ... Ex 40:24 4908
the hanging at the door of the *t* ... Ex 40:28 4908
offering by the door of the *t* of ... Ex 40:29 4908
up the court round about the *t* ... Ex 40:33 4908
glory of the LORD filled the *t* ... Ex 40:34 4908
glory of the LORD filled the *t* ... Ex 40:35 4908
was taken up from over the *t* ... Ex 40:36 4908
of the LORD was upon the *t* by day ... Ex 40:38 4908
out of the *t* of the congregation ... Lev 1:1 168
will at the door of the *t* of the ... Lev 1:3 168
door of the *t* of the congregation ... Lev 1:5 168
door of the *t* of the congregation ... Lev 3:2 168
kill it before the *t* of the ... Lev 3:8 168
kill it before the *t* of the ... Lev 3:13 168
bullock unto the door of the *t* of ... Lev 4:4 168
and bring it to the *t* of the ... Lev 4:5 168
LORD, which is in the *t* of the ... Lev 4:7 168
door of the *t* of the congregation ... Lev 4:7 168
before the *t* of the congregation ... Lev 4:14 168
to the *t* of the congregation ... Lev 4:16 168
the LORD, that is in the *t* of the ... Lev 4:18 168
door of the *t* of the congregation ... Lev 4:18 168
in the court of the *t* of the ... Lev 6:16 168
of the *t* of the congregation ... Lev 6:26 168
into the *t* of the congregation to ... Lev 6:30 168
door of the *t* of the congregation ... Lev 8:3 168
door of the *t* of the congregation ... Lev 8:4 168
anointing oil, and anointed the *t* ... Lev 8:10 4908
door of the *t* of the congregation ... Lev 8:31 168
t of the congregation in seven ... Lev 8:33 168
of the *t* of the congregation day ... Lev 8:35 168
before the *t* of the congregation ... Lev 9:5 168
into the *t* of the congregation ... Lev 9:23 168
door of the *t* of the congregation ... Lev 10:7 168
go into the *t* of the congregation ... Lev 10:9 168
door of the *t* of the congregation ... Lev 12:6 168
at the door of the *t* of the ... Lev 14:11 168
door of the *t* of the congregation ... Lev 14:23 168
door of the *t* of the congregation ... Lev 15:14 168
to the door of the *t* of the ... Lev 15:29 168
defile my *t* that is among them ... Lev 15:31 4908
door of the *t* of the congregation ... Lev 16:7 168
do for the *t* of the congregation ... Lev 16:16 168
the *t* of the congregation when he ... Lev 16:17 168
the *t* of the congregation, and the ... Lev 16:20 168
into the *t* of the congregation ... Lev 16:23 168
for the *t* of the congregation ... Lev 16:33 168
door of the *t* of the congregation ... Lev 17:4 168
the LORD before the *t* of the LORD ... Lev 17:4 4908
door of the *t* of the congregation ... Lev 17:5 168
door of the *t* of the congregation ... Lev 17:6 168
door of the *t* of the congregation ... Lev 17:9 168
door of the *t* of the congregation ... Lev 19:21 168
in the *t* of the congregation, ... Lev 24:3 168
And I will set my *t* among you ... Lev 26:11 4908
in the *t* of the congregation, on ... Num 1:1 168
Levites over the *t* of testimony ... Num 1:50 4908
they shall bear the *t*, and all the ... Num 1:50 4908
and shall encamp round about the *t* ... Num 1:50 4908
when the *t* setteth forward, the ... Num 1:51 4908
when the *t* is to be pitched, the ... Num 1:51 4908
round about the *t* of testimony ... Num 1:53 4908
the charge of the *t* of testimony ... Num 1:53 4908
far off about the *t* of the ... Num 2:2 168
Then the *t* of the congregation ... Num 2:17 168
before the *t* of the congregation ... Num 3:7 168
to do the service of the *t* ... Num 3:7 4908
of the *t* of the congregation ... Num 3:8 168
to do the service of the *t* ... Num 3:8 4908
shall pitch behind the *t* westward ... Num 3:23 4908
t of the congregation shall be ... Num 3:25 168
the congregation shall be the *t* ... Num 3:25 4908
door of the *t* of the congregation ... Num 3:25 168
of the court, which is by the *t* ... Num 3:26 4908
on the side of the *t* southward ... Num 3:29 4908
on the side of the *t* northward ... Num 3:35 4908
shall be the boards of the *t* ... Num 3:36 4908
before the *t* toward the east ... Num 3:38 4908
even before the *t* of the ... Num 3:38 168
work in the *t* of the congregation ... Num 4:3 168
in the *t* of the congregation ... Num 4:4 168
in the *t* of the congregation ... Num 4:15 168
and the oversight of all the *t* ... Num 4:16 4908
work in the *t* of the congregation ... Num 4:23 168
shall bear the curtains of the *t* ... Num 4:25 4908
the *t* of the congregation, his ... Num 4:25 168
door of the *t* of the congregation ... Num 4:25 168
of the court, which is by the *t* ... Num 4:26 4908
in the *t* of the congregation ... Num 4:28 168
work of the *t* of the congregation ... Num 4:30 168
in the *t* of the congregation ... Num 4:31 168
the boards of the *t*, and the bars ... Num 4:31 4908
in the *t* of the congregation, ... Num 4:33 168
work in the *t* of the congregation ... Num 4:35 168
in the *t* of the congregation ... Num 4:37 168
work in the *t* of the congregation ... Num 4:39 168
in the *t* of the congregation ... Num 4:41 168
work in the *t* of the congregation ... Num 4:43 168
in the *t* of the congregation ... Num 4:47 168
of the *t* the priest shall take ... Num 5:17 4908
to the door of the *t* of the ... Num 6:10 168
door of the *t* of the congregation ... Num 6:13 168
door of the *t* of the congregation ... Num 6:18 168
that Moses had fully set up the *t* ... Num 7:1 4908
and they brought them before the *t* ... Num 7:3 4908
of the *t* of the congregation ... Num 7:5 168
t of the congregation to speak ... Num 7:89 168
before the *t* of the congregation ... Num 8:9 168
of the *t* of the congregation ... Num 8:15 168

T

in the *t* of the congregation … Num 8:19 168
the *t* of the congregation before … Num 8:22 168
of the *t* of the congregation … Num 8:24 168
in the *t* of the congregation … Num 8:26 168
on the day that the *t* was reared … Num 9:15 4908
reared up the cloud covered the *t* … Num 9:15 4908
at even there was upon the *t* as … Num 9:15 4908
the cloud was taken up from the *t* … Num 9:17 168
the *t* they rested in their tents … Num 9:18 4908
tarried long upon the *t* many days … Num 9:19 4908
cloud was a few days upon the *t* … Num 9:20 4908
that the cloud tarried upon the *t* … Num 9:22 4908
door of the *t* of the congregation … Num 10:3 168
from off the *t* of the testimony … Num 10:11 4908
And the *t* was taken down … Num 10:17 4908
Merari set forward, bearing the *t* … Num 10:17 4908
set up the *t* against they came … Num 10:21 4908
unto the *t* of the congregation … Num 11:16 168
and set them round about the *t* … Num 11:24 168
but went not out unto the *t* … Num 11:26 168
unto the *t* of the congregation … Num 12:4 168
and stood in the door of the *t* … Num 12:5 168
the cloud departed from off the *t* … Num 12:10 168
of the LORD appeared in the *t* of … Num 14:10 168
the service of the *t* of the LORD … Num 16:9 4908
stood in the door of the *t* of the … Num 16:18 168
door of the *t* of the congregation … Num 16:19 168
you up from about the *t* of Korah … Num 16:24 4908
they gat up from the *t* of Korah … Num 16:27 4908
toward the *t* of the congregation … Num 16:42 168
before the *t* of the congregation … Num 16:43 168
door of the *t* of the congregation … Num 16:50 168
thou shalt lay them up in the *t* … Num 17:4 168
the LORD in the *t* of witness … Num 17:7 168
Moses went into the *t* of witness … Num 17:8 168
unto the *t* of the LORD shall die … Num 17:13 4908
minister before the *t* of witness … Num 18:2 168
and the charge of all the *t* … Num 18:3 168
of the *t* of the congregation … Num 18:4 168
for all the service of the *t* … Num 18:4 168
of the *t* of the congregation … Num 18:6 168
of the *t* of the congregation … Num 18:21 168
nigh the *t* of the congregation … Num 18:22 168
of the *t* of the congregation … Num 18:23 168
in the *t* of the congregation … Num 18:31 168
her blood directly before the *t* … Num 19:4 168
defileth the *t* of the LORD … Num 19:13 4908
door of the *t* of the congregation … Num 20:6 168
door of the *t* of the congregation … Num 25:6 168
by the door of the *t* of the … Num 27:2 168
the charge of the *t* of the LORD … Num 31:30 4908
the charge of the *t* of the LORD … Num 31:47 4908
it into the *t* of the congregation … Num 31:54 168
in the *t* of the congregation … Deut 31:14 168
in the *t* of the congregation … Deut 31:14 168
in the *t* in a pillar of a cloud … Deut 31:15 168
stood over the door of the *t* … Deut 31:15 168
set up the *t* of the congregation … Josh 18:1 168
at the door of the *t* of the … Josh 19:51 168
wherein the LORD's *t* dwelleth … Josh 22:19 4908
LORD our God that is before his *t* … Josh 22:29 4908
door of the *t* of the congregation … 1Sa 2:22 168
in the midst of the *t* that David … 2Sa 6:17 168
have walked in a tent and in a *t* … 2Sa 7:6 4908
took an horn of oil out of the *t* … 1Kin 1:39 168
Joab fled unto the *t* of the LORD … 1Kin 2:28 168
was fled unto the *t* of the LORD … 1Kin 2:29 168
Benaiah came to the *t* of the LORD … 1Kin 2:30 168
the *t* of the congregation, and all … 1Kin 8:4 168
holy vessels that were in the *t* … 1Kin 8:4 168
of the *t* of the congregation with … 1Chr 6:32 168
of the *t* of the house of God … 1Chr 6:48 4908
keepers of the gates of the *t* … 1Chr 9:19 168
door of the *t* of the congregation … 1Chr 9:21 168
LORD, namely, the house of the *t* … 1Chr 9:23 168
before the *t* of the LORD in the … 1Chr 16:39 4908
to tent, and from one *t* to another … 1Chr 17:5 4908
For the *t* of the LORD, which … 1Chr 21:29 4908
they shall no more carry the *t* … 1Chr 23:26 4908
of the *t* of the congregation … 1Chr 23:32 168
for there was the *t* of the … 2Chr 1:3 168
he put before the *t* of the LORD … 2Chr 1:5 4908
which was at the *t* of the … 2Chr 1:6 168
from before the *t* of the … 2Chr 1:13 168
the *t* of the congregation, and all … 2Chr 5:5 168
holy vessels that were in the *t* … 2Chr 5:5 168
of Israel, for the *t* of witness … 2Chr 24:6 168
know that thy *t* shall be in peace … Job 5:24 168
The light shall be dark in his *t* … Job 18:6 168
Shall be rooted out of his *t* … Job 18:14 168
It shall dwell in his *t*, because … Job 18:15 168
me, and encamp round about my *t* … Job 19:12 168
with him that is left in his *t* … Job 20:26 168
the secret of God was upon my *t* … Job 29:4 168
If the men of my *t* said not … Job 31:31 168
the clouds, or the noise of his *t* … Job 36:29 5521
Lord, who shall abide in thy *t* … Ps 15:1 168
them hath he set a *t* for the sun … Ps 19:4 168
secret of his *t* shall he hide me … Ps 27:5 168
offer in his *t* sacrifices of joy … Ps 27:6 168
I will abide in thy *t* for ever … Ps 61:4 168
In Salem also is his *t*, and his … Ps 76:2 5520
that he forsook the *t* of Shiloh … Ps 78:60 4908
he refused the *t* of Joseph … Ps 78:67 168
not come into the *t* of my house … Ps 132:3 168
but the *t* of the upright shall … Prov 14:11 168
there shall be a *t* for a shadow … Is 4:6 5521
it in truth in the *t* of David … Is 16:5 168
a *t* that shall not be taken down … Is 33:20 168
My *t* is spoiled, and all my cords … Jer 10:20 168
in the *t* of the daughter of Zion … Lam 2:4 168
hath violently taken away his *t* … Lam 2:6 7900
My *t* also shall be with them … Eze 37:27 4908
which was the breadth of the *t* … Eze 41:1 168
have borne the *t* of your Moloch … Amos 5:26 5522
up the *t* of David that is fallen … Amos 9:11 5521
Yea, ye took up the *t* of Moloch … Acts 7:43 *4633*
Our fathers had the *t* of witness … Acts 7:44 *4633*
desired to find a *t* for the God … Acts 7:46 *4638*
will build again the *t* of David … Acts 15:16 *4633*
house of this *t* were dissolved … 2Cor 5:1 *4636*
we that are in this *t* do groan … 2Cor 5:4 *4636*
the sanctuary, and of the true *t* … Heb 8:2 *4633*
when he was about to make the *t* … Heb 8:5 *4633*
For there was a *t* made … Heb 9:2 *4633*
the *t* which is called the Holiest … Heb 9:3 *4633*
went always into the first *t* … Heb 9:6 *4633*
as the first *t* was yet standing … Heb 9:8 *4633*
by a greater and more perfect *t* … Heb 9:11 *4633*
sprinkled with blood both the *t* … Heb 9:21 *4633*
no right to eat which serve the *t* … Heb 13:10 *4633*
meet, as long as I am in this *t* … 2Pet 1:13 *4638*
shortly I must put off this my *t* … 2Pet 1:14 *4638*
to blaspheme his name, and his *t* … Rev 13:6 *4633*
the temple of the *t* of the … Rev 15:5 *4633*
the *t* of God is with men, and he … Rev 21:3 *4633*

TABERNACLES
month shall be the feast of *t* for … Lev 23:34 5521
are thy tents, O Jacob, and thy *t* … Num 24:5 4908
observe the feast of *t* seven days … Deut 16:13 5521
of weeks, and in the feast of *t* … Deut 16:16 5521
of release, in the feast of *t* … Deut 31:10 5521
of weeks, and in the feast of *t* … 2Chr 8:13 5521
They kept also the feast of *t* … Ezr 3:4 5521
let not wickedness dwell in thy *t* … Job 11:14 168
The *t* of robbers prosper, and they … Job 12:6 168
shall consume the *t* of bribery … Job 15:34 168
put away iniquity far from thy *t* … Job 22:23 168
unto thy holy hill, and to thy *t* … Ps 43:3 4908
place of the *t* of the most High … Ps 46:4 4908
of their strength in the *t* of Ham … Ps 78:51 168
The *t* of Edom, and the Ishmaelites … Ps 83:6 168
How amiable are thy *t*, O LORD of … Ps 84:1 4908
is in the *t* of the righteous … Ps 118:15 168
We will go into his *t* … Ps 132:7 4908
he shall plant the *t* of his … Dan 11:45 168
thorns shall be in their *t* … Hos 9:6 168
will yet make thee to dwell in *t* … Hos 12:9 168
hosts, and to keep the feast of *t* … Zec 14:16 5521
not up to keep the feast of *t* … Zec 14:18 5521
not up to keep the feast of *t* … Zec 14:19 5521
scholar, out of the *t* of Jacob … Mal 2:12 168
wilt, let us make here three *t* … Mt 17:4 *4633*
and let us make three *t* … Mk 9:5 *4633*
and let us make three *t* … Lk 9:33 *4633*
the Jews' feast of *t* was at hand … Jn 7:2 *4634*
country, dwelling in *t* with Isaac … Heb 11:9 *4633*

TABITHA (*tab'-ith-ah*) *Woman raised from the dead by Peter.*
Joppa a certain disciple named *T* … Acts 9:36 *5000*
turning him to the body said, *T* … Acts 9:40 *5000*

TABLE
also make a *t* of shittim wood … Ex 25:23 7979
of the staves to bear the *t* … Ex 25:27 7979
that the *t* may be borne with them … Ex 25:28 7979
thou shalt set upon the *t* … Ex 25:30 7979
shalt set the *t* without the vail … Ex 26:35 7979
candlestick over against the *t* on … Ex 26:35 7979
shalt put the *t* on the north side … Ex 26:35 7979
And the *t* and all his vessels, and … Ex 30:27 7979
And the *t* and his furniture, and the … Ex 31:8 7979
The *t*, and his staves, and all his … Ex 35:13 7979
he made the *t* of shittim wood … Ex 37:10 7979
for the staves to bear the *t* … Ex 37:14 7979
them with gold, to bear the *t* … Ex 37:15 7979
the vessels which were upon the *t* … Ex 37:16 7979
The *t*, and all the vessels thereof … Ex 39:36 7979
And thou shalt bring in the *t* … Ex 40:4 7979
he put the *t* in the tent of the … Ex 40:22 7979
congregation, over against the *t* … Ex 40:24 7979
upon the pure *t* before the LORD … Lev 24:6 7979
charge shall be the ark, and the *t* … Num 3:31 7979
upon the *t* of shewbread they … Num 4:7 7979
gathered their meat under my *t* … Judg 1:7 7979
he cometh not unto the king's *t* … 1Sa 20:29 7979
arose from the *t* in fierce anger … 1Sa 20:34 7979
eat bread at my *t* continually … 2Sa 9:7 7979
son shall eat bread alway at my *t* … 2Sa 9:10 7979
the king, he shall eat at my *t* … 2Sa 9:11 7979
eat continually at the king's *t* … 2Sa 9:13 7979
them that did eat at thine own *t* … 2Sa 19:28 7979
be of those that eat at thy *t* … 1Kin 2:7 7979
that came unto king Solomon's *t* … 1Kin 4:27 7979
the *t* of gold, whereupon the … 1Kin 7:48 7979
And the meat of his *t*, and the … 1Kin 10:5 7979
to pass, as they sat at the *t* … 1Kin 13:20 7979
hundred, which eat at Jezebel's *t* … 1Kin 18:19 7979
set for him there a bed, and a *t* … 2Kin 4:10 7979
tables of shewbread, for every *t* … 1Chr 28:16 7979
And the meat of his *t*, and the … 2Chr 9:4 7979
set they in order upon the pure *t* … 2Chr 13:11 7979
thereof, and the shewbread *t* … 2Chr 29:18 7979
there were at my *t* an hundred … Neh 5:17 7979
thy *t* should be full of fatness … Job 36:16 7979
Thou preparest a *t* before me in … Ps 23:5 7979
Let their *t* become a snare before … Ps 69:22 7979
God furnish a *t* in the wilderness … Ps 78:19 7979
olive plants round about thy *t* … Ps 128:3 7979
them upon the *t* of thine heart … Prov 3:3 3871
them upon the *t* of thine heart … Prov 7:3 3871
she hath also furnished her *t* … Prov 9:2 7979
While the king sitteth at his *t* … Song 1:12 4524
Prepare the *t*, watch in the … Is 21:5 7979
go, write it before them in a *t* … Is 30:8 3871
that prepare a *t* for that troop … Is 65:11 7979
graven upon the *t* of their heart … Jer 17:1 3871
a *t* prepared before it, whereupon … Eze 23:41 7979
be filled at my *t* with horses … Eze 39:20 7979
This is the *t* that is before the … Eze 41:22 7979
and they shall come near to my *t* … Eze 44:16 7979
and they shall speak lies at one *t* … Dan 11:27 7979
The *t* of the LORD is contemptible … Mal 1:7 7979
The *t* of the LORD is polluted … Mal 1:12 7979
which fall from their masters' *t* … Mt 15:27 *5132*
yet the dogs under the *t* eat of … Mk 7:28 *5132*
And he asked for a writing *t* … Lk 1:63 *4093*
which fell from the rich man's *t* … Lk 16:21 *5132*
betrayeth me is with me on the *t* … Lk 22:21 *5132*
drink at my *t* in my kingdom, and … Lk 22:30 *5132*
them that sat at the *t* with him … Jn 12:2
Now no man at the *t* knew for what … Jn 13:28 *345*
Let their *t* be made a snare, and a … Rom 11:9 *5132*
be partakers of the Lord's *t* … 1Cor 10:21 *5132*
and of the *t* of devils … 1Cor 10:21 *5132*
was the candlestick, and the *t* … Heb 9:2 *5132*

TABLES
and I will give thee *t* of stone … Ex 24:12 3871
two *t* of testimony, *t* of … Ex 31:18 3871
t of stone, written with the … Ex 31:18 3871
the two *t* of the testimony were … Ex 32:15 3871
the *t* were written on both their … Ex 32:15 3871
the *t* were the work of God, and … Ex 32:16 3871
writing of God, graven upon the *t* … Ex 32:16 3871
he cast the *t* out of his hands … Ex 32:19 3871
Hew thee two *t* of stone like unto … Ex 34:1 3871
I will write upon these *t* the … Ex 34:1 3871
words that were in the first *t* … Ex 34:1 3871
he hewed two *t* of stone like unto … Ex 34:4 3871
in his hand the two *t* of stone … Ex 34:4 3871
he wrote upon the *t* the words of … Ex 34:28 3871
two *t* of testimony in Moses' hand … Ex 34:29 3871
he wrote them upon two *t* of stone … Deut 4:13 3871
he wrote them in two *t* of stone … Deut 5:22 3871
mount to receive the *t* of stone … Deut 9:9 3871
even the *t* of the covenant which … Deut 9:9 3871
two *t* of stone written with the … Deut 9:10 3871
LORD gave me the two *t* of stone … Deut 9:11 3871
even the *t* of the covenant … Deut 9:11 3871
the two *t* of the covenant were in … Deut 9:15 3871
And I took the two *t*, and cast them … Deut 9:17 3871
Hew thee two *t* of stone like unto … Deut 10:1 3871
I will write on the *t* the words … Deut 10:2 3871
in the first *t* which thou brakest … Deut 10:2 3871
hewed two *t* of stone like unto … Deut 10:3 3871
having the two *t* in mine hand … Deut 10:3 3871
And he wrote on the *t*, according … Deut 10:4 3871
put the *t* in the ark which I had … Deut 10:5 3871
the ark save the two *t* of stone … 1Kin 8:9 3871
gave gold for the *t* of shewbread … 1Chr 28:16 7979
silver for the *t* of silver … 1Chr 28:16 7979
He made also ten *t*, and placed … 2Chr 4:8 7979
the *t* whereon the shewbread was … 2Chr 4:19 7979
two *t* which Moses put therein at … 2Chr 5:10 3871
For all *t* are full of vomit and … Is 28:8 7979
the gate were two *t* on this side … Eze 40:39 7979
two *t* on that side, to slay … Eze 40:39 7979
of the north gate, were two *t* … Eze 40:40 7979
the porch of the gate, were two *t* … Eze 40:40 7979
Four *t* were on this side, and four … Eze 40:41 7979
four *t* on that side, by the side … Eze 40:41 7979
eight *t*, whereupon they slew … Eze 40:41 7979
the four *t* were of hewn stone for … Eze 40:42 7979
upon the *t* was the flesh of the … Eze 40:43 7979
vision, and make it plain upon *t* … Hab 2:2 3871
temple, and overthrew the *t* of the … Mt 21:12 *5132*
and pots, brasen vessels, and of *t* … Mk 7:4 *2825*
temple, and overthrew the *t* of the … Mk 11:15 *5132*
money, and overthrew the *t* … Jn 2:15 *5132*
leave the word of God, and serve *t* … Acts 6:2 *5132*
not in *t* of stone, but in fleshly … 2Cor 3:3 *4109*
but in fleshly *t* of the heart … 2Cor 3:3 *4109*
budded, and the *t* of the covenant … Heb 9:4 *4109*

TABLETS
and earrings, and rings, and *t* … Ex 35:22 3558
bracelets, rings, earrings, and *t* … Num 31:50 3558
legs, and the headbands, and the *t* … Is 3:20

TABOR (*ta'-bor*)
1. A mountain in Issachar and Zebulun.
And the coast reacheth to *T* … Josh 19:22 8396
saying, Go and draw toward mount *T* … Judg 4:6 8396
of Abinoam was gone up to mount *T* … Judg 4:12 8396
So Barak went down from mount *T* … Judg 4:14 8396
men were they whom ye slew at *T* … Judg 8:18 8396
T and Hermon shall rejoice in thy … Ps 89:12 8396
hosts, Surely as *T* is among the … Jer 46:18 8396
on Mizpah, and a net spread upon *T* … Hos 5:1 8396
2. A plain in Benjamin.
thou shalt come to the plain of *T* … 1Sa 10:3 8396
3. A Levitical city in Zebulun.
her suburbs, *T* with her suburbs … 1Chr 6:77 8396

TABRET
with mirth, and with songs, with *t* … Gen 31:27 8596
place with a psaltery, and a *t* … 1Sa 10:5 8596
and aforetime I was as a *t* … Job 17:6 8611
And the harp, and the viol, the *t* … Is 5:12 8596

TABRETS
to meet king Saul, with *t* … 1Sa 18:6 8596
The mirth of *t* ceaseth, the noise … Is 24:8 8596
lay upon him, it shall be with *t* … Is 30:32 8596
shalt again be adorned with thy *t* … Jer 31:4 8596
the workmanship of thy *t* and of … Eze 28:13 8596

TABRIMMON See TABRIMON.

TABRIMON (*tab'-rim-on*) *Father of Ben-hadad, king of Syria.*
them to Ben-hadad, the son of *T* … 1Kin 15:18 2886

TACHES
thou shalt make fifty t of gold Ex 26:6 7165
the curtains together with the t Ex 26:6 7165
thou shalt make fifty t of brass Ex 26:11 7165
put the t into the loops, and Ex 26:11 7165
hang up the vail under the t Ex 26:33 7165
his tent, and his covering, his t Ex 35:11 7165
And he made fifty t of gold Ex 36:13 7165
one unto another with the t Ex 36:13 7165
he made fifty t of brass to Ex 36:18 7165
tent, and all his furniture, his t Ex 39:33 7165

TACHMONITE (*tak'-mun-ite*) See HACHMONITE. *Family name of a "mighty man" of David.*
The T that sat in the seat, chief 2Sa 23:8 8461

TACKLING
our own hands the t of the ship Acts 27:19 4631

TACKLINGS
Thy t are loosed Is 33:23 2256

TADMOR (*tad'-mor*) *A city rebuilt by Solomon.*
T in the wilderness, in the land, 1Kin 9:18 8412
he built T in the wilderness, and 2Chr 8:4 8412

TAHAN (*ta'-han*) See TAHANITES.
1. A son of Ephraim.
of T, the family of the Tahanites Num 26:35 8465
2. A descendant of Ephraim.
and Telah his son, and T his son, 1Chr 7:25 8465

TAHANITES (*ta'-han-ites*) *Descendants of Tahan 1.*
of Tahan, the family of the T Num 26:35 8470

TAHAPANES (*ta-hap'-a-neze*) See TAHAPANHES. *A city in Egypt.*
T have broken the crown of thy Jer 2:16 8471

TAHASH See THAHASH.

TAHATH (*ta'-hath*)
1. An Israelite encampment in the wilderness.
from Makheloth, and encamped at T Num 33:26 8480
And they departed from T, and Num 33:27 8480
2. Father of Uriel.
T his son, Uriel his son, Uzziah 1Chr 6:24 8480
The son of T, the son of Assir, 1Chr 6:37 8480
3. Father of Eladah.
T his son, and Eladah his son, and 1Chr 7:20 8480
4. Son of Eladah.
and Eladah his son, and T his son, 1Chr 7:20 8480

TAHCHEMONITE See TACHMONITE.

TAHKEMONITE See TACHMONITE.

TAHPANHES (*tah'-pan-heze*) See TAHAPANES, TAHPENES, TEHAPHNEHES. *Same as Tahapanes.*
thus came they even to T Jer 43:7 8471
of the LORD unto Jeremiah in T Jer 43:8 8471
the entry of Pharaoh's house in T Jer 43:9 8471
which dwell at Migdol, and at T Jer 44:1 8471
and publish in Noph and in T Jer 46:14 8471

TAHPENES (*tah'-pe-neze*) See TAHPANHES. *Queen of a pharaoh.*
wife, the sister of T the queen 1Kin 11:19 8472
the sister of T bare him Genubath 1Kin 11:20 8472
whom T weaned in Pharaoh's house 1Kin 11:20 8472

TAHREA (*tah'-re-ah*) See TAREA. *Son of Micah.*
were, Pithon, and Melech, and T 1Chr 9:41 8475

TAHTIM-HODSHI (*tah''-tim-hod'-shi*) *A district north of Gilead in Bashan.*
to Gilead, and to the land of T 2Sa 24:6 8483

TAIL
thine hand, and take it by the t Ex 4:4 2180
make thee the head, and not the t Deut 28:13 2180
the head, and thou shalt be the t Deut 28:44 2180
firebrands, and turned t to t Judg 15:4 2180
He moveth his t like a cedar Job 40:17 2180
cut off from Israel head and t Is 9:14 2180
that teacheth lies, he is the t Is 9:15 2180
for Egypt, which the head or t Is 19:15 2180
his t drew the third part of the Rev 12:4 3769

TAILS
in the midst between two t Judg 15:4 2180
two t of these smoking firebrands Is 7:4 2180
they had t like unto scorpions, Rev 9:10 3769
and there were stings in their t Rev 9:10 3769
is in their mouth, and in their t Rev 9:19 3769
for their t were like unto Rev 9:19 3769

TAKE
t also of the tree of life, and Gen 3:22 3947
t thou unto thee of all food that Gen 6:21 3947
thou shalt t to thee by sevens Gen 7:2 3947
thy wife, t her, and go thy way Gen 12:19 3947
if thou wilt t the left hand, Gen 13:9 3947
and t the goods to thyself Gen 14:21 3947
That I will not t from a thread Gen 14:23 3947
that I will not t any thing that Gen 14:23 3947
let them t their portion Gen 14:24 3947
T me an heifer of three years old Gen 15:9 3947
t thy wife, and thy two daughters, Gen 19:15 3947
the mountain, lest some evil t me Gen 19:19 1692
ewe lambs shalt thou t of my hand Gen 21:30 3947
T now thy son, thine only son Gen 22:2 3947
t it of me, and I will bury my Gen 23:13 3947
that thou shalt not t a wife unto Gen 24:3 3947
t a wife unto my son Isaac Gen 24:4 3947
thou shalt t a wife unto my son Gen 24:7 3947
Thou shalt not t a wife to my son Gen 24:37 3947
kindred, and t a wife unto my son Gen 24:38 3947
thou shalt t a wife for my son of Gen 24:40 3947
t my master's brother's daughter Gen 24:48 3947
t her, and go, and let her be thy Gen 24:51 3947
Now therefore t, I pray thee, thy Gen 27:3 5375
the field, and t me some venison Gen 27:3 6679
if Jacob t a wife of the Gen 27:46 3947
Thou shalt not t a wife of the Gen 28:1 3947
t thee a wife from thence of the Gen 28:2 3947
to t him a wife from thence Gen 28:6 3947
Thou shalt not t a wife of the Gen 28:6 3947
wouldest thou t away my son's Gen 30:15 3947
T heed that thou speak not to Gen 31:24
T thou heed that thou speak not Gen 31:29
Peradventure thou wouldest t by Gen 31:31 1497
is thine with me, and t it to thee Gen 31:32 3947
or if thou shalt t other wives Gen 31:50 3947
T, I pray thee, my blessing that Gen 33:11 3947
Let us t our journey, and let us Gen 33:12
us, and t our daughters unto you Gen 34:9 3947
we will t your daughters to us, Gen 34:16 3947
then will we t our daughter Gen 34:17 3947
let us t their daughters to us Gen 34:21 3947
Let her t it to her, lest we be Gen 38:23 3947
t up the fifth part of the land Gen 41:34
t food for the famine of your Gen 42:33 3947
not, and ye will t Benjamin away Gen 42:36 3947
t of the best fruits in the land Gen 43:11 3947
t double money in your hand Gen 43:12 3947
T also your brother, and arise, go Gen 43:13 3947
t us for bondmen, and our asses Gen 43:18 3947
if ye t this also from me, and Gen 44:29 3947
t your father and your households, Gen 45:18 3947
t you wagons out of the land of Gen 45:19 3947
T this child away, and nurse it Ex 2:9 3212
thine hand, and t it by the tail Ex 4:4 270
that thou shalt t of the water of Ex 4:9 3947
thou shalt t this rod in thine Ex 4:17 3947
I will t you to me for a people, Ex 6:7 3947
T thy rod, and cast it before Ex 7:9 3947
shalt thou t in thine hand Ex 7:15 3947
T thy rod, and stretch out thine Ex 7:19 3947
that he may t away the frogs from Ex 8:8 5493
T to you handfuls of ashes of the Ex 9:8 3947
that he may t away from me this Ex 10:17 5493
for thereof must we t to serve Ex 10:26 3947
t heed to thyself, see my face no Ex 10:28
shall t to them every man a lamb Ex 12:3 3947
t it according to the number of Ex 12:4 3947
ye shall t it out from the sheep, Ex 12:5 3947
they shall t of the blood, and Ex 12:7 3947
t you a lamb according to your Ex 12:21 3947
ye shall t a bunch of hyssop, and Ex 12:22 3947
Also t your flocks and your herds, Ex 12:32 3947
sorrow shall t hold on the Ex 15:14 270
trembling shall t hold upon them Ex 15:15 270
t ye every man for them which are Ex 16:16 3947
T a pot, and put an omer full of Ex 16:33 3947
t with thee of the elders of Ex 17:5 3947
the river, t in thine hand, and go Ex 17:5 3947
T heed to yourselves, that ye go Ex 19:12
Thou shalt not t the name of the Ex 20:7 5375
If he t him another wife Ex 21:10 3947
thou shalt t him from mine altar, Ex 21:14 3947
If thou at all t thy neighbour's Ex 22:26 2254
And thou shalt t no gift Ex 23:8 3947
I will t sickness away from the Ex 23:25 5493
his heart ye shall t my offering Ex 25:2 3947
offering which ye shall t of them Ex 25:3 3947
that the loops may t hold one of Ex 26:5 6901
t thou unto thee Aaron thy Ex 28:1 7126
And they shall t gold, and blue, and Ex 28:5 3947
thou shalt t two onyx stones, and Ex 28:9 3947
T one young bullock, and two rams Ex 29:1 3947
thou shalt t the garments, and put Ex 29:5 3947
Then shalt thou t the anointing Ex 29:7 3947
thou shalt t of the blood of the Ex 29:12 3947
thou shalt t all the fat that Ex 29:13 3947
Thou shalt also t one ram Ex 29:15 3947
ram, and thou shalt t his blood Ex 29:16 3947
thou shalt t the other ram Ex 29:19 3947
t of his blood, and put it upon Ex 29:20 3947
thou shalt t of the blood that is Ex 29:21 3947
Also thou shalt t of the ram the Ex 29:22 3947
thou shalt t the breast of the Ex 29:26 3947
thou shalt t the ram of the Ex 29:31 3947
thou shalt t the atonement money Ex 30:16 3947
T thou also unto thee principal Ex 30:23 3947
T unto thee sweet spices, stacte, Ex 30:34 3947
I will t away mine hand, and thou Ex 33:23 5493
t us for thine inheritance Ex 34:9
T heed to thyself, lest thou make Ex 34:12
thou t of their daughters unto Ex 34:16 3947
T ye from among you an offering Ex 35:5 3947
thou shalt t the anointing oil, Ex 40:9 3947
he shall t thereout his handful Lev 2:2 7061
the priest shall t from the meat Lev 2:9 7311
the kidneys, it shall he t away Lev 3:4 5493
it shall he t off hard by the Lev 3:9 5493
the kidneys, it shall he t away Lev 3:10 5493
the kidneys, it shall he t away Lev 3:15 5493
shall t of the bullock's blood Lev 4:5 3947
he shall t off from it all the Lev 4:8 3318
the kidneys, it shall he t away Lev 4:9 5493
he shall t all his fat from him, Lev 4:19 7311
the priest shall t of the blood Lev 4:25 3947
the priest shall t of the blood Lev 4:30 3947
he shall t away all the fat Lev 4:31 5493
the priest shall t of the blood Lev 4:34 3947
he shall t away all the fat Lev 4:35 5493
the priest shall t his handful of Lev 5:12 7061
t up the ashes which the fire Lev 6:10 7311
he shall t of it his handful, of Lev 6:15 7311
the kidneys, it shall he t away Lev 7:4 5493
T Aaron and his sons with him, and Lev 8:2 3947
T thee a young calf for a sin Lev 9:2 3947
T ye a kid of the goats for a sin Lev 9:3 3947
left, T the meat offering that Lev 10:12 3947
shall the priest command to t for Lev 14:4 3947
the living bird, he shall t it Lev 14:6 3947
on the eighth day he shall t two Lev 14:10 3947
And the priest shall t one he lamb Lev 14:12 3947
the priest shall t some of the Lev 14:14 3947
the priest shall t some of the Lev 14:15 3947
then he shall t one lamb for a Lev 14:21 3947
the priest shall t the lamb of Lev 14:24 3947
the priest shall t some of the Lev 14:25 3947
t away the stones in which the Lev 14:40 2502
they shall t other stones, and put Lev 14:42 3947
he shall t other morter, and shall Lev 14:42 3947
he shall t to cleanse the house Lev 14:49 3947
he shall t the cedar wood, and the Lev 14:51 3947
he shall t to him two turtledoves Lev 15:14 3947
she shall t unto her two turtles Lev 15:29 3947
he shall t of the congregation of Lev 16:5 3947
he shall t the two goats, and Lev 16:7 3947
he shall t a censer full of Lev 16:12 3947
he shall t of the blood of the Lev 16:14 3947
shall t of the blood of the Lev 16:18 3947
shalt thou t her son's daughter Lev 18:17 3947
Neither shalt thou t a wife to Lev 18:18 3947
And if a man t a wife and her Lev 20:14 3947
And if a man shall t his sister Lev 20:17 3947
if a man shall t his brother's Lev 20:21 3947
They shall not t a wife that is a Lev 21:7 3947
neither shall they t a woman put Lev 21:7 3947
And he shall t a wife in her Lev 21:13 3947
an harlot, these shall he not t Lev 21:14 3947
but he shall t a virgin of his Lev 21:14 3947
man of whom he may t uncleanness Lev 22:5
ye shall t you on the first day Lev 23:40 3947
And thou shalt t fine flour Lev 24:5 3947
T thou no usury of him, or Lev 25:36 3947
ye shall t them as an inheritance Lev 25:46
T ye the sum of all the Num 1:2 5375
neither t the sum of them among Num 1:49 5375
the Levites shall t it down Num 1:51 3381
t the number of their names Num 3:40 5375
thou shalt t the Levites for me Num 3:41 3947
T the Levites instead of all the Num 3:45 3947
Thou shalt even t five shekels Num 3:47 3947
the sanctuary shalt thou t them Num 3:47 3947
T the sum of the sons of Kohath Num 4:2 5375
they shall t down the covering Num 4:5 3381
they shall t a cloth of blue, and Num 4:9 3947
they shall t all the instruments Num 4:12 3947
they shall t away the ashes from Num 4:13
T also the sum of the sons of Num 4:22 5375
the priest shall t holy water in Num 5:17 3947
the tabernacle the priest shall t Num 5:17 3947
Then the priest shall t the Num 5:25 3947
the priest shall t an handful of Num 5:26 7061
shall t the hair of the head of Num 6:18 3947
the priest shall t the sodden Num 6:19 3947
T it of them, that they may be to Num 7:5 3947
T the Levites from among the Num 8:6 3947
Then let them t a young bullock Num 8:8 3947
shalt thou t for a sin offering Num 8:8 3947
south side shall t their journey Num 10:6
I will t of the spirit which is Num 11:17 680
Ye t too much upon you, seeing Num 16:3
T you censers, Korah, and all his Num 16:6 3947
ye t too much upon you, ye sons Num 16:7
t every man his censer, and put Num 16:17 3947
that he t up the censers out of Num 16:37 7311
T a censer, and put fire therein Num 16:46 3947
t of every one of them a rod Num 17:2 3947
thou shalt quite t away their Num 17:10 3615
When ye t of the children of Num 18:26 3947
Eleazar the priest shall t of her Num 19:4 3947
And the priest shall t cedar wood Num 19:6 3947
shall t of the ashes of the burnt Num 19:17 3947
And a clean person shall t hyssop Num 19:18 3947
T the rod, and gather thou the Num 20:8 3947
T Aaron and Eleazar his son, and Num 20:25 3947
that he t away the serpents from Num 21:7 5493
Must I not t heed to speak that Num 23:12
T all the heads of the people, and Num 25:4 3947
T the sum of all the congregation Num 26:2 5375
T the sum of the people, from Num 26:4
T thee Joshua the son of Nun, a Num 27:18 3947
T the sum of the prey that was Num 31:26 5375
T it of their half, and give it Num 31:29 3947
thou shalt t one portion of fifty Num 31:30 3947
ye shall t one prince of every Num 34:18 3947
Moreover ye shall t no Num 35:31 3947
ye shall t no satisfaction for Num 35:32 3947
t your journey, and go to the Deut 1:7
T you wise men, and understanding, Deut 1:13 3051
you, and t your journey into the Deut 1:40
t ye good heed unto yourselves Deut 2:4
t your journey, and pass over the Deut 2:24
Only t heed to thyself, and keep Deut 4:9
T ye therefore good heed unto Deut 4:15
T heed unto yourselves, lest ye Deut 4:23
t him a nation from the midst of Deut 4:34 3947
Thou shalt not t the name of the Deut 5:11 5375
shalt thou t unto thy son Deut 7:3 3947
the LORD will t away from thee Deut 7:15 5493
nor t it unto thee, lest thou be Deut 7:25 3947
t thy journey before the people, Deut 10:11
T heed to yourselves, that your Deut 11:16
T heed to thyself that thou offer Deut 12:13
T heed to thyself that thou Deut 12:19
hast, and thy vows, thou shalt t Deut 12:26 5375
T heed to thyself that thou be Deut 12:30
Then thou shalt t an aul, and Deut 15:17 3947
respect persons, neither t a gift Deut 16:19 3947
the battle, and another man t her Deut 20:7 3947
shalt thou t unto thyself Deut 20:14 962
in making war against it to t it Deut 20:19 8610
of that city shall t an heifer Deut 21:3 3947

T

Context	Reference	Number
thou shalt not *t* the dam with the	Deut 22:6	3947
dam go, and *t* the young to thee	Deut 22:7	3947
If any man *t* a wife, and go in	Deut 22:13	3947
of the damsel, and her mother, *t*	Deut 22:15	3947
of that city shall *t* that man	Deut 22:18	3947
A man shall not *t* his father's	Deut 22:30	3947
may not *t* her again to be his	Deut 24:4	3947
No man shall *t* the nether or the	Deut 24:6	2254
T heed in the plague of leprosy,	Deut 24:8	
nor *t* a widow's raiment to pledge	Deut 24:17	2254
t her to him to wife, and perform	Deut 25:5	3947
like not to *t* his brother's wife	Deut 25:7	3947
it, and say, I like not to *t* her	Deut 25:8	3947
That thou shalt *t* of the first of	Deut 26:2	3947
the priest shall *t* the basket out	Deut 26:4	3947
T heed, and hearken, O Israel	Deut 27:9	5535
T this book of the law, and put it	Deut 31:26	3947
mine hand *t* hold on judgment	Deut 32:41	270
T up the ark of the covenant, and	Josh 3:6	5375
Now therefore *t* you twelve men	Josh 3:12	3947
T you twelve men out of the	Josh 4:2	3947
T you hence out of the midst of	Josh 4:3	5375
t you up every man of you a stone	Josh 4:5	7311
T up the ark of the covenant, and	Josh 6:6	5375
when ye *t* of the accursed thing,	Josh 6:18	3947
until ye *t* away the accursed	Josh 7:13	5493
shall *t* shall come by households	Josh 7:14	3920
shall *t* shall come man by man	Josh 7:14	3920
t all the people of war with thee	Josh 8:1	3947
shall ye *t* for a prey unto	Josh 8:2	
commanded that they should *t* his	Josh 8:29	3381
T victuals with you for the	Josh 9:11	3947
land did Joshua *t* at one time	Josh 10:42	3920
the kings of them, did Joshua *t*	Josh 11:12	3920
they shall *t* him into the city	Josh 20:4	622
But *t* diligent heed to do the	Josh 22:5	
and *t* possession among us	Josh 22:19	270
T good heed therefore unto	Josh 23:11	
t with thee ten thousand men of	Judg 4:6	3947
necks of them that *t* the spoil	Judg 5:30	
T the flesh and the unleavened	Judg 6:20	3947
T thy father's young bullock,	Judg 6:25	3947
t the second bullock, and offer a	Judg 6:26	3947
t before them the waters unto	Judg 7:24	3920
that thou goest to *t* a wife of	Judg 14:3	3947
after a time he returned to *t* her	Judg 14:8	3947
ye called us to *t* that we have	Judg 14:15	3423
t her, I pray thee, instead of	Judg 15:2	1961
t advice, and speak your minds	Judg 19:30	
we will *t* ten men of an hundred	Judg 20:10	3947
thou shouldest *t* knowledge of me	Ruth 2:10	
he that did *t* knowledge of thee	Ruth 2:19	
then *t* as much as thy soul	1Sa 2:16	3947
and if not, I will *t* it by force	1Sa 2:16	3947
t two milch kine, on which there	1Sa 6:7	3947
t the ark of the LORD, and lay it	1Sa 6:8	3947
He will *t* your sons, and appoint	1Sa 8:11	3947
he will *t* your daughters to be	1Sa 8:13	3947
he will *t* your fields, and your	1Sa 8:14	3947
he will *t* the tenth of your seed,	1Sa 8:15	
he will *t* your menservants, and	1Sa 8:16	3947
He will *t* the tenth of your sheep	1Sa 8:17	
T now one of the servants with	1Sa 9:3	3947
the asses, and *t* thought for us	1Sa 9:5	
T an heifer with thee, and say, I	1Sa 16:2	3947
T now for thy brethren an ephah	1Sa 17:17	3947
brethren fare, and *t* their pledge	1Sa 17:18	3947
thee, and *t* thine head from thee	1Sa 17:46	5493
t heed to thyself until the	1Sa 19:2	
Saul sent messengers to *t* David	1Sa 19:14	3947
Saul sent messengers to *t* David	1Sa 19:20	3947
are on this side of thee, *t* them	1Sa 20:21	3947
if thou wilt *t* that, *t* it	1Sa 21:9	3947
t knowledge of all the lurking	1Sa 23:23	
and his men round about to *t* them	1Sa 23:26	8610
yet thou huntest my soul to *t* it	1Sa 24:11	3947
Shall I then *t* my bread, and my	1Sa 25:11	3947
Abigail, to *t* her to him to wife	1Sa 25:39	3947
thee, to *t* thee to him to wife	1Sa 25:40	3947
t thou now the spear that is at	1Sa 26:11	3947
young men, and *t* thee his armour	2Sa 2:21	3947
t you away from the earth	2Sa 4:11	1197
Except thou *t* away the blind and	2Sa 5:6	5493
he spared to *t* of his own flock	2Sa 12:4	3947
I will *t* thy wives before thine	2Sa 12:11	3947
encamp against the city, and *t* it	2Sa 12:28	3920
lest I *t* the city, and it be	2Sa 12:28	3920
the king *t* the thing to his heart	2Sa 13:33	7760
thou, and *t* back thy brethren	2Sa 15:20	
I pray thee, and *t* off his head	2Sa 16:9	5493
the king should *t* it to his heart	2Sa 19:19	7760
unto the king, Yea, let him *t* all	2Sa 19:30	3947
t thou thy lord's servants, and	2Sa 20:6	3947
t away the iniquity of thy	2Sa 24:10	5674
David, Let my lord the king *t*	2Sa 24:22	3947
T with you the servants of your	1Kin 1:33	3947
If thy children *t* heed to their	1Kin 2:4	
that thou mayest *t* away the	1Kin 2:31	5493
thy children *t* heed to their way	1Kin 8:25	
to Jeroboam, *T* thee ten pieces	1Kin 11:31	3947
Howbeit I will not *t* the whole	1Kin 11:34	3947
But I will *t* the kingdom out of	1Kin 11:35	3947
And I will *t* thee, and thou shalt	1Kin 11:37	3947
t with thee ten loaves, and	1Kin 14:3	3947
will *t* away the remnant of the	1Kin 14:10	1197
I will *t* away the posterity of	1Kin 16:3	1197
unto them, *T* the prophets of Baal	1Kin 18:40	8610
now, O LORD, *t* away my life	1Kin 19:4	3947
they seek my life, to *t* it away	1Kin 19:10	3947
they seek my life, to *t* it away	1Kin 19:14	3947
it in their hand, and *t* it away	1Kin 20:6	3947
come out for peace, *t* them alive	1Kin 20:18	8610
be come out for war, *t* them alive	1Kin 20:18	8610
T the kings away, every man out	1Kin 20:24	5493
t possession of the vineyard of	1Kin 21:15	3423
Jezreelite, to *t* possession of it	1Kin 21:16	3423
will *t* away thy posterity, and	1Kin 21:21	1197
t it not out of the hand of the	1Kin 22:3	3947
T Micaiah, and carry him back unto	1Kin 22:26	3947
when the LORD would *t* up Elijah	2Kin 2:1	5927
t away thy master from thy head	2Kin 2:3	3947
t away thy master from thy head	2Kin 2:5	3947
the creditor is come to *t* unto	2Kin 4:1	3947
t my staff in thine hand, and go	2Kin 4:29	3947
unto him, he said, *T* up thy son	2Kin 4:36	5375
t a blessing of thy servant	2Kin 5:15	3947
And he urged him to *t* it	2Kin 5:16	3947
after him, and *t* somewhat of him	2Kin 5:20	3947
said, Be content, *t* two talents	2Kin 5:23	3947
t thence every man a beam, and let	2Kin 6:2	3947
said he, *T* it up to thee	2Kin 6:7	7311
hath sent to *t* away mine head	2Kin 6:32	5493
answered and said, Let some *t*	2Kin 7:13	3947
T a present in thine hand, and go,	2Kin 8:8	3947
t this box of oil in thine hand,	2Kin 9:1	3947
Then *t* the box of oil, and pour it	2Kin 9:3	3947
T an horseman, and send to meet	2Kin 9:17	3947
T up, and cast him in the portion	2Kin 9:25	5375
Now therefore *t* and cast him into	2Kin 9:26	5375
t ye the heads of the men your	2Kin 10:6	3947
And he said, *T* them alive	2Kin 10:14	8610
Let the priests *t* it to them	2Kin 12:5	3947
said unto him, *T* bow and arrows	2Kin 13:15	3947
And he said, *T* the arrows	2Kin 13:18	3947
t you away to a land like your	2Kin 18:32	3947
shall yet again *t* root downward	2Kin 19:30	3947
And Isaiah said, *T* a lump of figs	2Kin 20:7	3947
shalt beget, shall they *t* away	2Kin 20:18	3947
came down to *t* away their cattle	1Chr 7:21	3947
I will not *t* my mercy away from	1Chr 17:13	5493
T it to thee, and let my lord the	1Chr 21:23	3947
for I will not *t* that which is	1Chr 21:24	5375
T heed now	1Chr 28:10	7200
yet so that thy children *t* heed	2Chr 6:16	
T ye Micaiah, and carry him back	2Chr 18:25	3947
to the judges, *T* heed what ye do	2Chr 19:6	7200
t heed and do it	2Chr 19:7	
his people came to *t* away the	2Chr 20:25	962
that they might *t* the city	2Chr 32:18	3920
so that they will *t* heed to do	2Chr 33:8	
T heed now that ye fail not to do	Ezr 4:22	2095
those did Cyrus the king *t* out of	Ezr 5:14	5312
T these vessels, go, carry them	Ezr 5:15	5376
neither *t* their daughters unto	Ezr 9:12	5375
therefore we *t* up corn for them,	Neh 5:2	3947
let us *t* counsel together	Neh 6:7	
nor *t* their daughters for our	Neh 10:30	3947
when the Levites *t* tithes	Neh 10:38	
nor *t* their daughters unto your	Neh 13:25	5375
to *t* the spoil of them for a prey	Est 3:13	3947
to *t* away his sackcloth from him	Est 4:4	5493
t the apparel and the horse, as	Est 6:10	3947
to *t* the spoil of them for a prey	Est 8:11	
and *t* away mine iniquity	Job 7:21	5674
will not suffer me to *t* my breath	Job 9:18	
Let him *t* his rod away from me,	Job 9:34	5493
that I may *t* comfort a little,	Job 10:20	
thou shalt *t* thy rest in safety	Job 11:18	7901
Wherefore do I *t* my flesh in my	Job 13:14	5375
The gin shall *t* him by the heel,	Job 18:9	270
They *t* the timbrel and harp, and	Job 21:12	5375
But he knoweth the way that I *t*	Job 23:10	5978
they violently *t* away flocks	Job 24:2	1497
they *t* the widow's ox for a	Job 24:3	2254
breast, and *t* a pledge of the poor	Job 24:9	2254
they *t* away the sheaf from the	Job 24:10	5375
Terrors *t* hold on him as waters,	Job 27:20	5381
and my sinews *t* no rest	Job 30:17	7901
Surely I would *t* it upon my	Job 31:36	5375
my maker would soon *t* me away	Job 32:22	5375
and justice *t* hold on thee	Job 36:17	8551
beware lest he *t* thee away with	Job 36:18	5496
T heed, regard not iniquity	Job 36:21	
That it might *t* hold of the ends	Job 38:13	270
That thou shouldest *t* it to the	Job 38:20	3947
wilt thou *t* him for a servant for	Job 41:4	3947
Therefore *t* unto you now seven	Job 42:8	3947
the rulers *t* counsel together,	Ps 2:2	
enemy persecute my soul, and *t* it	Ps 7:5	5381
How long shall I *t* counsel in my	Ps 13:2	7896
nor *t* up their names into my lips	Ps 16:4	5375
me, then the LORD will *t* me up	Ps 27:10	622
they devised to *t* away my life	Ps 31:13	3947
T hold of shield and buckler, and	Ps 35:2	2388
I will *t* heed to my ways, that I	Ps 39:1	
I will *t* no bullock out of thy	Ps 50:9	3947
or that thou shouldest *t* my	Ps 50:16	5375
t not thy holy spirit from me	Ps 51:11	3947
he shall *t* thee away, and pluck	Ps 52:5	2846
he shall *t* them away as with a	Ps 58:9	8175
and I looked for some to *t* pity	Ps 69:20	
thy wrathful anger *t* hold of them	Ps 69:24	5381
for my soul *t* counsel together	Ps 71:10	
persecute and *t* him	Ps 71:11	8610
and didst cause it to *t* deep root	Ps 80:9	
T a psalm, and bring hither the	Ps 81:2	5375
Let us *t* to ourselves the houses	Ps 83:12	
will I not utterly *t* from him	Ps 89:33	6331
For thy servants *t* pleasure in	Ps 102:14	
t me not away in the midst of my	Ps 102:24	5927
and let another *t* his office	Ps 109:8	3947
I will *t* the cup of salvation, and	Ps 116:13	5375
t not the word of truth utterly	Ps 119:43	5337
If I *t* the wings of the morning,	Ps 139:9	5375
thine enemies *t* thy name in vain	Ps 139:20	5375
neither *t* they hold of the paths	Prov 2:19	5381
T fast hold of instruction	Prov 4:13	2388
her steps *t* hold on hell	Prov 5:5	8551
shall *t* the wicked himself	Prov 5:22	3920
neither let her *t* thee with her	Prov 6:25	3947
Can a man *t* fire in his bosom, and	Prov 6:27	2846
let us *t* our fill of love until	Prov 7:18	
T his garment that is surety for	Prov 20:16	3947
t a pledge of him for a strange	Prov 20:16	2254
why should he *t* away thy bed from	Prov 22:27	3947
T away the dross from the silver,	Prov 25:4	1898
T away the wicked from before the	Prov 25:5	1898
T his garment that is surety for	Prov 27:13	3947
t a pledge of him for a strange	Prov 27:13	2254
t the name of my God in vain	Prov 30:9	8610
shall *t* nothing of his labour,	Eccl 5:15	5375
to *t* his portion, and to rejoice	Eccl 5:19	5375
thou shouldest *t* hold of this	Eccl 7:18	270
Also *t* no heed unto all words	Eccl 7:21	5414
T us the foxes, the little foxes,	Song 2:15	270
I will *t* hold of the boughs	Song 7:8	270
thy dross, and *t* away all thy tin	Is 1:25	5493
doth *t* away from Jerusalem and	Is 3:1	5493
When a man shall *t* hold of his	Is 3:6	8610
will *t* away the bravery of their	Is 3:18	5493
women shall *t* hold of one man	Is 4:1	2388
thy name, to *t* away our reproach	Is 4:1	622
I will *t* away the hedge thereof,	Is 5:5	5493
t away the righteousness of the	Is 5:23	5493
say unto him, *T* heed, and be quiet	Is 7:4	
T thee a great roll, and write in	Is 8:1	3947
T counsel together, and it shall	Is 8:10	
to *t* away the right from the poor	Is 10:2	1497
to *t* the spoil, and to	Is 10:6	7997
to *t* the prey, and to tread them	Is 10:6	962
and sorrows shall *t* hold of them	Is 13:8	270
And the people shall *t* them	Is 14:2	3947
they shall *t* them captives, whose	Is 14:2	
That thou shalt *t* up this proverb	Is 14:4	5375
T counsel, execute judgment	Is 16:3	935
I will *t* my rest, and I will	Is 18:4	
t away and cut down the branches	Is 18:5	5493
T an harp, go about the city,	Is 23:16	3947
he *t* away from off all the earth	Is 25:8	5493
Or let him *t* hold of my strength,	Is 27:5	2388
them that come of Jacob to *t* root	Is 27:6	2388
all the fruit to *t* away his sin	Is 27:9	5493
it goeth forth it shall *t* you	Is 28:19	3947
that *t* counsel, but not of me	Is 30:1	6213
a sherd to *t* fire from the hearth	Is 30:14	2846
or to *t* water withal out of the	Is 30:14	2834
the lame *t* the prey	Is 33:23	962
t you away to a land like your	Is 36:17	3947
Judah shall again *t* root downward	Is 37:31	
Let them *t* a lump of figs, and lay	Is 38:21	5375
shall beget, shall they *t* away	Is 39:7	3947
shall not *t* root in the earth	Is 40:24	3947
the whirlwind shall *t* them away	Is 40:24	5375
for he will *t* thereof, and warm	Is 44:15	3947
let them *t* counsel together	Is 45:21	
T the millstones, and grind meal	Is 47:2	3947
I will *t* vengeance, and I will not	Is 47:3	3947
me, and *t* hold of my covenant	Is 56:4	2388
vanity shall *t* them	Is 57:13	3947
t up the stumblingblock out of	Is 57:14	7311
they delight in approaching to	Is 58:2	
If thou *t* away from the midst of	Is 58:9	5493
up himself to *t* hold of thee	Is 64:7	2388
I will also *t* of them for priests	Is 66:21	3947
t thee much sope, yet thine	Jer 2:22	
I will *t* you one of a city, and	Jer 3:14	3947
t away the foreskins of your	Jer 4:4	5493
t away her battlements	Jer 5:10	5493
t up a lamentation on high places	Jer 7:29	5375
T ye heed every one of his	Jer 9:4	
mountains will I *t* up a weeping	Jer 9:10	5375
t up a wailing for us, that our	Jer 9:18	5375
T the girdle that thou hast got,	Jer 13:4	3947
t the girdle from thence, which I	Jer 13:6	3947
shall not sorrows *t* thee, as a	Jer 13:21	270
t me not away in thy	Jer 15:15	3947
if thou *t* forth the precious from	Jer 15:19	3318
Thou shalt not *t* thee a wife	Jer 16:2	3947
T heed to yourselves, and bear no	Jer 17:21	
they have digged a pit to *t* me	Jer 18:22	3920
t of the ancients of the people,	Jer 19:1	
t them, and carry them to Babylon	Jer 20:5	3947
we shall *t* our revenge on him	Jer 20:10	3947
t all the families of the north,	Jer 25:9	3947
Moreover I will *t* from them the	Jer 25:10	6
T the wine cup of this fury at my	Jer 25:15	3947
if they refuse to *t* the cup at	Jer 25:28	3947
T ye wives, and beget sons and	Jer 29:6	3947
t wives for your sons, and give	Jer 29:6	3947
king of Babylon, and he shall *t* it	Jer 32:3	3920
T these evidences, this evidence	Jer 32:14	3947
are come unto the city to *t* it	Jer 32:24	3920
field for money, and *t* witnesses	Jer 32:25	5749
king of Babylon, and he shall *t* it	Jer 32:28	3920
t witnesses in the land of	Jer 32:44	5749
so that I will not *t* any of his	Jer 33:26	3947
t it, and burn it with fire	Jer 34:22	3920
T thee a roll of a book, and write	Jer 36:2	3947
T in thine hand the roll wherein	Jer 36:14	3947
to *t* Baruch the scribe and	Jer 36:26	3947
T thee again another roll, and	Jer 36:28	3947
t it, and burn it with fire	Jer 37:8	3920
Babylon's army, which shall *t* it	Jer 38:3	3920
T from hence thirty men with thee	Jer 38:10	3947
t up Jeremiah the prophet out of	Jer 38:10	3947
T him, and look well to him, and do	Jer 39:12	3947
T great stones in thine hand, and	Jer 43:9	3947
t Nebuchadrezzar the king of	Jer 43:10	3947
I will *t* the remnant of Judah,	Jer 44:12	3947
t balm, O virgin, the daughter of	Jer 46:11	3947
and their flocks shall they *t* away	Jer 49:29	3947
they shall *t* to themselves their	Jer 49:29	5375

Context	Reference	Number
t vengeance upon her	Jer 50:15	
t balm for her pain, if so be she	Jer 51:8	3947
they shall not *t* of thee a stone	Jer 51:26	3947
cause, and *t* vengeance for thee	Jer 51:36	
What thing shall I *t* to witness	Lam 2:13	
t thee a tile, and lay it before	Eze 4:1	3947
Moreover *t* thou unto thee an iron	Eze 4:3	3947
T thou also unto thee wheat, and	Eze 4:9	3947
t thee a sharp knife	Eze 5:1	3947
t thee a barber's razor, and cause	Eze 5:1	3947
then *t* thee balances to weigh, and	Eze 5:1	3947
thou shalt *t* a third part, and	Eze 5:2	3947
Thou shalt also *t* thereof a few	Eze 5:3	3947
Then *t* of them again, and cast	Eze 5:4	3947
T fire from between the wheels,	Eze 10:6	3947
they shall *t* away all the	Eze 11:18	5493
I will *t* the stony heart out of	Eze 11:19	5493
That I may *t* the house of Israel	Eze 14:5	8610
or will men *t* a pin of it to hang	Eze 15:3	3947
And of thy garments thou didst *t*	Eze 16:16	3947
shall *t* thy fair jewels, and leave	Eze 16:39	3947
I will also *t* of the highest	Eze 17:22	3947
Moreover *t* thou up a lamentation	Eze 19:1	5375
the diadem, and *t* off the crown	Eze 21:26	7311
thou shalt *t* thine inheritance in	Eze 22:16	
they shall *t* away thy nose and	Eze 23:25	5493
they shall *t* thy sons and thy	Eze 23:25	3947
and *t* away thy fair jewels	Eze 23:26	3947
shall *t* away all thy labour, and	Eze 23:29	3947
T the choice of the flock, and	Eze 24:5	3947
fury to come up to *t* vengeance	Eze 24:8	
I *t* away from thee the desire of	Eze 24:16	3947
when I *t* from them their strength	Eze 24:25	3947
they shall *t* up a lamentation for	Eze 26:17	5375
t up a lamentation for Tyrus	Eze 27:2	5375
shall *t* up a lamentation for thee	Eze 27:32	5375
t up a lamentation upon the king	Eze 28:12	5375
he shall *t* her multitude	Eze 29:19	5375
multitude, and *t* her spoil	Eze 29:19	7997
her spoil, and *t* her prey	Eze 29:19	962
they shall *t* away her multitude,	Eze 30:4	3947
t up a lamentation for Pharaoh	Eze 32:2	5375
the land *t* a man of their coasts	Eze 33:2	3947
t him away, his blood shall be	Eze 33:4	3947
t any person from among them, he	Eze 33:6	3947
For I will *t* you from among the	Eze 36:24	3947
I will *t* away the stony heart out	Eze 36:26	5493
t thee one stick, and write upon	Eze 37:16	3947
then *t* another stick, and write	Eze 37:16	3947
I will *t* the stick of Joseph,	Eze 37:19	3947
I will *t* the children of Israel	Eze 37:21	3947
To *t* a spoil, and to	Eze 38:12	7997
a spoil, and to *t* a prey	Eze 38:12	962
thee, Art thou come to *t* a spoil	Eze 38:13	7997
gathered thy company to *t* a prey	Eze 38:13	962
to *t* away cattle and goods, to	Eze 38:13	3947
and goods, to *t* a great spoil	Eze 38:13	3947
So that they shall *t* no wood out	Eze 39:10	5375
thou shalt *t* of the blood thereof	Eze 43:20	3947
Thou shalt *t* the bullock also of	Eze 43:21	3947
Neither shall they *t* for their	Eze 44:22	3947
but they shall *t* maidens of the	Eze 44:22	3947
t away your exactions from my	Eze 45:9	7311
thou shalt *t* a young bullock	Eze 45:18	3947
the priest shall *t* of the blood	Eze 45:19	3947
Moreover the prince shall not *t*	Eze 46:18	3947
should *t* Daniel up out of the den	Dan 6:23	5267
the most High shall *t* the kingdom	Dan 7:18	6902
they shall *t* away his dominion,	Dan 7:26	5709
and *t* the most fenced cities	Dan 11:15	3920
unto the isles, and shall *t* many	Dan 11:18	3920
shall *t* away the daily sacrifice,	Dan 11:31	5493
t unto thee a wife of whoredoms	Hos 1:2	3947
but I will utterly *t* them away	Hos 1:6	5375
t away my corn in the time	Hos 2:9	3947
For I will *t* away the names of	Hos 2:17	5493
left off to *t* heed to the LORD	Hos 4:10	
new wine *t* away the heart	Hos 4:11	3947
I will *t* away, and none shall	Hos 5:14	5375
that *t* off the yoke on their jaws	Hos 11:4	7311
T with you words, and turn to the	Hos 14:2	3947
T away all iniquity, and receive	Hos 14:2	5375
shall one *t* up a snare from the	Amos 3:5	5927
that he will *t* you away with	Amos 4:2	5375
word which I *t* up against you	Amos 5:1	5375
ye *t* from him burdens of wheat	Amos 5:11	3947
they *t* a bribe, and they turn	Amos 5:12	3947
T thou away from me the noise of	Amos 5:23	5493
And a man's uncle shall *t* him up	Amos 6:10	5375
thence shall mine hand *t* them	Amos 9:2	3947
will search and *t* them out thence	Amos 9:3	3947
T me up, and cast me forth into	Jonah 1:12	5375
Therefore now, O LORD, *t*, I	Jonah 4:3	3947
fields, and *t* them by violence	Mic 2:2	5375
and houses, and *t* them away	Mic 2:2	5375
In that day shall one *t* up a	Mic 2:4	5375
them, that they shall not *t* shame	Mic 2:6	5253
and thou shalt *t* hold, but shalt	Mic 6:14	5253
the LORD will *t* vengeance on his	Nah 1:2	
T ye the spoil of silver	Nah 2:9	962
t the spoil of gold	Nah 2:9	962
for they shall heap dust, and *t* it	Hab 1:10	3920
They *t* up all of them with the	Hab 1:15	5927
Shall not all these *t* up a	Hab 2:6	5375
for then I will *t* away out of the	Zeph 3:11	5493
I will *t* pleasure in it, and I	Hag 1:8	
the LORD of hosts, will I *t* thee	Hag 2:23	3947
did they not *t* hold of your	Zec 1:6	5381
T away the filthy garments from	Zec 3:4	5493
T of them of the captivity, even	Zec 6:10	3947
Then *t* silver and gold, and make	Zec 6:11	3947
that ten men shall *t* hold out of	Zec 8:23	2388
even shall *t* hold of the skirt of	Zec 8:23	2388
I will *t* away his blood out of	Zec 9:7	5493
T unto thee yet the instruments	Zec 11:15	3947
t of them, and seethe therein	Zec 14:21	3947
one shall *t* you away with it	Mal 2:3	5375
Therefore *t* heed to your spirit,	Mal 2:15	
therefore *t* heed to your spirit,	Mal 2:16	
fear not to *t* unto thee Mary thy	Mt 1:20	*3880*
t the young child and his mother,	Mt 2:13	*3880*
t the young child and his mother,	Mt 2:20	*3880*
t away thy coat, let him have thy	Mt 5:40	*2983*
T heed that ye do not your alms	Mt 6:1	
T no thought for your life, what	Mt 6:25	
why *t* ye thought for raiment	Mt 6:28	
Therefore *t* no thought, saying,	Mt 6:31	
T therefore no thought for the	Mt 6:34	
for the morrow shall *t* thought	Mt 6:34	
t up thy bed, and go unto thine	Mt 9:6	*142*
t no thought how or what ye shall	Mt 10:19	
and the violent *t* it by force	Mt 11:12	*726*
T my yoke upon you, and learn of	Mt 11:29	*142*
and said, It is not meet to *t* the	Mt 15:26	*2983*
they had forgotten to *t* bread	Mt 16:5	*2983*
T heed and beware of the leaven of	Mt 16:6	
t up his cross, and follow me	Mt 16:24	*142*
of the earth *t* custom or tribute	Mt 17:25	*2983*
t up the fish that first cometh	Mt 17:27	*142*
that *t*, and give unto them for me	Mt 17:27	*2983*
T heed that ye despise not one of	Mt 18:10	
then *t* with thee one or two more,	Mt 18:16	*3880*
which would *t* account of his	Mt 18:23	*4868*
T that thine is, and go thy way	Mt 20:14	*142*
t him away, and cast him into	Mt 22:13	*142*
T heed that no man deceive you	Mt 24:4	
to *t* any thing out of his house	Mt 24:17	*142*
return back to *t* his clothes	Mt 24:18	*142*
T therefore the talent from him,	Mt 25:28	*142*
they might *t* Jesus by subtilty	Mt 26:4	*2902*
it to the disciples, and said, *T*	Mt 26:26	*2983*
Sleep on now, and *t* your rest	Mt 26:45	
for all they that *t* the sword	Mt 26:52	*2983*
with swords and staves for to *t* me	Mt 26:55	*4815*
Arise, and *t* up thy bed, and walk	Mk 2:9	*142*
t up thy bed, and go thy way into	Mk 2:11	*142*
unto them, *T* heed what ye hear	Mk 4:24	
t nothing for their journey	Mk 6:8	*142*
meet to *t* the children's bread	Mk 7:27	*2983*
had forgotten to *t* bread, neither	Mk 8:14	*2983*
T heed, beware of the leaven of	Mk 8:15	
t up his cross, and follow me	Mk 8:34	*142*
t up the cross, and follow me	Mk 10:21	*142*
his brother should *t* his wife	Mk 12:19	*2983*
T heed lest any man deceive you	Mk 13:5	
But *t* heed to yourselves	Mk 13:9	
t no thought beforehand what ye	Mk 13:11	
to *t* any thing out of his house	Mk 13:15	*142*
again for to *t* up his garment	Mk 13:16	*142*
But *t* ye heed	Mk 13:23	
T ye heed, watch and pray	Mk 13:33	
how they might *t* him by craft	Mk 14:1	*2902*
it and gave to them, and said, *T*	Mk 14:22	*2983*
t away this cup from me	Mk 14:36	*3911*
Sleep on now, and *t* your rest	Mk 14:41	
t him, and lead him away safely	Mk 14:44	*2902*
swords and with staves to *t* me	Mk 14:48	*4815*
them, what every man should *t*	Mk 15:24	*142*
Elias will come to *t* him down	Mk 15:36	*2507*
They shall *t* up serpents	Mk 16:18	*142*
to *t* away my reproach among men	Lk 1:25	*851*
t up thy couch, and go into thine	Lk 5:24	*142*
into the house of God, and did *t*	Lk 6:4	*2983*
forbid not to *t* thy coat also	Lk 6:29	
T heed therefore how ye hear	Lk 8:18	
T nothing for your journey,	Lk 9:3	*142*
t up his cross daily, and follow	Lk 9:23	*142*
and said unto him, *T* care of him	Lk 10:35	
T heed therefore that the light	Lk 11:35	*4648*
t ye no thought how or what thing	Lk 12:11	
T heed, and beware of covetousness	Lk 12:15	
t thine ease, eat, drink, and be	Lk 12:19	
T no thought for your life, what	Lk 12:22	
why *t* ye thought for the rest	Lk 12:26	
with shame to *t* the lowest room	Lk 14:9	*2722*
T thy bill, and sit down quickly,	Lk 16:6	*1209*
T thy bill, and write fourscore	Lk 16:7	*1209*
T heed to yourselves	Lk 17:3	
him not come down to *t* it away	Lk 17:31	*142*
T from him the pound, and give it	Lk 19:24	*142*
that they might *t* hold of his	Lk 20:20	*1949*
they could not *t* hold of his	Lk 20:26	*1949*
his brother should *t* his wife	Lk 20:28	*2983*
T heed that ye be not deceived	Lk 21:8	
t heed to yourselves, lest at any	Lk 21:34	
T this, and divide it among	Lk 22:17	*2983*
that hath a purse, let him *t* it	Lk 22:36	*142*
sold doves, *T* these things hence	Jn 2:16	*142*
him, Rise, *t* up thy bed, and walk	Jn 5:8	*142*
unto me, *T* up thy bed, and walk	Jn 5:11	*142*
unto thee, *T* up thy bed, and walk	Jn 5:12	*142*
every one of them may *t* a little	Jn 6:7	*2983*
t him by force, to make him a	Jn 6:15	*726*
Then they sought to *t* him	Jn 7:30	*4084*
priests sent officers to *t* him	Jn 7:32	*4084*
my life, that I might *t* it again	Jn 10:17	*2983*
and I have power to *t* it again	Jn 10:18	*2983*
they sought again to *t* him	Jn 10:39	*4084*
Jesus said, *T* ye away the stone	Jn 11:39	*142*
t away both our place and nation	Jn 11:48	*142*
shew it, that they might *t* him	Jn 11:57	*4084*
said I, that he shall *t* of mine	Jn 16:15	*2983*
shouldest *t* them out of the world	Jn 17:15	*142*
T ye him, and judge him according	Jn 18:31	*2983*
them, *T* ye him, and crucify him	Jn 19:6	*2983*
he might *t* away the body of Jesus	Jn 19:38	*142*
laid him, and I will *t* him away	Jn 20:15	*142*
and his bishoprick let another *t*	Acts 1:20	*2983*
That he may *t* part of this	Acts 1:25	*2983*
t heed to yourselves what ye	Acts 5:35	
proceeded further to *t* Peter also	Acts 12:3	*4815*
to *t* out of them a people for his	Acts 15:14	*2983*
determined to *t* with them John	Acts 15:37	*4838*
not good to *t* him with them	Acts 15:38	*4838*
there intending to *t* in Paul	Acts 20:13	*353*
Wherefore I *t* you to record this	Acts 20:26	
T heed therefore unto yourselves,	Acts 20:28	
Them *t*, and purify thyself with	Acts 21:24	*3880*
saying, *T* heed what thou doest	Acts 22:26	
to *t* him by force from among them	Acts 23:10	*726*
of whom thyself mayest *t*	Acts 24:8	
Paul besought them all to *t* meat	Acts 27:33	*3335*
I pray you to *t* some meat	Acts 27:34	*4355*
t heed lest he also spare not	Rom 11:21	
when I shall *t* away their sins	Rom 11:27	*851*
Whensoever I *t* my journey into	Rom 15:24	
But let every man *t* heed how he	1Cor 3:10	
Why do ye not rather *t* wrong	1Cor 6:7	
shall I then *t* the members of	1Cor 6:15	*142*
But *t* heed lest by any means this	1Cor 8:9	
Doth God *t* care for oxen	1Cor 9:9	
he standeth *t* heed lest he fall	1Cor 10:12	
thanks, he brake it, and said, *T*	1Cor 11:24	*2983*
t upon us the fellowship of the	2Cor 8:4	
man devour you, if a man *t* of you	2Cor 11:20	*2983*
Therefore I *t* pleasure in	2Cor 12:10	
t heed that ye be not consumed	Gal 5:15	
Wherefore *t* unto you the whole	Eph 6:13	*353*
t the helmet of salvation, and the	Eph 6:17	*1209*
T heed to the ministry which thou	Col 4:17	
how shall he *t* care of the church	1Ti 3:5	
T heed unto thyself, and unto the	1Ti 4:16	
T Mark, and bring him with thee	2Ti 4:11	*353*
T heed, brethren, lest there be	Heb 3:12	
have a commandment to *t* tithes of	Heb 7:5	
and of goats should *t* away sins	Heb 10:4	*851*
which can never *t* away sins	Heb 10:11	*4014*
T, my brethren, the prophets, who	Jas 5:10	*2983*
faults, ye shall *t* it patiently	1Pet 2:20	
ye *t* it patiently, this is	1Pet 2:20	
ye do well that ye *t* heed	2Pet 1:19	
was manifested to *t* away our sins	1Jn 3:5	*142*
hast, that no man *t* thy crown	Rev 3:11	*2983*
Thou art worthy to *t* the book	Rev 5:9	*2983*
thereon to *t* peace from the earth	Rev 6:4	*2983*
t the little book which is open	Rev 10:8	*2983*
said unto me, *T* it, and eat it up	Rev 10:9	*2983*
let him *t* the water of life	Rev 22:17	*2902*
if any man shall *t* away from the	Rev 22:19	*851*
God shall *t* away his part out of	Rev 22:19	*851*

TAKEN

Context	Reference	Number
which the LORD God had *t* from man	Gen 2:22	3947
because she was *t* out of Man	Gen 2:23	3947
for out of it wast thou *t*	Gen 3:19	3947
the ground from whence he was *t*	Gen 3:23	3947
shall be *t* on him sevenfold	Gen 4:15	
the woman was *t* into Pharaoh's	Gen 12:15	3947
so I might have *t* her to me to	Gen 12:19	3947
that his brother was *t* captive	Gen 14:14	
I have *t* upon me to speak unto	Gen 18:27	2974
I have *t* upon me to speak unto	Gen 18:31	2974
for the woman which thou hast *t*	Gen 20:3	3947
servants had violently *t* away	Gen 21:25	1497
where is he that hath *t* venison	Gen 27:33	6679
and hath *t* away thy blessing	Gen 27:35	3947
now he hath *t* away my blessing	Gen 27:36	3947
that thou hast *t* my husband	Gen 30:15	3947
God hath *t* away my reproach	Gen 30:23	622
Jacob hath *t* away all that was	Gen 31:1	3947
Thus God hath *t* away the cattle	Gen 31:9	5337
which God hath *t* from our father	Gen 31:16	5337
as captives *t* with the sword	Gen 31:26	
Now Rachel had *t* the images	Gen 31:34	3947
hast thou *t* us away to die in the	Ex 14:11	3947
they shall not be *t* from it	Ex 25:15	5493
when the cloud was *t* up from over	Ex 40:36	5927
But if the cloud were not *t* up	Ex 40:37	5927
not till the day that it was *t* up	Ex 40:37	5927
As it was *t* off from the bullock	Lev 4:10	7311
as the fat is *t* away from off the	Lev 4:31	7311
as the fat of the lamb is *t* away	Lev 4:35	7311
or in a thing *t* away by violence,	Lev 6:2	1497
the heave shoulder have I *t* of	Lev 7:34	3947
that he hath *t* away the stones	Lev 14:43	2502
being *t* from the children of	Lev 24:8	
I have *t* the Levites from among	Num 3:12	3947
neither she be *t* with the manner	Num 5:13	8610
of Israel, have I *t* them unto me	Num 8:16	3947
I have *t* the Levites for all the	Num 8:18	3947
when the cloud was *t* up from the	Num 9:17	5927
the cloud was *t* up in the morning	Num 9:21	5927
by night that the cloud was *t* up	Num 9:21	5927
but when it was *t* up, they	Num 9:22	5927
that the cloud was *t* up from off	Num 10:11	5927
And the tabernacle was *t* down	Num 10:17	3381
I have not *t* one ass from them,	Num 16:15	5375
I have *t* your brethren the	Num 18:6	3947
t all his land out of his hand,	Num 21:26	3947
the sum of the prey that was *t*	Num 31:26	7628
Thy servants have *t* the sum of	Num 31:49	5375
(For the men of war had *t* spoil	Num 31:53	
be *t* from the inheritance of our	Num 36:3	1639
so shall it be *t* from the lot of	Num 36:3	1639
be *t* away from the inheritance of	Num 36:4	1639
But the LORD hath *t* you, and	Deut 4:20	3947
a wife, and hath not *t* her	Deut 20:7	3947
thou hast *t* them captive,	Deut 21:10	
When a man hath *t* a wife, and	Deut 24:1	3947
When a man hath *t* a new wife	Deut 24:5	3947
cheer up his wife which he hath *t*	Deut 24:5	3947
neither have I *t* away ought	Deut 26:14	1197

t away from before thy face ... Deut 28:31 1497
for they have even *t* of the ... Josh 7:11 3947
that he that is *t* with the ... Josh 7:15 3920
and the tribe of Judah was *t* ... Josh 7:16 3920
and Zabdi was *t* ... Josh 7:17 3920
of the tribe of Judah, was *t* ... Josh 7:18 3920
shall be, when ye have *t* the city ... Josh 8:8 8610
that the ambush had *t* the city ... Josh 8:21 3920
had heard how Joshua had *t* Ai ... Josh 10:1 3920
against Jerusalem, and had *t* it ... Judg 1:8 3920
forasmuch as the LORD hath *t* ... Judg 11:36 6213
he told not them that he had *t* ... Judg 14:9 7287
because he had *t* his wife ... Judg 15:6 3947
of silver that were *t* from thee ... Judg 17:2 3947
Ye have *t* away my gods which I ... Judg 18:24 3947
And the ark of God was *t* ... 1Sa 4:11 3947
are dead, and the ark of God is *t* ... 1Sa 4:17 3947
tidings that the ark of God was *t* ... 1Sa 4:19 3947
because the ark of God was *t* ... 1Sa 4:21 3947
for the ark of God is *t* ... 1Sa 4:22 3947
which the Philistines had *t* from ... 1Sa 7:14 3947
near, the tribe of Benjamin was *t* ... 1Sa 10:20 3920
the family of Matri was *t* ... 1Sa 10:21 3920
and Saul the son of Kish was *t* ... 1Sa 10:21 3920
whose ox have I *t* ... 1Sa 12:3 3947
or whose ass have I *t* ... 1Sa 12:3 3947
neither hast thou *t* ought of any ... 1Sa 12:4 3947
And Saul and Jonathan were *t* ... 1Sa 14:41 3920
And Jonathan was *t* ... 1Sa 14:42 3920
that was *t* from before the LORD, ... 1Sa 21:6 5493
in the day when it was *t* away ... 1Sa 21:6 3947
had *t* the women captives, that ... 1Sa 30:2
their daughters, were *t* captives ... 1Sa 30:3
David's two wives were *t* captives ... 1Sa 30:5
they had *t* out of the land of the ... 1Sa 30:16 3947
any thing that they had *t* to them ... 1Sa 30:19 3947
hast *t* his wife to be thy wife, ... 2Sa 12:9 3947
hast *t* the wife of Uriah the ... 2Sa 12:10 3947
have *t* the city of waters ... 2Sa 12:27 3920
thou art *t* in thy mischief, ... 2Sa 16:8
he was *t* up between the heaven and ... 2Sa 18:9 5414
Now Absalom in his lifetime had *t* ... 2Sa 18:18 3947
they cannot be *t* with hands ... 2Sa 23:6 3947
daughter, whom he had *t* to wife ... 1Kin 7:8 3947
have *t* hold upon other gods, and ... 1Kin 9:9 2388
t Gezer, and burnt it with fire, ... 1Kin 9:16 3920
Zimri saw that the city was *t* ... 1Kin 16:18 3920
thou killed, and also *t* possession ... 1Kin 21:19
the high places were not *t* away ... 1Kin 22:43 5493
before I be *t* away from thee ... 2Kin 2:9 3947
thou see me when I am *t* from thee ... 2Kin 2:10 3947
Spirit of the LORD hath *t* him up ... 2Kin 2:16 5375
And when he had *t* him, and brought ... 2Kin 4:20 5375
hast *t* captive with thy sword ... 2Kin 6:22
the high places were not *t* away ... 2Kin 12:3 5493
which he had *t* out of the hand of ... 2Kin 13:25 3947
the high places were not *t* away ... 2Kin 14:4 5493
king of Israel, Samaria was *t* ... 2Kin 18:10 3920
whose altars Hezekiah hath *t* away ... 2Kin 18:22 5493
for the king of Babylon had *t* ... 2Kin 24:7 3947
household being *t* for Eleazar ... 1Chr 24:6 270
for Eleazar, and one *t* for Ithamar ... 1Chr 24:6 270
which he had *t* from mount Ephraim ... 2Chr 15:8 3920
were not *t* away out of Israel ... 2Chr 15:17 5493
which Asa his father had *t* ... 2Chr 17:2 3920
in that thou hast *t* away the ... 2Chr 19:3 1197
the high places were not *t* away ... 2Chr 20:33 5493
which ye have *t* captive of your ... 2Chr 28:11
had *t* Beth-shemesh, and Ajalon, and ... 2Chr 28:18 3920
For the king had *t* counsel ... 2Chr 30:2
Hezekiah *t* away his high places ... 2Chr 32:12 5493
For they have *t* of their ... Ezr 9:2 5375
have *t* strange wives of the ... Ezr 10:2 3427
have *t* strange wives, to increase ... Ezr 10:10 3427
let all them which have *t* strange ... Ezr 10:14 3427
end with all the men that had *t* ... Ezr 10:17 3427
found that had *t* strange wives ... Ezr 10:18 3427
All these had *t* strange wives ... Ezr 10:44 5375
had *t* of them bread and wine, ... Neh 5:15 3947
his son Johanan had *t* the ... Neh 6:18 3947
who had *t* her for his daughter, ... Est 2:15 3947
So Esther was *t* unto king ... Est 2:16 3947
ring, which he had *t* from Haman ... Est 8:2 5674
gave, and the LORD hath *t* away ... Job 1:21 3947
he hath also *t* me by my neck, and ... Job 16:12 247
and *t* the crown from my head ... Job 19:9 5493
because he hath violently *t* away ... Job 20:19 1497
For thou hast *t* a pledge from thy ... Job 22:6 2254
they are *t* out of the way as all ... Job 24:24 7092
who hath *t* away my judgment ... Job 27:2 5493
Iron is *t* out of the earth, and ... Job 28:2 3947
of affliction have *t* hold upon me ... Job 30:16 270
God hath *t* away my judgment ... Job 34:5 5493
shall be *t* away without hand ... Job 34:20 5493
they hid is their own foot *t* ... Ps 9:15 3920
let them be *t* in the devices that ... Ps 10:2 8610
iniquities have *t* hold upon me ... Ps 40:12 5381
let them even be *t* in their pride ... Ps 59:12 3920
They have *t* crafty counsel ... Ps 83:3
Thou hast *t* away all thy wrath ... Ps 85:3 5375
Horror hath *t* hold upon me ... Ps 119:53 270
Thy testimonies have I *t* as an ... Ps 119:111
and anguish have *t* hold on me ... Ps 119:143 4672
shall keep thy foot from being *t* ... Prov 3:26 3921
and their sleep is *t* away, unless ... Prov 4:16 1497
thou art *t* with the words of thy ... Prov 6:2 3920
He hath *t* a bag of money with him ... Prov 7:20 3947
be *t* in their own naughtiness ... Prov 11:6 3920
which I had *t* under the sun ... Eccl 2:18 6001
to it, nor any thing *t* from it ... Eccl 3:14 1639
but the sinner shall be *t* by her ... Eccl 7:26 3920
fishes that are *t* in an evil net ... Eccl 9:12 270
which he had *t* with the tongs ... Is 6:6 3947
and thine iniquity is *t* away ... Is 6:7 5493
have *t* evil counsel against thee, ... Is 7:5
the spoil of Samaria shall be *t* ... Is 8:4 5375
be broken, and be snared, and be *t* ... Is 8:15 3920
that his burden shall be *t* away ... Is 10:27 5493
they have *t* up their lodging at ... Is 10:29 3885
And gladness is *t* away, and joy out ... Is 16:10 622
Damascus is *t* away from being a ... Is 17:1 5493
pangs have *t* hold upon me, as the ... Is 21:3 270
Who hath *t* this counsel against ... Is 23:8
the pit shall be *t* in the snare ... Is 24:18 3920
and be broken, and snared, and *t* ... Is 28:13 3920
that shall not be *t* down ... Is 33:20 6813
whose altars Hezekiah hath *t* away ... Is 36:7 5493
Thou whom I have *t* from the ends ... Is 41:9 2388
the prey be *t* from the mighty ... Is 49:24 3947
of the mighty shall be *t* away ... Is 49:25 3947
I have *t* out of thine hand the ... Is 51:22 3947
my people is *t* away for nought ... Is 52:5 3947
He was *t* from prison and from ... Is 53:8 3947
and merciful men are *t* away ... Is 57:1 622
that the righteous is *t* away from ... Is 57:1 622
like the wind, have *t* us away ... Is 64:6 5375
husband with the wife shall be *t* ... Jer 6:11 3920
anguish hath *t* hold of us ... Jer 6:24 2388
ashamed, they are dismayed and *t* ... Jer 8:9
astonishment hath *t* hold on me ... Jer 8:21 2388
them, yea, they have *t* root ... Jer 12:2
for I have *t* away my peace from ... Jer 16:5 622
of them shall be *t* up a curse by ... Jer 29:22 3947
his hand, but shalt surely be *t* ... Jer 34:3 8610
but shalt be *t* by the hand of the ... Jer 38:23 8610
the day that Jerusalem was *t* ... Jer 38:28 3920
he was there when Jerusalem was *t* ... Jer 38:28 3920
and when they had *t* him, they ... Jer 39:5 3947
when he had *t* him being bound in ... Jer 40:1 3947
in your cities that ye have *t* ... Jer 40:10 8610
Kiriathaim is confounded and *t* ... Jer 48:1 3920
treasures, thou shalt also be *t* ... Jer 48:7 3920
gladness is *t* from the plentiful ... Jer 48:33 622
Kerioth is *t*, and the strong holds ... Jer 48:41 3920
the pit shall be *t* in the snare ... Jer 48:44 3920
for thy sons are *t* captives ... Jer 48:46 3947
LORD, that he hath *t* against Edom ... Jer 49:20 3289
anguish and sorrows have *t* her ... Jer 49:24 270
hath *t* counsel against you ... Jer 49:30
say, Babylon is *t*, Bel is ... Jer 50:2 3920
from thence she shall be *t* ... Jer 50:9 3920
for thee, and thou art also *t* ... Jer 50:24 3920
that he hath *t* against Babylon ... Jer 50:45 3289
that his city is *t* at one end ... Jer 51:31 3920
How is Sheshach *t* ... Jer 51:41 3920
Babylon, and her mighty men are *t* ... Jer 51:56 3920
he hath violently *t* away his ... Lam 2:6
was *t* in their pits, of whom we ... Lam 4:20 3920
him, and he shall be *t* in my snare ... Eze 12:13 8610
Shall wood be *t* thereof to do any ... Eze 15:3 3947
Thou hast also *t* thy fair jewels ... Eze 16:17 3947
Moreover thou hast *t* thy sons ... Eze 16:20 3947
with whom thou hast *t* pleasure ... Eze 16:37
hath *t* the king thereof, and the ... Eze 17:12 3947
hath *t* of the king's seed, and ... Eze 17:13 3947
him, and hath *t* an oath of him ... Eze 17:13 935
he hath also *t* the mighty of the ... Eze 17:13 3947
him, and he shall be *t* in my snare ... Eze 17:20 8610
neither hath *t* any increase ... Eze 18:8 3947
upon usury, and hath *t* increase ... Eze 18:13 3947
That hath *t* off his hand from the ... Eze 18:17 7725
he was *t* in their pit, and they ... Eze 19:4 8610
he was *t* in their pit ... Eze 19:8 8610
the iniquity, that they may be *t* ... Eze 21:23 8610
ye shall be *t* with the hand ... Eze 21:24 8610
In thee have they *t* gifts to shed ... Eze 22:12 3947
thou hast *t* usury and increase, and ... Eze 22:12 3947
they have *t* the treasure and ... Eze 22:25 3947
and have *t* vengeance with a ... Eze 25:15
they have *t* cedars from Lebanon ... Eze 27:5 3947
he is *t* away in his iniquity ... Eze 33:6 3947
ye are *t* up in the lips of ... Eze 36:3 5927
his father Nebuchadnezzar had *t* ... Dan 5:2 5312
the golden vessels that were *t* ... Dan 5:3 5312
So Daniel was *t* up out of the den ... Dan 6:23 5267
they had their dominion *t* away ... Dan 7:12 5709
the daily sacrifice was *t* away ... Dan 8:11 7311
when he hath *t* away the multitude ... Dan 11:12 5375
daily sacrifice shall be *t* away ... Dan 12:11 5493
of the sea also shall be *t* away ... Hos 4:3 622
Because ye have *t* my silver ... Joel 3:5 3947
of his den, if he have *t* nothing ... Amos 3:4 3920
earth, and have *t* nothing at all ... Amos 3:5 3947
be *t* out that dwell in Samaria in ... Amos 3:12 5337
sword, and have *t* away your horses ... Amos 4:10 7628
Have we not *t* to us horns by our ... Amos 6:13 3947
have ye *t* away my glory for ever ... Mic 2:9 3947
for pangs have *t* thee as a woman ... Mic 4:9 2388
The LORD hath *t* away thy ... Zeph 3:15 5493
and the city shall be *t*, and the ... Zec 14:2 3947
that were *t* with divers diseases ... Mt 4:24 *4912*
bridegroom shall be *t* from them ... Mt 9:15 *522*
from him shall be *t* away even ... Mt 13:12 *142*
It is because we have *t* no bread ... Mt 16:7 *2983*
of God shall be *t* from you ... Mt 21:43 *142*
the one shall be *t*, and the other ... Mt 24:40 *3880*
the one shall be *t*, and the other ... Mt 24:41 *3880*
be *t* away even that which he hath ... Mt 25:29 *142*
And when Joseph had *t* the body ... Mt 27:59 *2983*
had *t* counsel, they gave large ... Mt 28:12 *2983*
shall be *t* away from them ... Mk 2:20 *522*
from him shall be *t* even that ... Mk 4:25 *142*
when he had *t* the five loaves and ... Mk 6:41 *2983*
when he had *t* him in his arms, he ... Mk 9:36 *1723*
Forasmuch as many have *t* in hand ... Lk 1:1 *2021*
mother was *t* with a great fever ... Lk 4:38 *4912*
all the night, and have *t* nothing ... Lk 5:5 *2983*
of the fishes which they had *t* ... Lk 5:9 *4815*
a man which was *t* with a palsy ... Lk 5:18
shall be *t* away from them ... Lk 5:35 *522*
the piece that was *t* out of the ... Lk 5:36
from him shall be *t* even that ... Lk 8:18 *142*
for they were *t* with great fear ... Lk 8:37 *4912*
there was *t* up of fragments that ... Lk 9:17 *142*
shall not be *t* away from her ... Lk 10:42 *851*
for ye have *t* away the key of ... Lk 11:52 *142*
the one shall be *t*, and the other ... Lk 17:34 *3880*
the one shall be *t*, and the other ... Lk 17:35 *3880*
the one shall be *t*, and the other ... Lk 17:36 *3880*
if I have *t* any thing from any ... Lk 19:8
he hath shall be *t* away from him ... Lk 19:26 *142*
And some of them would have *t* him ... Jn 7:44 *4084*
unto him a woman *t* in adultery ... Jn 8:3 *2638*
this woman was *t* in adultery ... Jn 8:4 *2638*
had *t* his garments, and was set ... Jn 13:12 *2983*
and that they might be *t* away ... Jn 19:31 *142*
seeth the stone *t* away from the ... Jn 20:1 *142*
They have *t* away the Lord out of ... Jn 20:2 *142*
Because they have *t* away my Lord ... Jn 20:13 *142*
the day in which he was *t* up ... Acts 1:2 *353*
while they beheld, he was *t* up ... Acts 1:9 *1869*
which is *t* up from you into ... Acts 1:11 *353*
same day that he was *t* up from us ... Acts 1:22 *353*
foreknowledge of God, ye have *t* ... Acts 2:23 *2983*
many *t* with palsies, and that were ... Acts 8:7
his judgment was *t* away ... Acts 8:33 *142*
for his life is *t* from the earth ... Acts 8:33 *142*
when they had *t* security of Jason ... Acts 17:9 *2983*
the third loft, and was *t* up dead ... Acts 20:9 *142*
when we had *t* our leave one of ... Acts 21:6 *782*
This man was *t* of the Jews ... Acts 23:27 *4815*
Which when they had *t* up, they ... Acts 27:17 *142*
should be saved was then *t* away ... Acts 27:20 *4014*
fasting, having *t* nothing ... Acts 27:33 *4355*
when they had *t* up the anchors, ... Acts 27:40 *4014*
word of God hath *t* none effect ... Rom 9:6
might be *t* away from among you ... 1Cor 5:2 *1808*
There hath no temptation *t* you ... 1Cor 10:13 *2983*
Lord, the vail shall be *t* away ... 2Cor 3:16 *4014*
being *t* from you for a short time ... 1Th 2:17 *642*
until he be *t* out of the way ... 2Th 2:7 *1096*
Let not a widow be *t* into the ... 1Ti 5:9 *2639*
who are *t* captive by him at his ... 2Ti 2:26 *2221*
For every high priest *t* from ... Heb 5:1 *2983*
brute beasts, made to be *t* ... 2Pet 2:12 *259*
And when he had *t* the book ... Rev 5:8 *2983*
because thou hast *t* to thee thy ... Rev 11:17 *2983*
And the beast was *t*, and with him ... Rev 19:20 *4084*

TAKER

as with the *t* of usury, so with ... Is 24:2

TAKEST

the water which thou *t* out of the ... Ex 4:9 3947
When thou *t* the sum of the ... Ex 30:12 5375
the journey that thou *t* shall not ... Judg 4:9 1980
if thou *t* heed to fulfil the ... 1Chr 22:13 8104
thou *t* away their breath, they ... Ps 104:29 622
that thou *t* knowledge of him ... Ps 144:3 3947
labour which thou *t* under the sun ... Eccl 9:9 6001
our soul, and thou *t* no knowledge ... Is 58:3
thou *t* up that thou layedst not ... Lk 19:21 *142*

TAKETH

guiltless that *t* his name in vain ... Ex 20:7 5375
guiltless that *t* his name in vain ... Deut 5:11 5375
not persons, nor *t* reward ... Deut 10:17 3947
for he *t* a man's life to pledge ... Deut 24:6 2254
her hand, and *t* him by the secrets ... Deut 25:11 2388
Cursed be he that *t* reward to ... Deut 27:25 3947
t them, beareth them on her wings ... Deut 32:11 3947
t shall come according to the ... Josh 7:14 [illegible]
t it, to him will I give Achsah ... Josh 15:16 3920
t it, to him will I give Achsah ... Judg 1:12 3920
t away the reproach from Israel ... 1Sa 17:26 5493
as a man *t* away dung, till it be ... 1Kin 14:10 1197
t it even out of the thorns, and ... Job 5:5 3947
He *t* the wise in their own ... Job 5:13 3920
he *t* away, who can hinder him ... Job 9:12 2862
t away the understanding of the ... Job 12:20 3947
He *t* away the heart of the chief ... Job 12:24 5493
trembling *t* hold on my flesh ... Job 21:6 270
gained, when God *t* away his soul ... Job 27:8 7953
He *t* it with his eyes ... Job 40:24 3947
nor *t* up a reproach against his ... Ps 15:3 5375
nor *t* reward against the innocent ... Ps 15:5 3947
The LORD *t* my part with them that ... Ps 118:7
Happy shall he be, that *t* ... Ps 137:9 270
he *t* not pleasure in the legs of ... Ps 147:10
The LORD *t* pleasure in them that ... Ps 147:11
For the LORD *t* pleasure in his ... Ps 149:4
which *t* away the life of the ... Prov 1:19 3947
his spirit than he that *t* a city ... Prov 16:32 3920
A wicked man *t* a gift out of the ... Prov 17:23 3947
As he that *t* away a garment in ... Prov 25:20 5710
is like one that *t* a dog by the ... Prov 26:17 2388
The spider *t* hold with her hands, ... Prov 30:28 8610
labour which he *t* under the sun ... Eccl 1:3 5998
his heart *t* not rest in the night ... Eccl 2:23
t under the sun all the days of ... Eccl 5:18 5998
and as a sheep that no man *t* up ... Is 13:14 6908
he *t* up the isles as a very ... Is 40:15 5190
t the cypress and the oak, which ... Is 44:14 3947
neither is there any that *t* her ... Is 51:18 2388
it, and *t* hold of my covenant ... Is 56:6 2388
which *t* strangers instead of her ... Eze 16:32 3947
of the trumpet, and *t* not warning ... Eze 33:4
But he that *t* warning shall ... Eze 33:5
As the shepherd *t* out of the ... Amos 3:12 5337
Then the devil *t* him up into the ... Mt 4:5 *3880*
the devil *t* him up into an ... Mt 4:8 *3880*
to fill it up *t* from the garment ... Mt 9:16 *142*
he that *t* not his cross, and ... Mt 10:38 *2983*

t with himself seven other Mt 12:45 3880
And after six days Jesus *t* Peter Mt 17:1 3880
filled it up *t* away from the old Mk 2:21 142
t away the word that was sown in Mk 4:15 142
he *t* the father and the mother of Mk 5:40 3880
six days Jesus *t* with him Peter Mk 9:2 3880
And wheresoever he *t* him, he Mk 9:18 2638
he *t* with him Peter and James and Mk 14:33 3880
him that *t* away thy cloke forbid Lk 6:29 142
of him that *t* away thy goods ask Lk 6:30 142
t away the word out of their Lk 8:12 142
And, lo, a spirit *t* him, and he Lk 9:39 2983
he *t* from him all his armour Lk 11:22 142
t to him seven other spirits more Lk 11:26 3880
for my lord *t* away from me the Lk 16:3 851
which *t* away the sin of the world Jn 1:29 142
No man *t* it from me, but I lay it Jn 10:18 142
that beareth not fruit he *t* away Jn 15:2 142
and your joy no man *t* from you Jn 16:22 142
t bread, and giveth them, and fish Jn 21:13 2983
God unrighteous who *t* vengeance Rom 3:5 2018
He *t* the wise in their own 1Cor 3:19 1405
For in eating every one *t* before 1Cor 11:21 4301
no man *t* this honour unto himself Heb 5:4 2983
He *t* away the first, that he may Heb 10:9 337

TAKING
of persons, nor *t* of gifts 2Chr 19:7 4727
I have seen the foolish *t* root Job 5:3
by *t* heed thereto according to Ps 119:9
At the noise of the *t* of Babylon Jer 50:46 8610
the house of Judah by *t* vengeance Eze 25:12
also to go, *t* them by their arms Hos 11:3 3947
Which of you by *t* thought can add Mt 6:27
man is as a man *t* a far journey Mk 13:34
t him up into an high mountain, Lk 4:5 321
which of you with *t* thought can Lk 12:25
t up that I laid not down, and Lk 19:22 142
had spoken of *t* of rest in sleep Jn 11:13
t occasion by the commandment, Rom 7:8 2983
t occasion by the commandment, Rom 7:11 2983
but *t* my leave of them, I went 2Cor 2:13
t wages of them, to do you 2Cor 11:8 2983
t the shield of faith, wherewith Eph 6:16 353
In flaming fire *t* vengeance on 2Th 1:8 1325
t the oversight thereof, not by 1Pet 5:2
t nothing of the Gentiles 3Jn 7 2983

TALE
the *t* of the bricks, which they Ex 5:8 4971
shall ye deliver the *t* of bricks Ex 5:18 8506
gave them in full *t* to the king 1Sa 18:27
should bring them in and out by *t* 1Chr 9:28 4557
our years as a *t* that is told Ps 90:9 1899

TALEBEARER
down as a *t* among thy people Lev 19:16 7400
A *t* revealeth secrets Prov 11:13
The words of a *t* are as wounds Prov 18:8 5372
about as a *t* revealeth secrets Prov 20:19 7400
so where there is no *t*, the Prov 26:20 5372
The words of a *t* are as wounds Prov 26:22 5372

TALENT
Of a *t* of pure gold shall he make Ex 25:39 3603
Of a *t* of pure gold made he it, Ex 37:24 3603
hundred talents, a *t* for a socket Ex 38:27 3603
the weight whereof was a *t* of 2Sa 12:30 3603
else thou shalt pay a *t* of silver 1Kin 20:39 3603
a *t* of silver, and two changes of 2Kin 5:22 3603
talents of silver, and a *t* of gold 2Kin 23:33 3603
and found it to weigh a *t* of gold 1Chr 20:2 3603
talents of silver and a *t* of gold 2Chr 36:3 3603
there was lifted up a *t* of lead Zec 5:7 3603
which had received the one *t* came Mt 25:24 5007
and went and hid thy *t* in the earth Mt 25:25 5007
Take therefore the *t* from him Mt 25:28 5007
stone about the weight of a *t* Rev 16:21 5006

TALENTS
offering, was twenty and nine *t* Ex 38:24 3603
the congregation was an hundred *t* Ex 38:25 3603
of the hundred *t* of silver were Ex 38:27 3603
hundred sockets of the hundred *t* Ex 38:27 3603
of the offering was seventy *t* Ex 38:29 3603
to the king sixscore *t* of gold 1Kin 9:14 3603
gold, four hundred and twenty *t* 1Kin 9:28 3603
twenty *t* of gold, and of spices 1Kin 10:10 3603
threescore and six *t* of gold, 1Kin 10:14 3603
of Shemer for two *t* of silver 1Kin 16:24 3603
and took with him ten *t* of silver 2Kin 5:5 3603
said, Be content, take two *t* 2Kin 5:23 3603
bound two *t* of silver in two bags 2Kin 5:23 3603
gave Pul a thousand *t* of silver 2Kin 15:19 3603
Judah three hundred *t* of silver 2Kin 18:14 3603
of silver and thirty *t* of gold 2Kin 18:14 3603
tribute of an hundred *t* of silver 2Kin 23:33 3603
of Ammon sent a thousand *t* of 1Chr 19:6 3603
an hundred thousand *t* of gold 1Chr 22:14 3603
a thousand thousand *t* of silver 1Chr 22:14 3603
Even three thousand *t* of gold 1Chr 29:4 3603
seven thousand *t* of refined 1Chr 29:4 3603
of God of gold five thousand *t* 1Chr 29:7 3603
and of silver ten thousand *t* 1Chr 29:7 3603
and of brass eighteen thousand *t* 1Chr 29:7 3603
and one hundred thousand *t* of iron 1Chr 29:7 3603
gold, amounting to six hundred *t* 2Chr 3:8 3603
fifty *t* of gold, and brought them 2Chr 8:18 3603
twenty *t* of gold, and of spices 2Chr 9:9 3603
and threescore and six *t* of gold 2Chr 9:13 3603
Israel for an hundred *t* of silver 2Chr 25:6 3603
shall we do for the hundred *t* 2Chr 25:9 3603
same year an hundred *t* of silver 2Chr 27:5 3603
land in an hundred *t* of silver 2Chr 36:3 3603
Unto an hundred *t* of silver Ezr 7:22 3604
fifty *t* of silver, and silver Ezr 8:26 3603
and silver vessels an hundred *t* Ezr 8:26 3603
and of gold an hundred *t* Ezr 8:26 3603
I will pay ten thousand *t* of Est 3:9 3603
which owed him ten thousand *t* Mt 18:24 5007
And unto one he gave five *t* Mt 25:15 5007
that had received the five *t* went Mt 25:16 5007
same, and made them other five *t* Mt 25:16 5007
he that had received five *t* came Mt 25:20 5007
came and brought other five *t* Mt 25:20 5007
thou deliveredst unto me five *t* Mt 25:20 5007
gained beside them five *t* more Mt 25:20 5007
also that had received two *t* came Mt 25:22 5007
thou deliveredst unto me two *t* Mt 25:22 5007
gained two other *t* beside them Mt 25:22 5007
give it unto him which hath ten *t* Mt 25:28 5007

TALES
men that carry *t* to shed blood Eze 22:9 7400
words seemed to them as idle *t* Lk 24:11 3026

TALITHA (*tal'-ith-ah*) *Aramaic for damsel.*
hand, and said unto her, *T* cumi Mk 5:41 5008

TALK
come down and *t* with thee there Num 11:17 1696
this day that God doth *t* with man Deut 5:24 1696
shalt *t* of them when thou sittest Deut 6:7 1696
T no more so exceeding proudly 1Sa 2:3 1696
t not with us in the Jews' 2Kin 18:26 1696
t ye of all his wondrous works 1Chr 16:9 7878
a man full of *t* be justified Job 11:2 8193
and *t* deceitfully for him Job 13:7 1696
he reason with unprofitable *t* Job 15:3 1697
they *t* to the grief of those whom Ps 69:26 5608
My tongue also shall *t* of thy Ps 71:24 1897
all thy work, and *t* of thy doings Ps 77:12 7878
t ye of all his wondrous works Ps 105:2 7878
so shall I *t* of thy wondrous Ps 119:27 7878
of thy kingdom, and *t* of thy power Ps 145:11 1696
awakest, it shall *t* with thee Prov 6:22 7878
but the *t* of the lips tendeth Prov 14:23 1697
and their lips *t* of mischief Prov 24:2 1696
the end of his *t* is mischievous Eccl 10:13 6310
yet let me *t* with thee of thy Jer 12:1 1696
and I will there *t* with thee Eze 3:22 1696
this my lord *t* with this my lord Dan 10:17 1696
they might entangle him in his *t* Mt 22:15 3056
I will not *t* much with you Jn 14:30 2980

TALKED
Cain *t* with Abel his brother Gen 4:8 559
and God *t* with him, saying, Gen 17:3 1696
in the place where he *t* with him Gen 35:13 1696
in the place where he *t* with him Gen 35:14 1696
that his brethren *t* with him Gen 45:15 1696
I have *t* with you from heaven Ex 20:22 1696
and the LORD *t* with Moses Ex 33:9 1696
face shone while he *t* with him Ex 34:29 1696
and Moses *t* with them Ex 34:31 1696
The LORD *t* with you face to face Deut 5:4 1696
he went down, and *t* with the woman Judg 14:7 1696
while Saul *t* unto the priest, 1Sa 14:19 1696
as he *t* with them, behold, there 1Sa 17:23 1696
lo, while she yet *t* with the king 1Kin 1:22 1696
pass, as they still went on, and *t* 2Kin 2:11 1696
And while he yet *t* with them 2Kin 6:33 1696
the king *t* with Gehazi the 2Kin 8:4 1696
as he *t* with him, that the king 2Chr 25:16 1696
hear that I have *t* with thee Jer 38:25 1696
t with me, and said, O Daniel, I Dan 9:22 1696
the angel that *t* with me said Zec 1:9 1696
that *t* with me with good words Zec 1:13 1696
unto the angel that *t* with me Zec 1:19 1696
the angel that *t* with me went Zec 2:3 1696
the angel that *t* with me came Zec 4:1 1696
spake to the angel that *t* with me Zec 4:4 1696
the angel that *t* with me answered Zec 4:5 1696
angel that *t* with me went forth Zec 5:5 1696
I to the angel that *t* with me Zec 5:10 1696
unto the angel that *t* with me Zec 6:4 1696
While he yet *t* to the people, Mt 12:46 2980
And immediately he *t* with them Mk 6:50 2980
there *t* with him two men, which Lk 9:30 4814
they *t* together of all these Lk 24:14 3656
while he *t* with us by the way, and Lk 24:32 2980
that he *t* with the woman Jn 4:27 2980
as he *t* with him, he went in, and Acts 10:27 4926
t a long while, even till break Acts 20:11 3656
they *t* between themselves, saying Acts 26:31 2980
t with me, saying unto me, Come Rev 17:1 2980
t with me, saying, Come hither, I Rev 21:9 2980
he that *t* with me had a golden Rev 21:15 2980

TALKERS
ye are taken up in the lips of *t* Eze 36:3 3956
there are many unruly and vain *t* Titus 1:10 3151

TALKEST
me a sign that thou *t* with me Judg 6:17 1696
while thou yet *t* there with the 1Kin 1:14 1696
or, Why *t* thou with her Jn 4:27 2980

TALKETH
and his tongue *t* of judgment Ps 37:30 1696
him, and it is he that *t* with thee Jn 9:37 2980

TALKING
And he left off *t* with him Gen 17:22 1696
either he is *t*, or he is pursuing 1Kin 18:27 7879
And while they were yet *t* with him Est 6:14 1696
The princes refrained *t*, and laid Job 29:9 4405
of thy people still are *t* against Eze 33:30 1696
them Moses and Elias *t* with him Mt 17:3 4814
and they were *t* with Jesus Mk 9:4 4814
Neither filthiness, nor foolish *t* Eph 5:4 3473
as it were of a trumpet *t* with me Rev 4:1 2980

TALL
a people great, and many, and *t* Deut 2:10 7311
A people great, and many, and *t* Deut 2:21 7311
A people great and *t*, the children Deut 9:2 7311
will cut down the *t* cedar trees 2Kin 19:23 6967
cut down the *t* cedars thereof Is 37:24 6967

TALLER
people is greater and *t* than we Deut 1:28 7311

TALMAI (*tal'-mahee*)
1. A son of Anak.
where Ahiman, Sheshai, and *T* Num 13:22 8526
of Anak, Sheshai, and Ahiman, and *T*.. Josh 15:14 8526
slew Sheshai, and Ahiman, and *T* Judg 1:10 8526
2. A king of Geshur.
the daughter of *T* king of Geshur 2Sa 3:3 8526
But Absalom fled, and went to *T* 2Sa 13:37 8526
the daughter of *T* king of Geshur 1Chr 3:2 8526

TALMON (*tal'-mon*) *A Levite in Jerusalem.*
were, Shallum, and Akkub, and *T* 1Chr 9:17 2929
of Ater, the children of *T* Ezr 2:42 2929
of Ater, the children of *T* Neh 7:45 2929
Moreover the porters, Akkub, *T* Neh 11:19 2929
Bakbukiah, Obadiah, Meshullam, *T* Neh 12:25 2929

TAMAH (*ta'-mah*) See THAMAH. *A family of exiles.*
of Sisera, the children of *T* Neh 7:55 8547

TAMAR (*ta'-mar*) See THAMAR.
1. Wife of Er.
his firstborn, whose name was *T* Gen 38:6 8559
Then said Judah to *T* his daughter Gen 38:11 8559
T went and dwelt in her father's Gen 38:11 8559
And it was told *T*, saying, Behold Gen 38:13 8559
T thy daughter in law hath played Gen 38:24 8559
whom *T* bare unto Judah, of the Ruth 4:12 8559
T his daughter in law bare him 1Chr 2:4 8559
2. A daughter of David.
a fair sister, whose name was *T* 2Sa 13:1 8559
he fell sick for his sister *T* 2Sa 13:2 8559
And Amnon said unto him, I love *T* 2Sa 13:4 8559
I pray thee, let my sister *T* come 2Sa 13:5 8559
let *T* my sister come, and make me 2Sa 13:6 8559
Then David sent home to *T* 2Sa 13:7 8559
So *T* went to her brother Amnon's 2Sa 13:8 8559
And Amnon said unto *T*, Bring the 2Sa 13:10 8559
T took the cakes which she had 2Sa 13:10 8559
T put ashes on her head, and rent 2Sa 13:19 8559
So *T* remained desolate in her 2Sa 13:20 8559
he had forced his sister *T* 2Sa 13:22 8559
day that he forced his sister *T* 2Sa 13:32 8559
the concubines, and *T* their sister 1Chr 3:9 8559
3. A daughter of Absalom.
and one daughter, whose name was *T*. 2Sa 14:27 8559
4. A city in Judah.
from *T* even to the waters of Eze 47:19 8559
T unto the waters of strife in Eze 48:28 8559

TAME
neither could any man *t* him Mk 5:4 1150
But the tongue can no man *t* Jas 3:8 1150

TAMED
and of things in the sea, is *t* Jas 3:7 1150
and hath been *t* of mankind Jas 3:7 1150

TAMMUZ (*tam'-muz*) *A Syrian god.*
there sat women weeping for *T* Eze 8:14 8542

TANACH (*ta'-nak*) See TAANACH. *Same as Taanach.*
Manasseh, *T* with her suburbs, and Josh 21:25 8590

TANHUMETH (*tan'-hu-meth*) *Father of Seraiah.*
the son of *T* the Netophathite 2Kin 25:23 8576
Kareah, and Seraiah the son of *T* Jer 40:8 8576

TANNER
days in Joppa with one Simon a *t* Acts 9:43 1033
He lodgeth with one Simon a *t* Acts 10:6 1033
of one Simon a *t* by the sea side Acts 10:32 1033

TAPESTRY
decked my bed with coverings of *t* Prov 7:16
She maketh herself coverings of *t* Prov 31:22

TAPHATH (*ta'-fath*) *A daughter of Solomon.*
which had *T* the daughter of 1Kin 4:11 2955

TAPPUAH (*tap'-pu-ah*)
1. A city in Judah.
The king of *T*, one Josh 12:17 8599
And Zanoah, and En-gannim, *T* Josh 15:34 8599
2. A city in Ephraim.
The border went out from *T* Josh 16:8 8599
Now Manasseh had the land of *T* Josh 17:8 8599
but *T* on the border of Manasseh Josh 17:8 8599
3. A son of Hebron.
Korah, and *T*, and Rekem, and Shema. 1Chr 2:43 8599

TARAH (*ta'-rah*) *An Israelite encampment in the wilderness.*
from Tahath, and pitched at *T* Num 33:27 8646
And they removed from *T*, and Num 33:28 8646

TARALAH (*tar'-a-lah*) *A city in Benjamin.*
And Rekem, and Irpeel, and *T* Josh 18:27 8634

TARE
t his garments, and lay on the 2Sa 13:31 7167
t forty and two children of them 2Kin 2:24 1234
him, straightway the spirit *t* him Mk 9:20 4682
devil threw him down, and *t* him Lk 9:42 4952

TAREA (*ta'-re-ah*) See TAHREA. *A son of Micah.*
were, Pithon, and Melech, and *T* 1Chr 8:35 8390

TARES
sowed *t* among the wheat, and went Mt 13:25 *2215*
fruit, then appeared the *t* also Mt 13:26 *2215*
from whence then hath it *t* Mt 13:27 *2215*
lest while ye gather up the *t* Mt 13:29 *2215*
Gather ye together first the *t* Mt 13:30 *2215*
the parable of the *t* of the field Mt 13:36 *2215*
but the *t* are the children of the Mt 13:38 *2215*
As therefore the *t* are gathered Mt 13:40 *2215*

TARGET
legs, and a *t* of brass between his 1Sa 17:6 3591
shekels of gold went to one *t* 1Kin 10:16 6793
of beaten gold went to one *t* 2Chr 9:15 6793

TARGETS
made two hundred *t* of beaten gold 1Kin 10:16 6793
made two hundred *t* of beaten gold 2Chr 9:15 6793
had an army of men that bare *t* 2Chr 14:8 6793

TARPELITES (*tar'-pel-ites*) *Foreigners resettled in Israel.*
the Apharsathchites, the *T* Ezr 4:9 2967

TARRIED
were with him, and *t* all night Gen 24:54 3885
t there all night, because the Gen 28:11 3885
and *t* all night in the mount Gen 31:54 3885
when the cloud *t* long upon the Num 9:19 748
that the cloud *t* upon the Num 9:22 748
they *t* till they were ashamed Judg 3:25 2342
And Ehud escaped while they *t* Judg 3:26 4102
they *t* until afternoon, and they Judg 19:8 4102
that she *t* a little in the house Ruth 2:7 3427
he *t* seven days, according to the 1Sa 13:8 3176
Saul *t* in the uttermost part of 1Sa 14:2 3427
But David *t* still at Jerusalem 2Sa 11:1 3427
t in a place that was far off 2Sa 15:17 5975
and they *t* there 2Sa 15:29 3427
but he *t* longer than the set time 2Sa 20:5 3186
(for he *t* at Jericho,) he said 2Kin 2:18 3427
But David *t* at Jerusalem 1Chr 20:1 3427
she that *t* at home divided the Ps 68:12 5116
While the bridegroom *t*, they all Mt 25:5 *5549*
marvelled that he *t* so long in Lk 1:21 *5549*
the child Jesus *t* behind in Lk 2:43 *5278*
there he *t* with them, and baptized Jn 3:22 *1304*
that he *t* many days in Joppa with Acts 9:43 *3306*
And after they had *t* there a space Acts 15:33 *4160*
Paul after this *t* there yet a Acts 18:18 *4357*
going before *t* for us at Troas Acts 20:5 *3306*
at Samos, and *t* at Trogyllium Acts 20:15 *3306*
disciples, we *t* there seven days Acts 21:4 *1961*
as we *t* there many days, there Acts 21:10 *1961*
when he had *t* among them more Acts 25:6 *1304*
the fourteenth day that ye have *t* Acts 27:33 *4328*
Syracuse, we *t* there three days Acts 28:12 *1961*

TARRIEST
And now why *t* thou Acts 22:16 *3195*

TARRIETH
his part be that *t* by the stuff 1Sa 30:24 3427
that *t* not for man, nor waiteth Mic 5:7 6960

TARRY
t all night, and wash your feet, Gen 19:2 3885
t with him a few days, until thy Gen 27:44 3427
found favour in thine eyes, *t* Gen 30:27
come down unto me, *t* not Gen 45:9 5975
out of Egypt, and could not *t* Ex 12:39 4102
T ye here for us, until we come Ex 24:14 3427
shall *t* abroad out of his tent Lev 14:8 3427
t ye also here this night, that I Num 22:19 3427
Why *t* the wheels of his chariots Judg 5:28 309
I will *t* until thou come again Judg 6:18 3427
t all night, and let thine heart Judg 19:6 3885
evening, I pray you *t* all night Judg 19:9 3885
the man would not *t* that night Judg 19:10 3885
Would ye *t* for them till they Ruth 1:13 7663
T this night, and it shall be in Ruth 3:13 3885
t until thou have weaned him 1Sa 1:23 3427
seven days shalt thou *t*, till I 1Sa 10:8 3176
unto us, *T* until we come to you 1Sa 14:9 1826
T at Jericho until your beards be 2Sa 10:5 3427
T here to day also, and to morrow 2Sa 11:12 3427
I will *t* in the plain of the 2Sa 15:28 4102
I may not *t* thus with thee 2Sa 18:14 3176
there will not *t* one with thee 2Sa 19:7 3885
unto Elisha, *T* here, I pray thee 2Kin 2:2 3427
him, Elisha, *t* here, I pray thee 2Kin 2:4 3427
And Elijah said unto him, *T* 2Kin 2:6 3427
if we *t* till the morning light, 2Kin 7:9 2442
open the door, and flee, and *t* not 2Kin 9:3 2442
glory of this, and *t* at home 2Kin 14:10 3427
T at Jericho until your beards be 1Chr 19:5 3427
lies shall not *t* in my sight Ps 101:7 3559
They that *t* long at the wine Prov 23:30 309
off, and my salvation shall not *t* Is 46:13 309
turneth aside to *t* for a night Jer 14:8 3885
though it *t*, wait for it Hab 2:3 4102
will surely come, it will not *t* Hab 2:3 309
t ye here, and watch with me Mt 26:38 *3306*
t ye here, and watch Mk 14:34 *3306*
And he went in to *t* with them Lk 24:29 *3306*
but *t* ye in the city of Jerusalem Lk 24:49 *2523*
him that he would *t* with them Jn 4:40 *3306*
If I will that he *t* till I come Jn 21:22 *3306*
If I will that he *t* till I come Jn 21:23 *3306*
prayed they him to *t* certain days Acts 10:48 *1961*
him to *t* longer time with them Acts 18:20 *3306*
were desired to *t* with them seven Acts 28:14 *1961*
to eat, *t* one for another 1Cor 11:33 *1551*
but I trust to *t* a while with you 1Cor 16:7 *1961*
But I will *t* at Ephesus until 1Cor 16:8 *1961*
But if I *t* long, that thou mayest 1Ti 3:15 *1019*
come will come, and will not *t* Heb 10:37 *5549*

TARRYING
make no *t*, O my God Ps 40:17 309
O LORD, make no *t* Ps 70:5 309

TARSHISH (*tar'-shish*) See THARSHISH.
1. A son of Javan.
Elishah, and *T*, Kittim, and Dodanim Gen 10:4 8659
Elishah, and *T*, Kittim, and Dodanim 1Chr 1:7 8659
2. Spain.
to *T* with the servants of Huram 2Chr 9:21 8659
came the ships of *T* bringing gold 2Chr 9:21 8659
with him to make ships to go to *T* 2Chr 20:36 8659
they were not able to go to *T* 2Chr 20:37 8659
the ships of *T* with an east wind Ps 48:7 8659
The kings of *T* and of the isles Ps 72:10 8659
And upon all the ships of *T* Is 2:16 8659
Howl, ye ships of *T* Is 23:1 8659
Pass ye over to *T* Is 23:6 8659
land as a river, O daughter of *T* Is 23:10 8659
Howl, ye ships of *T* Is 23:14 8659
for me, and the ships of *T* first Is 60:9 8659
of them unto the nations, to *T* Is 66:19 8659
into plates is brought from *T* Jer 10:9 8659
T was thy merchant by reason of Eze 27:12 8659
The ships of *T* did sing of thee Eze 27:25 8659
and Dedan, and the merchants of *T* Eze 38:13 8659
T from the presence of the LORD Jonah 1:3 8659
and he found a ship going to *T* Jonah 1:3 8659
to go with them unto *T* from the Jonah 1:3 8659
Therefore I fled before unto *T* Jonah 4:2 8659
3. A prince of Persia.
was Carshena, Shethar, Admatha, *T* Est 1:14 8659

TARSHISHAH See TARSHISH.

TARSUS (*tar'-sus*) *Capital of Roman province of Cilicia.*
Judas for one called Saul, of *T* Acts 9:11 *5018*
Caesarea, and sent him forth to *T* Acts 9:30 *5019*
Then departed Barnabas to *T* Acts 11:25 *5019*
I am a man which am a Jew of *T* Acts 21:39 *5018*
a man which am a Jew, born in *T* Acts 22:3 *5019*

TARTAK (*tar'-tak*) *A god of the Avites.*
And the Avites made Nibhaz and *T* 2Kin 17:31 8662

TARTAN (*tar'-tan*) *The commander of the Assyrian army.*
And the king of Assyria sent *T* 2Kin 18:17 8661
the year that *T* came unto Ashdod Is 20:1 8661

TASK
have ye not fulfilled your *t* in Ex 5:14 2706
from your bricks of your daily *t* Ex 5:19 1697

TASKMASTERS
they did set over them *t* to Ex 1:11
their cry by reason of their *t* Ex 3:7 5065
the same day the *t* of the people Ex 5:6 5065
the *t* of the people went out, and Ex 5:10 5065
the *t* hasted them, saying, Fulfil Ex 5:13 5065
which Pharaoh's *t* had set over Ex 5:14 5065

TASKS
Fulfil your works, your daily *t* Ex 5:13 1697

TASTE
the *t* of it was like wafers made Ex 16:31 2940
the *t* of it was as the Num 11:8 2940
of it was as the *t* of fresh oil Num 11:8 2940
I did but *t* a little honey with 1Sa 14:43 2938
if I *t* bread, or ought else, till 2Sa 3:35 2938
can thy servant *t* what I eat or 2Sa 19:35 2938
of is there any *t* in the white of Job 6:6 2940
cannot my *t* discern perverse Job 6:30 2441
and the mouth *t* his meat Job 12:11 2938
O *t* and see that the LORD is good Ps 34:8 2938
How sweet are thy words unto my *t* Ps 119:103 2441
which is sweet to thy *t* Prov 24:13 2441
and his fruit was sweet to my *t* Song 2:3 2441
therefore his *t* remained in him, Jer 48:11 2940
herd nor flock, *t* any thing Jonah 3:7 2938
here, which shall not *t* of death Mt 16:28 *1089*
here, which shall not *t* of death Mk 9:1 *1089*
here, which shall not *t* of death Lk 9:27 *1089*
were bidden shall *t* of my supper Lk 14:24 *1089*
saying, he shall never *t* of death Jn 8:52 *1089*
t not Col 2:21 *1089*
God should *t* death for every man Heb 2:9 *1089*

TASTED
So none of the people *t* any food 1Sa 14:24 2938
because I *t* a little of this 1Sa 14:29 2938
Belshazzar, whiles he *t* the wine Dan 5:2 2942
and when he had *t* thereof, he Mt 27:34 *1089*
t the water that was made wine Jn 2:9 *1089*
have *t* of the heavenly gift, and Heb 6:4 *1089*
have *t* the good word of God, and Heb 6:5 *1089*
If so be ye have *t* that the Lord 1Pet 2:3 *1089*

TASTETH
trieth words, as the mouth *t* meat Job 34:3 2938

TATNAI (*tat'-nahee*) *Persian governor of Samaria.*
At the same time came to them *T* Ezr 5:3 8674
The copy of the letter that *T* Ezr 5:6 8674
Now therefore, *T*, governor beyond Ezr 6:6 8674
Then *T*, governor on this side the Ezr 6:13 8674

TATTENAI See TATNAI.

TATTLERS
but *t* also and busybodies, 1Ti 5:13 *5397*

TAUGHT
Behold, I have *t* you statutes and Deut 4:5 3925
t it the children of Israel Deut 31:22 3925
with them he *t* the men of Succoth Judg 8:16 3045
t them how they should fear the 2Kin 17:28 3384
when thou hast *t* them the good 2Chr 6:27 3384
they *t* in Judah, and had the book 2Chr 17:9 3925
cities of Judah, and *t* the people 2Chr 17:9 3925
and such as *t* to sing praise 2Chr 23:13 3045
unto all the Levites that *t* the 2Chr 30:22 7919
the Levites that *t* all Israel 2Chr 35:3 4000
and the Levites that *t* the people Neh 8:9 995
thou hast *t* me from my youth Ps 71:17 3925
for thou hast *t* me Ps 119:102 3384
when thou hast *t* me thy statutes Ps 119:171 3925
He *t* me also, and said unto me, Prov 4:4 3384
I have *t* thee in the way of Prov 4:11 3384
prophecy that his mother *t* him Prov 31:1 3256
he still *t* the people knowledge Eccl 12:9 3925
me is *t* by the precept of men Is 29:13 3925
being his counsellor hath *t* him Is 40:13 3045
t him in the path of judgment, and Is 40:14 3925
t him knowledge, and shewed to him Is 40:14 3925
children shall be *t* of the LORD Is 54:13 3928
also *t* the wicked ones thy ways Jer 2:33 3925
they have *t* their tongue to speak Jer 9:5 3925
which their fathers *t* them Jer 9:14 3925
as they *t* my people to swear by Jer 12:16 3925
for thou hast *t* them to be Jer 13:21 3925
because thou hast *t* rebellion Jer 28:16 1696
because he hath *t* rebellion Jer 29:32 1696
though I *t* them, rising up early Jer 32:33 3925
that all women may be *t* not to do Eze 23:48 3256
Ephraim is as an heifer that is *t* Hos 10:11 3925
I *t* Ephraim also to go, taking Hos 11:3 8637
for man *t* me to keep cattle from Zec 13:5
his mouth, and *t* them, saying, Mt 5:2 *1321*
For he *t* them as one having Mt 7:29
he *t* them in their synagogue, Mt 13:54 *1321*
the money, and did as they were *t* Mt 28:15 *1321*
entered into the synagogue, and *t* Mk 1:21 *1321*
for he *t* them as one that had Mk 1:22
resorted unto him, and he *t* them Mk 2:13 *1321*
he *t* them many things by parables Mk 4:2 *1321*
they had done, and what they had *t* Mk 6:30 *1321*
For he *t* his disciples, and said Mk 9:31 *1321*
as he was wont, he *t* them again Mk 10:1 *1321*
And he *t*, saying unto them, Is it Mk 11:17 *1321*
while he *t* in the temple, How say Mk 12:35 *1321*
he *t* in their synagogues, being Lk 4:15 *1321*
t them on the sabbath days Lk 4:31
t the people out of the ship Lk 5:3 *1321*
entered into the synagogue and *t* Lk 6:6 *1321*
as John also *t* his disciples Lk 11:1 *1321*
thou hast *t* in our streets Lk 13:26 *1321*
And he *t* daily in the temple Lk 19:47
as he *t* the people in the temple, Lk 20:1 *1321*
And they shall be all *t* of God Jn 6:45 *1318*
synagogue, as he *t* in Capernaum Jn 6:59 *1321*
went up into the temple, and *t* Jn 7:14 *1321*
cried Jesus in the temple as he *t* Jn 7:28 *1321*
and he sat down, and *t* them Jn 8:2 *1321*
treasury, as he *t* in the temple Jn 8:20 *1321*
but as my Father hath *t* me Jn 8:28 *1321*
I ever *t* in the synagogue, and in Jn 18:20 *1321*
grieved that they *t* the people Acts 4:2 *1321*
temple early in the morning, and *t* Acts 5:21 *1321*
with the church, and *t* much people Acts 11:26 *1321*
had *t* many, they returned again Acts 14:21 *3100*
down from Judaea *t* the brethren Acts 15:1 *1321*
t diligently the things of the Acts 18:25 *1321*
have *t* you publickly, and from Acts 20:20 *1321*
t according to the perfect manner Acts 22:3 *3811*
it of man, neither was I *t* it Gal 1:12 *1321*
Let him that is *t* in the word Gal 6:6 *2727*
heard him, and have been *t* by him Eph 4:21 *1321*
in the faith, as ye have been *t* Col 2:7 *1321*
for ye yourselves are *t* of God to 1Th 4:9 *2312*
traditions which ye have been *t* 2Th 2:15 *1321*
faithful word as he hath been *t* Titus 1:9 *1322*
no lie, and even as it hath *t* you 1Jn 2:27 *1321*
of Balaam, who *t* Balac to cast a Rev 2:14 *1321*

TAUNT
be a reproach and a proverb, a *t* Jer 24:9 8148
So it shall be a reproach and a *t* Eze 5:15 1422

TAUNTING
a *t* proverb against him, and say, Hab 2:6 4426

TAVERNS
as Appii forum, and The three *t* Acts 28:15 *4999*

TAXATION
of every one according to his *t* 2Kin 23:35 6187

TAXED
but he *t* the land to give the 2Kin 23:35 6186
that all the world should be *t* Lk 2:1 *582*
And all went to be *t*, every one Lk 2:3 *582*
To be *t* with Mary his espoused Lk 2:5 *582*

TAXES
of *t* in the glory of the kingdom Dan 11:20 5065

TAXING
this *t* was first made when Lk 2:2 *583*
of Galilee in the days of the *t* Acts 5:37 *583*

TEACH
t thee what thou shalt say Ex 4:12 3384
will *t* you what ye shall do Ex 4:15 3384
thou shalt *t* them ordinances and Ex 18:20 2094
that thou mayest *t* them Ex 24:12 3384
put in his heart that he may *t* Ex 35:34 3384
that ye may *t* the children of Lev 10:11 3384
To *t* when it is unclean, and when Lev 14:57 3384
unto the judgments, which I *t* you Deut 4:1 3925
but *t* them thy sons, and thy sons' Deut 4:9 3045
that they may *t* their children Deut 4:10 3925
me at that time to *t* you statutes Deut 4:14 3925
which thou shalt *t* them, that Deut 5:31 3925

LORD your God commanded to t you ... Deut 6:1 3925
thou shalt t them diligently unto ... Deut 6:7 8150
ye shall t them your children, ... Deut 11:19 3925
the law which they shall t thee ... Deut 17:11 3384
That they t you not to do after ... Deut 20:18 3925
priests the Levites shall t you ... Deut 24:8 3384
t it the children of Israel ... Deut 31:19 3925
They shall t Jacob thy judgments, ... Deut 33:10 3384
to t them war, at the least such ... Judg 3:2 3925
t us what we shall do unto the ... Judg 13:8 3384
but I will t you the good and the ... 1Sa 12:23 3384
(Also he bade them t the children ... 2Sa 1:18 3925
that thou t them the good way ... 1Kin 8:36 3384
let him t them the manner of the ... 2Kin 17:27 3384
to t in the cities of Judah ... 2Chr 17:7 3925
to t in Israel statutes and ... Ezr 7:10 3925
t ye them that know them not ... Ezr 7:25 3046
T me, and I will hold my tongue ... Job 6:24 3384
Shall not they t thee, and tell ... Job 8:10 3384
the beasts, and they shall t thee ... Job 12:7 3384
to the earth, and it shall t thee ... Job 12:8 3384
Shall any t God knowledge ... Job 21:22 3925
I will t you by the hand of God ... Job 27:11 3384
of years should t wisdom ... Job 32:7 3045
peace, and I shall t thee wisdom ... Job 33:33 502
That which I see not t thou me ... Job 34:32 3384
T us what we shall say unto him ... Job 37:19 3045
t me thy paths ... Ps 25:4 3925
Lead me in thy truth, and t me ... Ps 25:5 3925
therefore will he t sinners in ... Ps 25:8 3384
and the meek will he t his way ... Ps 25:9 3925
him shall he t in the way that he ... Ps 25:12 3384
T me thy way, O LORD, and lead me ... Ps 27:11 3384
t thee in the way which thou ... Ps 32:8 3384
I will t you the fear of the LORD ... Ps 34:11 3925
hand shall t thee terrible things ... Ps 45:4 3384
Then will I t transgressors thy ... Ps 51:13 3925
Michtam of David, to t ... Ps 60:t 3925
T me thy way, O LORD ... Ps 86:11 3384
So t us to number our days, that ... Ps 90:12 3045
and t his senators wisdom ... Ps 105:22
t me thy statutes ... Ps 119:12 3925
t me thy statutes ... Ps 119:26 3925
T me, O LORD, the way of thy ... Ps 119:33 3384
t me thy statutes ... Ps 119:64 3925
T me good judgment and knowledge ... Ps 119:66 3925
t me thy statutes ... Ps 119:68 3925
O LORD, and t me thy judgments ... Ps 119:108 3925
thy mercy, and t me thy statutes ... Ps 119:124 3925
and t me thy statutes ... Ps 119:135 3925
my testimony that I shall t them ... Ps 132:12 3925
T me to do thy will ... Ps 143:10 3925
t a just man, and he will increase ... Prov 9:9 3045
he will t us of his ways, and we ... Is 2:3 3384
Whom shall he t knowledge ... Is 28:9 3384
him to discretion, and doth t him ... Is 28:26 3384
t your daughters wailing, and ... Jer 9:20 3925
they shall t no more every man ... Jer 31:34 3925
they shall t my people the ... Eze 44:23 3384
and whom they might t the learning ... Dan 1:4 3925
and the priests thereof t for hire ... Mic 3:11 3384
he will t us of his ways, and we ... Mic 4:2 3384
the dumb stone, Arise, it shall t ... Hab 2:19 3384
shall t men so, he shall be ... Mt 5:19 1321
t them, the same shall be called ... Mt 5:19 1321
he departed thence to t and to ... Mt 11:1 1321
t all nations, baptizing them in ... Mt 28:19 3100
began again to t by the sea side ... Mk 4:1 1321
he began to t in the synagogue ... Mk 6:2 1321
he began to t them many things ... Mk 6:34 1321
And he began to t them, that the ... Mk 8:31 1321
t us to pray, as John also taught ... Lk 11:1 1321
For the Holy Ghost shall t you in ... Lk 12:12 1321
the Gentiles, and t the Gentiles ... Jn 7:35 1321
born in sins, and dost thou t us ... Jn 9:34 1321
he shall t you all things, and ... Jn 14:26 1321
that Jesus began both to do and t ... Acts 1:1 1321
at all nor t in the name of Jesus ... Acts 4:18 1321
that ye should not t in this name ... Acts 5:28 1321
every house, they ceased not to t ... Acts 5:42 1321
t customs, which are not lawful ... Acts 16:21 2605
as I t every where in every ... 1Cor 4:17 1321
Doth not even nature itself t you ... 1Cor 11:14 1321
by my voice I might t others also ... 1Cor 14:19 2727
that they t no other doctrine ... 1Ti 1:3 2085
But I suffer not a woman to t ... 1Ti 2:12 1321
given to hospitality, apt to t ... 1Ti 3:2 1317
These things command and t ... 1Ti 4:11 1321
These things t and exhort ... 1Ti 6:2 1321
If any man t otherwise, and ... 1Ti 6:3 2085
shall be able to t others also ... 2Ti 2:2 1321
be gentle unto all men, apt to t ... 2Ti 2:24 1317
That they may t the young women ... Titus 2:4 4994
ye have need that one t you again ... Heb 5:12 1321
they shall not t every man his ... Heb 8:11 1321
and ye need not that any man t you ... 1Jn 2:27 1321
herself a prophetess, to t ... Rev 2:20 1321

TEACHER

the great, the t as the scholar ... 1Chr 25:8 995
a t of lies, that the maker of ... Hab 2:18 3384
that thou art a t come from God ... Jn 3:2 1320
a t of babes, which hast the form ... Rom 2:20 1320
a t of the Gentiles in faith and ... 1Ti 2:7 1320
apostle, and a t of the Gentiles ... 2Ti 1:11 1320

TEACHERS

more understanding than all my t ... Ps 119:99 3925
have not obeyed the voice of my t ... Prov 5:13 3384
yet shall not thy t be removed ... Is 30:20 3384
but thine eyes shall see thy t ... Is 30:20 3384
thy t have transgressed against ... Is 43:27 3887
at Antioch certain prophets and t ... Acts 13:1 1320
secondarily prophets, thirdly t ... 1Cor 12:28 1320
are all t? ... 1Cor 12:29 1320
and some, pastors and t ... Eph 4:11 1320
Desiring to be t of the law ... 1Ti 1:7 3547
shall they heap to themselves t ... 2Ti 4:3 1320
to much wine, t of good things ... Titus 2:3 2567
for the time ye ought to be t ... Heb 5:12 1320
there shall be false t among you ... 2Pet 2:1 5572

TEACHEST

O LORD, and t him out of thy law ... Ps 94:12 3925
t the way of God in truth, ... Mt 22:16 1321
but t the way of God in truth ... Mk 12:14 1321
t rightly, neither acceptest thou ... Lk 20:21 1321
but t the way of God truly ... Lk 20:21 1321
that thou t all the Jews which ... Acts 21:21 1321
Thou therefore which t another ... Rom 2:21 1321
t thou not thyself? ... Rom 2:21 1321

TEACHETH

He t my hands to war ... 2Sa 22:35 3925
Who t us more than the beasts of ... Job 35:11 502
who t like him ... Job 36:22 3384
He t my hands to war, so that a ... Ps 18:34 3925
he that t man knowledge, shall ... Ps 94:10 3925
which t my hands to war, and my ... Ps 144:1 3925
his feet, he t with his fingers ... Prov 6:13 3384
The heart of the wise t his mouth ... Prov 16:23 7919
and the prophet that t lies ... Is 9:15 3384
thy God which t thee to profit ... Is 48:17 3925
that t all men every where ... Acts 21:28 1321
or he that t, on teaching ... Rom 12:7 1321
in the words which man's wisdom t ... 1Cor 2:13 1318
but which the Holy Ghost t ... 1Cor 2:13 1318
him that t in all good things ... Gal 6:6 2727
anointing t you of all things ... 1Jn 2:27 1321

TEACHING

true God, and without a t priest ... 2Chr 15:3 3384
t them, yet they have not ... Jer 32:33 3925
t in their synagogues, and ... Mt 4:23 1321
t in their synagogues, and ... Mt 9:35 1321
t for doctrines the commandments ... Mt 15:9 1321
people came unto him as he was t ... Mt 21:23 1321
daily with you t in the temple ... Mt 26:55 1321
T them to observe all things ... Mt 28:20 1321
went round about the villages, t ... Mk 6:6 1321
t for doctrines the commandments ... Mk 7:7 1321
daily with you in the temple t ... Mk 14:49 1321
on a certain day, as he was t ... Lk 5:17 1321
he was t in one of the synagogues ... Lk 13:10 1321
through the cities and villages, t ... Lk 13:22 1321
day time he was t in the temple ... Lk 21:37 1321
t throughout all Jewry, beginning ... Lk 23:5 1321
in the temple, and t the people ... Acts 5:25 1321
Barnabas continued in Antioch, t ... Acts 15:35 1321
t the word of God among them ... Acts 18:11 1321
t those things which concern the ... Acts 28:31 1321
or he that teacheth, on t ... Rom 12:7 1319
t every man in all wisdom ... Col 1:28 1321
t and admonishing one another in ... Col 3:16 1321
t things which they ought not, ... Titus 1:11 1321
T us that, denying ungodliness and ... Titus 2:12 3811

TEAR

then I will t your flesh with the ... Judg 8:7 1758
Lest he t my soul like a lion, ... Ps 7:2 2963
they did t me, and ceased not ... Ps 35:15 7167
lest I t you in pieces, and there ... Ps 50:22 2963
sword to slay, and the dogs to t ... Jer 15:3 5498
Neither shall men t themselves ... Jer 16:7 6536
I will t them from your arms, and ... Eze 13:20 7167
Your kerchiefs also will I t ... Eze 13:21 7167
I, even I, will t and go away ... Hos 5:14 2963
the wild beast shall t them ... Hos 13:8 1234
and his anger did t perpetually ... Amos 1:11 2963
The lion did t in pieces enough ... Nah 2:12 2963
fat, and t their claws in pieces ... Zec 11:16 6561

TEARETH

t the arm with the crown of the ... Deut 33:20 2963
He t me in his wrath, who hateth ... Job 16:9 2963
He t himself in his anger ... Job 18:4 2963
t in pieces, and none can deliver ... Mic 5:8 2963
he taketh him, he t him ... Mk 9:18 4486
it t him that he foameth again, ... Lk 9:39 4682

TEARS

thy prayer, I have seen thy t ... 2Kin 20:5 1832
besought him with t to put away ... Est 8:3 1058
mine eye poureth out t unto God ... Job 16:20
I water my couch with my t ... Ps 6:6 1832
hold not thy peace at my t ... Ps 39:12 1832
My t have been my meat day and ... Ps 42:3 1832
put thou my t into thy bottle ... Ps 56:8 1832
feedest them with the bread of t ... Ps 80:5 1832
givest them t to drink in great ... Ps 80:5 1832
soul from death, mine eyes from t ... Ps 116:8 1832
They that sow in t shall reap in ... Ps 126:5 1832
behold the t of such as were ... Eccl 4:1 1832
I will water thee with my t ... Is 16:9 1832
wipe away t from off all faces ... Is 25:8 1832
thy prayer, I have seen thy t ... Is 38:5 1832
and mine eyes a fountain of t ... Jer 9:1 1832
that our eyes may run down with t ... Jer 9:18 1832
weep sore, and run down with t ... Jer 13:17 1832
mine eyes run down with t night ... Jer 14:17 1832
weeping, and thine eyes from t ... Jer 31:16 1832
night, and her t are on her cheeks ... Lam 1:2 1832
Mine eyes do fail with t, my ... Lam 2:11 1832
let t run down like a river day ... Lam 2:18 1832
neither shall thy t run down ... Eze 24:16 1832
the altar of the LORD with t ... Mal 2:13 1832
child cried out, and said with t ... Mk 9:24 1144
and began to wash his feet with t ... Lk 7:38 1144
she hath washed my feet with t ... Lk 7:44 1144
humility of mind, and with many t ... Acts 20:19 1144
every one night and day with t ... Acts 20:31 1144
I wrote unto you with many t ... 2Cor 2:4 1144
see thee, being mindful of thy t ... 2Ti 1:4 1144
t unto him that was able to save ... Heb 5:7 1144
he sought it carefully with t ... Heb 12:17 1144
wipe away all t from their eyes ... Rev 7:17 1144
wipe away all t from their eyes ... Rev 21:4 1144

TEATS

They shall lament for the t ... Is 32:12 7699
bruised the t of their virginity ... Eze 23:3 1717
youth, in bruising thy t by the ... Eze 23:21 1717

TEBAH (te'-bah) *A son of Nahor.*
name was Reumah, she bare also T ... Gen 22:24 2875

TEBALIAH (teb-a-li'-ah) *A sanctuary servant.*
T the third, Zechariah the fourth ... 1Chr 26:11 2882

TEBETH (te'-beth) *Tenth month of the Hebrew year.*
tenth month, which is the month T ... Est 2:16 2887

TEDIOUS

that I be not further t unto thee ... Acts 24:4 1465

TEETH

wine, and his t white with milk ... Gen 49:12 8127
the flesh was yet between their t ... Num 11:33 8127
send the t of beasts upon them ... Deut 32:24 8127
fleshhook of three t in his hand ... 1Sa 2:13 8127
the t of the young lions, are ... Job 4:10 8127
do I take my flesh in my t ... Job 13:14 8127
he gnasheth upon me with his t ... Job 16:9 8127
am escaped with the skin of my t ... Job 19:20 8127
and plucked the spoil out of his t ... Job 29:17 8127
his t are terrible round about ... Job 41:14 8127
hast broken the t of the ungodly ... Ps 3:7 8127
they gnashed upon me with their t ... Ps 35:16 8127
and gnasheth upon him with his t ... Ps 37:12 8127
whose t are spears and arrows, and ... Ps 57:4 8127
Break their t, O God, in their ... Ps 58:6 8127
the great t of the young lions ... Ps 58:6 4973
he shall gnash with his t ... Ps 112:10 8127
not given us as a prey to their t ... Ps 124:6 8127
As vinegar to the t, and as smoke ... Prov 10:26 8127
whose t are as swords, and their ... Prov 30:14 8127
swords, and their jaw t as knives ... Prov 30:14 4973
Thy t are like a flock of sheep ... Song 4:2 8127
Thy t are as a flock of sheep ... Song 6:6 8127
threshing instrument having t ... Is 41:15 6374
the children's t are set on edge ... Jer 31:29 8127
his t shall be set on edge ... Jer 31:30 8127
they hiss and gnash the t ... Lam 2:16 8127
broken my t with gravel stones ... Lam 3:16 8127
the children's t are set on edge ... Eze 18:2 8127
mouth of it between the t of it ... Dan 7:5 8128
and it had great iron t ... Dan 7:7 8128
whose t were of iron, and his ... Dan 7:19 8128
whose t are the ... Joel 1:6 8127
are the t of a lion ... Joel 1:6 8127
hath the cheek t of a great lion ... Joel 1:6 4973
cleanness of t in all your cities ... Amos 4:6 8127
err, that bite with their t ... Mic 3:5 8127
abominations from between his t ... Zec 9:7 8127
shall be weeping and gnashing of t ... Mt 8:12 3599
shall be wailing and gnashing of t ... Mt 13:42 3599
shall be wailing and gnashing of t ... Mt 13:50 3599
shall be weeping and gnashing of t ... Mt 22:13 3599
shall be weeping and gnashing of t ... Mt 24:51 3599
shall be weeping and gnashing of t ... Mt 25:30 3599
with him, cast the same in his t ... Mt 27:44 3679
foameth, and gnasheth with his t ... Mk 9:18 3599
shall be weeping and gnashing of t ... Lk 13:28 3599
they gnashed on him with their t ... Acts 7:54 3599
their t were as the ... Rev 9:8 3599
were as the t of lions ... Rev 9:8

TEHAPHNEHES (te-haf'-ne-heze) *Same as Tahpanhes.*
At T also the day shall be ... Eze 30:18 8471

TEHINNAH (te-hin'-nah) *A descendant of Judah.*
T the father of Ir-nahash ... 1Chr 4:12 8468

TEIL

as a t tree, and as an oak, whose ... Is 6:13 424

TEKEL (te'-kel) *Part of the "handwriting on the wall."*
that was written, MENE, MENE, T ... Dan 5:25 8625
T; Thou art weighed ... Dan 5:27 8625

TEKOA (te'-ko-ah) See TEKOAH, TEKOITE.
1. Son of Ashur.
bare him Ashur the father of T ... 1Chr 2:24 8620
the father of T had two wives ... 1Chr 4:5 8620
2. A city in Judah.
even Beth-lehem, and Etam, and T ... 2Chr 11:6 8620
forth into the wilderness of T ... 2Chr 20:20 8620
and blow the trumpet in T ... Jer 6:1 8620
who was among the herdmen of T ... Amos 1:1 8620

TEKOAH (te'-ko-ah) See TEKOA. *Same as Tekoa 2.*
And Joab sent to T, and fetched ... 2Sa 14:2 8620
the woman of T spake to the king ... 2Sa 14:4 8621
the woman of T said unto the king ... 2Sa 14:9 8621

TEKOITE (te'-ko-ite) See TEKOITES. *An inhabitant of Tekoa.*
Ira the son of Ikkesh the T ... 2Sa 23:26 8621
Ira the son of Ikkesh the T ... 1Chr 11:28 8621
was Ira the son of Ikkesh the T ... 1Chr 27:9 8621

TEKOITES (te'-ko-ites)
And next unto them the T repaired ... Neh 3:5 8621
After them the T repaired another ... Neh 3:27 8621

TEL-ABIB (tel-a'-bib) *Town on the River Chebar.*
to them of the captivity at T ... Eze 3:15 8512

T

TELAH (*te'-lah*) *Father of Tahan.*
T his son, and Tahan his son, 1Chr 7:25 8520

TELAIM (*tel'-a-im*) See TELEM. *A place in Judah.*
together, and numbered them in *T* 1Sa 15:4 2923

TELASSAR (*te-las'-sar*) See THELASAR. *A city in Mesopotamia.*
children of Eden which were in *T* Is 37:12 8515

TEL AVIV See TEL-ABIB.

TELEM (*te'-lem*) See TELAIM.
1. A city in Judah.
Ziph, and *T*, and Bealoth, Josh 15:24 2928
2. Married a foreigner in exile.
Shallum, and *T*, and Uri Ezr 10:24 2928

TEL-HARESHA (*tel-ha-re'-sha*) See TEL-HARSA. *A Babylonian settlement of exiles.*
went up also from Tel-melah, *T* Neh 7:61 8521

TEL-HARSA (*tel'-har-sah*) See TEL-HARESHA. *Same as Tel-haresha.*
which went up from Tel-melah, *T* Ezr 2:59 8521

TELL
why didst thou not *t* me that she Gen 12:18 5046
t the stars, if thou be able to Gen 15:5 5608
neither didst thou *t* me, neither Gen 21:26 5046
mountains which I will *t* thee of Gen 22:2 559
t me, I pray thee. Gen 24:23 5046
and truly with my master, *t* me Gen 24:49 5046
and if not, *t* me Gen 24:49 5046
the land which I shall *t* thee of Gen 26:2 559
t me, what shall thy wages be Gen 29:15 5046
and didst not *t* me, that I might Gen 31:27 5046
and I have sent to *t* my lord Gen 32:5 5046
T me, I pray thee, thy name Gen 32:29 5046
t me, I pray thee, where they Gen 37:16 5046
t me them, I pray you Gen 40:8 5608
as to *t* the man whether ye had Gen 43:6 5046
we cannot *t* who put our money in Gen 43:22 3045
ye shall *t* my father of all my Gen 45:13 5046
that I may *t* you that which shall Gen 49:1 5046
t him, Thus saith the LORD God of Ex 9:1 1696
that thou mayest *t* in the ears of Ex 10:2 5608
word that we did *t* thee in Egypt Ex 14:12 1696
and *t* the children of Israel Ex 19:3 5046
t the priest, saying, It seemeth Lev 14:35 5046
they will *t* it to the inhabitants Num 14:14 559
heard *t* that Israel came by the Num 21:1
he sheweth me I will *t* thee Num 23:3 5046
judgment which they shall *t* thee Deut 17:11 559
thy elders, and they will *t* thee Deut 32:7 559
t me now what thou hast done Josh 7:19 5046
my mother, and shall I *t* it thee Judg 14:16 5046
T me, I pray thee, wherein thy Judg 16:6 5046
now *t* me, I pray thee, wherewith Judg 16:10 5046
t me wherewith thou mightest be Judg 16:13 5046
T us, how was this wickedness Judg 20:3 1696
he will *t* thee what thou shalt do Ruth 3:4 5046
wilt not redeem it, then *t* me Ruth 4:4 5046
t us wherewith we shall send it 1Sa 6:2 3045
the man of God, to *t* us our way 1Sa 9:8 5046
T me, I pray thee, where the 1Sa 9:18 5046
will *t* thee all that is in thine 1Sa 9:19 5046
T me, I pray thee, what Samuel 1Sa 10:15 5046
T me what thou hast done 1Sa 14:43 5046
I will *t* thee what the LORD hath 1Sa 15:16 5046
soul liveth, O king, I cannot *t* 1Sa 17:55 3045
and what I see, that I will *t* thee 1Sa 19:3 5046
thee, then would not I *t* it thee 1Sa 20:9 5046
David to Jonathan, Who shall *t* me 1Sa 20:10 5046
that he would surely *t* Saul 1Sa 22:22 5046
I beseech thee, *t* thy servant 1Sa 23:11 5046
saying, Lest they should *t* on us 1Sa 27:11 5046
I pray thee, *t* me 2Sa 1:4 5046
T it not in Gath, publish it not 2Sa 1:20 5046
t my servant David, Thus saith 2Sa 7:5 559
to *t* him that the child was dead 2Sa 12:18 5046
if we *t* him that the child is 2Sa 12:18 559
Who can *t* whether GOD will be 2Sa 12:22 3045
wilt thou not *t* me 2Sa 13:4 5046
thou shalt *t* it to Zadok and 2Sa 15:35 5046
t David, saying, Lodge not this 2Sa 17:16 5046
Go *t* the king what thou hast seen 2Sa 18:21 5046
that thou shouldest *t* them who 1Kin 1:20 5046
he shall *t* thee what shall become 1Kin 14:3 5046
t Jeroboam, Thus saith the LORD 1Kin 14:7 559
t thy lord, Behold, Elijah is 1Kin 18:8 559
t thy lord, Behold, Elijah is 1Kin 18:11 559
t Ahab, and he cannot find thee, 1Kin 18:12 5046
t thy lord, Behold, Elijah is 1Kin 18:14 559
T my lord the king, All that thou 1Kin 20:9 559
T him, Let not him that girdeth 1Kin 20:11 1696
t me nothing but that which is 1Kin 22:16 1696
Did I not *t* thee that he would 1Kin 22:18 559
t me, what hast thou in the house 2Kin 4:2 5046
may go and *t* the king's household 2Kin 7:9 5046
T me, I pray thee, all the great 2Kin 8:4 5608
t us now 2Kin 9:12 5046
the city to go to *t* it in Jezreel 2Kin 9:15 5046
t Hezekiah the captain of my 2Kin 20:5 559
T the man that sent you to me, 2Kin 22:15 559
t David my servant, Thus saith 1Chr 17:4 559
Furthermore I *t* thee that the 1Chr 17:10 5046
t David, saying, Thus saith the 1Chr 21:10 1696
Did I not *t* thee that he would 2Chr 18:17 559
T ye the man that sent you to me, 2Chr 34:23 559
I only am escaped alone to *t* thee Job 1:15 5046
I only am escaped alone to *t* thee Job 1:16 5046
I only am escaped alone to *t* thee Job 1:17 5046
I only am escaped alone to *t* thee Job 1:19 5046
t thee, and utter words out of Job 8:10 559
of the air, and they shall *t* thee Job 12:7 5046
Let men of understanding *t* me Job 34:34 559
I may *t* all my bones Ps 22:17 5608
t of all thy wondrous works Ps 26:7 5608
t the towers thereof Ps 48:12 5608
that ye may *t* it to the Ps 48:13 5608
I were hungry, I would not *t* thee Ps 50:12 559
his son's name, if thou canst *t* Prov 30:4 3045
for who can *t* a man what shall be Eccl 6:12 5046
for who can *t* him when it shall Eccl 8:7 5046
a man cannot *t* what shall be Eccl 10:14 5046
shall be after him, who can *t* him Eccl 10:14 5046
hath wings shall *t* the matter Eccl 10:20 5046
T me, O thou whom my soul loveth, Song 1:7 5046
ye find my beloved, that ye *t* him Song 5:8 5046
I will *t* you what I will do to my Is 5:5 3045
t this people, Hear ye indeed, Is 6:9 559
and let them *t* thee now, and let Is 19:12 5046
they spring forth I *t* you of them Is 42:9 8085
T ye, and bring them near Is 45:21 5046
t this, utter it even to the end Is 48:20 8085
then thou shalt *t* them, Thus Jer 15:2 559
the words that I shall *t* thee Jer 19:2 1696
they *t* every man to his neighbour Jer 23:27 5608
hath a dream, let him *t* a dream Jer 23:28 5608
do *t* them, and cause my people to Jer 23:32 5608
t Hananiah, saying, Thus saith Jer 28:13 559
t him, Thus saith the LORD Jer 34:2 559
t the men of Judah and the Jer 35:13 559
We will surely *t* the king of all Jer 36:16 5046
T us now, How didst thou write Jer 36:17 5046
t ye it in Arnon, that Moab is Jer 48:20 5046
t them, Thus saith the Lord GOD Eze 3:11 559
T them therefore, Thus saith the Eze 12:23 559
t them, Behold, the king of Eze 17:12 559
Wilt thou not *t* us what these Eze 24:19 5046
t thy servants the dream, and we Dan 2:4 560
Let the king *t* his servants the Dan 2:7 560
therefore *t* me the dream, and I Dan 2:9 560
we will *t* the interpretation Dan 2:36 560
t me the visions of my dream that Dan 4:9 560
T ye your children of it, and let Joel 1:3 5608
your children *t* their children Joel 1:3
T us, we pray thee, for whose Jonah 1:8 5046
Who can *t* if God will turn and Jonah 3:9 3045
saith unto him, See thou *t* no man Mt 8:4 *2036*
What I *t* you in darkness, that Mt 10:27 *3004*
t no man that he was Jesus the Mt 16:20 *2036*
T the vision to no man, until the Mt 17:9 *2036*
t him his fault between thee and Mt 18:15 *1650*
hear them, *t* it unto the church Mt 18:17 *2036*
T ye the daughter of Sion, Behold, Mt 21:5 *2036*
you one thing, which if ye *t* me Mt 21:24 *2036*
I in like wise will *t* you by what Mt 21:24 *2046*
Jesus, and said, We cannot *t* Mt 21:27 *1492*
Neither *t* I you by what authority Mt 21:27 *3004*
T them which are bidden, Behold, Mt 22:4 *2036*
T us therefore, What thinkest Mt 22:17 *2036*
T us, when shall these things be Mt 24:3 *2036*
that thou *t* us whether thou be Mt 26:63 *2036*
t his disciples that he is risen Mt 28:7 *2036*
as they went to *t* his disciples Mt 28:9 *518*
go *t* my brethren that they go Mt 28:10 *518*
fever, and anon they *t* him of her Mk 1:30 *3004*
t them how great things the Lord Mk 5:19 *312*
them that they should *t* no man Mk 7:36 *2036*
nor *t* it to any in the town Mk 8:26 *2036*
that they should *t* no man of him Mk 8:30 *3004*
t no man what things they had Mk 9:9 *1334*
began to *t* them what things Mk 10:32 *3004*
I will *t* you by what authority I Mk 11:29 *2046*
and said unto Jesus, We cannot *t* Mk 11:33 *1492*
Neither do I *t* you by what Mk 11:33 *3004*
T us, when shall these things be Mk 13:4 *2036*
t his disciples and Peter that he Mk 16:7 *2036*
But I *t* you of a truth, many Lk 4:25 *3004*
And he charged him to *t* no man Lk 5:14 *2036*
t John what things ye have seen Lk 7:22 *518*
T me therefore, which of them Lk 7:42 *2036*
should *t* no man what was done Lk 8:56 *2036*
them to *t* no man that thing Lk 9:21 *2036*
But I *t* you of a truth, there be Lk 9:27 *3004*
For I *t* you, that many prophets Lk 10:24 *3004*
I *t* you, Nay Lk 12:51 *3004*
I *t* thee, thou shalt not depart Lk 12:59 *3004*
I *t* you, Nay Lk 13:3 *3004*
I *t* you, Nay Lk 13:5 *3004*
I *t* you, I know you not whence ye Lk 13:27 *3004*
t that fox, Behold, I cast out Lk 13:32 *2036*
I *t* you, in that night there Lk 17:34 *3004*
I *t* you that he will avenge them Lk 18:8 *3004*
I *t* you, this man went down to Lk 18:14 *3004*
I *t* you that, if these should Lk 19:40 *3004*
T us, by what authority doest Lk 20:2 *2036*
they could not *t* whence it was Lk 20:7 *1492*
Neither *t* I you by what authority Lk 20:8 *3004*
I *t* thee, Peter, the cock shall Lk 22:34 *3004*
Art thou the Christ? *t* us Lk 22:67 *2036*
And he said unto them, If I *t* you Lk 22:67 *2036*
but canst not *t* whence it cometh, Jn 3:8 *1492*
if I *t* you of heavenly things Jn 3:12 *2036*
is come, he will *t* us all things Jn 4:25 *312*
but ye cannot *t* whence I come Jn 8:14 *1492*
because I *t* you the truth, ye Jn 8:45 *3004*
thou be the Christ, *t* us plainly Jn 10:24 *2036*
and again Andrew and Philip *t* Jesus Jn 12:22 *3004*
Now I *t* you before it come, that, Jn 13:19 *3004*
Nevertheless I *t* you the truth Jn 16:7 *3004*
we cannot *t* what he saith Jn 16:18 *1492*
or did others *t* it thee of me Jn 18:34 *2036*
t me where thou hast laid him, and Jn 20:15 *2036*
T me whether ye sold the land for Acts 5:8 *2036*
he shall *t* thee what thou Acts 10:6 *2980*
Who shall *t* thee words, whereby Acts 11:14 *2980*
who shall also *t* you the same Acts 15:27 *518*
in nothing else, but either to *t* Acts 17:21 *3004*
unto him, *T* me, art thou a Roman Acts 22:27 *3004*
he hath a certain thing to *t* him Acts 23:17 *518*
What is that thou hast to *t* me Acts 23:19 *518*
See thou *t* no man that thou hast Acts 23:22 *1583*
(whether in the body, I cannot *t* 2Cor 12:2 *1492*
out of the body, I cannot *t* 2Cor 12:2 *1492*
or out of the body, I cannot *t* 2Cor 12:3 *1492*
because I *t* you the truth Gal 4:16 *226*
T me, ye that desire to be under Gal 4:21 *3004*
of the which I *t* you before Gal 5:21 *4302*
now *t* you even weeping, that they Phil 3:18 *3004*
time would fail me to *t* of Gedeon Heb 11:32 *1334*
I will *t* thee the mystery of the Rev 17:7 *2046*

TELLEST
Thou *t* my wanderings Ps 56:8 5608

TELLETH
Also the LORD *t* thee that he will 2Sa 7:11 5046
t the king of Israel the words 2Kin 6:12 5046
when he goeth abroad, he *t* it Ps 41:6 1696
he that *t* lies shall not tarry in Ps 101:7 1696
He *t* the number of the stars Ps 147:4 4487
the hands of him that *t* them Jer 33:13 4487
Philip cometh and *t* Andrew Jn 12:22 *3004*

TELLING
Gideon heard the *t* of the dream Judg 7:15 4557
When thou hast made an end of *t* 2Sa 11:19 1696
as he was *t* the king how he had 2Kin 8:5 5608

TEL-MELAH (*tel-me'-lah*) *A place where the exiles lived.*
were they which went up from *T* Ezr 2:59 8528
they which went up also from *T* Neh 7:61 8528

TEMA (*te'-mah*)
1. A son of Ishmael.
Hadar, and *T*, Jetur, Naphish, and Gen 25:15 8485
and Dumah, Massa, Hadad, and *T* 1Chr 1:30 8485
T brought water to him that was Is 21:14 8485
Dedan, and *T*, and Buz, and all that Jer 25:23 8485
2. A city in northern Arabia.
The troops of *T* looked, the Job 6:19 8485

TEMAH See THAMAH.

TEMAN (*te'-man*) See TEMANITE.
1. A son of Eliphaz.
And the sons of Eliphaz were *T* Gen 36:11 8487
duke *T*, duke Omar, duke Zepho, Gen 36:15 8487
Duke Kenaz, duke *T*, duke Mibzar, Gen 36:42 8487
T, and Omar, Zephi, and Gatam, 1Chr 1:36 8487
Duke Kenaz, duke *T*, duke Mibzar, 1Chr 1:53 8487
2. A race and district of Edom.
Is wisdom no more in *T* Jer 49:7 8487
against the inhabitants of *T* Jer 49:20 8487
and I will make it desolate from *T* Eze 25:13 8487
But I will send a fire upon *T* Amos 1:12 8487
And thy mighty men, O *T*, shall be Obad 9 8487
God came from *T*, and the Holy One Hab 3:3 8487

TEMANI (*te'-ma-ni*) See TEMANITE. *A son of Ashur.*
land of *T* reigned in his stead Gen 36:34 8489

TEMANITE (*te'-man-ite*) See TEMANI, TEMANITES. *An inhabitant of Teman 2.*
Eliphaz the *T*, and Bildad the Job 2:11 8489
Then Eliphaz the *T* answered Job 4:1 8489
Then answered Eliphaz the *T* Job 15:1 8489
Then Eliphaz the *T* answered Job 22:1 8489
the LORD said to Eliphaz the *T* Job 42:7 8489
So Eliphaz the *T* and Bildad the Job 42:9 8489

TEMANITES (*te'-man-ites*)
of the *T* reigned in his stead 1Chr 1:45 8489

TEMENI (*tem'-e-ni*) *A descendant of Caleb.*
bare him Ahuzam, and Hepher, and *T* 1Chr 4:6 8488

TEMPER
of oil, to *t* with the fine flour Eze 46:14 7450

TEMPERANCE
he reasoned of righteousness, *t* Acts 24:25 *1466*
Meekness, *t* Gal 5:23 *1466*
And to knowledge *t* 2Pet 1:6 *1466*
and to *t* patience 2Pet 1:6 *1466*

TEMPERATE
the mastery is *t* in all things 1Cor 9:25 *1467*
of good men, sober, just, holy, *t* Titus 1:8 *1468*
the aged men be sober, grave, *t* Titus 2:2 *4998*

TEMPERED
and cakes unleavened *t* with oil Ex 29:2 1101
t together, pure and holy Ex 30:35 4414
but God hath *t* the body together, 1Cor 12:24 *4786*

TEMPEST
For he breaketh me with a *t* Job 9:17 8183
a *t* stealeth him away in the Job 27:20 5492
and brimstone, and an horrible *t* Ps 11:6 7307
escape from the windy storm and *t* Ps 55:8 5591
So persecute them with thy *t* Ps 83:15 5591
strong one, which as a *t* of hail Is 28:2 2230
and great noise, with storm and *t* Is 29:6 5591
fire, with scattering, and *t* Is 30:30 2230
the wind, and a covert from the *t* Is 32:2 2230
O thou afflicted, tossed with *t* Is 54:11 5590
with a *t* in the day of the Amos 1:14 5591
there was a mighty *t* in the sea Jonah 1:4 5591
my sake this great *t* is upon you Jonah 1:12 5591
there arose a great *t* in the sea Mt 8:24 *4578*
being exceedingly tossed with a *t* Acts 27:18 *5492*
no small *t* lay on us, all hope Acts 27:20 *5494*
unto blackness, and darkness, and *t* Heb 12:18 *2366*
clouds that are carried with a *t* 2Pet 2:17 *2978*

TEMPESTUOUS
shall be very *t* round about him ... Ps 50:3 8175
for the sea wrought, and was *t* ... Jonah 1:11 5490
wrought, and was *t* against them ... Jonah 1:13 5490
there arose against it a *t* wind ... Acts 27:14 *5189*

TEMPLE
by a post of the *t* of the LORD ... 1Sa 1:9 1964
God went out in the *t* of the LORD ... 1Sa 3:3 1964
he did hear my voice out of his *t* ... 2Sa 22:7 1964
porch before the *t* of the house ... 1Kin 6:3 1964
house round about, both of the *t* ... 1Kin 6:5 1964
the *t* before it, was forty cubits ... 1Kin 6:17 1964
door of the *t* posts of olive tree ... 1Kin 6:33 1964
the pillars in the porch of the *t* ... 1Kin 7:21 1964
of the house, to wit, of the *t* ... 1Kin 7:50 1964
that were in the *t* of the LORD ... 2Kin 11:10 1004
the *t* to the left corner of the ... 2Kin 11:11 1004
to the left corner of the *t* ... 2Kin 11:11 1004
along by the altar and the *t* ... 2Kin 11:11 1004
the people into the *t* of the LORD ... 2Kin 11:13 1004
the doors of the *t* of the LORD ... 2Kin 18:16 1964
to bring forth out of the *t* of ... 2Kin 23:4 1964
had made in the *t* of the LORD ... 2Kin 24:13 1964
the priest's office in the *t* that ... 1Chr 6:10 1004
his head in the *t* of Dagon ... 1Chr 10:10 1004
up the pillars before the *t* ... 2Chr 3:17 1964
their form, and set them in the *t* ... 2Chr 4:7 1964
tables, and placed them in the *t* ... 2Chr 4:8 1964
the doors of the house of the *t* ... 2Chr 4:22 1964
from the right side of the *t* to ... 2Chr 23:10 1004
to the left side of the *t* ... 2Chr 23:10 1004
along by the altar and the *t* ... 2Chr 23:10 1004
went into the *t* of the LORD to ... 2Chr 26:16 1964
not into the *t* of the LORD ... 2Chr 27:2 1964
that they found in the *t* of the ... 2Chr 29:16 1964
when Josiah had prepared the *t* ... 2Chr 35:20 1004
and put them in his *t* at Babylon ... 2Chr 36:7 1964
But the foundation of the *t* of ... Ezr 3:6 1964
foundation of the *t* of the LORD ... Ezr 3:10 1964
the *t* unto the LORD God of Israel ... Ezr 4:1 1964
of the *t* that was in Jerusalem ... Ezr 5:14 1965
them into the *t* of Babylon ... Ezr 5:14 1965
king take out of the *t* of Babylon ... Ezr 5:14 1965
carry them into the *t* that is in ... Ezr 5:15 1965
of the *t* which is at Jerusalem ... Ezr 6:5 1965
unto the *t* which is at Jerusalem ... Ezr 6:5 1965
in the house of God, within the *t* ... Neh 6:10 1964
and let us shut the doors of the *t* ... Neh 6:10 1964
go into the *t* to save his life ... Neh 6:11 1964
will I worship toward thy holy *t* ... Ps 5:7 1964
The LORD is in his holy *t* ... Ps 11:4 1964
he heard my voice out of his *t* ... Ps 18:6 1964
the LORD, and to enquire in his *t* ... Ps 27:4 1964
in his *t* doth every one speak of ... Ps 29:9 1964
O God, in the midst of thy *t* ... Ps 48:9 1964
of thy house, even of thy holy *t* ... Ps 65:4 1964
Because of thy *t* at Jerusalem ... Ps 68:29 1964
thy holy *t* have they defiled ... Ps 79:1 1964
I will worship toward thy holy *t* ... Ps 138:2 1964
up, and his train filled the *t* ... Is 6:1 1964
and to the *t*, Thy foundation shall ... Is 44:28 1964
from the city, a voice from the *t* ... Is 66:6 1964
The *t* of the LORD ... Jer 7:4 1964
The *t* of the LORD ... Jer 7:4 1964
The *t* of the LORD, are these ... Jer 7:4 1964
were set before the *t* of the LORD ... Jer 24:1 1964
our God, the vengeance of his *t* ... Jer 50:28 1964
the LORD, the vengeance of his *t* ... Jer 51:11 1964
at the door of the *t* of the LORD ... Eze 8:16 1964
backs toward the *t* of the LORD ... Eze 8:16 1964
Afterward he brought me to the *t* ... Eze 41:1 1964
twenty cubits, before the *t* ... Eze 41:4 1964
hundred cubits, with the inner *t* ... Eze 41:15 1964
made, and on the wall of the *t* ... Eze 41:20 1964
The posts of the *t* were squared ... Eze 41:21 1964
And the *t* and the sanctuary had two .. Eze 41:23 1964
on them, on the doors of the *t* ... Eze 41:25 1964
before the *t* were an hundred ... Eze 42:8 1964
had taken out of the *t* which was ... Dan 5:2 1965
that were taken out of the *t* of ... Dan 5:3 1965
the songs of the *t* shall be ... Amos 8:3 1964
will look again toward thy holy *t* ... Jonah 2:4 1964
in unto thee, into thine holy *t* ... Jonah 2:7 1964
you, the Lord from his holy *t* ... Mic 1:2 1964
But the LORD is in his holy *t* ... Hab 2:20 1964
upon a stone in the *t* of the LORD ... Hag 2:15 1964
of the LORD's *t* was laid, ... Hag 2:18 1964
he shall build the *t* of the LORD ... Zec 6:12 1964
he shall build the *t* of the LORD ... Zec 6:13 1964
a memorial in the *t* of the LORD ... Zec 6:14 1964
and build in the *t* of the LORD ... Zec 6:15 1964
that the *t* might be built ... Zec 8:9 1964
shall suddenly come to his *t* ... Mal 3:1 1964
him on a pinnacle of the *t* ... Mt 4:5 *2411*
in the *t* profane the sabbath ... Mt 12:5 *2411*
place is one greater than the *t* ... Mt 12:6 *2411*
And Jesus went into the *t* of God ... Mt 21:12 *2411*
them that sold and bought in the *t* ... Mt 21:12 *2411*
and the lame came to him in the *t* ... Mt 21:14 *2411*
and the children crying in the *t* ... Mt 21:15 *2411*
And when he was come into the *t* ... Mt 21:23 *2411*
Whosoever shall swear by the *t* ... Mt 23:16 *3485*
shall swear by the gold of the *t* ... Mt 23:16 *3485*
or the *t* that sanctifieth the ... Mt 23:17 *3485*
And whoso shall swear by the *t* ... Mt 23:21 *3485*
whom ye slew between the *t* ... Mt 23:35 *3485*
went out, and departed from the *t* ... Mt 24:1 *2411*
shew him the buildings of the *t* ... Mt 24:1 *2411*
daily with you teaching in the *t* ... Mt 26:55 *2411*
I am able to destroy the *t* of God ... Mt 26:61 *3485*
the pieces of silver in the *t* ... Mt 27:5 *3485*
Thou that destroyest the *t* ... Mt 27:40 *3485*
the veil of the *t* was rent in ... Mt 27:51 *3485*
into Jerusalem, and into the *t* ... Mk 11:11 *2411*
and Jesus went into the *t*, and ... Mk 11:15 *2411*
them that sold and bought in the *t* ... Mk 11:15 *2411*
carry any vessel through the *t* ... Mk 11:16 *2411*
and as he was walking in the *t* ... Mk 11:27 *2411*
and said, while he taught in the *t* ... Mk 12:35 *2411*
And as he went out of the *t* ... Mk 13:1 *2411*
of Olives over against the *t* ... Mk 13:3 *2411*
daily with you in the *t* teaching ... Mk 14:49 *2411*
I will destroy this *t* that is ... Mk 14:58 *3485*
Ah, thou that destroyest the *t* ... Mk 15:29 *3485*
the veil of the *t* was rent in ... Mk 15:38 *3485*
he went into the *t* of the Lord ... Lk 1:9 *3485*
that he tarried so long in the *t* ... Lk 1:21 *3485*
he had seen a vision in the *t* ... Lk 1:22 *3485*
he came by the Spirit into the *t* ... Lk 2:27 *2411*
which departed not from the *t* ... Lk 2:37 *2411*
days they found him in the *t* ... Lk 2:46 *2411*
and set him on a pinnacle of the *t* ... Lk 4:9 *2411*
between the altar and the *t* ... Lk 11:51 *3624*
men went up into the *t* to pray ... Lk 18:10 *2411*
And he went into the *t*, and began ... Lk 19:45 *2411*
And he taught daily in the *t* ... Lk 19:47 *2411*
as he taught the people in the *t* ... Lk 20:1 *2411*
And as some spake of the *t* ... Lk 21:5 *2411*
day time he was teaching in the *t* ... Lk 21:37 *2411*
in the morning to him in the *t* ... Lk 21:38 *2411*
priests, and captains of the *t* ... Lk 22:52 *2411*
I was daily with you in the *t* ... Lk 22:53 *2411*
the veil of the *t* was rent in the ... Lk 23:45 *3485*
And were continually in the *t* ... Lk 24:53 *2411*
found in the *t* those that sold ... Jn 2:14 *2411*
he drove them all out of the *t* ... Jn 2:15 *2411*
and said unto them, Destroy this *t* ... Jn 2:19 *3485*
six years was this *t* in building ... Jn 2:20 *3485*
But he spake of the *t* of his body ... Jn 2:21 *3485*
Jesus findeth him in the *t* ... Jn 5:14 *2411*
feast Jesus went up into the *t* ... Jn 7:14 *2411*
cried Jesus in the *t* as he taught ... Jn 7:28 *2411*
morning he came again into the *t* ... Jn 8:2 *2411*
treasury, as he taught in the *t* ... Jn 8:20 *2411*
hid himself, and went out of the *t* ... Jn 8:59 *2411*
in the *t* in Solomon's porch ... Jn 10:23 *2411*
as they stood in the *t*, What ... Jn 11:56 *2411*
in the synagogue, and in the *t* ... Jn 18:20 *2411*
daily with one accord in the *t* ... Acts 2:46 *2411*
into the *t* at the hour of prayer ... Acts 3:1 *2411*
the *t* which is called Beautiful ... Acts 3:2 *2411*
of them that entered into the *t* ... Acts 3:2 *2411*
to go into the *t* asked an alms ... Acts 3:3 *2411*
and entered with them into the *t* ... Acts 3:8 *2411*
at the Beautiful gate of the *t* ... Acts 3:10 *2411*
priests, and the captain of the *t* ... Acts 4:1 *2411*
speak in the *t* to the people all ... Acts 5:20 *2411*
into the *t* early in the morning ... Acts 5:21 *2411*
priest and the captain of the *t* ... Acts 5:24 *2411*
in prison are standing in the *t* ... Acts 5:25 *2411*
And daily in the *t*, and in every ... Acts 5:42 *2411*
but also that the *t* of the great ... Acts 19:27 *2411*
with them entered into the *t* ... Acts 21:26 *2411*
Asia, when they saw him in the *t* ... Acts 21:27 *2411*
brought Greeks also into the *t* ... Acts 21:28 *2411*
that Paul had brought into the *t* ... Acts 21:29 *2411*
Paul, and drew him out of the *t* ... Acts 21:30 *2411*
even while I prayed in the *t* ... Acts 22:17 *2411*
hath gone about to profane the *t* ... Acts 24:6 *2411*
in the *t* disputing with any man ... Acts 24:12 *2411*
Asia found me purified in the *t* ... Acts 24:18 *2411*
the Jews, neither against the *t* ... Acts 25:8 *2411*
the Jews caught me in the *t* ... Acts 26:21 *2411*
ye not that ye are the *t* of God ... 1Cor 3:16 *3485*
If any man defile the *t* of God ... 1Cor 3:17 *3485*
for the *t* of God is holy, which ... 1Cor 3:17 *3485*
of God is holy, which *t* ye are ... 1Cor 3:17
ye not that your body is the *t* of ... 1Cor 6:19 *3485*
sit at meat in the idol's *t* ... 1Cor 8:10
live of the things of the *t* ... 1Cor 9:13 *2411*
hath the *t* of God with idols ... 2Cor 6:16 *3485*
for ye are the *t* of the living ... 2Cor 6:16 *3485*
unto an holy *t* in the Lord ... Eph 2:21 *3485*
he as God sitteth in the *t* of God ... 2Th 2:4 *3485*
make a pillar in the *t* of my God ... Rev 3:12 *3485*
serve him day and night in his *t* ... Rev 7:15 *3485*
Rise, and measure the *t* of God ... Rev 11:1 *3485*
which is without the *t* leave out ... Rev 11:2 *3485*
the *t* of God was opened in heaven ... Rev 11:19 *3485*
there was seen in his *t* the ark ... Rev 11:19 *3485*
another angel came out of the *t* ... Rev 14:15 *3485*
out of the *t* which is in heaven ... Rev 14:17 *3485*
the *t* of the tabernacle of the ... Rev 15:5 *3485*
seven angels came out of the *t* ... Rev 15:6 *3485*
the *t* was filled with smoke from ... Rev 15:8 *3485*
man was able to enter into the *t* ... Rev 15:8 *3485*
the *t* saying to the seven angels ... Rev 16:1 *3485*
voice out of the *t* of heaven ... Rev 16:17 *3485*
And I saw no *t* therein ... Rev 21:22 *3485*
and the Lamb are the *t* of it ... Rev 21:22 *3485*

TEMPLES
him, and smote the nail into his *t* ... Judg 4:21 7451
dead, and the nail was in his *t* ... Judg 4:22 7451
pierced and stricken through his *t* ... Judg 5:26 7451
thy *t* are like a piece of a ... Song 4:3 7451
are thy *t* within thy locks ... Song 6:7 7451
his Maker, and buildeth *t* ... Hos 8:14 1964
have carried into your *t* my ... Joel 3:5 1964
dwelleth not in *t* made with hands ... Acts 7:48 *3485*
dwelleth not in *t* made with hands ... Acts 17:24 *3485*

TEMPORAL
the things which are seen are *t* ... 2Cor 4:18 *4340*

TEMPT
things, that God did *t* Abraham ... Gen 22:1 5254
wherefore do ye *t* the LORD ... Ex 17:2 5254
Ye shall not *t* the LORD your God, ... Deut 6:16 5254
ask, neither will I *t* the LORD ... Is 7:12 5254
yea, they that *t* God are even ... Mal 3:15 974
Thou shalt not *t* the Lord thy God ... Mt 4:7 *1598*
Why *t* ye me, ye hypocrites ... Mt 22:18 *3985*
said unto them, Why *t* ye me ... Mk 12:15 *3985*
Thou shalt not *t* the Lord thy God ... Lk 4:12 *1598*
and said unto them, Why *t* ye me ... Lk 20:23 *3985*
to *t* the Spirit of the Lord ... Acts 5:9 *3985*
Now therefore why *t* ye God ... Acts 15:10 *3985*
that Satan *t* you not for your ... 1Cor 7:5 *3985*
Neither let us *t* Christ, as some ... 1Cor 10:9 *1598*

TEMPTATION
as in the day of *t* in the ... Ps 95:8 4531
And lead us not into *t*, but ... Mt 6:13 *3986*
and pray, that ye enter not into *t* ... Mt 26:41 *3986*
ye and pray, lest ye enter into *t* ... Mk 14:38 *3986*
the devil had ended all the *t* ... Lk 4:13 *3986*
and in time of *t* fall away ... Lk 8:13 *3986*
And lead us not into *t* ... Lk 11:4 *3986*
Pray that ye enter not into *t* ... Lk 22:40 *3986*
and pray, lest ye enter into *t* ... Lk 22:46 *3986*
There hath no *t* taken you but ... 1Cor 10:13 *3986*
but will with the *t* also make a ... 1Cor 10:13 *3986*
my *t* which was in my flesh ye ... Gal 4:14 *3986*
that will be rich fall into *t* ... 1Ti 6:9 *3986*
in the day of *t* in the wilderness ... Heb 3:8 *3986*
is the man that endureth *t* ... Jas 1:12 *3986*
will keep thee from the hour of *t* ... Rev 3:10 *3986*

TEMPTATIONS
the midst of another nation, by *t* ... Deut 4:34 4531
The great *t* which thine eyes saw, ... Deut 7:19 4531
The great *t* which thine eyes have ... Deut 29:3 4531
have continued with me in my *t* ... Lk 22:28 *3986*
of mind, and with many tears, and *t* ... Acts 20:19 *3986*
joy when ye fall into divers *t* ... Jas 1:2 *3986*
in heaviness through manifold *t* ... 1Pet 1:6 *3986*
how to deliver the godly out of *t* ... 2Pet 2:9 *3986*

TEMPTED
and because they *t* the LORD ... Ex 17:7 5254
have *t* me now these ten times, and ... Num 14:22 5254
your God, as ye *t* him in Massah ... Deut 6:16 5254
they *t* God in their heart by ... Ps 78:18 5254
t God, and limited the Holy One of ... Ps 78:41 5254
Yet they *t* and provoked the most ... Ps 78:56 5254
When your fathers *t* me, proved me ... Ps 95:9 5254
and *t* God in the desert ... Ps 106:14 5254
wilderness to be *t* of the devil ... Mt 4:1 *3985*
wilderness forty days, *t* of Satan ... Mk 1:13 *3985*
Being forty days *t* of the devil ... Lk 4:2 *3985*
t him, saying, Master, what shall ... Lk 10:25 *1598*
Christ, as some of them also *t* ... 1Cor 10:9 *3985*
to be *t* above that ye are able ... 1Cor 10:13 *3985*
thyself, lest thou also be *t* ... Gal 6:1 *3985*
some means the tempter have *t* you ... 1Th 3:5 *3985*
he himself hath suffered being *t* ... Heb 2:18 *3985*
able to succour them that are *t* ... Heb 2:18 *3985*
When your fathers *t* me, proved me ... Heb 3:9 *3985*
in all points *t* like as we are ... Heb 4:15 *3985*
they were sawn asunder, were *t* ... Heb 11:37 *3985*
when he is *t*, I am *t* of God ... Jas 1:13 *3985*
for God cannot be *t* with evil ... Jas 1:13 *551*
But every man is *t*, when he is ... Jas 1:14 *3985*

TEMPTER
when the *t* came to him, he said, ... Mt 4:3 *3985*
some means the *t* have tempted you ... 1Th 3:5 *3985*

TEMPTETH
with evil, neither *t* he any man ... Jas 1:13 *3985*

TEMPTING
t desired him that he would shew ... Mt 16:1 *3985*
t him, and saying unto him, Is it ... Mt 19:3 *3985*
him a question, *t* him, and saying, ... Mt 22:35 *3985*
of him a sign from heaven, *t* him ... Mk 8:11 *3985*
put away his wife? *t* him ... Mk 10:2 *3985*
t him, sought of him a sign from ... Lk 11:16 *3985*
t him, that they might have to ... Jn 8:6 *3985*

TEN
were nine hundred and *t* years ... Gen 5:14 6235
after Abram had dwelt *t* years in ... Gen 16:3 6235
Peradventure *t* shall be found ... Gen 18:32 6235
the servant took *t* camels of the ... Gen 24:10 6235
hands of *t* shekels weight of gold ... Gen 24:22 6235
us a few days, at the least *t* ... Gen 24:55 6218
me, and changed my wages *t* times ... Gen 31:7 6235
hast changed my wages *t* times ... Gen 31:41 6235
t bulls, twenty she asses ... Gen 32:15 6235
twenty she asses, and *t* foals ... Gen 32:15 6235
Joseph's *t* brethren went down to ... Gen 42:3 6235
t asses laden with the good ... Gen 45:23 6235
t she asses laden with corn and ... Gen 45:23 6235
into Egypt, were threescore and *t* ... Gen 46:27
for him threescore and *t* days ... Gen 50:3
lived an hundred and *t* years ... Gen 50:22 6235
being an hundred and *t* years old ... Gen 50:26 6235
and threescore and *t* palm trees ... Ex 15:27
t curtains of fine twined linen ... Ex 26:1 6235
T cubits shall be the length of a ... Ex 26:16 6235
pillars *t*, and their sockets *t* ... Ex 27:12 6235
the covenant, the *t* commandments ... Ex 34:28 6235
t curtains of fine twined linen ... Ex 36:8 6235
length of a board was *t* cubits ... Ex 36:21 6235
pillars *t*, and their sockets *t* ... Ex 38:12 6235
shall put *t* thousand to flight ... Lev 26:8 7233
t women shall bake your bread in ... Lev 26:26 6235
and for the female *t* shekels ... Lev 27:5 6235
and for the female *t* shekels ... Lev 27:7 6235
One spoon of *t* shekels of gold, ... Num 7:14 6235
One spoon of gold of *t* shekels ... Num 7:20 6235
One golden spoon of *t* shekels ... Num 7:26 6235
One golden spoon of *t* shekels ... Num 7:32 6235

One golden spoon of *t* shekels Num 7:38 6235
One golden spoon of *t* shekels Num 7:44 6235
One golden spoon of *t* shekels Num 7:50 6235
One golden spoon of *t* shekels Num 7:56 6235
One golden spoon of *t* shekels Num 7:62 6235
One golden spoon of *t* shekels Num 7:68 6235
One golden spoon of *t* shekels Num 7:74 6235
One golden spoon of *t* shekels Num 7:80 6235
weighing *t* shekels apiece, after Num 7:86 6235
nor five days, neither *t* days Num 11:19 6235
gathered least gathered *t* homers Num 11:32 6235
have tempted me now these *t* times Num 14:22 6235
And on the fourth day *t* bullocks Num 29:23 6235
and threescore and *t* palm trees Num 33:9
to perform, even *t* commandments Deut 4:13 6235
the *t* commandments, which the Deut 10:4 6235
with threescore and *t* persons Deut 10:22
two put *t* thousand to flight, Deut 32:30 7233
he came with *t* thousands of Deut 33:2 7233
they are the *t* thousands of Deut 33:17 7233
t cities with their villages Josh 15:57 6235
there fell *t* portions to Manasseh Josh 17:5 6235
half tribe of Manasseh, *t* cities Josh 21:5 6235
All the cities were *t* with their Josh 21:26 6235
And with him *t* princes, of each Josh 22:14 6235
being an hundred and *t* years old Josh 24:29 6235
of them in Bezek *t* thousand men Judg 1:4 6235
t kings, having their thumbs and Judg 1:7
being an hundred and *t* years old Judg 2:8 6235
at that time about *t* thousand men Judg 3:29 6235
take with thee *t* thousand men of Judg 4:6 6235
he went up with *t* thousand men at Judg 4:10 6235
and *t* thousand men after him Judg 4:14 6235
Then Gideon took *t* men of his Judg 6:27 6235
and there remained *t* thousand Judg 7:3 6235
t sons of his body begotten Judg 8:30
t persons, reign over you, or Judg 9:2
t pieces of silver out of the Judg 9:4
t persons, upon one stone Judg 9:5
t persons, upon one stone, and Judg 9:18
t sons of Jerubbaal might come, Judg 9:24
and he judged Israel *t* years Judg 12:11 6235
rode on threescore and *t* ass colts Judg 12:14
I will give thee *t* shekels of Judg 17:10 6235
we will take *t* men of an hundred Judg 20:10 6235
and a thousand out of *t* thousand Judg 20:10 7233
there came against Gibeah *t* Judg 20:34 6235
they dwelled there about *t* years Ruth 1:4 6235
he took *t* men of the elders of Ruth 4:2 6235
not I better to thee than *t* sons 1Sa 1:8 6235
thousand and threescore and *t* men 1Sa 6:19
and *t* thousand men of Judah 1Sa 15:4 6235
these *t* loaves, and run to the 1Sa 17:17 6235
carry these *t* cheeses unto the 1Sa 17:18 6235
and David his *t* thousands 1Sa 18:7 7233
ascribed unto David *t* thousands 1Sa 18:8 7233
and David his *t* thousands 1Sa 21:11 7233
And David sent out *t* young men 1Sa 25:5 6235
came to pass about *t* days after 1Sa 25:38 6235
and David his *t* thousands 1Sa 29:5 7233
And the king left *t* women, which 2Sa 15:16 6235
thou art worth *t* thousand of us 2Sa 18:3 6235
given thee *t* shekels of silver 2Sa 18:11 6235
t young men that bare Joab's 2Sa 18:15 6235
We have *t* parts in the king, and 2Sa 19:43 6235
the king took the *t* women his 2Sa 20:3 6235
T fat oxen, and twenty oxen out of 1Kin 4:23 6235
t thousand a month by courses 1Kin 5:14 6235
t thousand that bare burdens, and 1Kin 5:15
t cubits was the breadth thereof 1Kin 6:3 6235
of olive tree, each *t* cubits high 1Kin 6:23 6235
part of the other were *t* cubits 1Kin 6:24 6235
And the other cherub was *t* cubits 1Kin 6:25 6235
of the one cherub was *t* cubits 1Kin 6:26 6235
great stones, stones of *t* cubits 1Kin 7:10 6235
t cubits from the one brim to the 1Kin 7:23 6235
t in a cubit, compassing the sea 1Kin 7:24 6235
And he made *t* bases of brass 1Kin 7:27 6235
this manner he made the *t* bases 1Kin 7:37 6235
Then made he *t* lavers of brass 1Kin 7:38 6235
one of the *t* bases one laver 1Kin 7:38 6235
bases, and *t* lavers on the bases 1Kin 7:43 6235
to Jeroboam, Take thee *t* pieces 1Kin 11:31 6235
will give *t* tribes to thee 1Kin 11:31 6235
give it unto thee, even *t* tribes 1Kin 11:35 6235
And take with thee *t* loaves 1Kin 14:3 6235
took with him *t* talents of silver 2Kin 5:5 6235
of gold, and *t* changes of raiment 2Kin 5:5 6235
t chariots, and *t* thousand 2Kin 13:7 6235
in the valley of salt *t* thousand 2Kin 14:7 6235
reigned *t* years in Samaria 2Kin 15:17 6235
t degrees, or go back *t* degrees 2Kin 20:9 6235
the shadow to go down *t* degrees 2Kin 20:10 6235
shadow return backward *t* degrees 2Kin 20:10 6235
the shadow *t* degrees backward 2Kin 20:11 6235
even *t* thousand captives, and all 2Kin 24:14 6235
t men with him, and smote Gedaliah 2Kin 25:25 6235
of Manasseh, by lot, *t* cities 1Chr 6:61 6235
t thousand men that drew sword 1Chr 21:5
t thousand drams, and of silver 1Chr 29:7 7239
of silver *t* thousand talents, and 1Chr 29:7 6235
t thousand men to bear burdens, 2Chr 2:2
t thousand of them to be bearers 2Chr 2:18
t cubits the height thereof 2Chr 4:1 6235
sea of *t* cubits from brim to brim 2Chr 4:2 6235
t in a cubit, compassing the sea 2Chr 4:3 6235
He made also *t* lavers, and put 2Chr 4:6 6235
he made *t* candlesticks of gold 2Chr 4:7 6235
He made also *t* tables, and placed 2Chr 4:8 6235
days the land was quiet *t* years 2Chr 14:1 6235
the children of Seir *t* thousand 2Chr 25:11 6235
other *t* thousand left alive did 2Chr 25:12 6235
t thousand measures of wheat 2Chr 27:5 6235
and *t* thousand of barley 2Chr 27:5 6235
t bullocks, an hundred rams, and 2Chr 29:32
bullocks and *t* thousand sheep 2Chr 30:24 6235
months and *t* days in Jerusalem 2Chr 36:9 6235
to fulfil threescore and *t* years 2Chr 36:21
a second sort four hundred and *t* Ezr 1:10 6235
and with him an hundred and *t* males. Ezr 8:12 6235
t of their brethren with them, Ezr 8:24 6235
came, they said unto us *t* times Neh 4:12 6235
once in *t* days store of all sorts Neh 5:18 6235
to bring one of *t* to dwell in Neh 11:1 6235
I will pay *t* thousand talents of Est 3:9 6235
The *t* sons of Haman the son of Est 9:10 6235
palace, and the *t* sons of Haman Est 9:12 6235
let Haman's *t* sons be hanged upon Est 9:13 6235
and they hanged Haman's *t* sons Est 9:14 6235
These *t* times have ye reproached Job 19:3 6235
afraid of *t* thousands of people Ps 3:6 7233
and an instrument of *t* strings Ps 33:2 6218
years are threescore years and *t* Ps 90:10
t thousand at thy right hand Ps 91:7 7233
Upon an instrument of *t* strings Ps 92:3 6218
an instrument of *t* strings will I Ps 144:9 6218
t thousands in our streets Ps 144:13 7231
the wise more than *t* mighty men Eccl 7:19 6235
the chiefest among *t* thousand Song 5:10 7233
t acres of vineyard shall yield Is 5:10 6235
dial of Ahaz, *t* degrees backward Is 38:8 6235
So the sun returned *t* degrees Is 38:8 6235
even *t* men with him, came unto Jer 41:1 6235
the *t* men that were with him, and Jer 41:2 6235
But *t* men were found among them Jer 41:8 6235
And it came to pass after *t* days Jer 42:7 6235
the entry of the gate, *t* cubits Eze 40:11 6235
breadth of the door was *t* cubits Eze 41:2 6235
a walk of *t* cubits breadth inward Eze 42:4 6235
the breadth shall be *t* thousand Eze 45:1 6235
and the breadth of *t* thousand Eze 45:3 6235
the *t* thousand of breadth, shall Eze 45:5 6235
cor, which is an homer of *t* baths Eze 45:14 6235
for *t* baths are an homer Eze 45:14 6235
and of *t* thousand in breadth Eze 48:9 6235
toward the west *t* thousand in Eze 48:10 6235
toward the east *t* thousand in Eze 48:10 6235
length, and *t* thousand in breadth Eze 48:13 6235
and the breadth *t* thousand Eze 48:13 6235
shall be *t* thousand eastward Eze 48:18 6235
and *t* thousand westward Eze 48:18 6235
servants, I beseech thee, *t* days Dan 1:12 6235
matter, and proved them *t* days Dan 1:14 6235
at the end of *t* days their Dan 1:15 6235
he found them *t* times better than Dan 1:20 6235
and it had *t* horns Dan 7:7 6236
unto him, and *t* thousand times Dan 7:10 7240
t thousand stood before him Dan 7:10 7240
of the *t* horns that were in his Dan 7:20 6236
the *t* horns out of this kingdom Dan 7:24 6236
are *t* kings that shall arise Dan 7:24 6236
shall cast down many *t* thousands Dan 11:12 7239
forth by an hundred shall leave *t* Amos 5:3 6235
if there remain *t* men in one Amos 6:9 6235
or with *t* thousands of rivers of Mic 6:7 7233
twenty measures, there were but *t* Hag 2:16 6235
these threescore and *t* years Zec 1:12
and the breadth thereof *t* cubits Zec 5:2 6235
that *t* men shall take hold out of Zec 8:23 6235
which owed him *t* thousand talents Mt 18:24 *3463*
And when the *t* heard it, they were Mt 20:24 *1176*
heaven be likened unto *t* virgins Mt 25:1 *1176*
it unto him which hath *t* talents Mt 25:28 *1176*
And when the *t* heard it, they Mk 10:41 *1176*
whether he be able with *t* Lk 14:31 *1176*
woman having *t* pieces of silver Lk 15:8 *1176*
there met him *t* men that were Lk 17:12 *1176*
said, Were there not *t* cleansed Lk 17:17 *1176*
And he called his *t* servants Lk 19:13 *1176*
and delivered them *t* pounds Lk 19:13 *1176*
thy pound hath gained *t* pounds Lk 19:16 *1176*
have thou authority over *t* cities Lk 19:17 *1176*
give it to him that hath *t* pounds Lk 19:24 *1176*
unto him, Lord, he hath *t* pounds Lk 19:25 *1176*
and horsemen threescore and *t* Acts 23:23
among them more than *t* days Acts 25:6 *1176*
For though ye have *t* thousand 1Cor 4:15 *3463*
than *t* thousand words in an 1Cor 14:19 *3463*
the Lord cometh with *t* thousands Jude 14 *3461*
ye shall have tribulation *t* days Rev 2:10 *1176*
the number of them was *t* thousand Rev 5:11 *3461*
thousand times *t* thousand Rev 5:11 *3461*
t horns, and seven crowns upon his Rev 12:3 *1176*
t horns, and upon his horns Rev 13:1 *1176*
and upon his horns *t* crowns Rev 13:1 *1176*
having seven heads and *t* horns Rev 17:3 *1176*
hath the seven heads and *t* horns Rev 17:7 *1176*
the *t* horns which thou sawest are Rev 17:12 *1176*
which thou sawest are *t* kings Rev 17:12 *1176*
the *t* horns which thou sawest Rev 17:16 *1176*

TEND
diligent *t* only to plenteousness Prov 21:5

TENDER
unto the herd, and fetcht a calf *t* Gen 18:7 7390
Leah was *t* eyed Gen 29:17 7390
knoweth that the children are *t* Gen 33:13 7390
that the man that is *t* among you Deut 28:54 7390
The *t* and delicate woman among you. Deut 28:56 7390
as the small rain upon the *t* herb Deut 32:2
as the *t* grass springing out of 2Sa 23:4
Because thine heart was *t* 2Kin 22:19 7401
Solomon my son is young and *t* 1Chr 22:5 7390
hath chosen, is yet young and *t* 1Chr 29:1 7390
Because thine heart was *t* 2Chr 34:27 7401
that the *t* branch thereof will Job 14:7 3127
bud of the *t* herb to spring forth Job 38:27
O LORD, thy *t* mercies and thy Ps 25:6
not thou thy *t* mercies from me Ps 40:11
of thy *t* mercies blot out my Ps 51:1
to the multitude of thy *t* mercies Ps 69:16
he in anger shut up his *t* mercies Ps 77:9
let thy *t* mercies speedily Ps 79:8
with lovingkindness and *t* mercies Ps 103:4
Let thy *t* mercies come unto me, Ps 119:77
Great are thy *t* mercies, O LORD Ps 119:156
his *t* mercies are over all his Ps 145:9
For I was my father's son, *t* Prov 4:3 7390
but the *t* mercies of the wicked Prov 12:10
the *t* grass sheweth itself, and Prov 27:25
the vines with the *t* grape give a Song 2:13
for our vines have *t* grapes Song 2:15
whether the *t* grape appear, and Song 7:12
thou shalt no more be called *t* Is 47:1 7390
grow up before him as a *t* plant Is 53:2 3126
top of his young twigs a *t* one Eze 17:22 7390
t love with the prince of the Dan 1:9
in the *t* grass of the field Dan 4:15
in the *t* grass of the field Dan 4:23
When his branch is yet *t*, and Mt 24:32 *527*
When her branch is yet *t*, and Mk 13:28 *527*
Through the *t* mercy of our God Lk 1:78 *4698*
is very pitiful, and of *t* mercy Jas 5:11 *3629*

TENDERHEARTED
when Rehoboam was young and *t* 2Chr 13:7
And be ye kind one to another, *t* Eph 4:32 *2155*

TENDERNESS
the ground for delicateness and *t* Deut 28:56 7391

TENDETH
labour of the righteous *t* to life Prov 10:16
As righteousness *t* to life Prov 11:19
than is meet, but it *t* to poverty Prov 11:24
talk of the lips *t* only to penury Prov 14:23
The fear of the LORD *t* to life Prov 19:23

TENONS
Two *t* shall there be in one board Ex 26:17 3027
under one board for his two *t* Ex 26:19 3027
under another board for his two *t* Ex 26:19 3027
One board had two *t*, equally Ex 36:22 3027
under one board for his two *t* Ex 36:24 3027
under another board for his two *t* Ex 36:24 3027

TENOR
according to the *t* of these words Gen 43:7 6310
for after the *t* of these words I Ex 34:27 6310

TEN'S
I will not destroy it for *t* sake Gen 18:32 6235

TENS
rulers of fifties, and rulers of *t* Ex 18:21 6235
rulers of fifties, and rulers of *t* Ex 18:25 6235
over fifties, and captains over *t* Deut 1:15 6235

TENT
and he was uncovered within his *t* Gen 9:21 168
east of Beth-el, and pitched his *t* Gen 12:8 168
unto the place where his *t* had Gen 13:3 168
pitched his *t* toward Sodom Gen 13:12 167
Then Abram removed his *t*, and came Gen 13:18 167
he sat in the *t* door in the heat Gen 18:1 168
ran to meet them from the *t* door Gen 18:2 168
hastened into the *t* unto Sarah Gen 18:6 168
And he said, Behold, in the *t* Gen 18:9 168
And Sarah heard it in the *t* door Gen 18:10 168
her into his mother Sarah's *t* Gen 24:67 168
pitched his *t* in the valley of Gen 26:17
the LORD, and pitched his *t* there Gen 26:25 168
had pitched his *t* in the mount Gen 31:25 168
Jacob's *t*, and into Leah's *t* Gen 31:33 168
Then went he out of Leah's *t* Gen 31:33 168
and entered into Rachel's *t* Gen 31:33 168
And Laban searched all the *t* Gen 31:34 168
pitched his *t* before the city Gen 33:18
field, where he had spread his *t* Gen 33:19 168
spread his *t* beyond the tower of Gen 35:21 168
and they came into the *t* Ex 18:7 168
loops, and couple the *t* together Ex 26:11 168
of the curtains of the *t*, the Ex 26:12 168
length of the curtains of the *t* Ex 26:13 168
for the *t* of rams' skins dyed red Ex 26:14 168
an hanging for the door of the *t* Ex 26:36 168
and stood every man at his *t* door Ex 33:8 168
every man in his *t* door Ex 33:10 168
The tabernacle, his *t*, and his Ex 35:11 168
for the *t* over the tabernacle Ex 36:14 168
of brass to couple the *t* together Ex 36:18 168
for the *t* of rams' skins dyed red Ex 36:19 168
t of the congregation finished Ex 39:32 168
the tabernacle unto Moses, the *t* Ex 39:33 168
for the *t* of the congregation, Ex 39:40 168
of the *t* of the congregation Ex 40:2 168
of the *t* of the congregation Ex 40:6 168
between the *t* of the congregation Ex 40:7 168
abroad the *t* over the tabernacle Ex 40:19 168
covering of the *t* above upon it Ex 40:19 168
in the *t* of the congregation Ex 40:22 168
in the *t* of the congregation Ex 40:24 168
t of the congregation before the Ex 40:26 168
of the *t* of the congregation Ex 40:29 168
between the *t* of the congregation Ex 40:30 168
into the *t* of the congregation Ex 40:32 168
covered the *t* of the congregation Ex 40:34 168
into the *t* of the congregation Ex 40:35 168
abroad out of his *t* seven days Lev 14:8 168
shall be the tabernacle, and the *t* Num 3:25 168
namely, the *t* of the testimony Num 9:15 168
every man in the door of his *t* Num 11:10 168
the law, when a man dieth in a *t* Num 19:14 168
all that come into the *t*, and all Num 19:14 168
and all that is in the *t* Num 19:14 168
water, and sprinkle it upon the *t* Num 19:18 168

the man of Israel into the *t* ... Num 25:8 6898
in the earth in the midst of my *t* ... Josh 7:21 168
and they ran unto the *t* ... Josh 7:22 168
and, behold, it was hid in his *t* ... Josh 7:22 168
them out of the midst of the *t* ... Josh 7:23 168
his asses, and his sheep, and his *t* ... Josh 7:24 168
pitched his *t* unto the plain of ... Judg 4:11 168
fled away on his feet to the *t* of ... Judg 4:17 168
had turned in unto her into the *t* ... Judg 4:18 168
her, Stand in the door of the *t* ... Judg 4:20 168
Heber's wife took a nail of the *t* ... Judg 4:21 168
And when he came into her *t* ... Judg 4:22
shall she be above women in the *t* ... Judg 5:24 168
of Israel every man unto his *t* ... Judg 7:8 168
host of Midian, and came unto a *t* ... Judg 7:13 168
it, that the *t* lay along ... Judg 7:13 168
We will not any of us go to his *t* ... Judg 20:8 168
and they fled every man into his *t* ... 1Sa 4:10 168
people he sent every man to his *t* ... 1Sa 13:2 168
but he put his armour in his *t* ... 1Sa 17:54 168
this day, but have walked in a *t* ... 2Sa 7:6 168
So they spread Absalom a *t* upon ... 2Sa 16:22 168
Israel fled every one to his *t* ... 2Sa 18:17 168
had fled every man to his *t* ... 2Sa 19:8 168
from the city, every man to his *t* ... 2Sa 20:22 168
of the camp, they went into one *t* ... 2Kin 7:8 168
again, and entered into another *t* ... 2Kin 7:8 168
ark of God, and pitched for it a *t* ... 1Chr 15:1 168
set it in the midst of the *t* that ... 1Chr 16:1 168
but have gone from *t* to *t* ... 1Chr 17:5 168
pitched a *t* for it at Jerusalem ... 2Chr 1:4 168
and they fled every man to his *t* ... 2Chr 25:22 168
the *t* which he placed among men ... Ps 78:60 168
shall the Arabian pitch *t* there ... Is 13:20 167
removed from me as a shepherd's *t* ... Is 38:12 168
them out as a *t* to dwell in ... Is 40:22 168
Enlarge the place of thy *t* ... Is 54:2 168
to stretch forth my *t* any more ... Jer 10:20 168
they rise up every man in his *t* ... Jer 37:10 168

TENTH
continually until the *t* month ... Gen 8:5 6224
in the *t* month, on the first day ... Gen 8:5 6224
will surely give the *t* unto thee ... Gen 28:22 6237
In the *t* day of this month they ... Ex 12:3 6218
an omer is the *t* part of an ephah ... Ex 16:36 6224
with the one lamb a *t* deal of ... Ex 29:40 6241
bring for his offering the *t* part ... Lev 5:11 6224
the *t* part of an ephah of fine ... Lev 6:20 6224
three *t* deals of fine flour for a ... Lev 14:10 6241
one *t* deal of fine flour mingled ... Lev 14:21 6241
on the *t* day of the month, ye ... Lev 16:29 6218
two *t* deals of fine flour mingled ... Lev 23:13 6241
two wave loaves of two *t* deals ... Lev 23:17 6241
Also on the *t* day of this seventh ... Lev 23:27 6218
two *t* deals shall be in one cake ... Lev 24:5 6241
on the *t* day of the seventh month ... Lev 25:9 6218
the *t* shall be holy unto the LORD ... Lev 27:32 6224
the *t* part of an ephah of barley ... Num 5:15 6224
On the *t* day Ahiezer the son of ... Num 7:66 6224
t deal of flour mingled with the ... Num 15:4 6241
t deals of flour mingled with the ... Num 15:6 6241
a meat offering of three *t* deals ... Num 15:9 6241
t in Israel for an inheritance ... Num 18:21 4643
even a *t* part of the tithe ... Num 18:26 4643
a *t* part of an ephah of flour for ... Num 28:5 6224
two *t* deals of flour for a meat ... Num 28:9 6241
three *t* deals of flour for a meat ... Num 28:12 6241
two *t* deals of flour for a meat ... Num 28:12 6241
a several *t* deal of flour mingled ... Num 28:13 6241
three *t* deals shall ye offer for ... Num 28:20 6241
bullock, and two *t* deals for a ram ... Num 28:20 6241
A several *t* deal shalt thou offer ... Num 28:21 6241
three *t* deals unto one bullock, ... Num 28:28 6241
two *t* deals unto one ram, ... Num 28:28 6241
A several *t* deal unto one lamb, ... Num 28:29 6241
three *t* deals for a bullock ... Num 29:3 6241
and two *t* deals for a ram, ... Num 29:3 6241
And one *t* deal for one lamb, ... Num 29:4 6241
ye shall have on the *t* day of ... Num 29:7 6218
three *t* deals to a bullock ... Num 29:9 6241
and two *t* deals to one ram, ... Num 29:9 6241
A several *t* deal for one lamb, ... Num 29:10 6241
three *t* deals unto every bullock ... Num 29:14 6241
two *t* deals to each ram of the ... Num 29:14 6241
a several *t* deal to each lamb of ... Num 29:15 6241
even to his *t* generation shall he ... Deut 23:2 6224
even to their *t* generation shall ... Deut 23:3 6224
on the *t* day of the first month ... Josh 4:19 6218
he will take the *t* of your seed ... 1Sa 8:15 6237
He will take the *t* of your sheep ... 1Sa 8:17 6237
year of his reign, in the *t* month ... 2Kin 25:1 6218
in the *t* day of the month, that ... 2Kin 25:1 6218
Jeremiah the *t*, Machbanai the ... 1Chr 12:13 6224
to Jeshua, the *t* to Shecaniah, ... 1Chr 24:11 6224
The *t* to Shimei, he, his sons, and ... 1Chr 25:17 6224
The *t* captain for the *t* month ... 1Chr 27:13 6224
the *t* month to examine the matter ... Ezr 10:16 6224
his house royal in the *t* month ... Est 2:16 6224
But yet in it shall be a *t* ... Is 6:13 6224
Jeremiah from the LORD in the *t* ... Jer 32:1 6224
king of Judah, in the *t* month ... Jer 39:1 6224
year of his reign, in the *t* month ... Jer 52:4 6224
in the *t* day of the month, that ... Jer 52:4 6218
in the *t* day of the month, which ... Jer 52:12 6218
the *t* day of the month, that ... Eze 20:1 6218
in the ninth year, in the *t* month ... Eze 24:1 6224
in the *t* day of the month, the ... Eze 24:1 6218
In the *t* year, in the *t* month ... Eze 29:1 6224
of our captivity, in the *t* month ... Eze 33:21 6224
in the *t* day of the month, in the ... Eze 40:1 6218
contain the *t* part of an homer ... Eze 45:11 4643
the ephah the *t* part of an homer ... Eze 45:11 6224
ye shall offer the *t* part of a ... Eze 45:14 4643
the seventh, and the fast of the *t* ... Zec 8:19 6224
for it was about the *t* hour ... Jn 1:39 *1182*
also Abraham gave a *t* part of all ... Heb 7:2 *1181*
Abraham gave the *t* of the spoils ... Heb 7:4 *1181*
the *t* part of the city fell, and ... Rev 11:13 *1182*
the *t*, a chrysoprasus ... Rev 21:20 *1182*

TENTMAKERS
by their occupation they were *t* ... Acts 18:3 *4635*

TENTS
the father of such as dwell in *t* ... Gen 4:20 168
he shall dwell in the *t* of Shem ... Gen 9:27 168
Abram, had flocks, and herds, and *t* ... Gen 13:5 168
was a plain man, dwelling in *t* ... Gen 25:27 168
and into the two maidservants' *t* ... Gen 31:33 168
man for them which are in his *t* ... Ex 16:16 168
of Israel shall pitch their *t* ... Num 1:52
of Israel pitched their *t* ... Num 9:17
tabernacle they rested in their *t* ... Num 9:18
of the LORD they abode in their *t* ... Num 9:20
of Israel abode in their *t* ... Num 9:22
of the LORD they rested in the *t* ... Num 9:23
that they dwell in, whether in *t* ... Num 13:19 4264
from the *t* of these wicked men, ... Num 16:26 168
and stood in the door of their *t* ... Num 16:27 168
his *t* according to their tribes ... Num 24:2
How goodly are thy *t*, O Jacob, and ... Num 24:5 168
And ye murmured in your *t*, and said .. Deut 1:27 168
out a place to pitch your *t* in ... Deut 1:33
them, Get you into your *t* again ... Deut 5:30 168
and their households, and their *t* ... Deut 11:6 168
in the morning, and go unto thy *t* ... Deut 16:7 168
and, Issachar, in thy *t* ... Deut 33:18 168
the people removed from their *t* ... Josh 3:14 168
return ye, and get you unto your *t* ... Josh 22:4 168
and they went unto their *t* ... Josh 22:6 168
sent them away also unto their *t* ... Josh 22:7 168
with much riches unto your *t* ... Josh 22:8 168
up with their cattle and their *t* ... Judg 6:5 168
dwelt in *t* on the east of Nobah ... Judg 8:11 168
and they spoiled their *t* ... 1Sa 17:53 4264
and Israel, and Judah, abide in *t* ... 2Sa 11:11 5521
every man to his *t*, O Israel ... 2Sa 20:1 168
king, and went unto their *t* joyful ... 1Kin 8:66 168
to your *t*, O Israel ... 1Kin 12:16 168
So Israel departed unto their *t* ... 1Kin 12:16 168
in the twilight, and left their *t* ... 2Kin 7:7 168
asses tied, and the *t* as they were ... 2Kin 7:10 168
spoiled the *t* of the Syrians ... 2Kin 7:16 4264
and the people fled into their *t* ... 2Kin 8:21 168
of Israel dwelt in their *t* ... 2Kin 13:5 168
and they fled every man to their *t* ... 2Kin 14:12 168
king of Judah, and smote their *t* ... 1Chr 4:41 168
they dwelt in their *t* throughout ... 1Chr 5:10 168
sent the people away into their *t* ... 2Chr 7:10 168
every man to your *t*, O Israel, and ... 2Chr 10:16 168
So all Israel went to their *t* ... 2Chr 10:16 168
They smote also the *t* of cattle ... 2Chr 14:15 168
in the gates of the *t* of the LORD ... 2Chr 31:2 4264
and there abode we in *t* three days ... Ezr 8:15 2583
and let none dwell in their *t* ... Ps 69:25 168
of Israel to dwell in their *t* ... Ps 78:55 168
to dwell in the *t* of wickedness ... Ps 84:10 168
But murmured in their *t*, and ... Ps 106:25 168
that I dwell in the *t* of Kedar ... Ps 120:5 168
as the *t* of Kedar, as the ... Song 1:5 168
thy kids beside the shepherds' *t* ... Song 1:8 4908
suddenly are my *t* spoiled ... Jer 4:20 168
they shall pitch their *t* against ... Jer 6:3 168
again the captivity of Jacob's *t* ... Jer 30:18 168
all your days ye shall dwell in *t* ... Jer 35:7 168
But we have dwelt in *t*, and have ... Jer 35:10 168
Their *t* and their flocks shall ... Jer 49:29 168
I saw the *t* of Cushan in ... Hab 3:7 168
shall save the *t* of Judah first ... Zec 12:7 168
beasts that shall be in these *t* ... Zec 14:15 4264

TERAH (*te'-rah*) See THARA. *Father of Abraham.*
nine and twenty years, and begat *T* ... Gen 11:24 8646
lived after he begat *T* an hundred ... Gen 11:25 8646
T lived seventy years, and begat ... Gen 11:26 8646
these are the generations of *T* ... Gen 11:27 8646
T begat Abram, Nahor, and Haran ... Gen 11:27 8646
T in the land of his nativity ... Gen 11:28 8646
T took Abram his son, and Lot the ... Gen 11:31 8646
the days of *T* were two hundred and ... Gen 11:32 8646
and *T* died in Haran ... Gen 11:32 8646
of the flood in old time, even *T* ... Josh 24:2 8646
Serug, Nahor, *T*, ... 1Chr 1:26 8646

TERAPHIM
of gods, and made an ephod, and *t* ... Judg 17:5 8655
is in these houses an ephod, and *t* ... Judg 18:14 8655
image, and the ephod, and the *t* ... Judg 18:17 8655
carved image, the ephod, and the *t* ... Judg 18:18 8655
and he took the ephod, and the *t* ... Judg 18:20 8655
and without an ephod, and without *t* ... Hos 3:4 8655

TERESH (*te'-resh*) *A servant of King Ahasuerus.*
king's chamberlains, Bigthan and *T* ... Est 2:21 8657
had told of Bigthana and *T* ... Est 6:2 8657

TERMED
Thou shalt no more be *t* Forsaken ... Is 62:4 559
thy land any more be *t* Desolate ... Is 62:4 559

TERRACES
trees *t* to the house of the LORD ... 2Chr 9:11 4546

TERRESTRIAL
celestial bodies, and bodies *t* ... 1Cor 15:40 *1919*
and the glory of the *t* is another ... 1Cor 15:40 *1919*

TERRIBLE
for it is a *t* thing that I will ... Ex 34:10 3372
t wilderness, which ye saw by the ... Deut 1:19 3372
is among you, a mighty God and *t* ... Deut 7:21 3372
t wilderness, wherein were fiery ... Deut 8:15 3372
a great God, a mighty, and a *t* ... Deut 10:17 3372
t things, which thine eyes have ... Deut 10:21 3372
of an angel of God, very *t* ... Judg 13:6 3372
to do for you great things and *t* ... 2Sa 7:23 3372
t God, that keepeth covenant and ... Neh 1:5 3372
the LORD, which is great and *t* ... Neh 4:14 3372
great, the mighty, and the *t* God ... Neh 9:32 3372
with God is *t* majesty ... Job 37:22 3372
the glory of his nostrils is *t* ... Job 39:20 367
his teeth are *t* round about ... Job 41:14 367
hand shall teach thee *t* things ... Ps 45:4 3372
For the LORD most high is *t* ... Ps 47:2 3372
By *t* things in righteousness wilt ... Ps 65:5 3372
How *t* art thou in thy works ... Ps 66:3 3372
he is *t* in his doing toward the ... Ps 66:5 3372
thou art *t* out of thy holy places ... Ps 68:35 3372
he is *t* to the kings of the earth ... Ps 76:12 3372
them praise thy great and *t* name ... Ps 99:3 3372
Ham, and *t* things by the Red sea ... Ps 106:22 3372
speak of the might of thy *t* acts ... Ps 145:6 3372
t as an army with banners ... Song 6:4 366
t as an army with banners ... Song 6:10 366
lay low the haughtiness of the *t* ... Is 13:11 6184
peeled, to a people *t* from their ... Is 18:2 3372
from a people *t* from their ... Is 18:7 3372
from the desert, from a *t* land ... Is 21:1 3372
the city of the *t* nations shall ... Is 25:3 6184
when the blast of the *t* ones is ... Is 25:4 6184
the branch of the *t* ones shall be ... Is 25:5 6184
the multitude of the *t* ones shall ... Is 29:5 6184
For the *t* one is brought to ... Is 29:20 6184
the prey of the *t* shall be ... Is 49:25 6184
When thou didst *t* things which we ... Is 64:3 3372
thee out of the hand of the *t* ... Jer 15:21 6184
LORD is with me as a mighty *t* one ... Jer 20:11 6184
an oven because of the *t* famine ... Lam 5:10 2152
as the colour of the *t* crystal ... Eze 1:22 3372
upon thee, the *t* of the nations ... Eze 28:7 6184
the *t* of the nations, shall be ... Eze 30:11 6184
the *t* of the nations, have cut ... Eze 31:12 6184
the *t* of the nations, all of them ... Eze 32:12 6184
and the form thereof was *t* ... Dan 2:31 1763
a fourth beast, dreadful and *t* ... Dan 7:7 574
of the LORD is great and very *t* ... Joel 2:11 3372
the *t* day of the LORD come ... Joel 2:31 3372
They are *t* and dreadful ... Hab 1:7 366
The LORD will be *t* unto them ... Zeph 2:11 3372
so *t* was the sight, that Moses ... Heb 12:21 *5398*

TERRIBLENESS
outstretched arm, and with great *t* ... Deut 26:8 4172
thee a name of greatness and *t* ... 1Chr 17:21 3372
Thy *t* hath deceived thee, and the ... Jer 49:16 8606

TERRIBLY
he ariseth to shake *t* the earth ... Is 2:19 6206
he ariseth to shake *t* the earth ... Is 2:21 6206
the fir trees shall be *t* shaken ... Nah 2:3

TERRIFIED
neither be ye *t* because of them ... Deut 20:3 6206
of wars and commotions, be not *t* ... Lk 21:9 *4422*
But they were *t* and affrighted, and ... Lk 24:37 *4422*
in nothing *t* by your adversaries ... Phil 1:28 *4426*

TERRIFIEST
dreams, and *t* me through visions ... Job 7:14 1204

TERRIFY
let the blackness of the day *t* it ... Job 3:5 1204
from me, and let not his fear *t* me ... Job 9:34 1204
did the contempt of families *t* me ... Job 31:34 2865
as if I would *t* you by letters ... 2Cor 10:9 *1629*

TERROR
the *t* of God was upon the cities ... Gen 35:5 2847
I will even appoint over you *t* ... Lev 26:16 928
t within, shall destroy both the ... Deut 32:25 367
in all the great *t* which Moses ... Deut 34:12 4172
that your *t* is fallen upon us, and ... Josh 2:9 367
from God was a *t* to me, and by ... Job 31:23 6343
my *t* shall not make thee afraid, ... Job 33:7 367
not be afraid for the *t* by night ... Ps 91:5 6343
hosts, shall lop the bough with *t* ... Is 10:33 4637
of Judah shall be a *t* unto Egypt ... Is 19:17 2283
Thine heart shall meditate *t* ... Is 33:18 367
and from *t* ... Is 54:14 4288
Be not a *t* unto me ... Jer 17:17 4288
I will make thee a *t* to thyself ... Jer 20:4 4032
out arm, and with great *t* ... Jer 32:21 4172
which cause their *t* to be on all ... Eze 26:17 2851
I will make thee a *t*, and thou ... Eze 26:21 1091
thou shalt be a *t*, and never shalt ... Eze 27:36 1091
thou shalt be a *t*, and never shalt ... Eze 28:19 1091
which caused *t* in the land of the ... Eze 32:23 2851
which caused their *t* in the land ... Eze 32:24 2851
though their *t* was caused in the ... Eze 32:25 2851
though they caused their *t* in the ... Eze 32:26 2851
though they were the *t* of the ... Eze 32:27 2851
with their *t* they are ashamed of ... Eze 32:30 2851
For I have caused my *t* in the ... Eze 32:32 2851
rulers are not a *t* to good works ... Rom 13:3 *5401*
therefore the *t* of the Lord ... 2Cor 5:11 *5401*
and be not afraid of their *t* ... 1Pet 3:14 *5401*

TERRORS
stretched out arm, and by great *t* ... Deut 4:34 4172
the *t* of God do set themselves in ... Job 6:4 1161
T shall make him afraid on every ... Job 18:11 1091
shall bring him to the king of *t* ... Job 18:14 1091
t are upon him ... Job 20:25 367
they are in the *t* of the shadow ... Job 24:17 1091

T take hold on him as waters, a ... Job 27:20 1091
T are turned upon me ... Job 30:15 1091
the *t* of death are fallen upon me ... Ps 55:4 367
they are utterly consumed with *t* ... Ps 73:19 1091
I suffer thy *t* I am distracted ... Ps 88:15 367
thy *t* have cut me off ... Ps 88:16 1161
it suddenly, and *t* upon the city ... Jer 15:8 928
in a solemn day my *t* round about ... Lam 2:22 4032
t by reason of the sword shall be ... Eze 21:12 4048

TERTIUS (*tur'-she-us*) *An assistant of Paul.*
I *T*, who wrote this epistle, ... Rom 16:22 *5060*

TERTULLUS (*tur-tul'-lus*) *An orator who opposed Paul.*
and with a certain orator named *T* ... Acts 24:1 *5061*
T began to accuse him, saying, ... Acts 24:2 *5061*

TESTAMENT
For this is my blood of the new *t* ... Mt 26:28 *1242*
This is my blood of the new *t* ... Mk 14:24 *1242*
This cup is the new *t* in my blood ... Lk 22:20 *1242*
This cup is the new *t* in my blood ... 1Cor 11:25 *1242*
us able ministers of the new *t* ... 2Cor 3:6 *1242*
away in the reading of the old *t* ... 2Cor 3:14 *1242*
Jesus made a surety of a better *t* ... Heb 7:22 *1242*
he is the mediator of the new *t* ... Heb 9:15 *1242*
that were under the first *t* ... Heb 9:15 *1242*
For where a *t* is, there must also ... Heb 9:16 *1242*
For a *t* is of force after men are ... Heb 9:17 *1242*
t was dedicated without blood ... Heb 9:18
This is the blood of the *t* which ... Heb 9:20 *1248*
in his temple the ark of his *t* ... Rev 11:19 *1248*

TESTATOR
necessity be the death of the *t* ... Heb 9:16 *1303*
at all while the *t* liveth ... Heb 9:17 *1303*

TESTIFIED
and it hath been *t* to his owner ... Ex 21:29 5749
hath *t* falsely against his ... Deut 19:18 6030
seeing the LORD hath *t* against me ... Ruth 1:21 6030
for thy mouth hath *t* against thee ... 2Sa 1:16 6030
Yet the LORD *t* against Israel, and ... 2Kin 17:13 5749
which he *t* against them ... 2Kin 17:15 5749
and they *t* against them ... 2Chr 24:19 5749
slew thy prophets which *t* against ... Neh 9:26 5749
I *t* against them in the day ... Neh 13:15 5749
Then I *t* against them, and said ... Neh 13:21 5749
the saying of the woman, which *t* ... Jn 4:39 *3140*
For Jesus himself *t*, that a ... Jn 4:44 *3140*
he was troubled in spirit, and *t* ... Jn 13:21 *3140*
And they, when they had *t* and ... Acts 8:25 *1263*
t to the Jews that Jesus was ... Acts 18:5 *1263*
for as thou hast *t* of me in ... Acts 23:11 *1263*
t the kingdom of God, persuading ... Acts 28:23 *1263*
because we have *t* of God that he ... 1Cor 15:15 *3140*
we also have forewarned you and *t* ... 1Th 4:6 *1263*
for all, to be *t* in due time ... 1Ti 2:6 *3142*
But one in a certain place *t* ... Heb 2:6 *1263*
signify, when it *t* beforehand the ... 1Pet 1:11 *4303*
of God which he hath *t* of his Son ... 1Jn 5:9 *3140*
t of the truth that is in thee, ... 3Jn 3 *3140*

TESTIFIEDST
t against them, that thou ... Neh 9:29 5749
t against them by thy spirit in ... Neh 9:30 5749

TESTIFIETH
the pride of Israel *t* to his face ... Hos 7:10 6030
he hath seen and heard, that he *t* ... Jn 3:32 *3140*
disciple which *t* of these things ... Jn 21:24 *3140*
For he *t*, Thou art a priest for ... Heb 7:17 *3140*
He which *t* these things saith, ... Rev 22:20 *3140*

TESTIFY
but one witness shall not *t* ... Num 35:30 6030
I *t* against you this day that ye ... Deut 8:19 5749
rise up against any man to *t* ... Deut 19:16 6030
that this song shall *t* against ... Deut 31:21 6030
which I *t* among you this day ... Deut 32:46 5749
thou didst *t* against them ... Neh 9:34 5749
thine own lips *t* against thee ... Job 15:6 6030
Israel, and I will *t* against thee ... Ps 50:7 5749
my people, and I will *t* unto thee ... Ps 81:8 5749
thee, and our sins *t* against us ... Is 59:12 6030
our iniquities *t* against us ... Jer 14:7 6030
of Israel doth *t* to his face ... Hos 5:5 6030
t in the house of Jacob, saith ... Amos 3:13 5749
t against me ... Mic 6:3 6030
that he may *t* unto them, lest ... Lk 16:28 *1263*
not that any should *t* of man ... Jn 2:25 *3140*
do know, and *t* that we have seen ... Jn 3:11 *3140*
and they are they which *t* of me ... Jn 5:39 *3140*
me it hateth, because I *t* of it ... Jn 7:7 *3140*
from the Father, he shall *t* of me ... Jn 15:26 *3140*
And with many other words did he *t* ... Acts 2:40 *1263*
to *t* that it is he which was ... Acts 10:42 *1263*
to *t* the gospel of the grace of ... Acts 20:24 *1263*
the beginning, if they would *t* ... Acts 26:5 *3140*
For I *t* again to every man that ... Gal 5:3 *3143*
t in the Lord, that ye henceforth ... Eph 4:17 *3143*
do *t* that the Father sent the Son ... 1Jn 4:14 *3140*
to *t* unto you these things in the ... Rev 22:16 *3140*
For I *t* unto every man that ... Rev 22:18 *4828*

TESTIFYING
T both to the Jews, and also to ... Acts 20:21 *1263*
was righteous, God *t* of his gifts ... Heb 11:4 *3140*
t that this is the true grace of ... 1Pet 5:12 *1957*

TESTIMONIES
These are the *t*, and the statutes, ... Deut 4:45 5713
of the LORD your God, and his *t* ... Deut 6:17 5713
to come, saying, What mean the *t* ... Deut 6:20 5713
and his judgments, and his *t* ... 1Kin 2:3 5715
his *t* which he testified against ... 2Kin 17:15 5715
to keep his commandments and his *t* ... 2Kin 23:3 5715
to keep thy commandments, thy *t* ... 1Chr 29:19 5715
keep his commandments, and his *t* ... 2Chr 34:31 5715
unto thy commandments and thy *t* ... Neh 9:34 5715
as keep his covenant and his *t* ... Ps 25:10 5713
most high God, and kept not his *t* ... Ps 78:56 5713
Thy *t* are very sure ... Ps 93:5 5713
they kept his *t*, and the ordinance ... Ps 99:7 5713
Blessed are they that keep his *t* ... Ps 119:2 5713
have rejoiced in the way of thy *t* ... Ps 119:14 5715
for I have kept thy *t* ... Ps 119:22 5713
Thy *t* also are my delight, and my ... Ps 119:24 5713
I have stuck unto thy *t* ... Ps 119:31 5715
Incline my heart unto thy *t* ... Ps 119:36 5715
speak of thy *t* also before kings ... Ps 119:46 5713
and turned my feet unto thy *t* ... Ps 119:59 5713
and those that have known thy *t* ... Ps 119:79 5713
but I will consider thy *t* ... Ps 119:95 5713
for thy *t* are my meditation ... Ps 119:99 5715
Thy *t* have I taken as an heritage ... Ps 119:111 5715
therefore I love thy *t* ... Ps 119:119 5713
that I may know thy *t* ... Ps 119:125 5713
Thy *t* are wonderful ... Ps 119:129 5715
Thy *t* that thou hast commanded ... Ps 119:138 5713
of thy *t* is everlasting ... Ps 119:144 5715
save me, and I shall keep thy *t* ... Ps 119:146 5713
Concerning thy *t*, I have known of ... Ps 119:152 5713
yet do I not decline from thy *t* ... Ps 119:157 5715
My soul hath kept thy *t* ... Ps 119:167 5713
I have kept thy precepts and thy *t* ... Ps 119:168 5713
nor in his statutes, nor in his *t* ... Jer 44:23 5715

TESTIMONY
so Aaron laid it up before the *T* ... Ex 16:34 5715
ark the *t* which I shall give thee ... Ex 25:16 5715
put the *t* that I shall give thee ... Ex 25:21 5715
which are upon the ark of the *t* ... Ex 25:22 5715
within the vail the ark of the *t* ... Ex 26:33 5715
of the *t* in the most holy place ... Ex 26:34 5715
the vail, which is before the *t* ... Ex 27:21 5715
vail that is by the ark of the *t* ... Ex 30:6 5715
the mercy seat that is over the *t* ... Ex 30:6 5715
therewith, and the ark of the *t* ... Ex 30:26 5715
put of it before the *t* in the ... Ex 30:36 5715
congregation, and the ark of the *t* ... Ex 31:7 5715
upon mount Sinai, two tables of *t* ... Ex 31:18 5715
tables of the *t* were in his hand ... Ex 32:15 5715
two tables of *t* in Moses' hand ... Ex 34:29 5715
even of the tabernacle of *t* ... Ex 38:21 5715
The ark of the *t*, and the staves ... Ex 39:35 5715
put therein the ark of the *t* ... Ex 40:3 5715
incense before the ark of the *t* ... Ex 40:5 5715
put the *t* into the ark, and set ... Ex 40:20 5715
and covered the ark of the *t* ... Ex 40:21 5715
the mercy seat that is upon the *t* ... Lev 16:13 5715
Without the vail of the *t* ... Lev 24:3 5715
Levites over the tabernacle of *t* ... Num 1:50 5715
round about the tabernacle of *t* ... Num 1:53 5715
the charge of the tabernacle of *t* ... Num 1:53 5715
and cover the ark of *t* with it ... Num 4:5 5715
seat that was upon the ark of *t* ... Num 7:89 5715
namely, the tent of the *t* ... Num 9:15 5715
from off the tabernacle of the *t* ... Num 10:11 5715
of the congregation before the *t* ... Num 17:4 5715
Aaron's rod again before the *t* ... Num 17:10 5715
that bear the ark of the *t* ... Josh 4:16 5715
and this was a *t* in Israel ... Ruth 4:7 8584
crown upon him, and gave him the *t* ... 2Kin 11:12 5715
him the crown, and gave him the *t* ... 2Chr 23:11 5715
the *t* of the LORD is sure, making ... Ps 19:7 5715
For he established a *t* in Jacob ... Ps 78:5 5715
he ordained in Joseph for a *t* ... Ps 81:5 5715
shall I keep the *t* of thy mouth ... Ps 119:88 5715
unto the *t* of Israel, to give ... Ps 122:4 5715
my *t* that I shall teach them, ... Ps 132:12 5713
Bind up the *t*, seal the law among ... Is 8:16 8584
To the law and to the *t* ... Is 8:20 8584
commanded, for a *t* unto them ... Mt 8:4 *3142*
for a *t* against them and the ... Mt 10:18 *3142*
commanded, for a *t* unto them ... Mk 1:44 *3142*
your feet for a *t* against them ... Mk 6:11 *3142*
for my sake, for a *t* against them ... Mk 13:9 *3142*
commanded, for a *t* unto them ... Lk 5:14 *3142*
your feet for a *t* against them ... Lk 9:5 *3142*
And it shall turn to you for a *t* ... Lk 21:13 *3142*
and no man receiveth his *t* ... Jn 3:32 *3141*
He that hath received his *t* hath ... Jn 3:33 *3141*
But I receive not *t* from man ... Jn 5:34 *3141*
that the *t* of two men is true ... Jn 8:17 *3141*
and we know that his *t* is true ... Jn 21:24 *3141*
to whom also he gave *t*, and said, ... Acts 13:22 *3140*
which gave *t* unto the word of his ... Acts 14:3 *3140*
not receive thy *t* concerning me ... Acts 22:18 *3141*
Even as the *t* of Christ was ... 1Cor 1:6 *3142*
declaring unto you the *t* of God ... 1Cor 2:1 *3142*
the *t* of our conscience, that in ... 2Cor 1:12 *3142*
them that believe (because our *t* ... 2Th 1:10 *3142*
ashamed of the *t* of our Lord ... 2Ti 1:8 *3142*
for a *t* of those things which ... Heb 3:5 *3142*
his translation he had this *t* ... Heb 11:5 *3140*
of the *t* of Jesus Christ, and of ... Rev 1:2 *3141*
for the *t* of Jesus Christ ... Rev 1:9 *3141*
for the *t* which they held ... Rev 6:9 *3141*
they shall have finished their *t* ... Rev 11:7 *3141*
Lamb, and by the word of their *t* ... Rev 12:11 *3141*
have the *t* of Jesus Christ ... Rev 12:17 *3141*
of the *t* in heaven was opened ... Rev 15:5 *3142*
brethren that have the *t* of Jesus ... Rev 19:10 *3141*
for the *t* of Jesus is the spirit ... Rev 19:10 *3141*

TETRARCH
At that time Herod the *t* heard of ... Mt 14:1 *5076*
and Herod being *t* of Galilee ... Lk 3:1 *5075*
his brother Philip *t* of Ituraea ... Lk 3:1 *5075*
and Lysanias the *t* of Abilene ... Lk 3:1 *5075*
But Herod the *t*, being reproved ... Lk 3:19 *5076*
Now Herod the *t* heard of all that ... Lk 9:7 *5076*
been brought up with Herod the *t* ... Acts 13:1 *5076*

THADDAEUS (*thad-de'-us*) See JUDE, LEBBAEUS. *A disciple of Jesus.*
and Lebbaeus, whose surname was *T* ... Mt 10:3 *2280*
James the son of Alphaeus, and *T* ... Mk 3:18 *2280*

THAHASH (*tha'-hash*) *A son of Reumah.*
bare also Tebah, and Gaham, and *T* ... Gen 22:24 8477

THAMAH (*tha'-mah*) See TAMAH. *A family of exiles.*
of Sisera, the children of *T* ... Ezr 2:53 8547

THAMAR (*tha'-mar*) See TAMAR. *Mother of Phares and Zara; ancestor of Jesus.*
Judas begat Phares and Zara of *T* ... Mt 1:3 *2283*

THAN
t any beast of the field which ... Gen 3:1
is greater *t* I can bear ... Gen 4:13
deal worse with thee, *t* with them ... Gen 19:9
be stronger *t* the other people ... Gen 25:23
for thou art much mightier *t* we ... Gen 26:16
t that I should give her to ... Gen 29:19
he loved also Rachel more *t* Leah ... Gen 29:30
he was more honourable *t* all the ... Gen 34:19
For their riches were more *t* that ... Gen 36:7
Joseph more *t* all his children ... Gen 37:3
loved him more *t* all his brethren ... Gen 37:4
She hath been more righteous *t* I ... Gen 38:26
is none greater in this house *t* I ... Gen 39:9
throne will I be greater *t* thou ... Gen 41:40
brother shall be greater *t* he ... Gen 48:19
Israel are more and mightier *t* we ... Ex 1:9
t that we should die in the ... Ex 14:12
the LORD is greater *t* all gods ... Ex 18:11
not give less *t* half a shekel ... Ex 30:15
The people bring much more *t* ... Ex 36:5
be deeper *t* the skin of his flesh ... Lev 13:3
in sight be not deeper *t* the skin ... Lev 13:4
it be in sight lower *t* the skin ... Lev 13:20
and if it be not lower *t* the skin ... Lev 13:21 4480
it be in sight deeper *t* the skin ... Lev 13:25 4480
it be no lower *t* the other skin ... Lev 13:26 4480
it be in sight deeper *t* the skin ... Lev 13:30 4480
be not in sight deeper *t* the skin ... Lev 13:31 4480
be not in sight deeper *t* the skin ... Lev 13:32 4480
nor be in sight deeper *t* the skin ... Lev 13:34 4480
in sight are lower *t* the wall ... Lev 14:37 4480
if he be poorer *t* thy estimation ... Lev 27:8
which are more *t* the Levites ... Num 3:46 5921
for they are stronger *t* we ... Num 13:31 4480
greater nation and mightier *t* they ... Num 14:12 4480
more, and more honourable *t* they ... Num 22:15
his king shall be higher *t* Agag ... Num 24:7
people is greater and taller *t* we ... Deut 1:28
greater and mightier *t* thou art ... Deut 4:38
greater and mightier *t* thou ... Deut 7:1
were more in number *t* any people ... Deut 7:7
heart, These nations are more *t* I ... Deut 7:17
greater and mightier *t* thyself ... Deut 9:1
nation mightier and greater *t* they ... Deut 9:14
nations and mightier *t* yourselves ... Deut 11:23
chariots, and a people more *t* thou ... Deut 20:1
and because it was greater *t* Ai ... Josh 10:2 4480
t they whom the children of ... Josh 10:11
themselves more *t* their fathers ... Judg 2:19
better *t* the vintage of Abi-ezer ... Judg 8:2
better *t* Balak the son of Zippor ... Judg 11:25
down, What is sweeter *t* honey ... Judg 14:18
And what is stronger *t* a lion ... Judg 14:18
her younger sister fairer *t* she ... Judg 15:2
more blameless *t* the Philistines ... Judg 15:3
t they which he slew in his life ... Judg 16:30
the latter end *t* at the beginning ... Ruth 3:10 4480
there is a kinsman nearer *t* I ... Ruth 3:12
is better to thee *t* seven sons ... Ruth 4:15
not I better to thee *t* ten sons ... 1Sa 1:8
of Israel a goodlier person *t* he ... 1Sa 9:2
he was higher *t* any of the people ... 1Sa 9:2
he was higher *t* any of the people ... 1Sa 10:23
to obey is better *t* sacrifice ... 1Sa 15:22
to hearken *t* the fat of rams ... 1Sa 15:22
of thine, that is better *t* thou ... 1Sa 15:28
wisely *t* all the servants of Saul ... 1Sa 18:30
Thou art more righteous *t* I ... 1Sa 24:17
t that I should speedily escape ... 1Sa 27:1 3588
they were swifter *t* eagles ... 2Sa 1:23
they were stronger *t* lions ... 2Sa 1:23
And I will yet be more vile *t* thus ... 2Sa 6:22
but, being stronger *t* she ... 2Sa 13:14
he hated her was greater *t* the ... 2Sa 13:15
in sending me away is greater *t* ... 2Sa 13:16
t the counsel of Ahithophel ... 2Sa 17:14
that day *t* the sword devoured ... 2Sa 18:8
that will be worse unto thee *t* ... 2Sa 19:7
also more right in David *t* ye ... 2Sa 19:43
the men of Judah were fiercer *t* ... 2Sa 19:43
but he tarried longer *t* the set ... 2Sa 20:5 4480
do us more harm *t* did Absalom ... 2Sa 20:6 4480
was more honourable *t* the thirty ... 2Sa 23:23 4480
make his throne greater *t* the ... 1Kin 1:37
name of Solomon better *t* thy name ... 1Kin 1:47
his throne greater *t* thy throne ... 1Kin 1:47
men more righteous and better *t* he ... 1Kin 2:32
For he was wiser *t* all men ... 1Kin 4:31
t Ethan the Ezrahite, and Heman, ... 1Kin 4:31
be thicker *t* my father's loins ... 1Kin 12:10
did worse *t* all that were before ... 1Kin 16:25
t all the kings of Israel that ... 1Kin 16:33
for I am not better *t* my fathers ... 1Kin 19:4
therefore they were stronger *t* we ... 1Kin 20:23
we shall be stronger *t* they ... 1Kin 20:23
we shall be stronger *t* they ... 1Kin 20:25
for it a better vineyard *t* it ... 1Kin 21:2

Context	Reference	No.
better *t* all the waters of Israel	2Kin 5:12	
are more *t* they that be with them	2Kin 6:16	
found no more of her *t* the skull	2Kin 9:35	
seduced them to do more evil *t*	2Kin 21:9	4480
more honourable *t* his brethren	1Chr 4:9	
he was more honourable *t* the two	1Chr 11:21	
Eleazar *t* of the sons of Ithamar	1Chr 24:4	4480
be thicker *t* my father's loins	2Chr 10:10	
more *t* they could carry away	2Chr 20:25	
which were better *t* thyself	2Chr 21:13	
to give thee much more *t* this	2Chr 25:9	
sanctify themselves *t* the priests	2Chr 29:34	
otherwise *t* it was written	2Chr 30:18	
there be more with us *t* with him	2Chr 32:7	
err, and to do worse *t* the heathen	2Chr 33:9	4480
to the river *t* runneth to Ahava	Ezr 8:15	4480
us less *t* our iniquities deserve	Ezr 9:13	4480
unto another that is better *t* she	Est 1:19	
his sight more *t* all the virgins	Est 2:17	
king's house, more *t* all the Jews	Est 4:13	
to do honour more *t* to myself	Est 6:6	
dig for it more *t* for hid	Job 3:21	
mortal man be more just *t* God	Job 4:17	
a man be more pure *t* his maker	Job 4:17	
be heavier *t* the sand of the sea	Job 6:3	
are swifter *t* a weaver's shuttle	Job 7:6	
and death rather *t* my life	Job 7:15	
Now my days are swifter *t* a post	Job 9:25	4480
less *t* thine iniquity deserveth	Job 11:6	
deeper *t* hell	Job 11:8	4480
thereof is longer *t* the earth	Job 11:9	4480
the earth, and broader *t* the sea	Job 11:9	4480
shall be clearer *t* the noonday	Job 11:17	
aged men, much elder *t* thy father	Job 15:10	
stroke is heavier *t* my groaning	Job 23:2	5921
mouth more *t* my necessary food	Job 23:12	
younger *t* I have me in derision	Job 30:1	
they were viler *t* the earth	Job 30:8	4480
he justified himself rather *t* God	Job 32:2	4480
because they were elder *t* he	Job 32:4	
thee, that God is greater *t* man	Job 33:12	
shall be fresher *t* a child's	Job 33:25	
the rich more *t* the poor	Job 34:19	6440
not lay upon man more *t* right	Job 34:23	
My righteousness is more *t* God's	Job 35:2	
clouds which are higher *t* thou	Job 35:5	
Who teacheth us more *t* the beasts	Job 35:11	
maketh us wiser *t* the fowls of	Job 35:11	
thou chosen rather *t* affliction	Job 36:21	
end of Job more *t* his beginning	Job 42:12	
more *t* in the time that their	Ps 4:7	
him a little lower *t* the angels	Ps 8:5	
to be desired are they *t* gold	Ps 19:10	
gold, yea, *t* much fine gold	Ps 19:10	
sweeter also *t* honey and the	Ps 19:10	
t the riches of many wicked	Ps 37:16	
they are more *t* can be numbered	Ps 40:5	
they are more *t* the hairs of mine	Ps 40:12	
Thou art fairer *t* the children of	Ps 45:2	
me, and I shall be whiter *t* snow	Ps 51:7	
Thou lovest evil more *t* good	Ps 52:3	
and lying rather *t* to speak	Ps 52:3	
his mouth were smoother *t* butter	Ps 55:21	
his words were softer *t* oil	Ps 55:21	
me to the rock that is higher *t* I	Ps 61:2	
are altogether lighter *t* vanity	Ps 62:9	
lovingkindness is better *t* life	Ps 63:3	
are more *t* the hairs of mine head	Ps 69:4	
t an ox or bullock that hath	Ps 69:31	
they have more *t* heart could wish	Ps 73:7	
excellent *t* the mountains of prey	Ps 76:4	
thy courts is better *t* a thousand	Ps 84:10	
t to dwell in the tents of	Ps 84:10	
more *t* all the dwellings of Jacob	Ps 87:2	
higher *t* the kings of the earth	Ps 89:27	
t the noise of many waters	Ps 93:4	
t the mighty waves of the sea	Ps 93:4	
them stronger *t* their enemies	Ps 105:24	
LORD *t* to put confidence in man	Ps 118:8	
t to put confidence in princes	Ps 118:9	
unto me *t* thousands of gold	Ps 119:72	
hast made me wiser *t* mine enemies	Ps 119:98	
understanding *t* all my teachers	Ps 119:99	
I understand more *t* the ancients	Ps 119:100	
sweeter *t* honey to my mouth	Ps 119:103	
soul waiteth for the Lord more *t*	Ps 130:6	
more *t* they that watch for the	Ps 130:6	
are more in number *t* the sand	Ps 139:18	
for they are stronger *t* I	Ps 142:6	
t the merchandise of silver	Prov 3:14	
and the gain thereof *t* fine gold	Prov 3:14	
She is more precious *t* rubies	Prov 3:15	
and her mouth is smoother *t* oil	Prov 5:3	
and knowledge rather *t* choice gold	Prov 8:10	
For wisdom is better *t* rubies	Prov 8:11	
My fruit is better *t* gold	Prov 8:19	
gold, yea, *t* fine gold	Prov 8:19	
my revenue *t* choice silver	Prov 8:19	
that withholdeth more *t* is meet	Prov 11:24	
is better *t* he that honoureth	Prov 12:9	
is more excellent *t* his neighbour	Prov 12:26	
fear of the LORD *t* great treasure	Prov 15:16	
love is, *t* a stalled ox and hatred	Prov 15:17	
t great revenues without right	Prov 16:8	
better is it to get wisdom *t* gold	Prov 16:16	
rather to be chosen *t* silver	Prov 16:16	
t to divide the spoil with the	Prov 16:19	
to anger is better *t* the mighty	Prov 16:32	
spirit *t* he that taketh a city	Prov 16:32	
t an house full of sacrifices	Prov 17:1	
entereth more into a wise man *t*	Prov 17:10	
rather *t* a fool in his folly	Prov 17:12	
harder to be won *t* a strong city	Prov 18:19	
that sticketh closer *t* a brother	Prov 18:24	
t he that is perverse in his lips	Prov 19:1	
and a poor man is better *t* a liar	Prov 19:22	
to the LORD *t* sacrifice	Prov 21:3	
t with a brawling woman and in a	Prov 21:9	
t with a contentious and an angry	Prov 21:19	
to be chosen *t* great riches	Prov 22:1	
and loving favour rather *t* silver	Prov 22:1	
t that thou shouldest be put	Prov 25:7	
t with a brawling woman and in a	Prov 25:24	
is more hope of a fool *t* of him	Prov 26:12	
t seven men that can render a	Prov 26:16	
wrath is heavier *t* them both	Prov 27:3	
rebuke is better *t* secret love	Prov 27:5	
that is near *t* a brother far off	Prov 27:10	
t he that is perverse in his ways	Prov 28:6	
shall find more favour *t* he that	Prov 28:23	
is more hope of a fool *t* of him	Prov 29:20	
I am more brutish *t* any man	Prov 30:2	
have gotten more wisdom *t* all	Eccl 1:16	5921
increased more *t* all that were	Eccl 2:9	
wise more *t* of the fool for ever	Eccl 2:16	5973
t that he should eat and drink, and	Eccl 2:24	
can hasten hereunto, more *t* I	Eccl 2:25	
t that a man should rejoice in	Eccl 3:22	
which are already dead more *t* the	Eccl 4:2	4480
Yea, better is he *t* both they	Eccl 4:3	
t both the hands full with	Eccl 4:6	
Two are better *t* one	Eccl 4:9	
a poor and a wise child *t* an old	Eccl 4:13	
t to give the sacrifice of fools	Eccl 5:1	
t that thou shouldest vow and not	Eccl 5:5	
is higher *t* the highest regardeth	Eccl 5:8	5921
and there be higher *t* they	Eccl 5:8	5921
an untimely birth is better *t* he	Eccl 6:3	
this hath more rest *t* the other	Eccl 6:5	
hath the wise more *t* the fool	Eccl 6:8	4480
t the wandering of the desire	Eccl 6:9	
with him that is mightier *t* he	Eccl 6:10	
is better *t* precious ointment	Eccl 7:1	
the day of death *t* the day of	Eccl 7:1	
t to go to the house of feasting	Eccl 7:2	
Sorrow is better *t* laughter	Eccl 7:3	
t for a man to hear the song of	Eccl 7:5	
a thing *t* the beginning thereof	Eccl 7:8	
is better *t* the proud in spirit	Eccl 7:8	
former days were better *t* these	Eccl 7:10	
strengtheneth the wise more *t* ten	Eccl 7:19	
more bitter *t* death the woman	Eccl 7:26	
t to eat, and to drink, and to be	Eccl 8:15	
dog is better *t* a dead lion	Eccl 9:4	4480
I, Wisdom is better *t* strength	Eccl 9:16	
more *t* the cry of him that ruleth	Eccl 9:17	
Wisdom is better *t* weapons of war	Eccl 9:18	
for thy love is better *t* wine	Song 1:2	
remember thy love more *t* wine	Song 1:4	
much better is thy love *t* wine	Song 4:10	
of thine ointments *t* all spices	Song 4:10	
beloved more *t* another beloved	Song 5:9	
beloved more *t* another beloved	Song 5:9	
a man more precious *t* fine gold	Is 13:12	
even a man *t* the golden wedge of	Is 13:12	
For the bed is shorter *t* that a	Is 28:20	
the covering narrower *t* that he	Is 28:20	
speech *t* thou canst perceive	Is 33:19	
are counted to him less *t* nothing	Is 40:17	
was so marred more *t* any man	Is 52:14	
his form more *t* the sons of men	Is 52:14	
t the children of the married	Is 54:1	
heavens are higher *t* the earth	Is 55:9	
so are my ways higher *t* your ways	Is 55:9	
my thoughts *t* your thoughts	Is 55:9	
place and a name better *t* of sons	Is 56:5	
thyself to another *t* me, and art	Is 57:8	
for I am holier *t* thou	Is 65:5	
herself more *t* treacherous Judah	Jer 3:11	
his horses are swifter *t* eagles	Jer 4:13	
made their faces harder *t* a rock	Jer 5:3	
they did worse *t* their fathers	Jer 7:26	
death shall be chosen rather *t*	Jer 8:3	
ye have done worse *t* your fathers	Jer 16:12	
thou art stronger *t* I, and hast	Jer 20:7	
of him that was stronger *t* he	Jer 31:11	
they are more *t* the grasshoppers	Jer 46:23	
of my people is greater *t* the	Lam 4:6	
Her Nazarites were purer *t* snow	Lam 4:7	
they were whiter *t* milk	Lam 4:7	
were more ruddy in body *t* rubies	Lam 4:7	
Their visage is blacker *t* a coal	Lam 4:8	
t they that be slain with hunger	Lam 4:9	
t the eagles of the heaven	Lam 4:19	
As an adamant harder *t* flint have	Eze 3:9	
wickedness more *t* the nations	Eze 5:6	4480
my statutes more *t* the countries	Eze 5:6	4480
more *t* the nations that are round	Eze 5:7	4480
more desolate *t* the wilderness	Eze 6:14	
see greater abominations *t* these	Eze 8:15	
is the vine tree more *t* any tree	Eze 15:2	
or *t* a branch which is among the	Eze 15:2	
more *t* they in all thy ways	Eze 16:47	
thine abominations more *t* they	Eze 16:51	
committed more abominable *t* they	Eze 16:52	
they are more righteous *t* thou	Eze 16:52	
in her inordinate love *t* she	Eze 23:11	
in her whoredoms more *t* her	Eze 23:11	
Behold, thou art wiser *t* Daniel	Eze 28:3	
unto you *t* at your beginnings	Eze 36:11	
the galleries were higher *t* these	Eze 42:5	
t the lower, and	Eze 42:5	
t the middlemost of the building	Eze 42:5	
was straitened more *t* the lowest	Eze 42:6	
t the children which are of your	Dan 1:10	4480
fatter in flesh *t* all the	Dan 1:15	4480
times better *t* all the magicians	Dan 1:20	5921
that I have more *t* any living	Dan 2:30	4481
more *t* it was wont to be heated	Dan 3:19	1768
look was more stout *t* his fellows	Dan 7:20	4481
but one was higher *t* the other	Dan 8:3	4480
shall be far richer *t* they all	Dan 11:2	
years *t* the king of the north	Dan 11:8	
a multitude greater *t* the former	Dan 11:13	4480
then was it better with me *t* now	Hos 2:7	
of God more *t* burnt offerings	Hos 6:6	
be they better *t* these kingdoms	Amos 6:2	4480
border greater *t* your border	Amos 6:2	
is better for me to die *t* to live	Jonah 4:3	
is better for me to die *t* to live	Jonah 4:8	
wherein are more *t* sixscore	Jonah 4:11	
is sharper *t* a thorn hedge	Mic 7:4	
Art thou better *t* populous No	Nah 3:8	
also are swifter *t* the leopards	Hab 1:8	
are more fierce *t* the evening	Hab 1:8	
of purer eyes *t* to behold evil	Hab 1:13	
man that is more righteous *t* he	Hab 1:13	
shall be greater *t* of the former	Hag 2:9	
cometh after me is mightier *t* I	Mt 3:11	
is more *t* these cometh of evil	Mt 5:37	
only, what do ye more *t* others	Mt 5:47	
Is not the life more *t* meat	Mt 6:25	
and the body *t* raiment	Mt 6:25	
Are ye not much better *t* they	Mt 6:26	
day of judgment, *t* for that city	Mt 10:15	*2228*
are of more value *t* many sparrows	Mt 10:31	
more *t* me is not worthy of me	Mt 10:37	*5228*
more *t* me is not worthy of me	Mt 10:37	*5228*
say unto you, and more *t* a prophet	Mt 11:9	
a greater *t* John the Baptist	Mt 11:11	
kingdom of heaven is greater *t* he	Mt 11:11	
at the day of judgment, *t* for you	Mt 11:22	*2228*
the day of judgment, *t* for thee	Mt 11:24	*2228*
place is one greater *t* the temple	Mt 12:6	
then is a man better *t* a sheep	Mt 12:12	
a greater *t* Jonas is here	Mt 12:41	
a greater *t* Solomon is here	Mt 12:42	
spirits more wicked *t* himself	Mt 12:45	
of that man is worse *t* the first	Mt 12:45	
rather *t* having two hands or two	Mt 18:8	*2228*
rather *t* having two eyes to be	Mt 18:9	*2228*
t of the ninety and nine which	Mt 18:13	*2228*
t for a rich man to enter into	Mt 19:24	*2228*
other servants more *t* the first	Mt 21:36	
the child of hell *t* yourselves	Mt 23:15	
more *t* twelve legions of angels	Mt 26:53	*2228*
error shall be worse *t* the first	Mt 27:64	
cometh one mightier *t* I after me	Mk 1:7	
is less *t* all the seeds that be	Mk 4:31	
and becometh greater *t* all herbs	Mk 4:32	
day of judgment, *t* for that city	Mk 6:11	*2228*
ship with them more *t* one loaf	Mk 8:14	*1508*
t having two hands to go into	Mk 9:43	*2228*
t having two feet to be cast into	Mk 9:45	*2228*
t having two eyes to be cast into	Mk 9:47	*2228*
t for a rich man to enter into	Mk 10:25	*2228*
other commandment greater *t* these	Mk 12:31	
is more *t* all whole burnt	Mk 12:33	
t all they which have cast into	Mk 12:43	
for more *t* three hundred pence	Mk 14:5	*1883*
Exact no more *t* that which is	Lk 3:13	*3844*
but one mightier *t* I cometh	Lk 3:16	
you, and much more *t* a prophet	Lk 7:26	
prophet *t* John the Baptist	Lk 7:28	
kingdom of God is greater *t* he	Lk 7:28	
day for Sodom, *t* for that city	Lk 10:12	*2228*
Sidon at the judgment, *t* for you	Lk 10:14	*2228*
But when a stronger *t* he shall	Lk 11:22	*2228*
spirits more wicked *t* himself	Lk 11:26	
of that man is worse *t* the first	Lk 11:26	
a greater *t* Solomon is here	Lk 11:31	
a greater *t* Jonas is here	Lk 11:32	
are of more value *t* many sparrows	Lk 12:7	
The life is more *t* meat, and the	Lk 12:23	
and the body is more *t* raiment	Lk 12:23	
more are ye better *t* the fowls	Lk 12:24	
man *t* thou be bidden of him	Lk 14:8	
more *t* over ninety and nine just	Lk 15:7	*2228*
wiser *t* the children of light	Lk 16:8	*5228*
t one tittle of the law to fail	Lk 16:17	*2228*
t that he should offend one of	Lk 17:2	*2228*
justified rather *t* the other	Lk 18:14	*2228*
t for a rich man to enter into	Lk 18:25	*2228*
hath cast in more *t* they all	Lk 21:3	
shalt see greater things *t* these	Jn 1:50	
men loved darkness rather *t* light	Jn 3:19	*2228*
and baptized more disciples *t* John	Jn 4:1	*2228*
thou greater *t* our father Jacob	Jn 4:12	
shew him greater works *t* these	Jn 5:20	
greater witness *t* that of John	Jn 5:36	
will he do more miracles *t* these	Jn 7:31	
Art thou greater *t* our father	Jn 8:53	
gave them me, is greater *t* all	Jn 10:29	
of men more *t* the praise of God	Jn 12:43	*2260*
servant is not greater *t* his lord	Jn 13:16	
sent greater *t* he that sent him	Jn 13:16	
greater works *t* these shall he do	Jn 14:12	
for my Father is greater *t* I	Jn 14:28	
Greater love hath no man *t* this	Jn 15:13	
servant is not greater *t* his lord	Jn 15:20	
lovest thou me more *t* these	Jn 21:15	
hearken unto you more *t* unto God	Acts 4:19	*2228*
We ought to obey God rather *t* men	Acts 5:29	*2228*
burden *t* these necessary things	Acts 15:28	*4133*
noble *t* those in Thessalonica	Acts 17:11	
more blessed to give *t* to receive	Acts 20:35	
they were more *t* forty which had	Acts 23:13	
for him of them more *t* forty men	Acts 23:21	
among them more *t* ten days	Acts 25:6	*2228*
things *t* those which the prophets	Acts 26:22	
more *t* those things which were	Acts 27:11	*2228*
the creature more *t* the Creator	Rom 1:25	*3844*

T

are we better *t* they ... Rom 3:9
t conquerors through him that ... Rom 8:37 *5245*
more highly *t* he ought to think ... Rom 12:3
nearer *t* when we believed ... Rom 13:11 *2228*
foolishness of God is wiser *t* men ... 1Cor 1:25
weakness of God is stronger *t* men ... 1Cor 1:25
can no man lay *t* that is laid ... 1Cor 3:11 *3844*
it is better to marry *t* to burn ... 1Cor 7:9 *2228*
t that any man should make my ... 1Cor 9:15 *2228*
are we stronger *t* he ... 1Cor 10:22
t he that speaketh with tongues ... 1Cor 14:5 *2228*
speak with tongues more *t* ye all ... 1Cor 14:18
t ten thousand words in an ... 1Cor 14:19 *2228*
more abundantly *t* they all ... 1Cor 15:10
t what ye read or acknowledge ... 2Cor 1:13 *2228*
any other gospel unto you *t* that ... Gal 1:8 *3844*
unto you *t* that ye have received ... Gal 1:9 *3844*
hath many more children *t* she ... Gal 4:27 *2228*
who am less *t* the least of all ... Eph 3:8
esteem other better *t* themselves ... Phil 2:3
rather *t* godly edifying which is ... 1Ti 1:4 *2228*
faith, and is worse *t* an infidel ... 1Ti 5:8 *2228*
of pleasures more *t* lovers of God ... 2Ti 3:4 *2228*
thou wilt also do more *t* I say ... Philem 21 5228
made so much better *t* the angels ... Heb 1:4
a more excellent name *t* they ... Heb 1:4 *3844*
him a little lower *t* the angels ... Heb 2:7 *3844*
who was made a little lower *t* the ... Heb 2:9 *3844*
worthy of more glory *t* Moses ... Heb 3:3 *2228*
hath more honour *t* the house ... Heb 3:3
sharper *t* any twoedged sword, ... Heb 4:12 *5288*
and made higher *t* the heavens ... Heb 7:26
with better sacrifices *t* these ... Heb 9:23 *3844*
a more excellent sacrifice *t* Cain ... Heb 11:4 *3844*
t to enjoy the pleasures of sin ... Heb 11:25 *2228*
riches *t* the treasures in Egypt ... Heb 11:26
better things *t* that of Abel ... Heb 12:24 *3844*
precious *t* of gold that perisheth ... 1Pet 1:7
for well doing, *t* for evil doing ... 1Pet 3:17 *2228*
worse with them *t* the beginning ... 2Pet 2:20
known the way of righteousness, *t* ... 2Pet 2:21 *2228*
us, God is greater *t* our heart ... 1Jn 3:20
t he that is in the world ... 1Jn 4:4 *2228*
I have no greater joy *t* to hear ... 3Jn 4
the last to be more *t* the first ... Rev 2:19

THANK

the LORD, and to record, and to *t* ... 1Chr 16:4 3034
delivered first this psalm to *t* ... 1Chr 16:7 3034
And to stand every morning to *t* ... 1Chr 23:30 3034
we *t* thee, and praise thy glorious ... 1Chr 29:13 3034
t offerings into the house of the ... 2Chr 29:31 8426
in sacrifices and *t* offerings ... 2Chr 29:31 8426
t offerings, and commanded Judah ... 2Chr 33:16 8426
I *t* thee, and praise thee, O thou ... Dan 2:23 3029
I *t* thee, O Father, Lord of ... Mt 11:25 *1843*
which love you, what *t* have ye ... Lk 6:32 *5485*
do good to you, what *t* have ye ... Lk 6:33 *5485*
hope to receive, what *t* have ye ... Lk 6:34 *5485*
I *t* thee, O Father, Lord of ... Lk 10:21 *1843*
Doth he *t* that servant because he ... Lk 17:9
I *t* thee, that I am not as other ... Lk 18:11 *2168*
I *t* thee that thou hast heard me ... Jn 11:41 *2168*
I *t* my God through Jesus Christ ... Rom 1:8 *2168*
I *t* God through Jesus Christ our ... Rom 7:25 *2168*
I *t* my God always on your behalf, ... 1Cor 1:4 *2168*
I *t* God that I baptized none of ... 1Cor 1:14 *2168*
I *t* my God, I speak with tongues ... 1Cor 14:18 *2168*
I *t* my God upon every remembrance .. Phil 1:3 *2168*
For this cause also *t* we God ... 1Th 2:13 *2168*
We are bound to *t* God always for ... 2Th 1:3 *2168*
I *t* Christ Jesus our Lord, who ... 1Ti 1:12
I *t* God, whom I serve from my ... 2Ti 1:3
I *t* my God, making mention of ... Philem 4 *2168*

THANKED

and bowed himself, and *t* the king ... 2Sa 14:22 1288
he *t* God, and took courage ... Acts 28:15 *2168*
But God be *t*, that ye were the ... Rom 6:17 *5485*

THANKFUL

be *t* unto him, and bless his name ... Ps 100:4 3034
him not as God, neither were *t* ... Rom 1:21 *2168*
and be ye *t* ... Col 3:15 *2170*

THANKFULNESS

most noble Felix, with all *t* ... Acts 24:3 *2169*

THANKING

heard in praising and *t* the LORD ... 2Chr 5:13 3034

THANKS

Therefore I will give *t* unto thee ... 2Sa 22:50 3034
Give *t* unto the LORD, call upon ... 1Chr 16:8 3034
O give *t* unto the LORD ... 1Chr 16:34 3034
we may give *t* to thy holy name ... 1Chr 16:35 3034
to give *t* to the LORD, because ... 1Chr 16:41 3034
prophesied with a harp, to give *t* ... 1Chr 25:3 3034
to minister, and to give *t* ... 2Chr 31:2 3034
and giving *t* unto the LORD ... Ezr 3:11 3034
them, to praise and to give *t* ... Neh 12:24 3034
companies of them that gave *t* ... Neh 12:31 8426
gave *t* went over against them ... Neh 12:38 8426
that gave *t* in the house of God ... Neh 12:40 8426
the grave who shall give thee *t* ... Ps 6:5 3034
Therefore will I give *t* unto thee ... Ps 18:49 3034
give *t* at the remembrance of his ... Ps 30:4 3034
I will give *t* unto thee for ever ... Ps 30:12 3034
I will give thee *t* in the great ... Ps 35:18 3034
Unto thee, O God, do we give *t* ... Ps 75:1 3034
unto thee do we give *t* ... Ps 75:1 3034
pasture will give thee *t* for ever ... Ps 79:13 3034
thing to give *t* unto the LORD ... Ps 92:1 3034
give *t* at the remembrance of his ... Ps 97:12 3034
O give *t* unto the LORD ... Ps 105:1 3034
O give *t* unto the LORD ... Ps 106:1 3034
to give *t* unto thy holy name, and ... Ps 106:47 3034
O give *t* unto the LORD, for he is ... Ps 107:1 3034
O give *t* unto the LORD ... Ps 118:1 3034
O give *t* unto the LORD ... Ps 118:29 3034
give *t* unto thee because of thy ... Ps 119:62 3034
to give *t* unto the name of the ... Ps 122:4 3034
O Give *t* unto the LORD ... Ps 136:1 3034
O give *t* unto the God of gods ... Ps 136:2 3034
O give *t* to the Lord of lords ... Ps 136:3 3034
O give *t* unto the God of heaven ... Ps 136:26 3034
shall give *t* unto thy name ... Ps 140:13 3034
gave *t* before his God, as he did ... Dan 6:10 3029
loaves and the fishes, and gave *t* ... Mt 15:36 *2168*
And he took the cup, and gave *t* ... Mt 26:27 *2168*
took the seven loaves, and gave *t* ... Mk 8:6 *2168*
the cup, and when he had given *t* ... Mk 14:23 *2168*
gave *t* likewise unto the Lord ... Lk 2:38 *437*
face at his feet, giving him *t* ... Lk 17:16 *2168*
And he took the cup, and gave *t* ... Lk 22:17 *2168*
And he took bread, and gave *t* ... Lk 22:19 *2168*
and when he had given *t*, he ... Jn 6:11 *2168*
after that the Lord had given *t* ... Jn 6:23 *2168*
gave *t* to God in presence of them ... Acts 27:35 *2168*
to the Lord, for he giveth God *t* ... Rom 14:6 *2168*
he eateth not, and giveth God *t* ... Rom 14:6 *2168*
unto whom not only I give *t* ... Rom 16:4 *2168*
of for that for which I give *t* ... 1Cor 10:30 *2168*
And when he had given *t*, he brake ... 1Cor 11:24 *2168*
say Amen at thy giving of *t* ... 1Cor 14:16 *2169*
For thou verily givest *t* well ... 1Cor 14:17 *2168*
But *t* be to God, which giveth us ... 1Cor 15:57 *5485*
t may be given by many on our ... 2Cor 1:11 *2168*
Now *t* be unto God, which always ... 2Cor 2:14 *5485*
But *t* be to God, which put the ... 2Cor 8:16 *5485*
T be unto God for his unspeakable ... 2Cor 9:15 *5485*
Cease not to give *t* for you ... Eph 1:16 *2168*
but rather giving of *t* ... Eph 5:4 *2169*
Giving *t* always for all things ... Eph 5:20 *2168*
We give *t* to God and the Father of ... Col 1:3 *2168*
Giving *t* unto the Father, which ... Col 1:12 *2168*
the Lord Jesus, giving *t* to God ... Col 3:17 *2168*
We give *t* to God always for you ... 1Th 1:2 *2168*
For what *t* can we render to God ... 1Th 3:9 *2169*
In every thing give *t* ... 1Th 5:18 *2168*
to give *t* alway to God for you ... 2Th 2:13 *2168*
intercessions, and giving of *t* ... 1Ti 2:1 *2169*
of our lips giving *t* to his name ... Heb 13:15 *3670*
t to him that sat on the throne, ... Rev 4:9 *2169*
Saying, We give thee *t*, O Lord ... Rev 11:17 *2168*

THANKSGIVING

If he offer it for a *t*, then he ... Lev 7:12 8426
offer with the sacrifice of *t* ... Lev 7:12 8426
of *t* of his peace offerings ... Lev 7:13 8426
of his peace offerings for *t* ... Lev 7:15 8426
a sacrifice of *t* unto the LORD ... Lev 22:29 8426
to begin the *t* in prayer ... Neh 11:17 3034
Mattaniah, which was over the *t* ... Neh 12:8 1960
and songs of praise and *t* unto God ... Neh 12:46
I may publish with the voice of *t* ... Ps 26:7 3034
Offer unto God *t* ... Ps 50:14 8426
song, and will magnify him with *t* ... Ps 69:30 8426
come before his presence with *t* ... Ps 95:2 8426
Enter into his gates with *t* ... Ps 100:4 8426
sacrifice the sacrifices of *t* ... Ps 107:22 8426
offer to thee the sacrifice of *t* ... Ps 116:17 8426
Sing unto the LORD with *t* ... Ps 147:7 8426
shall be found therein, *t* ... Is 51:3 8426
And out of them shall proceed *t* ... Jer 30:19 8426
a sacrifice of *t* with leaven ... Amos 4:5 8426
unto thee with the voice of *t* ... Jonah 2:9 8426
grace might through the *t* of many ... 2Cor 4:15 *2169*
which causeth through us *t* to God ... 2Cor 9:11 *2169*
supplication with *t* let your ... Phil 4:6 *2169*
taught, abounding therein with *t* ... Col 2:7 *2169*
and watch in the same with *t* ... Col 4:2 *2169*
with *t* of them which believe ... 1Ti 4:3 *2169*
refused, if it be received with *t* ... 1Ti 4:4 *2169*
and glory, and wisdom, and *t* ... Rev 7:12 *2169*

THANKSGIVINGS

with gladness, both with *t* ... Neh 12:27 8426
abundant also by many *t* unto God ... 2Cor 9:12 *2169*

THANKWORTHY

For this is *t*, if a man for ... 1Pet 2:19 *5485*

THARA (*tha'-rah*) See TERAH. *Greek form of Terah.*

Abraham, which was the son of *T* ... Lk 3:34 *2291*

THARSHISH (*thar'-shish*) See TARSHISH.

1. Ships fitted for long voyages.

navy of *T* with the navy of Hiram ... 1Kin 10:22 8659
in three years came the navy of *T* ... 1Kin 10:22 8659
of *T* to go to Ophir for gold ... 1Kin 22:48 8659

2. Son of Bilhan.

and Chenaanah, and Zethan, and *T* ... 1Chr 7:10 8659

THAT See PREFACE.

THE See PREFACE.

THEATRE

rushed with one accord into the *t* ... Acts 19:29 *2302*
not adventure himself into the *t* ... Acts 19:31 *2302*

THEBES See THEBEZ.

THEBEZ (*the'-bez*) *A city in Ephraim.*

Then went Abimelech to *T*, and ... Judg 9:50 8405
to *T*, and encamped against *T* ... Judg 9:50 8405
from the wall, that he died in *T* ... 2Sa 11:21 8405

THEE See PREFACE.

THEE-WARD

works have been to *t* very good ... 1Sa 19:4

THEFT

then he shall be sold for his *t* ... Ex 22:3 1591
If the *t* be certainly found in ... Ex 22:4 1591

THEFTS

adulteries, fornications, *t* ... Mt 15:19 *2829*
T, covetousness, wickedness, ... Mk 7:22 *2829*
their fornication, nor of their *t* ... Rev 9:21 *2804*

THEIR See PREFACE.

THEIR'S

thing in Israel shall be *t* ... Eze 44:29 1992

THEIRS

stranger in a land that is not *t* ... Gen 15:13 1992
and every beast of *t* be ours ... Gen 34:23
five times so much as any of *t* ... Gen 43:34
be *t* for a perpetual statute ... Ex 29:9 1992
for *t* is thine own nakedness ... Lev 18:10 2007
wicked men, and touch nothing of *t* ... Num 16:26 1992
t, every meat offering of *t* ... Num 18:9
and every sin offering of *t* ... Num 18:9
and every trespass offering of *t* ... Num 18:9
for *t* was the first lot ... Josh 21:10 1992
for *t* was the lot ... 1Chr 6:54 1992
I pray thee, be like one of *t* ... 2Chr 18:12 1992
words shall stand, mine, or *t* ... Jer 44:28 1992
their multitude, nor of any of *t* ... Eze 7:11 1992
the dwellingplaces that are not *t* ... Hab 1:6
for *t* is the kingdom of heaven ... Mt 5:3 *846*
for *t* is the kingdom of heaven ... Mt 5:10 *846*
of Jesus Christ our Lord, both *t* ... 1Cor 1:2
unto all men, as *t* also was ... 2Ti 3:9

THELASAR (*the-la'-sar*) See TELASSAR. *Same as Telassar.*

children of Eden which were in *T* ... 2Kin 19:12 8515

THEM See PREFACE.

THEMSELVES

leaves together, and made *t* aprons ... Gen 3:7 1992
his wife hid *t* from the presence ... Gen 3:8
they separated *t* the one from the ... Gen 13:11
they wearied *t* to find the door ... Gen 19:11
seven ewe lambs of the flock by *t* ... Gen 21:28
lambs which thou hast set by *t* ... Gen 21:29
and he put his own flocks by *t* ... Gen 30:40 905
of his servants, every drove by *t* ... Gen 32:16 905
their children, and they bowed *t* ... Gen 33:6
children came near, and bowed *t* ... Gen 33:7
near and Rachel, and they bowed *t* ... Gen 33:7
they shall gather *t* together ... Gen 34:30
bowed down *t* before him with ... Gen 42:6
bowed *t* to him to the earth ... Gen 43:26
him by himself, and for them by *t* ... Gen 43:32 905
which did eat with him, by *t* ... Gen 43:32 905
let them go and gather straw for *t* ... Ex 5:7 1992
unto me, and bow down *t* unto me ... Ex 11:8
they prepared for *t* any victual ... Ex 12:39 1992
every small matter they judged *t* ... Ex 18:26 1992
come near to the LORD, sanctify *t* ... Ex 19:22
t, and six curtains by *t* ... Ex 26:9 905
gathered *t* together unto Aaron ... Ex 32:1
land of Egypt, have corrupted *t* ... Ex 32:7
Levi gathered *t* together unto him ... Ex 32:26
t of their ornaments by the mount ... Ex 33:6
t, and six curtains by *t* ... Ex 36:16 905
they shall both bathe *t* in water ... Lev 15:18
that they separate *t* from the ... Lev 22:2
to vow a vow of a Nazarite ... Num 6:2
to separate *t* unto the LORD ... Num 6:2
their clothes, and so make *t* clean ... Num 8:7 1992
t to thee at the door of the ... Num 10:3
Israel, shall gather *t* unto thee ... Num 10:4
abroad for *t* round about the camp ... Num 11:32 1992
they gathered *t* together against ... Num 16:3
they gathered *t* together against ... Num 20:2
t together against the LORD in ... Num 27:3
hide *t* from thee, be destroyed ... Deut 7:20
out of Egypt have corrupted *t* ... Deut 9:12
presented *t* in the tabernacle of ... Deut 31:14
they shall have eaten and filled *t* ... Deut 31:20
They have corrupted *t*, their spot ... Deut 32:5
should behave *t* strangely ... Deut 32:27
even our enemies *t* being judges ... Deut 32:31
Israel took for a prey unto *t* ... Josh 8:27 1992
That they gathered *t* together ... Josh 9:2
of Eglon, gathered *t* together ... Josh 10:5
had avenged *t* upon their enemies ... Josh 10:13
hid *t* in a cave at Makkedah ... Josh 10:16
of Israel took for a prey unto *t* ... Josh 11:14 1992
gathered *t* together at Shiloh ... Josh 22:12
and they presented *t* before God ... Josh 24:1
bowed *t* unto them, and provoked ... Judg 2:12
other gods, and bowed *t* unto them ... Judg 2:17
corrupted *t* more than their ... Judg 2:19
the people willingly offered *t* ... Judg 5:2
that offered *t* willingly among ... Judg 5:9
lest Israel vaunt *t* against me ... Judg 7:2
t together out of Naphtali ... Judg 7:23
of Ephraim gathered *t* together ... Judg 7:24
of Israel assembled *t* together ... Judg 10:17
of Ephraim gathered *t* together ... Judg 12:1
in Judah, and spread *t* in Lehi ... Judg 15:9
presented *t* in the assembly of ... Judg 20:2
children of Benjamin gathered *t* ... Judg 20:14
the men of Israel put *t* in array ... Judg 20:20
the men of Israel encouraged *t* ... Judg 20:22
they put *t* in array the first day ... Judg 20:22
put *t* in array against Gibeah, as ... Judg 20:30
put *t* in array at Baal-tamar ... Judg 20:33

and the liers in wait drew *t* along	Judg 20:37	
full have hired out *t* for bread	1Sa 2:5	
because his sons made *t* vile	1Sa 3:13	1992
the Philistines put *t* in array	1Sa 4:2	
of Israel gathered *t* together	1Sa 8:4	
the Philistines gathered *t*	1Sa 13:5	
the people did hide *t* in caves	1Sa 13:6	
gathered *t* together at Michmash	1Sa 13:11	
both of them discovered *t* unto	1Sa 14:11	
of the holes where they had hid *t*	1Sa 14:11	
that were with him assembled *t*	1Sa 14:20	
which had hid *t* in mount Ephraim	1Sa 14:22	
have kept *t* at least from women	1Sa 21:4	
discontented, gathered *t* unto him	1Sa 22:2	
Philistines gathered *t* together	1Sa 28:4	
gathered *t* together after Abner	2Sa 2:25	
spread *t* in the valley of Rephaim	2Sa 5:18	
spread *t* in the valley of Rephaim	2Sa 5:22	
and Maacah, were by *t* in the field	2Sa 10:8	905
Israel, they gathered *t* together	2Sa 10:15	
the Syrians set *t* in array	2Sa 10:17	
came weary, and refreshed *t* there	2Sa 16:14	
Strangers shall submit *t* unto me	2Sa 22:45	
t unto king Solomon at the feast	1Kin 8:2	
Yet if they shall bethink *t* in	1Kin 8:47	
let them choose one bullock for *t*	1Kin 18:23	1992
cut *t* after their manner with	1Kin 18:28	
they set *t* in array against the	1Kin 20:12	
bowed *t* to the ground before him	2Kin 2:15	
the camp to hide *t* in the field	2Kin 7:12	
of Judah, and made a king over *t*	2Kin 8:20	1992
sold *t* to do evil in the sight of	2Kin 17:17	
made unto *t* of the lowest of them	2Kin 17:32	
year such things as grow of *t*	2Kin 19:29	
gathered *t* to David unto Hebron	1Chr 11:1	
who strengthened *t* with him in	1Chr 11:10	
they set *t* in the midst of that	1Chr 11:14	
of the Gadites there separated *t*	1Chr 12:8	
that they may gather *t* unto us	1Chr 13:2	
spread *t* in the valley of Rephaim	1Chr 14:9	
spread *t* abroad in the valley	1Chr 14:13	
the Levites sanctified *t* to bring	1Chr 15:14	
they had made *t* odious to David	1Chr 19:6	
t together from their cities	1Chr 19:7	
were come were by *t* in the field	1Chr 19:9	905
they set *t* in array against the	1Chr 19:11	
and his four sons with him hid *t*	1Chr 21:20	
submitted *t* unto Solomon the king	1Chr 29:24	
spread *t* forth twenty cubits	2Chr 3:13	
t unto the king in the feast	2Chr 5:3	
Yet if they bethink *t* in the land	2Chr 6:37	
they bowed *t* with their faces to	2Chr 7:3	
called by my name, shall humble *t*	2Chr 7:14	
of Israel and the king humbled *t*	2Chr 12:6	
the LORD saw that they humbled *t*	2Chr 12:7	
saying, They have humbled *t*	2Chr 12:7	
have strengthened *t* against	2Chr 13:7	
that they could not recover *t*	2Chr 14:13	1992
So they gathered *t* together at	2Chr 15:10	
And Judah gathered *t* together	2Chr 20:4	
which they stripped off for *t*	2Chr 20:25	
t in the valley of Berachah	2Chr 20:26	
of Judah, and made *t* a king	2Chr 21:8	1992
their brethren, and sanctified *t*	2Chr 29:15	
were present with him bowed *t*	2Chr 29:29	
other priests had sanctified *t*	2Chr 29:34	
to sanctify *t* than the priests	2Chr 29:34	
had not sanctified *t* sufficiently	2Chr 30:3	
gathered *t* together to Jerusalem	2Chr 30:3	
Manasseh and of Zebulun humbled *t*	2Chr 30:11	
were ashamed, and sanctified *t*	2Chr 30:15	
and Zebulun, had not cleansed *t*	2Chr 30:18	
number of priests sanctified *t*	2Chr 30:24	
they sanctified *t* in holiness	2Chr 31:18	
the people rested *t* upon the	2Chr 32:8	
afterward they made ready for *t*	2Chr 35:14	1992
the Levites prepared for *t*	2Chr 35:14	1992
the people gathered *t* together as	Ezr 3:1	
brethren the priests, and for *t*	Ezr 6:20	1992
all such as had separated *t* unto	Ezr 6:21	
have not separated *t* from the	Ezr 9:1	
taken of their daughters for *t*	Ezr 9:2	1992
t with the people of those lands	Ezr 9:2	
gather *t* together unto Jerusalem	Ezr 10:7	
Benjamin gathered *t* together unto	Ezr 10:9	
will they fortify *t*	Neh 4:2	1992
all the people gathered *t*	Neh 8:1	
made *t* booths, every one upon the	Neh 8:16	1992
separated *t* from all strangers	Neh 9:2	
delighted *t* in thy great goodness	Neh 9:25	
all they that had separated *t*	Neh 10:28	
offered *t* to dwell at Jerusalem	Neh 11:2	
the singers gathered *t* together	Neh 12:28	
priests and the Levites purified *t*	Neh 12:30	
that they should cleanse *t*	Neh 13:22	
every city to gather *t* together	Est 8:11	
day to avenge *t* on their enemies	Est 8:13	
The Jews gathered *t* together in	Est 9:2	
that were in Shushan gathered *t*	Est 9:15	
provinces gathered *t* together	Est 9:16	
all such as joined *t* unto them	Est 9:27	
and as they had decreed for *t*	Est 9:31	5315
came to present *t* before the LORD	Job 1:6	
came to present *t* before the LORD	Job 2:1	
which built desolate places for *t*	Job 3:14	
God do set *t* in array against me	Job 6:4	
they have gathered *t* together	Job 16:10	
poor of the earth hide *t* together	Job 24:4	
had marked for *t* in the daytime	Job 24:16	
The young men saw me, and hid *t*	Job 29:8	
desolation they rolled *t* upon me	Job 30:14	
workers of iniquity may hide *t*	Job 34:22	
They bow *t*, they bring forth	Job 39:3	
they are firm in *t*	Job 41:23	
reason of breakings they purify *t*	Job 41:25	
The kings of the earth set *t*	Ps 2:2	
that have set *t* against me round	Ps 3:6	
nations may know *t* to be but men	Ps 9:20	
strangers shall submit *t* unto me	Ps 18:44	
rejoiced, and gathered *t* together	Ps 35:15	
gathered *t* together against me	Ps 35:15	
that magnify *t* against me	Ps 35:26	
shall delight *t* in the abundance	Ps 37:11	
they magnify *t* against me	Ps 38:16	
and they which hate us spoil for *t*	Ps 44:10	
boast *t* in the multitude of their	Ps 49:6	
t together, they hide *t*	Ps 56:6	
midst whereof they are fallen *t*	Ps 57:6	
prepare *t* without my fault	Ps 59:4	
They encourage *t* in an evil	Ps 64:5	
their own tongue to fall upon *t*	Ps 64:8	
thine enemies submit *t* unto thee	Ps 66:3	
let not the rebellious exalt *t*	Ps 66:7	
and our enemies laugh among *t*	Ps 80:6	
should have submitted *t* unto him	Ps 81:15	
the workers of iniquity boast *t*	Ps 94:4	
They gather *t* together against	Ps 94:21	
images, that boast *t* of idols	Ps 97:7	
ariseth, they gather *t* together	Ps 104:22	
They joined *t* also unto Baal-peor	Ps 106:28	
let them cover *t* with their own	Ps 109:29	
lest they exalt *t*	Ps 140:8	
for riches certainly make *t* wings	Prov 23:5	
When the wicked rise, men hide *t*	Prov 28:28	
might see that they *t* are beasts	Eccl 3:18	1992
they empty *t* upon the earth	Eccl 11:3	
and the strong men shall bow *t*	Eccl 12:3	
they please *t* in the children of	Is 2:6	
they have rewarded evil unto *t*	Is 3:9	1992
be hungry, they shall fret *t*	Is 8:21	
of Gebim gather *t* to flee	Is 10:31	
they shall gird *t* with sackcloth	Is 15:3	
shall set *t* in array at the gate	Is 22:7	
to strengthen *t* in the strength	Is 30:2	
but *t* are gone into captivity	Is 46:2	5315
they shall not deliver *t* from the	Is 47:14	5315
For they call *t* of the holy city	Is 48:2	
stay *t* upon the God of Israel	Is 48:2	
all these gather *t* together	Is 49:18	
that join *t* to the LORD, to serve	Is 56:6	
they cover *t* with their works	Is 59:6	
all they gather *t* together	Is 60:4	
that despised thee shall bow *t*	Is 60:14	
They that sanctify *t*, and purify	Is 66:17	
purify *t* in the gardens behind	Is 66:17	
that seek her will not weary *t*	Jer 2:24	
the nations shall bless *t* in him	Jer 4:2	
assembled *t* by troops in the	Jer 5:7	
though the waves thereof toss *t*	Jer 5:22	
do they not provoke *t* to the	Jer 7:19	
weary *t* to commit iniquity	Jer 9:5	
t to provoke me to anger in	Jer 11:17	1992
they have put *t* to pain, but	Jer 12:13	
men lament for them, nor cut *t*	Jer 16:6	
nor make *t* bald for them	Jer 16:6	
men tear *t* for them in mourning	Jer 16:7	
kings shall serve *t* of them also	Jer 25:14	
great kings shall serve *t* of him	Jer 27:7	
shall no more serve *t* of him	Jer 30:8	
And their nobles shall be of *t*	Jer 30:21	
should serve *t* of them any more	Jer 34:10	
clothes rent, and having cut *t*	Jer 41:5	
shall take to *t* their curtains	Jer 49:29	1992
they shall set *t* in array against	Jer 50:9	
they have girded *t* with sackcloth	Lam 2:10	
they have polluted *t* with blood	Lam 4:14	
they shall lothe *t* for the evils	Eze 6:9	6440
shall also gird *t* with sackcloth	Eze 7:18	
lifted up, these lifted up *t* also	Eze 10:17	
of Chebar, their appearances and *t*	Eze 10:22	6440
they only shall be delivered *t*	Eze 14:18	
shall clothe *t* with trembling	Eze 26:16	
they shall wallow *t* in the ashes	Eze 27:30	
they shall make *t* utterly bald	Eze 27:31	
waters exalt *t* for their height	Eze 31:14	
of Israel that do feed *t*	Eze 34:2	
my flock, but the shepherds fed *t*	Eze 34:8	
the shepherds feed *t* any more	Eze 34:10	853
of those that served *t* of them	Eze 34:27	
t any more with their idols	Eze 37:23	
and they shall consecrate *t*	Eze 43:26	3027
they shall not gird *t* with any	Eze 44:18	
at no dead person to defile *t*	Eze 44:25	
had no husband, they may defile *t*	Eze 44:25	
of the house, have for *t*, for a	Eze 45:5	1992
they shall mingle *t* with the seed	Dan 2:43	
them, so that they fled to hide *t*	Dan 10:7	
years they shall join *t* together	Dan 11:6	
exalt *t* to establish the vision	Dan 11:14	
appoint *t* one head, and they shall	Hos 1:11	1992
for *t* are separated with whores	Hos 4:14	1992
they assemble *t* for corn and wine	Hos 7:14	
They have deeply corrupted *t*	Hos 9:9	
separated *t* unto that shame	Hos 9:10	
shall bind *t* in their two furrows	Hos 10:10	
they lay *t* down upon clothes laid	Amos 2:8	
stretch *t* upon their couches, and	Amos 6:4	
invent to *t* instruments of musick	Amos 6:5	1992
anoint *t* with the chief ointments	Amos 6:6	
that stretched *t* shall be removed	Amos 6:7	
though they hide *t* in the top of	Amos 9:3	
behaved *t* ill in their doings	Mic 3:4	
their dignity shall proceed of *t*	Hab 1:7	
and their horsemen shall spread *t*	Hab 1:8	
shall weary *t* for very vanity	Hab 2:13	
magnified *t* against their border	Zeph 2:8	
magnified *t* against the people of	Zeph 2:10	
empty the golden oil out of *t*	Zec 4:12	
slay them, and hold *t* not guilty	Zec 11:5	
all that burden *t* with it shall	Zec 12:3	
do not magnify *t* against Judah	Zec 12:7	
of the scribes said within *t*	Mt 9:3	*1438*
works do shew forth *t* in him	Mt 14:2	
the villages, and buy *t* victuals	Mt 14:15	*1438*
And they reasoned among *t*, saying	Mt 16:7	*1438*
which have made *t* eunuchs for the	Mt 19:12	*1438*
And they reasoned with *t*, saying	Mt 21:25	*1438*
saw the son, they said among *t*	Mt 21:38	*1438*
but they *t* will not move them	Mt 23:4	
that they questioned among *t*	Mk 1:27	*848*
that they so reasoned within *t*	Mk 2:8	*1438*
And have no root in *t*, and so	Mk 4:17	*1438*
works do shew forth *t* in him	Mk 6:14	
gathered *t* together unto Jesus	Mk 6:30	
into the villages, and buy *t* bread	Mk 6:36	*1438*
sore amazed in *t* beyond measure	Mk 6:51	*1438*
And they reasoned among *t*, saying	Mk 8:16	*240*
into an high mountain apart by *t*	Mk 9:2	*3441*
any more, save Jesus only with *t*	Mk 9:8	*1438*
And they kept that saying with *t*	Mk 9:10	*1438*
the way they had disputed among *t*	Mk 9:34	*240*
out of measure, saying among *t*	Mk 10:26	*1438*
And they reasoned with *t*, saying	Mk 11:31	*1438*
But those husbandmen said among *t*	Mk 12:7	*1438*
that had indignation within *t*	Mk 14:4	*1438*
said among *t* with the scribes	Mk 15:31	*240*
And they said among *t*, Who shall	Mk 16:3	*1438*
were all amazed, and spake among *t*	Lk 4:36	*240*
the counsel of God against *t*	Lk 7:30	*1438*
with him began to say within *t*	Lk 7:49	*1438*
in *t* that they were righteous	Lk 18:9	*1438*
And they reasoned with *t*, saying	Lk 20:5	*1438*
saw him, they reasoned among *t*	Lk 20:14	*1438*
which should feign *t* just men	Lk 20:20	*1438*
And they began to enquire among *t*	Lk 22:23	*1438*
they were at enmity between *t*	Lk 23:12	*1438*
the linen clothes laid by *t*	Lk 24:12	*3441*
The Jews therefore strove among *t*	Jn 6:52	*240*
Then said the Jews among *t*	Jn 7:35	*1438*
before the passover, to purify *t*	Jn 11:55	*1438*
they for Jesus, and spake among *t*	Jn 11:56	*240*
Pharisees therefore said among *t*	Jn 12:19	*1438*
some of his disciples among *t*	Jn 16:17	*240*
might have my joy fulfilled in *t*	Jn 17:13	*848*
and they warmed *t*	Jn 18:18	
they *t* went not into the judgment	Jn 18:28	*846*
They said therefore among *t*	Jn 19:24	*240*
council, they conferred among *t*	Acts 4:15	*240*
men, about four hundred, joined *t*	Acts 5:36	
they assembled *t* with the church	Acts 11:26	
and Silas, being prophets also *t*	Acts 15:32	*846*
but let them come *t* and fetch us	Acts 16:37	*846*
And when they opposed *t*, and	Acts 18:6	
save only that they keep *t* from	Acts 21:25	
bound *t* under a curse, saying	Acts 23:12	*1438*
which have bound *t* with an oath	Acts 23:21	*1438*
God, which they *t* also allow	Acts 24:15	*846*
gone aside, they talked between *t*	Acts 26:31	*240*
they committed *t* unto the sea	Acts 27:40	
should cast *t* first into the sea	Acts 27:43	
on his hand, they said among *t*	Acts 28:4	*846*
And when they agreed not among *t*	Acts 28:25	*846*
and had great reasoning among *t*	Acts 28:29	*1438*
Professing *t* to be wise, they	Rom 1:22	
their own bodies between *t*	Rom 1:24	*1438*
receiving in *t* that recompence of	Rom 1:27	*1438*
not the law, are a law unto *t*	Rom 2:14	*1438*
have not submitted *t* unto the	Rom 10:3	
shall receive to *t* damnation	Rom 13:2	*1438*
nor abusers of *t* with mankind	1Cor 6:9	
that they have addicted *t* to the	1Cor 16:15	*1438*
should not henceforth live unto *t*	2Cor 5:15	*1438*
power they were willing of *t*	2Cor 8:3	*830*
with some that commend *t*	2Cor 10:12	*1438*
they measuring *t* by *t*	2Cor 10:12	*1438*
and comparing *t* among *t*	2Cor 10:12	*1438*
transforming *t* into the apostles	2Cor 11:13	
For neither they *t* who are	Gal 6:13	*846*
given *t* over unto lasciviousness	Eph 4:19	*1438*
each esteem other better than *t*	Phil 2:3	*1438*
For they *t* shew of us what manner	1Th 1:9	*846*
them that defile *t* with mankind	1Ti 1:10	
that women adorn *t* in modest	1Ti 2:9	*1438*
well purchase to *t* a good degree	1Ti 3:13	*1438*
pierced *t* through with many	1Ti 6:10	*1438*
Laying up in store for *t* a good	1Ti 6:19	*1438*
instructing those that oppose *t*	2Ti 2:25	
that they may recover *t* out of	2Ti 2:26	
shall they heap to *t* teachers	2Ti 4:3	*1438*
One of *t*, even a prophet of their	Titus 1:12	*846*
to *t* the Son of God afresh	Heb 6:6	*1438*
but the heavenly things *t* with	Heb 9:23	*846*
it was revealed, that not unto *t*	1Pet 1:12	*1438*
who trusted in God, adorned *t*	1Pet 3:5	*1438*
bring upon *t* swift destruction	2Pet 2:1	*1438*
sporting *t* with their own	2Pet 2:13	*1438*
they *t* are the servants of	2Pet 2:19	*846*
giving *t* over to fornication, and	Jude 7	
in those things they corrupt *t*	Jude 10	
with you, feeding *t* without fear	Jude 12	*1438*
These be they who separate *t*	Jude 19	*1438*
hid *t* in the dens and in the rocks	Rev 6:15	*1438*
trumpets prepared *t* to sound	Rev 8:6	*1438*

THEN

t your eyes shall be opened, and	Gen 3:5	
t began men to call upon the name	Gen 4:26	227
t he put forth his hand, and took	Gen 8:9	
the Canaanite was *t* in the land	Gen 12:6	227
Perizzite dwelled *t* in the land	Gen 13:7	227
hand, *t* I will go to the right	Gen 13:9	
hand, *t* I will go to the left	Gen 13:9	

T Lot chose him all the plain of Gen 13:11
t shall thy seed also be numbered Gen 13:16
T Abram removed his tent, and came Gen 13:18
T Abraham fell upon his face, and Gen 17:17
T Sarah denied, saying, I laughed Gen 18:15
t I will spare all the place for Gen 18:26
t the angels hastened Lot, saying Gen 19:15
T the LORD rained upon Sodom and Gen 19:24
T Abimelech called Abraham, and Gen 20:9
t Abimelech rose up, and Phichol Gen 21:32
T on the third day Abraham lifted Gen 22:4
t thou shalt be clear from this Gen 24:8
T shalt thou be clear from this Gen 24:41 227
T Laban and Bethuel answered and Gen 24:50
T again Abraham took a wife, and Gen 25:1
T Abraham gave up the ghost, and Gen 25:8
T Jacob gave Esau bread and Gen 25:34
T Isaac sowed in that land, and Gen 26:12
T Abimelech went to him from Gen 26:26
t will I slay my brother Jacob Gen 27:41
t I will send, and fetch thee from Gen 27:45
T went Esau unto Ishmael, and took Gen 28:9
t shall the LORD be my God Gen 28:21
T Jacob went on his journey, and Gen 29:1
t we water the sheep Gen 29:8
wherefore *t* hast thou beguiled me Gen 29:25
T Rachel said to Leah, Give me, I Gen 30:14
t all the cattle bare speckled Gen 31:8
t bare all the cattle ringstraked Gen 31:8
now *t*, whatsoever God hath said Gen 31:16
T Jacob rose up, and set his sons Gen 31:17
T Laban overtook Jacob Gen 31:25
T went he out of Leah's tent, and Gen 31:33
T Jacob offered sacrifice upon Gen 31:54
T Jacob was greatly afraid and Gen 32:7
t the other company which is left Gen 32:8
T thou shalt say, They be thy Gen 32:18
T the handmaidens came near, they Gen 33:6
t receive my present at my hand Gen 33:10
T will we give our daughters unto Gen 34:16
t will we take our daughter, and Gen 34:17
T Jacob said unto his household, Gen 35:2
T there passed by Midianites Gen 37:28
T said Judah to Tamar his Gen 38:11
T he asked the men of that place, Gen 38:21
how *t* can I do this great Gen 39:9
T spake the chief butler unto Gen 41:9
T Pharaoh sent and called Joseph, Gen 41:14
T Joseph commanded to fill their Gen 42:25
T shall I know that ye are no Gen 42:34
t shall ye bring down my gray Gen 42:38
t let me bear the blame for ever Gen 43:9
how *t* should we steal out of thy Gen 44:8
T they speedily took down every Gen 44:11
T they rent their clothes, and Gen 44:13
T Judah came near unto him, and Gen 44:18
be with us, *t* will we go down Gen 44:26
t I shall bear the blame to my Gen 44:32
T Joseph could not refrain Gen 45:1
T Joseph came and told Pharaoh, and Gen 47:1
t make them rulers over my cattle Gen 47:6
T Joseph said unto the people, Gen 47:23
t defiledst thou it Gen 49:4 227
it be a son, *t* ye shall kill him Ex 1:16
be a daughter, *t* she shall live Ex 1:16
T said his sister to Pharaoh's Ex 2:7
T Zipporah took a sharp stone, and Ex 4:25
t she said, A bloody husband thou Ex 4:26 227
t they bowed their heads and Ex 4:31
T the officers of the children of Ex 5:15
T the LORD said unto Moses, Now Ex 6:1
how *t* shall Pharaoh hear me, who Ex 6:12
t thou shalt say unto Aaron, Take Ex 7:9
T Pharaoh also called the wise Ex 7:11
T Pharaoh called for Moses and Ex 8:8
T the magicians said unto Pharaoh Ex 8:19
T the LORD said unto Moses, Go in Ex 9:1
T Pharaoh called for Moses and Ex 10:16
T Moses called for all the elders Ex 12:21
him, *t* shall he eat thereof Ex 12:44 227
t let him come near and keep it Ex 12:48 227
t thou shalt break his neck Ex 13:13
T sang Moses and the children of Ex 15:1 227
T the dukes of Edom shall be Ex 15:15 227
T said the LORD unto Moses, Ex 16:4
t ye shall know that the LORD Ex 16:6
t ye shall see the glory of the Ex 16:7
T came Amalek, and fought with Ex 17:8
T Jethro, Moses' father in law, Ex 18:2
t thou shalt be able to endure, Ex 18:23
t ye shall be a peculiar treasure Ex 19:5
t his wife shall go out with him Ex 21:3
T his master shall bring him unto Ex 21:6
t shall he let her be redeemed Ex 21:8
t shall she go out free without Ex 21:11
t I will appoint thee a place Ex 21:13
t shall he that smote him be quit Ex 21:19
t thou shalt give life for life, Ex 21:23
t the ox shall be surely stoned, Ex 21:28
t he shall give for the ransom of Ex 21:30
t they shall sell the live ox, and Ex 21:35
t he shall be sold for his theft Ex 22:3
t the master of the house shall Ex 22:8
T shall an oath of the LORD be Ex 22:11
t let him bring it for witness, Ex 22:13
t I will be an enemy unto thine Ex 23:22
T went up Moses, and Aaron, Nadab, Ex 24:9
T shalt thou take the anointing Ex 29:7
T shalt thou kill the ram, and Ex 29:20
t thou shalt burn the remainder Ex 29:34
t shall they give every man a Ex 30:12
t I cast it into the fire, and Ex 32:24
T Moses stood in the gate of the Ex 32:26
t shalt thou break his neck Ex 34:20

T wrought Bezaleel and Aholiab, and Ex 36:1
T a cloud covered the tent of the Ex 40:34
t they journeyed not till the day Ex 40:37
t he shall bring his offering of Lev 1:14
t shall he offer it before the Lev 3:7
t he shall offer it before the Lev 3:12
t let him bring for his sin, Lev 4:3
t the congregation shall offer a Lev 4:14
t he shall bring his offering, a Lev 4:28
t he shall bear his iniquity Lev 5:1
of it, *t* he shall be guilty Lev 5:3
t he shall be guilty in one of Lev 5:4
t he shall bring for his trespass Lev 5:7
t he that sinned shall bring for Lev 5:11
T shall he bring it to the priest Lev 5:12
t he shall bring for his trespass Lev 5:15
T it shall be, because he hath Lev 6:4
t he shall offer with the Lev 7:12
T Moses said unto Aaron, This is Lev 10:3
t she shall be unclean seven days Lev 12:2
she shall *t* continue in the blood Lev 12:4
t she shall be unclean two weeks, Lev 12:5
t she shall bring two turtles, or Lev 12:8
t he shall be brought unto Aaron Lev 13:2
t the priest shall shut up him Lev 13:4
t the priest shall shut him up Lev 13:5
t the priest shall pronounce him Lev 13:8
t he shall be brought unto the Lev 13:9
T the priest shall consider Lev 13:13
t the priest shall pronounce him Lev 13:17
t the priest shall shut him up Lev 13:21
t the priest shall pronounce him Lev 13:22
T the priest shall look upon it Lev 13:25
t the priest shall shut him up Lev 13:26
t the priest shall pronounce him Lev 13:27
T the priest shall see the plague Lev 13:30
t the priest shall pronounce him Lev 13:30
t the priest shall shut up him Lev 13:31
t the priest shall pronounce him Lev 13:34
T the priest shall look on him Lev 13:36
T the priest shall look Lev 13:39
T the priest shall look upon it Lev 13:43
T the priest shall command that Lev 13:54
t he shall rend it out of the Lev 13:56
t it shall be washed the second Lev 13:58
T shall the priest command to Lev 14:4
t he shall take one lamb for a Lev 14:21
T the priest shall command that Lev 14:36
T the priest shall go out of the Lev 14:38
T the priest shall command that Lev 14:40
T the priest shall come and look, Lev 14:44
t the priest shall pronounce the Lev 14:48
t he shall wash his clothes, and Lev 15:8
t he shall number to himself Lev 15:13
t he shall wash all his flesh in Lev 15:16
t she shall number to herself Lev 15:28
T shall he kill the goat of the Lev 16:15
t shall he be clean Lev 17:15
t he shall bear his iniquity Lev 17:16
t ye shall count the fruit Lev 19:23
T I will set my face against that Lev 20:5
t he shall put the fifth part Lev 22:14
t it shall be seven days under Lev 22:27
t ye shall bring a sheaf of the Lev 23:10
T ye shall sacrifice one kid of Lev 23:19
t shall the land keep a sabbath Lev 25:2
T shalt thou cause the trumpet of Lev 25:9
T I will command my blessing upon Lev 25:21
t shall he redeem that which his Lev 25:25
T let him count the years of the Lev 25:27
t that which is sold shall remain Lev 25:28
t he may redeem it within a whole Lev 25:29
t the house that is in the walled Lev 25:30
t the house that was sold, and the Lev 25:33
t thou shalt relieve him Lev 25:35
t shall he depart from thee, both Lev 25:41
t he shall count with him, and Lev 25:52
t he shall go out in the year of Lev 25:54
T I will give you rain in due Lev 26:4
t I will punish you seven times Lev 26:18
T will I also walk contrary unto Lev 26:24
T I will walk contrary unto you Lev 26:28
T shall the land enjoy her Lev 26:34 227
even *t* shall the land rest, and Lev 26:34 227
if *t* their uncircumcised hearts Lev 26:41 227
they *t* accept of the punishment Lev 26:41 227
T will I remember my covenant Lev 26:42
t thy estimation shall be thirty Lev 27:4
t thy estimation shall be of the Lev 27:5
t thy estimation shall be of the Lev 27:6
t thy estimation shall be fifteen Lev 27:7
t he shall present himself before Lev 27:8
t it and the exchange thereof Lev 27:10
t he shall present the beast Lev 27:11
t he shall add a fifth part Lev 27:13
t the priest shall estimate it, Lev 27:14
t he shall add the fifth part of Lev 27:15
t thy estimation shall be Lev 27:16
t the priest shall reckon unto Lev 27:18
t he shall add the fifth part of Lev 27:19
T the priest shall reckon unto Lev 27:23
t he shall redeem it according to Lev 27:27
t it shall be sold according to Lev 27:27
t both it and the change thereof Lev 27:33
T the tribe of Zebulun Num 2:7
T the tribe of Gad Num 2:14
T the tabernacle of the Num 2:17
T the tribe of Benjamin Num 2:22
T the tribe of Naphtali Num 2:29
T they shall confess their sin Num 5:7
T shall the man bring his wife Num 5:15
T the priest shall charge the Num 5:21
T the priest shall take the Num 5:25
t it shall come to pass, that, if Num 5:27

t she shall be free, and shall Num 5:28
T shall the man be guiltless from Num 5:31
t he shall shave his head in the Num 6:9
t he heard the voice of one Num 7:89
T let them take a young bullock Num 8:8
t after that the children of Num 9:17
t the children of Israel kept the Num 9:19
in the morning, *t* they journeyed Num 9:21
t the princes, which are heads of Num 10:4
t the camps that lie on the east Num 10:5
t the camps that lie on the south Num 10:6
t ye shall blow an alarm with the Num 10:9
T Moses heard the people weep Num 11:10
wherefore *t* were ye not afraid to Num 12:8
T Moses and Aaron fell on their Num 14:5
t he will bring us into this land Num 14:8
T the Egyptians shall hear it, Num 14:13
t the nations which have heard Num 14:15
T the Amalekites came down, and Num 14:45
T shall he that offereth his Num 15:4
T shall he bring with a bullock a Num 15:9
T it shall be, that, when ye eat Num 15:19
T it shall be, if ought be Num 15:24
t he shall bring a she goat of Num 15:27
wherefore *t* lift ye up yourselves Num 16:3
t the LORD hath not sent me Num 16:29
t ye shall understand that these Num 16:30
t ye shall offer up an heave Num 18:26
t it shall be counted unto the Num 18:30
T the priest shall wash his Num 19:7
t the seventh day he shall not be Num 19:12
T came the children of Israel, Num 20:1
of thy water, *t* I will pay for it Num 20:19
t he fought against Israel, and Num 21:1
t I will utterly destroy their Num 21:2
T Israel sang this song, Spring Num 21:17 227
T the LORD opened the eyes of Num 22:31
T came the daughters of Num 27:1
t ye shall cause his inheritance Num 27:8
t ye shall give his inheritance Num 27:9
t ye shall give his inheritance Num 27:10
t ye shall give his inheritance Num 27:11
t all her vows shall stand, and Num 30:4
t her vows shall stand, and her Num 30:7
t he shall make her vow which she Num 30:8
t all her vows shall stand, and Num 30:11
t whatsoever proceeded out of her Num 30:12
t he establisheth all her vows, Num 30:14
t he shall bear her iniquity Num 30:15
t afterward ye shall return, and Num 32:22
t ye shall give them the land of Num 32:29
T ye shall drive out all the Num 33:52
t it shall come to pass, that Num 33:55
T your south quarter shall be Num 34:3
T ye shall appoint you cities to Num 35:11
T the congregation shall judge Num 35:24
t shall their inheritance be Num 36:3
t shall their inheritance be put Num 36:4
T I said unto you, Dread not, Deut 1:29
T ye answered and said unto me, We Deut 1:41
T we turned, and took our journey Deut 2:1
T Sihon came out against us, he Deut 2:32
T we turned, and went up the way Deut 3:1
t shall ye return every man unto Deut 3:20
T Moses severed three cities on Deut 4:41 227
our God any more, *t* we shall die Deut 5:25
T beware lest thou forget the Deut 6:12
T thou shalt say unto thy son, We Deut 6:21
t thou shalt bless the LORD thy Deut 8:10
T thine heart be lifted up, and Deut 8:14
t I abode in the mount forty days Deut 9:9
t ye rebelled against the Deut 9:23
t the LORD's wrath be kindled Deut 11:17
T will the LORD drive out all Deut 11:23
T there shall be a place which Deut 12:11
t thou shalt kill of thy herd and Deut 12:21
T shalt thou enquire, and make Deut 13:14
T shalt thou turn it into money, Deut 14:25
t in the seventh year thou shalt Deut 15:12
T thou shalt take an aul, and Deut 15:17
T shalt thou bring forth that man Deut 17:5
t shalt thou arise, and get thee Deut 17:8
T he shall minister in the name Deut 18:7
t shalt thou add three cities Deut 19:9
T the elders of his city shall Deut 19:12
T both the men, between whom the Deut 19:17
T shall ye do unto him, as he had Deut 19:19
it, *t* proclaim peace unto it Deut 20:10
t it shall be, that all the Deut 20:11
thee, *t* thou shalt besiege it Deut 20:12
T thy elders and thy judges shall Deut 21:2
T thou shalt bring her home to Deut 21:12
t thou shalt let her go whither Deut 21:14
T it shall be, when he maketh his Deut 21:16
T shall his father and his mother Deut 21:19
t thou shalt bring it unto thine Deut 22:2
t thou shalt make a battlement Deut 22:8
T shall the father of the damsel, Deut 22:15
T they shall bring out the damsel Deut 22:21
t they shall both of them die, Deut 22:22
T ye shall bring them both out Deut 22:24
t the man only that lay with her Deut 22:25
T the man that lay with her shall Deut 22:29
t keep thee from every wicked Deut 23:9
t shall he go abroad out of the Deut 23:10
t thou mayest eat grapes thy fill Deut 23:24
t thou mayest pluck the ears with Deut 23:25
t let him write her a bill of Deut 24:1
t that thief shall die Deut 24:7
t they shall justify the Deut 25:1
t thy brother should seem vile Deut 25:3
t let his brother's wife go up to Deut 25:7
T the elders of his city shall Deut 25:8
T shall his brother's wife come Deut 25:9

Context	Reference	No.
T thou shalt cut off her hand,	Deut 25:12	
T thou shalt say before the LORD	Deut 26:13	
T the LORD will make thy plagues	Deut 28:59	
but *t* the anger of the LORD and	Deut 29:20	227
T men shall say, Because they	Deut 29:25	
That *t* the LORD thy God will turn	Deut 30:3	
T my anger shall be kindled	Deut 31:17	
t will they turn unto other gods,	Deut 31:20	
t he forsook God which made him,	Deut 32:15	
Israel *t* shall dwell in safety	Deut 33:28	
for *t* thou shalt make thy way	Josh 1:8	227
t thou shalt have good success	Josh 1:8	227
T Joshua commanded the officers	Josh 1:10	
t ye shall return unto the land	Josh 1:15	
T she let them down by a cord	Josh 2:15	
t we will be quit of thine oath	Josh 2:20	
t ye shall remove from your place	Josh 3:3	
T Joshua called the twelve men,	Josh 4:4	
T ye shall answer them, That the	Josh 4:7	
T ye shall let your children know	Josh 4:22	
t shall ye shout	Josh 6:10	
t I coveted them, and took them	Josh 7:21	
T ye shall rise up from the	Josh 8:7	
t they turned again, and slew the	Josh 8:21	
T Joshua built an altar unto the	Josh 8:30	227
T spake Joshua to the LORD in the	Josh 10:12	227
T said Joshua, Open the mouth of	Josh 10:22	
T Joshua passed from Makkedah, and	Josh 10:29	
T Horam king of Gezer came up to	Josh 10:33	227
T the children of Judah came unto	Josh 14:6	
as my strength was *t*, even so is	Josh 14:11	227
t I shall be able to drive them	Josh 14:12	
This *t* was the lot of the tribe	Josh 15:1	
t get thee up to the wood country	Josh 17:15	
t goeth out to Daberath, and goeth	Josh 19:12	
t the coast turneth to Ramah, and	Josh 19:29	
t the coast turneth westward to	Josh 19:34	
t they shall not deliver the	Josh 20:5	
t shall the slayer return, and	Josh 20:6	227
T came near the heads of the	Josh 21:1	
T Joshua called the Reubenites,	Josh 22:1	227
their tents, *t* he blessed them,	Josh 22:7	
t pass ye over unto the land of	Josh 22:19	
T the children of Reuben and the	Josh 22:21	
t shall the anger of the LORD be	Josh 23:16	
T Balak the son of Zippor, king	Josh 24:9	
t he will turn and do you hurt, and	Josh 24:20	
t the LORD was with the judge, and	Judg 2:18	
T Ehud went forth through the	Judg 3:23	
thou wilt go with me, *t* I will go	Judg 4:8	
not go with me, *t* I will not go	Judg 4:8	
T Jael Heber's wife took a nail	Judg 4:21	
T sang Deborah and Barak the son	Judg 5:1	
t was war in the gates	Judg 5:8	227
t shall the people of the LORD go	Judg 5:11	
T he made him that remaineth have	Judg 5:13	227
t fought the kings of Canaan in	Judg 5:19	227
T were the horsehoofs broken by	Judg 5:22	227
why *t* is all this befallen us	Judg 6:13	
t shew me a sign that thou	Judg 6:17	
T the angel of the LORD put forth	Judg 6:21	
T the angel of the LORD departed	Judg 6:21	
T Gideon built an altar there	Judg 6:24	
T Gideon took ten men of his	Judg 6:27	
T the men of the city said unto	Judg 6:30	
T all the Midianites and the	Judg 6:33	
t shall I know that thou wilt	Judg 6:37	
T Jerubbaal, who is Gideon, and	Judg 7:1	
T went he down with Phurah his	Judg 7:11	
t blow ye the trumpets also on	Judg 7:18	
T all the men of Ephraim gathered	Judg 7:24	
T their anger was abated toward	Judg 8:3	227
t I will tear your flesh with the	Judg 8:7	
T said he unto Zebah and Zalmunna,	Judg 8:18	
T Zebah and Zalmunna said, Rise	Judg 8:21	
T the men of Israel said unto	Judg 8:22	
T said the trees unto the vine,	Judg 9:12	
T said all the trees unto the	Judg 9:14	
t come and put your trust in my	Judg 9:15	
If ye *t* have dealt truly and	Judg 9:19	
t rejoice ye in Abimelech, and let	Judg 9:19	
T God sent an evil spirit between	Judg 9:23	
t would I remove Abimelech	Judg 9:29	
t mayest thou do to them as thou	Judg 9:33	
T said Zebul unto him, Where is	Judg 9:38	
T went Abimelech to Thebez, and	Judg 9:50	
T he called hastily unto the	Judg 9:54	
T the children of Ammon were	Judg 10:17	
T Jephthah fled from his brethren	Judg 11:3	
T Jephthah went with the elders	Judg 11:11	
T Israel sent messengers unto the	Judg 11:17	
T they went along through the	Judg 11:18	
T the Spirit of the LORD came	Judg 11:29	
T it shall be, that whatsoever	Judg 11:31	
wherefore *t* are ye come up unto	Judg 12:3	
T Jephthah gathered together all	Judg 12:4	
T said they unto him, Say now	Judg 12:6	
T they took him, and slew him at	Judg 12:6	
T died Jephthah the Gileadite, and	Judg 12:7	
T died Ibzan, and was buried at	Judg 12:10	
T the woman came and told her	Judg 13:6	
T Manoah intreated the LORD, and	Judg 13:8	
T Manoah knew that he was an	Judg 13:21	227
T his father and his mother said	Judg 14:3	
T went Samson down, and his father	Judg 14:5	
t I will give you thirty sheets	Judg 14:12	
t shall ye give me thirty sheets	Judg 14:13	
T the Philistines said, Who hath	Judg 15:6	
T the Philistines went up, and	Judg 15:9	
T three thousand men of Judah	Judg 15:11	
T went Samson to Gaza, and saw	Judg 16:1	
t shall I be weak, and be as	Judg 16:7	
T the lords of the Philistines	Judg 16:8	
t shall I be weak, and be as	Judg 16:11	
t my strength will go from me, and	Judg 16:17	
T the lords of the Philistines	Judg 16:18	
T the lords of the Philistines	Judg 16:23	
T his brethren and all the house	Judg 16:31	
T said Micah, Now know I that the	Judg 17:13	
T the five men departed, and came	Judg 18:7	
T answered the five men that went	Judg 18:14	
T said the priest unto them, What	Judg 18:18	
T came the woman in the dawning	Judg 19:26	
T the man took her up upon an ass	Judg 19:28	
T all the children of Israel went	Judg 20:1	
T said the children of Israel,	Judg 20:3	
T all the children of Israel, and	Judg 20:26	
T the elders of the congregation	Judg 21:16	
T they said, Behold, there is a	Judg 21:19	
t come ye out of the vineyards,	Judg 21:21	
T she arose with her daughters in	Ruth 1:6	
T she kissed them	Ruth 1:9	
t she left speaking unto her	Ruth 1:18	
why *t* call ye me Naomi, seeing	Ruth 1:21	
T said Boaz unto his servant that	Ruth 2:5	
T said Boaz unto Ruth, Hearest	Ruth 2:8	
T she fell on her face, and bowed	Ruth 2:10	
T she said, Let me find favour in	Ruth 2:13	
T Naomi her mother in law said	Ruth 3:1	
t will I do the part of a kinsman	Ruth 3:13	
T said she, Sit still, my	Ruth 3:18	
T went Boaz up to the gate, and	Ruth 4:1	
t tell me, that I may know	Ruth 4:4	
T said Boaz, What day thou buyest	Ruth 4:5	
T said Elkanah her husband to her	1Sa 1:8	
t I will give him unto the LORD	1Sa 1:11	
T Eli answered and said, Go in	1Sa 1:17	
t I will bring him, that he may	1Sa 1:22	
t take as much as thy soul	1Sa 2:16	
t he would answer him, Nay	1Sa 2:16	
T Samuel answered, Speak	1Sa 3:10	
T Eli called Samuel, and said,	1Sa 3:16	
t ye shall be healed, and it shall	1Sa 6:3	227
T said they, What shall be the	1Sa 6:4	
Wherefore *t* do ye harden your	1Sa 6:6	
t he hath done us this great evil	1Sa 6:9	
t we shall know that it is not	1Sa 6:9	
t put away the strange gods and	1Sa 7:3	
T the children of Israel did put	1Sa 7:4	
T Samuel took a stone, and set it	1Sa 7:12	
T all the elders of Israel	1Sa 8:4	
t they passed through the land of	1Sa 9:4	
T said Saul to his servant, But,	1Sa 9:7	
T said Saul to his servant, Well	1Sa 9:10	
T Saul drew near to Samuel in the	1Sa 9:18	
wherefore *t* speakest thou so to	1Sa 9:21	
T Samuel took a vial of oil, and	1Sa 10:1	
t thou shalt find two men by	1Sa 10:2	
T shalt thou go on forward from	1Sa 10:3	
t the people said one to another,	1Sa 10:11	
T Samuel told the people the	1Sa 10:25	
T Nahash the Ammonite	1Sa 11:1	
and *t*, if there be no man to save	1Sa 11:3	
T came the messengers to Gibeah	1Sa 11:4	
T said Samuel to the people, Come	1Sa 11:14	
t the LORD sent Moses and Aaron,	1Sa 12:8	
of the LORD *t* shall both ye	1Sa 12:14	
t shall the hand of the LORD be	1Sa 12:15	
for *t* should ye go after vain	1Sa 12:21	
t the people did hide themselves	1Sa 13:6	
T said Jonathan, Behold, we will	1Sa 14:8	
t we will stand still in our	1Sa 14:9	
t we will go up	1Sa 14:10	
T said Saul unto the people that	1Sa 14:17	
T answered one of the people, and	1Sa 14:28	
T said Jonathan, My father hath	1Sa 14:29	
T they told Saul, saying, Behold,	1Sa 14:33	
T said the priest, Let us draw	1Sa 14:36	
T said he unto all Israel, Be ye	1Sa 14:40	
T Saul said to Jonathan, Tell me	1Sa 14:43	
T Saul went up from following the	1Sa 14:46	
T came the word of the LORD unto	1Sa 15:10	
What meaneth *t* this bleating of	1Sa 15:14	
T Samuel said unto Saul, Stay, and	1Sa 15:16	
Wherefore *t* didst thou not obey	1Sa 15:19	
T he said, I have sinned	1Sa 15:30	
T said Samuel, Bring ye hither to	1Sa 15:32	
T Samuel went to Ramah	1Sa 15:34	
T Jesse called Abinadab, and made	1Sa 16:8	
T Jesse made Shammah to pass by	1Sa 16:9	
T Samuel took the horn of oil, and	1Sa 16:13	
T answered one of the servants,	1Sa 16:18	
t will we be your servants	1Sa 17:9	
t shall ye be our servants, and	1Sa 17:9	
T said David to the Philistine,	1Sa 17:45	
T Jonathan and David made a	1Sa 18:3	
T the princes of the Philistines	1Sa 18:30	
wherefore *t* wilt thou sin against	1Sa 19:5	
T went he also to Ramah, and came	1Sa 19:22	
T said Jonathan unto David,	1Sa 20:4	
t say, David earnestly asked	1Sa 20:6	
t be sure that evil is determined	1Sa 20:7	
t would not I tell it thee	1Sa 20:9	
T said David to Jonathan, Who	1Sa 20:10	
I *t* send not unto thee, and shew	1Sa 20:12	227
t I will shew it thee, and send	1Sa 20:13	
T Jonathan said to David, To	1Sa 20:18	
t thou shalt go down quickly, and	1Sa 20:19	
t come thou	1Sa 20:21	
T Saul's anger was kindled	1Sa 20:30	
T came David to Nob to Ahimelech	1Sa 21:1	
T said Achish unto his servants,	1Sa 21:14	
wherefore *t* have ye brought him	1Sa 21:14	
T David departed, and came into	1Sa 22:5	
T Saul said unto his servants	1Sa 22:7	
T answered Doeg the Edomite,	1Sa 22:9	
T the king sent to call Ahimelech	1Sa 22:11	
T Ahimelech answered the king, and	1Sa 22:14	
Did I *t* begin to enquire of God	1Sa 22:15	3117
T they told David, saying, Behold	1Sa 23:1	
how much more *t* if we come to	1Sa 23:3	3588
T David enquired of the LORD yet	1Sa 23:4	
T said David, O LORD God of	1Sa 23:10	
T said David, Will the men of	1Sa 23:12	
T David and his men, which were	1Sa 23:13	
T came up the Ziphites to Saul to	1Sa 23:19	
T Saul took three thousand chosen	1Sa 24:2	
T David arose, and cut off the	1Sa 24:4	
Shall I *t* take my bread, and my	1Sa 25:11	
T Abigail made haste, and took two	1Sa 25:18	
t remember thine handmaid	1Sa 25:31	
T Saul arose, and went down to the	1Sa 26:2	
T answered David and said to	1Sa 26:6	
T said Abishai to David, God hath	1Sa 26:8	
T David went over to the other	1Sa 26:13	
T Abner answered and said, Who art	1Sa 26:14	
wherefore *t* hast thou not kept	1Sa 26:15	
T said Saul, I have sinned	1Sa 26:21	
T Saul said to David, Blessed be	1Sa 26:25	
T Achish gave him Ziklag that day	1Sa 27:6	
T said Saul unto his servants,	1Sa 28:7	
wherefore *t* layest thou a snare	1Sa 28:9	
T said the woman, Whom shall I	1Sa 28:11	
T said Samuel, Wherefore	1Sa 28:16	
Wherefore *t* dost thou ask of me,	1Sa 28:16	
T Saul fell straightway all along	1Sa 28:20	
T they rose up, and went away that	1Sa 28:25	
T said the princes of the	1Sa 29:3	
T Achish called David, and said	1Sa 29:6	
T David and the people that were	1Sa 30:4	
T answered all the wicked men and	1Sa 30:22	
T said David, Ye shall not do so,	1Sa 30:23	
T said Saul unto his armourbearer	1Sa 31:4	
T David took hold on his clothes,	2Sa 1:11	
T there arose and went over by	2Sa 2:15	
T Abner looked behind him, and	2Sa 2:20	
how *t* should I hold up my face to	2Sa 2:22	
T Abner called to Joab, and said,	2Sa 2:26	
how long shall it be *t*, ere thou	2Sa 2:26	
surely *t* in the morning the	2Sa 2:27	
T was Abner very wroth for the	2Sa 3:8	
T said Abner unto him, Go, return	2Sa 3:16	
Now *t* do it	2Sa 3:18	
T Joab came to the king, and said,	2Sa 3:24	
T came all the tribes of Israel	2Sa 5:1	
that *t* thou shalt bestir thyself	2Sa 5:24	227
for *t* shall the LORD go out	2Sa 5:24	227
T David returned to bless his	2Sa 6:20	
T went king David in, and sat	2Sa 7:18	
T David put garrisons in Syria of	2Sa 8:6	
T Toi sent Joram his son unto	2Sa 8:10	
T king David sent, and fetched him	2Sa 9:5	
T the king called to Ziba, Saul's	2Sa 9:9	
T said Ziba unto the king,	2Sa 9:11	
T said David, I will shew	2Sa 10:2	
your beards be grown, and *t* return	2Sa 10:5	
for me, *t* thou shalt help me	2Sa 10:11	
t I will come and help thee	2Sa 10:11	
t fled they also before Abishai,	2Sa 10:14	
why *t* didst thou not go down unto	2Sa 11:10	
shall I *t* go into mine house, to	2Sa 11:11	
T Joab sent and told David all the	2Sa 11:18	
t say thou, Thy servant Uriah the	2Sa 11:21	
T David said unto the messenger,	2Sa 11:25	
how will he *t* vex himself	2Sa 12:18	
T David arose from the earth, and	2Sa 12:20	
t he came to his own house	2Sa 12:20	
T said his servants unto him,	2Sa 12:21	
T David sent home to Tamar,	2Sa 13:7	
T Amnon hated her exceedingly	2Sa 13:15	
T he called his servant that	2Sa 13:17	
T his servant brought her out, and	2Sa 13:18	
T said Absalom, If not, I pray	2Sa 13:26	
t kill him, fear not	2Sa 13:28	
T all the king's sons arose, and	2Sa 13:29	
T the king arose, and tare his	2Sa 13:31	
T said she, I pray thee, let the	2Sa 14:11	
T the woman said, Let thine	2Sa 14:12	
Wherefore *t* hast thou thought	2Sa 14:13	
T thine handmaid said, The word	2Sa 14:17	
T the king answered and said unto	2Sa 14:18	
T Joab arose, and came to Absalom	2Sa 14:31	
t Absalom called unto him, and	2Sa 15:2	
t I will serve the LORD	2Sa 15:8	
t ye shall say, Absalom reigneth	2Sa 15:10	
T said the king to Ittai the	2Sa 15:19	
t thou shalt be a burden unto me	2Sa 15:33	
t mayest thou for me defeat the	2Sa 15:34	
T said the king to Ziba, Behold,	2Sa 16:4	
T said Abishai the son of Zeruiah	2Sa 16:9	
Who shall *t* say, Wherefore hast	2Sa 16:10	
T said Absalom to Ahithophel,	2Sa 16:20	
t shall the hands of all that are	2Sa 16:21	
T said Absalom, Call now Hushai	2Sa 17:5	
t shall all Israel bring ropes to	2Sa 17:13	
T said Hushai unto Zadok and to	2Sa 17:15	
T David arose, and all the people	2Sa 17:22	
T David came to Mahanaim	2Sa 17:24	
T said Joab, I may not tarry thus	2Sa 18:14	
T said Ahimaaz the son of Zadok,	2Sa 18:19	
T said Joab to Cushi, Go tell the	2Sa 18:21	
T said Ahimaaz the son of Zadok	2Sa 18:22	
T Ahimaaz ran by the way of the	2Sa 18:23	
t it had pleased thee well	2Sa 19:6	227
T the king arose, and sat in the	2Sa 19:8	
wherefore *t* are ye the last to	2Sa 19:12	
wherefore *t* should thy servant be	2Sa 19:35	
T the king went on to Gilgal, and	2Sa 19:40	
wherefore *t* be ye angry for this	2Sa 19:42	
why *t* did ye despise us, that our	2Sa 19:43	
T said the king to Amasa,	2Sa 20:4	
T cried a wise woman out of the	2Sa 20:16	

T she said unto him, Hear the 2Sa 20:17
T she spake, saying, They were 2Sa 20:18
T the woman went unto all the 2Sa 20:22
T there was a famine in the days 2Sa 21:1
T the men of David sware unto him 2Sa 21:17 227
t Sibbechai the Hushathite slew 2Sa 21:18 227
T the earth shook and trembled 2Sa 22:8
T did I beat them as small as the 2Sa 22:43
David was *t* in an hold, and the 2Sa 23:14 227
Philistines was *t* in Beth-lehem 2Sa 23:14
T they came to Gilead, and to the 2Sa 24:6
T Adonijah the son of Haggith 1Kin 1:5
why *t* doth Adonijah reign 1Kin 1:13
T king David answered and said, 1Kin 1:28
T Bath-sheba bowed with her face 1Kin 1:31
T ye shall come up after him, 1Kin 1:35
T sat Solomon upon the throne of 1Kin 2:12
T she said, I desire one small 1Kin 2:20
T king Solomon sware by the LORD, 1Kin 2:23
T tidings came to Joab 1Kin 2:28
T Solomon sent Benaiah the son of 1Kin 2:29
Why *t* hast thou not kept the oath 1Kin 2:43
t I will lengthen thy days 1Kin 3:14
T came there two women, that were 1Kin 3:16 227
T said the king, The one saith, 1Kin 3:23
T spake the woman whose the 1Kin 3:26
T the king answered and said, Give 1Kin 3:27
t he built chambers against all 1Kin 6:10
t will I perform my word with 1Kin 6:12
T he made a porch for the throne 1Kin 7:7
T made he ten lavers of brass 1Kin 7:38
T Solomon assembled the elders of 1Kin 8:1 227
T spake Solomon, The LORD said 1Kin 8:12 227
T hear thou in heaven, and do, and 1Kin 8:32
T hear thou in heaven, and forgive 1Kin 8:34
T hear thou in heaven, and forgive 1Kin 8:36
T hear thou in heaven thy 1Kin 8:39
T hear thou in heaven their 1Kin 8:45
T hear thou their prayer and their 1Kin 8:49
T I will establish the throne of 1Kin 9:5
T will I cut off Israel out of 1Kin 9:7
that *t* king Solomon gave Hiram 1Kin 9:11 227
t did he build Millo 1Kin 9:24 227
T did Solomon build an high place 1Kin 11:7
T Pharaoh said unto him, But what 1Kin 11:22
three days, *t* come again to me 1Kin 12:5
t they will be thy servants for 1Kin 12:7
T king Rehoboam sent Adoram, who 1Kin 12:18
T Jeroboam built Shechem in mount 1Kin 12:25
t shall the heart of this people 1Kin 12:27
T he said unto him, Come home 1Kin 13:15
t bury me in the sepulchre 1Kin 13:31
T Asa took all the silver and the 1Kin 15:18
T king Asa made a proclamation 1Kin 15:22
T the word of the LORD came to 1Kin 16:1
T were the people of Israel 1Kin 16:21 227
but if Baal, *t* follow him 1Kin 18:21
T said Elijah unto the people, I, 1Kin 18:22
T the fire of the LORD fell, and 1Kin 18:38
T Jezebel sent a messenger unto 1Kin 19:2
t an angel touched him, and said 1Kin 19:5
mother, and *t* I will follow thee 1Kin 19:20
T he arose, and went after Elijah, 1Kin 19:21
T the king of Israel called all 1Kin 20:7
T he said, Who shall order the 1Kin 20:14
T he numbered the young men of 1Kin 20:15
T he said, Go ye, bring him 1Kin 20:33
T Ben-hadad came forth to him 1Kin 20:33
T said Ahab, I will send thee 1Kin 20:34
T said he unto him, Because thou 1Kin 20:36
T he found another man, and said, 1Kin 20:37
t shall thy life be for his life, 1Kin 20:39
t carry him out, and stone him, 1Kin 21:10
T they carried him forth out of 1Kin 21:13
T they sent to Jezebel, saying, 1Kin 21:14
T the king of Israel gathered the 1Kin 22:6
T the king of Israel called an 1Kin 22:9
There was *t* no king in Edom 1Kin 22:47
T said Ahaziah the son of Ahab 1Kin 22:49 227
T Moab rebelled against Israel 2Kin 1:1
T the king sent unto him a 2Kin 1:9
t let fire come down from heaven, 2Kin 1:10
T he took his eldest son that 2Kin 3:27
T he said, Go, borrow thee 2Kin 4:3
T she came and told the man of God 2Kin 4:7
What *t* is to be done for her 2Kin 4:14
on her knees till noon, and *t* died 2Kin 4:20
T she saddled an ass, and said to 2Kin 4:24
T she said, Did I desire a son of 2Kin 4:28
T he said to Gehazi, Gird up thy 2Kin 4:29
T he returned, and walked in the 2Kin 4:35
T she went in, and fell at his 2Kin 4:37
But he said, *T* bring meal 2Kin 4:41
how much rather *t*, when he saith 2Kin 5:13
T went he down, and dipped himself 2Kin 5:14
And Naaman said, Shall there not *t* 2Kin 5:17
T the king of Syria warred 2Kin 6:8
T he said, God do so and more also 2Kin 6:31
T Elisha said, Hear ye the word 2Kin 7:1
T a lord on whose hand the king 2Kin 7:2
t the famine is in the city, and 2Kin 7:4
T they said one to another, We do 2Kin 7:9
T spake Elisha unto the woman, 2Kin 8:1
Jehoshaphat being *t* king of Judah 2Kin 8:16
T Libnah revolted at the same 2Kin 8:22 227
T take the box of oil, and pour it 2Kin 9:3
T open the door, and flee, and 2Kin 9:3
T Jehu came forth to the servants 2Kin 9:11
T they hasted, and took every man 2Kin 9:13
t let none go forth nor escape 2Kin 9:15
T he sent out a second on 2Kin 9:19
T said Jehu to Bidkar his captain 2Kin 9:25
how *t* shall we stand 2Kin 10:4
T he wrote a letter the second 2Kin 10:6
T king Jehoash called for 2Kin 12:7
T Hazael king of Syria went up, 2Kin 12:17 227
T Elisha said, Shoot 2Kin 13:17
t hadst thou smitten Syria till 2Kin 13:19 227
T Amaziah sent messengers to 2Kin 14:8 227
T Menahem smote Tiphsah, and all 2Kin 15:16 227
T Rezin king of Syria and Pekah 2Kin 16:5 227
T the king of Assyria came up 2Kin 17:5
T the king of Assyria commanded, 2Kin 17:27
T one of the priests whom they 2Kin 17:28
How *t* wilt thou turn away the 2Kin 18:24
T said Eliakim the son of Hilkiah 2Kin 18:26
T Rab-shakeh stood and cried with 2Kin 18:28
t eat ye every man of his own 2Kin 18:31
T came Eliakim the son of Hilkiah 2Kin 18:37
T Isaiah the son of Amoz sent to 2Kin 19:20
T he turned his face to the wall, 2Kin 20:2
T came Isaiah the prophet unto 2Kin 20:14
T said Hezekiah unto Isaiah, Good 2Kin 20:19
T he said, What title is that 2Kin 23:17
t he turned and rebelled against 2Kin 24:1
t Kedar, and Adbeel, and Mibsam, 1Chr 1:29
t Abiah Hezron's wife bare him 1Chr 2:24
t they waited on their office 1Chr 6:32
t Zur, and Kish, and Baal, and Ner, 1Chr 9:36
T said Saul to his armourbearer, 1Chr 10:4
t they forsook their cities, and 1Chr 10:7
T all Israel gathered themselves 1Chr 11:1
David was *t* in the hold, and the 1Chr 11:16 227
garrison was *t* at Beth-lehem 1Chr 11:16 227
t Joash, the sons of Shemaah the 1Chr 12:3
T the spirit came upon Amasai, 1Chr 12:18
T David received them, and made 1Chr 12:18
T David said, God hath broken in 1Chr 14:11
that *t* thou shalt go out to 1Chr 14:15 227
T David said, None ought to carry 1Chr 15:2 227
T on that day David delivered 1Chr 16:7 227
T shall the trees of the wood 1Chr 16:33 227
T Nathan said unto David, Do all 1Chr 17:2
T David put garrisons in 1Chr 18:6
T there went certain, and told 1Chr 19:5
your beards be grown, and *t* return 1Chr 19:5
for me, *t* thou shalt help me 1Chr 19:12
for thee, *t* I will help thee 1Chr 19:12
T Joab came to Jerusalem 1Chr 19:15
why *t* doth my lord require this 1Chr 21:3
T David and the elders of Israel, 1Chr 21:16
T the angel of the LORD commanded 1Chr 21:18
T David said to Ornan, Grant me 1Chr 21:22
Jebusite, *t* he sacrificed there 1Chr 21:28
T David said, This is the house 1Chr 22:1
T he called for Solomon his son, 1Chr 22:6
T shalt thou prosper, if thou 1Chr 22:13 227
T for Zechariah his son, a wise 1Chr 26:14
T David the king stood up upon 1Chr 28:2
T David gave to Solomon his son 1Chr 28:11
who *t* is willing to consecrate 1Chr 29:5
T the chief of the fathers and 1Chr 29:6
T the people rejoiced, for that 1Chr 29:9
T Solomon sat on the throne of 1Chr 29:23
T Solomon spake unto all Israel, 2Chr 1:2
T Solomon came from his journey 2Chr 1:13
who am I *t*, that I should build 2Chr 2:6
T Huram the king of Tyre answered 2Chr 2:11
T Solomon began to build the 2Chr 3:1
T Solomon assembled the elders of 2Chr 5:2 227
and did not *t* wait by course 2Chr 5:11
that *t* the house was filled with 2Chr 5:13
T said Solomon, The LORD hath 2Chr 6:1 227
Now *t*, O LORD God of Israel, let 2Chr 6:17
T hear thou from heaven, and do, 2Chr 6:23
T hear thou from the heavens, and 2Chr 6:25
T hear thou from heaven, and 2Chr 6:27
T what prayer or what 2Chr 6:29
T hear thou from heaven thy 2Chr 6:30
T hear thou from the heavens, 2Chr 6:33
T hear thou from the heavens 2Chr 6:35
T hear thou from the heavens, 2Chr 6:39
T the king and all the people 2Chr 7:4
t will I hear from heaven, and 2Chr 7:14
T will I stablish the throne of 2Chr 7:18
T will I pluck them up by the 2Chr 7:20
T Solomon offered burnt offerings 2Chr 8:12 227
T went Solomon to Ezion-geber, and 2Chr 8:17 227
T king Rehoboam sent Hadoram that 2Chr 10:18
T came Shemaiah the prophet to 2Chr 12:5
T the men of Judah gave a shout 2Chr 13:15
T Asa went out against him, and 2Chr 14:10
T Asa brought out silver and gold 2Chr 16:2
T Asa the king took all Judah 2Chr 16:6
T Asa was wroth with the seer, and 2Chr 16:10
T he said, I did see all Israel 2Chr 18:16
T there came out a spirit, and 2Chr 18:20
T Zedekiah the son of Chenaanah 2Chr 18:23
T the king of Israel said, Take 2Chr 18:25
t hath not the LORD spoken by me 2Chr 18:27
T there came some that told 2Chr 20:2
t thou wilt hear and help 2Chr 20:9
T upon Jahaziel the son of 2Chr 20:14
T they returned, every man of 2Chr 20:27
T Eliezer the son of Dodavah of 2Chr 20:37
T Jehoram went forth with his 2Chr 21:9
T they brought out the king's son 2Chr 23:11
T Athaliah rent her clothes, and 2Chr 23:13
T Jehoiada the priest brought out 2Chr 23:14
T all the people went to the 2Chr 23:17
T the king hearkened unto them 2Chr 24:17
T Amaziah separated them, to wit, 2Chr 25:10
T the prophet forbare, and said, I 2Chr 25:16
T Amaziah king of Judah took 2Chr 25:17
T all the people of Judah took 2Chr 26:1
T Uzziah was wroth, and had a 2Chr 26:19
T certain of the heads of the 2Chr 28:12
t they returned to Samaria 2Chr 28:15
T the Levites arose, Mahath the 2Chr 29:12
T they went in to Hezekiah the 2Chr 29:18
T Hezekiah the king rose early, 2Chr 29:20
T Hezekiah answered and said, Now 2Chr 29:31
T they killed the passover on the 2Chr 30:15
T the priests the Levites arose 2Chr 30:27
T all the children of Israel 2Chr 31:1
T Hezekiah questioned with the 2Chr 31:9
T Hezekiah commanded to prepare 2Chr 31:11
T they cried with a loud voice in 2Chr 32:18
T Manasseh knew that the LORD he 2Chr 33:13
T Shaphan the scribe told the 2Chr 34:18
T the king sent and gathered 2Chr 34:29
T the people of the land took 2Chr 36:1
T rose up the chief of the Ezr 1:5
T stood up Jeshua the son of Ezr 3:2
T stood Jeshua with his sons and Ezr 3:9
T they came to Zerubbabel, and to Ezr 4:2
T the people of the land weakened Ezr 4:4
T wrote Rehum the chancellor, and Ezr 4:9 116
t will they not pay toll, tribute Ezr 4:13
T sent the king an answer unto Ezr 4:17
T ceased the work of the house of Ezr 4:24 116
T the prophets, Haggai the Ezr 5:1
T rose up Zerubbabel the son of Ezr 5:2 116
T said we unto them after this Ezr 5:4 116
t they returned answer by letter Ezr 5:5 116
T asked we those elders, and said Ezr 5:9 116
T came the same Sheshbazzar, and Ezr 5:16 116
T Darius the king made a decree, Ezr 6:1 116
T Tatnai, governor on this side Ezr 6:13 116
T sent I for Eliezer, for Ariel, Ezr 8:16
T I proclaimed a fast there, at Ezr 8:21
T I separated twelve of the chief Ezr 8:24
T we departed from the river of Ezr 8:31
T were assembled unto me every Ezr 9:4
T arose Ezra, and made the chief Ezr 10:5
T Ezra rose up from before the Ezr 10:6
T all the men of Judah and Ezr 10:9
T all the congregation answered Ezr 10:12
T I was very sore afraid, Neh 2:2
T the king said unto me, For what Neh 2:4
T I came to the governors beyond Neh 2:9
T I went on to the gate of the Neh 2:14
T went I up in the night by the Neh 2:15
T said I unto them, Ye see the Neh 2:17
T I told them of the hand of my Neh 2:18
T answered I them, and said unto Neh 2:20
T Eliashib the high priest rose Neh 3:1
stopped, *t* they were very wroth, Neh 4:7
T I consulted with myself, and I Neh 5:7
T held they their peace, and found Neh 5:8
T said they, We will restore them Neh 5:12
T I called the priests, and took Neh 5:12
T sent Sanballat his servant unto Neh 6:5
T I sent unto him, saying, There Neh 6:8
T he said unto them, Go your way, Neh 8:10
T stood up upon the stairs, of Neh 9:4
T the Levites, Jeshua, and Kadmiel Neh 9:5
T I brought up the princes of Neh 12:31
T I commanded, and they cleansed Neh 13:9
T contended I with the rulers, and Neh 13:11
T brought all Judah the tithe of Neh 13:12
T I contended with the nobles of Neh 13:17
T I testified against them, and Neh 13:21
Shall we *t* hearken unto you to do Neh 13:27
T the king said to the wise men, Est 1:13
T said the king's servants that Est 2:2
T thus came every maiden unto the Est 2:13
T the king made a great feast Est 2:18
t Mordecai sat in the king's gate Est 2:19
T the king's servants, which were Est 3:3
t was Haman full of wrath Est 3:5
T were the king's scribes called Est 3:12
T was the queen exceedingly Est 4:4
T called Esther for Hatach, one Est 4:5
T Mordecai commanded to answer Est 4:13
t shall there enlargement and Est 4:14
T Esther bade them return Est 4:15
T said the king unto her, What Est 5:3
T the king said, Cause Haman to Est 5:5
T answered Esther, and said, My Est 5:7
T went Haman forth that day Est 5:9
T said Zeresh his wife and all his Est 5:14
t go thou in merrily with the Est 5:14
T said the king's servants that Est 6:3
T the king said to Haman, Make Est 6:10
T took Haman the apparel and the Est 6:11
T said his wise men and Zeresh his Est 6:13
T Esther the queen answered and Est 7:3
T the king Ahasuerus answered and Est 7:5
T Haman was afraid before the Est 7:6
T the king returned out of the Est 7:8
T said the king, Will he force Est 7:8
T the king said, Hang him thereon Est 7:9
T was the king's wrath pacified Est 7:10
T the king held out the golden Est 8:4
T the king Ahasuerus said unto Est 8:7
T were the king's scribes called Est 8:9
T said Esther, If it please the Est 9:13
T Esther the queen, the daughter Est 9:29
T Satan answered the LORD, and Job 1:7
T Satan answered the LORD, and Job 1:9
T Job arose, and rent his mantle, Job 1:20
T said his wife unto him, Dost Job 2:9
t had I been at rest, Job 3:13 227
T Eliphaz the Temanite answered Job 4:1
T a spirit passed before my face Job 4:15
T should I yet have comfort Job 6:10
T thou scarest me with dreams, and Job 7:14
T answered Bildad the Shuhite, and Job 8:1
t it shall deny him, saying, I Job 8:18
T Job answered and said, Job 9:1
be wicked, why *t* labour I in vain Job 9:29

T would I speak, and not fear him	Job 9:35	
t thou markest me, and thou wilt	Job 10:14	
Wherefore *t* hast thou brought me	Job 10:18	
cease *t*, and let me alone, that I	Job 10:20	
T answered Zophar the Naamathite,	Job 11:1	
together, *t* who can hinder him	Job 11:10	
will he not *t* consider it	Job 11:11	
For *t* shalt thou lift up thy face	Job 11:15	227
t I will not hide myself from	Job 13:20	227
T call thou, and I will answer	Job 13:22	
T answered Eliphaz the Temanite,	Job 15:1	
T Job answered and said,	Job 16:1	
t I shall go the way whence I	Job 16:22	
T answered Bildad the Shuhite, and	Job 18:1	
T Job answered and said,	Job 19:1	
T answered Zophar the Naamathite,	Job 20:1	
How *t* comfort ye me in vain,	Job 21:34	
T Eliphaz the Temanite answered	Job 22:1	
T shalt thou lay up gold as dust,	Job 22:24	
For *t* shalt thou have thy delight	Job 22:26	227
t thou shalt say, There is	Job 22:29	
T Job answered and said,	Job 23:1	
T answered Bildad the Shuhite, and	Job 25:1	
How *t* can man be justified with	Job 25:4	
why *t* are ye thus altogether vain	Job 27:12	
Whence *t* cometh wisdom	Job 28:20	
T did he see it, and declare it	Job 28:27	227
the ear heard me, *t* it blessed me	Job 29:11	
T I said, I shall die in my nest,	Job 29:18	
for good, *t* evil came unto me	Job 30:26	
why *t* should I think upon a maid	Job 31:1	
T let me sow, and let another eat	Job 31:8	
T let my wife grind unto another,	Job 31:10	
What *t* shall I do when God riseth	Job 31:14	
T let mine arm fall from my	Job 31:22	
T was kindled the wrath of Elihu	Job 32:2	
men, *t* his wrath was kindled	Job 32:5	
T he openeth the ears of men, and	Job 33:16	227
T he is gracious unto him, and	Job 33:24	
quietness, who *t* can make trouble	Job 34:29	
his face, who *t* can behold him	Job 34:29	
T he sheweth them their work, and	Job 36:9	
t a great ransom cannot deliver	Job 36:18	
T the beasts go into dens, and	Job 37:8	
T the LORD answered Job out of	Job 38:1	
thou it, because thou wast *t* born	Job 38:21	227
T Job answered the LORD, and said,	Job 40:3	
T answered the LORD unto Job out	Job 40:6	
T will I also confess unto thee	Job 40:14	
who *t* is able to stand before me	Job 41:10	
T Job answered the LORD, and said,	Job 42:1	
T came there unto him all his	Job 42:11	
T shall he speak unto them in his	Ps 2:5	227
T the earth shook and trembled	Ps 18:7	
T the channels of waters were	Ps 18:15	
T did I beat them small as the	Ps 18:42	
t shall I be upright, and I shall	Ps 19:13	227
t the LORD will take me up	Ps 27:10	
t spake I with my tongue,	Ps 39:3	
T said I, Lo, I come	Ps 40:7	227
T will I go unto the altar of God	Ps 43:4	
t thou consentedst with him, and	Ps 50:18	
T will I teach transgressors thy	Ps 51:13	
T shalt thou be pleased with the	Ps 51:19	227
t shall they offer bullocks upon	Ps 51:19	227
for *t* would I fly away, and be at	Ps 55:6	
t would I wander far off, and	Ps 55:7	
t I could have borne it	Ps 55:12	
t I would have hid myself from	Ps 55:12	
t shall mine enemies turn back	Ps 56:9	227
T shall the earth yield her	Ps 67:6	
t I restored that which I took	Ps 69:4	227
t understood I their end	Ps 73:17	
he slew them, *t* they sought him	Ps 78:34	
T the Lord awaked as one out of	Ps 78:65	
Why hast thou *t* broken down her	Ps 80:12	
T thou spakest in vision to thy	Ps 89:19	227
T will I visit their	Ps 89:32	
t shall all the trees of the wood	Ps 96:12	227
T believed they his words	Ps 106:12	
T stood up Phinehas, and executed	Ps 106:30	
T they cried unto the LORD in	Ps 107:6	
T they cried unto the LORD in	Ps 107:13	
T they cry unto the LORD in their	Ps 107:19	
T they cry unto the LORD in their	Ps 107:28	
T are they glad because they be	Ps 107:30	
T called I upon the name of the	Ps 116:4	
T shall I not be ashamed, when I	Ps 119:6	227
I should *t* have perished in mine	Ps 119:92	227
T they had swallowed us up quick,	Ps 124:3	233
T the waters had overwhelmed us,	Ps 124:4	233
T the proud waters had gone over	Ps 124:5	233
T was our mouth filled with	Ps 126:2	227
t said they among the heathen,	Ps 126:2	227
within me, *t* thou knewest my path	Ps 142:3	
T shall they call upon me, but I	Prov 1:28	227
T shalt thou understand the fear	Prov 2:5	227
T shalt thou understand	Prov 2:9	227
T shalt thou walk in thy way	Prov 3:23	227
T I was by him, as one brought up	Prov 8:30	
When pride cometh, *t* cometh shame	Prov 11:2	
how much more *t* the hearts of the	Prov 15:11	
t cometh also contempt, and with	Prov 18:3	
he is gone his way, *t* he boasteth	Prov 20:14	227
how can a man *t* understand his	Prov 20:24	
t there shall be a reward, and thy	Prov 24:14	
T I saw, and considered it well	Prov 24:32	
T I looked on all the works that	Eccl 2:11	
T I saw that wisdom excelleth	Eccl 2:13	
T said I in my heart, As it	Eccl 2:15	
and why was I *t* more wise	Eccl 2:15	227
T I said in my heart, that this	Eccl 2:15	
T I returned, and I saw vanity	Eccl 4:7	
lie together, *t* they have heat	Eccl 4:11	
T I commended mirth, because a	Eccl 8:15	
T I beheld all the work of God,	Eccl 8:17	
T said I, Wisdom is better than	Eccl 9:16	
t must he put to more strength	Eccl 10:10	
T shall the dust return to the	Eccl 12:7	
t was I in his eyes as one that	Song 8:10	227
T shall the lambs feed after	Is 5:17	
T said I, Woe is me	Is 6:5	
T flew one of the seraphims unto	Is 6:6	
T said I, Here am I	Is 6:8	
T said I, Lord, how long	Is 6:11	
T said the LORD unto Isaiah, Go	Is 7:3	
T said the LORD to me, Call his	Is 8:3	
t shall his yoke depart from off	Is 14:25	
What shall one *t* answer the	Is 14:32	
T the moon shall be confounded,	Is 24:23	
t ye shall be trodden down by it	Is 28:18	
T shall he give the rain of thy	Is 30:23	
T shall the Assyrian fall with	Is 31:8	
T judgment shall dwell in the	Is 32:16	
t is the prey of a great spoil	Is 33:23	227
T the eyes of the blind shall be	Is 35:5	227
T shall the lame man leap as an	Is 35:6	227
T came forth unto him Eliakim,	Is 36:3	
How *t* wilt thou turn away the	Is 36:9	
T said Eliakim and Shebna and Joah	Is 36:11	
T Rabshakeh stood, and cried with	Is 36:13	
T came Eliakim, the son of	Is 36:22	
T Isaiah the son of Amoz sent	Is 37:21	
T the angel of the LORD went	Is 37:36	
T Hezekiah turned his face toward	Is 38:2	
T came the word of the LORD to	Is 38:4	
T came Isaiah the prophet unto	Is 39:3	
T said he, What have they seen in	Is 39:4	
T said Isaiah to Hezekiah, Hear	Is 39:5	
T said Hezekiah to Isaiah, Good	Is 39:8	
To whom *t* will ye liken God	Is 40:18	
To whom *t* will ye liken me, or	Is 40:25	
t let them speak	Is 41:1	227
T shall it be for a man to burn	Is 44:15	
t had thy peace been as a river,	Is 48:18	
T I said, I have laboured in vain	Is 49:4	
T shalt thou say in thine heart,	Is 49:21	
T shall thy light break forth as	Is 58:8	227
T shalt thou call, and the LORD	Is 58:9	227
t shall thy light rise in	Is 58:10	
T shalt thou delight thyself in	Is 58:14	227
T thou shalt see, and flow	Is 60:5	227
T he remembered the days of old,	Is 63:11	
t shall ye suck, ye shall be	Is 66:12	
T the word of the LORD came unto	Jer 1:4	
T said I, Ah, Lord GOD	Jer 1:6	
T the LORD put forth his hand, and	Jer 1:9	
T said the LORD unto me, Thou	Jer 1:12	
T the LORD said unto me, Out of	Jer 1:14	
how *t* art thou turned into the	Jer 2:21	
my sight, *t* shalt thou not remove	Jer 4:1	
T said I, Ah, Lord GOD	Jer 4:10	
they *t* committed adultery, and	Jer 5:7	
t shalt thou answer them, Like as	Jer 5:19	
T will I cause you to dwell in	Jer 7:7	
T will I cause to cease from the	Jer 7:34	
Why *t* is this people of Jerusalem	Jer 8:5	
why *t* is not the health of the	Jer 8:22	3588
T answered I, and said, So be it,	Jer 11:5	
T the LORD said unto me, Proclaim	Jer 11:6	
T shall the cities of Judah and	Jer 11:12	
thou doest evil, *t* thou rejoicest	Jer 11:15	227
t thou shewedst me their doings	Jer 11:18	227
t how canst thou contend with	Jer 12:5	
t how wilt thou do in the	Jer 12:5	
t shall they be built in the	Jer 12:16	
T I went to Euphrates, and digged,	Jer 13:7	
T the word of the LORD came unto	Jer 13:8	
T shalt thou say unto them, Thus	Jer 13:13	
t may ye also do good, that are	Jer 13:23	
T said the LORD unto me, Pray not	Jer 14:11	
T said I, Ah, Lord GOD	Jer 14:13	
T the LORD said unto me, The	Jer 14:14	
t behold the slain with the sword	Jer 14:18	
t behold them that are sick with	Jer 14:18	
T said the LORD unto me, Though	Jer 15:1	
t thou shalt tell them, Thus	Jer 15:2	
t will I bring thee again, and	Jer 15:19	
T shalt thou say unto them,	Jer 16:11	
T shall there enter into the	Jer 17:25	
t will I kindle a fire in the	Jer 17:27	
T I went down to the potter's	Jer 18:3	
T the word of the LORD came to me	Jer 18:5	
t I will repent of the good,	Jer 18:10	
T said they, Come, and let us	Jer 18:18	
T shalt thou break the bottle in	Jer 19:10	
T came Jeremiah from Tophet,	Jer 19:14	
T Pashur smote Jeremiah the	Jer 20:2	
T said Jeremiah unto him, The	Jer 20:3	
T I said, I will not make mention	Jer 20:9	
T said Jeremiah unto them, Thus	Jer 21:3	
t shall there enter in by the	Jer 22:4	
T they shall answer, Because they	Jer 22:9	
and *t* it was well with him	Jer 22:15	227
t it was well with him	Jer 22:16	227
surely *t* shalt thou be ashamed and	Jer 22:22	227
t they should have turned them	Jer 23:22	
thou shalt *t* say unto them, What	Jer 23:33	
T said the LORD unto me, What	Jer 24:3	
T took I the cup at the LORD's	Jer 25:17	
t shalt thou say unto them, Thus	Jer 25:28	
T will I make this house like	Jer 26:6	
t they came up from the king's	Jer 26:10	
T spake the priests and the	Jer 26:11	
T spake Jeremiah unto all the	Jer 26:12	
T said the princes and all the	Jer 26:16	
T rose up certain of the elders	Jer 26:17	
t many nations and great kings	Jer 27:7	
t will I bring them up, and	Jer 27:22	
T the prophet Jeremiah said unto	Jer 28:5	
t shall the prophet be known,	Jer 28:9	
T Hananiah the prophet took the	Jer 28:10	
T the word of the LORD came unto	Jer 28:12	
T said the prophet Jeremiah unto	Jer 28:15	
T shall ye call upon me, and ye	Jer 29:12	
T came the word of the LORD unto	Jer 29:30	
T shall the virgin rejoice in the	Jer 31:13	
t the seed of Israel also shall	Jer 31:36	
For *t* the king of Babylon's army	Jer 32:2	227
T I knew that this was the word	Jer 32:8	
T came the word of the LORD unto	Jer 32:26	
T may also my covenant be broken	Jer 33:21	
T will I cast away the seed of	Jer 33:26	1571
T Jeremiah the prophet spake all	Jer 34:6	
t they obeyed, and let them go	Jer 34:10	
T I took Jaazaniah the son of	Jer 35:3	
T came the word of the LORD unto	Jer 35:12	
T Jeremiah called Baruch the son	Jer 36:4	
T read Baruch in the book the	Jer 36:10	
T he went down into the king's	Jer 36:12	
T Michaiah declared unto them all	Jer 36:13	
T Baruch answered them, He	Jer 36:18	
T said the princes unto Baruch,	Jer 36:19	
T the word of the LORD came to	Jer 36:27	
T took Jeremiah another roll, and	Jer 36:32	
T Pharaoh's army was come forth	Jer 37:5	
T came the word of the LORD unto	Jer 37:6	
T Jeremiah went forth out of	Jer 37:12	
T said Jeremiah, It is false	Jer 37:14	
T Zedekiah the king sent, and took	Jer 37:17	
T Zedekiah the king commanded	Jer 37:21	
T Shephatiah the son of Mattan,	Jer 38:1	
T Zedekiah the king said, Behold,	Jer 38:5	
T took they Jeremiah, and cast him	Jer 38:6	
the king *t* sitting in the gate of	Jer 38:7	
T the king commanded Ebed-melech	Jer 38:10	
T Zedekiah the king sent, and took	Jer 38:14	
T Jeremiah said unto Zedekiah, If	Jer 38:15	
T said Jeremiah unto Zedekiah,	Jer 38:17	
t thy soul shall live, and this	Jer 38:17	
t shall this city be given into	Jer 38:18	
T said Zedekiah unto Jeremiah,	Jer 38:24	
T thou shalt say unto them, I	Jer 38:26	
T came all the princes unto	Jer 38:27	
t they fled, and went forth out of	Jer 39:4	
T the king of Babylon slew the	Jer 39:6	
T Nebuzar-adan the captain of the	Jer 39:9	
T went Jeremiah unto Gedaliah the	Jer 40:6	
T they came to Gedaliah to Mizpah	Jer 40:8	
T Johanan the son of Kareah spake	Jer 40:15	
T arose Ishmael the son of	Lam 41:2	
T Ishmael carried away captive	Jer 41:10	
T they took all the men, and went	Jer 41:12	
were with him, *t* they were glad	Jer 41:13	
T took Johanan the son of Kareah,	Jer 41:16	
T all the captains of the forces,	Jer 42:1	
T Jeremiah the prophet said unto	Jer 42:4	
T they said to Jeremiah, The LORD	Jer 42:5	
T called he Johanan the son of	Jer 42:8	
t will I build you, and not pull	Jer 42:10	
T it shall come to pass, that the	Jer 42:16	
T spake Azariah the son of	Jer 43:2	
T came the word of the LORD unto	Jer 43:8	
T all the men which knew that	Jer 44:15	
for *t* had we plenty of victuals,	Jer 44:17	
T Jeremiah said unto all the	Jer 44:20	
t the men shall cry, and all the	Jer 47:2	
why *t* doth their king inherit Gad	Jer 49:1	
t shall Israel be heir unto them	Jer 49:2	
T the heaven and the earth, and all	Jer 51:48	
T shalt thou say, O LORD, thou	Jer 51:62	
T the city was broken up, and all	Jer 52:7	
T they took the king, and carried	Jer 52:9	
T he put out the eyes of Zedekiah	Jer 52:11	
T Nebuzar-adan the captain of the	Jer 52:15	
t I said, I am cut off	Lam 3:54	
T did I eat it	Eze 3:3	
T the spirit took me up, and I	Eze 3:12	
T I came to them of the captivity	Eze 3:15	
T I arose, and went forth into the	Eze 3:23	
T the spirit entered into me, and	Eze 3:24	
T said I, Ah Lord GOD	Eze 4:14	
T he said unto me, Lo, I have	Eze 4:15	
t take thee balances to weigh, and	Eze 5:1	
T take of them again, and cast	Eze 5:4	
T shall ye know that I am the	Eze 6:13	
t shall they seek a vision of the	Eze 7:26	
T I beheld, and lo a likeness as	Eze 8:2	
T said he unto me, Son of man,	Eze 8:5	
T said he unto me, Son of man,	Eze 8:8	
T said he unto me, Son of man,	Eze 8:12	
T he brought me to the door of	Eze 8:14	
T said he unto me, Hast thou seen	Eze 8:15	
T he said unto me, Hast thou seen	Eze 8:17	
T they began at the ancient men	Eze 9:6	
T said he unto me, The iniquity	Eze 9:9	
T I looked, and, behold, in the	Eze 10:1	
T the glory of the LORD went up	Eze 10:4	
t he went in, and stood beside the	Eze 10:6	
T the glory of the LORD departed	Eze 10:18	
T said he unto me, Son of man,	Eze 11:2	
T fell I down upon my face, and	Eze 11:13	
T did the cherubims lift up their	Eze 11:22	
T I spake unto them of the	Eze 11:25	
T shalt thou bring forth thy	Eze 12:4	
T came certain of the elders of	Eze 14:1	
t will I stretch out mine hand	Eze 14:13	
T washed I thee with water	Eze 16:9	
t will I bring again the	Eze 16:53	
t thou and thy daughters shall	Eze 16:55	
T thou shalt remember thy ways,	Eze 16:61	
shall he *t* live	Eze 18:13	

t she took another of her whelps,	Eze 19:5	
T the nations set against him on	Eze 19:8	
T came the word of the LORD unto	Eze 20:2	
T said I unto them, Cast ye away	Eze 20:7	
t I said, I will pour out my fury	Eze 20:8	
t I said, I would pour out my	Eze 20:13	
t I said, I would pour out my	Eze 20:21	
t they saw every high hill, and	Eze 20:28	
T I said unto them, What is the	Eze 20:29	
T said I, Ah Lord GOD	Eze 20:49	
Seeing *t* that I will cut off from	Eze 21:4	
should we *t* make mirth	Eze 21:10	176
T say thou, Thus saith the Lord	Eze 22:3	
T I saw that she was defiled,	Eze 23:13	
t my mind was alienated from her,	Eze 23:18	
t they came the same day into my	Eze 23:39	
T said I unto her that was old in	Eze 23:43	
T set it empty upon the coals	Eze 24:11	
T I answered them, The word of	Eze 24:20	
T all the princes of the sea	Eze 26:16	
t shall they dwell in their land	Eze 28:25	
T will I leave thee upon the land	Eze 32:4	
T will I make their waters deep,	Eze 32:14	227
t shall they know that I am the	Eze 32:15	
T whosoever heareth the sound of	Eze 33:4	
in them, how should we *t* live	Eze 33:10	
T the word of the LORD came unto	Eze 33:23	
T shall they know that I am the	Eze 33:29	
t shall they know that a prophet	Eze 33:33	
T will I sprinkle clean water	Eze 36:25	
T shall ye remember your own evil	Eze 36:31	
T the heathen that are left round	Eze 36:36	
T said he unto me, Prophesy unto	Eze 37:9	
T he said unto me, Son of man,	Eze 37:11	
t shall ye know that I the LORD	Eze 37:14	
t take another stick, and write	Eze 37:16	
t shall he set up a sign by it,	Eze 39:15	
T shall they know that I am the	Eze 39:28	
T came he unto the gate which	Eze 40:6	
T measured he the porch of the	Eze 40:9	
He measured *t* the gate from the	Eze 40:13	
T brought he me into the outward	Eze 40:17	
T he measured the breadth from	Eze 40:19	
T went he inward, and measured the	Eze 41:3	
T he brought me forth into the	Eze 42:1	
T said he unto me, The north	Eze 42:13	
t shall they not go out of the	Eze 42:14	
T he brought me back the way of	Eze 44:1	
T said the LORD unto me	Eze 44:2	
T brought he me the way of the	Eze 44:4	
t he shall go forth	Eze 46:2	
one shall *t* open him the gate	Eze 46:12	
t he shall go forth	Eze 46:12	
t it shall be his to the year of	Eze 46:17	
T said he unto me, This is the	Eze 46:20	
T he brought me forth into the	Eze 46:21	
T said he unto me, These are the	Eze 46:24	
T brought he me out of the way of	Eze 47:2	
T he brought me, and caused me to	Eze 47:6	
T said he unto me, These waters	Eze 47:8	
t shall ye make me endanger my	Dan 1:10	
T said Daniel to Melzar, whom the	Dan 1:11	
T let our countenances be looked	Dan 1:13	
t the prince of the eunuchs	Dan 1:18	
T the king commanded to call the	Dan 2:2	
T spake the Chaldeans to the king	Dan 2:4	
T Daniel answered with counsel and	Dan 2:14	116
T Arioch made the thing known to	Dan 2:15	116
T Daniel went in, and desired of	Dan 2:16	
T Daniel went to his house, and	Dan 2:17	116
T was the secret revealed unto	Dan 2:19	116
T Daniel blessed the God of	Dan 2:19	116
T Arioch brought in Daniel before	Dan 2:25	116
T was the iron, the clay, the	Dan 2:35	116
T the king Nebuchadnezzar fell	Dan 2:46	116
T the king made Daniel a great	Dan 2:48	116
T Daniel requested of the king,	Dan 2:49	
T Nebuchadnezzar the king sent to	Dan 3:2	
T the princes, the governors, and	Dan 3:3	116
T an herald cried aloud, To you	Dan 3:4	
T Nebuchadnezzar in his rage and	Dan 3:13	116
T they brought these men before	Dan 3:13	116
T was Nebuchadnezzar full of fury	Dan 3:19	116
T these men were bound in their	Dan 3:21	116
T Nebuchadnezzar the king was	Dan 3:24	116
T Nebuchadnezzar came near to the	Dan 3:26	116
T Shadrach, Meshach, and Abed-nego	Dan 3:26	116
T Nebuchadnezzar spake, and said,	Dan 3:28	
T the king promoted Shadrach,	Dan 3:30	116
T came in the magicians, the	Dan 4:7	116
T Daniel, whose name was	Dan 4:19	116
T they brought the golden vessels	Dan 5:3	116
T the king's countenance was	Dan 5:6	116
T came in all the king's wise men	Dan 5:8	116
T was king Belshazzar greatly	Dan 5:9	116
T was Daniel brought in before	Dan 5:13	116
T Daniel answered and said before	Dan 5:17	116
T was the part of the hand sent	Dan 5:24	116
T commanded Belshazzar, and they	Dan 5:29	116
T this Daniel was preferred above	Dan 6:3	116
T the presidents and princes	Dan 6:4	116
T said these men, We shall not	Dan 6:5	116
T these presidents and princes	Dan 6:6	116
T these men assembled, and found	Dan 6:11	116
T they came near, and spake before	Dan 6:12	116
T answered they and said before	Dan 6:13	116
T the king, when he heard these	Dan 6:14	116
T these men assembled unto the	Dan 6:15	116
T the king commanded, and they	Dan 6:16	116
T the king went to his palace, and	Dan 6:18	116
T the king arose very early in	Dan 6:19	116
T said Daniel unto the king, O	Dan 6:21	116
T was the king exceeding glad for	Dan 6:23	116
T king Darius wrote unto all	Dan 6:25	116
t he wrote the dream, and told the	Dan 7:1	116
I beheld *t* because of the voice	Dan 7:11	116
T I would know the truth of the	Dan 7:19	116
T I lifted up mine eyes, and saw,	Dan 8:3	
T I heard one saint speaking, and	Dan 8:13	
t shall the sanctuary be cleansed	Dan 8:14	
and sought for the meaning, *t*	Dan 8:15	
T I lifted up mine eyes, and	Dan 10:5	
t was I in a deep sleep on my	Dan 10:9	
T said he unto me, Fear not,	Dan 10:12	
t I opened my mouth, and spake, and	Dan 10:16	
T there came again and touched me	Dan 10:18	
T said he, Knowest thou wherefore	Dan 10:20	
t shall he return, and be stirred	Dan 11:10	
T he shall turn his face toward	Dan 11:19	
T shall stand up in his estate a	Dan 11:20	
T shall he return into his land	Dan 11:28	
T I Daniel looked, and, behold,	Dan 12:5	
t said I, O my Lord, what shall	Dan 12:8	
T said God, Call his name Lo-ammi	Hos 1:9	
T shall the children of Judah and	Hos 1:11	
t shall she say, I will go and	Hos 2:7	
for *t* was it better with me than	Hos 2:7	227
T said the LORD unto me, Go yet,	Hos 3:1	
t went Ephraim to the Assyrian,	Hos 5:13	
T shall we know, if we follow on	Hos 6:3	
t the iniquity of Ephraim was	Hos 7:1	
what *t* should a king do to us	Hos 10:3	
t I loved him, and called my son	Hos 11:1	
t the children shall tremble from	Hos 11:10	
T will the LORD be jealous for	Joel 2:18	
Be glad *t*, ye children of Zion,	Joel 2:23	
t shall Jerusalem be holy, and	Joel 3:17	
t go down to Gath of the	Amos 6:2	
T shall he say, Hold thy tongue	Amos 6:10	
t I said, O Lord GOD, forgive, I	Amos 7:2	
T said I, O Lord GOD, cease, I	Amos 7:5	
T said the Lord, Behold, I will	Amos 7:8	
T Amaziah the priest of Beth-el	Amos 7:10	
T answered Amos, and said to	Amos 7:14	
T said the LORD unto me, The end	Amos 8:2	
T the mariners were afraid, and	Jonah 1:5	
T said they unto him, Tell us, we	Jonah 1:8	
T were the men exceedingly afraid	Jonah 1:10	
T said they unto him, What shall	Jonah 1:11	
T the men feared the LORD	Jonah 1:16	
T Jonah prayed unto the LORD his	Jonah 2:1	
T I said, I am cast out of thy	Jonah 2:4	
T said the LORD, Doest thou well	Jonah 4:4	
T said the LORD, Thou hast had	Jonah 4:10	
T shall they cry unto the LORD,	Mic 3:4	227
T shall the seers be ashamed, and	Mic 3:7	
t the remnant of his brethren	Mic 5:3	
t shall we raise against him	Mic 5:5	
T she that is mine enemy shall	Mic 7:10	
T shall his mind change, and he	Hab 1:11	227
For *t* will I turn to the people a	Zeph 3:9	227
for *t* I will take away out of the	Zeph 3:11	227
T came the word of the LORD by	Hag 1:3	
T Zerubbabel the son of Shealtiel	Hag 1:12	
T spake Haggai the LORD'S	Hag 1:13	
T said Haggai, If one that is	Hag 2:13	
T answered Haggai, and said, So is	Hag 2:14	
T said I, O my lord, what are	Zec 1:9	
T the angel of the LORD answered	Zec 1:12	
T lifted I up mine eyes, and saw,	Zec 1:18	
T said I, What come these to do	Zec 1:21	
T said I, Whither goest thou	Zec 2:2	
t thou shalt also judge my house,	Zec 3:7	
T the angel that talked with me	Zec 4:5	
T he answered and spake unto me	Zec 4:6	
T answered I, and said unto him,	Zec 4:11	
T said he, These are the two	Zec 4:14	
T I turned, and lifted up mine	Zec 5:1	
T said he unto me, This is the	Zec 5:3	
T the angel that talked with me	Zec 5:5	
T lifted I up mine eyes, and	Zec 5:9	
T said I to the angel that talked	Zec 5:10	
T I answered and said unto the	Zec 6:4	
T cried he upon me, and spake unto	Zec 6:8	
T take silver and gold, and make	Zec 6:11	
T came the word of the LORD of	Zec 7:4	
T said I, I will not feed you	Zec 11:9	
T I cut asunder mine other staff,	Zec 11:14	
t his father and his mother that	Zec 13:3	
T he shall answer, Those with	Zec 13:6	
T shall the LORD go forth, and	Zec 14:3	
if *t* I be a father, where is mine	Mal 1:6	
T shall the offering of Judah and	Mal 3:4	
T they that feared the LORD spake	Mal 3:16	
T shall ye return, and discern	Mal 3:18	
T Joseph her husband, being a	Mt 1:19	*1161*
T Joseph being raised from sleep	Mt 1:24	*1161*
T Herod, when he had privily	Mt 2:7	*5119*
T Herod, when he saw that he was	Mt 2:16	*5119*
T was fulfilled that which was	Mt 2:17	*5119*
T went out to him Jerusalem, and	Mt 3:5	*5119*
T cometh Jesus from Galilee to	Mt 3:13	*5119*
T he suffered him	Mt 3:15	*5119*
T was Jesus led up of the spirit	Mt 4:1	*5119*
T the devil taketh him up into	Mt 4:5	*5119*
T saith Jesus unto him, Get thee	Mt 4:10	*5119*
T the devil leaveth him, and,	Mt 4:11	*5119*
and *t* come and offer thy gift	Mt 5:24	*5119*
t shalt thou see clearly to cast	Mt 7:5	*5119*
If ye *t*, being evil, know how to	Mt 7:11	*3767*
t will I profess unto them, I	Mt 7:23	*5119*
T he arose, and rebuked the winds	Mt 8:26	*5119*
(*t* saith he to the sick of the	Mt 9:6	*5119*
T came to him the disciples of	Mt 9:14	*5119*
from them, and *t* shall they fast	Mt 9:15	*5119*
T touched he their eyes, saying,	Mt 9:29	*5119*
T saith he unto his disciples,	Mt 9:37	*5119*
T began he to upbraid the cities	Mt 11:20	*5119*
How much *t* is a man better than a	Mt 12:12	*3767*
T saith he to the man, Stretch	Mt 12:13	*5119*
T the Pharisees went out, and held	Mt 12:14	*1161*
T was brought unto him one	Mt 12:22	*5119*
how shall *t* his kingdom stand	Mt 12:26	*3767*
t the kingdom of God is come unto	Mt 12:28	*686*
t he will spoil his house	Mt 12:29	*5119*
T certain of the scribes and of	Mt 12:38	*5119*
T he saith, I will return into my	Mt 12:44	*5119*
T goeth he, and taketh with	Mt 12:45	*5119*
T one said unto him, Behold, thy	Mt 12:47	*5119*
t cometh the wicked one, and	Mt 13:19	
t appeared the tares also	Mt 13:26	*5119*
from whence *t* hath it tares	Mt 13:27	*3767*
Wilt thou *t* that we go and gather	Mt 13:28	*3767*
T Jesus sent the multitude away,	Mt 13:36	*5119*
T shall the righteous shine forth	Mt 13:43	*5119*
T said he unto them, Therefore	Mt 13:52	*1161*
Whence *t* hath this man all these	Mt 13:56	*3767*
T they that were in the ship came	Mt 14:33	*1161*
T came to Jesus scribes and	Mt 15:1	*5119*
T came his disciples, and said	Mt 15:12	*5119*
T answered Peter and said unto him	Mt 15:15	*1161*
T Jesus went thence, and departed	Mt 15:21	*2532*
T came she and worshipped him,	Mt 15:25	*1161*
T Jesus answered and said unto her	Mt 15:28	*5119*
T Jesus called his disciples unto	Mt 15:32	*1161*
T Jesus said unto them, Take heed	Mt 16:6	*1161*
T understood they how that he	Mt 16:12	*5119*
T charged he his disciples that	Mt 16:20	*5119*
T Peter took him, and began to	Mt 16:22	*2532*
T said Jesus unto his disciples,	Mt 16:24	*5119*
t he shall reward every man	Mt 16:27	*5119*
T answered Peter, and said unto	Mt 17:4	*1161*
Why *t* say the scribes that Elias	Mt 17:10	*3767*
T the disciples understood that	Mt 17:13	*5119*
T Jesus answered and said, O	Mt 17:17	*1161*
T came the disciples to Jesus	Mt 17:19	*5119*
unto him, *T* are the children free	Mt 17:26	*686*
t take with thee one or two more,	Mt 18:16	
T came Peter to him, and said,	Mt 18:21	*5119*
T the lord of that servant was	Mt 18:27	*1161*
T his lord, after that he had	Mt 18:32	*5119*
Why did Moses *t* command to give a	Mt 19:7	*3767*
T were there brought unto him	Mt 19:13	*5119*
T said Jesus unto his disciples,	Mt 19:23	*1161*
saying, Who *t* can be saved	Mt 19:25	*686*
T answered Peter and said unto him	Mt 19:27	*5119*
T came to him the mother of	Mt 20:20	*5119*
t sent Jesus two disciples,	Mt 21:1	*5119*
us, Why did ye not *t* believe him	Mt 21:25	*3767*
T saith he to his servants, The	Mt 22:8	*5119*
T said the king to the servants,	Mt 22:13	*5119*
T went the Pharisees, and took	Mt 22:15	*5119*
T saith he unto them, Render	Mt 22:21	*5119*
T one of them, which was a lawyer	Mt 22:35	*2532*
How *t* doth David in spirit call	Mt 22:43	*3767*
If David *t* call him Lord	Mt 22:45	*3767*
T spake Jesus to the multitude,	Mt 23:1	*5119*
Fill ye up *t* the measure of your	Mt 23:32	*2532*
T shall they deliver you up to be	Mt 24:9	*5119*
t shall many be offended, and	Mt 24:10	*5119*
and *t* shall the end come	Mt 24:14	*5119*
T let them which be in Judaea	Mt 24:16	*5119*
For *t* shall be great tribulation,	Mt 24:21	*5119*
T if any man shall say unto you,	Mt 24:23	*5119*
t shall appear the sign of the	Mt 24:30	*5119*
t shall all the tribes of the	Mt 24:30	*5119*
T shall two be in the field	Mt 24:40	*5119*
Who *t* is a faithful and wise	Mt 24:45	*686*
T shall the kingdom of heaven be	Mt 25:1	*5119*
T all those virgins arose, and	Mt 25:7	*5119*
T he that had received the five	Mt 25:16	*1161*
T he which had received the one	Mt 25:24	*1161*
t at my coming I should have	Mt 25:27	
t shall he sit upon the throne of	Mt 25:31	*5119*
T shall the King say unto them on	Mt 25:34	*5119*
T shall the righteous answer him,	Mt 25:37	*5119*
T shall he say also unto them on	Mt 25:41	*5119*
T shall they also answer him,	Mt 25:44	*5119*
T shall he answer them, saying,	Mt 25:45	*5119*
T assembled together the chief	Mt 26:3	*5119*
T one of the twelve, called Judas	Mt 26:14	*5119*
T Judas, which betrayed him,	Mt 26:25	*1161*
T saith Jesus unto them, All ye	Mt 26:31	*5119*
T cometh Jesus with them unto a	Mt 26:36	*5119*
T saith he unto them, My soul is	Mt 26:38	*5119*
T cometh he to his disciples, and	Mt 26:45	*5119*
T came they, and laid hands on	Mt 26:50	*5119*
T said Jesus unto him, Put up	Mt 26:52	*5119*
But how *t* shall the scriptures be	Mt 26:54	*3767*
T all the disciples forsook him,	Mt 26:56	*5119*
T the high priest rent his	Mt 26:65	*5119*
T did they spit in his face, and	Mt 26:67	*5119*
T began he to curse and to swear,	Mt 26:74	*5119*
T Judas, which had betrayeth him,	Mt 27:3	*5119*
T was fulfilled that which was	Mt 27:9	*5119*
T said Pilate unto him, Hearest	Mt 27:13	*5119*
they had *t* a notable prisoner,	Mt 27:16	*5119*
What shall I do *t* with Jesus	Mt 27:22	*3767*
T answered all the people, and	Mt 27:25	*2532*
T released he Barabbas unto them	Mt 27:26	*5119*
T the soldiers of the governor	Mt 27:27	*5119*
T were there two thieves	Mt 27:38	*5119*
T Pilate commanded the body to be	Mt 27:58	*5119*
T said Jesus unto them, Be not	Mt 28:10	*5119*
T the eleven disciples went away	Mt 28:16	*1161*
t shall they fast in those days	Mk 2:20	*5119*
t he will spoil his house	Mk 3:27	*5119*
There came *t* his brethren and his	Mk 3:31	*3767*
how *t* will ye know all parables	Mk 4:13	
t the ear, after that the full	Mk 4:28	*1534*
T came together unto him the	Mk 7:1	*2532*
T the Pharisees and scribes asked	Mk 7:5	*1899*

Context	Reference	Number
so *t* they are no more twain, but	Mk 10:8	
T Jesus beholding him loved him,	Mk 10:21	1161
themselves, Who *t* can be saved	Mk 10:26	
T Peter began to say unto him, Lo	Mk 10:28	2532
Why *t* did ye not believe him	Mk 11:31	3767
T come unto him the Sadducees,	Mk 12:18	2532
and whence is he *t* his son	Mk 12:37	
t let them that be in Judaea	Mk 13:14	5119
t if any man shall say to you, Lo	Mk 13:21	5119
t shall they see the Son of man	Mk 13:26	5119
t shall he send his angels, and	Mk 13:27	5119
T the high priest rent his	Mk 14:63	1161
What will ye *t* that I shall do	Mk 15:12	3767
T Pilate said unto them, Why,	Mk 15:14	1161
So *t* after the Lord had spoken	Mk 16:19	3767
T said Mary unto the angel, How	Lk 1:34	1161
T took he him up in his arms, and	Lk 2:28	2532
T said he to the multitude that	Lk 3:7	3767
him, saying, What shall we do *t*	Lk 3:10	3767
T came also publicans to be	Lk 3:12	1161
t shall they fast in those days	Lk 5:35	5119
t both the new maketh a rent, and	Lk 5:36	
T said Jesus unto them, I will	Lk 6:9	3767
t shalt thou see clearly to pull	Lk 6:42	5119
T Jesus went with them	Lk 7:6	1161
T Jesus answering said unto them,	Lk 7:22	2532
Whereunto *t* shall I liken the men	Lk 7:31	3767
t cometh the devil, and taketh	Lk 8:12	1534
T came to him his mother and his	Lk 8:19	1161
T he arose, and rebuked the wind	Lk 8:24	1161
T went the devils out of the man,	Lk 8:33	1161
T they went out to see what was	Lk 8:35	1161
T the whole multitude of the	Lk 8:37	2532
T he called his twelve disciples	Lk 9:1	1161
t came the twelve, and said unto	Lk 9:12	1161
T he took the five loaves and the	Lk 9:16	1161
T there arose a reasoning among	Lk 9:46	1161
T said Jesus unto him, Go, and do	Lk 10:37	3767
If ye *t*, being evil, know how to	Lk 11:13	3767
T goeth he, and taketh to him	Lk 11:26	5119
T answered one of the lawyers, and	Lk 11:45	1161
t whose shall those things be,	Lk 12:20	1161
If ye *t* be not able to do that	Lk 12:26	3767
If *t* God so clothe the grass,	Lk 12:28	1161
T Peter said unto him, Lord,	Lk 12:41	1161
Who *t* is that faithful and wise	Lk 12:42	686
T said he unto the dresser of his	Lk 13:7	1161
t after that thou shalt cut it	Lk 13:9	
The Lord *t* answered him, and said,	Lk 13:15	3767
T said he, Unto what is the	Lk 13:18	1161
T said one unto him, Lord, are	Lk 13:23	1161
T shall ye begin to say, We have	Lk 13:26	5119
t shalt thou have worship in the	Lk 14:10	5119
T said he also to him that bade	Lk 14:12	1161
T said he unto him, A certain man	Lk 14:16	1161
T the master of the house being	Lk 14:21	5119
T drew near unto him all the	Lk 15:1	1161
T the steward said within himself	Lk 16:3	1161
T said he to another, And how much	Lk 16:7	1899
T he said, I pray thee therefore,	Lk 16:27	1161
T said he unto the disciples, It	Lk 17:1	1161
heard it said, Who *t* can be saved	Lk 18:26	2532
T Peter said, Lo, we have left	Lk 18:28	1161
T he took unto him the twelve, and	Lk 18:31	1161
t he commanded these servants to	Lk 19:15	1532
T came the first, saying, Lord,	Lk 19:16	1161
Wherefore *t* gavest not thou my	Lk 19:23	2532
Why *t* believed ye him not	Lk 20:5	3767
T began he to speak to the people	Lk 20:9	1161
T said the lord of the vineyard,	Lk 20:13	1161
What is this *t* that is written,	Lk 20:17	3767
T came to him certain of the	Lk 20:27	1161
T certain of the scribes	Lk 20:39	1161
him Lord, how is he *t* his son	Lk 20:44	2532
T in the audience of all the	Lk 20:45	1161
T said he unto them, Nation shall	Lk 21:10	5119
t know that the desolation	Lk 21:20	5119
T let them which are in Judaea	Lk 21:21	5119
t shall they see the Son of man	Lk 21:27	5119
t look up, and lift up your heads	Lk 21:28	
T entered Satan into Judas	Lk 22:3	1161
T came the day of unleavened	Lk 22:7	1161
T said he unto them, But now, he	Lk 22:36	3767
T Jesus said unto the chief	Lk 22:52	1161
T took they him, and led him, and	Lk 22:54	1161
T said they all, Art thou	Lk 22:70	1161
Art thou *t* the Son of God	Lk 22:70	3767
T said Pilate to the chief	Lk 23:4	1161
T he questioned with him in many	Lk 23:9	1161
T shall they begin to say to the	Lk 23:30	5119
T said Jesus, Father, forgive	Lk 23:34	1161
T arose Peter, and ran unto the	Lk 24:12	1161
T he said unto them, O fools, and	Lk 24:25	1161
T opened he their understanding,	Lk 24:45	5119
And they asked him, What *t*	Jn 1:21	3767
T said they unto him, Who art	Jn 1:22	3767
unto him, Why baptizest thou *t*	Jn 1:25	3767
T Jesus turned, and saw them	Jn 1:38	1161
well drunk, *t* that which is worse	Jn 2:10	5119
T answered the Jews and said unto	Jn 2:18	3767
T said the Jews, Forty and six	Jn 2:20	3767
T there arose a question between	Jn 3:25	3767
T cometh he to a city of Samaria,	Jn 4:5	3767
T saith the woman of Samaria unto	Jn 4:9	3767
from whence *t* hast thou that	Jn 4:11	3767
The woman *t* left her waterpot, and	Jn 4:28	3767
T they went out of the city, and	Jn 4:30	3767
four months, and *t* cometh harvest	Jn 4:35	
T when he was come into Galilee,	Jn 4:45	3767
T said Jesus unto him, Except ye	Jn 4:48	3767
T enquired he of them the hour	Jn 4:52	3767
whosoever *t* first after the	Jn 5:4	3767
T asked they him, What man is	Jn 5:12	3767
T answered Jesus and said unto	Jn 5:19	3767
When Jesus *t* lifted up his eyes,	Jn 6:5	3767
T those men, when they had seen	Jn 6:14	3767
T they willingly received him	Jn 6:21	3767
T said they unto him, What shall	Jn 6:28	3767
him, What sign shewest thou *t*	Jn 6:30	3767
T Jesus said unto them, Verily,	Jn 6:32	3767
T said they unto him, Lord,	Jn 6:34	3767
The Jews *t* murmured at him,	Jn 6:41	3767
how is it *t* that he saith, I came	Jn 6:42	3767
T Jesus said unto them, Verily,	Jn 6:53	3767
T said Jesus unto the twelve,	Jn 6:67	3767
T Simon Peter answered him, Lord,	Jn 6:68	3767
T Jesus said unto them, My time	Jn 7:6	3767
t went he also up unto the feast,	Jn 7:10	5119
T the Jews sought him at the	Jn 7:11	3767
T said some of them of Jerusalem,	Jn 7:25	3767
T cried Jesus in the temple as he	Jn 7:28	3767
T they sought to take him	Jn 7:30	3767
T said Jesus unto them, Yet a	Jn 7:33	3767
t I go unto him that sent me	Jn 7:33	
T said the Jews among themselves,	Jn 7:35	3767
T came the officers to the chief	Jn 7:45	3767
T answered them the Pharisees,	Jn 7:47	3767
T spake Jesus again unto them,	Jn 8:12	3767
T said they unto him, Where is	Jn 8:19	3767
T said Jesus again unto them, I	Jn 8:21	3767
T said the Jews, Will he kill	Jn 8:22	3767
T said they unto him, Who art	Jn 8:25	3767
T said Jesus unto them, When ye	Jn 8:28	3767
t shall ye know that I am he, and	Jn 8:28	5119
T said Jesus to those Jews which	Jn 8:31	3767
t are ye my disciples indeed	Jn 8:31	
T said they to him, We be not	Jn 8:41	3767
T answered the Jews, and said unto	Jn 8:48	3767
T said the Jews unto him, Now we	Jn 8:52	3767
T said the Jews unto him, Thou	Jn 8:57	3767
T took they up stones to cast at	Jn 8:59	3767
T said they unto him, Where is he	Jn 9:12	3767
T again the Pharisees also asked	Jn 9:15	3767
how *t* doth he now see	Jn 9:19	3767
T again called they the man that	Jn 9:24	3767
T said they to him again, What	Jn 9:26	1161
T they reviled him, and said, Thou	Jn 9:28	3767
T said Jesus unto them again,	Jn 10:7	3767
T came the Jews round about him,	Jn 10:24	3767
T the Jews took up stones again	Jn 10:31	3767
T after that saith he to his	Jn 11:7	1899
T said his disciples, Lord, if he	Jn 11:12	3767
T said Jesus unto them plainly,	Jn 11:14	3767
T said Thomas, which is called	Jn 11:16	3767
T when Jesus came, he found that	Jn 11:17	3767
T Martha, as soon as she heard	Jn 11:20	3767
T said Martha unto Jesus, Lord,	Jn 11:21	3767
The Jews *t* which were with her in	Jn 11:31	3767
T when Mary was come where Jesus	Jn 11:32	3767
T said the Jews, Behold how he	Jn 11:36	3767
T they took away the stone from	Jn 11:41	3767
T many of the Jews which came to	Jn 11:45	3767
T gathered the chief priests and	Jn 11:47	3767
T from that day forth they took	Jn 11:53	3767
T sought they for Jesus, and spake	Jn 11:56	3767
T Jesus six days before the	Jn 12:1	3767
T took Mary a pound of ointment	Jn 12:3	3767
T saith one of his disciples,	Jn 12:4	3767
T said Jesus, Let her alone	Jn 12:7	3767
t remembered they that these	Jn 12:16	5119
T came there a voice from heaven,	Jn 12:28	3767
T Jesus said unto them, Yet a	Jn 12:35	3767
T cometh he to Simon Peter	Jn 13:6	3767
If I *t*, your Lord and Master, have	Jn 13:14	3767
T the disciples looked one on	Jn 13:22	3767
He *t* lying on Jesus' breast saith	Jn 13:25	1161
T said Jesus unto him, That thou	Jn 13:27	3767
He *t* having received the sop went	Jn 13:30	3767
and how sayest thou *t*, Shew us the	Jn 14:9	
T said some of his disciples	Jn 16:17	3767
Judas *t*, having received a band	Jn 18:3	3767
As soon *t* as he had said unto	Jn 18:6	3767
T asked he them again, Whom seek	Jn 18:7	3767
T Simon Peter having a sword drew	Jn 18:10	3767
T said Jesus unto Peter, Put up	Jn 18:11	3767
T the band and the captain and	Jn 18:12	3767
T went out that other disciple,	Jn 18:16	3767
T saith the damsel that kept the	Jn 18:17	3767
The high priest *t* asked Jesus of	Jn 18:19	3767
Peter *t* denied again	Jn 18:27	3767
T led they Jesus from Caiaphas	Jn 18:28	3767
Pilate *t* went out unto them, and	Jn 18:29	3767
T said Pilate unto them, Take ye	Jn 18:31	3767
T Pilate entered into the	Jn 18:33	3767
t would my servants fight, that I	Jn 18:36	
said unto him, Art thou a king *t*	Jn 18:37	3766
T cried they all again, saying,	Jn 18:40	3767
T Pilate therefore took Jesus, and	Jn 19:1	5119
T came Jesus forth, wearing the	Jn 19:5	3767
T saith Pilate unto him, Speakest	Jn 19:10	3767
T delivered he him therefore unto	Jn 19:16	5119
This title *t* read many of the	Jn 19:20	3767
T said the chief priests of the	Jn 19:21	3767
T the soldiers, when they had	Jn 19:23	3767
T saith he to the disciple,	Jn 19:27	1534
T came the soldiers, and brake the	Jn 19:32	3767
T took they the body of Jesus, and	Jn 19:40	3767
T she runneth, and cometh to Simon	Jn 20:2	3767
T cometh Simon Peter following	Jn 20:6	3767
T went in also that other	Jn 20:8	5119
T the disciples went away again	Jn 20:10	3767
T the same day at evening, being	Jn 20:19	3767
T were the disciples glad, when	Jn 20:20	3767
T said Jesus to them again, Peace	Jn 20:21	3767
t came Jesus, the doors being	Jn 20:26	3767
T saith he to Thomas, Reach	Jn 20:27	1534
T Jesus saith unto them, Children	Jn 21:5	3767
As soon *t* as they were come to	Jn 21:9	3767
Jesus *t* cometh, and taketh bread,	Jn 21:13	3767
T Peter, turning about, seeth the	Jn 21:20	1161
T went this saying abroad among	Jn 21:23	3767
T returned they unto Jerusalem	Acts 1:12	5119
T Peter said unto them, Repent,	Acts 2:38	1161
T they that gladly received his	Acts 2:41	3767
T Peter said, Silver and gold have	Acts 3:6	1161
T Peter, filled with the Holy	Acts 4:8	5119
T Peter said unto her, How is it	Acts 5:9	1161
T fell she down straightway at	Acts 5:10	1161
T the high priest rose up, and all	Acts 5:17	1161
T came one and told them, saying,	Acts 5:25	1161
T went the captain with the	Acts 5:26	5119
T Peter and the other apostles	Acts 5:29	1161
T stood there up one in the	Acts 5:34	1161
T the twelve called the multitude	Acts 6:2	1161
T there arose certain of the	Acts 6:9	1161
T they suborned men, which said,	Acts 6:11	5119
T said the high priest, Are these	Acts 7:1	1161
T came he out of the land of the	Acts 7:4	5119
T sent Joseph, and called his	Acts 7:14	1161
T fled Moses at this saying, and	Acts 7:29	1161
T Moses trembled, and durst not	Acts 7:32	1161
T said the Lord to him, Put off	Acts 7:33	1161
T God turned, and gave them up to	Acts 7:42	1161
T they cried out with a loud	Acts 7:57	1161
T Philip went down to the city of	Acts 8:5	1161
T Simon himself believed also	Acts 8:13	1161
T laid they their hands on them,	Acts 8:17	5119
T answered Simon, and said, Pray	Acts 8:24	1161
T the Spirit said unto Philip, Go	Acts 8:29	1161
T Philip opened his mouth, and	Acts 8:35	1161
T Ananias answered, Lord, I have	Acts 9:13	1161
T was Saul certain days with the	Acts 9:19	1161
T the disciples took him by night	Acts 9:25	1161
T had the churches rest	Acts 9:31	3767
T Peter arose and went with them	Acts 9:39	1161
T Peter went down to the men	Acts 10:21	1161
T called he them in, and lodged	Acts 10:23	3767
T Peter opened his mouth, and said	Acts 10:34	1161
T answered Peter,	Acts 10:46	5119
T prayed they him to tarry	Acts 10:48	5119
T remembered I the word of the	Acts 11:16	1161
Forasmuch *t* as God gave them the	Acts 11:17	3767
T hath God also to the Gentiles	Acts 11:18	686
T tidings of these things came	Acts 11:22	1161
T departed Barnabas to Tarsus,	Acts 11:25	1161
T the disciples, every man	Acts 11:29	1161
(*T* were the days of unleavened	Acts 12:3	1161
T said they, It is his angel	Acts 12:15	1161
T Saul, (who also is called Paul,	Acts 13:9	1161
T the deputy, when he saw what	Acts 13:12	5119
T Paul stood up, and beckoning	Acts 13:16	1161
T Paul and Barnabas waxed bold, and	Acts 13:46	1161
T the priest of Jupiter, which	Acts 14:13	1161
T all the multitude kept silence,	Acts 15:12	1161
T pleased it the apostles and	Acts 15:22	5119
T came he to Derbe and Lystra	Acts 16:1	1161
T he called for a light, and	Acts 16:29	1161
t immediately the brethren sent	Acts 17:14	5119
T certain philosophers of the	Acts 17:18	1161
T Paul stood in the midst of	Acts 17:22	1161
Forasmuch *t* as we are the	Acts 17:29	3767
T spake the Lord to Paul in the	Acts 18:9	1161
T all the Greeks took Sosthenes,	Acts 18:17	1161
t took his leave of the brethren,	Acts 18:18	
Unto what *t* were ye baptized	Acts 19:3	3767
T said Paul, John verily baptized	Acts 19:4	1161
T certain of the vagabond Jews,	Acts 19:13	1161
Seeing *t* that these things cannot	Acts 19:36	3767
T Paul answered, What mean ye to	Acts 21:13	1161
T Paul took the men, and the next	Acts 21:26	5119
T the chief captain came near, and	Acts 21:33	5119
t lifted up their voices, and said	Acts 22:22	
T the chief captain came, and said	Acts 22:27	1161
T straightway they departed from	Acts 22:29	3767
T said Paul unto him, God shall	Acts 23:3	5119
T said Paul, I wist not, brethren	Acts 23:5	5037
T Paul called one of the	Acts 23:17	1161
T the chief captain took him by	Acts 23:19	1161
So the chief captain *t* let the	Acts 23:22	
t came I with an army, and rescued	Acts 23:27	
T the soldiers, as it was	Acts 23:31	3767
T Paul, after that the governor	Acts 24:10	1161
T the high priest and the chief of	Acts 25:2	1161
T said Paul, I stand at Caesar's	Acts 25:10	1161
T Festus, when he had conferred	Acts 25:12	5119
T Agrippa said unto Festus, I	Acts 25:22	1161
T Agrippa said unto Paul, Thou	Acts 26:1	1161
T Paul stretched forth the hand,	Acts 26:1	5119
t to the Gentiles, that they	Acts 26:20	
T Agrippa said unto Paul, Almost	Acts 26:28	1161
T said Agrippa unto Festus, This	Acts 26:32	1161
should be saved was *t* taken away	Acts 27:20	3063
T fearing lest we should have	Acts 27:29	5037
T the soldiers cut off the ropes	Acts 27:32	5119
T were they all of good cheer, and	Acts 27:36	1161
t they knew that the island was	Acts 28:1	5119
What advantage *t* hath the Jew	Rom 3:1	3767
for *t* how shall God judge the	Rom 3:6	
What *t*? are we better	Rom 3:9	3767
Where is boasting *t*	Rom 3:27	3767
Do we *t* make void the law through	Rom 3:31	3767
What shall we say *t* that Abraham	Rom 4:1	3767
Cometh this blessedness *t* upon	Rom 4:9	3767
How was it *t* reckoned	Rom 4:10	3767
Much more *t*, being now justified	Rom 5:9	3767
What shall we say *t*	Rom 6:1	3767
What *t*? shall we sin	Rom 6:15	3767
Being *t* made free from sin, ye	Rom 6:18	1161
What fruit had ye *t* in those	Rom 6:21	3767
So *t* if, while her husband liveth	Rom 7:3	686
What shall we say *t*	Rom 7:7	3767
Was *t* that which is good made	Rom 7:13	3767

If *t* I do that which I would not, Rom 7:16 *1161*
Now *t* it is no more I that do it, Rom 7:17 *1161*
I find *t* a law, that, when I Rom 7:21 *686*
So *t* with the mind I myself serve Rom 7:25 *686*
So *t* they that are in the flesh Rom 8:8 *1161*
And if children, *t* heirs Rom 8:17 *2535*
t do we with patience wait for it Rom 8:25
What shall we *t* say to these Rom 8:31 *3767*
What shall we say *t* Rom 9:14 *3767*
So *t* it is not of him that Rom 9:16 *686*
Thou wilt say *t* unto me, Why doth Rom 9:19 *3767*
What shall we say *t* Rom 9:30 *3767*
How *t* shall they call on him in Rom 10:14 *3767*
So *t* faith cometh by hearing, and Rom 10:17 *686*
I say *t*, Hath God cast away his Rom 11:1 *3767*
Even so *t* at this present time Rom 11:5 *3767*
grace, *t* is it no more of works Rom 11:6
of works, *t* is it no more grace Rom 11:6
What *t*? Israel hath not Rom 11:7 *3767*
I say *t*, Have they stumbled that Rom 11:11 *3767*
Thou wilt say *t*, The branches Rom 11:19 *3767*
Having *t* gifts differing Rom 12:6 *1161*
Wilt thou *t* not be afraid of the Rom 13:3 *1161*
So *t* every one of us shall give Rom 14:12 *686*
Let not *t* your good be evil Rom 14:16 *3767*
We *t* that are strong ought to Rom 15:1 *1161*
Who *t* is Paul, and who is Apollos, 1Cor 3:5 *3767*
So *t* neither is he that planteth 1Cor 3:7
t shall every man have praise of 1Cor 4:5 *5119*
for *t* must ye needs go out of the 1Cor 5:10 *686*
If *t* ye have judgments of things 1Cor 6:4 *3767*
shall I *t* take the members of 1Cor 6:15 *3767*
So *t* he that giveth her in 1Cor 7:38 *2532*
What is my reward *t* 1Cor 9:18 *3767*
What say I *t* 1Cor 10:19 *3767*
t gifts of healings, helps, 1Cor 12:28 *1534*
t that which is in part shall be 1Cor 13:10 *5119*
but *t* face to face 1Cor 13:12 *5119*
but *t* shall I know even as also I 1Cor 13:12 *5119*
What is it *t* 1Cor 14:15 *3767*
How is it *t*, brethren 1Cor 14:26 *3767*
seen of Cephas, *t* of the twelve 1Cor 15:5 *1534*
t of all the apostles 1Cor 15:7 *1534*
the dead, *t* is Christ not risen 1Cor 15:13 *3761*
t is our preaching vain, and your 1Cor 15:14 *686*
rise not, *t* is not Christ raised 1Cor 15:16 *3761*
T they also which are fallen 1Cor 15:18 *686*
T cometh the end, when he shall 1Cor 15:24 *1534*
t shall the Son also himself be 1Cor 15:28 *5119*
why are they *t* baptized for the 1Cor 15:29
t shall be brought to pass the 1Cor 15:54 *5119*
who is he *t* that maketh me glad, 2Cor 2:2 *2532*
Seeing *t* that we have such hope, 2Cor 3:12 *3767*
So *t* death worketh in us, but 2Cor 4:12 *3303*
one died for all, *t* were all dead 2Cor 5:14 *686*
Now *t* we are ambassadors for 2Cor 5:20
We *t*, as workers together with 2Cor 6:1 *3767*
for when I am weak, *t* am I strong 2Cor 12:10
T after three years I went up to Gal 1:18 *1899*
T fourteen years after I went up Gal 2:1 *1899*
the law, *t* Christ is dead in vain Gal 2:21 *636*
So *t* they which be of faith are Gal 3:9
Wherefore *t* serveth the law Gal 3:19 *3767*
Is the law *t* against the promises Gal 3:21 *3767*
t are ye Abraham's seed, and heirs Gal 3:29 *686*
t an heir of God through Christ Gal 4:7 *2532*
Howbeit *t*, when ye knew not God, Gal 4:8 *5119*
Where is *t* the blessedness ye Gal 4:15 *3767*
But as *t* he that was born after Gal 4:29 *5119*
So *t*, brethren, we are not Gal 4:31 *686*
t is the offence of the cross Gal 5:11 *686*
This I say *t*, Walk in the Spirit, Gal 5:16 *1161*
t shall he have rejoicing in Gal 6:4 *5119*
See *t* that ye walk circumspectly, Eph 5:15 *3767*
What *t*? notwithstanding Phil 1:18 *1063*
If ye *t* be risen with Christ, Col 3:1 *3767*
t shall ye also appear with him Col 3:4 *5119*
Furthermore *t* we beseech you, 1Th 4:1 *3767*
T we which are alive and remain 1Th 4:17 *1899*
t sudden destruction cometh upon 1Th 5:3 *5119*
t shall that Wicked be revealed, 2Th 2:8 *5119*
For Adam was first formed, *t* Eve 1Ti 2:13 *1534*
A bishop *t* must be blameless, the 1Ti 3:2 *3767*
t let them use the office of a 1Ti 3:10 *1534*
Forasmuch *t* as the children are Heb 2:14 *3767*
t would he not afterward have Heb 4:8
Seeing *t* that we have a great Heb 4:14 *3767*
own sins, and *t* for the people's Heb 7:27 *1899*
t should no place have been Heb 8:7
T verily the first covenant had Heb 9:1 *3767*
a figure for the time *t* present Heb 9:9 *3588*
For *t* must he often have suffered Heb 9:26
For *t* would they not have ceased Heb 10:2
T said I, Lo, I come (in the Heb 10:7 *5119*
T said he, Lo, I come to do thy Heb 10:9 *5119*
t are ye bastards, and not sons Heb 12:8 *686*
Whose voice *t* shook the earth Heb 12:26 *5119*
T when lust hath conceived, it Jas 1:15 *1534*
Are ye not *t* partial in Jas 2:4 *2532*
Ye see *t* how that by works a man Jas 2:24 *5106*
t peaceable, gentle, and easy to Jas 3:17 *1899*
little time, and *t* vanisheth away Jas 4:14 *1899*
Forasmuch *t* as Christ hath 1Pet 4:1 *3767*
Whereby the world that *t* was 2Pet 3:6 *5119*
Seeing *t* that all these things 2Pet 3:11 *3767*
This *t* is the message which we 1Jn 1:5 *2532*
t have we confidence toward God 1Jn 3:21
So *t* because thou art lukewarm, Rev 3:16
T saith he unto me, See thou do Rev 22:9 *2532*

THENCE
from *t* it was parted, and became Gen 2:10 8033
t upon the face of all the earth Gen 11:8 8033
from *t* did the LORD scatter them Gen 11:9 8033
he removed from *t* unto a mountain Gen 12:8 8033
And the men rose up from *t* Gen 18:16 8033
the men turned their faces from *t* Gen 18:22 8033
Abraham journeyed from *t* toward Gen 20:1 8033
take a wife unto my son from *t* Gen 24:7 8033
And Isaac departed *t*, and pitched Gen 26:17 8033
And he removed from *t*, and digged Gen 26:22 8033
he went up from *t* to Beer-sheba Gen 26:23 8033
fetch me from *t* two good kids of Gen 27:9 8033
I will send, and fetch thee from *t* Gen 27:45 8033
take thee a wife from *t* of the Gen 28:2 8033
to take him a wife from *t* Gen 28:6 8033
removing from *t* all the speckled Gen 30:32 8033
thither, and buy for us from *t* Gen 42:2 8033
with the corn, and departed *t* Gen 42:26 8033
(from *t* is the shepherd, the Gen 49:24 8033
cut down from *t* a branch with one Num 13:23 8033
of Israel cut down from *t* Num 13:24 8033
From *t* they removed, and pitched Num 21:12 8033
From *t* they removed, and pitched Num 21:13 8033
And from *t* they went to Beer Num 21:16 8033
that *t* he might see the utmost Num 22:41 8033
and curse me them from *t* Num 23:13 8033
thou mayest curse me them from *t* Num 23:27 8033
But if from *t* thou shalt seek the Deut 4:29 8033
thee out *t* through a mighty hand Deut 5:15 8033
And he brought us out from *t* Deut 6:23 8033
From *t* they journeyed unto Deut 10:7 8033
city shall send and fetch him *t* Deut 19:12 8033
house, if any man fall from *t* Deut 22:8
the LORD thy God redeemed thee *t* Deut 24:18 8033
from *t* will the LORD thy God Deut 30:4 8033
from *t* will he fetch thee Deut 30:4 8033
house, and bring out *t* the woman Josh 6:22 8033
From *t* it passed toward Azmon, and Josh 15:4
Caleb drove *t* the three sons of Josh 15:14 8033
he went up *t* to the inhabitants Josh 15:15 8033
went over from *t* toward Luz Josh 18:13 8033
And the border was drawn *t* Josh 18:14
from *t* passeth on along on the Josh 19:13 8033
and goeth out from *t* to Hukkok Josh 19:34 8033
from *t* he went against the Judg 1:11 8033
he expelled *t* the three sons of Judg 1:20 8033
And he went up *t* to Penuel Judg 8:8 8033
there went from *t* of the family Judg 18:11 8033
they passed *t* unto mount Ephraim, Judg 18:13 8033
from *t* am I Judg 19:18 8033
of Israel departed *t* at that time Judg 21:24 8033
they went out from *t* every man to Judg 21:24 8033
that they might bring from *t* the 1Sa 4:4 8033
shalt thou go on forward from *t* 1Sa 10:3 8033
And they ran and fetched him *t* 1Sa 10:23 8033
took *t* a stone, and slang it, and 1Sa 17:49 8033
David therefore departed *t* 1Sa 22:1 8033
David went *t* to Mizpeh of Moab 1Sa 22:3 8033
And David went up from *t*, and dwelt 1Sa 23:29 8033
to bring up from *t* the ark of God 2Sa 6:2 8033
fetched *t* a wise woman, and said 2Sa 14:2 8033
t came out a man of the family of 2Sa 16:5 8033
up from *t* the bones of Saul 2Sa 21:13 8033
they are come up from *t* rejoicing 1Kin 1:45 8033
and go not forth *t* any whither 1Kin 2:36 8033
to Ophir, and fetched from *t* gold 1Kin 9:28 8033
and went out from *t*, and built 1Kin 12:25 8033
So he departed *t*, and found Elisha 1Kin 19:19 8033
there shall not be from *t* any 2Kin 2:21 8033
And he went up from *t* unto Beth-el 2Kin 2:23 8033
he went from *t* to mount Carmel, 2Kin 2:25 8033
from *t* he returned to Samaria 2Kin 2:25 8033
take *t* every man a beam, and let 2Kin 6:2 8033
eat and drink, and carried *t* silver 2Kin 7:8 8033
another tent, and carried *t* also 2Kin 7:8 8033
And when he was departed *t* 2Kin 10:15 8033
priests whom ye brought from *t* 2Kin 17:27 8033
whom they carried away from *t* 2Kin 17:33 8033
down, and brake them down from *t* 2Kin 23:12 8033
And he carried out *t* all the 2Kin 24:13 8033
to bring up *t* the ark of God the 1Chr 13:6 8033
took *t* four hundred and fifty 2Chr 8:18 8033
and they thrust him out from *t* 2Chr 26:20 8033
the river, be ye far from *t* Ezr 6:6 8536
yet will I gather them from *t* Neh 1:9 8033
From *t* she seeketh the prey, and Job 39:29 8033
ye, depart ye, go ye out from *t* Is 52:11 8033
be no more *t* an infant of days Is 65:20 8033
out *t* shall be torn in pieces Jer 5:6 2007
and take the girdle from *t* Jer 13:6 8033
hand, yet would I pluck thee *t* Jer 22:24 8033
shall cause to cease from *t* man Jer 36:29
to separate himself *t* in the Jer 37:12 8033
took *t* old cast clouts and old Jer 38:11 8033
he shall go forth from *t* in peace Jer 43:12 8033
I will bring thee down from *t* Jer 49:16 8033
and will destroy from *t* the king Jer 49:38 8033
from *t* she shall be taken Jer 50:9 8033
the abominations thereof from *t* Eze 11:18
give her her vineyards from *t* Hos 2:15 8033
from *t* go ye to Hamath the great Amos 6:2 8033
t shall mine hand take them Amos 9:2 8033
heaven, *t* will I bring them down Amos 9:2 8033
I will search and take them out *t* Amos 9:3 8033
t will I command the serpent, and Amos 9:3 8033
t will I command the sword, and it Amos 9:4 8033
t will I bring thee down, saith Obad 4 8033
And going on from *t*, he saw other Mt 4:21 *1564*
Thou shalt by no means come out *t* Mt 5:26 *1564*
And as Jesus passed forth from *t* Mt 9:9 *1564*
And when Jesus departed *t*, two Mt 9:27 *1564*
and there abide till ye go *t* Mt 10:11
disciples, he departed *t* to teach Mt 11:1 *1564*
And when he was departed *t* Mt 12:9 *1564*
it, he withdrew himself from *t* Mt 12:15 *1564*
these parables, he departed *t* Mt 13:53 *1564*
he departed *t* by ship into a Mt 14:13 *1564*
Then Jesus went *t*, and departed Mt 15:21 *1564*
And Jesus departed from *t*, and came Mt 15:29 *1564*
his hands on them, and departed *t* Mt 19:15 *1564*
he had gone a little farther *t* Mk 1:19 *1564*
And he went out from *t*, and came Mk 6:1 *1564*
nor hear you, when ye depart *t* Mk 6:11 *1564*
from *t* he arose, and went into the Mk 7:24 *1564*
And they departed *t*, and passed Mk 9:30 *1564*
And he arose from *t*, and cometh Mk 10:1 *1564*
into, there abide, and *t* depart Lk 9:4 *1564*
thee, thou shalt not depart *t* Lk 12:59 *1564*
to us, that would come from *t* Lk 16:26 *1564*
Now after two days he departed *t* Jn 4:43 *1564*
but went *t* unto a country near to Jn 11:54 *1564*
and from *t*, when his father was Acts 7:4 *1564*
from *t* they sailed to Cyprus Acts 13:4 *1564*
t sailed to Antioch, from whence Acts 14:26 *1564*
from *t* to Philippi, which is the Acts 16:12 *1564*
And he departed *t*, and entered into Acts 18:7 *1564*
sailed *t* into Syria, and with him Acts 18:18
And we sailed *t*, and came the next Acts 20:15 *1564*
Rhodes, and from *t* unto Patara Acts 21:1 *1564*
And when we had launched from *t* Acts 27:4 *1564*
part advised to depart *t* also Acts 27:12 *1564*
obtained their purpose, loosing *t* Acts 27:13 *1564*
from *t* we fetched a compass, and Acts 28:13 *3606*
And from *t*, when the brethren Acts 28:15 *1564*
I went from *t* into Macedonia 2Cor 2:13

THENCEFORTH
t it shall be accepted for an Lev 22:27 1973
the sight of all nations from *t* 2Chr 32:23
it is *t* good for nothing, but to Mt 5:13 *2089*
from *t* Pilate sought to release Jn 19:12

THEOPHILUS (*the-of'-il-us*) *To whom the gospel of Luke and the Acts of the Apostles are addressed.*
thee in order, most excellent *T* Lk 1:3 *2321*
former treatise have I made, O *T* Acts 1:1 *2321*

THERE
And God said, Let *t* be light Gen 1:3
and *t* was light Gen 1:3
Let *t* be a firmament in the midst Gen 1:6
Let *t* be lights in the firmament Gen 1:14
upon the earth, wherein *t* is life Gen 1:30
t was not a man to till the Gen 2:5
But *t* went up a mist from the Gen 2:6
t he put the man whom he had Gen 2:8 8033
land of Havilah, where *t* is gold Gen 2:11
t is bdellium and the onyx stone Gen 2:12 8033
but for Adam *t* was not found an Gen 2:20
to him also *t* was born a son Gen 4:26
T were giants in the earth in Gen 6:4
T went in two and two unto Noah Gen 7:9
neither shall *t* any more be a Gen 9:11
and they dwelt *t* Gen 11:2 8033
t confound their language, that Gen 11:7 8033
because the LORD did *t* confound Gen 11:9 8033
they came unto Haran, and dwelt *t* Gen 11:31 8033
t builded he an altar unto the Gen 12:7 8033
t he builded an altar unto the Gen 12:8 8033
t was a famine in the land Gen 12:10
went down into Egypt to sojourn *t* Gen 12:10 8033
which he had made *t* at the first Gen 13:4 8033
t Abram called on the name of the Gen 13:4 8033
t was a strife between the Gen 13:7
Let *t* be no strife, I pray thee, Gen 13:8
built *t* an altar unto the LORD Gen 13:18 8033
t went out the king of Sodom, and Gen 14:8
Sodom and Gomorrah fled, and fell *t* Gen 14:10 8033
t came one that had escaped, and Gen 14:13
Peradventure *t* be fifty righteous Gen 18:24
Peradventure *t* shall lack five of Gen 18:28
And he said, If I find *t* forty Gen 18:28 8033
t shall be forty found *t* Gen 18:29
t shall thirty be found *t* Gen 18:30 8033
not do it, if I find thirty *t* Gen 18:30 8033
t shall be twenty found *t* Gen 18:31 8033
Peradventure ten shall be found *t* Gen 18:32 8033
t came two angels to Sodom at Gen 19:1
t is not a man in the earth to Gen 19:31
because *t* they sware both of them Gen 21:31 8033
called *t* on the name of the LORD, Gen 21:33 8033
offer him *t* for a burnt offering Gen 22:2 8033
and Abraham built an altar *t* Gen 22:9 8033
of me, and I will bury my dead *t* Gen 23:13 8033
is *t* room in thy father's house Gen 24:23
t was set meat before him to eat Gen 24:33
t was Abraham buried, and Sarah Gen 25:10 8033
behold, *t* were twins in her womb Gen 25:24
t was a famine in the land, Gen 26:1
when he had been *t* a long time Gen 26:8 8033
the valley of Gerar, and dwelt *t* Gen 26:17 8033
found *t* a well of springing water Gen 26:19 8033
And he builded an altar *t*, and Gen 26:25 8033
the LORD, and pitched his tent *t* Gen 26:25 8033
t Isaac's servants digged a well Gen 26:25 8033
Let *t* be now an oath betwixt us, Gen 26:28
tarried *t* all night, because the Gen 28:11 8033
t were three flocks of sheep Gen 29:2 8033
unto him, Is *t* yet any portion or Gen 31:14
they did eat *t* upon the heap Gen 31:46 8033
with Laban, and stayed *t* until now Gen 32:4
he lodged *t* that same night Gen 32:13 8033
t wrestled a man with him until Gen 32:24
And he blessed him *t* Gen 32:29 8033
And he erected *t* an altar, and Gen 33:20 8033
go up to Beth-el, and dwell *t* Gen 35:1 8033
make *t* an altar unto God, that Gen 35:1 8033
I will make *t* an altar unto God, Gen 35:3 8033
And he built *t* an altar, and called Gen 35:7 8033
because *t* God appeared unto him, Gen 35:7 8033
t was but a little way to come to Gen 35:16

before *t* reigned any king over	Gen 36:31	
was empty, *t* was no water in it	Gen 37:24	
Then *t* passed by Midianites	Gen 37:28	
Judah saw *t* a daughter of a	Gen 38:2	8033
T was no harlot in this place	Gen 38:21	
that *t* was no harlot in this	Gen 38:22	
T is none greater in this house	Gen 39:9	
t was none of the men of the	Gen 39:11	
of the men of the house *t* within	Gen 39:11	8033
and he was *t* in the prison	Gen 39:20	8033
and whatsoever they did *t*, he was	Gen 39:22	8033
t is no interpreter of it	Gen 40:8	
in the uppermost basket *t* was of	Gen 40:17	
t came up out of the river seven	Gen 41:2	
but *t* was none that could	Gen 41:8	
t was *t* with us a young man,	Gen 41:12	8033
t is none that can interpret it	Gen 41:15	
t came up out of the river seven	Gen 41:18	
but *t* was none that could declare	Gen 41:24	
t come seven years of great	Gen 41:29	
t shall arise after them seven	Gen 41:30	
t is none so discreet and wise as	Gen 41:39	
all the land of Egypt *t* was bread	Gen 41:54	
saw that *t* was corn in Egypt	Gen 42:1	
heard that *t* is corn in Egypt	Gen 42:2	
whether *t* be any truth in you	Gen 42:16	
that they should eat bread *t*	Gen 43:25	8033
into his chamber, and wept *t*	Gen 43:30	8033
for he was yet *t*	Gen 44:14	8033
t stood no man with him, while	Gen 45:1	
yet *t* are five years, in the	Gen 45:6	
in the which *t* shall neither be	Gen 45:6	
And *t* will I nourish thee	Gen 45:11	8033
for yet *t* are five years of	Gen 45:11	
for I will *t* make of thee a great	Gen 46:3	8033
t was no bread in all the land	Gen 47:13	
t is not ought left in the sight	Gen 47:18	
when yet *t* was but a little way	Gen 48:7	
I buried her *t* in the way of	Gen 48:7	8033
T they buried Abraham and Sarah	Gen 49:31	8033
t they buried Isaac and Rebekah	Gen 49:31	8033
and *t* I buried Leah	Gen 49:31	8033
of Canaan, *t* shalt thou bury me	Gen 50:5	8033
t went up with him both chariots	Gen 50:9	
t they mourned with a great and	Gen 50:10	8033
Now *t* arose up a new king over	Ex 1:8	
when *t* falleth out any war, they	Ex 1:10	
t went a man of the house of Levi	Ex 2:1	
and when he saw that *t* was no man	Ex 2:12	
Let *t* more work be laid upon the	Ex 5:9	
daily tasks, as when *t* was straw	Ex 5:13	
T is no straw given unto thy	Ex 5:16	
for *t* shall no straw be given you	Ex 5:18	
that *t* may be blood throughout	Ex 7:19	
t was blood throughout all the	Ex 7:21	
that thou mayest know that *t* is	Ex 8:10	
Pharaoh saw that *t* was respite	Ex 8:15	
so *t* were lice upon man, and upon	Ex 8:18	
no swarms of flies shall be *t*	Ex 8:22	
t came a grievous swarm of flies	Ex 8:24	
t remained not one	Ex 8:31	
t shall be a very grievous	Ex 9:3	
t shall nothing die of all that	Ex 9:4	
t was not one of the cattle of	Ex 9:7	
that *t* is none like me in all the	Ex 9:14	
that *t* may be hail in all the	Ex 9:22	
So *t* was hail, and fire mingled	Ex 9:24	
such as *t* was none like it in all	Ex 9:24	
of Israel were, was *t* no hail	Ex 9:26	
LORD (for it is enough) that *t* be	Ex 9:28	
neither shall *t* be any more hail	Ex 9:29	
before them *t* were no such	Ex 10:14	
t remained not any green thing in	Ex 10:15	
t remained not one locust in all	Ex 10:19	
that *t* may be darkness over the	Ex 10:21	
t was a thick darkness in all the	Ex 10:22	
t shall not an hoof be left	Ex 10:26	
t shall be a great cry throughout	Ex 11:6	
such as *t* was none like it, nor	Ex 11:6	
in the first day *t* shall be an	Ex 12:16	
in the seventh day *t* shall be an	Ex 12:16	
Seven days shall *t* be no leaven	Ex 12:19	
t was a great cry in Egypt	Ex 12:30	
for *t* was not a house	Ex 12:30	
a house where *t* was not one dead	Ex 12:30	
T shall no stranger eat thereof	Ex 12:43	
t shall no leavened bread be	Ex 13:3	
t shall no leavened bread be seen	Ex 13:7	
neither shall *t* be leaven seen	Ex 13:7	
Because *t* were no graves in Egypt	Ex 14:11	
t remained not so much as one of	Ex 14:28	
t he made for them a statute and	Ex 15:25	8033
ordinance, and *t* he proved them,	Ex 15:25	8033
and they encamped *t* by the waters	Ex 15:27	8033
t lay a small round thing	Ex 16:14	
neither was *t* any worm therein	Ex 16:24	
sabbath, in it *t* shall be none	Ex 16:26	
that *t* went out some of the	Ex 16:27	
t was no water for the people to	Ex 17:1	
the people thirsted *t* for water	Ex 17:3	8033
thee *t* upon the rock in Horeb	Ex 17:6	8033
t shall come water out of it,	Ex 17:6	
t Israel camped before the mount	Ex 19:2	8033
T shall not an hand touch it, but	Ex 19:13	
morning, that *t* were thunders and	Ex 19:16	
If *t* be laid on him a sum of	Ex 21:30	
t shall no blood be shed for him	Ex 22:2	
t shall be blood shed for him	Ex 22:3	
T shall nothing cast their young,	Ex 23:26	
t was under his feet as it were a	Ex 24:10	
up to me into the mount, and be *t*	Ex 24:12	8033
t I will meet with thee, and I	Ex 25:22	
t shall be a knop under two	Ex 25:35	
tenons shall *t* be in one board	Ex 26:17	
side *t* shall be twenty boards	Ex 26:20	
for the south side southward *t*	Ex 27:9	
for the north side in length *t*	Ex 27:11	
t shall be an hole in the top of	Ex 28:32	
meet you, to speak *t* unto thee	Ex 29:42	8033
t I will meet with the children	Ex 29:43	8033
that *t* be no plague among them,	Ex 30:12	
of each shall *t* be a like weight	Ex 30:34	
T is a noise of war in the camp	Ex 32:17	
the fire, and *t* came out this calf	Ex 32:24	
t fell of the people that day	Ex 32:28	
for *t* shall no man see me, and	Ex 33:20	
t is a place by me, and thou shalt	Ex 33:21	
present thyself *t* to me in the	Ex 34:2	8033
in the cloud, and stood with him *t*	Ex 34:5	8033
he was *t* with the LORD forty days	Ex 34:28	8033
but on the seventh day *t* shall be	Ex 35:2	
And *t* were eight boards	Ex 36:30	
t was an hole in the midst of the	Ex 39:23	
and the altar, and put water *t*	Ex 40:30	8033
when *t* is sprinkled of the blood	Lev 6:27	
t is one law for them	Lev 7:7	
t eat it with the bread that is	Lev 8:31	8033
t came a fire out from before the	Lev 9:24	
t went out fire from the LORD, and	Lev 10:2	
wherein *t* is plenty of water,	Lev 11:36	
t be quick raw flesh in the	Lev 13:10	
of the boil *t* be a white rising	Lev 13:19	
t be no white hairs therein, and	Lev 13:21	
Or if *t* be any flesh, in the skin	Lev 13:24	
skin whereof *t* is a hot burning	Lev 13:24	
t be no white hair in the bright	Lev 13:26	
t be in it a yellow thin hair	Lev 13:30	
that *t* is no black hair in it	Lev 13:31	
t be in it no yellow hair, and the	Lev 13:32	
that *t* is black hair grown up	Lev 13:37	
if *t* be in the bald head, or bald	Lev 13:42	
It seemeth to me *t* is as it were	Lev 14:35	
And *t* shall be no man in the	Lev 16:17	
holy place, and shall leave them *t*	Lev 16:23	8033
What man soever *t* be of the house	Lev 17:3	
Whatsoever man *t* be of the house	Lev 17:8	
whatsoever man *t* be of the house	Lev 17:10	
whatsoever man *t* be of the	Lev 17:13	
that *t* be no wickedness among you	Lev 20:14	
T shall none be defiled for the	Lev 21:1	
T shall no stranger eat of the	Lev 22:10	
but *t* shall no stranger eat	Lev 22:13	
t shall be no blemish therein	Lev 22:21	
t shall be a day of atonement	Lev 23:27	
If *t* be yet many years behind,	Lev 25:51	
if *t* remain but few years unto	Lev 25:52	
with you *t* shall be a man of	Num 1:4	
that *t* be no wrath upon the	Num 1:53	
t be no witness against her,	Num 5:13	
t shall no razor come upon his	Num 6:5	
that *t* be no plague among the	Num 8:19	
t were certain men, who were	Num 9:6	
at even *t* was upon the tabernacle	Num 9:15	
t the children of Israel pitched	Num 9:17	8033
t is nothing at all, beside this	Num 11:6	
that they may stand *t* with thee	Num 11:16	8033
come down and talk with thee *t*	Num 11:17	8033
But *t* remained two of the men in	Num 11:26	
t ran a young man, and told Moses,	Num 11:27	
t went forth a wind from the LORD	Num 11:31	
because *t* they buried the people	Num 11:34	8033
If *t* be a prophet among you, I	Num 12:6	
whether *t* be wood therein, or not	Num 13:20	
we saw the children of Anak *t*	Num 13:28	
t we saw the giants, the sons of	Num 13:33	8033
be consumed, and *t* they shall die	Num 14:35	8033
the Canaanites are *t* before you	Num 14:43	8033
t came out a fire from the LORD,	Num 16:35	
for *t* is wrath gone out from the	Num 16:46	
that *t* be no wrath any more upon	Num 18:5	
and upon the persons that were *t*	Num 19:18	8033
and Miriam died *t*, and was buried	Num 20:1	8033
died *t*, and was buried *t*	Num 20:1	8033
And *t* was no water for the	Num 20:2	
we and our cattle should die *t*	Num 20:4	8033
neither is *t* any water to drink	Num 20:5	
unto his people, and shall die *t*	Num 20:26	8033
Aaron died *t* in the top of the	Num 20:28	8033
for *t* is no bread, neither is	Num 21:5	
no bread, neither is *t* any water	Num 21:5	
For *t* is a fire gone out of	Num 21:28	
out the Amorites that were *t*	Num 21:32	8033
until *t* was none left him alive	Num 21:35	
t is a people come out from Egypt	Num 22:5	
t is a people come out of Egypt,	Num 22:11	
I would *t* were a sword in mine	Num 22:29	
Surely *t* is no enchantment	Num 23:23	
neither is *t* any divination	Num 23:23	
t shall come a Star out of Jacob,	Num 24:17	
because *t* was no inheritance	Num 26:62	
But among these *t* was not a man	Num 26:64	
t was not left a man of them,	Num 26:65	
So *t* were delivered out of the	Num 31:5	
Peor, and *t* was a plague among the	Num 31:16	
t lacketh not one man of us	Num 31:49	
shall be *t* in the cities of	Num 32:26	8033
and they pitched *t*	Num 33:9	8033
of the LORD, and died *t*, in the	Num 33:38	8033
t shall be six cities for refuge	Num 35:6	
(*T* are eleven days' journey from	Deut 1:2	
seen the sons of the Anakims *t*	Deut 1:28	8033
Surely *t* shall not one of these	Deut 1:35	
unto the days that ye abode *t*	Deut 1:46	
t was not one city too strong for	Deut 2:36	
t was not a city which we took	Deut 3:4	
for what God is *t* in heaven or in	Deut 3:24	
For what nation is *t* so great	Deut 4:7	
And what nation is *t* so great	Deut 4:8	
t ye shall serve gods, the work	Deut 4:28	8033
whether *t* hath been any such	Deut 4:32	
t is none else beside him	Deut 4:35	
t is none else	Deut 4:39	
For who is *t* of all flesh, that	Deut 5:26	
O that *t* were such an heart in	Deut 5:29	
t shall not be male or female	Deut 7:14	
t shall no man be able to stand	Deut 7:24	
and drought, where *t* was no water	Deut 8:15	
t they be, as the LORD commanded	Deut 10:5	8033
t Aaron died, and *t* he was	Deut 10:6	8033
that *t* be no rain, and that the	Deut 11:17	
T shall no man be able to stand	Deut 11:25	
all your tribes to put his name *t*	Deut 12:5	8033
t ye shall eat before the LORD	Deut 12:7	8033
Then *t* shall be a place which the	Deut 12:11	
to cause his name to dwell *t*	Deut 12:11	8033
t thou shalt offer thy burnt	Deut 12:14	8033
t thou shalt do all that I	Deut 12:14	8033
his name *t* be too far from thee	Deut 12:21	8033
If *t* arise among you a prophet,	Deut 13:1	
God hath given thee to dwell *t*	Deut 13:12	
t shall cleave nought of the	Deut 13:17	
shall choose to place his name *t*	Deut 14:23	8033
shall choose to set his name *t*	Deut 14:24	8033
thou shalt eat *t* before the LORD	Deut 14:26	8033
Save when *t* shall be no poor	Deut 15:4	
If *t* be among you a poor man of	Deut 15:7	
Beware that *t* be not a thought in	Deut 15:9	
if *t* be any blemish therein, as	Deut 15:21	
shall choose to place his name *t*	Deut 16:2	8033
t shall be no leavened bread seen	Deut 16:4	
neither shall *t* any thing of the	Deut 16:4	
t thou shalt sacrifice the	Deut 16:6	8033
hath chosen to place his name *t*	Deut 16:11	8033
If *t* be found among you, within	Deut 17:2	
If *t* arise a matter too hard for	Deut 17:8	
t before the LORD thy God	Deut 17:12	8033
which stand *t* before the LORD	Deut 18:7	8033
T shall not be found among you	Deut 18:10	
What man is *t* that hath built a	Deut 20:5	
what man is *t* that hath betrothed	Deut 20:7	
What man is *t* that is fearful and	Deut 20:8	
the heifer's neck *t* in the valley	Deut 21:4	8033
t is in the damsel no sin worthy	Deut 22:26	
cried, and *t* was none to save her	Deut 22:27	
If *t* be among you any man, that	Deut 23:10	
T shall be no whore of the	Deut 23:17	
If *t* be a controversy between men	Deut 25:1	
shall choose to place his name *t*	Deut 26:2	8033
sojourned *t* with a few, and became	Deut 26:5	8033
became *t* a nation, great, mighty,	Deut 26:5	8033
t shalt thou build an altar unto	Deut 27:5	8033
peace offerings, and shalt eat *t*	Deut 27:7	8033
t shall be no might in thine hand	Deut 28:32	
t shalt thou serve other gods,	Deut 28:36	8033
t thou shalt serve other gods,	Deut 28:64	8033
give thee *t* a trembling heart	Deut 28:65	8033
t ye shall be sold unto your	Deut 28:68	8033
Lest *t* should be among you man,	Deut 29:18	
lest *t* should be among you a root	Deut 29:18	
that it may be *t* for a witness	Deut 31:26	8033
t was no strange god with him	Deut 32:12	
neither is *t* any understanding in	Deut 32:28	
t is none shut up, or left	Deut 32:36	
I, am he, and *t* is no god with me	Deut 32:39	
neither is *t* any that can deliver	Deut 32:39	
t they shall offer sacrifices of	Deut 33:19	8033
first part for himself, because *t*	Deut 33:21	8033
T is none like unto the God of	Deut 33:26	
LORD died *t* in the land of Moab	Deut 34:5	8033
t arose not a prophet since in	Deut 34:10	
T shall not any man be able to	Josh 1:5	
house, named Rahab, and lodged *t*	Josh 2:1	8033
t came men in hither to night of	Josh 2:2	
T came men unto me, but I wist	Josh 2:4	
neither did *t* remain any more	Josh 2:11	
and hide yourselves *t* three days	Josh 2:16	8033
abode *t* three days, until the	Josh 2:22	8033
lodged *t* before they passed over	Josh 3:1	8033
Yet *t* shall be a space between	Josh 3:4	
they lodged, and laid them down *t*	Josh 4:8	8033
and they are *t* unto this day	Josh 4:9	8033
neither was *t* spirit in them any	Josh 5:1	
t stood a man over against him	Josh 5:13	
So *t* went up thither of the	Josh 7:4	
T is an accursed thing in the	Josh 7:13	
now *t* was a valley between them	Josh 8:11	
but he wist not that *t* were liers	Josh 8:14	
t was not a man left in Ai or	Josh 8:17	
he wrote *t* upon the stones a copy	Josh 8:32	8033
T was not a word of all that	Josh 8:35	
t shall none of you be freed from	Josh 9:23	
t shall not a man of them stand	Josh 10:8	
t was no day like that before it	Josh 10:14	
t was not any left to breathe	Josh 11:11	
T was not a city that made peace	Josh 11:19	
T was none of the Anakims left in	Josh 11:22	
in Gath, and in Ashdod, *t* remained	Josh 11:22	
t remaineth yet very much land to	Josh 13:1	
that day how the Anakims were *t*	Josh 14:12	8033
T was also a lot for the tribe of	Josh 17:1	
T was also a lot for the rest of	Josh 17:2	
t fell ten portions to Manasseh,	Josh 17:5	
cut down for thyself *t* in the	Josh 17:15	8033
tabernacle of the congregation *t*	Josh 18:1	8033
t remained among the children of	Josh 18:2	
t Joshua divided the land unto	Josh 18:10	8033
t stood not a man of all their	Josh 21:44	
T failed not ought of any good	Josh 21:45	
built *t* an altar by Jordan	Josh 22:10	8033
although *t* was a plague in the	Josh 22:17	
set it up *t* under an oak, that	Josh 24:26	8033
him to Jerusalem, and *t* he died	Judg 1:7	8033

they sacrificed *t* unto the LORD	Judg 2:5	8033
t arose another generation after	Judg 2:10	
and *t* escaped not a man	Judg 3:29	
and *t* was not a man left	Judg 4:16	
for *t* was peace between Jabin the	Judg 4:17	
thee, and say, Is *t* any man here	Judg 4:20	
was *t* a shield or spear seen	Judg 5:8	
t shall they rehearse the	Judg 5:11	
Out of Ephraim was *t* a root of	Judg 5:14	
For the divisions of Reuben *t*	Judg 5:15	
For the divisions of Reuben *t*	Judg 5:16	
he bowed, *t* he fell down dead,	Judg 5:27	8033
t came an angel of the LORD, and	Judg 6:11	
t rose up fire out of the rock,	Judg 6:21	
built an altar *t* unto the LORD	Judg 6:24	8033
upon all the ground let *t* be dew	Judg 6:39	
t was dew on all the ground	Judg 6:40	
t returned of the people twenty	Judg 7:3	
and *t* remained ten thousand	Judg 7:3	
and I will try them for thee *t*	Judg 7:4	8033
t was a man that told a dream	Judg 7:13	
for *t* fell an hundred and twenty	Judg 8:10	
fled, and went to Beer, and dwelt *t*	Judg 9:21	8033
t come people down from the top	Judg 9:36	
See *t* come people down by the	Judg 9:37	
But *t* was a strong tower within	Judg 9:51	
after Abimelech *t* arose to defend	Judg 10:1	
t were gathered vain men to	Judg 11:3	
t fell at that time of the	Judg 12:6	
t was a certain man of Zorah, of	Judg 13:2	
Is *t* never a woman among the	Judg 14:3	
t was a swarm of bees and honey in	Judg 14:8	
and Samson made *t* a feast	Judg 14:10	8033
the jaw, and *t* came water thereout	Judg 15:19	
saw *t* an harlot, and went in unto	Judg 16:1	8033
Now *t* were men lying in wait,	Judg 16:9	
t were liers in wait abiding in	Judg 16:12	
T hath not come a razor upon mine	Judg 16:17	
lords of the Philistines were *t*	Judg 16:27	8033
t were upon the roof about three	Judg 16:27	
t was a man of mount Ephraim,	Judg 17:1	
In those days *t* was no king in	Judg 17:6	
And *t* was a young man out of	Judg 17:7	
was a Levite, and he sojourned *t*	Judg 17:7	8033
In those days *t* was no king in	Judg 18:1	
the house of Micah, they lodged *t*	Judg 18:2	8033
t was no magistrate in the land,	Judg 18:7	
a place where *t* is no want of any	Judg 18:10	
t went from thence of the family	Judg 18:11	
Do ye know that *t* is in these	Judg 18:14	
t was no deliverer, because it	Judg 18:28	
when *t* was no king in Israel,	Judg 19:1	
that *t* was a certain Levite	Judg 19:1	
and was *t* four whole months	Judg 19:2	8033
did eat and drink, and lodged *t*	Judg 19:4	8033
therefore he lodged *t* again	Judg 19:7	8033
t were with him two asses saddled	Judg 19:10	
for *t* was no man that took them	Judg 19:15	
t came an old man from his work	Judg 19:16	
t is no man that receiveth me to	Judg 19:18	
Yet *t* is both straw and provender	Judg 19:19	
t is bread and wine also for me,	Judg 19:19	
t is no want of any thing	Judg 19:19	
T was no such deed done nor seen	Judg 19:30	
Among all this people *t* were	Judg 20:16	
sat *t* before the LORD, and fasted	Judg 20:26	8033
of God was *t* in those days	Judg 20:27	8033
t came against Gibeah ten	Judg 20:34	
Now *t* was an appointed sign	Judg 20:38	
t fell of Benjamin eighteen	Judg 20:44	
T shall not any of us give his	Judg 21:1	
abode *t* till even before God, and	Judg 21:2	8033
that *t* should be to day one tribe	Judg 21:3	
built *t* an altar, and offered	Judg 21:4	8033
Who is *t* among all the tribes of	Judg 21:5	
T is one tribe cut off from	Judg 21:6	
What one is *t* of the tribes of	Judg 21:8	
t came none to the camp from	Judg 21:8	
t were none of the inhabitants of	Judg 21:9	
inhabitants of Jabesh-gilead *t*	Judg 21:9	8033
T must be an inheritance for them	Judg 21:17	
t is a feast of the LORD in	Judg 21:19	
In those days *t* was no king in	Judg 21:25	
that *t* was a famine in the land	Ruth 1:1	
country of Moab, and continued *t*	Ruth 1:2	8033
they dwelled *t* about ten years	Ruth 1:4	8033
are *t* yet any more sons in my	Ruth 1:11	
will I die, and *t* will I be buried	Ruth 1:17	8033
howbeit *t* is a kinsman nearer	Ruth 3:12	
up to the gate, and sat him down *t*	Ruth 4:1	8033
for *t* is none to redeem it beside	Ruth 4:4	
saying, *T* is a son born to Naomi	Ruth 4:17	
Now *t* was a certain man of	1Sa 1:1	
the priests of the LORD, were *t*	1Sa 1:3	8033
t shall no razor come upon his	1Sa 1:11	
the LORD, and *t* abide for ever	1Sa 1:22	8033
And he worshipped the LORD *t*	1Sa 1:28	8033
T is none holy as the LORD	1Sa 2:2	
for *t* is none beside thee	1Sa 2:2	
neither is *t* any rock like our	1Sa 2:2	
t came a man of God unto Eli, and	1Sa 2:27	
that *t* shall not be an old man in	1Sa 2:31	
t shall not be an old man in	1Sa 2:32	
t was no open vision	1Sa 3:1	
were *t* with the ark of the	1Sa 4:4	8033
for *t* hath not been such a thing	1Sa 4:7	
t was a very great slaughter	1Sa 4:10	
for *t* fell of Israel thirty	1Sa 4:10	
t ran a man of Benjamin out of	1Sa 4:12	
And he said, What is *t* done	1Sa 4:16	
and *t* hath been also a great	1Sa 4:17	
for *t* was a deadly destruction	1Sa 5:11	
the hand of God was very heavy *t*	1Sa 5:11	
on which *t* hath come no yoke, and	1Sa 6:7	
a Beth-shemite, and stood *t*	1Sa 6:14	8033
where *t* was a great stone	1Sa 6:14	
and fasted on that day, and said *t*	1Sa 7:6	
t was peace between Israel and the	1Sa 7:14	
for *t* was his house	1Sa 7:17	8033
and *t* he judged Israel	1Sa 7:17	8033
t he built an altar unto the LORD	1Sa 7:17	8033
Now *t* was a man of Benjamin,	1Sa 9:1	
t was not among the children of	1Sa 9:2	
of Shalim, and *t* they were not	1Sa 9:4	
t is in this city a man of God,	1Sa 9:6	
t is not a present to bring to	1Sa 9:7	
for *t* is a sacrifice of the	1Sa 9:12	
t shall meet thee three men going	1Sa 10:3	
that *t* is none like him among all	1Sa 10:24	
t went with him a band of men,	1Sa 10:26	
if *t* be no man to save us, we	1Sa 11:3	
T shall not a man be put to death	1Sa 11:13	
to Gilgal, and renew the kingdom *t*	1Sa 11:14	8033
t they made Saul king before the	1Sa 11:15	8033
t they sacrificed sacrifices of	1Sa 11:15	8033
t Saul and all the men of Israel	1Sa 11:15	8033
Now *t* was no smith found	1Sa 13:19	
that *t* was neither sword nor	1Sa 13:22	
with Jonathan his son was *t* found	1Sa 13:22	
t was a sharp rock on the one	1Sa 14:4	
for *t* is no restraint to the LORD	1Sa 14:6	
t was trembling in the host, in	1Sa 14:15	
and his armourbearer were not *t*	1Sa 14:17	
t was a very great discomfiture	1Sa 14:20	
t was honey upon the ground	1Sa 14:25	
for had *t* not been now a much	1Sa 14:30	
him that night, and slew them *t*	1Sa 14:34	8033
But *t* was not a man among all the	1Sa 14:39	
t shall not one hair of his head	1Sa 14:45	
t was sore war against the	1Sa 14:52	
T remaineth yet the youngest, and,	1Sa 16:11	
t was a valley between them	1Sa 17:3	
t went out a champion out of the	1Sa 17:4	
t came up the champion, the	1Sa 17:23	
Is *t* not a cause	1Sa 17:29	
t came a lion, and a bear, and took	1Sa 17:34	
know that *t* is a God in Israel	1Sa 17:46	
but *t* was no sword in the hand of	1Sa 17:50	
t was a javelin in Saul's hand	1Sa 18:10	
And *t* was war again	1Sa 19:8	
t was an image in the bed, with a	1Sa 19:16	
t is but a step between me and	1Sa 20:3	
for *t* is a yearly sacrifice	1Sa 20:6	
sacrifice *t* for all the family	1Sa 20:6	8033
if *t* be in me iniquity, slay me	1Sa 20:8	
if *t* be good toward David, and I	1Sa 20:12	
for *t* is peace to thee, and no	1Sa 20:21	
he hath commanded me to be *t*	1Sa 20:29	
mine hand, or what *t* is present	1Sa 21:3	
T is no common bread under mine	1Sa 21:4	
hand, but *t* is hallowed bread	1Sa 21:4	
for *t* was no bread	1Sa 21:6	
was no bread *t* but the shewbread	1Sa 21:6	8033
servants of Saul was *t* that day	1Sa 21:7	
is *t* not here under thine hand	1Sa 21:8	
for *t* is no other save that here	1Sa 21:9	
David said, *T* is none like that	1Sa 21:9	
t were with him about four	1Sa 22:2	
t is none that sheweth me that my	1Sa 22:8	
t is none of you that is sorry	1Sa 22:8	
day, when Doeg the Edomite was *t*	1Sa 22:22	8033
haunt is, and who hath seen him *t*	1Sa 23:22	8033
But *t* came a messenger unto Saul,	1Sa 23:27	
see that *t* is neither evil nor	1Sa 24:11	
t was a man in Maon, whose	1Sa 25:2	
neither was *t* ought missing unto	1Sa 25:7	
t be many servants now a days	1Sa 25:10	
t went up after David about four	1Sa 25:13	
surely *t* had not been left unto	1Sa 25:34	
for *t* came one of the people in	1Sa 26:15	
t is nothing better for me than	1Sa 27:1	
the country, that I may dwell *t*	1Sa 27:5	8033
t is a woman that hath a familiar	1Sa 28:7	
t shall no punishment happen to	1Sa 28:10	
and *t* was no strength in him	1Sa 28:20	
t escaped not a man of them, save	1Sa 30:17	
t was nothing lacking to them,	1Sa 30:19	
came to Jabesh, and burnt them *t*	1Sa 31:12	8033
let *t* be no dew, neither let	2Sa 1:21	
be no dew, neither let *t* be rain	2Sa 1:21	
for *t* the shield of the mighty is	2Sa 1:21	8033
t they anointed David king over	2Sa 2:4	8033
Then *t* arose and went over by	2Sa 2:15	
t was a very sore battle that day	2Sa 2:17	
t were three sons of Zeruiah	2Sa 2:18	
were three sons of Zeruiah *t*	2Sa 2:18	8033
and he fell down *t*, and died in the	2Sa 2:23	8033
t lacked of David's servants	2Sa 2:30	
Now *t* was long war between the	2Sa 3:1	
while *t* was war between the house	2Sa 3:6	
smote him *t* under the fifth rib,	2Sa 3:27	8033
let *t* not fail from the house of	2Sa 3:29	
Know ye not that *t* is a prince	2Sa 3:38	
were sojourners *t* until this day	2Sa 4:3	8033
t were yet sons and daughters born	2Sa 5:13	
and David smote them *t*, and said,	2Sa 5:20	8033
t they left their images, and	2Sa 5:21	8033
and God smote him *t* for his error	2Sa 6:7	8033
t he died by the ark of God	2Sa 6:7	8033
for *t* is none like thee	2Sa 7:22	
neither is *t* any God beside thee,	2Sa 7:22	
Is *t* yet any that is left of the	2Sa 9:1	
t was of the house of Saul a	2Sa 9:2	
is *t* not yet any of the house of	2Sa 9:3	
captain of their host, who died *t*	2Sa 10:18	8033
t followed him a mess of meat	2Sa 11:8	
t fell some of the people of the	2Sa 11:17	
T were two men in one city	2Sa 12:1	
t came a traveller unto the rich	2Sa 12:4	
she said unto him, *T* is no cause	2Sa 13:16	
t is not one of them left	2Sa 13:30	
t came much people by the way of	2Sa 13:34	
to Geshur, and was *t* three years	2Sa 13:38	8033
t was none to part them, but the	2Sa 14:6	
t shall not one hair of thy son	2Sa 14:11	
But in all Israel *t* was none to	2Sa 14:25	
his head *t* was no blemish in him	2Sa 14:25	
unto Absalom *t* were born three	2Sa 14:27	
is near mine, and he hath barley *t*	2Sa 14:30	8033
good for me to have been *t* still	2Sa 14:32	8033
if *t* be any iniquity in me, let	2Sa 14:32	
but *t* is no man deputed of the	2Sa 15:3	
t came a messenger to David,	2Sa 15:13	
even *t* also will thy servant be	2Sa 15:21	8033
until *t* come word from you to	2Sa 15:28	
and they tarried *t*	2Sa 15:29	8033
hast thou not *t* with thee Zadok	2Sa 15:35	8033
they have *t* with them their two	2Sa 15:36	8033
weary, and refreshed themselves *t*	2Sa 16:14	8033
T is a slaughter among the people	2Sa 17:9	
t shall not be left so much as	2Sa 17:12	
until *t* be not one small stone	2Sa 17:13	
be not one small stone found *t*	2Sa 17:13	8033
by the morning light *t* lacked not	2Sa 17:22	
t was *t* a great slaughter	2Sa 18:7	8033
For the battle was *t* scattered	2Sa 18:8	8033
not smite him *t* to the ground	2Sa 18:11	8033
for *t* is no matter hid from the	2Sa 18:13	
t is tidings in his mouth	2Sa 18:25	
t will not tarry one with thee	2Sa 19:7	
t were a thousand men of Benjamin	2Sa 19:17	
t went over a ferry boat to carry	2Sa 19:18	
shall *t* any man be put to death	2Sa 19:22	
And *t* happened to be *t* a man	2Sa 20:1	8033
t went out after him Joab's men,	2Sa 20:7	
Then *t* was a famine in the days	2Sa 21:1	
that *t* was again a battle with	2Sa 21:18	
t was again a battle in Gob with	2Sa 21:19	
t was yet a battle in Gath, where	2Sa 21:20	
T went up a smoke out of his	2Sa 22:9	
looked, but *t* was none to save	2Sa 22:42	
the Philistines that were *t*	2Sa 23:9	8033
t were in Israel eight hundred	2Sa 24:9	
or that *t* be three days'	2Sa 24:13	
t died of the people from Dan	2Sa 24:15	
David built *t* an altar unto the	2Sa 24:25	8033
Let *t* be sought for my lord the	1Kin 1:2	
thou yet talkest *t* with the king	1Kin 1:14	8033
anoint him *t* king over Israel	1Kin 1:34	8033
t shall not an hair of him fall	1Kin 1:52	
t shall not fail thee (said he) a	1Kin 2:4	
shall *t* be peace for ever from	1Kin 2:33	
an house in Jerusalem, and dwell *t*	1Kin 2:36	8033
because *t* was no house built unto	1Kin 3:2	
went to Gibeon to sacrifice *t*	1Kin 3:4	8033
so that *t* was none like thee	1Kin 3:12	
so that *t* shall not be any among	1Kin 3:13	
Then came *t* two women, that were	1Kin 3:16	
t was no stranger with us in the	1Kin 3:18	
t came of all people to hear the	1Kin 4:34	
so that *t* is neither adversary	1Kin 5:4	
for thou knowest that *t* is not	1Kin 5:6	
cause them to be discharged *t*	1Kin 5:9	8033
t was peace between Hiram and	1Kin 5:12	
so that *t* was neither hammer nor	1Kin 6:7	
t was no stone seen	1Kin 6:18	
to set *t* the ark of the covenant	1Kin 6:19	8033
t were windows in three rows, and	1Kin 7:4	
about *t* were knops compassing it	1Kin 7:24	
upon the ledges *t* was a base	1Kin 7:29	
t were four undersetters to the	1Kin 7:34	
in the top of the base was *t* a	1Kin 7:35	
and *t* they are unto this day	1Kin 8:8	8033
T was nothing in the ark save the	1Kin 8:9	
stone, which Moses put *t* at Horeb	1Kin 8:9	8033
I have set *t* a place for the ark,	1Kin 8:21	8033
t is no God like thee, in heaven	1Kin 8:23	
T shall not fail thee a man in my	1Kin 8:25	
hast said, My name shall be *t*	1Kin 8:29	8033
t is no rain, because they have	1Kin 8:35	
If *t* be in the land famine	1Kin 8:37	
if *t* be pestilence, blasting,	1Kin 8:37	
locust, or if *t* be caterpiller	1Kin 8:37	
plague, whatsoever sickness *t* be	1Kin 8:37	
(for *t* is no man that sinneth not	1Kin 8:46	
t hath not failed one word of all	1Kin 8:56	
is God, and that *t* is none else	1Kin 8:60	
for *t* he offered burnt offerings,	1Kin 8:64	8033
built, to put my name *t* for ever	1Kin 9:3	8033
mine heart shall be *t* perpetually	1Kin 9:3	8033
T shall not fail thee a man upon	1Kin 9:5	
t was not any thing hid from the	1Kin 10:3	
t was no more spirit in her	1Kin 10:5	
t came no more such abundance of	1Kin 10:10	
t came no such almug trees, nor	1Kin 10:12	
t were stays on either side on	1Kin 10:19	
lions stood *t* on the one side	1Kin 10:20	8033
t was not the like made in any	1Kin 10:20	
did Joab remain *t* with all Israel	1Kin 11:16	8033
I have chosen me to put my name *t*	1Kin 11:36	8033
t was none that followed the	1Kin 12:20	
t came a man of God out of Judah	1Kin 13:1	
Now *t* dwelt an old prophet in	1Kin 13:11	
eat no bread nor drink water *t*	1Kin 13:17	8033
t is Ahijah the prophet, which	1Kin 14:2	8033
because in him *t* is found some	1Kin 14:13	
of Israel, to put his name *t*	1Kin 14:21	8033
t were also sodomites in the land	1Kin 14:24	
t was war between Rehoboam and	1Kin 14:30	
t was war between Rehoboam and	1Kin 15:6	
t was war between Abijam and	1Kin 15:7	
t was war between Asa and Baasha	1Kin 15:16	

T is a league between me and thee, 1Kin 15:19
t was war between Asa and Baasha 1Kin 15:32
t shall not be dew nor rain these 1Kin 17:1
the ravens to feed thee *t* 1Kin 17:4 8033
because *t* had been no rain in the 1Kin 17:7
belongeth to Zidon, and dwell *t* 1Kin 17:9 8033
a widow woman *t* to sustain thee 1Kin 17:9 8033
woman was *t* gathering of sticks 1Kin 17:10 8033
that *t* was no breath left in him 1Kin 17:17
t was a sore famine in Samaria 1Kin 18:2
t is no nation or kingdom, 1Kin 18:10
and when they said, He is not *t* 1Kin 18:10
But *t* was no voice, nor any that 1Kin 18:26
that *t* was neither voice, nor any 1Kin 18:29
the brook Kishon, and slew them *t* 1Kin 18:40 8033
for *t* is a sound of abundance of 1Kin 18:41
and looked, and said, *T* is nothing 1Kin 18:43
t ariseth a little cloud out of 1Kin 18:44
and wind, and *t* was a great rain 1Kin 18:45
to Judah, and left his servant *t* 1Kin 19:3 8033
t was a cake baken on the coals, 1Kin 19:6
thither unto a cave, and lodged *t* 1Kin 19:9 8033
t came a voice unto him, and said, 1Kin 19:13
t were thirty and two kings with 1Kin 20:1
t came a prophet unto Ahab king 1Kin 20:13
T are men come out of Samaria 1Kin 20:17
t came a man of God, and spake 1Kin 20:28
t a wall fell upon twenty and 1Kin 20:30
as thy servant was busy here and *t* 1Kin 20:40 2008
t came in two men, children of 1Kin 21:13
But *t* was none like unto Ahab, 1Kin 21:25
Is *t* not here a prophet of the 1Kin 22:7
T is yet one man, Micaiah the son 1Kin 22:8
t came forth a spirit, and stood 1Kin 22:21 8033
t went a proclamation throughout 1Kin 22:36
T was then no king in Edom 1Kin 22:47
Is it not because *t* is not a God 2Kin 1:3
T came a man up to meet us, and 2Kin 1:6
Is it not because *t* is not a God 2Kin 1:6
t came down fire from heaven, and 2Kin 1:10
t came fire down from heaven, and 2Kin 1:14
is it not because *t* is no God in 2Kin 1:16
t appeared a chariot of fire, and 2Kin 2:11
t be with thy servants fifty 2Kin 2:16
the waters, and cast the salt in *t* 2Kin 2:21
t shall not be from thence any 2Kin 2:21
t came forth little children out 2Kin 2:23
t came forth two she bears out of 2Kin 2:24
t was no water for the host, and 2Kin 3:9
Is *t* not here a prophet of the 2Kin 3:11
t came water by the way of Edom, 2Kin 3:20
t was great indignation against 2Kin 3:27
Now *t* cried a certain woman of 2Kin 4:1
unto her, *T* is not a vessel more 2Kin 4:6
and let us set for him *t* a bed 2Kin 4:10 8033
turned into the chamber, and lay *t* 2Kin 4:11 8033
but *t* was neither voice, nor 2Kin 4:31
t was a dearth in the land 2Kin 4:38
man of God, *t* is death in the pot 2Kin 4:40
And *t* was no harm in the pot 2Kin 4:41
t came a man from Baal-shalisha, 2Kin 4:42
he shall know that *t* is a prophet 2Kin 5:8
now I know that *t* is no God in 2Kin 5:15
Shall *t* not then, I pray thee, be 2Kin 5:17
the house of Rimmon to worship *t* 2Kin 5:18 8033
even now *t* be come to me from 2Kin 5:22
beam, and let us make us a place *t* 2Kin 6:2 8033
warned him of, and saved himself *t* 2Kin 6:10 8033
t was a great famine in Samaria 2Kin 6:25
t cried a woman unto him, saying, 2Kin 6:26
t were four leprous men at the 2Kin 7:3
is in the city, and we shall die *t* 2Kin 7:4 8033
Syria, behold, *t* was no man *t* 2Kin 7:5 8033
and, behold, *t* was no man *t* 2Kin 7:10 8033
look out *t* Jehu the son of 2Kin 9:2 8033
t shall be none to bury her 2Kin 9:10
for Joram lay *t* 2Kin 9:16 8033
t stood a watchman on the tower 2Kin 9:17
So *t* went one on horseback to 2Kin 9:18
T is treachery, O Ahaziah 2Kin 9:23
And he fled to Megiddo, and died *t* 2Kin 9:27 8033
t looked out to him two or three 2Kin 9:32
t are with you chariots and horses 2Kin 10:2
t came a messenger, and told him, 2Kin 10:8
Know now that *t* shall fall unto 2Kin 10:10
so that *t* was not a man left that 2Kin 10:21
look that *t* be here with you none 2Kin 10:23
and *t* was she slain 2Kin 11:16 8033
when they saw that *t* was much 2Kin 12:10
Howbeit *t* were not made for the 2Kin 12:13
t remained the grove also in 2Kin 13:6
t passed by a wild beast that was 2Kin 14:9
him to Lachish, and slew him *t* 2Kin 14:19 8033
for *t* was not any shut up, nor 2Kin 14:26
back, and stayed not *t* in the land 2Kin 15:20 8033
Elath, and dwelt *t* unto this day 2Kin 16:6 8033
t they burnt incense in all the 2Kin 17:11 8033
t was none left but the tribe of 2Kin 17:18
the beginning of their dwelling *t* 2Kin 17:25 8033
and let them go and dwell *t* 2Kin 17:27 8033
t came out to them Eliakim the 2Kin 18:18
t is not strength to bring forth 2Kin 19:3
this city, nor shoot an arrow *t* 2Kin 19:32 8033
t was nothing in his house, nor 2Kin 20:13
t is nothing among my treasures 2Kin 20:15
Howbeit *t* was no reckoning made 2Kin 22:7
that were *t* in the mount, and sent 2Kin 23:16 8033
that were *t* upon the altars 2Kin 23:20 8033
Surely *t* was not holden such a 2Kin 23:22
like unto him was *t* no king 2Kin 23:25
after him arose *t* any like him 2Kin 23:25
which I said, My name shall be *t* 2Kin 23:27 8033
and he came to Egypt, and died *t* 2Kin 23:34 8033
t was no bread for the people of 2Kin 25:3
t came to Gedaliah to Mizpah, 2Kin 25:23
t he reigned seven years and six 1Chr 3:4 8033
t they dwelt with the king for 1Chr 4:23 8033
they of Ham had dwelt *t* of old 1Chr 4:40 8033
the habitations that were found *t* 1Chr 4:41
because *t* was pasture *t* for 1Chr 4:41 8033
escaped, and dwelt *t* unto this day 1Chr 4:43 8033
For *t* fell down many slain, 1Chr 5:22
t the Philistines were gathered 1Chr 11:13 8033
of the Gadites *t* separated 1Chr 12:8
t came of the children of 1Chr 12:16
seeing *t* is no wrong in mine 1Chr 12:17
t fell some of Manasseh to David, 1Chr 12:19
t fell to him of Manasseh, Adnah, 1Chr 12:20
day *t* came to David to help him 1Chr 12:22
t they were with David three days 1Chr 12:39 8033
for *t* was joy in Israel 1Chr 12:40
and *t* he died before God 1Chr 13:10 8033
and David smote them *t* 1Chr 14:11 8033
when they had left their gods *t* 1Chr 14:12 8033
So he left *t* before the ark of 1Chr 16:37 8033
t is none like thee, neither is 1Chr 17:20
neither is *t* any God beside thee, 1Chr 17:20
Then *t* went certain, and told 1Chr 19:5
t were precious stones in it 1Chr 20:2
that *t* arose war at Gezer with 1Chr 20:4
And *t* was war again with the 1Chr 20:5
yet again *t* was war at Gath, 1Chr 20:6
t fell of Israel seventy thousand 1Chr 21:14
David built *t* an altar unto the 1Chr 21:26 8033
Jebusite, then he sacrificed *t* 1Chr 21:28 8033
Moreover *t* are workmen with thee 1Chr 22:15
and the iron, *t* is no number 1Chr 22:16
t were more chief men found of 1Chr 24:4
Among the sons of Eleazar *t* were 1Chr 24:4
t were found among them mighty 1Chr 26:31
because *t* fell wrath for it 1Chr 27:24
t shall be with thee for all 1Chr 28:21
as a shadow, and *t* is none abiding 1Chr 29:15
for *t* was the tabernacle of the 2Chr 1:3 8033
neither shall *t* any after thee 2Chr 1:12
And *t* it is unto this day 2Chr 5:9 8033
T was nothing in the ark save the 2Chr 5:10
house in, that my name might be *t* 2Chr 6:5 8033
that my name might be *t* 2Chr 6:6 8033
t is no God like thee in the 2Chr 6:14
T shall not fail thee a man in my 2Chr 6:16
that thou wouldest put thy name *t* 2Chr 6:20 8033
t is no rain, because they have 2Chr 6:26
If *t* be dearth in the land 2Chr 6:28
if *t* be blasting, or mildew, 2Chr 6:28
sore or whatsoever sickness *t* be 2Chr 6:28
(for *t* is no man which sinneth 2Chr 6:36
for *t* he offered burnt offerings, 2Chr 7:7 8033
shut up heaven that *t* be no rain 2Chr 7:13
that my name may be *t* for ever 2Chr 7:16 8033
mine heart shall be *t* perpetually 2Chr 7:16 8033
T shall not fail thee a man to be 2Chr 7:18
the children of Israel to dwell *t* 2Chr 8:2 8033
t was nothing hid from Solomon 2Chr 9:2
t was no more spirit in her 2Chr 9:4
neither was *t* any such spice as 2Chr 9:9
t were none such seen before in 2Chr 9:11
t were six steps to the throne, 2Chr 9:18
lions stood *t* on the one side 2Chr 9:19 8033
T was not the like made in any 2Chr 9:19
of Israel, to put his name *t* 2Chr 12:13 8033
t were wars between Rehoboam and 2Chr 12:15
t was war between Abijah and 2Chr 13:2
t are gathered unto him vain men, 2Chr 13:7
t are with you golden calves, 2Chr 13:8
so *t* fell down slain of Israel 2Chr 13:17
t came out against them Zerah the 2Chr 14:9
for *t* was exceeding much spoil in 2Chr 14:14
in those times *t* was no peace to 2Chr 15:5
t was no more war unto the five 2Chr 15:19
T is a league between me and thee, 2Chr 16:3
as *t* was between my father and thy 2Chr 16:3
Is *t* not here a prophet of the 2Chr 18:6
T is yet one man, by whom we may 2Chr 18:7
Then *t* came out a spirit, and 2Chr 18:20
Nevertheless *t* are good things 2Chr 19:3
for *t* is no iniquity with the 2Chr 19:7
Then *t* came some that told 2Chr 20:2
T cometh a great multitude 2Chr 20:2
and in thine hand is *t* not power 2Chr 20:6
for *t* they blessed the LORD 2Chr 20:26 8033
t came a writing to him from 2Chr 21:12
so that *t* was never a son left 2Chr 21:17
the king's house, they slew her *t* 2Chr 23:15 8033
they saw that *t* was much money 2Chr 24:11
But *t* came a man of God to him, 2Chr 25:7
t passed by a wild beast that was 2Chr 25:18
Lachish after him, and slew him *t* 2Chr 25:27 8033
But a prophet of the LORD was *t* 2Chr 28:9 8033
but are *t* not with you, even with 2Chr 28:10
t is fierce wrath against Israel 2Chr 28:13
and they dwelt *t* 2Chr 28:18 8033
t assembled at Jerusalem much 2Chr 30:13
For *t* were many in the 2Chr 30:17
So *t* was great joy in Jerusalem 2Chr 30:26
t was not the like in Jerusalem 2Chr 30:26
So *t* was gathered much people 2Chr 32:4
for *t* be more with us than with 2Chr 32:7
Who was *t* among all the gods of 2Chr 32:14
bowels slew him *t* with the sword 2Chr 32:21 8033
therefore *t* was wrath upon him, 2Chr 32:25
and of the Levites *t* were scribes 2Chr 34:13
t was no passover like to that 2Chr 35:18
his people, till *t* was no remedy 2Chr 36:16
Who is *t* among you of all his 2Chr 36:23
Who is *t* among you of all his Ezr 1:3
till *t* stood up a priest with Ezr 2:63
of whom *t* were seven thousand Ezr 2:65
t were among them two hundred Ezr 2:65
T have been mighty kings also Ezr 4:20
let *t* be search made in the Ezr 5:17
which is *t* at Babylon, whether it Ezr 5:17 8536
t was found at Achmetha, in the Ezr 6:2
name to dwell *t* destroy all kings Ezr 6:12 8536
t went up some of the children of Ezr 7:7
for why should *t* be wrath against Ezr 7:23
t abode we in tents three days Ezr 8:15 8033
found *t* none of the sons of Levi Ezr 8:15 8033
Then I proclaimed a fast *t* Ezr 8:21 8033
lords, and all Israel *t* present Ezr 8:25
Jerusalem, and abode *t* three days Ezr 8:32 8033
so that *t* should be no remnant Ezr 9:14
t assembled unto him out of Ezr 10:1
yet now *t* is hope in Israel Ezr 10:2
t were found that had taken Ezr 10:18
t in the province are in great Neh 1:3 8033
though *t* were of you cast out Neh 1:9
I have chosen to set my name *t* Neh 1:9 8033
that *t* was come a man to seek the Neh 2:10
to Jerusalem, and was *t* three days Neh 2:11 8033
neither was *t* any beast with me, Neh 2:12
but *t* was no place for the beast Neh 2:14
is decayed, and *t* is much rubbish Neh 4:10
t was a great cry of the people Neh 5:1
For *t* were that said, We, our Neh 5:2
Some also *t* were that said, We Neh 5:3
T were also that said, We have Neh 5:4
Moreover *t* were at my table an Neh 5:17
that *t* was no breach left therein Neh 6:1
saying, *T* is a king in Judah Neh 6:7
T are no such things done as thou Neh 6:8
and who is *t*, that, being as I am, Neh 6:11
For *t* were many in Judah sworn Neh 6:18
till *t* stood up a priest with Neh 7:65
of whom *t* were seven thousand Neh 7:67
t was very great gladness Neh 8:17
Asaph of old *t* were chief of the Neh 12:46
T dwelt men of Tyre also therein, Neh 13:16
that *t* should no burden be Neh 13:19
nations was *t* no king like him Neh 13:26
Thus shall *t* arise too much Est 1:18
let *t* go a royal commandment from Est 1:19
Let *t* be fair young virgins Est 2:2
the palace *t* was a certain Jew Est 2:5
T is a certain people scattered Est 3:8
t was written according to all Est 3:12
t was great mourning among the Est 4:3
t is one law of his to put him to Est 4:11
then shall *t* enlargement and Est 4:14
T is nothing done for him Est 6:3
for he saw that *t* was evil Est 7:7
T was a man in the land of Uz, Job 1:1
t were born unto him seven sons Job 1:2
Now *t* was a day when the sons of Job 1:6
that *t* is none like him in the Job 1:8
t was a day when his sons and his Job 1:13
t came a messenger unto Job, and Job 1:14
t came also another, and said, The Job 1:16
t came also another, and said, The Job 1:17
t came also another, and said, Thy Job 1:18
t came a great wind from the Job 1:19
Again *t* was a day when the sons Job 2:1
that *t* is none like him in the Job 2:3
T is a man child conceived Job 3:3
T the wicked cease from troubling Job 3:17 8033
and *t* the weary be at rest Job 3:17 8033
T the prisoners rest together Job 3:18
The small and great are *t* Job 3:19 8033
t was silence, and I heard a voice Job 4:16
if *t* be any that will answer thee Job 5:1
neither is *t* any to deliver them Job 5:4
in seven *t* shall no evil touch Job 5:19
or is *t* any taste in the white of Job 6:6 8033
Is *t* iniquity in my tongue Job 6:30
Is *t* not an appointed time to man Job 7:1
Neither is *t* any daysman betwixt Job 9:33
t is none that can deliver out of Job 10:7
be secure, because *t* is hope Job 11:18
up a man, and *t* can be no opening Job 12:14
in a wilderness where *t* is no way Job 12:24
For *t* is hope of a tree, if it be Job 14:7
is *t* any secret thing with thee Job 15:11
Are *t* not mockers with me Job 17:2
I cry aloud, but *t* is no judgment Job 19:7
that ye may know *t* is a judgment Job 19:29
T shall none of his meat be left Job 20:21
as *t* are innumerable before him Job 21:33
answers *t* remaineth falsehood Job 21:34
thou shalt say, *T* is lifting up Job 22:29
T the righteous might dispute Job 23:7 8033
I go forward, but he is not *t* Job 23:8 8033
Is *t* any number of his armies Job 25:3
Surely *t* is a vein for the silver Job 28:1
T is a path which no fowl knoweth Job 28:7
waited for light, *t* came darkness Job 30:26
portion of God is *t* from above Job 31:2
When Elihu saw that *t* was no Job 32:5
But *t* is a spirit in man Job 32:8
t was none of you that convinced Job 32:12
neither is *t* iniquity in me Job 33:9
If *t* be a messenger with him, an Job 33:23
T is no darkness, nor shadow of Job 34:22
T they cry, but none giveth Job 35:12 8033
place, where *t* is no straitness Job 36:16
Because *t* is wrath, beware lest Job 36:18
wilderness, wherein *t* is no man Job 38:26
and where the slain are, *t* is she Job 39:30 8033
Upon earth *t* is not his like, who Job 41:33
Then came *t* unto him all his Job 42:11
Many *t* be which say of my soul, Ps 3:2
T is no help for him in God Ps 3:2
T be many that say, Who will shew Ps 4:6

For *t* is no faithfulness in their Ps 5:9
For in death *t* is no remembrance Ps 6:5
while *t* is none to deliver Ps 7:2
if *t* be iniquity in my hands Ps 7:3
said in his heart, *T* is no God Ps 14:1
t is none that doeth good Ps 14:1
to see if *t* were any that did Ps 14:2
t is none that doeth good, no, Ps 14:3
T were they in great fear Ps 14:5 8033
at thy right hand *t* are pleasures Ps 16:11
T went up a smoke out of his Ps 18:8
but *t* was none to save them Ps 18:41
T is no speech nor language, Ps 19:3
t is nothing hid from the heat Ps 19:6
keeping of them *t* is great reward Ps 19:11
for *t* is none to help Ps 22:11
What profit is *t* in my blood Ps 30:9
and in whose spirit *t* is no guile Ps 32:2
T is no king saved by the Ps 33:16
for *t* is no want to them that Ps 34:9
that *t* is no fear of God before Ps 36:1
T are the workers of iniquity Ps 36:12 8033
T is no soundness in my flesh Ps 38:3
neither is *t* any rest in my bones Ps 38:3
t is no soundness in my flesh Ps 38:7
of Tyre shall be *t* with a gift Ps 45:12
T is a river, the streams whereof Ps 46:4
Fear took hold upon them *t* Ps 48:6 8033
pieces, and *t* be none to deliver Ps 50:22
said in his heart, *T* is no God Ps 53:1
t is none that doeth good Ps 53:1
to see if *t* were any that did Ps 53:2
t is none that doeth good, no, Ps 53:3
T were they in great fear, where Ps 53:5 8033
for *t* were many with me Ps 55:18
Verily *t* is a reward for the Ps 58:11
t did we rejoice in him Ps 66:6 8033
T is little Benjamin with their Ps 68:27 8033
deep mire, where *t* is no standing Ps 69:2
some to take pity, but *t* was none Ps 69:20
that they may dwell *t*, and have it Ps 69:35
for *t* is none to deliver him Ps 71:11
T shall be an handful of corn in Ps 72:16
For *t* are no bands in their death Ps 73:4
is *t* knowledge in the most High Ps 73:11
t is none upon earth that I Ps 73:25
t is no more any prophet Ps 74:9
neither is *t* among us any that Ps 74:9
the hand of the LORD *t* is a cup Ps 75:8
T brake he the arrows of the bow, Ps 76:3 8033
and *t* was none to bury them Ps 79:3
T shall no strange god be in thee Ps 81:9
Among the gods *t* is none like Ps 86:8
neither are *t* any works like unto Ps 86:8
this man was born *t* Ps 87:4 8033
people, that this man was born *t* Ps 87:6 8033
players on instruments shall be *t* Ps 87:7
T shall no evil befall thee, Ps 91:10
t is no unrighteousness in him Ps 92:15
T go the ships Ps 104:26 8033
t is that leviathan, whom thou Ps 104:26
t came divers sorts of flies, and Ps 105:31
t was not one feeble person among Ps 105:37
t was not one of them left Ps 106:11
fell down, and *t* was none to help Ps 107:12
t he maketh the hungry to dwell, Ps 107:36 8033
the wilderness, where *t* is no way Ps 107:40
Let *t* be none to extend mercy Ps 109:12
neither let *t* be any to favour Ps 109:12
Unto the upright *t* ariseth light Ps 112:4
For *t* are set thrones of judgment Ps 122:5 8033
But *t* is forgiveness with thee, Ps 130:4
for with the LORD *t* is mercy Ps 130:7
T will I make the horn of David Ps 132:17 8033
for *t* the LORD commanded the Ps 133:3 8033
neither is *t* any breath in their Ps 135:17
t we sat down, yea, we wept, when Ps 137:1 8033
For *t* they that carried us away Ps 137:3 8033
For *t* is not a word in my tongue, Ps 139:4
ascend up into heaven, thou art *t* Ps 139:8 8033
bed in hell, behold, thou art *t* Ps 139:8
Even *t* shall thy hand lead me, and Ps 139:10 8033
when as yet *t* was none of them Ps 139:16
see if *t* be any wicked way in me, Ps 139:24
but *t* was no man that would know Ps 142:4
that *t* be no breaking in, nor Ps 144:14
that *t* be no complaining in our Ps 144:14
son of man, in whom *t* is no help Ps 146:3
t met him a woman with the attire Prov 7:10
t is nothing froward or perverse Prov 8:8
When *t* were no depths, I was Prov 8:24
when *t* were no fountains Prov 8:24
he prepared the heavens, I was *t* Prov 8:27 8033
knoweth not that the dead are *t* Prov 9:18 8033
of words *t* wanteth not sin Prov 10:19
the wicked perish, *t* is shouting Prov 11:10
of counsellors *t* is safety Prov 11:14
T is that scattereth, and yet Prov 11:24
t is that withholdeth more than Prov 11:24
T is that speaketh like the Prov 12:18
T shall no evil happen to the Prov 12:21
the pathway thereof *t* is no death Prov 12:28
T is that maketh himself rich, Prov 13:7
t is that maketh himself poor, Prov 13:7
but *t* is that is destroyed for Prov 13:23
among the righteous *t* is favour Prov 14:9
T is a way which seemeth right Prov 14:12
In all labour *t* is profit Prov 14:23
T is a way that seemeth right Prov 16:25
in his lips *t* is as a burning Prov 16:27
Wherefore is *t* a price in the Prov 17:16
t is a friend that sticketh Prov 18:24
Chasten thy son while *t* is hope Prov 19:18
T are many devices in a man's Prov 19:21
T is gold, and a multitude of Prov 20:15
T is treasure to be desired and Prov 21:20
T is no wisdom nor understanding Prov 21:30
T is a lion without, I shall be Prov 22:13
For surely *t* is an end Prov 23:18
of counsellors *t* is safety Prov 24:6
then *t* shall be a reward, and thy Prov 24:14
For *t* shall be no reward to the Prov 24:20
t shall come forth a vessel for Prov 25:4
t is more hope of a fool than of Prov 26:12
man saith, *T* is a lion in the way Prov 26:13
no wood is, *t* the fire goeth out Prov 26:20
so where *t* is no talebearer, the Prov 26:20
for *t* are seven abominations in Prov 26:25
men do rejoice, *t* is great glory Prov 28:12
of an evil man *t* is a snare Prov 29:6
he rage or laugh, *t* is no rest Prov 29:9
Where *t* is no vision, the people Prov 29:18
t is more hope of a fool than of Prov 29:20
T is a generation that curseth Prov 30:11
T is a generation that are pure Prov 30:12
T is a generation, O how lofty Prov 30:13
T is a generation, whose teeth Prov 30:14
T are three things that are never Prov 30:15
T be three things which are too Prov 30:18
T be four things which are little Prov 30:24
T be three things which go well, Prov 30:29
against whom *t* is no rising up Prov 30:31
t is no new thing under the sun Eccl 1:9
Is *t* any thing whereof it may be Eccl 1:10
T is no remembrance of former Eccl 1:11
neither shall *t* be any Eccl 1:11
t was no profit under the sun Eccl 2:11
For *t* is no remembrance of the Eccl 2:16
For *t* is a man whose labour is in Eccl 2:21
T is nothing better for a man, Eccl 2:24
To every thing *t* is a season Eccl 3:1
I know that *t* is no good in them, Eccl 3:12
judgment, that wickedness was *t* Eccl 3:16 8033
that iniquity was *t* Eccl 3:16 8033
for *t* is a time *t* Eccl 3:17 8033
perceive that *t* is nothing better Eccl 3:22
of their oppressors *t* was power Eccl 4:1
T is one alone, and *t* is not a Eccl 4:8
one alone, and *t* is not a second Eccl 4:8
yet is *t* no end of all his labour Eccl 4:8
T is no end of all the people, Eccl 4:16
many words *t* are also divers Eccl 5:7
and *t* be higher than they Eccl 5:8
what good is *t* to the owners Eccl 5:11
T is a sore evil which I have Eccl 5:13
son, and *t* is nothing in his hand Eccl 5:14
T is an evil which I have seen Eccl 6:1
Seeing *t* be many things that Eccl 6:11
by it *t* is profit to them that Eccl 7:11
t is a just man that perisheth in Eccl 7:15
t is a wicked man that prolongeth Eccl 7:15
For *t* is not a just man upon Eccl 7:20
the word of a king is, *t* is power Eccl 8:4
to every purpose *t* is time Eccl 8:6
T is no man that hath power over Eccl 8:8
t is no discharge in that war Eccl 8:8
t is a time wherein one man Eccl 8:9
T is a vanity which is done upon Eccl 8:14
that *t* be just men, unto whom it Eccl 8:14
t be wicked men, to whom it Eccl 8:14
(for also *t* is that neither day Eccl 8:16
t is one event to the righteous, Eccl 9:2
that *t* is one event unto all Eccl 9:3
to all the living *t* is hope Eccl 9:4
for *t* is no work, nor device, nor Eccl 9:10
T was a little city, and few men Eccl 9:14
t came a great king against it, Eccl 9:14
Now *t* was found in it a poor wise Eccl 9:15
T is an evil which I have seen Eccl 10:5
the tree falleth, *t* it shall be Eccl 11:3 8033
of making many books *t* is no end Eccl 12:12
whereon *t* hang a thousand Song 4:4
t is no spot in thee Song 4:7
t is not one barren among them Song 6:6
T are threescore queens, and Song 6:8
t will I give thee my loves Song 7:12
t thy mother brought thee forth Song 8:5
t she brought thee forth that Song 8:5
the head *t* is no soundness in it Is 1:6
neither is *t* any end of their Is 2:7
neither is *t* any end of their Is 2:7
of sweet smell *t* shall be stink Is 3:24
t shall be a tabernacle for a Is 4:6
but *t* shall come up briers and Is 5:6
till *t* be no place, that they may Is 5:8
t be a great forsaking in the Is 6:12
where *t* were a thousand vines at Is 7:23
t shall not come thither the fear Is 7:25
it is because *t* is no light in Is 8:20
peace *t* shall be no end, upon the Is 9:7
t was none that moved the wing, Is 10:14
t shall come forth a rod out of Is 11:1
in that day *t* shall be a root of Is 11:10
t shall be an highway for the Is 11:16
shall the Arabian pitch tent *t* Is 13:20 8033
the shepherds make their fold *t* Is 13:20 8033
beasts of the desert shall lie *t* Is 13:21 8033
and owls shall dwell *t*, and satyrs Is 13:21 8033
and satyrs shall dance *t* Is 13:21 8033
for *t* shall come from the north a Is 14:31
faileth, *t* is no green thing Is 15:6
in the vineyards *t* shall be no Is 16:10
neither shall *t* be shouting Is 16:10
and *t* shall be desolation Is 17:9
Neither shall *t* be any work for Is 19:15
In that day shall *t* be an altar Is 19:19
In that day shall *t* be a highway Is 19:23
t shalt thou die Is 22:18 8033
t the chariots of thy glory shall Is 22:18 8033
so that *t* is no house, no Is 23:1
t is no more strength Is 23:10
t also shalt thou have no rest Is 23:12 8033
T is a crying for wine in the Is 24:11
t shall be as the shaking of an Is 24:13
t shall the calf feed Is 27:10 8033
t shall he lie down, and consume Is 27:10 8033
so that *t* is no place clean Is 28:8
here a little, and *t* a little Is 28:10 8033
here a little, and *t* a little Is 28:13 8033
t shall be heaviness and sorrow Is 29:2
so that *t* shall not be found in Is 30:14
t shall be upon every high Is 30:25
t shall be a bridle in the jaws Is 30:28
But *t* the glorious LORD will be Is 33:21 8033
the kingdom, but none shall be *t* Is 34:12 8033
the screech owl also shall rest *t* Is 34:14 8033
T shall the great owl make her Is 34:15 8033
t shall the vultures also be Is 34:15 8033
And an highway shall be *t*, and a Is 35:8 8033
No lion shall be *t*, nor any Is 35:9 8033
thereon, it shall not be found *t* Is 35:9 8033
but the redeemed shall walk *t* Is 35:9
t is not strength to bring forth Is 37:3
this city, nor shoot an arrow *t* Is 37:33 8033
t was nothing in his house, nor Is 39:2
t is nothing among my treasures Is 39:4
For *t* shall be peace and truth in Is 39:8
t is no searching of his Is 40:28
t is none, and their tongue Is 41:17
t is none that sheweth, yea, Is 41:26
t is none that declareth, yea, Is 41:26
t is none that heareth your words Is 41:26
For I beheld, and *t* was no man Is 41:28
t was no counsellor, that, when I Is 41:28
before me *t* was no God formed, Is 43:10
neither shall *t* be after me Is 43:10
beside me *t* is no saviour Is 43:11
when *t* was no strange god among Is 43:12
t is none that can deliver out of Is 43:13
and beside me *t* is no God Is 44:6
Is *t* a God beside me Is 44:8
yea, *t* is no God Is 44:8
neither is *t* knowledge nor Is 44:19
Is *t* not a lie in my right hand Is 44:20
t is none else, *t* is no God Is 45:5
west, that *t* is none beside me Is 45:6
I am the LORD, and *t* is none else Is 45:6
t is none else, *t* is no God Is 45:14
and *t* is none else Is 45:18
t is no God else beside me Is 45:21
t is none beside me Is 45:21
for I am God, and *t* is none else Is 45:22
for I am God, and *t* is none else Is 46:9
I am God, and *t* is none like me, Is 46:9
t is no throne, O daughter of the Is 47:1
t shall not be a coal to warm at, Is 47:14
from the time that it was, *t* am I Is 48:16 8033
T is no peace, saith the LORD, Is 48:22
when I came, was *t* no man Is 50:2
I called, was *t* none to answer Is 50:2
because *t* is no water, and dieth Is 50:2
T is none to guide her among all Is 51:18
neither is *t* any that taketh her Is 51:18
for henceforth *t* shall no more Is 52:1
aforetime into Egypt to sojourn *t* Is 52:4 8033
t is no beauty that we should Is 53:2
yet saidst thou not, *T* is no hope Is 57:10
T is no peace, saith my God, to Is 57:21
t is no judgment in their goings Is 59:8
look for judgment, but *t* is none Is 59:11
him that *t* was no judgment Is 59:15
And he saw that *t* was no man Is 59:16
no man, and wondered that *t* was no Is 59:16
of the people *t* was none with me Is 63:3
I looked, and *t* was none to help Is 63:5
I wondered that *t* was none to Is 63:5
t is none that calleth upon thy Is 64:7
it, and my servants shall dwell *t* Is 65:9 8033
T shall be no more thence an Is 65:20
and see if *t* be such a thing Jer 2:10
but thou saidst, *T* is no hope Jer 2:25
t hath been no latter rain Jer 3:3
tree, and *t* hath played the harlot Jer 3:6 8033
t was no man, and all the birds of Jer 4:25
if *t* be any that executeth Jer 5:1
when *t* is no peace Jer 6:14
To what purpose cometh *t* to me Jer 6:20
proclaim *t* this word, and say, Jer 7:2 8033
in Tophet, till *t* be no place Jer 7:32
when *t* is no peace Jer 8:11
t shall be no grapes on the vine, Jer 8:13
cities, and let us be silent *t* Jer 8:14 8033
Is *t* no balm in Gilead Jer 8:22
is *t* no physician *t* Jer 8:22
Forasmuch as *t* is none like unto Jer 10:6
t is none like unto thee Jer 10:7
t is a multitude of waters in the Jer 10:13
and *t* is no breath in them Jer 10:14
t is none to stretch forth my Jer 10:20
t shall be no remnant of them Jer 11:23
hide it *t* in a hole of the rock Jer 13:4 8033
which I commanded thee to hide *t* Jer 13:6 8033
for *t* was no rain in the earth, Jer 14:4
it, because *t* was no grass Jer 14:5
did fail, because *t* was no grass Jer 14:6
us, and *t* is no healing for us Jer 14:19
looked for peace, and *t* is no good Jer 14:19
Are *t* any among the vanities of Jer 14:22
t shall ye serve other gods day Jer 16:13 8033
and things wherein *t* is no profit Jer 16:19
Then shall *t* enter into the gates Jer 17:25
t I will cause thee to hear my Jer 18:2 8033

And they said, *T* is no hope	Jer 18:12	
proclaim *t* the words that I shall	Jer 19:2	8033
till *t* be no place to bury	Jer 19:11	
t thou shalt die, and shalt be	Jer 20:6	8033
shalt die, and shalt be buried *t*	Jer 20:6	8033
of Judah, and speak *t* this word,	Jer 22:1	8033
then shall *t* enter in by the	Jer 22:4	
and *t* shall ye die	Jer 22:26	8033
t was also a man that prophesied	Jer 26:20	
t shall they be until the day	Jer 27:22	8033
that ye may be increased *t*	Jer 29:6	8033
T is none to plead thy cause,	Jer 30:13	
For *t* shall be a day, that the	Jer 31:6	
t is hope in thine end, saith the	Jer 31:17	
t shall dwell in Judah itself, and	Jer 31:24	
t shall he be until I visit him,	Jer 32:5	8033
t is nothing too hard for thee	Jer 32:17	
is *t* any thing too hard for me	Jer 32:27	
Again *t* shall be heard in this	Jer 33:10	
that *t* should not be day and night	Jer 33:20	
and, lo, all the princes sat *t*	Jer 36:12	8033
t was a fire on the hearth	Jer 36:22	
t were added besides unto them	Jer 36:32	
t remained but wounded men among	Jer 37:10	
a captain of the ward was *t*	Jer 37:13	8033
Jeremiah had remained *t* many days	Jer 37:16	8033
Is *t* any word from the LORD	Jer 37:17	
And Jeremiah said, *T* is	Jer 37:17	
Jonathan the scribe, lest I die *t*	Jer 37:20	8033
And in the dungeon *t* was no water	Jer 38:6	
for *t* is no more bread in the	Jer 38:9	
to Jonathan's house, to die *t*	Jer 38:26	8033
he was *t* when Jerusalem was taken	Jer 38:28	
t they did eat bread together in	Jer 41:1	8033
the Chaldeans that were found *t*	Jer 41:3	8033
That *t* came certain from Shechem,	Jer 41:5	
and *t* will we dwell	Jer 42:14	8033
into Egypt, and go to sojourn *t*	Jer 42:15	8033
shall overtake you *t* in the land	Jer 42:16	8033
follow close after you *t* in Egypt	Jer 42:16	8033
and *t* ye shall die	Jer 42:16	8033
to go into Egypt to sojourn *t*	Jer 42:17	8033
Go not into Egypt to sojourn *t*	Jer 43:2	8033
the land of Egypt to sojourn *t*	Jer 44:12	8033
the land of Egypt to sojourn *t*	Jer 44:14	8033
a desire to return to dwell *t*	Jer 44:14	8033
until *t* be an end of them	Jer 44:27	
the land of Egypt to sojourn *t*	Jer 44:28	8033
They did cry *t*, Pharaoh king of	Jer 46:17	8033
t hath he appointed it	Jer 47:7	8033
T shall be no more praise of Moab	Jer 48:2	
T shall be lamentation generally	Jer 48:38	
the LORD, no man shall abide *t*	Jer 49:18	8033
t is sorrow on the sea	Jer 49:23	
t shall no man abide *t*, nor	Jer 49:33	
t shall no man abide *t*	Jer 49:33	8033
t shall be no nation whither the	Jer 49:36	
For out of the north *t* cometh up	Jer 50:3	
be sought for, and *t* shall be none	Jer 50:20	
of the islands shall dwell *t*	Jer 50:39	
so shall no man abide *t*, neither	Jer 50:40	8033
t is a multitude of waters in the	Jer 51:16	
and *t* is no breath in them	Jer 51:17	
so that *t* was no bread for the	Jer 52:6	
t were ninety and six pomegranates	Jer 52:23	
t was a continual diet given him	Jer 52:34	
see if *t* be any sorrow like unto	Lam 1:12	
and *t* is none to comfort her	Lam 1:17	
bereaveth, at home *t* is as death	Lam 1:20	
t is none to comfort me	Lam 1:21	
if so be *t* may be hope	Lam 3:29	
They shall no more sojourn *t*	Lam 4:15	
t is none that doth deliver us	Lam 5:8	
hand of the LORD was *t* upon him	Eze 1:3	8033
t was a voice from the firmament	Eze 1:25	
yet shall know that *t* hath been	Eze 2:5	
and *t* was written therein	Eze 2:10	
remained *t* astonished among them	Eze 3:15	8033
hand of the LORD was *t* upon me	Eze 3:22	8033
plain, and I will *t* talk with thee	Eze 3:22	8033
the glory of the LORD stood *t*	Eze 3:23	8033
neither came *t* abominable flesh	Eze 4:14	
neither shall *t* be wailing for	Eze 7:11	
seek peace, and *t* shall be none	Eze 7:25	
of the Lord GOD fell *t* upon me	Eze 8:1	8033
glory of the God of Israel was *t*	Eze 8:4	8033
t stood before them seventy men	Eze 8:11	
t sat women weeping for Tammuz	Eze 8:14	8033
t appeared over them as it were a	Eze 10:1	
t appeared in the cherubims the	Eze 10:8	
not see it, though he shall die *t*	Eze 12:13	8033
For *t* shall be no more any vain	Eze 12:24	
T shall none of my words be	Eze 12:28	
and *t* was no peace	Eze 13:10	
t shall be an overflowing shower	Eze 13:11	
t shall be an overflowing shower	Eze 13:13	
t is no peace, saith the Lord GOD	Eze 13:16	
wherewith ye *t* hunt the souls to	Eze 13:20	8033
T was also another great eagle	Eze 17:7	
will plead with him *t* for his	Eze 17:20	8033
they offered *t* their sacrifices,	Eze 20:28	8033
t they presented the provocation	Eze 20:28	8033
t also they made their sweet	Eze 20:28	8033
and poured out *t* their drink	Eze 20:28	8033
t will I plead with you face to	Eze 20:35	8033
t shall all the house of Israel,	Eze 20:40	8033
t will I accept them	Eze 20:40	8033
t will I require your offerings,	Eze 20:40	8033
t shall ye remember your ways, and	Eze 20:43	8033
in my fury, and I will leave you *t*	Eze 22:20	8033
T is a conspiracy of her prophets	Eze 22:25	
t were two women, the daughters	Eze 23:2	
t were their breasts pressed, and	Eze 23:3	8033
t they bruised the teats of their	Eze 23:3	8033
t is no secret that they can hide	Eze 28:3	
t shall be no more a pricking	Eze 28:24	
they shall be *t* a base kingdom	Eze 29:14	8033
t shall be no more a prince of	Eze 30:13	
shall break *t* the yokes of Egypt	Eze 30:18	8033
Asshur is *t* and all her company	Eze 32:22	8033
T is Elam and all her multitude	Eze 32:24	8033
T is Meshech, Tubal, and all her	Eze 32:26	8033
T is Edom, her kings, and all her	Eze 32:29	8033
T be the princes of the north,	Eze 32:30	8033
because *t* is no shepherd	Eze 34:5	
because *t* was no shepherd,	Eze 34:8	
t shall they lie in a good fold,	Eze 34:14	8033
t shall be showers of blessing	Eze 34:26	
whereas the LORD was *t*	Eze 35:10	8033
t were very many in the open	Eze 37:2	
t was a noise, and behold a	Eze 37:7	
but *t* was no breath in them	Eze 37:8	
Surely in that day *t* shall be a	Eze 38:19	
Gog a place *t* of graves in Israel	Eze 39:11	8033
t shall they bury Gog and all his	Eze 39:11	8033
have left none of them any more *t*	Eze 39:28	8033
t was a man, whose appearance was	Eze 40:3	
t were narrow windows to the	Eze 40:16	
t were chambers, and a pavement	Eze 40:17	
t were windows in it and in the	Eze 40:25	
t were seven steps to go up to it	Eze 40:26	
t was a gate in the inner court	Eze 40:27	
t were windows in it and in the	Eze 40:29	
t were windows therein and in the	Eze 40:33	
t were pillars by the posts, one	Eze 40:49	
t was an enlarging, and a winding	Eze 41:7	
t were made on them, on the doors	Eze 41:25	
t were thick planks upon the face	Eze 41:25	
t were narrow windows and palm	Eze 41:26	
t shall they lay the most holy	Eze 42:13	8033
but *t* they shall lay their	Eze 42:14	8033
Of this *t* shall be for the	Eze 45:2	
t was a place on the two sides	Eze 46:19	8033
corner of the court *t* was a court	Eze 46:21	
t were courts joined of forty	Eze 46:22	
t was a row of building round	Eze 46:23	
t ran out waters on the right	Eze 47:2	
t shall be a very great multitude	Eze 47:9	
t shall ye give him his	Eze 47:23	8033
that day shall be, The LORD is *t*	Eze 48:35	8033
t is but one decree for you	Dan 2:9	
T is not a man upon the earth	Dan 2:10	
therefore *t* is no king, lord, nor	Dan 2:10	
t is none other that can shew it	Dan 2:11	
But *t* is a God in heaven that	Dan 2:28	
but *t* shall be in it of the	Dan 2:41	
T are certain Jews whom thou hast	Dan 3:12	
because *t* is no other God that	Dan 3:29	
t fell a voice from heaven,	Dan 4:31	
T is a man in thy kingdom, in	Dan 5:11	
neither was *t* any error or fault	Dan 6:4	
t came up among them another	Dan 7:8	
before whom *t* were three of the	Dan 7:8	
t was given him dominion, and	Dan 7:14	
t stood before the river a ram	Dan 8:3	
neither was *t* any that could	Dan 8:4	
t was no power in the ram to	Dan 8:7	
t was none that could deliver the	Dan 8:7	
behold, *t* stood before me as the	Dan 8:15	
t remained no strength in me	Dan 10:8	
I remained *t* with the kings of	Dan 10:13	8033
straightway *t* remained no	Dan 10:17	
neither is *t* breath left in me	Dan 10:17	
Then *t* came again and touched me	Dan 10:18	
t is none that holdeth with me in	Dan 10:21	
t shall stand up yet three kings	Dan 11:2	
in those times *t* shall many stand	Dan 11:14	
neither shall *t* be any strength	Dan 11:15	
t shall be a time of trouble,	Dan 12:1	
such as never was since *t* was a	Dan 12:1	
t stood other two, the one on	Dan 12:5	
t shall be a thousand two hundred	Dan 12:11	
t it shall be said unto them, Ye	Hos 1:10	
and she shall sing *t*, as in the	Hos 2:15	8033
because *t* is no truth, nor mercy,	Hos 4:1	
t shall be, like people, like	Hos 4:9	
t have they dealt treacherously	Hos 6:7	8033
t is the whoredom of Ephraim,	Hos 6:10	8033
t is none among them that calleth	Hos 7:7	
t upon him, yet he knoweth not	Hos 7:9	
that *t* shall not be a man left	Hos 9:12	
for *t* I hated them	Hos 9:15	8033
t they stood	Hos 10:9	8033
in Beth-el, and *t* he spake with us	Hos 12:4	8033
Is *t* iniquity in Gilead	Hos 12:11	
for *t* is no saviour beside me	Hos 13:4	
t will I devour them like a lion	Hos 13:8	8033
t hath not been ever the like,	Joel 2:2	
plead with them *t* for my people	Joel 3:2	8033
for *t* will I sit to judge all the	Joel 3:12	8033
t shall no strangers pass through	Joel 3:17	
shall *t* be evil in a city, and the	Amos 3:6	
An adversary *t* shall be even	Amos 3:11	
when *t* were yet three months to	Amos 4:7	
t is none to raise her up	Amos 5:2	
t be none to quench it in Beth-el	Amos 5:6	
if *t* remain ten men in one house,	Amos 6:9	
the house, Is *t* yet any with thee	Amos 6:10	
will one plow *t* with oxen	Amos 6:12	
t eat bread, and prophesy *t*	Amos 7:12	8033
t shall be many dead bodies in	Amos 8:3	
t is none understanding in him	Obad 7	
and *t* shall be holiness	Obad 17	
t shall not be any remaining of	Obad 18	
t was a mighty tempest in the sea	Jonah 1:4	
t made him a booth, and sat under	Jonah 4:5	8033
for *t* is no answer of God	Mic 3:7	
is *t* no king in thee	Mic 4:9	
t shalt thou be delivered	Mic 4:10	
t the LORD shall redeem thee from	Mic 4:10	8033
Are *t* yet the treasures of	Mic 6:10	
t is no cluster to eat	Mic 7:1	
t is none upright among men	Mic 7:2	
T is one come out of thee, that	Nah 1:11	
for *t* is none end of the store and	Nah 2:9	
t is a multitude of slain, and a	Nah 3:3	
t is none end of their corpses	Nah 3:3	
T shall the fire devour thee	Nah 3:15	8033
T is no healing of thy bruise	Nah 3:19	
t are that raise up strife and	Hab 1:3	
t is no breath at all in the	Hab 2:19	
t was the hiding of his power	Hab 3:4	8033
t shall be no herd in the stalls	Hab 3:17	
that *t* shall be the noise of a	Zeph 1:10	
mighty man shall cry *t* bitterly	Zeph 1:14	8033
that *t* shall be no inhabitant	Zeph 2:5	
I am, and *t* is none beside me	Zeph 2:15	
so that *t* is no man	Zeph 3:6	
that *t* is none inhabitant	Zeph 3:6	
ye clothe you, but *t* is none warm	Hag 1:6	
which they offer *t* is unclean	Hag 2:14	8033
twenty measures, *t* were but ten	Hag 2:16	
of the press, *t* were but twenty	Hag 2:16	
and behind him were *t* red horses	Zec 1:8	
t was lifted up a talent of lead	Zec 5:7	
t came out two women, and the wind	Zec 5:9	
and set *t* upon her own base	Zec 5:11	8033
t came four chariots out from	Zec 6:1	
T shall yet old men and old women	Zec 8:4	
these days *t* was no hire for man	Zec 8:10	
neither was *t* any peace to him	Zec 8:10	
that *t* shall come people, and the	Zec 8:20	
because *t* was no shepherd	Zec 10:2	
T is a voice of the howling of	Zec 11:3	
In that day shall *t* be a great	Zec 12:11	
In that day *t* shall be a fountain	Zec 13:1	
t shall be a very great valley	Zec 14:4	
in that day shall *t* be one LORD	Zec 14:9	
it, and *t* shall be no more utter	Zec 14:11	
t shall be the plague, wherewith	Zec 14:18	
In that day shall *t* be upon the	Zec 14:20	
in that day *t* shall be no more	Zec 14:21	
Who is *t* even among you that	Mal 1:10	
that *t* may be meat in mine house,	Mal 3:10	
that *t* shall not be room enough	Mal 3:10	
t came wise men from the east to	Mt 2:1	
be thou *t* until I bring thee word	Mt 2:13	*1563*
was *t* until the death of Herod	Mt 2:15	*1563*
In Rama was *t* a voice heard,	Mt 2:18	
t followed him great multitudes	Mt 4:25	
t rememberest that thy brother	Mt 5:23	*1563*
Leave *t* thy gift before the altar	Mt 5:24	*1563*
t will your heart be also	Mt 6:21	*1563*
Or what man is *t* of you, whom if	Mt 7:9	
many *t* be which go in thereat	Mt 7:13	
life, and few *t* be that find it	Mt 7:14	
t came a leper and worshipped him,	Mt 8:2	
t came unto him a centurion,	Mt 8:5	
t shall be weeping and gnashing of	Mt 8:12	*1563*
t arose a great tempest in the	Mt 8:24	
and *t* was a great calm	Mt 8:26	
t met him two possessed with	Mt 8:28	
t was a good way off from them an	Mt 8:30	
t came a certain ruler, and	Mt 9:18	*1563*
t abide till ye go thence	Mt 10:11	*1563*
for *t* is nothing covered, that	Mt 10:26	
them that are born of women *t*	Mt 11:11	
t was a man which had his hand	Mt 12:10	
What man shall *t* be among you	Mt 12:11	
t shall no sign be given to it,	Mt 12:39	
and they enter in and dwell *t*	Mt 12:45	*1563*
t shall be wailing and gnashing of	Mt 13:42	*1563*
t shall be wailing and gnashing of	Mt 13:50	*1563*
works *t* because of their unbelief	Mt 13:58	*1563*
evening was come, he was *t* alone	Mt 14:23	*1563*
up into a mountain, and sat down *t*	Mt 15:29	*1563*
t shall no sign be given unto it,	Mt 16:4	
T be some standing here, which	Mt 16:28	
t appeared unto them Moses and	Mt 17:3	
t came to him a certain man,	Mt 17:14	
t am I in the midst of them	Mt 18:20	*1563*
and he healed them *t*	Mt 19:2	*1563*
For *t* are some eunuchs, which	Mt 19:12	
t are some eunuchs, which were	Mt 19:12	
t be eunuchs, which have made	Mt 19:12	
Then were *t* brought unto him	Mt 19:13	
t is none good but one, that is,	Mt 19:17	
and he lodged *t*	Mt 21:17	*1563*
T was a certain householder,	Mt 21:33	
he saw *t* a man which had not on a	Mt 22:11	*1563*
t shall be weeping and gnashing of	Mt 22:13	*1563*
Sadducees, which say that *t* is no	Mt 22:23	
Now *t* were with us seven brethren	Mt 22:25	
T shall not be left here one	Mt 24:2	
and *t* shall be famines, and	Mt 24:7	
t should no flesh be saved	Mt 24:22	
you, Lo, here is Christ, or *t*	Mt 24:23	*5602*
For *t* shall arise false Christs,	Mt 24:24	
t will the eagles be gathered	Mt 24:28	*1563*
t shall be weeping and gnashing of	Mt 24:51	*1563*
at midnight *t* was a cry made,	Mt 25:6	
lest *t* be not enough for us and	Mt 25:9	
t thou hast that is thine	Mt 25:25	
t shall be weeping and gnashing of	Mt 25:30	*1563*
lest *t* be an uproar among the	Mt 26:5	
T came unto him a woman having an	Mt 26:7	
t shall also this, that this	Mt 26:13	
and said unto them that were *t*	Mt 26:71	*1563*
sitting down they watched him *t*	Mt 27:36	*1563*
Then were *t* two thieves crucified	Mt 27:38	
Now from the sixth hour *t* was	Mt 27:45	
Some of them that stood *t*	Mt 27:47	*1563*

many women were *t* beholding afar Mt 27:55 1563
t came a rich man of Arimathaea, Mt 27:57
t was Mary Magdalene, and the Mt 27:61 1563
behold, *t* was a great earthquake Mt 28:2
t shall ye see him Mt 28:7 1563
Galilee, and *t* shall they see me Mt 28:10 1563
t went out unto him all the land Mk 1:5
T cometh one mightier than I Mk 1:7
t came a voice from heaven, Mk 1:11
he was *t* in the wilderness forty Mk 1:13 1563
t was in their synagogue a man Mk 1:23
a solitary place, and *t* prayed Mk 1:35 1563
towns, that I may preach *t* also Mk 1:38 1563
t came a leper to him, beseeching Mk 1:40
insomuch that *t* was no room to Mk 2:2
But *t* were certain of the scribes Mk 2:6
certain of the scribes sitting *t* Mk 2:6 1563
for *t* were many, and they followed Mk 2:15
t was a man *t* which had a Mk 3:1 1563
T came then his brethren and his Mk 3:31
t was gathered unto him a great Mk 4:1
t went out a sower to sow Mk 4:3
For *t* is nothing hid, which shall Mk 4:22
t were also with him other little Mk 4:36
t arose a great storm of wind, and Mk 4:37
ceased, and *t* was a great calm Mk 4:39
immediately *t* met him out of the Mk 5:2
Now *t* was *t* nigh unto the Mk 5:11 1563
t cometh one of the rulers of the Mk 5:22
t came from the ruler of the Mk 5:35
he could *t* do no mighty work, Mk 6:5 1563
t abide till ye depart from that Mk 6:10 1563
for *t* were many coming and going, Mk 6:31
And many other things *t* be Mk 7:4
T is nothing from without a man, Mk 7:15
T shall no sign be given unto Mk 8:12
That *t* be some of them that stand Mk 9:1
t appeared unto them Elias with Mk 9:4
t was a cloud that overshadowed Mk 9:7
for *t* is no man which shall do a Mk 9:39
t came one running, and kneeled to Mk 10:17
t is none good but one, that is, Mk 10:18
T is no man that hath left house, Mk 10:29
them that stood *t* said unto them Mk 11:5 1563
t come to him the chief priests, Mk 11:27
which say *t* is no resurrection Mk 12:18
Now *t* were seven brethren Mk 12:20
T is none other commandment Mk 12:31
for *t* is one God Mk 12:32
and *t* is none other but he Mk 12:32
t came a certain poor widow, and Mk 12:42
t shall not be left one stone Mk 13:2
t shall be earthquakes in divers Mk 13:8
t shall be famines and troubles Mk 13:8
or, lo, he is *t* Mk 13:21 1563
lest *t* be an uproar of the people Mk 14:2
at meat, *t* came a woman having an Mk 14:3
t were some that had indignation Mk 14:4
t shall meet you a man bearing a Mk 14:13
t make ready for us Mk 14:15 1563
t followed him a certain young Mk 14:51
t arose certain, and bare false Mk 14:57
t cometh one of the maids of the Mk 14:66
t was one named Barabbas, which Mk 15:7
t was darkness over the whole Mk 15:33
T were also women looking on afar Mk 15:40
t shall ye see him, as he said Mk 16:7 1563
T was in the days of Herod, the Lk 1:5
t appeared unto him an angel of Lk 1:11
of his kingdom *t* shall be no end Lk 1:33
for *t* shall be a performance of Lk 1:45
T is none of thy kindred that is Lk 1:61
that *t* went out a decree from Lk 2:1
it was, that, while they were *t* Lk 2:6 1563
because *t* was no room for them in Lk 2:7
t were in the same country Lk 2:8
suddenly *t* was with the angel a Lk 2:13
t was a man in Jerusalem, whose Lk 2:25
t was one Anna, a prophetess, the Lk 2:36
t went out a fame of him through Lk 4:14
t was delivered unto him the book Lk 4:17
And in the synagogue *t* was a man Lk 4:33
more went *t* a fame abroad of him Lk 5:15
that *t* were Pharisees and doctors Lk 5:17
and *t* was a great company of Lk 5:29
t was a man whose right hand was Lk 6:6 1563
for *t* went virtue out of him, and Lk 6:19
t was a dead man carried out, the Lk 7:12
And *t* came a fear on all Lk 7:16
those that are born of women *t* is Lk 7:28
T was a certain creditor which Lk 7:41
t came down a storm of wind on Lk 8:23
and they ceased, and *t* was a calm Lk 8:24
t met him out of the city a Lk 8:27
t was *t* an herd of many swine Lk 8:32 1563
t came a man named Jairus, and he Lk 8:41
t cometh one from the ruler of Lk 8:49
t abide, and thence depart Lk 9:4 1563
t was taken up of fragments that Lk 9:17
t be some standing here, which Lk 9:27
t talked with him two men, which Lk 9:30
t came a cloud, and overshadowed Lk 9:34
t came a voice out of the cloud, Lk 9:35
Then *t* arose a reasoning among Lk 9:46
And if the son of peace be *t* Lk 10:6 1563
by chance *t* came down a certain Lk 10:31
and they enter in, and dwell *t* Lk 11:26 1563
t shall no sign be given it, but Lk 11:29
when *t* were gathered together an Lk 12:1
For *t* is nothing covered, that Lk 12:2
t will I bestow all my fruits and Lk 12:18 1563
t will your heart be also Lk 12:34 1563
For from henceforth *t* shall be Lk 12:52
ye say, *T* cometh a shower Lk 12:54

wind blow, ye say, *T* will be heat Lk 12:55
T were present at that season Lk 13:1
t was a woman which had a spirit Lk 13:11
T are six days in which men ought Lk 13:14
Lord, are *t* few that be saved Lk 13:23
T shall be weeping and gnashing of Lk 13:28 1563
t are last which shall be first, Lk 13:30
t are first which shall be last Lk 13:30
The same day *t* came certain of Lk 13:31
t was a certain man before him Lk 14:2
hast commanded, and yet *t* is room Lk 14:22
t went great multitudes with him Lk 14:25
t is joy in the presence of the Lk 15:10
t wasted his substance with Lk 15:13 1563
t arose a mighty famine in that Lk 15:14
T was a certain rich man, which Lk 16:1
T was a certain rich man, which Lk 16:19
t was a certain beggar named Lk 16:20
you *t* is a great gulf fixed Lk 16:26
t met him ten men that were Lk 17:12
said, Were *t* not ten cleansed Lk 17:17
T are not found that returned to Lk 17:18
Lo here! or, lo *t*! Lk 17:21 1563
See here; or, see *t* Lk 17:23 1563
in that night *t* shall be two men Lk 17:34
T was in a city a judge, which Lk 18:2
t was a widow in that city Lk 18:3
T is no man that hath left house, Lk 18:29
t was a man named Zacchaeus, Lk 19:2
which deny that *t* is any Lk 20:27
T were therefore seven brethren Lk 20:29
in the which *t* shall not be left Lk 21:6
what sign will *t* be when these Lk 21:7
signs shall *t* be from heaven Lk 21:11
But *t* shall not an hair of your Lk 21:18
for *t* shall be great distress in Lk 21:23
t shall be signs in the sun, and Lk 21:25
t shall a man meet you, bearing a Lk 22:10
t make ready Lk 22:12 1563
t was also a strife among them, Lk 22:24
t appeared an angel unto him from Lk 22:43
t followed him a great company of Lk 23:27
And *t* were also two others, Lk 23:32
t they crucified him, and the Lk 23:33 1563
t was a darkness over all the Lk 23:44
t was a man named Joseph, a Lk 23:50
are come to pass *t* in these days Lk 24:18
T was a man sent from God, whose Jn 1:6
but *t* standeth one among you, Jn 1:26
Can *t* any good thing come out of Jn 1:46
the third day *t* was a marriage in Jn 2:1
and the mother of Jesus was *t* Jn 2:1 1563
t were set *t* six waterpots of Jn 2:6 1563
and they continued *t* not many days Jn 2:12 1563
T was a man of the Pharisees, Jn 3:1
t he tarried with them, and Jn 3:22 1563
because *t* was much water *t* Jn 3:23 1563
Then *t* arose a question between Jn 3:25
Now Jacob's well was *t* Jn 4:6 1563
T cometh a woman of Samaria to Jn 4:7
T are yet four months, and then Jn 4:35
and he abode *t* two days Jn 4:40 1563
t was a certain nobleman, whose Jn 4:46
After this *t* was a feast of the Jn 5:1
Now *t* is at Jerusalem by the Jn 5:2
And a certain man was *t*, which had Jn 5:5 1563
T is another that beareth witness Jn 5:32
t is one that accuseth you, even Jn 5:45
t he sat with his disciples Jn 6:3 1563
T is a lad here, which hath five Jn 6:9
Now *t* was much grass in the place Jn 6:10
that *t* was none other boat *t* Jn 6:22 1563
(Howbeit *t* came other boats from Jn 6:23
saw that Jesus was not *t*, neither Jn 6:24 1563
But *t* are some of you that Jn 6:64
For *t* is no man that doeth any Jn 7:4
t was much murmuring among the Jn 7:12
So *t* was a division among the Jn 7:43
because *t* is no truth in him Jn 8:44
t is one that seeketh and judgeth Jn 8:50
t was a division among them Jn 9:16
t shall be one fold, and one Jn 10:16
T was a division therefore again Jn 10:19
and *t* he abode Jn 10:40 1563
And many believed on him *t* Jn 10:42 1563
Are *t* not twelve hours in the day Jn 11:9
because *t* is no light in him Jn 11:10
for your sakes that I was not *t* Jn 11:15 1563
goeth unto the grave to weep *t* Jn 11:31 1563
t continued with his disciples Jn 11:54 1563
T they made him a supper Jn 12:2 1563
Jews therefore knew that he was *t* Jn 12:9 1563
t were certain Greeks among them Jn 12:20
t shall also my servant be Jn 12:26 1563
Then came *t* a voice from heaven, Jn 12:28
Now *t* was leaning on Jesus' bosom Jn 13:23
that where I am, *t* ye may be also Jn 14:3
the servants and officers stood *t* Jn 18:18
Now *t* stood by the cross of Jesus Jn 19:25
Now *t* was set a vessel full of Jn 19:29
and forthwith came *t* out blood Jn 19:34
t came also Nicodemus, which at Jn 19:39
he was crucified *t* was a garden Jn 19:41
T laid they Jesus therefore Jn 19:42 1563
T were together Simon Peter, and Jn 21:2
land, they saw a fire of coals *t* Jn 21:9
for all *t* were so many, yet was Jn 21:11
t are also many other things Jn 21:25
suddenly *t* came a sound from Acts 2:2
t appeared unto them cloven Acts 2:3
t were dwelling at Jerusalem Jews Acts 2:5
the same day *t* were added unto Acts 2:41
Neither is *t* salvation in any Acts 4:12
for *t* is none other name under Acts 4:12

Neither was *t* any among them that Acts 4:34
T came also a multitude out of Acts 5:16
Then stood *t* up one in the Acts 5:34
t arose a murmuring of the Acts 6:1
Then *t* arose certain of the Acts 6:9
Now *t* came a dearth over all the Acts 7:11
heard that *t* was corn in Egypt Acts 7:12
expired, *t* appeared to him in the Acts 7:30
at that time *t* was a great Acts 8:1
t was great joy in that city Acts 8:8
But *t* was a certain man, called Acts 8:9
suddenly *t* shined round about him Acts 9:3
t was a certain disciple at Acts 9:10
immediately *t* fell from his eyes Acts 9:18
t he found a certain man named Acts 9:33 1563
Now *t* was at Joppa a certain Acts 9:36
had heard that Peter was *t* Acts 9:38
T was a certain man in Caesarea Acts 10:1
t came a voice to him, Rise, Acts 10:13
was surnamed Peter, were lodged *t* Acts 10:18 1759
immediately *t* were three men Acts 11:11
t stood up one of them named Acts 11:28
that *t* should be great dearth Acts 11:28
t was no small stir among the Acts 12:18
Judaea to Caesarea, and *t* abode Acts 12:19
Now *t* were in the church that was Acts 13:1
immediately *t* fell on him a mist Acts 13:11
t cometh one after me, whose Acts 13:25
when *t* was an assault made both Acts 14:5
t they preached the gospel Acts 14:7 1563
t sat a certain man at Lystra, Acts 14:8
t came thither certain Jews from Acts 14:19
t they abode long time with the Acts 14:28 1563
But *t* rose up certain of the sect Acts 15:5
when *t* had been much disputing, Acts 15:7
after they had tarried *t* a space Acts 15:33
it pleased Silas to abide *t* still Acts 15:34 847
behold, a certain disciple was *t* Acts 16:1 1563
T stood a man of Macedonia, and Acts 16:9
come into my house, and abide *t* Acts 16:15
suddenly *t* was a great earthquake Acts 16:26
saying that *t* is another king, Acts 17:7
Silas and Timotheus abode *t* still Acts 17:14 1563
strangers which were *t* spent Acts 17:21 1927
And he continued *t* a year and six Acts 18:11
this tarried *t* yet a good while Acts 18:18
came to Ephesus, and left them *t* Acts 18:19 847
And after he had spent some time *t* Acts 18:23
heard whether *t* be any Holy Ghost Acts 19:2
t were seven sons of one Sceva, a Acts 19:14
saying, After I have been *t* Acts 19:21 1563
the same time *t* arose no small Acts 19:23
what man is *t* that knoweth not Acts 19:35
law is open, and *t* are deputies Acts 19:38
t being no cause whereby we may Acts 19:40
And *t* abode three months Acts 20:3
t accompanied him into Asia Acts 20:4
t were many lights in the upper Acts 20:8
t sat in a window a certain young Acts 20:9
t intending to take in Paul Acts 20:13 1564
the things that shall befall me *t* Acts 20:22
for *t* the ship was to unlade her Acts 21:3 1566
we tarried *t* seven days Acts 21:4 847
And as we tarried *t* many days Acts 21:10
t came down from Judaea a certain Acts 21:10
T went with us also certain of Acts 21:16
of Jews *t* are which believe Acts 21:20
when *t* was made a great silence, Acts 21:40
which were *t* bound unto Jerusalem Acts 22:5 1566
suddenly *t* shone from heaven a Acts 22:6
t it shall be told thee of all Acts 22:10 1563
of all the Jews which dwelt *t* Acts 22:12
t arose a dissension between the Acts 23:7
say that *t* is no resurrection Acts 23:8
And *t* arose a great cry Acts 23:9
when *t* arose a great dissension, Acts 23:10
for *t* lie in wait for him of them Acts 23:21
that *t* are yet but twelve days Acts 24:11
that *t* shall be a resurrection of Acts 24:15
if *t* be any wickedness in him Acts 25:5
t be judged of these things Acts 25:9 1563
but if *t* be none of these things Acts 25:11
And when they had been *t* many days Acts 25:14 1563
T is a certain man left in bonds Acts 25:14
t be judged of these matters Acts 25:20 1563
t the centurion found a ship of Acts 27:6 1563
attain to Phenice, and *t* to winter Acts 27:12
But not long after *t* arose Acts 27:14
for *t* shall be no loss of any Acts 27:22
For *t* stood by me this night the Acts 27:23
for *t* shall not an hair fall from Acts 27:34
t came a viper out of the heat, Acts 28:3
Syracuse, we tarried *t* three days Acts 28:12
because *t* was no cause of death Acts 28:18
t came many to him into his Acts 28:23
For *t* is no respect of persons Rom 2:11
what profit is *t* of circumcision Rom 3:1
T is none righteous, no, not one Rom 3:10
T is none that understandeth, Rom 3:11
t is none that seeketh after God Rom 3:11
t is none that doeth good, no, Rom 3:12
T is no fear of God before their Rom 3:18
by the deeds of the law *t* shall Rom 3:20
for *t* is no difference Rom 3:22
no law is, *t* is no transgression Rom 4:15
is not imputed when *t* is no law Rom 5:13
T is therefore now no Rom 8:1
Is *t* unrighteousness with God Rom 9:14
t shall they be called the Rom 9:26 1563
For *t* is no difference between Rom 10:12
t is a remnant according to the Rom 11:5
T shall come out of Sion the Rom 11:26
For *t* is no power but of God Rom 13:1 1563
if *t* be any other commandment, it Rom 13:9

that *t* is nothing unclean of ... Rom 14:14
T shall be a root of Jesse, and he ... Rom 15:12
that *t* be no divisions among you ... 1Cor 1:10
that *t* are contentions among you ... 1Cor 1:11
for whereas *t* is among you ... 1Cor 3:3
that *t* is fornication among you ... 1Cor 5:1
that *t* is not a wise man among ... 1Cor 6:5
Now therefore *t* is utterly a ... 1Cor 6:7
T is difference also between a ... 1Cor 7:34
that *t* is none other God but one ... 1Cor 8:4
For though *t* be that are called ... 1Cor 8:5
(as *t* be gods many, and lords many ... 1Cor 8:5
But to us *t* is but one God, the ... 1Cor 8:6
Howbeit *t* is not in every man ... 1Cor 8:7
T hath no temptation taken you ... 1Cor 10:13
I hear that *t* be divisions among ... 1Cor 11:18
For *t* must be also heresies among ... 1Cor 11:19
Now *t* are diversities of gifts, ... 1Cor 12:4
And *t* are differences of ... 1Cor 12:5
t are diversities of operations, ... 1Cor 12:6
That *t* should be no schism in the ... 1Cor 12:25
but whether *t* be prophecies, they ... 1Cor 13:8
whether *t* be tongues, they shall ... 1Cor 13:8
whether *t* be knowledge, it shall ... 1Cor 13:8
T are, it may be, so many kinds ... 1Cor 14:10
and *t* come in those that are ... 1Cor 14:23
t come in one that believeth not, ... 1Cor 14:24
But if *t* be no interpreter, let ... 1Cor 14:28
how say some among you that *t* is ... 1Cor 15:12
But if *t* be no resurrection of ... 1Cor 15:13
but *t* is one kind of flesh of men ... 1Cor 15:39
T are also celestial bodies, and ... 1Cor 15:40
T is one glory of the sun, and ... 1Cor 15:41
T is a natural body ... 1Cor 15:44
and *t* is a spiritual body ... 1Cor 15:44
that *t* be no gatherings when I ... 1Cor 16:2
me, and *t* are many adversaries ... 1Cor 16:9
that with me *t* should be yea yea, ... 2Cor 1:17
of the Lord is, *t* is liberty ... 2Cor 3:17 *1563*
that as *t* was a readiness to will ... 2Cor 8:11
so *t* may be a performance also ... 2Cor 8:11
For if *t* be first a willing mind, ... 2Cor 8:12
that *t* may be equality ... 2Cor 8:14
t was given to me a thorn in the ... 2Cor 12:7
lest *t* be debates, envyings, ... 2Cor 12:20
but *t* be some that trouble you, ... Gal 1:7
for if *t* had been a law given ... Gal 3:21
T is neither Jew nor Greek ... Gal 3:28
t is neither bond nor free ... Gal 3:28
t is neither male nor female ... Gal 3:28
against such *t* is no law ... Gal 5:23
T is one body, and one Spirit, ... Eph 4:4
neither is *t* respect of persons ... Eph 6:9
If *t* be therefore any consolation ... Phil 2:1
if *t* be any virtue ... Phil 4:8
if *t* be any praise, think on ... Phil 4:8
Where *t* is neither Greek nor Jew, ... Col 3:11
t is no respect of persons ... Col 3:25
except *t* come a falling away ... 2Th 2:3
For we hear that *t* are some which ... 2Th 3:11
if *t* be any other thing that is ... 1Ti 1:10
For *t* is one God, and one mediator ... 1Ti 2:5
But in a great house *t* are not ... 2Ti 2:20
Henceforth *t* is laid up for me a ... 2Ti 4:8
For *t* are many unruly and vain ... Titus 1:10
for I have determined *t* to winter ... Titus 3:12 *1563*
T salute thee Epaphras, my ... Philem 23
lest *t* be in any of you an evil ... Heb 3:12
T remaineth therefore a rest to ... Heb 4:9
Neither is *t* any creature that is ... Heb 4:13
but *t* he receiveth them, of whom ... Heb 7:8 *1563*
what further need was *t* that ... Heb 7:11
t is made of necessity a change ... Heb 7:12
t ariseth another priest, ... Heb 7:15
For *t* is verily a disannulling of ... Heb 7:18
seeing that *t* are priests that ... Heb 8:4
For *t* was a tabernacle made ... Heb 9:2
t must also of necessity be the ... Heb 9:16
But in those sacrifices *t* is a ... Heb 10:3
t is no more offering for sin ... Heb 10:18
t remaineth no more sacrifice for ... Heb 10:26
Therefore sprang *t* even of one ... Heb 11:12
Lest *t* be any fornicator, or ... Heb 12:16
For if *t* come unto your assembly ... Jas 2:2
t come in also a poor man in vile ... Jas 2:2
and say to the poor, Stand thou *t* ... Jas 2:3 *1563*
Thou believest that *t* is one God ... Jas 2:19
t is confusion and every evil work ... Jas 3:16 *1563*
T is one lawgiver, who is able to ... Jas 4:12
such a city, and continue *t* a year ... Jas 4:13 *1563*
when *t* came such a voice to him ... 2Pet 1:17
But *t* were false prophets also ... 2Pet 2:1
even as *t* shall be false teachers ... 2Pet 2:1
that *t* shall come in the last ... 2Pet 3:3
t is none occasion of stumbling ... 1Jn 2:10
even now are *t* many antichrists ... 1Jn 2:18
T is no fear in love ... 1Jn 4:18
For *t* are three that bear record ... 1Jn 5:7
t are three that bear witness in ... 1Jn 5:8
T is a sin unto death ... 1Jn 5:16
t is a sin not unto death ... 1Jn 5:17
If *t* come any unto you, and bring ... 2Jn 10
For *t* are certain men crept in ... Jude 4
How that they told you *t* should ... Jude 18
because thou hast *t* them that ... Rev 2:14 *1563*
t was a rainbow round about the ... Rev 4:3
t were seven lamps of fire ... Rev 4:5
before the throne *t* was a sea of ... Rev 4:6
t went out another horse that was ... Rev 6:4
t was given unto him a great ... Rev 6:4
and, lo, *t* was a great earthquake ... Rev 6:12
t were sealed an hundred and forty ... Rev 7:4
t was silence in heaven about the ... Rev 8:1
t was given unto him much incense ... Rev 8:3
t were voices, and thunderings, and ... Rev 8:5
t followed hail and fire mingled ... Rev 8:7
t fell a great star from heaven, ... Rev 8:10
t arose a smoke out of the pit, ... Rev 9:2
t came out of the smoke locusts ... Rev 9:3
t were stings in their tails ... Rev 9:10
t come two woes more hereafter ... Rev 9:12
that *t* should be time no longer ... Rev 10:6
t was given me a reed like unto a ... Rev 11:1
the same hour was *t* a great ... Rev 11:13
t were great voices in heaven, ... Rev 11:15
t was seen in his temple the ark ... Rev 11:19
t were lightnings, and voices, and ... Rev 11:19
t appeared a great wonder in ... Rev 12:1
t appeared another wonder in ... Rev 12:3
feed her *t* a thousand two hundred ... Rev 12:6 *1563*
And *t* was war in heaven ... Rev 12:7
t was given unto him a mouth ... Rev 13:5
t followed another angel, saying, ... Rev 14:8
t fell a noisome and grievous sore ... Rev 16:2
t came a great voice out of the ... Rev 16:17
t were voices, and thunders, and ... Rev 16:18
t was a great earthquake, such as ... Rev 16:18
t fell upon men a great hail out ... Rev 16:21
t came one of the seven angels ... Rev 17:1
And *t* are seven kings ... Rev 17:10
t was found no place for them ... Rev 20:11
and *t* was no more sea ... Rev 21:1
t shall be no more death, neither ... Rev 21:4
neither shall *t* be any more pain ... Rev 21:4
t came unto me one of the seven ... Rev 21:9
for *t* shall be no night *t* ... Rev 21:25 *1563*
t shall in no wise enter into it ... Rev 21:27
was *t* the tree of life, which ... Rev 22:2
And *t* shall be no more curse ... Rev 22:3
And *t* shall be no night *t* ... Rev 22:5 *1563*

THEREABOUT
as they were much perplexed *t* ... Lk 24:4

THEREAT
wash their hands and their feet *t* ... Ex 30:19
their hands and their feet *t* ... Ex 40:31
and many there be which go in *t* ... Mt 7:13

THEREBY
t shall I know that thou hast ... Gen 24:14 2004
them, that ye should be defiled *t* ... Lev 11:43
t good shall come unto thee ... Job 22:21
is deceived *t* is not wise ... Prov 20:1
wood shall be endangered *t* ... Eccl 10:9
neither shall gallant ship pass *t* ... Is 33:21
passeth *t* shall be astonished ... Jer 18:16 5921
passeth *t* shall be astonished ... Jer 19:8 5921
doth any son of man pass *t* ... Jer 51:43 2004
in their sight, and carry out *t* ... Eze 12:5
through the wall to carry out *t* ... Eze 12:12
he shall not fall *t* in the day ... Eze 33:12
iniquity, he shall even die *t* ... Eze 33:18
lawful and right, he shall live *t* ... Eze 33:19
And Hamath also shall border *t* ... Zec 9:2
Son of God might be glorified *t* ... Jn 11:4
cross, having slain the enmity *t* ... Eph 2:16
unto them which are exercised *t* ... Heb 12:11
trouble you, and *t* many be defiled ... Heb 12:15
for *t* some have entertained ... Heb 13:2
of the word, that ye may grow *t* ... 1Pet 2:2

THEREFORE
T shall a man leave his father and ... Gen 2:24
T the LORD God sent him forth ... Gen 3:23
T whosoever slayeth Cain, ... Gen 4:15 *3767*
T is the name of it called Babel ... Gen 11:9
T it shall come to pass, when the ... Gen 12:12
now *t* behold thy wife, take her, ... Gen 12:19
Thou shalt keep my covenant *t* ... Gen 17:9
for *t* are ye come to your servant ... Gen 18:5
T Sarah laughed within herself, ... Gen 18:12
for *t* came they under the shadow ... Gen 19:8
T the name of the city was called ... Gen 19:22
t suffered I thee not to touch ... Gen 20:6
Now *t* restore the man his wife ... Gen 20:7
T Abimelech rose early in the ... Gen 20:8
Now *t* swear unto me here by God ... Gen 21:23
bury *t* thy dead ... Gen 23:15
t she took a vail, and covered ... Gen 24:65
t was his name called Edom ... Gen 25:30
t the name of the city is ... Gen 26:33
Now *t* take, I pray thee, thy ... Gen 27:3
Now *t*, my son, obey my voice ... Gen 27:8
T God give thee of the dew of ... Gen 27:28
Now *t*, my son, obey my voice ... Gen 27:43
shouldest thou *t* serve me for ... Gen 29:15
now *t* my husband will love me ... Gen 29:32 3588
he hath *t* given me this son also ... Gen 29:33 1571
t was his name called Levi ... Gen 29:34
t she called his name Judah ... Gen 29:35
t called she his name Dan ... Gen 30:6
T he shall lie with thee to night ... Gen 30:15 3651
Now *t* come thou, let us make a ... Gen 31:44
T was the name of it called ... Gen 31:48
T the children of Israel eat not ... Gen 32:32
for *t* I have seen thy face, as ... Gen 33:10
t the name of the place is called ... Gen 33:17
t let them dwell in the land, and ... Gen 34:21
Come now *t*, and let us slay him, ... Gen 37:20
t his name was called Pharez ... Gen 38:29
Now *t* let Pharaoh look out a man ... Gen 41:33
t is this distress come upon us ... Gen 42:21
t, behold, also his blood is ... Gen 42:22 1571
Now *t* when I come to thy servant ... Gen 44:30
Now *t*, I pray thee, let thy ... Gen 44:33
Now *t* be not grieved, nor angry ... Gen 45:5
now *t*, we pray thee, let thy ... Gen 47:4
Now *t* let me go up, I pray thee, ... Gen 50:5
Now *t* fear ye not ... Gen 50:21
T they did set over them ... Ex 1:11
T God dealt well with the ... Ex 1:20
Now *t*, behold, the cry of the ... Ex 3:9
Come now *t*, and I will send thee ... Ex 3:10
Now *t* go, and I will be with thy ... Ex 4:12
t they cry, saying, Let us go and ... Ex 5:8
t ye say, Let us go and do ... Ex 5:17
Go *t* now, and work ... Ex 5:18
Send *t* now, and gather thy cattle, ... Ex 9:19
Now *t* forgive, I pray thee, my ... Ex 10:17
t shall ye observe this day in ... Ex 12:17
Thou shalt *t* keep this ordinance ... Ex 13:10
t I sacrifice to the LORD all ... Ex 13:15
t the name of it was called Marah ... Ex 15:23
t he giveth you on the sixth day ... Ex 16:29
Now *t*, if ye will obey my voice ... Ex 19:5
Ye shall keep the sabbath *t* ... Ex 31:14
Now *t* let me alone, that my wrath ... Ex 32:10
T now go, lead the people unto ... Ex 32:34
t now put off thy ornaments from ... Ex 33:5
Now *t*, I pray thee, if I have ... Ex 33:13
T shall ye abide at the door of ... Lev 8:35
Aaron *t* went unto the altar, and ... Lev 9:8
ye shall *t* sanctify yourselves, ... Lev 11:44
ye shall *t* be holy, for I am holy ... Lev 11:45
He shall *t* burn that garment, ... Lev 13:52
t shall he wash his flesh in ... Lev 16:4
T I said unto the children of ... Lev 17:12
t I said unto the children of ... Lev 17:14
Ye shall *t* keep my statutes, and ... Lev 18:5
t I do visit the iniquity thereof ... Lev 18:25
Ye shall *t* keep my statutes and my ... Lev 18:26
T shall ye keep mine ordinance, ... Lev 18:30
T every one that eateth it shall ... Lev 19:8
T shall ye observe all my ... Lev 19:37
Sanctify yourselves *t*, and be ye ... Lev 20:7
Ye shall *t* keep all my statutes, ... Lev 20:22
things, and *t* I abhorred them ... Lev 20:23
Ye shall *t* put difference between ... Lev 20:25
t they shall be holy ... Lev 21:6
Thou shalt sanctify him *t* ... Lev 21:8
They shall *t* keep mine ordinance, ... Lev 22:9
they bear sin for it, and die *t* ... Lev 22:9
T shall ye keep my commandments, ... Lev 22:31
Ye shall not *t* oppress one ... Lev 25:17
t the Levites shall be mine ... Num 3:12
t the LORD will give you flesh, ... Num 11:18
t he hath slain them in the ... Num 14:16
t the LORD will not be with you ... Num 14:43
the LORD, *t* they are hallowed ... Num 16:38
T thou and thy sons with thee ... Num 18:7
t I have said unto them, Among ... Num 18:24
T thou shalt say unto them, When ... Num 18:30
t ye shall not bring this ... Num 20:12 3651
T the people came to Moses, and ... Num 21:7
He sent messengers *t* unto Balaam ... Num 22:5
Come now *t*, I pray thee, curse me ... Num 22:6
come *t*, I pray thee, curse me ... Num 22:17
Now *t*, I pray you, tarry ye also ... Num 22:19
now *t*, if it displease thee, I ... Num 22:34
T now flee thou to thy place ... Num 24:11
come *t*, and I will advertise thee ... Num 24:14
Give unto us *t* a possession among ... Num 27:4
Now *t* kill every male among the ... Num 31:17
We have *t* brought an oblation for ... Num 31:50
Defile not *t* the land which ye ... Num 35:34
ye good heed unto yourselves *t* ... Deut 2:4
Now *t* hearken, O Israel, unto the ... Deut 4:1
Keep *t* and do them ... Deut 4:6
Take ye *t* good heed unto ... Deut 4:15
t he chose their seed after them, ... Deut 4:37
Know *t* this day, and consider it ... Deut 4:39 *3767*
Thou shalt keep *t* his statutes ... Deut 4:40
t the LORD thy God commanded thee ... Deut 5:15
Now *t* why should we die ... Deut 5:25
Ye shall observe to do *t* as the ... Deut 5:32
Hear *t*, O Israel, and observe to ... Deut 6:3
Know *t* that the LORD thy God, he ... Deut 7:9
Thou shalt *t* keep the ... Deut 7:11
T thou shalt keep the ... Deut 8:6
Understand *t* this day, that the ... Deut 9:3
Understand *t*, that the LORD thy ... Deut 9:6
I prayed *t* unto the LORD, and said ... Deut 9:26
Circumcise *t* the foreskin of your ... Deut 10:16
Love ye *t* the stranger ... Deut 10:19
T thou shalt love the LORD thy ... Deut 11:1
T shall ye keep all the ... Deut 11:8
T shall ye lay up these my words ... Deut 11:18
t they are unclean unto you ... Deut 14:7
t I command thee, saying, Thou ... Deut 15:11
t I command thee this thing to ... Deut 15:15
Thou shalt *t* sacrifice the ... Deut 16:2
t thou shalt surely rejoice ... Deut 16:15
T shall they have no inheritance ... Deut 18:2
t shall thy camp be holy ... Deut 23:14
t I command thee to do this thing ... Deut 24:18
t I command thee to do this thing ... Deut 24:22
T it shall be, when the LORD thy ... Deut 25:19
thou shalt *t* keep and do them with ... Deut 26:16
T it shall be when ye be gone ... Deut 27:4
Thou shalt *t* obey the voice of ... Deut 27:10
T shalt thou serve thine enemies ... Deut 28:48
Keep *t* the words of this covenant ... Deut 29:9
t choose life, that both thou and ... Deut 30:19
Now *t* write ye this song for you, ... Deut 31:19
Moses *t* wrote this song the same ... Deut 31:22
now *t* arise, go over this Jordan, ... Josh 1:2
Now *t*, I pray you, swear unto me ... Josh 2:12
Now *t* take you twelve men out of ... Josh 3:12
Joshua *t* commanded the priests, ... Josh 4:17
T the children of Israel could ... Josh 7:12
In the morning *t* ye shall be ... Josh 7:14
t we will flee before them ... Josh 8:6
Joshua *t* sent them forth ... Josh 8:9

T

now *t* make ye a league with us... Josh 9:6
t now make ye a league with us... Josh 9:11
now *t* we may not touch them... Josh 9:19
Now *t* ye are cursed, and there... Josh 9:23
t we were sore afraid of our... Josh 9:24
T the five kings of the Amorites,... Josh 10:5
Joshua *t* came unto them suddenly,... Josh 10:9
Now *t* divide this land for an... Josh 13:7
t they gave no part unto the... Josh 14:4
Now *t* give me this mountain,... Josh 14:12
Hebron *t* became the inheritance... Josh 14:14
t he had Gilead and Bashan... Josh 17:1
T according to the commandment of... Josh 17:4
Ye shall *t* describe the land into... Josh 18:6
t the children of Simeon had... Josh 19:9
t the children of Dan went up to... Josh 19:47
t now return ye, and get you unto... Josh 22:4
T we said, Let us now prepare to... Josh 22:26
T said we, that it shall be, when... Josh 22:28
Be ye *t* very courageous to keep... Josh 23:6
Take good heed *t* unto yourselves,... Josh 23:11
T it shall come to pass, that as... Josh 23:15
t he blessed you still... Josh 24:10
Now *t* fear the LORD, and serve him... Josh 24:14
t will we also serve the LORD... Josh 24:18
Now *t* put away, said he, the... Josh 24:23
it shall be *t* a witness unto you,... Josh 24:27
T the LORD left those nations,... Judg 2:23
T the anger of the LORD was hot... Judg 3:8
t they took a key, and opened them... Judg 3:25
T on that day he called him... Judg 6:32
Now *t* go to, proclaim in the ears... Judg 7:3
T when the LORD hath delivered... Judg 8:7
Now *t*, if ye have done truly and... Judg 9:16
Now *t* up by night, thou and the... Judg 9:32
T we turn again to thee now, that... Judg 11:8
now *t* restore those lands again... Judg 11:13
why *t* did ye not recover them... Judg 11:26
Now *t* beware, I pray thee, and... Judg 13:4
now *t* get her for me to wife... Judg 14:2
t I gave her to thy companion... Judg 15:2
Delilah *t* took new ropes, and... Judg 16:12
now *t* I will restore it unto thee... Judg 17:3
now *t* consider what ye have to do... Judg 18:14
t he lodged there again... Judg 19:7
Now *t* deliver us the men, the... Judg 20:13
T they turned their backs before... Judg 20:42
T they commanded the children of... Judg 21:20
Wash thyself *t*, and anoint thee,... Ruth 3:3
spread *t* thy skirt over thine... Ruth 3:9
T the kinsman said unto Boaz, Buy... Ruth 4:8
t she wept, and did not eat... 1Sa 1:7
t Eli thought she had been... 1Sa 1:13
T also I have lent him to the... 1Sa 1:28
T Eli said unto Samuel, Go, lie... 1Sa 3:9
t I have sworn unto the house of... 1Sa 3:14
T neither the priests of Dagon,... 1Sa 5:5
They sent *t* and gathered all the... 1Sa 5:8
T they sent the ark of God to... 1Sa 5:10
Now *t* make a new cart, and take... 1Sa 6:7
Now *t* hearken unto their voice... 1Sa 8:9
Now *t* get you up... 1Sa 9:13
T it became a proverb, Is Saul... 1Sa 10:12
Now *t* present yourselves before... 1Sa 10:19
T they enquired of the LORD... 1Sa 10:22
T the men of Jabesh said, To... 1Sa 11:10
Now *t* stand still, that I may... 1Sa 12:7
Now *t* behold the king whom ye... 1Sa 12:13
Now *t* stand and see this great... 1Sa 12:16 1571
T said I, The Philistines will... 1Sa 13:12
I forced myself *t*, and offered a... 1Sa 13:12
T Saul said unto the LORD God of... 1Sa 14:41
now *t* hearken thou unto the voice... 1Sa 15:1
Now *t*, I pray thee, pardon my sin... 1Sa 15:25
T David ran, and stood upon the... 1Sa 17:51
T Saul removed him from him, and... 1Sa 18:13
now *t* be the king's son in law... 1Sa 18:22
now *t*, I pray thee, take heed to... 1Sa 19:2
T thou shalt deal kindly with thy... 1Sa 20:8
T he cometh not unto the king's... 1Sa 20:29
Now *t* what is under thine hand... 1Sa 21:3
David *t* departed thence, and... 1Sa 22:1
T David enquired of the LORD,... 1Sa 23:2
Now *t*, O king, come down... 1Sa 23:20
See *t*, and take knowledge of all... 1Sa 23:23
t they called that place... 1Sa 23:28
The LORD *t* be judge, and judge... 1Sa 24:15
Swear now *t* unto me by the LORD,... 1Sa 24:21
Now *t* know and consider what thou... 1Sa 25:17
Now *t*, my lord, as the LORD... 1Sa 25:26
David *t* sent out spies, and... 1Sa 26:4
now *t* let me smite him, I pray... 1Sa 26:8
Now *t*, I pray thee, let my lord... 1Sa 26:19
Now *t*, let not my blood fall to... 1Sa 26:20
t he shall be my servant for ever... 1Sa 27:12
T will I make thee keeper of mine... 1Sa 28:2
t I have called thee, that thou... 1Sa 28:15
t hath the LORD done this thing... 1Sa 28:18
Now *t*, I pray thee, hearken thou... 1Sa 28:22
T Saul took a sword, and fell upon... 1Sa 31:4
T now let your hands be... 2Sa 2:7
shall I not *t* now require his... 2Sa 4:11
T he called the name of that... 2Sa 5:20
t will I play before the LORD... 2Sa 6:21
T Michal the daughter of Saul had... 2Sa 6:23
Now *t* so shalt thou say unto my... 2Sa 7:8
t hath thy servant found in his... 2Sa 7:27
T now let it please thee to bless... 2Sa 7:29
Thou *t*, and thy sons, and thy... 2Sa 9:10
Now *t* the sword shall never... 2Sa 12:10
David *t* besought God for the... 2Sa 12:16
t David said unto his servants,... 2Sa 12:19
Now *t* gather the rest of the... 2Sa 12:28
Now *t*, I pray thee, speak unto... 2Sa 13:13
Now *t* let not my lord the king... 2Sa 13:33
Now *t* that I am come to speak of... 2Sa 14:15
t the LORD thy God will be with... 2Sa 14:17
go *t*, bring the young man Absalom... 2Sa 14:21
was heavy on him, *t* he polled it... 2Sa 14:26
T Absalom sent for Joab, to have... 2Sa 14:29
T he said unto his servants, See,... 2Sa 14:30
now *t* let me see the king's face... 2Sa 14:32
Zadok *t* and Abiathar carried the... 2Sa 15:29
t it shall be, that what thing... 2Sa 15:35
T I counsel that all Israel be... 2Sa 17:11
Now *t* send quickly, and tell David... 2Sa 17:16
t now it is better that thou... 2Sa 18:3
Now *t* arise, go forth, and speak... 2Sa 19:7
Now *t* why speak ye not a word of... 2Sa 19:10
t, behold, I am come the first... 2Sa 19:20
T the king said unto Shimei, Thou... 2Sa 19:23
do *t* what is good in thine eyes... 2Sa 19:27
What right *t* have I yet to cry... 2Sa 19:28
T the LORD hath recompensed me... 2Sa 22:25
T I will give thanks unto thee, O... 2Sa 22:50
t he would not drink it... 2Sa 23:17
t he was their captain... 2Sa 23:19
Now *t* come, let me, I pray thee,... 1Kin 1:12
be thou strong *t*, and shew thyself... 1Kin 2:2
Do *t* according to thy wisdom, and... 1Kin 2:6
Now *t* hold him not guiltless... 1Kin 2:9
Bath-sheba *t* went unto king... 1Kin 2:19
Now *t*, as the LORD liveth, which... 1Kin 2:24
Their blood shall *t* return upon... 1Kin 2:33
t the LORD shall return thy... 1Kin 2:44
Give *t* thy servant an... 1Kin 3:9
Now *t* command thou that they hew... 1Kin 5:6
T now, LORD God of Israel, keep... 1Kin 8:25
Let your heart *t* be perfect with... 1Kin 8:61
t hath the LORD brought upon them... 1Kin 9:9
t made he thee king, to do... 1Kin 10:9
Solomon sought *t* to kill Jeroboam... 1Kin 11:40
now *t* make thou the grievous... 1Kin 12:4
T king Rehoboam made speed to get... 1Kin 12:18
They hearkened *t* to the word of... 1Kin 12:24
t the LORD hath delivered him... 1Kin 13:26
T, behold, I will bring evil upon... 1Kin 14:10
Arise thou *t*, get thee to thine... 1Kin 14:12
Now *t* send, and gather to me all... 1Kin 18:19
Let them *t* give us two bullocks... 1Kin 18:23
t they were stronger than we... 1Kin 20:23
t will I deliver all this great... 1Kin 20:28
t thy life shall go for his life,... 1Kin 20:42
Hear thou *t* the word of the LORD... 1Kin 22:19 3651
Now *t*, behold, the LORD hath put... 1Kin 22:23
Now *t* thus saith the LORD, Thou... 2Kin 1:4 3651
t thou shalt not come down from... 2Kin 1:6 3651
t let my life now be precious in... 2Kin 1:14
t thou shalt not come down off... 2Kin 1:16
They sent *t* fifty men... 2Kin 2:17
now *t*, Moab, to the spoil... 2Kin 3:23
He went in *t*, and shut the door... 2Kin 4:33
now *t*, I pray thee, take a... 2Kin 5:15
The leprosy *t* of Naaman shall... 2Kin 5:27
T said he, Take it up to thee... 2Kin 6:7
T the heart of the king of Syria... 2Kin 6:11
T sent he thither horses, and... 2Kin 6:14
Now *t* come, and let us fall unto... 2Kin 7:4
now *t* come, that we may go and... 2Kin 7:9
t are they gone out of the camp... 2Kin 7:12
They took *t* two chariot horses... 2Kin 7:14
Now *t* take and cast him into the... 2Kin 9:26
Now *t* call unto me all the... 2Kin 10:19
now *t* receive no more money of... 2Kin 12:7
T Jehoash king of Israel went up... 2Kin 14:11
opened not to him, *t* he smote it... 2Kin 15:16
t the king of Assyria shut him up... 2Kin 17:4
T the LORD was very angry with... 2Kin 17:18
t the LORD sent lions among them,... 2Kin 17:25
t he hath sent lions among them,... 2Kin 17:26
Now *t*, I pray thee, give pledges... 2Kin 18:23
t they have destroyed them... 2Kin 19:18
Now *t*, O LORD our God, I beseech... 2Kin 19:19
T their inhabitants were of small... 2Kin 19:26
t I will put my hook in thy nose,... 2Kin 19:28
T thus saith the LORD concerning... 2Kin 19:32 3651
T thus saith the LORD God of... 2Kin 21:12 3651
t my wrath shall be kindled... 2Kin 22:17
Behold *t*, I will gather thee unto... 2Kin 22:20 3651
t he slew him, and turned the... 1Chr 10:14
T came all the elders of Israel... 1Chr 11:3
t they called it the city of... 1Chr 11:7
T he would not drink it... 1Chr 11:19
t they called the name of that... 1Chr 14:11
T David enquired again of God... 1Chr 14:14
David *t* did as God commanded him... 1Chr 14:16
Now *t* thus shalt thou say unto my... 1Chr 17:7
T now, LORD, let the thing that... 1Chr 17:23
t thy servant hath found in his... 1Chr 17:25
Now *t* let it please thee to bless... 1Chr 17:27
t he smote Israel... 1Chr 21:7
Now *t* advise thyself what word I... 1Chr 21:12
I will *t* now make preparation for... 1Chr 22:5
Arise *t*, and be doing, and the LORD... 1Chr 22:16
arise *t*, and build ye the... 1Chr 22:19
t they were in one reckoning,... 1Chr 23:11
t Eleazar and Ithamar executed the... 1Chr 24:2
Now *t*, in the sight of all Israel... 1Chr 28:8
Now *t*, our God, we thank thee, and... 1Chr 29:13
Send me now *t* a man cunning to... 2Chr 2:7
Now *t* the wheat, and the barley,... 2Chr 2:15
The LORD *t* hath performed his... 2Chr 6:10
Now *t*, O LORD God of Israel, keep... 2Chr 6:16
Have respect *t* to the prayer of... 2Chr 6:19
Hearken *t* unto the supplications... 2Chr 6:21
Now *t* arise, O LORD God, into thy... 2Chr 6:41
t hath he brought all this evil... 2Chr 7:22
t made he thee king over them, to... 2Chr 9:8
now *t* ease thou somewhat the... 2Chr 10:4
t have I also left you in the... 2Chr 12:5
t I will not destroy them, but I... 2Chr 12:7
T he said unto Judah, Let us... 2Chr 14:7
Be ye strong *t*, and let not your... 2Chr 15:7
t is the host of the king of... 2Chr 16:7
t from henceforth thou shalt have... 2Chr 16:9
T the LORD stablished the kingdom... 2Chr 17:5
T the king of Israel gathered... 2Chr 18:5
let thy word *t*, I pray thee, be... 2Chr 18:12
let them return *t* every man to... 2Chr 18:16
T hear the word of the LORD... 2Chr 18:18 3651
Now *t*, behold, the LORD hath put... 2Chr 18:22
T they compassed about him to... 2Chr 18:31
t he said to his chariot man,... 2Chr 18:33
t is wrath upon thee from before... 2Chr 19:2 2063
t the name of the same place was... 2Chr 20:26
Now hear me *t*, and deliver the... 2Chr 28:11
t will I sacrifice to them, that... 2Chr 28:23
who *t* gave them up to desolation,... 2Chr 30:7
t the Levites had the charge of... 2Chr 30:17
Now *t* let not Hezekiah deceive... 2Chr 32:15
t there was wrath upon him, and... 2Chr 32:25
t my wrath shall be poured out... 2Chr 34:25
t the Levites prepared for... 2Chr 35:14
His servants *t* took him out of... 2Chr 35:24
T he brought upon them the king... 2Chr 36:17
t were they, as polluted, put... Ezr 2:62
t have we sent and certified the... Ezr 4:14
Now *t*, if it seem good to the... Ezr 5:17
Now *t*, Tatnai, governor beyond... Ezr 6:6
Now *t* give not your daughters... Ezr 9:12
Now *t* let us make a covenant with... Ezr 10:3
Now *t* make confession unto the... Ezr 10:11
t we his servants will arise and... Neh 2:20
T set I in the lower places... Neh 4:13
In what place *t* ye hear the sound... Neh 4:20
t we take up corn for them, that... Neh 5:2
Come now *t*, and let us take... Neh 6:7
Now *t*, O God, strengthen my hands... Neh 6:9
T was he hired, that I should be... Neh 6:13
t were they, as polluted, put... Neh 7:64
T thou deliveredst them into the... Neh 9:27
t leftest thou them in the hand... Neh 9:28
t gavest thou them into the hand... Neh 9:30
Now *t*, our God, the great, the... Neh 9:32
t I cast forth all the household... Neh 13:8
t I chased him from me... Neh 13:28
t was the king very wroth, and his... Est 1:12
t they were both hanged on a tree... Est 2:23
t it is not for the king's profit... Est 3:8
T the Jews of the villages, that... Est 9:19
T for all the words of this... Est 9:26
t despise not thou the chastening... Job 5:17
t my words are swallowed up... Job 6:3
Now *t* be content, look upon me... Job 6:28
T I will not refrain my mouth... Job 7:11 1571
t I said it, He destroyeth the... Job 9:22
t see thou mine affliction... Job 10:15
Know *t* that God exacteth of thee... Job 11:6
t shalt thou not exalt them... Job 17:4
T do my thoughts cause me to... Job 20:2 3651
t shall no man look for his goods... Job 20:21
T they say unto God, Depart from... Job 21:14
T snares are round about thee, and... Job 22:10
T am I troubled at his presence... Job 23:15
T I said, Hearken to me... Job 32:10 3651
T hearken unto me, ye men of... Job 34:10 3651
T he knoweth their works, and he... Job 34:25 3651
t speak what thou knowest... Job 34:33
t trust thou in him... Job 35:14
T doth Job open his mouth in vain... Job 35:16
Men do *t* fear him... Job 37:24 3651
t have I uttered that I... Job 42:3 3651
T take unto you now seven... Job 42:8
T the ungodly shall not stand in... Ps 1:5
Be wise now *t*, O ye kings... Ps 2:10
for their sakes *t* return thou on... Ps 7:7
T my heart is glad, and my glory... Ps 16:9 3651
T hath the LORD recompensed me... Ps 18:24
T will I give thanks unto thee, O... Ps 18:49
T shalt thou make them turn their... Ps 21:12
t will he teach sinners in the... Ps 25:8
t I shall not slide... Ps 26:1
t will I offer in his tabernacle... Ps 27:6
t my heart greatly rejoiceth... Ps 28:7
t for thy name's sake lead me, and... Ps 31:3
t the children of men put their... Ps 36:7
t my heart faileth me... Ps 40:12
t will I remember thee from the... Ps 42:6
t God hath blessed thee for ever... Ps 45:2
t God, thy God, hath anointed... Ps 45:7
t shall the people praise thee... Ps 45:17
T will not we fear, though the... Ps 46:2
no changes, *t* they fear not God... Ps 55:19
Thou *t*, O LORD God of hosts, the... Ps 59:5
t in the shadow of thy wings will... Ps 63:7
T pride compasseth them about as... Ps 73:6
T his people return hither... Ps 73:10 3651
T the LORD heard this, and was... Ps 78:21 3651
T their days did he consume in... Ps 78:33
upon me, *t* will I deliver him... Ps 91:14
T he said that he would destroy... Ps 106:23
T he lifted up his hand against... Ps 106:26
T was the wrath of the LORD... Ps 106:40
T he brought down their heart... Ps 107:12
t shall he lift up the head... Ps 110:7
t will I call upon him as long as... Ps 116:2
I believed, *t* have I spoken... Ps 116:10 3588
t shall I see my desire upon them... Ps 118:7
t I hate every false way... Ps 119:104
t I love thy testimonies... Ps 119:119 3651
T I love thy commandments above... Ps 119:127
T I esteem all thy precepts... Ps 119:128

Context	Reference	Number
t doth my soul keep them	Ps 119:129	
t thy servant loveth it	Ps 119:140	
depart from me *t*, ye bloody men	Ps 139:19	
T is my spirit overwhelmed within	Ps 143:4	
T shall they eat of the fruit of	Prov 1:31	
t get wisdom	Prov 4:7	
Hear me now *t*, O ye children, and	Prov 5:7	
T shall his calamity come	Prov 6:15	
t he will not spare in the day of	Prov 6:34	
T came I forth to meet thee,	Prov 7:15	
Hearken unto me now *t*, O ye	Prov 7:24	
Now *t* hearken unto me, O ye	Prov 8:32	
t a cruel messenger shall be sent	Prov 17:11	
t leave off contention, before it	Prov 17:14	
t shall he beg in harvest, and	Prov 20:4	
t meddle not with him that	Prov 20:19	
thee with mirth, *t* enjoy pleasure	Eccl 2:1	
T I hated life	Eccl 2:17	
T I went about to cause my heart	Eccl 2:20	
t let thy words be few	Eccl 5:2	
t the misery of man is great upon	Eccl 8:6	
t the heart of the sons of men is	Eccl 8:11	
T remove sorrow from thy heart,	Eccl 11:10	
t do the virgins love thee	Song 1:3	
T saith the Lord, the LORD of	Is 1:24	3651
T thou hast forsaken thy people	Is 2:6	
t forgive them not	Is 2:9	
T the Lord will smite with a scab	Is 3:17	
T my people are gone into	Is 5:13	3651
T hell hath enlarged herself, and	Is 5:14	3651
T as the fire devoureth the	Is 5:24	3651
T is the anger of the LORD	Is 5:25	
T the Lord himself shall give you	Is 7:14	3651
Now *t*, behold, the Lord bringeth	Is 8:7	3651
T the LORD shall set up the	Is 9:11	
T the LORD will cut off from	Is 9:14	
T the Lord shall have no joy in	Is 9:17	
T shall the Lord, the Lord of	Is 10:16	3651
T thus saith the Lord GOD of	Is 10:24	3651
T with joy shall ye draw water	Is 12:3	
T shall all hands be faint, and	Is 13:7	
T I will shake the heavens, and	Is 13:13	
t the armed soldiers of Moab	Is 15:4	
T the abundance they have gotten,	Is 15:7	
T shall Moab howl for Moab, every	Is 16:7	3651
T I will bewail with the weeping	Is 16:9	
t shalt thou plant pleasant	Is 17:10	
T are my loins filled with pain	Is 21:3	
T said I, Look away from me	Is 22:4	
T hath the curse devoured the	Is 24:6	
t the inhabitants of the earth	Is 24:6	
T shall the strong people glorify	Is 25:3	
t hast thou visited and destroyed	Is 26:14	3651
By this *t* shall the iniquity of	Is 27:9	3651
t he that made them will not have	Is 27:11	
T thus saith the Lord GOD, Behold	Is 28:16	3651
Now *t* be ye not mockers, lest	Is 28:22	
T, behold, I will proceed to do a	Is 29:14	3651
T thus saith the LORD, who	Is 29:22	3651
T shall the strength of Pharaoh	Is 30:3	
t have I cried concerning this,	Is 30:7	3651
T this iniquity shall be to you	Is 30:13	3651
t shall ye flee	Is 30:16	
t shall they that pursue you be	Is 30:16	
t will the LORD wait, that he may	Is 30:18	3651
t will he be exalted, that he may	Is 30:18	3651
Now *t* give pledges, I pray thee,	Is 36:8	
t they have destroyed them	Is 37:19	
Now *t*, O LORD our God, save us	Is 37:20	
T their inhabitants were of small	Is 37:27	
t will I put my hook in thy nose,	Is 37:29	
T thus saith the LORD concerning	Is 37:33	3651
t we will sing my songs to the	Is 38:20	
T he hath poured upon him the	Is 42:25	
t will I give men for thee, and	Is 43:4	
t ye are my witnesses, saith the	Is 43:12	
T I have profaned the princes of	Is 43:28	
T hear now this, thou that art	Is 47:8	
T shall evil come upon thee	Is 47:11	
t shall I not be confounded	Is 50:7	
t have I set my face like a flint	Is 50:7	
T the redeemed of the LORD shall	Is 51:11	
T hear now this, thou afflicted,	Is 51:21	3651
Now *t*, what have I here, saith	Is 52:5	
T my people shall know my name	Is 52:6	3651
t they shall know in that day	Is 52:6	3651
T will I divide him a portion	Is 53:12	3651
t thou wast not grieved	Is 57:10	
T is judgment far from us,	Is 59:9	
t his arm brought salvation unto	Is 59:16	
T thy gates shall be open	Is 60:11	
t in their land they shall	Is 61:7	3651
t mine own arm brought salvation	Is 63:5	
t he was turned to be their enemy	Is 63:10	
t will I measure their former	Is 65:7	
T will I number you to the sword,	Is 65:12	
T thus saith the Lord GOD, Behold	Is 65:13	3651
Thou *t* gird up thy loins, and	Jer 1:17	
know *t* and see that it is an evil	Jer 2:19	
t hast thou also taught the	Jer 2:33	3651
T the showers have been	Jer 3:3	
T I said, Surely these are poor	Jer 5:4	
t they are become great, and waxen	Jer 5:27	
T I am full of the fury of the	Jer 6:11	
t they shall fall among them that	Jer 6:15	3651
T hear, ye nations, and know, O	Jer 6:18	3651
T thus saith the LORD, Behold, I	Jer 6:21	3651
T will I do unto this house,	Jer 7:14	
T pray not thou for this people,	Jer 7:16	
T thus saith the Lord GOD	Jer 7:20	3651
T thou shalt speak all these	Jer 7:27	
T, behold, the days come, saith	Jer 7:32	3651
T will I give their wives unto	Jer 8:10	3651
t shall they fall among them that	Jer 8:12	3651

Context	Reference	Number
T thus saith the LORD of hosts,	Jer 9:7	3651
T thus saith the LORD of hosts,	Jer 9:15	3651
t they shall not prosper, and all	Jer 10:21	
t I will bring upon them all the	Jer 11:8	
T thus saith the LORD, Behold, I	Jer 11:11	3651
T pray not thou for this people,	Jer 11:14	
T thus saith the LORD of the men	Jer 11:21	3651
T thus saith the LORD of hosts,	Jer 11:22	3651
t have I hated it	Jer 12:8	
T thou shalt speak unto them this	Jer 13:12	
T will I scatter them as the	Jer 13:24	
T will I discover thy skirts upon	Jer 13:26	
t the LORD doth not accept them	Jer 14:10	
T thus saith the LORD concerning	Jer 14:15	3651
T thou shalt say this word unto	Jer 14:17	
t we will wait upon thee	Jer 14:22	
t will I stretch out my hand	Jer 15:6	
T thus saith the LORD, If thou	Jer 15:19	3651
T will I cast you out of this	Jer 16:13	
T, behold, the days come, saith	Jer 16:14	3651
T, behold, I will this once cause	Jer 16:21	3651
Now *t* go to, speak to the men of	Jer 18:11	
T thus saith the LORD	Jer 18:13	3651
T deliver up their children to	Jer 18:21	3651
T, behold, the days come, saith	Jer 19:6	3651
t my persecutors shall stumble,	Jer 20:11	
T thus saith the LORD concerning	Jer 22:18	3651
T thus saith the LORD God of	Jer 23:2	3651
T, behold, the days come, saith	Jer 23:7	3651
T thus saith the LORD of hosts	Jer 23:15	3651
T, behold, I am against the	Jer 23:30	3651
t they shall not profit this	Jer 23:32	
t thus saith the LORD	Jer 23:38	3651
T, behold, I, even I, will	Jer 23:39	3651
T thus saith the LORD of hosts	Jer 25:8	3651
T thou shalt say unto them, Thus	Jer 25:27	
T prophesy thou against them all	Jer 25:30	
T now amend your ways and your	Jer 26:13	
T hearken not ye to your prophets	Jer 27:9	
T hearken not unto the words of	Jer 27:14	
T thus saith the LORD	Jer 28:16	3651
Hear ye *t* the word of the LORD,	Jer 29:20	
Now *t* why hast thou not reproved	Jer 29:27	
For *t* he sent unto us in Babylon,	Jer 29:28	
T thus saith the LORD	Jer 29:32	3651
T fear thou not, O my servant	Jer 30:10	
T all they that devour thee shall	Jer 30:16	3651
t with lovingkindness have I	Jer 31:3	
T they shall come and sing in the	Jer 31:12	
t my bowels are troubled for him	Jer 31:20	
t thou hast caused all this evil	Jer 32:23	
T thus saith the LORD	Jer 32:28	
now *t* thus saith the LORD, the	Jer 32:36	3651
T the word of the LORD came to	Jer 34:12	
T thus saith the LORD	Jer 34:17	3651
T thus saith the LORD God of	Jer 35:17	3651
T thus saith the LORD of hosts,	Jer 35:19	3651
T go thou, and read in the roll,	Jer 36:6	
T all the princes sent Jehudi the	Jer 36:14	
T thus saith the LORD of	Jer 36:30	3651
T hear now, I pray thee, O my	Jer 37:20	
T the princes said unto the king,	Jer 38:4	
t this thing is come upon you	Jer 40:3	
now *t* hear the word of the LORD,	Jer 42:15	3651
Now *t* know certainly that ye	Jer 42:22	
T now thus saith the LORD, the	Jer 44:7	
T thus saith the LORD of hosts,	Jer 44:11	3651
t is your land a desolation, and	Jer 44:22	
t this evil is happened unto you,	Jer 44:23	
T hear ye the word of the LORD,	Jer 44:26	3651
t his taste remained in him, and	Jer 48:11	
T, behold, the days come, saith	Jer 48:12	3651
T will I howl for Moab, and I will	Jer 48:31	
T mine heart shall sound for Moab	Jer 48:36	
T, behold, the days come, saith	Jer 49:2	3651
T hear the counsel of the LORD,	Jer 49:20	3651
T her young men shall fall in her	Jer 49:26	3651
T thus saith the LORD of hosts,	Jer 50:18	3651
T shall her young men fall in the	Jer 50:30	3651
T the wild beasts of the desert	Jer 50:39	3651
T hear ye the counsel of the LORD	Jer 50:45	3651
t the nations are mad	Jer 51:7	
T thus saith the LORD	Jer 51:36	3651
T, behold, the days come, that I	Jer 51:47	3651
t she is removed	Lam 1:8	
t she came down wonderfully	Lam 1:9	
t he made the rampart and the wall	Lam 2:8	
recall to my mind, *t* have I hope	Lam 3:21	
t will I hope in him	Lam 3:24	
t hear the word at my mouth, and	Eze 3:17	
T thou shalt set thy face toward	Eze 4:7	
T thus saith the Lord GOD	Eze 5:7	3651
T thus saith the Lord GOD	Eze 5:8	3651
T the fathers shall eat the sons	Eze 5:10	3651
t will I also diminish thee	Eze 5:11	
t have I set it far from them	Eze 7:20	
T will I also deal in fury	Eze 8:18	
T prophesy against them, prophesy	Eze 11:4	3651
T thus saith the Lord GOD	Eze 11:7	3651
T say, Thus saith the Lord GOD	Eze 11:16	3651
T say, Thus saith the Lord GOD	Eze 11:17	3651
T, thou son of man, prepare thee	Eze 12:3	
Tell them *t*, Thus saith the Lord	Eze 12:23	3651
T say unto them, Thus saith the	Eze 12:28	3651
T thus saith the Lord GOD	Eze 13:8	3651
spoken vanity, and seen lies, *t*	Eze 13:8	3651
T thus saith the Lord GOD	Eze 13:13	3651
T ye shall see no more vanity,	Eze 13:23	3651
T speak unto them, and say unto	Eze 14:4	3651
T say unto the house of Israel,	Eze 14:6	3651
T thus saith the Lord GOD	Eze 15:6	3651
t I have stretched out my hand	Eze 16:27	
unto thee, *t* thou art contrary	Eze 16:34	
t I will gather all thy lovers,	Eze 16:37	3651

Context	Reference	Number
t I also will recompense thy way	Eze 16:43	
t I took them away as I saw good	Eze 16:50	
T thus saith the Lord GOD	Eze 17:19	3651
T I will judge you, O house of	Eze 18:30	3651
T, son of man, speak unto the	Eze 20:27	3651
t shall my sword go forth out of	Eze 21:4	
Sigh *t*, thou son of man, with the	Eze 21:6	
smite *t* upon thy thigh	Eze 21:12	
Thou *t*, son of man, prophesy, and	Eze 21:14	
T thus saith the Lord GOD	Eze 21:24	3651
t have I made thee a reproach	Eze 22:4	3651
t I have smitten mine hand at thy	Eze 22:13	
T thus saith the Lord GOD	Eze 22:19	3651
t I will gather you into the	Eze 22:19	3651
T have I poured out mine	Eze 22:31	
T, O Aholibah, thus saith the	Eze 23:22	3651
t will I give her cup into thine	Eze 23:31	
T thus saith the Lord GOD	Eze 23:35	3651
t bear thou also thy lewdness and	Eze 23:35	
T thus saith the Lord GOD	Eze 24:9	3651
t I will deliver thee to the men	Eze 25:4	3651
t I will stretch out mine hand	Eze 25:7	3651
T, behold, I will open the side	Eze 25:9	3651
T thus saith the Lord GOD	Eze 25:13	3651
T thus saith the Lord GOD	Eze 25:16	3651
T thus saith the Lord GOD	Eze 26:3	3651
T thus saith the Lord GOD	Eze 28:6	3651
t I will bring strangers upon	Eze 28:7	3651
t I will cast thee as profane out	Eze 28:16	
t will I bring forth a fire from	Eze 28:18	
T thus saith the Lord GOD	Eze 29:8	3651
t I am against thee, and against	Eze 29:10	3651
T thus saith the Lord GOD	Eze 29:19	3651
T thus saith the Lord GOD	Eze 30:22	3651
T his height was exalted above	Eze 31:5	
T thus saith the Lord GOD	Eze 31:10	3651
I have *t* delivered him into the	Eze 31:11	
I will *t* spread out my net over	Eze 32:3	
t thou shalt hear the word at my	Eze 33:7	
T, O thou son of man, speak unto	Eze 33:10	
T, thou son of man, say unto the	Eze 33:12	
T, ye shepherds, hear the word of	Eze 34:7	3651
T, O ye shepherds, hear the word	Eze 34:9	3651
T thus saith the Lord GOD unto	Eze 34:20	3651
T will I save my flock, and they	Eze 34:22	
T, as I live, saith the Lord GOD,	Eze 35:6	3651
T, as I live, saith the Lord GOD,	Eze 35:11	3651
T prophesy and say, Thus saith the	Eze 36:3	3651
T, ye mountains of Israel, hear	Eze 36:4	3651
T thus saith the Lord GOD	Eze 36:5	3651
Prophesy *t* concerning the land of	Eze 36:6	3651
T thus saith the Lord GOD	Eze 36:7	3651
T thou shalt devour men no more,	Eze 36:14	3651
T say unto the house of Israel,	Eze 36:22	3651
T prophesy and say unto them, Thus	Eze 37:12	3651
T, son of man, prophesy and say	Eze 38:14	3651
T, thou son of man, prophesy	Eze 39:1	3651
t hid I my face from them, and	Eze 39:23	
T thus saith the Lord GOD	Eze 39:25	3651
t the breadth of the house was	Eze 41:7	
t the building was straitened	Eze 42:6	
in by it, *t* it shall be shut	Eze 44:2	
t have I lifted up mine hand	Eze 44:12	
t he requested of the prince of	Dan 1:8	
t stood they before the king	Dan 1:19	
t shew me the dream, and the	Dan 2:6	2006
t tell me the dream, and I shall	Dan 2:9	2006
t there is no king, lord, nor	Dan 2:10	
T Daniel went in unto Arioch,	Dan 2:24	
T at that time, when all the	Dan 3:7	
t he spake, and commanded that	Dan 3:19	
T because the king's commandment	Dan 3:22	
T I make a decree, That every	Dan 3:29	
T made I a decree to bring in all	Dan 4:6	
T the he goat waxed very great	Dan 8:8	
t the curse is poured upon us, and	Dan 9:11	
T hath the LORD watched upon the	Dan 9:14	
Now *t*, O our God, hear the prayer	Dan 9:17	
t understand the matter, and	Dan 9:23	
Know *t* and understand, that from	Dan 9:25	
T I was left alone, and saw this	Dan 10:8	
t he shall be grieved, and return,	Dan 11:30	
t he shall go forth with great	Dan 11:44	
let her *t* put away her whoredoms	Hos 2:2	
T, behold, I will hedge up thy	Hos 2:6	3651
T will I return, and take away my	Hos 2:9	3651
T, behold, I will allure her, and	Hos 2:14	3651
T shall the land mourn, and every	Hos 4:3	
T shalt thou fall in the day, and	Hos 4:5	
t will I change their glory into	Hos 4:7	
t your daughters shall commit	Hos 4:13	
t the people that doth not	Hos 4:14	
t shall Israel and Ephraim fall in	Hos 5:5	
t I will pour out my wrath upon	Hos 5:10	
T will I be unto Ephraim as a	Hos 5:12	
T have I hewed them by the	Hos 6:5	
t it is not God	Hos 8:6	
t he will remember their iniquity	Hos 9:9	
T shall a tumult arise among thy	Hos 10:14	
T turn thou to thy God	Hos 12:6	
t shall he leave his blood upon	Hos 12:14	
T they shall be as the morning	Hos 13:3	3651
t have they forgotten me	Hos 13:6	
T I will be unto them as a lion	Hos 13:7	
T also now, saith the LORD, turn	Joel 2:12	1571
T the flight shall perish from	Amos 2:14	
t I will punish you for all your	Amos 3:2	
T thus saith the Lord GOD	Amos 3:11	3651
T thus will I do unto thee, O	Amos 4:12	3651
Forasmuch *t* as your treading is	Amos 5:11	3651
T the prudent shall keep silence	Amos 5:13	3651
T the LORD, the God of hosts, the	Amos 5:16	3651
T will I cause you to go into	Amos 5:27	
T now shall they go captive with	Amos 6:7	3651

Context	Reference	No.
t will I deliver up the city with	Amos 6:8	
Now *t* hear thou the word of the	Amos 7:16	
T thus saith the LORD	Amos 7:17	3651
T I fled before unto Tarshish	Jonah 4:2	
T now, O LORD, take, I beseech	Jonah 4:3	
T I will make Samaria as an heap	Mic 1:6	
T I will wail and howl, I will go	Mic 1:8	
T shalt thou give presents to	Mic 1:14	3651
T thus saith the LORD	Mic 2:3	3651
T thou shalt have none that shall	Mic 2:5	3651
T night shall be unto you, that	Mic 3:6	3651
T shall Zion for your sake be	Mic 3:12	3651
T will he give them up, until the	Mic 5:3	3651
T also will I make thee sick in	Mic 6:13	
t ye shall bear the reproach of	Mic 6:16	
T I will look unto the LORD	Mic 7:7	
T the law is slacked, and judgment	Hab 1:4	
t wrong judgment proceedeth	Hab 1:4	
t they rejoice and are glad	Hab 1:15	
T they sacrifice unto their net,	Hab 1:16	
Shall they *t* empty their net, and	Hab 1:17	3651
T their goods shall become a	Zeph 1:13	
T as I live, saith the LORD of	Zeph 2:9	3651
T wait ye upon me, saith the LORD	Zeph 3:8	3651
Now *t* thus saith the LORD of	Hag 1:5	
T the heaven over you is stayed	Hag 1:10	
T say thou unto them, Thus saith	Zec 1:3	
T thus saith the LORD	Zec 1:16	3651
t came a great wrath from the	Zec 7:12	
T it is come to pass, that as he	Zec 7:13	
t love the truth and peace	Zec 8:19	
t they went their way as a flock,	Zec 10:2	
T have I also made you	Mal 2:9	
T take heed to your spirit, and	Mal 2:15	
t take heed to your spirit, that	Mal 2:16	
t ye sons of Jacob are not	Mal 3:6	
Bring forth *t* fruits meet for	Mt 3:8	3767
t every tree which bringeth not	Mt 3:10	3767
Whosoever *t* shall break one of	Mt 5:19	3767
T if thou bring thy gift to the	Mt 5:23	3767
Be ye *t* perfect, even as your	Mt 5:48	3767
T when thou doest thine alms, do	Mt 6:2	3767
Be not ye *t* like unto them	Mt 6:8	3767
After this manner *t* pray ye	Mt 6:9	3767
if *t* thine eye be single, thy	Mt 6:22	3767
If *t* the light that is in thee be	Mt 6:23	3767
T I say unto you, Take no thought	Mt 6:25	
T take no thought, saying, What	Mt 6:31	3767
Take *t* no thought for the morrow	Mt 6:34	3767
T all things whatsoever ye would	Mt 7:12	3767
T whosoever heareth these sayings	Mt 7:24	3767
Pray ye *t* the Lord of the harvest	Mt 9:38	3767
be ye *t* wise as serpents, and	Mt 10:16	3767
Fear them not *t*	Mt 10:26	3767
Fear ye not *t*, ye are of more	Mt 10:31	3767
Whosoever *t* shall confess me	Mt 10:32	3767
t they shall be your judges	Mt 12:27	
T speak I to them in parables	Mt 13:13	
Hear ye *t* the parable of the	Mt 13:18	3767
As *t* the tares are gathered and	Mt 13:40	3767
them, *T* every scribe which is	Mt 13:52	
t mighty works do shew forth	Mt 14:2	
Whosoever *t* shall humble himself	Mt 18:4	3767
T is the kingdom of heaven	Mt 18:23	
The servant *t* fell down, and	Mt 18:26	3767
What *t* God hath joined together,	Mt 19:6	3767
what shall we have *t*	Mt 19:27	686
When the lord *t* of the vineyard	Mt 21:40	3767
T say I unto you, The kingdom of	Mt 21:43	
Go ye *t* into the highways, and as	Mt 22:9	3767
Tell us *t*, What thinkest thou	Mt 22:17	3767
Render *t* unto Caesar the things	Mt 22:21	3767
T in the resurrection whose wife	Mt 22:28	3767
All *t* whatsoever they bid you	Mt 23:3	3767
t ye shall receive the greater	Mt 23:14	
Whoso *t* shall swear by the altar,	Mt 23:20	3767
When ye *t* shall see the	Mt 24:15	3767
Watch *t*: for ye know not	Mt 24:42	3767
T be ye also ready	Mt 24:44	
Watch *t*, for ye know neither the	Mt 25:13	3767
Thou oughtest *t* to have put my	Mt 25:27	3767
Take *t* the talent from him, and	Mt 25:28	3767
T when they were gathered	Mt 27:17	3767
Command *t* that the sepulchre be	Mt 27:64	3767
Go ye *t*, and teach all nations,	Mt 28:19	3767
for *t* came I forth	Mk 1:38	
t the Son of man is Lord also of	Mk 2:28	5620
t mighty works do shew forth	Mk 6:14	
T Herodias had a quarrel against	Mk 6:19	
Whosoever *t* shall be ashamed of	Mk 8:38	1063
What *t* God hath joined together,	Mk 10:9	3767
T I say unto you, What things	Mk 11:24	
Having yet *t* one son, his	Mk 12:6	3767
What shall *t* the lord of the	Mk 12:9	3767
In the resurrection *t*, when they	Mk 12:23	3747
said unto them, Do ye not *t* err	Mk 12:24	
ye *t* do greatly err	Mk 12:27	3767
David *t* himself calleth him Lord	Mk 12:37	3767
Watch ye *t*	Mk 13:35	3767
t also that holy thing which	Lk 1:35	1352
Bring forth *t* fruits worthy of	Lk 3:8	3767
every tree *t* which bringeth not	Lk 3:9	3767
If thou *t* wilt worship me, all	Lk 4:7	3767
for *t* am I sent	Lk 4:43	
Be ye *t* merciful, as your Father	Lk 6:36	3767
Tell me *t*, which of them will	Lk 7:42	3767
Take heed *t* how ye hear	Lk 8:18	3767
T said he unto them, The harvest	Lk 10:2	3767
pray ye *t* the Lord of the harvest	Lk 10:2	
bid her *t* that she help me	Lk 10:40	3767
t shall they be your judges	Lk 11:19	
t when thine eye is single, thy	Lk 11:34	3767
Take heed *t* that the light which	Lk 11:35	3767
thy whole body *t* be full of light	Lk 11:36	3767
T also said the wisdom of God, I	Lk 11:49	
T whatsoever ye have spoken in	Lk 12:3	
Fear not *t*	Lk 12:7	3767
T I say unto you, Take no thought	Lk 12:22	
Be ye *t* ready also	Lk 12:40	3767
in them *t* come and be healed, and	Lk 13:14	3767
a wife, and *t* I cannot come	Lk 14:20	
t came his father out, and	Lk 15:28	3767
If *t* ye have not been faithful in	Lk 16:11	3767
Then he said, I pray thee *t*	Lk 16:27	3767
He said *t*, A certain nobleman	Lk 19:12	3767
What *t* shall the lord of the	Lk 20:15	3767
Render *t* unto Caesar the things	Lk 20:25	5106
There were *t* seven brethren	Lk 20:29	3767
T in the resurrection whose wife	Lk 20:33	3767
David *t* calleth him Lord, how is	Lk 20:44	
go ye not *t* after them	Lk 21:8	3767
Settle it *t* in your hearts, not	Lk 21:14	3767
Watch ye *t*, and pray always, that	Lk 21:36	3767
I will *t* chastise him, and release	Lk 23:16	3767
Pilate *t*, willing to release	Lk 23:20	3767
I will *t* chastise him, and let him	Lk 23:22	3767
t am I come baptizing with water	Jn 1:31	
When *t* he was risen from the dead	Jn 2:22	3767
this my joy *t* is fulfilled	Jn 3:29	3767
When *t* the Lord knew how the	Jn 4:1	3767
Jesus *t*, being wearied with his	Jn 4:6	3767
T said the disciples one to	Jn 4:33	3767
The Jews *t* said unto him that was	Jn 5:10	3767
t did the Jews persecute Jesus,	Jn 5:16	
T the Jews sought the more to	Jn 5:18	
T they gathered them together, and	Jn 6:13	3767
When Jesus *t* perceived that they	Jn 6:15	3767
When the people *t* saw that Jesus	Jn 6:24	3767
They said *t* unto him, What sign	Jn 6:30	3767
Jesus *t* answered and said unto	Jn 6:43	3767
Every man *t* that hath heard, and	Jn 6:45	3767
The Jews *t* strove among	Jn 6:52	3767
Many *t* of his disciples, when	Jn 6:60	3767
T said I unto you, that no man	Jn 6:65	
His brethren *t* said unto him,	Jn 7:3	3767
Moses *t* gave unto you	Jn 7:22	
Many of the people *t*, when they	Jn 7:40	3767
The Pharisees *t* said unto him	Jn 8:13	3767
I said *t* unto you, that ye shall	Jn 8:24	3767
If the Son *t* shall make you free,	Jn 8:36	3767
ye *t* hear them not, because ye	Jn 8:47	
He went his way *t*, and washed, and	Jn 9:7	3767
The neighbours *t*, and they which	Jn 9:8	3767
T said they unto him, How were	Jn 9:10	3767
T said some of the Pharisees,	Jn 9:16	3767
T said his parents, He is of age	Jn 9:23	
t your sin remaineth	Jn 9:41	3767
T doth my Father love me, because	Jn 10:17	
There was a division *t* again	Jn 10:19	3767
T they sought again to take him	Jn 10:39	3767
T his sisters sent unto him,	Jn 11:3	3767
he had heard *t* that he was sick	Jn 11:6	3767
When Jesus *t* saw her weeping, and	Jn 11:33	3767
Jesus *t* again groaning in himself	Jn 11:38	3767
Jesus *t* walked no more openly	Jn 11:54	3767
the Jews *t* knew that he was there	Jn 12:9	3767
The people *t* that was with him	Jn 12:17	3767
The Pharisees *t* said among	Jn 12:19	3767
The same came *t* to Philip	Jn 12:21	3767
The people *t*, that stood by, and	Jn 12:29	3767
T they could not believe, because	Jn 12:39	
whatsoever I speak *t*, even as the	Jn 12:50	3767
t said he, Ye are not all clean	Jn 13:11	
Simon Peter *t* beckoned to him,	Jn 13:24	3767
T, when he was gone out, Jesus	Jn 13:31	3767
the world, *t* the world hateth you	Jn 15:19	
t said I, that he shall take of	Jn 16:15	
They said *t*, What is this that he	Jn 16:18	3767
And ye now *t* have sorrow	Jn 16:22	3767
Jesus *t*, knowing all things that	Jn 18:4	3767
if *t* ye seek me, let these go	Jn 18:8	3767
They said *t* unto him, Art not	Jn 18:25	3767
The Jews *t* said unto him, It is	Jn 18:31	3767
Pilate *t* said unto him, Art thou	Jn 18:37	3767
will ye *t* that I release unto you	Jn 18:39	3767
Then Pilate *t* took Jesus, and	Jn 19:1	3767
Pilate *t* went forth again, and	Jn 19:4	3767
When the chief priests *t* and	Jn 19:6	3767
When Pilate *t* heard that saying,	Jn 19:8	3767
t he that delivered me unto thee	Jn 19:11	
When Pilate *t* heard that saying,	Jn 19:13	3767
Then delivered he him *t* unto them	Jn 19:16	3767
They said *t* among themselves, Let	Jn 19:24	3767
These things *t* the soldiers did	Jn 19:24	3767
When Jesus *t* saw his mother, and	Jn 19:26	3767
When Jesus *t* had received the	Jn 19:30	3767
The Jews *t*, because it was the	Jn 19:31	3767
He came *t*, and took the body of	Jn 19:38	3767
they Jesus *t* because of the Jews'	Jn 19:42	3767
Peter *t* went forth, and that other	Jn 20:3	3767
other disciples *t* said unto him	Jn 20:25	3767
They cast *t*, and now they were not	Jn 21:6	3767
T that disciple whom Jesus loved	Jn 21:7	3767
When they *t* were come together,	Acts 1:6	3767
T did my heart rejoice, and my	Acts 2:26	
T being a prophet, and knowing	Acts 2:30	3767
T being by the right hand of God	Acts 2:33	3767
T let all the house of Israel	Acts 2:36	3767
Repent ye *t*, and be converted,	Acts 3:19	3767
T they that were scattered abroad	Acts 8:4	3767
Repent *t* of this thy wickedness,	Acts 8:22	3767
Arise *t*, and get thee down, and go	Acts 10:20	235
T came I unto you without	Acts 10:29	1352
I ask *t* for what intent ye have	Acts 10:29	3767
Send *t* to Joppa, and call hither	Acts 10:32	3767
Immediately *t* I sent to thee	Acts 10:33	3767
Now *t* are we all here present	Acts 10:33	3767
Peter *t* was kept in prison	Acts 12:5	3767
Be it known unto you *t*, men and	Acts 13:38	3767
Beware *t*, lest that come upon you	Acts 13:40	3767
Long time *t* abode they speaking	Acts 14:3	3767
When *t* Paul and Barnabas had no	Acts 15:2	3767
Now *t* why tempt ye God, to put a	Acts 15:10	3767
We have sent *t* Judas and Silas,	Acts 15:27	3767
T loosing from Troas, we came	Acts 16:11	3767
now *t* depart, and go in peace	Acts 16:36	3767
T many of them believed	Acts 17:12	3757
T disputed he in the synagogue	Acts 17:17	3767
we would know *t* what these things	Acts 17:20	3767
Whom *t* ye ignorantly worship, him	Acts 17:23	3767
Some *t* cried one thing, and some	Acts 19:32	3767
When he *t* was come up again, and	Acts 20:11	3767
Take heed *t* unto yourselves, and	Acts 20:28	3767
T watch, and remember, that by the	Acts 20:31	1352
What is it *t*	Acts 21:22	3767
Do *t* this that we say to thee	Acts 21:23	3767
Now *t* ye with the council signify	Acts 23:15	3767
Let them *t*, said he, which among	Acts 25:5	3767
T, when they were come hither,	Acts 25:17	3767
Having *t* obtained help of God, I	Acts 26:22	3767
For this cause *t* have I called	Acts 28:20	3767
Be it known *t* unto you, that the	Acts 28:28	3767
T thou art inexcusable, O man,	Rom 2:1	1352
Thou *t* which teachest another,	Rom 2:21	3767
T if the uncircumcision keep the	Rom 2:26	3767
T by the deeds of the law there	Rom 3:20	1360
T we conclude that a man is	Rom 3:28	3767
T it is of faith, that it might	Rom 4:16	
t it was imputed to him for	Rom 4:22	1352
T being justified by faith, we	Rom 5:1	3767
T as by the offence of one	Rom 5:18	
T we are buried with him by	Rom 6:4	3767
Let not sin *t* reign in your	Rom 6:12	3767
There is *t* now no condemnation to	Rom 8:1	686
T, brethren, we are debtors, not	Rom 8:12	
T hath he mercy on whom he will	Rom 9:18	
Behold *t* the goodness and severity	Rom 11:22	3767
I beseech you *t*, brethren, by the	Rom 12:1	3767
T if thine enemy hunger, feed him	Rom 12:20	3767
Whosoever *t* resisteth the power,	Rom 13:2	5620
Render *t* to all their dues	Rom 13:7	3767
t love is the fulfilling of the	Rom 13:10	3767
let us *t* cast off the works of	Rom 13:12	3767
whether we live *t*, or die, we are	Rom 14:8	3767
Let us not *t* judge one another	Rom 14:13	3767
Let us *t* follow after the things	Rom 14:19	
I have *t* whereof I may glory	Rom 15:17	3767
When *t* I have performed this, and	Rom 15:28	3767
I am glad *t* on your behalf	Rom 16:19	3767
T let no man glory in men	1Cor 3:21	5620
T judge nothing before the time,	1Cor 4:5	5620
Purge out *t* the old leaven, that	1Cor 5:7	3767
T let us keep the feast, not with	1Cor 5:8	5620
T put away from among yourselves	1Cor 5:13	
Now *t* there is utterly a fault	1Cor 6:7	3767
t glorify God in your body, and in	1Cor 6:20	1211
I say *t* to the unmarried and	1Cor 7:8	1160
I suppose *t* that this is good for	1Cor 7:26	3767
As concerning *t* the eating of	1Cor 8:4	3767
I *t* so run, not as uncertainly	1Cor 9:26	5106
Whether *t* ye eat, or drink, or	1Cor 10:31	3767
ye come together *t* into one place	1Cor 11:20	3767
is it *t* not of the body	1Cor 12:15	
is it *t* not of the body	1Cor 12:16	
T if I know not the meaning of	1Cor 14:11	3767
If *t* the whole church be come	1Cor 14:23	3767
T whether it were I or they, so	1Cor 15:11	3767
T, my beloved brethren, be ye	1Cor 15:58	5620
Let no man *t* despise him	1Cor 16:11	3767
t acknowledge ye them that are	1Cor 16:18	3767
When I *t* was thus minded, did I	2Cor 1:17	3767
T, seeing we have this ministry,	2Cor 4:1	
I believed, and *t* have I spoken	2Cor 4:13	1352
we also believe, and *t* speak	2Cor 4:13	1352
T we are always confident,	2Cor 5:6	3767
Knowing *t* the terror of the Lord,	2Cor 5:11	3767
T if any man be in Christ, he is	2Cor 5:17	5620
Having *t* these promises dearly	2Cor 7:1	3767
T we were comforted in your	2Cor 7:13	
I rejoice *t* that I have	2Cor 7:16	
T, as ye abound in every thing,	2Cor 8:7	235
Now *t* perform the doing of it	2Cor 8:11	2532
T I thought it necessary to	2Cor 9:5	3767
T it is no great thing if his	2Cor 11:15	3767
Most gladly *t* will I rather glory	2Cor 12:9	3767
T I take pleasure in infirmities,	2Cor 12:10	1352
T I write these things being	2Cor 13:10	
is *t* Christ the minister of sin	Gal 2:17	686
He *t* that ministereth to you the	Gal 3:5	3767
Know ye *t* that they which are of	Gal 3:7	686
Am I *t* become your enemy, because	Gal 4:16	5620
Stand fast *t* in the liberty	Gal 5:1	3767
As we have *t* opportunity, let us	Gal 6:10	
Now *t* ye are no more strangers and	Eph 2:19	686
I *t*, the prisoner of the Lord,	Eph 4:1	3767
This I say *t*, and testify in the	Eph 4:17	3767
Be ye *t* followers of God, as dear	Eph 5:1	3767
Be not ye *t* partakers with them	Eph 5:7	3767
T as the church is subject unto	Eph 5:24	235
Stand *t*, having your loins girt	Eph 6:14	3767
If there be *t* any consolation in	Phil 2:1	3767
Him *t* I hope to send presently,	Phil 2:23	3767
I sent him *t* the more carefully,	Phil 2:28	3767
Receive him *t* in the Lord with	Phil 2:29	3767
Let us *t*, as many as be perfect,	Phil 3:15	3767
T, my brethren dearly beloved and	Phil 4:1	5620
As ye have *t* received Christ	Col 2:6	3767
Let no man *t* judge you in meat,	Col 2:16	3767
Mortify *t* your members which are	Col 3:5	3767
Put on *t*, as the elect of God,	Col 3:12	3767
T, brethren, we were comforted	1Th 3:7	
He *t* that despiseth, despiseth	1Th 4:8	5105

T let us not sleep, as do others	1Th 5:6	
T, brethren, stand fast, and hold	2Th 2:15	
I exhort *t*, that, first of all,	1Ti 2:1	*3767*
I will *t* that men pray every	1Ti 2:8	*3767*
For *t* we both labour and suffer	1Ti 4:10	
I will *t* that the younger women	1Ti 5:14	*3767*
Be not thou *t* ashamed of the	2Ti 1:8	*3767*
Thou *t*, my son, be strong in the	2Ti 2:1	*3767*
Thou *t* endure hardness, as a good	2Ti 2:3	*3767*
T I endure all things for the	2Ti 2:10	
If a man *t* purge himself from	2Ti 2:21	*3767*
I charge thee *t* before God	2Ti 4:1	*3767*
thou *t* receive him, that is, mine	Philem 12	
For perhaps he *t* departed for a	Philem 15	
If thou count me *t* a partner	Philem 17	*3767*
t God, even thy God, hath	Heb 1:9	
T we ought to give the more	Heb 2:1	
Let us *t* fear, lest, a promise	Heb 4:1	*3767*
Seeing *t* it remaineth that some	Heb 4:6	*3767*
There remaineth *t* a rest to the	Heb 4:9	*686*
Let us labour *t* to enter into	Heb 4:11	*3767*
Let us *t* come boldly unto the	Heb 4:16	*3767*
T leaving the principles of the	Heb 6:1	
If *t* perfection were by the	Heb 7:11	*3767*
It was *t* necessary that the	Heb 9:23	*3767*
Having *t*, brethren, boldness to	Heb 10:19	*3767*
Cast not away *t* your confidence,	Heb 10:35	*3767*
T sprang there even of one, and	Heb 11:12	*1352*
Let us go forth *t* unto him	Heb 13:13	*5106*
By him *t* let us offer the	Heb 13:15	*3767*
whosoever *t* will be a friend of	Jas 4:4	*3767*
Submit yourselves *t* to God	Jas 4:7	*3767*
T to him that knoweth to do good,	Jas 4:17	*3767*
Be patient *t*, brethren, unto the	Jas 5:7	*3767*
Unto you *t* which believe he is	1Pet 2:7	*3767*
be ye *t* sober, and watch unto	1Pet 4:7	*3767*
Humble yourselves *t* under the	1Pet 5:6	*3767*
Ye *t*, beloved, seeing ye know	2Pet 3:17	*3767*
Let that *t* abide in you, which ye	1Jn 2:24	*3767*
t the world knoweth us not,	1Jn 3:1	
t speak they of the world, and the	1Jn 4:5	
We *t* ought to receive such, that	3Jn 8	*3767*
I will *t* put you in remembrance,	Jude 5	
Remember *t* from whence thou art	Rev 2:5	*3767*
Remember *t* how thou hast received	Rev 3:3	*3767*
If *t* thou shalt not watch, I will	Rev 3:3	*3767*
be zealous *t*, and repent	Rev 3:19	*3767*
T are they before the throne of	Rev 7:15	
T rejoice, ye heavens, and ye that	Rev 12:12	
T shall her plagues come in one	Rev 18:8	*5124*

THEREFROM

that ye turn not aside *t* to the	Josh 23:6	
he departed not *t*	2Kin 3:3	
he departed not *t*	2Kin 13:2	

THEREIN

in the earth, and multiply *t*	Gen 9:7	
the fifty righteous that are *t*	Gen 18:24	7130
I thee, and the cave that is *t*	Gen 23:11	
field, and the cave which was *t*	Gen 23:17	
the field, and the cave that is *t*	Gen 23:20	
dwell and trade ye *t*, and get you	Gen 34:10	
and get you possessions *t*	Gen 34:10	
dwell in the land, and trade *t*	Gen 34:21	
and they had possessions *t*	Gen 47:27	
of the cave that is *t* was from	Gen 49:32	
and with pitch, and put the child *t*	Ex 2:3	
the men, that they may labour *t*	Ex 5:9	
neither was there any worm *t*	Ex 16:24	
and put an omer full of manna *t*	Ex 16:33	8033
it, and an ox or an ass fall *t*	Ex 21:33	8033
sons' after him, to be anointed *t*	Ex 29:29	
altar, and thou shalt put water *t*	Ex 30:18	8033
for whosoever doeth any work *t*	Ex 31:14	
whosoever doeth work *t* shall be	Ex 35:2	
thou shalt put *t* the ark of the	Ex 40:3	8033
the altar, and shalt put water *t*	Ex 40:7	8033
the tabernacle, and all that is *t*	Ex 40:9	
these that a man doeth, sinning *t*	Lev 6:3	2007
he hath done in trespassing *t*	Lev 6:7	
the tabernacle and all that was *t*	Lev 8:10	
of them his censer, and put fire *t*	Lev 10:1	2004
behold, there be no white hairs *t*	Lev 13:21	
there is black hair grown up *t*	Lev 13:37	
keep mine ordinances, to walk *t*	Lev 18:4	
that ye defile not yourselves *t*	Lev 18:30	
whither I bring you to dwell *t*	Lev 20:22	
there shall be no blemish *t*	Lev 22:21	
ye shall do no work *t*	Lev 23:3	
ye shall do no servile work *t*	Lev 23:7	
ye shall do no servile work *t*	Lev 23:8	
ye shall do no servile work *t*	Lev 23:21	
Ye shall do no servile work *t*	Lev 23:25	
ye shall do no servile work *t*	Lev 23:35	
and ye shall do no servile work *t*	Lev 23:36	
your fill, and dwell *t* in safety	Lev 25:19	5921
your enemies which dwell *t* shall	Lev 26:32	
tabernacle, and of all that *t* is	Num 4:16	
and the people that dwelleth *t*	Num 13:18	5921
or lean, whether there be wood *t*	Num 13:20	
which I sware to make you dwell *t*	Num 14:30	
And put fire *t*, and put incense in	Num 16:7	2004
put fire *t* from off the altar, and	Num 16:46	5921
do no manner of servile work *t*	Num 28:18	
ye shall not do any work *t*	Num 29:7	
ye shall do no servile work *t*	Num 29:35	
and he dwelt *t*	Num 32:40	
of the land, and dwell *t*	Num 33:53	
of the blood that is shed *t*	Num 35:33	
The Emims dwelt *t* in times past	Deut 2:10	
giants dwelt *t* in old time	Deut 2:20	
unto thee, lest thou be snared *t*	Deut 7:25	
built goodly houses, and dwelt *t*	Deut 8:12	
earth also, with all that *t* is	Deut 10:14	
ye shall possess it, and dwell *t*	Deut 11:31	
it utterly, and all that is *t*	Deut 13:15	
And if there be any blemish *t*	Deut 15:21	
thou shalt do no work *t*	Deut 16:8	
possess it, and shalt dwell *t*	Deut 17:14	
he shall read *t* all the days of	Deut 17:19	
all the people that is found *t*	Deut 20:11	
and possessest it, and dwellest *t*	Deut 26:1	
house, and thou shalt not dwell *t*	Deut 28:30	
beareth, nor any grass groweth *t*	Deut 29:23	
but thou shalt meditate *t* day	Josh 1:8	
to all that is written *t*	Josh 1:8	
even it, and all that are *t*	Josh 6:17	
city with fire, and all that was *t*	Josh 6:24	
and all the souls that were *t*	Josh 10:28	
and all the souls that were *t*	Josh 10:30	
and all the souls that were *t*	Josh 10:32	
all the souls that were *t* he	Josh 10:35	
and all the souls that were *t*	Josh 10:37	
and all the souls that were *t*	Josh 10:37	
all the souls that were *t*	Josh 10:39	
were *t* with the edge of the sword	Josh 11:11	
and possessed it, and dwelt *t*	Josh 19:47	
and he built the city, and dwelt *t*	Josh 19:50	
and they possessed it, and dwelt *t*	Josh 21:43	
the way of the LORD to walk *t*	Judg 2:22	
did cast *t* every man the earrings	Judg 8:25	8033
and slew the people that was *t*	Judg 9:45	
upon all the people that were *t*	Judg 16:30	
and saw the people that were *t*	Judg 18:7	7130
And they built a city, and dwelt *t*	Judg 18:28	
the women captives, that were *t*	1Sa 30:2	
forth the people that were *t*	2Sa 12:31	
an house, that my name might be *t*	1Kin 8:16	8033
they went to Damascus, and dwelt *t*	1Kin 11:24	
in mount Ephraim, and dwelt *t*	1Kin 12:25	
me a new cruse, and put salt *t*	2Kin 2:20	8033
t all the money that was brought	2Kin 12:9	8033
who made Israel sin, but walked *t*	2Kin 13:6	
but he walked *t*	2Kin 13:11	
smote Tiphsah, and all that were *t*	2Kin 15:16	
all the women *t* that were with	2Kin 15:16	
fields rejoice, and all that is *t*	1Chr 16:32	
build an altar *t* unto the LORD	1Chr 21:22	
to build him an house to dwell *t*	2Chr 2:3	
tables which Moses put *t* at Horeb	2Chr 5:10	
And they dwelt *t*, and have built	2Chr 20:8	
thee a sanctuary *t* for thy name	2Chr 20:8	
and sedition have been made *t*	Ezr 4:19	
t was a record thus written	Ezr 6:2	1459
that there was no breach left *t*	Neh 6:1	
but the people were few *t*	Neh 7:4	
at the first, and found written *t*	Neh 7:5	
he read *t* before the street that	Neh 8:3	
earth, and all things that are *t*	Neh 9:6	5921
the seas, and all that is *t*	Neh 9:6	
t was found written, that the	Neh 13:1	
There dwelt men of Tyre also *t*	Neh 13:16	
let no joyful voice come *t*	Job 3:7	
be, and he shall not rejoice *t*	Job 20:18	
the world, and they that dwell *t*	Ps 24:1	
the land, and dwell *t* for ever	Ps 37:29	5921
Thy congregation hath dwelt *t*	Ps 68:10	
and every thing that moveth *t*	Ps 69:34	
that love his name shall dwell *t*	Ps 69:36	
field be joyful, and all that is *t*	Ps 96:12	
the world, and they that dwell *t*	Ps 98:7	
whom thou hast made to play *t*	Ps 104:26	
wickedness of them that dwell *t*	Ps 107:34	
of all them that have pleasure *t*	Ps 111:2	
for *t* do I delight	Ps 119:35	
earth, the sea, and all that *t* is	Ps 146:6	
but perverseness *t* is a breach in	Prov 15:4	
abhorred of the LORD shall fall *t*	Prov 22:14	8033
Whoso diggeth a pit shall fall *t*	Prov 26:27	
t shall he leave it for his	Eccl 2:21	
of it, and also made a winepress *t*	Is 5:2	8432
and let us make a breach *t* for us	Is 7:6	
and they that dwell *t* are desolate	Is 24:6	
the people that dwell *t* shall be	Is 33:24	
the earth hear, and all that is *t*	Is 34:1	4393
to generation shall they dwell *t*	Is 34:17	
though fools, shall not err *t*	Is 35:8	
it, and spirit to them that walk *t*	Is 42:5	
down to the sea, and all that is *t*	Is 42:10	4393
O forest, and every tree *t*	Is 44:23	
joy and gladness shall be found *t*	Is 51:3	
they that dwell *t* shall die in	Is 51:6	
whosoever goeth *t* shall not know	Is 59:8	
be forsaken, and not a man dwell *t*	Jer 4:29	2004
where is the good way, and walk *t*	Jer 6:16	
But they said, We will not walk *t*	Jer 6:16	
the city, and those that dwell *t*	Jer 8:16	
obeyed my voice, neither walked *t*	Jer 9:13	
wickedness of them that dwell *t*	Jer 12:4	
the sabbath day, to do no work *t*	Jer 17:24	
shall be driven on, and fall *t*	Jer 23:12	
and they shall till it, and dwell *t*	Jer 27:11	
write *t* all the words that I have	Jer 36:2	413
saying, Why hast thou written *t*	Jer 36:29	5921
who wrote *t* from the mouth of	Jer 36:32	5921
desolation, and no man dwelleth *t*	Jer 44:2	
the land, and all that is *t*	Jer 47:2	4393
the city, and them that dwell *t*	Jer 47:2	
desolate, without any to dwell *t*	Jer 48:9	2004
desolate, and none shall dwell *t*	Jer 50:3	
there, and the owls shall dwell *t*	Jer 50:39	
shall any son of man dwell *t*	Jer 50:40	
and the earth, and all that is *t*	Jer 51:48	
and, lo, a roll of a book was *t*	Eze 2:9	
there was written *t* lamentations	Eze 2:10	413
and of their detestable things *t*	Eze 7:20	
be desolate from all that is *t*	Eze 12:19	4393
violence of all them that dwell *t*	Eze 12:19	
t shall be left a remnant that	Eze 14:22	
to the north shall be burned *t*	Eze 20:47	
let them seethe the bones of it *t*	Eze 24:5	8432
city, to the pot whose scum is *t*	Eze 24:6	
And they shall dwell safely *t*	Eze 28:26	5921
the land waste, and all that is *t*	Eze 30:12	4393
shall smite all them that dwell *t*	Eze 32:15	
and they shall dwell *t*, even they,	Eze 37:25	
and there were windows *t* and in the	Eze 40:33	
When the priests enter *t*, then	Eze 42:14	
and for all that shall be done *t*	Eze 44:14	
and his concubines, might drink *t*	Dan 5:2	
that dwelleth *t* shall languish	Hos 4:3	
the transgressors shall fall *t*	Hos 14:9	
up the city with all that is *t*	Amos 6:8	4393
every one mourn that dwelleth *t*	Amos 8:8	
and all that dwell *t* shall mourn	Amos 9:5	
O earth, and all that *t* is	Mic 1:2	4393
because of them that dwell *t*	Mic 7:13	
the world, and all that dwell *t*	Nah 1:5	
the city, and of all that dwell *t*	Hab 2:8	
the city, and of all that dwell *t*	Hab 2:17	
the maker of his work trusteth *t*	Hab 2:18	5921
the multitude of men and cattle *t*	Zec 2:4	8432
The black horses which are *t* go	Zec 6:6	
two parts *t* shall be cut off and	Zec 13:8	
but the third shall be left *t*	Zec 13:8	
come and take of them, and seethe *t*	Zec 14:21	
by it, and by him that dwelleth *t*	Mt 23:21	
child, he shall not enter *t*	Mk 10:15	
into the house, neither enter *t*	Mk 13:15	
And heal the sick that are *t*	Lk 10:9	
child shall in no wise enter *t*	Lk 18:17	
to cast out them that sold *t*	Lk 19:45	
the bag, and bare what was put *t*	Jn 12:6	
desolate, and let no man dwell *t*	Acts 1:20	
the sea, and all things that are *t*	Acts 14:15	
made the world and all things *t*	Acts 17:24	
and he put us *t*	Acts 27:6	
For *t* is the righteousness of God	Rom 1:17	
dead to sin, live any longer *t*	Rom 6:2	
he is called, *t* abide with God	1Cor 7:24	
that *t* I may speak boldly, as I	Eph 6:20	
I *t* do rejoice, yea, and will	Phil 1:18	
abounding *t* with thanksgiving	Col 2:7	
remaineth that some must enter *t*	Heb 4:6	
not, neither hadst pleasure *t*	Heb 10:8	
them that have been occupied *t*	Heb 13:9	
law of liberty, and continueth *t*	Jas 1:25	
they are again entangled *t*	2Pet 2:20	*5125*
that are *t* shall be burned up	2Pet 3:10	
those things which are written *t*	Rev 1:3	
heaven, and the things that *t* are	Rev 10:6	
earth, and the things that *t* are	Rev 10:6	
sea, and the things which are *t*	Rev 10:6	
the altar, and them that worship *t*	Rev 11:1	
them which dwell *t* to worship the	Rev 13:12	
And I saw no temple *t*	Rev 21:22	

THEREINTO

that are in the countries enter *t*	Lk 21:21	

THEREOF

eatest *t* thou shalt surely die	Gen 2:17	
creature, that was the name *t*	Gen 2:19	
and closed up the flesh instead *t*	Gen 2:21	
know that in the day ye eat *t*	Gen 3:5	
one wise, she took of the fruit *t*	Gen 3:6	
of his flock and of the fat *t*	Gen 4:4	
ark shalt thou set in the side *t*	Gen 6:16	
But flesh with the life *t*	Gen 9:4	
which is the blood *t*	Gen 9:4	
the clusters *t* brought forth ripe	Gen 40:10	
This is the interpretation *t*	Gen 40:18	
of Egypt, and all the wise men *t*	Gen 41:8	
the fame *t* was heard in Pharaoh's	Gen 45:16	
of Egypt even to the other end *t*	Gen 47:21	
which I will do in the midst *t*	Ex 3:20	
ye shall not diminish ought *t*	Ex 5:8	
the foundation *t* even until now	Ex 9:18	
for *t* must we take to serve the	Ex 10:26	
legs, and with the purtenance *t*	Ex 12:9	
There shall no stranger eat *t*	Ex 12:43	
him, then shall he eat *t*	Ex 12:44	
an hired servant shall not eat *t*	Ex 12:45	
neither shall ye break a bone *t*	Ex 12:46	
uncircumcised person shall eat *t*	Ex 12:48	
of Israel called the name *t* Manna	Ex 16:31	
the smoke *t* ascended as the smoke	Ex 19:18	
and the owner of it shall accept *t*	Ex 22:11	
make restitution unto the owner *t*	Ex 22:12	
the owner *t* being not with it, he	Ex 22:14	
But if the owner *t* be with it	Ex 22:15	
and shalt gather in the fruits *t*	Ex 23:10	
pattern of all the instruments *t*	Ex 25:9	
and a half shall be the length *t*	Ex 25:10	
a cubit and a half the breadth *t*	Ex 25:10	
and a cubit and a half the height *t*	Ex 25:10	
and put them in the four corners *t*	Ex 25:12	
and a half shall be the length *t*	Ex 25:17	
a cubit and a half the breadth *t*	Ex 25:17	
the cherubims on the two ends *t*	Ex 25:19	
two cubits shall be the length *t*	Ex 25:23	
and a cubit the breadth *t*	Ex 25:23	
and a cubit and a half the height *t*	Ex 25:23	
crown to the border *t* round about	Ex 25:25	
that are on the four feet *t*	Ex 25:26	
the dishes *t*, and spoons *t*	Ex 25:29	
and covers *t*, and bowls *t*	Ex 25:29	
thou shalt make the seven lamps *t*	Ex 25:37	
and they shall light the lamps *t*	Ex 25:37	
And the tongs *t*, and the	Ex 25:38	
and the snuffdishes *t*	Ex 25:38	
according to the fashion *t* which	Ex 26:30	
the height *t* shall be three	Ex 27:1	

T

of it upon the four corners *t*	Ex 27:2
all the vessels *t* thou shalt make	Ex 27:3
rings in the four corners *t*	Ex 27:4
And the twenty pillars *t* and their	Ex 27:10
tabernacle in all the service *t*	Ex 27:19
and all the pins *t*	Ex 27:19
have the two shoulderpieces *t*	Ex 28:7
joined at the two edges *t*	Ex 28:7
the same, according to the work *t*	Ex 28:8
a span shall be the length *t*	Ex 28:16
and a span shall be the breadth *t*	Ex 28:16
the breastplate in the border *t*	Ex 28:26
underneath, toward the forepart *t*	Ex 28:27
over against the other coupling *t*	Ex 28:27
t unto the rings of the ephod	Ex 28:28
in the top of it, in the midst *t*	Ex 28:32
of scarlet, round about the hem *t*	Ex 28:33
but a stranger shall not eat *t*	Ex 29:33
according to the drink offering *t*	Ex 29:41
A cubit shall be the length *t*	Ex 30:2
and a cubit the breadth *t*	Ex 30:2
two cubits shall be the height *t*	Ex 30:2
the horns *t* shall be of the same	Ex 30:2
it with pure gold, the top *t*	Ex 30:3
the sides *t* round about, and the	Ex 30:3
round about, and the horns *t*	Ex 30:3
crown of it, by the two corners *t*	Ex 30:4
according to the composition *t*	Ex 30:37
The ark, and the staves *t*, with	Ex 35:12
and coupled together at the head *t*	Ex 36:29
cubits and a half was the length *t*	Ex 37:6
one cubit and a half the breadth *t*	Ex 37:6
the cherubims on the two ends *t*	Ex 37:8
two cubits was the length *t*	Ex 37:10
and a cubit the breadth *t*	Ex 37:10
and a cubit and a half the height *t*	Ex 37:10
gold for the border *t* round about	Ex 37:12
that were in the four feet *t*	Ex 37:13
branches going out of the sides *t*	Ex 37:18
candlestick out of the one side *t*	Ex 37:18
out of the other side *t*	Ex 37:18
made he it, and all the vessels *t*	Ex 37:24
the horns *t* were of the same	Ex 37:25
the sides *t* round about, and the	Ex 37:26
of gold for it under the crown *t*	Ex 37:27
of it, upon the two sides *t*	Ex 37:27
five cubits was the length *t*	Ex 38:1
and five cubits the breadth *t*	Ex 38:1
and three cubits the height *t*	Ex 38:1
he made the horns *t* on the four	Ex 38:2
the horns *t* were of the same	Ex 38:2
all the vessels *t* made he of	Ex 38:3
t beneath unto the midst of it	Ex 38:4
the same, according to the work *t*	Ex 39:5
a span was the length *t*, and a	Ex 39:9
and a span the breadth *t*	Ex 39:9
over against the other coupling *t*	Ex 39:20
of the testimony, and the staves *t*	Ex 39:35
The table, and all the vessels *t*	Ex 39:36
candlestick, with the lamps *t*	Ex 39:37
in order, and all the vessels *t*	Ex 39:37
candlestick, and light the lamps *t*	Ex 40:4
hallow it, and all the vessels *t*	Ex 40:9
sockets, and set up the boards *t*	Ex 40:18
and put in the bars *t*	Ex 40:18
the blood *t* shall be wrung out at	Lev 1:15
shall cleave it with the wings *t*	Lev 1:17
flour *t*, and of the oil *t*	Lev 2:2
with all the frankincense *t*	Lev 2:2
the meat offering a memorial *t*	Lev 2:9
of it, part of the beaten corn *t*	Lev 2:16
and part of the oil *t*	Lev 2:16
with all the frankincense *t*	Lev 2:16
t round about upon the altar	Lev 3:8
the fat *t*, and the whole rump, it	Lev 3:9
t upon the altar round about	Lev 3:13
And he shall offer *t* his offering	Lev 3:14
of the blood *t* with his finger	Lev 4:30
t at the bottom of the altar	Lev 4:30
he shall take away all the fat *t*	Lev 4:31
t at the bottom of the altar	Lev 4:34
he shall take away all the fat *t*	Lev 4:35
handful of it, even a memorial *t*	Lev 5:12
meat offering, and of the oil *t*	Lev 6:15
And the remainder *t* shall Aaron	Lev 6:16
the morning, and half *t* at night	Lev 6:20
touch the flesh *t* shall be holy	Lev 6:27
of the blood *t* upon any garment	Lev 6:27
among the priests shall eat *t*	Lev 6:29
the blood *t* shall he sprinkle	Lev 7:2
shall offer of it all the fat *t*	Lev 7:3
among the priests shall eat *t*	Lev 7:6
all that be clean shall eat *t*	Lev 7:19
he sprinkled *t* upon the altar	Lev 8:11
unto him, with the pieces *t*	Lev 9:13
offering, and took an handful *t*	Lev 9:17
he that toucheth the carcase *t*	Lev 11:39
the hair *t* be not turned white	Lev 13:4
in which, even in the skin *t*	Lev 13:18
the hair *t* be turned white	Lev 13:20
the stones of it, and the timber *t*	Lev 14:45
shall even pour out the blood *t*	Lev 17:13
the blood of it is for the life *t*	Lev 17:14
life of all flesh is the blood *t*	Lev 17:14
I do visit the iniquity *t* upon it	Lev 18:25
the fruit *t* as uncircumcised	Lev 19:23
t shall be holy to praise the	Lev 19:24
year shall ye eat of the fruit *t*	Lev 19:25
may yield unto you the increase *t*	Lev 19:25
but there shall no stranger eat *t*	Lev 22:13
put the fifth part *t* unto it	Lev 22:14
make any offering *t* in your land	Lev 22:24
you, and shall reap the harvest *t*	Lev 23:10
the meat offering *t* shall be two	Lev 23:13
drink offering *t* shall be of wine	Lev 23:13
flour, and bake twelve cakes *t*	Lev 24:5
and gather in the fruit *t*	Lev 25:3
shall all the increase *t* be meat	Lev 25:7
land unto all the inhabitants *t*	Lev 25:10
the increase *t* out of the field	Lev 25:12
thou shalt increase the price *t*	Lev 25:16
him count the years of the sale *t*	Lev 25:27
the exchange *t* shall be holy	Lev 27:10
fifth part *t* unto thy estimation	Lev 27:13
shall be according to the seed *t*	Lev 27:16
the possession *t* shall be the	Lev 27:21
add thereto the fifth part *t*	Lev 27:31
the change *t* shall be holy	Lev 27:33
and over all the vessels *t*	Num 1:50
tabernacle, and all the vessels *t*	Num 1:50
and those that were numbered *t*	Num 2:6
and those that were numbered *t*	Num 2:8
and those that were numbered *t*	Num 2:11
and the tent, the covering *t*	Num 3:25
cords of it for all the service *t*	Num 3:26
the hanging, and all the service *t*	Num 3:31
of the tabernacle, and the bars *t*	Num 3:36
pillars *t*, and the sockets *t*	Num 3:36
and all the vessels *t*	Num 3:36
and shall put in the staves *t*	Num 4:6
and shall put in the staves *t*	Num 4:8
and all the oil vessels *t*	Num 4:9
all the vessels *t* within a	Num 4:10
and shall put to the staves *t*	Num 4:11
put upon it all the vessels *t*	Num 4:14
sanctuary, and in the vessels *t*	Num 4:16
of the tabernacle, and the bars *t*	Num 4:31
the pillars *t*, and sockets *t*	Num 4:31
his trespass with the principal *t*	Num 5:7
and add unto it the fifth part *t*	Num 5:7
the offering, even the memorial *t*	Num 5:26
it, and all the instruments *t*	Num 7:1
the altar and all the vessels *t*	Num 7:1
the weight *t* was an hundred and	Num 7:13
he lighted the lamps *t* over	Num 8:3
shaft *t*, unto the flowers *t*	Num 8:4
cease waiting upon the service *t*	Num 8:25
according to all the ceremonies *t*	Num 9:3
and according to the manner *t*	Num 9:14
the colour *t* as the colour of	Num 11:7
that eateth up the inhabitants *t*	Num 13:32
ye shall give *t* the LORD's heave	Num 18:28
of the LORD, of all the best *t*	Num 18:29
the hallowed part *t* out of it	Num 18:29
ye have heaved the best *t* from it	Num 18:30
Heshbon, and in all the villages *t*	Num 21:25
and they took the villages *t*	Num 21:32
t be divided between many	Num 26:56
the drink offering *t* shall be the	Num 28:7
and as the drink offering *t*	Num 28:8
with oil, and the drink offering *t*	Num 28:9
offering, and the meat offering *t*	Num 29:19
with the cities *t* in the coasts	Num 32:33
went and took the small towns *t*	Num 32:41
and took Kenath, and the villages *t*	Num 32:42
land of Canaan with the coasts *t*	Num 34:2
the going forth *t* shall be from	Num 34:4
with the coasts *t* round about	Num 34:12
nine cubits was the length *t*	Deut 3:11
mount Gilead, and the cities *t*	Deut 3:12
also, and Jordan, and the coast *t*	Deut 3:17
I cast the dust *t* into the brook	Deut 9:21
unclean and the clean may eat *t*	Deut 12:15
that is therein, and the cattle *t*	Deut 13:15
it into the midst of the street *t*	Deut 13:16
and all the spoil *t* every whit	Deut 13:16
thou shalt not eat the blood *t*	Deut 15:23
male *t* with the edge of the sword	Deut 20:13
in the city, even all the spoil *t*	Deut 20:14
shalt not destroy the trees *t* by	Deut 20:19
I have not eaten *t* in my mourning	Deut 26:14
away ought *t* for any unclean use	Deut 26:14
nor given ought *t* for the dead	Deut 26:14
and shalt not gather the grapes *t*	Deut 28:30
eyes, and thou shalt not eat *t*	Deut 28:31
the whole land *t* is brimstone	Deut 29:23
things of the earth and fulness *t*	Deut 33:16
thine hand Jericho, and the king *t*	Josh 6:2
the foundation *t* in his firstborn	Josh 6:26
come according to the families *t*	Josh 7:14
only the spoil *t*, and the cattle	Josh 8:2
spoil *t*, and the cattle *t*	Josh 8:2
Hivite, and the Jebusite, heard *t*	Josh 9:1
Ai, and all the men *t* were mighty	Josh 10:2
the king *t* he utterly destroyed,	Josh 10:28
delivered it also, and the king *t*	Josh 10:30
but did unto the king *t* as he did	Josh 10:30
king *t*, and all the cities *t*	Josh 10:37
king *t*, and all the cities *t*	Josh 10:39
he did to Debir, and to the king *t*	Josh 10:39
smote the king *t* with the sword	Josh 11:10
was Jordan, and the border *t*	Josh 13:23
the cities and the villages *t*	Josh 13:23
the goings out *t* were at En-rogel	Josh 15:7
to the great sea, and the coast *t*	Josh 15:12
and the great sea, and the border *t*	Josh 15:47
the goings out *t* are at the sea	Josh 16:3
the goings out *t* were at the sea	Josh 16:8
the goings out *t* were at the	Josh 18:12
and the goings out *t* were at	Josh 18:14
by the coasts *t* round about	Josh 18:20
the outgoings *t* are in the valley	Josh 19:14
the outgoings *t* are at the sea	Josh 19:29
the outgoings *t* were at Jordan	Josh 19:33
with the suburbs *t* for our cattle	Josh 21:2
with the suburbs *t* round about it	Josh 21:11
of the city, and the villages *t*	Josh 21:12
half *t* gave Joshua among their	Josh 22:7
and not one thing hath failed *t*	Josh 23:14
Judah took Gaza with the coast *t*	Judg 1:18
and Askelon with the coast *t*	Judg 1:18
and Ekron with the coast *t*	Judg 1:18
a city, and called the name *t* Luz	Judg 1:26
which is the name *t* unto this day	Judg 1:26
such as before knew nothing *t*	Judg 3:2
ye bitterly the inhabitants *t*	Judg 5:23
dream, and the interpretation *t*	Judg 7:15
of Succoth, and the elders *t*	Judg 8:14
And Gideon made an ephod *t*	Judg 8:27
he took *t* in his hands, and went	Judg 14:9
he called the name *t* En-hakkore	Judg 15:19
who made *t* a graven image and a	Judg 17:4
even Ashdod and the coasts *t*	1Sa 5:6
in a coffer by the side *t*	1Sa 6:8
the coasts *t* did Israel deliver	1Sa 7:14
and drew it out of the sheath *t*	1Sa 17:51
shoot three arrows on the side *t*	1Sa 20:20
and did bake unleavened bread *t*	1Sa 28:24
upon his loins in the sheath *t*	2Sa 20:8
nevertheless he would not drink *t*	2Sa 23:16
my father David not knowing *t*	1Kin 2:32
she is the mother *t*	1Kin 3:27
the length *t* was threescore	1Kin 6:2
the breadth *t* twenty cubits, and	1Kin 6:2
the height *t* thirty cubits	1Kin 6:2
twenty cubits was the length *t*	1Kin 6:3
the breadth *t* before the house	1Kin 6:3
and twenty cubits in the height *t*	1Kin 6:20
throughout all the parts *t*	1Kin 6:38
the length *t* was an hundred	1Kin 7:2
the breadth *t* fifty cubits, and	1Kin 7:2
the height *t* thirty cubits, upon	1Kin 7:2
the length *t* was fifty cubits, and	1Kin 7:6
the breadth *t* thirty cubits	1Kin 7:6
and called the name *t* Jachin	1Kin 7:21
pillar, and called the name *t* Boaz	1Kin 7:21
the brim *t* was wrought like the	1Kin 7:26
and four cubits the breadth *t*	1Kin 7:27
four corners *t* had undersetters	1Kin 7:30
but the mouth *t* was round after	1Kin 7:31
the top of the base the ledges *t*	1Kin 7:35
the borders *t* were of the same	1Kin 7:35
For on the plates of the ledges *t*	1Kin 7:36
and on the borders *t*	1Kin 7:36
the ark and the staves *t* above	1Kin 8:7
him back from the way heard *t*	1Kin 13:26
came to pass, when Baasha heard *t*	1Kin 15:21
stones of Ramah, and the timber *t*	1Kin 15:22
he laid the foundation *t* in	1Kin 16:34
set up the gates *t* in his	1Kin 16:34
but make me *t* a little cake first	1Kin 17:13 8033
of Israel, and the horsemen *t*	2Kin 2:12
left they the stones *t*	2Kin 3:25
gathered *t* wild gourds his lap	2Kin 4:39
And they could not eat *t*	2Kin 4:40
full ears of corn in the husk *t*	2Kin 4:42
They shall eat, and shall leave *t*	2Kin 4:43
them, and they did eat, and left *t*	2Kin 4:44
thine eyes, but shalt not eat *t*	2Kin 7:2
thine eyes, but shalt not eat *t*	2Kin 7:19
of Israel, and the horsemen *t*	2Kin 13:14
and the coasts *t* from Tirzah	2Kin 15:16
to all the workmanship *t*	2Kin 16:10
Samaria, and dwelt in the cities *t*	2Kin 17:24
even unto Gaza, and the borders *t*	2Kin 18:8
cut down the tall cedar trees *t*	2Kin 19:23
and the choice fir trees *t*	2Kin 19:23
vineyards, and eat the fruits *t*	2Kin 19:29
place, and upon the inhabitants *t*	2Kin 22:16
and against the inhabitants *t*	2Kin 22:19
cast the powder *t* upon the graves	2Kin 23:6
them, with Kenath, and the towns *t*	1Chr 2:23
the suburbs *t* round about it	1Chr 6:55
of the city, and the villages *t*	1Chr 6:56
were, Beth-el and the towns *t*	1Chr 7:28
westward Gezer, with the towns *t*	1Chr 7:28
Shechem also and the towns *t*	1Chr 7:28
unto Gaza and the towns *t*	1Chr 7:28
Ono, and Lod, with the towns *t*	1Chr 8:12
the opening *t* every morning	1Chr 9:27
the sea roar, and the fulness *t*	1Chr 16:32
his sword again into the sheath *t*	1Chr 21:27
vessels of it for the service *t*	1Chr 23:26
of the porch, and of the houses *t*	1Chr 28:11
and of the treasuries *t*	1Chr 28:11
and of the upper chambers *t*	1Chr 28:11
and of the inner parlours *t*	1Chr 28:11
candlestick, and for the lamps *t*	1Chr 28:15
and also for the lamps *t*,	1Chr 28:15
the walls *t*, and the doors *t*	2Chr 3:7
the breadth *t* twenty cubits	2Chr 3:8
brass, twenty cubits the length *t*	2Chr 4:1
and twenty cubits the breadth *t*	2Chr 4:1
and ten cubits the height *t*	2Chr 4:1
and five cubits the height *t*	2Chr 4:2
the inner doors *t* for the most	2Chr 4:22
the ark and the staves *t* above	2Chr 5:8
of gold with the lamps *t*, to burn	2Chr 13:11
him, Beth-el with the towns *t*	2Chr 13:19
and Jeshanah with the towns *t*	2Chr 13:19
and Ephrain with the towns *t*	2Chr 13:19
stones of Ramah, and the timber *t*	2Chr 16:6
and Shocho with the villages *t*	2Chr 28:18
and Timnah with the villages *t*	2Chr 28:18
Gimzo also and the villages *t*	2Chr 28:18
offering, with all the vessels *t*	2Chr 29:18
table, with all the vessels *t*	2Chr 29:18
things, and the establishment *t*	2Chr 32:1
place, and upon the inhabitants *t*	2Chr 34:24
and against the inhabitants *t*	2Chr 34:27
burnt all the palaces *t* with fire	2Chr 36:19
all the goodly vessels *t*	2Chr 36:19

city, and have set up the walls *t* Ezr 4:12
again, and the walls *t* set up Ezr 4:16
foundations *t* be strongly laid Ezr 6:3
the height *t* threescore cubits, Ezr 6:3
the breadth *t* threescore cubits Ezr 6:3
and to repair the desolations *t* Ezr 9:9
of every city, and the judges *t* Ezr 10:14
the gates *t* are burned with fire Neh 1:3
the gates *t* are consumed with Neh 2:3
the gates *t* were consumed with Neh 2:13
the gates *t* are burned with fire Neh 2:17
build, who also laid the beams *t* Neh 3:3
and set up the doors *t* Neh 3:3
the locks *t*, and the bars *t* Neh 3:3
they laid the beams *t*, and set up Neh 3:6
and set up the doors *t* Neh 3:6
the locks *t*, and the bars *t* Neh 3:6
built it, and set up the doors *t* Neh 3:13
the locks *t*, and the bars *t* Neh 3:13
build it, and set up the doors *t* Neh 3:14
the locks *t*, and the bars *t* Neh 3:14
covered it, and set up the doors *t* Neh 3:15
the locks *t*, and the bars *t* Neh 3:15
joined together unto the half *t* Neh 4:6
that when all our enemies heard *t* Neh 6:16
the fruit *t* and the good *t* Neh 9:36
and in the villages *t*, and at Neh 11:25
and at Dibon, and in the villages *t* Neh 11:25
Jekabzeel, and in the villages *t* Neh 11:25
Beer-sheba, and in the villages *t* Neh 11:27
at Mekonah, and in the villages *t* Neh 11:28
at Lachish, and the fields *t* Neh 11:30
at Azekah, and in the villages *t* Neh 11:30
of my God, and for the offices *t* Neh 13:14
according to the writing *t* Est 1:22
the king *t* in Mordecai's name Est 2:22
according to the writing *t* Est 3:12
on the three and twentieth day *t* Est 8:9
according to the writing *t* Est 8:9
together on the thirteenth day *t* Est 9:18
and on the fourteenth *t* Est 9:18
stars of the twilight *t* be dark Job 3:9
and mine ear received a little *t* Job 4:12
I could not discern the form *t* Job 4:16
place, and the pillars *t* tremble Job 9:6
the faces of the judges *t* Job 9:24
The measure *t* is longer than the Job 11:9
tender branch *t* will not cease Job 14:7
Though the root *t* wax old in the Job 14:8
the stock *t* die in the ground Job 14:8
the perfection *t* upon the earth Job 15:29
take away flocks, and feed *t* Job 24:2
they know not the ways *t*, nor Job 24:13
nor abide in the paths *t* Job 24:13
the waters, and the inhabitants *t* Job 26:5
Man knoweth not the price *t* Job 28:13
silver be weighed for the price *t* Job 28:15
heard the fame *t* with our ears Job 28:22
God understandeth the way *t* Job 28:23
and he knoweth the place *t* Job 28:23
the fatherless hath not eaten *t* Job 31:17
the furrows likewise *t* complain Job 31:38
eaten the fruits *t* without money Job 31:39
the owners *t* to lose their life Job 31:39
rain according to the vapour *t* Job 36:27
The noise *t* sheweth concerning it Job 36:33
Who hath laid the measures *t* Job 38:5
are the foundations *t* fastened Job 38:6
or who laid the corner stone *t* Job 38:6
I made the cloud the garment *t* Job 38:9
darkness, where is the place *t* Job 38:19
shouldest take it to the bound *t* Job 38:20
know the paths to the house *t* Job 38:20
set the dominion *t* in the earth Job 38:33
is nothing hid from the heat *t* Ps 19:6
is the LORD's, and the fulness *t* Ps 24:1
the humble shall hear *t*, and be Ps 34:2
Though the waters *t* roar and be Ps 46:3
shake with the swelling *t* Ps 46:3
tell the towers *t* Ps 48:12
of the sun unto the going down *t* Ps 50:1
world is mine, and the fulness *t* Ps 50:12
they go about it upon the walls *t* Ps 55:10
Wickedness is in the midst *t* Ps 55:11
heal the breaches *t* Ps 60:2
waterest the ridges *t* abundantly Ps 65:10
thou settlest the furrows *t* Ps 65:10
thou blessest the springing *t* Ps 65:10
for I know not the numbers *t* Ps 71:15
the fruit *t* shall shake like Ps 72:16
carved work *t* at once with axes Ps 74:6
the inhabitants *t* are dissolved Ps 75:3
but the dregs *t*, all the wicked Ps 75:8
the boughs *t* were like the goodly Ps 80:10
when the waves *t* arise, thou Ps 89:9
as for the world and the fulness *t* Ps 89:11
the sea roar, and the fulness *t* Ps 96:11
the multitude of isles be glad *t* Ps 97:1
the sea roar, and the fulness *t* Ps 98:7
her stones, and favour the dust *t* Ps 102:14
the place *t* shall know it no more Ps 103:16
which lifteth up the waves *t* Ps 107:25
so that the waves *t* are still Ps 107:29
upon the willows in the midst *t* Ps 137:2
rase it, even to the foundation *t* Ps 137:7
away the life of the owners *t* Prov 1:19
the gain *t* than fine gold Prov 3:14
in the pathway *t* there is no Prov 12:28
but the end *t* are the ways of Prov 14:12
but the end *t* are the ways of Prov 16:25
whole disposing *t* is of the LORD Prov 16:33
love it shall eat the fruit *t* Prov 18:21
but the end *t* shall not be Prov 20:21
the strength of the confidence *t* Prov 21:22
and nettles had covered the face *t* Prov 24:31
the stone wall *t* was broken down Prov 24:31
know not what to do in the end *t* Prov 25:8
fig tree shall eat the fruit *t* Prov 27:18
of a land many are the princes *t* Prov 28:2
the state *t* shall be prolonged Prov 28:2
good is there to the owners *t* Eccl 5:11
for the owners *t* to their hurt Eccl 5:13
and hath given him power to eat *t* Eccl 5:19
God giveth him not power to eat *t* Eccl 6:2
of a thing than the beginning *t* Eccl 7:8
sendeth forth the smell *t* Song 1:12
He made the pillars *t* of silver Song 3:10
of silver, the bottom *t* of gold Song 3:10
the midst *t* being paved with love Song 3:10
that the spices *t* may flow out Song 4:16
I will take hold of the boughs *t* Song 7:8
the coals *t* are coals of fire, Song 8:6
every one for the fruit *t* was to Song 8:11
that keep the fruit *t* two hundred Song 8:12
of his people, and the princes *t* Is 3:14
midst *t* by the spirit of judgment Is 4:4
it, and gathered out the stones *t* Is 5:2
I will take away the hedge *t* Is 5:5
and break down the wall *t*, and it Is 5:5
is darkened in the heavens *t* Is 5:30
seed shall be the substance *t* Is 6:13
destroy the sinners *t* out of it Is 13:9
the constellations *t* shall not Is 13:10
and destroyed the cities *t* Is 14:17
the howling *t* unto Eglaim Is 15:8
the howling *t* unto Beer-elim Is 15:8
down the principal plants *t* Is 16:8
the outmost fruitful branches *t* Is 17:6
Egypt shall fail in the midst *t* Is 19:3
and I will destroy the counsel *t* Is 19:3
shall be broken in the purposes *t* Is 19:10
that are the stay of the tribes *t* Is 19:13
a perverse spirit in the midst *t* Is 19:14
Egypt to err in every work *t* Is 19:14
t shall be afraid in himself Is 19:17
at the border *t* to the LORD Is 19:19
all the sighing *t* have I made to Is 21:2
have not looked unto the maker *t* Is 22:11
to destroy the strong holds *t* Is 23:11
they set up the towers *t* Is 23:13
they raised up the palaces *t* Is 23:13
abroad the inhabitants *t* Is 24:1
defiled under the inhabitants *t* Is 24:5
the transgression *t* shall be Is 24:20
down, and consume the branches *t* Is 27:10
When the boughs *t* are withered Is 27:11
he hath made plain the face *t* Is 28:25
anger, and the burden *t* is heavy Is 30:27
the pile *t* is fire and much wood Is 30:33
for mount Zion, and for the hill *t* Is 31:4
stakes *t* shall ever be removed Is 33:20
any of the cords *t* be broken Is 33:20
the streams *t* shall be turned Is 34:9
the dust *t* into brimstone, and the Is 34:9
the land *t* shall become burning Is 34:9
the smoke *t* shall go up for ever Is 34:10
call the nobles *t* to the kingdom Is 34:12
and brambles in the fortresses *t* Is 34:13
I will cut down the tall cedars *t* Is 37:24
and the choice fir trees *t* Is 37:24
vineyards, and eat the fruit *t* Is 37:30
all the goodliness *t* is as the Is 40:6
nor the beasts *t* sufficient for a Is 40:16
and the inhabitants *t* are as Is 40:22
called thee from the chief men *t* Is 41:9
the isles, and the inhabitants *t* Is 42:10
the cities *t* lift up their voice, Is 42:11
for he will take *t*, and warm Is 44:15
He burneth part *t* in the fire Is 44:16
with part *t* he eateth flesh Is 44:16
the residue *t* he maketh a god, Is 44:17
have baked bread upon the coals *t* Is 44:19
make the residue *t* an abomination Is 44:19
raise up the decayed places *t* Is 44:26
of thy bowels like the gravel *t* Is 48:19
t go forth as brightness, and the Is 62:1
the salvation *t* as a lamp that Is 62:1
the face *t* is toward the north Jer 1:13
all the walls *t* round about Jer 1:15
of Judah, against the princes *t* Jer 1:18
against the priests *t* Jer 1:18
fruit *t* and the goodness *t* Jer 2:7
all the cities *t* were broken down Jer 4:26
and seek in the broad places *t* Jer 5:1
the waves *t* toss themselves Jer 5:22
and what will ye do in the end *t* Jer 5:31
We have heard the fame *t* Jer 6:24
destroy the tree with the fruit *t* Jer 11:19
mourneth, and the gates *t* languish Jer 14:2
the saviour *t* in time of trouble, Jer 14:8
I kindle a fire in the gates *t* Jer 17:27
hiss because of all the plagues *t* Jer 19:8
the LORD, and to the inhabitants *t* Jer 19:12
this city, and all the labours *t* Jer 20:5
and all the precious things *t* Jer 20:5
kindle a fire in the forest *t* Jer 21:14
and the inhabitants *t* as Gomorrah Jer 23:14
and against the inhabitants *t* Jer 25:9
kings *t*, and the princes *t* Jer 25:18
city, and upon the inhabitants *t* Jer 26:15
for in the peace *t* shall ye have Jer 29:7
shall remain after the manner *t* Jer 30:18
land of Judah and in the cities *t* Jer 31:23
and in all the cities *t* together Jer 31:24
the sea when the waves *t* roar Jer 31:35
Thus saith the LORD the maker *t* Jer 33:2
beast, and in all the cities *t* Jer 33:12
and against all the cities *t* Jer 34:1
and passed between the parts *t* Jer 34:18
the city and the inhabitants *t* Jer 46:8
The voice *t* shall go like a Jer 46:22
for the cities *t* shall be Jer 48:9
of Moab, and in the streets *t* Jer 48:38
all the cities *t* shall be Jer 49:13
shall hiss at all the plagues *t* Jer 49:17
and the neighbour cities *t* Jer 49:18
at the cry the noise *t* was heard Jer 49:21
their calamity from all sides *t* Jer 49:32
let none *t* escape Jer 50:29
and the neighbour cities *t* Jer 50:40
of the Medes, the captains *t* Jer 51:28
and all the rulers *t* Jer 51:28
with the multitude of the waves *t* Jer 51:42
the thickness *t* was four fingers Jer 52:21
the kingdom and the princes *t* Lam 2:2
hath devoured the foundations *t* Lam 4:11
out of the midst *t* as the colour Eze 1:4
Also out of the midst *t* came the Eze 1:5
one vessel, and make thee bread *t* Eze 4:9
and ninety days shalt thou eat *t* Eze 4:9
shalt also take *t* a few in number Eze 5:3
for *t* shall a fire come forth Eze 5:4
wrath is upon all the multitude *t* Eze 7:12
is touching the whole multitude *t* Eze 7:13
wrath is upon all the multitude *t* Eze 7:14
that be done in the midst *t* Eze 9:4
between the cherubims, and took *t* Eze 10:7
the streets *t* with the slain Eze 11:6
will bring you out of the midst *t* Eze 11:9
ye be the flesh in the midst *t* Eze 11:11
away all the detestable things *t* Eze 11:18
the abominations *t* from thence Eze 11:18
foundation *t* shall be discovered Eze 13:14
shall be consumed in the midst *t* Eze 13:14
break the staff of the bread *t* Eze 14:13
wood be taken *t* to do any work Eze 15:3
the roots *t* were under him Eze 17:6
shall he not pull up the roots *t* Eze 17:9
and cut off the fruit *t* Eze 17:9
to pluck it up by the roots *t* Eze 17:9
king *t*, and the princes *t* Eze 17:12
the branches *t* shall they dwell Eze 17:23
was desolate, and the fulness *t* Eze 19:7
the name *t* is called Bamah unto Eze 20:29
ye shall be melted in the midst *t* Eze 22:21
shall ye be melted in the midst *t* Eze 22:22
of her prophets in the midst *t* Eze 22:25
her many widows in the midst *t* Eze 22:25
Her princes in the midst *t* are Eze 22:27
and thou shalt break the sherds *t* Eze 23:34
Gather the pieces *t* into it Eze 24:4
set it empty upon the coals *t* Eze 24:11
the wise men *t* were in thee thy Eze 27:9
him, and I restrained the floods *t* Eze 31:15
heaven, and make the stars *t* dark Eze 32:7
all the multitude *t* shall be Eze 32:12
destroy also all the beasts *t* Eze 32:13
with all the young lions *t* Eze 38:13
the east, and went up the stairs *t* Eze 40:6
and the posts *t*, two cubits Eze 40:9
length *t*, and the breadth *t* Eze 40:20
the little chambers *t* were three Eze 40:21
and the posts *t* and the arches Eze 40:21
the arches *t* were after the Eze 40:21
the length *t* was fifty cubits, and Eze 40:21
the arches *t* were before them Eze 40:22
and he measured the posts *t* Eze 40:24
the arches *t* according to these Eze 40:24
it and in the arches *t* round about Eze 40:25
the arches *t* were before them Eze 40:26
on that side, upon the posts *t* Eze 40:26
And the little chambers *t*, and the Eze 40:29
posts *t*, and the arches *t* Eze 40:29
it and in the arches *t* round about Eze 40:29
the arches *t* were toward the Eze 40:31
palm trees were upon the posts *t* Eze 40:31
And the little chambers *t*, and the Eze 40:33
chambers *t*, and the posts *t* Eze 40:33
posts *t*, and the arches *t* Eze 40:33
and in the arches *t* round about Eze 40:33
the arches *t* were toward the Eze 40:34
palm trees were upon the posts *t* Eze 40:34
The little chambers *t*, the posts Eze 40:36
posts *t*, and the arches *t* Eze 40:36
the posts *t* were toward the utter Eze 40:37
palm trees were upon the posts *t* Eze 40:37
the entries *t* were by the posts Eze 40:38
and he measured the length *t* Eze 41:2
So he measured the length *t* Eze 41:4
the length *t* ninety cubits Eze 41:12
and the building, with the walls *t* Eze 41:13
the galleries *t* on the one side Eze 41:15
high, and the length *t* two cubits Eze 41:22
and the corners *t*, and the length Eze 41:22
length *t*, and the walls *t* Eze 41:22
the length *t* was fifty cubits Eze 42:7
of the house, and the fashion *t* Eze 43:11
and the goings out *t* Eze 43:11
and the comings in *t* Eze 43:11
and all the forms *t* Eze 43:11
and all the ordinances *t* Eze 43:11
and all the forms *t* Eze 43:11
and all the laws *t* Eze 43:11
they may keep the whole form *t* Eze 43:11
and all the ordinances *t* Eze 43:11
t round about shall be most holy Eze 43:12
the border *t* by the edge *t* Eze 43:13
square in the four squares *t* Eze 43:16
broad in the four squares *t* Eze 43:17
the bottom *t* shall be a cubit Eze 43:17
And thou shalt take of the blood *t* Eze 43:20
of the LORD, and all the laws *t* Eze 44:5

the house, for all the service *t*	Eze 44:14	
in all the borders *t* round about	Eze 45:1	
round about for the suburbs *t*	Eze 45:2	
the measure *t* shall be after the	Eze 45:11	
and he shall go forth by the way *t*	Eze 46:8	
the inheritance *t* shall be his	Eze 46:16	
But the miry places *t* and the	Eze 47:11	
the marishes *t* shall not be	Eze 47:11	
And by the river upon the bank *t*	Eze 47:12	
shall the fruit *t* be consumed	Eze 47:12	
the fruit *t* shall be for meat, and	Eze 47:12	
meat, and the leaf *t* for medicine	Eze 47:12	
the LORD shall be in the midst *t*	Eze 48:10	
the city shall be in the midst *t*	Eze 48:15	
And these shall be the measures *t*	Eze 48:16	
the increase *t* shall be for food	Eze 48:18	
the house shall be in the midst *t*	Eze 48:21	
that at the end *t* they might	Dan 1:5	
dream, with the interpretation *t*	Dan 2:5	
dream, and the interpretation *t*	Dan 2:6	
dream, and the interpretation *t*	Dan 2:6	
can shew me the interpretation *t*	Dan 2:9	
seen, and the interpretation *t*	Dan 2:26	
and the form *t* was terrible	Dan 2:31	
interpretation *t* before the king	Dan 2:36	
and the interpretation *t* sure	Dan 2:45	
and the breadth *t* six cubits	Dan 3:1	
unto me the interpretation *t*	Dan 4:7	
seen, and the interpretation *t*	Dan 4:9	
earth, and the height *t* was great	Dan 4:10	
the height *t* reached unto heaven,	Dan 4:11	
the sight *t* to the end of all the	Dan 4:11	
The leaves *t* were fair, and the	Dan 4:12	
were fair, and the fruit *t* much	Dan 4:12	
the heaven dwelt in the boughs *t*	Dan 4:12	
declare the interpretation *t*	Dan 4:18	
dream, or the interpretation *t*	Dan 4:19	
interpretation *t* to thine enemies	Dan 4:19	
the sight *t* to all the earth	Dan 4:20	
were fair, and the fruit *t* much	Dan 4:21	
stump of the roots *t* in the earth	Dan 4:23	
and shew me the interpretation *t*	Dan 5:7	
to the king the interpretation *t*	Dan 5:8	
unto me the interpretation *t*	Dan 5:15	
known to me the interpretation *t*	Dan 5:16	
till the wings *t* were plucked	Dan 7:4	
the end *t* shall be with a flood,	Dan 9:26	
take away my corn in the time *t*	Hos 2:9	
and my wine in the season *t*	Hos 2:9	
because the shadow *t* is good	Hos 4:13	
and it shall devour the palaces *t*	Hos 8:14	
all that eat *t* shall be polluted	Hos 9:4	
for the people *t* shall mourn over	Hos 10:5	
the priests *t* that rejoiced on it	Hos 10:5	
rejoiced on it, for the glory *t*	Hos 10:5	
the scent *t* shall be as the wine	Hos 14:7	
the branches *t* are made white	Joel 1:7	
not turn away the punishment *t*	Amos 1:3	
not turn away the punishment *t*	Amos 1:6	
which shall devour the palaces *t*	Amos 1:7	
not turn away the punishment *t*	Amos 1:9	
which shall devour the palaces *t*	Amos 1:10	
not turn away the punishment *t*	Amos 1:11	
not turn away the punishment *t*	Amos 1:13	
and it shall devour the palaces *t*	Amos 1:14	
not turn away the punishment *t*	Amos 2:1	
off the judge from the midst *t*	Amos 2:3	
slay all the princes *t* with him	Amos 2:3	
not turn away the punishment *t*	Amos 2:4	
not turn away the punishment *t*	Amos 2:6	
the great tumults in the midst *t*	Amos 3:9	
and the oppressed in the midst *t*	Amos 3:9	
the end *t* as a bitter day	Amos 8:10	
and close up the breaches *t*	Amos 9:11	
vineyards, and drink the wine *t*	Amos 9:14	
so he paid the fare *t*, and went	Jonah 1:3	
down the stones *t* into the valley	Mic 1:6	
I will discover the foundations *t*	Mic 1:6	
all the graven images *t* shall be	Mic 1:7	
all the hires *t* shall be burned	Mic 1:7	
all the idols *t* will I lay	Mic 1:7	
The heads *t* judge for reward, and	Mic 3:11	
the priests *t* teach for hire, and	Mic 3:11	
the prophets *t* divine for money	Mic 3:11	
land of Nimrod in the entrances *t*	Mic 5:6	
For the rich men *t* are full of	Mic 6:12	
the inhabitants *t* have spoken	Mic 6:12	
and the inhabitants *t* an hissing	Mic 6:16	
make an utter end of the place *t*	Nah 1:8	
shall make haste to the wall *t*	Nah 2:5	
that the maker *t* hath graven it	Hab 2:18	
but not drink the wine *t*	Zeph 1:13	
The just LORD is in the midst *t*	Zeph 3:5	
to see what is the breadth *t*	Zec 2:2	
and what is the length *t*	Zec 2:2	
I will engrave the graving *t*	Zec 3:9	
lamps, which are upon the top *t*	Zec 4:2	
and the other upon the left side *t*	Zec 4:3	
the headstone *t* with shoutings	Zec 4:7	
and upon the left side *t*	Zec 4:11	
the length *t* is twenty cubits	Zec 5:2	
and the breadth *t* ten cubits	Zec 5:2	
timber *t* and the stones *t*	Zec 5:4	
weight of lead upon the mouth *t*	Zec 5:8	
the cities *t* round about her,	Zec 7:7	
and girls playing in the streets *t*	Zec 8:5	
and Damascus shall be the rest *t*	Zec 9:1	
in the midst *t* toward the east	Zec 14:4	
and the fruit *t*, even his meat, is	Mal 1:12	
Bethlehem, and in all the coasts *t*	Mt 2:16	*846*
unto the day is the evil *t*	Mt 6:34	*846*
account *t* in the day of judgment	Mt 12:36	
come and lodge in the branches *t*	Mt 13:32	*846*
he hideth, and for joy *t* goeth	Mt 13:44	*846*
and when the people had heard *t*	Mt 14:13	
bringing forth the fruits *t*	Mt 21:43	*846*
But when the king heard *t*	Mt 22:7	
and when he had tasted *t*, he would	Mt 27:34	
But when Herod heard *t*, he said,	Mk 6:16	
the owners *t* said unto them, Why	Lk 19:33	
that the desolation *t* is nigh	Lk 21:20	*846*
you, I will not any more eat *t*	Lk 22:16	
and thou hearest the sound *t*	Jn 3:8	*846*
drank *t* himself, and his children,	Jn 4:12	
from heaven, that a man may eat *t*	Jn 6:50	
of it, that the works *t* are evil	Jn 7:7	
and I will build again the ruins *t*	Acts 15:16	*846*
ye should obey it in the lusts *t*	Rom 6:12	*846*
the flesh, to fulfil the lusts *t*	Rom 13:14	
and eateth not of the fruit *t*	1Cor 9:7	*846*
I might be partaker *t* with you	1Cor 9:23	*846*
is the Lord's, and the fulness *t*	1Cor 10:26	*846*
is the Lord's, and the fulness *t*	1Cor 10:28	*846*
but denying the power *t*	2Ti 3:5	*846*
weakness and unprofitableness *t*	Heb 7:18	*846*
grass, and the flower *t* falleth	Jas 1:11	*846*
the flower *t* falleth away	1Pet 1:24	*846*
among you, taking the oversight *t*	1Pet 5:2	
world passeth away, and the lust *t*	1Jn 2:17	*846*
the book, and to loose the seals *t*	Rev 5:2	*846*
and to loose the seven seals *t*	Rev 5:5	*846*
the book, and to open the seals *t*	Rev 5:9	*846*
the water *t* was dried up, that	Rev 16:12	*846*
for the plague *t* was exceeding	Rev 16:21	*846*
the gates *t*, and the wall *t*	Rev 21:15	*846*
And he measured the wall *t*	Rev 21:17	*846*
it, and the Lamb is the light *t*	Rev 21:23	*846*

THEREON

and he poured a drink offering *t*	Gen 35:14	5921
and he poured oil *t*	Gen 35:14	5921
and put it under him, and he sat *t*	Ex 17:12	5921
shalt sacrifice *t* thy burnt	Ex 20:24	5921
thy nakedness be not discovered *t*	Ex 20:26	5921
Aaron shall burn *t* sweet incense	Ex 30:7	5921
shall offer no strange incense *t*	Ex 30:9	5921
shall ye pour drink offering *t*	Ex 30:9	5921
And he burnt sweet incense *t*	Ex 40:27	5921
because the cloud abode *t*	Ex 40:35	5921
upon it, and put frankincense *t*	Lev 2:1	5921
part it in pieces, and pour oil *t*	Lev 2:6	5921
upon it, and lay frankincense *t*	Lev 2:15	5921
shall he put any frankincense *t*	Lev 5:11	5921
he shall burn *t* the fat of the	Lev 6:12	5921
fire therein, and put incense *t*	Lev 10:1	5921
any part of their carcase fall *t*	Lev 11:38	5921
shall put *t* the covering of	Num 4:6	5921
put *t* the dishes, and the spoons,	Num 4:7	5921
and the continual bread shall be *t*	Num 4:7	5921
altar, and spread a purple cloth *t*	Num 4:13	5921
upon it, nor put frankincense *t*	Num 5:15	5921
upon the tabernacle, remaining *t*	Num 9:22	5921
fire in them, and laid incense *t*	Num 16:18	5921
offerings *t* unto the LORD thy God	Deut 27:6	5921
raise *t* a great heap of stones,	Josh 8:29	5921
they offered *t* burnt offerings	Josh 8:31	5921
or if to offer *t* burnt offering	Josh 22:23	5921
or if to offer peace offerings *t*	Josh 22:23	5921
mouth, and spread ground corn *t*	2Sa 17:19	5921
me an ass, that I may ride *t*	2Sa 19:26	5921
And he carved *t* cherubims and palm	1Kin 6:35	
and he rode *t*,	1Kin 13:13	5921
to the altar, and offered *t*	2Kin 16:12	5921
the God of our fathers look *t*	1Chr 12:17	
their shoulders with the staves *t*	1Chr 15:15	5921
set *t* palm trees and chains	2Chr 3:5	5921
linen, and wrought cherubims *t*	2Chr 3:14	5921
sacrificed *t* peace offerings and	2Chr 33:16	5921
to offer burnt offerings *t*	Ezr 3:2	5921
burnt offerings *t* unto the LORD	Ezr 3:3	5921
being set up, let him be hanged *t*	Ezr 6:11	5921
that Mordecai may be hanged *t*	Est 5:14	5921
Then the king said, Hang him *t*	Est 7:9	5921
and perverseness, and stay *t*	Is 30:12	5921
any ravenous beast shall go up *t*	Is 35:9	
a pin of it to hang any vessel *t*	Eze 15:3	5921
to slay *t* the burnt offering and	Eze 40:39	5921
it, to offer burnt offerings *t*	Eze 43:18	5921
and to sprinkle blood *t*	Eze 43:18	5921
top of it, and his seven lamps *t*	Zec 4:2	5921
their clothes, and they set him *t*	Mt 21:7	
he came to it, and found nothing *t*	Mt 21:19	
by it, and by all things *t*	Mt 23:20	
of God, and by him that sitteth *t*	Mt 23:22	
haply he might find any thing *t*	Mk 11:13	
And when he thought *t*, he wept	Mk 14:72	*1911*
and he came and sought fruit *t*	Lk 13:6	
the colt, and they set Jesus *t*	Lk 19:35	*1913*
he had found a young ass, sat *t*	Jn 12:14	
of coals there, and fish laid *t*	Jn 21:9	*1945*
foundation, and another buildeth *t*	1Cor 3:10	*2026*
open the book, neither to look *t*	Rev 5:3	*846*
read the book, neither to look *t*	Rev 5:4	*846*
t to take peace from the earth	Rev 6:4	
twelve angels, and names written *t*	Rev 21:12	*1924*

THEREOUT

he shall take *t* his handful of	Lev 2:2	8033
in the jaw, and there came water *t*	Judg 15:19	

THERETO

make *t* a crown of gold round	Ex 25:24	
shalt do *t* according to the meat	Ex 29:41	
make like unto that, to smell *t*	Ex 30:38	
and shall add the fifth part *t*	Lev 5:16	5921
shall add the fifth part more *t*	Lev 6:5	5921
before a beast to lie down *t*	Lev 18:23	
unto any beast, and lie down *t*	Lev 20:16	
and shall add a fifth part of it *t*	Lev 27:27	5921
he shall add *t* the fifth part	Lev 27:31	5921
thereof, and all that serveth *t*	Num 3:36	
water shall be put *t* in a vessel	Num 19:17	5921
thou shalt not add *t*, nor	Deut 12:32	5921
king of Edom would not hearken *t*	Judg 11:17	
and thou mayest add *t*	1Chr 22:14	5921
your yoke heavy, but I will add *t*	2Chr 10:14	5921
fornication, and compelled Judah *t*	2Chr 21:11	
by taking heed *t* according to thy	Ps 119:9	
a graven image, and falleth down *t*	Is 44:15	
and thy speech agreeth *t*	Mk 14:70	
no man disannulleth, or addeth *t*	Gal 3:15	*1928*

THEREUNTO

it, and have sacrificed *t*, and said	Ex 32:8	
he made *t* four pillars of shittim	Ex 36:36	
made *t* a crown of gold round	Ex 37:11	
Also he made *t* a border of an	Ex 37:12	
and unto all the places nigh *t*	Deut 1:7	
watching *t* with all perseverance	Eph 6:18	
know that we are appointed *t*	1Th 3:3	
make the comers *t* perfect	Heb 10:1	*4334*
knowing that ye are *t* called	1Pet 3:9	

THEREUPON

and the mercy seat that is *t*	Ex 31:7	
colours, and playedst the harlot *t*	Eze 16:16	
they shall feed *t*	Zeph 2:7	
man take heed how he buildeth *t*	1Cor 3:10	*2026*
work abide which he hath built *t*	1Cor 3:14	*2026*

THEREWITH

corn, or the field, be consumed *t*	Ex 22:6	
tabernacle of the congregation *t*	Ex 30:26	
t he made the sockets to the door	Ex 38:30	
maketh atonement *t* shall have it	Lev 7:7	
the ephod, and bound it unto him *t*	Lev 8:7	
goeth from him, and is defiled *t*	Lev 15:32	
any beast to defile thyself *t*	Lev 18:23	
shall not eat to defile himself *t*	Lev 22:8	
shalt thou eat unleavened bread *t*	Deut 16:3	5921
thyself abroad, thou shalt dig *t*	Deut 23:13	
took it, and slew a thousand men *t*	Judg 15:15	
took new ropes, and bound him *t*	Judg 16:12	
any bribe to blind mine eyes *t*	1Sa 12:3	
slew him, and cut off his head *t*	1Sa 17:51	
thy sword, and thrust me through *t*	1Sa 31:4	
so he smote him *t* in the fifth	2Sa 20:10	
I have *t* sent Naaman my servant	2Kin 5:6	
repaired *t* the house of the LORD	2Kin 12:14	
thy sword, and thrust me through *t*	1Chr 10:4	
I made, said David, to praise *t*	1Chr 23:5	
and he built *t* Geba and Mizpah	2Chr 16:6	
than great treasure and trouble *t*	Prov 15:16	
is, than a stalled ox and hatred *t*	Prov 15:17	
is a dry morsel, and quietness *t*	Prov 17:1	
for thee, lest thou be filled *t*	Prov 25:16	
the sons of man to be exercised *t*	Eccl 1:13	
to water *t* the wood that bringeth	Eccl 2:6	
removeth stones shall be hurt *t*	Eccl 10:9	
itself against him that heweth *t*	Is 10:15	
and thou shalt prepare thy bread *t*	Eze 4:15	5921
oil, and ye shall be satisfied *t*	Joel 2:19	854
state I am, *t* to be content	Phil 4:11	
and raiment let us be *t* content	1Ti 6:8	*5125*
T bless we God, even the Father	Jas 3:9	
t curse we men, which are made	Jas 3:9	
and not content *t*, neither doth he	3Jn 10	

THESE

T are the generations of the	Gen 2:4	428
T are the generations of Noah	Gen 6:9	428
T are the three sons of Noah	Gen 9:19	428
Now *t* are the generations of the	Gen 10:1	428
By *t* were the isles of the	Gen 10:5	428
T are the sons of Ham, after	Gen 10:20	428
all *t* were the sons of Joktan	Gen 10:29	428
T are the sons of Shem, after	Gen 10:31	428
T are the families of the sons of	Gen 10:32	428
by *t* were the nations divided in	Gen 10:32	428
T are the generations of Shem	Gen 11:10	428
Now *t* are the generations of	Gen 11:27	428
That *t* made war with Bera king of	Gen 14:2	
All *t* were joined together in the	Gen 14:3	428
t were confederate with Abram	Gen 14:13	1992
After *t* things the word of the	Gen 15:1	428
And he took unto him all *t*	Gen 15:10	428
only unto *t* men do nothing	Gen 19:8	428
told all *t* things in their ears	Gen 20:8	428
What mean *t* seven ewe lambs which	Gen 21:29	
For *t* seven ewe lambs shalt thou	Gen 21:30	
And it came to pass after *t* things	Gen 22:1	
And it came to pass after *t* things	Gen 22:20	
t eight Milcah did bear to Nahor,	Gen 22:23	
t were the years of the life of	Gen 23:1	
of her mother's house *t* things	Gen 24:28	
All *t* were the children of	Gen 25:4	428
t are the days of the years of	Gen 25:7	428
Now *t* are the generations of	Gen 25:12	428
t are the names of the sons of	Gen 25:13	428
T are the sons of Ishmael, and	Gen 25:16	428
t are their names, by their towns	Gen 25:16	428
t are the years of the life of	Gen 25:17	428
t are the generations of Isaac,	Gen 25:19	428
seed, I will give all *t* countries	Gen 26:3	411
unto thy seed all *t* countries	Gen 26:4	411
he hath supplanted me *t* two times	Gen 27:36	2088
t words of Esau her elder son	Gen 27:42	
such as *t* which are of the	Gen 27:46	428
And he told Laban all *t* things	Gen 29:13	428
T daughters are my daughters, and	Gen 31:43	
t children are my children, and	Gen 31:43	
t cattle are my cattle, and all	Gen 31:43	
I do this day unto *t* my daughters	Gen 31:43	
and whose are *t* before thee	Gen 32:17	428
T are to find grace in the sight	Gen 33:8	

T men are peaceable with us	Gen 34:21	428
t are the sons of Jacob, which	Gen 35:26	428
Now *t* are the generations of Esau	Gen 36:1	428
t are the sons of Esau, which	Gen 36:5	428
t are the generations of Esau the	Gen 36:9	428
T are the names of Esau's sons	Gen 36:10	428
t were the sons of Adah Esau's	Gen 36:12	428
And *t* are the sons of Reuel	Gen 36:13	428
t were the sons of Bashemath	Gen 36:13	428
t were the sons of Aholibamah,	Gen 36:14	428
T were dukes of the sons of Esau	Gen 36:15	428
t are the dukes that came of	Gen 36:16	428
t were the sons of Adah	Gen 36:16	428
t are the sons of Reuel Esau's	Gen 36:17	428
t are the dukes that came of	Gen 36:17	428
t are the sons of Bashemath	Gen 36:17	428
t are the sons of Aholibamah	Gen 36:18	428
t were the dukes that came of	Gen 36:18	428
T are the sons of Esau, who is	Gen 36:19	428
who is Edom, and *t* are their dukes	Gen 36:19	428
T are the sons of Seir the Horite	Gen 36:20	428
t are the dukes of the Horites,	Gen 36:21	428
And the children of Shobal were *t*	Gen 36:23	428
t are the children of Zibeon	Gen 36:24	428
And the children of Anah were *t*	Gen 36:25	428
t are the children of Dishon	Gen 36:26	428
The children of Ezer are *t*	Gen 36:27	428
The children of Dishan are *t*	Gen 36:28	428
T are the dukes that came of the	Gen 36:29	428
t are the dukes that came of Hori	Gen 36:30	428
t are the kings that reigned in	Gen 36:31	428
t are the names of the dukes that	Gen 36:40	428
t be the dukes of Edom, according	Gen 36:43	428
T are the generations of Jacob	Gen 37:2	428
saying, By the man, whose *t* are	Gen 38:25	428
Discern, I pray thee, whose are *t*	Gen 38:25	428
And it came to pass after *t* things	Gen 39:7	428
unto him according to *t* words	Gen 39:17	428
And it came to pass after *t* things	Gen 40:1	428
all *t* things are against me	Gen 42:36	
according to the tenor of *t* words	Gen 43:7	428
Bring *t* men home, and slay, and	Gen 43:16	
for *t* men shall dine with me at	Gen 43:16	
he spake unto them *t* same words	Gen 44:6	411
Wherefore saith my lord *t* words	Gen 44:7	428
For *t* two years hath the famine	Gen 45:6	2088
t are the names of the children	Gen 46:8	428
T be the sons of Leah, which she	Gen 46:15	428
T are the sons of Zilpah, whom	Gen 46:18	428
t she bare unto Jacob, even	Gen 46:18	428
T are the sons of Rachel, which	Gen 46:22	428
T are the sons of Bilhah, which	Gen 46:25	428
and she bare *t* unto Jacob	Gen 46:25	428
And it came to pass after *t* things	Gen 48:1	428
Joseph's sons, and said, Who are *t*	Gen 48:8	428
All *t* are the twelve tribes of	Gen 49:28	428
Now *t* are the names of the	Ex 1:1	428
will not believe also *t* two signs	Ex 4:9	428
T be the heads of their fathers'	Ex 6:14	428
t be the families of Reuben	Ex 6:14	428
t are the families of Simeon	Ex 6:15	428
t are the names of the sons of	Ex 6:16	428
t are the families of Levi	Ex 6:19	428
t are the families of the	Ex 6:24	428
t are the heads of the fathers of	Ex 6:25	428
T are that Aaron and Moses, to	Ex 6:26	1931
T are they which spake to Pharaoh	Ex 6:27	1992
t are that Moses and Aaron	Ex 6:27	
that I might shew *t* my signs	Ex 10:1	428
all *t* thy servants shall come	Ex 11:8	428
Aaron did all *t* wonders before	Ex 11:10	428
but it gave light by night to *t*	Ex 14:20	
put none of *t* diseases upon thee	Ex 15:26	
T are the words which thou shalt	Ex 19:6	
laid before their faces all *t*	Ex 19:7	428
And God spake all *t* words, saying,	Ex 20:1	428
Now *t* are the judgments which	Ex 21:1	428
if he do not *t* three unto her,	Ex 21:11	428
with you concerning all *t* words	Ex 24:8	428
he make it, with all *t* vessels	Ex 25:39	428
t are the garments which they	Ex 28:4	428
t sweet spices with pure	Ex 30:34	
T be thy gods, O Israel, which	Ex 32:4	428
T be thy gods, O Israel, which	Ex 32:8	428
the people heard *t* evil tidings	Ex 33:4	
I will write upon *t* tables the	Ex 34:1	
unto Moses, Write thou *t* words	Ex 34:27	428
for after the tenor of *t* words I	Ex 34:27	428
T are the words which the LORD	Ex 35:1	428
is made of *t* things unto the LORD	Lev 2:8	428
he shall be guilty in one of *t*	Lev 5:4	428
be guilty in one of *t* things	Lev 5:5	428
that he hath sinned in one of *t*	Lev 5:13	428
commit any of *t* things which are	Lev 5:17	
in any of all *t* that a man doeth,	Lev 6:3	
T are the beasts which ye shall	Lev 11:2	2063
Nevertheless *t* shall ye not eat	Lev 11:4	2088
T shall ye eat of all that are in	Lev 11:9	2088
t are they which ye shall have in	Lev 11:13	428
Yet *t* may ye eat of every flying	Lev 11:21	2088
Even *t* of them ye may eat	Lev 11:22	428
for *t* ye shall be unclean	Lev 11:24	428
T also shall be unclean unto you	Lev 11:29	2088
T are unclean to you among all	Lev 11:31	2088
t are holy garments	Lev 16:4	1992
ye yourselves in any of *t* things	Lev 18:24	428
for in all *t* the nations are	Lev 18:24	428
not commit any of *t* abominations	Lev 18:26	428
(For all *t* abominations have the	Lev 18:27	411
commit any of *t* abominations	Lev 18:29	428
any one of *t* abominable customs	Lev 18:30	
for they committed all *t* things	Lev 20:23	428
or an harlot, *t* shall he not take	Lev 21:14	428
shall not offer *t* unto the LORD	Lev 22:22	428
the bread of your God of any of *t*	Lev 22:25	428
even *t* are my feasts	Lev 23:2	428
T are the feasts of the LORD,	Lev 23:4	428
T are the feasts of the LORD,	Lev 23:37	428
if he be not redeemed in *t* years	Lev 25:54	428
and will not do all *t* commandments	Lev 26:14	428
not be reformed by me by *t* things	Lev 26:23	428
T are the statutes and judgments	Lev 26:46	428
T are the commandments, which the	Lev 27:34	428
t are the names of the men that	Num 1:5	428
T were the renowned of the	Num 1:16	428
Aaron took *t* men which are	Num 1:17	428
T are those that were numbered,	Num 1:44	428
T shall first set forth	Num 2:9	
T are those which were numbered	Num 2:32	428
T also are the generations of	Num 3:1	428
t are the names of the sons of	Num 3:2	428
T are the names of the sons of	Num 3:3	428
t were the sons of Levi by their	Num 3:17	428
t are the names of the sons of	Num 3:18	428
T are the families of the Levites	Num 3:20	428
t are the families of the	Num 3:21	428
t are the families of the	Num 3:27	428
t are the families of Merari	Num 3:33	428
t shall pitch on the side of the	Num 3:35	
T things are the burden of the	Num 4:15	428
T were they that were numbered of	Num 4:37	428
T are they that were numbered of	Num 4:41	428
T be those that were numbered of	Num 4:45	428
shall write *t* curses in a book	Num 5:23	428
And *t* were their names	Num 13:4	428
T are the names of the men which	Num 13:16	428
have tempted me now *t* ten times	Num 14:22	2088
Moses told *t* sayings unto all the	Num 14:39	428
do *t* things after this manner	Num 15:13	428
not observed all *t* commandments	Num 15:22	428
thou put out the eyes of *t* men	Num 16:14	1992
from the tents of *t* wicked men	Num 16:26	428
hath sent me to do all *t* works	Num 16:28	428
If *t* men die the common death of	Num 16:29	428
that *t* men have provoked the LORD	Num 16:30	
an end of speaking all *t* words	Num 16:31	428
The censers of *t* sinners against	Num 16:38	428
And Israel took all *t* cities	Num 21:25	428
and said, What men are *t* with thee	Num 22:9	428
hast smitten me *t* three times	Num 22:28	2088
smitten thine ass *t* three times	Num 22:32	2088
and turned from me *t* three times	Num 22:33	2088
blessed them *t* three times	Num 24:10	2088
T are the families of the	Num 26:7	428
T are the families of the	Num 26:14	428
T are the families of the	Num 26:18	428
T are the families of Judah	Num 26:22	428
T are the families of Issachar	Num 26:25	428
T are the families of the	Num 26:27	428
T are the sons of Gilead	Num 26:30	428
T are the families of Manasseh,	Num 26:34	428
T are the sons of Ephraim after	Num 26:35	428
t are the sons of Shuthelah	Num 26:36	428
T are the families of the sons of	Num 26:37	428
T are the sons of Joseph after	Num 26:37	428
T are the sons of Benjamin after	Num 26:41	428
T are the sons of Dan after their	Num 26:42	428
T are the families of Dan after	Num 26:42	428
T are the families of the sons of	Num 26:47	428
T are the families of Naphtali	Num 26:50	428
T were the numbered of the	Num 26:51	428
Unto *t* the land shall be divided	Num 26:53	428
t are they that were numbered of	Num 26:57	428
T are the families of the Levites	Num 26:58	428
T are they that were numbered by	Num 26:63	428
But among *t* there was not a man	Num 26:64	428
t are the names of his daughters	Num 27:1	428
Ye shall offer *t* beside the burnt	Num 28:23	428
T things ye shall do unto the	Num 29:39	428
T are the statutes, which the	Num 30:16	428
t caused the children of Israel,	Num 31:16	2007
T are the journeys of the	Num 33:1	428
t are their journeys according to	Num 33:2	428
T are the names of the men which	Num 34:17	428
And the names of the men are *t*	Num 34:19	428
T are they whom the LORD	Num 34:29	428
of *t* cities which ye shall give	Num 35:13	
T six cities shall be a refuge,	Num 35:15	428
of blood according to *t* judgments	Num 35:24	428
So *t* things shall be for a	Num 35:29	428
T are the commandments and the	Num 36:13	428
T be the words which Moses spake	Deut 1:1	428
Surely there shall not one of *t*	Deut 1:35	428
t forty years the LORD thy God	Deut 2:7	2088
All *t* cities were fenced with	Deut 3:5	428
God hath done unto *t* two kings	Deut 3:21	428
which shall hear all *t* statutes	Deut 4:6	428
all *t* things are come upon thee,	Deut 4:30	428
one of *t* cities he might live	Deut 4:42	411
T are the testimonies, and the	Deut 4:45	428
T words the LORD spake unto all	Deut 5:22	428
Now *t* are the commandments, the	Deut 6:1	2063
t words, which I command thee	Deut 6:6	
commanded us to do all *t* statutes	Deut 6:24	428
if we observe to do all *t*	Deut 6:25	2063
if ye hearken to *t* judgments	Deut 7:12	428
T nations are more than I	Deut 7:17	428
t forty years in the wilderness	Deut 8:2	2088
did thy foot swell, *t* forty years	Deut 8:4	2088
but for the wickedness of *t*	Deut 9:4	428
but for the wickedness of *t*	Deut 9:5	428
that hath done for thee *t* great	Deut 10:21	428
lay up *t* my words in your heart	Deut 11:18	438
t commandments which I command	Deut 11:22	2063
out all *t* nations from before you	Deut 11:23	428
T are the statutes and judgments,	Deut 12:1	428
hear all *t* words which I command	Deut 12:28	428
How did *t* nations serve their	Deut 12:30	428
T are the beasts which ye shall	Deut 14:4	2063
Nevertheless *t* ye shall not eat	Deut 14:7	2088
T ye shall eat of all that are in	Deut 14:9	2088
But *t* are they of which ye shall	Deut 14:12	2088
thy God, to observe to do all *t*	Deut 15:5	2063
shalt observe and do *t* statutes	Deut 16:12	428
law and *t* statutes, to do them	Deut 17:19	428
For all that do *t* things are an	Deut 18:12	428
because of *t* abominations the	Deut 18:12	428
For *t* nations, which thou shalt	Deut 18:14	428
If thou shalt keep all *t*	Deut 19:9	2063
more for thee, beside *t* three	Deut 19:9	
and fleeth into one of *t* cities	Deut 19:11	411
not of the cities of *t* nations	Deut 20:15	
But of the cities of *t* people	Deut 20:16	428
yet *t* are the tokens of my	Deut 22:17	428
for even both *t* are abomination	Deut 23:18	
beat him above *t* with many	Deut 25:3	
commanded thee to do *t* statutes	Deut 26:16	428
that ye shall set up *t* stones	Deut 27:4	428
T shall stand upon mount Gerizim	Deut 27:12	428
t shall stand upon mount Ebal to	Deut 27:13	428
all *t* blessings shall come on	Deut 28:2	428
that all *t* curses shall come upon	Deut 28:15	428
Moreover all *t* curses shall come	Deut 28:45	428
among *t* nations shalt thou find	Deut 28:65	1992
T are the words of the covenant,	Deut 29:1	428
go and serve the gods of *t* nations	Deut 29:18	1992
when all *t* things are come upon	Deut 30:1	428
all *t* curses upon thine enemies	Deut 30:7	428
spake *t* words unto all Israel	Deut 31:1	428
he will destroy *t* nations from	Deut 31:3	428
Are not *t* evils come upon us,	Deut 31:17	428
that I may speak *t* words in their	Deut 31:28	428
all *t* words to all Israel	Deut 32:45	428
as soon as we had heard *t* things	Josh 2:11	
saying, What mean ye by *t* stones	Josh 4:6	428
t stones shall be for a memorial	Josh 4:7	428
come, saying, What mean *t* stones	Josh 4:21	428
t bottles of wine, which we	Josh 9:13	428
t our garments and our shoes are	Josh 9:13	428
But *t* five kings fled, and hid	Josh 10:16	428
feet upon the necks of *t* kings	Josh 10:24	428
all *t* kings and their land did	Josh 10:42	428
when all *t* kings were met	Josh 11:5	428
And all the spoil of *t* cities	Josh 11:14	428
Now *t* are the kings of the land,	Josh 12:1	428
t are the kings of the country	Josh 12:7	428
for *t* did Moses smite, and cast	Josh 13:12	
T are the countries which Moses	Josh 13:32	428
t are the countries which the	Josh 14:1	428
t forty and five years, even since	Josh 14:10	2088
t were the male children of	Josh 17:2	428
t are the names of his daughters,	Josh 17:3	428
t cities of Ephraim are among the	Josh 17:9	428
about *t* cities to Baalath-beer	Josh 19:8	428
t cities with their villages	Josh 19:16	428
t cities with their villages	Josh 19:31	428
t cities with their villages	Josh 19:48	428
T are the inheritances, which	Josh 19:51	428
T were the cities appointed for	Josh 20:9	428
t cities and their suburbs	Josh 21:3	428
t cities with their suburbs	Josh 21:8	428
t cities which are here mentioned	Josh 21:9	428
T cities were every one with	Josh 21:42	428
thus were all *t* cities	Josh 21:42	428
t many days unto this day	Josh 22:3	428
unto all *t* nations because of you	Josh 23:3	428
you by lot *t* nations that remain	Josh 23:4	428
That ye come not among *t* nations	Josh 23:7	428
t that remain among you	Josh 23:7	428
unto the remnant of *t* nations	Josh 23:12	428
even *t* that remain among you, and	Josh 23:12	428
any of *t* nations from before you	Josh 23:13	428
Joshua wrote *t* words in the book	Josh 24:26	428
And it came to pass after *t* things	Josh 24:29	428
the angel of the LORD spake *t*	Judg 2:4	428
Now *t* are the nations which the	Judg 3:1	428
the men of Shechem all *t* words	Judg 9:3	428
he have shewed us all *t* things	Judg 13:23	428
have told us such things as *t*	Judg 13:23	2063
thou hast mocked me *t* three times	Judg 16:15	2088
there is in *t* houses an ephod	Judg 18:14	428
t went into Micah's house, and	Judg 18:18	428
of *t* places to lodge all night	Judg 19:13	
all *t* were men of war	Judg 20:17	2088
all *t* drew the sword	Judg 20:25	428
all *t* drew the sword	Judg 20:35	428
all *t* were men of valour	Judg 20:44	428
all *t* were men of valour	Judg 20:46	428
T six measures of barley gave he	Ruth 3:17	428
Now *t* are the generations of	Ruth 4:18	428
out of the hand of *t* mighty Gods	1Sa 4:8	428
t are the Gods that smote the	1Sa 4:8	428
t are the golden emerods which	1Sa 6:17	428
when *t* signs are come unto thee,	1Sa 10:7	428
the garrison of *t* uncircumcised	1Sa 14:6	428
we will pass over unto *t* men	1Sa 14:8	
names of his two daughters were *t*	1Sa 14:49	
Jesse, The LORD hath not chosen *t*	1Sa 16:10	428
t ten loaves, and run to the camp	1Sa 17:17	2088
carry *t* ten cheeses unto the	1Sa 17:18	428
unto Saul, I cannot go with *t*	1Sa 17:39	428
his servants told David *t* words	1Sa 18:26	428
kept from us about *t* three days	1Sa 21:5	
David laid up *t* words in his	1Sa 21:12	428
Shall I go and smite *t* Philistines	1Sa 23:2	428
stayed his servants with *t* words	1Sa 24:7	
end of speaking *t* words unto Saul	1Sa 24:16	428
and his wife had told him *t* things	1Sa 25:37	
What do *t* Hebrews here	1Sa 29:3	428
which hath been with me *t* days	1Sa 29:3	2088
or *t* years, and I have found no	1Sa 29:3	2088
it not be with the heads of *t* men	1Sa 29:4	1992

lest *t* uncircumcised come and	1Sa 31:4	428
T were born to David in Hebron	2Sa 3:5	428
t men the sons of Zeruiah be too	2Sa 3:39	428
t be the names of those that were	2Sa 5:14	428
According to all *t* words, and	2Sa 7:17	428
hast thou done all *t* great things	2Sa 7:21	2063
king David heard of all *t* things	2Sa 13:21	428
he put all *t* words in the mouth	2Sa 14:19	428
unto Ziba, What meanest thou by *t*	2Sa 16:2	428
T four were born to the giant in	2Sa 21:22	428
Now *t* be the last words of David	2Sa 23:1	428
T be the names of the mighty men	2Sa 23:8	428
T things did *t* three mighty	2Sa 23:17	428
T things did Benaiah the son of	2Sa 23:22	428
but *t* sheep, what have they done	2Sa 24:17	428
All *t* things did Araunah, as a	2Sa 24:23	
t were the princes which he had	1Kin 4:2	428
And *t* are their names	1Kin 4:8	428
All *t* were of costly stones,	1Kin 7:9	428
all *t* vessels, which Hiram made	1Kin 7:45	428
let *t* my words, wherewith I have	1Kin 8:59	428
What cities are *t* which thou hast	1Kin 9:13	428
T were the chief of the officers	1Kin 9:23	428
happy are *t* thy servants, which	1Kin 10:8	428
such abundance of spices as *t*	1Kin 10:10	1931
Solomon clave unto *t* in love	1Kin 11:2	1992
shall not be dew nor rain *t* years	1Kin 17:1	428
And it came to pass after *t* things	1Kin 17:17	428
done all *t* things at thy word	1Kin 18:36	428
So *t* young men of the princes of	1Kin 20:19	428
And it came to pass after *t* things	1Kin 21:1	428
With *t* shalt thou push the	1Kin 22:11	428
the LORD said, *T* have no master	1Kin 22:17	428
the mouth of all *t* thy prophets	1Kin 22:23	428
to meet you, and told you *t* words	2Kin 1:7	428
the life of *t* fifty thy servants,	2Kin 1:13	428
the LORD, I have healed *t* waters	2Kin 2:21	428
called *t* three kings together	2Kin 3:10	428
called *t* three kings together	2Kin 3:13	428
LORD, open the eyes of *t* men	2Kin 6:20	428
when *t* lepers came to the	2Kin 7:8	428
but who slew all *t*	2Kin 10:9	428
So *t* nations feared the LORD, and	2Kin 17:41	428
and to thee, to speak *t* words	2Kin 18:27	428
and said unto him, What said *t* men	2Kin 20:14	428
of Judah hath done *t* abominations	2Kin 21:11	428
who proclaimed *t* words	2Kin 23:16	428
proclaimed *t* things that thou	2Kin 23:17	428
the brass of all *t* vessels was	2Kin 25:16	428
like unto *t* had the second pillar	2Kin 25:17	428
captain of the guard took *t*	2Kin 25:20	
All *t* were the sons of Joktan	1Chr 1:23	428
T are their generations	1Chr 1:29	428
T are the sons of Ishmael	1Chr 1:31	
All *t* are the sons of Keturah	1Chr 1:33	428
Now *t* are the kings that reigned	1Chr 1:43	428
T are the dukes of Edom	1Chr 1:54	428
T are the sons of Israel	1Chr 2:1	428
her sons are *t*	1Chr 2:18	428
All *t* belonged to the sons of	1Chr 2:23	428
T were the sons of Jerahmeel	1Chr 2:33	428
T were the sons of Caleb the son	1Chr 2:50	428
T are the Kenites that came of	1Chr 2:55	1992
Now *t* were the sons of David,	1Chr 3:1	428
T six were born unto him in	1Chr 3:4	
t were born unto him in Jerusalem	1Chr 3:5	428
T were all the sons of David,	1Chr 3:9	
T are the families of the	1Chr 4:2	428
t were of the father of Etam	1Chr 4:3	428
T are the sons of Hur, the	1Chr 4:4	428
T were the sons of Naarah	1Chr 4:6	428
T are the men of Recah	1Chr 4:12	428
t are the sons of Bithiah the	1Chr 4:18	428
And *t* are ancient things	1Chr 4:22	
T were the potters, and those that	1Chr 4:23	1992
T were their cities unto the	1Chr 4:31	428
T were their habitations, and	1Chr 4:33	2063
T mentioned by their names were	1Chr 4:38	428
t written by name came in the	1Chr 4:41	428
T are the children of Abihail the	1Chr 5:14	428
All *t* were reckoned by	1Chr 5:17	
t were the heads of the house of	1Chr 5:24	428
t be the names of the sons of	1Chr 6:17	428
t are the families of the Levites	1Chr 6:19	428
t are they whom David set over	1Chr 6:31	
t are they that waited with their	1Chr 6:33	428
And *t* are the sons of Aaron	1Chr 6:50	428
Now *t* are their dwelling places	1Chr 6:54	428
t cities with their suburbs	1Chr 6:64	
t cities, which are called by	1Chr 6:65	
All *t* are the sons of Becher	1Chr 7:8	428
All *t* the sons of Jediael, by the	1Chr 7:11	428
T were the sons of Gilead, the	1Chr 7:17	428
In *t* dwelt the children of Joseph	1Chr 7:29	428
T are the children of Japhlet	1Chr 7:33	428
All *t* were the children of Asher,	1Chr 7:40	428
And *t* are the sons of Ehud	1Chr 8:6	428
t are the heads of the fathers of	1Chr 8:6	
T were his sons, heads of the	1Chr 8:10	428
T were heads of the fathers, by	1Chr 8:28	428
T dwelt in Jerusalem	1Chr 8:28	
t also dwelt with their brethren	1Chr 8:32	1992
had six sons, whose names are *t*	1Chr 8:38	428
All *t* were the sons of Azel	1Chr 8:38	428
All *t* are of the sons of Benjamin	1Chr 8:40	428
All *t* men were chief of the	1Chr 9:9	428
All *t* which were chosen to be	1Chr 9:22	
T were reckoned by their	1Chr 9:22	1992
For *t* Levites, the four chief	1Chr 9:26	1992
t are the singers, chief of the	1Chr 9:33	428
T chief fathers of the Levites	1Chr 9:34	428
t dwelt at Jerusalem	1Chr 9:34	
had six sons, whose names are *t*	1Chr 9:44	428
t were the sons of Azel	1Chr 9:44	428
lest *t* uncircumcised come and	1Chr 10:4	428
T also are the chief of the	1Chr 11:10	428
shall I drink the blood of *t* men	1Chr 11:19	428
T things did *t* three	1Chr 11:19	428
T things did Benaiah the son of	1Chr 11:24	428
Now *t* are they that came to David	1Chr 12:1	428
T were of the sons of Gad,	1Chr 12:14	428
T are they that went over Jordan	1Chr 12:15	
t are the numbers of the bands	1Chr 12:23	428
All *t* men of war, that could keep	1Chr 12:38	428
Now *t* are the names of his	1Chr 14:4	428
According to all *t* words, and	1Chr 17:15	428
making known all *t* great things	1Chr 17:19	
he brought from all *t* nations	1Chr 18:11	
T were born unto the giant in	1Chr 20:8	411
but as for *t* sheep, what have	1Chr 21:17	428
T were the chief of the fathers	1Chr 23:9	428
T four were the sons of Shimei	1Chr 23:10	428
T were the sons of Levi after the	1Chr 23:24	428
Now *t* are the divisions of the	1Chr 24:1	
T were the orderings of them in	1Chr 24:19	428
rest of the sons of Levi were *t*	1Chr 24:20	
T were the sons of the Levites	1Chr 24:30	428
T likewise cast lots over against	1Chr 24:31	1992
All *t* were the sons of Heman the	1Chr 25:5	428
All *t* were under the hands of	1Chr 25:6	428
All *t* of the sons of Obed-edom	1Chr 26:8	428
Among *t* were the divisions of the	1Chr 26:12	428
T are the divisions of the	1Chr 26:19	428
T were the princes of the tribes	1Chr 27:22	428
All *t* were the rulers of the	1Chr 27:31	428
willingly offered all *t* things	1Chr 29:17	428
statutes, and to do all *t* things	1Chr 29:19	
Now *t* are the things wherein	2Chr 3:3	428
The wings of *t* cherubims spread	2Chr 3:13	428
Thus Solomon made all *t* vessels	2Chr 4:18	428
t did the priests and the Levites	2Chr 5:5	
And *t* were the chief of king	2Chr 8:10	428
happy are *t* thy servants, which	2Chr 9:7	428
unto Judah, Let us build *t* cities	2Chr 14:7	428
all *t* were mighty men of valour	2Chr 14:8	428
And when Asa heard *t* words	2Chr 15:8	428
t are the numbers of them	2Chr 17:14	428
T waited on the king, beside	2Chr 17:19	428
With *t* thou shalt push Syria	2Chr 18:10	428
the LORD said, *T* have no master	2Chr 18:16	428
in the mouth of *t* thy prophets	2Chr 18:22	428
all *t* were the sons of	2Chr 21:2	428
t are they that conspired against	2Chr 24:26	428
all *t* were for a burnt offering	2Chr 29:32	428
After *t* things, and the	2Chr 32:1	428
t were of the king's substance	2Chr 35:7	428
all *t* he brought to Babylon	2Chr 36:18	
All *t* did Sheshbazzar bring up	Ezr 1:11	
Now *t* are the children of the	Ezr 2:1	428
t were they which went up from	Ezr 2:59	428
T sought their register among	Ezr 2:62	428
to cause *t* men to cease, and that	Ezr 4:21	479
this house, and to make up *t* walls	Ezr 5:9	1836
that was builded *t* many years ago	Ezr 5:11	1836
Take *t* vessels, go, carry them	Ezr 5:15	412
ye shall do to the elders of *t*	Ezr 6:8	479
expences be given unto *t* men	Ezr 6:8	479
Now after *t* things, in the reign	Ezr 7:1	428
T are now the chief of their	Ezr 8:1	428
of Adonikam, whose names are *t*	Ezr 8:13	428
Now when *t* things were done, the	Ezr 9:1	428
with the people of *t* abominations	Ezr 9:14	428
All *t* had taken strange wives	Ezr 10:44	428
to pass, when I heard *t* words	Neh 1:4	428
Now *t* are thy servants and thy	Neh 1:10	1992
and said, What do *t* feeble Jews	Neh 4:2	
when I heard their cry and *t* words	Neh 5:6	428
their king, according to *t* words	Neh 6:6	428
to the king according to *t* words	Neh 6:7	428
according to *t* their works	Neh 6:14	428
that were about us saw *t* things	Neh 6:16	
T are the children of the	Neh 7:6	428
t were they which went up also	Neh 7:61	428
T sought their register among	Neh 7:64	428
t were the priests	Neh 10:8	428
Now *t* are the chief of the	Neh 11:3	428
t are the sons of Benjamin	Neh 11:7	428
Now *t* are the priests and the	Neh 12:1	428
T were the chief of the priests	Neh 12:7	428
T were in the days of Joiakim the	Neh 12:26	428
king of Israel sin by *t* things	Neh 13:26	
when *t* days were expired, the	Est 1:5	428
After *t* things, when the wrath of	Est 2:1	428
After *t* things did king Ahasuerus	Est 3:1	428
in unto the king *t* thirty days	Est 4:11	2088
And Mordecai wrote *t* things	Est 9:20	428
Wherefore they called *t* days	Est 9:26	428
that they would keep *t* two days	Est 9:27	428
that *t* days should be remembered	Est 9:28	428
that *t* days of Purim should not	Est 9:28	428
To confirm *t* days of Purim in	Est 9:31	428
confirmed *t* matters of Purim	Est 9:32	428
How long wilt thou speak *t* things	Job 8:2	428
t things hast thou hid in thine	Job 10:13	428
who knoweth not such things as *t*	Job 12:3	428
Who knoweth not in all *t* that the	Job 12:9	428
T ten times have ye reproached me	Job 19:3	2088
Lo, *t* are parts of his ways	Job 26:14	428
So *t* three men ceased to answer	Job 32:1	428
in the mouth of *t* three men	Job 32:5	
Lo, all *t* things worketh God	Job 33:29	428
LORD had spoken *t* words unto Job	Job 42:7	428
He that doeth *t* things shall	Ps 15:5	428
When I remember *t* things, I pour	Ps 42:4	428
T things hast thou done, and I	Ps 50:21	428
until *t* calamities be overpast	Ps 57:1	
t are the ungodly, who prosper in	Ps 73:12	428
T wait all upon thee	Ps 104:27	
T see the works of the LORD, and	Ps 107:24	1992
is wise, and will observe *t* things	Ps 107:43	428
T six things doth the LORD hate	Prov 6:16	2007
T things also belong to the wise	Prov 24:23	428
T are also proverbs of Solomon,	Prov 25:1	428
former days were better than *t*	Eccl 7:10	428
that for all *t* things God will	Eccl 11:9	428
And further, by *t*, my son, be	Eccl 12:12	1992
two tails of *t* smoking firebrands	Is 7:4	428
no one of *t* shall fail, none	Is 34:16	2007
and to thee to speak *t* words	Is 36:12	428
among all the gods of *t* lands	Is 36:20	428
by *t* things men live, and in all	Is 38:16	5921
in all *t* things is the life of my	Is 38:16	
and said unto him, What said *t* men	Is 39:3	428
behold who hath created *t* things	Is 40:26	428
T things will I do unto them, and	Is 42:16	428
Remember *t*, O Jacob and Israel	Is 44:21	428
I the LORD do all *t* things	Is 45:7	428
not lay *t* things to thy heart	Is 47:7	428
But *t* two things shall come to	Is 47:9	428
save thee from *t* things that	Is 47:13	
among them hath declared *t* things	Is 48:14	428
Behold, *t* shall come from far	Is 49:12	428
t from the north and from the west	Is 49:12	428
and *t* from the land of Sinim	Is 49:12	428
all *t* gather themselves together,	Is 49:18	
heart, Who hath begotten me *t*	Is 49:21	428
and who hath brought up *t*	Is 49:21	2004
t, where had they been	Is 49:21	428
T two things are come unto thee	Is 51:19	2007
Should I receive comfort in *t*	Is 57:6	428
Who are *t* that fly as a cloud, and	Is 60:8	428
thou refrain thyself for *t* things	Is 64:12	428
T are a smoke in my nose, a fire	Is 65:5	428
by secret search, but upon all *t*	Jer 2:34	428
after she had done all *t* things	Jer 3:7	428
proclaim *t* words toward the north	Jer 3:12	428
have procured *t* things unto thee	Jer 4:18	428
I said, Surely *t* are poor	Jer 5:4	1992
but *t* have altogether broken the	Jer 5:5	1992
Shall I not visit for *t* things	Jer 5:9	428
LORD our God all *t* things unto us	Jer 5:19	428
have turned away *t* things	Jer 5:25	428
Shall I not visit for *t* things	Jer 5:29	428
that enter in at *t* gates to	Jer 7:2	428
The temple of the LORD, are *t*	Jer 7:4	1992
to do all *t* abominations	Jer 7:10	428
because ye have done all *t* works	Jer 7:13	428
shalt speak all *t* words unto them	Jer 7:27	428
I not visit them for *t* things	Jer 9:9	428
for in *t* things I delight, saith	Jer 9:24	428
for all *t* nations are	Jer 9:26	
earth, and from under *t* heavens	Jer 10:11	429
Proclaim all *t* words in the	Jer 11:6	428
Wherefore come *t* things upon me	Jer 13:22	428
for thou hast made all *t* things	Jer 14:22	428
shew this people all *t* words	Jer 16:10	428
that enter in by *t* gates	Jer 17:20	428
that Jeremiah prophesied *t* things	Jer 20:1	428
people that enter in by *t* gates	Jer 22:2	428
But if ye will not hear *t* words	Jer 22:5	428
I have not sent *t* prophets	Jer 23:21	
Like *t* good figs, so will I	Jer 24:5	428
against all *t* nations round about	Jer 25:9	428
t nations shall serve the king of	Jer 25:11	428
thou against them all *t* words	Jer 25:30	428
t words in the house of the LORD	Jer 26:7	428
princes of Judah heard *t* things	Jer 26:10	428
to speak all *t* words in your ears	Jer 26:15	428
now have I given all *t* lands into	Jer 27:6	428
of Judah according to all *t* words	Jer 27:12	428
upon the neck of all *t* nations	Jer 28:14	428
Now *t* are the words of the letter	Jer 29:1	428
t are the words that the LORD	Jer 30:4	428
I have done *t* things unto thee	Jer 30:15	428
turn again to *t* thy cities	Jer 31:21	428
Take *t* evidences, this evidence	Jer 32:14	428
all *t* words unto Zedekiah king of	Jer 34:6	428
for *t* defenced cities remained of	Jer 34:7	2007
tell the king of all *t* words	Jer 36:16	428
write all *t* words at his mouth	Jer 36:17	428
He pronounced all *t* words unto me	Jer 36:18	428
servants that heard all *t* words	Jer 36:24	428
t men have done evil in all that	Jer 38:9	428
Put now *t* old cast clouts and	Jer 38:12	
hand of *t* men that seek thy life	Jer 38:16	428
Let no man know of *t* words	Jer 38:24	428
to all *t* words that the king had	Jer 38:27	428
him to them, even all *t* words	Jer 43:1	428
upon *t* stones that I have hid	Jer 43:10	428
when he had written *t* words in a	Jer 45:1	
even all *t* words that are written	Jer 51:60	428
see, and shalt read all *t* words	Jer 51:61	428
the brass of all *t* vessels was	Jer 52:20	428
the pomegranates were like unto *t*	Jer 52:22	428
For *t* things I weep	Lam 1:16	428
for *t* pine away, stricken through	Lam 4:9	1992
for *t* things our eyes are dim	Lam 5:17	428
When those went, *t* went	Eze 1:21	
and when those stood, *t* stood	Eze 1:21	
see greater abominations than *t*	Eze 8:15	428
When they stood, *t* stood	Eze 10:17	
t lifted up themselves also	Eze 10:17	
t are the men that devise	Eze 11:2	428
t men have set up their idols in	Eze 14:3	428
Though *t* three men, Noah, Daniel,	Eze 14:14	428
Though *t* three men were in it, as	Eze 14:16	428
Though *t* three men were in it, as	Eze 14:18	428
thee, to do any of *t* unto thee	Eze 16:5	428
t hast thou sacrificed unto them	Eze 16:20	
seeing thou doest all *t* things	Eze 16:30	428
hast fretted me in all *t* things	Eze 16:43	428
Know ye not what *t* things mean	Eze 17:12	428

hand, and hath done all *t* things	Eze 17:18	428
the like to any one of *t* things	Eze 18:10	428
he hath done all *t* abominations	Eze 18:13	428
T discovered her nakedness	Eze 23:10	1992
I will do *t* things unto thee,	Eze 23:30	428
tell us what *t* things are to us	Eze 24:19	428
in *t* were they thy merchants	Eze 27:21	
T were thy merchants in all sorts	Eze 27:24	1992
t cities shall go into captivity	Eze 30:17	2007
T two nations and *t* two	Eze 35:10	
T are the people of the LORD, and	Eze 36:20	428
me, Son of man, can *t* bones live	Eze 37:3	428
unto me, Prophesy upon *t* bones	Eze 37:4	428
saith the Lord GOD unto *t* bones	Eze 37:5	428
O breath, and breathe upon *t* slain	Eze 37:9	428
t bones are the whole house of	Eze 37:11	428
shew us what thou meanest by *t*	Eze 37:18	428
thereof according to *t* measures	Eze 40:24	428
gate according to *t* measures	Eze 40:28	428
thereof, according to *t* measures	Eze 40:29	428
the gate according to *t* measures	Eze 40:32	428
were according to *t* measures	Eze 40:33	428
it according to *t* measures	Eze 40:35	428
t are the sons of Zadok among the	Eze 40:46	1992
the galleries were higher than *t*	Eze 42:5	2007
from under *t* chambers was the	Eze 42:9	428
t are the measures of the altar	Eze 43:13	428
T are the ordinances of the altar	Eze 43:18	428
when *t* days are expired, it shall	Eze 43:27	
t four corners were of one	Eze 46:22	
T are the places of them that	Eze 46:24	428
T waters issue out toward the	Eze 47:8	428
because *t* waters shall come	Eze 47:9	428
Now *t* are the names of the tribes	Eze 48:1	428
for *t* are his sides east and west	Eze 48:1	
t shall be the measures thereof	Eze 48:16	428
t are their portions, saith the	Eze 48:29	428
t are the goings out of the city	Eze 48:30	428
Now among *t* were of the children	Dan 1:6	1992
As for *t* four children, God gave	Dan 1:17	428
of thy head upon thy bed, are *t*	Dan 2:28	1836
and as iron that breaketh all *t*	Dan 2:40	459
in the days of *t* kings shall the	Dan 2:44	581
pieces and consume all *t* kingdoms	Dan 2:44	459
t men, O king, have not regarded	Dan 3:12	479
Then they brought *t* men before	Dan 3:13	479
Then *t* men were bound in their	Dan 3:21	479
t three men, Shadrach, Meshach,	Dan 3:23	479
gathered together, saw *t* men	Dan 3:27	479
And over *t* three presidents	Dan 6:2	4481
Then said *t* men, We shall not	Dan 6:5	479
Then *t* presidents and princes	Dan 6:6	459
Then *t* men assembled, and found	Dan 6:11	479
the king, when he heard *t* words	Dan 6:14	
Then *t* men assembled unto the	Dan 6:15	479
T great beasts, which are four,	Dan 7:17	459
that holdeth with me in *t* things	Dan 10:21	428
that strengtheneth her in *t* times	Dan 11:6	
both *t* kings' hearts shall be to	Dan 11:27	
but *t* shall escape out of his	Dan 11:41	428
it be to the end of *t* wonders	Dan 12:6	
all *t* things shall be finished	Dan 12:7	428
what shall be the end of *t* things	Dan 12:8	428
T are my rewards that my lovers	Hos 2:12	1992
and he shall understand *t* things	Hos 14:9	428
be they better than *t* kingdoms	Amos 6:2	428
are *t* his doings	Mic 2:7	428
Shall not all *t* take up a parable	Hab 2:6	428
by a dead body touch any of *t*	Hag 2:13	428
said I, O my lord, what are *t*	Zec 1:9	428
me, I will shew thee what *t* be	Zec 1:9	428
T are they whom the LORD hath	Zec 1:10	428
hast had indignation *t* threescore	Zec 1:12	2088
that talked with me, What be *t*	Zec 1:19	428
T are the horns which have	Zec 1:19	428
Then said I, What come *t* to do	Zec 1:21	428
T are the horns which have	Zec 1:21	428
but *t* are come to fray them, to	Zec 1:21	428
to walk among *t* that stand by	Zec 3:7	428
with me, saying, What are *t*	Zec 4:4	428
me, Knowest thou not what *t* be	Zec 4:5	428
What are *t* two olive trees upon	Zec 4:11	428
What be *t* two olive branches	Zec 4:12	
said, Knowest thou not what *t* be	Zec 4:13	428
T are the two anointed ones, that	Zec 4:14	428
Whither do *t* bear the ephah	Zec 5:10	1992
that talked with me, What are *t*	Zec 6:4	428
T are the four spirits of the	Zec 6:5	428
t that go toward the north	Zec 6:8	
as I have done *t* so many years	Zec 7:3	2088
remnant of this people in *t* days	Zec 8:6	1992
ye that hear in *t* days	Zec 8:9	428
days *t* words by the mouth of the	Zec 8:9	428
For before *t* days there was no	Zec 8:10	1992
people to possess all *t* things	Zec 8:12	428
So again have I thought in *t* days	Zec 8:15	428
T are the things that ye shall do	Zec 8:16	428
for all *t* are things that I hate,	Zec 8:17	428
What are *t* wounds in thine hands	Zec 13:6	428
beasts that shall be in *t* tents	Zec 14:15	1992
But while he thought on *t* things	Mt 1:20	*5023*
Herod the king had heard *t* things	Mt 2:3	
that God is able of *t* stones to	Mt 3:9	*5130*
command that *t* stones be made	Mt 4:3	*3778*
All *t* things will I give thee, if	Mt 4:9	*5023*
break one of *t* least commandments	Mt 5:19	*5130*
is more than *t* cometh of evil	Mt 5:37	*5130*
was not arrayed like one of *t*	Mt 6:29	*5130*
(For after all *t* things do the	Mt 6:32	*5023*
that ye have need of all *t* things	Mt 6:32	*5130*
all *t* things shall be added unto	Mt 6:33	*5023*
heareth *t* sayings of mine	Mt 7:24	*5128*
that heareth *t* sayings of mine	Mt 7:26	*5128*
when Jesus had ended *t* sayings	Mt 7:28	*5128*
While he spake *t* things unto them	Mt 9:18	*5023*
of the twelve apostles are *t*	Mt 10:2	*5023*
T twelve Jesus sent forth, and	Mt 10:5	*5128*
t little ones a cup of cold water	Mt 10:42	*5130*
hast hid *t* things from the wise	Mt 11:25	*5023*
All *t* things spake Jesus unto the	Mt 13:34	*5023*
Have ye understood all *t* things	Mt 13:51	*5023*
Jesus had finished *t* parables	Mt 13:53	*5025*
this wisdom, and *t* mighty works	Mt 13:54	*3588*
then hath this man all *t* things	Mt 13:56	*5023*
T are the things which defile a	Mt 15:20	*5023*
But whoso shall offend one of *t*	Mt 18:6	*5130*
despise not one of *t* little ones	Mt 18:10	*5130*
that one of *t* little ones should	Mt 18:14	*5130*
when Jesus had finished *t* sayings	Mt 19:1	*5128*
All *t* things have I kept from my	Mt 19:20	*5023*
T last have wrought but one hour,	Mt 20:12	*3778*
Grant that *t* my two sons may sit,	Mt 20:21	*3778*
unto him, Hearest thou what *t* say	Mt 21:16	*3778*
authority doest thou *t* things	Mt 21:23	*5023*
by what authority I do *t* things	Mt 21:24	*5023*
by what authority I do *t* things	Mt 21:27	*5023*
When they had heard *t* words	Mt 22:22	
On *t* two commandments hang all	Mt 22:40	*5025*
t ought ye to have done, and not	Mt 23:23	*5023*
All *t* things shall come upon this	Mt 23:36	*5023*
them, See ye not all *t* things	Mt 24:2	*5023*
Tell us, when shall *t* things be	Mt 24:3	*5023*
for all *t* things must come to	Mt 24:6	
All *t* are the beginning of	Mt 24:8	*5023*
when ye shall see all *t* things	Mt 24:33	*5023*
till all *t* things be fulfilled	Mt 24:34	*5023*
one of the least of *t* my brethren	Mt 25:40	*5130*
it not to one of the least of *t*	Mt 25:45	*5130*
t shall go away into everlasting	Mt 25:46	*3778*
Jesus had finished all *t* sayings	Mt 26:1	*5128*
what is it which *t* witness	Mt 26:62	*3778*
Why reason ye *t* things in your	Mk 2:8	*5023*
all *t* things are done in parables	Mk 4:11	*3588*
t are they by the way side, where	Mk 4:15	*3778*
t are they likewise which are	Mk 4:16	*3778*
t are they which are sown among	Mk 4:18	*3778*
t are they which are sown on good	Mk 4:20	*3778*
whence hath this man *t* things	Mk 6:2	*5023*
All *t* evil things come from	Mk 7:23	*5023*
t men with bread here in the	Mk 8:4	*5128*
whosoever shall offend one of *t*	Mk 9:42	*3588*
all *t* have I observed from my	Mk 10:20	*5023*
authority doest thou *t* things	Mk 11:28	*5023*
this authority to do *t* things	Mk 11:28	*5023*
by what authority I do *t* things	Mk 11:29	*5023*
by what authority I do *t* things	Mk 11:33	*5023*
other commandment greater than *t*	Mk 12:31	*5130*
t shall receive greater damnation	Mk 12:40	*3778*
Seest thou *t* great buildings	Mk 13:2	*5025*
Tell us, when shall *t* things be	Mk 13:4	*5023*
all *t* things shall be fulfilled	Mk 13:4	*5023*
t are the beginnings of sorrows	Mk 13:8	*5023*
when ye shall see *t* things come	Mk 13:29	*5023*
till all *t* things be done	Mk 13:30	*5023*
what is it which *t* witness	Mk 14:60	*3778*
t signs shall follow them that	Mk 16:17	*5023*
and to shew thee *t* glad tidings	Lk 1:19	*5023*
until the day that *t* things shall	Lk 1:20	*5023*
all *t* sayings were noised abroad	Lk 1:65	*5023*
But Mary kept all *t* things	Lk 2:19	*5023*
kept all *t* sayings in her heart	Lk 2:51	*5023*
That God is able of *t* stones to	Lk 3:8	*5130*
when they heard *t* things	Lk 4:28	*5023*
after *t* things he went forth, and	Lk 5:27	*5023*
When Jesus heard *t* things	Lk 7:9	*5023*
John shewed him of all *t* things	Lk 7:18	*5130*
And when he had said *t* things	Lk 8:8	*5023*
t have no root, which for a while	Lk 8:13	*3778*
my brethren are *t* which hear the	Lk 8:21	*3778*
an eight days after *t* sayings	Lk 9:28	*5128*
Let *t* sayings sink down into your	Lk 9:44	*5128*
After *t* things the Lord appointed	Lk 10:1	*5023*
that thou hast hid *t* things from	Lk 10:21	*5023*
Which now of *t* three, thinkest	Lk 10:36	*5130*
to pass, as he spake *t* things	Lk 11:27	*5023*
t ought ye to have done, and not	Lk 11:42	*5023*
as he said *t* things unto them,	Lk 11:53	*5023*
was not arrayed like one of *t*	Lk 12:27	*5130*
For all *t* things do the nations	Lk 12:30	*5023*
that ye have need of *t* things	Lk 12:30	*5130*
all *t* things shall be added unto	Lk 12:31	*5023*
Suppose ye that *t* Galilaeans were	Lk 13:2	*3778*
t three years I come seeking	Lk 13:7	
t eighteen years, be loosed from	Lk 13:16	
And when he had said *t* things	Lk 13:17	*5023*
not answer him again to *t* things	Lk 14:6	*5023*
at meat with him heard *t* things	Lk 14:15	*5023*
came, and shewed his lord *t* things	Lk 14:21	*5023*
asked what *t* things meant	Lk 15:26	*5023*
t many years do I serve thee,	Lk 15:29	*5118*
were covetous, heard all *t* things	Lk 16:14	*5023*
offend one of *t* little ones	Lk 17:2	*5130*
All *t* have I kept from my youth	Lk 18:21	*5023*
Now when Jesus heard *t* things	Lk 18:22	*5023*
they understood none of *t* things	Lk 18:34	*5130*
And as they heard *t* things	Lk 19:11	*5023*
then he commanded *t* servants to	Lk 19:15	*5128*
if *t* should hold their peace, the	Lk 19:40	*3778*
authority doest thou *t* things	Lk 20:2	*5023*
by what authority I do *t* things	Lk 20:8	*5023*
destroy *t* husbandmen, and shall	Lk 20:16	*5128*
For all *t* have of their abundance	Lk 21:4	*3778*
As for *t* things which ye behold,	Lk 21:6	*5023*
but when shall *t* things be	Lk 21:7	*5023*
when *t* things shall come to pass	Lk 21:7	*5023*
for *t* things must first come to	Lk 21:9	*5023*
But before all *t*, they shall lay	Lk 21:12	*5130*
For *t* be the days of vengeance,	Lk 21:22	*3778*
when *t* things begin to come to	Lk 21:28	*5130*
when ye see *t* things come to pass	Lk 21:31	*5023*
t things that shall come to pass	Lk 21:36	*5023*
For if they do *t* things in a	Lk 23:31	*5023*
afar off, beholding *t* things	Lk 23:49	*5023*
told all *t* things unto the eleven	Lk 24:9	*5023*
which told *t* things unto the	Lk 24:10	*5023*
all *t* things which had happened	Lk 24:14	*5130*
are *t* that ye have one to another	Lk 24:17	*3778*
are come to pass there in *t* days	Lk 24:18	*5025*
day since *t* things were done	Lk 24:21	*5023*
Christ to have suffered *t* things	Lk 24:26	*5023*
T are the words which I spake	Lk 24:44	*3778*
And ye are witnesses of *t* things	Lk 24:48	*5130*
T things were done in Bethabara	Jn 1:28	*5023*
shalt see greater things than *t*	Jn 1:50	*5130*
sold doves, Take *t* things hence	Jn 2:16	*5023*
seeing that thou doest *t* things	Jn 2:18	*5023*
for no man can do *t* miracles that	Jn 3:2	*5023*
unto him, How can *t* things be	Jn 3:9	*5023*
Israel, and knowest not *t* things	Jn 3:10	*5023*
After *t* things came Jesus and his	Jn 3:22	*5023*
In *t* lay a great multitude of	Jn 5:3	*5025*
because he had done *t* things on	Jn 5:16	*5023*
t also doeth the Son likewise	Jn 5:19	*5023*
shew him greater works than *t*	Jn 5:20	*5130*
but *t* things I say, that ye might	Jn 5:34	*5023*
After *t* things Jesus went over	Jn 6:1	*5023*
we buy bread, that *t* may eat	Jn 6:5	*3778*
T things said he in the synagogue	Jn 6:59	*5023*
After *t* things Jesus walked in	Jn 7:1	*5023*
If thou do *t* things, shew thyself	Jn 7:4	*5023*
he had said *t* words unto them	Jn 7:9	*5023*
than *t* which this man hath done	Jn 7:31	*5130*
T words spake Jesus in the	Jn 8:20	*5023*
hath taught me, I speak *t* things	Jn 8:28	*5023*
As he spake *t* words, many	Jn 8:30	*5023*
T words spake his parents,	Jn 9:22	*5023*
which were with him heard *t* words	Jn 9:40	*5023*
among the Jews for *t* sayings	Jn 10:19	*5128*
T are not the words of him that	Jn 10:21	*5023*
T things said he	Jn 11:11	*5023*
T things understood not his	Jn 12:16	*5023*
then remembered they that *t*	Jn 12:16	*5023*
they had done *t* things unto him	Jn 12:16	*5023*
T things spake Jesus, and departed	Jn 12:36	*5023*
T things said Esaias, when he saw	Jn 12:41	*5023*
If ye know *t* things, happy are ye	Jn 13:17	*5023*
greater works than *t* shall he do	Jn 14:12	*5130*
T things have I spoken unto you,	Jn 14:25	*5023*
T things have I spoken unto you,	Jn 15:11	*5023*
T things I command you, that ye	Jn 15:17	*5023*
But all *t* things will they do	Jn 15:21	*5023*
T things have I spoken unto you,	Jn 16:1	*5023*
t things will they do unto you,	Jn 16:3	*5023*
But *t* things have I told you,	Jn 16:4	*5023*
t things I said not unto you at	Jn 16:4	*5023*
I have said *t* things unto you	Jn 16:6	*5023*
T things have I spoken unto you	Jn 16:25	*5023*
T things I have spoken unto you,	Jn 16:33	*5023*
T words spake Jesus, and lifted up	Jn 17:1	*5023*
but *t* are in the world, and I come	Jn 17:11	*3778*
t things I speak in the world,	Jn 17:13	*5023*
Neither pray I for *t* alone	Jn 17:20	*5130*
t have known that thou hast sent	Jn 17:25	*3778*
When Jesus had spoken *t* words	Jn 18:1	*5023*
ye seek me, let *t* go their way	Jn 18:8	*5128*
T things therefore the soldiers	Jn 19:24	*5023*
For *t* things were done, that the	Jn 19:36	*5023*
he had spoken *t* things unto her	Jn 20:18	*5023*
But *t* are written, that ye might	Jn 20:31	*5023*
After *t* things Jesus shewed	Jn 21:1	*5023*
Jonas, lovest thou me more than *t*	Jn 21:15	*5130*
which testifieth of *t* things	Jn 21:24	*5130*
and wrote *t* things	Jn 21:24	*5023*
And when he had spoken *t* things	Acts 1:9	*5023*
T all continued with one accord	Acts 1:14	*3778*
Wherefore of *t* men which have	Acts 1:21	*5130*
shew whether of *t* two thou hast	Acts 1:24	*5130*
are not all *t* which speak	Acts 2:7	*3778*
T men are full of new wine	Acts 2:13	
For *t* are not drunken, as ye	Acts 2:15	*3778*
Ye men of Israel, hear *t* words	Acts 2:22	*5128*
have likewise foretold of *t* days	Acts 3:24	*5025*
Saying, What shall we do to *t* men	Acts 4:16	*5125*
Ananias hearing *t* words fell down	Acts 5:5	*5128*
on all them that heard *t* things	Acts 5:5	*5023*
and upon as many as heard *t* things	Acts 5:11	*5023*
the chief priests heard *t* things	Acts 5:24	*5128*
we are his witnesses of *t* things	Acts 5:32	*5130*
ye intend to do as touching *t* men	Acts 5:35	*5125*
For before *t* days rose up Theudas	Acts 5:36	*5130*
say unto you, Refrain from *t* men	Acts 5:38	*5130*
the high priest, Are *t* things so	Acts 7:1	*5023*
not my hand made all *t* things	Acts 7:50	*5023*
When they heard *t* things, they	Acts 7:54	*5023*
that none of *t* things which ye	Acts 8:24	
declared all *t* things unto them	Acts 10:8	
While Peter yet spake *t* words	Acts 10:44	*5023*
that *t* should not be baptized,	Acts 10:47	*5128*
Moreover *t* six brethren	Acts 11:12	*3778*
When they heard *t* things, they	Acts 11:18	*5023*
Then tidings of *t* things came	Acts 11:22	*846*
in *t* days came prophets from	Acts 11:27	*5125*
Go shew *t* things unto James, and	Acts 12:17	*5023*
the Gentiles besought that *t*	Acts 13:42	*5023*
saying, Sirs, why do ye *t* things	Acts 14:15	*5130*
t vanities unto the living God	Acts 14:15	*5023*
with *t* sayings scarce restrained	Acts 14:18	*5023*
the Lord, who doeth all *t* things	Acts 15:17	*5023*
burden than *t* necessary things	Acts 15:28	*5130*
T men are the servants of the	Acts 16:17	*3778*
T men, being Jews, do exceedingly	Acts 16:20	*3778*
the serjeants told *t* words unto	Acts 16:38	*5023*

T

T that have turned the world Acts 17:6 3778
t all do contrary to the decrees Acts 17:7 3778
city, when they heard *t* things Acts 17:8 5023
T were more noble than those in Acts 17:11 3778
know therefore what *t* things mean Acts 17:20 5023
After *t* things Paul departed from Acts 18:1 5023
After *t* things were ended, Paul Acts 19:21 5023
And when they heard *t* sayings Acts 19:28
Seeing then that *t* things cannot Acts 19:36 5130
For ye have brought hither *t* men Acts 19:37 5128
T going before tarried for us at Acts 20:5 3778
But none of *t* things move me, Acts 20:24
that *t* hands have ministered unto Acts 20:34 3778
And when we heard *t* things Acts 21:12 5023
which before *t* days madest an Acts 21:38 5130
thou hast shewed *t* things to me Acts 23:22 5023
take knowledge of all *t* things Acts 24:8 5130
saying that *t* things were so Acts 24:9 5023
Or else let *t* same here say, if Acts 24:20 3778
And when Felix heard *t* things Acts 24:22 5023
be judged of *t* things before me Acts 25:9 5130
t things whereof *t* accuse me Acts 25:11 3778
and there be judged of *t* matters Acts 25:20 5130
a witness both of *t* things which Acts 26:16
For *t* causes the Jews caught me Acts 26:21 5130
For the king knoweth of *t* things Acts 26:26 5130
of *t* things are hidden from him Acts 26:26 5130
such as I am, except *t* bonds Acts 26:29 5130
Except *t* abide in the ship, ye Acts 27:31 3778
And when he had said *t* words Acts 28:29 5023
things contained in the law, *t* Rom 2:14 3778
shall we then say to *t* things Rom 8:31 5023
in all *t* things we are more than Rom 8:37 5125
t are not the children of God Rom 9:8 5023
how much more shall *t*, which be Rom 11:24 3778
Even so have *t* also now not Rom 11:31 3778
For he that in *t* things serveth Rom 14:18 5125
having no more place in *t* parts Rom 15:23 5125
having a great desire *t* many Rom 15:23
t things, brethren, I have in a 1Cor 4:6 5023
I write not *t* things to shame you 1Cor 4:14 5023
Say I *t* things as a man 1Cor 9:8 5023
But I have used none of *t* things 1Cor 9:15 5130
neither have I written *t* things 1Cor 9:15 5023
Now *t* things were our examples, 1Cor 10:6 5023
Now all *t* things happened unto 1Cor 10:11 5023
carried away unto *t* dumb idols 1Cor 12:2
But all *t* worketh that one and the 1Cor 12:11 5023
upon *t* we bestow more abundant 1Cor 12:23 5125
faith, hope, charity, *t* three 1Cor 13:13 5023
but the greatest of *t* is charity 1Cor 13:13 5130
And who is sufficient for *t* things 2Cor 2:16 5023
Having therefore *t* promises 2Cor 7:1 5025
Therefore I write *t* things being 2Cor 13:10 5023
But of *t* who seemed to be Gal 2:6
for *t* are the two covenants Gal 4:24 3778
t are contrary the one to the Gal 5:17 5023
flesh are manifest, which are *t* Gal 5:19
for because of *t* things cometh Eph 5:6 5023
be any praise, think on *t* things Phil 4:8 5023
But now ye also put off all *t* Col 3:8 5023
above all *t* things put on charity Col 3:14 5125
T only are my fellow workers unto Col 4:11 3778
should be moved by *t* afflictions 1Th 3:3 5025
comfort one another with *t* words 1Th 4:18 5125
yet with you, I told you *t* things 2Th 2:5 5023
let *t* also first be proved 1Ti 3:10 3778
T things write I unto thee, 1Ti 3:14 5023
in remembrance of *t* things 1Ti 4:6 5023
T things command and teach 1Ti 4:11 5023
Meditate upon *t* things 1Ti 4:15 5023
t things give in charge, that 1Ti 5:7 5023
that thou observe *t* things 1Ti 5:21 5023
T things teach and exhort 1Ti 6:2 5023
thou, O man of God, flee *t* things 1Ti 6:11 5023
cause I also suffer *t* things 2Ti 1:12 5023
Of *t* things put them in 2Ti 2:14 5023
therefore purge himself from *t* 2Ti 2:21 5130
so do *t* also resist the truth 2Ti 3:8 3778
T things speak, and exhort, and Titus 2:15 5023
t things I will that thou affirm Titus 3:8 5130
T things are good and profitable Titus 3:8 5023
Hath in *t* last days spoken unto Heb 1:2 5130
For he of whom *t* things are Heb 7:13 5023
Now when *t* things were thus Heb 9:6 5130
heavens should be purified with *t* Heb 9:23 5125
with better sacrifices than *t* Heb 9:23 5025
Now where remission of *t* is Heb 10:18 5130
T all died in faith, not having Heb 11:13 3778
t all, having obtained a good Heb 11:39 3778
t things ought not so to be Jas 3:10 5023
manifest in *t* last times for you 1Pet 1:20 3588
that by *t* ye might be partakers 2Pet 1:4 5130
For if *t* things be in you, and 2Pet 1:8 5023
he that lacketh *t* things is blind 2Pet 1:9 5023
for if ye do *t* things, ye shall 2Pet 1:10 5023
always in remembrance of *t* things 2Pet 1:12 5130
t things always in remembrance 2Pet 1:15 5130
But *t*, as natural brute beasts, 2Pet 2:12 3778
T are wells without water, clouds 2Pet 2:17 3778
Seeing then that all *t* things 2Pet 3:11 5130
speaking in them of *t* things 2Pet 3:16 5130
seeing ye know *t* things before 2Pet 3:17
t things write we unto you, that 1Jn 1:4 5023
t things write I unto you, that 1Jn 2:1 5023
T things have I written unto you 1Jn 2:26 5023
and *t* three are one 1Jn 5:7 3778
and *t* three agree in one 1Jn 5:8 3778
T things have I written unto you 1Jn 5:13 5023
Likewise also *t* filthy dreamers Jude 8 3778
But *t* speak evil of those things Jude 10 3778
T are spots in your feasts of Jude 12 3778
from Adam, prophesied of *t* Jude 14 5125
T are murmurers, complainers, Jude 16 3778
T be they who separate themselves Jude 19 3778
T things saith he that holdeth Rev 2:1 3592
T things saith the first and the Rev 2:8 3592
T things saith he which hath the Rev 2:12 3592
T things saith the Son of God, Rev 2:18 3592
T things saith he that hath the Rev 3:1 3592
T things saith he that is holy, Rev 3:7 3592
T things saith the Amen, the Rev 3:14 3592
after *t* things I saw four angels Rev 7:1 5023
What are *t* which are arrayed in Rev 7:13 3778
T are they which came out of Rev 7:14 3778
By *t* three was the third part of Rev 9:18 5130
men which were not killed by *t* Rev 9:20 5025
T are the two olive trees, and the Rev 11:4 3778
T have power to shut heaven, that Rev 11:6 3778
because *t* two prophets tormented Rev 11:10 3778
T are they which were not defiled Rev 14:4 3778
T are they which follow the Lamb Rev 14:4 3778
T were redeemed from among men, Rev 14:4 3778
which hath power over *t* plagues Rev 16:9 5025
T have one mind, and shall give Rev 17:13 3778
T shall make war with the Lamb, Rev 17:14 3778
t shall hate the whore, and shall Rev 17:16 3778
after *t* things I saw another Rev 18:1 5023
The merchants of *t* things Rev 18:15 5130
after *t* things I heard a great Rev 19:1 5023
T are the true sayings of God Rev 19:9 3778
T both were cast alive into a Rev 19:20 3588
for *t* words are true and faithful Rev 21:5 3778
T sayings are faithful and true Rev 22:6 3778
And I John saw *t* things, and heard Rev 22:8 5023
angel which shewed me *t* things Rev 22:8 5023
unto you *t* things in the churches Rev 22:16 5023
any man shall add unto *t* things Rev 22:18 5023
which testifieth *t* things saith Rev 22:20 5023

THESSALONIANS (*thes-sa-lo'-ne-uns*) *The inhabitants of Thessalonica.*
and of the *T*, Aristarchus and Acts 20:4 2331
unto the church of the *T* which is 1Th 1:1 2331
the *T* was written from Athens 1Th *s* 2331
church of the *T* in God our Father 2Th 1:1 2331
to the *T* was written from Athens 2Th *s* 2331

THESSALONICA (*thes-sa-lo-ni'-cah*) *A city in Macedonia.*
and Apollonia, they came to *T* Acts 17:1 2332
were more noble than those in *T* Acts 17:11 2332
But when the Jews of *T* had Acts 17:13 2332
Aristarchus, a Macedonian of *T* Acts 27:2 2331
For even in *T* ye sent once and Phil 4:16 2332
world, and is departed unto *T* 2Ti 4:10 2332

THEUDAS (*thew'-das*) *A false Jewish Messiah.*
For before these days rose up *T* Acts 5:36 2333

THEY See PREFACE.

THICK
there was a *t* darkness in all the Ex 10:22 653
Lo, I come unto thee in a *t* cloud Ex 19:9 5645
a *t* cloud upon the mount, and the Ex 19:16 3515
unto the *t* darkness where God was Ex 20:21
trees, and the boughs of *t* trees Lev 23:40 5687
darkness, clouds, and *t* darkness Deut 4:11
of the *t* darkness, with a great Deut 5:22
art waxen fat, thou art grown *t* Deut 32:15 5666
under the *t* boughs of a great oak 2Sa 18:9
waters, and *t* clouds of the skies 2Sa 22:12
the *t* beam were before them 1Kin 7:6
And it was an hand breadth *t* 1Kin 7:26 5672
he would dwell in the *t* darkness 1Kin 8:12
morrow, that he took a *t* cloth 2Kin 8:15
he would dwell in the *t* darkness 2Chr 6:1
branches, and branches of *t* trees Neh 8:15 5687
upon the *t* bosses of his bucklers Job 15:26 5672
T clouds are a covering to him, Job 22:14
up the waters in his *t* clouds Job 26:8
watering he wearieth the *t* cloud Job 37:11
t darkness a swaddlingband for it Job 38:9
waters and *t* clouds of the skies Ps 18:11
before him his *t* clouds passed Ps 18:12
lifted up axes upon the *t* trees Ps 74:5 5441
as a *t* cloud, thy transgressions, Is 44:22
green tree, and under every *t* oak Eze 6:13 5687
a *t* cloud of incense went up Eze 8:11 6282
was exalted among the *t* branches Eze 19:11 5688
high hill, and all the *t* trees Eze 20:28 5687
and his top was among the *t* boughs Eze 31:3 5688
up his top among the *t* boughs Eze 31:10 5688
up their top among the *t* boughs Eze 31:14 5688
was five cubits *t* round about Eze 41:12 7341
there were *t* planks upon the face Eze 41:25 5645
of the house, and *t* planks Eze 41:26
of *t* darkness, as the morning Joel 2:2
that ladeth himself with *t* clay Hab 2:6
a day of clouds and *t* darkness, Zeph 1:15
people were gathered *t* together Lk 11:29

THICKER
shall be *t* than my father's loins 1Kin 12:10 5666
shall be *t* than my father's loins 2Chr 10:10 5666

THICKET
a ram caught in a *t* by his horns Gen 22:13 5442
The lion is come up from his *t* Jer 4:7 5441

THICKETS
hide themselves in caves, and in *t* 1Sa 13:6 2337
kindle in the *t* of the forest Is 9:18 5442
he shall cut down the *t* of the Is 10:34 5442
they shall go into *t*, and climb up Jer 4:29 5645

THICKNESS
the *t* of it was an handbreadth, 2Chr 4:5 5672
the *t* thereof was four fingers Jer 52:21 5672
The *t* of the wall, which was for Eze 41:9 7341
The chambers were in the *t* of the Eze 42:10 7341

THIEF
If a *t* be found breaking up, and Ex 22:2 1590
if the *t* be found, let him pay Ex 22:7 1590
If the *t* be not found, then the Ex 22:8 1590
then that *t* shall die Deut 24:7 1590
needy, and in the night is as a *t* Job 24:14 1590
cried after them as after a *t* Job 30:5 1590
When thou sawest a *t*, then thou Ps 50:18 1590
Men do not despise a *t*, if he Prov 6:30 1590
with a *t* hateth his own soul Prov 29:24 1590
As the *t* is ashamed when he is Jer 2:26 1590
the *t* cometh in, and the troop of Hos 7:1 1590
enter in at the windows like a *t* Joel 2:9 1590
enter into the house of the *t* Zec 5:4 1590
in what watch the *t* would come Mt 24:43 2812
out as against a *t* with swords Mt 26:55 3027
Are ye come out, as against a *t* Mk 14:48 3027
where no *t* approacheth, neither Lk 12:33 2812
known what hour the *t* would come Lk 12:39 2812
Be ye come out, as against a *t* Lk 22:52 3027
some other way, the same is a *t* Jn 10:1 2812
The *t* cometh not, but for to Jn 10:10 2812
but because he was a *t*, and had Jn 12:6 2812
so cometh as a *t* in the night 1Th 5:2 2812
day should overtake you as a *t* 1Th 5:4 2812
suffer as a murderer, or as a *t* 1Pet 4:15 2812
will come as a *t* in the night 2Pet 3:10 2812
watch, I will come on thee as a *t* Rev 3:3 2812
Behold, I come as a *t* Rev 16:15 2812

THIEVES
rebellious, and companions of *t* Is 1:23 1590
was he found among *t* Jer 48:27 1590
if *t* by night, they will destroy Jer 49:9 1590
If *t* came to thee, if robbers by Obad 5 1590
where *t* break through and steal Mt 6:19 2812
where *t* do not break through nor Mt 6:20 2812
but ye have made it a den of *t* Mt 21:13 3027
there two *t* crucified with him Mt 27:38 3027
The *t* also, which were crucified Mt 27:44 3027
but ye have made it a den of *t* Mk 11:17 3027
And with him they crucify two *t* Mk 15:27 3027
to Jericho, and fell among *t* Lk 10:30 3027
unto him that fell among the *t* Lk 10:36 3027
but ye have made it a den of *t* Lk 19:46 3027
that ever came before me are *t* Jn 10:8 2812
Nor *t*, nor covetous, nor 1Cor 6:10 2812

THIGH
I pray thee, thy hand under my *t* Gen 24:2 3409
under the *t* of Abraham his master Gen 24:9 3409
he touched the hollow of his *t* Gen 32:25 3409
of Jacob's *t* was out of joint Gen 32:25 3409
upon him, and he halted upon his *t* Gen 32:31 3409
which is upon the hollow of the *t* Gen 32:32 3409
t in the sinew that shrank Gen 32:32 3409
I pray thee, thy hand under my *t* Gen 47:29 3409
the LORD doth make thy *t* to rot Num 5:21 3409
belly to swell, and thy *t* to rot Num 5:22 3409
shall swell, and her *t* shall rot Num 5:27 3409
his raiment upon his right *t* Judg 3:16 3409
took the dagger from his right *t* Judg 3:21 3409
hip and *t* with a great slaughter Judg 15:8 3409
Gird thy sword upon thy *t* Ps 45:3 3409
man hath his sword upon his *t* Song 3:8 3409
make bare the leg, uncover the *t* Is 47:2 7785
was instructed, I smote upon my *t* Jer 31:19 3409
smite therefore upon thy *t* Eze 21:12 3409
it, even every good piece, the *t* Eze 24:4 3409
on his *t* a name written, KING OF Rev 19:16 3382

THIGHS
even unto the *t* they shall reach Ex 28:42 3409
joints of thy *t* are like jewels Song 7:1 3409
his belly and his *t* of brass, Dan 2:32 3410

THIMNATHAH (*thim'-nath-ah*) See TIMNAH. *A city in Dan.*
And Elon, and *T*, and Ekron, Josh 19:43 8553

THIN
And, behold, seven *t* ears and Gen 41:6 1851
the seven *t* ears devoured the Gen 41:7 1851
behold, seven ears, withered, *t* Gen 41:23 1851
the *t* ears devoured the seven Gen 41:24 1851
And the seven *t* and ill favoured Gen 41:27 7534
did beat the gold into *t* plates Ex 39:3
and there be in it a yellow *t* hair Lev 13:30 1851
certain additions made of *t* work 1Kin 7:29 4174
glory of Jacob shall be made *t* Is 17:4 1809

THINE
from him, Lift up now *t* eyes Gen 13:14
which hath delivered *t* enemies Gen 14:20
will not take any thing that is *t* Gen 14:23
saying, This shall not be *t* heir Gen 15:4
t own bowels shall be *t* heir Gen 15:4
die, thou, and all that are *t* Gen 20:7
up the lad, and hold him in *t* hand Gen 21:18
t only son Isaac, whom thou Gen 22:2
Lay not *t* hand upon the lad, Gen 22:12
thy son, *t* only son from me Gen 22:12
not withheld thy son, *t* only son Gen 22:16
if I have found favour in *t* eyes Gen 30:27
And he said, Lift up now *t* eyes Gen 31:12
discern thou what is *t* with me Gen 31:32
and thy staff that is in *t* hand Gen 38:18
days shall Pharaoh lift up *t* head Gen 40:13
let not *t* anger burn against thy Gen 44:18
shall put his hand upon *t* eyes Gen 46:4
shall we die before *t* eyes Gen 47:19
begettest after them, shall be *t* Gen 48:6
shall be in the neck of *t* enemies Gen 49:8
unto him, What is that in *t* hand Ex 4:2
said unto Moses, Put forth *t* hand Ex 4:4
Put now *t* hand into thy bosom Ex 4:6
Put *t* hand into thy bosom again Ex 4:7

shalt take this rod in *t* hand ... Ex 4:17
which I have put in *t* hand ... Ex 4:21
but the fault is in *t* own people ... Ex 5:16
serpent shalt thou take in *t* hand ... Ex 7:15
stretch out *t* hand upon the ... Ex 7:19
shall go up and come into *t* house ... Ex 8:3
into *t* ovens, and into thy ... Ex 8:3
Stretch forth *t* hand with thy rod ... Ex 8:5
send all my plagues upon *t* heart ... Ex 9:14
Stretch forth *t* hand toward ... Ex 9:22
Stretch out *t* hand over the land ... Ex 10:12
Stretch out *t* hand toward heaven, ... Ex 10:21
for a sign unto thee upon *t* hand ... Ex 13:9
and for a memorial between *t* eyes ... Ex 13:9
shall be for a token upon *t* hand ... Ex 13:16
and for frontlets between *t* eyes ... Ex 13:16
stretch out *t* hand over the sea, ... Ex 14:16
Stretch out *t* hand over the sea, ... Ex 14:26
in the greatness of *t* excellency ... Ex 15:7
by the greatness of *t* arm they ... Ex 15:16
in the mountain of *t* inheritance ... Ex 15:17
smotest the river, take in *t* hand ... Ex 17:5
offerings, thy sheep, and *t* oxen ... Ex 20:24
shalt thou do with *t* oxen ... Ex 22:30
put not *t* hand with the wicked to ... Ex 23:1
If thou meet *t* enemy's ox or his ... Ex 23:4
that *t* ox and *t* ass may rest, ... Ex 23:12
I will be an enemy unto *t* enemies ... Ex 23:22
an adversary unto *t* adversaries ... Ex 23:22
I will make all *t* enemies turn ... Ex 23:27
whom thou swarest by *t* own self ... Ex 32:13
sin, and take us for *t* inheritance ... Ex 34:9
with all *t* offerings thou shalt ... Lev 2:13
and it shall be *t*, and thy sons' ... Lev 10:15
for theirs is *t* own nakedness ... Lev 18:10
she is *t* aunt ... Lev 18:14
not hate thy brother in *t* heart ... Lev 19:17
he shall give *t* estimation in ... Lev 27:23
it according to *t* estimation ... Lev 27:27
lain with thee beside *t* husband ... Num 5:20
let *t* enemies be scattered ... Num 10:35
This shall be *t* of the most holy ... Num 18:9
And this is *t* ... Num 18:11
bring unto the LORD, shall be *t* ... Num 18:13
clean in *t* house shall eat of it ... Num 18:13
devoted in Israel shall be *t* ... Num 18:14
be of men or beasts, shall be *t* ... Num 18:15
redeem, according to *t* estimation ... Num 18:16
And the flesh of them shall be *t* ... Num 18:18
and as the right shoulder are *t* ... Num 18:18
t inheritance among the children ... Num 18:20
said unto Balaam, Am not I *t* ass ... Num 22:30
ever since I was *t* unto this day ... Num 22:30
smitten *t* ass these three times ... Num 22:32
spirit, and lay *t* hand upon him ... Num 27:18
put some of *t* honour upon him ... Num 27:20
I have given into *t* hand Sihon ... Deut 2:24
T eyes have seen all that the ... Deut 3:21
lift up *t* eyes westward, and ... Deut 3:27
and behold it with *t* eyes ... Deut 3:27
the things which *t* eyes have seen ... Deut 4:9
thou lift up *t* eyes unto heaven ... Deut 4:19
day, and consider it in *t* heart ... Deut 4:39
nor *t* ox, nor *t* ass, nor any ... Deut 5:14
the LORD thy God with all *t* heart ... Deut 6:5
this day, shall be in *t* heart ... Deut 6:6
them when thou sittest in *t* house ... Deut 6:7
bind them for a sign upon *t* hand ... Deut 6:8
be as frontlets between *t* eyes ... Deut 6:8
To cast out all *t* enemies from ... Deut 6:19
t oil, the increase of thy kine, ... Deut 7:13
t eye shall have no pity upon ... Deut 7:16
If thou shalt say in *t* heart ... Deut 7:17
temptations which *t* eyes saw ... Deut 7:19
deliver their kings into *t* hand ... Deut 7:24
bring an abomination into *t* house ... Deut 7:26
thee, to know what was in *t* heart ... Deut 8:2
shalt also consider in *t* heart ... Deut 8:5
Then *t* heart be lifted up, and ... Deut 8:14
And thou say in *t* heart, My power ... Deut 8:17
Speak not thou in *t* heart ... Deut 9:4
or for the uprightness of *t* heart ... Deut 9:5
t inheritance, which thou hast ... Deut 9:26
t inheritance, which thou ... Deut 9:29
things, which *t* eyes have seen ... Deut 10:21
thy corn, and thy wine, and *t* oil ... Deut 11:14
them when thou sittest in *t* house ... Deut 11:19
upon the door posts of *t* house ... Deut 11:20
or heave offering of *t* hand ... Deut 12:17
that thou puttest *t* hands unto ... Deut 12:18
friend, which is as *t* own soul ... Deut 13:6
neither shall *t* eye pity him ... Deut 13:8
t hand shall be first upon him to ... Deut 13:9
of the cursed thing to *t* hand ... Deut 13:17
of *t* oil, and the firstlings of ... Deut 14:23
and bind up the money in *t* hand ... Deut 14:25
rejoice, thou, and *t* household, ... Deut 14:26
tithe of *t* increase the same year ... Deut 14:28
work of *t* hand which thou doest ... Deut 14:29
but that which is *t* with thy ... Deut 15:3
thy brother *t* hand shall release ... Deut 15:3
thou shalt not harden *t* heart ... Deut 15:7
nor shut *t* hand from thy poor ... Deut 15:7
shalt open *t* hand wide unto him ... Deut 15:8
t eye be evil against thy poor ... Deut 15:9
t heart shall not be grieved when ... Deut 15:10
all that thou puttest *t* hand unto ... Deut 15:10
Thou shalt open *t* hand wide unto ... Deut 15:11
t house, because he is well with ... Deut 15:16
of a freewill offering of *t* hand ... Deut 16:10
bless thee in all *t* increase ... Deut 16:15
and in all the works of *t* hands ... Deut 16:15
of *t* oil, and the first of the ... Deut 18:4
And if thou say in *t* heart ... Deut 18:21

T eye shall not pity him, but ... Deut 19:13
time have set in *t* inheritance ... Deut 19:14
And *t* eye shall not pity ... Deut 19:21
out to battle against *t* enemies ... Deut 20:1
hath delivered it into *t* hands ... Deut 20:13
shalt eat the spoil of *t* enemies ... Deut 20:14
forth to war against *t* enemies ... Deut 21:10
hath delivered them into *t* hands ... Deut 21:10
shalt bring her home to *t* house ... Deut 21:12
her, and shall remain in *t* house ... Deut 21:13
shalt bring it unto *t* own house ... Deut 22:2
thou bring not blood upon *t* house ... Deut 22:8
goeth forth against *t* enemies ... Deut 23:9
to give up *t* enemies before thee ... Deut 23:14
t hand to in the land whither ... Deut 23:20
grapes thy fill at *t* own pleasure ... Deut 23:24
mayest pluck the ears with *t* hand ... Deut 23:25
down *t* harvest in thy field ... Deut 24:19
thee in all the work of *t* hands ... Deut 24:19
When thou beatest *t* olive tree ... Deut 24:20
hand, *t* eye shall not pity her ... Deut 25:12
have in *t* house divers measures ... Deut 25:14
from all *t* enemies round about ... Deut 25:19
take the basket out of *t* hand ... Deut 26:4
unto *t* house, thou, and the Levite ... Deut 26:11
of *t* increase the third year ... Deut 26:12
keep and do them with all *t* heart ... Deut 26:16
The LORD shall cause *t* enemies ... Deut 28:7
all that thou settest *t* hand unto ... Deut 28:8
to bless all the work of *t* hand ... Deut 28:12
settest *t* hand unto for to do ... Deut 28:20
to be smitten before *t* enemies ... Deut 28:25
T ox shall be slain before ... Deut 28:31
ox shall be slain before *t* eyes ... Deut 28:31
t ass shall be violently taken ... Deut 28:31
shall be given unto *t* enemies ... Deut 28:31
t eyes shall look, and fail with ... Deut 28:32
there shall be no might in *t* hand ... Deut 28:32
of *t* eyes which thou shalt see ... Deut 28:34
for *t* olive shall cast his fruit ... Deut 28:40
Therefore shalt thou serve *t* ... Deut 28:48
shalt eat the fruit of *t* own body ... Deut 28:53
wherewith *t* enemies shall ... Deut 28:53
wherewith *t* enemies shall ... Deut 28:55
wherewith *t* enemy shall distress ... Deut 28:57
for the fear of *t* heart wherewith ... Deut 28:67
for the sight of *t* eyes which ... Deut 28:67
which *t* eyes have seen, the signs ... Deut 29:3
and thy children, with all *t* heart ... Deut 30:2
If any of *t* be driven out unto ... Deut 30:4
thy God will circumcise *t* heart ... Deut 30:6
the LORD thy God with all *t* heart ... Deut 30:6
all these curses upon *t* enemies ... Deut 30:7
plenteous in every work of *t* hand ... Deut 30:9
the LORD thy God with all *t* heart ... Deut 30:10
But if *t* heart turn away, so that ... Deut 30:17
burnt sacrifice upon *t* altar ... Deut 33:10
t enemies shall be found liars ... Deut 33:29
caused thee to see it with *t* eyes ... Deut 34:4
which are entered into *t* house ... Josh 2:3
t oath which thou hast made us ... Josh 2:17
then we will be quit of *t* oath ... Josh 2:20
I have given into *t* hand Jericho ... Josh 6:2
canst not stand before *t* enemies ... Josh 7:13
for I will give it into *t* hand ... Josh 8:18
And now, behold, we are in *t* hand ... Josh 9:25
I have delivered them into *t* hand ... Josh 10:8
trodden shall be *t* inheritance ... Josh 14:9
But the mountain shall be *t* ... Josh 17:18
and the outgoings of it shall be *t* ... Josh 17:18
and I will deliver him into *t* hand ... Judg 4:7
takest shall not be for *t* honour ... Judg 4:9
hath delivered Sisera into *t* hand ... Judg 4:14
So let all *t* enemies perish, O ... Judg 5:31
Let not *t* anger be hot against me ... Judg 6:39
the Midianites into *t* hand ... Judg 7:7
I have delivered it into *t* hand ... Judg 7:9
afterward shall *t* hands be ... Judg 7:11
Zebah and Zalmunna now in *t* hand ... Judg 8:6
we should give bread unto *t* army ... Judg 8:6
Zebah and Zalmunna now in *t* hand ... Judg 8:15
to Abimelech, Increase *t* army ... Judg 9:29
vengeance for thee of *t* enemies ... Judg 11:36
we will burn *t* house upon thee ... Judg 12:1
when *t* heart is not with me ... Judg 16:15
lay *t* hand upon thy mouth, and go ... Judg 18:19
Comfort *t* heart with a morsel of ... Judg 19:5
night, and let *t* heart be merry ... Judg 19:6
father said, Comfort *t* heart ... Judg 19:8
that *t* heart may be merry ... Judg 19:9
the man that came into *t* house ... Judg 19:22
I will deliver them into *t* hand ... Judg 20:28
Let *t* eyes be on the field that ... Ruth 2:9
Why have I found grace in *t* eyes ... Ruth 2:10
law since the death of *t* husband ... Ruth 2:11
spoken friendly unto *t* handmaid ... Ruth 2:13
like unto one of *t* handmaidens ... Ruth 2:13
answered, I am Ruth *t* handmaid ... Ruth 3:9
thy skirt over *t* handmaid ... Ruth 3:9
is come into *t* house like Rachel ... Ruth 4:11
life, and a nourisher of *t* old age ... Ruth 4:15
on the affliction of *t* handmaid ... 1Sa 1:11
me, and not forget *t* handmaid ... 1Sa 1:11
but wilt give unto *t* handmaid a ... 1Sa 1:11
Count not *t* handmaid for a ... 1Sa 1:16
Let *t* handmaid find grace in thy ... 1Sa 1:18
come, that I will cut off *t* arm ... 1Sa 2:31
not be an old man in *t* house ... 1Sa 2:31
be an old man in *t* house for ever ... 1Sa 2:32
And the man of *t*, whom I shall not ... 1Sa 2:33
altar, shall be to consume *t* eyes ... 1Sa 2:33
and to grieve *t* heart ... 1Sa 2:33
all the increase of *t* house shall ... 1Sa 2:33
is left in *t* house shall come ... 1Sa 2:36

tell thee all that is in *t* heart ... 1Sa 9:19
as for *t* asses that were lost ... 1Sa 9:20
him, Do all that is in *t* heart ... 1Sa 14:7
unto the priest, Withdraw *t* hand ... 1Sa 14:19
thou wast little in *t* own sight ... 1Sa 15:17
hath given it to a neighbour of *t* ... 1Sa 15:28
fill *t* horn with oil, and go, I ... 1Sa 16:1
and the naughtiness of *t* heart ... 1Sa 17:28
thee, and take *t* head from thee ... 1Sa 17:46
that I have found grace in *t* eyes ... 1Sa 20:3
if I have found favour in *t* eyes ... 1Sa 20:29
son of Jesse to *t* own confusion ... 1Sa 20:30
therefore what is under *t* hand ... 1Sa 21:3
here under *t* hand spear or sword ... 1Sa 21:8
and is honourable in *t* house ... 1Sa 22:14
the Philistines into *t* hand ... 1Sa 23:4
deliver *t* enemy into *t* hand ... 1Sa 24:4
this day *t* eyes have seen how ... 1Sa 24:10
and deliver me out of *t* hand ... 1Sa 24:15
LORD had delivered me into *t* hand ... 1Sa 24:18
shall be established in *t* hand ... 1Sa 24:20
to thee, and peace be to *t* house ... 1Sa 25:6
young men find favour in *t* eyes ... 1Sa 25:8
whatsoever cometh to *t* hand unto ... 1Sa 25:8
let *t* handmaid, I pray thee, ... 1Sa 25:24
I pray thee, speak in *t* audience ... 1Sa 25:24
and hear the words of *t* handmaid ... 1Sa 25:24
but I *t* handmaid saw not the ... 1Sa 25:25
t own hand, now let *t* enemies ... 1Sa 25:26
now this blessing which *t* ... 1Sa 25:27
the trespass of *t* handmaid ... 1Sa 25:28
and the souls of *t* enemies ... 1Sa 25:29
my lord, then remember *t* handmaid ... 1Sa 25:31
her, Go up in peace to *t* house ... 1Sa 25:35
let *t* handmaid be a servant to ... 1Sa 25:41
t enemy into *t* hand this day ... 1Sa 26:8
was precious in *t* eyes this day ... 1Sa 26:21
I have now found grace in *t* eyes ... 1Sa 27:5
from thee, and is become *t* enemy ... 1Sa 28:16
rent the kingdom out of *t* hand ... 1Sa 28:17
t handmaid hath obeyed thy voice, ... 1Sa 28:21
also unto the voice of *t* handmaid ... 1Sa 28:22
t hand to destroy the LORD's ... 2Sa 1:14
thou wast slain in *t* high places ... 2Sa 1:25
over all that *t* heart desireth ... 2Sa 3:21
the son of Saul *t* enemy, which ... 2Sa 4:8
the Philistines into *t* hand ... 2Sa 5:19
Go, do all that is in *t* heart ... 2Sa 7:3
have cut off all *t* enemies out of ... 2Sa 7:9
thee to rest from all *t* enemies ... 2Sa 7:11
t house and thy kingdom shall be ... 2Sa 7:16
sake, and according to *t* own heart ... 2Sa 7:21
thou not go down unto *t* house ... 2Sa 11:10
shall never depart from *t* house ... 2Sa 12:10
against thee out of *t* own house ... 2Sa 12:11
will take thy wives before *t* eyes ... 2Sa 12:11
chamber, that I may eat of *t* hand ... 2Sa 13:10
is risen against *t* handmaid ... 2Sa 14:7
unto the woman, Go to *t* house ... 2Sa 14:8
Let *t* handmaid, I pray thee, ... 2Sa 14:12
Then *t* handmaid said, The word of ... 2Sa 14:17
words in the mouth of *t* handmaid ... 2Sa 14:19
t are all that pertained unto ... 2Sa 16:4
thou go to battle in *t* own person ... 2Sa 17:11
In that thou lovest *t* enemies ... 2Sa 19:6
therefore what is good in *t* eyes ... 2Sa 19:27
them that did eat at *t* own table ... 2Sa 19:28
him, Hear the words of *t* handmaid ... 2Sa 20:17
but *t* eyes are upon the haughty, ... 2Sa 22:28
three months before *t* enemies ... 2Sa 24:13
stay now *t* hand ... 2Sa 24:16
let *t* hand, I pray thee, be ... 2Sa 24:17
that thou mayest save *t* own life ... 1Kin 1:12
O king, swear unto *t* handmaid ... 1Kin 1:13
the LORD thy God unto *t* handmaid ... 1Kin 1:17
said unto him, Go to *t* house ... 1Kin 1:53
to Anathoth, unto *t* own fields ... 1Kin 2:26
blood shall be upon *t* own head ... 1Kin 2:37
which *t* heart is privy to ... 1Kin 2:44
thy wickedness upon *t* own head ... 1Kin 2:44
hast asked the life of *t* enemies ... 1Kin 3:11
while *t* handmaid slept, and laid ... 1Kin 3:20
Let it be neither mine nor *t* ... 1Kin 3:26
Whereas it was in *t* heart to ... 1Kin 8:18
didst well that it was in *t* heart ... 1Kin 8:18
and hast fulfilled it with *t* hand ... 1Kin 8:24
That *t* eyes may be open toward ... 1Kin 8:29
come before *t* altar in this house ... 1Kin 8:31
t inheritance, which thou ... 1Kin 8:51
That *t* eyes may be open unto the ... 1Kin 8:52
to be *t* inheritance, as thou ... 1Kin 8:53
seekest to go to *t* own country ... 1Kin 11:22
now see to *t* own house, David ... 1Kin 12:16
If thou wilt give me half *t* house ... 1Kin 13:8
him back with thee into *t* house ... 1Kin 13:18
get thee to *t* own house ... 1Kin 14:12
thee, a morsel of bread in *t* hand ... 1Kin 17:11
covenant, thrown down *t* altars ... 1Kin 19:10
covenant, thrown down *t* altars ... 1Kin 19:14
according to thy saying, I am *t* ... 1Kin 20:4
and they shall search *t* house ... 1Kin 20:6
whatsoever is pleasant in *t* eyes ... 1Kin 20:6
deliver it into *t* hand this day ... 1Kin 20:13
this great multitude into *t* hand ... 1Kin 20:28
bread, and let *t* heart be merry ... 1Kin 21:7
shall dogs lick thy blood, even *t* ... 1Kin 21:19 859
will make *t* house like the house ... 1Kin 21:22
of his chariot, Turn *t* hand ... 1Kin 22:34
T handmaid hath not any thing in ... 2Kin 4:2
God, do not lie unto *t* handmaid ... 2Kin 4:16
loins, and take my staff in *t* hand ... 2Kin 4:29
thou shalt see it with *t* eyes ... 2Kin 7:2
thou shalt see it with *t* eyes ... 2Kin 7:19
thou and *t* household, and sojourn ... 2Kin 8:1

Hazael, Take a present in *t* hand.......... 2Kin 8:8
and take this box of oil in *t* hand.......... 2Kin 9:1
thou that which is good in *t* eyes.......... 2Kin 10:5
Is *t* heart right, as my heart is.......... 2Kin 10:15
If it be, give me *t* hand.......... 2Kin 10:15
Israel, Put *t* hand upon the bow.......... 2Kin 13:16
t heart hath lifted thee up.......... 2Kin 14:10
LORD, bow down *t* ear, and hear.......... 2Kin 19:16
open, LORD, *t* eyes, and see.......... 2Kin 19:16
and lifted up *t* eyes on high.......... 2Kin 19:22
the LORD, Set *t* house in order.......... 2Kin 20:1
What have they seen in *t* house.......... 2Kin 20:15
come, that all that is in *t* house.......... 2Kin 20:17
Because *t* heart was tender, and.......... 2Kin 22:19
t eyes shall not see all the evil.......... 2Kin 22:20
that *t* hand might be with me, and.......... 1Chr 4:10
T are we, David, and on thy side,.......... 1Chr 12:18
thee, and peace be to *t* helpers.......... 1Chr 12:18
I will deliver them into *t* hand.......... 1Chr 14:10
David, Do all that is in *t* heart.......... 1Chr 17:2
have cut off all *t* enemies from.......... 1Chr 17:8
I will subdue all *t* enemies.......... 1Chr 17:10
this was a small thing in *t* eyes.......... 1Chr 17:17
sake, and according to *t* own heart.......... 1Chr 17:19
thou make *t* own people for ever.......... 1Chr 17:22
of *t* enemies overtaketh thee.......... 1Chr 21:12
It is enough, stay now *t* hand.......... 1Chr 21:15
let *t* hand, I pray thee, O LORD.......... 1Chr 21:17
take that which is *t* for the LORD.......... 1Chr 21:24
T, O LORD, is the greatness, and.......... 1Chr 29:11
the heaven and in the earth is *t*.......... 1Chr 29:11
t is the kingdom, O LORD, and thou.......... 1Chr 29:11
in *t* hand is power and might.......... 1Chr 29:12
in *t* hand it is to make great, and.......... 1Chr 29:12
of *t* own have we given thee.......... 1Chr 29:14
t holy name cometh of *t* hand.......... 1Chr 29:16
Because this was in *t* heart.......... 2Chr 1:11
honour, nor the life of *t* enemies.......... 2Chr 1:11
Forasmuch as it was in *t* heart to.......... 2Chr 6:8
well in that it was in *t* heart.......... 2Chr 6:8
and hast fulfilled it with *t* hand.......... 2Chr 6:15
That *t* eyes may be open upon this.......... 2Chr 6:20
come before *t* altar in this house.......... 2Chr 6:22
t eyes be open, and let *t* ears.......... 2Chr 6:40
not away the face of *t* anointed.......... 2Chr 6:42
heard in mine own land of *t* acts.......... 2Chr 9:5
and now, David, see to *t* own house.......... 2Chr 10:16
of Syria escaped out of *t* hand.......... 2Chr 16:7
he delivered them into *t* hand.......... 2Chr 16:8
to his chariot man, Turn *t* hand.......... 2Chr 18:33
hast prepared *t* heart to seek God.......... 2Chr 19:3
in *t* hand is there not power and.......... 2Chr 20:6
their own people out of *t* hand.......... 2Chr 25:15
t heart lifteth thee up to boast.......... 2Chr 25:19
shouldest thou meddle to *t* hurt.......... 2Chr 25:19
neither shall it be for *t* honour.......... 2Chr 26:18
Because *t* heart was tender, and.......... 2Chr 34:27
neither shall *t* eyes see all the.......... 2Chr 34:28
law of thy God which is in *t* hand.......... Ezr 7:14
of thy God, that is in *t* hand.......... Ezr 7:25
Let *t* ear now be attentive, and.......... Neh 1:6
t eyes open, that thou mayest.......... Neh 1:6
let now *t* ear be attentive to the.......... Neh 1:11
feignest them out of *t* own heart.......... Neh 6:8
But put forth *t* hand now, and.......... Job 1:11
upon himself put not forth *t* hand.......... Job 1:12
But put forth *t* hand now, and.......... Job 2:5
Satan, Behold, he is in *t* hand.......... Job 2:6
thou still retain *t* integrity.......... Job 2:9
t offspring as the grass of the.......... Job 5:25
t eyes are upon me, and I am not.......... Job 7:8
shouldest set *t* heart upon him.......... Job 7:17
despise the work of *t* hands.......... Job 10:3
that can deliver out of *t* hand.......... Job 10:7
T hands have made me and fashioned.......... Job 10:8
things hast thou hid in *t* heart.......... Job 10:13
increasest *t* indignation upon me.......... Job 10:17
is pure, and I am clean in *t* eyes.......... Job 11:4
less than *t* iniquity deserveth.......... Job 11:6
If thou prepare *t* heart, and.......... Job 11:13
stretch out *t* hands toward him.......... Job 11:13
If iniquity be in *t* hand, put it.......... Job 11:14
t age shall be clearer than the.......... Job 11:17
Withdraw *t* hand far from me.......... Job 13:21
face, and holdest me for *t* enemy.......... Job 13:24
dost thou open *t* eyes upon such.......... Job 14:3
a desire to the work of *t* hands.......... Job 14:15
For thy mouth uttereth *t* iniquity.......... Job 15:5
T own mouth condemneth thee, and.......... Job 15:6
t own lips testify against thee.......... Job 15:6
Why doth *t* heart carry thee away.......... Job 15:12
and *t* iniquities infinite.......... Job 22:5
and lay up his words in *t* heart.......... Job 22:22
by the pureness of *t* hands.......... Job 22:30
or what receiveth he of *t* hand.......... Job 35:7
t own right hand can save thee.......... Job 40:14
Lay *t* hand upon him, remember the.......... Job 41:8
the heathen for *t* inheritance.......... Ps 2:8
O lord, rebuke me not in *t* anger.......... Ps 6:1
in *t* anger, lift up thyself.......... Ps 7:6
strength because of *t* enemies.......... Ps 8:2
O God, lift up *t* hand.......... Ps 10:12
thou wilt cause *t* ear to hear.......... Ps 10:17
neither wilt thou suffer *t* Holy.......... Ps 16:10
let *t* eyes behold the things that.......... Ps 17:2
incline *t* ear unto me, and hear my.......... Ps 17:6
thee according to *t* own heart.......... Ps 20:4
T hand shall find out all.......... Ps 21:8
hand shall find out all *t* enemies.......... Ps 21:8
fiery oven in the time of *t* anger.......... Ps 21:9
when thou shalt make ready *t*.......... Ps 21:12
exalted, LORD, in *t* own strength.......... Ps 21:13
so will I compass *t* altar.......... Ps 26:6
the place where *t* honour dwelleth.......... Ps 26:8
and he shall strengthen *t* heart.......... Ps 27:14
people, and bless *t* inheritance.......... Ps 28:9
Bow down *t* ear to me.......... Ps 31:2
Into *t* hand I commit my spirit.......... Ps 31:5
I am cut off from before *t* eyes.......... Ps 31:22
give thee the desires of *t* heart.......... Ps 37:4
For *t* arrows stick fast in me, and.......... Ps 38:2
in my flesh because of *t* anger.......... Ps 38:3
am consumed by the blow of *t* hand.......... Ps 39:10
t arm, and the light of thy.......... Ps 44:3
T arrows are sharp in the heart.......... Ps 45:5
and consider, and incline *t* ear.......... Ps 45:10
forget also *t* own people, and thy.......... Ps 45:10
thou slanderest *t* own mother's.......... Ps 50:20
set them in order before *t* eyes.......... Ps 50:21
they offer bullocks upon *t* altar.......... Ps 51:19
in *t* anger cast down the people,.......... Ps 56:7
greatness of thy power shall *t*.......... Ps 66:3
thou didst confirm *t* inheritance.......... Ps 68:9
dipped in the blood of *t* enemies.......... Ps 68:23
For the zeal of *t* house hath.......... Ps 69:9
Pour out *t* indignation upon them,.......... Ps 69:24
incline *t* ear unto me, and save me.......... Ps 71:2
thy righteousness, even of *t* only.......... Ps 71:16
why doth *t* anger smoke against.......... Ps 74:1
the rod of *t* inheritance, which.......... Ps 74:2
T enemies roar in the midst of.......... Ps 74:4
day is *t*, the night also is *t*.......... Ps 74:16
Arise, O God, plead *t* own cause.......... Ps 74:22
Forget not the voice of *t* enemies.......... Ps 74:23
Thou hast with *t* arm redeemed thy.......... Ps 77:15
t arrows also went abroad.......... Ps 77:17
are come into *t* inheritance.......... Ps 79:1
For, lo, *t* enemies make a tumult.......... Ps 83:2
even *t* altars, O LORD of hosts,.......... Ps 84:3
look upon the face of *t* anointed.......... Ps 84:9
from the fierceness of *t* anger.......... Ps 85:3
cause *t* anger toward us to cease.......... Ps 85:4
wilt thou draw out *t* anger to all.......... Ps 85:5
Bow down *t* ear, O LORD, hear me.......... Ps 86:1
and save the son of *t* handmaid.......... Ps 86:16
incline *t* ear unto my cry.......... Ps 88:2
thou hast scattered *t* enemies.......... Ps 89:10
The heavens are *t*.......... Ps 89:11
the earth also is *t*.......... Ps 89:11
hast been wroth with *t* anointed.......... Ps 89:38
Wherewith *t* enemies have.......... Ps 89:51
the footsteps of *t* anointed.......... Ps 89:51
For we are consumed by *t* anger.......... Ps 90:7
Who knoweth the power of *t* anger.......... Ps 90:11
Only with *t* eyes shalt thou.......... Ps 91:8
t enemies, O LORD.......... Ps 92:9
for, lo, *t* enemies shall perish.......... Ps 92:9
holiness becometh *t* house.......... Ps 93:5
O LORD, and afflict *t* heritage.......... Ps 94:5
incline *t* ear unto me.......... Ps 102:2
Because of *t* indignation and thy.......... Ps 102:10
Who forgiveth all *t* iniquities.......... Ps 103:3
thou openest *t* hand, they are.......... Ps 104:28
I may glory with *t* inheritance.......... Ps 106:5
until I make *t* enemies thy.......... Ps 110:1
thou in the midst of *t* enemies.......... Ps 110:2
servant, and the son of *t* handmaid.......... Ps 116:16
day according to *t* ordinances.......... Ps 119:91
I am *t*, save me.......... Ps 119:94
Let *t* hand help me.......... Ps 119:173
shalt eat the labour of *t* hands.......... Ps 128:2
vine by the sides of *t* house.......... Ps 128:3
let *t* ears be attentive to the.......... Ps 130:2
not away the face of *t* anointed.......... Ps 132:10
thou shalt stretch forth *t* hand.......... Ps 138:7
not the works of *t* own hands.......... Ps 138:8
and before, and laid *t* hand upon me.......... Ps 139:5
T eyes did see my substance, yet.......... Ps 139:16
t enemies take thy name in vain.......... Ps 139:20
shoot out *t* arrows, and destroy.......... Ps 144:6
Send *t* hand from above.......... Ps 144:7
Thou openest *t* hand, and.......... Ps 145:16
thou incline *t* ear unto wisdom.......... Prov 2:2
apply *t* heart to understanding.......... Prov 2:2
When wisdom entereth into *t* heart.......... Prov 2:10
but let *t* heart keep my.......... Prov 3:1
them upon the table of *t* heart.......... Prov 3:3
in the LORD with all *t* heart.......... Prov 3:5
lean not unto *t* own understanding.......... Prov 3:5
Be not wise in *t* own eyes.......... Prov 3:7
the firstfruits of all *t* increase.......... Prov 3:9
let not them depart from *t* eyes.......... Prov 3:21
in the power of *t* hand to do it.......... Prov 3:27
Let *t* heart retain my words.......... Prov 4:4
She shall give to *t* head an.......... Prov 4:9
incline *t* ear unto my sayings.......... Prov 4:20
Let them not depart from *t* eyes.......... Prov 4:21
keep them in the midst of *t* heart.......... Prov 4:21
Let *t* eyes look right on, and let.......... Prov 4:25
let *t* eyelids look straight.......... Prov 4:25
bow *t* ear to my understanding.......... Prov 5:1
Lest thou give *t* honour unto.......... Prov 5:9
Drink waters out of *t* own cistern.......... Prov 5:15
running waters out of *t* own well.......... Prov 5:15
Let them be only *t* own, and not.......... Prov 5:17
Give not sleep to *t* eyes, nor.......... Prov 6:4
eyes, nor slumber to *t* eyelids.......... Prov 6:4
them continually upon *t* heart.......... Prov 6:21
not after her beauty in *t* heart.......... Prov 6:25
and my law as the apple of *t* eye.......... Prov 7:2
them upon the table of *t* heart.......... Prov 7:3
Let not *t* heart decline to her.......... Prov 7:25
open *t* eyes, and thou shalt be.......... Prov 20:13
Bow down *t* ear, and hear the words.......... Prov 22:17
apply *t* heart unto my knowledge.......... Prov 22:17
cease from *t* own wisdom.......... Prov 23:4
Wilt thou set *t* eyes upon that.......... Prov 23:5
Apply *t* heart unto instruction,.......... Prov 23:12
t ears to the words of knowledge.......... Prov 23:12
if *t* heart be wise, my heart.......... Prov 23:15
Let not *t* heart envy sinners.......... Prov 23:17
t expectation shall not be cut.......... Prov 23:18
wise, and guide *t* heart in the way.......... Prov 23:19
My son, give me *t* heart, and let.......... Prov 23:26
let *t* eyes observe my ways.......... Prov 23:26
T eyes shall behold strange women.......... Prov 23:33
t heart shall utter perverse.......... Prov 23:33
Rejoice not when *t* enemy falleth.......... Prov 24:17
let not *t* heart be glad when he.......... Prov 24:17
and afterwards build *t* house.......... Prov 24:27
the prince whom *t* eyes have seen.......... Prov 25:7
shame, and *t* infamy turn not away.......... Prov 25:10
If *t* enemy be hungry, give him.......... Prov 25:21
praise thee, and not *t* own mouth.......... Prov 27:2
a stranger, and not *t* own lips.......... Prov 27:2
T own friend, and thy father's.......... Prov 27:10
lay *t* hand upon thy mouth.......... Prov 30:32
let not *t* heart be hasty to utter.......... Eccl 5:2
and destroy the work of *t* hands.......... Eccl 5:6
from this withdraw not *t* hand.......... Eccl 7:18
For oftentimes also *t* own heart.......... Eccl 7:22
the evening withhold not *t* hand.......... Eccl 11:6
and walk in the ways of *t* heart.......... Eccl 11:9
and in the sight of *t* eyes.......... Eccl 11:9
my heart with one of *t* eyes.......... Song 4:9
the smell of *t* ointments than all.......... Song 4:10
Turn away *t* eyes from me, for.......... Song 6:5
t eyes like the fishpools in.......... Song 7:4
T head upon thee is like Carmel,.......... Song 7:5
the hair of *t* head like purple.......... Song 7:5
Set me as a seal upon *t* heart.......... Song 8:6
as a seal upon *t* arm.......... Song 8:6
t iniquity is taken away, and thy.......... Is 6:7
t anger is turned away, and thou.......... Is 12:1
For thou hast said in *t* heart.......... Is 14:13
the fire of *t* enemies shall.......... Is 26:11
but *t* eyes shall see thy teachers.......... Is 30:20
t ears shall hear a word behind.......... Is 30:21
T eyes shall see the king in his.......... Is 33:17
T heart shall meditate terror.......... Is 33:18
t eyes shall see Jerusalem a.......... Is 33:20
Incline *t* ear, O LORD, and hear.......... Is 37:17
open *t* eyes, O LORD, and see.......... Is 37:17
and lifted up *t* eyes on high.......... Is 37:23
the LORD, Set *t* house in order.......... Is 38:1
What have they seen in *t* house.......... Is 39:4
come, that all that is in *t* house.......... Is 39:6
and will hold *t* hand, and will.......... Is 42:6
hast wearied me with *t* iniquities.......... Is 43:24
and my blessing upon *t* offspring.......... Is 44:3
unto thee, and they shall be *t*.......... Is 45:14
and given them into *t* hand.......... Is 47:6
that sayest in *t* heart, I am, and.......... Is 47:8
great abundance of *t* enchantments.......... Is 47:9
and thou hast said in *t* heart.......... Is 47:10
Stand now with *t* enchantments.......... Is 47:12
time that *t* ear was not opened.......... Is 48:8
Lift up *t* eyes round about, and.......... Is 49:18
other, shall say again in *t* ears.......... Is 49:20
Then shalt thou say in *t* heart.......... Is 49:21
I have taken out of *t* hand the.......... Is 51:22
the curtains of *t* habitations.......... Is 54:2
For thy Maker is *t* husband.......... Is 54:5
hast found the life of *t* hand.......... Is 57:10
hide not thyself from *t* own flesh.......... Is 58:7
t health shall spring forth.......... Is 58:8
honour him, not doing *t* own ways.......... Is 58:13
nor finding *t* own pleasure.......... Is 58:13
nor speaking *t* own words.......... Is 58:13
Lift up *t* eyes round about, and.......... Is 60:4
t heart shall fear, and be.......... Is 60:5
and *t* exactors righteousness.......... Is 60:17
LORD shall be *t* everlasting light.......... Is 60:20
thy corn to be meat for *t* enemies.......... Is 62:8
art thou red in *t* apparel.......... Is 63:2
sake, the tribes of *t* inheritance.......... Is 63:17
We are *t*.......... Is 63:19
thy name known to *t* adversaries.......... Is 64:2
youth, the love of *t* espousals.......... Jer 2:2
T own wickedness shall correct.......... Jer 2:19
yet *t* iniquity is marked before.......... Jer 2:22
him, and *t* hands upon *t* head.......... Jer 2:37
Lift up *t* eyes unto the high.......... Jer 3:2
Only acknowledge *t* iniquity.......... Jer 3:13
and if thou wilt put away *t*.......... Jer 4:1
wash *t* heart from wickedness,.......... Jer 4:14
because it reacheth unto *t* heart.......... Jer 4:18
are not *t* eyes upon the truth.......... Jer 5:3
And they shall eat up *t* harvest.......... Jer 5:17
eat up thy flocks and *t* herds.......... Jer 5:17
turn back *t* hand as a.......... Jer 6:9
Cut off *t* hair, O Jerusalem, and.......... Jer 7:29
T habitation is in the midst of.......... Jer 9:6
not in *t* anger, lest thou bring.......... Jer 10:24
And if thou say in *t* heart.......... Jer 13:22
For the greatness of *t* iniquity.......... Jer 13:22
I have seen *t* adulteries, and thy.......... Jer 13:27
t abominations on the hills in.......... Jer 13:27
I will make thee to pass with *t*.......... Jer 15:14
shalt discontinue from *t* heritage.......... Jer 17:4
I will cause thee to serve *t*.......... Jer 17:4
with them in the time of *t* anger.......... Jer 18:23
and *t* eyes shall behold it.......... Jer 20:4
all that dwell in *t* house shall.......... Jer 20:6
But *t* eyes and *t* heart are not.......... Jer 22:17
take the cup at *t* hand to drink.......... Jer 25:28
this word that I speak in *t* ears.......... Jer 28:7
for the multitude of *t* iniquity.......... Jer 30:14
Why criest thou for *t* affliction.......... Jer 30:15
for the multitude of *t* iniquity.......... Jer 30:15
all *t* adversaries, every one of.......... Jer 30:16
weeping, and *t* eyes from tears.......... Jer 31:16

And there is hope in *t* end ... Jer 31:17
set *t* heart toward the highway, ... Jer 31:21
t uncle shall come unto thee ... Jer 32:7
of redemption is *t* to buy it ... Jer 32:7
for the right of inheritance is *t* ... Jer 32:8
and the redemption is *t* ... Jer 32:8
for *t* eyes are open upon all the ... Jer 32:19
t eyes shall behold the eyes of ... Jer 34:3
Take in *t* hand the roll wherein ... Jer 36:14
rotten rags under *t* armholes ... Jer 38:12
and thou shalt live, and *t* house ... Jer 38:17
the chains which were upon *t* hand ... Jer 40:4
of many, as *t* eyes do behold us ... Jer 42:2
Take great stones in *t* hand ... Jer 43:9
thee, and the pride of *t* heart ... Jer 49:16
t end is come, and the measure of ... Jer 51:13
have not discovered *t* iniquity ... Lam 2:14
All *t* enemies have opened their ... Lam 2:16
he hath caused *t* enemy to rejoice ... Lam 2:17
set up the horn of *t* adversaries ... Lam 2:17
let not the apple of *t* eye cease ... Lam 2:18
of the watches pour out *t* heart ... Lam 2:19
slain them in the day of *t* anger ... Lam 2:21
hide not *t* ear at my breathing, ... Lam 3:56
The punishment of *t* iniquity is ... Lam 4:22
he will visit *t* iniquity, O ... Lam 4:22
t heart, and hear with *t* ears ... Eze 3:10
blood will I require at *t* hand ... Eze 3:18
blood will I require at *t* hand ... Eze 3:20
Go, shut thyself within *t* house ... Eze 3:24
t arm shall be uncovered, and thou ... Eze 4:7
and cause it to pass upon *t* head ... Eze 5:1
because of all *t* abominations, ... Eze 5:9
and with all *t* abominations, ... Eze 5:11
Smite with *t* hand, and stamp with ... Eze 6:11
upon thee all *t* abominations ... Eze 7:3
t abominations shall be in the ... Eze 7:4
thee for all *t* abominations ... Eze 7:8
t abominations that are in the ... Eze 7:9
lift up *t* eyes now the way toward ... Eze 8:5
fill *t* hand with coals of fire ... Eze 10:2
saw thee polluted in *t* own blood ... Eze 16:6
t hair is grown, whereas thou ... Eze 16:7
forehead, and earrings in *t* ears ... Eze 16:12
and a beautiful crown upon *t* head ... Eze 16:12
thou didst trust in *t* own beauty ... Eze 16:15
in all *t* abominations and thy ... Eze 16:22
have diminished *t* ordinary food ... Eze 16:27
How weak is *t* heart, saith the ... Eze 16:30
In that thou buildest *t* eminent ... Eze 16:31
makest *t* high place in every ... Eze 16:31
shall throw down *t* eminent place ... Eze 16:39
they shall burn *t* houses with ... Eze 16:41
recompense thy way upon *t* head ... Eze 16:43
lewdness above all *t* abominations ... Eze 16:43
t elder sister is Samaria, she and ... Eze 16:46
but thou hast multiplied *t* ... Eze 16:51
t abominations which thou hast ... Eze 16:51
bear *t* own shame for thy sins ... Eze 16:52
That thou mayest bear *t* own shame ... Eze 16:54
t abominations, saith the LORD ... Eze 16:58
sisters, *t* elder and thy younger ... Eze 16:61
smite *t* hands together, and let ... Eze 21:14
hast defiled thyself in *t* idols ... Eze 22:4
Can *t* heart endure ... Eze 22:14
or can *t* hands be strong, in the ... Eze 22:14
thou shalt take *t* inheritance in ... Eze 22:16
take away thy nose and *t* ears ... Eze 23:25
not lift up *t* eyes unto them ... Eze 23:27
will I give her cup into *t* hand ... Eze 23:31
and pluck off *t* own breasts ... Eze 23:34
desire of *t* eyes with a stroke ... Eze 24:16
bind the tire of *t* head upon thee ... Eze 24:17
cause thee to hear it with *t* ears ... Eze 24:26
Because thou hast clapped *t* hands ... Eze 25:6
of Bashan have they made *t* oars ... Eze 27:6
of Lud and of Phut were in *t* army ... Eze 27:10
The men of Arvad with *t* army were ... Eze 27:11
were the merchandise of *t* hand ... Eze 27:15
Because *t* heart is lifted up, and ... Eze 28:2
though thou set *t* heart as the ... Eze 28:2
with *t* understanding thou hast ... Eze 28:4
t heart is lifted up because of ... Eze 28:5
Because thou hast set *t* heart as ... Eze 28:6
T heart was lifted up because of ... Eze 28:17
by the multitude of *t* iniquities ... Eze 28:18
blood will I require at *t* hand ... Eze 33:8
will even do according to *t* anger ... Eze 35:11
according to *t* envy which thou ... Eze 35:11
they shall become one in *t* hand ... Eze 37:17
be in *t* hand before their eyes ... Eze 37:20
all *t* army, horses and horsemen, ... Eze 38:4
to turn *t* hand upon the desolate ... Eze 38:12
will cause *t* arrows to fall out ... Eze 39:3
Son of man, behold with *t* eyes ... Eze 40:4
and hear with *t* ears ... Eze 40:4
set *t* heart upon all that I shall ... Eze 40:4
mark well, and behold with *t* eyes ... Eze 44:5
hear with *t* ears all that I say ... Eze 44:5
the blessing to rest in *t* house ... Eze 44:30
heaven hath he given into *t* hand ... Dan 2:38
he will deliver us out of *t* hand ... Dan 3:17
thereof to *t* enemies ... Dan 4:19
t iniquities by shewing mercy to ... Dan 4:27
hast not humbled *t* heart ... Dan 5:22
let *t* anger and thy fury be turned ... Dan 9:16
O my God, incline *t* ear, and hear ... Dan 9:18
open *t* eyes, and behold our ... Dan 9:18
not, for *t* own sake, O my God ... Dan 9:19
didst set *t* heart to understand ... Dan 10:12
for the multitude of *t* iniquity ... Hos 9:7
but in me is *t* help ... Hos 13:9
thou hast fallen by *t* iniquity ... Hos 14:1
give not *t* heritage to reproach, ... Joel 2:17
The pride of *t* heart hath ... Obad 3
shall return upon *t* own head ... Obad 15
What is *t* occupation ... Jonah 1:8
in unto thee, into *t* holy temple ... Jonah 2:7
thee from the hand of *t* enemies ... Mic 4:10
for I will make *t* horn iron ... Mic 4:13
T hand shall be lifted up upon ... Mic 5:9
be lifted up upon *t* adversaries ... Mic 5:9
all *t* enemies shall be cut off ... Mic 5:9
cut off witchcrafts out of *t* hand ... Mic 5:12
more worship the work of *t* hands ... Mic 5:13
thy rod, the flock of *t* heritage ... Mic 7:14
be set wide open unto *t* enemies ... Nah 3:13
was *t* anger against the rivers ... Hab 3:8
thou didst ride upon *t* horses ... Hab 3:8
at the light of *t* arrows they ... Hab 3:11
for salvation with *t* anointed ... Hab 3:13
through the sea with *t* horses ... Hab 3:15
he hath cast out *t* enemy ... Zeph 3:15
to Zion, Let not *t* hands be slack ... Zeph 3:16
I have caused *t* iniquity to pass ... Zec 3:4
said unto me, Lift up now *t* eyes ... Zec 5:5
What are these wounds in *t* hands ... Zec 13:6
Agree with *t* adversary quickly, ... Mt 5:25 *4675*
perform unto the Lord *t* oaths ... Mt 5:33 *4675*
thy neighbour, and hate *t* enemy ... Mt 5:43 *4675*
Therefore when thou doest *t* alms ... Mt 6:2
That *t* alms may be in secret ... Mt 6:4 *4675*
For *t* is the kingdom, and the ... Mt 6:13 *4675*
when thou fastest, anoint *t* head ... Mt 6:17 *4675*
if therefore *t* eye be single, thy ... Mt 6:22 *4675*
But if *t* eye be evil, thy whole ... Mt 6:23 *4675*
not the beam that is in *t* own eye ... Mt 7:3 *4674*
me pull out the mote out of *t* eye ... Mt 7:4 *4675*
behold, a beam is in *t* own eye ... Mt 7:4 *4675*
out the beam out of *t* own eye ... Mt 7:5 *4675*
up thy bed, and go unto *t* house ... Mt 9:6 *4675*
to the man, Stretch forth *t* hand ... Mt 12:13 *4675*
if *t* eye offend thee, pluck it ... Mt 18:9 *4675*
Take that *t* is, and go thy way ... Mt 20:14 *4674*
Is *t* eye evil, because I am good ... Mt 20:15 *4675*
till I make *t* enemies thy ... Mt 22:44 *4675*
lo, there thou hast that is *t* ... Mt 25:25 *4674*
bed, and go thy way into *t* house ... Mk 2:11 *4675*
the man, Stretch forth *t* hand ... Mk 3:5 *4675*
if *t* eye offend thee, pluck it ... Mk 9:47 *4675*
till I make *t* enemies thy ... Mk 12:36 *4675*
wilt worship me, all shall be *t* ... Lk 4:7 *4675*
up thy couch, and go into *t* house ... Lk 5:24 *4675*
but *t* eat and drink ... Lk 5:33 *4674*
not the beam that is in *t* own eye ... Lk 6:41 *2398*
out the mote that is in *t* eye ... Lk 6:42 *4675*
not the beam that is in *t* own eye ... Lk 6:42 *4675*
first the beam out of *t* own eye ... Lk 6:42 *4675*
I entered into *t* house, thou ... Lk 7:44 *4675*
Return to *t* own house, and shew ... Lk 8:39 *4675*
therefore when *t* eye is single ... Lk 11:34 *4675*
but when *t* eye is evil, thy body ... Lk 11:34 *4675*
take *t* ease, eat, drink, and be ... Lk 12:19
When thou goest with *t* adversary ... Lk 12:58 *4675*
thou art loosed from *t* infirmity ... Lk 13:12 *4675*
with me, and all that I have is *t* ... Lk 15:31 *4674*
Out of *t* own mouth will I judge ... Lk 19:22 *4675*
but now they are hid from *t* eyes ... Lk 19:42 *4675*
that *t* enemies shall cast a ... Lk 19:43 *4675*
Till I make *t* enemies thy ... Lk 20:43 *4675*
nevertheless not my will, but *t* ... Lk 22:42 *4674*
The zeal of *t* house hath eaten me ... Jn 2:17 *4675*
Woman, where are those *t* accusers ... Jn 8:10 *4675*
unto him, How were *t* eyes opened ... Jn 9:10 *4675*
him, that he hath opened *t* eyes ... Jn 9:17 *4675*
how opened he *t* eyes ... Jn 9:26 *4675*
glorify thou me with *t* own self ... Jn 17:5 *4572*
t they were, and thou gavest them ... Jn 17:6 *4671*
for they are *t* ... Jn 17:9 *4671*
And all mine are *t*, and *t* are ... Jn 17:10 *4674*
all mine are *t*, and *t* are mine ... Jn 17:10
keep through *t* own name those ... Jn 17:11 *4675*
T own nation and the chief priests ... Jn 18:35 *4674*
neither wilt thou suffer *t* Holy ... Acts 2:27 *4675*
stretching forth *t* hand to heal ... Acts 4:30 *4675*
why hath Satan filled *t* heart to ... Acts 5:3 *4675*
it remained, was it not *t* own ... Acts 5:4 *4671*
sold, was it not in *t* own power ... Acts 5:4
conceived this thing in *t* heart ... Acts 5:4 *4675*
if perhaps the thought of *t* heart ... Acts 8:22 *4675*
thou believest with all *t* heart ... Acts 8:37 *3588*
t alms are come up for a memorial ... Acts 10:4 *3588*
t alms are had in remembrance in ... Acts 10:31 *4675*
Thou shalt not suffer *t* Holy One ... Acts 13:35 *4675*
when *t* accusers are also come ... Acts 23:35 *4675*
on this wise, Say not in *t* heart ... Rom 10:6 *4675*
shalt believe in *t* heart that God ... Rom 10:9 *4675*
prophets, and digged down *t* altars ... Rom 11:3 *4675*
Therefore if *t* enemy hunger ... Rom 12:20 *4675*
Conscience, I say, not *t* own ... 1Cor 10:29 *1438*
sake and *t* often infirmities ... 1Ti 5:23 *4675*
unto me even *t* own self besides ... Philem 19 *4572*
heavens are the works of *t* hands ... Heb 1:10 *4675*
until I make *t* enemies thy ... Heb 1:13 *4675*
anoint *t* eyes with eyesalve, that ... Rev 3:18 *4675*

THING

his kind, cattle, and creeping *t* ... Gen 1:24
every *t* that creepeth upon the ... Gen 1:25
over every creeping *t* that ... Gen 1:26
over every living *t* that moveth ... Gen 1:28
to every *t* that creepeth upon the ... Gen 1:30
God saw every *t* that he had made, ... Gen 1:31
man, and beast, and the creeping *t* ... Gen 6:7
every *t* that is in the earth ... Gen 6:17
And of every living *t* of all flesh ... Gen 6:19
of every creeping *t* of the earth ... Gen 6:20
of every *t* that creepeth upon the ... Gen 7:8
every creeping *t* that creepeth ... Gen 7:14
of every creeping *t* that creepeth ... Gen 7:21
Noah, and every living *t*, and all ... Gen 8:1
every living *t* that is with thee ... Gen 8:17
of every creeping *t* that creepeth ... Gen 8:17
Every beast, every creeping *t* ... Gen 8:19
smite any more every *t* living ... Gen 8:21
Every moving *t* that liveth shall ... Gen 9:3
will not take any *t* that is thine ... Gen 14:23
Is any *t* too hard for the LORD ... Gen 18:14 1697
from Abraham that *t* which I do ... Gen 18:17
thee concerning this *t* also ... Gen 19:21 1697
for I cannot do any *t* till thou ... Gen 19:22
thou, that thou hast done this *t* ... Gen 20:10 1697
the *t* was very grievous in ... Gen 21:11 1697
I wot not who hath done this *t* ... Gen 21:26 1697
neither do thou any *t* unto him ... Gen 22:12
for because thou hast done this *t* ... Gen 22:16 1697
The *t* proceedeth from the LORD ... Gen 24:50 1697
Thou shalt not give me any *t* ... Gen 30:31 1697
if thou wilt do this *t* for me ... Gen 30:31 1697
which *t* ought not to be done ... Gen 34:7 3651
unto them, We cannot do this *t* ... Gen 34:14 1697
man deferred not to do the *t* ... Gen 34:19 1697
the *t* which he did displeased the ... Gen 38:10
kept back any *t* from me but thee ... Gen 39:9 3972
to any *t* that was under his hand ... Gen 39:23 3972
This is the *t* which I have spoken ... Gen 41:28 1697
it is because the *t* is ... Gen 41:32 1697
the *t* was good in the eyes of ... Gen 41:37 1697
should do according to this *t* ... Gen 44:7 1697
them, Why have ye done this *t* ... Ex 1:18 1697
and said, Surely this *t* is known ... Ex 2:14 1697
Now when Pharaoh heard this *t* ... Ex 2:15 1697
LORD shall do this *t* in the land ... Ex 9:5 1697
the LORD did that *t* on the morrow ... Ex 9:6 1697
not any green *t* in the trees ... Ex 10:15
ye shall observe this *t* for an ... Ex 12:24 1697
there lay a small round *t* ... Ex 16:14
This is the *t* which the LORD hath ... Ex 16:16 1697
This is the *t* which the LORD ... Ex 16:32 1697
for in the *t* wherein they dealt ... Ex 18:11 1697
What is this *t* that thou doest to ... Ex 18:14 1697
The *t* that thou doest is not good ... Ex 18:17 1697
for this *t* is too heavy for thee ... Ex 18:18 1697
If thou shalt do this *t*, and God ... Ex 18:23 1697
or any likeness of any *t* that is ... Ex 20:4
nor any *t* that is thy neighbour's ... Ex 20:17
or for any manner of lost *t* ... Ex 22:9
if it be an hired *t*, it came for ... Ex 22:15
this is the *t* that thou shalt do ... Ex 29:1 1697
I will do this *t* also that thou ... Ex 33:17 1697
for it is a terrible *t* that I ... Ex 34:10
This is the *t* which the LORD ... Ex 35:4 1697
it is a *t* most holy of the ... Lev 2:3
it is a *t* most holy of the ... Lev 2:10
the *t* be hid from the eyes of the ... Lev 4:13 1697
Or if a soul touch any unclean *t* ... Lev 5:2 1697
that he hath sinned in that *t* ... Lev 5:5
that he hath done in the holy *t* ... Lev 5:16
or in a *t* taken away by violence, ... Lev 6:2
away, or the *t* which he hath ... Lev 6:4
or the lost *t* which he found, ... Lev 6:4
any *t* of all that he hath done in ... Lev 6:7
any unclean *t* shall not be eaten ... Lev 7:19
that shall touch any unclean *t* ... Lev 7:21
or any abominable unclean *t* ... Lev 7:21
This is the *t* which the LORD ... Lev 8:5 1697
This is the *t* which the LORD ... Lev 9:6 1697
of any living *t* which is in the ... Lev 11:10 5315
t that goeth upon all four ... Lev 11:21
every *t* whereupon any part of ... Lev 11:35
every creeping *t* that creepeth ... Lev 11:41
with any creeping *t* that creepeth ... Lev 11:43
with any manner of creeping *t* ... Lev 11:44
she shall touch no hallowed *t* ... Lev 12:4
a skin, or in any *t* made of skin ... Lev 13:48 4399
in the woof, or in any *t* of skin ... Lev 13:49 3627
or any *t* of skin, wherein the ... Lev 13:52 3627
in the woof, or in any *t* of skin ... Lev 13:53 3627
wash the *t* wherein the plague is ... Lev 13:54
in the woof, or in any *t* of skin ... Lev 13:57 3627
or whatsoever *t* of skin it be ... Lev 13:58 3627
or any *t* of skins, to pronounce ... Lev 13:59 3627
and every *t*, whereon he sitteth, ... Lev 15:4 3627
he that sitteth on any *t* whereon ... Lev 15:6 3627
whosoever toucheth any *t* that was ... Lev 15:10
every *t* that she lieth upon in ... Lev 15:20
every *t* also that she sitteth ... Lev 15:20
whosoever toucheth any *t* that she ... Lev 15:22 3627
or on any *t* whereon she sitteth, ... Lev 15:23 3627
This is the *t* which the LORD hath ... Lev 17:2 1697
the hallowed *t* of the LORD ... Lev 19:8
not eat any *t* with the blood ... Lev 19:26
it is a wicked *t* ... Lev 20:17
wife, it is an unclean *t* ... Lev 20:21
or by any manner of living *t* that ... Lev 20:25
flat nose, or any *t* superfluous, ... Lev 21:18
whoso toucheth any *t* that is ... Lev 22:4
whosoever toucheth any creeping *t* ... Lev 22:5
no stranger eat of the holy *t* ... Lev 22:10
shall not eat of the holy *t* ... Lev 22:10
man eat of the holy *t* unwittingly ... Lev 22:14
unto the priest with the holy *t* ... Lev 22:14
t superfluous or lacking in his ... Lev 22:23
offerings, every *t* upon his day ... Lev 23:37 1697
as a holy *t* unto the LORD ... Lev 27:23
Notwithstanding no devoted *t* ... Lev 27:28
every devoted *t* is most holy unto ... Lev 27:28
they shall not touch any holy *t* ... Num 4:15
Seemeth it but a small *t* unto you ... Num 16:9
Is it a small *t* that thou hast ... Num 16:13
But if the LORD make a new *t* ... Num 16:30
Whosoever cometh any *t* near unto ... Num 17:13

office for every *t* of the altar	Num 18:7	1697
Every *t* devoted in Israel shall	Num 18:14	
Every *t* that openeth the matrix	Num 18:15	
only, without doing any *t* else	Num 20:19	1697
now any power at all to say any *t*	Num 22:38	3972
This is the *t* which the LORD hath	Num 30:1	1697
Every *t* that may abide the fire	Num 31:23	1697
unto them, If ye will do this *t*	Num 32:20	1697
him any *t* without laying of wait	Num 35:22	3627
This is the *t* which the LORD doth	Num 36:6	1697
The *t* which thou hast spoken is	Deut 1:14	1697
Yet in this *t* ye did not believe	Deut 1:32	1697
The likeness of any *t* that	Deut 4:18	
image, or the likeness of any *t*	Deut 4:23	
image, or the likeness of any *t*	Deut 4:25	
any such *t* as this great *t* is	Deut 4:32	1697
or any likeness of any *t* that is	Deut 5:8	
or any *t* that is thy neighbour's	Deut 5:21	
lest thou be a cursed *t* like it	Deut 7:26	
for it is a cursed *t*	Deut 7:26	
thou shalt not lack any *t* in it	Deut 8:9	
What *t* soever I command you	Deut 12:32	1697
and the *t* certain, that such	Deut 13:14	1697
of the cursed *t* to thine hand	Deut 13:17	
shalt not eat any abominable *t*	Deut 14:3	
every creeping *t* that flieth is	Deut 14:19	
eat of any *t* that dieth of itself	Deut 14:21	
because that for this *t* the LORD	Deut 15:10	1697
I command thee this *t* to day	Deut 15:15	1697
shall there any *t* of the flesh	Deut 16:4	
true, and the *t* certain, that such	Deut 17:4	1697
have committed that wicked *t*	Deut 17:5	1697
if the *t* follow not, nor come to	Deut 18:22	1697
that is the *t* which the LORD hath	Deut 18:22	1697
But if this *t* be true, and the	Deut 22:20	1697
keep thee from every wicked *t*	Deut 23:9	1697
that he see no unclean *t* in thee	Deut 23:14	1697
usury of any *t* that is lent upon	Deut 23:19	1697
thou dost lend thy brother any *t*	Deut 24:10	4859
I command thee to do this *t*	Deut 24:18	1697
I command thee to do this *t*	Deut 24:22	1697
t which the LORD thy God hath	Deut 26:11	
which have not known any *t*	Deut 31:13	
For it is not a vain *t* for you	Deut 32:47	1697
through this *t* ye shall prolong	Deut 32:47	1697
until every *t* was finished that	Josh 4:10	1697
yourselves from the accursed *t*	Josh 6:18	
when ye take of the accursed *t*	Josh 6:18	
a trespass in the accursed *t*	Josh 7:1	
of Judah, took of the accursed *t*	Josh 7:1	
have even taken of the accursed *t*	Josh 7:11	
accursed *t* in the midst of thee	Josh 7:13	
the accursed *t* from among you	Josh 7:13	
t shall be burnt with fire	Josh 7:15	
of you, and have done this *t*	Josh 9:24	1697
Thou knowest the *t* that the LORD	Josh 14:6	1697
failed not ought of any good *t*	Josh 21:45	1697
a trespass in the accursed *t*	Josh 22:20	
rather done it for fear of this *t*	Josh 22:24	1697
the *t* pleased the children of	Josh 22:33	1697
that not one *t* hath failed of all	Josh 23:14	1697
not one *t* hath failed thereof	Josh 23:14	1697
to another, Who hath done this *t*	Judg 6:29	1697
the son of Joash hath done this *t*	Judg 6:29	1697
which *t* became a snare unto	Judg 8:27	
now art thou any *t* better than	Judg 11:25	
Let this *t* be done for me	Judg 11:37	1697
drink, and eat not any unclean *t*	Judg 13:4	
drink, neither eat any unclean *t*	Judg 13:7	
She may not eat of any *t* that	Judg 13:14	
drink, nor eat any unclean *t*	Judg 13:14	
might put them to shame in any *t*	Judg 18:7	1697
of any *t* that is in the earth	Judg 18:10	1697
there is no want of any *t*	Judg 19:19	1697
unto this man do not so vile a *t*	Judg 19:24	1697
But now this shall be the *t* which	Judg 20:9	1697
this is the *t* that ye shall do	Judg 21:11	1697
he have finished the *t* this day	Ruth 3:18	1697
Behold, I will do a *t* in Israel	1Sa 3:11	1697
What is the *t* that the LORD hath	1Sa 3:17	1697
if thou hide any *t* from me of all	1Sa 3:17	1697
hath not been such a *t* heretofore	1Sa 4:7	
But the *t* displeased Samuel, when	1Sa 8:6	1697
stand and see this great *t*	1Sa 12:16	1697
up to us, and we will shew you a *t*	1Sa 14:12	1697
but every *t* that was vile and	1Sa 15:9	4399
told Saul, and the *t* pleased him	1Sa 18:20	1697
light *t* to be a king's son in law	1Sa 18:23	
my father hide this *t* from me	1Sa 20:2	1697
Saul spake not any *t* that day	1Sa 20:26	
But the lad knew not any *t*	1Sa 20:39	
Let no man know any *t* of the	1Sa 21:2	1697
impute any *t* unto his servant	1Sa 22:15	1697
I should do this *t* unto my master	1Sa 24:6	1697
not hurt, neither missed we any *t*	1Sa 25:15	
This *t* is not good that thou hast	1Sa 26:16	1697
happen to thee for this *t*	1Sa 28:10	1697
done this *t* unto thee this day	1Sa 28:18	1697
nor any *t* that they had taken to	1Sa 30:19	
because ye have done this *t*	2Sa 2:6	1697
but one *t* I require of thee, that	2Sa 3:13	1697
was yet a small *t* in thy sight	2Sa 7:19	
soul liveth, I will not do this *t*	2Sa 11:11	1697
Let not this *t* displease thee	2Sa 11:25	1697
But the *t* that David had done	2Sa 11:27	1697
hath done this *t* shall surely die	2Sa 12:5	
fourfold, because he did this *t*	2Sa 12:6	1697
will do this *t* before all Israel	2Sa 12:12	1697
What *t* is this that thou hast	2Sa 12:21	1697
hard for him to do any *t* to her	2Sa 13:2	
for no such *t* ought to be done in	2Sa 13:12	3651
regard not this *t*	2Sa 13:20	1697
the king take the *t* to his heart	2Sa 13:33	1697
a *t* against the people of God	2Sa 14:13	
this *t* as one which is faulty	2Sa 14:13	1697
of this *t* unto my lord the king	2Sa 14:15	1697
the *t* that I shall ask thee	2Sa 14:18	1697
hath thy servant Joab done this *t*	2Sa 14:20	1697
Behold now, I have done this *t*	2Sa 14:21	1697
and they knew not any *t*	2Sa 15:11	1697
that what *t* soever thou shalt	2Sa 15:35	1697
unto me every *t* that ye can hear	2Sa 15:36	1697
and the *t* was not known	2Sa 17:19	1697
lord the king delight in this *t*	2Sa 24:3	1697
Is this *t* done by my lord the	1Kin 1:27	1697
that Solomon had asked this *t*	1Kin 3:10	1697
Because thou hast asked this *t*	1Kin 3:11	1697
was not any *t* hid from the king	1Kin 10:3	1697
commanded him concerning this *t*	1Kin 11:10	1697
for this *t* is from me	1Kin 12:24	1697
And this *t* became a sin	1Kin 12:30	1697
After this *t* Jeroboam returned	1Kin 13:33	1697
this *t* became sin unto the house	1Kin 13:34	1697
to ask a *t* of thee for her son	1Kin 14:5	1697
t toward the LORD God of Israel	1Kin 14:13	1697
turned not aside from any *t* that	1Kin 15:5	
as if it had been a light *t* for	1Kin 16:31	
but this *t* I may not do	1Kin 20:9	1697
And do this *t*, Take the kings away	1Kin 20:24	1697
whether any *t* would come from him	1Kin 20:33	
he said, Thou hast asked a hard *t*	2Kin 2:10	
this is but a light *t* in the	2Kin 3:18	
hath not any *t* in the house	2Kin 4:2	
had bid thee do some great *t*	2Kin 5:13	1697
In this *t* the LORD pardon thy	2Kin 5:18	1697
LORD pardon thy servant in this *t*	2Kin 5:18	1697
was sore troubled for this *t*	2Kin 6:11	1697
in heaven, might this *t* be	2Kin 7:2	1697
in heaven, might such a *t* be	2Kin 7:19	1697
even of every good *t* of Damascus	2Kin 8:9	
that he should do this great *t*	2Kin 8:13	1697
This is the *t* that ye shall do	2Kin 11:5	1697
unto them, Ye shall not do this *t*	2Kin 17:12	1697
will do the *t* that he hath spoken	2Kin 20:9	1697
It is a light *t* for the shadow to	2Kin 20:10	
transgressed in the *t* accursed	1Chr 2:7	
it me, that I should do this *t*	1Chr 11:19	
for the *t* was right in the eyes	1Chr 13:4	1697
this was a small *t* in thine eyes	1Chr 17:17	
let the *t* that thou hast spoken	1Chr 17:23	1697
then doth my lord require this *t*	1Chr 21:3	
And God was displeased with this *t*	1Chr 21:7	1697
because I have done this *t*	1Chr 21:8	1697
and whosoever had dedicated any *t*	1Chr 26:28	
it was not any *t* accounted of in	2Chr 9:20	
for this *t* is done of me	2Chr 11:4	1697
a rage with him because of this *t*	2Chr 16:10	
This is the *t* that ye shall do	2Chr 23:4	1697
unclean in any *t* should enter in	2Chr 23:19	1697
for the *t* was done suddenly	2Chr 29:36	1697
the *t* pleased the king and all the	2Chr 30:4	1697
which hath put such a *t* as this	Ezr 7:27	
And when I heard this *t*, I rent my	Ezr 9:3	1697
hope in Israel concerning this *t*	Ezr 10:2	
that have transgressed in this *t*	Ezr 10:13	1697
said, What is this *t* that ye do	Neh 2:19	1697
What evil *t* is this that ye do	Neh 13:17	1697
And the *t* pleased the king	Est 2:4	1697
the *t* was known to Mordecai, who	Est 2:22	1697
And the *t* pleased Haman	Est 5:14	1697
every *t* that had befallen him	Est 6:13	
the *t* seem right before the king	Est 8:5	1697
For the *t* which I greatly feared	Job 3:25	
Now a *t* was secretly brought to	Job 4:12	1697
grant me the *t* that I long for	Job 6:8	
For now ye are no *t*	Job 6:21	
This is one *t*, therefore I said	Job 9:22	
is the soul of every living *t*	Job 12:10	
And he, as a rotten *t*, consumeth	Job 13:28	
bring a clean *t* out of an unclean	Job 14:4	
is there any secret *t* with thee	Job 15:11	1697
Thou shalt also decree a *t*	Job 22:28	562
For he performeth the *t* that is	Job 23:14	
declared the *t* as it is	Job 26:3	
and his eye seeth every precious *t*	Job 28:10	
the *t* that is hid bringeth he	Job 28:11	
If thou hast any *t* to say	Job 33:32	
he searcheth after every green *t*	Job 39:8	
I know that thou canst do every *t*	Job 42:2	
spoken of me the *t* that is right	Job 42:7	
spoken of me the *t* which is right	Job 42:8	
and the people imagine a vain *t*	Ps 2:1	
One *t* have I desired of the LORD	Ps 27:4	
An horse is a vain *t* for safety	Ps 33:17	
LORD shall not want any good *t*	Ps 34:10	
I follow the *t* that good is	Ps 38:20	
every *t* that moveth therein	Ps 69:34	
no good *t* will he withhold from	Ps 84:11	
nor alter the *t* that is gone out	Ps 89:34	
It is a good *t* to give thanks	Ps 92:1	
set no wicked *t* before mine eyes	Ps 101:3	1697
not my heart to any evil *t*	Ps 141:4	1697
the desire of every living *t*	Ps 145:16	
Let every *t* that hath breath	Ps 150:6	
Wisdom is the principal *t*	Prov 4:7	
findeth a wife findeth a good *t*	Prov 18:22	
For it is a pleasant *t* if thou	Prov 22:18	
the glory of God to conceal a *t*	Prov 25:2	1697
soul every bitter *t* is sweet	Prov 27:7	
The *t* that hath been, it is that	Eccl 1:9	
there is no new *t* under the sun	Eccl 1:9	
Is there any *t* whereof it may be	Eccl 1:10	1697
To every *t* there is a season, and	Eccl 3:1	
He hath made every *t* beautiful in	Eccl 3:11	
to it, nor any *t* taken from it	Eccl 3:14	
even one *t* befalleth them	Eccl 3:19	
hasty to utter any *t* before God	Eccl 5:2	1697
not seen the sun, nor known any *t*	Eccl 6:5	
Better is the end of a *t* than the	Eccl 7:8	1697
knoweth the interpretation of a *t*	Eccl 8:1	1697
stand not in an evil *t*	Eccl 8:3	1697
commandment shall feel no evil *t*	Eccl 8:5	1697
hath no better *t* under the sun	Eccl 8:15	
but the dead know not any *t*	Eccl 9:5	
any *t* that is done under the sun	Eccl 9:6	
a pleasant *t* it is for the eyes	Eccl 11:7	
judgment, with every secret *t*	Eccl 12:14	
Is it a small *t* for you to weary	Is 7:13	
faileth, there is no green *t*	Is 15:6	
like a rolling *t* before the	Is 17:13	
every *t* sown by the brooks, shall	Is 19:7	
or shall the *t* framed say of him	Is 29:16	
aside the just for a *t* of nought	Is 29:21	
do this *t* that he hath spoken	Is 38:7	1697
up the isles as a very little *t*	Is 40:15	
as nothing, and as a *t* of nought	Is 41:12	
Behold, I will do a new *t*	Is 43:19	
It is a light *t* that thou	Is 49:6	
from thence, touch no unclean *t*	Is 52:11	
in the *t* whereto I sent it	Is 55:11	
But we are all as an unclean *t*	Is 64:6	
Who hath heard such a *t*	Is 66:8	
and see if there be such a *t*	Jer 2:10	
and see that it is an evil *t*	Jer 2:19	
horrible *t* is committed in the	Jer 5:30	
But this *t* commanded I them	Jer 7:23	1697
set up altars to that shameful *t*	Jer 11:13	
a *t* of nought, and the deceit of	Jer 14:14	
hath done a very horrible *t*	Jer 18:13	
For if ye do this *t* indeed	Jer 22:4	1697
of Jerusalem an horrible *t*	Jer 23:14	
hath created a new *t* in the earth	Jer 31:22	
is there any *t* too hard for me	Jer 32:27	1697
that I will perform that good *t*	Jer 33:14	1697
he that can do any *t* against you	Jer 38:5	1697
Jeremiah, I will ask thee a *t*	Jer 38:14	1697
therefore this *t* is come upon you	Jer 40:3	1697
Kareah, Thou shalt not do this *t*	Jer 40:16	1697
may walk, and the *t* that we may do	Jer 42:3	1697
that whatsoever *t* the LORD shall	Jer 42:4	1697
nor any *t* for the which he hath	Jer 42:21	
not this abominable *t* that I hate	Jer 44:4	1697
t goeth forth out of our own	Jer 44:17	1697
What *t* shall I take to witness	Lam 2:13	
what *t* shall I liken to thee, O	Lam 2:13	
Is it a light *t* to the house of	Eze 8:17	
deceived when he hath spoken a *t*	Eze 14:9	1697
as if that were a very little *t*	Eze 16:47	
Seemeth it a small *t* unto you to	Eze 34:18	
with any *t* that causeth sweat	Eze 44:18	
every dedicated *t* in Israel shall	Eze 44:29	
of any *t* that is dead of itself	Eze 44:31	
that every *t* that liveth, which	Eze 47:9	5315
every *t* shall live whither the	Eze 47:9	
t most holy by the border of the	Eze 48:12	
Chaldeans, The *t* is gone from me	Dan 2:5	4406
ye see the *t* is gone from me	Dan 2:8	4406
it is a rare *t* that the king	Dan 2:11	4406
Arioch made the *t* known to Daniel	Dan 2:15	4406
made the *t* known to Hananiah	Dan 2:17	4406
which speak any *t* amiss against	Dan 3:29	
The same hour was the *t* fulfilled	Dan 4:33	4406
shew the interpretation of the *t*	Dan 5:15	4406
is the interpretation of the *t*	Dan 5:26	4406
The *t* is true, according to the	Dan 6:12	4406
a *t* was revealed unto Daniel	Dan 10:1	1697
the *t* was true, but the time	Dan 10:1	1697
and he understood the *t*, and had	Dan 10:1	1697
horrible *t* in the house of Israel	Hos 6:10	
hath cast off the *t* that is good	Hos 8:3	
they were counted as a strange *t*	Hos 8:12	
Ye which rejoice in a *t* of nought	Amos 6:13	1697
herd nor flock, taste any *t*	Jonah 3:7	
unto the Lord a corrupt *t*	Mal 1:14	
into the city, and told every *t*	Mt 8:33	
any *t* that they shall ask	Mt 18:19	*4229*
what good *t* shall I do, that I	Mt 19:16	
and desiring a certain *t* of him	Mt 20:20	
them, I also will ask you one *t*	Mt 21:24	*3056*
to take any *t* out of his house	Mt 24:17	
saying, What *t* is this	Mk 1:27	
neither was any *t* kept secret	Mk 4:22	
to see her that had done this *t*	Mk 5:32	
that whatsoever *t* from without	Mk 7:18	
but if thou canst do any *t*	Mk 9:22	
said unto him, One *t* thou lackest	Mk 10:21	
haply he might find any *t* thereon	Mk 11:13	
to take any *t* out of his house	Mk 13:15	
neither said they any *t* to any	Mk 16:8	
and if they drink any deadly *t*	Mk 16:18	
therefore also that holy *t* which	Lk 1:35	
see this *t* which is come to pass	Lk 2:15	*4487*
unto them, I will ask you one *t*	Lk 6:9	
neither any *t* hid, that shall not	Lk 8:17	
them to tell no man that *t*	Lk 9:21	
But one *t* is needful	Lk 10:42	
how or what *t* ye shall answer	Lk 12:11	
able to do that *t* which is least	Lk 12:26	
unto him, Yet lackest thou one *t*	Lk 18:22	
if I have taken any *t* from any	Lk 19:8	
them, I will also ask you one *t*	Lk 20:3	*3056*
them it was that should do this *t*	Lk 22:23	
scrip, and shoes, lacked ye any *t*	Lk 22:35	
was not any *t* made that was made	Jn 1:3	
Can there any good *t* come out of	Jn 1:46	
lest a worse *t* come unto thee	Jn 5:14	
no man that doeth any *t* in secret	Jn 7:4	
one *t* I know, that, whereas I was	Jn 9:25	
Why herein is a marvellous *t*	Jn 9:30	
If ye shall ask any *t* in my name	Jn 14:14	
Sayest thou this *t* of thyself	Jn 18:34	
conceived this *t* in thine heart	Acts 5:4	*4229*

any *t* that is common or unclean ... Acts 10:14
t for a man that is a Jew to keep ... Acts 10:28
And when he had considered the *t* ... Acts 12:12
to tell, or to hear some new *t* ... Acts 17:21
hands, as though he needed any *t* ... Acts 17:25
Some therefore cried one *t* ... Acts 19:32
But if ye enquire any *t* ... Acts 19:39
that they observe no such *t* ... Acts 21:25
And some cried one *t*, some another ... Acts 21:34
he hath a certain *t* to tell him ... Acts 23:17
have I offended any *t* at all ... Acts 25:8
committed any *t* worthy of death ... Acts 25:11
certain *t* to write unto my lord ... Acts 25:26
thought a *t* incredible with you ... Acts 26:8
Which *t* I also did in Jerusalem ... Acts 26:10
for this *t* was not done in a ... Acts 26:26
in my flesh,) dwelleth no good *t* ... Rom 7:18
Who shall lay any *t* to the charge ... Rom 8:33
Shall the *t* formed say to him ... Rom 9:20 *4110*
continually upon this very *t* ... Rom 13:6
Owe no man any *t*, but to love one ... Rom 13:8
esteemeth any *t* to be unclean ... Rom 14:14
nor any *t* whereby thy brother ... Rom 14:21
in that *t* which he alloweth ... Rom 14:22
That in every *t* ye are enriched ... 1Cor 1:5
that ye all speak the same *t* ... 1Cor 1:10
not to know any *t* among you ... 1Cor 2:2
neither is he that planteth any *t* ... 1Cor 3:7
t that I should be judged of you ... 1Cor 4:3
man think that he knoweth any *t* ... 1Cor 8:2
it as a *t* offered unto an idol ... 1Cor 8:7
is it a great *t* if we shall reap ... 1Cor 9:11
For if I do this *t* willingly ... 1Cor 9:17
that the idol is any *t*, or that ... 1Cor 10:19
in sacrifice to idols is any *t* ... 1Cor 10:19
If any *t* be revealed to another ... 1Cor 14:30
And if they will learn any *t* ... 1Cor 14:35
To whom ye forgive any *t*, I ... 2Cor 2:10
for if I forgave any *t*, to whom I ... 2Cor 2:10
to think any *t* as of ourselves ... 2Cor 3:5
us for the selfsame *t* is God ... 2Cor 5:5
Giving no offence in any *t* ... 2Cor 6:3
Lord, and touch not the unclean *t* ... 2Cor 6:17
For behold this selfsame *t* ... 2Cor 7:11
have boasted any *t* to him of you ... 2Cor 7:14
as ye abound in every *t*, in ... 2Cor 8:7
in every *t* to all bountifulness ... 2Cor 9:11
every high *t* that exalteth itself ... 2Cor 10:5 *5313*
great *t* if his ministers also be ... 2Cor 11:15
For this *t* I besought the Lord ... 2Cor 12:8
affected always in a good *t* ... Gal 4:18
circumcision availeth any *t* ... Gal 5:6
circumcision availeth any *t* ... Gal 6:15
his hands the *t* which is good ... Eph 4:28
to their own husbands in every *t* ... Eph 5:24
spot, or wrinkle, or any such *t* ... Eph 5:27
whatsoever good *t* any man doeth ... Eph 6:8
Being confident of this very *t* ... Phil 1:6
but this one *t* I do, forgetting ... Phil 3:13 *1520*
if in any *t* ye be otherwise ... Phil 3:15
same rule, let us mind the same *t* ... Phil 3:16
but in every *t* by prayer and ... Phil 4:6
that we need not to speak any *t* ... 1Th 1:8
In every *t* give thanks ... 1Th 5:18
t with God to recompense ... 2Th 1:6
if there be any other *t* that is ... 1Ti 1:10
That good *t* which was committed ... 2Ti 1:14
having no evil *t* to say of you ... Titus 2:8
t which is in you in Christ Jesus ... Philem 6
he was sanctified, an unholy *t* ... Heb 10:29
It is a fearful *t* to fall into ... Heb 10:31
provided some better *t* for us ... Heb 11:40
For it is a good *t* that the heart ... Heb 13:9
shall receive any *t* of the Lord ... Jas 1:7
some strange *t* happened unto you ... 1Pet 4:12
be not ignorant of this one *t* ... 2Pet 3:8
which *t* is true in him and in you ... 1Jn 2:8
if we ask any *t* according to his ... 1Jn 5:14
the Nicolaitanes, which *t* I hate ... Rev 2:15
of the earth, neither any green *t* ... Rev 9:4
enter into it any *t* that defileth ... Rev 21:27

THINGS

man, and cattle, and the creeping *t* ... Gen 7:23
green herb have I given you all *t* ... Gen 9:3
After these *t* the word of the ... Gen 15:1 1697
and told all these *t* in their ears ... Gen 20:8 1697
And it came to pass after these *t* ... Gen 22:1 1697
And it came to pass after these *t* ... Gen 22:20 1697
LORD had blessed Abraham in all *t* ... Gen 24:1
of her mother's house these *t* ... Gen 24:28 1697
and to her mother precious *t* ... Gen 24:53
told Isaac all *t* that he had done ... Gen 24:66 1697
And he told Laban all these *t* ... Gen 29:13 1697
And it came to pass after these *t* ... Gen 39:7 1697
And it came to pass after these *t* ... Gen 40:1 1697
all these *t* are against me ... Gen 42:36
laden with the good *t* of Egypt ... Gen 45:23
And it came to pass after these *t* ... Gen 48:1 1697
what *t* I have wrought in Egypt, ... Ex 10:2
unto them such *t* as they required ... Ex 12:36
in all *t* that I have said unto ... Ex 23:13
of all *t* which I will give thee ... Ex 25:22
bear the iniquity of the holy *t* ... Ex 28:38
they shall eat those *t* wherewith ... Ex 29:33
according to all *t* which I have ... Ex 29:35
set in order the *t* that are to be ... Ex 40:4
is made of these *t* unto the LORD ... Lev 2:8
of the LORD concerning *t* which ... Lev 4:2
of the LORD concerning *t* which ... Lev 4:13
t which should not be done ... Lev 4:22
of the LORD concerning *t* which ... Lev 4:27
the carcase of unclean creeping *t* ... Lev 5:2
shall be guilty in one of these *t* ... Lev 5:5
in the holy *t* of the LORD ... Lev 5:15
commit any of these *t* which are ... Lev 5:17
his sons did all *t* which the LORD ... Lev 8:36 1697
and such *t* have befallen me ... Lev 10:19
But all other flying creeping *t* ... Lev 11:23
t that creep upon the earth ... Lev 11:29
t that creep upon the earth ... Lev 11:42
is to be made clean, and those *t* ... Lev 14:11
of those *t* shall wash his clothes ... Lev 15:10
toucheth those *t* shall be unclean ... Lev 15:27
ye yourselves in any of these *t* ... Lev 18:24
for they committed all these *t* ... Lev 20:23
themselves from the holy *t* of the ... Lev 22:2
those *t* which they hallow unto me ... Lev 22:2
that goeth unto the holy *t* ... Lev 22:3
he shall not eat of the holy *t* ... Lev 22:4
and shall not eat of the holy *t* ... Lev 22:6
shall afterward eat of the holy *t* ... Lev 22:7
eat of an offering of the holy *t* ... Lev 22:12
holy *t* of the children of Israel ... Lev 22:15
when they eat their holy *t* ... Lev 22:16
not be reformed by me by these *t* ... Lev 26:23
over all *t* that belong to it ... Num 1:50
about the most holy *t* ... Num 4:4
These *t* are the burden of the ... Num 4:15
approach unto the most holy *t* ... Num 4:19
see when the holy *t* are covered ... Num 4:20
holy *t* of the children of Israel ... Num 5:9
man's hallowed *t* shall be his ... Num 5:10
do these *t* after this manner ... Num 15:13
t of the children of Israel ... Num 18:8
shall be thine of the most holy *t* ... Num 18:9
the heave offerings of the holy *t* ... Num 18:19
holy *t* of the children of Israel ... Num 18:32
These *t* ye shall do unto the LORD ... Num 29:39
hair, and all *t* made of wood ... Num 31:20
So these *t* shall be for a statute ... Num 35:29
time all the *t* which ye should do ... Deut 1:18 1697
all *t* that we call upon him for ... Deut 4:7
lest thou forget the *t* which ... Deut 4:9 1697
all these *t* are come upon thee, ... Deut 4:30 1697
And houses full of all good *t* ... Deut 6:11
thee these great and terrible *t* ... Deut 10:21
the *t* that we do here this day ... Deut 12:8
Only thy holy *t* which thou hast, ... Deut 12:26
For all that do these *t* are an ... Deut 18:12
with all lost *t* of thy brother's, ... Deut 22:3
For all that do such *t*, and all ... Deut 25:16
the hallowed *t* out of mine house ... Deut 26:13
heart, for the abundance of all *t* ... Deut 28:47
in nakedness, and in want of all *t* ... Deut 28:48
of all *t* secretly in the siege ... Deut 28:57
The secret *t* belong unto the LORD ... Deut 29:29
but those *t* which are revealed ... Deut 29:29
when all these *t* are come upon ... Deut 30:1 1697
the *t* that shall come upon them ... Deut 32:35
for the precious *t* of heaven ... Deut 33:13
for the precious *t* put forth by ... Deut 33:14
for the chief *t* of the ancient ... Deut 33:15
for the precious *t* of the lasting ... Deut 33:15
for the precious *t* of the earth ... Deut 33:16
we hearkened unto Moses in all *t* ... Josh 1:17
as soon as we had heard these *t* ... Josh 2:11
told him all *t* that befell them ... Josh 2:23
king of Hazor had heard those *t* ... Josh 11:1
hath failed of all the good *t* ... Josh 23:14 1697
that as all good *t* are come upon ... Josh 23:15 1697
LORD bring upon you all evil *t* ... Josh 23:15 1697
And it came to pass after these *t* ... Josh 24:29 1697
he have shewed us all these *t* ... Judg 13:23
time have told us such *t* as these ... Judg 13:23
they took the *t* which Micah had ... Judg 18:27
changing, for to confirm all *t* ... Ruth 4:7
said unto them, Why do ye such *t* ... 1Sa 2:23 1697
t which I have spoken concerning ... 1Sa 3:12
all the *t* that he said unto thee ... 1Sa 3:17
then should ye go after vain *t* ... 1Sa 12:21
how great *t* he hath done for you ... 1Sa 12:24
the chief of the *t* which should ... 1Sa 15:21
Jonathan shewed him all those *t* ... 1Sa 19:7 1697
and his wife had told him these *t* ... 1Sa 25:37 1697
thou shalt both do great *t* ... 1Sa 26:25
hast thou done all these great *t* ... 2Sa 7:21
a name, and to do for you great *t* ... 2Sa 7:23
all the *t* concerning the war ... 2Sa 11:18 1697
given unto thee such and such *t* ... 2Sa 12:8
king David heard of all these *t* ... 2Sa 13:21 1697
to know all *t* that are in the ... 2Sa 14:20
covenant, ordered in all *t* ... 2Sa 23:5
These *t* did these three mighty ... 2Sa 23:17
These *t* did Benaiah the son of ... 2Sa 23:22
the LORD, I offer thee three *t* ... 2Sa 24:12
All these *t* did Araunah, as a ... 2Sa 24:23
and of fowl, and of creeping *t* ... 1Kin 4:33
I have considered the *t* which ... 1Kin 5:8
Solomon brought in the *t* which ... 1Kin 7:51
he brought in the *t* which his ... 1Kin 15:15
the *t* which himself had dedicated ... 1Kin 15:15
And it came to pass after these *t* ... 1Kin 17:17 1697
have done all these *t* at thy word ... 1Kin 18:36 1697
And it came to pass after these *t* ... 1Kin 21:1 1697
according to all *t* as did the ... 1Kin 21:26
all the great *t* that Elisha hath ... 2Kin 8:4
to all *t* that Jehoiada the priest ... 2Kin 11:9
t that is brought into the house ... 2Kin 12:4
the hallowed *t* that Jehoshaphat ... 2Kin 12:18
dedicated, and his own hallowed *t* ... 2Kin 12:18
to all *t* as Joash his father did ... 2Kin 14:3
of Israel did secretly those *t* ... 2Kin 17:9 1697
wrought wicked *t* to provoke the ... 2Kin 17:11 1697
year such *t* as grow of themselves ... 2Kin 19:29
all the house of his precious *t* ... 2Kin 20:13
All the *t* that are in mine house ... 2Kin 20:15
proclaimed these *t* that thou hast ... 2Kin 23:17 1697
such *t* as were of gold, in gold, ... 2Kin 25:15
And these are ancient *t* ... 1Chr 4:22 1697
the *t* that were made in the pans ... 1Chr 9:31
These *t* did these three mightiest ... 1Chr 11:19
These *t* did Benaiah the son of ... 1Chr 11:24
in making known all these great *t* ... 1Chr 17:19
the LORD, I offer thee three *t* ... 1Chr 21:10
should sanctify the most holy *t* ... 1Chr 23:13
and in the purifying of all holy *t* ... 1Chr 23:28
the treasures of the dedicated *t* ... 1Chr 26:20
the treasures of the dedicated *t* ... 1Chr 26:26
the treasuries of the dedicated *t* ... 1Chr 28:12
of gold by weight for *t* of gold ... 1Chr 28:14
the gold for *t* to be made of gold ... 1Chr 29:2
and the silver for *t* of silver ... 1Chr 29:2
and the brass for *t* of brass ... 1Chr 29:2
of brass, the iron for *t* of iron ... 1Chr 29:2
of iron, and wood for *t* of wood ... 1Chr 29:2
The gold for *t* of gold, and the ... 1Chr 29:5
and the silver for *t* of silver ... 1Chr 29:5
for all *t* come of thee, and of ... 1Chr 29:14
willingly offered all these *t* ... 1Chr 29:17
statutes, and to do all these *t* ... 1Chr 29:19
Now these are the *t* wherein ... 2Chr 3:3
such *t* as they offered for the ... 2Chr 4:6
the *t* that David his father had ... 2Chr 5:1
and also in Judah *t* went well ... 2Chr 12:12 1697
into the house of God the *t* that ... 2Chr 15:18
there are good *t* found in thee ... 2Chr 19:3 1697
and of gold, and of precious *t* ... 2Chr 21:3
t that Jehoiada the priest had ... 2Chr 23:8
also all the dedicated *t* of the ... 2Chr 24:7
the consecrated *t* were six ... 2Chr 29:33
the tithe of all *t* brought they ... 2Chr 31:5
the tithe of holy *t* which were ... 2Chr 31:6
and the dedicated *t* faithfully ... 2Chr 31:12
of the LORD, and the most holy *t* ... 2Chr 31:14
After these *t*, and the ... 2Chr 32:1 1697
with beasts, and with precious *t* ... Ezr 1:6
should not eat of the most holy *t* ... Ezr 2:63
Now after these *t*, in the reign ... Ezr 7:1 1697
Now when these *t* were done ... Ezr 9:1
There are no such *t* done as thou ... Neh 6:8 1697
that were about us saw these *t* ... Neh 6:16
should not eat of the most holy *t* ... Neh 7:65
all *t* that are therein, the seas, ... Neh 9:6
the set feasts, and for the holy *t* ... Neh 10:33
holy *t* unto the Levites ... Neh 12:47
king of Israel sin by these *t* ... Neh 13:26
After these *t*, when the wrath of ... Est 2:1 1697
let their *t* for purification be ... Est 2:3
gave her her *t* for purification ... Est 2:9
with such *t* as belonged to her, ... Est 2:9
with other *t* for the purifying of ... Est 2:12
After these *t* did king Ahasuerus ... Est 3:1 1697
all the *t* wherein the king had ... Est 5:11
And Mordecai wrote these *t* ... Est 9:20 1697
Which doeth great *t* and ... Job 5:9
marvellous *t* without number ... Job 5:9
The *t* that my soul refused to ... Job 6:7
my taste discern perverse *t* ... Job 6:30
How long wilt thou speak these *t* ... Job 8:2
doeth great *t* past finding out ... Job 9:10
these *t* hast thou hid in thine ... Job 10:13
who knoweth not such *t* as these ... Job 12:3
deep *t* out of darkness, and ... Job 12:22
Only do not two *t* unto me ... Job 13:20
thou writest bitter *t* against me ... Job 13:26
thou washest away the *t* which ... Job 14:19
I have heard many such *t* ... Job 16:2
filled their houses with good *t* ... Job 22:18
and many such *t* are with him ... Job 23:14
Dead *t* are formed from under the ... Job 26:5
Lo, all these *t* worketh God ... Job 33:29
great *t* doeth he, which we cannot ... Job 37:5
sharp pointed *t* upon the mire ... Job 41:30
He beholdeth all high *t* ... Job 41:34
t too wonderful for me, which I ... Job 42:3
hast put all *t* under his feet ... Ps 8:6
the tongue that speaketh proud *t* ... Ps 12:3
He that doeth these *t* shall never ... Ps 15:5
eyes behold the *t* that are equal ... Ps 17:2
which speak grievous *t* proudly ... Ps 31:18
to my charge *t* that I knew not ... Ps 35:11
seek my hurt speak mischievous *t* ... Ps 38:12
When I remember these *t*, I pour ... Ps 42:4
I speak of the *t* which I have ... Ps 45:1
hand shall teach thee terrible *t* ... Ps 45:4
These *t* hast thou done, and I kept ... Ps 50:21
God that performeth all *t* for me ... Ps 57:2
hast shewed thy people hard *t* ... Ps 60:3
By terrible *t* in righteousness ... Ps 65:5
very high, who hast done great *t* ... Ps 71:19
Israel, who only doeth wondrous *t* ... Ps 72:18
Marvellous *t* did he in the sight ... Ps 78:12
art great, and doest wondrous *t* ... Ps 86:10
Glorious *t* are spoken of thee, O ... Ps 87:3
shall they utter and speak hard *t* ... Ps 94:4
for he hath done marvellous *t* ... Ps 98:1
satisfieth thy mouth with good *t* ... Ps 103:5
wide sea, wherein are *t* creeping ... Ps 104:25
which had done great *t* in Egypt ... Ps 106:21
terrible *t* by the Red sea ... Ps 106:22
is wise, and will observe these *t* ... Ps 107:43
behold the *t* that are in heaven ... Ps 113:6
behold wondrous *t* out of thy law ... Ps 119:18
concerning all *t* to be right ... Ps 119:128
LORD hath done great *t* for them ... Ps 126:2
The LORD hath done great *t* for us ... Ps 126:3
matters, or in *t* too high for me ... Ps 131:1
creeping *t*, and flying fowl ... Ps 148:10
the man that speaketh froward *t* ... Prov 2:12
all the *t* thou canst desire are ... Prov 3:15
These six *t* doth the LORD hate ... Prov 6:16

for I will speak of excellent *t* Prov 8:6
of my lips shall be right *t* Prov 8:6
all the *t* that may be desired are Prov 8:11
of the wicked poureth out evil *t* Prov 15:28
LORD hath made all *t* for himself Prov 16:4
his eyes to devise froward *t* Prov 16:30
to thee excellent *t* in counsels Prov 22:20
when thy lips speak right *t* Prov 23:16
heart shall utter perverse *t* Prov 23:33
These *t* also belong to the wise Prov 24:23
all *t* both rewardeth the fool Prov 26:10
seek the LORD understand all *t* Prov 28:5
shall have good *t* in possession Prov 28:10
Two *t* have I required of thee Prov 30:7
There are three *t* that are never Prov 30:15
four *t* say not, It is enough Prov 30:15
There be three *t* which are too Prov 30:18
For three *t* the earth is Prov 30:21
There be four *t* which are little Prov 30:24
There be three *t* which go well Prov 30:29
All *t* are full of labour Eccl 1:8 1697
is no remembrance of former *t* Eccl 1:11
of *t* that are to come with those Eccl 1:11
all *t* that are done under heaven Eccl 1:13
be many *t* that increase vanity Eccl 6:11 1697
All *t* have I seen in the days of Eccl 7:15
out wisdom, and the reason of *t* Eccl 7:25
All *t* come alike to all Eccl 9:2
This is an evil among all *t* that Eccl 9:3
but money answereth all *t* Eccl 10:19
that for all these *t* God will Eccl 11:9
for he hath done excellent *t* Is 12:5
for thou hast done wonderful *t* Is 25:1
unto all people a feast of fat *t* Is 25:6
of fat *t* full of marrow, of wines Is 25:6
Surely your turning of *t* upside Is 29:16
Prophesy not unto us right *t* Is 30:10
speak unto us smooth *t* Is 30:10
the liberal deviseth liberal *t* Is 32:8
by liberal *t* shall he stand Is 32:8
all *t* that come forth of it Is 34:1
O Lord, by these *t* men live Is 38:16
in all these *t* is the life of my Is 38:16
them the house of his precious *t* Is 39:2
behold who hath created these *t* Is 40:26
let them shew the former *t* Is 41:22
or declare us *t* for to come Is 41:22
Shew the *t* that are to come Is 41:23
the former *t* are come to pass, and Is 42:9
to pass, and new *t* do I declare Is 42:9
them, and crooked *t* straight Is 42:16
These *t* will I do unto them, and Is 42:16 1697
Seeing many *t*, but thou observest Is 42:20
declare this, and shew us former *t* Is 43:9
Remember ye not the former *t* Is 43:18
neither consider the *t* of old Is 43:18
the *t* that are coming, and shall Is 44:7
delectable *t* shall not profit Is 44:9
I am the LORD that maketh all *t* Is 44:24
I the LORD do all these *t* Is 45:7
Ask me of *t* to come concerning my Is 45:11
I declare *t* that are right Is 45:19
Remember the former *t* of old Is 46:9
times the *t* that are not yet done Is 46:10
not lay these *t* to thy heart Is 47:7
But these two *t* shall come to Is 47:9
save thee from these *t* that shall Is 47:13
the former *t* from the beginning Is 48:3
shewed thee new *t* from this time Is 48:6
from this time, even hidden *t* Is 48:6
among them hath declared these *t* Is 48:14
These two *t* are come unto thee Is 51:19
choose the *t* that please me, and Is 56:4
as the garden causeth the *t* that Is 61:11
t which we looked not for Is 64:3
all our pleasant *t* are laid waste Is 64:11
thou refrain thyself for these *t* Is 64:12
abominable *t* is in their vessels Is 65:4
For all those *t* hath mine hand Is 66:2
made, and all those *t* have been Is 66:2
who hath seen such *t* Is 66:8
walked after *t* that do not profit Jer 2:8
done evil *t* as thou couldest Jer 3:5
after she had done all these *t* Jer 3:7
have procured these *t* unto thee Jer 4:18
Shall I not visit for these *t* Jer 5:9
LORD our God all these *t* unto us Jer 5:19
have turned away these *t*, and your Jer 5:25
have withholden good *t* from you Jer 5:25
Shall I not visit for these *t* Jer 5:29
the *t* that I have given them Jer 8:13
I not visit them for these *t* Jer 9:9
for in these *t* I delight, saith Jer 9:24
for he is the former of all *t* Jer 10:16
Wherefore come these *t* upon me Jer 13:22
for thou hast made all these *t* Jer 14:22
their detestable and abominable *t* Jer 16:18
t wherein there is no profit Jer 16:19
heart is deceitful above all *t* Jer 17:9
heathen, who hath heard such *t* Jer 18:13
that Jeremiah prophesied these *t* Jer 20:1 1697
and all the precious *t* thereof Jer 20:5
shall devour all *t* round about it Jer 21:14
princes of Judah heard these *t* Jer 26:10 1697
I have done these *t* unto thee Jer 30:15
and shall eat them as common *t* Jer 31:5
and shew thee great and mighty *t* Jer 33:3
t for the which the LORD thy God Jer 42:5 1697
unto her, we have wanted all *t* Jer 44:18
seekest thou great *t* for thyself Jer 45:5
for he is the former of all *t* Jer 51:19
her miseries all her pleasant *t* Lam 1:7
his hand upon all her pleasant *t* Lam 1:10
t for meat to relieve the soul Lam 1:11
For these *t* I weep Lam 1:16
seen vain and foolish *t* for thee Lam 2:14
for these *t* our eyes are dim Lam 5:17
with all thy detestable *t* Eze 5:11
and of their detestable *t* therein Eze 7:20
behold every form of creeping *t* Eze 8:10
for I know the *t* that come into Eze 11:5
away all the detestable *t* thereof Eze 11:18
the heart of their detestable *t* Eze 11:21
the *t* that the LORD had shewed me Eze 11:25 1697
the like *t* shall not come, Eze 16:16
seeing thou doest all these *t* Eze 16:30
hast fretted me in all these *t* Eze 16:43
Know ye not what these *t* mean Eze 17:12
shall he escape that doeth such *t* Eze 17:15
hand, and hath done all these *t* Eze 17:18
the like to any one of these *t* Eze 18:10
oblations, with all your holy *t* Eze 20:40
Thou hast despised mine holy *t* Eze 22:8
taken the treasure and precious *t* Eze 22:25
law, and have profaned mine holy *t* Eze 22:26
I will do these *t* unto thee Eze 23:30
tell us what these *t* are to us Eze 24:19
thy merchants in all sorts of *t* Eze 27:24
nor with their detestable *t* Eze 37:23
time shall *t* come into thy mind Eze 38:10 1697
all creeping *t* that creep upon Eze 38:20
LORD shall eat the most holy *t* Eze 42:13
shall they lay the most holy *t* Eze 42:13
shall approach to those *t* which Eze 42:14
kept the charge of mine holy *t* Eze 44:8
to come near to any of my holy *t* Eze 44:13
of all the firstfruits of all *t* Eze 44:30
that asked such *t* at any magician Dan 2:10
He revealeth the deep and secret *t* Dan 2:22
in pieces and subdueth all *t* Dan 2:40
man, and a mouth speaking great *t* Dan 7:8
know the interpretation of the *t* Dan 7:16 4406
a mouth that spake very great *t* Dan 7:20
that holdeth with me in these *t* Dan 10:21
shall speak marvellous *t* against Dan 11:36
precious stones, and pleasant *t* Dan 11:38
over all the precious *t* of Egypt Dan 11:43
all these *t* shall be finished Dan 12:7
what shall be the end of these *t* Dan 12:8
with the creeping *t* of the ground Hos 2:18
to him the great *t* of my law Hos 8:12
shall eat unclean *t* in Assyria Hos 9:3
and he shall understand these *t* Hos 14:9
up, because he hath done great *t* Joel 2:20
for the LORD will do great *t* Joel 2:21
your temples my goodly pleasant *t* Joel 3:5
How are the *t* of Esau searched Obad 6
how are his hidden *t* sought up Obad 6
will I shew unto him marvellous *t* Mic 7:15
of the sea, as the creeping *t* Hab 1:14
consume all *t* from off the land Zeph 1:2
hath despised the day of small *t* Zec 4:10
people to possess all these *t* Zec 8:12
These are the *t* that ye shall do Zec 8:16
for all these are *t* that I hate Zec 8:17
But while he thought on these *t* Mt 1:20
Herod the king had heard these *t* Mt 2:3
All these *t* will I give thee, if Mt 4:9
knoweth what *t* ye have need of Mt 6:8
all these *t* do the Gentiles seek Mt 6:32
that ye have need of all these *t* Mt 6:32
all these *t* shall be added unto Mt 6:33
take thought for the *t* of itself Mt 6:34
give good *t* to them that ask him Mt 7:11
Therefore all *t* whatsoever ye Mt 7:12
While he spake these *t* unto them Mt 9:18
again those *t* which ye do hear Mt 11:4
hast hid these *t* from the wise Mt 11:25
All *t* are delivered unto me of my Mt 11:27
can ye, being evil, speak good *t* Mt 12:34
the heart bringeth forth good *t* Mt 12:35
treasure bringeth forth evil *t* Mt 12:35
he spake many *t* unto them in Mt 13:3
to see those *t* which ye see Mt 13:17
and to hear those *t* which ye hear Mt 13:17
All these *t* spake Jesus unto the Mt 13:34
I will utter *t* which have been Mt 13:35
of his kingdom all *t* that offend Mt 13:41
Have ye understood all these *t* Mt 13:51
forth out of his treasure *t* new Mt 13:52
then hath this man all these *t* Mt 13:56
But those *t* which proceed out of Mt 15:18
These are the *t* which defile a Mt 15:20
suffer many *t* of the elders and Mt 16:21
not the *t* that be of God, but Mt 16:23
first come, and restore all *t* Mt 17:11
All these *t* have I kept from my Mt 19:20
but with God all *t* are possible Mt 19:26
saw the wonderful *t* that he did Mt 21:15
And all *t*, whatsoever ye shall ask Mt 21:22
what authority doest thou these *t* Mt 21:23
by what authority I do these *t* Mt 21:24
by what authority I do these *t* Mt 21:27
are killed, and all *t* are ready Mt 22:4
Caesar the *t* which are Caesar's Mt 22:21
unto God the *t* that are God's Mt 22:21
by it, and by all *t* thereon Mt 23:20
All these *t* shall come upon this Mt 23:36
unto them, See ye not all these *t* Mt 24:2
Tell us, when shall these *t* be Mt 24:3
for all these *t* must come to pass Mt 24:6
ye, when ye shall see all these *t* Mt 24:33
till all these *t* be fulfilled Mt 24:34
hast been faithful over a few *t* Mt 25:21
will make thee ruler over many *t* Mt 25:21
hast been faithful over a few *t* Mt 25:23
will make thee ruler over many *t* Mt 25:23
many *t* they witness against thee Mt 27:13
for I have suffered many *t* this Mt 27:19
those *t* that were done, they Mt 27:54
priests all the *t* that were done Mt 28:11
Teaching them to observe all *t* Mt 28:20
those *t* which Moses commanded Mk 1:44
reason ye these *t* in your hearts Mk 2:8
had heard what great *t* he did Mk 3:8
he taught them many *t* by parables Mk 4:2
all these *t* are done in parables Mk 4:11
the lusts of other *t* entering in Mk 4:19
expounded all *t* to his disciples Mk 4:34
tell them how great *t* the Lord Mk 5:19
great *t* Jesus had done for him Mk 5:20
had suffered many *t* of many Mk 5:26
From whence hath this man these *t* Mk 6:2
when he heard him, he did many *t* Mk 6:20
unto Jesus, and told him all *t* Mk 6:30
and he began to teach them many *t* Mk 6:34
And many other *t* there be, which Mk 7:4
and many other such like *t* ye do Mk 7:8
and many such like *t* do ye Mk 7:13
but the *t* which come out of him, Mk 7:15
All these evil *t* come from within Mk 7:23
saying, He hath done all *t* well Mk 7:37
the Son of man must suffer many *t* Mk 8:31
not the *t* that be of God, but the Mk 8:33
of God, but the *t* that be of men Mk 8:33
tell no man what *t* they had seen Mk 9:9
cometh first, and restoreth all *t* Mk 9:12
man, that he must suffer many *t* Mk 9:12
all *t* are possible to him that Mk 9:23
for with God all *t* are possible Mk 10:27
what *t* should happen unto him Mk 10:32
had looked round about upon all *t* Mk 11:11
t which he saith shall come to Mk 11:23
What *t* soever ye desire, when ye Mk 11:24
what authority doest thou these *t* Mk 11:28
thee this authority to do these *t* Mk 11:28
by what authority I do these *t* Mk 11:29
by what authority I do these *t* Mk 11:33
to Caesar the *t* that are Caesar's Mk 12:17
to God the *t* that are God's Mk 12:17
Tell us, when shall these *t* be Mk 13:4
all these *t* shall be fulfilled Mk 13:4
for such *t* must needs be Mk 13:7
behold, I have foretold you all *t* Mk 13:23
ye shall see these *t* come to pass Mk 13:29
pass, till all these *t* be done Mk 13:30
all *t* are possible unto thee Mk 14:36
priests accused him of many *t* Mk 15:3
behold how many *t* they witness Mk 15:4
t which are most surely believed Lk 1:1 *4229*
of all *t* from the very first Lk 1:3
know the certainty of those *t* Lk 1:4 *3056*
that these *t* shall be performed Lk 1:20
t which were told her from the Lk 1:45
is mighty hath done to me great *t* Lk 1:49
filled the hungry with good *t* Lk 1:53
t which were told them by the Lk 2:18
But Mary kept all these *t* Lk 2:19 *4487*
for all the *t* that they had heard Lk 2:20
those *t* which were spoken of him Lk 2:33
all *t* according to the law of the Lk 2:39
many other *t* in his exhortation Lk 3:18
when they heard these *t*, were Lk 4:28
We have seen strange *t* to day Lk 5:26
after these *t* he went forth, and Lk 5:27
Lord, and do not the *t* which I say Lk 6:46
When Jesus heard these *t*, he Lk 7:9
of John shewed him of all these *t* Lk 7:18
and tell John what *t* ye have seen Lk 7:22
And when he had said these *t* Lk 8:8
shew how great *t* God hath done Lk 8:39
great *t* Jesus had done unto him Lk 8:39
is this, of whom I hear such *t* Lk 9:9
The Son of man must suffer many *t* Lk 9:22
of those *t* which they had seen Lk 9:36
one at all *t* which Jesus did Lk 9:43
After these *t* the Lord appointed Lk 10:1
and drinking such *t* as they give Lk 10:7
eat such *t* as are set before you Lk 10:8
hast hid these *t* from the wise Lk 10:21
All *t* are delivered to me of my Lk 10:22
eyes which see the *t* that ye see Lk 10:23
to see those *t* which ye see Lk 10:24
and to hear those *t* which ye hear Lk 10:24
careful and troubled about many *t* Lk 10:41
came to pass, as he spake these *t* Lk 11:27
give alms of such *t* as ye have Lk 11:41
behold, all *t* are clean unto you Lk 11:41
And as he said these *t* unto them Lk 11:53
to provoke him to speak of many *t* Lk 11:53
of the *t* which he possesseth Lk 12:15
then whose shall those *t* be Lk 12:20
For all these *t* do the nations of Lk 12:30
that ye have need of these *t* Lk 12:30
all these *t* shall be added unto Lk 12:31
did commit *t* worthy of stripes, Lk 12:48
because they suffered such *t* Lk 13:2
And when he had said these *t* Lk 13:17
glorious *t* that were done by him Lk 13:17
not answer him again to these *t* Lk 14:6
at meat with him heard these *t* Lk 14:15
for all *t* are now ready Lk 14:17
came, and shewed his lord these *t* Lk 14:21
and asked what these *t* meant Lk 15:26
were covetous, heard all these *t* Lk 16:14
lifetime receivedst thy good *t* Lk 16:25
and likewise Lazarus evil *t* Lk 16:25
did the *t* that were commanded him Lk 17:9
those *t* which are commanded you Lk 17:10
But first must he suffer many *t* Lk 17:25
Now when Jesus heard these *t* Lk 18:22
The *t* which are impossible with Lk 18:27

all *t* that are written by the Lk 18:31
they understood none of these *t* Lk 18:34
knew they the *t* which were spoken Lk 18:34
And as they heard these *t*, he Lk 19:11
the *t* which belong unto thy peace Lk 19:42
what authority doest thou these *t* Lk 20:2
by what authority I do these *t* Lk 20:8
Caesar the *t* which be Caesar's Lk 20:25
unto God the *t* which be God's Lk 20:25
As for these *t* which ye behold, Lk 21:6
Master, but when shall these *t* be Lk 21:7
when these *t* shall come to pass Lk 21:7
for these *t* must first come to Lk 21:9
that all *t* which are written may Lk 21:22
for looking after those *t* which Lk 21:26
when these *t* begin to come to Lk 21:28
when ye see these *t* come to pass Lk 21:31
these *t* that shall come to pass Lk 21:36
for the *t* concerning me have an Lk 22:37
many other *t* blasphemously spake Lk 22:65
he had heard many *t* of him Lk 23:8
those *t* whereof ye accuse him Lk 23:14
they do these *t* in a green tree Lk 23:31
beholding the *t* which were done, Lk 23:48
stood afar off, beholding these *t* Lk 23:49
told all these *t* unto the eleven, Lk 24:9
which told these *t* unto the Lk 24:10
of all these *t* which had happened Lk 24:14
hast not known the *t* which are Lk 24:18
And he said unto them, What *t* Lk 24:19
third day since these *t* were done Lk 24:21
Christ to have suffered these *t* Lk 24:26
the *t* concerning himself Lk 24:27
they told what *t* were done in the Lk 24:35
that all *t* must be fulfilled, Lk 24:44
And ye are witnesses of these *t* Lk 24:48
All *t* were made by him Jn 1:3
These *t* were done in Bethabara Jn 1:28
shalt see greater *t* than these Jn 1:50
sold doves, Take these *t* hence Jn 2:16
seeing that thou doest these *t* Jn 2:18
said unto him, How can these *t* be Jn 3:9
of Israel, and knowest not these *t* Jn 3:10
If I have told you earthly *t* Jn 3:12
if I tell you of heavenly *t* Jn 3:12
After these *t* came Jesus and his Jn 3:22
and hath given all *t* into his hand Jn 3:35
he is come, he will tell us all *t* Jn 4:25
told me all *t* that ever I did Jn 4:29
having seen all the *t* that he did Jn 4:45
done these *t* on the sabbath day Jn 5:16
for what *t* soever he doeth, these Jn 5:19
sheweth him all *t* that himself Jn 5:20
but these *t* I say, that ye might Jn 5:34
After these *t* Jesus went over the Jn 6:1
These *t* said he in the synagogue, Jn 6:59
After these *t* Jesus walked in Jn 7:1
If thou do these *t*, shew thyself Jn 7:4
murmured such *t* concerning him Jn 7:32
I have many *t* to say and to judge Jn 8:26
those *t* which I have heard of him Jn 8:26
hath taught me, I speak these *t* Jn 8:28
do always those *t* that please him Jn 8:29
but they understood not what *t* Jn 10:6
but all *t* that John spake of this Jn 10:41
These *t* said he Jn 11:11 *5023*
had seen the *t* which Jesus did, Jn 11:45
told them what *t* Jesus had done Jn 11:46
These *t* understood not his Jn 12:16
that these *t* were written of him Jn 12:16
they had done these *t* unto him Jn 12:16
These *t* spake Jesus, and departed, Jn 12:36
These *t* said Esaias, when he saw Jn 12:41
had given all *t* into his hands Jn 13:3
If ye know these *t*, happy are ye Jn 13:17
Buy those *t* that we have need of Jn 13:29
These *t* have I spoken unto you, Jn 14:25
my name, he shall teach you all *t* Jn 14:26
bring all *t* to your remembrance, Jn 14:26
These *t* have I spoken unto you, Jn 15:11
for all *t* that I have heard of my Jn 15:15
These *t* I command you, that ye Jn 15:17
But all these *t* will they do unto Jn 15:21
These *t* have I spoken unto you, Jn 16:1
these *t* will they do unto you, Jn 16:3
But these *t* have I told you, that Jn 16:4
these *t* I said not unto you at Jn 16:4
I have said these *t* unto you Jn 16:6
I have yet many *t* to say unto you Jn 16:12
and he will shew you *t* to come Jn 16:13
All *t* that the Father hath are Jn 16:15
These *t* have I spoken unto you in Jn 16:25
we sure that thou knowest all *t* Jn 16:30
These *t* I have spoken unto you, Jn 16:33
Now they have known that all *t* Jn 17:7
these *t* I speak in the world, Jn 17:13
knowing all *t* that should come Jn 18:4
These *t* therefore the soldiers Jn 19:24
that all *t* were now accomplished Jn 19:28
For these *t* were done, that the Jn 19:36
he had spoken these *t* unto her Jn 20:18
After these *t* Jesus shewed Jn 21:1
him, Lord, thou knowest all *t* Jn 21:17
which testifieth of these *t* Jn 21:24
and wrote these *t* Jn 21:24
also many other *t* which Jesus did Jn 21:25
speaking of the *t* pertaining to Acts 1:3
And when he had spoken these *t* Acts 1:9
together, and had all *t* common Acts 2:44
But those *t*, which God before had Acts 3:18
the times of restitution of all *t* Acts 3:21
him shall ye hear in all *t* Acts 3:22
speak the *t* which we have seen Acts 4:20
and the people imagine vain *t* Acts 4:25

any of them that ought of the *t* Acts 4:32
but they had all *t* common Acts 4:32
prices of the *t* that were sold Acts 4:34
on all them that heard these *t* Acts 5:5
and upon as many as heard these *t* Acts 5:11
the chief priests heard these *t* Acts 5:24 *3056*
we are his witnesses of these *t* Acts 5:32 *4487*
the high priest, Are these *t* so Acts 7:1
Hath not my hand made all these *t* Acts 7:50
When they heard these *t*, they Acts 7:54
unto those *t* which Philip spake Acts 8:6
t concerning the kingdom of God Acts 8:12
that none of these *t* which ye Acts 8:24
t he must suffer for my name's Acts 9:16
declared all these *t* unto them Acts 10:8
and wild beasts, and creeping *t* Acts 10:12
to hear all *t* that are commanded Acts 10:33
we are witnesses of all *t* which Acts 10:39
and wild beasts, and creeping *t* Acts 11:6
When they heard these *t*, they Acts 11:18
Then tidings of these *t* came unto Acts 11:22
said, Go shew these *t* unto James Acts 12:17
believe are justified from all *t* Acts 13:39
spake against those *t* which were Acts 13:45
saying, Sirs, why do ye these *t* Acts 14:15
sea, and all *t* that are therein Acts 14:15
they declared all *t* that God had Acts 15:4
the Lord, who doeth all these *t* Acts 15:17
from *t* strangled, and from blood Acts 15:20
also tell you the same *t* by mouth Acts 15:27
burden than these necessary *t* Acts 15:28
from *t* strangled, and from Acts 15:29
the *t* which were spoken of Paul Acts 16:14
the city, when they heard these *t* Acts 17:8
daily, whether those *t* were so Acts 17:11
certain strange *t* to our ears Acts 17:20
know therefore what these *t* mean Acts 17:20
I perceive that in all *t* ye are Acts 17:22
all *t* therein, seeing that he is Acts 17:24
to all life, and breath, and all *t* Acts 17:25
After these *t* Paul departed from Acts 18:1
Gallio cared for none of those *t* Acts 18:17
diligently the *t* of the Lord Acts 18:25
persuading the *t* concerning the Acts 19:8
After these *t* were ended, Paul Acts 19:21
Seeing then that these *t* cannot Acts 19:36
not knowing the *t* that shall Acts 20:22
But none of these *t* move me Acts 20:24 *3056*
men arise, speaking perverse *t* Acts 20:30
I have shewed you all *t*, how that Acts 20:35
And when we heard these *t*, both we Acts 21:12
what *t* God had wrought among the Acts 21:19
and all may know that those *t* Acts 21:24
from *t* offered to idols, and from Acts 21:25
it shall be told thee of all *t* Acts 22:10
thou hast shewed these *t* to me Acts 23:22
take knowledge of all these *t* Acts 24:8
saying that these *t* were so Acts 24:9
the *t* whereof they now accuse me Acts 24:13
believing all *t* which are written Acts 24:14
And when Felix heard these *t* Acts 24:22
be judged of these *t* before me Acts 25:9
these *t* whereof these accuse me Acts 25:11
of such *t* as I supposed Acts 25:18
the *t* whereof I am accused of the Acts 26:2
that I ought to do many *t* Acts 26:9
of these *t* which thou hast seen Acts 26:16
of those *t* in the which I will Acts 26:16
saying none other *t* than those Acts 26:22
For the king knoweth of these *t* Acts 26:26
of these *t* are hidden from him Acts 26:26
more than those *t* which were Acts 27:11
us with such *t* as were necessary Acts 28:10
believed the *t* which were spoken Acts 28:24
teaching those *t* which concern Acts 28:31
For the invisible *t* of him from Rom 1:20
understood by the *t* that are made Rom 1:20
fourfooted beasts, and creeping *t* Rom 1:23
to do those *t* which are not Rom 1:28
boasters, inventors of evil *t* Rom 1:30
commit such *t* are worthy of death Rom 1:32
that judgest doest the same *t* Rom 2:1
against them which commit such *t* Rom 2:2
that judgest them which do such *t* Rom 2:3
do by nature the *t* contained in Rom 2:14
approvest the *t* that are more Rom 2:18
that what *t* soever the law saith Rom 3:19
calleth those *t* which be not as Rom 4:17
t whereof ye are now ashamed Rom 6:21
for the end of those *t* is death Rom 6:21
flesh do mind the *t* of the flesh Rom 8:5
the Spirit the *t* of the Spirit Rom 8:5
we know that all *t* work together Rom 8:28
What shall we then say to these *t* Rom 8:31
him also freely give us all *t* Rom 8:32
in all these *t* we are more than Rom 8:37
nor *t* present, nor *t* to come Rom 8:38
doeth those *t* shall live by them Rom 10:5
and bring glad tidings of good *t* Rom 10:15 *18*
through him, and to him, are all *t* Rom 11:36
Mind not high *t*, but condescend Rom 12:16
Provide *t* honest in the sight of Rom 12:17
believeth that he may eat all *t* Rom 14:2
For he that in these *t* serveth Rom 14:18
after the *t* which make for peace Rom 14:19
t wherewith one may edify another Rom 14:19
All *t* indeed are pure Rom 14:20
For whatsoever *t* were written Rom 15:4
in those *t* which pertain to God Rom 15:17
t which Christ hath not wrought Rom 15:18
partakers of their spiritual *t* Rom 15:27
to minister unto them in carnal *t* Rom 15:27
t of the world to confound the 1Cor 1:27
God hath chosen the weak *t* of the 1Cor 1:27

confound the *t* which are mighty 1Cor 1:27
base *t* of the world 1Cor 1:28
t which are despised, hath God 1Cor 1:28
t which are not, to bring to 1Cor 1:28
to bring to nought *t* that are 1Cor 1:28
the *t* which God hath prepared for 1Cor 2:9
for the Spirit searcheth all *t* 1Cor 2:10
yea, the deep *t* of God 1Cor 2:10
what man knoweth the *t* of a man 1Cor 2:11
even so the *t* of God knoweth no 1Cor 2:11
that we might know the *t* that are 1Cor 2:12
Which *t* also we speak, not in the 1Cor 2:13
spiritual *t* with spiritual 1Cor 2:13
not the *t* of the Spirit of God 1Cor 2:14
that is spiritual judgeth all *t* 1Cor 2:15
For all *t* are yours 1Cor 3:21
or *t* present, or *t* to come 1Cor 3:22
to light the hidden *t* of darkness 1Cor 4:5
And these *t*, brethren, I have in a 1Cor 4:6
of all *t* unto this day 1Cor 4:13
I write not these *t* to shame you 1Cor 4:14
how much more *t* that pertain to 1Cor 6:3
of *t* pertaining to this life 1Cor 6:4
All *t* are lawful unto me, but all 1Cor 6:12
but all *t* are not expedient 1Cor 6:12
all *t* are lawful for me, but I 1Cor 6:12
Now concerning the *t* whereof ye 1Cor 7:1
for the *t* that belong to the Lord 1Cor 7:32
for the *t* that are of the world 1Cor 7:33
careth for the *t* of the Lord 1Cor 7:34
careth for the *t* of the world 1Cor 7:34
Now as touching *t* offered unto 1Cor 8:1
t that are offered in sacrifice 1Cor 8:4
the Father, of whom are all *t* 1Cor 8:6
Jesus Christ, by whom are all *t* 1Cor 8:6
t which are offered to idols 1Cor 8:10
Say I these *t* as a man 1Cor 9:8
we have sown unto you spiritual *t* 1Cor 9:11
if we shall reap your carnal *t* 1Cor 9:11
but suffer all *t*, lest we should 1Cor 9:12
holy *t* live of the *t* of the 1Cor 9:13
But I have used none of these *t* 1Cor 9:15
neither have I written these *t* 1Cor 9:15
I am made all *t* to all men 1Cor 9:22
the mastery is temperate in all *t* 1Cor 9:25
Now these *t* were our examples, to 1Cor 10:6
we should not lust after evil *t* 1Cor 10:6
Now all these *t* happened unto 1Cor 10:11
that the *t* which the Gentiles 1Cor 10:20
All *t* are lawful for me, but all 1Cor 10:23
but all *t* are not expedient 1Cor 10:23
all *t* are lawful for me, but all 1Cor 10:23
for me, but all *t* edify not 1Cor 10:23
Even as I please all men in all *t* 1Cor 10:33
that ye remember me in all *t* 1Cor 11:2
but all *t* of God 1Cor 11:12
Beareth all *t*, believeth all 1Cor 13:7
all *t*, hopeth all *t*, 1Cor 13:7
hopeth all *t*, endureth all *t* 1Cor 13:7
a man, I put away childish *t* 1Cor 13:11
even *t* without life giving sound, 1Cor 14:7
Let all *t* be done unto edifying 1Cor 14:26
let him acknowledge that the *t* 1Cor 14:37
Let all *t* be done decently and in 1Cor 14:40
he hath put all *t* under his feet 1Cor 15:27
he saith all *t* are put under him 1Cor 15:27
which did put all *t* under him 1Cor 15:27
when all *t* shall be subdued unto 1Cor 15:28
unto him that put all *t* under him 1Cor 15:28
Let all your *t* be done with 1Cor 16:14
we write none other *t* unto you 2Cor 1:13
or the *t* that I purpose, do I 2Cor 1:17
whether ye be obedient in all *t* 2Cor 2:9
And who is sufficient for these *t* 2Cor 2:16
the hidden *t* of dishonesty 2Cor 4:2
For all *t* are for your sakes, 2Cor 4:15
look not at the *t* which are seen 2Cor 4:18
but at the *t* which are not seen 2Cor 4:18
for the *t* which are seen are 2Cor 4:18
but the *t* which are not seen are 2Cor 4:18
receive the *t* done in his body 2Cor 5:10
old *t* are passed away 2Cor 5:17
behold, all *t* are become new 2Cor 5:17
all *t* are of God, who hath 2Cor 5:18
But in all *t* approving ourselves 2Cor 6:4
nothing, and yet possessing all *t* 2Cor 6:10
In all *t* ye have approved 2Cor 7:11
as we spake all *t* to you in truth 2Cor 7:14
I have confidence in you in all *t* 2Cor 7:16
Providing for honest *t*, not only 2Cor 8:21
proved diligent in many *t* 2Cor 8:22
having all sufficiency in all *t* 2Cor 9:8
Do ye look on *t* after the outward 2Cor 10:7
boast of *t* without our measure 2Cor 10:13
Not boasting of *t* without our 2Cor 10:15
line of *t* made ready to our hand 2Cor 10:16
made manifest among you in all *t* 2Cor 11:6
in all *t* I have kept myself from 2Cor 11:9
Beside those *t* that are without, 2Cor 11:28
I will glory of the *t* which 2Cor 11:30
but we do all *t*, dearly beloved, 2Cor 12:19
I write these *t* being absent 2Cor 13:10
Now the *t* which I write unto you, Gal 1:20
again the *t* which I destroyed Gal 2:18
ye suffered so many *t* in vain Gal 3:4
t which are written in the book Gal 3:10
Which *t* are an allegory Gal 4:24
ye cannot do the *t* that ye would Gal 5:17
that they which do such *t* shall Gal 5:21
him that teacheth in all good *t* Gal 6:6
together in one all *t* in Christ Eph 1:10
t after the counsel of his own Eph 1:11
hath put all *t* under his feet, and Eph 1:22
the head over all *t* to the church Eph 1:22

T

who created all *t* by Jesus Christ	Eph 3:9	
heavens, that he might fill all *t*	Eph 4:10	
may grow up into him in all *t*	Eph 4:15	
for because of these *t* cometh the	Eph 5:6	
those *t* which are done of them in	Eph 5:12	
But all *t* that are reproved are	Eph 5:13	
thanks always for all *t* unto God	Eph 5:20	
masters, do the same *t* unto them	Eph 6:9	
shall make known to you all *t*	Eph 6:21	
may approve *t* that are excellent	Phil 1:10	
that the *t* which happened unto me	Phil 1:12	
Look not every man on his own *t*	Phil 2:4	
every man also on the *t* of others	Phil 2:4	
of *t* in heaven	Phil 2:10	
t in earth, and *t* under the	Phil 2:10	
Do all *t* without murmurings and	Phil 2:14	
not the *t* which are Jesus	Phil 2:21	
To write the same *t* to you	Phil 3:1	
But what *t* were gain to me, those	Phil 3:7	
I count all *t* but loss for the	Phil 3:8	
I have suffered the loss of all *t*	Phil 3:8	
those *t* which are behind, and	Phil 3:13	
unto those *t* which are before	Phil 3:13	
their shame, who mind earthly *t*	Phil 3:19	
even to subdue all *t* unto himself	Phil 3:21	
brethren, whatsoever *t* are true	Phil 4:8	
whatsoever *t* are honest	Phil 4:8	
whatsoever *t* are just	Phil 4:8	
whatsoever *t* are pure	Phil 4:8	
whatsoever *t* are lovely	Phil 4:8	
whatsoever *t* are of good report	Phil 4:8	
be any praise, think on these *t*	Phil 4:8	
Those *t*, which ye have both	Phil 4:9	
in all *t* I am instructed both to	Phil 4:12	
I can do all *t* through Christ	Phil 4:13	
the *t* which were sent from you	Phil 4:18	
For by him were all *t* created	Col 1:16	
all *t* were created by him, and for	Col 1:16	
And he is before all *t*, and by him	Col 1:17	
and by him all *t* consist	Col 1:17	
that in all *t* he might have the	Col 1:18	
to reconcile all *t* unto himself	Col 1:20	
t in earth, or *t* in heaven	Col 1:20	
Which are a shadow of *t* to come	Col 2:17	
intruding into those *t* which he	Col 2:18	
Which *t* have indeed a shew of	Col 2:23	
seek those *t* which are above,	Col 3:1	
Set your affection on *t* above	Col 3:2	
not on *t* on the earth	Col 3:2	
above all these *t* put on charity	Col 3:14	
obey your parents in all *t*	Col 3:20	
obey in all *t* your masters	Col 3:22	
you all *t* which are done here	Col 4:9	
like *t* of your own countrymen	1Th 2:14	
Prove all *t*	1Th 5:21	
yet with you, I told you these *t*	2Th 2:5	
will do the *t* which we command	2Th 3:4	
sober, faithful in all *t*	1Ti 3:11	
These *t* write I unto thee, hoping	1Ti 3:14	
in remembrance of these *t*	1Ti 4:6	
is profitable unto all *t*, having	1Ti 4:8	
These *t* command and teach	1Ti 4:11	
Meditate upon these *t*	1Ti 4:15	
these *t* give in charge, that they	1Ti 5:7	
speaking *t* which they ought not	1Ti 5:13	
that thou observe these *t* without	1Ti 5:21	
These *t* teach and exhort	1Ti 6:2	
thou, O man of God, flee these *t*	1Ti 6:11	
of God, who quickeneth all *t*	1Ti 6:13	
giveth us richly all *t* to enjoy	1Ti 6:17	
which cause I also suffer these *t*	2Ti 1:12	
in how many *t* he ministered unto	2Ti 1:18	
the *t* that thou hast heard of me	2Ti 2:2	
give thee understanding in all *t*	2Ti 2:7	
all *t* for the elect's sakes	2Ti 2:10	
Of these *t* put them in	2Ti 2:14	
in the *t* which thou hast learned	2Ti 3:14	
But watch thou in all *t*, endure	2Ti 4:5	
in order the *t* that are wanting	Titus 1:5	
teaching *t* which they ought not,	Titus 1:11	
Unto the pure all *t* are pure	Titus 1:15	
But speak thou the *t* which become	Titus 2:1	
to much wine, teachers of good *t*	Titus 2:3	
In all *t* shewing thyself a	Titus 2:7	
and to please them well in all *t*	Titus 2:9	
of God our Saviour in all *t*	Titus 2:10	
These *t* speak, and exhort, and	Titus 2:15	
these *t* I will that thou affirm	Titus 3:8	
These *t* are good and profitable	Titus 3:8	
he hath appointed heir of all *t*	Heb 1:2	
upholding all *t* by the word of	Heb 1:3	
heed to the *t* which we have heard	Heb 2:1	
Thou hast put all *t* in subjection	Heb 2:8	
see not yet all *t* put under him	Heb 2:8	
it became him, for whom are all *t*	Heb 2:10	
and by whom are all *t*	Heb 2:10	
Wherefore in all *t* it behoved him	Heb 2:17	
priest in *t* pertaining to God	Heb 2:17	
but he that built all *t* is God	Heb 3:4	
for a testimony of those *t* which	Heb 3:5	
but all *t* are naked and opened	Heb 4:13	
for men in *t* pertaining to God	Heb 5:1	
by the *t* which he suffered	Heb 5:8	
Of whom we have many *t* to say	Heb 5:11	
we are persuaded better *t* of you	Heb 6:9	
t that accompany salvation,	Heb 6:9	
That by two immutable *t*, in which	Heb 6:18	
For he of whom these *t* are spoken	Heb 7:13	*4229*
Now of the *t* which we have spoken	Heb 8:1	
example and shadow of heavenly *t*	Heb 8:5	
that thou make all *t* according to	Heb 8:5	
Now when these *t* were thus	Heb 9:6	
an high priest of good *t* to come	Heb 9:11	
almost all *t* are by the law	Heb 9:22	
of *t* in the heavens should be	Heb 9:23	
but the heavenly *t* themselves	Heb 9:23	
having a shadow of good *t* to come	Heb 10:1	
and not the very image of the *t*	Heb 10:1	*4229*
is the substance of *t* hoped for	Heb 11:1	*4229*
the evidence of *t* not seen	Heb 11:1	
so that *t* which are seen were not	Heb 11:3	
not made of *t* which do appear	Heb 11:3	
of God of *t* not seen as yet	Heb 11:7	
For they that say such *t* declare	Heb 11:14	
and Esau concerning *t* to come	Heb 11:20	
better *t* than that of Abel	Heb 12:24	
of those *t* that are shaken	Heb 12:27	
as of *t* that are made, that those	Heb 12:27	
that those *t* which cannot be	Heb 12:27	
be content with such *t* as ye have	Heb 13:5	
in all *t* willing to live honestly	Heb 13:18	
ye give them not those *t* which	Jas 2:16	
For in many *t* we offend all	Jas 3:2	
member, and boasteth great *t*	Jas 3:5	
of *t* in the sea, is tamed, and	Jas 3:7	
these *t* ought not so to be	Jas 3:10	
But above all *t*, my brethren,	Jas 5:12	
unto us they did minister the *t*	1Pet 1:12	*846*
which *t* the angels desire to look	1Pet 1:12	
not redeemed with corruptible *t*	1Pet 1:18	
But the end of all *t* is at hand	1Pet 4:7	
above all *t* have fervent charity	1Pet 4:8	
that God in all *t* may be	1Pet 4:11	
us all *t* that pertain unto life	2Pet 1:3	
For if these *t* be in you, and	2Pet 1:8	
he that lacketh these *t* is blind	2Pet 1:9	
for if ye do these *t*, ye shall	2Pet 1:10	
always in remembrance of these *t*	2Pet 1:12	
these *t* always in remembrance	2Pet 1:15	
speak evil of the *t* that they	2Pet 2:12	
all *t* continue as they were from	2Pet 3:4	
all these *t* shall be dissolved	2Pet 3:11	
seeing that ye look for such *t*	2Pet 3:14	
speaking in them of these *t*	2Pet 3:16	
in which are some *t* hard to be	2Pet 3:16	
seeing ye know these *t* before	2Pet 3:17	
these *t* write we unto you, that	1Jn 1:4	
these *t* write I unto you, that ye	1Jn 2:1	
neither the *t* that are in the	1Jn 2:15	
the Holy One, and ye know all *t*	1Jn 2:20	
These *t* have I written unto you	1Jn 2:26	
anointing teacheth you of all *t*	1Jn 2:27	
than our heart, and knoweth all *t*	1Jn 3:20	
do those *t* that are pleasing in	1Jn 3:22	
These *t* have I written unto you	1Jn 5:13	
not those *t* which we have wrought	2Jn 8	
Having many *t* to write unto you,	2Jn 12	
I wish above all *t* that thou	3Jn 2	
I had many *t* to write, but I will	3Jn 13	
of those *t* which they know not	Jude 10	
beasts, in those *t* they corrupt	Jude 10	
to shew unto his servants *t* which	Rev 1:1	
Christ, and of all *t* that he saw	Rev 1:2	
keep those *t* which are written	Rev 1:3	
Write the *t* which thou hast seen,	Rev 1:19	
the *t* which are	Rev 1:19	
the *t* which shall be hereafter	Rev 1:19	
These *t* saith he that holdeth the	Rev 2:1	
These *t* saith the first and the	Rev 2:8	
Fear none of those *t* which thou	Rev 2:10	
These *t* saith he which hath the	Rev 2:12	
But I have a few *t* against thee	Rev 2:14	
to eat *t* sacrificed unto idols,	Rev 2:14	
These *t* saith the Son of God, who	Rev 2:18	
I have a few *t* against thee	Rev 2:20	
to eat *t* sacrificed unto idols	Rev 2:20	
These *t* saith he that hath the	Rev 3:1	
and strengthen the *t* which remain	Rev 3:2	
These *t* saith he that is holy, he	Rev 3:7	
These *t* saith the Amen, the	Rev 3:14	
I will shew thee *t* which must be	Rev 4:1	
for thou hast created all *t*	Rev 4:11	
after these *t* I saw four angels	Rev 7:1	
Seal up those *t* which the seven	Rev 10:4	
the *t* that therein are, and the	Rev 10:6	
the *t* that therein are, and the	Rev 10:6	
the *t* which are therein, that	Rev 10:6	
unto him a mouth speaking great *t*	Rev 13:5	
after these *t* I saw another angel	Rev 18:1	
all *t* which were dainty and goodly	Rev 18:14	
The merchants of these *t*, which	Rev 18:15	
after these *t* I heard a great	Rev 19:1	
dead were judged out of those *t*	Rev 20:12	
for the former *t* are passed away	Rev 21:4	
said, Behold, I make all *t* new	Rev 21:5	
overcometh shall inherit all *t*	Rev 21:7	
the *t* which must shortly be done	Rev 22:6	
And I John saw these *t*, and heard	Rev 22:8	
the angel which shewed me these *t*	Rev 22:8	
unto you these *t* in the churches	Rev 22:16	
If any man shall add unto these *t*	Rev 22:18	
from the *t* which are written in	Rev 22:19	
He which testifieth these *t* saith	Rev 22:20	

THINGS'

For which *t* sake the wrath of God	Col 3:6	

THINK

But *t* on me when it shall be well	Gen 40:14	2142
them marry to whom they *t* best	Num 36:6	5869
to *t* that all the king's sons are	2Sa 13:33	559
now ye *t* to withstand the kingdom	2Chr 13:8	559
T upon me, my God, for good,	Neh 5:19	2142
that thou and the Jews *t* to rebel	Neh 6:6	2803
t thou upon Tobiah and Sanballat	Neh 6:14	2142
T not with thyself that thou	Est 4:13	1819
why then should I *t* upon a maid	Job 31:1	995
one would *t* the deep to be hoary	Job 41:32	2803
though a wise man *t* to know it	Eccl 8:17	559
so, neither doth his heart *t* so	Is 10:7	2803
Which *t* to cause my people to	Jer 23:27	2803
the thoughts that I *t* toward you	Jer 29:11	2803
thou shalt *t* an evil thought	Eze 38:10	2803
t to change times and laws	Dan 7:25	5452
if so be that God will *t* upon us	Jonah 1:6	6245
And I said unto them, If ye *t* good	Zec 11:12	5869
t not to say within yourselves,	Mt 3:9	*1380*
T not that I am come to destroy	Mt 5:17	*3543*
for they *t* that they shall be	Mt 6:7	*1380*
Wherefore *t* ye evil in your	Mt 9:4	*1760*
T not that I am come to send	Mt 10:34	*3543*
How *t* ye?	Mt 18:12	*1380*
But what *t* ye	Mt 21:28	*1380*
Saying, What *t* ye of Christ	Mt 22:42	*1380*
as ye *t* not the Son of man cometh	Mt 24:44	*1380*
What *t* ye?	Mt 26:66	*1380*
what *t* ye?	Mk 14:64	*5316*
cometh at an hour when ye *t* not	Lk 12:40	*1380*
t ye that they were sinners above	Lk 13:4	*1380*
for in them ye *t* ye have eternal	Jn 5:39	*1380*
Do not *t* that I will accuse you	Jn 5:45	*1380*
stood in the temple, What *t* ye	Jn 11:56	*1380*
will *t* that he doeth God service	Jn 16:2	*1380*
he said, Whom *t* ye that I am	Acts 13:25	*5282*
we ought not to *t* that the	Acts 17:29	*3543*
I *t* myself happy, king Agrippa,	Acts 26:2	*2233*
not to *t* of himself more highly	Rom 12:3	*5252*
more highly than he ought to *t*	Rom 12:3	*5426*
but to *t* soberly, according as	Rom 12:3	*5426*
to *t* of men above that which is	1Cor 4:6	*5426*
For I *t* that God hath set forth	1Cor 4:9	*1380*
But if any man *t* that he behaveth	1Cor 7:36	*3543*
I *t* also that I have the Spirit	1Cor 7:40	*1380*
if any man *t* that he knoweth any	1Cor 8:2	*1380*
which we *t* to be less honourable,	1Cor 12:23	*1380*
If any man *t* himself to be a	1Cor 14:37	*1380*
to *t* any thing as of ourselves	2Cor 3:5	*3049*
wherewith I *t* to be bold against	2Cor 10:2	*3049*
which *t* of us as if we walked	2Cor 10:2	*3049*
let him of himself *t* this again	2Cor 10:7	*3049*
Let such an one *t* this, that,	2Cor 10:11	*3049*
say again, Let no man *t* me a fool	2Cor 11:16	*1380*
lest any man should *t* of me above	2Cor 12:6	*3049*
t ye that we excuse ourselves	2Cor 12:19	*1380*
For if a man *t* himself to be	Gal 6:3	*1380*
above all that we ask or *t*	Eph 3:20	*3539*
meet for me to *t* this of you all	Phil 1:7	*5426*
be any praise, *t* on these things	Phil 4:8	*3049*
For let not that man *t* that he	Jas 1:7	*3633*
Do ye *t* that the scripture saith	Jas 4:5	*1380*
Wherein they *t* it strange that ye	1Pet 4:4	
t it not strange concerning the	1Pet 4:12	
I *t* it meet, as long as I am in	2Pet 1:13	*2233*

THINKEST

T thou that David doth honour thy	2Sa 10:3	5869
T thou that David doth honour thy	1Chr 19:3	5869
T thou this to be right, that	Job 35:2	2803
him, saying, What *t* thou, Simon	Mt 17:25	*1380*
Tell us therefore, What *t* thou	Mt 22:17	*1380*
T thou that I cannot now pray to	Mt 26:53	*1380*
t thou, was neighbour unto him	Lk 10:36	*1380*
to hear of thee what thou *t*	Acts 28:22	*5426*
t thou this, O man, that judgest	Rom 2:3	*3049*

THINKETH

Me *t* the running of the foremost	2Sa 18:27	7200
yet the Lord *t* upon me	Ps 40:17	2803
For as he *t* in his heart, so is	Prov 23:7	8176
Wherefore let him that *t* he	1Cor 10:12	*1380*
is not easily provoked, *t* no evil	1Cor 13:5	*3049*
If any other man *t* that he hath	Phil 3:4	*1380*

THINKING

t to have brought good tidings, I	2Sa 4:10	
t, David cannot come in	2Sa 5:6	559

THIRD

and the morning were the *t* day	Gen 1:13	7992
the name of the *t* river is	Gen 2:14	7992
t stories shalt thou make it	Gen 6:16	7992
Then on the *t* day Abraham lifted	Gen 22:4	7992
on the *t* day that Jacob was fled	Gen 31:22	7992
commanded he the second, and the *t*	Gen 32:19	7992
And it came to pass on the *t* day	Gen 34:25	7992
And it came to pass the *t* day	Gen 40:20	7992
Joseph said unto them the *t* day	Gen 42:18	7992
children of the *t* generation	Gen 50:23	8029
In the *t* month, when the children	Ex 19:1	7992
And be ready against the *t* day	Ex 19:11	7992
for the *t* day the LORD will come	Ex 19:11	7992
Be ready against the *t* day	Ex 19:15	7969
pass on the *t* day in the morning	Ex 19:16	7992
upon the children unto the *t*	Ex 20:5	8029
the *t* row a ligure, an agate, and	Ex 28:19	7992
children's children, unto the *t*	Ex 34:7	8029
And the *t* row, a ligure, an agate,	Ex 39:12	7992
t day shall be burnt with fire	Lev 7:17	7992
be eaten at all on the *t* day	Lev 7:18	7992
if ought remain until the *t* day	Lev 19:6	7992
it be eaten at all on the *t* day	Lev 19:7	7992
shall go forward in the *t* rank	Num 2:24	7992
On the *t* day Eliab the son of	Num 7:24	7992
upon the children unto the *t*	Num 14:18	8029
with the *t* part of an hin of oil	Num 15:6	7992
the *t* part of an hin of wine	Num 15:7	7992
himself with it on the *t* day	Num 19:12	7992
he purify not himself the *t* day	Num 19:12	7992
upon the unclean on the *t* day	Num 19:19	7992
the *t* part of an hin unto a ram,	Num 28:14	7992
on the *t* day eleven bullocks, two	Num 29:20	7992
and your captives on the *t* day	Num 31:19	7992
upon the children unto the *t*	Deut 5:9	8029
of the LORD in their *t* generation	Deut 23:8	7992
of thine increase the *t* year	Deut 26:12	7992

unto their cities on the *t* day ... Josh 9:17 7992
the *t* lot came up for the ... Josh 19:10 7992
children of Benjamin on the *t* day ... Judg 20:30 7992
called Samuel again the *t* time ... 1Sa 3:8 7992
him Abinadab, and the *t* Shammah ... 1Sa 17:13 7992
sent messengers again the *t* time ... 1Sa 19:21 7992
the field unto the *t* day at even ... 1Sa 20:5 7992
to morrow any time, or the *t* day ... 1Sa 20:12 7992
were come to Ziklag on the *t* day ... 1Sa 30:1 7992
It came even to pass on the *t* day ... 2Sa 1:2 7992
and the *t*, Absalom the son of ... 2Sa 3:3 7992
David sent forth a *t* part of the ... 2Sa 18:2 7992
a *t* part under the hand of ... 2Sa 18:2 7992
a *t* part under the hand of Ittai ... 2Sa 18:2 7992
it came to pass the *t* day after ... 1Kin 3:18 7992
the *t* was seven cubits broad ... 1Kin 6:6 7992
and out of the middle into the *t* ... 1Kin 6:8 7992
people came to Rehoboam the *t* day ... 1Kin 12:12 7992
Come to me again the *t* day ... 1Kin 12:12 7992
Even in the *t* year of Asa king of ... 1Kin 15:28 7969
In the *t* year of Asa king of ... 1Kin 15:33 7969
LORD came to Elijah in the *t* year ... 1Kin 18:1 7992
And he said, Do it the *t* time ... 1Kin 18:34 8027
And they did it the *t* time ... 1Kin 18:34 8027
And it came to pass in the *t* year ... 1Kin 22:2 7992
of the *t* fifty with his fifty ... 2Kin 1:13 7992
the *t* captain of fifty went up, ... 2Kin 1:13 7992
A *t* part of you that enter in on ... 2Kin 11:5 7992
a *t* part shall be at the gate of ... 2Kin 11:6 7992
a *t* part at the gate behind the ... 2Kin 11:6 7992
Now it came to pass in the *t* year ... 2Kin 18:1 7969
in the *t* year sow ye, and reap, and ... 2Kin 19:29 7992
on the *t* day thou shalt go up ... 2Kin 20:5 7992
the house of the LORD the *t* day ... 2Kin 20:8 7992
the second, and Shimma the *t* ... 1Chr 2:13 7992
The *t*, Absalom the son of Maachah ... 1Chr 3:2 7992
the *t* Zedekiah, the fourth ... 1Chr 3:15 7992
the second, and Aharah the *t* ... 1Chr 8:1 7992
the second, and Eliphelet the *t* ... 1Chr 8:39 7992
Obadiah the second, Eliab the *t* ... 1Chr 12:9 7992
the second, Jahaziel the *t* ... 1Chr 23:19 7992
The *t* to Harim, the fourth to ... 1Chr 24:8 7992
the second, Jahaziel the *t* ... 1Chr 24:23 7992
The *t* to Zaccur, he, his sons, and ... 1Chr 25:10 7992
the second, Zebadiah the *t* ... 1Chr 26:2 7992
Jehozabad the second, Joah the *t* ... 1Chr 26:4 7992
the second, Tebaliah the *t* ... 1Chr 26:11 7992
The *t* captain of the host for the ... 1Chr 27:5 7992
captain of the host for the *t* ... 1Chr 27:5 7992
came to Rehoboam on the *t* day ... 2Chr 10:12 7992
Come again to me on the *t* day ... 2Chr 10:12 7992
at Jerusalem in the *t* month ... 2Chr 15:10 7992
Also in the *t* year of his reign ... 2Chr 17:7 7969
A *t* part of you entering on the ... 2Chr 23:4 7992
a *t* part shall be at the king's ... 2Chr 23:5 7992
a *t* part at the gate of the ... 2Chr 23:5 7992
both the second year, and the *t* ... 2Chr 27:5 7992
In the *t* month they began to lay ... 2Chr 31:7 7992
on the *t* day of the month Adar ... Ezr 6:15 8531
the *t* part of a shekel for the ... Neh 10:32 7992
In the *t* year of his reign, he ... Est 1:3 7969
Now it came to pass on the *t* day ... Est 5:1 7992
at that time in the *t* month ... Est 8:9 7992
and the name of the *t*, ... Job 42:14 7992
shall Israel be the *t* with Egypt ... Is 19:24 7992
in the *t* year sow ye, and reap, and ... Is 37:30 7992
t entry that is in the house of ... Jer 38:14 7992
Thou shalt burn with fire a *t* ... Eze 5:2 7992
and thou shalt take a *t* part ... Eze 5:2 7992
a *t* part thou shalt scatter in ... Eze 5:2 7992
A *t* part of thee shall die with ... Eze 5:12 7992
a *t* part shall fall by the sword ... Eze 5:12 7992
I will scatter a *t* part into all ... Eze 5:12 7992
the *t* the face of a lion, and the ... Eze 10:14 7992
the sword be doubled the *t* time ... Eze 21:14 7992
the eleventh year, in the *t* month ... Eze 31:1 7992
the *t* part of an hin of oil, to ... Eze 46:14 7992
In the *t* year of the reign of ... Dan 1:1 7969
another *t* kingdom of brass, which ... Dan 2:39 8523
shall be the *t* ruler in the ... Dan 5:7 8523
shalt be the *t* ruler in the ... Dan 5:16 8531
be the *t* ruler in the kingdom ... Dan 5:29 8531
In the *t* year of the reign of ... Dan 8:1 7969
In the *t* year of Cyrus king of ... Dan 10:1 7969
in the *t* day he will raise us up, ... Hos 6:2 7992
in the *t* chariot white horses ... Zec 6:3 7992
but the *t* shall be left therein ... Zec 13:8 7992
I will bring the *t* part through ... Zec 13:9 7992
and be raised again the *t* day ... Mt 16:21 5154
the *t* day he shall be raised ... Mt 17:23 5154
And he went out about the *t* hour ... Mt 20:3 5154
the *t* day he shall rise again ... Mt 20:19 5154
the second also, and the *t* ... Mt 22:26 5154
away again, and prayed the *t* time ... Mt 26:44 5154
be made sure until the *t* day ... Mt 27:64 5154
killed, he shall rise the *t* day ... Mk 9:31 5154
the *t* day he shall rise again ... Mk 10:34 5154
and the *t* likewise ... Mk 12:21 5154
And he cometh the *t* time, and saith ... Mk 14:41 5154
And it was the *t* hour, and they ... Mk 15:25 5154
be slain, and be raised the *t* day ... Lk 9:22 5154
watch, or come in the *t* watch ... Lk 12:38 5154
the *t* day I shall be perfected ... Lk 13:32 5154
the *t* day he shall rise again ... Lk 18:33 5154
And again he sent a *t* ... Lk 20:12 5154
And the *t* took her ... Lk 20:31 5154
And he said unto them the *t* time ... Lk 23:22 5154
and the *t* day rise again ... Lk 24:7 5154
to day is the *t* day since these ... Lk 24:21 5154
to rise from the dead the *t* day ... Lk 24:46 5154
the *t* day there was a marriage in ... Jn 2:1 5154
This is now the *t* time that Jesus ... Jn 21:14 5154
He saith unto him the *t* time ... Jn 21:17 5154
he said unto him the *t* time ... Jn 21:17 5154
it is but the *t* hour of the day ... Acts 2:15 5154
Him God raised up the *t* day ... Acts 10:40 5154
and fell down from the *t* loft ... Acts 20:9 5152
at the *t* hour of the night ... Acts 23:23 5154
the *t* day we cast out with our ... Acts 27:19 5154
that he rose again the *t* day ... 1Cor 15:4 5154
an one caught up to the *t* heaven ... 2Cor 12:2 5154
the *t* time I am ready to come to ... 2Cor 12:14 5154
This is the *t* time I am coming to ... 2Cor 13:1 5154
the *t* beast had a face as a man, ... Rev 4:7 5154
And when he had opened the *t* seal ... Rev 6:5 5154
I heard the *t* beast say ... Rev 6:5 5154
the *t* part of trees was burnt up, ... Rev 8:7 5154
the *t* part of the sea became ... Rev 8:8 5154
the *t* part of the creatures which ... Rev 8:9 5154
the *t* part of the ships were ... Rev 8:9 5154
the *t* angel sounded, and there ... Rev 8:10 5154
it fell upon the *t* part of the ... Rev 8:10 5154
the *t* part of the waters became ... Rev 8:11 5154
the *t* part of the sun was smitten ... Rev 8:12 5154
the *t* part of the moon, and the ... Rev 8:12 5154
moon, and the *t* part of the stars ... Rev 8:12 5154
so as the *t* part of them was ... Rev 8:12 5154
day shone not for a *t* part of it ... Rev 8:12 5154
for to slay the *t* part of men ... Rev 9:15 5154
was the *t* part of men killed ... Rev 9:18 5154
behold, the *t* woe cometh quickly ... Rev 11:14 5154
his tail drew the *t* part of the ... Rev 12:4 5154
the *t* angel followed them, saying ... Rev 14:9 5154
the *t* angel poured out his vial ... Rev 16:4 5154
the *t*, a chalcedony ... Rev 21:19 5154

THIRDLY

t teachers, after that miracles, ... 1Cor 12:28 5154

THIRST

our children and our cattle with *t* ... Ex 17:3 6772
against thee, in hunger, and in *t* ... Deut 28:48 6772
heart, to add drunkenness to *t* ... Deut 29:19 6771
and now shall I die for *t*, and fall ... Judg 15:18 6772
to die by famine and by *t*, saying, ... 2Chr 32:11 6772
them out of the rock for their *t* ... Neh 9:15 6772
and gavest them water for their *t* ... Neh 9:20 6772
their winepresses, and suffer *t* ... Job 24:11 6770
in my *t* they gave me vinegar to ... Ps 69:21 6772
the wild asses quench their *t* ... Ps 104:11 6772
their multitude dried up with *t* ... Is 5:13 6772
and their tongue faileth for *t* ... Is 41:17 6772
They shall not hunger nor *t* ... Is 49:10 6770
there is no water, and dieth for *t* ... Is 50:2 6772
unshod, and thy throat from *t* ... Jer 2:25 6773
down from thy glory, and sit in *t* ... Jer 48:18 6772
to the roof of his mouth for *t* ... Lam 4:4 6772
a dry land, and slay her with *t* ... Hos 2:3 6772
nor a *t* for water, but of hearing ... Amos 8:11 6772
virgins and young men faint for *t* ... Amos 8:13 6772
hunger and *t* after righteousness ... Mt 5:6 1372
of this water shall *t* again ... Jn 4:13 1372
I shall give him shall never *t* ... Jn 4:14 1372
give me this water, that I *t* not ... Jn 4:15 1372
believeth on me shall never *t* ... Jn 6:35 1372
and cried, saying, If any man *t* ... Jn 7:37 1372
might be fulfilled, saith, I *t* ... Jn 19:28 1372
if he *t*, give him drink ... Rom 12:20 1372
present hour we both hunger, and *t* ... 1Cor 4:11 1372
watchings often, in hunger and *t* ... 2Cor 11:27 1373
no more, neither *t* any more ... Rev 7:16 1372

THIRSTED

the people *t* there for water ... Ex 17:3 6770
they *t* not when he led them ... Is 48:21 6770

THIRSTETH

My soul *t* for God, for the living ... Ps 42:2 6770
my soul *t* for thee, my flesh ... Ps 63:1 6770
my soul *t* after thee, as a ... Ps 143:6
Ho, every one that *t*, come ye to ... Is 55:1 6771

THIRSTY

for I am *t* ... Judg 4:19 6770
people is hungry, and weary, and *t* ... 2Sa 17:29 6771
t land, where no water is ... Ps 63:1
Hungry and *t*, their soul fainted ... Ps 107:5 6771
thirsteth after thee, as a *t* land ... Ps 143:6
and if he be *t*, give him water to ... Prov 25:21 6771
As cold waters to a *t* soul ... Prov 25:25
brought water to him that was *t* ... Is 21:14 6771
or as when a *t* man dreameth ... Is 29:8 6771
cause the drink of the *t* to fail ... Is 32:6 6771
the *t* land springs of water ... Is 35:7 6774
pour water upon him that is *t* ... Is 44:3 6771
shall drink, but ye shall be *t* ... Is 65:13 6770
wilderness, in a dry and *t* ground ... Eze 19:13 6772
I was *t*, and ye gave me drink ... Mt 25:35 1372
or *t*, and gave thee drink ... Mt 25:37 1372
I was *t*, and ye gave me no drink ... Mt 25:42 1372

THIRTEEN

Ishmael his son was *t* years old ... Gen 17:25
two hundred and threescore and *t* ... Num 3:43 7969
t of the firstborn of the ... Num 3:46 7969
t young bullocks, two rams, and ... Num 29:13
every bullock of the *t* bullocks ... Num 29:14
t cities and their villages ... Josh 19:6
the tribe of Benjamin, *t* cities ... Josh 21:4
of Manasseh in Bashan, *t* cities ... Josh 21:6
were *t* cities with their suburbs ... Josh 21:19
to their families were *t* cities ... Josh 21:33
building his own house *t* years ... 1Kin 7:1
their families were *t* cities ... 1Chr 6:60
of Manasseh in Bashan, *t* cities ... 1Chr 6:62
sons and brethren of Hosah were *t* ... 1Chr 26:11
the length of the gate, *t* cubits ... Eze 40:11

THIRTEENTH

in the *t* year they rebelled ... Gen 14:4
The *t* to Huppah, the fourteenth ... 1Chr 24:13
The *t* to Shubael, he, his sons, ... 1Chr 25:20
on the *t* day of the first month ... Est 3:12
even upon the *t* day of the ... Est 3:13
upon the *t* day of the twelfth ... Est 8:12
on the *t* day of the same, when ... Est 9:1
On the *t* day of the month Adar ... Est 9:17
together on the *t* day thereof ... Est 9:18
in the *t* year of his reign ... Jer 1:2
From the *t* year of Josiah the son ... Jer 25:3

THIRTIETH

t year of Uzziah king of Judah ... 2Kin 15:13 7970
t year of Azariah king of Judah ... 2Kin 15:17 7970
t year of the captivity of ... 2Kin 25:27 7970
t year of the reign of Asa ... 2Chr 15:19 7970
t year of the reign of Asa Baasha ... 2Chr 16:1 7970
t year of Artaxerxes the king, ... Neh 5:14 7970
t year of Artaxerxes king of ... Neh 13:6 7970
t year of the captivity of ... Jer 52:31 7970
Now it came to pass in the *t* year ... Eze 1:1 7970

THIRTY

t years, and begat a son in his ... Gen 5:3 7970
were nine hundred and *t* years ... Gen 5:5 7970
t years, and begat sons and ... Gen 5:16 7970
and the height of it *t* cubits ... Gen 6:15 7970
five and *t* years, and begat Salah ... Gen 11:12 7970
And Salah lived *t* years, and begat ... Gen 11:14 7970
four and *t* years, and begat Peleg ... Gen 11:16 7970
t years, and begat sons and ... Gen 11:17 7970
And Peleg lived *t* years, and begat ... Gen 11:18 7970
two and *t* years, and begat Serug ... Gen 11:20 7970
And Serug lived *t* years, and begat ... Gen 11:22 7970
there shall *t* be found there ... Gen 18:30 7970
will not do it, if I find *t* there ... Gen 18:30 7970
life of Ishmael, an hundred and *t* ... Gen 25:17 7970
T milch camels with their colts, ... Gen 32:15 7970
Joseph was *t* years old when he ... Gen 41:46 7970
his sons and his daughters were *t* ... Gen 46:15 7970
are an hundred and *t* years ... Gen 47:9 7970
life of Levi were an hundred *t* ... Ex 6:16 7970
life of Kohath were an hundred *t* ... Ex 6:18 7970
of Amram were an hundred and *t* ... Ex 6:20 7970
was four hundred and *t* years ... Ex 12:40 7970
t years, even the selfsame day it ... Ex 12:41 7970
their master *t* shekels of silver ... Ex 21:32 7970
of one curtain shall be *t* cubits ... Ex 26:8 7970
of one curtain was *t* cubits ... Ex 36:15 7970
t shekels, after the shekel of ... Ex 38:24 7970
of her purifying three and *t* days ... Lev 12:4 7970
thy estimation shall be *t* shekels ... Lev 27:4 7970
of the tribe of Manasseh, were *t* ... Num 1:35 7970
of the tribe of Benjamin, were *t* ... Num 1:37 7970
were numbered of them, were *t* ... Num 2:21 7970
were numbered of them, were *t* ... Num 2:23 7970
From *t* years old and upward even ... Num 4:3 7970
From *t* years old and upward until ... Num 4:23 7970
From *t* years old and upward even ... Num 4:30 7970
From *t* years old and upward even ... Num 4:35 7970
From *t* years old and upward even ... Num 4:39 7970
two thousand and six hundred and *t* ... Num 4:40 7970
From *t* years old and upward even ... Num 4:43 7970
From *t* years old and upward even ... Num 4:47 7970
t shekels, one silver bowl of ... Num 7:13 7970
t shekels, one silver bowl of ... Num 7:19 7970
t shekels, one silver bowl of ... Num 7:25 7970
t shekels, one silver bowl of ... Num 7:31 7970
t shekels, one silver bowl of ... Num 7:37 7970
t shekels, a silver bowl of ... Num 7:43 7970
t shekels, one silver bowl of ... Num 7:49 7970
t shekels, one silver bowl of ... Num 7:55 7970
t shekels, one silver bowl of ... Num 7:61 7970
t shekels, one silver bowl of ... Num 7:67 7970
t shekels, one silver bowl of ... Num 7:73 7970
t shekels, one silver bowl of ... Num 7:79 7970
t shekels, each bowl seventy ... Num 7:85 7970
they mourned for Aaron *t* days ... Num 20:29 7970
thousand and seven hundred and *t* ... Num 26:7 7970
that were numbered of them, *t* ... Num 26:37 7970
and a thousand seven hundred and *t* ... Num 26:51 7970
And *t* and two thousand persons in ... Num 31:35 7970
t thousand and five hundred sheep ... Num 31:36 7970
And the beeves were *t* and six ... Num 31:38 7970
And the asses were *t* thousand ... Num 31:39 7970
of which the LORD's tribute was *t* ... Num 31:40 7970
t thousand and seven thousand and ... Num 31:43 7970
And *t* and six thousand beeves, ... Num 31:44 7970
t thousand asses and five hundred, ... Num 31:45 7970
come over the brook Zered, was *t* ... Deut 2:14 7970
in the plains of Moab *t* days ... Deut 34:8 7970
men of Ai smote of them about *t* ... Josh 7:5 7970
Joshua chose out *t* thousand ... Josh 8:3 7970
all the kings *t* and one ... Josh 12:24 7970
he had *t* sons that rode ... Judg 10:4 7970
sons that rode on *t* ass colts ... Judg 10:4 7970
ass colts, and they had *t* cities ... Judg 10:4 7970
And he had *t* sons ... Judg 12:9 7970
t daughters, whom he sent abroad, ... Judg 12:9 7970
took in *t* daughters from abroad ... Judg 12:9 7970
sons and *t* nephews, that rode on ... Judg 12:14 7970
that they brought *t* companions to ... Judg 14:11 7970
then I will give you *t* sheets ... Judg 14:12 7970
sheets and *t* change of garments ... Judg 14:12 7970
then shall ye give me *t* sheets ... Judg 14:13 7970
sheets and *t* change of garments ... Judg 14:13 7970
slew *t* men of them, and took their ... Judg 14:19 7970
the field, about *t* men of Israel ... Judg 20:31 7970
the men of Israel about *t* persons ... Judg 20:39 7970
fell of Israel *t* thousand footmen ... 1Sa 4:10 7970
which were about *t* persons ... 1Sa 9:22 7970
and the men of Judah *t* thousand ... 1Sa 11:8 7970
t thousand chariots, and six ... 1Sa 13:5 7970
David was *t* years old when he ... 2Sa 5:4 7970
and in Jerusalem he reigned *t* ... 2Sa 5:5 7970
chosen men of Israel, *t* thousand ... 2Sa 6:1 7970

three of the *t* chief went down,	2Sa 23:13	7970
He was more honourable than the *t*	2Sa 23:23	7970
brother of Joab was one of the *t*	2Sa 23:24	7970
t and seven in all	2Sa 23:39	7970
years reigned he in Hebron, and *t*	1Kin 2:11	7970
day was *t* measures of fine flour	1Kin 4:22	7970
and the levy was *t* thousand men	1Kin 5:13	7970
and the height thereof *t* cubits	1Kin 6:2	7970
and the height thereof *t* cubits	1Kin 7:2	7970
and the breadth thereof *t* cubits	1Kin 7:6	7970
a line of *t* cubits did compass it	1Kin 7:23	7970
In the *t* and first year of Asa	1Kin 16:23	7970
And in the *t* and eighth year of Asa	1Kin 16:29	7970
and there were *t* and two kings with	1Kin 20:1	7970
and they were two hundred and *t* two.	1Kin 20:15	7970
pavilions, he and the kings, the *t*	1Kin 20:16	7970
the king of Syria commanded his *t*	1Kin 22:31	7970
Jehoshaphat was *t* and five years	1Kin 22:42	7970
T and two years old was he when he	2Kin 8:17	7970
In the *t* and seventh year of Joash	2Kin 13:10	7970
In the *t* and eighth year of	2Kin 15:8	7970
of silver and *t* talents of gold	2Kin 18:14	7970
began to reign, and he reigned *t*	2Kin 22:1	7970
and in Jerusalem he reigned *t*	1Chr 3:4	7970
for war, six and *t* thousand men	1Chr 7:4	7970
twenty and two thousand and *t*	1Chr 7:7	7970
Now three of the *t* captains went	1Chr 11:15	7970
he was honourable among the *t*	1Chr 11:25	7970
of the Reubenites, and *t* with him,	1Chr 11:42	7970
among the *t*, and over the *t*	1Chr 12:4	7970
with them with shield and spear *t*	1Chr 12:34	7970
and his brethren an hundred and *t*	1Chr 15:7	7970
So they hired *t* and two thousand	1Chr 19:7	7970
numbered from the age of *t* years	1Chr 23:3	7970
by their polls, man by man, was *t*	1Chr 23:3	7970
among the *t*, and above the *t*	1Chr 27:6	7970
years reigned he in Hebron, and *t*	1Chr 29:27	7970
before the house two pillars of *t*	2Chr 3:15	7970
a line of *t* cubits did compass it	2Chr 4:2	7970
And Asa in the *t* and ninth year of	2Chr 16:12	7970
he was *t* and five years old when	2Chr 20:31	7970
Jehoram was *t* and two years old	2Chr 21:5	7970
T and two years old was he when he	2Chr 21:20	7970
t years old was he when he died	2Chr 24:15	7970
in Jerusalem one and *t* years	2Chr 34:1	7970
to the number of *t* thousand	2Chr 35:7	7970
t chargers of gold, a thousand	Ezr 1:9	7970
T basons of gold, silver basons	Ezr 1:10	7970
thousand and six hundred and *t*	Ezr 2:35	7970
of Shobai, in all an hundred *t*	Ezr 2:42	7970
seven thousand three hundred *t*	Ezr 2:65	7970
Their horses were seven hundred *t*	Ezr 2:66	7970
Their camels, four hundred *t*	Ezr 2:67	7970
three thousand nine hundred and *t*	Neh 7:38	7970
children of Shobai, an hundred *t*	Neh 7:45	7970
seven thousand three hundred *t*	Neh 7:67	7970
Their horses, seven hundred *t*	Neh 7:68	7970
Their camels, four hundred *t*	Neh 7:69	7970
hundred and *t* priests' garments	Neh 7:70	7970
in unto the king these *t* days	Est 4:11	7970
Take from hence *t* men with thee	Jer 38:10	7970
from Jerusalem eight hundred *t*	Jer 52:29	7970
t chambers were upon the pavement	Eze 40:17	7970
one over another, and *t* in order	Eze 41:6	7970
of forty cubits long and *t* broad	Eze 46:22	7970
of any God or man for *t* days	Dan 6:7	8533
of any God or man within *t* days	Dan 6:12	8533
three hundred and five and *t* days	Dan 12:12	7970
for my price *t* pieces of silver	Zec 11:12	7970
I took the *t* pieces of silver, and	Zec 11:13	7970
hundredfold, some sixty, some *t*	Mt 13:23	5144
with him for *t* pieces of silver	Mt 26:15	5144
brought again the *t* pieces of	Mt 27:3	5144
they took the *t* pieces of silver,	Mt 27:9	5144
and brought forth, some *t*, and some	Mk 4:8	5144
began to be about *t* years of age	Lk 3:23	5144
there, which had an infirmity *t*	Jn 5:5	5144
five and twenty or *t* furlongs	Jn 6:19	5144
t years after, cannot disannul,	Gal 3:17	5144

THIRTYFOLD

some sixtyfold, some *t*	Mt 13:8	5144
it, and bring forth fruit, some *t*	Mk 4:20	5144

THIS

T is now bone of my bones, and	Gen 2:23	2063
What is *t* that thou hast done	Gen 3:13	2063
serpent, Because thou hast done *t*	Gen 3:14	2063
thou hast driven me out *t* day	Gen 4:14	
T is the book of the generations	Gen 5:1	2088
saying, *T* same shall comfort us	Gen 5:29	2088
t is the fashion which thou shalt	Gen 6:15	2088
before me in *t* generation	Gen 7:1	2088
T is the token of the covenant	Gen 9:12	2063
T is the token of the covenant,	Gen 9:17	
and *t* they begin to do	Gen 11:6	2088
Unto thy seed will I give *t* land	Gen 12:7	2063
they shall say, *T* is his wife	Gen 12:12	2063
What is *t* that thou hast done	Gen 12:18	2063
my house is *t* Eliezer of Damascus	Gen 15:2	1931
T shall not be thine heir	Gen 15:4	2088
to give thee *t* land to inherit it	Gen 15:7	2063
Unto thy seed have I given *t* land	Gen 15:18	2063
T is my covenant, which ye shall	Gen 17:10	2063
at *t* set time in the next year	Gen 17:21	2088
from thee to do after *t* manner	Gen 18:25	2088
and I will speak yet but *t* once	Gen 18:32	6471
men which came in to thee *t* night	Gen 19:5	
T one fellow came in to sojourn,	Gen 19:9	
city, bring them out of *t* place	Gen 19:12	
For we will destroy *t* place	Gen 19:13	2088
said, Up, get you out of *t* place	Gen 19:14	2088
for the LORD will destroy *t* city	Gen 19:14	
t city is near to flee unto, and	Gen 19:20	2063
thee concerning *t* thing also	Gen 19:21	2088
that I will not overthrow *t* city	Gen 19:21	
make him drink wine *t* night also	Gen 19:34	
father of the Moabites unto *t* day	Gen 19:37	
the children of Ammon unto *t* day	Gen 19:38	
of my hands have I done *t*	Gen 20:5	2063
I know that thou didst *t* in the	Gen 20:6	2063
thou, that thou hast done *t* thing	Gen 20:10	2088
the fear of God is not in *t* place	Gen 20:11	2088
T is thy kindness which thou	Gen 20:13	2088
Cast out *t* bondwoman and her son	Gen 21:10	2063
for the son of *t* bondwoman shall	Gen 21:10	2063
I wot not who hath done *t* thing	Gen 21:26	2088
me, that I have digged *t* well	Gen 21:30	
as it is said to *t* day, In the	Gen 22:14	
because thou hast done *t* thing	Gen 22:16	
And after *t*, Abraham buried Sarah	Gen 23:19	
willing to follow me unto *t* land	Gen 24:5	
Unto thy seed will I give *t* land	Gen 24:7	
shalt be clear from *t* my oath	Gen 24:8	
thee, send me good speed *t* day	Gen 24:12	
thou be clear from *t* my oath	Gen 24:41	
I came *t* day unto the well, and	Gen 24:42	
unto her, Wilt thou go with *t* man	Gen 24:58	2088
What man is *t* that walketh in the	Gen 24:65	1976
Sell me *t* day thy birthright	Gen 25:31	
what profit shall *t* birthright do	Gen 25:32	2088
And Jacob said, Swear to me *t* day	Gen 25:33	
Sojourn in *t* land, and I will be	Gen 26:3	2063
What is *t* thou hast done unto us	Gen 26:10	2063
He that toucheth *t* man or his	Gen 26:11	2088
the city is Beer-sheba unto *t* day	Gen 26:33	2088
will bring thee again into *t* land	Gen 28:15	2063
Surely the LORD is in *t* place	Gen 28:16	2088
and said, How dreadful is *t* place	Gen 28:17	2088
t is none other but the house of	Gen 28:17	2088
God, and *t* is the gate of heaven	Gen 28:17	2088
will keep me in *t* way that I go	Gen 28:20	2088
t stone, which I have set for a	Gen 28:22	2063
What is *t* thou hast done unto me	Gen 29:25	2063
we will give thee *t* also for the	Gen 29:27	2063
therefore given me *t* son also	Gen 29:33	2088
Now *t* time will my husband be	Gen 29:34	
if thou wilt do *t* thing for me	Gen 30:31	2088
hath he gotten all *t* glory	Gen 31:1	2088
arise, get thee out from *t* land	Gen 31:13	2063
T twenty years have I been with	Gen 31:38	2088
what can I do *t* day unto these my	Gen 31:43	
T heap is a witness between me and	Gen 31:48	2088
witness between me and thee *t* day	Gen 31:48	
said to Jacob, Behold *t* heap	Gen 31:51	2088
and behold *t* pillar	Gen 31:51	
T heap be witness, and *t* pillar	Gen 31:52	2088
will not pass over *t* heap to thee	Gen 31:52	2088
thou shalt not pass over *t* heap	Gen 31:52	2088
t pillar unto me, for harm	Gen 31:52	2063
them, he said, *T* is God's host	Gen 32:2	2088
my staff I passed over *t* Jordan	Gen 32:10	2088
On *t* manner shall ye speak unto	Gen 32:19	2088
hollow of the thigh, unto *t* day	Gen 32:32	2088
thou by all *t* drove which I met	Gen 33:8	2088
saying, Get me *t* damsel to wife	Gen 34:4	2063
unto them, We cannot do *t* thing	Gen 34:14	2088
But in *t* will we consent unto you	Gen 34:15	2063
thou shalt have *t* son also	Gen 35:17	2088
of Rachel's grave unto *t* day	Gen 35:20	
t was that Anah that found the	Gen 36:24	1931
t dream which I have dreamed	Gen 37:6	2088
What is *t* dream that thou hast	Gen 37:10	2088
another, Behold, *t* dreamer cometh	Gen 37:19	1976
but cast him into *t* pit that is	Gen 37:22	2088
and said, *T* have we found	Gen 37:32	2063
There was no harlot in *t* place	Gen 38:21	2088
there was no harlot in *t* place	Gen 38:22	2088
behold, I sent *t* kid, and thou	Gen 38:23	2088
thread, saying, *T* came out first	Gen 38:28	2088
t breach be upon thee	Gen 38:29	
is none greater in *t* house than I	Gen 39:9	2088
then can I do *t* great wickedness	Gen 39:9	2063
And it came to pass about *t* time	Gen 39:11	2088
After *t* manner did thy servant to	Gen 39:19	428
T is the interpretation of it	Gen 40:12	2088
and bring me out of *t* house	Gen 40:14	2088
T is the interpretation thereof	Gen 40:18	2088
I do remember my faults *t* day	Gen 41:9	
I told *t* unto the magicians	Gen 41:24	
T is the thing which I have	Gen 41:28	
Let Pharaoh do *t*, and let him	Gen 41:34	
Can we find such a one as *t* is	Gen 41:38	2088
as God hath shewed thee all *t*	Gen 41:39	2063
the youngest is *t* day with our	Gen 42:13	
them the third day, *T* do, and live	Gen 42:18	2063
therefore is *t* distress come upon	Gen 42:21	2063
What is *t* that God hath done unto	Gen 42:28	2063
the youngest is *t* day with our	Gen 42:32	
now we had returned *t* second time	Gen 43:10	2088
them, If it must be so now, do *t*	Gen 43:11	2063
Is *t* your younger brother, of	Gen 43:29	2088
Is not *t* it in which my lord	Gen 44:5	2088
should do according to *t* thing	Gen 44:7	2088
What deed is *t* that ye have done	Gen 44:15	
if ye take *t* also from me, and	Gen 44:29	2088
Say unto thy brethren, *T* do ye	Gen 45:17	2063
Now thou art commanded, *t* do ye	Gen 45:19	2063
his father he sent after *t* manner	Gen 45:23	2063
Behold, I have bought you *t* day	Gen 47:23	
over the land of Egypt unto *t* day	Gen 47:26	2088
will give *t* land to thy seed	Gen 48:4	2063
whom God hath given me in *t* place	Gen 48:9	2088
me all my life long unto *t* day	Gen 48:15	
for *t* is the firstborn	Gen 48:18	2088
t is it that their father spake	Gen 49:28	2063
T is a grievous mourning to the	Gen 50:11	2088
to bring to pass, as it is *t* day	Gen 50:20	2088
bring you out of *t* land unto the	Gen 50:24	2063
them, Why have ye done *t* thing	Ex 1:18	2088
T is one of the Hebrews' children	Ex 2:6	2088
Take *t* child away, and nurse it	Ex 2:9	2088
And he looked *t* way and that way,	Ex 2:12	3541
and said, Surely *t* thing is known	Ex 2:14	
Now when Pharaoh heard *t* thing	Ex 2:15	2088
see *t* great sight, why the bush	Ex 3:3	2088
t shall be a token unto thee,	Ex 3:12	
shall serve God upon *t* mountain	Ex 3:12	
t is my name for ever	Ex 3:15	2088
t is my memorial unto all	Ex 3:15	2088
I will give *t* people favour in	Ex 3:21	
thou shalt take *t* rod in thine	Ex 4:17	2088
thou so evil entreated *t* people	Ex 5:22	2088
he hath done evil to *t* people	Ex 5:23	2088
In *t* thou shalt know that I am	Ex 7:17	2063
did he set his heart to *t* also	Ex 7:23	2063
Pharaoh, *T* is the finger of God	Ex 8:19	1931
to morrow shall *t* sign be	Ex 8:23	2088
hardened his heart at *t* time also	Ex 8:32	2063
LORD shall do *t* thing in the land	Ex 9:5	2088
For I will at *t* time send all my	Ex 9:14	2063
in very deed for *t* cause have I	Ex 9:16	2063
to morrow about *t* time I will	Ex 9:18	
unto them, I have sinned *t* time	Ex 9:27	
were upon the earth unto *t* day	Ex 10:6	2088
How long shall *t* man be a snare	Ex 10:7	2088
I pray thee, my sin only *t* once	Ex 10:17	
take away from me *t* death only	Ex 10:17	2088
T month shall be unto you the	Ex 12:2	2088
In the tenth day of *t* month they	Ex 12:3	2088
through the land of Egypt *t* night	Ex 12:12	2088
t day shall be unto you for a	Ex 12:14	2088
for in *t* selfsame day have I	Ex 12:17	2088
therefore shall ye observe *t* day	Ex 12:17	
ye shall observe *t* thing for an	Ex 12:24	2088
that ye shall keep *t* service	Ex 12:25	
you, What mean ye by *t* service	Ex 12:26	2063
t is that night of the LORD to be	Ex 12:42	2088
T is the ordinance of the	Ex 12:43	
unto the people, Remember *t* day	Ex 13:3	2088
LORD brought you out from *t* place	Ex 13:3	2088
T day came ye out in the month	Ex 13:4	
keep *t* service in *t* month	Ex 13:5	2088
T is done because of that which	Ex 13:8	
Thou shalt therefore keep *t*	Ex 13:10	2063
time to come, saying, What is *t*	Ex 13:14	2063
and they said, Why have we done *t*	Ex 14:5	2063
Is not *t* the word that we did	Ex 14:12	2088
of Israel *t* song unto the LORD	Ex 15:1	2063
us forth into *t* wilderness	Ex 16:3	2088
to kill *t* whole assembly with	Ex 16:3	2088
T shall be, when the LORD shall	Ex 16:8	
T is the bread which the LORD	Ex 16:15	1931
T is the thing which the LORD	Ex 16:16	2088
T is that which the LORD hath	Ex 16:23	1931
T is the thing which the LORD	Ex 16:32	2088
Wherefore is *t* that thou hast	Ex 17:3	2088
What shall I do unto *t* people	Ex 17:4	2088
Write *t* for a memorial in a book,	Ex 17:14	2063
What is *t* thing that thou doest	Ex 18:14	2088
t people that is with thee	Ex 18:18	2088
for *t* thing is too heavy for thee	Ex 18:18	
If thou shalt do *t* thing, and God	Ex 18:23	2088
all *t* people shall also go to	Ex 18:23	2088
according to *t* judgment shall it	Ex 21:31	2088
t is the offering which ye shall	Ex 25:3	2063
sides of the tabernacle on *t* side	Ex 26:13	2088
t shall be the first row	Ex 28:17	
t is the thing that thou shalt do	Ex 29:1	2088
Now *t* is that which thou shalt	Ex 29:38	2088
T shall be a continual burnt	Ex 29:42	
T they shall give, every one that	Ex 30:13	2088
T shall be an holy anointing oil	Ex 30:31	2088
for as for *t* Moses, the man that	Ex 32:1	2088
unto Moses, I have seen *t* people	Ex 32:9	2088
repent of *t* evil against thy	Ex 32:12	
all *t* land that I have spoken of	Ex 32:13	2063
What did *t* people unto thee, that	Ex 32:21	2088
for as for *t* Moses, the man that	Ex 32:23	2088
fire, and there came out *t* calf	Ex 32:24	
bestow upon you a blessing *t* day	Ex 32:29	
t people have sinned a great sin,	Ex 32:31	2088
sayest unto me, Bring up *t* people	Ex 33:12	2088
consider that *t* nation is thy	Ex 33:13	
I will do *t* thing also that thou	Ex 33:17	2088
that which I command thee *t* day	Ex 34:11	
T is the thing which the LORD	Ex 35:4	2088
One cherub on the end on *t* side	Ex 37:8	2088
on *t* hand and that hand, were	Ex 38:15	2088
T is the sum of the tabernacle,	Ex 38:21	428
t was the first row	Ex 39:10	
offering, so shall he do with *t*	Lev 4:20	
T is the law of the burnt	Lev 6:9	2063
t is the law of the meat offering	Lev 6:14	2063
T is the offering of Aaron and of	Lev 6:20	2088
T is the law of the sin offering	Lev 6:25	2063
Likewise *t* is the law of the	Lev 7:1	2063
t is the law of the sacrifice of	Lev 7:11	2063
T is the portion of the anointing	Lev 7:35	2063
T is the law of the burnt	Lev 7:37	2063
T is the thing which the LORD	Lev 8:5	2088
As he hath done *t* day, so the	Lev 8:34	2088
T is the thing which the LORD	Lev 9:6	2088
T is it that the LORD spake,	Lev 10:3	1931
t day have they offered their sin	Lev 10:19	
T is the law of the beasts, and of	Lev 11:46	2063
T is the law for her that hath	Lev 12:7	2063
T is the law of the plague of	Lev 13:59	2063
T shall be the law of the leper	Lev 14:2	2063
T is the law of him in whom is	Lev 14:32	2063
T is the law for all manner of	Lev 14:54	2063
t is the law of leprosy	Lev 14:57	2063
t shall be his uncleanness in his	Lev 15:3	2063

T is the law of him that hath an	Lev 15:32	2063
t shall be a statute for ever	Lev 16:29	
t shall be an everlasting statute	Lev 16:34	2063
T is the thing which the LORD	Lev 17:2	2063
T shall be a statute for ever	Lev 17:7	2063
Also on the tenth day of *t*	Lev 23:27	2088
The fifteenth day of *t* seventh	Lev 23:34	2088
t son of the Israelitish woman and	Lev 24:10	
In the year of *t* jubile ye shall	Lev 25:13	2063
I also will do *t* unto you	Lev 26:16	
not yet for all *t* hearken unto me	Lev 26:18	428
not for all *t* hearken unto me	Lev 26:27	2063
T shall be the service of the	Num 4:4	2063
T is the service of the families	Num 4:24	2063
T is the service of the families	Num 4:28	2063
t is the charge of their burden,	Num 4:31	2063
T is the service of the families	Num 4:33	2063
be thou free from *t* bitter water	Num 5:19	
t water that causeth the curse	Num 5:22	
T is the law of jealousies, when	Num 5:29	2063
shall execute upon her all *t* law	Num 5:30	2063
t woman shall bear her iniquity	Num 5:31	1931
t is the law of the Nazarite,	Num 6:13	2063
t is holy for the priest, with	Num 6:20	1931
T is the law of the Nazarite who	Num 6:21	2063
On *t* wise ye shall bless the	Num 6:23	3541
t was the offering of Nahshon the	Num 7:17	2088
t was the offering of Nethaneel	Num 7:23	2088
t was the offering of Eliab the	Num 7:29	2088
t was the offering of Elizur the	Num 7:35	2088
t was the offering of Shelumiel	Num 7:41	2088
t was the offering of Eliasaph	Num 7:47	2088
t was the offering of Elishama	Num 7:53	2088
t was the offering of Gamaliel	Num 7:59	2088
t was the offering of Abidan the	Num 7:65	2088
t was the offering of Ahiezer the	Num 7:71	2088
t was the offering of Pagiel the	Num 7:77	2088
t was the offering of Ahira the	Num 7:83	2088
T was the dedication of the altar	Num 7:84	2063
T was the dedication of the altar	Num 7:88	2063
t work of the candlestick was of	Num 8:4	2088
T is it that belongeth unto the	Num 8:24	2063
In the fourteenth day of *t* month	Num 9:3	2088
is nothing at all, beside *t* manna	Num 11:6	
burden of all *t* people upon me	Num 11:11	2088
Have I conceived all *t* people	Num 11:12	2088
flesh to give unto all *t* people	Num 11:13	2088
able to bear all *t* people alone	Num 11:14	2088
it were a day's journey on *t* side	Num 11:31	3541
Get you up *t* way southward, and go	Num 13:17	2088
and *t* is the fruit of it	Num 13:27	2088
God we had died in *t* wilderness	Num 14:2	2088
the LORD brought us unto *t* land	Num 14:3	2063
then he will bring us into *t* land	Num 14:8	2063
How long will *t* people provoke me	Num 14:11	2088
(for thou broughtest up *t* people	Num 14:13	2088
it to the inhabitants of *t* land	Num 14:14	2063
that thou LORD art among *t* people	Num 14:14	2088
kill all *t* people as one man	Num 14:15	2088
t people into the land which he	Num 14:16	2088
thee, the iniquity of *t* people	Num 14:19	2088
and as thou hast forgiven *t* people	Num 14:19	2088
I bear with *t* evil congregation	Num 14:27	2063
shall fall in *t* wilderness	Num 14:29	2088
they shall fall in *t* wilderness	Num 14:32	2088
it unto all *t* evil congregation	Num 14:35	2063
in *t* wilderness they shall be	Num 14:35	2088
do these things after *t* manner	Num 15:13	
T do; Take you censers	Num 16:6	2063
from among *t* congregation	Num 16:21	2063
you up from among *t* congregation	Num 16:45	2063
T shall be thine of the most holy	Num 18:9	2088
And *t* is thine	Num 18:11	2088
t your heave offering shall be	Num 18:27	
T is the ordinance of the law	Num 19:2	2063
T is the law, when a man dieth in	Num 19:14	2063
of the LORD into *t* wilderness	Num 20:4	2088
to bring us in unto *t* evil place	Num 20:5	2088
we fetch you water out of *t* rock	Num 20:10	2088
t congregation into the land	Num 20:12	2088
T is the water of Meribah	Num 20:13	1992
deliver *t* people into my hand	Num 21:2	2088
our soul loatheth *t* light bread	Num 21:5	
Then Israel sang *t* song, Spring	Num 21:17	2088
Moab on *t* side Jordan by Jericho	Num 22:1	
Now shall *t* company lick up all	Num 22:4	
I pray thee, curse me *t* people	Num 22:6	2088
unto them, Lodge here *t* night	Num 22:8	
I pray thee, curse me *t* people	Num 22:17	2088
you, tarry ye also here *t* night	Num 22:19	
vineyards, a wall being on *t* side	Num 22:24	2088
ever since I was thine unto *t* day	Num 22:30	2088
according to *t* time it shall be	Num 23:23	
I will advertise thee what *t*	Num 24:14	2088
who shall live when God doeth *t*	Num 24:23	
T is that Dathan and Abiram, which	Num 26:9	1931
Get thee up into *t* mount Abarim	Num 27:12	2088
T is the offering made by fire	Num 28:3	
T is the burnt offering of every	Num 28:10	
t is the burnt offering of every	Num 28:14	2063
day of *t* month is the feast	Num 28:17	2088
After *t* manner ye shall offer	Num 28:24	428
day of *t* seventh month an holy	Num 29:7	2088
T is the thing which the LORD	Num 30:1	2088
T is the ordinance of the law	Num 31:21	2063
let *t* land be given unto thy	Num 32:5	2063
and ye shall destroy all *t* people	Num 32:15	2088
to us on *t* side Jordan eastward	Num 32:19	
unto them, If ye will do *t* thing	Num 32:20	2088
t land shall be your possession	Num 32:22	2063
of our inheritance on *t* side	Num 32:32	
(*t* is the land that shall fall	Num 34:2	2063
t shall be your west border	Num 34:6	2088
t shall be your north border	Num 34:7	2088
t shall be your north border	Num 34:9	2088
t shall be your land with the	Num 34:12	2063
T is the land which ye shall	Num 34:13	2063
on *t* side Jordan near Jericho	Num 34:15	
t shall be to them the suburbs of	Num 35:5	2088
three cities on *t* side Jordan	Num 35:14	
T is the thing which the LORD	Num 36:6	2088
t side Jordan in the wilderness	Deut 1:1	
On *t* side Jordan, in the land of	Deut 1:5	
began Moses to declare *t* law	Deut 1:5	2063
have dwelt long enough in *t* mount	Deut 1:6	2088
ye are *t* day as the stars of	Deut 1:10	
went, until ye came into *t* place	Deut 1:31	
Yet in *t* thing ye did not believe	Deut 1:32	2088
t evil generation see that good	Deut 1:35	2088
Ye have compassed *t* mountain long	Deut 2:3	2088
through *t* great wilderness	Deut 2:7	2088
Ar, the coast of Moab, *t* day	Deut 2:18	
in their stead even unto *t* day	Deut 2:22	2088
T day will I begin to put the	Deut 2:25	2088
into thy hand, as appeareth *t* day	Deut 2:30	2088
land that was on *t* side Jordan	Deut 3:8	
t land, which we possessed at	Deut 3:12	2063
Bashan-havoth-jair, unto *t* day	Deut 3:14	2088
given you *t* land to possess it	Deut 3:18	2063
speak no more unto me of *t* matter	Deut 3:26	2088
thou shalt not go over *t* Jordan	Deut 3:27	2088
he shall go over before *t* people	Deut 3:28	2088
are alive every one of you *t* day	Deut 4:4	
for *t* is your wisdom and your	Deut 4:6	1931
Surely *t* great nation is a wise	Deut 4:6	2088
so righteous as all *t* law	Deut 4:8	2063
which I set before you *t* day	Deut 4:8	
of inheritance, as ye are *t* day	Deut 4:20	2088
But I must die in *t* land, I must	Deut 4:22	2088
to witness against you *t* day	Deut 4:26	
such thing as *t* great thing is	Deut 4:32	2088
an inheritance, as it is *t* day	Deut 4:38	2088
Know therefore *t* day, and consider	Deut 4:39	
which I command thee *t* day	Deut 4:40	
on *t* side Jordan toward the	Deut 4:41	
t is the law which Moses set	Deut 4:44	2063
On *t* side Jordan, in the valley	Deut 4:46	
which were on *t* side Jordan	Deut 4:47	
all the plain on *t* side Jordan	Deut 4:49	
which I speak in your ears *t* day	Deut 5:1	
The LORD made not *t* covenant with	Deut 5:3	2063
are all of us here alive *t* day	Deut 5:3	
we have seen *t* day that God doth	Deut 5:24	2088
for *t* great fire will consume us	Deut 5:25	2063
voice of the words of *t* people	Deut 5:28	2088
words, which I command thee *t* day	Deut 6:6	
us alive, as it is at *t* day	Deut 6:24	2088
which I command thee *t* day	Deut 7:11	
which I command thee *t* day shall	Deut 8:1	
which I command thee *t* day	Deut 8:11	
mine hand hath gotten me *t* wealth	Deut 8:17	2088
unto thy fathers, as it is *t* day	Deut 8:18	2088
I testify against you *t* day that	Deut 8:19	
art to pass over Jordan *t* day	Deut 9:1	
Understand therefore *t* day	Deut 9:3	
brought me in to possess *t* land	Deut 9:4	2088
LORD thy God giveth thee not *t*	Deut 9:6	2063
Egypt, until ye came unto *t* place	Deut 9:7	2088
me, saying, I have seen *t* people	Deut 9:13	2088
unto the stubbornness of *t* people	Deut 9:27	2088
to bless in his name, unto *t* day	Deut 10:8	2088
I command thee *t* day for thy good	Deut 10:13	
above all people, as it is *t* day	Deut 10:15	2088
And know ye *t* day	Deut 11:2	
hath destroyed them unto *t* day	Deut 11:4	2088
until ye came into *t* place	Deut 11:5	
which I command you *t* day	Deut 11:8	
which I command you *t* day	Deut 11:13	
I set before you *t* day a blessing	Deut 11:26	
God, which I command you *t* day	Deut 11:27	
the way which I command you *t* day	Deut 11:28	
which I set before you *t* day	Deut 11:32	
the things that we do here *t* day	Deut 12:8	
such wickedness as *t* is among you	Deut 13:11	2088
which I command thee *t* day	Deut 13:18	
t is the manner of the release	Deut 15:2	2088
which I command thee *t* day	Deut 15:5	
because that for *t* thing the LORD	Deut 15:10	2088
I command thee *t* thing to day	Deut 15:15	2088
he shall write him a copy of *t*	Deut 17:18	2063
to keep all the words of *t* law	Deut 17:19	2063
t shall be the priest's due from	Deut 18:3	2088
neither let me see *t* great fire	Deut 18:16	2063
t is the case of the slayer,	Deut 19:4	2088
them, which I command thee *t* day	Deut 19:9	
ye approach *t* day unto battle	Deut 20:3	
Our hands have not shed *t* blood	Deut 21:7	2088
city, *T* our son is stubborn and	Deut 21:20	2088
upon her, and say, I took *t* woman	Deut 22:14	2063
my daughter unto *t* man to wife	Deut 22:16	2088
But if *t* thing be true, and the	Deut 22:20	2088
slayeth him, even so is *t* matter	Deut 22:26	2088
I command thee to do *t* thing	Deut 24:18	2088
I command thee to do *t* thing	Deut 24:22	2088
I profess *t* day unto the LORD thy	Deut 26:3	
he hath brought us into *t* place	Deut 26:9	2088
and hath given us *t* land	Deut 26:9	2063
T day the LORD thy God hath	Deut 26:16	2088
the LORD *t* day to be thy God	Deut 26:17	
the LORD hath avouched thee *t* day	Deut 26:18	
which I command you *t* day	Deut 27:1	
upon them all the words of *t* law	Deut 27:3	2063
stones, which I command you *t* day	Deut 27:4	
the words of *t* law very plainly	Deut 27:8	2063
t day thou art become the people	Deut 27:9	2088
which I command thee *t* day	Deut 27:10	
all the words of *t* law to do them	Deut 27:26	2063
which I command thee *t* day	Deut 28:1	
God, which I command thee *t* day	Deut 28:13	
words which I command thee *t* day	Deut 28:14	
which I command thee *t* day	Deut 28:15	
of *t* law that are written	Deut 28:58	2063
law that are written in *t* book	Deut 28:58	2088
that thou mayest fear *t* glorious	Deut 28:58	2088
not written in the book of *t* law	Deut 28:61	2063
see, and ears to hear, unto *t* day	Deut 29:4	2088
And when ye came unto *t* place	Deut 29:7	2088
therefore the words of *t* covenant	Deut 29:9	2063
Ye stand *t* day all of you before	Deut 29:10	
thy God maketh with thee *t* day	Deut 29:12	
do I make *t* covenant and *t* oath	Deut 29:14	2063
us *t* day before the LORD our God	Deut 29:15	
that is not here with us *t* day	Deut 29:15	
whose heart turneth away *t* day	Deut 29:18	
he heareth the words of *t* curse	Deut 29:19	2063
in *t* book shall lie upon him	Deut 29:20	2088
are written in *t* book of the law	Deut 29:21	2088
the LORD done thus unto *t* land	Deut 29:24	2063
meaneth the heat of *t* great anger	Deut 29:24	2088
LORD was kindled against *t* land	Deut 29:27	1931
curses that are written in *t* book	Deut 29:27	2088
into another land, as it is *t* day	Deut 29:28	2088
we may do all the words of *t* law	Deut 29:29	2063
to all that I command thee *t* day	Deut 30:2	
which I command thee *t* day	Deut 30:8	
are written in *t* book of the law	Deut 30:10	2088
For *t* commandment which	Deut 30:11	2063
which I command thee *t* day	Deut 30:11	
I have set before thee *t* day life	Deut 30:15	
In that I command thee *t* day to	Deut 30:16	
I denounce unto you *t* day	Deut 30:18	
earth to record *t* day against you	Deut 30:19	
hundred and twenty years old *t* day	Deut 31:2	
Thou shalt not go over *t* Jordan	Deut 31:2	2088
for thou must go with *t* people	Deut 31:7	2088
And Moses wrote *t* law, and	Deut 31:9	2063
thou shalt read *t* law before all	Deut 31:11	2063
to do all the words of *t* law	Deut 31:12	2063
t people will rise up, and go a	Deut 31:16	2088
therefore write ye *t* song for you	Deut 31:19	2063
that *t* song may be a witness for	Deut 31:19	2063
that *t* song shall testify against	Deut 31:21	2063
wrote *t* song the same day	Deut 31:22	2063
the words of *t* law in a book	Deut 31:24	2063
Take *t* book of the law, and put it	Deut 31:26	2088
I am yet alive with you *t* day	Deut 31:27	
of Israel the words of *t* song	Deut 31:30	2063
and the LORD hath not done all *t*	Deut 32:27	2063
were wise, that they understood *t*	Deut 32:29	2063
Is not *t* laid up in store with me	Deut 32:34	1931
spake all the words of *t* song in	Deut 32:44	2063
which I testify among you *t* day	Deut 32:46	2063
to do, all the words of *t* law	Deut 32:46	2063
through *t* thing ye shall prolong	Deut 32:47	2088
thee up into *t* mountain Abarim	Deut 32:49	2088
t is the blessing, wherewith	Deut 33:1	2063
t is the blessing of Judah	Deut 33:7	2063
T is the land which I sware unto	Deut 34:4	2063
of his sepulchre unto *t* day	Deut 34:6	2088
therefore arise, go over *t* Jordan	Josh 1:2	
all *t* people, unto the land which	Josh 1:2	2088
t Lebanon even unto the great	Josh 1:4	2088
for unto *t* people shalt thou	Josh 1:6	2088
T book of the law shall not	Josh 1:8	2088
days ye shall pass over *t* Jordan	Josh 1:11	2088
rest, and hath given you *t* land	Josh 1:13	2063
Moses gave you on *t* side Jordan	Josh 1:14	
you on *t* side Jordan toward the	Josh 1:15	
if ye utter not *t* our business	Josh 2:14	2088
We will be blameless of *t* thine	Josh 2:17	2088
thou shalt bind *t* line of scarlet	Josh 2:18	2088
And if thou utter *t* our business	Josh 2:20	2088
have not passed *t* way heretofore	Josh 3:4	
T day will I begin to magnify	Josh 3:7	2088
where ye shall lodge *t* night	Josh 4:3	
That *t* may be a sign among you,	Josh 4:6	2063
and they are there unto *t* day	Josh 4:9	2063
Israel came over *t* Jordan on dry	Josh 4:22	2088
t is the cause why Joshua did	Josh 5:4	2088
T day have I rolled away the	Josh 5:9	
place is called Gilgal unto *t* day	Josh 5:9	2088
in Israel even unto *t* day	Josh 6:25	2088
up and buildeth *t* city Jericho	Josh 6:26	2063
all brought *t* people over Jordan	Josh 7:7	2088
the LORD shall trouble thee *t* day	Josh 7:25	2088
a great heap of stones unto *t* day	Josh 7:26	2088
The valley of Achor, unto *t* day	Josh 7:26	2088
power to flee *t* way or that way	Josh 8:20	2007
midst of Israel, some on *t* side	Josh 8:22	2088
even a desolation unto *t* day	Josh 8:28	2088
stones, that remaineth unto *t* day	Josh 8:29	2088
stood on *t* side the ark and on	Josh 8:33	2088
kings which were on *t* side Jordan	Josh 9:1	
T our bread we took hot for our	Josh 9:12	2088
T we will do to them	Josh 9:20	2063
of you, and have done *t* thing	Josh 9:24	2088
of the LORD, even unto *t* day	Josh 9:27	2088
Is not *t* written in the book of	Josh 10:13	1931
which remain until *t* very day	Josh 10:27	2088
for to morrow about *t* time will I	Josh 11:6	2063
on *t* side Jordan on the west	Josh 12:7	
T is the land that yet remaineth	Josh 13:2	2063
Now therefore divide *t* land for	Josh 13:7	2063
among the Israelites until *t* day	Josh 13:13	2088
T was the inheritance of the	Josh 13:23	2063
T is the inheritance of the	Josh 13:28	2063
t was the possession of the half	Josh 13:29	
the LORD spake *t* word unto Moses	Josh 14:10	2088
I am *t* day fourscore and five	Josh 14:10	
As yet I am as strong *t* day as I	Josh 14:11	
Now therefore give me *t* mountain	Josh 14:12	2088
Jephunneh the Kenezite unto *t* day	Josh 14:14	2088

T then was the lot of the tribe	Josh 15:1	
t shall be your south coast	Josh 15:4	2088
T is the coast of the children of	Josh 15:12	2088
T is the inheritance of the tribe	Josh 15:20	2063
of Judah at Jerusalem unto *t* day	Josh 15:63	2088
T is the inheritance of the tribe	Josh 16:8	2063
among the Ephraimites unto *t* day	Josh 16:10	2088
t was the west quarter	Josh 18:14	2063
t was the south coast	Josh 18:19	2088
T was the inheritance of the	Josh 18:20	2063
T is the inheritance of the	Josh 18:28	2063
T is the inheritance of the tribe	Josh 19:8	2063
T is the inheritance of the	Josh 19:16	2063
T is the inheritance of the tribe	Josh 19:23	2063
T is the inheritance of the tribe	Josh 19:31	2063
T is the inheritance of the tribe	Josh 19:39	2063
T is the inheritance of the tribe	Josh 19:48	2063
these many days unto *t* day	Josh 22:3	2088
on *t* side Jordan westward	Josh 22:7	
What trespass is *t* that ye have	Josh 22:16	2088
to turn away *t* day from following	Josh 22:16	
that ye might rebel *t* day against	Josh 22:16	
we are not cleansed until *t* day	Josh 22:17	2088
But that ye must turn away *t* day	Josh 22:18	
the LORD, (save us not *t* day	Josh 22:22	2088
done it for fear of *t* thing	Josh 22:24	2063
turn *t* day from following the	Josh 22:29	
T day we perceive that the LORD	Josh 22:31	
t trespass against the LORD	Josh 22:31	2088
God, as ye have done unto *t* day	Josh 23:8	2088
to stand before you unto *t* day	Josh 23:9	2088
until ye perish from off *t* good	Josh 23:13	2063
t day I am going the way of all	Josh 23:14	
t good land which the LORD your	Josh 23:15	2063
choose you *t* day whom ye will	Josh 24:15	
t stone shall be a witness unto	Josh 24:27	2063
Benjamin in Jerusalem unto *t* day	Judg 1:21	2088
is the name thereof unto *t* day	Judg 1:26	2088
with the inhabitants of *t* land	Judg 2:2	2063
why have ye done *t*	Judg 2:2	2063
Because that *t* people hath	Judg 2:20	2088
for *t* is the day in which the	Judg 4:14	2088
us, why then is all *t* befallen us	Judg 6:13	2063
Go in *t* thy might, and thou shalt	Judg 6:14	2088
cakes, and lay them upon *t* rock	Judg 6:20	1975
unto *t* day it is yet in Ophrah of	Judg 6:24	2088
thy God upon the top of *t* rock	Judg 6:26	2088
to another, Who hath done *t* thing	Judg 6:29	2088
son of Joash hath done *t* thing	Judg 6:29	2088
me, and I will speak but *t* once	Judg 6:39	
but *t* once with the fleece	Judg 6:39	
T shall go with thee, the same	Judg 7:4	2088
T shall not go with thee, the	Judg 7:4	2088
T is nothing else save the sword	Judg 7:14	2063
peace, I will break down *t* tower	Judg 8:9	
against my father's house *t* day	Judg 9:18	
Jerubbaal and with his house *t* day	Judg 9:19	2088
would to God *t* people were under	Judg 9:29	2088
is not *t* the people that thou	Judg 9:38	2088
are called Havoth-jair unto *t* day	Judg 10:4	2088
us only, we pray thee, *t* day	Judg 10:15	2088
t day between the children of	Judg 11:27	
Let *t* thing be done for me	Judg 11:37	2088
then are ye come up unto me *t* day	Judg 12:3	2088
nor would as at *t* time have told	Judg 13:23	
Philistines said, Who hath done *t*	Judg 15:6	2063
unto them, Though ye have done *t*	Judg 15:7	2063
what is *t* that thou hast done	Judg 15:11	2063
and said, Thou hast given *t* great	Judg 15:18	2063
which is in Lehi unto *t* day	Judg 15:19	2063
saying, Come up *t* once, for he	Judg 16:18	
me, I pray thee, only *t* once	Judg 16:28	2088
and what makest thou in *t* place	Judg 18:3	6311
that place Mahaneh-dan unto *t* day	Judg 18:12	2088
what is *t* that ye say unto me,	Judg 18:24	2088
let us turn in into *t* city of the	Judg 19:11	2063
seeing that *t* man is come into	Judg 19:23	2088
into mine house, do not *t* folly	Judg 19:23	2063
but unto *t* man do not so vile a	Judg 19:24	2088
of the land of Egypt unto *t* day	Judg 19:30	2088
Tell us, how was *t* wickedness	Judg 20:3	2063
But now *t* shall be the thing	Judg 20:9	2063
What wickedness is *t* that is done	Judg 20:12	2063
Among all *t* people there were	Judg 20:16	2088
why is *t* come to pass in Israel,	Judg 21:3	2063
tribe cut off from Israel *t* day	Judg 21:6	
t is the thing that ye shall do,	Judg 21:11	2063
did not give unto them at *t* time	Judg 21:22	
them, and they said, Is *t* Naomi	Ruth 1:19	2063
the reapers, Whose damsel is *t*	Ruth 2:5	2063
Tarry *t* night, and it shall be in	Ruth 3:13	
he have finished the thing *t* day	Ruth 3:18	
Now *t* was the manner in former	Ruth 4:7	2063
t was a testimony in Israel	Ruth 4:7	2063
people, Ye are witnesses *t* day	Ruth 4:9	
ye are witnesses *t* day	Ruth 4:10	
shall give thee of *t* young woman	Ruth 4:12	2063
left thee *t* day without a kinsman	Ruth 4:14	
t man went up out of his city	1Sa 1:3	1931
For *t* child I prayed	1Sa 1:27	2088
The LORD give thee seed of *t*	1Sa 2:20	2063
evil dealings by all *t* people	1Sa 2:23	428
t shall be a sign unto thee, that	1Sa 2:34	2088
What meaneth the noise of *t* great	1Sa 4:6	2063
meaneth the noise of *t* tumult	1Sa 4:14	2088
of Dagon in Ashdod unto *t* day	1Sa 5:5	2088
then he hath done us *t* great evil	1Sa 6:9	2063
unto *t* day in the field of Joshua	1Sa 6:18	2088
to stand before *t* holy LORD God	1Sa 6:20	2088
up out of Egypt even unto *t* day	1Sa 8:8	2088
T will be the manner of the king	1Sa 8:11	2088
there is in *t* city a man of God,	1Sa 9:6	2063
for about *t* time ye shall find	1Sa 9:13	
To morrow about *t* time I will	1Sa 9:16	
t same shall reign over my people	1Sa 9:17	2088
for unto *t* time hath it been kept	1Sa 9:24	
What is *t* that is come unto the	1Sa 10:11	2088
ye have *t* day rejected your God,	1Sa 10:19	
said, How shall *t* man save us	1Sa 10:27	2088
On *t* condition will I make a	1Sa 11:2	2063
not a man be put to death *t* day	1Sa 11:13	2088
you from my childhood unto *t* day	1Sa 12:2	2088
and his anointed is witness *t* day	1Sa 12:5	2088
and made them dwell in *t* place	1Sa 12:8	
see *t* great thing, which the LORD	1Sa 12:16	2088
added unto all our sins *t* evil	1Sa 12:19	
ye have done all *t* wickedness	1Sa 12:20	2063
t shall be a sign unto us	1Sa 14:10	2088
man that eateth any food *t* day	1Sa 14:28	
I tasted a little of *t* honey	1Sa 14:29	2088
roll a great stone unto me *t* day	1Sa 14:33	
wherein *t* sin hath been *t* day	1Sa 14:38	2088
die, who hath wrought *t* great	1Sa 14:45	2088
he hath wrought with God *t* day	1Sa 14:45	2088
What meaneth then *t* bleating of	1Sa 15:14	2088
the LORD hath said to me *t* night	1Sa 15:16	
kingdom of Israel from thee *t* day	1Sa 15:28	
Neither hath the LORD chosen *t*	1Sa 16:8	2088
Neither hath the LORD chosen *t*	1Sa 16:9	2088
for *t* is he	1Sa 16:12	2088
I defy the armies of Israel *t* day	1Sa 17:10	2088
an ephah of *t* parched corn	1Sa 17:17	2088
Have ye seen *t* man that is come	1Sa 17:25	2088
the man that killeth *t* Philistine	1Sa 17:26	1975
for who is *t* uncircumcised	1Sa 17:26	2088
answered him after *t* manner	1Sa 17:27	2088
go and fight with *t* Philistine	1Sa 17:32	2088
t Philistine to fight with him	1Sa 17:33	2088
t uncircumcised Philistine shall	1Sa 17:36	2088
out of the hand of *t* Philistine	1Sa 17:37	2088
T day will the LORD deliver thee	1Sa 17:46	2088
t day unto the fowls of the air	1Sa 17:46	2088
all *t* assembly shall know that	1Sa 17:47	2088
host, Abner, whose son is *t* youth	1Sa 17:55	2088
Thou shalt *t* day be my son in law	1Sa 18:21	
saying, On *t* manner spake David	1Sa 18:24	428
my father hide *t* thing from me	1Sa 20:2	2088
he saith, Let not Jonathan know *t*	1Sa 20:3	2063
the arrows are on *t* side of thee	1Sa 20:21	2007
sanctified *t* day in the vessel	1Sa 21:5	
Is not *t* David the king of the	1Sa 21:11	2088
that ye have brought *t* fellow to	1Sa 21:15	2088
shall *t* fellow come into my house	1Sa 21:15	2088
me, to lie in wait, as at *t* day	1Sa 22:8	2088
me, to lie in wait, as at *t* day	1Sa 22:13	2088
thy servant knew nothing of all *t*	1Sa 22:15	2063
Saul went on *t* side of the	1Sa 23:26	2088
should do *t* thing unto my master	1Sa 24:6	2088
t day thine eyes have seen how	1Sa 24:10	
Is *t* thy voice, my son David	1Sa 24:16	2088
thou hast shewed *t* day how that	1Sa 24:18	
that thou hast done unto me *t* day	1Sa 24:19	2088
in vain have I kept all that *t*	1Sa 25:21	2088
lord, upon me let *t* iniquity be	1Sa 25:24	
regard *t* man of Belial, even	1Sa 25:25	2088
now *t* blessing which thine	1Sa 25:27	2063
That *t* shall be no grief unto	1Sa 25:31	2063
which sent thee *t* day to meet me	1Sa 25:32	2088
which hath kept me *t* day from	1Sa 25:33	2088
thine enemy into thine hand *t* day	1Sa 26:8	
T thing is not good that thou	1Sa 26:16	2088
Is *t* thy voice, my son David	1Sa 26:17	2088
me out *t* day from abiding in the	1Sa 26:19	
was precious in thine eyes *t* day	1Sa 26:21	2088
much set by *t* day in mine eyes	1Sa 26:24	2088
the kings of Judah unto *t* day	1Sa 27:6	2088
happen to thee for *t* thing	1Sa 28:10	2088
done *t* thing unto thee *t* day	1Sa 28:18	2088
the Philistines, Is not *t* David	1Sa 29:3	2088
since he fell unto me unto *t* day	1Sa 29:3	2088
Make *t* fellow return, that he may	1Sa 29:4	
Is not *t* David, of whom they sang	1Sa 29:5	2088
of thy coming unto me unto *t* day	1Sa 29:6	2088
I have been with thee unto *t* day	1Sa 29:8	2088
Shall I pursue after *t* troop	1Sa 30:8	2088
thou bring me down to *t* company	1Sa 30:15	2088
will bring thee down to *t* company	1Sa 30:15	2088
and said, *T* is David's spoil	1Sa 30:20	2088
will hearken unto you in *t* matter	1Sa 30:24	2088
ordinance for Israel unto *t* day	1Sa 30:25	2088
David lamented with *t* lamentation	2Sa 1:17	2063
And it came to pass after *t*	2Sa 2:1	3651
that ye have shewed *t* kindness	2Sa 2:5	2088
also will requite you *t* kindness	2Sa 2:6	2088
because ye have done *t* thing	2Sa 2:6	2088
t day unto the house of Saul thy	2Sa 3:8	
with a fault concerning *t* woman	2Sa 3:8	
great man fallen *t* day in Israel	2Sa 3:38	2088
I am *t* day weak, though anointed	2Sa 3:39	
were sojourners there until *t* day	2Sa 4:3	2088
my lord the king *t* day of Saul	2Sa 4:8	2088
of the place Perez-uzzah to *t* day	2Sa 6:8	2088
out of Egypt, even to *t* day	2Sa 7:6	2088
and according to all *t* vision	2Sa 7:17	2088
t was yet a small thing in thy	2Sa 7:19	2063
is *t* the manner of man, O Lord	2Sa 7:19	2063
heart to pray *t* prayer unto thee	2Sa 7:27	2063
thou hast promised *t* goodness	2Sa 7:28	2088
after *t* it came to pass, that	2Sa 8:1	3651
And it came to pass after *t*	2Sa 10:1	3651
Is not *t* Bath-sheba, the daughter	2Sa 11:3	2063
liveth, I will not do *t* thing	2Sa 11:11	2088
Let not *t* thing displease thee,	2Sa 11:25	2088
done *t* thing shall surely die	2Sa 12:5	2063
fourfold, because he did *t* thing	2Sa 12:6	2088
thy wives in the sight of *t* sun	2Sa 12:11	2063
but I will do *t* thing before all	2Sa 12:12	2088
because by *t* deed thou hast given	2Sa 12:14	2088
What thing is *t* that thou hast	2Sa 12:21	2088
And it came to pass after *t*	2Sa 13:1	3651
do not thou *t* folly	2Sa 13:12	2063
t evil in sending me away is	2Sa 13:16	2063
Put now *t* woman out from me, and	2Sa 13:17	2063
regard not *t* thing	2Sa 13:20	2063
t hath been determined from the	2Sa 13:32	
speak on *t* manner unto him	2Sa 14:3	2088
for the king doth speak *t* thing	2Sa 14:13	2088
that I am come to speak of *t*	2Sa 14:15	2088
hand of Joab with thee in all *t*	2Sa 14:19	2063
To fetch about *t* form of speech	2Sa 14:20	
thy servant Joab done *t* thing	2Sa 14:20	2088
Behold now, I have done *t* thing	2Sa 14:21	2088
And it came to pass after *t*	2Sa 15:1	3651
on *t* manner did Absalom to all	2Sa 15:6	2088
should I *t* day make thee go up and	2Sa 15:20	
Why should *t* dead dog curse my	2Sa 16:9	2088
more now may *t* Benjamite do it	2Sa 16:11	
me good for his cursing *t* day	2Sa 16:12	2088
Is *t* thy kindness to thy friend	2Sa 16:17	2088
t people, and all the men of	2Sa 16:18	2088
and pursue after David *t* night	2Sa 17:1	
hath spoken after *t* manner	2Sa 17:6	2088
hath given is not good at *t* time	2Sa 17:7	2063
Lodge not *t* night in the plains	2Sa 17:16	
and it is called unto *t* day	2Sa 18:18	2088
Thou shalt not bear tidings *t* day	2Sa 18:20	2088
but *t* day thou shalt bear no	2Sa 18:20	2088
t day of all them that rose up	2Sa 18:31	
said Thou hast shamed *t* day the	2Sa 19:5	
which *t* day have saved thy life,	2Sa 19:5	
For thou hast declared *t* day	2Sa 19:6	
for *t* day I perceive, that if	2Sa 19:6	
lived, and all we had died *t* day	2Sa 19:6	
not tarry one with thee *t* night	2Sa 19:7	
so that they sent *t* word unto the	2Sa 19:14	
I am come the first *t* day of all	2Sa 19:20	
not Shimei be put to death for *t*	2Sa 19:21	2063
Zeruiah, that ye should *t* day be	2Sa 19:22	
be put to death *t* day in Israel	2Sa 19:22	
that I am *t* day king over Israel	2Sa 19:22	
I am *t* day fourscore years old	2Sa 19:35	
then be ye angry for *t* matter	2Sa 19:42	2088
And it came to pass after *t*	2Sa 21:18	3651
unto the LORD the words of *t* song	2Sa 22:1	2063
for *t* is all my salvation, and all	2Sa 23:5	
me, O LORD, that I should do *t*	2Sa 23:17	2063
is not *t* the blood of the men	2Sa 23:17	
lord the king delight in *t* thing	2Sa 24:3	2088
For he is gone down *t* day	1Kin 1:25	
Is *t* thing done by my lord the	1Kin 1:27	2088
even so will I certainly do *t* day	1Kin 1:30	2088
Wherefore is *t* noise of the city	1Kin 1:41	
T is the noise that ye have heard	1Kin 1:45	1931
one to sit on my throne *t* day	1Kin 1:48	
t word against his own life	1Kin 2:23	2088
shall be put to death *t* day	1Kin 2:24	
but I will not at *t* time put thee	1Kin 2:26	2088
kept for him *t* great kindness	1Kin 3:6	2088
sit on his throne, as it is *t* day	1Kin 3:6	2088
to judge *t* thy so great a people	1Kin 3:9	2088
that Solomon had asked *t* thing	1Kin 3:10	2088
Because thou hast asked *t* thing	1Kin 3:11	2088
t woman dwell in one house	1Kin 3:17	2063
that *t* woman was delivered also	1Kin 3:18	2063
t woman's child died in the night	1Kin 3:19	2063
And *t* said, No	1Kin 3:22	2063
T is my son that liveth, and thy	1Kin 3:23	2063
the region on *t* side the river	1Kin 4:24	
all the kings on *t* side the river	1Kin 4:24	
said, Blessed be the LORD *t* day	1Kin 5:7	
a wise son over *t* great people	1Kin 5:7	2088
Concerning *t* house which thou art	1Kin 6:12	2088
taken to wife, like unto *t* porch	1Kin 7:8	2088
work of the bases was on *t* manner	1Kin 7:28	2088
After *t* manner he made the ten	1Kin 7:37	2063
and there they are unto *t* day	1Kin 8:8	2088
with thine hand, as it is *t* day	1Kin 8:24	2088
how much less *t* house that I have	1Kin 8:27	2088
may be open toward *t* house night	1Kin 8:29	2088
servant shall make toward *t* place	1Kin 8:29	2088
they shall pray toward *t* place	1Kin 8:30	2088
before thine altar in *t* house	1Kin 8:31	2088
supplication unto thee in *t* house	1Kin 8:33	2088
if they pray toward *t* place	1Kin 8:35	2088
forth his hands toward *t* house	1Kin 8:38	2088
shall come and pray toward *t* house	1Kin 8:42	2088
that they may know that *t* house	1Kin 8:43	2088
an end of praying all *t* prayer	1Kin 8:54	2063
his commandments, as at *t* day	1Kin 8:61	2088
I have hallowed *t* house, which	1Kin 9:3	2088
t house, which I have hallowed	1Kin 9:7	
at *t* house, which is high, every	1Kin 9:8	2088
unto *t* land, and to *t* house	1Kin 9:8	
LORD brought upon them all *t* evil	1Kin 9:9	2063
them the land of Cabul unto *t* day	1Kin 9:13	2088
t is the reason of the levy which	1Kin 9:15	2088
tribute of bondservice unto *t* day	1Kin 9:21	2088
trees, nor were seen unto *t* day	1Kin 10:12	2088
commanded him concerning *t* thing	1Kin 11:10	2088
Forasmuch as *t* is done of thee,	1Kin 11:11	2063
t was the cause that he lifted up	1Kin 11:27	2088
I will for *t* afflict the seed of	1Kin 11:39	2063
advise that I may answer *t* people	1Kin 12:6	2088
a servant unto *t* people *t* day	1Kin 12:7	2088
ye that we may answer *t* people	1Kin 12:9	2088
Thus shalt thou speak unto *t*	1Kin 12:10	2088
the house of David unto *t* day	1Kin 12:19	2088
for *t* thing is from me	1Kin 12:24	2088
If *t* people go up to do sacrifice	1Kin 12:27	2088
then shall the heart of *t* people	1Kin 12:27	2088
And *t* thing became a sin	1Kin 12:30	2088
T is the sign which the LORD hath	1Kin 13:3	2088

bread nor drink water in *t* place	1Kin 13:8	2088
drink water with thee in *t* place	1Kin 13:16	2088
After *t* thing Jeroboam returned	1Kin 13:33	2088
t thing became sin unto the house	1Kin 13:34	2088
I should be king over *t* people	1Kin 14:2	2088
root up Israel out of *t* good land	1Kin 14:15	2063
let *t* child's soul come into him	1Kin 17:21	2088
Now by *t* I know that thou art a	1Kin 17:24	2088
let it be known *t* day that thou	1Kin 18:36	2088
that *t* people may know that thou	1Kin 18:37	2088
of them by to morrow about *t* time	1Kin 19:2	
unto thee to morrow about *t* time	1Kin 20:6	
see how *t* man seeketh mischief	1Kin 20:7	2088
but *t* thing I may not do	1Kin 20:9	2088
when Ben-hadad heard *t* message	1Kin 20:12	2088
thou seen all *t* great multitude	1Kin 20:13	2088
deliver it into thine hand *t* day	1Kin 20:13	2088
do *t* thing, Take the kings away,	1Kin 20:24	2088
therefore will I deliver all *t*	1Kin 20:28	2088
send thee away with *t* covenant	1Kin 20:34	
man unto me, and said, Keep *t* man	1Kin 20:39	2088
And one said on *t* manner, and	1Kin 22:20	3541
Put *t* fellow in the prison, and	1Kin 22:27	2088
I shall recover of *t* disease	2Kin 1:2	2088
situation of *t* city is pleasant	2Kin 2:19	2088
the waters were healed unto *t* day	2Kin 2:22	2088
Make *t* valley full of ditches	2Kin 3:16	2088
t is but a light thing in the	2Kin 3:18	2063
And they said, *T* is blood	2Kin 3:23	2088
I perceive that *t* is an holy man	2Kin 4:9	1931
his servant, Call *t* Shunammite	2Kin 4:12	2063
careful for us with all *t* care	2Kin 4:13	2063
About *t* season, according to the	2Kin 4:16	2088
and said, Call *t* Shunammite	2Kin 4:36	2063
should I set *t* before an hundred	2Kin 4:43	2088
Now when *t* letter is come unto	2Kin 5:6	2088
that *t* man doth send unto me to	2Kin 5:7	2088
In *t* thing the LORD pardon thy	2Kin 5:18	2088
pardon thy servant in *t* thing	2Kin 5:18	2088
hath spared Naaman *t* Syrian	2Kin 5:20	2088
was sore troubled for *t* thing	2Kin 6:11	2088
Smite *t* people, I pray thee, with	2Kin 6:18	2088
T is not the way	2Kin 6:19	
the way, neither is *t* the city	2Kin 6:19	2090
And it came to pass after *t*	2Kin 6:24	3651
T woman said unto me, Give thy	2Kin 6:28	2063
Shaphat shall stand on him *t* day	2Kin 6:31	
See ye how *t* son of a murderer	2Kin 6:32	
Behold, *t* evil is of the LORD	2Kin 6:33	2063
To morrow about *t* time shall a	2Kin 7:1	
in heaven, might *t* thing be	2Kin 7:2	2088
t day is a day of good tidings,	2Kin 7:9	1931
shall be to morrow about *t* time	2Kin 7:18	
t is the woman	2Kin 8:5	2063
t is her son, whom Elisha	2Kin 8:5	2088
Shall I recover of *t* disease	2Kin 8:8	2088
Shall I recover of *t* disease	2Kin 8:9	2088
that he should do *t* great thing	2Kin 8:13	2088
the hand of Judah unto *t* day	2Kin 8:22	
take *t* box of oil in thine hand,	2Kin 9:1	2088
wherefore came *t* mad fellow to	2Kin 9:11	2088
the LORD laid *t* burden upon him	2Kin 9:25	2088
and I will requite thee in *t* plat	2Kin 9:26	2063
Ahaziah the king of Judah saw *t*	2Kin 9:27	
see now *t* cursed woman, and bury	2Kin 9:34	2063
T is the word of the LORD, which	2Kin 9:36	1931
they shall not say, *T* is Jezebel	2Kin 9:37	2063
Now as soon as *t* letter cometh to	2Kin 10:2	2088
me to Jezreel by to morrow *t* time	2Kin 10:6	
it a draught house unto *t* day	2Kin 10:27	2088
T is the thing that ye shall do	2Kin 11:5	2088
name of it Joktheel unto *t* day	2Kin 14:7	2088
glory of *t*, and tarry at home	2Kin 14:10	
T was the word of the LORD which	2Kin 15:12	1931
Elath, and dwelt there unto *t* day	2Kin 16:6	2088
them, Ye shall not do *t* thing	2Kin 17:12	2088
own land to Assyria unto *t* day	2Kin 17:23	2088
Unto *t* day they do after the	2Kin 17:34	2088
fathers, so do they unto *t* day	2Kin 17:41	2088
What confidence is *t* wherein thou	2Kin 18:19	2088
upon the staff of *t* bruised reed	2Kin 18:21	2088
before *t* altar in Jerusalem	2Kin 18:22	2088
against *t* place to destroy it	2Kin 18:25	2088
said to me, Go up against *t* land	2Kin 18:25	2063
t city shall not be delivered	2Kin 18:30	2063
T day is a day of trouble, and of	2Kin 19:3	2088
T is the word that the LORD hath	2Kin 19:21	2088
t shall be a sign unto thee, Ye	2Kin 19:29	2088
Ye shall eat *t* year such things	2Kin 19:29	
of the LORD of hosts shall do *t*	2Kin 19:31	2063
He shall not come into *t* city	2Kin 19:32	
and shall not come into *t* city	2Kin 19:33	2063
For I will defend *t* city, to save	2Kin 19:34	2063
t city out of the hand of the	2Kin 20:6	2063
I will defend *t* city for mine own	2Kin 20:6	
T sign shalt thou have of the	2Kin 20:9	2088
have laid up in store unto *t* day	2Kin 20:17	2088
In *t* house, and in Jerusalem,	2Kin 21:7	2088
out of Egypt, even unto *t* day	2Kin 21:15	2088
the words of *t* book that is found	2Kin 22:13	2088
unto the words of *t* book, to do	2Kin 22:13	2088
I will bring evil upon *t* place	2Kin 22:16	2088
shall be kindled against *t* place	2Kin 22:17	2088
what I spake against *t* place	2Kin 22:19	2088
which I will bring upon *t* place	2Kin 22:20	2088
to perform the words of *t*	2Kin 23:3	2063
that were written in *t* book	2Kin 23:3	2088
written in the book of *t* covenant	2Kin 23:21	2088
wherein *t* passover was holden to	2Kin 23:23	2088
will cast off *t* city Jerusalem	2Kin 23:27	2063
of the LORD came *t* upon Judah	2Kin 24:3	
destroyed them utterly unto *t* day	1Chr 4:41	
and dwelt there unto *t* day	1Chr 4:43	2088
and to the river Gozan, unto *t* day	1Chr 5:26	2088
t is the number of the mighty men	1Chr 11:11	428
it me, that I should do *t* thing	1Chr 11:19	2063
is called Perez-uzza to *t* day	1Chr 13:11	2088
t psalm to thank the LORD into	1Chr 16:7	
I brought up Israel unto *t* day	1Chr 17:5	2088
and according to all *t* vision	1Chr 17:15	2088
yet *t* was a small thing in thine	1Chr 17:17	2063
hast thou done all *t* greatness	1Chr 17:19	2063
hast promised *t* goodness unto thy	1Chr 17:26	2063
Now after *t* it came to pass, that	1Chr 18:1	3651
Now it came to pass after *t*	1Chr 19:1	3651
And it came to pass after *t*	1Chr 20:4	3651
then doth my lord require *t* thing	1Chr 21:3	2063
God was displeased with *t* thing	1Chr 21:7	2088
because I have done *t* thing	1Chr 21:8	2088
me the place of *t* threshingfloor	1Chr 21:22	
T is the house of the LORD God,	1Chr 22:1	2088
t is the altar of the burnt	1Chr 22:1	2088
among them of Israel on *t* side	1Chr 26:30	
T is that Benaiah, who was mighty	1Chr 27:6	1931
and my judgments, as at *t* day	1Chr 28:7	2088
that ye may possess *t* good land	1Chr 28:8	
All *t*, said David, the LORD made	1Chr 28:19	
even all the works of *t* pattern	1Chr 28:19	
his service *t* day unto the LORD	1Chr 29:5	
offer so willingly after *t* sort	1Chr 29:14	2063
all *t* store that we have prepared	1Chr 29:16	2088
fathers, keep *t* for ever in the	1Chr 29:18	2063
go out and come in before *t* people	2Chr 1:10	2088
for who can judge *t* thy people	2Chr 1:10	2088
Because *t* was in thine heart, and	2Chr 1:11	2063
T is an ordinance for ever to	2Chr 2:4	2063
And there it is unto *t* day	2Chr 5:9	2088
with thine hand, as it is *t* day	2Chr 6:15	
how much less *t* house which I	2Chr 6:18	2088
eyes may be open upon *t* house day	2Chr 6:20	2088
servant prayeth toward *t* place	2Chr 6:20	2088
they shall make toward *t* place	2Chr 6:21	2088
before thine altar in *t* house	2Chr 6:22	2088
before thee in *t* house	2Chr 6:24	2088
yet if they pray toward *t* place	2Chr 6:26	2088
spread forth his hands in *t* house	2Chr 6:29	2088
if they come and pray in *t* house	2Chr 6:32	2088
may know that *t* house which I	2Chr 6:33	2088
they pray unto thee toward *t* city	2Chr 6:34	2063
prayer that is made in *t* place	2Chr 6:40	2088
have chosen *t* place to myself for	2Chr 7:12	2088
prayer that is made in *t* place	2Chr 7:15	2088
I chosen and sanctified *t* house	2Chr 7:16	2088
t house, which I have sanctified	2Chr 7:20	2088
t house, which is high, shall be	2Chr 7:21	2088
the LORD done thus unto *t* land	2Chr 7:21	2063
unto *t* land, and unto *t* house	2Chr 7:21	2088
he brought all *t* evil upon them	2Chr 7:22	2063
make to pay tribute until *t* day	2Chr 8:8	2088
me to return answer to *t* people	2Chr 10:6	2088
If thou be kind to *t* people	2Chr 10:7	2088
we may return answer to *t* people	2Chr 10:9	2088
the house of David unto *t* day	2Chr 10:19	2088
for *t* thing is done of me	2Chr 11:4	2088
name we go against *t* multitude	2Chr 14:11	2088
rage with him because of *t* thing	2Chr 16:10	2063
one spake saying after *t* manner	2Chr 18:19	3602
Put *t* fellow in the prison, and	2Chr 18:26	2088
t do, and ye shall not trespass	2Chr 19:10	3541
It came to pass after *t* also	2Chr 20:1	3651
beyond the sea on *t* side Syria	2Chr 20:2	
drive out the inhabitants of *t*	2Chr 20:7	2063
famine, we stand before *t* house	2Chr 20:9	2088
(for thy name is in *t* house	2Chr 20:9	2088
t great company that cometh	2Chr 20:12	2088
by reason of *t* great multitude	2Chr 20:15	2088
not need to fight in *t* battle	2Chr 20:17	2063
valley of Berachah, unto *t* day	2Chr 20:26	2088
after *t* did Jehoshaphat king of	2Chr 20:35	3651
the hand of Judah unto *t* day	2Chr 21:10	2088
after all *t* the LORD smote him in	2Chr 21:18	2063
T is the thing that ye shall do	2Chr 23:4	2088
And it came to pass after *t*	2Chr 24:4	3651
Jerusalem for *t* their trespass	2Chr 24:18	2063
to give thee much more than *t*	2Chr 25:9	2088
thee, because thou hast done *t*	2Chr 25:16	2063
t is that king Ahaz	2Chr 28:22	1931
our wives are in captivity for *t*	2Chr 29:9	2088
all *t* continued until the burnt	2Chr 29:28	
they shall come again into *t* land	2Chr 30:9	2063
Now when all *t* was finished	2Chr 31:1	2063
which is left is *t* great store	2Chr 31:10	2088
After *t* did Sennacherib king of	2Chr 32:9	2088
you, nor persuade you on *t* manner	2Chr 32:15	2063
for *t* cause Hezekiah the king, and	2Chr 32:20	2063
T same Hezekiah also stopped the	2Chr 32:30	1931
In *t* house, and in Jerusalem,	2Chr 33:7	2088
Now after *t* he built a wall	2Chr 33:14	3651
all that is written in *t* book	2Chr 34:21	2088
I will bring evil upon *t* place	2Chr 34:24	2088
shall be poured out upon *t* place	2Chr 34:25	2088
his words against *t* place	2Chr 34:27	2088
that I will bring upon *t* place	2Chr 34:28	2088
which are written in *t* book	2Chr 34:31	2088
of Josiah was *t* passover kept	2Chr 35:19	2088
After all *t*, when Josiah had	2Chr 35:20	2063
I come not against thee *t* day	2Chr 35:21	
in their lamentations to *t* day	2Chr 35:25	
And *t* is the number of them	Ezr 1:9	428
when the foundation of *t* house	Ezr 3:12	2088
to Artaxerxes the king in *t* sort	Ezr 4:8	3660
rest that are on *t* side the river	Ezr 4:10	
T is the copy of the letter that	Ezr 4:11	1836
the men on *t* side the river	Ezr 4:11	
if *t* city be builded, and the	Ezr 4:13	1791
know that *t* city is a rebellious	Ezr 4:15	1791
which cause was *t* city destroyed	Ezr 4:15	1791
if *t* city be builded again, and	Ezr 4:16	1791
by *t* means thou shalt have no	Ezr 4:16	1836
no portion on *t* side the river	Ezr 4:16	
it is found that *t* city of old	Ezr 4:19	1791
that *t* city be not builded, until	Ezr 4:21	1791
heed now that ye fail not to do *t*	Ezr 4:22	1836
governor on *t* side the river, and	Ezr 5:3	
commanded you to build *t* house	Ezr 5:3	1836
and to make up *t* wall	Ezr 5:3	1836
said we unto them after *t* manner	Ezr 5:4	3660
of the men that make *t* building	Ezr 5:4	1836
by letter concerning *t* matter	Ezr 5:5	1836
governor on *t* side the river, and	Ezr 5:6	
which were on *t* side the river,	Ezr 5:6	
and *t* work goeth fast on, and	Ezr 5:8	1791
commanded you to build *t* house	Ezr 5:9	1836
Chaldean, who destroyed *t* house	Ezr 5:12	1836
a decree to build *t* house of God	Ezr 5:13	1836
build *t* house of God at Jerusalem	Ezr 5:17	1791
to us concerning *t* matter	Ezr 5:17	1836
Let the work of *t* house of God	Ezr 6:7	1791
build *t* house of God in his place	Ezr 6:7	1791
the building of *t* house of God	Ezr 6:8	1791
that whosoever shall alter *t* word	Ezr 6:11	1836
house be made a dunghill for *t*	Ezr 6:11	1836
to destroy *t* house of God which	Ezr 6:12	1791
governor on *t* side the river,	Ezr 6:13	
t house was finished on the third	Ezr 6:15	1836
of *t* house of God with joy	Ezr 6:16	1836
of *t* house of God an hundred	Ezr 6:17	1836
T Ezra went up from Babylon	Ezr 7:6	1931
Now *t* is the copy of the letter	Ezr 7:11	2088
speedily with *t* money bullocks	Ezr 7:17	1836
or ministers of *t* house of God	Ezr 7:24	1836
a thing as *t* in the king's heart	Ezr 7:27	2063
t is the genealogy of them that	Ezr 8:1	428
fasted and besought our God for *t*	Ezr 8:23	2063
all *t* was a burnt offering unto	Ezr 8:35	
the governors on *t* side the river	Ezr 8:36	
hath been chief in *t* trespass	Ezr 9:2	2088
And when I heard *t* thing, I rent	Ezr 9:3	2088
in a great trespass unto *t* day	Ezr 9:7	2088
confusion of face, as it is *t* day	Ezr 9:7	2088
God, what shall we say after *t*	Ezr 9:10	2063
given us such deliverance as *t*	Ezr 9:13	2063
yet escaped, as it is *t* day	Ezr 9:15	2063
stand before thee because of *t*	Ezr 9:15	2063
hope in Israel concerning *t* thing	Ezr 10:2	2063
for *t* matter belongeth unto thee	Ezr 10:4	
should do according to *t* word	Ezr 10:5	2088
trembling because of *t* matter	Ezr 10:9	
neither is *t* a work of one day or	Ezr 10:13	
that have transgressed in *t* thing	Ezr 10:13	2088
for *t* matter be turned from us	Ezr 10:14	2088
were employed about *t* matter	Ezr 10:15	2063
I pray thee, thy servant *t* day	Neh 1:11	
him mercy in the sight of *t* man	Neh 1:11	2088
t is nothing else but sorrow of	Neh 2:2	2088
their hands for *t* good work	Neh 2:18	
What is *t* thing that ye do	Neh 2:19	2088
the governor on *t* side the river	Neh 3:7	
you, let us leave off *t* usury	Neh 5:10	2088
I pray you, to them, even *t* day	Neh 5:11	
should do according to *t* promise	Neh 5:12	2088
that performeth not *t* promise	Neh 5:13	2088
people did according to *t* promise	Neh 5:13	2088
I continued in the work of *t* wall	Neh 5:16	2063
yet for all *t* required not I the	Neh 5:18	2063
bondage was heavy upon *t* people	Neh 5:18	2088
all that I have done for *t* people	Neh 5:19	2088
unto me four times after *t* sort	Neh 6:4	2088
pronounced *t* prophecy against me	Neh 6:12	
for they perceived that *t* work	Neh 6:16	2063
men of the people of Israel was *t*	Neh 7:7	
T day is holy unto the LORD your	Neh 8:9	
for *t* day is holy unto our Lord	Neh 8:10	
fourth day of *t* month the	Neh 9:1	2088
get thee a name, as it is *t* day	Neh 9:10	2088
T is thy God that brought thee up	Neh 9:18	2088
the kings of Assyria unto *t* day	Neh 9:32	2088
Behold, we are servants *t* day	Neh 9:36	
because of all *t* we make a sure	Neh 9:38	2063
And before *t*, Eliashib the priest,	Neh 13:4	2088
But in all *t* time was not I at	Neh 13:6	2088
me, O my God, concerning *t*	Neh 13:14	2088
What evil thing is *t* that ye do	Neh 13:17	2088
our God bring all *t* evil upon us	Neh 13:18	2088
upon us, and upon *t* city	Neh 13:18	2063
me, O my God, concerning *t* also	Neh 13:22	2063
unto you to do all *t* great evil	Neh 13:27	2063
(*t* is Ahasuerus which reigned	Est 1:1	1931
For *t* deed of the queen shall	Est 1:17	
Media say *t* day unto all the	Est 1:18	2088
holdest thy peace at *t* time	Est 4:14	2063
the kingdom for such a time as *t*	Est 4:14	2063
them return Mordecai *t* answer	Est 4:15	
Haman come *t* day unto the banquet	Est 5:4	
Yet all *t* availeth me nothing, so	Est 5:13	2088
hath been done to Mordecai for *t*	Est 6:3	2088
let *t* apparel and horse be	Est 6:9	
and enemy is *t* wicked Haman	Est 7:6	2088
for *t* man Mordecai waxed greater	Est 9:4	
according unto *t* day's decree	Est 9:13	
To stablish *t* among them, that	Est 9:21	
for all the words of *t* letter	Est 9:26	
they had seen concerning *t* matter	Est 9:26	3602
to confirm *t* second letter of	Est 9:29	2063
so that *t* man was the greatest of	Job 1:3	1931
In all *t* Job sinned not, nor	Job 1:22	2063
In all *t* did not Job sin with his	Job 2:10	2063
three friends heard of all *t* evil	Job 2:11	2063
After *t* opened Job his mouth, and	Job 3:1	3651
Is not *t* thy fear, thy confidence	Job 4:6	
Lo *t*, we have searched it, so it	Job 5:27	2063
t is the joy of his way, and out	Job 8:19	1931

T is one thing, therefore I said	Job 9:22	1931
I know that *t* is with thee	Job 10:13	2063
hand of the LORD hath wrought *t*	Job 12:9	2063
Lo, mine eye hath seen all *t*	Job 13:1	
men shall be astonied at *t*	Job 17:8	2063
t is the place of him that	Job 18:21	2088
my skin worms destroy *t* body	Job 19:26	2063
to answer, and for *t* I make haste	Job 20:2	
Knowest thou not *t* of old	Job 20:4	2063
T is the portion of a wicked man	Job 20:29	2088
let *t* be your consolations	Job 21:2	2063
T is the portion of a wicked man	Job 27:13	2088
For *t* is an heinous crime	Job 31:11	1931
T also were an iniquity to be	Job 31:28	1931
Behold, in *t* thou art not just	Job 33:12	2063
thou hast understanding, hear *t*	Job 34:16	2063
Thinkest thou *t* to be right	Job 35:2	2063
for *t* hast thou chosen rather	Job 36:21	2088
At *t* also my heart trembleth, and	Job 37:1	2063
Hearken unto *t*, O Job	Job 37:14	2063
Who is *t* that darkeneth counsel	Job 38:2	2088
After *t* lived Job an hundred and	Job 42:16	2063
t day have I begotten thee	Ps 2:7	
O LORD my God, if I have done *t*	Ps 7:3	2063
t shall be the portion of their	Ps 11:6	
them from *t* generation for ever	Ps 12:7	2098
have their portion in *t* life	Ps 17:14	
unto the LORD the words of *t* song	Ps 18:*t*	2063
be born, that he hath done *t*	Ps 22:31	
T is the generation of them that	Ps 24:6	2088
Who is *t* King of glory	Ps 24:8	2088
Who is *t* King of glory	Ps 24:10	2088
me, in *t* will I be confident	Ps 27:3	2063
For *t* shall every one that is	Ps 32:6	2063
T poor man cried, and the LORD	Ps 34:6	2088
T thou hast seen, O LORD	Ps 35:22	
By *t* I know that thou favourest	Ps 41:11	2063
All *t* is come upon us	Ps 44:17	2063
Shall not God search *t* out	Ps 44:21	2063
For *t* God is our God for ever and	Ps 48:14	2088
Hear *t*, all ye people	Ps 49:1	2063
T their way is their folly	Ps 49:13	2088
Now consider *t*, ye that forget	Ps 50:22	2063
and done *t* evil in thy sight	Ps 51:4	
t is the man that made not God	Ps 52:7	
t I know	Ps 56:9	2088
twice have I heard *t*	Ps 62:11	2098
t is the hill which God desireth	Ps 68:16	
T also shall please the LORD	Ps 69:31	
The humble shall see *t*, and be	Ps 69:32	
thy strength unto *t* generation	Ps 71:18	
When I thought to know *t*, it was	Ps 73:16	2063
t mount Zion, wherein thou hast	Ps 74:2	2088
Remember *t*, that the enemy hath	Ps 74:18	2063
And I said, *T* is my infirmity	Ps 77:10	1931
Therefore the LORD heard *t*	Ps 78:21	
For all *t* they sinned still, and	Ps 78:32	2063
even to *t* mountain, which his	Ps 78:54	2088
When God heard *t*, he was wroth,	Ps 78:59	
and behold, and visit *t* vine	Ps 80:14	2063
For *t* was a statute for Israel,	Ps 81:4	1931
T he ordained in Joseph for a	Ps 81:5	
t man was born there	Ps 87:4	2088
And of Zion it shall be said, *T*	Ps 87:5	
that *t* man was born there	Ps 87:6	2088
neither doth a fool understand *t*	Ps 92:6	2063
was I grieved with *t* generation	Ps 95:10	
T shall be written for the	Ps 102:18	2088
So is *t* great and wide sea,	Ps 104:25	2088
Let *t* be the reward of mine	Ps 109:20	2063
they may know that *t* is thy hand	Ps 109:27	2063
of the LORD from *t* time forth	Ps 113:2	
bless the LORD from *t* time forth	Ps 115:18	
T gate of the LORD, into which	Ps 118:20	2088
T is the LORD's doing	Ps 118:23	2063
T is the day which the LORD hath	Ps 118:24	2088
T is my comfort in my affliction	Ps 119:50	
T I had, because I kept thy	Ps 119:56	
They continue *t* day according to	Ps 119:91	
thy coming in from *t* time forth	Ps 121:8	
T is my rest for ever	Ps 132:14	
t honour have all his saints	Ps 149:9	1931
Do *t* now, my son, and deliver	Prov 6:3	2063
t day have I payed my vows	Prov 7:14	
I have made known to thee *t* day	Prov 22:19	
it may be said, See, *t* is new	Eccl 1:10	2088
t sore travail hath God given to	Eccl 1:13	1931
I perceived that *t* also is	Eccl 1:17	2088
and, behold, *t* also is vanity	Eccl 2:1	1931
t was my portion of all my labour	Eccl 2:10	2088
my heart, that *t* also is vanity	Eccl 2:15	2088
T is also vanity	Eccl 2:19	2088
T also is vanity and a great evil	Eccl 2:21	2088
T is also vanity	Eccl 2:23	
T also I saw, that it was from	Eccl 2:24	2088
T also is vanity and vexation of	Eccl 2:26	2088
that for *t* a man is envied of his	Eccl 4:4	1931
T is also vanity and vexation of	Eccl 4:4	2088
T is also vanity, yea, it is a	Eccl 4:8	2088
Surely *t* also is vanity and	Eccl 4:16	2088
t is also vanity	Eccl 5:10	2088
t also is a sore evil, that in	Eccl 5:16	2090
t is the gift of God	Eccl 5:19	2090
t is vanity, and it is an evil	Eccl 6:2	2088
t hath more rest than the other	Eccl 6:5	2088
t is also vanity and vexation of	Eccl 6:9	2088
what is good for man in *t* life	Eccl 6:12	
t also is vanity	Eccl 7:6	2088
not enquire wisely concerning *t*	Eccl 7:10	2088
thou shouldest take hold of *t*	Eccl 7:18	2088
also from *t* withdraw not thine	Eccl 7:18	2088
All *t* have I proved by wisdom	Eccl 7:23	2090
t have I found, saith the	Eccl 7:27	2088
t only have I found, that God	Eccl 7:29	2088
All *t* have I seen, and applied my	Eccl 8:9	2088
t is also vanity	Eccl 8:10	2088
I said that *t* also is vanity	Eccl 8:14	2088
For all *t* I considered in my	Eccl 9:1	2088
in my heart even to declare all *t*	Eccl 9:1	2088
T is an evil among all things	Eccl 9:3	2088
for that is thy portion in *t* life	Eccl 9:9	
T wisdom have I seen also under	Eccl 9:13	2090
either *t* or that, or whether they	Eccl 11:6	2088
for *t* is the whole duty of man	Eccl 12:13	2088
Who is *t* that cometh out of the	Song 3:6	2063
T is my beloved	Song 5:16	2088
t is my friend, O daughters of	Song 5:16	2088
T thy stature is like to a palm	Song 7:7	2063
Who is *t* that cometh up from the	Song 8:5	2063
who hath required *t* at your hand	Is 1:12	2063
let *t* ruin be under thy hand	Is 3:6	2063
For all *t* his anger is not turned	Is 5:25	2063
said, Lo, *t* hath touched thy lips	Is 6:7	2088
tell *t* people, Hear ye indeed,	Is 6:9	2088
Make the heart of *t* people fat	Is 6:10	2088
Forasmuch as *t* people refuseth	Is 8:6	2088
not walk in the way of *t* people	Is 8:11	2088
them to whom *t* people shall say	Is 8:12	2088
speak not according to *t* word	Is 8:20	2088
but *t* shall be with burning and	Is 9:5	
the LORD of hosts will perform *t*	Is 9:7	2063
For all *t* his anger is not turned	Is 9:12	2063
For the leaders of *t* people cause	Is 9:16	2088
For all *t* his anger is not turned	Is 9:17	2063
For all *t* his anger is not turned	Is 9:21	2063
For all *t* his anger is not turned	Is 10:4	2063
t is known in all the earth	Is 12:5	2063
That thou shalt take up *t* proverb	Is 14:4	2088
Is *t* the man that made the earth	Is 14:16	2088
T is the purpose that is purposed	Is 14:26	2063
t is the hand that is stretched	Is 14:26	2063
that king Ahaz died was *t* burden	Is 14:28	2088
T is the word that the LORD hath	Is 16:13	2008
T is the portion of them that	Is 17:14	2088
the inhabitant of *t* isle shall	Is 20:6	2088
Surely *t* iniquity shall not be	Is 22:14	2088
Go, get thee unto *t* treasurer	Is 22:15	2088
Is *t* your joyous city, whose	Is 23:7	2063
Who hath taken *t* counsel against	Is 23:8	2063
t people was not, til the	Is 23:13	2088
for the LORD hath spoken *t* word	Is 24:3	2088
in *t* mountain shall the LORD of	Is 25:6	2088
he will destroy in *t* mountain the	Is 25:7	2088
in that day, Lo, *t* is our God	Is 25:9	2088
t is the LORD	Is 25:9	2088
For in *t* mountain shall the hand	Is 25:10	2088
In that day shall *t* song be sung	Is 26:1	2088
By *t* therefore shall the iniquity	Is 27:9	2063
t is all the fruit to take away	Is 27:9	2088
tongue will he speak to *t* people	Is 28:11	2088
T is the rest wherewith ye may	Is 28:12	2063
and *t* is the refreshing	Is 28:12	2063
that rule *t* people which is in	Is 28:14	2088
T also cometh forth from the LORD	Is 28:29	2088
that is learned, saying, Read *t*	Is 29:11	2088
is not learned, saying, Read *t*	Is 29:12	2088
Forasmuch as *t* people draw near	Is 29:13	
a marvellous work among *t* people	Is 29:14	2088
have I cried concerning *t*	Is 30:7	2063
That *t* is a rebellious people,	Is 30:9	1931
Israel, Because ye despise *t* word	Is 30:12	2088
Therefore *t* iniquity shall be to	Is 30:13	2088
T is the way, walk ye in it, when	Is 30:21	2088
What confidence is *t* wherein thou	Is 36:4	2088
in the staff of *t* broken reed	Is 36:6	2088
Ye shall worship before *t* altar	Is 36:7	2088
LORD against *t* land to destroy it	Is 36:10	2063
unto me, Go up against *t* land	Is 36:10	2063
t city shall not be delivered	Is 36:15	2063
T day is a day of trouble, and of	Is 37:3	2088
T is the word which the LORD hath	Is 37:22	2088
t shall be a sign unto thee, Ye	Is 37:30	2088
Ye shall eat *t* year such as	Is 37:30	
of the LORD of hosts shall do *t*	Is 37:32	2063
He shall not come into *t* city	Is 37:33	2063
and shall not come into *t* city	Is 37:34	2063
For I will defend *t* city to save	Is 37:35	2063
t city out of the hand of the	Is 38:6	2063
and I will defend *t* city	Is 38:6	2063
t shall be a sign unto thee from	Is 38:7	2088
that the LORD will do *t* thing	Is 38:7	2088
shall praise thee, as I do *t* day	Is 38:19	
have laid up in store until *t* day	Is 39:6	2088
the hand of the LORD hath done *t*	Is 41:20	2063
But *t* is a people robbed and	Is 42:22	1931
Who among you will give ear to *t*	Is 42:23	2063
who among them can declare *t*	Is 43:9	2063
T people have I formed for myself	Is 43:21	2098
hath declared *t* from ancient time	Is 45:21	2063
Remember *t*, and shew yourselves	Is 46:8	2063
Therefore hear now *t*, thou that	Is 47:8	2063
Hear ye *t*, O house of Jacob,	Is 48:1	2063
Thou hast heard, see all *t*	Is 48:6	
thee new things from *t* time	Is 48:6	
Come ye near unto me, hear ye *t*	Is 48:16	2063
of singing declare ye, tell *t*	Is 48:20	2063
T shall ye have of mine hand	Is 50:11	2063
Therefore hear now *t*, thou	Is 51:21	2063
For *t* is as the waters of Noah	Is 54:9	2063
T is the heritage of the servants	Is 54:17	2063
Blessed is the man that doeth *t*	Is 56:2	2063
and to morrow shall be as *t* day	Is 56:12	2088
ye shall not fast as ye do *t* day	Is 58:4	
wilt thou call *t* a fast, and an	Is 58:5	2088
Is not *t* the fast that I have	Is 58:6	2088
t is my covenant with them, saith	Is 59:21	2063
Who is *t* that cometh from Edom,	Is 63:1	2088
t that is glorious in his apparel	Is 63:1	2088
but to *t* man will I look, even to	Is 66:2	2088
And when ye see *t*, your heart	Is 66:14	
I have *t* day set thee over the	Jer 1:10	2088
I have made thee *t* day a defenced	Jer 1:18	
Be astonished, O ye heavens, at *t*	Jer 2:12	2063
thou not procured *t* unto thyself	Jer 2:17	2063
thou not from *t* time cry unto me	Jer 3:4	
yet for all *t* her treacherous	Jer 3:10	2063
from our youth even unto *t* day	Jer 3:25	2088
For *t* gird you with sackcloth	Jer 4:8	2063
hast greatly deceived *t* people	Jer 4:10	2088
time shall it be said to *t* people	Jer 4:11	2088
t is thy wickedness, because it	Jer 4:18	2063
For *t* shall the earth mourn, and	Jer 4:28	2063
How shall I pardon thee for *t*	Jer 5:7	2063
be avenged on such a nation as *t*	Jer 5:9	2088
of hosts, Because ye speak *t* word	Jer 5:14	2088
t people wood, and it shall devour	Jer 5:14	2088
Declare *t* in the house of Jacob,	Jer 5:20	2063
Hear now *t*, O foolish people, and	Jer 5:21	2063
But *t* people hath a revolting and	Jer 5:23	2088
be avenged on such a nation as *t*	Jer 5:29	
t is the city to be visited	Jer 6:6	1931
I will bring evil upon *t* people	Jer 6:19	2088
stumblingblocks before *t* people	Jer 6:21	2088
house, and proclaim there *t* word	Jer 7:2	2088
cause you to dwell in *t* place	Jer 7:3	2088
not innocent blood in *t* place	Jer 7:6	2088
I cause you to dwell in *t* place	Jer 7:7	2088
and stand before me in *t* house	Jer 7:10	2088
Is *t* house, which is called by my	Jer 7:11	2088
Therefore will I do unto *t* house	Jer 7:14	
pray not thou for *t* people	Jer 7:16	2088
shall be poured out upon *t* place	Jer 7:20	2088
But *t* thing commanded I them,	Jer 7:23	2088
t day I have even sent unto you	Jer 7:25	2088
T is a nation that obeyeth not	Jer 7:28	2088
the carcases of *t* people shall be	Jer 7:33	2088
them that remain of *t* evil family	Jer 8:3	2063
Why then is *t* people of Jerusalem	Jer 8:5	2088
be avenged on such a nation as *t*	Jer 9:9	2088
wise man, that may understand *t*	Jer 9:12	2063
even *t* people, with wormwood, and	Jer 9:15	2088
let him that glorieth glory in *t*	Jer 9:24	2063
inhabitants of the land at *t* once	Jer 10:18	2063
Truly *t* is a grief, and I must	Jer 10:19	2063
Hear ye the words of *t* covenant	Jer 11:2	2088
not the words of *t* covenant	Jer 11:3	2088
milk and honey, as it is *t* day	Jer 11:5	2088
Hear ye the words of *t* covenant	Jer 11:6	2088
land of Egypt, even unto *t* day	Jer 11:7	2088
them all the words of *t* covenant	Jer 11:8	2088
pray not thou for *t* people	Jer 11:14	2088
After *t* manner will I mar the	Jer 13:9	
T evil people, which refuse to	Jer 13:10	2088
them, shall even be as *t* girdle	Jer 13:10	2088
thou shalt speak unto them *t* word	Jer 13:12	2088
all the inhabitants of *t* land	Jer 13:13	
T is thy lot, the portion of thy	Jer 13:25	2088
Thus saith the LORD unto *t* people	Jer 14:10	2088
Pray not for *t* people for their	Jer 14:11	2088
give you assured peace in *t* place	Jer 14:13	2088
and famine shall not be in *t* land	Jer 14:15	2063
thou shalt say *t* word unto them	Jer 14:17	2088
mind could not be toward *t* people	Jer 15:1	2088
I will make thee unto *t* people a	Jer 15:20	2088
have sons or daughters in *t* place	Jer 16:2	2088
that are born in *t* place, and	Jer 16:3	2088
fathers that begat them in *t* land	Jer 16:3	2088
taken away my peace from *t* people	Jer 16:5	2088
and the small shall die in *t* land	Jer 16:6	2063
cease out of *t* place in your eyes	Jer 16:9	2088
when thou shalt shew *t* people all	Jer 16:10	2088
all *t* great evil against us	Jer 16:10	2063
will I cast you out of *t* land	Jer 16:13	2063
I will *t* once cause them to know,	Jer 16:21	2063
of *t* city on the sabbath day	Jer 17:24	2063
into the gates of *t* city kings	Jer 17:25	2063
t city shall remain for ever	Jer 17:25	2088
cannot I do with you as *t* potter	Jer 18:6	2088
I will bring evil upon *t* place	Jer 19:3	2088
me, and have estranged *t* place	Jer 19:4	2088
have filled *t* place with the	Jer 19:4	2088
that *t* place shall no more be	Jer 19:6	2088
of Judah and Jerusalem in *t* place	Jer 19:7	2088
I will make *t* city desolate, and	Jer 19:8	2063
Even so will I break *t* people	Jer 19:11	2088
t city, as one breaketh a	Jer 19:11	2063
Thus will I do unto *t* place	Jer 19:12	2088
even make *t* city as Tophet	Jer 19:12	2063
Behold, I will bring upon *t* city	Jer 19:15	
all the strength of *t* city	Jer 20:5	2063
them into the midst of *t* city	Jer 21:4	2063
smite the inhabitants of *t* city	Jer 21:6	2063
such as are left in *t* city from	Jer 21:7	2063
unto *t* people thou shalt say,	Jer 21:8	2088
He that abideth in *t* city shall	Jer 21:9	2063
my face against *t* city for evil	Jer 21:10	2063
of Judah, and speak there *t* word	Jer 22:1	2088
shed innocent blood in *t* place	Jer 22:3	2088
For if ye do *t* thing indeed	Jer 22:4	2088
of *t* house kings sitting upon the	Jer 22:4	2088
that *t* house shall become a	Jer 22:5	2088
many nations shall pass by *t* city	Jer 22:8	2063
LORD done thus unto *t* great city	Jer 22:8	2063
which went forth out of *t* place	Jer 22:11	2088
and shall see *t* land no more	Jer 22:12	2063
was not *t* to know me	Jer 22:16	1931
T hath been thy manner from thy	Jer 22:21	2088
Is *t* man Coniah a despised broken	Jer 22:28	2088
Write ye *t* man childless, a man	Jer 22:30	2088
t is his name whereby he shall be	Jer 23:6	2088
How long shall *t* be in the heart	Jer 23:26	
shall not profit *t* people at all	Jer 23:32	2088

when *t* people, or the prophet, or	Jer 23:33	2088
Because ye say *t* word, The burden	Jer 23:38	2088
whom I have sent out of *t* place	Jer 24:5	2088
I will bring them again to *t* land	Jer 24:6	2063
Jerusalem, that remain in *t* land	Jer 24:8	2063
king of Judah, even unto *t* day	Jer 25:3	2088
and will bring them against *t* land	Jer 25:9	2063
And *t* whole land shall be a	Jer 25:11	2063
all that is written in *t* book	Jer 25:13	2088
the wine cup of *t* fury at my hand	Jer 25:15	2063
as it is *t* day	Jer 25:18	2088
Judah came *t* word from the LORD	Jer 26:1	2088
Then will I make *t* house like	Jer 26:6	2088
will make *t* city a curse to all	Jer 26:6	2063
T house shall be like Shiloh, and	Jer 26:9	2088
t city shall be desolate without	Jer 26:9	2063
saying, *T* man is worthy to die	Jer 26:11	2088
he hath prophesied against *t* city	Jer 26:11	2063
me to prophesy against *t* house	Jer 26:12	2088
against *t* city all the words that	Jer 26:12	2063
upon yourselves, and upon *t* city	Jer 26:15	2063
T man is not worthy to die	Jer 26:16	2088
who prophesied against *t* city	Jer 26:20	2063
against *t* land according to all	Jer 26:20	2063
t word unto Jeremiah from the	Jer 27:1	2088
to the priests and to all *t* people	Jer 27:16	2088
wherefore should *t* city be laid	Jer 27:17	2063
the vessels that remain in *t* city	Jer 27:19	2063
up, and restore them to *t* place	Jer 27:22	2008
t place all the vessels of the	Jer 28:3	2008
of Babylon took away from *t* place	Jer 28:3	2008
I will bring again to *t* place	Jer 28:4	2008
from Babylon into *t* place	Jer 28:6	2008
Nevertheless hear thou now *t* word	Jer 28:7	2008
but thou makest *t* people to trust	Jer 28:15	2008
t year thou shalt die, because	Jer 28:16	
causing you to return to *t* place	Jer 29:10	2088
people that dwelleth in *t* city	Jer 29:16	2063
saying, *T* captivity is long	Jer 29:28	1931
Zephaniah the priest read *t*	Jer 29:29	
a man to dwell among *t* people	Jer 29:32	2088
T is Zion, whom no man seeketh	Jer 30:17	1931
for who is *t* that engaged his	Jer 30:21	
As yet they shall use *t* speech in	Jer 31:23	2088
Upon *t* I awaked, and beheld	Jer 31:26	2063
But *t* shall be the covenant that	Jer 31:33	2063
I will give *t* city into the hand	Jer 32:3	2063
Then I knew that *t* was the word	Jer 32:8	1931
t evidence of the purchase, both	Jer 32:14	2088
and *t* evidence which is open	Jer 32:14	2088
be possessed again in *t* land	Jer 32:15	2063
land of Egypt, even unto *t* day	Jer 32:20	2088
made thee a name, as at *t* day	Jer 32:20	2088
And hast given them *t* land	Jer 32:22	2063
all *t* evil to come upon them	Jer 32:23	2063
I will give *t* city into the hand	Jer 32:28	2063
that fight against *t* city	Jer 32:29	2063
shall come and set fire on *t* city	Jer 32:29	2063
For *t* city hath been to me as a	Jer 32:31	2063
they built it even unto *t* day	Jer 32:31	2088
that they should do *t* abomination	Jer 32:35	2063
God of Israel, concerning *t* city	Jer 32:36	2063
bring them again unto *t* place	Jer 32:37	
I will plant them in *t* land	Jer 32:41	2063
Like as I have brought all *t*	Jer 32:42	2063
all *t* great evil upon *t* people	Jer 32:42	2088
fields shall be bought in *t* land	Jer 32:43	2063
concerning the houses of *t* city	Jer 33:4	2063
I have hid my face from *t* city	Jer 33:5	2063
there shall be heard in *t* place	Jer 33:10	2088
Again in *t* place, which is	Jer 33:12	2088
t is the name wherewith she shall	Jer 33:16	2088
not what *t* people have spoken	Jer 33:24	2088
I will give *t* city into the hand	Jer 34:2	2063
T is the word that came unto	Jer 34:8	
and cause them to return to *t* city	Jer 34:22	2063
for unto *t* day they drink none,	Jer 35:14	2088
but *t* people hath not hearkened	Jer 35:16	2088
that *t* word came unto Jeremiah	Jer 36:1	2088
days of Josiah, even into *t* day	Jer 36:2	2088
hath pronounced against *t* people	Jer 36:7	2088
Thou hast burned *t* roll, saying,	Jer 36:29	2063
certainly come and destroy *t* land	Jer 36:29	2063
again, and fight against *t* city	Jer 37:8	2063
tent, and burn *t* city with fire	Jer 37:10	2063
thy servants, or against *t* people	Jer 37:18	2088
against you, nor against *t* land	Jer 37:19	2063
He that remaineth in *t* city shall	Jer 38:2	2063
T city shall surely be given into	Jer 38:3	2063
let *t* man be put to death	Jer 38:4	2088
men of war that remain in *t* city	Jer 38:4	2063
for *t* man seeketh not the welfare	Jer 38:4	2088
not the welfare of *t* people	Jer 38:4	2088
LORD liveth, that made us *t* soul	Jer 38:16	2063
t city shall not be burned with	Jer 38:17	2063
then shall *t* city be given into	Jer 38:18	2063
t is the word that the LORD hath	Jer 38:21	2088
thou shalt cause *t* city to be	Jer 38:23	2063
my words upon *t* city for evil	Jer 39:16	2063
pronounced *t* evil upon	Jer 40:2	2063
evil upon *t* place	Jer 40:2	2088
therefore *t* thing is come upon	Jer 40:3	2088
I loose thee *t* day from the	Jer 40:4	
Kareah, Thou shalt not do *t* thing	Jer 40:16	2088
thy God, even for all *t* remnant	Jer 42:2	2063
If ye will still abide in *t* land	Jer 42:10	2063
say, We will not dwell in *t* land	Jer 42:13	2063
ye shall see *t* place no more	Jer 42:18	2088
that I have admonished you *t* day	Jer 42:19	
now I have *t* day declared it to	Jer 42:21	
t day they are a desolation, and	Jer 44:2	2088
do not *t* abominable thing that I	Jer 44:4	2088
wasted and desolate, as at *t* day	Jer 44:6	2088
Wherefore commit ye *t* great evil	Jer 44:7	

are not humbled even unto *t* day	Jer 44:10	2088
an inhabitant, as at *t* day	Jer 44:22	2088
therefore *t* evil is happened unto	Jer 44:23	2063
is happened unto you, as at *t* day	Jer 44:23	2088
t shall be a sign unto you, saith	Jer 44:29	2063
that I will punish you in *t* place	Jer 44:29	2088
will pluck up, even *t* whole land	Jer 45:4	1931
Who is *t* that cometh up as a	Jer 46:7	2088
For *t* is the day of the Lord GOD	Jer 46:10	1931
last *t* Nebuchadrezzar king of	Jer 50:17	2088
for *t* is the work of the Lord GOD	Jer 50:25	1931
for *t* is the time of the LORD's	Jer 51:6	1931
t Seraiah was a quiet prince	Jer 51:59	
thou hast spoken against *t* place	Jer 51:62	2088
made an end of reading *t* book	Jer 51:63	2088
T is the people whom	Jer 52:28	2088
Is *t* the city that men call The	Lam 2:15	2088
certainly *t* is the day that we	Lam 2:16	2088
consider to whom thou hast done *t*	Lam 2:20	3541
T I recall to my mind, therefore	Lam 3:21	2063
For *t* our heart is faint	Lam 5:17	2088
And *t* was their appearance	Eze 1:5	2088
had two, which covered on *t* side	Eze 1:23	2007
T was the appearance of the	Eze 1:28	1931
against me, even unto *t* very day	Eze 2:3	2088
eat *t* roll, and go speak unto the	Eze 3:1	2063
fill thy bowels with *t* roll that	Eze 3:3	2063
T shall be a sign to the house of	Eze 4:3	1931
T is Jerusalem	Eze 5:5	2063
that I would do *t* evil unto them	Eze 6:10	2063
at the gate of the altar *t* image	Eze 8:5	2088
said he unto me, Hast thou seen *t*	Eze 8:15	
he said unto me, Hast thou seen *t*	Eze 8:17	
T is the living creature that I	Eze 10:15	1931
T is the living creature that I	Eze 10:20	1931
and give wicked counsel in *t* city	Eze 11:2	2063
t city is the caldron, and we be	Eze 11:3	1931
multiplied your slain in *t* city	Eze 11:6	2063
flesh, and *t* city is the caldron	Eze 11:7	1931
T city shall not be your caldron,	Eze 11:11	1931
unto us is *t* land given in	Eze 11:15	1931
T burden concerneth the prince in	Eze 12:10	2088
I will make *t* proverb to cease,	Eze 12:23	2088
Is *t* of thy whoredoms a small	Eze 16:20	
thou shalt not commit *t* lewdness	Eze 16:43	
shall use *t* proverb against thee	Eze 16:44	
t was the iniquity of thy sister	Eze 16:49	2088
t vine did bend her roots toward	Eze 17:7	2063
that ye use *t* proverb concerning	Eze 18:2	2088
more to use *t* proverb in Israel	Eze 18:3	2088
T is a lamentation, and shall be	Eze 19:14	1931
Yet in *t* your fathers have	Eze 20:27	2063
is called Bamah unto *t* day	Eze 20:29	2088
all your idols, even unto *t* day	Eze 20:31	
t sword is sharpened, and it is	Eze 21:11	1931
t shall not be the same	Eze 21:26	2063
And when her sister Aholibah saw *t*	Eze 23:11	
Moreover *t* they have done unto me	Eze 23:38	2063
of the day, even of *t* same day	Eze 24:2	2088
against Jerusalem *t* same day	Eze 24:2	2088
when *t* cometh, ye shall know that	Eze 24:24	
T is Pharaoh and all his multitude	Eze 31:18	1931
T is the lamentation wherewith	Eze 32:16	1931
when *t* cometh to pass, (lo, it	Eze 33:33	
I do not *t* for your sakes, O	Eze 36:22	
Not for your sakes do I *t*	Eze 36:32	
T land that was desolate is	Eze 36:35	1977
I will yet for *t* be enquired of	Eze 36:37	
t is the day whereof I have	Eze 39:8	1931
eastward were three on *t* side	Eze 40:10	6311
posts had one measure on *t* side	Eze 40:10	6311
chambers was one cubit on *t* side	Eze 40:12	
were six cubits on *t* side	Eze 40:12	6311
thereof were three on *t* side	Eze 40:21	6311
it had palm trees, one on *t* side	Eze 40:26	6311
on *t* side, and on that side	Eze 40:34	6311
on *t* side, and on that side	Eze 40:37	6311
gate were two tables on *t* side	Eze 40:39	6311
Four tables were on *t* side	Eze 40:41	6311
T chamber, whose prospect is	Eze 40:45	2090
the porch, five cubits on *t* side	Eze 40:48	6311
gate was three cubits on *t* side	Eze 40:48	6311
by the posts, one on *t* side	Eze 40:49	6311
unto me, *T* is the most holy place	Eze 41:4	2088
T is the table that is before the	Eze 41:22	2088
T is the law of the house	Eze 43:12	2063
t is the law of the house	Eze 43:12	2063
t shall be the higher place of	Eze 43:13	2088
T gate shall be shut, it shall	Eze 44:2	2088
T shall be holy in all the	Eze 45:1	1931
Of *t* there shall be for the	Eze 45:2	2088
of *t* measure shalt thou measure	Eze 45:3	2063
T is the oblation that ye shall	Eze 45:13	2063
give *t* oblation for the prince in	Eze 45:16	2063
of *t* gate before the LORD in the	Eze 46:3	1931
T is the place where the priests	Eze 46:20	2088
me, Son of man, hast thou seen *t*	Eze 47:6	
on *t* side and on that side, shall	Eze 47:12	2088
T shall be the border, whereby ye	Eze 47:13	2088
t land shall fall unto you for	Eze 47:14	2063
t shall be the border of the land	Eze 47:15	2088
And *t* is the north side	Eze 47:17	
And *t* is the east side	Eze 47:18	
t is the south side southward	Eze 47:19	
T is the west side	Eze 47:20	2063
So shall ye divide *t* land unto	Eze 47:21	2063
priests, shall be *t* holy oblation	Eze 48:10	
t oblation of the land that is	Eze 48:12	
T is the land which ye shall	Eze 48:29	2063
he consented to them in *t* matter	Dan 1:14	2088
For *t* cause the king was angry and	Dan 2:12	1836
God of heaven concerning *t* secret	Dan 2:18	1836
t secret is not revealed to me	Dan 2:30	1836
T great image, whose brightness	Dan 2:31	1797

T image's head was of fine gold,	Dan 2:32	1931
T is the dream	Dan 2:36	1836
Thou art *t* head of gold	Dan 2:38	1931
thou couldst reveal *t* secret	Dan 2:47	1836
to answer thee in *t* matter	Dan 3:16	1836
God that can deliver after *t* sort	Dan 3:29	1836
T matter is by the decree of the	Dan 4:17	
T dream I king Nebuchadnezzar	Dan 4:18	1836
T is the interpretation, O king,	Dan 4:24	1836
t is the decree of the most High,	Dan 4:24	1931
All *t* came upon the king	Dan 4:28	
Is not *t* great Babylon, that I	Dan 4:30	1668
Whosoever shall read *t* writing	Dan 5:7	1836
that they should read *t* writing	Dan 5:15	1836
heart, though thou knewest all *t*	Dan 5:22	1836
and *t* writing was written	Dan 5:24	1836
t is the writing that was written	Dan 5:25	1836
T is the interpretation of the	Dan 5:26	1836
Then *t* Daniel was preferred above	Dan 6:3	1836
any occasion against *t* Daniel	Dan 6:5	1836
So *t* Daniel prospered in the	Dan 6:28	1836
After *t* I beheld, and lo another,	Dan 7:6	1836
After *t* I saw in the night	Dan 7:7	1836
in *t* horn were eyes like the eyes	Dan 7:8	1668
and asked him the truth of all *t*	Dan 7:16	1836
the ten horns out of *t* kingdom	Dan 7:24	
make *t* man to understand the	Dan 8:16	1975
confusion of faces, as at *t* day	Dan 9:7	2088
all *t* evil is come upon us	Dan 9:13	2063
gotten thee renown, as at *t* day	Dan 9:15	
saw *t* great vision, and there	Dan 10:8	
when he had spoken *t* word unto me	Dan 10:11	2088
t my lord talk with *t* my lord	Dan 10:17	2088
After *t* shall he turn his face	Dan 11:18	
the one on *t* side of the bank of	Dan 12:5	2008
Hear ye *t*, O priests	Hos 5:1	2063
their God, nor seek him for all *t*	Hos 7:10	2063
t shall be their derision in the	Hos 7:16	2097
Hear *t*, ye old men, and give ear,	Joel 1:2	2063
Hath *t* been in your days, or even	Joel 1:2	2063
Proclaim ye *t* among the Gentiles	Joel 3:9	2063
Hear *t* word that the LORD hath	Amos 3:1	2088
Hear *t* word, ye kine of Bashan,	Amos 4:1	2088
for *t* liketh you, O ye children	Amos 4:5	3651
and because I will do *t* unto thee	Amos 4:12	2063
Hear ye *t* word which I take up	Amos 5:1	2088
The LORD repented for *t*	Amos 7:3	2063
The LORD repented for *t*	Amos 7:6	2063
T also shall not be, saith the	Amos 7:6	1931
Hear *t*, O ye that swallow up the	Amos 8:4	2063
Shall not the land tremble for *t*	Amos 8:8	2063
name, saith the LORD that doeth *t*	Amos 9:12	2063
the captivity of *t* host of the	Obad 20	2088
for whose cause *t* evil is upon us	Jonah 1:7	2063
for whose cause *t* evil is upon us	Jonah 1:8	2063
unto him, Why hast thou done *t*	Jonah 1:10	2063
sake *t* great tempest is upon you	Jonah 1:12	
us not perish for *t* man's life	Jonah 1:14	2088
was not *t* my saying, when I was	Jonah 4:2	2088
transgression of Jacob is all *t*	Mic 1:5	2063
against *t* family do I devise an	Mic 2:3	2063
for *t* time is evil	Mic 2:3	1931
for *t* is not your rest	Mic 2:10	2063
even be the prophet of *t* people	Mic 2:11	2088
Hear *t*, I pray you, ye heads of	Mic 3:9	2063
t man shall be the peace, when	Mic 5:5	2088
imputing *t* his power unto his god	Hab 1:11	2098
the remnant of Baal from *t* place	Zeph 1:4	
T shall they have for their pride	Zeph 2:10	2063
T is the rejoicing city that	Zeph 2:15	2063
T people say, The time is not	Hag 1:2	2088
houses, and *t* house lie waste	Hag 1:4	2088
saw *t* house in her first glory	Hag 2:3	2088
I will fill *t* house with glory,	Hag 2:7	2088
The glory of *t* latter house shall	Hag 2:9	2088
in *t* place will I give peace,	Hag 2:9	2088
So is *t* people, and so	Hag 2:14	2088
so is *t* nation before me, saith	Hag 2:14	2088
I pray you, consider from *t* day	Hag 2:15	2088
Consider now from *t* day and upward	Hag 2:18	2088
from *t* day will I bless you	Hag 2:19	2088
speak to *t* young man, saying,	Zec 2:4	1975
is not *t* a brand plucked out of	Zec 3:2	2088
T is the word of the LORD unto	Zec 4:6	2088
laid the foundation of *t* house	Zec 4:9	2088
T is the curse that goeth forth	Zec 5:3	2063
off as on *t* side according to it	Zec 5:3	2088
see what is *t* that goeth forth	Zec 5:5	2063
T is an ephah that goeth forth	Zec 5:6	2063
T is their resemblance through	Zec 5:6	2063
t is a woman that sitteth in the	Zec 5:7	2063
And he said, *T* is wickedness	Zec 5:8	2063
t shall come to pass, if ye will	Zec 6:15	
remnant of *t* people in these days	Zec 8:6	2088
of *t* people as in the former days	Zec 8:11	2088
of *t* people to possess all these	Zec 8:12	2088
t shall be the plague wherewith	Zec 14:12	2063
be in these tents, as *t* plague	Zec 14:15	2063
T shall be the punishment of	Zec 14:19	2063
t hath been by your means	Mal 1:9	2063
should I accept *t* of your hand	Mal 1:13	
priests, *t* commandment is for you	Mal 2:1	2063
have sent *t* commandment unto you	Mal 2:4	2063
will cut off the man that doeth *t*	Mal 2:12	
t have ye done again, covering	Mal 2:13	
robbed me, even *t* whole nation	Mal 3:9	
feet in the day that I shall do *t*	Mal 4:3	
of Jesus Christ was on *t* wise	Mt 1:18	*3779*
Now all *t* was done, that it might	Mt 1:22	*5124*
For *t* is he that was spoken of by	Mt 3:3	*3773*
T is my beloved Son, in whom I am	Mt 3:17	*3773*
After *t* manner therefore pray ye	Mt 6:9	*3779*
Give us *t* day our daily bread	Mt 6:11	*4594*
for *t* is the law and the prophets	Mt 7:12	*3778*

and I say to *t* man, Go, and he	Mt 8:9	5129
and to my servant, Do *t*, and he	Mt 8:9	5124
saying, What manner of man is *t*	Mt 8:27	3778
themselves, *T* man blasphemeth	Mt 9:3	3778
Believe ye that I am able to do *t*	Mt 9:28	5124
when they persecute you in *t* city	Mt 10:23	5026
For *t* is he, of whom it is	Mt 11:10	3778
t is Elias, which was for to come	Mt 11:14	
shall I liken *t* generation	Mt 11:16	5026
would have remained until *t* day	Mt 11:23	4594
That in *t* place is one greater	Mt 12:6	5602
if ye had known what *t* meaneth	Mt 12:7	
Is not *t* the son of David	Mt 12:23	3778
T fellow doth not cast out devils	Mt 12:24	3778
forgiven him, neither in *t* world	Mt 12:32	5129
in judgment with *t* generation	Mt 12:41	5026
in the judgment with *t* generation	Mt 12:42	5026
be also unto *t* wicked generation	Mt 12:45	5026
For *t* people's heart is waxed	Mt 13:15	5127
T is he which received seed by	Mt 13:19	3778
and the care of *t* world, and the	Mt 13:22	5127
unto them, An enemy hath done *t*	Mt 13:28	5124
shall it be in the end of *t* world	Mt 13:40	5127
Whence hath *t* man	Mt 13:54	5129
man *t* wisdom, and	Mt 13:54	3778
Is not *t* the carpenter's son	Mt 13:55	3778
Whence then hath *t* man all these	Mt 13:56	5129
servants, *T* is John the Baptist	Mt 14:2	3778
T is a desert place, and the time	Mt 14:15	3588
T people draweth nigh unto me	Mt 15:8	3778
of the mouth, *t* defileth a man	Mt 15:11	5124
after they heard *t* saying	Mt 15:12	3588
him, Declare unto us *t* parable	Mt 15:15	5026
upon *t* rock I will build my	Mt 16:18	5026
t shall not be unto thee	Mt 16:22	5124
T is my beloved Son, in whom I am	Mt 17:5	3778
ye shall say unto *t* mountain	Mt 17:20	5129
Howbeit *t* kind goeth not out but	Mt 17:21	5124
humble himself as *t* little child	Mt 18:4	5124
For *t* cause shall a man leave	Mt 19:5	5127
All men cannot receive *t* saying	Mt 19:11	5126
them, With men *t* is impossible	Mt 19:26	5124
I will give unto *t* last, even as	Mt 20:14	5129
All *t* was done, that it might be	Mt 21:4	5124
city was moved, saying, Who is *t*	Mt 21:10	3778
T is Jesus the prophet of	Mt 21:11	3778
ye shall not only do *t* which is	Mt 21:21	3588
if ye shall say unto *t* mountain	Mt 21:21	5129
and who gave thee *t* authority	Mt 21:23	5026
among themselves, *T* is the heir	Mt 21:38	3778
t is the Lord's doing, and it is	Mt 21:42	3778
fall on *t* stone shall be broken	Mt 21:44	5126
saith unto them, Whose is *t* image	Mt 22:20	3778
And when the multitude heard *t*	Mt 22:33	
T is the first and great	Mt 22:38	3778
shall come upon *t* generation	Mt 23:36	5026
t gospel of the kingdom shall be	Mt 24:14	5124
beginning of the world to *t* time	Mt 24:21	3568
T generation shall not pass, till	Mt 24:34	3778
But know *t*, that if the goodman	Mt 24:43	1565
To what purpose is *t* waste	Mt 26:8	3778
For *t* ointment might have been	Mt 26:9	5124
hath poured *t* ointment on my body	Mt 26:12	5124
Wheresoever *t* gospel shall be	Mt 26:13	5124
whole world, there shall also *t*	Mt 26:13	3778
that *t* woman hath done, be told	Mt 26:13	3778
t is my body	Mt 26:26	5124
For *t* is my blood of the new	Mt 26:28	5124
henceforth of *t* fruit of the vine	Mt 26:29	5127
be offended because of me *t* night	Mt 26:31	5026
That *t* night, before the cock	Mt 26:34	5026
possible, let *t* cup pass from me	Mt 26:39	5124
if *t* cup may not pass away from	Mt 26:42	5124
But all *t* was done, that the	Mt 26:56	5124
T fellow said, I am able to	Mt 26:61	3778
T fellow was also with Jesus of	Mt 26:71	3778
The field of blood, unto *t* day	Mt 27:8	4594
t day in a dream because of him	Mt 27:19	4594
of the blood of *t* just person	Mt 27:24	5127
T IS JESUS THE	Mt 27:37	3778
said, *T* man calleth for Elias	Mt 27:47	3778
Truly *t* was the Son of God	Mt 27:54	3778
if *t* come to the governor's ears	Mt 28:14	5124
t saying is commonly reported	Mt 28:15	3778
among the Jews until *t* day	Mt 28:15	4594
saying, What thing is *t*	Mk 1:27	3778
what new doctrine is *t*	Mk 1:27	5124
Why doth *t* man thus speak	Mk 2:7	3778
We never saw it on *t* fashion	Mk 2:12	3779
unto them, Know ye not *t* parable	Mk 4:13	5026
And the cares of *t* world, and the	Mk 4:19	3588
another, What manner of man is *t*	Mk 4:41	3778
to see her that had done *t* thing	Mk 5:32	5124
unto them, Why make ye *t* ado	Mk 5:39	
whence hath *t* man these things	Mk 6:2	5129
what wisdom is *t* which is given	Mk 6:2	3588
Is not *t* the carpenter, the son	Mk 6:3	3778
T is a desert place, and now the	Mk 6:35	3588
T people honoureth me with their	Mk 7:6	3778
unto her, For *t* saying go thy way	Mk 7:29	5126
Why doth *t* generation seek after	Mk 8:12	3778
sign be given unto *t* generation	Mk 8:12	5026
me and of my words in *t* adulterous	Mk 8:38	5026
saying, *T* is my beloved Son	Mk 9:7	3778
is it ago since *t* came unto him	Mk 9:21	5124
T kind can come forth by nothing	Mk 9:29	5124
your heart he wrote you *t* precept	Mk 10:5	5026
For *t* cause shall a man leave his	Mk 10:7	5127
an hundredfold now in *t* time	Mk 10:30	5129
any man say unto you, Why do ye *t*	Mk 11:3	5124
shall say unto *t* mountain	Mk 11:23	5129
who gave thee *t* authority to do	Mk 11:28	5026
among themselves, *T* is the heir	Mk 12:7	3778
And have ye not read *t* scripture	Mk 12:10	5026
T was the Lord's doing, and it is	Mk 12:11	3778
saith unto them, Whose is *t* image	Mk 12:16	3778
t is the first commandment	Mk 12:30	3778
And the second is like, namely *t*	Mk 12:31	3778
That *t* poor widow hath cast more	Mk 12:43	3778
which God created unto *t* time	Mk 13:19	3568
that *t* generation shall not pass,	Mk 13:30	3778
Why was *t* waste of the ointment	Mk 14:4	3778
Wheresoever *t* gospel shall be	Mk 14:9	5124
t also that she hath done shall	Mk 14:9	
t is my body	Mk 14:22	5124
them, *T* is my blood of the new	Mk 14:24	5124
be offended because of me *t* night	Mk 14:27	5026
I say unto thee, That *t* day	Mk 14:30	4594
even in *t* night	Mk 14:30	5026
take away *t* cup from me	Mk 14:36	5124
I will destroy *t* temple that is	Mk 14:58	5126
that stood by, *T* is one of them	Mk 14:69	3778
I know not *t* man of whom ye speak	Mk 14:71	5126
Truly *t* man was the Son of God	Mk 15:39	3778
the angel, Whereby shall I know *t*	Lk 1:18	5124
manner of salutation *t* should be	Lk 1:29	3778
unto the angel, How shall *t* be	Lk 1:34	5124
t is the sixth month with her,	Lk 1:36	3778
And whence is *t* to me, that the	Lk 1:43	5124
kindred that is called by *t* name	Lk 1:61	5129
What manner of child shall *t* be	Lk 1:66	5124
t taxing was first made when	Lk 2:2	3778
For unto you is born *t* day in the	Lk 2:11	4594
t shall be a sign unto you	Lk 2:12	5124
see *t* thing which is come to pass	Lk 2:15	5124
was told them concerning *t* child	Lk 2:17	5127
t child is set for the fall and	Lk 2:34	3778
Added yet *t* above all, that he	Lk 3:20	5124
command *t* stone that it be made	Lk 4:3	5129
All *t* power will I give thee, and	Lk 4:6	5026
unto them, *T* day is	Lk 4:21	4594
is *t* scripture fulfilled	Lk 4:21	3778
they said, Is not *t* Joseph's son	Lk 4:22	3778
will surely say unto me *t* proverb	Lk 4:23	5026
saying, What a word is *t*	Lk 4:36	3778
And when they had *t* done, they	Lk 5:6	5124
saying, Who is *t* which speaketh	Lk 5:21	3778
Have ye not read so much as *t*	Lk 6:3	5124
worthy for whom he should do *t*	Lk 7:4	5124
and to my servant, Do *t*, and he	Lk 7:8	5124
t rumour of him went forth	Lk 7:17	3778
T is he, of whom it is written,	Lk 7:27	3778
I liken the men of *t* generation	Lk 7:31	5026
T man, if he were a prophet,	Lk 7:39	3778
of woman *t* is that toucheth him	Lk 7:39	3588
unto Simon, Seest thou *t* woman	Lk 7:44	5026
but *t* woman since the time I came	Lk 7:45	3778
but *t* woman hath anointed my feet	Lk 7:46	3778
Who is *t* that forgiveth sins also	Lk 7:49	3778
saying, What might *t* parable be	Lk 8:9	3778
Now the parable is *t*	Lk 8:11	3778
and riches and pleasures of *t* life	Lk 8:14	3588
another, What manner of man is *t*	Lk 8:25	3778
but who is *t*, of whom I hear such	Lk 9:9	3778
go and buy meat for all *t* people	Lk 9:13	5126
saying, *T* is my beloved Son	Lk 9:35	3778
But they understood not *t* saying	Lk 9:45	5127
Whosoever shall receive *t* child	Lk 9:48	5124
his disciples James and John saw *t*	Lk 9:54	
first say, Peace be to *t* house	Lk 10:5	5129
notwithstanding be ye sure of *t*	Lk 10:11	5124
Notwithstanding in *t* rejoice not	Lk 10:20	5129
t do, and thou shalt live	Lk 10:28	5124
to say, *T* is an evil generation	Lk 11:29	3778
the Son of man be to *t* generation	Lk 11:30	5026
with the men of *t* generation	Lk 11:31	5026
in the judgment with *t* generation	Lk 11:32	5026
may be required of *t* generation	Lk 11:50	5026
shall be required of *t* generation	Lk 11:51	5026
And he said, *T* will I do	Lk 12:18	5124
t night thy soul shall be	Lk 12:20	5026
t know, that if the goodman of	Lk 12:39	5124
speakest thou *t* parable unto us,	Lk 12:41	5026
it that ye do not discern *t* time	Lk 12:56	5126
He spake also *t* parable	Lk 13:6	5026
come seeking fruit on *t* fig tree	Lk 13:7	5026
Lord, let it alone *t* year also	Lk 13:8	5124
And ought not *t* woman, being a	Lk 13:16	5026
be loosed from *t* bond on the	Lk 13:16	5127
and say to thee, Give *t* man place	Lk 14:9	5129
T man began to build, and was not	Lk 14:30	3778
T man receiveth sinners, and	Lk 15:2	3778
he spake *t* parable unto them,	Lk 15:3	5026
For *t* my son was dead, and is	Lk 15:24	3778
But as soon as *t* thy son was come	Lk 15:30	3778
for *t* thy brother was dead, and is	Lk 15:32	3778
How is it that I hear *t* of thee	Lk 16:2	5124
for the children of *t* world are	Lk 16:8	5127
for I am tormented in *t* flame	Lk 16:24	5026
And beside all *t*, between us and	Lk 16:26	5125
also come into *t* place of torment	Lk 16:28	5126
ye might say unto *t* sycamine tree	Lk 17:6	5026
glory to God, save *t* stranger	Lk 17:18	3778
and be rejected of *t* generation	Lk 17:25	5026
a parable unto them to *t* end	Lk 18:1	3588
Yet because *t* widow troubleth me,	Lk 18:5	5026
he spake *t* parable unto certain	Lk 18:9	5026
adulterers, or even as *t* publican	Lk 18:11	3778
t man went down to his house	Lk 18:14	3778
And when he heard *t*, he was very	Lk 18:23	5023
manifold more in *t* present time	Lk 18:30	5129
t saying was hid from them,	Lk 18:34	5124
T day is salvation come to	Lk 19:9	4594
day is salvation come to *t* house	Lk 19:9	5129
We will not have *t* man to reign	Lk 19:14	5126
even thou, at least in *t* thy day	Lk 19:42	5026
is he that gave thee *t* authority	Lk 20:2	5026
to speak to the people *t* parable	Lk 20:9	5026
themselves, saying, *T* is the heir	Lk 20:14	3778
What is *t* then that is written,	Lk 20:17	5124
had spoken *t* parable against them	Lk 20:19	5026
The children of *t* world marry	Lk 20:34	5126
that *t* poor widow hath cast in	Lk 21:3	3778
the land, and wrath upon *t* people	Lk 21:23	5129
T generation shall not pass away,	Lk 21:32	3778
drunkenness, and cares of *t* life	Lk 21:34	
eat *t* passover with you before I	Lk 22:15	5124
and gave thanks, and said, Take *t*	Lk 22:17	5124
T is my body which is given for	Lk 22:19	5124
t do in remembrance of me	Lk 22:19	5124
T cup is the new testament in my	Lk 22:20	5124
it was that should do *t* thing	Lk 22:23	5124
the cock shall not crow *t* day	Lk 22:34	4594
that *t* that is written must yet	Lk 22:37	5124
be willing, remove *t* cup from me	Lk 22:42	5124
but *t* is your hour, and the power	Lk 22:53	3778
and said, *T* man was also with him	Lk 22:56	3778
Of a truth *t* fellow also was with	Lk 22:59	3778
We found *t* fellow perverting the	Lk 23:2	5126
people, I find no fault in *t* man	Lk 23:4	5129
beginning from Galilee to *t* place	Lk 23:5	5602
Ye have brought *t* man unto me	Lk 23:14	5129
have found no fault in *t* man	Lk 23:14	5126
at once, saying, Away with *t* man	Lk 23:18	5126
T IS THE KING OF THE JEWS	Lk 23:38	3778
but *t* man hath done nothing amiss	Lk 23:41	3778
Certainly *t* was a righteous man	Lk 23:47	3778
T man went unto Pilate, and begged	Lk 23:52	3778
and beside all *t*, to day is the	Lk 24:21	5125
T was he of whom I spake, He that	Jn 1:15	3778
t is the record of John, when the	Jn 1:19	3778
T is he of whom I said, After me	Jn 1:30	3778
bare record that *t* is the Son of	Jn 1:34	3778
T beginning of miracles did Jesus	Jn 2:11	5026
After *t* he went down to Capernaum	Jn 2:12	5124
said unto them, Destroy *t* temple	Jn 2:19	5126
six years was *t* temple in	Jn 2:20	3778
that he had said *t* unto them	Jn 2:22	5124
t is the condemnation, that light	Jn 3:19	3778
t my joy therefore is fulfilled	Jn 3:29	3778
Whosoever drinketh of *t* water	Jn 4:13	5127
unto him, Sir, give me *t* water	Jn 4:15	5124
fathers worshipped in *t* mountain	Jn 4:20	5129
ye shall neither in *t* mountain	Jn 4:21	5129
upon *t* came his disciples, and	Jn 4:27	5129
is not *t* the Christ	Jn 4:29	3778
know that *t* is indeed the Christ,	Jn 4:42	3778
T is again the second miracle	Jn 4:54	5124
After *t* there was a feast of the	Jn 5:1	5023
Marvel not at *t*	Jn 5:28	5124
And *t* he said to prove him	Jn 6:6	5124
T is of a truth that prophet that	Jn 6:14	3778
T is the work of God, that ye	Jn 6:29	5124
Lord, evermore give us *t* bread	Jn 6:34	5126
t is the Father's will which hath	Jn 6:39	5124
t is the will of him that sent me	Jn 6:40	5124
And they said, Is not *t* Jesus	Jn 6:42	3778
T is the bread which cometh down	Jn 6:50	3778
if any man eat of *t* bread	Jn 6:51	5127
How can *t* man give us his flesh	Jn 6:52	3778
T is that bread which came down	Jn 6:58	3778
he that eateth of *t* bread shall	Jn 6:58	5126
disciples, when they had heard *t*	Jn 6:60	
T is an hard saying	Jn 6:60	3778
said unto them, Doth *t* offend you	Jn 6:61	5124
Go ye up unto *t* feast	Jn 7:8	5026
I go not up yet unto *t* feast	Jn 7:8	5026
saying, How knoweth *t* man letters	Jn 7:15	3778
of them of Jerusalem, Is not *t* he	Jn 7:25	3778
indeed that *t* is the very Christ	Jn 7:26	3778
Howbeit we know *t* man whence he	Jn 7:27	5126
than these which *t* man hath done	Jn 7:31	3778
of saying is *t* that he said	Jn 7:36	3778
(But *t* spake he of the Spirit,	Jn 7:39	5124
when they heard *t* saying	Jn 7:40	3588
Of a truth *t* is the Prophet	Jn 7:40	3778
Others said, *T* is the Christ	Jn 7:41	3778
Never man spake like *t* man	Jn 7:46	3778
But *t* people who knoweth not the	Jn 7:49	3778
t woman was taken in adultery, in	Jn 8:4	3778
T they said, tempting him, that	Jn 8:6	5124
ye are of *t* world	Jn 8:23	5127
I am not of *t* world	Jn 8:23	5127
t did not Abraham	Jn 8:40	5124
t man, or his parents, that he	Jn 9:2	3778
Neither hath *t* man sinned	Jn 9:3	3778
Is not *t* he that sat and begged	Jn 9:8	3778
Some said, *T* is he	Jn 9:9	3778
T man is not of God, because he	Jn 9:16	3778
Is *t* your son, who ye say was	Jn 9:19	3778
said, We know that *t* is our son	Jn 9:20	3778
we know that *t* man is a sinner	Jn 9:24	3778
as for *t* fellow, we know not from	Jn 9:29	5126
If *t* man were not of God, he	Jn 9:33	3778
judgment I am come into *t* world	Jn 9:39	5126
T parable spake Jesus unto them	Jn 10:6	
I have, which are not of *t* fold	Jn 10:16	5026
T commandment have I received of	Jn 10:18	5026
John spake of *t* man were true	Jn 10:41	5127
T sickness is not unto death, but	Jn 11:4	3778
he seeth the light of *t* world	Jn 11:9	5127
Believest thou *t*	Jn 11:26	5124
of them said, Could not *t* man	Jn 11:37	3778
have caused that even *t* man	Jn 11:37	3778
him, Lord, by *t* time he stinketh	Jn 11:39	2235
for *t* man doeth many miracles	Jn 11:47	3778
t spake he not of himself	Jn 11:51	5124
Why was not *t* ointment sold for	Jn 12:5	5124
T he said, not that he cared for	Jn 12:6	5124
day of my burying hath she kept *t*	Jn 12:7	846
For *t* cause the people also met	Jn 12:18	5124
heard that he had done *t* miracle	Jn 12:18	5124

he that hateth his life in *t*	Jn 12:25	5129
Father, save me from *t* hour	Jn 12:27	5026
but for *t* cause came I unto	Jn 12:27	5124
cause came I unto *t* hour	Jn 12:27	5026
T voice came not because of me,	Jn 12:30	3778
Now is the judgment of *t* world	Jn 12:31	5127
the prince of *t* world be cast out	Jn 12:31	5127
T he said, signifying what death	Jn 12:33	5124
who is *t* Son of man	Jn 12:34	3778
out of *t* world unto the Father	Jn 13:1	5127
what intent he spake *t* unto him	Jn 13:28	5124
By *t* shall all men know that ye	Jn 13:35	5129
for the prince of *t* world cometh	Jn 14:30	3127
T is my commandment, That ye love	Jn 15:12	3778
Greater love hath no man than *t*	Jn 15:13	5026
But *t* cometh to pass, that the	Jn 15:25	
the prince of *t* world is judged	Jn 16:11	5127
What is *t* that he saith unto us,	Jn 16:17	5124
What is *t* that he saith, A little	Jn 16:18	5124
by *t* we believe that thou camest	Jn 16:30	5129
t is life eternal, that they	Jn 17:3	3778
also one of *t* man's disciples	Jn 18:17	5127
accusation bring ye against *t* man	Jn 18:29	5127
Sayest thou *t* thing of thyself,	Jn 18:34	5124
My kingdom is not of *t* world	Jn 18:36	5127
if my kingdom were of *t* world	Jn 18:36	5127
To *t* end was I born	Jn 18:37	5124
for *t* cause came I into the world	Jn 18:37	5124
And when he had said *t*, he went	Jn 18:38	5124
they all again, saying, Not *t* man	Jn 18:40	5126
out, saying, If thou let *t* man go	Jn 19:12	5126
T title then read many of the	Jn 19:20	5126
After *t*, Jesus knowing that all	Jn 19:28	5124
after *t* Joseph of Arimathaea,	Jn 19:38	5023
And when he had said *t*, he	Jn 20:22	5124
which are not written in *t* book	Jn 20:30	5129
on *t* wise shewed he himself	Jn 21:1	3779
T is now the third time that	Jn 21:14	5124
T spake he, signifying by what	Jn 21:19	5124
And when he had spoken *t*, he saith	Jn 21:19	5124
Lord, and what shall *t* man do	Jn 21:21	3778
Then went *t* saying abroad among	Jn 21:23	3778
T is the disciple which	Jn 21:24	3778
wilt thou at *t* time restore again	Acts 1:6	5129
t same Jesus, which is taken up	Acts 1:11	3778
t scripture must needs have been	Acts 1:16	5026
had obtained part of *t* ministry	Acts 1:17	5026
Now *t* man purchased a field with	Acts 1:18	3778
he may take part of *t* ministry	Acts 1:25	5026
Now when *t* was noised abroad, the	Acts 2:6	5026
one to another, What meaneth *t*	Acts 2:12	5124
be *t* known unto you, and hearken	Acts 2:14	5124
But *t* is that which was spoken by	Acts 2:16	5124
sepulchre is with us unto *t* day	Acts 2:29	5026
He seeing *t* before spake of the	Acts 2:31	
T Jesus hath God raised up,	Acts 2:32	5126
Holy Ghost, he hath shed forth *t*	Acts 2:33	5124
Now when they heard *t*, they were	Acts 2:37	
from *t* untoward generation	Acts 2:40	5026
men of Israel, why marvel ye at *t*	Acts 3:12	5129
we had made *t* man to walk	Acts 3:12	846
his name hath made *t* man strong	Acts 3:16	5026
him *t* perfect soundness in the	Acts 3:16	5126
or by what name, have ye done *t*	Acts 4:7	5124
If we *t* day be examined of the	Acts 4:9	4594
even by him doth *t* man stand here	Acts 4:10	3778
T is the stone which was set at	Acts 4:11	3778
henceforth to no man in *t* name	Acts 4:17	5129
on whom *t* miracle of healing was	Acts 4:22	5124
conceived *t* thing in thine heart	Acts 5:4	5124
people all the words of *t* life	Acts 5:20	5026
of them whereunto *t* would grow	Acts 5:24	5124
ye should not teach in *t* name	Acts 5:28	5129
intend to bring *t* man's blood	Acts 5:28	5127
After *t* man rose up Judas of	Acts 5:37	5126
for if *t* counsel or	Acts 5:38	3778
counsel or *t* work be of men	Acts 5:38	5124
we may appoint over *t* business	Acts 6:3	5026
T man ceaseth not to speak	Acts 6:13	5127
words against *t* holy place	Acts 6:13	3778
that *t* Jesus of Nazareth shall	Acts 6:14	5126
of Nazareth shall destroy *t* place	Acts 6:14	3778
dead, he removed him into *t* land	Acts 7:4	5026
And God spake on *t* wise, That his	Acts 7:6	3779
forth, and serve me in *t* place	Acts 7:7	5129
Then fled Moses at *t* saying	Acts 7:29	5129
T Moses whom they refused, saying	Acts 7:35	5126
T is that Moses, which said unto	Acts 7:37	3778
T is he, that was in the church	Acts 7:38	3778
for as for *t* Moses, which brought	Acts 7:40	3778
lay not *t* sin to their charge	Acts 7:60	5026
And when he had said *t*, he fell	Acts 7:60	5124
T man is the great power of God	Acts 8:10	3778
Saying, Give me also *t* power	Acts 8:19	5026
neither part nor lot in *t* matter	Acts 8:21	5129
therefore of *t* thy wickedness	Acts 8:22	5026
and join thyself to *t* chariot	Acts 8:29	5129
the scripture which he read was *t*	Acts 8:32	3778
of whom speaketh the prophet *t*	Acts 8:34	5124
that if he found any of *t* way	Acts 9:2	3588
I have heard by many of *t* man	Acts 9:13	5127
Is not *t* he that destroyed them	Acts 9:21	3778
called on *t* name in Jerusalem	Acts 9:21	5124
proving that *t* is very Christ	Acts 9:22	3778
t woman was full of good works and	Acts 9:36	3778
T was done thrice	Acts 10:16	5124
Peter doubted in himself what *t*	Acts 10:17	3588
ago I was fasting until *t* hour	Acts 10:30	5026
And *t* was done three times	Acts 11:10	5124
The God of *t* people of Israel	Acts 13:17	5127
Of *t* man's seed hath God	Acts 13:23	5127
is the word of *t* salvation sent	Acts 13:26	5026
t day have I begotten thee	Acts 13:33	4594
to corruption, he said on *t* wise	Acts 13:34	3779
that through *t* man is preached	Acts 13:38	5127
And when the Gentiles heard *t*	Acts 13:48	
and elders about *t* question	Acts 15:2	5127
for to consider of *t* matter	Acts 15:6	5127
to *t* agree the words of the	Acts 15:15	5129
After *t* I will return, and will	Acts 15:16	5023
letters by them after *t* manner	Acts 15:23	3592
And *t* did she many days	Acts 16:18	5124
the prison told *t* saying to Paul	Acts 16:36	5128
that *t* Jesus, whom I preach unto	Acts 17:3	3778
said, What will *t* babbler say	Acts 17:18	3778
May we know what *t* new doctrine	Acts 17:19	3778
found an altar with *t* inscription	Acts 17:23	3739
the times of *t* ignorance God	Acts 17:30	3588
will hear thee again of *t* matter	Acts 17:32	5127
for I have much people in *t* city	Acts 18:10	5026
T fellow persuadeth men to	Acts 18:13	3778
Paul after *t* tarried there yet a	Acts 18:18	
I must by all means keep *t* feast	Acts 18:21	3588
T man was instructed in the way	Acts 18:25	3778
When they heard *t*, they were	Acts 19:5	
t continued by the space of two	Acts 19:10	5124
t was known to all the Jews and	Acts 19:17	5124
ye know that by *t* craft we have	Acts 19:25	5026
t Paul hath persuaded and turned	Acts 19:26	3778
So that not only *t* our craft is	Acts 19:27	5124
in question for *t* day's uproar	Acts 19:40	4594
give an account of *t* concourse	Acts 19:40	5026
I take you to record *t* day	Acts 20:26	4594
For I know *t*, that after my	Acts 20:29	5124
bind the man that owneth *t* girdle	Acts 21:11	3778
Do therefore *t* that we say to	Acts 21:23	5124
T is the man, that teacheth all	Acts 21:28	3778
people, and the law, and *t* place	Acts 21:28	5126
and hath polluted *t* holy place	Acts 21:28	5127
yet brought up in *t* city at the	Acts 22:3	5026
toward God, as ye all are *t* day	Acts 22:3	4594
I persecuted *t* way unto the death	Acts 22:4	5026
gave him audience unto *t* word	Acts 22:22	5127
for *t* man is a Roman	Acts 22:26	3778
a great sum obtained I *t* freedom	Acts 22:28	5026
conscience before God until *t* day	Acts 23:1	5026
saying, We find no evil in *t* man	Acts 23:9	5129
forty which had made *t* conspiracy	Acts 23:13	5026
Bring *t* young man unto the chief	Acts 23:17	5126
prayed me to bring *t* young man	Acts 23:18	5126
he wrote a letter after *t* manner	Acts 23:25	5126
T man was taken of the Jews, and	Acts 23:27	5126
unto *t* nation by thy providence	Acts 24:2	5129
For we have found *t* man a	Acts 24:5	5126
many years a judge unto *t* nation	Acts 24:10	5129
But *t* I confess unto thee, that	Acts 24:14	5124
Except it be for *t* one voice	Acts 24:21	5026
called in question by you *t* day	Acts 24:21	4594
answered, Go thy way for *t* time	Acts 24:25	3568
go down with me, and accuse *t* man	Acts 25:5	846
present with us, ye see *t* man	Acts 25:24	5126
I shall answer for myself *t* day	Acts 26:2	4594
appeared unto thee for *t* purpose	Acts 26:16	5124
of God, I continue unto *t* day	Acts 26:22	5026
for *t* thing was not done in a	Acts 26:26	5124
but also all that hear me *t* day	Acts 26:29	4594
T man doeth nothing worthy of	Acts 26:31	3778
T man might have been set at	Acts 26:32	3778
I perceive that *t* voyage will be	Acts 27:10	3588
Crete, and to have gained *t* harm	Acts 27:21	5026
For there stood by me *t* night the	Acts 27:23	5026
T day is the fourteenth day that	Acts 27:33	4594
for *t* is for your health	Acts 27:34	5124
No doubt *t* man is a murderer,	Acts 28:4	3778
So when *t* was done, others also,	Acts 28:9	5127
For *t* cause therefore have I	Acts 28:20	5026
of Israel I am bound with *t* chain	Acts 28:20	5026
for as concerning *t* sect, we know	Acts 28:22	5026
Saying, Go unto *t* people, and say,	Acts 28:26	5126
For the heart of *t* people is	Acts 28:27	5127
For *t* cause God gave them up unto	Rom 1:26	5124
And thinkest thou *t*, O man, that	Rom 2:3	5124
at *t* time his righteousness	Rom 3:26	
Cometh *t* blessedness then upon	Rom 4:9	3778
into *t* grace wherein we stand	Rom 5:2	5026
Knowing *t*, that our old man is	Rom 6:6	5124
me from the body of *t* death	Rom 7:24	5127
t present time are not worthy to	Rom 8:18	3588
For *t* is the word of promise, At	Rom 9:9	3778
At *t* time will I come, and Sarah	Rom 9:9	5126
And not only *t*	Rom 9:10	
Even for *t* same purpose have I	Rom 9:17	5124
is of faith speaketh on *t* wise	Rom 10:6	3779
Even so then at *t* present time	Rom 11:5	3588
not hear;) unto *t* day	Rom 11:8	4594
should be ignorant of *t* mystery	Rom 11:25	5124
For *t* is my covenant unto them,	Rom 11:27	3778
And be not conformed to *t* world	Rom 12:2	5129
For for *t* cause pay ye tribute	Rom 13:6	5124
continually upon *t* very thing	Rom 13:6	5124
For *t*, Thou shalt not commit	Rom 13:9	3588
briefly comprehended in *t* saying	Rom 13:9	5129
For to *t* end Christ both died, and	Rom 14:9	5124
but judge *t* rather, that no man	Rom 14:13	5124
For *t* cause I will confess to	Rom 15:9	5124
When therefore I have performed *t*	Rom 15:28	5124
and have sealed to them *t* fruit	Rom 15:28	5126
I Tertius, who wrote *t* epistle	Rom 16:22	3588
Now *t* I say, that every one of	1Cor 1:12	5124
where is the disputer of *t* world	1Cor 1:20	5127
foolish the wisdom of *t* world	1Cor 1:20	5127
yet not the wisdom of *t* world	1Cor 2:6	5127
nor of the princes of *t* world	1Cor 2:6	5127
of the princes of *t* world knew	1Cor 2:8	5127
man build upon *t* foundation gold	1Cor 3:12	5126
you seemeth to be wise in *t* world	1Cor 3:18	5129
For the wisdom of *t* world is	1Cor 3:19	5127
Even unto *t* present hour we both	1Cor 4:11	3588
of all things unto *t* day	1Cor 4:13	737
For *t* cause have I sent unto you	1Cor 4:17	5124
that he that hath done *t* deed	1Cor 5:2	5124
him that hath so done *t* deed	1Cor 5:3	5124
with the fornicators of *t* world	1Cor 5:10	5127
things that pertain to *t* life	1Cor 6:3	
of things pertaining to *t* life	1Cor 6:4	
But I speak *t* by permission, and	1Cor 7:6	5124
gift of God, one after *t* manner	1Cor 7:7	3779
that *t* is good for the present	1Cor 7:26	5124
But *t* I say, brethren, the time	1Cor 7:29	5124
And they that use *t* world, as not	1Cor 7:31	5127
fashion of *t* world passeth away	1Cor 7:31	5129
t I speak for your own profit	1Cor 7:35	5124
conscience of the idol unto *t*	1Cor 8:7	737
means *t* liberty of yours become a	1Cor 8:9	3778
to them that do examine me is *t*	1Cor 9:3	3778
our sakes, no doubt, *t* is written	1Cor 9:10	
be partakers of *t* power over you	1Cor 9:12	3588
we have not used *t* power	1Cor 9:12	5026
For if I do *t* thing willingly, I	1Cor 9:17	5124
t I do for the gospel's sake,	1Cor 9:23	5124
T is offered in sacrifice unto	1Cor 10:28	5124
For *t* cause ought the woman to	1Cor 11:10	5124
Now in *t* that I declare unto you	1Cor 11:17	5124
t is not to eat the Lord's supper	1Cor 11:20	
shall I praise you in *t*	1Cor 11:22	5129
t is my body, which is broken for	1Cor 11:24	5124
t do in remembrance of me	1Cor 11:24	5124
T cup is the new testament in my	1Cor 11:25	5124
t do ye, as oft as ye drink it,	1Cor 11:25	5124
For as often as ye eat *t* bread	1Cor 11:26	5126
bread, and drink *t* cup	1Cor 11:26	5124
whosoever shall eat *t* bread	1Cor 11:27	5126
and drink *t* cup of the Lord,	1Cor 11:27	5126
For *t* cause many are weak and	1Cor 11:30	5124
lips will I speak unto *t* people	1Cor 14:21	5129
part remain unto *t* present	1Cor 15:6	
If in *t* life only we have hope in	1Cor 15:19	5126
I speak *t* to your shame	1Cor 15:34	
Now *t* I say, brethren, that flesh	1Cor 15:50	5124
For *t* corruptible must put on	1Cor 15:53	5124
t mortal must put on immortality	1Cor 15:53	5124
So when *t* corruptible shall have	1Cor 15:54	5124
t mortal shall have put on	1Cor 15:54	5124
was not at all to come at *t* time	1Cor 16:12	3568
For our rejoicing is *t*, the	2Cor 1:12	3778
in *t* confidence I was minded to	2Cor 1:15	5026
But I determined *t* with myself	2Cor 2:1	5124
I wrote *t* same unto you, lest,	2Cor 2:3	5124
to such a man is *t* punishment	2Cor 2:6	3778
For to *t* end also did I write,	2Cor 2:9	5124
had no glory in *t* respect	2Cor 3:10	5129
for until *t* day remaineth the	2Cor 3:14	4594
But even unto *t* day, when Moses	2Cor 3:15	4594
seeing we have *t* ministry	2Cor 4:1	5026
In whom the god of *t* world hath	2Cor 4:4	5127
But we have *t* treasure in earthen	2Cor 4:7	5126
of *t* tabernacle were dissolved	2Cor 5:1	3588
For in *t* we groan, earnestly	2Cor 5:2	5129
For we that are in *t* tabernacle	2Cor 5:4	3588
I speak not *t* to condemn you	2Cor 7:3	
For behold *t* selfsame thing, that	2Cor 7:11	5124
to be clear in *t* matter	2Cor 7:11	3588
t they did, not as we hoped, but	2Cor 8:5	
that ye abound in *t* grace also	2Cor 8:7	5124
for *t* is expedient for you, who	2Cor 8:10	5124
that now at *t* time your abundance	2Cor 8:14	
to travel with us with *t* grace	2Cor 8:19	5124
Avoiding *t*, that no man should	2Cor 8:20	5124
that no man should blame us in *t*	2Cor 8:20	5026
you should be in vain in *t* behalf	2Cor 9:3	5129
in *t* same confident boasting	2Cor 9:4	3588
But *t* I say, He which soweth	2Cor 9:6	5124
For the administration of *t*	2Cor 9:12	5026
Whiles by the experiment of *t*	2Cor 9:13	5026
let him of himself think *t* again	2Cor 10:7	5124
Let such an one think *t*, that,	2Cor 10:11	5124
no man shall stop me of *t*	2Cor 11:10	3778
in *t* confidence of boasting	2Cor 11:17	5026
For *t* thing I besought the Lord	2Cor 12:8	5127
forgive me *t* wrong	2Cor 12:13	5026
T is the third time I am coming	2Cor 13:1	5124
t also we wish, even your	2Cor 13:9	5124
us from *t* present evil world	Gal 1:4	3588
T only would I learn of you,	Gal 3:2	5124
t I say, that the covenant, that	Gal 3:17	5124
For *t* Agar is mount Sinai in	Gal 4:25	3588
T persuasion cometh not of him	Gal 5:8	3588
fulfilled in one word, even in *t*	Gal 5:14	3588
T I say then, Walk in the Spirit,	Gal 5:16	
many as walk according to *t* rule	Gal 6:16	5129
is named, not only in *t* world	Eph 1:21	3588
to the course of *t* world,	Eph 2:2	5127
For *t* cause I Paul, the prisoner	Eph 3:1	5127
is *t* grace given, that I should	Eph 3:8	3778
For *t* cause I bow my knees unto	Eph 3:14	5127
T I say therefore, and testify in	Eph 4:17	5124
For *t* ye know, that no	Eph 5:5	5124
For *t* cause shall a man leave his	Eph 5:31	5127
T is a great mystery	Eph 5:32	5124
for *t* is right	Eph 6:1	5124
rulers of the darkness of *t* world	Eph 6:12	5127
Being confident of *t* very thing	Phil 1:6	5124
meet for me to think *t* of you all	Phil 1:7	5124
t I pray, that your love may	Phil 1:9	5124
For I know that *t* shall turn to	Phil 1:19	5124
t is the fruit of my labour	Phil 1:22	5124
having *t* confidence, I know that	Phil 1:25	5124
Let *t* mind be in you, which was	Phil 2:5	5124
but *t* one thing I do, forgetting	Phil 3:13	
God shall reveal even *t* unto you	Phil 3:15	5124
For *t* cause we also, since the	Col 1:9	5124
of *t* mystery among the Gentiles	Col 1:27	5127

t I say, lest any man should ... Col 2:4 5124
for *t* is well pleasing unto the ... Col 3:20 5124
when *t* epistle is read among you, ... Col 4:16 3588
For *t* cause also thank we God ... 1Th 2:13 5124
For *t* cause, when I could no ... 1Th 3:5 5124
For *t* is the will of God, even ... 1Th 4:3 5124
For *t* we say unto you by the word ... 1Th 4:15 5124
for *t* is the will of God in ... 1Th 5:18 5124
t epistle be read unto all the ... 1Th 5:27 3588
count you worthy of *t* calling ... 2Th 1:11 3588
for *t* cause God shall send them ... 2Th 2:11 5124
t we commanded you, that if any ... 2Th 3:10 5124
obey not our word by *t* epistle ... 2Th 3:14 3588
Knowing *t*, that the law is not ... 1Ti 1:9 5124
T is a faithful saying, and worthy ... 1Ti 1:15 3588
Howbeit for *t* cause I obtained ... 1Ti 1:16 5124
T charge I commit unto thee, son ... 1Ti 1:18 5026
For *t* is good and acceptable in ... 1Ti 2:3 5124
T is a true saying, If a man ... 1Ti 3:1
T is a faithful saying and worthy ... 1Ti 4:9 3588
for in doing *t* thou shalt both ... 1Ti 4:16 5124
we brought nothing into *t* world ... 1Ti 6:7 3588
That thou keep *t* commandment ... 1Ti 6:14 3588
them that are rich in *t* world ... 1Ti 6:17
T thou knowest, that all they ... 2Ti 1:15 5124
with the affairs of *t* life ... 2Ti 2:4
God standeth sure, having *t* seal ... 2Ti 2:19 5026
T know also, that in the last ... 2Ti 3:1 5124
For of *t* sort are they which ... 2Ti 3:6 5130
having loved *t* present world, and ... 2Ti 4:10 3588
For *t* cause left I thee in Crete, ... Titus 1:5 5127
T witness is true ... Titus 1:13 3778
and godly, in *t* present world ... Titus 2:12 3588
T is a faithful saying, and these ... Titus 3:8 3588
t day have I begotten thee ... Heb 1:5 4594
For *t* man was counted worthy of ... Heb 3:3 3778
of the seventh day on *t* wise ... Heb 4:4 3779
in *t* place again, If they shall ... Heb 4:5 5129
no man taketh *t* honour unto ... Heb 5:4 3588
t will we do, if God permit ... Heb 6:3 5124
For *t* Melchisedec, king of Salem, ... Heb 7:1 3778
Now consider how great *t* man was ... Heb 7:4 3778
but *t* with an oath by him that ... Heb 7:21
But *t* man, because he continueth ... Heb 7:24
for *t* he did once, when he ... Heb 7:27 5124
which we have spoken *t* is the sum ... Heb 8:1
it is of necessity that *t* man ... Heb 8:3 5126
For *t* is the covenant that I will ... Heb 8:10 3778
The Holy Ghost *t* signifying ... Heb 9:8 5124
that is to say, not of *t* building ... Heb 9:11 5026
for *t* cause he is the mediator of ... Heb 9:15 5124
T is the blood of the testament ... Heb 9:20 5124
to die, but after *t* the judgment ... Heb 9:27 5124
But *t* man, after he had offered ... Heb 10:12 3778
T is the covenant that I will ... Heb 10:16 3778
translation he had *t* testimony ... Heb 11:5
t word, Yet once more, signifieth ... Heb 12:27 3588
I beseech you the rather to do *t* ... Heb 13:19 5124
Knowing *t*, that the trying of ... Jas 1:3
t man shall be blessed in his ... Jas 1:25 3778
heart, *t* man's religion is vain ... Jas 1:26 5127
before God and the Father is *t* ... Jas 1:27 3778
the poor of *t* world rich in faith ... Jas 2:5 5127
T wisdom descendeth not from ... Jas 3:15 3778
Lord will, we shall live, and do *t* ... Jas 4:15 5124
t is the word which by the gospel ... 1Pet 1:25 5124
For *t* is thankworthy, if a man ... 1Pet 2:19 5124
t is acceptable with God ... 1Pet 2:20 5124
For after *t* manner in the old ... 1Pet 3:5 3779
For for *t* cause was the gospel ... 1Pet 4:6 5124
let him glorify God on *t* behalf ... 1Pet 4:16 5129
testifying that *t* is the true ... 1Pet 5:12 5026
And beside *t*, giving all diligence ... 2Pet 1:5 5124
as long as I am in *t* tabernacle ... 2Pet 1:13 5129
I must put off *t* my tabernacle ... 2Pet 1:14 3588
T is my beloved Son, in whom I am ... 2Pet 1:17 3778
t voice which came from heaven we ... 2Pet 1:18 5026
Knowing *t* first, that no prophecy ... 2Pet 1:20 5124
T second epistle, beloved, I now ... 2Pet 3:1 5026
Knowing *t* first, that there shall ... 2Pet 3:3 5124
For *t* they willingly are ignorant ... 2Pet 3:5 5124
be not ignorant of *t* one thing ... 2Pet 3:8 5124
T then is the message which we ... 1Jn 1:5 3778
t is the promise that he hath ... 1Jn 2:25 3778
every man that hath *t* hope in him ... 1Jn 3:3 5026
For *t* purpose the Son of God was ... 1Jn 3:8 5124
In *t* the children of God are ... 1Jn 3:10 5129
For *t* is the message that ye ... 1Jn 3:11 2778
But whoso hath *t* world's good ... 1Jn 3:17 3588
t is his commandment, That we ... 1Jn 3:23 3778
t is that spirit of antichrist ... 1Jn 4:3 5124
In *t* was manifested the love of ... 1Jn 4:9 5129
as he is, so are we in *t* world ... 1Jn 4:17 5129
t commandment have we from him, ... 1Jn 4:21 5026
By *t* we know that we love the ... 1Jn 5:2 5129
For *t* is the love of God, that we ... 1Jn 5:3 3778
t is the victory that overcometh ... 1Jn 5:4 3778
T is he that came by water and ... 1Jn 5:6 3778
for *t* is the witness of God which ... 1Jn 5:9 3778
t is the record, that God hath ... 1Jn 5:11 3778
life, and *t* life is in his Son ... 1Jn 5:11 3778
t is the confidence that we have ... 1Jn 5:14 3778
T is the true God, and eternal ... 1Jn 5:20 3778
t is love, that we walk after his ... 2Jn 6 3778
T is the commandment, That, as ye ... 2Jn 6 3778
T is a deceiver and an antichrist ... 2Jn 7 3778
unto you, and bring not *t* doctrine ... 2Jn 10 5026
of old ordained to *t* condemnation ... Jude 4 5124
though ye once knew *t*, how that ... Jude 5 5124
that hear the words of *t* prophecy ... Rev 1:3 3588
But *t* thou hast, that thou hatest ... Rev 2:6 5124
as many as have not *t* doctrine ... Rev 2:24 5026
After *t* I looked, and, behold, a ... Rev 4:1 5023
After *t* I beheld, and, lo, a great ... Rev 7:9 5023
he must in *t* manner be killed ... Rev 11:5 3779
The kingdoms of *t* world are ... Rev 11:15 5026
city is like unto *t* great city ... Rev 18:18
T is the first resurrection ... Rev 20:5 3778
T is the second death ... Rev 20:14 3778
sayings of the prophecy of *t* book ... Rev 22:7 5127
which keep the sayings of *t* book ... Rev 22:9 5127
sayings of the prophecy of *t* book ... Rev 22:10 5127
words of the prophecy of *t* book ... Rev 22:18 5127
that are written in *t* book ... Rev 22:18 5129
words of the book of *t* prophecy ... Rev 22:19 5129
which are written in *t* book ... Rev 22:19 5026

THISTLE
The *t* that was in Lebanon sent to ... 2Kin 14:9 2336
in Lebanon, and trode down the *t* ... 2Kin 14:9 2336
The *t* that was in Lebanon sent to ... 2Chr 25:18 2336
in Lebanon, and trode down the *t* ... 2Chr 25:18 2336
the *t* shall come up on their ... Hos 10:8 1863

THISTLES
t shall it bring forth to thee ... Gen 3:18 1863
Let *t* grow instead of wheat, and ... Job 31:40 2336
grapes of thorns, or figs of *t* ... Mt 7:16 5146

THITHER
Oh, let me escape *t*, (is it not a ... Gen 19:20
Haste thee, escape *t* ... Gen 19:22
do any thing till thou be come *t* ... Gen 19:22
thou bring not my son *t* again ... Gen 24:6
only bring not my son *t* again ... Gen 24:8 8033
t were all the flocks gathered ... Gen 29:3 8033
which had brought him down *t* ... Gen 39:1 8033
get you down *t*, and buy for us ... Gen 42:2 8033
serve the LORD, until we come *t* ... Ex 10:26 8033
that thou mayest bring in *t* ... Ex 26:33 8033
the manslayer, that he may flee *t* ... Num 35:6 8033
that the slayer may flee *t* ... Num 35:11 8033
any person unawares may flee *t* ... Num 35:15 8033
Thou also shalt not go in *t* ... Deut 1:37 8033
before thee, he shall go in *t* ... Deut 1:38 8033
good and evil, they shall go in *t* ... Deut 1:39 8033
That the slayer might flee *t* ... Deut 4:42 8033
ye seek, and *t* thou shalt come ... Deut 12:5 8033
t ye shall bring your burnt ... Deut 12:6 8033
t shall ye bring all that I ... Deut 12:11 8033
that every slayer may flee *t* ... Deut 19:3 8033
of the slayer, which shall flee *t* ... Deut 19:4 8033
but thou shalt not go *t* unto the ... Deut 32:52 8033
but thou shalt not go over *t* ... Deut 34:4 8033
not all the people to labour *t* ... Josh 7:3 8033
So there went up *t* of the people ... Josh 7:4 8033
and unwittingly may flee *t* ... Josh 20:3 8033
person at unawares might flee *t* ... Josh 20:9 8033
all Israel went *t* a whoring after ... Judg 8:27 8033
t fled all the men and women, and ... Judg 9:51 8033
and they turned in *t*, and said unto ... Judg 18:3 8033
the land went up, and came in *t* ... Judg 18:17 8033
And they turned aside *t*, to go in ... Judg 19:15 8033
the congregation sent *t* twelve ... Judg 21:10 8033
all the Israelites that came *t* ... 1Sa 2:14 8033
ark of the God of Israel about *t* ... 1Sa 5:8 8033
now let us go *t* ... 1Sa 9:6 8033
when thou art come *t* to the city ... 1Sa 10:5 8033
And when they came *t* to the hill ... 1Sa 10:10 8033
if the man should yet come *t* ... 1Sa 10:22 1988
he went *t* to Naioth in Ramah ... 1Sa 19:23 8033
heard it, they went down *t* to him ... 1Sa 22:1 8033
Abiathar brought *t* the ephod to ... 1Sa 30:7 8033
So David went up *t*, and his two ... 2Sa 2:2 8033
they came *t* into the midst of the ... 2Sa 4:6 8033
ready before it was brought *t* ... 1Kin 6:7 8033
he came *t* unto a cave, and lodged ... 1Kin 19:9 8033
and they were divided hither and *t* ... 2Kin 2:8 2008
waters, they parted hither and *t* ... 2Kin 2:14 2008
by, he turned in *t* to eat bread ... 2Kin 4:8 8033
to us, that he shall turn in *t* ... 2Kin 4:10 8033
it fell on a day, that he came *t* ... 2Kin 4:11 8033
cut down a stick, and cast it in *t* ... 2Kin 6:6 8033
for *t* the Syrians are come down ... 2Kin 6:9 8033
Therefore sent he *t* horses ... 2Kin 6:14 8033
And when thou comest *t*, look out ... 2Kin 9:2 8033
Carry *t* one of the priests whom ... 2Kin 17:27 8033
Solomon went up *t* to the brasen ... 2Chr 1:6 8033
and when he came *t*, he did eat no ... Ezr 10:6 8033
the trumpet, resort ye *t* unto us ... Neh 4:20 8033
were gathered *t* unto the work ... Neh 5:16 8033
t brought I again the vessels of ... Neh 13:9 8033
womb, and naked shall I return *t* ... Job 1:21 8033
they came *t*, and were ashamed ... Job 6:20 5704
rivers come, *t* they return again ... Eccl 1:7 8033
and with bows shall men come *t* ... Is 7:24 8033
not come *t* the fear of briers ... Is 7:25 8033
that send forth *t* the feet of the ... Is 32:20 8033
from heaven, and returneth not *t* ... Is 55:10 8033
even *t* wentest thou up to offer ... Is 57:7 8033
He shall not return *t* any more ... Jer 22:11 8033
return, *t* shall they not return ... Jer 22:27 8033
a great company shall return *t* ... Jer 31:8 2008
convenient for thee to go, *t* go ... Jer 40:4 8033
went, *t* was their spirit to go ... Eze 1:20 8033
And they shall come *t*, and they ... Eze 11:18 8033
was upon me, and brought me, *t* ... Eze 40:1 8033
And he brought me *t*, and, behold, ... Eze 40:3 8033
because these waters shall come *t* ... Eze 47:9 8033
t cause thy mighty ones to come ... Joel 3:11 8033
Herod, he was afraid to go *t* ... Mt 2:22 1563
ran afoot *t* out of all cities, and ... Mk 6:33 1563
t will the eagles be gathered ... Lk 17:37 1563
poor widow casting in *t* two mites ... Lk 21:2 1563
and where I am, *t* ye cannot come ... Jn 7:34
and where I am, *t* ye cannot come ... Jn 7:36
and goest thou *t* again ... Jn 11:8 1563
resorted *t* with his disciples ... Jn 18:2 1563
cometh *t* with lanterns and torches ... Jn 18:3 1563
And Philip ran *t* to him, and heard ... Acts 8:30 4370
there came *t* certain Jews from ... Acts 14:19 1904
unto the women which resorted *t* ... Acts 16:13
who coming *t* went into the ... Acts 17:10 3854
Paul at Berea, they came *t* also ... Acts 17:13 1563
he himself would depart shortly *t* ... Acts 25:4

THITHERWARD
And they turned *t*, and came to the ... Judg 18:15 8033
way to Zion with their faces *t* ... Jer 50:5 2008
to be brought on my way *t* by you ... Rom 15:24 1563

THOMAS (*tom'-us*) See DIDYMUS. *One of the twelve apostles.*
T, and Matthew the publican ... Mt 10:3 2381
and Matthew, and *T* ... Mk 3:18 2381
Matthew and *T*, James the son of ... Lk 6:15 2381
Then said *T*, which is called ... Jn 11:16 2381
T saith unto him, Lord, we know ... Jn 14:5 2381
But *T*, one of the twelve, called ... Jn 20:24 2381
were within, and *T* with them ... Jn 20:26 2381
Then saith he to *T*, Reach hither ... Jn 20:27 2381
T answered and said unto him, My ... Jn 20:28 2381
Jesus saith unto him, *T*, because ... Jn 20:29 2381
T called Didymus, and Nathanael of ... Jn 21:2 2381
and John, and Andrew, Philip, and *T* ... Acts 1:13 2381

THONGS
And as they bound him with *t* ... Acts 22:25 2438

THORN
or bore his jaw through with a *t* ... Job 41:2 2336
As a *t* goeth up into the hand of ... Prov 26:9 2336
Instead of the the *t* shall come ... Is 55:13 5285
nor any grieving *t* of all that ... Eze 28:24 6975
the *t* and the thistle shall come ... Hos 10:8 6975
upright is sharper than a *t* hedge ... Mic 7:4 4534
was given to me a *t* in the flesh ... 2Cor 12:7 4647

THORNS
T also and thistles shall it bring ... Gen 3:18 6975
If fire break out, and catch in *t* ... Ex 22:6 6975
t in your sides, and shall vex you ... Num 33:55 6975
t in your eyes, until ye perish ... Josh 23:13 6975
they shall be as *t* in your sides ... Judg 2:3
with the *t* of the wilderness ... Judg 8:7 6975
t of the wilderness and briers, and ... Judg 8:16 6975
be all of them as *t* thrust away ... 2Sa 23:6 6975
which took Manasseh among the *t* ... 2Chr 33:11 2336
and taketh it even out of the *t* ... Job 5:5 6791
Before your pots can feel the *t* ... Ps 58:9 329
are quenched as the fire of *t* ... Ps 118:12 6975
slothful man is as an hedge of *t* ... Prov 15:19 2312
T and snares are in the way of the ... Prov 22:5 6791
lo, it was all grown over with *t* ... Prov 24:31 7063
as the crackling of *t* under a pot ... Eccl 7:6 5518
As the lily among *t*, so is my ... Song 2:2 2336
there shall come up briers and *t* ... Is 5:6 7898
holes of the rocks, and upon all *t* ... Is 7:19 5285
it shall even be for briers and *t* ... Is 7:23 7898
the land shall become briers and *t* ... Is 7:24 7898
thither the fear of briers and *t* ... Is 7:25 7898
it shall devour the briers and *t* ... Is 9:18 7898
and it shall burn and devour his *t* ... Is 10:17 7898
briers and *t* against me in battle ... Is 27:4 7898
land of my people shall come up *t* ... Is 32:13 6975
as *t* cut up shall they be burned ... Is 33:12 6975
t shall come up in her palaces, ... Is 34:13 5518
fallow ground, and sow not among *t* ... Jer 4:3 6975
have sown wheat, but shall reap *t* ... Jer 12:13 6975
t be with thee, and thou dost ... Eze 2:6 5544
I will hedge up thy way with *t* ... Hos 2:6 5518
t shall be in their tabernacles ... Hos 9:6 2336
they be folden together as *t* ... Nah 1:10 5518
Do men gather grapes of *t* ... Mt 7:16 173
And some fell among *t* ... Mt 13:7 173
the *t* sprung up, and choked them ... Mt 13:7 173
the *t* is he that heareth the word ... Mt 13:22 173
they had platted a crown of *t* ... Mt 27:29 173
And some fell among *t*, and the ... Mk 4:7 173
the *t* grew up, and choked it, and ... Mk 4:7 173
are they which are sown among *t* ... Mk 4:18 173
purple, and platted a crown of *t* ... Mk 15:17 174
For of *t* men do not gather figs, ... Lk 6:44 173
And some fell among *t* ... Lk 8:7 173
the *t* sprang up with it, and ... Lk 8:7 173
that which fell among *t* are they ... Lk 8:14 173
the soldiers platted a crown of *t* ... Jn 19:2 173
forth, wearing the crown of *t* ... Jn 19:5 174
But that which beareth *t* and ... Heb 6:8 173

THOROUGHLY
and shall cause him to be healed ... Ex 21:19 7495
his images brake they in pieces *t* ... 2Kin 11:18 3190

THOSE
giants in the earth in *t* days ... Gen 6:4 1992
lamp that passed between *t* pieces ... Gen 15:17 428
And he overthrew *t* cities, and all ... Gen 19:25 411
the gate of *t* which hate them ... Gen 24:60
and said, Who are *t* with thee ... Gen 33:5 428
food of *t* good years that come ... Gen 41:35 428
to buy corn among *t* that came ... Gen 42:5
the days of *t* which are embalmed ... Gen 50:3
And it came to pass in *t* days ... Ex 2:11 1992
see that thou do all *t* wonders ... Ex 4:21
they shall eat *t* things wherewith ... Ex 29:33
of *t* that devise cunning work ... Ex 35:35
all four, *t* are unclean unto you ... Lev 11:27 1992
t things, before the LORD, at the ... Lev 14:11
put them in the place of *t* stones ... Lev 14:42
he that beareth any of *t* things ... Lev 15:10
whosoever toucheth *t* things shall ... Lev 15:27
profane not my holy name in *t* ... Lev 22:2
T that were numbered of them, ... Num 1:21
t that were numbered of them, ... Num 1:22
T that were numbered of them, ... Num 1:23

T that were numbered of them, Num 1:25
T that were numbered of them, Num 1:27
T that were numbered of them, Num 1:29
T that were numbered of them, Num 1:31
T that were numbered of them, Num 1:33
T that were numbered of them, Num 1:35
T that were numbered of them, Num 1:37
T that were numbered of them, Num 1:39
T that were numbered of them, Num 1:41 1992
T that were numbered of them, Num 1:43
These are *t* that were numbered, Num 1:44
So were all *t* that were numbered Num 1:45
t that were numbered of them, Num 2:4
t that do pitch next unto him Num 2:5
t that were numbered thereof, Num 2:6
t that were numbered thereof, Num 2:8
t that were numbered thereof, Num 2:11
t which pitch by him shall be the Num 2:12
t that were numbered of them, Num 2:13
t that were numbered of them, Num 2:15
t that were numbered of them, Num 2:19
t that were numbered of them, Num 2:21
t that were numbered of them, Num 2:23
t that were numbered of them, Num 2:26
t that encamp by him shall be the Num 2:27
t that were numbered of them, Num 2:28
t that were numbered of them, Num 2:30
These are *t* which were numbered Num 2:32
all *t* that were numbered of the Num 2:32
T that were numbered of them, Num 3:22
even *t* that were numbered of them Num 3:22
t that were numbered of them, Num 3:34
But *t* that encamp before the Num 3:38
of *t* that were numbered of them, Num 3:43
for *t* that are to be redeemed of Num 3:46
t that were numbered of them by Num 4:36
t that were numbered of the sons Num 4:38
Even *t* that were numbered of them Num 4:40
t that were numbered of the Num 4:42
Even *t* that were numbered of them Num 4:44
These be *t* that were numbered of Num 4:45
All *t* that were numbered of the Num 4:46
Even *t* that were numbered of them Num 4:48
t men said unto him, We are Num 9:7 1992
all *t* men were heads of the Num 13:3
Because all *t* men which have seen Num 14:22 582
Even *t* men that did bring up the Num 14:37 582
t that are to be redeemed from a Num 18:16
t that died in the plague were Num 25:9
to *t* that were numbered of them Num 26:18
to *t* that were numbered of them Num 26:22
of Issachar according to *t* that Num 26:25
to *t* that were numbered of them Num 26:27
t that were numbered of them, Num 26:34
to *t* that were numbered of them Num 26:37
according to *t* that were numbered Num 26:43
to *t* that were numbered of them Num 26:47
be given according to *t* that were Num 26:54
t that were numbered of them were Num 26:62
that *t* which ye let remain of Num 33:55
t nations before thee by little Deut 7:22 411
the judge that shall be in *t* days Deut 17:9 1992
the abominations of *t* nations Deut 18:9 1992
shall flee unto one of *t* cities Deut 19:5 428
judges, which shall be in *t* days Deut 19:17 1992
t which remain shall hear, and Deut 19:20
priest that shall be in *t* days Deut 26:3 1992
the signs, and *t* great miracles Deut 29:3 1992
but *t* things which are revealed Deut 29:29
with *t* which are not a people Deut 32:21
t that came down toward the sea Josh 3:16
t twelve stones, which they took Josh 4:20 428
bring out *t* five kings unto me Josh 10:22 428
brought forth *t* five kings unto Josh 10:23 428
brought out *t* kings unto Joshua Josh 10:24 428
king of Hazor had heard *t* things Josh 11:1
was the head of all *t* kingdoms Josh 11:10 428
And all the cities of *t* kings Josh 11:12 428
war a long time with all *t* kings Josh 11:18 428
out the inhabitants of *t* cities Josh 17:12 428
of *t* cities shall stand at the Josh 20:4 428
priest that shall be in *t* days Josh 20:6
nine cities out of *t* two tribes Josh 21:16 428
which did *t* great signs in our Josh 24:17 428
the hand of *t* that spoiled them Judg 2:16
Therefore the LORD left *t* nations Judg 2:23 428
retained *t* three hundred men Judg 7:8
restore *t* lands again peaceably Judg 11:13
that when *t* Ephraimites which Judg 12:5
In *t* days there was no king in Judg 17:6 1992
In *t* days there was no king in Judg 18:1 1992
in *t* days the tribe of the Judg 18:1 1992
And it came to pass in *t* days Judg 19:1 1992
of God was there in *t* days Judg 20:27 1992
Aaron, stood before it in *t* days Judg 20:28 1992
In *t* days there was no king in Judg 21:25 1992
the LORD was precious in *t* days 1Sa 3:1 1992
and judged Israel in all *t* places 1Sa 7:16 428
all *t* signs came to pass that day 1Sa 10:9 428
upon Saul when he heard *t* tidings 1Sa 11:6 428
all Israel heard *t* words of the 1Sa 17:11 428
with whom hast thou left *t* few 1Sa 17:28 2007
Saul's servants spake *t* words in 1Sa 18:23 428
Jonathan shewed him all *t* things 1Sa 19:7 428
all *t* words in the name of David 1Sa 25:9 428
and came and told him all *t* sayings 1Sa 25:12 428
for *t* nations were of the old the 1Sa 27:8 2007
And it came to pass in *t* days 1Sa 28:1 1992
Saul had put away *t* that had 1Sa 28:3 1992
how he hath cut off *t* that have 1Sa 28:9
where *t* that were left behind 1Sa 30:9
they drave before *t* other cattle 1Sa 30:20 1931
of *t* that went with David, and 1Sa 30:22
these be the names of *t* that were 2Sa 5:14

which he counselled in *t* days 2Sa 16:23 1992
let them be of *t* that eat at thy 1Kin 2:7
name of the LORD, until *t* days 1Kin 3:2 1992
t officers provided victual for 1Kin 4:27 428
even *t* did the priests and the 1Kin 8:4
upon *t* did Solomon levy a tribute 1Kin 9:21
to pass, when Ahab heard *t* words 1Kin 21:27 428
shalt pour out into all *t* vessels 2Kin 4:4 428
wouldest thou smite *t* whom thou 2Kin 6:22
In *t* days the LORD began to cut 2Kin 10:32 1992
In *t* days the LORD began to send 2Kin 15:37 1992
t things that were not right 2Kin 17:9
for unto *t* days the children of 2Kin 18:4 1992
In *t* days was Hezekiah sick unto 2Kin 20:1 1992
t carried he into captivity from 2Kin 24:15
t that dwelt among plants and 1Chr 4:23
cymbals for *t* that should make a 1Chr 16:42
rest, and he had no war in *t* years 2Chr 14:6 428
in *t* times there was no peace to 2Chr 15:5 1992
beside *t* whom the king put in the 2Chr 17:19
all the kingdoms of *t* countries 2Chr 20:29
t lands any ways able to deliver 2Chr 32:13
t nations that my fathers utterly 2Chr 32:14 428
In *t* days Hezekiah was sick to 2Chr 32:24 1992
Even *t* did Cyrus king of Persia Ezr 1:8
of *t* which had been carried away, Ezr 2:1
sought their register among *t* Ezr 2:62
of the people of *t* countries Ezr 3:3
Then asked we *t* elders, and said Ezr 5:9 479
t did Cyrus the king take out of Ezr 5:14 1994
t deliver thou before the God of Ezr 7:19
Also the children of *t* that had Ezr 8:35
with the people of *t* lands Ezr 9:2
of *t* that had been carried away Ezr 9:4
lord, and of *t* that tremble at the Ezr 10:3
from the congregation of *t* that Ezr 10:8
with *t* that laded, every one with Neh 4:17
beside *t* that came unto us from Neh 5:17
Moreover in *t* days the nobles of Neh 6:17 1992
of *t* that had been carried away, Neh 7:6
sought their register among *t* Neh 7:64
women, and *t* that could understand Neh 8:3
Now *t* that sealed were, Nehemiah, Neh 10:1
In *t* days saw I in Judah some Neh 13:15 1992
In *t* days also saw I Jews that Neh 13:23 1992
That in *t* days, when the king Est 1:2 1992
In *t* days, while Mordecai sat in Est 2:21 1992
of *t* which kept the door, were Est 2:21
of silver to the hands of *t* that Est 3:9
they would unto *t* that hated them Est 9:5
On that day the number of *t* that Est 9:11
To set up on high *t* that be low Job 5:11
that *t* which mourn may be exalted Job 5:11
seeing he judgeth *t* that are high Job 21:22
They are of *t* that rebel against Job 24:13
the grave *t* which have sinned Job 24:19
T that remain of him shall be Job 27:15
But let all *t* that put their Ps 5:11
t that trouble me rejoice when I Ps 13:4
from *t* that rise up against them Ps 17:7
to all *t* that trust in him Ps 18:30
me *t* that rose up against me Ps 18:39
above *t* that rise up against me Ps 18:48
shall find out *t* that hate thee Ps 21:8
but *t* that wait upon the LORD, Ps 37:9
Let all *t* that seek thee rejoice Ps 40:16
t that have made a covenant with Ps 50:5
heritage of *t* that fear thy name Ps 61:5
But *t* that seek my soul, to Ps 63:9
he bringeth out *t* which are bound Ps 68:6
company of *t* that published it Ps 68:11
let not *t* that seek thee be Ps 69:6
grief of *t* whom thou hast wounded Ps 69:26
Let all *t* that seek thee rejoice Ps 70:4
the tumult of *t* that rise up Ps 74:23
thou *t* that are appointed to die Ps 79:11
T that be planted in the house of Ps 92:13
to loose *t* that are appointed to Ps 102:20
and to *t* that remember his Ps 103:18
all *t* that carried them captives Ps 106:46
to save him from *t* that condemn Ps 109:31
Let *t* that fear thee turn unto me Ps 119:79
t that have known thy testimonies Ps 119:79
to do unto *t* that love thy name Ps 119:132
scorning of *t* that are at ease Ps 123:4
unto *t* that be good, and to them Ps 125:4
am not I grieved with *t* that rise Ps 139:21
As for the head of *t* that compass Ps 140:9
as *t* that have been long dead Ps 143:3
raiseth up all *t* that be bowed Ps 145:14
in *t* that hope in his mercy Ps 147:11
as *t* that go down into the pit Prov 1:12
are life unto *t* that find them Prov 4:22
t that seek me early shall find Prov 8:17
That I may cause *t* that love me Prov 8:21
the soul of *t* that spoiled them Prov 22:23
t that are ready to be slain Prov 24:11
A lying tongue hateth *t* that are Prov 26:28
wine unto *t* that be of heavy Prov 31:6
come with *t* that shall come after Eccl 1:11
But *t* riches perish by evil Eccl 5:14 1931
among all *t* have I not found Eccl 7:28 428
deliver *t* that are given to it Eccl 8:8
t that look out of the windows be Eccl 12:3
causing the lips of *t* that are Song 7:9
t that keep the fruit thereof two Song 8:12
the raiment of *t* that are slain Is 14:19
as he smote *t* that smote him Is 27:7
but it shall be for *t* Is 35:8
In *t* days was Hezekiah sick unto Is 38:1 1992
shall gently lead *t* that are with Is 40:11
beside *t* that are gathered unto Is 56:8
t nations shall be utterly wasted Is 60:12
t that remember thee in thy ways Is 64:5

in *t* is continuance, and we shall Is 64:5 1992
For all *t* things hath mine hand Is 66:2 428
all *t* things have been, saith the Is 66:2 428
I will send *t* that escape of them Is 66:19 1992
in *t* days, saith the LORD, they Jer 3:16 1992
In *t* days the house of Judah Jer 3:18 1992
Even a full wind from *t* places Jer 4:12 428
Nevertheless in *t* days, saith the Jer 5:18 1992
the city, and *t* that dwell therein Jer 8:16
famine shall *t* prophets be Jer 14:15 1992
into the hand of *t* that seek Jer 21:7
t will I let remain still in Jer 27:11
In *t* days they shall say no more, Jer 31:29 1992
After *t* days, saith the LORD, I Jer 31:33 1992
If *t* ordinances depart from Jer 31:36 428
In *t* days, and at that time, will Jer 33:15 1992
In *t* days shall Judah be saved, Jer 33:16 1992
t women shall say, Thy friends Jer 38:22 2007
t that fell away, that fell to Jer 39:9
hand of *t* that seek their lives Jer 46:26
from all *t* that be about thee Jer 49:5
scatter them toward all *t* winds Jer 49:36 428
In *t* days, and in that time, saith Jer 50:4 1992
In *t* days, and in that time, saith Jer 50:20 1992
t that fell away, that fell to Jer 52:15
t that I have swaddled and brought Lam 2:22
The lips of *t* that rose up Lam 3:62
When *t* went, these went Eze 1:21
when *t* stood, these stood Eze 1:21
when *t* were lifted up from the Eze 1:21
And that doeth not any of *t* duties Eze 18:11 428
T that be near Eze 22:5
t that be far from thee, shall Eze 22:5
executed judgments upon all *t* Eze 28:26
they that inhabit *t* wastes of the Eze 33:24 428
them out of the hand of *t* that Eze 34:27
which prophesied in *t* days many Eze 38:17 1992
they shall spoil *t* that spoiled Eze 39:10
rob *t* that robbed them, saith the Eze 39:10
to bury with the passengers *t* Eze 39:14
round about, like *t* windows Eze 40:25 428
shall approach to *t* things which Eze 42:14
slew *t* men that took up Shadrach Dan 3:22 479
t that walk in pride he is able Dan 4:37 1768
they brought *t* men which had Dan 6:24 479
In *t* days I Daniel was mourning Dan 10:2 1992
up, even for others beside *t* Dan 11:4 428
in *t* times there shall many stand Dan 11:14 1992
and *t* that suck the breasts Joel 2:16
upon the handmaids in *t* days will Joel 2:29 1992
in *t* days, and in that time, when Joel 3:1 1992
to cut off *t* of his that did Obad 14
thou have delivered up *t* of his Obad 14
t that have not sought the LORD, Zeph 1:6
all *t* that leap on the threshold Zeph 1:9
Since *t* days were, when one came Hag 2:16
chariots, and *t* that ride in them Hag 2:22
spake unto *t* that stood before Zec 3:4
hand of Zerubbabel with *t* seven Zec 4:10 428
even *t* seventy years, did ye at Zec 7:5 2088
In *t* days it shall come to pass, Zec 8:23 1992
shall not visit *t* that be cut off Zec 11:16
T with which I was wounded in the Zec 13:6
forth, and fight against *t* nations Zec 14:3 1992
against *t* that oppress the Mal 3:5
In *t* days came John the Baptist, Mt 3:1 *1565*
t which were possessed with Mt 4:24 *3588*
t which were lunatick Mt 4:24
lunatick, and *t* that had the palsy Mt 4:24
shew John again *t* things which ye Mt 11:4
to see *t* things which ye see Mt 13:17
to hear *t* things which ye hear, Mt 13:17
But *t* things which proceed out of Mt 15:18 *3588*
having with them *t* that were lame Mt 15:30
be of God, but *t* that be of men Mt 16:23 *3588*
what will he do unto *t* husbandmen Mt 21:40 *1565*
miserably destroy *t* wicked men Mt 21:41 *846*
armies, and destroyed *t* murderers Mt 22:7 *1565*
So *t* servants went out into the Mt 22:10 *1565*
to them that give suck in *t* days Mt 24:19 *1565*
except *t* days should be shortened Mt 24:22 *1565*
sake *t* days shall be shortened Mt 24:22 *1565*
after the tribulation of *t* days Mt 24:29 *1565*
Then all *t* virgins arose, and Mt 25:7 *1565*
the lord of *t* servants cometh Mt 25:19 *1565*
t things that were done, they Mt 27:54 *3588*
And it came to pass in *t* days Mk 1:9 *1565*
offer for thy cleansing *t* things Mk 1:44
and then shall they fast in *t* days Mk 2:20 *1565*
about in beds *t* that were sick Mk 6:55 *3588*
t are they that defile the man Mk 7:15 *1565*
In *t* days the multitude being Mk 8:1 *1565*
rebuked *t* that brought them Mk 10:13 *3588*
but shall believe that *t* things Mk 11:23
But *t* husbandmen said among Mk 12:7 *1565*
to them that give suck in *t* days Mk 13:17 *1565*
For in *t* days shall be affliction Mk 13:19 *1565*
the Lord had shortened *t* days Mk 13:20 *3588*
But in *t* days, after that Mk 13:24 *3588*
of *t* things which are most surely Lk 1:1 *3588*
know the certainty of *t* things Lk 1:4
after *t* days his wife Elisabeth Lk 1:24 *5025*
And Mary arose in *t* days, and went Lk 1:39 *5025*
t things which were told her from Lk 1:45 *3588*
And it came to pass in *t* days Lk 2:1 *1565*
t things which were told them by Lk 2:18
his mother marvelled at *t* things Lk 2:33 *3588*
in *t* days he did eat nothing Lk 4:2 *1565*
and then shall they fast in *t* days Lk 5:35 *1565*
And it came to pass in *t* days Lk 6:12 *5025*
also love *t* that love them Lk 6:32 *3588*
Among *t* that are born of women Lk 7:28
T by the way side are they that Lk 8:12 *3588*
told no man in *t* days any of Lk 9:36 *1565*

of *t* things which they had seen Lk 9:36
to see *t* things which ye see Lk 10:24
to hear *t* things which ye hear, Lk 10:24
then whose shall *t* things be Lk 12:20
Blessed are *t* servants, whom the Lk 12:37 *1565*
them so, blessed are *t* servants Lk 12:38 *1565*
Or *t* eighteen, upon whom the Lk 13:4 *1565*
a parable to *t* which were bidden Lk 14:7 *3588*
That none of *t* men which were Lk 14:24 *1565*
when ye shall have done all *t* Lk 17:10 *3588*
But *t* mine enemies, which would Lk 19:27 *1565*
to pass, that on one of *t* days Lk 20:1 *1565*
to them that give suck, in *t* days Lk 21:23 *1565*
for looking after *t* things which Lk 21:26
t things whereof ye accuse him Lk 23:14
in the temple *t* that sold oxen Jn 2:14 *3588*
Then *t* men, when they had seen Jn 6:14 *3588*
where are *t* thine accusers Jn 8:10 *1565*
I speak to the world *t* things Jn 8:26 *5023*
for I do always *t* things that Jn 8:29 *3588*
Then said Jesus to *t* Jews which Jn 8:31 *3588*
for which of *t* works do ye stone Jn 10:32 *846*
Buy *t* things that we have need of Jn 13:29
name *t* whom thou hast given me Jn 17:11 *846*
t that thou gavest me I have kept Jn 17:12 *846*
in *t* days Peter stood up in the Acts 1:15 *5025*
pour out in *t* days of my Spirit Acts 2:18 *1565*
But *t* things, which God before Acts 3:18
t that follow after, as many as Acts 3:24 *3588*
in *t* days, when the number of the Acts 6:1 *5025*
And they made a calf in *t* days Acts 7:41 *1565*
unto *t* things which Philip spake Acts 8:6 *3588*
And it came to pass in *t* days Acts 9:37 *1565*
spake against *t* things which were Acts 13:45 *3588*
the Jews which were in *t* quarters Acts 16:3 *1565*
serjeants, saying, Let *t* men go Acts 16:35 *1565*
more noble than *t* in Thessalonica Acts 17:11 *3588*
daily, whether *t* things were so Acts 17:11 *5023*
Gallio cared for none of *t* things Acts 18:17
And when he had gone over *t* parts Acts 20:2 *1565*
when we had accomplished *t* days Acts 21:5 *3588*
after *t* days we took up our Acts 21:15 *5025*
and all may know that *t* things Acts 21:24
of *t* things in the which I will Acts 26:16
things than *t* which the prophets Acts 26:22
more than *t* things which were Acts 27:11 *3588*
teaching *t* things which concern Acts 28:31 *3588*
to do *t* things which are not Rom 1:28 *3588*
calleth *t* things which be not as Rom 4:17 *3588*
as *t* that are alive from the dead Rom 6:13
in *t* things whereof ye are now Rom 6:21
for the end of *t* things is death Rom 6:21 *1565*
That the man which doeth *t* things Rom 10:5 *846*
in *t* things which pertain to God Rom 15:17 *3588*
not dare to speak of any of *t* Rom 15:18
therefore the eating of *t* things 1Cor 8:4 *3588*
eat *t* things which are offered to 1Cor 8:10 *3588*
much more *t* members of the body, 1Cor 12:22 *3588*
t members of the body, which we 1Cor 12:23
and there come in *t* that are 1Cor 14:23
that comforteth *t* that are cast 2Cor 7:6 *3588*
Beside *t* things that are without, 2Cor 11:28 *3588*
t things which are done of them Eph 5:12 *3588*
t I counted loss for Christ Phil 3:7 *5023*
forgetting *t* things which are Phil 3:13 *3588*
reaching forth unto *t* things Phil 3:13 *3588*
help *t* women which laboured with Phil 4:3
T things, which ye have both Phil 4:9 *5023*
intruding into *t* things which he Col 2:18
seek *t* things which are above, Col 3:1 *3588*
men, specially of *t* that believe 1Ti 4:10
specially for *t* of his own house, 1Ti 5:8 *3588*
t that oppose themselves 2Ti 2:25 *3588*
despisers of *t* that are good, 2Ti 3:3
for a testimony of *t* things which Heb 3:5 *3588*
even *t* who by reason of use have Heb 5:14 *3588*
For it is impossible for *t* who Heb 6:4 *3588*
(For *t* priests were made without Heb 7:21 *3588*
as *t* high priests, to offer up Heb 7:27 *3588*
the house of Israel after *t* days Heb 8:10 *1565*
can never with *t* sacrifices which Heb 10:1
But in *t* sacrifices there is a Heb 10:3 *846*
will make with them after *t* days Heb 10:16 *1565*
of *t* things that are shaken Heb 12:27 *3588*
that *t* things which cannot be Heb 12:27 *3588*
For the bodies of *t* beasts Heb 13:11 *5130*
ye give them not *t* things which Jas 2:16 *3588*
making them an ensample unto *t* 2Pet 2:6 *3588*
t that were clean escaped from 2Pet 2:18 *3588*
do *t* things that are pleasing in 1Jn 3:22 *3588*
that we lose not *t* things which 2Jn 8
But these speak evil of *t* things Jude 10 *3745*
beasts, in *t* things they corrupt Jude 10 *5125*
keep *t* things which are written Rev 1:3 *3588*
Fear none of *t* things which thou Rev 2:10 *3588*
even in *t* days wherein Antipas Rev 2:13 *3588*
when *t* beasts give glory and Rev 4:9 *3588*
but only *t* men which have not the Rev 9:4 *3588*
in *t* days shall men seek death, Rev 9:6 *1565*
Seal up *t* things which the seven Rev 10:4
on the earth by the means of *t* Rev 13:14 *3588*
the dead were judged out of *t* Rev 20:12 *3588*

THOU See PREFACE.

THOUGH
t thou wouldest needs be gone, Gen 31:30
as *t* I had seen the face of God, Gen 33:10
and it was as *t* it budded, and her Gen 40:10
t he wist it not, yet is he Lev 5:17
t he divide the hoof, and be Lev 11:7
yea, *t* he be a stranger, or a Lev 25:35
as *t* it were the corn of the Num 18:27
t I walk in the imagination of Deut 29:19 3588
t they have iron chariots, and Josh 17:18 3588
chariots, and *t* they be strong Josh 17:18 3588
T thou detain me, I will not eat Judg 13:16 518
t I do them a displeasure Judg 15:3 3588
T ye have done this, yet will I Judg 15:7 518
t I be not like unto one of thine Ruth 2:13
t it be in Jonathan my son, he 1Sa 14:39
thereof, as *t* I shot at a mark 1Sa 20:20
t it were sanctified this day in 1Sa 21:5 3588
as *t* he had not been anointed 2Sa 1:21
am this day weak, *t* anointed king 2Sa 3:39
as *t* they would have fetched 2Sa 4:6
T I should receive a thousand 2Sa 18:12 3863
t he turned not after Absalom 1Kin 2:28
(for *t* he was not the firstborn, 1Chr 26:10
t he be not cleansed according to 2Chr 30:19
t there were of you cast out unto Neh 1:9 518
(*t* at that time I had not set up Neh 6:1 1571
(*t* it was turned to the contrary, Est 9:1
T thy beginning was small, yet Job 8:7
t I were righteous, yet would I Job 9:15 518
T I were perfect, yet would I not Job 9:21
have been as *t* I had not been Job 10:19
t man be born like a wild ass's Job 11:12
T he slay me, yet will I trust in Job 13:15
T the root thereof wax old in the Job 14:8 518
T I speak, my grief is not Job 16:6 518
t I forbear, what am I eased Job 16:6
t I intreated for the children's Job 19:17
t after my skin worms destroy Job 19:26
t my reins be consumed within me Job 19:27
T his excellency mount up to the Job 20:6
T wickedness be sweet in his Job 20:12 518
t he hide it under his tongue Job 20:12
T he spare it, and forsake it not, Job 20:13
T it be given him to be in safety Job 24:23
t he hath gained, when God taketh Job 27:8 3588
T he heap up silver as the dust, Job 27:16 518
t they cry in his destruction Job 30:24 518
ones, as *t* they were not hers Job 39:16
t I walk through the valley of Ps 23:4 3588
T an host should encamp against Ps 27:3 518
t war should rise against me, in Ps 27:3 518
I behaved myself as *t* he had been Ps 35:14
T he fall, he shall not be Ps 37:24 3588
T thou hast sore broken us in the Ps 44:19 3588
t the earth be removed Ps 46:2
t the mountains be carried into Ps 46:2
T the waters thereof roar and be Ps 46:3
t the mountains shake with the Ps 46:3
T while he lived he blessed his Ps 49:18 3588
T ye have lien among the pots, Ps 68:13 518
T he had commanded the clouds Ps 78:23
t thou tookest vengeance of their Ps 99:8
T the LORD be high, yet hath he Ps 138:6 3588
T I walk in the midst of trouble, Ps 138:7 518
content, *t* thou givest many gifts Prov 6:35 3588
T hand join in hand, the wicked Prov 11:21
t hand join in hand, he shall not Prov 16:5
T thou shouldest bray a fool in a Prov 27:22 518
in his ways, *t* he be rich Prov 28:6
for *t* he understand he will not Prov 29:19
t he live a thousand years twice Eccl 6:6
T a sinner do evil an hundred Eccl 8:12
because *t* a man labour to seek it Eccl 8:17 834
t a wise man think to know it, Eccl 8:17 518
t your sins be as scarlet, they Is 1:18 518
t they be red like crimson, they Is 1:18 518
For *t* thy people Israel be as the Is 10:22 518
t thou wast angry with me, thine Is 12:1 3588
t the Lord give you the bread of Is 30:20
t fools, shall not err therein Is 35:8
thee, *t* thou hast not known me Is 45:4
thee, *t* thou hast not known me Is 45:5
T Israel be not gathered, yet Is 49:5
t Abraham be ignorant of us, and Is 63:16 3588
For *t* thou wash thee with nitre, Jer 2:22 518
T thou clothest thyself with Jer 4:30 3588
crimson, *t* thou deckest thee with Jer 4:30 3588
t thou rentest thy face with Jer 4:30 3588
t they say, The LORD liveth Jer 5:2 518
and *t* the waves thereof toss Jer 5:22
t they roar, yet can they not Jer 5:22
t they shall cry unto me, I will Jer 11:11
t they speak fair words unto thee Jer 12:6 3588
t our iniquities testify against Jer 14:7 518
T Moses and Samuel stood before me Jer 15:1 518
t Coniah the son of Jehoiakim Jer 22:24 518
t I make a full end of all Jer 30:11 3588
t ye fight with the Chaldeans, ye Jer 32:5 3588
t I taught them, rising up early Jer 32:33
For *t* ye had smitten the whole Jer 37:10 518
the LORD, *t* it cannot be searched Jer 46:23
t thou shouldest make thy nest as Jer 49:16 3588
t their land was filled with sin Jer 51:5 3588
T Babylon should mount up to Jer 51:53 3588
t she should fortify the height Jer 51:53 3588
But *t* he cause grief, yet will he Lam 3:32 518
t briers and thorns be with thee, Eze 2:6 3588
t they be a rebellious house Eze 2:6 3588
t they be a rebellious house Eze 3:9
t they cry in mine ears with a Eze 8:18
t they be a rebellious house Eze 12:3 3518
not see it, *t* he shall die there Eze 12:13
T these three men, Noah, Daniel, Eze 14:14
T these three men were in it, as Eze 14:16
T these three men were in it, as Eze 14:18
T Noah, Daniel, and Job, were in Eze 14:20
t thou be sought for, yet shalt Eze 26:21
t thou set thine heart as the Eze 28:2
t their terror was caused in the Eze 32:25 3588
t they caused their terror in the Eze 32:26 3588
t they were the terror of the Eze 32:27 3588
heart, *t* thou knewest all this Dan 5:22
t we have rebelled against him Dan 9:9 3588
T thou, Israel, play the harlot, Hos 4:15 518
t I have been a rebuker of them Hos 5:2
t I have redeemed them, yet they Hos 7:13
T I have bound and strengthened Hos 7:15
t they have hired among the Hos 8:10 3588
T they bring up their children, Hos 9:12
t they bring forth, yet will I Hos 9:16 3588
t they called them to the most Hos 11:7
T he be fruitful among his Hos 13:15 3588
T ye offer me burnt offerings and Amos 5:22
T they dig into hell, thence Amos 9:2 518
t they climb up to heaven, thence Amos 9:2 518
t they hide themselves in the top Amos 9:3 518
t they be hid from my sight in Amos 9:3 518
t they go into captivity before Amos 9:4 518
T thou exalt thyself as the eagle Obad 4 518
t thou set thy nest among the Obad 4 518
they shall be as *t* they had not Obad 16
t thou be little among the Mic 5:2
T they be quiet, and likewise many Nah 1:12 518
T I have afflicted thee, I will Nah 1:12
not believe, *t* it be told you Hab 1:5 3588
t it tarry, wait for it Hab 2:3 518
and Zidon, *t* it be very wise Zec 9:2 3588
they shall be as *t* I had not cast Zec 10:6 834
t all the people of the earth be Zec 12:3
T all men shall be offended Mt 26:33 *1499*
T I should die with thee, yet Mt 26:35 *2579*
t many false witnesses came, yet Mt 26:60
because his face was as *t* he Lk 9:53
T he will not rise and give him, Lk 11:8 *1499*
t one rose from the dead Lk 16:31 *1437*
T I fear not God, nor regard man Lk 18:4 *1499*
him, *t* he bear long with them Lk 18:7 *2532*
he made as *t* he would have gone Lk 24:28
(*T* Jesus himself baptized not, Jn 4:2 *2544*
ground, as *t* he heard them not Jn 8:6
T I bear record of myself, yet my Jn 8:14 *2579*
t ye believe not me, believe the Jn 10:38 *2579*
t he were dead, yet shall he live Jn 11:25 *2579*
But *t* he had done so many Jn 12:37
as *t* by our own power or holiness Acts 3:12
t they found no cause of death in Acts 13:28
t a man declare it unto you Acts 13:41 *1437*
as *t* he needed any thing, seeing Acts 17:25
t he be not far from every one of Acts 17:27 *2544*
as *t* ye would enquire something Acts 23:15
as *t* they would enquire somewhat Acts 23:20
under colour as *t* they would have Acts 27:30
t he hath escaped the sea, yet Acts 28:4
t I have committed nothing Acts 28:17
t they be not circumcised Rom 4:11 *1223*
which be not as *t* they were Rom 4:17
t she be married to another man Rom 7:3
Not as *t* the word of God hath Rom 9:6 *3754*
T the number of the children of Rom 9:27 *1437*
For *t* ye have ten thousand 1Cor 4:15 *1437*
as *t* I would not come to you 1Cor 4:18
as *t* I were present, concerning 1Cor 5:3
have wives be as *t* they had none 1Cor 7:29
that weep, as *t* they wept not 1Cor 7:30
rejoice, as *t* they rejoiced not 1Cor 7:30
that buy, as *t* they possessed not 1Cor 7:30
For *t* there be that are called 1Cor 8:5 *1512*
For *t* I preach the gospel, I have 1Cor 9:16 *1437*
For *t* I be free from all men, yet 1Cor 9:19
T I speak with the tongues of men 1Cor 13:1 *1437*
t I have the gift of prophecy, and 1Cor 13:2 *1437*
t I have all faith, so that I 1Cor 13:2 *1437*
t I bestow all my goods to feed 1Cor 13:3 *1437*
t I give my body to be burned, and 1Cor 13:3 *1437*
but *t* our outward man perish, yet 2Cor 4:16 *1499*
t we have known Christ after the 2Cor 5:16 *1499*
as *t* God did beseech you by us 2Cor 5:20
For *t* I made you sorry with a 2Cor 7:8 *1499*
I do not repent, *t* I did repent 2Cor 7:8 *1499*
t it were but for a season 2Cor 7:8 *1499*
t I wrote unto you, I did it not 2Cor 7:12 *1499*
t he was rich, yet for your sakes 2Cor 8:9
For *t* we walk in the flesh, we do 2Cor 10:3
For *t* I should boast somewhat 2Cor 10:8 *1437*
as *t* we reached not unto you 2Cor 10:14
But *t* I be rude in speech, yet 2Cor 11:6 *1499*
reproach, as *t* we had been weak 2Cor 11:21 *3754*
For *t* I would desire to glory, I 2Cor 12:6 *1437*
chiefest apostles, *t* I be nothing 2Cor 12:11 *1499*
t the more abundantly I love you, 2Cor 12:15 *1499*
For *t* he was crucified through 2Cor 13:4 *1487*
is honest, *t* we be as reprobates 2Cor 13:7
But *t* we, or an angel from heaven Gal 1:8 *1437*
T it be but a man's covenant, yet Gal 3:15 *3676*
a servant, *t* he be lord of all Gal 4:1
T I might also have confidence in Phil 3:4 *2539*
Not as *t* I had already attained, Phil 3:12 *3754*
For *t* I be absent in the flesh, Col 2:5 *1499*
as *t* living in the world, are ye Col 2:20
t I might be much bold in Christ Philem 8
T he were a Son, yet learned he Heb 5:8 *2539*
salvation, *t* we thus speak Heb 6:9 *1499*
t they come out of the loins of Heb 7:5 *2539*
t he sought it carefully with Heb 12:17 *2539*
t a man say he hath faith, and Jas 2:14 *1437*
which *t* they be so great, and are Jas 3:4
t now for a season, if need be, 1Pet 1:6
t it be tried with fire, might be 1Pet 1:7
t now ye see him not, yet 1Pet 1:8
as *t* some strange thing happened 1Pet 4:12
t ye know them, and be established 2Pet 1:12 *2539*
lady, not as *t* I wrote a new 2Jn 5
t ye once knew this, how that the Jude 5

THOUGHT
And Abraham said, Because I *t* Gen 20:11 559
saw her, he *t* her to be an harlot Gen 38:15 2803

I had not *t* to see thy face	Gen 48:11	6419
as for you, ye *t* evil against me	Gen 50:20	2803
which he *t* to do unto his people	Ex 32:14	1696
I *t* to promote thee unto great	Num 24:11	559
unto you, as I *t* to do unto them	Num 33:56	1819
be not a *t* in thy wicked heart	Deut 15:9	1697
as he had *t* to have done unto his	Deut 19:19	2161
I verily *t* that thou hadst	Judg 15:2	559
by night, and *t* to have slain me	Judg 20:5	1819
I *t* to advertise thee, saying,	Ruth 4:4	559
therefore Eli *t* she had been	1Sa 1:13	2803
for the asses, and take *t* for us	1Sa 9:5	1672
But Saul *t* to make David fall by	1Sa 18:25	2803
for he *t*, Something hath befallen	1Sa 20:26	559
who *t* that I would have given him	2Sa 4:10	
Amnon *t* it hard for him to do any	2Sa 13:2	5869
Wherefore then hast thou *t* such a	2Sa 14:13	2803
and to do what he *t* good	2Sa 19:18	5869
new sword, *t* to have slain David	2Sa 21:16	559
went away, and said, Behold, I *t*	2Kin 5:11	559
for he *t* to make him king	2Chr 11:22	
t to win them for himself	2Chr 32:1	559
But they *t* to do me mischief	Neh 6:2	2803
he *t* scorn to lay hands on	Est 3:6	5869
Now Haman *t* in his heart, To whom	Est 6:6	559
in the *t* of him that is at ease	Job 12:5	6248
that no *t* can be withholden from	Job 42:2	4209
We have *t* of thy lovingkindness,	Ps 48:9	1819
Their inward *t* is, that their	Ps 49:11	
both the inward *t* of every one of	Ps 64:6	
When I *t* to know this, it was too	Ps 73:16	2803
I *t* on my ways, and turned my feet	Ps 119:59	2803
thou understandest my *t* afar off	Ps 139:2	7454
The *t* of foolishness is sin	Prov 24:9	2154
thyself, or if thou hast *t* evil	Prov 30:32	2161
not the king, no not in thy *t*	Eccl 10:20	4093
sworn, saying, Surely as I have *t*	Is 14:24	1819
the evil that I *t* to do unto them	Jer 18:8	2803
and thou shalt think an evil *t*	Eze 38:10	4284
I *t* it good to shew the signs and	Dan 4:2	
the king *t* to set him over the	Dan 6:3	6246
declareth unto man what is his *t*	Amos 4:13	7807
the LORD of hosts *t* to do unto us	Zec 1:6	2161
As I *t* to punish you, when your	Zec 8:14	2161
So again have I *t* in these days	Zec 8:15	2161
the LORD, and that *t* upon his name	Mal 3:16	2803
But while he *t* on these things,	Mt 1:20	*1760*
Take no *t* for your life, what ye	Mt 6:25	*3309*
Which of you by taking *t* can add	Mt 6:27	*3309*
And why take ye *t* for raiment	Mt 6:28	*3309*
Therefore take no *t*, saying, What	Mt 6:31	*3309*
therefore no *t* for the morrow	Mt 6:34	*3309*
take *t* for the things of itself	Mt 6:34	*3309*
take no *t* how or what ye shall	Mt 10:19	*3309*
take no *t* beforehand what ye	Mk 13:11	*4305*
And when he *t* thereon, he wept	Mk 14:72	*1911*
Wherefore neither *t* I myself	Lk 7:7	
perceiving the *t* of their heart	Lk 9:47	*1261*
take ye no *t* how or what thing ye	Lk 12:11	*3309*
he *t* within himself, saying, What	Lk 12:17	*1260*
Take no *t* for your life, what ye	Lk 12:22	*3309*
which of you with taking *t* can	Lk 12:25	*3309*
why take ye *t* for the rest	Lk 12:26	*3309*
because they *t* that the kingdom	Lk 19:11	*1380*
but they *t* that he had spoken of	Jn 11:13	*1380*
For some of them *t*, because Judas	Jn 13:29	*1380*
because thou hast *t* that the gift	Acts 8:20	*3543*
if perhaps the *t* of thine heart	Acts 8:22	*1963*
While Peter *t* on the vision, the	Acts 10:19	*1760*
but *t* he saw a vision	Acts 12:9	*1380*
But Paul *t* not good to take him	Acts 15:38	
Why should it be *t* a thing	Acts 26:8	*2919*
I verily *t* with myself, that I	Acts 26:9	*1380*
as a child, I *t* as a child	1Cor 13:11	*3049*
Therefore I *t* it necessary to	2Cor 9:5	*2233*
t to the obedience of Christ	2Cor 10:5	*3540*
t it not robbery to be equal with	Phil 2:6	*2233*
we *t* it good to be left at Athens	1Th 3:1	*2106*
suppose ye, shall he be *t* worthy	Heb 10:29	

THOUGHTEST

thou *t* that I was altogether such	Ps 50:21	1819

THOUGHTS

the *t* of his heart was only evil	Gen 6:5	4284
there were great *t* of heart	Judg 5:15	2711
all the imaginations of the *t*	1Chr 28:9	4284
the *t* of the heart of thy people	1Chr 29:18	4284
In *t* from the visions of the	Job 4:13	5587
off, even the *t* of my heart	Job 17:11	4180
Therefore do my *t* cause me to	Job 20:2	5587
Behold, I know your *t*, and the	Job 21:27	4284
God is not in all his *t*	Ps 10:4	4209
the *t* of his heart to all	Ps 33:11	4284
thy *t* which are to us-ward	Ps 40:5	4284
all their *t* are against me for	Ps 56:5	4284
and thy *t* are very deep	Ps 92:5	4284
The LORD knoweth the *t* of man	Ps 94:11	4284
In the multitude of my *t* within	Ps 94:19	8312
I hate vain *t*	Ps 119:113	5588
precious also are thy *t* unto me	Ps 139:17	7454
try me, and know my *t*	Ps 139:23	8312
in that very day his *t* perish	Ps 146:4	6250
The *t* of the righteous are right	Prov 12:5	4284
The *t* of the wicked are an	Prov 15:26	4284
thy *t* shall be established	Prov 16:3	4284
The *t* of the diligent tend only	Prov 21:5	4284
way, and the unrighteous man his *t*	Is 55:7	4284
For my *t* are not your *t*,	Is 55:8	4284
ways, and my *t* than your *t*	Is 55:9	4284
their *t* are *t* of iniquity	Is 59:7	4284
was not good, after their own *t*	Is 65:2	4284
For I know their works and their *t*	Is 66:18	4284
thy vain *t* lodge within thee	Jer 4:14	4284
people, even the fruit of their *t*	Jer 6:19	4284
have performed the *t* of his heart	Jer 23:20	4209
For I know the *t* that I think	Jer 29:11	4284
t of peace, and not of evil, to	Jer 29:11	4284
thy *t* came into thy mind upon thy	Dan 2:29	7476
mightest know the *t* of thy heart	Dan 2:30	7476
the *t* upon my bed and the visions	Dan 4:5	2031
one hour, and his *t* troubled him	Dan 4:19	7476
his *t* troubled him, so that the	Dan 5:6	7476
let not thy *t* trouble thee, nor	Dan 5:10	7476
they know not the *t* of the LORD	Mic 4:12	4284
And Jesus knowing their *t* said	Mt 9:4	*1761*
And Jesus knew their *t*, and said	Mt 12:25	*1761*
out of the heart proceed evil *t*	Mt 15:19	*1261*
the heart of men, proceed evil *t*	Mk 7:21	*1261*
that the *t* of many hearts may be	Lk 2:35	*1261*
But when Jesus perceived their *t*	Lk 5:22	*1261*
But he knew their *t*, and said to	Lk 6:8	*1261*
But he, knowing their *t*, said	Lk 11:17	*1270*
why do *t* arise in your hearts	Lk 24:38	*1261*
their *t* the mean while accusing	Rom 2:15	*3053*
Lord knoweth the *t* of the wise	1Cor 3:20	*1261*
and is a discerner of the *t*	Heb 4:12	*1761*
and are become judges of evil *t*	Jas 2:4	*1261*

THOUSAND

thy brother a *t* pieces of silver	Gen 20:16	505
about six hundred *t* on foot that	Ex 12:37	505
people that day about three *t* men	Ex 32:28	505
a *t* seven hundred and threescore	Ex 38:25	505
six hundred *t* and three *t*	Ex 38:26	505
of the *t* seven hundred seventy and	Ex 38:28	505
was seventy talents, and two *t*	Ex 38:29	505
of you shall put ten *t* to flight	Lev 26:8	7233
of Reuben, were forty and six *t*	Num 1:21	505
of Simeon, were fifty and nine *t*	Num 1:23	505
five *t* six hundred and fifty	Num 1:25	505
were threescore and fourteen *t*	Num 1:27	505
of Issachar, were fifty and four *t*	Num 1:29	505
of Zebulun, were fifty and seven *t*	Num 1:31	505
tribe of Ephraim, were forty *t*	Num 1:33	505
of Manasseh, were thirty and two *t*	Num 1:35	505
Benjamin, were thirty and five *t*	Num 1:37	505
of Dan, were threescore and two *t*	Num 1:39	505
of Asher, were forty and one *t*	Num 1:41	505
Naphtali, were fifty and three *t*	Num 1:43	505
were numbered were six hundred *t*	Num 1:46	505
six hundred *t* and three *t*	Num 1:46	505
were threescore and fourteen *t*	Num 2:4	505
thereof, were fifty and four *t*	Num 2:6	505
thereof, were fifty and seven *t*	Num 2:8	505
camp of Judah were an hundred *t*	Num 2:9	505
and fourscore *t* and six *t*	Num 2:9	505
thereof, were forty and six *t*	Num 2:11	505
of them, were fifty and nine *t*	Num 2:13	505
of them, were forty and five *t*	Num 2:15	505
camp of Reuben were an hundred *t*	Num 2:16	505
t and fifty and one *t*	Num 2:16	505
numbered of them, were forty *t*	Num 2:19	505
of them, were thirty and two *t*	Num 2:21	505
of them, were thirty and five *t*	Num 2:23	505
an hundred *t* and eight *t*	Num 2:24	505
of them, were threescore and two *t*	Num 2:26	505
of them, were forty and one *t*	Num 2:28	505
of them, were fifty and three *t*	Num 2:30	505
the camp of Dan were an hundred *t*	Num 2:31	505
and fifty and seven *t*	Num 2:31	505
six hundred *t* and three *t*	Num 2:32	505
numbered of them were seven *t*	Num 3:22	505
month old and upward, were eight *t*	Num 3:28	505
a month old and upward, were six *t*	Num 3:34	505
and upward, were twenty and two *t*	Num 3:39	505
two *t* two hundred and threescore	Num 3:43	505
a *t* three hundred and threescore	Num 3:50	505
families were two *t* seven hundred	Num 4:36	505
of their fathers, were two *t*	Num 4:40	505
their families, were three *t*	Num 4:44	505
numbered of them, were eight *t*	Num 4:48	505
the silver vessels weighed two *t*	Num 7:85	505
I am, are six hundred *t* footmen	Num 11:21	505
in the plague were fourteen *t*	Num 16:49	505
the plague were twenty and four *t*	Num 25:9	505
of them were forty and three *t*	Num 26:7	505
the Simeonites, twenty and two *t*	Num 26:14	505
were numbered of them, forty *t*	Num 26:18	505
of them, threescore and sixteen *t*	Num 26:22	505
of them, threescore and four *t*	Num 26:25	505
numbered of them, threescore *t*	Num 26:27	505
numbered of them, fifty and two *t*	Num 26:34	505
numbered of them, thirty and two *t*	Num 26:37	505
of them were forty and five *t*	Num 26:41	505
them, were threescore and four *t*	Num 26:43	505
who were fifty and three *t*	Num 26:47	505
of them were forty and five *t*	Num 26:50	505
children of Israel, six hundred *t*	Num 26:51	505
a *t* seven hundred and thirty	Num 26:51	505
of them were twenty and three *t*	Num 26:62	505
Of every tribe a *t*, throughout	Num 31:4	505
a *t* of every tribe, twelve	Num 31:5	505
tribe, twelve *t* armed for war	Num 31:5	505
a *t* of every tribe, them and	Num 31:6	505
war had caught, was six hundred *t*	Num 31:32	505
seventy *t* and five *t* sheep,	Num 31:32	505
And threescore and twelve *t* beeves	Num 31:33	505
And threescore and one *t* asses,	Num 31:34	505
two *t* persons in all, of women	Num 31:35	505
was in number three hundred *t*	Num 31:36	505
and seven and thirty *t*	Num 31:36	505
the beeves were thirty and six *t*	Num 31:38	505
And the asses were thirty *t*	Num 31:39	505
And the persons were sixteen *t*	Num 31:40	505
congregation was three hundred *t*	Num 31:43	505
and thirty *t* and seven *t*	Num 31:43	505
And thirty and six *t* beeves,	Num 31:44	505
And thirty *t* asses and five hundred	Num 31:45	505
And sixteen *t* persons	Num 31:46	505
was sixteen *t* seven hundred and	Num 31:52	505
outward a *t* cubits round about	Num 35:4	505
on the east side two *t* cubits	Num 35:5	505
and on the south side two *t* cubits	Num 35:5	505
and on the west side two *t* cubits	Num 35:5	505
and on the north side two *t* cubits	Num 35:5	505
a *t* times so many more as ye are	Deut 1:11	505
commandments to a *t* generations	Deut 7:9	505
How should one chase a *t*, and two	Deut 32:30	505
and two put ten *t* to flight	Deut 32:30	505
about two *t* cubits by measure	Josh 3:4	505
About forty *t* prepared for war	Josh 4:13	505
about two or three *t* men go up	Josh 7:3	505
of the people about three *t* men	Josh 7:4	505
out thirty *t* mighty men of valour	Josh 8:3	505
And he took about five *t* men	Josh 8:12	505
of men and women, were twelve *t*	Josh 8:25	505
One man of you shall chase a *t*	Josh 23:10	505
slew of them in Bezek ten *t* men	Judg 1:4	505
Moab at that time about ten *t* men	Judg 3:29	505
take with thee ten *t* men of the	Judg 4:6	505
up with ten *t* men at his feet	Judg 4:10	505
Tabor, and ten *t* men after him	Judg 4:14	505
seen among forty *t* in Israel	Judg 5:8	505
of the people twenty and two *t*	Judg 7:3	505
and there remained ten *t*	Judg 7:3	505
with them, about fifteen *t* men	Judg 8:10	505
twenty *t* men that drew sword	Judg 8:10	505
that he requested was a *t*	Judg 8:26	505
Shechem died also, about a *t* men	Judg 9:49	505
of the Ephraimites forty and two *t*	Judg 12:6	505
Then three *t* men of Judah went to	Judg 15:11	505
it, and slew a *t* men therewith	Judg 15:15	505
of an ass have I slain a *t* men	Judg 15:16	505
upon the roof about three *t* men	Judg 16:27	505
four hundred *t* footmen that drew	Judg 20:2	505
of Israel, and an hundred of a *t*	Judg 20:10	505
and a *t* out of ten *t*	Judg 20:10	7233
six *t* men that drew sword, beside	Judg 20:15	505
hundred *t* men that drew sword	Judg 20:17	505
that day twenty and two *t* men	Judg 20:21	505
of Israel again eighteen *t* men	Judg 20:25	505
t chosen men out of all Israel	Judg 20:34	505
that day twenty and five *t*	Judg 20:35	505
fell of Benjamin eighteen *t* men	Judg 20:44	505
them in the highways five *t* men	Judg 20:45	505
Gidom, and slew two *t* men of them	Judg 20:45	505
five *t* men that drew the sword	Judg 20:46	505
sent thither twelve *t* men of the	Judg 21:10	505
in the field about four *t* men	1Sa 4:2	505
fell of Israel thirty *t* footmen	1Sa 4:10	505
he smote of the people fifty *t*	1Sa 6:19	505
of Israel were three hundred *t*	1Sa 11:8	505
and the men of Judah thirty *t*	1Sa 11:8	505
chose him three *t* men of Israel	1Sa 13:2	505
whereof two *t* were with Saul in	1Sa 13:2	505
a *t* were with Jonathan in Gibeah	1Sa 13:2	505
thirty *t* chariots, and six	1Sa 13:5	505
six *t* horsemen, and people as the	1Sa 13:5	505
in Telaim, two hundred *t* footmen	1Sa 15:4	505
footmen, and ten *t* men of Judah	1Sa 15:4	505
coat was five *t* shekels of brass	1Sa 17:5	505
unto the captain of their *t*	1Sa 17:18	505
and made him his captain over a *t*	1Sa 18:13	505
Then Saul took three *t* chosen men	1Sa 24:2	505
great, and he had three *t* sheep	1Sa 25:2	505
sheep, and a *t* goats	1Sa 25:2	505
having three *t* chosen men of	1Sa 26:2	505
chosen men of Israel, thirty *t*	2Sa 6:1	505
David took from him a *t* chariots	2Sa 8:4	505
horsemen, and twenty *t* footmen	2Sa 8:4	505
the Syrians two and twenty *t* men	2Sa 8:5	505
of salt, being eighteen *t* men	2Sa 8:13	505
twenty *t* footmen, and of king	2Sa 10:6	505
and of king Maacah a *t* men	2Sa 10:6	505
and of Ish-tob twelve *t* men	2Sa 10:6	505
forty *t* horsemen, and smote	2Sa 10:18	505
me now choose out twelve *t* men	2Sa 17:1	505
now thou art worth ten *t* of us	2Sa 18:3	505
that day of twenty *t* men	2Sa 18:7	505
Though I should receive a *t*	2Sa 18:12	505
there were a *t* men of Benjamin	2Sa 19:17	505
were in Israel eight hundred *t* men	2Sa 24:9	505
of Judah were five hundred *t* men	2Sa 24:9	505
even to Beer-sheba seventy *t* men	2Sa 24:15	505
a *t* burnt offerings did Solomon	1Kin 3:4	505
Solomon had forty *t* stalls of	1Kin 4:26	505
chariots, and twelve *t* horsemen	1Kin 4:26	505
And he spake three *t* proverbs	1Kin 4:32	505
and his songs were a *t* and five	1Kin 4:32	505
Solomon gave Hiram twenty *t*	1Kin 5:11	505
and the levy was thirty *t* men	1Kin 5:13	505
Lebanon, ten *t* a month by courses	1Kin 5:14	505
ten *t* that bare burdens, and	1Kin 5:15	505
fourscore *t* hewers in the	1Kin 5:15	505
which were over the work, three *t*	1Kin 5:16	505
it contained two *t* baths	1Kin 7:26	505
the LORD, two and twenty *t* oxen	1Kin 8:63	505
and an hundred and twenty *t* sheep	1Kin 8:63	505
and he had a *t* and four hundred	1Kin 10:26	505
twelve *t* horsemen, whom he	1Kin 10:26	505
fourscore *t* chosen men, which	1Kin 12:21	505
I have left me seven *t* in Israel	1Kin 19:18	505
children of Israel, being seven *t*	1Kin 20:15	505
an hundred *t* footmen in one day	1Kin 20:29	505
seven *t* of the men that were left	1Kin 20:30	505
king of Israel an hundred *t* lambs	2Kin 3:4	505
lambs, and an hundred *t* rams	2Kin 3:4	505
six *t* pieces of gold, and ten	2Kin 5:5	505
and ten chariots, and ten *t* footmen	2Kin 13:7	505
Edom in the valley of salt ten *t*	2Kin 14:7	505
gave Pul a *t* talents of silver	2Kin 15:19	505
I will deliver thee two *t* horses	2Kin 18:23	505

an hundred fourscore and five *t* ... 2Kin 19:35 505
of valour, even ten *t* captives ... 2Kin 24:14 505
the men of might, even seven *t* ... 2Kin 24:16 505
and craftsmen and smiths a *t* ... 2Kin 24:16 505
four and forty *t* seven hundred and ... 1Chr 5:18 505
of their camels fifty *t*, and of ... 1Chr 5:21 505
fifty *t*, and of asses two *t* ... 1Chr 5:21 505
and of men an hundred *t* ... 1Chr 5:21 505
the days of David two and twenty *t* ... 1Chr 7:2 505
for war, six and thirty *t* men ... 1Chr 7:4 505
genealogies fourscore and seven *t* ... 1Chr 7:5 505
their genealogies twenty and two *t* ... 1Chr 7:7 505
men of valour, was twenty *t* ... 1Chr 7:9 505
men of valour, were seventeen *t* ... 1Chr 7:11 505
to battle was twenty and six *t* men ... 1Chr 7:40 505
the house of their fathers, a *t* ... 1Chr 9:13 505
hundred, and the greatest over a *t* ... 1Chr 12:14 505
bare shield and spear were six *t* ... 1Chr 12:24 505
of valour for the war, seven *t* ... 1Chr 12:25 505
Of the children of Levi four *t* ... 1Chr 12:26 505
and with him were three *t* ... 1Chr 12:27 505
the kindred of Saul, three *t* ... 1Chr 12:29 505
the children of Ephraim twenty *t* ... 1Chr 12:30 505
half tribe of Manasseh eighteen *t* ... 1Chr 12:31 505
all instruments of war, fifty *t* ... 1Chr 12:33 505
And of Naphtali a *t* captains ... 1Chr 12:34 505
shield and spear thirty and seven *t* ... 1Chr 12:34 505
expert in war twenty and eight *t* ... 1Chr 12:35 505
to battle, expert in war, forty *t* ... 1Chr 12:36 505
battle, an hundred and twenty *t* ... 1Chr 12:37 505
he commanded to a *t* generations ... 1Chr 16:15 505
David took from him a *t* chariots ... 1Chr 18:4 505
seven *t* horsemen, and twenty ... 1Chr 18:4 505
horsemen, and twenty *t* footmen ... 1Chr 18:4 505
the Syrians two and twenty *t* men ... 1Chr 18:5 505
in the valley of salt eighteen *t* ... 1Chr 18:12 505
the children of Ammon sent a *t* ... 1Chr 19:6 505
two *t* chariots, and the king of ... 1Chr 19:7 505
t men which fought in chariots ... 1Chr 19:18 505
forty *t* footmen, and killed ... 1Chr 19:18 505
they of Israel were a *t t* ... 1Chr 21:5 505
an hundred *t* men that drew sword ... 1Chr 21:5 505
ten *t* men that drew sword ... 1Chr 21:5 505
fell of Israel seventy *t* men ... 1Chr 21:14 505
LORD an hundred *t* talents of gold ... 1Chr 22:14 505
a *t t* talents of silver ... 1Chr 22:14 505
man by man, was thirty and eight *t* ... 1Chr 23:3 505
four *t* were to set forward the ... 1Chr 23:4 505
six *t* were officers and judges ... 1Chr 23:4 505
Moreover four *t* were porters ... 1Chr 23:5 505
four *t* praised the LORD with the ... 1Chr 23:5 505
his brethren, men of valour, a *t* ... 1Chr 26:30 505
men of valour, were two *t* ... 1Chr 26:32 505
course were twenty and four *t* ... 1Chr 27:1 505
his course were twenty and four *t* ... 1Chr 27:2 505
likewise were twenty and four *t* ... 1Chr 27:4 505
his course were twenty and four *t* ... 1Chr 27:5 505
his course were twenty and four *t* ... 1Chr 27:7 505
his course were twenty and four *t* ... 1Chr 27:8 505
his course were twenty and four *t* ... 1Chr 27:9 505
his course were twenty and four *t* ... 1Chr 27:10 505
his course were twenty and four *t* ... 1Chr 27:11 505
his course were twenty and four *t* ... 1Chr 27:12 505
his course were twenty and four *t* ... 1Chr 27:13 505
his course were twenty and four *t* ... 1Chr 27:14 505
his course were twenty and four *t* ... 1Chr 27:15 505
Even three *t* talents of gold, of ... 1Chr 29:4 505
seven *t* talents of refined silver ... 1Chr 29:4 505
of God of gold five *t* talents ... 1Chr 29:7 505
ten *t* drams, and of silver ten ... 1Chr 29:7 7239
drams, and of silver ten *t* talents ... 1Chr 29:7 505
and of brass eighteen *t* talents ... 1Chr 29:7 505
one hundred *t* talents of iron ... 1Chr 29:7 505
even a *t* bullocks, a *t* ... 1Chr 29:21 505
a *t* rams, and a *t* lambs, ... 1Chr 29:21 505
offered a *t* burnt offerings upon ... 2Chr 1:6 505
and he had a *t* and four hundred ... 2Chr 1:14 505
twelve *t* horsemen, which he ... 2Chr 1:14 505
ten *t* men to bear burdens, and ... 2Chr 2:2 505
fourscore *t* to hew in the ... 2Chr 2:2 505
hew in the mountain, and three *t* ... 2Chr 2:2 505
twenty *t* measures of beaten wheat ... 2Chr 2:10 505
twenty *t* measures of barley, and ... 2Chr 2:10 505
twenty *t* baths of wine, and twenty ... 2Chr 2:10 505
of wine, and twenty *t* baths of oil ... 2Chr 2:10 505
and fifty *t* and three *t* ... 2Chr 2:17 505
ten *t* of them to be bearers of ... 2Chr 2:18 505
fourscore *t* to be hewers in the ... 2Chr 2:18 505
in the mountain, and three *t* ... 2Chr 2:18 505
it received and held three *t* baths ... 2Chr 4:5 505
two *t* oxen, and an hundred and ... 2Chr 7:5 505
and an hundred and twenty *t* sheep ... 2Chr 7:5 505
Solomon had four *t* stalls for ... 2Chr 9:25 505
and chariots, and twelve *t* horsemen ... 2Chr 9:25 505
fourscore *t* chosen men, which ... 2Chr 11:1 505
and threescore *t* horsemen ... 2Chr 12:3 505
even four hundred *t* chosen men ... 2Chr 13:3 505
with eight hundred *t* chosen men ... 2Chr 13:3 505
Israel five hundred *t* chosen men ... 2Chr 13:17 505
out of Judah three hundred *t* ... 2Chr 14:8 505
bows, two hundred and fourscore *t* ... 2Chr 14:8 505
with an host of a *t t* ... 2Chr 14:9 505
hundred oxen and seven *t* sheep ... 2Chr 15:11 505
brought him flocks, seven *t* ... 2Chr 17:11 505
and seven hundred rams, and seven *t* ... 2Chr 17:11 505
men of valour three hundred *t* ... 2Chr 17:14 505
him two hundred and fourscore *t* ... 2Chr 17:15 505
hundred *t* mighty men of valour ... 2Chr 17:16 505
with bow and shield two hundred *t* ... 2Chr 17:17 505
fourscore *t* ready prepared for ... 2Chr 17:18 505
them three hundred *t* choice men ... 2Chr 25:5 505
He hired also an hundred *t* mighty ... 2Chr 25:6 505
of the children of Seir ten *t* ... 2Chr 25:11 505
other ten *t* left alive did the ... 2Chr 25:12 505
and smote three *t* of them ... 2Chr 25:13 505
mighty men of valour were two *t* ... 2Chr 26:12 505
three hundred *t* and seven *t* ... 2Chr 26:13 505
ten *t* measures of wheat, and ten ... 2Chr 27:5 505
of wheat, and ten *t* of barley ... 2Chr 27:5 505
twenty *t* in one day, which were ... 2Chr 28:6 505
of their brethren two hundred *t* ... 2Chr 28:8 505
six hundred oxen and three *t* sheep ... 2Chr 29:33 505
to the congregation a *t* bullocks ... 2Chr 30:24 505
bullocks and seven *t* sheep ... 2Chr 30:24 505
to the congregation a *t* bullocks ... 2Chr 30:24 505
t bullocks and ten *t* sheep ... 2Chr 30:24 505
to the number of thirty *t* ... 2Chr 35:7 505
and three *t* bullocks ... 2Chr 35:7 505
for the passover offerings two *t* ... 2Chr 35:8 505
offerings five *t* small cattle ... 2Chr 35:9 505
a *t* chargers of silver, nine and ... Ezr 1:9 505
and ten, and other vessels a *t* ... Ezr 1:10 505
of gold and of silver were five *t* ... Ezr 1:11 505
two *t* an hundred seventy and two ... Ezr 2:3 505
two *t* eight hundred and twelve ... Ezr 2:6 505
a *t* two hundred fifty and four ... Ezr 2:7 505
a *t* two hundred twenty and two ... Ezr 2:12 505
of Bigvai, two *t* fifty and six ... Ezr 2:14 505
a *t* two hundred fifty and four ... Ezr 2:31 505
The children of Senaah, three *t* ... Ezr 2:35 505
of Immer, a *t* fifty and two ... Ezr 2:37 505
a *t* two hundred forty and seven ... Ezr 2:38 505
The children of Harim, a *t* ... Ezr 2:39 505
two *t* three hundred and threescore ... Ezr 2:64 505
were seven *t* three hundred thirty ... Ezr 2:65 505
six *t* seven hundred and twenty ... Ezr 2:67 505
one *t* drams of gold, and five ... Ezr 2:69 505
five *t* pound of silver, and one ... Ezr 2:69 505
basons of gold, of a *t* drams ... Ezr 8:27 505
a *t* cubits on the wall unto the ... Neh 3:13 505
two *t* an hundred seventy and two ... Neh 7:8 505
children of Jeshua and Joab, two *t* ... Neh 7:11 505
a *t* two hundred fifty and four ... Neh 7:12 505
two *t* three hundred twenty and two ... Neh 7:17 505
two *t* threescore and seven ... Neh 7:19 505
a *t* two hundred fifty and four ... Neh 7:34 505
three *t* nine hundred and thirty ... Neh 7:38 505
of Immer, a *t* fifty and two ... Neh 7:40 505
a *t* two hundred forty and seven ... Neh 7:41 505
The children of Harim, a *t* ... Neh 7:42 505
two *t* three hundred and threescore ... Neh 7:66 505
were seven *t* three hundred thirty ... Neh 7:67 505
six *t* seven hundred and twenty ... Neh 7:69 505
to the treasure a *t* drams of gold ... Neh 7:70 505
the work twenty *t* drams of gold ... Neh 7:71 7239
of gold, and two *t* ... Neh 7:71 505
gave was twenty *t* drams of gold ... Neh 7:72 505
two *t* pounds of silver, and ... Neh 7:72 7239
I will pay ten *t* talents of ... Est 3:9 505
of their foes seventy and five *t* ... Est 9:16 505
substance also was seven *t* sheep ... Job 1:3 505
three *t* camels, and five hundred ... Job 1:3 505
he cannot answer him one of a *t* ... Job 9:3 505
an interpreter, one among a *t* ... Job 33:23 505
for he had fourteen *t* sheep ... Job 42:12 505
six *t* camels, and a *t* yoke ... Job 42:12 505
yoke of oxen, and a *t* she asses ... Job 42:12 505
and the cattle upon a *t* hills ... Ps 50:10 505
in the valley of salt twelve *t* ... Ps 60:t 505
The chariots of God are twenty *t* ... Ps 68:17 7239
in thy courts is better than a *t* ... Ps 84:10 505
For a *t* years in thy sight are ... Ps 90:4 505
A *t* shall fall at thy side, and ... Ps 91:7 505
side, and ten *t* at thy right hand ... Ps 91:7 7233
he commanded to a *t* generations ... Ps 105:8 505
he live a *t* years twice told ... Eccl 6:6 505
one man among a *t* have I found ... Eccl 7:28 505
whereon there hang a *t* bucklers ... Song 4:4 505
ruddy, the chiefest among ten *t* ... Song 5:10 7233
was to bring a *t* pieces of silver ... Song 8:11 505
thou, O Solomon, must have a *t* ... Song 8:12 505
t vines at a *t* silverlings ... Is 7:23 505
One *t* shall flee at the rebuke of ... Is 30:17 505
and I will give thee two *t* horses ... Is 36:8 505
an hundred and fourscore and five *t* ... Is 37:36 505
A little one shall become a *t* ... Is 60:22 505
in the seventh year three *t* Jews ... Jer 52:28 505
all the persons were four *t* ... Jer 52:30 505
length of five and twenty *t* reeds ... Eze 45:1 505
and the breadth shall be ten *t* ... Eze 45:1 505
the length of five and twenty *t* ... Eze 45:3 505
and the breadth of ten *t* ... Eze 45:3 505
twenty *t* of length, and the ten ... Eze 45:5 505
the ten *t* of breadth, shall also ... Eze 45:5 505
of the city five *t* broad, and five ... Eze 45:6 505
broad, and five and twenty *t* long ... Eze 45:6 505
eastward, he measured a *t* cubits ... Eze 47:3 505
Again he measured a *t*, and brought ... Eze 47:4 505
Again he measured a *t*, and brought ... Eze 47:4 505
Afterward he measured a *t* ... Eze 47:5 505
twenty *t* reeds in breadth, and in ... Eze 48:8 505
twenty *t* in length, and of ten ... Eze 48:9 505
in length, and of ten *t* in breadth ... Eze 48:9 505
twenty *t* in length, and toward the ... Eze 48:10 505
toward the west ten *t* in breadth ... Eze 48:10 505
toward the east ten *t* in breadth ... Eze 48:10 505
south five and twenty *t* in length ... Eze 48:10 505
twenty *t* in length, and ten ... Eze 48:13 505
in length, and ten *t* in breadth ... Eze 48:13 505
length shall be five and twenty *t* ... Eze 48:13 505
and the breadth ten *t* ... Eze 48:13 505
And the five *t*, that are left in ... Eze 48:15 505
over against the five and twenty *t* ... Eze 48:15 505
the north side four *t* and five ... Eze 48:16 505
hundred, and the south side four *t* ... Eze 48:16 505
and on the east side four *t* ... Eze 48:16 505
hundred, and the west side four *t* ... Eze 48:16 505
portion shall be ten *t* eastward ... Eze 48:18 505
eastward, and ten *t* westward ... Eze 48:18 505
twenty *t* by five and twenty ... Eze 48:20 505
by five and twenty *t* ... Eze 48:20 505
twenty *t* of the oblation toward ... Eze 48:21 505
twenty *t* toward the west border, ... Eze 48:21 505
city on the north side, four *t* ... Eze 48:30 505
And at the east side four *t* ... Eze 48:32 505
And at the south side four *t* ... Eze 48:33 505
At the west side four *t* and five ... Eze 48:34 505
round about eighteen *t* measures ... Eze 48:35 505
a great feast to a *t* of his lords ... Dan 5:1 506
lords, and drank wine before the *t* ... Dan 5:1 506
t thousands ministered unto him, ... Dan 7:10 506
ten *t* times ten *t* stood ... Dan 7:10 7240
And he said unto me, Unto two *t* ... Dan 8:14 505
there shall be a *t* two hundred ... Dan 12:11 505
and cometh to the *t* three hundred ... Dan 12:12 505
out by a *t* shall leave an hundred ... Amos 5:3 505
t persons that cannot discern ... Jonah 4:11 7239
had eaten were about five *t* men ... Mt 14:21 4000
they that did eat were four *t* men ... Mt 15:38 5070
the five loaves of the five *t* ... Mt 16:9 4000
the seven loaves of the four *t* ... Mt 16:10 5070
him, which owed him ten *t* talents ... Mt 18:24 3463
the sea, (they were about two *t* ... Mk 5:13 1367
the loaves were about five *t* men ... Mk 6:44 4000
that had eaten were about four *t* ... Mk 8:9 5070
the five loaves among five *t* ... Mk 8:19 4000
And when the seven among four *t* ... Mk 8:20 5070
For they were about five *t* men ... Lk 9:14 4000
whether he be able with ten *t* to ... Lk 14:31 5505
cometh against him with twenty *t* ... Lk 14:31 5505
sat down, in number about five *t* ... Jn 6:10 4000
unto them about three *t* souls ... Acts 2:41 5153
of the men was about five *t* ... Acts 4:4 5505
found it fifty *t* pieces of silver ... Acts 19:19 3461
four *t* men that were murderers ... Acts 21:38 5070
reserved to myself seven *t* men ... Rom 11:4 2035
have ten *t* instructers in Christ ... 1Cor 4:15 3463
fell in one day three and twenty *t* ... 1Cor 10:8 5505
than ten *t* words in an unknown ... 1Cor 14:19 3463
day is with the Lord as a *t* years ... 2Pet 3:8 5507
years, and a *t* years as one day ... 2Pet 3:8 5507
them was ten *t* times ten *t* ... Rev 5:11 3461
four *t* of all the tribes of the ... Rev 7:4 5505
of Juda were sealed twelve *t* ... Rev 7:5 5505
of Reuben were sealed twelve *t* ... Rev 7:5 5505
tribe of Gad were sealed twelve *t* ... Rev 7:5 5505
of Aser were sealed twelve *t* ... Rev 7:6 5505
of Nepthalim were sealed twelve *t* ... Rev 7:6 5505
of Manasses were sealed twelve *t* ... Rev 7:6 5505
of Simeon were sealed twelve *t* ... Rev 7:7 5505
of Levi were sealed twelve *t* ... Rev 7:7 5505
of Issachar were sealed twelve *t* ... Rev 7:7 5505
of Zabulon were sealed twelve *t* ... Rev 7:8 5505
of Joseph were sealed twelve *t* ... Rev 7:8 5505
of Benjamin were sealed twelve *t* ... Rev 7:8 5505
were two hundred *t t* ... Rev 9:16 3461
shall prophesy a *t* two hundred ... Rev 11:3 5507
were slain of men seven *t* ... Rev 11:13 5505
feed her there a *t* two hundred ... Rev 12:6 5507
him an hundred forty and four *t* ... Rev 14:1 5505
the hundred and forty and four *t* ... Rev 14:3 5505
bridles, by the space of a *t* ... Rev 14:20 5507
and Satan, and bound him a *t* years ... Rev 20:2 5507
till the *t* years should be ... Rev 20:3 5507
and reigned with Christ a *t* years ... Rev 20:4 5507
until the *t* years were finished ... Rev 20:5 5507
and shall reign with him a *t* years ... Rev 20:6 5507
when the *t* years are expired, ... Rev 20:7 5507
with the reed, twelve *t* furlongs ... Rev 21:16 5505

THOUSANDS

thou the mother of *t* of millions ... Gen 24:60 505
such over them, to be rulers of *t* ... Ex 18:21 505
over the people, rulers of *t* ... Ex 18:25 505
shewing mercy unto *t* of them that ... Ex 20:6 505
Keeping mercy for *t*, forgiving ... Ex 34:7 505
fathers, heads of *t* in Israel ... Num 1:16 505
are heads of the *t* of Israel ... Num 10:4 505
O LORD, unto the many *t* of Israel ... Num 10:36 505
delivered out of the *t* of Israel ... Num 31:5 505
host, with the captains over *t* ... Num 31:14 505
which were over *t* of the host ... Num 31:48 505
of the host, the captains of *t* ... Num 31:48 505
to the LORD, of the captains of *t* ... Num 31:52 505
the gold of the captains of *t* ... Num 31:54 505
heads over you, captains over *t* ... Deut 1:15 505
shewing mercy unto *t* of them that ... Deut 5:10 505
and he came with ten *t* of saints ... Deut 33:2 7233
and they are the ten *t* of Ephraim ... Deut 33:17 7233
and they are the *t* of Manasseh ... Deut 33:17 505
fathers among the *t* of Israel ... Josh 22:14 505
unto the heads of the *t* of Israel ... Josh 22:21 505
heads of the *t* of Israel which ... Josh 22:30 505
will appoint him captains over *t* ... 1Sa 8:12 505
LORD by your tribes, and by your *t* ... 1Sa 10:19 505
his *t*, and David his ten *t* ... 1Sa 18:7 505
have ascribed unto David ten *t* ... 1Sa 18:8 7233
and to me they have ascribed but *t* ... 1Sa 18:8 505
saying, Saul hath slain his *t* ... 1Sa 21:11 505
and David his ten *t* ... 1Sa 21:11 7233
and make you all captains of *t* ... 1Sa 22:7 505
out throughout all the *t* of Judah ... 1Sa 23:23 505
passed on by hundreds, and by *t* ... 1Sa 29:2 505
dances, saying, Saul slew his *t* ... 1Sa 29:5 7233
and David his ten *t* ... 1Sa 29:5 505
with him, and set captains of *t* ... 2Sa 18:1 505
came out by hundreds and by *t* ... 2Sa 18:4 505
captains of the *t* that were of ... 1Chr 12:20 505
consulted with the captains of *t* ... 1Chr 13:1 505
of Israel, and the captains over *t* ... 1Chr 15:25 505
fathers, the captains over *t* ... 1Chr 26:26 505
chief fathers and captains of *t* ... 1Chr 27:1 505

and the captains over the *t* 1Chr 28:1 505
of Israel, and the captains of *t* 1Chr 29:6 505
all Israel, to the captains of *t* 2Chr 1:2 505
Of Judah, the captains of *t* 2Chr 17:14 505
and made them captains over *t* 2Chr 25:5 505
not be afraid of ten *t* of people Ps 3:6 7233
twenty thousand, even *t* of angels Ps 68:17 505
is better unto me than *t* of gold Ps 119:72 505
that our sheep may bring forth *t* Ps 144:13 503
and ten *t* in our streets Ps 144:13 7232
shewest lovingkindness unto *t* Jer 32:18 505
thousand *t* ministered unto him, Dan 7:10 506
and he shall cast down many ten *t* Dan 11:12 7239
be little among the *t* of Judah Mic 5:2 505
LORD be pleased with *t* of rams Mic 6:7 505
or with ten *t* of rivers of oil Mic 6:7 7233
how many *t* of Jews there are Acts 21:20 *3461*
cometh with ten *t* of his saints Jude 14 *3461*
ten thousand, and *t* of *t* Rev 5:11 *5505*

THREAD
from a *t* even to a shoelatchet Gen 14:23 2339
bound upon his hand a scarlet *t* Gen 38:28
had the scarlet *t* upon his hand Gen 38:30
t in the window which thou didst Josh 2:18 2339
as a *t* of tow is broken when it Judg 16:9 6616
them from off his arms like a *t* Judg 16:12 2339
Thy lips are like a *t* of scarlet Song 4:3 2339

THREATEN
people, let us straitly *t* them Acts 4:17 *546*

THREATENED
So when they had further *t* them Acts 4:21 *4324*
when he suffered, he *t* not 1Pet 2:23 *546*

THREATENING
things unto them, forbearing *t* Eph 6:9 *547*

THREATENINGS
And now, Lord, behold their *t* Acts 4:29 *547*
And Saul, yet breathing out *t* Acts 9:1 *547*

THREE
begat Methuselah *t* hundred years Gen 5:22 7969
of Enoch were *t* hundred sixty Gen 5:23 7969
And Noah begat *t* sons, Shem, Ham, Gen 6:10 7969
the ark shall be *t* hundred cubits Gen 6:15 7969
the *t* wives of his sons with them Gen 7:13 7969
These are the *t* sons of Noah Gen 9:19 7969
lived after the flood *t* hundred Gen 9:28 7969
t years, and begat sons and Gen 11:13 7969
t years, and begat sons and Gen 11:15 7969
t hundred and eighteen, and pursued Gen 14:14 7969
Take me an heifer of *t* years old Gen 15:9 8027
old, and a she goat of *t* years old Gen 15:9 8027
a ram of *t* years old, and a Gen 15:9 8027
and, lo, *t* men stood by him Gen 18:2 7969
Make ready quickly *t* measures of Gen 18:6 7969
there were *t* flocks of sheep Gen 29:2 7969
because I have born him *t* sons Gen 29:34 7969
he set *t* days' journey betwixt Gen 30:36 7969
came to pass about *t* months after Gen 38:24 7969
And in the vine were *t* branches Gen 40:10 7969
The *t* branches are *t* days Gen 40:12 7969
Yet within *t* days shall Pharaoh Gen 40:13 7969
I had *t* white baskets on my head Gen 40:16 7969
The *t* baskets are *t* days Gen 40:18 7969
Yet within *t* days shall Pharaoh Gen 40:19 7969
all together into ward *t* days Gen 42:17 7969
but to Benjamin he gave *t* hundred Gen 45:22 7969
and his daughters were thirty and *t* Gen 46:15 7969
child, she hid him *t* months Ex 2:2 7969
thee, *t* days' journey into the Ex 3:18 7969
t days' journey into the desert, Ex 5:3 7969
were an hundred thirty and *t* years Ex 6:18 7969
t years old, when they spake unto Ex 7:7 7969
We will go *t* days' journey into Ex 8:27 7969
in all the land of Egypt *t* days Ex 10:22 7969
any from his place for *t* days Ex 10:23 7969
and they went *t* days in the Ex 15:22 7969
And if he do not these *t* unto her Ex 21:11 7969
T times thou shalt keep a feast Ex 23:14 7969
T times in the year all thy males Ex 23:17 7969
t branches of the candlestick out Ex 25:32 7969
t branches of the candlestick out Ex 25:32 7969
T bowls made like unto almonds, Ex 25:33 7969
t bowls made like almonds in the Ex 25:33 7969
height thereof shall be *t* cubits Ex 27:1 7969
pillars *t*, and their sockets *t* Ex 27:14 7969
pillars *t*, and their sockets *t* Ex 27:15 7969
that day about *t* thousand men Ex 32:28 7969
t branches of the candlestick out Ex 37:18 7969
t branches of the candlestick out Ex 37:18 7969
T bowls made after the fashion of Ex 37:19 7969
t bowls made like almonds in Ex 37:19 7969
t cubits the height thereof Ex 38:1 7969
pillars *t*, and their sockets *t* Ex 38:14 7969
pillars *t*, and their sockets *t* Ex 38:15 7969
t thousand and five hundred and Ex 38:26 7969
in the blood of her purifying *t* Lev 12:4 7969
t tenth deals of fine flour for a Lev 14:10 7969
t years shall it be as Lev 19:23 7969
bring forth fruit for *t* years Lev 25:21 7969
shall be *t* shekels of silver Lev 27:6 7969
and nine thousand and *t* hundred Num 1:23 7969
t thousand and four hundred Num 1:43 7969
t thousand and five hundred and Num 1:46 7969
and nine thousand and *t* hundred Num 2:13 7969
t thousand and four hundred Num 2:30 7969
t thousand and five hundred and Num 2:32 7969
a thousand *t* hundred and Num 3:50 7969
were *t* thousand and two hundred Num 4:44 7969
mount of the LORD *t* days' journey Num 10:33 7969
them in the *t* days' journey Num 10:33 7969
Come out ye *t* unto the tabernacle Num 12:4 7969
And they *t* came out Num 12:4 7969
of *t* tenth deals of flour mingled Num 15:9 7969
hast smitten me these *t* times Num 22:28 7969
smitten thine ass these *t* times Num 22:32 7969
and turned from me these *t* times Num 22:33 7969
blessed them these *t* times Num 24:10 7969
t thousand and seven hundred and Num 26:7 7969
and four thousand and *t* hundred Num 26:25 7969
t thousand and four hundred Num 26:47 7969
t thousand, all males from a Num 26:62 7969
t tenth deals of flour for a meat Num 28:12 7969
t tenth deals shall ye offer for Num 28:20 7969
t tenth deals unto one bullock, Num 28:28 7969
t tenth deals for a bullock, and Num 29:3 7969
t tenth deals to a bullock, and Num 29:9 7969
t tenth deals unto every bullock Num 29:14 7969
was in number *t* hundred thousand Num 31:36 7969
was *t* hundred thousand and thirty Num 31:43 7969
went *t* days' journey in the Num 33:8 7969
t years old when he died in mount Num 33:39 7969
Ye shall give *t* cities on this Num 35:14 7969
t cities shall ye give in the Num 35:14 7969
Then Moses severed *t* cities on Deut 4:41 7969
At the end of *t* years thou shalt Deut 14:28 7969
T times in a year shall all thy Deut 16:16 7969
or *t* witnesses, shall he that is Deut 17:6 7969
Thou shalt separate *t* cities for Deut 19:2 7969
into *t* parts, that every slayer Deut 19:3 8027
shalt separate *t* cities for thee Deut 19:7 7969
then shalt thou add *t* cities more Deut 19:9 7969
more for thee, beside these *t* Deut 19:9 7969
or at the mouth of *t* witnesses Deut 19:15 7969
for within *t* days ye shall pass Josh 1:11 7969
and hide yourselves there *t* days Josh 2:16 7969
mountain, and abode there *t* days Josh 2:22 7969
And it came to pass after *t* days Josh 3:2 7969
about two or *t* thousand men go up Josh 7:3 7969
the people about *t* thousand men Josh 7:4 7969
of *t* days after they had made a Josh 9:16 7969
drove thence the *t* sons of Anak Josh 15:14 7969
and her towns, even *t* countries Josh 17:11 7969
among you *t* men for each tribe Josh 18:4 7969
with her suburbs; *t* cities Josh 21:32 7969
thence the *t* sons of Anak Judg 1:20 7969
their mouth, were *t* hundred men Judg 7:6 7969
By the *t* hundred men that lapped Judg 7:7 7969
and retained those *t* hundred men Judg 7:8 7969
he divided the *t* hundred men into Judg 7:16 7969
hundred men into *t* companies Judg 7:16 7969
the *t* companies blew the trumpets Judg 7:20 7969
the *t* hundred blew the trumpets, Judg 7:22 7969
the *t* hundred men that were with Judg 8:4 7969
had reigned *t* years over Israel Judg 9:22 7969
and divided them into *t* companies Judg 9:43 7969
t years, and died, and was buried Judg 10:2 7969
coasts of Arnon, *t* hundred years Judg 11:26 7969
they could not in *t* days expound Judg 14:14 7969
caught *t* hundred foxes, and took Judg 15:4 7969
Then *t* thousand men of Judah went Judg 15:11 7969
thou hast mocked me these *t* times Judg 16:15 7969
the roof about *t* thousand men Judg 16:27 7969
and he abode with him *t* days Judg 19:4 7969
with *t* bullocks, and one ephah of 1Sa 1:24 7969
fleshhook of *t* teeth in his hand 1Sa 2:13 7969
she conceived, and bare *t* sons 1Sa 2:21 7969
asses that were lost *t* days ago 1Sa 9:20 7969
there shall meet thee *t* men going 1Sa 10:3 7969
to Beth-el, one carrying *t* kids 1Sa 10:3 7969
carrying *t* loaves of bread 1Sa 10:3 7969
of Israel were *t* hundred thousand 1Sa 11:8 7969
put the people in *t* companies 1Sa 11:11 7969
Saul chose him *t* thousand men of 1Sa 13:2 7969
of the Philistines in *t* companies 1Sa 13:17 7969
the *t* eldest sons of Jesse went 1Sa 17:13 7969
the names of his *t* sons that went 1Sa 17:13 7969
the *t* eldest followed Saul 1Sa 17:14 7969
And when thou hast stayed *t* days 1Sa 20:19 8027
I will shoot *t* arrows on the side 1Sa 20:20 7969
ground, and bowed himself *t* times 1Sa 20:41 7969
kept from us about these *t* days 1Sa 21:5 8032
Then Saul took *t* thousand chosen 1Sa 24:2 7969
he had *t* thousand sheep, and a 1Sa 25:2 7969
having *t* thousand chosen men of 1Sa 26:2 7969
any water, *t* days and *t* nights 1Sa 30:12 7969
because *t* days agone I fell sick 1Sa 30:13 7969
his *t* sons, and his armourbearer, 1Sa 31:6 7969
his *t* sons fallen in mount Gilboa 1Sa 31:8 7969
there were *t* sons of Zeruiah 2Sa 2:18 7969
of Abner's men, so that *t* hundred 2Sa 2:31 7969
t years over all Israel and Judah 2Sa 5:5 7969
of Obed-edom the Gittite *t* months 2Sa 6:11 7969
to Geshur, and was there *t* years 2Sa 13:38 7969
Absalom there were born *t* sons 2Sa 14:27 7969
he took *t* darts in his hand, and 2Sa 18:14 7969
me the men of Judah within *t* days 2Sa 20:4 7969
in the days of David *t* years 2Sa 21:1 7969
t hundred shekels of brass in 2Sa 21:16 7969
one of the *t* mighty men with 2Sa 23:9 7969
t of the thirty chief went down, 2Sa 23:13 7991
the *t* mighty men brake through 2Sa 23:16 7969
things did these *t* mighty men 2Sa 23:17 7969
son of Zeruiah, was chief among *t* 2Sa 23:18 7992
up his spear against *t* hundred 2Sa 23:18 7969
them, and had the name among *t* 2Sa 23:18 7969
Was he not most honourable of *t* 2Sa 23:19 7969
he attained not unto the first *t* 2Sa 23:19 7969
had the name among *t* mighty men 2Sa 23:22 7969
he attained not to the first *t* 2Sa 23:23 7969
the LORD, I offer thee *t* things 2Sa 24:12 7969
or wilt thou flee *t* months before 2Sa 24:13 7969
or that there be *t* days' 2Sa 24:13 7969
t years reigned he in Jerusalem 1Kin 2:11 7969
to pass at the end of *t* years 1Kin 2:39 7969
he spake *t* thousand proverbs 1Kin 4:32 7969
t thousand and *t* hundred, 1Kin 5:16 7969
court with *t* rows of hewed stone 1Kin 6:36 7969
And there were windows in *t* rows 1Kin 7:4 7969
was against light in *t* ranks 1Kin 7:4 7969
was against light in *t* ranks 1Kin 7:5 7969
was with *t* rows of hewed stones 1Kin 7:12 7969
t looking toward the north, and 1Kin 7:25 7969
t looking toward the west, and 1Kin 7:25 7969
t looking toward the south, and 1Kin 7:25 7969
t looking toward the east 1Kin 7:25 7969
t cubits the height of it 1Kin 7:27 7969
t times in a year did Solomon 1Kin 9:25 7969
he made *t* hundred shields of 1Kin 10:17 7969
t pound of gold went to one 1Kin 10:17 7969
once in *t* years came the navy of 1Kin 10:22 7969
and *t* hundred concubines 1Kin 11:3 7969
unto them, Depart yet for *t* days 1Kin 12:5 7969
T years reigned he in Jerusalem 1Kin 15:2 7969
himself upon the child *t* times 1Kin 17:21 7969
they continued *t* years without 1Kin 22:1 7969
and they sought *t* days, but found 2Kin 2:17 7969
called these *t* kings together 2Kin 3:10 7969
called these *t* kings together 2Kin 3:13 7969
out to him two or *t* eunuchs 2Kin 9:32 7969
But it was so, that in the *t* 2Kin 12:6 7969
In the *t* and twentieth year of 2Kin 13:1 7969
T times did Joash beat him, and 2Kin 13:25 7969
Samaria, and besieged it *t* years 2Kin 17:5 7969
at the end of *t* years they took 2Kin 18:10 7969
Judah *t* hundred talents of silver 2Kin 18:14 7969
t years old when he began to 2Kin 23:31 7969
he reigned *t* months in Jerusalem 2Kin 23:31 7969
became his servant *t* years 2Kin 24:1 7969
he reigned in Jerusalem *t* months 2Kin 24:8 7969
height of the chapiter *t* cubits 2Kin 25:17 7969
the *t* keepers of the door 2Kin 25:18 7969
which *t* were born unto him of the 1Chr 2:3 7969
Abishai, and Joab, and Asahel, *t* 1Chr 2:16 7969
And Segub begat Jair, who had *t* 1Chr 2:22 7969
he reigned thirty and *t* years 1Chr 3:4 7969
and Hezekiah, and Azrikam, *t* 1Chr 3:23 7969
Bela, and Becher, and Jediael, *t* 1Chr 7:6 7969
his *t* sons, and all his house died 1Chr 10:6 7969
t hundred slain by him at one 1Chr 11:11 7969
who was one of the *t* mighties 1Chr 11:12 7969
Now *t* of the thirty captains went 1Chr 11:15 7969
the *t* brake through the host of 1Chr 11:18 7969
things did these *t* mightiest 1Chr 11:19 7969
of Joab, he was chief of the *t* 1Chr 11:20 7969
up his spear against *t* hundred 1Chr 11:20 7969
them, and had a name among the *t* 1Chr 11:20 7969
Of the *t*, he was more honourable 1Chr 11:21 7969
he attained not to the first *t* 1Chr 11:21 7969
had the name among the *t* mighties 1Chr 11:24 7969
but attained not to the first *t* 1Chr 11:25 7969
and with him were *t* thousand 1Chr 12:27 7969
the kindred of Saul, *t* thousand 1Chr 12:29 7969
there they were with David *t* days 1Chr 12:39 7969
Obed-edom in his house *t* months 1Chr 13:14 7969
the LORD, I offer thee *t* things 1Chr 21:10 7969
Either *t* years' famine 1Chr 21:12 7969
or *t* months to be destroyed 1Chr 21:12 7969
or else *t* days the sword of the 1Chr 21:12 7969
was Jehiel, and Zetham, and Joel, *t* 1Chr 23:8 7969
Shelomith, and Haziel, and Haran, *t* 1Chr 23:9 7969
Mahli, and Eder, and Jeremoth, *t* 1Chr 23:23 7969
The *t* and twentieth to Delaiah, 1Chr 24:18 7969
fourteen sons and *t* daughters 1Chr 25:5 7969
The *t* and twentieth to Mahazioth, 1Chr 25:30 7969
Even *t* thousand talents of gold, 1Chr 29:4 7969
t years reigned he in Jerusalem 1Chr 29:27 7969
t thousand and six hundred to 2Chr 2:2 7969
t thousand and six hundred 2Chr 2:17 7969
t thousand and six hundred 2Chr 2:18 7969
t looking toward the north, and 2Chr 4:4 7969
t looking toward the west, and 2Chr 4:4 7969
t looking toward the south, and 2Chr 4:4 7969
t looking toward the east 2Chr 4:4 7969
received and held *t* thousand baths 2Chr 4:5 7969
t cubits high, and had set it in 2Chr 6:13 7969
And on the *t* and twentieth day of 2Chr 7:10 7969
t times in the year, even in the 2Chr 8:13 7969
t hundred shields made he of 2Chr 9:16 7969
t hundred shekels of gold went to 2Chr 9:16 7969
every *t* years once came the ships 2Chr 9:21 7969
Come again unto me after *t* days 2Chr 10:5 7969
son of Solomon strong, *t* years 2Chr 11:17 7969
for *t* years they walked in the 2Chr 11:17 7969
He reigned *t* years in Jerusalem 2Chr 13:2 7969
out of Judah *t* hundred thousand 2Chr 14:8 7969
thousand, and *t* hundred chariots 2Chr 14:9 7969
men of valour *t* hundred thousand 2Chr 17:14 7969
they were *t* days in gathering of 2Chr 20:25 7969
found them *t* hundred thousand 2Chr 25:5 7969
smote *t* thousand of them, and took 2Chr 25:13 7969
t hundred thousand and seven 2Chr 26:13 7969
hundred oxen and *t* thousand sheep 2Chr 29:33 7969
from *t* years old and upward, even 2Chr 31:16 7969
thousand, and *t* thousand bullocks 2Chr 35:7 7969
small cattle, and *t* hundred oxen 2Chr 35:8 7969
t years old when he began to 2Chr 36:2 7969
he reigned *t* months in Jerusalem 2Chr 36:2 7969
to reign, and he reigned *t* months 2Chr 36:9 7969
t hundred seventy and two Ezr 2:4 7969
of Bebai, six hundred twenty and *t* Ezr 2:11 7969
Bezai, *t* hundred twenty and *t* Ezr 2:17 7969
Hashum, two hundred twenty and *t* Ezr 2:19 7969
an hundred twenty and *t* Ezr 2:21 7969
seven hundred and forty and *t* Ezr 2:25 7969
and Ai, two hundred twenty and *t* Ezr 2:28 7969
of Harim, *t* hundred and twenty Ezr 2:32 7969
Jericho, *t* hundred forty and five Ezr 2:34 7969
t thousand and six hundred and Ezr 2:35 7969
Jeshua, nine hundred seventy and *t* Ezr 2:36 7969
were *t* hundred ninety and two Ezr 2:58 7969

forty and two thousand *t* hundred........ Ezr 2:64 7969
seven thousand *t* hundred thirty.......... Ezr 2:65 7969
With *t* rows of great stones, and a........ Ezr 6:4 8532
and with him *t* hundred males.............. Ezr 8:5 7969
and there abode we in tents *t* days........ Ezr 8:15 7969
Jerusalem, and abode there *t* days........ Ezr 8:32 7969
would not come within *t* days.............. Ezr 10:8 7969
unto Jerusalem within *t* days.............. Ezr 10:9 7969
to Jerusalem, and was there *t* days........ Neh 2:11 7969
t hundred seventy and two.................. Neh 7:9 7969
two thousand *t* hundred twenty and.... Neh 7:17 7969
t hundred twenty and eight.................. Neh 7:22 7969
Bezai, *t* hundred twenty and four......... Neh 7:23 7969
Beeroth, seven hundred forty and *t*........ Neh 7:29 7969
and Ai, an hundred twenty and *t*........ Neh 7:32 7969
of Harim, *t* hundred and twenty............ Neh 7:35 7969
Jericho, *t* hundred forty and five.......... Neh 7:36 7969
t thousand nine hundred and thirty..... Neh 7:38 7969
Jeshua, nine hundred seventy and *t*..... Neh 7:39 7969
were *t* hundred ninety and two............ Neh 7:60 7969
forty and two thousand *t* hundred......... Neh 7:66 7969
seven thousand *t* hundred thirty.......... Neh 7:67 7969
and neither eat nor drink *t* days.......... Est 4:16 7969
is, the month Sivan, on the *t*.............. Est 8:9 7969
slew *t* hundred men at Shushan............ Est 9:15 7969
him seven sons and *t* daughters............ Job 1:2 7969
t thousand camels, and five................. Job 1:3 7969
called for their *t* sisters to eat............ Job 1:4 7969
The Chaldeans made out *t* bands........... Job 1:17 7969
Now when Job's *t* friends heard of....... Job 2:11 7969
So these *t* men ceased to answer.......... Job 32:1 7969
Also against his *t* friends was............ Job 32:3 7969
in the mouth of these *t* men................ Job 32:5 7969
also seven sons and *t* daughters............ Job 42:13 7969
There are *t* things that are never......... Prov 30:15 7969
There be *t* things which are too........... Prov 30:18 7969
For *t* things the earth is.................... Prov 30:21 7969
There be *t* things which go well,.......... Prov 30:29 7969
Zoar, an heifer of *t* years old.............. Is 15:5 7992
spoken, saying, Within *t* years............. Is 16:14 7969
two or *t* berries in the top of.............. Is 17:6 7969
barefoot *t* years for a sign and............. Is 20:3 7969
even unto this day, that is the *t*.......... Jer 25:3 7969
Jehudi had read *t* or four leaves........... Jer 36:23 7969
as an heifer of *t* years old.................. Jer 48:34 7992
the *t* keepers of the door.................... Jer 52:24 7969
year *t* thousand Jews and *t*................ Jer 52:28 7969
In the *t* and twentieth year of.............. Jer 52:30 7969
days, *t* hundred and ninety days............ Eze 4:5 7969
t hundred and ninety days shalt............ Eze 4:9 7969
Though these *t* men, Noah, Daniel,...... Eze 14:14 7969
Though these *t* men were in it, as........ Eze 14:16 7969
Though these *t* men were in it, as........ Eze 14:18 7969
gate eastward were *t* on this side......... Eze 40:10 7969
on this side, and *t* on that side........... Eze 40:10 7969
they *t* were of one measure.................. Eze 40:10 7969
thereof were *t* on this side.................. Eze 40:21 7969
on this side and *t* on that side............. Eze 40:21 7969
gate was *t* cubits on this side.............. Eze 40:48 7969
side, and *t* cubits on that side............. Eze 40:48 7969
And the side chambers were *t*.............. Eze 41:6 7969
round about on their *t* stories............. Eze 41:16 7969
altar of wood was *t* cubits high............ Eze 41:22 7969
against gallery in *t* stories................. Eze 42:3 7992
For they were in *t* stories................... Eze 42:6 8027
t gates northward................................ Eze 48:31 7969
five hundred: and *t* gates..................... Eze 48:32 7969
hundred measures: and *t* gates.............. Eze 48:33 7969
five hundred, with their *t* gates........... Eze 48:34 7969
so nourishing them *t* years.................. Dan 1:5 7969
And these *t* men, Shadrach, Meshach.. Dan 3:23 8532
Did not we cast *t* men bound into........ Dan 3:24 8532
And over these *t* presidents................. Dan 6:2 8532
upon his knees *t* times a day............... Dan 6:10 8532
maketh his petition *t* times a day......... Dan 6:13 8532
it had *t* ribs in the mouth of it............ Dan 7:5 8532
before whom there were *t* of the........... Dan 7:8 8532
came up, and before whom *t* fell........... Dan 7:20 8532
first, and he shall subdue *t* kings......... Dan 7:24 8532
two thousand and *t* hundred days........... Dan 8:14 7969
Daniel was mourning *t* full weeks......... Dan 10:2 7969
till *t* whole weeks were fulfilled.......... Dan 10:3 7969
stand up yet *t* kings in Persia.............. Dan 11:2 7969
cometh to the thousand *t* hundred......... Dan 12:12 7969
For *t* transgressions of Damascus,........ Amos 1:3 7969
For *t* transgressions of Gaza, and......... Amos 1:6 7969
For *t* transgressions of Tyrus, and....... Amos 1:9 7969
For *t* transgressions of Edom, and........ Amos 1:11 7969
For *t* transgressions of the................. Amos 1:13 7969
For *t* transgressions of Moab, and......... Amos 2:1 7969
For *t* transgressions of Judah, and........ Amos 2:4 7969
For *t* transgressions of Israel,............. Amos 2:6 7969
and your tithes after *t* years............... Amos 4:4 7969
when there were yet *t* months to........... Amos 4:7 7969
So two or *t* cities wandered unto.......... Amos 4:8 7969
the fish *t* days and *t* nights................. Jonah 1:17 7969
great city of *t* days' journey............... Jonah 3:3 7969
T shepherds also I cut off in one......... Zec 11:8 7969
For as Jonas was *t* days...................... Mt 12:40 5140
t nights in the whale's belly................. Mt 12:40 5140
so shall the Son of man be *t* days......... Mt 12:40 5140
t nights in the heart of the.................. Mt 12:40 5140
hid in *t* measures of meal, till.............. Mt 13:33 5140
they continue with me now *t* days......... Mt 15:32 5140
let us make here *t* tabernacles............. Mt 17:4 5140
or *t* witnesses every word may be.......... Mt 18:16 5140
For where two or *t* are gathered........... Mt 18:20 5140
of God, and to build it in *t* days........... Mt 26:61 5140
temple, and buildest it in *t* days........... Mt 27:40 5140
After *t* days I will rise again................ Mt 27:63 5140
they have now been with me *t* days........ Mk 8:2 5140
and after *t* days rise again.................. Mk 8:31 5140
and let us make *t* tabernacles.............. Mk 9:5 5140
for more than *t* hundred pence.............. Mk 14:5 5145
within *t* days I will build..................... Mk 14:58 5140
temple, and buildest it in *t* days........... Mk 15:29 5140
abode with her about *t* months............. Lk 1:56 5140
that after *t* days they found him........... Lk 2:46 5140
the heaven was shut up *t* years............. Lk 4:25 5140
and let us make *t* tabernacles.............. Lk 9:33 5140
Which now of these *t*, thinkest............. Lk 10:36 5140
him, Friend, lend me *t* loaves.............. Lk 11:5 5140
t against two, and two against.............. Lk 12:52 5140
against two, and two against *t*.............. Lk 12:52 5140
these *t* years I come seeking................ Lk 13:7 5140
hid in *t* measures of meal, till.............. Lk 13:21 5140
two or *t* firkins apiece........................ Jn 2:6 5140
in *t* days I will raise it up................... Jn 2:19 5140
and wilt thou rear it up in *t* days.......... Jn 2:20 5140
ointment sold for *t* hundred pence......... Jn 12:5 5145
fishes, an hundred and fifty and *t*......... Jn 21:11 5140
unto them about *t* thousand souls.......... Acts 2:41 5153
about the space of *t* hours after........... Acts 5:7 5140
up in his father's house *t* months.......... Acts 7:20 5140
he was *t* days without sight, and........... Acts 9:9 5140
unto him, Behold, *t* men seek thee........ Acts 10:19 5140
And this was done *t* times................... Acts 11:10 5151
immediately there were *t* men.............. Acts 11:11 5140
t sabbath days reasoned with them....... Acts 17:2 5140
boldly for the space of *t* months........... Acts 19:8 5140
And there abode *t* months.................... Acts 20:3 5140
that by the space of *t* years I.............. Acts 20:31 5148
after *t* days he ascended from.............. Acts 25:1 5140
lodged us *t* days courteously................ Acts 28:7 5140
after *t* months we departed in a............ Acts 28:11 5140
Syracuse, we tarried there *t* days......... Acts 28:12 5140
as Appii forum, and The *t* taverns......... Acts 28:15 5140
that after *t* days Paul called the........... Acts 28:17 5140
committed, and fell in one day *t*........... 1Cor 10:8 5140
faith, hope, charity, these *t*................. 1Cor 13:13 5140
it be by two, or at the most by *t*.......... 1Cor 14:27 5140
Let the prophets speak two or *t*............ 1Cor 14:29 5140
In the mouth of two or *t*..................... 2Cor 13:1 5140
Then after *t* years I went up to............. Gal 1:18 5140
but before two or *t* witnesses.............. 1Ti 5:19 5140
mercy under two or *t* witnesses............ Heb 10:28 5140
was hid *t* months of his parents,........... Heb 11:23 5150
the earth by the space of *t* years.......... Jas 5:17 5140
For there are *t* that bear record............ 1Jn 5:7 5140
and these *t* are one.............................. 1Jn 5:7 5140
there are *t* that bear witness in............ 1Jn 5:8 5140
and these *t* agree in one...................... 1Jn 5:8 5140
t measures of barley for a penny........... Rev 6:6 5140
of the trumpet of the *t* angels............... Rev 8:13 5140
By these *t* was the third part of............ Rev 9:18 5140
see their dead bodies *t* days................. Rev 11:9 5140
And after *t* days and an half the........... Rev 11:11 5140
I saw *t* unclean spirits like.................. Rev 16:13 5140
city was divided into *t* parts................. Rev 16:19 5140
On the east *t* gates............................. Rev 21:13 5140
on the north *t* gates............................ Rev 21:13 5140
on the south *t* gates............................ Rev 21:13 5140
and on the west *t* gates........................ Rev 21:13 5140

THREEFOLD

a *t* cord is not quickly broken................ Eccl 4:12 8027

THREESCORE

life which he lived, an hundred *t*.......... Gen 25:7 7657
Isaac was *t* years old when she............. Gen 25:26 8346
sons' wives, all the souls were *t*............ Gen 46:26 8346
which came into Egypt, were *t*.............. Gen 46:27 7657
the Egyptians mourned for him *t*........... Gen 50:3 7657
were twelve wells of water, and *t*......... Ex 15:27 7657
and a thousand seven hundred and *t*... Ex 38:25 7657
in the blood of her purifying *t*.............. Lev 12:5 8346
of the tribe of Judah, were *t*.............. Num 1:27 7657
even of the tribe of Dan, were *t*........... Num 1:39 8346
were numbered of them, were *t*............ Num 2:4 7657
were numbered of them, were *t*............ Num 2:26 8346
and two thousand two hundred and *t*.. Num 3:43 7657
redeemed of the two hundred and *t*...... Num 3:46 7657
a thousand three hundred and *t*............ Num 3:50 8346
that were numbered of them, *t*.............. Num 26:22 7657
that were numbered of them, *t*.............. Num 26:25 8346
t thousand and five hundred................. Num 26:27 8346
were numbered of them, were *t*............ Num 26:43 8346
And *t* and twelve thousand beeves,...... Num 31:33 7657
And *t* and one thousand asses,............. Num 31:34 8346
of the sheep was six hundred and *t*...... Num 31:37 7657
of which the LORD's tribute was *t*......... Num 31:38 7657
of which the LORD's tribute was *t*......... Num 31:39 8346
twelve fountains of water, and *t*.......... Num 33:9 7657
t cities, all the region of Argob........... Deut 3:4 8346
went down into Egypt with *t*................. Deut 10:22 7657
which are in Bashan, *t* cities................ Josh 13:30 8346
And Adoni-bezek said, *T* and ten.......... Judg 1:7 7657
and the elders thereof, even *t*............. Judg 8:14 7657
And Gideon had *t* and ten sons of......... Judg 8:30 7657
sons of Jerubbaal, which are *t*............. Judg 9:2 7657
And they gave him *t* and ten pieces...... Judg 9:4 7657
the sons of Jerubbaal, being *t*............. Judg 9:5 7657
day, and have slain his sons, *t*............ Judg 9:18 7657
That the cruelty done to the *t*.............. Judg 9:24 7657
and thirty nephews, that rode on *t*........ Judg 12:14 7657
of the people fifty thousand and *t*........ 1Sa 6:19 7657
that three hundred and *t* men died......... 2Sa 2:31 8346
t great cities with walls and................. 1Kin 4:13 8346
flour, and *t* measures of meal,.............. 1Kin 4:22 8346
And Solomon had *t* and ten thousand. 1Kin 5:15 7657
the length thereof was *t* cubits............. 1Kin 6:2 8346
in one year was six hundred *t*............... 1Kin 10:14 8346
t men of the people of the land............. 2Kin 25:19 8346
married when he was *t* years old........... 1Chr 2:21 8346
the towns thereof, even *t* cities............. 1Chr 2:23 8346
forty thousand seven hundred and *t*....... 1Chr 5:18 8346
a thousand and seven hundred and *t*.... 1Chr 9:13 8346
Obed-edom with their brethren, *t*.......... 1Chr 16:38 8346
and Judah was four hundred *t*............... 1Chr 21:5 7657
strength for the service, were *t*............ 1Chr 26:8 8346
And Solomon told out *t* and ten............. 2Chr 2:2 7657
And he set *t* and ten thousand of.......... 2Chr 2:18 7657
the first measure was *t* cubits............. 2Chr 3:3 8346
in one year was six hundred and *t*........ 2Chr 9:13 8346
eighteen wives, and *t* concubines......... 2Chr 11:21 8346
and eight sons, and *t* daughters........... 2Chr 11:21 8346
chariots, and *t* thousand horsemen........ 2Chr 12:3 8346
the congregation brought, was *t*............ 2Chr 29:32 7657
she kept sabbath, to fulfil *t*.................. 2Chr 36:21 7657
of Zaccai, seven hundred and *t*............. Ezr 2:9 8346
two thousand three hundred and *t*........ Ezr 2:64 8346
unto the treasure of the work *t*........... Ezr 2:69 7239
the height thereof *t* cubits................... Ezr 6:3 8361
and the breadth thereof *t* cubits............ Ezr 6:3 8361
and with him an hundred and *t* males. Ezr 8:10 8346
and Shemaiah, and with them *t* males. Ezr 8:13 8346
of Zaccai, seven hundred and *t*............. Neh 7:14 8346
of Adonikam, six hundred *t*.................. Neh 7:18 8346
of Bigvai, two thousand *t*.................... Neh 7:19 8346
two thousand three hundred and *t*........ Neh 7:66 8346
thousand pounds of silver, and *t*........... Neh 7:72 8346
at Jerusalem were four hundred *t*.......... Neh 11:6 8346
The days of our years are *t* years.......... Ps 90:10 7657
t valiant men are about it, of................ Song 3:7 7657
There are *t* queens, and fourscore......... Song 6:8 7657
and within *t* and five years shall........... Is 7:8 7657
t men of the people of the land,............ Jer 52:25 7657
He made also posts of *t* cubits.............. Eze 40:14 7657
gold, whose height was *t* cubits............. Dan 3:1 8361
took the kingdom, being about *t*............ Dan 5:31 8361
Prince shall be seven weeks, and *t*........ Dan 9:25 8346
And after *t* and two weeks shall............ Dan 9:26 8346
thou hast had indignation these *t*......... Zec 1:12 7657
from Jerusalem about *t* furlongs........... Lk 24:13 1835
to him, and all his kindred, *t*............... Acts 7:14 1440
to go to Caesarea, and horsemen *t*........ Acts 23:23 1440
in all in the ship two hundred *t*............ Acts 27:37 1440
into the number under *t* years old........ 1Ti 5:9 1835
t days, clothed in sackcloth.................. Rev 11:3 1835
a thousand two hundred and *t* days....... Rev 12:6 1835
and his number is six hundred *t*........... Rev 13:18 5516

THRESH

thou shalt *t* the mountains, and............ Is 41:15 1758
it is time to *t* her................................ Jer 51:33 1869
Arise and *t*, O daughter of Zion............. Mic 4:13 1758
thou didst *t* the heathen in anger.......... Hab 3:12 1758

THRESHED

his son Gideon *t* wheat by the............... Judg 6:11 2251
For the fitches are not *t* with a............. Is 28:27 1758
because they have *t* Gilead with............ Amos 1:3 1758

THRESHETH

that he that *t* in hope should be........... 1Cor 9:10 248

THRESHING

your *t* shall reach unto the................... Lev 26:5 1786
and *t* instruments and other.................. 2Sa 24:22 4173
had made them like the dust by *t*........... 2Kin 13:7 1758
Now Ornan was *t* wheat....................... 1Chr 21:20 1758
the *t* instruments for wood, and............ 1Chr 21:23 4173
O my *t*, and the corn of my floor........... Is 21:10 4098
not threshed with a *t* instrument............ Is 28:27 2742
because he will not ever be *t* it.............. Is 28:28 1758
sharp *t* instrument having teeth............. Is 41:15 4173
Gilead with *t* instruments of iron........... Amos 1:3 2742

THRESHINGFLOOR

And they came to the *t* of Atad............. Gen 50:10 1637
ye do the heave offering of the *t*.......... Num 15:20 1637
though it were the corn of the *t*........... Num 18:27 1637
Levites as the increase of the *t*............ Num 18:30 1637
barley to night in the *t*........................ Ruth 3:2 1637
And when they came to Nachon's *t*........ 2Sa 6:6 1637
in the *t* of Araunah the Jebusite............ 2Sa 24:18 1637
David said, To buy the *t* of thee............ 2Sa 24:21 1637
So David bought the *t* and the oxen....... 2Sa 24:24 1637
they came unto the *t* of Chidon.............. 1Chr 13:9 1637
by the *t* of Ornan the Jebusite............... 1Chr 21:15 1637
in the *t* of Ornan the Jebusite................ 1Chr 21:18 1637
saw David, and went out of the *t*........... 1Chr 21:21 1637
Grant me the place of this *t*.................. 1Chr 21:22 1637
in the *t* of Ornan the Jebusite................ 1Chr 21:28 1637
in the *t* of Ornan the Jebusite................ 2Chr 3:1 1637
daughter of Babylon is like a *t*.............. Jer 51:33 1637

THRESHINGFLOORS

against Keilah, and they rob the *t*.......... 1Sa 23:1 1637
like the chaff of the summer *t*............... Dan 2:35 147

THRESHINGPLACE

by the *t* of Araunah the Jebusite........... 2Sa 24:16 1637

THRESHOLD

and her hands were upon the *t*............... Judg 19:27 5592
his hands were cut off upon the *t*........... 1Sa 5:4 4670
tread on the *t* of Dagon in Ashdod......... 1Sa 5:5 4670
she came to the *t* of the door............... 1Kin 14:17 5592
he was, to the *t* of the house................ Eze 9:3 4670
and stood over the *t* of the house.......... Eze 10:4 4670
from off the *t* of the house.................... Eze 10:18 4670
and measured the *t* of the gate............. Eze 40:6 5592
the other *t* of the gate, which............... Eze 40:6 5592
the *t* of the gate by the porch of........... Eze 40:7 5592
of their *t* by my thresholds................... Eze 43:8 5592
worship at the *t* of the gate.................. Eze 46:2 4670
under the *t* of the house eastward......... Eze 47:1 4670
all those that leap on the *t*.................. Zeph 1:9 4670

THRESHOLDS

the ward at the *t* of the gates.............. Neh 12:25 624
of their threshold by my *t*.................... Eze 43:8 5592
desolation shall be in the *t*.................. Zeph 2:14 5592

THREW

t stones at him, and cast dust.............. 2Sa 16:13 5619
So they *t* her down............................. 2Kin 9:33 8058

t down the high places and the ... 2Chr 31:1 5422
she *t* in two mites, which make a ... Mk 12:42 *906*
a coming, the devil *t* him down ... Lk 9:42 *4952*
clothes, and *t* dust into the air, ... Acts 22:23 *906*

THREWEST

persecutors thou *t* into the deeps ... Neh 9:11 7993

THRICE

T in the year shall all your men ... Ex 34:23
the LORD thy God *t* in the year ... Ex 34:24
And he smote *t*, and stayed ... 2Kin 13:18
now thou shalt smite Syria but *t* ... 2Kin 13:19
cock crow, thou shalt deny me *t* ... Mt 26:34 *5151*
cock crow, thou shalt deny me *t* ... Mt 26:75 *5151*
crow twice, thou shalt deny me *t* ... Mk 14:30 *5151*
crow twice, thou shalt deny me *t* ... Mk 14:72 *5151*
before that thou shalt *t* deny ... Lk 22:34 *5151*
cock crow, thou shalt deny me *t* ... Lk 22:61 *5151*
crow, till thou hast denied me *t* ... Jn 13:38 *5151*
This was done *t* ... Acts 10:16 *5151*
T was I beaten with rods, once ... 2Cor 11:25 *5151*
t I suffered shipwreck, a night ... 2Cor 11:25 *5151*
this thing I besought the Lord *t* ... 2Cor 12:8 *5151*

THROAT

their *t* is an open sepulchre ... Ps 5:9 1627
my *t* is dried ... Ps 69:3 1627
speak they through their *t* ... Ps 115:7 1627
And put a knife to thy *t*, if thou ... Prov 23:2 3930
unshod, and thy *t* from thirst ... Jer 2:25 1627
on him, and took him by the *t* ... Mt 18:28 *4155*
Their *t* is an open sepulchre ... Rom 3:13 *2995*

THRONE

only in the *t* will I be greater ... Gen 41:40 3678
Pharaoh that sitteth upon his *t* ... Ex 11:5 3678
his *t* unto the firstborn of the ... Ex 12:29 3678
sitteth upon the *t* of his kingdom ... Deut 17:18 3678
make them inherit the *t* of glory ... 1Sa 2:8 3678
to set up the *t* of David over ... 2Sa 3:10 3678
I will stablish the *t* of his ... 2Sa 7:13 3678
thy *t* shall be established for ... 2Sa 7:16 3678
and the king and his *t* be guiltless ... 2Sa 14:9 3678
me, and he shall sit upon my *t* ... 1Kin 1:13 3678
me, and he shall sit upon my *t* ... 1Kin 1:17 3678
t of my lord the king after him ... 1Kin 1:20 3678
me, and he shall sit upon my *t* ... 1Kin 1:24 3678
who should sit on the *t* of my ... 1Kin 1:27 3678
shall sit upon my *t* in my stead ... 1Kin 1:30 3678
that he may come and sit upon my *t* ... 1Kin 1:35 3678
make his *t* greater than the ... 1Kin 1:37 3678
than the *t* of my lord king David ... 1Kin 1:37 3678
sitteth on the *t* of the kingdom ... 1Kin 1:46 3678
his *t* greater than thy *t* ... 1Kin 1:47 3678
given one to sit on my *t* this day ... 1Kin 1:48 3678
said he) a man on the *t* of Israel ... 1Kin 2:4 3678
upon the *t* of David his father ... 1Kin 2:12 3678
unto her, and sat down on his *t* ... 1Kin 2:19 3678
set me on the *t* of David my ... 1Kin 2:24 3678
and upon his house, and upon his *t* ... 1Kin 2:33 3678
and the *t* of David shall be ... 1Kin 2:45 3678
given him a son to sit on his *t* ... 1Kin 3:6 3678
I will set upon thy *t* in thy room ... 1Kin 5:5 3678
for the *t* where he might judge ... 1Kin 7:7 3678
father, and sit on the *t* of Israel ... 1Kin 8:20 3678
sight to sit on the *t* of Israel ... 1Kin 8:25 3678
Then I will establish the *t* of ... 1Kin 9:5 3678
thee a man upon the *t* of Israel ... 1Kin 9:5 3678
to set thee on the *t* of Israel ... 1Kin 10:9 3678
the king made a great *t* of ivory ... 1Kin 10:18 3678
The *t* had six steps, and the top ... 1Kin 10:19 3678
the top of the *t* was round behind ... 1Kin 10:19 3678
reign, as soon as he sat on his *t* ... 1Kin 16:11 3678
king of Judah sat each on his *t* ... 1Kin 22:10 3678
I saw the LORD sitting on his *t* ... 1Kin 22:19 3678
and set him on his father's *t* ... 2Kin 10:3 3678
shall sit on the *t* of Israel ... 2Kin 10:30 3678
And he sat on the *t* of the kings ... 2Kin 11:19 3678
and Jeroboam sat upon his *t* ... 2Kin 13:13 3678
the *t* of Israel unto the fourth ... 2Kin 15:12 3678
set his *t* above the *t* of the ... 2Kin 25:28 3678
and I will stablish his *t* for ever ... 1Chr 17:12 3678
his *t* shall be established for ... 1Chr 17:14 3678
I will establish the *t* of his ... 1Chr 22:10 3678
Solomon my son to sit upon the *t* ... 1Chr 28:5 3678
Then Solomon sat on the *t* of the ... 1Chr 29:23 3678
and am set on the *t* of Israel ... 2Chr 6:10 3678
sight to sit upon the *t* of Israel ... 2Chr 6:16 3678
I stablish the *t* of thy kingdom ... 2Chr 7:18 3678
in thee to set thee on his *t* ... 2Chr 9:8 3678
the king made a great *t* of ivory ... 2Chr 9:17 3678
And there were six steps to the *t* ... 2Chr 9:18 3678
which were fastened to the *t* ... 2Chr 9:18 3678
Judah sat either of them on his *t* ... 2Chr 18:9 3678
I saw the LORD sitting upon his *t* ... 2Chr 18:18 3678
king upon the *t* of the kingdom ... 2Chr 23:20 3678
unto the *t* of the governor on ... Neh 3:7 3678
sat on the *t* of his kingdom ... Est 1:2 3678
his royal *t* in the royal house ... Est 5:1 3678
He holdeth back the face of his *t* ... Job 26:9 3678
but with kings are they on the *t* ... Job 36:7 3678
satest in the *t* judging right ... Ps 9:4 3678
hath prepared his *t* for judgment ... Ps 9:7 3678
the LORD's *t* is in heaven ... Ps 11:4 3678
Thy *t*, O God, is for ever and ever ... Ps 45:6 3678
upon the *t* of his holiness ... Ps 47:8 3678
build up thy *t* to all generations ... Ps 89:4 3678
are the habitation of thy *t* ... Ps 89:14 3678
his *t* as the days of heaven ... Ps 89:29 3678
his *t* as the sun before me ... Ps 89:36 3678
cast his *t* down to the ground ... Ps 89:44 3678
Thy *t* is established of old ... Ps 93:2 3678
Shall the *t* of iniquity have ... Ps 94:20 3678
are the habitation of his *t* ... Ps 97:2 3678
prepared his *t* in the heavens ... Ps 103:19 3678
of thy body will I set upon thy *t* ... Ps 132:11 3678
also sit upon thy *t* for evermore ... Ps 132:12 3678
for the *t* is established by ... Prov 16:12 3678
A king that sitteth in the *t* of ... Prov 20:8 3678
his *t* is upholden by mercy ... Prov 20:28 3678
his *t* shall be established in ... Prov 25:5 3678
his *t* shall be established for ... Prov 29:14 3678
also the Lord sitting upon a *t* ... Is 6:1 3678
be no end, upon the *t* of David ... Is 9:7 3678
I will exalt my *t* above the stars ... Is 14:13 3678
mercy shall the *t* be established ... Is 16:5 3678
glorious *t* to his father's house ... Is 22:23 3678
there is no *t*, O daughter of the ... Is 47:1 3678
the LORD, The heaven is my *t* ... Is 66:1 3678
they shall set every one his *t* at ... Jer 1:15 3678
call Jerusalem the *t* of the LORD ... Jer 3:17 3678
the kings that sit upon David's *t* ... Jer 13:13 3678
not disgrace the *t* of thy glory ... Jer 14:21 3678
A glorious high *t* from the ... Jer 17:12 3678
sitting upon the *t* of David ... Jer 17:25 3678
that sittest upon the *t* of David ... Jer 22:2 3678
kings sitting upon the *t* of David ... Jer 22:4 3678
sitting upon the *t* of David ... Jer 22:30 3678
that sitteth upon the *t* of David ... Jer 29:16 3678
upon the *t* of the house of Israel ... Jer 33:17 3678
have a son to reign upon his *t* ... Jer 33:21 3678
none to sit upon the *t* of David ... Jer 36:30 3678
will set his *t* upon these stones ... Jer 43:10 3678
And I will set my *t* in Elam ... Jer 49:38 3678
set his *t* above the *t* of the ... Jer 52:32 3678
thy *t* from generation to ... Lam 5:19 3678
heads was the likeness of a *t* ... Eze 1:26 3678
of the *t* was the likeness as the ... Eze 1:26 3678
appearance of the likeness of a *t* ... Eze 10:1 3678
me, Son of man, the place of my *t* ... Eze 43:7 3678
he was deposed from his kingly *t* ... Dan 5:20 3764
his *t* was like the fiery flame, ... Dan 7:9 3764
Nineveh, and he arose from his *t* ... Jonah 3:6 3678
will overthrow the *t* of kingdoms ... Hag 2:22 3678
and shall sit and rule upon his *t* ... Zec 6:13 3678
he shall be a priest upon his *t* ... Zec 6:13 3678
for it is God's *t* ... Mt 5:34 *2362*
shall sit in the *t* of his glory ... Mt 19:28 *2362*
heaven, sweareth by the *t* of God ... Mt 23:22 *2362*
he sit upon the *t* of his glory ... Mt 25:31 *2362*
him the *t* of his father David ... Lk 1:32 *2362*
raise up Christ to sit on his *t* ... Acts 2:30 *2362*
Heaven is my *t*, and earth is my ... Acts 7:49 *2362*
in royal apparel, sat upon his *t* ... Acts 12:21 *968*
But unto the Son he saith, Thy *t* ... Heb 1:8 *2362*
come boldly unto the *t* of grace ... Heb 4:16 *2362*
t of the Majesty in the heavens ... Heb 8:1 *2362*
at the right hand of the *t* of God ... Heb 12:2 *2362*
Spirits which are before his *t* ... Rev 1:4 *2362*
I grant to sit with me in my *t* ... Rev 3:21 *2362*
set down with my Father in his *t* ... Rev 3:21 *2362*
a *t* was set in heaven, and one sat ... Rev 4:2 *2362*
in heaven, and one sat on the *t* ... Rev 4:2 *2362*
was a rainbow round about the *t* ... Rev 4:3 *2362*
And round about the *t* were four ... Rev 4:4 *2362*
out of the *t* proceeded lightnings ... Rev 4:5 *2362*
of fire burning before the *t* ... Rev 4:5 *2362*
before the *t* there was a sea of ... Rev 4:6 *2362*
and in the midst of the *t*, and ... Rev 4:6 *2362*
and round about the *t* ... Rev 4:6 *2362*
thanks to him that sat on the *t* ... Rev 4:9 *2362*
down before him that sat on the *t* ... Rev 4:10 *2362*
and cast their crowns before the *t* ... Rev 4:10 *2362*
on the *t* a book written within ... Rev 5:1 *2362*
and, lo, in the midst of the *t* ... Rev 5:6 *2362*
hand of him that sat upon the *t* ... Rev 5:7 *2362*
of many angels round about the *t* ... Rev 5:11 *2362*
unto him that sitteth upon the *t* ... Rev 5:13 *2362*
face of him that sitteth on the *t* ... Rev 6:16 *2362*
and tongues, stood before the *t* ... Rev 7:9 *2362*
our God which sitteth upon the *t* ... Rev 7:10 *2362*
angels stood round about the *t* ... Rev 7:11 *2362*
fell before the *t* on their faces ... Rev 7:11 *2362*
are they before the *t* of God ... Rev 7:15 *2362*
on the *t* shall dwell among them ... Rev 7:15 *2362*
midst of the *t* shall feed them ... Rev 7:17 *2362*
altar which was before the *t* ... Rev 8:3 *2362*
caught up unto God, and to his *t* ... Rev 12:5 *2362*
it were a new song before the *t* ... Rev 14:3 *2362*
without fault before the *t* of God ... Rev 14:5 *2362*
the temple of heaven, from the *t* ... Rev 16:17 *2362*
worshipped God that sat on the *t* ... Rev 19:4 *2362*
And a voice came out of the *t* ... Rev 19:5 *2362*
And I saw a great white *t*, and him ... Rev 20:11 *2362*
And he that sat upon the *t* said ... Rev 21:5 *2362*
proceeding out of the *t* of God ... Rev 22:1 *2362*
but the *t* of God and of the Lamb ... Rev 22:3 *2362*

THRONES

For there are set *t* of judgment ... Ps 122:5 3678
the *t* of the house of David ... Ps 122:5 3678
t all the kings of the nations ... Is 14:9 3678
sea shall come down from their *t* ... Eze 26:16 3678
beheld till the *t* were cast down ... Dan 7:9 3764
ye also shall sit upon twelve *t* ... Mt 19:28 *2362*
sit on *t* judging the twelve ... Lk 22:30 *2362*
and invisible, whether they be *t* ... Col 1:16 *2362*
And I saw *t*, and they sat upon them ... Rev 20:4 *2362*

THRONG

multitude, lest they should *t* him ... Mk 3:9 *2346*
Master, the multitude *t* thee ... Lk 8:45 *4912*

THRONGED

people followed him, and *t* him ... Mk 5:24 *4918*
But as he went the people *t* him ... Lk 8:42 *4846*

THRONGING

Thou seest the multitude *t* thee ... Mk 5:31 *4918*

THROUGH

is filled with violence *t* them ... Gen 6:13 6440
Abram passed *t* the land unto the ... Gen 12:6
walk *t* the land in the length of ... Gen 13:17
I will pass *t* all thy flock to ... Gen 30:32
the land perish not *t* the famine ... Gen 41:36
field, *t* all the land of Egypt ... Ex 10:15
For I will pass *t* the land of ... Ex 12:12
pass *t* to smite the Egyptians ... Ex 12:23
that God led them not *t* the way ... Ex 13:17
t the way of the wilderness of ... Ex 13:18
dry ground *t* the midst of the sea ... Ex 14:16 8432
Egyptians *t* the pillar of fire ... Ex 14:24
shall surely be stoned, or shot *t* ... Ex 19:13
lest they break *t* unto the LORD ... Ex 19:21
the people break *t* to come up ... Ex 19:24
shall bore his ear *t* with an aul ... Ex 21:6
t the boards from the one end to ... Ex 36:33 8432
If a soul shall sin *t* ignorance ... Lev 4:2
of Israel sin *t* ignorance ... Lev 4:13
done somewhat *t* ignorance against ... Lev 4:22
the common people sin *t* ignorance ... Lev 4:27
sin *t* ignorance, in the holy ... Lev 5:15
seed pass *t* the fire to Molech ... Lev 18:21
shall the sword go *t* your land ... Lev 26:6
t which we have gone to search it ... Num 13:32
which we passed *t* to search it ... Num 14:7
And if any soul sin *t* ignorance ... Num 15:27
for him that sinneth *t* ignorance ... Num 15:29
pass, I pray thee, *t* thy country ... Num 20:17
we will not pass *t* the fields ... Num 20:17
or *t* the vineyards, neither will ... Num 20:17
any thing else, go *t* on my feet ... Num 20:19 5674
And he said, Thou shalt not go *t* ... Num 20:20 5674
give Israel passage *t* his border ... Num 20:21
Let me pass *t* thy land ... Num 21:22
Israel to pass *t* his border ... Num 21:23
pierce them *t* with his arrows ... Num 24:8
tent, and thrust both of them *t* ... Num 25:8
Israel, and the woman *t* her belly ... Num 25:8 413
t the counsel of Balaam, to ... Num 31:16
ye shall make it go *t* the fire ... Num 31:23
fire ye shall make go *t* the water ... Num 31:23
passed *t* the midst of the sea ... Num 33:8 8432
we went *t* all that great and ... Deut 1:19
Ye are to pass *t* the coast of ... Deut 2:4
walking *t* this great wilderness ... Deut 2:7
t the way of the plain from Elath ... Deut 2:8
Thou art to pass over *t* Ar ... Deut 2:18
Let me pass *t* thy land ... Deut 2:27
only I will pass *t* on my feet ... Deut 2:28
thee out thence *t* a mighty hand ... Deut 5:15
Who led thee *t* that great ... Deut 8:15
hast redeemed *t* thy greatness ... Deut 9:26
thrust it *t* his ear unto the door ... Deut 15:17
his daughter to pass *t* the fire ... Deut 18:10
how we came *t* the nations which ... Deut 29:16 7130
to anger *t* the work of your hands ... Deut 31:29
t this thing ye shall prolong ... Deut 32:47
smite *t* the loins of them that ... Deut 33:11
Pass *t* the host, and command the ... Josh 1:11 7130
them down by a cord *t* the window ... Josh 2:15 1157
that the officers went *t* the host ... Josh 3:2 7130
go *t* the land, and describe it ... Josh 18:4
walk *t* the land, and describe it, ... Josh 18:8
passed *t* the land, and described ... Josh 18:9
went up *t* the mountains westward ... Josh 18:12
all the people *t* whom we passed ... Josh 24:17 7130
That *t* them I may prove Israel, ... Judg 2:22
Then Ehud went forth *t* the porch ... Judg 3:23
and the travellers walked *t* byways ... Judg 5:6
pierced and stricken *t* his temples ... Judg 5:26
cried *t* the lattice, Why is his ... Judg 5:28 1157
And his young man thrust him *t* ... Judg 9:54
walked *t* the wilderness unto the ... Judg 11:16
me, I pray thee, pass *t* thy land ... Judg 11:17
they went along *t* the wilderness ... Judg 11:18
thee, *t* thy land into my place ... Judg 11:19
not Israel to pass *t* his coast ... Judg 11:20
men *t* all the tribe of Benjamin ... Judg 20:12
he passed *t* mount Ephraim, and ... 1Sa 9:4
passed *t* the land of Shalisha, ... 1Sa 9:4
then they passed *t* the land of ... 1Sa 9:4
he passed *t* the land of the ... 1Sa 9:4
Michal let David down *t* a window ... 1Sa 19:12 1157
sword, and thrust me *t* therewith ... 1Sa 31:4
uncircumcised come and thrust me *t* ... 1Sa 31:4
walked all that night *t* the plain ... 2Sa 2:29
went *t* all Bithron, and they came ... 2Sa 2:29
gat them away *t* the plain all ... 2Sa 4:7 1870
Saul's daughter looked *t* a window ... 2Sa 6:16 1157
and made them pass *t* the brickkiln ... 2Sa 12:31
thrust them *t* the heart of ... 2Sa 18:14
he went *t* all the tribes of ... 2Sa 20:14
T the brightness before him were ... 2Sa 22:13
For by thee I have run *t* a troop ... 2Sa 22:30
the three mighty men brake *t* the ... 2Sa 23:16 1234
Go now *t* all the tribes of Israel ... 2Sa 24:2 7751
when they had gone *t* all the land ... 2Sa 24:8
Ahaziah fell down *t* a lattice in ... 2Kin 1:2 1157
The way *t* the wilderness of Edom ... 2Kin 3:8
to break *t* even unto the king of ... 2Kin 3:26 1234
And Jehu sent *t* all Israel ... 2Kin 10:21
made his son to pass *t* the fire ... 2Kin 16:3
daughters to pass *t* the fire ... 2Kin 17:17
he made his son pass *t* the fire ... 2Kin 21:6
to pass *t* the fire to Molech ... 2Kin 23:10
For *t* the anger of the LORD it ... 2Kin 24:20 5921
sword, and thrust me *t* therewith ... 1Chr 10:4
the three brake *t* the host of the ... 1Chr 11:18 1234
he went out again *t* the people ... 2Chr 19:4

T

they came *t* the high gate into 2Chr 23:20 8432
they made a proclamation *t* Judah 2Chr 24:9
to city *t* the country of Ephraim 2Chr 30:10
daughters, *t* all the congregation 2Chr 31:18 5674
the brook that ran *t* the midst of 2Chr 32:4 8432
t the fire in the valley of the 2Chr 33:6
they prospered *t* the prophesying Ezr 6:14
so that they went *t* the midst of Neh 9:11 8432
t the street of the city, and Est 6:9
t the street of the city, and Est 6:11
and terrifiest me *t* visions Job 7:14
Yet *t* the scent of water it will Job 14:9
bow of steel shall strike him *t* Job 20:24
can he judge *t* the dark cloud Job 22:13
In the dark they dig *t* houses Job 24:16 2864
he smiteth *t* the proud Job 26:12
by his light I walked *t* darkness Job 29:3
I went out to the gate *t* the city Job 29:7 5921
his nose pierceth *t* snares Job 40:24
or bore his jaw *t* with a thorn Job 41:2
whatsoever passeth *t* the paths of Ps 8:8
t the pride of his countenance, Ps 10:4
For by thee I have run *t* a troop Ps 18:29
line is gone out *t* all the earth Ps 19:4
t the mercy of the most High he Ps 21:7
though I walk *t* the valley of the Ps 23:4
my bones waxed old *t* my roaring Ps 32:3
T thee will we push down our Ps 44:5
t thy name will we tread them Ps 44:5
T God we shall do valiantly Ps 60:12
t the greatness of thy power Ps 66:3
they went *t* the flood on foot Ps 66:6
we went *t* fire and *t* water Ps 66:12
thou didst march *t* the wilderness Ps 68:7
their tongue walketh *t* the earth Ps 73:9
the sea, and caused them to pass *t* Ps 78:13
when he went out *t* the land of Ps 81:5 5921
Who passing *t* the valley of Baca Ps 84:6
hast made me glad *t* thy work Ps 92:4
so he led them *t* the depths Ps 106:9
the depths, as *t* the wilderness Ps 106:9
and brought low *t* oppression Ps 107:39
T God we shall do valiantly Ps 108:13
My knees are weak *t* fasting Ps 109:24
t kings in the day of his wrath Ps 110:5
neither speak they *t* their throat Ps 115:7
Thou *t* thy commandments hast made Ps 119:98
T thy precepts I get Ps 119:104
Israel to pass *t* the midst of it Ps 136:14 8432
led his people *t* the wilderness Ps 136:16
my house I looked *t* my casement Prov 7:6
Passing *t* the street near her Prov 7:8
Till a dart strike *t* his liver Prov 7:23
but *t* knowledge shall the just be Prov 11:9
T desire a man, having separated Prov 18:1
T wisdom is an house builded Prov 24:3
For a dream cometh *t* the Eccl 5:3
t idleness of the hands the house Eccl 10:18
of the hands the house droppeth *t* Eccl 10:18 1811
shewing himself *t* the lattice Song 2:9 4480
And he shall pass *t* Judah Is 8:8
And they shall pass *t* it, hardly Is 8:21
T the wrath of the LORD of hosts Is 9:19
that is found shall be thrust *t* Is 13:15 1856
thrust *t* with a sword, that go Is 14:19 2944
they wandered *t* the wilderness Is 16:8
As whirlwinds in the south pass *t* Is 21:1
Pass *t* thy land as a river, O Is 23:10
I would go *t* them, I would burn Is 27:4
But they also have erred *t* wine Is 28:7
t strong drink are out of the way Is 28:7
prophet have erred *t* strong drink Is 28:7
are out of the way *t* strong drink Is 28:7 4480
overflowing scourge shall pass *t* Is 28:15
overflowing scourge shall pass *t* Is 28:18
For *t* the voice of the LORD shall Is 30:31
none shall pass *t* it for ever Is 34:10
When thou passest *t* the waters Is 43:2
t the rivers, they shall not Is 43:2
when thou walkest *t* the fire Is 43:2 1119
when he led them *t* the deserts Is 48:21
hated, so that no man went *t* thee Is 60:15 5674
Go *t*, go *t* the gates Is 62:10 5674
That led them *t* the deep, as an Is 63:13
that led us *t* the wilderness, Jer 2:6
t a land of deserts and of pits, Jer 2:6
t a land of drought, and of the Jer 2:6
t a land that no man passed Jer 2:6
a land that no man passed *t* Jer 2:6
it came to pass *t* the lightness Jer 3:9
fro *t* the streets of Jerusalem, Jer 5:1
t deceit they refuse to know me, Jer 9:6
up, so that none can pass *t* them Jer 9:10
a wilderness, that none passeth *t* Jer 9:12
all high places *t* the wilderness Jer 12:12
to bring in no burden *t* the gates Jer 17:24
to pass *t* the fire unto Molech Jer 32:35
that are thrust *t* in her streets Jer 51:4 1856
t all her land the wounded shall Jer 51:52
For *t* the anger of the LORD it Jer 52:3 5921
that our prayer should not pass *t* Lam 3:44
stricken *t* for want of the fruits Lam 4:9
cup also shall pass *t* unto thee Lam 4:21
and blood shall pass *t* thee Eze 5:17
be scattered *t* the countries Eze 6:8
Go *t* the midst of the city, Eze 9:4 5674
t the midst of Jerusalem, and set Eze 9:4
Go ye after him *t* the city Eze 9:5
Dig thou *t* the wall in their Eze 12:5
in the even I digged *t* the wall Eze 12:7
they shall dig *t* the wall to Eze 12:12
estranged from me *t* their idols Eze 14:5
noisome beasts to pass *t* the land Eze 14:15
that no man may pass *t* because of Eze 14:15

and say, Sword, go *t* the land Eze 14:17
it was perfect *t* my comeliness Eze 16:14
them to pass *t* the fire for them Eze 16:21
thy nakedness discovered *t* thy Eze 16:36
thrust thee *t* with their swords Eze 16:40
and disperse them *t* the countries Eze 20:23
in that they caused to pass *t* the Eze 20:26
make your sons to pass *t* the fire Eze 20:31
me, to pass for them *t* the fire Eze 23:37
No foot of man shall pass *t* it Eze 29:11
nor foot of beast shall pass *t* it Eze 29:11
disperse them *t* the countries Eze 29:12
disperse them *t* the countries Eze 30:23
desolate, that none shall pass *t* Eze 33:28
wandered *t* all the mountains Eze 34:6
were dispersed *t* the countries Eze 36:19
passing *t* the land to bury with Eze 39:14
passengers that pass *t* the land Eze 39:15
it was made *t* all the house round Eze 41:19 413
After he brought me *t* the entry Eze 46:19
and he brought me *t* the waters Eze 47:3 5674
and brought me *t* the waters Eze 47:4 5674
a thousand, and brought me *t* Eze 47:4 5674
t his policy also he shall cause Dan 8:25 5921
t all the countries whither thou Dan 9:7
by his strength *t* his riches he Dan 11:2
come, and overflow, and pass *t* Dan 11:10
no strangers pass *t* her any more Joel 3:17
you forty years *t* the wilderness Amos 2:10
for I will pass *t* thee, saith the Amos 5:17 7130
published *t* Nineveh by the decree Jonah 3:7
up, and have passed *t* the gate Mic 2:13
who, if he go *t*, both treadeth Mic 5:8 5674
be cut down, when he shall pass *t* Nah 1:12
wicked shall no more pass *t* thee Nah 1:15
selleth nations *t* her whoredoms Nah 3:4
families *t* her witchcrafts Nah 3:4
which shall march *t* the breadth Hab 1:6
Thou didst march *t* the land in Hab 3:12
Thou didst strike *t* with his Hab 3:14
Thou didst walk *t* the sea with Hab 3:15
t the heap of great waters Hab 3:15
to walk to and fro *t* the earth Zec 1:10
fro *t* the earth, and, behold, all Zec 1:11
My cities *t* prosperity shall yet Zec 1:17
run to and fro *t* the whole earth Zec 4:10
t the two golden pipes empty the Zec 4:12 3027
their resemblance *t* all the earth Zec 5:6
might walk to and fro *t* the earth Zec 6:7
hence, walk to and fro *t* the earth Zec 6:7
they walked to and fro *t* the earth Zec 6:7
that no man passed *t* nor returned Zec 7:14
shall pass *t* them any more Zec 9:8
drink, and make a noise as *t* wine Zec 9:15
heart shall rejoice as *t* wine Zec 10:7
he shall pass *t* the sea with Zec 10:11
thrust him *t* when he prophesieth Zec 13:3
bring the third part *t* the fire Zec 13:9
corrupt, and where thieves break *t* Mt 6:19 *1358*
thieves do not break *t* nor steal Mt 6:20 *1358*
He casteth out devils *t* the Mt 9:34 *1722*
on the sabbath day *t* the corn Mt 12:1 *1223*
of a man, he walketh *t* dry places Mt 12:43 *1223*
camel to go *t* the eye of a needle Mt 19:24 *1223*
that he went *t* the corn fields on Mk 2:23 *1223*
ran *t* that whole region round Mk 6:55 *4063*
of none effect *t* your tradition Mk 7:13
t the midst of the coasts of Mk 7:31 *303*
thence, and passed *t* Galilee Mk 9:30 *1223*
camel to go *t* the eye of a needle Mk 10:25 *1223*
carry any vessel *t* the temple Mk 11:16 *1223*
T the tender mercy of our God Lk 1:78 *1223*
shall pierce *t* thy own soul also Lk 2:35 *1330*
him *t* all the region round about Lk 4:14 *2596*
But he passing *t* the midst of Lk 4:30 *1223*
let him down *t* the tiling with Lk 5:19 *1223*
that he went *t* the corn fields Lk 6:1 *1223*
went *t* the towns, preaching the Lk 9:6 *2596*
are subject unto us *t* thy name Lk 10:17 *1722*
He casteth out devils *t* Beelzebub Lk 11:15 *1722*
I cast out devils *t* Beelzebub Lk 11:18 *1722*
of a man, he walketh *t* dry places Lk 11:24 *1223*
suffered his house to be broken *t* Lk 12:39 *1358*
he went *t* the cities and villages, Lk 13:22 *2569*
woe unto him, *t* whom they come Lk 17:1 *1223*
that he passed *t* the midst of Lk 17:11 *1223*
a camel to go *t* a needle's eye Lk 18:25 *1223*
Jesus entered and passed *t* Jericho Lk 19:1 *1330*
that all men *t* him might believe Jn 1:7 *1223*
the world *t* him might be saved Jn 3:17 *1223*
And he must needs go *t* Samaria Jn 4:4 *1223*
going *t* the midst of them, and so Jn 8:59 *1223*
Now ye are clean *t* the word which Jn 15:3 *1223*
keep *t* thine own name those whom Jn 17:11 *1722*
Sanctify them *t* thy truth Jn 17:17 *1722*
might be sanctified *t* the truth Jn 17:19 *1722*
shall believe on me *t* their word Jn 17:20 *1223*
ye might have life *t* his name Jn 20:31 *1722*
after that he *t* the Holy Ghost Acts 1:2 *1223*
his name *t* faith in his name hath Acts 3:16 *1909*
I wot that *t* ignorance ye did it, Acts 3:17 *2596*
preached *t* Jesus the resurrection Acts 4:2 *1722*
when Simon saw that *t* laying on Acts 8:18 *1223*
passing *t* he preached in all the Acts 8:40 *1223*
that *t* his name whosoever Acts 10:43 *1223*
out, and passed on *t* one street Acts 12:10
when they had gone *t* the isle Acts 13:6 *1330*
that *t* this man is preached unto Acts 13:38 *1223*
that we must *t* much tribulation Acts 14:22 *1223*
the church, they passed *t* Phenice Acts 15:3 *1330*
But we believe that *t* the grace Acts 15:11 *1223*
And he went *t* Syria and Cilicia, Acts 15:41 *1350*
And as they went *t* the cities Acts 16:4 *1279*
when they had passed *t* Amphipolis Acts 17:1 *1653*

much which had believed *t* grace Acts 18:27 *1223*
Paul having passed *t* the upper Acts 19:1 *1330*
when he had passed *t* Macedonia Acts 19:21 *1330*
he purposed to return *t* Macedonia Acts 20:3 *1223*
who said to Paul *t* the Spirit Acts 21:4 *1223*
I thank my God *t* Jesus Christ for Rom 1:8 *1223*
gave them up to uncleanness *t* the Rom 1:24 *1722*
t breaking the law dishonourest Rom 2:23 *1223*
among the Gentiles *t* you, as it Rom 2:24 *1223*
abounded *t* my lie unto his glory Rom 3:7 *1722*
grace *t* the redemption that is in Rom 3:24 *1223*
propitiation *t* faith in his blood Rom 3:25 *1223*
past, *t* the forbearance of God Rom 3:25 *1722*
faith, and uncircumcision *t* faith Rom 3:30 *1223*
we then make void the law *t* faith Rom 3:31 *1223*
t the law, but *t* the Rom 4:13 *1223*
at the promise of God *t* unbelief Rom 4:20
with God *t* our Lord Jesus Christ Rom 5:1 *1223*
shall be saved from wrath *t* him Rom 5:9 *1223*
in God *t* our Lord Jesus Christ Rom 5:11 *1223*
For if *t* the offence of one many Rom 5:15
even so might grace reign *t* Rom 5:21 *1223*
but alive unto God *t* Jesus Christ Rom 6:11 *1722*
life *t* Jesus Christ our Lord Rom 6:23 *1722*
I thank God *t* Jesus Christ our Rom 7:25 *1223*
in that it was weak *t* the flesh Rom 8:3 *1223*
but if ye *t* the Spirit do mortify Rom 8:13
conquerors *t* him that loved us Rom 8:37 *1223*
but rather *t* their fall salvation Rom 11:11
obtained mercy *t* their unbelief Rom 11:30
that *t* your mercy they also may Rom 11:31
t him, and to him, are all things Rom 11:36 *1223*
t the grace given unto me, to Rom 12:3 *1223*
that we *t* patience and comfort of Rom 15:4 *1223*
t the power of the Holy Ghost Rom 15:13 *1722*
t Jesus Christ in those things Rom 15:17 *1722*
T mighty signs and wonders, by the Rom 15:19 *1722*
be glory *t* Jesus Christ for ever Rom 16:27 *1223*
of Jesus Christ *t* the will of God 1Cor 1:1 *1223*
I have begotten you *t* the gospel 1Cor 4:15 *1223*
t thy knowledge shall the weak 1Cor 8:11 *1909*
cloud, and all passed *t* the sea 1Cor 10:1 *1223*
For now we see *t* a glass, darkly 1Cor 13:12 *1223*
victory *t* our Lord Jesus Christ 1Cor 15:57 *1223*
when I shall pass *t* Macedonia 1Cor 16:5 *1330*
for I do pass *t* Macedonia 1Cor 16:5 *1330*
have we *t* Christ to God-ward 2Cor 3:4 *1223*
might *t* the thanksgiving of many 2Cor 4:15 *1223*
that ye *t* his poverty might be 2Cor 8:9
which causeth *t* us thanksgiving 2Cor 9:11 *1223*
but mighty *t* God to the pulling 2Cor 10:4
beguiled Eve *t* his subtilty 2Cor 11:3 *1722*
t a window in a basket was I let 2Cor 11:33 *1223*
measure *t* the abundance of the 2Cor 12:7
he was crucified *t* weakness 2Cor 13:4 *1537*
For I *t* the law am dead to the Gal 2:19 *1223*
would justify the heathen *t* faith Gal 3:8 *1537*
on the Gentiles *t* Jesus Christ Gal 3:14 *1722*
the promise of the Spirit *t* faith Gal 3:14 *1223*
son, then an heir of God *t* Christ Gal 4:7 *1223*
Ye know how *t* infirmity of the Gal 4:13 *1223*
For we *t* the Spirit wait for the Gal 5:5
have confidence in you *t* the Lord Gal 5:10 *1722*
we have redemption *t* his blood Eph 1:7 *1223*
kindness toward us *t* Christ Jesus Eph 2:7 *1722*
For by grace are ye saved *t* faith Eph 2:8 *1223*
For *t* him we both have access by Eph 2:18 *1223*
an habitation of God *t* the Spirit Eph 2:22 *1722*
all, and *t* all, and in you all Eph 4:6 *1223*
t the ignorance that is in them Eph 4:18 *1223*
to my salvation *t* your prayer Phil 1:19 *1223*
be done *t* strife or vainglory Phil 2:3 *2596*
but that which is *t* the faith of Phil 3:9 *1223*
hearts and minds *t* Christ Jesus Phil 4:7 *1722*
I can do all things *t* Christ Phil 4:13 *1722*
we have redemption *t* his blood Col 1:14 *1223*
having made peace *t* the blood of Col 1:20 *1223*
In the body of his flesh *t* death Col 1:22 *1223*
any man spoil you *t* philosophy Col 2:8 *1223*
also ye are risen with him *t* the Col 2:12 *1223*
chosen you to salvation *t* 2Th 2:13 *1722*
consolation and good hope *t* grace 2Th 2:16 *1722*
themselves *t* with many sorrows 1Ti 6:10 *4044*
immortality to light *t* the gospel 2Ti 1:10 *1223*
make thee wise unto salvation *t* 2Ti 3:15 *1223*
manifested his word *t* preaching Titus 1:3 *1722*
t Jesus Christ our Saviour Titus 3:6 *1223*
for I trust that *t* your prayers I Philem 22 *1223*
salvation perfect *t* sufferings Heb 2:10 *1223*
that *t* death he might destroy him Heb 2:14 *1223*
deliver them who *t* fear of death Heb 2:15
t the deceitfulness of sin Heb 3:13
but followers of them who *t* faith Heb 6:12 *1223*
who *t* the eternal Spirit offered Heb 9:14 *1223*
t the offering of the body of Heb 10:10 *1223*
t the veil, that is to say, his Heb 10:20 *1223*
T faith we understand that the Heb 11:3
T faith also Sara herself Heb 11:11
T faith he kept the passover, and Heb 11:28
By faith they passed *t* the Red Heb 11:29 *1224*
Who *t* faith subdued kingdoms, Heb 11:33 *1223*
obtained a good report *t* faith Heb 11:39 *1223*
stoned, or thrust *t* with a dart Heb 12:20 *2700*
t the blood of the everlasting Heb 13:20 *1722*
in his sight, *t* Jesus Christ Heb 13:21 *1223*
t sanctification of the Spirit, 1Pet 1:2 *1722*
are kept by the power of God *t* 1Pet 1:5 *1223*
ye are in heaviness *t* manifold 1Pet 1:6 *1722*
t the Spirit unto unfeigned love 1Pet 1:22 *1223*
may be glorified *t* Jesus Christ 1Pet 4:11 *1223*
us *t* the righteousness of God 2Pet 1:1 *1722*
unto you *t* the knowledge of God 2Pet 1:2 *1722*
t the knowledge of him that hath 2Pet 1:3 *1223*
that is in the world *t* lust 2Pet 1:4 *1722*

t covetousness shall they with 2Pet 2:3 1722
they allure t the lusts of the 2Pet 2:18 1722
t much wantonness, those that 2Pet 2:18
world t the knowledge of the Lord 2Pet 2:20 1722
world, that we might live t him 1Jn 4:9 1223
flying t the midst of heaven Rev 8:13 1722
of the earth are waxed rich t the Rev 18:3 1537
may enter in t the gates into the Rev 22:14

THROUGHLY
let us make brick, and burn them t Gen 11:3
O that my grief were t weighed Job 6:2
Wash me t from mine iniquity, and Ps 51:2 7235
They shall t glean the remnant of Jer 6:9
For if ye t amend your ways and Jer 7:5
if ye t execute judgment between Jer 7:5
he shall t plead their cause, Jer 50:34
I t washed away thy blood from Eze 16:9
he will t purge his floor, and Mt 3:12 1245
he will t purge his floor, and Lk 3:17 1245
but we have been t made manifest 2Cor 11:6
t furnished unto all good works 2Ti 3:17 1822

THROUGHOUT
plenty t all the land of Egypt Gen 41:29
went t all the land of Egypt Gen 41:46
a ruler t all the land of Egypt Gen 45:8
people were scattered abroad t Ex 5:12
be blood t all the land of Egypt Ex 7:19
there was blood t all the land of Ex 7:21
lice t all the land of Egypt Ex 8:16
lice t all the land of Egypt Ex 8:17
beast, t all the land of Egypt Ex 9:9
may be declared t all the earth Ex 9:16
of the field, t the land of Egypt Ex 9:22
the hail smote t all the land of Ex 9:25
great cry t all the land of Egypt Ex 11:6
to the LORD t your generations Ex 12:14
be a continual burnt offering t Ex 29:42
the LORD t your generations Ex 30:8
upon it t your generations Ex 30:10
to his seed t their generations Ex 30:21
oil unto me t your generations Ex 30:31
me and you t your generations Ex 31:13
the sabbath t their generations Ex 31:16
out from gate to gate t the camp Ex 32:27
any man be seen t all the mount Ex 34:3
Ye shall kindle no fire t your Ex 35:3
it to be proclaimed t the camp Ex 36:6
so t the six branches going out Ex 37:19
priesthood t their generations Ex 40:15
of Israel, t all their journeys Ex 40:38
generations t all your dwellings Lev 3:17
for ever t their generations Lev 7:36
for ever t your generations Lev 10:9
unto them t their generations Lev 17:7
t your generations in all your Lev 23:14
your dwellings t your generations Lev 23:21
t your generations in all your Lev 23:31
the trumpet sound t all your land Lev 25:9
proclaim liberty t all the land Lev 25:10
that bought it t his generations Lev 25:30
t their generations, after their Num 1:42
his own standard, t their hosts Num 1:52
of Judah pitch t their armies Num 2:3
and four hundred, t their armies Num 2:9
hundred and fifty, t their armies Num 2:16
and an hundred, t their armies Num 2:24
t their hosts were six hundred Num 2:32
t their families, all the males Num 3:39
t the houses of their fathers, by Num 4:22
t their families, and by the house Num 4:38
t their families, by the house of Num 4:40
t their families, by the house of Num 4:42
for ever t your generations Num 10:8
of all the camps t their hosts Num 10:25
the people weep t their families Num 11:10
garments t their generations Num 15:38
for ever t your generations Num 18:23
t their fathers' house, all that Num 26:2
month t the months of the year Num 28:14
for every lamb, t the seven lambs Num 28:21
t the seven days, the meat of the Num 28:24
unto one lamb, t the seven lambs Num 28:29
for one lamb, t the seven lambs Num 29:4
for one lamb, t the seven lambs Num 29:10
t all the tribes of Israel, shall Num 31:4
t your generations in all your Num 35:29
thy God giveth thee, t thy tribes Deut 16:18
have olive trees t all thy coasts Deut 28:40
thou trustedst, t all thy land Deut 28:52
in all thy gates t all thy land Deut 28:52
sought them t all the way Josh 2:22
fame was noised t all the country Josh 6:27
up from Jericho t mount Beth-el Josh 16:1
prince t all the tribes of Israel Josh 22:14
led him t all the land of Canaan, Josh 24:3
he sent messengers t all Manasseh Judg 6:35
his fellow, even t all the host Judg 7:22
messengers t all mount Ephraim Judg 7:24
sent her t all the country of the Judg 20:6
t all the tribes of Israel Judg 20:10
deadly destruction t all the city 1Sa 5:11
sent them t all the coasts of 1Sa 11:7
blew the trumpet t all the land 1Sa 13:3
found t all the land of Israel 1Sa 13:19
out t all the thousands of Judah 1Sa 23:23
t all Edom put he garrisons, and 2Sa 8:14
But Absalom sent spies t all the 2Sa 15:10
strife t all the tribes of Israel 2Sa 19:9
damsel t all the coasts of Israel 1Kin 1:3
finished t all the parts thereof 1Kin 6:38
made a proclamation t all Judah 1Kin 15:22
land between them to pass t it 1Kin 18:6
there went a proclamation t the 1Kin 22:36
of Assyria came up t all the land 2Kin 17:5
they dwelt in their tents t all 1Chr 5:10 5921
t their castles in their coasts 1Chr 6:54
All their cities t their families 1Chr 6:60
to the sons of Gershom t their 1Chr 6:62
t their families, out of the 1Chr 6:63
the number t the genealogy of 1Chr 7:40
were chief t their generations 1Chr 9:34
famous t the house of their 1Chr 12:30
went t all Israel, and came to 1Chr 21:4
t all the coasts of Israel 1Chr 21:12
fame and of glory t all countries 1Chr 22:5
that ruled t the house of their 1Chr 26:6
went out month by month t all the 1Chr 27:1
t all the land of his dominion 2Chr 8:6
t all the countries of Judah 2Chr 11:23
fro t the whole earth, to shew 2Chr 16:9
went about t all the cities of 2Chr 17:9
in the fenced cities t all Judah 2Chr 17:19
he set judges in the land t all 2Chr 19:5
and proclaimed a fast t all Judah 2Chr 20:3 5921
fathers, t all Judah and Benjamin 2Chr 25:5
for them t all the host shields 2Chr 26:14
to make proclamation t all Israel 2Chr 30:5
king and his princes t all Israel 2Chr 30:6
they did eat t the feast seven 2Chr 30:22
And thus did Hezekiah t all Judah 2Chr 31:20
idols t all the land of Israel 2Chr 34:7
a proclamation t all his kingdom 2Chr 36:22
a proclamation t all his kingdom Ezr 1:1
And they made proclamation t Judah Ezr 10:7
be published t all his empire Est 1:20
t the whole kingdom of Ahasuerus Est 3:6
together in their cities t all Est 9:2
fame went out t all the provinces Est 9:4
kept t every generation, every Est 9:28
and moon endure, t all generations Ps 72:5
thy years are t all generations Ps 102:24
O LORD, t all generations Ps 135:13
endureth t all generations Ps 145:13
places for sin, t all thy borders Jer 17:3
against him t all my mountains Eze 38:21
And his fame went t all Syria Mt 4:24 1519
his fame spread abroad t all the Mk 1:28 1519
in their synagogues t all Galilee Mk 1:39 1519
be preached t the whole world Mk 14:9 1519
sayings were noised abroad t all Lk 1:65 1722
great famine was t all the land Lk 4:25 1909
of him went forth t all Judaea Lk 7:17 1722
t all the region round about Lk 7:17 1722
that he went t every city Lk 8:1 2596
published t the whole city how Lk 8:39 2596
teaching t all Jewry, beginning Lk 23:5 2596
seam, woven from the top t Jn 19:23
abroad t the regions of Judaea Acts 8:1 2596
the churches rest t all Judaea Acts 9:31 2596
as Peter passed t all quarters Acts 9:32 1223
And it was known t all Joppa Acts 9:42 2596
which was published t all Judaea Acts 10:37 2596
be great dearth t all the world Acts 11:28 1909
was published t all the region Acts 13:49 1223
after they had passed t Pisidia Acts 14:24 1330
Now when they had gone t Phrygia Acts 16:6 1330
at Ephesus, but almost t all Asia Acts 19:26
among all the Jews t the world Acts 24:5 2596
t all the coasts of Judaea, and Acts 26:20 1519
is spoken of t the whole world Rom 1:8 1722
might be declared t all the earth Rom 9:17 1722
in the gospel t all the churches 2Cor 8:18 1223
church by Christ Jesus t all ages Eph 3:21 1519
the strangers scattered t Pontus 1Pet 1:1

THROW
ye shall t down their altars Judg 2:2 5422
t down the altar of Baal that thy Judg 6:25 2040
battered the wall, to t it down 2Sa 20:15 5307
And he said, T her down 2Kin 9:33 8058
to t down, to build, and to plant Jer 1:10 2040
to t down, and to destroy, and to Jer 31:28 2040
they shall t down thine eminent Eze 16:39 2040
t down all thy strong holds Mic 5:11 2040
shall build, but I will t down Mal 1:4 2040

THROWING
And if he smite him with t a stone Num 35:17 3027

THROWN
his rider hath he t into the sea Ex 15:1 7411
his rider hath he t into the sea Ex 15:21
because he hath t down his altar Judg 6:32 5422
his head shall be t to thee over 2Sa 20:21 7993
t down thine altars, and slain thy 1Kin 19:10 2040
t down thine altars, and slain thy 1Kin 19:14 2040
nor t down any more for ever Jer 31:40 2040
which are t down by the mounts, Jer 33:4 5422
are fallen, her walls are t down Jer 50:15 2040
he hath t down in his wrath the Lam 2:2 2040
he hath t down, and hath not Lam 2:17 2040
I will leave thee t into the Eze 29:5
and the mountains shall be t down Eze 38:20 2040
and the rocks are t down by him Nah 1:6 5422
another, that shall not be t down Mt 24:2 2647
another, that shall not be t down Mk 13:2 2647
the devil had t him in the midst Lk 4:35 4496
another, that shall not be t down Lk 21:6 2647
that great city Babylon be t down Rev 18:21 906

THRUST
he shall surely t you out hence Ex 11:1 1644
because they were t out of Egypt Ex 12:39 1644
she t herself unto the wall, and Num 22:25 3905
t both of them through, the man Num 25:8 1856
But if he t him of hatred, or Num 35:20 1920
But if he t him suddenly without Num 35:22 1920
to t thee out of the way which Deut 13:5 5080
because he hath sought to t thee Deut 13:10 5080
t it through his ear unto the Deut 15:17 5414
he shall t out the enemy from Deut 33:27 1644
thigh, and t it into his belly Judg 3:21 8628
t the fleece together, and wringed Judg 6:38 2115
Zebul t out Gaal and his brethren, Judg 9:41 1644
And his young man t him through Judg 9:54 1856
they t out Jephthah, and said unto Judg 11:2 1644
that I may t out all your right 1Sa 11:2 5365
sword, and t me through therewith 1Sa 31:4 1856
t me through, and abuse me 1Sa 31:4 1856
t his sword in his fellow's side 2Sa 2:16
t them through the heart of 2Sa 18:14 8628
be all of them as thorns t away 2Sa 23:6 5074
So Solomon t out Abiathar from 1Kin 2:27 1644
Gehazi came near to t her away 2Kin 4:27 1920
sword, and t me through therewith 1Chr 10:4 1856
they t him out from thence 2Chr 26:20 926
Thou hast t sore at me that I Ps 118:13 1760
that is found shall be t through Is 13:15 1856
t through with a sword, that go Is 14:19 2944
they that are t through in her Jer 51:4 1856
t thee through with their swords Eze 16:40 1333
Because ye have t with side Eze 34:21 1920
to t them out of their possession Eze 46:18 3238
Neither shall one t another Joel 2:8 1766
t him through when he prophesieth Zec 13:3 1856
t him out of the city, and led him Lk 4:29 1544
prayed him that he would t out a Lk 5:3 1877
heaven, shalt be t down to hell Lk 10:15 2601
of God, and you yourselves t out Lk 13:28 1544
t my hand into his side, I will Jn 20:25 906
thy hand, and t it into my side Jn 20:27 906
his neighbour wrong t him away Acts 7:27 683
but t him from them, and in their Acts 7:39 683
t them into the inner prison, and Acts 16:24 906
now do they t us out privily Acts 16:37 1544
were possible, to t in the ship Acts 27:39 1856
stoned, or t through with a dart Heb 12:20 2700
cloud, T in thy sickle, and reap Rev 14:15 3992
he that sat on the cloud t in his Rev 14:16 906
T in thy sharp sickle, and gather Rev 14:18 3992
the angel t in his sickle into Rev 14:19 906

THRUSTETH
God t him down, not man Job 32:13 5086

THUMB
upon the t of their right hand, Ex 29:20 931
upon the t of his right hand, and Lev 8:23 931
upon the t of his right hand, and Lev 14:14 931
upon the t of his right hand, and Lev 14:17 931
upon the t of his right hand, and Lev 14:25 931
upon the t of his right hand, and Lev 14:28 931

THUMBS
upon the t of their right hands, Lev 8:24 931
and caught him, and cut off his t Judg 1:6
and ten kings, having their t Judg 1:7

THUMMIM *(thum'-mim) A symbolic object in the High Priest's breastplate.*
of judgment the Urim and the T Ex 28:30 8550
the breastplate the Urim and the T Lev 8:8 8550
And of Levi he said, Let thy T Deut 33:8 8550
up a priest with Urim and with T Ezr 2:63 8550
stood up a priest with Urim and T Neh 7:65 8550

THUNDER
and the LORD sent t and hail, and Ex 9:23 6963
the t shall cease, neither shall Ex 9:29 6963
of heaven shall he t upon them 1Sa 2:10 7481
a great t on that day upon the 1Sa 7:10 6963
unto the LORD, and he shall send t 1Sa 12:17 6963
and the LORD sent t and rain that 1Sa 12:18 6963
but the t of his power who can Job 26:14 7482
a way for the lightning of the t Job 28:26 6963
or a way for the lightning of t Job 38:25 6963
hast thou clothed his neck with t Job 39:19 7483
the t of the captains, and the Job 39:25 7482
or canst thou t with a voice like Job 40:9 7481
The voice of thy t was in the Ps 77:18 7482
thee in the secret place of t Ps 81:7 7482
voice of thy t they hasted away Ps 104:7 7482
of the LORD of hosts with t Is 29:6 7482
which is, The sons of t Mk 3:17 1027
heard, as it were the noise of t Rev 6:1 1027
and as the voice of a great t Rev 14:2 1027

THUNDERBOLTS
hail, and their flocks to hot t Ps 78:48 7565

THUNDERED
but the LORD t with a great 1Sa 7:10 7481
The LORD t from heaven, and the 2Sa 22:14 7481
The LORD also t in the heavens, Ps 18:13 7481
by, and heard it, said that it t Jn 12:29

THUNDERETH
he t with the voice of his Job 37:4 7481
God t marvellously with his voice Job 37:5 7481
the God of glory t Ps 29:3 7481

THUNDERINGS
that there be no more mighty t Ex 9:28 6963
And all the people saw the t Ex 20:18 6963
throne proceeded lightnings and t Rev 4:5 1027
and there were voices, and t Rev 8:5 1027
were lightnings, and voices, and t Rev 11:19 1027
and as the voice of mighty t Rev 19:6 1027

THUNDERS
and the t and hail ceased, and the Ex 9:33 6963
the t were ceased, he sinned yet Ex 9:34 6963
in the morning, that there were t Ex 19:16 6963
seven t uttered their voices Rev 10:3 1027
when the seven t had uttered Rev 10:4 1027
things which the seven t uttered Rev 10:4 1027
And there were voices, and t Rev 16:18 1027

THUS

T the heavens and the earth were	Gen 2:1	
T did Noah	Gen 6:22	
T were both the daughters of Lot	Gen 19:36	
t she was reproved	Gen 20:16	
T they made a covenant at	Gen 21:32	3541
saying, *T* spake the man unto me	Gen 24:30	3541
she said, If it be so, why am I *t*	Gen 25:22	2088
t Esau despised his birthright	Gen 25:34	
If he said *t*, The speckled shall	Gen 31:8	3541
and if he said *t*, The ringstraked	Gen 31:8	3541
T God hath taken away the cattle	Gen 31:9	
T I was	Gen 31:40	
T have I been twenty years in thy	Gen 31:41	2088
T shall ye speak unto my lord	Gen 32:4	3541
Thy servant Jacob saith *t*	Gen 32:4	3541
T dwelt Esau in mount Seir	Gen 36:8	
T his father wept for him	Gen 37:35	
and *t* did he unto them	Gen 42:25	3651
T saith thy son Joseph, God hath	Gen 45:9	3541
T shalt thou say unto the	Ex 3:14	3541
T shalt thou say unto the	Ex 3:15	3541
T saith the LORD, Israel is my	Ex 4:22	3541
T saith the LORD God of Israel,	Ex 5:1	3541
T saith Pharaoh, I will not give	Ex 5:10	3541
dealest thou *t* with thy servants	Ex 5:15	3541
T saith the LORD, In this thou	Ex 7:17	3541
T saith the LORD, Let my people	Ex 8:1	3541
T saith the LORD, Let my people	Ex 8:20	3541
T saith the LORD God of the	Ex 9:1	3541
T saith the LORD God of the	Ex 9:13	3541
T saith the LORD God of the	Ex 10:3	3541
T saith the LORD, About midnight	Ex 11:4	3541
And *t* shall ye eat it	Ex 12:11	3602
T did all the children of Israel	Ex 12:50	
hast thou dealt *t* with us	Ex 14:11	2063
T the LORD saved Israel that day	Ex 14:30	
T shalt thou say to the house of	Ex 19:3	3541
T thou shalt say unto the	Ex 20:22	3541
t shalt thou make for all the	Ex 26:17	3651
t shall it be for them both	Ex 26:24	3651
t shalt thou do unto Aaron, and to	Ex 29:35	
T saith the LORD God of Israel,	Ex 32:27	3541
t did he make for all the boards	Ex 36:22	3651
t he did to both of them in both	Ex 36:29	3651
T was all the work of the	Ex 39:32	
T did Moses	Ex 40:16	
T shall ye separate the children	Lev 15:31	
T shall Aaron come into the holy	Lev 16:3	2063
But *t* do unto them, that they may	Num 4:19	
t were they numbered of him, as	Num 4:49	
t shalt thou do unto them, to	Num 8:7	3541
T shalt thou separate the Levites	Num 8:14	
T shalt thou do unto the Levites	Num 8:26	3602
T were the journeyings of the	Num 10:28	428
And if thou deal *t* with me	Num 11:15	3602
T shall it be done for one	Num 15:11	3602
T speak unto the Levites, and say	Num 18:26	
T ye also shall offer an heave	Num 18:28	3651
T saith thy brother Israel, Thou	Num 20:14	3541
T Edom refused to give Israel	Num 20:21	
T Israel dwelt in the land of the	Num 21:31	
T saith Balak the son of Zippor,	Num 22:16	3541
unto Balak, and *t* thou shalt speak	Num 23:5	3541
Go again unto Balak, and say *t*	Num 23:16	3541
T did your fathers, when I sent	Num 32:8	3541
But *t* shall ye deal with them	Deut 7:5	3541
T I fell down before the LORD	Deut 9:25	
T shalt thou do unto all the	Deut 20:15	3651
the LORD done *t* unto this land	Deut 29:24	3662
Do ye *t* requite the LORD, O	Deut 32:6	2063
two men, and hid them, and said *t*	Josh 2:4	3651
T shalt thou do six days	Josh 6:3	3541
liest thou *t* upon thy face	Josh 7:10	2088
for *t* saith the LORD God of	Josh 7:13	3541
the LORD God of Israel, and *t*	Josh 7:20	2063
and *t* have I done	Josh 7:20	2063
for *t* shall the LORD do to all	Josh 10:25	3602
according to their families was *t*	Josh 16:5	
T they gave to the children of	Josh 21:13	
t were all these cities	Josh 21:42	3651
T saith the whole congregation of	Josh 22:16	3541
T saith the LORD God of Israel,	Josh 24:2	3541
T saith the LORD God of Israel, I	Judg 6:8	3541
him, Why hast thou served us *t*	Judg 8:1	
T was Midian subdued before the	Judg 8:28	
T God rendered the wickedness of	Judg 9:56	
T saith Jephthah, Israel took not	Judg 11:15	3541
T the children of Ammon were	Judg 11:33	
Why askest thou *t* after my name	Judg 13:18	2088
And he said unto them, *T* and	Judg 18:4	2090
t dealeth Micah with me, and hath	Judg 18:4	2088
T they inclosed the Benjamites	Judg 20:43	
T saith the LORD, Did I plainly	1Sa 2:27	3541
t he spake, Come, and let us go to	1Sa 9:9	3541
T saith the LORD God of Israel, I	1Sa 10:18	3541
T shall ye say unto the men of	1Sa 11:9	3541
If they say *t* unto us, Tarry	1Sa 14:9	3541
But if they say *t*, Come up unto	1Sa 14:10	3541
T saith the LORD of hosts, I	1Sa 15:2	3541
T shall ye say to David, The king	1Sa 18:25	3541
If he say *t*, It is well	1Sa 20:7	3541
But if I say *t* unto the young man	1Sa 20:22	3541
t shall ye say to him that liveth	1Sa 25:6	3541
Wherefore doth my lord *t* pursue	1Sa 26:18	2088
And I will yet be more vile than *t*	2Sa 6:22	2063
T saith the LORD, Shalt thou	2Sa 7:5	3541
T saith the LORD of hosts, I took	2Sa 7:8	3541
T shalt thou say unto Joab, Let	2Sa 11:25	3541
T saith the LORD God of Israel, I	2Sa 12:7	3541
T saith the LORD, Behold, I will	2Sa 12:11	3541
t did he unto all the cities of	2Sa 12:31	3651
But if he *t* say, I have no	2Sa 15:26	3541
t said Shimei when he cursed,	2Sa 16:7	3541
and to Abiathar the priests, *T*	2Sa 17:15	2063
t did Ahithophel counsel Absalom	2Sa 17:15	2063
and *t* and *t* have I counselled	2Sa 17:15	2063
for *t* hath Ahithophel counselled	2Sa 17:21	3602
Joab, I may not tarry *t* with thee	2Sa 18:14	3651
t he said, O my son Absalom, my	2Sa 18:33	3541
T saith the LORD, I offer thee	2Sa 24:12	3541
also *t* said the king, Blessed be	1Kin 1:48	3602
T saith the king, Come forth	1Kin 2:30	3541
T said Joab, and *t* he answered	1Kin 2:30	3541
T they spake before the king	1Kin 3:22	
t gave Solomon to Hiram year by	1Kin 5:11	3541
the LORD done *t* unto this land	1Kin 9:8	3602
for *t* saith the LORD, the God of	1Kin 11:31	3541
T shalt thou speak unto this	1Kin 12:10	3541
t shalt thou say unto them, My	1Kin 12:10	3541
T saith the LORD, Ye shall not go	1Kin 12:24	3541
O altar, altar, *t* saith the LORD	1Kin 13:2	3541
T saith the LORD, Forasmuch as	1Kin 13:21	3541
t and *t* shalt thou say unto her	1Kin 14:5	2090
t shalt thou say unto her	1Kin 14:5	2088
T saith the LORD God of Israel,	1Kin 14:7	3541
T did Zimri destroy all the house	1Kin 16:12	
For *t* saith the LORD God of	1Kin 17:14	3541
said unto him, *T* saith Ben-hadad,	1Kin 20:2	3541
T speaketh Ben-hadad, saying,	1Kin 20:5	3541
T saith the LORD, Hast thou seen	1Kin 20:13	3541
T saith the LORD, Even by the	1Kin 20:14	3541
T saith the LORD, Because the	1Kin 20:28	3541
T saith the LORD, Because thou	1Kin 20:42	3541
T saith the LORD, Hast thou	1Kin 21:19	3541
T saith the LORD, In the place	1Kin 21:19	3541
T saith the LORD, With these	1Kin 22:11	3541
T saith the king, Put this fellow	1Kin 22:27	3541
Now therefore *t* saith the LORD,	2Kin 1:4	3541
T saith the LORD, Is it not	2Kin 1:6	3541
man of God, *t* hath the king said	2Kin 1:11	3541
T saith the LORD, Forasmuch as	2Kin 1:16	3541
T saith the LORD, I have healed	2Kin 2:21	3541
T saith the LORD, Make this	2Kin 3:16	3541
For *t* saith the LORD, Ye shall	2Kin 3:17	3541
for *t* saith the LORD, They shall	2Kin 4:43	3541
in, and told his lord, saying, *T*	2Kin 5:4	2063
t said the maid that is of the	2Kin 5:4	2063
T saith the LORD, To morrow about	2Kin 7:1	3541
T saith the LORD, I have anointed	2Kin 9:3	3541
T saith the LORD God of Israel, I	2Kin 9:6	3541
And he said, *T* and *t* spake he to	2Kin 9:12	2063
T saith the LORD, I have anointed	2Kin 9:12	3541
T saith the king, Is it peace	2Kin 9:18	3541
T saith the king, Is it peace	2Kin 9:19	3541
T Jehu destroyed Baal out of	2Kin 10:28	3541
T did Urijah the priest,	2Kin 16:16	
T saith the great king, the king	2Kin 18:19	3541
T saith the king, Let not	2Kin 18:29	3541
for *t* saith the king of Assyria,	2Kin 18:31	3541
T saith Hezekiah, This day is a	2Kin 19:3	3541
T shall ye say to your master,	2Kin 19:6	3541
T saith the LORD, Be not afraid	2Kin 19:6	3541
T shall ye speak to Hezekiah king	2Kin 19:10	3541
T saith the LORD God of Israel,	2Kin 19:20	3541
Therefore *t* saith the LORD	2Kin 19:32	3541
T saith the LORD, Set thine house	2Kin 20:1	3541
T saith the LORD, the God of	2Kin 20:5	3541
Therefore *t* saith the LORD God of	2Kin 21:12	3541
T saith the LORD God of Israel,	2Kin 22:15	3541
T saith the LORD, Behold, I will	2Kin 22:16	3541
t shall ye say to him, *T* saith	2Kin 22:18	3541
T saith the LORD God of Israel,	2Kin 22:18	3541
T all Israel brought up the ark	1Chr 15:28	
T saith the LORD, Thou shalt not	1Chr 17:4	3541
Now therefore *t* shalt thou say	1Chr 17:7	3541
T saith the LORD of hosts, I took	1Chr 17:7	3541
T the LORD preserved David	1Chr 18:6	
T the LORD preserved David	1Chr 18:13	
T saith the LORD, I offer thee	1Chr 21:10	3541
T saith the LORD, Choose thee	1Chr 21:11	3541
and *t* were they divided	1Chr 24:4	
T were they divided by lot, one	1Chr 24:5	
T David the son of Jesse reigned	1Chr 29:26	
T Solomon made all these vessels	2Chr 4:18	
T all the work that Solomon made	2Chr 5:1	
T Solomon finished the house of	2Chr 7:11	
the LORD done *t* unto this land	2Chr 7:21	3602
T shalt thou answer the people	2Chr 10:10	3541
t shalt thou say unto them, My	2Chr 10:10	3541
T saith the LORD, Ye shall not go	2Chr 11:4	3541
T saith the LORD, Ye have	2Chr 12:5	3541
T the children of Israel were	2Chr 13:18	
T saith the LORD, With these thou	2Chr 18:10	3541
T saith the king, Put this fellow	2Chr 18:26	3541
T shall ye do in the fear of the	2Chr 19:9	3541
T saith the LORD unto you, Be not	2Chr 20:15	3541
T saith the LORD God of David thy	2Chr 21:12	3541
T they did day by day, and	2Chr 24:11	3541
T saith God, Why transgress ye	2Chr 24:20	3541
T Joash the king remembered not	2Chr 24:22	
t did Hezekiah throughout all	2Chr 31:20	2063
T saith Sennacherib king of	2Chr 32:10	3541
T the LORD saved Hezekiah and the	2Chr 32:22	
T saith the LORD God of Israel,	2Chr 34:23	3541
T saith the LORD, Behold, I will	2Chr 34:24	3541
T saith the LORD God of Israel	2Chr 34:26	3541
T saith Cyrus king of Persia, All	2Chr 36:23	3541
T saith Cyrus king of Persia, The	Ezr 1:2	3541
said *t* unto them, Who hath	Ezr 5:3	3652
unto him, wherein was written *t*	Ezr 5:7	1836
those elders, and said unto them *t*	Ezr 5:9	3660
t they returned us answer, saying	Ezr 5:11	3660
and therein was a record *t* written	Ezr 6:2	3652
even *t* be he shaken out, and	Neh 5:13	3602
Did not your fathers *t*, and did	Neh 13:18	3541
T cleansed I them from all	Neh 13:30	
T shall there arise too much	Est 1:18	
Then *t* came every maiden unto the	Est 2:13	2088
T shall it be done to the man	Est 6:9	3602
T shall it be done unto the man	Est 6:11	3602
T the Jews smote all their	Est 9:5	
T did Job continually	Job 1:5	3602
why then are ye *t* altogether vain	Job 27:12	2088
T I was as a man that heareth not	Ps 38:14	
T will I bless thee while I live	Ps 63:4	3651
If I say, I will speak *t*	Ps 73:15	3644
T my heart was grieved, and I was	Ps 73:21	3588
T they changed their glory into	Ps 106:20	
T they provoked him to anger with	Ps 106:29	
T were they defiled with their	Ps 106:39	
that *t* shall the man be blessed	Ps 128:4	3651
T saith the Lord GOD, It shall	Is 7:7	3541
For the LORD spake *t* to me with a	Is 8:11	3541
Therefore *t* saith the Lord GOD of	Is 10:24	3541
For *t* hath the Lord said unto me,	Is 21:6	3541
For *t* hath the Lord said unto me,	Is 21:16	3541
T saith the Lord GOD of hosts, Go	Is 22:15	3541
When *t* it shall be in the midst	Is 24:13	3541
Therefore *t* saith the Lord GOD,	Is 28:16	3541
Therefore *t* saith the LORD, who	Is 29:22	3541
Wherefore *t* saith the Holy One of	Is 30:12	3541
For *t* saith the Lord GOD, the	Is 30:15	3541
For *t* hath the LORD spoken unto	Is 31:4	3541
T saith the great king, the king	Is 36:4	3541
T saith the king, Let not	Is 36:14	3541
for *t* saith the king of Assyria,	Is 36:16	3541
T saith Hezekiah, This day is a	Is 37:3	3541
T shall ye say unto your master,	Is 37:6	3541
T saith the LORD, Be not afraid	Is 37:6	3541
T shall ye speak to Hezekiah king	Is 37:10	3541
T saith the LORD God of Israel,	Is 37:21	3541
Therefore *t* saith the LORD	Is 37:33	3541
T saith the LORD, Set thine house	Is 38:1	3541
T saith the LORD, the God of	Is 38:5	3541
T saith God the LORD, he that	Is 42:5	3541
But now *t* saith the LORD that	Is 43:1	3541
T saith the LORD, your redeemer,	Is 43:14	3541
T saith the LORD, which maketh a	Is 43:16	3541
T saith the LORD that made thee,	Is 44:2	3541
T saith the LORD the King of	Is 44:6	3541
T saith the LORD, thy redeemer,	Is 44:24	3541
T saith the LORD to his anointed,	Is 45:1	3541
T saith the LORD, the Holy One of	Is 45:11	3541
T saith the LORD, The labour of	Is 45:14	3541
For *t* saith the LORD that created	Is 45:18	3541
T shall they be unto thee with	Is 47:15	3651
T saith the LORD, thy Redeemer,	Is 48:17	3541
T saith the LORD, the Redeemer of	Is 49:7	3541
T saith the LORD, In an	Is 49:8	3541
T saith the Lord GOD, Behold, I	Is 49:22	3541
But *t* saith the LORD, Even the	Is 49:25	3541
T saith the LORD, Where is the	Is 50:1	3541
T saith thy Lord the LORD, and thy	Is 51:22	3541
For *t* saith the LORD, Ye have	Is 52:3	3541
For *t* saith the Lord GOD, My	Is 52:4	3541
T saith the LORD, Keep ye	Is 56:1	3541
For *t* saith the LORD unto the	Is 56:4	3541
For *t* saith the high and lofty One	Is 57:15	3541
T saith the LORD, As the new wine	Is 65:8	3541
Therefore *t* saith the Lord GOD,	Is 65:13	3541
T saith the LORD, The heaven is	Is 66:1	3541
For *t* saith the LORD, Behold, I	Is 66:12	3541
saying, *T* saith the LORD	Jer 2:2	3541
T saith the LORD, What iniquity	Jer 2:5	3541
For *t* saith the LORD to the men	Jer 4:3	3541
For *t* hath the LORD said, The	Jer 4:27	3541
t shall it be done unto them	Jer 5:13	3541
Wherefore *t* saith the LORD God of	Jer 5:14	3541
For *t* hath the LORD of hosts said	Jer 6:6	3541
T saith the LORD of hosts, They	Jer 6:9	3541
T saith the LORD, Stand ye in the	Jer 6:16	3541
Therefore *t* saith the LORD,	Jer 6:21	3541
T saith the LORD, Behold, a	Jer 6:22	3541
T saith the LORD of hosts, the	Jer 7:3	3541
Therefore *t* saith the Lord GOD	Jer 7:20	3541
T saith the LORD of hosts, the	Jer 7:21	3541
say unto them, *T* saith the LORD	Jer 8:4	3541
Therefore *t* saith the LORD of	Jer 9:7	3541
Therefore *t* saith the LORD of	Jer 9:15	3541
T saith the LORD of hosts,	Jer 9:17	3541
T saith the LORD, Even the	Jer 9:22	3541
T saith the LORD, Let not the	Jer 9:23	3541
T saith the LORD, Learn not the	Jer 10:2	3541
T shall ye say unto them, The	Jer 10:11	1836
For *t* saith the LORD, Behold, I	Jer 10:18	3541
T saith the LORD God of Israel	Jer 11:3	3541
Therefore *t* saith the LORD,	Jer 11:11	3541
Therefore *t* saith the LORD of the	Jer 11:21	3541
Therefore *t* saith the LORD of	Jer 11:22	3541
T saith the LORD against all mine	Jer 12:14	3541
T saith the LORD unto me, Go and	Jer 13:1	3541
T saith the LORD, After this	Jer 13:9	3541
T saith the LORD God of Israel,	Jer 13:12	3541
T saith the LORD, Behold, I will	Jer 13:13	3541
T saith the LORD unto this people	Jer 14:10	3541
T have they loved to wander, they	Jer 14:10	3651
Therefore *t* saith the LORD	Jer 14:15	3541
shalt tell them, *T* saith the LORD	Jer 15:2	3541
Therefore *t* saith the LORD, If	Jer 15:19	3541
For *t* saith the LORD concerning	Jer 16:3	3541
For *t* saith the LORD, Enter not	Jer 16:5	3541
For *t* saith the LORD of hosts,	Jer 16:9	3541
T saith the LORD	Jer 17:5	3541
T said the LORD unto me	Jer 17:19	3541
T saith the LORD	Jer 17:21	3541
saying, *T* saith the LORD	Jer 18:11	3541
Therefore *t* saith the LORD	Jer 18:13	3541
deal *t* with them in the time of	Jer 18:23	
T saith the LORD, Go and get a	Jer 19:1	3541
T saith the LORD of hosts, the	Jer 19:3	3541
T saith the LORD of hosts	Jer 19:11	3541

T will I do unto this place, Jer 19:12 3651
T saith the LORD of hosts, the Jer 19:15 3541
For *t* saith the LORD, Behold, I Jer 20:4 3541
T shall ye say to Zedekiah Jer 21:3 3541
T saith the LORD God of Israel Jer 21:4 3541
thou shalt say, *T* saith the LORD Jer 21:8 3541
house of David, *t* saith the LORD Jer 21:12 3541
T saith the LORD Jer 22:1 3541
T saith the LORD Jer 22:3 3541
For *t* saith the LORD unto the Jer 22:6 3541
LORD done *t* unto this great city Jer 22:8 3602
For *t* saith the LORD touching Jer 22:11 3541
Therefore *t* saith the LORD Jer 22:18 3541
T saith the LORD, Write ye this Jer 22:30 3541
Therefore *t* saith the LORD God of Jer 23:2 3541
Therefore *t* saith the LORD of Jer 23:15 3541
T saith the LORD of hosts, Jer 23:16 3541
T shall ye say every one to his Jer 23:35 3541
T shalt thou say to the prophet, Jer 23:37 3541
therefore *t* saith the LORD Jer 23:38 3541
T saith the LORD, the God of Jer 24:5 3541
surely *t* saith the LORD, So will Jer 24:8 3541
Therefore *t* saith the LORD of Jer 25:8 3541
For *t* saith the LORD God of Jer 25:15 3541
T saith the LORD of hosts, the Jer 25:27 3541
T saith the LORD of hosts Jer 25:28 3541
T saith the LORD of hosts, Behold Jer 25:32 3541
T saith the LORD Jer 26:2 3541
say unto them, *T* saith the LORD Jer 26:4 3541
T saith the LORD of hosts Jer 26:18 3541
T might we procure great evil Jer 26:19 3541
T saith the LORD to me Jer 27:2 3541
T saith the LORD of hosts, the Jer 27:4 3541
T shall ye say unto your masters Jer 27:4 3541
people, saying, *T* saith the LORD Jer 27:16 3541
For *t* saith the LORD of hosts Jer 27:19 3541
t saith the LORD of hosts, the Jer 27:21 3541
T speaketh the LORD of hosts, the Jer 28:2 3541
people, saying, *T* saith the LORD Jer 28:11 3602
saying, *T* saith the LORD Jer 28:13 3541
For *t* saith the LORD of hosts, Jer 28:14 3541
Therefore *t* saith the LORD Jer 28:16 3541
T saith the LORD of hosts, the Jer 29:4 3541
For *t* saith the LORD of hosts, Jer 29:8 3541
For *t* saith the LORD, That after Jer 29:10 3541
Know that *t* saith the LORD of the Jer 29:16 3541
T saith the LORD of hosts Jer 29:17 3541
T saith the LORD of hosts, the Jer 29:21 3541
T shalt thou also speak to Jer 29:24
T speaketh the LORD of hosts, the Jer 29:25 3541
T saith the LORD concerning Jer 29:31 3541
Therefore *t* saith the LORD Jer 29:32 3541
T speaketh the LORD God of Israel Jer 30:2 3541
For *t* saith the LORD Jer 30:5 3541
For *t* saith the LORD, Thy bruise Jer 30:12 3541
T saith the LORD Jer 30:18 3541
T saith the LORD, The people Jer 31:2 3541
For *t* saith the LORD Jer 31:7 3541
T saith the LORD Jer 31:15 3541
T saith the LORD Jer 31:16 3541
heard Ephraim bemoaning himself *t* Jer 31:18
T saith the LORD of hosts, the Jer 31:23 3541
T saith the LORD, which giveth Jer 31:35 3541
T saith the LORD Jer 31:37 3541
T saith the LORD, Behold, I will Jer 32:3 3541
T saith the LORD of hosts, the Jer 32:14 3541
For *t* saith the LORD of hosts, Jer 32:15 3541
Therefore *t* saith the LORD Jer 32:28 3541
now therefore *t* saith the LORD, Jer 32:36 3541
For *t* saith the LORD Jer 32:42 3541
T saith the LORD the maker Jer 33:2 3541
For *t* saith the LORD, the God of Jer 33:4 3541
T saith the LORD Jer 33:10 3541
T saith the LORD of hosts Jer 33:12 3541
For *t* saith the LORD Jer 33:17 3541
T saith the LORD Jer 33:20 3541
t they have despised my people, Jer 33:24
T saith the LORD Jer 33:25 3541
T saith the LORD, the God of Jer 34:2 3541
and tell him, *T* saith the LORD Jer 34:2 3541
T saith the LORD of thee, Thou Jer 34:4 3541
T saith the LORD, the God of Jer 34:13 3541
Therefore *t* saith the LORD Jer 34:17 3541
T have we obeyed the voice of Jer 35:8
T saith the LORD of hosts, the Jer 35:13 3541
Therefore *t* saith the LORD God of Jer 35:17 3541
T saith the LORD of hosts, the Jer 35:18 3541
Therefore *t* saith the LORD of Jer 35:19 3541
king of Judah, *T* saith the LORD Jer 36:29 3541
Therefore *t* saith the LORD of Jer 36:30 3541
T saith the LORD, the God of Jer 37:7 3541
T shall ye say to the king of Jer 37:7 3541
T saith the LORD Jer 37:9 3541
T Jeremiah remained in the court Jer 37:21
T saith the LORD, He that Jer 38:2 3541
T saith the LORD, This city shall Jer 38:3 3541
for *t* he weakeneth the hands of Jer 38:4
T saith the LORD of hosts, the Jer 39:16 3541
T saith the LORD, the God of Jer 42:9 3541
T saith the LORD of hosts, the Jer 42:15 3541
For *t* saith the LORD of hosts, Jer 42:18 3541
t came they even to Tahpanhes Jer 43:7
T saith the LORD of hosts, the Jer 43:10 3541
T saith the LORD of hosts, the Jer 44:2 3541
Therefore now *t* saith the LORD, Jer 44:7 3541
Therefore *t* saith the LORD of Jer 44:11 3541
T saith the LORD of hosts, the Jer 44:25 3541
T saith the LORD Jer 44:30 3541
T saith the LORD, the God of Jer 45:2 3541
T shalt thou say unto him, The Jer 45:4 3541
say unto him, The LORD saith *t* Jer 45:4 3541
T saith the LORD Jer 47:2 3541
Against Moab *t* saith the LORD of Jer 48:1 3541
For *t* saith the LORD Jer 48:40 3541
T far is the judgment of Moab Jer 48:47 2008
The Ammonites, *t* saith the LORD Jer 49:1 3541
t saith the LORD of hosts Jer 49:7 3541
For *t* saith the LORD Jer 49:12 3541
shall smite, *t* saith the LORD Jer 49:28 3541
T saith the LORD of hosts Jer 49:35 3541
Therefore *t* saith the LORD of Jer 50:18 3541
T saith the LORD of hosts Jer 50:33 3541
T saith the LORD Jer 51:1 3541
T the slain shall fall in the Jer 51:4
For *t* saith the LORD of hosts, Jer 51:33 3541
Therefore *t* saith the LORD Jer 51:36 3541
T saith the LORD of hosts Jer 51:58 3541
T shall Babylon sink, and shall Jer 51:64 3602
T far are the words of Jeremiah Jer 51:64 2008
T Judah was carried away captive Jer 52:27
T were their faces Eze 1:11
unto them, *T* saith the Lord GOD Eze 2:4 3541
tell them, *T* saith the Lord GOD Eze 3:11 3541
unto them, *T* saith the Lord GOD Eze 3:27 3541
Even *t* shall the children of Eze 4:13 3602
T saith the Lord GOD Eze 5:5 3541
Therefore *t* saith the Lord GOD Eze 5:7 3541
Therefore *t* saith the Lord GOD Eze 5:8 3541
T shall mine anger be Eze 5:13
T saith the Lord GOD to the Eze 6:3 3541
T saith the Lord GOD Eze 6:11 3541
t will I accomplish my fury upon Eze 6:12
t saith the Lord GOD unto the Eze 7:2 3541
T saith the Lord GOD Eze 7:5 3541
T saith the LORD Eze 11:5 3541
T have ye said, O house of Israel Eze 11:5 3651
Therefore *t* saith the Lord GOD Eze 11:7 3541
say, *T* saith the Lord GOD Eze 11:16 3541
say, *T* saith the Lord GOD Eze 11:17 3541
unto them, *T* saith the Lord GOD Eze 12:10 3541
T saith the Lord GOD of the Eze 12:19 3541
therefore, *T* saith the Lord GOD Eze 12:23 3541
unto them, *T* saith the Lord GOD Eze 12:28 3541
T saith the Lord GOD Eze 13:3 3541
Therefore *t* saith the Lord GOD Eze 13:8 3541
Therefore *t* saith the Lord GOD Eze 13:13 3541
T will I accomplish my wrath upon Eze 13:15
And say, *T* saith the Lord GOD Eze 13:18 3541
Wherefore *t* saith the Lord GOD Eze 13:20 3541
unto them, *T* saith the Lord GOD Eze 14:4 3541
of Israel, *T* saith the Lord GOD Eze 14:6 3541
For *t* saith the Lord GOD Eze 14:21 3541
Therefore *t* saith the Lord GOD Eze 15:6 3541
T saith the Lord GOD unto Eze 16:3 3541
T wast thou decked with gold and Eze 16:13
t it was, saith the Lord GOD Eze 16:19
T saith the Lord GOD Eze 16:36 3541
For *t* saith the Lord GOD Eze 16:59 3541
And say, *T* saith the Lord GOD Eze 17:3 3541
Say thou, *T* saith the Lord GOD Eze 17:9 3541
Therefore *t* saith the Lord GOD Eze 17:19 3541
T saith the Lord GOD Eze 17:22 3541
unto them, *T* saith the Lord GOD Eze 20:3 3541
unto them, *T* saith the Lord GOD Eze 20:5 3541
unto them, *T* saith the Lord GOD Eze 20:27 3541
of Israel, *T* saith the Lord GOD Eze 20:30 3541
of Israel, *t* saith the Lord GOD Eze 20:39 3541
T saith the Lord GOD Eze 20:47 3541
land of Israel, *T* saith the LORD Eze 21:3 3541
and say, *T* saith the LORD Eze 21:9 3541
Therefore *t* saith the Lord GOD Eze 21:24 3541
T saith the Lord GOD Eze 21:26 3541
T saith the Lord GOD concerning Eze 21:28 3541
T saith the Lord GOD, The city Eze 22:3 3541
Therefore *t* saith the Lord GOD Eze 22:19 3541
T saith the Lord GOD, when the Eze 22:28 3541
T were their names Eze 23:4
T she committed her whoredoms Eze 23:7
T thou calledst to remembrance Eze 23:21
O Aholibah, *t* saith the Lord GOD Eze 23:22 3541
T will I make thy lewdness to Eze 23:27
For *t* saith the Lord GOD Eze 23:28 3541
T saith the Lord GOD Eze 23:32 3541
Therefore *t* saith the Lord GOD Eze 23:35 3541
t have they done in the midst of Eze 23:39 3541
For *t* saith the Lord GOD Eze 23:46 3541
T will I cause lewdness to cease Eze 23:48
unto them, *T* saith the Lord GOD Eze 24:3 3541
Wherefore *t* saith the Lord GOD Eze 24:6 3541
Therefore *t* saith the Lord GOD Eze 24:9 3541
of Israel, *T* saith the Lord GOD Eze 24:21 3541
T Ezekiel is unto you a sign Eze 24:24
T saith the Lord GOD Eze 25:3 3541
For *t* saith the Lord GOD Eze 25:6 3541
T saith the Lord GOD Eze 25:8 3541
T saith the Lord GOD Eze 25:12 3541
Therefore *t* saith the Lord GOD Eze 25:13 3541
T saith the Lord GOD Eze 25:15 3541
Therefore *t* saith the Lord GOD Eze 25:16 3541
Therefore *t* saith the Lord GOD Eze 26:3 3541
For *t* saith the Lord GOD Eze 26:7 3541
T saith the Lord GOD to Tyrus Eze 26:15 3541
For *t* saith the Lord GOD Eze 26:19 3541
many isles, *T* saith the Lord GOD Eze 27:3 3541
of Tyrus, *T* saith the Lord GOD Eze 28:2 3541
Therefore *t* saith the Lord GOD Eze 28:6 3541
unto him, *T* saith the Lord GOD Eze 28:12 3541
And say, *T* saith the Lord GOD Eze 28:22 3541
T saith the Lord GOD Eze 28:25 3541
and say, *T* saith the Lord GOD Eze 29:3 3541
Therefore *t* saith the Lord GOD Eze 29:8 3541
Yet *t* saith the Lord GOD Eze 29:13 3541
Therefore *t* saith the Lord GOD Eze 29:19 3541
and say, *T* saith the Lord GOD Eze 30:2 3541
T saith the LORD Eze 30:6 3541
T saith the Lord GOD Eze 30:10 3541
T saith the Lord GOD Eze 30:13 3541
T will I execute judgments in Eze 30:19
Therefore *t* saith the Lord GOD Eze 30:22 3541
T was he fair in his greatness, Eze 31:7
Therefore *t* saith the Lord GOD Eze 31:10 3541
T saith the Lord GOD Eze 31:15
To whom art thou *t* like in glory Eze 31:18 3602
T saith the Lord GOD Eze 32:3 3541
For *t* saith the Lord GOD Eze 32:11 3541
T ye speak, saying, If our Eze 33:10 3651
unto them, *T* saith the Lord GOD Eze 33:25 3541
Say thou *t* unto them, *T* saith Eze 33:27 3541
T saith the Lord GOD unto the Eze 34:2 3541
T saith the Lord GOD Eze 34:10 3541
For *t* saith the Lord GOD Eze 34:11 3541
O my flock, *t* saith the Lord GOD Eze 34:17 3541
Therefore *t* saith the Lord GOD Eze 34:20 3541
T shall they know that I the LORD Eze 34:30
say unto it, *T* saith the Lord GOD Eze 35:3 3541
T will I make mount Seir most Eze 35:7
T with your mouth ye have boasted Eze 35:13
T saith the Lord GOD Eze 35:14 3541
T saith the Lord GOD Eze 36:2 3541
and say, *T* saith the Lord GOD Eze 36:3 3541
T saith the Lord GOD to the Eze 36:4 3541
Therefore *t* saith the Lord GOD Eze 36:5 3541
the valleys, *T* saith the Lord GOD Eze 36:6 3541
Therefore *t* saith the Lord GOD Eze 36:7 3541
T saith the Lord GOD Eze 36:13 3541
of Israel, *T* saith the Lord GOD Eze 36:22 3541
T saith the Lord GOD Eze 36:33 3541
T saith the Lord GOD Eze 36:37 3541
T saith the Lord GOD unto these Eze 37:5 3541
to the wind, *T* saith the Lord GOD Eze 37:9 3541
unto them, *T* saith the Lord GOD Eze 37:12 3541
unto them, *T* saith the Lord GOD Eze 37:19 3541
unto them, *T* saith the Lord GOD Eze 37:21 3541
And say, *T* saith the Lord GOD Eze 38:3 3541
T saith the Lord GOD Eze 38:10 3541
unto Gog, *T* saith the Lord GOD Eze 38:14 3541
T saith the Lord GOD Eze 38:17 3541
T will I magnify myself, and Eze 38:23
Gog, and say, *T* saith the Lord GOD Eze 39:1 3541
T shall they cleanse the land Eze 39:16
son of man, *t* saith the Lord GOD Eze 39:17 3541
T ye shall be filled at my table Eze 39:20
Therefore *t* saith the Lord GOD Eze 39:25 3541
Son of man, *t* saith the Lord GOD Eze 43:18 3541
t shalt thou cleanse and purge it Eze 43:20
of Israel, *T* saith the Lord GOD Eze 44:6 3541
T saith the Lord GOD Eze 44:9 3541
T saith the Lord GOD Eze 45:9 3541
T saith the Lord GOD Eze 45:18 3541
T saith the Lord GOD Eze 46:1 3541
T shall they prepare the lamb, and Eze 46:15
T saith the Lord GOD Eze 46:16 3541
T saith the Lord GOD Eze 47:13 3541
T Melzar took away the portion of Dan 1:16
he went and said *t* unto him Dan 2:24 3652
said *t* unto him, I have found a Dan 2:25 3652
T were the visions of mine head Dan 4:10
He cried aloud, and said *t* Dan 4:14 3652
said *t* unto him, King Darius, Dan 6:6 3652
and they said *t* unto it, Arise, Dan 7:5 3652
T he said, The fourth beast shall Dan 7:23 3652
t shall he do Dan 11:17
T shall he do in the most strong Dan 11:39
t judgment springeth up as Hos 10:4
T saith the LORD Amos 1:3 3541
T saith the LORD Amos 1:6 3541
T saith the LORD Amos 1:9
T saith the LORD Amos 1:11 3541
T saith the LORD Amos 1:13 3541
T saith the LORD Amos 2:1 3541
T saith the LORD Amos 2:4 3541
T saith the LORD Amos 2:6 3541
Is it not even *t*, O ye children Amos 2:11 2063
Therefore *t* saith the Lord GOD Amos 3:11 3541
T saith the LORD Amos 3:12 3541
Therefore *t* will I do unto thee, Amos 4:12 3541
For *t* saith the Lord GOD Amos 5:3 3541
For *t* saith the LORD unto the Amos 5:4 3541
God of hosts, the Lord, saith *t* Amos 5:16 3541
T hath the Lord GOD shewed unto Amos 7:1 3541
T hath the Lord GOD shewed unto Amos 7:4 3541
T he shewed me Amos 7:7 3541
For *t* Amos saith, Jeroboam shall Amos 7:11 3541
Therefore *t* saith the LORD Amos 7:17 3541
T hath the Lord GOD shewed unto Amos 8:1 3541
T saith the Lord GOD concerning Obad 1 3541
Therefore *t* saith the LORD Mic 2:3 3541
T saith the LORD concerning the Mic 3:5 3541
t shall he deliver us from the Mic 5:6
T saith the LORD Nah 1:12 3541
yet *t* shall they be cut down, Nah 1:12 3651
T speaketh the LORD of hosts, Hag 1:2 3541
Now therefore *t* saith the LORD of Hag 1:5 3541
T saith the LORD of hosts Hag 1:7 3541
For *t* saith the LORD of hosts Hag 2:6 3541
T saith the LORD of hosts Hag 2:11 3541
T saith the LORD of hosts Zec 1:3 3541
T saith the LORD of hosts Zec 1:4 3541
T saith the LORD of hosts Zec 1:14 3541
Therefore *t* saith the LORD Zec 1:16 3541
T saith the LORD of hosts Zec 1:17 3541
For *t* saith the LORD of hosts Zec 2:8 3541
T saith the LORD of hosts Zec 3:7 3541
T speaketh the LORD of hosts, Zec 6:12 3541
T speaketh the LORD of hosts, Zec 7:9 3541
T the land was desolate after Zec 7:14
T saith the LORD of hosts Zec 8:2 3541
T saith the LORD Zec 8:3 3541
T saith the LORD of hosts Zec 8:4 3541
T saith the LORD of hosts Zec 8:6 3541
T saith the LORD of hosts Zec 8:7 3541
T saith the LORD of hosts Zec 8:9 3541

For *t* saith the LORD of hosts ... Zec 8:14 3541
T saith the LORD of hosts ... Zec 8:19 3541
T saith the LORD of hosts ... Zec 8:20 3541
T saith the LORD of hosts ... Zec 8:23 3541
T saith the LORD my God ... Zec 11:4 3541
t saith the LORD of hosts, They ... Mal 1:4 3541
t ye brought an offering ... Mal 1:13 3541
for *t* it is written by the ... Mt 2:5 3779
for *t* it becometh us to fulfil ... Mt 3:15 3779
T have ye made the commandment of ... Mt 15:6 2532
be fulfilled, that *t* it must be ... Mt 26:54 3779
doth this man *t* speak blasphemies ... Mk 2:7 3779
T hath the Lord dealt with me in ... Lk 1:25 3779
why hast thou *t* dealt with us ... Lk 2:48 3779
While he *t* spake, there came a ... Lk 9:34 5023
t saying thou reproachest us also ... Lk 11:45 5023
Even *t* shall it be in the day ... Lk 17:30
prayed *t* with himself, God, I ... Lk 18:11 5023
And when he had *t* spoken, he went ... Lk 19:28 5023
t shall ye say unto him, Because ... Lk 19:31 3779
answered and said, Suffer ye *t* far ... Lk 22:51 5127
and having said *t*, he gave up the ... Lk 23:46 5023
And as they *t* spake, Jesus himself ... Lk 24:36 5023
And when he had *t* spoken, he ... Lk 24:40 5124
T it is written, and *t* it ... Lk 24:46 3779
his journey, sat *t* on the well ... Jn 4:6 3779
When he had *t* spoken, he spat on ... Jn 9:6 5023
when he *t* had spoken, he cried ... Jn 11:43 5023
If we let him *t* alone, all men ... Jn 11:48 3779
When Jesus had *t* said, he was ... Jn 13:21 5023
And when he had *t* spoken, one of ... Jn 18:22 5023
And when she had *t* said, she ... Jn 20:14 5023
And when he had *t* spoken, he ... Acts 19:41 5023
And when he had *t* spoken, he ... Acts 20:36 5023
T saith the Holy Ghost, So shall ... Acts 21:11 3592
as he *t* spake for himself, Festus ... Acts 26:24 5023
And when he had *t* spoken, the king ... Acts 26:30 5023
And when he had *t* spoken, he took ... Acts 27:35 5023
it, Why hast thou made me *t* ... Rom 9:20 3779
t are the secrets of his heart ... 1Cor 14:25 3779
When I therefore was *t* minded ... 2Cor 1:17 5124
because we *t* judge, that if one ... 2Cor 5:14 5124
many as be perfect, be *t* minded ... Phil 3:15 5124
salvation, though we *t* speak ... Heb 6:9 3779
when these things were *t* ordained ... Heb 9:6 3779
t I saw the horses in the vision ... Rev 9:17 3779
be, because thou hast judged *t* ... Rev 16:5 5023
T with violence shall that great ... Rev 18:21 3779

THY See PREFACE.

THYATIRA (*thi-a-ti'-rah*) *A city in Lydia in Asia Minor.*
of purple, of the city of *T* ... Acts 16:14 2363
and unto Pergamos, and unto *T* ... Rev 1:11 2363
angel of the church in *T* write ... Rev 2:18 2363
you I say, and unto the rest in *T* ... Rev 2:24 2363

THYINE
all *t* wood, and all manner vessels ... Rev 18:12 2367

THYSELF
separate *t*, I pray thee, from me ... Gen 13:9
persons, and take the goods to *t* ... Gen 14:21
and submit *t* under her hands ... Gen 16:9
keep that thou hast unto *t* ... Gen 33:9
exaltest thou *t* against my people ... Ex 9:17
thou refuse to humble *t* before me ... Ex 10:3
Get thee from me, take heed to *t* ... Ex 10:28
why sittest thou *t* alone, and all ... Ex 18:14 859
not able to perform it *t* alone ... Ex 18:18
so shall it be easier for *t* ... Ex 18:22
Thou shalt not bow down *t* to them ... Ex 20:5
present *t* there to me in the top ... Ex 34:2
Take heed to *t*, lest thou make a ... Ex 34:12
and make an atonement for *t* ... Lev 9:7
wife, to defile *t* with her ... Lev 18:20
any beast to defile *t* therewith ... Lev 18:23
shalt love thy neighbour as *t* ... Lev 19:18
you, and thou shalt love him as *t* ... Lev 19:34
that thou bear it not *t* alone ... Num 11:17
except thou make *t* altogether a ... Num 16:13
Only take heed to *t*, and keep thy ... Deut 4:9
shalt not bow down *t* unto them ... Deut 5:9
greater and mightier than *t* ... Deut 9:1
Take heed to *t* that thou offer ... Deut 12:13
Take heed to *t* that thou forsake ... Deut 12:19
Take heed to *t* that thou be not ... Deut 12:30
thereof, shalt thou take unto *t* ... Deut 20:14
go astray, and hide *t* from them ... Deut 22:1
thou mayest not hide *t* ... Deut 22:3
by the way, and hide *t* from them ... Deut 22:4
wherewith thou coverest *t* ... Deut 22:12
be, when thou wilt ease *t* abroad ... Deut 23:13
shalt not anoint *t* with the oil ... Deut 28:40
cut down for *t* there in the land ... Josh 17:15
Wash *t* therefore, and anoint thee, ... Ruth 3:3
but make not *t* known unto the man ... Ruth 3:3
redeem thou my right to *t* ... Ruth 4:6
take heed to *t* until the morning, ... 1Sa 19:2
in a secret place, and hide *t* ... 1Sa 19:2
be in me iniquity, slay me *t* ... 1Sa 20:8 859
t when the business was in hand ... 1Sa 20:19
from avenging *t* with thine own ... 1Sa 25:26
that then thou shalt bestir *t* ... 2Sa 5:24
to *t* thy people Israel to be a ... 2Sa 7:24
down on thy bed, and make *t* sick ... 2Sa 13:5
feign *t* to be a mourner, and put ... 2Sa 14:2
apparel, and anoint not *t* with oil ... 2Sa 14:2
thou *t* wouldest have set *t* ... 2Sa 18:13 859
wouldest have set *t* against me ... 2Sa 18:13
thou wilt shew *t* merciful ... 2Sa 22:26
man thou wilt shew *t* upright ... 2Sa 22:26
the pure thou wilt shew *t* pure ... 2Sa 22:27
thou wilt shew *t* unsavoury ... 2Sa 22:27
strong therefore, and shew *t* a man ... 1Kin 2:2
and whithersoever thou turnest *t* ... 1Kin 2:3
and hast not asked for *t* long life ... 1Kin 3:11
neither hast asked riches for *t* ... 1Kin 3:11
but hast asked for *t* ... 1Kin 3:11
Come home with me, and refresh *t* ... 1Kin 13:7
Arise, I pray thee, and disguise *t* ... 1Kin 14:2
why feignest thou *t* to be another ... 1Kin 14:6
hide *t* by the brook Cherith, that ... 1Kin 17:3
saying, Go, shew *t* unto Ahab ... 1Kin 18:1
said unto him, Go, strengthen *t* ... 1Kin 20:22
t hast decided it ... 1Kin 20:40
because thou hast sold *t* to work ... 1Kin 21:20
into an inner chamber to hide *t* ... 1Kin 22:25
hast humbled *t* before the LORD ... 2Kin 22:19
Now therefore advise *t* what word ... 1Chr 21:12
asked wisdom and knowledge for *t* ... 2Chr 1:11
into an inner chamber to hide *t* ... 2Chr 18:24
thou hast joined *t* with Ahaziah ... 2Chr 20:37
house, which were better than *t* ... 2Chr 21:13
and thou didst humble *t* before God ... 2Chr 34:27
thereof, and humbledst *t* before me ... 2Chr 34:27
Think not with *t* that thou shalt ... Est 4:13 5315
prepare *t* to the search of their ... Job 8:8
thou shewest *t* marvellous upon me ... Job 10:16
and dost thou restrain wisdom to *t* ... Job 15:8 413
Acquaint now *t* with him, and be at ... Job 22:21
hand thou opposest *t* against me ... Job 30:21
Deck *t* now with majesty and ... Job 40:10
array *t* with glory and beauty ... Job 40:10
lift up *t* because of the rage of ... Ps 7:6
why hidest thou *t* in times of ... Ps 10:1
thou wilt shew *t* merciful ... Ps 18:25
man thou wilt shew *t* upright ... Ps 18:25
the pure thou wilt shew *t* pure ... Ps 18:26
froward thou wilt shew *t* froward ... Ps 18:26
Stir up *t*, and awake to my ... Ps 35:23
Fret not *t* because of evildoers, ... Ps 37:1
Delight *t* also in the LORD ... Ps 37:4
fret not *t* because of him who ... Ps 37:7
fret not *t* in any wise to do evil ... Ps 37:8
thee, when thou doest well to *t* ... Ps 49:18
I was altogether such an one as *t* ... Ps 50:21
Why boastest thou *t* in mischief ... Ps 52:1
hide not *t* from my supplication ... Ps 55:1
O turn *t* to us again ... Ps 60:1
that thou madest strong for *t* ... Ps 80:15
man whom thou madest strong for *t* ... Ps 80:17
thou hast turned *t* from the ... Ps 85:3
wilt thou hide *t* for ever ... Ps 89:46
whom vengeance belongeth, shew *t* ... Ps 94:1
Lift up *t*, thou judge of the ... Ps 94:2
Who coverest *t* with light as with ... Ps 104:2
Do this now, my son, and deliver *t* ... Prov 6:3
go, humble *t*, and make sure thy ... Prov 6:3
Deliver *t* as a roe from the hand ... Prov 6:5
be wise, thou shalt be wise for *t* ... Prov 9:12
Fret not *t* because of evil men, ... Prov 24:19
and make it fit for *t* in the field ... Prov 24:27
Put not forth *t* in the presence ... Prov 25:6
Boast not *t* of to morrow ... Prov 27:1
done foolishly in lifting up *t* ... Prov 30:32
neither make *t* over wise ... Eccl 7:16
why shouldest thou destroy *t* ... Eccl 7:16
t likewise hast cursed others ... Eccl 7:22 859
hide *t* as it were for a little ... Is 26:20
at the lifting up of *t* the ... Is 33:3
thou art a God that hidest *t* ... Is 45:15
Shake *t* from the dust ... Is 52:2
loose *t* from the bands of thy ... Is 52:2
discovered *t* to another than me ... Is 57:8
didst debase *t* even unto hell ... Is 57:9
that thou hide not *t* from thine ... Is 58:7
shalt thou delight *t* in the LORD ... Is 58:14
to make *t* a glorious name ... Is 63:14
thou refrain *t* for these things ... Is 64:12
Which say, Stand by *t*, come not ... Is 65:5
thou not procured this unto *t* ... Jer 2:17
thou clothest *t* with crimson ... Jer 4:30
in vain shalt thou make *t* fair ... Jer 4:30
sackcloth, and wallow *t* in ashes ... Jer 6:26
And thou, even *t*, shalt ... Jer 17:4
I will make thee a terror to *t* ... Jer 20:4
because thou closest *t* in cedar ... Jer 22:15
buy it for *t* ... Jer 32:8
seekest thou great things for *t* ... Jer 45:5
furnish *t* to go into captivity ... Jer 46:19
how long wilt thou cut *t* ... Jer 47:5
put up *t* into thy scabbard, rest, ... Jer 47:6
give *t* no rest ... Lam 2:18
Thou hast covered *t* with a cloud ... Lam 3:44
be drunken, and shalt make *t* naked ... Lam 4:21
shut *t* within thine house ... Eze 3:24
madest to *t* images of men, and ... Eze 16:17
hast defiled *t* in thine idols ... Eze 22:4
in *t* in the sight of the heathen ... Eze 22:16
for whom thou didst wash *t* ... Eze 23:40
deckedst *t* with ornaments, ... Eze 23:40
thou hast lifted up *t* in height ... Eze 31:10
thou prepared, and prepare for *t* ... Eze 38:7
the king, Let thy gifts be to *t* ... Dan 5:17
But hast lifted up *t* against the ... Dan 5:23
to chasten *t* before thy God, thy ... Dan 10:12
O Israel, thou hast destroyed *t* ... Hos 13:9
Though thou exalt *t* as the eagle ... Obad 4
of Aphrah roll *t* in the dust ... Mic 1:10
Now gather *t* in troops, O ... Mic 5:1
make *t* many as the cankerworm, ... Nah 3:15
make *t* many as the locusts ... Nah 3:15
Deliver *t*, O Zion, that dwellest ... Zec 2:7
be the Son of God, cast *t* down ... Mt 4:6 4572
time, Thou shalt not forswear *t* ... Mt 5:33
shew *t* to the priest, and offer ... Mt 8:4 4572
shalt love thy neighbour as *t* ... Mt 19:19 4572
shalt love thy neighbour as *t* ... Mt 22:39 4572
buildest it in three days, save *t* ... Mt 27:40 4572
shew *t* to the priest, and offer ... Mk 1:44 4572
shalt love thy neighbour as *t* ... Mk 12:31 4572
Save *t*, and come down from the ... Mk 15:30 4572
of God, cast *t* down from hence ... Lk 4:9 4572
this proverb, Physician, heal *t* ... Lk 4:23 4572
shew *t* to the priest, and offer ... Lk 5:14 4572
when thou *t* beholdest not the ... Lk 6:42 846
unto him, Lord, trouble not *t* ... Lk 7:6
and thy neighbour as *t* ... Lk 10:27 4572
wherewith I may sup, and gird *t* ... Lk 17:8
be the king of the Jews, save *t* ... Lk 23:37 4572
saying, If thou be Christ, save *t* ... Lk 23:39 4572
What sayest thou of *t* ... Jn 1:22 4572
these things, shew *t* to the world ... Jn 7:4 4572
him, Thou bearest record of *t* ... Jn 8:13 4572
whom makest thou *t* ... Jn 8:53 4572
thou, being a man, makest *t* God ... Jn 10:33 4572
that thou wilt manifest *t* unto us ... Jn 14:22 4572
him, Sayest thou this thing of *t* ... Jn 18:34 1438
thou wast young, thou girdedst *t* ... Jn 21:18 4572
near, and join *t* to this chariot ... Acts 8:29
the angel said unto him, Gird *t* ... Acts 12:8
loud voice, saying, Do *t* no harm ... Acts 16:28 4572
purify *t* with them, and be at ... Acts 21:24
but that thou *t* also walkest ... Acts 21:24 846
by examining of whom *t* mayest ... Acts 24:8 846
Thou art permitted to speak for *t* ... Acts 26:1 4572
voice, Paul, thou art beside *t* ... Acts 26:24
another, thou condemnest *t* ... Rom 2:1 4572
heart treasurest up unto *t* wrath ... Rom 2:5 4572
art confident that thou *t* art a ... Rom 2:19 4572
another, teachest thou not *t* ... Rom 2:21 4572
shalt love thy neighbour as *t* ... Rom 13:9 1438
have it to *t* before God ... Rom 14:22 4572
shalt love thy neighbour as *t* ... Gal 5:14 1438
considering *t*, lest thou also be ... Gal 6:1 4572
to behave *t* in the house of God ... 1Ti 3:15
exercise *t* rather unto godliness ... 1Ti 4:7 4572
give *t* wholly to them ... 1Ti 4:15
Take heed unto *t*, and unto the ... 1Ti 4:16 4572
doing this thou shalt both save *t* ... 1Ti 4:16 4572
keep *t* pure ... 1Ti 5:22 4572
from such withdraw *t* ... 1Ti 6:5
Study to shew *t* approved unto God ... 2Ti 2:15 4572
In all things shewing *t* a pattern ... Titus 2:7 4572
shalt love thy neighbour as *t* ... Jas 2:8 4572

TIARAS See HOODS.

TIBERIAS (*ti-be'-re-as*) *A city on the Sea of Galilee.*
of Galilee, which is the sea of *T* ... Jn 6:1 5085
there came other boats from *T* ... Jn 6:23 5085
to the disciples at the sea of *T* ... Jn 21:1 5085

TIBERIUS (*ti-be'-re-us*) See CAESAR. *A Roman emperor.*
year of the reign of *T* Caesar ... Lk 3:1 5086

TIBHATH (*tib'-hath*) *A city in Aram Zobah.*
Likewise from *T*, and from Chun, ... 1Chr 18:8 2880

TIBNI (*tib'-ni*) *Son of Ginath.*
followed *T* the son of Ginath ... 1Kin 16:21 8402
that followed *T* the son of Ginath ... 1Kin 16:22 8402
so *T* died, and Omri reigned ... 1Kin 16:22 8402

TIDAL (*ti'-dal*) *A king of Goyim.*
of Elam, and *T* king of nations ... Gen 14:1 8413
with *T* king of nations, and ... Gen 14:9 8413

TIDINGS
when Laban heard the *t* of Jacob ... Gen 29:13 8088
the people heard these evil *t* ... Ex 33:4 1697
when she heard the *t* that the ark ... 1Sa 4:19 8052
told the *t* in the ears of the ... 1Sa 11:4 1697
they told him the *t* of the men of ... 1Sa 11:5 1697
upon Saul when he heard those *t* ... 1Sa 11:6 1697
woman alive, to bring *t* to Gath ... 1Sa 27:11
years old when the *t* came of Saul ... 2Sa 4:4 8052
thinking to have brought good *t* ... 2Sa 4:10 1319
have given him a reward for his *t* ... 2Sa 4:10 1309
that *t* came to David, saying, ... 2Sa 13:30 8052
me now run, and bear the king *t* ... 2Sa 18:19 1319
Thou shalt not bear *t* this day ... 2Sa 18:20 1309
but thou shalt bear *t* another day ... 2Sa 18:20 1319
but this day thou shalt bear no *t* ... 2Sa 18:20 1319
seeing that thou hast no *t* ready ... 2Sa 18:22 1309
be alone, there is *t* in his mouth ... 2Sa 18:25 1309
the king said, He also bringeth *t* ... 2Sa 18:26 1319
a good man, and cometh with good *t* ... 2Sa 18:27 1309
and Cushi said, *T*, my lord the ... 2Sa 18:31 1319
a valiant man, and bringest good *t* ... 1Kin 1:42 1319
Then *t* came to Joab ... 1Kin 2:28 8052
I am sent to thee with heavy *t* ... 1Kin 14:6
this day is a day of good *t* ... 2Kin 7:9 1309
to carry *t* unto their idols, and ... 1Chr 10:9 1319
He shall not be afraid of evil *t* ... Ps 112:7 8052
O Zion, that bringest good *t* ... Is 40:9 1319
O Jerusalem, that bringest good *t* ... Is 40:9 1319
one that bringeth good *t* ... Is 41:27 1319
feet of him that bringeth good *t* ... Is 52:7 1319
that bringeth good *t* of good ... Is 52:7 1319
me to preach good *t* unto the meek ... Is 61:1 1319
man who brought *t* to my father ... Jer 20:15 1319
Jerusalem heard of *t* of them ... Jer 37:5 8088
for they have heard evil *t* ... Jer 49:23 8052
that thou shalt answer, For the *t* ... Eze 21:7 8052
But *t* out of the east and out of ... Dan 11:44 8052
feet of him that bringeth good *t* ... Nah 1:15 1319
and to shew thee these glad *t* ... Lk 1:19 2097
I bring you good *t* of great joy ... Lk 2:10 2097
shewing the glad *t* of the kingdom ... Lk 8:1 2097
Then *t* of these things came unto ... Acts 11:22 3056
And we declare unto you glad *t* ... Acts 13:32 2097
t came unto the chief captain of ... Acts 21:31 5334

bring glad *t* of good things ... Rom 10:15 2097
brought us good *t* of your faith ... 1Th 3:6 2097

TIE
t the kine to the cart, and bring ... 1Sa 6:7 631
heart, and *t* them about thy neck ... Prov 6:21 6029

TIED
they *t* unto it a lace of blue, to ... Ex 39:31 5414
t them to the cart, and shut up ... 1Sa 6:10 631
voice of man, but horses *t* ... 2Kin 7:10 631
man, but horses *t*, and asses *t* ... 2Kin 7:10 631
ye shall find an ass *t*, and a colt ... Mt 21:2 1210
into it, ye shall find a colt *t* ... Mk 11:2 1210
found the colt *t* by the door ... Mk 11:4 1210
entering ye shall find a colt *t* ... Lk 19:30 1210

TIGLATH-PILESER (*tig''-lath-pi-le'-zur*) See TILGATH-PILNESER. *An Assyrian king.*
of Israel came *T* king of Assyria ... 2Kin 15:29 8407
messengers to *T* king of Assyria ... 2Kin 16:7 8407
to meet *T* king of Assyria ... 2Kin 16:10 8407

TIGRIS See HIDDEKEL.

TIKVAH (*tik'-vah*) See TIKVATH.
1. Father-in-law of Huldah.
the wife of Shallum the son of *T* ... 2Kin 22:14 8616
2. Father of Jahaziah.
Jahaziah the son of *T* were ... Ezr 10:15 8616

TIKVATH (*tik'-vath*) See TIKVAH. *Same as Tikvah 1.*
the wife of Shallum the son of *T* ... 2Chr 34:22 8616

TIL
t the Assyrian founded it for ... Is 23:13

TILE
also, son of man, take thee a *t* ... Eze 4:1 3843

TILGATH-PILNESER (*til''-gath-pil-ne'-zur*) See TIGLATH-PILESER. *Same as Tiglath-pileser.*
whom *T* king of Assyria carried ... 1Chr 5:6 8407
the spirit of *T* king of Assyria, ... 1Chr 5:26 8407
T king of Assyria came unto him, ... 2Chr 28:20 8407

TILING
let him down through the *t* with ... Lk 5:19 2766

TILL
was not a man to *t* the ground ... Gen 2:5 5647
t thou return unto the ground ... Gen 3:19 5704
to *t* the ground from whence he ... Gen 3:23 5647
any thing *t* thou be come thither ... Gen 19:22 5704
t they roll the stone from the ... Gen 29:8
house, *t* Shelah my son be grown ... Gen 38:11 5704
give me a pledge, *t* thou send it ... Gen 38:17 5704
t thy people pass over, O LORD, ... Ex 15:16 5704
t the people pass over, which ... Ex 15:16 5704
no man leave of it *t* the morning ... Ex 16:19 5704
And they laid it up *t* the morning ... Ex 16:24 5704
t Moses had done speaking with ... Ex 34:33
then they journeyed not *t* the day ... Ex 40:37 5704
the people journeyed not *t* Miriam ... Num 12:15 5704
them with stones, *t* they die ... Deut 17:5
thee, *t* thou be destroyed ... Deut 28:45 5704
t all the people that were men of ... Josh 5:6 5704
in the camp, *t* they were whole ... Josh 5:8 5704
us) *t* we have drawn them from the ... Josh 8:6 5704
t they were consumed, that the ... Josh 10:20 5704
they tarried *t* they were ashamed ... Judg 3:25 5704
t thou come unto Gaza, and left no ... Judg 6:4 5704
even *t* thou come to Minnith, even ... Judg 11:33 5704
And Samson lay *t* midnight, and ... Judg 16:3 5704
her lord was, *t* it was light ... Judg 19:26 5704
abode there *t* even before God, and ... Judg 21:2 5704
tarry for them *t* they were grown ... Ruth 1:13 5704
t I come to thee, and shew thee ... 1Sa 10:8 5704
not sit down *t* he come hither ... 1Sa 16:11 5704
t I know what God will do for me ... 1Sa 22:3 5704
or ought else, *t* the sun be down ... 2Sa 3:35 6440
shall *t* the land for him, and thou ... 2Sa 9:10 5647
away dung, *t* it be all gone ... 1Kin 14:10 5704
t the blood gushed out upon them ... 1Kin 18:28 5704
they urged him *t* he was ashamed ... 2Kin 2:17 5704
he sat on her knees *t* noon ... 2Kin 4:20 5704
if we tarry *t* the morning light ... 2Kin 7:9 5704
t he had destroyed him, according ... 2Kin 10:17 5704
t thou have consumed them ... 2Kin 13:17 5704
Syria *t* thou hadst consumed it ... 2Kin 13:19 5704
t he had filled Jerusalem from ... 2Kin 21:16 5704
helped, *t* he was strong ... 2Chr 26:15
t the work was ended, and until ... 2Chr 29:34 5704
his people, *t* there was no remedy ... 2Chr 36:16 5704
t there stood up a priest with ... Ezr 2:63 5704
t the matter came to Darius ... Ezr 5:5 5705
with us *t* thou hadst consumed us ... Ezr 9:14 5704
me over *t* I come into Judah ... Neh 2:7 5704
t we come in the midst among them ... Neh 4:11 5704
the morning *t* the stars appeared ... Neh 4:21 5704
t there stood up a priest with ... Neh 7:65 5704
not be opened *t* after the sabbath ... Neh 13:19 5704
nor let me alone *t* I swallow down ... Job 7:19 5704
T he fill thy mouth with laughing ... Job 8:21 5704
t he shall accomplish, as an ... Job 14:6 5704
t the heavens be no more, they ... Job 14:12 5704
will I wait, *t* my change come ... Job 14:14 5704
t I die I will not remove mine ... Job 27:5 5704
Elihu had waited *t* Job had spoken ... Job 32:4
his wickedness *t* thou find none ... Ps 10:15
I turn again *t* they were consumed ... Ps 18:37 5704
t every one submit himself with ... Ps 68:30
T a dart strike through his liver ... Prov 7:23 5704
man keepeth it in *t* afterwards ... Prov 29:11
t I might see what was that good ... Eccl 2:3 5704
nor awake my love, *t* he please ... Song 2:7 5704
nor awake my love, *t* he please ... Song 3:5 5704
t there be no place, that they ... Is 5:8 5704
until night, *t* wine inflame them ... Is 5:11
not be purged from you *t* ye die ... Is 22:14 5704
t ye be left as a beacon upon the ... Is 30:17
I reckoned *t* morning, that, as a ... Is 38:13 5704
t he have set judgment in the ... Is 42:4 5704
t he establish, and *t* he make ... Is 62:7 5704
in Tophet, *t* there be no place ... Jer 7:32
them, *t* I have consumed them ... Jer 9:16 5704
t there be no place to bury ... Jer 19:11
t he have performed the thoughts ... Jer 23:20 5704
t they be consumed from off the ... Jer 24:10 5704
and they shall *t* it, and dwell ... Jer 27:11 5647
will destroy *t* they have enough ... Jer 49:9 5704
them, *t* I have consumed them ... Jer 49:37 5704
t he had cast them out from his ... Jer 52:3 5704
put him in prison *t* the day of ... Jer 52:11 5704
T the LORD look down, and behold ... Lam 3:50 5704
t thou hast ended the days of thy ... Eze 4:8 5704
for from my youth up even *t* now ... Eze 4:14 5704
t I have caused my fury to rest ... Eze 24:13 5704
t iniquity was found in thee ... Eze 28:15 5704
t ye have scattered them abroad ... Eze 34:21 5704
t the buriers have buried it in ... Eze 39:15 5704
And ye shall eat fat *t* ye be full ... Eze 39:19
drink blood *t* ye be drunken, of ... Eze 39:19
t a man come over against Hamath ... Eze 47:20 5704
before me, *t* the time be changed ... Dan 2:9 5704
Thou sawest *t* that a stone was ... Dan 2:34 5704
t seven times pass over him ... Dan 4:23 5704
t thou know that the most High ... Dan 4:25 5704
t his hairs were grown like ... Dan 4:33 5704
t he knew that the most high God ... Dan 5:21 5704
he laboured *t* the going down of ... Dan 6:14 5704
I beheld *t* the wings thereof were ... Dan 7:4 5704
I beheld *t* the thrones were cast ... Dan 7:9 5704
I beheld even *t* the beast was ... Dan 7:11 5704
at all, *t* three whole weeks were ... Dan 10:3 5704
shall prosper *t* the indignation ... Dan 11:36 5704
sealed *t* the time of the end ... Dan 12:9 5704
But go thou thy way *t* the end be ... Dan 12:13
t they acknowledge their offence, ... Hos 5:15 5704
t he come and rain righteousness ... Hos 10:12 5704
not have stolen *t* they had enough ... Obad 5
t he might see what would become ... Jonah 4:5 5704
gnaw not the bones *t* the morrow ... Zeph 3:3
knew her not *t* she had brought ... Mt 1:25 2193
t it came and stood over where the ... Mt 2:9 2193
T heaven and earth pass, one jot ... Mt 5:18 2193
from the law, *t* all be fulfilled ... Mt 5:18 2193
t thou hast paid the uttermost ... Mt 5:26 2193
there abide *t* ye go thence ... Mt 10:11 2193
Israel, *t* the Son of man be come ... Mt 10:23 2193
t he send forth judgment unto ... Mt 12:20 2193
of meal, *t* the whole was leavened ... Mt 13:33 2193
t they see the Son of man coming ... Mt 16:28 2193
t seven times? ... Mt 18:21 2193
prison, *t* he should pay the debt ... Mt 18:30 2193
t he should pay all that was due ... Mt 18:34 2193
t I make thine enemies thy ... Mt 22:44 2193
t ye shall say, Blessed is he ... Mt 23:39 2193
t all these things be fulfilled ... Mt 24:34 2193
there abide *t* ye depart from that ... Mk 6:10 2193
t they have seen the kingdom of ... Mk 9:1 2193
t the Son of man were risen from ... Mk 9:9
t I make thine enemies thy ... Mk 12:36 2193
t all these things be done ... Mk 13:30 3360
was in the deserts *t* the day of ... Lk 1:80 2193
t they see the kingdom of God ... Lk 9:27 2193
I straitened *t* it be accomplished ... Lk 12:50 2193
t thou hast paid the very last ... Lk 12:59 2193
t I shall dig about it, and dung ... Lk 13:8 2193
of meal, *t* the whole was leavened ... Lk 13:21 2193
and seek diligently *t* she find it ... Lk 15:8 2193
t I have eaten and drunken ... Lk 17:8 2193
said unto them, Occupy *t* I come ... Lk 19:13 2193
T I make thine enemies thy ... Lk 20:43 2193
not pass away, *t* all be fulfilled ... Lk 21:32 2193
t thou hast denied me thrice ... Jn 13:38 2193
If I will that he tarry *t* I come ... Jn 21:22 2193
If I will that he tarry *t* I come ... Jn 21:23 2193
T another king arose, which knew ... Acts 7:18
the cities, *t* he came to Caesarea ... Acts 8:40 2193
even *t* break of day, so he ... Acts 20:11 891
t we were out of the city ... Acts 21:5 2193
nor drink *t* they had killed Paul ... Acts 23:12 2193
nor drink *t* they have killed him ... Acts 23:21 2193
kept *t* I might send him to Caesar ... Acts 25:21 2193
prophets, from morning *t* evening ... Acts 28:23 2193
shew the Lord's death *t* he come ... 1Cor 11:26
t he hath put all enemies under ... 1Cor 15:25
t the seed should come to whom ... Gal 3:19
T we all come in the unity of the ... Eph 4:13 3360
without offence *t* the day of ... Phil 1:10 1519
T I come, give attendance to ... 1Ti 4:13 2193
t his enemies be made his ... Heb 10:13 2193
have already hold fast *t* I come ... Rev 2:25 891
t we have sealed the servants of ... Rev 7:3 891
t the seven plagues of the seven ... Rev 15:8 891
t the thousand years should be ... Rev 20:3 891

TILLAGE
did the work of the field for *t* ... 1Chr 27:26 5656
tithes in all the cities of our *t* ... Neh 10:37 5656
Much food is in the *t* of the poor ... Prov 13:23 5215

TILLED
turn unto you, and ye shall be *t* ... Eze 36:9 5647
And the desolate land shall be *t* ... Eze 36:34 5647

TILLER
but Cain was a *t* of the ground ... Gen 4:2 5647

TILLEST
When thou *t* the ground, it shall ... Gen 4:12 5647

TILLETH
He that *t* his land shall be ... Prov 12:11 5647
He that *t* his land shall have ... Prov 28:19 5647

TILON (*ti'-lon*) *A descendant of Judah.*
Rinnah, Ben-hanan, and *T* ... 1Chr 4:20 8436

TIMAEUS (*ti-me'-us*) See BARTIMAEUS. *Father of Bartimaeus.*
blind Bartimaeus, the son of *T* ... Mk 10:46 5090

TIMBER
to set them, and in carving of *t* ... Ex 31:5 6086
the *t* thereof, and all the morter ... Lev 14:45 6086
to hew *t* like unto the Sidonians ... 1Kin 5:6 6086
thy desire concerning *t* of cedar ... 1Kin 5:8 6086
of cedar, and concerning *t* of fir ... 1Kin 5:8 6086
so they prepared *t* and stones to ... 1Kin 5:18 6086
on the house with *t* of cedar ... 1Kin 6:10 6086
the *t* thereof, wherewith Baasha ... 1Kin 15:22 6086
and hewers of stone, and to buy *t* ... 2Kin 12:12 6086
builders, and masons, and to buy *t* ... 2Kin 22:6 6086
t of cedars, with masons and ... 1Chr 14:1 6086
t also and stone have I prepared ... 1Chr 22:14 6086
hewers and workers of stone and *t* ... 1Chr 22:15 6086
can skill to cut *t* in Lebanon ... 2Chr 2:8 6086
Even to prepare me *t* in abundance ... 2Chr 2:9 6086
servants, the hewers that cut *t* ... 2Chr 2:10 6086
brass, in iron, in stone, and in *t* ... 2Chr 2:14 6086
the *t* thereof, wherewith Baasha ... 2Chr 16:6 6086
t for couplings, and to floor the ... 2Chr 34:11 6086
t is laid in the walls, and this ... Ezr 5:8 636
great stones, and a row of new *t* ... Ezr 6:4 636
let *t* be pulled down from his ... Ezr 6:11 636
that he may give me *t* to make ... Neh 2:8 6086
shall lay thy stones and thy *t* ... Eze 26:12 6086
beam out of the *t* shall answer it ... Hab 2:11 6086
consume it with the *t* thereof ... Zec 5:4 6086

TIMBREL
of Aaron, took a *t* in her hand ... Ex 15:20 8596
They take the *t* and harp, and ... Job 21:12 8596
a psalm, and bring hither the *t* ... Ps 81:2 8596
sing praises unto him with the *t* ... Ps 149:3 8596
Praise him with the *t* and dance ... Ps 150:4 8596

TIMBRELS
women went out after her with *t* ... Ex 15:20 8596
came out to meet him with *t* ... Judg 11:34 8596
harps, and on psalteries, and on *t* ... 2Sa 6:5 8596
and with psalteries, and with *t* ... 1Chr 13:8 8596
were the damsels playing with *t* ... Ps 68:25 8608

TIME
in process of *t* it came to pass, ... Gen 4:3 3117
at this set *t* in the next year ... Gen 17:21
thee according to the *t* of life ... Gen 18:10 6256
At the *t* appointed I will return ... Gen 18:14
thee, according to the *t* of life ... Gen 18:14 6256
at the set *t* of which God had ... Gen 21:2
And it came to pass at that *t* ... Gen 21:22 6256
out of heaven the second *t* ... Gen 22:15 6256
of water at the *t* of the evening ... Gen 24:11 6256
even the *t* that women go out to ... Gen 24:11 6256
when he had been there a long *t* ... Gen 26:8 3117
neither is it *t* that the cattle ... Gen 29:7 6256
Now this *t* will my husband be ... Gen 29:34 6471
answer for me in *t* to come ... Gen 30:33 3117
it came to pass at the *t* that the ... Gen 31:10 6256
And it came to pass at that *t* ... Gen 38:1 6256
in process of *t* the daughter of ... Gen 38:12 3117
to pass in the *t* of her travail ... Gen 38:27 6256
it came to pass from the *t* that ... Gen 39:5
And it came to pass about this *t* ... Gen 39:11 3117
he slept and dreamed the second *t* ... Gen 41:5
now we had returned this second *t* ... Gen 43:10 6471
at the first *t* are we brought in ... Gen 43:18 8462
down at the first *t* to buy food ... Gen 43:20 8462
the *t* drew nigh that Israel must ... Gen 47:29 3117
it came to pass in process of *t* ... Ex 2:23 3117
hardened his heart at this *t* also ... Ex 8:32 6471
And the LORD appointed a set *t* ... Ex 9:5
For I will at this *t* send all my ... Ex 9:14 6471
to morrow about this *t* I will ... Ex 9:18 6256
unto them, I have sinned this *t* ... Ex 9:27 6471
thy son asketh thee in *t* to come ... Ex 13:14 4279
shall pay for the loss of his *t* ... Ex 21:19 7674
to push with his horn in *t* past ... Ex 21:29
ox hath used to push in *t* past ... Ex 21:36
in the *t* appointed of the month ... Ex 23:15
in the *t* of the month Abib ... Ex 34:18 4150
in earing *t* and in harvest thou ... Ex 34:21
it shall be washed the second *t* ... Lev 13:58
out of the *t* of her separation ... Lev 15:25 6256
beyond the *t* of her separation ... Lev 15:25 6256
beside the other in her life *t* ... Lev 18:18
may the Levites redeem at any *t* ... Lev 25:32
according to the *t* of an hired ... Lev 25:50
shall reach unto the sowing *t* ... Lev 26:5
ye blow an alarm the second *t* ... Num 10:6
Now the *t* was the *t* of the ... Num 13:20 3117
we have dwelt in Egypt a long *t* ... Num 20:15 3117
king of the Moabites at that *t* ... Num 22:4 6256
according to this *t* it shall be ... Num 23:23 6256
what *t* the fire devoured two ... Num 26:10
anger was kindled the same *t* ... Num 32:10 3117
t come without the border of the ... Num 35:26
And I spake unto you at that *t* ... Deut 1:9 6256
I charged your judges at that *t* ... Deut 1:16 6256
I commanded you at that *t* all the ... Deut 1:18
giants dwelt therein in old *t* ... Deut 2:20
we took all his cities at that *t* ... Deut 2:34 6256

Context	Reference	Strong's
we took all his cities at that *t*	Deut 3:4	6256
we took at that *t* out of the hand	Deut 3:8	6256
which we possessed at that *t*	Deut 3:12	6256
And I commanded you at that *t*	Deut 3:18	6256
And I commanded Joshua at that *t*	Deut 3:21	6256
And I besought the LORD at that *t*	Deut 3:23	6256
at that *t* to teach you statutes	Deut 4:14	6256
between the LORD and you at that *t*	Deut 5:5	6256
thy son asketh thee in *t* to come	Deut 6:20	4279
hearkened unto me at that *t* also	Deut 9:19	6471
prayed for Aaron also the same *t*	Deut 9:20	6256
At that *t* the LORD said unto me,	Deut 10:1	6256
At that *t* the LORD separated the	Deut 10:8	6256
mount, according to the first *t*	Deut 10:10	3117
hearkened unto me at that *t* also	Deut 10:10	6471
the seven weeks from such *t* as	Deut 16:9	
whom he hated not in *t* past	Deut 19:4	
as he hated him not in *t* past	Deut 19:6	
which they of old *t* have set in	Deut 19:14	
shalt besiege a city a long *t*	Deut 20:19	3117
their foot shall slide in due *t*	Deut 32:35	6256
the *t* of shutting of the gate	Josh 2:5	
his banks all the *t* of harvest	Josh 3:15	3117
ask their fathers in *t* to come	Josh 4:6	4279
ask their fathers in *t* to come	Josh 4:21	4279
At that *t* the LORD said unto	Josh 5:2	6256
children of Israel the second *t*	Josh 5:2	
it came to pass at the seventh *t*	Josh 6:16	6471
And Joshua adjured them at that *t*	Josh 6:26	6256
at a *t* appointed, before the	Josh 8:14	
it came to pass at the *t* of the	Josh 10:27	6256
land did Joshua take at one *t*	Josh 10:42	6471
for to morrow about this *t* will I	Josh 11:6	6256
And Joshua at that *t* turned back	Josh 11:10	6256
war a long *t* with all those kings	Josh 11:18	3117
at that *t* came Joshua, and cut off	Josh 11:21	6256
In *t* to come your children might	Josh 22:24	4279
say to our children in *t* to come	Josh 22:27	4279
to our generations in *t* to come	Josh 22:28	4279
it came to pass a long *t* after	Josh 23:1	3117
other side of the flood in old *t*	Josh 24:2	5769
at that *t* about ten thousand men	Judg 3:29	6256
she judged Israel at that *t*	Judg 4:4	6256
The trees went forth on a *t* to	Judg 9:8	
you in the *t* of your tribulation	Judg 10:14	6256
it came to pass in process of *t*	Judg 11:4	3117
ye not recover them within that *t*	Judg 11:26	6256
there fell at that *t* of the	Judg 12:6	6256
nor would as at this *t* have told	Judg 13:23	6256
for at that *t* the Philistines had	Judg 14:4	6256
after a *t* he returned to take her	Judg 14:8	3117
in the *t* of wheat harvest, that	Judg 15:1	3117
all the *t* that the house of God	Judg 18:31	
that *t* out of the cities twenty	Judg 20:15	
And Benjamin came again at that *t*	Judg 21:14	6256
did not give unto them at this *t*	Judg 21:22	6256
Israel departed thence at that *t*	Judg 21:24	
this was the manner in former *t*	Ruth 4:7	6440
when the *t* was that Elkanah	1Sa 1:4	3117
when the *t* was come about after	1Sa 1:20	3117
And it came to pass at that *t*	1Sa 3:2	3117
called Samuel again the third *t*	1Sa 3:8	
about the *t* of her death the	1Sa 4:20	6256
that the *t* was long	1Sa 7:2	3117
for about this *t* ye shall find	1Sa 9:13	3117
To morrow about this *t* I will	1Sa 9:16	6256
for unto this *t* hath it been kept	1Sa 9:24	4150
by that *t* the sun be hot, ye	1Sa 11:9	
according to the set *t* that	1Sa 13:8	
t with the children of Israel	1Sa 14:18	3117
the Philistines before that *t*	1Sa 14:21	8032
the *t* when Merab Saul's daughter	1Sa 18:19	6256
sent messengers again the third *t*	1Sa 19:21	
my father about to morrow any *t*	1Sa 20:12	6256
at the *t* appointed with David	1Sa 20:35	
I will not smite him the second *t*	1Sa 26:8	
the *t* that David dwelt in the	1Sa 27:7	
the *t* that David was king in	2Sa 2:11	
Also in *t* past, when Saul was	2Sa 5:2	
dwelt in any house since the *t*	2Sa 7:6	3117
as since the *t* that I commanded	2Sa 7:11	3117
at the *t* when kings go forth to	2Sa 11:1	6256
had a long *t* mourned for the dead	2Sa 14:2	3117
when he sent again the second *t*	2Sa 14:29	
hath given is not good at this *t*	2Sa 17:7	6471
set *t* which he had appointed him	2Sa 20:5	
They were wont to speak in old *t*	2Sa 20:18	
hundred, whom he slew at one *t*	2Sa 23:8	6471
t unto the cave of Adullam	2Sa 23:13	
the midst of a pit in *t* of snow	2Sa 23:20	3117
morning even to the *t* appointed	2Sa 24:15	6256
displeased him at any *t* in saying	1Kin 1:6	3117
not at this *t* put thee to death	1Kin 2:26	3117
at that *t* Solomon held a feast,	1Kin 8:65	6256
appeared to Solomon the second *t*	1Kin 9:2	
it came to pass at that *t* when	1Kin 11:29	6256
the *t* that Solomon reigned in	1Kin 11:42	3117
At that *t* Abijah the son of	1Kin 14:1	6256
Nevertheless in the *t* of his old	1Kin 15:23	6256
they prophesied until the *t* of	1Kin 18:29	
And he said, Do it the second *t*	1Kin 18:34	
And they did it the second *t*	1Kin 18:34	
And he said, Do it the third *t*	1Kin 18:34	
And they did it the third *t*	1Kin 18:34	
it came to pass at the *t* of the	1Kin 18:36	
it came to pass at the seventh *t*	1Kin 18:44	
of them by to morrow about this *t*	1Kin 19:2	6256
the LORD came again the second *t*	1Kin 19:7	
unto thee to morrow about this *t*	1Kin 20:6	6256
went out of Samaria the same *t*	2Kin 3:6	3117
according to the *t* of life	2Kin 4:16	6256
her, according to the *t* of life	2Kin 4:17	6256
Is it a *t* to receive money, and to	2Kin 5:26	6256
To morrow about this *t* shall a	2Kin 7:1	6256
this *t* in the gate of Samaria	2Kin 7:18	6256
Libnah revolted at the same *t*	2Kin 8:22	6256
a letter the second *t* to them	2Kin 10:6	
me to Jezreel by to morrow this *t*	2Kin 10:6	6256
the *t* that Jehu reigned over	2Kin 10:36	3117
At that *t* Rezin king of Syria	2Kin 16:6	6256
At that *t* did Hezekiah cut off	2Kin 18:16	6256
At that *t* Berodach-baladan, the	2Kin 20:12	6256
At that *t* the servants of	2Kin 24:10	6256
was the ruler over them in *t* past	1Chr 9:20	6440
days from *t* to *t* with them	1Chr 9:25	6256
And moreover in *t* past, even when	1Chr 11:2	8543
hundred slain by him at one *t*	1Chr 11:11	6471
For at that *t* day by day there	1Chr 12:22	6256
since the *t* that I commanded	1Chr 17:10	3117
at the *t* that kings go out to	1Chr 20:1	6256
at which *t* Sibbechai the	1Chr 20:4	227
At that *t* when David saw that the	1Chr 21:28	6256
son of David king the second *t*	1Chr 29:22	
the *t* that he reigned over Israel	1Chr 29:27	3117
Also at the same *t* Solomon kept	2Chr 7:8	6256
were brought under at that *t*	2Chr 13:18	6256
offered unto the LORD the same *t*	2Chr 15:11	3117
at that *t* Hanani the seer came to	2Chr 16:7	6256
some of the people the same *t*	2Chr 16:10	6256
about the *t* of the sun going down	2Chr 18:34	6256
The same *t* also did Libnah revolt	2Chr 21:10	6256
to pass, that in process of *t*	2Chr 21:19	3117
that at what *t* the chest was	2Chr 24:11	6256
Now after the *t* that Amaziah did	2Chr 25:27	6256
At that *t* did king Ahaz send unto	2Chr 28:16	6256
in the *t* of his distress did he	2Chr 28:22	6256
they could not keep it at that *t*	2Chr 30:3	6256
t in such sort as it was written	2Chr 30:5	
for since the *t* of Solomon the	2Chr 30:26	3117
kept the passover at that *t*	2Chr 35:17	6256
side the river, and at such a *t*	Ezr 4:10	
side the river, and at such a *t*	Ezr 4:11	
sedition within the same of old *t*	Ezr 4:15	3118
the river, Peace, and at such a *t*	Ezr 4:17	
t hath made insurrection against	Ezr 4:19	3118
At the same *t* came to them Tatnai	Ezr 5:3	2166
since that *t* even until now hath	Ezr 5:16	116
perfect peace, and at such a *t*	Ezr 7:12	
the weight was written at that *t*	Ezr 8:34	6256
it is a *t* of much rain, and we are	Ezr 10:13	6256
and I set him a *t*	Neh 2:6	2165
it came to pass from that *t* forth	Neh 4:16	3117
Likewise at the same *t* said I	Neh 4:22	6256
Moreover from the *t* that I was	Neh 5:14	3117
(though at that *t* I had not set	Neh 6:1	6256
me in like manner the fifth *t*	Neh 6:5	6471
in the *t* of their trouble, when	Neh 9:27	6256
since the *t* of the kings of	Neh 9:32	3117
at that *t* were some appointed	Neh 12:44	3117
But in all this *t* was not I at	Neh 13:6	
From that *t* forth came they no	Neh 13:21	6256
gathered together the second *t*	Est 2:19	
holdest thy peace at this *t*	Est 4:14	6256
the kingdom for such a *t* as this	Est 4:14	6256
at that *t* in the third month	Est 8:9	6256
to their appointed *t* every year	Est 9:27	2165
What *t* they wax warm, they vanish	Job 6:17	6256
an appointed *t* to man upon earth	Job 7:1	6635
who shall set me a *t* to plead	Job 9:19	
thou wouldest appoint me a set *t*	Job 14:13	
of my appointed *t* will I wait	Job 14:14	6635
be accomplished before his *t*	Job 15:32	3117
Which were cut down out of *t*	Job 22:16	6256
wilderness in former *t* desolate	Job 30:3	570
reserved against the *t* of trouble	Job 38:23	6256
Knowest thou the *t* when the wild	Job 39:1	6256
or knowest thou the *t* when they	Job 39:2	6256
What *t* she lifteth up herself on	Job 39:18	6256
than in the *t* that their corn	Ps 4:7	6256
oven in the *t* of thine anger	Ps 21:9	6256
For in the *t* of trouble he shall	Ps 27:5	3117
in a *t* when thou mayest be found	Ps 32:6	6256
not be ashamed in the evil *t*	Ps 37:19	6256
strength in the *t* of trouble	Ps 37:39	6256
will deliver him in *t* of trouble	Ps 41:1	3117
What *t* I am afraid, I will trust	Ps 56:3	3117
thee, O LORD, in an acceptable *t*	Ps 69:13	6256
me not off in the *t* of old age	Ps 71:9	6256
many a *t* turned he his anger away	Ps 78:38	
in the *t* appointed, on our solemn	Ps 81:3	
but their *t* should have endured	Ps 81:15	6256
Remember how short my *t* is	Ps 89:47	
for the *t* to favour her, yea, the	Ps 102:13	6256
to favour her, yea, the set *t*	Ps 102:13	
Until the *t* that his word came	Ps 105:19	6256
of the LORD from this *t* forth	Ps 113:2	
bless the LORD from this *t* forth	Ps 115:18	6258
It is *t* for thee, LORD, to work	Ps 119:126	6256
thy coming in from this *t* forth	Ps 121:8	
Many a *t* have they afflicted me	Ps 129:1	7227
Many a *t* have they afflicted me	Ps 129:2	7227
cold of snow in the *t* of harvest	Prov 25:13	3117
in an unfaithful man in *t* of	Prov 25:19	3117
and she shall rejoice in *t* to come	Prov 31:25	3117
it hath been already of old *t*	Eccl 1:10	
a *t* to every purpose under the	Eccl 3:1	6256
A *t* to be born, and a *t* to die	Eccl 3:2	6256
a *t* to plant, and a *t* to pluck	Eccl 3:2	6256
A *t* to kill, and a *t* to heal	Eccl 3:3	6256
a *t* to break down	Eccl 3:3	6256
and a *t* to build up	Eccl 3:3	6256
A *t* to weep, and a *t* to laugh	Eccl 3:4	6256
a *t* to mourn, and a *t* to dance	Eccl 3:4	6256
A *t* to cast away stones, and a	Eccl 3:5	6256
a *t* to gather stones together	Eccl 3:5	6256
a *t* to embrace	Eccl 3:5	6256
a *t* to refrain from embracing	Eccl 3:5	6256
A *t* to get, and a *t* to lose	Eccl 3:6	6256
t to keep, and a *t* to cast away	Eccl 3:6	6256
A *t* to rend, and a *t* to sew	Eccl 3:7	6256
a *t* to keep silence	Eccl 3:7	6256
and a *t* to speak	Eccl 3:7	6256
A *t* to love, and a *t* to hate	Eccl 3:8	6256
a *t* of war, and a *t* of peace	Eccl 3:8	6256
every thing beautiful in his *t*	Eccl 3:11	6256
for there is a *t* there for every	Eccl 3:17	6256
shouldest thou die before thy *t*	Eccl 7:17	6256
man's heart discerneth both *t*	Eccl 8:5	6256
to every purpose there is *t*	Eccl 8:6	6256
there is a *t* wherein one man	Eccl 8:9	6256
but *t* and chance happeneth to them	Eccl 9:11	6256
For man also knoweth not his *t*	Eccl 9:12	6256
sons of men snared in an evil *t*	Eccl 9:12	6256
the *t* of the singing of birds is	Song 2:12	6256
t to recover the remnant of his	Is 11:11	6256
her *t* is near to come, and her	Is 13:22	6256
concerning Moab since that *t*	Is 16:13	227
In that *t* shall the present be	Is 18:7	6256
At the same *t* spake the LORD by	Is 20:2	6256
near the *t* of her delivery	Is 26:17	
From the *t* that it goeth forth it	Is 28:19	1767
may be for the *t* to come for ever	Is 30:8	3117
also in the *t* of trouble	Is 33:2	6256
At that *t* Merodach-baladan, the	Is 39:1	6256
I have long *t* holden my peace	Is 42:14	
hearken and hear for the *t* to come	Is 42:23	268
have not I told thee from that *t*	Is 44:8	227
hath declared this from ancient *t*	Is 45:21	
who hath told it from that *t*	Is 45:21	227
thee new things from this *t*	Is 48:6	6258
from that *t* that thine ear was	Is 48:8	227
from the *t* that it was, there am	Is 48:16	6256
In an acceptable *t* have I heard	Is 49:8	6256
the LORD will hasten it in his *t*	Is 60:22	6256
LORD came unto me the second *t*	Jer 1:13	
For of old *t* I have broken thy	Jer 2:20	
but in the *t* of their trouble	Jer 2:27	6256
save thee in the *t* of thy trouble	Jer 2:28	6256
thou not from this *t* cry unto me	Jer 3:4	6258
At that *t* they shall call	Jer 3:17	6256
At that *t* shall it be said to	Jer 4:11	6256
at the *t* that I visit them they	Jer 6:15	6256
At that *t*, saith the LORD, they	Jer 8:1	6256
observe the *t* of their coming	Jer 8:7	6256
in the *t* of their visitation they	Jer 8:12	6256
for a *t* of health, and behold	Jer 8:15	6256
in the *t* of their visitation they	Jer 10:15	6256
at all in the *t* of their trouble	Jer 11:12	6256
t that they cry unto me for their	Jer 11:14	6256
LORD came unto me the second *t*	Jer 13:3	
saviour thereof in *t* of trouble	Jer 14:8	6256
for the *t* of healing, and behold	Jer 14:19	6256
thee well in the *t* of evil	Jer 15:11	6256
of evil and in the *t* of affliction	Jer 15:11	6256
with them in the *t* of thine anger	Jer 18:23	6256
until the very *t* of his land come	Jer 27:7	6256
it is even the *t* of Jacob's	Jer 30:7	6256
At the same *t*, saith the LORD,	Jer 31:1	6256
came unto Jeremiah the second *t*	Jer 33:1	
In those days, and at that *t*	Jer 33:15	6256
vineyards and fields at the same *t*	Jer 39:10	3117
he hath passed the *t* appointed	Jer 46:17	
the *t* of their visitation	Jer 46:21	6256
the *t* that I will visit him	Jer 49:8	6256
and who will appoint me the *t*	Jer 49:19	
In those days, and in that *t*	Jer 50:4	6256
the sickle in the *t* of harvest	Jer 50:16	6256
In those days, and in that *t*	Jer 50:20	6256
the *t* of their visitation	Jer 50:27	6256
the *t* that I will visit thee	Jer 50:31	6256
and who will appoint me the *t*	Jer 50:44	
for this is the *t* of the LORD's	Jer 51:6	6256
in the *t* of their visitation they	Jer 51:18	6256
it is *t* to thresh her	Jer 51:33	6256
the *t* of her harvest shall come	Jer 51:33	6256
for ever, and forsake us so long *t*	Lam 5:20	3117
from *t* to *t* shalt thou eat it	Eze 4:10	6256
from *t* to *t* shalt thou drink	Eze 4:11	6256
the *t* is come, the day of trouble	Eze 7:7	6256
The *t* is come, the day draweth	Eze 7:12	6256
thy *t* was the *t* of love	Eze 16:8	6256
as at the *t* of thy reproach of	Eze 16:57	6256
the sword be doubled the third *t*	Eze 21:14	
midst of it, that her *t* may come	Eze 22:3	6256
the pit, with the people of old *t*	Eze 26:20	
In the *t* when thou shalt be	Eze 27:34	6256
it shall be the *t* of the heathen	Eze 30:3	6256
sword in the *t* of their calamity	Eze 35:5	6256
in the *t* that their iniquity had	Eze 35:5	6256
that at the same *t* shall things	Eze 38:10	3117
t by my servants the prophets of	Eze 38:17	3117
shall come to pass at the same *t*	Eze 38:18	3117
that ye would gain the *t*, because	Dan 2:8	5732
before me, till the *t* be changed	Dan 2:9	5732
the king that he would give him *t*	Dan 2:16	2166
That at what *t* ye hear the sound	Dan 3:5	5732
Therefore at that *t*, when all the	Dan 3:7	2166
Wherefore at that *t* certain	Dan 3:8	2166
t ye hear the sound of the cornet	Dan 3:15	5732
At the same *t* my reason returned	Dan 4:36	2166
were prolonged for a season and *t*	Dan 7:12	5732
the *t* came that the saints	Dan 7:22	2166
be given into his hand until a *t*	Dan 7:25	5732
and times and the dividing of *t*	Dan 7:25	5732
for at the *t* of the end shall be	Dan 8:17	6256
for at the *t* appointed the end	Dan 8:19	
in the latter *t* of their kingdom,	Dan 8:23	
touched me about the *t* of the	Dan 9:21	6256
but the *t* appointed was long	Dan 10:1	
the strong holds, even for a *t*	Dan 11:24	6256
end shall be at the *t* appointed	Dan 11:27	
At the *t* appointed he shall	Dan 11:29	

white, even to the *t* of the end	Dan 11:35	6256
it is yet for a *t* appointed	Dan 11:35	
at the *t* of the end shall the	Dan 11:40	6256
at that *t* shall Michael stand up,	Dan 12:1	6256
and there shall be a *t* of trouble	Dan 12:1	6256
was a nation even to that same *t*	Dan 12:1	6256
at that *t* thy people shall be	Dan 12:1	6256
book, even to the *t* of the end	Dan 12:4	6256
for ever that it shall be for a *t*	Dan 12:7	4150
and sealed till the *t* of the end	Dan 12:9	6256
from the *t* that the daily	Dan 12:11	6256
away my corn in the *t* thereof	Hos 2:9	6256
in the fig tree at her first *t*	Hos 9:10	7225
for it is *t* to seek the LORD,	Hos 10:12	6256
in those days, and in that *t*	Joel 3:1	6256
shall keep silence in that *t*	Amos 5:13	6256
for it is an evil *t*	Amos 5:13	6256
LORD came unto Jonah the second *t*	Jonah 3:1	
for this *t* is evil	Mic 2:3	6256
hide his face from them at that *t*	Mic 3:4	6256
until the *t* that she which	Mic 5:3	6256
shall not rise up the second *t*	Nah 1:9	6471
vision is yet for an appointed *t*	Hab 2:3	
it shall come to pass at that *t*	Zeph 1:12	6256
at that *t* I will undo all that	Zeph 3:19	6256
At that *t* will I bring you again,	Zeph 3:20	6256
even in the *t* that I gather you	Zeph 3:20	6256
The *t* is not come	Hag 1:2	6256
the *t* that the LORD's house	Hag 1:2	6256
Is it *t* for you, O ye, to dwell	Hag 1:4	6256
rain in the *t* of the latter rain	Zec 10:1	6256
that at evening *t* it shall be	Zec 14:7	6256
fruit before the *t* in the field	Mal 3:11	
about the *t* they were carried	Mt 1:11	1909
what *t* the star appeared	Mt 2:7	5550
according to the *t* which he had	Mt 2:16	5550
lest at any *t* thou dash thy foot	Mt 4:6	3379
From that *t* Jesus began to preach	Mt 4:17	5119
that it was said by them of old *t*	Mt 5:21	744
lest at any *t* the adversary	Mt 5:25	3379
that it was said by them of old *t*	Mt 5:27	744
hath been said by them of old *t*	Mt 5:33	744
hither to torment us before the *t*	Mt 8:29	2540
At that *t* Jesus answered and said,	Mt 11:25	2540
At that *t* Jesus went on the	Mt 12:1	2540
lest at any *t* they should see	Mt 13:15	3379
in the *t* of harvest I will say to	Mt 13:30	2540
At that *t* Herod the tetrarch	Mt 14:1	2540
place, and the *t* is now past	Mt 14:15	5610
From that *t* forth began Jesus to	Mt 16:21	5119
At the same *t* came the disciples	Mt 18:1	5610
when the *t* of the fruit drew near	Mt 21:34	2540
beginning of the world to this *t*	Mt 24:21	2540
After a long *t* the lord of those	Mt 25:19	5550
from that *t* he sought opportunity	Mt 26:16	5119
The Master saith, My *t* is at hand	Mt 26:18	2540
He went away again the second *t*	Mt 26:42	
away again, and prayed the third *t*	Mt 26:44	
The *t* is fulfilled, and the	Mk 1:15	2540
lest at any *t* they should be	Mk 4:12	3379
and so endure but for a *t*	Mk 4:17	4340
place, and now the *t* is far passed	Mk 6:35	5610
an hundredfold now in this *t*	Mk 10:30	2540
for the *t* of figs was not yet	Mk 11:13	2540
which God created unto this *t*	Mk 13:19	3568
for ye know not when the *t* is	Mk 13:33	2540
And he cometh the third *t*, and	Mk 14:41	
the second *t* the cock crew	Mk 14:72	
without at the *t* of incense	Lk 1:10	5610
Now Elisabeth's full *t* came that	Lk 1:57	5550
of the world in a moment of *t*	Lk 4:5	5550
lest at any *t* thou dash thy foot	Lk 4:11	3379
in the *t* of Eliseus the prophet	Lk 4:27	1909
but this woman since the *t* I came	Lk 7:45	
in *t* of temptation fall away	Lk 8:13	2540
man, which had devils long *t*	Lk 8:27	5550
when the *t* was come that he	Lk 9:51	2250
In the mean *t*, when there were	Lk 12:1	
it that ye do not discern this *t*	Lk 12:56	2540
until the *t* come when ye shall	Lk 13:35	
sent his servant at supper *t* to	Lk 14:17	5610
I at any *t* thy commandment	Lk 15:29	
since that *t* the kingdom of God	Lk 16:16	5119
manifold more in this present *t*	Lk 18:30	2540
not the *t* of thy visitation	Lk 19:44	2540
into a far country for a long *t*	Lk 20:9	5550
and the *t* draweth near	Lk 21:8	2540
lest at any *t* your hearts be	Lk 21:34	3379
in the day *t* he was teaching in	Lk 21:37	2250
also was at Jerusalem at that *t*	Lk 23:7	2250
And he said unto them the third *t*	Lk 23:22	
No man hath seen God at any *t*	Jn 1:18	4455
second *t* into his mother's womb	Jn 3:4	1208
been now a long *t* in that case	Jn 5:6	5550
neither heard his voice at any *t*	Jn 5:37	4455
From that *t* many of his disciples	Jn 6:66	
unto them, My *t* is not yet come	Jn 7:6	2540
but your *t* is alway ready	Jn 7:6	2540
for my *t* is not yet full come	Jn 7:8	2540
him, Lord, by this *t* he stinketh	Jn 11:39	2235
Have I been so long *t* with you	Jn 14:9	5550
the *t* cometh, that whosoever	Jn 16:2	5610
you, that when the *t* shall come	Jn 16:4	5610
but the *t* cometh, when I shall no	Jn 16:25	5610
This is now the third *t* that	Jn 21:14	
saith to him again the second *t*	Jn 21:16	
He saith unto him the third *t*	Jn 21:17	
he said unto him the third *t*	Jn 21:17	
wilt thou at this *t* restore again	Acts 1:6	5550
the *t* that the Lord Jesus went in	Acts 1:21	5550
at the second *t* Joseph was made	Acts 7:13	
But when the *t* of the promise	Acts 7:17	5550
In which *t* Moses was born, and was	Acts 7:20	2540
at that *t* there was a great	Acts 8:1	2250
because that of long *t* he had	Acts 8:11	5550
spake unto him again the second *t*	Acts 10:15	
at any *t* entered into my mouth	Acts 11:8	
Now about that *t* Herod the king	Acts 12:1	2540
about the *t* of forty years	Acts 13:18	5550
Long *t* therefore abode they	Acts 14:3	5550
abode long *t* with the disciples	Acts 14:28	5550
For Moses of old *t* hath in every	Acts 15:21	1074
spent their *t* in nothing else	Acts 17:21	2119
him to tarry longer *t* with them	Acts 18:20	5550
after he had spent some *t* there	Acts 18:23	5550
the same *t* there arose no small	Acts 19:23	2540
he would not spend the *t* in Asia	Acts 20:16	5551
answered, Go thy way for this *t*	Acts 24:25	3568
Now when much *t* was spent	Acts 27:9	5550
at this *t* his righteousness	Rom 3:26	2540
in due *t* Christ died for the	Rom 5:6	2540
t are not worthy to be compared	Rom 8:18	2540
At this *t* will I come, and Sarah	Rom 9:9	2540
present *t* also there is a remnant	Rom 11:5	2540
And that, knowing the *t*, that now	Rom 13:11	2540
that now it is high *t* to awake	Rom 13:11	5610
judge nothing before the *t*	1Cor 4:5	2540
except it be with consent for a *t*	1Cor 7:5	2540
I say, brethren, the *t* is short	1Cor 7:29	2540
warfare any *t* at his own charges	1Cor 9:7	4218
also, as of one born out of due *t*	1Cor 15:8	
was not at all to come at this *t*	1Cor 16:12	3598
when he shall have convenient *t*	1Cor 16:12	2119
I have heard thee in a *t* accepted	2Cor 6:2	2540
behold, now is the accepted *t*	2Cor 6:2	2540
that now at this *t* your abundance	2Cor 8:14	2540
the third *t* I am ready to come to	2Cor 12:14	
This is the third *t* I am coming	2Cor 13:1	
if I were present, the second *t*	2Cor 13:2	
in *t* past in the Jews' religion	Gal 1:13	4218
governors until the *t* appointed	Gal 4:2	4287
the fulness of the *t* was come	Gal 4:4	5550
as I have also told you in *t* past	Gal 5:21	
Wherein in *t* past ye walked	Eph 2:2	4218
that ye being in *t* past Gentiles	Eph 2:11	4218
That at that *t* ye were without	Eph 2:12	2540
Redeeming the *t*, because the days	Eph 5:16	2540
the which ye also walked some *t*	Col 3:7	4218
that are without, redeeming the *t*	Col 4:5	2540
For neither at any *t* used we	1Th 2:5	4218
you for a short *t* in presence	1Th 2:17	2540
he might be revealed in his *t*	2Th 2:6	2540
for all, to be testified in due *t*	1Ti 2:6	2540
foundation against the *t* to come	1Ti 6:19	3195
For the *t* will come when they	2Ti 4:3	2540
the *t* of my departure is at hand	2Ti 4:6	2540
brought before Nero the second *t*	2Ti s	
Which in *t* past was to thee	Philem 11	4218
in divers manners spake in *t* past	Heb 1:1	3819
of the angels said he at any *t*	Heb 1:5	4218
lest at any *t* we should let them	Heb 2:1	4218
David, To day, after so long a *t*	Heb 4:7	5550
find grace to help in *t* of need	Heb 4:16	2121
For when for the *t* ye ought to be	Heb 5:12	5550
a figure for the *t* then present	Heb 9:9	2540
them until the *t* of reformation	Heb 9:10	2540
t without sin unto salvation	Heb 9:28	
for the *t* would fail me to tell	Heb 11:32	5550
that appeareth for a little *t*	Jas 4:14	
to be revealed in the last *t*	1Pet 1:5	2540
or what manner of *t* the Spirit of	1Pet 1:11	2540
pass the *t* of your sojourning	1Pet 1:17	5550
Which in *t* past were not a people	1Pet 2:10	4218
in the old *t* the holy women also	1Pet 3:5	4218
should live the rest of his *t* in	1Pet 4:2	5550
For the *t* past of our life may	1Pet 4:3	5550
For the *t* is come that judgment	1Pet 4:17	2540
that he may exalt you in due *t*	1Pet 5:6	2540
not in old *t* by the will of man	2Pet 1:21	4218
now of a long *t* lingereth not	2Pet 2:3	1597
Little children, it is the last *t*	1Jn 2:18	5610
we know that it is the last *t*	1Jn 2:18	5610
No man hath seen God at any *t*	1Jn 4:12	4455
should be mockers in the last *t*	Jude 18	5550
for the *t* is at hand	Rev 1:3	2540
that there should be *t* no longer	Rev 10:6	5550
the *t* of the dead, that they	Rev 11:18	2540
that he hath but a short *t*	Rev 12:12	2540
for a *t*, and times, and half a *t*	Rev 12:14	2540
for the *t* is come for thee to	Rev 14:15	5610
for the *t* is at hand	Rev 22:10	2540

TIMES

he hath supplanted me these two *t*	Gen 27:36	6471
me, and changed my wages ten *t*	Gen 31:7	4489
thou hast changed my wages ten *t*	Gen 31:41	4489
himself to the ground seven *t*	Gen 33:3	6471
five *t* so much as any of theirs	Gen 43:34	3027
Three *t* thou shalt keep a feast	Ex 23:14	
Three *t* in the year all thy males	Ex 23:17	6471
the blood seven *t* before the LORD	Lev 4:6	6471
it seven *t* before the LORD	Lev 4:17	6471
thereof upon the altar seven *t*	Lev 8:11	6471
cleansed from the leprosy seven *t*	Lev 14:7	6471
finger seven *t* before the LORD	Lev 14:16	6471
left hand seven *t* before the LORD	Lev 14:27	6471
and sprinkle the house seven *t*	Lev 14:51	6471
that he come not at all *t* into	Lev 16:2	6256
the blood with his finger seven *t*	Lev 16:14	6471
upon it with his finger seven *t*	Lev 16:19	6471
ye use enchantment, nor observe *t*	Lev 19:26	
unto thee, seven *t* seven years	Lev 25:8	6471
you seven *t* more for your sins	Lev 26:18	
I will bring seven *t* more plagues	Lev 26:21	
you yet seven *t* for your sins	Lev 26:24	
you seven *t* for your sins	Lev 26:28	
have tempted me now these ten *t*	Num 14:22	
of the congregation seven *t*	Num 19:4	
hast smitten me these three *t*	Num 22:28	
smitten thine ass these three *t*	Num 22:32	
and turned from me these three *t*	Num 22:33	
he went not, as at other *t*	Num 24:1	6471
blessed them these three *t*	Num 24:10	
thousand *t* so many more as ye are	Deut 1:11	6471
The Emims dwelt therein in *t* past	Deut 2:10	
and hated him not in *t* past	Deut 4:42	8543
Three *t* in a year shall all thy	Deut 16:16	6471
divination, or an observer of *t*	Deut 18:10	
hearkened unto observers of *t*	Deut 18:14	
ye shall compass the city seven *t*	Josh 6:4	6471
after the same manner seven *t*	Josh 6:15	6471
they compassed the city seven *t*	Josh 6:15	6471
at *t* in the camp of Dan between	Judg 13:25	
thou hast mocked me these three *t*	Judg 16:15	6471
will go out as at other *t* before	Judg 16:20	6471
against Gibeah, as at other *t*	Judg 20:30	6471
people, and kill, as at other *t*	Judg 20:31	6471
and stood, and called as at other *t*	1Sa 3:10	6471
with his hand, as at other *t*	1Sa 18:10	3117
was in his presence, as in *t* past	1Sa 19:7	
sat upon his seat, as at other *t*	1Sa 20:25	6471
ground, and bowed himself three *t*	1Sa 20:41	6471
Ye sought for David in *t* past to	2Sa 3:17	8543
of his people Israel at all *t*	1Kin 8:59	3117
three *t* in a year did Solomon	1Kin 9:25	6471
himself upon the child three *t*	1Kin 17:21	6471
And he said, Go again seven *t*	1Kin 18:43	6471
How many *t* shall I adjure thee	1Kin 22:16	6471
and the child sneezed seven *t*	2Kin 4:35	6471
Go and wash in Jordan seven *t*	2Kin 5:10	6471
dipped himself seven *t* in Jordan	2Kin 5:14	6471
have smitten five or six *t*	2Kin 13:19	6471
Three *t* did Joash beat him, and	2Kin 13:25	6471
of ancient *t* that I have formed	2Kin 19:25	3117
through the fire, and observed *t*	2Kin 21:6	
that had understanding of the *t*	1Chr 12:32	
hundred *t* so many more as they be	1Chr 21:3	6471
the *t* that went over him, and over	1Chr 29:30	
three *t* in the year, even in the	2Chr 8:13	6471
in those *t* there was no peace to	2Chr 15:5	
How many *t* shall I adjure thee	2Chr 18:15	6471
also he observed *t*, and used	2Chr 33:6	
in our cities come at appointed *t*	Ezr 10:14	6256
came, they said unto us ten *t*	Neh 4:12	6471
unto me four *t* after this sort	Neh 6:4	6471
many *t* didst thou deliver them	Neh 9:28	6256
at *t* appointed year by year, to	Neh 10:34	6256
at *t* appointed, and for the	Neh 13:31	6256
to the wise men, which knew the *t*	Est 1:13	6256
of Purim in their *t* appointed	Est 9:31	2165
These ten *t* have ye reproached me	Job 19:3	6471
seeing *t* are not hidden from the	Job 24:1	6256
a refuge in *t* of trouble	Ps 9:9	6256
thou thyself in *t* of trouble	Ps 10:1	6256
of earth, purified seven *t*	Ps 12:6	
My *t* are in thy hand	Ps 31:15	6256
I will bless the LORD at all *t*	Ps 34:1	6256
in their days, in the *t* of old	Ps 44:1	3117
Trust in him at all *t*	Ps 62:8	6256
of old, the years of ancient *t*	Ps 77:5	
that doeth righteousness at all *t*	Ps 106:3	6256
Many *t* did he deliver them	Ps 106:43	6471
hath unto thy judgments at all *t*	Ps 119:20	6256
Seven *t* a day do I praise thee	Ps 119:164	
her breasts satisfy thee at all *t*	Prov 5:19	6256
A friend loveth at all *t*, and a	Prov 17:17	6256
For a just man falleth seven *t*	Prov 24:16	
a sinner do evil an hundred *t*	Eccl 8:12	
shall be alone in his appointed *t*	Is 14:31	4151
shall be the stability of thy *t*	Is 33:6	6256
and of ancient *t*, that I have	Is 37:26	3117
from ancient *t* the things that	Is 46:10	
heaven knoweth her appointed *t*	Jer 8:7	6256
of the *t* that are far off	Eze 12:27	6256
he found them ten *t* better than	Dan 1:20	
And he changeth the *t* and the	Dan 2:21	5732
heat the furnace one seven *t* more	Dan 3:19	
let seven *t* pass over him	Dan 4:16	5732
till seven *t* pass over him	Dan 4:23	5732
seven *t* shall pass over thee,	Dan 4:25	5732
seven *t* shall pass over thee,	Dan 4:32	5732
upon his knees three *t* a day	Dan 6:10	2166
maketh his petition three *t* a day	Dan 6:13	2166
ten thousand *t* ten thousand stood	Dan 7:10	
most High, and think to change *t*	Dan 7:25	2166
into his hand until a time and *t*	Dan 7:25	5732
and the wall, even in troublous *t*	Dan 9:25	6256
that strengthened her in these *t*	Dan 11:6	6256
in those *t* there shall many stand	Dan 11:14	6256
that it shall be for a time, *t*	Dan 12:7	4150
ye not discern the signs of the *t*	Mt 16:3	2540
till seven *t*	Mt 18:21	2034
say not unto thee, Until seven *t*	Mt 18:22	2034
but, Until seventy *t* seven	Mt 18:22	1441
against thee seven *t* in a day	Lk 17:4	2034
seven *t* in a day turn again to	Lk 17:4	2034
until the *t* of the Gentiles be	Lk 21:24	2540
you to know the *t* or the seasons	Acts 1:7	5550
when the *t* of refreshing shall	Acts 3:19	2540
t of restitution of all things	Acts 3:21	5550
And this was done three *t*	Acts 11:10	5151
Who in *t* past suffered all	Acts 14:16	1074
determined the *t* before appointed	Acts 17:26	2540
the *t* of this ignorance God	Acts 17:30	5550
For as ye in *t* past have not	Rom 11:30	4218
Of the Jews five *t* received I	2Cor 11:24	3999
in *t* past now preacheth the faith	Gal 1:23	4218
Ye observe days, and months, and *t*	Gal 4:10	2540
dispensation of the fulness of *t*	Eph 1:10	2540
t past in the lusts of our flesh	Eph 2:3	4218
But of the *t* and the seasons,	1Th 5:1	2540
that in the latter *t* some shall	1Ti 4:1	5550

Which in his t he shall shew, who 1Ti 6:15 5550
last days perilous t shall come 2Ti 3:1 5550
But hath in due t manifested his Titus 1:3 5550
God, who at sundry t and in divers Heb 1:1
of the angels said he at any t Heb 1:13
manifest in these last t for you 1Pet 1:20 5550
was ten thousand t ten thousand Rev 5:11
she is nourished for a time, and t Rev 12:14 2540

TIMNA (*tim'-nah*) See TIMNATH.
1. Concubine of Eliphaz.
T was concubine to Eliphaz Esau's Gen 36:12 8555
2. Daughter of Seir.
and Lotan's sister was T Gen 36:22 8555
and T was Lotan's sister 1Chr 1:39 8555
3. A son of Eliphaz.
Zephi, and Gatam, Kenaz, and T 1Chr 1:36 8555

TIMNAH (*tim'-nah*) See TIMNA, TIMNATH.
1. A chief of Edom.
duke T, duke Alvah, duke Jetheth, Gen 36:40 8555
duke T, duke Aliah, duke Jetheth, 1Chr 1:51 8555
2. A city in Judah.
Cain, Gibeah, and T Josh 15:57 8553
3. A city in Dan.
Beth-shemesh, and passed on to T Josh 15:10 8553
T with the villages thereof, 2Chr 28:18 8553

TIMNATH (*tim'-nath*) See THIMNATHAH, TIMNAH.
1. Same as Timnah 2.
up unto his sheepshearers to T Gen 38:12 8553
goeth up to T to shear his sheep Gen 38:13 8553
place, which is by the way to T Gen 38:14 8553
2. Same as Timnah 3.
And Samson went down to T Judg 14:1 8553
saw a woman in T of the daughters Judg 14:1 8553
I have seen a woman in T of the Judg 14:2 8553
and his father and his mother, to T Judg 14:5 8553
and came to the vineyards of T Judg 14:5 8553

TIMNATH-HERES (*tim''-nath-he'-rez*) See TIMNATH-SERAH. *Land near Mount Ephraim.*
border of his inheritance in T Judg 2:9 8556

TIMNATH-SERAH (*tim''-nath-se'-rah*) See TIMANTH-HERES. *Same as Timnath-heres.*
he asked, even T in mount Ephraim Josh 19:50 8556
border of his inheritance in T Josh 24:30 8556

TIMNITE (*tim'-nite*) *An inhabitant of Timnath.*
Samson, the son in law of the T Judg 15:6 8554

TIMON (*ti'-mon*) *A leader in the Jerusalem church.*
and Prochorus, and Nicanor, and T Acts 6:5 5096

TIMOTHEOUS
and Fortunatus, and Achaicus, and T 1Cor s 5095

TIMOTHEUS (*tim-o'-the-us*) See TIMOTHY.
Same as Timothy.
disciple was there, named T Acts 16:1 5095
but Silas and T abode there still Acts 17:14 5095
T for to come to him with all Acts 17:15 5095
T were come from Macedonia, Paul Acts 18:5 5095
them that ministered unto him, T Acts 19:22 5095
and Gaius of Derbe, and T Acts 20:4 5095
T my workfellow, and Lucius, and Rom 16:21 5095
this cause have I sent unto you T 1Cor 4:17 5095
Now if T come, see that he may be 1Cor 16:10 5095
us, even by me and Silvanus and T 2Cor 1:19 5095
Paul and T, the servants of Jesus Phil 1:1 5095
Jesus to send T shortly unto you Phil 2:19 5095
will of God, and T our brother, Col 1:1 5095
Paul, and Silvanus, and T, unto the 1Th 1:1 5095
And sent T, our brother, and 1Th 3:2 5095
But now when T came from you unto. 1Th 3:6 5095
Paul, and Silvanus, and T, unto the 2Th 1:1 5095
The second epistle unto T 2Ti s 5095

TIMOTHY (*tim'-o-thy*) See TIMOTHEUS. *A co-worker with Paul.*
T our brother, unto the church of 2Cor 1:1 5095
Unto T, my own son in the faith 1Ti 1:2 5095
charge I commit unto thee, son T 1Ti 1:18 5095
O T, keep that which is committed 1Ti 6:20 5095
The first to T was written from 1Ti s 5095
To T, my dearly beloved son 2Ti 1:2 5095
T our brother, unto Philemon our Philem 1 5095
our brother T is set at liberty Heb 13:23 5095
to the Hebrews from Italy by T Heb s 5095

TIN
the brass, the iron, the t Num 31:22 913
thy dross, and take away all thy t Is 1:25 913
all they are brass, and t, and iron Eze 22:18 913
and brass, and iron, and lead, and t Eze 22:20 913
with silver, iron, t, and lead, Eze 27:12 913

TINGLE
every one that heareth it shall t 1Sa 3:11 6750
of it, both his ears shall t 2Kin 21:12 6750
heareth, his ears shall t Jer 19:3 6750

TINKLING
making a t with their feet Is 3:16 5913
t ornaments about their feet Is 3:18
as sounding brass, or a t cymbal 1Cor 13:1 214

TIP
put it upon the t of the right Ex 29:20 8571
upon the t of the right ear of Ex 29:20 8571
put it upon the t of Aaron's Lev 8:23 8571
upon the t of their right ear Lev 8:24 8571
priest shall put it upon the t of Lev 14:14 8571
shall the priest put upon the t Lev 14:17 8571
put it upon the t of the right Lev 14:25 8571
that is in his hand upon the t of Lev 14:28 8571
that he may dip the t of his Lk 16:24 206

TIPHSAH (*tif'-sah*)
1. A city on the Euphrates River.
from T even to Azzah, over all 1Kin 4:24 8607
2. A city in Judah.
Then Menahem smote T, and all that 2Kin 15:16 8607

TIRAS (*Ti'-ras*) *A son of Japheth.*
Javan, and Tubal, and Meshech, and T Gen 10:2 8493
Javan, and Tubal, and Meshech, and T 1Chr 1:5 8493

TIRATHITES (*ti'-rath-ites*) *A family of scribes.*
the T, the Shimeathites, and 1Chr 2:55 8654

TIRE
bind the t of thine head upon Eze 24:17 6287

TIRED
t her head, and looked out at a 2Kin 9:30 3190

TIRES
their round t like the moon, Is 3:18 7720
your t shall be upon your heads, Eze 24:23 6287

TIRHAKAH (*tur-ha'-kah*) *A king of Ethiopia.*
heard say of T king of Ethiopia 2Kin 19:9 8640
say concerning T king of Ethiopia Is 37:9 8640

TIRHANAH (*tur-ha'-nah*) *A son of Caleb.*
concubine, bare Sheber, and T 1Chr 2:48 8647

TIRIA (*tir'-e-ah*) *A descendant of Judah.*
Ziph, and Ziphah, T, and Asareel 1Chr 4:16 8493

TIRSHATHA (*tur'-sha-thah*) *Persian governors of Judah.*
the T said unto them, that they Ezr 2:63 8660
the T said unto them, that they Neh 7:65 8660
The T gave to the treasure a Neh 7:70 8660
And Nehemiah, which is the T Neh 8:9 8660
that sealed were, Nehemiah, the T Neh 10:1 8660

TIRZAH (*tur'-zah*)
1. A daughter of Zelophehad.
and Noah, Hoglah, Milcah, and T Num 26:33 8656
Noah, and Hoglah, and Milcah, and T Num 27:1 8656
For Mahlah, T, and Hoglah, and Num 36:11 8656
and Noah, Hoglah, Milcah, and T Josh 17:3 8656
2. A city in Ephraim.
The king of T, one Josh 12:24 8656
arose, and departed, and came to T 1Kin 14:17 8656
building of Ramah, and dwelt in T 1Kin 15:21 8656
to reign over all Israel in T 1Kin 15:33 8656
his fathers, and was buried in T 1Kin 16:6 8656
Baasha to reign over Israel in T 1Kin 16:8 8656
against him, as he was in T 1Kin 16:9 8656
of Arza steward of his house in T 1Kin 16:9 8656
did Zimri reign seven days in T 1Kin 16:15 8656
with him, and they besieged T 1Kin 16:17 8656
six years reigned he in T 1Kin 16:23 8656
the son of Gadi went up from T 2Kin 15:14 8656
and the coasts thereof from T 2Kin 15:16 8656
art beautiful, O my love, as T Song 6:4 8656

TISHBE See TISHBITE.

TISHBITE (*tish'-bite*) *An inhabitant of Tishbeh.*
And Elijah the T, who was of the 1Kin 17:1 8664
of the LORD came to Elijah the T 1Kin 21:17 8664
of the LORD came to Elijah the T 1Kin 21:28 8664
of the LORD said to Elijah the T 2Kin 1:3 8664
And he said, It is Elijah the T 2Kin 1:8 8664
spake by his servant Elijah the T 2Kin 9:36 8664

TITHE
all the t of the land, whether of Lev 27:30 4643
And concerning the t of the herd Lev 27:32 4643
LORD, even a tenth part of the t Num 18:26 4643
thy gates the t of thy corn Deut 12:17 4643
Thou shalt truly t all the Deut 14:22 6237
the t of thy corn, of thy wine, Deut 14:23 4643
thou shalt bring forth all the t Deut 14:28 4643
the t of all things brought they 2Chr 31:5 4643
also brought in the t of oxen 2Chr 31:6 4643
the t of holy things which were 2Chr 31:6 4643
the Levites shall bring up the t Neh 10:38 4643
all Judah the t of the corn Neh 13:12 4643
for ye pay t of mint and anise and Mt 23:23 586
for ye t mint and rue and all Lk 11:42 586

TITHES
And he gave him t of all Gen 14:20 4643
will at all redeem ought of his t Lev 27:31 4643
But the t of the children of Num 18:24 4643
the t which I have given you from Num 18:26 4643
unto the LORD of all your t Num 18:28 4643
and your sacrifices, and your t Deut 12:6 4643
and your sacrifices, your t Deut 12:11 4643
the t of thine increase the third Deut 26:12 4643
brought in the offerings and the t 2Chr 31:12 4643
the t of our ground unto the Neh 10:37 4643
the t in all the cities of our Neh 10:37 6237
Levites, when the Levites take t Neh 10:38 6237
the t unto the house of our God Neh 10:38 4643
for the firstfruits, and for the t Neh 12:44 4643
the t of the corn, the new wine, Neh 13:5 4643
and your t after three years Amos 4:4 4643
In t and offerings Mal 3:8 4643
Bring ye all the t into the Mal 3:10 4643
I give t of all that I possess Lk 18:12 586
have a commandment to take t of Heb 7:5 586
from them received t of Abraham Heb 7:6 1183
And here men that die receive t Heb 7:8 1181
say, Levi also, who receiveth t Heb 7:9 1183
payed t in Abraham Heb 7:9 1183

TITHING
end of t all the tithes of thine Deut 26:12 6237
year, which is the year of t Deut 26:12 4643

TITIUS See JUSTUS.

TITIUS JUSTUS See JUSTUS.

TITLE
What t is that that I see 2Kin 23:17 6725
And Pilate wrote a t, and put it on Jn 19:19 5102
This t then read many of the Jews Jn 19:20 5102

TITLES
let me give flattering t unto man Job 32:21
I know not to give flattering t Job 32:22

TITTLE
one jot or one t shall in no wise Mt 5:18 2762
than one t of the law to fail Lk 16:17 2762

TITUS (*ti'-tus*) *A co-worker with Paul.*
because I found not T my brother 2Cor 2:13 5103
comforted us by the coming of T 2Cor 7:6 5103
more joyed we for the joy of T 2Cor 7:13 5103
boasting, which I made before T 2Cor 7:14 5103
Insomuch that we desired T 2Cor 8:6 5103
care into the heart of T for you 2Cor 8:16 5103
Whether any do enquire of T 2Cor 8:23 5103
I desired T, and with him I sent a 2Cor 12:18 5103
Did T make a gain of you 2Cor 12:18 5103
a city of Macedonia, by T 2Cor s 5103
Barnabas, and took T with me also Gal 2:1 5103
But neither T, who was with me, Gal 2:3 5103
to Galatia, T unto Dalmatia 2Ti 4:10 5103
To T, mine own son after the Titus 1:4 5103
It was written to T, ordained the Titus s 5103

TIZITE (*ti'-zite*) *Family name of Joha.*
and Joha his brother, the T 1Chr 11:45 8491

TO See PREFACE.

TOAH (*to'-ah*) See NAHATH, TOHU. *An ancestor of Samuel.*
the son of Eliel, the son of T 1Chr 6:34 8430

TOB (*tob*) *A district in Syria.*
and dwelt in the land of T Judg 11:3 2897
Jephthah out of the land of T Judg 11:5 2897

TOB-ADONIJAH (*tob''-ad-o-ni'-jah*) *A Levite messenger of King Jehoshaphat.*
and Adonijah, and Tobijah, and T 2Chr 17:8 2899

TOBIAH (*to-bi'-ah*) See TOBIJAH.
1. A family of exiles.
of Delaiah, the children of T Ezr 2:60 2900
of Delaiah, the children of T Neh 7:62 2900
2. An Ammonite who opposed Nehemiah.
T the servant, the Ammonite, Neh 2:10 2900
T the servant, the Ammonite, and Neh 2:19 2900
T the Ammonite was by him, and Neh 4:3 2900
pass, that when Sanballat, and T Neh 4:7 2900
to pass, when Sanballat, and T Neh 6:1 2900
for T and Sanballat had hired him Neh 6:12 2900
My God, think thou upon T Neh 6:14 2900
of Judah sent many letters unto T Neh 6:17 2900
the letters of T came unto them Neh 6:17 2900
T sent letters to put me in fear Neh 6:19 2900
of our God, was allied unto T Neh 13:4 2900
the evil that Eliashib did for T Neh 13:7 2900
stuff of T out of the chamber Neh 13:8 2900

TOBIJAH (*to-bi'-jah*) See TOBIAH.
1. A Levite messenger of King Jehoshaphat.
and Jehonathan, and Adonijah, and T. 2Chr 17:8 2900
2. A clan leader of exiles.
captivity, even of Heldai, of T Zec 6:10 2900
crowns shall be to Helem, and to T Zec 6:14 2900

TOCHEN (*to'-ken*) *A city in Simeon.*
were, Etam, and Ain, Rimmon, and T 1Chr 4:32 8507

TODAY
glorious was the king of Israel t 2Sa 6:20
T thy servant knoweth that I have 2Sa 14:22
T shall the house of Israel 2Sa 16:3

TOE
upon the great t of their right Ex 29:20 931
upon the great t of his right Lev 8:23 931
upon the great t of his right Lev 14:14 931
upon the great t of his right Lev 14:17 931
upon the great t of his right Lev 14:25 931
upon the great t of his right Lev 14:28 931

TOES
upon the great t of their right Lev 8:24 931
cut off his thumbs and his great t Judg 1:6
thumbs and their great t cut off Judg 1:7
fingers, and on every foot six t 2Sa 21:20 676
t were four and twenty, six on 1Chr 20:6 676
whereas thou sawest the feet and t Dan 2:41 677
as the t of the feet were part of Dan 2:42 677

TOGARMAH (*to-gar'-mah*) *A son of Gomer.*
Ashkenaz, and Riphath, and T Gen 10:3 8425
Ashchenaz, and Riphath, and T 1Chr 1:6 8425
They of the house of T traded in Eze 27:14 8425
the house of T of the north Eze 38:6 8425

TOGETHER
be gathered t unto one place Gen 1:9
the gathering t of the waters Gen 1:10
and they sewed fig leaves t Gen 3:7
them, that they might dwell t Gen 13:6 3162
so that they could not dwell t Gen 13:6 3162
joined t in the vale of Siddim Gen 14:3
and they went both of them t Gen 22:6 3162
so they went both of them t Gen 22:8 3162
rose up and went t to Beer-sheba Gen 22:19 3162
children struggled t within her Gen 25:22
the cattle should be gathered t Gen 29:7
all the flocks be gathered t Gen 29:8
Laban gathered t all the men of Gen 29:22
gather themselves t against me Gen 34:30

more than that they might dwell *t* ... Gen 36:7 3162
he put them all *t* into ward three ... Gen 42:17
and said, Gather yourselves *t* ... Gen 49:1
Gather yourselves *t*, and hear, ye ... Gen 49:2
two men of the Hebrews strove *t* ... Ex 2:13
and gather the elders of Israel *t* ... Ex 3:16
gathered *t* all the elders of the ... Ex 4:29
they gathered them *t* upon heaps ... Ex 8:14
the waters were gathered *t* ... Ex 15:8
And all the people answered *t* ... Ex 19:8 3162
And if men strive *t*, and one smite ... Ex 21:18
shall be coupled *t* one to another ... Ex 26:3
the curtains *t* with the taches ... Ex 26:6
the loops, and couple the tent *t* ... Ex 26:11
they shall be coupled *t* beneath ... Ex 26:24
they shall be coupled *t* above the ... Ex 26:24 3162
and so it shall be joined *t* ... Ex 28:7
art of the apothecary, tempered *t* ... Ex 30:35
gathered themselves *t* unto Aaron ... Ex 32:1
gathered themselves *t* unto him ... Ex 32:26
of the children of Israel *t* ... Ex 35:1
of brass to couple the tent *t* ... Ex 36:18
coupled *t* at the head thereof, to ... Ex 36:29 3162
for it, to couple it *t* ... Ex 39:4
by the two edges was it coupled *t* ... Ex 39:4
thou all the congregation *t* unto ... Lev 8:3
the assembly was gathered *t* unto ... Lev 8:4
of Israel strove *t* in the camp ... Lev 24:10
are gathered *t* within your cities ... Lev 26:25
t on the first day of the second ... Num 1:18
of the children of Israel *t* ... Num 8:9
congregation is to be gathered *t* ... Num 10:7
of the sea be gathered *t* for them ... Num 11:22
that are gathered *t* against me ... Num 14:35
themselves *t* against Moses ... Num 16:3
are gathered *t* against the LORD ... Num 16:11
themselves *t* against Moses ... Num 20:2
and gather thou the assembly *t* ... Num 20:8
congregation *t* before the rock ... Num 20:10
unto Moses, Gather the people *t* ... Num 21:16
Sihon gathered all his people *t* ... Num 21:23
Balaam, and he smote his hands *t* ... Num 24:10 3162
and swallowed them up *t* with Korah .. Num 26:10
them that gathered themselves *t* ... Num 27:3
unto me, Gather me the people *t* ... Deut 4:10
not plow with an ox and an ass *t* ... Deut 22:10 3162
sorts, as of woollen and linen *t* ... Deut 22:11 3162
If brethren dwell *t*, and one of ... Deut 25:5 3162
When men strive *t* one with ... Deut 25:11 3162
Gather the people *t*, men, and ... Deut 31:12
tribes of Israel were gathered *t* ... Deut 33:5 3162
people *t* to the ends of the earth ... Deut 33:17 3162
called *t* to pursue after them ... Josh 8:16
That they gathered themselves *t* ... Josh 9:2 3162
of Eglon, gathered themselves *t* ... Josh 10:5
are gathered *t* against us ... Josh 10:6
when all these kings were met *t* ... Josh 11:5 3162
pitched *t* at the waters of Merom, ... Josh 11:5 3162
they met *t* in Asher on the north, ... Josh 17:10
of Israel assembled *t* at Shiloh ... Josh 18:1
gathered themselves *t* at Shiloh ... Josh 22:12
Sisera gathered *t* all his ... Judg 4:13
of the east were gathered *t* ... Judg 6:33 3162
morrow, and thrust the fleece *t* ... Judg 6:38
themselves *t* out of Naphtali ... Judg 7:23
of Ephraim gathered themselves *t* ... Judg 7:24
all the men of Shechem gathered *t* ... Judg 9:6
tower of Shechem were gathered *t* ... Judg 9:47
children of Ammon were gathered *t* ... Judg 10:17
of Israel assembled themselves *t* ... Judg 10:17
Sihon gathered all his people *t* ... Judg 11:20
of Ephraim gathered themselves *t* ... Judg 12:1
gathered *t* all the men of Gilead ... Judg 12:4
the Philistines gathered them *t* ... Judg 16:23
to Micah's house were gathered *t* ... Judg 18:22
did eat and drink both of them *t* ... Judg 19:6 3162
t with her bones, into twelve ... Judg 19:29
was gathered *t* as one man ... Judg 20:1
the city, knit *t* as one man ... Judg 20:11
t out of the cities unto Gibeah ... Judg 20:14
gathered *t* all the lords of the ... 1Sa 5:11
And they gathered *t* to Mizpeh ... 1Sa 7:6
Israel were gathered *t* to Mizpeh ... 1Sa 7:7
of Israel gathered themselves *t* ... 1Sa 8:4
people *t* unto the LORD to Mizpeh ... 1Sa 10:17
that two of them were not left *t* ... 1Sa 11:11 3162
called *t* after Saul to Gilgal ... 1Sa 13:4
themselves *t* to fight with Israel ... 1Sa 13:5
gathered themselves *t* at Michmash ... 1Sa 13:11
And Saul gathered the people *t* ... 1Sa 15:4
gathered *t* their armies to battle ... 1Sa 17:1
and were gathered *t* at Shochoh ... 1Sa 17:1
the men of Israel were gathered *t* ... 1Sa 17:2 3162
me a man, that we may fight *t* ... 1Sa 17:10 3162
called all the people *t* to war ... 1Sa 23:8 3162
the Israelites were gathered *t* ... 1Sa 25:1
their armies *t* for warfare ... 1Sa 28:1
Philistines gathered themselves *t* ... 1Sa 28:4
and Saul gathered all Israel *t* ... 1Sa 28:4
t with the woman, compelled him ... 1Sa 28:23
t all their armies to Aphek ... 1Sa 29:1
and all his men, that same day *t* ... 1Sa 31:6 3162
met *t* by the pool of Gibeon ... 2Sa 2:13 3162
so they fell down *t* ... 2Sa 2:16 3162
gathered themselves *t* after Abner ... 2Sa 2:25
he had gathered all the people *t* ... 2Sa 2:30
David gathered *t* all the chosen ... 2Sa 6:1
they gathered themselves *t* ... 2Sa 10:15 3162
David, he gathered all Israel *t* ... 2Sa 10:17
and it grew up *t* with him, and with ... 2Sa 12:3 3162
gather the rest of the people *t* ... 2Sa 12:28
David gathered all the people *t* ... 2Sa 12:29
and they two strove *t* in the field ... 2Sa 14:6
my son *t* out of the inheritance ... 2Sa 14:16 3162

and they were gathered *t*, and went ... 2Sa 20:14
and they fell all seven *t*, and were ... 2Sa 21:9 3162
were there gathered *t* to battle ... 2Sa 23:9
were gathered *t* into a troop ... 2Sa 23:11
and we were *t* ... 1Kin 3:18 3162
and they two made a league *t* ... 1Kin 5:12
And Solomon gathered *t* chariots ... 1Kin 10:26
t with the daughter of Pharaoh, ... 1Kin 11:1
the prophets *t* unto mount Carmel ... 1Kin 18:20
of Syria gathered all his host *t* ... 1Kin 20:1
of Israel gathered the prophets *t* ... 1Kin 22:6
took his mantle, and wrapped it *t* ... 2Kin 2:8
hath called these three kings *t* ... 2Kin 3:10
hath called these three kings *t* ... 2Kin 3:13
thou rode *t* after Ahab his father ... 2Kin 9:25 6776
And Jehu gathered all the people *t* ... 2Kin 10:18
sons, and all his house died *t* ... 1Chr 10:6 3162
were gathered *t* to battle ... 1Chr 11:13
So David gathered all Israel *t* ... 1Chr 13:5
all Israel *t* to Jerusalem ... 1Chr 15:3
of our salvation, and gather us *t* ... 1Chr 16:35
themselves *t* from their cities ... 1Chr 19:7
David commanded to gather *t* the ... 1Chr 22:2
he gathered *t* all the princes of ... 1Chr 23:2
that were gathered *t* to Jerusalem ... 2Chr 12:5
So they gathered themselves *t* at ... 2Chr 15:10
the king of Israel gathered *t* of ... 2Chr 18:5
And Judah gathered themselves *t* ... 2Chr 20:4
And he gathered *t* the priests ... 2Chr 24:5
Moreover Amaziah gathered Judah *t* ... 2Chr 25:5
Ahaz gathered *t* the vessels of ... 2Chr 28:24
gathered them *t* into the east ... 2Chr 29:4
themselves *t* to Jerusalem ... 2Chr 30:3
there was gathered much people *t* ... 2Chr 32:4
gathered them *t* to him in the ... 2Chr 32:6
they have gathered *t* the money ... 2Chr 34:17
gathered *t* all the elders of ... 2Chr 34:29
whole congregation *t* was forty ... Ezr 2:64 259
t as one man to Jerusalem ... Ezr 3:1
and his sons, the sons of Judah, *t* ... Ezr 3:9 259
they sang *t* by course in praising ... Ezr 3:11
but we ourselves *t* will build ... Ezr 4:3 3162
and the Levites were purified *t* ... Ezr 6:20 259
I gathered *t* out of Israel chief ... Ezr 7:28
I gathered them *t* to the river ... Ezr 8:15
themselves *t* unto Jerusalem ... Ezr 10:7
t unto Jerusalem within three ... Ezr 10:9
joined *t* unto the half thereof ... Neh 4:6
conspired all of them *t* to come ... Neh 4:8 3162
let us meet *t* in some one of the ... Neh 6:2 3162
and let us take counsel *t* ... Neh 6:7 3162
Let us meet *t* in the house of God ... Neh 6:10
mine heart to gather *t* the nobles ... Neh 7:5
whole congregation *t* was forty ... Neh 7:66 259
the people gathered themselves *t* ... Neh 8:1
t the chief of the fathers of all ... Neh 8:13
the singers gathered themselves *t* ... Neh 12:28
And I gathered them *t*, and set them ... Neh 13:11
that they may gather *t* all the ... Est 2:3
t unto Shushan the palace ... Est 2:8
were gathered *t* the second time ... Est 2:19
gather *t* all the Jews that are ... Est 4:16
every city to gather themselves *t* ... Est 8:11
The Jews gathered themselves *t* in ... Est 9:2
t on the fourteenth day also of ... Est 9:15
provinces gathered themselves *t* ... Est 9:16
t on the thirteenth day thereof ... Est 9:18
t to come to mourn with him ... Job 2:11 3162
There the prisoners rest *t* ... Job 3:18 3162
calamity laid in the balances *t* ... Job 6:2 3162
and we should come *t* in judgment ... Job 9:32 3162
me and fashioned me *t* round about ... Job 10:8 3162
cut off, and shut up, or gather *t* ... Job 11:10
gathered themselves *t* against me ... Job 16:10 3162
when our rest *t* is in the dust ... Job 17:16 3162
His troops come *t*, and raise up ... Job 19:12 3162
of the earth hide themselves *t* ... Job 24:4 3162
the nettles they were gathered *t* ... Job 30:7
All flesh shall perish *t*, and man ... Job 34:15 3162
When the morning stars sang *t* ... Job 38:7 3162
and the clods cleave fast *t* ... Job 38:38
Hide them in the dust *t* ... Job 40:13 3162
of his stones are wrapped *t* ... Job 40:17
shut up *t* as with a close seal ... Job 41:15
one to another, they stick *t* ... Job 41:17
flakes of his flesh are joined *t* ... Job 41:23
and the rulers take counsel *t* ... Ps 2:2 3162
they are all *t* become filthy ... Ps 14:3 3162
they took counsel *t* against me ... Ps 31:13 3162
waters of the sea *t* as an heap ... Ps 33:7
me, and let us exalt his name *t* ... Ps 34:3 3162
and gathered themselves *t* ... Ps 35:15
gathered themselves *t* against me ... Ps 35:15
brought to confusion *t* that ... Ps 35:26 3162
shall be destroyed *t* ... Ps 37:38 3162
confounded *t* that seek after my ... Ps 40:14 3162
that hate me whisper *t* against me ... Ps 41:7 3162
of the people are gathered *t* ... Ps 47:9 3162
were assembled, they passed by *t* ... Ps 48:4 3162
Both low and high, rich and poor, *t* ... Ps 49:2 3162
Gather my saints *t* unto me ... Ps 50:5
We took sweet counsel *t*, and ... Ps 55:14 3162
They gather themselves *t*, they ... Ps 56:6
wait for my soul take counsel *t* ... Ps 71:10 3162
hearts, Let us destroy them *t* ... Ps 74:8 3162
have consulted *t* with one consent ... Ps 83:5 3162
Mercy and truth are met *t* ... Ps 85:10
they compassed me about *t* ... Ps 88:17 3162
They gather themselves *t* against ... Ps 94:21
let the hills be joyful *t* ... Ps 98:8 3162
When the people are gathered *t* ... Ps 102:22 3162
ariseth, they gather themselves *t* ... Ps 104:22
as a city that is compact *t* ... Ps 122:3 3162
for brethren to dwell *t* in unity ... Ps 133:1 3162

are they gathered *t* for war ... Ps 140:2
he gathereth *t* the outcasts of ... Ps 147:2
The rich and poor meet *t* ... Prov 22:2
poor and the deceitful man meet *t* ... Prov 29:13
and a time to gather stones *t* ... Eccl 3:5
The fool foldeth his hands *t* ... Eccl 4:5
Again, if two lie *t*, then they ... Eccl 4:11
Come now, and let us reason *t* ... Is 1:18
and of the sinners shall be *t* ... Is 1:28 3162
spark, and they shall both burn *t* ... Is 1:31 3162
Take counsel *t*, and it shall come ... Is 8:10
him, and join his enemies *t* ... Is 9:11
they *t* shall be against Judah ... Is 9:21 3162
the young lion and the fatling *t* ... Is 11:6 3162
their young ones shall lie down *t* ... Is 11:7 3162
gather *t* the dispersed of Judah ... Is 11:12
shall spoil them of the east *t* ... Is 11:14 3162
kingdoms of nations gathered *t* ... Is 13:4
They shall be left *t* unto the ... Is 18:6 3162
All thy rulers are fled *t* ... Is 22:3 3162
are found in thee are bound *t* ... Is 22:3 3162
ye gathered *t* the waters of the ... Is 22:9
And they shall be gathered *t* ... Is 24:22
t with the spoils of their hands ... Is 25:11
t with my dead body shall they ... Is 26:19
through them, I would burn them *t* ... Is 27:4 3162
down, and they all shall fail *t* ... Is 31:3 3162
shall be rolled *t* as a scroll ... Is 34:4
and all flesh shall see it *t* ... Is 40:5 3162
let us come near *t* to judgment ... Is 41:1 3162
and the pine, and the box tree *t* ... Is 41:19 3162
and consider, and understand *t* ... Is 41:20 3162
may be dismayed, and behold it *t* ... Is 41:23 3162
Let all the nations be gathered *t* ... Is 43:9 3162
they shall lie down *t*, they shall ... Is 43:17 3162
let us plead *t* ... Is 43:26 3162
let them all be gathered *t* ... Is 44:11
fear, and they shall be ashamed *t* ... Is 44:11 3162
and let righteousness spring up *t* ... Is 45:8 3162
t that are makers of idols ... Is 45:16 3162
draw near *t*, ye that are escaped ... Is 45:20 3162
yea, let them take counsel *t* ... Is 45:21 3162
They stoop, they bow down *t* ... Is 46:2 3162
I call unto them, they stand up *t* ... Is 48:13 3162
all these gather themselves *t* ... Is 49:18
let us stand *t* ... Is 50:8 3162
with the voice *t* shall they sing ... Is 52:8 3162
Break forth into joy, sing *t* ... Is 52:9 3162
they shall surely gather *t* ... Is 54:15
whosoever shall gather *t* against ... Is 54:15
all they gather themselves *t* ... Is 60:4
Then thou shalt see, and flow *t* ... Is 60:5
shall be gathered *t* unto thee ... Is 60:7
tree, the pine tree, and the box *t* ... Is 60:13 3162
they that have brought it *t* shall ... Is 62:9
the iniquities of your fathers *t* ... Is 65:7 3162
The wolf and the lamb shall feed *t* ... Is 65:25 259
and the mouse, shall be consumed *t* ... Is 66:17 3162
they shall come *t* out of the land ... Jer 3:18 3162
cry, gather *t*, and say, Assemble ... Jer 4:5
upon the assembly of young men *t* ... Jer 6:11 3162
with their fields and wives *t* ... Jer 6:12 3162
the sons *t* shall fall upon them ... Jer 6:21 3162
even the fathers and the sons *t* ... Jer 13:14 3162
her that travaileth with child *t* ... Jer 31:8 3162
shall flow *t* to the goodness of ... Jer 31:12
dance, both young men and old *t* ... Jer 31:13 3162
and in all the cities thereof *t* ... Jer 31:24 3162
they did eat bread *t* in Mizpah ... Jer 41:1 3162
mighty, and they are fallen both *t* ... Jer 46:12 3162
turned back, and are fled away *t* ... Jer 46:21 3162
with his priests and his princes *t* ... Jer 48:7 3162
and his priests and his princes *t* ... Jer 49:3 3162
the heathen, saying, Gather ye *t* ... Jer 49:14
they and the children of Judah *t* ... Jer 50:4 3162
Call *t* the archers against ... Jer 50:29
of Judah were oppressed *t* ... Jer 50:33 3162
call *t* against her the kingdoms ... Jer 51:27
They shall roar *t* like lions ... Jer 51:38 3162
not flow *t* any more unto him ... Jer 51:44
they languished *t* ... Lam 2:8 3162
prophesy, and smite thine hands *t* ... Eze 21:14
I will also smite mine hands *t* ... Eze 21:17
thou shalt not be brought *t* ... Eze 29:5
a shaking, and the bones came *t* ... Eze 37:7
and the gold, broken to pieces *t* ... Dan 2:35 2298
king sent to gather *t* the princes ... Dan 3:2
were gathered *t* unto the ... Dan 3:3
counsellors, being gathered *t* ... Dan 3:27
princes assembled *t* to the king ... Dan 6:6
have consulted *t* to establish a ... Dan 6:7
they shall join themselves *t* ... Dan 11:6
children of Israel be gathered *t* ... Hos 1:11 3162
me, my repentings are kindled *t* ... Hos 11:8 3162
gather yourselves *t* round about ... Joel 3:11
captivity, he and his princes *t* ... Amos 1:15 3162
Can two walk *t*, except they be ... Amos 3:3 3162
I will put them *t* as the sheep of ... Mic 2:12 3162
while they be folden *t* as thorns ... Nah 1:10
melteth, and the knees smite *t* ... Nah 2:10
Gather yourselves *t*, yea, gather ... Zeph 2:1
t, yea, gather *t*, O nation ... Zeph 2:1
bow, out of him every oppressor *t* ... Zec 10:4 3162
earth be gathered *t* against it ... Zec 12:3
round about shall be gathered *t* ... Zec 14:14
to Joseph, before they came *t* ... Mt 1:18 *4905*
and scribes of the people *t* ... Mt 2:4 *4863*
were gathered *t* unto him, so that ... Mt 13:2 *4863*
Let both grow *t* until the harvest ... Mt 13:30 *4886*
Gather ye *t* first the tares, and ... Mt 13:30 *4816*
three are gathered *t* in my name ... Mt 18:20 *4863*
What therefore God hath joined *t* ... Mt 19:6 *4801*
gathered *t* all as many as they ... Mt 22:10 *4863*
to silence, they were gathered *t* ... Mt 22:34

T

the Pharisees were gathered *t* Mt 22:41 *4863*
I have gathered thy children *t* Mt 23:37 *1996*
will the eagles be gathered *t* Mt 24:28 *4863*
they shall gather *t* his elect Mt 24:31 *1996*
Then assembled *t* the chief Mt 26:3 *4863*
when they were gathered *t* Mt 27:17 *4863*
and Pharisees came *t* unto Pilate Mt 27:62 *4863*
city was gathered *t* at the door Mk 1:33 *1996*
straightway many were gathered *t* Mk 2:2 *4863*
and sinners sat also *t* with Jesus Mk 2:15 *4873*
And the multitude cometh *t* again Mk 3:20 *4905*
gathered themselves *t* unto Jesus Mk 6:30 *4863*
outwent them, and came *t* unto him Mk 6:33 *4905*
Then came *t* unto him the Mk 7:1 *4863*
that the people came running *t* Mk 9:25 *1998*
What therefore God hath joined *t* Mk 10:9 *4801*
and having heard them reasoning *t* Mk 12:28 *4802*
shall gather *t* his elect from the Mk 13:27 *1996*
but their witness agreed not *t* Mk 14:56
so did their witness agree *t* Mk 14:59
they call *t* the whole band Mk 15:16 *4779*
great multitudes came *t* to hear Lk 5:15 *4905*
pressed down, and shaken *t* Lk 6:38
when much people were gathered *t* Lk 8:4 *4896*
he called his twelve disciples *t* Lk 9:1 *4779*
the people were gathered thick *t* Lk 11:29 *1865*
when there were gathered *t* an Lk 12:1 *1996*
eighteen years, and was bowed *t* Lk 13:11 *4794*
I have gathered thy children *t* Lk 13:34 *1996*
he calleth *t* his friends and Lk 15:6 *4779*
her friends and her neighbours *t* Lk 15:9 *4779*
the younger son gathered all *t* Lk 15:13 *4863*
Two women shall be grinding *t* Lk 17:35
will the eagles be gathered *t* Lk 17:37 *4863*
of the hall, and were set down *t* Lk 22:55 *4776*
priests and the scribes came *t* Lk 22:66 *4863*
and Herod were made friends *t* Lk 23:12
he had called *t* the chief priests Lk 23:13 *4779*
people that came *t* to that sight Lk 23:48 *4836*
they talked *t* of all these things Lk 24:14
pass, that, while they communed *t* Lk 24:15
and found the eleven gathered *t* Lk 24:33 *4867*
and he that reapeth may rejoice *t* Jn 4:36 *3674*
Therefore they gathered them *t* Jn 6:13 *4863*
but that also he should gather *t* Jn 11:52 *4863*
counsel *t* for to put him to death Jn 11:53 *4853*
So they ran both *t* Jn 20:4 *3674*
but wrapped *t* in a place by Jn 20:7 *1794*
There were *t* Simon Peter, and Jn 21:2 *3674*
And, being assembled *t* with them Acts 1:4 *4811*
When they therefore were come *t* Acts 1:6 *4905*
(the number of names *t* were about Acts 1:15
abroad, the multitude came *t* Acts 2:6 *4905*
And all that believed were *t* Acts 2:44
John went up *t* into the temple at Acts 3:1
all the people ran *t* unto them in Acts 3:11
were gathered *t* at Jerusalem Acts 4:6 *4863*
were gathered *t* against the Lord Acts 4:26
people of Israel, were gathered *t* Acts 4:27 *4863*
where they were assembled *t* Acts 4:31 *4863*
How is it that ye have agreed *t* Acts 5:9 *4856*
with him, and called the council *t* Acts 5:21 *4779*
had called *t* his kinsmen and near Acts 10:24 *4779*
and found many that were come *t* Acts 10:27 *4905*
many were gathered *t* praying Acts 12:12 *4867*
city *t* to hear the word of God Acts 13:44 *4863*
that they went both *t* into the Acts 14:1
and had gathered the church *t* Acts 14:27 *4863*
elders came *t* for to consider of Acts 15:6 *4863*
they had gathered the multitude *t* Acts 15:30 *4863*
multitude rose up *t* against them Acts 16:22 *4911*
arts brought their books *t* Acts 19:19 *4851*
Whom he called *t* with the workmen Acts 19:25 *4867*
not wherefore they were come *t* Acts 19:32 *4897*
disciples came *t* to break bread Acts 20:7 *4863*
where they were gathered *t* Acts 20:8 *4863*
the multitude must needs come *t* Acts 21:22 *4905*
was moved, and the people ran *t* Acts 21:30 *4890*
day, certain of the Jews banded *t* Acts 23:12 *4966*
called the chief of the Jews *t* Acts 28:17 *4779*
and when they were come *t*, he said Acts 28:17 *4905*
that I may be comforted *t* with Rom 1:12 *4837*
they are *t* become unprofitable Rom 3:12 *260*
For if we have been planted *t* in Rom 6:5 *4854*
that we may be also glorified *t* Rom 8:17 *4888*
and travaileth in pain *t* until now Rom 8:22 *4944*
we know that all things work *t* Rom 8:28 *4903*
that ye strive *t* with me in your Rom 15:30 *4865*
joined *t* in the same mind 1Cor 1:10 *2675*
For we are labourers *t* with God 1Cor 3:9 *4904*
Christ, when ye are gathered *t* 1Cor 5:4 *4863*
come *t* again, that Satan tempt 1Cor 7:5
that ye come *t* not for the better 1Cor 11:17 *4905*
when ye come *t* in the church, I 1Cor 11:18 *4905*
When ye come *t* therefore into one 1Cor 11:20 *4905*
brethren, when ye come *t* to eat 1Cor 11:33 *4905*
that ye come not *t* unto 1Cor 11:34 *4905*
but God hath tempered the body *t* 1Cor 12:24 *4786*
church be come *t* into one place 1Cor 14:23 *4905*
when ye come *t*, every one of you 1Cor 14:26 *4905*
Ye also helping *t* by prayer for 2Cor 1:11 *4943*
We then, as workers *t* with him 2Cor 6:1 *4903*
yoked *t* with unbelievers 2Cor 6:14 *2086*
of times he might gather *t* in one Eph 1:10 *346*
hath quickened us *t* with Christ Eph 2:5 *4806*
And hath raised us up *t*, and made Eph 2:6 *4891*
made us sit *t* in heavenly places Eph 2:6 *4776*
all the building fitly framed *t* Eph 2:21 *4883*
t for an habitation of God Eph 2:22 *4925*
the whole body fitly joined *t* Eph 4:16 *4883*
with one mind striving *t* for the Phil 1:27 *4866*
Brethren, be followers *t* of me Phil 3:17 *4831*
comforted, being knit *t* in love Col 2:2 *4822*
hath he quickened *t* with him Col 2:13 *4806*
nourishment ministered, and knit *t* Col 2:19 *4822*
up *t* with them in the clouds 1Th 4:17 *260*
sleep, we should live *t* with him 1Th 5:10 *260*
Wherefore comfort yourselves *t* 1Th 5:11 *240*
and by our gathering *t* unto him 2Th 2:1 *1997*
the assembling of ourselves *t* Heb 10:25 *1997*
treasure *t* for the last days Jas 5:3
as being heirs *t* of the grace of 1Pet 3:7 *4789*
elected *t* with you, saluteth you 1Pet 5:13 *4899*
as a scroll when it is rolled *t* Rev 6:14
he gathered them *t* into a place Rev 16:16 *4863*
gather yourselves *t* unto the Rev 19:17 *4863*
gathered *t* to make war against Rev 19:19 *4863*
Magog, to gather them *t* to battle Rev 20:8 *4863*

TOHU (*to'-hu*) See NAHATH, TOAH. *An ancestor of Samuel.*
the son of Elihu, the son of *T* 1Sa 1:1 8459

TOI (*to'-i*) See TOU. *King of Hamath.*
When *T* king of Hamath heard that 2Sa 8:9 8583
Then *T* sent Joram his son unto 2Sa 8:10 8583
for Hadadezer had wars with *T* 2Sa 8:10 8583

TOIL
t of our hands, because of the Gen 5:29 6093
he, hath made me forget all my *t* Gen 41:51 5999
they *t* not, neither do they spin Mt 6:28 *2872*
they *t* not, they spin not Lk 12:27 *2872*

TOILED
we have *t* all the night, and have Lk 5:5 *2872*

TOILING
And he saw them *t* in rowing Mk 6:48 *928*

TOKEN
This is the *t* of the covenant Gen 9:12 226
it shall be for a *t* of a covenant Gen 9:13 226
This is the *t* of the covenant, Gen 9:17 226
it shall be a *t* of the covenant Gen 17:11 226
and this shall be a *t* unto thee Ex 3:12 226
a *t* upon the houses where ye are Ex 12:13 226
shall be for a *t* upon thine hand Ex 13:16 226
to be kept for a *t* against the Num 17:10 226
house, and give me a true *t* Josh 2:12 226
Shew me a *t* for good Ps 86:17 226
betrayed him had given them a *t* Mk 14:44 *4953*
to them an evident *t* of perdition Phil 1:28 *1732*
Which is a manifest *t* of the 2Th 1:5 *1730*
which is the *t* in every epistle 2Th 3:17 *4592*

TOKENS
bring forth the *t* of the damsel's Deut 22:15
yet these are the *t* of my Deut 22:17
the *t* of virginity be not found Deut 22:20
and do ye not know their *t* Job 21:29 226
parts are afraid at thy *t* Ps 65:8 226
Who sent *t* and wonders into the Ps 135:9 226
frustrateth the *t* of the liars Is 44:25 226

TOKHATH See TIKVATH.

TOLA (*to'-lah*) See TOLAITES.
1. A son of Issachar.
T, and Phuvah, and Job, and Shimron Gen 46:13 8439
of *T*, the family of the Tolaites Num 26:23 8439
Now the sons of Issachar were, *T* 1Chr 7:1 8439
And the sons of *T* 1Chr 7:2 8439
father's house, to wit, of *T* 1Chr 7:2 8439
2. A judge of Israel.
defend Israel *T* the son of Puah Judg 10:1 8439

TOLAD (*to'-lad*) See EL-TOLAD. *A city in Simeon.*
And at Bilhah, and at Ezem, and at *T* 1Chr 4:29 8434

TOLAITES (*to'-lah-ites*) *Descendants of Tola.*
of Tola, the family of the *T* Num 26:23 8440

TOLD
Who *t* thee that thou wast naked Gen 3:11 5046
t his two brethren without Gen 9:22 5046
escaped, and *t* Abram the Hebrew Gen 14:13 5046
t all these things in their ears Gen 20:8 1696
the place of which God had *t* him Gen 22:3 559
the place which God had *t* him of Gen 22:9 559
things, that it was *t* Abraham Gen 22:20 5046
t them of her mother's house Gen 24:28 5046
eat, until I have *t* mine errand Gen 24:33 1696
the servant *t* Isaac all things Gen 24:66 5608
t him concerning the well which Gen 26:32 5046
her elder son were *t* to Rebekah Gen 27:42 5046
Jacob *t* Rachel that he was her Gen 29:12 5046
and she ran and *t* her father Gen 29:12 5046
he *t* Laban all these things Gen 29:13 5608
in that he *t* him not that he fled Gen 31:20 5046
it was *t* Laban on the third day Gen 31:22 5046
a dream, and he *t* it his brethren Gen 37:5 5046
t it his brethren, and said, Gen 37:9 5608
he *t* it to his father, and to his Gen 37:10 5608
And it was *t* Tamar, saying, Behold Gen 38:13 5046
months after, that it was *t* Judah Gen 38:24 5046
the chief butler *t* his dream to Gen 40:9 5608
and Pharaoh *t* them his dream Gen 41:8 5608
we *t* him, and he interpreted to us Gen 41:12 5608
I *t* this unto the magicians Gen 41:24 559
t him all that befell unto them Gen 42:29 5046
we *t* him according to the tenor Gen 43:7 5046
we *t* him the words of my lord Gen 44:24 5046
t him, saying, Joseph is yet Gen 45:26 5046
they *t* him all the words of Gen 45:27 1696
t Pharaoh, and said, My father and Gen 47:1 5046
these things, that one *t* Joseph Gen 48:1 559
one *t* Jacob, and said, Behold, thy Gen 48:2 5046
Moses *t* Aaron all the words of Ex 4:28 5046
t Pharaoh, Thus saith the LORD Ex 5:1 559
it was *t* the king of Egypt that Ex 14:5 5046
the congregation came and *t* Moses Ex 16:22 5046
Moses *t* his father in law all Ex 18:8 5608
Moses *t* the words of the people Ex 19:9 5046
t the people all the words of the Ex 24:3 5608
Moses *t* it unto Aaron, and to his Lev 21:24 1696
t the people the words of the Num 11:24 1696
t Moses, and said, Eldad and Medad Num 11:27 5046
And they *t* him, and said, We came Num 13:27 5608
Moses *t* these sayings unto all Num 14:39 1696
T not I thee, saying, All that Num 23:26 1696
Moses *t* the children of Israel Num 29:40 559
And it be *t* thee, and thou hast Deut 17:4 5046
it was *t* the king of Jericho, Josh 2:2 559
t him all things that befell them Josh 2:23 5608
it was certainly *t* thy servants Josh 9:24 5046
And it was *t* Joshua, saying, The Josh 10:17 5046
which our fathers *t* us of Judg 6:13 5608
there was a man that *t* a dream Judg 7:13 5608
when they *t* it to Jotham, he went Judg 9:7 5046
and it was *t* Abimelech Judg 9:25 5046
and they *t* Abimelech Judg 9:42 5046
it was *t* Abimelech, that all the Judg 9:47 5046
t her husband, saying, A man of Judg 13:6 559
he was, neither *t* he me his name Judg 13:6 5046
have *t* us such things as these Judg 13:23 8085
t his father and his mother, and Judg 14:2 5046
but he *t* not his father or his Judg 14:6 5046
but he *t* not them that he had Judg 14:9 5046
of my people, and hast not *t* it me Judg 14:16 5046
I have not *t* it my father nor my Judg 14:16 5046
on the seventh day, that he *t* her Judg 14:17 5046
she *t* the riddle to the children Judg 14:17 5046
it was *t* the Gazites, saying, Judg 16:2
thou hast mocked me, and *t* me lies Judg 16:10 1696
thou hast mocked me, and *t* me lies Judg 16:13 1696
hast not *t* me wherein thy great Judg 16:15 5046
That he *t* her all his heart, and Judg 16:17 5046
that he had *t* her all his heart Judg 16:18 5046
she *t* her all that the man had Ruth 3:16 5046
For I have *t* him that I will 1Sa 3:13 5046
Samuel *t* him every whit, and hid 1Sa 3:18 5046
t it, all the city cried out 1Sa 4:13 5046
the man came in hastily, and *t* Eli 1Sa 4:14 5046
Samuel *t* all the words of the 1Sa 8:10 559
Now the LORD had *t* Samuel in his 1Sa 9:15 1540
He *t* us plainly that the asses 1Sa 10:16 5046
Samuel spake, he *t* him not 1Sa 10:16 5046
Then Samuel *t* the people the 1Sa 10:25 1696
t the tidings in the ears of the 1Sa 11:4 1696
they *t* him the tidings of the men 1Sa 11:5 5608
But he *t* not his father 1Sa 14:1 5046
Then they *t* Saul, saying, Behold, 1Sa 14:33 5046
And Jonathan *t* him, and said, I did 1Sa 14:43 5046
in the morning, it was *t* Samuel 1Sa 15:12 5046
and they *t* Saul, and the thing 1Sa 18:20 5046
And the servants of Saul *t* him 1Sa 18:24 5046
his servants *t* David these words 1Sa 18:26 5046
and Jonathan *t* David, saying, Saul 1Sa 19:2 5046
and Michal David's wife *t* him 1Sa 19:11 5046
t him all that Saul had done to 1Sa 19:18 5046
And it was *t* Saul, saying, Behold, 1Sa 19:19 5046
And when it was *t* Saul, he sent 1Sa 19:21 5046
Then they *t* David, saying, Behold 1Sa 23:1 5046
it was *t* Saul that David was come 1Sa 23:7 5046
it was *t* Saul that David was 1Sa 23:13 5046
for it is *t* me that he dealeth 1Sa 23:22 559
And they *t* David 1Sa 23:25 5046
Philistines, that it was *t* him 1Sa 24:1 5046
came and *t* him all those sayings 1Sa 25:12 5046
one of the young men *t* Abigail 1Sa 25:14 5046
But she *t* not her husband Nabal 1Sa 25:19 5046
wherefore she *t* him nothing 1Sa 25:36 5046
his wife had *t* him these things, 1Sa 25:37 5046
it was *t* Saul that David was fled 1Sa 27:4 5046
unto the young man that *t* him 2Sa 1:5 5046
And the young man that *t* him said 2Sa 1:6 5046
unto the young man that *t* him 2Sa 1:13 5046
they *t* David, saying, That the 2Sa 2:4 5046
with him were come, they *t* Joab 2Sa 3:23 5046
When one *t* me, saying, Behold, 2Sa 4:10 5046
it was *t* king David, saying, The 2Sa 6:12 5046
When they *t* it unto David, he 2Sa 10:5 5046
And when it was *t* David, he 2Sa 10:17 5046
t David, and said, I am with child 2Sa 11:5 5046
And when they had *t* David, saying, 2Sa 11:10 5046
t David all the things concerning 2Sa 11:18 5046
Joab came to the king, and *t* him 2Sa 14:33 5046
one *t* David, saying, Ahithophel 2Sa 15:31 5046
and a wench went and *t* them 2Sa 17:17 5046
and they went and *t* king David 2Sa 17:17 5046
a lad saw them, and *t* Absalom 2Sa 17:18 5046
t king David, and said unto David, 2Sa 17:21 5046
t Joab, and said, Behold, I saw 2Sa 18:10 5046
Joab said unto the man that *t* him 2Sa 18:11 5046
the watchman cried, and *t* the king 2Sa 18:25 5046
And it was *t* Joab, Behold, the 2Sa 19:1 5046
they *t* unto all the people, 2Sa 19:8 5046
it was *t* David what Rizpah the 2Sa 21:11 5046
t him, and said unto him, Shall 2Sa 24:13 5046
they *t* the king, saying, Behold 1Kin 1:23 5046
it was *t* Solomon, saying, Behold, 1Kin 1:51 5046
it was *t* king Solomon that Joab 1Kin 2:29 5046
they *t* Shimei, saying, Behold, 1Kin 2:39 5046
it was *t* Solomon that Shimei had 1Kin 2:41 5046
that could not be *t* nor numbered 1Kin 8:5 5608
Solomon *t* her all her questions 1Kin 10:3 5046
from the king, which he *t* her not 1Kin 10:3 5046
and, behold, the half was not *t* me 1Kin 10:7 5046
t him all the works that the man 1Kin 13:11 5608
them they *t* also to their father 1Kin 13:11 5608
t it in the city where the old 1Kin 13:25 1696
which *t* me that I should be king 1Kin 14:2 1696
Was it not *t* my lord what I did 1Kin 18:13 5046
went to meet Ahab, and *t* him 1Kin 18:16 5046
Ahab *t* Jezebel all that Elijah 1Kin 19:1 5046
Ben-hadad sent out, and they *t* him 1Kin 20:17 5046

to meet you, and *t* you these words ... 2Kin 1:7 1696
Then she came and *t* the man of God.. 2Kin 4:7 5046
hid it from me, and hath not *t* me ... 2Kin 4:27 5046
t him, saying, The child is not ... 2Kin 4:31 5046
t his lord, saying, Thus and thus ... 2Kin 5:4 5046
place which the man of God *t* him ... 2Kin 6:10 559
And it was *t* him, saying, Behold, ... 2Kin 6:13 5046
and they *t* them, saying, We came ... 2Kin 7:10 5046
they *t* it to the king's house ... 2Kin 7:11 5046
returned, and *t* the king ... 2Kin 7:15 5046
king asked the woman, she *t* him ... 2Kin 8:6 5608
and it was *t* him, saying, The man ... 2Kin 8:7 5046
He *t* me that thou shouldest ... 2Kin 8:14 559
And the watchman *t*, saying, The ... 2Kin 9:18 5046
And the watchman *t*, saying, He ... 2Kin 9:20 5046
they came again, and *t* him ... 2Kin 9:36 5046
t him, saying, They have brought ... 2Kin 10:8 5046
t the money that was found in the ... 2Kin 12:10 4487
And they gave the money, being *t* ... 2Kin 12:11 8505
t him the words of Rab-shakeh ... 2Kin 18:37 5046
And the men of the city *t* him ... 2Kin 23:17 559
hast *t* thy servant that thou wilt ... 1Chr 17:25 1540
t David how the men were served ... 1Chr 19:5 5046
And it was *t* David ... 1Chr 19:17 5046
Solomon *t* out threescore and ten ... 2Chr 2:2 5608
which could not be *t* nor numbered ... 2Chr 5:6 5608
Solomon *t* her all her questions ... 2Chr 9:2 5046
from Solomon which he *t* her not ... 2Chr 9:2 5046
of thy wisdom was not *t* me ... 2Chr 9:6 5046
came some that *t* Jehoshaphat ... 2Chr 20:2 5046
Shaphan the scribe *t* the king ... 2Chr 34:18 5046
I *t* them what they should say ... Ezr 8:17
neither *t* I any man what my God ... Neh 2:12 5046
had I as yet *t* it to the Jews ... Neh 2:16 5046
Then I *t* them of the hand of my ... Neh 2:18 5046
who *t* it unto Esther the queen ... Est 2:22 5046
not unto them, that they *t* Haman ... Est 3:4 5046
for he had *t* them that he was a ... Est 3:4 5046
her chamberlains came and *t* it her ... Est 4:4 5046
Mordecai *t* him of all that had ... Est 4:7 5046
t Esther the words of Mordecai ... Est 4:9 5046
they *t* to Mordecai Esther's words ... Est 4:12 5046
Haman *t* them of the glory of his ... Est 5:11 5608
that Mordecai had *t* of Bigthana ... Est 6:2 5046
Haman *t* Zeresh his wife and all ... Est 6:13 5608
for Esther had *t* what he was unto ... Est 8:1 5046
men have *t* from their fathers ... Job 15:18 5046
Shall it be *t* him that I speak ... Job 37:20 5608
O God, our fathers have *t* us ... Ps 44:1 5608
t Saul, and said unto him, David ... Ps 52:*t* 5046
known, and our fathers have *t* us ... Ps 78:3 5608
our years as a tale that is *t* ... Ps 90:9
he live a thousand years twice *t* ... Eccl 6:6
it was *t* the house of David, ... Is 7:2 5046
t him the words of Rabshakeh ... Is 36:22 5046
hath it not been *t* you from the ... Is 40:21 5046
have not I *t* thee from that time, ... Is 44:8 8085
who hath *t* it from that time ... Is 45:21 5046
not been *t* them shall they see ... Is 52:15 5608
t all the words in the ears of ... Jer 36:20 5046
he *t* them according to all these ... Jer 38:27 5046
I *t* the dream before them ... Dan 4:7 560
and before him I *t* the dream ... Dan 4:8 560
and *t* the sum of the matters ... Dan 7:1 560
So he *t* me, and made me know the ... Dan 7:16 560
the morning which was *t* is true ... Dan 8:26 560
the LORD, because he had *t* them ... Jonah 1:10 5046
not believe, though it be *t* you ... Hab 1:5 5608
a lie, and have *t* false dreams ... Zec 10:2 1696
t every thing, and what was ... Mt 8:33 518
and said unto him that *t* him ... Mt 12:48 2036
and buried it, and went and *t* Jesus ... Mt 14:12 518
t unto their lord all that was ... Mt 18:31 1285
Behold, I have *t* you before ... Mt 24:25 4280
be *t* for a memorial of her ... Mt 26:13 2980
lo, I have *t* you ... Mt 28:7 2036
t it in the city, and in the ... Mk 5:14 312
they that saw it *t* them how it ... Mk 5:16 1334
him, and *t* him all the truth ... Mk 5:33 2036
t him all things, both what they ... Mk 6:30 518
t them, Elias verily cometh first ... Mk 9:12 2036
t them that had been with him, as ... Mk 16:10 518
went and *t* it unto the residue ... Mk 16:13 518
which were *t* her from the Lord ... Lk 1:45 2980
was *t* them concerning this child ... Lk 2:17 2980
were *t* them by the shepherds ... Lk 2:18 2980
and seen, as it was *t* unto them ... Lk 2:20 2980
it was *t* him by certain which ... Lk 8:20 518
t it in the city and in the ... Lk 8:34 518
They also which saw it *t* them by ... Lk 8:36 518
t him all that they had done ... Lk 9:10 1334
t no man in those days any of ... Lk 9:36 518
some that *t* him of the Galilaeans ... Lk 13:1 518
And they *t* him, that Jesus of ... Lk 18:37 518
t all these things unto the ... Lk 24:9 518
which *t* these things unto the ... Lk 24:10 3004
they *t* what things were done in ... Lk 24:35 1834
If I have *t* you earthly things, ... Jn 3:12 2036
which *t* me all things that ever I ... Jn 4:29 2036
He *t* me all that ever I did ... Jn 4:39 2036
t him, saying, Thy son liveth ... Jn 4:51 518
t the Jews that it was Jesus, ... Jn 5:15 312
a man that hath *t* you the truth ... Jn 8:40 2980
I have *t* you already, and ye did ... Jn 9:27 2036
I *t* you, and ye believed not ... Jn 10:25 2036
t them what things Jesus had done ... Jn 11:46 2036
were not so, I would have *t* you ... Jn 14:2 2036
now I have *t* you before it come ... Jn 14:29 2046
But these things have I *t* you ... Jn 16:4 2980
may remember that I *t* you of them ... Jn 16:4 2036
I have *t* you that I am he ... Jn 18:8 2036
t the disciples that she had seen ... Jn 20:18 513
the prison, they returned, and *t* ... Acts 5:22 513
t them, saying, Behold, the men ... Acts 5:25 513
it shall be *t* thee what thou must ... Acts 9:6 2980
t how Peter stood before the gate ... Acts 12:14 518
the prison *t* this saying to Paul ... Acts 16:36 518
the serjeants *t* these words unto ... Acts 16:38 312
there it shall be *t* thee of all ... Acts 22:10 2980
t the chief captain, saying, Take ... Acts 22:26 518
into the castle, and *t* Paul ... Acts 23:16 518
when it was *t* me how that the ... Acts 23:30 3377
it shall be even as it was *t* me ... Acts 27:25 2980
when he *t* us your earnest desire, ... 2Cor 7:7 312
I *t* you before, and foretell you, ... 2Cor 13:2 4280
as I have also *t* you in time past ... Gal 5:21 4277
walk, of whom I have *t* you often ... Phil 3:18 3004
we *t* you before that we should ... 1Th 3:4 4302
with you, I *t* you these things ... 2Th 2:5 3004
How that they *t* you there should ... Jude 18 3004

TOLERABLE
It shall be more *t* for the land ... Mt 10:15 414
you, It shall be more *t* for Tyre ... Mt 11:22 414
That it shall be more *t* for the ... Mt 11:24 414
you, It shall be more *t* for Sodom ... Mk 6:11 414
be more *t* in that day for Sodom ... Lk 10:12 414
But it shall be more *t* for Tyre ... Lk 10:14 414

TOLL
again, then will they not pay *t* ... Ezr 4:13 4061
and *t*, tribute, and custom, was ... Ezr 4:20 4061
shall not be lawful to impose *t* ... Ezr 7:24 4061

TOMB
grave, and shall remain in the *t* ... Job 21:32 1430
And laid it in his own new *t* ... Mt 27:60 3419
up his corpse, and laid it in a *t* ... Mk 6:29 3419

TOMBS
with devils, coming out of the *t* ... Mt 8:28 3419
ye build the *t* of the prophets ... Mt 23:29 5028
there met him out of the *t* a man ... Mk 5:2 3419
Who had his dwelling among the *t* ... Mk 5:3 3419
was in the mountains, and in the *t* ... Mk 5:5 3418
abode in any house, but in the *t* ... Lk 8:27 3418

TONGS
the *t* thereof, and the snuffdishes ... Ex 25:38 4457
the light, and his lamps, and his *t* ... Num 4:9 4457
and the lamps, and the *t* of gold, ... 1Kin 7:49 4457
flowers, and the lamps, and the *t* ... 2Chr 4:21 4457
with the *t* from off the altar ... Is 6:6 4457
The smith with the *t* both worketh ... Is 44:12 4621

TONGUE
every one after his *t*, after ... Gen 10:5 3956
am slow of speech, and of a slow *t* ... Ex 4:10 3956
Israel shall not a dog move his *t* ... Ex 11:7 3956
a nation whose *t* thou shalt not ... Deut 28:49 3956
none moved his *t* against any of ... Josh 10:21 3956
lappeth of the water with his *t* ... Judg 7:5 3956
by me, and his word was in my *t* ... 2Sa 23:2 3956
was written in the Syrian *t* ... Ezr 4:7 762
and interpreted in the Syrian *t* ... Ezr 4:7 762
and bondwomen, I had held my *t* ... Est 7:4 2790
be hid from the scourge of the *t* ... Job 5:21 3956
Teach me, and I will hold my *t* ... Job 6:24 2790
Is there iniquity in my *t* ... Job 6:30 3956
for now, if I hold my *t*, I shall ... Job 13:19 2790
thou choosest the *t* of the crafty ... Job 15:5 3956
though he hide it under his *t* ... Job 20:12 3956
the viper's *t* shall slay him ... Job 20:16 3956
wickedness, nor my *t* utter deceit ... Job 27:4 3956
their *t* cleaved to the roof of ... Job 29:10 3956
my *t* hath spoken in my mouth ... Job 33:2 3956
or his *t* with a cord which thou ... Job 41:1 3956
they flatter with their *t* ... Ps 5:9 3956
under his *t* is mischief and vanity ... Ps 10:7 3956
the *t* that speaketh proud things ... Ps 12:3 3956
With our *t* will we prevail ... Ps 12:4 3956
He that backbiteth not with his *t* ... Ps 15:3 3956
and my *t* cleaveth to my jaws ... Ps 22:15 3956
Keep thy *t* from evil, and thy lips ... Ps 34:13 3956
And my *t* shall speak of thy ... Ps 35:28 3956
his *t* talketh of judgment ... Ps 37:30 3956
my ways, that I sin not with my *t* ... Ps 39:1 3956
then spake I with my *t*, ... Ps 39:3 3956
my *t* is the pen of a ready writer ... Ps 45:1 3956
to evil, and thy *t* frameth deceit ... Ps 50:19 3956
my *t* shall sing aloud of thy ... Ps 51:14 3956
Thy *t* deviseth mischiefs ... Ps 52:2 3956
words, O thou deceitful *t* ... Ps 52:4 3956
arrows, and their *t* a sharp sword ... Ps 57:4 3956
Who whet their *t* like a sword ... Ps 64:3 3956
own *t* to fall upon themselves ... Ps 64:8 3956
and he was extolled with my *t* ... Ps 66:17 3956
the *t* of thy dogs in the same ... Ps 68:23 3956
My *t* also shall talk of thy ... Ps 71:24 3956
their *t* walketh through the earth ... Ps 73:9 3956
spoken against me with a lying *t* ... Ps 109:2 3956
My *t* shall speak of thy word ... Ps 119:172 3956
lying lips, and from a deceitful *t* ... Ps 120:2 3956
be done unto thee, thou false *t* ... Ps 120:3 3956
laughter, and our *t* with singing ... Ps 126:2 3956
let my *t* cleave to the roof of my ... Ps 137:6 3956
For there is not a word in my *t* ... Ps 139:4 3956
A proud look, a lying *t*, and hands ... Prov 6:17 3956
of the *t* of a strange woman ... Prov 6:24 3956
The *t* of the just is as choice ... Prov 10:20 3956
but the froward *t* shall be cut ... Prov 10:31 3956
but the *t* of the wise is health ... Prov 12:18 3956
but a lying *t* is but for a moment ... Prov 12:19 3956
The *t* of the wise useth knowledge ... Prov 15:2 3956
A wholesome *t* is a tree of life ... Prov 15:4 3956
in man, and the answer of the *t* ... Prov 16:1 3956
a liar giveth ear to a naughty *t* ... Prov 17:4 3956
perverse *t* falleth into mischief ... Prov 17:20 3956
and life are in the power of the *t* ... Prov 18:21 3956
a lying *t* is a vanity tossed to ... Prov 21:6 3956
his *t* keepeth his soul from ... Prov 21:23 3956
a soft *t* breaketh the bone ... Prov 25:15 3956
angry countenance a backbiting *t* ... Prov 25:23 3956
A lying *t* hateth those that are ... Prov 26:28 3956
he that flattereth with the *t* ... Prov 28:23 3956
in her *t* is the law of kindness ... Prov 31:26 3956
honey and milk are under thy *t* ... Song 4:11 3956
because their *t* and their doings ... Is 3:8 3956
destroy the *t* of the Egyptian sea ... Is 11:15 3956
another *t* will he speak to this ... Is 28:11 3956
his *t* as a devouring fire ... Is 30:27 3956
the *t* of the stammerers shall be ... Is 32:4 3956
of a stammering *t*, that thou ... Is 33:19 3956
hart, and the *t* of the dumb sing ... Is 35:6 3956
their *t* faileth for thirst, I the ... Is 41:17 3956
shall bow, every *t* shall swear ... Is 45:23 3956
given me the *t* of the learned ... Is 50:4 3956
every *t* that shall rise against ... Is 54:17 3956
a wide mouth, and draw out the *t* ... Is 57:4 3956
your *t* hath muttered perverseness ... Is 59:3 3956
have taught their *t* to speak lies ... Jer 9:5 3956
Their *t* is as an arrow shot out ... Jer 9:8 3956
and let us smite him with the *t* ... Jer 18:18 3956
The *t* of the sucking child ... Lam 4:4 3956
I will make thy *t* cleave to the ... Eze 3:26 3956
and the *t* of the Chaldeans ... Dan 1:4 3956
the sword for the rage of their *t* ... Hos 7:16 3956
Then shall he say, Hold thy *t* ... Amos 6:10 2013
their *t* is deceitful in their ... Mic 6:12 3956
holdest thy *t* when the wicked ... Hab 1:13 2790
t be found in their mouth ... Zeph 3:13 3956
their *t* shall consume away in ... Zec 14:12 3956
and he spit, and touched his *t* ... Mk 7:33 1100
and the string of his *t* was loosed ... Mk 7:35 1100
his *t* loosed, and he spake, and ... Lk 1:64 1100
his finger in water, and cool my *t* ... Lk 16:24 1100
called in the Hebrew *t* Bethesda ... Jn 5:2 1447
field is called in their proper *t* ... Acts 1:19 1258
hear we every man in our own *t* ... Acts 2:8 1258
heart rejoice, and my *t* was glad ... Acts 2:26 1100
spake unto them in the Hebrew *t* ... Acts 21:40 1258
he spake in the Hebrew *t* to them ... Acts 22:2 1258
me, and saying in the Hebrew *t* ... Acts 26:14 1258
every *t* shall confess to God ... Rom 14:11 1100
unknown *t* speaketh not unto men ... 1Cor 14:2 1100
in an unknown *t* edifieth himself ... 1Cor 14:4 1100
except ye utter by the *t* words ... 1Cor 14:9 1100
t pray that he may interpret ... 1Cor 14:13 1100
For if I pray in an unknown *t* ... 1Cor 14:14 1100
thousand words in an unknown *t* ... 1Cor 14:19 1100
psalm, hath a doctrine, hath a *t* ... 1Cor 14:26 1100
If any man speak in an unknown *t* ... 1Cor 14:27 1100
that every *t* should confess that ... Phil 2:11 1100
religious, and bridleth not his *t* ... Jas 1:26 1100
Even so the *t* is a little member, ... Jas 3:5 1100
the *t* is a fire, a world of ... Jas 3:6 1100
so is the *t* among our members, ... Jas 3:6 1100
But the *t* can no man tame ... Jas 3:8 1100
let him refrain his *t* from evil ... 1Pet 3:10 1100
us not love in word, neither in *t* ... 1Jn 3:18 1100
blood out of every kindred, and *t* ... Rev 5:9 1100
name in the Hebrew *t* is Abaddon ... Rev 9:11 1447
but in the Greek *t* hath his name ... Rev 9:11
to every nation, and kindred, and *t* ... Rev 14:6 1100
called in the Hebrew *t* Armageddon ... Rev 16:16 1447

TONGUES
their families, after their *t* ... Gen 10:20 3956
their families, after their *t* ... Gen 10:31 3956
a pavilion from the strife of *t* ... Ps 31:20 3956
O Lord, and divide their *t* ... Ps 55:9 3956
they lied unto him with their *t* ... Ps 78:36 3956
sharpened their *t* like a serpent ... Ps 140:3 3956
I will gather all nations and *t* ... Is 66:18 3956
they bend their *t* like their bow ... Jer 9:3 3956
saith the LORD, that use their *t* ... Jer 23:31 3956
they shall speak with new *t* ... Mk 16:17 1100
them cloven *t* like as of fire ... Acts 2:3 1100
and began to speak with other *t* ... Acts 2:4 1100
our *t* the wonderful works of God ... Acts 2:11 1100
For they heard them speak with *t* ... Acts 10:46 1100
and they spake with *t*, and ... Acts 19:6 1100
with their *t* they have used ... Rom 3:13 1100
to another divers kinds of *t* ... 1Cor 12:10 1100
another the interpretation of *t* ... 1Cor 12:10 1100
governments, diversities of *t* ... 1Cor 12:28 1100
do all speak with *t* ... 1Cor 12:30 1100
Though I speak with the *t* of men ... 1Cor 13:1 1100
whether there be *t*, they shall ... 1Cor 13:8 1100
I would that ye all spake with *t* ... 1Cor 14:5 1100
than he that speaketh with *t* ... 1Cor 14:5 1100
I come unto you speaking with *t* ... 1Cor 14:6 1100
I speak with *t* more than ye all ... 1Cor 14:18 1100
is written, With men of other *t* ... 1Cor 14:21 2084
Wherefore *t* are for a sign, not ... 1Cor 14:22 1100
one place, and all speak with *t* ... 1Cor 14:23 1100
and forbid not to speak with *t* ... 1Cor 14:39 1100
and kindreds, and people, and *t* ... Rev 7:9 1100
many peoples, and nations, and *t* ... Rev 10:11 1100
of the people and kindreds and *t* ... Rev 11:9 1100
given him over all kindreds, and *t* ... Rev 13:7 1100
and they gnawed their *t* for pain ... Rev 16:10 1100
and multitudes, and nations, and *t* ... Rev 17:15 1100

TOO
Is any thing *t* hard for the LORD ... Gen 18:14
be *t* little for the lamb, let him ... Ex 12:4
this thing is *t* heavy for thee ... Ex 18:18
the work to make it, and *t* much ... Ex 36:7 3498
because it is *t* heavy for me ... Num 11:14
Ye take *t* much upon you, seeing ... Num 16:3
ye take *t* much upon you, ye sons ... Num 16:7
for they are *t* mighty for me ... Num 22:6
the cause that is *t* hard for you ... Deut 1:17
was not one city *t* strong for us ... Deut 2:36
his name there be *t* far from thee ... Deut 12:21 7368

T

And if the way be *t* long for thee ... Deut 14:24
if the place be *t* far from thee ... Deut 14:24
If there arise a matter *t* hard ... Deut 17:8
Ephraim be *t* narrow for thee ... Josh 17:15
of Judah was *t* much for them ... Josh 19:9
of Dan went out *t* little for them ... Josh 19:47
iniquity of Peor *t* little for us ... Josh 22:17
are *t* many for me to give the ... Judg 7:2
Gideon, The people are yet *t* many ... Judg 7:4
that they were *t* strong for him ... Judg 18:26
for I am *t* old to have an husband ... Ruth 1:12
sons of Zeruiah be *t* hard for me ... 2Sa 3:39
If the Syrians be *t* strong for me ... 2Sa 10:11
of Ammon be *t* strong for thee ... 2Sa 10:11
and if that had been *t* little ... 2Sa 12:8
for they were *t* strong for me ... 2Sa 22:18
God of my lord the king say so *t* ... 1Kin 1:36
was *t* little to receive the burnt ... 1Kin 8:64
It is *t* much for you to go up to ... 1Kin 12:28
the journey is *t* great for thee ... 1Kin 19:7
the battle was *t* sore for him ... 2Kin 3:26
with thee is *t* strait for us ... 2Kin 6:1
If the Syrians be *t* strong for me ... 1Chr 19:12
of Ammon be *t* strong for thee ... 1Chr 19:12
But the priests were *t* few ... 2Chr 29:34
shall there arise *t* much contempt ... Est 1:18 1767
things *t* wonderful for me, which ... Job 42:3
for they were *t* strong for me ... Ps 18:17
from him that is *t* strong for him ... Ps 35:10
burden they are *t* heavy for me ... Ps 38:4
this, it was *t* painful for me ... Ps 73:16
or in things *t* high for me ... Ps 131:1
knowledge is *t* wonderful for me ... Ps 139:6
Wisdom is *t* high for a fool ... Prov 24:7
which are *t* wonderful for me ... Prov 30:18
shall even now be *t* narrow by ... Is 49:19
The place is *t* strait for me ... Is 49:20
there is nothing *t* hard for thee ... Jer 32:17
is there any thing *t* hard for me ... Jer 32:27
all things ye are *t* superstitious ... Acts 17:22 *1174*

TOOK

And the LORD God *t* the man ... Gen 2:15 3947
he *t* one of his ribs, and closed ... Gen 2:21 3947
she *t* of the fruit thereof, and ... Gen 3:6 3947
Lamech *t* unto him two wives ... Gen 4:19 3947
for God *t* him ... Gen 5:24 3947
they *t* them wives of all which ... Gen 6:2 3947
t her, and pulled her in unto him ... Gen 8:9 3947
t of every clean beast, and of ... Gen 8:20 3947
Japheth *t* a garment, and laid it ... Gen 9:23 3947
And Abram and Nahor *t* them wives ... Gen 11:29 3947
Terah *t* Abram his son, and Lot the ... Gen 11:31 3947
Abram *t* Sarai his wife, and Lot ... Gen 12:5 3947
they *t* all the goods of Sodom and ... Gen 14:11 3947
And they *t* Lot, Abram's brother's ... Gen 14:12 3947
he *t* unto him all these, and ... Gen 15:10 3947
Sarai Abram's wife *t* Hagar her ... Gen 16:3 3947
Abraham *t* Ishmael his son, and all ... Gen 17:23 3947
he *t* butter, and milk, and the calf ... Gen 18:8 3947
king of Gerar sent, and *t* Sarah ... Gen 20:2 3947
And Abimelech *t* sheep, and oxen, and ... Gen 20:14 3947
t bread, and a bottle of water, and ... Gen 21:14 3947
his mother *t* him a wife out of ... Gen 21:21 3947
And Abraham *t* sheep and oxen, and ... Gen 21:27 3947
t two of his young men with him, ... Gen 22:3 3947
Abraham *t* the wood of the burnt ... Gen 22:6 3947
he *t* the fire in his hand, and a ... Gen 22:6 3947
t the knife to slay his son ... Gen 22:10 3947
t the ram, and offered him up for ... Gen 22:13 3947
which *t* me from my father's house ... Gen 24:7 3947
the servant *t* ten camels of the ... Gen 24:10 3947
that the man *t* a golden earring ... Gen 24:22 3947
and the servant *t* Rebekah, and went ... Gen 24:61 3947
therefore she *t* a vail, and ... Gen 24:65 3947
t Rebekah, and she became his wife ... Gen 24:67 3947
Then again Abraham *t* a wife ... Gen 25:1 3947
old when he *t* Rebekah to wife ... Gen 25:20 3947
his hand *t* hold on Esau's heel ... Gen 25:26
was forty years old when he *t* to ... Gen 26:34 3947
Rebekah *t* goodly raiment of her ... Gen 27:15 3947
he *t* away my birthright ... Gen 27:36 3947
t unto the wives which he had ... Gen 28:9 3947
he *t* of the stones of that place, ... Gen 28:11 3947
t the stone that he had put for ... Gen 28:18 3947
that he *t* Leah his daughter, and ... Gen 29:23 3947
she *t* Zilpah her maid, and gave ... Gen 30:9 3947
Jacob *t* him rods of green poplar, ... Gen 30:37 3947
he *t* his brethren with him, and ... Gen 31:23 3947
Jacob *t* a stone, and set it up for ... Gen 31:45 3947
they *t* stones, and made an heap ... Gen 31:46 3947
t of that which came to his hand ... Gen 32:13 3947
t his two wives, and his two ... Gen 32:22 3947
he *t* them, and sent them over the ... Gen 32:23 3947
And he urged him, and he *t* it ... Gen 33:11 3947
he *t* her, and lay with her, and ... Gen 34:2 3947
t each man his sword, and came ... Gen 34:25 3947
t Dinah out of Shechem's house, ... Gen 34:26 3947
They *t* their sheep, and their oxen ... Gen 34:28 3947
their wives *t* they captive, and ... Gen 34:29
Esau *t* his wives of the daughters ... Gen 36:2 3947
Esau *t* his wives, and his sons, and ... Gen 36:6 3947
And they *t* him, and cast him into a ... Gen 37:24 3947
they *t* Joseph's coat, and killed a ... Gen 37:31 3947
he *t* her, and went in unto her ... Gen 38:2 3947
Judah *t* a wife for Er his ... Gen 38:6 3947
and the midwife *t* and bound upon ... Gen 38:28 3947
And Joseph's master *t* him, and put ... Gen 39:20 3947
I *t* the grapes, and pressed them ... Gen 40:11 3947
Pharaoh *t* off his ring from his ... Gen 41:42 5493
t from them Simeon, and bound him ... Gen 42:24 3947
t us for spies of the country ... Gen 42:30 5414
the men *t* that present, and they ... Gen 43:15 3947
they *t* double money in their hand ... Gen 43:15 3947

And he *t* and sent messes unto them ... Gen 43:34 5375
Then they speedily *t* down every ... Gen 44:11 3381
Israel *t* his journey with all ... Gen 46:1
they *t* their cattle, and their ... Gen 46:6 3947
he *t* some of his brethren, even ... Gen 47:2 3947
he *t* with him his two sons, ... Gen 48:1 3947
Joseph *t* them both, Ephraim in ... Gen 48:13 3947
which I *t* out of the hand of the ... Gen 48:22 3947
Joseph *t* an oath of the children ... Gen 50:25
t to wife a daughter of Levi ... Ex 2:1 3947
she *t* for him an ark of bulrushes ... Ex 2:3 3947
And the woman *t* the child, and ... Ex 2:9 3947
and when he *t* it out, behold, his ... Ex 4:6 3318
Moses *t* his wife and his sons, and ... Ex 4:20 3947
Moses *t* the rod of God in his ... Ex 4:20 3947
Then Zipporah *t* a sharp stone ... Ex 4:25 3947
Amram *t* him Jochebed his father's ... Ex 6:20 3947
Aaron *t* him Elisheba, daughter of ... Ex 6:23 3947
Eleazar Aaron's son *t* him one of ... Ex 6:25 3947
they *t* ashes of the furnace, and ... Ex 9:10 3947
which *t* away the locusts, and cast ... Ex 10:19 5375
the people *t* their dough before ... Ex 12:34 5375
Moses *t* the bones of Joseph with ... Ex 13:19 3947
they *t* their journey from Succoth ... Ex 13:20
He *t* not away the pillar of the ... Ex 13:22 4185
chariot, and *t* his people with him ... Ex 14:6 3947
he *t* six hundred chosen chariots, ... Ex 14:7 3947
t off their chariot wheels, that ... Ex 14:25 5493
of Aaron, *t* a timbrel in her hand ... Ex 15:20 3947
they *t* their journey from Elim, ... Ex 16:1
they *t* a stone, and put it under ... Ex 17:12 3947
t Zipporah, Moses' wife, after he ... Ex 18:2 3947
t a burnt offering and sacrifices ... Ex 18:12 3947
Moses *t* half of the blood, and put ... Ex 24:6 3947
he *t* the book of the covenant, and ... Ex 24:7 3947
Moses *t* the blood, and sprinkled ... Ex 24:8 3947
he *t* the calf which they had made ... Ex 32:20 3947
Moses *t* the tabernacle, and ... Ex 33:7 3947
t in his hand the two tables of ... Ex 34:4 3947
he *t* the vail off, until he came ... Ex 34:34 5493
And he *t* and put the testimony into ... Ex 40:20 3947
that which he *t* violently away ... Lev 6:4
Moses *t* the anointing oil, and ... Lev 8:10 3947
Moses *t* the blood, and put it upon ... Lev 8:15 3947
he *t* all the fat that was upon ... Lev 8:16 3947
Moses *t* of the blood of it, and ... Lev 8:23 3947
he *t* the fat, and the rump, and all ... Lev 8:25 3947
he *t* one unleavened cake, and a ... Lev 8:26 3947
Moses *t* them from off their hands ... Lev 8:28 3947
Moses *t* the breast, and waved it ... Lev 8:29 3947
Moses *t* of the anointing oil, and ... Lev 8:30 3947
t the goat, which was the sin ... Lev 9:15 3947
t an handful thereof, and burnt it ... Lev 9:17
t either of them his censer, and ... Lev 10:1 3947
Aaron *t* these men which are ... Num 1:17 3947
Moses *t* the redemption money of ... Num 3:49 3947
children of Israel *t* he the money ... Num 3:50 3947
Moses *t* the wagons and the oxen, ... Num 7:6 3947
the children of Israel *t* their ... Num 10:12
they first *t* their journey ... Num 10:13
t of the spirit that was upon him ... Num 11:25 680
of Peleth, sons of Reuben, *t* men ... Num 16:1 3947
they *t* every man his censer, and ... Num 16:18 3947
the priest *t* the brasen censers ... Num 16:39 3947
Aaron *t* as Moses commanded, and ... Num 16:47 3947
looked, and *t* every man his rod ... Num 17:9 3947
Moses *t* the rod from before the ... Num 20:9 3947
and *t* some of them prisoners ... Num 21:1
Israel *t* all these cities ... Num 21:25 3947
they *t* the villages thereof, and ... Num 21:32 3920
the morrow, that Balak *t* Balaam ... Num 22:41 3947
he *t* up his parable, and said, ... Num 23:7 5375
I *t* thee to curse mine enemies, ... Num 23:11 3947
he *t* up his parable, and said, ... Num 23:18 5375
he *t* up his parable, and said, ... Num 24:3 5375
he *t* up his parable, and said, ... Num 24:15 5375
he *t* up his parable, and said, ... Num 24:20 5375
t up his parable, and said, Strong ... Num 24:21 5375
he *t* up his parable, and said, ... Num 24:23 5375
and *t* a javelin in his hand ... Num 25:7 3947
he *t* Joshua, and set him before ... Num 27:22 3947
the children of Israel *t* all the ... Num 31:9
t the spoil of all their cattle, ... Num 31:9
they *t* all the spoil, and all the ... Num 31:11 3947
them that *t* the war upon them ... Num 31:27 8610
Moses *t* one portion of fifty, ... Num 31:47 3947
the priest *t* the gold of them ... Num 31:51 3947
Eleazar the priest *t* the gold of ... Num 31:54 3947
t it, and dispossessed the Amorite ... Num 32:39 3920
t the small towns thereof, and ... Num 32:41 3920
t Kenath, and the villages thereof ... Num 32:42 3920
they *t* their journey out of the ... Num 33:12 5265
So I *t* the chief of your tribes, ... Deut 1:15 3947
I *t* twelve men of you, one of a ... Deut 1:23 3947
they *t* of the fruit of the land ... Deut 1:25 3947
t our journey into the wilderness ... Deut 2:1 5265
we *t* all his cities at that time, ... Deut 2:34 3920
Only the cattle we *t* for a prey ... Deut 2:35
spoil of the cities which we *t*, ... Deut 2:35 3920
we *t* all his cities at that time, ... Deut 3:4 3920
a city which we *t* not from them ... Deut 3:4 3947
we *t* for a prey to ourselves ... Deut 3:7
we *t* at that time out of the hand ... Deut 3:8 3947
Jair the son of Manasseh *t* all ... Deut 3:14 3947
I *t* the two tables, and cast them ... Deut 9:17 8610
I *t* your sin, the calf which ye ... Deut 9:21 3947
the children of Israel *t* their ... Deut 10:6
I *t* this woman, and when I came to ... Deut 22:14 3947
which *t* her to be his wife ... Deut 24:3 3947
we *t* their land, and gave it for ... Deut 29:8 3947
the woman *t* the two men, and hid ... Josh 2:4 3947
they *t* up the ark of the covenant ... Josh 3:6 5375
t up twelve stones out of the ... Josh 4:8 5375
which they *t* out of Jordan, did ... Josh 4:20 3947

the priests *t* up the ark of the ... Josh 6:12 5375
before him, and they *t* the city ... Josh 6:20 3920
of Judah, *t* of the accursed thing ... Josh 7:1 3947
he *t* the family of the Zarhites ... Josh 7:17 3920
then I coveted them, and *t* them ... Josh 7:21 3947
they *t* them out of the midst of ... Josh 7:23 3947
t Achan the son of Zerah, and the ... Josh 7:24 3947
he *t* about five thousand men, and ... Josh 8:12 3947
t it, and hasted and set the city ... Josh 8:19 3920
And the king of Ai they *t* alive ... Josh 8:23 8610
t for a prey unto themselves ... Josh 8:27
t old sacks upon their asses, and ... Josh 9:4 3947
This our bread we *t* hot for our ... Josh 9:12
the men *t* of their victuals, and ... Josh 9:14 3947
they *t* them down off the trees, ... Josh 10:27 3381
And that day Joshua *t* Makkedah ... Josh 10:28 3920
which *t* it on the second day, and ... Josh 10:32 3920
they *t* it on that day, and smote ... Josh 10:35 3920
And they *t* it, and smote it with ... Josh 10:37 3920
And he *t* it, and the king thereof, ... Josh 10:39 3920
t Hazor, and smote the king ... Josh 11:10 3920
the children of Israel *t* for a ... Josh 11:14
So Joshua *t* all that land, the ... Josh 11:16 3947
and all their kings he *t*, and smote ... Josh 11:17 3920
all other they *t* in battle ... Josh 11:19 3947
So Joshua *t* the whole land, ... Josh 11:23 3947
Kenaz, the brother of Caleb, *t* it ... Josh 15:17 3920
and Ephraim, *t* their inheritance ... Josh 16:4
t it, and smote it with the edge ... Josh 19:47 3920
I *t* your father Abraham from the ... Josh 24:3 3947
t a great stone, and set it up ... Josh 24:26 3947
Caleb's younger brother, *t* it ... Judg 1:13 3920
Also Judah *t* Gaza with the coast ... Judg 1:18 3920
they *t* their daughters to be ... Judg 3:6 3947
t the dagger from his right thigh ... Judg 3:21 3947
therefore they *t* a key, and opened ... Judg 3:25 3947
t the fords of Jordan toward Moab ... Judg 3:28 3920
Heber's wife *t* a nail of the tent ... Judg 4:21 3947
t an hammer in her hand, and went ... Judg 4:21 7760
they *t* no gain of money ... Judg 5:19 3947
Then Gideon *t* ten men of his ... Judg 6:27 3947
So the people *t* victuals in their ... Judg 7:8 3947
t the waters unto Beth-barah and ... Judg 7:24 3920
they *t* two princes of the ... Judg 7:25 3920
t the two kings of Midian, Zebah ... Judg 8:12 3920
he *t* the elders of the city, and ... Judg 8:16 3947
t away the ornaments that were on ... Judg 8:21 3947
he *t* the people, and divided them ... Judg 9:43 3947
he *t* the city, and slew the people ... Judg 9:45 3920
Abimelech *t* an axe in his hand, ... Judg 9:48 3947
t it, and laid it on his shoulder, ... Judg 9:48 5375
encamped against Thebez, and *t* it ... Judg 9:50 3920
Because Israel *t* away my land ... Judg 11:13 3947
Israel *t* not away the land of ... Judg 11:15 3947
the Gileadites *t* the passages of ... Judg 12:5 3920
Then they *t* him, and slew him at ... Judg 12:6 270
t in thirty daughters from abroad ... Judg 12:9 935
So Manoah *t* a kid with a meat ... Judg 13:19 3947
he *t* thereof in his hands, and ... Judg 14:9 7287
t their spoil, and gave change of ... Judg 14:19 3947
t firebrands, and turned tail to ... Judg 15:4 3947
t it, and slew a thousand men ... Judg 15:15 3947
t the doors of the gate of the ... Judg 16:3 270
Delilah therefore *t* new ropes ... Judg 16:12 3947
But the Philistines *t* him ... Judg 16:21 270
Samson *t* hold of the two middle ... Judg 16:29
t him, and brought him up, and ... Judg 16:31 5375
I *t* it ... Judg 17:2 3947
his mother *t* two hundred shekels ... Judg 17:4 3947
t the graven image, and the ephod, ... Judg 18:17 3947
he *t* the ephod, and the teraphim, ... Judg 18:20 3947
they *t* the things which Micah had ... Judg 18:27 3947
who *t* to him a concubine out of ... Judg 19:1 3947
for there was no man that *t* them ... Judg 19:15 622
so the man *t* his concubine, and ... Judg 19:25 2388
Then the man *t* her up upon an ass ... Judg 19:28 3947
he *t* a knife, and laid hold on his ... Judg 19:29 3947
I *t* my concubine, and cut her in ... Judg 20:6 270
t them wives, according to their ... Judg 21:23 5375
they *t* them wives of the women of ... Ruth 1:4 5375
she *t* it up, and went into the ... Ruth 2:18 5375
he *t* ten men of the elders of the ... Ruth 4:2 3947
So Boaz *t* Ruth, and she was his ... Ruth 4:13 3947
Naomi *t* the child, and laid it in ... Ruth 4:16 3947
she *t* him up with her, with three ... 1Sa 1:24 5927
up the priest *t* for himself ... 1Sa 2:14 3947
the Philistines *t* the ark of God ... 1Sa 5:1 3947
the Philistines *t* the ark of God ... 1Sa 5:2 3947
they *t* Dagon, and set him in his ... 1Sa 5:3 3947
t two milch kine, and tied them to ... 1Sa 6:10 3947
the kine *t* the straight way to ... 1Sa 6:12
the Levites *t* down the ark of the ... 1Sa 6:15 3381
Samuel *t* a sucking lamb, and ... 1Sa 7:9 3947
Then Samuel *t* a stone, and set it ... 1Sa 7:12 3947
t bribes, and perverted judgment ... 1Sa 8:3 3947
And Samuel *t* Saul and his servant, ... 1Sa 9:22 3947
the cook *t* up the shoulder, and ... 1Sa 9:24 7311
Then Samuel *t* a vial of oil, and ... 1Sa 10:1 3947
he *t* a yoke of oxen, and hewed ... 1Sa 11:7 3947
t sheep, and oxen, and calves, and ... 1Sa 14:32 3947
So Saul *t* the kingdom over Israel ... 1Sa 14:47 3920
valiant man, he *t* him unto him ... 1Sa 14:52 622
he *t* Agag the king of the ... 1Sa 15:8 8610
But the people *t* of the spoil ... 1Sa 15:21 3947
Then Samuel *t* the horn of oil, and ... 1Sa 16:13 3947
Jesse *t* an ass laden with bread, ... 1Sa 16:20 3947
upon Saul, that David *t* an harp ... 1Sa 16:23 3947
the sheep with a keeper, and *t* ... 1Sa 17:20 5375
t a lamb out of the flock ... 1Sa 17:34 5375
he *t* his staff in his hand, and ... 1Sa 17:40 3947
t thence a stone, and slang it, and ... 1Sa 17:49 3947
t his sword, and drew it out of ... 1Sa 17:51 3947
And David *t* the head of the ... 1Sa 17:54 3947
of the Philistine, Abner *t* him ... 1Sa 17:57 3947

Saul *t* him that day, and would let	1Sa 18:2	3947
Michal *t* an image, and laid it in	1Sa 19:13	3947
Then Saul *t* three thousand chosen	1Sa 24:2	3947
t two hundred loaves, and two	1Sa 25:18	3947
David also *t* Ahinoam of Jezreel	1Sa 25:43	3947
So David *t* the spear and the cruse	1Sa 26:12	3947
t away the sheep, and the oxen, and	1Sa 27:9	3947
t flour, and kneaded it, and did	1Sa 28:24	3947
David *t* all the flocks and the	1Sa 30:20	3947
Therefore Saul *t* a sword, and fell	1Sa 31:4	3947
t the body of Saul and the bodies	1Sa 31:12	3947
they *t* their bones, and buried	1Sa 31:13	3947
I *t* the crown that was upon his	2Sa 1:10	3947
Then David *t* hold on his clothes,	2Sa 1:11	
t Ish-bosheth the son of Saul, and	2Sa 2:8	3947
they *t* up Asahel, and buried him	2Sa 2:32	5375
t her from her husband, even from	2Sa 3:15	3947
Joab *t* him aside in the gate to	2Sa 3:27	
And all the people *t* notice of it	2Sa 3:36	5384
of Jezreel, and his nurse *t* him up	2Sa 4:4	5375
t his head, and gat them away	2Sa 4:7	3947
I *t* hold of him, and slew him in	2Sa 4:10	
But they *t* the head of	2Sa 4:12	3947
Nevertheless David *t* the strong	2Sa 5:7	3920
David *t* him more concubines and	2Sa 5:13	3947
the ark of God, and *t* hold of it	2Sa 6:6	
I *t* thee from the sheepcote, from	2Sa 7:8	3947
as I *t* it from Saul, whom I put	2Sa 7:15	5493
David *t* Metheg-ammah out of the	2Sa 8:1	3947
David *t* from him a thousand	2Sa 8:4	3920
David *t* the shields of gold that	2Sa 8:7	3947
king David *t* exceeding much brass	2Sa 8:8	3947
Wherefore Hanun *t* David's	2Sa 10:4	3947
David sent messengers, and *t* her	2Sa 11:4	3947
but *t* the poor man's lamb, and	2Sa 12:4	3947
of Ammon, and *t* the royal city	2Sa 12:26	3920
and fought against it, and *t* it	2Sa 12:29	3920
he *t* their king's crown from off	2Sa 12:30	3947
she *t* flour, and kneaded it, and	2Sa 13:8	3947
she *t* a pan, and poured them out	2Sa 13:9	3947
Tamar *t* the cakes which she had	2Sa 13:10	3947
he *t* hold of her, and said unto	2Sa 13:11	
his hand, and *t* him, and kissed him	2Sa 15:5	2388
And the woman *t* and spread a	2Sa 17:19	3947
he *t* three darts in his hand, and	2Sa 18:14	3947
they *t* Absalom, and cast him into	2Sa 18:17	3947
the king *t* the ten women his	2Sa 20:3	3947
Joab *t* Amasa, by the beard with	2Sa 20:9	270
But Amasa *t* no heed to the sword	2Sa 20:10	
But the king *t* the two sons of	2Sa 21:8	3947
the daughter of Aiah *t* sackcloth	2Sa 21:10	3947
t the bones of Saul and the bones	2Sa 21:12	3947
He sent from above, he *t* me	2Sa 22:17	3947
t it, and brought it to David	2Sa 23:16	5375
Zadok the priest *t* an horn of oil	1Kin 1:39	3947
t Pharaoh's daughter, and brought	1Kin 3:1	3947
t my son from beside me, while	1Kin 3:20	3947
he also *t* Basmath the daughter of	1Kin 4:15	3947
came, and the priests *t* up the ark	1Kin 8:3	5375
they *t* men with them out of Paran	1Kin 11:18	3947
Whereupon the king *t* counsel	1Kin 12:28	
the prophet *t* up the carcase of	1Kin 13:29	5375
he *t* away the treasures of the	1Kin 14:26	3947
he even *t* away all	1Kin 14:26	3947
he *t* away all the shields of gold	1Kin 14:26	3947
he *t* away the sodomites out of	1Kin 15:12	5674
Then Asa *t* all the silver and the	1Kin 15:18	3947
they *t* away the stones of Ramah,	1Kin 15:22	5375
that he *t* to wife Jezebel the	1Kin 16:31	3947
he *t* him out of her bosom, and	1Kin 17:19	3947
Elijah *t* the child, and brought	1Kin 17:23	3947
that Obadiah *t* an hundred	1Kin 18:4	3947
he *t* an oath of the kingdom and	1Kin 18:10	
they *t* the bullock which was	1Kin 18:26	3947
Elijah *t* twelve stones, according	1Kin 18:31	3947
And they *t* them	1Kin 18:40	8610
t a yoke of oxen, and slew them,	1Kin 19:21	3947
which my father *t* from thy father	1Kin 20:34	3947
t the ashes away from his face	1Kin 20:41	
father Asa, he *t* out of the land	1Kin 22:46	1197
Elijah *t* his mantle, and wrapped	2Kin 2:8	3947
he *t* hold of his own clothes, and	2Kin 2:12	
He *t* up also the mantle of Elijah	2Kin 2:13	7311
he *t* the mantle of Elijah that	2Kin 2:14	3947
he *t* with him seven hundred men	2Kin 3:26	3947
Then he *t* his eldest son that	2Kin 3:27	3947
t up her son, and went out	2Kin 4:37	5375
t with him ten talents of silver,	2Kin 5:5	3947
he *t* them from their hand, and	2Kin 5:24	3947
And he put out his hand, and *t* it	2Kin 6:7	3947
t counsel with his servants,	2Kin 6:8	
They *t* therefore two chariot	2Kin 7:14	3947
t a present with him, even of	2Kin 8:9	3947
that he *t* a thick cloth, and	2Kin 8:15	3947
t every man his garment, and put	2Kin 9:13	3947
that they *t* the king's sons, and	2Kin 10:7	3947
they *t* them alive, and slew them	2Kin 10:14	8610
he *t* him up to him into the	2Kin 10:15	5927
But Jehu *t* no heed to walk in the	2Kin 10:31	
t Joash the son of Ahaziah, and	2Kin 11:2	3947
t an oath of them in the house of	2Kin 11:4	
they *t* every man his men that	2Kin 11:9	3947
he *t* the rulers over hundreds, and	2Kin 11:19	3947
But Jehoiada the priest *t* a chest	2Kin 12:9	3947
and fought against Gath, and *t* it	2Kin 12:17	3920
Jehoash king of Judah *t* all the	2Kin 12:18	3947
he *t* unto him bow and arrows	2Kin 13:15	3947
And he *t* them	2Kin 13:18	3947
t again out of the hand of	2Kin 13:25	3947
t Selah by war, and called the	2Kin 14:7	8610
of Israel *t* Amaziah king of Judah	2Kin 14:13	8610
he *t* all the gold and silver, and	2Kin 14:14	3947
all the people of Judah *t* Azariah	2Kin 14:21	3947
t Ijon, and Abel-beth-maachah, and	2Kin 15:29	3947
Ahaz *t* the silver and gold that	2Kin 16:8	3947
t it, and carried the people of it	2Kin 16:9	8610
t down the sea from off the	2Kin 16:17	3381
the king of Assyria *t* Samaria	2Kin 17:6	3920
the end of three years they *t* it	2Kin 18:10	3920
fenced cities of Judah, and *t* them	2Kin 18:13	8610
And they *t* and laid it on the boil,	2Kin 20:7	3947
he *t* away the horses that the	2Kin 23:11	7673
t the bones out of the sepulchres	2Kin 23:16	3947
the LORD to anger, Josiah *t* away	2Kin 23:19	5493
the people of the land *t* Jehoahaz	2Kin 23:30	3947
to Jehoiakim, and *t* Jehoahaz away	2Kin 23:34	3947
the king of Babylon *t* him in the	2Kin 24:12	3947
So they *t* the king, and brought	2Kin 25:6	8610
they ministered, *t* they away	2Kin 25:14	3947
the captain of the guard *t* away	2Kin 25:15	3947
guard *t* Seraiah the chief priest	2Kin 25:18	3947
out of the city he *t* an officer	2Kin 25:19	3947
captain of the guard *t* these	2Kin 25:20	3947
Caleb *t* unto him Ephrath, which	1Chr 2:19	3947
he *t* Geshur, and Aram, with the	1Chr 2:23	3947
of Pharaoh, which Mered *t*	1Chr 4:18	3947
And they *t* away their cattle	1Chr 5:21	
Machir *t* to wife the sister of	1Chr 7:15	3947
So Saul *t* a sword, and fell upon	1Chr 10:4	3947
they *t* his head, and his armour,	1Chr 10:9	5375
t away the body of Saul, and the	1Chr 10:12	5375
David *t* the castle of Zion	1Chr 11:5	3920
t it, and brought it to David	1Chr 11:18	5375
David *t* more wives at Jerusalem	1Chr 14:3	3947
I *t* thee from the sheepcote, even	1Chr 17:7	3947
as I *t* it from him that was	1Chr 17:13	5493
t Gath and her towns out of the	1Chr 18:1	3947
David *t* from him a thousand	1Chr 18:4	3920
David *t* the shields of gold that	1Chr 18:7	3947
Wherefore Hanun *t* David's	1Chr 19:4	3947
David *t* the crown of their king	1Chr 20:2	3947
brethren the sons of Kish *t* them	1Chr 23:22	5375
But David *t* not the number of	1Chr 27:23	5375
and the Levites *t* up the ark	2Chr 5:4	5375
t thence four hundred and fifty	2Chr 8:18	3947
king Rehoboam *t* counsel with the	2Chr 10:6	
t counsel with the young men that	2Chr 10:8	
Rehoboam *t* him Mahalath the	2Chr 11:18	3947
after her he *t* Maachah the	2Chr 11:20	3947
(for he *t* eighteen wives, and	2Chr 11:21	5375
he *t* the fenced cities which	2Chr 12:4	3920
t away the treasures of the house	2Chr 12:9	3947
he *t* all	2Chr 12:9	3947
t cities from him, Beth-el with	2Chr 13:19	3920
For he *t* away the altars of the	2Chr 14:3	5493
Also he *t* away out of all the	2Chr 14:5	5493
he *t* courage, and put away the	2Chr 15:8	
Then Asa the king *t* all Judah	2Chr 16:6	3947
moreover he *t* away the high	2Chr 17:6	
t Joash the son of Ahaziah, and	2Chr 22:11	3947
t the captains of hundreds,	2Chr 23:1	3947
t every man his men that were to	2Chr 23:8	3947
he *t* the captains of hundreds, and	2Chr 23:20	3947
Jehoiada *t* for him two wives	2Chr 24:3	5375
t it, and carried it to his place	2Chr 24:11	5375
thousand of them, and *t* much spoil	2Chr 25:13	
Amaziah king of Judah *t* advice	2Chr 25:17	
of Israel *t* Amaziah king of Judah	2Chr 25:23	8610
he *t* all the gold and the silver,	2Chr 25:24	
all the people of Judah *t* Uzziah	2Chr 26:1	3947
t also away much spoil from them,	2Chr 28:8	
t the captives, and with the spoil	2Chr 28:15	2388
For Ahaz *t* away a portion out of	2Chr 28:21	
And the Levites *t* it, to carry it	2Chr 29:16	6901
t away the altars that were in	2Chr 30:14	
altars for incense *t* they away	2Chr 30:14	
the whole assembly *t* counsel to	2Chr 30:23	
He *t* counsel with his princes and	2Chr 32:3	
which *t* Manasseh among the thorns	2Chr 33:11	3920
he *t* away the strange gods, and	2Chr 33:15	
And Josiah *t* away all the	2Chr 34:33	
His servants therefore *t* him out	2Chr 35:24	5674
land *t* Jehoahaz the son of Josiah	2Chr 36:1	3947
Necho *t* Jehoahaz his brother, and	2Chr 36:4	3947
which *t* a wife of the daughters	Ezr 2:61	3947
which Nebuchadnezzar *t* out of the	Ezr 5:14	5312
which Nebuchadnezzar *t* forth out	Ezr 6:5	5312
So *t* the priests and the Levites	Ezr 8:30	6901
I *t* up the wine, and gave it unto	Neh 2:1	5375
t great indignation, and mocked	Neh 4:1	
t an oath of them, that they	Neh 5:12	
which *t* one of the daughters of	Neh 7:63	3947
they *t* strong cities, and a fat	Neh 9:25	3920
were dead, *t* for his own daughter	Est 2:7	3947
the king *t* his ring from his hand	Est 3:10	5493
Then *t* Haman the apparel and the	Est 6:11	3947
the king *t* off his ring, which he	Est 8:2	5493
t upon them, and upon their seed,	Est 9:27	6901
fell upon them, and *t* them away	Job 1:15	3947
he *t* him a potsherd to scrape	Job 2:8	3947
He sent from above, he *t* me	Ps 18:16	3947
art he that *t* me out of the womb	Ps 22:9	1518
while they *t* counsel together	Ps 31:13	
Fear *t* hold upon them there, and	Ps 48:6	
We *t* sweet counsel together, and	Ps 55:14	
the Philistines *t* him in Gath	Ps 56:*t*	270
restored that which I *t* not away	Ps 69:4	1497
thou art he that *t* me out of my	Ps 71:6	1491
t him from the sheepfolds	Ps 78:70	3947
not that which he *t* in hunting	Prov 12:27	
labour which I *t* under the sun	Eccl 2:20	
the walls *t* away my veil from me	Song 5:7	5375
I *t* unto me faithful witnesses to	Is 8:2	
and fought against Ashdod, and *t* it	Is 20:1	3920
cities of Judah, and *t* them	Is 36:1	8610
With whom *t* he counsel, and who	Is 40:14	
t the girdle from the place where	Jer 13:7	3947
Then *t* I the cup at the LORD's	Jer 25:17	3947
prophets and all the people *t* him	Jer 26:8	8610
king of Babylon *t* not, when he	Jer 27:20	3947
of Babylon *t* away from this place	Jer 28:3	3947
Then Hananiah the prophet *t* the	Jer 28:10	3947
t them by the hand to bring them	Jer 31:32	2388
t witnesses, and weighed him the	Jer 32:10	
So I *t* the evidence of the	Jer 32:11	3947
Then I *t* Jaazaniah the son of	Jer 35:3	3947
of Neriah *t* the roll in his hand	Jer 36:14	3947
he *t* it out of Elishama the	Jer 36:21	3947
Then *t* Jeremiah another roll, and	Jer 36:32	3947
he *t* Jeremiah the prophet, saying	Jer 37:13	8610
so Irijah *t* Jeremiah, and brought	Jer 37:14	8610
the king sent, and *t* him out	Jer 37:17	3947
Then *t* they Jeremiah, and cast him	Jer 38:6	3947
So Ebed-melech *t* the men with him	Jer 38:11	3947
t thence old cast clouts and old	Jer 38:11	3947
t him up out of the dungeon	Jer 38:13	5927
t Jeremiah the prophet unto him	Jer 38:14	3947
t Jeremiah out of the court of	Jer 39:14	3947
captain of the guard *t* Jeremiah	Jer 40:2	3947
Then they *t* all the men, and went	Jer 41:12	3947
Then *t* Johanan the son of Kareah,	Jer 41:16	3947
t all the remnant of Judah, that	Jer 43:5	3947
all that *t* them captives held	Jer 50:33	
anguish *t* hold of him, and pangs	Jer 50:43	
Then they *t* the king, and carried	Jer 52:9	8610
they ministered, *t* they away	Jer 52:18	3947
t the captain of the guard away	Jer 52:19	3947
guard *t* Seraiah the chief priest	Jer 52:24	3947
He *t* also out of the city an	Jer 52:25	3947
the captain of the guard *t* them	Jer 52:26	3947
They *t* the young men to grind, and	Lam 5:13	5375
Then the spirit *t* me up, and I	Eze 3:12	5375
me up, and *t* me away, and I went in	Eze 3:14	3947
t me by a lock of mine head	Eze 8:3	3947
t thereof, and put it into the	Eze 10:7	5375
who *t* it, and went out	Eze 10:7	3947
Afterwards the spirit *t* me up	Eze 11:24	5375
therefore I *t* them away as I saw	Eze 16:50	5493
t the highest branch of the cedar	Eze 17:3	3947
He *t* also of the seed of the land	Eze 17:5	3947
then she *t* another of her whelps,	Eze 19:5	3947
they *t* her sons and her daughters,	Eze 23:10	3947
that they *t* both one way,	Eze 23:13	
When they *t* hold of thee by thy	Eze 29:7	8610
of the trumpet, and *t* not warning	Eze 33:5	
So the spirit *t* me up, and brought	Eze 43:5	5375
Thus Melzar *t* away the portion of	Dan 1:16	5375
slew those men that *t* up Shadrach	Dan 3:22	5267
they *t* his glory from him	Dan 5:20	5709
Darius the Median *t* the kingdom	Dan 5:31	6902
t Gomer the daughter of Diblaim	Hos 1:3	3947
He *t* his brother by the heel in	Hos 12:3	
anger, and *t* him away in my wrath	Hos 13:11	3947
the LORD *t* me as I followed the	Amos 7:15	3947
So they *t* up Jonah, and cast him	Jonah 1:15	5375
And I *t* unto me two staves	Zec 11:7	3947
I *t* my staff, even Beauty, and cut	Zec 11:10	3947
I *t* the thirty pieces of silver,	Zec 11:13	3947
him, and *t* unto him his wife	Mt 1:24	*3880*
he *t* the young child and his	Mt 2:14	*3880*
t the young child and his mother,	Mt 2:21	*3880*
Himself *t* our infirmities, and	Mt 8:17	*2983*
t her by the hand, and the maid	Mt 9:25	*2902*
of mustard seed, which a man *t*	Mt 13:31	*2983*
like unto leaven, which a woman *t*	Mt 13:33	*2983*
t up the body, and buried it, and	Mt 14:12	*142*
t the five loaves, and the two	Mt 14:19	*2983*
they *t* up of the fragments that	Mt 14:20	*142*
he *t* the seven loaves and the	Mt 15:36	*2983*
they *t* up of the broken meat that	Mt 15:37	*142*
t ship, and came into the coasts	Mt 15:39	
and how many baskets ye *t* up	Mt 16:9	*2983*
and how many baskets ye *t* up	Mt 16:10	*2983*
Then Peter *t* him, and began to	Mt 16:22	*4355*
t him by the throat, saying, Pay	Mt 18:28	*2902*
Jesus going up to Jerusalem *t* the	Mt 20:17	*3880*
And the husbandmen *t* his servants	Mt 21:35	*2983*
because they *t* him for a prophet	Mt 21:46	*2192*
the remnant *t* his servants, and	Mt 22:6	*2902*
t counsel how they might entangle	Mt 22:15	*2983*
flood came, and *t* them all away	Mt 24:39	*142*
which *t* their lamps, and went	Mt 25:1	*2983*
that were foolish *t* their lamps	Mt 25:3	*2983*
lamps, and *t* no oil with them	Mt 25:3	*2983*
But the wise *t* oil in their	Mt 25:4	*2983*
and straightway *t* his journey	Mt 25:15	*589*
I was a stranger, and ye *t* me in	Mt 25:35	*4863*
we thee a stranger, and *t* thee in	Mt 25:38	*4863*
was a stranger, and ye *t* me not in	Mt 25:43	*4863*
they were eating, Jesus *t* bread	Mt 26:26	*2983*
he *t* the cup, and gave thanks, and	Mt 26:27	*2983*
he *t* with him Peter and the two	Mt 26:37	*3880*
and laid hands on Jesus, and *t* him	Mt 26:50	*2902*
elders of the people *t* counsel	Mt 27:1	*2983*
chief priests *t* the silver pieces	Mt 27:6	*2983*
they *t* counsel, and bought with	Mt 27:7	*2983*
they *t* the thirty pieces of	Mt 27:9	*2983*
he *t* water, and washed his hands	Mt 27:24	*2983*
t Jesus into the common hall	Mt 27:27	*3880*
t the reed, and smote him on the	Mt 27:30	*2983*
they *t* the robe off from him, and	Mt 27:31	*1562*
t a spunge, and filled it with	Mt 27:48	*2983*
So they *t* the money, and did as	Mt 28:15	*2983*
t her by the hand, and lifted her	Mk 1:31	*2902*
t up the bed, and went forth	Mk 2:12	*142*
straightway *t* counsel with the	Mk 3:6	*4160*
they *t* him even as he was in the	Mk 4:36	*3880*
he *t* the damsel by the hand, and	Mk 5:41	*2902*
t up his corpse, and laid it in a	Mk 6:29	*142*
they *t* up twelve baskets full of	Mk 6:43	*142*
he *t* him aside from the multitude	Mk 7:33	*618*
he *t* the seven loaves, and gave	Mk 8:6	*2983*

T

they *t* up of the broken meat that Mk 8:8 *142*
baskets full of fragments *t* ye up Mk 8:19 *142*
baskets full of fragments *t* ye up Mk 8:20 *142*
he *t* the blind man by the hand, Mk 8:23 *1949*
And Peter *t* him, and began to Mk 8:32 *4355*
But Jesus *t* him by the hand, and Mk 9:27 *2902*
he *t* a child, and set him in the Mk 9:36 *2983*
he *t* them up in his arms, put his Mk 10:16 *1723*
he *t* again the twelve, and began Mk 10:32 *3880*
And they *t* him, and killed him, and Mk 12:8 *2983*
and the first *t* a wife, and dying Mk 12:20 *2983*
And the second *t* her, and died, Mk 12:21 *2983*
And as they did eat, Jesus *t* bread Mk 14:22 *2983*
he *t* the cup, and when he had Mk 14:23 *2983*
laid their hands on him, and *t* him Mk 14:46 *2902*
temple teaching, and ye *t* me not Mk 14:49 *2902*
they *t* off the purple from him, Mk 15:20 *1562*
t him down, and wrapped him in the Mk 15:46 *2507*
Then *t* he him up in his arms, and Lk 2:28 *1209*
t up that whereon he lay, and Lk 5:25 *142*
t her by the hand, and called, Lk 8:54 *2902*
And he *t* them, and went aside Lk 9:10 *3880*
Then he *t* the five loaves and the Lk 9:16 *2983*
he *t* Peter and John and James, and Lk 9:28 *3880*
t a child, and set him by him, Lk 9:47 *1949*
him to an inn, and *t* care of him Lk 10:34 *1959*
he *t* out two pence, and gave them Lk 10:35 *1544*
of mustard seed, which a man *t* Lk 13:19 *2983*
is like leaven, which a woman *t* Lk 13:21 *2983*
he *t* him, and healed him, and let Lk 14:4 *1949*
t his journey into a far country, Lk 15:13 *589*
Then he *t* unto him the twelve, and Lk 18:31 *3830*
and the first *t* a wife, and died Lk 20:29 *2983*
the second *t* her to wife, and he Lk 20:30 *2983*
And the third *t* her Lk 20:31 *2983*
he *t* the cup, and gave thanks, and Lk 22:17 *1209*
he *t* bread, and gave thanks, and Lk 22:19 *2983*
Then *t* they him, and led him, and Lk 22:54 *4815*
he *t* it down, and wrapped it in Lk 23:53 *2507*
he *t* bread, and blessed it, and Lk 24:30 *2983*
And he *t* it, and did eat before Lk 24:43 *2983*
whole, and *t* up his bed, and walked Jn 5:9 *142*
And Jesus *t* the loaves Jn 6:11 *2983*
disciples, they also *t* shipping Jn 6:24
Then *t* they up stones to cast at Jn 8:59 *142*
Then the Jews *t* up stones again Jn 10:31 *941*
Then they *t* away the stone from Jn 11:41 *142*
Then from that day forth they *t* Jn 11:53 *4823*
Then *t* Mary a pound of ointment Jn 12:3 *2983*
T branches of palm trees, and went Jn 12:13 *2983*
t a towel, and girded himself Jn 13:4 *2983*
and officers of the Jews *t* Jesus Jn 18:12 *4815*
Then Pilate therefore *t* Jesus Jn 19:1 *2983*
they *t* Jesus, and led him away Jn 19:16 *3880*
t his garments, and made four Jn 19:23 *2983*
disciple *t* her unto his own home Jn 19:27 *2983*
therefore, and *t* the body of Jesus Jn 19:38 *142*
Then *t* they the body of Jesus, and Jn 19:40 *2983*
was guide to them that *t* Jesus Acts 1:16 *4815*
he *t* him by the right hand, and Acts 3:7 *4084*
they *t* knowledge of them, that Acts 4:13 *1921*
heart, and *t* counsel to slay them Acts 5:33 *1011*
out, Pharaoh's daughter *t* him up Acts 7:21 *337*
ye *t* up the tabernacle of Moloch, Acts 7:43 *353*
the Jews *t* counsel to kill him Acts 9:23 *4823*
Then the disciples *t* him by night Acts 9:25 *2983*
But Barnabas *t* him, and brought Acts 9:27 *1949*
But Peter *t* him up, saying, Stand Acts 10:26 *1453*
t with them John, whose surname Acts 12:25 *4838*
they *t* him down from the tree, and Acts 13:29 *2507*
and so Barnabas *t* Mark, and sailed Acts 15:39 *3880*
and *t* and circumcised him because Acts 16:3 *2983*
he *t* them the same hour of the Acts 16:33 *3880*
t unto them certain lewd fellows Acts 17:5 *4355*
And they *t* him, and brought him Acts 17:19 *1949*
Then all the Greeks *t* Sosthenes Acts 18:17 *1949*
then *t* his leave of the brethren, Acts 18:18 *657*
heard, they *t* him unto them, and Acts 18:26 *4355*
t upon them to call over them Acts 19:13 *2021*
we *t* him in, and came to Mitylene Acts 20:14 *353*
leave one of another, we *t* ship Acts 21:6
he *t* Paul's girdle, and bound his Acts 21:11 *142*
those days we *t* up our carriages Acts 21:15 *643*
Then Paul *t* the men, and the next Acts 21:26 *3880*
and they *t* Paul, and drew him out Acts 21:30 *1949*
Who immediately *t* soldiers Acts 21:32 *3880*
t him, and commanded him to be Acts 21:33 *1949*
So he *t* him, and brought him to Acts 23:18 *3880*
chief captain *t* him by the hand Acts 23:19 *1949*
t Paul, and brought him by night Acts 23:31 *353*
whom we *t*, and would have judged Acts 24:6 *2902*
with great violence *t* him away Acts 24:7 *520*
he *t* bread, and gave thanks to God Acts 27:35 *2983*
cheer, and they also *t* some meat Acts 27:36 *4355*
saw, he thanked God, and *t* courage Acts 28:15 *2983*
in which he was betrayed *t* bread 1Cor 11:23 *2983*
the same manner also he *t* the cup 1Cor 11:25
Barnabas, and *t* Titus with me also Gal 2:1 *4838*
t upon him the form of a servant, Phil 2:7 *2983*
t it out of the way, nailing it Col 2:14 *142*
likewise *t* part of the same Heb 2:14 *3348*
For verily he *t* not on him the Heb 2:16 *1949*
but he *t* on him the seed of Heb 2:16 *1949*
in the day when I *t* them by the Heb 8:9 *1949*
he *t* the blood of calves and of Heb 9:19 *2983*
t joyfully the spoiling of your Heb 10:34 *4327*
t the book out of the right hand Rev 5:7 *2983*
the angel *t* the censer, and filled Rev 8:5 *2983*
I *t* the little book out of the Rev 10:10 *2983*
a mighty angel *t* up a stone like Rev 18:21 *142*

TOOKEST
though thou *t* vengeance of their Ps 99:8
t thy broidered garments, and Eze 16:18 3947

TOOL
for if thou lift up thy *t* upon it Ex 20:25 2719
and fashioned it with a graving *t* Ex 32:4
not lift up any iron *t* upon them Deut 27:5
any *t* of iron heard in the house 1Kin 6:7 3627

TOOTH
Eye for eye, *t* for *t*, hand Ex 21:24 8127
he smite out his manservant's *t* Ex 21:27 8127
or his maidservant's *t* Ex 21:27 8127
breach, eye for eye, *t* for *t* Lev 24:20 8127
life, eye for eye, *t* for *t* Deut 19:21 8127
of trouble is like a broken *t* Prov 25:19 8127
for an eye, and a *t* for a *t* Mt 5:38 *3599*

TOOTH'S
let him go free for his *t* sake Ex 21:27 8127

TOP
whose *t* may reach unto heaven Gen 11:4 7218
the *t* of it reached to heaven Gen 28:12 7218
and poured oil upon the *t* of it Gen 28:18 7218
to morrow I will stand on the *t* Ex 17:9 7218
Hur went up to the *t* of the hill Ex 17:10 7218
Sinai, on the *t* of the mount Ex 19:20 7218
Moses up to the *t* of the mount Ex 19:20 7218
was like devouring fire on the *t* Ex 24:17 7218
shall be an hole in the *t* of it Ex 28:32 7218
the *t* thereof, and the sides Ex 30:3 1406
there to me in the *t* of the mount Ex 34:2 7218
with pure gold, both the *t* of it Ex 37:26 1406
up into the *t* of the mountain Num 14:40 7218
presumed to go up unto the hill *t* Num 14:44 7218
died there in the *t* of the mount Num 20:28 7218
to the *t* of Pisgah, which looketh Num 21:20 7218
For from the *t* of the rocks I see Num 23:9 7218
to the *t* of Pisgah, and built Num 23:14 7218
brought Balaam unto the *t* of Peor Num 23:28 7218
Get thee up into the *t* of Pisgah Deut 3:27 7218
thy foot unto the *t* of thy head Deut 28:35 6936
upon the *t* of the head of him Deut 33:16 6936
to the *t* of Pisgah, that is over Deut 34:1 7218
the border went up to the *t* of Josh 15:8 7218
t of the hill unto the fountain Josh 15:9 7218
thy God upon the *t* of this rock Judg 6:26 7218
stood in the *t* of mount Gerizim, Judg 9:7 7218
for him in the *t* of the mountains Judg 9:25 7218
down from the *t* of the mountains Judg 9:36 7218
gat them up to the *t* of the tower Judg 9:51 1406
dwelt in the *t* of the rock Etam Judg 15:8 5585
went to the *t* of the rock Etam Judg 15:11 5585
carried them up to the *t* of an Judg 16:3 7218
with Saul upon the *t* of the house 1Sa 9:25 1406
called Saul to the *t* of the house 1Sa 9:26 1406
stood on the *t* of an hill afar 1Sa 26:13 7218
and stood on the *t* of an hill 2Sa 2:25 7218
was come to the *t* of the mount 2Sa 15:32 7218
a little past the *t* of the hill 2Sa 16:1 7218
a tent upon the *t* of the house 2Sa 16:22 1406
were upon the *t* of the pillars 1Kin 7:17 7218
chapiters that were upon the *t* 1Kin 7:18 7218
the *t* of the pillars were of lily 1Kin 7:19 7218
upon the *t* of the pillars was 1Kin 7:22 7218
in the *t* of the base was there a 1Kin 7:35 7218
on the *t* of the base the ledges 1Kin 7:35 7218
were on the *t* of the two pillars 1Kin 7:41 7218
were upon the *t* of the pillars 1Kin 7:41 7218
the *t* of the throne was round 1Kin 10:19 7218
Elijah went up to the *t* of Carmel 1Kin 18:42 7218
he sat on the *t* of an hill 2Kin 1:9 7218
under him on the *t* of the stairs 2Kin 9:13 1634
the altars that were on the *t* of 2Kin 23:12 1406
the chapiter that was on the *t* of 2Chr 3:15 7218
were on the *t* of the two pillars 2Chr 4:12 7218
were on the *t* of the pillars 2Chr 4:12 7218
them unto the *t* of the rock 2Chr 25:12 7218
them down from the *t* of the rock 2Chr 25:12 7218
touched the *t* of the sceptre Est 5:2 7218
earth upon the *t* of the mountains Ps 72:16 7218
a sparrow alone upon the house *t* Ps 102:7 1406
standeth in the *t* of high places Prov 8:2 7218
that lieth upon the *t* of a mast Prov 23:34 7218
look from the *t* of Amana, from Song 4:8 7218
from the *t* of Shenir and Hermon, Song 4:8 7218
in the *t* of the mountains Is 2:2 7218
in the *t* of the uppermost bough Is 17:6 7218
a beacon upon the *t* of a mountain Is 30:17 7218
shout from the *t* of the mountains Is 42:11 7218
hunger in the *t* of every street Lam 2:19 7218
out in the *t* of every street Lam 4:1 7218
off the *t* of his young twigs Eze 17:4 7218
I will crop off from the *t* of his Eze 17:22 7218
she set it upon the *t* of a rock Eze 24:7 6706
her blood upon the *t* of a rock Eze 24:8 6706
and make her like the *t* of a rock Eze 26:4 6706
make thee like the *t* of a rock Eze 26:14 6706
his *t* was among the thick boughs Eze 31:3 6788
he hath shot up his *t* among the Eze 31:10 6788
up their *t* among the thick boughs Eze 31:14 6788
Upon the *t* of the mountain the Eze 43:12 7218
the *t* of Carmel shall wither Amos 1:2 7218
themselves in the *t* of Carmel Amos 9:3 7218
in the *t* of the mountains Mic 4:1 7218
at the *t* of all the streets Nah 3:10 7218
with a bowl upon the *t* of it Zec 4:2 7218
which are upon the *t* thereof Zec 4:2 7218
in twain from the *t* to the bottom Mt 27:51 *509*
in twain from the *t* to the bottom Mk 15:38 *509*
seam, woven from the *t* throughout Jn 19:23 *509*
leaning upon the *t* of his staff Heb 11:21 *206*

TOPAZ
first row shall be a sardius, a *t* Ex 28:17 6357
the first row was a sardius, a *t* Ex 39:10 6357
The *t* of Ethiopia shall not equal Job 28:19 6357
was thy covering, the sardius, *t* Eze 28:13 6357
the ninth, a *t* Rev 21:20 *5116*

TOPHEL (*to'-fel*) *A place in the Sinai wilderness.*
the Red sea, between Paran, and *T* Deut 1:1 8603

TOPHET (*to'-fet*) See TOPHETH. *A place in the valley of Hinnom.*
For *T* is ordained of old Is 30:33 8613
have built the high places of *T* Jer 7:31 8612
that it shall no more be called *T* Jer 7:32 8612
for they shall bury in *T*, till Jer 7:32 8612
place shall no more be called *T* Jer 19:6 8612
and they shall bury them in *T* Jer 19:11 8612
and even make this city as *T* Jer 19:12 8612
be defiled as the place of *T* Jer 19:13 8612
Then came Jeremiah from *T* Jer 19:14 8612

TOPHETH (*to'-feth*) See TOPHET. *Same as Tophet.*
And he defiled *T*, which is in the 2Kin 23:10 8612

TOPS
were the *t* of the mountains seen Gen 8:5 7218
in the *t* of the mulberry trees 2Sa 5:24 7218
to set upon the *t* of the pillars 1Kin 7:16 7218
herb, as the grass on the house *t* 2Kin 19:26 1406
in the *t* of the mulberry trees 1Chr 14:15 7218
cut off as the *t* of the ears of Job 24:24 7218
into the *t* of the ragged rocks, Is 2:21 5585
on the *t* of their houses, and in Is 15:3 1406
in all the *t* of the mountains, and Eze 6:13 7218
upon the *t* of the mountains Hos 4:13 7218
t of mountains shall they leap Joel 2:5 7218

TORCH
like a *t* of fire in a sheaf Zec 12:6 3940

TORCHES
t in the day of his preparation Nah 2:3 6393
they shall seem like *t*, they Nah 2:4 3940
cometh thither with lanterns and *t* Jn 18:3 *2985*

TORMENT
hither to *t* us before the time Mt 8:29 *928*
thee by God, that thou *t* me not Mk 5:7 *928*
I beseech thee, *t* me not Lk 8:28 *928*
also come into this place of *t* Lk 16:28 *931*
because fear hath *t* 1Jn 4:18 *2851*
their *t* was as the *t* of a Rev 9:5 *929*
was as the *t* of a scorpion Rev 9:5 *929*
the smoke of their *t* ascendeth up Rev 14:11 *929*
and lived deliciously, so much *t* Rev 18:7 *929*
afar off for the fear of her *t* Rev 18:10 *929*
afar off for the fear of her *t* Rev 18:15 *929*

TORMENTED
sick of the palsy, grievously *t* Mt 8:6 *928*
for I am *t* in this flame Lk 16:24 *3600*
he is comforted, and thou art *t* Lk 16:25 *3600*
being destitute, afflicted, *t* Heb 11:37 *2558*
that they should be *t* five months Rev 9:5 *928*
because these two prophets *t* them Rev 11:10 *928*
and he shall be *t* with fire Rev 14:10 *928*
prophet are, and shall be *t* day Rev 20:10 *928*

TORMENTORS
wroth, and delivered him to the *t* Mt 18:34 *930*

TORMENTS
taken with divers diseases and *t* Mt 4:24 *931*
he lift up his eyes, being in *t* Lk 16:23 *931*

TORN
That which was *t* of beasts I Gen 31:39 2966
I said, Surely he is *t* in pieces Gen 44:28 2963
If it be *t* in pieces, then let Ex 22:13 2963
not make good that which was *t* Ex 22:13 2966
that is *t* of beasts in the field Ex 22:31 2966
of that which is *t* with beasts Lev 7:24 2966
or that which was *t* with beasts Lev 17:15 2966
or is *t* with beasts, he shall not Lev 22:8 2966
unto the lion, which hath *t* him 1Kin 13:26 7665
eaten the carcase, nor *t* the ass 1Kin 13:28 7665
their carcases were *t* in the Is 5:25 5478
out thence shall be *t* in pieces Jer 5:6 2963
of itself, or is *t* in pieces Eze 4:14 2966
that is dead of itself, or *t* Eze 44:31 2966
for he hath *t*, and he will heal us Hos 6:1 2963
and ye brought that which was *t* Mal 1:13 1497
when the unclean spirit had *t* him Mk 1:26 *4682*

TORTOISE
mouse, and the *t* after his kind, Lev 11:29 6632

TORTURED
and others were *t*, not accepting Heb 11:35 *5178*

TOSS
t thee like a ball into a large Is 22:18 6802
the waves thereof *t* themselves Jer 5:22 1607

TOSSED
I am *t* up and down as the locust Ps 109:23 5287
a lying tongue is a vanity *t* to Prov 21:6 5086
t with tempest, and not comforted, Is 54:11
midst of the sea, *t* with waves Mt 14:24 *928*
exceedingly *t* with a tempest Acts 27:18 *5492*
t to and fro, and carried about Eph 4:14 *2831*
the sea driven with the wind and *t* Jas 1:6 *4494*

TOSSINGS
and I am full of *t* to and fro unto Job 7:4 5076

TOTTERING
wall shall ye be, and as a *t* fence Ps 62:3 1760

TOU (*to'-u*) See TOI. *Same as Toi.*
Now when *T* king of Hamath heard 1Chr 18:9 8583
(for Hadarezer had war with *T* 1Chr 18:10 8583

TOUCH

eat of it, neither shall ye *t* it ... Gen 3:3 5060
suffered I thee not to *t* her ... Gen 20:6 5060
the mount, or *t* the border of it ... Ex 19:12 5060
There shall not an hand *t* it ... Ex 19:13 5060
Or if a soul *t* any unclean thing, ... Lev 5:2 5060
Or if he *t* the uncleanness of man ... Lev 5:3 5060
Whatsoever shall *t* the flesh ... Lev 6:27 5060
that shall *t* any unclean thing ... Lev 7:21 5060
and their carcase shall ye not *t* ... Lev 11:8 5060
whosoever doth *t* them, when they ... Lev 11:31 5060
she shall *t* no hallowed thing, ... Lev 12:4 5060
they shall not *t* any holy thing ... Num 4:15 5060
t nothing of theirs, lest ye be ... Num 16:26 5060
flesh, nor *t* their dead carcase ... Deut 14:8 5060
now therefore we may not *t* them ... Josh 9:19 5060
men that they shall not *t* thee ... Ruth 2:9 5060
he shall not *t* thee any more ... 2Sa 14:10 5060
Beware that none *t* the young man ... 2Sa 18:12
But the man that shall *t* them ... 2Sa 23:7 5060
T not mine anointed, and do my ... 1Chr 16:22 5060
t all that he hath, and he will ... Job 1:11 5060
t his bone and his flesh, and he ... Job 2:5 5060
seven there shall no evil *t* thee ... Job 5:19 5060
to *t* are as my sorrowful meat ... Job 6:7 5060
T not mine anointed, and do my ... Ps 105:15 5060
t the mountains, and they shall ... Ps 144:5 5060
from thence, *t* no unclean thing ... Is 52:11 5060
that *t* the inheritance which I ... Jer 12:14 5060
men could not *t* their garments ... Lam 4:14 5060
depart, depart, *t* not ... Lam 4:15 5060
and with his skirt do *t* bread ... Hag 2:12 5060
by a dead body *t* any of these ... Hag 2:13 5060
If I may but *t* his garment ... Mt 9:21 680
only *t* the hem of his garment ... Mt 14:36 680
pressed upon him for to *t* him ... Mk 3:10 680
If I may *t* but his clothes, I ... Mk 5:28 680
t if it were but the border of ... Mk 6:56 680
him, and besought him to *t* him ... Mk 8:22 680
to him, that he should *t* them ... Mk 10:13 680
whole multitude sought to *t* him ... Lk 6:19 680
ye yourselves *t* not the burdens ... Lk 11:46 4379
infants, that he would *t* them ... Lk 18:15 680
Jesus saith unto her, *T* me not ... Jn 20:17 680
good for a man not to *t* a woman ... 1Cor 7:1 680
Lord, and *t* not the unclean thing ... 2Cor 6:17 680
T not; taste not ... Col 2:21 680
the firstborn should *t* them ... Heb 11:28 2345
so much as a beast *t* the mountain ... Heb 12:20 2345

TOUCHED

us no hurt, as we have not *t* thee ... Gen 26:29 5060
he *t* the hollow of his thigh ... Gen 32:25 5060
because he *t* the hollow of ... Gen 32:32 5060
The soul which hath *t* any such ... Lev 22:6 5060
there, and upon him that *t* a bone ... Num 19:18 5060
and whosoever hath *t* any slain ... Num 31:19 5060
t the flesh and the unleavened ... Judg 6:21 5060
of men, whose hearts God had *t* ... 1Sa 10:26 5060
wing of the one *t* the one wall ... 1Kin 6:27 5060
the other cherub *t* the other wall ... 1Kin 6:27 5060
their wings *t* one another in the ... 1Kin 6:27 5060
tree, behold, then an angel *t* him ... 1Kin 19:5 5060
t him, and said, Arise and eat ... 1Kin 19:7 5060
t the bones of Elisha, he revived ... 2Kin 13:21 5060
near, and *t* the top of the sceptre ... Est 5:2 5060
for the hand of God hath *t* me ... Job 19:21 5060
and said, Lo, this hath *t* thy lips ... Is 6:7 5060
put forth his hand, and *t* my mouth ... Jer 1:9 5060
creatures that *t* one another ... Eze 3:13 5401
whole earth, and *t* not the ground ... Dan 8:5 5060
but he *t* me, and set me upright ... Dan 8:18 5060
t me about the time of the ... Dan 9:21 5060
And, behold, an hand *t* me, which ... Dan 10:10 5060
of the sons of men *t* my lips ... Dan 10:16 5060
t me one like the appearance of a ... Dan 10:18 5060
hand, and *t* him, saying, I will ... Mt 8:3 680
he *t* her hand, and the fever left ... Mt 8:15 680
him, and *t* the hem of his garment ... Mt 9:20 680
Then *t* he their eyes, saying, ... Mt 9:29 680
as many as *t* were made perfectly ... Mt 14:36 680
t them, and said, Arise, and be not ... Mt 17:7 680
on them, and *t* their eyes ... Mt 20:34 680
t him, and saith unto him, I will ... Mk 1:41 680
press behind, and *t* his garment ... Mk 5:27 680
press, and said, Who *t* my clothes ... Mk 5:30 680
thee, and sayest thou, Who *t* me ... Mk 5:31 680
as many as *t* him were made whole ... Mk 6:56 680
ears, and he spit, and *t* his tongue ... Mk 7:33 680
hand, and *t* him, saying, I will ... Lk 5:13 680
And he came and *t* the bier ... Lk 7:14 680
t the border of his garment ... Lk 8:44 680
And Jesus said, Who *t* me ... Lk 8:45 680
thee, and sayest thou, Who *t* me ... Lk 8:45 680
And Jesus said, Somebody hath *t* me ... Lk 8:46 680
for what cause she had *t* him ... Lk 8:47 680
he *t* his ear, and healed him ... Lk 22:51 680
And the next day we *t* at Sidon ... Acts 27:3 2609
be *t* with the feeling of our ... Heb 4:15 4834
unto the mount that might be *t* ... Heb 12:18 5584

TOUCHETH

He that *t* this man or his wife ... Gen 26:11 5060
whosoever *t* the mount shall be ... Ex 19:12 5060
whatsoever *t* the altar shall be ... Ex 29:37 5060
whatsoever *t* them shall be holy ... Ex 30:29 5060
every one that *t* them shall be ... Lev 6:18 5060
the flesh that *t* any unclean ... Lev 7:19 5060
whosoever *t* the carcase of them ... Lev 11:24 5060
every one that *t* them shall be ... Lev 11:26 5060
whoso *t* their carcase shall be ... Lev 11:27 5060
but that which *t* their carcase ... Lev 11:36 5060
he that *t* the carcase thereof ... Lev 11:39 5060
whosoever *t* his bed shall wash ... Lev 15:5 5060
he that *t* the flesh of him that ... Lev 15:7 5060
whosoever *t* any thing that was ... Lev 15:10 5060
whomsoever he *t* that hath the ... Lev 15:11 5060
that he *t* which hath the issue, ... Lev 15:12 5060
whosoever *t* her shall be unclean ... Lev 15:19 5060
whosoever *t* her bed shall wash ... Lev 15:21 5060
whosoever *t* any thing that she ... Lev 15:22 5060
whereon she sitteth, when he *t* it ... Lev 15:23 5060
whosoever *t* those things shall be ... Lev 15:27 5060
whoso *t* any thing that is unclean ... Lev 22:4 5060
Or whosoever *t* any creeping thing ... Lev 22:5 5060
He that *t* the dead body of any ... Num 19:11 5060
Whosoever *t* the dead body of any ... Num 19:13 5060
whosoever *t* one that is slain ... Num 19:16 5060
he that *t* the water of separation ... Num 19:21 5060
unclean person *t* shall be unclean ... Num 19:22 5060
the soul that *t* it shall be ... Num 19:22 5060
tow is broken when it *t* the fire ... Judg 16:9 7306
it *t* thee, and thou art troubled ... Job 4:5 5060
he *t* the hills, and they smoke ... Ps 104:32 5060
whosoever *t* her shall not be ... Prov 6:29 5060
wither, when the east wind *t* it ... Eze 17:10 5060
they break out, and blood *t* blood ... Hos 4:2 5060
of hosts is he that *t* the land ... Amos 9:5 5060
for he that *t* you ... Zec 2:8 5060
you *t* the apple of his eye ... Zec 2:8 5060
of woman this is that *t* him ... Lk 7:39 680
and that wicked one *t* him not ... 1Jn 5:18 680

TOUCHING

as *t* thee, doth comfort himself, ... Gen 27:42
make an atonement for him as *t* ... Lev 5:13 413
unto the Levites *t* their charge ... Num 8:26
as *t* the matter which thou and I ... 1Sa 20:23
As *t* the words which thou hast ... 2Kin 22:18
that *t* any of the priests and ... Ezr 7:24
T the Almighty, we cannot find ... Job 37:23
which I have made *t* the king ... Ps 45:1
song of my beloved *t* his vineyard ... Is 5:1
them *t* all their wickedness ... Jer 1:16 5921
t the house of the king of Judah, ... Jer 21:11
For thus saith the LORD *t* Shallum ... Jer 22:11 413
for the vision is *t* the whole ... Eze 7:13 413
t any thing that they shall ask ... Mt 18:19 4012
But as *t* the resurrection of the ... Mt 22:31 4012
as *t* the dead, that they rise ... Mk 12:26 4012
t those things whereof ye accuse ... Lk 23:14
ye intend to do as *t* these men ... Acts 5:35 1909
As *t* the Gentiles which believe, ... Acts 21:25 4012
T the resurrection of the dead I ... Acts 24:21 4012
t all the things whereof I am ... Acts 26:2 4012
but as *t* the election, they are ... Rom 11:28 2596
Now as *t* things offered unto ... 1Cor 8:1 4012
As *t* our brother Apollos, I ... 1Cor 16:12 4012
For as *t* the ministering to the ... 2Cor 9:1 4012
as *t* the law, a Pharisee ... Phil 3:5 2596
t the righteousness which is in ... Phil 3:6 2596
(*t* whom ye received commandments ... Col 4:10 4012
But as *t* brotherly love ye need ... 1Th 4:9 4012
have confidence in the Lord *t* you ... 2Th 3:4 1909

TOW

as a thread of *t* is broken when ... Judg 16:9 5296
And the strong shall be as *t* ... Is 1:31 5296
extinct, they are quenched as *t* ... Is 43:17 6594

TOWARD

which goeth *t* the east of Assyria ... Gen 2:14
going on still *t* the south ... Gen 12:9
and pitched his tent *t* Sodom ... Gen 13:12 5704
and said, Look now *t* heaven ... Gen 15:5
and bowed himself *t* the ground ... Gen 18:2
up from thence, and looked *t* Sodom ... Gen 18:16
from thence, and went *t* Sodom ... Gen 18:22
with his face *t* the ground ... Gen 19:1
looked *t* Sodom and Gomorrah ... Gen 19:28
t all the land of the plain, and ... Gen 19:28
from thence *t* the south country ... Gen 20:1
Egypt, as thou goest *t* Assyria ... Gen 25:18
from Beer-sheba, and went *t* Haran ... Gen 28:10
of the flocks *t* the ringstraked ... Gen 30:40 413
it was not *t* him as before ... Gen 31:2
that it is not *t* me as before ... Gen 31:5
set his face *t* the mount Gilead ... Gen 31:21
right hand *t* Israel's left hand ... Gen 48:13
left hand *t* Israel's right hand ... Gen 48:13
let Moses sprinkle it *t* the ... Ex 9:8
and Moses sprinkled it up *t* heaven ... Ex 9:10
Stretch forth thine hand *t* heaven ... Ex 9:22
stretched forth his rod *t* heaven ... Ex 9:23
Stretch out thine hand *t* heaven ... Ex 10:21
stretched forth his hand *t* heaven ... Ex 10:22
that they looked *t* the wilderness ... Ex 16:10 413
t the mercy seat shall the faces ... Ex 25:20
of the tabernacle *t* the south ... Ex 26:35
t the forepart thereof, over ... Ex 28:27 4136
and bowed his head *t* the earth ... Ex 34:8
which is *t* the north corner, he ... Ex 36:25
t the forepart of it, over ... Ex 39:20 4136
lifted up his hand *t* the people ... Lev 9:22 413
the part of his head *t* his face ... Lev 13:41
on the east side *t* the rising of ... Num 2:3
before the tabernacle *t* the east ... Num 3:38
that they looked *t* the tabernacle ... Num 16:42 413
is before Moab, *t* the sunrising ... Num 21:11
Pisgah, which looketh *t* Jeshimon ... Num 21:20
of Peor, that looketh *t* Jeshimon ... Num 23:28
he set his face *t* the wilderness ... Num 24:1 413
fierce anger of the LORD *t* Israel ... Num 32:14 413
Jericho eastward, *t* the sunrising ... Num 34:15
this side Jordan *t* the sunrising ... Deut 4:41
this side Jordan *t* the sunrising ... Deut 4:47
eye shall be evil *t* his brother ... Deut 28:54
t the wife of his bosom, and ... Deut 28:54
t the remnant of his children ... Deut 28:54
her eye shall be evil *t* the ... Deut 28:56
t her son, and *t* her daughter ... Deut 28:56
t her young one that cometh out ... Deut 28:57
t her children which she shall ... Deut 28:57
unto the great sea *t* the going ... Josh 1:4
this side Jordan *t* the sunrising ... Josh 1:15
came down *t* the sea of the plain ... Josh 3:16 5921
spear that is in thy hand *t* Ai ... Josh 8:18 413
he had in his hand *t* the city ... Josh 8:18 413
Jordan *t* the rising of the sun ... Josh 12:1
t the sunrising, from Baal-gad ... Josh 13:5
From thence it passed *t* Azmon ... Josh 15:4
the border went up *t* Debir from ... Josh 15:7
and so northward, looking *t* Gilgal ... Josh 15:7 413
the border passed *t* the waters of ... Josh 15:7 413
t the coast of Edom southward ... Josh 15:21 413
the border went out *t* the sea to ... Josh 16:6
went over from thence *t* Luz ... Josh 18:13
and went forth *t* Geliloth ... Josh 18:17 413
passed along *t* the side over ... Josh 18:18 413
And their border went up *t* the sea ... Josh 19:11
turned from Sarid eastward *t* the ... Josh 19:12
And their border was *t* Jezreel ... Josh 19:18
turneth *t* the sunrising to ... Josh 19:27
t the north side of Beth-emek ... Josh 19:27
Judah upon Jordan *t* the sunrising ... Josh 19:34
took the fords of Jordan *t* Moab ... Judg 3:28
draw *t* mount Tabor, and take with ... Judg 4:6
My heart is *t* the governors of ... Judg 5:9
even the righteous acts *t* the ... Judg 5:11
Then their anger was abated *t* him ... Judg 8:3
when the flame went up *t* heaven ... Judg 13:20
now the day draweth *t* evening ... Judg 19:9
t the side of mount Ephraim ... Judg 19:18 5704
against Gibeah *t* the sunrising ... Judg 20:43
fled *t* the wilderness unto the ... Judg 20:45
valley of Zeboim *t* the wilderness ... 1Sa 13:18
And he turned from him *t* another ... 1Sa 17:30
ran *t* the army to meet the ... 1Sa 17:48
behold, if there be good *t* David ... 1Sa 20:12 413
arose out of a place *t* the south ... 1Sa 20:41 681
the king's heart was *t* Absalom ... 2Sa 14:1 5921
t the way of the wilderness ... 2Sa 15:23
of the river of Gad, and *t* Jazer ... 2Sa 24:5
and his servants coming on *t* him ... 2Sa 24:20 5921
on the outside *t* the great court ... 1Kin 7:9 5704
oxen, three looking *t* the north ... 1Kin 7:25
and three looking *t* the west ... 1Kin 7:25
and three looking *t* the south ... 1Kin 7:25
and three looking *t* the east ... 1Kin 7:25
spread forth his hands *t* heaven ... 1Kin 8:22
may be open *t* this house night ... 1Kin 8:29 413
even *t* the place of which thou ... 1Kin 8:29 413
servant shall make *t* this place ... 1Kin 8:29 413
when they shall pray *t* this place ... 1Kin 8:30 413
if they pray *t* this place ... 1Kin 8:35 413
forth his hands *t* this house ... 1Kin 8:38 413
shall come and pray *t* this house ... 1Kin 8:42 413
shall pray unto the LORD *t* the ... 1Kin 8:44 1870
t the house that I have built for ... 1Kin 8:44
and pray unto thee *t* their land ... 1Kin 8:48 1870
t the LORD God of Israel in the ... 1Kin 14:13 413
Go up now, look *t* the sea ... 1Kin 18:43 1870
of Judah, I would not look *t* thee ... 2Kin 3:14 413
the king went the way *t* the plain ... 2Kin 25:4 1870
t the east, west, north, and south ... 1Chr 9:24
both *t* the east, and *t* the ... 1Chr 12:15
t the east, and *t* the west ... 1Chr 12:15
a day, and *t* Asuppim two and two ... 1Chr 26:17
oxen, three looking *t* the north ... 2Chr 4:4
and three looking *t* the west ... 2Chr 4:4
and three looking *t* the south ... 2Chr 4:4
and three looking *t* the east ... 2Chr 4:4
spread forth his hands *t* heaven ... 2Chr 6:13
thy servant prayeth *t* this place ... 2Chr 6:20 413
they shall make *t* this place ... 2Chr 6:21 413
yet if they pray *t* this place ... 2Chr 6:26 413
they pray unto thee *t* this city ... 2Chr 6:34 1870
pray *t* their land, which thou ... 2Chr 6:38 1870
t the city which thou hast chosen ... 2Chr 6:38
t the house which I have built ... 2Chr 6:38
them whose heart is perfect *t* him ... 2Chr 16:9 413
when Judah came *t* the watch tower ... 2Chr 20:24 5921
done good in Israel, both *t* God ... 2Chr 24:16 5973
God, and *t* his house ... 2Chr 24:16
the Levite, the porter *t* the east ... 2Chr 31:14
mercy endureth for ever *t* Israel ... Ezr 3:11 5921
against the water gate *t* the east ... Neh 3:26
upon the wall *t* the dung gate ... Neh 12:31
king's manner *t* all that knew law ... Est 1:13 6440
out the golden sceptre *t* Esther ... Est 8:4
dust upon their heads *t* heaven ... Job 2:12
and stretch out thine hands *t* him ... Job 11:13 413
and stretch her wings *t* the south ... Job 39:26
will I worship *t* thy holy temple ... Ps 5:7 413
Mine eyes are ever *t* the LORD ... Ps 25:15 413
up my hands *t* thy holy oracle ... Ps 28:2 413
his doing *t* the children of men ... Ps 66:5 5921
cause thine anger *t* us to cease ... Ps 85:4 5973
For great is thy mercy *t* me ... Ps 86:13 5921
his truth *t* the house of Israel ... Ps 98:3
is his mercy *t* them that fear him ... Ps 103:11 5921
LORD for all his benefits *t* me ... Ps 116:12 5921
merciful kindness is great *t* us ... Ps 117:2 5921
I will worship *t* thy holy temple, ... Ps 138:2 413
king's favour is *t* a wise servant ... Prov 14:35
fly away as an eagle *t* heaven ... Prov 23:5
The wind goeth *t* the south ... Eccl 1:6 413
and if the tree fall *t* the south ... Eccl 11:3
or *t* the north, in the place ... Eccl 11:3
Lebanon which looketh *t* Damascus ... Song 7:4
beloved's, and his desire is *t* me ... Song 7:10 5921
went up *t* Jerusalem to war ... Is 7:1
of the Philistines *t* the west ... Is 11:14
their fear *t* me is taught by the ... Is 29:13 854

turned his face *t* the wall	Is 38:2	413
thee with their face *t* the earth	Is 49:23	
the great goodness *t* the house of	Is 63:7	
thy bowels and of thy mercies *t* me	Is 63:15	413
shall be known *t* his servants	Is 66:14	854
and his indignation *t* his enemies	Is 66:14	854
the face thereof is *t* the north	Jer 1:13	6440
proclaim these words *t* the north	Jer 3:12	
Set up the standard *t* Zion	Jer 4:6	
t the daughter of my people	Jer 4:11	
me, and tried mine heart *t* thee	Jer 12:3	854
mind could not be *t* this people	Jer 15:1	413
and perform my good word *t* you	Jer 29:10	5921
the thoughts that I think *t* you	Jer 29:11	5921
set thine heart *t* the highway	Jer 31:21	
of the horse gate *t* the east	Jer 31:40	
fall *t* the north by the river	Jer 46:6	
scatter them *t* all those winds	Jer 49:36	
lift up thy hands *t* him for the	Lam 2:19	5921
straight, the one *t* the other	Eze 1:23	413
thy face *t* the siege of Jerusalem	Eze 4:7	413
set thy face *t* the mountains of	Eze 6:2	413
than the wilderness *t* Diblath	Eze 6:14	
gate, that looketh *t* the north	Eze 8:3	
eyes now the way *t* the north	Eze 8:5	
up mine eyes the way *t* the north	Eze 8:5	
house which was *t* the north	Eze 8:14	5921
with their backs *t* the temple of	Eze 8:16	413
LORD, and their faces *t* the east	Eze 8:16	
worshipped the sun *t* the east	Eze 8:16	
gate, which lieth *t* the north	Eze 9:2	
I will scatter *t* every wind all	Eze 12:14	
I make my fury *t* thee to rest	Eze 16:42	
when I am pacified *t* thee for all	Eze 16:63	
whose branches turned *t* him	Eze 17:6	413
vine did bend her roots *t* him	Eze 17:7	5921
and shot forth her branches *t* him	Eze 17:7	5921
shall be scattered *t* all winds	Eze 17:21	
of man, set thy face *t* the south	Eze 20:46	1870
and drop thy word *t* the south	Eze 20:46	413
of man, set thy face *t* Jerusalem	Eze 21:2	413
drop thy word *t* the holy places,	Eze 21:2	413
and mourn one *t* another	Eze 24:23	413
and lift up your eyes *t* your idols	Eze 33:25	413
the gate which looketh *t* the east	Eze 40:6	1870
court that looked *t* the north	Eze 40:20	1870
the gate that looketh *t* the east	Eze 40:22	1870
t the north, and *t* the east	Eze 40:23	
that he brought me *t* the south	Eze 40:24	1870
and behold a gate *t* the south	Eze 40:24	1870
in the inner court *t* the south	Eze 40:27	1870
t the south an hundred cubits	Eze 40:27	1870
thereof were *t* the utter court	Eze 40:31	413
into the inner court *t* the east	Eze 40:32	1870
thereof were *t* the outward court	Eze 40:34	
thereof were *t* the utter court	Eze 40:37	
and their prospect was *t* the south	Eze 40:44	1870
having the prospect *t* the north	Eze 40:44	1870
whose prospect is *t* the south	Eze 40:45	1870
is *t* the north is for the priests	Eze 40:46	1870
were *t* the place that was left	Eze 41:11	1870
one door *t* the north, and another	Eze 41:11	1870
and another door *t* the south	Eze 41:11	1870
end *t* the west was seventy cubits	Eze 41:12	1870
of the separate place *t* the east	Eze 41:14	
t the palm tree on the one side	Eze 41:19	413
the face of a young lion *t* the	Eze 41:19	413
utter court, the way *t* the north	Eze 42:1	1870
before the building *t* the north	Eze 42:1	413
and their doors *t* the north	Eze 42:4	
t the utter court on the forepart	Eze 42:7	1870
the wall of the court *t* the east	Eze 42:10	1870
chambers which were *t* the north	Eze 42:11	1870
t the south was a door in the	Eze 42:12	1870
before the wall *t* the east	Eze 42:12	1870
he brought me forth *t* the gate	Eze 42:15	1870
gate whose prospect is *t* the east	Eze 42:15	1870
the gate that looketh *t* the east	Eze 43:1	1870
gate whose prospect is *t* the east	Eze 43:4	1870
his stairs shall look *t* the east	Eze 43:17	
which looketh *t* the east	Eze 44:1	
t the east shall be shut the six	Eze 46:1	
the gate that looketh *t* the east	Eze 46:12	
priests, which looked *t* the north	Eze 46:19	
of the house stood *t* the east	Eze 47:1	
issue out *t* the east country	Eze 47:8	
of the land *t* the north side	Eze 47:15	
t the north five and twenty	Eze 48:10	
t the west ten thousand in	Eze 48:10	
t the east ten thousand in	Eze 48:10	
t the south five and twenty	Eze 48:10	
shall be *t* the north two hundred	Eze 48:17	
t the south two hundred and fifty,	Eze 48:17	
t the east two hundred and fifty,	Eze 48:17	
t the west two hundred and fifty	Eze 48:17	
of the oblation *t* the east border	Eze 48:21	5704
twenty thousand *t* the west border	Eze 48:21	5921
to the river *t* the great sea	Eze 48:28	5921
the high God hath wrought *t* me	Dan 4:2	5974
open in his chamber *t* Jerusalem	Dan 6:10	5049
ones *t* the four winds of heaven	Dan 8:8	
t the south, and *t* the east,	Dan 8:9	413
the east, and *t* the pleasant land	Dan 8:9	413
sleep on my face *t* the ground	Dan 8:18	
my face, and my face *t* the ground	Dan 10:9	
me, I set my face *t* the ground	Dan 10:15	
shall be divided *t* the four winds	Dan 11:4	
face *t* the fort of his own land	Dan 11:19	
shall return, and come *t* the south	Dan 11:29	
the LORD *t* the children of Israel	Hos 3:1	854
for judgment is *t* you, because ye	Hos 5:1	
with his face *t* the east sea	Joel 2:20	413
his hinder part *t* the utmost sea	Joel 2:20	413
will look again *t* thy holy temple	Jonah 2:4	413
go forth *t* the south country	Zec 6:6	413
these that go *t* the north country	Zec 6:8	413
of Israel, shall be *t* the LORD	Zec 9:1	
in the midst thereof *t* the east	Zec 14:4	
t the west, and there shall be a	Zec 14:4	
mountain shall remove *t* the north	Zec 14:4	
north, and half of it *t* the south	Zec 14:4	
half of them *t* the former sea, and	Zec 14:8	413
half of them *t* the hinder sea	Zec 14:8	413
forth his hand *t* his disciples	Mt 12:49	*1909*
was moved with compassion *t* them	Mt 14:14	*1909*
as it began to dawn *t* the first	Mt 28:1	*1519*
was moved with compassion *t* them	Mk 6:34	*1909*
on earth peace, good will *t* men	Lk 2:14	*1722*
for himself, and is not rich *t* God	Lk 12:21	*1519*
and journeying *t* Jerusalem	Lk 13:22	*1519*
for it is *t* evening, and the day	Lk 24:29	*4314*
and went over the sea *t* Capernaum	Jn 6:17	*1519*
stedfastly *t* heaven as he went up	Acts 1:10	*1519*
go *t* the south unto the way that	Acts 8:26	*2596*
to the Greeks, repentance *t* God	Acts 20:21	*1519*
faith *t* our Lord Jesus Christ	Acts 20:21	*1519*
the fathers, and was zealous *t* God	Acts 22:3	
And have hope *t* God, which they	Acts 24:15	*1519*
conscience void of offence *t* God	Acts 24:16	*4314*
God, and *t* men	Acts 24:16	
lieth *t* the south west and north	Acts 27:12	*2596*
to the wind, and made *t* shore	Acts 27:40	*1519*
and so we went *t* Rome	Acts 28:14	*1519*
in their lust one *t* another	Rom 1:27	*1519*
But God commendeth his love *t* us	Rom 5:8	*1519*
but *t* thee, goodness, if thou	Rom 11:22	*1909*
Be of the same mind one *t* another	Rom 12:16	*1519*
one *t* another according to Christ	Rom 15:5	*1722*
himself uncomely *t* his virgin	1Cor 7:36	*1909*
to be brought on my way *t* Judaea	2Cor 1:16	*1519*
our word *t* you was not yea and nay	2Cor 1:18	*4314*
ye would confirm your love *t* him	2Cor 2:8	*1519*
is my boldness of speech *t* you	2Cor 7:4	*4314*
mourning, your fervent mind *t* me	2Cor 7:7	*5228*
affection is more abundant *t* you	2Cor 7:15	*1519*
to make all grace abound *t* you	2Cor 9:8	*1519*
but being absent am bold *t* you	2Cor 10:1	*1519*
him by the power of God *t* you	2Cor 13:4	*1519*
was mighty in me *t* the Gentiles	Gal 2:8	*1519*
hath abounded *t* us in all wisdom	Eph 1:8	*1519*
t us through Christ Jesus	Eph 2:7	*1909*
supply your lack of service *t* me	Phil 2:30	*4314*
I press *t* the mark for the prize	Phil 3:14	*2596*
Walk in wisdom *t* them that are	Col 4:5	*4314*
and abound in love one *t* another	1Th 3:12	*1519*
t all men, even as we do *t*	1Th 3:12	*1519*
all men, even as we do *t* you	1Th 3:12	*1519*
indeed ye do it *t* all the	1Th 4:10	*1519*
honestly *t* them that are without	1Th 4:12	*4314*
the weak, be patient *t* all men	1Th 5:14	*4314*
of you all *t* each other aboundeth	2Th 1:3	*1519*
of God our Saviour *t* man appeared	Titus 3:4	*4314*
which thou hast *t* the Lord Jesus	Philem 5	*4314*
the Lord Jesus, and *t* all saints	Philem 5	*1519*
dead works, and of faith *t* God	Heb 6:1	*1909*
which ye have shewed *t* his name	Heb 6:10	*1519*
for conscience *t* God endure grief	1Pet 2:19	
answer of a good conscience *t* God	1Pet 3:21	*1519*
then have we confidence *t* God	1Jn 3:21	*4314*
manifested the love of God *t* us	1Jn 4:9	*1722*

TOWEL

and took a *t*, and girded himself	Jn 13:4	*3012*
to wipe them with the *t* wherewith	Jn 13:5	*3012*

TOWER

to, let us build us a city and a *t*	Gen 11:4	4026
down to see the city and the *t*	Gen 11:5	4026
his tent beyond the *t* of Edar	Gen 35:21	4026
peace, I will break down this *t*	Judg 8:9	4026
And he beat down the *t* of Penuel	Judg 8:17	4026
of the *t* of Shechem heard that	Judg 9:46	4026
that all the men of the *t* of	Judg 9:47	4026
men of the *t* of Shechem died also	Judg 9:49	4026
was a strong *t* within the city	Judg 9:51	4026
gat them up to the top of the *t*	Judg 9:51	4026
And Abimelech came unto the *t*	Judg 9:52	4026
of the *t* to burn it with fire	Judg 9:52	4026
horn of my salvation, my high *t*	2Sa 22:3	4869
He is the *t* of salvation for his	2Sa 22:51	1431
And when he came to the *t*, he took	2Kin 5:24	6076
a watchman on the *t* in Jezreel	2Kin 9:17	4026
from the *t* of the watchmen to the	2Kin 17:9	4026
from the *t* of the watchmen to the	2Kin 18:8	4026
the watch *t* in the wilderness	2Chr 20:24	
even unto the *t* of Meah they	Neh 3:1	4026
it, unto the *t* of Hananeel	Neh 3:1	4026
piece, and the *t* of the furnaces	Neh 3:11	4026
the *t* which lieth out from the	Neh 3:25	4026
the east, and the *t* that lieth out	Neh 3:26	4026
the great *t* that lieth out	Neh 3:27	4026
from beyond the *t* of the furnaces	Neh 12:38	4026
the *t* of Hananeel	Neh 12:39	4026
the *t* of Meah, even unto the	Neh 12:39	4026
of my salvation, and my high *t*	Ps 18:2	4869
a strong *t* from the enemy	Ps 61:3	4026
my high *t*, and my deliverer	Ps 144:2	4869
name of the LORD is a strong *t*	Prov 18:10	4026
Thy neck is like the *t* of David	Song 4:4	4026
Thy neck is as a *t* of ivory	Song 7:4	4026
thy nose is as the *t* of Lebanon	Song 7:4	4026
And upon every high *t*, and upon	Is 2:15	4026
built a *t* in the midst of it, and	Is 5:2	4026
I have set thee for a *t* and a	Jer 6:27	969
t of Hananeel unto the gate of	Jer 31:38	4026
from the *t* of Syene even unto the	Eze 29:10	4024
from the *t* of Syene shall they	Eze 30:6	4024
O *t* of the flock, the strong hold	Mic 4:8	4026
my watch, and set me upon the *t*	Hab 2:1	4692
from the *t* of Hananeel unto the	Zec 14:10	4026
a winepress in it, and built a *t*	Mt 21:33	*4444*
for the winefat, and built a *t*	Mk 12:1	*4444*
upon whom the *t* in Siloam fell,	Lk 13:4	*4444*
of you, intending to build a *t*	Lk 14:28	*4444*

TOWERS

and make about them walls, and *t*	2Chr 14:7	4026
Moreover Uzziah built *t* in	2Chr 26:9	4026
Also he built *t* in the desert	2Chr 26:10	4026
by cunning men, to be on the *t*	2Chr 26:15	4026
the forests he built castles and *t*	2Chr 27:4	4026
broken, and raised it up to the *t*	2Chr 32:5	4026
tell the *t* thereof	Ps 48:12	4026
I am a wall, and my breasts like *t*	Song 8:10	4026
they set up the *t* thereof	Is 23:13	971
great slaughter, when the *t* fall	Is 30:25	4026
t shall be for dens for ever, a	Is 32:14	975
where is he that counted the *t*	Is 33:18	4026
of Tyrus, and break down her *t*	Eze 26:4	4026
axes he shall break down thy *t*	Eze 26:9	4026
and the Gammadims were in thy *t*	Eze 27:11	4026
cities, and against the high *t*	Zeph 1:16	6438
their *t* are desolate	Zeph 3:6	6438

TOWN

for her house was upon the *t* wall	Josh 2:15	7023
the elders of the *t* trembled at	1Sa 16:4	7023
entering into a *t* that hath gates	1Sa 23:7	5892
a place in some *t* in the country	1Sa 27:5	5892
him that buildeth a *t* with blood	Hab 2:12	5892
city or *t* ye shall enter, enquire	Mt 10:11	*2968*
the hand, and led him out of the *t*	Mk 8:23	*2968*
saying, Neither go into the *t*	Mk 8:26	*2968*
nor tell it to any in the *t*	Mk 8:26	*2968*
come out of every *t* of Galilee	Lk 5:17	*2968*
out of the *t* of Bethlehem, where	Jn 7:42	*2968*
the *t* of Mary and her sister	Jn 11:1	*2968*
Jesus was not yet come into the *t*	Jn 11:30	*2968*

TOWNCLERK

when the *t* had appeased the	Acts 19:35	*1122*

TOWNS

these are their names, by their *t*	Gen 25:16	2691
went and took the small *t* thereof	Num 32:41	2333
beside unwalled *t* a great many	Deut 3:5	5892
of Bashan, and all the *t* of Jair	Josh 13:30	2333
Ekron, with her *t* and her villages	Josh 15:45	1323
Ashdod with her *t* and her villages	Josh 15:47	1323
and her villages, Gaza with her *t*	Josh 15:47	1323
and in Asher Beth-shean and her *t*	Josh 17:11	1323
and Ibleam and her *t*	Josh 17:11	1323
the inhabitants of Dor and her *t*	Josh 17:11	1323
inhabitants of En-dor and her *t*	Josh 17:11	1323
inhabitants of Taanach and her *t*	Josh 17:11	1323
inhabitants of Megiddo and her *t*	Josh 17:11	1323
who are of Beth-shean and her *t*	Josh 17:16	1323
of Beth-shean and her *t*, nor	Judg 1:27	1323
nor Taanach and her *t*	Judg 1:27	1323
the inhabitants of Dor and her *t*	Judg 1:27	1323
inhabitants of Ibleam and her *t*	Judg 1:27	1323
inhabitants of Megiddo and her *t*	Judg 1:27	1323
Israel dwelt in Heshbon and her *t*	Judg 11:26	1323
and in Aroer and her *t*	Judg 11:26	1323
to him pertained the *t* of Jair	1Kin 4:13	2333
and Aram, with the *t* of Jair	1Chr 2:23	2333
the *t* thereof, even threescore	1Chr 2:23	1323
in Gilead in Bashan, and in her *t*	1Chr 5:16	1323
the *t* thereof, and eastward Naaran	1Chr 7:28	1323
Gezer, with the *t* thereof	1Chr 7:28	1323
unto Gaza and the *t* thereof	1Chr 7:28	1323
of Manasseh, Beth-shean and her *t*	1Chr 7:29	
Taanach and her *t*	1Chr 7:29	
Megiddo and her *t*	1Chr 7:29	
Dor and her *t*	1Chr 7:29	
Ono, and Lod, with the *t* thereof	1Chr 8:12	1323
her *t* out of the hand of the	1Chr 18:1	1323
him, Beth-el with the *t* thereof	2Chr 13:19	1323
and Jeshanah with the *t* thereof	2Chr 13:19	1323
and Ephrain with the *t* thereof	2Chr 13:19	1323
that dwelt in the unwalled *t*	Est 9:19	5892
upon all her *t* all the evil that	Jer 19:15	5892
t without walls for the multitude	Zec 2:4	6519
them, Let us go into the next *t*	Mk 1:38	*2969*
into the *t* of Caesarea Philippi	Mk 8:27	*2968*
departed, and went through the *t*	Lk 9:6	*2968*
away, that they may go into the *t*	Lk 9:12	*2968*

TRACHONITIS (*trak-o-ni'-tis*) *A rocky district east of the Jordan.*

of Ituraea and of the region of *T*	Lk 3:1	*5139*

TRADE

dwell and *t* ye therein, and get you	Gen 34:10	5503
dwell in the land, and *t* therein	Gen 34:21	5503
for their *t* hath been to feed	Gen 46:32	582
Thy servants' *t* hath been about	Gen 46:34	582
sailors, and as many as *t* by sea	Rev 18:17	*2038*

TRADED

tin, and lead, they *t* in thy fairs	Eze 27:12	5414
they *t* the persons of men and	Eze 27:13	5414
t in thy fairs with horses	Eze 27:14	5414
they *t* in thy market wheat of	Eze 27:17	5414
t with the same, and made them	Mt 25:16	*2038*

TRADING

much every man had gained by *t*	Lk 19:15	*1281*

TRADITION

transgress the *t* of the elders	Mt 15:2	*3862*
the commandment of God by your *t*	Mt 15:3	*3862*
of God of none effect by your *t*	Mt 15:6	*3862*
holding the *t* of the elders	Mk 7:3	*3862*
according to the *t* of the elders	Mk 7:5	*3862*
of God, ye hold the *t* of men	Mk 7:8	*3862*
God, that ye may keep your own *t*	Mk 7:9	*3862*

God of none effect through your *t* ... Mk 7:13 *3862*
vain deceit, after the *t* of men ... Col 2:8 *3862*
not after the *t* which he received ... 2Th 3:6 *3862*
received by *t* from your fathers ... 1Pet 1:18 *3862*

TRADITIONS
zealous of the *t* of my fathers ... Gal 1:14 *3862*
hold the *t* which ye have been ... 2Th 2:15 *3862*

TRAFFICK
and ye shall *t* in the land ... Gen 42:34 5503
of the *t* of the spice merchants, ... 1Kin 10:15 4536
and carried it into a land of *t* ... Eze 17:4 3667
by thy *t* hast thou increased thy ... Eze 28:5 7404
by the iniquity of thy *t* ... Eze 28:18 7404

TRAFFICKERS
whose *t* are the honourable of the ... Is 23:8 3669

TRAIN
to Jerusalem with a very great *t* ... 1Kin 10:2 2428
T up a child in the way he should ... Prov 22:6 2596
up, and his *t* filled the temple ... Is 6:1 7757

TRAINED
captive, he armed his *t* servants ... Gen 14:14 2593

TRAITOR
Iscariot, which also was the *t* ... Lk 6:16 *4273*

TRAITORS
T, heady, highminded, lovers of ... 2Ti 3:4 *4273*

TRAMPLE
dragon shalt thou *t* under feet ... Ps 91:13 7429
mine anger, and *t* them in my fury ... Is 63:3 7429
lest they *t* them under their feet ... Mt 7:6 *2662*

TRANCE
of the Almighty, falling into a *t* ... Num 24:4
of the Almighty, falling into a *t* ... Num 24:16
they made ready, he fell into a *t* ... Acts 10:10 *1611*
in a *t* I saw a vision, A certain ... Acts 11:5 *1611*
in the temple, I was in a *t* ... Acts 22:17 *1611*

TRANQUILITY
it may be a lengthening of thy *t* ... Dan 4:27 7963

TRANSFERRED
I have in a figure *t* to myself ... 1Cor 4:6 *3345*

TRANSFIGURED
And was *t* before them ... Mt 17:2 *3339*
and he was *t* before them ... Mk 9:2 *3339*

TRANSFORMED
but be ye *t* by the renewing of ... Rom 12:2 *3339*
for Satan himself is *t* into an ... 2Cor 11:14 *3345*
also be *t* as the ministers of ... 2Cor 11:15 *3345*

TRANSFORMING
t themselves into the apostles of ... 2Cor 11:13 *3345*

TRANSGRESS
Wherefore now do ye *t* the ... Num 14:41 5674
ye make the LORD's people to *t* ... 1Sa 2:24 5674
Why *t* ye the commandments of the ... 2Chr 24:20 5674
servant Moses, saying, If ye *t* ... Neh 1:8 4603
to *t* against our God in marrying ... Neh 13:27 4603
that my mouth shall not *t* ... Ps 17:3 5674
be ashamed which *t* without cause ... Ps 25:3 898
a piece of bread that man will *t* ... Prov 28:21 6586
and thou saidst, I will not *t* ... Jer 2:20 5647
rebels, and them that *t* against me ... Eze 20:38 6586
Come to Beth-el, and *t* ... Amos 4:4 6586
Why do thy disciples *t* the ... Mt 15:2 *3845*
Why do ye also *t* the commandment ... Mt 15:3 *3845*
and circumcision dost *t* the law ... Rom 2:27 *3848*

TRANSGRESSED
I have not *t* thy commandments, ... Deut 26:13 5674
they have also *t* my covenant ... Josh 7:11 5674
because he hath *t* the covenant of ... Josh 7:15 5674
When ye have *t* the covenant of ... Josh 23:16 5674
t my covenant which I commanded ... Judg 2:20 5674
And he said, Ye have *t* ... 1Sa 14:33 898
for I have *t* the commandment of ... 1Sa 15:24 5674
wherein they have *t* against thee ... 1Kin 8:50 6586
but *t* his covenant, and all that ... 2Kin 18:12 5674
who *t* in the thing accursed ... 1Chr 2:7 4603
they *t* against the God of their ... 1Chr 5:25 4603
they had *t* against the LORD ... 2Chr 12:2 4603
for he *t* against the LORD his God ... 2Chr 26:16 4603
naked, and *t* sore against the LORD ... 2Chr 28:19 4603
t very much after all the ... 2Chr 36:14 4603
up, and said unto them, Ye have *t* ... Ezr 10:10 4603
many that have *t* in this thing ... Ezr 10:13 6586
because they have *t* the laws ... Is 24:5 5674
and thy teachers have *t* against me ... Is 43:27 6586
of the men that have *t* against me ... Is 66:24 6586
the pastors also *t* against me ... Jer 2:8 6586
ye all have *t* against me, saith ... Jer 2:29 6586
that thou hast *t* against the LORD ... Jer 3:13 6586
and whereby they have *t* against me ... Jer 33:8 6586
the men that have *t* my covenant ... Jer 34:18 5674
We have *t* and have rebelled ... Lam 3:42 6586
their fathers have *t* against me ... Eze 2:3 6586
transgressions, whereby ye have *t* ... Eze 18:31 6586
Yea, all Israel have *t* thy law ... Dan 9:11 5674
they like men have *t* the covenant ... Hos 6:7 5674
because they have *t* against me ... Hos 7:13 6586
because they have *t* my covenant ... Hos 8:1 5674
wherein thou hast *t* against me ... Zeph 3:11 6586
neither *t* I at any time thy ... Lk 15:29 *3928*

TRANSGRESSEST
Why *t* thou the king's commandment . Est 3:3 5674

TRANSGRESSETH
his mouth *t* not in judgment ... Prov 16:10 4603
Yea also, because he *t* by wine ... Hab 2:5 898
committeth sin *t* also the law ... 1Jn 3:4
Whosoever *t*, and abideth not in ... 2Jn 9 *3845*

TRANSGRESSING
LORD thy God, in *t* his covenant, ... Deut 17:2 5674
In *t* and lying against the LORD, ... Is 59:13 6586

TRANSGRESSION
forgiving iniquity and *t* and sin, ... Ex 34:7 6588
mercy, forgiving iniquity and *t* ... Num 14:18 6588
or if in *t* against the LORD, ... Josh 22:22 4604
neither evil nor *t* in mine hand ... 1Sa 24:11 6588
away to Babylon for their *t* ... 1Chr 9:1 4604
So Saul died for his *t* which he ... 1Chr 10:13 4604
his reign did cast away in his *t* ... 2Chr 29:19 4604
because of the *t* of those that ... Ezr 9:4 4604
t of them that had been carried ... Ezr 10:6 4604
And why dost thou not pardon my *t* ... Job 7:21 6588
have cast them away for their *t* ... Job 8:4 6588
make me to know my *t* and my sin ... Job 13:23 6588
My *t* is sealed up in a bag, and ... Job 14:17 6588
I am clean without *t*, I am ... Job 33:9 6588
my wound is incurable without *t* ... Job 34:6 6588
be innocent from the great *t* ... Ps 19:13 6588
Blessed is he whose *t* is forgiven ... Ps 32:1 6588
The *t* of the wicked saith within ... Ps 36:1 6588
not for my *t*, nor for my sin, O ... Ps 59:3 6588
will I visit their *t* with the rod ... Ps 89:32 6588
Fools, because of their *t* ... Ps 107:17 6588
is snared by the *t* of his lips ... Prov 12:13 6588
He that covereth a *t* seeketh love ... Prov 17:9 6588
He loveth *t* that loveth strife ... Prov 17:19 6588
it is his glory to pass over a *t* ... Prov 19:11 6588
For the *t* of a land many are the ... Prov 28:2 6588
his mother, and saith, It is no *t* ... Prov 28:24 6588
In the *t* of an evil man there is ... Prov 29:6 6588
are multiplied, *t* increaseth ... Prov 29:16 6588
and a furious man aboundeth in *t* ... Prov 29:22 6588
the *t* thereof shall be heavy upon ... Is 24:20 6588
for the *t* of my people was he ... Is 53:8 6588
are ye not children of *t*, a seed ... Is 57:4 6588
and shew my people their *t* ... Is 58:1 6588
them that turn from *t* in Jacob ... Is 59:20 6588
deliver him in the day of his *t* ... Eze 33:12 6588
daily sacrifice by reason of *t* ... Dan 8:12 6588
the *t* of desolation, to give both ... Dan 8:13 6588
thy holy city, to finish the *t* ... Dan 9:24 6588
at Gilgal multiply *t* ... Amos 4:4 6586
For the *t* of Jacob is all this, ... Mic 1:5 6588
What is the *t* of Jacob ... Mic 1:5 6588
to declare unto Jacob his *t* ... Mic 3:8 6588
I give my firstborn for my *t* ... Mic 6:7 6588
passeth by the *t* of the remnant ... Mic 7:18 6588
from which Judas by *t* fell ... Acts 1:25 *3845*
where no law is, there is no *t* ... Rom 4:15 *3847*
after the similitude of Adam's *t* ... Rom 5:14 *3847*
woman being deceived was in the *t* ... 1Ti 2:14 *3847*
angels was stedfast, and every *t* ... Heb 2:2 *3847*
for sin is the *t* of the law ... 1Jn 3:4 *458*

TRANSGRESSIONS
for he will not pardon your *t* ... Ex 23:21 6588
because of their *t* in all their ... Lev 16:16 6588
all their *t* in all their sins, ... Lev 16:21 6588
not forgive your *t* nor your sins ... Josh 24:19 6588
all their *t* wherein they have ... 1Kin 8:50 6588
If I covered my *t* as Adam ... Job 31:33 6588
or if thy *t* be multiplied, what ... Job 35:6 6588
their *t* that they have exceeded ... Job 36:9 6588
out in the multitude of their *t* ... Ps 5:10 6588
the sins of my youth, nor my *t* ... Ps 25:7 6588
I will confess my *t* unto the LORD ... Ps 32:5 6588
Deliver me from all my *t* ... Ps 39:8 6588
thy tender mercies blot out my *t* ... Ps 51:1 6588
For I acknowledge my *t* ... Ps 51:3 6588
as for our *t*, thou shalt purge ... Ps 65:3 6588
far hath he removed our *t* from us ... Ps 103:12 6588
out thy *t* for mine own sake ... Is 43:25 6588
out, as a thick cloud, thy *t* ... Is 44:22 6588
for your *t* is your mother put ... Is 50:1 6588
But he was wounded for our *t* ... Is 53:5 6588
For our *t* are multiplied before ... Is 59:12 6588
for our *t* are with us ... Is 59:12 6588
because their *t* are many, and ... Jer 5:6 6588
her for the multitude of her *t* ... Lam 1:5 6588
The yoke of my *t* is bound by his ... Lam 1:14 6588
hast done unto me for all my *t* ... Lam 1:22 6588
any more with all their *t* ... Eze 14:11 6588
All his *t* that he hath committed, ... Eze 18:22 6588
all his *t* that he hath committed ... Eze 18:28 6588
turn yourselves from all your *t* ... Eze 18:30 6588
Cast away from you all your *t* ... Eze 18:31 6588
in that your *t* are discovered, so ... Eze 21:24 6588
Thus ye speak, saying, If our *t* ... Eze 33:10 6588
things, nor with any of their *t* ... Eze 37:23 6588
according to their *t* have I done ... Eze 39:24 6588
For three *t* of Damascus, and for ... Amos 1:3 6588
For three *t* of Gaza, and for four, ... Amos 1:6 6588
For three *t* of Tyrus, and for four ... Amos 1:9 6588
For three *t* of Edom, and for four, ... Amos 1:11 6588
For three *t* of the children of ... Amos 1:13 6588
For three *t* of Moab, and for four, ... Amos 2:1 6588
For three *t* of Judah, and for four ... Amos 2:4 6588
For three *t* of Israel, and for ... Amos 2:6 6588
t of Israel upon him I will also ... Amos 3:14 6588
For I know your manifold *t* ... Amos 5:12 6588
for the *t* of Israel were found in ... Mic 1:13 6588
It was added because of *t* ... Gal 3:19 *3847*
the *t* that were under the first ... Heb 9:15 *3847*

TRANSGRESSOR
and the *t* for the upright ... Prov 21:18 898
overthroweth the words of the *t* ... Prov 22:12 898
and wast called a *t* from the womb ... Is 48:8 6586
I destroyed, I make myself a *t* ... Gal 2:18 *3848*
thou art become a *t* of the law ... Jas 2:11 *3848*

TRANSGRESSORS
But the *t* shall be destroyed ... Ps 37:38 6586
Then will I teach *t* thy ways ... Ps 51:13 6586
be not merciful to any wicked *t* ... Ps 59:5 898
I beheld the *t*, and was grieved ... Ps 119:158 898
the *t* shall be rooted out of it ... Prov 2:22 898
of *t* shall destroy them ... Prov 11:3 898
but *t* shall be taken in their own ... Prov 11:6 898
soul of the *t* shall eat violence ... Prov 13:2 898
but the way of *t* is hard ... Prov 13:15 898
and increaseth the *t* among men ... Prov 23:28 898
the fool, and rewardeth *t* ... Prov 26:10 5674
And the destruction of the *t* ... Is 1:28 6586
bring it again to mind, O ye *t* ... Is 46:8 6586
and he was numbered with the *t* ... Is 53:12 6586
and made intercession for the *t* ... Is 53:12 6586
when the *t* are come to the full, ... Dan 8:23 6586
but the *t* shall fall therein ... Hos 14:9 6586
And he was numbered with the *t* ... Mk 15:28 *459*
And he was reckoned among the *t* ... Lk 22:37 *459*
and are convinced of the law as *t* ... Jas 2:9 *3848*

TRANSLATE
To *t* the kingdom from the house ... 2Sa 3:10 5674

TRANSLATED
hath *t* us into the kingdom of his ... Col 1:13 *3179*
By faith Enoch was *t* that he ... Heb 11:5 *3346*
not found, because God had *t* him ... Heb 11:5 *3346*

TRANSLATION
for before his *t* he had this ... Heb 11:5 *3331*

TRANSPARENT
was pure gold, as it were *t* glass ... Rev 21:21 *1307*

TRAP
ground, and a *t* for him in the way ... Job 18:10 4434
their welfare, let it become a *t* ... Ps 69:22 4170
they set a *t*, they catch men ... Jer 5:26 4889
table be made a snare, and a *t* ... Rom 11:9 *2339*

TRAPS
t unto you, and scourges in your ... Josh 23:13 4170

TRAVAIL
came to pass in the time of her *t* ... Gen 38:27 3205
all the *t* that had come upon them ... Ex 18:8 8513
and pain, as of a woman in *t* ... Ps 48:6 3205
this sore *t* hath God given to the ... Eccl 1:13 6045
days are sorrows, and his *t* grief ... Eccl 2:23 6045
but to the sinner he giveth *t* ... Eccl 2:26 6045
I have seen the *t*, which God hath ... Eccl 3:10 6045
Again, I considered all *t* ... Eccl 4:4 5999
than both the hands full with *t* ... Eccl 4:6 5999
also vanity, yea, it is a sore *t* ... Eccl 4:8 6045
But those riches perish by evil *t* ... Eccl 5:14 6045
I *t* not, nor bring forth children ... Is 23:4 2342
He shall see of the *t* of his soul ... Is 53:11 5999
thou that didst not *t* with child ... Is 54:1 2342
heard a voice as of a woman in *t* ... Jer 4:31 2470
us, and pain, as of a woman in *t* ... Jer 6:24 3205
take thee, as a woman in *t* ... Jer 13:21 3205
thee, the pain as of a woman in *t* ... Jer 22:23 3205
whether a man doth *t* with child ... Jer 30:6 3205
on his loins, as a woman in *t* ... Jer 30:6 3205
have taken her, as a woman in *t* ... Jer 49:24 3205
him, and pangs as of a woman in *t* ... Jer 50:43 3205
have taken thee as a woman in *t* ... Mic 4:9 3205
of Zion, like a woman in *t* ... Mic 4:10 3205
when she is in *t* hath sorrow ... Jn 16:21 *5088*
of whom I *t* in birth again until ... Gal 4:19 *5605*
brethren, our labour and *t* ... 1Th 2:9 *3449*
as *t* upon a woman with child ... 1Th 5:3 *5604*
t night and day, that we might not ... 2Th 3:8 *3449*

TRAVAILED
and Rachel *t*, and she had hard ... Gen 35:16 3205
And it came to pass, when she *t* ... Gen 38:28 3205
were dead, she bowed herself and *t* ... 1Sa 4:19 3205
Before she *t*, she brought forth ... Is 66:7 2342
for as soon as Zion *t*, she ... Is 66:8 2342

TRAVAILEST
forth and cry, thou that *t* not ... Gal 4:27 *5605*

TRAVAILETH
The wicked man *t* with pain all ... Job 15:20 2342
he *t* with iniquity, and hath ... Ps 7:14 2254
be in pain as a woman that *t* ... Is 13:8 3205
as the pangs of a woman that *t* ... Is 21:3 3205
her that *t* with child together ... Jer 31:8 3205
she which *t* hath brought forth ... Mic 5:3 3205
t in pain together until now ... Rom 8:22 *4944*

TRAVAILING
now will I cry like a *t* woman ... Is 42:14 3205
The sorrows of a *t* woman shall ... Hos 13:13 3205
t in birth, and pained to be ... Rev 12:2 *5605*

TRAVEL
Thou knowest all the *t* that hath ... Num 20:14 8513
and compassed me with gall and *t* ... Lam 3:5 8513
Macedonia, Paul's companions in *t* ... Acts 19:29 *4898*
to *t* with us with this grace ... 2Cor 8:19 *4898*

TRAVELERS
the *t* walked through byways ... Judg 5:6

TRAVELLED
about Stephen *t* as far as Phenice ... Acts 11:19 *1330*

TRAVELLER
there came a *t* unto the rich man, ... 2Sa 12:4 1982
but I opened my doors to the *t* ... Job 31:32 734

TRAVELLETH
thy poverty come as one that *t* ... Prov 6:11 1980
thy poverty come as one that *t* ... Prov 24:34 1980

T

TRAVELLING
O ye *t* companies of Dedanim ... Is 21:13 736
t in the greatness of his ... Is 63:1 6808
is as a man *t* into a far country ... Mt 25:14 *589*

TRAVERSING
art a swift dromedary *t* her ways ... Jer 2:23 8308

TREACHEROUS
the *t* dealer dealeth ... Is 21:2 898
the *t* dealers have dealt ... Is 24:16 898
the *t* dealers have dealt very ... Is 24:16 898
her *t* sister Judah saw it ... Jer 3:7 901
yet her *t* sister Judah feared not ... Jer 3:8 898
yet for all this her *t* sister ... Jer 3:10 901
herself more than *t* Judah ... Jer 3:11 898
adulterers, an assembly of *t* men ... Jer 9:2 898
prophets are light and *t* persons ... Zeph 3:4 900

TREACHEROUSLY
of Shechem dealt *t* with Abimelech ... Judg 9:23 898
the treacherous dealer dealeth *t* ... Is 21:2 898
treacherous dealers have dealt *t* ... Is 24:16 898
dealers have dealt very *t* ... Is 24:16 898
and dealest *t*, and they dealt not ... Is 33:1 898
and they dealt not *t* with thee ... Is 33:1 898
thou shalt make an end to deal *t* ... Is 33:1 898
they shall deal *t* with thee ... Is 33:1 898
that thou wouldest deal very *t* ... Is 48:8 898
Surely as a wife *t* departeth from ... Jer 3:20 898
so have ye dealt *t* with me ... Jer 3:20 898
have dealt very *t* against me ... Jer 5:11 898
all they happy that deal very *t* ... Jer 12:1 898
even they have dealt *t* with thee ... Jer 12:6 898
her friends have dealt *t* with her ... Lam 1:2 898
They have dealt *t* against the ... Hos 5:7 898
have they dealt *t* against me ... Hos 6:7 898
thou upon them that deal *t* ... Hab 1:13 898
why do we deal *t* every man ... Mal 2:10 898
Judah hath dealt *t*, and an ... Mal 2:11 898
against whom thou hast dealt *t* ... Mal 2:14 898
let none deal *t* against the wife ... Mal 2:15 898
your spirit, that ye deal not *t* ... Mal 2:16 898

TREACHERY
and said to Ahaziah, There is *t* ... 2Kin 9:23 4820

TREAD
your feet shall *t* shall be yours ... Deut 11:24 1869
all the land that ye shall *t* upon ... Deut 11:25 1869
thou shalt *t* upon their high ... Deut 33:29 1869
sole of your foot shall *t* upon ... Josh 1:3 1869
t on the threshold of Dagon in ... 1Sa 5:5 1869
t their winepresses, and suffer ... Job 24:11 1869
t down the wicked in their place ... Job 40:12 1915
let him *t* down my life upon the ... Ps 7:5 7429
through thy name will we *t* them ... Ps 44:5 947
is that shall *t* down our enemies ... Ps 60:12 947
Thou shalt *t* upon the lion and ... Ps 91:13 1869
is that shall *t* down our enemies ... Ps 108:13 947
this at your hand, to *t* my courts ... Is 1:12 7429
to *t* them down like the mire of ... Is 10:6 4823
my mountains *t* him under foot ... Is 14:25 947
the treaders shall *t* out no wine ... Is 16:10 1869
The foot shall *t* it down, even ... Is 26:6 7429
for I will *t* them in mine anger, ... Is 63:3 1869
I will *t* down the people in mine ... Is 63:6 947
shout, as they that *t* the grapes ... Jer 25:30 1869
none shall *t* with shouting ... Jer 48:33 1869
shall he *t* down all thy streets ... Eze 26:11 7429
but ye must *t* down with your feet ... Eze 34:18 7429
shall *t* it down, and break it in ... Dan 7:23 1759
and loveth to *t* out the corn ... Hos 10:11 1758
t upon the high places of the ... Mic 1:3 1869
when he shall *t* in our palaces, ... Mic 5:5 1869
thou shalt *t* the olives, but thou ... Mic 6:15 1869
t the morter, make strong the ... Nah 3:14 7429
which *t* down their enemies in the ... Zec 10:5 947
ye shall *t* down the wicked ... Mal 4:3 6072
unto you power to *t* on serpents ... Lk 10:19 *3961*
shall they *t* under foot forty ... Rev 11:2 *3961*

TREADER
the *t* of grapes him that soweth ... Amos 9:13 1869

TREADERS
the *t* shall tread out no wine in ... Is 16:10 1869

TREADETH
the ox when he *t* out the corn ... Deut 25:4 1758
t upon the waves of the sea ... Job 9:8 1869
morter, and as the potter *t* clay ... Is 41:25 7429
like him that *t* in the winefat ... Is 63:2 1869
t upon the high places of the ... Amos 4:13 1869
when he *t* within our borders ... Mic 5:6 1869
if he go through, both *t* down ... Mic 5:8 7429
of the ox that *t* out the corn ... 1Cor 9:9 *248*
muzzle the ox that *t* out the corn ... 1Ti 5:18 *248*
he *t* the winepress of the ... Rev 19:15 *3961*

TREADING
some *t* winepresses on the sabbath ... Neh 13:15 1869
for the *t* of lesser cattle ... Is 7:25 4823
of *t* down, and of perplexity by ... Is 22:5 4001
as your *t* is upon the poor ... Amos 5:11 1318

TREASON
his *t* that he wrought, are they ... 1Kin 16:20 7195
rent her clothes, and cried, *T*. ... 2Kin 11:14 7195
her clothes, and cried, *T*, *T* ... 2Kin 11:14 7195
rent her clothes, and said, *T* ... 2Chr 23:13 7195
her clothes, and said, *T*, *T* ... 2Chr 23:13 7195

TREASURE
hath given you *t* in your sacks ... Gen 43:23 4301
they built for Pharaoh *t* cities ... Ex 1:11 4543
t unto me above all people ... Ex 19:5
shall open unto thee his good *t* ... Deut 28:12 214
to the *t* of the house of the LORD ... 1Chr 29:8 214
unto the *t* of the work threescore ... Ezr 2:69 214
search made in the king's *t* house ... Ezr 5:17 1596
it out of the king's *t* house ... Ezr 7:20 1596
to the *t* a thousand drams of gold ... Neh 7:70 214
of the fathers gave to the *t* of ... Neh 7:71 214
to the chambers, into the *t* house ... Neh 10:38 214
belly thou fillest with thy hid *t* ... Ps 17:14
and Israel for his peculiar *t* ... Ps 135:4
house of the righteous is much *t* ... Prov 15:6 2633
the fear of the LORD than great *t* ... Prov 15:16 214
There is *t* to be desired and oil ... Prov 21:20 214
gold, and the peculiar *t* of kings ... Eccl 2:8
the fear of the LORD is his *t* ... Is 33:6 214
they have taken the *t* and precious ... Eze 22:25 2633
into the *t* house of his god ... Dan 1:2 214
he shall spoil the *t* of all ... Hos 13:15 214
For where your *t* is, there will ... Mt 6:21 *2344*
A good man out of the good *t* of ... Mt 12:35 *2344*
evil *t* bringeth forth evil things ... Mt 12:35 *2344*
is like unto *t* hid in a field ... Mt 13:44 *2344*
forth out of his *t* things new ... Mt 13:52 *2344*
and thou shalt have *t* in heaven ... Mt 19:21 *2344*
and thou shalt have *t* in heaven ... Mk 10:21 *2344*
A good man out of the good *t* of ... Lk 6:45 *2344*
t of his heart bringeth forth ... Lk 6:45 *2344*
he that layeth up *t* for himself ... Lk 12:21 *2343*
a *t* in the heavens that faileth ... Lk 12:33 *2344*
For where your *t* is, there will ... Lk 12:34 *2344*
and thou shalt have *t* in heaven ... Lk 18:22 *2344*
who had the charge of all her *t* ... Acts 8:27 *1047*
But we have this *t* in earthen ... 2Cor 4:7 *2344*
Ye have heaped *t* together for the ... Jas 5:3 *2343*

TREASURED
it shall not be *t* nor laid up ... Is 23:18 686

TREASURER
by the hand of Mithredath the *t* ... Ezr 1:8 1489
hosts, Go, get thee unto this *t* ... Is 22:15 5532

TREASURERS
the *t* which are beyond the river ... Ezr 7:21 1490
I made *t* over the treasuries, ... Neh 13:13 686
the captains, the judges, the *t* ... Dan 3:2 1411
and captains, the judges, the *t* ... Dan 3:3 1411

TREASURES
with me, and sealed up among my *t* ... Deut 32:34 214
the seas, and of *t* hid in the sand ... Deut 33:19 8226
did he put among the *t* of the ... 1Kin 7:51 214
he took away the *t* of the house ... 1Kin 14:26 214
the *t* of the king's house ... 1Kin 14:26 214
in the *t* of the house of the LORD ... 1Kin 15:18 214
the *t* of the king's house, and ... 1Kin 15:18 214
in the *t* of the house of the LORD ... 2Kin 12:18 214
in the *t* of the king's house, and ... 2Kin 14:14 214
in the *t* of the king's house, and ... 2Kin 16:8 214
in the *t* of the king's house ... 2Kin 18:15 214
and all that was found in his *t* ... 2Kin 20:13 214
there is nothing among my *t* that ... 2Kin 20:15 214
the *t* of the house of the LORD ... 2Kin 24:13 214
the *t* of the king's house, and cut ... 2Kin 24:13 214
over the *t* of the house of God ... 1Chr 26:20 214
over the *t* of the dedicated ... 1Chr 26:20 214
which were over the *t* of the ... 1Chr 26:22 214
son of Moses, was ruler of the *t* ... 1Chr 26:24 214
all the *t* of the dedicated things ... 1Chr 26:26 214
over the king's *t* was Azmaveth ... 1Chr 27:25 214
put he among the *t* of the house ... 2Chr 5:1 214
any matter, or concerning the *t* ... 2Chr 8:15 214
took away the *t* of the house of ... 2Chr 12:9 214
the *t* of the king's house ... 2Chr 12:9 214
gold out of the *t* of the house of ... 2Chr 16:2 214
the *t* of the king's house, the ... 2Chr 25:24 214
the *t* of the house of the LORD, ... 2Chr 36:18 214
the *t* of the king, and of his ... 2Chr 36:18 214
where the *t* were laid up in ... Ezr 6:1 1596
over the chambers for the *t* ... Neh 12:44 214
and dig for it more than for hid *t* ... Job 3:21 4301
entered into the *t* of the snow ... Job 38:22 214
hast thou seen the *t* of the hail ... Job 38:22 214
and searchest for her as for hid *t* ... Prov 2:4 4301
and I will fill their *t* ... Prov 8:21 214
T of wickedness profit nothing ... Prov 10:2 214
The getting of *t* by a lying ... Prov 21:6 214
is there any end of their *t* ... Is 2:7 214
people, and have robbed their *t* ... Is 10:13 6259
their *t* upon the bunches of ... Is 30:6 214
and all that was found in his *t* ... Is 39:2 214
there is nothing among my *t* that ... Is 39:4 214
will give thee the *t* of darkness ... Is 45:3 214
forth the wind out of his *t* ... Jer 10:13 214
thy *t* will I give to the spoil ... Jer 15:13 214
all thy *t* to the spoil, and thy ... Jer 17:3 214
all the *t* of the kings of Judah ... Jer 20:5 214
for we have *t* in the field, of ... Jer 41:8 4301
trusted in thy works and in thy *t* ... Jer 48:7 214
that trusted in her *t*, saying, ... Jer 49:4 214
a sword is upon her *t* ... Jer 50:37 214
upon many waters, abundant in *t* ... Jer 51:13 214
forth the wind out of his *t* ... Jer 51:16 214
gotten gold and silver into thy *t* ... Eze 28:4 214
have power over the *t* of gold ... Dan 11:43 4362
Are there yet the *t* of wickedness ... Mic 6:10 214
and when they had opened their *t* ... Mt 2:11 *2344*
up for yourselves *t* upon earth ... Mt 6:19 *2344*
lay up for yourselves *t* in heaven ... Mt 6:20 *2344*
whom are hid all the *t* of wisdom ... Col 2:3 *2344*
riches than the *t* in Egypt ... Heb 11:26 *2344*

TREASUREST
impenitent heart *t* up unto ... Rom 2:5 *2343*

TREASURIES
chambers and *t* of the house of God ... 1Chr 9:26 214
of the *t* thereof, and of the upper ... 1Chr 28:11 1597
of the *t* of the house of God, and ... 1Chr 28:12 214
of the *t* of the dedicated things ... 1Chr 28:12 214
and he made himself *t* for silver ... 2Chr 32:27 214
new wine and the oil unto the *t* ... Neh 13:12 214
And I made treasurers over the *t* ... Neh 13:13 214
to bring it into the king's *t* ... Est 3:9 1595
pay to the king's *t* for the Jews ... Est 4:7 1595
he bringeth the wind out of his *t* ... Ps 135:7 214

TREASURY
shall come into the *t* of the LORD ... Josh 6:19 214
they put into the *t* of the house ... Josh 6:24 214
the house of the king under the *t* ... Jer 38:11 214
lawful for to put them into the *t* ... Mt 27:6 *2878*
And Jesus sat over against the *t* ... Mk 12:41 *1049*
the people cast money into the *t* ... Mk 12:41 *1049*
they which have cast into the *t* ... Mk 12:43 *1049*
casting their gifts into the *t* ... Lk 21:1 *1049*
These words spake Jesus in the *t* ... Jn 8:20 *1049*

TREATISE
The former *t* have I made, O ... Acts 1:1 *3056*

TREE
the fruit *t* yielding fruit after ... Gen 1:11 6086
the *t* yielding fruit, whose seed ... Gen 1:12 6086
face of all the earth, and every *t* ... Gen 1:29 6086
is the fruit of a *t* yielding seed ... Gen 1:29 6086
t that is pleasant to the sight ... Gen 2:9 6086
the *t* of life also in the midst ... Gen 2:9 6086
the *t* of knowledge of good and ... Gen 2:9 6086
Of every *t* of the garden thou ... Gen 2:16 6086
But of the *t* of the knowledge of ... Gen 2:17 6086
not eat of every *t* of the garden ... Gen 3:1 6086
But of the fruit of the *t* which ... Gen 3:3 6086
saw that the *t* was good for food ... Gen 3:6 6086
a *t* to be desired to make one ... Gen 3:6 6086
Hast thou eaten of the *t*, whereof ... Gen 3:11 6086
be with me, she gave me of the *t* ... Gen 3:12 6086
thy wife, and hast eaten of the *t* ... Gen 3:17 6086
and take also of the *t* of life ... Gen 3:22 6086
to keep the way of the *t* of life ... Gen 3:24 6086
and rest yourselves under the *t* ... Gen 18:4 6086
and he stood by them under the *t* ... Gen 18:8 6086
and of the hazel and chesnut *t* ... Gen 30:37
thee, and shall hang thee on a *t* ... Gen 40:19 6086
brake every *t* of the field ... Ex 9:25 6086
shall eat every *t* which groweth ... Ex 10:5 6086
and the LORD shewed him a *t* ... Ex 15:25 6086
land, or of the fruit of the *t* ... Lev 27:30 6086
that is made of the vine *t* ... Num 6:4
the hills, and under every green *t* ... Deut 12:2 6086
with the axe to cut down the *t* ... Deut 19:5 6086
not cut them down (for the *t* of ... Deut 20:19 6086
to death, and thou hang him on a *t* ... Deut 21:22 6086
not remain all night upon the *t* ... Deut 21:23 6086
before thee in the way in any *t* ... Deut 22:6 6086
When thou beatest thine olive *t* ... Deut 24:20
he hanged on a *t* until eventide ... Josh 8:29 6086
take his carcase down from the *t* ... Josh 8:29 6086
palm *t* of Deborah between Ramah ... Judg 4:5
and they said unto the olive *t* ... Judg 9:8
But the olive *t* said unto them, ... Judg 9:9
And the trees said to the fig *t* ... Judg 9:10 6086
But the fig *t* said unto them, ... Judg 9:11 6086
pomegranate *t* which is in Migron ... 1Sa 14:2
in Gibeah under a *t* in Ramah ... 1Sa 22:6 815
buried them under a *t* at Jabesh ... 1Sa 31:13 815
under his vine and under his fig *t* ... 1Kin 4:25
from the cedar *t* that is in ... 1Kin 4:33 6086
he made two cherubims of olive *t* ... 1Kin 6:23 6086
oracle he made doors of olive *t* ... 1Kin 6:31 6086
two doors also were of olive *t* ... 1Kin 6:32 6086
of the temple posts of olive *t* ... 1Kin 6:33 6086
And the two doors were of fir *t* ... 1Kin 6:34 6086
high hill, and under every green *t* ... 1Kin 14:23 6086
and sat down under a juniper *t* ... 1Kin 19:4
he lay and slept under a juniper *t* ... 1Kin 19:5
city, and shall fell every good *t* ... 2Kin 3:19 6086
the hills, and under every green *t* ... 2Kin 16:4 6086
high hill, and under every green *t* ... 2Kin 17:10 6086
vine, and every one of his fig *t* ... 2Kin 18:31
house he cieled with fir *t* ... 2Chr 3:5 6086
the hills, and under every green *t* ... 2Chr 28:4 6086
they were both hanged on a *t* ... Est 2:23 6086
For there is hope of a *t*, if it ... Job 14:7 6086
hope hath he removed like a *t* ... Job 19:10 6086
wickedness shall be broken as a *t* ... Job 24:20 6086
he shall be like a *t* planted by ... Ps 1:3 6086
himself like a green bay *t* ... Ps 37:35
green olive *t* in the house of God ... Ps 52:8
shall flourish like the palm *t* ... Ps 92:12
She is a *t* of life to them that ... Prov 3:18 6086
of the righteous is a *t* of life ... Prov 11:30 6086
desire cometh, it is a *t* of life ... Prov 13:12 6086
A wholesome tongue is a *t* of life ... Prov 15:4 6086
Whoso keepeth the fig *t* shall eat ... Prov 27:18
if the *t* fall toward the south, ... Eccl 11:3 6086
in the place where the *t* falleth ... Eccl 11:3 6086
the almond *t* shall flourish, and ... Eccl 12:5
As the apple *t* among the trees of ... Song 2:3 6086
The fig *t* putteth forth her green ... Song 2:13
thy stature is like to a palm *t* ... Song 7:7
said, I will go up to the palm *t* ... Song 7:8
raised thee up under the apple *t* ... Song 8:5
as a teil *t*, and as an oak, whose ... Is 6:13
it, as the shaking of an olive *t* ... Is 17:6
be as the shaking of an olive *t* ... Is 24:13
as a falling fig from the fig *t* ... Is 34:4
vine, and every one of his fig *t* ... Is 36:16
chooseth a *t* that will not rot ... Is 40:20 6086
the cedar, the shittah *t*, and the ... Is 41:19 6086
t, and the myrtle, and the oil *t* ... Is 41:19 6086
will set in the desert the fir *t* ... Is 41:19
the pine, and the box *t* together ... Is 41:19
I fall down to the stock of a *t* ... Is 44:19 6086

O forest, and every *t* therein Is 44:23 6086
the thorn shall come up the fir *t* Is 55:13
brier shall come up the myrtle *t* Is 55:13
eunuch say, Behold, I am a dry *t* Is 56:3 6086
with idols under every green *t* Is 57:5 6086
shall come unto thee, the fir *t* Is 60:13
thee, the fir *t*, the pine *t* Is 60:13
for as the days of a *t* are the Is 65:22 6086
gardens behind one *t* in the midst Is 66:17
said, I see a rod of an almond *t* Jer 1:11
every green *t* thou wanderest Jer 2:20 6086
mountain and under every green *t* Jer 3:6 6086
the strangers under every green *t* Jer 3:13 6086
the vine, nor figs on the fig *t* Jer 8:13
one cutteth a *t* out of the forest Jer 10:3 6086
They are upright as the palm *t* Jer 10:5
called thy name, A green olive *t* Jer 11:16
Let us destroy the *t* with the Jer 11:19 6086
For he shall be as a *t* planted by Jer 17:8 6086
mountains, and under every green *t* Eze 6:13 6086
is the vine *t* more than any *t* Eze 15:2 6086
As the vine *t* among the trees of Eze 15:6 6086
waters, and set it as a willow *t* Eze 17:5
LORD have brought down the high *t* Eze 17:24 6086
have exalted the low *t* Eze 17:24 6086
t, have dried up the green *t* Eze 17:24 6086
have made the dry *t* to flourish Eze 17:24 6086
devour every green *t* in thee Eze 20:47 6086
and every dry *t* Eze 20:47 6086
the rod of my son, as every *t* Eze 21:10 6086
nor any *t* in the garden of God Eze 31:8 6086
the *t* of the field shall yield Eze 34:27 6086
will multiply the fruit of the *t* Eze 36:30 6086
so that a palm *t* was between a Eze 41:18
toward the palm *t* on the one side Eze 41:19
the palm *t* on the other side Eze 41:19
behold a *t* in the midst of the Dan 4:10 363
The *t* grew, and was strong, and the Dan 4:11 363
and said thus, Hew down the *t* Dan 4:14 363
The *t* that thou sawest, which Dan 4:20 363
heaven, and saying, Hew the *t* down Dan 4:23 363
to leave the stump of the *t* roots Dan 4:26 363
in the fig *t* at her first time Hos 9:10
beauty shall be as the olive *t* Hos 14:6
I am like a green fir *t* Hos 14:8
my vine waste, and barked my fig *t* Joel 1:7
up, and the fig *t* languisheth Joel 1:12
pomegranate *t*, the palm *t* also Joel 1:12
also, and the apple *t* Joel 1:12
for the *t* beareth her fruit, the Joel 2:22 6086
beareth her fruit, the fig *t* Joel 2:22
under his vine and under his fig *t* Mic 4:4
Although the fig *t* shall not Hab 3:17
as yet the vine, and the fig *t* Hag 2:19
the pomegranate, and the olive *t* Hag 2:19 6086
under the vine and under the fig *t* Zec 3:10
Howl, fir *t* Zec 11:2
therefore every *t* which bringeth Mt 3:10 *1186*
Even so every good *t* bringeth Mt 7:17 *1186*
but a corrupt *t* bringeth forth Mt 7:17 *1186*
A good *t* cannot bring forth evil Mt 7:18 *1186*
neither can a corrupt *t* bring Mt 7:18 *1186*
Every *t* that bringeth not forth Mt 7:19 *1186*
Either make the *t* good, and his Mt 12:33 *1186*
or else make the *t* corrupt Mt 12:33 *1186*
for the *t* is known by his fruit Mt 12:33 *1186*
among herbs, and becometh a *t* Mt 13:32 *1186*
And when he saw a fig *t* in the way Mt 21:19 *4808*
presently the fig *t* withered away Mt 21:19 *4808*
soon is the fig *t* withered away Mt 21:20 *4808*
this which is done to the fig *t* Mt 21:21 *4808*
Now learn a parable of the fig *t* Mt 24:32 *4808*
seeing a fig *t* afar off having Mk 11:13 *4808*
they saw the fig *t* dried up from Mk 11:20 *4808*
the fig *t* which thou cursedst is Mk 11:21 *4808*
Now learn a parable of the fig *t* Mk 13:28 *4808*
every *t* therefore which bringeth Lk 3:9 *1186*
For a good *t* bringeth not forth Lk 6:43 *1186*
corrupt *t* bring forth good fruit Lk 6:43 *1186*
For every *t* is known by his own Lk 6:44 *1186*
a fig *t* planted in his vineyard Lk 13:6 *4808*
come seeking fruit on this fig *t* Lk 13:7 *4808*
and it grew, and waxed a great *t* Lk 13:19 *1186*
ye might say unto this sycamine *t* Lk 17:6
up into a sycomore *t* to see him Lk 19:4 *4809*
Behold the fig *t*, and all the Lk 21:29 *4808*
they do these things in a green *t* Lk 23:31 *3586*
when thou wast under the fig *t* Jn 1:48 *4808*
thee, I saw thee under the fig *t* Jn 1:50 *4808*
whom ye slew and hanged on a *t* Acts 5:30 *3586*
whom they slew and hanged on a *t* Acts 10:39 *3586*
they took him down from the *t* Acts 13:29 *3586*
and thou, being a wild olive *t* Rom 11:17 *65*
root and fatness of the olive *t* Rom 11:17
olive *t* which is wild by nature Rom 11:24 *65*
to nature into a good olive *t* Rom 11:24 *2565*
be graffed into their own olive *t* Rom 11:24
is every one that hangeth on a *t* Gal 3:13 *3586*
Can the fig *t*, my brethren, bear Jas 3:12 *4808*
our sins in his own body on the *t* 1Pet 2:24 *3586*
I give to eat of the *t* of life Rev 2:7 *3586*
even as a fig *t* casteth her Rev 6:13 *4808*
nor on the sea, nor on any *t* Rev 7:1 *1186*
any green thing, neither any *t* Rev 9:4 *1186*
river, was there the *t* of life Rev 22:2 *3586*
the leaves of the *t* were for the Rev 22:2 *3586*
may have right to the *t* of life Rev 22:14 *3586*

TREES

the fruit of the *t* of the garden Gen 3:2 6086
God amongst the *t* of the garden Gen 3:8 6086
all the *t* that were in the field, Gen 23:17 6086
all the fruit of the *t* which the Ex 10:15 6086
not any green thing in the *t* Ex 10:15 6086
and threescore and ten palm *t* Ex 15:27
planted all manner of *t* for food Lev 19:23 6086
first day the boughs of goodly *t* Lev 23:40 6086
branches of palm *t* Lev 23:40
and the boughs of thick *t* Lev 23:40 6086
the *t* of the field shall yield Lev 26:4 6086
neither shall the *t* of the land Lev 26:20 6086
as the *t* of lign aloes which the Num 24:6
as cedar *t* beside the waters Num 24:6
and threescore and ten palm *t* Num 33:9
not, vineyards and olive *t* Deut 6:11
and barley, and vines, and fig *t* Deut 8:8
not plant thee a grove of any *t* Deut 16:21 6086
the *t* thereof by forcing an ax Deut 20:19 6086
Only the *t* which thou knowest Deut 20:20 6086
that they be not *t* for meat Deut 20:20 6086
Thou shalt have olive *t* Deut 28:40
All thy *t* and fruit of thy land Deut 28:42 6086
of Jericho, the city of palm *t* Deut 34:3
them, and hanged them on five *t* Josh 10:26 6086
upon the *t* until the evening Josh 10:26 6086
and they took them down off the *t* Josh 10:27 6086
t with the children of Judah into Judg 1:16
and possessed the city of palm *t* Judg 3:13
The *t* went forth on a time to Judg 9:8 6086
and go to be promoted over the *t* Judg 9:9 6086
the *t* said to the fig tree, Come Judg 9:10 6086
and go to be promoted over the *t* Judg 9:11 6086
Then said the *t* unto the vine Judg 9:12 6086
and go to be promoted over the *t* Judg 9:13 6086
said all the *t* unto the bramble Judg 9:14 6086
And the bramble said unto the *t* Judg 9:15 6086
and cut down a bough from the *t* Judg 9:48 6086
messengers to David, and cedar *t* 2Sa 5:11 6086
them over against the mulberry *t* 2Sa 5:23
in the tops of the mulberry *t* 2Sa 5:24
And he spake of *t*, from the cedar 1Kin 4:33 6086
hew me cedar *t* out of Lebanon 1Kin 5:6
So Hiram gave Solomon cedar *t* 1Kin 5:10 6086
fir *t* according to all his desire 1Kin 5:10 6086
figures of cherubims and palm *t* 1Kin 6:29
carvings of cherubims and palm *t* 1Kin 6:32
the cherubims, and upon the palm *t* 1Kin 6:32
thereon cherubims and palm *t* 1Kin 6:35
cherubims, lions, and palm *t* 1Kin 7:36
Solomon with cedar *t* and fir *t* 1Kin 9:11 6086
Ophir great plenty of almug *t* 1Kin 10:11 6086
the king made of the almug *t* 1Kin 10:12 6086
there came no such almug *t* 1Kin 10:12 6086
sycomore *t* that are in the vale 1Kin 10:27
water, and felled all the good *t* 2Kin 3:25 6086
cut down the tall cedar *t* thereof 2Kin 19:23
and the choice fir *t* thereof 2Kin 19:23
them over against the mulberry *t* 1Chr 14:14
in the tops of the mulberry *t* 1Chr 14:15
Then shall the *t* of the wood sing 1Chr 16:33 6086
Also cedar *t* in abundance 1Chr 22:4 6086
And over the olive *t* and the 1Chr 27:28
the sycomore *t* that were in the 1Chr 27:28
cedar *t* made he as the sycomore 2Chr 1:15
t that are in the vale for 2Chr 1:15
Send me also cedar *t* 2Chr 2:8 6086
fir *t*, and algum *t* 2Chr 2:8
fine gold, and set thereon palm *t* 2Chr 3:5
gold from Ophir, brought algum *t* 2Chr 9:10 6086
the king made of the algum *t* 2Chr 9:11 6086
cedar *t* made he as the sycomore 2Chr 9:27
t that are in the low plains in 2Chr 9:27
to Jericho, the city of palm *t* 2Chr 28:15
to bring cedar *t* from Lebanon to Ezr 3:7 6086
branches, and branches of thick *t* Neh 8:15 6086
and fruit *t* in abundance Neh 9:25 6086
firstfruits of all fruit of all *t* Neh 10:35 6086
and the fruit of all manner of *t* Neh 10:37 6086
He lieth under the shady *t* Job 40:21
The shady *t* cover him with their Job 40:22
lifted up axes upon the thick *t* Ps 74:5 6086
and their sycomore *t* with frost Ps 78:47
then shall all the *t* of the wood Ps 96:12 6086
The *t* of the LORD are full of sap Ps 104:16 6086
stork, the fir *t* are her house Ps 104:17
their vines also and their fig *t* Ps 105:33
brake the *t* of their coasts Ps 105:33 6086
fruitful *t*, and all cedars Ps 148:9 6086
I planted *t* in them of all kind Eccl 2:5 6086
the wood that bringeth forth *t* Eccl 2:6 6086
tree among the *t* of the wood Song 2:3 6086
with all *t* of frankincense Song 4:14 6086
as the *t* of the wood are moved Is 7:2 6086
the rest of the *t* of his forest Is 10:19 6086
the fir *t* rejoice at thee, and the Is 14:8
and the choice fir *t* thereof Is 37:24
himself among the *t* of the forest Is 44:14 6086
all the *t* of the field shall clap Is 55:12 6086
be called *t* of righteousness Is 61:3 352
eat up thy vines and thy fig *t* Jer 5:17
LORD of hosts said, Hew ye down *t* Jer 6:6 6097
upon the *t* of the field, and upon Jer 7:20 6086
the green *t* upon the high hills Jer 17:2 6086
is among the *t* of the forest Eze 15:2 6086
tree among the *t* of the forest Eze 15:6 6086
all the *t* of the field shall know Eze 17:24 6086
high hill, and all the thick *t* Eze 20:28 6086
thy ship boards of fir *t* of Senir Eze 27:5
unto all the *t* of the field Eze 31:4 6086
above all the *t* of the field Eze 31:5 6086
the fir *t* were not like his Eze 31:8
the chesnut *t* were not like his Eze 31:8
so that all the *t* of Eden Eze 31:9 6086
t by the waters exalt themselves Eze 31:14 6086
neither their *t* stand up in their Eze 31:14 352
all the *t* of the field fainted Eze 31:15 6086
and all the *t* of Eden, the choice Eze 31:16 6086
in greatness among the *t* of Eden Eze 31:18 6086
t of Eden unto the nether parts Eze 31:18 6086
and upon each post were palm *t* Eze 40:16
and their arches, and their palm *t* Eze 40:22
and it had palm *t*, one on this Eze 40:26
palm *t* were upon the posts Eze 40:31
palm *t* were upon the posts Eze 40:34
palm *t* were upon the posts Eze 40:37
was made with cherubims and palm *t* Eze 41:18
were cherubims and palm *t* made Eze 41:20
the temple, cherubims and palm *t* Eze 41:25
palm *t* on the one side and on the Eze 41:26
were very many *t* on the one side Eze 47:7 6086
side, shall grow all *t* for meat Eze 47:12 6086
destroy her vines and her fig *t* Hos 2:12
tree, even all the *t* of the field Joel 1:12 6086
burned all the *t* of the field Joel 1:19 6086
and your vineyards and your fig *t* Amos 4:9
and your olive *t* increased Amos 4:9
the fir *t* shall be terribly Nah 2:3
fig *t* with the firstripe figs Nah 3:12
myrtle *t* that were in the bottom Zec 1:8
stood among the myrtle *t* answered Zec 1:10
that stood among the myrtle *t* Zec 1:11
And two olive *t* by it, one upon Zec 4:3
What are these two olive *t* upon Zec 4:11
ax is laid unto the root of the *t* Mt 3:10 *1186*
cut down branches from the *t* Mt 21:8 *1186*
up, and said, I see men as *t* Mk 8:24 *1186*
cut down branches off the *t* Mk 11:8 *1186*
is laid unto the root of the *t* Lk 3:9 *1186*
Behold the fig tree, and all the *t* Lk 21:29 *1186*
Took branches of palm *t*, and went Jn 12:13
t whose fruit withereth, without Jude 12 *1186*
earth, neither the sea, nor the *t* Rev 7:3 *1186*
the third part of *t* was burnt up Rev 8:7 *1186*
These are the two olive *t* Rev 11:4

TREMBLE

hear report of thee, and shall *t* Deut 2:25 7264
faint, fear not, and do not *t* Deut 20:3 2648
lord, and of those that *t* at the Ezr 10:3 2730
place, and the pillars thereof *t* Job 9:6 6426
The pillars of heaven *t*, and are Job 26:11 7322
Thou hast made the earth to *t* Ps 60:2 7493
let the people *t* Ps 99:1 7264
T, thou earth, at the presence of Ps 114:7 2342
the keepers of the house shall *t* Eccl 12:3 2111
and the hills did *t*, and their Is 5:25 7264
the man that made the earth to *t* Is 14:16 7264
T, ye women that are at ease Is 32:11 2729
the nations may *t* at thy presence Is 64:2 7264
the LORD, ye that *t* at his word Is 66:5 2730
will ye not *t* at my presence, Jer 5:22 2342
at his wrath the earth shall *t* Jer 10:10 7493
t for all the goodness and for all Jer 33:9 7264
And the land shall *t* and sorrow Jer 51:29 7493
shall *t* at every moment, and be Eze 26:16 2729
Now shall the isles *t* in the day Eze 26:18 2729
they shall *t* at every moment, Eze 32:10 2729
dominion of my kingdom men *t* Dan 6:26 2112
children shall *t* from the west Hos 11:10 2729
They shall *t* as a bird out of Hos 11:11 2729
all the inhabitants of the land *t* Joel 2:1 7264
the heavens shall *t* Joel 2:10 7493
Shall not the land *t* for this Amos 8:8 7264
of the land of Midian did *t* Hab 3:7 7264
the devils also believe, and *t* Jas 2:19 *5425*

TREMBLED

Isaac *t* very exceedingly, and said Gen 27:33 2729
the people that was in the camp *t* Ex 19:16 2729
of the field of Edom, the earth *t* Judg 5:4 7493
for his heart *t* for the ark of 1Sa 4:13 2730
and the spoilers, they also *t* 1Sa 14:15 2729
of the town *t* at his coming 1Sa 16:4 2729
afraid, and his heart greatly *t* 1Sa 28:5 2729
Then the earth shook and *t* 2Sa 22:8 7493
unto me every one that *t* at the Ezr 9:4 2730
Then the earth shook and *t* Ps 18:7 7493
the earth *t* and shook Ps 77:18 7264
the earth saw, and *t* Ps 97:4 2342
the mountains, and, lo, they *t* Jer 4:24 7493
the whole land *t* at the sound of Jer 8:16 7493
people, nations, and languages, *t* Dan 5:19 2112
The mountains saw thee, and they *t* Hab 3:10 2342
When I heard, my belly *t* Hab 3:16 7364
I *t* in myself, that I might rest Hab 3:16 7264
for they *t* and were amazed Mk 16:8
Then Moses *t*, and durst not behold Acts 7:32
and judgment to come, Felix *t* Acts 24:25

TREMBLETH

At this also my heart *t*, and is Job 37:1 2729
He looketh on the earth, and it *t* Ps 104:32 7460
My flesh *t* for fear of thee Ps 119:120 5568
contrite spirit, and *t* at my word Is 66:2 2730

TREMBLING

t shall take hold upon them Ex 15:15 7460
shall give thee there a *t* heart Deut 28:65 7268
and all the people followed him *t* 1Sa 13:7 2729
there was *t* in the host, in the 1Sa 14:15 2731
so it was a very great *t* 1Sa 14:15 2731
t because of this matter, and for Ezr 10:9 7460
Fear came upon me, and *t*, which Job 4:14 7460
t taketh hold on my flesh Job 21:6 6427
LORD with fear, and rejoice with *t* Ps 2:11 7460
t are come upon me, and horror Ps 55:5 7460
drunken the dregs of the cup of *t* Is 51:17 8653
out of thine hand the cup of *t* Is 51:22 8653
We have heard a voice of *t* Jer 30:5 2731
and drink thy water with *t* Eze 12:18 7269
shall clothe themselves with *t* Eze 26:16 2731
this word unto me, I stood *t* Dan 10:11 7460
When Ephraim spake *t*, he exalted Hos 13:1 7578
I will make Jerusalem a cup of *t* Zec 12:2 7478

But the woman fearing and *t* Mk 5:33 *5141*
that she was not hid, she came *t* Lk 8:47 *5141*
And he *t* and astonished said, Lord, Acts 9:6 *5141*
a light, and sprang in, and came *t* Acts 16:29
and in fear, and in much *t* 1Cor 2:3 *5156*
with fear and *t* ye received him 2Cor 7:15 *5156*
to the flesh, with fear and *t* Eph 6:5 *5156*
your own salvation with fear and *t* Phil 2:12 *5156*

TRENCH

and he came to the *t*, as the host 1Sa 17:20 4570
and Saul lay in the *t*, and the 1Sa 26:5 4570
Saul lay sleeping within the *t* 1Sa 26:7 4570
the city, and it stood in the *t* 2Sa 20:15 2426
he made a *t* about the altar, as 1Kin 18:32 8585
he filled the *t* also with water 1Kin 18:35 8565
up the water that was in the *t* 1Kin 18:38 8565
enemies shall cast a *t* about thee Lk 19:43 *5482*

TRESPASS

and said to Laban, What is my *t* Gen 31:36 6588
the *t* of thy brethren, and their Gen 50:17 6588
forgive the *t* of the servants of Gen 50:17 6588
For all manner of *t*, whether it Ex 22:9 6588
he shall bring his *t* offering Lev 5:6 817
then he shall bring for his *t* Lev 5:7 817
If a soul commit a *t*, and sin Lev 5:15 4604
his *t* unto the LORD a ram without Lev 5:15 817
the sanctuary, for a *t* offering Lev 5:15 817
with the ram of the *t* offering Lev 5:16 817
for a *t* offering, unto the priest Lev 5:18 817
It is a *t* offering Lev 5:19 817
commit a *t* against the LORD, and Lev 6:2 4604
in the day of his *t* offering Lev 6:5 819
he shall bring his *t* offering Lev 6:6 817
for a *t* offering, unto the priest Lev 6:6 817
offering, and as the *t* offering Lev 6:17 817
this is the law of the *t* offering Lev 7:1 817
shall they kill the *t* offering Lev 7:2 817
it is a *t* offering Lev 7:5 817
offering is, so is the *t* offering Lev 7:7 817
of the *t* offering, and of the Lev 7:37 817
and offer him for a *t* offering Lev 14:12 817
priest's, so is the *t* offering Lev 14:13 817
of the blood of the *t* offering Lev 14:14 817
upon the blood of the *t* offering Lev 14:17 817
lamb for a *t* offering to be waved Lev 14:21 817
take the lamb of the *t* offering Lev 14:24 817
kill the lamb of the *t* offering Lev 14:25 817
of the blood of the *t* offering Lev 14:25 817
of the blood of the *t* offering Lev 14:28 817
he shall bring his *t* offering Lev 19:21 817
even a ram for a *t* offering Lev 19:21 817
for him with the ram of the *t* Lev 19:22 817
them to bear the iniquity of *t* Lev 22:16 819
fathers, with their *t* which they Lev 26:40 4604
to do a *t* against the LORD, and Num 5:6 4604
he shall recompense his *t* with Num 5:7 817
kinsman to recompense the *t* unto Num 5:8 817
let the *t* be recompensed unto the Num 5:8 817
aside, and commit a *t* against him, Num 5:12 4604
have done *t* against her husband, Num 5:27 4604
the first year for a *t* offering Num 6:12 817
every *t* offering of theirs, which Num 18:9 817
to commit *t* against the LORD in Num 31:16 4604
a *t* in the accursed thing Josh 7:1 4604
What *t* is this that ye have Josh 22:16 4604
commit a *t* in the accursed thing Josh 22:20 4604
committed this *t* against the LORD Josh 22:31 4604
any wise return him a *t* offering 1Sa 6:3 817
What shall be the *t* offering 1Sa 6:4 817
ye return him for a *t* offering 1Sa 6:8 817
for a *t* offering unto the LORD 1Sa 6:17 817
forgive the *t* of thine handmaid 1Sa 25:28 6588
If any man *t* against his 1Kin 8:31 2398
The *t* money and sin money was not 2Kin 12:16 817
will he be a cause of *t* to Israel 1Chr 21:3 819
that they *t* not against the LORD 2Chr 19:10 816
this do, and ye shall not *t* 2Chr 19:10 816
and Jerusalem for this their *t* 2Chr 24:18 819
add more to our sins and to our *t* 2Chr 28:13 819
for our *t* is great, and there is 2Chr 28:13 819
he *t* yet more against the LORD 2Chr 28:22 4603
of him, and all his sin, and his *t* 2Chr 33:19 4604
rulers hath been chief in this *t* Ezr 9:2 4604
our *t* is grown up unto the Ezr 9:6 819
been in a great *t* unto this day Ezr 9:7 819
evil deeds, and for our great *t* Ezr 9:13 819
to increase the *t* of Israel Ezr 10:10 819
a ram of the flock for their *t* Ezr 10:19 819
because they have committed a *t* Eze 15:8 4604
plead with him there for his *t* Eze 17:20 4604
in his *t* that he hath trespassed, Eze 18:24 4604
have committed a *t* against me Eze 20:27 4604
sin offering and the *t* offering Eze 40:39 817
sin offering, and the *t* offering Eze 42:13 817
sin offering, and the *t* offering Eze 44:29 817
priests shall boil the *t* offering Eze 46:20 817
because of their *t* that they have Dan 9:7 4604
thy brother shall *t* against thee Mt 18:15 *264*
If thy brother *t* against thee Lk 17:3 *264*
if he *t* against thee seven times Lk 17:4 *264*

TRESPASSED

hath certainly *t* against the LORD Lev 5:19 816
trespass which they *t* against me Lev 26:40 4604
unto him against whom he hath *t* Num 5:7 816
Because ye *t* against me among the Deut 32:51 4603
for thou hast *t* 2Chr 26:18 4603
For our fathers have *t*, and done 2Chr 29:6 4603
which *t* against the LORD God of 2Chr 30:7 4603
but Amon *t* more and more 2Chr 33:23 819
We have *t* against our God, and Ezr 10:2 4603
that he hath *t* against me Eze 17:20 4603
in his trespass that he hath *t* Eze 18:24 4604
because they *t* against me Eze 39:23 4603
whereby they have *t* against me Eze 39:26 4603
that they have *t* against thee Dan 9:7 4603
my covenant, and *t* against my law Hos 8:1

TRESPASSES

we are before thee in our *t* Ezr 9:15 819
an one as goeth on still in his *t* Ps 68:21 817
all their *t* whereby they have Eze 39:26 4604
For if ye forgive men their *t* Mt 6:14 *3900*
But if ye forgive not men their *t* Mt 6:15 *3900*
will your Father forgive your *t* Mt 6:15 *3900*
not every one his brother their *t* Mt 18:35 *3900*
in heaven may forgive you your *t* Mk 11:25 *3900*
which is in heaven forgive your *t* Mk 11:26 *3900*
not imputing their *t* unto them 2Cor 5:19 *3900*
he quickened, who were dead in *t* Eph 2:1 *3900*
him, having forgiven you all *t* Col 2:13 *3900*

TRESPASSING

that he hath done in *t* therein Lev 6:7 819
against me by *t* grievously Eze 14:13 4603

TRIAL

laugh at the *t* of the innocent Job 9:23 4531
Because it is a *t*, and what if the Eze 21:13 974
How that in a great *t* of 2Cor 8:2 *1382*
others had *t* of cruel mockings and Heb 11:36 *3984*
That the *t* of your faith, being 1Pet 1:7 *1383*
the fiery *t* which is to try you 1Pet 4:12

TRIBE

the son of Hur, of the *t* of Judah Ex 31:2 4294
son of Ahisamach, of the *t* of Dan Ex 31:6 4294
the son of Hur, of the *t* of Judah Ex 35:30 4294
son of Ahisamach, of the *t* of Dan Ex 35:34 4294
of the *t* of Judah, made all that Ex 38:22 4294
son of Ahisamach, of the *t* of Dan Ex 38:23 4294
of Dibri, of the *t* of Dan Lev 24:11 4294
there shall be a man of every *t* Num 1:4 4294
of the *t* of Reuben Num 1:5
of them, even of the *t* of Reuben Num 1:21 4294
of them, even of the *t* of Simeon Num 1:23 4294
of them, even of the *t* of Gad Num 1:25 4294
of them, even of the *t* of Judah Num 1:27 4294
them, even of the *t* of Issachar Num 1:29 4294
of them, even of the *t* of Zebulun Num 1:31 4294
of them, even of the *t* of Ephraim Num 1:33 4294
them, even of the *t* of Manasseh Num 1:35 4294
them, even of the *t* of Benjamin Num 1:37 4294
of them, even of the *t* of Dan Num 1:39 4294
of them, even of the *t* of Asher Num 1:41 4294
them, even of the *t* of Naphtali Num 1:43 4294
the *t* of their fathers were not Num 1:47
shalt not number the *t* of Levi Num 1:49 4294
him shall be the *t* of Issachar Num 2:5 4294
Then the *t* of Zebulun Num 2:7 4294
by him shall be the *t* of Simeon Num 2:12 4294
Then the *t* of Gad Num 2:14 4294
by him shall be the *t* of Manasseh Num 2:20 4294
Then the *t* of Benjamin Num 2:22 4294
by him shall be the *t* of Asher Num 2:27 4294
Then the *t* of Naphtali Num 2:29 4294
Bring the *t* of Levi near, and Num 3:6 4294
Cut ye not off the *t* of the Num 4:18 7626
of Amminadab, of the *t* of Judah Num 7:12 4294
over the host of the *t* of the Num 10:15 4294
over the host of the *t* of the Num 10:16 4294
over the host of the *t* of the Num 10:19 4294
over the host of the *t* of the Num 10:20 4294
over the host of the *t* of the Num 10:23 4294
over the host of the *t* of the Num 10:24 4294
over the host of the *t* of the Num 10:26 4294
over the host of the *t* of the Num 10:27 4294
of every *t* of their fathers shall Num 13:2 4294
of the *t* of Reuben, Shammua the Num 13:4 4294
Of the *t* of Simeon, Shaphat the Num 13:5 4294
Of the *t* of Judah, Caleb the son Num 13:6 4294
Of the *t* of Issachar, Igal the Num 13:7 4294
Of the *t* of Ephraim, Oshea the Num 13:8 4294
Of the *t* of Benjamin, Palti the Num 13:9 4294
Of the *t* of Zebulun, Gaddiel the Num 13:10 4294
Of the *t* of Joseph, namely, of Num 13:11 4294
of the *t* of Manasseh, Gaddi the Num 13:11 4294
Of the *t* of Dan, Ammiel the son Num 13:12 4294
Of the *t* of Asher, Sethur the son Num 13:13 4294
Of the *t* of Naphtali, Nahbi the Num 13:14 4294
Of the *t* of Gad, Geuel the son of Num 13:15 4294
brethren also of the *t* of Levi Num 18:2 4294
the *t* of thy father, bring thou Num 18:2 7626
Of every *t* a thousand, throughout Num 31:4 4294
of Israel, a thousand of every *t* Num 31:5 4294
to the war, a thousand of every *t* Num 31:6 4294
unto half the *t* of Manasseh the Num 32:33 7626
the nine tribes, and to the half *t* Num 34:13 4294
For the *t* of the children of Num 34:14 4294
the *t* of the children of Gad Num 34:14 4294
half the *t* of Manasseh have Num 34:14 4294
the half *t* have received their Num 34:15 4294
shall take one prince of every *t* Num 34:18 4294
Of the *t* of Judah, Caleb the son Num 34:19 4294
of the *t* of the children of Num 34:20 4294
Of the *t* of Benjamin, Elidad the Num 34:21 4294
the prince of the *t* of the Num 34:22 4294
for the *t* of the children of Num 34:23 4294
the prince of the *t* of the Num 34:24 4294
the prince of the *t* of the Num 34:25 4294
the prince of the *t* of the Num 34:26 4294
the prince of the *t* of the Num 34:27 4294
the prince of the *t* of the Num 34:28 4294
the *t* whereunto they are received Num 36:3 4294
the *t* whereunto they are received Num 36:4 4294
of the *t* of our fathers Num 36:4 4294
The *t* of the sons of Joseph hath Num 36:5 4294
only to the family of the *t* of Num 36:6 4294
of Israel remove from *t* to *t* Num 36:7 4294
of the *t* of his fathers Num 36:7 4294
an inheritance in any *t* of the Num 36:8 4294
the family of the *t* of her father Num 36:8 4294
from one *t* to another *t* Num 36:9 4294
inheritance remained in the *t* of Num 36:12 4294
twelve men of you, one of a *t* Deut 1:23 7626
I unto the half *t* of Manasseh Deut 3:13 7626
the LORD separated the *t* of Levi Deut 10:8 7626
the Levites, and all the *t* of Levi Deut 18:1 7626
and to the half *t* of Manasseh Deut 29:8 7626
man, or woman, or family, or *t* Deut 29:18 7626
and to half the *t* of Manasseh Josh 1:12 7626
of Israel, out of every *t* a man Josh 3:12 7626
the people, out of every *t* a man Josh 4:2 7626
of Israel, out of every *t* a man Josh 4:4 7626
half the *t* of Manasseh, passed Josh 4:12 7626
of the *t* of Judah, took of the Josh 7:1 4294
that the *t* which the LORD taketh Josh 7:14 7626
and the *t* of Judah was taken Josh 7:16 7626
of the *t* of Judah, was taken Josh 7:18 4294
and the half *t* of Manasseh Josh 12:6 7626
and the half *t* of Manasseh, Josh 13:7 7626
Only unto the *t* of Levi he gave Josh 13:14 7626
Moses gave unto the *t* of the Josh 13:15 4294
inheritance unto the *t* of Gad Josh 13:24 4294
unto the half *t* of Manasseh Josh 13:29 7626
t of the children of Manasseh by Josh 13:29 4294
But unto the *t* of Levi Moses gave Josh 13:33 7626
nine tribes, and for the half *t* Josh 14:2 4294
an half *t* on the other side Josh 14:3 4294
the *t* of the children of Judah by Josh 15:1 4294
of the *t* of the children of Judah Josh 15:20 4294
the uttermost cities of the *t* of Josh 15:21 4294
t of the children of Ephraim by Josh 16:8 4294
also a lot for the *t* of Manasseh Josh 17:1 4294
among you three men for each *t* Josh 18:4 7626
half the *t* of Manasseh, have Josh 18:7 7626
the lot of the *t* of the children Josh 18:11 4294
Now the cities of the *t* of the Josh 18:21 4294
even for the *t* of the children of Josh 19:1 4294
the *t* of the children of Simeon Josh 19:8 4294
the *t* of the children of Issachar Josh 19:23 4294
the *t* of the children of Asher Josh 19:24 4294
of the *t* of the children of Asher Josh 19:31 4294
of the *t* of the children of Naphtali Josh 19:39 4294
for the *t* of the children of Dan Josh 19:40 4294
of the *t* of the children of Dan Josh 19:48 4294
the plain out of the *t* of Reuben Josh 20:8 4294
in Gilead out of the *t* of Gad Josh 20:8 4294
Bashan out of the *t* of Manasseh Josh 20:8 4294
had by lot out of the *t* of Judah Josh 21:4 4294
Judah, and out of the *t* of Simeon Josh 21:4 4294
out of the *t* of Benjamin, Josh 21:4 4294
the families of the *t* of Ephraim Josh 21:5 4294
Ephraim, and out of the *t* of Dan Josh 21:5 4294
and out of the half *t* of Manasseh Josh 21:5 4294
the families of the *t* of Issachar Josh 21:6 4294
and out of the *t* of Asher Josh 21:6 4294
out of the *t* of Naphtali, and out Josh 21:6 4294
out of the half *t* of Manasseh in Josh 21:6 4294
had out of the *t* of Reuben Josh 21:7 4294
of Reuben, and out of the *t* of Gad Josh 21:7 4294
Gad, and out of the *t* of Zebulun Josh 21:7 4294
they gave out of the *t* of the Josh 21:9 4294
out of the *t* of the children of Josh 21:9 4294
out of the *t* of Benjamin, Gibeon Josh 21:17 4294
their lot out of the *t* of Ephraim Josh 21:20 4294
And out of the *t* of Dan, Eltekeh Josh 21:23 4294
And out of the half *t* of Manasseh Josh 21:25 4294
out of the other half *t* of Josh 21:27 4294
out of the *t* of Issachar, Kishon Josh 21:28 4294
And out of the *t* of Asher, Mishal Josh 21:30 4294
out of the *t* of Naphtali, Kedesh Josh 21:32 4294
Levites, out of the *t* of Zebulun Josh 21:34 4294
And out of the *t* of Reuben Josh 21:36
And out of the *t* of Gad, Ramoth in Josh 21:38 4294
and the half *t* of Manasseh, Josh 22:1 4294
Now to the one half of the *t* of Josh 22:7 7626
the half *t* of Manasseh returned, Josh 22:9 7626
the half *t* of Manasseh built Josh 22:10 7626
the half *t* of Manasseh have built Josh 22:11 7626
Gad, and to the half *t* of Manasseh Josh 22:13 7626
Gad, and to the half *t* of Manasseh Josh 22:15 7626
the half *t* of Manasseh answered, Josh 22:21 7626
in those days the *t* of the Judg 18:1 7626
or that thou be a priest unto a *t* Judg 18:19 7626
the *t* of Dan until the day of the Judg 18:30 7626
men through all the *t* of Benjamin Judg 20:12 7626
be to day one *t* lacking in Israel Judg 21:3 7626
There is one *t* cut off from Judg 21:6 7626
that a *t* be not destroyed out of Judg 21:17 7626
at that time, every man to his *t* Judg 21:24 7626
the families of the *t* of Benjamin 1Sa 9:21 7626
the *t* of Benjamin was taken 1Sa 10:20 7626
When he had caused the *t* of 1Sa 10:21 7626
widow's son of the *t* of Naphtali 1Kin 7:14 4294
but will give one *t* to thy son 1Kin 11:13 7626
(But he shall have one *t* for my 1Kin 11:32 7626
And unto his son will I give one *t* 1Kin 11:36 7626
of David, but the *t* of Judah only 1Kin 12:20 7626
with the *t* of Benjamin, an 1Kin 12:21 7626
none left but the *t* of Judah only 2Kin 17:18 7626
half the *t* of Manasseh, of 1Chr 5:18 7626
the children of the half *t* of 1Chr 5:23 7626
the half *t* of Manasseh, and 1Chr 5:26 7626
And out of the *t* of Benjamin 1Chr 6:60 4294
were left of the family of that *t* 1Chr 6:61 4294
cities given out of the half *t* 1Chr 6:61 4294
out of the half *t* of Manasseh 1Chr 6:61
families out of the *t* of Issachar 1Chr 6:62 4294
and out of the *t* of Asher 1Chr 6:62 4294
out of the *t* of Naphtali, and out 1Chr 6:62 4294
out of the *t* of Manasseh in 1Chr 6:62 4294
families, out of the *t* of Reuben 1Chr 6:63 4294

of Reuben, and out of the *t* of Gad 1Chr 6:63 4294
Gad, and out of the *t* of Zebulun 1Chr 6:63 4294
of the *t* of the children of Judah 1Chr 6:65 4294
out of the *t* of the children of 1Chr 6:65 4294
out of the *t* of the children of 1Chr 6:65 4294
coasts out of the *t* of Ephraim 1Chr 6:66 4294
And out of the half *t* of Manasseh 1Chr 6:70 4294
family of the half *t* of Manasseh 1Chr 6:71 4294
And out of the *t* of Issachar 1Chr 6:72 4294
And out of the *t* of Asher 1Chr 6:74 4294
And out of the *t* of Naphtali 1Chr 6:76 4294
given out of the *t* of Zebulun 1Chr 6:77 4294
given them out of the *t* of Reuben 1Chr 6:78 4294
And out of the *t* of Gad 1Chr 6:80 4294
of the half *t* of Manasseh 1Chr 12:31 4294
and of the half *t* of Manasseh 1Chr 12:37 7626
sons were named of the *t* of Levi 1Chr 23:14 7626
the half *t* of Manasseh, for every 1Chr 26:32 7626
of the half *t* of Manasseh 1Chr 27:20 7626
Of the half *t* of Manasseh in 1Chr 27:21
and chose not the *t* of Ephraim Ps 78:67 7626
But chose the *t* of Judah, the Ps 78:68 7626
that in what *t* the stranger Eze 47:23 7626
of Phanuel, of the *t* of Aser Lk 2:36 *5443*
Cis, a man of the *t* of Benjamin Acts 13:21 *5443*
of Abraham, of the *t* of Benjamin Rom 11:1 *5443*
of the *t* of Benjamin, an Hebrew Phil 3:5 *5443*
spoken pertaineth to another *t* Heb 7:13 *5443*
of which *t* Moses spake nothing Heb 7:14 *5443*
behold, the Lion of the *t* of Juda Rev 5:5 *5443*
Of the *t* of Juda were sealed Rev 7:5 *5443*
Of the *t* of Reuben were sealed Rev 7:5 *5443*
Of the *t* of Gad were sealed Rev 7:5 *5443*
Of the *t* of Aser were sealed Rev 7:6 *5443*
Of the *t* of Nepthalim were sealed Rev 7:6 *5443*
Of the *t* of Manasses were sealed Rev 7:6 *5443*
Of the *t* of Simeon were sealed Rev 7:7 *5443*
Of the *t* of Levi were sealed Rev 7:7 *5443*
Of the *t* of Issachar were sealed Rev 7:7 *5443*
Of the *t* of Zabulon were sealed Rev 7:8 *5443*
Of the *t* of Joseph were sealed Rev 7:8 *5443*
Of the *t* of Benjamin were sealed Rev 7:8 *5443*

TRIBES
people, as one of the *t* of Israel Gen 49:16 7626
these are the twelve *t* of Israel Gen 49:28 7626
to the twelve *t* of Israel Ex 24:4 7626
they be according to the twelve *t* Ex 28:21 7626
name, according to the twelve *t* Ex 39:14 7626
princes of the *t* of their fathers Num 1:16 4294
who were the princes of the *t* Num 7:2 4294
in his tents according to their *t* Num 24:2 7626
the *t* of their fathers they shall Num 26:55 4294
the *t* concerning the children of Num 30:1 4294
throughout all the *t* of Israel Num 31:4 4294
the chief fathers of the *t* of the Num 32:28 4294
according to the *t* of your Num 33:54 4294
commanded to give unto the nine *t* Num 34:13 4294
The two *t* and the half tribe have Num 34:15 4294
other *t* of the children of Israel Num 36:3 7626
but every one of the *t* of the Num 36:9 4294
and known among your *t*, and I will Deut 1:13 7626
So I took the chief of your *t* Deut 1:15 7626
tens, and officers among your *t* Deut 1:15 7626
me, even all the heads of your *t* Deut 5:23 7626
all your *t* to put his name there Deut 12:5 7626
LORD shall choose in one of thy *t* Deut 12:14 7626
God giveth thee, throughout thy *t* Deut 16:18 7626
hath chosen him out of all thy *t* Deut 18:5 7626
your captains of your *t*, your Deut 29:10 7626
evil out of all the *t* of Israel Deut 29:21 7626
unto me all the elders of your *t* Deut 31:28 7626
the *t* of Israel were gathered Deut 33:5 7626
twelve men out of the *t* of Israel Josh 3:12 7626
unto the number of the *t* of the Josh 4:5 7626
the *t* of the children of Israel Josh 4:8 7626
be brought according to your *t* Josh 7:14 7626
and brought Israel by their *t* Josh 7:16 7626
to their divisions by their *t* Josh 11:23 7626
the *t* of Israel for a possession Josh 12:7 7626
an inheritance unto the nine *t* Josh 13:7 7626
the *t* of the children of Israel Josh 14:1 4294
the hand of Moses, for the nine *t* Josh 14:2 4294
given the inheritance of two *t* Josh 14:3 4294
the children of Joseph were two *t* Josh 14:4 4294
the children of Israel seven *t* Josh 18:2 7626
the *t* of the children of Israel Josh 19:51 4294
the *t* of the children of Israel Josh 21:1 4294
nine cities out of those two *t* Josh 21:16 7626
throughout all the *t* of Israel Josh 22:14 4294
to be an inheritance for your *t* Josh 23:4 7626
all the *t* of Israel to Shechem Josh 24:1 7626
unto them among the *t* of Israel Judg 18:1 7626
even of all the *t* of Israel Judg 20:2 7626
throughout all the *t* of Israel Judg 20:10 7626
the *t* of Israel sent men through Judg 20:12 7626
Who is there among all the *t* of Judg 21:5 7626
What one is there of the *t* of Judg 21:8 7626
made a breach in the *t* of Israel Judg 21:15 7626
the *t* of Israel to be my priest 1Sa 2:28 7626
the smallest of the *t* of Israel 1Sa 9:21 7626
before the LORD by your *t* 1Sa 10:19 7626
all the *t* of Israel to come near 1Sa 10:20 7626
made the head of the *t* of Israel 1Sa 15:17 7626
Then came all the *t* of Israel to 2Sa 5:1 7626
word with any of the *t* of Israel 2Sa 7:7 7626
is of one of the *t* of Israel 2Sa 15:2 7626
throughout all the *t* of Israel 2Sa 15:10 7626
throughout all the *t* of Israel 2Sa 19:9 7626
all the *t* of Israel unto Abel 2Sa 20:14 7626
now through all the *t* of Israel 2Sa 24:2 7626
Israel, and all the heads of the *t* 1Kin 8:1 4294
the *t* of Israel to build an house 1Kin 8:16 7626
and will give ten *t* to thee 1Kin 11:31 7626
chosen out of all the *t* of Israel 1Kin 11:32 7626
give it unto thee, even ten *t* 1Kin 11:35 7626
choose out of all the *t* of Israel 1Kin 14:21 7626
of the *t* of the sons of Jacob 1Kin 18:31 7626
chosen out of all *t* of Israel 2Kin 21:7 7626
Furthermore over the *t* of Israel 1Chr 27:16 7626
the princes of the *t* of Israel 1Chr 27:22 7626
of Israel, the princes of the *t* 1Chr 28:1 7626
and princes of the *t* of Israel 1Chr 29:6 7626
Israel, and all the heads of the *t* 2Chr 5:2 4294
I chose no city among all the *t* 2Chr 6:5 7626
after them out of all the *t* of 2Chr 11:16 7626
chosen out of all the *t* of Israel 2Chr 12:13 7626
chosen before all the *t* of Israel 2Chr 33:7 7626
to the number of the *t* of Israel Ezr 6:17 7625
made the *t* of Israel to dwell in Ps 78:55 7626
one feeble person among their *t* Ps 105:37 7626
Whither the *t* go up, the *t* Ps 122:4 7626
the *t* of the LORD, unto the Ps 122:4 7626
are the stay of the *t* thereof Is 19:13 7626
to raise up the *t* of Jacob Is 49:6 7626
the *t* of thine inheritance Is 63:17 7626
the *t* of Israel his fellows, and Eze 37:19 7626
of Israel according to their *t* Eze 45:8 7626
to the twelve *t* of Israel Eze 47:13 7626
you according to the *t* of Israel Eze 47:21 7626
with you among the *t* of Israel Eze 47:22 7626
Now these are the names of the *t* Eze 48:1 7626
it out of all the *t* of Israel Eze 48:19 7626
As for the rest of the *t*, from Eze 48:23 7626
the *t* of Israel for inheritance Eze 48:29 7626
the names of the *t* of Israel Eze 48:31 7626
among the *t* of Israel have I made Hos 5:9 7626
according to the oaths of the *t* Hab 3:9 4294
of man, as of all the *t* of Israel Zec 9:1 7626
judging the twelve *t* of Israel Mt 19:28 *5443*
all the *t* of the earth mourn Mt 24:30 *5443*
judging the twelve *t* of Israel Lk 22:30 *5443*
Unto which promise our twelve *t* Acts 26:7 *1429*
to the twelve *t* which are Jas 1:1 *5443*
four thousand of all the *t* of the Rev 7:4 *5443*
t of the children of Israel Rev 21:12 *5443*

TRIBULATION
When thou art in *t*, and all these Deut 4:30 6862
deliver you in the time of your *t* Judg 10:14 6869
let him deliver me out of all *t* 1Sa 26:24 6869
for when *t* or persecution ariseth Mt 13:21 *2347*
For then shall be great *t* Mt 24:21 *2347*
Immediately after the *t* of those Mt 24:29 *2347*
But in those days, after that *t* Mk 13:24 *2347*
In the world ye shall have *t* Jn 16:33 *2347*
that we must through much *t* enter Acts 14:22 *2347*
T and anguish, upon every soul of Rom 2:9 *2347*
knowing that *t* worketh patience Rom 5:3 *2347*
shall *t*, or distress, or Rom 8:35 *2347*
patient in *t* Rom 12:12 *2347*
Who comforteth us in all our *t* 2Cor 1:4 *2347*
am exceeding joyful in all our *t* 2Cor 7:4 *2347*
before that we should suffer *t* 1Th 3:4 *2346*
t to them that trouble you 2Th 1:6 *2347*
your brother, and companion in *t* Rev 1:9 *2347*
I know thy works, and *t*, and Rev 2:9 *2347*
and ye shall have *t* ten days Rev 2:10 *2347*
adultery with her into great *t* Rev 2:22 *2347*
they which came out of great *t* Rev 7:14 *2347*

TRIBULATIONS
of all your adversities and your *t* 1Sa 10:19 6869
only so, but we glory in *t* also Rom 5:3 *2347*
that ye faint not at my *t* for you Eph 3:13 *2347*
persecutions and *t* that ye endure 2Th 1:4 *2347*

TRIBUTARIES
therein shall be *t* unto thee Deut 20:11 4522
dwelt among them, and became *t* Judg 1:30 4522
of Beth-anath became *t* unto them Judg 1:33 4522
prevailed, so that they became *t* Judg 1:35 4522

TRIBUTARY
provinces, how is she become *t* Lam 1:1 4522

TRIBUTE
bear, and became a servant unto *t* Gen 49:15 4522
levy a *t* unto the LORD of the men Num 31:28 4371
the LORD's *t* of the sheep was six Num 31:37 4371
which the LORD's *t* was threescore Num 31:38 4371
which the LORD's *t* was threescore Num 31:39 4371
of which the LORD's *t* was thirty Num 31:40 4371
And Moses gave the *t*, which was Num 31:41 4371
unto the LORD thy God with a *t* of Deut 16:10 4530
unto this day, and serve under *t* Josh 16:10 4522
that they put the Canaanites to *t* Josh 17:13 4522
that they put the Canaanites to *t* Judg 1:28 4522
And Adoram was over the *t* 2Sa 20:24 4522
the son of Abda was over the *t* 1Kin 4:6 4522
a *t* of bondservice unto this day 1Kin 9:21 4522
sent Adoram, who was over the *t* 1Kin 12:18 4522
put the land to a *t* of an hundred 2Kin 23:33 6066
make to pay *t* until this day 2Chr 8:8 4522
sent Hadoram that was over the *t* 2Chr 10:18 4522
Jehoshaphat presents, and *t* silver 2Chr 17:11 4853
then will they not pay toll, *t* Ezr 4:13 1093
and toll, *t*, and custom, was paid Ezr 4:20 1093
even of the *t* beyond the river Ezr 6:8 4061
not be lawful to impose toll, *t* Ezr 7:24 1093
borrowed money for the king's *t* Neh 5:4 4060
Ahasuerus laid a *t* upon the land Est 10:1 4522
but the slothful shall be under *t* Prov 12:24 4522
they that received *t* money came Mt 17:24 *1323*
said, Doth not your master pay *t* Mt 17:24 *1323*
of the earth take custom or *t* Mt 17:25 *2778*
it lawful to give *t* unto Caesar Mt 22:17 *2778*
Shew me the *t* money Mt 22:19 *2778*
Is it lawful to give *t* to Caesar Mk 12:14 *2778*
for us to give *t* unto Caesar Lk 20:22 *5411*
and forbidding to give *t* to Caesar Lk 23:2 *5411*
For for this cause pay ye *t* also Rom 13:6 *5411*
t to whom *t* is due Rom 13:7 *5411*

TRICKLETH
Mine eye *t* down, and ceaseth not, Lam 3:49 5064

TRIED
controversy and every stroke be *t* Deut 21:5
the word of the LORD is *t* 2Sa 22:31 6884
when he hath *t* me, I shall come Job 23:10 974
is that Job may be *t* unto the end Job 34:36 974
as silver *t* in a furnace of earth Ps 12:6 6884
thou hast *t* me, and shalt find Ps 17:3 6884
the word of the LORD is *t* Ps 18:30 6884
hast *t* us, as silver is *t* Ps 66:10 6884
the word of the LORD *t* him Ps 105:19 6884
a *t* stone, a precious corner Is 28:16 976
me, and *t* mine heart toward thee Jer 12:3 974
be purified, and made white, and *t* Dan 12:10 6884
and will try them as gold is *t* Zec 13:9 974
By faith Abraham, when he was *t* Heb 11:17 *3985*
for when he is *t*, he shall Jas 1:12 *1384*
though it be *t* with fire 1Pet 1:7 *1381*
thou hast *t* them which say they Rev 2:2 *3985*
you into prison, that ye may be *t* Rev 2:10 *3985*
to buy of me gold *t* in the fire Rev 3:18 *4448*

TRIEST
my God, that thou *t* the heart 1Chr 29:17 974
that *t* the reins and the heart, Jer 11:20 974
that *t* the righteous, and seest Jer 20:12 974

TRIETH
For the ear *t* words, as the mouth Job 34:3 974
the righteous God *t* the hearts Ps 7:9 974
The LORD *t* the righteous Ps 11:5 974
but the LORD *t* the hearts Prov 17:3 974
men, but God, which *t* our hearts 1Th 2:4 *1381*

TRIMMED
nor *t* his beard, nor washed his 2Sa 19:24 6213
virgins arose, and *t* their lamps Mt 25:7 *2885*

TRIMMEST
Why *t* thou thy way to seek love Jer 2:33 3190

TRIUMPH
daughters of the uncircumcised *t* 2Sa 1:20 5937
let not mine enemies *t* over me Ps 25:2 5970
mine enemy doth not *t* over me Ps 41:11 7321
unto God with the voice of *t* Ps 47:1 7440
Philistia, *t* thou because of me Ps 60:8 7321
I will *t* in the works of thy Ps 92:4 7442
how long shall the wicked *t* Ps 94:3 5937
holy name, and to *t* in thy praise Ps 106:47 7623
over Philistia will I *t* Ps 108:9 7321
always causeth us to *t* in Christ 2Cor 2:14 *2358*

TRIUMPHED
LORD, for he hath *t* gloriously Ex 15:1 1342
LORD, for he hath *t* gloriously Ex 15:21 1342

TRIUMPHING
That the *t* of the wicked is short Job 20:5 7445
of them openly, *t* over them in it Col 2:15 *2358*

TROAS (*tro'-as*) *A seaport of Phrygia in Asia Minor.*
passing by Mysia came down to *T* Acts 16:8 5174
Therefore loosing from *T*, we came Acts 16:11 *5174*
going before tarried for us at *T* Acts 20:5 *5174*
came unto them to *T* in five days Acts 20:6 *5174*
when I came to *T* to preach 2Cor 2:12 *5174*
that I left at *T* with Carpus 2Ti 4:13 *5174*

TRODDEN
give the land that he hath *t* upon Deut 1:36 1869
have *t* shall be thine inheritance Josh 14:9 1869
thou hast *t* down strength Judg 5:21 1869
old way which wicked men have *t* Job 22:15 1869
The lion's whelps have not *t* it Job 28:8 1869
Thou hast *t* down all them that Ps 119:118 5541
thereof, and it shall be *t* down Is 5:5 4823
as a carcase *t* under feet Is 14:19 947
t down, whose land the rivers Is 18:2 4001
t under foot, whose land the Is 18:7 4001
Moab shall be *t* down under him, Is 25:10 1758
even as straw is *t* down for the Is 25:10 1758
of Ephraim, shall be *t* under feet Is 28:3 7429
then ye shall be *t* down by it Is 28:18 4823
I have *t* the winepress alone Is 63:3 1869
have *t* down thy sanctuary Is 63:18 947
they have *t* my portion under foot Jer 12:10 947
The Lord hath *t* under foot all my Lam 1:15 5541
the Lord hath *t* the virgin Lam 1:15 1869
which ye have *t* with your feet Eze 34:19 7429
and the host to be *t* under foot Dan 8:13 4823
now shall she be *t* down as the Mic 7:10 4823
to be *t* under foot of men Mt 5:13 *2662*
and it was *t* down, and the fowls of Lk 8:5 *2662*
Jerusalem shall be *t* down of the Lk 21:24 *3961*
who hath *t* under foot the Son of Heb 10:29 *2662*
winepress was *t* without the city Rev 14:20 *3961*

TRODE
t the grapes, and made merry, and Judg 9:27 1869
t them down with ease over Judg 20:43 1869
the people *t* upon him in the gate 2Kin 7:17 7429
for the people *t* upon him in the 2Kin 7:20 7429
and he *t* her under foot 2Kin 9:33 7429
in Lebanon, and *t* down the thistle 2Kin 14:9 7429
in Lebanon, and *t* down the thistle 2Chr 25:18 7429
that they *t* one upon another Lk 12:1 *2662*

TROGYLLIUM (*tro-jil'-le-um*) *A coastal town in Ionia in Asia Minor.*
arrived at Samos, and tarried at *T* Acts 20:15 *5175*

T

TROOP
And Leah said, A *t* cometh ... Gen 30:11 1409
Gad, a *t* shall overcome him ... Gen 49:19 1416
Shall I pursue after this *t* ... 1Sa 30:8 1416
after Abner, and became one *t* ... 2Sa 2:25 92
and Joab came from pursuing a *t* ... 2Sa 3:22 1416
by thee I have run through a *t* ... 2Sa 22:30 1416
were gathered together into a *t* ... 2Sa 23:11 2416
the *t* of the Philistines pitched ... 2Sa 23:13 2416
by thee I have run through a *t* ... Ps 18:29 1416
that prepare a table for that *t* ... Is 65:11 1409
bring a *t* suddenly upon them ... Jer 18:22 1416
the *t* of robbers spoileth without ... Hos 7:1 1416
hath founded his *t* in the earth ... Amos 9:6 92

TROOPS
The *t* of Tema looked, the ... Job 6:19 734
His *t* come together, and raise up ... Job 19:12 1416
by *t* in the harlots' houses ... Jer 5:7
as *t* of robbers wait for a man, ... Hos 6:9 1416
in *t*, O daughter of *t* ... Mic 5:1 1416
he will invade them with his *t* ... Hab 3:16

TROPHIMUS (*trof'-im-us*) *A companion of Paul.*
and of Asia, Tychicus and *T* ... Acts 20:4 *5161*
him in the city *T* an Ephesian ... Acts 21:29 *5161*
but *T* have I left at Miletum sick ... 2Ti 4:20 *5161*

TROUBLE
camp of Israel a curse, and *t* it ... Josh 6:18 5916
the LORD shall *t* thee this day ... Josh 7:25 5916
and thou art one of them that *t* me ... Judg 11:35 5916
Hezekiah, This day is a day of *t* ... 2Kin 19:3 6869
in my *t* I have prepared for the ... 1Chr 22:14 6040
But when they in their *t* did turn ... 2Chr 15:4 6862
and he hath delivered them to *t* ... 2Chr 29:8 2189
to affright them, and to *t* them ... 2Chr 32:18 926
and in the time of their *t* ... Neh 9:27 6869
let not all the *t* seem little ... Neh 9:32 8513
yet *t* came ... Job 3:26 7267
neither doth *t* spring out of the ... Job 5:6 5999
Yet man is born unto *t*, as the ... Job 5:7 5999
is of few days, and full of *t* ... Job 14:1 7267
T and anguish shall make him ... Job 15:24 6862
his cry when *t* cometh upon him ... Job 27:9 6869
not I weep for him that was in *t* ... Job 30:25
quietness, who then can make *t* ... Job 34:29 7561
reserved against the time of *t* ... Job 38:23 6862
how are they increased that *t* me ... Ps 3:1 6862
oppressed, a refuge in times of *t* ... Ps 9:9 6869
consider my *t* which I suffer of ... Ps 9:13 6040
hidest thou thyself in times of *t* ... Ps 10:1 6869
those that *t* me rejoice when I am ... Ps 13:4 6862
LORD hear thee in the day of *t* ... Ps 20:1 6869
for *t* is near ... Ps 22:11 6869
For in the time of *t* he shall ... Ps 27:5 7451
for thou hast considered my *t* ... Ps 31:7 6040
upon me, O LORD, for I am in *t* ... Ps 31:9 6887
thou shalt preserve me from *t* ... Ps 32:7 6862
their strength in the time of *t* ... Ps 37:39 6869
will deliver him in time of *t* ... Ps 41:1 7451
a very present help in *t* ... Ps 46:1 6869
And call upon me in the day of *t* ... Ps 50:15 6869
he hath delivered me out of all *t* ... Ps 54:7 6869
and refuge in the day of my *t* ... Ps 59:16 6862
Give us help from *t* ... Ps 60:11 6862
hath spoken, when I was in *t* ... Ps 66:14 6862
for I am in *t* ... Ps 69:17 6887
They are not in *t* as other men ... Ps 73:5 5999
In the day of my *t* I sought the ... Ps 77:2 6869
in vanity, and their years in *t* ... Ps 78:33 928
wrath, and indignation, and *t* ... Ps 78:49 6869
Thou calledst in *t*, and I ... Ps 81:7 6869
In the day of my *t* I will call ... Ps 86:7 6869
I will be with him in *t* ... Ps 91:15 6869
from me in the day when I am in *t* ... Ps 102:2 6862
cried unto the LORD in their *t* ... Ps 107:6 6862
cried unto the LORD in their *t* ... Ps 107:13 6862
they cry unto the LORD in their *t* ... Ps 107:19 6862
their soul is melted because of *t* ... Ps 107:26 7451
they cry unto the LORD in their *t* ... Ps 107:28 6862
Give us help from *t* ... Ps 108:12 6862
I found *t* and sorrow ... Ps 116:3 6869
T and anguish have taken hold on ... Ps 119:143 6862
Though I walk in the midst of *t* ... Ps 138:7 6869
I shewed before him my *t* ... Ps 142:2 6869
sake bring my soul out of *t* ... Ps 143:11 6869
righteous is delivered out of *t* ... Prov 11:8 6869
but the just shall come out of *t* ... Prov 12:13 6869
the revenues of the wicked is *t* ... Prov 15:6 5916
great treasure and *t* therewith ... Prov 15:16 4103
time of *t* is like a broken tooth ... Prov 25:19 6869
they are a *t* unto me ... Is 1:14 2960
and behold *t* and darkness, dimness ... Is 8:22 6869
And behold at eveningtide *t* ... Is 17:14 1091
For it is a day of *t*, and of ... Is 22:5 4103
in *t* have they visited thee ... Is 26:16 6862
into the land of *t* and anguish, ... Is 30:6 6869
salvation also in the time of *t* ... Is 33:2 6869
Hezekiah, This day is a day of *t* ... Is 37:3 6869
answer, nor save him out of his *t* ... Is 46:7 6869
in vain, nor bring forth for *t* ... Is 65:23 928
the time of their *t* they will say ... Jer 2:27 7451
save thee in the time of thy *t* ... Jer 2:28 7451
for a time of health, and behold *t* ... Jer 8:15 1205
at all in the time of their *t* ... Jer 11:12 7451
that they cry unto me for their *t* ... Jer 11:14 7451
the saviour thereof in time of *t* ... Jer 14:8 6869
the time of healing, and behold *t* ... Jer 14:19 1205
it is even the time of Jacob's *t* ... Jer 30:7 6869
for in the day of *t* they shall be ... Jer 51:2 7451
mine enemies have heard of my *t* ... Lam 1:21 7451
is come, the day of *t* is near ... Eze 7:7 4103
the foot of man *t* them any more ... Eze 32:13 4103
nor the hoofs of beasts *t* them ... Eze 32:13 1804
interpretation thereof, *t* thee ... Dan 4:19 927
let not thy thoughts *t* thee ... Dan 5:10 927
and out of the north shall *t* him ... Dan 11:44 926
and there shall be a time of *t* ... Dan 12:1 6869
a strong hold in the day of *t* ... Nah 1:7 6869
that I might rest in the day of *t* ... Hab 3:16 6869
day is a day of wrath, a day of *t* ... Zeph 1:15 6869
unto them, Why *t* ye the woman ... Mt 26:10 *3930*
why *t* ye her ... Mk 14:6 *3930*
unto him, Lord, *t* not thyself ... Lk 7:6 *4660*
t not the Master ... Lk 8:49 *4660*
shall answer and say, *T* me not ... Lk 11:7 *2873*
that we *t* not them, which from ... Acts 15:19 *3926*
Jews, do exceedingly *t* our city ... Acts 16:20 *1613*
him said, *T* not yourselves ... Acts 20:10 *2350*
such shall have *t* in the flesh ... 1Cor 7:28 *2347*
comfort them which are in any *t* ... 2Cor 1:4 *2347*
of our *t* which came to us in Asia ... 2Cor 1:8 *2347*
but there be some that *t* you ... Gal 1:7 *5015*
were even cut off which *t* you ... Gal 5:12 *387*
From henceforth let no man *t* me ... Gal 6:17
tribulation to them that *t* you ... 2Th 1:6 *2346*
Wherein I suffer *t*, as an evil ... 2Ti 2:9 *2553*
of bitterness springing up *t* you ... Heb 12:15 *1776*

TROUBLED
Ye have *t* me to make me to stink ... Gen 34:30 5916
the morning that his spirit was *t* ... Gen 41:8 6470
for they were *t* at his presence ... Gen 45:3 926
t the host of the Egyptians, ... Ex 14:24 2000
Joshua said, Why hast thou *t* us ... Josh 7:25 5916
My father hath *t* the land ... 1Sa 14:29 5916
evil spirit from the LORD *t* him ... 1Sa 16:14 1204
Saul, and saw that he was sore *t* ... 1Sa 28:21 926
and all the Israelites were *t* ... 2Sa 4:1 926
he answered, I have not *t* Israel ... 1Kin 18:18 5916
Syria was sore *t* for this thing ... 2Kin 6:11 5590
of Judah, and *t* them in building, ... Ezr 4:4 1089
it toucheth thee, and thou art *t* ... Job 4:5 926
so, why should not my spirit be *t* ... Job 21:4 7114
Therefore am I *t* at his presence ... Job 23:15 926
the people shall be *t* at midnight ... Job 34:20 1607
didst hide thy face, and I was *t* ... Ps 30:7 926
I am *t* ... Ps 38:6 5753
the waters thereof roar and be *t* ... Ps 46:3 2560
they were *t*, and hasted away ... Ps 48:5 926
I remembered God, and was *t* ... Ps 77:3 1993
I am so *t* that I cannot speak ... Ps 77:4 6470
the depths also were *t* ... Ps 77:16 7264
them be confounded and *t* for ever ... Ps 83:17 926
anger, and by thy wrath are we *t* ... Ps 90:7 926
Thou hidest thy face, they are *t* ... Ps 104:29 926
the wicked is as a *t* fountain ... Prov 25:26 7515
Many days and years shall ye be *t* ... Is 32:10 7264
be *t*, ye careless ones ... Is 32:11 7264
But the wicked are like the *t* sea ... Is 57:20 1644
therefore my bowels are *t* for him ... Jer 31:20 1993
my bowels are *t* ... Lam 1:20 2560
fail with tears, my bowels are *t* ... Lam 2:11 2560
the people of the land shall be *t* ... Eze 7:27 926
sea shall be *t* at thy departure ... Eze 26:18 926
afraid, they shall be *t* in their ... Eze 27:35 7481
wherewith his spirit was *t* ... Dan 2:1 6470
my spirit was *t* to know the dream ... Dan 2:3 6470
and the visions of my head *t* me ... Dan 4:5 927
one hour, and his thoughts *t* him ... Dan 4:19 927
changed, and his thoughts *t* him ... Dan 5:6 927
was king Belshazzar greatly *t* ... Dan 5:9 927
and the visions of my head *t* me ... Dan 7:15 927
Daniel, my cogitations much *t* me ... Dan 7:28 927
their way as a flock, they were *t* ... Zec 10:2 6031
had heard these things, he was *t* ... Mt 2:3 *5015*
walking on the sea, they were *t* ... Mt 14:26 *5015*
see that ye be not *t* ... Mt 24:6 *2360*
For they all saw him, and were *t* ... Mk 6:50 *5015*
and rumours of wars, be ye not *t* ... Mk 13:7 *2360*
when Zacharias saw him, he was *t* ... Lk 1:12 *5015*
she was *t* at his saying, and cast ... Lk 1:29 *1298*
careful and *t* about many things ... Lk 10:41 *5182*
he said unto them, Why are ye *t* ... Lk 24:38 *5015*
into the pool, and *t* the water ... Jn 5:4 *5015*
have no man, when the water is *t* ... Jn 5:7 *5015*
groaned in the spirit, and was *t* ... Jn 11:33
Now is my soul *t* ... Jn 12:27 *5015*
he was *t* in spirit, and testified, ... Jn 13:21 *5015*
Let not your heart be *t* ... Jn 14:1 *5015*
Let not your heart be *t*, neither ... Jn 14:27 *5015*
out from us have *t* you with words ... Acts 15:24 *5015*
they *t* the people and the rulers ... Acts 17:8 *5015*
We are *t* on every side, yet not ... 2Cor 4:8 *2346*
but we were *t* on every side ... 2Cor 7:5 *2346*
And to you who are *t* rest with us ... 2Th 1:7 *2346*
not soon shaken in mind, or be *t* ... 2Th 2:2 *2360*
of their terror, neither be *t* ... 1Pet 3:14 *5015*

TROUBLEDST
t the waters with thy feet, and ... Eze 32:2 1804

TROUBLER
the *t* of Israel, who transgressed ... 1Chr 2:7 5916

TROUBLES
many evils and *t* shall befall them ... Deut 31:17 6869
t are befallen them, that this ... Deut 31:21 6869
He shall deliver thee in six *t* ... Job 5:19 6869
The *t* of my heart are enlarged ... Ps 25:17 6869
Israel, O God, out of all his *t* ... Ps 25:22 6869
and saved him out of all his *t* ... Ps 34:6 6869
them out of all their *t* ... Ps 34:17 6869
hast shewed me great and sore *t* ... Ps 71:20 6869
For my soul is full of *t* ... Ps 88:3 7451
tongue keepeth his soul from *t* ... Prov 21:23 6869
the former *t* are forgotten ... Is 65:16 6869
and there shall be famines and *t* ... Mk 13:8 *5016*

TROUBLEST
why *t* thou the Master any further ... Mk 5:35 *4660*

TROUBLETH
an evil spirit from God *t* thee ... 1Sa 16:15 1204
him, Art thou he that *t* Israel ... 1Kin 18:17 5916
about thee, and sudden fear *t* thee ... Job 22:10 926
heart soft, and the Almighty *t* me ... Job 23:16 926
he that is cruel *t* his own flesh ... Prov 11:17 5916
He that *t* his own house shall ... Prov 11:29 5916
is greedy of gain *t* his own house ... Prov 15:27 5916
is in thee, and no secret *t* thee ... Dan 4:9 598
Yet because this widow *t* me ... Lk 18:5
but he that *t* you shall bear his ... Gal 5:10 *5015*

TROUBLING
There the wicked cease from *t* ... Job 3:17 7267
the *t* of the water stepped in was ... Jn 5:4 *5015*

TROUBLOUS
and the wall, even in *t* times ... Dan 9:25 5916

TROUGH
and emptied her pitcher into the *t* ... Gen 24:20 8268

TROUGHS
t when the flocks came to drink ... Gen 30:38 8268
filled the *t* to water their ... Ex 2:16 7298

TROW
I *t* not ... Lk 17:9 *1380*

TRUCEBREAKERS
Without natural affection, *t* ... 2Ti 3:3 *786*

TRUE
we are *t* men, thy servants are no ... Gen 42:11 3651
If ye be *t* men, let one of your ... Gen 42:19 3651
And we said unto him, We are *t* men ... Gen 42:31 3651
shall I know that ye are *t* men ... Gen 42:33 3651
no spies, but that ye are *t* men ... Gen 42:34 3651
diligently, and, behold, it be *t* ... Deut 17:4 571
But if this thing be *t*, and the ... Deut 22:20 571
house, and give me a *t* token ... Josh 2:12 571
now it is *t* that I am thy near ... Ruth 3:12 551
art that God, and thy words be *t* ... 2Sa 7:28 571
It was a *t* report that I heard in ... 1Kin 10:6 571
is *t* in the name of the LORD ... 1Kin 22:16 571
It was a *t* report which I heard ... 2Chr 9:5 571
hath been without the *t* God ... 2Chr 15:3 571
and *t* laws, good statutes and ... Neh 9:13 571
the judgments of the LORD are *t* ... Ps 19:9 571
Thy word is *t* from the beginning ... Ps 119:160 571
A *t* witness delivereth souls ... Prov 14:25 571
But the LORD is the *t* God ... Jer 10:10 571
said to Jeremiah, The LORD be a *t* ... Jer 42:5 571
hath executed *t* judgment between ... Eze 18:8 571
spake and said unto them, Is it *t* ... Dan 3:14 6656
answered and said unto the king, *T* ... Dan 3:24 3330
answered and said, The thing is *t* ... Dan 6:12 3330
the morning which was told is *t* ... Dan 8:26 571
and the thing was *t*, but the time ... Dan 10:1 571
Execute *t* judgment, and shew mercy ... Zec 7:9 571
Master, we know that thou art *t* ... Mt 22:16 *227*
Master, we know that thou art *t* ... Mk 12:14 *227*
commit to your trust the *t* riches ... Lk 16:11 *228*
That was the *t* Light, which ... Jn 1:9 *228*
set to his seal that God is *t* ... Jn 3:33 *227*
when the *t* worshippers shall ... Jn 4:23 *228*
And herein is that saying *t* ... Jn 4:37 *228*
of myself, my witness is not *t* ... Jn 5:31 *227*
which he witnesseth of me is *t* ... Jn 5:32 *227*
you the *t* bread from heaven ... Jn 6:32 *228*
that sent him, the same is *t* ... Jn 7:18 *227*
myself, but he that sent me is *t* ... Jn 7:28 *228*
thy record is not *t* ... Jn 8:13 *227*
of myself, yet my record is *t* ... Jn 8:14 *227*
yet if I judge, my judgment is *t* ... Jn 8:16 *227*
the testimony of two men is *t* ... Jn 8:17 *227*
but he that sent me is *t* ... Jn 8:26 *227*
John spake of this man were *t* ... Jn 10:41 *227*
I am the *t* vine, and my Father is ... Jn 15:1 *228*
might know thee the only *t* God ... Jn 17:3 *228*
bare record, and his record is *t* ... Jn 19:35 *228*
and he knoweth that he saith *t* ... Jn 19:35 *2227*
we know that his testimony is *t* ... Jn 21:24 *227*
wist not that it was *t* which was ... Acts 12:9 *227*
yea, let God be *t*, but every man ... Rom 3:4 *227*
But as God is *t*, our word toward ... 2Cor 1:18 *4103*
as deceivers, and yet *t* ... 2Cor 6:8 *227*
in righteousness and *t* holiness ... Eph 4:24
t yokefellow, help those women ... Phil 4:3 *1103*
brethren, whatsoever things are *t* ... Phil 4:8 *227*
to serve the living and *t* God ... 1Th 1:9 *228*
This is a *t* saying, If a man ... 1Ti 3:1 *4103*
This witness is *t* ... Titus 1:13 *227*
of the *t* tabernacle, which the ... Heb 8:2 *228*
which are the figures of the *t* ... Heb 9:24 *228*
Let us draw near with a *t* heart ... Heb 10:22 *228*
testifying that this is the *t* ... 1Pet 5:12 *227*
them according to the *t* proverb ... 2Pet 2:22 *227*
unto you, which thing is *t* in him ... 1Jn 2:8 *227*
past, and the *t* light now shineth ... 1Jn 2:8 *228*
that we may know him that is *t* ... 1Jn 5:20 *228*
and we are in him that is *t* ... 1Jn 5:20 *228*
This is the *t* God, and eternal ... 1Jn 5:20 *228*
and ye know that our record is *t* ... 3Jn 12 *227*
he that is holy, he that is *t* ... Rev 3:7 *228*
t witness, the beginning of the ... Rev 3:14 *228*
How long, O Lord, holy and *t* ... Rev 6:10 *228*
t are thy ways, thou King of ... Rev 15:3 *228*
Even so, Lord God Almighty, *t* ... Rev 16:7 *228*
For *t* and righteous are his ... Rev 19:2 *228*
These are the *t* sayings of God ... Rev 19:9 *228*
upon him was called Faithful and *T* ... Rev 19:11 *228*
for these words are *t* and faithful ... Rev 21:5 *228*
These sayings are faithful and *t* ... Rev 22:6 *228*

TRULY

- *t* Lamech seventy and sevenfold ... Gen 4:24 571
- *t* with my master, tell me ... Gen 24:49 571
- and deal kindly and *t* with me ... Gen 47:29 571
- but *t* his younger brother shall ... Gen 48:19 199
- But as *t* as I live, all the earth ... Num 14:21 199
- As *t* as I live, saith the LORD, ... Num 14:28
- Thou shalt *t* tithe all the ... Deut 14:22
- will deal kindly and *t* with thee ... Josh 2:14 571
- *T* the LORD hath delivered into ... Josh 2:24 3588
- Now therefore, if ye have done *t* ... Judg 9:16 571
- If ye then have dealt *t* and ... Judg 9:19 571
- but *t* as the LORD liveth, and as ... 1Sa 20:3 199
- For *t* my words shall not be false ... Job 36:4 551
- *T* my soul waiteth upon God ... Ps 62:1 389
- *T* God is good to Israel, even to ... Ps 73:1 389
- O LORD, *t* I am thy servant ... Ps 116:16 577
- they that deal *t* are his delight ... Prov 12:22 530
- *T* the light is sweet, and a ... Eccl 11:7
- *T* in vain is salvation hoped for ... Jer 3:23 403
- *t* in the LORD our God is the ... Jer 3:23 403
- *T* this is a grief, and I must bear ... Jer 10:19 389
- that the LORD hath *t* sent him ... Jer 28:9 571
- hath kept my judgments, to deal *t* ... Eze 18:9 571
- But *t* I am full of power by the ... Mic 3:8 199
- The harvest *t* is plenteous, but ... Mt 9:37 *3303*
- Elias *t* shall first come, and ... Mt 17:11 *3303*
- *T* this was the Son of God ... Mt 27:54 *230*
- The spirit *t* is ready, but the ... Mk 14:38 *3303*
- *T* this man was the Son of God ... Mk 15:39 *230*
- unto them, The harvest *t* is great ... Lk 10:2 *3303*
- *T* ye bear witness that ye allow ... Lk 11:48 *686*
- but teachest the way of God *t* ... Lk 20:21
- *t* the Son of man goeth, as it was ... Lk 22:22 *3303*
- in that saidst thou *t* ... Jn 4:18 *227*
- many other signs *t* did Jesus in ... Jn 20:30 *3303*
- For John *t* baptized with water ... Acts 1:5 *3303*
- For Moses *t* said unto the fathers ... Acts 3:22 *3303*
- The prison *t* found we shut with ... Acts 5:23 *3303*
- *T* the signs of an apostle were ... 2Cor 12:12 *3303*
- they *t* were many priests, because ... Heb 7:23 *3303*
- And *t*, if they had been mindful of ... Heb 11:15 *3303*
- *t* our fellowship is with the ... 1Jn 1:3 *1161*

TRUMP

- O my soul, the sound of the *t* ... Jer 4:19 7782
- in Gibeah, and the *t* in Ramah ... Hos 5:8 2689
- of an eye, at the last *t* ... 1Cor 15:52 *4536*
- archangel, and with the *t* of God ... 1Th 4:16 *4536*

TRUMPET

- when the *t* soundeth long, they ... Ex 19:13 3104
- the voice of the *t* exceeding loud ... Ex 19:16 7782
- the voice of the *t* sounded long ... Ex 19:19 7782
- lightnings, and the noise of the *t* ... Ex 20:18 7782
- Then shalt thou cause the *t* of ... Lev 25:9 7782
- *t* sound throughout all your land ... Lev 25:9 7782
- And if they blow but with one *t* ... Num 10:4
- when ye hear the sound of the *t* ... Josh 6:5 7782
- people heard the sound of the *t* ... Josh 6:20 7782
- that he blew a *t* in the mountain ... Judg 3:27 7782
- came upon Gideon, and he blew a *t* ... Judg 6:34 7782
- he put a *t* in every man's hand ... Judg 7:16 7782
- When I blow with a *t*, I and all ... Judg 7:18 7782
- Saul blew the *t* throughout all ... 1Sa 13:3 7782
- So Joab blew a *t*, and all the ... 2Sa 2:28 7782
- and with the sound of the *t* ... 2Sa 6:15 7782
- as ye hear the sound of the *t* ... 2Sa 15:10 7782
- And Joab blew the *t*, and the people ... 2Sa 18:16 7782
- and he blew a *t*, and said, We have ... 2Sa 20:1 7782
- And he blew a *t*, and they retired ... 2Sa 20:22 7782
- and blow ye with the *t*, and say, ... 1Kin 1:34 7782
- And they blew the *t* ... 1Kin 1:39 7782
- Joab heard the sound of the *t* ... 1Kin 1:41 7782
- he that sounded the *t* was by me ... Neh 4:18 7782
- ye hear the sound of the *t* ... Neh 4:20 7782
- he that it is the sound of the *t* ... Job 39:24 7782
- the LORD with the sound of a *t* ... Ps 47:5 7782
- Blow up the *t* in the new moon, in ... Ps 81:3 7782
- him with the sound of the *t* ... Ps 150:3 7782
- and when he bloweth a *t*, hear ye ... Is 18:3 7782
- that the great *t* shall be blown ... Is 27:13 7782
- not, lift up thy voice like a *t* ... Is 58:1 7782
- and say, Blow ye the *t* in the land ... Jer 4:5 7782
- and hear the sound of the *t* ... Jer 4:21 7782
- Jerusalem, and blow the *t* in Tekoa ... Jer 6:1 7782
- Hearken to the sound of the *t* ... Jer 6:17 7782
- war, nor hear the sound of the *t* ... Jer 42:14 7782
- blow the *t* among the nations, ... Jer 51:27 7782
- They have blown the *t*, even to ... Eze 7:14 8628
- come upon the land, he blow the *t* ... Eze 33:3 7782
- heareth the sound of the *t* ... Eze 33:4 7782
- He heard the sound of the *t* ... Eze 33:5 7782
- the sword come, and blow not the *t* ... Eze 33:6 7782
- Set the *t* to thy mouth ... Hos 8:1 7782
- Blow ye the *t* in Zion, and sound ... Joel 2:1 7782
- Blow the *t* in Zion, sanctify a ... Joel 2:15 7782
- and with the sound of the *t* ... Amos 2:2 7782
- Shall a *t* be blown in the city, ... Amos 3:6 7782
- A day of the *t* and alarm against ... Zeph 1:16 7782
- and the Lord GOD shall blow the *t* ... Zec 9:14 7782
- do not sound a *t* before thee ... Mt 6:2 *4537*
- angels with a great sound of a *t* ... Mt 24:31 *4536*
- For if the *t* give an uncertain ... 1Cor 14:8 *4536*
- for the *t* shall sound, and the ... 1Cor 15:52
- And the sound of a *t*, and the voice ... Heb 12:19 *4536*
- me a great voice, as of a *t* ... Rev 1:10 *4536*
- as it were of a *t* talking with me ... Rev 4:1 *4536*
- of the *t* of the three angels ... Rev 8:13 *4536*
- the sixth angel which had the *t* ... Rev 9:14 *4536*

TRUMPETERS

- the *t* by the king, and all the ... 2Kin 11:14 2689
- It came even to pass, as the *t* ... 2Chr 5:13 2689
- singers sang, and the *t* sounded ... 2Chr 29:28 2690
- and musicians, and of pipers, and *t* ... Rev 18:22 *4538*

TRUMPETS

- a memorial of blowing of *t* ... Lev 23:24
- Make thee two *t* of silver ... Num 10:2 2689
- priests, shall blow with the *t* ... Num 10:8 2689
- ye shall blow an alarm with the *t* ... Num 10:9 2689
- ye shall blow with the *t* over ... Num 10:10 2689
- a day of blowing the *t* unto you ... Num 29:1
- the *t* to blow in his hand ... Num 31:6 2689
- the ark seven *t* of rams' horns ... Josh 6:4 7782
- the priests shall blow with the *t* ... Josh 6:4 7782
- let seven priests bear seven *t* of ... Josh 6:6 7782
- *t* of rams' horns passed on before ... Josh 6:8 7782
- the LORD, and blew with the *t* ... Josh 6:8 7782
- the priests that blew with the *t* ... Josh 6:9 7782
- going on, and blowing with the *t* ... Josh 6:9 7782
- seven priests bearing seven *t* of ... Josh 6:13 7782
- continually, and blew with the *t* ... Josh 6:13 7782
- going on, and blowing with the *t* ... Josh 6:13 7782
- when the priests blew with the *t* ... Josh 6:16 7782
- when the priests blew with the *t* ... Josh 6:20 7782
- in their hand, and their *t* ... Judg 7:8 7782
- then blow ye the *t* also on every ... Judg 7:18 7782
- and they blew the *t*, and brake the ... Judg 7:19 7782
- And the three companies blew the *t* ... Judg 7:20 7782
- the *t* in their right hands to ... Judg 7:20 7782
- And the three hundred blew the *t* ... Judg 7:22 7782
- top of the stairs, and blew with *t* ... 2Kin 9:13 7782
- the land rejoiced, and blew with *t* ... 2Kin 11:14
- of silver, snuffers, basons, *t* ... 2Kin 12:13 2689
- and with cymbals, and with *t* ... 1Chr 13:8 2689
- did blow with the *t* before the ... 1Chr 15:24 2689
- sound of the cornet, and with *t* ... 1Chr 15:28 2689
- Jahaziel the priests with *t* ... 1Chr 16:6 2689
- them Heman and Jeduthun with *t* ... 1Chr 16:42 2689
- and twenty priests sounding with *t* ... 2Chr 5:12 2689
- lifted up their voice with the *t* ... 2Chr 5:13
- the priests sounded *t* before them ... 2Chr 7:6
- *t* to cry alarm against you ... 2Chr 13:12 2689
- and the priests sounded with the *t* ... 2Chr 13:14 2689
- and with shouting, and with *t* ... 2Chr 15:14 2689
- *t* unto the house of the LORD ... 2Chr 20:28 2689
- the princes and the *t* by the king ... 2Chr 23:13 2689
- land rejoiced, and sounded with *t* ... 2Chr 23:13 2689
- David, and the priests with the *t* ... 2Chr 29:26 2689
- of the LORD began also with the *t* ... 2Chr 29:27 2689
- priests in their apparel with *t* ... Ezr 3:10 2689
- of the priests' sons with *t* ... Neh 12:35 2689
- Zechariah, and Hananiah, with *t* ... Neh 12:41 2689
- He saith among the *t*, Ha, ha ... Job 39:25 7782
- With *t* and sound of cornet make a ... Ps 98:6 2689
- and to them were given seven *t* ... Rev 8:2 *4536*
- angels which had the seven *t* ... Rev 8:6 *4536*

TRUST

- come and put your *t* in my shadow ... Judg 9:15 2620
- whose wings thou art come to *t* ... Ruth 2:12 2620
- in him will I *t* ... 2Sa 22:3 2620
- buckler to all them that *t* in him ... 2Sa 22:31 2620
- Now on whom dost thou *t*, that ... 2Kin 18:20 982
- of Egypt unto all that *t* on him ... 2Kin 18:21 982
- unto me, We *t* in the LORD our God ... 2Kin 18:22 982
- put thy *t* on Egypt for chariots ... 2Kin 18:24 982
- Hezekiah make you *t* in the LORD ... 2Kin 18:30 982
- because they put their *t* in him ... 1Chr 5:20 982
- king of Assyria, Whereon do ye *t* ... 2Chr 32:10 982
- he put no *t* in his servants ... Job 4:18 539
- whose *t* shall be a spider's web ... Job 8:14 4009
- he slay me, yet will I *t* in him ... Job 13:15 3176
- he putteth no *t* in his saints ... Job 15:15 539
- him that is deceived *t* in vanity ... Job 15:31 539
- therefore *t* thou in him ... Job 35:14 2342
- Wilt thou *t* him, because his ... Job 39:11 982
- all they that put their *t* in him ... Ps 2:12 2620
- and put your *t* in the LORD ... Ps 4:5 982
- that put their *t* in thee rejoice ... Ps 5:11 2620
- my God, in thee do I put my *t* ... Ps 7:1 2620
- thy name will put their *t* in thee ... Ps 9:10 982
- In the LORD put I my *t* ... Ps 11:1 2620
- for in thee do I put my *t* ... Ps 16:1 2620
- *t* in thee from those that rise up ... Ps 17:7 2620
- my strength, in whom I will *t* ... Ps 18:2 2620
- to all those that *t* in him ... Ps 18:30 2620
- Some *t* in chariots, and some in ... Ps 20:7
- O my God, I *t* in thee ... Ps 25:2 982
- for I put my *t* in thee ... Ps 25:20 2620
- In thee, O LORD, do I put my *t* ... Ps 31:1 2620
- but I *t* in the LORD ... Ps 31:6 982
- *t* in thee before the sons of men ... Ps 31:19 2620
- none of them that *t* in him shall ... Ps 34:22 2620
- *t* under the shadow of thy wings ... Ps 36:7 2620
- *T* in the LORD, and do good ... Ps 37:3 982
- *t* also in him ... Ps 37:5 982
- save them, because they *t* in him ... Ps 37:40 2620
- and fear, and shall *t* in the LORD ... Ps 40:3 982
- man that maketh the LORD his *t* ... Ps 40:4 4009
- For I will not *t* in my bow ... Ps 44:6 982
- They that *t* in their wealth, and ... Ps 49:6 982
- I *t* in the mercy of God for ever ... Ps 52:8 982
- but I will *t* in thee ... Ps 55:23 982
- I am afraid, I will *t* in thee ... Ps 56:3 982
- his word, in God I have put my *t* ... Ps 56:4 982
- In God have I put my *t* ... Ps 56:11 982
- I will *t* in the covert of thy ... Ps 61:4 2620
- *T* in him at all times ... Ps 62:8 982
- *T* not in oppression, and become ... Ps 62:10 982
- in the LORD, and shall *t* in him ... Ps 64:10 2620
- In thee, O LORD, do I put my *t* ... Ps 71:1 2620
- thou art my *t* from my youth ... Ps 71:5 4004
- I have put my *t* in the Lord GOD, ... Ps 73:28 4268
- in him will I *t* ... Ps 91:2 982
- and under his wings shalt thou *t* ... Ps 91:4 2620
- O Israel, *t* thou in the LORD ... Ps 115:9 982
- O house of Aaron, *t* in the LORD ... Ps 115:10 982
- that fear the LORD, *t* in the LORD ... Ps 115:11 982
- It is better to *t* in the LORD ... Ps 118:8 2620
- It is better to *t* in the LORD ... Ps 118:9 2620
- for I *t* in thy word ... Ps 119:42 982
- They that *t* in the LORD shall be ... Ps 125:1 982
- in thee is my *t* ... Ps 141:8 2620
- for in thee do I *t* ... Ps 143:8 982
- my shield, and he in whom I *t* ... Ps 144:2 2620
- Put not your *t* in princes ... Ps 146:3 982
- *T* in the LORD with all thine ... Prov 3:5 982
- That thy *t* may be in the LORD, I ... Prov 22:19 4009
- but he that putteth his *t* in the ... Prov 28:25 982
- but whoso putteth his *t* in the ... Prov 29:25 982
- unto them that put their *t* in him ... Prov 30:5 2620
- her husband doth safely *t* in her ... Prov 31:11 982
- I will *t*, and not be afraid ... Is 12:2 982
- poor of his people shall *t* in it ... Is 14:32 2620
- *T* ye in the LORD for ever ... Is 26:4 982
- to *t* in the shadow of Egypt ... Is 30:2 2620
- the *t* in the shadow of Egypt your ... Is 30:3 2622
- *t* in oppression and perverseness, ... Is 30:12 982
- *t* in chariots, because they are ... Is 31:1 982
- now on whom dost thou *t*, that ... Is 36:5 982
- of Egypt to all that *t* in him ... Is 36:6 982
- to me, We *t* in the LORD our God ... Is 36:7 982
- put thy *t* on Egypt for chariots ... Is 36:9 982
- Hezekiah make you *t* in the LORD ... Is 36:15 982
- that *t* in graven images, that say ... Is 42:17 982
- let him *t* in the name of the LORD ... Is 50:10 982
- me, and on mine arm shall they *t* ... Is 51:5 3176
- but he that putteth his *t* in me ... Is 57:13 2620
- they *t* in vanity, and speak lies ... Is 59:4 982
- *T* ye not in lying words, saying, ... Jer 7:4 982
- ye *t* in lying words, that cannot ... Jer 7:8 982
- called by my name, wherein ye *t* ... Jer 7:14 982
- and *t* ye not in any brother ... Jer 9:4 982
- makest this people to *t* in a lie ... Jer 28:15 982
- and he caused you to *t* in a lie ... Jer 29:31 982
- because thou hast put thy *t* in me ... Jer 39:18 982
- and all them that *t* in him ... Jer 46:25 982
- and let thy widows *t* in me ... Jer 49:11 982
- But thou didst *t* in thine own ... Eze 16:15 982
- if he *t* to his own righteousness, ... Eze 33:13 982
- because thou didst *t* in thy way ... Hos 10:13 982
- *t* in the mountain of Samaria, ... Amos 6:1 982
- *T* ye not in a friend, put ye not ... Mic 7:5 539
- and he knoweth them that *t* in him ... Nah 1:7 2620
- they shall *t* in the name of the ... Zeph 3:12 2620
- in his name shall the Gentiles *t* ... Mt 12:21 *1679*
- *t* in riches to enter into the ... Mk 10:24 *3982*
- commit to your *t* the true riches ... Lk 16:11 *4100*
- you, even Moses, in whom ye *t* ... Jn 5:45 *1679*
- in him shall the Gentiles *t* ... Rom 15:12 *1679*
- for I *t* to see you in my journey, ... Rom 15:24 *1679*
- but I *t* to tarry a while with you ... 1Cor 16:7 *1679*
- that we should not *t* in ourselves ... 2Cor 1:9 *3982*
- in whom we *t* that he will yet ... 2Cor 1:10 *1679*
- I *t* ye shall acknowledge even to ... 2Cor 1:13 *1679*
- such *t* have we through Christ to ... 2Cor 3:4 *4006*
- I *t* also are made manifest in ... 2Cor 5:11 *1679*
- If any man *t* to himself that he ... 2Cor 10:7 *3982*
- But I *t* that ye shall know that ... 2Cor 13:6 *1679*
- But I *t* in the Lord Jesus to send ... Phil 2:19 *1679*
- But I *t* in the Lord that I also ... Phil 2:24 *3892*
- whereof he might *t* in the flesh ... Phil 3:4 *3982*
- to be put in *t* with the gospel ... 1Th 2:4 *4100*
- God, which was committed to my *t* ... 1Ti 1:11 *4100*
- because we *t* in the living God, ... 1Ti 4:10 *1679*
- nor *t* in uncertain riches, but in ... 1Ti 6:17 *1679*
- that which is committed to thy *t* ... 1Ti 6:20
- for I *t* that through your prayers ... Philem 22 *1679*
- And again, I will put my *t* in him ... Heb 2:13 *3982*
- for we *t* we have a good ... Heb 13:18 *3982*
- but I *t* to come unto you, and ... 2Jn 12 *1679*
- But I *t* I shall shortly see thee, ... 3Jn 14 *1679*

TRUSTED

- gods, their rock in whom they *t* ... Deut 32:37 2620
- But Sihon *t* not Israel to pass ... Judg 11:20 539
- because they *t* unto the liers in ... Judg 20:36 982
- He *t* in the LORD God of Israel ... 2Kin 18:5 982
- But I have *t* in thy mercy ... Ps 13:5 982
- Our fathers *t* in thee ... Ps 22:4 982
- they *t*, and thou didst deliver ... Ps 22:4 982
- they *t* in thee, and were not ... Ps 22:5 982
- He *t* on the LORD that he would ... Ps 22:8 1556
- I have *t* also in the LORD ... Ps 26:1 982
- my heart *t* in him, and I am helped ... Ps 28:7 982
- But I *t* in thee, O LORD ... Ps 31:14 982
- because we have *t* in his holy ... Ps 33:21 982
- own familiar friend, in whom I *t* ... Ps 41:9 982
- but *t* in the abundance of his ... Ps 52:7 982
- in God, and *t* not in his salvation ... Ps 78:22 982
- For thou hast *t* in thy wickedness ... Is 47:10 982
- forgotten me, and *t* in falsehood ... Jer 13:25 982
- because thou hast *t* in thy works ... Jer 48:7 982
- that *t* in her treasures, saying, ... Jer 49:4 982
- his servants that *t* in him ... Dan 3:28 7365
- she *t* not in the LORD ... Zeph 3:2 982
- He *t* in God ... Mt 27:43 *3982*
- him all his armour wherein he *t* ... Lk 11:22 *3982*
- *t* in themselves that they were ... Lk 18:9 *3982*
- But we *t* that it had been he ... Lk 24:21 *1679*
- his glory, who first *t* in Christ ... Eph 1:12 *4276*
- In whom ye also *t*, after that ye ... Eph 1:13
- who *t* in God, adorned themselves, ... 1Pet 3:5 *1679*

TRUSTEDST

- walls come down, wherein thou *t* ... Deut 28:52 982
- thy fenced cities, wherein thou *t* ... Jer 5:17 982
- the land of peace, wherein thou *t* ... Jer 12:5 982

TRUSTEST

- confidence is this wherein thou *t* ... 2Kin 18:19 982
- thou *t* upon the staff of this ... 2Kin 18:21 982

God in whom thou *t* deceive thee ... 2Kin 19:10 982
confidence is this wherein thou *t* ... Is 36:4 982
thou *t* in the staff of this ... Is 36:6 982
Let not thy God, in whom thou *t* ... Is 37:10 982

TRUSTETH
he *t* that he can draw up Jordan ... Job 40:23 982
For the king *t* in the LORD ... Ps 21:7 982
but he that *t* in the LORD ... Ps 32:10 982
blessed is the man that *t* in him ... Ps 34:8 2620
for my soul *t* in thee ... Ps 57:1 2620
blessed is the man that *t* in thee ... Ps 84:12 982
save thy servant that *t* in thee ... Ps 86:2 982
so is every one that *t* in them ... Ps 115:8 982
so is every one that *t* in them ... Ps 135:18 982
He that *t* in his riches shall ... Prov 11:28 982
whoso *t* in the LORD, happy is he ... Prov 16:20 982
He that *t* in his own heart is a ... Prov 28:26 982
because he *t* in thee ... Is 26:3 982
Cursed be the man that *t* in man ... Jer 17:5 982
is the man that *t* in the LORD ... Jer 17:7 982
the maker of his work *t* therein ... Hab 2:18 982
t in God, and continueth in ... 1Ti 5:5 *1679*

TRUSTING
his heart is fixed, *t* in the LORD ... Ps 112:7 982

TRUSTY
removeth away the speech of the *t* ... Job 12:20 539

TRUTH
my master of his mercy and his *t* ... Gen 24:27 571
all the mercies, and of all the *t* ... Gen 32:10 571
whether there be any *t* in you ... Gen 42:16 571
men, such as fear God, men of *t* ... Ex 18:21 571
and abundant in goodness and *t* ... Ex 34:6 571
and, behold, if it be *t*, and the ... Deut 13:14 571
a God of *t* and without iniquity ... Deut 32:4 530
and serve him in sincerity and in *t* ... Josh 24:14 571
If in *t* ye anoint me king over ... Judg 9:15 571
serve him in *t* with all your ... 1Sa 12:24 571
Of a *t* women have been kept from ... 1Sa 21:5
LORD shew kindness and *t* unto you ... 2Sa 2:6 571
mercy and *t* be with thee ... 2Sa 15:20 571
me in *t* with all their heart ... 1Kin 2:4 571
as he walked before thee in *t* ... 1Kin 3:6 571
of the LORD in thy mouth is *t* ... 1Kin 17:24 571
Of a *t*, LORD, the kings of ... 2Kin 19:17 551
I have walked before thee in *t* ... 2Kin 20:3 571
good, if peace and *t* be in my days ... 2Kin 20:19 571
t to me in the name of the LORD ... 2Chr 18:15 571
t before the LORD his God ... 2Chr 31:20 571
with words of peace and *t* ... Est 9:30 571
I know it is so of a *t* ... Job 9:2 551
and speaketh the *t* in his heart ... Ps 15:2 571
Lead me in thy *t*, and teach me ... Ps 25:5 571
t unto such as keep his covenant ... Ps 25:10 571
and I have walked in thy *t* ... Ps 26:3 571
shall it declare thy *t* ... Ps 30:9 571
hast redeemed me, O LORD God of *t* ... Ps 31:5 571
and all his works are done in *t* ... Ps 33:4 530
thy *t* from the great congregation ... Ps 40:10 571
thy *t* continually preserve me ... Ps 40:11 571
O send out thy light and thy *t* ... Ps 43:3 571
ride prosperously because of *t* ... Ps 45:4 571
thou desirest *t* in the inward ... Ps 51:6 571
cut them off in thy *t* ... Ps 54:5 571
send forth his mercy and his *t* ... Ps 57:3 571
heavens, and thy *t* unto the clouds ... Ps 57:10 571
may be displayed because of the *t* ... Ps 60:4 7189
O prepare mercy and *t*, which may ... Ps 61:7 571
in the *t* of thy salvation ... Ps 69:13 571
with the psaltery, even thy *t* ... Ps 71:22 571
Mercy and *t* are met together ... Ps 85:10 571
T shall spring out of the earth ... Ps 85:11 571
I will walk in thy *t* ... Ps 86:11 571
and plenteous in mercy and *t* ... Ps 86:15 571
t shall go before thy face ... Ps 89:14 571
thou swarest unto David in thy *t* ... Ps 89:49 530
his *t* shall be thy shield and ... Ps 91:4 571
and the people with his *t* ... Ps 96:13 530
his *t* toward the house of Israel ... Ps 98:3 530
his *t* endureth to all generations ... Ps 100:5 530
thy *t* reacheth unto the clouds ... Ps 108:4 571
ever and ever, and are done in *t* ... Ps 111:8 571
the *t* of the LORD endureth for ... Ps 117:2 571
I have chosen the way of *t* ... Ps 119:30 530
take not the word of *t* utterly ... Ps 119:43 571
and thy law is the *t* ... Ps 119:142 571
and all thy commandments are *t* ... Ps 119:151 571
LORD hath sworn in *t* unto David ... Ps 132:11 571
thy lovingkindness and for thy *t* ... Ps 138:2 571
to all that call upon him in *t* ... Ps 145:18 571
which keepeth *t* for ever ... Ps 146:6 571
Let not mercy and *t* forsake thee ... Prov 3:3 571
For my mouth shall speak *t* ... Prov 8:7 571
He that speaketh *t* sheweth forth ... Prov 12:17 530
The lip of *t* shall be established ... Prov 12:19 571
t shall be to them that devise ... Prov 14:22 571
By mercy and *t* iniquity is purged ... Prov 16:6 571
Mercy and *t* preserve the king ... Prov 20:28 571
the certainty of the words of *t* ... Prov 22:21 571
of *t* to them that send unto thee ... Prov 22:21 571
Buy the *t*, and sell it not ... Prov 23:23 571
was upright, even words of *t* ... Eccl 12:10 571
Of a *t* many houses shall be ... Is 5:9
the Holy One of Israel, in *t* ... Is 10:20 571
he shall sit upon it in *t* in the ... Is 16:5 571
of old are faithfulness and *t* ... Is 25:1 544
which keepeth the *t* may enter in ... Is 26:2 529
Of a *t*, LORD, the kings of ... Is 37:18 551
I have walked before thee in *t* ... Is 38:3 571
the pit cannot hope for thy *t* ... Is 38:18 571
children shall make known thy *t* ... Is 38:19 571
shall be peace and *t* in my days ... Is 39:8 571
shall bring forth judgment unto *t* ... Is 42:3 571
or let them hear, and say, It is *t* ... Is 43:9 571
the God of Israel, but not in *t* ... Is 48:1 571
justice, nor any pleadeth for *t* ... Is 59:4 530
for *t* is fallen in the street, and ... Is 59:14 571
Yea, *t* faileth ... Is 59:15 571
and I will direct their work in *t* ... Is 61:8 571
bless himself in the God of *t* ... Is 65:16 548
earth shall swear by the God of *t* ... Is 65:16 548
swear, The LORD liveth, in *t* ... Jer 4:2 571
judgment, that seeketh the *t* ... Jer 5:1 530
are not thine eyes upon the *t* ... Jer 5:3 530
t is perished, and is cut off from ... Jer 7:28 530
valiant for the *t* upon the earth ... Jer 9:3 530
and will not speak the *t* ... Jer 9:5 571
for of a *t* the LORD hath sent me ... Jer 26:15 571
them the abundance of peace and *t* ... Jer 33:6 571
Of a *t* it is, that your God is a ... Dan 2:47 7187
of heaven, all whose works are *t* ... Dan 4:37 7187
and asked him the *t* of all this ... Dan 7:16 3330
know the *t* of the fourth beast ... Dan 7:19 3321
it cast down the *t* to the ground ... Dan 8:12 571
iniquities, and understand thy *t* ... Dan 9:13 571
is noted in the scripture of *t* ... Dan 10:21 571
And now will I shew thee the *t* ... Dan 11:2 571
the land, because there is no *t* ... Hos 4:1 571
Thou wilt perform the *t* to Jacob ... Mic 7:20 571
shall be called a city of *t* ... Zec 8:3 571
and I will be their God, in *t* ... Zec 8:8 571
every man the *t* to his neighbour ... Zec 8:16 571
execute the judgment of *t* ... Zec 8:16 571
therefore love the *t* and peace ... Zec 8:19 571
The law of *t* was in his mouth, and ... Mal 2:6 571
Of a *t* thou art the Son of God ... Mt 14:33 *230*
And she said, *T*, Lord ... Mt 15:27 *3483*
and teachest the way of God in *t* ... Mt 22:16 *225*
before him, and told him all the *t* ... Mk 5:33 *225*
but teachest the way of God in *t* ... Mk 12:14 *225*
Master, thou hast said the *t* ... Mk 12:32 *225*
But I tell you of a *t*, many ... Lk 4:25 *225*
But I tell you of a *t*, there be ... Lk 9:27 *230*
Of a *t* I say unto you, that he ... Lk 12:44 *230*
Of a *t* I say unto you, that this ... Lk 21:3 *230*
Of a *t* this fellow also was with ... Lk 22:59 *225*
the Father,) full of grace and *t* ... Jn 1:14 *225*
grace and *t* came by Jesus Christ ... Jn 1:17 *225*
But he that doeth *t* cometh to the ... Jn 3:21 *225*
the Father in spirit and in *t* ... Jn 4:23 *225*
worship him in spirit and in *t* ... Jn 4:24 *225*
and he bare witness unto the *t* ... Jn 5:33 *225*
This is of a *t* that prophet that ... Jn 6:14 *230*
Of a *t* this is the Prophet ... Jn 7:40 *230*
And ye shall know the *t*, and the ... Jn 8:32 *225*
the *t* shall make you free ... Jn 8:32 *225*
a man that hath told you the *t* ... Jn 8:40 *225*
beginning, and abode not in the *t* ... Jn 8:44 *225*
because there is no *t* in him ... Jn 8:44 *225*
And because I tell you the *t* ... Jn 8:45 *225*
And if I say the *t*, why do ye not ... Jn 8:46 *225*
unto him, I am the way, the *t* ... Jn 14:6 *225*
Even the Spirit of *t* ... Jn 14:17 *225*
the Father, even the Spirit of *t* ... Jn 15:26 *225*
Nevertheless I tell you the *t* ... Jn 16:7 *225*
Howbeit when he, the Spirit of *t* ... Jn 16:13 *225*
he will guide you into all *t* ... Jn 16:13 *225*
Sanctify them through thy *t* ... Jn 17:17 *225*
thy word is *t* ... Jn 17:17 *225*
might be sanctified through the *t* ... Jn 17:19 *225*
I should bear witness unto the *t* ... Jn 18:37 *225*
that is of the *t* heareth my voice ... Jn 18:37 *225*
Pilate saith unto him, What is *t* ... Jn 18:38 *225*
For of a *t* against thy holy child ... Acts 4:27 *225*
Of a *t* I perceive that God is no ... Acts 10:34 *225*
but speak forth the words of *t* ... Acts 26:25 *225*
who hold the *t* in unrighteousness ... Rom 1:18 *225*
Who changed the *t* of God into a ... Rom 1:25 *225*
t against them which commit such ... Rom 2:2 *225*
contentious, and do not obey the *t* ... Rom 2:8 *225*
knowledge and of the *t* in the law ... Rom 2:20 *225*
For if the *t* of God hath more ... Rom 3:7 *225*
I say the *t* in Christ, I lie not ... Rom 9:1 *225*
the circumcision for the *t* of God ... Rom 15:8 *225*
bread of sincerity and *t* ... 1Cor 5:8 *225*
iniquity, but rejoiceth in the *t* ... 1Cor 13:6 *225*
report that God is in you of a *t* ... 1Cor 14:25 *3689*
but by manifestation of the *t* ... 2Cor 4:2 *225*
By the word of *t*, by the power of ... 2Cor 6:7 *225*
we spake all things to you in *t* ... 2Cor 7:14 *225*
I made before Titus, is found a *t* ... 2Cor 7:14 *225*
As the *t* of Christ is in me, no ... 2Cor 11:10 *225*
for I will say the *t* ... 2Cor 12:6 *225*
against the *t*, but for the *t* ... 2Cor 13:8 *225*
that the *t* of the gospel might ... Gal 2:5 *225*
according to the *t* of the gospel ... Gal 2:14 *225*
that ye should not obey the *t* ... Gal 3:1 *225*
enemy, because I tell you the *t* ... Gal 4:16 *226*
you that ye should not obey the *t* ... Gal 5:7 *225*
after that ye heard the word of *t* ... Eph 1:13 *225*
But speaking the *t* in love ... Eph 4:15 *226*
by him, as the *t* is in Jesus ... Eph 4:21 *225*
speak every man *t* with his ... Eph 4:25 *226*
goodness and righteousness and *t* ... Eph 5:9 *226*
your loins girt about with *t* ... Eph 6:14 *226*
way, whether in pretence, or in *t* ... Phil 1:18 *226*
the word of the *t* of the gospel ... Col 1:5 *226*
it, and knew the grace of God in *t* ... Col 1:6 *226*
word of men, but as it is in *t* ... 1Th 2:13 *230*
received not the love of the *t* ... 2Th 2:10 *225*
be damned who believed not the *t* ... 2Th 2:12 *225*
of the Spirit and belief of the *t* ... 2Th 2:13 *225*
come unto the knowledge of the *t* ... 1Ti 2:4 *225*
apostle, (I speak the *t* in Christ ... 1Ti 2:7 *225*
the pillar and ground of the *t* ... 1Ti 3:15 *225*
them which believe and know the *t* ... 1Ti 4:3 *225*
minds, and destitute of the *t* ... 1Ti 6:5 *225*
rightly dividing the word of *t* ... 2Ti 2:15 *225*
Who concerning the *t* have erred ... 2Ti 2:18 *225*
to the acknowledging of the *t* ... 2Ti 2:25 *225*
to come to the knowledge of the *t* ... 2Ti 3:7 *225*
so do these also resist the *t* ... 2Ti 3:8 *225*
turn away their ears from the *t* ... 2Ti 4:4 *225*
of the *t* which is after godliness ... Titus 1:1 *225*
of men, that turn from the *t* ... Titus 1:14 *225*
received the knowledge of the *t* ... Heb 10:26 *225*
begat he us with the word of *t* ... Jas 1:18 *225*
not, and lie not against the *t* ... Jas 3:14 *225*
if any of you do err from the *t* ... Jas 5:19 *225*
the *t* through the Spirit unto ... 1Pet 1:22 *225*
be established in the present *t* ... 2Pet 1:12 *225*
way of *t* shall be evil spoken of ... 2Pet 2:2 *225*
darkness, we lie, and do not the *t* ... 1Jn 1:6 *225*
ourselves, and the *t* is not in us ... 1Jn 1:8 *225*
is a liar, and the *t* is not in him ... 1Jn 2:4 *225*
you because ye know not the *t* ... 1Jn 2:21 *225*
it, and that no lie is of the *t* ... 1Jn 2:21 *225*
you of all things, and is *t* ... 1Jn 2:27 *227*
but in deed and in *t* ... 1Jn 3:18 *225*
we know that we are of the *t* ... 1Jn 3:19 *225*
Hereby know we the spirit of *t* ... 1Jn 4:6 *225*
witness, because the Spirit is *t* ... 1Jn 5:6 *225*
children, whom I love in the *t* ... 2Jn 1 *225*
all they that have known the *t* ... 2Jn 1 *225*
the Son of the Father, in *t* ... 2Jn 3 *225*
of thy children walking in *t* ... 2Jn 4 *225*
Gaius, whom I love in the *t* ... 3Jn 1 *225*
of the *t* that is in thee, even as ... 3Jn 3 *225*
even as thou walkest in the *t* ... 3Jn 3 *225*
hear that my children walk in *t* ... 3Jn 4 *225*
might be fellowhelpers to the *t* ... 3Jn 8 *225*
of all men, and of the *t* itself ... 3Jn 12 *225*

TRUTH'S
for thy mercy, and for thy *t* sake ... Ps 115:1 571
For the *t* sake, which dwelleth in ... 2Jn 2 *225*

TRY
I will *t* them for thee there ... Judg 7:4 6884
to *t* him, that he might know all ... 2Chr 32:31 5254
morning, and *t* him every moment ... Job 7:18 974
Doth not the ear *t* words ... Job 12:11 974
his eyes behold, his eyelids *t* ... Ps 11:4 974
t my reins and my heart ... Ps 26:2 6884
t me, and know my thoughts ... Ps 139:23 974
thou mayest know and *t* their way ... Jer 6:27 974
I will melt them, and *t* them ... Jer 9:7 974
I *t* the reins, even to give every ... Jer 17:10 974
t our ways, and turn again to the ... Lam 3:40 2713
to *t* them, and to purge, and to ... Dan 11:35 6884
will *t* them as gold is tried ... Zec 13:9 974
the fire shall *t* every man's work ... 1Cor 3:13 *1381*
the fiery trial which is to *t* you ... 1Pet 4:12
but *t* the spirits whether they ... 1Jn 4:1 *1381*
to *t* them that dwell upon the ... Rev 3:10 *3985*

TRYING
that the *t* of your faith worketh ... Jas 1:3 *1383*

TRYPHAENA See TRYPHENA.

TRYPHENA (*tri-fe'-nah*) *A Christian in Rome.*
Salute *T* and Tryphosa, who labour ... Rom 16:12 *5170*

TRYPHOSA (*tri-fo'-sah*) *A Christian in Rome.*
Salute Tryphena and *T*, who labour ... Rom 16:12 *5173*

TUBAL (*tu'-bal*)
1. A son of Japheth.
Magog, and Madai, and Javan, and *T* ... Gen 10:2 8422
Magog, and Madai, and Javan, and *T* ... 1Chr 1:5 8422
2. Migrants to Sicily and Spain.
and Lud, that draw the bow, to *T* ... Is 66:19 8422
Javan, *T*, and Meshech, they were ... Eze 27:13 8422
There is Meshech, *T*, and all her ... Eze 32:26 8422
the chief prince of Meshech and *T* ... Eze 38:2 8422
the chief prince of Meshech and *T* ... Eze 38:3 8422
the chief prince of Meshech and *T* ... Eze 39:1 8422

TUBAL-CAIN (*tu'-bal-cain*) *Son of Lamech.*
And Zillah, she also bare *T* ... Gen 4:22 8423
and the sister of *T* was Naamah ... Gen 4:22 8423

TUMBLED
a cake of barley bread *t* into the ... Judg 7:13 2015

TUMULT
What meaneth the noise of this *t* ... 1Sa 4:14 1995
me thy servant, I saw a great *t* ... 2Sa 18:29 1995
thy *t* is come up into mine ears ... 2Kin 19:28 7600
waves, and the *t* of the people ... Ps 65:7 1995
the *t* of those that rise up ... Ps 74:23 7588
For, lo, thine enemies make a *t* ... Ps 83:2 1993
noise of the *t* the people fled ... Is 33:3 1995
thy rage against me, and thy *t* ... Is 37:29 7600
with the noise of a great *t* he ... Jer 11:16 1999
Therefore shall a *t* arise among ... Hos 10:14 7588
and Moab shall die with *t*, with ... Amos 2:2 7588
that a great *t* from the LORD ... Zec 14:13 4103
but that rather a *t* was made ... Mt 27:24 *2351*
of the synagogue, and seeth the *t* ... Mk 5:38 *2351*
not know the certainty for the *t* ... Acts 21:34 *2351*
with multitude, nor with *t* ... Acts 24:18 *2351*

TUMULTS
behold the great *t* in the midst ... Amos 3:9 4103
stripes, in imprisonments, in *t* ... 2Cor 6:5 *181*
whisperings, swellings, *t* ... 2Cor 12:20 *181*

TUMULTUOUS
a *t* noise of the kingdoms of ... Is 13:4 7588
of stirs, a *t* city, a joyous city ... Is 22:2 1993
crown of the head of the *t* ones ... Jer 48:45

TURN
t in, I pray you, into your ... Gen 19:2 5493
that I may *t* to the right hand ... Gen 24:49 6437

until thy brother's fury *t* away	Gen 27:44	7725
brother's anger *t* away from thee	Gen 27:45	7725
And Moses said, I will now *t* aside	Ex 3:3	5493
children of Israel, that they *t*	Ex 14:2	7725
enemies *t* their backs unto thee	Ex 23:27	
T from thy fierce wrath, and	Ex 32:12	7725
Or if the raw flesh *t* again	Lev 13:16	7725
T ye not unto idols, nor make to	Lev 19:4	6437
To morrow *t* you, and get you into	Num 14:25	6437
we will not *t* to the right hand	Num 20:17	5186
we will not *t* into the fields, or	Num 21:22	5186
the ass, to *t* her into the way	Num 22:23	5186
where was no way to *t* either to	Num 22:26	5186
For if ye *t* away from after him,	Num 32:15	7725
your border shall *t* from the	Num 34:4	5437
T you, and take your journey, and	Deut 1:7	6437
t you, and take your journey into	Deut 1:40	6437
t you northward	Deut 2:3	6437
I will neither *t* unto the right	Deut 2:27	5493
if thou *t* to the LORD thy God, and	Deut 4:30	7725
ye shall not *t* aside to the right	Deut 5:32	5493
For they will *t* away thy son from	Deut 7:4	5493
ye *t* aside, and serve other gods,	Deut 11:16	5493
but *t* aside out of the way which	Deut 11:28	5493
because he hath spoken to *t* you	Deut 13:5	5627
that the LORD may *t* from the	Deut 13:17	7725
Then shalt thou *t* it into money	Deut 14:25	5414
thou shalt *t* in the morning, and	Deut 16:7	6437
that his heart *t* not away	Deut 17:17	5493
that he *t* not aside from the	Deut 17:20	5493
dig therewith, and shalt *t* back	Deut 23:13	7725
in thee, and *t* away from thee	Deut 23:14	7725
LORD thy God will *t* thy captivity	Deut 30:3	7725
if thou *t* unto the LORD thy God	Deut 30:10	7725
But if thine heart *t* away	Deut 30:17	6437
then will they *t* unto other gods,	Deut 31:20	6437
t aside from the way which I have	Deut 31:29	5493
t not from it to the right hand	Josh 1:7	5493
to *t* away this day from following	Josh 22:16	7725
But that ye must *t* away this day	Josh 22:18	7725
to *t* from following the LORD	Josh 22:23	7725
t this day from following the	Josh 22:29	7725
that ye *t* not aside therefrom to	Josh 23:6	5493
strange gods, then he will *t*	Josh 24:20	7725
T in, my lord, *t* in to me	Judg 4:18	5493
Therefore we *t* again to thee now,	Judg 11:8	7725
let us *t* in into this city of the	Judg 19:11	5493
We will not *t* aside hither into	Judg 19:12	5493
we any of us *t* into his house	Judg 20:8	5493
Naomi said, *T* again, my daughters	Ruth 1:11	7725
T again, my daughters, go your	Ruth 1:12	7725
t aside, sit down here	Ruth 4:1	5493
yet *t* not aside from following	1Sa 12:20	5493
And *t* ye not aside	1Sa 12:21	5493
t thee; behold, I am	1Sa 14:7	5186
t again with me, that I may	1Sa 15:25	7725
t again with me, that I may	1Sa 15:30	7725
footmen that stood about him, *T*	1Sa 22:17	5437
T thou, and fall upon the priests	1Sa 22:18	5437
T thee aside to thy right hand or	2Sa 2:21	5186
But Asahel would not *t* aside from	2Sa 2:21	5493
T thee aside from following me	2Sa 2:22	5493
Howbeit he refused to *t* aside	2Sa 2:23	5493
none can *t* to the right hand or	2Sa 14:19	
Let him *t* to his own house, and	2Sa 14:24	5437
t the counsel of Ahithophel into	2Sa 15:31	
unto him, *T* aside, and stand here	2Sa 18:30	5437
t back again, that I may die in	2Sa 19:37	7725
shall *t* again to thee, and confess	1Kin 8:33	7725
t from their sin, when thou	1Kin 8:35	7725
shall at all *t* from following me	1Kin 9:6	7725
for surely they will *t* away your	1Kin 11:2	5186
people *t* again unto their lord	1Kin 12:27	7725
nor *t* again by the same way that	1Kin 13:9	7725
nor *t* again to go by the way that	1Kin 13:17	7725
t thee eastward, and hide thyself	1Kin 17:3	6437
T thine hand, and carry me out of	1Kin 22:34	2015
t again unto the king that sent	2Kin 1:6	7725
to us, that he shall *t* in thither	2Kin 4:10	5493
t thee behind me	2Kin 9:18	5437
t thee behind me	2Kin 9:19	5437
T ye from your evil ways, and keep	2Kin 17:13	7725
How then wilt thou *t* away the	2Kin 18:24	7725
I will *t* thee back by the way by	2Kin 19:28	7725
T again, and tell Hezekiah the	2Kin 20:5	7725
to *t* the kingdom of Saul to him,	1Chr 12:23	5437
t away from them, and come upon	1Chr 14:14	5437
t from their sin, when thou dost	2Chr 6:26	7725
they are carried captive, and *t*	2Chr 6:37	7725
t not away the face of thine	2Chr 6:42	7725
face, and *t* from their wicked ways	2Chr 7:14	7725
But if ye *t* away, and forsake my	2Chr 7:19	7725
did *t* unto the LORD God of Israel	2Chr 15:4	7725
T thine hand, that thou mayest	2Chr 18:33	2015
t away from following the LORD	2Chr 25:27	5493
fierce wrath may *t* away from us	2Chr 29:10	7725
t again unto the LORD God of	2Chr 30:6	7725
of his wrath may *t* away from you	2Chr 30:8	7725
For if ye *t* again unto the LORD,	2Chr 30:9	7725
will not *t* away his face from you	2Chr 30:9	5493
would not *t* his face from him	2Chr 35:22	5437
But if ye *t* unto me, and keep my	Neh 1:9	7725
t their reproach upon their own	Neh 4:4	7725
against them to *t* them to thee	Neh 9:26	7725
Now when every maid's *t* was come	Est 2:12	8447
Now when the *t* of Esther, the	Est 2:15	8447
which of the saints wilt thou *t*	Job 5:1	6437
T from him, that he may rest,	Job 14:6	8159
is in one mind, and who can *t* him	Job 23:13	7725
They *t* the needy out of the way	Job 24:4	5186
man shall *t* again unto dust	Job 34:15	7725
how long will ye *t* my glory into	Ps 4:2	
If he *t* not, he will whet his	Ps 7:12	7725
neither did I *t* again till they	Ps 18:37	7725
shalt thou make them *t* their back	Ps 21:12	
shall remember and *t* unto the LORD	Ps 22:27	7725
T thee unto me, and have mercy	Ps 25:16	6437
nor such as *t* aside to lies	Ps 40:4	7750
Thou makest us to *t* back from the	Ps 44:10	7725
then shall mine enemies *t* back	Ps 56:9	7725
O *t* thyself to us again	Ps 60:1	7725
t unto me according to the	Ps 69:16	6437
T us again, O God, and cause thy	Ps 80:3	7725
T us again, O God of hosts, and	Ps 80:7	7725
T us again, O LORD God of hosts,	Ps 80:19	7725
T us, O God of our salvation, and	Ps 85:4	7725
but let them not *t* again to folly	Ps 85:8	7725
O *t* unto me, and have mercy upon	Ps 86:16	6437
the work of them that *t* aside	Ps 101:3	7750
that they *t* not again to cover	Ps 104:9	7725
to *t* away his wrath, lest he	Ps 106:23	7725
T away mine eyes from beholding	Ps 119:37	5674
T away my reproach which I fear	Ps 119:39	5674
those that fear thee *t* unto me	Ps 119:79	7725
As for such as *t* aside unto their	Ps 125:5	5186
T again our captivity, O LORD, as	Ps 126:4	7725
sake *t* not away the face of thine	Ps 132:10	7725
he will not *t* from it	Ps 132:11	7725
T you at my reproof	Prov 1:23	7725
by it, *t* from it, and pass away	Prov 4:15	7847
T not to the right hand nor to	Prov 4:27	5186
is simple, let him *t* in hither	Prov 9:4	5493
is simple, let him *t* in hither	Prov 9:16	5493
he *t* away his wrath from him	Prov 24:18	7725
shame, and thine infamy *t* not away	Prov 25:10	7725
but wise men *t* away wrath	Prov 29:8	7725
the dust, and all *t* to dust again	Eccl 3:20	7725
and the shadows flee away, *t*	Song 2:17	5437
T away thine eyes from me, for	Song 6:5	5437
I will *t* my hand upon thee, and	Is 1:25	7725
To *t* aside the needy from	Is 10:2	5186
every man *t* to his own people	Is 13:14	6437
out, and who shall *t* it back	Is 14:27	7725
they shall *t* the rivers far away	Is 19:6	2186
He will surely violently *t*	Is 22:18	6801
she shall *t* to her hire, and shall	Is 23:17	7725
that *t* the battle to the gate	Is 28:6	7725
t aside the just for a thing of	Is 29:21	5186
t aside out of the path, cause	Is 30:11	5186
when ye *t* to the right hand, and	Is 30:21	
hand, and when ye *t* to the left	Is 30:21	
T ye unto him from whom the	Is 31:6	7725
How then wilt thou *t* away the	Is 36:9	7725
I will *t* thee back by the way by	Is 37:29	7725
If thou *t* away thy foot from the	Is 58:13	7725
to Zion, and unto them that *t* from	Is 59:20	7725
her occasion who can *t* her away	Jer 2:24	7725
surely his anger shall *t* from me	Jer 2:35	7725
all these things, *T* thou unto me	Jer 3:7	7725
T, O backsliding children, saith	Jer 3:14	7725
and shalt not *t* away from me	Jer 3:19	7725
neither will I *t* back from it	Jer 4:28	7725
t back thine hand as a	Jer 6:9	7725
shall he *t* away, and not return	Jer 8:4	7725
he *t* it into the shadow of death,	Jer 13:16	7760
t from their evil, I will repent	Jer 18:8	7725
to *t* away thy wrath from them	Jer 18:20	7725
I will *t* back the weapons of war	Jer 21:4	5437
T ye again now every one from his	Jer 25:5	7725
t every man from his evil way,	Jer 26:3	7725
I will *t* away your captivity, and	Jer 29:14	7725
for I will *t* their mourning into	Jer 31:13	2015
t thou me, and I shall be turned	Jer 31:18	7725
t again, O virgin of Israel	Jer 31:21	7725
t again to these thy cities	Jer 31:21	7725
that I will not *t* away from them	Jer 32:40	7725
ear to *t* from their wickedness	Jer 44:5	7725
t back, dwell deep, O inhabitants	Jer 49:8	6437
shall *t* every one to his people	Jer 50:16	6437
iniquity, to *t* away thy captivity	Lam 2:14	7725
To *t* aside the right of a man	Lam 3:35	5186
our ways, and *t* again to the LORD	Lam 3:40	7725
T thou us unto thee, O LORD, and	Lam 5:21	7725
he *t* not from his wickedness, nor	Eze 3:19	7725
man doth *t* from his righteousness	Eze 3:20	7725
thou shalt not *t* thee from one	Eze 4:8	2015
My face will I *t* also from them	Eze 7:22	5437
but *t* thee yet again, and thou	Eze 8:6	7725
T thee yet again, and thou shalt	Eze 8:13	7725
t thee yet again, and thou shalt	Eze 8:15	7725
t yourselves from your idols	Eze 14:6	7725
t away your faces from all your	Eze 14:6	7725
But if the wicked will *t* from all	Eze 18:21	7725
t yourselves from all your	Eze 18:30	7725
wherefore *t* yourselves, and live	Eze 18:32	7725
wicked of his way to *t* from it	Eze 33:9	7725
if he do not *t* from his way	Eze 33:9	7725
that the wicked *t* from his way	Eze 33:11	7725
t ye, *t* ye from your evil ways	Eze 33:11	7725
if he *t* from his sin, and do that	Eze 33:14	7725
But if the wicked *t* from his	Eze 33:19	7725
I will *t* unto you, and ye shall be	Eze 36:9	6437
I will *t* thee back, and put hooks	Eze 38:4	7725
to *t* thine hand upon the desolate	Eze 38:12	7725
I will *t* thee back, and leave but	Eze 39:2	7725
our God, that we might *t* from our	Dan 9:13	7725
After this shall he *t* his face	Dan 11:18	7725
he shall cause it to *t* upon him	Dan 11:18	7725
Then he shall *t* his face toward	Dan 11:19	7725
they that *t* many to righteousness	Dan 12:3	
their doings to *t* unto their God	Hos 5:4	7725
Therefore *t* thou to thy God	Hos 12:6	7725
with you words, and *t* to the LORD	Hos 14:2	7725
t ye even to me with all your	Joel 2:12	7725
and *t* unto the LORD your God	Joel 2:13	7725
I will not *t* away the punishment	Amos 1:3	7725
I will not *t* away the punishment	Amos 1:6	7725
I will *t* mine hand against Ekron	Amos 1:8	7725
I will not *t* away the punishment	Amos 1:9	7725
I will not *t* away the punishment	Amos 1:11	7725
I will not *t* away the punishment	Amos 1:13	7725
I will not *t* away the punishment	Amos 2:1	7725
I will not *t* away the punishment	Amos 2:4	7725
I will not *t* away the punishment	Amos 2:6	7725
t aside the way of the meek	Amos 2:7	5186
who *t* judgment to wormwood	Amos 5:7	2015
they *t* aside the poor in the gate	Amos 5:12	5186
I will *t* your feasts into	Amos 8:10	2015
let them *t* every one from his	Jonah 3:8	7725
Who can tell if God will *t*	Jonah 3:9	7725
t away from his fierce anger,	Jonah 3:9	7725
He will *t* again, he will have	Mic 7:19	7725
them, and *t* away their captivity	Zeph 2:7	7725
For then will I *t* to the people a	Zeph 3:9	2015
when I *t* back your captivity	Zeph 3:20	7725
T ye unto me, saith the LORD of	Zec 1:3	7725
I will *t* unto you, saith the LORD	Zec 1:3	7725
T ye now from your evil ways, and	Zec 1:4	7725
T you to the strong hold, ye	Zec 9:12	7725
with their children, and *t* again	Zec 10:9	7725
I will *t* mine hand upon the	Zec 13:7	7725
did *t* many away from iniquity	Mal 2:6	7725
that *t* aside the stranger from	Mal 3:5	5186
he shall *t* the heart of the	Mal 4:6	7725
cheek, *t* to him the other also	Mt 5:39	*4762*
borrow of thee *t* not thou away	Mt 5:42	*654*
feet, and *t* again and rend you	Mt 7:6	*4762*
him that is in the field not *t*	Mk 13:16	*1994*
shall he *t* to the Lord their God	Lk 1:16	*1994*
to *t* the hearts of the fathers to	Lk 1:17	*1994*
if not, it shall *t* to you again	Lk 10:6	*344*
times in a day *t* again to thee	Lk 17:4	*1994*
it shall *t* to you for a testimony	Lk 21:13	*576*
seeking to *t* away the deputy from	Acts 13:8	*1294*
life, lo, we *t* to the Gentiles	Acts 13:46	*4762*
t from these vanities unto the	Acts 14:15	*1994*
to *t* them from darkness to light,	Acts 26:18	*1994*
t to God, and do works meet for	Acts 26:20	*1994*
shall *t* away ungodliness from	Rom 11:26	*654*
when it shall *t* to the Lord	2Cor 3:16	*1994*
how *t* ye again to the weak and	Gal 4:9	*1994*
For I know that this shall *t* to	Phil 1:19	*576*
from such *t* away	2Ti 3:5	*665*
they shall *t* away their ears from	2Ti 4:4	*654*
of men, that *t* from the truth	Titus 1:14	*654*
if we *t* away from him that	Heb 12:25	*654*
we *t* about their whole body	Jas 3:3	*3329*
to *t* from the holy commandment	2Pet 2:21	*1994*
over waters to *t* them to blood	Rev 11:6	*4762*

TURNED

a flaming sword which *t* every way	Gen 3:24	2015
the men *t* their faces from thence	Gen 18:22	6437
they *t* in unto him, and entered	Gen 19:3	5493
t in to a certain Adullamite,	Gen 38:1	5186
he *t* unto her by the way, and said	Gen 38:16	5186
he *t* himself about from them, and	Gen 42:24	5437
LORD saw that he *t* aside to see	Ex 3:4	5493
it was *t* again as his other flesh	Ex 4:7	7725
the rod which was *t* to a serpent	Ex 7:15	2015
and they shall be *t* to blood	Ex 7:17	2015
were in the river were *t* to blood	Ex 7:20	2015
And Pharaoh *t* and went into his	Ex 7:23	6437
he *t* himself, and went out from	Ex 10:6	6437
the LORD *t* a mighty strong west	Ex 10:19	2015
servants was *t* against the people	Ex 14:5	2015
They have *t* aside quickly out of	Ex 32:8	5493
And Moses *t*, and went down from the	Ex 32:15	6437
And he *t* again into the camp	Ex 33:11	7725
the hair in the plague is *t* white	Lev 13:3	2015
the hair thereof be not *t* white	Lev 13:4	2015
it have *t* the hair white, and	Lev 13:10	2015
it is all *t* white	Lev 13:13	2015
if the plague be *t* into white	Lev 13:17	2015
and the hair thereof be *t* white	Lev 13:20	2015
in the bright spot be *t* white	Lev 13:25	2015
because ye are *t* away from the	Num 14:43	7725
wherefore Israel *t* away from him	Num 20:21	5186
And they *t* and went up by the way	Num 21:33	6437
the ass *t* aside out of the way,	Num 22:23	5186
t from me these three times	Num 22:33	5186
unless she had *t* from me, surely	Num 22:33	5186
LORD may be *t* away from Israel	Num 25:4	7725
hath *t* my wrath away from the	Num 25:11	7725
t again unto Pi-hahiroth, which	Num 33:7	7725
And they *t* and went up into the	Deut 1:24	6437
Then we *t*, and took our journey	Deut 2:1	6437
Elath, and from Ezion-gaber, we *t*	Deut 2:8	6437
Then we *t*, and went up the way to	Deut 3:1	6437
they are quickly *t* aside out of	Deut 9:12	5493
So I *t* and came down from the	Deut 9:15	6437
ye had *t* aside quickly out of the	Deut 9:16	5493
I *t* myself and came down from the	Deut 10:5	6437
but the LORD thy God *t* the curse	Deut 23:5	2015
that they are *t* unto other gods	Deut 31:18	6437
but *t* their backs before their	Josh 7:12	6437
So the LORD *t* from the fierceness	Josh 7:26	7725
t back upon the pursuers	Josh 8:20	2015
city ascended, then they *t* again	Josh 8:21	7725
And Joshua at that time *t* back	Josh 11:10	7725
t from Sarid eastward toward the	Josh 19:12	7725
they *t* quickly out of the way	Judg 2:17	5493
But he himself *t* again from the	Judg 3:19	7725
when he had *t* in unto her into	Judg 4:18	5493
the children of Israel *t* again	Judg 8:33	7725
he *t* aside to see the carcase of	Judg 14:8	5493
and *t* tail to tail, and put a	Judg 15:4	6437
they *t* in thither, and said unto	Judg 18:3	5493
they *t* thitherward, and came to	Judg 18:15	5493
So they *t* and departed, and put the	Judg 18:21	6437
they *t* their faces, and said unto	Judg 18:23	5437
were too strong for him, he *t*	Judg 18:26	6437

they *t* aside thither, to go in and	Judg 19:15	5493
And when the men of Israel *t* again	Judg 20:41	2015
Therefore they *t* their backs	Judg 20:42	6437
And they *t* and fled toward the	Judg 20:45	6437
But six hundred men *t* and fled to	Judg 20:47	6437
the men of Israel *t* again upon	Judg 20:48	7725
the man was afraid, and *t* himself	Ruth 3:8	3943
And he *t* aside, and sat down	Ruth 4:1	5493
t not aside to the right hand or	1Sa 6:12	5493
but *t* aside after lucre, and took	1Sa 8:3	5186
shalt be *t* into another man	1Sa 10:6	2015
that when he had *t* his back to go	1Sa 10:9	6437
one company *t* unto the way that	1Sa 13:17	6437
another company *t* the way to	1Sa 13:18	6437
another company *t* to the way of	1Sa 13:18	6437
even they also *t* to be with the	1Sa 14:21	
and whithersoever he *t* himself	1Sa 14:47	6437
for he is *t* back from following	1Sa 15:11	7725
as Samuel *t* about to go away, he	1Sa 15:27	5437
So Samuel *t* again after Saul	1Sa 15:31	7725
he *t* from him toward another, and	1Sa 17:30	5437
And Doeg the Edomite *t*, and he fell	1Sa 22:18	5437
So David's young men *t* their way	1Sa 25:12	2015
the bow of Jonathan *t* not back	2Sa 1:22	7734
in going he *t* not to the right	2Sa 2:19	5186
he *t* aside, and stood still	2Sa 18:30	5437
the victory that day was *t* into	2Sa 19:2	
t not again until I had consumed	2Sa 22:38	7725
howbeit the kingdom is *t* about	1Kin 2:15	5437
for Joab had *t* after Adonijah	1Kin 2:28	5186
though he *t* not after Absalom	1Kin 2:28	5186
the king *t* his face about, and	1Kin 8:14	5437
So she *t* and went to her own	1Kin 10:13	6437
his wives *t* away his heart	1Kin 11:3	5186
that his wives *t* away his heart	1Kin 11:4	5186
because his heart was *t* from the	1Kin 11:9	5186
t not aside from any thing that	1Kin 15:5	5493
that thou hast *t* their heart back	1Kin 18:37	5437
and, behold, a man *t* aside	1Kin 20:39	5493
t away his face, and would eat no	1Kin 21:4	5437
they *t* aside to fight against him	1Kin 22:32	5493
that they *t* back from pursuing	1Kin 22:33	7725
he *t* not aside from it, doing	1Kin 22:43	5493
the messengers *t* back unto him	2Kin 1:5	7725
unto them, Why are ye now *t* back	2Kin 1:5	7725
he *t* back, and looked on them, and	2Kin 2:24	6437
he *t* in thither to eat bread	2Kin 4:8	5493
he *t* into the chamber, and lay	2Kin 4:11	5493
So he *t* and went away in a rage	2Kin 5:12	6437
when the man *t* again from his	2Kin 5:26	2015
Joram *t* his hands, and fled, and	2Kin 9:23	2015
So the king of Assyria *t* back	2Kin 15:20	7725
t he from the house of the LORD	2Kin 16:18	5437
Then he *t* his face to the wall	2Kin 20:2	5437
t not aside to the right hand or	2Kin 22:2	5493
And as Josiah *t* himself, he spied	2Kin 23:16	6437
that *t* to the LORD with all his	2Kin 23:25	7725
Notwithstanding the LORD *t* not	2Kin 23:26	7725
t his name to Jehoiakim, and took	2Kin 23:34	5437
then he *t* and rebelled against him	2Kin 24:1	7725
t the kingdom unto David the son	1Chr 10:14	5437
And Ornan *t* back, and saw the angel	1Chr 21:20	7725
And the king *t* his face, and	2Chr 6:3	5437
So she *t*, and went away to her own	2Chr 9:12	2015
the wrath of the LORD *t* from him	2Chr 12:12	7725
they *t* back again from pursuing	2Chr 18:32	7725
Egypt, but they *t* from them, and	2Chr 20:10	5493
have *t* away their faces from the	2Chr 29:6	5437
of the LORD, and *t* their backs	2Chr 29:6	5414
and *t* his name to Jehoiakim	2Chr 36:4	5437
t the heart of the king of	Ezr 6:22	5437
God for this matter be *t* from us	Ezr 10:14	7725
t back, and entered by the gate of	Neh 2:15	7725
neither *t* they from their wicked	Neh 9:35	7725
howbeit our God *t* the curse into	Neh 13:2	2015
(though it was *t* to the contrary	Est 9:1	2015
the month which was *t* unto them	Est 9:22	2015
paths of their way are *t* aside	Job 6:18	3943
t me over into the hands of the	Job 16:11	3399
whom I loved are *t* against me	Job 19:19	2015
Yet his meat in his bowels is *t*	Job 20:14	2015
under it is *t* up as it were fire	Job 28:5	2015
Terrors are *t* upon me	Job 30:15	2015
My harp also is *t* to mourning	Job 30:31	
If my step hath *t* out of the way	Job 31:7	5186
Because they *t* back from him, and	Job 34:27	5493
it is *t* round about by his	Job 37:12	2015
It is *t* as clay to the seal	Job 38:14	2015
sorrow is *t* into joy before him	Job 41:22	1750
slingstones are *t* with him into	Job 41:28	2015
the LORD *t* the captivity of Job	Job 42:10	7725
When mine enemies are *t* back	Ps 9:3	7725
The wicked shall be *t* into hell	Ps 9:17	7725
Thou hast *t* for me my mourning	Ps 30:11	2015
my moisture is *t* into the drought	Ps 32:4	2015
let them be *t* back and brought to	Ps 35:4	5472
Our heart is not *t* back, neither	Ps 44:18	5472
He *t* the sea into dry land	Ps 66:6	2015
which hath not *t* away my prayer	Ps 66:20	5493
let them be *t* backward, and put to	Ps 70:2	5472
Let them be *t* back for a reward	Ps 70:3	7725
t back in the day of battle	Ps 78:9	2015
many a time *t* he his anger away	Ps 78:38	7725
Yea, they *t* back and tempted God	Ps 78:41	7725
had *t* their rivers into blood	Ps 78:44	2015
But *t* back, and dealt unfaithfully	Ps 78:57	5472
they were *t* aside like a	Ps 78:57	2015
and *t* my hand against their	Ps 81:14	7725
thou hast *t* thyself from the	Ps 85:3	7725
Thou hast also *t* the edge of his	Ps 89:43	7725
He *t* their heart to hate his	Ps 105:25	2015
He *t* their waters into blood, and	Ps 105:29	2015
Which *t* the rock into a standing	Ps 114:8	2015
t my feet unto thy testimonies	Ps 119:59	7725
When the LORD *t* again the	Ps 126:1	7725
and *t* back that hate Zion	Ps 129:5	5472
I *t* myself to behold wisdom, and	Eccl 2:12	6437
whither is thy beloved *t* aside	Song 6:1	6437
all this his anger is not *t* away	Is 5:25	7725
all this his anger is not *t* away	Is 9:12	7725
all this his anger is not *t* away	Is 9:17	7725
all this his anger is not *t* away	Is 9:21	7725
all this his anger is not *t* away	Is 10:4	7725
with me, thine anger is *t* away	Is 12:1	7725
hath he *t* into fear unto me	Is 21:4	7760
wheel *t* about upon the cummin	Is 28:27	5437
Lebanon shall be *t* into a	Is 29:17	7725
thereof shall be *t* into pitch	Is 34:9	2015
Then Hezekiah *t* his face toward	Is 38:2	5437
They shall be *t* back, they shall	Is 42:17	5472
a deceived heart hath *t* him aside	Is 44:20	5186
rebellious, neither *t* away back	Is 50:5	5472
we have *t* every one to his own	Is 53:6	6437
judgment is *t* away backward, and	Is 59:14	5253
therefore he was *t* to be their	Is 63:10	2015
how then art thou *t* into the	Jer 2:21	2015
for they have *t* their back unto	Jer 2:27	6437
sister Judah hath not *t* unto me	Jer 3:10	7725
of the LORD is not *t* back from us	Jer 4:8	7725
have *t* away these things, and your	Jer 5:25	5186
houses shall be *t* unto others	Jer 6:12	5437
every one *t* to his course, as the	Jer 8:6	7725
They are *t* back to the iniquities	Jer 11:10	7725
then they should have *t* them from	Jer 23:22	7725
and all faces are *t* into paleness	Jer 30:6	2015
turn thou me, and I shall be *t*	Jer 31:18	7725
Surely after that I was *t*	Jer 31:19	7725
they have *t* unto me the back, and	Jer 32:33	6437
But afterward they *t*, and caused	Jer 34:11	7725
And ye were now *t*, and had done	Jer 34:15	7725
But ye *t* and polluted my name, and	Jer 34:16	7725
the mire, and they are *t* away back	Jer 38:22	5472
seen them dismayed and *t* away back	Jer 46:5	5472
for they also are *t* back, and are	Jer 46:21	6437
how hath Moab *t* the back with	Jer 48:39	6437
they have *t* them away on the	Jer 50:6	7725
for my feet, he hath *t* me back	Lam 1:13	7725
mine heart is *t* within me	Lam 1:20	2015
Surely against me is he *t*	Lam 3:3	7725
He hath *t* aside my ways, and	Lam 3:11	5493
Our inheritance is *t* to strangers	Lam 5:2	2015
our dance is *t* into mourning	Lam 5:15	2015
thee, O LORD, and we shall be *t*	Lam 5:21	7725
they *t* not when they went	Eze 1:9	5437
they *t* not when they went	Eze 1:12	5437
they *t* not when they went	Eze 1:17	5437
they *t* not as they went, but to	Eze 10:11	5437
they *t* not as they went	Eze 10:11	5437
also *t* not from beside them	Eze 10:16	5437
whose branches *t* toward him	Eze 17:6	6437
she is *t* unto me	Eze 26:2	5437
He *t* about to the west side, and	Eze 42:19	5437
thy fury be *t* away from thy city	Dan 9:16	7725
was *t* in me into corruption	Dan 10:8	2015
vision my sorrows are *t* upon me	Dan 10:16	2015
Ephraim is a cake not *t*	Hos 7:8	2015
mine heart is *t* within me	Hos 11:8	2015
for mine anger is *t* away from him	Hos 14:4	7725
The sun shall be *t* into darkness	Joel 2:31	2015
for ye have *t* judgment into gall	Amos 6:12	2015
that they *t* from their evil way	Jonah 3:10	7725
For the LORD hath *t* away the	Nah 2:2	7725
right hand shall be *t* unto thee	Hab 2:16	5437
them that are *t* back from the	Zeph 1:6	5472
yet ye *t* not to me, saith the	Hag 2:17	
Then I *t*, and lifted up mine eyes	Zec 5:1	7725
And I *t*, and lifted up mine eyes	Zec 6:1	7725
All the land shall be *t* as a	Zec 14:10	5437
he *t* aside into the parts of	Mt 2:22	*402*
But Jesus *t* him about, and when he	Mt 9:22	*1994*
But he *t*, and said unto Peter, Get	Mt 16:23	*4672*
t him about in the press, and said	Mk 5:30	*1994*
But when he had *t* about and looked	Mk 8:33	*1994*
they *t* back again to Jerusalem	Lk 2:45	*5290*
t him about, and said unto the	Lk 7:9	*4762*
he *t* to the woman, and said unto	Lk 7:44	*4762*
But he *t*, and rebuked them, and	Lk 9:55	*4762*
he *t* him unto his disciples, and	Lk 10:23	*4762*
and he *t*, and said unto them	Lk 14:25	*4762*
t back, and with a loud voice	Lk 17:15	*5290*
And the Lord *t*, and looked upon	Lk 22:61	*4762*
Then Jesus *t*, and saw them	Jn 1:38	*4762*
your sorrow shall be *t* into joy	Jn 16:20	*1096*
she *t* herself back, and saw Jesus	Jn 20:14	*4762*
She *t* herself, and saith unto him	Jn 20:16	*4762*
The sun shall be *t* into darkness	Acts 2:20	*4762*
in their hearts *t* back again into	Acts 7:39	*4762*
Then God *t*, and gave them up to	Acts 7:42	*4762*
Saron saw him, and *t* to the Lord	Acts 9:35	*1994*
believed, and *t* unto the Lord	Acts 11:21	*1994*
among the Gentiles are *t* to God	Acts 15:19	*1994*
But Paul, being grieved, *t*	Acts 16:18	*1994*
These that have *t* the world	Acts 17:6	*387*
t away much people, saying that	Acts 19:26	*3179*
how ye *t* to God from idols to	1Th 1:9	*1994*
have *t* aside unto vain jangling	1Ti 1:6	*1824*
are already *t* aside after Satan	1Ti 5:15	*1824*
are in Asia be *t* away from me	2Ti 1:15	*654*
truth, and shall be *t* unto fables	2Ti 4:4	*654*
t to flight the armies of the	Heb 11:34	*2827*
which is lame be *t* out of the way	Heb 12:13	*1624*
yet are they *t* about with a very	Jas 3:4	*3329*
your laughter be *t* to mourning	Jas 4:9	*3344*
The dog is *t* to his own vomit	2Pet 2:22	*1994*
I *t* to see the voice that spake	Rev 1:12	*1994*
And being *t*, I saw seven golden	Rev 1:12	*1994*

TURNEST

and whithersoever thou *t* thyself	1Kin 2:3	6437
That thou *t* thy spirit against	Job 15:13	7725
Thou *t* man to destruction	Ps 90:3	7725

TURNETH

the soul that *t* after such as	Lev 20:6	6437
whose heart *t* away this day from	Deut 29:18	6437
when Israel *t* their backs before	Josh 7:8	2015
t toward the sunrising to	Josh 19:27	7725
And then the coast *t* to Ramah	Josh 19:29	7725
and the coast *t* to Hosah	Josh 19:29	7725
then the coast *t* westward to	Josh 19:34	7725
neither *t* he back from the sword	Job 39:22	7725
He *t* rivers into a wilderness, and	Ps 107:33	7760
He *t* the wilderness into a	Ps 107:35	7760
of the wicked he *t* upside down	Ps 146:9	5791
A soft answer *t* away wrath	Prov 15:1	7725
whithersoever it *t*, it prospereth	Prov 17:8	6437
he *t* it whithersoever he will	Prov 21:1	5186
As the door *t* upon his hinges, so	Prov 26:14	5437
He that *t* away his ear from	Prov 28:9	5493
beasts, and *t* not away for any	Prov 30:30	7725
south, and *t* about unto the north	Eccl 1:6	5437
that *t* aside by the flocks of thy	Song 1:7	5844
For the people *t* not unto him	Is 9:13	7725
t it upside down, and scattereth	Is 24:1	5753
that *t* wise men backward, and	Is 44:25	7725
as a wayfaring man that *t* aside	Jer 14:8	5186
t herself to flee, and fear hath	Jer 49:24	6437
yea, she sigheth, and *t* backward	Lam 1:8	7725
he *t* his hand against me all the	Lam 3:3	7725
But when the righteous *t* away	Eze 18:24	7725
When a righteous man *t* away from	Eze 18:26	7725
when the wicked man *t* away from	Eze 18:27	7725
and *t* away from all his	Eze 18:28	7725
day that he *t* from his wickedness	Eze 33:12	7725
When the righteous *t* from his	Eze 33:18	7725
t the shadow of death into the	Amos 5:8	2015

TURNING

wiping it, and *t* it upside down	2Kin 21:13	2015
gate, and at the *t* of the wall, and	2Chr 26:9	4740
hardened his heart from *t* unto	2Chr 36:13	7257
the armoury at the *t* of the wall	Neh 3:19	4740
from the *t* of the wall unto the	Neh 3:20	4740
of Azariah unto the *t* of the wall	Neh 3:24	4740
over against the *t* of the wall	Neh 3:25	4740
For the *t* away of the simple	Prov 1:32	4878
Surely your *t* of things upside	Is 29:16	2017
two leaves apiece, two *t* leaves	Eze 41:24	4142
t away he hath divided our fields	Mic 2:4	7725
But Jesus *t* unto them said	Lk 23:28	*4762*
t about, seeth the disciple whom	Jn 21:20	*1994*
in *t* away every one of you from	Acts 3:26	*654*
t him to the body said, Tabitha	Acts 9:40	*1994*
variableness, neither shadow of *t*	Jas 1:17	*5157*
t the cities of Sodom and Gomorrah	2Pet 2:6	*5077*
t the grace of our God into	Jude 4	*3346*

TURTLE

the voice of the *t* is heard in	Song 2:12	8449
and the *t* and the crane and the	Jer 8:7	8449

TURTLEDOVE

a ram of three years old, and a *t*	Gen 15:9	8449
and a young pigeon, or a *t*	Lev 12:6	8449
thy *t* unto the multitude of the	Ps 74:19	8449

TURTLEDOVES

he shall bring his offering of *t*	Lev 1:14	8449
which he hath committed, two *t*	Lev 5:7	8449
if he be not able to bring two *t*	Lev 5:11	8449
And two *t*, or two young pigeons	Lev 14:22	8449
he shall offer the one of the *t*	Lev 14:30	8449
day he shall take to him two *t*	Lev 15:14	8449
the law of the Lord, A pair of *t*	Lk 2:24	*5167*

TURTLES

lamb, then she shall bring two *t*	Lev 12:8	8449
day she shall take unto her two *t*	Lev 15:29	8449
eighth day he shall bring two *t*	Num 6:10	8449

TUTORS

But is under *t* and governors until	Gal 4:2	*2012*

TWAIN

my son in law in the one of the *t*	1Sa 18:21	8147
and shut the door upon them *t*	2Kin 4:33	8147
with *t* he covered his face, and	Is 6:2	8147
with *t* he covered his feet, and	Is 6:2	8147
his feet, and with *t* he did fly	Is 6:2	8147
me, when they cut the calf in *t*	Jer 34:18	8147
both *t* shall come forth out of	Eze 21:19	8147
thee to go a mile, go with him *t*	Mt 5:41	*1417*
they *t* shall be one flesh	Mt 19:5	*1417*
Wherefore they are no more *t*	Mt 19:6	*1417*
Whether of them *t* did the will of	Mt 21:31	*1417*
Whether of the *t* will ye that I	Mt 27:21	*1417*
in *t* from the top to the bottom	Mt 27:51	*1417*
they *t* shall be one flesh	Mk 10:8	*1417*
so then they are no more *t*	Mk 10:8	*1417*
in *t* from the top to the bottom	Mk 15:38	*1417*
make in himself of *t* one new man	Eph 2:15	*1417*

TWELFTH

On the *t* day Ahira the son of	Num 7:78	
oxen before him, and he with the *t*	1Kin 19:19	
In the *t* year of Joram the son of	2Kin 8:25	
In the *t* year of Ahaz king of	2Kin 17:1	
king of Judah, in the *t* month	2Kin 25:27	
to Eliashib, the *t* to Jakim	1Chr 24:12	
The *t* to Hashabiah, he, his sons	1Chr 25:19	
The *t* captain for the *t*	1Chr 27:15	
in the *t* year he began to purge	2Chr 34:3	
on the *t* day of the first month	Ezr 8:31	
in the *t* year of king Ahasuerus	Est 3:7	
month to month, to the *t* month	Est 3:7	

the thirteenth day of the *t* month	Est 3:13	
the thirteenth day of the *t* month	Est 8:12	
Now in the *t* month, that is, the	Est 9:1	
king of Judah, in the *t* month	Jer 52:31	
in the *t* day of the month, the	Eze 29:1	
the *t* year, in the *t* month	Eze 32:1	
came to pass also in the *t* year	Eze 32:17	
in the *t* year of our captivity	Eze 33:21	
the *t*, an amethyst	Rev 21:20	*1428*

TWELVE

Seth were nine hundred and *t* years	Gen 5:8	
T years they served Chedorlaomer,	Gen 14:4	
t princes shall he beget, and I	Gen 17:20	
t princes according to their	Gen 25:16	
Now the sons of Jacob were *t*	Gen 35:22	
said, Thy servants are *t* brethren	Gen 42:13	
We be *t* brethren, sons of our	Gen 42:32	
these are the *t* tribes of Israel	Gen 49:28	
where were *t* wells of water, and	Ex 15:27	
t pillars, according to the	Ex 24:4	
to the *t* tribes of Israel	Ex 24:4	
of the children of Israel, *t*	Ex 28:21	
they be according to the *t* tribes	Ex 28:21	
of the children of Israel, *t*	Ex 39:14	
name, according to the *t* tribes	Ex 39:14	
flour, and bake *t* cakes thereof	Lev 24:5	
princes of Israel, being *t* men	Num 1:44	
six covered wagons, and *t* oxen	Num 7:3	
t chargers of silver	Num 7:84	
t silver bowls, *t* spoons of	Num 7:84	
The golden spoons were *t*, full of	Num 7:86	
were *t* bullocks, the rams *t*	Num 7:87	
the lambs of the first year *t*	Num 7:87	
of the goats for sin offering *t*	Num 7:87	
the house of their fathers *t* rods	Num 17:2	
fathers' houses, even *t* rods	Num 17:6	
ye shall offer *t* young bullocks	Num 29:17	
tribe, *t* thousand armed for war	Num 31:5	
threescore and *t* thousand beeves,	Num 31:33	8147
tribute was threescore and *t*	Num 31:38	8147
in Elim were *t* fountains of water	Num 33:9	
I took *t* men of you, one of a	Deut 1:23	
Now therefore take you *t* men out	Josh 3:12	
Take you *t* men out of the people,	Josh 4:2	
t stones, and ye shall carry them	Josh 4:3	
Then Joshua called the *t* men	Josh 4:4	
took up *t* stones out of the midst	Josh 4:8	
Joshua set up *t* stones in the	Josh 4:9	
those *t* stones, which they took	Josh 4:20	
were *t* thousand, even all the men	Josh 8:25	
t cities with their villages	Josh 18:24	
t cities with their villages	Josh 19:15	
of the tribe of Zebulun, *t* cities	Josh 21:7	
were by their lot *t* cities	Josh 21:40	
into *t* pieces, and sent her into	Judg 19:29	
the congregation sent thither *t*	Judg 21:10	
went over by number *t* of Benjamin	2Sa 2:15	
t of the servants of David	2Sa 2:15	
of Ish-tob *t* thousand men	2Sa 10:6	
me now choose out *t* thousand men	2Sa 17:1	
Solomon had *t* officers over all	1Kin 4:7	
chariots, and *t* thousand horsemen	1Kin 4:26	
a line of *t* cubits did compass	1Kin 7:15	
It stood upon *t* oxen, three	1Kin 7:25	
one sea, and *t* oxen under the sea	1Kin 7:44	
t lions stood there on the one	1Kin 10:20	
t thousand horsemen, whom he	1Kin 10:26	
on him, and rent it in *t* pieces	1Kin 11:30	
to reign over Israel, *t* years	1Kin 16:23	
And Elijah took *t* stones,	1Kin 18:31	
who was plowing with *t* yoke of	1Kin 19:19	
king of Judah, and reigned *t* years	2Kin 3:1	
Manasseh was *t* years old when he	2Kin 21:1	
of the tribe of Zebulun, *t* cities	1Chr 6:63	
the gates were two hundred and *t*	1Chr 9:22	
and his brethren an hundred and *t*	1Chr 15:10	
with his brethren and sons were *t*	1Chr 25:9	
his sons, and his brethren, were *t*	1Chr 25:10	
his sons, and his brethren, were *t*	1Chr 25:11	
his sons, and his brethren, were *t*	1Chr 25:12	
his sons, and his brethren, were *t*	1Chr 25:13	
his sons, and his brethren, were *t*	1Chr 25:14	
his sons, and his brethren, were *t*	1Chr 25:15	
his sons, and his brethren, were *t*	1Chr 25:16	
his sons, and his brethren, were *t*	1Chr 25:17	
his sons, and his brethren, were *t*	1Chr 25:18	
his sons, and his brethren, were *t*	1Chr 25:19	
his sons, and his brethren, were *t*	1Chr 25:20	
his sons, and his brethren, were *t*	1Chr 25:21	
his sons, and his brethren, were *t*	1Chr 25:22	
his sons, and his brethren, were *t*	1Chr 25:23	
his sons, and his brethren, were *t*	1Chr 25:24	
his sons, and his brethren, were *t*	1Chr 25:25	
his sons, and his brethren, were *t*	1Chr 25:26	
his sons, and his brethren, were *t*	1Chr 25:27	
his sons, and his brethren, were *t*	1Chr 25:28	
his sons, and his brethren, were *t*	1Chr 25:29	
his sons, and his brethren, were *t*	1Chr 25:30	
his sons, and his brethren, were *t*	1Chr 25:31	
t thousand horsemen, which he	2Chr 1:14	
It stood upon *t* oxen, three	2Chr 4:4	
One sea, and *t* oxen under it	2Chr 4:15	
t lions stood there on the one	2Chr 9:19	
chariots, and *t* thousand horsemen	2Chr 9:25	
With *t* hundred chariots, and	2Chr 12:3	505
Manasseh was *t* years old when he	2Chr 33:1	
two thousand eight hundred and *t*	Ezr 2:6	
of Jorah, an hundred and *t*	Ezr 2:18	
t he goats, according to the	Ezr 6:17	
Then I separated *t* of the chief	Ezr 8:24	
t bullocks for all Israel, ninety	Ezr 8:35	
t he goats for a sin offering	Ezr 8:35	
t years, I and my brethren have	Neh 5:14	
of Hariph, an hundred and *t*	Neh 7:24	
after that she had been *t* months	Est 2:12	
in the valley of salt *t* thousand	Ps 60:*t*	
t brasen bulls that were under	Jer 52:20	
a fillet of *t* cubits did compass	Jer 52:21	
the altar shall be *t* cubits long	Eze 43:16	
t broad, square in the four	Eze 43:16	
to the *t* tribes of Israel	Eze 47:13	
At the end of *t* months he walked	Dan 4:29	
with an issue of blood *t* years	Mt 9:20	*1427*
called unto him his *t* disciples	Mt 10:1	*1427*
names of the *t* apostles are these	Mt 10:2	*1427*
These *t* Jesus sent forth, and	Mt 10:5	*1427*
end of commanding his *t* disciples	Mt 11:1	*1427*
that remained *t* baskets full	Mt 14:20	*1427*
ye also shall sit upon *t* thrones	Mt 19:28	*1427*
judging the *t* tribes of Israel	Mt 19:28	*1427*
the *t* disciples apart in the way	Mt 20:17	*1427*
Then one of the *t*, called Judas	Mt 26:14	*1427*
was come, he sat down with the *t*	Mt 26:20	*1427*
spake, lo, Judas, one of the *t*	Mt 26:47	*1427*
me more than *t* legions of angels	Mt 26:53	*1427*
And he ordained *t*, that they	Mk 3:14	*1427*
the *t* asked of him the parable	Mk 4:10	*1427*
had an issue of blood *t* years	Mk 5:25	*1427*
for she was of the age of *t* years	Mk 5:42	*1427*
And he called unto him the *t*	Mk 6:7	*1427*
they took up *t* baskets full of	Mk 6:43	*1427*
They say unto him, *T*	Mk 8:19	*1427*
And he sat down, and called the *t*	Mk 9:35	*1427*
And he took again the *t*, and began	Mk 10:32	*1427*
went out unto Bethany with the *t*	Mk 11:11	*1427*
And Judas Iscariot, one of the *t*	Mk 14:10	*1427*
the evening he cometh with the *t*	Mk 14:17	*1427*
unto them, It is one of the *t*	Mk 14:20	*1427*
spake, cometh Judas, one of the *t*	Mk 14:43	*1427*
And when he was *t* years old	Lk 2:42	*1427*
and of them he chose *t*, whom also	Lk 6:13	*1427*
and the *t* were with him,	Lk 8:1	*1427*
about *t* years of age, and she lay	Lk 8:42	*1427*
having an issue of blood *t* years	Lk 8:43	*1427*
called his *t* disciples together	Lk 9:1	*1427*
to wear away, then came the *t*	Lk 9:12	*1427*
that remained to them *t* baskets	Lk 9:17	*1427*
Then he took unto him the *t*	Lk 18:31	*1427*
being of the number of the *t*	Lk 22:3	*1427*
down, and the *t* apostles with him	Lk 22:14	*1427*
judging the *t* tribes of Israel	Lk 22:30	*1427*
was called Judas, one of the *t*	Lk 22:47	*1427*
filled *t* baskets with the	Jn 6:13	*1427*
Then said Jesus unto the *t*	Jn 6:67	*1427*
them, Have not I chosen you *t*	Jn 6:70	*1427*
betray him, being one of the *t*	Jn 6:71	*1427*
Are there not *t* hours in the day	Jn 11:9	*1427*
But Thomas, one of the *t*, called	Jn 20:24	*1427*
Then the *t* called the multitude	Acts 6:2	*1427*
and Jacob begat the *t* patriarchs	Acts 7:8	*1427*
And all the men were about *t*	Acts 19:7	*1177*
that there are yet but *t* days	Acts 24:11	*1177*
Unto which promise our *t* tribes	Acts 26:7	*1429*
was seen of Cephas, then of the *t*	1Cor 15:5	*1427*
to the *t* tribes which are	Jas 1:1	*1427*
of Juda were sealed *t* thousand	Rev 7:5	*1427*
of Reuben were sealed *t* thousand	Rev 7:5	*1427*
of Gad were sealed *t* thousand	Rev 7:5	*1427*
of Aser were sealed *t* thousand	Rev 7:6	*1427*
Nepthalim were sealed *t* thousand	Rev 7:6	*1427*
Manasses were sealed *t* thousand	Rev 7:6	*1427*
of Simeon were sealed *t* thousand	Rev 7:7	*1427*
of Levi were sealed *t* thousand	Rev 7:7	*1427*
Issachar were sealed *t* thousand	Rev 7:7	*1427*
of Zabulon were sealed *t* thousand	Rev 7:8	*1427*
of Joseph were sealed *t* thousand	Rev 7:8	*1427*
Benjamin were sealed *t* thousand	Rev 7:8	*1427*
upon her head a crown of *t* stars	Rev 12:1	*1427*
had *t* gates, and at the gates	Rev 21:12	*1427*
gates, and at the gates *t* angels	Rev 21:12	*1427*
the *t* tribes of the children of	Rev 21:12	*1427*
of the city had *t* foundations	Rev 21:14	*1427*
of the *t* apostles of the Lamb	Rev 21:14	*1427*
the reed, *t* thousand furlongs	Rev 21:16	*1427*
the *t* gates were *t* pearls	Rev 21:21	*1427*
which bare *t* manner of fruits, and	Rev 22:2	*1427*

TWENTIETH

t day of the month, was the earth	Gen 8:14	6242
t day of the month at even	Ex 12:18	6242
it came to pass on the *t* day of	Num 10:11	6242
in the *t* year of Jeroboam king of	1Kin 15:9	6242
t year of king Jehoash the	2Kin 12:6	6242
t year of Joash the son of	2Kin 13:1	6242
in the *t* year of Jotham the son	2Kin 15:30	6242
seven and *t* day of the month, that	2Kin 25:27	6242
to Pethahiah, the *t* to Jehezekel,	1Chr 24:16	6242
t to Jachin, the two and	1Chr 24:17	6242
to Jachin, the two and *t* to Gamul,	1Chr 24:17	6242
t to Delaiah, the four and	1Chr 24:18	6242
Delaiah, the four and *t* to Maaziah	1Chr 24:18	6242
The *t* to Eliathah, he, his sons,	1Chr 25:27	6242
t to Hothir, he, his sons, and his	1Chr 25:28	6242
t to Giddalti, he, his sons, and	1Chr 25:29	6242
t to Mahazioth, he, his sons, and	1Chr 25:30	6242
t to Romamti-ezer, he, his sons,	1Chr 25:31	6242
t day of the seventh month he	2Chr 7:10	6242
on the *t* day of the month	Ezr 10:9	6242
the month Chisleu, in the *t* year	Neh 1:1	6242
in the *t* year of Artaxerxes the	Neh 2:1	6242
from the *t* year even unto the two	Neh 5:14	6242
on the three and *t* day thereof	Est 8:9	6242
t year, the word of the LORD hath	Jer 25:3	6242
three and *t* year of Nebuchadrezzar	Jer 52:30	6242
five and *t* day of the month, that	Jer 52:31	6242
t year, in the first month, in	Eze 29:17	6242
t year of our captivity, in the	Eze 40:1	6242
t day of the first month, as I	Dan 10:4	6242
t day of the sixth month, in the	Hag 1:15	6242
t day of the month, came the word	Hag 2:1	6242
t day of the ninth month, in the	Hag 2:10	6242
t day of the ninth month, even	Hag 2:18	6242
t day of the month, saying,	Hag 2:20	6242
t day of the eleventh month,	Zec 1:7	6242

TWENTY

shall be an hundred and *t* years	Gen 6:3	6242
nine and *t* years, and begat Terah	Gen 11:24	6242
there shall be *t* found there	Gen 18:31	6242
hundred and seven and *t* years old	Gen 23:1	6242
This *t* years have I been with	Gen 31:38	6242
Thus have I been *t* years in thy	Gen 31:41	6242
t he goats, two hundred ewes, and	Gen 32:14	6242
two hundred ewes, and *t* rams,	Gen 32:14	6242
t she asses, and ten foals	Gen 32:15	6242
for *t* pieces of silver	Gen 37:28	6242
t cubits, and the breadth of one	Ex 26:2	6242
t boards on the south side	Ex 26:18	6242
of silver under the *t* boards	Ex 26:19	6242
side there shall be *t* boards	Ex 26:20	6242
the *t* pillars thereof and their	Ex 27:10	6242
their *t* sockets shall be of brass	Ex 27:10	6242
his *t* pillars and their *t*	Ex 27:11	6242
shall be an hanging of *t* cubits	Ex 27:16	6242
(a shekel is *t* gerahs	Ex 30:13	6242
from *t* years old and above, shall	Ex 30:14	6242
The length of one curtain was *t*	Ex 36:9	6242
t boards for the south side	Ex 36:23	6242
silver he made under the *t* boards	Ex 36:24	6242
north corner, he made *t* boards	Ex 36:25	6242
Their pillars were *t*, and their	Ex 38:10	6242
and their brasen sockets *t*	Ex 38:10	6242
cubits, their pillars were *t*	Ex 38:11	6242
and their sockets of brass *t*	Ex 38:11	6242
t cubits was the length, and the	Ex 38:18	6242
the gold of the offering, was *t*	Ex 38:24	6242
from *t* years old and upward, for	Ex 38:26	6242
shall be of the male from *t* years	Lev 27:3	6242
years old even unto *t* years old	Lev 27:5	6242
shall be of the male *t* shekels	Lev 27:5	6242
t gerahs shall be the shekel	Lev 27:25	6242
From *t* years old and upward, all	Num 1:3	6242
from *t* years old and upward, by	Num 1:18	6242
every male from *t* years old	Num 1:20	6242
every male from *t* years old	Num 1:22	6242
from *t* years old and upward, all	Num 1:24	6242
from *t* years old and upward, all	Num 1:26	6242
from *t* years old and upward, all	Num 1:28	6242
from *t* years old and upward, all	Num 1:30	6242
from *t* years old and upward, all	Num 1:32	6242
from *t* years old and upward, all	Num 1:34	6242
from *t* years old and upward, all	Num 1:36	6242
from *t* years old and upward, all	Num 1:38	6242
from *t* years old and upward, all	Num 1:40	6242
from *t* years old and upward, all	Num 1:42	6242
from *t* years old and upward, all	Num 1:45	6242
a month old and upward, were *t*	Num 3:39	6242
were numbered of them, were *t*	Num 3:43	6242
(the shekel is *t* gerahs	Num 3:47	6242
was an hundred and *t* shekels	Num 7:86	6242
of the peace offerings were *t*	Num 7:88	6242
from *t* and five years old and	Num 8:24	6242
neither ten days, nor *t* days	Num 11:19	6242
from *t* years old and upward, which	Num 14:29	6242
the sanctuary, which is *t* gerahs	Num 18:16	6242
that died in the plague were *t*	Num 25:9	6242
from *t* years old and upward,	Num 26:2	6242
from *t* years old and upward	Num 26:4	6242
the families of the Simeonites, *t*	Num 26:14	6242
that were numbered of them were *t*	Num 26:62	6242
from *t* years old and upward, shall	Num 32:11	6242
And Aaron was an hundred and *t*	Num 33:39	6242
hundred and *t* years old this day	Deut 31:2	6242
and *t* years old when he died	Deut 34:7	6242
all the cities are *t* and nine,	Josh 15:32	6242
t and two cities with their	Josh 19:30	6242
t years he mightily oppressed the	Judg 4:3	6242
And there returned of the people *t*	Judg 7:3	6242
t thousand men that drew sword	Judg 8:10	6242
And he judged Israel *t* and three	Judg 10:2	6242
a Gileadite, and judged Israel *t*	Judg 10:3	6242
even *t* cities, and unto the plain	Judg 11:33	6242
days of the Philistines *t* years	Judg 15:20	6242
And he judged Israel *t* years	Judg 16:31	6242
at that time out of the cities *t*	Judg 20:15	6242
of the Israelites that day *t*	Judg 20:21	6242
of the Benjamites that day *t*	Judg 20:35	6242
fell that day of Benjamin were *t*	Judg 20:46	6242
for it was *t* years	1Sa 7:2	6242
made, was about *t* men, within as	1Sa 14:14	6242
to Hebron, and *t* men with him	2Sa 3:20	6242
horsemen, and *t* thousand footmen	2Sa 8:4	6242
the Syrians two and *t* thousand men	2Sa 8:5	6242
had fifteen sons and *t* servants	2Sa 9:10	6242
t thousand footmen, and of king	2Sa 10:6	6242
that day of *t* thousand men	2Sa 18:7	6242
sons and his *t* servants with him	2Sa 19:17	6242
six toes, four and *t* in number	2Sa 21:20	6242
the end of nine months and *t* days	2Sa 24:8	6242
t oxen out of the pastures, and an	1Kin 4:23	6242
Solomon gave Hiram *t* thousand	1Kin 5:11	6242
and *t* measures of pure oil	1Kin 5:11	6242
and the breadth thereof *t* cubits	1Kin 6:2	6242
t cubits was the length thereof,	1Kin 6:3	6242
he built *t* cubits on the sides of	1Kin 6:16	6242
forepart was *t* cubits in length	1Kin 6:20	6242
t cubits in breadth	1Kin 6:20	6242
t cubits in the height thereof	1Kin 6:20	6242
t thousand oxen, and an hundred and	1Kin 8:63	6242
and an hundred and *t* thousand sheep	1Kin 8:63	6242
to pass at the end of *t* years	1Kin 9:10	6242

T

then king Solomon gave Hiram *t* ... 1Kin 9:11 6242
t talents, and brought it to king ... 1Kin 9:28 6242
t talents of gold, and of spices ... 1Kin 10:10 6242
reigned were two and *t* years ... 1Kin 14:20 6242
over all Israel in Tirzah, *t* ... 1Kin 15:33 6242
In the *t* and sixth year of Asa ... 1Kin 16:8 6242
him, and killed him, in the *t* ... 1Kin 16:10 6242
In the *t* and seventh year of Asa ... 1Kin 16:15 6242
reigned over Israel in Samaria *t* ... 1Kin 16:29 6242
and there a wall fell upon *t* ... 1Kin 20:30 6242
and he reigned *t* and five years in ... 1Kin 22:42 6242
t loaves of barley, and full ears ... 2Kin 4:42 6242
t years old was Ahaziah when he ... 2Kin 8:26 6242
over Israel in Samaria was *t* ... 2Kin 10:36 6242
He was *t* and five years old when ... 2Kin 14:2 6242
he began to reign, and reigned *t* ... 2Kin 14:2 6242
In the *t* and seventh year of ... 2Kin 15:1 6242
in Samaria, and reigned *t* years ... 2Kin 15:27 6242
t years old was he when he began ... 2Kin 15:33 6242
T years old was Ahaz when he ... 2Kin 16:2 6242
T and five years old was he when ... 2Kin 18:2 6242
and he reigned *t* and nine years in ... 2Kin 18:2 6242
Amon was *t* and two years old when ... 2Kin 21:19 6242
Jehoahaz was *t* and three years old ... 2Kin 23:31 6242
Jehoiakim was *t* and five years old ... 2Kin 23:36 6242
Zedekiah was *t* and one years old ... 2Kin 24:18 6242
t cities in the land of Gilead ... 1Chr 2:22 6242
t thousand and six hundred ... 1Chr 7:2 6242
reckoned by their genealogies *t* ... 1Chr 7:7 6242
was *t* thousand and two hundred ... 1Chr 7:9 6242
apt to the war and to battle was *t* ... 1Chr 7:40 6242
and of his father's house *t* ... 1Chr 12:28 6242
children of Ephraim *t* thousand ... 1Chr 12:30 6242
And of the Danites expert in war *t* ... 1Chr 12:35 6242
battle, an hundred and *t* thousand ... 1Chr 12:37 6242
and his brethren an hundred and *t* ... 1Chr 15:5 6242
and his brethren two hundred and *t* ... 1Chr 15:6 6242
horsemen, and *t* thousand footmen ... 1Chr 18:4 6242
the Syrians two and *t* thousand men ... 1Chr 18:5 6242
fingers and toes were four and *t* ... 1Chr 20:6 6242
Of which, *t* and four thousand were ... 1Chr 23:4 6242
the LORD, from the age of *t* years ... 1Chr 23:24 6242
were numbered from *t* years old ... 1Chr 23:27 6242
the year, of every course were *t* ... 1Chr 27:1 6242
and in his course were *t* and four ... 1Chr 27:2 6242
in his course likewise were *t* ... 1Chr 27:4 6242
and in his course were *t* and four ... 1Chr 27:5 6242
and in his course were *t* and four ... 1Chr 27:7 6242
and in his course were *t* and four ... 1Chr 27:8 6242
and in his course were *t* and four ... 1Chr 27:9 6242
and in his course were *t* and four ... 1Chr 27:10 6242
and in his course were *t* and four ... 1Chr 27:11 6242
and in his course were *t* and four ... 1Chr 27:12 6242
and in his course were *t* and four ... 1Chr 27:13 6242
and in his course were *t* and four ... 1Chr 27:14 6242
and in his course were *t* and four ... 1Chr 27:15 6242
number of them from *t* years old ... 1Chr 27:23 6242
t thousand measures of beaten ... 2Chr 2:10 6242
t thousand measures of barley, and ... 2Chr 2:10 6242
t thousand baths of wine, and ... 2Chr 2:10 6242
wine, and *t* thousand baths of oil ... 2Chr 2:10 6242
cubits, and the breadth *t* cubits ... 2Chr 3:3 6242
t cubits, and the height was an ... 2Chr 3:4 6242
and the height was an hundred and *t* ... 2Chr 3:4 6242
t cubits, and the breadth thereof ... 2Chr 3:8 6242
and the breadth thereof *t* cubits ... 2Chr 3:8 6242
the cherubims were *t* cubits long ... 2Chr 3:11 6242
spread themselves forth *t* cubits ... 2Chr 3:13 6242
t cubits the length thereof, and ... 2Chr 4:1 6242
t cubits the breadth thereof, and ... 2Chr 4:1 6242
t priests sounding with trumpets ... 2Chr 5:12 6242
Solomon offered a sacrifice of *t* ... 2Chr 7:5 6242
and an hundred and *t* thousand sheep. 2Chr 7:5 6242
to pass at the end of *t* years ... 2Chr 8:1 6242
t talents of gold, and of spices ... 2Chr 9:9 6242
and begat *t* and eight sons, and ... 2Chr 11:21 6242
fourteen wives, and begat *t* ... 2Chr 13:21 6242
began to reign, and he reigned *t* ... 2Chr 20:31 6242
Amaziah was *t* and five years old ... 2Chr 25:1 6242
began to reign, and he reigned *t* ... 2Chr 25:1 6242
he numbered them from *t* years old ... 2Chr 25:5 6242
Jotham was *t* and five years old ... 2Chr 27:1 6242
t years old when he began to ... 2Chr 27:8 6242
Ahaz was *t* years old when he ... 2Chr 28:1 6242
t thousand in one day, which were ... 2Chr 28:6 6242
t years old, and he reigned nine ... 2Chr 29:1 6242
nine and *t* years in Jerusalem ... 2Chr 29:1 6242
and the Levites from *t* years old ... 2Chr 31:17 6242
t years old when he began to ... 2Chr 33:21 6242
Jehoahaz was *t* and three years old ... 2Chr 36:2 6242
Jehoiakim was *t* and five years old ... 2Chr 36:5 6242
t years old when he began to ... 2Chr 36:11 6242
of silver, nine and *t* knives ... Ezr 1:9 6242
children of Bebai, six hundred *t* ... Ezr 2:11 6242
Azgad, a thousand two hundred *t* ... Ezr 2:12 6242
of Bezai, three hundred *t* ... Ezr 2:17 6242
children of Hashum, two hundred *t* ... Ezr 2:19 6242
of Beth-lehem, an hundred *t* ... Ezr 2:21 6242
The men of Anathoth, an hundred *t* ... Ezr 2:23 6242
of Ramah and Gaba, six hundred *t* ... Ezr 2:26 6242
The men of Michmas, an hundred *t* ... Ezr 2:27 6242
of Beth-el and Ai, two hundred *t* ... Ezr 2:28 6242
of Harim, three hundred and *t* ... Ezr 2:32 6242
Hadid, and Ono, seven hundred *t* ... Ezr 2:33 6242
children of Asaph, an hundred *t* ... Ezr 2:41 6242
six thousand seven hundred and *t* ... Ezr 2:67 6242
from *t* years old and upward, to ... Ezr 3:8 6242
the son of Bebai, and with him *t* ... Ezr 8:11 6242
his brethren and their sons, *t* ... Ezr 8:19 6242
two hundred and *t* Nethinims ... Ezr 8:20 6242
Also *t* basons of gold, of a ... Ezr 8:27 6242
So the wall was finished in the *t* ... Neh 6:15 6242
children of Bebai, six hundred *t* ... Neh 7:16 6242
two thousand three hundred *t* ... Neh 7:17 6242
of Hashum, three hundred *t* ... Neh 7:22 6242
of Bezai, three hundred *t* ... Neh 7:23 6242
The men of Anathoth, an hundred *t* ... Neh 7:27 6242
of Ramah and Gaba, six hundred *t* ... Neh 7:30 6242
men of Michmas, an hundred and *t* ... Neh 7:31 6242
of Beth-el and Ai, an hundred *t* ... Neh 7:32 6242
of Harim, three hundred and *t* ... Neh 7:35 6242
Hadid, and Ono, seven hundred *t* ... Neh 7:37 6242
thousand seven hundred and *t* asses ... Neh 7:69 6242
the work *t* thousand drams of gold ... Neh 7:71 7239
gave was *t* thousand drams of gold ... Neh 7:72 7239
Now in the *t* and fourth day of ... Neh 9:1 6242
Gabbai, Sallai, nine hundred *t* ... Neh 11:8 6242
of the house were eight hundred *t* ... Neh 11:12 6242
men of valour, an hundred *t* ... Neh 11:14 6242
hundred and seven and *t* provinces ... Est 1:1 6242
India unto Ethiopia, an hundred *t* ... Est 8:9 6242
all the Jews, to the hundred *t* ... Est 9:30 6242
chariots of God are *t* thousand ... Ps 68:17 7239
t years old when he began to ... Jer 52:1 6242
three thousand Jews and three and *t* ... Jer 52:28 6242
be by weight, *t* shekels a day ... Eze 4:10 6242
t men, with their backs toward ... Eze 8:16 6242
door of the gate five and *t* men ... Eze 11:1 6242
t cubits, door against door ... Eze 40:13 6242
and the breadth five and *t* cubits ... Eze 40:21 6242
and the breadth five and *t* cubits ... Eze 40:25 6242
long, and five and *t* cubits broad ... Eze 40:29 6242
t cubits long, and five cubits ... Eze 40:30 6242
long, and five and *t* cubits broad ... Eze 40:33 6242
and the breadth five and *t* cubits ... Eze 40:36 6242
length of the porch was *t* cubits ... Eze 40:49 6242
and the breadth, *t* cubits ... Eze 41:2 6242
the length thereof, *t* cubits ... Eze 41:4 6242
t cubits, before the temple ... Eze 41:4 6242
chambers was the wideness of *t* ... Eze 41:10 6242
Over against the *t* cubits which ... Eze 42:3 6242
t thousand reeds, and the breadth ... Eze 45:1 6242
t thousand, and the breadth of ten ... Eze 45:3 6242
t thousand of length, and the ten ... Eze 45:5 6242
for a possession for *t* chambers ... Eze 45:5 6242
t thousand long, over against the ... Eze 45:6 6242
And the shekel shall be *t* gerahs ... Eze 45:12 6242
t shekels, five and *t* shekels ... Eze 45:12 6242
t thousand reeds in breadth, and ... Eze 48:8 6242
t thousand in length, and of ten ... Eze 48:9 6242
t thousand in length, and toward ... Eze 48:10 6242
five and *t* thousand in length ... Eze 48:10 6242
t thousand in length, and ten ... Eze 48:13 6242
t thousand, and the breadth ten ... Eze 48:13 6242
t thousand, shall be a profane ... Eze 48:15 6242
t thousand by five and ... Eze 48:20 6242
thousand by five and *t* thousand ... Eze 48:20 6242
t thousand of the oblation toward ... Eze 48:21 6242
t thousand toward the west border ... Eze 48:21 6242
t princes, which should be over ... Dan 6:1 6243
Persia withstood me one and *t* days ... Dan 10:13 6242
one came to an heap of *t* measures ... Hag 2:16 6242
of the press, there were but *t* ... Hag 2:16 6242
the length thereof is *t* cubits ... Zec 5:2 6242
against him with *t* thousand ... Lk 14:31 *1501*
t or thirty furlongs, they see ... Jn 6:19 *1501*
were about an hundred and *t* ... Acts 1:15 *1501*
And sounded, and found it *t* fathoms ... Acts 27:28 *1501*
in one day three and *t* thousand ... 1Cor 10:8 *1501*
the throne were four and *t* seats ... Rev 4:4 *1501*
t elders sitting, clothed in ... Rev 4:4 *1501*
t elders fall down before him ... Rev 4:10 *1501*
t elders fell down before the ... Rev 5:8 *1501*
t elders fell down and worshipped ... Rev 5:14 *1501*
t elders, which sat before God on ... Rev 11:16 *1501*
t elders and the four beasts fell ... Rev 19:4 *1501*

TWENTY'S

I will not destroy it for *t* sake ... Gen 18:31 6242

TWICE

dream was doubled unto Pharaoh *t* ... Gen 41:32 6471
it shall be *t* as much as they ... Ex 16:5 4932
day they gathered *t* as much bread ... Ex 16:22 4932
with his rod he smote the rock *t* ... Num 20:11 6471
avoided out of his presence *t* ... 1Sa 18:11 6471
which had appeared unto him *t* ... 1Kin 11:9 6471
himself there, not once nor *t* ... 2Kin 6:10 8147
without Jerusalem once or *t* ... Neh 13:20 8147
For God speaketh once, yea *t* ... Job 33:14 8147
will not answer: yea, *t* ... Job 40:5 8147
also the LORD gave Job *t* as much ... Job 42:10 4932
t have I heard this ... Ps 62:11 8147
he live a thousand years *t* told ... Eccl 6:6 6471
night, before the cock crow *t* ... Mk 14:30 *1364*
unto him, Before the cock crow *t* ... Mk 14:72 *1364*
I fast *t* in the week, I give ... Lk 18:12 *1364*
t dead, plucked up by the roots ... Jude 12 *1364*

TWIGS

off the top of his young *t* ... Eze 17:4 3242
top of his young *t* a tender one ... Eze 17:22 3127

TWILIGHT

David smote them from the *t* even ... 1Sa 30:17 5399
And they rose up in the *t*, to go ... 2Kin 7:5 5399
they arose and fled in the *t* ... 2Kin 7:7 5399
stars of the *t* thereof be dark ... Job 3:9 5399
the adulterer waiteth for the *t* ... Job 24:15 5399
In the *t*, in the evening, in the ... Prov 7:9 5399
and carry it forth in the *t* ... Eze 12:6 5939
I brought it forth in the *t* ... Eze 12:7 5939
bear upon his shoulder in the *t* ... Eze 12:12 5939

TWINED

with ten curtains of fine *t* linen ... Ex 26:1 7806
fine *t* linen of cunning work ... Ex 26:31 7806
fine *t* linen, wrought with ... Ex 26:36 7806
hangings for the court of fine *t* ... Ex 27:9 7806
fine *t* linen, wrought with ... Ex 27:16 7806
five cubits of fine *t* linen ... Ex 27:18 7806
fine *t* linen, with cunning work ... Ex 28:6 7806
and scarlet, and fine *t* linen ... Ex 28:8 7806
and of scarlet, and of fine *t* linen ... Ex 28:15 7806
made ten curtains of fine *t* linen ... Ex 36:8 7806
and scarlet, and fine *t* linen ... Ex 36:35 7806
fine *t* linen, of needlework ... Ex 36:37 7806
of the court were of fine *t* linen ... Ex 38:9 7806
round about were of fine *t* linen ... Ex 38:16 7806
and scarlet, and fine *t* linen ... Ex 38:18 7806
and scarlet, and fine *t* linen ... Ex 39:2 7806
and scarlet, and fine *t* linen ... Ex 39:5 7806
and scarlet, and fine *t* linen ... Ex 39:8 7806
and purple, and scarlet, and *t* linen ... Ex 39:24 7806
and linen breeches of fine *t* linen ... Ex 39:28 7806
And a girdle of fine *t* linen ... Ex 39:29 7806

TWINKLING

in the *t* of an eye, at the last ... 1Cor 15:52 *4493*

TWINS

behold, there were *t* in her womb ... Gen 25:24 8380
that, behold, *t* were in her womb ... Gen 38:27 8380
whereof every one bear *t*, and none ... Song 4:2 8382
like two young roes that are *t* ... Song 4:5 8380
whereof every one beareth *t* ... Song 6:6 8382
like two young roes that are *t* ... Song 7:3 8380

TWO

And God made *t* great lights ... Gen 1:16 8147
And Lamech took unto him *t* wives ... Gen 4:19 8147
t years, and he begat Enoch ... Gen 5:18 8147
nine hundred sixty and *t* years ... Gen 5:20 8147
t years, and begat sons and ... Gen 5:26 8147
eighty and *t* years, and begat a son ... Gen 5:28 8147
t of every sort shalt thou bring ... Gen 6:19 8147
t of every sort shall come unto ... Gen 6:20 8147
of beasts that are not clean by *t* ... Gen 7:2 8147
There went in *t* and *t* unto Noah ... Gen 7:9 8147
went in unto Noah into the ark, *t* ... Gen 7:15 8147
t of all flesh, wherein is the ... Gen 7:15 8147
told his *t* brethren without ... Gen 9:22 8147
And unto Eber were born *t* sons ... Gen 10:25 8147
begat Arphaxad *t* years after the ... Gen 11:10 8147
after he begat Reu *t* hundred ... Gen 11:19 8147
And Reu lived *t* and thirty years, ... Gen 11:20 8147
after he begat Serug *t* hundred ... Gen 11:21 8147
he begat Nahor *t* hundred years ... Gen 11:23 8147
the days of Terah were *t* hundred ... Gen 11:32 8147
there came *t* angels to Sodom at ... Gen 19:1 8147
I have *t* daughters which have not ... Gen 19:8 8147
thy *t* daughters, which are here ... Gen 19:15 8147
upon the hand of his *t* daughters ... Gen 19:16 8147
and his *t* daughters with him ... Gen 19:30 8147
in a cave, he and his *t* daughters ... Gen 19:30 8147
took *t* of his young men with him, ... Gen 22:3 8147
t bracelets for her hands of ten ... Gen 24:22 8147
T nations are in thy womb ... Gen 25:23 8147
t manner of people shall be ... Gen 25:23 8147
fetch me from thence *t* good kids ... Gen 27:9 8147
hath supplanted me these *t* times ... Gen 27:36 6471
And Laban had *t* daughters ... Gen 29:16 8147
into the *t* maidservants' tents ... Gen 31:33 8147
years for thy *t* daughters ... Gen 31:41 8147
and the camels, into *t* bands ... Gen 32:7 8147
and now I am become *t* bands ... Gen 32:10 8147
T hundred she goats, and twenty he ... Gen 32:14
t hundred ewes, and twenty rams, ... Gen 32:14
that night, and took his *t* wives ... Gen 32:22 8147
his *t* womenservants, and his ... Gen 32:22 8147
Rachel, and unto the *t* handmaids ... Gen 33:1 8147
that *t* of the sons of Jacob, ... Gen 34:25 8147
wroth against *t* of his officers ... Gen 40:2 8147
pass at the end of *t* full years ... Gen 41:1
unto Joseph were born *t* sons ... Gen 41:50 8147
father, saying, Slay my *t* sons ... Gen 42:37 8147
know that my wife bare me *t* sons ... Gen 44:27 8147
For these *t* years hath the famine ... Gen 45:6
born him in Egypt, were *t* souls ... Gen 46:27 8147
and he took with him his *t* sons ... Gen 48:1 8147
And now thy *t* sons, Ephraim and ... Gen 48:5 8147
couching down between *t* burdens ... Gen 49:14
t men of the Hebrews strove ... Ex 2:13 8147
not believe also these *t* signs ... Ex 4:9 8147
and strike it on the *t* side posts ... Ex 12:7 8147
the *t* side posts with the blood ... Ex 12:22 8147
on the *t* side posts, the LORD ... Ex 12:23 8147
much bread, *t* omers for one man ... Ex 16:22 8147
the sixth day the bread of *t* days ... Ex 16:29 8147
And her *t* sons ... Ex 18:3 8147
thy wife, and her *t* sons with her ... Ex 18:6 8147
if he continue a day or *t* ... Ex 21:21
t cubits and a half shall be the ... Ex 25:10
t rings shall be in the one side ... Ex 25:12 8147
t rings in the other side of it ... Ex 25:12 8147
t cubits and a half shall be the ... Ex 25:17
thou shalt make *t* cherubims of ... Ex 25:18 8147
in the *t* ends of the mercy seat ... Ex 25:18 8147
cherubims on the *t* ends thereof ... Ex 25:19 8147
from between the *t* cherubims ... Ex 25:22 8147
t cubits shall be the length ... Ex 25:23
knop under *t* branches of the same ... Ex 25:35 8147
a knop under *t* branches of the ... Ex 25:35 8147
a knop under *t* branches of the ... Ex 25:35 8147
T tenons shall there be in one ... Ex 26:17 8147
t sockets under one board for his ... Ex 26:19 8147
under one board for his *t* tenons ... Ex 26:19 8147
t sockets under another board for ... Ex 26:19 8147
another board for his *t* tenons ... Ex 26:19 8147
t sockets under one board ... Ex 26:21 8147
t sockets under another board ... Ex 26:21 8147
t boards shalt thou make for the ... Ex 26:23 8147
of the tabernacle in the *t* sides ... Ex 26:23
they shall be for the *t* corners ... Ex 26:24 8147
t sockets under one board ... Ex 26:25 8147

t sockets under another board ... Ex 26:25 8147
for the *t* sides westward ... Ex 26:27
be upon the *t* sides of the altar ... Ex 27:7 8147
It shall have the *t* ... Ex 28:7 8147
joined at the *t* edges thereof ... Ex 28:7 8147
And thou shalt take *t* onyx stones ... Ex 28:9 8147
shalt thou engrave the *t* stones ... Ex 28:11 8147
thou shalt put the *t* stones upon ... Ex 28:12 8147
his *t* shoulders for a memorial ... Ex 28:12 8147
t chains of pure gold at the ends ... Ex 28:14 8147
the breastplate *t* rings of gold ... Ex 28:23 8147
shalt put the *t* rings ... Ex 28:23 8147
on the *t* ends of the breastplate ... Ex 28:23 8147
thou shalt put the *t* wreathen ... Ex 28:24 8147
t rings which are on the ends of ... Ex 28:24 8147
the other *t* ends of the *t* ... Ex 28:25 8147
thou shalt fasten in the *t* ouches ... Ex 28:25 8147
thou shalt make *t* rings of gold ... Ex 28:26 8147
thou shalt put them upon the *t* ... Ex 28:26 8147
t other rings of gold thou shalt ... Ex 28:27 8147
shalt put them on the *t* sides of ... Ex 28:27 8147
and *t* rams without blemish, ... Ex 29:1 8147
with the bullock and the *t* rams ... Ex 29:3 8147
the *t* kidneys, and the fat that is ... Ex 29:13 8147
the *t* kidneys, and the fat that is ... Ex 29:22 8147
t lambs of the first year day by ... Ex 29:38 8147
t cubits shall be the height ... Ex 30:2
t golden rings shalt thou make to ... Ex 30:4 8147
by the *t* corners thereof, upon ... Ex 30:4 8147
upon the *t* sides of it shalt thou ... Ex 30:4 8147
even *t* hundred and fifty shekels, ... Ex 30:23
and of sweet calamus *t* hundred ... Ex 30:23
t tables of testimony, tables of ... Ex 31:18 8147
the *t* tables of the testimony ... Ex 32:15 8147
Hew thee *t* tables of stone like ... Ex 34:1 8147
he hewed *t* tables of stone like ... Ex 34:4 8147
in his hand the *t* tables of stone ... Ex 34:4 8147
t tables of testimony in Moses' ... Ex 34:29 8147
One board had *t* tenons, equally ... Ex 36:22 8147
t sockets under one board for his ... Ex 36:24 8147
under one board for his *t* tenons ... Ex 36:24 8147
t sockets under another board for ... Ex 36:24 8147
another board for his *t* tenons ... Ex 36:24 8147
t sockets under one board ... Ex 36:26 8147
t sockets under another board ... Ex 36:26 8147
t boards made he for the corners ... Ex 36:28 8147
of the tabernacle in the *t* sides ... Ex 36:28
under every board *t* sockets ... Ex 36:30 8147
t cubits and a half was the length ... Ex 37:1
even *t* rings upon the one side of ... Ex 37:3 8147
t rings upon the other side of it ... Ex 37:3 8147
t cubits and a half was the length ... Ex 37:6
he made *t* cherubims of gold, ... Ex 37:7 8147
on the *t* ends of the mercy seat ... Ex 37:7 8147
cherubims on the *t* ends thereof ... Ex 37:8 8147
t cubits was the length thereof, ... Ex 37:10
a knop under *t* branches of the ... Ex 37:21 8147
a knop under *t* branches of the ... Ex 37:21 8147
a knop under *t* branches of the ... Ex 37:21 8147
t cubits was the height of it ... Ex 37:25
he made *t* rings of gold for it ... Ex 37:27 8147
by the *t* corners of it, upon the ... Ex 37:27 8147
upon the *t* sides thereof, to be ... Ex 37:27 8147
t thousand and four hundred ... Ex 38:29
by the *t* edges was it coupled ... Ex 39:4 8147
they made *t* ouches of gold, and ... Ex 39:16 8147
ouches of gold, and *t* gold rings ... Ex 39:16 8147
put the *t* rings in the *t* ends ... Ex 39:16 8147
they put the *t* wreathen chains of ... Ex 39:17 8147
in the *t* rings on the ends of the ... Ex 39:17 8147
the *t* ends of the *t* wreathen ... Ex 39:18 8147
they fastened in the *t* ouches ... Ex 39:18 8147
they made *t* rings of gold, and put ... Ex 39:19 8147
put them on the *t* ends of the ... Ex 39:19 8147
they made *t* other golden rings, ... Ex 39:20 8147
put them on the *t* sides of the ... Ex 39:20 8147
the *t* kidneys, and the fat that is ... Lev 3:4 8147
the *t* kidneys, and the fat that is ... Lev 3:10 8147
the *t* kidneys, and the fat that is ... Lev 3:15 8147
the *t* kidneys, and the fat that is ... Lev 4:9 8147
t turtledoves, or *t* young ... Lev 5:7 8147
not able to bring *t* turtledoves ... Lev 5:11 8147
or *t* young pigeons, then he that ... Lev 5:11 8147
the *t* kidneys, and the fat that is ... Lev 7:4 8147
t rams, and a basket of unleavened ... Lev 8:2 8147
the *t* kidneys, and their fat, and ... Lev 8:16 8147
the *t* kidneys, and their fat, and ... Lev 8:25 8147
then she shall be unclean *t* weeks ... Lev 12:5
t turtles, or *t* young pigeons ... Lev 12:8 8147
is to be cleansed *t* birds alive ... Lev 14:4 8147
take *t* he lambs without blemish ... Lev 14:10 8147
t turtledoves, or *t* young ... Lev 14:22 8147
take to cleanse the house *t* birds ... Lev 14:49 8147
shall take to him *t* turtledoves ... Lev 15:14 8147
or *t* young pigeons, and come ... Lev 15:14 8147
she shall take unto her *t* turtles ... Lev 15:29 8147
or *t* young pigeons, and bring them ... Lev 15:29 8147
the death of the *t* sons of Aaron ... Lev 16:1 8147
of the children of Israel *t* kids ... Lev 16:5 8147
And he shall take the *t* goats ... Lev 16:7 8147
shall cast lots upon the *t* goats ... Lev 16:8 8147
be *t* tenth deals of fine flour ... Lev 23:13 8147
t wave loaves of *t* tenth deals ... Lev 23:17 8147
and one young bullock, and *t* rams ... Lev 23:18 8147
t lambs of the first year for a ... Lev 23:19 8147
before the LORD, with the *t* lambs ... Lev 23:20 8147
t tenth deals shall be in one ... Lev 24:5 8147
And thou shalt set them in *t* rows ... Lev 24:6 8147
t thousand and *t* hundred ... Num 1:35 8147
t thousand and seven hundred ... Num 1:39 8147
t thousand and *t* hundred ... Num 2:21 8147
and *t* thousand and *t* hundred ... Num 2:21
t thousand and seven hundred ... Num 2:26 8147
were six thousand and *t* hundred ... Num 3:34

upward, were twenty and *t* thousand ... Num 3:39 8147
t thousand *t* hundred and ... Num 3:43 8147
to be redeemed of the *t* hundred ... Num 3:46
were *t* thousand seven hundred ... Num 4:36
were *t* thousand and six hundred and ... Num 4:40
were three thousand and *t* hundred ... Num 4:44
day he shall bring *t* turtles ... Num 6:10 8147
or *t* young pigeons, to the priest ... Num 6:10 8147
a wagon for *t* of the princes, and ... Num 7:3 8147
T wagons and four oxen he gave ... Num 7:7 8147
t oxen, five rams, five he goats, ... Num 7:17 8147
t oxen, five rams, five he goats, ... Num 7:23 8147
t oxen, five rams, five he goats, ... Num 7:29 8147
t oxen, five rams, five he goats, ... Num 7:35 8147
t oxen, five rams, five he goats, ... Num 7:41 8147
t oxen, five rams, five he goats, ... Num 7:47 8147
t oxen, five rams, five he goats, ... Num 7:53 8147
t oxen, five rams, five he goats, ... Num 7:59 8147
t oxen, five rams, five he goats, ... Num 7:65 8147
t oxen, five rams, five he goats, ... Num 7:71 8147
t oxen, five rams, five he goats, ... Num 7:77 8147
t oxen, five rams, five he goats, ... Num 7:83 8147
silver vessels weighed *t* thousand ... Num 7:85
from between the *t* cherubims ... Num 7:89 8147
Or whether it were *t* days ... Num 9:22
Make thee *t* trumpets of silver ... Num 10:2 8147
nor *t* days, nor five days, ... Num 11:19
But there remained *t* of the men ... Num 11:26 8147
as it were *t* cubits high upon the ... Num 11:31
bare it between *t* upon a staff ... Num 13:23 8147
prepare for a meat offering *t* ... Num 15:6 8147
t hundred and fifty princes of the ... Num 16:2
t hundred and fifty censers ... Num 16:17
LORD, and consumed the *t* hundred ... Num 16:35
his *t* servants were with him ... Num 22:22 8147
time the fire devoured *t* hundred ... Num 26:10
t thousand and *t* hundred ... Num 26:14 8147
t thousand and seven hundred ... Num 26:34 8147
t thousand and five hundred ... Num 26:37 8147
t lambs of the first year without ... Num 28:3 8147
on the sabbath day *t* lambs of the ... Num 28:9 8147
t tenth deals of flour for a meat ... Num 28:9 8147
t young bullocks, and one ram, ... Num 28:11 8147
t tenth deals of flour for a meat ... Num 28:12 8147
t young bullocks, and one ram, and ... Num 28:19 8147
and *t* tenth deals for a ram ... Num 28:20 8147
t young bullocks, one ram, seven ... Num 28:27 8147
t tenth deals unto one ram, ... Num 28:28 8147
and *t* tenth deals for a ram, ... Num 29:3 8147
t tenth deals to one ram, ... Num 29:9 8147
t rams, and fourteen lambs of the ... Num 29:13 8147
t tenth deals to each ram of the ... Num 29:14 8147
deals to each ram of the *t* rams ... Num 29:14 8147
t rams, fourteen lambs of the ... Num 29:17 8147
t rams, fourteen lambs of the ... Num 29:20 8147
t rams, and fourteen lambs of the ... Num 29:23 8147
t rams, and fourteen lambs of the ... Num 29:26 8147
t rams, and fourteen lambs of the ... Num 29:29 8147
t rams, and fourteen lambs of the ... Num 29:32 8147
And divide the prey into *t* parts ... Num 31:27 8147
t thousand persons in all, of ... Num 31:35 8147
tribute was thirty and *t* persons ... Num 31:40 8147
The *t* tribes and the half tribe ... Num 34:15 8147
the east side *t* thousand cubits ... Num 35:5
the south side *t* thousand cubits ... Num 35:5
the west side *t* thousand cubits ... Num 35:5
the north side *t* thousand cubits ... Num 35:5
ye shall add forty and *t* cities ... Num 35:6 8147
time out of the hand of the *t* ... Deut 3:8 8147
God hath done unto these *t* kings ... Deut 3:21 8147
wrote them upon *t* tables of stone ... Deut 4:13 8147
t kings of the Amorites, which ... Deut 4:47 8147
wrote them in *t* tables of stone ... Deut 5:22 8147
the LORD delivered unto me *t* ... Deut 9:10 8147
gave me the *t* tables of stone ... Deut 9:11 8147
the *t* tables of the covenant were ... Deut 9:15 8147
the covenant were in my *t* hands ... Deut 9:15 8147
And I took the *t* tables, and cast ... Deut 9:17 8147
and cast them out of my *t* hands ... Deut 9:17 8147
Hew thee *t* tables of stone like ... Deut 10:1 8147
hewed *t* tables of stone like unto ... Deut 10:3 8147
having the *t* tables in mine hand ... Deut 10:3 8147
cleaveth the cleft into *t* claws ... Deut 14:6 8147
At the mouth of *t* witnesses ... Deut 17:6 8147
and the *t* cheeks, and the maw ... Deut 18:3 8147
at the mouth of *t* witnesses ... Deut 19:15 8147
If a man have *t* wives, one ... Deut 21:15 8147
t put ten thousand to flight, ... Deut 32:30 8147
of Shittim *t* men to spy secretly ... Josh 2:1 8147
And the woman took the *t* men ... Josh 2:4 8147
what ye did unto the *t* kings of ... Josh 2:10 8147
So the *t* men returned, and ... Josh 2:23 8147
about *t* thousand cubits by ... Josh 3:4
the *t* men that had spied out the ... Josh 6:22 8147
but let about *t* or three thousand ... Josh 7:3
t hundred shekels of silver, and a ... Josh 7:21 8147
to the *t* kings of the Amorites ... Josh 9:10 8147
given the inheritance of *t* tribes ... Josh 14:3 8147
children of Joseph were *t* tribes ... Josh 14:4 8147
t cities with their villages ... Josh 15:60 8147
t cities with their villages ... Josh 19:30 8147
nine cities out of those *t* tribes ... Josh 21:16 8147
with her suburbs; *t* cities ... Josh 21:25 8147
with her suburbs; *t* cities ... Josh 21:27 8147
even the *t* kings of the Amorites ... Josh 24:12 8147
him a dagger which had *t* edges ... Judg 3:16 8147
to every man a damsel or *t* ... Judg 5:30
the people twenty and *t* thousand ... Judg 7:3 8147
they took *t* princes of the ... Judg 7:25 8147
took the *t* kings of Midian, Zebah ... Judg 8:12 8147
the *t* other companies ran upon ... Judg 9:44 8147
judged Israel twenty and *t* years ... Judg 10:3 8147
let me alone *t* months, that I may ... Judg 11:37 8147
And he sent her away for *t* months ... Judg 11:38 8147

to pass at the end of *t* months ... Judg 11:39 8147
Ephraimites forty and *t* thousand ... Judg 12:6 8147
in the midst between *t* tails ... Judg 15:4 8147
they bound him with *t* new cords ... Judg 15:13 8147
the *t* posts, and went away with ... Judg 16:3 8147
of the Philistines for my *t* eyes ... Judg 16:28 8147
Samson took hold of the *t* middle ... Judg 16:29 8147
his mother took *t* hundred shekels ... Judg 17:4
were with him *t* asses saddled ... Judg 19:10 6771
that day twenty and *t* thousand men ... Judg 20:21 8147
slew *t* thousand men of them ... Judg 20:45
he, and his wife, and his *t* sons ... Ruth 1:1 8147
and the name of his *t* sons Mahlon ... Ruth 1:2 8147
and she was left, and her *t* sons ... Ruth 1:3 8147
the woman was left of her *t* sons ... Ruth 1:5 8147
her *t* daughters in law with her ... Ruth 1:7 8147
said unto her *t* daughters in law ... Ruth 1:8 8147
So they *t* went until they came to ... Ruth 1:19 8147
which *t* did build the house of ... Ruth 4:11 8147
And he had *t* wives ... 1Sa 1:2 8147
the *t* sons of Eli, Hophni and ... 1Sa 1:3 8147
and bare three sons and *t* daughters ... 1Sa 2:21 8147
that shall come upon thy *t* sons ... 1Sa 2:34 8147
the *t* sons of Eli, Hophni and ... 1Sa 4:4 8147
the *t* sons of Eli, Hophni and ... 1Sa 4:11 8147
thy *t* sons also, Hophni and ... 1Sa 4:17 8147
take *t* milch kine, on which there ... 1Sa 6:7 8147
took *t* milch kine, and tied them ... 1Sa 6:10 8147
then thou shalt find *t* men by ... 1Sa 10:2 8147
give thee *t* loaves of bread ... 1Sa 10:4 8147
so that *t* of them were not left ... 1Sa 11:11 8147
had reigned *t* years over Israel ... 1Sa 13:1 8147
whereof *t* thousand were with Saul ... 1Sa 13:2
the names of his *t* daughters were ... 1Sa 14:49 8147
t hundred thousand footmen, and ... 1Sa 15:4
of the Philistines *t* hundred men ... 1Sa 18:27
they *t* made a covenant before the ... 1Sa 23:18 8147
t hundred abode by the stuff ... 1Sa 25:13
took *t* hundred loaves ... 1Sa 25:18
t bottles of wine, and five sheep ... 1Sa 25:18 8147
t hundred cakes of figs, and laid ... 1Sa 25:18
even David with his *t* wives ... 1Sa 27:3 8147
t men with him, and they came to ... 1Sa 28:8 8147
David's *t* wives were taken ... 1Sa 30:5 8147
for *t* hundred abode behind, which ... 1Sa 30:10
of figs, and *t* clusters of raisins ... 1Sa 30:12 8147
and David rescued his *t* wives ... 1Sa 30:18 8147
David came to the *t* hundred men ... 1Sa 30:21
David had abode *t* days in Ziklag ... 2Sa 1:1 8147
his *t* wives also, Ahinoam the ... 2Sa 2:2 8147
over Israel, and reigned *t* years ... 2Sa 2:10 8147
Saul's son had *t* men that were ... 2Sa 4:2 8147
even with *t* lines measured he to ... 2Sa 8:2 8147
David slew of the Syrians *t* ... 2Sa 8:5 8147
There were *t* men in one city ... 2Sa 12:1 8147
came to pass after *t* full years ... 2Sa 13:23
And thy handmaid had *t* sons ... 2Sa 14:6 8147
they *t* strove together in the ... 2Sa 14:6 8147
at *t* hundred shekels after the ... 2Sa 14:26 8147
So Absalom dwelt *t* full years in ... 2Sa 14:28
with Absalom went *t* hundred men ... 2Sa 15:11
your *t* sons with you, Ahimaaz thy ... 2Sa 15:27 8147
have there with them their *t* sons ... 2Sa 15:36 8147
upon them *t* hundred loaves of ... 2Sa 16:1
And David sat between the *t* gates ... 2Sa 18:24 8147
But the king took the *t* sons of ... 2Sa 21:8 8147
he slew *t* lionlike men of Moab ... 2Sa 23:20 8147
what he did to the *t* captains of ... 1Kin 2:5 8147
head, who fell upon *t* men more ... 1Kin 2:32 8147
that *t* of the servants of Shimei ... 1Kin 2:39 8147
Then came there *t* women, that ... 1Kin 3:16 8147
the house, save we *t* in the house ... 1Kin 3:18 8147
Divide the living child in *t* ... 1Kin 3:25 8147
they *t* made a league together ... 1Kin 5:12 8147
in Lebanon, and *t* months at home ... 1Kin 5:14 8147
he made *t* cherubims of olive tree ... 1Kin 6:23 8147
The *t* doors also were of olive ... 1Kin 6:32 8147
the *t* doors were of fir tree ... 1Kin 6:34 8147
the *t* leaves of the one door were ... 1Kin 6:34 8147
the *t* leaves of the other door ... 1Kin 6:34 8147
For he cast *t* pillars of brass, ... 1Kin 7:15 8147
he made *t* chapiters of molten ... 1Kin 7:16 8147
t rows round about upon the one ... 1Kin 7:18 8147
the chapiters upon the *t* pillars ... 1Kin 7:20 8147
the pomegranates were *t* hundred ... 1Kin 7:20
the knops were cast in *t* rows ... 1Kin 7:24 8147
it contained *t* thousand baths ... 1Kin 7:26
The *t* pillars, and the *t* bowls ... 1Kin 7:41 8147
were on the top of the *t* pillars ... 1Kin 7:41 8147
the *t* networks, to cover ... 1Kin 7:41 8147
to cover the *t* bowls of the ... 1Kin 7:41 8147
pomegranates for the *t* networks ... 1Kin 7:42 8147
even *t* rows of pomegranates for ... 1Kin 7:42 8147
to cover the *t* bowls of the ... 1Kin 7:42 8147
cherubims spread forth their *t* ... 1Kin 8:7
ark save the *t* tables of stone ... 1Kin 8:9 8147
which he offered unto the LORD, *t* ... 1Kin 8:63 8147
Solomon had built the *t* houses ... 1Kin 9:10 8147
king Solomon made *t* hundred ... 1Kin 10:16
t lions stood beside the stays ... 1Kin 10:19 8147
they *t* were alone in the field ... 1Kin 11:29 8147
made *t* calves of gold, and said ... 1Kin 12:28 8147
which Jeroboam reigned were *t* ... 1Kin 14:20 8147
and reigned over Israel *t* years ... 1Kin 15:25 8147
over Israel in Tirzah, *t* years ... 1Kin 16:8
of Israel divided into *t* parts ... 1Kin 16:21 2677
of Shemer for *t* talents of silver ... 1Kin 16:24
in Samaria twenty and *t* years ... 1Kin 16:29 8147
behold, I am gathering *t* sticks ... 1Kin 17:12 8147
long halt ye between *t* opinions ... 1Kin 18:21 8147
them therefore give us *t* bullocks ... 1Kin 18:23 8147
would contain *t* measures of seed ... 1Kin 18:32
t kings with him, and horses, and ... 1Kin 20:1 8147
they were *t* hundred and thirty *t* ... 1Kin 20:15 8147

T

thirty and *t* kings that helped him 1Kin 20:16 8147
them like *t* little flocks of kids 1Kin 20:27 8147
And set *t* men, sons of Belial, 1Kin 21:10 8147
And there came in *t* men, children 1Kin 21:13 8147
t captains that had rule over his 1Kin 22:31 8147
reigned *t* years over Israel 1Kin 22:51
burnt up the *t* captains of the 2Kin 1:14 8147
And they *t* went on 2Kin 2:6 8147
and they *t* stood by Jordan 2Kin 2:7 8147
so that they *t* went over on dry 2Kin 2:8 8147
clothes, and rent them in *t* pieces 2Kin 2:12 8147
there came forth *t* she bears out 2Kin 2:24 8147
tare forty and *t* children of them 2Kin 2:24 8147
unto him my *t* sons to be bondmen 2Kin 4:1 8147
servant *t* mules' burden of earth 2Kin 5:17
t young men of the sons of the 2Kin 5:22 8147
silver, and *t* changes of garments 2Kin 5:22 8147
said, Be content, take *t* talents 2Kin 5:23
t talents of silver in *t* bags 2Kin 5:23 8147
with *t* changes of garments, and 2Kin 5:23 8147
laid them upon *t* of his servants 2Kin 5:23 8147
t measures of barley for a shekel 2Kin 7:1
took therefore *t* chariot horses 2Kin 7:14 8147
t measures of barley for a shekel 2Kin 7:16
T measures of barley for a shekel 2Kin 7:18
t years old was he when he began 2Kin 8:17 8147
T and twenty years old was Ahaziah 2Kin 8:26 8147
out to him *t* or three eunuchs 2Kin 9:32 8147
t kings stood not before him 2Kin 10:4 8147
Lay ye them in *t* heaps at the 2Kin 10:8 8147
pit of the shearing house, even *t* 2Kin 10:14 8147
t parts of all you that go forth 2Kin 11:7 8147
began to reign, and he reigned *t* 2Kin 15:2 8147
in Samaria, and reigned *t* years 2Kin 15:23 8147
In the *t* and fiftieth year of 2Kin 15:27 8147
even *t* calves, and made a grove, 2Kin 17:16 8147
deliver thee *t* thousand horses 2Kin 18:23
all the host of heaven in the *t* 2Kin 21:5 8147
t years old when he began to 2Kin 21:19 8147
he reigned *t* years in Jerusalem 2Kin 21:19 8147
which Manasseh had made in the *t* 2Kin 23:12 8147
way of the gate between *t* walls 2Kin 25:4 8147
The *t* pillars, one sea, and the 2Kin 25:16 8147
And unto Eber were born *t* sons 1Chr 1:19 8147
the father of Tekoa had *t* wives 1Chr 4:5 8147
thousand, and of sheep *t* hundred 1Chr 5:21
thousand, and of asses *t* thousand 1Chr 5:21
number was in the days of David *t* 1Chr 7:2 8147
t thousand and thirty and four 1Chr 7:7 8147
was twenty thousand and *t* hundred 1Chr 7:9
t hundred soldiers, fit to go out 1Chr 7:11
in the gates were *t* hundred 1Chr 9:22
he was more honourable than the *t* 1Chr 11:21 8147
he slew *t* lionlike men of Moab 1Chr 11:22 8147
house twenty and *t* captains 1Chr 12:28 8147
the heads of them were *t* hundred 1Chr 12:32
chief, and his brethren *t* hundred 1Chr 15:6
chief, and his brethren *t* hundred 1Chr 15:8
David slew of the Syrians *t* 1Chr 18:5
t thousand chariots, and the king 1Chr 19:7 8147
one and twentieth to Jachin, the *t* 1Chr 24:17 8147
was *t* hundred fourscore and eight 1Chr 25:7
The *t* and twentieth to Giddalti, 1Chr 25:29 8147
were threescore and *t* of Obed-edom 1Chr 26:8 8147
a day, and toward Asuppim *t* and *t* 1Chr 26:17 8147
at the causeway, and *t* at Parbar 1Chr 26:18 8147
were *t* thousand and seven hundred 1Chr 26:32
he made *t* cherubims of image work 2Chr 3:10 8147
the house *t* pillars of thirty 2Chr 3:15 8147
T rows of oxen were cast, when it 2Chr 4:3 8147
the *t* pillars, and the pommels, and 2Chr 4:12 8147
were on the top of the *t* pillars 2Chr 4:12 8147
the *t* wreaths to cover the *t* 2Chr 4:12 8147
pomegranates on the *t* wreaths 2Chr 4:13 8147
t rows of pomegranates on each 2Chr 4:13 8147
to cover the *t* pommels of the 2Chr 4:13 8147
t tables which Moses put therein 2Chr 5:10 8147
t thousand oxen, and an hundred and 2Chr 7:5 8147
even *t* hundred and fifty, that 2Chr 8:10
king Solomon made *t* hundred 2Chr 9:15
t lions standing by the stays 2Chr 9:18 8147
t sons, and sixteen daughters 2Chr 13:21 8147
t hundred and fourscore thousand 2Chr 14:8
captain, and with him *t* hundred 2Chr 17:15
with him *t* hundred thousand 2Chr 17:16
shield *t* hundred thousand 2Chr 17:17
t years old when he began to 2Chr 21:5 8147
of time, after the end of *t* years 2Chr 21:19 8147
t years old was he when he began 2Chr 21:20 8147
t years old was Ahaziah when he 2Chr 22:2 8147
And Jehoiada took for him *t* wives 2Chr 24:3 8147
fifty and *t* years in Jerusalem 2Chr 26:3 8147
men of valour were *t* thousand 2Chr 26:12
their brethren *t* hundred thousand 2Chr 28:8
hundred rams, and *t* hundred lambs 2Chr 29:32
all the host of heaven in the *t* 2Chr 33:5 8147
Amon was *t* and twenty years old 2Chr 33:21
reigned *t* years in Jerusalem 2Chr 33:21
the passover offerings *t* thousand 2Chr 35:8
t thousand an hundred seventy and Ezr 2:3
thousand an hundred seventy and *t* Ezr 2:3 8147
three hundred seventy and *t* Ezr 2:4
t thousand eight hundred and Ezr 2:6
a thousand *t* hundred fifty and Ezr 2:7
of Bani, six hundred forty and *t* Ezr 2:10 8147
thousand *t* hundred twenty and *t* Ezr 2:12 8147
Bigvai, *t* thousand fifty and six Ezr 2:14
t hundred twenty and three Ezr 2:19
children of Azmaveth, forty and *t* Ezr 2:24 8147
Michmas, an hundred twenty and *t* Ezr 2:27 8147
t hundred twenty and three Ezr 2:28
The children of Nebo, fifty and *t* Ezr 2:29 8147
a thousand *t* hundred fifty and Ezr 2:31
of Immer, a thousand fifty and *t* Ezr 2:37 8147
a thousand *t* hundred forty and Ezr 2:38
were three hundred ninety and *t* Ezr 2:58 8147
of Nekoda, six hundred fifty and *t* Ezr 2:60 8147
t thousand three hundred and Ezr 2:64
among them *t* hundred singing men Ezr 2:65
mules, *t* hundred forty and five Ezr 2:66
t hundred rams, four hundred Ezr 6:17
and with him *t* hundred males Ezr 8:4
of Jehiel, and with him *t* hundred Ezr 8:9
t hundred and twenty Nethinims Ezr 8:20
t vessels of fine copper, Ezr 8:27 8147
is this a work of one day or *t* Ezr 10:13 8147
twentieth year even unto the *t* Neh 5:14 8147
month Elul, in fifty and *t* days Neh 6:15 8147
t thousand an hundred seventy and Neh 7:8 8147
thousand an hundred seventy and *t* Neh 7:8 8147
three hundred seventy and *t* Neh 7:9 8147
of Arah, six hundred fifty and *t* Neh 7:10 8147
t thousand and eight hundred and Neh 7:11
a thousand *t* hundred fifty and Neh 7:12
t thousand three hundred twenty Neh 7:17 8147
three hundred twenty and *t* Neh 7:17 8147
t thousand threescore and seven Neh 7:19
men of Beth-azmaveth, forty and *t* Neh 7:28 8147
an hundred and twenty and *t* Neh 7:31 8147
men of the other Nebo, fifty and *t* Neh 7:33 8147
a thousand *t* hundred fifty and Neh 7:34
of Immer, a thousand fifty and *t* Neh 7:40 8147
a thousand *t* hundred forty and Neh 7:41
were three hundred ninety and *t* Neh 7:60 8147
of Nekoda, six hundred forty and *t* Neh 7:62 8147
t thousand three hundred and Neh 7:66
they had *t* hundred forty and five Neh 7:67
mules, *t* hundred forty and five Neh 7:68
t thousand and *t* hundred pounds Neh 7:71
t thousand pounds of silver, and Neh 7:72
were eight hundred twenty and *t* Neh 11:12 8147
fathers, *t* hundred forty and *t* Neh 11:13 8147
city were *t* hundred fourscore Neh 11:18
were an hundred seventy and *t* Neh 11:19 8147
appointed *t* great companies of Neh 12:31 8147
So stood the *t* companies of them Neh 12:40 8147
for in the *t* and thirtieth year of Neh 13:6 8147
t of the king's chamberlains, Est 2:21 8147
t of the king's chamberlains, the Est 6:2 8147
that they would keep these *t* days Est 9:27 8147
Only do not *t* things unto me Job 13:20 8147
thee, and against thy *t* friends Job 42:7 8147
T things have I required of thee Prov 30:7 8147
The horseleach hath *t* daughters Prov 30:15 8147
T are better than one Eccl 4:9 8147
if *t* lie together, then they have Eccl 4:11 8147
him, *t* shall withstand him Eccl 4:12 8147
Thy *t* breasts are like *t* young Song 4:5 8147
it were the company of *t* armies Song 6:13
Thy *t* breasts are like *t* young Song 7:3 8147
keep the fruit thereof *t* hundred Song 8:12
for the *t* tails of these smoking Is 7:4 8147
nourish a young cow, and *t* sheep Is 7:21 8147
t or three berries in the top of Is 17:6 8147
made also a ditch between the *t* Is 22:11
will give thee *t* thousand horses Is 36:8
before him the *t* leaved gates Is 45:1
But these *t* things shall come to Is 47:9 8147
These *t* things are come unto thee Is 51:19 8147
my people have committed *t* evils Jer 2:13 8147
t of a family, and I will bring Jer 3:14 8147
t baskets of figs were set before Jer 24:1 8147
Within *t* full years will I bring Jer 28:3
within the space of *t* full years Jer 28:11
The *t* families which the LORD Jer 33:24 8147
by the gate betwixt the *t* walls Jer 39:4 8147
of the gate between the *t* walls Jer 52:7 8147
The *t* pillars, one sea, and twelve Jer 52:20 8147
eight hundred thirty and *t* persons Jer 52:29 8147
t wings of every one were joined Eze 1:11 8147
and *t* covered their bodies Eze 1:11 8147
every one had *t*, which covered on Eze 1:23 8147
on this side, and every one had *t* Eze 1:23 8147
son of man, appoint thee *t* ways Eze 21:19 8147
way, at the head of the *t* ways Eze 21:21 8147
Son of man, there were *t* women Eze 23:2 8147
These *t* nations and these *t* Eze 35:10 8147
they shall be no more *t* nations Eze 37:22 8147
into *t* kingdoms any more at all Eze 37:22 8147
and the posts thereof, *t* cubits Eze 40:9 8147
gate were *t* tables on this side Eze 40:39 8147
t tables on that side, to slay Eze 40:39
of the north gate, were *t* tables Eze 40:40 8147
porch of the gate, were *t* tables Eze 40:40 8147
the post of the door, *t* cubits Eze 41:3 8147
and every cherub had *t* faces Eze 41:18 8147
and the length thereof *t* cubits Eze 41:22 8147
and the sanctuary had *t* doors Eze 41:23 8147
And the doors had *t* leaves apiece Eze 41:24 8147
leaves apiece, *t* turning leaves Eze 41:24 8147
t leaves for the one door Eze 41:24 8147
t leaves for the other door Eze 41:24 8147
lower settle shall be *t* cubits Eze 43:14 8147
out of *t* hundred, out of the fat Eze 45:15
a place on the *t* sides westward Eze 46:19
Joseph shall have *t* portions Eze 47:13
be toward the north *t* hundred Eze 48:17
and toward the south *t* hundred Eze 48:17
and toward the east *t* hundred Eze 48:17
and toward the west *t* hundred Eze 48:17
about threescore and *t* years old Dan 5:31 8648
the river a ram which had *t* horns Dan 8:3
and the *t* horns were high Dan 8:3
came to the ram that had *t* horns Dan 8:6
the ram, and brake his *t* horns Dan 8:7 8147
Unto *t* thousand and three hundred Dan 8:14
t horns are the kings of Media Dan 8:20
weeks, and threescore and *t* weeks Dan 9:25 8147
t weeks shall Messiah be cut off, Dan 9:26 8147
and, behold, there stood other *t* Dan 12:5 8147
shall be a thousand *t* hundred Dan 12:11
After *t* days will he revive us Hos 6:2
themselves in their *t* furrows Hos 10:10 8147
t years before the earthquake Amos 1:1
Can *t* walk together, except they Amos 3:3 8147
of the mouth of the lion *t* legs Amos 3:12 8147
So *t* or three cities wandered Amos 4:8 8147
t olive trees by it, one upon the Zec 4:3 8147
What are these *t* olive trees upon Zec 4:11 8147
What be these *t* olive branches Zec 4:12 8147
branches which through the *t* Zec 4:12 8147
he, These are the *t* anointed ones Zec 4:14 8147
behold, there came out *t* women Zec 5:9 8147
out from between *t* mountains Zec 6:1 8147
And I took unto me *t* staves Zec 11:7 8147
t parts therein shall be cut off Zec 13:8 8147
from *t* years old and under, Mt 2:16 *1332*
saw *t* brethren, Simon called Mt 4:18 *1417*
thence, he saw other *t* brethren Mt 4:21 *1417*
No man can serve *t* masters Mt 6:24 *1417*
there met him *t* possessed with Mt 8:28 *1417*
t blind men followed him, crying, Mt 9:27 *1417*
for your journey, neither *t* coats Mt 10:10 *1417*
Are not *t* sparrows sold for a Mt 10:29 *1417*
he sent *t* of his disciples, Mt 11:2 *1417*
here but five loaves, and *t* fishes Mt 14:17 *1417*
the *t* fishes, and looking up to Mt 14:19 *1417*
rather than having *t* hands or *t* Mt 18:8 *1417*
rather than having *t* eyes to be Mt 18:9 *1417*
then take with thee one or *t* more Mt 18:16 *1417*
that in the mouth of *t* or three Mt 18:16 *1417*
That if *t* of you shall agree on Mt 18:19 *1417*
For where *t* or three are gathered Mt 18:20 *1417*
that these my *t* sons may sit Mt 20:21 *1417*
against the *t* brethren Mt 20:24 *1417*
t blind men sitting by the way Mt 20:30 *1417*
then sent Jesus *t* disciples Mt 21:1 *1417*
A certain man had *t* sons Mt 21:28 *1417*
On these *t* commandments hang all Mt 22:40 *1417*
Then shall *t* be in the field Mt 24:40 *1417*
T women shall be grinding at the Mt 24:41 *1417*
gave five talents, to another *t* Mt 25:15 *1417*
likewise he that had received *t* Mt 25:17 *1417*
he also gained other *t* Mt 25:17 *1417*
that had received *t* talents came Mt 25:22 *1417*
deliveredst unto me *t* talents Mt 25:22 *1417*
I have gained *t* other talents Mt 25:22 *1417*
Ye know that after *t* days is the Mt 26:2 *1417*
the *t* sons of Zebedee, and began Mt 26:37 *1417*
the last came *t* false witnesses Mt 26:60 *1417*
Then were there *t* thieves Mt 27:38 *1417*
sea, (they were about *t* thousand Mk 5:13 *1367*
to send them forth by *t* and *t* Mk 6:7 *1417*
and not put on *t* coats Mk 6:9 *1417*
buy *t* hundred pennyworth of bread Mk 6:37 *1250*
knew, they say, Five, and *t* fishes Mk 6:38 *1417*
the *t* fishes, he looked up to Mk 6:41 *1417*
the *t* fishes divided he among Mk 6:41 *1417*
than having *t* hands to go into Mk 9:43 *1417*
than having *t* feet to be cast Mk 9:45 *1417*
than having *t* eyes to be cast Mk 9:47 *1417*
sendeth forth *t* of his disciples Mk 11:1 *1417*
in a place where *t* ways met Mk 11:4 *296*
widow, and she threw in *t* mites Mk 12:42 *1417*
After *t* days was the feast of the Mk 14:1 *1417*
sendeth forth *t* of his disciples Mk 14:13 *1417*
with him they crucify *t* thieves Mk 15:27 *1417*
in another form unto *t* of them Mk 16:12 *1417*
turtledoves, or *t* young pigeons Lk 2:24 *1417*
unto them, He that hath *t* coats Lk 3:11 *1417*
saw *t* ships standing by the lake Lk 5:2 *1417*
John calling unto him *t* of his Lk 7:19 *1417*
creditor which had *t* debtors Lk 7:41 *1417*
neither have *t* coats apiece Lk 9:3 *1417*
more but five loaves and *t* fishes Lk 9:13 *1417*
the *t* fishes, and looking up to Lk 9:16 *1417*
there talked with him *t* men Lk 9:30 *1417*
the *t* men that stood with him Lk 9:32 *1417*
seventy also, and sent them *t* Lk 10:1
t before his face into every city Lk 10:1 *1417*
he departed, he took out *t* pence Lk 10:35 *1417*
sparrows sold for *t* farthings Lk 12:6 *1417*
house divided, three against *t* Lk 12:52 *1417*
against *t*, and *t* against three Lk 12:52 *1417*
he said, A certain man had *t* sons Lk 15:11 *1417*
No servant can serve *t* masters Lk 16:13 *1417*
there shall be *t* men in one bed Lk 17:34 *1417*
T women shall be grinding Lk 17:35 *1417*
T men shall be in the field Lk 17:36 *1417*
T men went up into the temple to Lk 18:10 *1417*
he sent *t* of his disciples, Lk 19:29 *1417*
widow casting in thither *t* mites Lk 21:2 *1417*
Lord, behold, here are *t* swords Lk 22:38 *1417*
And there were also *t* others Lk 23:32 *1417*
t men stood by them in shining Lk 24:4 *1417*
t of them went that same day to a Lk 24:13 *1417*
John stood, and *t* of his disciples Jn 1:35 *1417*
the *t* disciples heard him speak, Jn 1:37 *1417*
One of the *t* which heard John Jn 1:40 *1417*
containing *t* or three firkins Jn 2:6 *1417*
and he abode there *t* days Jn 4:40 *1417*
Now after *t* days he departed Jn 4:43 *1417*
T hundred pennyworth of bread is Jn 6:7 *1250*
barley loaves, and *t* small fishes Jn 6:9 *1417*
the testimony of *t* men is true Jn 8:17 *1417*
he abode *t* days still in the same Jn 11:6 *1417*
t others with him, on either side Jn 19:18 *1417*
seeth *t* angels in white sitting, Jn 20:12 *1417*
and *t* other of his disciples Jn 21:2 *1417*
but as it were *t* hundred cubits Jn 21:8 *1250*
t men stood by them in white Acts 1:10 *1417*
And they appointed *t*, Joseph Acts 1:23 *1417*

of these t thou hast chosen Acts 1:24 1417
of Madian, where he begat t sons Acts 7:29 1417
there, they sent unto him t men Acts 9:38 1417
he called t of his household Acts 10:7 1417
was sleeping between t soldiers Acts 12:6 1417
t soldiers, bound with t chains Acts 12:6 1417
continued by the space of t years Acts 19:10 1417
So he sent into Macedonia t of Acts 19:22 1417
the space of t hours cried out Acts 19:34 1417
him to be bound with t chains Acts 21:33 1417
he called unto him t centurions Acts 23:23 1417
Make ready t hundred soldiers to Acts 23:23 1250
and ten, and spearmen t hundred Acts 23:23 1250
But after t years Porcius Festus Acts 24:27 1333
in the ship t hundred threescore Acts 27:37 1250
into a place where t seas met Acts 27:41 1337
Paul dwelt t whole years in his Acts 28:30 1333
for t, saith he, shall be one 1Cor 6:16 1417
an unknown tongue, let it be by t 1Cor 14:27 1417
Let the prophets speak t or three 1Cor 14:29 1417
In the mouth of t or three 2Cor 13:1 1417
written, that Abraham had t sons Gal 4:22 1417
for these are the t covenants Gal 4:24 1417
they t shall be one flesh Eph 5:31 1417
For I am in a strait betwixt t Phil 1:23 1417
but before t or three witnesses 1Ti 5:19 1417
That by t immutable things, in Heb 6:18 1417
mercy under t or three witnesses Heb 10:28 1417
hath the sharp sword with t edges Rev 2:12 1366
there come t woes more hereafter Rev 9:12 1417
were t hundred thousand thousand Rev 9:16 1417
under foot forty and t months Rev 11:2 1417
give power unto my t witnesses Rev 11:3 1417
prophesy a thousand t hundred Rev 11:3 1250
These are the t olive trees Rev 11:4 1417
the t candlesticks standing Rev 11:4 1417
because these t prophets Rev 11:10 1417
her there a thousand t hundred Rev 12:6 1417
given t wings of a great eagle Rev 12:14 1417
him to continue forty and t months Rev 13:5 1417
he had t horns like a lamb, and he Rev 13:11 1417

TWOEDGED
mouth, and a t sword in their hand Ps 149:6 6374
as wormwood, sharp as a t sword Prov 5:4 6310
and sharper than any t sword Heb 4:12 1366
of his mouth went a sharp t sword Rev 1:16 1366

TWOFOLD
ye make him t more the child of Mt 23:15 1366

TYCHICUS (*tik'-ik-us*) *A co-worker with Paul.*
and of Asia, T and Trophimus Acts 20:4 5190
know my affairs, and how I do, T Eph 6:21 5190
from Rome unto the Ephesians by T Eph s 5190
my state shall T declare unto you Col 4:7 5190
from Rome to the Colossians by T Col s 5190
And T have I sent to Ephesus 2Ti 4:12 5190
send Artemas unto thee, or T Titus 3:12 5190

TYRANNUS (*ti-ran'-nus*) *An Ephesian schoolmaster.*
daily in the school of one T Acts 19:9 5181

TYRE (*tire*) See TYRUS. *A coastal city of Phoenicia.*
to Ramah, and to the strong city T Josh 19:29 6865
Hiram king of T sent messengers 2Sa 5:11 6865
And came to the strong hold of T 2Sa 24:7 6865
Hiram king of T sent his servants 1Kin 5:1 6865
sent and fetched Hiram out of T 1Kin 7:13 6865
and his father was a man of T 1Kin 7:14 6876
(Now Hiram the king of T had 1Kin 9:11 6865
Hiram came out from T to see the 1Kin 9:12 6865
Now Hiram king of T sent 1Chr 14:1 6865
they of T brought much cedar wood 1Chr 22:4 6876
sent to Huram the king of T 2Chr 2:3 6865
the king of T answered in writing 2Chr 2:11 6865
Dan, and his father was a man of T 2Chr 2:14 6876
them of Zidon, and to them of T Ezr 3:7 6876
There dwelt men of T also therein Neh 13:16 6876
the daughter of T shall be there Ps 45:12 6865
with the inhabitants of T Ps 83:7 6865
behold Philistia, and T, with Ps 87:4 6865
The burden of T Is 23:1 6865
sorely pained at the report of T Is 23:5 6865
hath taken this counsel against T Is 23:8 6865
that T shall be forgotten seventy Is 23:15 6865
years shall T sing as an harlot Is 23:15 6865
years, that the LORD will visit T Is 23:17 6865
what have ye to do with me, O T Joel 3:4 6865
done in you, had been done in T Mt 11:21 5184
It shall be more tolerable for T Mt 11:22 5184
and departed into the coasts of T Mt 15:21 5184
and they about T and Sidon, a great Mk 3:8 5184
and went into the borders of T Mk 7:24 5184
departing from the coasts of T Mk 7:31 5184
and from the sea coast of T Lk 6:17 5184
mighty works had been done in T Lk 10:13 5184
it shall be more tolerable for T Lk 10:14 5184
highly displeased with them of T Acts 12:20 5185
sailed into Syria, and landed at T Acts 21:3 5184
we had finished our course from T Acts 21:7 5184

TYRIAN See TYRE.

TYRUS (*ti'-rus*) See TYRE. *Same as Tyre.*
And all the kings of T, and all the Jer 25:22 6865
Ammonites, and to the king of T Jer 27:3 6865
Philistines, and to cut off from T Jer 47:4 6865
because that T hath said against Eze 26:2 6865
Behold, I am against thee, O T Eze 26:3 6865
they shall destroy the walls of T Eze 26:4 6865
Behold, I will bring upon T Eze 26:7 6865
Thus saith the Lord GOD to T Eze 26:15 6865
man, take up a lamentation for T Eze 27:2 6865
And say unto T, O thou that art Eze 27:3 6865
O T, thou hast said, I am of Eze 27:3 6865
thy wise men, O T, that were in Eze 27:8 6865
thee, saying, What city is like T Eze 27:32 6865
of man, say unto the prince of T Eze 28:2 6865
a lamentation upon the king of T Eze 28:12 6865
serve a great service against T Eze 29:18 6865
he no wages, nor his army, for T Eze 29:18 6865
Ephraim, as I saw T, is planted Hos 9:13 6865
For three transgressions of T Amos 1:9 6865
will send a fire on the wall of T Amos 1:10 6865
T, and Zidon, though it be very Zec 9:2 6865
T did build herself a strong hold Zec 9:3 6865

U

UCAL (*u'-cal*) *An obscure name.*
Ithiel, even unto Ithiel and U Prov 30:1 401

UEL (*u'-el*) *Married a foreigner in exile.*
Maadai, Amram, and U, Ezr 10:34 177

ULAI (*u'-lahee*) *A river near Susa.*
and I was by the river of U Dan 8:2 195
voice between the banks of U Dan 8:16 195

ULAM (*u'-lam*)
1. A son of Sheresh.
and his sons were U and Rakem 1Chr 7:16 198
And the sons of U 1Chr 7:17 198
2. A son of Eshek.
U his firstborn, Jehush the 1Chr 8:39 198
the sons of U were mighty men of 1Chr 8:40 198

ULLA (*ul'-la*) *An Asherite chief.*
And the sons of U 1Chr 7:39 5925

UMMAH (*um'-mah*) *A city in Asher.*
U also, and Aphek, and Rehob Josh 19:30 5981

UNACCUSTOMED
as a bullock u to the yoke Jer 31:18

UNADVISEDLY
so that he spake u with his lips Ps 106:33 981

UNAWARES
Jacob stole away u to Laban the Gen 31:20
thou hast stolen away u to me Gen 31:26
which killeth any person at u Num 35:11 7684
any person u may flee thither Num 35:15 7684
which should kill his neighbour u Deut 4:42
slayer that killeth any person u Josh 20:3 7684
person at u might flee thither Josh 20:9 7684
destruction come upon him at u Ps 35:8 3045
and so that day come upon you u Lk 21:34 160
of false brethren u brought in Gal 2:4 3920
some have entertained angels u Heb 13:2 2990
there are certain men crept in u Jude 4 3921

UNBELIEF
works there because of their u Mt 13:58 570
said unto them, Because of your u Mt 17:20 570
he marvelled because of their u Mk 6:6 570
help thou mine u Mk 9:24 570
and upbraided them with their u Mk 16:14 570
shall their u make the faith of Rom 3:3 570
at the promise of God through u Rom 4:20 570
because of u they were broken off Rom 11:20 570
if they abide not still in u Rom 11:23 570
obtained mercy through their u Rom 11:30 543
God hath concluded them all in u Rom 11:32 543
because I did it ignorantly in u 1Ti 1:13 570
in any of you an evil heart of u Heb 3:12 570
could not enter in because of u Heb 3:19 570
entered not in because of u Heb 4:6 543
fall after the same example of u Heb 4:11 543

UNBELIEVERS
him his portion with the u Lk 12:46 571
brother, and that before the u 1Cor 6:6 571
in those that are unlearned, or u 1Cor 14:23 571
unequally yoked together with u 2Cor 6:14 571

UNBELIEVING
But the u Jews stirred up the Acts 14:2 544
For the u husband is sanctified 1Cor 7:14 571
the u wife is sanctified by the 1Cor 7:14 571
But if the u depart, let him 1Cor 7:15 571
are defiled and u is nothing pure Titus 1:15 571
But the fearful, and u, and the Rev 21:8 571

UNBLAMEABLE
death, to present you holy and u Col 1:22 299
hearts u in holiness before God 1Th 3:13 299

UNBLAMEABLY
u we behaved ourselves among you 1Th 2:10 274

UNCERTAIN
if the trumpet give an u sound 1Cor 14:8 82
highminded, nor trust in u riches 1Ti 6:17 83

UNCERTAINLY
I therefore so run, not as u 1Cor 9:26 82

UNCHANGEABLE
ever, hath an u priesthood Heb 7:24 531

UNCIRCUMCISED
the u man child whose flesh of Gen 17:14 6189
give our sister to one that is u Gen 34:14 6190
Pharaoh hear me, who am of u lips Ex 6:12 6189
the LORD, Behold, I am of u lips Ex 6:30 6189
for no u person shall eat thereof Ex 12:48 6189
count the fruit thereof as u Lev 19:23 6189
years shall it be as u unto you Lev 19:23 6189
if then their u hearts be humbled Lev 26:41 6189
for they were u, because they had Josh 5:7 6189
take a wife of the u Philistines Judg 14:3 6189
and fall into the hand of the u Judg 15:18 6189
over unto the garrison of these u 1Sa 14:6 6189
for who is this u Philistine 1Sa 17:26 6189
this u Philistine shall be as one 1Sa 17:36 6189
lest these u come and thrust me 1Sa 31:4 6189
the daughters of the u triumph 2Sa 1:20 6189
lest these u come and abuse me 1Chr 10:4 6189
no more come into thee the u Is 52:1 6189
behold, their ear is u, and they Jer 6:10 6189
which are circumcised with the u Jer 9:25 6190
for all these nations are u Jer 9:26 6189
of Israel are u in the heart Jer 9:26 6189
of the u by the hand of strangers Eze 28:10 6189
shalt lie in the midst of the u Eze 31:18 6189
down, and be thou laid with the u Eze 32:19 6189
they are gone down, they lie u Eze 32:21 6189
which are gone down u into the Eze 32:24 6189
all of them u, slain by the sword Eze 32:25 6189
all of them u, slain by the sword Eze 32:26 6189
mighty that are fallen of the u Eze 32:27 6189
be broken in the midst of the u Eze 32:28 6189
they shall lie with the u Eze 32:29 6189
they lie u with them that be Eze 32:30 6189
be laid in the midst of the u Eze 32:32 6189
u in heart, and u in flesh Eze 44:7 6189
u in heart, nor u in flesh Eze 44:9 6189
u in heart and ears, ye do always Acts 7:51 564
Saying, Thou wentest in to men u Acts 11:3
faith which he had yet being u Rom 4:11
Abraham, which he had being yet u Rom 4:12
let him not become u 1Cor 7:18 1986

UNCIRCUMCISION
law, thy circumcision is made u Rom 2:25 203
Therefore if the u keep the Rom 2:26 203
shall not his u be counted for Rom 2:26 203
shall not u which is by nature, Rom 2:27 203
by faith, and u through faith Rom 3:30 203
only, or upon the u also Rom 4:9 203
he was in circumcision, or in u Rom 4:10 203
Not in circumcision, but in u Rom 4:10 203
Is any called in u 1Cor 7:18 203
u is nothing, but the keeping of 1Cor 7:19 203
of the u was committed unto me Gal 2:7 203
availeth any thing, nor u Gal 5:6 203
availeth any thing, nor u Gal 6:15 203
who are called U by that which is Eph 2:11 203
the u of your flesh, hath he Col 2:13 203
Greek nor Jew, circumcision nor u Col 3:11 203

UNCLE
the sons of Uzziel the u of Aaron Lev 10:4 1730
Either his u, or his uncle's son, Lev 25:49 1730
Saul's u said unto him and to his 1Sa 10:14 1730
And Saul's u said, Tell me, I pray 1Sa 10:15 1730
And Saul said unto his u, He told 1Sa 10:16 1730
Abner, the son of Ner, Saul's u 1Sa 14:50 1730
David's u was a counsellor 1Chr 27:32 1730
of Abihail the u of Mordecai Est 2:15 1730
thine u shall come unto thee Jer 32:7 1730
a man's u shall take him up, and Amos 6:10 1730

UNCLEAN
Or if a soul touch any u thing Lev 5:2 2931
it be a carcase of an u beast Lev 5:2 2931
or a carcase of u cattle Lev 5:2 2931
the carcase of u creeping things Lev 5:2 2931
he also shall be u, and guilty Lev 5:2 2931
any u thing shall not be eaten Lev 7:19 2931
soul that shall touch any u thing Lev 7:21 2932
of man, or any u beast, or any Lev 7:21 2931
or any abominable u thing Lev 7:21 2931
holy and unholy, and between u Lev 10:10 2931
he is u unto you Lev 11:4 2931
he is u unto you Lev 11:5 2931
he is u unto you Lev 11:6 2931
he is u to you Lev 11:7 2931
they are u to you Lev 11:8 2931
And for these ye shall be u Lev 11:24 2930
of them shall be u until the even Lev 11:24 2930
clothes, and be u until the even Lev 11:25 2930
cheweth the cud, are u unto you Lev 11:26 2931
one that toucheth them shall be u Lev 11:26 2930
on all four, those are u unto you Lev 11:27 2931
carcase shall be u until the even Lev 11:27 2930
clothes, and be u until the even Lev 11:28 2930
they are u unto you Lev 11:28 2931
These also shall be u unto you Lev 11:29 2931
These are u to you among all that Lev 11:31 2931
shall be u until the even Lev 11:31 2930
dead, doth fall, it shall be u Lev 11:32 2930

it shall be *u* until the even Lev 11:32 2930
whatsoever is in it shall be *u* Lev 11:33 2930
such water cometh shall be *u* Lev 11:34 2930
in every such vessel shall be *u* Lev 11:34 2930
their carcase falleth shall be *u* Lev 11:35 2930
for they are *u*, and shall be Lev 11:35 2931
and shall be *u* unto you Lev 11:35 2931
toucheth their carcase shall be *u* Lev 11:36 2930
thereon, it shall be *u* unto you Lev 11:38 2931
thereof shall be *u* until the even Lev 11:39 2930
clothes, and be *u* until the even Lev 11:40 2930
clothes, and be *u* until the even Lev 11:40 2930
ye make yourselves *u* with them Lev 11:43 2930
make a difference between the *u* Lev 11:47 2931
then she shall be *u* seven days Lev 12:2 2930
for her infirmity shall she be *u* Lev 12:2 2930
then she shall be *u* two weeks Lev 12:5 2930
look on him, and pronounce him *u* Lev 13:3 2930
the priest shall pronounce him *u* Lev 13:8 2930
the priest shall pronounce him *u* Lev 13:11 2930
for he is *u* Lev 13:11 2931
appeareth in him, he shall be *u* Lev 13:14 2930
flesh, and pronounce him to be *u* Lev 13:15 2930
for the raw flesh is *u* Lev 13:15 2931
the priest shall pronounce him *u* Lev 13:20 2930
the priest shall pronounce him *u* Lev 13:22 2930
the priest shall pronounce him *u* Lev 13:25 2930
the priest shall pronounce him *u* Lev 13:27 2930
the priest shall pronounce him *u* Lev 13:30 2930
he is *u* Lev 13:36 2931
He is a leprous man, he is *u* Lev 13:44 2931
shall pronounce him utterly *u* Lev 13:44 2930
lip, and shall cry, *U*, *u* Lev 13:45 2931
he is *u* Lev 13:46 2931
it is *u* Lev 13:51 2931
it is *u* Lev 13:55 2931
it clean, or to pronounce it *u* Lev 13:59 2930
is in the house be not made *u* Lev 14:36 2930
into an *u* place without the city Lev 14:40 2931
without the city into an *u* place Lev 14:41 2931
it is *u* Lev 14:44 2931
out of the city into an *u* place Lev 14:45 2931
shut up shall be *u* until the even Lev 14:46 2930
To teach when it is *u*, and when it Lev 14:57 2931
because of his issue he is *u* Lev 15:2 2931
lieth that hath the issue, is *u* Lev 15:4 2930
whereon he sitteth, shall be *u* Lev 15:4 2930
in water, and be *u* until the even Lev 15:5 2930
in water, and be *u* until the even Lev 15:6 2930
in water, and be *u* until the even Lev 15:7 2930
in water, and be *u* until the even Lev 15:8 2930
that hath the issue shall be *u* Lev 15:9 2930
him shall be *u* until the even Lev 15:10 2930
in water, and be *u* until the even Lev 15:10 2930
in water, and be *u* until the even Lev 15:11 2930
in water, and be *u* until the even Lev 15:16 2930
water, and be *u* until the even Lev 15:17 2930
in water, and be *u* until the even Lev 15:18 2930
her shall be *u* until the even Lev 15:19 2930
upon in her separation shall be *u* Lev 15:20 2930
that she sitteth upon shall be *u* Lev 15:20 2930
in water, and be *u* until the even Lev 15:21 2930
in water, and be *u* until the even Lev 15:22 2930
he shall be *u* until the even Lev 15:23
him, he shall be *u* seven days Lev 15:24 2930
bed whereon he lieth shall be *u* Lev 15:24 2930
she shall be *u* Lev 15:25 2931
she sitteth upon shall be *u* Lev 15:26 2931
toucheth those things shall be *u* Lev 15:27 2930
in water, and be *u* until the even Lev 15:27 2930
him that lieth with her that is *u* Lev 15:33 2931
in water, and be *u* until the even Lev 17:15 2930
brother's wife, it is an *u* thing Lev 20:21 5079
between clean beasts and *u* Lev 20:25 2931
and between *u* fowls Lev 20:25 2931
I have separated from you as *u* Lev 20:25 2930
any thing that is *u* by the dead Lev 22:4 2931
thing, whereby he may be made *u* Lev 22:5 2930
any such shall be *u* until even Lev 22:6 2930
And if it be any *u* beast, of which Lev 27:11 2931
And if it be of an *u* beast Lev 27:27 2931
not make himself *u* for his father Num 6:7 2930
be *u* by reason of a dead body Num 9:10 2931
the firstling of *u* beasts shalt Num 18:15 2931
priest shall be *u* until the even Num 19:7 2930
shall be *u* until the even Num 19:8 2930
clothes, and be *u* until the even Num 19:10 2930
of any man shall be *u* seven days Num 19:11 2930
sprinkled upon him, he shall be *u* Num 19:13 2931
the tent, shall be *u* seven days Num 19:14 2930
no covering bound upon it, is *u* Num 19:15 2931
or a grave, shall be *u* seven days Num 19:16 2930
for an *u* person they shall take Num 19:17 2931
upon the *u* on the third day Num 19:19 2931
But the man that shall be *u* Num 19:20 2930
he is *u* Num 19:20 2931
separation shall be *u* until even Num 19:21 2930
whatsoever the *u* person toucheth Num 19:22 2931
person toucheth shall be *u* Num 19:22 2930
toucheth it shall be *u* until even Num 19:22 2930
the *u* and the clean may eat Deut 12:15 2931
the *u* and the clean shall eat of Deut 12:22 2931
therefore they are *u* unto you Deut 14:7 2931
not the cud, it is *u* unto you Deut 14:8 2931
it is *u* unto you Deut 14:10 2931
thing that flieth is *u* unto you Deut 14:19 2931
the *u* and the clean person shall Deut 15:22 2931
that he see no *u* thing in thee Deut 23:14 6172
away ought thereof for any *u* use Deut 26:14 2931
the land of your possession be *u* Josh 22:19 2931
drink, and eat not any *u* thing Judg 13:4 2931
drink, neither eat any *u* thing Judg 13:7 2932
strong drink, nor eat any *u* thing Judg 13:14 2932
that none which was *u* in any 2Chr 23:19 2931
is an *u* land with the filthiness Ezr 9:11 5079
bring a clean thing out of an *u* Job 14:4 2931
and their life is among the *u* Job 36:14 6945
good and to the clean, and to the *u* Eccl 9:2 2931
because I am a man of *u* lips Is 6:5 2931
the midst of a people of *u* lips Is 6:5 2931
the *u* shall not pass over it Is 35:8 2931
thee the uncircumcised and the *u* Is 52:1 2931
out from thence, touch no *u* thing Is 52:11 2931
But we are all as an *u* thing Is 64:6 2931
it is *u* Lam 4:15 2931
shewed difference between the *u* Eze 22:26 2931
them to discern between the *u* Eze 44:23 2931
they shall eat *u* things in Hos 9:3 2931
If one that is *u* by a dead body Hag 2:13 2931
touch any of these, shall it be *u* Hag 2:13 2930
answered and said, It shall be *u* Hag 2:13 2930
that which they offer there is *u* Hag 2:14 2931
the *u* spirit to pass out of the Zec 13:2 2932
gave them power against *u* spirits Mt 10:1 169
When the *u* spirit is gone out of Mt 12:43 169
synagogue a man with an *u* spirit Mk 1:23 169
when the *u* spirit had torn him, Mk 1:26 169
commandeth he even the *u* spirits Mk 1:27 169
u spirits, when they saw him, Mk 3:11 169
they said, He hath an *u* spirit Mk 3:30 169
the tombs a man with an *u* spirit Mk 5:2 169
out of the man, thou *u* spirit Mk 5:8 169
the *u* spirits went out, and Mk 5:13 169
and gave them power over *u* spirits Mk 6:7 169
young daughter had an *u* spirit Mk 7:25 169
which had a spirit of an *u* devil Lk 4:33 169
power he commandeth the *u* spirits Lk 4:36 169
that were vexed with *u* spirits Lk 6:18 169
(For he had commanded the *u* Lk 8:29 169
And Jesus rebuked the *u* spirit Lk 9:42 169
When the *u* spirit is gone out of Lk 11:24 169
which were vexed with *u* spirits Acts 5:16 169
For *u* spirits, crying with loud Acts 8:7 169
any thing that is common or *u* Acts 10:14 169
not call any man common or *u* Acts 10:28 169
for nothing common or *u* hath at Acts 11:8 169
that there is nothing *u* of itself Rom 14:14 2839
that esteemeth any thing to be *u* Rom 14:14 2839
to him it is *u* Rom 14:14 2839
else were your children *u* 1Cor 7:14 169
Lord, and touch not the *u* thing 2Cor 6:17 169
nor *u* person, nor covetous man, Eph 5:5 169
of an heifer sprinkling the *u* Heb 9:13 2840
I saw three *u* spirits like frogs Rev 16:13 169
foul spirit, and a cage of every *u* Rev 18:2 169

UNCLEANNESS

Or if he touch the *u* of man Lev 5:3 2932
whatsoever *u* it be that a man Lev 5:3 2932
the LORD, having his *u* upon him Lev 7:20 2932
unclean thing, as the *u* of man Lev 7:21 2932
that is to be cleansed from his *u* Lev 14:19 2932
this shall be his *u* in his issue Lev 15:3 2932
from his issue, it is his *u* Lev 15:3 2932
her *u* shall be as the days of her Lev 15:25 2932
as the *u* of her separation Lev 15:26 2932
the LORD for the issue of her *u* Lev 15:30 2932
children of Israel from their *u* Lev 15:31 2932
that they die not in their *u* Lev 15:31 2932
because of the *u* of the children Lev 16:16 2932
them in the midst of their *u* Lev 16:16 2932
hallow it from the *u* of the Lev 16:19 2932
as she is put apart for her *u* Lev 18:19 2932
the LORD, having his *u* upon him Lev 22:3 2932
or a man of whom he may take *u* Lev 22:5 2930
whatsoever *u* he hath Lev 22:5 2932
to *u* with another instead of thy Num 5:19 2932
his *u* is yet upon him Num 19:13 2932
of *u* that chanceth him by night Deut 23:10 7137
he hath found some *u* in her Deut 24:1 6172
for she was purified from her *u* 2Sa 11:4 2932
brought out all the *u* that they 2Chr 29:16 2932
one end to another with their *u* Ezr 9:11 2932
me as the *u* of a removed woman Eze 36:17 2932
According to their *u* and according Eze 39:24 2932
of Jerusalem for sin and for *u* Zec 13:1 5079
of dead men's bones, and of all *u* Mt 23:27 167
God also gave them up to *u* Rom 1:24 167
your members servants to *u* Rom 6:19 167
and have not repented of the *u* 2Cor 12:21 167
Adultery, fornication, *u*, Gal 5:19 167
to work all *u* with greediness Eph 4:19 167
But fornication, and all *u* Eph 5:3 167
fornication, *u*, inordinate Col 3:5 167
was not of deceit, nor of *u* 1Th 2:3 167
For God hath not called us unto *u* 1Th 4:7 167
after the flesh in the lust of *u* 2Pet 2:10 3394

UNCLEANNESSES

also save you from all your *u* Eze 36:29 2932

UNCLE'S

a man shall lie with his *u* wife Lev 20:20 1733
he hath uncovered his *u* nakedness Lev 20:20 1730
Either his uncle, or his *u* son Lev 25:49 1733
that is, Esther, his *u* daughter Est 2:7 1733
So Hanameel mine *u* son came to me Jer 32:8 1733
the field of Hanameel my *u* son Jer 32:9 1733
the sight of Hanameel mine *u* son Jer 32:12 1733

UNCLOTHED

not for that we would be *u* 2Cor 5:4 1562

UNCOMELY

himself *u* toward his virgin 1Cor 7:36 807
our *u* parts have more abundant 1Cor 12:23 809

UNCONDEMNED

They have beaten us openly *u* Acts 16:37 178
a man that is a Roman, and *u* Acts 22:25 178

UNCORRUPTIBLE

changed the glory of the *u* God Rom 1:23 862

UNCORRUPTNESS

in doctrine shewing *u*, gravity, Titus 2:7 90

UNCOVER

U not your heads, neither rend Lev 10:6 6544
kin to him, to *u* their nakedness Lev 18:6 1540
of thy mother, shalt thou not *u* Lev 18:7 1540
thou shalt not *u* her nakedness Lev 18:7 1540
father's wife shalt thou not *u* Lev 18:8 1540
their nakedness thou shalt not *u* Lev 18:9 1540
their nakedness thou shalt not *u* Lev 18:10 1540
thou shalt not *u* her nakedness Lev 18:11 1540
Thou shalt not *u* the nakedness of Lev 18:12 1540
Thou shalt not *u* the nakedness of Lev 18:13 1540
Thou shalt not *u* the nakedness of Lev 18:14 1540
Thou shalt not *u* the nakedness of Lev 18:15 1540
thou shalt not *u* her nakedness Lev 18:15 1540
Thou shalt not *u* the nakedness of Lev 18:16 1540
Thou shalt not *u* the nakedness of Lev 18:17 1540
daughter, to *u* her nakedness Lev 18:17 1540
to *u* her nakedness, beside the Lev 18:18 1540
unto a woman to *u* her nakedness Lev 18:19 1540
and shall *u* her nakedness Lev 20:18 1540
thou shalt not *u* the nakedness of Lev 20:19 1540
garments, shall not *u* his head Lev 21:10 6544
u the woman's head, and put the Num 5:18 6544
u his feet, and lay thee down Ruth 3:4 1540
u thy locks, make bare the leg, Is 47:2 1540
u the thigh, pass over the rivers Is 47:2 1540
for he shall *u* the cedar work Zeph 2:14 6168

UNCOVERED

and he was *u* within his tent Gen 9:21 1540
hath *u* his father's nakedness Lev 20:11 1540
he hath *u* his sister's nakedness Lev 20:17 1540
she hath *u* the fountain of her Lev 20:18 1540
he hath *u* his uncle's nakedness Lev 20:20 1540
he hath *u* his brother's nakedness Lev 20:21 1540
u his feet, and laid her down Ruth 3:7 1540
of Israel today, who *u* himself 2Sa 6:20 1540
even with their buttocks *u* Is 20:4 2834
and horsemen, and Kir *u* the shield Is 22:6 6168
Thy nakedness shall be *u*, yea, Is 47:3 1540
I have *u* his secret places, and he Jer 49:10 1540
and thine arm shall be *u*, and thou Eze 4:7 2834
also, and let thy foreskin be *u* Hab 2:16
they *u* the roof where he was Mk 2:4 648
her head *u* dishonoureth her head 1Cor 11:5 177
that a woman pray unto God *u* 1Cor 11:13 177

UNCOVERETH

for he *u* his near kin Lev 20:19 6168
because he *u* his father's skirt Deut 27:20 1540
fellows shamelessly *u* himself 2Sa 6:20 1540

UNCTION

But ye have an *u* from the Holy 1Jn 2:20 5545

UNDEFILED

Blessed are the *u* in the way Ps 119:1 8549
my sister, my love, my dove, my *u* Song 5:2 8535
My dove, my *u* is but one Song 6:9 8535
us, who is holy, harmless, *u* Heb 7:26 283
honourable in all, and the bed *u* Heb 13:4 283
u before God and the Father is Jas 1:27 283
inheritance incorruptible, and *u* 1Pet 1:4 283

UNDER

u the firmament from the waters Gen 1:7 8478
Let the waters *u* the heaven be Gen 1:9 8478
the breath of life, from *u* heaven Gen 6:17 8478
that were *u* the whole heaven, Gen 7:19 8478
and submit thyself *u* her hands Gen 16:9 8478
and rest yourselves *u* the tree Gen 18:4 8478
and he stood by them *u* the tree Gen 18:8 8478
came they *u* the shadow of my roof Gen 19:8
the child *u* one of the shrubs Gen 21:15 8478
I pray thee, thy hand *u* my thigh Gen 24:2 8478
the servant put his hand *u* the Gen 24:9 8478
Jacob hid them *u* the oak which Gen 35:4 8478
buried beneath Beth-el *u* an oak Gen 35:8 8478
to any thing that was *u* his hand Gen 39:23
lay up corn *u* the hand of Pharaoh Gen 41:35 8478
I pray thee, thy hand *u* my thigh Gen 47:29 8478
of the deep that lieth *u*, Gen 49:25 8478
I will bring you out from *u* the Ex 6:6 8478
which bringeth you out from *u* the Ex 6:7 8478
took a stone, and put it *u* him Ex 17:12 8478
of Amalek from *u* heaven Ex 17:14 8478
from *u* the hand of the Egyptians Ex 18:10 8478
that is in the water *u* the earth Ex 20:4 8478
with a rod, and he die *u* his hand Ex 21:20 8478
hateth thee lying *u* his burden Ex 23:5 8478
and builded an altar *u* the hill Ex 24:4 8478
there was *u* his feet as it were a Ex 24:10 8478
there shall be a knop *u* two Ex 25:35 8478
a knop *u* two branches of the same Ex 25:35 8478
a knop *u* two branches of the same Ex 25:35 8478
of silver *u* the twenty boards Ex 26:19 8478
two sockets *u* one board for his Ex 26:19 8478
two sockets *u* another board for Ex 26:19 8478
two sockets *u* one board Ex 26:21 8478
two sockets *u* another board Ex 26:21 8478
two sockets *u* one board Ex 26:25 8478
two sockets *u* another board Ex 26:25 8478
hang up the vail *u* the taches Ex 26:33 8478
thou shalt put it *u* the compass Ex 27:5 8478
thou make to it *u* the crown of it Ex 30:4 8478
he made *u* the twenty boards Ex 36:24 8478
two sockets *u* one board for his Ex 36:24 8478
two sockets *u* another board for Ex 36:24 8478
two sockets *u* one board Ex 36:26 8478
two sockets *u* another board Ex 36:26 8478
u every board two sockets Ex 36:30 8478

a knop *u* two branches of the same	Ex 37:21	8478
a knop *u* two branches of the same	Ex 37:21	8478
a knop *u* two branches of the same	Ex 37:21	8478
gold for it *u* the crown thereof	Ex 37:27	8478
u the compass thereof beneath	Ex 38:4	8478
toucheth any thing that was *u* him	Lev 15:10	8478
it shall be seven days *u* the dam	Lev 22:27	8478
of whatsoever passeth *u* the rod	Lev 27:32	8478
u the custody and charge of the	Num 3:36	
their charge shall be *u* the hand	Num 4:28	
u the hand of Ithamar the son of	Num 4:33	
is *u* the sacrifice of the peace	Num 6:18	8478
u the hand of Ithamar the son of	Num 7:8	
clave asunder that was *u* them	Num 16:31	8478
the LORD, she fell down *u* Balaam	Num 22:27	8478
men of war which are *u* our charge	Num 31:49	
their armies *u* the hand of Moses	Num 33:1	
that are *u* the whole heaven	Deut 2:25	8478
u Ashdoth-pisgah eastward	Deut 3:17	8478
came near and stood *u* the mountain	Deut 4:11	8478
all nations *u* the whole heaven	Deut 4:19	8478
plain, *u* the springs of Pisgah	Deut 4:49	8478
destroy their name from *u* heaven	Deut 7:24	8478
blot out their name from *u* heaven	Deut 9:14	8478
the hills, and *u* every green tree	Deut 12:2	8478
of Amalek from *u* heaven	Deut 25:19	8478
the earth that is *u* thee shall be	Deut 28:23	8478
blot out his name from *u* heaven	Deut 29:20	8478
of my tent, and the silver *u* it	Josh 7:21	8478
in his tent, and the silver *u* it	Josh 7:22	8478
to the Hivite *u* Hermon in the	Josh 11:3	8478
valley of Lebanon *u* mount Hermon	Josh 11:17	8478
from the south, *u* Ashdoth-pisgah	Josh 12:3	8478
from Baal-gad *u* mount Hermon unto	Josh 13:5	8478
unto this day, and serve *u* tribute	Josh 16:10	
and set it up there *u* an oak	Josh 24:26	8478
gathered their meat *u* my table	Judg 1:7	8478
he did gird it *u* his raiment upon	Judg 3:16	8478
that day *u* the hand of Israel	Judg 3:30	8478
she dwelt *u* the palm tree of	Judg 4:5	8478
sat *u* an oak which was in Ophrah,	Judg 6:11	8478
brought it out unto him *u* the oak	Judg 6:19	8478
to God this people were *u* my hand	Judg 9:29	
u whose wings thou art come to	Ruth 2:12	8478
them, until they came *u* Beth-car	1Sa 7:11	8478
u a pomegranate tree which is in	1Sa 14:2	8478
therefore what is *u* thine hand	1Sa 21:3	8478
is no common bread *u* mine hand	1Sa 21:4	8478
is there not here *u* thine hand	1Sa 21:8	8478
abode in Gibeah *u* a tree in Ramah	1Sa 22:6	8478
buried them *u* a tree at Jabesh,	1Sa 31:13	8478
spear smote him *u* the fifth rib	2Sa 2:23	413
smote him there *u* the fifth rib	2Sa 3:27	
and they smote him *u* the fifth rib	2Sa 4:6	413
were therein, and put them *u* saws	2Sa 12:31	
u harrows of iron, and *u* axes	2Sa 12:31	
of the people *u* the hand of Joab	2Sa 18:2	
a third part *u* the hand of	2Sa 18:2	
a third part *u* the hand of Ittai	2Sa 18:2	
the mule went *u* the thick boughs	2Sa 18:9	8478
the mule that was *u* him went away	2Sa 18:9	8478
and darkness was *u* his feet	2Sa 22:10	8478
Thou hast enlarged my steps *u* me	2Sa 22:37	8478
yea, they are fallen *u* my feet	2Sa 22:39	8478
against me hast thou subdued *u* me	2Sa 22:40	8478
bringeth down the people *u* me	2Sa 22:48	8478
safely, every man *u* his vine	1Kin 4:25	8478
u his fig tree, from Dan even to	1Kin 4:25	8478
put them *u* the soles of his feet	1Kin 5:3	8478
u the brim of it round about	1Kin 7:24	8478
u the laver were undersetters	1Kin 7:30	8478
u the borders were four wheels	1Kin 7:32	8478
one sea, and twelve oxen *u* the sea	1Kin 7:44	8478
even *u* the wings of the cherubims	1Kin 8:6	
and found him sitting *u* an oak	1Kin 13:14	8478
high hill, and *u* every green tree	1Kin 14:23	8478
lay it on wood, and put no fire *u*	1Kin 18:23	
lay it on wood, and put no fire *u*	1Kin 18:23	
of your gods, but put no fire *u*	1Kin 18:25	
sat down *u* a juniper tree	1Kin 19:4	8478
slept *u* a juniper tree, behold,	1Kin 19:5	8478
revolted from *u* the hand of Judah	2Kin 8:20	8478
Yet Edom revolted from *u* the hand	2Kin 8:22	8478
put it *u* him on the top of the	2Kin 9:13	8478
and he trode her *u* foot	2Kin 9:33	
from *u* the hand of the Syrians	2Kin 13:5	8478
the name of Israel from *u* heaven	2Kin 14:27	8478
the hills, and *u* every green tree	2Kin 16:4	8478
the brasen oxen that were *u* it	2Kin 16:17	8478
from *u* the hand of Pharaoh king	2Kin 17:7	8478
high hill, and *u* every green tree	2Kin 17:10	8478
their bones *u* the oak in Jabesh	1Chr 10:12	8478
of the LORD remaineth *u* curtains	1Chr 17:1	8478
u Aaron their father, as the LORD	1Chr 24:19	
the sons of Asaph *u* the hands of	1Chr 25:2	5921
u the hands of their father	1Chr 25:3	5921
All these were *u* the hands of	1Chr 25:6	5921
it was *u* the hand of Shelomith,	1Chr 26:28	5921
them from twenty years old and *u*	1Chr 27:23	4295
u it was the similitude of oxen,	2Chr 4:3	8478
One sea, and twelve oxen *u* it	2Chr 4:15	8478
even *u* the wings of the cherubims	2Chr 5:7	8478
were brought *u* at that time	2Chr 13:18	
from *u* the dominion of Judah	2Chr 21:8	8478
So the Edomites revolted from *u*	2Chr 21:10	8478
did Libnah revolt from *u* his hand	2Chr 21:10	8478
u the hand of Hananiah, one of	2Chr 26:11	5921
u their hand was an army, three	2Chr 26:13	5921
the hills, and *u* every green tree	2Chr 28:4	8478
to keep *u* the children of Judah	2Chr 28:10	
were overseers *u* the hand of	2Chr 31:13	
the beast that was *u* me to pass	Neh 2:14	8478
made booths, and sat *u* the booths	Neh 8:17	
the proud helpers do stoop *u* him	Job 9:13	8478
though he hide it *u* his tongue	Job 20:12	8478
are formed from *u* the waters	Job 26:5	8478
and the cloud is not rent *u* them	Job 26:8	5921
u it is turned up as it were fire	Job 28:5	8478
and seeth *u* the whole heaven	Job 28:24	8478
u the nettles they were gathered	Job 30:7	8478
He directeth it *u* the whole	Job 37:3	8478
He lieth *u* the shady trees, in	Job 40:21	8478
whatsoever is *u* the whole heaven	Job 41:11	8478
Sharp stones are *u* him	Job 41:30	8478
hast put all things *u* his feet	Ps 8:6	8478
u his tongue is mischief and	Ps 10:7	8478
hide me *u* the shadow of thy wings	Ps 17:8	
and darkness was *u* his feet	Ps 18:9	8478
Thou hast enlarged my steps *u* me	Ps 18:36	8478
they are fallen *u* my feet	Ps 18:38	8478
thou hast subdued *u* me those that	Ps 18:39	8478
me, and subdueth the people *u* me	Ps 18:47	8478
trust *u* the shadow of thy wings	Ps 36:7	
them *u* that rise up against us	Ps 44:5	
whereby the people fall *u* thee	Ps 45:5	8478
He shall subdue the people *u* us	Ps 47:3	8478
us, and the nations *u* our feet	Ps 47:3	8478
u the shadow of the Almighty	Ps 91:1	
u his wings shalt thou trust	Ps 91:4	8478
dragon shalt thou trample *u* feet	Ps 91:13	
into subjection *u* their hand	Ps 106:42	8478
adders' poison is *u* their lips	Ps 140:3	8478
who subdueth my people *u* me	Ps 144:2	8478
the slothful shall be *u* tribute	Prov 12:24	
he take away thy bed from *u* thee	Prov 22:27	8478
labour which he taketh *u* the sun	Eccl 1:3	8478
there is no new thing *u* the sun	Eccl 1:9	8478
all things that are done *u* heaven	Eccl 1:13	8478
the works that are done *u* the sun	Eccl 1:14	8478
which they should do *u* the heaven	Eccl 2:3	8478
and there was no profit *u* the sun	Eccl 2:11	8478
the work that is wrought *u* the	Eccl 2:17	8478
which I had taken *u* the sun	Eccl 2:18	8478
have shewed myself wise *u* the sun	Eccl 2:19	8478
the labour which I took *u* the sun	Eccl 2:20	8478
he hath laboured *u* the sun	Eccl 2:22	8478
to every purpose *u* the heaven	Eccl 3:1	8478
moreover I saw *u* the sun the	Eccl 3:16	8478
that are done *u* the sun	Eccl 4:1	8478
evil work that is done *u* the sun	Eccl 4:3	8478
and I saw vanity *u* the sun	Eccl 4:7	8478
the living which walk *u* the sun	Eccl 4:15	8478
evil which I have seen *u* the sun	Eccl 5:13	8478
u the sun all the days of his	Eccl 5:18	8478
evil which I have seen *u* the sun	Eccl 6:1	8478
what shall be after him *u* the sun	Eccl 6:12	8478
the crackling of thorns *u* a pot	Eccl 7:6	8478
every work that is done *u* the sun	Eccl 8:9	8478
hath no better thing *u* the sun	Eccl 8:15	8478
which God giveth him *u* the sun	Eccl 8:15	8478
the work that is done *u* the sun	Eccl 8:17	8478
things that are done *u* the sun	Eccl 9:3	8478
any thing that is done *u* the sun	Eccl 9:6	8478
he hath given thee *u* the sun	Eccl 9:9	8478
which thou takest *u* the sun	Eccl 9:9	8478
saw *u* the sun, that the race is	Eccl 9:11	8478
wisdom have I seen also *u* the sun	Eccl 9:13	8478
evil which I have seen *u* the sun	Eccl 10:5	8478
I sat down *u* his shadow with	Song 2:3	
His left hand is *u* my head	Song 2:6	8478
honey and milk are *u* thy tongue	Song 4:11	8478
His left hand should be *u* my head	Song 8:3	8478
I raised thee up *u* the apple tree	Song 8:5	8478
and let this ruin be *u* thy hand	Is 3:6	8478
shall bow down *u* the prisoners	Is 10:4	8478
and they shall fall *u* the slain	Is 10:4	8478
u his glory he shall kindle a	Is 10:16	8478
the worm is spread *u* thee	Is 14:11	8478
as a carcase trodden *u* feet	Is 14:19	
my mountains tread him *u* foot	Is 14:25	
meted out and trodden *u* foot	Is 18:7	
defiled *u* the inhabitants thereof	Is 24:5	8478
Moab shall be trodden down *u* him	Is 25:10	8478
Ephraim, shall be trodden *u* feet	Is 28:3	
u falsehood have we hid ourselves	Is 28:15	
and hatch, and gather *u* her shadow	Is 34:15	
with idols *u* every green tree	Is 57:5	8478
valleys *u* the clifts of the rocks	Is 57:5	8478
spread sackcloth and ashes *u* him	Is 58:5	
u every green tree thou wanderest	Jer 2:20	8478
u every green tree, and there hath	Jer 3:6	
the strangers *u* every green tree	Jer 3:13	8478
earth, and from *u* these heavens	Jer 10:11	8460
have trodden my portion *u* foot	Jer 12:10	
that will not put their neck *u*	Jer 27:8	
nations that bring their neck *u*	Jer 27:11	
Bring your necks *u* the yoke of	Jer 27:12	
shall the flocks pass again *u* the	Jer 33:13	5921
house of the king *u* the treasury	Jer 38:11	
u thine armholes *u* the cords	Jer 38:12	8478
They that fled stood *u* the shadow	Jer 48:45	
bulls that were *u* the bases	Jer 52:20	8478
The Lord hath trodden *u* foot all	Lam 1:15	
To crush *u* his feet all the	Lam 3:34	8478
from *u* the heavens of the LORD	Lam 3:66	8478
U his shadow we shall live among	Lam 4:20	
Our necks are *u* persecution	Lam 5:5	5921
and the children fell *u* the wood	Lam 5:13	
they had the hands of a man *u*	Eze 1:8	8478
u the firmament were their wings	Eze 1:23	8478
u every green tree	Eze 6:13	8478
u every thick oak, the place	Eze 6:13	8478
even *u* the cherub, and fill thine	Eze 10:2	
of a man's hand *u* their wings	Eze 10:8	8478
u the God of Israel by the river	Eze 10:20	8478
hands of a man was *u* their wings	Eze 10:21	8478
and the roots thereof were *u* him	Eze 17:6	8478
u it shall dwell all fowl of	Eze 17:23	8478
will cause you to pass *u* the rod	Eze 20:37	8478
and burn also the bones *u* it	Eze 24:5	8478
u his branches did all the beasts	Eze 31:6	8478
u his shadow dwelt all great	Eze 31:6	
that dwelt *u* his shadow in the	Eze 31:17	
laid their swords *u* their heads	Eze 32:27	8478
from *u* these chambers was the	Eze 42:9	8478
places *u* the rows round about	Eze 46:23	8478
waters issued out from *u* the	Eze 47:1	8478
the waters came down from *u* from	Eze 47:1	8478
of the field had shadow *u* it	Dan 4:12	8460
let the beasts get away from *u* it	Dan 4:14	8478
u which the beasts of the field	Dan 4:21	8460
of the kingdom *u* the whole heaven	Dan 7:27	8460
and the host to be trodden *u* foot	Dan 8:13	
for *u* the whole heaven hath not	Dan 9:12	8478
gone a whoring from *u* their God	Hos 4:12	8478
u oaks and poplars and elms,	Hos 4:13	8478
They that dwell *u* his shadow	Hos 14:7	
The seed is rotten *u* their clods	Joel 1:17	8478
Behold, I am pressed *u* you	Amos 2:13	8478
bread have laid a wound *u* thee	Obad 7	8478
sat *u* it in the shadow, till he	Jonah 4:5	8478
mountains shall be molten *u* him	Mic 1:4	8478
u his vine and *u* his fig tree	Mic 4:4	8478
man his neighbour *u* the vine	Zec 3:10	8478
u the vine and *u* the fig tree	Zec 3:10	8478
for they shall be ashes *u* the	Mal 4:3	8478
thereof, from two years old and *u*	Mt 2:16	*2736*
and to be trodden *u* foot of men	Mt 5:13	*2662*
put it *u* a bushel, but on a	Mt 5:15	*5259*
they trample them *u* their feet	Mt 7:6	*1722*
thou shouldest come *u* my roof	Mt 8:8	*5259*
For I am a man *u* authority	Mt 8:9	*5259*
authority, having soldiers *u* me	Mt 8:9	*5259*
her chickens *u* her wings, and ye	Mt 23:37	*5259*
be put *u* a bushel, or *u* a bed	Mk 4:21	*5259*
air may lodge *u* the shadow of it	Mk 4:32	*5259*
shake off the dust *u* your feet	Mk 6:11	*5270*
yet the dogs *u* the table eat of	Mk 7:28	*5270*
thou shouldest enter *u* my roof	Lk 7:6	*5259*
I also am a man set *u* authority	Lk 7:8	*5259*
having *u* me soldiers, and I say	Lk 7:8	*5259*
a vessel, or putteth it *u* a bed	Lk 8:16	*5270*
neither *u* a bushel, but on a	Lk 11:33	*5259*
doth gather her brood *u* her wings	Lk 13:34	*5259*
out of the one part *u* heaven	Lk 17:24	*5259*
unto the other part *u* heaven	Lk 17:24	*5259*
when thou wast *u* the fig tree	Jn 1:48	*5259*
I saw thee *u* the fig tree,	Jn 1:50	*5273*
men, out of every nation *u* heaven	Acts 2:5	*5259*
name *u* heaven given among men	Acts 4:12	*5259*
an eunuch of great authority *u*	Acts 8:27	
and bound themselves *u* a curse	Acts 23:12	*332*
bound ourselves *u* a great curse	Acts 23:14	*332*
from thence, we sailed *u* Cyprus	Acts 27:4	*5284*
suffering us, we sailed *u* Crete	Acts 27:7	*5284*
running *u* a certain island which	Acts 27:16	*5295*
u colour as though they would	Acts 27:30	
Gentiles, that they are all *u* sin	Rom 3:9	*5259*
poison of asps is *u* their lips	Rom 3:13	*5259*
saith to them who are *u* the law	Rom 3:19	*1722*
not *u* the law, but *u* grace	Rom 6:14	*5259*
not *u* the law, but *u* grace	Rom 6:15	*5259*
but I am carnal, sold *u* sin	Rom 7:14	*5259*
bruise Satan *u* your feet shortly	Rom 16:20	*5259*
not be brought *u* the power of any	1Cor 6:12	*5259*
is not *u* bondage in such cases	1Cor 7:15	
to them that are *u* the law	1Cor 9:20	*5259*
as *u* the law, that I might gain	1Cor 9:20	*5259*
gain them that are *u* the law	1Cor 9:20	*5259*
but *u* the law to Christ,) that I	1Cor 9:21	*1772*
But I keep *u* my body, and bring it	1Cor 9:27	*5299*
all our fathers were *u* the cloud	1Cor 10:1	*5259*
are commanded to be *u* obedience	1Cor 14:34	*5293*
hath put all enemies *u* his feet	1Cor 15:25	*5259*
he hath put all things *u* his feet	1Cor 15:27	*5259*
he saith all things are put *u* him	1Cor 15:27	*5259*
which did put all things *u* him	1Cor 15:27	*5293*
him that put all things *u* him	1Cor 15:28	*5293*
In Damascus the governor *u* Aretas	2Cor 11:32	
works of the law are *u* the curse	Gal 3:10	*5259*
hath concluded all *u* sin, that	Gal 3:22	*5259*
came, we were kept *u* the law	Gal 3:23	*5259*
we are no longer *u* a schoolmaster	Gal 3:25	*5259*
But is *u* tutors and governors	Gal 4:2	*5259*
were in bondage *u* the elements of	Gal 4:3	*5259*
made of a woman, made *u* the law,	Gal 4:4	*5259*
redeem them that were *u* the law	Gal 4:5	*5259*
ye that desire to be *u* the law	Gal 4:21	*5259*
the Spirit, ye are not *u* the law	Gal 5:18	*5259*
And hath put all things *u* his feet	Eph 1:22	*5259*
in earth, and things *u* the earth	Phil 2:10	*2709*
every creature which is *u* heaven	Col 1:23	*5259*
the number *u* threescore years old	1Ti 5:9	*1640*
as are *u* the yoke count their own	1Ti 6:1	*5259*
things in subjection *u* his feet	Heb 2:8	*5270*
he put all in subjection *u* him	Heb 2:8	
nothing that is not put *u* him	Heb 2:8	*506*
see not yet all things put *u* him	Heb 2:8	*5293*
(for *u* it the people received the	Heb 7:11	*1909*
that were *u* the first testament	Heb 9:15	*1909*
mercy *u* two or three witnesses	Heb 10:28	*1909*
who hath trodden *u* foot the Son	Heb 10:29	*2662*
or sit here *u* my footstool	Jas 2:3	*5259*
u the mighty hand of God, that he	1Pet 5:6	*5259*
u darkness unto the judgment of	Jude 6	*5259*
neither *u* the earth, was able to	Rev 5:3	*5270*
u the earth, and such as are in	Rev 5:13	*5270*
I saw *u* the altar the souls of	Rev 6:9	*5270*
shall they tread *u* foot forty	Rev 11:2	
the sun, and the moon *u* her feet	Rev 12:1	*5270*

UNDERGIRDING		
up, they used helps, *u* the ship	Acts 27:17	*5269*

UNDERNEATH		
on the two sides of the ephod *u*	Ex 28:27	4295
on the two sides of the ephod *u*	Ex 39:20	4295
u are the everlasting arms	Deut 33:27	8478

UNDERSETTERS		
and the four corners thereof had *u*	1Kin 7:30	3802
under the laver were *u* molten	1Kin 7:30	3802
there were four *u* to the four	1Kin 7:34	3802
the *u* were of the very base	1Kin 7:34	3802

UNDERSTAND		
that they may not *u* one another's	Gen 11:7	8085
that thou canst *u* a dream to	Gen 41:15	8085
then ye shall *u* that these men	Num 16:30	3045
U therefore this day, that the	Deut 9:3	3045
U therefore, that the LORD thy	Deut 9:6	3045
whose tongue thou shalt not *u*	Deut 28:49	8085
for we *u* it	2Kin 18:26	8085
the LORD made me *u* in writing by	1Chr 28:19	7919
the women, and those that could *u*	Neh 8:3	995
caused the people to *u* the law	Neh 8:7	995
and caused them to *u* the reading	Neh 8:8	995
even to *u* the words of the law	Neh 8:13	7919
cause me to *u* wherein I have	Job 6:24	995
u what he would say unto me	Job 23:5	995
thunder of his power who can *u*	Job 26:14	995
neither do the aged *u* judgment	Job 32:9	995
Also can any *u* the spreadings of	Job 36:29	995
see if there were any that did *u*	Ps 14:2	7919
Who can *u* his errors	Ps 19:12	995
see if there were any that did *u*	Ps 53:2	7919
know not, neither will they *u*	Ps 82:5	995
neither doth a fool *u* this	Ps 92:6	995
U, ye brutish among the people	Ps 94:8	995
things, even they shall *u* the	Ps 107:43	995
Make me to *u* the way of thy	Ps 119:27	995
I *u* more than the ancients,	Ps 119:100	995
To *u* a proverb, and the	Prov 1:6	995
Then shalt thou *u* the fear of the	Prov 2:5	995
Then shalt thou *u* righteousness	Prov 2:9	995
O ye simple, *u* wisdom	Prov 8:5	995
of the prudent is to *u* his way	Prov 14:8	995
and he will *u* knowledge	Prov 19:25	995
how can a man then *u* his own way	Prov 20:24	995
Evil men *u* not judgment	Prov 28:5	995
that seek the LORD *u* all things	Prov 28:5	995
for though he *u* he will not	Prov 29:19	995
people, Hear ye indeed, but *u* not	Is 6:9	995
u with their heart, and convert,	Is 6:10	995
whom shall he make to *u* doctrine	Is 28:9	995
a vexation only to *u* the report	Is 28:19	995
of the rash shall *u* knowledge	Is 32:4	995
tongue, that thou canst not *u*	Is 33:19	998
for we *u* it	Is 36:11	8085
u together, that the hand of the	Is 41:20	7919
and believe me, and *u* that I am he	Is 43:10	995
their hearts, that they cannot *u*	Is 44:18	7919
they are shepherds that cannot *u*	Is 56:11	995
is the wise man, that may *u* this	Jer 9:12	995
whose words thou canst not *u*	Eze 3:6	8085
make this man to *u* the vision	Dan 8:16	995
but he said unto me, *U*, O son of	Dan 8:17	995
our iniquities, and *u* thy truth	Dan 9:13	7919
therefore *u* the matter, and	Dan 9:23	995
Know therefore and *u*, that from	Dan 9:25	7919
u the words that I speak unto	Dan 10:11	995
thou didst set thine heart to *u*	Dan 10:12	995
Now I am come to make thee *u* what	Dan 10:14	995
they that *u* among the people	Dan 11:33	7919
and none of the wicked shall *u*	Dan 12:10	995
but the wise shall *u*	Dan 12:10	995
people that doth not *u* shall fall	Hos 4:14	995
wise, and he shall *u* these things	Hos 14:9	995
neither *u* they his counsel	Mic 4:12	995
they hear not, neither do they *u*	Mt 13:13	*4920*
ye shall hear, and shall not *u*	Mt 13:14	*4920*
should *u* with their heart, and	Mt 13:15	*4920*
and said unto them, Hear, and *u*	Mt 15:10	*4920*
Do not ye yet *u*, that whatsoever	Mt 15:17	*3539*
Do ye not yet *u*, neither remember	Mt 16:9	*3539*
How is it that ye do not *u* that I	Mt 16:11	*3539*
place, (whoso readeth, let him *u*	Mt 24:15	*3539*
hearing they may hear, and not *u*	Mk 4:12	*4920*
unto me every one of you, and *u*	Mk 7:14	*4920*
perceive ye not yet, neither *u*	Mk 8:17	*4920*
them, How is it that ye do not *u*	Mk 8:21	*4920*
not, (let him that readeth *u*	Mk 13:14	*3539*
neither *u* I what thou sayest	Mk 14:68	*1987*
see, and hearing they might not *u*	Lk 8:10	*4920*
that they might *u* the scriptures	Lk 24:45	*4920*
Why do ye not *u* my speech	Jn 8:43	*1097*
nor *u* with their heart, and be	Jn 12:40	*3539*
Because that thou mayest *u*	Acts 24:11	*1097*
ye shall hear, and shall not *u*	Acts 28:26	*4920*
u with their heart, and should be	Acts 28:27	*4920*
they that have not heard shall *u*	Rom 15:21	*4920*
Wherefore I give you to *u*	1Cor 12:3	*1107*
u all mysteries, and all knowledge	1Cor 13:2	*1492*
ye may *u* my knowledge in the	Eph 3:4	*3539*
But I would ye should *u*, brethren	Phil 1:12	*1097*
Through faith we *u* that the	Heb 11:3	*3539*
of the things that they *u* not	2Pet 2:12	*50*

UNDERSTANDEST		
what *u* thou, which is not in us	Job 15:9	995
thou *u* my thought afar off	Ps 139:2	995
not, neither *u* what they say	Jer 5:15	8085
and said, *U* thou what thou readest	Acts 8:30	*1097*

UNDERSTANDETH		
u all the imaginations of the	1Chr 28:9	995
God *u* the way thereof, and he	Job 28:23	995
u not, is like the beasts that	Ps 49:20	995
They are all plain to him that *u*	Prov 8:9	995
knowledge is easy unto him that *u*	Prov 14:6	995
glorieth glory in this, that he *u*	Jer 9:24	7919
u it not, then cometh the wicked	Mt 13:19	*4920*
he that heareth the word, and *u* it	Mt 13:23	*4920*
There is none that *u*, there is	Rom 3:11	*4920*
for no man *u* him	1Cor 14:2	*191*
seeing he *u* not what thou sayest	1Cor 14:16	*1492*

UNDERSTANDING		
spirit of God, in wisdom, and in *u*	Ex 31:3	8394
spirit of God, in wisdom, in *u*	Ex 35:31	8394
u to know how to work all manner	Ex 36:1	8394
Take you wise men, and *u*	Deut 1:13	995
your *u* in the sight of the	Deut 4:6	998
nation is a wise and *u* people	Deut 4:6	995
neither is there any *u* in them	Deut 32:28	8394
and she was a woman of good *u*	1Sa 25:3	7922
an *u* heart to judge thy people	1Kin 3:9	8085
for thyself *u* to discern judgment	1Kin 3:11	995
given thee a wise and an *u* heart	1Kin 3:12	995
u exceeding much, and largeness of	1Kin 4:29	8394
he was filled with wisdom, and *u*	1Kin 7:14	8394
were men that had *u* of the times	1Chr 12:32	998
the LORD give thee wisdom and *u*	1Chr 22:12	998
son, endued with prudence and *u*	2Chr 2:12	998
sent a cunning man, endued with *u*	2Chr 2:13	998
who had *u* in the visions of God	2Chr 26:5	995
and for Elnathan, men of *u*	Ezr 8:16	995
us they brought us a man of *u*	Ezr 8:18	7922
and all that could hear with *u*	Neh 8:2	995
one having knowledge, and having *u*	Neh 10:28	995
But I have *u* as well as you	Job 12:3	3824
and in length of days *u*	Job 12:12	8394
and strength, he hath counsel and *u*	Job 12:13	8394
and taketh away the *u* of the aged	Job 12:20	2940
thou hast hid their heart from *u*	Job 17:4	7922
the spirit of my *u* causeth me to	Job 20:3	998
by his *u* he smiteth through the	Job 26:12	8394
and where is the place of *u*	Job 28:12	998
and where is the place of *u*	Job 28:20	998
and to depart from evil is *u*	Job 28:28	998
of the Almighty giveth them *u*	Job 32:8	995
hearken unto me, ye men of *u*	Job 34:10	3824
If now thou hast *u*, hear this	Job 34:16	998
Let men of *u* tell me, and let a	Job 34:34	3824
declare, if thou hast *u*	Job 38:4	998
or who hath given *u* to the heart	Job 38:36	998
neither hath he imparted to her *u*	Job 39:17	998
or as the mule, which have no *u*	Ps 32:9	995
sing ye praises with *u*	Ps 47:7	7919
of my heart shall be of *u*	Ps 49:3	8394
a good *u* have all they that do	Ps 111:10	7922
Give me *u*, and I shall keep thy	Ps 119:34	995
give me *u*, that I may learn thy	Ps 119:73	995
I have more *u* than all my	Ps 119:99	7919
Through thy precepts I get *u*	Ps 119:104	995
give me *u*, that I may know thy	Ps 119:125	995
it giveth *u* unto the simple	Ps 119:130	995
give me *u*, and I shall live	Ps 119:144	995
give me *u* according to thy word	Ps 119:169	995
his *u* is infinite	Ps 147:5	8394
to perceive the words of *u*	Prov 1:2	998
a man of *u* shall attain unto wise	Prov 1:5	995
wisdom, and apply thine heart to *u*	Prov 2:2	8394
and liftest up thy voice for *u*	Prov 2:3	8394
his mouth cometh knowledge and *u*	Prov 2:6	8394
preserve thee, *u* shall keep thee	Prov 2:11	8394
good *u* in the sight of God and man	Prov 3:4	7922
and lean not unto thine own *u*	Prov 3:5	998
wisdom, and the man that getteth *u*	Prov 3:13	8394
by *u* hath he established the	Prov 3:19	8394
of a father, and attend to know *u*	Prov 4:1	998
Get wisdom, get *u*	Prov 4:5	998
and with all thy getting get *u*	Prov 4:7	998
wisdom, and bow thine ear to my *u*	Prov 5:1	8394
adultery with a woman lacketh *u*	Prov 6:32	3820
and call *u* thy kinswoman	Prov 7:4	998
the youths, a young man void of *u*	Prov 7:7	3820
and *u* put forth her voice	Prov 8:1	8394
and, ye fools, be ye of an *u* heart	Prov 8:5	995
I am *u*	Prov 8:14	998
as for him that wanteth *u*	Prov 9:4	3820
and go in the way of *u*	Prov 9:6	998
and the knowledge of the holy is *u*	Prov 9:10	998
and as for him that wanteth *u*	Prov 9:16	3820
him that hath *u* wisdom is found	Prov 10:13	995
the back of him that is void of *u*	Prov 10:13	3820
but a man of *u* hath wisdom	Prov 10:23	8394
but a man of *u* holdeth his peace	Prov 11:12	8394
vain persons is void of *u*	Prov 12:11	3820
Good *u* giveth favour	Prov 13:15	7922
is slow to wrath is of great *u*	Prov 14:29	8394
in the heart of him that hath *u*	Prov 14:33	995
him that hath *u* seeketh knowledge	Prov 15:14	995
but a man of *u* walketh uprightly	Prov 15:21	8394
he that heareth reproof getteth *u*	Prov 15:32	3820
to get *u* rather to be chosen than	Prov 16:16	998
U is a wellspring of life unto	Prov 16:22	7922
A man void of *u* striketh hands,	Prov 17:18	3820
Wisdom is before him that hath *u*	Prov 17:24	995
a man of *u* is of an excellent	Prov 17:27	8394
his lips is esteemed a man of *u*	Prov 17:28	995
A fool hath no delight in *u*	Prov 18:2	8394
he that keepeth *u* shall find good	Prov 19:8	8394
and reprove one that hath *u*	Prov 19:25	995
but a man of *u* will draw it out	Prov 20:5	8394
the way of *u* shall remain in the	Prov 21:16	7919
There is no wisdom nor *u* nor	Prov 21:30	8394
also wisdom, and instruction, and *u*	Prov 23:23	998
and by *u* it is established	Prov 24:3	8394
the vineyard of the man void of *u*	Prov 24:30	3820
but by a man of *u* and knowledge	Prov 28:2	995
that hath *u* searcheth him out	Prov 28:11	995
The prince that wanteth *u* is also	Prov 28:16	8394
man, and have not the *u* of a man	Prov 30:2	998
wise, nor yet riches to men of *u*	Eccl 9:11	995
him, the spirit of wisdom and *u*	Is 11:2	998
quick *u* in the fear of the LORD	Is 11:3	7306
for it is a people of no *u*	Is 27:11	998
the *u* of their prudent men shall	Is 29:14	998
him that framed it, He had no *u*	Is 29:16	995
erred in spirit shall come to *u*	Is 29:24	998
and shewed to him the way of *u*	Is 40:14	8394
there is no searching of his *u*	Is 40:28	8394
is there knowledge nor *u* to say	Is 44:19	8394
feed you with knowledge and *u*	Jer 3:15	7919
children, and they have none *u*	Jer 4:22	995
O foolish people, and without *u*	Jer 5:21	3820
stretched out the heaven by his *u*	Jer 51:15	8394
with thine *u* thou hast gotten	Eze 28:4	8394
u science, and such as had ability	Dan 1:4	995
Daniel had *u* in all visions and	Dan 1:17	995
And in all matters of wisdom and *u*	Dan 1:20	998
and knowledge to them that know *u*	Dan 2:21	999
mine *u* returned unto me, and I	Dan 4:34	4486
the days of thy father light and *u*	Dan 5:11	7924
spirit, and knowledge, and *u*	Dan 5:12	7924
is in thee, and that light and *u*	Dan 5:14	7924
u dark sentences, shall stand up	Dan 8:23	995
forth to give thee skill and *u*	Dan 9:22	998
the thing, and had *u* of the vision	Dan 10:1	998
And some of them of *u* shall fall	Dan 11:35	7919
and idols according to their own *u*	Hos 13:2	8394
there is none *u* in him	Obad 7	8394
u out of the mount of Esau	Obad 8	8394
said, Are ye also yet without *u*	Mt 15:16	*801*
them, Are ye so without *u* also	Mk 7:18	*801*
all the heart, and with all the *u*	Mk 12:33	*4907*
having had perfect *u* of all	Lk 1:3	*3877*
him were astonished at his *u*	Lk 2:47	*4907*
Then opened he their *u*, that they	Lk 24:45	*3563*
Without *u*, covenantbreakers,	Rom 1:31	*801*
to nothing the *u* of the prudent	1Cor 1:19	*4907*
prayeth, but my *u* is unfruitful	1Cor 14:14	*3563*
and I will pray with the *u* also	1Cor 14:15	*3563*
and I will sing with the *u* also	1Cor 14:15	*3563*
rather speak five words with my *u*	1Cor 14:19	*3563*
Brethren, be not children in *u*	1Cor 14:20	*5424*
be ye children, but in *u* be men	1Cor 14:20	*5424*
The eyes of your *u* being	Eph 1:18	*1271*
Having the *u* darkened, being	Eph 4:18	*1271*
but *u* what the will of the Lord	Eph 5:17	*4920*
peace of God, which passeth all *u*	Phil 4:7	*3563*
will in all wisdom and spiritual *u*	Col 1:9	*4907*
riches of the full assurance of *u*	Col 2:2	*4907*
u neither what they say, nor	1Ti 1:7	*4920*
Lord give thee *u* in all things	2Ti 2:7	*4907*
is come, and hath given us an *u*	1Jn 5:20	*1271*
Let him that hath *u* count the	Rev 13:18	*3563*

UNDERSTOOD		
they knew not that Joseph *u* them	Gen 42:23	8085
they were wise, that they *u* this	Deut 32:29	7919
they *u* that the ark of the LORD	1Sa 4:6	3045
u that Saul was come in very deed	1Sa 26:4	3045
all Israel *u* that day that it was	2Sa 3:37	3045
because they had *u* the words that	Neh 8:12	995
u of the evil that Eliashib did	Neh 13:7	995
this, mine ear hath heard and *u* it	Job 13:1	995
have I uttered that I *u* not	Job 42:3	995
then *u* I their end	Ps 73:17	995
I heard a language that I *u* not	Ps 81:5	3045
Our fathers *u* not thy wonders in	Ps 106:7	7919
have ye not *u* from the	Is 40:21	995
They have not known nor *u*	Is 44:18	995
at the vision, but none *u* it	Dan 8:27	995
u by books the number of the	Dan 9:2	995
and he *u* the thing, and had	Dan 10:1	995
And I heard, but I *u* not	Dan 12:8	995
Have ye *u* all these things	Mt 13:51	*4920*
Then *u* they how that he bade them	Mt 16:12	*4920*
Then the disciples *u* that he	Mt 17:13	*4920*
When Jesus *u* it, he said unto	Mt 26:10	*1097*
But they *u* not that saying, and	Mk 9:32	*50*
they *u* not the saying which he	Lk 2:50	*4920*
But they *u* not this saying, and it	Lk 9:45	*50*
they *u* none of these things	Lk 18:34	*4920*
They *u* not that he spake to them	Jn 8:27	*1097*
but they *u* not what things they	Jn 10:6	*1097*
These things *u* not his disciples	Jn 12:16	*1097*
his brethren would have *u* how	Acts 7:25	*4920*
but they *u* not	Acts 7:25	*4920*
having *u* that he was a Roman	Acts 23:27	*3129*
when he *u* that he was of Cilicia	Acts 23:34	*4441*
being *u* by the things that are	Rom 1:20	*3539*
I *u* as a child, I thought as a	1Cor 13:11	*5426*
by the tongue words easy to be *u*	1Cor 14:9	*2154*
are some things hard to be *u*	2Pet 3:16	*1425*

UNDERTAKE		
oppressed; *u* for me	Is 38:14	6148

UNDERTOOK		
the Jews *u* to do as they had	Est 9:23	6901

UNDO		
to *u* the heavy burdens, and to let	Is 58:6	5425
at that time I will *u* all that	Zeph 3:19	6213

UNDONE		
thou art *u*, O people of Chemosh	Num 21:29	6
he left nothing *u* of all that the	Josh 11:15	5493
for I am *u*	Is 6:5	1820
done, and not to leave the other *u*	Mt 23:23	
done, and not to leave the other *u*	Lk 11:42	

UNDRESSED		
gather the grapes of thy vine *u*	Lev 25:5	5139
the grapes in it of thy vine *u*	Lev 25:11	5139

UNEQUAL
- are not your ways *u* Eze 18:25
- are not your ways *u* Eze 18:29

UNEQUALLY
- Be ye not *u* yoked together with 2Cor 6:14 *2086*

UNFAITHFUL
- Confidence in an *u* man in time of Prov 25:19 898

UNFAITHFULLY
- dealt *u* like their fathers Ps 78:57 898

UNFEIGNED
- by the Holy Ghost, by love *u* 2Cor 6:6 *505*
- a good conscience, and of faith *u* 1Ti 1:5 *505*
- the *u* faith that is in thee 2Ti 1:5 *505*
- unto *u* love of the brethren 1Pet 1:22 *505*

UNFRUITFUL
- choke the word, and he becometh *u* Mt 13:22 *175*
- choke the word, and it becometh *u* Mk 4:19 *175*
- but my understanding is *u* 1Cor 14:14 *175*
- with the *u* works of darkness Eph 5:11 *175*
- uses, that they be not *u* Titus 3:14 *175*
- *u* in the knowledge of our Lord 2Pet 1:8 *175*

UNGIRDED
- he *u* his camels, and gave straw and Gen 24:32 6605

UNGODLINESS
- from heaven against all *u* Rom 1:18 *763*
- and shall turn away *u* from Jacob Rom 11:26 *763*
- they will increase unto more *u* 2Ti 2:16 *763*
- Teaching us that, denying *u* Titus 2:12 *763*

UNGODLY
- the floods of *u* men made me 2Sa 22:5 1100
- Shouldest thou help the *u* 2Chr 19:2 7563
- God hath delivered me to the *u* Job 16:11 5760
- and to princes, Ye are *u* Job 34:18 7563
- not in the counsel of the *u* Ps 1:1 7563
- The *u* are not so Ps 1:4 7563
- Therefore the *u* shall not stand Ps 1:5 7563
- but the way of the *u* shall perish Ps 1:6 7563
- hast broken the teeth of the *u* Ps 3:7 7563
- the floods of *u* men made me Ps 18:4 1100
- my cause against an *u* nation Ps 43:1
- Behold, these are the *u*, who Ps 73:12 7563
- An *u* man diggeth up evil Prov 16:27 1100
- An *u* witness scorneth judgment Prov 19:28 1100
- on him that justifieth the *u* Rom 4:5 *765*
- in due time Christ died for the *u* Rom 5:6 *765*
- lawless and disobedient, for the *u* 1Ti 1:9 *765*
- be saved, where shall the *u* 1Pet 4:18 *765*
- the flood upon the world of the *u* 2Pet 2:5 *765*
- those that after should live *u* 2Pet 2:6 *764*
- of judgment and perdition of *u* men 2Pet 3:7 *765*
- *u* men, turning the grace of our Jude 4 *765*
- to convince all that are *u* among Jude 15 *763*
- *u* deeds which they have Jude 15 *763*
- deeds which they have *u* committed Jude 15 *764*
- all their hard speeches which *u* Jude 15 *765*
- walk after their own *u* lusts Jude 18 *763*

UNHOLY
- put difference between holy and *u* Lev 10:10 2455
- the ungodly and for sinners, for *u* 1Ti 1:9 *462*
- to parents, unthankful, *u* 2Ti 3:2 *462*
- an *u* thing, and hath done despite Heb 10:29 *2839*

UNICORN
- as it were the strength of a *u* Num 23:22 7214
- as it were the strength of a *u* Num 24:8 7214
- Will the *u* be willing to serve Job 39:9 7214
- Canst thou bind the *u* with his Job 39:10 7214
- Lebanon and Sirion like a young *u* Ps 29:6 7214
- thou exalt like the horn of an *u* Ps 92:10 7214

UNICORNS
- his horns are like the horns of *u* Deut 33:17 7214
- heard me from the horns of the *u* Ps 22:21 7214
- the *u* shall come down with them, Is 34:7 7214

UNITE
- *u* my heart to fear thy name Ps 86:11 3161

UNITED
- mine honour, be not thou *u* Gen 49:6 3161

UNITY
- brethren to dwell together in *u* Ps 133:1 3162
- Endeavouring to keep the *u* of the Eph 4:3 *1775*
- we all come in the *u* of the faith Eph 4:13 *1775*

UNJUST
- me from the deceitful and *u* man Ps 43:1 5766
- the hope of *u* men perisheth Prov 11:7 205
- *u* gain increaseth his substance, Prov 28:8 8636
- An *u* man is an abomination to the Prov 29:27 5766
- but the *u* knoweth no shame Zeph 3:5 5767
- rain on the just and on the *u* Mt 5:45 *94*
- the lord commended the *u* steward Lk 16:8 *93*
- he that is *u* in the least is Lk 16:10 *94*
- in the least is *u* also in much Lk 16:10 *94*
- said, Hear what the *u* judge saith Lk 18:6 *93*
- as other men are, extortioners, *u* Lk 18:11 *94*
- the dead, both of the just and *u* Acts 24:15 *94*
- another, go to law before the *u* 1Cor 6:1 *94*
- for sins, the just for the *u* 1Pet 3:18 *94*
- to reserve the *u* unto the day of 2Pet 2:9 *94*
- He that is *u*, let him be *u* Rev 22:11 *91*

UNJUSTLY
- How long will ye judge *u*, and Ps 82:2 5766
- of uprightness will he deal *u* Is 26:10 5765

UNKNOWN
- this inscription, TO THE *U* GOD Acts 17:23 *57*
- For he that speaketh in an *u* 1Cor 14:2
- He that speaketh in an *u* tongue 1Cor 14:4
- in an *u* tongue pray that he may 1Cor 14:13
- For if I pray in an *u* tongue 1Cor 14:14
- ten thousand words in an *u* tongue 1Cor 14:19
- If any man speak in an *u* tongue 1Cor 14:27
- As *u*, and yet well known 2Cor 6:9 *50*
- was *u* by face unto the churches Gal 1:22 *50*

UNLADE
- the ship was to *u* her burden Acts 21:3 *670*

UNLAWFUL
- Ye know how that it is an *u* thing Acts 10:28 *111*
- day to day with their *u* deeds 2Pet 2:8 *459*

UNLEARNED
- and perceived that they were *u* Acts 4:13 *62*
- the *u* say Amen at thy giving of 1Cor 14:16 *2399*
- and there come in those that are *u* 1Cor 14:23 *2399*
- one that believeth not, or one *u* 1Cor 14:24 *2399*
- *u* questions avoid, knowing that 2Ti 2:23 *521*
- understood, which they that are *u* 2Pet 3:16 *261*

UNLEAVENED
- them a feast, and did bake *u* bread Gen 19:3 4682
- roast with fire, and *u* bread Ex 12:8 4682
- Seven days shall ye eat *u* bread Ex 12:15 4682
- observe the feast of *u* bread Ex 12:17 4682
- at even, ye shall eat *u* bread Ex 12:18 4682
- habitations shall ye eat *u* bread Ex 12:20 4682
- they baked *u* cakes of the dough Ex 12:39 4682
- Seven days thou shalt eat *u* bread Ex 13:6 4682
- *U* bread shall be eaten seven days Ex 13:7 4682
- shalt keep the feast of *u* bread Ex 23:15 4682
- (thou shalt eat *u* bread seven Ex 23:15 4682
- *u* bread, and cakes *u* Ex 29:2 4682
- wafers *u* anointed with oil Ex 29:2 4682
- *u* bread that is before the LORD Ex 29:23 4682
- The feast of *u* bread shalt thou Ex 34:18 4682
- Seven days thou shalt eat *u* bread Ex 34:18 4682
- it shall be *u* cakes of fine flour Lev 2:4 4682
- or *u* wafers anointed with oil Lev 2:4 4682
- pan, it shall be of fine flour *u* Lev 2:5 4682
- with *u* bread shall it be eaten in Lev 6:16 4682
- *u* cakes mingled with oil, and Lev 7:12 4682
- *u* wafers anointed with oil, and Lev 7:12 4682
- two rams, and a basket of *u* bread Lev 8:2 4682
- And out of the basket of *u* bread Lev 8:26 4682
- the LORD, he took one *u* cake Lev 8:26 4682
- feast of *u* bread unto the LORD Lev 23:6 4682
- seven days ye must eat *u* bread Lev 23:6 4682
- And a basket of *u* bread, cakes of Num 6:15 4682
- wafers of *u* bread anointed with Num 6:15 4682
- LORD, with the basket of *u* bread Num 6:17 4682
- one *u* cake out of the basket, and Num 6:19 4682
- one *u* wafer, and shall put them Num 6:19 4682
- keep it, and eat it with *u* bread Num 9:11 4682
- seven days shall *u* bread be eaten Num 28:17 4682
- shalt thou eat *u* bread therewith Deut 16:3 4682
- Six days thou shalt eat *u* bread Deut 16:8 4682
- in the feast of *u* bread, and in Deut 16:16 4682
- *u* cakes, and parched corn in the Josh 5:11 4682
- *u* cakes of an ephah of flour Judg 6:19 4682
- the *u* cakes, and lay them upon Judg 6:20 4682
- touched the flesh and the *u* cakes Judg 6:21 4682
- consumed the flesh and the *u* cakes Judg 6:21 4682
- it, and did bake *u* bread thereof 1Sa 28:24 4682
- but they did eat of the *u* bread 2Kin 23:9 4682
- meat offering, and for the *u* cakes 1Chr 23:29 4682
- even in the feast of *u* bread 2Chr 8:13 4682
- of *u* bread in the second month 2Chr 30:13 4682
- of *u* bread seven days with great 2Chr 30:21 4682
- the feast of *u* bread seven days 2Chr 35:17 4682
- kept the feast of *u* bread seven Ezr 6:22 4682
- *u* bread shall be eaten Eze 45:21 4682
- of *u* bread the disciples came to Mt 26:17 *106*
- of the passover, and of *u* bread Mk 14:1 *106*
- And the first day of *u* bread Mk 14:12 *106*
- the feast of *u* bread drew nigh Lk 22:1 *106*
- Then came the day of *u* bread Lk 22:7 *106*
- (Then were the days of *u* bread Acts 12:3 *106*
- after the days of *u* bread Acts 20:6 *106*
- ye may be a new lump, as ye are *u* 1Cor 5:7 *106*
- but with the *u* bread of sincerity 1Cor 5:8 *106*

UNLESS
- *u* he wash his flesh with water Lev 22:6
- *u* she had turned from me, surely Num 22:33 194
- *u* thou hadst spoken, surely then 2Sa 2:27
- *u* I had believed to see the Ps 27:13 3884
- *U* the LORD had been my help, my Ps 94:17 3884
- *U* thy law had been my delights, I Ps 119:92 3884
- *u* they cause some to fall Prov 4:16
- *u* ye have believed in vain 1Cor 15:2

UNLOOSE
- am not worthy to stoop down and *u* Mk 1:7 *3089*
- whose shoes I am not worthy to *u* Lk 3:16 *3089*
- latchet I am not worthy to *u* Jn 1:27 *3089*

UNMARRIED
- I say therefore to the *u* and 1Cor 7:8 *22*
- if she depart, let her remain *u* 1Cor 7:11 *22*
- He that is *u* careth for the 1Cor 7:32 *22*
- The *u* woman careth for the things 1Cor 7:34 *22*

UNMERCIFUL
- natural affection, implacable, *u* Rom 1:31 *415*

UNMINDFUL
- Rock that begat thee thou art *u* Deut 32:18 7876

UNMOVABLE
- brethren, be ye stedfast, *u* 1Cor 15:58 *277*

UNMOVEABLE
- stuck fast, and remained *u* Acts 27:41 *761*

UNNI (*un'-nee*) A Levite.
- and Shemiramoth, and Jehiel, and *U* 1Chr 15:18 6042
- and Shemiramoth, and Jehiel, and *U* 1Chr 15:20 6042
- Also Bakbukiah and *U*, their Neh 12:9 6042

UNOCCUPIED
- days of Jael, the highways were *u* Judg 5:6 2308

UNPERFECT
- did see my substance, yet being *u* Ps 139:16

UNPREPARED
- come with me, and find you *u* 2Cor 9:4 *532*

UNPROFITABLE
- Should he reason with *u* talk Job 15:3 5532
- cast ye the *u* servant into outer Mt 25:30 *888*
- you, say, We are *u* servants Lk 17:10 *888*
- way, they are together become *u* Rom 3:12 *889*
- for they are *u* and vain Titus 3:9 *512*
- Which in time past was to thee *u* Philem 11 *890*
- for that is *u* for you Heb 13:17 *255*

UNPROFITABLENESS
- for the weakness and *u* thereof Heb 7:18 *512*

UNPUNISHED
- hand, the wicked shall not be *u* Prov 11:21 5352
- join in hand, he shall not be *u* Prov 16:5 5352
- glad at calamities shall not be *u* Prov 17:5 5352
- A false witness shall not be *u* Prov 19:5 5352
- A false witness shall not be *u* Prov 19:9 5352
- name, and should ye be utterly *u* Jer 25:29 5352
- Ye shall not be *u* Jer 25:29 5352
- will not leave thee altogether *u* Jer 30:11 5352
- will I not leave thee wholly *u* Jer 46:28 5352
- he that shall altogether go *u* Jer 49:12 5352
- thou shalt not go *u*, but thou Jer 49:12 5352

UNQUENCHABLE
- burn up the chaff with *u* fire Mt 3:12 *762*
- chaff he will burn with fire *u* Lk 3:17 *762*

UNREASONABLE
- to me *u* to send a prisoner Acts 25:27 *249*
- that we may be delivered from *u* 2Th 3:2 *824*

UNREBUKEABLE
- this commandment without spot, *u* 1Ti 6:14 *423*

UNREPROVEABLE
- and unblameable and *u* in his sight Col 1:22 *410*

UNRIGHTEOUS
- the wicked to be an *u* witness Ex 23:1 2555
- riseth up against me as the *u* Job 27:7 5767
- wicked, out of the hand of the *u* Ps 71:4 5765
- unto them that decree *u* decrees Is 10:1 205
- way, and the *u* man his thoughts Is 55:7 205
- not been faithful in the *u* mammon Lk 16:11 *94*
- Is God *u* who taketh vengeance Rom 3:5 *94*
- Know ye not that the *u* shall not 1Cor 6:9 *94*
- For God is not *u* to forget your Heb 6:10 *94*

UNRIGHTEOUSLY
- do such things, and all that do *u* Deut 25:16 5766

UNRIGHTEOUSNESS
- Ye shall do no *u* in judgment Lev 19:15 5766
- Ye shall do no *u* in judgment Lev 19:35 5766
- my rock, and there is no *u* in him Ps 92:15 5766
- him that buildeth his house by *u* Jer 22:13
- friends of the mammon of *u* Lk 16:9 *93*
- same is true, and no *u* is in him Jn 7:18 *93*
- *u* of men, who hold the truth in Rom 1:18 *93*
- of men, who hold the truth in *u* Rom 1:18 *93*
- Being filled with all *u*, Rom 1:29 *93*
- do not obey the truth, but obey *u* Rom 2:8 *93*
- But if our *u* commend the Rom 3:5 *93*
- as instruments of *u* unto sin Rom 6:13 *93*
- Is there *u* with God Rom 9:14 *93*
- hath righteousness with *u* 2Cor 6:14 *458*
- of *u* in them that perish 2Th 2:10 *93*
- the truth, but had pleasure in *u* 2Th 2:12 *93*
- For I will be merciful to their *u* Heb 8:12 *93*
- And shall receive the reward of *u* 2Pet 2:13 *93*
- Bosor, who loved the wages of *u* 2Pet 2:15 *93*
- sins, and to cleanse us from all *u* 1Jn 1:9 *93*
- All *u* is sin 1Jn 5:17 *93*

UNRIPE
- shake off his *u* grape as the vine Job 15:33 1154

UNRULY
- brethren, warn them that are *u* 1Th 5:14 *813*
- children not accused of riot or *u* Titus 1:6 *506*
- For there are many *u* and vain Titus 1:10 *506*
- it is an *u* evil, full of deadly Jas 3:8 *183*

UNSATIABLE
- Assyrians, because thou wast *u* Eze 16:28

UNSAVOURY
- froward thou wilt shew thyself *u* 2Sa 22:27 6617
- Can that which is *u* be eaten Job 6:6 8602

UNSEARCHABLE
- Which doeth great things and *u* Job 5:9
- and his greatness is *u* Ps 145:3
- depth, and the heart of kings is *u* Prov 25:3
- how *u* are his judgments, and his Rom 11:33 *419*
- Gentiles the *u* riches of Christ Eph 3:8 *421*

UNSEEMLY
- with men working that which is *u* Rom 1:27 *808*
- Doth not behave itself *u*, seeketh 1Cor 13:5

UNSHOD
- Withhold thy foot from being *u* Jer 2:25 *3182*

UNSKILFUL
- is *u* in the word of righteousness Heb 5:13 *552*

UNSPEAKABLE
- Thanks be unto God for his *u* gift 2Cor 9:15 *411*
- into paradise, and heard *u* words 2Cor 12:4 *731*
- believing, ye rejoice with joy *u* 1Pet 1:8 *412*

UNSPOTTED
to keep himself *u* from the world Jas 1:27 *784*

UNSTABLE
U as water, thou shalt not excel Gen 49:4 6349
minded man is *u* in all his ways Jas 1:8 *182*
beguiling *u* souls 2Pet 2:14 *793*
u wrest, as they do also the 2Pet 3:16 *793*

UNSTOPPED
the ears of the deaf shall be *u* Is 35:5 6605

UNTAKEN
day remaineth the same vail *u* 2Cor 3:14 *3361*

UNTEMPERED
others daubed it with *u* morter Eze 13:10 8602
them which daub it with *u* morter Eze 13:11 8602
that ye have daubed with *u* morter Eze 13:14 8602
that have daubed it with *u* morter Eze 13:15 8602
have daubed them with *u* morter Eze 22:28 8602

UNTHANKFUL
for he is kind unto the *u* Lk 6:35 *884*
disobedient to parents, *u* 2Ti 3:2 *884*

UNTIL
continually *u* the tenth month Gen 8:5 5704
u the waters were dried up from Gen 8:7 5704
u they have done drinking Gen 24:19
u I have told mine errand Gen 24:33
grew *u* he became very great Gen 26:13 5704
u thy brother's fury turn away Gen 27:44
U thy brother's anger turn away Gen 27:45 5704
u I have done that which I have Gen 28:15
u all the flocks be gathered Gen 29:8 5704
with Laban, and stayed there *u* now Gen 32:4 5704
him *u* the breaking of the day Gen 32:24 5704
u he came near to his brother Gen 33:3 5704
u I come unto my lord unto Seir Gen 33:14 5704
held his peace *u* they were come Gen 34:5 5704
by her, *u* his lord came home Gen 39:16 5704
very much, *u* he left numbering Gen 41:49 5704
cattle from our youth even *u* now Gen 46:34 5704
between his feet, *u* Shiloh come Gen 49:10
the foundation thereof even *u* now Ex 9:18 5704
serve the LORD, *u* we come thither Ex 10:26 5704
ye shall keep it up *u* the Ex 12:6 5704
of it remain *u* the morning Ex 12:10 5704
that which remaineth of it *u* the Ex 12:10 5704
the first day *u* the seventh day Ex 12:15 5704
u the one and twentieth day of the Ex 12:18 5704
door of his house *u* the morning Ex 12:22 5704
of them left of it *u* the morning Ex 16:20 5704
for you to be kept *u* the morning Ex 16:23 5704
u they came to a land inhabited Ex 16:35 5704
u they came unto the borders of Ex 16:35 5704
his hands were steady *u* the going Ex 17:12 5704
my sacrifice remain *u* the morning Ex 23:18 5704
u thou be increased, and inherit Ex 23:30 5704
for us, *u* we come again unto you Ex 24:14 5704
u he was gone into the tabernacle Ex 33:8 5704
took the vail off, *u* he came out Ex 34:34 5704
u he went in to speak with him Ex 34:35 5704
not leave any of it *u* the morning Lev 7:15 5704
u the days of your consecration Lev 8:33 5704
them shall be unclean *u* the even Lev 11:24 5704
clothes, and be unclean *u* the even Lev 11:25 5704
shall be unclean *u* the even Lev 11:27 5704
clothes, and be unclean *u* the even Lev 11:28 5704
dead, shall be unclean *u* the even Lev 11:31 5704
and it shall be unclean *u* the even Lev 11:32 5704
shall be unclean *u* the even Lev 11:39 5704
clothes, and be unclean *u* the even Lev 11:40 5704
clothes, and be unclean *u* the even Lev 11:40 5704
u the days of her purifying be Lev 12:4 5704
up shall be unclean *u* the even Lev 14:46 5704
water, and be unclean *u* the even Lev 15:5 5704
water, and be unclean *u* the even Lev 15:6 5704
water, and be unclean *u* the even Lev 15:7 5704
water, and be unclean *u* the even Lev 15:8
him shall be unclean *u* the even Lev 15:10 5704
water, and be unclean *u* the even Lev 15:10 5704
water, and be unclean *u* the even Lev 15:11
water, and be unclean *u* the even Lev 15:16 5704
water, and be unclean *u* the even Lev 15:17 5704
water, and be unclean *u* the even Lev 15:18 5704
her shall be unclean *u* the even Lev 15:19 5704
water, and be unclean *u* the even Lev 15:21 5704
water, and be unclean *u* the even Lev 15:22 5704
he shall be unclean *u* the even Lev 15:23 5704
water, and be unclean *u* the even Lev 15:27 5704
u he come out, and have made an Lev 16:17 5704
water, and be unclean *u* the even Lev 17:15 5704
if ought remain *u* the third day Lev 19:6 5704
with thee all night *u* the morning Lev 19:13 5704
of the holy things, *u* he be clean Lev 22:4 5704
any such shall be unclean *u* even Lev 22:6 5704
leave none of it *u* the morrow Lev 22:30 5704
u the selfsame day that ye have Lev 23:14 5704
yet of old fruit *u* the ninth year Lev 25:22 5704
u her fruits come in ye shall eat Lev 25:22 5704
bought it *u* the year of jubile Lev 25:28 5704
upward even *u* fifty years old, Num 4:3 5704
upward *u* fifty years old shalt Num 4:23 5704
u the days be fulfilled, in the Num 6:5 5704
appearance of fire, *u* the morning Num 9:15 5704
u it come out at your nostrils, Num 11:20 5704
people, from Egypt even *u* now Num 14:19 5704
u your carcases be wasted in the Num 14:33 5704
shall be unclean *u* the even Num 19:7 5704
and shall be unclean *u* the even Num 19:8 5704
clothes, and be unclean *u* the even Num 19:10 5704
shall be unclean *u* even Num 19:21 5704
it shall be unclean *u* even Num 19:22 5704
u we have passed thy borders Num 20:17 5704
way, *u* we be past thy borders Num 21:22 5704
u there was none left him alive Num 21:35 5704
not lie down *u* he eat of the prey Num 23:24 5704
u Asshur shall carry thee away Num 24:22 5704
u all the generation, that had Num 32:13 5704
u we have brought them unto their Num 32:17 5704
u the children of Israel have Num 32:18 5704
u he hath driven out his enemies Num 32:21 5704
die not, *u* he stand before the Num 35:12 5704
in the city of his refuge *u* the Num 35:28 5704
u the death of the priest Num 35:32 5704
u ye came into this place Deut 1:31 5704
u we were come over the brook Deut 2:14 5704
u all the generation of the men Deut 2:14 5704
the host, *u* they were consumed Deut 2:15 5704
u I shall pass over Jordan into Deut 2:29 5704
we smote him *u* none was left to Deut 3:3 5704
U the LORD have given rest unto Deut 3:20 5704
u they also possess the land Deut 3:20
u they that are left, and hide Deut 7:20 5704
destruction, *u* they be destroyed Deut 7:23 5704
u thou have destroyed them Deut 7:24 5704
u ye came unto this place, ye Deut 9:7 5704
even *u* it was as small as dust Deut 9:21 5704
u ye came into this place Deut 11:5 5704
remain all night *u* the morning Deut 16:4
war with thee, *u* it be subdued Deut 20:20 5704
it shall be with thee *u* thy Deut 22:2 5704
u thou be destroyed Deut 28:20 5704
and *u* thou perish quickly Deut 28:20 5704
u he have consumed thee from off Deut 28:21 5704
shall pursue thee *u* thou perish Deut 28:22 5704
upon thee, *u* thou be destroyed Deut 28:24 5704
neck, *u* he have destroyed thee Deut 28:48 5704
of thy land, *u* thou be destroyed Deut 28:51 5704
sheep, *u* he have destroyed thee Deut 28:51 5704
u thy high and fenced walls come Deut 28:52 5704
upon thee, *u* thou be destroyed Deut 28:61 5704
in a book, *u* they were finished Deut 31:24 5704
of this song, *u* they were ended Deut 31:30 5704
U the LORD have given your Josh 1:15 5704
u the pursuers be returned Josh 2:16 5704
u the pursuers were returned Josh 2:22 5704
u all the people were passed Josh 3:17 5704
u every thing was finished that Josh 4:10 5704
u ye were passed over, as the Josh 4:23 5704
before us, *u* we were gone over Josh 4:23 5704
u we were passed over, that their Josh 5:1 5704
u the day I bid you shout Josh 6:10 5704
ark of the LORD *u* the eventide Josh 7:6 5704
u ye take away the accursed thing Josh 7:13 5704
u they were consumed, that all Josh 8:24 5704
u he had utterly destroyed all Josh 8:26 5704
Ai he hanged on a tree *u* eventide Josh 8:29 5704
stayed, *u* the people had avenged Josh 10:13 5704
upon the trees *u* the evening Josh 10:26 5704
which remain *u* this very day Josh 10:27 5704
u he had left him none remaining Josh 10:33 5704
u they left them none remaining Josh 11:8 5704
u they had destroyed them, Josh 11:14 5704
among the Israelites *u* this day Josh 13:13 5704
that city, *u* he stand before the Josh 20:6 5704
u the death of the high priest Josh 20:6 5704
of blood, *u* he stood before the Josh 20:9 5704
we are not cleansed *u* this day Josh 22:17 5704
u ye perish from off this good Josh 23:13 5704
u he have destroyed you from off Josh 23:15 5704
u they had destroyed Jabin king Judg 4:24 5704
u that I Deborah arose, that I Judg 5:7 5704
u I come unto thee, and bring Judg 6:18 5704
I will tarry *u* thou come again Judg 6:18 5704
u we shall have made ready a kid Judg 13:15 5704
priests to the tribe of Dan *u* the Judg 18:30 5704
And they tarried *u* afternoon Judg 19:8 5704
her all the night *u* the morning Judg 19:25 5704
up and wept before the LORD *u* even Judg 20:23 5704
LORD, and fasted that day *u* even Judg 20:26 5704
So they two went *u* they came to Ruth 1:19 5704
even from the morning *u* now Ruth 2:7 5704
she gleaned in the field *u* even Ruth 2:17 5704
u they have ended all my harvest Ruth 2:21
u he shall have done eating and Ruth 3:3 5704
lie down *u* the morning Ruth 3:13 5704
she lay at his feet *u* the morning Ruth 3:14 5704
u thou know how the matter will Ruth 3:18
u he have finished the thing this Ruth 3:18
I will not go up *u* the child be 1Sa 1:22 5704
tarry *u* thou have weaned him 1Sa 1:23 5704
her son suck *u* she weaned him 1Sa 1:23 5704
Samuel lay *u* the morning, and 1Sa 3:15 5704
u they came under Beth-car 1Sa 7:11 5704
the people will not eat *u* he come 1Sa 9:13 5704
slew the Ammonites *u* the heat of 1Sa 11:11 5704
unto us, Tarry *u* we come to you 1Sa 14:9 5704
that eateth any food *u* evening 1Sa 14:24 5704
spoil them *u* the morning light, 1Sa 14:36 5704
Havilah *u* thou comest to Shur 1Sa 15:7
against them *u* they be consumed 1Sa 15:18 5704
see Saul *u* the day of his death 1Sa 15:35 5704
u thou come to the valley, and to 1Sa 17:52 5704
heed to thyself *u* the morning 1Sa 19:2 5704
u he came to Naioth in Ramah 1Sa 19:23 5704
with another, *u* David exceeded 1Sa 20:41 5704
less or more, *u* the morning light 1Sa 25:36 5704
u they had no more power to weep 1Sa 30:4
and wept, and fasted *u* even 2Sa 1:12 5704
were sojourners there *u* this day 2Sa 4:3 5704
from Geba *u* thou come to Gazer 2Sa 5:25 5704
Tarry at Jericho *u* your beards be 2Sa 10:5 5704
u all the people had done passing 2Sa 15:24 5704
u there come word from you to 2Sa 15:28 5704
u there be not one small stone 2Sa 17:13
befell thee from thy youth *u* now 2Sa 19:7 5704
u the day he came again in peace 2Sa 19:24 5704
from the beginning of harvest *u* 2Sa 21:10 5704
turned not again *u* I had consumed 2Sa 22:38 5704
Philistines *u* his hand was weary 2Sa 23:10
u he had made an end of building 1Kin 3:1 5704
name of the LORD, *u* those days 1Kin 3:2 5704
u the LORD put them under the 1Kin 5:3 5704
u he had finished all the house 1Kin 6:22 5704
u I came, and mine eyes had seen 1Kin 10:7 5704
u he had cut off every male in 1Kin 11:16 5704
was in Egypt *u* the death of 1Kin 11:40 5704
u he had destroyed him, according 1Kin 15:29 5704
u the day that the LORD sendeth 1Kin 17:14 5704
of Baal from morning even *u* noon 1Kin 18:26 5704
they prophesied *u* the time of the 1Kin 18:29 5704
u thou have consumed them 1Kin 22:11 5704
of affliction, *u* I come in peace 1Kin 22:27 5704
u an ass's head was sold for 2Kin 6:25 5704
another, Why sit we here *u* we die 2Kin 7:3 5704
she left the land, even *u* now 2Kin 8:6 5704
stedfastly, *u* he was ashamed 2Kin 8:11 5704
in of the gate *u* the morning 2Kin 10:8 5704
u he left him none remaining 2Kin 10:11 5704
u he had cast them out of his 2Kin 17:20 5704
U the LORD removed Israel out of 2Kin 17:23 5704
U I come and take you away to a 2Kin 18:32 5704
u he had cast them out from his 2Kin 24:20 5704
in their steads *u* the captivity 1Chr 5:22 5704
u Solomon had built the house of 1Chr 6:32 5704
u it was a great host, like the 1Chr 12:22 5704
Tarry at Jericho *u* your beards be 1Chr 19:5 5704
u thou hast finished all the work 1Chr 28:20 5704
make to pay tribute *u* this day 2Chr 8:8 5704
of the LORD, and *u* it was finished 2Chr 8:16 5704
u I came, and mine eyes had seen 2Chr 9:6 5704
u his disease was exceeding great 2Chr 16:12 5704
push Syria *u* they be consumed 2Chr 18:10 5704
affliction, *u* I return in peace 2Chr 18:26 5704
against the Syrians *u* the even 2Chr 18:34 5704
u thy bowels fall out by reason 2Chr 21:15 5704
the chest, *u* they had made an end 2Chr 24:10 5704
all this continued *u* the burnt 2Chr 29:28 5704
ended, and *u* the other priests had 2Chr 29:34 5704
u they had utterly destroyed them 2Chr 31:1 5704
offerings and the fat *u* night 2Chr 35:14 5704
u the wrath of the LORD arose 2Chr 36:16 5704
his sons *u* the reign of the 2Chr 36:20 5704
u the land had enjoyed her 2Chr 36:21 5704
even *u* the reign of Darius king Ezr 4:5 5704
u another commandment shall be Ezr 4:21 5704
since that time even *u* now hath Ezr 5:16 5704
u ye weigh them before the chief Ezr 8:29 5704
I sat astonied *u* the evening Ezr 9:4 5704
u the fierce wrath of our God for Ezr 10:14 5704
be opened *u* the sun be hot Neh 7:3 5704
gate from the morning *u* midday Neh 8:3 5704
even *u* the days of Johanan the Neh 12:23 5704
u thy wrath be past, that thou Job 14:13 5704
u the day and night come to an end Job 26:10 5704
u his iniquity be found to be Ps 36:2
u these calamities be overpast Ps 57:1 5704
u I have shewed thy strength unto Ps 71:18 5704
U I went into the sanctuary of Ps 73:17 5704
u the pit be digged for the Ps 94:13 5704
and to his labour *u* the evening Ps 104:23 5704
U the time that his word came Ps 105:19 5704
u I make thine enemies thy Ps 110:1 5704
u he see his desire upon his Ps 112:8 5704
u that he have mercy upon us Ps 123:2 5704
U I find out a place for the LORD Ps 132:5 5704
our fill of love *u* the morning Prov 7:18 5704
U the day break, and the shadows Song 2:17 5704
u I had brought him into my Song 3:4 5704
U the day break, and the shadows Song 4:6 5704
nor awake my love, *u* he please Song 8:4 5704
that continue *u* night, till wine Is 5:11
U the cities be wasted without Is 6:11 5704
u the indignation be overpast Is 26:20 5704
U the spirit be poured upon us Is 32:15 5704
U I come and take you away to a Is 36:17 5704
have laid up in store *u* this day Is 39:6 5704
u the righteousness thereof go Is 62:1 5704
u he have executed, and till he Jer 23:20 5704
u the very time of his land come Jer 27:7 5704
u I have consumed them by his Jer 27:8 5704
there shall they be *u* the day Jer 27:22 5704
u he have done it Jer 30:24 5704
u he have performed the intents Jer 30:24 5704
there shall he be *u* I visit him Jer 32:5 5704
u all the roll was consumed in Jer 36:23 5704
u all the bread in the city were Jer 37:21 5704
u the day that Jerusalem was Jer 38:28 5704
u there be an end of them Jer 44:27 5704
every day a portion *u* the day of Jer 52:34 5704
u he come whose right it is Eze 21:27 5704
u he came to me in the morning Eze 33:22 5704
shall not be shut *u* the evening Eze 46:2 5704
u thou know that the most High Dan 4:32 5704
U the Ancient of days came, and Dan 7:22 5704
be given into his hand *u* a time Dan 7:25 5704
even *u* the consummation, and that Dan 9:27 5704
the dough, *u* it be leavened Hos 7:4 5704
u the time that she which Mic 5:3 5704
u he plead my cause, and execute Mic 7:9 5704
u the day that I rise up to the Zeph 3:8
from David *u* the carrying away Mt 1:17 *2193*
be thou there *u* I bring thee word Mt 2:13 *2193*
was there *u* the death of Herod Mt 2:15 *2193*
u now the kingdom of heaven Mt 11:12 *2193*
and the law prophesied *u* John Mt 11:13 *2193*
it would have remained *u* this day Mt 11:23 *3360*
both grow together *u* the harvest Mt 13:30 *3360*
u the Son of man be risen again Mt 17:9 *2193*
say not unto thee, *U* seven times Mt 18:22 *2193*
but, *U* seventy times seven Mt 18:22 *2193*
u the day that Noe entered into Mt 24:38 *891*

knew not *u* the flood came, and — Mt 24:39 — *2193*
u that day when I drink it new — Mt 26:29 — *2193*
be made sure *u* the third day — Mt 27:64 — *2193*
among the Jews *u* this day — Mt 28:15 — *3360*
u that day that I drink it new in — Mk 14:25 — *2193*
the whole land *u* the ninth hour — Mk 15:33 — *2193*
u the day that these things shall — Lk 1:20 — *891*
u the time come when ye shall say — Lk 13:35 — *2193*
that which is lost, *u* he find it — Lk 15:4 — *2193*
law and the prophets were *u* John — Lk 16:16 — *2193*
u the day that Noe entered into — Lk 17:27 — *891*
u the times of the Gentiles be — Lk 21:24 — *891*
u it be fulfilled in the kingdom — Lk 22:16 — *2193*
u the kingdom of God shall come — Lk 22:18 — *2193*
all the earth *u* the ninth hour — Lk 23:44 — *2193*
u ye be endued with power from on — Lk 24:49 — *2193*
hast kept the good wine *u* now — Jn 2:10 — *2193*
u they called the parents of him — Jn 9:18 — *2193*
U the day in which he was taken — Acts 1:2 — *891*
U I make thy foes thy footstool — Acts 2:35 — *2193*
Whom the heaven must receive *u* — Acts 3:21 — *891*
ago I was fasting *u* this hour — Acts 10:30 — *3360*
fifty years, *u* Samuel the prophet — Acts 13:20 — *2193*
continued his speech *u* midnight — Acts 20:7 — *3360*
u that an offering should be — Acts 21:26 — *2193*
conscience before God *u* this day — Acts 23:1 — *891*
eat nothing *u* we have slain Paul — Acts 23:14 — *2193*
(For *u* the law sin was in the — Rom 5:13 — *891*
travaileth in pain together *u* now — Rom 8:22 — *891*
u the fulness of the Gentiles be — Rom 11:25 — *891*
u the Lord come, who both will — 1Cor 4:5 — *2193*
will tarry at Ephesus *u* Pentecost — 1Cor 16:8 — *2193*
for *u* this day remaineth the same — 2Cor 3:14 — *891*
governors *u* the time appointed of — Gal 4:2 — *891*
again *u* Christ be formed in you — Gal 4:19 — *891*
the earnest of our inheritance *u* — Eph 1:14 — *1519*
gospel from the first day *u* now — Phil 1:5 — *891*
it *u* the day of Jesus Christ — Phil 1:6 — *891*
u he be taken out of the way — 2Th 2:7 — *2193*
u the appearing of our Lord Jesus — 1Ti 6:14 — *3360*
u I make thine enemies thy — Heb 1:13 — *2193*
imposed on them *u* the time of — Heb 9:10 — *3360*
u he receive the early and latter — Jas 5:7 — *2193*
u the day dawn, and the day star — 2Pet 1:19 — *2193*
is in darkness even *u* now — 1Jn 2:9 — *2193*
u their fellowservants also and — Rev 6:11 — *2193*
u the words of God shall be — Rev 17:17 — *891*
again *u* the thousand years were — Rev 20:5 — *2193*

UNTIMELY
Or as an hidden *u* birth I had not — Job 3:16 — 5309
like the *u* birth of a woman, that — Ps 58:8 — 5309
that an *u* birth is better than he — Eccl 6:3 — 5309
as a fig tree casteth her *u* figs — Rev 6:13 — *3653*

UNTO See PREFACE.

UNTOWARD
yourselves from this *u* generation — Acts 2:40 — *4646*

UNWALLED
beside *u* towns a great many — Deut 3:5 — 6521
that dwelt in the *u* towns — Est 9:19 — 6519
go up to the land of *u* villages — Eze 38:11

UNWASHEN
but to eat with *u* hands defileth — Mt 15:20 — *449*
defiled, that is to say, with *u* — Mk 7:2 — *449*
but eat bread with *u* hands — Mk 7:5 — *449*

UNWEIGHED
And Solomon left all the vessels *u* — 1Kin 7:47

UNWISE
the LORD, O foolish people and *u* — Deut 32:6
he is an *u* son — Hos 13:13
both to the wise, and to the *u* — Rom 1:14 — *453*
Wherefore be ye not *u*, but — Eph 5:17 — *878*

UNWITTINGLY
if a man eat of the holy thing *u* — Lev 22:14 — 7684
unawares and *u* may flee thither — Josh 20:3
because he smote his neighbour *u* — Josh 20:5

UNWORTHILY
and drink this cup of the Lord, *u* — 1Cor 11:27 — *371*
For he that eateth and drinketh *u* — 1Cor 11:29 — *371*

UNWORTHY
judge yourselves *u* of everlasting — Acts 13:46
are ye *u* to judge the smallest — 1Cor 6:2 — *370*

UP See PREFACE.

UPBRAID
Zalmunna, with whom ye did *u* me — Judg 8:15 — 2778
Then began he to *u* the cities — Mt 11:20 — *3679*

UPBRAIDED
u them with their unbelief and — Mk 16:14 — *3679*

UPBRAIDETH
to all men liberally, and *u* not — Jas 1:5 — *3679*

UPHARSIN (*u-far'-sin*) See PERES. *Part of the "handwriting on the wall."*
MENE, TEKEL, *U* — Dan 5:25 — 6537

UPHAZ (*u'-faz*) *A place in southern Arabia.*
from Tarshish, and gold from *U* — Jer 10:9 — 210
were girded with fine gold of *U* — Dan 10:5 — 210

UPHELD
and my fury, it *u* me — Is 63:5 — 5564

UPHOLD
u me with thy free spirit — Ps 51:12 — 5564
Lord is with them that *u* my soul — Ps 54:4 — 5564
U me according unto thy word — Ps 119:116 — 5564
but honour shall *u* the humble in — Prov 29:23 — 8551
I will *u* thee with the right hand — Is 41:10 — 8551
Behold my servant, whom I *u* — Is 42:1 — 8551
wondered that there was none to *u* — Is 63:5 — 5564
They also that *u* Egypt shall fall — Eze 30:6 — 5564

UPHOLDEN
Thy words have *u* him that was — Job 4:4 — 6965
and his throne is *u* by mercy — Prov 20:28 — 5582

UPHOLDEST
thou *u* me in mine integrity, and — Ps 41:12 — 8551

UPHOLDETH
but the LORD *u* the righteous — Ps 37:17 — 5564
for the LORD *u* him with his hand — Ps 37:24 — 5564
thy right hand *u* me — Ps 63:8 — 8551
The LORD *u* all that fall, and — Ps 145:14 — 5564

UPHOLDING
u all things by the word of his — Heb 1:3 — *5342*

UPON See PREFACE.

UPPER
on the *u* door post of the houses — Ex 12:7 — 4947
put a covering upon his *u* lip — Lev 13:45 — 8222
or the *u* millstone to pledge — Deut 24:6 — 7393
And he gave her the *u* springs — Josh 15:19 — 5942
unto Beth-horon the *u* — Josh 16:5 — 5945
And Caleb gave her the *u* springs — Judg 1:15 — 5942
his *u* chamber that was in Samaria — 2Kin 1:2 — 5944
by the conduit of the *u* pool — 2Kin 18:17 — 5945
the top of the *u* chamber of Ahaz — 2Kin 23:12 — 5944
Beth-horon the nether, and the *u* — 1Chr 7:24 — 5945
of the *u* chambers thereof, and of — 1Chr 28:11 — 5944
he overlaid the *u* chambers with — 2Chr 3:9 — 5944
Also he built Beth-horon the *u* — 2Chr 8:5 — 5945
the *u* watercourse of Gihon — 2Chr 32:30 — 5945
the *u* pool in the highway of the — Is 7:3 — 5945
the *u* pool in the highway of the — Is 36:2 — 5945
Now the *u* chambers were shorter — Eze 42:5 — 5945
lodge in the *u* lintels of it — Zeph 2:14 — 3730
shew you a large *u* room furnished — Mk 14:15 — *508*
shew you a large *u* room furnished — Lk 22:12 — *508*
in, they went up into an *u* room — Acts 1:13 — *5253*
they laid her in an *u* chamber — Acts 9:37 — *5253*
brought him into the *u* chamber — Acts 9:39 — *5253*
the *u* coasts came to Ephesus — Acts 19:1 — *510*
were many lights in the *u* chamber — Acts 20:8 — *5250*

UPPERMOST
in the *u* basket there was of all — Gen 40:17 — 5945
berries in the top of the *u* bough — Is 17:6
an *u* branch, which they left — Is 17:9
love the *u* rooms at feasts, and — Mt 23:6 — *4411*
and the *u* rooms at feasts — Mk 12:39 — *4411*
for ye love the *u* seats in the — Lk 11:43 — *4410*

UPRIGHT
my sheaf arose, and also stood *u* — Gen 37:7
the floods stood *u* as an heap — Ex 15:8
of your yoke, and made you go *u* — Lev 26:13 — 6968
the LORD liveth, thou hast been *u* — 1Sa 29:6 — 3477
I was also *u* before him, and have — 2Sa 22:24 — 8549
with the *u* man thou wilt shew — 2Sa 22:26 — 8549
man thou wilt shew thyself *u* — 2Sa 22:26 — 8552
for the Levites were more *u* in — 2Chr 29:34 — 3477
and that man was perfect and *u* — Job 1:1 — 3477
an *u* man, one that feareth God — Job 1:8 — 3477
an *u* man, one that feareth God — Job 2:3 — 3477
If thou wert pure and *u* — Job 8:6 — 3477
the just *u* man is laughed to — Job 12:4 — 8549
U men shall be astonied at this — Job 17:8 — 3477
God, which saveth the *u* in heart — Ps 7:10 — 3477
privily shoot at the *u* in heart — Ps 11:2 — 3477
his countenance doth behold the *u* — Ps 11:7 — 3477
I was also *u* before him, and I — Ps 18:23 — 8549
with an *u* man thou wilt shew — Ps 18:25 — 8549
man thou wilt shew thyself *u* — Ps 18:25
then shall I be *u*, and I shall be — Ps 19:13 — 8552
but we are risen, and stand *u* — Ps 20:8
Good and *u* is the LORD — Ps 25:8 — 3477
joy, all ye that are *u* in heart — Ps 32:11 — 3477
for praise is comely for the *u* — Ps 33:1 — 3477
righteousness to the *u* in heart — Ps 36:10 — 3477
slay such as be of *u* conversation — Ps 37:14 — 3477
LORD knoweth the days of the *u* — Ps 37:18 — 8549
the perfect man, and behold the *u* — Ps 37:37 — 3477
the *u* shall have dominion over — Ps 49:14 — 3477
all the *u* in heart shall glory — Ps 64:10 — 3477
To shew that the LORD is *u* — Ps 92:15 — 3477
all the *u* in heart shall follow — Ps 94:15 — 3477
and gladness for the *u* in heart — Ps 97:11 — 3477
heart, in the assembly of the *u* — Ps 111:1 — 3477
of the *u* shall be blessed — Ps 112:2 — 3477
Unto the *u* there ariseth light in — Ps 112:4 — 3477
O LORD, and *u* are thy judgments — Ps 119:137 — 3477
them that are *u* in their hearts — Ps 125:4 — 3477
the *u* shall dwell in thy presence — Ps 140:13 — 3477
For the *u* shall dwell in the land — Prov 2:21 — 3477
of the LORD is strength to the *u* — Prov 10:29 — 8537
of the *u* shall guide them — Prov 11:3 — 3477
of the *u* shall deliver them — Prov 11:6 — 3477
of the *u* the city is exalted — Prov 11:11 — 3477
but such as are *u* in their way — Prov 11:20 — 8549
mouth of the *u* shall deliver them — Prov 12:6 — 3477
keepeth him that is *u* in the way — Prov 13:6 — 8537
of the *u* shall flourish — Prov 14:11 — 3477
prayer of the *u* is his delight — Prov 15:8 — 3477
The highway of the *u* is to depart — Prov 16:17 — 3477
and the transgressor for the *u* — Prov 21:18 — 3477
but as for the *u*, he directeth — Prov 21:29 — 3477
but the *u* shall have good things — Prov 28:10 — 8549
The bloodthirsty hate the *u* — Prov 29:10 — 8535
he that is *u* in the way is — Prov 29:27 — 3477
I found, that God hath made man *u* — Eccl 7:29 — 3477
and that which was written was *u* — Eccl 12:10 — 3476
the *u* love thee — Song 1:4 — 4339
thou, most *u*, dost weigh the path — Is 26:7 — 3477
They are *u* as the palm tree, but — Jer 10:5 — 4749
but he touched me, and set me *u* — Dan 8:18 — 5977
I speak unto thee, and stand *u* — Dan 10:11 — 5977
whole kingdom, and *u* ones with him — Dan 11:17 — 3477
and there is none *u* among men — Mic 7:2 — 3477
the most *u* is sharper than a — Mic 7:4 — 3477
is lifted up is not *u* in him — Hab 2:4 — 3474
a loud voice, Stand *u* on thy feet — Acts 14:10 — *3717*

UPRIGHTLY
He that walketh *u*, and worketh — Ps 15:2 — 8549
do ye judge *u*, O ye sons of men — Ps 58:1 — 4339
the congregation I will judge *u* — Ps 75:2 — 4339
he withhold from them that walk *u* — Ps 84:11 — 8549
is a buckler to them that walk *u* — Prov 2:7 — 8537
He that walketh *u* walketh surely — Prov 10:9 — 8537
a man of understanding walketh *u* — Prov 15:21 — 3474
Whoso walketh *u* shall be saved — Prov 28:18 — 8549
righteously, and speaketh *u* — Is 33:15 — 4339
and they abhor him that speaketh *u* — Amos 5:10 — 8549
do good to him that walketh *u* — Mic 2:7 — 3477
u according to the truth of the — Gal 2:14 — *3716*

UPRIGHTNESS
or for the *u* of thine heart, dost — Deut 9:5 — 3476
and in *u* of heart with thee — 1Kin 3:6 — 3483
in integrity of heart, and in *u* — 1Kin 9:4 — 3476
the heart, and hast pleasure in *u* — 1Chr 29:17 — 3476
in the *u* of mine heart I have — 1Chr 29:17 — 4339
thy hope, and the *u* of thy ways — Job 4:6 — 8537
shall be of the *u* of my heart — Job 33:3 — 3476
thousand, to shew unto man his *u* — Job 33:23 — 3476
judgment to the people in *u* — Ps 9:8 — 4339
Let integrity and *u* preserve me — Ps 25:21 — 3476
ever, and are done in truth and *u* — Ps 111:8 — 3477
will praise thee with *u* of heart — Ps 119:7 — 3476
lead me into the land of *u* — Ps 143:10 — 4334
Who leave the paths of *u*, to walk — Prov 2:13 — 3476
walketh in his *u* feareth the LORD — Prov 14:2 — 3476
is the poor that walketh in his *u* — Prov 28:6 — 8537
The way of the just is *u* — Is 26:7 — 4339
in the land of *u* will he deal — Is 26:10 — 5229
beds, each one walking in his *u* — Is 57:2 — 5228

UPRISING
knowest my downsitting and mine *u* — Ps 139:2 — 6965

UPROAR
noise of the city being in an *u* — 1Kin 1:41 — 1993
there be an *u* among the people — Mt 26:5 — *2351*
lest there be an *u* of the people — Mk 14:2 — *2351*
and set all the city on an *u* — Acts 17:5 — *2350*
in question for this day's *u* — Acts 19:40 — *4714*
after the *u* was ceased, Paul — Acts 20:1 — *2351*
that all Jerusalem was in an *u* — Acts 21:31 — *4797*
before these days madest an *u* — Acts 21:38 — *387*

UPSIDE
wiping it, and turning it *u* down — 2Kin 21:13
of the wicked he turneth *u* down — Ps 146:9
it waste, and turneth it *u* down — Is 24:1
u down shall be esteemed as the — Is 29:16
world *u* down are come hither also — Acts 17:6 — *389*

UPWARD
Fifteen cubits *u* did the waters — Gen 7:20 — 4605
from twenty years old and *u* — Ex 38:26 — 4605
From twenty years old and *u* — Num 1:3 — 4605
names, from twenty years old and *u* — Num 1:18 — 4605
male from twenty years old and *u* — Num 1:20 — 4605
male from twenty years old and *u* — Num 1:22 — 4605
names, from twenty years old and *u* — Num 1:24 — 4605
names, from twenty years old and *u* — Num 1:26 — 4605
names, from twenty years old and *u* — Num 1:28 — 4605
names, from twenty years old and *u* — Num 1:30 — 4605
names, from twenty years old and *u* — Num 1:32 — 4605
names, from twenty years old and *u* — Num 1:34 — 4605
names, from twenty years old and *u* — Num 1:36 — 4605
names, from twenty years old and *u* — Num 1:38 — 4605
names, from twenty years old and *u* — Num 1:40 — 4605
names, from twenty years old and *u* — Num 1:42 — 4605
from twenty years old and *u* — Num 1:45 — 4605
old and *u* shalt thou number them — Num 3:15 — 4605
the males, from a month old and *u* — Num 3:22 — 4605
the males, from a month old and *u* — Num 3:28 — 4605
the males, from a month old and *u* — Num 3:34 — 4605
the males from a month old and *u* — Num 3:39 — 4605
of Israel from a month old and *u* — Num 3:40 — 4605
of names, from a month old and *u* — Num 3:43 — 4605
u even until fifty years old, all — Num 4:3 — 4605
u until fifty years old shalt — Num 4:23 — 4605
u even unto fifty years old shalt — Num 4:30 — 4605
u even unto fifty years old — Num 4:35 — 4605
u even unto fifty years old — Num 4:39 — 4605
u even unto fifty years old — Num 4:43 — 4605
u even unto fifty years old — Num 4:47 — 4605
u they shall go in to wait upon — Num 8:24 — 4605
from twenty years old and *u* — Num 14:29 — 4605
from twenty years old and *u* — Num 26:2 — 4605
from twenty years old and *u* — Num 26:4 — 4605
all males from a month old and *u* — Num 26:62 — 4605
Egypt, from twenty years old and *u* — Num 32:11 — 4605
to Akrabbim, from the rock, and *u* — Judg 1:36 — 4605
u he was higher than any of the — 1Sa 9:2 — 4605
people from his shoulders and *u* — 1Sa 10:23 — 4605
were able to put on armour, and *u* — 2Kin 3:21 — 4605
root downward, and bear fruit *u* — 2Kin 19:30 — 4605
from the age of thirty years and *u* — 1Chr 23:3 — 4605
from the age of twenty years and *u* — 1Chr 23:24 — 4605
males, from three years old and *u* — 2Chr 31:16 — 4605
from twenty years old and *u* — 2Chr 31:17 — 4605
from twenty years old and *u* — Ezr 3:8 — 4605
unto trouble, as the sparks fly *u* — Job 5:7 — 1361
the spirit of man that goeth *u* — Eccl 3:21 — 4605
king and their God, and look *u* — Is 8:21 — 4605
root downward, and bear fruit *u* — Is 37:31 — 4605
mine eyes fail with looking *u* — Is 38:14 — 4791
and their wings were stretched *u* — Eze 1:11 — 4605
appearance of his loins even *u* — Eze 1:27 — 4605

and from his loins even *u*, as the Eze 8:2 4605
still *u* to the side chambers Eze 41:7 4605
still *u* round about the house Eze 41:7 4605
breadth of the house was still *u* Eze 41:7 4605
altar and *u* shall be four horns Eze 43:15 4605
you, consider from this day and *u* Hag 2:15 4605
Consider now from this day and *u* Hag 2:18 4605

UR (*ur*)
1. A district in Mesopotamia.
nativity, in *U* of the Chaldees Gen 11:28 218
with them from *U* of the Chaldees Gen 11:31 218
thee out of *U* of the Chaldees Gen 15:7 218
forth out of *U* of the Chaldees Neh 9:7 218
2. Father of Eliphal.
Hararite, Eliphal the son of *U* 1Chr 11:35 218

URBANE (*ur'-bane*) *A Christian in Rome.*
Salute *U*, our helper in Christ, Rom 16:9 3779

URBANUS See URBANE.

URGE
began to *u* him vehemently Lk 11:53 *1758*

URGED
And he *u* him, and he took it Gen 33:11 6484
u him, so that his soul was vexed Judg 16:16 509
depart, his father in law *u* him Judg 19:7 6484
when they *u* him till he was 2Kin 2:17 6484
And he *u* him to take it 2Kin 5:16 6484
he *u* him, and bound two talents of 2Kin 5:23 6555

URGENT
Egyptians were *u* upon the people Ex 12:33 2388
the king's commandment was *u* Dan 3:22 2685

URI (*u'-ri*)
1. Father of Bezaleel.
by name Bezaleel the son of *U* Ex 31:2 221
by name Bezaleel the son of *U* Ex 35:30 221
And Bezaleel the son of *U*, the son Ex 38:22 221
And Hur begat *U* 1Chr 2:20 221
and *U* begat Bezaleel 1Chr 2:20 221
altar, that Bezaleel the son of *U* 2Chr 1:5 221
2. Father of Geber.
Geber the son of *U* was in the 1Kin 4:19 221
Shallum, and Telem, and *U* Ezr 10:24 221

URIAH (*u-ri'-ah*) See URIAH'S, URIAS, URIJAH.
1. Husband of Bathsheba.
Eliam, the wife of *U* the Hittite 2Sa 11:3 223
saying, Send me *U* the Hittite 2Sa 11:6 223
And Joab sent *U* to David 2Sa 11:6 223
when *U* was come unto him, David 2Sa 11:7 223
And David said to *U*, Go down to 2Sa 11:8 223
U departed out of the king's 2Sa 11:8 223
But *U* slept at the door of the 2Sa 11:9 223
U went not down unto his house, 2Sa 11:10 223
unto his house, David said unto *U* 2Sa 11:10 223
U said unto David, The ark, and 2Sa 11:11 223
And David said to *U*, Tarry here to 2Sa 11:12 223
So *U* abode in Jerusalem that day, 2Sa 11:12 223
Joab, and sent it by the hand of *U* 2Sa 11:14 223
Set ye *U* in the forefront of the 2Sa 11:15 223
that he assigned *U* unto a place 2Sa 11:16 223
and *U* the Hittite died also 2Sa 11:17 223
Thy servant *U* the Hittite is dead 2Sa 11:21 223
thy servant *U* the Hittite is dead 2Sa 11:24 223
when the wife of *U* heard that 2Sa 11:26 223
heard that *U* her husband was dead 2Sa 11:26 223
thou hast killed *U* the Hittite 2Sa 12:9 223
hast taken the wife of *U* the 2Sa 12:10 223
U the Hittite 2Sa 23:39 223
in the matter of *U* the Hittite 1Kin 15:5 223
U the Hittite, Zabad the son of 1Chr 11:41 223
2. A rebuilder of Jerusalem's wall.
Meremoth the son of *U* the priest Ezr 8:33 223
3. A priest who aided Isaiah.
U the priest, and Zechariah the Is 8:2 223

URIAH'S (*u-ri'-ahz*) *Refers to Uriah 1.*
child that *U* wife bare unto David 2Sa 12:15 223

URIAS (*u-ri'-as*) *Greek form of Uriah 1.*
her that had been the wife of *U* Mt 1:6 *3774*

URIEL (*u'-re-el*)
1. Son of Tahath.
U his son, Uzziah his son, and 1Chr 6:24 222
U the chief, and his brethren an 1Chr 15:5 222
and for the Levites, for *U* 1Chr 15:11 222
2. Father of Micaiah.
the daughter of *U* of Gibeah 2Chr 13:2 222

URIJAH (*u-ri'-jah*) See URIAH.
1. A priest in Jerusalem.
king Ahaz sent to *U* the priest 2Kin 16:10 223
U the priest built an altar 2Kin 16:11 223
so *U* the priest made it against 2Kin 16:11 223
king Ahaz commanded *U* the priest 2Kin 16:15 223
Thus did *U* the priest, according 2Kin 16:16 223
2. A priest who rebuilt the wall.
repaired Meremoth the son of *U* Neh 3:4 223
of *U* the son of Koz another piece Neh 3:21 223
3. A priest who aided Ezra.
and Shema, and Anaiah, and *U* Neh 8:4 223
4. A prophet killed by Jehoiakim.
LORD, *U* the son of Shemaiah of Jer 26:20 223
but when *U* heard it, he was Jer 26:21 223
they fetched forth *U* out of Egypt Jer 26:23 223

URIM (*u'-rim*) *A symbolic object in the High Priest's breastplate.*
the breastplate of judgment the *U* Ex 28:30 224
he put in the breastplate the *U* Lev 8:8 224
the judgment of *U* before the LORD Num 27:21 224
thy *U* be with thy holy one, whom Deut 33:8 224
not, neither by dreams, nor by *U* 1Sa 28:6 224
there stood up a priest with *U* Ezr 2:63 224
there stood up a priest with *U* Neh 7:65 224

US See PREFACE.

USE
may be used in any other *u* Lev 7:24 4399
neither shall ye *u* enchantment Lev 19:26 5172
that thou mayest *u* them for the Num 10:2
after which ye *u* to go a whoring Num 15:39
ought thereof for any unclean *u* Deut 26:14
of Judah the *u* of the bow 2Sa 1:18
could *u* both the right hand and 1Chr 12:2 3231
according to the *u* of every 1Chr 28:15 5656
that *u* their tongues, and say, He Jer 23:31 3947
As yet they shall *u* this speech Jer 31:23 559
vain shalt thou *u* many medicines Jer 46:11
they shall no more *u* it as a Eze 12:23 4912
shall *u* this proverb against thee Eze 16:44 4911
that ye *u* this proverb concerning Eze 18:2 4911
more to *u* this proverb in Israel Eze 18:3 4911
of the two ways, to *u* divination Eze 21:21 7080
for them which despitefully *u* you Mt 5:44 *1908*
u not vain repetitions, as the Mt 6:7
for them which despitefully *u* you Lk 6:28 *1908*
to *u* them despitefully, and to Acts 14:5 *5195*
u into that which is against Rom 1:26 *5540*
the natural *u* of the woman Rom 1:27 *5540*
mayest be made free, *u* it rather 1Cor 7:21 *5530*
they that *u* this world, as not 1Cor 7:31 *5530*
thus minded, did I *u* lightness 2Cor 1:17 *5530*
we *u* great plainness of speech 2Cor 3:12 *5530*
present I should *u* sharpness 2Cor 13:10 *5530*
only *u* not liberty for an Gal 5:13
is good to the *u* of edifying Eph 4:29 *5532*
is good, if a man *u* it lawfully 1Ti 1:8 *5530*
then let them *u* the office of a 1Ti 3:10
but *u* a little wine for thy 1Ti 5:23 *5530*
and meet for the master's *u* 2Ti 2:21
even those who by reason of *u* Heb 5:14 *1838*
U hospitality one to another 1Pet 4:9 *5382*

USED
ox hath *u* to push in time past Ex 21:36
may be *u* in any other use Lev 7:24 6213
for so *u* the young men to do Judg 14:10
whom he had *u* as his friend Judg 14:20
u divination and enchantments, and 2Kin 17:17
u enchantments, and dealt with 2Kin 21:6
times, and *u* enchantments, and *u* 2Chr 33:6
u witchcraft, and dealt with a 2Chr 33:6
A wild ass *u* to the wilderness, Jer 2:24 3928
of the land have *u* oppression Eze 22:29
to thine envy which thou hast *u* Eze 35:11 6213
u similitudes, by the ministry of Hos 12:10
and of the Pharisees *u* to fast Mk 2:18 *1510*
in the same city *u* sorcery Acts 8:9 *3096*
Many of them also which *u* curious Acts 19:19 *4238*
they *u* helps, undergirding the Acts 27:17 *5530*
their tongues they have *u* deceit Rom 3:13 *1387*
we have not *u* this power 1Cor 9:12 *5530*
But I have *u* none of these things 1Cor 9:15 *5530*
at any time *u* we flattering words 1Th 2:5
For they that have *u* the office 1Ti 3:13 *1247*
companions of them that were so *u* Heb 10:33 *390*

USES
good works for necessary *u* Titus 3:14 *5532*

USEST
as thou *u* to do unto those that Ps 119:132 4941

USETH
or that *u* divination, or an Deut 18:10
brought which the king *u* to wear Est 6:8
of the wise *u* knowledge aright Prov 15:2
The poor *u* intreaties Prov 18:23 1696
that *u* his neighbour's service Jer 22:13
every one that *u* proverbs shall Eze 16:44
For every one that *u* milk is Heb 5:13 *3348*

USING
all are to perish with the *u* Col 2:22 *671*
not *u* your liberty for a cloke of 1Pet 2:16 *2192*

USURER
thou shalt not be to him as a *u* Ex 22:25 5383

USURP
nor to *u* authority over the man, 1Ti 2:12 *831*

USURY
neither shalt thou lay upon him *u* Ex 22:25 5392
Take thou no *u* of him, or Lev 25:36 5392
not give him thy money upon *u* Lev 25:37 5392
not lend upon *u* to thy brother Deut 23:19 5391
u of money, *u* of victuals, Deut 23:19 5392
u of any thing that is lent upon Deut 23:19 5392
of any thing that is lent upon *u* Deut 23:19 5391
stranger thou mayest lend upon *u* Deut 23:20 5391
thou shalt not lend upon *u* Deut 23:20 5391
and said unto them, Ye exact *u* Neh 5:7 5383
pray you, let us leave off this *u* Neh 5:10 5383
putteth not out his money to *u* Ps 15:5 5392
He that by *u* and unjust gain Prov 28:8 5392
as with the taker of *u* Is 24:2 5383
so with the giver of *u* to him Is 24:2 5378
I have neither lent on *u* Jer 15:10 5383
nor men have lent to me on *u* Jer 15:10 5383
that hath not given forth upon *u* Eze 18:8 5392
Hath given forth upon *u*, and hath Eze 18:13 5392
hath not received *u* nor increase Eze 18:17 5392
thou hast taken *u* and increase, and Eze 22:12 5392
have received mine own with *u* Mt 25:27 *5110*
have required mine own with *u* Lk 19:23 *5110*

US-WARD
and thy thoughts which are to *u* Ps 40:5 413
of his power to *u* who believe Eph 1:19
but is longsuffering to *u* 2Pet 3:9

UTHAI (*u'-thahee*)
1. Son of Ammihud.
U the son of Ammihud, the son of 1Chr 9:4 5793
2. A clan leader with Ezra.
U, and Zabbud, and with them Ezr 8:14 5793

UTMOST
of my progenitors unto the *u* Gen 49:26
of Arnon, which is in the *u* coast Num 22:36 7097
see the *u* part of the people Num 22:41 7097
shalt see but the *u* part of them Num 23:13 7097
the land of Judah, unto the *u* sea Deut 34:2 314
and all that are in the *u* corners Jer 9:26 7112
and all that are in the *u* corners Jer 25:23 7112
them that are in the *u* corners Jer 49:32 7112
against her from the *u* border Jer 50:26 7093
his hinder part toward the *u* sea Joel 2:20 314
for she came from the *u* parts of Lk 11:31 *4009*

UTTER
if he do not *u* it, then he shall Lev 5:1 5046
if ye *u* not this our business Josh 2:14 5046
if thou *u* this our business, then Josh 2:20 5046
awake, awake, *u* a song Judg 5:12 1696
whom I appointed to *u* destruction 1Kin 20:42
u words out of their heart Job 8:10 3318
a wise man *u* vain knowledge Job 15:2 6030
nor my tongue *u* deceit Job 27:4 1897
my lips shall *u* knowledge clearly Job 33:3 4448
I will *u* dark sayings of old Ps 78:2 5042
How long shall they *u* and speak Ps 94:4 5042
Who can *u* the mighty acts of the Ps 106:2 4448
My lips shall *u* praise, when thou Ps 119:171 5042
They shall abundantly *u* the Ps 145:7 5042
but a false witness will *u* lies Prov 14:5 6315
heart shall *u* perverse things Prov 23:33 1696
man cannot *u* it Eccl 1:8 1696
hasty to *u* any thing before God Eccl 5:2 3318
to *u* error against the LORD, to Is 32:6 1696
u it even to the end of the earth Is 48:20 3318
I will *u* my judgments against Jer 1:16 1696
u his voice from his holy Jer 25:30 5414
u a parable unto the rebellious Eze 24:3 4911
thereof were toward the *u* court Eze 40:31 2435
thereof were toward the *u* court Eze 40:37 2435
brought me forth into the *u* court Eze 42:1 2435
which was for the *u* court Eze 42:3 2435
toward the *u* court on the Eze 42:7 2435
in the *u* court was fifty cubits Eze 42:8 2435
goeth into them from the *u* court Eze 42:9 2435
the holy place into the *u* court Eze 42:14 2435
they go forth into the *u* court Eze 44:19 2435
even into the *u* court to the Eze 44:19 2435
them not out into the *u* court Eze 46:20 2435
brought me forth into the *u* court Eze 46:21 2435
u gate by the way that looketh Eze 47:2 2531
the LORD shall *u* his voice before Joel 2:11 5414
u his voice from Jerusalem Joel 3:16 5414
u his voice from Jerusalem Amos 1:2 5414
flood he will make an *u* end of Nah 1:8 3617
he will make an *u* end Nah 1:9 3617
shall be no more *u* destruction Zec 14:11
I will *u* things which have been Mt 13:35 *2044*
except ye *u* by the tongue words 1Cor 14:9 *1325*
it is not lawful for a man to *u* 2Cor 12:4 *2980*

UTTERANCE
as the Spirit gave them *u* Acts 2:4 *669*
ye are enriched by him, in all *u* 1Cor 1:5 *3056*
in every thing, in faith, and *u* 2Cor 8:7 *3056*
that *u* may be given unto me, that Eph 6:19 *3056*
would open unto us a door of *u* Col 4:3 *3056*

UTTERED
or *u* ought out of her lips, Num 30:6 4008
and that which she *u* with her lips Num 30:8 4008
Jephthah *u* all his words before Judg 11:11 1696
and the most High *u* his voice 2Sa 22:14 5414
before me, and *u* my words to him Neh 6:19 3318
To whom hast thou *u* words Job 26:4 5046
therefore have I *u* that I Job 42:3 5046
he *u* his voice, the earth melted Ps 46:6 5414
Which my lips have *u*, and my mouth Ps 66:14 4475
have they *u* their voice, from Jer 48:34 5414
a noise of their voice is *u* Jer 51:55 5414
the deep *u* his voice, and lifted Hab 3:10 5414
with groanings which cannot be *u* Rom 8:26 *215*
things to say, and hard to be *u* Heb 5:11 *3004*
seven thunders *u* their voices Rev 10:3 *2980*
seven thunders had *u* their voices Rev 10:4 *2980*
things which the seven thunders *u* Rev 10:4 *2980*

UTTERETH
For thy mouth *u* thine iniquity, Job 15:5 502
Day unto day *u* speech, and night Ps 19:2 5042
she *u* her voice in the streets Prov 1:20 5414
in the city she *u* her words Prov 1:21 559
he that *u* a slander, is a fool Prov 10:18 3318
A fool *u* all his mind Prov 29:11 3318
When he *u* his voice, there is a Jer 10:13 5414
When he *u* his voice, there is a Jer 51:16 5414
he *u* his mischievous desire Mic 7:3 1696

UTTERING
u from the heart words of Is 59:13 1897

UTTERLY
for I will *u* put out the Ex 17:14
If her father *u* refuse to give Ex 22:17
only, he shall be *u* destroyed Ex 22:20
but thou shalt *u* overthrow them Ex 23:24
shall pronounce him *u* unclean Lev 13:44
I abhor them, to destroy them *u* Lev 26:44 3615
that soul shall *u* be cut off Num 15:31
then I will *u* destroy their Num 21:2
they *u* destroyed them and their Num 21:3
But if her husband hath *u* made Num 30:12

u destroyed the men, and the women.. Deut 2:34
we *u* destroyed them, as we did.......... Deut 3:6
u destroying the men, women, and....... Deut 3:6
that ye shall soon *u* perish from.......... Deut 4:26
upon it, but shall *u* be destroyed.......... Deut 4:26
smite them, and *u* destroy them.......... Deut 7:2
but thou shalt *u* detest it.......... Deut 7:26
and thou shalt *u* abhor it.......... Deut 7:26
Ye shall *u* destroy all the places.......... Deut 12:2
of the sword, destroying it *u*.......... Deut 13:15
But thou shalt *u* destroy them.......... Deut 20:17
ye will *u* corrupt yourselves.......... Deut 31:29
Sihon and Og, whom ye *u* destroyed.... Josh 2:10
they *u* destroyed all that was in.......... Josh 6:21
until he had *u* destroyed all the.......... Josh 8:26
taken Ai, and had *u* destroyed it.......... Josh 10:1
the king thereof he *u* destroyed.......... Josh 10:28
therein he *u* destroyed that day.......... Josh 10:35
but destroyed it *u*, and all the.......... Josh 10:37
u destroyed all the souls that.......... Josh 10:39
but *u* destroyed all that breathed.......... Josh 10:40
of the sword, *u* destroying them.......... Josh 11:11
he *u* destroyed them, as Moses the...... Josh 11:12
that he might destroy them *u*.......... Josh 11:20
them *u* with their cities.......... Josh 11:21
but did not *u* drive them out.......... Josh 17:13
Zephath, and *u* destroyed it.......... Judg 1:17
and did not *u* drive them out.......... Judg 1:28
that thou hadst *u* hated her.......... Judg 15:2
Ye shall *u* destroy every male, and...... Judg 21:11
u destroy all that they have, and.......... 1Sa 15:3
u destroyed all the people with.......... 1Sa 15:8
good, and would not *u* destroy them.... 1Sa 15:9
and refuse, that they destroyed *u*.......... 1Sa 15:9
and the rest we have *u* destroyed.......... 1Sa 15:15
u destroy the sinners the.......... 1Sa 15:18
have *u* destroyed the Amalekites.......... 1Sa 15:20
should have been *u* destroyed.......... 1Sa 15:21
his people Israel *u* to abhor him.......... 1Sa 27:12
the heart of a lion, shall *u* melt.......... 2Sa 17:10
they shall be *u* burned with fire.......... 2Sa 23:7
also were not able *u* to destroy.......... 1Kin 9:21
all lands, by destroying them *u*.......... 2Kin 19:11
and destroyed them *u* unto this day..... 1Chr 4:41
u to slay and destroy them.......... 2Chr 20:23
until they had *u* destroyed them.......... 2Chr 31:1
that my fathers *u* destroyed.......... 2Chr 32:14
thou didst not *u* consume them.......... Neh 9:31
fall, he shall not be *u* cast down.......... Ps 37:24
they are *u* consumed with terrors.......... Ps 73:19
will I not *u* take from him.......... Ps 89:33
O forsake me not *u*.......... Ps 119:8 3966
word of truth *u* out of my mouth.......... Ps 119:43 3966
for love, it would *u* be contemned.......... Song 8:7
And the idols he shall *u* abolish.......... Is 2:18 3632
man, and the land be *u* desolate.......... Is 6:11
the LORD shall *u* destroy the.......... Is 11:15
be *u* emptied, and *u* spoiled.......... Is 24:3
The earth is *u* broken down.......... Is 24:19
he hath *u* destroyed them, he hath...... Is 34:2
to all lands by destroying them *u*.......... Is 37:11
and the young men shall *u* fall.......... Is 40:30
The LORD hath *u* separated me from.... Is 56:3
those nations shall be *u* wasted.......... Is 60:12
for every brother will *u* supplant.......... Jer 9:4
I will *u* pluck up and destroy that....... Jer 12:17
Hast thou *u* rejected Judah.......... Jer 14:19
will *u* forget you, and I will.......... Jer 23:39
will *u* destroy them, and make them..... Jer 25:9
and should ye be *u* unpunished.......... Jer 25:29
u destroy after them, saith the.......... Jer 50:21
her up as heaps, and destroy her *u*.......... Jer 50:26
destroy ye *u* all her host.......... Jer 51:3
of Babylon shall be *u* broken.......... Jer 51:58
But thou hast *u* rejected us.......... Lam 5:22
Slay *u* old and young, both maids,.......... Eze 9:6
shall it not *u* wither, when the.......... Eze 17:10
make themselves *u* bald for thee.......... Eze 27:31
make the land of Egypt *u* waste.......... Eze 29:10
destroy, and *u* to make away many...... Dan 11:44
but I will *u* take them away.......... Hos 1:6
the king of Israel *u* be cut off.......... Hos 10:15
saving that I will not *u* destroy.......... Amos 9:8
and say, We be *u* spoiled.......... Mic 2:4 7703
he is *u* cut off.......... Nah 1:15 3605
I will *u* consume all things from.......... Zeph 1:2
his right eye shall be *u* darkened.......... Zec 11:17
there is *u* a fault among you.......... 1Cor 6:7 *3654*
shall *u* perish in their own.......... 2Pet 2:12 *2704*
she shall be *u* burned with fire.......... Rev 18:8 *2618*

UTTERMOST
in the *u* edge of another curtain.......... Ex 26:4 7020
in the *u* side of another curtain.......... Ex 36:11 7020
the *u* edge of the curtain in the.......... Ex 36:17 7020
were in the *u* parts of the camp.......... Num 11:1 7097
a city in the *u* of thy border.......... Num 20:16 7097
even unto the *u* sea shall your.......... Deut 11:24 314
was the *u* part of the south coast.......... Josh 15:1 7097
the sea at the *u* part of Jordan.......... Josh 15:5 7097
the *u* cities of the tribe of the.......... Josh 15:21 7097
Saul tarried in the *u* part of.......... 1Sa 14:2 7097
from the *u* part of the one wing.......... 1Kin 6:24 7098
the *u* part of the other were ten.......... 1Kin 6:24 7098
the *u* part of the camp of Syria.......... 2Kin 7:5 7097
came to the *u* part of the camp.......... 2Kin 7:8 7097
out unto the *u* part of the heaven.......... Neh 1:9 7097
the *u* parts of the earth for thy.......... Ps 2:8 657
They also that dwell in the *u*.......... Ps 65:8 7098
dwell in the *u* parts of the sea.......... Ps 139:9 319
the *u* part of the rivers of Egypt.......... Is 7:18 7097
From the *u* part of the earth have.......... Is 24:16 3671
thou hast paid the *u* farthing.......... Mt 5:26 *2078*
for she came from the *u* parts of.......... Mt 12:42 *4009*
from the *u* part of the earth to.......... Mk 13:27 *206*
the earth to the *u* part of heaven.......... Mk 13:27 *206*
unto the *u* part of the earth.......... Acts 1:8 *2078*
I will know the *u* of your matter.......... Acts 24:22 *1231*
wrath is come upon them to the *u*.......... 1Th 2:16 *5056*
the *u* that come unto God by him.......... Heb 7:25 *3838*

UZ (*uz*) *A son of Aram.*
U, and Hul, and Gether, and Mash.......... Gen 10:23 5780
are these; *U*, and Aran.......... Gen 36:28 5780
Arphaxad, and Lud, and Aram, and *U*. 1Chr 1:17 5780
of Dishan; *U*, and Aran.......... 1Chr 1:42 5780
There was a man in the land of *U*.......... Job 1:1 5780
and all the kings of the land of *U*.......... Jer 25:20 5780
that dwellest in the land of *U*.......... Lam 4:21 5780

UZAI (*u'-zahee*) *Father of Palal.*
Palal the son of *U*, over against.......... Neh 3:25 186

UZAL (*u'-zal*) *A son of Joktan.*
And Hadoram, and *U*, and Diklah,.......... Gen 10:27 187
Hadoram also, and *U*, and Diklah,.......... 1Chr 1:21 187

UZZA (*uz'-zah*) See UZZAH.
1. Name of the burial ground of Manasseh and Amon.
his own house, in the garden of *U*.......... 2Kin 21:18 5798
his sepulchre in the garden of *U*.......... 2Kin 21:26 5798
2. Son of Shimei.
son, Shimei his son, *U* his son,.......... 1Chr 6:29 5798
3. A brother of Ahihud.
Gera, he removed them, and begat *U*... 1Chr 8:7 5798
4. Touched the Ark and died.
and *U* and Ahio drave the cart.......... 1Chr 13:7 5798
U put forth his hand to hold the.......... 1Chr 13:9 5798
of the LORD was kindled against *U*.......... 1Chr 13:10 5798
the LORD had made a breach upon *U*... 1Chr 13:11 5798
5. A family of Nethinims.
The children of *U*, the children.......... Ezr 2:49 5798
of Gazzam, the children of *U*.......... Neh 7:51 5798

UZZAH (*uz'-zah*) See UZZA. *Same as Uzza 4.*
and *U* and Ahio, the sons of.......... 2Sa 6:3 5798
U put forth his hand to the ark.......... 2Sa 6:6 5798
of the LORD was kindled against *U*.......... 2Sa 6:7 5798
the LORD had made a breach upon *U*... 2Sa 6:8 5798

UZZEN-SHEERAH See UZZEN-SHERH.

UZZEN-SHEERAH (*uz''-zen-she'-rah*) *A city in Ephraim.*
the nether, and the upper, and *U*.......... 1Chr 7:24 242

UZZI (*uz'-zi*)
1. A son of Bukki.
begat Bukki, and Bukki begat *U*.......... 1Chr 6:5 5813
U begat Zerahiah, and Zerahiah.......... 1Chr 6:6 5813
U his son, Zerahiah his son,.......... 1Chr 6:51 5813
The son of Zerahiah, the son of *U*.......... Ezr 7:4 5813
2. Father of Izrahiah.
U, and Rephaiah, and Jeriel, and.......... 1Chr 7:2 5813
And the sons of *U*.......... 1Chr 7:3 5813
3. Son of Bela.
Ezbon, and *U*, and Uzziel, and.......... 1Chr 7:7 5813
4. A family of exiles.
of Jeroham, and Elah the son of *U*.......... 1Chr 9:8 5813
5. An overseer of Levites.
Jerusalem was *U* the son of Bani.......... Neh 11:22 5813
6. A priest descended from Jedaiah.
of Jedaiah, *U*.......... Neh 12:19 5813
and Shemaiah, and Eleazar, and *U*.......... Neh 12:42 5813

UZZIA (*uz-zi'-ah*) *A "mighty man" of David.*
U the Ashterathite, Shama and.......... 1Chr 11:44 5814

UZZIAH (*uz-zi'-ah*)
1. A king of Judah.
thirtieth year of *U* king of Judah.......... 2Kin 15:13 5818
year of Jotham the son of *U*.......... 2Kin 15:30 5818
son of *U* king of Judah to reign.......... 2Kin 15:32 5818
to all that his father *U* had done.......... 2Kin 15:34 5818
all the people of Judah took *U*.......... 2Chr 26:1 5818
Sixteen years old was *U* when he.......... 2Chr 26:3 5818
And the Ammonites gave gifts to *U*.......... 2Chr 26:8 5818
Moreover *U* built towers in.......... 2Chr 26:9 5818
Moreover *U* had an host of.......... 2Chr 26:11 5818
U prepared for them throughout.......... 2Chr 26:14 5818
And they withstood *U* the king.......... 2Chr 26:18 5818
It appertaineth not unto thee, *U*.......... 2Chr 26:18 5818
Then *U* was wroth, and had a censer... 2Chr 26:19 5818
U the king was a leper unto the.......... 2Chr 26:21 5818
Now the rest of the acts of *U*.......... 2Chr 26:22 5818
So *U* slept with his fathers, and.......... 2Chr 26:23 5818
to all that his father *U* did.......... 2Chr 27:2 5818
and Jerusalem in the days of *U*.......... Is 1:1 5818
In the year that king *U* died I.......... Is 6:1 5818
the son of Jotham, the son of *U*.......... Is 7:1 5818
son of Beeri, in the days of *U*.......... Hos 1:1 5818
in the days of *U* king of Judah.......... Amos 1:1 5818
in the days of *U* king of Judah.......... Zec 14:5 5818
2. Son of Uriel.
U his son, and Shaul his son.......... 1Chr 6:24 5818
3. Father of Jehonathan.
was Jehonathan the son of *U*.......... 1Chr 27:25 5818
4. Married a foreigner in exile.
and Shemaiah, and Jehiel, and *U*.......... Ezr 10:21 5818
5. A family of exiles.
Athaiah the son of *U*, the son of.......... Neh 11:4 5818

UZZIEL (*uz-zi'-el*)
1. A son of Kohath.
Amram, and Izhar, and Hebron, and *U* Ex 6:18 5816
And the sons of *U*.......... Ex 6:22 5816
the sons of *U* the uncle of Aaron,.......... Lev 10:4 5816
Amram, and Izehar, Hebron, and *U*.......... Num 3:19 5816
shall be Elizaphan the son of *U*.......... Num 3:30 5816
Amram, Izhar, and Hebron, and *U*.......... 1Chr 6:2 5816
Amram, and Izhar, and Hebron, and *U* 1Chr 6:18 5816
Of the sons of *U*.......... 1Chr 15:10 5816
Amram, Izhar, Hebron, and *U*.......... 1Chr 23:12 5816
Of the sons of *U*.......... 1Chr 23:20 5816
Of the sons of *U*.......... 1Chr 24:24 5816
2. A son of Ishi.
and Neariah, and Rephaiah, and *U*.......... 1Chr 4:42 5816
3. A son of Bela.
Ezbon, and Uzzi, and *U*, and Jerimoth. 1Chr 7:7 5816
4. A sanctuary servant.
Bukkiah, Mattaniah, *U*, Shebuel,.......... 1Chr 25:4 5816
5. A Levite who cleansed the Temple.
Shemaiah, and *U*.......... 2Chr 29:14 5816
6. A repairer of Jerusalem's wall.
repaired *U* the son of Harhaiah.......... Neh 3:8 5816

UZZIELITES (*uz-zi'-el-ites*) *Descendants of Uzziel 1.*
and the family of the *U*.......... Num 3:27 5817
the Hebronites, and the *U*.......... 1Chr 26:23 5817

V

VAGABOND
a *v* shalt thou be in the earth.......... Gen 4:12 5110
be a fugitive and a *v* in the earth.......... Gen 4:14 5110
Then certain of the *v* Jews.......... Acts 19:13 *4022*

VAGABONDS
Let his children be continually *v*.......... Ps 109:10 5128

VAIL
therefore she took a *v*, and.......... Gen 24:65 6809
from her, and covered her with a *v*.......... Gen 38:14 6809
away, and laid by her *v* from her.......... Gen 38:19 6809
And thou shalt make a *v* of blue.......... Ex 26:31 6532
hang up the *v* under the taches.......... Ex 26:33 6532
the *v* the ark of the testimony.......... Ex 26:33 6532
the *v* shall divide unto you.......... Ex 26:33 6532
shalt set the table without the *v*.......... Ex 26:35 6532
of the congregation without the *v*.......... Ex 27:21 6532
the *v* that is by the ark of the.......... Ex 30:6 6532
with them, he put a *v* on his face.......... Ex 34:33 4533
speak with him, he took the *v* off.......... Ex 34:34 4533
Moses put the *v* upon his face.......... Ex 34:35 4533
seat, and the *v* of the covering,.......... Ex 35:12 6532
And he made a *v* of blue, and purple... Ex 36:35 6532
and the sockets of the *v*.......... Ex 38:27 6532
skins, and the *v* of the covering,.......... Ex 39:34 6532
and cover the ark with the *v*.......... Ex 40:3 6532
set up the *v* of the covering, and.......... Ex 40:21 6532
northward, without the *v*.......... Ex 40:22 6532
of the congregation before the *v*.......... Ex 40:26 6532
before the *v* of the sanctuary.......... Lev 4:6 6532
the LORD, even before the *v*.......... Lev 4:17 6532
the *v* before the mercy seat.......... Lev 16:2 6532
small, and bring it within the *v*.......... Lev 16:12 6532
and bring his blood within the *v*.......... Lev 16:15 6532
he shall not go in unto the *v*.......... Lev 21:23 6532
Without the *v* of the testimony,.......... Lev 24:3 6532
shall take down the covering *v*.......... Num 4:5 6532
of the altar, and within the *v*.......... Num 18:7 6532
Bring the *v* that thou hast upon.......... Ruth 3:15 4304
And he made the *v* of blue, and.......... 2Chr 3:14 6532
the *v* that is spread over all.......... Is 25:7 4541
which put a *v* over his face, that.......... 2Cor 3:13 *2571*
this day remaineth the same *v*.......... 2Cor 3:14 *2571*
which *v* is done away in Christ.......... 2Cor 3:14
the *v* is upon their heart.......... 2Cor 3:15 *2571*
the *v* shall be taken away.......... 2Cor 3:16 *2571*

VAILS
linen, and the hoods, and the *v*.......... Is 3:23 7289

VAIN
and let them not regard *v* words.......... Ex 5:9 8267
the name of the LORD thy God in *v*.......... Ex 20:7 7723
that taketh his name in *v*.......... Ex 20:7 7723
and ye shall sow your seed in *v*.......... Lev 26:16 7385
your strength shall be spent in *v*.......... Lev 26:20 7385
the name of the LORD thy God in *v*.......... Deut 5:11 7723
that taketh his name in *v*.......... Deut 5:11 7723
For it is not a *v* thing for you.......... Deut 32:47 7386
wherewith Abimelech hired *v*.......... Judg 9:4 7386
were gathered *v* men to Jephthah.......... Judg 11:3 7386

then should ye go after *v* things	1Sa 12:21	8414
for they are *v*	1Sa 12:21	8414
Surely in *v* have I kept all that	1Sa 25:21	8267
servants, as one of the *v* fellows	2Sa 6:20	7386
they followed vanity, and became *v*	2Kin 17:15	1891
sayest, (but they are but *v* words	2Kin 18:20	8193
there are gathered unto him *v* men	2Chr 13:7	7386
be wicked, why then labour I in *v*	Job 9:29	1892
For he knoweth *v* men	Job 11:11	7723
For *v* man would be wise, though	Job 11:12	5014
a wise man utter *v* knowledge	Job 15:2	7307
Shall *v* words have an end	Job 16:3	7307
How then comfort ye me in *v*	Job 21:34	1892
why then are ye thus altogether *v*	Job 27:12	1891
doth Job open his mouth in *v*	Job 35:16	1892
her labour is in *v* without fear	Job 39:16	7385
Behold, the hope of him is in *v*	Job 41:9	3576
and the people imagine a *v* thing	Ps 2:1	7385
I have not sat with *v* persons	Ps 26:4	7723
An horse is a *v* thing for safety	Ps 33:17	8267
every man walketh in a *v* shew	Ps 39:6	
surely they are disquieted in *v*	Ps 39:6	1892
for *v* is the help of man	Ps 60:11	7723
and become not *v* in robbery	Ps 62:10	1891
I have cleansed my heart in *v*	Ps 73:13	7385
hast thou made all men in *v*	Ps 89:47	7723
for *v* is the help of man	Ps 108:12	7723
I hate *v* thoughts	Ps 119:113	
they labour in *v* that build it	Ps 127:1	7723
the watchman waketh but in *v*	Ps 127:1	7723
It is *v* for you to rise up early	Ps 127:2	7723
thine enemies take thy name in *v*	Ps 139:20	7723
Surely in *v* the net is spread in	Prov 1:17	2600
followeth *v* persons is void of	Prov 12:11	7386
v persons shall have poverty	Prov 28:19	7386
and take the name of my God in *v*	Prov 30:9	
is deceitful, and beauty is *v*	Prov 31:30	1892
all the days of his *v* life which	Eccl 6:12	1892
Bring no more *v* oblations	Is 1:13	7723
For the Egyptians shall help in *v*	Is 30:7	1892
(but they are but *v* words) I have	Is 36:5	8193
it, he created it not in *v*	Is 45:18	8414
seed of Jacob, Seek ye me in *v*	Is 45:19	8414
Then I said, I have laboured in *v*	Is 49:4	7385
my strength for nought, and in *v*	Is 49:4	1892
They shall not labour in *v*	Is 65:23	7385
after vanity, and are become *v*	Jer 2:5	1891
In *v* have I smitten your children	Jer 2:30	7723
Truly in *v* is salvation hoped for	Jer 3:23	8267
How long shall thy *v* thoughts	Jer 4:14	205
in *v* shalt thou make thyself fair	Jer 4:30	7723
the founder melteth in *v*	Jer 6:29	7723
Lo, certainly in *v* made he it	Jer 8:8	8267
the pen of the scribes is in *v*	Jer 8:8	8267
the customs of the people are *v*	Jer 10:3	1892
they make you *v*	Jer 23:16	1891
in *v* shalt thou use many	Jer 46:11	7723
none shall return in *v*	Jer 50:9	7387
and the people shall labour in *v*	Jer 51:58	7385
Thy prophets have seen *v* and	Lam 2:14	7723
eyes as yet failed for our *v* help	Lam 4:17	1892
that I have not said in *v* that I	Eze 6:10	2600
more any *v* vision nor flattering	Eze 12:24	7723
Have ye not seen a *v* vision	Eze 13:7	7723
they comfort in *v*	Zec 10:2	1892
have said, It is *v* to serve God	Mal 3:14	7723
use not *v* repetitions, as the	Mt 6:7	
But in *v* they do worship me,	Mt 15:9	*3155*
Howbeit in *v* do they worship me,	Mk 7:7	*3155*
and the people imagine *v* things	Acts 4:25	*2756*
but became *v* in their	Rom 1:21	*3154*
for he beareth not the sword in *v*	Rom 13:4	*1500*
of the wise, that they are *v*	1Cor 3:20	*3152*
you, unless ye have believed in *v*	1Cor 15:2	*1500*
was bestowed upon me was not in *v*	1Cor 15:10	*2756*
risen, then is our preaching *v*	1Cor 15:14	*2756*
and your faith is also *v*	1Cor 15:14	*2756*
be not raised, your faith is *v*	1Cor 15:17	*3152*
labour is not in *v* in the Lord	1Cor 15:58	*2756*
receive not the grace of God in *v*	2Cor 6:1	*2756*
you should be in *v* in this behalf	2Cor 9:3	*2761*
I should run, or had run, in *v*	Gal 2:2	*2756*
the law, then Christ is dead in *v*	Gal 2:21	*1432*
ye suffered so many things in *v*	Gal 3:4	*1500*
if it be yet in *v*	Gal 3:4	*1500*
bestowed upon you labour in *v*	Gal 4:11	*1500*
Let us not be desirous of *v* glory	Gal 5:26	*2755*
no man deceive you with *v* words	Eph 5:6	*2756*
Christ, that I have not run in *v*	Phil 2:16	*2756*
neither laboured in *v*	Phil 2:16	*2756*
v deceit, after the tradition of	Col 2:8	*2756*
in unto you, that it was not in *v*	1Th 2:1	*2756*
you, and our labour be in *v*	1Th 3:5	*2756*
have turned aside unto *v* jangling	1Ti 1:6	*3150*
v babblings, and oppositions of	1Ti 6:20	*2757*
But shun profane and *v* babblings	2Ti 2:16	*2757*
v talkers and deceivers, specially	Titus 1:10	*3151*
for they are unprofitable and *v*	Titus 3:9	*3152*
heart, this man's religion is *v*	Jas 1:26	*3152*
O *v* man, that faith without works	Jas 2:20	*2756*
that the scripture saith in *v*	Jas 4:5	*2761*
from your *v* conversation received	1Pet 1:18	*3152*

VAINGLORY

be done through strife or *v*	Phil 2:3	*2754*

VAINLY

v puffed up by his fleshly mind,	Col 2:18	*1500*

VAIZATHA See VAJEZATHA.

VAJEZATHA (*va-jez'-a-thah*) *A son of Haman.*

and Arisai, and Aridai, and *V*	Est 9:9	2055

VALE

together in the *v* of Siddim	Gen 14:3	6010
with them in the *v* of Siddim	Gen 14:8	6010
the *v* of Siddim was full of	Gen 14:10	6010
sent him out of the *v* of Hebron	Gen 37:14	6010
plain, in the hills, and in the *v*	Deut 1:7	8219
and of the south, and of the *v*	Josh 10:40	8219
sycomore trees that are in the *v*	1Kin 10:27	8219
that are in the *v* for abundance	2Chr 1:15	8219
mountains, in the cities of the *v*	Jer 33:13	8219

VALIANT

saw any strong man, or any *v* man	1Sa 14:52	2428
in playing, and a mighty *v* man	1Sa 16:18	2428
only be thou *v* for me, and fight	1Sa 18:17	
to Abner, Art not thou a *v* man	1Sa 26:15	
All the *v* men arose, and went all	1Sa 31:12	2428
hands be strengthened, and be ye *v*	2Sa 2:7	
where he knew that *v* men were	2Sa 11:16	2428
be courageous, and be *v*	2Sa 13:28	
And he also that is *v*, whose heart	2Sa 17:10	
they which be with him are *v* men	2Sa 17:10	2428
of Jehoiada, the son of a *v* man	2Sa 23:20	2428
v men that drew the sword	2Sa 24:9	2428
for thou art a *v* man, and bringest	1Kin 1:42	2428
of *v* men, men able to bear	1Chr 5:18	2428
they were *v* men of might in their	1Chr 7:2	1368
of Issachar were *v* men of might	1Chr 7:5	1368
They arose, all the *v* men	1Chr 10:12	2428
the son of a *v* man of Kabzeel	1Chr 11:22	2428
Also the *v* men of the armies were	1Chr 11:26	1368
mighty men, and with all the *v* men	1Chr 28:1	2428
with an army of *v* men of war	2Chr 13:3	1368
of the LORD, that were *v* men	2Chr 26:17	2428
in one day, which were all *v* men	2Chr 28:6	2428
hundred threescore and eight *v* men	Neh 11:6	2428
threescore *v* men are about it, of	Song 3:7	1368
are about it, of the *v* of Israel	Song 3:7	1368
down the inhabitants like a *v* man	Is 10:13	3524
their *v* ones shall cry without	Is 33:7	691
but they are not *v* for the truth	Jer 9:3	1396
Why are thy *v* men swept away	Jer 46:15	47
red, the *v* men are in scarlet	Nah 2:3	2428
waxed *v* in fight, turned to	Heb 11:34	*2478*

VALIANTEST

twelve thousand men of the *v*	Judg 21:10	

VALIANTLY

and Israel shall do *v*	Num 24:18	2428
behave ourselves *v* for our people	1Chr 19:13	2388
Through God we shall do *v*	Ps 60:12	2428
Through God we shall do *v*	Ps 108:13	2428
right hand of the LORD doeth *v*	Ps 118:15	2428
right hand of the LORD doeth *v*	Ps 118:16	2428

VALLEY

at the *v* of Shaveh, which is the	Gen 14:17	6010
his tent in the *v* of Gerar	Gen 26:17	5158
Isaac's servants digged in the *v*	Gen 26:19	5158
and the Canaanites dwelt in the *v*	Num 14:25	6010
and pitched in the *v* of Zared	Num 21:12	5158
And from Bamoth in the *v*, that is	Num 21:20	1516
they went up unto the *v* of Eshcol	Num 32:9	5158
and came unto the *v* of Eshcol	Deut 1:24	5158
unto the river Arnon half the *v*	Deut 3:16	5158
So we abode in the *v* over against	Deut 3:29	1516
in the *v* over against Beth-peor,	Deut 4:46	1516
down the heifer unto a rough *v*	Deut 21:4	5158
the heifer's neck there in the *v*	Deut 21:4	5158
heifer that is beheaded in the *v*	Deut 21:6	5158
and the plain of the *v* of Jericho	Deut 34:3	1237
he buried him in a *v* in the land	Deut 34:6	1516
brought them unto the *v* of Achor	Josh 7:24	6010
The *v* of Achor, unto this day	Josh 7:26	6010
now there was a *v* between them	Josh 8:11	1516
night into the midst of the *v*	Josh 8:13	6010
and thou, Moon, in the *v* of Ajalon	Josh 10:12	6010
south of Chinneroth, and in the *v*	Josh 11:2	8219
unto the *v* of Mizpeh eastward	Josh 11:8	1237
all the land of Goshen, and the *v*	Josh 11:16	8219
of Israel, and the *v* of the same	Josh 11:16	8219
even unto Baal-gad in the *v* of	Josh 11:17	1237
from Baal-gad in the *v* of Lebanon	Josh 12:7	1237
in the mount of the *v*,	Josh 13:19	6010
And in the *v*, Beth-aram, and	Josh 13:27	6010
toward Debir from the *v* of Achor	Josh 15:7	6010
the border went up by the *v* of	Josh 15:8	1516
before the *v* of Hinnom westward	Josh 15:8	1516
of the *v* of the giants northward	Josh 15:8	6010
And in the *v*, Eshtaol, and Zoreah,	Josh 15:33	8219
of the *v* have chariots of iron	Josh 17:16	6010
they who are of the *v* of Jezreel	Josh 17:16	6010
before the *v* of the son of Hinnom	Josh 18:16	1516
which is in the *v* of the giants	Josh 18:16	6010
and descended to the *v* of Hinnom	Josh 18:16	1516
Beth-hoglah, and the *v* of Keziz,	Josh 18:21	6010
are in the *v* of Jiphthah-el	Josh 19:14	1516
to the *v* of Jiphthah-el toward	Josh 19:27	1516
and in the south, and in the *v*	Judg 1:9	8219
out the inhabitants of the *v*	Judg 1:19	6010
suffer them to come down to the *v*	Judg 1:34	6010
he was sent on foot into the *v*	Judg 5:15	6010
and pitched in the *v* of Jezreel	Judg 6:33	6010
by the hill of Moreh, in the *v*	Judg 7:1	6010
Midian was beneath him in the *v*	Judg 7:8	6010
of the east lay along in the *v*	Judg 7:12	6010
loved a woman in the *v* of Sorek	Judg 16:4	5158
it was in the *v* that lieth by	Judg 18:28	6010
their wheat harvest in the *v*	1Sa 6:13	6010
the border that looketh to the *v*	1Sa 13:18	1516
of Amalek, and laid wait in the *v*	1Sa 15:5	5158
and pitched by the *v* of Elah	1Sa 17:2	6010
there was a *v* between them	1Sa 17:3	1516
of Israel, were in the *v* of Elah	1Sa 17:19	6010
until thou come to the *v*	1Sa 17:52	1516
thou slewest in the *v* of Elah	1Sa 21:9	6010
were on the other side of the *v*	1Sa 31:7	6010
themselves in the *v* of Rephaim	2Sa 5:18	6010
themselves in the *v* of Rephaim	2Sa 5:22	6010
of the Syrians in the *v* of salt	2Sa 8:13	1516
pitched in the *v* of Rephaim	2Sa 23:13	6010
some mountain, or into some *v*	2Kin 2:16	1516
Make this *v* full of ditches	2Kin 3:16	5158
yet that *v* shall be filled with	2Kin 3:17	5158
in the *v* of salt ten thousand	2Kin 14:7	1516
which is in the *v* of the children	2Kin 23:10	1516
the father of the *v* of Charashim	1Chr 4:14	1516
even unto the east side of the *v*	1Chr 4:39	1516
were in the *v* saw that they fled	1Chr 10:7	6010
encamped in the *v* of Rephaim	1Chr 11:15	6010
themselves in the *v* of Rephaim	1Chr 14:9	6010
spread themselves abroad in the *v*	1Chr 14:13	6010
the *v* of salt eighteen thousand	1Chr 18:12	1516
in the *v* of Zephathah at Mareshah	2Chr 14:10	1516
themselves in the *v* of Berachah	2Chr 20:26	6010
The *v* of Berachah, unto this day	2Chr 20:26	6010
people, and went to the *v* of salt	2Chr 25:11	1516
the corner gate, and at the *v* gate	2Chr 26:9	1516
in the *v* of the son of Hinnom	2Chr 28:3	1516
in the *v* of the son of Hinnom	2Chr 33:6	1516
the west side of Gihon, in the *v*	2Chr 33:14	5158
came to fight in the *v* of Megiddo	2Chr 35:22	1237
out by night by the gate of the *v*	Neh 2:13	1516
and entered by the gate of the *v*	Neh 2:15	1516
The *v* gate repaired Hanun, and the	Neh 3:13	1516
Beer-sheba unto the *v* of Hinnom	Neh 11:30	1516
Lod, and Ono, the *v* of craftsmen	Neh 11:35	1516
The clods of the *v* shall be sweet	Job 21:33	5158
He paweth in the *v*, and rejoiceth	Job 39:21	6010
the *v* of the shadow of death	Ps 23:4	1516
smote of Edom in the *v* of salt	Ps 60:*t*	1516
and mete out the *v* of Succoth	Ps 60:6	6010
the *v* of Baca make it a well	Ps 84:6	6010
and mete out the *v* of Succoth	Ps 108:7	6010
ravens of the *v* shall pick it out	Prov 30:17	5158
nuts to see the fruits of the *v*	Song 6:11	5158
ears in the *v* of Rephaim	Is 17:5	6010
The burden of the *v* of vision	Is 22:1	1516
GOD of hosts in the *v* of vision	Is 22:5	1516
which is on the head of the fat *v*	Is 28:4	1516
be wroth as in the *v* of Gibeon	Is 28:21	6010
Every *v* shall be exalted, and	Is 40:4	1516
As a beast goeth down into the *v*	Is 63:14	1237
the *v* of Achor a place for the	Is 65:10	6010
see thy way in the *v*, know what	Jer 2:23	1516
which is in the *v* of the son of	Jer 7:31	1516
nor the *v* of the son of Hinnom,	Jer 7:32	1516
of Hinnom, but the *v* of slaughter	Jer 7:32	1516
go forth unto the *v* of the son of	Jer 19:2	1516
nor The *v* of the son of Hinnom,	Jer 19:6	1516
of Hinnom, but The *v* of slaughter	Jer 19:6	1516
thee, O inhabitant of the *v*	Jer 21:13	6010
the whole *v* of the dead bodies,	Jer 31:40	6010
which are in the *v* of the son of	Jer 32:35	1516
and in the cities of the *v*	Jer 32:44	8219
off with the remnant of their *v*	Jer 47:5	6010
the *v* also shall perish, and the	Jer 48:8	6010
in the valleys, thy flowing *v*	Jer 49:4	6010
of the *v* which was full of bones	Eze 37:1	1237
were very many in the open *v*	Eze 37:2	1237
the *v* of the passengers on the	Eze 39:11	1516
shall call it The *v* of Hamon-gog	Eze 39:11	1516
buried it in the *v* of Hamon-gog	Eze 39:15	1516
bow of Israel in the *v* of Jezreel	Hos 1:5	6010
the *v* of Achor for a door of hope	Hos 2:15	6010
down into the *v* of Jehoshaphat	Joel 3:2	6010
come up to the *v* of Jehoshaphat	Joel 3:12	6010
multitudes in the *v* of decision	Joel 3:14	6010
LORD is near in the *v* of decision	Joel 3:14	6010
and shall water the *v* of Shittim	Joel 3:18	5158
the stones thereof into the *v*	Mic 1:6	1516
Hadadrimmon in the *v* of Megiddon	Zec 12:11	1237
and there shall be a very great *v*	Zec 14:4	1516
flee to the *v* of the mountains	Zec 14:5	1516
for the *v* of the mountains shall	Zec 14:5	1516
Every *v* shall be filled, and every	Lk 3:5	*5327*

VALLEYS

As the *v* are they spread forth,	Num 24:6	5158
and depths that spring out of *v*	Deut 8:7	1237
it, is a land of hills and *v*	Deut 11:11	1237
Jordan, in the hills, and in the *v*	Josh 9:1	8219
In the mountains, and in the *v*	Josh 12:8	8219
hills, but he is not God of the *v*	1Kin 20:28	6010
put to flight all them of the *v*	1Chr 12:15	6010
v was Shaphat the son of Adlai	1Chr 27:29	6010
To dwell in the cliffs of the *v*	Job 30:6	5158
will he harrow the *v* after thee	Job 39:10	6010
the *v* also are covered over with	Ps 65:13	6010
they go down by the *v* unto the	Ps 104:8	1237
He sendeth the springs into the *v*	Ps 104:10	5158
of Sharon, and the lily of the *v*	Song 2:1	6010
all of them in the desolate *v*	Is 7:19	5158
that thy choicest *v* shall be full	Is 22:7	6010
are on the head of the fat *v* of	Is 28:1	1516
fountains in the midst of the *v*	Is 41:18	1237
slaying the children in the *v*	Is 57:5	5158
Wherefore gloriest thou in the *v*	Jer 49:4	6010
hills, to the rivers, and to the *v*	Eze 6:3	1516
the mountains like doves of the *v*	Eze 7:16	1516
in all the *v* his branches are	Eze 31:12	1516
fill the *v* with thy height	Eze 32:5	1516
in thy hills, and in thy *v*	Eze 35:8	1516
hills, to the rivers, and to the *v*	Eze 36:4	1516
hills, to the rivers, and to the *v*	Eze 36:6	1516
the *v* shall be cleft, as wax	Mic 1:4	6010

VALOUR

armed, all the mighty men of *v*	Josh 1:14	2428
thereof, and the mighty men of *v*	Josh 6:2	2428
thirty thousand mighty men of *v*	Josh 8:3	2428
him, and all the mighty men of *v*	Josh 10:7	2428
men, all lusty, and all men of *v*	Judg 3:29	2428
with thee, thou mighty man of *v*	Judg 6:12	2428

Gileadite was a mighty man of v ... Judg 11:1 2428
men from their coasts, men of v ... Judg 18:2 2428
all these were men of v ... Judg 20:44 2428
all these were men of v ... Judg 20:46 2428
Jeroboam was a mighty man of v ... 1Kin 11:28 2428
he was also a mighty man in v ... 2Kin 5:1 2428
and all the mighty men of v ... 2Kin 24:14 2428
and Jahdiel, mighty men of v ... 1Chr 5:24 2428
of their fathers, mighty men of v ... 1Chr 7:7 2428
of their fathers, mighty men of v ... 1Chr 7:9 2428
of their fathers, mighty men of v ... 1Chr 7:11 2428
house, choice and mighty men of v ... 1Chr 7:40 2428
sons of Ulam were mighty men of v ... 1Chr 8:40 2428
for they were all mighty men of v ... 1Chr 12:21 2428
mighty men of v for the war ... 1Chr 12:25 2428
And Zadok, a young man mighty of v. 1Chr 12:28 2428
and eight hundred, mighty men of v ... 1Chr 12:30 2428
for they were mighty men of v ... 1Chr 26:6 2428
and his brethren, men of v ... 1Chr 26:30 2428
men of v at Jazer of Gilead ... 1Chr 26:31 2428
And his brethren, men of v ... 1Chr 26:32 2428
chosen men, being mighty men of v ... 2Chr 13:3 2428
all these were mighty men of v ... 2Chr 14:8 2428
the men of war, mighty men of v ... 2Chr 17:13 2428
men of v three hundred thousand ... 2Chr 17:14 2428
hundred thousand mighty men of v ... 2Chr 17:16 2428
Eliada a mighty man of v, and with ... 2Chr 17:17 2428
of v out of Israel for an hundred ... 2Chr 25:6 2428
mighty men of v were two thousand ... 2Chr 26:12 2428
cut off all the mighty men of v ... 2Chr 32:21 2428
their brethren, mighty men of v ... Neh 11:14 2428

VALUE
priest, and the priest shall v him ... Lev 27:8 6186
that vowed shall the priest v him ... Lev 27:8 6186
And the priest shall v it, whether ... Lev 27:12 6186
ye are all physicians of no v ... Job 13:4 457
ye are of more v than many ... Mt 10:31 *1308*
of the children of Israel did v ... Mt 27:9 *5091*
ye are of more v than many ... Lk 12:7 *1308*

VALUED
be v at fifty shekels of silver ... Lev 27:16
It cannot be v with the gold of ... Job 28:16 5541
shall it be v with pure gold ... Job 28:19 5541
the price of him that was v ... Mt 27:9 *5091*

VALUEST
as thou v it, who art the priest, ... Lev 27:12 6187

VANIAH (va-ni'-ah) *Married a foreigner in exile.*
V, Meremoth, Eliashib, ... Ezr 10:36 2057

VANISH
What time they wax warm, they v ... Job 6:17 6789
heavens shall v away like smoke ... Is 51:6 4414
be knowledge, it shall v away ... 1Cor 13:8 *2673*
and waxeth old is ready to v away ... Heb 8:13 *854*

VANISHED
is their wisdom v ... Jer 49:7 5628
and he v out of their sight ... Lk 24:31

VANISHETH
the cloud is consumed and v away ... Job 7:9 3212
for a little time, and then v away ... Jas 4:14 *853*

VANITIES
provoked me to anger with their v ... Deut 32:21 1892
of Israel to anger with their v ... 1Kin 16:13 1892
of Israel to anger with their v ... 1Kin 16:26 1892
hated them that regard lying v ... Ps 31:6 1892
Vanity of v, saith the Preacher, ... Eccl 1:2 1892
saith the Preacher, vanity of v ... Eccl 1:2 1892
words there are also divers v ... Eccl 5:7 1892
Vanity of v, saith the preacher ... Eccl 12:8 1892
graven images, and with strange v ... Jer 8:19 1892
the stock is a doctrine of v ... Jer 10:8 1892
Are there any among the v of the ... Jer 14:22 1892
lying v forsake their own mercy ... Jonah 2:8 1892
from these v unto the living God ... Acts 14:15 *3152*

VANITY
and they followed v, and became ... 2Kin 17:15 1892
am I made to possess months of v ... Job 7:3 7723
for my days are v ... Job 7:16 1892
him that is deceived trust in v ... Job 15:31 7723
for v shall be his recompence ... Job 15:31 7723
mischief, and bring forth v ... Job 15:35 205
If I have walked with v, or if my ... Job 31:5 7723
Surely God will not hear v ... Job 35:13 7723
how long will ye love v, and seek ... Ps 4:2 7385
under his tongue is mischief and v ... Ps 10:7 205
They speak v every one with his ... Ps 12:2 7723
not lifted up his soul unto v ... Ps 24:4 7723
at his best state is altogether v ... Ps 39:5 1892
surely every man is v ... Ps 39:11 1892
he come to see me, he speaketh v ... Ps 41:6 7723
Surely men of low degree are v ... Ps 62:9 1892
are altogether lighter than v ... Ps 62:9 1892
their days did he consume in v ... Ps 78:33 1892
thoughts of man, that they are v ... Ps 94:11 1892
away mine eyes from beholding v ... Ps 119:37 7723
Man is like to v ... Ps 144:4 1892
Whose mouth speaketh v, and their ... Ps 144:8 7723
children, whose mouth speaketh v ... Ps 144:11 7723
Wealth gotten by v shall be ... Prov 13:11 1892
a lying tongue is a v tossed to ... Prov 21:6 1892
that soweth iniquity shall reap v ... Prov 22:8 205
Remove far from me v and lies ... Prov 30:8 7723
V of vanities, saith the Preacher ... Eccl 1:2 1892
saith the Preacher, V of vanities ... Eccl 1:2 1892
all is v ... Eccl 1:2 1892
and, behold, all is v and vexation ... Eccl 1:14 1892
and, behold, this also is v ... Eccl 2:1 1892
and, behold, all was v and vexation ... Eccl 2:11 1892
in my heart, that this also is v ... Eccl 2:15 1892
for all is v and vexation of ... Eccl 2:17 1892
This is also v ... Eccl 2:19 1892
This also is v and a great evil ... Eccl 2:21 1892
This is also v ... Eccl 2:23 1892
This also is v and vexation of ... Eccl 2:26 1892
for all is v ... Eccl 3:19 1892
This is also v and vexation of ... Eccl 4:4 1892
and I saw v under the sun ... Eccl 4:7 1892
This is also v, yea, it is a sore ... Eccl 4:8 1892
Surely this also is v and vexation ... Eccl 4:16 1892
this is also v ... Eccl 5:10 1892
this is v, and it is an evil ... Eccl 6:2 1892
For he cometh in with v, and ... Eccl 6:4 1892
this is also v and vexation of ... Eccl 6:9 1892
be many things that increase v ... Eccl 6:11 1892
this also is v ... Eccl 7:6 1892
have I seen in the days of my v ... Eccl 7:15 1892
this is also v ... Eccl 8:10 1892
There is a v which is done upon ... Eccl 8:14 1892
I said that this also is v ... Eccl 8:14 1892
all the days of the life of thy v ... Eccl 9:9 1892
the sun, all the days of thy v ... Eccl 9:9 1892
All that cometh is v ... Eccl 11:8 1892
for childhood and youth are v ... Eccl 11:10 1892
V of vanities, saith the preacher ... Eccl 12:8 1892
all is v ... Eccl 12:8 1892
draw iniquity with cords of v ... Is 5:18 7723
the nations with the sieve of v ... Is 30:28 7723
to him less than nothing, and v ... Is 40:17 8414
the judges of the earth as v ... Is 40:23 8414
Behold, they are all v ... Is 41:29 205
a graven image are all of them v ... Is 44:9 8414
v shall take them ... Is 57:13 1892
of the finger, and speaking v ... Is 58:9 205
they trust in v, and speak lies ... Is 59:4 8414
from me, and have walked after v ... Jer 2:5 1892
They are v, and the work of errors ... Jer 10:15 1892
fathers have inherited lies, v ... Jer 16:19 1892
me, they have burned incense to v ... Jer 18:15 7723
They are v, the work of errors ... Jer 51:18 1892
They have seen v and lying ... Eze 13:6 7723
Because ye have spoken v, and seen ... Eze 13:8 7723
be upon the prophets that see v ... Eze 13:9 7723
Therefore ye shall see no more v ... Eze 13:23 7723
Whiles they see v unto thee ... Eze 21:29 7723
with untempered morter, seeing v ... Eze 22:28 7723
surely they are v ... Hos 12:11 7723
shall weary themselves for very v ... Hab 2:13 7385
For the idols have spoken v ... Zec 10:2 205
creature was made subject to v ... Rom 8:20 *3153*
walk, in the v of their mind, ... Eph 4:17 *3153*
speak great swelling words of v ... 2Pet 2:18 *3153*

VAPORS
he causeth the v to ascend from ... Jer 10:13 5387
he causeth the v to ascend from ... Jer 51:16 5387

VAPOUR
rain according to the v thereof ... Job 36:27 108
the cattle also concerning the v ... Job 36:33 5927
blood, and fire, and v of smoke ... Acts 2:19 *822*
It is even a v, that appeareth ... Jas 4:14 *822*

VAPOURS
He causeth the v to ascend from ... Ps 135:7 5387
and hail; snow, and v ... Ps 148:8 7008

VARIABLENESS
of lights, with whom is no v ... Jas 1:17 3883

VARIANCE
set a man at v against his father ... Mt 10:35 *1369*
Idolatry, witchcraft, hatred, v ... Gal 5:20 *2054*

VASHNI (vash'-ni) *A son of Samuel.*
the firstborn V, and Abiah ... 1Chr 6:28 2059

VASHTI (vash'-ti) *A Persian queen, succeeded by Esther.*
Also V the queen made a feast for ... Est 1:9 2060
To bring V the queen before the ... Est 1:11 2060
But the queen V refused to come ... Est 1:12 2060
unto the queen V according to law ... Est 1:15 2060
V the queen hath not done wrong ... Est 1:16 2060
V the queen to be brought in ... Est 1:17 2060
That V come no more before king ... Est 1:19 2060
was appeased, he remembered V ... Est 2:1 2060
the king be queen instead of V ... Est 2:4 2060
and made her queen instead of V ... Est 2:17 2060

VAUNT
lest Israel v themselves against ... Judg 7:2 6286

VAUNTETH
charity v not itself, is not ... 1Cor 13:4 *4068*

VEDAN See DAN.

VEHEMENT
fire, which hath a most v flame ... Song 8:6 3050
that God prepared a v east wind ... Jonah 4:8 2759
what v desire, yea, what zeal, ... 2Cor 7:11 *1972*

VEHEMENTLY
But he spake the more v, If I ... Mk 14:31
the stream beat v upon that house ... Lk 6:48 *4366*
which the stream did beat v ... Lk 6:49 *4366*
the Pharisees began to urge him v ... Lk 11:53 *1171*
and scribes stood and v accused him ... Lk 23:10 *2159*

VEIL
the walls took away my v from me ... Song 5:7 7289
the v of the temple was rent in ... Mt 27:51 *2665*
the v of the temple was rent in ... Mk 15:38 *2665*
the v of the temple was rent in ... Lk 23:45 *2665*
entereth into that within the v ... Heb 6:19 *2665*
And after the second v, the ... Heb 9:3 *2665*
consecrated for us, through the v ... Heb 10:20 *2665*

VEIN
there is a v for the silver ... Job 28:1 4161

VENGEANCE
v shall be taken on him sevenfold ... Gen 4:15 5358
To me belongeth v, and recompence ... Deut 32:35 5359
I will render v to mine enemies, ... Deut 32:41 5359
will render v to his adversaries, ... Deut 32:43 5359
as the LORD hath taken v for thee ... Judg 11:36 5360
shall rejoice when he seeth the v ... Ps 58:10 5359
O LORD God, to whom v belongeth ... Ps 94:1 5360
to whom v belongeth, shew thyself ... Ps 94:1 5360
tookest v of their inventions ... Ps 99:8 5358
To execute v upon the heathen, and ... Ps 149:7 5360
he will not spare in the day of v ... Prov 6:34 5359
For it is the day of the LORD's v ... Is 34:8 5359
behold, your God will come with v ... Is 35:4 5359
I will take v, and I will not meet ... Is 47:3 5359
on the garments of v for clothing ... Is 59:17 5359
LORD, and the day of v of our God ... Is 61:2 5359
For the day of v is in mine heart ... Is 63:4 5359
heart, let me see thy v on them ... Jer 11:20 5360
heart, let me see thy v on them ... Jer 20:12 5360
the Lord GOD of hosts, a day of v ... Jer 46:10 5360
for it is the v of the LORD ... Jer 50:15 5360
take v upon her ... Jer 50:15 5358
in Zion the v of the LORD our God ... Jer 50:28 5360
LORD our God, the v of his temple ... Jer 50:28 5360
this is the time of the LORD's v ... Jer 51:6 5360
because it is the v of the LORD ... Jer 51:11 5360
of the LORD, the v of his temple ... Jer 51:11 5360
thy cause, and take v for thee ... Jer 51:36 5360
Thou hast seen all their v ... Lam 3:60 5360
cause fury to come up to take v ... Eze 24:8 5359
the house of Judah by taking v ... Eze 25:12 5359
I will lay my v upon Edom by the ... Eze 25:14 5360
and they shall know my v, saith ... Eze 25:14 5360
have taken v with a despiteful ... Eze 25:15 5359
I will execute great v upon them ... Eze 25:17 5360
when I shall lay my v upon them ... Eze 25:17 5360
And I will execute v in anger ... Mic 5:15 5359
will take v on his adversaries ... Nah 1:2 5358
For these be the days of v ... Lk 21:22 *1557*
yet v suffereth not to live ... Acts 28:4 *1349*
Is God unrighteous who taketh v ... Rom 3:5 *3709*
for it is written, V is mine ... Rom 12:19 *1557*
In flaming fire taking v on them ... 2Th 1:8 *1557*
V belongeth unto me, I will ... Heb 10:30 *1557*
suffering the v of eternal fire ... Jude 7 *1349*

VENISON
Esau, because he did eat of his v ... Gen 25:28 6718
to the field, and take me some v ... Gen 27:3 6720
went to the field to hunt for v ... Gen 27:5 6718
Bring me v, and make me savoury ... Gen 27:7 6718
I pray thee, sit and eat of my v ... Gen 27:19 6718
me, and I will eat of my son's v ... Gen 27:25 6718
arise, and eat of his son's v ... Gen 27:31 6718
where is he that hath taken v ... Gen 27:33 6718

VENOM
dragons, and the cruel v of asps ... Deut 32:33 7219

VENOMOUS
saw the v beast hang on his hand ... Acts 28:4

VENT
belly is as wine which hath no v ... Job 32:19 6605

VENTURE
a certain man drew a bow at a v ... 1Kin 22:34 8537
a certain man drew a bow at a v ... 2Chr 18:33 8537

VERIFIED
so shall your words be v, and ye ... Gen 42:20 539
let thy word, I pray thee, be v ... 1Kin 8:26 539
God of Israel, let thy word be v ... 2Chr 6:17 539

VERILY
We are v guilty concerning our ... Gen 42:21 61
V my sabbaths ye shall keep ... Ex 31:13 389
I v thought that thou hadst ... Judg 15:2 559
V our lord king David hath made ... 1Kin 1:43 61
V she hath no child, and her ... 2Kin 4:14 61
but I will v buy it for the full ... 1Chr 21:24 7069
are v estranged from me ... Job 19:13 389
the land, and v thou shalt be fed ... Ps 37:3 530
v every man at his best state is ... Ps 39:5 389
V there is a reward for the ... Ps 58:11 389
v he is a God that judgeth in the ... Ps 58:11 389
But v God hath heard me ... Ps 66:19 403
V I have cleansed my heart in ... Ps 73:13 389
V thou art a God that hidest ... Is 45:15 403
V it shall be well with thy ... Jer 15:11
v I will cause the enemy to ... Jer 15:11 518
For v I say unto you, Till heaven ... Mt 5:18 *281*
V I say unto thee, Thou shalt by ... Mt 5:26 *281*
V I say unto you, They have their ... Mt 6:2 *281*
V I say unto you, They have their ... Mt 6:5 *281*
V I say unto you, They have their ... Mt 6:16 *281*
V I say unto you, I have not ... Mt 8:10 *281*
V I say unto you, It shall be ... Mt 10:15 *281*
for v I say unto you, Ye shall ... Mt 10:23 *281*
v I say unto you, he shall in no ... Mt 10:42 *281*
V I say unto you, Among them that ... Mt 11:11 *281*
For v I say unto you, That many ... Mt 13:17 *281*
V I say unto you, There be some ... Mt 16:28 *281*
for v I say unto you, If ye have ... Mt 17:20 *281*
V I say unto you, Except ye be ... Mt 18:3 *281*
v I say unto you, he rejoiceth ... Mt 18:13 *281*
V I say unto you, Whatsoever ye ... Mt 18:18 *281*
V I say unto you, That a rich man ... Mt 19:23 *281*
V I say unto you, That ye which ... Mt 19:28 *281*
V I say unto you, If ye have ... Mt 21:21 *281*
V I say unto you, That the ... Mt 21:31 *281*
V I say unto you, All these ... Mt 23:36 *281*
v I say unto you, There shall not ... Mt 24:2 *281*
V I say unto you, This generation ... Mt 24:34 *281*

V I say unto you, That he shall ... Mt 24:47 281
V I say unto you, I know you not ... Mt 25:12 281
V I say unto you, Inasmuch as ye ... Mt 25:40 281
V I say unto you, Inasmuch as ye ... Mt 25:45 281
V I say unto you, Wheresoever ... Mt 26:13 281
V I say unto you, that one of you ... Mt 26:21 281
V I say unto thee, That this ... Mt 26:34 281
V I say unto you, All sins shall ... Mk 3:28 281
V I say unto you, It shall be ... Mk 6:11 281
v I say unto you, There shall no ... Mk 8:12 281
V I say unto you, That there be ... Mk 9:1 281
them, Elias v cometh first, and ... Mk 9:12 3303
v I say unto you, he shall not ... Mk 9:41 281
V I say unto you, Whosoever shall ... Mk 10:15 281
V I say unto you, There is no man ... Mk 10:29 281
For v I say unto you, That ... Mk 11:23 281
V I say unto you, That this poor ... Mk 12:43 281
V I say unto you, that this ... Mk 13:30 281
V I say unto you, Wheresoever ... Mk 14:9 281
V I say unto you, One of you ... Mk 14:18 281
V I say unto you, I will drink no ... Mk 14:25 281
V I say unto thee, That this day ... Mk 14:30 281
V I say unto you, No prophet is ... Lk 4:24 281
v I say unto you, It shall be ... Lk 11:51 3483
v I say unto you, that he shall ... Lk 12:37 281
v I say unto you, Ye shall not ... Lk 13:35 281
V I say unto you, Whosoever shall ... Lk 18:17 281
V I say unto you, There is no man ... Lk 18:29 281
V I say unto you, This generation ... Lk 21:32 281
V I say unto thee, To day shalt ... Lk 23:43 281
And he saith unto him, V, v, ... Jn 1:51 281
and said unto him, V, v ... Jn 3:3 281
Jesus answered, V, v ... Jn 3:5 281
V, v, I say unto thee, We ... Jn 3:11 281
and said unto them, V, v ... Jn 5:19 281
V, v, I say unto you, He ... Jn 5:24 281
V, v, I say unto you, The ... Jn 5:25 281
answered them and said, V, v ... Jn 6:26 281
Jesus said unto them, V, v ... Jn 6:32 281
V, v, I say unto you, He ... Jn 6:47 281
Jesus said unto them, V, v ... Jn 6:53 281
Jesus answered them, V, v ... Jn 8:34 281
V, v, I say unto you, If a ... Jn 8:51 281
Jesus said unto them, V, v ... Jn 8:58 281
V, v, I say unto you, He ... Jn 10:1 281
Jesus unto them again, V, v ... Jn 10:7 281
V, v, I say unto you, Except ... Jn 12:24 281
V, v, I say unto you, The ... Jn 13:16 281
V, v, I say unto you, He ... Jn 13:20 281
and testified, and said, V, v ... Jn 13:21 281
V, v, I say unto thee, The ... Jn 13:38 281
V, v, I say unto you, He ... Jn 14:12 281
V, v, I say unto you, That ... Jn 16:20 281
V, v, I say unto you, ... Jn 16:23 281
V, v, I say unto thee, When ... Jn 21:18 281
nay v; but let them ... Acts 16:37 1063
John v baptized with the baptism ... Acts 19:4 3303
I am v a man which am a Jew, born ... Acts 22:3 3303
I v thought with myself, that I ... Acts 26:9
For circumcision v profiteth ... Rom 2:25 3303
Yes v, their sound went into all ... Rom 10:18 3304
It hath pleased them v ... Rom 15:27 1063
For I v, as absent in body, but ... 1Cor 5:3 3303
V that, when I preach the gospel, ... 1Cor 9:18
For thou v givest thanks well, ... 1Cor 14:17 3303
v righteousness should have been ... Gal 3:21 3689
For v, when we were with you, we ... 1Th 3:4 2532
For v he took not on him the ... Heb 2:16 1222
Moses v was faithful in all his ... Heb 3:5 3303
For men v swear by the greater ... Heb 6:16 3303
v they that are of the sons of ... Heb 7:5 3303
For there is v a disannulling of ... Heb 7:18 3303
Then v the first covenant had ... Heb 9:1 3303
For they v for a few days ... Heb 12:10 3303
Who v was foreordained before the ... 1Pet 1:20 3303
in him v is the love of God ... 1Jn 2:5 230

VERITY

The works of his hands are v ... Ps 111:7 571
of the Gentiles in faith and v ... 1Ti 2:7 225

VERMILION

with cedar, and painted with v ... Jer 22:14 8350
the Chaldeans pourtrayed with v ... Eze 23:14 8350

VERY

made, and, behold, it was v good ... Gen 1:31 3966
And Cain was v wroth, and his ... Gen 4:5 3966
the woman that she was v fair ... Gen 12:14 3966
Abram was v rich in cattle, in ... Gen 13:2 3966
because their sin is v grievous ... Gen 18:20 3966
the thing was v grievous in ... Gen 21:11 3966
the damsel was v fair to look ... Gen 24:16 3966
and grew until he became v great ... Gen 26:13 3966
thou be my v son Esau or not ... Gen 27:21 2088
he said, Art thou my v son Esau ... Gen 27:24 2088
And Isaac trembled v exceedingly ... Gen 27:33 1419
grieved, and they were v wroth ... Gen 34:7 3966
v ill favoured and leanfleshed, ... Gen 41:19 3966
for it shall be v grievous ... Gen 41:31 3966
v much, until he left numbering ... Gen 41:49 3966
for the famine was v sore ... Gen 47:13 3966
and it was a v great company ... Gen 50:9 3966
a great and v sore lamentation ... Gen 50:10 3966
multiplied, and waxed v mighty ... Ex 1:20 3966
only ye shall not go v far away ... Ex 8:28
shall be a v grievous murrain ... Ex 9:3 3966
in v deed for this cause have I ... Ex 9:16 199
it to rain a v grievous hail ... Ex 9:18 3966
v grievous, such as there was ... Ex 9:24 3966
v grievous were they ... Ex 10:14 3966
was v great in the land of Egypt ... Ex 11:3 3966
and herds, even v much cattle ... Ex 12:38 3966
shalt beat some of it v small ... Ex 30:36 1854
if any man die v suddenly by him, ... Num 6:9 6621
the people with a v great plague ... Num 11:33 3966
(Now the man Moses was v meek ... Num 12:3 3966
the cities are walled, and v great ... Num 13:28 3966
And Moses was v wroth, and said ... Num 16:15 3966
promote thee unto v great honour ... Num 22:17 3966
had a v great multitude of cattle ... Num 32:1 3966
the LORD was v angry with Aaron ... Deut 9:20 3966
stamped it, and ground it v small ... Deut 9:21 3190
which are v far off from thee ... Deut 20:15 3966
the words of this law v plainly ... Deut 27:8 3190
shall get up above thee v high ... Deut 28:43 4605
and thou shalt come down v low ... Deut 28:43 4295
v delicate, his eye shall be evil ... Deut 28:54 3966
But the word is v nigh unto thee ... Deut 30:14 3966
for they are a v froward ... Deut 32:20
v courageous, that thou mayest ... Josh 1:7 3966
rose up upon an heap v far from ... Josh 3:16 3966
go not v far from the city, but ... Josh 8:4 3966
From a v far country thy servants ... Josh 9:9 3966
by reason of the v long journey ... Josh 9:13 3966
us, saying, We are v far from you ... Josh 9:22 3966
them with a v great slaughter ... Josh 10:20 3966
which remain until this v day ... Josh 10:27 6106
with horses and chariots v many ... Josh 11:4 3966
there remaineth yet v much land ... Josh 13:1 3966
with v much cattle, with silver, ... Josh 22:8 3966
with iron, and with v much raiment ... Josh 22:8 3966
Be ye therefore v courageous to ... Josh 23:6 3966
and Eglon was a v fat man ... Judg 3:17 3966
with a v great slaughter ... Judg 11:33 3966
thou hast brought me v low ... Judg 11:35
of an angel of God, v terrible ... Judg 13:6 3966
land, and, behold, it is v good ... Judg 18:9 3966
hath dealt v bitterly with me ... Ruth 1:20 3966
men was v great before the LORD ... 1Sa 2:17 3966
Now Eli was v old, and heard all ... 1Sa 2:22 3966
there was a v great slaughter ... 1Sa 4:10 3966
city with a v great destruction ... 1Sa 5:9 3966
the hand of God was v heavy there ... 1Sa 5:11 3966
so it was a v great trembling ... 1Sa 14:15 430
there was a v great discomfiture ... 1Sa 14:20 3966
and the people were v faint ... 1Sa 14:31 3966
And Saul was v wroth, and the ... 1Sa 18:8 3966
that he behaved himself v wisely ... 1Sa 18:15 3966
have been to thee-ward v good ... 1Sa 19:4 3966
but if he be v wroth, then be ... 1Sa 20:7
me that he dealeth v subtilly ... 1Sa 23:22
and the man was v great, and he had .. 1Sa 25:2 3966
But the men were v good unto us ... 1Sa 25:15 3966
For in v deed, as the LORD God of ... 1Sa 25:34 199
within him for he was v drunken ... 1Sa 25:36
that Saul was come in v deed ... 1Sa 26:4 3559
v pleasant hast thou been unto me ... 2Sa 1:26 3966
there was a v sore battle that ... 2Sa 2:17 3966
Then was Abner v wroth for the ... 2Sa 3:8 3966
the woman was v beautiful to look ... 2Sa 11:2 3966
bare unto David, and it was v sick ... 2Sa 12:15
and Jonadab was a v subtil man ... 2Sa 13:3 3966
all these things, he was v wroth ... 2Sa 13:21 3966
and all his servants wept v sore ... 2Sa 13:36 3966
laid a v great heap of stones ... 2Sa 18:17 3966
Now Barzillai was a v aged man ... 2Sa 19:32 3966
for he was a v great man ... 2Sa 19:32 3966
for I have done v foolishly ... 2Sa 24:10 3966
And the damsel was v fair, and ... 1Kin 1:4 3966
and he also was a v goodly man ... 1Kin 1:6 3966
and the king was v old ... 1Kin 1:15 3966
were of the v base itself ... 1Kin 7:34
to Jerusalem with a v great train ... 1Kin 10:2 3966
v much gold, and precious stones ... 1Kin 10:2 3966
of spices v great store, and ... 1Kin 10:10 3966
I have been v jealous for the ... 1Kin 19:10
I have been v jealous for the ... 1Kin 19:14
he did v abominably in following ... 1Kin 21:26 3966
of Israel, that it was v bitter ... 2Kin 14:26 3966
the LORD was v angry with Israel ... 2Kin 17:18 3966
shed innocent blood v much ... 2Kin 21:16 3966
v able men for the work of the ... 1Chr 9:13
brought David v much brass ... 1Chr 18:8 3966
for I have done v foolishly ... 1Chr 21:8 3966
for v great are his mercies ... 1Chr 21:13 3966
the sons of Rehabiah were v many ... 1Chr 23:17 4605
But will God in v deed dwell with ... 2Chr 6:18 552
a v great congregation, from the ... 2Chr 7:8 3966
with a v great company, and camels ... 2Chr 9:1 3966
and they carried away v much spoil ... 2Chr 14:13 3966
with v many chariots and horsemen ... 2Chr 16:8 3966
they made a v great burning for ... 2Chr 16:14 3966
of Israel, who did v wickedly ... 2Chr 20:35
the LORD delivered a v great host ... 2Chr 24:24 3966
month, a v great congregation ... 2Chr 30:13 3966
had given him substance v much ... 2Chr 32:29 3966
and raised it up a v great height ... 2Chr 33:14 3966
transgressed v much after all the ... 2Chr 36:14
unto him out of Israel a v great ... Ezr 10:1 3966
for the people wept v sore ... Ezr 10:1
We have dealt v corruptly against ... Neh 1:7
Then I was v sore afraid, ... Neh 2:2 3966
stopped, then they were v wroth ... Neh 4:7 3966
I was v angry when I heard their ... Neh 5:6 3966
there was v great gladness ... Neh 8:17 3966
therefore was the king v wroth ... Est 1:12 3966
she asses, and a v great household ... Job 1:3 3966
saw that his grief was v great ... Job 2:13 3966
v aged men, much elder than thy ... Job 15:10 3453
said, I am young, and ye are v old ... Job 32:6 3453
their inward part is v wickedness ... Ps 5:9 1942
into that v destruction let him ... Ps 35:8
a v present help in trouble ... Ps 46:1 3966
it shall be v tempestuous round ... Ps 50:3 3966
is v high, who hast done great ... Ps 71:19 5704
for we are brought v low ... Ps 79:8 3966
thou establish in the v heavens ... Ps 89:2
and thy thoughts are v deep ... Ps 92:5 3966
Thy testimonies are v sure ... Ps 93:5 3966
O LORD my God, thou art v great ... Ps 104:1 3966
v few, and strangers in it ... Ps 105:12
I am afflicted v much ... Ps 119:107
are righteous and v faithful ... Ps 119:138 3966
Thy word is v pure ... Ps 119:140 3966
for I am brought v low ... Ps 142:6 3966
in that v day his thoughts perish ... Ps 146:4
his word runneth v swiftly ... Ps 147:15 5704
a matter separateth v friends ... Prov 17:9
dropping in a v rainy day ... Prov 27:15 5464
left unto us a v small remnant ... Is 1:9 4592
a vineyard in a v fruitful hill ... Is 5:1
For yet a v little while, and the ... Is 10:25 4213
he is v proud ... Is 16:6 3966
and the remnant shall be v small ... Is 16:14 4213
have dealt v treacherously ... Is 24:16 899
Is it not yet a v little while ... Is 29:17 4213
he will be v gracious unto thee ... Is 30:19
because they are v strong ... Is 31:1 3966
behold the land that is v far off ... Is 33:17 4801
up the isles as a v little thing ... Is 40:15 1851
hast thou v heavily laid thy yoke ... Is 47:6 3966
wouldest deal v treacherously ... Is 48:8 898
exalted and extolled, and be v high ... Is 52:13 3966
Be not wroth v sore, O LORD, ... Is 64:9 3966
thy peace, and afflict us v sore ... Is 64:12 3966
be ye v desolate, saith the LORD ... Jer 2:12 3966
I am pained at my v heart ... Jer 4:19 7023
dealt v treacherously against me ... Jer 5:11
happy that deal v treacherously ... Jer 12:1 899
breach, with a v grievous blow ... Jer 14:17 3966
hath done a v horrible thing ... Jer 18:13 3966
making him v glad ... Jer 20:15
One basket had v good figs ... Jer 24:2 3966
other basket had v naughty figs ... Jer 24:2 3966
the good figs, v good ... Jer 24:3 3966
v evil, that cannot be eaten, ... Jer 24:3 3966
until the v time of his land come ... Jer 27:7
wine and summer fruits v much ... Jer 40:12 3966
Egypt is like a v fair heifer ... Jer 46:20 3304
thou art v wroth against us ... Lam 5:22
against me, even unto this v day ... Eze 2:3 6106
as if that were a v little thing ... Eze 16:47 6985
made v glorious in the midst of ... Eze 27:25 3966
thou art unto them as a v lovely ... Eze 33:32 5690
there were v many in the open ... Eze 37:2 3966
and, lo, they were v dry ... Eze 37:2 3966
and set me upon a v high mountain ... Eze 40:2 3966
were v many trees on the one side ... Eze 47:7 3966
and there shall be a v great ... Eze 47:9 3966
v furious, and commanded to ... Dan 2:12 7690
Then the king arose v early in ... Dan 6:19
a mouth that spake v great things ... Dan 7:20 7260
the he goat waxed v great ... Dan 8:8
up to battle with a v great ... Dan 11:25
for his camp is v great ... Joel 2:11 3966
the LORD is great and v terrible ... Joel 2:11 3966
even v dark, and no brightness in ... Amos 5:20 651
exceedingly, and he was v angry ... Jonah 4:1
people shall labour in the v fire ... Hab 2:13 1767
weary themselves for v vanity ... Hab 2:13 1767
I am v sore displeased with the ... Zec 1:15
his staff in his hand for v age ... Zec 8:4 7230
and Zidon, though it be v wise ... Zec 9:2 3966
it, and be v sorrowful, and Ekron ... Zec 9:5 3966
there shall be a v great valley ... Zec 14:4 3966
But the v hairs of your head are ... Mt 10:30 2532
was made whole from that v hour ... Mt 15:28 1565
child was cured from that v hour ... Mt 17:18 1565
what was done, they were v sorry ... Mt 18:31 4970
a v great multitude spread their ... Mt 21:8 4118
they shall deceive the v elect ... Mt 24:24 2532
box of v precious ointment ... Mt 26:7 927
began to be sorrowful and v heavy ... Mt 26:37 85
days the multitude being v great ... Mk 8:1 3827
ointment of spikenard v precious ... Mk 14:3 4185
be sore amazed, and to be v heavy ... Mk 14:33 85
v early in the morning the first ... Mk 16:2 3029
for it was v great ... Mk 16:4 4970
of all things from the v first ... Lk 1:3
shake off the v dust from your ... Lk 9:5 2532
Even the v dust of your city, ... Lk 10:11
But even the v hairs of your head ... Lk 12:7 2532
thou hast paid the v last mite ... Lk 12:59
he heard this, he was v sorrowful ... Lk 18:23 4970
for he was v rich ... Lk 18:23 4970
Jesus saw that he was v sorrowful ... Lk 18:24 4036
hast been faithful in a v little ... Lk 19:17 1646
were v attentive to hear him ... Lk 19:48 1582
v early in the morning, they came ... Lk 24:1
indeed that this is the v Christ ... Jn 7:26 230
taken in adultery, in the v act ... Jn 8:4 1888
v costly, and anointed the feet of ... Jn 12:3 4186
believe me for the v works' sake ... Jn 14:11
proving that this is v Christ ... Acts 9:22 846
And he became v hungry, and would ... Acts 10:10 4361
that v worthy deeds are done unto ... Acts 24:2 2735
no wrong, as thou v well knowest ... Acts 25:10 2566
But Esaias is v bold, and saith, I ... Rom 10:20 662
continually upon this v thing ... Rom 13:6 846
But with me it is a v small thing ... 1Cor 4:3 1646
and your zeal hath provoked v many ... 2Cor 9:2 4119
behind the v chiefest apostles ... 2Cor 11:5 5228
I behind the v chiefest apostles ... 2Cor 12:11 3029
I will v gladly spend and be spent ... 2Cor 12:15 2236
Being confident of this v thing ... Phil 1:6 846
to esteem them v highly in love ... 1Th 5:13 5228
the v God of peace sanctify you ... 1Th 5:23 846
he sought me out v diligently ... 2Ti 1:17 4708
at Ephesus, thou knowest v well ... 2Ti 1:18 957
not the v image of the things, ... Heb 10:1 846
turned about with a v small helm ... Jas 3:4 1646
that the Lord is v pitiful ... Jas 5:11 4184

VESSEL
But the earthen *v* wherein it is ... Lev 6:28 3627
whether it be any *v* of wood ... Lev 11:32 3627
skin, or sack, whatsoever *v* it be ... Lev 11:32 3627
And every earthen *v*, whereinto any ... Lev 11:33 3627
in every such *v* shall be unclean ... Lev 11:34 3627
an earthen *v* over running water ... Lev 14:5 3627
an earthen *v* over running water ... Lev 14:50 3627
the *v* of earth, that he toucheth ... Lev 15:12 3627
every *v* of wood shall be rinsed ... Lev 15:12 3627
take holy water in an earthen *v* ... Num 5:17 3627
And every open *v*, which hath no ... Num 19:15 3627
water shall be put thereto in a *v* ... Num 19:17 3627
thou shalt not put any in thy *v* ... Deut 23:24 3627
were sanctified this day in the *v* ... 1Sa 21:5 3627
pray thee, a little water in a *v* ... 1Kin 17:10 3627
unto her son, Bring me yet a *v* ... 2Kin 4:6 3627
unto her, There is not a *v* more ... 2Kin 4:6 3627
them in pieces like a potter's *v* ... Ps 2:9 3627
I am like a broken *v* ... Ps 31:12 3627
come forth a *v* for the finer ... Prov 25:4 3627
v that is broken in pieces ... Is 30:14 5035
v into the house of the LORD ... Is 66:20 3627
the *v* that he made of clay was ... Jer 18:4 3627
so he made it again another *v* ... Jer 18:4 3627
as one breaketh a potter's *v* ... Jer 19:11 3627
is he a *v* wherein is no pleasure ... Jer 22:28 3627
ye shall fall like a pleasant *v* ... Jer 25:34 3627
and put them in an earthen *v* ... Jer 32:14 3627
not been emptied from *v* to *v* ... Jer 48:11 3627
like a *v* wherein is no pleasure ... Jer 48:38 3627
me, he hath made me an empty *v* ... Jer 51:34 3627
and fitches, and put them in one *v* ... Eze 4:9 3627
a pin of it to hang any *v* thereon ... Eze 15:3 3627
as a *v* wherein is no pleasure ... Hos 8:8 3627
carry any *v* through the temple ... Mk 11:16 *4632*
a candle, covereth it with a *v* ... Lk 8:16 *4632*
there was set a *v* full of vinegar ... Jn 19:29 *4632*
for he is a chosen *v* unto me ... Acts 9:15 *4632*
a certain *v* descending unto him, ... Acts 10:11 *4632*
the *v* was received up again into ... Acts 10:16 *4632*
saw a vision, A certain *v* descend ... Acts 11:5 *4632*
lump to make one *v* unto honour ... Rom 9:21 *4632*
possess his *v* in sanctification ... 1Th 4:4 *4632*
he shall be a *v* unto honour ... 2Ti 2:21 *4632*
the wife, as unto the weaker *v* ... 1Pet 3:7 *4632*

VESSELS
best fruits in the land in your *v* ... Gen 43:11 3627
v of wood, and in *v* of stone ... Ex 7:19
he make it, with all these *v* ... Ex 25:39 3627
all the *v* thereof thou shalt make ... Ex 27:3 3627
All the *v* of the tabernacle in ... Ex 27:19 3627
And the table and all his *v* ... Ex 30:27 3627
and the candlestick and his *v* ... Ex 30:27 3627
of burnt offering with all his *v* ... Ex 30:28 3627
and his staves, and all his *v* ... Ex 35:13 3627
grate, his staves, and all his *v* ... Ex 35:16 3627
he made the *v* which were upon the ... Ex 37:16 3627
made he it, and all the *v* thereof ... Ex 37:24 3627
And he made all the *v* of the altar ... Ex 38:3 3627
all the *v* thereof made he of ... Ex 38:3 3627
it, and all the *v* of the altar, ... Ex 38:30 3627
The table, and all the *v* thereof ... Ex 39:36 3627
in order, and all the *v* thereof ... Ex 39:37 3627
brass, his staves, and all his *v* ... Ex 39:39 3627
all the *v* of the service of the ... Ex 39:40 3627
hallow it, and all the *v* thereof ... Ex 40:9 3627
the burnt offering, and all his *v* ... Ex 40:10 3627
anointed the altar and all his *v* ... Lev 8:11 3627
and over all the *v* thereof ... Num 1:50 3627
tabernacle, and all the *v* thereof ... Num 1:50 3627
the *v* of the sanctuary wherewith ... Num 3:31 3627
thereof, and all the *v* thereof ... Num 3:36 3627
and all the oil *v* thereof ... Num 4:9 3627
all the *v* thereof within a ... Num 4:10 3627
put upon it all the *v* thereof ... Num 4:14 3627
basons, all the *v* of the altar ... Num 4:14 3627
all the *v* of the sanctuary, as ... Num 4:15 3627
sanctuary, and in the *v* thereof ... Num 4:16 3627
the altar and all the *v* thereof ... Num 7:1 3627
all the silver *v* weighed two ... Num 7:85 3627
come nigh the *v* of the sanctuary ... Num 18:3 3627
upon the tent, and upon all the *v* ... Num 19:18 3627
gold, and *v* of brass and iron, are ... Josh 6:19 3627
the *v* of brass and of iron, they ... Josh 6:24 3627
thou art athirst, go unto the *v* ... Ruth 2:9 3627
for the bread is spent in our *v* ... 1Sa 9:7 3627
the *v* of the young men are holy, ... 1Sa 21:5 3627
brought with him *v* of silver ... 2Sa 8:10 3627
and *v* of gold, and *v* of brass ... 2Sa 8:10 3627
beds, and basons, and earthen *v* ... 2Sa 17:28 3627
and all these *v*, which Hiram made ... 1Kin 7:45 3627
Solomon left all the *v* unweighed ... 1Kin 7:47 3627
Solomon made all the *v* that ... 1Kin 7:48 3627
the silver, and the gold, and the *v* ... 1Kin 7:51 3627
all the holy *v* that were in the ... 1Kin 8:4 3627
Solomon's drinking *v* were of gold ... 1Kin 10:21 3627
all the *v* of the house of the ... 1Kin 10:21 3627
v of silver, and *v* of gold, ... 1Kin 10:25 3627
the LORD, silver, and gold, and *v* ... 1Kin 15:15 3627
borrow thee *v* abroad of all thy ... 2Kin 4:3 3627
all thy neighbours, even empty *v* ... 2Kin 4:3 3627
shalt pour out into all those *v* ... 2Kin 4:4 3627
sons, who brought the *v* to her ... 2Kin 4:5
when the *v* were full, that she ... 2Kin 4:6 3627
the way was full of garments and *v* ... 2Kin 7:15 3627
any *v* of gold ... 2Kin 12:13 3627
or *v* of silver, of the money that ... 2Kin 12:13 3627
all the *v* that were found in the ... 2Kin 14:14 3627
all the *v* that were made for Baal ... 2Kin 23:4 3627
cut in pieces all the *v* of gold ... 2Kin 24:13 3627
all the *v* of brass wherewith they ... 2Kin 25:14 3627
of all these *v* was without weight ... 2Kin 25:16 3627
the charge of the ministering *v* ... 1Chr 9:28 3627
were appointed to oversee the *v* ... 1Chr 9:29 3627
and the pillars, and the *v* of brass ... 1Chr 18:8 3627
with him all manner of *v* of gold ... 1Chr 18:10 3627
of the LORD, and the holy *v* of God ... 1Chr 22:19 3627
nor any *v* of it for the service ... 1Chr 23:26 3627
for all the *v* of service in the ... 1Chr 28:13 3627
all these *v* in great abundance ... 2Chr 4:18 3627
Solomon made all the *v* that were ... 2Chr 4:19 3627
all the holy *v* that were in the ... 2Chr 5:5 3627
all the drinking *v* of king ... 2Chr 9:20 3627
all the *v* of the house of the ... 2Chr 9:20 3627
v of silver, and *v* of gold, ... 2Chr 9:24 3627
dedicated, silver, and gold, and *v* ... 2Chr 15:18 3627
whereof were made *v* for the house ... 2Chr 24:14 3627
even *v* to minister, and to offer ... 2Chr 24:14 3627
and spoons, and *v* of gold and silver ... 2Chr 24:14 3627
all the *v* that were found in the ... 2Chr 25:24 3627
the *v* of the house of God ... 2Chr 28:24 3627
cut in pieces the *v* of the house ... 2Chr 28:24 3627
offering, with all the *v* thereof ... 2Chr 29:18 3627
table, with all the *v* thereof ... 2Chr 29:18 3627
Moreover all the *v*, which king ... 2Chr 29:19 3627
also carried of the *v* of the ... 2Chr 36:7 3627
with the goodly *v* of the house of ... 2Chr 36:10 3627
all the *v* of the house of God, ... 2Chr 36:18 3627
all the goodly *v* thereof ... 2Chr 36:19 3627
their hands with *v* of silver ... Ezr 1:6 3627
the *v* of the house of the LORD ... Ezr 1:7 3627
and ten, and other *v* a thousand ... Ezr 1:10 3627
All the *v* of gold and of silver ... Ezr 1:11 3627
the *v* also of gold and silver of ... Ezr 5:14 3984
And said unto him, Take these *v* ... Ezr 5:15 3984
silver *v* of the house of God, ... Ezr 6:5 3984
The *v* also that are given thee ... Ezr 7:19 3984
the silver, and the gold, and the *v* ... Ezr 8:25 3627
silver *v* an hundred talents, and ... Ezr 8:26 3627
two *v* of fine copper, precious as ... Ezr 8:27 3627
the *v* are holy also ... Ezr 8:28 3627
the silver, and the gold, and the *v* ... Ezr 8:30 3627
the *v* weighed in the house of our ... Ezr 8:33 3627
where are the *v* of the sanctuary, ... Neh 10:39 3627
the frankincense, and the *v* ... Neh 13:5 3627
I again the *v* of the house of God ... Neh 13:9 3627
they gave them drink in *v* of gold ... Est 1:7 3627
(the *v* being diverse one from ... Est 1:7 3627
even in *v* of bulrushes upon the ... Is 18:2 3627
all *v* of small quantity, from the ... Is 22:24 3627
quantity, from the *v* of cups ... Is 22:24 3627
even to all the *v* of flagons ... Is 22:24 3627
that bear the *v* of the LORD ... Is 52:11 3627
abominable things is in their *v* ... Is 65:4 3627
they returned with their *v* empty ... Jer 14:3 3627
the *v* of the LORD's house shall ... Jer 27:16 3627
that the *v* which are left in the ... Jer 27:18 3627
of the *v* that remain in this city ... Jer 27:19 3627
concerning the *v* that remain in ... Jer 27:21 3627
all the *v* of the LORD's house ... Jer 28:3 3627
to bring again the *v* of the ... Jer 28:6 3627
and oil, and put them in your *v* ... Jer 40:10 3627
to wander, and shall empty his *v* ... Jer 48:12 3627
their curtains, and all their *v* ... Jer 49:29 3627
all the *v* of brass wherewith they ... Jer 52:18 3627
of all these *v* was without weight ... Jer 52:20 3627
men and *v* of brass in thy market ... Eze 27:13 3627
with part of the *v* of the house ... Dan 1:2 3627
he brought the *v* into the ... Dan 1:2 3627
silver *v* which his father ... Dan 5:2 3984
v that were taken out of the ... Dan 5:3 3984
they have brought the *v* of his ... Dan 5:23 3984
with their precious *v* of silver ... Dan 11:8 3627
the treasure of all pleasant *v* ... Hos 13:15 3627
draw out fifty *v* out of the press ... Hag 2:16
down, and gathered the good into *v* ... Mt 13:48 *30*
oil in their *v* with their lamps ... Mt 25:4 *30*
of cups, and pots, brasen *v* ... Mk 7:4
with much longsuffering the *v* of ... Rom 9:22 *4632*
of his glory on the *v* of mercy ... Rom 9:23 *4632*
have this treasure in earthen *v* ... 2Cor 4:7 *4632*
there are not only *v* of gold ... 2Ti 2:20 *4632*
all the *v* of the ministry ... Heb 9:21 *4632*
as the *v* of a potter shall they ... Rev 2:27 *4632*
wood, and all manner *v* of ivory ... Rev 18:12 *4632*
all manner *v* of most precious ... Rev 18:12 *4632*

VESTMENTS
Bring forth *v* for all the ... 2Kin 10:22 3830
And he brought them forth *v* ... 2Kin 10:22 4403

VESTRY
said unto him that was over the *v* ... 2Kin 10:22 4458

VESTURE
upon the four quarters of thy *v* ... Deut 22:12 3682
them, and cast lots upon my *v* ... Ps 22:18 3830
as a *v* shalt thou change them, and ... Ps 102:26 3830
upon my *v* did they cast lots ... Mt 27:35 *2441*
for my *v* they did cast lots ... Jn 19:24 *2441*
as a *v* shalt thou fold them up, ... Heb 1:12 *4018*
clothed with a *v* dipped in blood ... Rev 19:13 *2440*
And he hath on his *v* and on his ... Rev 19:16 *2440*

VESTURES
and arrayed him in *v* of fine linen ... Gen 41:42 899

VEX
Thou shalt neither *v* a stranger ... Ex 22:21 3238
sister, to *v* her, to uncover her ... Lev 18:18 6887
in your land, ye shall not *v* him ... Lev 19:33 3238
V the Midianites, and smite them ... Num 25:17 6887
For they *v* you with their wiles, ... Num 25:18 6887
shall *v* you in the land wherein ... Num 33:55 6887
how will he then *v* himself ... 2Sa 12:18
for God did *v* them with all ... 2Chr 15:6 2000
How long will ye *v* my soul ... Job 19:2 3013
v them in his sore displeasure ... Ps 2:5 926
v it, and let us make a breach ... Is 7:6 6973
and Judah shall not *v* Ephraim ... Is 11:13 6887
I will also *v* the hearts of many ... Eze 32:9 3707
thee, and awake that shall *v* thee ... Hab 2:7 2111
hands to *v* certain of the church ... Acts 12:1 *2559*

VEXATION
shall send upon thee cursing, *v* ... Deut 28:20 4103
all is vanity and *v* of spirit ... Eccl 1:14 7469
that this also is *v* of spirit ... Eccl 1:17 7475
v of spirit, and there was no ... Eccl 2:11 7469
for all is vanity and *v* of spirit ... Eccl 2:17 7469
of the *v* of his heart, wherein he ... Eccl 2:22 7475
also is vanity and *v* of spirit ... Eccl 2:26 7469
is also vanity and *v* of spirit ... Eccl 4:4 7469
full with travail and *v* of spirit ... Eccl 4:6 7469
also is vanity and *v* of spirit ... Eccl 4:16 7475
is also vanity and *v* of spirit ... Eccl 6:9 7469
shall not be such as was in her *v* ... Is 9:1 4164
and it shall be a *v* only to ... Is 28:19 2113
and shall howl for *v* of spirit ... Is 65:14 7667

VEXATIONS
but great *v* were upon all the ... 2Chr 15:5 4103

VEXED
and the Egyptians *v* us, and our ... Num 20:15 7489
that oppressed them and *v* them ... Judg 2:18 1766
And that year they *v* and oppressed ... Judg 10:8 7492
so that his soul was *v* unto death ... Judg 16:16 7114
he turned himself, he *v* them ... 1Sa 14:47 7561
And Amnon was so *v*, that he fell ... 2Sa 13:2 3334
for her soul is *v* within her ... 2Kin 4:27 4843
hand of their enemies, who *v* them ... Neh 9:27 6887
the Almighty, who hath *v* my soul ... Job 27:2 4843
for my bones are *v* ... Ps 6:2 926
My soul is also sore *v* ... Ps 6:3 926
mine enemies be ashamed and sore *v* ... Ps 6:10 926
rebelled, and *v* his holy Spirit ... Is 63:10 6087
which art infamous and much *v* ... Eze 22:5 4103
thee have they *v* the fatherless ... Eze 22:7 3238
and have *v* the poor and needy ... Eze 22:29 3238
is grievously *v* with a devil ... Mt 15:22 *1139*
for he is lunatick, and sore *v* ... Mt 17:15 *3958*
they that were *v* with unclean ... Lk 6:18 *3791*
them which were *v* with unclean ... Acts 5:16 *3791*
v with the filthy conversation of ... 2Pet 2:7 *2669*
v his righteous soul from day to ... 2Pet 2:8 *928*

VIAL
Then Samuel took a *v* of oil ... 1Sa 10:1 6378
poured out his *v* upon the earth ... Rev 16:2 *5357*
poured out his *v* upon the sea ... Rev 16:3 *5357*
poured out his *v* upon the rivers ... Rev 16:4 *5357*
poured out his *v* upon the sun ... Rev 16:8 *5357*
his *v* upon the seat of the beast ... Rev 16:10 *5357*
v upon the great river Euphrates ... Rev 16:12 *5357*
poured out his *v* into the air ... Rev 16:17 *5357*

VIALS
golden *v* full of odours, which ... Rev 5:8 *5357*
golden *v* full of the wrath of God ... Rev 15:7 *5357*
pour out the *v* of the wrath of ... Rev 16:1 *5357*
angels which had the seven *v* ... Rev 17:1 *5357*
angels which had the seven *v* full ... Rev 21:9 *5357*

VICTORY
the *v* that day was turned into ... 2Sa 19:2 8668
LORD wrought a great *v* that day ... 2Sa 23:10 8668
and the LORD wrought a great *v* ... 2Sa 23:12 8668
the power, and the glory, and the *v* ... 1Chr 29:11 5331
holy arm, hath gotten him the *v* ... Ps 98:1 3467
He will swallow up death in *v* ... Is 25:8 5331
he send forth judgment unto *v* ... Mt 12:20 *3534*
Death is swallowed up in *v* ... 1Cor 15:54 *3534*
O grave, where is thy *v* ... 1Cor 15:55 *3534*
which giveth us the *v* through our ... 1Cor 15:57 *3534*
this is the *v* that overcometh the ... 1Jn 5:4 *3529*
had gotten the *v* over the beast ... Rev 15:2 *3528*

VICTUAL
prepared for themselves any *v* ... Ex 12:39 6720
to fetch *v* for the people, that ... Judg 20:10 6720
provided *v* for king Solomon ... 1Kin 4:27 3557
captains in them, and store of *v* ... 2Chr 11:11 3978
and he gave them *v* in abundance ... 2Chr 11:23 4202

VICTUALS
Sodom and Gomorrah, and all their *v* ... Gen 14:11 400
nor lend him thy *v* for increase ... Lev 25:37 400
usury of money, usury of *v* ... Deut 23:19 400
the people, saying, Prepare you *v* ... Josh 1:11 6720
Take *v* with you for the journey, ... Josh 9:11 6720
And the men took of their *v* ... Josh 9:14 6718
the people took *v* in their hand ... Judg 7:8 6720
and a suit of apparel, and thy *v* ... Judg 17:10 4241
the LORD for him, and gave him *v* ... 1Sa 22:10 6720
which provided *v* for the king ... 1Kin 4:7 3557
him an house, and appointed him *v* ... 1Kin 11:18 3899
any *v* on the sabbath day to sell ... Neh 10:31 7668
in the day wherein they sold *v* ... Neh 13:15 6718
captain of the guard gave him *v* ... Jer 40:5 737
for then had we plenty of *v* ... Jer 44:17 3899
the villages, and buy themselves *v* ... Mt 14:15 *1033*
round about, and lodge, and get *v* ... Lk 9:12 *1979*

VIEW
Go *v* the land, even Jericho ... Josh 2:1 7200
saying, Go up and *v* the country ... Josh 7:2 7270
went, and stood to *v* afar off ... 2Kin 2:7 5048
were to *v* at Jericho saw him ... 2Kin 2:15 5048

VIEWED
And the men went up and *v* Ai ... Josh 7:2 7370
I *v* the people, and the priests, ... Ezr 8:15 995
v the walls of Jerusalem, which ... Neh 2:13 7663
v the wall, and turned back, and ... Neh 2:15 7663

VIGILANT

the husband of one wife, *v*.... 1Ti 3:2 *3524*
Be sober, be *v*.... 1Pet 5:8 *1127*

VILE

brother should seem *v* unto thee.... Deut 25:3 7034
unto this man do not so *v* a thing.... Judg 19:24 5039
his sons made themselves *v*.... 1Sa 3:13 7043
but every thing that was *v*.... 1Sa 15:9 5240
And I will yet be more *v* than thus.... 2Sa 6:22 7043
and reputed *v* in your sight.... Job 18:3 2933
Behold, I am *v*.... Job 40:4 7043
In whose eyes a *v* person is.... Ps 15:4 959
The *v* person shall be no more.... Is 32:5 5036
For the *v* person will speak.... Is 32:6 5036
forth the precious from the *v*.... Jer 15:19 2151
and will make them like *v* figs.... Jer 29:17 8182
for I am become *v*.... Lam 1:11 2151
estate shall stand up a *v* person.... Dan 11:21 959
for thou art *v*.... Nah 1:14 7043
filth upon thee, and make thee *v*.... Nah 3:6 5034
gave them up unto *v* affections.... Rom 1:26 *819*
Who shall change our *v* body.... Phil 3:21 *5014*
in also a poor man in *v* raiment.... Jas 2:2 *4508*

VILELY

of the mighty is *v* cast away.... 2Sa 1:21 1602

VILER

they were *v* than the earth.... Job 30:8 5217

VILEST

when the *v* men are exalted.... Ps 12:8 2149

VILLAGE

Go into the *v* over against you.... Mt 21:2 *2968*
way into the *v* over against you.... Mk 11:2 *2968*
went throughout every city and *v*.... Lk 8:1 *2968*
went, and entered into a *v* of the.... Lk 9:52 *2968*
And they went to another *v*.... Lk 9:56 *2968*
that he entered into a certain *v*.... Lk 10:38 *2968*
And as he entered into a certain *v*.... Lk 17:12 *2968*
Go ye into the *v* over against you.... Lk 19:30 *2968*
same day to a *v* called Emmaus.... Lk 24:13 *2968*
And they drew nigh unto the *v*.... Lk 24:28 *2968*

VILLAGES

out of the houses, out of the *v*.... Ex 8:13 2691
But the houses of the *v* which.... Lev 25:31 2691
Heshbon, and in all the *v* thereof.... Num 21:25 1323
and they took the *v* thereof.... Num 21:32 1323
the *v* thereof, and called it Nobah.... Num 32:42 1323
the cities and the *v* thereof.... Josh 13:23 2691
families, the cities, and their *v*.... Josh 13:28 2691
are twenty and nine, with their *v*.... Josh 15:32 2691
fourteen cities with their *v*.... Josh 15:36 2691
sixteen cities with their *v*.... Josh 15:41 2691
nine cities with their *v*.... Josh 15:44 2691
Ekron, with her towns and her *v*.... Josh 15:45 2691
lay near Ashdod, with their *v*.... Josh 15:46 2691
Ashdod with her towns and her *v*.... Josh 15:47 2691
Gaza with her towns and her *v*.... Josh 15:47 2691
eleven cities with their *v*.... Josh 15:51 2691
nine cities with their *v*.... Josh 15:54 2691
ten cities with their *v*.... Josh 15:57 2691
six cities with their *v*.... Josh 15:59 2691
two cities with their *v*.... Josh 15:60 2691
six cities with their *v*.... Josh 15:62 2691
all the cities with their *v*.... Josh 16:9 2691
twelve cities with their *v*.... Josh 18:24 2691
fourteen cities with their *v*.... Josh 18:28 2691
thirteen cities and their *v*.... Josh 19:6 2691
four cities and their *v*.... Josh 19:7 2691
all the *v* that were round about.... Josh 19:8 2691
twelve cities with their *v*.... Josh 19:15 2691
these cities with their *v*.... Josh 19:16 2691
sixteen cities with their *v*.... Josh 19:22 2691
families, the cities and their *v*.... Josh 19:23 2691
twenty and two cities with their *v*.... Josh 19:30 2691
these cities with their *v*.... Josh 19:31 2691
nineteen cities with their *v*.... Josh 19:38 2691
families, the cities and their *v*.... Josh 19:39 2691
these cities with their *v*.... Josh 19:48 2691
the *v* thereof, gave they to Caleb.... Josh 21:12 2691
The inhabitants of the *v* ceased.... Judg 5:7 6520
inhabitants of his *v* in Israel.... Judg 5:11 6520
of fenced cities, and of country *v*.... 1Sa 6:18 3724
And their *v* were, Etam, and Ain,.... 1Chr 4:32 2691
all their *v* that were round about.... 1Chr 4:33 2691
the *v* thereof, they gave to Caleb.... 1Chr 6:56 2691
that dwelt in the *v* of the.... 1Chr 9:16 2691
by their genealogy in their *v*.... 1Chr 9:22 2691
brethren, which were in their *v*.... 1Chr 9:25 2691
in the cities, and in the *v*.... 1Chr 27:25 3723
and Shocho with the *v* thereof.... 2Chr 28:18 1323
and Timnah with the *v* thereof.... 2Chr 28:18 1323
Gimzo also and the *v* thereof.... 2Chr 28:18 1323
one of the *v* in the plain of Ono.... Neh 6:2 3715
And for the *v*, with their fields,.... Neh 11:25 2691
in the *v* thereof, and at Dibon, and.... Neh 11:25 2691
in the *v* thereof, and at Jekabzeel.... Neh 11:25 1323
Jekabzeel, and in the *v* thereof,.... Neh 11:25 1323
Beer-sheba, and in the *v* thereof,.... Neh 11:27 1323
at Mekonah, and in the *v* thereof,.... Neh 11:28 1323
Zanoah, Adullam, and in their *v*.... Neh 11:30 2691
at Azekah, and in the *v* thereof.... Neh 11:30 1323
Aija, and Beth-el, and in their *v*.... Neh 11:31 1323
and from the *v* of Netophathi.... Neh 12:28 2691
them *v* round about Jerusalem.... Neh 12:29 2691
Therefore the Jews of the *v*.... Est 9:19 6521
in the lurking places of the *v*.... Ps 10:8 2691
let us lodge in the *v*.... Song 7:11 3723
the *v* that Kedar doth inhabit.... Is 42:11 2691
go up to the land of unwalled *v*.... Eze 38:11 6519
with his staves the head of his *v*.... Hab 3:14 6518
went about all the cities and *v*.... Mt 9:35 *2968*
away, that they may go into the *v*.... Mt 14:15 *2968*
And he went round about the *v*.... Mk 6:6 *2968*
round about, and into the *v*.... Mk 6:36 *2968*
whithersoever he entered, into *v*.... Mk 6:56 *2968*
he went through the cities and *v*.... Lk 13:22 *2968*
in many *v* of the Samaritans.... Acts 8:25 *2968*

VILLANY

For the vile person will speak *v*.... Is 32:6 5039
they have committed *v* in Israel.... Jer 29:23 5039

VINE

dream, behold, a *v* was before me.... Gen 40:9 1612
in the *v* were three branches.... Gen 40:10 1612
Binding his foal unto the *v*.... Gen 49:11 1612
his ass's colt unto the choice *v*.... Gen 49:11 8321
the grapes of thy *v* undressed.... Lev 25:5 5139
grapes in it of thy *v* undressed.... Lev 25:11 5139
that is made of the *v* tree.... Num 6:4 3196
their *v* is of the *v* of Sodom.... Deut 32:32 1612
Then said the trees unto the *v*.... Judg 9:12 1612
the *v* said unto them, Should I.... Judg 9:13 1612
of any thing that cometh of the *v*.... Judg 13:14 1612
safely, every man under his *v*.... 1Kin 4:25 1612
gather herbs, and found a wild *v*.... 2Kin 4:39 1612
eat ye every man of his own *v*.... 2Kin 18:31 1612
v dressers in the mountains, and.... 2Chr 26:10 3755
off his unripe grape as the *v*.... Job 15:33 1612
hast brought a *v* out of Egypt.... Ps 80:8 1612
and behold, and visit this *v*.... Ps 80:14 1612
v by the sides of thine house.... Ps 128:3 1612
to see whether the *v* flourished.... Song 6:11 1612
shall be as clusters of the *v*.... Song 7:8 1612
let us see if the *v* flourish.... Song 7:12 1612
and planted it with the choicest *v*.... Is 5:2 8321
languish, and the *v* of Sibmah.... Is 16:8 1612
weeping of Jazer the *v* of Sibmah.... Is 16:9 1612
the *v* languisheth, all the.... Is 24:7 1612
fields, for the fruitful *v*.... Is 32:12 1612
the leaf falleth off from the *v*.... Is 34:4 1612
and eat ye every one of his *v*.... Is 36:16 1612
Yet I had planted thee a noble *v*.... Jer 2:21 8321
plant of a strange *v* unto me.... Jer 2:21 1612
the remnant of Israel as a *v*.... Jer 6:9 1612
there shall be no grapes on the *v*.... Jer 8:13 1612
O *v* of Sibmah, I will weep for.... Jer 48:32 1612
What is the *v* tree more than any.... Eze 15:2 1612
As the *v* tree among the trees of.... Eze 15:6 1612
a spreading *v* of low stature.... Eze 17:6 1612
so it became a *v*, and brought.... Eze 17:6 1612
this *v* did bend her roots toward.... Eze 17:7 1612
that it might be a goodly *v*.... Eze 17:8 1612
mother is like a *v* in thy blood.... Eze 19:10 1612
Israel is an empty *v*, he bringeth.... Hos 10:1 1612
as the corn, and grow as the *v*.... Hos 14:7 1612
He hath laid my *v* waste, and.... Joel 1:7 1612
The *v* is dried up, and the fig.... Joel 1:12 1612
the *v* do yield their strength.... Joel 2:22 1612
shall sit every man under his *v*.... Mic 4:4 1612
out, and marred their *v* branches.... Nah 2:2 2156
yea, as yet the *v*, and the fig.... Hag 2:19 1612
man his neighbour under the *v*.... Zec 3:10 1612
the *v* shall give her fruit, and.... Zec 8:12 1612
neither shall your *v* cast her.... Mal 3:11 1612
henceforth of this fruit of the *v*.... Mt 26:29 *288*
no more of the fruit of the *v*.... Mk 14:25 *288*
not drink of the fruit of the *v*.... Lk 22:18 *288*
I am the true *v*, and my Father is.... Jn 15:1 *288*
itself, except it abide in the *v*.... Jn 15:4 *288*
I am the *v*, ye are the branches.... Jn 15:5 *288*
either a *v*, figs?.... Jas 3:12 *288*
clusters of the *v* of the earth.... Rev 14:18 *288*
and gathered the *v* of the earth.... Rev 14:19 *288*

VINEDRESSERS

of the poor of the land to be *v*.... 2Kin 25:12 3755
shall be your plowmen and your *v*.... Is 61:5 3755
of the poor of the land for *v*.... Jer 52:16 3755
howl, O ye *v*, for the wheat and.... Joel 1:11 3755

VINEGAR

and shall drink no *v* of wine.... Num 6:3 2558
or *v* of strong drink, neither.... Num 6:3 2558
bread, and dip thy morsel in the *v*.... Ruth 2:14 2558
my thirst they gave me *v* to drink.... Ps 69:21 2558
As *v* to the teeth, and as smoke to.... Prov 10:26 2558
as *v* upon nitre, so is he that.... Prov 25:20 2558
They gave him *v* to drink mingled.... Mt 27:34 *3690*
a spunge, and filled it with *v*.... Mt 27:48 *3690*
ran and filled a spunge full of *v*.... Mk 15:36 *3690*
coming to him, and offering him *v*.... Lk 23:36 *3690*
there was set a vessel full of *v*.... Jn 19:29 *3690*
and they filled a spunge with *v*.... Jn 19:29 *3690*
therefore had received the *v*.... Jn 19:30 *3690*

VINES

of seed, or of figs, or of *v*.... Num 20:5 1612
A land of wheat, and barley, and *v*.... Deut 8:8 1612
He destroyed their *v* with hail.... Ps 78:47 1612
He smote their *v* also and their.... Ps 105:33 1612
the *v* with the tender grape give.... Song 2:13 1612
little foxes, that spoil the *v*.... Song 2:15 3754
for our *v* have tender grapes.... Song 2:15 3754
v at a thousand silverlings.... Is 7:23 1612
they shall eat up thy *v* and thy.... Jer 5:17 1612
Thou shalt yet plant *v* upon the.... Jer 31:5 3754
And I will destroy her *v* and her.... Hos 2:12 1612
neither shall fruit be in the *v*.... Hab 3:17 1612

VINEYARD

an husbandman, and he planted a *v*.... Gen 9:20 3754
cause a field or *v* to be eaten.... Ex 22:5 3754
and of the best of his own *v*.... Ex 22:5 3754
manner thou shalt deal with thy *v*.... Ex 23:11 3754
And thou shalt not glean thy *v*.... Lev 19:10 3754
thou gather every grape of thy *v*.... Lev 19:10 3754
six years thou shalt prune thy *v*.... Lev 25:3 3754
sow thy field, nor prune thy *v*.... Lev 25:4 3754
man is he that hath planted a *v*.... Deut 20:6 3754
not sow thy *v* with divers seeds.... Deut 22:9 3754
hast sown, and the fruit of thy *v*.... Deut 22:9 3754
comest into thy neighbour's *v*.... Deut 23:24 3754
gatherest the grapes of thy *v*.... Deut 24:21 3754
thou shalt plant a *v*, and shalt.... Deut 28:30 3754
Naboth the Jezreelite had a *v*.... 1Kin 21:1 3754
Naboth, saying, Give me thy *v*.... 1Kin 21:2 3754
thee for it a better *v* than it.... 1Kin 21:2 3754
unto him, Give me thy *v* for money.... 1Kin 21:6 3754
I will give thee another *v* for it.... 1Kin 21:6 3754
I will not give thee my *v*.... 1Kin 21:6 3754
I will give thee the *v* of Naboth.... 1Kin 21:7 3754
take possession of the *v* of.... 1Kin 21:15 3754
to the *v* of Naboth the Jezreelite.... 1Kin 21:16 3754
behold, he is in the *v* of Naboth.... 1Kin 21:18 3754
the *v* which thy right hand hath.... Ps 80:15 3657
by the *v* of the man void of.... Prov 24:30 3754
of her hands she planteth a *v*.... Prov 31:16 3754
but mine own *v* have I not kept.... Song 1:6 3754
Solomon had a *v* at Baal-hamon.... Song 8:11 3754
he let out the *v* unto keepers.... Song 8:11 3754
My *v*, which is mine, is before me.... Song 8:12 3754
Zion is left as a cottage in a *v*.... Is 1:8 3754
for ye have eaten up the *v*.... Is 3:14 3754
song of my beloved touching his *v*.... Is 5:1 3754
My wellbeloved hath a *v* in a very.... Is 5:1 3754
I pray you, betwixt me and my *v*.... Is 5:3 3754
could have been done more to my *v*.... Is 5:4 3754
tell you what I will do to my *v*.... Is 5:5 3754
For the *v* of the LORD of hosts is.... Is 5:7 3754
ten acres of *v* shall yield one.... Is 5:10 3754
sing ye unto her, A *v* of red wine.... Is 27:2 3754
Many pastors have destroyed my *v*.... Jer 12:10 3754
house, nor sow seed, nor plant *v*.... Jer 35:7 3754
neither have we *v*, nor field, nor.... Jer 35:9 3754
the field, and as plantings of a *v*.... Mic 1:6 3754
to hire labourers into his *v*.... Mt 20:1 *290*
a day, he sent them into his *v*.... Mt 20:2 *290*
Go ye also into the *v*, and.... Mt 20:4 *290*
unto them, Go ye also into the *v*.... Mt 20:7 *290*
the lord of the *v* saith unto his.... Mt 20:8 *290*
said, Son, go work to day in my *v*.... Mt 21:28 *290*
householder, which planted a *v*.... Mt 21:33 *290*
him, and cast him out of the *v*.... Mt 21:39 *290*
lord therefore of the *v* cometh.... Mt 21:40 *290*
will let out his *v* unto other.... Mt 21:41 *290*
A certain man planted a *v*.... Mk 12:1 *290*
husbandmen of the fruit of the *v*.... Mk 12:2 *290*
him, and cast him out of the *v*.... Mk 12:8 *290*
therefore the lord of the *v* do.... Mk 12:9 *290*
and will give the *v* unto others.... Mk 12:9 *290*
had a fig tree planted in his *v*.... Lk 13:6 *290*
said he unto the dresser of his *v*.... Lk 13:7 *289*
A certain man planted a *v*.... Lk 20:9 *290*
give him of the fruit of the *v*.... Lk 20:10 *290*
Then said the lord of the *v*.... Lk 20:13 *290*
So they cast him out of the *v*.... Lk 20:15 *290*
the lord of the *v* do unto them.... Lk 20:15 *290*
and shall give the *v* to others.... Lk 20:16 *290*
who planteth a *v*, and eateth not.... 1Cor 9:7 *290*

VINEYARDS

us inheritance of fields and *v*.... Num 16:14 3754
the fields, or through the *v*.... Num 20:17 3754
into the fields, or into the *v*.... Num 21:22 3754
the LORD stood in a path of the *v*.... Num 22:24 3754
which thou diggedst not, *v*.... Deut 6:11 3754
Thou shalt plant *v*, and dress them.... Deut 28:39 3754
of the *v* and oliveyards which ye.... Josh 24:13 3754
the fields, and gathered their *v*.... Judg 9:27 3754
and unto the plain of the *v*.... Judg 11:33 3754
and came to the *v* of Timnath.... Judg 14:5 3754
the standing corn, with the *v*.... Judg 15:5 3754
Go and lie in wait in the *v*.... Judg 21:20 3754
dances, then come ye out of the *v*.... Judg 21:21 3754
will take your fields, and your *v*.... 1Sa 8:14 3754
tenth of your seed, and of your *v*.... 1Sa 8:15 3754
give every one of you fields and *v*.... 1Sa 22:7 3754
garments, and oliveyards, and *v*.... 2Kin 5:26 3754
and wine, a land of bread and *v*.... 2Kin 18:32 3754
year sow ye, and reap, and plant *v*.... 2Kin 19:29 3754
over the *v* was Shimei the.... 1Chr 27:27 3754
over the increase of the *v* for.... 1Chr 27:27 3754
We have mortgaged our lands, *v*.... Neh 5:3 3754
and that upon our lands and *v*.... Neh 5:4 3754
for other men have our lands and *v*.... Neh 5:5 3754
this day, their lands, their *v*.... Neh 5:11 3754
of all goods, wells digged, *v*.... Neh 9:25 3754
he beholdeth not the way of the *v*.... Job 24:18 3754
And sow the fields, and plant *v*.... Ps 107:37 3754
I planted me *v*.... Eccl 2:4 3754
they made me the keeper of the *v*.... Song 1:6 3754
of camphire in the *v* of En-gedi.... Song 1:14 3754
Let us get up early to the *v*.... Song 7:12 3754
in the *v* there shall be no.... Is 16:10 3754
and wine, a land of bread and *v*.... Is 36:17 3754
year sow ye, and reap, and plant *v*.... Is 37:30 3754
and they shall plant *v*, and eat the.... Is 65:21 3754
v shall be possessed again in.... Jer 32:15 3754
the land of Judah, and gave them *v*.... Jer 39:10 3754
and shall build houses, and plant *v*.... Eze 28:26 3754
I will give her her *v* from thence.... Hos 2:15 3754
when your gardens and your *v*.... Amos 4:9 3754
ye have planted pleasant *v*.... Amos 5:11 3754
in all *v* shall be wailing.... Amos 5:17 3754
and they shall plant *v*, and drink.... Amos 9:14 3754
and they shall plant *v*, but not.... Zeph 1:13 3754

VINTAGE

threshing shall reach unto the *v*.... Lev 26:5 1210
the *v* shall reach unto the sowing.... Lev 26:5 1210
better than the *v* of Abi-ezer.... Judg 8:2 1210
they gather the *v* of the wicked.... Job 24:6 3754
made their *v* shouting to cease.... Is 16:10

grapes when the *v* is done ... Is 24:13 1210
for the *v* shall fail, the ... Is 32:10 1210
thy summer fruits and upon thy *v* ... Jer 48:32 1210
as the grapegleanings of the *v* ... Mic 7:1 1210
the forest of the *v* is come down ... Zec 11:2 1208

VIOL
And the harp, and the *v*, the tabret ... Is 5:12 5035
That chant to the sound of the *v* ... Amos 6:5 5035

VIOLATED
Her priests have *v* my law ... Eze 22:26 2554

VIOLENCE
and the earth was filled with *v* ... Gen 6:11 2555
is filled with *v* through them ... Gen 6:13 2555
or in a thing taken away by *v* ... Lev 6:2 1498
thou savest me from *v* ... 2Sa 22:3 2555
him that loveth *v* his soul hateth ... Ps 11:5 2555
for I have seen *v* and strife in ... Ps 55:9 2555
ye weigh the *v* of your hands in ... Ps 58:2 2555
their soul from deceit and *v* ... Ps 72:14 2555
v covereth them as a garment ... Ps 73:6 2555
and drink the wine of *v* ... Prov 4:17 2555
but *v* covereth the mouth of the ... Prov 10:6 2555
but *v* covereth the mouth of the ... Prov 10:11 2555
of the transgressors shall eat *v* ... Prov 13:2 2555
A man that doeth *v* to the blood ... Prov 28:17 6231
because he had done no *v*, neither ... Is 53:9 2555
the act of *v* is in their hands ... Is 59:6 2555
V shall no more be heard in thy ... Is 60:18 2555
v and spoil is heard in her ... Jer 6:7 2555
I spake, I cried out, I cried *v* ... Jer 20:8 2555
do no *v* to the stranger, the ... Jer 22:3 2554
and for oppression, and for *v* ... Jer 22:17 4835
The *v* done to me and to my flesh ... Jer 51:35 2555
v in the land, ruler against ... Jer 51:46 2555
V is risen up into a rod of ... Eze 7:11 2555
crimes, and the city is full of *v* ... Eze 7:23 2555
they have filled the land with *v* ... Eze 8:17 2555
because of the *v* of all them that ... Eze 12:19 2555
pledge, hath spoiled none by *v* ... Eze 18:7 1500
poor and needy, hath spoiled by *v* ... Eze 18:12 1500
pledge, neither hath spoiled by *v* ... Eze 18:16 1500
spoiled his brother by *v* ... Eze 18:18 1499
filled the midst of thee with *v* ... Eze 28:16 2555
remove *v* and spoil, and execute ... Eze 45:9 2555
for the *v* against the children of ... Joel 3:19 2555
saith the LORD, who store up *v* ... Amos 3:10 2555
cause the seat of *v* to come near ... Amos 6:3 2555
For thy *v* against thy brother ... Obad 10 2555
from the *v* that is in their hands ... Jonah 3:8 2555
covet fields, and take them by *v* ... Mic 2:2 1497
rich men thereof are full of *v* ... Mic 6:12 2555
even cry out unto thee of *v* ... Hab 1:2 2555
for spoiling and *v* are before me ... Hab 1:3 2555
They shall come all for *v* ... Hab 1:9 2555
for the *v* of the land, of the ... Hab 2:8 2555
For the *v* of Lebanon shall cover ... Hab 2:17 2555
for the *v* of the land, of the ... Hab 2:17 2555
fill their masters' houses with *v* ... Zeph 1:9 2555
they have done *v* to the law ... Zeph 3:4 2554
one covereth *v* with his garment ... Mal 2:16 2555
the kingdom of heaven suffereth *v* ... Mt 11:12 *971*
Do *v* to no man, neither accuse ... Lk 3:14 *1286*
and brought them without *v* ... Acts 5:26 *970*
soldiers for the *v* of the people ... Acts 21:35 *970*
with great *v* took him away out of ... Acts 24:7 *970*
broken with the *v* of the waves ... Acts 27:41 *970*
Quenched the *v* of fire, escaped ... Heb 11:34 *1411*
Thus with *v* shall that great city ... Rev 18:21 *3731*

VIOLENT
hast delivered me from the *v* man ... 2Sa 22:49 2555
his *v* dealing shall come down ... Ps 7:16 2555
hast delivered me from the *v* man ... Ps 18:48 2555
the assemblies of *v* men have ... Ps 86:14 6184
preserve me from the *v* man ... Ps 140:1 2555
preserve me from the *v* man ... Ps 140:4 2555
evil shall hunt the *v* man to ... Ps 140:11 2555
A *v* man enticeth his neighbour, ... Prov 16:29 2555
v perverting of judgment and ... Eccl 5:8 1499
and the *v* take it by force ... Mt 11:12 *973*

VIOLENTLY
servants had *v* taken away ... Gen 21:25 1497
restore that which he took *v* away ... Lev 6:4 1500
thine ass shall be *v* taken away ... Deut 28:31 1497
because he hath *v* taken away an ... Job 20:19 1497
they *v* take away flocks, and feed ... Job 24:2 1497
He will surely *v* turn and toss ... Is 22:18
And he hath *v* taken away his ... Lam 2:6 2554
the whole herd of swine ran *v* ... Mt 8:32
the herd ran *v* down a steep place ... Mk 5:13
the herd ran *v* down a steep place ... Lk 8:33

VIOLS
the grave, and the noise of thy *v* ... Is 14:11 5035
will not hear the melody of thy *v* ... Amos 5:23 5035

VIPER
come the young and old lion, the *v* ... Is 30:6 660
is crushed breaketh out into a *v* ... Is 59:5 660
there came a *v* out of the heat, ... Acts 28:3 *2191*

VIPER'S
the *v* tongue shall slay him ... Job 20:16 660

VIPERS
said unto them, O generation of *v* ... Mt 3:7 *2191*
O generation of *v*, how can ye, ... Mt 12:34 *2191*
Ye serpents, ye generation of *v* ... Mt 23:33 *2191*
of him, O generation of *v* ... Lk 3:7 *2191*

VIRGIN
was very fair to look upon, a *v* ... Gen 24:16 1330
that when the *v* cometh forth to ... Gen 24:43 5959
And for his sister a *v*, that is ... Lev 21:3 1330
but he shall take a *v* of his own ... Lev 21:14 1330
an evil name upon a *v* of Israel ... Deut 22:19 1330
If a damsel that is a *v* be ... Deut 22:23 1330
a man find a damsel that is a *v* ... Deut 22:28 1330
both the young man and the *v* ... Deut 32:25 1330
for she was a *v* ... 2Sa 13:2 1330
for my lord the king a young *v* ... 1Kin 1:2 1330
The *v* the daughter of Zion hath ... 2Kin 19:21 1330
a *v* shall conceive, and bear a son ... Is 7:14 5959
more rejoice, O thou oppressed *v* ... Is 23:12 1330
The *v*, the daughter of Zion, hath ... Is 37:22 1330
O *v* daughter of Babylon, sit on ... Is 47:1 1330
For as a young man marrieth a *v* ... Is 62:5 1330
for the *v* daughter of my people ... Jer 14:17 1330
the *v* of Israel hath done a very ... Jer 18:13 1330
shalt be built, O *v* of Israel ... Jer 31:4 1330
Then shall the *v* rejoice in the ... Jer 31:13 1330
O *v* of Israel, turn again to ... Jer 31:21 1330
up into Gilead, and take balm, O *v* ... Jer 46:11 1330
the Lord hath trodden the *v* ... Lam 1:15 1330
thee, O *v* daughter of Zion ... Lam 2:13 1330
Lament like a *v* girded with ... Joel 1:8 1330
The *v* of Israel is fallen ... Amos 5:2 1330
a *v* shall be with child, and shall ... Mt 1:23 *3933*
To a *v* espoused to a man whose ... Lk 1:27 *3933*
if a *v* marry, she hath not sinned ... 1Cor 7:28 *3933*
also between a wife and a *v* ... 1Cor 7:34 *3933*
himself uncomely toward his *v* ... 1Cor 7:36 *3933*
his heart that he will keep his *v* ... 1Cor 7:37 *3933*
you as a chaste *v* to Christ ... 2Cor 11:2 *3933*

VIRGINITY
And he shall take a wife in her *v* ... Lev 21:13 1331
the tokens of the damsel's *v* unto ... Deut 22:15 1331
are the tokens of my daughter's *v* ... Deut 22:17 1331
the tokens of *v* be not found for ... Deut 22:20 1331
the mountains, and bewail my *v* ... Judg 11:37 1331
bewailed her *v* upon the mountains ... Judg 11:38 1331
they bruised the teats of their *v* ... Eze 23:3 1331
they bruised the breasts of her *v* ... Eze 23:8 1331
an husband seven years from her *v* ... Lk 2:36 *3932*

VIRGIN'S
and the *v* name was Mary ... Lk 1:27 *3933*

VIRGINS
money according to the dowry of *v* ... Ex 22:17 1330
four hundred young *v*, that had ... Judg 21:12 1330
daughters that were *v* apparelled ... 2Sa 13:18 1330
fair young *v* sought for the king ... Est 2:2 1330
young *v* unto Shushan the palace ... Est 2:3 1330
in his sight more than all the *v* ... Est 2:17 1330
when the *v* were gathered together ... Est 2:19 1330
the *v* her companions that follow ... Ps 45:14 1330
therefore do the *v* love thee ... Song 1:3 5959
concubines, and *v* without number ... Song 6:8 5959
up young men, nor bring up *v* ... Is 23:4 1330
her *v* are afflicted, and she is in ... Lam 1:4 1330
my *v* and my young men are gone ... Lam 1:18 1330
the *v* of Jerusalem hang down ... Lam 2:10 1330
my *v* and my young men are fallen ... Lam 2:21 1330
In that day shall the fair *v* ... Amos 8:13 1330
of heaven be likened unto ten *v* ... Mt 25:1 *3933*
Then all those *v* arose, and ... Mt 25:7 *3933*
Afterward came also the other *v* ... Mt 25:11 *3933*
same man had four daughters, *v* ... Acts 21:9 *3933*
Now concerning *v* I have no ... 1Cor 7:25 *3933*
for they are *v* ... Rev 14:4 *3933*

VIRTUE
that *v* had gone out of him ... Mk 5:30 *1411*
for there went *v* out of him ... Lk 6:19 *1411*
perceive that *v* is gone out of me ... Lk 8:46 *1411*
if there be any *v*, and if there be ... Phil 4:8 *703*
that hath called us to glory and *v* ... 2Pet 1:3 *703*
diligence, add to your faith *v* ... 2Pet 1:5 *703*
and to *v* knowledge ... 2Pet 1:5 *703*

VIRTUOUS
doth know that thou art a *v* woman ... Ruth 3:11 2428
A *v* woman is a crown to her ... Prov 12:4 2428
Who can find a *v* woman ... Prov 31:10 2428

VIRTUOUSLY
Many daughters have done *v* ... Prov 31:29 2428

VISAGE
his *v* was so marred more than any ... Is 52:14 4758
Their *v* is blacker than a coal ... Lam 4:8 8389
the form of his *v* was changed ... Dan 3:19 600

VISIBLE
heaven, and that are in earth, *v* ... Col 1:16 *3707*

VISION
the LORD came unto Abram in a *v* ... Gen 15:1 4236
make myself known unto him in a *v* ... Num 12:6 4758
which saw the *v* of the Almighty, ... Num 24:4 4236
which saw the *v* of the Almighty, ... Num 24:16 4236
there was no open *v* ... 1Sa 3:1 2377
Samuel feared to shew Eli the *v* ... 1Sa 3:15 4758
words, and according to all this *v* ... 2Sa 7:17 2384
words, and according to all this *v* ... 1Chr 17:15 2377
in the *v* of Isaiah the prophet ... 2Chr 32:32 2377
chased away as a *v* of the night ... Job 20:8 2384
in a *v* of the night, when deep ... Job 33:15 2384
thou spakest in *v* to thy holy one ... Ps 89:19 2377
Where there is no *v*, the people ... Prov 29:18 2377
The *v* of Isaiah the son of Amoz, ... Is 1:1 2377
A grievous *v* is declared unto me ... Is 21:2 2380
The burden of the valley of *v* ... Is 22:1 2384
GOD of hosts in the valley of *v* ... Is 22:5 2384
they err in *v*, they stumble in ... Is 28:7 7203
shall be as a dream of a night *v* ... Is 29:7 2377
the *v* of all is become unto you ... Is 29:11 2380
they prophesy unto you a false *v* ... Jer 14:14 2377
they speak a *v* of their own heart ... Jer 23:16 2377
also find no *v* from the LORD ... Lam 2:9 2377
for the *v* is touching the whole ... Eze 7:13 2377
they seek a *v* of the prophet ... Eze 7:26 2377
according to the *v* that I saw in ... Eze 8:4 4758
brought me in a *v* by the Spirit ... Eze 11:24 4758
So the *v* that I had seen went up ... Eze 11:24 4758
are prolonged, and every *v* faileth ... Eze 12:22 2377
at hand, and the effect of every *v* ... Eze 12:23 2377
vain *v* nor flattering divination ... Eze 12:24 2377
The *v* that he seeth is for many ... Eze 12:27 2377
Have ye not seen a vain *v* ... Eze 13:7 4236
appearance of the *v* which I saw ... Eze 43:3 4758
even according to the *v* that I ... Eze 43:3 4758
the visions were like the *v* that ... Eze 43:3 4758
revealed unto Daniel in a night *v* ... Dan 2:19 2376
and said, I saw in my *v* by night ... Dan 7:2 2376
Belshazzar a *v* appeared unto me ... Dan 8:1 2377
And I saw in a *v* ... Dan 8:2 2377
and I saw in a *v*, and I was by the ... Dan 8:2 2377
spake, How long shall be the *v* ... Dan 8:13 2377
I, even I Daniel, had seen the *v* ... Dan 8:15 2377
make this man to understand the *v* ... Dan 8:16 4758
time of the end shall be the *v* ... Dan 8:17 4758
the *v* of the evening and the ... Dan 8:26 4758
wherefore shut thou up the *v* ... Dan 8:26 2377
and I was astonished at the *v* ... Dan 8:27 4758
seen in the *v* at the beginning ... Dan 9:21 2377
the matter, and consider the *v* ... Dan 9:23 2377
and to seal up the *v* and prophecy, ... Dan 9:24 2377
and had understanding of the *v* ... Dan 10:1 4758
And I Daniel alone saw the *v* ... Dan 10:7 4759
that were with me saw not the *v* ... Dan 10:7 4759
left alone, and saw this great *v* ... Dan 10:8 4759
for yet the *v* is for many days ... Dan 10:14 2377
by the *v* my sorrows are turned ... Dan 10:16 4758
themselves to establish the *v* ... Dan 11:14 2377
The *v* of Obadiah ... Obad 1 2377
you, that ye shall not have a *v* ... Mic 3:6 2377
The book of the *v* of Nahum the ... Nah 1:1 2377
answered me, and said, Write the *v* ... Hab 2:2 2377
For the *v* is yet for an appointed ... Hab 2:3 2377
be ashamed every one of his *v* ... Zec 13:4 2384
Tell the *v* to no man, until the ... Mt 17:9 *3705*
he had seen a *v* in the temple ... Lk 1:22 *3701*
they had also seen a *v* of angels ... Lk 24:23 *3701*
and to him said the Lord in a *v* ... Acts 9:10 *3705*
hath seen in a *v* a man named ... Acts 9:12 *3705*
He saw in a *v* evidently about the ... Acts 10:3 *3705*
doubted in himself what this *v* ... Acts 10:17 *3705*
While Peter thought on the *v* ... Acts 10:19 *3705*
and in a trance I saw a *v*, A ... Acts 11:5 *3705*
but thought he saw a *v* ... Acts 12:9 *3705*
a *v* appeared to Paul in the night ... Acts 16:9 *3705*
And after he had seen the *v* ... Acts 16:10 *3705*
Lord to Paul in the night by a *v* ... Acts 18:9 *3705*
disobedient unto the heavenly *v* ... Acts 26:19 *3705*
And thus I saw the horses in the *v* ... Rev 9:17 *3706*

VISIONS
unto Israel in the *v* of the night ... Gen 46:2 4759
in the *v* of Iddo the seer against ... 2Chr 9:29 2378
had understanding in the *v* of God ... 2Chr 26:5 7200
thoughts from the *v* of the night ... Job 4:13 2384
and terrifiest me through *v* ... Job 7:14 2384
were opened, and I saw *v* of God ... Eze 1:1 4759
brought me in the *v* of God to ... Eze 8:3 4759
which see *v* of peace for her, and ... Eze 13:16 2377
In the *v* of God brought he me ... Eze 40:2 4759
the *v* were like the vision that I ... Eze 43:3 4759
Daniel had understanding in all *v* ... Dan 1:17 2377
the *v* of thy head upon thy bed, ... Dan 2:28 2376
the *v* of my head troubled me ... Dan 4:5 2376
tell me the *v* of my dream that I ... Dan 4:9 2376
Thus were the *v* of mine head in ... Dan 4:10 2376
I saw in the *v* of my head upon my ... Dan 4:13 2376
v of his head upon his bed ... Dan 7:1 2376
After this I saw in the night *v* ... Dan 7:7 2376
I saw in the night *v*, and, behold, ... Dan 7:13 2376
the *v* of my head troubled me ... Dan 7:15 2376
prophets, and I have multiplied *v* ... Hos 12:10 2377
your young men shall see *v* ... Joel 2:28 2384
and your young men shall see *v* ... Acts 2:17 *3706*
I will come to *v* and revelations ... 2Cor 12:1 *3701*

VISIT
and God will surely *v* you, and ... Gen 50:24 6485
saying, God will surely *v* you ... Gen 50:25 6485
saying, God will surely *v* you ... Ex 13:19 6485
I *v* I will *v* their sin upon ... Ex 32:34 6485
therefore I do *v* the iniquity ... Lev 18:25 6485
thou shalt *v* thy habitation, and ... Job 5:24 6485
shouldest *v* him every morning ... Job 7:18 6485
awake to *v* all the heathen ... Ps 59:5 6485
heaven, and behold, and *v* this vine ... Ps 80:14 6485
Then will I *v* their transgression ... Ps 89:32 6485
O *v* me with thy salvation ... Ps 106:4 6485
years, that the LORD will *v* Tyre ... Is 23:17 6485
neither shall they *v* it ... Jer 3:16 6485
Shall I not *v* for these things ... Jer 5:9 6485
Shall I not *v* for these things ... Jer 5:29 6485
at the time that I *v* them they ... Jer 6:15 6485
Shall I not *v* them for these ... Jer 9:9 6485
their iniquity, and *v* their sins ... Jer 14:10 6485
v me, and revenge me of my ... Jer 15:15 6485
I will *v* upon you the evil of ... Jer 23:2 6485
be until the day that I *v* them ... Jer 27:22 6485
at Babylon I will *v* you, and ... Jer 29:10 6485
there shall he be until I *v* him ... Jer 32:5 6485
him, the time that I will *v* him ... Jer 49:8 6485
come, the time that I will *v* thee ... Jer 50:31 6485
he will *v* thine iniquity, O ... Lam 4:22 6485
I will *v* upon her the days of ... Hos 2:13 6485
their iniquity, and *v* their sins ... Hos 8:13 6485
iniquity, he will *v* their sins ... Hos 9:9 6485
v the transgressions of Israel ... Amos 3:14 6485
will also *v* the altars of Beth-el ... Amos 3:14 6485
the LORD their God shall *v* them ... Zeph 2:7 6485

which shall not *v* those that be ... Zec 11:16 6485
it came into his heart to *v* his ... Acts 7:23 *1980*
at the first did *v* the Gentiles ... Acts 15:14 *1980*
v our brethren in every city ... Acts 15:36 *1980*
To *v* the fatherless and widows in ... Jas 1:27 *1980*

VISITATION

be visited after the *v* of all men ... Num 16:29 6486
thy *v* hath preserved my spirit ... Job 10:12 6486
what will ye do in the day of *v* ... Is 10:3 6486
in the time of their *v* they shall ... Jer 8:12 6486
time of their *v* they shall perish ... Jer 10:15 6486
even the year of their *v* ... Jer 11:23 6486
them, even the year of their *v* ... Jer 23:12 6486
upon them, and the time of their *v* ... Jer 46:21 6486
upon Moab, the year of their *v* ... Jer 48:44 6486
day is come, the time of their *v* ... Jer 50:27 6486
time of their *v* they shall perish ... Jer 51:18 6486
The days of *v* are come, the days ... Hos 9:7 6486
of thy watchmen and thy *v* cometh ... Mic 7:4 6486
knewest not the time of thy *v* ... Lk 19:44 *1984*
glorify God in the day of *v* ... 1Pet 2:12 *1984*

VISITED

the LORD *v* Sarah as he had said ... Gen 21:1 6485
me, saying, I have surely *v* you ... Ex 3:16 6485
LORD had *v* the children of Israel ... Ex 4:31 6485
or if they be *v* after the ... Num 16:29 6485
that Samson *v* his wife with a kid ... Judg 15:1 6485
of Moab how that the LORD had *v* ... Ruth 1:6 6485
And the LORD *v* Hannah, so that she ... 1Sa 2:21 6485
is not so, he hath *v* in his anger ... Job 35:15 6485
thou hast *v* me in the night ... Ps 17:3 6485
he shall not be *v* with evil ... Prov 19:23 6485
after many days shall they be *v* ... Is 24:22 6485
therefore hast thou *v* and ... Is 26:14 6485
LORD, in trouble have they *v* thee ... Is 26:16 6485
Thou shalt be *v* of the LORD of ... Is 29:6 6485
this is the city to be *v* ... Jer 6:6 6485
them away, and have not *v* them ... Jer 23:2 6485
After many days thou shalt be *v* ... Eze 38:8 6485
for the LORD of hosts hath *v* his ... Zec 10:3 6485
I was sick, and ye *v* me ... Mt 25:36 *1980*
and in prison, and ye *v* me not ... Mt 25:43 *1980*
for he hath *v* and redeemed his ... Lk 1:68 *1980*
dayspring from on high hath *v* us ... Lk 1:78 *1980*
and, That God hath *v* his people ... Lk 7:16 *1980*

VISITEST

the son of man, that thou *v* him ... Ps 8:4 6485
Thou *v* the earth, and waterest it ... Ps 65:9 6485
the son of man, that thou *v* him ... Heb 2:6 *1980*

VISITETH

and when he *v*, what shall I answer ... Job 31:14 6485

VISITING

v the iniquity of the fathers ... Ex 20:5 6485
v the iniquity of the fathers ... Ex 34:7 6485
v the iniquity of the fathers ... Num 14:18 6485
v the iniquity of the fathers ... Deut 5:9 6485

VOCATION

of the *v* wherewith ye are called ... Eph 4:1 *2821*

VOICE

they heard the *v* of the LORD God ... Gen 3:8 6963
I heard thy *v* in the garden, and I ... Gen 3:10 6963
hearkened unto the *v* of thy wife ... Gen 3:17 6963
the *v* of thy brother's blood ... Gen 4:10 6963
wives, Adah and Zillah, Hear my *v* ... Gen 4:23 6963
Abram hearkened to the *v* of Sarai ... Gen 16:2 6963
unto thee, hearken unto her *v* ... Gen 21:12 6963
against him, and lift up her *v* ... Gen 21:16 6963
And God heard the *v* of the lad ... Gen 21:17 6963
the *v* of the lad where he is ... Gen 21:17 6963
because thou hast obeyed my *v* ... Gen 22:18 6963
Because that Abraham obeyed my *v* ... Gen 26:5 6963
obey my *v* according to that which ... Gen 27:8 6963
only obey my *v*, and go fetch me ... Gen 27:13 6963
and said, The *v* is Jacob's *v* ... Gen 27:22 6963
And Esau lifted up his *v*, and wept ... Gen 27:38 6963
Now therefore, my son, obey my *v* ... Gen 27:43 6963
kissed Rachel, and lifted up his *v* ... Gen 29:11 6963
me, and hath also heard my *v* ... Gen 30:6 6963
with me, and I cried with a loud *v* ... Gen 39:14 6963
he heard that I lifted up my *v* ... Gen 39:15 6963
came to pass, as I lifted up my *v* ... Gen 39:18 6963
And they shall hearken to thy *v* ... Ex 3:18 6963
believe me, nor hearken unto my *v* ... Ex 4:1 6963
to the *v* of the first sign ... Ex 4:8 6963
believe the *v* of the latter sign ... Ex 4:8 6963
signs, neither hearken unto thy *v* ... Ex 4:9 6963
obey his *v* to let Israel go ... Ex 5:2 6963
to the *v* of the LORD thy God ... Ex 15:26 6963
Hearken now unto my *v*, I will ... Ex 18:19 6963
to the *v* of his father in law ... Ex 18:24 6963
if ye will obey my *v* indeed ... Ex 19:5 6963
the *v* of the trumpet exceeding ... Ex 19:16 6963
when the *v* of the trumpet sounded ... Ex 19:19 6963
spake, and God answered him by a *v* ... Ex 19:19 6963
Beware of him, and obey his *v* ... Ex 23:21 6963
if thou shalt indeed obey his *v* ... Ex 23:22 6963
the people answered with one *v* ... Ex 24:3 6963
It is not the *v* of them that ... Ex 32:18 6963
neither is it the *v* of them that ... Ex 32:18 6963
hear the *v* of swearing, and is a ... Lev 5:1 6963
then he heard the *v* of one ... Num 7:89 6963
congregation lifted up their *v* ... Num 14:1 6963
and have not hearkened to my *v* ... Num 14:22 6963
unto the LORD, he heard our *v* ... Num 20:16 6963
LORD hearkened to the *v* of Israel ... Num 21:3 6963
LORD heard the *v* of your words ... Deut 1:34 6963
LORD would not hearken to your *v* ... Deut 1:45 6963
ye heard the *v* of the words ... Deut 4:12 6963
only ye heard a *v* ... Deut 4:12 6963
and shalt be obedient unto his *v* ... Deut 4:30 6963
Did ever people hear the *v* of God ... Deut 4:33 6963
heaven he made thee to hear his *v* ... Deut 4:36 6963
thick darkness, with a great *v* ... Deut 5:22 6963
when ye heard the *v* out of the ... Deut 5:23 6963
we have heard his *v* out of the ... Deut 5:24 6963
if we hear the *v* of the LORD our ... Deut 5:25 6963
that hath heard the *v* of the ... Deut 5:26 6963
LORD heard the *v* of your words ... Deut 5:28 6963
I have heard the *v* of the words ... Deut 5:28 6963
unto the *v* of the LORD your God ... Deut 8:20 6963
him not, nor hearkened to his *v* ... Deut 9:23 6963
his commandments, and obey his *v* ... Deut 13:4 6963
to the *v* of the LORD thy God ... Deut 13:18 6963
unto the *v* of the LORD thy God ... Deut 15:5 6963
again the *v* of the LORD my God ... Deut 18:16 6963
will not obey the *v* of his father ... Deut 21:18 6963
or the *v* of his mother, and that, ... Deut 21:18 6963
he will not obey our *v* ... Deut 21:20 6963
our fathers, the LORD heard our *v* ... Deut 26:7 6963
to the *v* of the LORD my God ... Deut 26:14 6963
and to hearken unto his *v* ... Deut 26:17 6963
obey the *v* of the LORD thy God ... Deut 27:10 6963
the men of Israel with a loud *v* ... Deut 27:14 6963
unto the *v* of the LORD thy God ... Deut 28:1 6963
unto the *v* of the LORD thy God ... Deut 28:2 6963
unto the *v* of the LORD thy God ... Deut 28:15 6963
unto the *v* of the LORD thy God ... Deut 28:45 6963
obey the *v* of the LORD thy God ... Deut 28:62 6963
shalt obey his *v* according to all ... Deut 30:2 6963
obey the *v* of the LORD, and do all ... Deut 30:8 6963
unto the *v* of the LORD thy God ... Deut 30:10 6963
and that thou mayest obey his *v* ... Deut 30:20 6963
the *v* of Judah, and bring him unto ... Deut 33:7 6963
they obeyed not the *v* of the LORD ... Josh 5:6 6963
nor make any noise with your *v* ... Josh 6:10 6963
hearkened unto the *v* of a man ... Josh 10:14 6963
have obeyed my *v* in all that I ... Josh 22:2 6963
we serve, and his *v* will we obey ... Josh 24:24 6963
but ye have not obeyed my *v* ... Judg 2:2 6963
that the people lifted up their *v* ... Judg 2:4 6963
and have not hearkened unto my *v* ... Judg 2:20 6963
but ye have not obeyed my *v* ... Judg 6:10 6963
mount Gerizim, and lifted up his *v* ... Judg 9:7 6963
God hearkened to the *v* of Manoah ... Judg 13:9 6963
they knew the *v* of the young man ... Judg 18:3 6963
Let not thy *v* be heard among us ... Judg 18:25 6963
would not hearken to the *v* of ... Judg 20:13 6963
and they lifted up their *v* ... Ruth 1:9 6963
And they lifted up their *v* ... Ruth 1:14 6963
moved, but her *v* was not heard ... 1Sa 1:13 6963
not unto the *v* of their father ... 1Sa 2:25 6963
Hearken unto the *v* of the people ... 1Sa 8:7 6963
therefore hearken unto their *v* ... 1Sa 8:9 6963
refused to obey the *v* of Samuel ... 1Sa 8:19 6963
to Samuel, Hearken unto their *v* ... 1Sa 8:22 6963
I have hearkened unto your *v* in ... 1Sa 12:1 6963
LORD, and serve him, and obey his *v* ... 1Sa 12:14 6963
will not obey the *v* of the LORD ... 1Sa 12:15 6963
the *v* of the words of the LORD ... 1Sa 15:1 6963
thou not obey the *v* of the LORD ... 1Sa 15:19 6963
I have obeyed the *v* of the LORD ... 1Sa 15:20 6963
as in obeying the *v* of the LORD ... 1Sa 15:22 6963
the people, and obeyed their *v* ... 1Sa 15:24 6963
hearkened unto the *v* of Jonathan ... 1Sa 19:6 6963
that Saul said, Is this thy *v* ... 1Sa 24:16 6963
And Saul lifted up his *v*, and wept ... 1Sa 24:16 6963
see, I have hearkened to thy *v* ... 1Sa 25:35 6963
And Saul knew David's *v* ... 1Sa 26:17 6963
and said, Is this thy *v* ... 1Sa 26:17 6963
And David said, It is my *v* ... 1Sa 26:17 6963
Samuel, she cried with a loud *v* ... 1Sa 28:12 6963
obeyedst not the *v* of the LORD ... 1Sa 28:18 6963
thine handmaid hath obeyed thy *v* ... 1Sa 28:21 6963
also unto the *v* of thine handmaid ... 1Sa 28:22 6963
and he hearkened unto their *v* ... 1Sa 28:23 6963
were with him lifted up their *v* ... 1Sa 30:4 6963
and the king lifted up his *v* ... 2Sa 3:32 6963
he would not hearken unto our *v* ... 2Sa 12:18 6963
he would not hearken unto her *v* ... 2Sa 13:14 6963
sons came, and lifted up their *v* ... 2Sa 13:36 6963
the country wept with a loud *v* ... 2Sa 15:23 6963
and the king cried with a loud *v* ... 2Sa 19:4 6963
any more the *v* of singing men ... 2Sa 19:35 6963
he did hear my *v* out of his ... 2Sa 22:7 6963
and the most High uttered his *v* ... 2Sa 22:14 6963
of Israel with a loud *v*, saying ... 1Kin 8:55 6963
And the LORD heard the *v* of Elijah ... 1Kin 17:22 6963
But there was no *v*, nor any that ... 1Kin 18:26 6963
that there was neither *v* ... 1Kin 18:29 6963
and after the fire a still small *v* ... 1Kin 19:12 6963
behold, there came a *v* unto him ... 1Kin 19:13 6963
And he hearkened unto their *v* ... 1Kin 20:25 6963
hast not obeyed the *v* of the LORD ... 1Kin 20:36 6963
but there was neither *v*, nor ... 2Kin 4:31 6963
no man there, neither *v* of man ... 2Kin 7:10 6963
and if ye will hearken unto my *v* ... 2Kin 10:6 6963
not the *v* of the LORD their God ... 2Kin 18:12 6963
cried with a loud *v* in the Jews' ... 2Kin 18:28 6963
whom hast thou exalted thy *v* ... 2Kin 19:22 6963
by lifting up the *v* with joy ... 1Chr 15:16 6963
up their *v* with the trumpets ... 2Chr 5:13 6963
sware unto the LORD with a loud *v* ... 2Chr 15:14 6963
of Israel with a loud *v* on high ... 2Chr 20:19 6963
their *v* was heard, and their ... 2Chr 30:27 6963
Then they cried with a loud *v* in ... 2Chr 32:18 6963
their eyes, wept with a loud *v* ... Ezr 3:12 6963
answered and said with a loud *v* ... Ezr 10:12 6963
cried with a loud *v* unto the LORD ... Neh 9:4 6963
him not, they lifted up their *v* ... Job 2:12 6963
let no joyful *v* come therein ... Job 3:7
hear not the *v* of the oppressor ... Job 3:18 6963
the *v* of the fierce lion, and the ... Job 4:10 6963
there was silence, and I heard a *v* ... Job 4:16 6963
that he had hearkened unto my *v* ... Job 9:16 6963
into the *v* of them that weep ... Job 30:31 6963
I have heard the *v* of thy words ... Job 33:8 6963
hearken to the *v* of my words ... Job 34:16 6963
attentively the noise of his *v* ... Job 37:2 6963
After it a *v* roareth ... Job 37:4 6963
with the *v* of his excellency ... Job 37:4 6963
not stay them when his *v* is heard ... Job 37:4 6963
marvellously with his *v* ... Job 37:5 6963
thou lift up thy *v* to the clouds ... Job 38:34 6963
thou thunder with a *v* like him ... Job 40:9 6963
I cried unto the LORD with my *v* ... Ps 3:4 6963
Hearken unto the *v* of my cry ... Ps 5:2 6963
My *v* shalt thou hear in the ... Ps 5:3 6963
hath heard the *v* of my weeping ... Ps 6:8 6963
he heard my *v* out of his temple ... Ps 18:6 6963
and the Highest gave his *v* ... Ps 18:13 6963
where their *v* is not heard ... Ps 19:3 6963
with the *v* of thanksgiving ... Ps 26:7 6963
O LORD, when I cry with my *v* ... Ps 27:7 6963
Hear the *v* of my supplications ... Ps 28:2 6963
heard the *v* of my supplications ... Ps 28:6 6963
The *v* of the LORD is upon the ... Ps 29:3 6963
The *v* of the LORD is powerful ... Ps 29:4 6963
the *v* of the LORD is full of ... Ps 29:4 6963
The *v* of the LORD breaketh the ... Ps 29:5 6963
The *v* of the LORD divideth the ... Ps 29:7 6963
The *v* of the LORD shaketh the ... Ps 29:8 6963
The *v* of the LORD maketh the ... Ps 29:9 6963
the *v* of my supplications when I ... Ps 31:22 6963
house of God, with the *v* of joy ... Ps 42:4 6963
For the *v* of him that reproacheth ... Ps 44:16 6963
he uttered his *v*, the earth ... Ps 46:6 6963
unto God with the *v* of triumph ... Ps 47:1 6963
Because of the *v* of the enemy ... Ps 55:3 6963
and he shall hear my *v* ... Ps 55:17 6963
not hearken to the *v* of charmers ... Ps 58:5 6963
Hear my *v*, O God, in my prayer ... Ps 64:1 6963
make the *v* of his praise to be ... Ps 66:8 6963
attended to the *v* of my prayer ... Ps 66:19 6963
out his *v*, and that a mighty *v* ... Ps 68:33 6963
Forget not the *v* of thine enemies ... Ps 74:23 6963
I cried unto God with my *v* ... Ps 77:1 6963
even unto God with my *v* ... Ps 77:1 6963
The *v* of thy thunder was in the ... Ps 77:18 6963
people would not hearken to my *v* ... Ps 81:11 6963
and attend to the *v* of my ... Ps 86:6 6963
the floods have lifted up their *v* ... Ps 93:3 6963
To day if ye will hear his *v* ... Ps 95:7 6963
the harp, and the *v* of a psalm ... Ps 98:5 6963
By reason of the *v* of my groaning ... Ps 102:5 6963
hearkening unto the *v* of his word ... Ps 103:20 6963
at the *v* of thy thunder they ... Ps 104:7 6963
not unto the *v* of the LORD ... Ps 106:25 6963
LORD, because he hath heard my *v* ... Ps 116:1 6963
The *v* of rejoicing and salvation ... Ps 118:15 6963
Hear my *v* according unto thy ... Ps 119:149 6963
Lord, hear my *v* ... Ps 130:2 6963
to the *v* of my supplications ... Ps 130:2 6963
hear the *v* of my supplications, O ... Ps 140:6 6963
give ear unto my *v*, when I cry ... Ps 141:1 6963
I cried unto the LORD with my *v* ... Ps 142:1 6963
with my *v* unto the LORD did I ... Ps 142:1 6963
she uttereth her *v* in the streets ... Prov 1:20 6963
and liftest up thy *v* for ... Prov 2:3 6963
not obeyed the *v* of my teachers ... Prov 5:13 6963
and understanding put forth her *v* ... Prov 8:1 6963
my *v* is to the sons of man ... Prov 8:4 6963
blesseth his friend with a loud *v* ... Prov 27:14 6963
a fool's *v* is known by multitude ... Eccl 5:3 6963
should God be angry at thy *v* ... Eccl 5:6 6963
bird of the air shall carry the *v* ... Eccl 10:20 6963
rise up at the *v* of the bird ... Eccl 12:4 6963
The *v* of my beloved ... Song 2:8 6963
the *v* of the turtle is heard in ... Song 2:12 6963
countenance, let me hear thy *v* ... Song 2:14 6963
for sweet is thy *v*, and thy ... Song 2:14 6963
it is the *v* of my beloved that ... Song 5:2 6963
the companions hearken to thy *v* ... Song 8:13 6963
moved at the *v* of him that cried ... Is 6:4 6963
Also I heard the *v* of the Lord ... Is 6:8 6963
Lift up thy *v*, O daughter of ... Is 10:30 6963
mountain, exalt the *v* unto them ... Is 13:2 6963
their *v* shall be heard even unto ... Is 15:4 6963
They shall lift up their *v* ... Is 24:14 6963
Give ye ear, and hear my *v* ... Is 28:23 6963
thy *v* shall be, as of one that ... Is 29:4 6963
unto thee at the *v* of thy cry ... Is 30:19 6963
cause his glorious *v* to be heard ... Is 30:30 6963
For through the *v* of the LORD ... Is 30:31 6963
he will not be afraid of their *v* ... Is 31:4 6963
hear my *v*, ye careless daughters ... Is 32:9 6963
cried with a loud *v* in the Jews' ... Is 36:13 6963
whom hast thou exalted thy *v* ... Is 37:23 6963
The *v* of him that crieth in the ... Is 40:3 6963
The *v* said, Cry ... Is 40:6 6963
lift up thy *v* with strength ... Is 40:9 6963
nor cause his *v* to be heard in ... Is 42:2 6963
cities thereof lift up their *v* ... Is 42:11
with a *v* of singing declare ye ... Is 48:20 6963
that obeyeth the *v* of his servant ... Is 50:10 6963
thanksgiving, and the *v* of melody ... Is 51:3 6963
Thy watchmen shall lift up the *v* ... Is 52:8 6963
with the *v* together shall they ... Is 52:8 6963
lift up thy *v* like a trumpet, and ... Is 58:1 6963
to make your *v* to be heard on ... Is 58:4 6963
the *v* of weeping shall be no more ... Is 65:19 6963
heard in her, nor the *v* of crying ... Is 65:19 6963
A *v* of noise from the city ... Is 66:6 6963
a *v* from the temple ... Is 66:6 6963
a *v* of the LORD that rendereth ... Is 66:6 6963
tree, and ye have not obeyed my *v* ... Jer 3:13 6963
A *v* was heard upon the high ... Jer 3:21 6963
obeyed the *v* of the LORD our God ... Jer 3:25 6963
For a *v* declareth from Dan, and ... Jer 4:15 6963

give out their v against the... Jer 4:16 6963
For I have heard a v as of a... Jer 4:31 6963
the v of the daughter of Zion,... Jer 4:31 6963
their v roareth like the sea... Jer 6:23 6963
I them, saying, Obey my v... Jer 7:23 6963
not the v of the LORD their God... Jer 7:28 6963
the v of mirth... Jer 7:34 6963
the v of gladness... Jer 7:34 6963
the v of the bridegroom... Jer 7:34 6963
and the v of the bride... Jer 7:34 6963
Behold the v of the cry of the... Jer 8:19 6963
can men hear the v of the cattle... Jer 9:10 6963
them, and have not obeyed my v... Jer 9:13 6963
For a v of wailing is heard out... Jer 9:19 6963
When he uttereth his v, there is... Jer 10:13 6963
iron furnace, saying, Obey my v... Jer 11:4 6963
and protesting, saying, Obey my v... Jer 11:7 6963
the v of mirth... Jer 16:9 6963
the v of gladness... Jer 16:9 6963
the v of the bridegroom... Jer 16:9 6963
and the v of the bride... Jer 16:9 6963
my sight, that it obey not my v... Jer 18:10 6963
hearken to the v of them that... Jer 18:19 6963
and lift up thy v in Bashan... Jer 22:20 6963
that thou obeyedst not my v... Jer 22:21 6963
take from them the v of mirth... Jer 25:10 6963
the v of gladness... Jer 25:10 6963
the v of the bridegroom... Jer 25:10 6963
the v of the bride... Jer 25:10 6963
utter his v from his holy... Jer 25:30 6963
A v of the cry of the shepherds,... Jer 25:36 6963
obey the v of the LORD your God... Jer 26:13 6963
We have heard a v of trembling... Jer 30:5 6963
the v of them that make merry... Jer 30:19 6963
A v was heard in Ramah,... Jer 31:15 6963
Refrain thy v from weeping, and... Jer 31:16 6963
but they obeyed not thy v... Jer 32:23 6963
The v of joy... Jer 33:11 6963
the v of gladness... Jer 33:11 6963
the v of the bridegroom... Jer 33:11 6963
the v of the bride... Jer 33:11 6963
the v of them that shall say,... Jer 33:11 6963
Thus have we obeyed the v of... Jer 35:8 6963
the v of the LORD, which I speak... Jer 38:20 6963
LORD, and have not obeyed his v... Jer 40:3 6963
we will obey the v of the LORD... Jer 42:6 6963
when we obey the v of the LORD... Jer 42:6 6963
neither obey the v of the LORD... Jer 42:13 6963
obeyed the v of the LORD your God... Jer 42:21 6963
obeyed not the v of the LORD... Jer 43:4 6963
they obeyed not the v of the LORD... Jer 43:7 6963
have not obeyed the v of the LORD... Jer 44:23 6963
The v thereof shall go like a... Jer 46:22 6963
A v of crying shall be from... Jer 48:3 6963
Jahaz, have they uttered their v... Jer 48:34 6963
The v of them that flee and escape... Jer 50:28 6963
their v shall roar like the sea,... Jer 50:42 6963
When he uttereth his v, there is... Jer 51:16 6963
destroyed out of her the great v... Jer 51:55 6963
a noise of their v is uttered... Jer 51:55 6963
Thou hast heard my v... Lam 3:56 6963
as the v of the Almighty, the... Eze 1:24 6963
the v of speech, as the noise of... Eze 1:24 6963
there was a v from the firmament... Eze 1:25 6963
I heard a v of one that spake... Eze 1:28 6963
behind me a v of a great rushing... Eze 3:12 6963
cry in mine ears with a loud v... Eze 8:18 6963
also in mine ears with a loud v... Eze 9:1 6963
as the v of the Almighty God when... Eze 10:5 6963
my face, and cried with a loud v... Eze 11:13 6963
that his v should no more be... Eze 19:9 6963
to lift up the v with shouting... Eze 21:22 6963
a v of a multitude being at ease... Eze 23:42 6963
shall cause their v to be heard... Eze 27:30 6963
of one that hath a pleasant v... Eze 33:32 6963
his v was like a noise of many... Eze 43:2 6963
mouth, there fell a v from heaven... Dan 4:31 7032
with a lamentable v unto Daniel... Dan 6:20 7032
v of the great words which the... Dan 7:11 7032
I heard a man's v between the... Dan 8:16 6963
obeyed the v of the LORD our God... Dan 9:10 6963
that they might not obey thy v... Dan 9:11 6963
for we obeyed not his v... Dan 9:14 6963
the v of his words like the... Dan 10:6 6963
words like the v of a multitude... Dan 10:6 6963
Yet heard I the v of his words... Dan 10:9 6963
when I heard the v of his words... Dan 10:9 6963
shall utter his v before his army... Joel 2:11 6963
utter his v from Jerusalem... Joel 3:16 6963
utter his v from Jerusalem... Amos 1:2 6963
cried I, and thou heardest my v... Jonah 2:2 6963
thee with the v of thanksgiving... Jonah 2:9 6963
and let the hills hear thy v... Mic 6:1 6963
The LORD's v crieth unto the city... Mic 6:9 6963
lead her as with the v of doves... Nah 2:7 6963
the v of thy messengers shall no... Nah 2:13 6963
the deep uttered his v, and lifted... Hab 3:10 6963
my lips quivered at the v... Hab 3:16 6963
even the v of the day of the LORD... Zeph 1:14 6963
their v shall sing in the windows... Zeph 2:14 6963
She obeyed not the v... Zeph 3:2 6963
obeyed the v of the LORD their... Hag 1:12 6963
obey the v of the LORD your God... Zec 6:15 6963
There is a v of the howling of... Zec 11:3 6963
a v of the roaring of young lions... Zec 11:3 6963
In Rama was there a v heard... Mt 2:18 5456
The v of one crying in the... Mt 3:3 5456
lo a v from heaven, saying, This... Mt 3:17 5456
any man hear his v in the streets... Mt 12:19 5456
behold a v out of the cloud,... Mt 17:5 5456
hour Jesus cried with a loud v... Mt 27:46 5456
he had cried again with a loud v... Mt 27:50 5456
The v of one crying in the... Mk 1:3 5456
And there came a v from heaven... Mk 1:11 5456
torn him, and cried with a loud v... Mk 1:26 5456
And cried with a loud v, and said,... Mk 5:7 5456
a v came out of the cloud, saying... Mk 9:7 5456
hour Jesus cried with a loud v... Mk 15:34 5456
And Jesus cried with a loud v... Mk 15:37 5456
And she spake out with a loud v... Lk 1:42 5456
For, lo, as soon as the v of thy... Lk 1:44 5456
The v of one crying in the... Lk 3:4 5456
a v came from heaven, which said,... Lk 3:22 5456
devil, and cried out with a loud v... Lk 4:33 5456
before him, and with a loud v said... Lk 8:28 5456
there came a v out of the cloud,... Lk 9:35 5456
And when the v was past, Jesus was... Lk 9:36 5456
of the company lifted up her v... Lk 11:27 5456
with a loud v glorified God,... Lk 17:15 5456
praise God with a loud v for all... Lk 19:37 5456
Jesus had cried with a loud v... Lk 23:46 5456
I am the v of one crying in the... Jn 1:23 5456
because of the bridegroom's v... Jn 3:29 5456
hear the v of the Son of God... Jn 5:25 5456
in the graves shall hear his v... Jn 5:28 5456
neither heard his v at any time... Jn 5:37 5456
and the sheep hear his v... Jn 10:3 5456
for they know his v... Jn 10:4 5456
they know not the v of strangers... Jn 10:5 5456
bring, and they shall hear my v... Jn 10:16 5456
My sheep hear my v, and I know... Jn 10:27 5456
spoken, he cried with a loud v... Jn 11:43 5456
Then came there a v from heaven... Jn 12:28 5456
This v came not because of me,... Jn 12:30 5456
that is of the truth heareth my v... Jn 18:37 5456
with the eleven, lifted up his v... Acts 2:14 5456
they lifted up their v to God... Acts 4:24 5456
the v of the Lord came unto him,... Acts 7:31 5456
Then they cried out with a loud v... Acts 7:57 5456
down, and cried with a loud v... Acts 7:60 5456
spirits, crying with loud v... Acts 8:7 5456
heard a v saying unto him, Saul,... Acts 9:4 5456
him stood speechless, hearing a v... Acts 9:7 5456
And there came a v to him, Rise,... Acts 10:13 5456
the v spake unto him again the... Acts 10:15 5456
I heard a v saying unto me, Arise... Acts 11:7 5456
But the v answered me again from... Acts 11:9 5456
And when she knew Peter's v... Acts 12:14 5456
saying, It is the v of a god... Acts 12:22 5456
Said with a loud v, Stand upright... Acts 14:10 5456
But Paul cried with a loud v... Acts 16:28 5456
all with one v about the space of... Acts 19:34 5456
heard a v saying unto me, Saul,... Acts 22:7 5456
but they heard not the v of him... Acts 22:9 5456
shouldest hear the v of his mouth... Acts 22:14 5456
Except it be for this one v... Acts 24:21 5456
death, I gave my v against them... Acts 26:10 5586
I heard a v speaking unto me, and... Acts 26:14 5456
Festus said with a loud v... Acts 26:24 5456
I know not the meaning of the v... 1Cor 14:11 5456
that by my v I might teach others... 1Cor 14:19
with you now, and to change my v... Gal 4:20 5456
with the v of the archangel, and... 1Th 4:16 5456
To day if ye will hear his v... Heb 3:7 5456
To day if ye will hear his v... Heb 3:15 5456
To day if ye will hear his v... Heb 4:7 5456
of a trumpet, and the v of words... Heb 12:19 5456
which v they that heard intreated... Heb 12:19
Whose v then shook the earth... Heb 12:26 5456
when there came such a v to him... 2Pet 1:17 5456
this v which came from heaven we... 2Pet 1:18 5456
man's v forbad the madness of the... 2Pet 2:16 5456
day, and heard behind me a great v... Rev 1:10 5456
to see the v that spake with me... Rev 1:12 5456
his v as the sound of many waters... Rev 1:15 5456
if any man hear my v, and open the... Rev 3:20 5456
the first v which I heard was as... Rev 4:1 5456
angel proclaiming with a loud v... Rev 5:2 5456
I heard the v of many angels... Rev 5:11 5456
Saying with a loud v, Worthy is... Rev 5:12 5456
I heard a v in the midst of the... Rev 6:6 5456
I heard the v of the fourth beast... Rev 6:7 5456
And they cried with a loud v... Rev 6:10 5456
with a loud v to the four angels... Rev 7:2 5456
And cried with a loud v, saying,... Rev 7:10 5456
of heaven, saying with a loud v... Rev 8:13 5456
I heard a v from the four horns... Rev 9:13 5456
And cried with a loud v, as when a... Rev 10:3 5456
I heard a v from heaven saying... Rev 10:4 5456
of the v of the seventh angel... Rev 10:7 5456
the v which I heard from heaven... Rev 10:8 5456
they heard a great v from heaven... Rev 11:12 5456
I heard a loud v saying in heaven... Rev 12:10 5456
I heard a v from heaven... Rev 14:2 5456
as the v of many waters... Rev 14:2 5456
as the v of a great thunder... Rev 14:2 5456
I heard the v of harpers harping... Rev 14:2 5456
Saying with a loud v, Fear God,... Rev 14:7 5456
them, saying with a loud v... Rev 14:9 5456
I heard a v from heaven saying... Rev 14:13 5456
crying with a loud v to him that... Rev 14:15 5456
I heard a great v out of the... Rev 16:1 5456
there came a great v out of the... Rev 16:17 5456
he cried mightily with a strong v... Rev 18:2 5456
And I heard another v from heaven... Rev 18:4 5456
the v of harpers, and musicians,... Rev 18:22 5456
the v of the bridegroom and of the... Rev 18:23 5456
great v of much people in heaven... Rev 19:1 5456
a v came out of the throne,... Rev 19:5 5456
were the v of a great multitude... Rev 19:6 5456
as the v of many waters... Rev 19:6 5456
as the v of mighty thunderings,... Rev 19:6 5456
and he cried with a loud v... Rev 19:17 5456
I heard a great v out of heaven... Rev 21:3 5456

VOICES

before God, and lifted up their v... Judg 21:2 6963
all the people lifted up their v... 1Sa 11:4 6963
And they lifted up their v... Lk 17:13 5456
And they were instant with loud v... Lk 23:23 5456
the v of them and of the chief... Lk 23:23 5456
nor yet the v of the prophets... Acts 13:27 5456
had done, they lifted up their v... Acts 14:11 5456
word, and then lifted up their v... Acts 22:22 5456
so many kinds of v in the world... 1Cor 14:10 5456
lightnings and thunderings and v... Rev 4:5 5456
and there were v, and thunderings,... Rev 8:5 5456
v of the trumpet of the three... Rev 8:13 5456
seven thunders uttered their v... Rev 10:3 5456
thunders had uttered their v... Rev 10:4 5456
and there were great v in heaven... Rev 11:15 5456
and there were lightnings, and v... Rev 11:19 5456
And there were v, and thunders, and... Rev 16:18 5456

VOID

the earth was without form, and v... Gen 1:2 922
them v on the day he heard them... Num 30:12 6565
her husband hath made them v... Num 30:12 6565
it, or her husband may make it v... Num 30:13 6565
v after that he hath heard them... Num 30:15 6565
they are a nation v of counsel... Deut 32:28 6
in a v place in the entrance of... 1Kin 22:10 1637
they sat in a v place at the... 2Chr 18:9 1637
Thou hast made v the covenant of... Ps 89:39 5010
for they have made v thy law... Ps 119:126 6565
a young man v of understanding,... Prov 7:7 2638
of him that is v of understanding... Prov 10:13 2638
He that is v of wisdom despiseth... Prov 11:12 2638
persons is v of understanding... Prov 12:11 2638
A man v of understanding striketh... Prov 17:18 2638
of the man v of understanding... Prov 24:30 2638
it shall not return unto me v... Is 55:11 7387
and, lo, it was without form, and v... Jer 4:23 922
I will make v the counsel of... Jer 19:7 1238
She is empty, and v, and waste... Nah 2:10 4003
v of offence toward God, and... Acts 24:16 677
Do we then make v the law through... Rom 3:31 2673
the law be heirs, faith is made v... Rom 4:14 2758
any man should make my glorying v... 1Cor 9:15 2758

VOLUME

in the v of the book it is... Ps 40:7 4039
I come (in the v of the book it... Heb 10:7 2777

VOLUNTARILY

peace offerings v unto the LORD... Eze 46:12 5071

VOLUNTARY

his own v will at the door of the... Lev 1:3 7522
or a v offering, it shall be... Lev 7:16 5071
a v burnt offering or peace... Eze 46:12 5071
of your reward in a v humility... Col 2:18 2309

VOMIT

and he shall v them up again... Job 20:15 6958
thou hast eaten shalt thou v up... Prov 23:8 6958
thou be filled therewith, and v it... Prov 25:16 6958
As a dog returneth to his v... Prov 26:11 6892
a drunken man staggereth in his v... Is 19:14 6892
For all tables are full of v... Is 28:8 6892
Moab also shall wallow in his v... Jer 48:26 6892
dog is turned to his own v again... 2Pet 2:22 1829

VOMITED

it v out Jonah upon the dry land... Jonah 2:10 6958

VOMITETH

the land itself v out her... Lev 18:25 6958

VOPHSI (vof'-si) *A spy sent to the Promised Land.*

of Naphtali, Nahbi the son of V... Num 13:14 2058

VOW

And Jacob vowed a v, saying, If... Gen 28:20 5088
and where thou vowedst a v unto me.. Gen 31:13 5088
sacrifice of his offering be a v... Lev 7:16 5088
unto the LORD to accomplish his v... Lev 22:21 5088
but for a v it shall not be... Lev 22:23 5088
a man shall make a singular v... Lev 27:2 5088
separate themselves to v... Num 6:2 5087
a v of a Nazarite, to... Num 6:2 5088
All the days of the v of his... Num 6:5 5088
according to the v which he vowed... Num 6:21 5088
or a sacrifice in performing a v... Num 15:3 5088
for a sacrifice in performing a v... Num 15:8 5088
And Israel vowed a v unto the LORD... Num 21:2 5088
If a man v a... Num 30:2 5087
a v unto the LORD... Num 30:2 5088
If a woman also v a... Num 30:3 5087
a v unto the LORD... Num 30:3 5088
And her father hear her v, and her... Num 30:4 5088
shall make her v which she vowed... Num 30:8 5088
But every v of a widow, and of her... Num 30:9 5088
Every v, and every binding oath to... Num 30:13 5088
vows which ye v unto the LORD... Deut 12:11 5087
of the LORD thy God for any v... Deut 23:18 5088
When thou shalt v a... Deut 23:21 5087
a v unto the LORD thy God... Deut 23:21 5088
But if thou shalt forbear to v... Deut 23:22 5087
Jephthah vowed a v unto the LORD... Judg 11:30 5088
to his v which he had vowed... Judg 11:39 5088
And she vowed a v, and said, O LORD.. 1Sa 1:11 5088
the yearly sacrifice, and his v... 1Sa 1:21 5088
pray thee, let me go and pay my v... 2Sa 15:7 5088
For thy servant vowed a v while I... 2Sa 15:8 5088
thee shall the v be performed... Ps 65:1 5088
V, and pay unto the LORD your God... Ps 76:11 5087
When thou vowest a v unto God... Eccl 5:4 5088
is it that thou shouldest not v... Eccl 5:5 5087
than that thou shouldest v... Eccl 5:5 5087
oblation; yea, they shall v... Is 19:21 5087
a v unto the LORD... Is 19:21 5088
for he had a v... Acts 18:18 2171
four men which have a v on them... Acts 21:23 2171

V

VOWED
And Jacob *v* a vow, saying, If God ... Gen 28:20 5087
that *v* shall the priest value him ... Lev 27:8 5087
law of the Nazarite who hath *v* ... Num 6:21 5087
according to the vow which he *v* ... Num 6:21 5087
Israel *v* a vow unto the LORD, and ... Num 21:2 5087
had at all an husband, when she *v* ... Num 30:6 5088
he shall make her vow which she *v* ... Num 30:8 5088
if she *v* in her husband's house, ... Num 30:10 5087
thou hast *v* unto the LORD thy God ... Deut 23:23 5087
Jephthah *v* a vow unto the LORD, ... Judg 11:30 5087
to his vow which he had *v* ... Judg 11:39 5087
she *v* a vow, and said, O LORD of ... 1Sa 1:11 5087
which I have *v* unto the LORD, in ... 2Sa 15:7 5087
For thy servant *v* a vow while I ... 2Sa 15:8 5087
v unto the mighty God of Jacob ... Ps 132:2 5087
pay that which thou hast *v* ... Eccl 5:4 5087
perform our vows that we have *v* ... Jer 44:25 5087
I will pay that that I have *v* ... Jonah 2:9 5087

VOWEDST
where thou *v* a vow unto me ... Gen 31:13 5087

VOWEST
nor any of thy vows which thou *v* ... Deut 12:17 5087
When thou *v* a vow unto God, defer ... Eccl 5:4 5087

VOWETH
hath in his flock a male, and *v* ... Mal 1:14 5087

VOWS
offer his oblation for all his *v* ... Lev 22:18 5088
your gifts, and beside all your *v* ... Lev 23:38 5088
in your set feasts, beside your *v* ... Num 29:39 5088
then all her *v* shall stand ... Num 30:4 5088
not any of her *v*, or of her bonds ... Num 30:5 5088
then her *v* shall stand, and her ... Num 30:7 5088
then all her *v* shall stand ... Num 30:11 5088
out of her lips concerning her *v* ... Num 30:12 5088
then he establisheth all her *v* ... Num 30:14 5088
offerings of your hand, and your *v* ... Deut 12:6 5088
all your choice *v* which ye vow ... Deut 12:11 5088
nor any of thy *v* which thou ... Deut 12:17 5088
things which thou hast, and thy *v* ... Deut 12:26 5088
thee, and thou shalt pay thy *v* ... Job 22:27 5088
I will pay my *v* before them that ... Ps 22:25 5088
pay thy *v* unto the most High ... Ps 50:14 5088
Thy *v* are upon me, O God ... Ps 56:12 5088
For thou, O God, hast heard my *v* ... Ps 61:5 5088
that I may daily perform my *v* ... Ps 61:8 5088
I will pay thee my *v*, ... Ps 66:13 5088
I will pay my *v* unto the LORD now ... Ps 116:14 5088
I will pay my *v* unto the LORD now ... Ps 116:18 5088
this day have I payed my *v* ... Prov 7:14 5088
holy, and after *v* to make enquiry ... Prov 20:25 5088
and what, the son of my *v* ... Prov 31:2 5088
perform our *v* that we have vowed ... Jer 44:25 5088
ye will surely accomplish your *v* ... Jer 44:25 5088
and surely perform your *v* ... Jer 44:25 5088
unto the LORD, and made *v* ... Jonah 1:16 5088
thy solemn feasts, perform thy *v* ... Nah 1:15 5088

VOYAGE
that this *v* will be with hurt ... Acts 27:10 *4144*

VULTURE
And the *v*, and the kite after his ... Lev 11:14 1676
kite, and the *v* after his kind, ... Deut 14:13 1772

VULTURE'S
which the *v* eye hath not seen ... Job 28:7 344

VULTURES
there shall the *v* also be ... Is 34:15 1772

WADI ZERED See ZARED.

WAFER
one *w* out of the basket of the ... Ex 29:23 7550
a cake of oiled bread, and one *w* ... Lev 8:26 7550
the basket, and one unleavened *w* ... Num 6:19 7550

WAFERS
of it was like *w* made with honey ... Ex 16:31 6838
w unleavened anointed with oil ... Ex 29:2 7550
or unleavened *w* anointed with oil ... Lev 2:4 7550
unleavened *w* anointed with oil, ... Lev 7:12 7550
w of unleavened bread anointed ... Num 6:15 7550

WAG
be astonished, and *w* his head ... Jer 18:16 5110
w their head at the daughter of ... Lam 2:15 5128
by her shall hiss, and *w* his hand ... Zeph 2:15 5128

WAGES
tell me, what shall thy *w* be ... Gen 29:15 4909
And he said, Appoint me thy *w* ... Gen 30:28 7939
me, and changed my *w* ten times ... Gen 31:7 4909
thus, The speckled shall be thy *w* ... Gen 31:8 7939
thou hast changed my *w* ten times ... Gen 31:41 4909
for me, and I will give thee thy *w* ... Ex 2:9 7939
the *w* of him that is hired shall ... Lev 19:13 6468
his neighbour's service without *w* ... Jer 22:13 2600
yet had he no *w*, nor his army, ... Eze 29:18 7939
and it shall be the *w* for his army ... Eze 29:19 7939
he that earneth *w* earneth *w* ... Hag 1:6 7936
oppress the hireling in his *w* ... Mal 3:5 7939
and be content with your *w* ... Lk 3:14 *3800*
And he that reapeth receiveth *w* ... Jn 4:36 *3408*
For the *w* of sin is death ... Rom 6:23 *3800*
taking *w* of them, to do you ... 2Cor 11:8 *3800*
son of Bosor, who loved the *w* of ... 2Pet 2:15 *3408*

WAGGING
by reviled him, *w* their heads, ... Mt 27:39 *2795*
w their heads, and saying, Ah, ... Mk 15:29 *2795*

WAGON
a *w* for two of the princes, and ... Num 7:3 5699

WAGONS
take you *w* out of the land of ... Gen 45:19 5699
and Joseph gave them *w*, according ... Gen 45:21 5699
when he saw the *w* which Joseph ... Gen 45:27 5699
in the *w* which Pharaoh had sent ... Gen 46:5 5699
before the LORD, six covered *w* ... Num 7:3 5699
And Moses took the *w* and the oxen, ... Num 7:6 5699
Two *w* and four oxen he gave unto ... Num 7:7 5699
And four *w* and eight oxen he gave ... Num 7:8 5699
against thee with chariots, *w* ... Eze 23:24 7393

WAHEB See DID.

WAIL
w for the multitude of Egypt, and ... Eze 32:18 5091
Therefore I will *w* and howl, I ... Mic 1:8 5594
the earth shall *w* because of him ... Rev 1:7 *2875*

WAILED
and them that wept and *w* greatly ... Mk 5:38 *214*

WAILING
and fasting, and weeping, and *w* ... Est 4:3 4553
will I take up a weeping and *w* ... Jer 9:10 5092
make haste, and take up a *w* for us ... Jer 9:18 5092
For a voice of *w* is heard out of ... Jer 9:19 5092
mouth, and teach your daughters *w* ... Jer 9:20 5092
neither shall there be *w* for them ... Eze 7:11 5089
bitterness of heart and bitter *w* ... Eze 27:31 4553
in their *w* they shall take up a ... Eze 27:32 5204
W shall be in all streets ... Amos 5:16 4553
are skilful of lamentation to *w* ... Amos 5:16 4553
And in all vineyards shall be *w* ... Amos 5:17 4553
I will make a *w* like the dragons, ... Mic 1:8 4553
there shall be *w* and gnashing of ... Mt 13:42 *2805*
there shall be *w* and gnashing of ... Mt 13:50 *2805*
fear of her torment, weeping and *w* ... Rev 18:15 *3996*
heads, and cried, weeping and *w* ... Rev 18:19 *3996*

WAIT
And if a man lie not in *w*, but God ... Ex 21:13 6658
they shall *w* on their priest's ... Num 3:10 8104
in to *w* upon the service of the ... Num 8:24 6633
or hurl at him by laying of *w* ... Num 35:20 6660
him any thing without laying of *w* ... Num 35:22 6660
lie in *w* for him, and rise up ... Deut 19:11 693
ye shall lie in *w* against the ... Josh 8:4 693
their liers in *w* on the west of ... Josh 8:13 6119
in *w* for him in the top of the ... Judg 9:25 693
thee, and lie in *w* in the field ... Judg 9:32 693
they laid *w* against Shechem in ... Judg 9:34 693
were with him, from lying in *w* ... Judg 9:35 3993
laid *w* in the field, and looked, ... Judg 9:43 693
laid *w* for him all night in the ... Judg 16:2 693
Now there were men lying in *w* ... Judg 16:9 693
there were liers in *w* abiding in ... Judg 16:12 693
set liers in *w* round about Gibeah ... Judg 20:29 693
the liers in *w* of Israel came ... Judg 20:33 693
in *w* which they had set beside ... Judg 20:36 693
And the liers in *w* hasted, and ... Judg 20:37 693
the liers in *w* drew themselves ... Judg 20:37 693
men of Israel and the liers in *w* ... Judg 20:38 693
lie in *w* in the vineyards ... Judg 21:20 693
how he laid *w* for him in the way, ... 1Sa 15:2
Amalek, and laid *w* in the valley ... 1Sa 15:5 693
servant against me, to lie in *w* ... 1Sa 22:8 693
rise against me, to lie in *w* ... 1Sa 22:13 693
what should I *w* for the LORD any ... 2Kin 6:33 3176
Because their office was to *w* on ... 1Chr 23:28 3027
and did not then *w* by course ... 2Chr 5:11 8104
the Levites *w* upon their business ... 2Chr 13:10
and of such as lay in *w* by the way ... Ezr 8:31 693
of my appointed time will I *w* ... Job 14:14 3176
If I *w*, the grave is mine house ... Job 17:13 6960
or if I have laid *w* at my ... Job 31:9 693
abide in the covert to lie in *w* ... Job 38:40 693
He lieth in *w* secretly as a lion ... Ps 10:9 693
he lieth in *w* to catch the poor ... Ps 10:9 693
let none that *w* on thee be ... Ps 25:3 6960
on thee do I *w* all the day ... Ps 25:5 6960
for I *w* on thee ... Ps 25:21 6960
W on the LORD ... Ps 27:14 6960
w, I say, on the LORD ... Ps 27:14 6960
the LORD, and *w* patiently for him ... Ps 37:7 2342
but those that *w* upon the LORD ... Ps 37:9 6960
W on the LORD, and keep his way, ... Ps 37:34 6960
And now, Lord, what *w* I for ... Ps 39:7 6960
and I will *w* on thy name ... Ps 52:9 6960
my steps, when they *w* for my soul ... Ps 56:6 6960
lo, they lie in *w* for my soul ... Ps 59:3 693
his strength will I *w* upon thee ... Ps 59:9 8104
My soul, *w* thou only upon God ... Ps 62:5 1826
eyes fail while I *w* for my God ... Ps 69:3 3176
Let not them that *w* on thee ... Ps 69:6 6960
they that lay *w* for my soul take ... Ps 71:10 8104
These *w* all upon thee ... Ps 104:27 7663
so our eyes *w* upon the LORD our ... Ps 123:2
w for the LORD, my soul doth *w* ... Ps 130:5 6960
The eyes of all *w* upon thee ... Ps 145:15 7663
with us, let us lay *w* for blood ... Prov 1:11 693
they lay *w* for their own blood ... Prov 1:18 693
lieth in *w* at every corner ... Prov 7:12 693
wicked are to lie in *w* for blood ... Prov 12:6 693
but *w* on the LORD, and he shall ... Prov 20:22 6960
She also lieth in *w* as for a prey ... Prov 23:28 693
Lay not *w*, O wicked man, against ... Prov 24:15 693
I will *w* upon the LORD, that ... Is 8:17 2442
And therefore will the LORD *w* ... Is 30:18 2442
are all they that *w* for him ... Is 30:18 2442
But they that *w* upon the LORD ... Is 40:31 6960
and the isles shall *w* for his law ... Is 42:4 3176
not be ashamed that *w* for me ... Is 49:23 6960
the isles shall *w* upon me ... Is 51:5 6960
we *w* for light, but behold ... Is 59:9 6960
Surely the isles shall *w* for me ... Is 60:9 6960
they lay *w*, as he that setteth ... Jer 5:26 7789
but in heart he layeth his *w* ... Jer 9:8 696
therefore we will *w* upon thee ... Jer 14:22 6960
was unto me as a bear lying in *w* ... Lam 3:10 693
is good unto them that *w* for him ... Lam 3:25 6960
quietly *w* for the salvation of ... Lam 3:26 1748
they laid *w* for us in the ... Lam 4:19 693
as troops of robbers *w* for a man ... Hos 6:9 2442
an oven, whiles they lie in *w* ... Hos 7:6 693
and *w* on thy God continually ... Hos 12:6 6960
they all lie in *w* for blood ... Mic 7:2 693
I will *w* for the God of my ... Mic 7:7 3176
though it tarry, *w* for it ... Hab 2:3 2442
Therefore *w* ye upon me, saith the ... Zeph 3:8 2442
that a small ship should *w* on him ... Mk 3:9 *4342*
Laying *w* for him, and seeking to ... Lk 11:54 *1748*
unto men that *w* for their lord ... Lk 12:36 *4327*
but *w* for the promise of the ... Acts 1:4 *4037*
And when the Jews laid *w* for him ... Acts 20:3
me by the lying in *w* of the Jews ... Acts 20:19 *1917*
son heard of their lying in *w* ... Acts 23:16 *1747*
for there lie in *w* for him of ... Acts 23:21 *1748*
that the Jews laid *w* for the man ... Acts 23:30 *1917*
laying *w* in the way to kill him ... Acts 25:3
then do we with patience *w* for it ... Rom 8:25 *553*
let us *w* on our ministering ... Rom 12:7
they which *w* at the altar are ... 1Cor 9:13 *4332*
For we through the Spirit *w* for ... Gal 5:5 *553*
whereby they lie in *w* to deceive ... Eph 4:14 *3180*
to *w* for his Son from heaven, ... 1Th 1:10 *362*

WAITED
I have *w* for thy salvation, O ... Gen 49:18 6960
w for the king by the way, and ... 1Kin 20:38 5975
and she *w* on Naaman's wife ... 2Kin 5:2
then they *w* on their office ... 1Chr 6:32 5975
they that *w* with their children ... 1Chr 6:33 5975
Who hitherto *w* in the king's gate ... 1Chr 9:18
the priests *w* on their offices ... 2Chr 7:6 5975
These *w* on the king, beside those ... 2Chr 17:19 8334
the porters *w* at every gate ... 2Chr 35:15
priests and for the Levites that *w* ... Neh 12:44 5975
the companies of Sheba *w* for them ... Job 6:19 6960
and he is *w* for of the sword ... Job 15:22 6822
Unto me men gave ear, and *w* ... Job 29:21 3176
they *w* for me as for the rain ... Job 29:23 3176
when I *w* for light, there came ... Job 30:26 3176
Now Elihu had *w* till Job had ... Job 32:4 2442
Behold, I *w* for your words ... Job 32:11 3176
When I had *w*, (for they spake not ... Job 32:16 3176
I *w* patiently for the LORD ... Ps 40:1 6960
they *w* not for his counsel ... Ps 106:13 2442
The wicked have *w* for me to ... Ps 119:95 6960
we have *w* for him, and he will ... Is 25:9 6960
we have *w* for him, we will be ... Is 25:9 6960
O LORD, have we *w* for thee ... Is 26:8 6960
we have *w* for thee ... Is 33:2 6960
Now when she saw that she had *w* ... Eze 19:5 3176
of Maroth *w* carefully for good ... Mic 1:12 2342
w upon me knew that it was the ... Zec 11:11 8104
which also *w* for the kingdom of ... Mk 15:43 *4327*
the people *w* for Zacharias, and ... Lk 1:21 *4328*
who also himself *w* for the ... Lk 23:51 *4327*
of them that *w* on him continually ... Acts 10:7 *4342*
And Cornelius *w* for them, and had ... Acts 10:24 *4328*
Now while Paul *w* for them at ... Acts 17:16 *1551*
of God *w* in the days of Noah ... 1Pet 3:20 *1551*

WAITETH
the adulterer *w* for the twilight ... Job 24:15 8104
Our soul *w* for the LORD ... Ps 33:20 2442
Truly my soul *w* upon God ... Ps 62:1 1747
Praise *w* for thee, O God in Sion ... Ps 65:1 1747
My soul *w* for the Lord more than ... Ps 130:6
so he that *w* on his master shall ... Prov 27:18 8104
prepared for him that *w* for him ... Is 64:4 2442
Blessed is he that *w*, and cometh ... Dan 12:12 2442
nor *w* for the sons of men ... Mic 5:7 3176
expectation of the creature *w* for ... Rom 8:19 *553*
the husbandman *w* for the precious ... Jas 5:7 *1551*

WAITING

cease *w* upon the service thereof	Num 8:25	6635
w at the posts of my doors	Prov 8:34	8104
w for the consolation of Israel	Lk 2:25	*4327*
for they were all *w* for him	Lk 8:40	*4328*
w for the moving of the water	Jn 5:3	*1551*
w for the adoption, to wit, the	Rom 8:23	*553*
w for the coming of our Lord	1Cor 1:7	*553*
and into the patient *w* for Christ	2Th 3:5	

WAKE

sleep a perpetual sleep, and not *w*	Jer 51:39	6974
sleep a perpetual sleep, and not *w*	Jer 51:57	6974
w up the mighty men, let all the	Joel 3:9	5782
us, that, whether we *w* or sleep	1Th 5:10	*1127*

WAKED

w me, as a man that is wakened	Zec 4:1	5782

WAKENED

Let the heathen be *w*, and come up	Joel 3:12	5782
a man that is *w* out of his sleep	Zec 4:1	5782

WAKENETH

he *w* morning by morning	Is 50:4	5782
he *w* mine ear to hear as the	Is 50:4	5782

WAKETH

city, the watchman *w* but in vain	Ps 127:1	8245
I sleep, but my heart *w*	Song 5:2	5782

WAKING

Thou holdest mine eyes *w*	Ps 77:4	8109

WALK

w through the land in the length	Gen 13:17	1980
w before me, and be thou perfect	Gen 17:1	1980
me, The LORD, before whom I *w*	Gen 24:40	1980
my fathers Abraham and Isaac did *w*	Gen 48:15	1980
whether they will *w* in my law	Ex 16:4	3212
them the way wherein they must *w*	Ex 18:20	3212
w abroad upon his staff, then	Ex 21:19	1980
neither shall ye *w* in their	Lev 18:3	3212
mine ordinances, to *w* therein	Lev 18:4	3212
ye shall not *w* in the manners of	Lev 20:23	3212
If ye *w* in my statutes, and keep	Lev 26:3	3212
I will *w* among you, and will be	Lev 26:12	1980
if ye *w* contrary unto me, and will	Lev 26:21	3212
but will *w* contrary unto me	Lev 26:23	1980
Then will I also *w* contrary unto	Lev 26:24	1980
unto me, but *w* contrary unto me	Lev 26:27	1980
Then I will *w* contrary unto you	Lev 26:28	1980
Ye shall *w* in all the ways which	Deut 5:33	3212
to *w* in his ways, and to fear him	Deut 8:6	3212
w after other gods, and serve them	Deut 8:19	1980
to *w* in all his ways, and to love	Deut 10:12	3212
to *w* in all his ways, and to	Deut 11:22	3212
Ye shall *w* after the LORD your	Deut 13:4	3212
thy God commanded thee to *w* in	Deut 13:5	3212
thy God, and to *w* ever in his ways	Deut 19:9	3212
to *w* in his ways, and to keep his	Deut 26:17	3212
LORD thy God, and *w* in his ways	Deut 28:9	1980
though I *w* in the imagination of	Deut 29:19	3212
to *w* in his ways, and to keep his	Deut 30:16	3212
w through the land, and describe	Josh 18:8	1980
to *w* in all his ways, and to keep	Josh 22:5	3212
the way of the LORD to *w* therein	Judg 2:22	3212
sit in judgment, and *w* by the way	Judg 5:10	1980
should *w* before me for ever	1Sa 2:30	1980
he shall *w* before mine anointed	1Sa 2:35	1980
thy sons *w* not in thy ways	1Sa 8:5	1980
to *w* in his ways, to keep his	1Kin 2:3	3212
to *w* before me in truth with all	1Kin 2:4	3212
And if thou wilt *w* in my ways	1Kin 3:14	3212
as thy father David did *w*	1Kin 3:14	1980
if thou wilt *w* in my statutes, and	1Kin 6:12	3212
all my commandments to *w* in them	1Kin 6:12	3212
that *w* before thee with all their	1Kin 8:23	1980
that they *w* before me as thou	1Kin 8:25	3212
good way wherein they should *w*	1Kin 8:36	3212
to *w* in all his ways, and to keep	1Kin 8:58	3212
to *w* in his statutes, and to keep	1Kin 8:61	3212
And if thou wilt *w* before me	1Kin 9:4	3212
wilt *w* in my ways, and do that is	1Kin 11:38	1980
been a light thing for him to *w*	1Kin 16:31	3212
But Jehu took no heed to *w* in the	2Kin 10:31	3212
to *w* after the LORD, and to keep	2Kin 23:3	3212
that *w* before thee with all their	2Chr 6:14	1980
heed to their way to *w* in my law	2Chr 6:16	3212
good way, wherein they should *w*	2Chr 6:27	3212
to *w* in thy ways, so long as they	2Chr 6:31	3212
thee, if thou wilt *w* before me	2Chr 7:17	3212
to *w* after the LORD, and to keep	2Chr 34:31	3212
ought ye not to *w* in the fear of	Neh 5:9	3212
to *w* in God's law, which was	Neh 10:29	3212
The wicked *w* on every side, when	Ps 12:8	1980
though I *w* through the valley of	Ps 23:4	3212
I will *w* in mine integrity	Ps 26:11	3212
W about Zion, and go round about	Ps 48:12	5437
that I may *w* before God in the	Ps 56:13	1980
God, and refused to *w* in his law	Ps 78:10	3212
they *w* on in darkness	Ps 82:5	1980
from them that *w* uprightly	Ps 84:11	1980
I will *w* in thy truth	Ps 86:11	1980
they shall *w*, O LORD, in the	Ps 89:15	1980
my law, and *w* not in my judgments	Ps 89:30	3212
I will *w* within my house with a	Ps 101:2	1980
feet have they, but they *w* not	Ps 115:7	1980
I will *w* before the LORD in the	Ps 116:9	1980
who *w* in the law of the LORD	Ps 119:1	1980
they *w* in his ways	Ps 119:3	1980
And I will *w* at liberty	Ps 119:45	1980
Though I *w* in the midst of	Ps 138:7	3212
know the way wherein I should *w*	Ps 143:8	3212
w not thou in the way with them	Prov 1:15	3212
buckler to them that *w* uprightly	Prov 2:7	1980
to *w* in the ways of darkness	Prov 2:13	3212
That thou mayest *w* in the way of	Prov 2:20	3212
Then shalt thou *w* in thy way	Prov 3:23	3212
the living which *w* under the sun	Eccl 4:15	1980
that knoweth to *w* before the	Eccl 6:8	1980
w in the ways of thine heart, and	Eccl 11:9	1980
ways, and we will *w* in his paths	Is 2:3	3212
let us *w* in the light of the LORD	Is 2:5	3212
w with stretched forth necks and	Is 3:16	3212
not *w* in the way of this people	Is 8:11	3212
That *w* to go down into Egypt, and	Is 30:2	1980
w ye in it, when ye turn to the	Is 30:21	3212
but the redeemed shall *w* there	Is 35:9	1980
and they shall *w*, and not faint	Is 40:31	3212
and spirit to them that *w* therein	Is 42:5	1980
for they would not *w* in his ways	Is 42:24	1980
w in the light of your fire, and	Is 50:11	3212
brightness, but we *w* in darkness	Is 59:9	1980
neither shall they *w* any more	Jer 3:17	3212
shall *w* with the house of Israel	Jer 3:18	3212
w therein, and ye shall find rest	Jer 6:16	3212
they said, We will not *w* therein	Jer 6:16	3212
into the field, nor *w* by the way	Jer 6:25	3212
neither *w* after other gods to	Jer 7:6	3212
w after other gods whom ye know	Jer 7:9	1980
w ye in all the ways that I have	Jer 7:23	1980
neighbour will *w* with slanders	Jer 9:4	1980
which *w* in the imagination of	Jer 13:10	1980
w after other gods, to serve them	Jer 13:10	1980
behold, ye *w* every one after the	Jer 16:12	1980
but we will *w* after our own	Jer 18:12	1980
to *w* in paths, in a way not cast	Jer 18:15	1980
commit adultery, and *w* in lies	Jer 23:14	1980
to *w* in my law, which I have set	Jer 26:4	1980
I will cause them to *w* by the	Jer 31:9	1980
shew us the way wherein we may *w*	Jer 42:3	1980
is desolate, the foxes *w* upon it	Lam 5:18	1980
That they may *w* in my statutes	Eze 11:20	3212
W ye not in the statutes of your	Eze 20:18	3212
w in my statutes, and keep my	Eze 20:19	3212
w in the statutes of life	Eze 33:15	1980
I will cause men to *w* upon you	Eze 36:12	3212
cause you to *w* in my statutes, and	Eze 36:27	3212
they shall also *w* in my judgments	Eze 37:24	3212
before the chambers was a *w* of	Eze 42:4	4109
those that *w* in pride he is able	Dan 4:37	1981
to *w* in his laws, which he set	Dan 9:10	3212
They shall *w* after the LORD	Hos 11:10	3212
and the just shall *w* in them	Hos 14:9	3212
they shall *w* every one in his	Joel 2:8	3212
Can two *w* together, except they	Amos 3:3	3212
ways, and we will *w* in his paths	Mic 4:2	3212
For all people will *w* every one	Mic 4:5	3212
we will *w* in the name of the LORD	Mic 4:5	3212
and to *w* humbly with thy God	Mic 6:8	3212
Ahab, and ye *w* in their counsels	Mic 6:16	3212
they shall stumble in their *w*	Nah 2:5	1979
Thou didst *w* through the sea with	Hab 3:15	1869
he will make me to *w* upon mine	Hab 3:19	1869
that they shall *w* like blind men	Zeph 1:17	1980
whom the LORD hath sent to *w* to	Zec 1:10	1980
If thou wilt *w* in my ways	Zec 3:7	3212
to *w* among these that stand by	Zec 3:7	4108
sought to go that they might *w* to	Zec 6:7	1980
w to and fro through the earth	Zec 6:7	1980
and they shall *w* up and down in his	Zec 10:12	1980
or to say, Arise, and *w*	Mt 9:5	*4043*
their sight, and the lame *w*	Mt 11:5	*4043*
maimed to be whole, the lame to *w*	Mt 15:31	*4043*
Arise, and take up thy bed, and *w*	Mk 2:9	*4043*
Why *w* not thy disciples according	Mk 7:5	*4043*
or to say, Rise up and *w*	Lk 5:23	*4043*
that the blind see, the lame *w*	Lk 7:22	*4043*
the men that *w* over them are not	Lk 11:44	*4043*
Nevertheless I must *w* to day	Lk 13:33	*4198*
which desire to *w* in long robes	Lk 20:46	*4043*
ye have one to another, as ye *w*	Lk 24:17	*4043*
him, Rise, take up thy bed, and *w*	Jn 5:8	*4043*
unto me, Take up thy bed, and *w*	Jn 5:11	*4043*
unto thee, Take up thy bed, and *w*	Jn 5:12	*4043*
for he would not *w* in Jewry	Jn 7:1	*4043*
me shall not *w* in darkness	Jn 8:12	*4043*
If any man *w* in the day, he	Jn 11:9	*4043*
But if a man *w* in the night	Jn 11:10	*4043*
W while ye have the light, lest	Jn 12:35	*4043*
Christ of Nazareth rise up and *w*	Acts 3:6	*4043*
we had made this man to *w*	Acts 3:12	*4043*
nations to *w* in their own ways	Acts 14:16	*4198*
neither to *w* after the customs	Acts 21:21	*4043*
but who also *w* in the steps of	Rom 4:12	*4748*
also should *w* in newness of life	Rom 6:4	*4043*
who *w* not after the flesh, but	Rom 8:1	*4043*
who *w* not after the flesh, but	Rom 8:4	*4043*
Let us *w* honestly, as in the day	Rom 13:13	*4043*
are ye not carnal, and *w* as men	1Cor 3:3	*4043*
called every one, so let him *w*	1Cor 7:17	*4043*
(For we *w* by faith, not by sight	2Cor 5:7	*4043*
will dwell in them, and *w* in them	2Cor 6:16	*1704*
For though we *w* in the flesh	2Cor 10:3	*4043*
W in the Spirit, and ye shall not	Gal 5:16	*4043*
let us also *w* in the Spirit	Gal 5:25	*4743*
as many as *w* according to this	Gal 6:16	*4743*
ordained that we should *w* in them	Eph 2:10	*4043*
beseech you that ye *w* worthy of	Eph 4:1	*4043*
w not as other Gentiles *w*	Eph 4:17	*4043*
w in love, as Christ also hath	Eph 5:2	*4043*
w as children of light	Eph 5:8	*4043*
See then that ye *w* circumspectly	Eph 5:15	*4043*
let us *w* by the same rule, let us	Phil 3:16	*4748*
mark them which *w* so as ye have	Phil 3:17	*4043*
(For many *w*, of whom I have told	Phil 3:18	*4043*
That ye might *w* worthy of the	Col 1:10	*4043*
Jesus the Lord, so *w* ye in him	Col 2:6	*4043*
W in wisdom toward them that are	Col 4:5	*4043*
That ye would *w* worthy of God	1Th 2:12	*4043*
received of us how ye ought to *w*	1Th 4:1	*4043*
That ye may *w* honestly toward	1Th 4:12	*4043*
some which *w* among you disorderly	2Th 3:11	*4043*
But chiefly them that *w* after the	2Pet 2:10	*4198*
w in darkness, we lie, and do not	1Jn 1:6	*4043*
But if we *w* in the light, as he	1Jn 1:7	*4043*
in him ought himself also so to *w*	1Jn 2:6	*4043*
that we *w* after his commandments	2Jn 6	*4043*
the beginning, ye should *w* in it	2Jn 6	*4043*
hear that my children *w* in truth	3Jn 4	*4043*
who should *w* after their own	Jude 18	*4198*
they shall *w* with me in white	Rev 3:4	*4043*
neither can see, nor hear, nor *w*	Rev 9:20	*4043*
his garments, lest he *w* naked	Rev 16:15	*4043*
saved shall *w* in the light of it	Rev 21:24	*4043*

WALKED

Enoch *w* with God after he begat	Gen 5:22	1980
And Enoch *w* with God	Gen 5:24	1980
generations, and Noah *w* with God	Gen 6:9	1980
her maidens *w* along by the	Ex 2:5	1980
But the children of Israel *w* upon	Ex 14:29	1980
also they have *w* contrary unto me	Lev 26:40	1980
that I also have *w* contrary unto	Lev 26:41	3212
For the children of Israel *w*	Josh 5:6	1980
the way which their fathers *w* in	Judg 2:17	1980
the travellers *w* through byways	Judg 5:6	3212
w through the wilderness unto the	Judg 11:16	3212
his sons *w* not in his ways, but	1Sa 8:3	1980
I have *w* before you from my	1Sa 12:2	1980
his men *w* all that night through	2Sa 2:29	1980
but have *w* in a tent and in a	2Sa 7:6	1980
all the places wherein I have *w*	2Sa 7:7	1980
w upon the roof of the king's	2Sa 11:2	1980
according as he *w* before thee in	1Kin 3:6	1980
me as thou hast *w* before me	1Kin 8:25	1980
before me, as David thy father *w*	1Kin 9:4	1980
have not *w* in my ways, to do that	1Kin 11:33	1980
he *w* in all the sins of his	1Kin 15:3	3212
w in the way of his father, and in	1Kin 15:26	3212
w in the way of Jeroboam, and in	1Kin 15:34	3212
thou hast *w* in the way of	1Kin 16:2	3212
For he *w* in all the way of	1Kin 16:26	3212
he *w* in all the ways of Asa his	1Kin 22:43	3212
w in the way of his father, and in	1Kin 22:52	3212
and *w* in the house to and fro	2Kin 4:35	3212
he *w* in the way of the kings of	2Kin 8:18	3212
he *w* in the way of the house of	2Kin 8:27	3212
made Israel sin, but *w* therein	2Kin 13:6	1980
but he *w* therein	2Kin 13:11	1980
But he *w* in the way of the kings	2Kin 16:3	3212
w in the statutes of the heathen	2Kin 17:8	3212
but *w* in the statutes of Israel	2Kin 17:19	3212
For the children of Israel *w* in	2Kin 17:22	3212
how I have *w* before thee in truth	2Kin 20:3	1980
he *w* in all the way that his	2Kin 21:21	3212
all the way that his father *w* in	2Kin 21:21	1980
w not in the way of the LORD	2Kin 21:22	1980
w in all the way of David his	2Kin 22:2	3212
I have *w* with all Israel, spake I	1Chr 17:6	1980
thee whithersoever thou hast *w*	1Chr 17:8	
my law, as thou hast *w* before me	2Chr 6:16	3212
before me, as David thy father *w*	2Chr 7:17	1980
years they *w* in the way of David	2Chr 11:17	1980
because he *w* in the first ways of	2Chr 17:3	1980
w in his commandments, and not	2Chr 17:4	1980
he *w* in the way of Asa his father	2Chr 20:32	3212
he *w* in the way of the kings of	2Chr 21:6	3212
Because thou hast not *w* in the	2Chr 21:12	1980
But hast *w* in the way of the	2Chr 21:13	3212
He also *w* in the ways of the	2Chr 22:3	1980
He *w* also after their counsel, and	2Chr 22:5	1980
For he *w* in the ways of the kings	2Chr 28:2	3212
w in the ways of David his father	2Chr 34:2	3212
Mordecai *w* every day before the	Est 2:11	1980
by his light I *w* through darkness	Job 29:3	3212
If I have *w* with vanity, or if my	Job 31:5	1980
mine heart *w* after mine eyes, and	Job 31:7	1980
or hast thou *w* in the search of	Job 38:16	1980
for I have *w* in mine integrity	Ps 26:1	1980
and I have *w* in thy truth	Ps 26:3	1980
w unto the house of God in	Ps 55:14	1980
they *w* in their own counsels	Ps 81:12	3212
me, and Israel had *w* in my ways	Ps 81:13	1980
In the way wherein I *w* have they	Ps 142:3	1980
The people that *w* in darkness	Is 9:2	1980
as my servant Isaiah hath *w* naked	Is 20:3	1980
how I have *w* before thee in truth	Is 38:3	1980
have *w* after vanity, and are	Jer 2:5	3212
w after things that do not profit	Jer 2:8	1980
but *w* in the counsels and in the	Jer 7:24	3212
served, and after whom they have *w*	Jer 8:2	1980
my voice, neither *w* therein	Jer 9:13	1980
But have *w* after the imagination	Jer 9:14	3212
their ear, but *w* every one in the	Jer 11:8	3212
have *w* after other gods, and have	Jer 16:11	3212
thy voice, neither *w* in thy law	Jer 32:23	1980
nor *w* in my law, nor in my	Jer 44:10	1980
nor *w* in his law, nor in his	Jer 44:23	1980
statutes, they have not *w* in them	Eze 5:6	1980
have not *w* in my statutes	Eze 5:7	1980
for ye have not *w* in my statutes	Eze 11:12	1980
hast thou not *w* after their ways	Eze 16:47	1980
Hath *w* in my statutes, and hath	Eze 18:9	1980
judgments, hath *w* in my statutes	Eze 18:17	1980
they *w* not in my statutes, and	Eze 20:13	1980
w not in my statutes, but	Eze 20:16	1980
they *w* not in my statutes	Eze 20:21	1980
Thou hast *w* in the way of thy	Eze 23:31	1980
thou hast *w* up and down in the	Eze 28:14	1980
At the end of twelve months he *w*	Dan 4:29	1981
because he willingly *w* after the	Hos 5:11	1980
the which their fathers have *w*	Amos 2:4	1980
the lion, even the old lion, *w*	Nah 2:11	1980

W

trees, and said, We have w to ... Zec 1:11 1980
So they w to and fro through the ... Zec 6:7 1980
he w with me in peace and equity, ... Mal 2:6 1980
that we have w mournfully before ... Mal 3:14 1980
he w on the water, to go to Jesus ... Mt 14:29 *4043*
Now as he w by the sea of Galilee ... Mk 1:16 *4043*
the damsel arose, and w ... Mk 5:42 *4043*
form unto two of them, as they w ... Mk 16:12 *4043*
And looking upon Jesus as he w ... Jn 1:36 *4043*
whole, and took up his bed, and w ... Jn 5:9 *4043*
went back, and w no more with him ... Jn 6:66 *4043*
these things Jesus w in Galilee ... Jn 7:1 *4043*
And Jesus w in the temple in ... Jn 10:23 *4043*
Jesus therefore w no more openly ... Jn 11:54 *4043*
And he leaping up stood, and w ... Acts 3:8 *4043*
mother's womb, who never had w ... Acts 14:8 *4043*
And he leaped and w ... Acts 14:10 *4043*
as if we w according to the flesh ... 2Cor 10:2 *4043*
w we not in the same spirit ... 2Cor 12:18 *4043*
w we not in the same steps ... 2Cor 12:18 *4043*
But when I saw that they w not ... Gal 2:14 *3716*
Wherein in time past ye w ... Eph 2:2 *4043*
In the which ye also w some time ... Col 3:7 *4043*
when we w in lasciviousness, ... 1Pet 4:3 *4198*
also so to walk, even as he w ... 1Jn 2:6 *4043*

WALKEDST

and w whither thou wouldest ... Jn 21:18 *4043*

WALKEST

when thou w by the way, and when ... Deut 6:7 3212
when thou w by the way, when thou .. Deut 11:19 3212
w abroad any whither, that thou ... 1Kin 2:42 1980
when thou w through the fire, ... Is 43:2 3212
that thou thyself also w orderly ... Acts 21:24 *4748*
now w thou not charitably ... Rom 14:15 *4043*
thee, even as thou w in the truth ... 3Jn 3 *4043*

WALKETH

What man is this that w in the ... Gen 24:65 1980
For the LORD thy God w in the ... Deut 23:14 1980
behold, the king w before you ... 1Sa 12:2 1980
own feet, and he w upon a snare ... Job 18:8 1980
he w in the circuit of heaven ... Job 22:14 1980
of iniquity, and w with wicked men ... Job 34:8 3212
Blessed is the man that w not in ... Ps 1:1 1980
He that w uprightly, and worketh ... Ps 15:2 1980
Surely every man w in a vain shew ... Ps 39:6 1980
their tongue w through the earth ... Ps 73:9 1980
the pestilence that w in darkness ... Ps 91:6 1980
he that w in a perfect way, he ... Ps 101:6 1980
who w upon the wings of the wind ... Ps 104:3 1980
that w in his ways ... Ps 128:1 1980
man, w with a froward mouth ... Prov 6:12 1980
that w uprightly w surely ... Prov 10:9 3212
He that w with wise men shall be ... Prov 13:20 1980
He that w in his uprightness ... Prov 14:2 1980
man of understanding w uprightly ... Prov 15:21 1980
the poor that w in his integrity ... Prov 19:1 1980
The just man w in his integrity ... Prov 20:7 1980
poor that w in his uprightness ... Prov 28:6 1980
Whoso w uprightly shall be saved ... Prov 28:18 1980
but whoso w wisely, he shall be ... Prov 28:26 1980
but the fool w in darkness ... Eccl 2:14 1980
he that is a fool w by the way ... Eccl 10:3 1980
He that w righteously, and ... Is 33:15 1980
that w in darkness, and hath no ... Is 50:10 1980
which w in a way that was not ... Is 65:2 1980
in man that w to direct his steps ... Jer 10:23 1980
w after the imagination of his ... Jer 23:17 1980
heart w after the heart of their ... Eze 11:21 1980
do good to him that w uprightly ... Mic 2:7 1980
he w through dry places, seeking ... Mt 12:43 *1330*
he w through dry places, seeking ... Lk 11:24 *1330*
for he that w in darkness knoweth ... Jn 12:35 *4043*
every brother that w disorderly ... 2Th 3:6 *4043*
w about, seeking whom he may ... 1Pet 5:8 *4043*
w in darkness, and knoweth not ... 1Jn 2:11 *4043*
who w in the midst of the seven ... Rev 2:1 *4043*

WALKING

w in the garden in the cool of ... Gen 3:8 1980
he knoweth thy w through this ... Deut 2:7 3212
w in the statutes of David his ... 1Kin 3:3 3212
in w in the way of Jeroboam, and ... 1Kin 16:19 3212
and fro in the earth, and from w up ... Job 1:7 1980
and fro in the earth, and from w up ... Job 2:2 1980
or the moon w in brightness ... Job 31:26 1980
princes w as servants upon the ... Eccl 10:7 1980
forth necks and wanton eyes, w ... Is 3:16 1980
And he did so, w naked and barefoot ... Is 20:2 1980
each one w in his uprightness ... Is 57:2 1980
revolters, w with slanders ... Jer 6:28 1980
w in the midst of the fire, and ... Dan 3:25 1981
If a man w in the spirit and ... Mic 2:11 1980
w by the sea of Galilee, saw two ... Mt 4:18 *4043*
went unto them, w on the sea ... Mt 14:25 *4043*
disciples saw him w on the sea ... Mt 14:26 *4043*
w upon the sea, and would have ... Mk 6:48 *4043*
when they saw him w upon the sea ... Mk 6:49 *4043*
and said, I see men as trees, w ... Mk 8:24 *4043*
as he was w in the temple, there ... Mk 11:27 *4043*
w in all the commandments and ... Lk 1:6 *4198*
they see Jesus w on the sea ... Jn 6:19 *4043*
with them into the temple, w ... Acts 3:8 *4043*
And all the people saw him w ... Acts 3:9 *4043*
w in the fear of the Lord, and in ... Acts 9:31 *4198*
not w in craftiness, nor handling ... 2Cor 4:2 *4043*
w after their own lusts, ... 2Pet 3:3 *4198*
found of thy children w in truth ... 2Jn 4 *4043*
w after their own lusts ... Jude 16 *4198*

WALL

selfwill they digged down a w ... Gen 49:6 7794
whose branches run over the w ... Gen 49:22 7791
the waters were a w unto them on ... Ex 14:22 2346
the waters were a w unto them on ... Ex 14:29 2346
in sight are lower than the w ... Lev 14:37 7023
no w round about them shall be ... Lev 25:31 2346
a w being on this side, and a w ... Num 22:24 1447
she thrust herself unto the w ... Num 22:25 7023
Balaam's foot against the w ... Num 22:25 7023
reach from the w of the city ... Num 35:4 7023
for her house was upon the town w ... Josh 2:15 2346
and she dwelt upon the w ... Josh 2:15 2346
the w of the city shall fall down ... Josh 6:5 2346
that the w fell down flat, so ... Josh 6:20 2346
smite David even to the w with it ... 1Sa 18:11 7023
even to the w with the javelin ... 1Sa 19:10 7023
he smote the javelin into the w ... 1Sa 19:10 7023
times, even upon a seat by the w ... 1Sa 20:25 7023
They were a w unto us both by ... 1Sa 25:16 2346
any that pisseth against the w ... 1Sa 25:22 7023
any that pisseth against the w ... 1Sa 25:34 2346
his body to the w of Beth-shan ... 1Sa 31:10 7023
his sons from the w of Beth-shan ... 1Sa 31:12 2346
that they would shoot from the w ... 2Sa 11:20 2346
a millstone upon him from the w ... 2Sa 11:21 2346
why went ye nigh the w ... 2Sa 11:21 2346
from off the w upon thy servants ... 2Sa 11:24 2346
the roof over the gate unto the w ... 2Sa 18:24 2346
were with Joab battered the w ... 2Sa 20:15 2346
be thrown to thee over the w ... 2Sa 20:21 2346
by my God have I leaped over a w ... 2Sa 22:30 7791
the w of Jerusalem round about ... 1Kin 3:1 2346
that springeth out of the w ... 1Kin 4:33 7023
against the w of the house he ... 1Kin 6:5 7023
for without in the w of the house ... 1Kin 6:6
wing of the one touched the one w ... 1Kin 6:27 7023
other cherub touched the other w ... 1Kin 6:27 7023
posts were a fifth part of the w ... 1Kin 6:31
tree, a fourth part of the w ... 1Kin 6:33
the w of Jerusalem, and Hazor, and ... 1Kin 9:15 2346
him that pisseth against the w ... 1Kin 14:10 7023
not one that pisseth against a w ... 1Kin 16:11 7023
there a w fell upon twenty and ... 1Kin 20:30 2346
him that pisseth against the w ... 1Kin 21:21 7023
eat Jezebel by the w of Jezreel ... 1Kin 21:23 2426
for a burnt offering upon the w ... 2Kin 3:27 2346
chamber, I pray thee, on the w ... 2Kin 4:10 7023
Israel was passing by upon the w ... 2Kin 6:26 2346
and he passed by upon the w ... 2Kin 6:30 2346
him that pisseth against the w ... 2Kin 9:8 7023
her blood was sprinkled on the w ... 2Kin 9:33 7023
brake down the w of Jerusalem ... 2Kin 14:13 2346
of the people that are on the w ... 2Kin 18:26 2346
me to the men which sit on the w ... 2Kin 18:27 2346
Then he turned his face to the w ... 2Kin 20:2 7023
reaching to the w of the house ... 2Chr 3:11 7023
reaching to the w of the house ... 2Chr 3:12 7023
brake down the w of Jerusalem ... 2Chr 25:23 2346
and brake down the w of Gath ... 2Chr 26:6 2346
the w of Jabneh, and the ... 2Chr 26:6 2346
the w of Ashdod, and built cities ... 2Chr 26:6 2346
gate, and at the turning of the w ... 2Chr 26:9
on the w of Ophel he built much ... 2Chr 27:3 2346
up all the w that was broken ... 2Chr 32:5 2346
the towers, and another w without ... 2Chr 32:5 2346
of Jerusalem that were on the w ... 2Chr 32:18 2346
a w without the city of David ... 2Chr 33:14 2346
and brake down the w of Jerusalem ... 2Chr 36:19 2346
this house, and to make up this w ... Ezr 5:3 846
and to give us a w in Judah ... Ezr 9:9 1447
the w of Jerusalem also is broken ... Neh 1:3 2346
for the w of the city, and for the ... Neh 2:8 2346
by the brook, and viewed the w ... Neh 2:15 2346
us build up the w of Jerusalem ... Neh 2:17 2346
Jerusalem unto the broad w ... Neh 3:8 2346
on the w unto the dung gate ... Neh 3:13 2346
the w of the pool of Siloah by ... Neh 3:15 2346
armoury at the turning of the w ... Neh 3:19
from the turning of the w unto ... Neh 3:20
Azariah unto the turning of the w ... Neh 3:24
over against the turning of the w ... Neh 3:25
out, even unto the w of Ophel ... Neh 3:27 2346
heard that we builded the w ... Neh 4:1 2346
even break down their stone w ... Neh 4:3 2346
So built we the w ... Neh 4:6 2346
all the w was joined together ... Neh 4:6 2346
we are not able to build the w ... Neh 4:10 2346
in the lower places behind the w ... Neh 4:13 2346
we returned all of us to the w ... Neh 4:15 2346
They which builded on the w ... Neh 4:17 2346
and we are separated upon the w ... Neh 4:19 2346
I continued in the work of this w ... Neh 5:16 2346
heard that I had builded the w ... Neh 6:1 2346
which cause thou buildest the w ... Neh 6:6 2346
So the w was finished in the ... Neh 6:15 2346
when the w was built, and I had ... Neh 7:1 2346
at the dedication of the w of ... Neh 12:27 2346
people, and the gates, and the w ... Neh 12:30 2346
the princes of Judah upon the w ... Neh 12:31 2346
upon the w toward the dung gate ... Neh 12:31 2346
David, at the going up of the w ... Neh 12:37 2346
the half of the people upon the w ... Neh 12:38 2346
furnaces even unto the broad w ... Neh 12:38 2346
them, Why lodge ye about the w ... Neh 13:21 2346
by my God have I leaped over a w ... Ps 18:29 7791
as a bowing w shall ye be ... Ps 62:3 7023
as an high w in his own conceit ... Prov 18:11 2346
the stone w thereof was broken ... Prov 24:31 1444
behold, he standeth behind our w ... Song 2:9 3796
If she be a w, we will build upon ... Song 8:9 2346
I am a w, and my breasts like ... Song 8:10 2346
tower, and upon every fenced w ... Is 2:15 2346
and break down the w thereof ... Is 5:5 1447
ye broken down to fortify the w ... Is 22:10 2346
ones is as a storm against the w ... Is 25:4 7023
to fall, swelling out in a high w ... Is 30:13 2346
of the people that are on the w ... Is 36:11 2346
me to the men that sit upon the w ... Is 36:12 2346
turned his face toward the w ... Is 38:2 7023
We grope for the w like the blind ... Is 59:10 7023
this people a fenced brasen w ... Jer 15:20 2346
a fire in the w of Damascus ... Jer 49:27 2346
the w of Babylon shall fall ... Jer 51:44 2346
the w of the daughter of Zion ... Lam 2:8 2346
the rampart and the w to lament ... Lam 2:8 2346
O w of the daughter of Zion, let ... Lam 2:18 2346
set it for a w of iron between ... Eze 4:3 7023
I looked, behold a hole in the w ... Eze 8:7 7023
me, Son of man, dig now in the w ... Eze 8:8 7023
and when I had digged in the w ... Eze 8:8 7023
pourtrayed upon the w round about ... Eze 8:10 7023
thou through the w in their sight ... Eze 12:5 7023
through the w with mine hand ... Eze 12:7 7023
the w to carry out thereby ... Eze 12:12 7023
and one built up a w, and, lo, ... Eze 13:10 2434
when the w is fallen, shall it ... Eze 13:12 7023
the w that ye have daubed with ... Eze 13:14 7023
I accomplish my wrath upon the w ... Eze 13:15 7023
The w is no more, neither they ... Eze 13:15 7023
she saw men pourtrayed upon the w ... Eze 23:14 7023
every w shall fall to the ground ... Eze 38:20 2346
behold a w on the outside of the ... Eze 40:5 2346
he measured the w of the house ... Eze 41:5 7023
they entered into the w which was ... Eze 41:6 7023
not hold in the w of the house ... Eze 41:6 7023
The thickness of the w, which was ... Eze 41:9 7023
the w of the building was five ... Eze 41:12 7023
by all the w round about within ... Eze 41:17 7023
made, and on the w of the temple ... Eze 41:20 7023
the w that was without over ... Eze 42:7 1447
w of the court toward the east ... Eze 42:10 1444
before the w toward the east ... Eze 42:12 1448
it had a w round about, five ... Eze 42:20 2346
the w between me and them, they ... Eze 43:8 7023
of the w of the king's palace ... Dan 5:5 3797
shall be built again, and the w ... Dan 9:25 2742
thy way with thorns, and make a w ... Hos 2:6 1447
shall climb the w like men of war ... Joel 2:7 2346
they shall run upon the w ... Joel 2:9 2346
will send a fire on the w of Gaza ... Amos 1:7 2346
send a fire on the w of Tyrus ... Amos 1:10 2346
kindle a fire in the w of Rabbah ... Amos 1:14 2346
and leaned his hand on the w ... Amos 5:19 7023
upon a w made by a plumbline ... Amos 7:7 2346
shall make haste to the w thereof ... Nah 2:5 2346
sea, and her w was from the sea ... Nah 3:8 2346
the stone shall cry out of the w ... Hab 2:11 7023
will be unto her a w of fire ... Zec 2:5 2346
let him down by the w in a basket ... Acts 9:25 *5038*
shall smite thee, thou whited w ... Acts 23:3 *5109*
a basket was I let down by the w ... 2Cor 11:33 *5038*
middle w of partition between us ... Eph 2:14
And had a w great and high, and had .. Rev 21:12 *5038*
the w of the city had twelve ... Rev 21:14 *5038*
gates thereof, and the w thereof ... Rev 21:15 *5038*
And he measured the w thereof ... Rev 21:17 *5038*
of the w of it was of jasper ... Rev 21:18 *5038*
the foundations of the w of the ... Rev 21:19 *5038*

WALLED

sell a dwelling house in a w city ... Lev 25:29 2346
w city shall be established for ... Lev 25:30 2346
in the land, and the cities are w ... Num 13:28 1219
are great and w up to heaven ... Deut 1:28 1219

WALLOW

sackcloth, and w thyself in ashes ... Jer 6:26 6428
w yourselves in the ashes, ye ... Jer 25:34 6428
Moab also shall w in his vomit ... Jer 48:26 5606
they shall w themselves in the ... Eze 27:30 6428

WALLOWED

Amasa w in blood in the midst of ... 2Sa 20:12 1556
fell on the ground, and w foaming ... Mk 9:20 *2947*

WALLOWING

was washed to her w in the mire ... 2Pet 2:22 *2946*

WALLS

if the plague be in the w of the ... Lev 14:37 7023
be spread in the w of the house ... Lev 14:39 7023
cities were fenced with high w ... Deut 3:5 2346
fenced w come down, wherein thou ... Deut 28:52 2346
threescore great cities with w ... 1Kin 4:13 2346
against the w of the house round ... 1Kin 6:5 7023
be fastened in the w of the house ... 1Kin 6:6 7023
he built the w of the house ... 1Kin 6:15 7023
house, and the w of the cieling ... 1Kin 6:15 7023
the w with boards of cedar ... 1Kin 6:16 7023
he carved all the w of the house ... 1Kin 6:29 7023
the way of the gate between two w ... 2Kin 25:4 2346
brake down the w of Jerusalem ... 2Kin 25:10 2346
to overlay the w of the houses ... 1Chr 29:4 7023
the w thereof, and the doors ... 2Chr 3:7 7023
and graved cherubims on the w ... 2Chr 3:7 7023
the nether, fenced cities, with w ... 2Chr 8:5 2346
cities, and make about them w ... 2Chr 14:7 2346
and have set up the w thereof ... Ezr 4:12 7791
the w set up again, then will ... Ezr 4:13 7791
the w thereof set up, by this ... Ezr 4:16 7791
and timber is laid in the w ... Ezr 5:8 3797
this house, and to make up these w ... Ezr 5:9 846
viewed the w of Jerusalem, which ... Neh 2:13 2346
heard that the w of Jerusalem ... Neh 4:7 2346
Which make oil within their w ... Job 24:11 7791
build thou the w of Jerusalem ... Ps 51:18 2346
go about it upon the w thereof ... Ps 55:10 2346
Peace be within thy w, and ... Ps 122:7 2426
that is broken down, and without w ... Prov 25:28 2346
the keepers of the w took away my ... Song 5:7 2346
of vision, breaking down the w ... Is 22:5 7023
also a ditch between the two w ... Is 22:11 2346
fort of thy w shall he bring down ... Is 25:12 2346

salvation will God appoint for *w* Is 26:1 2346
thy *w* are continually before me Is 49:16 2346
mine house and within my *w* a place Is 56:5 2346
of strangers shall build up thy *w* Is 60:10 2346
thou shalt call thy *w* Salvation Is 60:18 2346
I have set watchmen upon thy *w* Is 62:6 2346
against all the *w* thereof round Jer 1:15 2346
brasen *w* against the whole land, Jer 1:18 2346
Go ye up upon her *w*, and destroy Jer 5:10 8284
which besiege you without the *w* Jer 21:4 2346
by the gate betwixt the two *w* Jer 39:4 2346
and brake down the *w* of Jerusalem Jer 39:8 2346
are fallen, her *w* are thrown down Jer 50:15 2346
standard upon the *w* of Babylon Jer 51:12 2346
The broad *w* of Babylon shall be Jer 51:58 2346
way of the gate between the two *w* Jer 52:7 2346
brake down all the *w* of Jerusalem Jer 52:14 2346
of the enemy the *w* of her palaces Lam 2:7 2346
they shall destroy the *w* of Tyrus Eze 26:4 2346
set engines of war against thy *w* Eze 26:9 2346
thy *w* shall shake at the noise of Eze 26:10 2346
and they shall break down thy *w* Eze 26:12 2346
army were upon thy *w* round about Eze 27:11 2346
shields upon thy *w* round about Eze 27:11 2346
are talking against thee by the *w* Eze 33:30 7023
all of them dwelling without *w* Eze 38:11 2346
the building, with the *w* thereof Eze 41:13 7023
the *w* thereof, were of wood Eze 41:22 7023
like as were made upon the *w* Eze 41:25 7023
day that thy *w* are to be built Mic 7:11 1447
w for the multitude of men Zec 2:4
By faith the *w* of Jericho fell Heb 11:30 *5038*

WANDER
when God caused me to *w* from my Gen 20:13 8582
your children shall *w* in the Num 14:33 7462
he made them *w* in the wilderness Num 32:13 5128
the blind to *w* out of the way Deut 27:18 7686
causeth them to *w* in a wilderness Job 12:24 8582
unto God, they *w* for lack of meat Job 38:41 8582
Lo, then would I *w* far off Ps 55:7 5074
Let them *w* up and down for meat, Ps 59:15 5128
and causeth them to *w* in the Ps 107:40 8582
O let me not *w* from thy Ps 119:10 7686
they shall *w* every one to his Is 47:15 8582
people, Thus have they loved to *w* Jer 14:10 5128
that shall cause him to *w* Jer 48:12 6808
they shall *w* from sea to sea, and Amos 8:12 5128

WANDERED
w in the wilderness of Beer-sheba Gen 21:14 8582
of Israel *w* in the wilderness Josh 14:10 1980
They *w* in the wilderness in a Ps 107:4 8582
they *w* through the wilderness Is 16:8 8582
They have *w* as blind men in the Lam 4:14 5128
when they fled away and *w*, they Lam 4:15 5128
My sheep *w* through all the Eze 34:6 7686
or three cities *w* unto one city Amos 4:8 5128
they *w* about in sheepskins and Heb 11:37 *4022*
they *w* in deserts, and in Heb 11:38 *4105*

WANDERERS
LORD, that I will send unto him *w* Jer 48:12 6808
they shall be *w* among the nations Hos 9:17 5074

WANDEREST
and under every green tree thou *w* Jer 2:20 6808

WANDERETH
He *w* abroad for bread, saying, Job 15:23 5074
The man that *w* out of the way of Prov 21:16 8582
As a bird that *w* from her nest Prov 27:8 5074
so is a man that *w* from his place Prov 27:8 5074
bewray not him that *w* Is 16:3 5074
none shall gather up him that *w* Jer 49:5 5074

WANDERING
and, behold, he was *w* in the field Gen 37:15 8582
As the bird by *w*, as the swallow Prov 26:2 5110
the eyes than the *w* of the desire Eccl 6:9 1981
as a *w* bird cast out of the nest, Is 16:2 5074
w about from house to house 1Ti 5:13 *4022*
w stars, to whom is reserved the Jude 13 *4107*

WANDERINGS
Thou tellest my *w* Ps 56:8 5112

WANT
nakedness, and in *w* of all things Deut 28:48 2640
for she shall eat them for *w* of Deut 28:57 2640
a place where there is no *w* of Judg 18:10 4270
there is no *w* of any thing Judg 19:19 4270
the rock for *w* of a shelter Job 24:8 1097
For *w* and famine they were Job 30:3 2639
seen any perish for *w* of clothing Job 31:19 1097
I shall not *w* Ps 23:1 2637
for there is no *w* to them that Ps 34:9 4270
LORD shall not *w* any good thing Ps 34:10 2637
and thy *w* as an armed man Prov 6:11 4270
but fools die for *w* of wisdom Prov 10:21 2638
is destroyed for *w* of judgment Prov 13:23 3808
the belly of the wicked shall *w* Prov 13:25 2637
but in the *w* of people is the Prov 14:28 657
every one that is hasty only to *w* Prov 21:5 4270
the rich, shall surely come to *w* Prov 22:16 4270
and thy *w* as an armed man Prov 24:34 4270
shall fail, none shall *w* her mate Is 34:16 6485
David shall never *w* a man to sit Jer 33:17 3772
shall the priests the Levites *w* a Jer 33:18 3772
the son of Rechab shall not *w* a Jer 35:19 3772
stricken through for *w* of the Lam 4:9
That they may *w* bread and water, Eze 4:17 2637
w of bread in all your places Amos 4:6 2640
but she of her *w* did cast in all Mk 12:44 *5304*
and he began to be in *w* Lk 15:14 *5302*
may be a supply for their *w* 2Cor 8:14 *5303*
also may be a supply for your *w* 2Cor 8:14 *5303*
supplieth the *w* of the saints 2Cor 9:12 *5303*
Not that I speak in respect of *w* Phil 4:11 *5304*

WANTED
we have *w* all things, and have Jer 44:18 2637
And when they *w* wine, the mother Jn 2:3 *5302*
when I was present with you, and *w* 2Cor 11:9 *5302*

WANTETH
for his need, in that which he *w* Deut 15:8 2637
as for him that *w* understanding Prov 9:4 2638
as for him that *w* understanding Prov 9:16 2638
of words there *w* not sin Prov 10:19 2308
The prince that *w* understanding Prov 28:16 2638
so that he *w* nothing for his soul Eccl 6:2 2638
round goblet, which *w* not liquor Song 7:2 2637

WANTING
let none be *w* 2Kin 10:19 6485
whosoever shall be *w*, he shall 2Kin 10:19 6485
with words, yet they are *w* to him Prov 19:7 3808
that which is *w* cannot be Eccl 1:15 2642
in the balances, and art found *w* Dan 5:27 2627
in order the things that are *w* Titus 1:5 *3007*
that nothing be *w* unto them Titus 3:13 *3007*
be perfect and entire, *w* nothing Jas 1:4 *3007*

WANTON
w eyes, walking and mincing as Is 3:16 8265
begun to wax *w* against Christ 1Ti 5:11 *2691*
pleasure on the earth, and been *w* Jas 5:5 *4684*

WANTONNESS
not in chambering and *w*, not in Rom 13:13 *766*
of the flesh, through much *w* 2Pet 2:18 *766*

WANTS
let all thy *w* lie upon me Judg 19:20 4270
and he that ministered to my *w* Phil 2:25 *5532*

WAR
That these made *w* with Bera king Gen 14:2 4421
when there falleth out any *w* Ex 1:10 4421
the people repent when they see *w* Ex 13:17 4421
The LORD is a man of *w* Ex 15:3 4421
sworn that the LORD will have *w* Ex 17:16 4421
There is a noise of *w* in the camp Ex 32:17 4421
able to go forth to *w* in Israel Num 1:3 6635
that were able to go forth to *w* Num 1:20 6635
that were able to go forth to *w* Num 1:22 6635
that were able to go forth to *w* Num 1:24 6635
that were able to go forth to *w* Num 1:26 6635
that were able to go forth to *w* Num 1:28 6635
that were able to go forth to *w* Num 1:30 6635
that were able to go forth to *w* Num 1:32 6635
that were able to go forth to *w* Num 1:34 6635
that were able to go forth to *w* Num 1:36 6635
that were able to go forth to *w* Num 1:38 6635
that were able to go forth to *w* Num 1:40 6635
that were able to go forth to *w* Num 1:42 6635
able to go forth to *w* in Israel Num 1:45 6635
if ye go to *w* in your land Num 10:9 4421
are able to go to *w* in Israel Num 26:2 6635
Arm some of yourselves unto the *w* Num 31:3 6635
of Israel, shall ye send to the *w* Num 31:4 6635
twelve thousand armed for *w* Num 31:5 6635
And Moses sent them to the *w* Num 31:6 6635
of Eleazar the priest, to the *w* Num 31:6 6635
men of *w* which went to the battle Num 31:21 6635
them that took the *w* upon them Num 31:27 4421
men of *w* which went out to battle Num 31:28 4421
which the men of *w* had caught Num 31:32 6635
of them that went out to *w* Num 31:36 6635
of *w* which are under our charge Num 31:49 4421
(For the men of *w* had taken spoil Num 31:53 6635
Shall your brethren go to *w* Num 32:6 4421
go armed before the LORD to *w* Num 32:20 4421
pass over, every man armed for *w* Num 32:27 6635
on every man his weapons of *w* Deut 1:41 4421
the generation of the men of *w* Deut 2:14 4421
all the men of *w* were consumed Deut 2:16 4421
all that are meet for the *w* Deut 3:18 2438
by signs, and by wonders, and by *w* Deut 4:34 4421
but will make *w* against thee Deut 20:12 4421
in making *w* against it to take it Deut 20:19 3898
the city that maketh *w* with thee Deut 20:20 4421
forth to *w* against thine enemies Deut 21:10 4421
wife, he shall not go out to *w* Deut 24:5 6635
for *w* passed over before the LORD Josh 4:13 6635
were males, even all the men of *w* Josh 5:4 4421
all the people that were men of *w* Josh 5:6 4421
compass the city, all ye men of *w* Josh 6:3 4421
all the people of *w* with thee Josh 8:1 4421
arose, and all the people of *w* Josh 8:3 4421
people of *w* that were with him Josh 8:11 4421
Gibeon, and made *w* against it Josh 10:5 3898
and all the people of *w* with him Josh 10:7 4421
the men of *w* which went with him Josh 10:24 4421
and all the people of *w* with him Josh 11:7 4421
Joshua made *w* a long time with Josh 11:18 4421
And the land rested from *w* Josh 11:23 4421
even so is my strength now, for *w* Josh 14:11 4421
And the land had rest from *w* Josh 14:15 4421
because he was a man of *w* Josh 17:1 4421
to go up to *w* against them Josh 22:12 6635
might know, to teach them *w* Judg 3:2 4421
judged Israel, and went out to *w* Judg 3:10 4421
then was *w* in the gates Judg 5:8 3901
of Ammon made *w* against Israel Judg 11:4 3898
of Ammon made *w* against Israel Judg 11:5 3898
doest me wrong to *w* against me Judg 11:27 3898
men appointed with weapons of *w* Judg 18:11 4421
appointed with their weapons of *w* Judg 18:16 4421
were appointed with weapons of *w* Judg 18:17 4421
all these were men of *w* Judg 20:17 4421
not to each man his wife in the *w* Judg 21:22 4421
and to make his instruments of *w* 1Sa 8:12 4421
there was sore *w* against the 1Sa 14:52 4421
mighty valiant man, and a man of *w* 1Sa 16:18 4421
he a man of *w* from his youth 1Sa 17:33 4421
and Saul set him over the men of *w* 1Sa 18:5 4421
And there was *w* again 1Sa 19:8 4421
all the people together to *w* 1Sa 23:8 4421
the Philistines make *w* against me 1Sa 28:15 3898
and the weapons of *w* perished 2Sa 1:27 4421
Now there was long *w* between the 2Sa 3:1 4421
while there was *w* between the 2Sa 3:6 4421
did, and how the *w* prospered 2Sa 11:7 4421
all the things concerning the *w* 2Sa 11:18 4421
matters of the *w* unto the king 2Sa 11:19 4421
and thy father is a man of *w* 2Sa 17:8 4421
had yet *w* again with Israel 2Sa 21:15 4421
He teacheth my hands to *w* 2Sa 22:35 4421
and shed the blood of *w* in peace 1Kin 2:5 4421
put the blood of *w* upon his 1Kin 2:5 4421
but they were men of *w*, and his 1Kin 9:22 4421
there was *w* between Rehoboam and 1Kin 14:30 4421
there was *w* between Rehoboam and 1Kin 15:6 4421
there was *w* between Abijam and 1Kin 15:7 4421
there was *w* between Asa and Baasha 1Kin 15:16 4421
there was *w* between Asa and Baasha 1Kin 15:32 4421
or whether they be come out for *w* 1Kin 20:18 4421
years without *w* between Syria 1Kin 22:1 4421
Joram the son of Ahab to the *w* 2Kin 8:28 4421
hand of Jehoahaz his father by *w* 2Kin 13:25 4421
ten thousand, and took Selah by *w* 2Kin 14:7 4421
Israel came up to Jerusalem to *w* 2Kin 16:5 4421
counsel and strength for the *w* 2Kin 18:20 4421
all that were strong and apt for *w* 2Kin 24:16 4421
all the men of *w* fled by night by 2Kin 25:4 4421
that was set over the men of *w* 2Kin 25:19 4421
they made *w* with the Hagarites 1Chr 5:10 4421
shoot with bow, and skilful in *w* 1Chr 5:18 4421
that went out to the *w* 1Chr 5:18 6635
they made *w* with the Hagarites, 1Chr 5:19 4421
slain, because the *w* was of God 1Chr 5:22 4421
were bands of soldiers for *w* 1Chr 7:4 4421
soldiers, fit to go out for *w* 1Chr 7:11 6635
of them that were apt to the *w* 1Chr 7:40 6635
the mighty men, helpers of the *w* 1Chr 12:1 4421
men of *w* fit for the battle, that 1Chr 12:8 6635
that were ready armed to the *w* 1Chr 12:23 6635
hundred, ready armed to the *w* 1Chr 12:24 6635
mighty men of valour for the *w* 1Chr 12:25 6635
went forth to battle, expert in *w* 1Chr 12:33 4421
with all instruments of *w* 1Chr 12:33 4421
of the Danites expert in *w* twenty 1Chr 12:35 4421
went forth to battle, expert in *w* 1Chr 12:36 4421
instruments of *w* for the battle 1Chr 12:37 6635
All these men of *w*, that could 1Chr 12:38 4421
(for Hadarezer had *w* with Tou 1Chr 18:10 4421
that there arose *w* at Gezer with 1Chr 20:4 4421
there was *w* again with the 1Chr 20:5 4421
And yet again there was *w* at Gath 1Chr 20:6 4421
because thou hast been a man of *w* 1Chr 28:3 4421
If thy people go out to *w* against 2Chr 6:34 4421
but they were men of *w*, and chief 2Chr 8:9 4421
there was *w* between Abijah and 2Chr 13:2 4421
with an army of valiant men of *w* 2Chr 13:3 4421
he had no *w* in those years 2Chr 14:6 4421
there was no more *w* unto the five 2Chr 15:19 4421
made no *w* against Jehoshaphat 2Chr 17:10 3898
and the men of *w*, mighty men of 2Chr 17:13 4421
thousand ready prepared for the *w* 2Chr 17:18 6635
and we will be with thee in the *w* 2Chr 18:3 4421
son of Ahab king of Israel to *w* 2Chr 22:5 4421
choice men, able to go forth to *w* 2Chr 25:5 6635
men, that went out to *w* by bands 2Chr 26:11 6635
that made *w* with mighty power, to 2Chr 26:13 4421
against them that came from the *w* 2Chr 28:12 6635
set captains of *w* over the people 2Chr 32:6 4421
put captains of *w* in all the 2Chr 33:14 2428
the house wherewith I have *w* 2Chr 35:21 4421
in *w* from the power of the sword Job 5:20 4421
changes and *w* are against me Job 10:17 6635
against the day of battle and *w* Job 38:23 4421
He teacheth my hands to *w* Ps 18:34 4421
though *w* should rise against me, Ps 27:3 4421
butter, but *w* was in his heart Ps 55:21 7128
thou the people that delight in *w* Ps 68:30 7128
but when I speak, they are for *w* Ps 120:7 4421
are they gathered together for *w* Ps 140:2 4421
which teacheth my hands to *w* Ps 144:1
and with good advice make *w* Prov 20:18 4421
counsel thou shalt make thy *w* Prov 24:6 4421
a time of *w*, and a time of peace Eccl 3:8 4421
there is no discharge in that *w* Eccl 8:8 4421
is better than weapons of *w* Eccl 9:18 7128
hold swords, being expert in *w* Song 3:8 4421
shall they learn *w* any more Is 2:4 4421
The mighty man, and the man of *w* Is 3:2 4421
the sword, and thy mighty in the *w* Is 3:25 4421
toward Jerusalem to *w* against it Is 7:1 4421
and from the grievousness of *w* Is 21:15 4421
I have counsel and strength for *w* Is 36:5 4421
is come forth to make *w* with thee Is 37:9 3898
they that *w* against thee shall be Is 41:12 4421
stir up jealousy like a man of *w* Is 42:13 4421
of the trumpet, the alarm of *w* Jer 4:19 4421
Prepare ye *w* against her Jer 6:4 4421
array as men for *w* against thee Jer 6:23 4421
of Babylon maketh *w* against us Jer 21:2 3898
of *w* that are in your hands Jer 21:4 4421
and against great kingdoms, of *w* Jer 28:8 4421
the hands of the men of *w* that Jer 38:4 4421
saw them, and all the men of *w* Jer 39:4 4421
were found there, and the men of *w* Jer 41:3 4421
of Ahikam, even mighty men of *w* Jer 41:16 4421
of Egypt, where we shall see no *w* Jer 42:14 4421
mighty and strong men for the *w* Jer 48:14 4421
of *w* to be heard in Rabbah of the Jer 49:2 4421
all the men of *w* shall be cut off Jer 49:26 4421

all her men of *w* shall be cut off Jer 50:30 4421
art my battle ax and weapons of *w* Jer 51:20 4421
the men of *w* are affrighted Jer 51:32 4421
up, and all the men of *w* fled Jer 52:7 4421
had the charge of the men of *w* Jer 52:25 4421
company make for him in the *w* Eze 17:17 4421
engines of *w* against thy walls Eze 26:9 6904
were in thine army, thy men of *w* Eze 27:10 4421
merchandise, and all thy men of *w* Eze 27:27 4421
to hell with their weapons of *w* Eze 32:27 4421
mighty men, and with all men of *w* Eze 39:20 4421
same horn made *w* with the saints Dan 7:21 7129
unto the end of the *w* desolations Dan 9:26 4421
climb the wall like men of *w* Joel 2:7 4421
Prepare *w*, wake up the mighty men Joel 3:9 4421
let all the men of *w* draw near Joel 3:9 4421
by securely as men averse from *w* Mic 2:8 4421
they even prepare *w* against him Mic 3:5 4421
shall they learn *w* any more Mic 4:3 4421
going to make *w* against another Lk 14:31 4171
his men of *w* set him at nought Lk 23:11 4753
we do not *w* after the flesh 2Cor 10:3 4754
by them mightest *w* a good warfare 1Ti 1:18 4754
your lusts that *w* in your members Jas 4:1 4754
ye fight and *w*, yet ye have not, Jas 4:2 4170
lusts, which *w* against the soul 1Pet 2:11 4754
pit shall make *w* against them Rev 11:7 4171
And there was *w* in heaven Rev 12:7 4171
went to make *w* with the remnant Rev 12:17 4171
who is able to make *w* with him Rev 13:4 4170
him to make *w* with the saints Rev 13:7 4171
These shall make *w* with the Lamb Rev 17:14 4170
he doth judge and make *w* Rev 19:11 4170
gathered together to make *w* Rev 19:19 4171

WARD
he put them in *w* in the house of Gen 40:3 4929
and they continued a season in *w* Gen 40:4 4929
him in the *w* of his lord's house Gen 40:7 4929
put me in *w* in the captain of the Gen 41:10 4929
all together into *w* three days Gen 42:17 4929
And they put him in *w*, that the Lev 24:12 4929
And they put him in *w*, because it Num 15:34 4929
keep the house, and put them in *w* 2Sa 20:3 4931
kept the *w* of the house of Saul 1Chr 12:29 4931
And they cast lots, *w* against 1Chr 25:8 4931
against *w*, as well 1Chr 25:8 4929
of the going up, *w* against *w* 1Chr 26:16 4929
man of God, *w* over against *w* Neh 12:24 4929
were porters keeping the *w* at the Neh 12:25 4929
porters kept the *w* of their God Neh 12:45 4931
the *w* of the purification, Neh 12:45 4931
and I am set in my *w* whole nights Is 21:8 4931
a captain of the *w* was there Jer 37:13 6488
And they put him in *w* in chains Eze 19:9 5474
past the first and the second *w* Acts 12:10 5438

WARDROBE
son of Harhas, keeper of the *w* 2Kin 22:14 899
son of Hasrah, keeper of the *w* 2Chr 34:22 899

WARDS
the house of the tabernacle, by *w* 1Chr 9:23 4931
having *w* one against another, to 1Chr 26:12 4931
appointed the *w* of the priests and Neh 13:30 4931

WARE
w or any victuals on the sabbath Neh 10:31 4728
brought fish, and all manner of *w* Neh 13:16 4377
sellers of all kind of *w* lodged Neh 13:20 4465
w no clothes, neither abode in Lk 8:27 1737
They were *w* of it, and fled unto Acts 14:6 4894
Of whom be thou *w* also 2Ti 4:15 5442

WARES
Gather up thy *w* out of the land, Jer 10:17 3666
multitude of the *w* of thy making Eze 27:16 4639
multitude of the *w* of thy making Eze 27:18 4639
When thy *w* went forth out of the Eze 27:33 5801
cast forth the *w* that were in the Jonah 1:5 3627

WARFARE
their armies together for *w* 1Sa 28:1 6635
that her *w* is accomplished, that Is 40:2 6635
Who goeth a *w* any time at his own 1Cor 9:7 4754
weapons of our *w* are not carnal 2Cor 10:4 4752
by them mightest war a good *w* 1Ti 1:18 4752

WARM
and the flesh of the child waxed *w* 2Kin 4:34 2552
What time they wax *w*, they vanish Job 6:17 2215
How thy garments are *w*, when he Job 37:17 2525
but how can one be *w* alone Eccl 4:11 3179
will take thereof, and *w* himself Is 44:15 2552
himself, and saith, Aha, I am *w* Is 44:16 2552
there shall not be a coal to *w* at Is 47:14 2552
clothe you, but there is none *w* Hag 1:6 2527

WARMED
if he were not *w* with the fleece Job 31:20 2552
and *w* himself at the fire Mk 14:54 2328
and they *w* themselves Jn 18:18 2328
stood with them, and *w* himself Jn 18:18 2328
And Simon Peter stood and *w* himself. Jn 18:25 2328
them, Depart in peace, be ye *w* Jas 2:16 2328

WARMETH
the earth, and *w* them in the dust, Job 39:14 2552
he *w* himself, and saith, Aha, I am Is 44:16 2552

WARMING
And when she saw Peter *w* himself Mk 14:67 2328

WARN
ye shall even *w* them that they 2Chr 19:10 2094
nor speakest to *w* the wicked from Eze 3:18 2094
Yet if thou *w* the wicked, and he Eze 3:19 2094
if thou *w* the righteous man Eze 3:21 2094
blow the trumpet, and *w* the people Eze 33:3 2094
at my mouth, and *w* them from me Eze 33:7 2094
to *w* the wicked from his way Eze 33:8 2094
if thou *w* the wicked of his way Eze 33:9 2094
I ceased not to *w* every one night Acts 20:31 3560
but as my beloved sons I *w* you 1Cor 4:14 3560
w them that are unruly, comfort 1Th 5:14 3560

WARNED
w him of, and saved himself there, 2Kin 6:10 2094
Moreover by them is thy servant *w* Ps 19:11 2094
surely live, because he is *w* Eze 3:21 2094
trumpet, and the people be not *w* Eze 33:6 2094
being *w* of God in a dream that Mt 2:12 5537
being *w* of God in a dream, he Mt 2:22 5537
who hath *w* you to flee from the Mt 3:7 5263
who hath *w* you to flee from the Lk 3:7 5263
was *w* from God by an holy angel Acts 10:22 5537
being *w* of God of things not seen Heb 11:7 5537

WARNING
To whom shall I speak, and give *w* Jer 6:10 5749
my mouth, and give them *w* from me Eze 3:17 2094
and thou givest him not *w*, nor Eze 3:18 2094
because thou hast not given him *w* Eze 3:20 2094
of the trumpet, and taketh not *w* Eze 33:4 2094
of the trumpet, and took not *w* Eze 33:5 2094
But he that taketh *w* shall Eze 33:5 2094
w every man, and teaching every Col 1:28 3560

WARP
Whether it be in the *w*, or woof Lev 13:48 8359
or in the skin, either in the *w* Lev 13:49 8359
in the garment, either in the *w* Lev 13:51 8359
that garment, whether *w* or woof Lev 13:52 8359
in the garment, either in the *w* Lev 13:53 8359
out of the skin, or out of the *w* Lev 13:56 8359
in the garment, either in the *w* Lev 13:57 8359
And the garment, either *w*, or woof Lev 13:58 8359
woollen or linen, either in the *w* Lev 13:59 8359

WARRED
they *w* against the Midianites, as Num 31:7 6633
Moses divided from the men that *w* Num 31:42 6633
w against Israel, and sent and Josh 24:9 3898
of the acts of Jeroboam, how he *w* 1Kin 14:19 3898
besieged Samaria, and *w* against it 1Kin 20:1 3898
might that he shewed, and how he *w* 1Kin 22:45 3898
king of Syria *w* against Israel 2Kin 6:8 3898
he did, and his might, how he *w* 2Kin 14:28 3898
w against the Philistines, and 2Chr 26:6 3898

WARRETH
No man that *w* entangleth himself 2Ti 2:4 4754

WARRING
king of Assyria *w* against Libnah 2Kin 19:8 3898
king of Assyria *w* against Libnah Is 37:8 3898
w against the law of my mind, and Rom 7:23 497

WARRIOR
of the *w* is with confused noise Is 9:5 5431

WARRIORS
thousand chosen men, which were *w* 1Kin 12:21
thousand chosen men, which were *w* 2Chr 11:1

WARS
in the book of the *w* of the LORD Num 21:14 4421
had not known all the *w* of Canaan Judg 3:1 4421
for Hadadezer had *w* with Toi 2Sa 8:10 4421
of the LORD his God for the *w* 1Kin 5:3 4421
abundantly, and hast made great *w* 1Chr 22:8 4421
there were *w* between Rehoboam and. 2Chr 12:15 4421
from henceforth thou shalt have *w* 2Chr 16:9 4421
the acts of Jotham, and all his *w* 2Chr 27:7 4421
He maketh *w* to cease unto the end Ps 46:9 4421
hear of *w* and rumours of *w* Mt 24:6 4171
hear of *w* and rumours of *w* Mk 13:7 4171
But when ye shall hear of *w* Lk 21:9 4171
From whence come *w* and fightings Jas 4:1 4171

WAS See PREFACE.

WASH
w your feet, and rest yourselves Gen 18:4 7364
w your feet, and ye shall rise up Gen 19:2 7364
camels, and water to *w* his feet Gen 24:32 7364
down to *w* herself at the river Ex 2:5 7364
let them *w* their clothes, Ex 19:10 3526
and shalt *w* them with water Ex 29:4 7364
w the inwards of him, and his legs Ex 29:17 7364
foot also of brass, to *w* withal Ex 30:18 7364
and his sons shall *w* their hands Ex 30:19 7364
they shall *w* with water, that Ex 30:20 7364
So they shall *w* their hands Ex 30:21 7364
and *w* them with water Ex 40:12 7364
and put water there, to *w* withal Ex 40:30 7364
and his legs shall he *w* in water Lev 1:9 7364
But he shall *w* the inwards Lev 1:13 7364
thou shalt *w* that whereon it was Lev 6:27 3526
he did *w* the inwards and the legs, Lev 9:14 7364
of them shall *w* his clothes Lev 11:25 3526
of them shall *w* his clothes Lev 11:28 3526
carcase of it shall *w* his clothes Lev 11:40 3526
carcase of it shall *w* his clothes Lev 11:40 3526
he shall *w* his clothes, and be Lev 13:6 3526
he shall *w* his clothes, and be Lev 13:34 3526
priest shall command that they *w* Lev 13:54 3526
of skin it be, which thou shalt *w* Lev 13:58 3526
be cleansed shall *w* his clothes Lev 14:8 3526
w himself in water, that he may Lev 14:8 7364
he shall *w* his clothes, also he Lev 14:9 3526
also he shall *w* his flesh in Lev 14:9 7364
in the house shall *w* his clothes Lev 14:47 3526
in the house shall *w* his clothes Lev 14:47 3526
his bed shall *w* his clothes Lev 15:5 3526
the issue shall *w* his clothes Lev 15:6 3526
the issue shall *w* his clothes Lev 15:7 3526
then he shall *w* his clothes Lev 15:8 3526
those things shall *w* his clothes Lev 15:10 3526
he shall *w* his clothes, and bathe Lev 15:11 3526
w his clothes, and bathe his flesh Lev 15:13 3526
then he shall *w* all his flesh in Lev 15:16 7364
her bed shall *w* his clothes Lev 15:21 3526
she sat upon shall *w* his clothes Lev 15:22 3526
shall *w* his clothes, and bathe Lev 15:27 3526
shall he *w* his flesh in water Lev 16:4 7364
he shall *w* his flesh with water Lev 16:24 7364
the scapegoat shall *w* his clothes Lev 16:26 3526
burneth them shall *w* his clothes Lev 16:28 3526
he shall both *w* his clothes Lev 17:15 3526
But if he *w* them not, nor bathe Lev 17:16 3526
unless he *w* his flesh with water Lev 22:6 7364
let them *w* their clothes, and so Num 8:7 3526
the priest shall *w* his clothes Num 19:7 3526
her shall *w* his clothes in water Num 19:8 3526
of the heifer shall *w* his clothes Num 19:10 3526
w his clothes, and bathe himself Num 19:19 3526
of separation shall *w* his clothes Num 19:21 3526
ye shall *w* your clothes on the Num 31:24 3526
shall *w* their hands over the Deut 21:6 7364
he shall *w* himself with water Deut 23:11 7364
W thyself therefore, and anoint Ruth 3:3 7364
w the feet of the servants of my 1Sa 25:41 7364
down to thy house, and *w* thy feet 2Sa 11:8 7364
w in Jordan seven times, and thy 2Kin 5:10 7364
may I not *w* in them, and be clean 2Kin 5:12 7364
then, when he saith to thee, *W* 2Kin 5:13 7364
and five on the left, to *w* in them 2Chr 4:6 7364
sea was for the priests to *w* in 2Chr 4:6 7364
If I *w* myself with snow water, and Job 9:30 7364
I will *w* mine hands in innocency Ps 26:6 7364
W me throughly from mine iniquity Ps 51:2 3526
w me, and I shall be whiter than Ps 51:7 3526
he shall *w* his feet in the blood Ps 58:10 7364
W you, make you clean Is 1:16 7364
For though thou *w* thee with nitre Jer 2:22 3526
w thine heart from wickedness, Jer 4:14 3526
for whom thou didst *w* thyself Eze 23:40 7364
anoint thine head, and *w* thy face Mt 6:17 3538
for they *w* not their hands when Mt 15:2 3538
except they *w* their hands oft, Mk 7:3 3538
from the market, except they *w* Mk 7:4 907
began to *w* his feet with tears, Lk 7:38 1026
w in the pool of Siloam, (which Jn 9:7 3538
Go to the pool of Siloam, and *w* Jn 9:11 3538
began to *w* the disciples' feet, Jn 13:5 3538
him, Lord, dost thou *w* my feet Jn 13:6 3538
him, Thou shalt never *w* my feet Jn 13:8 3538
If I *w* thee not, thou hast no Jn 13:8 3538
needeth not save to *w* his feet Jn 13:10 3538
ye also ought to *w* one another's Jn 13:14 3538
w away thy sins, calling on the Acts 22:16 628

WASHED
them water, and they *w* their feet Gen 43:24 7364
he *w* his face, and went out, and Gen 43:31 7364
he *w* his garments in wine, and his Gen 49:11 3526
and they *w* their clothes Ex 19:14 3526
his sons *w* their hands and their Ex 40:31 7364
came near unto the altar, they *w* Ex 40:32 7364
and his sons, and *w* them with water Lev 8:6 7364
he *w* the inwards and the legs in Lev 8:21 7364
on the plague, after that it is *w* Lev 13:55 3526
it shall be *w* the second time Lev 13:58 3526
shall be *w* with water, and be Lev 15:17 3526
purified, and they *w* their clothes Num 8:21 3526
they *w* their feet, and did eat and Judg 19:21 7364
David arose from the earth, and *w* 2Sa 12:20 7364
nor *w* his clothes, from the day 2Sa 19:24 3526
one *w* the chariot in the pool of 1Kin 22:38 7857
and they *w* his armour 1Kin 22:38 7364
the burnt offering they *w* in them 2Chr 4:6 1740
When I *w* my steps with butter, and Job 29:6 7364
vain, and *w* my hands in innocency Ps 73:13 7364
eyes, and yet is not *w* from their Prov 30:12 7364
I have *w* my feet Song 5:3 7364
w with milk, and fitly set Song 5:12 7364
When the Lord shall have *w* away Is 4:4 7364
neither wast thou *w* in water to Eze 16:4 7364
Then *w* I thee with water Eze 16:9 7364
I throughly *w* away thy blood from Eze 16:9 7857
where they *w* the burnt offering Eze 40:38 1740
w his hands before the multitude, Mt 27:24 633
but she hath *w* my feet with tears Lk 7:44 1026
he had not first *w* before dinner Lk 11:38 907
He went his way therefore, and *w* Jn 9:7 3538
and I went and *w*, and I received Jn 9:11 3538
put clay upon mine eyes, and I *w* Jn 9:15 3538
He that is *w* needeth not save to Jn 13:10 3068
So after he had *w* their feet Jn 13:12 3538
Lord and Master, have *w* your feet Jn 13:14 3538
whom when they had *w*, they laid Acts 9:37 3068
of the night, and *w* their stripes Acts 16:33 3068
but ye are *w*, but ye are 1Cor 6:11 628
if she have *w* the saints' feet, 1Ti 5:10 3538
our bodies *w* with pure water Heb 10:22 3068
the sow that was *w* to her 2Pet 2:22 3068
w us from our sins in his own Rev 1:5 3068
have *w* their robes, and made them Rev 7:14 4150

WASHEST
thou *w* away the things which grow Job 14:19 7857

WASHING
somewhat dark after the *w* of it Lev 13:56 3526
the roof he saw a woman *w* herself 2Sa 11:2 7364
that every one put them off for *w* Neh 4:23 4325
shorn, which came up from the *w* Song 4:2 7367
of sheep which go up from the *w* Song 6:6 7367
as the *w* of cups, and pots, brasen Mk 7:4 909
of men, as the *w* of pots and cups Mk 7:8 909
out of them, and were *w* their nets Lk 5:2 637
cleanse it with the *w* of water by Eph 5:26 3067

by the w of regeneration, and ... Titus 3:5 *3067*

WASHINGS
in meats and drinks, and divers w ... Heb 9:10 *909*

WASHPOT
Moab is my w ... Ps 60:8
Moab is my w ... Ps 108:9

WAST
Who told thee that thou w naked ... Gen 3:11
for out of it w thou taken ... Gen 3:19
of God, and thou w pleased with me ... Gen 33:10
manner when thou w his butler ... Gen 40:13 1961
remember that thou w a servant in ... Deut 5:15 1961
thou shalt remember that thou w a ... Deut 15:15 1961
that thou w a bondman in Egypt ... Deut 16:12 1961
because thou w a stranger in his ... Deut 23:7 1961
that thou w a bondman in Egypt ... Deut 24:18 1961
thou shalt remember that thou w a ... Deut 24:22 1961
behind thee, when thou w faint ... Deut 25:18
of Egypt, which thou w afraid of ... Deut 28:60
with whose maidens thou w ... Ruth 3:2
When thou w little in thine own ... 1Sa 15:17
w thou not made the head of the ... 1Sa 15:17
How w thou not afraid to stretch ... 2Sa 1:14
thou w slain in thine high places ... 2Sa 1:25
thou w he that leddest out and ... 2Sa 5:2 1961
thou w he that leddest out and ... 1Chr 11:2
or w thou made before the hills ... Job 15:7
Where w thou when I laid the ... Job 38:4 1961
thou it, because thou w then born ... Job 38:21
thou w a God that forgavest them, ... Ps 99:8 1961
Jordan, that thou w driven back ... Ps 114:5
though thou w angry with me, ... Is 12:1
wherein thou w made to serve ... Is 14:3
spoilest, and thou w not spoiled ... Is 33:1
Since thou w precious in my sight ... Is 43:4
w called a transgressor from the ... Is 48:8
of youth, when thou w refused ... Is 54:6
therefore thou w not grieved ... Is 57:10
as thou w ashamed of Assyria ... Jer 2:36
O Babylon, and thou w not aware ... Jer 50:24
in the day thou w born thy navel ... Eze 16:4
neither w thou washed in water to ... Eze 16:4
thou w not salted at all, nor ... Eze 16:4
but thou w cast out in the open ... Eze 16:5
in the day that thou w born ... Eze 16:5
thee when thou w in thy blood ... Eze 16:6
thee when thou w in thy blood ... Eze 16:6
is grown, whereas thou w naked ... Eze 16:7
Thus w thou decked with gold and ... Eze 16:13
thou w exceeding beautiful, and ... Eze 16:13
of thy youth, when thou w naked ... Eze 16:22 1961
bare, and w polluted in thy blood ... Eze 16:22 1961
because thou w unsatiable ... Eze 16:28
yet thou w not satisfied herewith ... Eze 16:29
thou w corrupted more than they ... Eze 16:47
in the place where thou w created ... Eze 21:30
thou w not purged, thou shalt not ... Eze 24:13
that w inhabited of seafaring men ... Eze 26:17
which w strong in the sea, she and ... Eze 26:17
thou w replenished, and made very ... Eze 27:25
in the day that thou w created ... Eze 28:13
thou w upon the holy mountain of ... Eze 28:14 1961
Thou w perfect in thy ways from ... Eze 28:15
from the day that thou w created ... Eze 28:15
even thou w as one of them ... Obad 11
Thou also w with Jesus of Galilee ... Mt 26:69 *2258*
thou also w with Jesus of ... Mk 14:67 *2258*
when thou w under the fig tree, I ... Jn 1:48 *5607*
Thou w altogether born in sins, ... Jn 9:34
say unto thee, When thou w young ... Jn 21:18 *2258*
for thou w slain, and hast ... Rev 5:9
God Almighty, which art, and w ... Rev 11:17 *2258*
O Lord, which art, and w, and ... Rev 16:5 *2258*

WASTE
And I will make your cities w ... Lev 26:31 2723
be desolate, and your cities w ... Lev 26:33 2723
have laid them w even unto Nophah ... Num 21:30 8074
in the w howling wilderness ... Deut 32:10 8414
The barrel of meal shall not w ... 1Kin 17:14 3615
lay w fenced cities into ruinous ... 2Kin 19:25 7582
of wickedness w them any more ... 1Chr 17:9 1086
my fathers' sepulchres, lieth w ... Neh 2:3 2720
we are in, how Jerusalem lieth w ... Neh 2:17 2720
in former time desolate and w ... Job 30:3 4875
satisfy the desolate and w ground ... Job 38:27 4875
laid w his dwelling place ... Ps 79:7 8074
boar out of the wood doth w it ... Ps 80:13 3765
And I will lay it w ... Is 5:6 1326
the w places of the fat ones ... Is 5:17 2723
in the night Ar of Moab is laid w ... Is 15:1 7703
the night Kir of Moab is laid w ... Is 15:1 7703
for it is laid w, so that there ... Is 23:1 7703
for your strength is laid w ... Is 23:14 7703
the earth empty, and maketh it w ... Is 24:1 1110
The highways lie w, the wayfaring ... Is 33:8 8074
to generation it shall lie w ... Is 34:10 2717
have laid w all the nations ... Is 37:18 2717
w defenced cities into ruinous ... Is 37:26 7582
I will make w mountains and hills, ... Is 42:15 2717
they that made thee w shall go ... Is 49:17 2717
For thy w and thy desolate places, ... Is 49:19 2723
he will comfort all her w places ... Is 51:3 2723
ye w places of Jerusalem ... Is 52:9 2723
thee shall build the old w places ... Is 58:12 2723
and they shall repair the w cities ... Is 61:4 2721
our pleasant things are laid w ... Is 64:11 2723
yelled, and they made his land w ... Jer 2:15 8047
and thy cities shall be laid w ... Jer 4:7 5327
should this city be laid w ... Jer 27:17 2723
for Noph shall be w and desolate ... Jer 46:19 8047
a desolation, a reproach, a w ... Jer 49:13 2721
w and utterly destroy after them, ... Jer 50:21 2717
Moreover I will make thee w ... Eze 5:14 2723
the cities shall be laid w ... Eze 6:6 2717
that your altars may be laid w ... Eze 6:6 2717
are inhabited shall be laid w ... Eze 12:20 2717
and he laid w their cities ... Eze 19:7 2717
be replenished, now she is laid w ... Eze 26:2 2717
of Egypt shall be desolate and w ... Eze 29:9 2723
make the land of Egypt utterly w ... Eze 29:10 2723
w shall be desolate forty years ... Eze 29:12 2717
and I will make the land w ... Eze 30:12 8074
I will lay thy cities w, and thou ... Eze 35:4 2723
and the w and desolate and ruined ... Eze 36:35 2720
so shall the w cities be filled ... Eze 36:38 2720
Israel, which have been always w ... Eze 38:8 2723
He hath laid my vine w, and barked ... Joel 1:7 8047
of Israel shall be laid w ... Amos 7:9 2717
and they shall build the w cities ... Amos 9:14 8074
they shall w the land of Assyria ... Mic 5:6 7489
She is empty, and void, and w ... Nah 2:10 1110
thee, and say, Nineveh is laid w ... Nah 3:7 7703
I made their streets w, that none ... Zeph 3:6 2717
houses, and this house lie w ... Hag 1:4 2720
Because of mine house that is w ... Hag 1:9 2720
his heritage w for the dragons of ... Mal 1:3 8077
saying, To what purpose is this w ... Mt 26:8 *684*
Why was this w of the ointment ... Mk 14:4 *684*

WASTED
carcases be w in the wilderness ... Num 14:33 8552
the Kenite shall be w, until ... Num 24:22 1197
of the men of war were w out from ... Deut 2:14 8552
And the barrel of meal w not ... 1Kin 17:16 3615
w the country of the children of ... 1Chr 20:1 7843
they that w us required of us ... Ps 137:3 8437
cities be w without inhabitant ... Is 6:11 7582
the sea, and the river shall be w ... Is 19:5 2717
those nations shall be utterly w ... Is 60:12 2717
and they are w and desolate, as at ... Jer 44:6 2723
midst of the cities that are w ... Eze 30:7 2717
The field is w, the land mourneth ... Joel 1:10 7703
for the corn is w ... Joel 1:10 7703
there w his substance with ... Lk 15:13 *1287*
unto him that he had w his goods ... Lk 16:1 *1287*
the church of God, and w it ... Gal 1:13 *4199*

WASTENESS
trouble and distress, a day of w ... Zeph 1:15 7722

WASTER
brother to him that is a great w ... Prov 18:9 7843
I have created the w to destroy ... Is 54:16 7843

WASTES
And they shall build the old w ... Is 61:4 2723
thereof shall be perpetual w ... Jer 49:13 2723
they that inhabit those w of the ... Eze 33:24 2723
in the w shall fall by the sword ... Eze 33:27 2723
to the valleys, to the desolate w ... Eze 36:4 2723
and the w shall be builded ... Eze 36:10 2723
cities, and the w shall be builded ... Eze 36:33 2723

WASTETH
But man dieth, and w away ... Job 14:10 2522
the destruction that w at noonday ... Ps 91:6 7736
He that w his father, and chaseth ... Prov 19:26 7703

WASTING
w and destruction are in their ... Is 59:7 7701
w nor destruction within thy ... Is 60:18 7701

WATCH
The LORD w between me and thee, ... Gen 31:49 6822
that in the morning w the LORD ... Ex 14:24 821
in the beginning of the middle w ... Judg 7:19 821
and they had but newly set the w ... Judg 7:19 8104
of the host in the morning w ... 1Sa 11:11 821
to w him, and to slay him in the ... 1Sa 19:11 8104
kept the w lifted up his eyes ... 2Sa 13:34 6822
of the w of the king's house ... 2Kin 11:5 4931
shall ye keep the w of the house ... 2Kin 11:6 4931
even they shall keep the w of the ... 2Kin 11:7 4931
the w tower in the wilderness ... 2Chr 20:24 4707
shall keep the w of the LORD ... 2Chr 23:6 4931
W ye, and keep them, until ye ... Ezr 8:29 8245
set a w against them day and night ... Neh 4:9 4929
of Jerusalem, every one in his w ... Neh 7:3 4929
that thou settest a w over me ... Job 7:12 4929
dost thou not w over my sin ... Job 14:16 8104
is past, and as a w in the night ... Ps 90:4 821
I w, and am as a sparrow alone ... Ps 102:7 8245
than they that w for the morning ... Ps 130:6 8104
than they that w for the morning ... Ps 130:6 8104
Set a w, O LORD, before my mouth ... Ps 141:3 8108
w in the watchtower, eat, drink ... Is 21:5 6822
all that w for iniquity are cut ... Is 29:20 8245
a leopard shall w over their ... Jer 5:6 8245
so will I w over them, to build, ... Jer 31:28 8245
I will w over them for evil, and ... Jer 44:27 8245
of Babylon, make the w strong ... Jer 51:12 4929
w the way, make thy loins strong, ... Nah 2:1 6822
I will stand upon my w, and set me ... Hab 2:1 4931
will w to see what he will say ... Hab 2:1 6822
in the fourth w of the night ... Mt 14:25 *5438*
W therefore ... Mt 24:42 *1127*
in what w the thief would come ... Mt 24:43 *5438*
W therefore, for ye know neither ... Mt 25:13 *1127*
tarry ye here, and w with me ... Mt 26:38 *1127*
could ye not w with me one hour ... Mt 26:40 *1127*
W and pray, that ye enter not into ... Mt 26:41 *1127*
said unto them, Ye have a w ... Mt 27:65 *2892*
sealing the stone, and setting a w ... Mt 27:66 *2892*
some of the w came into the city, ... Mt 28:11 *2892*
about the fourth w of the night ... Mk 6:48 *5438*
Take ye heed, w and pray ... Mk 13:33 *69*
and commanded the porter to w ... Mk 13:34 *1127*
W ye therefore ... Mk 13:35 *1127*
I say unto you I say unto all, W ... Mk 13:37 *1127*
tarry ye here, and w ... Mk 14:34 *1127*
couldest not thou w one hour ... Mk 14:37 *1127*
W ye and pray, lest ye enter into ... Mk 14:38 *1127*
keeping w over their flock by ... Lk 2:8 *5438*
if he shall come in the second w ... Lk 12:38 *5438*
or come in the third w ... Lk 12:38 *5438*
W ye therefore, and pray always, ... Lk 21:36 *69*
Therefore w, and remember, that by ... Acts 20:31 *1127*
W ye, stand fast in the faith, ... 1Cor 16:13 *1127*
w in the same with thanksgiving ... Col 4:2 *1127*
but let us w and be sober ... 1Th 5:6 *1127*
But w thou in all things, endure ... 2Ti 4:5 *3525*
for they w for your souls, as ... Heb 13:17 *69*
therefore sober, and w unto prayer ... 1Pet 4:7 *3525*
If therefore thou shalt not w ... Rev 3:3 *1127*

WATCHED
they w the house to kill him ... Ps 59:t 8104
All my familiars w for my halting ... Jer 20:10 8104
that like as I have w over them ... Jer 31:28 8245
in our watching we have w for a ... Lam 4:17 6822
hath the LORD w upon the evil ... Dan 9:14 8245
thief would come, he would have w ... Mt 24:43 *1127*
And sitting down they w him there ... Mt 27:36 *5083*
And they w him, whether he would ... Mk 3:2 *3906*
And the scribes and Pharisees w him ... Lk 6:7 *3906*
thief would come, he would have w ... Lk 12:39 *1127*
the sabbath day, that they w him ... Lk 14:1 *3906*
And they w him, and sent forth ... Lk 20:20 *3906*
they w the gates day and night to ... Acts 9:24 *3906*

WATCHER
head upon my bed, and, behold, a w ... Dan 4:13 5894
And whereas the king saw a w ... Dan 4:23 5894

WATCHERS
that w come from a far country, ... Jer 4:16 5341
matter is by the decree of the w ... Dan 4:17 5894

WATCHES
appoint w of the inhabitants of ... Neh 7:3 4931
were over against them in the w ... Neh 12:9 4931
meditate on thee in the night w ... Ps 63:6 821
Mine eyes prevent the night w ... Ps 119:148 821
in the beginning of the w pour ... Lam 2:19 821

WATCHETH
The wicked w the righteous, and ... Ps 37:32 6822
it w for thee ... Eze 7:6 6974
Blessed is he that w, and keepeth ... Rev 16:15 *1127*

WATCHFUL
Be w, and strengthen the things ... Rev 3:2 *1127*

WATCHING
sat upon a seat by the wayside w ... 1Sa 4:13 6822
w daily at my gates, waiting at ... Prov 8:34 8245
in our w we have watched for a ... Lam 4:17 6822
w Jesus, saw the earthquake, and ... Mt 27:54 *5083*
lord when he cometh shall find w ... Lk 12:37 *1127*
w thereunto with all perseverance ... Eph 6:18 *69*

WATCHINGS
in tumults, in labours, in w ... 2Cor 6:5 *70*
in w often, in hunger and thirst, ... 2Cor 11:27 *70*

WATCHMAN
the w went up to the roof over ... 2Sa 18:24 6822
the w cried, and told the king ... 2Sa 18:25 6822
the w saw another man running ... 2Sa 18:26 6822
the w called unto the porter, and ... 2Sa 18:26 6822
the w said, Me thinketh the ... 2Sa 18:27 6822
there stood a w on the tower in ... 2Kin 9:17 6822
the w told, saying, The messenger ... 2Kin 9:18 6822
the w told, saying, He came even ... 2Kin 9:20 6822
city, the w waketh but in vain ... Ps 127:1 8104
Lord said unto me, Go, set a w ... Is 21:6 6822
He calleth to me out of Seir, W ... Is 21:11 8104
W, what of the night ... Is 21:11 8104
The w said, The morning cometh, ... Is 21:12 8104
I have made thee a w unto the ... Eze 3:17 6822
coasts, and set him for their w ... Eze 33:2 6822
But if the w see the sword come, ... Eze 33:6 6822
I have set thee a w unto the ... Eze 33:7 6822
The w of Ephraim was with my God ... Hos 9:8 6822

WATCHMAN'S
will I require at the w hand ... Eze 33:6 6822

WATCHMEN
the w of Saul in Gibeah of ... 1Sa 14:16 6822
tower of the w to the fenced city ... 2Kin 17:9 5341
tower of the w to the fenced city ... 2Kin 18:8 5341
The w that go about the city ... Song 3:3 8104
The w that went about the city ... Song 5:7 8104
Thy w shall lift up the voice ... Is 52:8 6822
His w are blind ... Is 56:10 6822
I have set w upon thy walls, O ... Is 62:6 8104
Also I set w over you, saying, ... Jer 6:17 6822
that the w upon the mount Ephraim ... Jer 31:6 5341
the watch strong, set up the w ... Jer 51:12 8104
the day of thy w and thy ... Mic 7:4 6822

WATCHTOWER
Prepare the table, watch in the w ... Is 21:5 6844
upon the w in the daytime ... Is 21:8 4707

WATER
went out of Eden to w the garden ... Gen 2:10 8248
a fountain of w in the wilderness ... Gen 16:7 4325
Let a little w, I pray you, be ... Gen 18:4 4325
and took bread, and a bottle of w ... Gen 21:14 4325
the w was spent in the bottle, and ... Gen 21:15 4325
her eyes, and she saw a well of w ... Gen 21:19 4325
went, and filled the bottle with w ... Gen 21:19 4325
Abimelech because of a well of w ... Gen 21:25 4325
of w at the time of the evening ... Gen 24:11 4325
time that women go out to draw w ... Gen 24:11
I stand here by the well of w ... Gen 24:13 4325
of the city come out to draw w ... Gen 24:13 4325

W

drink a little *w* of thy pitcher	Gen 24:17	4325
I will draw *w* for thy camels also	Gen 24:19	4325
ran again unto the well to draw *w*	Gen 24:20	4325
w to wash his feet, and the men's	Gen 24:32	4325
Behold, I stand by the well of *w*	Gen 24:43	4325
the virgin cometh forth to draw *w*	Gen 24:43	
a little *w* of thy pitcher to	Gen 24:43	4325
down unto the well, and drew *w*	Gen 24:45	4325
Isaac digged again the wells of *w*	Gen 26:18	4325
found there a well of springing *w*	Gen 26:19	4325
herdmen, saying, The *w* is ours	Gen 26:20	4325
and said unto him, We have found *w*	Gen 26:32	4325
w ye the sheep, and go and feed	Gen 29:7	8248
then we *w* the sheep	Gen 29:8	8248
was empty, there was no *w* in it	Gen 37:24	4325
Joseph's house, and gave them *w*	Gen 43:24	4325
Unstable as *w*, thou shalt not	Gen 49:4	4325
Because I drew him out of the *w*	Ex 2:10	4325
and they came and drew *w*, and filled	Ex 2:16	
troughs to *w* their father's flock	Ex 2:16	8248
also drew *w* enough for us, and	Ex 2:19	
shalt take of the *w* of the river	Ex 4:9	4325
the *w* which thou takest out of	Ex 4:9	4325
lo, he goeth out unto the *w*	Ex 7:15	4325
to drink of the *w* of the river	Ex 7:18	4325
and upon all their pools of *w*	Ex 7:19	4325
not drink of the *w* of the river	Ex 7:21	4325
about the river for *w* to drink	Ex 7:24	4325
not drink of the *w* of the river	Ex 7:24	4325
lo, he cometh forth to the *w*	Ex 8:20	4325
it raw, nor sodden at all with *w*	Ex 12:9	4325
in the wilderness, and found no *w*	Ex 15:22	4325
where were twelve wells of *w*	Ex 15:27	4325
there was no *w* for the people to	Ex 17:1	4325
Give us *w* that we may drink	Ex 17:2	4325
the people thirsted there for *w*	Ex 17:3	4325
and there shall come *w* out of it	Ex 17:6	4325
that is in the *w* under the earth	Ex 20:4	4325
shall bless thy bread, and thy *w*	Ex 23:25	4325
and shalt wash them with *w*	Ex 29:4	4325
and thou shalt put *w* therein	Ex 30:18	4325
they shall wash with *w*, that	Ex 30:20	4325
powder, and strawed it upon the *w*	Ex 32:20	4325
neither eat bread, nor drink *w*	Ex 34:28	4325
the altar, and shalt put *w* therein	Ex 40:7	4325
congregation, and wash them with *w*	Ex 40:12	4325
put *w* there, to wash withal	Ex 40:30	4325
and his legs shall he wash in *w*	Lev 1:9	4325
the inwards and the legs with *w*	Lev 1:13	4325
be both scoured, and rinsed in *w*	Lev 6:28	4325
his sons, and washed them with *w*	Lev 8:6	4325
the inwards and the legs in *w*	Lev 8:21	4325
is done, it must be put into *w*	Lev 11:32	4325
that on which such *w* cometh shall	Lev 11:34	4325
pit, wherein there is plenty of *w*	Lev 11:36	4325
But if any *w* be put upon the seed	Lev 11:38	4325
an earthen vessel over running *w*	Lev 14:5	4325
was killed over the running *w*	Lev 14:6	4325
his hair, and wash himself in *w*	Lev 14:8	4325
also he shall wash his flesh in *w*	Lev 14:9	4325
an earthen vessel over running *w*	Lev 14:50	4325
slain bird, and in the running *w*	Lev 14:51	4325
the bird, and with the running *w*	Lev 14:52	4325
clothes, and bathe himself in *w*	Lev 15:5	4325
clothes, and bathe himself in *w*	Lev 15:6	4325
clothes, and bathe himself in *w*	Lev 15:7	4325
clothes, and bathe himself in *w*	Lev 15:8	4325
clothes, and bathe himself in *w*	Lev 15:10	4325
and hath not rinsed his hands in *w*	Lev 15:11	4325
clothes, and bathe himself in *w*	Lev 15:11	4325
of wood shall be rinsed in *w*	Lev 15:12	4325
and bathe his flesh in running *w*	Lev 15:13	4325
he shall wash all his flesh in *w*	Lev 15:16	4325
shall be washed with *w*, and be	Lev 15:17	4325
shall both bathe themselves in *w*	Lev 15:18	4325
clothes, and bathe himself in *w*	Lev 15:21	4325
clothes, and bathe himself in *w*	Lev 15:22	4325
clothes, and bathe himself in *w*	Lev 15:27	4325
shall he wash his flesh in *w*	Lev 16:4	4325
flesh with *w* in the holy place	Lev 16:24	4325
clothes, and bathe his flesh in *w*	Lev 16:26	4325
clothes, and bathe his flesh in *w*	Lev 16:28	4325
clothes, and bathe himself in *w*	Lev 17:15	4325
unless he wash his flesh with *w*	Lev 22:6	4325
take holy *w* in an earthen vessel	Num 5:17	4325
shall take, and put it into the *w*	Num 5:17	4325
bitter *w* that causeth the curse	Num 5:18	4325
bitter *w* that causeth the curse	Num 5:19	4325
this *w* that causeth the curse	Num 5:22	4325
blot them out with the bitter *w*	Num 5:23	4325
bitter *w* that causeth the curse	Num 5:24	4325
the *w* that causeth the curse	Num 5:24	4325
cause the woman to drink the *w*	Num 5:26	4325
he hath made her to drink the *w*	Num 5:27	4325
that the *w* that causeth the curse	Num 5:27	4325
Sprinkle *w* of purifying upon them	Num 8:7	4325
and he shall bathe his flesh in *w*	Num 19:7	4325
her shall wash his clothes in *w*	Num 19:8	4325
and bathe his flesh in *w*	Num 19:8	4325
of Israel for a *w* of separation	Num 19:9	4325
because the *w* of separation was	Num 19:13	4325
running *w* shall be put thereto in	Num 19:17	4325
take hyssop, and dip it in the *w*	Num 19:18	4325
clothes, and bathe himself in *w*	Num 19:19	4325
the *w* of separation hath not been	Num 19:20	4325
that he that sprinkleth the *w* of	Num 19:21	4325
he that toucheth the *w* of	Num 19:21	4325
And there was no *w* for the	Num 20:2	4325
neither is there any *w* to drink	Num 20:5	4325
and it shall give forth his *w*	Num 20:8	4325
forth to them *w* out of the rock	Num 20:8	4325
we fetch you *w* out of this rock	Num 20:10	4325
the *w* came out abundantly, and the	Num 20:11	4325
This is the *w* of Meribah	Num 20:13	4325
we drink of the *w* of the wells	Num 20:17	4325
if I and my cattle drink of thy *w*	Num 20:19	4325
my word at the *w* of Meribah	Num 20:24	4325
no bread, neither is there any *w*	Num 21:5	4325
together, and I will give them *w*	Num 21:16	4325
He shall pour the *w* out of his	Num 24:7	4325
me at the *w* before their eyes	Num 27:14	4325
that is the *w* of Meribah in	Num 27:14	4325
purified with the *w* of separation	Num 31:23	4325
ye shall make go through the *w*	Num 31:23	4325
Elim were twelve fountains of *w*	Num 33:9	4325
where was no *w* for the people to	Num 33:14	4325
also buy *w* of them for money	Deut 2:6	4325
give me *w* for money, that I may	Deut 2:28	4325
good land, a land of brooks of *w*	Deut 8:7	4325
and drought, where there was no *w*	Deut 8:15	4325
who brought thee forth *w* out of	Deut 8:15	4325
neither did eat bread nor drink *w*	Deut 9:9	4325
neither eat bread, nor drink *w*	Deut 9:18	4325
how he made the *w* of the Red sea	Deut 11:4	4325
drinketh *w* of the rain of heaven	Deut 11:11	4325
shall pour it upon the earth as *w*	Deut 12:16	4325
shalt pour it upon the earth as *w*	Deut 12:24	4325
pour it upon the ground as *w*	Deut 15:23	4325
with *w* in the way, when ye came	Deut 23:4	4325
on, he shall wash himself with *w*	Deut 23:11	4325
thy wood unto the drawer of thy *w*	Deut 29:11	4325
up the *w* of the Red sea for you	Josh 2:10	4325
to the brink of the *w* of Jordan	Josh 3:8	4325
were dipped in the brim of the *w*	Josh 3:15	4325
the people melted, and became as *w*	Josh 7:5	4325
drawers of *w* unto all the	Josh 9:21	4325
drawers of *w* for the house of my	Josh 9:23	4325
drawers of *w* for the congregation	Josh 9:27	4325
the fountain of the *w* of Nephtoah	Josh 15:9	4325
give me also springs of *w*	Josh 15:19	4325
unto the *w* of Jericho on the east	Josh 16:1	4325
give me also springs of *w*	Judg 1:15	4325
I pray thee, a little *w* to drink	Judg 4:19	4325
the clouds also dropped *w*	Judg 5:4	4325
in the places of drawing *w*	Judg 5:11	
He asked *w*, and she gave him milk	Judg 5:25	4325
of the fleece, a bowl full of *w*	Judg 6:38	4325
bring them down unto the *w*	Judg 7:4	4325
down the people unto the *w*	Judg 7:5	4325
lappeth of the *w* with his tongue	Judg 7:5	4325
down upon their knees to drink *w*	Judg 7:6	4325
the jaw, and there came *w* thereout	Judg 15:19	4325
together to Mizpeh, and drew *w*	1Sa 7:6	4325
young maidens going out to draw *w*	1Sa 9:11	4325
I then take my bread, and my *w*	1Sa 25:11	4325
at his bolster, and the cruse of *w*	1Sa 26:11	4325
the cruse of *w* from Saul's	1Sa 26:12	4325
the cruse of *w* that was at his	1Sa 26:16	4325
and they made him drink *w*	1Sa 30:11	4325
eaten no bread, nor drunk any *w*	1Sa 30:12	4325
are as *w* spilt on the ground,	2Sa 14:14	4325
They be gone over the brook of *w*	2Sa 17:20	4325
Arise, and pass quickly over the *w*	2Sa 17:21	4325
the beginning of harvest until *w*	2Sa 21:10	4325
the *w* of the well of Beth-lehem	2Sa 23:15	4325
drew *w* out of the well of	2Sa 23:16	4325
bread nor drink *w* in this place	1Kin 13:8	4325
saying, Eat no bread, nor drink *w*	1Kin 13:9	4325
drink *w* with thee in this place	1Kin 13:16	4325
eat no bread nor drink *w* there	1Kin 13:17	4325
that he may eat bread and drink *w*	1Kin 13:18	4325
bread in his house, and drank *w*	1Kin 13:19	4325
drunk *w* in the place, of the	1Kin 13:22	4325
thee, Eat no bread, and drink no *w*	1Kin 13:22	4325
as a reed is shaken in the *w*	1Kin 14:15	4325
a little *w* in a vessel, that I	1Kin 17:10	4325
cave, and fed them with bread and *w*	1Kin 18:4	4325
the land, unto all fountains of *w*	1Kin 18:5	4325
cave, and fed them with bread and *w*	1Kin 18:13	4325
and said, Fill four barrels with *w*	1Kin 18:33	4325
the *w* ran round about the altar	1Kin 18:35	4325
he filled the trench also with *w*	1Kin 18:35	4325
licked up the *w* that was in the	1Kin 18:38	4325
and a cruse of *w* at his head	1Kin 19:6	4325
with *w* of affliction, until I	1Kin 22:27	4325
but the *w* is naught, and the	2Kin 2:19	4325
and there was no *w* for the host	2Kin 3:9	4325
which poured *w* on the hands of	2Kin 3:11	4325
valley shall be filled with *w*	2Kin 3:17	4325
good tree, and stop all wells of *w*	2Kin 3:19	4325
there came *w* by the way of Edom,	2Kin 3:20	4325
and the country was filled with *w*	2Kin 3:20	4325
and the sun shone upon the *w*	2Kin 3:22	4325
the Moabites saw the *w* on the	2Kin 3:22	4325
they stopped all the wells of *w*	2Kin 3:25	4325
beam, the ax head fell into the *w*	2Kin 6:5	4325
w before them, that they may eat	2Kin 6:22	4325
a thick cloth, and dipped it in *w*	2Kin 8:15	4325
brought *w* into the city, are they	2Kin 20:20	4325
the *w* of the well of Beth-lehem	1Chr 11:17	4325
drew *w* out of the well of	1Chr 11:18	4325
with *w* of affliction, until I	2Chr 18:26	4325
of Assyria come, and find much *w*	2Chr 32:4	4325
he did eat no bread, nor drink *w*	Ezr 10:6	4325
the *w* gate toward the east	Neh 3:26	4325
street that was before the *w* gate	Neh 8:1	4325
the *w* gate from the morning until	Neh 8:3	4325
and in the street of the *w* gate	Neh 8:16	4325
broughtest forth *w* for them out	Neh 9:15	4325
gavest them *w* for their thirst	Neh 9:20	4325
even unto the *w* gate eastward	Neh 12:37	4325
of Israel with bread and with *w*	Neh 13:2	4325
can the flag grow without *w*	Job 8:11	4325
If I wash myself with snow *w*	Job 9:30	1119
the scent of *w* it will bud	Job 14:9	4325
which drinketh iniquity like *w*	Job 15:16	4325
Thou hast not given *w* to the	Job 22:7	4325
who drinketh up scorning like *w*	Job 34:7	4325
he maketh small the drops of *w*	Job 36:27	4325
a tree planted by the rivers of *w*	Ps 1:3	4325
I *w* my couch with my tears	Ps 6:6	4529
I am poured out like *w*, and all my	Ps 22:14	4325
hart panteth after the *w* brooks	Ps 42:1	4325
and thirsty land, where no *w* is	Ps 63:1	4325
river of God, which is full of *w*	Ps 65:9	4325
we went through fire and through *w*	Ps 66:12	4325
as showers that *w* the earth	Ps 72:6	2222
The clouds poured out *w*	Ps 77:17	4325
shed like *w* round about Jerusalem	Ps 79:3	4325
came round about me daily like *w*	Ps 88:17	4325
the wilderness into a standing *w*	Ps 107:35	4325
it come into his bowels like *w*	Ps 109:18	4325
turned the rock into a standing *w*	Ps 114:8	4325
no fountains abounding with *w*	Prov 8:24	4325
is as when one letteth out *w*	Prov 17:14	4325
the heart of man is like deep *w*	Prov 20:5	4325
of the LORD, as the rivers of *w*	Prov 21:1	4325
be thirsty, give him *w* to drink	Prov 25:21	4325
As in *w* face answereth to face,	Prov 27:19	4325
earth that is not filled with *w*	Prov 30:16	4325
I made me pools of *w*	Eccl 2:6	4325
to *w* therewith the wood that	Eccl 2:6	8248
dross, thy wine mixed with *w*	Is 1:22	4325
and as a garden that hath no *w*	Is 1:30	4325
of bread, and the whole stay of *w*	Is 3:1	4325
with joy shall ye draw *w* out of	Is 12:3	4325
for the bittern, and pools of *w*	Is 14:23	4325
I will *w* thee with my tears, O	Is 16:9	7301
brought *w* to him that was thirsty	Is 21:14	4325
walls for the *w* of the old pool	Is 22:11	4325
I will *w* it every moment	Is 27:3	8248
or to take *w* withal out of the	Is 30:14	4325
the *w* of affliction, yet shall	Is 30:20	4325
as rivers of *w* in a dry place, as	Is 32:2	4325
and the thirsty land springs of *w*	Is 35:7	4325
I have digged, and drunk *w*	Is 37:25	4325
When the poor and needy seek *w*	Is 41:17	4325
make the wilderness a pool of *w*	Is 41:18	4325
and the dry land springs of *w*	Is 41:18	4325
For I will pour *w* upon him that	Is 44:3	4325
as willows by the *w* courses	Is 44:4	4325
he drinketh no *w*, and is faint	Is 44:12	4325
springs of *w* shall he guide them	Is 49:10	4325
stinketh, because there is no *w*	Is 50:2	4325
garden, and like a spring of *w*	Is 58:11	4325
arm, dividing the *w* before them	Is 63:12	4325
cisterns, that can hold no *w*	Jer 2:13	4325
given us *w* of gall to drink,	Jer 8:14	4325
give them *w* of gall to drink	Jer 9:15	4325
thy loins, and put it not in *w*	Jer 13:1	4325
came to the pits, and found no *w*	Jer 14:3	4325
and make them drink the *w* of gall	Jer 23:15	4325
And in the dungeon there was no *w*	Jer 38:6	4325
eye, mine eye runneth down with *w*	Lam 1:16	4325
pour out thine heart like *w*	Lam 2:19	4325
of *w* for the destruction of the	Lam 3:48	4325
We have drunken our *w* for money	Lam 5:4	4325
shalt drink also *w* by measure	Eze 4:11	4325
and they shall drink *w* by measure	Eze 4:16	4325
That they may want bread and *w*	Eze 4:17	4325
and all knees shall be weak as *w*	Eze 7:17	4325
drink thy *w* with trembling and	Eze 12:18	4325
drink their *w* with astonishment,	Eze 12:19	4325
thou washed in *w* to supple thee	Eze 16:4	4325
Then washed I thee with *w*	Eze 16:9	4325
that he might *w* it by the furrows	Eze 17:7	8248
and all knees shall be weak as *w*	Eze 21:7	4325
set it on, and also pour *w* into it	Eze 24:3	4325
and thy dust in the midst of the *w*	Eze 26:12	4325
in their height, all that drink *w*	Eze 31:14	4325
best of Lebanon, all that drink *w*	Eze 31:16	4325
I will also *w* with thy blood the	Eze 32:6	8248
will I sprinkle clean *w* upon you	Eze 36:25	4325
us pulse to eat, and *w* to drink	Dan 1:12	4325
that give me my bread and my *w*	Hos 2:5	4325
out my wrath upon them like *w*	Hos 5:10	4325
is cut off as the foam upon the *w*	Hos 10:7	4325
shall *w* the valley of Shittim	Joel 3:18	8248
unto one city, to drink *w*	Amos 4:8	4325
of bread, nor a thirst for *w*	Amos 8:11	4325
let them not feed, nor drink *w*	Jonah 3:7	4325
is of old like a pool of *w*	Nah 2:8	4325
overflowing of the *w* passed by	Hab 3:10	4325
out of the pit wherein is no *w*	Zec 9:11	4325
you with *w* unto repentance	Mt 3:11	5204
went up straightway out of the *w*	Mt 3:16	5204
w only in the name of a disciple	Mt 10:42	
bid me come unto thee on the *w*	Mt 14:28	5204
of the ship, he walked on the *w*	Mt 14:29	5204
into the fire, and oft into the *w*	Mt 17:15	5204
a tumult was made, he took *w*	Mt 27:24	5204
I indeed have baptized you with *w*	Mk 1:8	5204
coming up out of the *w*, he saw	Mk 1:10	5204
a cup of *w* to drink in my name	Mk 9:41	5204
you a man bearing a pitcher of *w*	Mk 14:13	5204
all, I indeed baptize you with *w*	Lk 3:16	5204
thou gavest me no *w* for my feet	Lk 7:44	5204
and they were filled with *w*	Lk 8:23	
the wind and the raging of the *w*	Lk 8:24	5204
even the winds and *w*	Lk 8:25	5204
dip the tip of his finger in *w*	Lk 16:24	5204
meet you, bearing a pitcher of *w*	Lk 22:10	5204
them, saying, I baptize with *w*	Jn 1:26	5204
am I come baptizing with *w*	Jn 1:31	5204
he that sent me to baptize with *w*	Jn 1:33	5204
them, Fill the waterpots with *w*	Jn 2:7	5204
tasted the *w* that was made wine	Jn 2:9	5204
servants which drew the *w* knew	Jn 2:9	5204
thee, Except a man be born of *w*	Jn 3:5	5204
because there was much *w* there	Jn 3:23	5204
a woman of Samaria to draw *w*	Jn 4:7	5204
he would have given thee living *w*	Jn 4:10	5204

then hast thou that living *w*	Jn 4:11	*5204*
of this *w* shall thirst again	Jn 4:13	*5204*
the *w* that I shall give him shall	Jn 4:14	*5204*
but the *w* that I shall give him	Jn 4:14	*5204*
w springing up into everlasting	Jn 4:14	*5204*
unto him, Sir, give me this *w*	Jn 4:15	*5204*
Galilee, where he made the *w* wine	Jn 4:46	*5204*
waiting for the moving of the *w*	Jn 5:3	*5204*
into the pool, and troubled the *w*	Jn 5:4	*5204*
after the troubling of the *w*	Jn 5:4	*5204*
when the *w* is troubled, to put me	Jn 5:7	*5204*
shall flow rivers of living *w*	Jn 7:38	*5204*
that he poureth *w* into a bason	Jn 13:5	*5204*
came there out blood and *w*	Jn 19:34	*5204*
For John truly baptized with *w*	Acts 1:5	*5204*
way, they came unto a certain *w*	Acts 8:36	*5204*
the eunuch said, See, here is *w*	Acts 8:36	*5204*
and they went down both into the *w*	Acts 8:38	*5204*
they were come up out of the *w*	Acts 8:39	*5204*
Can any man forbid *w*, that these	Acts 10:47	*5204*
said, John indeed baptized with *w*	Acts 11:16	*5204*
with the washing of *w* by the word	Eph 5:26	*5204*
Drink no longer *w*, but use a	1Ti 5:23	*5202*
of calves and of goats, with *w*	Heb 9:19	*5204*
and our bodies washed with pure *w*	Heb 10:22	*5204*
forth at the same place sweet *w*	Jas 3:11	
can no fountain both yield salt *w*	Jas 3:12	*5204*
is, eight souls were saved by *w*	1Pet 3:20	*5204*
These are wells without *w*	2Pet 2:17	*504*
out of the *w* and in the *w*	2Pet 3:5	*5204*
then was, being overflowed with *w*	2Pet 3:6	*5204*
This is he that came by *w*	1Jn 5:6	*5204*
not by *w* only, but by *w*	1Jn 5:6	*5204*
in earth, the spirit, and the *w*	1Jn 5:8	*5204*
clouds they are without *w*	Jude 12	*504*
w as a flood after the woman	Rev 12:15	*5204*
the *w* thereof was dried up, that	Rev 16:12	*5204*
fountain of the *w* of life freely	Rev 21:6	*5204*
me a pure river of *w* of life	Rev 22:1	*5204*
let him take the *w* of life freely	Rev 22:17	*5204*

WATERCOURSE

also stopped the upper *w* of Gihon	2Chr 32:30	
Who hath divided a *w* for the	Job 38:25	8585

WATERED

w the whole face of the ground	Gen 2:6	8248
that it was well *w* every where	Gen 13:10	4945
of that well they *w* the flocks	Gen 29:2	8248
w the sheep, and put the stone	Gen 29:3	8248
w the flock of Laban his mother's	Gen 29:10	8248
and helped them, and *w* their flock	Ex 2:17	8248
enough for us, and *w* the flock	Ex 2:19	8248
watereth shall be *w* also himself	Prov 11:25	3384
and thou shalt be like a *w* garden	Is 58:11	7302
their soul shall be as a *w* garden	Jer 31:12	7302
I have planted, Apollos *w*	1Cor 3:6	*4222*

WATEREDST

w it with thy foot, as a garden	Deut 11:10	8248

WATEREST

Thou visitest the earth, and *w* it	Ps 65:9	7783
Thou *w* the ridges thereof	Ps 65:10	7301

WATERETH

He *w* the hills from his chambers	Ps 104:13	8248
he that *w* shall be watered also	Prov 11:25	7301
but *w* the earth, and maketh it	Is 55:10	7301
any thing, neither he that *w*	1Cor 3:7	*4222*
planteth and he that *w* are one	1Cor 3:8	*4222*

WATERFLOOD

Let not the *w* overflow me	Ps 69:15	

WATERING

flocks in the gutters in the *w*	Gen 30:38	4325
Also by *w* he wearieth the thick	Job 37:11	7377
the stall, and lead him away to *w*	Lk 13:15	*4222*

WATERPOT

The woman then left her *w*	Jn 4:28	*5201*

WATERPOTS

were set there six *w* of stone	Jn 2:6	*5201*
unto them, Fill the *w* with water	Jn 2:7	*5201*

WATERS

God moved upon the face of the *w*	Gen 1:2	4325
a firmament in the midst of the *w*	Gen 1:6	4325
it divide the *w* from the *w*	Gen 1:6	4325
divided the *w* which were under	Gen 1:7	4325
under the firmament from the *w*	Gen 1:7	4325
Let the *w* under the heaven be	Gen 1:9	4325
together of the *w* called he Seas	Gen 1:10	4325
Let the *w* bring forth abundantly	Gen 1:20	4325
which the *w* brought forth	Gen 1:21	4325
fill the *w* in the seas, and let	Gen 1:22	4325
bring a flood of *w* upon the earth	Gen 6:17	4325
the flood of *w* was upon the earth	Gen 7:6	4325
because of the *w* of the flood	Gen 7:7	4325
that the *w* of the flood were upon	Gen 7:10	4325
the *w* increased, and bare up the	Gen 7:17	4325
And the *w* prevailed, and were	Gen 7:18	4325
ark went upon the face of the *w*	Gen 7:18	4325
the *w* prevailed exceedingly upon	Gen 7:19	4325
cubits upward did the *w* prevail	Gen 7:20	4325
the *w* prevailed upon the earth an	Gen 7:24	4325
over the earth, and the *w* asswaged	Gen 8:1	4325
the *w* returned from off the earth	Gen 8:3	4325
and fifty days the *w* were abated	Gen 8:3	4325
the *w* decreased continually until	Gen 8:5	4325
until the *w* were dried up from	Gen 8:7	4325
to see if the *w* were abated from	Gen 8:8	4325
for the *w* were on the face of the	Gen 8:9	4325
so Noah knew that the *w* were	Gen 8:11	4325
the *w* were dried up from off the	Gen 8:13	4325
off any more by the *w* of a flood	Gen 9:11	4325
the *w* shall no more become a	Gen 9:15	4325
upon the *w* which are in the river	Ex 7:17	4325
thine hand upon the *w* of Egypt	Ex 7:19	4325
smote the *w* that were in the	Ex 7:20	4325
all the *w* that were in the river	Ex 7:20	4325
out his hand over the *w* of Egypt	Ex 8:6	4325
dry land, and the *w* were divided	Ex 14:21	4325
the *w* were a wall unto them on	Ex 14:22	4325
that the *w* may come again upon	Ex 14:26	4325
the *w* returned, and covered the	Ex 14:28	4325
the *w* were a wall unto them on	Ex 14:29	4325
the *w* were gathered together	Ex 15:8	4325
they sank as lead in the mighty *w*	Ex 15:10	4325
again the *w* of the sea upon them	Ex 15:19	4325
could not drink of the *w* of Marah	Ex 15:23	4325
which when he had cast into the *w*	Ex 15:25	4325
the *w* were made sweet	Ex 15:25	4325
and they encamped there by the *w*	Ex 15:27	4325
ye eat of all that are in the *w*	Lev 11:9	4325
hath fins and scales in the *w*	Lev 11:9	4325
rivers, of all that move in the *w*	Lev 11:10	4325
living thing which is in the *w*	Lev 11:10	4325
hath no fins nor scales in the *w*	Lev 11:12	4325
creature that moveth in the *w*	Lev 11:46	4325
not drink of the *w* of the well	Num 21:22	4325
and as cedar trees beside the *w*	Num 24:6	4325
and his seed shall be in many *w*	Num 24:7	4325
is in the *w* beneath the earth	Deut 4:18	4325
is in the *w* beneath the earth	Deut 5:8	4325
to Jotbath, a land of rivers of *w*	Deut 10:7	4325
eat of all that are in the *w*	Deut 14:9	4325
Israel at the *w* of Meribah-kadesh	Deut 32:51	4325
didst strive at the *w* of Meribah	Deut 33:8	4325
shall rest in the *w* of Jordan	Josh 3:13	4325
that the *w* of Jordan shall be cut	Josh 3:13	4325
the *w* that come down from above	Josh 3:13	4325
That the *w* which came down from	Josh 3:16	4325
That the *w* of Jordan were cut off	Josh 4:7	4325
the *w* of Jordan were cut off	Josh 4:7	4325
that the *w* of Jordan returned	Josh 4:18	4325
the *w* of Jordan from before you	Josh 4:23	4325
the *w* of Jordan from before the	Josh 5:1	4325
together at the *w* of Merom	Josh 11:5	4325
them by the *w* of Merom suddenly	Josh 11:7	4325
passed toward the *w* of En-shemesh	Josh 15:7	4325
out to the well of *w* of Nephtoah	Josh 18:15	4325
in Taanach by the *w* of Megiddo	Judg 5:19	4325
before them the *w* unto Beth-barah	Judg 7:24	4325
took the *w* unto Beth-barah and	Judg 7:24	4325
before me, as the breach of *w*	2Sa 5:20	4325
and have taken the city of *w*	2Sa 12:27	4325
pavilions round about him, dark *w*	2Sa 22:12	4325
he drew me out of many *w*	2Sa 22:17	4325
it together, and smote the *w*	2Kin 2:8	4325
fell from him, and smote the *w*	2Kin 2:14	4325
and when he also had smitten the *w*	2Kin 2:14	4325
forth unto the spring of the *w*	2Kin 2:21	4325
the LORD, I have healed these *w*	2Kin 2:21	4325
So the *w* were healed unto this	2Kin 2:22	4325
better than all the *w* of Israel	2Kin 5:12	4325
ye every one the *w* of his cistern	2Kin 18:31	4325
I have digged and drunk strange *w*	2Kin 19:24	4325
hand like the breaking forth of *w*	1Chr 14:11	4325
his mighty men to stop the *w* of	2Chr 32:3	4325
as a stone into the mighty *w*	Neh 9:11	4325
are poured out like the *w*	Job 3:24	4325
sendeth *w* upon the fields	Job 5:10	4325
remember it as *w* that pass away	Job 11:16	4325
Behold, he withholdeth the *w*	Job 12:15	4325
As the *w* fail from the sea, and	Job 14:11	4325
The *w* wear the stones	Job 14:19	4325
and abundance of *w* cover thee	Job 22:11	4325
He is swift as the *w*	Job 24:18	4325
and heat consume the snow *w*	Job 24:19	4325
are formed from under the *w*	Job 26:5	4325
He bindeth up the *w* in his thick	Job 26:8	4325
hath compassed the *w* with bounds	Job 26:10	4325
Terrors take hold on him as *w*	Job 27:20	4325
even the *w* forgotten of the foot	Job 28:4	
and he weigheth the *w* by measure	Job 28:25	4325
My root was spread out by the *w*	Job 29:19	4325
me as a wide breaking in of *w*	Job 30:14	
breadth of the *w* is straitened	Job 37:10	4325
for the overflowing of *w*, or a	Job 38:25	
The *w* are hid as with a stone, and	Job 38:30	4325
abundance of *w* may cover thee	Job 38:34	4325
round about him were dark *w*	Ps 18:11	4325
Then the channels of *w* were seen	Ps 18:15	4325
took me, he drew me out of many *w*	Ps 18:16	4325
he leadeth me beside the still *w*	Ps 23:2	4325
voice of the LORD is upon the *w*	Ps 29:3	4325
the LORD is upon many *w*	Ps 29:3	4325
w they shall not come nigh unto	Ps 32:6	4325
He gathereth the *w* of the sea	Ps 33:7	4325
Though the *w* thereof roar and be	Ps 46:3	4325
away as *w* which run continually	Ps 58:7	4325
for the *w* are come in unto my	Ps 69:1	4325
I am come into deep *w*, where the	Ps 69:2	4325
hate me, and out of the deep *w*	Ps 69:14	4325
w of a full cup are wrung out to	Ps 73:10	4325
the heads of the dragons in the *w*	Ps 74:13	4325
The *w* saw thee, O God, the *w*	Ps 77:16	4325
sea, and thy path in the great *w*	Ps 77:19	4325
he made the *w* to stand as an heap	Ps 78:13	4325
caused *w* to run down like rivers	Ps 78:16	4325
that the *w* gushed out, and the	Ps 78:20	4325
I proved thee at the *w* of Meribah	Ps 81:7	4325
mightier than the noise of many *w*	Ps 93:4	4325
beams of his chambers in the *w*	Ps 104:3	4325
the *w* stood above the mountains	Ps 104:6	4325
He turned their *w* into blood	Ps 105:29	4325
the rock, and the *w* gushed out	Ps 105:41	4325
the *w* covered their enemies	Ps 106:11	4325
him also at the *w* of strife	Ps 106:32	4325
that do business in great *w*	Ps 107:23	4325
the flint into a fountain of *w*	Ps 114:8	4325
Rivers of *w* run down mine eyes,	Ps 119:136	4325
Then the *w* had overwhelmed us,	Ps 124:4	4325
Then the proud *w* had gone over	Ps 124:5	4325
out the earth above the *w*	Ps 136:6	4325
me, and deliver me out of great *w*	Ps 144:7	4325
his wind to blow, and the *w* flow	Ps 147:18	4325
ye *w* that be above the heavens	Ps 148:4	4325
Drink *w* out of thine own cistern,	Prov 5:15	4325
running *w* out of thine own well	Prov 5:15	
rivers of *w* in the streets	Prov 5:16	4325
that the *w* should not pass his	Prov 8:29	4325
Stolen *w* are sweet, and bread	Prov 9:17	4325
of a man's mouth are as deep *w*	Prov 18:4	4325
As cold *w* to a thirsty soul, so	Prov 25:25	4325
who hath bound the *w* in a garment	Prov 30:4	4325
Cast thy bread upon the *w*	Eccl 11:1	4325
of gardens, a well of living *w*	Song 4:15	4325
eyes of doves by the rivers of *w*	Song 5:12	4325
Many *w* cannot quench love,	Song 8:7	4325
the *w* of Shiloah that go softly	Is 8:6	4325
up upon them the *w* of the river	Is 8:7	4325
the LORD, as the *w* cover the sea	Is 11:9	4325
For the *w* of Nimrim shall be	Is 15:6	4325
For the *w* of Dimon shall be full	Is 15:9	4325
like the rushing of mighty *w*	Is 17:12	4325
rush like the rushing of many *w*	Is 17:13	4325
vessels of bulrushes upon the *w*	Is 18:2	4325
the *w* shall fail from the sea, and	Is 19:5	4325
nets upon the *w* shall languish	Is 19:8	4325
together the *w* of the lower pool	Is 22:9	4325
by great *w* the seed of Sihor, the	Is 23:3	4325
a flood of mighty *w* overflowing	Is 28:2	4325
the *w* shall overflow the hiding	Is 28:17	4325
streams of *w* in the day of the	Is 30:25	4325
are ye that sow beside all *w*	Is 32:20	4325
his *w* shall be sure	Is 33:16	4325
the wilderness shall *w* break out	Is 35:6	4325
one the *w* of his own cistern	Is 36:16	4325
Who hath measured the *w* in the	Is 40:12	4325
When thou passest through the *w*	Is 43:2	4325
sea, and a path in the mighty *w*	Is 43:16	4325
because I give *w* in the	Is 43:20	4325
come forth out of the *w* of Judah	Is 48:1	4325
he caused the *w* to flow out of	Is 48:21	4325
rock also, and the *w* gushed out	Is 48:21	4325
the sea, the *w* of the great deep	Is 51:10	4325
this is as the *w* of Noah unto me	Is 54:9	4325
for as I have sworn that the *w* of	Is 54:9	4325
that thirsteth, come ye to the *w*	Is 55:1	4325
whose *w* cast up mire and dirt	Is 57:20	4325
spring of water, whose *w* fail not	Is 58:11	4325
the fire causeth the *w* to boil	Is 64:2	4325
me the fountain of living *w*	Jer 2:13	4325
of Egypt, to drink the *w* of Sihor	Jer 2:18	4325
to drink the *w* of the river	Jer 2:18	4325
As a fountain casteth out her *w*	Jer 6:7	4325
Oh that my head were *w*, and mine	Jer 9:1	4325
and our eyelids gush out with *w*	Jer 9:18	4325
a multitude of *w* in the heavens	Jer 10:13	4325
sent their little ones to the *w*	Jer 14:3	4325
me as a liar, and as *w* that fail	Jer 15:18	4325
be as a tree planted by the *w*	Jer 17:8	4325
LORD, the fountain of living *w*	Jer 17:13	4325
or shall the cold flowing *w* that	Jer 18:14	4325
the rivers of *w* in a straight way	Jer 31:9	4325
by the great *w* that are in Gibeon	Jer 41:12	4325
whose *w* are moved as the rivers	Jer 46:7	4325
his *w* are moved like the rivers	Jer 46:8	4325
w rise up out of the north, and	Jer 47:2	4325
for the *w* also of Nimrim shall be	Jer 48:34	4325
A drought is upon her *w*	Jer 50:38	4325
O thou that dwellest upon many *w*	Jer 51:13	4325
a multitude of *w* in the heavens	Jer 51:16	4325
her waves do roar like great *w*	Jer 51:55	4325
W flowed over mine head	Lam 3:54	4325
wings, like the noise of great *w*	Eze 1:24	4325
he placed it by great *w*, and set	Eze 17:5	4325
planted in a good soil by great *w*	Eze 17:8	4325
in thy blood, planted by the *w*	Eze 19:10	4325
of branches by reason of many *w*	Eze 19:10	4325
thee, and great *w* shall cover thee	Eze 26:19	4325
have brought thee into great *w*	Eze 27:26	4325
depths of the *w* thy merchandise	Eze 27:34	4325
The *w* made him great, the deep	Eze 31:4	4325
because of the multitude of *w*	Eze 31:5	4325
for his root was by great *w*	Eze 31:7	4325
the *w* exalt themselves for their	Eze 31:14	4325
and the great *w* were stayed	Eze 31:15	4325
and troubledst the *w* with thy feet	Eze 32:2	4325
thereof from beside the great *w*	Eze 32:13	4325
Then will I make their *w* deep	Eze 32:14	4325
and to have drunk of the deep *w*	Eze 34:18	4325
voice was like a noise of many *w*	Eze 43:2	4325
w issued out from under the	Eze 47:1	4325
the *w* came down from under from	Eze 47:1	4325
there ran out *w* on the right side	Eze 47:2	4325
and he brought me through the *w*	Eze 47:3	4325
the *w* were to the ancles	Eze 47:3	4325
and brought me through the *w*	Eze 47:4	4325
the *w* were to the knees	Eze 47:4	4325
the *w* were to the loins	Eze 47:4	4325
for the *w* were risen	Eze 47:5	4325
w to swim in, a river that could	Eze 47:5	4325
These *w* issue out toward the east	Eze 47:8	4325
the sea, the *w* shall be healed	Eze 47:8	4325
because these *w* shall come	Eze 47:9	4325
because their *w* they they issued	Eze 47:12	4325
even to the *w* of strife in Kadesh	Eze 47:19	4325
unto the *w* of strife in Kadesh	Eze 48:28	4325
which was upon the *w* of the river	Dan 12:6	4325
which was upon the *w* of the river	Dan 12:7	4325
for the rivers of *w* are dried up	Joel 1:20	4325
rivers of Judah shall flow with *w*	Joel 3:18	4325

that calleth for the *w* of the sea … Amos 5:8 4325
But let judgment run down as *w* … Amos 5:24 4325
that calleth for the *w* of the sea … Amos 9:6 4325
The *w* compassed me about, even to … Jonah 2:5 4325
as the *w* that are poured down a … Mic 1:4 4325
that had the *w* round about it, … Nah 3:8 4325
Draw thee *w* for the siege, … Nah 3:14 4325
the LORD, as the *w* cover the sea … Hab 2:14 4325
through the heap of great *w* … Hab 3:15 4325
that living *w* shall go out from … Zec 14:8 4325
the sea, and perished in the *w* … Mt 8:32 *5204*
him into the fire, and into the *w* … Mk 9:22 *5204*
journeyings often, in perils of *w* … 2Cor 11:26 *4215*
his voice as the sound of many *w* … Rev 1:15 *5204*
them unto living fountains of *w* … Rev 7:17 *5204*
and upon the fountains of *w* … Rev 8:10 *5204*
part of the *w* became wormwood … Rev 8:11 *5204*
and many men died of the *w* … Rev 8:11 *5204*
have power over *w* to turn them to … Rev 11:6 *5204*
heaven, as the voice of many *w* … Rev 14:2 *5204*
and the sea, and the fountains of *w* … Rev 14:7 *5204*
upon the rivers and fountains of *w* … Rev 16:4 *5204*
And I heard the angel of the *w* say … Rev 16:5 *5204*
whore that sitteth upon many *w* … Rev 17:1 *5204*
The *w* which thou sawest, where … Rev 17:15 *5204*
and as the voice of many *w* … Rev 19:6 *5204*

WATERSPOUTS
unto deep at the noise of thy *w* … Ps 42:7 6794

WATERSPRINGS
and the *w* into dry ground … Ps 107:33
water, and dry ground into *w* … Ps 107:35

WAVE
shalt *w* them for a … Ex 29:24 5130
them for a *w* offering … Ex 29:24 8573
and *w* it for a … Ex 29:26 5130
it for a *w* offering before … Ex 29:26 8573
the breast of the *w* offering … Ex 29:27 8573
for a *w* offering before the LORD … Lev 7:30 8573
For the *w* breast and the heave … Lev 7:34 8573
waved them for a *w* offering … Lev 8:27 8573
waved it for a *w* offering before … Lev 8:29 8573
for a *w* offering before the LORD … Lev 9:21 8573
the *w* breast and heave shoulder … Lev 10:14 8573
the *w* breast shall they bring … Lev 10:15 8573
to *w* it for a *w* offering … Lev 10:15 5130
w them for a … Lev 14:12 5130
them for a *w* offering before … Lev 14:12 8573
the priest shall *w* them for a … Lev 14:24 5130
for a *w* offering before the LORD … Lev 14:24 8573
he shall *w* the sheaf before the … Lev 23:11 5130
the sabbath the priest shall *w* it … Lev 23:11 5130
ye *w* the sheaf an he lamb without … Lev 23:12 5130
the sheaf of the *w* offering … Lev 23:15 8573
two *w* loaves of two tenth deals … Lev 23:17 8573
the priest shall *w* them with the … Lev 23:20 5130
for a *w* offering before the LORD … Lev 23:20 8573
shall *w* the offering before the … Num 5:25 5130
the priest shall *w* them for a … Num 6:20 5130
for a *w* offering before the LORD … Num 6:20 8573
for the priest, with the *w* breast … Num 6:20 8573
with all the *w* offerings of the … Num 18:11 8573
shall be thine, as the *w* breast … Num 18:18 8573
For he that wavereth is like a *w* … Jas 1:6 *2830*

WAVED
of the heave offering, which is *w* … Ex 29:27 5130
that the breast may be *w* for a … Lev 7:30 5130
w them for a wave offering before … Lev 8:27 5130
w it for a wave offering before … Lev 8:29 5130
the right shoulder Aaron *w* for a … Lev 9:21 5130
for a trespass offering to be *w* … Lev 14:21 8573

WAVERETH
For he that *w* is like a wave of … Jas 1:6 *1252*

WAVERING
profession of our faith without *w* … Heb 10:23 *186*
let him ask in faith, nothing *w* … Jas 1:6 *1252*

WAVES
When the *w* of death compassed me, … 2Sa 22:5 4867
and treadeth upon the *w* of the sea … Job 9:8 1116
here shall thy proud *w* be stayed … Job 38:11 1530
all thy *w* and thy billows are gone … Ps 42:7 4867
of the seas, the noise of their *w* … Ps 65:7 1530
hast afflicted me with all thy *w* … Ps 88:7 4867
when the *w* thereof arise, thou … Ps 89:9 1530
the floods lift up their *w* … Ps 93:3 1796
yea, than the mighty *w* of the sea … Ps 93:4 4867
which lifteth up the *w* thereof … Ps 107:25 1530
so that the *w* thereof are still … Ps 107:29 1530
righteousness as the *w* of the sea … Is 48:18 1530
divided the sea, whose *w* roared … Is 51:15 1530
though the *w* thereof toss … Jer 5:22 1530
the sea when the *w* thereof roar … Jer 31:35 1530
the multitude of the *w* thereof … Jer 51:42 1530
when her *w* do roar like great … Jer 51:55 1530
the sea causeth his *w* to come up … Eze 26:3 1530
billows and thy *w* passed over me … Jonah 2:3 1530
and shall smite the *w* in the sea … Zec 10:11 1530
the ship was covered with the *w* … Mt 8:24 *2949*
midst of the sea, tossed with *w* … Mt 14:24 *2949*
the *w* beat into the ship, so that … Mk 4:37 *2949*
the sea and the *w* roaring … Lk 21:25 *4535*
broken with the violence of the *w* … Acts 27:41 *2949*
Raging *w* of the sea, foaming out … Jude 13 *2949*

WAX
And my wrath shall *w* hot, and I … Ex 22:24
my wrath may *w* hot against them … Ex 32:10
why doth thy wrath *w* hot against … Ex 32:11
not the anger of my lord *w* hot … Ex 32:22
or stranger *w* rich by thee … Lev 25:47
that dwelleth by him *w* poor … Lev 25:47
place, and his eyes began to *w* dim … 1Sa 3:2
What time they *w* warm, they … Job 6:17
root thereof *w* old in the earth … Job 14:8
my heart is like *w* … Ps 22:14 1749
as *w* melteth before the fire, so … Ps 68:2 1749
The hills melted like *w* at the … Ps 97:5 1749
all of them shall *w* old like a … Ps 102:26
fatness of his flesh shall *w* lean … Is 17:4
neither shall his face now *w* pale … Is 29:22
they all shall *w* old as a garment … Is 50:9
the earth shall *w* old like a … Is 51:6
our hands *w* feeble … Jer 6:24
as *w* before the fire, and as the … Mic 1:4 1749
the love of many shall *w* cold … Mt 24:12 *5594*
yourselves bags which *w* not old … Lk 12:33 *3822*
begun to *w* wanton against Christ … 1Ti 5:11 *2691*
men and seducers shall *w* worse … 2Ti 3:13 *4298*
they all shall *w* old as doth a … Heb 1:11 *3822*

WAXED
After I am *w* old shall I have … Gen 18:12
And the man *w* great, and went … Gen 26:13
the famine *w* sore in the land of … Gen 41:56
multiplied, and *w* exceeding mighty … Ex 1:7
multiplied, and *w* very mighty … Ex 1:20
and when the sun *w* hot, it melted … Ex 16:21
w louder and louder, Moses spake, … Ex 19:19
and Moses' anger *w* hot, and he cast … Ex 32:19
Moses, Is the LORD's hand *w* short … Num 11:23
Thy raiment *w* not old upon thee, … Deut 8:4
But Jeshurun *w* fat, and kicked … Deut 32:15
round about, that Joshua *w* old … Josh 23:1
hath many children is *w* feeble … 1Sa 2:5
but David *w* stronger and stronger, … 2Sa 3:1 1980
and the house of Saul *w* weaker … 2Sa 3:1 1980
and David *w* faint … 2Sa 21:15
and the flesh of the child *w* warm … 2Kin 4:34
So David *w* greater and greater … 1Chr 11:9 1980
But Abijah *w* mighty, and married … 2Chr 13:21
Jehoshaphat *w* great exceedingly … 2Chr 17:12 1980
But Jehoiada *w* old, and was full … 2Chr 24:15
their clothes *w* not old, and their … Neh 9:21
for this man Mordecai *w* greater … Est 9:4 1980
my bones *w* old through my roaring … Ps 32:3
Damascus is *w* feeble, and turneth … Jer 49:24
of them, and his hands *w* feeble … Jer 50:43
the he goat *w* very great … Dan 8:8
which *w* exceeding great, toward … Dan 8:9
it *w* great, even to the host of … Dan 8:10
this people's heart is *w* gross … Mt 13:15 *3975*
w strong in spirit, and was in the … Lk 1:80 *2901*
w strong in spirit, filled with … Lk 2:40 *2901*
and it grew, and *w* a great tree … Lk 13:19 *1096*
Then Paul and Barnabas *w* bold … Acts 13:46 *3955*
heart of this people is *w* gross … Acts 28:27 *3975*
w valiant in fight, turned to … Heb 11:34 *1096*
w rich through the abundance of … Rev 18:3 *4147*

WAXEN
because the cry of them is *w* … Gen 19:13
If thy brother be *w* poor, and hath … Lev 25:25
And if thy brother be *w* poor … Lev 25:35
that dwelleth by thee be *w* poor … Lev 25:39
clothes are not *w* old upon you … Deut 29:5
thy shoe is not *w* old upon thy … Deut 29:5
and filled themselves, and *w* fat … Deut 31:20
thou art *w* fat, thou art grown … Deut 32:15
children of Israel were *w* strong … Josh 17:13
they are become great, and *w* rich … Jer 5:27
They are *w* fat, they shine … Jer 5:28
w great, and thou art come to … Eze 16:7

WAXETH
It *w* old because of all mine … Ps 6:7
w old is ready to vanish away … Heb 8:13 *1095*

WAXING
w confident by my bonds, are much … Phil 1:14 *3982*

WAY
sword which turned every *w* … Gen 3:24
to keep the *w* of the tree of life … Gen 3:24
corrupted his *w* upon the earth … Gen 6:12
thy wife, take her, and go thy *w* … Gen 12:19
their victuals, and went their *w* … Gen 14:11 3212
by the fountain in the *w* to Shur … Gen 16:7 1870
with them to bring them on the *w* … Gen 18:16 7971
they shall keep the *w* of the LORD … Gen 18:19 1870
And the LORD went his *w*, as soon … Gen 18:33 3212
over against him a good *w* off … Gen 21:16
I being in the *w*, the LORD led me … Gen 24:27 1870
angel with thee, and prosper thy *w* … Gen 24:40 1870
thou do prosper my *w* which I go … Gen 24:42 1870
w to take my master's brother's … Gen 24:48 1870
the LORD hath prospered my *w* … Gen 24:56 1870
took Rebekah, and went his *w* … Gen 24:61 3212
Isaac came from the *w* of the well … Gen 24:62 935
drink, and rose up, and went his *w* … Gen 25:34 3212
will keep me in this *w* that I go … Gen 28:20 1870
And Jacob went on his *w*, and the … Gen 32:1 1870
that day on his *w* unto Seir … Gen 33:16 1870
was with me in the *w* which I went … Gen 35:3 1870
but a little *w* to come to Ephrath … Gen 35:16 776
and was buried in the *w* to Ephrath … Gen 35:19 1870
which is by the *w* to Timnath … Gen 38:14 1870
And he turned unto her by the *w* … Gen 38:16 1870
that was openly by the *w* side … Gen 38:21 1870
to give them provision for the *w* … Gen 42:25 1870
him by the *w* in the which ye go … Gen 42:38 1870
and gave them provision for the *w* … Gen 45:21 1870
and meat for his father by the *w* … Gen 45:23 1870
See that ye fall not out by the *w* … Gen 45:24 1870
me in the land of Canaan in the *w* … Gen 48:7 1870
a little *w* to come unto Ephrath … Gen 48:7 776
her there in the *w* of Ephrath … Gen 48:7 1870
Dan shall be a serpent by the *w* … Gen 49:17 1870
And he looked this *w* and that *w*, … Ex 2:12 3541
came to pass by the *w* in the inn … Ex 4:24 1870
and Aaron, who stood in the *w* … Ex 5:20 7125
God led them not through the *w* of … Ex 13:17 1870
through the *w* of the wilderness … Ex 13:18 1870
of a cloud, to lead them the *w* … Ex 13:21 1870
that had come upon them by the *w* … Ex 18:8 1870
shalt shew them the *w* wherein … Ex 18:20 1870
he went his *w* into his own land … Ex 18:27
thee, to keep thee in the *w* … Ex 23:20 1870
of the *w* which I commanded them … Ex 32:8 1870
lest I consume thee in the *w* … Ex 33:3 1870
in thy sight, shew me now thy *w* … Ex 33:13 1870
them, Get you up this *w* southward … Num 13:17
by the *w* of the Red sea … Num 14:25 1870
we will go by the king's high *w* … Num 20:17 1870
him, We will go by the high *w* … Num 20:19
Israel came by the *w* of the spies … Num 21:1 1870
mount Hor by the *w* of the Red sea … Num 21:4 1870
much discouraged because of the *w* … Num 21:4 1870
go along by the king's high *w* … Num 21:22 1870
and went up by the *w* of Bashan … Num 21:33 1870
w for an adversary against him … Num 22:22 1870
of the LORD standing in the *w* … Num 22:23 1870
the ass turned aside out of the *w* … Num 22:23 1870
the ass, to turn her into the *w* … Num 22:23 1870
where was no *w* to turn either to … Num 22:26 1870
of the LORD standing in the *w* … Num 22:31 1870
because thy *w* is perverse before … Num 22:32 1870
thou stoodest in the *w* against me … Num 22:34 1870
and Balak also went his *w* … Num 24:25 1870
Horeb by the *w* of mount Seir unto … Deut 1:2 1870
which ye saw by the *w* of the … Deut 1:19 1870
again by what *w* we must go up … Deut 1:22 1870
in all the *w* that ye went, until … Deut 1:31 1870
Who went in the *w* before you … Deut 1:33 1870
shew you by what *w* ye should go … Deut 1:33 1870
by the *w* of the Red sea … Deut 1:40 1870
by the *w* of the Red sea, as the … Deut 2:1 1870
through the *w* of the plain from … Deut 2:8 1870
passed by the *w* of the wilderness … Deut 2:8 1870
I will go along by the high *w* … Deut 2:27 1870
and went up the *w* to Bashan … Deut 3:1 1870
and when thou walkest by the *w* … Deut 6:7 1870
thou shalt remember all the *w* … Deut 8:2 1870
of the *w* which I commanded them … Deut 9:12 1870
w which the LORD had commanded … Deut 9:16 1870
and when thou walkest by the *w* … Deut 11:19 1870
but turn aside out of the *w* which … Deut 11:28 1870
by the *w* where the sun goeth down … Deut 11:30 1870
of the *w* which the LORD thy God … Deut 13:5 1870
if the *w* be too long for thee, so … Deut 14:24 1870
henceforth return no more that *w* … Deut 17:16 1870
Thou shalt prepare thee a *w* … Deut 19:3 1870
him, because the *w* is long … Deut 19:6 1870
ass or his ox fall down by the *w* … Deut 22:4 1870
before thee in the *w* in any tree … Deut 22:6 1870
with bread and with water in the *w* … Deut 23:4 1870
thy God did unto Miriam by the *w* … Deut 24:9 1870
Amalek did unto thee by the *w* … Deut 25:17 1870
How he met thee by the *w*, and … Deut 25:18 1870
the blind to wander out of the *w* … Deut 27:18 1870
shall come out against thee one *w* … Deut 28:7 1870
shalt go out one *w* against them … Deut 28:25 1870
by the *w* whereof I spake unto … Deut 28:68 1870
turn aside from the *w* which I … Deut 31:29 1870
thou shalt make thy *w* prosperous … Josh 1:8 1870
the *w* to Jordan unto the fords … Josh 2:7 1870
and afterward may ye go your *w* … Josh 2:16 1870
sought them throughout all the *w* … Josh 2:22 1870
know the *w* by which ye must go … Josh 3:4 1870
have not passed this *w* heretofore … Josh 3:4 1870
died in the wilderness by the *w* … Josh 5:4 1870
born in the wilderness by the *w* … Josh 5:5 1870
had not circumcised them by the *w* … Josh 5:7 1870
fled by the *w* of the wilderness … Josh 8:15 1870
power to flee this *w* or that *w* … Josh 8:20 2008
chased them along the *w* that … Josh 10:10 1870
the east, the *w* to Beth-jeshimoth … Josh 12:3 1870
I am going the *w* of all the earth … Josh 23:14 1870
us in all the *w* wherein we went … Josh 24:17 1870
w which their fathers walked in … Judg 2:17 1870
doings, nor from their stubborn *w* … Judg 2:19 1870
whether they will keep the *w* of … Judg 2:22 1870
sit in judgment, and walk by the *w* … Judg 5:10 1870
Gideon went up by the *w* of them … Judg 8:11 1870
that came along that *w* by them … Judg 9:25 1870
that we may know whether our *w* … Judg 18:5 1870
the LORD is your *w* wherein ye go … Judg 18:6 1870
when they were a good *w* from the … Judg 18:22
the children of Dan went their *w* … Judg 18:26 1870
of bread, and afterward go your *w* … Judg 19:5
to morrow get you early on your *w* … Judg 19:9 1870
And they passed on and went their *w* … Judg 19:14 3212
house, and went out to go his *w* … Judg 19:27 1870
unto the *w* of the wilderness … Judg 20:42 1870
they went on the *w* to return unto … Ruth 1:7 1870
again, my daughters, go your *w* … Ruth 1:12 1870
So the woman went her *w*, and did … 1Sa 1:18 1870
up by the *w* of his own coast to … 1Sa 6:9 1870
w to the *w* of Beth-shemesh … 1Sa 6:12 1870
shew us our *w* that we should go … 1Sa 9:6 1870
the man of God, to tell us our *w* … 1Sa 9:8 1870
teach you the good and the right *w* … 1Sa 12:23 1870
unto the *w* that leadeth to Ophrah … 1Sa 13:17 1870
turned the *w* to Beth-horon … 1Sa 13:18 1870
w of the border that looketh to … 1Sa 13:18 1870
how he laid wait for him in the *w* … 1Sa 15:2 1870
have gone the *w* which the LORD … 1Sa 15:20 1870
fell down by the *w* to Shaaraim … 1Sa 17:52 1870
go thy *w* … 1Sa 20:22 3212
came to the sheepcotes by the *w* … 1Sa 24:3 1870
out of the cave, and went on his *w* … 1Sa 24:7 1870
David's young men turned their *w* … 1Sa 25:12 1870
is before Jeshimon, by the *w* … 1Sa 26:3 1870

So David went on his *w*, and Saul ... 1Sa 26:25 1870
when thou goest on thy *w* ... 1Sa 28:22 1870
them away, and went on their *w* ... 1Sa 30:2 1870
the *w* of the wilderness of Gibeon ... 2Sa 2:24 1870
to pass, while they were in the *w* ... 2Sa 13:30 1870
the *w* of the hill side behind him ... 2Sa 13:34 1870
and stood beside the *w* of the gate ... 2Sa 15:2 1870
toward the *w* of the wilderness ... 2Sa 15:23 1870
as David and his men went by the *w* ... 2Sa 16:13 1870
Ahimaaz ran by the *w* of the plain ... 2Sa 18:23 1870
w over Jordan with the king ... 2Sa 19:36 1870
As for God, his *w* is perfect ... 2Sa 22:31 1870
and he maketh my *w* perfect ... 2Sa 22:33 1870
rose up, and went every man his *w* ... 1Kin 1:49 1870
I go the *w* of all the earth ... 1Kin 2:2 1870
thy children take heed to their *w* ... 1Kin 2:4 1870
thy children take heed to their *w* ... 1Kin 8:25 1870
to bring his *w* upon his head ... 1Kin 8:32 1870
good *w* wherein they should walk ... 1Kin 8:36 1870
the Shilonite found him in the *w* ... 1Kin 11:29 1870
by the same *w* that thou camest ... 1Kin 13:9 1870
So he went another *w*, and returned ... 1Kin 13:10 1870
returned not by the *w* that he ... 1Kin 13:10 1870
said unto them, What *w* went he ... 1Kin 13:12 1870
seen what *w* the man of God went ... 1Kin 13:12 1870
to go by the *w* that thou camest ... 1Kin 13:17 1870
was gone, a lion met him by the *w* ... 1Kin 13:24 1870
and his carcase was cast in the *w* ... 1Kin 13:24 1870
and saw the carcase cast in the *w* ... 1Kin 13:25 1870
him back from the *w* heard thereof ... 1Kin 13:26 1870
found his carcase cast in the *w* ... 1Kin 13:28 1870
returned not from his evil *w* ... 1Kin 13:33 1870
and walked in the *w* of his father ... 1Kin 15:26 1870
and walked in the *w* of Jeroboam ... 1Kin 15:34 1870
hast walked in the *w* of Jeroboam ... 1Kin 16:2 1870
in walking in the *w* of Jeroboam ... 1Kin 16:19 1870
For he walked in all the *w* of ... 1Kin 16:26 1870
Ahab went one *w* by himself ... 1Kin 18:6 1870
Obadiah went another *w* by himself ... 1Kin 18:6 1870
And as Obadiah was in the *w* ... 1Kin 18:7 1870
return on thy *w* to the wilderness ... 1Kin 19:15 1870
and waited for the king by the *w* ... 1Kin 20:38 1870
Which *w* went the Spirit of the ... 1Kin 22:24 2088
and walked in the *w* of his father ... 1Kin 22:52 1870
in the *w* of his mother, and in the ... 1Kin 22:52 1870
in the *w* of Jeroboam the son of ... 1Kin 22:52 1870
and as he was going up by the *w* ... 2Kin 2:23 1870
he said, Which *w* shall we go up ... 2Kin 3:8 1870
The *w* through the wilderness of ... 2Kin 3:8 1870
there came water by the *w* of Edom ... 2Kin 3:20 1870
staff in thine hand, and go thy *w* ... 2Kin 4:29 1870
he departed from him a little *w* ... 2Kin 5:19 776
said unto them, This is not the *w* ... 2Kin 6:19 1870
all the *w* was full of garments and ... 2Kin 7:15 1870
he walked in the *w* of the kings ... 2Kin 8:18 1870
he walked in the *w* of the house ... 2Kin 8:27 1870
he fled by the *w* of the garden ... 2Kin 9:27 1870
at the shearing house in the *w* ... 2Kin 10:12 1870
she went by the *w* by the which ... 2Kin 11:16 1870
came by the *w* of the gate of the ... 2Kin 11:19 1870
But he walked in the *w* of the ... 2Kin 16:3 1870
by the *w* by which thou camest ... 2Kin 19:28 1870
By the *w* that he came, by the ... 2Kin 19:33 1870
he walked in all the *w* that his ... 2Kin 21:21 1870
walked not in the *w* of the LORD ... 2Kin 21:22 1870
walked in all the *w* of David his ... 2Kin 22:2 1870
w of the gate between two walls ... 2Kin 25:4 1870
king went the *w* toward the plain ... 2Kin 25:4 1870
heed to their *w* to walk in my law ... 2Chr 6:16 1870
his *w* upon his own head ... 2Chr 6:23 1870
thou hast taught them the good *w* ... 2Chr 6:27 1870
the *w* that thou shalt send them ... 2Chr 6:34 1870
they walked in the *w* of David ... 2Chr 11:17 1870
Which *w* went the Spirit of the ... 2Chr 18:23 1870
he walked in the *w* of Asa his ... 2Chr 20:32 1870
he walked in the *w* of the kings ... 2Chr 21:6 1870
in the *w* of the kings of Israel ... 2Chr 21:13 1870
to seek of him a right *w* for us ... Ezr 8:21 1870
us against the enemy in the *w* ... Ezr 8:22 1870
of such as lay in wait by the *w* ... Ezr 8:31 1870
Then he said unto them, Go your *w* ... Neh 8:10 1870
the people went their *w* to eat ... Neh 8:12 1870
in the *w* wherein they should go ... Neh 9:12 1870
by day, to lead them in the *w* ... Neh 9:19 1870
the *w* wherein they should go ... Neh 9:19 1870
So Mordecai went his *w*, and did ... Est 4:17
given to a man whose *w* is hid ... Job 3:23 1870
paths of their *w* are turned aside ... Job 6:18 1870
Behold, this is the joy of his *w* ... Job 8:19 1870
a wilderness where there is no *w* ... Job 12:24 1870
then I shall go the *w* whence I ... Job 16:22 734
also shall hold on his *w*, and he ... Job 17:9 1870
and a trap for him in the *w* ... Job 18:10 5410
fenced up my *w* that I cannot pass ... Job 19:8 734
and raise up their *w* against me ... Job 19:12 1870
not asked them that go by the *w* ... Job 21:29 1870
shall declare his *w* to his face ... Job 21:31 1870
Hast thou marked the old *w* which ... Job 22:15 734
But he knoweth the *w* that I take ... Job 23:10 1870
his *w* have I kept, and not ... Job 23:11 1870
They turn the needy out of the *w* ... Job 24:4 1870
not the *w* of the vineyards ... Job 24:18 1870
taken out of the *w* as all other ... Job 24:24 1870
God understandeth the *w* thereof ... Job 28:23 1870
a *w* for the lightning of the ... Job 28:26 1870
I chose out their *w*, and sat chief ... Job 29:25 1870
my step hath turned out of the *w* ... Job 31:7 1870
Who hath enjoined him his *w* ... Job 36:23 1870
Where is the *w* where light ... Job 38:19 1870
By what *w* is the light parted, ... Job 38:24 1870
or a *w* for the lightning of ... Job 38:25 1870
nor standeth in the *w* of sinners ... Ps 1:1 1870
knoweth the *w* of the righteous ... Ps 1:6 1870
but the *w* of the ungodly shall ... Ps 1:6 1870
be angry, and ye perish from the *w* ... Ps 2:12 1870
make thy *w* straight before my ... Ps 5:8 1870
As for God, his *w* is perfect ... Ps 18:30 1870
strength, and maketh my *w* perfect ... Ps 18:32 1870
will he teach sinners in the *w* ... Ps 25:8 1870
and the meek will he teach his *w* ... Ps 25:9 1870
in the *w* that he shall choose ... Ps 25:12 1870
Teach me thy *w*, O LORD, and lead ... Ps 27:11 1870
teach thee in the *w* which thou ... Ps 32:8 1870
stop the *w* against them that ... Ps 35:3
Let their *w* be dark and slippery ... Ps 35:6 1870
himself in a *w* that is not good ... Ps 36:4 1870
Commit thy *w* unto the LORD ... Ps 37:5 1870
of him who prospereth in his *w* ... Ps 37:7 1870
and he delighteth in his *w* ... Ps 37:23 1870
Wait on the LORD, and keep his *w* ... Ps 37:34 1870
our steps declined from thy *w* ... Ps 44:18 734
This their *w* is their folly ... Ps 49:13 1870
That thy *w* may be known upon ... Ps 67:2 1870
Thy *w*, O God, is in the sanctuary ... Ps 77:13 1870
Thy *w* is in the sea, and thy path ... Ps 77:19 1870
He made a *w* to his anger ... Ps 78:50 5410
which pass by the *w* do pluck her ... Ps 80:12 1870
set us in the *w* of his steps ... Ps 85:13 1870
Teach me thy *w*, O LORD ... Ps 86:11 1870
All that pass by the *w* spoil him ... Ps 89:41 1870
myself wisely in a perfect *w* ... Ps 101:2 1870
he that walketh in a perfect *w* ... Ps 101:6 1870
He weakened my strength in the *w* ... Ps 102:23 1870
in the wilderness in a solitary *w* ... Ps 107:4 1870
he led them forth by the right *w* ... Ps 107:7 1870
wilderness, where there is no *w* ... Ps 107:40 1870
shall drink of the brook in the *w* ... Ps 110:7 1870
are the undefiled in the *w* ... Ps 119:1 1870
shall a young man cleanse his *w* ... Ps 119:9 734
in the *w* of thy testimonies ... Ps 119:14 1870
understand the *w* of thy precepts ... Ps 119:27 1870
Remove from me the *w* of lying ... Ps 119:29 1870
I have chosen the *w* of truth ... Ps 119:30 1870
I will run the *w* of thy ... Ps 119:32 1870
me, O LORD, the *w* of thy statutes ... Ps 119:33 1870
and quicken thou me in thy *w* ... Ps 119:37 1870
my feet from every evil *w* ... Ps 119:101 734
therefore I hate every false *w* ... Ps 119:104 734
and I hate every false *w* ... Ps 119:128 734
if there be any wicked *w* in me ... Ps 139:24 1870
and lead me in the *w* everlasting ... Ps 139:24 1870
In the *w* wherein I walked have ... Ps 142:3 734
cause me to know the *w* wherein I ... Ps 143:8 1870
but the *w* of the wicked he ... Ps 146:9 1870
walk not thou in the *w* with them ... Prov 1:15 1870
eat of the fruit of their own *w* ... Prov 1:31 1870
and preserveth the *w* of his saints ... Prov 2:8 1870
thee from the *w* of the evil man ... Prov 2:12 1870
mayest walk in the *w* of good men ... Prov 2:20 1870
shalt thou walk in thy *w* safely ... Prov 3:23 1870
taught thee in the *w* of wisdom ... Prov 4:11 1870
and go not in the *w* of evil men ... Prov 4:14 1870
The *w* of the wicked is as ... Prov 4:19 1870
Remove thy *w* far from her, and ... Prov 5:8 1870
of instruction are the *w* of life ... Prov 6:23 1870
he went the *w* to her house, ... Prov 7:8 1870
Her house is the *w* to hell ... Prov 7:27 1870
by the *w* in the places of the ... Prov 8:2 1870
and arrogancy, and the evil *w* ... Prov 8:13 1870
I lead in the *w* of righteousness, ... Prov 8:20 734
me in the beginning of his *w* ... Prov 8:22 1870
go in the *w* of understanding ... Prov 9:6 1870
He is in the *w* of life that ... Prov 10:17 734
The *w* of the LORD is strength to ... Prov 10:29 1870
of the perfect shall direct his *w* ... Prov 11:5 1870
in their *w* are his delight ... Prov 11:20 1870
The *w* of a fool is right in his ... Prov 12:15 1870
but the *w* of the wicked seduceth ... Prov 12:26 1870
In the *w* of righteousness is life ... Prov 12:28 734
him that is upright in the *w* ... Prov 13:6 1870
but the *w* of transgressors is ... Prov 13:15 1870
prudent is to understand his *w* ... Prov 14:8 1870
There is a *w* which seemeth right ... Prov 14:12 1870
The *w* of the wicked is an ... Prov 15:9 1870
unto him that forsaketh the *w* ... Prov 15:10 734
The *w* of the slothful man is as ... Prov 15:19 1870
but the *w* of the righteous is ... Prov 15:19 734
The *w* of life is above to the ... Prov 15:24 734
A man's heart deviseth his *w* ... Prov 16:9 1870
keepeth his *w* preserveth his soul ... Prov 16:17 1870
There is a *w* that seemeth right ... Prov 16:25 1870
him into the *w* that is not good ... Prov 16:29 1870
found in the *w* of righteousness ... Prov 16:31 1870
of man perverteth his *w* ... Prov 19:3 1870
but when he is gone his *w* ... Prov 20:14
a man then understand his own *w* ... Prov 20:24 1870
Every *w* of a man is right in his ... Prov 21:2 1870
The *w* of man is froward and ... Prov 21:8 1870
w of understanding shall remain ... Prov 21:16 1870
the upright, he directeth his *w* ... Prov 21:29 1870
are in the *w* of the froward ... Prov 22:5 1870
up a child in the *w* he should go ... Prov 22:6 1870
and guide thine heart in the *w* ... Prov 23:19 1870
saith, There is a lion in the *w* ... Prov 26:13 1870
to go astray in an evil *w* ... Prov 28:10 1870
he that is upright in the *w* is ... Prov 29:27 1870
The *w* of an eagle in the air ... Prov 30:19 1870
the *w* of a serpent upon a rock ... Prov 30:19 1870
the *w* of a ship in the midst of ... Prov 30:19 1870
the *w* of a man with a maid ... Prov 30:19 1870
Such is the *w* of an adulterous ... Prov 30:20 1870
Go thy *w*, eat thy bread with joy, ... Eccl 9:7
that is a fool walketh by the *w* ... Eccl 10:3 1870
not what is the *w* of the spirit ... Eccl 11:5 1870
high, and fears shall be in the *w* ... Eccl 12:5 1870
go thy *w* forth by the footsteps ... Song 1:8 1870
destroy the *w* of thy paths ... Is 3:12 1870
not walk in the *w* of this people ... Is 8:11 1870
afflict her by the *w* of the sea ... Is 9:1 1870
for in the *w* of Horonaim they ... Is 15:5 1870
The *w* of the just is uprightness ... Is 26:7 734
in the *w* of thy judgments, O LORD ... Is 26:8 734
strong drink are out of the *w* ... Is 28:7 8582
they are out of the *w* through ... Is 28:7 8582
Get you out of the *w*, turn aside ... Is 30:11 1870
thee, saying, This is the *w* ... Is 30:21 1870
an highway shall be there, and a *w* ... Is 35:8 1870
shall be called The *w* of holiness ... Is 35:8 1870
by the *w* by which thou camest ... Is 37:29 1870
By the *w* that he came, by the ... Is 37:34 1870
Prepare ye the *w* of the LORD ... Is 40:3 1870
to him the *w* of understanding ... Is 40:14 1870
My *w* is hid from the LORD, and my ... Is 40:27 1870
even by the *w* that he had not ... Is 41:3 734
blind by a *w* that they knew not ... Is 42:16 1870
LORD, which maketh a *w* in the sea ... Is 43:16 1870
even make a *w* in the wilderness ... Is 43:19 1870
and he shall make his *w* prosperous ... Is 48:15 1870
by the *w* that thou shouldest go ... Is 48:17 1870
I will make all my mountains a *w* ... Is 49:11 1870
made the depths of the sea a *w* ... Is 51:10 1870
turned every one to his own *w* ... Is 53:6 1870
Let the wicked forsake his *w* ... Is 55:7 1870
they all look to their own *w* ... Is 56:11 1870
wearied in the greatness of thy *w* ... Is 57:10 1870
ye up, cast ye up, prepare the *w* ... Is 57:14 1870
out of the *w* of my people ... Is 57:14 1870
frowardly in the *w* of his heart ... Is 57:17 1870
The *w* of peace they know not ... Is 59:8 1870
prepare ye the *w* of the people ... Is 62:10 1870
walketh in a *w* that was not good ... Is 65:2 1870
God, when he led thee by the *w* ... Jer 2:17 1870
hast thou to do in the *w* of Egypt ... Jer 2:18 1870
thou to do in the *w* of Assyria ... Jer 2:18 1870
see thy *w* in the valley, know ... Jer 2:23 1870
trimmest thou thy *w* to seek love ... Jer 2:33 1870
about so much to change thy *w* ... Jer 2:36 1870
for they have perverted their *w* ... Jer 3:21 1870
of the Gentiles is on his *w* ... Jer 4:7 5265
Thy *w* and thy doings have procured ... Jer 4:18 1870
they know not the *w* of the LORD ... Jer 5:4 1870
they have known the *w* of the LORD ... Jer 5:5 1870
old paths, where is the good *w* ... Jer 6:16 1870
into the field, nor walk by the *w* ... Jer 6:25 1870
thou mayest know and try their *w* ... Jer 6:27 1870
Learn not the *w* of the heathen, ... Jer 10:2 1870
I know that the *w* of man is not ... Jer 10:23 1870
Wherefore doth the *w* of the ... Jer 12:1 1870
ye now every one from his evil *w* ... Jer 18:11 1870
walk in paths, in a *w* not cast up ... Jer 18:15 1870
w of life, and the *w* of death ... Jer 21:8 1870
Wherefore their *w* shall be unto ... Jer 23:12 1870
turned them from their evil *w* ... Jer 23:22 1870
now every one from his evil *w* ... Jer 25:5 1870
shepherds shall have no *w* to flee ... Jer 25:35 4498
and turn every man from his evil *w* ... Jer 26:3 1870
the prophet Jeremiah went his *w* ... Jer 28:11 1870
rivers of waters in a straight *w* ... Jer 31:9 1870
even the *w* which thou wentest ... Jer 31:21 1870
give them one heart, and one *w* ... Jer 32:39 1870
ye now every man from his evil *w* ... Jer 35:15 1870
return every man from his evil *w* ... Jer 36:3 1870
return every one from his evil *w* ... Jer 36:7 1870
by the *w* of the king's garden, by ... Jer 39:4 1870
and he went out the *w* of the plain ... Jer 39:4 1870
shew us the *w* wherein we may walk ... Jer 42:3 1870
of Aroer, stand by the *w*, and espy ... Jer 48:19 1870
They shall ask the *w* to Zion with ... Jer 50:5 1870
the *w* of the gate between the two ... Jer 52:7 1870
they went by the *w* of the plain ... Jer 52:7 1870
warn the wicked from his wicked *w* ... Eze 3:18 1870
wickedness, nor from his wicked *w* ... Eze 3:19 1870
I will do unto them after their *w* ... Eze 7:27 1870
eyes now the *w* toward the north ... Eze 8:5 1870
mine eyes the *w* toward the north ... Eze 8:5 1870
from the *w* of the higher gate ... Eze 9:2 1870
their *w* upon their head ... Eze 9:10 1870
their *w* upon their own heads ... Eze 11:21 1870
not return from his wicked *w* ... Eze 13:22 1870
unto you, and ye shall see their *w* ... Eze 14:22 1870
high place at every head of the *w* ... Eze 16:25 1870
which are ashamed of thy lewd *w* ... Eze 16:27 1870
place in the head of every *w* ... Eze 16:31 1870
recompense thy *w* upon thine head ... Eze 16:43 1870
The *w* of the Lord is not equal ... Eze 18:25 1870
Is not my *w* equal ... Eze 18:25 1870
The *w* of the Lord is not equal ... Eze 18:29 1870
Go thee one *w* or other, either on ... Eze 21:16
at the head of the *w* to the city ... Eze 21:19 1870
Appoint a *w*, that the sword may ... Eze 21:20 1870
stood at the parting of the *w* ... Eze 21:21 1870
their own *w* have I recompensed ... Eze 22:31 1870
that they took both one *w* ... Eze 23:13 1870
walked in the *w* of thy sister ... Eze 23:31 1870
to warn the wicked from his *w* ... Eze 33:8 1870
wicked of his *w* to turn from it ... Eze 33:9 1870
if he do not turn from his *w* ... Eze 33:9 1870
that the wicked turn from his *w* ... Eze 33:11 1870
The *w* of the Lord is not equal ... Eze 33:17 1870
as for them, their *w* is not equal ... Eze 33:17 1870
The *w* of the Lord is not equal ... Eze 33:20 1870
they defiled it by their own *w* ... Eze 36:17 1870
their *w* was before me as the ... Eze 36:17 1870
according to their *w* and according ... Eze 36:19 1870
court, the *w* toward the north ... Eze 42:1 1870
breadth inward, a *w* of one cubit ... Eze 42:4 1870
the *w* before them was like the ... Eze 42:11 1870
was a door in the head of the *w* ... Eze 42:12 1870
even the *w* directly before the ... Eze 42:12 1870
came from the *w* of the east ... Eze 43:2 1870
w of the gate whose prospect is ... Eze 43:4 1870
the *w* of the gate of the outward ... Eze 44:1 1870

he shall enter by the *w* of the	Eze 44:3	1870
shall go out by the *w* of the same	Eze 44:3	1870
Then brought he me the *w* of the	Eze 44:4	1870
the *w* of the porch of that gate	Eze 46:2	1870
he shall go in by the *w* of the	Eze 46:8	1870
shall go forth by the *w* thereof	Eze 46:8	1870
he that entereth in by the *w* of	Eze 46:9	1870
go out by the *w* of the south gate	Eze 46:9	1870
he that entereth by the *w* of the	Eze 46:9	1870
forth by the *w* of the north gate	Eze 46:9	1870
he shall not return by the *w* of	Eze 46:9	1870
of the *w* of the gate northward	Eze 47:2	1870
led me about the *w* without unto	Eze 47:2	1870
by the *w* that looketh eastward	Eze 47:2	1870
the *w* of Hethlon, as men go to	Eze 47:15	1870
to the coast of the *w* of Hethlon	Eze 48:1	1870
And he said, Go thy *w*, Daniel	Dan 12:9	
But go thou thy *w* till the end be	Dan 12:13	1870
I will hedge up thy *w* with thorns	Hos 2:6	1870
murder in the *w* by consent	Hos 6:9	1870
because thou didst trust in thy *w*	Hos 10:13	1870
by the *w* will I observe them	Hos 13:7	1870
and turn aside the *w* of the meek	Amos 2:7	1870
turn every one from his evil *w*	Jonah 3:8	1870
they turned from their evil *w*	Jonah 3:10	1870
LORD hath his *w* in the whirlwind	Nah 1:3	1870
keep the munition, watch the *w*	Nah 2:1	1870
they went their *w* as a flock	Zec 10:2	
But ye are departed out of the *w*	Mal 2:8	1870
he shall prepare the *w* before me	Mal 3:1	1870
into their own country another *w*	Mt 2:12	*3598*
Prepare ye the *w* of the Lord	Mt 3:3	*3598*
by the *w* of the sea, beyond	Mt 4:15	*3598*
before the altar, and go thy *w*	Mt 5:24	
whiles thou art in the *w* with him	Mt 5:25	*3598*
is the gate, and broad is the *w*	Mt 7:13	*3598*
is the gate, and narrow is the *w*	Mt 7:14	*3598*
but go thy *w*, shew thyself to the	Mt 8:4	
said unto the centurion, Go thy *w*	Mt 8:13	
that no man might pass by that *w*	Mt 8:28	*3598*
there was a good *w* off from them	Mt 8:30	*3112*
Go not into the *w* of the Gentiles	Mt 10:5	*3598*
shall prepare thy *w* before thee	Mt 11:10	*3598*
some seeds fell by the *w* side	Mt 13:4	*3598*
which received seed by the *w* side	Mt 13:19	*3598*
among the wheat, and went his *w*	Mt 13:25	
fasting, lest they faint in the *w*	Mt 15:32	*3598*
And they went their *w*	Mt 20:4	
Take that thine is, and go thy *w*	Mt 20:14	
twelve disciples apart in the *w*	Mt 20:17	*3598*
blind men sitting by the *w* side	Mt 20:30	*3598*
spread their garments in the *w*	Mt 21:8	*3598*
trees, and strawed them in the *w*	Mt 21:8	*3598*
when he saw a fig tree in the *w*	Mt 21:19	*3598*
you in the *w* of righteousness	Mt 21:32	*3598*
teachest the *w* of God in truth,	Mt 22:16	*3598*
and left him, and went their *w*	Mt 22:22	
go your *w*, make it as sure as ye	Mt 27:65	
shall prepare thy *w* before thee	Mk 1:2	*3598*
Prepare ye the *w* of the Lord	Mk 1:3	*3598*
but go thy *w*, shew thyself to the	Mk 1:44	
go thy *w* into thine house	Mk 2:11	
he sowed, some fell by the *w* side	Mk 4:4	*3598*
And these are they by the *w* side	Mk 4:15	*3598*
her, For this saying go thy *w*	Mk 7:29	
houses, they will faint by the *w*	Mk 8:3	*3598*
by the *w* he asked his disciples,	Mk 8:27	*3598*
among yourselves by the *w*	Mk 9:33	*3598*
for by the *w* they had disputed	Mk 9:34	*3598*
when he was gone forth into the *w*	Mk 10:17	*3598*
go thy *w*, sell whatsoever thou	Mk 10:21	
they were in the *w* going up to	Mk 10:32	*3598*
And Jesus said unto him, Go thy *w*	Mk 10:52	
sight, and followed Jesus in the *w*	Mk 10:52	*3598*
Go your *w* into the village over	Mk 11:2	
And they went their *w*, and found	Mk 11:4	
spread their garments in the *w*	Mk 11:8	*3598*
trees, and strawed them in the *w*	Mk 11:8	*3598*
and they left him, and went their *w*	Mk 12:12	
teachest the *w* of God in truth	Mk 12:14	*3598*
But go your *w*, tell his disciples	Mk 16:7	
our feet into the *w* of peace	Lk 1:79	*3598*
Prepare ye the *w* of the Lord	Lk 3:4	*3598*
the midst of them went his *w*	Lk 4:30	
they could not find by what *w*	Lk 5:19	
said unto them, Go your *w*	Lk 7:22	
shall prepare thy *w* before thee	Lk 7:27	*3598*
he sowed, some fell by the *w* side	Lk 8:5	*3598*
Those by the *w* side are they that	Lk 8:12	*3598*
And he went his *w*, and published	Lk 8:39	
pass, that, as they went in the *w*	Lk 9:57	*3598*
and salute no man by the *w*	Lk 10:4	*3598*
came down a certain priest that *w*	Lk 10:31	*3598*
magistrate, as thou art in the *w*	Lk 12:58	*3598*
the other is yet a great *w* off	Lk 14:32	*4206*
But when he was yet a great *w* off	Lk 15:20	*3112*
he said unto him, Arise, go thy *w*	Lk 17:19	
man sat by the *w* side begging	Lk 18:35	*3598*
for he was to pass that *w*	Lk 19:4	
they that were sent went their *w*	Lk 19:32	
spread their clothes in the *w*	Lk 19:36	*3598*
but teachest the *w* of God truly	Lk 20:21	*3598*
And he went his *w*, and communed	Lk 22:4	
while he talked with us by the *w*	Lk 24:32	*3598*
what things were done in the *w*	Lk 24:35	*3598*
Make straight the *w* of the Lord	Jn 1:23	*3598*
went her *w* into the city, and	Jn 4:28	
Jesus saith unto him, Go thy *w*	Jn 4:50	
spoken unto him, and he went his *w*	Jn 4:50	
Jesus again unto them, I go my *w*	Jn 8:21	
He went his *w* therefore, and	Jn 9:7	
but climbeth up some other *w*	Jn 10:1	
she had so said, she went her *w*	Jn 11:28	
I go ye know, and the *w* ye know	Jn 14:4	*3598*
and how can we know the *w*	Jn 14:5	*3598*
Jesus saith unto him, I am the *w*	Jn 14:6	*3598*
But now I go my *w* to him that	Jn 16:5	
ye seek me, let these go their *w*	Jn 18:8	
go toward the south unto the *w*	Acts 8:26	*3598*
And as they went on their *w*	Acts 8:36	*3598*
and he went on his *w* rejoicing	Acts 8:39	*3598*
that if he found any of this *w*	Acts 9:2	*3598*
the Lord said unto him, Go thy *w*	Acts 9:15	
And Ananias went his *w*, and entered	Acts 9:17	
unto thee in the *w* as thou camest	Acts 9:17	*3598*
how he had seen the Lord in the *w*	Acts 9:27	*3598*
brought on their *w* by the church	Acts 15:3	*4311*
shew unto us the *w* of salvation	Acts 16:17	*3598*
instructed in the *w* of the Lord	Acts 18:25	*3598*
him the *w* of God more perfectly	Acts 18:26	*3598*
of that *w* before the multitude	Acts 19:9	*3598*
arose no small stir about that *w*	Acts 19:23	*3598*
days, we departed and went our *w*	Acts 21:5	*4311*
and they all brought us on our *w*	Acts 21:5	*4311*
persecuted this *w* unto the death	Acts 22:4	*3598*
that after the *w* which they call	Acts 24:14	*3598*
more perfect knowledge of that *w*	Acts 24:22	*3598*
answered, Go thy *w* for this time	Acts 24:25	
laying wait in the *w* to kill him	Acts 25:3	*3598*
I saw in the *w* a light from	Acts 26:13	*3598*
Much every *w*: chiefly	Rom 3:2	*5158*
They are all gone out of the *w*	Rom 3:12	
the *w* of peace have they not	Rom 3:17	*3598*
to fall in his brother's *w*	Rom 14:13	
on my *w* thitherward by you	Rom 15:24	*4311*
also make a *w* to escape, that ye	1Cor 10:13	*1545*
I unto you a more excellent *w*	1Cor 12:31	*3598*
I will not see you now by the *w*	1Cor 16:7	*3938*
be brought on my *w* toward Judaea	2Cor 1:16	*4311*
notwithstanding, every *w*, whether	Phil 1:18	*5158*
to us, and took it out of the *w*	Col 2:14	*3319*
Christ, direct our *w* unto you	1Th 3:11	*3598*
until he be taken out of the *w*	2Th 2:7	*3319*
and on them that are out of the *w*	Heb 5:2	*4105*
that the *w* into the holiest of	Heb 9:8	*3598*
By a new and living *w*, which he	Heb 10:20	*3598*
is lame be turned out of the *w*	Heb 12:13	*1624*
beholdeth himself, and goeth his *w*	Jas 1:24	
and had sent them out another *w*	Jas 2:25	*3598*
w shall save a soul from death	Jas 5:20	*3598*
by reason of whom the *w* of truth	2Pet 2:2	*3598*
Which have forsaken the right *w*	2Pet 2:15	*3598*
following the *w* of Balaam the son	2Pet 2:15	*3598*
have known the *w* of righteousness	2Pet 2:21	*3598*
pure minds by *w* of remembrance	2Pet 3:1	*1722*
they have gone in the *w* of Cain	Jude 11	*3598*
that the *w* of the kings of the	Rev 16:12	*3598*

WAYFARING

he saw a *w* man in the street of	Judg 19:17	732
to dress for the *w* man that was	2Sa 12:4	732
lie waste, the *w* man ceaseth	Is 33:8	
the *w* men, though fools, shall	Is 35:8	
a lodging place of *w* men	Jer 9:2	732
as a *w* man that turneth aside to	Jer 14:8	732

WAYMARKS

Set thee up *w*, make thee high	Jer 31:21	6725

WAYS

rise up early, and go on your *w*	Gen 19:2	1870
w hide their eyes from the man	Lev 20:4	
your high *w* shall be desolate	Lev 26:22	1870
But if he shall any *w* make them	Num 30:15	
Ye shall walk in all the *w* which	Deut 5:33	1870
LORD thy God, to walk in his *w*	Deut 8:6	1870
thy God, to walk in all his *w*	Deut 10:12	1870
your God, to walk in all his *w*	Deut 11:22	1870
thy God, and to walk ever in his *w*	Deut 19:9	1870
be thy God, and to walk in his *w*	Deut 26:17	1870
way, and flee before thee seven *w*	Deut 28:7	1870
LORD thy God, and walk in his *w*	Deut 28:9	1870
them, and flee seven *w* before them	Deut 28:25	1870
thou shalt not prosper in thy *w*	Deut 28:29	1870
LORD thy God, to walk in his *w*	Deut 30:16	1870
for all his *w* are judgment	Deut 32:4	1870
your God, and to walk in all his *w*	Josh 22:5	1870
And his sons walked not in his *w*	1Sa 8:3	1870
and thy sons walk not in thy *w*	1Sa 8:5	1870
himself wisely in all his *w*	1Sa 18:14	1870
For I have kept the *w* of the LORD	2Sa 22:22	1870
LORD thy God, to walk in his *w*	1Kin 2:3	1870
And if thou wilt walk in my *w*	1Kin 3:14	1870
to every man according to his *w*	1Kin 8:39	1870
unto him, to walk in all his *w*	1Kin 8:58	1870
and have not walked in my *w*	1Kin 11:33	1870
thee, and wilt walk in my *w*	1Kin 11:38	1870
in all the *w* of Asa his father	1Kin 22:43	1870
saying, Turn ye from your evil *w*	2Kin 17:13	1870
man according unto all his *w*	2Chr 6:30	1870
may fear thee, to walk in thy *w*	2Chr 6:31	1870
face, and turn from their wicked *w*	2Chr 7:14	1870
of the acts of Abijah, and his *w*	2Chr 13:22	1870
the first *w* of his father David	2Chr 17:3	1870
lifted up in the *w* of the LORD	2Chr 17:6	1870
the *w* of Jehoshaphat thy father	2Chr 21:12	1870
nor in the *w* of Asa king of Judah	2Chr 21:12	1870
in the *w* of the house of Ahab	2Chr 22:3	1870
his *w* before the LORD his God	2Chr 27:6	1870
Jotham, and all his wars, and his *w*	2Chr 27:7	1870
For he walked in the *w* of the	2Chr 28:2	1870
rest of his acts and of all his *w*	2Chr 28:26	1870
the nations of those lands any *w*	2Chr 32:13	
walked in the *w* of David his	2Chr 34:2	1870
hope, and the uprightness of thy *w*	Job 4:6	1870
maintain mine own *w* before him	Job 13:15	1870
desire not the knowledge of thy *w*	Job 21:14	1870
that thou makest thy *w* perfect	Job 22:3	1870
the light shall shine upon thy *w*	Job 22:28	1870
they know not the *w* thereof	Job 24:13	1870
yet his eyes are upon their *w*	Job 24:23	1870
Lo, these are parts of his *w*	Job 26:14	1870
me the *w* of their destruction	Job 30:12	734
Doth not he see my *w*, and count	Job 31:4	1870
man to find according to his *w*	Job 34:11	734
his eyes are upon the *w* of man	Job 34:21	1870
would not consider any of his *w*	Job 34:27	1870
He is the chief of the *w* of God	Job 40:19	1870
His *w* are always grievous	Ps 10:5	1870
For I have kept the *w* of the LORD	Ps 18:21	1870
Shew me thy *w*, O LORD	Ps 25:4	1870
I said, I will take heed to my *w*	Ps 39:1	1870
will I teach transgressors thy *w*	Ps 51:13	1870
me, and Israel had walked in my *w*	Ps 81:13	1870
in whose heart are the *w* of them	Ps 84:5	4546
thee, to keep thee in all thy *w*	Ps 91:11	1870
and they have not known my *w*	Ps 95:10	1870
He made known his *w* unto Moses	Ps 103:7	1870
they walk in his *w*	Ps 119:3	1870
O that my *w* were directed to keep	Ps 119:5	1870
and have respect unto thy *w*	Ps 119:15	734
I have declared my *w*, and thou	Ps 119:26	1870
I thought on my *w*, and turned my	Ps 119:59	1870
for all my *w* are before thee	Ps 119:168	1870
turn aside unto their crooked *w*	Ps 125:5	
that walketh in his *w*	Ps 128:1	1870
shall sing in the *w* of the LORD	Ps 138:5	1870
and art acquainted with all my *w*	Ps 139:3	1870
LORD is righteous in all his *w*	Ps 145:17	1870
So are the *w* of every one that is	Prov 1:19	734
to walk in the *w* of darkness	Prov 2:13	1870
Whose *w* are crooked, and they	Prov 2:15	734
In all thy *w* acknowledge him, and	Prov 3:6	1870
Her *w* are *w* of pleasantness,	Prov 3:17	1870
and choose none of his *w*	Prov 3:31	1870
let all thy *w* be established	Prov 4:26	1870
her *w* are moveable, that thou	Prov 5:6	4570
For the *w* of man are before the	Prov 5:21	1870
consider her *w*, and be wise	Prov 6:6	1870
not thine heart decline to her *w*	Prov 7:25	1870
blessed are they that keep my *w*	Prov 8:32	1870
who go right on their *w*	Prov 9:15	734
perverteth his *w* shall be known	Prov 10:9	1870
perverse in his *w* despiseth him	Prov 14:2	1870
end thereof are the *w* of death	Prov 14:12	1870
shall be filled with his own *w*	Prov 14:14	1870
All the *w* of a man are clean in	Prov 16:2	1870
When a man's *w* please the LORD,	Prov 16:7	1870
end thereof are the *w* of death	Prov 16:25	1870
to pervert the *w* of judgment	Prov 17:23	734
he that despiseth his *w* shall die	Prov 19:16	1870
Lest thou learn his *w*, and get a	Prov 22:25	734
and let thine eyes observe my *w*	Prov 23:26	1870
than he that is perverse in his *w*	Prov 28:6	1870
in his *w* shall fall at once	Prov 28:18	1870
women, nor thy *w* to that which	Prov 31:3	1870
well to the *w* of her household	Prov 31:27	1979
walk in the *w* of thine heart, and	Eccl 11:9	1870
in the broad *w* I will seek him	Song 3:2	7339
and he will teach us of his *w*	Is 2:3	1870
for they would not walk in his *w*	Is 42:24	1870
and I will direct all his *w*	Is 45:13	1870
They shall feed in the *w*, and	Is 49:9	1870
neither are your *w* my *w*	Is 55:8	1870
so are my *w* higher than your *w*	Is 55:9	1870
I have seen his *w*, and will heal	Is 57:18	1870
me daily, and delight to know my *w*	Is 58:2	1870
honour him, not doing thine own *w*	Is 58:13	1870
thou made us to err from thy *w*	Is 63:17	1870
those that remember thee in thy *w*	Is 64:5	1870
Yea, they have chosen their own *w*	Is 66:3	1870
swift dromedary traversing her *w*	Jer 2:23	1870
also taught the wicked ones thy *w*	Jer 2:33	1870
In the *w* hast thou sat for them,	Jer 3:2	1870
hast scattered thy *w* to the	Jer 3:13	1870
saith the LORD, Stand ye in the *w*	Jer 6:16	1870
the God of Israel, Amend your *w*	Jer 7:3	1870
For if ye throughly amend your *w*	Jer 7:5	1870
walk ye in all the *w* that I have	Jer 7:23	1870
learn the *w* of my people, to	Jer 12:16	1870
they return not from their *w*	Jer 15:7	1870
mine eyes are upon all their *w*	Jer 16:17	1870
give every man according to his *w*	Jer 17:10	1870
from his evil way, and make your *w*	Jer 18:11	1870
in their *w* from the ancient paths	Jer 18:15	1870
as slippery *w* in the darkness	Jer 23:12	
Therefore now amend your *w*	Jer 26:13	1870
upon all the *w* of the sons of men	Jer 32:19	1870
give every one according to his *w*	Jer 32:19	1870
The *w* of Zion do mourn, because	Lam 1:4	1870
inclosed my *w* with hewn stone	Lam 3:9	1870
He hath turned aside my *w*	Lam 3:11	1870
Let us search and try our *w*	Lam 3:40	1870
judge thee according to thy *w*	Eze 7:3	1870
I will recompense thy *w* upon thee	Eze 7:4	1870
judge thee according to thy *w*	Eze 7:8	1870
thee according to thy *w* and thine	Eze 7:9	1870
comfort you, when ye see their *w*	Eze 14:23	1870
thou not walked after their *w*	Eze 16:47	1870
more than they in all thy *w*	Eze 16:47	1870
Then thou shalt remember thy *w*	Eze 16:61	1870
that he should return from his *w*	Eze 18:23	1870
are not your *w* unequal	Eze 18:25	1870
of Israel, are not my *w* equal	Eze 18:29	1870
are not your *w* unequal	Eze 18:29	1870
every one according to his *w*	Eze 18:30	1870
And there shall ye remember your *w*	Eze 20:43	1870
not according to your wicked *w*	Eze 20:44	1870
son of man, appoint thee two *w*	Eze 21:19	1870
the way, at the head of the two *w*	Eze 21:21	1870
according to thy *w*, and according	Eze 24:14	1870
Thou wast perfect in thy *w* from	Eze 28:15	1870
turn ye, turn ye from your evil *w*	Eze 33:11	1870

judge you every one after his *w* Eze 33:20 1870
shall ye remember your own evil *w* Eze 36:31 1870
and confounded for your own *w* Eze 36:32 1870
are truth, and his *w* judgment Dan 4:37 735
breath is, and whose are all thy *w* Dan 5:23 735
and I will punish them for their *w* Hos 4:9 1870
a snare of a fowler in all his *w* Hos 9:8 1870
punish Jacob according to his *w* Hos 12:2 1870
for the *w* of the LORD are right, Hos 14:9 1870
shall march every one on his *w* Joel 2:7 1870
and he will teach us of his *w* Mic 4:2 1870
against another in the broad *w* Nah 2:4
his *w* are everlasting Hab 3:6 1979
Consider your *w* Hag 1:5 1870
Consider your *w* Hag 1:7 1870
Turn ye now from your evil *w* Zec 1:4 1870
to do unto us, according to our *w* Zec 1:6 1870
If thou wilt walk in my *w* Zec 3:7 1870
as ye have not kept my *w*, but Mal 2:9 1870
went their *w* into the city, and Mt 8:33
made light of it, and went their *w* Mt 22:5
in a place where two *w* met Mk 11:4 *296*
face of the Lord to prepare his *w* Lk 1:76 *3598*
the rough *w* shall be made smooth Lk 3:5 *3598*
Go your *w* Lk 10:3
go your *w* out into the streets of Lk 10:10
went their *w* to the Pharisees Jn 11:46
made known to me the *w* of life Acts 2:28 *3598*
pervert the right *w* of the Lord Acts 13:10 *3598*
nations to walk in their own *w* Acts 14:16 *3598*
and misery are in their *w* Rom 3:16 *3598*
and his *w* past finding out Rom 11:33 *3598*
of my *w* which be in Christ 1Cor 4:17 *3598*
and they have not known my *w* Heb 3:10 *3598*
man is unstable in all his *w* Jas 1:8 *3598*
the rich man fade away in his *w* Jas 1:11 *4197*
shall follow their pernicious *w* 2Pet 2:2 *684*
just and true are thy *w*, thou King Rev 15:3 *3598*
to the seven angels, Go your *w* Rev 16:1

WAYSIDE
sat upon a seat by the *w* watching 1Sa 4:13
they have spread a net by the *w* Ps 140:5

WE See PREFACE.

WEAK
whether they be strong or *w* Num 13:18 7504
never dried, then shall I be *w* Judg 16:7 2470
were occupied, then shall I be *w* Judg 16:11 2470
go from me, and I shall become *w* Judg 16:17 2470
And I am this day *w*, though 2Sa 3:39 7390
w handed, and will make him afraid 2Sa 17:2 7504
and let not your hands be *w* 2Chr 15:7 7503
hast strengthened the *w* hands Job 4:3 7504
for I am *w* Ps 6:2 536
My knees are *w* through fasting Ps 109:24 3782
Art thou also become *w* as we Is 14:10 2470
Strengthen ye the *w* hands Is 35:3 7504
and all knees shall be *w* as water Eze 7:17 3212
How *w* is thine heart, saith the Eze 16:30 535
and all knees shall be *w* as water Eze 21:7 3212
let the *w* say, I am strong Joel 3:10 2523
is willing, but the flesh is *w* Mt 26:41 *772*
is ready, but the flesh is *w* Mk 14:38 *772*
ye ought to support the *w* Acts 20:35 *770*
And being not *w* in faith, he Rom 4:19 *770*
in that it was *w* through the Rom 8:3 *770*
Him that is *w* in the faith Rom 14:1 *770*
another, who is *w*, eateth herbs Rom 14:2 *770*
or is offended, or is made *w* Rom 14:21 *770*
to bear the infirmities of the *w* Rom 15:1 *102*
God hath chosen the *w* things of 1Cor 1:27 *772*
we are *w*, but ye are strong 1Cor 4:10 *772*
conscience being *w* is defiled 1Cor 8:7 *772*
stumblingblock to them that are *w* 1Cor 8:9 *770*
is *w* be emboldened to eat those 1Cor 8:10 *772*
shall the *w* brother perish 1Cor 8:11 *770*
and wound their *w* conscience 1Cor 8:12 *770*
To the *w* became I as *w* 1Cor 9:22 *770*
as *w*, that I might gain the *w* 1Cor 9:22 *770*
For this cause many are *w* 1Cor 11:30 *770*
but his bodily presence is *w* 2Cor 10:10 *770*
reproach, as though we had been *w* 2Cor 11:21 *770*
Who is *w*, and I am not *w* 2Cor 11:29 *770*
for when I am *w*, then am I strong 2Cor 12:10 *770*
in me, which to you-ward is not *w* 2Cor 13:3 *770*
For we also are *w* in him, but we 2Cor 13:4 *770*
For we are glad, when we are *w* 2Cor 13:9 *770*
God, how turn ye again to the *w* Gal 4:9 *772*
the feebleminded, support the *w* 1Th 5:14 *772*

WEAKEN
ground, which didst *w* the nations Is 14:12 2522

WEAKENED
land *w* the hands of the people of Ezr 4:4 7503
hands shall be *w* from the work Neh 6:9 7503
He *w* my strength in the way Ps 102:23 6031

WEAKENETH
w the strength of the mighty Job 12:21 7503
for thus he *w* the hands of the Jer 38:4 7503

WEAKER
house of Saul waxed *w* and *w* 2Sa 3:1 1800
the wife, as unto the *w* vessel 1Pet 3:7 *772*

WEAKNESS
the *w* of God is stronger than men 1Cor 1:25 *772*
And I was with you in *w*, and in 1Cor 2:3 *769*
it is sown in *w* 1Cor 15:43 *769*
my strength is made perfect in *w* 2Cor 12:9 *769*
though he was crucified through *w* 2Cor 13:4 *769*
going before for the *w* and Heb 7:18 *772*
out of *w* were made strong, waxed Heb 11:34 *769*

WEALTH
And all their *w*, and all their Gen 34:29 2428
mine hand hath gotten me this *w* Deut 8:17 2428
that giveth thee power to get *w* Deut 8:18 2428
her husband's, a mighty man of *w* Ruth 2:1 2428
in all the *w* which God shall give 1Sa 2:32
even of all the mighty men of *w* 2Kin 15:20 2428
and thou hast not asked riches, *w* 2Chr 1:11 5233
and I will give thee riches, and *w* 2Chr 1:12 5233
their peace or their *w* for ever Ezr 9:12 2896
seeking the *w* of his people, and Est 10:3 2896
They spend their days in *w* Job 21:13 2896
I rejoiced because my *w* was great Job 31:25 2428
not increase thy *w* by their price Ps 44:12
They that trust in their *w* Ps 49:6 2428
and leave their *w* to others Ps 49:10 2428
W and riches shall be in his house Ps 112:3 1952
strangers be filled with thy *w* Prov 5:10 3581
The rich man's *w* is his strong Prov 10:15 1952
W gotten by vanity shall be Prov 13:11 1952
the *w* of the sinner is laid up Prov 13:22 2428
The rich man's *w* is his strong Prov 18:11 1952
W maketh many friends Prov 19:4 1952
whom God hath given riches and *w* Eccl 5:19 5233
to whom God hath given riches, *w* Eccl 6:2 5233
the *w* of all the heathen round Zec 14:14 2428
that by this craft we have our *w* Acts 19:25 *2142*
own, but every man another's *w* 1Cor 10:24

WEALTHY
broughtest us out into a *w* place Ps 66:12 7310
get you up unto the *w* nation Jer 49:31 7961

WEANED
And the child grew, and was *w* Gen 21:8 1580
the same day that Isaac was *w* Gen 21:8 1580
not go up until the child be *w* 1Sa 1:22 1580
tarry until thou have *w* him 1Sa 1:23 1580
gave her son suck until she *w* him 1Sa 1:23 1580
And when she had *w* him, she took 1Sa 1:24 1580
whom Tahpenes *w* in Pharaoh's 1Kin 11:20 1580
a child that is *w* of his mother Ps 131:2 1580
my soul is even as a *w* child Ps 131:2 1580
the *w* child shall put his hand on Is 11:8 1580
them that are *w* from the milk Is 28:9 1580
Now when she had *w* Lo-ruhamah Hos 1:8 1580

WEAPON
smite him with an hand *w* of wood Num 35:18 3627
shalt have a paddle upon thy *w* Deut 23:13 240
man having his *w* in his hand 2Chr 23:10 7973
and with the other hand held a *w* Neh 4:17 7973
He shall flee from the iron *w* Job 20:24 5402
No *w* that is formed against thee Is 54:17 3627
with his destroying *w* in his hand Eze 9:1 3627
man a slaughter *w* in his hand Eze 9:2 3627

WEAPONS
take, I pray thee, thy *w*, thy Gen 27:3 3627
girded on every man his *w* of war Deut 1:41 3627
men appointed with *w* of war Judg 18:11 3627
men appointed with their *w* of war Judg 18:16 3627
that were appointed with *w* of war Judg 18:17 3627
brought my sword nor my *w* with me 1Sa 21:8 3627
fallen, and the *w* of war perished 2Sa 1:27 3627
every man with his *w* in his hand 2Kin 11:8 3627
every man with his *w* in his hand 2Kin 11:11 3627
every man with his *w* in his hand 2Chr 23:7 3627
Wisdom is better than *w* of war Eccl 9:18 3627
the *w* of his indignation, to Is 13:5 3627
I will turn back the *w* of war Jer 21:4 3627
thee, every one with his *w* Jer 22:7 3627
forth the *w* of his indignation Jer 50:25 3627
Thou art my battle ax and *w* of war Jer 51:20 3627
down to hell with their *w* of war Eze 32:27 3627
shall set on fire and burn the *w* Eze 39:9 5402
they shall burn the *w* with fire Eze 39:10 5402
with lanterns and torches and *w* Jn 18:3 *3696*
(For the *w* of our warfare are not 2Cor 10:4 *3696*

WEAR
Thou wilt surely *w* away, both Ex 18:18 5034
The woman shall not *w* that which Deut 22:5 1961
Thou shalt not *w* a garment of Deut 22:11 3847
incense, to *w* an ephod before me 1Sa 2:28 5375
persons that did *w* a linen ephod 1Sa 22:18 5375
brought which the king useth to *w* Est 6:8 3847
The waters *w* the stones Job 14:19 7833
own bread, and *w* our own apparel Is 4:1 3847
shall *w* out the saints of the Dan 7:25 1080
neither shall they *w* a rough Zec 13:4 3847
they that *w* soft clothing are in Mt 11:8 *5409*
And when the day began to *w* away Lk 9:12 *2827*

WEARETH
to him that *w* the gay clothing Jas 2:3 *5409*

WEARIED
so that they *w* themselves to find Gen 19:11 3811
offering, nor *w* thee with incense Is 43:23 3021
thou hast *w* me with thine Is 43:24 3021
Thou art *w* in the multitude of Is 47:13 3811
Thou art *w* in the greatness of Is 57:10 3021
for my soul is *w* because of Jer 4:31 5888
the footmen, and they have *w* thee Jer 12:5 3811
thou trustedst, they *w* thee Jer 12:5
She hath *w* herself with lies, and Eze 24:12 3811
and wherein have I *w* thee Mic 6:3 3811
Ye have *w* the LORD with your Mal 2:17 3021
Yet ye say, Wherein have we *w* him Mal 2:17 3021
being *w* with his journey, sat Jn 4:6 *2872*
against himself, lest ye be *w* Heb 12:3 *2577*

WEARIETH
by watering he *w* the thick cloud Job 37:11 2959
the foolish *w* every one of them Eccl 10:15 3021

WEARINESS
and much study is a *w* of the flesh Eccl 12:12 3024
said also, Behold, what a *w* is it Mal 1:13 4972
In *w* and painfulness, in watchings 2Cor 11:27 *2873*

WEARING
priest in Shiloh, *w* an ephod 1Sa 14:3 5375
w the crown of thorns, and the Jn 19:5 *5409*
of *w* of gold, or of putting on of 1Pet 3:3 *4025*

WEARISOME
w nights are appointed to me Job 7:3 5999

WEARY
I am *w* of my life because of the Gen 27:46 6973
thee, when thou wast faint and *w* Deut 25:18 3023
for he was fast asleep and *w* Judg 4:21 5774
bread unto thy men that are *w* Judg 8:15 3286
people that were with him, came *w* 2Sa 16:14 5889
will come upon him while he is *w* 2Sa 17:2 3023
said, The people is hungry, and *w* 2Sa 17:29 5889
Philistines until his hand was *w* 2Sa 23:10 3021
and there the *w* be at rest Job 3:17 3019
My soul is *w* of my life Job 10:1 5354
But now he hath made me *w* Job 16:7 3811
not given water to the *w* to drink Job 22:7 5889
I am *w* with my groaning Ps 6:6 3021
thine inheritance, when it was *w* Ps 68:9 3811
I am *w* of my crying Ps 69:3 3021
neither be *w* of his correction Prov 3:11 6973
lest he be *w* of thee, and so hate Prov 25:17 7646
I am *w* to bear them Is 1:14 3811
None shall be *w* nor stumble among Is 5:27 5889
it a small thing for you to *w* men Is 7:13 3811
but will ye *w* my God also Is 7:13 3811
that Moab is *w* on the high place Is 16:12 3811
ye may cause the *w* to rest Is 28:12 5889
of a great rock in a *w* land Is 32:2 5889
earth, fainteth not, neither is *w* Is 40:28 3021
the youths shall faint and be *w* Is 40:30 3021
they shall run, and not be *w* Is 40:31 3021
but thou hast been *w* of me Is 43:22 3021
they are a burden to the *w* beast Is 46:1 5889
a word in season to him that is *w* Is 50:4 3287
seek her will not *w* themselves Jer 2:24 3286
I am *w* with holding in Jer 6:11 3811
w themselves to commit iniquity Jer 9:5 3811
I am *w* with repenting Jer 15:6 3811
I was *w* with forbearing, and I Jer 20:9 3811
For I have satiated the *w* soul Jer 31:25 5889
in the fire, and they shall be *w* Jer 51:58 3286
and they shall be *w* Jer 51:64 3286
the people shall *w* themselves for Hab 2:13 3286
by her continual coming she *w* me Lk 18:5 *5299*
And let us not be *w* in well doing Gal 6:9 *1573*
brethren, be not *w* in well doing 2Th 3:13 *1573*

WEASEL
the *w*, and the mouse, and the Lev 11:29 2467

WEATHER
Fair *w* cometh out of the north Job 37:22 2091
taketh away a garment in cold *w* Prov 25:20 3117
ye say, It will be fair *w* Mt 16:2 *2105*
morning, It will be foul *w* to day Mt 16:3 *5494*

WEAVE
flax, and they that *w* networks Is 19:9 707
eggs, and *w* the spider's web Is 59:5 707

WEAVER
and in fine linen, and of the *w* Ex 35:35 707
I have cut off like a *w* my life Is 38:12 707

WEAVER'S
of his spear was like a *w* beam 1Sa 17:7 707
of whose spear was like a *w* beam 2Sa 21:19 707
hand was a spear like a *w* beam 1Chr 11:23 707
spear staff was like a *w* beam 1Chr 20:5 707
days are swifter than a *w* shuttle Job 7:6

WEAVEST
If thou *w* the seven locks of my Judg 16:13 707

WEB
seven locks of my head with the *w* Judg 16:13 4545
pin of the beam, and with the *w* Judg 16:14 4545
whose trust shall be a spider's *w* Job 8:14 1004
eggs, and weave the spider's *w* Is 59:5 6980

WEBS
Their *w* shall not become garments Is 59:6 6980

WEDDING
them that were bidden to the *w* Mt 22:3 *1062*
The *w* is ready, but they which Mt 22:8 *1062*
the *w* was furnished with guests Mt 22:10 *1062*
man which had not on a *w* garment Mt 22:11 *1062*
in hither not having a *w* garment Mt 22:12 *1062*
when he will return from the *w* Lk 12:36 *1062*
thou art bidden of any man to a *w* Lk 14:8 *1062*

WEDGE
a *w* of gold of fifty shekels Josh 7:21 3956
the *w* of gold, and his sons, and Josh 7:24 3956
a man than the golden *w* of Ophir Is 13:12

WEDLOCK
judge thee, as women that break *w* Eze 16:38 5003

WEEDS
the *w* were wrapped about my head Jonah 2:5 5488

WEEK
Fulfil her *w*, and we will give Gen 29:27 7620
Jacob did so, and fulfilled her *w* Gen 29:28 7620
the covenant with many for one *w* Dan 9:27 7620
in the midst of the *w* he shall Dan 9:27 7620
toward the first day of the *w* Mt 28:1 *4521*
morning the first day of the *w* Mk 16:2 *4521*
early the first day of the *w* Mk 16:9 *4521*
I fast twice in the *w*, I give Lk 18:12 *4521*

Now upon the first day of the *w* Lk 24:1 *4521*
The first day of the *w* cometh Jn 20:1 *4521*
being the first day of the *w* Jn 20:19 *4521*
And upon the first day of the *w* Acts 20:7 *4521*
Upon the first day of the *w* let 1Cor 16:2 *4521*

WEEKS
thou shalt observe the feast of *w* Ex 34:22 7620
then she shall be unclean two *w* Lev 12:5 7620
the LORD, after your *w* be out Num 28:26 7620
Seven *w* shalt thou number unto Deut 16:9 7620
seven *w* from such time as thou Deut 16:9 7620
of *w* unto the LORD thy God with a Deut 16:10 7620
bread, and in the feast of *w* Deut 16:16 7620
bread, and in the feast of *w* 2Chr 8:13 7620
us the appointed *w* of the harvest Jer 5:24 7620
Seventy *w* are determined upon thy Dan 9:24 7620
the Prince shall be seven *w* Dan 9:25 7620
and threescore and two *w* Dan 9:25 7620
two *w* shall Messiah be cut off Dan 9:26 7620
Daniel was mourning three full *w* Dan 10:2 7620
till three whole *w* were fulfilled Dan 10:3 7620

WEEP
mourn for Sarah, and to *w* for her Gen 23:2 1058
and he sought where to *w* Gen 43:30 1058
w throughout their families Num 11:10 1058
for they *w* unto me, saying, Give Num 11:13 1058
aileth the people that they *w* 1Sa 11:5 1058
until they had no more power to *w* 1Sa 30:4 1058
w over Saul, who clothed you in 2Sa 1:24 1058
w for the child, while it was 2Sa 12:21 1058
rend thy clothes, and *w* before me 2Chr 34:27 1058
mourn not, nor *w* Neh 8:9 1058
and his widows shall not *w* Job 27:15 1058
Did not I *w* for him that was in Job 30:25 1058
into the voice of them that *w* Job 30:31 1058
A time to *w*, and a time to laugh Eccl 3:4 1058
to Dibon, the high places, to *w* Is 15:2 1065
I will *w* bitterly, labour not to Is 22:4 1065
thou shalt *w* no more Is 30:19 1058
of peace shall *w* bitterly Is 33:7 1058
of tears, that I might *w* day Jer 9:1 1058
my soul shall *w* in secret places Jer 13:17 1058
and mine eye shall *w* sore, and run Jer 13:17 1830
W ye not for the dead, neither Jer 22:10 1058
but *w* sore for him that goeth Jer 22:10 1058
I will *w* for thee with the Jer 48:32 1058
For these things I *w* Lam 1:16 1058
neither shalt thou mourn nor *w* Eze 24:16 1058
ye shall not mourn nor *w* Eze 24:23 1058
they shall *w* for thee with Eze 27:31 1058
Awake, ye drunkards, and *w* Joel 1:5 1058
w between the porch and the altar, Joel 2:17 1058
it not at Gath, *w* ye not at all Mic 1:10 1058
Should I *w* in the fifth month, Zec 7:3 1058
them, Why make ye this ado, and *w* Mk 5:39 *2799*
Blessed are ye that *w* now Lk 6:21 *2799*
for ye shall mourn and *w* Lk 6:25 *2799*
on her, and said unto her, *W* not Lk 7:13 *2799*
but he said, *W* not Lk 8:52 *2799*
w not for me, but *w* for Lk 23:28 *2799*
goeth unto the grave to *w* there Jn 11:31 *2799*
I say unto you, That ye shall *w* Jn 16:20 *2799*
Paul answered, What mean ye to *w* Acts 21:13 *2799*
rejoice, and *w* with them that *w* Rom 12:15 *2799*
And they that *w*, as though they 1Cor 7:30 *2799*
Be afflicted, and mourn, and *w* Jas 4:9 *2799*
Go to now, ye rich men, *w* Jas 5:1 *2799*
the elders saith unto me, *W* not Rev 5:5 *2799*
merchants of the earth shall *w* Rev 18:11 *2799*

WEEPEST
to her, Hannah, why *w* thou 1Sa 1:8 1058
say unto her, Woman, why *w* thou Jn 20:13 *2799*
saith unto her, Woman, why *w* thou Jn 20:15 *2799*

WEEPETH
was told Joab, Behold, the king *w* 2Sa 19:1 1058
And Hazael said, Why *w* my lord 2Kin 8:12 1058
He that goeth forth and *w*, bearing Ps 126:6 1058
She *w* sore in the night, and her Lam 1:2 1058

WEEPING
who were *w* before the door of the Num 25:6 1058
so the days of *w* and mourning for Deut 34:8 1065
her along *w* behind her to Bahurim 2Sa 3:16 1058
they went up, *w* as they went up 2Sa 15:30 1058
the noise of the *w* of the people Ezr 3:13 1065
and when he had confessed, *w* Ezr 10:1 1058
among the Jews, and fasting, and *w* Est 4:3 1065
My face is foul with *w*, and on my Job 16:16 1065
LORD hath heard the voice of my *w* Ps 6:8 1065
w may endure for a night, but joy Ps 30:5 1065
bread, and mingled my drink with *w* Ps 102:9 1065
one shall howl, *w* abundantly Is 15:3 1065
Luhith with *w* shall they go it up Is 15:5 1065
I will bewail with the *w* of Jazer Is 16:9 1065
the Lord GOD of hosts call to *w* Is 22:12 1065
the voice of *w* shall be no more Is 65:19 1065
was heard upon the high places, *w* Jer 3:21 1065
the mountains will I take up a *w* Jer 9:10 1065
They shall come with *w*, and with Jer 31:9 1065
Ramah, lamentation, and bitter *w* Jer 31:15 1065
Rahel *w* for her children refused Jer 31:15 1058
Refrain thy voice from *w*, and Jer 31:16 1065
meet them, *w* all along as he went Jer 41:6 1058
of Luhith continual *w* shall go up Jer 48:5 1065
weep for thee with the *w* of Jazer Jer 48:32 1065
of Judah together, going and *w* Jer 50:4 1058
there sat women *w* for Tammuz Eze 8:14 1058
heart, and with fasting, and with *w* Joel 2:12 1065
of the LORD with tears, with *w* Mal 2:13 1065
a voice heard, lamentation, and *w* Mt 2:18 *2805*
Rachel *w* for her children, and Mt 2:18 *2799*
there shall be *w* and gnashing of Mt 8:12 *2805*
there shall be *w* and gnashing of Mt 22:13 *2805*
there shall be *w* and gnashing of Mt 24:51 *2805*
there shall be *w* and gnashing of Mt 25:30 *2805*
And stood at his feet behind him *w* Lk 7:38 *2799*
There shall be *w* and gnashing of Lk 13:28 *2805*
When Jesus therefore saw her *w* Jn 11:33 *2799*
the Jews also *w* which came with Jn 11:33 *2799*
stood without at the sepulchre *w* Jn 20:11 *2799*
and all the widows stood by him *w* Acts 9:39 *2799*
you often, and now tell you even *w* Phil 3:18 *2799*
for the fear of her torment, *w* Rev 18:15 *2799*
dust on their heads, and cried, *w* Rev 18:19 *2799*

WEIGH
found it to *w* a talent of gold, 1Chr 20:2 4948
until ye *w* them before the chief Ezr 8:29 8254
ye *w* the violence of your hands Ps 58:2 6424
dost *w* the path of the just Is 26:7 6424
w silver in the balance, and hire Is 46:6 8254
then take thee balances to *w* Eze 5:1 4948

WEIGHED
Abraham *w* to Ephron the silver, Gen 23:16 8254
the silver vessels *w* two thousand Num 7:85
and by him actions are *w* 1Sa 2:3 8505
his spear's head *w* six hundred 1Sa 17:7
he *w* the hair of his head at two 2Sa 14:26 8254
the weight of whose spear *w* three 2Sa 21:16
w unto them the silver, and the Ezr 8:25 8254
I even *w* unto their hand six Ezr 8:26 8254
the vessels *w* in the house of our Ezr 8:33 8254
O that my grief were throughly *w* Job 6:2 8254
silver be *w* for the price thereof Job 28:15 8254
Let me be *w* in an even balance, Job 31:6 8254
w the mountains in scales, and the Is 40:12 8254
w him the money, even seventeen Jer 32:9 8254
w him the money in the balances Jer 32:10 8254
Thou art *w* in the balances, and Dan 5:27 8625
So they *w* for my price thirty Zec 11:12 8254

WEIGHETH
he *w* the waters by measure Job 28:25 8505
but the LORD *w* the spirits Prov 16:2 8505

WEIGHING
charger of silver *w* an hundred Num 7:85
w ten shekels apiece, after the Num 7:86

WEIGHT
golden earring of half a shekel *w* Gen 24:22 4948
hands of ten shekels *w* of gold Gen 24:22 4948
of his sack, our money in full *w* Gen 43:21 4948
of each shall there be a like *w* Ex 30:34
in judgment, in meteyard, in *w* Lev 19:35 4948
deliver you your bread again by *w* Lev 26:26 4948
the *w* thereof was an hundred and Num 7:13
the *w* whereof was an hundred and Num 7:19
the *w* whereof was an hundred and Num 7:25
charger of the *w* of an hundred Num 7:31 4948
the *w* whereof was an hundred and Num 7:37 4948
charger of the *w* of an hundred Num 7:43 4948
the *w* whereof was an hundred and Num 7:49 4948
charger of the *w* of an hundred Num 7:55 4948
the *w* whereof was an hundred and Num 7:61 4948
the *w* whereof was an hundred and Num 7:67 4948
the *w* whereof was an hundred and Num 7:73 4948
the *w* whereof was an hundred and Num 7:79 4948
shalt have a perfect and just *w* Deut 25:15 68
wedge of gold of fifty shekels *w* Josh 7:21 4948
the *w* of the golden earrings that Judg 8:26 4948
the *w* of the coat was five 1Sa 17:5 4948
the *w* whereof was a talent of 2Sa 12:30 4948
shekels after the king's *w* 2Sa 14:26 68
the *w* of whose spear weighed 2Sa 21:16 4948
hundred shekels of brass in *w* 2Sa 21:16 4948
neither was the *w* of the brass 1Kin 7:47 4948
Now the *w* of gold that came to 1Kin 10:14 4948
all these vessels was without *w* 2Kin 25:16 4948
six hundred shekels of gold by *w* 1Chr 21:25 4948
and brass in abundance without *w* 1Chr 22:3 4948
and of brass and iron without *w* 1Chr 22:14 4948
of gold by *w* for things of gold 1Chr 28:14 4948
all instruments of silver by *w* 1Chr 28:14 4948
Even the *w* for the candlesticks 1Chr 28:15 4948
by *w* for every candlestick, and 1Chr 28:15 4948
the candlesticks of silver by *w* 1Chr 28:15 4948
by *w* he gave gold for the tables 1Chr 28:16 4948
he gave gold by *w* for every bason 1Chr 28:17 4948
likewise silver by *w* for every 1Chr 28:17 4948
of incense refined gold by *w* 1Chr 28:18 4948
the *w* of the nails was fifty 2Chr 3:9 4948
for the *w* of the brass could not 2Chr 4:18 4948
Now the *w* of gold that came to 2Chr 9:13 4948
the Levites the *w* of the silver Ezr 8:30 4948
By number and by *w* of every one Ezr 8:34 4948
all the *w* was written at that Ezr 8:34 4948
To make the *w* for the winds Job 28:25 4948
but a just *w* is his delight Prov 11:1 68
A just *w* and balance are the Prov 16:11 6425
all these vessels was without *w* Jer 52:20 4948
thou shalt eat shall be by *w* Eze 4:10 4946
and they shall eat bread by *w* Eze 4:16 4948
he cast the *w* of lead upon the Zec 5:8 68
aloes, about an hundred pound *w* Jn 19:39
exceeding and eternal *w* of glory 2Cor 4:17 *922*
let us lay aside every *w* Heb 12:1 *3591*
stone about the *w* of a talent Rev 16:21 *5006*

WEIGHTIER
have omitted the *w* matters of the Mt 23:23 *926*

WEIGHTS
Just balances, just *w*, a just Lev 19:36 68
not have in thy bag divers *w* Deut 25:13 68
all the *w* of the bag are his work Prov 16:11 68
Divers *w*, and divers measures, Prov 20:10 68
Divers *w* are an abomination unto Prov 20:23 68
and with the bag of deceitful *w* Mic 6:11 68

WEIGHTY
A stone is heavy, and the sand *w* Prov 27:3 5192
For his letters, say they, are *w* 2Cor 10:10 *926*

WELFARE
And he asked them of their *w* Gen 43:27 7965
they asked each other of their *w* Ex 18:7 7965
king David, to enquire of his *w* 1Chr 18:10 7965
the *w* of the children of Israel Neh 2:10 2896
my *w* passeth away as a cloud Job 30:15 3444
should have been for their *w* Ps 69:22 7965
seeketh not the *w* of this people Jer 38:4 7965

WELL
If thou doest *w*, shalt thou not Gen 4:7 3190
and if thou doest not *w*, sin lieth Gen 4:7 3190
that it may be *w* with me for thy Gen 12:13 3190
he entreated Abram *w* for her sake Gen 12:16 3190
that it was *w* watered every where Gen 13:10
Wherefore the *w* was called Gen 16:14 875
were old and *w* stricken in age Gen 18:11
her eyes, and she saw a *w* of water Gen 21:19 875
Abimelech because of a *w* of water Gen 21:25 875
me, that I have digged this *w* Gen 21:30 875
was old, and *w* stricken in age Gen 24:1
down without the city by a *w* of Gen 24:11 875
I stand here by the *w* of water Gen 24:13 5869
and she went down to the *w* Gen 24:16 5869
again unto the *w* to draw water Gen 24:20 875
ran out unto the man, unto the *w* Gen 24:29 5869
he stood by the camels at the *w* Gen 24:30 5869
And I came this day unto the *w* Gen 24:42 5869
Behold, I stand by the *w* of water Gen 24:43 5869
and she went down unto the *w* Gen 24:45 5869
from the way of the *w* Lahai-roi Gen 24:62
and Isaac dwelt by the *w* Lahai-roi Gen 25:11 883
found there a *w* of springing Gen 26:19 875
he called the name of the *w* Esek Gen 26:20 875
And they digged another *w*, and Gen 26:21 875
from thence, and digged another *w* Gen 26:22 875
there Isaac's servants digged a *w* Gen 26:25 875
the *w* which they had digged Gen 26:32 875
behold a *w* in the field, and, lo, Gen 29:2 875
for out of that *w* they watered Gen 29:2 875
And he said unto them, Is he *w* Gen 29:6 7965
And they said, He is *w* Gen 29:6 7965
was beautiful and *w* favoured Gen 29:17 3303
and I will deal *w* with thee Gen 32:9 3190
whether it be *w* with thy brethren Gen 37:14 7965
and *w* with the flocks Gen 37:14 7965
a goodly person, and *w* favoured Gen 39:6 3303
me when it shall be *w* with thee Gen 40:14 3190
the river seven *w* favoured kine Gen 41:2 3303
did eat up the seven *w* favoured Gen 41:4 3303
kine, fatfleshed and *w* favoured Gen 41:18 3303
and said, Is your father *w* Gen 43:27 7965
and it pleased Pharaoh *w*, and his Gen 45:16
even a fruitful bough by a *w* Gen 49:22 5869
God dealt *w* with the midwives Ex 1:20 3190
and he sat down by a *w* Ex 2:15 875
I know that he can speak *w* Ex 4:14
And Moses said, Thou hast spoken *w* Ex 10:29 3651
as *w* the stranger, as he that is Lev 24:16
as *w* for the stranger, as for one Lev 24:22
for it was *w* with us in Egypt Num 11:18 2895
for we are *w* able to overcome it Num 13:30
that is the *w* whereof the LORD Num 21:16 875
sang this song, Spring up, O *w* Num 21:17 875
The princes digged the *w*, the Num 21:18 875
not drink of the waters of the *w* Num 21:22 875
of the sons of Joseph hath said *w* Num 36:5 3651
hear the small as *w* as the great Deut 1:17
And the saying pleased me *w* Deut 1:23
as *w* as unto you, and until they Deut 3:20
day, that it may go *w* with thee Deut 4:40 3190
maidservant may rest as *w* as thou Deut 5:14
and that it may go *w* with thee Deut 5:16 3190
they have *w* said all that they Deut 5:28 3190
that it might be *w* with them Deut 5:29 3190
and that it may be *w* with you Deut 5:33 2895
that it may be *w* with thee Deut 6:3 3190
that it may be *w* with thee Deut 6:18 3190
but shalt *w* remember what the Deut 7:18
that it may go *w* with thee Deut 12:25 3190
thee, that it may go *w* with thee Deut 12:28 3190
house, because he is *w* with thee Deut 15:16 2895
They have *w* spoken that which Deut 18:17 3190
that it may go *w* with thee Deut 19:13 2895
heart faint as *w* as his heart Deut 20:8
that it may be *w* with thee Deut 22:7 3190
as *w* the stranger, as he that was Josh 8:33
went out to the *w* of waters of Josh 18:15 4599
and pitched beside the *w* of Harod Judg 7:1 5878
if ye have dealt *w* with Jerubbaal Judg 9:16 2895
for she pleaseth me *w* Judg 14:3
and she pleased Samson *w* Judg 14:7
as *w* the men of every city, as Judg 20:48 3190
thee, that it may be *w* with thee Ruth 3:1 3190
thee the part of a kinsman, *w* Ruth 3:13 2896
said Saul to his servant, *W* said 1Sa 9:10 2896
with his hand, and thou shalt be *w* 1Sa 16:16 2895
me now a man that can play *w* 1Sa 16:17 3190
so Saul was refreshed, and was *w* 1Sa 16:23 2895
it pleased David *w* to be the 1Sa 18:26
came to a great *w* that is in 1Sa 19:22 953
If he say thus, It is *w* 1Sa 20:7 2896
that thou hast dealt *w* with me 1Sa 24:18 2896
enemy, will he let him go *w* away 1Sa 24:19 2896
I know *w* that thou shalt surely 1Sa 24:20
shall have dealt *w* with my lord 1Sa 25:31 3190
And he said, *W* 2Sa 3:13 2896
him again from the *w* of Sirah 2Sa 3:26 953
as *w* to the women as men, to 2Sa 6:19

devoureth one as w as another 2Sa 11:25 2090
And the saying pleased Absalom w 2Sa 17:4
which had a w in his court 2Sa 17:18 375
that they came up out of the w 2Sa 17:21 375
and said unto the king, All is w 2Sa 18:28 7965
day, then it had pleased thee w 2Sa 19:6
the water of the w of Beth-lehem 2Sa 23:15 953
water out of the w of Beth-lehem 2Sa 23:16 953
And Bath-sheba said, W 1Kin 2:18 2896
thou didst w that it was in thine 1Kin 8:18 3190
answered and said, It is w spoken 1Kin 18:24 2896
And she said, It shall be w 2Kin 4:23 7965
say unto her, Is it w with thee 2Kin 4:26 7965
is it w with thy husband 2Kin 4:26 7965
is it w with the child 2Kin 4:26 7965
And she answered, It is w 2Kin 4:26 7965
to meet him, and said, Is all w 2Kin 5:21 7965
And he said, All is w 2Kin 5:22 7965
said one to another, We do not w 2Kin 7:9 3651
and one said unto him, Is all w 2Kin 9:11 7965
Because thou hast done w in 2Kin 10:30 2895
and it shall be w with you 2Kin 25:24 3190
the water of the w of Beth-lehem 1Chr 11:17 953
water out of the w of Beth-lehem 1Chr 11:18 953
as w the small as the great, the 1Chr 25:8
as w the small as the great, 1Chr 26:13
thou didst w in that it was in 2Chr 6:8 2895
and also in Judah things went w 2Chr 12:12 2896
as w to the great as to the small 2Chr 31:15
valley, even before the dragon w Neh 2:13 5869
I have understanding as w as you Job 12:3 71
Mark w, O Job, hearken unto me Job 33:31 7181
Mark ye w her bulwarks, consider Ps 48:13
when thou doest w to thyself Ps 49:18 3190
my steps had w nigh slipped Ps 73:2 369
So they did eat, and were w filled Ps 78:29 3966
the valley of Baca make it a w Ps 84:6 4599
As w the singers as the players Ps 87:7
Thou hast dealt w with thy Ps 119:65 2896
be, and it shall be w with thee Ps 128:2 2896
and that my soul knoweth right w Ps 139:14
running waters out of thine own w Prov 5:15 875
of a righteous man is a w of life Prov 10:11 4726
When it goeth w with the Prov 11:10 2898
but with the w advised is wisdom Prov 13:10
man looketh w to his going Prov 14:15 995
Then I saw, and considered it w Prov 24:32 3190
flocks, and look w to thy herds Prov 27:23
There be three things which go w Prov 30:29 3190
She looketh w to the ways of her Prov 31:27 6822
be w with them that fear God Eccl 8:12 2896
it shall not be w with the wicked Eccl 8:13 2896
a w of living waters, and streams Song 4:15 875
Learn to do w Is 1:17 3190
that it shall be w with him Is 3:10 2896
instead of w set hair baldness Is 3:24 4639
of wines on the lees w refined Is 25:6
they could not w strengthen their Is 33:23 3651
The LORD is w pleased for his Is 42:21 2654
LORD unto me, Thou hast w seen Jer 1:12 3190
you, that it may be w unto you Jer 7:23 3190
it shall be w with thy remnant Jer 15:11 2896
thee w in the time of evil Jer 15:11
and then it was w with him Jer 22:15 2896
then it was w with him Jer 22:16 2896
so it shall be w unto thee Jer 38:20 3190
look w to him, and do him no harm Jer 39:12
and I will look w unto thee Jer 40:4
and it shall be w with you Jer 40:9 3190
that it may be w with us, when we Jer 42:6 2896
we plenty of victuals, and were w Jer 44:17 2896
bones under it, and make it boil w Eze 24:5 7571
consume the flesh, and spice it w Eze 24:10
can play w on an instrument Eze 33:32
said unto me, Son of man, mark w Eze 44:5
mark w the entering in of the Eze 44:5
inherit it, one as w as another Eze 47:14
but w favoured, and skilful in all Dan 1:4 2896
which I have made; w Dan 3:15
LORD, Doest thou w to be angry Jonah 4:4 3190
Doest thou w to be angry for the Jonah 4:9 3190
I do w to be angry, even unto Jonah 4:9 3190
these days to do w unto Jerusalem Zec 8:15 3190
Son, in whom I am w pleased Mt 3:17 2106
to do w on the sabbath days Mt 12:12 2573
in whom my soul is w pleased Mt 12:18 2106
w did Esaias prophesy of you, Mt 15:7 2573
Son, in whom I am w pleased Mt 17:5 2106
W done, thou good and faithful Mt 25:21 2095
W done, good and faithful servant Mt 25:23 2095
Son, in whom I am w pleased Mk 1:11 2106
W hath Esaias prophesied of you Mk 7:6 2573
Full w ye reject the commandment Mk 7:9 2573
saying, He hath done all things w Mk 7:37 2573
that he had answered them w Mk 12:28 2573
And the scribe said unto him, W Mk 12:32 2573
both were now w stricken in years Lk 1:7 4260
my wife w stricken in years Lk 1:18 4260
in thee I am w pleased Lk 3:22 2106
when all men shall speak w of you Lk 6:26 2573
And if it bear fruit, w Lk 13:9 2573
And he said unto him, W, thou good Lk 19:17 2095
said, Master, thou hast w said Lk 20:39 2573
and when men have w drunk, then Jn 2:10 3184
Now Jacob's w was there Jn 4:6 4077
his journey, sat thus on the w Jn 4:6 4077
to draw with, and the w is deep Jn 4:11 5421
father Jacob, which gave us the w Jn 4:12 5421
a w of water springing up into Jn 4:14 4077
said unto her, Thou hast w said Jn 4:17 2573
Say we not w that thou art a Jn 8:48 2573
Lord, if he sleep, he shall do w Jn 11:12 4982
and ye say w Jn 13:13 2573
but if w, why smitest thou me Jn 18:23 2573
thou hast w done that thou art Acts 10:33 2573
the Holy Ghost as w as we Acts 10:47 2532
ye keep yourselves, ye shall do w Acts 15:29 2095
Fare ye w Acts 15:29 2095
Which was w reported of by the Acts 16:2 3140
no wrong, as thou very w knowest Acts 25:10 2573
W spake the Holy Ghost by Esaias Acts 28:25 2573
in w doing seek for glory Rom 2:7 18
W; because of unbelief Rom 11:20 2573
he will keep his virgin, doeth w 1Cor 7:37 2573
giveth her in marriage doeth w 1Cor 7:38 2573
as w as other apostles, and as the 1Cor 9:5 2532
of them God was not w pleased 1Cor 10:5 2106
For thou verily givest thanks w 1Cor 14:17 2573
As unknown, and yet w known 2Cor 6:9 1921
ye might w bear with him 2Cor 11:4 2573
zealously affect you, but not w Gal 4:17 2573
Ye did run w Gal 5:7 2573
And let us not be weary in w doing Gal 6:9 2570
That it may be w with thee Eph 6:3 2095
Notwithstanding ye have w done Phil 4:14 2573
for this is w pleasing unto the Col 3:20 2101
brethren, be not weary in w doing 2Th 3:13 2569
One that ruleth w his own house 1Ti 3:4 2573
children and their own houses w 1Ti 3:12 2573
used the office of a deacon w 1Ti 3:13 2573
W reported of for good works 1Ti 5:10 3140
Let the elders that rule w be 1Ti 5:17 2573
at Ephesus, thou knowest very w 2Ti 1:18 957
and to please them w in all things Titus 2:9
preached, as w as unto them Heb 4:2 2509
such sacrifices God is w pleased Heb 13:16 2100
thy neighbour as thyself, ye do w Jas 2:8 2573
thou doest w Jas 2:19 2573
for the praise of them that do w 1Pet 2:14 17
that with w doing ye may put to 1Pet 2:15 15
but if, when ye do w, and suffer 1Pet 2:20 15
ye are, as long as ye do w 1Pet 3:6 15
be so, that ye suffer for w doing 1Pet 3:17 15
of their souls to him in w doing 1Pet 4:19 16
Son, in whom I am w pleased 2Pet 1:17 2106
whereunto ye do w that ye take 2Pet 1:19 2573
a godly sort, thou shalt do w 3Jn 6 2573

WELLBELOVED

A bundle of myrrh is my w unto me Song 1:13 1730
Now will I sing to my w a song of Is 5:1 3039
My w hath a vineyard in a very Is 5:1 3039
yet therefore one son, his w Mk 12:6 27
Salute my w Epaenetus, who is the Rom 16:5 27
The elder unto the w Gaius 3Jn 1 27

WELLFAVOURED

of the whoredoms of the w harlot Nah 3:4

WELLPLEASING

a sacrifice acceptable, w to God Phil 4:18 2101
you that which is w in his sight Heb 13:21 2101

WELL'S

great stone was upon the w mouth Gen 29:2 875
rolled the stone from the w mouth Gen 29:3 875
upon the w mouth in his place Gen 29:3 875
roll the stone from the w mouth Gen 29:8 875
rolled the stone from the w mouth Gen 29:10 875
a covering over the w mouth 2Sa 17:19 875

WELLS

For all the w which his father's Gen 26:15 875
Isaac digged again the w of water Gen 26:18 875
where were twelve w of water Ex 15:27 5869
we drink of the water of the w Num 20:17 875
w digged, which thou diggedst not Deut 6:11 953
good tree, and stop all w of water 2Kin 3:19 4599
they stopped all the w of water 2Kin 3:25 4599
in the desert, and digged many w 2Chr 26:10 953
goods, w digged, vineyards, and Neh 9:25 953
water out of the w of salvation Is 12:3 4599
These are w without water, clouds 2Pet 2:17 4077

WELLSPRING

Understanding is a w of life unto Prov 16:22 4726
the w of wisdom as a flowing Prov 18:4 4726

WEN

broken, or maimed, or having a w Lev 22:22 2990

WENCH

and a w went and told them 2Sa 17:17 8198

WENT

But there w up a mist from the Gen 2:6 5927
a river w out of Eden to water Gen 2:10 3318
Cain w out from the presence of Gen 4:16 3318
And Noah w in, and his sons, and his Gen 7:7 935
There w in two and two unto Noah Gen 7:9 935
they w in unto Noah into the ark, Gen 7:15 935
And they that w in, w in male Gen 7:16 935
the ark w upon the face of the Gen 7:18 3212
which w forth to and fro, until Gen 8:7 3318
Noah w forth, and his sons, and his Gen 8:18 3318
kinds, w forth out of the ark Gen 8:19 3318
that w forth of the ark, were Gen 9:18 3318
w backward, and covered the Gen 9:23 3212
Out of that land w forth Asshur Gen 10:11 3318
they w forth with them from Ur of Gen 11:31 3318
and Lot w with him Gen 12:4 3212
they w forth to go into the land Gen 12:5 3318
Abram w down into Egypt to Gen 12:10 3381
Abram w up out of Egypt, he, and Gen 13:1 5927
he w on his journeys from the Gen 13:3 3212
which w with Abram, had flocks, Gen 13:5 1980
there w out the king of Sodom, and Gen 14:8 3318
their victuals, and w their way Gen 14:11 3212
the king of Sodom w out to meet Gen 14:17 3318
of the men which w with me Gen 14:24 1980
pass, that, when the sun w down Gen 15:17 935
he w in unto Hagar, and she Gen 16:4 935
him, and God w up from Abraham Gen 17:22 5927
Abraham w with them to bring them Gen 18:16 1980
from thence, and w toward Sodom Gen 18:22 3212
And the LORD w his way, as soon as Gen 18:33 3212
Lot w out at the door unto them, Gen 19:6 3318
And Lot w out, and spake unto his Gen 19:14 3318
the smoke of the country w up as Gen 19:28 5927
Lot w up out of Zoar, and dwelt in Gen 19:30 5927
and the firstborn w in, and lay Gen 19:33 935
And she w, and sat her down over Gen 21:16 3212
and she w, and filled the bottle Gen 21:19 3212
w unto the place of which God had Gen 22:3 3212
they w both of them together Gen 22:6 3212
so they w both of them together Gen 22:8 3212
Abraham w and took the ram Gen 22:13 3212
up and w together to Beer-sheba Gen 22:19 3212
even of all that w in at the gate Gen 23:10 935
before all that w in at the gate Gen 23:18 935
w to Mesopotamia, unto the city Gen 24:10 3212
she w down to the well, and filled Gen 24:16 3381
she w down unto the well, and drew Gen 24:45 3381
took Rebekah, and w his way Gen 24:61 3212
Isaac w out to meditate in the Gen 24:63 3318
she w to enquire of the LORD Gen 25:22 3212
drink, and rose up, and w his way Gen 25:34 3212
Isaac w unto Abimelech king of Gen 26:1 3212
w forward, and grew until he Gen 26:13 3212
he w up from thence to Beer-sheba Gen 26:23 5927
Then Abimelech w to him from Gen 26:26 1980
Esau w to the field to hunt for Gen 27:5 3212
And he w, and fetched, and brought Gen 27:14 3212
Jacob w near unto Isaac his Gen 27:22 5066
he w to Padan-aram unto Laban, Gen 28:5 3212
Then w Esau unto Ishmael, and took Gen 28:9 3212
Jacob w out from Beer-sheba, and Gen 28:10 3318
Beer-sheba, and w toward Haran Gen 28:10 3212
Then Jacob w on his journey, and Gen 29:1
brother, that Jacob w near Gen 29:10 5066
and he w in unto her Gen 29:23 935
he w in also unto Rachel, and he Gen 29:30 935
and Jacob w in unto her Gen 30:4 935
Reuben w in the days of wheat Gen 30:14 3212
Leah w out to meet him, and said, Gen 30:16 3318
Laban w to shear his sheep Gen 31:19 1980
Laban w into Jacob's tent, and Gen 31:33 935
Then w he out of Leah's tent, and Gen 31:33 3318
Jacob w on his way, and the angels Gen 32:1 1980
So w the present over before him Gen 32:21 5674
w out to see the daughters of the Gen 34:1 3318
Hamor the father of Shechem w out Gen 34:6 3318
his son hearkened all that w out Gen 34:24 3318
all that w out of the gate of his Gen 34:24 3318
out of Shechem's house, and w out Gen 34:26 3318
was with me in the way which I w Gen 35:3 1980
God w up from him in the place Gen 35:13 5927
dwelt in that land, that Reuben w Gen 35:22 3212
w into the country from the face Gen 36:6 3212
his brethren w to feed their Gen 37:12 3212
Joseph w after his brethren, and Gen 37:17 3212
that Judah w down from his Gen 38:1 3381
and he took her, and w in unto her Gen 38:2 935
when he w in unto his brother's Gen 38:9 935
And Tamar w and dwelt in her Gen 38:11 3212
w up unto his sheepshearers to Gen 38:12 5927
w away, and laid by her vail from Gen 38:19 3212
that Joseph w into the house to Gen 39:11 935
Joseph w out over all the land of Gen 41:45 3318
Joseph w out from the presence of Gen 41:46 3318
w throughout all the land of Gen 41:46 5674
Joseph's ten brethren w down to Gen 42:3 3381
w down to Egypt, and stood before Gen 43:15 3381
w out, and refrained himself, and Gen 43:31 3318
the one w out from me, and I said, Gen 44:28 3318
they w up out of Egypt, and came Gen 45:25 5927
w up to meet Israel his father, Gen 46:29 5927
w out from before Pharaoh Gen 47:10 3318
he w up to my couch Gen 49:4 5927
Joseph w up to bury his father Gen 50:7 5927
with him w up all the servants of Gen 50:7 5927
there w up with him both chariots Gen 50:9 5927
all that w up with him to bury Gen 50:14 5927
And his brethren also w and fell Gen 50:18 3212
there w a man of the house of Ex 2:1 3212
And the maid w and called the Ex 2:8 3212
that he w out unto his brethren, Ex 2:11 3318
when he w out the second day, Ex 2:13 3318
And Moses w and returned to Jethro Ex 4:18 3212
And he w, and met him in the mount Ex 4:27 3212
And Moses and Aaron w and gathered Ex 4:29 3212
And afterward Moses and Aaron w in Ex 5:1 935
taskmasters of the people w out Ex 5:10 3318
Aaron w in unto Pharaoh, and they Ex 7:10 935
w into his house, neither did he Ex 7:23 935
Moses and Aaron w out from Pharaoh Ex 8:12 3318
Moses w out from Pharaoh, and Ex 8:30 3318
Moses w out of the city from Ex 9:33 3318
himself, and w out from Pharaoh Ex 10:6 3318
the locusts w up over all the Ex 10:14 5927
he w out from Pharaoh, and Ex 10:18 3318
he w out from Pharaoh in a great Ex 11:8 3318
And the children of Israel w away Ex 12:28 3212
multitude w up also with them Ex 12:38 5927
LORD w out from the land of Egypt Ex 12:41 3318
the children of Israel w up Ex 13:18 5927
the LORD w before them by day in Ex 13:21 1980
of Israel w out with an high hand Ex 14:8 3318
which w before the camp of Israel Ex 14:19 1980
removed and w behind them Ex 14:19 3212
cloud w from before their face Ex 14:19 5265
the children of Israel w into the Ex 14:22 935
w in after them to the midst of Ex 14:23 935
of Pharaoh w in with his chariots Ex 15:19 935
but the children of Israel w on Ex 15:19 1980
all the women w out after her Ex 15:20 3318

W

they *w* out into the wilderness of ... Ex 15:22 3318
and they *w* three days in the ... Ex 15:22 3212
that there *w* out some of the ... Ex 16:27 3318
Hur *w* up to the top of the hill ... Ex 17:10 5927
Moses *w* out to meet his father in ... Ex 18:7 3318
he *w* his way into his own land ... Ex 18:27 3212
Moses *w* up unto God, and the LORD ... Ex 19:3 5927
Moses *w* down from the mount unto ... Ex 19:14 3381
and Moses *w* up ... Ex 19:20 5927
So Moses *w* down unto the people, ... Ex 19:25 3381
Then *w* up Moses, and Aaron, Nadab, ... Ex 24:9 5927
Moses *w* up into the mount of God ... Ex 24:13 5927
Moses *w* up into the mount, and a ... Ex 24:15 5927
Moses *w* into the midst of the ... Ex 24:18 935
w down from the mount, and the two ... Ex 32:15 3381
w out unto the tabernacle of the ... Ex 33:7 3318
when Moses *w* out unto the ... Ex 33:8 3318
w up unto mount Sinai, as the ... Ex 34:4 5927
But when Moses *w* in before the ... Ex 34:34 935
until he *w* in to speak with him ... Ex 34:35 935
every one that *w* to be numbered ... Ex 38:26 5674
When they *w* into the tent of the ... Ex 40:32 935
the children of Israel *w* onward ... Ex 40:36 5265
Aaron therefore *w* unto the altar ... Lev 9:8 7121
Aaron *w* into the tabernacle of ... Lev 9:23 935
there *w* out fire from the LORD, ... Lev 10:2 3318
So they *w* near, and carried them ... Lev 10:5 7126
on when he *w* into the holy place ... Lev 16:23 935
w out among the children of ... Lev 24:10 3318
after that *w* the Levites in to do ... Num 8:22 935
In the first place *w* the standard ... Num 10:14 5265
w before them in the three days' ... Num 10:33 5265
when they *w* out of the camp ... Num 10:34 5265
And the people *w* about, and ... Num 11:8 7751
And Moses *w* out, and told the ... Num 11:24 3318
but *w* not out unto the tabernacle ... Num 11:26 3318
there *w* forth a wind from the ... Num 11:31 5265
So they *w* up, and searched the ... Num 13:21 5927
they *w* and came to Moses ... Num 13:26 3212
the men that *w* up with him said ... Num 13:31 5927
into the land whereinto he *w* ... Num 14:24 935
the men that *w* to search the land ... Num 14:38 1980
up and *w* unto Dathan and Abiram ... Num 16:25 3212
w down alive into the pit, and the ... Num 16:33 3381
that on the morrow Moses *w* into ... Num 17:8 935
Aaron *w* from the presence of the ... Num 20:6 935
How our fathers *w* down into Egypt ... Num 20:15 3381
they *w* up into mount Hor in the ... Num 20:27 5927
And from thence they *w* to Beer ... Num 21:16
the wilderness they *w* to Mattanah ... Num 21:18
w out against Israel into the ... Num 21:23 3318
w up by the way of Bashan ... Num 21:33 5927
king of Bashan *w* out against them ... Num 21:33 3318
they *w* unto Balak, and said, ... Num 22:14 935
w with the princes of Moab ... Num 22:21 3212
anger was kindled because he *w* ... Num 22:22 1980
of the way, and *w* into the field ... Num 22:23 3212
the angel of the LORD *w* further ... Num 22:26 5674
I *w* out to withstand thee, ... Num 22:32 3318
So Balaam *w* with the princes of ... Num 22:35 3212
he *w* out to meet him unto a city ... Num 22:36 3318
Balaam *w* with Balak, and they came ... Num 22:39 3212
And he *w* to an high place ... Num 23:3 3212
he *w* not, as at other times, to ... Num 24:1 1980
And Balaam rose up, and *w* and ... Num 24:25 3212
and Balak also *w* his way ... Num 24:25 1980
he *w* after the man of Israel into ... Num 25:8 935
which *w* forth out of the land of ... Num 26:4 3318
w forth to meet them without the ... Num 31:13 3318
men of war which *w* to the battle ... Num 31:21 935
who *w* out to battle, and between ... Num 31:27 3318
men of war which *w* out to battle ... Num 31:28 3318
portion of them that *w* out to war ... Num 31:36 3318
For when they *w* up unto the ... Num 32:9 5927
the son of Manasseh *w* to Gilead ... Num 32:39 3212
And Jair the son of Manasseh *w* ... Num 32:41 1980
Nobah *w* and took Kenath ... Num 32:42 1980
which *w* forth out of the land of ... Num 33:1 3318
w out with an high hand in the ... Num 33:3 3318
w three days' journey in the ... Num 33:8 3212
they *w* from Kehelathah, and ... Num 33:23 5265
they *w* from Mithcah, and pitched ... Num 33:29 5265
they *w* from Hor-hagidgad, and ... Num 33:33 5265
Aaron the priest *w* up into mount ... Num 33:38 5927
we *w* through all that great and ... Deut 1:19 3212
w up into the mountain, and came ... Deut 1:24 5927
his son, in all the way that ye *w* ... Deut 1:31 1980
Who *w* in the way before you, to ... Deut 1:33 1980
w presumptuously up into the hill ... Deut 1:43 5927
we *w* over the brook Zered ... Deut 2:13 5674
turned, and *w* up the way to Bashan ... Deut 3:1 5927
fire, and *w* not up into the mount ... Deut 5:5 5927
w up into the mount, having the ... Deut 10:3 5927
Thy fathers *w* down into Egypt ... Deut 10:22 3381
and he *w* down into Egypt, and ... Deut 26:5 3381
For they *w* and served other gods, ... Deut 29:26 3212
And Moses *w* and spake these words ... Deut 31:1 3212
And Moses and Joshua *w*, and ... Deut 31:14 3212
from his right hand *w* a fiery law ... Deut 33:2
Moses *w* up from the plains of ... Deut 34:1 5927
And they *w*, and came into an ... Josh 2:1 3212
it was dark, that the men *w* out ... Josh 2:5 3318
whither the men *w* I wot not ... Josh 2:5 1980
And they *w*, and came unto the ... Josh 2:22 3212
the officers *w* through the host ... Josh 3:2 5974
covenant, and *w* before the people ... Josh 3:6 3212
Joshua *w* unto him, and said unto ... Josh 5:13 3212
none *w* out, and none came in ... Josh 6:1 3318
the armed men *w* before the ... Josh 6:9 1980
ark of the LORD *w* on continually ... Josh 6:13 1980
and the armed men *w* before them ... Josh 6:13 1980
the people *w* up into the city ... Josh 6:20 5927
young men that were spies *w* in ... Josh 6:23 935
And the men *w* up and viewed Ai ... Josh 7:2 5927

So there *w* up thither of the ... Josh 7:4 5927
they *w* to lie in ambush, and abode ... Josh 8:9 3212
w up, he and the elders of Israel, ... Josh 8:10 5927
w up, and drew nigh, and came ... Josh 8:11 5927
Joshua *w* that night into the ... Josh 8:13 3212
the men of the city *w* out against ... Josh 8:14 3318
that *w* not out after Israel ... Josh 8:17 3318
They did work wilily, and *w* ... Josh 9:4 3212
they *w* to Joshua unto the camp at ... Josh 9:6 3212
w up, they and all their hosts, and ... Josh 10:5 5927
w up from Gilgal all night ... Josh 10:9 5927
the men of war which *w* with him ... Josh 10:24 1980
Joshua *w* up from Eglon, and all ... Josh 10:36 5927
And they *w* out, they and all their ... Josh 11:4 3318
w up with me made the heart of ... Josh 14:8 5927
it *w* out to the south side to ... Josh 15:3 3318
w up to Adar, and fetched a ... Josh 15:3 5927
w out unto the river of Egypt ... Josh 15:4 3318
the border *w* up to Beth-hogla, and ... Josh 15:6 5927
the border *w* up to the stone of ... Josh 15:6 5927
the border *w* up toward Debir from ... Josh 15:7 5927
the border *w* up by the valley of ... Josh 15:8 5927
the border *w* up to the top of the ... Josh 15:8 5927
w out to the cities of mount ... Josh 15:9 3318
w down to Beth-shemesh, and passed ... Josh 15:10 3381
the border *w* out unto the side of ... Josh 15:11 3318
Baalah, and *w* out unto Jabneel ... Josh 15:11 3318
he *w* up thence to the inhabitants ... Josh 15:15 5927
the border *w* out toward the sea ... Josh 16:6 3318
the border *w* about eastward unto ... Josh 16:6 5437
it *w* down from Janohah to Ataroth ... Josh 16:7 3381
to Jericho, and *w* out at Jordan ... Josh 16:7 3318
The border *w* out from Tappuah ... Josh 16:8 3212
the border *w* along on the right ... Josh 17:7 1980
And the men arose, and *w* away ... Josh 18:8 3212
them that *w* to describe the land ... Josh 18:8 1980
And the men *w* and passed through ... Josh 18:9 3212
the border *w* up to the side of ... Josh 18:12 5927
w up through the mountains ... Josh 18:12 5927
the border *w* over from thence ... Josh 18:13 5674
the border *w* out on the west, and ... Josh 18:15 3318
w out to the well of waters of ... Josh 18:15 3318
w forth to En-shemesh, and *w* ... Josh 18:17 3318
northward, and *w* down unto Arabah ... Josh 18:18 3381
their border *w* up toward the sea, ... Josh 19:11 5927
of Dan *w* out too little for them ... Josh 19:47 3318
Dan *w* up to fight against Leshem ... Josh 19:47 5927
and they *w* unto their tents ... Josh 22:6 3212
his children *w* down into Egypt ... Josh 24:4 3381
ye *w* over Jordan, and came unto ... Josh 24:11 5674
us in all the way wherein we *w* ... Josh 24:17 1980
So Simeon *w* with him ... Judg 1:3 3212
And Judah *w* up ... Judg 1:4 5927
Judah *w* down to fight against the ... Judg 1:9 3381
Judah *w* against the Canaanites ... Judg 1:10 3212
from thence he *w* against the ... Judg 1:11 3212
w up out of the city of palm ... Judg 1:16 5927
and they *w* and dwelt among the ... Judg 1:16 3212
Judah *w* with Simeon his brother, ... Judg 1:17 3212
they also *w* up against Beth-el ... Judg 1:22 5927
the man *w* into the land of the ... Judg 1:26 3212
the children of Israel *w* every ... Judg 2:6 3212
Whithersoever they *w* out, the ... Judg 2:15 3318
but they *w* a whoring after other ... Judg 2:17
he judged Israel, and *w* out to war ... Judg 3:10 3318
Ammon and Amalek, and *w* ... Judg 3:13 3212
that stood by him *w* out from him ... Judg 3:19 3318
the haft also *w* in after the ... Judg 3:22 935
Then Ehud *w* forth through the ... Judg 3:23 3318
the children of Israel *w* down ... Judg 3:27 3381
they *w* down after him, and took ... Judg 3:28 3381
arose, and *w* with Barak to Kedesh ... Judg 4:9 3212
he *w* up with ten thousand men at ... Judg 4:10 5927
and Deborah *w* up with him ... Judg 4:10 5927
So Barak *w* down from mount Tabor, ... Judg 4:14 3381
Jael *w* out to meet Sisera, and ... Judg 4:18 3318
w softly unto him, and smote the ... Judg 4:21 935
And Gideon *w* in, and made ready a ... Judg 6:19 935
w over, and pitched in the valley ... Judg 6:33 5674
Then *w* he down with Phurah his ... Judg 7:11 3381
he *w* up thence to Penuel, and ... Judg 8:8 5927
Gideon *w* up by the way of them ... Judg 8:11 5927
all Israel *w* thither a whoring ... Judg 8:27
And Jerubbaal the son of Joash *w* ... Judg 8:29 3212
w a whoring after Baalim, and made ... Judg 8:33
w to Shechem unto his mother's ... Judg 9:1 3212
he *w* unto his father's house at ... Judg 9:5 935
and all the house of Millo, and *w* ... Judg 9:6 3212
when they told it to Jotham, he *w* ... Judg 9:7 3212
The trees *w* forth on a time to ... Judg 9:8 1980
w to Beer, and dwelt there, for ... Judg 9:21 3212
brethren, and *w* over to Shechem ... Judg 9:26 5674
they *w* out into the fields, and ... Judg 9:27 3318
w into the house of their god, and ... Judg 9:27 935
And Gaal the son of Ebed *w* out ... Judg 9:35 3318
Gaal *w* out before the men of ... Judg 9:39 3318
that the people *w* out into the ... Judg 9:42 3318
Then *w* Abimelech to Thebez, and ... Judg 9:50 3212
w hard unto the door of the tower ... Judg 9:52 5066
to Jephthah, and *w* out with him ... Judg 11:3 3318
the elders of Gilead *w* to fetch ... Judg 11:5 3212
Then Jephthah *w* with the elders ... Judg 11:11 3212
Then they *w* along through the ... Judg 11:18 3212
she *w* with her companions, and ... Judg 11:38 3212
That the daughters of Israel *w* ... Judg 11:40 3212
w northward, and said unto ... Judg 12:1 5674
w after his wife, and came to the ... Judg 13:11 3212
when the flame *w* up toward heaven ... Judg 13:20 5927
Samson *w* down to Timnath, and saw ... Judg 14:1 3381
Then *w* Samson down, and his father ... Judg 14:5 3381
he *w* down, and talked with the ... Judg 14:7 3381
w on eating, and came to his ... Judg 14:9 3212
So his father *w* down unto the ... Judg 14:10 3381
seventh day before the sun *w* down ... Judg 14:18 935

he *w* down to Ashkelon, and slew ... Judg 14:19 3381
he *w* up to his father's house ... Judg 14:19 5927
And Samson *w* and caught three ... Judg 15:4 3212
he *w* down and dwelt in the top of ... Judg 15:8 3381
Then the Philistines *w* up ... Judg 15:9 5927
w to the top of the rock Etam ... Judg 15:11 3381
Then *w* Samson to Gaza, and saw ... Judg 16:1 3212
there an harlot, and *w* in unto her ... Judg 16:1 935
w away with them, bar and all, and ... Judg 16:3 5265
w away with the pin of the beam, ... Judg 16:14 5265
him, and his strength *w* from him ... Judg 16:19 5493
So the Levite *w* in ... Judg 17:10 3212
there *w* from thence of the family ... Judg 18:11 5265
And they *w* up, and pitched in ... Judg 18:12 5927
w to spy out the country of Laish ... Judg 18:14 1980
w to spy out the land *w* up ... Judg 18:17 5927
these *w* into Micah's house, and ... Judg 18:18 935
w in the midst of the people ... Judg 18:20 935
the children of Dan *w* their way ... Judg 18:26 3212
turned and *w* back unto his house ... Judg 18:26 7725
w away from him unto her father's ... Judg 19:2 3212
w after her, to speak friendly ... Judg 19:3 3212
And they passed on and *w* their way ... Judg 19:14 3212
the sun *w* down upon them when ... Judg 19:14 935
and when he *w* in, he sat him down ... Judg 19:15 935
I *w* to Beth-lehem-judah, but I am ... Judg 19:18 3212
w out unto them, and said unto ... Judg 19:23 3318
the house, and *w* out to go his way ... Judg 19:27 3318
all the children of Israel *w* out ... Judg 20:1 3318
w up to the house of God, and ... Judg 20:18 5927
the men of Israel *w* out to battle ... Judg 20:20 3318
(And the children of Israel *w* up ... Judg 20:23 5927
Benjamin *w* forth against them out ... Judg 20:25 3318
w up, and came unto the house of ... Judg 20:26 5927
the children of Israel *w* up ... Judg 20:30 5927
Benjamin *w* out against the people ... Judg 20:31 3318
and they *w* and returned unto their ... Judg 21:23 3212
they *w* out from thence every man ... Judg 21:24 3318
w to sojourn in the country of ... Ruth 1:1 3212
Wherefore she *w* forth out of the ... Ruth 1:7 3318
they *w* on the way to return unto ... Ruth 1:7 3212
So they two *w* until they came to ... Ruth 1:19 3212
I *w* out full, and the LORD hath ... Ruth 1:21 1980
And she *w*, and came, and gleaned in ... Ruth 2:3 3212
took it up, and *w* into the city ... Ruth 2:18 935
she *w* down unto the floor, and did ... Ruth 3:6 3381
he *w* to lie down at the end of ... Ruth 3:7 935
and she *w* into the city ... Ruth 3:15 935
Then *w* Boaz up to the gate, and ... Ruth 4:1 5927
when he *w* in unto her, the LORD ... Ruth 4:13 935
this man *w* up out of his city ... 1Sa 1:3 5927
when she *w* up to the house of the ... 1Sa 1:7 5927
So the woman *w* her way, and did ... 1Sa 1:18 3212
w up to offer unto the LORD the ... 1Sa 1:21 5927
But Hannah *w* not up ... 1Sa 1:22 5927
Elkanah *w* to Ramah to his house ... 1Sa 2:11 3212
they *w* unto their own home ... 1Sa 2:20 1980
ere the lamp of God *w* out in the ... 1Sa 3:3 3518
And he *w* and lay down ... 1Sa 3:5 3212
w to Eli, and said, Here am I ... 1Sa 3:6 3212
w to Eli, and said, Here am I ... 1Sa 3:8 3212
So Samuel *w* and lay down in his ... 1Sa 3:9 3212
Now Israel *w* out against the ... 1Sa 4:1 3318
cry of the city *w* up to heaven ... 1Sa 5:12 5927
w along the highway, lowing as ... 1Sa 6:12 1980
the highway, lowing as they *w* ... 1Sa 6:12 1980
the lords of the Philistines *w* ... 1Sa 6:12 1980
Philistines *w* up against Israel ... 1Sa 7:7 5927
the men of Israel *w* out of Mizpeh ... 1Sa 7:11 3318
he *w* from year to year in circuit ... 1Sa 7:16 1980
when a man *w* to enquire of God, ... 1Sa 9:9 3212
So they *w* unto the city where the ... 1Sa 9:10 3212
as they *w* up the hill to the city ... 1Sa 9:11 5927
And they *w* up into the city ... 1Sa 9:14 5927
they *w* out both of them, he and ... 1Sa 9:26 3318
and to his servant, Whither *w* ye ... 1Sa 10:14 1980
Saul also *w* home to Gibeah ... 1Sa 10:26 1980
there *w* with him a band of men, ... 1Sa 10:26 3212
And all the people *w* to Gilgal ... 1Sa 11:15 3212
some of the Hebrews *w* over Jordan ... 1Sa 13:7 5674
Saul *w* out to meet him, that he ... 1Sa 13:10 3318
But all the Israelites *w* down to ... 1Sa 13:20 3381
w out to the passage of Michmash ... 1Sa 13:23 3318
they *w* on beating down one ... 1Sa 14:16 3212
the host of the Philistines *w* on ... 1Sa 14:19 3212
which *w* up with them into the ... 1Sa 14:21 5927
Then Saul *w* up from following the ... 1Sa 14:46 5927
the Philistines *w* to their own ... 1Sa 14:46 1980
Then Samuel *w* to Ramah ... 1Sa 15:34 3212
Saul *w* up to his house to Gibeah ... 1Sa 15:34 5927
So Samuel rose up, and *w* to Ramah ... 1Sa 16:13 3212
there *w* out a champion out of the ... 1Sa 17:4 3318
one bearing a shield *w* before him ... 1Sa 17:7 1980
the man *w* among men for an old ... 1Sa 17:12 935
the three eldest sons of Jesse *w* ... 1Sa 17:13 3212
w to the battle were Eliab the ... 1Sa 17:13 1980
But David *w* and returned from Saul ... 1Sa 17:15 1980
with a keeper, and took, and *w* ... 1Sa 17:20 3212
I *w* out after him, and smote him, ... 1Sa 17:35 3318
that bare the shield *w* before him ... 1Sa 17:41
David *w* out whithersoever Saul ... 1Sa 18:5 3318
he *w* out and came in before the ... 1Sa 18:13 3318
loved David, because he *w* out ... 1Sa 18:16 3318
Wherefore David arose and *w* ... 1Sa 18:27 3212
of the Philistines *w* forth ... 1Sa 18:30 3318
came to pass, after they *w* forth ... 1Sa 18:30 3318
and David *w* out, and fought with ... 1Sa 19:8 3318
and he *w*, and fled, and escaped ... 1Sa 19:12 3212
And he and Samuel *w* and dwelt in ... 1Sa 19:18 3212
Then *w* he also to Ramah, and came ... 1Sa 19:22 3212
he *w* thither to Naioth in Ramah ... 1Sa 19:23 3212
God was upon him also, and he *w* on ... 1Sa 19:23 3212
they *w* out both of them into the ... 1Sa 20:11 3318
that Jonathan *w* out into the ... 1Sa 20:35 3318

and Jonathan *w* into the city	1Sa 20:42	935
w to Achish the king of Gath	1Sa 21:10	935
they *w* down thither to him	1Sa 22:1	3381
David *w* thence to Mizpeh of Moab	1Sa 22:3	3212
his men *w* to Keilah, and fought	1Sa 23:5	3212
w whithersoever they could go	1Sa 23:13	1980
w to David into the wood, and	1Sa 23:16	3212
wood, and Jonathan *w* to his house	1Sa 23:18	1980
arose, and *w* to Ziph before Saul	1Sa 23:24	3212
also and his men *w* to seek him	1Sa 23:25	3212
Saul *w* on this side of the	1Sa 23:26	3212
w against the Philistines	1Sa 23:28	3212
David *w* up from thence, and dwelt	1Sa 23:29	5927
w to seek David and his men upon	1Sa 24:2	3212
Saul *w* in to cover his feet	1Sa 24:3	935
out of the cave, and *w* on his way	1Sa 24:7	3212
w out of the cave, and cried after	1Sa 24:8	3318
And Saul *w* home	1Sa 24:22	3212
w down to the wilderness of Paran	1Sa 25:1	3381
w again, and came and told him all	1Sa 25:12	7725
there *w* up after David about four	1Sa 25:13	5927
damsels of hers that *w* after her	1Sa 25:42	1980
she *w* after the messengers of	1Sa 25:42	3212
w down to the wilderness of Ziph,	1Sa 26:2	3381
Then David *w* over to the other	1Sa 26:13	5674
So David *w* on his way, and Saul	1Sa 26:25	3212
And David and his men *w* up, and	1Sa 27:8	5927
and put on other raiment, and he *w*	1Sa 28:8	3212
rose up, and *w* away that night	1Sa 28:25	3212
the Philistines *w* up to Jezreel	1Sa 29:11	5927
them away, and *w* on their way	1Sa 30:2	3212
So David *w*, he and the six hundred	1Sa 30:9	3212
they *w* forth to meet David, and to	1Sa 30:21	3318
of those that *w* with David	1Sa 30:22	1980
said, Because they *w* not with us	1Sa 30:22	1980
the battle *w* sore against Saul,	1Sa 31:3	
w all night, and took the body of	1Sa 31:12	3212
said unto him, How *w* the matter	2Sa 1:4	1961
So David *w* up thither, and his two	2Sa 2:2	5927
w out from Mahanaim to Gibeon	2Sa 2:12	3318
w out, and met together by the	2Sa 2:13	3318
w over by number twelve of	2Sa 2:15	5674
the sun *w* down when they were	2Sa 2:24	935
w through all Bithron, and they	2Sa 2:29	3212
his men *w* all night, and they came	2Sa 2:32	3212
her husband *w* with her along	2Sa 3:16	3212
Abner *w* also to speak in the ears	2Sa 3:19	3212
and he *w* in peace	2Sa 3:21	3212
Beerothite, Rechab and Baanah, *w*	2Sa 4:5	3212
his men *w* to Jerusalem unto the	2Sa 5:6	3212
And David *w* on, and grew great, and	2Sa 5:10	3212
of it, and *w* down to the hold	2Sa 5:17	3381
w with all the people that were	2Sa 6:2	3212
and Ahio *w* before the ark	2Sa 6:4	1980
So David *w* and brought up the ark	2Sa 6:12	3212
Then *w* king David in, and sat	2Sa 7:18	935
whom God *w* to redeem for a people	2Sa 7:23	1980
as he *w* to recover his border at	2Sa 8:3	3212
David whithersoever he *w*	2Sa 8:6	1980
David whithersoever he *w*	2Sa 8:14	1980
host of Hadarezer *w* before them	2Sa 10:16	
lord, and *w* not down to his house	2Sa 11:9	3381
Uriah *w* not down unto his house,	2Sa 11:10	3381
at even he *w* out to lie on his	2Sa 11:13	3318
but *w* not down to his house	2Sa 11:13	3381
And the men of the city *w* out	2Sa 11:17	3318
why *w* ye nigh the wall	2Sa 11:21	5066
So the messenger *w*, and came and	2Sa 11:22	3212
w in, and lay all night upon the	2Sa 12:16	935
w to him, to raise him up from	2Sa 12:17	
w in unto her, and lay with her	2Sa 12:24	935
w to Rabbah, and fought against it	2Sa 12:29	3212
So Tamar *w* to her brother Amnon's	2Sa 13:8	3212
they *w* out every man from him	2Sa 13:9	3318
hand on her head, and *w* on crying	2Sa 13:19	3212
w to Talmai, the son of Ammihud,	2Sa 13:37	3212
w to Geshur, and was there three	2Sa 13:38	3212
w to Geshur, and brought Absalom	2Sa 14:23	3212
So he arose, and *w* to Hebron	2Sa 15:9	3212
with Absalom *w* two hundred men	2Sa 15:11	1980
they *w* in their simplicity, and	2Sa 15:11	1980
And the king *w* forth, and all his	2Sa 15:16	3318
And the king *w* forth, and all the	2Sa 15:17	3318
and Abiathar *w* up, until all the	2Sa 15:24	5927
David *w* up by the ascent of mount	2Sa 15:30	5927
mount Olivet, and wept as he *w* up	2Sa 15:30	5927
head covered, and he *w* barefoot	2Sa 15:30	1980
w up, weeping as they *w* up	2Sa 15:30	5927
his men *w* by the way, Shimei *w*	2Sa 16:13	3212
against him, and cursed as he *w*	2Sa 16:13	1980
Absalom *w* in unto his father's	2Sa 16:22	935
and a wench *w* and told them	2Sa 17:17	980
and they *w* and told king David	2Sa 17:17	3212
but they *w* both of them away	2Sa 17:18	3212
whither they *w* down	2Sa 17:18	3381
came up out of the well, and *w*	2Sa 17:21	3212
that *w* in to Abigail the daughter	2Sa 17:25	935
So the people *w* out into the	2Sa 18:6	3318
the mule *w* under the thick boughs	2Sa 18:9	935
mule that was under him *w* away	2Sa 18:9	5674
the watchman *w* up to the roof	2Sa 18:24	3212
w up to the chamber over the gate	2Sa 18:33	5927
and as he *w*, thus he said, O my	2Sa 18:33	3212
they *w* over Jordan before the	2Sa 19:17	6743
there *w* over a ferry boat to	2Sa 19:18	5674
lord the king *w* out of Jerusalem	2Sa 19:19	3318
w over Jordan with the king, to	2Sa 19:31	5674
And all the people *w* over Jordan	2Sa 19:39	5674
Then the king *w* on to Gilgal	2Sa 19:40	5674
and Chimham *w* on with him	2Sa 19:40	5674
of Israel *w* up from after David	2Sa 20:2	5927
fed them, but *w* not in unto them	2Sa 20:3	935
So Amasa *w* to assemble the men of	2Sa 20:5	3212
there *w* out after him Joab's men,	2Sa 20:7	3318
they *w* out of Jerusalem, to	2Sa 20:7	3318
is in Gibeon, Amasa *w* before them	2Sa 20:8	935
as he *w* forth it fell out	2Sa 20:8	3318
all the people *w* on after Joab	2Sa 20:13	5674
he *w* through all the tribes of	2Sa 20:14	5674
together, and *w* also after him	2Sa 20:14	935
Then the woman *w* unto all the	2Sa 20:22	935
And David *w* and took the bones of	2Sa 21:12	3212
and David *w* down, and his servants	2Sa 21:15	3381
There *w* up a smoke out of his	2Sa 22:9	5927
three of the thirty chief *w* down	2Sa 23:13	3381
that *w* in jeopardy of their lives	2Sa 23:17	1980
he *w* down also and slew a lion in	2Sa 23:20	3381
but he *w* down to him with a staff	2Sa 23:21	3381
the captains of the host *w* out	2Sa 24:4	3318
they *w* out to the south of Judah,	2Sa 24:7	3318
w up as the LORD commanded	2Sa 24:19	5927
and Araunah *w* out, and bowed	2Sa 24:20	3318
Bath-sheba *w* in unto the king	1Kin 1:15	935
w down, and caused Solomon to ride	1Kin 1:38	3381
rose up, and *w* every man his way	1Kin 1:49	3212
of Solomon, and arose, and *w*	1Kin 1:50	3212
in the day when I *w* to Mahanaim	1Kin 2:8	3212
therefore *w* unto king Solomon	1Kin 2:19	935
Benaiah the son of Jehoiada *w* up	1Kin 2:34	5927
w to Gath to Achish to seek his	1Kin 2:40	3212
and Shimei *w*, and brought his	1Kin 2:40	3212
which *w* out, and fell upon him,	1Kin 2:46	3318
the king *w* to Gibeon to sacrifice	1Kin 3:4	3212
they *w* up with winding stairs	1Kin 6:8	5927
w unto their tents joyful and glad	1Kin 8:66	3212
his ascent by which he *w* up unto	1Kin 10:5	5927
w to her own country, she and her	1Kin 10:13	3212
shekels of gold *w* to one target	1Kin 10:16	5927
pound of gold *w* to one shield	1Kin 10:17	5927
w out of Egypt for six hundred	1Kin 10:29	3318
For Solomon *w* after Ashtoreth the	1Kin 11:5	3212
w not fully after the LORD, as	1Kin 11:6	
they *w* to Damascus, and dwelt	1Kin 11:24	3212
when Jeroboam *w* out of Jerusalem	1Kin 11:29	3318
And Rehoboam *w* to Shechem	1Kin 12:1	3212
w out from thence, and built	1Kin 12:25	3318
for the people *w* to worship	1Kin 12:30	3212
So he *w* another way, and returned	1Kin 13:10	3212
said unto them, What way *w* he	1Kin 13:12	1980
seen what way the man of God *w*	1Kin 13:12	1980
w after the man of God, and found	1Kin 13:14	3212
So he *w* back with him, and did eat	1Kin 13:19	7725
And he *w* and found his carcase cast	1Kin 13:28	3212
w to Shiloh, and came to the house	1Kin 14:4	3212
when the king *w* into the house of	1Kin 14:28	935
king of Israel *w* up against Judah	1Kin 15:17	5927
And Zimri *w* in and smote him, and	1Kin 16:10	935
Omri *w* up from Gibbethon, and all	1Kin 16:17	5927
that he *w* into the palace of the	1Kin 16:18	935
king of the Zidonians, and *w*	1Kin 16:31	3212
So he *w* and did according unto the	1Kin 17:5	3212
for he *w* and dwelt by the brook	1Kin 17:5	3212
So he arose and *w* to Zarephath	1Kin 17:10	3212
And she *w* and did according to the	1Kin 17:15	3212
Elijah *w* to shew himself unto	1Kin 18:2	3212
Ahab *w* one way by himself, and	1Kin 18:6	1980
Obadiah *w* another way by himself	1Kin 18:6	1980
So Obadiah *w* to meet Ahab, and	1Kin 18:16	3212
and Ahab *w* to meet Elijah	1Kin 18:16	3212
So Ahab *w* up to eat and to drink	1Kin 18:42	5927
Elijah *w* up to the top of Carmel	1Kin 18:42	5927
And he *w* up, and looked, and said,	1Kin 18:43	5927
And Ahab rode, and *w* to Jezreel	1Kin 18:45	3212
w for his life, and came to	1Kin 19:3	3212
But he himself *w* a day's journey	1Kin 19:4	1980
w in the strength of that meat	1Kin 19:8	3212
w out, and stood in the entering	1Kin 19:13	3318
w after Elijah, and ministered	1Kin 19:21	3212
and he *w* up and besieged Samaria,	1Kin 20:1	5927
And they *w* out at noon	1Kin 20:16	3318
of the provinces *w* out first	1Kin 20:17	3318
And the king of Israel *w* out	1Kin 20:21	3318
w up to Aphek, to fight against	1Kin 20:26	5927
all present, and *w* against them	1Kin 20:27	3212
Thy servant *w* out into the midst	1Kin 20:39	3318
of Israel *w* to his house heavy	1Kin 20:43	3212
and lay in sackcloth, and *w* softly	1Kin 21:27	1980
the son of Chenaanah *w* near	1Kin 22:24	5674
Which way *w* the Spirit of the	1Kin 22:24	5674
of Judah *w* up to Ramoth-gilead	1Kin 22:29	5927
himself, and *w* into the battle	1Kin 22:30	935
there *w* a proclamation throughout	1Kin 22:36	5674
but they *w* not	1Kin 22:48	1980
And he *w* up to him	2Kin 1:9	5927
the third captain of fifty *w* up	2Kin 1:13	5927
w down with him unto the king	2Kin 1:15	3381
that Elijah *w* with Elisha from	2Kin 2:1	3212
So they *w* down to Beth-el	2Kin 2:2	3381
And they two *w* on	2Kin 2:6	3212
men of the sons of the prophets *w*	2Kin 2:7	1980
so that they two *w* over on dry	2Kin 2:8	5674
came to pass, as they still *w* on	2Kin 2:11	1980
Elijah *w* up by a whirlwind into	2Kin 2:11	5927
w back, and stood by the bank of	2Kin 2:13	7725
and Elisha *w* over	2Kin 2:14	5674
he *w* forth unto the spring of the	2Kin 2:21	3318
he *w* up from thence unto Beth-el	2Kin 2:23	5927
he *w* from thence to mount Carmel,	2Kin 2:25	3212
king Jehoram *w* out of Samaria the	2Kin 3:6	3318
And he *w* and sent to Jehoshaphat	2Kin 3:7	3212
So the king of Israel *w*, and the	2Kin 3:9	3212
and the king of Edom *w* down to him	2Kin 3:12	3381
but they *w* forward smiting the	2Kin 3:24	5221
howbeit the slingers *w* about it	2Kin 3:25	5437
So she *w* from him, and shut the	2Kin 4:5	3212
that he *w* out to his father to	2Kin 4:18	3318
And she *w* up, and laid him on the	2Kin 4:21	5927
shut the door upon him, and *w* out	2Kin 4:21	3318
So she *w* and came unto the man of	2Kin 4:25	3212
Wherefore he *w* again to meet him,	2Kin 4:31	7725
He *w* in therefore, and shut the	2Kin 4:33	935
And he *w* up, and lay upon the child	2Kin 4:34	5927
w up, and stretched himself upon	2Kin 4:35	5927
Then she *w* in, and fell at his	2Kin 4:37	935
and took up her son, and *w* out	2Kin 4:37	3318
one *w* out into the field to	2Kin 4:39	3318
And one *w* in, and told his lord,	2Kin 5:4	935
w away, and said, Behold, I	2Kin 5:11	3212
So he turned and *w* away in a rage	2Kin 5:12	3212
Then *w* he down, and dipped himself	2Kin 5:14	3381
But he *w* in, and stood before his	2Kin 5:25	935
he said, Thy servant *w* no whither	2Kin 5:25	1980
W not mine heart with thee, when	2Kin 5:26	1980
he *w* out from his presence a	2Kin 5:27	3318
So he *w* with them	2Kin 6:4	3212
away, and they *w* to their master	2Kin 6:23	3212
w up, and besieged Samaria	2Kin 6:24	5927
they *w* into one tent, and did eat	2Kin 7:8	935
silver, and gold, and raiment, and *w*	2Kin 7:8	3212
and carried thence also, and *w*	2Kin 7:8	3212
they *w* after them unto Jordan	2Kin 7:15	3212
And the people *w* out, and spoiled	2Kin 7:16	3318
she *w* with her household, and	2Kin 8:2	3212
she *w* forth to cry unto the king	2Kin 8:3	3318
So Hazael *w* to meet him, and took	2Kin 8:9	3212
So Joram *w* over to Zair, and all	2Kin 8:21	5674
he *w* with Joram the son of Ahab	2Kin 8:28	3212
king Joram *w* back to be healed in	2Kin 8:29	7725
w down to see Joram the son of	2Kin 8:29	3381
the prophet, *w* to Ramoth-gilead	2Kin 9:4	3212
And he arose, and *w* into the house	2Kin 9:6	935
in a chariot, and *w* to Jezreel	2Kin 9:16	3212
So there *w* one on horseback to	2Kin 9:18	3212
and Ahaziah king of Judah *w* out	2Kin 9:21	3318
they *w* out against Jehu, and met	2Kin 9:21	3318
the arrow *w* out at his heart, and	2Kin 9:24	3318
And they *w* to bury her	2Kin 9:35	3212
in the morning, that he *w* out	2Kin 10:9	3318
And Jehu *w*, and Jehonadab the son	2Kin 10:23	935
And when they *w* in to offer	2Kin 10:24	935
w to the city of the house of	2Kin 10:25	3212
she *w* by the way by the which the	2Kin 11:16	935
the land *w* into the house of Baal	2Kin 11:18	935
Then Hazael king of Syria *w* up	2Kin 12:17	5927
and he *w* away from Jerusalem	2Kin 12:18	5927
so that they *w* out from under the	2Kin 13:5	3318
Jehoash king of Israel *w* up	2Kin 14:11	5927
the son of Gadi *w* up from Tirzah	2Kin 15:14	5927
of Assyria *w* up against Damascus	2Kin 16:9	5927
king Ahaz *w* to Damascus to meet	2Kin 16:10	3212
w up to Samaria, and besieged it	2Kin 17:5	5927
w after the heathen that were	2Kin 17:15	3212
whithersoever he *w* forth	2Kin 18:7	3318
And they *w* up and came to Jerusalem	2Kin 18:17	5927
w into the house of the LORD	2Kin 19:1	935
Hezekiah *w* up into the house of	2Kin 19:14	5927
that the angel of the LORD *w* out	2Kin 19:35	3318
king of Assyria departed, and *w*	2Kin 19:36	3212
w unto Huldah the prophetess, the	2Kin 22:14	3212
the king *w* up into the house of	2Kin 23:2	5927
Pharaoh-nechoh king of Egypt *w* up	2Kin 23:29	5927
and king Josiah *w* against him	2Kin 23:29	3212
w out to the king of Babylon	2Kin 24:12	3318
the king *w* the way toward the	2Kin 25:4	3212
afterward Hezron *w* in to the	1Chr 2:21	935
they *w* to the entrance of Gedor,	1Chr 4:39	3212
w to mount Seir, having for their	1Chr 4:42	1980
threescore, that *w* out to the war	1Chr 5:18	3318
w a whoring after the gods of the	1Chr 5:25	
Jehozadak *w* into captivity, when	1Chr 6:15	1980
when he *w* in to his wife, she	1Chr 7:23	935
because it *w* evil with his house	1Chr 7:23	1961
the battle *w* sore against Saul,	1Chr 10:3	
all Israel *w* to Jerusalem, which	1Chr 11:4	3212
the son of Zeruiah *w* first up	1Chr 11:6	5927
w down to the rock to David	1Chr 11:15	3381
also he *w* down and slew a lion in	1Chr 11:22	3381
he *w* down to him with a staff, and	1Chr 11:23	3381
These are they that *w* over Jordan	1Chr 12:15	5674
David *w* out to meet them, and	1Chr 12:17	3318
As he *w* to Ziklag, there fell to	1Chr 12:20	3212
such as *w* forth to battle, expert	1Chr 12:33	3318
such as *w* forth to battle, expert	1Chr 12:36	3318
And David *w* up, and all Israel, to	1Chr 13:6	5927
Philistines *w* up to seek David	1Chr 14:8	5927
of it, and *w* out against them	1Chr 14:8	3318
the fame of David *w* out into all	1Chr 14:17	3318
w to bring up the ark of the	1Chr 15:25	1980
when they *w* from nation to nation	1Chr 16:20	1980
whom God *w* to redeem to be his	1Chr 17:21	1980
as he *w* to stablish his dominion	1Chr 18:3	3212
David whithersoever he *w*	1Chr 18:6	1980
David whithersoever he *w*	1Chr 18:13	1980
Then there *w* certain, and told	1Chr 19:5	3212
host of Hadarezer *w* before them	1Chr 19:16	
w throughout all Israel, and came	1Chr 21:4	1980
David *w* up at the saying of Gad,	1Chr 21:19	5927
w out of the threshingfloor, and	1Chr 21:21	3318
w out month by month throughout	1Chr 27:1	3318
and the times that *w* over him	1Chr 29:30	5674
w to the high place that was at	2Chr 1:3	3212
Solomon *w* up thither to the	2Chr 1:6	5927
Solomon *w* to Hamath-zobah, and	2Chr 8:3	3212
Then *w* Solomon to Ezion-geber, and	2Chr 8:17	1980
they *w* with the servants of	2Chr 8:18	935
his ascent by which he *w* up into	2Chr 9:4	5927
w away to her own land, she and	2Chr 9:12	3212
of beaten gold *w* to one target	2Chr 9:15	5927
shekels of gold *w* to one shield	2Chr 9:16	5927
For the king's ships *w* to	2Chr 9:21	1980
And Rehoboam *w* to Shechem	2Chr 10:1	3212
So all Israel *w* to their tents	2Chr 10:16	3212

and also in Judah things *w* well 2Chr 12:12 1961
Then Asa *w* out against him, and 2Chr 14:10 3318
he *w* out to meet Asa, and said 2Chr 15:2 3318
was no peace to him that *w* out 2Chr 15:5 3318
w about throughout all the cities 2Chr 17:9 5437
after certain years he *w* down to 2Chr 18:2 3381
the messenger that *w* to call 2Chr 18:12 1980
Which way *w* the Spirit of the 2Chr 18:23 5674
of Judah *w* up to Ramoth-gilead 2Chr 18:28 5927
and they *w* to the battle 2Chr 18:29 935
Hanani the seer *w* out to meet him 2Chr 19:2 3318
he *w* out again through the people 2Chr 19:4 3318
w forth into the wilderness of 2Chr 20:20 3318
and as they *w* forth, Jehoshaphat 2Chr 20:20 3318
as they *w* out before the army, and 2Chr 20:21 3318
Then Jehoram *w* forth with his 2Chr 21:9 5674
w with Jehoram the son of Ahab 2Chr 22:5 3212
son of Jehoram king of Judah *w* 2Chr 22:6 3381
he *w* out with Jehoram against 2Chr 22:7 3318
they *w* about in Judah, and 2Chr 23:2 5437
Then all the people *w* to the 2Chr 23:17 935
w to the valley of salt, and smote 2Chr 25:11 3212
So Joash the king of Israel *w* up 2Chr 25:21 5927
he *w* forth and warred against the 2Chr 26:6 3318
that *w* out to war by bands, 2Chr 26:11 3318
w into the temple of the LORD to 2Chr 26:16 935
Azariah the priest *w* in after him 2Chr 26:17 935
he *w* out before the host that 2Chr 28:9 3318
the priests *w* into the inner part 2Chr 29:16 935
Then they *w* in to Hezekiah the 2Chr 29:18 935
w up to the house of the LORD 2Chr 29:20 5927
So the posts *w* with the letters 2Chr 30:6 3212
w out to the cities of Judah 2Chr 31:1 3318
w to Huldah the prophetess, the 2Chr 34:22 3212
the king *w* up into the house of 2Chr 34:30 5927
and Josiah *w* out against him 2Chr 35:20 3318
that *w* up out of the captivity Ezr 2:1 5927
they which *w* up from Tel-melah Ezr 2:59 5927
they *w* up in haste to Jerusalem Ezr 4:23 236
that we *w* into the province of Ezr 5:8 236
This Ezra *w* up from Babylon Ezr 7:6 5927
there *w* up some of the children Ezr 7:7 5927
that *w* up with me from Babylon Ezr 8:1 5927
w into the chamber of Johanan the Ezr 10:6 3212
I *w* out by night by the gate of Neh 2:13 3318
Then I *w* on to the gate of the Neh 2:14 5674
Then *w* I up in the night by the Neh 2:15 5927
the rulers knew not whither I *w* Neh 2:16 1980
that *w* up out of the captivity, Neh 7:6 5927
these were they which *w* up also Neh 7:61 5927
all the people *w* their way to eat Neh 8:12 3212
So the people *w* forth, and brought Neh 8:16 3318
so that they *w* through the midst Neh 9:11 5674
So the children *w* in and possessed Neh 9:24 935
the Levites that *w* up with Neh 12:1 5927
whereof one *w* on the right hand Neh 12:31 1980
And after them *w* Hoshaiah, and half Neh 12:32 3212
they *w* up by the stairs of the Neh 12:37 5927
gave thanks *w* over against them Neh 12:38 1980
In the evening she *w*, and on the Est 2:14 935
The posts *w* out, being hastened Est 3:15 3318
w out into the midst of the city, Est 4:1 3318
So Hatach *w* forth to Mordecai Est 4:6 3318
So Mordecai *w* his way, and did Est 4:17 5674
Then *w* Haman forth that day Est 5:9 3318
wrath *w* into the palace garden Est 7:7
As the word *w* out of the king's Est 7:8 3318
rode upon mules and camels *w* out Est 8:14 3318
Mordecai *w* out from the presence Est 8:15 3318
his fame *w* out throughout all the Est 9:4 1980
And his sons *w* and feasted in their Job 1:4 1980
So Satan *w* forth from the Job 1:12 3318
So *w* Satan forth from the Job 2:7 3318
as they that *w* before were Job 18:20 6923
When I *w* out to the gate through Job 29:7 3318
I *w* mourning without the sun Job 30:28 1980
silence, and *w* not out of the door Job 31:34 3318
and Zophar the Naamathite *w* Job 42:9 3212
There *w* up a smoke out of his Ps 18:8 5927
I *w* with them to the house of God Ps 42:4 1718
they *w* through the flood on foot Ps 66:6 5674
we *w* through fire and through Ps 66:12 935
The singers *w* before, the players Ps 68:25 6923
Until I *w* into the sanctuary of Ps 73:17 935
thine arrows also *w* abroad Ps 77:17 1980
when he *w* out through the land of Ps 81:5 3318
When they *w* from one nation to Ps 105:13 1980
so that it *w* ill with Moses for Ps 106:32
w a whoring with their own Ps 106:39
When Israel *w* out of Egypt, the Ps 114:1 3318
Before I was afflicted I *w* astray Ps 119:67 7683
that *w* down to the skirts of his Ps 133:2 3381
he *w* the way to her house, Prov 7:8 6805
I *w* by the field of the slothful, Prov 24:30 5674
Therefore I *w* about to cause my Eccl 2:20 5437
The watchmen that *w* about the Song 5:7 5437
I *w* down into the garden of nuts Song 6:11 3381
w up toward Jerusalem to war Is 7:1 5927
And I *w* unto the prophetess Is 8:3 7126
w into the house of the LORD Is 37:1 935
Hezekiah *w* up unto the house of Is 37:14 5927
the angel of the LORD *w* forth Is 37:36 3318
king of Assyria departed, and *w* Is 37:37 3212
they *w* forth out of my mouth, and Is 48:3 3318
the street, to them that *w* over Is 51:23 5674
My people *w* down aforetime into Is 52:4 3381
he *w* on frowardly in the way of Is 57:17 3212
so that no man *w* through thee Is 60:15 5674
sister Judah feared not, but *w* Jer 3:8 3212
w backward, and not forward Jer 7:24 1961
they *w* after other gods to serve Jer 11:10 1980
So I *w*, and hid it by Euphrates, Jer 13:5 3212
Then I *w* to Euphrates, and digged, Jer 13:7 3212
Then I *w* down to the potter's Jer 18:3 3381

which *w* forth out of this place Jer 22:11 3318
afraid, and fled, and *w* into Egypt Jer 26:21 935
that *w* into Babylon, saith the Jer 28:4 935
And the prophet Jeremiah *w* his way Jer 28:11 3212
when I *w* to cause him to rest Jer 31:2 1980
Then he *w* down into the king's Jer 36:12 3381
they *w* in to the king into the Jer 36:20 935
came in and *w* out among the people Jer 37:4 3318
Then Jeremiah *w* forth out of Jer 37:12 3318
Ebed-melech *w* forth out of the Jer 38:8 3318
w into the house of the king Jer 38:11 935
w forth out of the city by night, Jer 39:4 3318
he *w* out the way of the plain Jer 39:4 3318
Then *w* Jeremiah unto Gedaliah the Jer 40:6 935
Ishmael the son of Nethaniah *w* Jer 41:6 3318
them, weeping all along as he *w* Jer 41:6 1980
w to fight with Ishmael the son Jer 41:12 3212
w unto Johanan the son of Kareah Jer 41:14 3212
eight men, and *w* to the Ammonites Jer 41:15 3212
in that they *w* to burn incense, Jer 44:3 3212
when he *w* with Zedekiah the king Jer 51:59 3212
w forth out of the city by night Jer 52:7 3318
they *w* by the way of the plain Jer 52:7 3212
they turned not when they *w* Eze 1:9 3212
they *w* every one straight forward Eze 1:9 3212
they *w* every one straight forward Eze 1:12 3212
the spirit was to go, they *w* Eze 1:12 3212
and they turned not when they *w* Eze 1:12 3212
it *w* up and down among the living Eze 1:13 1980
out of the fire *w* forth lightning Eze 1:13 3318
When they *w*, they *w* upon their Eze 1:17 3212
and they turned not when they *w* Eze 1:17 3212
And when the living creatures *w* Eze 1:19 3212
the wheels *w* by them Eze 1:19 3212
the spirit was to go, they *w* Eze 1:20 3212
When those *w*, these *w* Eze 1:21 3212
And when they *w*, I heard the noise Eze 1:24 3212
I *w* in bitterness, in the heat of Eze 3:14 3212
arose, and *w* forth into the plain Eze 3:23 3318
So I *w* in and saw Eze 8:10 935
and a thick cloud of incense *w* up Eze 8:11 5927
and they *w* in, and stood beside the Eze 9:2 935
they *w* forth, and slew in the city Eze 9:7 3318
And he *w* in in my sight Eze 10:2 935
of the house, when the man *w* in Eze 10:3 935
of the LORD *w* up from the cherub Eze 10:4 7311
then he *w* in, and stood beside the Eze 10:6 935
who took it, and *w* out Eze 10:7 3318
When they *w*, they *w* upon their Eze 10:11 3212
they turned not as they *w* Eze 10:11 3212
they turned not as they *w* Eze 10:11 3212
And when the cherubims *w* Eze 10:16 3212
the wheels *w* by them Eze 10:16 3212
when they *w* out, the wheels also Eze 10:19 3318
they *w* every one straight forward Eze 10:22 3212
the glory of the LORD *w* up from Eze 11:23 5927
that I had seen *w* up from me Eze 11:24 5927
thy renown *w* forth among the Eze 16:14 3318
And he *w* up and down among the Eze 19:6 1980
for their heart *w* after their Eze 20:16 1980
Yet they *w* in unto her, as they Eze 23:44 935
so *w* they in unto Aholah and unto Eze 23:44 935
her great scum *w* not forth out of Eze 24:12 3318
when they *w* into captivity Eze 25:3
When thy wares *w* forth out of the Eze 27:33 3318
In the day when he *w* down to the Eze 31:15 3381
They also *w* down into hell with Eze 31:17 3381
unto the heathen, whither they *w* Eze 36:20 935
among the heathen, whither they *w* Eze 36:21 935
among the heathen, whither ye *w* Eze 36:22 935
Israel *w* into captivity for their Eze 39:23
w up the stairs thereof, and Eze 40:6 5927
they *w* up unto it by seven steps Eze 40:22 5927
the steps whereby they *w* up to it Eze 40:49 5927
Then *w* he inward, and measured the Eze 41:3 935
w still upward round about the Eze 41:7
far from me, when Israel *w* astray Eze 44:10 8582
which *w* astray away from me after Eze 44:10 8582
of Israel *w* astray from me Eze 44:15 8582
line in his hand *w* forth eastward Eze 47:3 3318
which *w* not astray when the Eze 48:11 8582
the children of Israel *w* astray Eze 48:11 8582
as the Levites *w* astray Eze 48:11 8582
the decree *w* forth that the wise Dan 2:13 5312
Then Daniel *w* in, and desired of Dan 2:16 5954
Then Daniel *w* to his house, and Dan 2:17 236
Therefore Daniel *w* in unto Arioch Dan 2:24 5954
he *w* and said thus unto him Dan 2:24 236
was signed, he *w* into his house Dan 6:10 5954
Then the king *w* to his palace Dan 6:18 236
and his sleep *w* from him Dan 6:18 5075
w in haste unto the den of lions Dan 6:19 236
So he *w* and took Gomer the Hos 1:3 3212
she *w* after her lovers, and forgat Hos 2:13 3212
then *w* Ephraim to the Assyrian, Hos 5:13 3212
but they *w* to Baal-peor, and Hos 9:10 935
called them, so they *w* from them Hos 11:2 1980
The city that *w* out by a thousand Amos 5:3 3318
that which *w* forth by an hundred Amos 5:3 3318
or *w* into the house, and leaned Amos 5:19 935
of the LORD, and *w* down to Joppa Jonah 1:3 3381
w down into it, to go with them Jonah 1:3 3381
I *w* down to the bottoms of the Jonah 2:6 3381
w unto Nineveh, according to the Jonah 3:3 3212
So Jonah *w* out of the city, and Jonah 4:5 3318
away, she *w* into captivity Nah 3:10 1980
Before him *w* the pestilence, and Hab 3:5 3212
burning coals *w* forth at his feet Hab 3:5 3318
the light of thine arrows they *w* Hab 3:11 1980
angel that talked with me *w* forth Zec 2:3 3318
another angel *w* out to meet him, Zec 2:3 3318
angel that talked with me *w* forth Zec 5:5 3318
And the bay *w* forth, and sought to Zec 6:7 3318
w out or came in because of the Zec 8:10 3318

therefore they *w* their way as a Zec 10:2 5265
w before them, till it came and Mt 2:9 *4254*
Then *w* out to him Jerusalem, and Mt 3:5 *1607*
w up straightway out of the water Mt 3:16 *305*
Jesus *w* about all Galilee, Mt 4:23 *4013*
his fame *w* throughout all Syria Mt 4:24 *565*
he *w* up into a mountain Mt 5:1 *305*
they *w* into the herd of swine Mt 8:32 *565*
w their ways into the city, and Mt 8:33 *565*
people were put forth, he *w* in Mt 9:25 *1525*
the fame hereof *w* abroad into all Mt 9:26 *1831*
As they *w* out, behold, they Mt 9:32 *1831*
Jesus *w* about all the cities and Mt 9:35 *4013*
What *w* ye out into the wilderness Mt 11:7 *1831*
But what *w* ye out for to see Mt 11:8 *1831*
But what *w* ye out for to see Mt 11:9 *1831*
At that time Jesus *w* on the Mt 12:1 *4198*
he *w* into their synagogue Mt 12:9 *2064*
Then the Pharisees *w* out, and held Mt 12:14 *1831*
The same day *w* Jesus out of the Mt 13:1 *1831*
so that he *w* into a ship, and sat Mt 13:2 *1684*
Behold, a sower *w* forth to sow Mt 13:3 *1831*
among the wheat, and *w* his way Mt 13:25 *565*
away, and *w* into the house Mt 13:36 *2064*
found one pearl of great price, *w* Mt 13:46 *565*
up the body, and buried it, and *w* Mt 14:12 *2064*
And Jesus *w* forth, and saw a great Mt 14:14 *1831*
he *w* up into a mountain apart to Mt 14:23 *305*
of the night Jesus *w* unto them Mt 14:25 *565*
Then Jesus *w* thence, and departed Mt 15:21 *1831*
w up into a mountain, and sat down Mt 15:29 *305*
ninety and nine which *w* not astray Mt 18:13 *4105*
But the same servant *w* out Mt 18:28 *1831*
but *w* and cast him into prison, Mt 18:30 *565*
that saying, he *w* away sorrowful Mt 19:22 *565*
which *w* out early in the morning Mt 20:1 *1821*
he *w* out about the third hour, and Mt 20:3 *1821*
And they *w* their way Mt 20:4 *565*
Again he *w* out about the sixth and Mt 20:5 *1831*
about the eleventh hour he *w* out Mt 20:6 *1831*
And the disciples *w*, and did as Mt 21:6 *4198*
And the multitudes that *w* before Mt 21:9 *4254*
Jesus *w* into the temple of God, Mt 21:12 *1525*
w out of the city into Bethany Mt 21:17 *1831*
but afterward he repented, and *w* Mt 21:29 *565*
I go sir: and *w* not Mt 21:30 *565*
and *w* into a far country Mt 21:33 *589*
w their ways, one to his farm, Mt 22:5 *565*
So those servants *w* out into the Mt 22:10 *1831*
Then *w* the Pharisees, and took Mt 22:15 *4198*
and left him, and *w* their way Mt 22:22 *565*
And Jesus *w* out, and departed from Mt 24:1 *1831*
w forth to meet the bridegroom Mt 25:1 *1831*
And while they *w* to buy, the Mt 25:10 *565*
they that were ready *w* in with Mt 25:10 *1525*
had received the five talents *w* Mt 25:16 *4198*
But he that had received one *w* Mt 25:18 *565*
And I was afraid, and *w* and hid thy Mt 25:25 *565*
w unto the chief priests, Mt 26:14 *4198*
they *w* out into the mount of Mt 26:30 *1831*
he *w* a little farther, and fell on Mt 26:39 *4281*
He *w* away again the second time, Mt 26:42 *565*
w away again, and prayed the third Mt 26:44 *565*
w in, and sat with the servants, Mt 26:58 *1525*
he *w* out, and wept bitterly Mt 26:75 *1831*
in the temple, and departed, and *w* Mt 27:5 *565*
w into the holy city, and appeared Mt 27:53 *1525*
He *w* to Pilate, and begged the Mt 27:58 *4344*
So they *w*, and made the sepulchre Mt 27:66 *4198*
as they *w* to tell his disciples, Mt 28:9 *4198*
disciples *w* away into Galilee Mt 28:16 *4198*
there *w* out unto him all the land Mk 1:5 *1607*
hired servants, and *w* after him Mk 1:20 *565*
And they *w* into Capernaum Mk 1:21 *1531*
he *w* out, and departed into a Mk 1:35 *1831*
But he *w* out, and began to publish Mk 1:45 *1831*
bed, and *w* forth before them all Mk 2:12 *1831*
he *w* forth again by the sea side Mk 2:13 *1831*
that he *w* through the corn fields Mk 2:23 *3899*
and his disciples began, as they *w* Mk 2:23
How he *w* into the house of God in Mk 2:26 *1525*
And the Pharisees *w* forth, and Mk 3:6 *1831*
and they *w* into an house Mk 3:19 *2064*
they *w* out to lay hold on him Mk 3:21 *1831*
there *w* out a sower to sow Mk 4:3 *1831*
And the unclean spirits *w* out Mk 5:13 *1831*
they *w* out to see what it was Mk 5:14 *1831*
And Jesus *w* with him Mk 5:24 *565*
he *w* out from thence, and came Mk 6:1 *1831*
he *w* round about the villages, Mk 6:6 *4013*
And they *w* out, and preached that Mk 6:12 *1831*
she *w* forth, and said unto her Mk 6:24 *1831*
and he *w* and beheaded him in the Mk 6:27 *565*
he *w* up unto them into the ship Mk 6:51 *305*
w into the borders of Tyre and Mk 7:24 *565*
And Jesus *w* out, and his disciples, Mk 8:27 *1831*
at that saying, and *w* away grieved Mk 10:22 *565*
and Jesus *w* before them Mk 10:32 *4254*
as he *w* out of Jericho with his Mk 10:46 *1607*
they *w* their way, and found the Mk 11:4 *565*
And they that *w* before, and they Mk 11:9 *4254*
he *w* out unto Bethany with the Mk 11:11 *1831*
Jesus *w* into the temple, and began Mk 11:15 *1525*
was come, he *w* out of the city Mk 11:19 *1607*
and *w* into a far country Mk 12:1 *589*
and they left him, and *w* their way Mk 12:12 *565*
as he *w* out of the temple, one of Mk 13:1 *1607*
w unto the chief priests, to Mk 14:10 *565*
And his disciples *w* forth, and came Mk 14:16 *1831*
they *w* out into the mount of Mk 14:26 *1831*
he *w* forward a little, and fell on Mk 14:35 *4281*
again he *w* away, and prayed Mk 14:39 *565*
And he *w* out into the porch Mk 14:68 *1831*
w in boldly unto Pilate, and Mk 15:43 *1525*

they *w* out quickly, and fled from ... Mk 16:8 1831
And she *w* and told them that had ... Mk 16:10 4198
walked, and *w* into the country ... Mk 16:12 4198
And they *w* and told it unto the ... Mk 16:13 565
they *w* forth, and preached every ... Mk 16:20 1831
he *w* into the temple of the Lord ... Lk 1:9 1525
w into the hill country with ... Lk 1:39 4198
that there *w* out a decree from ... Lk 2:1 1831
all *w* to be taxed, every one into ... Lk 2:3 4198
Joseph also *w* up from Galilee, ... Lk 2:4 305
Now his parents *w* to Jerusalem ... Lk 2:41 4198
they *w* up to Jerusalem after the ... Lk 2:42 305
in the company, *w* a day's journey ... Lk 2:44 2064
he *w* down with them, and came to ... Lk 2:51 2597
there *w* out a fame of him through ... Lk 4:14 1831
he *w* into the synagogue on the ... Lk 4:16 1525
the midst of them *w* his way ... Lk 4:30 4198
the fame of him *w* out into every ... Lk 4:37 1607
departed and *w* into a desert place ... Lk 4:42 4198
But so much the more *w* there a ... Lk 5:15 1330
they *w* upon the housetop, and let ... Lk 5:19 305
And after these things he *w* forth ... Lk 5:27 1831
that he *w* through the corn fields ... Lk 6:1 1279
How he *w* into the house of God, ... Lk 6:4 1525
that he *w* out into a mountain to ... Lk 6:12 1831
for there *w* virtue out of him, and ... Lk 6:19 1831
Then Jesus *w* with them ... Lk 7:6 4198
that he *w* into a city called Nain ... Lk 7:11 4198
many of his disciples *w* with him ... Lk 7:11 4848
this rumour of him *w* forth ... Lk 7:17 1831
What *w* ye out into the wilderness ... Lk 7:24 1831
But what *w* ye out for to see ... Lk 7:25 1831
But what *w* ye out for to see ... Lk 7:26 1831
he *w* into the Pharisee's house, ... Lk 7:36 1525
that he *w* throughout every city ... Lk 8:1 1353
out of whom *w* seven devils, ... Lk 8:2 1831
A sower *w* out to sow his seed ... Lk 8:5 1831
that he *w* into a ship with his ... Lk 8:22 1684
when he *w* forth to land, there ... Lk 8:27 1831
Then *w* the devils out of the man, ... Lk 8:33 1831
what was done, they fled, and *w* ... Lk 8:34 565
Then they *w* out to see what was ... Lk 8:35 1831
he *w* up into the ship, and ... Lk 8:37 1681
w his way, and published ... Lk 8:39 565
But as he *w* the people thronged ... Lk 8:42 5217
w through the towns, preaching ... Lk 9:6 1330
w aside privately into a desert ... Lk 9:10 5298
w up into a mountain to pray ... Lk 9:28 305
and they *w*, and entered into a ... Lk 9:52 4198
they *w* to another village ... Lk 9:56 4198
as they *w* in the way, a certain ... Lk 9:57 4198
A certain man *w* down from ... Lk 10:30 2597
w to him, and bound up his wounds, ... Lk 10:34 4334
Now it came to pass, as they *w* ... Lk 10:38 4198
and he *w* in, and sat down to meat ... Lk 11:37 1525
he *w* through the cities and ... Lk 13:22 1279
as he *w* into the house of one of ... Lk 14:1 2064
there *w* great multitudes with him ... Lk 14:25 4848
And he *w* and joined himself to a ... Lk 15:15 4198
but if one *w* unto them from the ... Lk 16:30 4198
as he *w* to Jerusalem, that he ... Lk 17:11 4198
it came to pass, that, as they *w* ... Lk 17:14 5217
But the same day that Lot *w* out ... Lk 17:29 1831
Two men *w* up into the temple to ... Lk 18:10 305
this man *w* down to his house ... Lk 18:14 2597
they which *w* before rebuked him, ... Lk 18:39 4254
A certain nobleman *w* into a far ... Lk 19:12 4198
he *w* before, ascending up to ... Lk 19:28 4198
they that were sent *w* their way ... Lk 19:32 565
And as he *w*, they spread their ... Lk 19:36 4198
he *w* into the temple, and began to ... Lk 19:45 1525
w into a far country for a long ... Lk 20:9 589
and at night he *w* out, and abode in ... Lk 21:37 1831
he *w* his way, and communed with ... Lk 22:4 565
And they *w*, and found as he had ... Lk 22:13 565
And he came out, and *w*, as he was ... Lk 22:39 4198
w before them, and drew near unto ... Lk 22:47 4281
And Peter *w* out, and wept bitterly ... Lk 22:62 1831
This man *w* unto Pilate, and begged ... Lk 23:52 4344
two of them *w* that same day to a ... Lk 24:13 4198
himself drew near, and *w* with them ... Lk 24:15 4848
were with us *w* to the sepulchre ... Lk 24:24 565
unto the village, whither they *w* ... Lk 24:28 4198
he *w* in to tarry with them ... Lk 24:29 1525
After this he *w* down to Capernaum ... Jn 2:12 2597
hand, and Jesus *w* up to Jerusalem, ... Jn 2:13 305
w her way into the city, and saith ... Jn 4:28 565
Then they *w* out of the city, and ... Jn 4:30 1831
thence, and *w* into Galilee ... Jn 4:43 565
for they also *w* unto the feast ... Jn 4:45 2064
he *w* unto him, and besought him ... Jn 4:47 565
spoken unto him, and he *w* his way ... Jn 4:50 4198
and Jesus *w* up to Jerusalem ... Jn 5:1 305
For an angel *w* down at a certain ... Jn 5:4 2597
Jesus *w* over the sea of Galilee ... Jn 6:1 565
Jesus *w* up into a mountain, and ... Jn 6:3 424
his disciples *w* down unto the sea ... Jn 6:16 2597
w over the sea toward Capernaum ... Jn 6:17 2064
was at the land whither they *w* ... Jn 6:21 5217
that Jesus *w* not with his ... Jn 6:22 4897
time many of his disciples *w* back ... Jn 6:66 565
then *w* he also up unto the feast, ... Jn 7:10 305
feast Jesus *w* up into the temple ... Jn 7:14 305
every man *w* unto his own house ... Jn 7:53 4198
Jesus *w* unto the mount of Olives ... Jn 8:1 4198
w out one by one, beginning at ... Jn 8:9 1831
w out of the temple, going ... Jn 8:59 1831
He *w* his way therefore, and ... Jn 9:7 565
and I *w* and washed, and I received ... Jn 9:11 565
w away again beyond Jordan into ... Jn 10:40 565
heard that Jesus was coming, *w* ... Jn 11:20 5221
she *w* her way, and called Mary her ... Jn 11:28 565
w out, followed her, saying, She ... Jn 11:31 1831
But some of them *w* their ways to ... Jn 11:46 565
but *w* thence unto a country near ... Jn 11:54 565
many *w* out of the country up to ... Jn 11:55 305
of him many of the Jews *w* away ... Jn 12:11 5217
w forth to meet him, and cried, ... Jn 12:13 1831
he was come from God, and *w* to God ... Jn 13:3 5217
the sop *w* immediately out ... Jn 13:30 1831
he *w* forth with his disciples ... Jn 18:1 1831
w forth, and said unto them, Whom ... Jn 18:4 1831
they *w* backward, and fell to the ... Jn 18:6 565
w in with Jesus into the palace ... Jn 18:15 4897
Then *w* out that other disciple, ... Jn 18:16 1831
they themselves *w* not into the ... Jn 18:28 1525
Pilate then *w* out unto them, and ... Jn 18:29 1831
he *w* out again unto the Jews, and ... Jn 18:38 1831
Pilate therefore *w* forth again ... Jn 19:4 1831
w again into the judgment hall, ... Jn 19:9 1525
he bearing his cross *w* forth into ... Jn 19:17 1831
Peter therefore *w* forth, and that ... Jn 20:3 1831
yet *w* he not in ... Jn 20:5 1525
w into the sepulchre, and seeth ... Jn 20:6 1525
Then *w* in also that other ... Jn 20:8 1525
Then the disciples *w* away again ... Jn 20:10 565
They *w* forth, and entered into a ... Jn 21:3 1831
Simon Peter *w* up, and drew the net ... Jn 21:11 305
Then *w* this saying abroad among ... Jn 21:23 1831
toward heaven as he *w* up, behold, ... Acts 1:10 4198
they *w* up into an upper room, ... Acts 1:13 305
the time that the Lord Jesus *w* in ... Acts 1:21
John *w* up together into the ... Acts 3:1 305
they *w* to their own company, and ... Acts 4:23 2064
Then *w* the captain with the ... Acts 5:26 565
So Jacob *w* down into Egypt, and ... Acts 7:15 2597
w every where preaching the word ... Acts 8:4 1330
Then Philip *w* down to the city of ... Acts 8:5 2718
And he arose and *w* ... Acts 8:27 4198
as they *w* on their way, they came ... Acts 8:36 4198
they *w* down both into the water, ... Acts 8:38 2597
he *w* on his way rejoicing ... Acts 8:39 4198
the Lord, *w* unto the high priest, ... Acts 9:1 4334
And Ananias *w* his way, and entered ... Acts 9:17 565
but they *w* about to slay him ... Acts 9:29 2021
Then Peter arose and *w* with them ... Acts 9:39 4905
as they *w* on their journey, and ... Acts 10:9 3596
Peter *w* up upon the housetop to ... Acts 10:9 305
Then Peter *w* down to the men ... Acts 10:21 2597
the morrow Peter *w* away with them ... Acts 10:23 1831
And as he talked with him, he *w* in ... Acts 10:27 1525
who *w* about doing good, and ... Acts 10:38 1330
he *w* out, and followed him ... Acts 12:9 1831
and they *w* out, and passed on ... Acts 12:10 1831
departed, and *w* into another place ... Acts 12:17 4198
he *w* down from Judaea to Caesarea ... Acts 12:19 2718
he *w* about seeking some to lead ... Acts 13:11 4013
w into the synagogue on the ... Acts 13:14 1525
that they *w* both together into ... Acts 14:1 1525
Perga, they *w* down into Attalia ... Acts 14:25 2597
that certain which *w* out from us ... Acts 15:24 1831
w not with them to the work ... Acts 15:38 4905
he *w* through Syria and Cilicia, ... Acts 15:41 1330
as they *w* through the cities, ... Acts 16:4 1279
on the sabbath we *w* out of the ... Acts 16:13 1831
as we *w* to prayer, a certain ... Acts 16:16 4198
they *w* out of the prison, and ... Acts 16:40 1831
w in unto them, and three sabbath ... Acts 17:2 1525
who coming thither *w* into the ... Acts 17:10 549
the church, he *w* down to Antioch ... Acts 18:22 2597
w over all the country of Galatia ... Acts 18:23 1330
he *w* into the synagogue, and spake ... Acts 19:8 1525
and the evil spirits *w* out of them ... Acts 19:12 1831
And Paul *w* down, and fell on him, ... Acts 20:10 2597
we *w* before to ship, and sailed ... Acts 20:13 4281
we *w* aboard, and set forth ... Acts 21:2 1910
days, we departed and *w* our way ... Acts 21:5 4198
carriages, and *w* up to Jerusalem ... Acts 21:15 305
There *w* with us also certain of ... Acts 21:16 4905
Paul *w* in with us unto James ... Acts 21:18 1524
as they *w* about to kill him, ... Acts 21:31 2212
w to Damascus, to bring them ... Acts 22:5 4198
the centurion heard that, he *w* ... Acts 22:26 4334
of their lying in wait, he *w* ... Acts 23:16 3854
w with him aside privately, and ... Acts 23:19 402
w up to Jerusalem for to worship ... Acts 24:11 305
ten days, he *w* down unto Caesarea ... Acts 25:6 2597
Whereupon as I *w* to Damascus with ... Acts 26:12 4198
the temple, and *w* about to kill me ... Acts 26:21 3987
and so we *w* toward Rome ... Acts 28:14 2064
their sound *w* into all the earth, ... Rom 10:18 1831
I *w* from thence into Macedonia ... 2Cor 2:13 1831
of his own accord he *w* unto you ... 2Cor 8:17 1831
Neither *w* I up to Jerusalem to ... Gal 1:17 424
but I *w* into Arabia, and returned ... Gal 1:17 565
Then after three years I *w* up to ... Gal 1:18 424
I *w* up again to Jerusalem with ... Gal 2:1 305
And I *w* up by revelation, and ... Gal 2:2 305
when I *w* into Macedonia, that ... 1Ti 1:3 4198
prophecies which *w* before on thee ... 1Ti 1:18 4254
the priests *w* always into the ... Heb 9:6 1524
But into the second *w* the high ... Heb 9:7
he *w* out, not knowing whither he ... Heb 11:8 1831
out, not knowing whither he *w* ... Heb 11:8 2064
By which also he *w* and preached ... 1Pet 3:19 4198
They *w* out from us, but they were ... 1Jn 2:19 1831
but they *w* out, that they might ... 1Jn 2:19
for his name's sake they *w* forth ... 3Jn 7 1831
out of his mouth *w* a sharp ... Rev 1:16 1607
he *w* forth conquering, and to ... Rev 6:2 1831
there *w* out another horse that ... Rev 6:4 1831
I *w* unto the angel, and said unto ... Rev 10:9 565
w to make war with the remnant of ... Rev 12:17 565
And the first *w*, and poured out his ... Rev 16:2 565
they *w* up on the breadth of the ... Rev 20:9 305

WENTEST

because thou *w* up to thy father's ... Gen 49:4 5927
when thou *w* out of Seir, when ... Judg 5:4 3318
when thou *w* to fight with the ... Judg 8:1 1980
which thou *w* to seek are found ... 1Sa 10:2 1980
with thee whithersoever thou *w* ... 2Sa 7:9 1980
why *w* thou not with thy friend ... 2Sa 16:17 1980
Wherefore *w* not thou with me, ... 2Sa 19:25 1980
when thou *w* forth before thy ... Ps 68:7 3318
even thither *w* thou up to offer ... Is 57:7 5927
thou *w* to the king with ointment, ... Is 57:9 7788
when thou *w* after me in the ... Jer 2:2 3212
even the way which thou *w* ... Jer 31:21 1980
Thou *w* forth for the salvation of ... Hab 3:13 3318
Thou *w* in to men uncircumcised, ... Acts 11:3 1525

WEPT

him, and lift up her voice, and *w* ... Gen 21:16 1058
And Esau lifted up his voice, and *w* ... Gen 27:38 1058
and lifted up his voice, and *w* ... Gen 29:11 1058
and they *w* ... Gen 33:4 1058
Thus his father *w* for him ... Gen 37:35 1058
himself about from them, and *w* ... Gen 42:24 1058
into his chamber, and *w* there ... Gen 43:30 1058
And he *w* aloud ... Gen 45:2
his brother Benjamin's neck, and *w* ... Gen 45:14 1058
and Benjamin *w* upon his neck ... Gen 45:14 1058
all his brethren, and *w* upon them ... Gen 45:15 1058
w on his neck a good while ... Gen 46:29 1058
w upon him, and kissed him ... Gen 50:1 1058
Joseph *w* when they spake unto him ... Gen 50:17 1058
and, behold, the babe *w* ... Ex 2:6 1058
children of Israel also *w* again ... Num 11:4 1058
for ye have *w* in the ears of the ... Num 11:18 1058
have *w* before him, saying, Why ... Num 11:20 1058
and the people *w* that night ... Num 14:1 1058
ye returned and *w* before the LORD ... Deut 1:45 1058
the children of Israel *w* for ... Deut 34:8 1058
lifted up their voice, and *w* ... Judg 2:4 1058
And Samson's wife *w* before him ... Judg 14:16 1058
she *w* before him the seven days, ... Judg 14:17 1058
w before the LORD until even, and ... Judg 20:23 1058
came unto the house of God, and *w* ... Judg 20:26 1058
lifted up their voices, and *w* sore ... Judg 21:2 1058
they lifted up their voice, and *w* ... Ruth 1:9 1058
lifted up their voice, and *w* again ... Ruth 1:14 1058
therefore she *w*, and did not eat ... 1Sa 1:7 1058
prayed unto the LORD, and *w* sore ... 1Sa 1:10 1058
lifted up their voices, and *w* ... 1Sa 11:4 1058
w one with another, until David ... 1Sa 20:41 1058
And Saul lifted up his voice, and *w* ... 1Sa 24:16 1058
him lifted up their voice and *w* ... 1Sa 30:4 1058
And they mourned, and *w*, and fasted ... 2Sa 1:12 1058
voice, and *w* at the grave of Abner ... 2Sa 3:32 1058
and all the people *w* ... 2Sa 3:32 1058
all the people *w* again over him ... 2Sa 3:34 1058
was yet alive, I fasted and *w* ... 2Sa 12:22 1058
and lifted up their voice and *w* ... 2Sa 13:36 1058
and all his servants *w* very sore ... 2Sa 13:36 1058
all the country *w* with a loud ... 2Sa 15:23 1058
w as he went up, and had his head ... 2Sa 15:30 1058
the chamber over the gate, and *w* ... 2Sa 18:33 1058
and the man of God *w* ... 2Kin 8:11 1058
w over his face, and said, O my ... 2Kin 13:14 1058
And Hezekiah *w* sore ... 2Kin 20:3 1058
rent thy clothes, and *w* before me ... 2Kin 22:19 1058
their eyes, *w* with a loud voice ... Ezr 3:12 1058
for the people *w* very sore ... Ezr 10:1 1058
these words, that I sat down and *w* ... Neh 1:4 1058
For all the people *w*, when they ... Neh 8:9 1058
they lifted up their voice, and *w* ... Job 2:12 1058
When I *w*, and chastened my soul ... Ps 69:10 1058
there we sat down, yea, we *w* ... Ps 137:1 1058
And Hezekiah *w* sore ... Is 38:3 1058
he *w*, and made supplication unto ... Hos 12:4 1058
And he went out, and *w* bitterly ... Mt 26:75 2799
seeth the tumult, and them that *w* ... Mk 5:38 2799
And when he thought thereon, he *w* ... Mk 14:72 2799
with him, as they mourned and *w* ... Mk 16:10 2799
mourned to you, and ye have not *w* ... Lk 7:32 2799
And all *w*, and bewailed her ... Lk 8:52 2799
he beheld the city, and *w* over it, ... Lk 19:41 2799
And Peter went out, and *w* bitterly ... Lk 22:62 2799
Jesus *w* ... Jn 11:35 1145
and as she *w*, she stooped down, and ... Jn 20:11 2799
And they all *w* sore, and fell on ... Acts 20:37
that weep, as though they *w* not ... 1Cor 7:30 2799
I *w* much, because no man was ... Rev 5:4 2799

WERE See PREFACE.

WERT

If thou *w* pure and upright ... Job 8:6
O that thou *w* as my brother, that ... Song 8:1
w graffed in among them, and with ... Rom 11:17
For if thou *w* cut out of the ... Rom 11:24
w graffed contrary to nature into ... Rom 11:24
I would thou *w* cold or hot ... Rev 3:15 1498

WEST

his tent, having Beth-el on the *w* ... Gen 12:8 3220
thou shalt spread abroad to the *w* ... Gen 28:14 3220
turned a mighty strong *w* wind ... Ex 10:19 3220
w side shall be hangings of fifty ... Ex 27:12 3220
for the *w* side were hangings of ... Ex 38:12 3220
On the *w* side shall be the ... Num 2:18 3220
this shall be your *w* border ... Num 34:6 3220
on the *w* side two thousand cubits ... Num 35:5 3220
of the LORD, possess thou the *w* ... Deut 33:23 3220
and Ai, on the *w* side of Ai ... Josh 8:9 3220
on the *w* side of the city ... Josh 8:12 3220
in wait on the *w* of the city ... Josh 8:13 3220
and in the borders of Dor on the *w* ... Josh 11:2 3220
Canaanite on the east and on the *w* ... Josh 11:3 3220
on this side Jordan on the *w* ... Josh 12:7 3220
the *w* border was to the great sea ... Josh 15:12 3220

this was the *w* quarter Josh 18:14 3220
and the border went out on the *w* Josh 18:15 3220
reacheth to Asher on the *w* side Josh 19:34 3220
and three looking toward the *w* 1Kin 7:25 3220
the porters, toward the east, *w* 1Chr 9:24 3220
toward the east, and toward the *w* 1Chr 12:15 4628
and three looking toward the *w* 2Chr 4:4 3220
the *w* side of the city of David 2Chr 32:30 4628
on the *w* side of Gihon, in the 2Chr 33:14 4628
from the east, nor from the *w* Ps 75:6 4628
As far as the east is from the *w* Ps 103:12 4628
from the east, and from the *w* Ps 107:3 4628
of the Philistines toward the *w* Is 11:14 3220
east, and gather thee from the *w* Is 43:5 4628
rising of the sun, and from the *w* Is 45:6 4628
from the north and from the *w* Is 49:12 3220
the name of the LORD from the *w* Is 59:19 4628
the *w* was seventy cubits broad Eze 41:12 3220
He turned about to the *w* side Eze 42:19 3220
from the *w* side westward, and from Eze 45:7 3220
from the *w* border unto the east Eze 45:7 3220
The *w* side also shall be the Eze 47:20 3220
This is the *w* side Eze 47:20 3220
for these are his sides east and *w* Eze 48:1 3220
the east side unto the *w* side Eze 48:2 3220
east side even unto the *w* side Eze 48:3 3220
the east side unto the *w* side Eze 48:4 3220
the east side unto the *w* side Eze 48:5 3220
east side even unto the *w* side Eze 48:6 3220
the east side unto the *w* side Eze 48:7 3220
the east side unto the *w* side Eze 48:8 3220
the east side unto the *w* side Eze 48:8 3220
toward the *w* ten thousand in Eze 48:10 3220
the *w* side four thousand and five Eze 48:16 3220
toward the *w* two hundred and fifty Eze 48:17 3220
thousand toward the *w* border Eze 48:21 3220
the east side unto the *w* side Eze 48:23 3220
the east side unto the *w* side Eze 48:24 3220
the east side unto the *w* side Eze 48:25 3220
the east side unto the *w* side Eze 48:26 3220
the east side unto the *w* side Eze 48:27 3220
At the *w* side four thousand and Eze 48:34 3220
an he goat came from the *w* on the Dan 8:5 4628
children shall tremble from the *w* Hos 11:10 3220
country, and from the *w* country Zec 8:7
toward the east and toward the *w* Zec 14:4 3220
shall come from the east and *w* Mt 8:11 *1424*
east, and shineth even unto the *w* Mt 24:27 *1424*
ye see a cloud rise out of the *w* Lk 12:54 *1424*
come from the east, and from the *w* Lk 13:29 *1424*
and lieth toward the south *w* Acts 27:12 *3047*
and north *w* Acts 27:12 *5566*
and on the *w* three gates Rev 21:13 *1424*

WESTERN

And as for the *w* border, ye shall Num 34:6 3220

WESTWARD

and southward, and eastward, and *w* Gen 13:14 3220
w thou shalt make six boards Ex 26:22 3220
tabernacle, for the two sides *w* Ex 26:27 3220
tabernacle *w* he made six boards Ex 36:27 3220
of the tabernacle for the sides *w* Ex 36:32 3220
pitch behind the tabernacle *w* Num 3:23 3220
Pisgah, and lift up thine eyes *w* Deut 3:27 3220
were on the side of Jordan *w* Josh 5:1 3220
before the valley of Hinnom *w* Josh 15:8 3220
from Baalah *w* unto mount Seir Josh 15:10 3220
goeth down *w* to the coast of Josh 16:3 3220
Tappuah *w* unto the river Kanah Josh 16:8 3220
went up through the mountains *w* Josh 18:12 3220
and reacheth to Carmel *w*, and to Josh 19:26 3220
coast turneth *w* to Aznoth-tabor Josh 19:34 3220
brethren on this side Jordan *w* Josh 22:7 3220
off, even unto the great sea *w* Josh 23:4
w Gezer, with the towns thereof 1Chr 7:28 4628
and Hosah the lot came forth *w* 1Chr 26:16 4628
At Parbar *w*, four at the causeway 1Chr 26:18 4628
of Israel on this side Jordan *w* 1Chr 26:30 4628
of the city, from the west side *w* Eze 45:7 3220
was a place on the two sides *w* Eze 46:19 3220
eastward, and ten thousand *w* Eze 48:18 3220
w over against the five and twenty Eze 48:21 3220
I saw the ram pushing *w*, and Dan 8:4 3220

WET

They are *w* with the showers of Job 24:8 7372
let it be *w* with the dew of Dan 4:15 6647
let it be *w* with the dew of Dan 4:23 6647
they shall *w* thee with the dew of Dan 4:25 6647
his body was *w* with the dew of Dan 4:33 6647
his body was *w* with the dew of Dan 5:21 6647

WHALE

Am I a sea, or a *w*, that thou Job 7:12 8577
and thou art as a *w* in the seas Eze 32:2 8565

WHALE'S

and three nights in the *w* belly Mt 12:40 *2785*

WHALES

And God created great *w*, and every Gen 1:21 8577

WHAT

Adam to see *w* he would call them Gen 2:19 4100
W is this that thou hast done Gen 3:13 4100
And he said, *W* hast thou done Gen 4:10 4100
knew *w* his younger son had done Gen 9:24
W is this that thou hast done Gen 12:18 4100
w wilt thou give me, seeing I go Gen 15:2 4100
him, *W* hast thou done unto us Gen 20:9 4100
w have I offended thee, that thou Gen 20:9 4100
W sawest thou, that thou hast Gen 20:10 4100
unto her, *W* aileth thee, Hagar Gen 21:17 4100
W mean these seven ewe lambs Gen 21:29 4100
w is that betwixt me and thee Gen 23:15 4100
W man is this that walketh in the Gen 24:65 4310
w profit shall this birthright do Gen 25:32 4100
W is this thou hast done unto us Gen 26:10 4100
w shall I do now unto thee, my Gen 27:37 4100
w good shall my life do me Gen 27:46 4100
tell me, *w* shall thy wages be Gen 29:15 4100
W is this thou hast done unto me Gen 29:25 4100
And he said, *W* shall I give thee Gen 30:31 4100
W hast thou done, that thou hast Gen 31:26 4100
discern thou *w* is thine with me Gen 31:32 4100
said to Laban, *W* is my trespass Gen 31:36 4100
w is my sin, that thou hast so Gen 31:36 4100
w hast thou found of all thy Gen 31:37 4100
w can I do this day unto these my Gen 31:43 4100
he said unto him, *W* is thy name Gen 32:27 4100
W meanest thou by all this drove Gen 33:8 4310
And he said, *W* needeth it Gen 33:15 4100
w ye shall say unto me I will Gen 34:11 834
W is this dream that thou hast Gen 37:10 4100
asked him, saying, *W* seekest thou Gen 37:15 4100
we shall see *w* will become of his Gen 37:20 4100
W profit is it if we slay our Gen 37:26 4100
W wilt thou give me, that thou Gen 38:16 4100
W pledge shall I give thee Gen 38:18 834
my master wotteth not *w* is with Gen 39:8 4100
Pharaoh *w* he is about to do Gen 41:25
W God is about to do he sheweth Gen 41:28 834
w he saith to you, do Gen 41:55 834
W is this that God hath done unto Gen 42:28 4100
W deed is this that ye have done Gen 44:15 4100
W shall we say unto my lord Gen 44:16 4100
w shall we speak Gen 44:16 4100
shall say, *W* is your occupation Gen 46:33 4100
brethren, *W* is your occupation Gen 47:3 4100
to wit *w* would be done to him Ex 2:4 4100
shall say to me, *W* is his name Ex 3:13 4100
w shall I say unto them Ex 3:13 4100
unto him, *W* is that in thine hand Ex 4:2 4100
teach thee *w* thou shalt say Ex 4:12 834
and will teach you *w* ye shall do Ex 4:15
Now shalt thou see *w* I will do to Ex 6:1
w things I have wrought in Egypt, Ex 10:2
we know not with *w* we must serve Ex 10:26 4100
W mean ye by this service Ex 12:26 4100
time to come, saying, *W* is this Ex 13:14 4100
Moses, saying, *W* shall we drink Ex 15:24 4100
w are we, that ye murmur against Ex 16:7 4100
and *w* are we Ex 16:8 4100
for they wist not *w* it was Ex 16:15 4100
W shall I do unto this people Ex 17:4 4100
W is this thing that thou doest Ex 18:14 4100
Ye have seen *w* I did unto the Ex 19:4 834
w they leave the beasts of the Ex 23:11
we wot not *w* is become of him Ex 32:1 4100
W did this people unto thee, that Ex 32:21 4100
we wot not *w* is become of him Ex 32:23 4100
that I may know *w* to do unto thee Ex 33:5 4100
w saddle soever he rideth upon Lev 15:9 834
W man soever there be of the Lev 17:3 376
W man soever of the seed of Aaron Lev 22:4 376
W shall we eat the seventh year Lev 25:20 4100
I will hear *w* the LORD will Num 9:8 4100
that *w* goodness the LORD shall do Num 10:32 834
And see the land, *w* it is Num 13:18 4100
w the land is that they dwell in, Num 13:19 4100
w cities they be that they dwell Num 13:19 4100
w the land is, whether it be fat Num 13:20 4100
declared *w* should be done to him Num 15:34 4100
w is Aaron, that ye murmur Num 16:11 4100
W he did in the Red sea, and in Num 21:14 853
W men are these with thee Num 22:9 4310
that I may know *w* the LORD will Num 22:19 4100
W have I done unto thee, that Num 22:28 4100
Balaam, *W* hast thou done unto me Num 23:11 4100
unto him, *W* hath the LORD spoken Num 23:17 4100
and of Israel, *W* hath God wrought Num 23:23 4100
but *w* the LORD saith, that will I Num 24:13 834
I will advertise thee *w* this Num 24:14 834
w time the fire devoured two Num 26:10
w every man hath gotten, of Num 31:50 834
word again by *w* way we must go up Deut 1:22 834
into *w* cities we shall come Deut 1:22 853
to shew you by *w* way ye should go Deut 1:33 834
for *w* God is there in heaven or Deut 3:24 4310
Your eyes have seen *w* the LORD Deut 4:3
For *w* nation is there so great, Deut 4:7 4310
w nation is there so great, that Deut 4:8 4310
W mean the testimonies, and the Deut 6:20 4100
but shalt well remember *w* the Deut 7:18
to know *w* was in thine heart, Deut 8:2
w doth the LORD thy God require Deut 10:12 4100
w he did unto the army of Egypt, Deut 11:4 834
And *w* he did unto you in the Deut 11:5 834
w he did unto Dathan and Abiram, Deut 11:6 834
W thing soever I command you, Deut 12:32 853
W man is there that hath built a Deut 20:5 4310
w man is he that hath planted a Deut 20:6 4310
And *w* man is there that hath Deut 20:7 4310
W man is there that is fearful and Deut 20:8 4310
Remember *w* the LORD thy God did Deut 24:9
Remember *w* Amalek did unto thee Deut 25:17
w meaneth the heat of this great Deut 29:24 4100
I will see *w* their end shall be Deut 32:20 4100
w ye did unto the two kings of Josh 2:10 834
W mean ye by these stones Josh 4:6 4100
come, saying, *W* mean these stones Josh 4:21 4100
W saith my lord unto his servant Josh 5:14 4100
w shall I say, when Israel Josh 7:8 4100
w wilt thou do unto thy great Josh 7:9 4100
tell me now *w* thou hast done Josh 7:19 4100
w Joshua had done unto Jericho Josh 9:3
said unto her, *W* wouldest thou Josh 15:18 4100
W trespass is this that ye have Josh 22:16 4100
W have ye to do with the LORD God Josh 22:24 4100
your eyes have seen *w* I have done Josh 24:7
Caleb said unto her, *W* wilt thou Judg 1:14 4100
And thou shalt hear *w* they say Judg 7:11 4100
W have I done now in comparison Judg 8:2 4100
w was I able to do in comparison Judg 8:3 4100
W manner of men were they Judg 8:18 375
W ye have seen me do, make haste, Judg 9:48 4100
W man is he that will begin to Judg 10:18 4310
W hast thou to do with me, that Judg 11:12 4100
teach us *w* we shall do unto the Judg 13:8 4100
W is thy name, that when thy Judg 13:17 4310
or his mother *w* he had done Judg 14:6
down, *W* is sweeter than honey Judg 14:18 4100
w is stronger than a lion Judg 14:18 4100
w is this that thou hast done Judg 15:11 4100
by *w* means we may prevail against Judg 16:5 4100
w makest thou in this place Judg 18:3 4100
and *w* hast thou here Judg 18:3 4100
brethren said unto them, *W* say ye Judg 18:8 4100
consider *w* ye have to do Judg 18:14 4100
the priest unto them, *W* do ye Judg 18:18 4100
W aileth thee, that thou comest Judg 18:23 4100
and *w* have I more Judg 18:24 4100
w is this that ye say Judg 18:24 4100
W aileth thee Judg 18:24 4100
do with them *w* seemeth good unto Judg 19:24
W wickedness is this that is done Judg 20:12 4100
W one is there of the tribes of Judg 21:8 4310
in law saw *w* she had gleaned Ruth 2:18
he will tell thee *w* thou shalt do Ruth 3:4
W day thou buyest the field of Ruth 4:5
unto her, Do *w* seemeth thee good 1Sa 1:23
W is the thing that the LORD hath 1Sa 3:17 4100
let him do *w* seemeth him good 1Sa 3:18
W meaneth the noise of this great 1Sa 4:6 4100
W meaneth the noise of this 1Sa 4:14 4100
he said, *W* is there done, my son 1Sa 4:16 4100
W shall we do with the ark of the 1Sa 5:8 4100
W shall we do to the ark of the 1Sa 6:2 4100
W shall be the trespass offering 1Sa 6:4 4100
we go, *w* shall we bring the man 1Sa 9:7 4100
w have we 1Sa 9:7 4100
saying, *W* shall I do for my son 1Sa 10:2 4100
shew thee *w* thou shalt do 1Sa 10:8
W is this that is come unto the 1Sa 10:11 4100
pray thee, *w* Samuel said unto you 1Sa 10:15 4100
W aileth the people that they 1Sa 11:5 4100
And Samuel said, *W* hast thou done 1Sa 13:11 4100
Do *w* seemeth good unto thee 1Sa 14:40
Tell me *w* thou hast done 1Sa 14:43 4100
W meaneth then this bleating of 1Sa 15:14 4100
I will tell thee *w* the LORD hath 1Sa 15:16
I will shew thee *w* thou shalt do 1Sa 16:3
W shall be done to the man that 1Sa 17:26 4100
And David said, *W* have I now done 1Sa 17:29 4100
w can he have more but the 1Sa 18:8
w is my life, or my father's 1Sa 18:18 4310
w I see, that I will tell thee 1Sa 19:3 4100
before Jonathan, *W* have I done 1Sa 20:1 4100
w is mine iniquity 1Sa 20:1 4100
w is my sin before thy father, 1Sa 20:1 4100
or *w* if thy father answer thee 1Sa 20:10 4100
w hath he done 1Sa 20:32 4100
thee, and *w* I have commanded thee 1Sa 21:2 834
Now therefore *w* is under thine 1Sa 21:3 4100
mine hand, or *w* there is present 1Sa 21:3
till I know *w* God will do for me 1Sa 22:3 4100
know and consider *w* thou wilt do 1Sa 25:17 4100
for *w* have I done 1Sa 26:18 4100
or *w* evil is in mine hand 1Sa 26:18 4100
shalt know *w* thy servant can do 1Sa 28:2
thou knowest *w* Saul hath done, 1Sa 28:9
for *w* sawest thou 1Sa 28:13 4100
he said unto her, *W* form is he of 1Sa 28:14 4100
make known unto me *w* I shall do 1Sa 28:15 4100
W do these Hebrews here 1Sa 29:3 4100
unto Achish, But *w* have I done 1Sa 29:8 4100
w hast thou found in thy servant 1Sa 29:8 4100
king, and said, *W* hast thou done 2Sa 3:24 4100
w is my house, that thou hast 2Sa 7:18 4310
w can David say more unto thee 2Sa 7:20 4100
w one nation in the earth is like 2Sa 7:23 4310
W is thy servant, that thou 2Sa 9:8 4100
W thing is this that thou hast 2Sa 12:21 4100
king said unto her, *W* aileth thee 2Sa 14:5 4100
him, and said, Of *w* city art thou 2Sa 15:2 4310
surely in *w* place my lord the 2Sa 15:21 834
that *w* thing soever thou shalt 2Sa 15:35 3605
Ziba, *W* meanest thou by these 2Sa 16:2 4100
W have I to do with you, ye sons 2Sa 16:10 4100
counsel among you *w* we shall do 2Sa 16:20 4100
let us hear likewise *w* he saith 2Sa 17:5 4100
W seemeth you best I will do 2Sa 18:4 834
Go tell the king *w* thou hast seen 2Sa 18:21 834
tumult, but I knew not *w* it was 2Sa 18:29 4100
and to do *w* he thought good 2Sa 19:18
W have I to do with you, ye sons 2Sa 19:22 4100
do therefore *w* is good in thine 2Sa 19:27
W right therefore have I yet to 2Sa 19:28 4100
taste *w* I eat or *w* I drink 2Sa 19:35
do to him *w* shall seem good unto 2Sa 19:37
Gibeonites, *W* shall I do for you 2Sa 21:3 4100
W ye shall say, that will I do 2Sa 21:4 4100
it was told David *w* Rizpah the 2Sa 21:11
see *w* answer I shall return to 2Sa 24:13 4100
but these sheep, *w* have they done 2Sa 24:17 4100
offer up *w* seemeth good unto him 2Sa 24:22
And the king said, *W* wouldest thou 1Kin 1:16 4100
Moreover thou knowest also *w* Joab 1Kin 2:5
w he did to the two captains of 1Kin 2:5 834
knowest *w* thou oughtest to do 1Kin 2:9
God said, Ask *w* I shall give thee 1Kin 3:5 4100
W prayer and supplication soever 1Kin 8:38 3605
W cities are these which thou 1Kin 9:13 4100
But *w* hast thou lacked with me, 1Kin 11:22 4100

W counsel give ye that we may 1Kin 12:9 4100
W portion have we in David 1Kin 12:16 4100
said unto them, *W* way went he 1Kin 13:12
For his sons had seen *w* way the 1Kin 13:12 834
he shall tell thee *w* shall become 1Kin 14:3 4100
but *w*? even now. 1Kin 14:14 4100
w he did, and his might, are they 1Kin 16:5 834
W have I to do with thee, O thou 1Kin 17:18 4100
W have I sinned, that thou 1Kin 18:9 4100
Was it not told my lord *w* I did 1Kin 18:13
W doest thou here, Elijah 1Kin 19:9 4100
W doest thou here, Elijah 1Kin 19:13 4100
for *w* have I done to thee 1Kin 19:20 4100
and mark, and see *w* thou doest 1Kin 20:22
w the LORD saith unto me, that 1Kin 22:14
W manner of man was he which came 2Kin 1:7 4100
Ask *w* I shall do for thee, before 2Kin 2:9 4100
Israel, *W* have I to do with thee 2Kin 3:13 4100
unto her, *W* shall I do for thee 2Kin 4:2 4100
tell me, *w* hast thou in the house 2Kin 4:2 4100
w is to be done for thee 2Kin 4:13 4100
W then is to be done for her 2Kin 4:14 4100
And his servitor said, *W*, should I 2Kin 4:43 4100
king said unto her, *W* aileth thee 2Kin 6:28 4100
w should I wait for the LORD any 2Kin 6:33 4100
I will now shew you *w* the Syrians 2Kin 7:12
And Hazael said, But *w*, is thy 2Kin 8:13 4100
to him, *W* said Elisha to thee 2Kin 8:14 4100
W hast thou to do with peace 2Kin 9:18 4100
W hast thou to do with peace 2Kin 9:19 4100
W peace, so long as the whoredoms 2Kin 9:22 4100
W confidence is this wherein thou 2Kin 18:19 4100
thou hast heard *w* the kings of 2Kin 19:11
W shall be the sign that the LORD 2Kin 20:8 4100
said unto him, *W* said these men 2Kin 20:14 4100
W have they seen in thine house 2Kin 20:15 4100
when thou heardest *w* I spake 2Kin 22:19 834
W title is that that I see 2Kin 23:17 4100
to know *w* Israel ought to do 1Chr 12:32 4100
w is mine house, that thou hast 1Chr 17:16 4310
W can David speak more to thee 1Chr 17:18 4100
w one nation in the earth is like 1Chr 17:21 4310
Now therefore advise thyself *w* 1Chr 21:12 4100
for these sheep, *w* have they done 1Chr 21:17 4100
w is my people, that we should be 1Chr 29:14 4310
unto him, Ask *w* I shall give thee 2Chr 1:7 4100
Then *w* prayer or *w* 2Chr 6:29 834
W counsel give ye me to return 2Chr 10:6 349
W advice give ye that we may 2Chr 10:9 4100
W portion have we in David 2Chr 10:16 4100
even *w* my God saith, that will I 2Chr 18:13
to the judges, Take heed *w* ye do 2Chr 19:6 4100
w cause soever shall come to you 2Chr 19:10 3602
neither know we *w* to do 2Chr 20:12 4100
that at *w* time the chest was 2Chr 24:11
But *w* shall we do for the hundred 2Chr 25:9 4100
Know ye not *w* I and my fathers 2Chr 32:13 4100
W have I to do with thee, thou 2Chr 35:21 4100
W are the names of the men that Ezr 5:4 4479
Moreover I make a decree *w* ye Ezr 6:8
I told them *w* they should say Ezr 8:17 1697
w shall we say after this Ezr 9:10 4100
For *w* dost thou make request Neh 2:4 4100
neither told I any man *w* my God Neh 2:12 4100
not whither I went, or *w* I did Neh 2:16 4100
W is this thing that ye do Neh 2:19 4100
and said, *W* do these feeble Jews Neh 4:2 4100
In *w* place therefore ye hear the Neh 4:20 834
W evil thing is this that ye do, Neh 13:17 4100
W shall we do unto the queen Est 1:15 4100
w she had done, and *w* was Est 2:1
did, and *w* should become of her Est 2:11 4100
she required nothing but *w* Hegai Est 2:15
to Mordecai, to know *w* it was Est 4:5 4100
W wilt thou, queen Esther Est 5:3 4100
and *w* is thy request Est 5:3 4100
of wine, *W* is thy petition Est 5:6 4100
and *w* is thy request Est 5:6 4100
W honour and dignity hath been Est 6:3 4100
W shall be done unto the man whom Est 6:6 4100
W is thy petition, queen Esther Est 7:2 4100
and *w* is thy request Est 7:2 4100
Esther had told *w* he was unto her Est 8:1 4100
did *w* they would unto those that Est 9:5 4100
w have they done in the rest of Est 9:12 4100
now *w* is thy petition Est 9:12 4100
or *w* is thy request further Est 9:12 4100
W? shall we receive good Job 2:10 1571
W is my strength, that I should Job 6:11 4100
w is mine end, that I should Job 6:11 4100
W time they wax warm, they vanish Job 6:17
but *w* doth your arguing reprove Job 6:25 4100
W is man, that thou shouldest Job 7:17 4100
w shall I do unto thee, O thou Job 7:20 4100
will say unto him, *W* doest thou Job 9:12 4100
w canst thou do Job 11:8 4100
w canst thou know Job 11:8 4100
W ye know, the same do I know Job 13:2
speak, and let come on me *w* will Job 13:13 4100
W knowest thou, that we know not Job 15:9 4100
w understandest thou, which is Job 15:9
and *w* do thy eyes wink at, Job 15:12 4100
W is man, that he should be clean Job 15:14 4100
or *w* emboldeneth thee that thou Job 16:3 4100
and though I forbear, *w* am I eased Job 16:6 4100
W is the Almighty, that we should Job 21:15 4100
w profit should we have, if we Job 21:15 4100
For *w* pleasure hath he in his Job 21:21 4100
shall repay him *w* he hath done Job 21:31
w can the Almighty do for them Job 22:17 4100
understand *w* he would say unto me Job 23:5 4100
w his soul desireth, even that he Job 23:13
For *w* is the hope of the Job 27:8 4100
For *w* portion of God is there Job 31:2 4100

w inheritance of the Almighty Job 31:2
W then shall I do when God riseth Job 31:14 4100
he visiteth, *w* shall I answer him Job 31:14 4100
whilst ye searched out *w* to say Job 32:11
us know among ourselves *w* is good Job 34:4 4100
W man is like Job, who drinketh Job 34:7 4310
therefore speak *w* thou knowest Job 34:33 4100
W advantage will it be unto thee Job 35:3 4100
W profit shall I have, if I be Job 35:3 4100
sinnest, *w* doest thou against him Job 35:6 4100
multiplied, *w* doest thou unto him Job 35:6 4100
be righteous, *w* givest thou him Job 35:7 4100
or *w* receiveth he of thine hand Job 35:7 4100
Teach us *w* we shall say unto him Job 37:19 4100
By *w* way is the light parted, Job 38:24
W time she lifteth up herself on Job 39:18
w shall I answer thee Job 40:4 4100
W is man, that thou art mindful Ps 8:4 4100
destroyed, *w* can the righteous do Ps 11:3 4100
W man is he that feareth the LORD Ps 25:12 4310
W profit is there in my blood, Ps 30:9 4100
W man is he that desireth life, Ps 34:12 4310
the measure of my days, *w* it is Ps 39:4 4310
And now, Lord, *w* wait I for Ps 39:7 4100
w work thou didst in their days, Ps 44:1
w desolations he hath made in the Ps 46:8 834
W hast thou to do to declare my Ps 50:16 4100
W time I am afraid, I will trust Ps 56:3
I will not fear *w* flesh can do Ps 56:4 4100
be afraid *w* man can do unto me Ps 56:11 4100
I will declare *w* he hath done for Ps 66:16 834
I will hear *w* God the LORD will Ps 85:8 4100
W man is he that liveth, and shall Ps 89:48 4310
W ailed thee, O thou sea, that Ps 114:5 4100
W shall I render unto the LORD Ps 116:12 4100
w can man do unto me Ps 118:6 4100
W shall be given unto thee Ps 120:3 4100
or *w* shall be done unto thee, Ps 120:3 4100
w is man, that thou takest Ps 144:3 4100
they know not at *w* they stumble Prov 4:19 4100
righteous know *w* is acceptable Prov 10:32
diligently *w* is before thee Prov 23:1
lest thou know not *w* to do in the Prov 25:8 4100
for thou knowest not *w* a day may Prov 27:1 4100
w is his name, and *w* is his Prov 30:4 4100
W, my son Prov 31:2 4100
and *w*, the son of my womb Prov 31:2 4100
and *w*, the son of my vows Prov 31:2 4100
W profit hath a man of all his Eccl 1:3 4100
and of mirth, *W* doeth it Eccl 2:2 4100
till I might see *w* was that good Eccl 2:3 335
for *w* can the man do that cometh Eccl 2:12 4100
For *w* hath man of all his labour, Eccl 2:22 4100
W profit hath he that worketh in Eccl 3:9 4100
him to see *w* shall be after him Eccl 3:22 4100
w good is there to the owners Eccl 5:11 4100
w profit hath he that hath Eccl 5:16 4100
For *w* hath the wise more than the Eccl 6:8 4100
w hath the poor, that knoweth to Eccl 6:8 4100
vanity, *w* is man the better Eccl 6:11 4100
For who knoweth *w* is good for man Eccl 6:12 4100
for who can tell a man *w* shall be Eccl 6:12 4100
W is the cause that the former Eccl 7:10 4100
may say unto him, *W* doest thou Eccl 8:4 4100
a man cannot tell *w* shall be Eccl 10:14 4100
w shall be after him, who can Eccl 10:14 4100
for thou knowest not *w* evil shall Eccl 11:2 4100
As thou knowest not *w* is the way Eccl 11:5 4100
W is thy beloved more than Song 5:9 4100
w is thy beloved more than Song 5:9 4100
W will ye see in the Shulamite Song 6:13 4100
w shall we do for our sister in Song 8:8 4100
To *w* purpose is the multitude of Is 1:11 4100
W mean ye that ye beat my people Is 3:15 4100
W could have been done more to my Is 5:4 4100
I will tell you *w* I will do to my Is 5:5
w will ye do in the day of Is 10:3 4100
W shall one then answer the Is 14:32 4100
let them know *w* the LORD of hosts Is 19:12 4100
let him declare *w* he seeth Is 21:6 834
of Seir, Watchman, *w* of the night Is 21:11 4100
Watchman, *w* of the night Is 21:11 4100
W aileth thee now, that thou art Is 22:1 4100
W hast thou here Is 22:16 4100
that are far off, *w* I have done Is 33:13 834
W confidence is this wherein thou Is 36:4
thou hast heard *w* the kings of Is 37:11 834
W shall I say Is 38:15 4100
W is the sign that I shall go up Is 38:22 4100
said unto him, *W* said these men Is 39:3 4100
W have they seen in thine house Is 39:4 4100
And he said, *W* shall I cry Is 40:6 4100
or *w* likeness will ye compare Is 40:18 4100
forth, and shew us *w* shall happen Is 41:22
w they be, that we may consider Is 41:22 4100
that fashioneth it, *W* makest thou Is 45:9 4100
unto his father, *W* begettest thou Is 45:10 4100
W hast thou brought forth Is 45:10 4100
w have I here, saith the LORD, Is 52:5 4100
w he hath prepared for him that Is 64:4
saying, Jeremiah, *w* seest thou Jer 1:11 4100
second time, saying, *W* seest thou Jer 1:13 4100
W iniquity have your fathers Jer 2:5 4100
now *w* hast thou to do in the way Jer 2:18 4100
or *w* hast thou to do in the way Jer 2:18 4100
the valley, know *w* thou hast done Jer 2:23 4100
thou art spoiled, *w* wilt thou do Jer 4:30 4100
neither understandest *w* they say Jer 5:15 4100
w will ye do in the end thereof Jer 5:31 4100
O congregation, *w* is among them Jer 6:18
To *w* purpose cometh there to me Jer 6:20 4100
see *w* I did to it for the Jer 7:12
Seest thou not *w* they do in the Jer 7:17 4100
wickedness, saying, *W* have I done Jer 8:6 4100

and *w* wisdom is in them Jer 8:9 4100
for *w* the land perisheth and is Jer 9:12 4100
W hath my beloved to do in mine Jer 11:15 4100
W wilt thou say when he shall Jer 13:21 4100
or *w* is our iniquity Jer 16:10 4100
or *w* is our sin that we have Jer 16:10 4100
At *w* instant I shall speak Jer 18:7
at *w* instant I shall speak Jer 18:9
I have heard *w* the prophets said, Jer 23:25
W is the chaff to the wheat Jer 23:28 4100
W is the burden of the LORD Jer 23:33 4100
then say unto them, *W* burden Jer 23:33 4100
brother, *W* hath the LORD answered Jer 23:35 4100
and, *W* hath the LORD spoken Jer 23:35 4100
W hath the LORD answered thee Jer 23:37 4100
and, *W* hath the LORD spoken Jer 23:37 4100
unto me, *W* seest thou, Jeremiah Jer 24:3 4100
w thou hast spoken is come to Jer 32:24 834
Considerest thou not *w* this Jer 33:24 4100
W have I offended against thee, Jer 37:18 4100
Declare unto us now *w* thou hast Jer 38:25 4100
also *w* the king said unto thee Jer 38:25 4100
that escapeth, and say, *W* is done Jer 48:19 4100
W thing shall I take to witness Lam 2:13 4100
w thing shall I liken to thee, O Lam 2:13 4100
w shall I equal to thee, that I Lam 2:13 4100
O LORD, *w* is come upon us Lam 5:1 4100
of man, hear *w* I say unto thee Eze 2:8
Son of man, seest thou *w* they do Eze 8:6 4100
hast thou seen *w* the ancients of Eze 8:12 834
said unto thee, *W* doest thou Eze 12:9 4100
w is that proverb that ye have in Eze 12:22 4100
W is the vine tree more than any Eze 15:2 4100
Know ye not *w* these things mean Eze 17:12 4100
W mean ye, that ye use this Eze 18:2 4100
And say, *W* is thy mother Eze 19:2 4100
W is the high place whereunto ye Eze 20:29 4100
w if the sword contemn even the Eze 21:13 4100
Wilt thou not tell us *w* these Eze 24:19 4100
W city is like Tyrus, like the Eze 27:32 4100
hear *w* is the word that cometh Eze 33:30 4100
shew us *w* thou meanest by these Eze 37:18 4100
that in *w* tribe the stranger Eze 47:23 834
he knoweth *w* is in the darkness, Dan 2:22 4101
unto me now *w* we desired of thee Dan 2:23 1768
to the king Nebuchadnezzar *w* Dan 2:28 4101
w should come to pass hereafter Dan 2:29 4101
to thee *w* shall come to pass Dan 2:29 4101
w shall come to pass hereafter Dan 2:45 4101
That at *w* time ye hear the sound Dan 3:5 1768
Now if ye be ready that at *w* time Dan 3:15 1768
or say unto him, *W* doest thou Dan 4:35 4101
I will make thee know *w* shall be Dan 8:19
w shall befall thy people in the Dan 10:14
w shall be the end of these Dan 12:8 4100
O Ephraim, *w* shall I do unto thee Hos 6:4 4100
O Judah, *w* shall I do unto thee Hos 6:4 4100
W will ye do in the solemn day, Hos 9:5 4100
w wilt thou give Hos 9:14 4100
w then should a king do to us Hos 10:3 4100
W have I to do any more with Hos 14:8 4100
w have ye to do with me, O Tyre, Joel 3:4 4100
unto man *w* is his thought Amos 4:13 4100
to *w* end is it for you Amos 5:18 4100
said unto me, Amos, *w* seest thou Amos 7:8 4100
And he said, Amos, *w* seest thou Amos 8:2 4100
W meanest thou, O sleeper Jonah 1:6 4100
W is thine occupation Jonah 1:8 4100
w is thy country Jonah 1:8 4100
and of *w* people art thou Jonah 1:8
W shall we do unto thee, that the Jonah 1:11 4100
till he might see *w* would become Jonah 4:5 4100
W is the transgression of Jacob Mic 1:5 4310
w are the high places of Judah Mic 1:5 4310
Hear ye now *w* the LORD saith Mic 6:1 834
people, *w* have I done unto thee Mic 6:3 4100
remember now *w* Balak king of Moab Mic 6:5 4100
w Balaam the son of Beor answered Mic 6:5 4100
shewed thee, O man, *w* is good Mic 6:8 4100
w doth the LORD require of thee, Mic 6:8 4100
W do ye imagine against the LORD Nah 1:9 4100
will watch to see *w* he will say Hab 2:1 4100
w I shall answer when I am Hab 2:1 4100
W profiteth the graven image that Hab 2:18 4100
said I, O my lord, *w* are these Zec 1:9 4100
me, I will shew thee *w* these be Zec 1:9 4100
that talked with me, *W* be these Zec 1:19 4100
Then said I, *W* come these to do Zec 1:21 4100
to see *w* is the breadth thereof, Zec 2:2 4100
and *w* is the length thereof Zec 2:2 4100
And said unto me, *W* seest thou Zec 4:2 4100
me, saying, *W* are these, my lord Zec 4:4 4100
me, Knowest thou not *w* these be Zec 4:5 4100
W are these two olive trees upon Zec 4:11 4100
W be these two olive branches Zec 4:12 4100
said, Knowest thou not *w* these be Zec 4:13 4100
And he said unto me, *W* seest thou Zec 5:2 4100
see *w* is this that goeth forth Zec 5:5 4100
And I said, *W* is it Zec 5:6 4100
with me, *W* are these, my lord Zec 6:4 4100
W are these wounds in thine hands Zec 13:6 4100
also, Behold, *w* a weariness is it Mal 1:13
W have we spoken so much against Mal 3:13 4100
w profit is it that we have kept Mal 3:14 4100
w time the star appeared Mt 2:7 *3588*
which love you, *w* reward have ye Mt 5:46 *5101*
only, *w* do ye more than others Mt 5:47 *5101*
hand know *w* thy right hand doeth Mt 6:3 *5101*
knoweth *w* things ye have need of Mt 6:8 *3739*
w ye shall eat, or *w* ye shall Mt 6:25 *5101*
for your body, *w* ye shall put on Mt 6:25 *5101*
thought, saying, *W* shall we eat Mt 6:31 *5101*
or, *W* shall we drink Mt 6:31 *5101*
For with *w* judgment ye judge, ye Mt 7:2 *3739*

with *w* measure ye mete, it shall	Mt 7:2	5101
Or *w* man is there of you, whom if	Mt 7:9	5101
W manner of man is this, that	Mt 8:27	4217
W have we to do with thee, Jesus,	Mt 8:29	5101
w was befallen to the possessed	Mt 8:33	3588
learn *w* that meaneth, I will have	Mt 9:13	5101
thought how or *w* ye shall speak	Mt 10:19	5101
that same hour *w* ye shall speak	Mt 10:19	5101
W I tell you in darkness, that	Mt 10:27	3739
w ye hear in the ear, that preach	Mt 10:27	3739
W went ye out into the wilderness	Mt 11:7	5101
But *w* went ye out for to see	Mt 11:8	5101
But *w* went ye out for to see	Mt 11:9	5101
Have ye not read *w* David did	Mt 12:3	5101
if ye had known *w* this meaneth	Mt 12:7	5101
W man shall there be among you,	Mt 12:11	5101
For *w* is a man profited, if he	Mt 16:26	5101
or *w* shall a man give in exchange	Mt 16:26	5101
saying, *W* thinkest thou, Simon	Mt 17:25	5101
his fellowservants saw *w* was done	Mt 18:31	3588
W therefore God hath joined	Mt 19:6	3739
w good thing shall I do, that I	Mt 19:16	5101
w lack I yet	Mt 19:20	5101
w shall we have therefore	Mt 19:27	5101
me to do *w* I will with mine own	Mt 20:15	3739
And he said unto her, *W* wilt thou	Mt 20:21	5101
and said, Ye know not *w* ye ask	Mt 20:22	5101
W will ye that I shall do unto	Mt 20:32	5101
him, Hearest thou *w* these say	Mt 21:16	5101
By *w* authority doest thou these	Mt 21:23	4169
by *w* authority I do these things	Mt 21:24	4169
Neither tell I you by *w* authority	Mt 21:27	4169
But *w* think ye	Mt 21:28	5101
cometh, *w* will he do unto those	Mt 21:40	5101
us therefore, *W* thinkest thou	Mt 22:17	5101
Saying, *W* think ye of Christ	Mt 22:42	5101
w shall be the sign of thy coming	Mt 24:3	5101
for ye know not *w* hour your Lord	Mt 24:42	4169
of the house had known in *w* watch	Mt 24:43	4169
To *w* purpose is this waste	Mt 26:8	5101
W will ye give me, and I will	Mt 26:15	5101
asleep, and saith unto Peter, *W*	Mt 26:40	3779
w is it which these witness	Mt 26:62	5101
w further need have we of	Mt 26:65	5101
W think ye	Mt 26:66	5101
saying, I know not *w* thou sayest	Mt 26:70	5101
And they said, *W* is that to us	Mt 27:4	5101
W shall I do then with Jesus	Mt 27:22	5101
said, Why, *w* evil hath he done	Mt 27:23	5101
w have we to do with thee, thou	Mk 1:24	5101
saying, *W* thing is this	Mk 1:27	5101
w new doctrine is this	Mk 1:27	5101
Have ye never read *w* David did	Mk 2:25	5101
had heard *w* great things he did	Mk 3:8	3745
unto them, Take heed *w* ye hear	Mk 4:24	3739
with *w* measure ye mete, it shall	Mk 4:24	5101
or with *w* comparison shall we	Mk 4:30	4169
W manner of man is this, that	Mk 4:41	
W have I to do with thee, Jesus,	Mk 5:7	5101
And he asked him, *W* is thy name	Mk 5:9	5101
out to see *w* it was that was done	Mk 5:14	5101
knowing *w* was done in her, came	Mk 5:33	3739
w wisdom is this which is given	Mk 6:2	5101
In *w* place soever ye enter into a	Mk 6:10	3699
unto her mother, *W* shall I ask	Mk 6:24	5101
both *w* they had done	Mk 6:30	3745
and *w* they had taught	Mk 6:30	3745
For *w* shall it profit a man, if	Mk 8:36	5101
Or *w* shall a man give in exchange	Mk 8:37	5101
For he wist not *w* to say	Mk 9:6	5101
no man *w* things they had seen	Mk 9:9	3739
questioning one with another *w*	Mk 9:10	5101
scribes, *W* question ye with them	Mk 9:16	5101
W was it that ye disputed among	Mk 9:33	5101
them, *W* did Moses command you	Mk 10:3	5101
W therefore God hath joined	Mk 10:9	3739
w shall I do that I may inherit	Mk 10:17	5101
began to tell them *w* things	Mk 10:32	3588
W would ye that I should do for	Mk 10:36	5101
unto them, Ye know not *w* ye ask	Mk 10:38	5101
W wilt thou that I should do unto	Mk 10:51	5101
W do ye, loosing the colt	Mk 11:5	5101
W things soever ye desire, when	Mk 11:24	3745
By *w* authority doest thou these	Mk 11:28	4169
I will tell you by *w* authority I	Mk 11:29	4169
Neither do I tell you by *w*	Mk 11:33	4169
W shall therefore the lord of the	Mk 12:9	5101
see *w* manner of stones	Mk 13:1	4217
and *w* buildings are here	Mk 13:1	4217
w shall be the sign when all	Mk 13:4	5101
beforehand *w* ye shall speak	Mk 13:11	5101
w I say unto you I say unto all,	Mk 13:37	3739
She hath done *w* she could	Mk 14:8	3739
not *w* I will, but *w* thou wilt	Mk 14:36	5101
neither wist they *w* to answer him	Mk 14:40	5101
w is it which these witness	Mk 14:60	5101
W need we any further witnesses	Mk 14:63	5101
w think ye	Mk 14:64	5101
understand I *w* thou sayest	Mk 14:68	5101
W will ye then that I shall do	Mk 15:12	5101
them, Why, *w* evil hath he done	Mk 15:14	5101
them, *w* every man should take	Mk 15:24	5101
cast in her mind *w* manner of	Lk 1:29	4217
W manner of child shall this be	Lk 1:66	
him, saying, *W* shall we do then	Lk 3:10	5101
unto him, Master, *w* shall we do	Lk 3:12	5101
of him, saying, And *w* shall we do	Lk 3:14	5101
w have we to do with thee, thou	Lk 4:34	5101
saying, *W* a word is this	Lk 4:36	5101
by *w* way they might bring him in	Lk 5:19	4169
W reason ye in your hearts	Lk 5:22	5101
w David did, when himself was an	Lk 6:3	3739
another *w* they might do to Jesus	Lk 6:11	5101
which love you, *w* thank have ye	Lk 6:32	4169
do good to you, *w* thank have ye	Lk 6:33	4169
hope to receive, *w* thank have ye	Lk 6:34	4169
tell John *w* things ye have seen	Lk 7:22	3739
W went ye out into the wilderness	Lk 7:24	5101
But *w* went ye out for to see	Lk 7:25	5101
But *w* went ye out for to see	Lk 7:26	5101
and to *w* are they like	Lk 7:31	5101
w manner of woman this is that	Lk 7:39	4217
saying, *W* might this parable be	Lk 8:9	5101
another, *W* manner of man is this	Lk 8:25	
W have I to do with thee, Jesus,	Lk 8:28	5101
asked him, saying, *W* is thy name	Lk 8:30	5101
they that fed them saw *w* was done	Lk 8:34	3588
they went out to see *w* was done	Lk 8:35	3588
w means he that was possessed of	Lk 8:36	4459
for *w* cause she had touched him	Lk 8:47	3739
should tell no man *w* was done	Lk 8:56	3588
For *w* is a man advantaged, if he	Lk 9:25	5101
not knowing *w* he said	Lk 9:33	3739
Ye know not *w* manner of spirit ye	Lk 9:55	3634
w shall I do to inherit eternal	Lk 10:25	5101
unto him, *W* is written in the law	Lk 10:26	5101
how or *w* thing ye shall answer	Lk 12:11	5101
shall answer, or *w* ye shall say	Lk 12:11	5101
the same hour *w* ye ought to say	Lk 12:12	3739
W shall I do, because I have no	Lk 12:17	5101
for your life, *w* ye shall eat	Lk 12:22	5101
for the body, *w* ye shall put on	Lk 12:22	5101
seek not ye *w* ye shall eat, or	Lk 12:29	5101
or *w* ye shall drink, neither be	Lk 12:29	5101
known *w* hour the thief would come	Lk 12:39	4169
w will I, if it be already	Lk 12:49	5101
judge ye not *w* is right	Lk 12:57	3588
Unto *w* is the kingdom of God like	Lk 13:18	5101
Or *w* king, going to make war	Lk 14:31	5101
W man of you, having an hundred	Lk 15:4	5101
Either *w* woman having ten pieces	Lk 15:8	5101
asked *w* these things meant	Lk 15:26	5101
said within himself, *W* shall I do	Lk 16:3	5101
I am resolved *w* to do, that, when	Lk 16:4	5101
Hear *w* the unjust judge saith	Lk 18:6	5101
w shall I do to inherit eternal	Lk 18:18	5101
pass by, he asked *w* it meant	Lk 18:36	5101
W wilt thou that I shall do unto	Lk 18:41	5101
And could not find *w* they might do	Lk 19:48	5101
by *w* authority doest thou these	Lk 20:2	4169
Neither tell I you by *w* authority	Lk 20:8	4169
of the vineyard, *W* shall I do	Lk 20:13	5101
W therefore shall the lord of the	Lk 20:15	5101
W is this then that is written,	Lk 20:17	5101
w sign will there be when these	Lk 21:7	5101
meditate before *w* ye shall answer	Lk 21:14	
were about him saw *w* would follow	Lk 22:49	3588
Man, I know not *w* thou sayest	Lk 22:60	3739
W need we any further witness	Lk 22:71	5101
time, Why, *w* evil hath he done	Lk 23:22	5101
w shall be done in the dry	Lk 23:31	5101
for they know not *w* they do	Lk 23:34	5101
when the centurion saw *w* was done	Lk 23:47	3588
W manner of communications are	Lk 24:17	5101
And he said unto them, *W* things	Lk 24:19	4169
they told *w* things were done in	Lk 24:35	3588
And they asked him, *W* then	Jn 1:21	5101
W sayest thou of thyself	Jn 1:22	5101
and saith unto them, *W* seek ye	Jn 1:38	5101
Woman, *w* have I to do with thee	Jn 2:4	5101
W sign shewest thou unto us,	Jn 2:18	5101
for he knew *w* was in man	Jn 2:25	5101
w he hath seen and heard, that he	Jn 3:32	3739
Ye worship ye know not *w*	Jn 4:22	3739
we know *w* we worship	Jn 4:22	3739
yet no man said, *W* seekest thou	Jn 4:27	5101
W man is that which said unto	Jn 5:12	3739
but *w* he seeth the Father do	Jn 5:19	5100
for *w* things soever he doeth,	Jn 5:19	5100
for he himself knew *w* he would do	Jn 6:6	5101
but *w* are they among so many	Jn 6:9	5101
W shall we do, that we might work	Jn 6:28	5101
W sign shewest thou then, that we	Jn 6:30	5101
w dost thou work	Jn 6:30	5101
W and if ye shall see the Son of	Jn 6:62	
W manner of saying is this that	Jn 7:36	5101
it hear him, and know *w* he doeth	Jn 7:51	5101
but *w* sayest thou	Jn 8:5	5101
W sayest thou of him, that he	Jn 9:17	5101
But by *w* means he now seeth, we	Jn 9:21	4459
to him again, *W* did he to thee	Jn 9:26	5101
but they understood not *w* things	Jn 10:6	5101
told them *w* things Jesus had done	Jn 11:46	3739
a council, and said, *W* do we	Jn 11:47	5101
W think ye, that he will not come	Jn 11:56	5101
bag, and bare *w* was put therein	Jn 12:6	3588
and *w* shall I say	Jn 12:27	5101
signifying *w* death he should die	Jn 12:33	4169
w I should say, and *w* I should	Jn 12:49	5101
W I do thou knowest not now	Jn 13:7	3739
Know ye *w* I have done to you	Jn 13:12	5101
no man at the table knew for *w*	Jn 13:28	5101
in you, ye shall ask *w* ye will	Jn 15:7	3739
knoweth not *w* his lord doeth	Jn 15:15	5101
W is this that he saith unto us,	Jn 16:17	5101
W is this that he saith, A little	Jn 16:18	5101
we cannot tell *w* he saith	Jn 16:18	5101
heard me, *w* I have said unto them	Jn 18:21	5101
behold, they know *w* I said	Jn 18:21	3739
W accusation bring ye against	Jn 18:29	5101
signifying *w* death he should die	Jn 18:32	4169
w hast thou done	Jn 18:35	5101
Pilate saith unto him, *W* is truth	Jn 18:38	5101
W I have written I have written	Jn 19:22	3739
signifying by *w* death he should	Jn 21:19	4169
Lord, and *w* shall this man do	Jn 21:21	5101
till I come, *w* is that to thee	Jn 21:22	5101
till I come, *w* is that to thee	Jn 21:23	5101
one to another, *W* meaneth this	Acts 2:12	5101
Men and brethren, *w* shall we do	Acts 2:37	5101
By *w* power, or by *w* name	Acts 4:7	4169
by *w* means he is made whole	Acts 4:9	5101
W shall we do to these men	Acts 4:16	5101
his wife, not knowing *w* was done	Acts 5:7	3588
take heed to yourselves *w* ye	Acts 5:35	5101
we wot not *w* is become of him	Acts 7:40	5101
w house will ye build me	Acts 7:49	4169
or *w* is the place of my rest	Acts 7:49	5101
Understandest thou *w* thou readest	Acts 8:30	3739
w doth hinder me to be baptized	Acts 8:36	5101
w wilt thou have me to do	Acts 9:6	5101
shall be told thee *w* thou must do	Acts 9:6	5101
afraid, and said, *W* is it, Lord	Acts 10:4	5101
he shall tell thee *w* thou	Acts 10:6	5101
W God hath cleansed, that call	Acts 10:15	3739
w this vision which he had seen	Acts 10:17	5101
w is the cause wherefore ye are	Acts 10:21	5101
I ask therefore for *w* intent ye	Acts 10:29	5101
W God hath cleansed, that call	Acts 11:9	3739
w was I, that I could withstand	Acts 11:17	5101
soldiers, *w* was become of Peter	Acts 12:18	
deputy, when he saw *w* was done	Acts 13:12	3588
the people saw *w* Paul had done	Acts 14:11	3739
and Paul, declaring *w* miracles	Acts 15:12	3745
Sirs, *w* must I do to be saved	Acts 16:30	5101
said, *W* will this babbler say	Acts 17:18	5101
May we know *w* this new doctrine,	Acts 17:19	5101
therefore *w* these things mean	Acts 17:20	5101
Unto *w* then were ye baptized	Acts 19:3	5101
w man is there that knoweth not	Acts 19:35	5101
after *w* manner I have been with	Acts 20:18	4459
W mean ye to weep and to break	Acts 21:13	5101
he declared particularly *w* things	Acts 21:19	3739
W is it therefore	Acts 21:22	5101
who he was, and *w* he had done	Acts 21:33	5101
And I said, *W* shall I do, Lord	Acts 22:10	5101
unto all men of *w* thou hast seen	Acts 22:15	3739
saying, Take heed *w* thou doest	Acts 22:26	5101
W is that thou hast to tell me	Acts 23:19	5101
thee *w* they had against him	Acts 23:30	3588
he asked of *w* province he was	Acts 23:34	4169
to hear of thee *w* thou thinkest	Acts 28:22	3739
W advantage then hath the Jew	Rom 3:1	5101
or *w* profit is there of	Rom 3:1	5101
For *w* if some did not believe	Rom 3:3	5101
of God, *w* shall we say	Rom 3:5	5101
W then?	Rom 3:9	5101
Now we know that *w* things soever	Rom 3:19	3745
w law?	Rom 3:27	4169
W shall we say then that Abraham	Rom 4:1	5101
For *w* saith the scripture	Rom 4:3	5101
w he had promised, he was able	Rom 4:21	3739
W shall we say then	Rom 6:1	5101
W then?	Rom 6:15	5101
W fruit had ye then in those	Rom 6:21	5101
W shall we say then	Rom 7:7	5101
for *w* I would, that do I not	Rom 7:15	3739
but *w* I hate, that do I	Rom 7:15	3739
For *w* the law could not do, in	Rom 8:3	3588
for *w* a man seeth, why doth he	Rom 8:24	
for we know not *w* we should pray	Rom 8:26	5101
w is the mind of the Spirit	Rom 8:27	5101
W shall we then say to these	Rom 8:31	5101
W shall we say then	Rom 9:14	5101
W if God, willing to shew his	Rom 9:22	
W shall we say then	Rom 9:30	5101
But *w* saith it	Rom 10:8	5101
Wot ye not *w* the scripture saith	Rom 11:2	5101
But *w* saith the answer of God	Rom 11:4	5101
W then?	Rom 11:7	5101
w shall the receiving of them be,	Rom 11:15	5101
that ye may prove *w* is that good	Rom 12:2	5101
For *w* man knoweth the things of a	1Cor 2:11	5101
every man's work of *w* sort it is	1Cor 3:13	3697
w hast thou that thou didst not	1Cor 4:7	5101
W will ye	1Cor 4:21	5101
For *w* have I to do to judge them	1Cor 5:12	5101
W? know ye not	1Cor 6:16	2228
W? know ye not	1Cor 6:19	2228
For *w* knowest thou, O wife,	1Cor 7:16	5101
so require, let him do *w* he will	1Cor 7:36	3739
W is my reward then	1Cor 9:18	5101
judge ye *w* I say	1Cor 10:15	3739
W say I then	1Cor 10:19	5101
W? have ye not	1Cor 11:22	1063
W shall I say to you	1Cor 11:22	5101
w shall I profit you, except I	1Cor 14:6	5101
it be known *w* is piped or harped	1Cor 14:7	3588
how shall it be known *w* is spoken	1Cor 14:9	3588
W is it then	1Cor 14:15	5101
understandeth not *w* thou sayest	1Cor 14:16	5101
W? came the word	1Cor 14:36	2228
in memory *w* I preached unto you	1Cor 15:2	5101
by the grace of God I am *w* I am	1Cor 15:10	3739
Else *w* shall they do which are	1Cor 15:29	5101
w advantageth it me, if the dead	1Cor 15:32	5101
and with *w* body do they come	1Cor 15:35	4169
than *w* ye read or acknowledge	2Cor 1:13	5101
for *w* fellowship hath	2Cor 6:14	5101
w communion hath light with	2Cor 6:14	5101
w concord hath Christ with Belial	2Cor 6:15	5101
or *w* part hath he that believeth	2Cor 6:15	5101
w agreement hath the temple of	2Cor 6:16	5101
w carefulness it wrought in you,	2Cor 7:11	4214
w clearing of yourselves, yea,	2Cor 7:11	
w indignation, yea, *w* fear,	2Cor 7:11	
w vehement desire, yea, *w* zeal	2Cor 7:11	
zeal, yea, *w* revenge	2Cor 7:11	
But *w* I do, that I will do, that	2Cor 11:12	5101
For *w* is it wherein ye were	2Cor 12:13	5101
Nevertheless *w* saith the	Gal 4:30	5101
that ye may know *w* is the hope of	Eph 1:18	5101

w the riches of the glory of his	Eph 1:18	*5101*
w is the exceeding greatness of	Eph 1:19	*5101*
to make all men see *w* is the	Eph 3:9	*5101*
with all saints *w* is the breadth	Eph 3:18	*5101*
w is it but that he also	Eph 4:9	*5101*
Proving *w* is acceptable unto the	Eph 5:10	*5101*
but understanding *w* the will of	Eph 5:17	*5101*
W then?	Phil 1:18	*5101*
yet *w* I shall choose I wot not	Phil 1:22	*5101*
But *w* things were gain to me,	Phil 3:7	*3748*
God would make known *w* is	Col 1:27	*5101*
For I would that ye knew *w* great	Col 2:1	*2245*
as ye know *w* manner of men we	1Th 1:5	*3634*
us *w* manner of entering in we had	1Th 1:9	*3697*
For *w* is our hope, or joy, or	1Th 2:19	*5101*
For *w* thanks can we render to God	1Th 3:9	*5101*
For ye know *w* commandments we	1Th 4:2	*5101*
now ye know *w* withholdeth that he	2Th 2:6	*3588*
understanding neither *w* they say	1Ti 1:7	*3739*
Consider *w* I say	2Ti 2:7	*3739*
w persecutions I endured	2Ti 3:11	*3634*
W is man, that thou art mindful	Heb 2:6	*5101*
w further need was there that	Heb 7:11	*5101*
And *w* shall I more say	Heb 11:32	*5101*
for *w* son is he whom the father	Heb 12:7	*5101*
I will not fear *w* man shall do	Heb 13:6	*5101*
forgetteth *w* manner of man he was	Jas 1:24	*3697*
W doth it profit, my brethren,	Jas 2:14	*5101*
w doth it profit	Jas 2:16	*5101*
Whereas ye know not *w* shall be on	Jas 4:14	*3588*
For *w* is your life	Jas 4:14	*4169*
Searching *w*, or	1Pet 1:11	
or *w* manner of time the Spirit of	1Pet 1:11	*4169*
For *w* glory is it, if, when ye be	1Pet 2:20	*4169*
w shall the end be of them that	1Pet 4:17	*5101*
w manner of persons ought ye to	2Pet 3:11	*4217*
w manner of love the Father hath	1Jn 3:1	*4217*
doth not yet appear *w* we shall be	1Jn 3:2	*5101*
but *w* they know naturally, as	Jude 10	*3745*
W thou seest, write in a book, and	Rev 1:11	*3739*
let him hear *w* the Spirit saith	Rev 2:7	*5101*
let him hear *w* the Spirit saith	Rev 2:11	*5101*
let him hear *w* the Spirit saith	Rev 2:17	*5101*
let him hear *w* the Spirit saith	Rev 2:29	*5101*
thou shalt not know *w* hour I will	Rev 3:3	*4169*
let him hear *w* the Spirit saith	Rev 3:6	*5101*
let him hear *w* the Spirit saith	Rev 3:13	*5101*
let him hear *w* the Spirit saith	Rev 3:22	*5101*
W are these which are arrayed in	Rev 7:13	*5101*
W city is like unto this great	Rev 18:18	*5101*

WHATSOEVER

w Adam called every living	Gen 2:19	
w creepeth upon the earth, after	Gen 8:19	3605
w thou hast in the city, bring	Gen 19:12	
w God hath said unto thee, do	Gen 31:16	
w they did there, he was the doer	Gen 39:22	
w openeth the womb among the	Ex 13:2	3605
of his life *w* is laid upon him	Ex 21:30	
w toucheth the altar shall be	Ex 29:37	3605
w toucheth them shall be holy	Ex 30:29	3605
w uncleanness it be that a man	Lev 5:3	3605
do good, *w* it be that a man shall	Lev 5:4	
W shall touch the flesh thereof	Lev 6:27	3605
W soul it be that eateth any	Lev 7:27	3605
W parteth the hoof, and is	Lev 11:3	3605
w hath fins and scales in the	Lev 11:9	3605
W hath no fins nor scales in the	Lev 11:12	3605
w goeth upon his paws, among all	Lev 11:27	3605
upon *w* any of them, when they are	Lev 11:32	3605
w vessel it be, wherein any work	Lev 11:32	3605
w is in it shall be unclean	Lev 11:33	3605
W goeth upon the belly, and	Lev 11:42	3605
w goeth upon all four, or	Lev 11:42	3605
or *w* hath more feet among all	Lev 11:42	3605
or *w* thing of skin it be, which	Lev 13:58	3605
w she sitteth upon shall be	Lev 15:26	
W man there be of the house of	Lev 17:8	
w man there be of the house of	Lev 17:10	
w man there be of the children of	Lev 17:13	
For *w* man he be that hath a	Lev 21:18	3605
w uncleanness he hath	Lev 22:5	3605
W he be of the house of Israel,	Lev 22:18	
But *w* hath a blemish, that shall	Lev 22:20	3605
For *w* soul it be that shall not	Lev 23:29	3605
w soul it be that doeth any work	Lev 23:30	3605
even of *w* passeth under the rod,	Lev 27:32	3605
w any man giveth the priest, it	Num 5:10	834
w is first ripe in the land,	Num 18:13	
w the unclean person toucheth	Num 19:22	3605
I will do *w* thou sayest unto me	Num 22:17	
w he sheweth me I will tell thee	Num 23:3	
then *w* proceeded out of her lips	Num 30:12	3605
nor unto *w* the LORD our God	Deut 2:37	3605
every man *w* is right in his own	Deut 12:8	3605
w thy soul lusteth after,	Deut 12:15	3605
flesh, *w* thy soul lusteth after	Deut 12:20	3605
gates *w* thy soul lusteth after	Deut 12:21	3605
w hath not fins and scales ye may	Deut 14:10	
for *w* thy soul lusteth after	Deut 14:26	
or for *w* thy soul desireth	Deut 14:26	
do thou unto us *w* seemeth good	Judg 10:15	3605
that *w* cometh forth of the doors	Judg 11:31	834
Do *w* seemeth good unto thee	1Sa 14:36	3605
W thy soul desireth, I will even	1Sa 20:4	4100
w cometh to thine hand unto thy	1Sa 25:8	
as *w* the king did pleased all the	2Sa 3:36	
thy servants are ready to do *w* my	2Sa 15:15	
w thou shalt require of me, that	2Sa 19:38	
w plague, *w* sickness	1Kin 8:37	3605
w she asked, beside that which	1Kin 10:13	834
that *w* is pleasant in thine eyes,	1Kin 20:6	3605
w sore or *w* sickness	2Chr 6:28	3605
w she asked, beside that which	2Chr 9:12	3605
w shall seem good to thee, and to	Ezr 7:18	
w more shall be needful for the	Ezr 7:20	
that *w* Ezra the priest, the	Ezr 7:21	
W is commanded by the God of	Ezr 7:23	
w she desired was given her to go	Est 2:13	
that they may do *w* he commandeth	Job 37:12	
w is under the whole heaven is	Job 41:11	
and *w* he doeth shall prosper	Ps 1:3	
w passeth through the paths of	Ps 8:8	
he hath done *w* he hath pleased	Ps 115:3	
W the LORD pleased, that did he	Ps 135:6	
w mine eyes desired I kept not	Eccl 2:10	
w God doeth, it shall be for ever	Eccl 3:14	
for he doeth *w* pleaseth him	Eccl 8:3	
W thy hand findeth to do, do it	Eccl 9:10	
w I command thee thou shalt speak	Jer 1:7	
that *w* thing the LORD shall	Jer 42:4	3605
But we will certainly do *w* thing	Jer 44:17	
for *w* is more than these cometh	Mt 5:37	*3588*
Therefore all things *w* ye would	Mt 7:12	
into *w* city or town ye shall	Mt 10:11	
oath to give her *w* she would ask	Mt 14:7	
by *w* thou mightest be profited by	Mt 15:5	
that *w* entereth in at the mouth	Mt 15:17	*3956*
w thou shalt bind on earth shall	Mt 16:19	
w thou shalt loose on earth shall	Mt 16:19	*1437*
have done unto him *w* they listed	Mt 17:12	*3745*
W ye shall bind on earth shall be	Mt 18:18	
w ye shall loose on earth shall	Mt 18:18	
w is right I will give you	Mt 20:4	
w is right, that shall ye receive	Mt 20:7	
w ye shall ask in prayer,	Mt 21:22	
All therefore *w* they bid you	Mt 23:3	
all things *w* I have commanded you	Mt 28:20	*3745*
the damsel, Ask of me *w* thou wilt	Mk 6:22	
W thou shalt ask of me, I will	Mk 6:23	
by *w* thou mightest be profited by	Mk 7:11	*1437*
that *w* thing from without	Mk 7:18	*3956*
have done unto him *w* they listed	Mk 9:13	*3745*
sell *w* thou hast, and give to the	Mk 10:21	*3745*
do for us *w* we shall desire	Mk 10:35	
he shall have *w* he saith	Mk 11:23	
but *w* shall be given you in that	Mk 13:11	
w we have heard done in Capernaum	Lk 4:23	*3745*
w house ye enter into, there	Lk 9:4	
into *w* house ye enter, first say,	Lk 10:5	
into *w* city ye enter, and they	Lk 10:8	
But into *w* city ye enter, and they	Lk 10:10	
w thou spendest more, when I come	Lk 10:35	
Therefore *w* ye have spoken in	Lk 12:3	*3745*
W he saith unto you, do it	Jn 2:5	
made whole of *w* disease he had	Jn 5:4	*1221*
w thou wilt ask of God, God will	Jn 11:22	
w I speak therefore, even as the	Jn 12:50	*3739*
w ye shall ask in my name, that	Jn 14:13	
w I have said unto you	Jn 14:26	*3739*
friends, if ye do *w* I command you	Jn 15:14	*3745*
that *w* ye shall ask of the Father	Jn 15:16	
but *w* he shall hear, that shall	Jn 16:13	*3745*
W ye shall ask the Father in my	Jn 16:23	
w thou hast given me are of thee	Jn 17:7	*3745*
things *w* he shall say unto you	Acts 3:22	
For to do *w* thy hand and thy	Acts 4:28	*3745*
for *w* is not of faith is sin	Rom 14:23	*3956*
For *w* things were written	Rom 15:4	*3745*
that ye assist her in *w* business	Rom 16:2	
W is sold in the shambles, that	1Cor 10:25	*3956*
w is set before you, eat, asking	1Cor 10:27	*3956*
or *w* ye do, do all to the glory	1Cor 10:31	*5100*
(*w* they were, it maketh no matter	Gal 2:6	
for *w* a man soweth, that shall he	Gal 6:7	
for *w* doth make manifest is light	Eph 5:13	*3956*
Knowing that *w* good thing any man	Eph 6:8	
w things are true	Phil 4:8	*3745*
w things are honest	Phil 4:8	*3745*
w things are just	Phil 4:8	*3745*
w things are pure	Phil 4:8	*3745*
w things are lovely	Phil 4:8	*3745*
w things are of good report	Phil 4:8	*3745*
in *w* state I am, therewith to be	Phil 4:11	
w ye do in word or deed, do all	Col 3:17	
w ye do, do it heartily, as to	Col 3:23	
w we ask, we receive of him,	1Jn 3:22	
For *w* is born of God overcometh	1Jn 5:4	*3956*
w we ask, we know that we have	1Jn 5:15	
thou doest faithfully *w* thou	3Jn 5	
of *w* craft he be, shall be found	Rev 18:22	*3956*
neither *w* worketh abomination, or	Rev 21:27	

WHEAT

went in the days of *w* harvest	Gen 30:14	2406
But the *w* and the rie were not	Ex 9:32	2406
of the firstfruits of *w* harvest	Ex 34:22	2406
the best of the wine, and of the *w*	Num 18:12	1715
A land of *w*, and barley, and vines,	Deut 8:8	2406
with the fat of kidneys of *w*	Deut 32:14	2406
threshed *w* by the winepress	Judg 6:11	2406
after, in the time of *w* harvest	Judg 15:1	2406
of barley harvest and of *w* harvest	Ruth 2:23	2406
their *w* harvest in the valley	1Sa 6:13	2406
Is it not *w* harvest to day	1Sa 12:17	2406
though they would have fetched *w*	2Sa 4:6	2406
basons, and earthen vessels, and *w*	2Sa 17:28	2406
of *w* for food to his household	1Kin 5:11	2406
Now Ornan was threshing *w*	1Chr 21:20	2406
the *w* for the meat offering	1Chr 21:23	2406
thousand measures of beaten *w*	2Chr 2:10	2406
Now therefore the *w*, and the	2Chr 2:15	2406
and ten thousand measures of *w*	2Chr 27:5	2406
offerings of the God of heaven, *w*	Ezr 6:9	2591
and to an hundred measures of *w*	Ezr 7:22	2591
Let thistles grow instead of *w*	Job 31:40	2406
also with the finest of the *w*	Ps 81:16	2406
thee with the finest of the *w*	Ps 147:14	2406
in a mortar among *w* with a pestle	Prov 27:22	7383
heap of *w* set about with lilies	Song 7:2	2406
and cast in the principal *w*	Is 28:25	2406
They have sown *w*, but shall reap	Jer 12:13	2406
What is the chaff to the *w*	Jer 23:28	1250
the goodness of the LORD, for *w*	Jer 31:12	1715
have treasures in the field, of *w*	Jer 41:8	2406
Take thou also unto thee *w*	Eze 4:9	2406
traded in thy market *w* of Minnith	Eze 27:17	2406
part of an ephah of an homer of *w*	Eze 45:13	2406
O ye vinedressers, for the *w*	Joel 1:11	2406
And the floors shall be full of *w*	Joel 2:24	1250
and ye take from him burdens of *w*	Amos 5:11	1250
sabbath, that we may set forth *w*	Amos 8:5	1250
yea, and sell the refuse of the *w*	Amos 8:6	1250
gather his *w* into the garner	Mt 3:12	*4621*
came and sowed tares among the *w*	Mt 13:25	*4621*
ye root up also the *w* with them	Mt 13:29	*4621*
but gather the *w* into my barn	Mt 13:30	*4621*
will gather the *w* into his garner	Lk 3:17	*4621*
he said, An hundred measures of *w*	Lk 16:7	*4621*
you, that he may sift you as *w*	Lk 22:31	*4621*
Except a corn of *w* fall into the	Jn 12:24	*4621*
and cast out the *w* into the sea	Acts 27:38	*4621*
bare grain, it may chance of *w*	1Cor 15:37	*4621*
say, A measure of *w* for a penny	Rev 6:6	*4621*
wine, and oil, and fine flour, and *w*	Rev 18:13	*4621*

WHEATEN

of *w* flour shalt thou make them	Ex 29:2	2406

WHEEL

and the height of a *w* was a cubit	1Kin 7:32	212
was like the work of a chariot *w*	1Kin 7:33	212
O my God, make them like a *w*	Ps 83:13	1534
and bringeth the *w* over them	Prov 20:26	212
or the *w* broken at the cistern	Eccl 12:6	1534
neither is a cart *w* turned about	Is 28:27	212
break it with the *w* of his cart	Is 28:28	1536
behold one *w* upon the earth by	Eze 1:15	212
were a *w* in the middle of a *w*	Eze 1:16	212
one *w* by one cherub, and another	Eze 10:9	212
another *w* by another cherub	Eze 10:9	212
as if a *w* had been in the midst	Eze 10:10	212
had been in the midst of a *w*	Eze 10:10	212
unto them in my hearing, O *w*	Eze 10:13	1534

WHEELS

And took off their chariot *w*	Ex 14:25	212
Why tarry the *w* of his chariots	Judg 5:28	6471
And every base had four brasen *w*	1Kin 7:30	212
And under the borders were four *w*	1Kin 7:32	212
the axletrees of the *w* were	1Kin 7:32	212
the work of the *w* was like the	1Kin 7:33	212
and their *w* like a whirlwind	Is 5:28	1534
he wrought a work on the *w*	Jer 18:3	70
and at the rumbling of his *w*	Jer 47:3	1534
The appearance of the *w* and their	Eze 1:16	212
went, the *w* went by them	Eze 1:19	212
the earth, the *w* were lifted up	Eze 1:19	212
the *w* were lifted up over against	Eze 1:20	212
the living creature was in the *w*	Eze 1:20	212
the *w* were lifted up over against	Eze 1:21	212
the living creature was in the *w*	Eze 1:21	212
the noise of the *w* over against	Eze 3:13	212
and said, Go in between the *w*	Eze 10:2	1534
Take fire from between the *w*	Eze 10:6	1534
he went in, and stood beside the *w*	Eze 10:6	212
looked, behold the four *w* by the	Eze 10:9	212
the appearance of the *w* was as	Eze 10:9	212
hands, and their wings, and the *w*	Eze 10:12	212
even the *w* that they four had	Eze 10:12	212
As for the *w*, it was cried unto	Eze 10:13	212
went, the *w* went by them	Eze 10:16	212
the same *w* also turned not from	Eze 10:16	212
the *w* also were beside them, and	Eze 10:19	212
their wings, and the *w* beside them	Eze 11:22	212
thee with chariots, wagons, and *w*	Eze 23:24	1534
of the horsemen, and of the *w*	Eze 26:10	1534
flame, and his *w* as burning fire	Dan 7:9	1535
noise of the rattling of the *w*	Nah 3:2	212

WHELP

Judah is a lion's *w*	Gen 49:9	1482
of Dan he said, Dan is a lion's *w*	Deut 33:22	1482
old lion, walked, and the lion's *w*	Nah 2:11	1482

WHELPS

bear robbed of her *w* in the field	2Sa 17:8	
the stout lion's *w* are scattered	Job 4:11	1121
The lion's *w* have not trodden it,	Job 28:8	1121
a bear robbed of her *w* meet a man	Prov 17:12	
they shall yell as lions' *w*	Jer 51:38	1484
nourished her *w* among young lions	Eze 19:2	1482
And she brought up one of her *w*	Eze 19:3	1482
then she took another of her *w*	Eze 19:5	1482
a bear that is bereaved of her *w*	Hos 13:8	
tear in pieces enough for his *w*	Nah 2:12	1484

WHEN

of the earth *w* they were created,	Gen 2:4	
w the woman saw that the tree was	Gen 3:6	
w they were in the field, that	Gen 4:8	
W thou tillest the ground, it	Gen 4:12	3588
in the day *w* they were created	Gen 5:2	
w men began to multiply on the	Gen 6:1	3588
w the sons of God came in unto	Gen 6:4	834
w the flood of waters was upon	Gen 7:6	
w I bring a cloud over the earth,	Gen 9:14	
five years old *w* he departed out	Gen 12:4	
w he was come near to enter into	Gen 12:11	834
w the Egyptians shall see thee,	Gen 12:12	3588
w Abram was come into Egypt, the	Gen 12:14	
w Abram heard that his brother	Gen 14:14	3588
w the fowls came down upon the	Gen 15:11	
w the sun was going down, a deep	Gen 15:12	1961
w the sun went down, and it was	Gen 15:17	1961

W

w she saw that she had conceived, Gen 16:4
w she saw that she had conceived, Gen 16:5
w Sarai dealt hardly with her, Gen 16:6
w Hagar bare Ishmael to Abram Gen 16:16
w Abram was ninety years old and Gen 17:1 1961
w he was circumcised in the flesh Gen 17:24
w he was circumcised in the flesh Gen 17:25
w he saw them, he ran to meet Gen 18:2
w the morning arose, then the Gen 19:15 3644
w they had brought them forth Gen 19:17
the earth *w* Lot entered into Zoar Gen 19:23
w God destroyed the cities of the Gen 19:29
w he overthrew the cities in the Gen 19:29
he perceived not *w* she lay down Gen 19:33
she lay down, nor *w* she arose Gen 19:33
he perceived not *w* she lay down Gen 19:35
she lay down, nor *w* she arose Gen 19:35
w God caused me to wander from my Gen 20:13 834
w his son Isaac was born unto him Gen 21:5
w she had done giving him drink, Gen 24:19 3588
w he saw the earring and bracelets Gen 24:30 3588
w he heard the words of Rebekah Gen 24:30 3588
a son to my master *w* she was old Gen 24:36 310
w thou comest to my kindred Gen 24:41 3588
that *w* the virgin cometh forth to Gen 24:43 3588
w Abraham's servant heard their Gen 24:52
w she saw Isaac, she lighted off Gen 24:64
old *w* he took Rebekah to wife Gen 25:20
w her days to be delivered were Gen 25:24
years old *w* she bare them Gen 25:26
w he had been there a long time, Gen 26:8 3588
Esau was forty years old *w* he Gen 26:34 3588
that *w* Isaac was old, and his eyes Gen 27:1 3588
Rebekah heard *w* Isaac spake to Gen 27:5 3588
w Esau heard the words of his Gen 27:34
it shall come to pass *w* thou Gen 27:40 834
W Esau saw that Isaac had blessed Gen 28:6
w Jacob saw Rachel the daughter Gen 29:10 834
w Laban heard the tidings of Gen 29:13
w the LORD saw that Leah was Gen 29:31
w Rachel saw that she bare Jacob Gen 30:1
W Leah saw that she had left Gen 30:9
w Rachel had born Joseph, that Gen 30:25 834
now *w* shall I provide for mine Gen 30:30 4970
w it shall come for my hire Gen 30:33 3588
w the flocks came to drink Gen 30:38 3588
conceive *w* they came to drink Gen 30:38
But *w* the cattle were feeble, he Gen 30:42
w we are absent one from another Gen 31:49 3588
w Jacob saw them, he said, This Gen 32:2 834
W Esau my brother meeteth thee, Gen 32:17 3588
ye speak unto Esau, *w* ye find him Gen 32:19
w he saw that he prevailed not Gen 32:25
w he came from Padan-aram Gen 33:18
w Shechem the son of Hamor the Gen 34:2
out of the field *w* they heard it Gen 34:7
w they were sore, that two of the Gen 34:25
that appeared unto thee *w* thou Gen 35:1
w he fled from the face of his Gen 35:7
w he came out of Padan-aram, and Gen 35:9
w she was in hard labour, that Gen 35:17
w Israel dwelt in that land, that Gen 35:22
w his brethren saw that their Gen 37:4
w they saw him afar off, even Gen 37:18
w Joseph was come unto his Gen 37:23 834
he was at Chezib, *w* she bare him Gen 38:5
w he went in unto his brother's Gen 38:9 518
W Judah saw her, he thought her Gen 38:15
W she was brought forth, she sent Gen 38:25
w she travailed, that the one put Gen 38:28
w she saw that he had left his Gen 39:13
w he heard that I lifted up my Gen 39:15
w his master heard the words of Gen 39:19
manner *w* thou wast his butler Gen 40:13 834
But think on me *w* it shall be Gen 40:14 834
W the chief baker saw that the Gen 40:16
w they had eaten them up, it Gen 41:21
Joseph was thirty years old *w* he Gen 41:46
w all the land of Egypt was Gen 41:55
Now *w* Jacob saw that there was Gen 42:1
w he besought us, and we would not Gen 42:21
w both they and their father saw Gen 42:35
w they had eaten up the corn Gen 43:2 834
w Joseph saw Benjamin with them, Gen 43:16 3588
w we came to the inn, that we Gen 43:21 3588
w Joseph came home, they brought Gen 43:26
w they were gone out of the city, Gen 44:4
w thou dost overtake them, say Gen 44:4
it came to pass *w* we came up unto Gen 44:24 3588
Now therefore *w* I come to thy Gen 44:30
w he seeth that the lad is not Gen 44:31
w he saw the wagons which Joseph Gen 45:27
w Pharaoh shall call you, and Gen 46:33 3588
w money failed in the land of Gen 47:15
W that year was ended, they came Gen 47:18
w I came from Padan, Rachel died Gen 48:7
w yet there was but a little way Gen 48:7 5750
w Joseph saw that his father laid Gen 48:17
w Jacob had made an end of Gen 49:33
w the days of his mourning were Gen 50:4
w the inhabitants of the land, Gen 50:11
w Joseph's brethren saw that Gen 50:15
Joseph wept *w* they spake unto him Gen 50:17
w there falleth out any war, they Ex 1:10 3588
W ye do the office of a midwife Ex 1:16
w she saw him that he was a Ex 2:2 3588
w she could not longer hide him, Ex 2:3 3588
w she saw the ark among the flags Ex 2:5
w she had opened it, she saw the Ex 2:6
w Moses was grown, that he went Ex 2:11
w he saw that there was no man, Ex 2:12
w he went out the second day, Ex 2:13
Now *w* Pharaoh heard this thing, Ex 2:15
w they came to Reuel their father Ex 2:18
w the LORD saw that he turned Ex 3:4
W thou hast brought forth the Ex 3:12
w I come unto the children of Ex 3:13
w ye go, ye shall not go empty Ex 3:21 3588
w he took it out, behold, his Ex 4:6
w he seeth thee, he will be glad Ex 4:14
W thou goest to return into Egypt Ex 4:21
w they heard that the LORD had Ex 4:31
daily tasks, as *w* there was straw Ex 5:13 834
it came to pass on the day *w* the Ex 6:28
w I stretch forth mine hand upon Ex 7:5
w they spake unto Pharaoh Ex 7:7
W Pharaoh shall speak unto you, Ex 7:9 3588
w shall I intreat for thee, and Ex 8:9 4970
But *w* Pharaoh saw that there was Ex 8:15
w Pharaoh saw that the rain and Ex 9:34
w it was morning, the east wind Ex 10:13
w he shall let you go, he shall Ex 11:1
w I see the blood, I will pass Ex 12:13
w I smite the land of Egypt Ex 12:13
w he seeth the blood upon the Ex 12:23
w ye be come to the land which Ex 12:25 3588
w your children shall say unto Ex 12:26 3588
w he smote the Egyptians, and Ex 12:27
w thou hast circumcised him, then Ex 12:44
w a stranger shall sojourn with Ex 12:48 3588
it shall be *w* the LORD shall Ex 13:5 3588
me *w* I came forth out of Egypt Ex 13:8
it shall be *w* the LORD shall Ex 13:11 3588
it shall be *w* thy son asketh thee Ex 13:14 3588
w Pharaoh would hardly let us go, Ex 13:15 3588
w Pharaoh had let the people go, Ex 13:17
the people repent *w* they see war Ex 13:17
w Pharaoh drew nigh, the children Ex 14:10
w I have gotten me honour upon Ex 14:18
strength *w* the morning appeared Ex 14:27
w they came to Marah, they could Ex 15:23
which *w* he had cast into the Ex 15:25
w we sat by the flesh pots, and Ex 16:3
w we did eat bread to the full Ex 16:3
w the LORD shall give you in the Ex 16:8
w the dew that lay was gone up, Ex 16:14
w the children of Israel saw it, Ex 16:15
w they did mete it with an omer, Ex 16:18
w the sun waxed hot, it melted Ex 16:21
w I brought you forth from the Ex 16:32
w Moses held up his hand, that Ex 17:11 834
w he let down his hand, Amalek Ex 17:11 834
W Jethro, the priest of Midian, Ex 18:1 3588
w Moses' father in law saw all Ex 18:14
W they have a matter, they come Ex 18:16 3588
w the children of Israel were Ex 19:1
may hear *w* I speak with thee Ex 19:9
w the trumpet soundeth long, they Ex 19:13
w the voice of the trumpet Ex 19:19 1961
w the people saw it, they removed Ex 20:18
w he crieth unto me, that I will Ex 22:27 3588
w thou hast gathered in thy Ex 23:16
w he goeth in unto the holy place Ex 28:29
w he goeth in before the LORD Ex 28:30
his sound shall be heard *w* he Ex 28:35
w he cometh out, that he die not Ex 28:35
his sons, *w* they come in unto the Ex 28:43
or *w* they come near unto the Ex 28:43
w he cometh into the tabernacle Ex 29:30 834
w thou hast made an atonement for Ex 29:36
w he dresseth the lamps, he shall Ex 30:7
w Aaron lighteth the lamps at Ex 30:8
W thou takest the sum of the Ex 30:12 3588
the LORD, *w* thou numberest them Ex 30:12
among them, *w* thou numberest them. Ex 30:12
w they give an offering unto the Ex 30:15
W they go into the tabernacle of Ex 30:20
or *w* they come near to the altar Ex 30:20
w he had made an end of communing. Ex 31:18
w the people saw that Moses Ex 32:1
w Aaron saw it, he built an altar Ex 32:5
w Joshua heard the noise of the Ex 32:17
w Moses saw that the people were Ex 32:25
nevertheless in the day *w* I visit Ex 32:34
w the people heard these evil Ex 33:4
w Moses went out unto the Ex 33:8
w thou shalt go up to appear Ex 34:24
w Moses came down from mount Ex 34:29
w he came down from the mount, Ex 34:29
w Aaron and all the children of Ex 34:30
But *w* Moses went in before the Ex 34:34
W they went into the tent of the Ex 40:32
w they came near unto the altar, Ex 40:32
w the cloud was taken up from Ex 40:36
w any will offer a meat offering Lev 2:1
w it is presented unto the priest Lev 2:8
W the sin, which they have sinned Lev 4:14
W a ruler hath sinned, and done Lev 4:22 834
w he knoweth of it, then he shall Lev 5:3
w he knoweth of it, then he shall Lev 5:4
w he shall be guilty in one of Lev 5:5 3588
LORD in the day *w* he is anointed Lev 6:20
w it is baken, thou shalt bring Lev 6:21
w there is sprinkled of the blood Lev 6:27 834
in the day *w* he presented them to Lev 7:35
which *w* all the people saw, they Lev 9:24
w ye go into the tabernacle of Lev 10:9
w Moses heard that, he was Lev 10:20
w they be dead, shall be unclean Lev 11:31
w they are dead, doth fall, it Lev 11:32 3588
w the days of her purifying are Lev 12:6
W a man shall have in the skin of Lev 13:2 3588
w the hair in the plague is Lev 13:3
W the plague of leprosy is in a Lev 13:9 3588
But *w* raw flesh appeareth in him, Lev 13:14 3117
w the priest seeth it, behold, it Lev 13:20
W ye be come into the land of Lev 14:34 3588
To teach *w* it is unclean Lev 14:57 3117
and *w* it is clean Lev 14:57 3117
W any man hath a running issue Lev 15:2 3588
w he that hath an issue is Lev 15:13 3588
w he toucheth it, he shall be Lev 15:23 3588
w they defile my tabernacle that Lev 15:31
w they offered before the LORD, Lev 16:1
w he goeth in to make an Lev 16:17
And *w* he hath made an end of Lev 16:20
which he put on *w* he went into Lev 16:23
w ye defile it, as it spued out Lev 18:28
w ye reap the harvest of your Lev 19:9
w ye shall come into the land, and Lev 19:23 3588
w he giveth of his seed unto Lev 20:4
w the sun is down, he shall be Lev 22:7
w they eat their holy things Lev 22:16
W a bullock, or a sheep, or a Lev 22:27
w ye will offer a sacrifice of Lev 22:29 3588
W ye be come into the land which Lev 23:10 3588
ye shall offer that day *w* ye wave Lev 23:12
w ye reap the harvest of your Lev 23:22
of thy field *w* thou reapest Lev 23:22
w ye have gathered in the fruit Lev 23:39
w I brought them out of the land Lev 23:43
w he blasphemeth the name of the Lev 24:16
W ye come into the land which I Lev 25:2 3588
ye shall flee *w* none pursueth you Lev 26:17
w ye are gathered together within Lev 26:25
w I have broken the staff of your Lev 26:26
your sabbaths, *w* ye dwelt upon it Lev 26:35
they shall fall *w* none pursueth Lev 26:36
before a sword, *w* none pursueth Lev 26:37
w they be in the land of their Lev 26:44
W a man shall make a singular vow Lev 27:2 3588
w a man shall sanctify his house Lev 27:14 3588
w it goeth out in the jubile, Lev 27:21
w the tabernacle setteth forward, Num 1:51 3588
w the tabernacle is to be pitched Num 1:51 3588
w they offered strange fire Num 3:4
w the camp setteth forward, Aaron Num 4:5
w Aaron and his sons have made an Num 4:15
w they approach unto the most Num 4:19
see *w* the holy things are covered Num 4:20
W a man or woman shall commit any. Num 5:6 3588
w the LORD doth make thy thigh to Num 5:21
w he hath made her to drink the Num 5:27
w a wife goeth aside to another Num 5:29 834
Or *w* the spirit of jealousy Num 5:30 834
W either man or woman shall Num 6:2 3588
or for his sister, *w* they die Num 6:7
w the days of his separation are Num 6:13
in the day *w* it was anointed, by Num 7:84
w Moses was gone into the Num 7:89
W thou lightest the lamps, the Num 8:2
w the children of Israel come Num 8:19
w the cloud was taken up from the Num 9:17 6310
w the cloud tarried long upon the Num 9:19 3588
w the cloud was a few days upon Num 9:20 834
w the cloud abode from even unto Num 9:21 834
but *w* it was taken up, they Num 9:22
w they shall blow with them, all Num 10:3
W ye blow an alarm, then the Num 10:5
W ye blow an alarm the second Num 10:6
But *w* the congregation is to be Num 10:7
their armies, *w* they set forward Num 10:28
w they went out of the camp Num 10:34
w the ark set forward, that Moses Num 10:35
w it rested, he said, Return, O Num 10:36
w the people complained, it Num 11:1
w Moses prayed unto the LORD, the Num 11:2
w the dew fell upon the camp in Num 11:9
w the spirit rested upon them, Num 11:25
w he cometh out of his mother's Num [illegible] [illegible]
W ye be come into the land of Num 15:2 3588
w thou preparest a bullock for a Num 15:8 3588
W ye come into the land whither I Num 15:18
w ye eat of the bread of the land Num 15:19
w he sinneth by ignorance before Num 15:28
w Moses heard it, he fell upon Num 16:4
w the congregation was gathered Num 16:42
W ye take of the children of Num 18:26 3588
W ye have heaved the best thereof Num 18:30
w ye have heaved from it the best Num 18:32
the law, *w* a man dieth in a tent Num 19:14 3588
Would God that we had died *w* our Num 20:3
w we cried unto the LORD, he Num 20:16
w all the congregation saw that Num 20:29
w king Arad the Canaanite, which Num 21:1
w he looketh upon it, shall live Num 21:8
w he beheld the serpent of brass, Num 21:9
w the ass saw the angel of the Num 22:25
w the ass saw the angel of the Num 22:27
w Balak heard that Balaam was Num 22:36
w he came to him, behold, he Num 23:17
w Balaam saw that it pleased the Num 24:1
w he looked on Amalek, he took up Num 24:20
who shall live *w* God doeth this Num 24:23
w Phinehas, the son of Eleazar, Num 25:7
w they strove against the LORD Num 26:9
w that company died, what time Num 26:10
w they offered strange fire Num 26:61
w they numbered the children of Num 26:64 834
w thou hast seen it, thou also Num 27:13
w ye bring a new meat offering Num 28:26
w she vowed, or uttered ought out Num 30:6
w they saw the land of Jazer, and Num 32:1
w I sent them from Kadesh-barnea Num 32:8
For *w* they went up unto the Num 32:9
three years old *w* he died in Num 33:39
W ye are passed over Jordan into Num 33:51 3588
W ye come into the land of Canaan Num 34:2 3588
W ye be come over Jordan into the Num 35:10 3588
w he meeteth him, he shall slay Num 35:19
the murderer, *w* he meeteth him Num 35:21
w the jubile of the children of Num 36:4 518

w we departed from Horeb, we went... Deut 1:19
w ye had girded on every man his........ Deut 1:41
w we passed by from our brethren....... Deut 2:8
w they had destroyed them from.......... Deut 2:12
w all the men of war were...................... Deut 2:16 834
w thou comest nigh over against........ Deut 2:19
w he destroyed the Horims from.......... Deut 2:22 834
w the LORD said unto me, Gather......... Deut 4:10
w thou seest the sun, and the moon..... Deut 4:19
W thou shalt beget children, and......... Deut 4:25 3588
W thou art in tribulation, and all.......... Deut 4:30
w ye heard the voice out of the........... Deut 5:23
of your words, *w* ye spake unto me...... Deut 5:28
shalt talk of them *w* thou sittest.......... Deut 6:7
w thou walkest by the way, and........... Deut 6:7
w thou liest down.................................... Deut 6:7
and *w* thou risest up.............................. Deut 6:7
w the LORD thy God shall have............ Deut 6:10 3588
w thou shalt have eaten and be............ Deut 6:11
w thy son asketh thee in time to......... Deut 6:20 3588
W the LORD thy God shall bring............ Deut 7:1 3588
w the LORD thy God shall deliver.......... Deut 7:2
W thou hast eaten and art full,............. Deut 8:10
Lest *w* thou hast eaten and art.............. Deut 8:12
w thy herds and thy flocks..................... Deut 8:13
W I was gone up into the mount to...... Deut 9:9
Likewise *w* the LORD sent you from...... Deut 9:23
speaking of them *w* thou sittest............ Deut 11:19
w thou walkest by the way.................... Deut 11:19
w thou liest down.................................... Deut 11:19
and *w* thou risest up.............................. Deut 11:19
w the LORD thy God hath brought......... Deut 11:29 3588
But *w* ye go over Jordan, and dwell..... Deut 12:10
w he giveth you rest from all................ Deut 12:10
W the LORD thy God shall enlarge........ Deut 12:20 3588
w thou shalt do that which is................ Deut 12:25 3588
w thou doest that which is good............ Deut 12:28 3588
W the LORD thy God shall cut off........... Deut 12:29 3588
W thou shalt hearken to the voice....... Deut 13:18 3588
w the LORD thy God hath blessed......... Deut 14:24 3588
Save *w* there shall be no poor............... Deut 15:4 3588
be grieved *w* thou givest unto him........ Deut 15:10
w thou sendest him out free from......... Deut 15:13 3588
w thou sendest him away free from...... Deut 15:18
w thou camest forth out of the.............. Deut 16:3
W thou art come unto the land............. Deut 17:14 3588
w he sitteth upon the throne of............. Deut 17:18
W thou art come into the land.............. Deut 18:9 3588
W a prophet speaketh in the name......... Deut 18:22 834
W the LORD thy God hath cut off........... Deut 19:1 3588
As *w* a man goeth into the wood........... Deut 19:5 834
W thou goest out to battle...................... Deut 20:1 3588
w ye are come nigh unto the................. Deut 20:2
w the officers have made an end........... Deut 20:9
W thou comest nigh unto a city to........ Deut 20:10 3588
w the LORD thy God hath delivered...... Deut 20:13
W thou shalt besiege a city a................. Deut 20:19 3588
w thou shalt do that which is................. Deut 21:9 3588
W thou goest forth to war against........ Deut 21:10 3588
w he maketh his sons to inherit............ Deut 21:16 3117
w they have chastened him, will........... Deut 21:18
W thou buildest a new house, then...... Deut 22:8 3588
w I came to her, I found her not........... Deut 22:14
for as *w* a man riseth against his.......... Deut 22:26
w ye came forth out of Egypt................ Deut 23:4
W the host goeth forth against............... Deut 23:9 3588
w evening cometh on, he shall............... Deut 23:11
w the sun is down, he shall come......... Deut 23:11
w thou wilt ease thyself abroad,............. Deut 23:13
W thou shalt vow a vow unto the......... Deut 23:21 3588
W thou comest into thy.......................... Deut 23:24 3588
W thou comest into the standing.......... Deut 23:25 3588
W a man hath taken a wife, and........... Deut 24:1 3588
w she is departed out of his................... Deut 24:2
W a man hath taken a new wife, he..... Deut 24:5 3588
W thou dost lend thy brother any......... Deut 24:10 3588
pledge again *w* the sun goeth down..... Deut 24:13
W thou cuttest down thine harvest...... Deut 24:19 3588
W thou beatest thine olive tree,........... Deut 24:20 3588
W thou gatherest the grapes of............. Deut 24:21 3588
the ox *w* he treadeth out the corn........ Deut 25:4
W men strive together one with........... Deut 25:11 3588
w ye were come forth out of Egypt...... Deut 25:17
w thou wast faint and weary................. Deut 25:18
w the LORD thy God hath given............. Deut 25:19
w thou art come in unto the land.......... Deut 26:1 3588
w we cried unto the LORD God of.......... Deut 26:7
W thou hast made an end of.................. Deut 26:12 3588
it shall be on the day *w* ye shall............ Deut 27:2 834
w thou art passed over, that thou........ Deut 27:3
Therefore it shall be *w* ye be................. Deut 27:4
w ye are come over Jordan.................... Deut 27:12
shalt thou be *w* thou comest in............. Deut 28:6
shalt thou be *w* thou goest out.............. Deut 28:6
shalt thou be *w* thou comest in............. Deut 28:19
shalt thou be *w* thou goest out.............. Deut 28:19
w ye came unto this place, Sihon.......... Deut 29:7
w he heareth the words of this.............. Deut 29:19
w they see the plagues of that.............. Deut 29:22
which he made with them *w* he............. Deut 29:25
w all these things are come upon......... Deut 30:1 3588
W all Israel is come to appear............... Deut 31:11
For *w* I shall have brought them.......... Deut 31:20 3588
w many evils and troubles are.............. Deut 31:21 3588
w Moses had made an end of................ Deut 31:24
W the Most High divided to the............ Deut 32:8
w he separated the sons of Adam,......... Deut 32:8
w the LORD saw it, he abhorred............ Deut 32:19
w he seeth that their power is.............. Deut 32:36 3588
w the heads of the people and the........ Deut 33:5
and twenty years old *w* he died............ Deut 34:7
w it was dark, that the men went......... Josh 2:5
for you, *w* ye came out of Egypt........... Josh 2:10
w the LORD hath given us the land....... Josh 2:14
w we come into the land, thou.............. Josh 2:18
W ye see the ark of the covenant......... Josh 3:3
W ye are come to the brink of the........ Josh 3:8
w the people removed from their.......... Josh 3:14
w all the people were clean.................. Josh 4:1 834
that *w* your children ask their.............. Josh 4:6 3588
w it passed over Jordan, the................. Josh 4:7
w all the people were clean.................. Josh 4:11 834
w the priests that bare the ark............. Josh 4:18
W your children shall ask their............. Josh 4:21 834
w all the kings of the Amorites,............ Josh 5:1
w they had done circumcising all.......... Josh 5:8 834
w Joshua was by Jericho, that he......... Josh 5:13
that *w* they make a long blast............... Josh 6:5
w ye hear the sound of the................... Josh 6:5
w Joshua had spoken unto the.............. Josh 6:8
w the priests blew with the.................. Josh 6:16
w ye take of the accursed thing,........... Josh 6:18
So the people shouted *w* the................. Josh 6:20
w the people heard the sound of.......... Josh 6:20
w Israel turneth their backs.................. Josh 7:8 6310
W I saw among the spoils a goodly...... Josh 7:21
w they come out against us, as at......... Josh 8:5 3588
w ye have taken the city, that ye.......... Josh 8:8
w they had set the people, even........... Josh 8:13
w the king of Ai saw it, that................. Josh 8:14
w the men of Ai looked behind............. Josh 8:20
w Joshua and all Israel saw that........... Josh 8:21
w Israel had made an end of................. Josh 8:24
w they were all fallen on the................. Josh 8:24
w all the kings which were on.............. Josh 9:1
w the inhabitants of Gibeon heard....... Josh 9:3
w ye dwell among us............................ Josh 9:22
w Adoni-zedek king of Jerusalem......... Josh 10:1 3588
day *w* the LORD delivered up the........... Josh 10:12
w Joshua and the children of............... Josh 10:20
w they brought out those kings........... Josh 10:24
w Jabin king of Hazor had heard.......... Josh 11:1
w all these kings were met.................. Josh 11:5
Forty years old was I *w* Moses the....... Josh 14:7
w the children of Israel were................ Josh 17:13 3588
W they had made an end of.................. Josh 19:49
w he that doth flee unto one of............. Josh 20:4
w Joshua sent them away also unto..... Josh 22:7 3588
w they came unto the borders of......... Josh 22:10
w the children of Israel heard of.......... Josh 22:12
w they should so say to us or to.......... Josh 22:28 3588
w Phinehas the priest, and the............ Josh 22:30
W ye have transgressed the................. Josh 23:16
w they cried unto the LORD, he............ Josh 24:7
w she came to him, that she moved..... Judg 1:14
w he shewed them the entrance........... Judg 1:25
w Israel was strong, that they.............. Judg 1:28
w the angel of the LORD spake.............. Judg 2:4
w Joshua had let the people go,........... Judg 2:6
w the LORD raised them up judges,....... Judg 2:18 3588
w the judge was dead, that they........... Judg 2:19
which Joshua left *w* he died................. Judg 2:21
w the children of Israel cried............... Judg 3:9
But *w* the children of Israel................... Judg 3:15
w he had made an end to offer the....... Judg 3:18 834
W he was gone out, his servants.......... Judg 3:24
w they saw that, behold, the............... Judg 3:24
w he was come, that he blew a............ Judg 3:27
of the LORD, *w* Ehud was dead............. Judg 4:1
w he had turned in unto her into.......... Judg 4:18
w any man doth come and enquire of. Judg 4:20 518
w he came into her tent, behold,......... Judg 4:22
w the people willingly offered............. Judg 5:2
w thou wentest out of Seir.................. Judg 5:4
w thou marchedst out of the field......... Judg 5:4
w she had pierced and stricken........... Judg 5:26
sun *w* he goeth forth in his might........ Judg 5:31
w Israel had sown, that the................ Judg 6:3 518
w the children of Israel cried............... Judg 6:7 3588
w Gideon perceived that he was an...... Judg 6:22
w the men of the city arose early......... Judg 6:28
w they enquired and asked, they.......... Judg 6:29
w Gideon was come, behold, there........ Judg 7:13
w Gideon heard the telling of the......... Judg 7:15
w I come to the outside of the.............. Judg 7:17
W I blow with a trumpet, I and all....... Judg 7:18
w thou wentest to fight with the.......... Judg 8:1 3588
toward him, *w* he had said that............. Judg 8:3
Therefore *w* the LORD hath.................... Judg 8:7
W I come again in peace, I will............. Judg 8:9
w Zebah and Zalmunna fled, he........... Judg 8:12
w they told it to Jotham, he went......... Judg 9:7
W Abimelech had reigned three........... Judg 9:22
w Zebul the ruler of the city............... Judg 9:30
w he and the people that is with.......... Judg 9:33
w Gaal saw the people, he said to........ Judg 9:36
w all the men of the tower of.............. Judg 9:46
w the men of Israel saw that............... Judg 9:55
that *w* the children of Ammon made.... Judg 11:5 834
unto me now *w* ye are in distress........ Judg 11:7 834
w they came up out of Egypt, from....... Judg 11:13
But *w* Israel came up from Egypt,......... Judg 11:16
w I return in peace from the.............. Judg 11:31
w he saw her, that he rent his............. Judg 11:35
w I called you, ye delivered me........... Judg 12:2
w I saw that ye delivered me not,......... Judg 12:3
that *w* those Ephraimites which............. Judg 12:5
that *w* thy sayings come to pass.......... Judg 13:17 3588
w the flame went up toward heaven.... Judg 13:20
w they saw him, that they brought....... Judg 14:11
w he had set the brands on fire........... Judg 15:5
And *w* he came unto Lehi, the.............. Judg 15:14
w he had made an end of speaking,..... Judg 15:17
w he had drunk, his spirit came.......... Judg 15:19
w it is day, we shall kill him................. Judg 16:2 5704
is broken *w* it toucheth the fire........... Judg 16:9
w thine heart is not with me............... Judg 16:15
w she pressed him daily with her......... Judg 16:16 3588
w Delilah saw that he had told............ Judg 16:18
w the people saw him, they................. Judg 16:24
w their hearts were merry, that........... Judg 16:25 3588
w he had restored the eleven.............. Judg 17:3
who *w* they came to mount Ephraim,.. Judg 18:2
W they were by the house of Micah.... Judg 18:3
W ye go, ye shall come unto a............. Judg 18:10
w they were a good way from the....... Judg 18:22
w Micah saw that they were too........... Judg 18:26
w there was no king in Israel,.............. Judg 19:1
w the father of the damsel saw........... Judg 19:3
w they arose early in the morning....... Judg 19:5
w the man rose up to depart, his.......... Judg 19:7
w the man rose up to depart, he,......... Judg 19:9
w they were by Jebus, the day was...... Judg 19:11
upon them *w* they were by Gibeah........ Judg 19:14
w he went in, he sat him down in........ Judg 19:15
w he had lifted up his eyes, he............. Judg 19:17
w the day began to spring, they........... Judg 19:25
w he was come into his house, he........ Judg 19:29
w they come to Gibeah of Benjamin..... Judg 20:10
w the men of Israel retired in.............. Judg 20:39
But *w* the flame began to arise up....... Judg 20:40
w the men of Israel turned again,......... Judg 20:41
w their fathers or their brethren.......... Judg 21:22 3588
in the days *w* the judges ruled............. Ruth 1:1
W she saw that she was stedfastly....... Ruth 1:18
w they were come to Beth-lehem,......... Ruth 1:19
w thou art athirst, go unto the............. Ruth 2:9
w she was risen up to glean, Boaz....... Ruth 2:15
w he lieth down, that thou shalt........... Ruth 3:4
w Boaz had eaten and drunk, and his.. Ruth 3:7
w she held it, he measured six............. Ruth 3:15
w she came to her mother in law,......... Ruth 3:16
w he went in unto her, the LORD.......... Ruth 4:13
w the time was that Elkanah................ 1Sa 1:4
w she went up to the house of the....... 1Sa 1:7 1767
w the time was come about after.......... 1Sa 1:20
w she had weaned him, she took......... 1Sa 1:24 834
w any man offered sacrifice, the........... 1Sa 2:13
w she came up with her husband to..... 1Sa 2:19
w they were in Egypt in Pharaoh's....... 1Sa 2:27
w Eli was laid down in his place,......... 1Sa 3:2
w I begin, I will also make an............... 1Sa 3:12
w they joined battle, Israel was............ 1Sa 4:2
w the people were come into the.......... 1Sa 4:3
w it cometh among us, it may save...... 1Sa 4:3
w the ark of the covenant of the.......... 1Sa 4:5
w the Philistines heard the noise.......... 1Sa 4:6
w he came, lo, Eli sat upon a............... 1Sa 4:13
w the man came into the city, and........ 1Sa 4:13
w Eli heard the noise of the................. 1Sa 4:14
w he made mention of the ark of.......... 1Sa 4:18
w she heard the tidings that the........... 1Sa 4:19
W the Philistines took the ark of.......... 1Sa 5:2
w they of Ashdod arose early on........... 1Sa 5:3
w they arose early on the morrow........ 1Sa 5:4
w the men of Ashdod saw that it........... 1Sa 5:7
w he had wrought wonderfully.............. 1Sa 6:6 834
And *w* the five lords of the................... 1Sa 6:16
w the Philistines heard that the............ 1Sa 7:7
w the children of Israel heard it............ 1Sa 7:7
w Samuel was old, that he made.......... 1Sa 8:1 834
w they said, Give us a king to.............. 1Sa 8:6 834
w they were come to the land of......... 1Sa 9:5
w a man went to enquire of God,......... 1Sa 9:9
w they were come into the city,............ 1Sa 9:14
w Samuel saw Saul, the LORD said....... 1Sa 9:17
w they were come down from the......... 1Sa 9:25
W thou art departed from me to........... 1Sa 10:2
w thou art come thither to the............. 1Sa 10:5
w these signs are come unto thee,........ 1Sa 10:7 3588
that *w* he had turned his back to........... 1Sa 10:9
w they came thither to the hill,............. 1Sa 10:10
w all that knew him beforetime............. 1Sa 10:11
And *w* he had made an end of............... 1Sa 10:13
w we saw that they were no where,....... 1Sa 10:14
w Samuel had caused all the................ 1Sa 10:20
W he had caused the tribe of................ 1Sa 10:21
w they sought him, he could not........... 1Sa 10:21
w he stood among the people, he......... 1Sa 10:23
Saul *w* he heard those tidings.............. 1Sa 11:6
w he numbered them in Bezek, the....... 1Sa 11:8
W Jacob was come into Egypt, and...... 1Sa 12:8 834
w they forgat the LORD their God,......... 1Sa 12:9
w ye saw that Nahash the king of........ 1Sa 12:12
w the LORD your God was your king... 1Sa 12:12
w he had reigned two years over......... 1Sa 13:1
W the men of Israel saw that they....... 1Sa 13:6
w they had numbered, behold,.............. 1Sa 14:17
w they heard that the Philistines.......... 1Sa 14:22
w the people were come into the......... 1Sa 14:26
But Jonathan heard not *w* his............... 1Sa 14:27
w Saul saw any strong man, or any..... 1Sa 14:52
the way, *w* he came up from Egypt...... 1Sa 15:2
w they came up out of Egypt............... 1Sa 15:6
w Samuel rose early to meet Saul........ 1Sa 15:12
W thou wast little in thine own............. 1Sa 15:17 518
w they were come, that he looked........ 1Sa 16:6
w the evil spirit from God is.................. 1Sa 16:16
w the evil spirit from God was.............. 1Sa 16:23
W Saul and all Israel heard those........ 1Sa 17:11
w they saw the man, fled from him...... 1Sa 17:24
heard *w* he spake unto the men............ 1Sa 17:28
w the words were heard which............. 1Sa 17:31
w he arose against me, I caught........... 1Sa 17:35
w the Philistine looked about, and........ 1Sa 17:42
w the Philistine arose, and came.......... 1Sa 17:48 3588
w the Philistines saw their..................... 1Sa 17:51
W Saul saw David go forth against....... 1Sa 17:55
w he had made an end of speaking...... 1Sa 18:1
w David was returned from the............ 1Sa 18:6
Wherefore *w* Saul saw that he............. 1Sa 18:15
w Merab Saul's daughter should........... 1Sa 18:19

W

w his servants told David these... 1Sa 18:26
w Saul sent messengers to take... 1Sa 19:14
w the messengers were come in,... 1Sa 19:16
w they saw the company of the... 1Sa 19:20
w it was told Saul, he sent other... 1Sa 19:21
w I have sounded my father about... 1Sa 20:12 3588
not *w* the LORD hath cut off the... 1Sa 20:15
w thou hast stayed three days,... 1Sa 20:19
w the business was in hand... 1Sa 20:19
w the new moon was come, the king... 1Sa 20:24
w the lad was come to the place... 1Sa 20:37
in the day *w* it was taken away... 1Sa 21:6
w his brethren and all his... 1Sa 22:1
W Saul heard that David was... 1Sa 22:6
and because they knew *w* he fled... 1Sa 22:17 3588
w Doeg the Edomite was there,... 1Sa 22:22 3588
w Abiathar the son of Ahimelech... 1Sa 23:6
w Saul heard that, he pursued... 1Sa 23:25
to pass, *w* Saul was returned from... 1Sa 24:1 834
w Saul looked behind him, David... 1Sa 24:8
w David had made an end of... 1Sa 24:16
forasmuch as *w* the LORD had... 1Sa 24:18
w David's young men came, they... 1Sa 25:9
them, *w* we were in the fields... 1Sa 25:15
w Abigail saw David, she hasted,... 1Sa 25:23
w the LORD shall have done to my... 1Sa 25:30 3588
but *w* the LORD shall have dealt... 1Sa 25:31
w the wine was gone out of Nabal,... 1Sa 25:37
w David heard that Nabal was dead... 1Sa 25:39
w the servants of David were come... 1Sa 25:40
as *w* one doth hunt a partridge in... 1Sa 26:20 834
w Saul saw the host of the... 1Sa 28:5
w Saul enquired of the LORD, the... 1Sa 28:6
w the woman saw Samuel, she cried... 1Sa 28:12
strength, *w* thou goest on thy way... 1Sa 28:22 3588
w David and his men were come to... 1Sa 30:1
w he had eaten, his spirit came... 1Sa 30:12
w he had brought him down, behold... 1Sa 30:16
w David came near to the people,... 1Sa 30:21
w David came to Ziklag, he sent... 1Sa 30:26
w his armourbearer saw that Saul... 1Sa 31:5
w the men of Israel that were on... 1Sa 31:7
w the Philistines came to strip... 1Sa 31:8
And *w* the inhabitants of... 1Sa 31:11
w David was returned from the... 2Sa 1:1
w he came to David, that he fell... 2Sa 1:2
w he looked behind him, he saw me... 2Sa 1:7
w he began to reign over Israel... 2Sa 2:10
the sun went down *w* they were... 2Sa 2:24
w he had gathered all the people... 2Sa 2:30
w thou comest to see my face... 2Sa 3:13
W Joab and all the host that was... 2Sa 3:23
w Joab was come out from David,... 2Sa 3:26
w Abner was returned to Hebron,... 2Sa 3:27
afterward *w* David heard it, he... 2Sa 3:28
w all the people came to cause... 2Sa 3:35
w Saul's son heard that Abner was... 2Sa 4:1
He was five years old *w* the... 2Sa 4:4
For *w* they came into the house,... 2Sa 4:7
W one told me, saying, Behold,... 2Sa 4:10
w wicked men have slain a... 2Sa 4:11 3588
w Saul was king over us, thou... 2Sa 5:2
years old *w* he began to reign... 2Sa 5:4 3588
But *w* the Philistines heard that... 2Sa 5:17
w David enquired of the LORD, he... 2Sa 5:23
w thou hearest the sound of a... 2Sa 5:24
And *w* they came to Nachon's... 2Sa 6:6
that *w* they that bare the ark of... 2Sa 6:13 3588
w the king sat in his house, and... 2Sa 7:1 3588
w thy days be fulfilled, and thou... 2Sa 7:12 3588
w the Syrians of Damascus came to... 2Sa 8:5
W Toi king of Hamath heard that... 2Sa 8:9
David gat him a name *w* he... 2Sa 8:13
w they had called him unto David,... 2Sa 9:2
Now *w* Mephibosheth, the son of... 2Sa 9:6
W they told it unto David, he... 2Sa 10:5
w the children of Ammon saw that... 2Sa 10:6
w David heard of it, he sent Joab... 2Sa 10:7
W Joab saw that the front of the... 2Sa 10:9
w the children of Ammon saw that... 2Sa 10:14
w the Syrians saw that they were... 2Sa 10:15
w it was told David, he gathered... 2Sa 10:17
w all the kings that were... 2Sa 10:19
at the time *w* kings go forth to... 2Sa 11:1
w Uriah was come unto him, David... 2Sa 11:7
w they had told David, saying,... 2Sa 11:10
w David had called him, he did... 2Sa 11:13 3588
w Joab observed the city, that he... 2Sa 11:16
W thou hast made an end of... 2Sa 11:19
nigh unto the city *w* ye did fight... 2Sa 11:20
w the wife of Uriah heard that... 2Sa 11:26
w the mourning was past, David... 2Sa 11:27
But *w* David saw that his servants... 2Sa 12:19
w he required, they set bread... 2Sa 12:20
but *w* the child was dead, thou... 2Sa 12:21 834
w thy father cometh to see thee,... 2Sa 13:5
w the king was come to see him,... 2Sa 13:6
w she had brought them unto him... 2Sa 13:11
But *w* king David heard of all... 2Sa 13:21
Mark ye now *w* Amnon's heart is... 2Sa 13:28
w I say unto you, Smite Amnon... 2Sa 13:28
w the woman of Tekoah spake to... 2Sa 14:4
w he polled his head, (for it was... 2Sa 14:26
w he sent again the second time,... 2Sa 14:29
w he had called for Absalom, he... 2Sa 14:33
that *w* any man that had a... 2Sa 15:2
that *w* any man came nigh to him... 2Sa 15:5
that *w* David was come to the top... 2Sa 15:32
w David was a little past the top... 2Sa 16:1
w king David came to Bahurim,... 2Sa 16:5
And thus said Shimei *w* he cursed... 2Sa 16:7
w Hushai the Archite, David's... 2Sa 16:16 834
w Hushai was come to Absalom,... 2Sa 17:6
w some of them be overthrown at... 2Sa 17:9
w Absalom's servants came to the... 2Sa 17:20
w they had sought and could not... 2Sa 17:20
w Ahithophel saw that his counsel... 2Sa 17:23
w David was come to Mahanaim,... 2Sa 17:27
all the people heard *w* the king... 2Sa 18:5
W Joab sent the king's servant,... 2Sa 18:29
steal away *w* they flee in battle... 2Sa 19:3
w he was come to Jerusalem to... 2Sa 19:25 3588
w the king was come over, the... 2Sa 19:39
W they were at the great stone... 2Sa 20:8
w the man saw that all the people... 2Sa 20:12
w he saw that every one that came... 2Sa 20:12
W he was removed out of the... 2Sa 20:13
w he was come near unto her, the... 2Sa 20:17
w the Philistines had slain Saul... 2Sa 21:12 3117
w he defied Israel, Jonathan the... 2Sa 21:21
W the waves of death compassed me... 2Sa 22:5 3588
w the sun riseth, even a morning... 2Sa 23:4
w they defied the Philistines... 2Sa 23:9
So *w* they had gone through all... 2Sa 24:8
For *w* David was up in the morning... 2Sa 24:11
w the angel stretched out his... 2Sa 24:16
David spake unto the LORD *w* he... 2Sa 24:17
w my lord the king shall sleep... 1Kin 1:21
w he was come in before the king,... 1Kin 1:23
w Joab heard the sound of the... 1Kin 1:41
for so they came to me *w* I fled... 1Kin 2:7
in the day *w* I went to Mahanaim... 1Kin 2:8
w I rose in the morning to give... 1Kin 3:21
but *w* I had considered it in the... 1Kin 3:21
w Hiram heard the words of... 1Kin 5:7
w it was in building, was built... 1Kin 6:7
cast in two rows, *w* it was cast... 1Kin 7:24
w the LORD made a covenant with... 1Kin 8:9 834
w they came out of the land of... 1Kin 8:9
w the priests were come out of... 1Kin 8:10
w he brought them out of the land... 1Kin 8:21
w they shall pray toward this... 1Kin 8:30 834
and *w* thou hearest, forgive... 1Kin 8:30
W thy people Israel be smitten... 1Kin 8:33
W heaven is shut up, and there is... 1Kin 8:35
their sin, *w* thou afflictest them... 1Kin 8:35 3588
w he shall come and pray toward... 1Kin 8:42
w thou broughtest our fathers out... 1Kin 8:53
that *w* Solomon had made an end of... 1Kin 8:54
w Solomon had finished the... 1Kin 9:1
w Solomon had built the two... 1Kin 9:10
w the queen of Sheba heard of the... 1Kin 10:1
w she was come to Solomon, she... 1Kin 10:2
w the queen of Sheba had seen all... 1Kin 10:4
w Solomon was old, that his wives... 1Kin 11:4 6256
w David was in Edom, and Joab the... 1Kin 11:15
w Hadad heard in Egypt that David... 1Kin 11:21
w David slew them of Zobah... 1Kin 11:24
it came to pass at that time *w*... 1Kin 11:29
w Jeroboam the son of Nebat, who... 1Kin 12:2
So *w* all Israel saw that the king... 1Kin 12:16
w all Israel heard that Jeroboam... 1Kin 12:20
w Rehoboam was come to Jerusalem,... 1Kin 12:21
w king Jeroboam heard the saying... 1Kin 13:4
w he was gone, a lion met him by... 1Kin 13:24
w the prophet that brought him... 1Kin 13:26
W I am dead, then bury me in the... 1Kin 13:31
w she cometh in, that she shall... 1Kin 14:5
w Ahijah heard the sound of her... 1Kin 14:6
w thy feet enter into the city,... 1Kin 14:12
w she came to the threshold of... 1Kin 14:17
one years old *w* he began to reign... 1Kin 14:21
w the king went into the house of... 1Kin 14:28 1767
w Baasha heard thereof, that he... 1Kin 15:21
w he reigned, that he smote all... 1Kin 15:29
w he began to reign, as soon as... 1Kin 16:11
w Zimri saw that the city was... 1Kin 16:18
w he came to the gate of the city... 1Kin 17:10
w Jezebel cut off the prophets of... 1Kin 18:4
w they said, He is not there... 1Kin 18:10
so *w* I come and tell Ahab, and he... 1Kin 18:12
w Jezebel slew the prophets of... 1Kin 18:13
w Ahab saw Elijah, that Ahab said... 1Kin 18:17
w midday was past, and they... 1Kin 18:29
w all the people saw it, they... 1Kin 18:39
w he saw that, he arose, and went... 1Kin 19:3
w Elijah heard it, that he... 1Kin 19:13
w thou comest, anoint Hazael to... 1Kin 19:15
w Ben-hadad heard this message,... 1Kin 20:12
w Jezebel heard that Naboth was... 1Kin 21:15
w Ahab heard that Naboth was dead... 1Kin 21:16 3588
w Ahab heard those words, that he... 1Kin 21:27
w thou shalt go into an inner... 1Kin 22:25 834
w the captains of the chariots... 1Kin 22:32
w the captains of the chariots... 1Kin 22:33
five years old *w* he began to... 1Kin 22:42
w the messengers turned back unto... 2Kin 1:5
w the LORD would take up Elijah... 2Kin 2:1
w they were gone over, that... 2Kin 2:9
if thou see me *w* I am taken from... 2Kin 2:10
w he also had smitten the waters,... 2Kin 2:14
w the sons of the prophets which... 2Kin 2:15
w they urged him till he was... 2Kin 2:17
w they came again to him, (for he... 2Kin 2:18
w Ahab was dead, that the king of... 2Kin 3:5
w the minstrel played, that the... 2Kin 3:15
w the meat offering was offered,... 2Kin 3:20
w all the Moabites heard that the... 2Kin 3:21
w they came to the camp of Israel... 2Kin 3:24
w the king of Moab saw that the... 2Kin 3:26
w thou art come in, thou shalt... 2Kin 4:4
w the vessels were full, that she... 2Kin 4:6
w he cometh to us, that he shall... 2Kin 4:10
w he had called her, she stood... 2Kin 4:12
w he had called her, she stood in... 2Kin 4:15
w the child was grown, it fell on... 2Kin 4:18
w he had taken him, and brought... 2Kin 4:20
w the man of God saw her afar off... 2Kin 4:25
w she came to the man of God to... 2Kin 4:27
w Elisha was come into the house,... 2Kin 4:32
w she was come in unto him, he... 2Kin 4:36
Now *w* this letter is come unto... 2Kin 5:6
w the king of Israel had read the... 2Kin 5:7
w Elisha the man of God had heard... 2Kin 5:8
w he saith to thee, Wash, and be... 2Kin 5:13 3588
that *w* my master goeth into the... 2Kin 5:18
w I bow down myself in the house... 2Kin 5:18
w Naaman saw him running after... 2Kin 5:21
w he came to the tower, he took... 2Kin 5:24
w the man turned again from his... 2Kin 5:26
w they came to Jordan, they cut... 2Kin 6:4
w the servant of the man of God... 2Kin 6:15
w they came down to him, Elisha... 2Kin 6:18
w they were come into Samaria,... 2Kin 6:20
w he saw them, My father, shall I... 2Kin 6:21
w they had eaten and drunk, he... 2Kin 6:23
w the king heard the words of the... 2Kin 6:30
w the messenger cometh, shut the... 2Kin 6:32
w they were come to the uttermost... 2Kin 7:5
w these lepers came to the... 2Kin 7:8 3588
W they come out of the city, we... 2Kin 7:12 3588
who spake *w* the king came down to... 2Kin 7:17
w the king asked the woman, she... 2Kin 8:6
old was he *w* he began to reign... 2Kin 8:17
was Ahaziah *w* he began to reign... 2Kin 8:26
w he fought against Hazael king... 2Kin 8:29
w thou comest thither, look out... 2Kin 9:2
w he came, behold, the captains... 2Kin 9:5 3588
w he fought with Hazael king of... 2Kin 9:15
w Joram saw Jehu, that he said,... 2Kin 9:22
w I and thou rode together after... 2Kin 9:25
But *w* Ahaziah the king of Judah... 2Kin 9:27
w Jehu was come to Jezreel,... 2Kin 9:30
w he was come in, he did eat and... 2Kin 9:34
w the letter came to them, that... 2Kin 10:7
w he was departed thence, he... 2Kin 10:15
w he came to Samaria, he slew all... 2Kin 10:17
And *w* they went in to offer... 2Kin 10:24 3588
w Athaliah the mother of Ahaziah... 2Kin 11:1
w Athaliah heard the noise of the... 2Kin 11:13
w she looked, behold, the king... 2Kin 11:14
was Jehoash *w* he began to reign... 2Kin 11:21
w they saw that there was much... 2Kin 12:10
w the man was let down, and... 2Kin 13:21
five years old *w* he began to... 2Kin 14:2
old was he *w* he began to reign... 2Kin 15:2
old was he *w* he began to reign... 2Kin 15:33
old was Ahaz *w* he began to reign... 2Kin 16:2
w the king was come from Damascus... 2Kin 16:12
old was he *w* he began to reign... 2Kin 18:2
w they were come up, they came and... 2Kin 18:17
w they had called to the king,... 2Kin 18:18
w he persuadeth you, saying, The... 2Kin 18:32 3588
w king Hezekiah heard it, that he... 2Kin 19:1
w he heard say of Tirhakah king... 2Kin 19:9
w they arose early in the morning... 2Kin 19:35
years old *w* he began to reign... 2Kin 21:1
two years old *w* he began to reign... 2Kin 21:19
years old *w* he began to reign... 2Kin 22:1
w the king had heard the words of... 2Kin 22:11
w thou heardest what I spake... 2Kin 22:19
him at Megiddo, *w* he had seen him... 2Kin 23:29
three years old *w* he began to... 2Kin 23:31
five years old *w* he began to... 2Kin 23:36
years old *w* he began to reign... 2Kin 24:8
one years old *w* he began to reign... 2Kin 24:18
w all the captains of the armies,... 2Kin 25:23
w Bela was dead, Jobab the son of... 1Chr 1:44
w Jobab was dead, Husham of the... 1Chr 1:45
w Husham was dead, Hadad the son... 1Chr 1:46
w Hadad was dead, Samlah of... 1Chr 1:47
w Samlah was dead, Shaul of... 1Chr 1:48
w Shaul was dead, Baal-hanan the... 1Chr 1:49
w Baal-hanan was dead, Hadad... 1Chr 1:50
w Azubah was dead, Caleb took... 1Chr 2:19
Gilead, whom he married *w* he was... 1Chr 2:21
w the genealogy of their... 1Chr 5:7
w the LORD carried away Judah and... 1Chr 6:15
w he went in to his wife, she... 1Chr 7:23 3588
w his armourbearer saw that Saul... 1Chr 10:5
w all the men of Israel that were... 1Chr 10:7
w the Philistines came to strip... 1Chr 10:8
w they had stripped him, they... 1Chr 10:9
w all Jabesh-gilead heard all... 1Chr 10:11
even *w* Saul was king, thou wast... 1Chr 11:2
w it had overflown all his banks... 1Chr 12:15
w he came with the Philistines... 1Chr 12:19
And *w* they came unto the... 1Chr 13:9
w the Philistines heard that... 1Chr 14:8
w they had left their gods there,... 1Chr 14:12
w thou shalt hear a sound of... 1Chr 14:15
w God helped the Levites that... 1Chr 15:26
w David had made an end of... 1Chr 16:2
W ye were but few, even a few, and... 1Chr 16:19
w they went from nation to nation... 1Chr 16:20
w thy days be expired that thou... 1Chr 17:11 3588
w the Syrians of Damascus came to... 1Chr 18:5
Now *w* Tou king of Hamath heard... 1Chr 18:9
w the children of Ammon saw that... 1Chr 19:6
w David heard of it, he sent Joab... 1Chr 19:8
Now *w* Joab saw that the battle... 1Chr 19:10
w the children of Ammon saw that... 1Chr 19:15
w the Syrians saw that they were... 1Chr 19:16
So *w* David had put the battle in... 1Chr 19:17
w the servants of Hadarezer saw... 1Chr 19:19
But *w* he defied Israel, Jonathan... 1Chr 20:7
At that time *w* David saw that the... 1Chr 21:28
So *w* David was old and full of... 1Chr 23:1
of oxen were cast, *w* it was cast... 2Chr 4:3
w the LORD made a covenant with... 2Chr 5:10 834
Israel, *w* they came out of Egypt... 2Chr 5:10
w the priests were come out of... 2Chr 5:11

w they lifted up their voice with	2Chr 5:13	
and *w* thou hearest, forgive	2Chr 6:21	
W the heaven is shut up, and there	2Chr 6:26	
sin, *w* thou dost afflict them	2Chr 6:26	3588
w thou hast taught them the good	2Chr 6:27	3588
w every one shall know his own	2Chr 6:29	834
Now *w* Solomon had made an end of	2Chr 7:1	
w all the children of Israel saw	2Chr 7:3	
w David praised by their ministry	2Chr 7:6	
w the queen of Sheba heard of the	2Chr 9:1	
w she was come to Solomon, she	2Chr 9:1	
w the queen of Sheba had seen the	2Chr 9:3	
w Jeroboam the son of Nebat, who	2Chr 10:2	
w all Israel saw that the king	2Chr 10:16	
w Rehoboam was come to Jerusalem,	2Chr 11:1	
w Rehoboam had established the	2Chr 12:1	
w the LORD saw that they humbled	2Chr 12:7	
w the king entered into the house	2Chr 12:11	1767
w he humbled himself, the wrath	2Chr 12:12	
forty years old *w* he began to	2Chr 12:13	
w Rehoboam was young and	2Chr 13:7	
w Judah looked back, behold, the	2Chr 13:14	
But *w* they in their trouble did	2Chr 15:4	
w Asa heard these words, and the	2Chr 15:8	
w they saw that the LORD his God	2Chr 15:9	
w Baasha heard it, that he left	2Chr 16:5	
w he was come to the king, the	2Chr 18:14	
thou shalt see on that day *w* thou	2Chr 18:24	834
w the captains of the chariots	2Chr 18:31	
w the captains of the chariots	2Chr 18:32	
w they returned to Jerusalem	2Chr 19:8	
w evil cometh upon us, as the	2Chr 20:9	
w they came out of the land of	2Chr 20:10	
w he had consulted with the	2Chr 20:21	
w they began to sing and to praise	2Chr 20:22	6256
w they had made an end of the	2Chr 20:23	
w Judah came toward the watch	2Chr 20:24	
w Jehoshaphat and his people came	2Chr 20:25	
w they had heard that the LORD	2Chr 20:29	
five years old *w* he began to	2Chr 20:31	
Now *w* Jehoram was risen up to the	2Chr 21:4	
two years old *w* he began to reign	2Chr 21:5	
old was he *w* he began to reign	2Chr 21:20	
was Ahaziah *w* he began to reign	2Chr 22:2	
w he fought with Hazael king of	2Chr 22:6	
for *w* he was come, he went out	2Chr 22:7	
w Jehu was executing judgment	2Chr 22:8	
w they had slain him, they buried	2Chr 22:9	
But *w* Athaliah the mother of	2Chr 22:10	
ye with the king *w* he cometh in	2Chr 23:7	
he cometh in, and *w* he goeth out	2Chr 23:7	
Now *w* Athaliah heard the noise of	2Chr 23:12	
w she was come to the entering of	2Chr 23:15	
years old *w* he began to reign	2Chr 24:1	
w they saw that there was much	2Chr 24:11	3588
w they had finished it, they	2Chr 24:14	
and was full of days *w* he died	2Chr 24:15	
thirty years old was he *w* he died	2Chr 24:15	
w he died, he said, The LORD look	2Chr 24:22	
w they were departed from him,	2Chr 24:25	
five years old *w* he began to	2Chr 25:1	
w the kingdom was established to	2Chr 25:3	834
was Uzziah *w* he began to reign	2Chr 26:3	
But *w* he was strong, his heart	2Chr 26:16	
five years old *w* he began to	2Chr 27:1	
twenty years old *w* he began to	2Chr 27:8	
years old *w* he began to reign	2Chr 28:1	
began to reign *w* he was five	2Chr 29:1	
w they had killed the rams, they	2Chr 29:22	
w the burnt offering began, the	2Chr 29:27	6256
w they had made an end of	2Chr 29:29	
Now *w* all this was finished, all	2Chr 31:1	
w Hezekiah and the princes came and	2Chr 31:8	
w Hezekiah saw that Sennacherib	2Chr 32:2	
w he was come into the house of	2Chr 32:21	
years old *w* he began to reign	2Chr 33:1	
w he was in affliction, he	2Chr 33:12	
twenty years old *w* he began to	2Chr 33:21	
years old *w* he began to reign	2Chr 34:1	
w he had broken down the altars	2Chr 34:7	
w he had purged the land, and the	2Chr 34:8	
w they came to Hilkiah the high	2Chr 34:9	
w they brought out the money that	2Chr 34:14	
w the king had heard the words of	2Chr 34:19	
w thou heardest his words against	2Chr 34:27	
w Josiah had prepared the temple,	2Chr 35:20	834
three years old *w* he began to	2Chr 36:2	
five years old *w* he began to	2Chr 36:5	
years old *w* he began to reign	2Chr 36:9	
w the year was expired, king	2Chr 36:10	
twenty years old *w* he began to	2Chr 36:11	
w they came to the house of the	Ezr 2:68	
w the seventh month was come, and	Ezr 3:1	
And *w* the builders laid the	Ezr 3:10	
w they praised the LORD, because	Ezr 3:11	
w the foundation of this house	Ezr 3:12	3588
Now *w* the adversaries of Judah and	Ezr 4:1	
Now *w* the copy of king	Ezr 4:23	
Now *w* these things were done, the	Ezr 9:1	3588
w I heard this thing, I rent my	Ezr 9:3	3588
Now *w* Ezra had prayed	Ezr 10:1	
w he had confessed, weeping and	Ezr 10:1	
w he came thither, he did eat no	Ezr 10:6	
w I heard these words, that I sat	Neh 1:4	
w the city, the place of my	Neh 2:3	834
and *w* wilt thou return	Neh 2:6	4970
W Sanballat the Horonite, and	Neh 2:10	
But *w* Sanballat the Horonite, and	Neh 2:19	
that *w* Sanballat heard that we	Neh 4:1	834
that *w* Sanballat, and Tobiah, and	Neh 4:7	834
that *w* the Jews which dwelt by	Neh 4:12	834
w our enemies heard that it was	Neh 4:15	834
I was very angry *w* I heard their	Neh 5:6	834
w Sanballat, and Tobiah, and Geshem	Neh 6:1	834
that *w* all our enemies heard	Neh 6:16	834
w the wall was built, and I had	Neh 7:1	834
w the seventh month came, the	Neh 7:73	
w he opened it, all the people	Neh 8:5	
w they heard the words of the law	Neh 8:9	
w they had made them a molten	Neh 9:18	3588
w they cried unto thee, thou	Neh 9:27	
yet *w* they returned, and cried	Neh 9:28	
w the Levites take tithes	Neh 10:38	
w they had heard the law, that	Neh 13:3	
that *w* the gates of Jerusalem	Neh 13:19	834
w the king Ahasuerus sat on the	Est 1:2	
W he shewed the riches of his	Est 1:4	
w these days were expired, the	Est 1:5	
w the heart of the king was merry	Est 1:10	
w it shall be reported, The king	Est 1:17	
w the king's decree which he	Est 1:20	
w the wrath of king Ahasuerus was	Est 2:1	
w her father and mother were dead,	Est 2:7	
w the king's commandment and his	Est 2:8	
w many maidens were gathered	Est 2:8	
Now *w* every maid's turn was come	Est 2:12	
Now *w* the turn of Esther, the	Est 2:15	
w the virgins were gathered	Est 2:19	
like as *w* she was brought up with	Est 2:20	
w inquisition was made of the	Est 2:23	
w they spake daily unto him, and	Est 3:4	
w Haman saw that Mordecai bowed	Est 3:5	
W Mordecai perceived all that was	Est 4:1	
w the king saw Esther the queen	Est 5:2	
but *w* Haman saw Mordecai in the	Est 5:9	
w he came home, he sent and called	Est 5:10	
w the king's commandment and his	Est 9:1	834
But *w* Esther came before the king	Est 9:25	
w the days of their feasting were	Job 1:5	3588
Now there was a day *w* the sons of	Job 1:6	
And there was a day *w* his sons	Job 1:13	
Again there was a day *w* the sons	Job 2:1	
Now *w* Job's three friends heard	Job 2:11	
w they lifted up their eyes afar	Job 2:12	
ghost *w* I came out of the belly	Job 3:11	
w they can find the grave	Job 3:22	3588
w deep sleep falleth on men,	Job 4:13	
afraid of destruction *w* it cometh	Job 5:21	3588
the wild ass bray *w* he hath grass	Job 6:5	
w it is hot, they are consumed	Job 6:17	
W I lie down, I say	Job 7:4	4970
W shall I arise, and the night be	Job 7:4	4970
W I say, My bed shall comfort me,	Job 7:13	3588
w thou mockest, shall no man make	Job 11:3	
W a few years are come, then I	Job 16:22	3588
w our rest together is in the	Job 17:16	518
W he is about to fill his belly,	Job 20:23	
Even *w* I remember I am afraid, and	Job 21:6	518
w the number of his months is cut	Job 21:21	
W men are cast down, then thou	Job 22:29	3588
w he hath tried me, I shall come	Job 23:10	
w I consider, I am afraid of him	Job 23:15	
w God taketh away his soul	Job 27:8	3588
Will God hear his cry *w* trouble	Job 27:9	3588
W he made a decree for the rain,	Job 28:26	
as in the days *w* God preserved me	Job 29:2	
W his candle shined upon my head,	Job 29:3	
w by his light I walked through	Job 29:3	
w the secret of God was upon my	Job 29:4	
W the Almighty was yet with me,	Job 29:5	5750
w my children were about me	Job 29:5	
W I washed my steps with butter,	Job 29:6	
W I went out to the gate through	Job 29:7	
w I prepared my seat in the	Job 29:7	
W the ear heard me, then it	Job 29:11	3588
w the eye saw me, it gave witness	Job 29:11	
W I looked for good, then evil	Job 30:26	3588
w I waited for light, there came	Job 30:26	
w they contended with me	Job 31:13	
then shall I do *w* God riseth up	Job 31:14	3588
w he visiteth, what shall I	Job 31:14	3588
w I saw my help in the gate	Job 31:21	3588
If I beheld the sun *w* it shined	Job 31:26	3588
lifted up myself *w* evil found him	Job 31:29	3588
W Elihu saw that there was no	Job 32:5	
W I had waited, (for they spake	Job 32:16	
w deep sleep falleth upon men, in	Job 33:15	
W he giveth quietness, who then	Job 34:29	
w he hideth his face, who then	Job 34:29	
they cry not *w* he bindeth them	Job 36:13	3588
w people are cut off in their	Job 36:20	
stay them *w* his voice is heard	Job 37:4	3588
Dost thou know *w* God disposed	Job 37:15	
w he quieteth the earth by the	Job 37:17	3588
Where wast thou *w* I laid the	Job 38:4	
W the morning stars sang together	Job 38:7	
w it brake forth, as if it had	Job 38:8	
W I made the cloud the garment	Job 38:9	
W the dust groweth into hardness,	Job 38:38	
W they couch in their dens, and	Job 38:40	3588
w his young ones cry unto God,	Job 38:41	3588
Knowest thou the time *w* the wild	Job 39:1	
thou mark *w* the hinds do calve	Job 39:1	
thou the time *w* they bring forth	Job 39:2	
W he raiseth up himself, the	Job 41:25	
w he prayed for his friends	Job 42:10	
w his wrath is kindled but a	Ps 2:12	3588
w he fled from Absalom his son	Ps 3:*t*	
Hear me *w* I call, O God of my	Ps 4:1	
enlarged me *w* I was in distress	Ps 4:1	
LORD will hear *w* I call unto him	Ps 4:3	
W I consider thy heavens, the	Ps 8:3	3588
W mine enemies are turned back,	Ps 9:3	
W he maketh inquisition for blood	Ps 9:12	3588
w he draweth him into his net	Ps 10:9	
w the vilest men are exalted	Ps 12:8	
trouble me rejoice *w* I am moved	Ps 13:4	3588
w the LORD bringeth back the	Ps 14:7	
w I awake, with thy likeness	Ps 17:15	
let the king hear us *w* we call	Ps 20:9	
w thou shalt make ready thine	Ps 21:12	
thou didst make me hope *w* I was	Ps 22:9	
but *w* he cried unto him, he heard	Ps 22:24	
W the wicked, even mine enemies	Ps 27:2	
O LORD, *w* I cry with my voice	Ps 27:7	
W thou saidst, Seek ye my face	Ps 27:8	
W my father and my mother forsake	Ps 27:10	3588
w I cry unto thee	Ps 28:2	
w I lift up my hands toward thy	Ps 28:2	
my blood, *w* I go down to the pit	Ps 30:9	
supplications *w* I cried unto thee	Ps 31:22	
W I kept silence, my bones waxed	Ps 32:3	3588
in a time *w* thou mayest be found	Ps 32:6	
w he changed his behaviour before	Ps 34:*t*	
w they were sick, my clothing was	Ps 35:13	
nor condemn him *w* he is judged	Ps 37:33	
w the wicked are cut off, thou	Ps 37:34	
w my foot slippeth, they magnify	Ps 38:16	
W thou with rebukes dost correct	Ps 39:11	
W shall he die, and his name	Ps 41:5	4970
w he goeth abroad, he telleth it	Ps 41:6	
w shall I come and appear before	Ps 42:2	4970
W I remember these things, I pour	Ps 42:4	
w the iniquity of my heels shall	Ps 49:5	
thou afraid *w* one is made rich	Ps 49:16	3588
w the glory of his house is	Ps 49:16	3588
For *w* he dieth he shall carry	Ps 49:17	3588
w thou doest well to thyself	Ps 49:18	3588
W thou sawest a thief, then thou	Ps 50:18	518
w Nathan the prophet came unto	Ps 51:*t*	
be justified *w* thou speakest	Ps 51:4	
and be clear *w* thou judgest	Ps 51:4	
w Doeg the Edomite came and told	Ps 52:*t*	
W God bringeth back the captivity	Ps 53:6	
w the Ziphims came and said to	Ps 54:*t*	
w the Philistines took him in	Ps 56:*t*	
my steps, *w* they wait for my soul	Ps 56:6	834
W I cry unto thee, then shall	Ps 56:9	
w he fled from Saul in the cave	Ps 57:*t*	
w he bendeth his bow to shoot his	Ps 58:7	
rejoice *w* he seeth the vengeance	Ps 58:10	3588
w Saul sent, and they watched the	Ps 59:*t*	
w he strove with Aram-naharaim and	Ps 60:*t*	
w Joab returned, and smote of Edom	Ps 60:*t*	
w my heart is overwhelmed	Ps 61:2	
w he was in the wilderness of	Ps 63:*t*	3588
W I remember thee upon my bed, and	Ps 63:6	518
w thou hast so provided for it	Ps 65:9	
hath spoken, *w* I was in trouble	Ps 66:14	
w thou wentest forth before thy	Ps 68:7	
w thou didst march through the	Ps 68:7	
thine inheritance, *w* it was weary	Ps 68:9	
W the Almighty scattered kings in	Ps 68:14	
W I wept, and chastened my soul	Ps 69:10	
forsake me not *w* my strength	Ps 71:9	
Now also *w* I am old and greyheaded	Ps 71:18	5704
rejoice *w* I sing unto thee	Ps 71:23	3588
deliver the needy *w* he crieth	Ps 72:12	
w I saw the prosperity of the	Ps 73:3	
W I thought to know this, it was	Ps 73:16	
As a dream *w* one awaketh	Ps 73:20	
w thou awakest, thou shalt	Ps 73:20	
W I shall receive the	Ps 75:2	3588
thy sight *w* once thou art angry	Ps 76:7	
W God arose to judgment, to save	Ps 76:9	
W he slew them, then they sought	Ps 78:34	518
nor the day *w* he delivered them	Ps 78:42	834
W God heard this, he was wroth,	Ps 78:59	
w he went out through the land of	Ps 81:5	
w he writeth up the people, that	Ps 87:6	
w the waves thereof arise, thou	Ps 89:9	
are but as yesterday *w* it is past	Ps 90:4	3588
W the wicked spring as the grass,	Ps 92:7	
w all the workers of iniquity do	Ps 92:7	
and ye fools, *w* will ye be wise	Ps 94:8	4970
W I said, My foot slippeth	Ps 94:18	518
W your fathers tempted me, proved	Ps 95:9	834
O *w* wilt thou come unto me	Ps 101:2	4970
w he is overwhelmed, and poureth	Ps 102:*t*	3588
me in the day *w* I am in trouble	Ps 102:2	
in the day *w* I call answer me	Ps 102:2	
W the LORD shall build up Zion,	Ps 102:16	3588
W the people are gathered	Ps 102:22	
W they were but a few men in	Ps 105:12	
W they went from one nation to	Ps 105:13	
Egypt was glad *w* they departed	Ps 105:38	
affliction, *w* he heard their cry	Ps 106:44	
W he shall be judged, let him be	Ps 109:7	
like the shadow *w* it declineth	Ps 109:23	
w they looked upon me they shaked	Ps 109:25	
w they arise, let them be ashamed	Ps 109:28	
W Israel went out of Egypt, the	Ps 114:1	
w I have respect unto all thy	Ps 119:6	
w I shall have learned thy	Ps 119:7	
w thou shalt enlarge my heart	Ps 119:32	3588
thee will be glad *w* they see me	Ps 119:74	
saying, *W* wilt thou comfort me	Ps 119:82	4970
w wilt thou execute judgment on	Ps 119:84	4970
w thou hast taught me thy	Ps 119:171	3588
but *w* I speak, they are for war	Ps 120:7	3588
I was glad *w* they said unto me,	Ps 122:1	
side, *w* men rose up against us	Ps 124:2	
w their wrath was kindled against	Ps 124:3	
W the LORD turned again the	Ps 126:1	
we wept, *w* we remembered Zion	Ps 137:1	
In the day *w* I cried thou	Ps 138:3	
w they hear the words of thy	Ps 138:4	3588
w I was made in secret, and	Ps 139:15	834
w as yet there was none of them	Ps 139:16	
w I awake, I am still with thee	Ps 139:18	
unto my voice, *w* I cry unto thee	Ps 141:1	
W their judges are overthrown in	Ps 141:6	

as *w* one cutteth and cleaveth wood	Ps 141:7	
A Prayer *w* he was in the cave	Ps 142:*t*	
W my spirit was overwhelmed	Ps 142:3	
I will mock *w* your fear cometh	Prov 1:26	
W your fear cometh as desolation,	Prov 1:27	
w distress and anguish cometh upon	Prov 1:27	
W wisdom entereth into thine	Prov 2:10	3588
W thou liest down, thou shalt not	Prov 3:24	518
of the wicked, *w* it cometh	Prov 3:25	3588
w it is in the power of thine	Prov 3:27	
w thou hast it by thee	Prov 3:28	
honour, *w* thou dost embrace her	Prov 4:8	3588
W thou goest, thy steps shall not	Prov 4:12	
w thou runnest, thou shalt not	Prov 4:12	518
w thy flesh and thy body are	Prov 5:11	
w thou art come into the hand of	Prov 6:3	3588
w wilt thou arise out of thy	Prov 6:9	4970
W thou goest, it shall lead thee	Prov 6:22	
w thou sleepest, it shall keep	Prov 6:22	
w thou awakest, it shall talk	Prov 6:22	
satisfy his soul *w* he is hungry	Prov 6:30	3588
W there were no depths, I was	Prov 8:24	
w there were no fountains	Prov 8:24	
W he prepared the heavens, I was	Prov 8:27	
w he set a compass upon the face	Prov 8:27	
W he established the clouds above	Prov 8:28	
w he strengthened the fountains	Prov 8:28	
W he gave to the sea his decree,	Prov 8:29	
w he appointed the foundations of	Prov 8:29	
W pride cometh, then cometh shame	Prov 11:2	
W a wicked man dieth, his	Prov 11:7	
W it goeth well with the	Prov 11:10	
w the wicked perish, there is	Prov 11:10	
but *w* the desire cometh, it is a	Prov 13:12	
w thou perceivest not in him the	Prov 14:7	
W a man's ways please the LORD,	Prov 16:7	
is as *w* one letteth out water	Prov 17:14	
w he holdeth his peace, is	Prov 17:28	
W the wicked cometh, then cometh	Prov 18:3	
but *w* he is gone his way, then he	Prov 20:14	
W the scorner is punished, the	Prov 21:11	
w the wise is instructed, he	Prov 21:11	
w he bringeth it with a wicked	Prov 21:27	3588
w he is old, he will not depart	Prov 22:6	3588
W thou sittest to eat with a	Prov 23:1	3588
w thy lips speak right things	Prov 23:16	
not thy mother *w* she is old	Prov 23:22	3588
thou upon the wine *w* it is red	Prov 23:31	3588
w it giveth his colour in the cup	Prov 23:31	3588
w it moveth itself aright	Prov 23:31	
w shall I awake	Prov 23:35	4970
w thou hast found it, then there	Prov 24:14	518
Rejoice not *w* thine enemy falleth	Prov 24:17	
heart be glad *w* he stumbleth	Prov 24:17	
w thy neighbour hath put thee to	Prov 25:8	
W he speaketh fair, believe him	Prov 26:25	3588
The wicked flee *w* no man pursueth	Prov 28:1	
W righteous men do rejoice, there	Prov 28:12	
but *w* the wicked rise, a man is	Prov 28:12	
W the wicked rise, men hide	Prov 28:28	
but *w* they perish, the righteous	Prov 28:28	
W the righteous are in authority,	Prov 29:2	
but *w* the wicked beareth rule,	Prov 29:2	
W the wicked are multiplied,	Prov 29:16	
For a servant *w* he reigneth	Prov 30:22	3588
a fool *w* he is filled with meat	Prov 30:22	3588
an odious woman *w* she is married	Prov 30:23	3588
w he sitteth among the elders of	Prov 31:23	
to him that is alone *w* he falleth	Eccl 4:10	
Keep thy foot *w* thou goest to the	Eccl 5:1	834
W thou vowest a vow unto God,	Eccl 5:4	834
W goods increase, they are	Eccl 5:11	
who can tell him *w* it shall be	Eccl 8:7	
W I applied mine heart to know	Eccl 8:16	834
w it falleth suddenly upon them	Eccl 9:12	
w he that is a fool walketh by	Eccl 10:3	
w thy king is a child, and thy	Eccl 10:16	
w thy king is the son of nobles,	Eccl 10:17	
w thou shalt say, I have no	Eccl 12:1	834
In the day *w* the keepers of the	Eccl 12:3	
w the sound of the grinding is	Eccl 12:4	
Also *w* they shall be afraid of	Eccl 12:5	
my soul failed *w* he spake	Song 5:6	
w I should find thee without, I	Song 8:1	
the day *w* she shall be spoken for	Song 8:8	
W ye come to appear before me,	Is 1:12	3588
w ye spread forth your hands, I	Is 1:15	
w ye make many prayers, I will	Is 1:15	3588
w he ariseth to shake terribly	Is 2:19	
w he ariseth to shake terribly	Is 2:21	
W a man shall take hold of his	Is 3:6	3588
W the Lord shall have washed away	Is 4:4	518
w I looked that it should bring	Is 5:4	
in them, *w* they cast their leaves	Is 6:13	834
w they shall say unto you, Seek	Is 8:19	3588
that *w* they shall be hungry, they	Is 8:21	3588
w at the first he lightly	Is 9:1	6256
as men rejoice *w* they divide the	Is 9:3	
that *w* the Lord hath performed	Is 10:12	3588
and they shall be as *w* a	Is 10:18	
shall be as *w* God overthrew Sodom	Is 13:19	
w it is seen that Moab is weary	Is 16:12	3588
it shall be as *w* the harvestman	Is 17:5	
w he lifteth up an ensign on the	Is 18:3	
w he bloweth a trumpet, hear ye	Is 18:3	
w the bud is perfect, and the sour	Is 18:5	3588
(*w* Sargon the king of Assyria	Is 20:1	
W thus it shall be in the midst	Is 24:13	3588
grapes *w* the vintage is done	Is 24:13	518
w the LORD of hosts shall reign	Is 24:23	3588
w the blast of the terrible ones	Is 25:4	3588
for *w* thy judgments are in the	Is 26:9	834
w thy hand is lifted up, they	Is 26:11	
they poured out a prayer *w* thy	Is 26:16	
w it shooteth forth, thou wilt	Is 27:8	
w he maketh all the stones of the	Is 27:9	
W the boughs thereof are withered	Is 27:11	
which *w* he that looketh upon it	Is 28:4	
w the overflowing scourge shall	Is 28:15	3588
w the overflowing scourge shall	Is 28:18	3588
W he hath made plain the face	Is 28:25	518
It shall even be as *w* an hungry	Is 29:8	834
or as *w* a thirsty man dreameth,	Is 29:8	834
But *w* he seeth his children, the	Is 29:23	3588
w he shall hear it, he will	Is 30:19	
w ye turn to the right hand	Is 30:21	3588
and *w* ye turn to the left	Is 30:21	3588
slaughter, *w* the towers fall	Is 30:25	
a song, as in the night *w* a holy	Is 30:29	
as *w* one goeth with a pipe to	Is 30:29	
W the LORD shall stretch out his	Is 31:3	
w a multitude of shepherds is	Is 31:4	834
even *w* the needy speaketh right	Is 32:7	
W it shall hail, coming down on	Is 32:19	
w thou shalt cease to spoil, thou	Is 33:1	
w thou shalt make an end to deal	Is 33:1	
w king Hezekiah heard it, that he	Is 37:1	
w he heard it, he sent messengers	Is 37:9	
w they arose early in the morning	Is 37:36	
w he had been sick, and was	Is 38:9	
W the poor and needy seek water,	Is 41:17	
w I asked of them, could answer a	Is 41:28	
W thou passest through the waters	Is 43:2	3588
w thou walkest through the fire,	Is 43:2	3588
w there was no strange god among	Is 43:12	
even before the day *w* thou	Is 48:7	
w I call unto them, they stand up	Is 48:13	
they thirsted not *w* he led them	Is 48:21	
w I came, was there no man	Is 50:2	
w I called, was there none to	Is 50:2	
w the LORD shall bring again Zion	Is 52:8	
w we shall see him, there is no	Is 53:2	
w thou shalt make his soul an	Is 53:10	518
w thou wast refused, saith thy	Is 54:6	3588
W thou criest, let thy companies	Is 57:13	
w it cannot rest, whose waters	Is 57:20	3588
w thou seest the naked, that thou	Is 58:7	3588
W the enemy shall come in like a	Is 59:19	3588
As *w* the melting fire burneth,	Is 64:2	
W thou didst terrible things	Is 64:3	
because *w* I called, ye did not	Is 65:12	
w I spake, ye did not hear	Is 65:12	
because *w* I called, none did	Is 66:4	
w I spake, they did not hear	Is 66:4	
w ye see this, your heart shall	Is 66:14	
w thou wentest after me in the	Jer 2:2	
but *w* ye entered, ye defiled my	Jer 2:7	
thy God, *w* he led thee by the way	Jer 2:17	6256
w upon every high hill and under	Jer 2:20	3588
thief is ashamed *w* he is found	Jer 2:26	3588
w for all the causes whereby	Jer 3:8	3588
w ye be multiplied and increased	Jer 3:16	3588
w thou art spoiled, what wilt	Jer 4:30	
w I had fed them to the full,	Jer 5:7	
w ye shall say, Wherefore doeth	Jer 5:19	3588
w there is no peace	Jer 6:14	
Were they ashamed *w* they had	Jer 6:15	3588
w there is no peace	Jer 8:11	
Were they ashamed *w* they had	Jer 8:12	3588
W I would comfort myself against	Jer 8:18	
W he uttereth his voice, there is	Jer 10:13	
w thou doest evil, then thou	Jer 11:15	3588
thou, O LORD, *w* I plead with thee	Jer 12:1	3588
What wilt thou say *w* he shall	Jer 13:21	3588
w shall it once be	Jer 13:27	
W they fast, I will not hear	Jer 14:12	3588
w they offer burnt offering and an	Jer 14:12	3588
w thou shalt shew this people all	Jer 16:10	3588
and shall not see *w* good cometh	Jer 17:6	3588
and shall not see *w* heat cometh	Jer 17:8	3588
w thou shalt bring a troop	Jer 18:22	3588
w king Zedekiah sent unto him	Jer 21:1	
thou be *w* pangs come upon thee	Jer 22:23	
w this people, or the prophet, or	Jer 23:33	3588
w seventy years are accomplished,	Jer 25:12	
w Jeremiah had made an end of	Jer 26:8	
W the princes of Judah heard	Jer 26:10	
w Jehoiakim the king, with all	Jer 26:21	
but *w* Urijah heard it, he was	Jer 26:21	
w he carried away captive	Jer 27:20	
w the word of the prophet shall	Jer 28:9	
w ye shall search for me with all	Jer 29:13	3588
w I went to cause him to rest	Jer 31:2	
w I shall bring again their	Jer 31:23	
the sea *w* the waves thereof roar	Jer 31:35	
Now *w* I had delivered the	Jer 32:16	
w Nebuchadnezzar king of Babylon,	Jer 34:1	
W the king of Babylon's army	Jer 34:7	
Now *w* all the princes, and all the	Jer 34:10	
w he hath served thee six years,	Jer 34:14	
w they cut the calf in twain, and	Jer 34:18	
w Nebuchadrezzar king of Babylon	Jer 35:11	
W Michaiah the son of Gemariah,	Jer 36:11	
w Baruch read the book in the	Jer 36:13	
w they had heard all the words,	Jer 36:16	
that *w* Jehudi had read three or	Jer 36:23	
w the Chaldeans that besieged	Jer 37:5	
that *w* the army of the Chaldeans	Jer 37:11	
w he was in the gate of Benjamin,	Jer 37:13	
W Jeremiah was entered into the	Jer 37:16	3588
Now *w* Ebed-melech the Ethiopian,	Jer 38:7	
he was there *w* Jerusalem was	Jer 38:28	834
that *w* Zedekiah the king of Judah	Jer 39:4	834
w they had taken him, they	Jer 39:5	
w he had taken him being bound in	Jer 40:1	
Now *w* all the captains of the	Jer 40:7	
Likewise *w* all the Jews that were	Jer 40:11	
w they came into the midst of the	Jer 41:7	
But *w* Johanan the son of Kareah,	Jer 41:11	
that *w* all the people which were	Jer 41:13	
w we obey the voice of the LORD	Jer 42:6	3588
w ye shall enter into Egypt	Jer 42:18	
w ye sent me unto the LORD your	Jer 42:20	3588
that *w* Jeremiah had made an end	Jer 43:1	
w he cometh, he shall smite the	Jer 43:11	
w we burned incense to the queen	Jer 44:19	3588
w he had written these words in a	Jer 45:1	
W he uttereth his voice, there is	Jer 51:16	
w her waves do roar like great	Jer 51:55	
w he went with Zedekiah the king	Jer 51:59	
W thou comest to Babylon, and	Jer 51:61	
w thou hast made an end of	Jer 51:63	
twenty years old *w* he began to	Jer 52:1	
w her people fell into the hand	Lam 1:7	
w they swooned as the wounded in	Lam 2:12	
w their soul was poured out into	Lam 2:12	
Also *w* I cry and shout, he	Lam 3:8	3588
w the Lord commandeth it not	Lam 3:37	
w they fled away and wandered,	Lam 4:15	3588
they turned not *w* they went	Eze 1:9	
and they turned not *w* they went	Eze 1:12	
W they went, they went upon their	Eze 1:17	
and they turned not *w* they went	Eze 1:17	
w the living creatures went, the	Eze 1:19	
w the living creatures were	Eze 1:19	
W those went, these went	Eze 1:21	
w those stood, these stood	Eze 1:21	
w those were lifted up from the	Eze 1:21	
w they went, I heard the noise of	Eze 1:24	
w they stood, they let down their	Eze 1:24	
w they stood, and had let down	Eze 1:25	
w I saw it, I fell upon my face,	Eze 1:28	
into me *w* he spake unto me	Eze 2:2	834
w I looked, behold, an hand was	Eze 2:9	
W I say unto the wicked, Thou	Eze 3:18	
W a righteous man doth turn from	Eze 3:20	
But *w* I speak with thee, I will	Eze 3:27	
w thou hast accomplished them,	Eze 4:6	
w the days of the siege are	Eze 5:2	
w I have accomplished my fury in	Eze 5:13	
w I shall execute judgments in	Eze 5:15	
W I shall send upon them the evil	Eze 5:16	
w ye shall be scattered through	Eze 6:8	
w their slain men shall be among	Eze 6:13	
w I looked, behold a hole in the	Eze 8:7	
w I had digged in the wall,	Eze 8:8	
of the house, *w* the man went in	Eze 10:3	
of the Almighty God *w* he speaketh	Eze 10:5	
that *w* he had commanded the man	Eze 10:6	
w I looked, behold the four	Eze 10:9	
W they went, they went upon their	Eze 10:11	
w the cherubims went, the wheels	Eze 10:16	
w the cherubims lifted up their	Eze 10:16	
W they stood, these stood	Eze 10:17	
w they were lifted up, these	Eze 10:17	
w they went out, the wheels also	Eze 10:19	
w I prophesied, that Pelatiah the	Eze 11:13	
w I shall scatter them among the	Eze 12:15	
w the wall is fallen, shall it	Eze 13:12	
deceived *w* he hath spoken a thing	Eze 14:9	3588
w the land sinneth against me by	Eze 14:13	3588
How much more *w* I send my four	Eze 14:21	3588
w ye see their ways and their	Eze 14:23	
w it was whole, it was meet for	Eze 15:5	
w the fire hath devoured it, and	Eze 15:5	3588
w I set my face against them	Eze 15:7	
w I passed by thee, and saw thee	Eze 16:6	
I said unto thee *w* thou wast in	Eze 16:6	
I said unto thee *w* thou wast in	Eze 16:6	
Now *w* I passed by thee, and looked	Eze 16:8	
w thou wast naked and bare, and	Eze 16:22	
W I shall bring again their	Eze 16:53	
W thy sisters, Sodom and her	Eze 16:55	
w thou shalt receive thy sisters,	Eze 16:61	
w I am pacified toward thee for	Eze 16:63	
w the east wind toucheth it	Eze 17:10	
oath by breaking the covenant, *w*	Eze 17:18	
W the son hath done that which is	Eze 18:19	
But *w* the righteous turneth away	Eze 18:24	
W a righteous man turneth away	Eze 18:26	
w the wicked man turneth away	Eze 18:27	
Now *w* she saw that she had waited	Eze 19:5	
In the day *w* I chose Israel, and	Eze 20:5	
w I lifted up mine hand unto them	Eze 20:5	
For *w* I had brought them into the	Eze 20:28	
For *w* ye offer your gifts	Eze 20:31	
w ye make your sons to pass	Eze 20:31	
w I bring you out from the people	Eze 20:41	
w I shall bring you into the land	Eze 20:42	
w I have wrought with you for my	Eze 20:44	3588
w they say unto thee, Wherefore	Eze 21:7	3588
w iniquity shall have an end,	Eze 21:25	6256
w their iniquity shall have an	Eze 21:29	6256
w the LORD hath not spoken	Eze 22:28	
played the harlot *w* she was mine	Eze 23:5	
w her sister Aholibah saw this,	Eze 23:11	3588
for *w* she saw men pourtrayed upon	Eze 23:14	
For *w* they had slain their	Eze 23:39	
w this cometh, ye shall know that	Eze 24:24	
shall it not be in the day *w* I	Eze 24:25	
my sanctuary, *w* it was profaned	Eze 25:3	3588
land of Israel, *w* it was desolate	Eze 25:3	3588
w they went into captivity	Eze 25:3	3588
w I shall lay my vengeance upon	Eze 25:17	
w he shall enter into thy gates,	Eze 26:10	
w the wounded cry	Eze 26:15	
w the slaughter is made in the	Eze 26:15	
W I shall make thee a desolate	Eze 26:19	
w I shall bring up the deep upon	Eze 26:19	
W I shall bring thee down with	Eze 26:20	
W thy wares went forth out of the	Eze 27:33	
In the time *w* thou shalt be	Eze 27:34	

w I shall have executed judgments Eze 28:22
W I shall have gathered the house Eze 28:25
w I have executed judgments upon Eze 28:26
W they took hold of thee by thy Eze 29:7
w they leaned upon thee, thou Eze 29:7
w they shall look after them Eze 29:16 3588
w the slain shall fall in Egypt, Eze 30:4
w I have set a fire in Egypt, and Eze 30:8
w all her helpers shall be Eze 30:8
w I shall break there the yokes Eze 30:18
w I shall put my sword into the Eze 30:25
of waters, *w* he shot forth Eze 31:5
In the day *w* he went down to the Eze 31:15
w I cast him down to hell with Eze 31:16
w I shall put thee out, I will Eze 32:7
w I shall bring thy destruction Eze 32:9
w I shall brandish my sword Eze 32:10
W I shall make the land of Egypt Eze 32:15
w I shall smite all them that Eze 32:15
W I bring the sword upon a land, Eze 33:2 3588
If *w* he seeth the sword come upon Eze 33:3
W I say unto the wicked, O wicked Eze 33:8
W I shall say to the righteous, Eze 33:13
w I say unto the wicked, Thou Eze 33:14
W the righteous turneth from his Eze 33:18
w I have laid the land most Eze 33:29
w this cometh to pass, (lo, it Eze 33:33
the field, *w* they were scattered Eze 34:5
w I have broken the bands of Eze 34:27
among them, *w* I have judged thee Eze 35:11 834
W the whole earth rejoiceth, I Eze 35:14
w the house of Israel dwelt in Eze 36:17
w they entered unto the heathen, Eze 36:20
w they said to them, These are Eze 36:20
w I shall be sanctified in you Eze 36:23
w I beheld, lo, the sinews and the Eze 37:8
w I have opened your graves, O my Eze 37:13
w the children of thy people Eze 37:18 3588
w my sanctuary shall be in the Eze 37:28
In that day *w* my people of Israel Eze 38:14
w I shall be sanctified in thee, Eze 38:16
come to pass at the same time *w* Eze 38:18 3117
w any seeth a man's bone, then Eze 39:15
w they dwelt safely in their land Eze 39:26
W I have brought them again from Eze 39:27
W the priests enter therein, then Eze 42:14
Now *w* he had made an end of Eze 42:15
to the vision that I saw *w* I came Eze 43:3
in the day *w* they shall make it Eze 43:18
W thou hast made an end of Eze 43:23
w these days are expired, it Eze 43:27
w ye offer my bread, the fat and Eze 44:7
w Israel went astray, which went Eze 44:10
w the children of Israel went Eze 44:15
that *w* they enter in at the gates Eze 44:17
w they go forth into the utter Eze 44:19
w they enter into the inner court Eze 44:21
w ye shall divide by lot the land Eze 45:1
w the prince shall enter, he Eze 46:8
But *w* the people of the land Eze 46:9
w they go in, shall go in Eze 46:10
w they go forth, shall go forth Eze 46:10
Now *w* the prince shall prepare a Eze 46:12 3588
w the man that had the line in Eze 47:3
Now *w* I had returned, behold, at Eze 47:7
which went not astray *w* the Eze 48:11
w all the people heard the sound Dan 3:7 1768
But *w* his heart was lifted up, and Dan 5:20 1768
Now *w* Daniel knew that the Dan 6:10 1768
w he heard these words, was sore Dan 6:14 1768
w he came to the den, he cried Dan 6:20
w I saw, that I was at Shushan in Dan 8:2
w he was strong, the great horn Dan 8:8
w I, even I Daniel, had seen the Dan 8:15
w he came, I was afraid, and fell Dan 8:17
w the transgressors are come to Dan 8:23
w I heard the voice of his words, Dan 10:9
w he had spoken this word unto me Dan 10:11
w he had spoken such words unto Dan 10:15
w he had spoken unto me, I was Dan 10:19
w I am gone forth, lo, the prince Dan 10:20
w he shall stand up, his kingdom Dan 11:4
And *w* he hath taken away the Dan 11:12
Now *w* they shall fall, they shall Dan 11:34
w he held up his right hand and Dan 12:7
w he shall have accomplished to Dan 12:7
Now *w* she had weaned Lo-ruhamah, Hos 1:8
as in the day *w* she came up out Hos 2:15
daughters *w* they commit whoredom Hos 4:14 3588
nor your spouses *w* they commit Hos 4:14 3588
W Ephraim saw his sickness, and Hos 5:13
w I returned the captivity of my Hos 6:11
W I would have healed Israel, Hos 7:1
W they shall go, I will spread my Hos 7:12 834
w they howled upon their beds Hos 7:14 3588
woe also to them *w* I depart from Hos 9:12
w they shall bind themselves in Hos 10:10
W Israel was a child, then I Hos 11:1 3588
w he shall roar, then the Hos 11:10 3588
W Ephraim spake trembling, he Hos 13:1
but *w* he offended in Baal, he Hos 13:1
w they fall upon the sword, they Joel 2:8
w I shall bring again the Joel 3:1 834
in the forest, *w* he hath no prey Amos 3:4
w there were yet three months to Amos 4:7
w your gardens and your vineyards Amos 4:9
that *w* they had made an end of Amos 7:2 518
W will the new moon be gone, that Amos 8:5 4970
W my soul fainted within me I Jonah 2:7
w I was yet in my country Jonah 4:2 5704
But God prepared a worm *w* the Jonah 4:7
w the sun did arise, that God Jonah 4:8
w the morning is light, they Mic 2:1
w the Assyrian shall come into Mic 5:5 3588

w he shall tread in our palaces, Mic 5:5 3588
w he cometh into our land, and Mic 5:6 3588
w he treadeth within our borders Mic 5:6 3588
for I am as *w* they have gathered Mic 7:1
w I fall, I shall arise Mic 7:8 3588
w I sit in darkness, the LORD Mic 7:8
cut down, *w* he shall pass through Nah 1:12 3588
but *w* the sun ariseth they flee Nah 3:17
holdest thy tongue *w* the wicked Hab 1:13
I shall answer *w* I am reproved Hab 2:1 5921
W I heard, my belly trembled Hab 3:16
w he cometh up unto the people, Hab 3:16
w I turn back your captivity Zeph 3:20
w ye brought it home, I did blow Hag 1:9
with you *w* ye came out of Egypt Hag 2:5
w one came to an heap of twenty Hag 2:16
w one came to the pressfat for to Hag 2:16
W they had sent unto the house of Zec 7:2
W ye fasted and mourned in the Zec 7:5 3588
w ye did eat Zec 7:6 3588
w ye did drink, did not ye eat Zec 7:6 3588
w Jerusalem was inhabited and in Zec 7:7
w men inhabited the south and the Zec 7:7
w your fathers provoked me to Zec 8:14
w the eyes of man, as of all the Zec 9:1 3588
W I have bent Judah for me, Zec 9:13 3588
w they shall be in the siege both Zec 12:2
that *w* any shall yet prophesy, Zec 13:3 3588
him through *w* he prophesieth Zec 13:3
his vision, *w* he hath prophesied Zec 13:4
as *w* he fought in the day of Zec 14:3 3117
W ye say, Every one that doeth Mal 2:17
and who shall stand *w* he appeareth Mal 3:2
in that day *w* I make up my jewels Mal 3:17 834
W as his mother Mary was espoused Mt 1:18
Now *w* Jesus was born in Bethlehem Mt 2:1
W Herod the king had heard these Mt 2:3
w he had gathered all the chief Mt 2:4
w he had privily called the wise Mt 2:7
w ye have found him, bring me Mt 2:8 *1875*
W they had heard the king, they Mt 2:9
W they saw the star, they Mt 2:10
w they were come into the house, Mt 2:11
w they had opened their treasures Mt 2:11
w they were departed, behold, the Mt 2:13
W he arose, he took the young Mt 2:14
w he saw that he was mocked of Mt 2:16
But *w* Herod was dead, behold, an Mt 2:19
But *w* he heard that Archelaus did Mt 2:22
But *w* he saw many of the Mt 3:7
w he was baptized, went up Mt 3:16
w he had fasted forty days and Mt 4:2
w the tempter came to him, he Mt 4:3
Now *w* Jesus had heard that John Mt 4:12
w he was set, his disciples came Mt 5:1
w men shall revile you, and Mt 5:11 *3752*
Therefore *w* thou doest thine alms Mt 6:2 *3752*
But *w* thou doest alms, let not Mt 6:3
w thou prayest, thou shalt not be Mt 6:5 *3752*
w thou prayest, enter into thy Mt 6:6 *3752*
w thou hast shut thy door, pray Mt 6:6
But *w* ye pray, use not vain Mt 6:7
Moreover *w* ye fast, be not, as Mt 6:16 *3752*
w thou fastest, anoint thine head Mt 6:17
w Jesus had ended these sayings, Mt 7:28 *3753*
W he was come down from the Mt 8:1
And *w* Jesus was entered into Mt 8:5
W Jesus heard it, he marvelled, Mt 8:10
w Jesus was come into Peter's Mt 8:14
W the even was come, they brought Mt 8:16
Now *w* Jesus saw great multitudes Mt 8:18
w he was entered into a ship, his Mt 8:23
w he was come to the other side Mt 8:28
w they were come out, they went Mt 8:32
w they saw him, they besought him Mt 8:34
But *w* the multitudes saw it, they Mt 9:8
w the Pharisees saw it, they said Mt 9:11
But *w* Jesus heard that, he said Mt 9:12
w the bridegroom shall be taken Mt 9:15 *3752*
w he saw her, he said, Daughter, Mt 9:22
w Jesus came into the ruler's Mt 9:23
But *w* the people were put forth, Mt 9:25 *3753*
w Jesus departed thence, two Mt 9:27
w he was come into the house, the Mt 9:28
w they were departed, spread Mt 9:31
w the devil was cast out, the Mt 9:33
But *w* he saw the multitudes, he Mt 9:36
w he had called unto him his Mt 10:1
w ye come into an house, salute Mt 10:12
w ye depart out of that house or Mt 10:14
But *w* they deliver you up, take Mt 10:19 *3752*
But *w* they persecute you in this Mt 10:23 *3752*
w Jesus had made an end of Mt 11:1 *3753*
Now *w* John had heard in the Mt 11:2
But *w* the Pharisees saw it, they Mt 12:2
w he was an hungred, and they that Mt 12:3 *3753*
w he was departed thence, he went Mt 12:9
But *w* Jesus knew it, he withdrew Mt 12:15
But *w* the Pharisees heard it, Mt 12:24
W the unclean spirit is gone out Mt 12:43 *3752*
w he is come, he findeth it empty Mt 12:44
w he sowed, some seeds fell by Mt 13:4
w the sun was up, they were Mt 13:6
W any one heareth the word of the Mt 13:19
for *w* tribulation or persecution Mt 13:21
But *w* the blade was sprung up, and Mt 13:26 *3753*
but *w* it is grown, it is the Mt 13:32 *3752*
the which *w* a man hath found, he Mt 13:44
w he had found one pearl of great Mt 13:46
w it was full, they drew to shore Mt 13:48 *3753*
that *w* Jesus had finished these Mt 13:53 *3753*
w he was come into his own Mt 13:54
w he would have put him to death, Mt 14:5
But *w* Herod's birthday was kept, Mt 14:6

W Jesus heard of it, he departed Mt 14:13
w the people had heard thereof, Mt 14:13
w it was evening, his disciples Mt 14:15
w he had sent the multitudes away Mt 14:23
w the evening was come, he was Mt 14:23
w the disciples saw him walking Mt 14:26
w Peter was come down out of the Mt 14:29
But *w* he saw the wind boisterous, Mt 14:30
w they were come into the ship, Mt 14:32
w they were gone over, they came Mt 14:34
w the men of that place had Mt 14:35
not their hands *w* they eat bread Mt 15:2 *3752*
w they saw the dumb to speak, the Mt 15:31
W it is evening, ye say, It will Mt 16:2
w his disciples were come to the Mt 16:5
Which *w* Jesus perceived, he said Mt 16:8
W Jesus came into the coasts of Mt 16:13
w the disciples heard it, they Mt 17:6
w they had lifted up their eyes, Mt 17:8
w they were come to the multitude Mt 17:14
w they were come to Capernaum, Mt 17:24
w he was come into the house, Mt 17:25 *3753*
w thou hast opened his mouth, Mt 17:27
w he had begun to reckon, one was Mt 18:24
So *w* his fellowservants saw what Mt 18:31
that *w* Jesus had finished these Mt 19:1 *3753*
But *w* the young man heard that Mt 19:22
W his disciples heard it, they Mt 19:25
in the regeneration *w* the Son of Mt 19:28 *3752*
And *w* he had agreed with the Mt 20:2
So *w* even was come, the lord of Mt 20:8
w they came that were hired about Mt 20:9
But *w* the first came, they Mt 20:10
w they had received it, they Mt 20:11
w the ten heard it, they were Mt 20:24
w they heard that Jesus passed by Mt 20:30
w they drew nigh unto Jerusalem, Mt 21:1 *3753*
w he was come into Jerusalem, all Mt 21:10
w the chief priests and scribes Mt 21:15
w he saw a fig tree in the way, Mt 21:19
w the disciples saw it, they Mt 21:20
w he was come into the temple, Mt 21:23
w ye had seen it, repented not Mt 21:32
w the time of the fruit drew near Mt 21:34 *3753*
But *w* the husbandmen saw the son, Mt 21:38
W the lord therefore of the Mt 21:40 *3752*
w the chief priests and Pharisees Mt 21:45
But *w* they sought to lay hands on Mt 21:46
But *w* the king heard thereof, he Mt 22:7
w the king came in to see the Mt 22:11
W they had heard these words, Mt 22:22
w he had married a wife, deceased Mt 22:25
w the multitude heard this, they Mt 22:33
But *w* the Pharisees had heard Mt 22:34
w he is made, ye make him twofold Mt 23:15 *3752*
Tell us, *w* shall these things be Mt 24:3 *4218*
W ye therefore shall see the Mt 24:15 *3752*
W his branch is yet tender, and Mt 24:32 *3752*
w ye shall see all these things, Mt 24:33 *3752*
whom his lord *w* he cometh shall Mt 24:46
in a day *w* he looketh not for him Mt 24:50
W the Son of man shall come in Mt 25:31 *3752*
W saw we thee an hungred, and fed Mt 25:37 *4218*
W saw we thee a stranger, and took Mt 25:38 *4218*
Or *w* saw we thee sick, or in Mt 25:39 *4218*
w saw we thee an hungred, or Mt 25:44 *4218*
w Jesus had finished all these Mt 26:1 *3753*
Now *w* Jesus was in Bethany, in Mt 26:6
But *w* his disciples saw it, they Mt 26:8
W Jesus understood it, he said Mt 26:10
until that day *w* I drink it new Mt 26:29 *3752*
w they had sung an hymn, they Mt 26:30
w he was gone out into the porch, Mt 26:71
W the morning was come, all the Mt 27:1
w they had bound him, they led Mt 27:2
w he saw that he was condemned, Mt 27:3
w he was accused of the chief Mt 27:12
Therefore *w* they were gathered Mt 27:17
W he was set down on the judgment Mt 27:19
W Pilate saw that he could Mt 27:24
w he had scourged Jesus, he Mt 27:26
w they had platted a crown of Mt 27:29
w they were come unto a place Mt 27:33
w he had tasted thereof, he would Mt 27:34
w they heard that, said, This man Mt 27:47
w he had cried again with a loud Mt 27:50
Now *w* the centurion, and they that Mt 27:54
W the even was come, there came a Mt 27:57
w Joseph had taken the body, he Mt 27:59
Now *w* they were going, behold, Mt 28:11 *3752*
w they were assembled with the Mt 28:12
w they saw him, they worshipped Mt 28:17
w he had gone a little farther Mk 1:19
w the unclean spirit had torn him Mk 1:26
w they were come out of the Mk 1:29
w the sun did set, they brought Mk 1:32 *3753*
w they had found him, they said Mk 1:37
w they could not come nigh unto Mk 2:4
w they had broken it up, they let Mk 2:4
W Jesus saw their faith, he said Mk 2:5
immediately *w* Jesus perceived in Mk 2:8
w the scribes and Pharisees saw Mk 2:16
W Jesus heard it, he saith unto Mk 2:17
w the bridegroom shall be taken Mk 2:20 *3752*
w he had need, and was an hungred, Mk 2:25 *3753*
w he had looked round about on Mk 3:5
w they had heard what great Mk 3:8
w they saw him, fell down before Mk 3:11 *3752*
w his friends heard of it, they Mk 3:21
But *w* the sun was up, it was Mk 4:6
w he was alone, they that were Mk 4:10 *3753*
but *w* they have heard, Satan Mk 4:15 *3752*
w they have heard the word, Mk 4:16 *3752*
w affliction or persecution Mk 4:17

But *w* the fruit is brought forth, Mk 4:29 3752
w it is sown in the earth, is Mk 4:31 3752
But *w* it is sown, it groweth up, Mk 4:32 3752
w they were alone, he expounded Mk 4:34
w the even was come, he saith Mk 4:35
And *w* they had sent away the Mk 4:36
w he was come out of the ship, Mk 5:2
But *w* he saw Jesus afar off, he Mk 5:6
w he was come into the ship, he Mk 5:18
w Jesus was passed over again by Mk 5:21
w he saw him, he fell at his feet Mk 5:22
W she had heard of Jesus, came in Mk 5:27
w he was come in, he saith unto Mk 5:39
But *w* he had put them all out, he Mk 5:40
w the sabbath day was come, he Mk 6:2
w ye depart thence, shake off the Mk 6:11
But *w* Herod heard thereof, he Mk 6:16
w he heard him, he did many Mk 6:20
w a convenient day was come, that Mk 6:21
w the daughter of the said Mk 6:22
w his disciples heard of it, they Mk 6:29
w he came out, saw much people, Mk 6:34
w the day was now far spent, his Mk 6:35
w they knew, they say, Five, and Mk 6:38
w he had taken the five loaves and Mk 6:41
w he had sent them away, he Mk 6:46
w even was come, the ship was in Mk 6:47
But *w* they saw him walking upon Mk 6:49
w they had passed over, they came Mk 6:53
w they were come out of the ship, Mk 6:54
w they saw some of his disciples Mk 7:2
w they come from the market, Mk 7:4
w he had called all the people Mk 7:14
w he was entered into the house Mk 7:17 3753
w she was come to her house, she Mk 7:30
w Jesus knew it, he saith unto Mk 8:17
W I brake the five loaves among Mk 8:19 3753
w the seven among four thousand, Mk 8:20 3753
w he had spit on his eyes, and put Mk 8:23
But *w* he had turned about and Mk 8:33
w he had called the people unto Mk 8:34
w he cometh in the glory of his Mk 8:38 3752
w they had looked round about, Mk 9:8
w he came to his disciples, he Mk 9:14
w they beheld him, were greatly Mk 9:15
w he saw him, straightway the Mk 9:20
W Jesus saw that the people came Mk 9:25
w he was come into the house, his Mk 9:28
w he had taken him in his arms, Mk 9:36
But *w* Jesus saw it, he was much Mk 10:14
w he was gone forth into the way, Mk 10:17
w the ten heard it, they began to Mk 10:41
w he heard that it was Jesus of Mk 10:47
w they came nigh to Jerusalem, Mk 11:1 3753
w he had looked round about upon Mk 11:11
w they were come from Bethany, he Mk 11:12
w he came to it, he found nothing Mk 11:13
w even was come, he went out of Mk 11:19 3753
w ye pray, believe that ye Mk 11:24
w ye stand praying, forgive, if Mk 11:25 3752
w they were come, they say unto Mk 12:14
w they shall rise, whose wife Mk 12:23 3752
For *w* they shall rise from the Mk 12:25 3752
w Jesus saw that he answered Mk 12:34
Tell us, *w* shall these things be Mk 13:4 4218
what shall be the sign *w* all Mk 13:4 3752
w ye shall hear of wars and Mk 13:7 3752
But *w* they shall lead you, and Mk 13:11 3752
But *w* ye shall see the Mk 13:14 3752
W her branch is yet tender, and Mk 13:28 3752
w ye shall see these things come Mk 13:29 3752
for ye know not *w* the time is Mk 13:33 4218
for ye know not *w* the master of Mk 13:35 4218
w they heard it, they were glad, Mk 14:11
w they killed the passover, his Mk 14:12 3753
w he had given thanks, he gave it Mk 14:23
w they had sung an hymn, they Mk 14:26
w he returned, he found them Mk 14:40
w she saw Peter warming himself, Mk 14:67
w he thought thereon, he wept Mk 14:72
w he had scourged him, to be Mk 15:15
w they had mocked him, they took Mk 15:20 3753
w they had crucified him, they Mk 15:24
w the sixth hour was come, there Mk 15:33
w they heard it said, Behold, he Mk 15:35
w the centurion, which stood over Mk 15:39
w he was in Galilee, followed him Mk 15:41 3753
now *w* the even was come, because Mk 15:42
w he knew it of the centurion, he Mk 15:45
w the sabbath was past, Mary Mk 16:1
w they looked, they saw that the Mk 16:4
Now *w* Jesus was risen early the Mk 16:9
w they had heard that he was Mk 16:11
his lot was to burn incense *w* he Lk 1:9
w Zacharias saw him, he was Lk 1:12
w he came out, he could not speak Lk 1:22
w she saw him, she was troubled Lk 1:29
w Elisabeth heard the salutation Lk 1:41 5613
this taxing was first made *w* Lk 2:2
w they had seen it, they made Lk 2:17
w eight days were accomplished Lk 2:21 3753
w the days of her purification Lk 2:22 3753
w the parents brought in the Lk 2:27
w they had performed all things Lk 2:39 5613
w he was twelve years old, they Lk 2:42 3753
w they had fulfilled the days, as Lk 2:43
w they found him not, they turned Lk 2:45
w they saw him, they were amazed Lk 2:48
Now *w* all the people were Lk 3:21
w they were ended, he afterward Lk 4:2 3752
w the devil had ended all the Lk 4:13 3752
w he had opened the book, he Lk 4:17
w the heaven was shut up three Lk 4:25 3753
w great famine was throughout all Lk 4:25 5613

w they heard these things, were Lk 4:28
w the devil had thrown him in the Lk 4:35
Now *w* the sun was setting, all Lk 4:40
w it was day, he departed and went Lk 4:42
Now *w* he had left speaking, he Lk 5:4 5613
w they had this done, they Lk 5:6
W Simon Peter saw it, he fell Lk 5:8
w they had brought their ships to Lk 5:11
w he was in a certain city, Lk 5:12
w they could not find by what way Lk 5:19
w he saw their faith, he said Lk 5:20
But *w* Jesus perceived their Lk 5:22
w the bridegroom shall be taken Lk 5:35 3752
w himself was an hungred, and they Lk 6:3 3698
w it was day, he called unto him Lk 6:13 3753
w men shall hate you Lk 6:22 3752
w they shall separate you from Lk 6:22 3752
w all men shall speak well of you Lk 6:26 3752
w thou thyself beholdest not the Lk 6:42
w the flood arose, the stream Lk 6:48
Now *w* he had ended all his Lk 7:1 1893
w he heard of Jesus, he sent unto Lk 7:3
w they came to Jesus, they Lk 7:4
w he was now not far from the Lk 7:6
W Jesus heard these things, he Lk 7:9
Now *w* he came nigh to the gate of Lk 7:12 5613
w the Lord saw her, he had Lk 7:13
W the men were come unto him, Lk 7:20
w the messengers of John were Lk 7:24
w she knew that Jesus sat at meat Lk 7:37
Now *w* the Pharisee which had Lk 7:39
w they had nothing to pay, he Lk 7:42
w much people were gathered Lk 8:4
w he had said these things, he Lk 8:8
w they hear, receive the word Lk 8:13 3752
w they have heard, go forth, and Lk 8:14
w he hath lighted a candle, Lk 8:16
w he went forth to land, there Lk 8:27
W he saw Jesus, he cried out, and Lk 8:28
W they that fed them saw what was Lk 8:34
w Jesus was returned, the people Lk 8:40
W all denied, Peter and they that Lk 8:45
w the woman saw that she was not Lk 8:47
But *w* Jesus heard it, he answered Lk 8:50
w he came into the house, he Lk 8:51
w ye go out of that city, shake Lk 9:5
w they were returned, told him Lk 9:10
w they knew it, followed him Lk 9:11
w the day began to wear away, Lk 9:12
w he shall come in his own glory, Lk 9:26 3752
w they were awake, they saw his Lk 9:32
w the voice was past, Jesus was Lk 9:36
w they were come down from the Lk 9:37
w the time was come that he Lk 9:51
w his disciples James and John saw Lk 9:54
w he saw him, he passed by on the Lk 10:31
w he was at the place, came and Lk 10:32
w he saw him, he had compassion Lk 10:33
And on the morrow *w* he departed Lk 10:35
w I come again, I will repay thee Lk 10:35
w he ceased, one of his disciples Lk 11:1 5613
W ye pray, say, Our Father which Lk 11:2 3752
w the devil was gone out, the Lk 11:14
W a strong man armed keepeth his Lk 11:21 3752
But *w* a stronger than he shall Lk 11:22 1875
W the unclean spirit is gone out Lk 11:24 3752
w he cometh, he findeth it swept Lk 11:25
w the people were gathered thick Lk 11:29
w he hath lighted a candle, Lk 11:33
therefore *w* thine eye is single, Lk 11:34 1875
but *w* thine eye is evil, thy body Lk 11:34 3752
as *w* the bright shining of a Lk 11:36 3752
w the Pharisee saw it, he Lk 11:38
w there were gathered together an Lk 12:1
w they bring you unto the Lk 12:11 3752
w he will return from the wedding Lk 12:36 4218
that *w* he cometh and knocketh, Lk 12:36
whom the lord *w* he cometh shall Lk 12:37
cometh at an hour *w* ye think not Lk 12:40
whom his lord *w* he cometh shall Lk 12:43
in a day *w* he looketh not for him Lk 12:46
at an hour *w* he is not aware, and Lk 12:46
W ye see a cloud rise out of the Lk 12:54 3752
w ye see the south wind blow, ye Lk 12:55 3753
W thou goest with thine adversary Lk 12:58 5613
w Jesus saw her, he called her to Lk 13:12
w he had said these things, all Lk 13:17
W once the master of the house is Lk 13:25
w ye shall see Abraham, and Isaac, Lk 13:28 3752
the time come *w* ye shall say Lk 13:35 3753
w he marked how they chose out Lk 14:7
W thou art bidden of any man to a Lk 14:8 3752
But *w* thou art bidden, go and sit Lk 14:10 3752
that *w* he that bade thee cometh, Lk 14:10 3752
W thou makest a dinner or a Lk 14:12 3752
But *w* thou makest a feast, call Lk 14:13 3752
w one of them that sat at meat Lk 14:15
w he hath found it, he layeth it Lk 15:5
w he cometh home, he calleth Lk 15:6
w she hath found it, she calleth Lk 15:9
w he had spent all, there arose a Lk 15:14
w he came to himself, he said, Lk 15:17
But *w* he was yet a great way off, Lk 15:20
w I am put out of the stewardship Lk 16:4 3752
w ye fail, they may receive you Lk 16:9 3752
w he is come from the field, Go Lk 17:7
w ye shall have done all those Lk 17:10 3752
w he saw them, he said unto them, Lk 17:14
w he saw that he was healed, Lk 17:15
And *w* he was demanded of the Lk 17:20
w the kingdom of God should come, Lk 17:20 4218
w ye shall desire to see one of Lk 17:22 3753
day *w* the Son of man is revealed Lk 17:30
Nevertheless *w* the Son of man Lk 18:8

but *w* his disciples saw it, they Lk 18:15
Now *w* Jesus heard these things, Lk 18:22
w he heard this, he was very Lk 18:23
w Jesus saw that he was very Lk 18:24
w he was come near, he asked him, Lk 18:40
w they saw it, gave praise unto Lk 18:43
w Jesus came to the place, he Lk 19:5 5618
w they saw it, they all murmured, Lk 19:7
that *w* he was returned, having Lk 19:15
w he had thus spoken, he went Lk 19:28
w he was come nigh to Bethphage Lk 19:29 5613
w he was come nigh, even now at Lk 19:37
w he was come near, he beheld the Lk 19:41 5613
will reverence him *w* they see him Lk 20:13
But *w* the husbandmen saw him, Lk 20:14
w they heard it, they said, God Lk 20:16
w he calleth the Lord the God of Lk 20:37 5618
but *w* shall these things be Lk 21:7 4218
what sign will there be *w* these Lk 21:7 3752
But *w* ye shall hear of wars and Lk 21:9 3752
And *w* ye shall see Jerusalem Lk 21:20 3752
w these things begin to come to Lk 21:28
W they now shoot forth, ye see and Lk 21:30 3752
w ye see these things come to Lk 21:31 3752
w the passover must be killed Lk 22:7
w ye are entered into the city, Lk 22:10
w the hour was come, he sat down, Lk 22:14
w thou art converted, strengthen Lk 22:32 4218
W I sent you without purse, and Lk 22:35 3753
w he was at the place, he said Lk 22:40
w he rose up from prayer, and was Lk 22:45
W they which were about him saw Lk 22:49
W I was daily with you in the Lk 22:53
w they had kindled a fire in the Lk 22:55
w they had blindfolded him, they Lk 22:64
W Pilate heard of Galilee, he Lk 23:6
w Herod saw Jesus, he was Lk 23:8
w he had called together the Lk 23:13
w they were come to the place, Lk 23:33 3753
remember me *w* thou comest into Lk 23:42 3752
w Jesus had cried with a loud Lk 23:46
Now *w* the centurion saw what was Lk 23:47
unto you *w* he was yet in Galilee Lk 24:6
w they found not his body, they Lk 24:23
w he had thus spoken, he shewed Lk 24:40
w the Jews sent priests and Jn 1:19 3753
w Jesus beheld him, he said, Thou Jn 1:42
w thou wast under the fig tree, I Jn 1:48
w they wanted wine, the mother of Jn 2:3
W the ruler of the feast had Jn 2:9 5613
w men have well drunk, then that Jn 2:10 3752
w he had made a scourge of small Jn 2:15
W therefore he was risen from the Jn 2:22 3753
Now *w* he was in Jerusalem at the Jn 2:23 5613
w they saw the miracles which he Jn 2:23
How can a man be born *w* he is old Jn 3:4
W therefore the Lord knew how the Jn 4:1 5613
w ye shall neither in this Jn 4:21 3753
w the true worshippers shall Jn 4:23 3753
w he is come, he will tell us all Jn 4:25 3752
So *w* the Samaritans were come Jn 4:40 5613
Then *w* he was come into Galilee, Jn 4:45 3753
W he heard that Jesus was come Jn 4:47
them the hour *w* he began to amend Jn 4:52
w he was come out of Judaea into Jn 4:54
W Jesus saw him lie, and knew that Jn 5:6
w the water is troubled, to put Jn 5:7 3752
w the dead shall hear the voice Jn 5:25 3753
W Jesus then lifted up his eyes, Jn 6:5
w he had given thanks, he Jn 6:11
W they were filled, he said unto Jn 6:12 5613
w they had seen the miracle that Jn 6:14
W Jesus therefore perceived that Jn 6:15
And *w* even was now come, his Jn 6:16 5613
So *w* they had rowed about five and Jn 6:19
w the people which stood on the Jn 6:22
W the people therefore saw that Jn 6:24 3753
w they had found him on the other Jn 6:25 4218
him, Rabbi, *w* camest thou hither Jn 6:25
w they had heard this, said, This Jn 6:60
W Jesus knew in himself that his Jn 6:61
W he had said these words unto Jn 7:9
But *w* his brethren were gone up, Jn 7:10 5613
but *w* Christ cometh, no man Jn 7:27 3752
W Christ cometh, will he do more Jn 7:31 3752
w they heard this saying, said, Jn 7:40 3752
w they had set her in the midst, Jn 8:3
So *w* they continued asking him, Jn 8:7 5613
W Jesus had lifted up himself, and Jn 8:10
W ye have lifted up the Son of Jn 8:28 3752
W he speaketh a lie, he speaketh Jn 8:44 3752
night cometh, *w* no man can work Jn 9:4 3753
W he had thus spoken, he spat on Jn 9:6
sabbath day *w* Jesus made the clay Jn 9:14 3753
w he had found him, he said unto Jn 9:35
w he putteth forth his own sheep, Jn 10:4 3752
W Jesus heard that, he said, This Jn 11:4
W he had heard therefore that he Jn 11:6 5613
Then *w* Jesus came, he found that Jn 11:17
w she had so said, she went her Jn 11:28
w they saw Mary, that she rose up Jn 11:31
Then *w* Mary was come where Jesus Jn 11:32 5613
W Jesus therefore saw her weeping Jn 11:33 5613
w he thus had spoken, he cried Jn 11:43
w they heard that Jesus was Jn 12:12
w he had found a young ass, sat Jn 12:14
but *w* Jesus was glorified, then Jn 12:16 3753
therefore that was with him *w* he Jn 12:17 3753
w he saw his glory, and spake of Jn 12:41 3753
w Jesus knew that his hour was Jn 13:1
w it is come to pass, ye may Jn 13:19 3752
W Jesus had thus said, he was Jn 13:21
give a sop, *w* I have dipped it Jn 13:26
w he had dipped the sop, he gave Jn 13:26 3753

w he was gone out, Jesus said, Jn 13:31 3753
w it is come to pass, ye might Jn 14:29 3752
But *w* the Comforter is come, whom Jn 15:26 3752
that *w* the time shall come, ye Jn 16:4 3752
w he is come, he will reprove the Jn 16:8
Howbeit *w* he, the Spirit of truth Jn 16:13 3752
A woman *w* she is in travail hath Jn 16:21 3752
w I shall no more speak unto you Jn 16:25 3753
W Jesus had spoken these words, Jn 18:1
w he had thus spoken, one of the Jn 18:22
w he had said this, he went out Jn 18:38
W the chief priests therefore and Jn 19:6 3753
W Pilate therefore heard that Jn 19:8 3753
W Pilate therefore heard that Jn 19:13 3753
w they had crucified Jesus, took Jn 19:23 3753
W Jesus therefore saw his mother, Jn 19:26
W Jesus therefore had received Jn 19:30 3753
But *w* they came to Jesus, and saw Jn 19:33 5613
w it was yet dark, unto the Jn 20:1
w she had thus said, she turned Jn 20:14
w the doors were shut where the Jn 20:19
w he had so said, he shewed unto Jn 20:20
glad, *w* they saw the Lord Jn 20:20
w he had said this, he breathed Jn 20:22
was not with them *w* Jesus came Jn 20:24 3753
But *w* the morning was now come, Jn 21:4
Now *w* Simon Peter heard that it Jn 21:7
So *w* they had dined, Jesus saith Jn 21:15 3753
W thou wast young, thou girdedst Jn 21:18 3753
but *w* thou shalt be old, thou Jn 21:18 3752
w he had spoken this, he saith Jn 21:19
W they therefore were come Acts 1:6
w he had spoken these things, Acts 1:9
w they were come in, they went up Acts 1:13 3753
w the day of Pentecost was fully Acts 2:1
Now *w* this was noised abroad, the Acts 2:6
Now *w* they heard this, they were Acts 2:37
w Peter saw it, he answered unto Acts 3:12
w he was determined to let him go Acts 3:13
w the times of refreshing shall Acts 3:19 3704
w they had set them in the midst, Acts 4:7
Now *w* they saw the boldness of Acts 4:13
But *w* they had commanded them to Acts 4:15
So *w* they had further threatened Acts 4:21
w they heard that, they lifted up Acts 4:24
w they had prayed, the place was Acts 4:31
w his wife, not knowing what was Acts 5:7
w they heard that, they entered Acts 5:21
But *w* the officers came, and found Acts 5:22
but *w* we had opened, we found no Acts 5:23
Now *w* the high priest and the Acts 5:24 5613
w they had brought them, they set Acts 5:27
W they heard that, they were cut Acts 5:33
w they had called the apostles, Acts 5:40
w the number of the disciples was Acts 6:1
w they had prayed, they laid Acts 6:6
w he was in Mesopotamia, before Acts 7:2
w his father was dead, he removed Acts 7:4 3326
him, *w* as yet he had no child Acts 7:5
But *w* Jacob heard that there was Acts 7:12
But *w* the time of the promise Acts 7:17 2531
w he was cast out, Pharaoh's Acts 7:21
w he was full forty years old, it Acts 7:23 5613
w forty years were expired, there Acts 7:30
W Moses saw it, he wondered at Acts 7:31
W they heard these things, they Acts 7:54
w he had said this, he fell Acts 7:60
But *w* they believed Philip Acts 8:12 3753
w he was baptized, he continued Acts 8:13
Now *w* the apostles which were at Acts 8:14
w they were come down, prayed for Acts 8:15
w Simon saw that through laying Acts 8:18
w they had testified and preached Acts 8:25
w they were come up out of the Acts 8:39 3753
w his eyes were opened, he saw no Acts 9:8
w he had received meat, he was Acts 9:19
w Saul was come to Jerusalem, he Acts 9:26
Which *w* the brethren knew, they Acts 9:30
whom *w* they had washed, they laid Acts 9:37
W he was come, they brought him Acts 9:39
w she saw Peter, she sat up Acts 9:40
w he had called the saints and Acts 9:41
w he looked on him, he was afraid Acts 10:4
w the angel which spake unto Acts 10:7 5613
w he had declared all these Acts 10:8
w he cometh, shall speak unto Acts 10:32
w Peter was come up to Jerusalem, Acts 11:2 3753
Upon the which *w* I had fastened Acts 11:6
W they heard these things, they Acts 11:18
w they were come to Antioch, Acts 11:20
w he came, and had seen the grace Acts 11:23
w he had found him, he brought Acts 11:26
w he had apprehended him, he put Acts 12:4
w Herod would have brought him Acts 12:6 3753
W they were past the first and the Acts 12:10
w Peter was come to himself, he Acts 12:11
w he had considered the thing, he Acts 12:12
w she knew Peter's voice, she Acts 12:14
w they had opened the door, and Acts 12:16
w Herod had sought for him, and Acts 12:19
w they had fulfilled their Acts 12:25
w they had fasted and prayed, and Acts 13:3
w they were at Salamis, they Acts 13:5
w they had gone through the isle Acts 13:6
w he saw what was done, believed, Acts 13:12
Now *w* Paul and his company loosed Acts 13:13
But *w* they departed from Perga, Acts 13:14
exalted the people *w* they dwelt Acts 13:17
w he had destroyed seven nations Acts 13:19
w he had removed him, he raised Acts 13:22
W John had first preached before Acts 13:24
w they had fulfilled all that was Acts 13:29 5613
w the Jews were gone out of the Acts 13:42
Now *w* the congregation was broken Acts 13:43
But *w* the Jews saw the multitudes Acts 13:45
w the Gentiles heard this, they Acts 13:48
w there was an assault made both Acts 14:5 5613
w the people saw what Paul had Acts 14:11
Which *w* the apostles, Barnabas and Acts 14:14 3752
w they had preached the gospel to Acts 14:21
w they had ordained them elders Acts 14:23
w they had preached the word in Acts 14:25
w they were come, and had gathered Acts 14:27
W therefore Paul and Barnabas had Acts 15:2
w they were come to Jerusalem, Acts 15:4
w there had been much disputing, Acts 15:7
So *w* they were dismissed, they Acts 15:30
w they had gathered the multitude Acts 15:30
Which *w* they had read, they Acts 15:31
Now *w* they had gone throughout Acts 16:6
w she was baptized, and her Acts 16:15 5613
w her masters saw that the hope Acts 16:19
w they had laid many stripes upon Acts 16:23
w he had brought them into his Acts 16:34
w it was day, the magistrates Acts 16:35
w they heard that they were Acts 16:38
w they had seen the brethren, Acts 16:40
Now *w* they had passed through Acts 17:1
w they found them not, they drew Acts 17:6
w they heard these things Acts 17:8
w they had taken security of Acts 17:9
But *w* the Jews of Thessalonica Acts 17:13 5613
w he saw the city wholly given to Acts 17:16
w they heard of the resurrection Acts 17:32
w Silas and Timotheus were come Acts 18:5 5613
w they opposed themselves, and Acts 18:6
w Gallio was the deputy of Achaia Acts 18:12
w Paul was now about to open his Acts 18:14
W they desired him to tarry Acts 18:20
w he had landed at Caesarea, and Acts 18:22
whom *w* Aquila and Priscilla had Acts 18:26
w he was disposed to pass into Acts 18:27
w he was come, helped them much Acts 18:27
W they heard this, they were Acts 19:5
w Paul had laid his hands upon Acts 19:6
But *w* divers were hardened, and Acts 19:9 5613
w he had passed through Macedonia Acts 19:21
w they heard these sayings, they Acts 19:28
w Paul would have entered in unto Acts 19:30
But *w* they knew that he was a Jew Acts 19:34
w the townclerk had appeased the Acts 19:35
And *w* he had thus spoken, he Acts 19:41
w he had gone over those parts, Acts 20:2
w the Jews laid wait for him, as Acts 20:3
w the disciples came together to Acts 20:7
W he therefore was come up again, Acts 20:11
w he met with us at Assos, we Acts 20:14 5613
w they were come to him, he said Acts 20:18 5613
w he had thus spoken, he kneeled Acts 20:36
Now *w* we had discovered Cyprus, Acts 21:3
w we had accomplished those days, Acts 21:5 3753
w we had taken our leave one of Acts 21:6
w we had finished our course from Acts 21:7
w he was come unto us, he took Acts 21:11
w we heard these things, both we, Acts 21:12 5613
w he would not be persuaded, we Acts 21:14
w we were come to Jerusalem, the Acts 21:17
w he had saluted them, he Acts 21:19
w they heard it, they glorified Acts 21:20
w the seven days were almost Acts 21:27 5613
w they saw him in the temple, Acts 21:27
w they saw the chief captain and Acts 21:32
w he could not know the certainty Acts 21:34
w he came upon the stairs, so it Acts 21:35 3753
w he had given him licence, Paul Acts 21:40
w there was made a great silence, Acts 21:40
w they heard that he spake in the Acts 22:2
w I could not see for the glory Acts 22:11 5613
w I was come again to Jerusalem, Acts 22:17
w the blood of thy martyr Stephen Acts 22:20 3753
W the centurion heard that, he Acts 22:26
But *w* Paul perceived that the one Acts 23:6
w he had so said, there arose a Acts 23:7
w there arose a great dissension, Acts 23:10
w it was day, certain of the Jews Acts 23:12
w Paul's sister's son heard of Acts 23:16
w I would have known the cause Acts 23:28
w it was told me how that the Acts 23:30
w they came to Caesarea, and Acts 23:33
w the governor had read the Acts 23:34
w he understood that he was of Acts 23:34
w thine accusers are also come Acts 23:35 3752
w he was called forth, Tertullus Acts 24:2
w Felix heard these things, Acts 24:22
W Lysias the chief captain shall Acts 24:22 3752
w Felix came with his wife Acts 24:24
w I have a convenient season, I Acts 24:25
Now *w* Festus was come into the Acts 25:1
w he had tarried among them more Acts 25:6
w he was come, the Jews which Acts 25:7
w he had conferred with the Acts 25:12
w they had been there many days, Acts 25:14 5613
w I was at Jerusalem, the chief Acts 25:15
w they were come hither, without Acts 25:17
Against whom *w* the accusers stood Acts 25:18
But *w* Paul had appealed to be Acts 25:21
w Agrippa was come, and Bernice, Acts 25:23
But *w* I found that he had Acts 25:25
w they were put to death, I gave Acts 26:10
w we were all fallen to the earth Acts 26:14
w he had thus spoken, the king Acts 26:30
w they were gone aside, they Acts 26:31
w it was determined that we Acts 27:1 5613
w we had launched from thence, we Acts 27:4
w we had sailed over the sea of Acts 27:5
w we had sailed slowly many days, Acts 27:7
Now *w* much time was spent, and Acts 27:9
w sailing was now dangerous, Acts 27:9
w the south wind blew softly, Acts 27:13
w the ship was caught, and could Acts 27:15
Which *w* they had taken up, they Acts 27:17
w neither sun nor stars in many Acts 27:20
But *w* the fourteenth night was Acts 27:27 5613
w they had gone a little further, Acts 27:28
w they had let down the boat into Acts 27:30 3752
w he had thus spoken, he took Acts 27:35
w he had broken it, he began to Acts 27:35
w they had eaten enough, they Acts 27:38
w it was day, they knew not the Acts 27:39 3753
w they had taken up the anchors, Acts 27:40
w they were escaped, then they Acts 28:1
w Paul had gathered a bundle of Acts 28:3
w the barbarians saw the venomous Acts 28:4 5613
Howbeit they looked *w* he should Acts 28:6
So *w* this was done, others also, Acts 28:9
w we departed, they laded us with Acts 28:10
w the brethren heard of us, they Acts 28:15
whom *w* Paul saw, he thanked God, Acts 28:15
w we came to Rome, the centurion Acts 28:16 3753
w they were come together, he Acts 28:17
w they had examined me, would Acts 28:18
But *w* the Jews spake against it, Acts 28:19
w they had appointed him a day, Acts 28:23
And *w* they agreed not among Acts 28:25 3752
w he had said these words, the Acts 28:29
w they knew God, they glorified Rom 1:21
For *w* the Gentiles, which have Rom 2:14 3752
In the day *w* God shall judge the Rom 2:16 3753
overcome *w* thou art judged Rom 3:4
w he was in circumcision, or in Rom 4:10
w he was about an hundred years Rom 4:19
For *w* we were yet without Rom 5:6
w we were enemies, we were Rom 5:10
is not imputed *w* there is no law Rom 5:13
For *w* ye were the servants of sin Rom 6:20 3753
For *w* we were in the flesh, the Rom 7:5 3753
but *w* the commandment came, sin Rom 7:9
w I would do good, evil is Rom 7:21
but *w* Rebecca also had conceived Rom 9:10
w I shall take away their sins Rom 11:27 3752
nearer than *w* we believed Rom 13:11 3753
W therefore I have performed this Rom 15:28
w I come unto you, I shall come Rom 15:29
w I came to you, came not with 1Cor 2:1
w ye are gathered together, and my 1Cor 5:4
But *w* ye sin so against the 1Cor 8:12
w I preach the gospel, I may make 1Cor 9:18
w I have preached to others, I 1Cor 9:27
w ye come together in the church, 1Cor 11:18
W ye come together therefore into 1Cor 11:20
w he had given thanks, he brake 1Cor 11:24
w he had supped, saying, This cup 1Cor 11:25 3326
But *w* we are judged, we are 1Cor 11:32
w ye come together to eat, tarry 1Cor 11:33
rest will I set in order *w* I come 1Cor 11:34 5613
But *w* that which is perfect is 1Cor 13:10 3752
W I was a child, I spake as a 1Cor 13:11 3753
but *w* I became a man, I put away 1Cor 13:11 3753
Else *w* thou shalt bless with the 1Cor 14:16 1437
w ye come together, every one of 1Cor 14:26 3752
w he shall have delivered up the 1Cor 15:24 3752
w he shall have put down all rule 1Cor 15:24 3752
But *w* he saith all things are put 1Cor 15:27 3752
w all things shall be subdued 1Cor 15:28 3752
So *w* this corruptible shall have 1Cor 15:54 3752
there be no gatherings *w* I come 1Cor 16:2 3752
w I come, whomsoever ye shall 1Cor 16:3 3752
w I shall pass through Macedonia 1Cor 16:5 3752
but he will come *w* he shall have 1Cor 16:12 3752
W I therefore was thus minded, 2Cor 1:17
w I came, I should have sorrow 2Cor 2:3
w I came to Troas to preach 2Cor 2:12
w Moses is read, the vail is upon 2Cor 3:15 2259
Nevertheless *w* it shall turn to 2Cor 3:16 2259
w we were come into Macedonia, 2Cor 7:5
w he told us your earnest desire, 2Cor 7:7
be bold *w* I am present with that 2Cor 10:2
w your obedience is fulfilled 2Cor 10:6 3752
word by letters *w* we are absent 2Cor 10:11
be also in deed *w* we are present 2Cor 10:11
w your faith is increased, that 2Cor 10:15
w I was present with you, and 2Cor 11:9
for *w* I am weak, then am I strong 2Cor 12:10 3752
w I come, I shall not find you 2Cor 12:20
w I come again, my God will 2Cor 12:21
w we are weak, and ye are strong 2Cor 13:9 3752
But *w* it pleased God, who Gal 1:15 3753
w they saw that the gospel of the Gal 2:7
w James, Cephas, and John, who Gal 2:9
But *w* Peter was come to Antioch, Gal 2:11 3753
but *w* they were come, he withdrew Gal 2:12 3753
But *w* I saw that they walked not Gal 2:14 3753
w we were children, were in Gal 4:3 3753
But *w* the fulness of the time was Gal 4:4 3753
w ye knew not God, ye did service Gal 4:8
not only *w* I am present with you Gal 4:18
w he is nothing, he deceiveth Gal 6:3
w he raised him from the dead, and Eph 1:20
Even *w* we were dead in sins, hath Eph 2:5
w ye read, ye may understand my Eph 3:4
W he ascended up on high, he led Eph 4:8 3752
good comfort, *w* I know your state Phil 2:19
w ye see him again, ye may Phil 2:28
w I departed from Macedonia, no Phil 4:15 3753
W Christ, who is our life, shall Col 3:4 3752
some time, *w* ye lived in them Col 3:7 3753
w this epistle is read among you, Col 4:16 3752
w we might have been burdensome, 1Th 2:6
w ye received the word of God 1Th 2:13
Wherefore *w* we could no longer 1Th 3:1
w we were with you, we told you 1Th 3:4 3753
w I could no longer forbear, I 1Th 3:5

But now *w* Timotheus came from you. 1Th 3:6
For *w* they shall say, Peace and 1Th 5:3 *3752*
w the Lord Jesus shall be 2Th 1:7
W he shall come to be glorified 2Th 1:10 *3752*
w I was yet with you, I told you 2Th 2:5
For even *w* we were with you, this 2Th 3:10 *3753*
w I went into Macedonia, that 1Ti 1:3
for *w* they have begun to wax 1Ti 5:11 *3752*
W I call to remembrance the 2Ti 1:5
w he was in Rome, he sought me 2Ti 1:17
For the time will come *w* they 2Ti 4:3 *3753*
w thou comest, bring with thee, 2Ti 4:13
w Paul was brought before Nero 2Ti *s* *3752*
W I shall send Artemas unto thee, Titus 3:12 *3752*
w he had by himself purged our Heb 1:3
And again, *w* he bringeth in the Heb 1:6 *3752*
W your fathers tempted me, proved Heb 3:9 *3756*
w they had heard, did provoke Heb 3:16
w he had offered up prayers and Heb 5:7
For *w* for the time ye ought to be Heb 5:12
For *w* God made promise to Abraham. Heb 6:13
his father, *w* Melchisedec met him Heb 7:10 *3753*
did once, *w* he offered up himself Heb 7:27
of God *w* he was about to make the Heb 8:5
w I will make a new covenant with Heb 8:8
in the day *w* I took them by the Heb 8:9
Now *w* these things were thus Heb 9:6
For *w* Moses had spoken every Heb 9:19
Wherefore *w* he cometh into the Heb 10:5
Above *w* he said, Sacrifice and Heb 10:8
w he was called to go out into a Heb 11:8
of a child *w* she was past age Heb 11:11
w he was tried, offered up Isaac Heb 11:17
w he was a dying, blessed both Heb 11:21
w he died, made mention of the Heb 11:22
w he was born, was hid three Heb 11:23
w he was come to years, refused Heb 11:24
w she had received the spies with Heb 11:31
nor faint *w* thou art rebuked of Heb 12:5
w he would have inherited the Heb 12:17
count it all joy *w* ye fall into Jas 1:2 *3752*
for *w* he is tried, he shall Jas 1:12
Let no man say *w* he is tempted Jas 1:13
w he is drawn away of his own Jas 1:14
Then *w* lust hath conceived, it Jas 1:15
w it is finished, bringeth forth Jas 1:15
w he had offered Isaac his son Jas 2:21
w she had received the messengers Jas 2:25
w it testified beforehand the 1Pet 1:11
w ye be buffeted for your faults, 1Pet 2:20
w ye do well, and suffer for it, 1Pet 2:20
w he was reviled, reviled not 1Pet 2:23
w he suffered, he threatened not 1Pet 2:23
w once the longsuffering of God 1Pet 3:20 *3753*
w we walked in lasciviousness, 1Pet 4:3
w his glory shall be revealed, ye 1Pet 4:13
w the chief Shepherd shall appear 1Pet 5:4
w we made known unto you the 2Pet 1:16
w there came such a voice to him 2Pet 1:17
w we were with him in the holy 2Pet 1:18
For *w* they speak great swelling 2Pet 2:18
w he shall appear, we may have 1Jn 2:28 *3752*
w he shall appear, we shall be 1Jn 3:2 *1437*
w we love God, and keep his 1Jn 5:2 *3752*
w the brethren came and testified 3Jn 3
w I gave all diligence to write Jude 3
w contending with the devil he Jude 9 *3753*
w they feast with you, feeding Jude 12
w I saw him, I fell at his feet Rev 1:17 *3753*
w those beasts give glory and Rev 4:9 *3752*
w he had taken the book, the four Rev 5:8 *3753*
I saw *w* the Lamb opened one of Rev 6:1 *3753*
w he had opened the second seal, Rev 6:3 *3753*
w he had opened the third seal, I Rev 6:5 *3753*
w he had opened the fourth seal, Rev 6:7 *3753*
w he had opened the fifth seal, I Rev 6:9 *3753*
I beheld *w* he had opened the Rev 6:12 *3753*
w she is shaken of a mighty wind Rev 6:13
a scroll *w* it is rolled together Rev 6:14
w he had opened the seventh seal, Rev 8:1 *3753*
a scorpion, *w* he striketh a man Rev 9:5 *3752*
a loud voice, as *w* a lion roareth Rev 10:3
w he had cried, seven thunders Rev 10:3 *3753*
w the seven thunders had uttered Rev 10:4 *3753*
w he shall begin to sound, the Rev 10:7 *3752*
w they shall have finished their Rev 11:7 *3752*
w the dragon saw that he was cast Rev 12:13 *3753*
w I saw her, I wondered with Rev 17:6
w they behold the beast that was, Rev 17:8
w he cometh, he must continue a Rev 17:10 *3752*
w they shall see the smoke of her Rev 18:9 *3752*
cried *w* they saw the smoke of her Rev 18:18
w the thousand years are expired, Rev 20:7 *3752*
w I had heard and seen, I fell Rev 22:8 *3753*

WHENCE
the ground from *w* he was taken Gen 3:23
Sarai's maid, *w* camest thou Gen 16:8 335
unto the land from *w* thou camest Gen 24:5 370
unto them, My brethren, *w* be ye Gen 29:4 370
and he said unto them, *W* come ye Gen 42:7 370
W should I have flesh to give Num 11:13 370
from *w* thou mayest see them Num 23:13
Lest the land *w* thou broughtest Deut 9:28
from *w* ye came out, where thou Deut 11:10
me, but I wist not *w* they were Josh 2:4 370
and from *w* come ye Josh 9:8 370
unto the city from *w* he fled Josh 20:6
but I asked him not *w* he was Judg 13:6
said unto him, *W* comest thou Judg 17:9 370
and *w* comest thou Judg 19:17 370
men, whom I know not *w* they be 1Sa 25:11
and *w* art thou 1Sa 30:13
said unto him, From *w* comest thou 2Sa 1:3
man that told him, *W* art thou 2Sa 1:13
unto him, *W* comest thou, Gehazi 2Kin 5:25 370
help thee, *w* shall I help thee 2Kin 6:27 370
from *w* came they unto thee 2Kin 20:14 370
From all places *w* ye shall return Neh 4:12 370
said unto Satan, *W* comest thou Job 1:7 370
unto Satan, From *w* comest thou Job 2:2
Before I go *w* I shall not return, Job 10:21
go the way *w* I shall not return, Job 16:22
W then cometh wisdom Job 28:20 370
the hills, from *w* cometh my help Ps 121:1 370
the place from *w* the rivers come Eccl 1:7
from *w* come the young and old lion Is 30:6 1992
from *w* came they unto thee Is 39:3 370
shalt not know from *w* it riseth Is 47:11 370
look unto the rock *w* ye are hewn Is 51:1
hole of the pit *w* ye are digged Is 51:1
bring you again into the place *w* Jer 29:14
and *w* comest thou Jonah 1:8 370
w shall I seek comforters for Nah 3:7 370
into my house from *w* I came out Mt 12:44 *3606*
from *w* then hath it tares Mt 13:27 *4159*
W hath this man this wisdom, and Mt 13:54 *4159*
W then hath this man all these Mt 13:56 *4159*
W should we have so much bread in Mt 15:33 *4159*
The baptism of John, *w* was it Mt 21:25 *4159*
From *w* hath this man these things Mk 6:2 *4159*
From *w* can a man satisfy these Mk 8:4 *4159*
and *w* is he then his son Mk 12:37 *4159*
w is this to me, that the mother Lk 1:43 *4159*
return unto my house *w* I came out Lk 11:24 *3606*
unto you, I know you not *w* ye are Lk 13:25 *4159*
tell you, I know you not *w* ye are Lk 13:27 *4159*
that they could not tell *w* it was Lk 20:7 *4159*
saith unto him, *W* knowest thou me Jn 1:48 *4159*
made wine, and knew not *w* it was Jn 2:9 *4159*
but canst not tell *w* it cometh Jn 3:8 *4159*
from *w* then hast thou that living Jn 4:11 *4159*
W shall we buy bread, that these Jn 6:5 *4159*
Howbeit we know this man *w* he is Jn 7:27 *4159*
cometh, no man knoweth *w* he is Jn 7:27 *4159*
both know me, and ye know *w* I am Jn 7:28 *4159*
for I know *w* I came, and whither I Jn 8:14 *4159*
but ye cannot tell *w* I come Jn 8:14 *4159*
fellow, we know not from *w* he is Jn 9:29 *4159*
that ye know not from *w* he is Jn 9:30 *4159*
and saith unto Jesus, *W* art thou Jn 19:9 *4159*
from *w* they had been recommended Acts 14:26 *3606*
from *w* also we look for the Phil 3:20 *3739*
that country from *w* they came out Heb 11:15 *3739*
from *w* also he received him in a Heb 11:19 *3606*
From *w* come wars and fightings Jas 4:1 *4159*
therefore from *w* thou art fallen Rev 2:5 *4159*
and *w* came they Rev 7:13 *4159*

WHENSOEVER
w the stronger cattle did Gen 30:41 3605
w ye will ye may do them good Mk 14:7 *3752*
W I take my journey into Spain, I Rom 15:24

WHERE
land of Havilah, *w* there is gold Gen 2:11
and said unto him, *W* art thou Gen 3:9 335
unto Cain, *W* is Abel thy brother Gen 4:9 335
unto the place *w* his tent had Gen 13:3 834
that it was well watered every *w* Gen 13:10
the place *w* thou art northward Gen 13:14 834
unto him, *W* is Sarah thy wife Gen 18:9 346
W are the men which came in to Gen 19:5 346
place *w* he stood before the LORD Gen 19:27 834
dwell *w* it pleaseth thee Gen 20:15
the voice of the lad *w* he is Gen 21:17 834
but *w* is the lamb for a burnt Gen 22:7 834
w is he that hath taken venison, Gen 27:33 645
w thou anointedst the pillar, and Gen 31:13 834
w thou vowedst a vow unto me Gen 31:13 834
w he had spread his tent, at the Gen 33:19 834
in the place *w* he talked with him Gen 35:13 834
in the place *w* he talked with him Gen 35:14 834
of the place *w* God spake with him Gen 35:15 834
w Abraham and Isaac sojourned Gen 35:27 834
thee, *w* they feed their flocks Gen 37:16 375
W is the harlot, that was openly Gen 38:21 346
a place *w* the king's prisoners Gen 39:20 834
the place *w* Joseph was bound Gen 40:3 834
and he sought *w* to weep Gen 43:30
unto his daughters, And *w* is he Ex 2:20 346
get you straw *w* ye can find it Ex 5:11 834
w the children of Israel were, Ex 9:26 834
a token upon the houses *w* ye are Ex 12:13 834
a house *w* there was not one dead Ex 12:30 834
w were twelve wells of water, and Ex 15:27 8033
w he encamped at the mount of God Ex 18:5
unto the thick darkness *w* God was Ex 20:21
in all places *w* I record my name Ex 20:24 834
and the breadth fifty every *w* Ex 27:18 834
w I will meet you, to speak there Ex 29:42
w I will meet with thee Ex 30:6
w I will meet with thee Ex 30:36
w the ashes are poured out, and Lev 4:12 413
w the ashes are poured out shall Lev 4:12 5921
kill it in the place *w* they kill Lev 4:24 834
w they kill the burnt offering Lev 4:33 834
In the place *w* the burnt offering Lev 6:25 834
In the place *w* they kill the Lev 7:2 834
slay the lamb in the place *w* he Lev 14:13 834
in the place *w* the cloud abode, Num 9:17 834
w Ahiman, Sheshai, and Talmai, the Num 13:22 8033
testimony, *w* I will meet with you Num 17:4
w was no way to turn either to Num 22:26 834
w was no water for the people to Num 33:14 8033
be in the place *w* his lot falleth Num 33:54
w thou hast seen how that the Deut 1:31 834
and drought, *w* there was no water Deut 8:15 834
w thou sowedst thy seed, and Deut 11:10 834
by the way *w* the sun goeth down, Deut 11:30
w he sojourned, and come with all Deut 18:6
thy gates, *w* it liketh him best Deut 23:16
W are their gods, their rock in Deut 32:37 335
out of the place *w* the priests' Josh 4:3
w ye shall lodge this night Josh 4:3 834
them unto the place *w* they lodged Josh 4:8 413
in the place *w* the feet of the Josh 4:9
w he bowed, there he fell down Judg 5:27 834
w be all his miracles which our Judg 6:13 346
W is now thy mouth, wherewith Judg 9:38 346
sojourn *w* he could find a place Judg 17:8 834
I go to sojourn *w* I may find a Judg 17:9 834
a place *w* there is no want of any Judg 18:10 834
of the man's house *w* her lord was Judg 19:26
again in array in the place *w* Judg 20:22
forth out of the place *w* she was Ruth 1:7
w thou lodgest, I will lodge Ruth 1:16 834
W thou diest, will I die, and Ruth 1:17 834
W hast thou gleaned to day Ruth 2:19 645
and *w* wroughtest thou Ruth 2:19 375
mark the place *w* he shall lie Ruth 3:4
w the ark of God was, and Samuel 1Sa 3:3
w there was a great stone 1Sa 6:14 8033
the city *w* the man of God was 1Sa 9:10
pray thee, *w* the seer's house is 1Sa 9:18
of God, *w* is the garrison of the 1Sa 10:5
when we saw that they were no *w* 1Sa 10:14 370
holes *w* they had hid themselves 1Sa 14:11
my father in the field *w* thou art 1Sa 19:3 834
and said, *W* are Samuel and David 1Sa 19:22 375
come to the place *w* thou didst 1Sa 20:19
and see his place *w* his haunt is 1Sa 23:22 834
places *w* he hideth himself 1Sa 23:23
by the way, *w* was a cave 1Sa 24:3 8033
to the place *w* Saul had pitched 1Sa 26:5
David beheld the place *w* Saul lay 1Sa 26:5
now see *w* the king's spear is, and 1Sa 26:16 335
w those that were left behind 1Sa 30:9
to all the places *w* David himself 1Sa 30:31
to the place *w* Asahel fell down 2Sa 2:23
the king said unto him, *W* is he 2Sa 9:4 375
w he knew that valiant men were 2Sa 11:16 834
w he worshipped God, behold, 2Sa 15:32
said, And *w* is thy master's son 2Sa 16:3 346
in some place *w* he shall be found 2Sa 17:12
said, *W* is Ahimaaz and Jonathan 2Sa 17:20 346
W the people of Israel were slain 2Sa 18:7 8033
w the Philistines had hanged them 2Sa 21:12
w Elhanan the son of Jaare-oregim 2Sa 21:19
w was a man of great stature, 2Sa 21:20
w was a piece of ground full of 2Sa 23:11 8033
the place *w* the officers were 1Kin 4:28
for the throne *w* he might judge 1Kin 7:7
his house *w* he dwelt had another 1Kin 7:8
told it in the city *w* the old 1Kin 13:25 834
w he abode, and laid him upon his 1Kin 17:19
In the place *w* dogs licked the 1Kin 21:19 834
W is the LORD God of Elijah 2Kin 2:14 346
to Shunem, *w* was a great woman 2Kin 4:8 8033
the place *w* we dwell with thee is 2Kin 6:1
us a place there, *w* we may dwell 2Kin 6:2 8033
And the man of God said, *W* fell it 2Kin 6:6 575
spy *w* he is, that I may send and 2Kin 6:13 351
W are the gods of Hamath, and of 2Kin 18:34 346
w are the gods of Sepharvaim, 2Kin 18:34 346
W is the king of Hamath, and the 2Kin 19:13 346
w the women wove hangings for the 2Kin 23:7
defiled the high places *w* the 2Kin 23:8 8033
w the Jebusites were, the 1Chr 11:4 8033
w was a parcel of ground full of 1Chr 11:13 834
abroad unto our brethren every *w* 1Chr 13:2
w was a man of great stature, 1Chr 20:6
w the LORD appeared unto David 2Chr 3:1 834
w the LORD commanded, saying, The 2Chr 25:4 834
w they were servants to him and 2Chr 36:20
in any place *w* he sojourneth Ezr 1:4
w the treasures were laid up in Ezr 6:1 8536
builded, the place *w* they offered Ezr 6:3 1768
w are the vessels of the Neh 10:39 8033
w aforetime they laid the meat Neh 13:5 8033
W were white, green, and blue, Est 1:6
w is he, that durst presume in Est 7:5 335
or *w* were the righteous cut off Job 4:7 375
if not, *w*, and who is he Job 9:24 645
w the light is as darkness Job 10:22
in a wilderness *w* there is no way Job 12:24
giveth up the ghost, and *w* is he Job 14:10 834
abroad for bread, saying, *W* is it Job 15:23 346
And *w* is now my hope Job 17:15
have seen him shall say, *W* is he Job 20:7 335
W is the house of the prince Job 21:28 346
w are the dwelling places of the Job 21:28 346
Oh that I knew *w* I might find him Job 23:3
w he doth work, but I cannot Job 23:9
a place for gold *w* they fine it Job 28:1
But *w* shall wisdom be found Job 28:12 370
w is the place of understanding Job 28:12
w is the place of understanding Job 28:20 335
w the workers of iniquity may Job 34:22 8033
W is God my maker, who giveth Job 35:10 335
place, *w* there is no straitness Job 36:16
W wast thou when I laid the Job 38:4 375
W is the way *w* light dwelleth Job 38:19 335
darkness, *w* is the place thereof, Job 38:19 335
to rain on the earth, *w* no man is Job 38:26
w the slain are, there is she Job 39:30 834
w all the beasts of the field Job 40:20 8033
w their voice is not heard Ps 19:3
the place *w* thine honour dwelleth Ps 26:8
say unto me, *W* is thy God Ps 42:3 346
say daily unto me, *W* is thy God Ps 42:10 346
they in great fear, *w* no fear was Ps 53:5
and thirsty land, *w* no water is Ps 63:1

deep mire, *w* there is no standing	Ps 69:2	
waters, *w* the floods overflow me	Ps 69:2	
the heathen say, *W* is their God	Ps 79:10	346
w I heard a language that I	Ps 81:5	
w she may lay her young, even	Ps 84:3	834
w are thy former lovingkindnesses	Ps 89:49	346
W the birds make their nests	Ps 104:17	
the wilderness, *w* there is no way	Ps 107:40	
heathen say, *W* is now their God	Ps 115:2	346
W no counsel is, the people fall	Prov 11:14	
W no oxen are, the crib is clean	Prov 14:4	
is a dinner of herbs *w* love is	Prov 15:17	8033
W no wood is, there the fire	Prov 26:20	657
so *w* there is no talebearer, the	Prov 26:20	
W there is no vision, the people	Prov 29:18	
hasteth to his place *w* he arose	Eccl 1:5	8033
W the word of a king is, there is	Eccl 8:4	834
in the city *w* they had so done	Eccl 8:10	834
in the place *w* the tree falleth,	Eccl 11:3	
w thou feedest, *w* thou makest	Song 1:7	349
w there were a thousand vines at	Is 7:23	834
w will ye leave your glory	Is 10:3	575
W are they	Is 19:12	335
w are thy wise men	Is 19:12	645
to Ariel, the city *w* David dwelt	Is 29:1	
in every place *w* the grounded	Is 30:32	
W is the scribe	Is 33:18	346
w is the receiver	Is 33:18	346
w is he that counted the towers	Is 33:18	346
w each lay, shall be grass with	Is 35:7	
W are the gods of Hamath and	Is 36:19	346
w are the gods of Sepharvaim	Is 36:19	346
W is the king of Hamath, and the	Is 37:13	346
these, *w* had they been	Is 49:21	375
W is the bill of your mother's	Is 50:1	335
w is the fury of the oppressor	Is 51:13	346
their bed *w* thou sawest it	Is 57:8	3027
W is he that brought them up out	Is 63:11	346
w is he that put his holy Spirit	Is 63:11	346
w is thy zeal and thy strength,	Is 63:15	346
w our fathers praised thee, is	Is 64:11	834
w is the house that ye build unto	Is 66:1	335
w is the place of my rest	Is 66:1	335
W is the LORD that brought us up	Jer 2:6	346
passed through, and *w* no man dwelt	Jer 2:6	8033
priests said not, *W* is the LORD	Jer 2:8	346
But *w* are thy gods that thou hast	Jer 2:28	346
see *w* thou hast not been lien	Jer 3:2	375
w is the good way, and walk	Jer 6:16	335
w I set my name at the first, and	Jer 7:12	
from the place *w* I had hid it	Jer 13:7	
w is the flock that was given	Jer 13:20	346
w I will not shew you favour	Jer 16:13	834
W is the word of the LORD	Jer 17:15	346
country, *w* ye were not born	Jer 22:26	
in the land *w* ye be strangers	Jer 35:7	
and let no man know *w* ye be	Jer 36:19	375
W are now your prophets which	Jer 37:19	346
for hunger in the place *w* he is	Jer 38:9	8478
w he gave judgment upon him	Jer 39:5	
w we shall see no war, nor hear	Jer 42:14	834
w he gave judgment upon him	Jer 52:9	
their mothers, *W* is corn and wine	Lam 2:12	346
I sat *w* they sat, and remained	Eze 3:15	8033
the place *w* they did offer sweet	Eze 6:13	
w was the seat of the image of	Eze 8:3	
the countries *w* they shall come	Eze 11:16	
w ye have been scattered, and I	Eze 11:17	834
W is the daubing wherewith ye	Eze 13:12	346
wither in the furrows *w* it grew	Eze 17:10	5921
surely in the place *w* the king	Eze 17:16	
out of the country *w* they sojourn	Eze 20:38	
in the place *w* thou wast created	Eze 21:30	834
deliver them out of all places *w*	Eze 34:12	
w they washed the burnt offering	Eze 40:38	8033
w the priests that approach unto	Eze 42:13	
w I will dwell in the midst of	Eze 43:7	
This is the place *w* the priests	Eze 46:20	
w they shall bake the meat	Eze 46:20	834
w the ministers of the house	Eze 46:24	
So he came near *w* I stood	Dan 8:17	
that in the place *w* it was said	Hos 1:10	834
w is any other that may save thee	Hos 13:10	645
among the people, *W* is their God	Joel 2:17	346
the earth, *w* no gin is for him	Amos 3:5	
unto me, *W* is the LORD thy God	Mic 7:10	346
W is the dwelling of the lions,	Nah 2:11	346
w the lion, even the old lion,	Nah 2:11	
place is not known *w* they are	Nah 3:17	335
fame in every land *w* they have	Zeph 3:19	
Your fathers, *w* are they	Zec 1:5	346
I be a father, *w* is mine honour	Mal 1:6	346
and if I be a master, *w* is my fear	Mal 1:6	346
or, *W* is the God of judgment	Mal 2:17	346
W is he that is born King of the	Mt 2:2	*4226*
he demanded of them *w* Christ	Mt 2:4	*4226*
stood over *w* the young child was	Mt 2:9	*3757*
w moth and rust doth corrupt, and	Mt 6:19	*3699*
w thieves break through and steal	Mt 6:19	*3699*
w neither moth nor rust doth	Mt 6:20	*3699*
w thieves do not break through	Mt 6:20	*3699*
For *w* your treasure is, there	Mt 6:21	*3699*
of man hath not *w* to lay his head	Mt 8:20	*4226*
w they had not much earth	Mt 13:5	*3699*
For *w* two or three are gathered	Mt 18:20	*3757*
reaping *w* thou hast not sown, and	Mt 25:24	*3699*
gathering *w* thou hast not strawed	Mt 25:24	*3606*
knewest that I reap *w* I sowed not	Mt 25:26	*3699*
gather *w* I have not strawed	Mt 25:26	*3606*
W wilt thou that we prepare for	Mt 26:17	*4226*
w the scribes and the elders were	Mt 26:57	*3699*
see the place *w* the Lord lay	Mt 28:6	*3699*
into a mountain *w* Jesus had	Mt 28:16	*3757*
they uncovered the roof *w* he was	Mk 2:4	*3699*
ground, *w* it had not much earth	Mk 4:5	*3699*
the way side, *w* the word is sown	Mk 4:15	*3699*
entereth in *w* the damsel was	Mk 5:40	*3699*
were sick, *w* they heard he was	Mk 6:55	*3699*
W their worm dieth not, and the	Mk 9:44	*3699*
W their worm dieth not, and the	Mk 9:46	*3699*
W their worm dieth not, and the	Mk 9:48	*3699*
without in a place *w* two ways met	Mk 11:4	*296*
standing *w* it ought not, (let him	Mk 13:14	*3699*
W wilt thou that we go and prepare	Mk 14:12	*4226*
W is the guestchamber	Mk 14:14	*4226*
w I shall eat the passover with	Mk 14:14	*3699*
of Joses beheld *w* he was laid	Mk 15:47	*4226*
behold the place *w* they laid him	Mk 16:6	*3699*
went forth, and preached every *w*	Mk 16:20	*3837*
w he had been brought up	Lk 4:16	*3757*
found the place *w* it was written	Lk 4:17	*3757*
said unto them, *W* is your faith	Lk 8:25	*4226*
the gospel, and healing every *w*	Lk 9:6	*3837*
of man hath not *w* to lay his head	Lk 9:58	*4226*
as he journeyed, came *w* he was	Lk 10:33	*2596*
no room *w* to bestow my fruits	Lk 12:17	*4226*
w no thief approacheth, neither	Lk 12:33	*3699*
For *w* your treasure is, there	Lk 12:34	*3699*
but *w* are the nine	Lk 17:17	*4226*
they answered and said unto him, *W*	Lk 17:37	*4226*
W wilt thou that we prepare	Lk 22:9	*4226*
into the house *w* he entereth in	Lk 22:10	*3757*
W is the guestchamber	Lk 22:11	*4226*
w I shall eat the passover with	Lk 22:11	*3699*
Jordan, *w* John was baptizing	Jn 1:28	*3699*
Master,) *w* dwellest thou	Jn 1:38	*4226*
saw *w* he dwelt, and abode with him	Jn 1:39	*4226*
The wind bloweth *w* it listeth	Jn 3:8	*3699*
the place *w* men ought to worship	Jn 4:20	*3699*
Galilee, *w* he made the water wine	Jn 4:46	*3699*
the place *w* they did eat bread	Jn 6:23	*3699*
of man ascend up *w* he was before	Jn 6:62	*3699*
at the feast, and said, *W* is he	Jn 7:11	*4226*
w I am, thither ye cannot come	Jn 7:34	*3699*
w I am, thither ye cannot come	Jn 7:36	*3699*
town of Bethlehem, *w* David was	Jn 7:42	*3699*
w are those thine accusers	Jn 8:10	*4226*
they unto him, *W* is thy Father	Jn 8:19	*4226*
Then said they unto him, *W* is he	Jn 9:12	*4226*
place *w* John at first baptized	Jn 10:40	*3699*
still in the same place *w* he was	Jn 11:6	
in that place *w* Martha met him	Jn 11:30	*3699*
when Mary was come *w* Jesus was	Jn 11:32	*3699*
And said, *W* have ye laid him	Jn 11:34	*4226*
the place *w* the dead was laid	Jn 11:41	*3757*
that, if any man knew *w* he were	Jn 11:57	*4226*
w Lazarus was which had been dead	Jn 12:1	*3699*
w I am, there shall also my	Jn 12:26	*3699*
that *w* I am, there ye may be also	Jn 14:3	*3699*
hast given me, be with me *w* I am	Jn 17:24	*3699*
w was a garden, into the which he	Jn 18:1	*3699*
W they crucified him, and two	Jn 19:18	*3699*
for the place *w* Jesus was	Jn 19:20	*3699*
Now in the place *w* he was	Jn 19:41	*3699*
we know not *w* they have laid him	Jn 20:2	*4226*
w the body of Jesus had lain	Jn 20:12	*3699*
I know not *w* they have laid him	Jn 20:13	*4226*
tell me *w* thou hast laid him, and	Jn 20:15	*4226*
when the doors were shut *w* the	Jn 20:19	*3699*
w abode both Peter, and James, and	Acts 1:13	*3757*
all the house *w* they were sitting	Acts 2:2	*3757*
the place was shaken *w* they were	Acts 4:31	
of Madian, *w* he begat two sons	Acts 7:29	*3757*
for the place *w* thou standest is	Acts 7:33	
went every *w* preaching the word	Acts 8:4	*1330*
come unto the house *w* I was	Acts 11:11	
w many were gathered together	Acts 12:12	*3757*
our brethren in every city *w* we	Acts 15:36	
w prayer was wont to be made	Acts 16:13	
w was a synagogue of the Jews	Acts 17:1	*3699*
all men every *w* to repent	Acts 17:30	*3837*
w we abode seven days	Acts 20:6	*3757*
w they were gathered together	Acts 20:8	*3757*
men every *w* against the people	Acts 21:28	*3838*
seat, *w* I ought to be judged	Acts 25:10	*3757*
into a place *w* two seas met	Acts 27:41	*1337*
W we found brethren, and were	Acts 28:14	*3757*
we know that every *w* it is spoken	Acts 28:22	*3837*
W is boasting then	Rom 3:27	*4226*
for *w* no law is, there is no	Rom 4:15	*3757*
But *w* sin abounded, grace did	Rom 5:20	*3757*
that in the place *w* it was said	Rom 9:26	*3757*
not *w* Christ was named, lest I	Rom 15:20	*3699*
W is the wise	1Cor 1:20	*4226*
w is the scribe	1Cor 1:20	*4226*
w is the disputer of this world	1Cor 1:20	*4226*
I teach every *w* in every church	1Cor 4:17	*3837*
were an eye, *w* were the hearing	1Cor 12:17	*4226*
were hearing, *w* were the smelling	1Cor 12:17	*4226*
all one member, *w* were the body	1Cor 12:19	*4226*
O death, *w* is thy sting	1Cor 15:55	*4226*
O grave, *w* is thy victory	1Cor 15:55	*4226*
w the Spirit of the Lord is,	2Cor 3:17	*3757*
W is then the blessedness ye	Gal 4:15	*5101*
every *w* and in all things I am	Phil 4:12	
w Christ sitteth on the right	Col 3:1	*3757*
W there is neither Greek nor Jew,	Col 3:11	*3699*
therefore that men pray every *w*	1Ti 2:8	
For *w* a testament is, there must	Heb 9:16	*3699*
Now *w* remission of these is,	Heb 10:18	*3699*
For *w* envying and strife is, there	Jas 3:16	*3699*
w shall the ungodly and the sinner	1Pet 4:18	*4226*
W is the promise of his coming	2Pet 3:4	*4226*
w thou dwellest	Rev 2:13	*4226*
even *w* Satan's seat is	Rev 2:13	*3699*
slain among you, *w* Satan dwelleth	Rev 2:13	*3699*
w also our Lord was crucified	Rev 11:8	*3699*
w she hath a place prepared of	Rev 12:6	*3699*
w she is nourished for a time, and	Rev 12:14	*3699*
w the whore sitteth, are peoples,	Rev 17:15	*3757*
w the beast and the false prophet	Rev 20:10	*3699*

WHEREABOUT

of the business *w* I send thee	1Sa 21:2	834

WHEREAS

W thou hast searched all my stuff	Gen 31:37	3588
w he was not worthy of death,	Deut 19:6	
w ye were as the stars of heaven	Deut 28:62	834
w I have rewarded thee evil	1Sa 24:17	
W I have not dwelt in any house	2Sa 7:6	3588
W thou camest but yesterday,	2Sa 15:20	
W it was in thine heart to build	1Kin 8:18	
now *w* my father did lade you with	1Kin 12:11	
W now thou shalt smite Syria but	2Kin 13:19	6258
For *w* my father put a heavy yoke	2Chr 10:11	6258
for *w* we have offended against	2Chr 28:13	3588
W our substance is not cut down,	Job 22:20	518
w also he that is born in his	Eccl 4:14	3588
W thou hast prayed to me against	Is 37:21	834
W thou hast been forsaken and	Is 60:15	8478
w the sword reacheth unto the	Jer 4:10	
w ye say, The LORD saith it	Eze 13:7	
w thou wast naked and bare	Eze 16:7	
w none followeth thee to commit	Eze 16:34	
w the LORD was there	Eze 35:10	
w it lay desolate in the sight of	Eze 36:34	
w thou sawest the feet and toes,	Dan 2:41	1768
w thou sawest iron mixed with	Dan 2:43	1768
w the king saw a watcher and an	Dan 4:23	1768
w they commanded to leave the	Dan 4:26	1768
w four stood up for it, four	Dan 8:22	
W Edom saith, We are impoverished	Mal 1:4	3588
that, *w* I was blind, now I see	Jn 9:25	
for *w* there is among you envying,	1Cor 3:3	*3699*
W ye know not what shall be on	Jas 4:14	*3748*
w they speak against you as	1Pet 2:12	
w they speak evil of you, as of	1Pet 3:16	
W angels, which are greater in	2Pet 2:11	*3699*

WHEREBY

w shall I know that I shall	Gen 15:8	4100
drinketh, and *w* indeed he divineth	Gen 44:5	
w he may be made unclean, or a	Lev 22:5	834
w an atonement shall be made for	Num 5:8	834
w they murmur against you	Num 17:5	834
w the LORD thy God brought thee	Deut 7:19	834
doings, *w* thou hast forsaken me	Deut 28:20	834
w Jonathan knew that it was	1Sa 20:33	
w the people fall under thee	Ps 45:5	
w they have made thee glad	Ps 45:8	4482
w thou didst confirm thine	Ps 68:9	
when for all the causes *w*	Jer 3:8	834
w the kings of Judah come in, and	Jer 17:19	834
this is his name *w* he shall be	Jer 23:6	834
w they have sinned against me	Jer 33:8	834
w they have sinned	Jer 33:8	834
w they have transgressed against	Jer 33:8	834
w ye have transgressed	Eze 18:31	834
judgments *w* they should not live	Eze 20:25	
all their trespasses *w* they have	Eze 39:26	834
by the steps *w* they went up to it	Eze 40:49	834
the way of the gate *w* he came in	Eze 46:9	834
w ye shall inherit the land	Eze 47:13	834
w they have reproached my people,	Zeph 2:8	834
the angel, *W* shall I know this	Lk 1:18	
w the dayspring from on high hath	Lk 1:78	
among men, *w* we must be saved	Acts 4:12	
w thou and all thy house shall be	Acts 11:14	
there being no cause *w* we may	Acts 19:40	
adoption, *w* we cry, Abba, Father	Rom 8:15	
nor any thing *w* thy brother	Rom 14:21	
W, when ye read, ye may	Eph 3:4	
w they lie in wait to deceive	Eph 4:14	*3739*
w ye are sealed unto the day of	Eph 4:30	
according to the working *w* he is	Phil 3:21	*3588*
w we may serve God acceptably	Heb 12:28	
W are given unto us exceeding	2Pet 1:4	
W the world that then was, being	2Pet 3:6	
w we know that it is the last	1Jn 2:18	

WHEREFORE

w it is said, Even as Nimrod the	Gen 10:9	
W the well was called	Gen 16:14	
W did Sarah laugh, saying, Shall	Gen 18:13	4100
W she said unto Abraham, Cast out	Gen 21:10	
W he called that place Beer-sheba	Gen 21:31	4100
w standest thou without	Gen 24:31	4100
W come ye to me, seeing ye hate	Gen 26:27	4069
w then hast thou beguiled me	Gen 29:25	
W didst thou flee away secretly,	Gen 31:27	4100
yet *w* hast thou stolen my gods	Gen 31:30	4100
W is it that thou dost ask after	Gen 32:29	4100
w he slew him also	Gen 38:10	
W look ye so sadly to day	Gen 40:7	4069
W dealt ye so ill with me, as to	Gen 43:6	4100
W have ye rewarded evil for good	Gen 44:4	4100
W saith my lord these words	Gen 44:7	4100
W shall we die before thine eyes,	Gen 47:19	4100
w they sold not their lands	Gen 47:22	
w the name of it was called	Gen 50:11	
W smitest thou thy fellow	Ex 2:13	4100
W do ye, Moses and Aaron, let the	Ex 5:4	4100
W have ye not fulfilled your task	Ex 5:14	4069
W dealest thou thus with thy	Ex 5:15	4100
w hast thou so evil entreated	Ex 5:22	4100
W say unto the children of Israel	Ex 6:6	3651
w hast thou dealt thus with us,	Ex 14:11	
unto Moses, *W* criest thou unto me	Ex 14:15	4100
W the people did chide with Moses	Ex 17:2	
w do ye tempt the LORD	Ex 17:2	4100
W is this that thou hast brought	Ex 17:3	4100
w the LORD blessed the sabbath	Ex 20:11	
W the children of Israel shall	Ex 31:16	

W should the Egyptians speak, and...... Ex 32:12 4100
W have ye not eaten the sin ...... Lev 10:17 4069
w the priest shall pronounce him...... Lev 13:25
W ye shall do my statutes, and...... Lev 25:18
w are we kept back, that we may...... Num 9:7 4100
W hast thou afflicted thy servant...... Num 11:11 4100
w have I not found favour in thy...... Num 11:11 4100
w then were ye not afraid to...... Num 12:8 4069
w hath the LORD brought us unto...... Num 14:3 4100
W now do ye transgress the...... Num 14:41 4100
w then lift ye up yourselves...... Num 16:3 4069
w have ye made us to come up out...... Num 20:5 4100
w Israel turned away from him...... Num 20:21
W have ye brought us up out of...... Num 21:5 4100
W it is said in the book of the...... Num 21:14
W they that speak in proverbs say...... Num 21:27
W hast thou smitten thine ass...... Num 22:32 4100
w camest thou not unto me...... Num 22:37 4100
W say, Behold, I give unto him my...... Num 25:12 3651
W, said they, if we have found...... Num 32:5
w discourage ye the heart of the...... Num 32:7 4100
W it shall come to pass, if ye...... Deut 7:12
W Levi hath no part nor...... Deut 10:9
W I command thee, saying, Thou...... Deut 19:7
W hath the LORD done thus unto...... Deut 29:24
W the name of the place is called...... Josh 5:9
w the hearts of the people melted...... Josh 7:5
w hast thou at all brought this...... Josh 7:7 4100
w liest thou thus upon thy face...... Josh 7:10 4100
W the name of that place was...... Josh 7:26
W our elders and all the...... Josh 9:11
W have ye beguiled us, saying, We...... Josh 9:22 4100
W Adoni-zedek king of Jerusalem...... Josh 10:3
W I also said, I will not drive...... Judg 2:3
w I will deliver you no more...... Judg 10:13 3651
W I have not sinned against thee,...... Judg 11:27
W passedst thou over to fight...... Judg 12:1 4069
w then are ye come up unto me...... Judg 12:3 4100
w he called the name thereof...... Judg 15:19 4100
w they called that place...... Judg 18:12
W she went forth out of the place...... Ruth 1:7
W it came to pass, when the time...... 1Sa 1:20
W the sin of the young men was...... 1Sa 2:17
W kick ye at my sacrifice and at...... 1Sa 2:29 4100
W the LORD God of Israel saith, I...... 1Sa 2:30 3651
W hath the LORD smitten us to day...... 1Sa 4:3 4100
W ye shall make images of your...... 1Sa 6:5
W then do ye harden your hearts,...... 1Sa 6:6 4100
w then speakest thou so to me...... 1Sa 9:21 4100
w he put forth the end of the rod...... 1Sa 14:27
W then didst thou not obey the...... 1Sa 15:19 4100
W Saul sent messengers unto Jesse...... 1Sa 16:19
W when Saul saw that he behaved...... 1Sa 18:15
W Saul said to David, Thou shalt...... 1Sa 18:21
W David arose and went, he and his...... 1Sa 18:27
w then wilt thou sin against...... 1Sa 19:5 4100
W they say, Is Saul also among...... 1Sa 19:24
W cometh not the son of Jesse to...... 1Sa 20:27 4069
W now send and fetch him unto me,...... 1Sa 20:31
unto him, *W* shall he be slain...... 1Sa 20:32 4100
w then have ye brought him to me...... 1Sa 21:14 4100
w he came down into a rock, and...... 1Sa 23:25
W Saul returned from pursuing...... 1Sa 23:28
W hearest thou men's words,...... 1Sa 24:9 4100
w the LORD reward thee good for...... 1Sa 24:19
W let the young men find favour...... 1Sa 25:8
w she told him nothing, less or...... 1Sa 25:36
w then hast thou not kept thy...... 1Sa 26:15 4100
W doth my lord thus pursue after...... 1Sa 26:18 4100
w Ziklag pertaineth unto the...... 1Sa 27:6 3651
w then layest thou a snare for my...... 1Sa 28:9 4100
W then dost thou ask of me,...... 1Sa 28:16 4100
W now return, and go in peace,...... 1Sa 29:7
W now rise up early in the...... 1Sa 29:10
w that place was called...... 2Sa 2:16
w should I smite thee to the...... 2Sa 2:22 4100
w Abner with the hinder end of...... 2Sa 2:23
W hast thou gone in unto my...... 2Sa 3:7 4069
W they said, The blind and the...... 2Sa 5:8 4100
W thou art great, O LORD God...... 2Sa 7:22
W Hanun took David's servants, and...... 2Sa 10:4
W approached ye so nigh unto the...... 2Sa 11:20 4069
W hast thou despised the...... 2Sa 12:9 4069
now he is dead, *w* should I fast...... 2Sa 12:23 4100
W then hast thou thought such a...... 2Sa 14:13 4100
W have thy servants set my field...... 2Sa 14:31 4100
to say, *W* am I come from Geshur...... 2Sa 14:32 4100
W goest thou also with us...... 2Sa 15:19 4100
then say, *W* hast thou done so...... 2Sa 16:10 4069
W wilt thou run, my son, seeing...... 2Sa 18:22
w then are ye the last to bring...... 2Sa 19:12 4100
W wentest not thou with me,...... 2Sa 19:25 4100
w then should thy servant be yet...... 2Sa 19:35 4100
w then be ye angry for this...... 2Sa 19:42 4100
W David said unto the Gibeonites,...... 2Sa 21:3
W is my lord the king come to his...... 2Sa 24:21 4069
W his servants said unto him, Let...... 1Kin 1:2
W Nathan spake unto Bath-sheba...... 1Kin 1:11
W is this noise of the city being...... 1Kin 1:41 4069
W the LORD said unto Solomon,...... 1Kin 11:11 4100
W the king hearkened not unto the...... 1Kin 12:15 4100
w all Israel made Omri, the...... 1Kin 16:16
W he said unto the messengers of...... 1Kin 20:9
w he said unto the driver of his...... 1Kin 22:34
W wilt thou go to him to day...... 2Kin 4:23 4069
W he went again to meet him, and...... 2Kin 4:31
w consider, I pray you, and see...... 2Kin 5:7
W hast thou rent thy clothes...... 2Kin 5:8 4100
W they arose and fled in the...... 2Kin 7:7
w came this mad fellow to thee...... 2Kin 9:11 4069
W they came again, and told him...... 2Kin 9:36
W they spake to the king of...... 2Kin 17:26
w lift up thy prayer for the...... 2Kin 19:4
w that place is called Perez-uzza...... 1Chr 13:11 4100

W Hanun took David's servants, and...... 1Chr 19:4
W Joab departed, and went...... 1Chr 21:4
W David blessed the LORD before...... 1Chr 29:10
W all the men of Israel assembled...... 2Chr 5:3
W now let the fear of the LORD be...... 2Chr 19:7
W he did evil in the sight of the...... 2Chr 22:4
w their anger was greatly kindled...... 2Chr 25:10
W the anger of the LORD was...... 2Chr 25:15
W the LORD his God delivered him...... 2Chr 28:5
W the wrath of the LORD was upon...... 2Chr 29:8
w their brethren the Levites did...... 2Chr 29:34
W the LORD brought upon them the...... 2Chr 33:11
W the king said unto me, Why is...... Neh 2:2
w Haman sought to destroy all the...... Est 3:6
W they called these days Purim...... Est 9:26
W is light given to him that is...... Job 3:20 4100
shew me *w* thou contendest with me...... Job 10:2
W then hast thou brought me forth...... Job 10:18 4100
W do I take my flesh in my teeth,...... Job 13:14
W hidest thou thy face, and...... Job 13:24 4100
W are we counted as beasts, and...... Job 18:3 4069
W do the wicked live, become old,...... Job 21:7 4069
w I was afraid, and durst not shew...... Job 32:6
W, Job, I pray thee, hear my...... Job 33:1 199
W I abhor myself, and repent in...... Job 42:6
W doth the wicked contemn God...... Ps 10:13
W hidest thou thy face, and...... Ps 44:24 4100
W should I fear in the days of...... Ps 49:5 4100
W should the heathen say, Where...... Ps 79:10 4100
w hast thou made all men in vain...... Ps 89:47 4100
W should the heathen say, Where...... Ps 115:2 4100
W is there a price in the hand of...... Prov 17:16
W I perceive that there is...... Eccl 3:22 4100
W I praised the dead which are...... Eccl 4:2
w should God be angry at thy...... Eccl 5:6 4100
w, when I looked that it should...... Is 5:4 4069
W it shall come to pass, that...... Is 10:12
W my bowels shall sound like an...... Is 16:11
W glorify ye the LORD in the...... Is 24:15
W hear the word of the LORD, ye...... Is 28:14 3651
W the Lord said, Forasmuch as...... Is 29:13
W thus saith the Holy One of...... Is 30:12 3651
w lift up thy prayer for the...... Is 37:4
W, when I came, was there no man...... Is 50:2 4069
W do ye spend money for that...... Is 55:2 4100
W have we fasted, say they, and...... Is 58:3 4100
w have we afflicted our soul, and...... Is 58:3
W art thou red in thine apparel,...... Is 63:2 4069
W I will yet plead with you,...... Jer 2:9 3651
W will ye plead with me...... Jer 2:29 4100
w say my people, We are lords...... Jer 2:31 4069
W a lion out of the forest shall...... Jer 5:6
W thus saith the LORD God of...... Jer 5:14 3651
W doeth the LORD our God all...... Jer 5:19
W doth the way of the wicked...... Jer 12:1 4069
w are all they happy that deal...... Jer 12:1
W come these things upon me...... Jer 13:22 4069
W hath the LORD pronounced all...... Jer 16:10
W came I forth out of the womb to...... Jer 20:18 4100
W hath the LORD done thus unto...... Jer 22:8
w are they cast out, he and his...... Jer 22:28 4069
W their way shall be unto them as...... Jer 23:12 3651
w should this city be laid waste...... Jer 27:17 4100
w do I see every man with his...... Jer 30:6 4069
W dost thou prophesy, and say,...... Jer 32:3 4069
W the princes were wroth with...... Jer 37:15
w should he slay thee, that all...... Jer 40:15 4100
W my fury and mine anger was...... Jer 44:6
W commit ye this great evil...... Jer 44:7 4100
W have I seen them dismayed and...... Jer 46:5 4069
W gloriest thou in the valleys,...... Jer 49:4 4100
W, behold, the days come, saith...... Jer 51:52 3651
W doth a living man complain, a...... Lam 3:39 4100
W dost thou forget us for ever,...... Lam 5:20 4100
W, as I live, saith the Lord GOD...... Eze 5:11 3651
W I will bring the worst of the...... Eze 7:24
W thus saith the Lord GOD...... Eze 13:20 3651
W, O harlot, hear the word of the...... Eze 16:35 3651
w turn yourselves, and live ye...... Eze 18:32
W I caused them to go forth out...... Eze 20:10
W I gave them also statutes that...... Eze 20:25
W say unto the house of Israel,...... Eze 20:30 3651
say unto thee, *W* sighest thou...... Eze 21:7
W I have delivered her into the...... Eze 23:9 3651
W thus saith the Lord GOD...... Eze 24:6 3651
W say unto them, Thus saith the...... Eze 33:25 3651
W I poured my fury upon them for...... Eze 36:18
w I have consumed them in mine...... Eze 43:8
W at that time certain Chaldeans...... Dan 3:8
W, O king, let my counsel be...... Dan 4:27 3861
W king Darius signed the writing...... Dan 6:9
w shut thou up the vision...... Dan 8:26
Knowest thou *w* I come unto thee...... Dan 10:20 4100
w should they say among the...... Joel 2:17 4100
W they cried unto the LORD, and...... Jonah 1:14
w lookest thou upon them that...... Hab 1:13 4100
Yet ye say, *W*...... Mal 2:14 4100
And *w* one...... Mal 2:15 4100
W, if God so clothe the grass of...... Mt 6:30 *1161*
W by their fruits ye shall know...... Mt 7:20
W think ye evil in your hearts...... Mt 9:4
W it is lawful to do well on the...... Mt 12:12 *5620*
W I say unto you, All manner of...... Mt 12:31
little faith, *w* didst thou doubt...... Mt 14:31
W if thy hand or thy foot offend...... Mt 18:8 *1161*
W they are no more twain, but one...... Mt 19:6 *5620*
W ye be witnesses unto yourselves...... Mt 23:31 *5620*
W, behold, I send unto you...... Mt 23:34
W if they shall say unto you,...... Mt 24:26 *3767*
unto him, Friend, *w* art thou come...... Mt 26:50
W that field was called, The...... Mt 27:8 *1352*
W neither thought I myself worthy...... Lk 7:7 *1352*
W I say unto thee, Her sins,...... Lk 7:47
W then gavest not thou my money...... Lk 19:23 *1302*

w would ye hear it again...... Jn 9:27 *5101*
W of these men which have...... Acts 1:21 *3767*
W, brethren, look ye out among...... Acts 6:3 *3767*
what is the cause *w* ye are come...... Acts 10:21
W he saith also in another psalm,...... Acts 13:35 *1352*
W my sentence is, that we trouble...... Acts 15:19 *1352*
the more part knew not *w* they...... Acts 19:32
W if Demetrius, and the craftsmen...... Acts 19:38
W I take you to record this day,...... Acts 20:26 *1352*
that he might know *w* they cried...... Acts 22:24
w he was accused of the Jews...... Acts 22:30 *5101*
the cause *w* they accused him...... Acts 23:28
w he sent for him the oftener, and...... Acts 24:26 *1352*
W I have brought him forth before...... Acts 25:26 *1352*
w I beseech thee to hear me...... Acts 26:3 *1352*
W, sirs, be of good cheer...... Acts 27:25 *1352*
W I pray you to take some meat...... Acts 27:34 *1352*
W God also gave them up to...... Rom 1:24 *1352*
W, as by one man sin entered into...... Rom 5:12
W, my brethren, ye also are...... Rom 7:4 *5620*
W the law is holy, and the...... Rom 7:12 *5620*
W? Because they sought...... Rom 9:32 *1302*
W ye must needs be subject, not...... Rom 13:5 *1352*
W receive ye one another, as...... Rom 15:7 *1352*
W I beseech you, be ye followers...... 1Cor 4:16 *3767*
W, if meat make my brother to...... 1Cor 8:13 *1355*
W let him that thinketh he...... 1Cor 10:12 *5620*
W, my dearly beloved, flee from...... 1Cor 10:14 *1355*
W whosoever shall eat this bread,...... 1Cor 11:27 *5620*
W, my brethren, when ye come...... 1Cor 11:33 *5620*
W I give you to understand, that...... 1Cor 12:3 *1352*
W let him that speaketh in an...... 1Cor 14:13 *1355*
W tongues are for a sign, not to...... 1Cor 14:22 *5620*
W, brethren, covet to prophesy,...... 1Cor 14:39 *5620*
W I beseech you that ye would...... 2Cor 2:8 *1352*
W we labour, that, whether...... 2Cor 5:9 *1352*
W henceforth know we no man after...... 2Cor 5:16 *5620*
W come out from among them...... 2Cor 6:17 *1352*
W, though I wrote unto you, I did...... 2Cor 7:12 *686*
W shew ye to them, and before the...... 2Cor 8:24 *3767*
W? because I love...... 2Cor 11:11 *1302*
W then serveth the law...... Gal 3:19 *5101*
W the law was our schoolmaster to...... Gal 3:24 *5620*
W thou art no more a servant, but...... Gal 4:7 *5620*
W I also, after I heard of your...... Eph 1:15
W remember, that ye being in time...... Eph 2:11 *1352*
W I desire that ye faint not at...... Eph 3:13 *1352*
W he saith, When he ascended up...... Eph 4:8 *1352*
W putting away lying, speak every...... Eph 4:25 *1352*
W he saith, Awake thou that...... Eph 5:14 *1352*
W be ye not unwise, but...... Eph 5:17
W take unto you the whole armour...... Eph 6:13
W God also hath highly exalted...... Phil 2:9 *1352*
W, my beloved, as ye have always...... Phil 2:12 *5620*
W if ye be dead with Christ from...... Col 2:20 *3767*
W we would have come unto you,...... 1Th 2:18 *1352*
W when we could no longer forbear...... 1Th 3:1 *1352*
W comfort one another with these...... 1Th 4:18 *5620*
W comfort yourselves together, and...... 1Th 5:11 *1352*
W also we pray always for you,...... 2Th 1:11
W I put thee in remembrance that...... 2Ti 1:6
W rebuke them sharply, that they...... Titus 1:13
W, though I might be much bold in...... Philem 8 *1352*
W in all things it behoved him to...... Heb 2:17 *3606*
W, holy brethren, partakers of...... Heb 3:1 *3606*
W (as the Holy Ghost saith, To...... Heb 3:7 *1352*
W I was grieved with that...... Heb 3:10 *1352*
W he is able also to save them to...... Heb 7:25 *3606*
w it is of necessity that this...... Heb 8:3 *3606*
W when he cometh into the world,...... Heb 10:5 *1352*
w God is not ashamed to be called...... Heb 11:16 *1352*
W seeing we also are compassed...... Heb 12:1 *5105*
W lift up the hands which hang...... Heb 12:12 *1352*
W we receiving a kingdom which...... Heb 12:28 *1352*
W Jesus also, that he might...... Heb 13:12 *1352*
W, my beloved brethren, let every...... Jas 1:19 *5620*
W lay apart all filthiness and...... Jas 1:21 *1352*
W he saith, God resisteth the...... Jas 4:6 *1352*
W gird up the loins of your mind,...... 1Pet 1:13 *1352*
W laying aside all malice, and all...... 1Pet 2:1 *3767*
W also it is contained in the...... 1Pet 2:6 *1352*
W let them that suffer according...... 1Pet 4:19 *5620*
W the rather, brethren, give...... 2Pet 1:10 *1352*
W I will not be negligent to put...... 2Pet 1:12 *1352*
W, beloved, seeing that ye look...... 2Pet 3:14 *1352*
And *w* slew he him...... 1Jn 3:12
W, if I come, I will remember his...... 3Jn 10
said unto me, *W* didst thou marvel...... Rev 17:7 *1302*

WHEREIN

w there is life, I have given...... Gen 1:30 834
w is the breath of life, from...... Gen 6:17 834
flesh, *w* is the breath of life...... Gen 7:15 834
the land *w* thou art a stranger,...... Gen 17:8
to the land *w* thou hast sojourned...... Gen 21:23 834
the land *w* thou art a stranger...... Gen 28:4
the land *w* they were strangers...... Gen 36:7
Jacob dwelt in the land *w* his...... Gen 37:1
w they made them serve, was with...... Ex 1:14 834
pilgrimage, *w* they were strangers...... Ex 6:4 834
the houses, *w* they shall eat it...... Ex 12:7 834
for in the thing *w* they dealt...... Ex 18:11 834
them the way *w* they must walk...... Ex 18:20
w shall he sleep...... Ex 22:27 4100
For *w* shall it be known here that...... Ex 33:16 4100
w he hath sinned, come to his...... Lev 4:23 834
his ignorance *w* he erred and wist...... Lev 5:18 834
But the earthen vessel *w* it is...... Lev 6:28 834
w any work is done, it must be...... Lev 11:32 834
w there is plenty of water, shall...... Lev 11:36
All the days *w* the plague shall...... Lev 13:46 834
thing of skin, *w* the plague is...... Lev 13:52 834
wash the thing *w* the plague is...... Lev 13:54 834
thou shalt burn that *w* the plague...... Lev 13:57 834

w ye dwelt, shall ye not do	Lev 18:3	834
w we have done foolishly	Num 12:11	834
and *w* we have sinned	Num 12:11	834
w is no blemish, and upon which	Num 19:2	834
all their cities *w* they dwelt	Num 31:10	
vex you in the land *w* ye dwell	Num 33:55	834
not pollute the land *w* ye are	Num 35:33	834
which ye shall inhabit, *w* I dwell	Num 35:34	834
A land *w* thou shalt eat bread	Deut 8:9	834
w were fiery serpents, and	Deut 8:15	
w the nations which ye shall	Deut 12:2	
w the LORD thy God hath blessed	Deut 12:7	834
or sheep, *w* is blemish, or any	Deut 17:1	834
w thou trustedst, throughout all	Deut 28:52	
the wilderness *w* they chased them	Josh 8:24	834
into the cave *w* they had been hid	Josh 10:27	
w the LORD's tabernacle dwelleth,	Josh 22:19	
to destroy the land *w* the	Josh 22:33	834
us in all the way *w* we went	Josh 24:17	834
see *w* his great strength lieth,	Judg 16:5	4100
w thy great strength lieth, and	Judg 16:6	4100
hast not told me *w* thy great	Judg 16:15	4100
the LORD is your way *w* ye go	Judg 18:6	834
w the jewels of gold were, and put	1Sa 6:15	834
see *w* this sin hath been this day	1Sa 14:38	4100
In all the places *w* I have walked	2Sa 7:7	834
in all *w* my father was afflicted	1Kin 2:26	834
w is the covenant of the LORD,	1Kin 8:21	
the good way *w* they should walk	1Kin 8:36	834
all their transgressions *w* they	1Kin 8:50	834
w the man of God is buried	1Kin 13:31	834
w Jehoiada the priest instructed	2Kin 12:2	834
w the LORD commanded, saying, The	2Kin 14:6	834
in their cities *w* they dwelt	2Kin 17:29	
is this *w* thou trustest	2Kin 18:19	834
w this passover was holden to the	2Kin 23:23	
Now these are the things *w*	2Chr 3:3	
w is the covenant of the LORD,	2Chr 6:11	
the good way, *w* they should walk	2Chr 6:27	834
w Solomon had built the house of	2Chr 8:1	834
the places *w* he built high places	2Chr 33:19	834
unto him, *w* was written thus	Ezr 5:7	1459
W was written, It is reported	Neh 6:6	
light in the way *w* they should go	Neh 9:12	834
and the way *w* they should go	Neh 9:19	834
in the day *w* they sold victuals	Neh 13:15	
all the things *w* the king had	Est 5:11	834
W the king granted the Jews which	Est 8:11	834
As the days *w* the Jews rested	Est 9:22	834
Let the day perish *w* I was born	Job 3:3	
of the ice, and *w* the snow is hid	Job 6:16	
me to understand *w* I have erred	Job 6:24	4100
the wilderness, *w* there is no man	Job 38:26	
mount Zion, *w* thou hast dwelt	Ps 74:2	
the days *w* thou hast afflicted us	Ps 90:15	
the years *w* we have seen evil	Ps 90:15	
w all the beasts of the forest do	Ps 104:20	
w are things creeping innumerable	Ps 104:25	8033
In the way *w* I walked have they	Ps 142:3	2098
to know the way *w* I should walk	Ps 143:8	2098
all my labour *w* I have laboured	Eccl 2:19	
w I have shewed myself wise under	Eccl 2:19	
w he hath laboured under the sun	Eccl 2:22	
worketh in that *w* he laboureth	Eccl 3:9	834
there is a time *w* one man ruleth	Eccl 8:9	834
for *w* is he to be accounted of	Is 2:22	4100
from the hard bondage *w* thou wast	Is 14:3	834
w shall go no galley with oars,	Is 33:21	
is this *w* thou trustest	Is 36:4	834
w thou hast laboured from thy	Is 47:12	834
did choose that *w* I delighted not	Is 65:12	834
w thou trustedst, with the sword	Jer 5:17	834
w ye trust, and unto the place	Jer 7:14	834
w thou trustedst, they wearied	Jer 12:5	
things *w* there is no profit	Jer 16:19	
Cursed be the day *w* I was born	Jer 20:14	834
let not the day *w* my mother bare	Jer 20:14	834
is he a vessel *w* is no pleasure	Jer 22:28	
way, *w* they shall not stumble	Jer 31:9	
Take in thine hand the roll *w*	Jer 36:14	834
Now the pit *w* Ishmael had cast	Jer 41:9	834
may shew us the way *w* we may walk	Jer 42:3	834
like a vessel *w* is no pleasure	Jer 48:38	
a land *w* no man dwelleth, neither	Jer 51:43	834
the countries *w* ye are scattered	Eze 20:34	834
w ye have been scattered	Eze 20:41	
doings, *w* ye have been defiled	Eze 20:43	834
w she had played the harlot in	Eze 23:19	834
into a city *w* is made a breach	Eze 26:10	
blood the land *w* thou swimmest	Eze 32:6	
w they have sinned, and will	Eze 37:23	834
w your fathers have dwelt	Eze 37:25	834
their garments *w* they minister	Eze 42:14	834
their garments *w* they ministered	Eze 44:19	834
w she burned incense to them, and	Hos 2:13	834
as a vessel *w* is no pleasure	Hos 8:8	
w are more than sixscore thousand	Jonah 4:11	
and *w* have I wearied thee	Mic 6:3	4100
w thou hast transgressed against	Zeph 3:11	834
out of the pit *w* is no water	Zec 9:11	
Yet ye say, *W* hast thou loved us	Mal 1:2	4100
W have we despised thy name	Mal 1:6	4100
ye say, *W* have we polluted thee	Mal 1:7	4100
Yet ye say, *W* have we wearied him	Mal 2:17	4100
But ye said, *W* shall we return	Mal 3:7	4100
But ye say, *W* have we robbed thee	Mal 3:8	4100
w most of his mighty works were	Mt 11:20	
the hour *w* the Son of man cometh	Mt 25:13	
they let down the bed *w* the sick	Mk 2:4	
w thou hast been instructed	Lk 1:4	
me in the days *w* he looked on me	Lk 1:25	*3739*
him all his armour *w* he trusted	Lk 11:22	
w never man before was laid	Lk 23:53	*3757*
w was never man yet laid	Jn 19:41	
in our own tongue, *w* we were born	Acts 2:8	
into this land, *w* ye now dwell	Acts 7:4	
W were all manner of fourfooted	Acts 10:12	
for *w* thou judgest another, thou	Rom 2:1	
faith into this grace *w* we stand	Rom 5:2	
that being dead *w* we were held	Rom 7:6	
the same calling *w* he was called	1Cor 7:20	
w he is called, therein abide	1Cor 7:24	
ye have received, and *w* ye stand	1Cor 15:1	
that *w* they glory, they may be	2Cor 11:12	
For what is it *w* ye were inferior	2Cor 12:13	*3757*
w he hath made us accepted in the	Eph 1:6	
W he hath abounded toward us in	Eph 1:8	*3757*
W in time past ye walked	Eph 2:2	
not drunk with wine, *w* is excess	Eph 5:18	
w ye were also careful, but ye	Phil 4:10	
w also ye are risen with him	Col 2:12	
W I suffer trouble, as an evil	2Ti 2:9	
W God, willing more abundantly to	Heb 6:17	
w was the candlestick, and the	Heb 9:2	
w was the golden pot that had	Heb 9:4	
W ye greatly rejoice, though now	1Pet 1:6	
w few, that is, eight souls were	1Pet 3:20	
W they think it strange that ye	1Pet 4:4	
the true grace of God *w* ye stand	1Pet 5:12	
w the heavens being on fire shall	2Pet 3:12	
earth, *w* dwelleth righteousness	2Pet 3:13	
even in those days *w* Antipas was	Rev 2:13	
w were made rich all that had	Rev 18:19	

WHEREINSOEVER

Howbeit *w* any is bold, (I speak	2Cor 11:21	

WHEREINTO

w any of them falleth, whatsoever	Lev 11:33	
I bring into the land *w* he went	Num 14:24	
save that one *w* his disciples	Jn 6:22	

WHEREOF

w I commanded thee that thou	Gen 3:11	834
w any of the blood is brought	Lev 6:30	834
in the skin *w* there is a hot	Lev 13:24	
w men bring an offering unto the	Lev 27:9	834
camps, in the midst *w* I dwell	Num 5:3	834
the weight *w* was an hundred and	Num 7:19	
the weight *w* was an hundred and	Num 7:25	834
the weight *w* was an hundred and	Num 7:37	
the weight *w* was an hundred and	Num 7:49	
the weight *w* was an hundred and	Num 7:61	
the weight *w* was an hundred and	Num 7:67	
the weight *w* was an hundred and	Num 7:73	
the weight *w* was an hundred and	Num 7:79	
that is the well *w* the LORD spake	Num 21:16	834
w he spake unto thee, saying, Let	Deut 13:2	834
w thou canst not be healed	Deut 28:27	834
by the way *w* I spake unto thee,	Deut 28:68	834
w the LORD spake in that day	Josh 14:12	834
w I spake unto you by the hand of	Josh 20:2	834
w they were possessed, according	Josh 22:9	834
w Samuel spake, he told him not	1Sa 10:16	834
w two thousand were with Saul in	1Sa 13:2	
the weight *w* was a talent of gold	2Sa 12:30	
sick of his sickness *w* he died	2Kin 13:14	834
w the LORD had said unto them, Ye	2Kin 17:12	834
the length *w* was according to the	2Chr 3:8	
upon the place *w* thou hast said	2Chr 6:20	834
w were made vessels for the house	2Chr 24:14	
w the LORD had said, In Jerusalem	2Chr 33:4	834
w one went on the right hand upon	Neh 12:31	
the poison *w* drinketh up my	Job 6:4	834
the streams *w* shall make glad the	Ps 46:4	
into the midst *w* they are fallen	Ps 57:6	
w we are glad	Ps 126:3	
there any thing *w* it may be said	Eccl 1:10	
w every one bear twins, and none	Song 4:2	
w every one beareth twins, and	Song 6:6	
w ye say, It shall be delivered	Jer 32:36	834
w ye say, It is desolate without	Jer 32:43	834
w ye were afraid, shall follow	Jer 42:16	834
destitute of that *w* it was full	Eze 32:15	
this is the day *w* I have spoken	Eze 39:8	834
w the word of the LORD came to	Dan 9:2	834
w she hath said, These are my	Hos 2:12	834
those things *w* ye accuse him	Lk 23:14	
raised up, *w* we all are witnesses	Acts 2:32	*3739*
w we are witnesses	Acts 3:15	*3739*
new doctrine, *w* thou speakest, is	Acts 17:19	
w he hath given assurance unto	Acts 17:31	
w they were informed concerning	Acts 21:24	
all these things, *w* we accuse him	Acts 24:8	*3739*
the things *w* they now accuse me	Acts 24:13	
of these things *w* these accuse me	Acts 25:11	*3739*
things *w* I am accused of the Jews	Acts 26:2	*3739*
by works, he hath *w* to glory	Rom 4:2	
those things *w* ye are now ashamed	Rom 6:21	
I have therefore *w* I may glory	Rom 15:17	
the things *w* ye wrote unto me	1Cor 7:1	
w ye had notice before, that the	2Cor 9:5	
W I was made a minister,	Eph 3:7	*3739*
w he might trust in the flesh	Phil 3:4	
w ye heard before in the word of	Col 1:5	*3739*
w I Paul am made a minister	Col 1:23	*3739*
W I am made a minister, according	Col 1:25	*3739*
what they say, nor *w* they affirm	1Ti 1:7	
w cometh envy, strife, railings,	1Ti 6:4	
the world to come, *w* we speak	Heb 2:5	
W the Holy Ghost also is a	Heb 10:15	
w all are partakers, then are ye	Heb 12:8	*3739*
w they have no right to eat which	Heb 13:10	
w ye have heard that it should	1Jn 4:3	*3739*

WHEREON

the land *w* thou liest, to thee	Gen 28:13	
for the place *w* thou standest is	Ex 3:5	
and also the ground *w* they are	Ex 8:21	
thou shalt wash that *w* it was	Lev 6:27	
w he lieth that hath the issue,	Lev 15:4	
w he sitteth, shall be unclean	Lev 15:4	
w he sat that hath the issue	Lev 15:6	
w is the seed of copulation,	Lev 15:17	
or on any thing *w* she sitteth	Lev 15:23	
all the bed *w* he lieth shall be	Lev 15:24	
Every bed *w* she lieth all the	Lev 15:26	
Every place *w* the soles of your	Deut 11:24	834
for the place *w* thou standest is	Josh 5:15	
Surely the land *w* thy feet have	Josh 14:9	834
w they set down the ark of the	1Sa 6:18	
the tables *w* the shewbread was	2Chr 4:19	5921
W do ye trust, that ye abide in	2Chr 32:10	
fallen upon the bed *w* Esther was	Est 7:8	
him to be in safety, *w* he resteth	Job 24:23	
w there hang a thousand bucklers,	Song 4:4	5921
w if a man lean, it will go into	Is 36:6	
the sticks *w* thou writest shall	Eze 37:20	
find a colt tied, *w* never man sat	Mk 11:2	
the hill *w* their city was built	Lk 4:29	
them, and took up that *w* he lay	Lk 5:25	
a colt tied, *w* yet never man sat	Lk 19:30	
reap that *w* ye bestowed no labour	Jn 4:38	*3739*

WHERESOEVER

to his foot, *w* the priest looketh	Lev 13:12	3605
sojourn *w* thou canst sojourn	2Kin 8:1	834
w any breach shall be found	2Kin 12:5	
W I have walked with all Israel,	1Chr 17:6	
or go *w* it seemeth convenient	Jer 40:5	
w the children of men dwell, the	Dan 2:38	
For *w* the carcase is, there will	Mt 24:28	
W this gospel shall be preached	Mt 26:13	
w he taketh him, he teareth him	Mk 9:18	
W this gospel shall be preached	Mk 14:9	
w he shall go in, say ye to the	Mk 14:14	
W the body is, thither will the	Lk 17:37	*3699*

WHERETO

w might the strength of their	Job 30:2	4100
prosper in the thing *w* I sent it	Is 55:11	834
w we have already attained, let	Phil 3:16	

WHEREUNTO

of the tribe *w* they are received	Num 36:3	*5101*
of the tribe *w* they are received	Num 36:4	834
perish from off the land *w* ye go	Deut 4:26	834
w the ark of the LORD hath come	2Chr 8:11	834
w the king advanced him, are they	Est 10:2	834
w I may continually resort	Ps 71:3	
But to the land *w* they desire to	Jer 22:27	834
w I will not do any more the like	Eze 5:9	834
What is the high place *w* ye go	Eze 20:29	
But *w* shall I liken this	Mt 11:16	*5101*
W shall we liken the kingdom of	Mk 4:30	*5101*
W then shall I liken the men of	Lk 7:31	*5101*
and *w* shall I resemble it	Lk 13:18	*5101*
W shall I liken the kingdom of	Lk 13:20	*5101*
doubted of them *w* this would grow	Acts 5:24	*5101*
Saul for the work *w* I have called	Acts 13:2	*3739*
nigh *w* was the city of Lasea	Acts 27:8	*3739*
w ye desire again to be in	Gal 4:9	*3739*
W I also labour, striving	Col 1:29	
W he called you by our gospel, to	2Th 2:14	
W I am ordained a preacher, and an	1Ti 2:7	
doctrine, *w* thou hast attained	1Ti 4:6	*3739*
w thou art also called, and hast	1Ti 6:12	
W I am appointed a preacher, and	2Ti 1:11	
w also they were appointed	1Pet 2:8	
The like figure *w* even baptism	1Pet 3:21	*3739*
w ye do well that ye take heed,	2Pet 1:19	*3739*

WHEREUPON

every thing *w* any part of their	Lev 11:35	
the pillars *w* the house standeth	Judg 16:26	
of gold, *w* the shewbread was,	1Kin 7:48	
W the king took counsel, and made	1Kin 12:28	
W the princes of Israel and the	2Chr 12:6	
W are the foundations thereof	Job 38:6	
w he was, to the threshold of the	Eze 9:3	
w thou hast set mine incense and	Eze 23:41	5921
that *w* they set their minds,	Eze 24:25	
w they slew their sacrifices	Eze 40:41	413
w also they laid the instruments	Eze 40:42	413
the piece *w* it rained not	Amos 4:7	
W he promised with an oath to	Mt 14:7	*3606*
W certain Jews from Asia found me	Acts 24:18	
W as I went to Damascus with	Acts 26:12	
W, O king Agrippa, I was not	Acts 26:19	*3606*
W neither the first testament was	Heb 9:18	*3606*

WHEREWITH

blessing *w* his father blessed him	Gen 27:41	834
w the Egyptians oppress them	Ex 3:9	834
thine hand, *w* thou shalt do signs	Ex 4:17	834
the bread *w* I have fed you in the	Ex 16:32	834
w thou smotest the river, take in	Ex 17:5	834
things *w* the atonement was made	Ex 29:33	834
of the sanctuary *w* they minister	Num 3:31	834
w the odd number of them is to be	Num 3:48	
thereof, *w* they minister unto it	Num 4:9	834
w they minister in the sanctuary,	Num 4:12	834
w they minister about it, even	Num 4:14	834
w they that were burnt had	Num 16:39	834
w they have beguiled you in the	Num 25:18	834
her bond *w* she hath bound her	Num 30:4	834
every bond *w* she hath bound her	Num 30:4	834
or of her bonds *w* she hath bound	Num 30:5	834
of her lips, *w* she bound her soul	Num 30:6	834
her bonds *w* she bound her soul	Num 30:7	834
w she bound her soul, of none	Num 30:8	834
w they have bound their souls,	Num 30:9	834
every bond *w* she bound her soul	Num 30:11	834
w he may die, and he die, he is a	Num 35:17	834
w he may die, and he die, he is a	Num 35:18	834
w a man may die, seeing him not,	Num 35:23	834

w the LORD was wroth against you Deut 9:19 834
of that *w* the LORD thy God hath Deut 15:14 834
vesture, *w* thou coverest thyself Deut 22:12 834
w thine enemies shall distress Deut 28:53 834
w thine enemies shall distress Deut 28:55 834
w thine enemy shall distress thee Deut 28:57 834
of thine heart *w* thou shalt fear Deut 28:67 834
w Moses the man of God blessed Deut 33:1 834
w he stretched out the spear, Josh 8:26 834
Oh my Lord, *w* shall I save Israel Judg 6:15 4100
w Abimelech hired vain and light Judg 9:4
w by me they honour God and man, Judg 9:9 834
w thou saidst, Who is Abimelech, Judg 9:38 834
w thou mightest be bound to Judg 16:6 4100
thee, *w* thou mightest be bound Judg 16:10 4100
tell me *w* thou mightest be bound Judg 16:13 834
tell us *w* we shall send it to his 1Sa 6:2 4100
w they have forsaken me, and 1Sa 8:8
for *w* should he reconcile himself 1Sa 29:4 4100
so that the hatred *w* he hated her 2Sa 13:15 834
than the love *w* he had loved her 2Sa 13:15 834
w shall I make the atonement, 2Sa 21:3 4100
w I have made supplication before 1Kin 8:59 834
thereof, *w* Baasha had builded 1Kin 15:22 834
in his sin *w* he made Israel to 1Kin 15:26 834
by his provocation *w* he provoked 1Kin 15:30 834
in his sin *w* he made Israel to 1Kin 15:34 834
in his sin *w* he made Israel to 1Kin 16:26 834
for the provocation *w* thou hast 1Kin 21:22 834
And the LORD said unto him, *W* 1Kin 22:22 4100
his might *w* he fought against 2Kin 13:12 834
beside his sin *w* he made Judah to 2Kin 21:16 834
w his anger was kindled against 2Kin 23:26 834
of brass *w* they ministered 2Kin 25:14 834
w Solomon made the brasen sea, and 1Chr 18:8
after the numbering *w* David his 2Chr 2:17 834
thereof, *w* Baasha was building 2Chr 16:6 834
And the LORD said unto him, *W* 2Chr 18:20 4100
against the house *w* I have war 2Chr 35:21
w thou didst testify against them Neh 9:34 834
or with speeches *w* he can do no Job 15:3
w they have reproached thee, O Ps 79:12 834
W thine enemies have reproached, Ps 89:51 834
w they have reproached the Ps 89:51 834
w he hath girded himself Ps 93:1
for a girdle *w* he is girded Ps 109:19
So shall I have *w* to answer him Ps 119:42 1697
W the mower filleth not his hand Ps 129:7
king Solomon with the crown *w* his Song 3:11
This is the rest *w* ye may cause Is 28:12 834
w the servants of the king of Is 37:6 834
w I said I would benefit them Jer 18:10 834
w their enemies, and they that Jer 19:9 834
w ye fight against the king of Jer 21:4 834
this is the name *w* she shall be Jer 33:16 834
of brass *w* they ministered Jer 52:18 834
w the LORD hath afflicted me in Lam 1:12 834
the daubing *w* ye have daubed it Eze 13:12 834
w ye there hunt the souls to make Eze 13:20 834
w I fed thee, thou hast even set Eze 16:19
his labour *w* he served against it Eze 29:20 834
w they shall lament her Eze 32:16
for their idols *w* they had Eze 36:18
w they slew the burnt offering Eze 40:42 834
w his spirit was troubled, and his Dan 2:1
W shall I come before the LORD, Mic 6:6 4100
this shall be the plague *w* the Zec 14:12 834
w the LORD will smite the heathen Zec 14:18 834
him for the fear *w* he feared me Mal 2:5
his savour, *w* shall it be salted Mt 5:13
blasphemies *w* soever they shall Mk 3:28 *3745*
his saltness, *w* will ye season it Mk 9:50
savour, *w* shall it be seasoned Lk 14:34
unto him, Make ready *w* I may sup Lk 17:8 *5101*
with the towel *w* he was girded Jn 13:5 *3739*
that the love *w* thou hast loved Jn 17:26 *3739*
things *w* one may edify another Rom 14:19
by the comfort *w* we ourselves are 2Cor 1:4 *3739*
but by the consolation *w* he was 2Cor 7:7 *3739*
w I think to be bold against some 2Cor 10:2 *3739*
w Christ hath made us free Gal 5:1 *3739*
for his great love *w* he loved us Eph 2:4 *3739*
of the vocation *w* ye are called Eph 4:1 *3739*
w ye shall be able to quench all Eph 6:16
for all the joy *w* we joy for your 1Th 3:9 *3739*
w he was sanctified, an unholy Heb 10:29

WHEREWITHAL

W shall a young man cleanse his Ps 119:9
or, *W* shall we be clothed Mt 6:31 *5101*

WHET

If I *w* my glittering sword, and Deut 32:41 8150
he turn not, he will *w* his sword Ps 7:12 3913
Who *w* their tongue like a sword, Ps 64:3 8150
be blunt, and he do not *w* the edge Eccl 10:10 7043

WHETHER

see *w* they have done altogether Gen 18:21
to wit *w* the LORD had made his Gen 24:21 518
w thou be my very son Esau or not Gen 27:21
w stolen by day, or stolen by Gen 31:39
see *w* it be well with thy Gen 37:14
know now *w* it be thy son's coat Gen 37:32
w there be any truth in you Gen 42:16
as to tell the man *w* ye had yet a Gen 43:6 5750
Egypt, and see *w* they be yet alive Ex 4:18 5750
w he be a stranger, or born in Ex 12:19
w they will walk in my law, or no Ex 16:4
w it be beast or man, it shall Ex 19:13 518
W he have gored a son, or have Ex 21:31 176
w it be ox, or ass, or sheep Ex 22:4 5704
to see *w* he have put his hand Ex 22:8
w it be for ox, for ass, for Ex 22:9
w ox or sheep, that is male Ex 34:19
w it be a male or female, he Lev 3:1 518
w he hath seen or known of it Lev 5:1 176
w it be a carcase of an unclean Lev 5:2 176
w it be of fowl or of beast, in Lev 7:26
w it be any vessel of wood, or Lev 11:32
w it be oven, or ranges for pots, Lev 11:35
w it be a woollen garment, or a Lev 13:47
W it be in the warp, or woof Lev 13:48 176
w in a skin, or in any thing made Lev 13:48 176
w warp or woof, in woollen or in Lev 13:52 176
w it be bare within or without Lev 13:55
w his flesh run with his issue, Lev 15:3
w it be one of your own country, Lev 16:29
w it be one of your own country, Lev 17:15
w she be born at home, or born Lev 18:9
w it be cow or ewe, ye shall not Lev 22:28 518
value it, *w* it be good or bad Lev 27:12 996
estimate it, *w* it be good or bad Lev 27:14 996
w it be ox, or sheep Lev 27:26 518
w of the seed of the land, or of Lev 27:30
not search *w* it be good or bad Lev 27:33 996
w it was by day or by night that Num 9:21 176
Or *w* it were two days, or a month Num 9:22 176
thou shalt see now *w* my word Num 11:23
w they be strong or weak, few or Num 13:18
dwell in, *w* it be good or bad Num 13:19
w in tents, or in strong holds Num 13:19
w it be fat or lean Num 13:20
w there be wood therein, or not Num 13:20
w he be born in the land, or a Num 15:30 4480
w it be of men or beasts, shall Num 18:15
w there hath been any such thing Deut 4:32
heart, *w* thou wouldest keep his Deut 8:2
to know *w* ye love the LORD your Deut 13:3
a sacrifice, *w* it be ox or sheep Deut 18:3 518
w they be young ones, or eggs, and Deut 22:6
w he be of thy brethren, or of Deut 24:14
w the gods which your fathers Josh 24:15 518
w they will keep the way of the Judg 2:22
to know *w* they would hearken unto Judg 3:4
W is better for you, either that Judg 9:2 4100
that we may know *w* our way which Judg 18:5
not young men, *w* poor or rich Ruth 3:10 518
Who can tell *w* GOD will be 2Sa 12:22
w in death or life, even there 2Sa 15:21 518
W they be come out for peace, 1Kin 20:18 518
or *w* they be come out for war, 1Kin 20:18 518
w any thing would come from him 1Kin 20:33
of Baal-zebub the god of Ekron *w* 2Kin 1:2 518
w with many, or with them that 2Chr 14:11 996
w small or great 2Chr 15:13 4480
w man or woman 2Chr 15:13
their seed, *w* they were of Israel Ezr 2:59 518
w it be so, that a decree was Ezr 5:17 2006
w it be unto death, or to Ezr 7:26 2006
their seed, *w* they were of Israel Neh 7:61 518
to see *w* Mordecai's matters would Est 3:4
w man or woman, shall come unto Est 4:11
who knoweth *w* thou art come to Est 4:14 518
w it be done against a nation, or Job 34:29
w thou refuse, or *w* thou Job 34:33 3588
w for correction, or for his land Job 37:13 518
w his work be pure Prov 20:11 518
and *w* it be right Prov 20:11 518
w he rage or laugh, there is no Prov 29:9 518
who knoweth *w* he shall be a wise Eccl 2:19
is sweet, *w* he eat little or much Eccl 5:12 518
thou knowest not *w* shall prosper Eccl 11:6 335
or *w* they both shall be alike Eccl 11:6 518
w it be good, or *w* it be Eccl 12:14 518
to see *w* the vine flourished, and Song 6:11
w the tender grape appear, and the Song 7:12
see *w* a man doth travail with Jer 30:6 518
W it be good, or *w* it be Jer 42:6 518
w they will hear, or *w* they Eze 2:5 518
w they will hear, or *w* they Eze 2:7 518
w they will hear, or *w* they Eze 3:11 518
or torn, *w* it be fowl or beast Eze 44:31 4480
For *w* is easier, to say, Thy sins Mt 9:5 *5101*
W of them twain did the will of Mt 21:31 *5101*
for *w* is greater, the gold, or Mt 23:17 *5101*
for *w* is greater, the gift, or Mt 23:19 *5101*
that thou tell us *w* thou be the Mt 26:63 *1487*
W of the twain will ye that I Mt 27:21 *5101*
let us see *w* Elias will come to Mt 27:49 *1487*
W is it easier to say to the sick Mk 2:9 *5101*
w he would heal him on the Mk 3:2 *1487*
let us see *w* Elias will come to Mk 15:36 *1487*
he asked him *w* he had been any Mk 15:44 *1487*
w he were the Christ, or not Lk 3:15 *3379*
W is easier, to say, Thy sins be Lk 5:23 *5101*
w he would heal on the sabbath Lk 6:7 *1487*
w he have sufficient to finish it Lk 14:28 *1487*
consulteth *w* he be able with ten Lk 14:31 *1487*
For *w* is greater, he that sitteth Lk 22:27 *5101*
he asked *w* the man were a Lk 23:6 *1487*
w it be of God Jn 7:17 *4220*
or *w* I speak of myself Jn 7:17
W he be a sinner or no, I know Jn 9:25 *1487*
shew *w* of these two thou hast Acts 1:24
W it be right in the sight of God Acts 4:19 *1487*
Tell me *w* ye sold the land for so Acts 5:8 *1487*
w they were men or women, he Acts 9:2 *5037*
And called, and asked *w* Simon Acts 10:18 *1487*
daily, *w* those things were so Acts 17:11 *1487*
heard *w* there be any Holy Ghost Acts 19:2 *1487*
I asked him *w* he would go to Acts 25:20 *1487*
w of sin unto death, or of Rom 6:16 *2273*
w prophecy, let us prophesy Rom 12:6 *1535*
For *w* we live, we live unto the Rom 14:8
w we die, we die unto the Lord Rom 14:8
w we live therefore, or die, we Rom 14:8
I know not *w* I baptized any other 1Cor 1:16 *1487*
W Paul, or Apollos, or Cephas, or 1Cor 3:22 *1535*
w thou shalt save thy husband 1Cor 7:16 *1487*
w thou shalt save thy wife 1Cor 7:16 *1487*
w in heaven or in earth, (as 1Cor 8:5 *1535*
W therefore ye eat, or drink, or 1Cor 10:31 *1535*
w we be Jews or Gentiles 1Cor 12:13 *1535*
w we be bond or free 1Cor 12:13 *1535*
w one member suffer, all the 1Cor 12:26 *1535*
but *w* there be prophecies, they 1Cor 13:8 *1535*
w there be tongues, they shall 1Cor 13:8 *1535*
w there be knowledge, it shall 1Cor 13:8 *1535*
w pipe or harp, except they give 1Cor 14:7 *1535*
Therefore *w* it were I or they, so 1Cor 15:11 *1535*
w we be afflicted, it is for your 2Cor 1:6 *1535*
or *w* we be comforted, it is for 2Cor 1:6 *1535*
w ye be obedient in all things 2Cor 2:9 *1487*
w present or absent, we may be 2Cor 5:9 *1535*
he hath done, *w* it be good or bad 2Cor 5:10 *1535*
For *w* we be beside ourselves, it 2Cor 5:13 *1535*
or *w* we be sober, it is for your 2Cor 5:13 *1535*
W any do enquire of Titus, he is 2Cor 8:23 *1535*
(*w* in the body, I cannot tell 2Cor 12:2 *1535*
or *w* out of the body, I cannot 2Cor 12:2 *1535*
(*w* in the body, or out of the 2Cor 12:3 *1535*
yourselves, *w* ye be in the faith 2Cor 13:5 *1487*
of the Lord, *w* he be bond or free Eph 6:8 *1535*
w in pretence, or in truth, Phil 1:18 *1535*
w it be by life, or by death Phil 1:20 *1535*
that *w* I come and see you, or else Phil 1:27 *1535*
w they be thrones, or dominions, Col 1:16 *1535*
w they be things in earth, or Col 1:20 *1535*
w we wake or sleep, we should 1Th 5:10 *1535*
w by word, or our epistle 2Th 2:15 *1535*
w it be to the king, as supreme 1Pet 2:13 *1535*
try the spirits *w* they are of God 1Jn 4:1 *1487*

WHICH

divided the waters *w* were under Gen 1:7 834
waters *w* were above the firmament Gen 1:7 834
w the waters brought forth Gen 1:21 834
w is upon the face of all the Gen 1:29 834
in the *w* is the fruit of a tree Gen 1:29 834
God ended his work *w* he had made Gen 2:2 834
from all his work *w* he had made Gen 2:2 834
from all his work *w* God created Gen 2:3 834
that is it *w* compasseth the whole Gen 2:11
that is it *w* goeth toward the Gen 2:14
w the LORD God had taken from man Gen 2:22 834
the field *w* the LORD God had made Gen 3:1 834
But of the fruit of the tree *w* is Gen 3:3 834
of *w* I commanded thee, saying, Gen 3:17 834
a flaming sword *w* turned every Gen 3:24
w hath opened her mouth to Gen 4:11 834
the ground *w* the LORD hath cursed Gen 5:29 834
them wives of all *w* they chose Gen 6:2 834
became mighty men *w* were of old Gen 6:4 834
this is the fashion *w* thou shalt Gen 6:15 834
living substance was destroyed *w* Gen 7:23 834
window of the ark *w* he had made Gen 8:6 834
w went forth to and fro, until the Gen 8:7
w returned not again unto him any Gen 8:12
w is the blood thereof, shall ye Gen 9:4
the covenant *w* I make between me Gen 9:12 834
w is between me and you and every Gen 9:15 834
w I have established between me Gen 9:17 834
w the children of men builded Gen 11:5 834
w they have imagined to do Gen 11:6
w he had made there at the first Gen 13:4 834
w went with Abram, had flocks, and Gen 13:5
For all the land *w* thou seest Gen 13:15 834
w is in Hebron, and built there an Gen 13:18 834
and the king of Bela, *w* is Zoar Gen 14:2 1931
vale of Siddim, *w* is the Salt Sea Gen 14:3 1931
El-paran, *w* is by the wilderness Gen 14:6 834
w is Kadesh, and smote all the Gen 14:7 834
w is on the left hand of Damascus Gen 14:15 834
of Shaveh, *w* is the king's dale Gen 14:17 1931
w hath delivered thine enemies Gen 14:20 834
Save only that *w* the young men Gen 14:24 834
portion of the men *w* went with me Gen 14:24 834
son's name, *w* Hagar bare, Ishmael Gen 16:15 834
w ye shall keep, between me and Gen 17:10 834
stranger, *w* is not of thy seed Gen 17:12 834
w Sarah shall bear unto thee at Gen 17:21 834
the calf *w* he had dressed, and set Gen 18:8 834
the tent door, *w* was behind him Gen 18:10 1931
a surety bear a child, *w* am old Gen 18:13 589
from Abraham that thing *w* I do Gen 18:17 834
that *w* he hath spoken of him Gen 18:19 834
the cry of it, *w* is come unto me Gen 18:21
the Lord, *w* am but dust and ashes Gen 18:27 595
Where are the men *w* came in to Gen 19:5 834
daughters *w* have not known man Gen 19:8 834
w married his daughters, and said, Gen 19:14
and thy two daughters, *w* are here Gen 19:15
w thou hast shewed unto me in Gen 19:19 834
for the *w* thou hast spoken Gen 19:21 834
that *w* grew upon the ground Gen 19:25
the cities in the *w* Lot dwelt Gen 19:29 834
for the woman *w* thou hast taken Gen 20:3 834
This is thy kindness *w* thou shalt Gen 20:13 834
at the set time of *w* God had Gen 21:2 834
w she had born unto Abraham, Gen 21:9 834
w Abimelech's servants had Gen 21:25 834
w thou hast set by themselves Gen 21:29 834
mountains *w* I will tell thee of Gen 22:2 834
the place of *w* God had told him Gen 22:3 834
the place *w* God had told him of Gen 22:9 834
as the sand *w* is upon the sea Gen 22:17 834
w he hath Gen 23:9 834
w is in the end of his field Gen 23:9 834
w he had named in the audience of Gen 23:16 834
w was in Machpelah Gen 23:17 834
w was before Mamre, the field, and Gen 23:17 834
the cave *w* was therein, and all Gen 23:17 834

the sin offering *w* is for himself	Lev 16:11	834
w he put on when he went into the	Lev 16:23	834
This is the thing *w* the LORD hath	Lev 17:2	834
w they offer in the open field,	Lev 17:5	834
the strangers *w* sojourn among you	Lev 17:8	834
w hunteth and catcheth any beast	Lev 17:13	834
that eateth that *w* died of itself	Lev 17:15	
or that *w* was torn with beasts,	Lev 17:15	
w if a man do, he shall live in	Lev 18:5	834
defiled *w* I cast out before you	Lev 18:24	834
w were before you, and the land is	Lev 18:27	834
w were committed before you, and	Lev 18:30	834
LORD for his sin *w* he hath done	Lev 19:22	834
the sin *w* he hath done shall be	Lev 19:22	
w brought you out of the land of	Lev 19:36	834
I am the LORD *w* sanctify you	Lev 20:8	
nation, *w* I cast out before you	Lev 20:23	834
w have separated you from other	Lev 20:24	834
w I have separated from you as	Lev 20:25	834
unto him, *w* hath had no husband	Lev 21:3	834
the LORD, *w* sanctify you, am holy	Lev 21:8	
things *w* they hallow unto me	Lev 22:2	834
w the children of Israel hallow	Lev 22:3	834
The soul *w* hath touched any such	Lev 22:6	834
That *w* dieth of itself, or is	Lev 22:8	
w they offer unto the LORD	Lev 22:15	834
w they will offer unto the LORD	Lev 22:18	834
unto the LORD that *w* is bruised	Lev 22:24	
I am the LORD *w* hallow you	Lev 22:32	834
w ye shall proclaim to be holy	Lev 23:2	834
w ye shall proclaim in their	Lev 23:4	834
into the land *w* I give unto you	Lev 23:10	834
w ye shall proclaim to be holy	Lev 23:37	834
w ye give unto the LORD	Lev 23:38	834
come into the land *w* I give you	Lev 25:2	834
That *w* groweth of its own accord	Lev 25:5	
neither reap that *w* groweth of	Lev 25:11	
he redeem that *w* his brother sold	Lev 25:25	
then that *w* is sold shall remain	Lev 25:28	
w have no wall round about them	Lev 25:31	834
w brought you forth out of the	Lev 25:38	834
w I brought forth out of the land	Lev 25:42	834
w thou shalt have, shall be of	Lev 25:44	834
w they begat in your land	Lev 25:45	
w brought you forth out of the	Lev 26:13	834
w shall rob you of your children,	Lev 26:22	
your enemies *w* dwell therein	Lev 26:32	
with their trespass *w* they	Lev 26:40	834
w the LORD made between him and	Lev 26:46	834
beast, of *w* they do not offer a	Lev 27:11	834
the LORD a field *w* he hath bought	Lev 27:22	
w is not of the fields of his	Lev 27:22	834
w should be the LORD's firstling,	Lev 27:26	834
w shall be devoted of men, shall	Lev 27:29	834
w the LORD commanded Moses for	Lev 27:34	834
Aaron took these men *w* are	Num 1:17	834
w Moses and Aaron numbered	Num 1:44	834
those *w* pitch by him shall be the	Num 2:12	
These are those *w* were numbered	Num 2:32	
the priests *w* were anointed, whom	Num 3:3	
w is by the tabernacle, and by the	Num 3:26	834
w Moses and Aaron numbered at the	Num 3:39	834
w are more than the Levites	Num 3:46	
w is by the tabernacle and by the	Num 4:26	834
w Moses and Aaron did number	Num 4:37	834
their sin *w* they have done	Num 5:7	834
w they bring unto the priest,	Num 5:9	834
w is the jealousy offering	Num 5:18	1958
in the *w* he separateth himself	Num 6:5	834
put it in the fire *w* is under the	Num 6:18	834
according to the vow *w* he vowed	Num 6:21	834
w the LORD had shewed Moses	Num 8:4	834
w are heads of the thousands of	Num 10:4	
w was the rereward of all the	Num 10:25	
unto the place of *w* the LORD said	Num 10:29	834
w we did eat in Egypt freely	Num 11:5	834
unto the land *w* thou swarest unto	Num 11:12	834
take of the spirit *w* is upon thee	Num 11:17	834
despised the LORD *w* is among you	Num 11:20	834
above all the men *w* were upon the	Num 12:3	834
w I give unto the children of	Num 13:2	834
w Moses sent to spy out the land	Num 13:16	834
of the cluster of grapes *w* the	Num 13:24	834
land *w* they had searched unto the	Num 13:32	834
through *w* we have gone to search	Num 13:32	834
of Anak, *w* come of the giants	Num 13:33	
w were of them that searched the	Num 14:6	
w we passed through to search it,	Num 14:7	834
a land *w* floweth with milk and	Num 14:8	834
for all the signs *w* I have shewed	Num 14:11	834
then the nations *w* have heard the	Num 14:15	834
the land *w* he sware unto them	Num 14:16	834
those men *w* have seen my glory	Num 14:22	
w I did in Egypt and in the	Num 14:22	834
land *w* I sware unto their fathers	Num 14:23	
congregation, *w* murmur against me	Num 14:27	834
Israel, *w* they murmur against me	Num 14:27	834
w have murmured against me,	Num 14:29	834
concerning *w* I sware to make you	Num 14:30	834
w ye said should be a prey, them	Num 14:31	
know the land *w* ye have despised	Num 14:31	834
days in *w* ye searched the land	Num 14:34	834
w Moses sent to search the land,	Num 14:36	834
w were of the men that went to	Num 14:38	
place *w* the LORD hath promised	Num 14:40	834
the Canaanites *w* dwelt in that	Num 14:45	
habitations, *w* I give unto you,	Num 15:2	834
w the LORD hath spoken unto Moses	Num 15:22	834
after *w* ye use to go a whoring	Num 15:39	834
w brought you out of the land of	Num 15:41	834
For *w* cause both thou and all thy	Num 16:11	
w said, We will not come up	Num 16:12	
w is not of the seed of Aaron,	Num 16:40	834
w they shall render unto me,	Num 18:9	834
the firstfruits of them *w* they	Num 18:12	834
w they shall bring unto the LORD,	Num 18:13	834
w they bring unto the LORD,	Num 18:15	834
the sanctuary, *w* is twenty gerahs	Num 18:16	1958
w the children of Israel offer	Num 18:19	834
for their service *w* they serve	Num 18:21	834
w they offer as an heave offering	Num 18:24	834
children of Israel the tithes *w* I	Num 18:26	834
w ye receive of the children of	Num 18:28	834
the law *w* the LORD hath commanded	Num 19:2	834
and upon *w* never came yoke	Num 19:2	834
w hath no covering bound upon it,	Num 19:15	834
into the land *w* I have given them	Num 20:12	834
shall not enter into the land *w* I	Num 20:24	834
w dwelt in the south, heard tell	Num 21:1	
the wilderness *w* is before Moab	Num 21:11	834
w is in the wilderness that	Num 21:13	834
w looketh toward Jeshimon	Num 21:20	
Nophah, *w* reacheth unto Medeba	Num 21:30	834
the Amorites, *w* dwelt at Heshbon	Num 21:34	834
w is by the river of the land of	Num 22:5	834
w covereth the face of the earth	Num 22:11	
but yet the word *w* I shall say	Num 22:20	834
upon *w* thou hast ridden ever	Num 22:30	834
w is in the border of Arnon,	Num 22:36	834
w is in the utmost coast	Num 22:36	834
w the LORD hath put in my mouth	Num 23:12	834
w heard the words of	Num 24:4	834
w saw the vision of the Almighty,	Num 24:4	
aloes *w* the LORD hath planted	Num 24:6	
messengers *w* thou sentest unto me	Num 24:12	834
w heard the words of God, and knew	Num 24:16	
w saw the vision of the Almighty,	Num 24:16	
w was slain in the day of the	Num 25:18	
w went forth out of the land of	Num 26:4	
w were famous in the congregation	Num 26:9	
see the land *w* I have given unto	Num 27:12	834
W may go out before them, and	Num 27:17	834
w may go in before them	Num 27:17	834
w may lead them out	Num 27:17	834
and *w* may bring them in	Num 27:17	834
not as sheep *w* have no shepherd	Num 27:17	834
w ye shall offer unto the LORD	Num 28:3	834
w was ordained in mount Sinai for	Num 28:6	
w is for a continual burnt	Num 28:23	834
This is the thing *w* the LORD hath	Num 30:1	834
he shall make her vow *w* she vowed	Num 30:8	834
that *w* she uttered with her lips,	Num 30:8	
or all her bonds, *w* are upon her	Num 30:14	834
w the LORD commanded Moses,	Num 30:16	834
w are by Jordan near Jericho	Num 31:12	834
hundreds, *w* came from the battle	Num 31:14	
men of war *w* went to the battle	Num 31:21	
law *w* the LORD commanded Moses	Num 31:21	834
men of war *w* went out to battle	Num 31:28	
Levites, *w* keep the charge of the	Num 31:30	
prey *w* the men of war had caught	Num 31:32	834
w was the portion of them that	Num 31:36	
of *w* the LORD's tribute was	Num 31:38	
of *w* the LORD's tribute was	Num 31:39	
of *w* the LORD's tribute was	Num 31:40	
w was the LORD's heave offering,	Num 31:41	
w Moses divided from the men that	Num 31:42	834
Levites, *w* kept the charge of the	Num 31:47	
And the officers *w* were over	Num 31:48	834
men of war *w* are under our charge	Num 31:49	834
Even the country *w* the LORD smote	Num 32:4	834
land *w* the LORD hath given them	Num 32:7	834
land *w* the LORD had given them	Num 32:9	834
shall see the land *w* I sware unto	Num 32:11	834
do that *w* hath proceeded out of	Num 32:24	
unto the cities *w* they builded	Num 32:38	834
the Amorite *w* was in it	Num 32:39	834
w went forth out of the land of	Num 33:1	834
w the LORD had smitten among them	Num 33:4	834
in Etham, *w* is in the edge of the	Num 33:6	834
w is before Baal-zephon	Num 33:7	834
wilderness of Zin, *w* is Kadesh	Num 33:36	1958
w dwelt in the south in the land	Num 33:40	834
that those *w* ye let remain of	Num 33:55	834
This is the land *w* ye shall	Num 34:13	834
w the LORD commanded to give unto	Num 34:13	834
w shall divide the land unto you	Num 34:17	834
w ye shall give unto the Levites,	Num 35:4	834
among the cities *w* ye shall give	Num 35:6	834
w ye shall appoint for the	Num 35:6	834
So all the cities *w* ye shall give	Num 35:7	834
the cities *w* ye shall give shall	Num 35:8	834
his inheritance *w* he inheriteth	Num 35:8	834
w killeth any person at unawares	Num 35:11	
of these cities *w* ye shall give	Num 35:13	834
w shall be cities of refuge	Num 35:14	
w was anointed with the holy oil	Num 35:25	834
a murderer, *w* is guilty of death	Num 35:31	834
the land *w* ye shall inhabit	Num 35:34	834
This is the thing *w* the LORD doth	Num 36:6	834
w the LORD commanded by the hand	Num 36:13	834
These be the words *w* Moses spake	Deut 1:1	834
w dwelt in Heshbon, and Og the	Deut 1:4	834
w dwelt at Astaroth in Edrei	Deut 1:4	834
possess the land *w* the LORD sware	Deut 1:8	834
The thing *w* thou hast spoken is	Deut 1:14	834
all the things *w* ye should do	Deut 1:18	834
w ye saw by the way of the	Deut 1:19	834
w the LORD our God doth give unto	Deut 1:20	834
It is a good land *w* the LORD our	Deut 1:25	834
LORD your God *w* goeth before you	Deut 1:30	
w I sware to give unto your	Deut 1:35	834
w standeth before thee, he shall	Deut 1:38	
w ye said should be a prey, and	Deut 1:39	834
w in that day had no knowledge	Deut 1:39	834
w dwelt in that mountain, came	Deut 1:44	
children of Esau, *w* dwell in Seir	Deut 2:4	
w dwelt in Seir, through the way	Deut 2:8	
W also were accounted giants, as	Deut 2:11	1992
w the LORD gave unto them	Deut 2:12	834
the space in *w* we came from	Deut 2:14	834
of Esau, *w* dwelt in Seir, when he	Deut 2:22	
the Avims *w* dwelt in Hazerim,	Deut 2:23	
w came forth out of Caphtor,	Deut 2:23	
children of Esau *w* dwell in Seir	Deut 2:29	
and the Moabites *w* dwell in Ar	Deut 2:29	
land *w* the LORD our God giveth us	Deut 2:29	834
the spoil of the cities *w* we took	Deut 2:35	834
w is by the brink of the river of	Deut 2:36	834
the Amorites, *w* dwelt at Heshbon	Deut 3:2	834
there was not a city *w* we took	Deut 3:4	834
(*W* Hermon the Sidonians call	Deut 3:9	
w we possessed at that time, from	Deut 3:12	
w is by the river Arnon, and half	Deut 3:12	834
w was called the land of giants	Deut 3:13	1931
w is the border of the children	Deut 3:16	
in your cities *w* I have given you	Deut 3:19	834
they also possess the land *w* the	Deut 3:20	834
possession, *w* I have given you	Deut 3:20	834
inherit the land *w* thou shalt see	Deut 3:28	834
w I teach you, for to do them,	Deut 4:1	834
possess the land *w* the LORD God	Deut 4:1	834
add unto the word *w* I command you	Deut 4:2	834
the LORD your God *w* I command you	Deut 4:2	834
w shall hear all these statutes,	Deut 4:6	834
w I set before you this day	Deut 4:8	834
the things *w* thine eyes have seen	Deut 4:9	834
w he commanded you to perform,	Deut 4:13	834
w the LORD thy God hath divided	Deut 4:19	834
w the LORD thy God giveth thee	Deut 4:21	834
w he made with you, and make you a	Deut 4:23	834
w the LORD thy God hath forbidden	Deut 4:23	834
w neither see, nor hear, nor eat,	Deut 4:28	834
thy fathers *w* he sware unto them	Deut 4:31	834
w were before thee, since the day	Deut 4:32	834
w I command thee this day, that	Deut 4:40	834
w the LORD thy God giveth thee,	Deut 4:40	834
w should kill his neighbour	Deut 4:42	834
this is the law *w* Moses set	Deut 4:44	834
w Moses spake unto the children	Deut 4:45	834
w were on this side Jordan toward	Deut 4:47	834
w is by the bank of the river	Deut 4:48	834
even unto mount Sion *w* is Hermon	Deut 4:48	834
judgments *w* I speak in your ears	Deut 5:1	834
w brought thee out of the land of	Deut 5:6	834
in the land *w* the LORD thy God	Deut 5:16	834
w they have spoken unto thee	Deut 5:28	834
w thou shalt teach them, that	Deut 5:31	834
land *w* I give them to possess it	Deut 5:31	834
the ways *w* the LORD your God hath	Deut 5:33	834
in the land *w* ye shall possess	Deut 5:33	834
w the LORD your God commanded to	Deut 6:1	834
w I command thee, thou, and thy	Deut 6:2	834
w I command thee this day, shall	Deut 6:6	834
land *w* he sware unto thy fathers	Deut 6:10	834
cities, *w* thou buildedst not,	Deut 6:10	834
w thou filledst not, and wells	Deut 6:11	834
w thou diggedst not, vineyards and	Deut 6:11	834
olive trees, *w* thou plantedst not	Deut 6:11	834
w brought thee forth out of the	Deut 6:12	834
the people *w* are round about you	Deut 6:14	834
w he hath commanded thee	Deut 6:17	834
And thou shalt do that *w* is right	Deut 6:18	834
possess the good land *w* the LORD	Deut 6:18	834
w the LORD our God hath commanded	Deut 6:20	834
to give us the land *w* he sware	Deut 6:23	834
w he had sworn unto your fathers	Deut 7:8	834
w keepeth covenant and mercy with	Deut 7:9	834
w I command thee this day, to do	Deut 7:11	834
the mercy *w* he swore unto thy	Deut 7:12	834
in the land *w* he sware unto thy	Deut 7:13	834
w thou knowest, upon thee	Deut 7:15	834
shalt consume all the people *w*	Deut 7:16	834
temptations *w* thine eyes saw	Deut 7:19	834
All the commandments *w* I command	Deut 8:1	834
possess the land *w* the LORD sware	Deut 8:1	834
w the LORD thy God led thee these	Deut 8:2	834
w thou knewest not, neither did	Deut 8:3	834
good land *w* he hath given thee	Deut 8:10	834
w I command thee this day	Deut 8:11	834
w brought thee forth out of the	Deut 8:14	
w thy fathers knew not, that he	Deut 8:16	834
w he sware unto thy fathers	Deut 8:18	834
As the nations *w* the LORD	Deut 8:20	834
is he *w* goeth over before thee	Deut 9:3	
that he may perform the word *w*	Deut 9:5	834
covenant *w* the LORD made with you	Deut 9:9	834
w the LORD spake with you in the	Deut 9:10	834
for thy people *w* thou hast	Deut 9:12	834
out of the way *w* I commanded them	Deut 9:12	834
way *w* the LORD had commanded you	Deut 9:16	834
of all your sins *w* ye sinned	Deut 9:18	834
the calf *w* ye had made, and burnt	Deut 9:21	834
the land *w* I have given you	Deut 9:23	834
w thou hast redeemed through thy	Deut 9:26	834
w thou hast brought forth out of	Deut 9:26	834
into the land *w* he promised them	Deut 9:28	834
w thou broughtest out by thy	Deut 9:29	834
the first tables *w* thou brakest	Deut 10:2	834
w the LORD spake unto you in the	Deut 10:4	834
tables in the ark *w* I had made	Deut 10:5	834
w I sware unto their fathers to	Deut 10:11	834
w I command thee this day for thy	Deut 10:13	834
w regardeth not persons, nor	Deut 10:17	834
things, *w* thine eyes have seen	Deut 10:21	834
your children *w* have not known	Deut 11:2	834
w have not seen the chastisement	Deut 11:2	834
w he did in the midst of Egypt	Deut 11:3	834
great acts of the LORD *w* he did	Deut 11:7	834
w I command you this day, that ye	Deut 11:8	834
w the LORD sware unto your	Deut 11:9	834
A land *w* the LORD thy God careth	Deut 11:12	834

Context	Reference	Strong's
w I command you this day, to love	Deut 11:13	834
good land *w* the LORD giveth you	Deut 11:17	834
in the land *w* the LORD sware unto	Deut 11:21	834
commandments *w* I command you	Deut 11:22	834
God, *w* I command you this day	Deut 11:27	834
the way *w* I command you this day	Deut 11:28	834
other gods, *w* ye have not known	Deut 11:28	834
w dwell in the champaign over	Deut 11:30	
w the LORD your God giveth you	Deut 11:31	834
judgments *w* I set before you this	Deut 11:32	834
w ye shall observe to do in the	Deut 12:1	834
w the LORD God of thy fathers	Deut 12:1	834
wherein the nations *w* ye shall	Deut 12:2	834
But unto the place *w* the LORD	Deut 12:5	834
w the LORD your God giveth you	Deut 12:9	834
dwell in the land *w* the LORD your	Deut 12:10	834
Then there shall be a place *w* the	Deut 12:11	834
vows *w* ye vow unto the LORD	Deut 12:11	834
But in the place *w* the LORD shall	Deut 12:14	834
LORD thy God *w* he hath given thee	Deut 12:15	834
nor any of thy vows *w* thou vowest	Deut 12:17	834
w the LORD thy God shall choose	Deut 12:18	834
If the place *w* the LORD thy God	Deut 12:21	834
w the LORD hath given thee, as I	Deut 12:21	834
when thou shalt do that *w* is	Deut 12:25	
Only thy holy things *w* thou hast	Deut 12:26	834
go unto the place *w* the LORD	Deut 12:26	834
all these words *w* I command thee	Deut 12:28	834
when thou doest that *w* is good	Deut 12:28	
w he hateth, have they done unto	Deut 12:31	834
w thou hast not known, and let us	Deut 13:2	834
w brought you out of the land of	Deut 13:5	
to thrust thee out of the way *w*	Deut 13:5	834
w is as thine own soul, entice	Deut 13:6	834
w thou hast not known, thou, nor	Deut 13:6	834
the people *w* are round about you	Deut 13:7	834
w brought thee out of the land of	Deut 13:10	
w the LORD thy God hath given	Deut 13:12	834
other gods, *w* ye have not known	Deut 13:13	834
w I command thee this day	Deut 13:18	834
to do that *w* is right in the eyes	Deut 13:18	
are the beasts *w* ye shall eat	Deut 14:4	834
are they of *w* ye shall not eat	Deut 14:12	834
in the place *w* he shall choose to	Deut 14:23	834
w the LORD thy God shall choose	Deut 14:24	834
shalt go unto the place *w* the	Deut 14:25	834
w are within thy gates, shall	Deut 14:29	834
work of thine hand *w* thou doest	Deut 14:29	834
but that *w* is thine with thy	Deut 15:3	834
w the LORD thy God giveth thee	Deut 15:4	834
w I command thee this day	Deut 15:5	834
w the LORD thy God giveth thee	Deut 15:7	834
his need, in that *w* he wanteth	Deut 15:8	834
the place *w* the LORD shall choose	Deut 15:20	834
in the place *w* the LORD shall	Deut 16:2	834
w thou sacrificedst the first day	Deut 16:4	834
w the LORD thy God giveth thee	Deut 16:5	834
But at the place *w* the LORD thy	Deut 16:6	834
eat it in the place *w* the LORD	Deut 16:7	834
w thou shalt give unto the LORD	Deut 16:10	834
in the place *w* the LORD thy God	Deut 16:11	834
the place *w* the LORD shall choose	Deut 16:15	834
in the place *w* he shall choose	Deut 16:16	834
LORD thy God *w* he hath given thee	Deut 16:17	834
w the LORD thy God giveth thee,	Deut 16:18	834
That *w* is altogether just shalt	Deut 16:20	
inherit the land *w* the LORD thy	Deut 16:20	834
thy God, *w* thou shalt make thee	Deut 16:21	834
w the LORD thy God hateth	Deut 16:22	834
within any of thy gates *w* the	Deut 17:2	834
of heaven, *w* I have not commanded	Deut 17:3	834
w have committed that wicked	Deut 17:5	834
get thee up into the place *w* the	Deut 17:8	834
w they of that place *w* the	Deut 17:10	834
the law *w* they shall teach thee	Deut 17:11	834
judgment *w* they shall tell thee	Deut 17:11	834
sentence *w* they shall shew thee	Deut 17:11	834
thou art come unto the land *w* the	Deut 17:14	834
over thee, *w* is not thy brother	Deut 17:15	834
that *w* is before the priests the	Deut 17:18	
the place *w* the LORD shall choose	Deut 18:6	834
w stand there before the LORD	Deut 18:7	
beside that *w* cometh of the sale	Deut 18:8	
thou art come into the land *w* the	Deut 18:9	834
w thou shalt possess, hearkened	Deut 18:14	834
spoken that *w* they have spoken	Deut 18:17	834
words *w* he shall speak in my name	Deut 18:19	834
w shall presume to speak a word	Deut 18:20	834
w I have not commanded him to	Deut 18:20	
word *w* the LORD hath not spoken	Deut 18:21	834
that is the thing *w* the LORD hath	Deut 18:22	834
w the LORD thy God giveth thee to	Deut 19:2	834
w the LORD thy God giveth thee to	Deut 19:3	834
w shall flee thither, that he may	Deut 19:4	834
give thee all the land *w* he	Deut 19:8	834
w I command thee this day, to	Deut 19:9	834
w the LORD thy God giveth thee	Deut 19:10	834
w they of old time have set in	Deut 19:14	834
w thou shalt inherit in the land	Deut 19:14	834
against him that *w* is wrong	Deut 19:16	
judges, *w* shall be in those days	Deut 19:17	834
those *w* remain shall hear, and	Deut 19:20	
w brought thee up out of the land	Deut 20:1	834
w the LORD thy God hath given	Deut 20:14	834
w are very far off from thee	Deut 20:15	
w are not of the cities of these	Deut 20:15	834
w the LORD thy God doth give thee	Deut 20:16	834
w they have done unto their gods	Deut 20:18	834
Only the trees *w* thou knowest	Deut 20:20	834
one be found slain in the land *w*	Deut 21:1	834
w are round about him that is	Deut 21:2	834
that the city *w* is next unto the	Deut 21:3	
w hath not been wrought with, and	Deut 21:3	834
w hath not drawn in the yoke	Deut 21:3	834
w is neither eared nor sown, and	Deut 21:4	834
when thou shalt do that *w* is	Deut 21:9	
sons to inherit that *w* he hath	Deut 21:16	834
w is indeed the firstborn	Deut 21:16	
w will not obey the voice of his	Deut 21:18	
w the LORD thy God giveth thee	Deut 21:23	834
w he hath lost, and thou hast	Deut 22:3	834
wear that *w* pertaineth unto a man	Deut 22:5	
of thy seed *w* thou hast sown	Deut 22:9	834
w is not betrothed, and lay hold	Deut 22:28	834
cover that *w* cometh from thee	Deut 23:13	834
unto his master the servant *w* is	Deut 23:15	834
in that place *w* he shall choose	Deut 23:16	834
That *w* is gone out of thy lips	Deut 23:23	834
w thou hast promised with thy	Deut 23:23	
w took her to be his wife	Deut 24:3	834
w sent her away, may not take her	Deut 24:4	834
w the LORD thy God giveth thee	Deut 24:4	834
cheer up his wife *w* he hath taken	Deut 24:5	834
that the firstborn *w* she beareth	Deut 25:6	
the name of his brother *w* is dead	Deut 25:6	
w the LORD thy God giveth thee	Deut 25:15	834
in the land *w* the LORD thy God	Deut 25:19	834
w the LORD thy God giveth thee	Deut 26:1	834
w thou shalt bring of thy land	Deut 26:2	834
shalt go unto the place *w* the	Deut 26:2	834
w the LORD sware unto our fathers	Deut 26:3	834
w thou, O LORD, hast given me	Deut 26:10	834
w the LORD thy God hath given	Deut 26:11	834
w is the year of tithing, and hast	Deut 26:12	
w thou hast commanded me	Deut 26:13	834
the land *w* thou hast given us, as	Deut 26:15	834
above all nations *w* he hath made	Deut 26:19	834
w I command you this day	Deut 27:1	834
w the LORD thy God giveth thee	Deut 27:2	834
w the LORD thy God giveth thee	Deut 27:3	834
w I command you this day, in	Deut 27:4	834
w I command thee this day	Deut 27:10	834
w I command thee this day	Deut 28:1	834
w the LORD thy God giveth thee	Deut 28:8	834
in the land *w* the LORD sware unto	Deut 28:11	834
w I command thee this day, to	Deut 28:13	834
words *w* I command thee this day	Deut 28:14	834
his statutes *w* I command thee	Deut 28:15	834
shall a nation *w* thou knowest not	Deut 28:33	834
of thine eyes *w* thou shalt see	Deut 28:34	834
thy king *w* thou shalt set over	Deut 28:36	834
unto a nation *w* neither thou nor	Deut 28:36	
his statutes *w* he commanded thee	Deut 28:45	834
w the LORD shall send against	Deut 28:48	834
w shall not regard the person of	Deut 28:50	834
w also shall not leave thee	Deut 28:51	834
w the LORD thy God hath given	Deut 28:52	834
w the LORD thy God hath given	Deut 28:53	834
of his children *w* he shall leave	Deut 28:54	834
w would not adventure to set the	Deut 28:56	834
her children *w* she shall bear	Deut 28:57	834
of Egypt, *w* thou wast afraid of	Deut 28:60	834
w is not written in the book of	Deut 28:61	834
w neither thou nor thy fathers	Deut 28:64	834
of thine eyes *w* thou shalt see	Deut 28:67	834
w the LORD commanded Moses to	Deut 29:1	834
beside the covenant *w* he made	Deut 29:1	834
w thine eyes have seen, the signs	Deut 29:3	834
w the LORD thy God maketh with	Deut 29:12	834
the nations *w* ye passed by	Deut 29:16	834
silver and gold, *w* were among them	Deut 29:17	834
the sicknesses *w* the LORD hath	Deut 29:22	834
w the LORD overthrew in his anger	Deut 29:23	834
w he made with them when he	Deut 29:25	834
but those things *w* are revealed	Deut 29:29	
w I have set before thee, and thou	Deut 30:1	834
the land *w* thy fathers possessed	Deut 30:5	834
that hate thee, *w* persecuted thee	Deut 30:7	834
w I command thee this day	Deut 30:8	834
his statutes *w* are written in	Deut 30:10	
For this commandment *w* I command.	Deut 30:11	834
thou mayest dwell in the land *w*	Deut 30:20	834
w I have commanded you	Deut 31:5	834
w the LORD hath sworn unto their	Deut 31:7	834
w bare the ark of the covenant of	Deut 31:9	
in the place *w* he shall choose	Deut 31:11	834
w have not known any thing, may	Deut 31:13	834
break my covenant *w* I have made	Deut 31:16	834
evils *w* they shall have wrought	Deut 31:18	834
land *w* I sware unto their fathers	Deut 31:20	834
their imagination *w* they go about	Deut 31:21	834
them into the land *w* I sware	Deut 31:21	834
into the land *w* I sware unto them	Deut 31:23	834
w bare the ark of the covenant of	Deut 31:25	834
the way *w* I have commanded you	Deut 31:29	834
then he forsook God *w* made him	Deut 32:15	
jealousy with that *w* is not God	Deut 32:21	
with those *w* are not a people	Deut 32:21	
W did eat the fat of their	Deut 32:38	834
w I testify among you this day	Deut 32:46	834
w ye shall command your children	Deut 32:46	834
w is in the land of Moab, that is	Deut 32:49	834
w I give unto the children of	Deut 32:49	834
not go thither unto the land *w* I	Deut 32:52	834
This is the land *w* I sware unto	Deut 34:4	834
w the LORD sent him to do in the	Deut 34:11	834
in all the great terror *w* Moses	Deut 34:12	834
unto the land *w* I do give to them	Josh 1:2	834
w I sware unto their fathers to	Josh 1:6	834
w Moses my servant commanded thee	Josh 1:7	834
w the LORD your God giveth you to	Josh 1:11	834
Remember the word *w* Moses the	Josh 1:13	834
shall remain in the land *w* Moses	Josh 1:14	834
also have possessed the land *w*	Josh 1:15	834
w Moses the LORD's servant gave	Josh 1:15	834
w are entered into thine house	Josh 2:3	834
w she had laid in order upon the	Josh 2:6	
as soon as they *w* pursued after	Josh 2:7	834
oath *w* thou hast made us swear	Josh 2:17	834
w thou didst let us down by	Josh 2:18	834
oath *w* thou hast made us to swear	Josh 2:20	834
may know the way by *w* ye must go	Josh 3:4	834
That the waters *w* came down from	Josh 3:16	
w bare the ark of the covenant	Josh 4:9	
For the priests *w* bare the ark	Josh 4:10	
w they took out of Jordan, did	Josh 4:20	834
w he dried up from before us,	Josh 4:23	834
w were on the side of Jordan	Josh 5:1	834
w were by the sea, heard that the	Josh 5:1	834
w came out of Egypt, were	Josh 5:6	
w the LORD sware unto their	Josh 5:6	834
w Joshua sent to spy out Jericho	Josh 6:25	834
w is beside Beth-aven, on the	Josh 7:2	834
my covenant *w* I commanded them	Josh 7:11	834
that the tribe *w* the LORD taketh	Josh 7:14	834
the family *w* the LORD shall take	Josh 7:14	834
the household *w* the LORD shall	Josh 7:14	834
of the LORD *w* he commanded Joshua.	Josh 8:27	834
over *w* no man hath lift up any	Josh 8:31	834
w he wrote in the presence of the	Josh 8:32	834
w bare the ark of the covenant of	Josh 8:33	
w Joshua read not before all the	Josh 8:35	834
when all the kings *w* were on this	Josh 9:1	834
of Bashan, *w* was at Ashtaroth	Josh 9:10	834
of wine, *w* we filled, were new	Josh 9:13	834
of the oath *w* we sware unto them	Josh 9:20	834
in the place *w* he should choose	Josh 9:27	834
they were more *w* died with	Josh 10:11	834
that the rest *w* remained of them	Josh 10:20	
of the men of war *w* went with him	Josh 10:24	
w remain until this very day	Josh 10:27	
w took it on the second day, and	Josh 10:32	
w the children of Israel smote,	Josh 12:1	834
w is upon the bank of the river	Josh 12:2	834
w is the border of the children	Josh 12:2	
w was of the remnant of the	Josh 12:4	
the kings of the country *w* Joshua	Josh 12:7	834
w Joshua gave unto the tribes of	Josh 12:7	
of Ai, *w* is beside Beth-el, one	Josh 12:9	834
w is before Egypt, even unto the	Josh 13:3	834
w is counted to the Canaanite	Josh 13:3	
w Moses gave them, beyond Jordan	Josh 13:8	834
w reigned in Heshbon, unto the	Josh 13:10	834
w reigned in Ashtaroth and in	Josh 13:12	834
w reigned in Heshbon, whom Moses	Josh 13:21	834
w were dukes of Sihon, dwelling	Josh 13:21	
w are in Bashan, threescore	Josh 13:30	834
These are the countries *w* Moses	Josh 13:32	834
w the children of Israel	Josh 14:1	834
w Eleazar the priest, and Joshua	Josh 14:1	
w Arba was a great man among the	Josh 14:15	
w is on the south side of the	Josh 15:7	834
w is at the end of the valley of	Josh 15:8	834
to Baalah, *w* is Kirjath-jearim	Josh 15:9	1958
w is Chesalon, on the north side,	Josh 15:10	834
father of Anak, *w* city is Hebron	Josh 15:13	1958
Kerioth, and Hezron, *w* is Hazor,	Josh 15:25	1958
and Kirjath-sannah, *w* is Debir,	Josh 15:49	1958
w is Hebron, and Zior	Josh 15:54	1958
w is Kirjath-jearim, and Rabbah	Josh 15:60	1958
w were on the other side Jordan	Josh 17:5	834
w had not yet received their	Josh 18:2	834
w the LORD God of your fathers	Josh 18:3	834
w Moses the servant of the LORD	Josh 18:7	834
of Luz, *w* is Beth-el, southward	Josh 18:13	1958
w is Kirjath-jearim, a city of	Josh 18:14	1958
w is in the valley of the giants	Josh 18:16	834
w is over against the going up of	Josh 18:17	834
w is Jerusalem, Gibeath, and	Josh 18:28	1958
they gave him the city *w* he asked	Josh 19:50	834
w Eleazar the priest, and Joshua	Josh 19:51	834
w is Hebron, in the mountain of	Josh 20:7	1958
w were of the Levites, had by lot	Josh 21:4	
these cities *w* are here mentioned	Josh 21:9	834
W the children of Aaron, being of	Josh 21:10	
w city is Hebron, in the hill	Josh 21:11	1958
the Levites *w* remained of the	Josh 21:20	
w were remaining of the families	Josh 21:40	
w he sware to give unto their	Josh 21:43	834
not ought of any good thing *w* the	Josh 21:45	834
w Moses the servant of the LORD	Josh 22:4	834
w Moses the servant of the LORD	Josh 22:5	834
w is in the land of Canaan, to go	Josh 22:9	834
from *w* we are not cleansed until	Josh 22:17	834
w our fathers made, not for burnt	Josh 22:28	834
of Israel *w* were with him	Josh 22:30	834
w the LORD your God hath given	Josh 23:13	834
things *w* the LORD your God spake	Josh 23:14	834
w the LORD your God promised you	Josh 23:15	834
you from off this good land *w* the	Josh 23:15	834
w he commanded you, and have gone.	Josh 23:16	834
land *w* he hath given unto you	Josh 23:16	834
to that *w* I did among them	Josh 24:5	834
w dwelt on the other side Jordan	Josh 24:8	
w drave them out from before you,	Josh 24:12	
a land for *w* ye did not labour	Josh 24:13	834
cities *w* ye built not, and ye	Josh 24:13	834
oliveyards *w* ye planted not do ye	Josh 24:13	834
put away the gods *w* your fathers	Josh 24:14	834
whether the gods *w* your fathers	Josh 24:15	834
w did those great signs in our	Josh 24:17	834
the Amorites *w* dwelt in the land	Josh 24:18	
the strange gods *w* are among you	Josh 24:23	834
of the LORD *w* he spake unto us	Josh 24:27	834
w is in mount Ephraim, on the	Josh 24:30	834
w had known all the works of the	Josh 24:31	834
w the children of Israel brought	Josh 24:32	834
in a parcel of ground *w* Jacob	Josh 24:32	834
w was given him in mount Ephraim	Josh 24:33	834
w lieth in the south of Arad	Judg 1:16	834
w is the name thereof unto this	Judg 1:26	1931
land *w* I sware unto your fathers	Judg 2:1	834

w knew not the Lord	Judg 2:10	834
nor yet the works *w* he had done	Judg 2:10	834
w brought them out of the land of	Judg 2:12	
w delivered them out of the hand	Judg 2:16	
the way *w* their fathers walked in	Judg 2:17	834
w I commanded their fathers	Judg 2:20	834
w Joshua left when he died	Judg 2:21	834
are the nations *w* the Lord left	Judg 3:1	834
w he commanded their fathers by	Judg 3:4	834
made him a dagger *w* had two edges	Judg 3:16	
w he had for himself alone	Judg 3:20	834
w slew of the Philistines six	Judg 3:31	
w dwelt in Harosheth of the	Judg 4:2	
w was of the children of Hobab	Judg 4:11	
plain of Zaanaim, *w* is by Kedesh	Judg 4:11	834
for this is the day in *w* the Lord	Judg 4:14	834
the dens *w* are in the mountains	Judg 6:2	834
w said unto them, Thus saith the	Judg 6:8	
sat under an oak *w* was in Ophrah	Judg 6:11	834
miracles *w* our fathers told us of	Judg 6:13	834
the grove *w* thou shalt cut down	Judg 6:26	834
w thing became a snare unto	Judg 8:27	
w he had shewed unto Israel	Judg 8:35	835
w are threescore and ten persons,	Judg 9:2	
and light persons, *w* followed him	Judg 9:4	
w cheereth God and man, and go to	Judg 9:13	
their brother, *w* slew them	Judg 9:24	834
w aided him in the killing of his	Judg 9:24	834
w he did unto his father, in	Judg 9:56	834
w are called Havoth-jair unto	Judg 10:4	
w are in the land of Gilead	Judg 10:4	834
of the Amorites, *w* is in Gilead	Judg 10:8	834
unto the gods *w* ye have chosen	Judg 10:14	834
Wilt not thou possess that *w*	Judg 11:24	834
words of Jephthah *w* he sent him	Judg 11:28	834
do to me according to that *w* hath	Judg 11:36	834
to his vow *w* he had vowed	Judg 11:39	834
Ephraimites *w* were escaped said	Judg 12:5	
let the man of God *w* thou didst	Judg 13:8	834
unto them *w* expounded the riddle	Judg 14:19	
w is in Lehi unto this day	Judg 15:19	834
green withs *w* had not been dried	Judg 16:8	834
of our country, *w* slew many of us	Judg 16:24	834
pillars upon *w* the house stood	Judg 16:29	834
on *w* it was borne up, of the one	Judg 16:29	
So the dead *w* he slew at his	Judg 16:30	834
than they *w* he slew in his life	Judg 16:30	834
about *w* thou cursedst, and spakest	Judg 17:2	
but every man did that *w* was	Judg 17:6	
way *w* we go shall be prosperous	Judg 18:5	834
w were of the children of Dan,	Judg 18:16	834
have taken away my gods *w* I made	Judg 18:24	834
took the things *w* Micah had made	Judg 18:27	834
and the priest *w* he had	Judg 18:27	834
w he made, all the time that the	Judg 18:31	834
against Jebus, *w* is Jerusalem	Judg 19:10	1958
Gibeah, *w* belongeth to Benjamin	Judg 19:14	834
w was also of mount Ephraim	Judg 19:16	
for the young man *w* is with thy	Judg 19:19	
the thing *w* we will do to Gibeah	Judg 20:9	834
w are in Gibeah, that we may put	Judg 20:13	834
w were numbered seven hundred	Judg 20:15	
W of us shall go up first to the	Judg 20:18	4310
of *w* one goeth up to the house of	Judg 20:31	834
wait *w* they had set beside Gibeah	Judg 20:36	834
them *w* came out of the cities	Judg 20:42	834
So that all *w* fell that day of	Judg 20:46	
w is in the land of Canaan	Judg 21:12	834
they gave them wives *w* they had	Judg 21:14	834
in Shiloh yearly in a place *w* is	Judg 21:19	834
every man did that *w* was right in	Judg 21:25	
w returned out of the country of	Ruth 1:22	
drink of that *w* the young men	Ruth 2:9	834
art come unto a people *w* thou	Ruth 2:11	834
w was our brother Elimelech's	Ruth 4:3	834
w two did build the house of	Ruth 4:11	834
of the seed *w* the Lord shall give	Ruth 4:12	834
w hath not left thee this day	Ruth 4:14	834
w loveth thee, *w* is better to	Ruth 4:15	834
me my petition *w* I asked of him	1Sa 1:27	834
the loan *w* is lent to the Lord	1Sa 2:20	834
w I have commanded in my	1Sa 2:29	834
in all the wealth *w* God shall	1Sa 2:32	834
to that *w* is in mine heart	1Sa 2:35	834
at *w* both the ears of every one	1Sa 3:11	834
w I have spoken concerning his	1Sa 3:12	834
for the iniquity *w* he knoweth	1Sa 3:13	834
w dwelleth between the cherubims	1Sa 4:4	
offering *w* we shall return to him	1Sa 6:4	834
on *w* there hath come no yoke, and	1Sa 6:7	834
w ye return him for a trespass	1Sa 6:8	834
these are the golden emerods *w*	1Sa 6:17	834
w stone remaineth unto this day	1Sa 6:18	
the cities *w* the Philistines had	1Sa 7:14	834
According to all the works *w* they	1Sa 8:8	834
king *w* ye shall have chosen you	1Sa 8:18	834
w were about thirty persons	1Sa 9:22	
Bring the portion *w* I gave thee	1Sa 9:23	834
of *w* I said unto thee, Set it by	1Sa 9:23	834
that *w* was upon it, and set it	1Sa 9:24	
said, Behold that *w* is left	1Sa 9:24	
The asses *w* thou wentest to seek	1Sa 10:2	834
w thou shalt receive of their	1Sa 10:4	
that they *w* remained were	1Sa 11:11	
w he did to you and to your	1Sa 12:7	834
w brought forth your fathers out	1Sa 12:8	
w the Lord will do before your	1Sa 12:16	834
w ye have done in the sight of	1Sa 12:17	834
w cannot profit nor deliver	1Sa 12:21	834
people as the sand *w* is on the	1Sa 13:5	834
Lord thy God, *w* he commanded thee.	1Sa 13:13	834
that *w* the Lord commanded thee	1Sa 13:14	834
a pomegranate tree *w* is in Migron	1Sa 14:2	834
by *w* Jonathan sought to go over	1Sa 14:4	834
w Jonathan and his armourbearer	1Sa 14:14	834
w a yoke of oxen might plow	1Sa 14:14	
w went up with them into the camp	1Sa 14:21	834
w had hid themselves in mount	1Sa 14:22	
of their enemies *w* they found	1Sa 14:30	834
w saveth Israel, though it be in	1Sa 14:39	
I remember that *w* Amalek did to	1Sa 15:2	834
the lowing of the oxen *w* I hear	1Sa 15:14	834
gone the way *w* the Lord sent me	1Sa 15:20	834
the chief of the things *w* should	1Sa 15:21	
Samuel did that *w* the Lord spake	1Sa 16:4	834
w are before thee, to seek out a	1Sa 16:16	
thy son, *w* is with the sheep	1Sa 16:19	834
w belongeth to Judah, and pitched	1Sa 17:1	834
words were heard *w* David spake	1Sa 17:31	834
them in a shepherd's bag *w* he had	1Sa 17:40	834
And as touching the matter *w* thou	1Sa 20:23	834
w was the second day of the month	1Sa 20:27	
find out now the arrows *w* I shoot	1Sa 20:36	834
of the arrow *w* Jonathan had shot	1Sa 20:37	834
w was set over the servants of	1Sa 22:9	1931
w is the king's son in law, and	1Sa 22:14	
w were about six hundred, arose	1Sa 23:13	
w is on the south of Jeshimon	1Sa 23:19	834
Behold the day of *w* the Lord said	1Sa 24:4	834
now thy shepherds *w* were with us	1Sa 25:7	834
now this blessing *w* thine	1Sa 25:27	834
w sent thee this day to meet me	1Sa 25:32	834
w hast kept me this day from	1Sa 25:33	834
w hath kept me back from hurting	1Sa 25:34	834
hand that *w* she had brought him	1Sa 25:35	834
the son of Laish, *w* was of Gallim	1Sa 25:44	834
of Hachilah, *w* is before Jeshimon	1Sa 26:1	834
w is before Jeshimon, by the way	1Sa 26:3	834
thy words *w* thou spakest unto me	1Sa 28:21	834
by a fountain *w* is in Jezreel	1Sa 29:1	834
w hath been with me these days,	1Sa 29:3	834
place *w* thou hast appointed him	1Sa 29:4	834
w were so faint that they could	1Sa 30:10	834
upon the coast *w* belongeth to	1Sa 30:14	834
w rode upon camels, and fled	1Sa 30:17	834
w they drave before those other	1Sa 30:20	
w were so faint that they could	1Sa 30:21	834
with that *w* the Lord hath given	1Sa 30:23	834
To them *w* were in Beth-el, and to	1Sa 30:27	834
to them *w* were in south Ramoth,	1Sa 30:27	834
to them *w* were in Jattir,	1Sa 30:27	834
to them *w* were in Aroer, and to	1Sa 30:28	834
to them *w* were in Siphmoth, and to	1Sa 30:28	834
to them *w* were in Eshtemoa,	1Sa 30:28	834
to them *w* were in Rachal, and to	1Sa 30:29	834
to them *w* were in the cities of	1Sa 30:29	834
to them *w* were in the cities of	1Sa 30:29	834
to them *w* were in Hormah, and to	1Sa 30:30	834
to them *w* were in Chor-ashan, and	1Sa 30:30	834
to them *w* were in Athach,	1Sa 30:30	834
to them *w* were in Hebron, and to	1Sa 30:31	
w the Philistines had done to	1Sa 31:11	
w pertained to Ish-bosheth the	2Sa 2:15	
Helkath-hazzurim, *w* is in Gibeon	2Sa 2:16	834
his father, *w* was in Beth-lehem	2Sa 2:32	834
w against Judah do shew kindness	2Sa 3:8	834
w I espoused to me for an hundred	2Sa 3:14	834
w brought him again from the well	2Sa 3:26	
thine enemy, *w* sought thy life	2Sa 4:8	834
w spake unto David, saying,	2Sa 5:6	
house of Abinadab *w* was at Gibeah	2Sa 6:4	834
w chose me before thy father, and	2Sa 6:21	834
w thou hast spoken of, of them	2Sa 6:22	834
w shall proceed out of thy bowels	2Sa 7:12	834
w thou redeemedst to thee from	2Sa 7:23	834
W also king David did dedicate	2Sa 8:11	
of all nations *w* he subdued	2Sa 8:11	834
yet a son, *w* is lame on his feet	2Sa 9:3	
Lord do that *w* seemeth him good	2Sa 10:12	
w he had bought and nourished up	2Sa 12:3	834
took the cakes *w* she had made	2Sa 13:10	834
Baal-hazor, *w* is beside Ephraim	2Sa 13:23	834
shall quench my coal *w* is left	2Sa 14:7	834
this thing as one *w* is faulty	2Sa 14:13	
w cannot be gathered up again	2Sa 14:14	834
that every man *w* hath any suit or	2Sa 15:4	834
w I have vowed unto the Lord, in	2Sa 15:7	834
w were concubines, to keep the	2Sa 15:16	
six hundred men *w* came after him	2Sa 15:18	834
w came forth of my bowels,	2Sa 16:11	834
w he hath left to keep the house	2Sa 16:21	834
w he counselled in those days,	2Sa 16:23	834
they *w* be with him are valiant	2Sa 17:10	834
w had a well in his court	2Sa 17:18	
w Amasa was a man's son, whose	2Sa 17:25	
a pillar, *w* is in the king's dale	2Sa 18:18	834
w hath delivered up the men that	2Sa 18:28	834
w this day have saved thy life,	2Sa 19:5	
w was of Bahurim, hasted and came	2Sa 19:16	834
neither do thou remember that *w*	2Sa 19:19	834
I will do to him that *w* shall	2Sa 19:38	
set time *w* he had appointed him	2Sa 20:5	834
at the great stone *w* is in Gibeon	2Sa 20:8	834
w had stolen them from the street	2Sa 21:12	834
w was of the sons of the giant,	2Sa 21:16	834
w was of the sons of the giant	2Sa 21:18	834
a people *w* I knew not shall serve	2Sa 22:44	
of Beth-lehem, *w* is by the gate	2Sa 23:15	834
w was with him, Go now through	2Sa 24:2	834
of that *w* doth cost me nothing	2Sa 24:24	834
the mighty men *w* belonged to	1Kin 1:8	834
w is by En-rogel, and called all	1Kin 1:9	834
w hath given one to sit on my	1Kin 1:48	834
his word *w* he spake concerning me	1Kin 2:4	834
w cursed me with a grievous curse	1Kin 2:8	1931
w hath established me, and set me	1Kin 2:24	834
w he spake concerning the house	1Kin 2:27	834
w Joab shed, from me, and from the	1Kin 2:31	834
w thine heart is privy to	1Kin 2:44	834
w went out, and fell upon him,	1Kin 2:46	
of thy people *w* thou hast chosen	1Kin 3:8	834
thee that *w* thou hast not asked	1Kin 3:13	834
it was not my son, *w* I did bear	1Kin 3:21	834
judgment *w* the king had judged	1Kin 3:28	834
these were the princes *w* he had	1Kin 4:2	834
w provided victuals for the king	1Kin 4:7	
w had Taphath the daughter of	1Kin 4:11	
w is by Zartanah beneath Jezreel,	1Kin 4:12	
son of Manasseh, *w* are in Gilead	1Kin 4:13	834
w is in Bashan, threescore great	1Kin 4:13	834
only officer *w* was in the land	1Kin 4:19	834
as the sand *w* is by the sea in	1Kin 4:20	834
w had heard of his wisdom	1Kin 4:34	834
w were about him on every side	1Kin 5:3	834
w hath given unto David a wise	1Kin 5:7	834
things *w* thou sentest to me for	1Kin 5:8	834
officers *w* were over the work	1Kin 5:16	834
w ruled over the people that	1Kin 5:16	
w is the second month, that he	1Kin 6:1	1931
the house *w* king Solomon built	1Kin 6:2	834
this house *w* thou art in building	1Kin 6:12	834
w I spake unto David thy father	1Kin 6:12	834
covered the altar *w* was of cedar	1Kin 6:20	
w is the eighth month, was the	1Kin 6:38	1931
the porch, *w* was of the like work	1Kin 7:8	
for the chapiters *w* were upon the	1Kin 7:17	834
the belly *w* was by the network	1Kin 7:20	834
w were upon the top of the	1Kin 7:41	834
w Hiram made to king Solomon for	1Kin 7:45	834
Solomon brought in the things *w*	1Kin 7:51	
of the city of David, *w* is Zion	1Kin 8:1	1958
Ethanim, *w* is the seventh month	1Kin 8:2	1931
w Moses put there at Horeb, when	1Kin 8:9	834
w spake with his mouth unto David	1Kin 8:15	834
w he made with our fathers, when	1Kin 8:21	834
w thou spakest unto thy servant	1Kin 8:26	834
w thy servant prayeth before thee	1Kin 8:28	834
the place of *w* thou hast said	1Kin 8:29	834
w thy servant shall make toward	1Kin 8:29	834
w thou gavest unto their fathers	1Kin 8:34	834
w thou hast given to thy people	1Kin 8:36	834
w shall know every man the plague	1Kin 8:38	834
w thou gavest unto our fathers	1Kin 8:40	834
w I have builded, is called by	1Kin 8:43	834
the city *w* thou hast chosen	1Kin 8:44	834
w led them away captive, and pray	1Kin 8:48	834
w thou gavest unto their fathers,	1Kin 8:48	834
the city *w* thou hast chosen, and	1Kin 8:48	834
the house *w* I have built for thy	1Kin 8:48	834
w thou broughtest forth out of	1Kin 8:51	834
w he promised by the hand of	1Kin 8:56	834
w he commanded our fathers	1Kin 8:58	834
w he offered unto the Lord, two	1Kin 8:63	834
desire *w* he was pleased to do	1Kin 9:1	834
w thou hast built, to put my name	1Kin 9:3	834
my statutes *w* I have set before	1Kin 9:6	834
of the land *w* I have given them	1Kin 9:7	834
w I have hallowed for my name,	1Kin 9:7	834
w is high, every one that passeth	1Kin 9:8	
cities *w* Solomon had given him	1Kin 9:12	834
are these *w* thou hast given me	1Kin 9:13	834
of the levy *w* king Solomon raised	1Kin 9:15	834
that *w* Solomon desired to build	1Kin 9:19	834
w were not of the children of	1Kin 9:20	834
w bare rule over the people that	1Kin 9:23	
house *w* Solomon had built for her	1Kin 9:24	834
altar *w* he built unto the Lord	1Kin 9:25	834
w is beside Eloth, on the shore	1Kin 9:26	834
from the king, *w* he told her not	1Kin 10:3	834
his ascent by *w* he went up unto	1Kin 10:5	834
exceedeth the fame *w* I heard	1Kin 10:7	834
w stand continually before thee,	1Kin 10:8	
w delighted in thee, to set thee	1Kin 10:9	834
abundance of spices as these *w*	1Kin 10:10	834
beside that *w* Solomon gave her of	1Kin 10:13	834
w God had put in his heart	1Kin 10:24	834
Of the nations concerning *w* the	1Kin 11:2	834
w burnt incense and sacrificed	1Kin 11:8	
w had appeared unto him twice	1Kin 11:9	
not that *w* the Lord commanded	1Kin 11:10	834
w I have commanded thee, I will	1Kin 11:11	834
Jerusalem's sake *w* I have chosen	1Kin 11:13	834
w gave him an house, and appointed	1Kin 11:18	
w fled from his lord Hadadezer	1Kin 11:23	834
the city *w* I have chosen out of	1Kin 11:32	834
to do that *w* is right in mine	1Kin 11:33	
the city *w* I have chosen me to	1Kin 11:36	834
his heavy yoke *w* he put upon us	1Kin 12:4	834
old men, *w* they had given him, and	1Kin 12:8	834
with him, and *w* stood before him	1Kin 12:8	834
Make the yoke *w* thy father did	1Kin 12:9	834
w the Lord spake by Ahijah the	1Kin 12:15	834
w dwelt in the cities of Judah	1Kin 12:17	
w were warriors, to fight against	1Kin 12:21	
w brought thee up out of the land	1Kin 12:28	834
w were not of the sons of Levi	1Kin 12:31	834
of the high places *w* he had made	1Kin 12:32	834
w he had made in Beth-el the	1Kin 12:33	834
even in the month *w* he had	1Kin 12:33	834
This is the sign *w* the Lord hath	1Kin 13:3	834
w had cried against the altar in	1Kin 13:4	834
w he put forth against him, dried	1Kin 13:4	834
according to the sign *w* the man	1Kin 13:5	834
the words *w* he had spoken unto	1Kin 13:11	834
of God went, *w* came from Judah	1Kin 13:12	834
hast not kept the commandment *w*	1Kin 13:21	834
of the *w* the Lord did say to thee	1Kin 13:22	834
w hath torn him, and slain him,	1Kin 13:26	
of the Lord, *w* he spake unto him	1Kin 13:26	834
For the saying *w* he cried by the	1Kin 13:32	834
w are in the cities of Samaria	1Kin 13:32	834
w told me that I should be king	1Kin 14:2	1931

to do that only *w* was right in	1Kin 14:8	1931
w he gave to their fathers, and	1Kin 14:15	834
w he spake by the hand of his	1Kin 14:18	834
the days *w* Jeroboam reigned were	1Kin 14:20	834
the city *w* the LORD did choose	1Kin 14:21	834
their sins *w* they had committed	1Kin 14:22	834
w the LORD cast out before the	1Kin 14:24	834
of gold *w* Solomon had made	1Kin 14:26	834
w kept the door of the king's	1Kin 14:27	
father, *w* he had done before him	1Kin 15:3	834
Because David did that *w* was	1Kin 15:5	
Asa did that *w* was right in the	1Kin 15:11	
things *w* his father had dedicated	1Kin 15:15	
and the things *w* himself had	1Kin 15:15	
w he had against the cities of	1Kin 15:20	834
he did, and the cities *w* he built	1Kin 15:23	834
w belonged to the Philistines	1Kin 15:27	834
w he spake by his servant Ahijah	1Kin 15:29	834
the sins of Jeroboam *w* he sinned	1Kin 15:30	834
w he made Israel sin, by his	1Kin 15:30	834
w he spake against Baasha by Jehu	1Kin 16:12	834
by *w* they sinned	1Kin 16:13	834
by *w* they made Israel to sin, in	1Kin 16:13	834
w belonged to the Philistines	1Kin 16:15	834
For his sins *w* he sinned in doing	1Kin 16:19	834
Jeroboam, and in his sin *w* he did	1Kin 16:19	834
the name of the city *w* he built	1Kin 16:24	834
rest of the acts of Omri *w* he did	1Kin 16:27	834
w he had built in Samaria	1Kin 16:32	834
w he spake by Joshua the son of	1Kin 16:34	834
w belongeth to Zidon, and dwell	1Kin 17:9	834
of the LORD, *w* he spake by Elijah	1Kin 17:16	834
w was the governor of his house	1Kin 18:3	834
hundred, *w* eat at Jezebel's table	1Kin 18:19	
took the bullock *w* was given them	1Kin 18:26	
leaped upon the altar *w* was made	1Kin 18:26	834
w belongeth to Judah, and left his	1Kin 19:3	834
all the knees *w* have not bowed	1Kin 19:18	834
every mouth *w* hath not kissed him	1Kin 19:18	834
city, and the army *w* followed them	1Kin 20:19	834
w my father took from thy father,	1Kin 20:34	834
w was in Jezreel, hard by the	1Kin 21:1	834
word *w* Naboth the Jezreelite had	1Kin 21:4	834
letters *w* she had sent unto them	1Kin 21:11	834
w he refused to give thee for	1Kin 21:15	834
king of Israel, *w* is in Samaria	1Kin 21:18	834
w did sell himself to work	1Kin 21:25	834
of them, and speak that *w* is good	1Kin 22:13	
thou tell me nothing but that *w*	1Kin 22:16	
W way went the Spirit of the LORD	1Kin 22:24	
the word of the LORD *w* he spake	1Kin 22:38	834
did, and the ivory house *w* he made	1Kin 22:39	834
doing that *w* was right in the	1Kin 22:43	
w remained in the days of his	1Kin 22:46	
that bed on *w* thou art gone up	2Kin 1:4	834
that bed on *w* thou art gone up	2Kin 1:6	834
man was he *w* came up to meet you	2Kin 1:7	834
that bed on *w* thou art gone up	2Kin 1:16	834
of the LORD *w* Elijah had spoken	2Kin 1:17	834
of the acts of Ahaziah *w* he did	2Kin 1:18	834
when the sons of the prophets *w*	2Kin 2:15	834
the saying of Elisha *w* he spake	2Kin 2:22	834
of Nebat, *w* made Israel to sin	2Kin 3:3	834
And he said, *W* way shall we go up	2Kin 3:8	
w poured water on the hands of	2Kin 3:11	834
shalt set aside that *w* is full	2Kin 4:4	
w passeth by us continually	2Kin 4:9	
at his hands that *w* he brought	2Kin 5:20	834
place *w* the man of God told him	2Kin 6:10	834
Will ye not shew me *w* of us is	2Kin 6:11	4310
w are left in the city, (behold,	2Kin 7:13	834
w the Syrians had cast away in	2Kin 7:15	834
smote the Edomites *w* compassed	2Kin 8:21	
w the Syrians had given him at	2Kin 8:29	834
And Jehu said, Unto *w* of all us	2Kin 9:5	4310
w the Syrians had given him	2Kin 9:15	834
w came to them, and said, Thus	2Kin 9:19	
going up to Gur, *w* is by Ibleam	2Kin 9:27	834
w he spake by his servant Elijah	2Kin 9:36	834
do thou that *w* is good in thine	2Kin 10:5	
of the city, *w* brought them up	2Kin 10:6	
w the LORD spake concerning the	2Kin 10:10	834
for the LORD hath done that *w* he	2Kin 10:10	834
of the LORD, *w* he spake to Elijah	2Kin 10:17	834
that *w* is right in mine eyes	2Kin 10:30	
of Jeroboam, *w* made Israel to sin	2Kin 10:31	834
w is by the river Arnon, even	2Kin 10:33	834
the king's sons *w* were slain	2Kin 11:2	
she went by the way by the *w* the	2Kin 11:16	
Jehoash did that *w* was right in	2Kin 12:2	
of Millo, *w* goeth down to Silla	2Kin 12:20	
he did that *w* was evil in the	2Kin 13:2	
of Nebat, *w* made Israel to sin	2Kin 13:2	
he did that *w* was evil in the	2Kin 13:11	
w he had taken out of the hand of	2Kin 13:25	834
he did that *w* was right in the	2Kin 14:3	
that he slew his servants *w* had	2Kin 14:5	834
according unto that *w* is written	2Kin 14:6	
w belongeth to Judah	2Kin 14:11	834
of the acts of Jehoash *w* he did	2Kin 14:15	834
w was sixteen years old, and made	2Kin 14:21	1931
he did that *w* was evil in the	2Kin 14:24	
w he spake by the hand of his	2Kin 14:25	834
the prophet, *w* was of Gath-hepher	2Kin 14:25	834
w belonged to Judah, for Israel,	2Kin 14:28	
he did that *w* was right in the	2Kin 15:3	
he did that *w* was evil in the	2Kin 15:9	
of the LORD *w* he spake unto Jehu	2Kin 15:12	834
and his conspiracy *w* he made	2Kin 15:15	834
he did that *w* was evil in the	2Kin 15:18	
he did that *w* was evil in the	2Kin 15:24	
he did that *w* was evil in the	2Kin 15:28	
he did that *w* was right in the	2Kin 15:34	
did not that *w* was right in the	2Kin 16:2	
of Israel, *w* rise up against me	2Kin 16:7	
w was before the LORD, from the	2Kin 16:14	834
rest of the acts of Ahaz *w* he did	2Kin 16:19	834
he did that *w* was evil in the	2Kin 17:2	
w had brought them up out of the	2Kin 17:7	
kings of Israel, *w* they had made	2Kin 17:8	834
law *w* I commanded your fathers	2Kin 17:13	834
w I sent to you by my servants	2Kin 17:13	834
his testimonies *w* he testified	2Kin 17:15	834
statutes of Israel *w* they made	2Kin 17:19	834
all the sins of Jeroboam *w* he did	2Kin 17:22	834
among them, *w* slew some of them	2Kin 17:25	
The nations *w* thou hast removed,	2Kin 17:26	834
places *w* the Samaritans had made	2Kin 17:29	834
w sacrificed for them in the	2Kin 17:32	1961
commandment *w* the LORD	2Kin 17:34	834
w he wrote for you, ye shall	2Kin 17:37	834
he did that *w* was right in the	2Kin 18:3	
w the LORD commanded Moses	2Kin 18:6	834
w was the seventh year of Hoshea	2Kin 18:9	1958
that *w* thou puttest on me will I	2Kin 18:14	834
from the pillars *w* Hezekiah king	2Kin 18:16	834
w is in the highway of the	2Kin 18:17	834
w was over the household, and	2Kin 18:18	834
on *w* if a man lean, it will go	2Kin 18:21	834
me to the men *w* sit on the wall	2Kin 18:27	
w was over the household, and	2Kin 18:37	834
w was over the household, and	2Kin 19:2	834
will reprove the words *w* the LORD	2Kin 19:4	834
of the words *w* thou hast heard	2Kin 19:6	834
with *w* the servants of the king	2Kin 19:6	834
them *w* my fathers have destroyed	2Kin 19:12	834
of Eden *w* were in Thelasar	2Kin 19:12	834
w dwellest between the cherubims,	2Kin 19:15	
w hath sent him to reproach the	2Kin 19:16	834
That *w* thou hast prayed to me	2Kin 19:20	834
back by the way by *w* thou camest	2Kin 19:28	834
year that *w* springeth of the same	2Kin 19:29	
have done that *w* is good in thy	2Kin 20:3	
by *w* it had gone down in the dial	2Kin 20:11	834
that *w* thy fathers have laid up	2Kin 20:17	834
w thou shalt beget, shall they	2Kin 20:18	834
of the LORD *w* thou hast spoken	2Kin 20:19	834
he did that *w* was evil in the	2Kin 21:2	834
places *w* Hezekiah his father had	2Kin 21:3	834
of *w* the LORD said, In Jerusalem	2Kin 21:4	834
of *w* the LORD said to David, and	2Kin 21:7	834
w I have chosen out of all tribes	2Kin 21:7	834
the land *w* I gave their fathers	2Kin 21:8	834
w were before him, and hath made	2Kin 21:11	834
done that *w* was evil in my sight	2Kin 21:15	
in doing that *w* was evil in the	2Kin 21:16	
he did that *w* was evil in the	2Kin 21:20	
rest of the acts of Amon *w* he did	2Kin 21:25	834
he did that *w* was right in the	2Kin 22:2	
that he may sum the silver *w* is	2Kin 22:4	
w the keepers of the door have	2Kin 22:4	834
w is in the house of the LORD	2Kin 22:5	834
that *w* is written concerning us	2Kin 22:13	
w the king of Judah hath read	2Kin 22:16	834
But to the king of Judah *w* sent	2Kin 22:18	
the words *w* thou hast heard	2Kin 22:18	834
w I will bring upon this place	2Kin 22:20	834
of the book of the covenant *w* was	2Kin 23:2	
w were on a man's left hand at	2Kin 23:8	834
w is in the valley of the	2Kin 23:10	834
w was in the suburbs, and burned	2Kin 23:11	834
w the kings of Judah had made, and	2Kin 23:12	834
the altars *w* Manasseh had made in	2Kin 23:12	834
w were on the right hand of the	2Kin 23:13	834
w Solomon the king of Israel had	2Kin 23:13	834
the high place *w* Jeroboam the son	2Kin 23:15	834
to the word of the LORD *w* the man	2Kin 23:16	834
w came from Judah, and proclaimed	2Kin 23:17	834
w the kings of Israel had made to	2Kin 23:19	834
perform the words of the law *w*	2Kin 23:24	
city Jerusalem *w* I have chosen	2Kin 23:27	834
and the house of *w* I said	2Kin 23:27	834
he did that *w* was evil in the	2Kin 23:32	
he did that *w* was evil in the	2Kin 23:37	
w he spake by his servants the	2Kin 24:2	834
w the LORD would not pardon	2Kin 24:4	
he did that *w* was evil in the	2Kin 24:9	
pieces all the vessels of gold *w*	2Kin 24:13	834
he did that *w* was evil in the	2Kin 24:19	
w is by the king's garden	2Kin 25:4	834
w is the nineteenth year of king	2Kin 25:8	1958
the bases *w* Solomon had made for	2Kin 25:16	834
w were found in the city, and the	2Kin 25:19	834
w mustered the people of the land	2Kin 25:19	
w smote Midian in the field of	1Chr 1:46	
w three were born unto him of the	1Chr 2:3	
unto him Ephrath, *w* bare him Hur	1Chr 2:19	
w was the father of Ziph	1Chr 2:42	1931
of the scribes *w* dwelt at Jabez	1Chr 2:55	
w were born unto him in Hebron	1Chr 3:1	834
granted him that *w* he requested	1Chr 4:10	834
w was the father of Eshton	1Chr 4:11	1931
daughter of Pharaoh, *w* Mered took	1Chr 4:18	834
w were left of the family of that	1Chr 6:61	
w are called by their names	1Chr 6:65	834
All these *w* were chosen to be	1Chr 9:22	
w were in their villages, were to	1Chr 9:25	
w he committed against the LORD	1Chr 10:13	834
w he kept not, and also for asking	1Chr 10:13	834
went to Jerusalem, *w* is Jebus	1Chr 11:4	1958
of Zion, *w* is the city of David	1Chr 11:5	1958
w were expressed by name, to come	1Chr 12:31	834
w were men that had understanding	1Chr 12:32	834
fifty thousand, *w* could keep rank	1Chr 12:33	
Levites *w* are in their cities and	1Chr 13:2	
w belonged to Judah, to bring up	1Chr 13:6	834
children *w* he had in Jerusalem	1Chr 14:4	834
place, *w* he had prepared for it	1Chr 15:3	834
the word *w* he commanded to a	1Chr 16:15	834
covenant *w* he made with Abraham	1Chr 16:16	834
the LORD, *w* he commanded Israel	1Chr 16:40	834
thee, *w* shall be of thy sons	1Chr 17:11	834
do that *w* is good in his sight	1Chr 19:13	
thousand men *w* fought in chariots	1Chr 19:18	
at *w* time Sibbechai the	1Chr 20:4	227
w he spake in the name of the	1Chr 21:19	834
do that *w* is good in his eyes	1Chr 21:23	
take that *w* is thine for the LORD	1Chr 21:24	834
w Moses made in the wilderness,	1Chr 21:29	834
judgments *w* the LORD charged	1Chr 22:13	834
Of *w*, twenty and four thousand	1Chr 23:4	428
with the instruments *w* I made	1Chr 23:5	834
for that *w* is baked in the pan,	1Chr 23:29	
and for that *w* is fried	1Chr 23:29	834
w prophesied according to the	1Chr 25:2	
w were over the treasures of the	1Chr 26:22	
W Shelomith and his brethren were	1Chr 26:26	1931
w David the king, and the chief	1Chr 26:26	834
w came in and went out month by	1Chr 27:1	
the substance *w* was king David's	1Chr 27:31	834
w I have given to the house of my	1Chr 29:3	
w are present here, to offer	1Chr 29:17	
for the *w* I have made provision	1Chr 29:19	834
w Moses the servant of the LORD	2Chr 1:3	834
place *w* David had prepared for it	2Chr 1:4	
w was at the tabernacle of the	2Chr 1:6	
w he placed in the chariot cities	2Chr 1:14	
the house *w* I build is great	2Chr 2:5	834
for the house *w* I am about to	2Chr 2:9	834
w he sent to Solomon, Because the	2Chr 2:11	
device *w* shall be put to him	2Chr 2:14	834
w my lord hath spoken of, let him	2Chr 2:15	834
w he overlaid with fine gold, and	2Chr 3:5	
w did compass it round about	2Chr 4:3	
the chapiters *w* were on the top	2Chr 4:12	
two pommels of the chapiters *w*	2Chr 4:12	834
chapiters *w* were upon the pillars	2Chr 4:13	834
of the city of David, *w* is Zion	2Chr 5:2	1958
feast *w* was in the seventh month	2Chr 5:3	1931
w could not be told nor numbered	2Chr 5:6	834
w Moses put therein at Horeb	2Chr 5:10	834
the Levites *w* were the singers	2Chr 5:12	
w he spake with his mouth to my	2Chr 6:4	834
but thy son *w* shall come forth	2Chr 6:9	
w keepest covenant, and shewest	2Chr 6:14	
Thou *w* hast kept with thy servant	2Chr 6:15	
that *w* thou hast promised him	2Chr 6:15	834
that *w* thou hast promised him	2Chr 6:16	834
w thou hast spoken unto thy	2Chr 6:17	834
less this house *w* I have built	2Chr 6:18	834
the prayer *w* thy servant prayeth	2Chr 6:19	834
to hearken unto the prayer *w* thy	2Chr 6:20	834
w they shall make toward this	2Chr 6:21	834
the land *w* thou gavest to them	2Chr 6:25	834
w thou hast given unto thy people	2Chr 6:27	834
w thou gavest unto our fathers	2Chr 6:31	834
w is not of thy people Israel,	2Chr 6:32	834
may know that this house *w* I have	2Chr 6:33	834
this city *w* thou hast chosen	2Chr 6:34	834
the house *w* I have built for thy	2Chr 6:34	834
for there is no man *w* sinneth not	2Chr 6:36	834
w thou gavest unto their fathers,	2Chr 6:38	834
toward the city *w* thou hast	2Chr 6:38	834
toward the house *w* I have built	2Chr 6:38	834
forgive thy people *w* have sinned	2Chr 6:39	834
w David the king had made to	2Chr 7:6	834
because the brasen altar *w*	2Chr 7:7	834
w are called by my name, shall	2Chr 7:14	834
w I have set before you, and shall	2Chr 7:19	834
of my land *w* I have given them	2Chr 7:20	834
w I have sanctified for my name,	2Chr 7:20	834
house, *w* is high, shall be an	2Chr 7:21	834
w brought them forth out of the	2Chr 7:22	834
That the cities *w* Huram had	2Chr 8:2	834
cities, *w* he built in Hamath	2Chr 8:4	834
Jebusites, *w* were not of Israel,	2Chr 8:7	834
w he had built before the porch,	2Chr 8:12	834
from Solomon *w* he told her not	2Chr 9:2	834
his ascent by *w* he went up into	2Chr 9:4	834
It was a true report *w* I heard in	2Chr 9:5	834
w stand continually before thee,	2Chr 9:7	
w delighted in thee to set thee	2Chr 9:8	834
w brought gold from Ophir,	2Chr 9:10	834
beside that *w* she had brought	2Chr 9:12	834
Beside that *w* chapmen and	2Chr 9:14	
w were fastened to the throne, and	2Chr 9:18	
counsel *w* the old men gave him	2Chr 10:8	834
w have spoken to me, saying, Ease	2Chr 10:9	834
w he spake by the hand of Ahijah	2Chr 10:15	834
w were warriors, to fight against	2Chr 11:1	
w are in Judah and in Benjamin	2Chr 11:10	834
and for the calves *w* he had made	2Chr 11:15	834
W bare him children	2Chr 11:19	
w bare him Abijah, and Attai, and	2Chr 11:20	
cities *w* pertained to Judah	2Chr 12:4	834
of gold *w* Solomon had made	2Chr 12:9	834
Instead of *w* king Rehoboam made	2Chr 12:10	
the city *w* the LORD had chosen	2Chr 12:13	834
w is in mount Ephraim, and said,	2Chr 13:4	834
w Jeroboam made you for gods	2Chr 13:8	834
w minister unto the LORD, are the	2Chr 13:10	
And Asa did that *w* was good	2Chr 14:2	
out of the cities *w* he had taken	2Chr 15:8	834
of the spoil *w* they had brought,	2Chr 15:11	
w he had made for himself in the	2Chr 16:14	834
laid him in the bed *w* was filled	2Chr 16:14	834
w Asa his father had taken	2Chr 17:2	834
W way went the Spirit of the LORD	2Chr 18:23	
be in Hazazon-tamar, *w* is En-gedi	2Chr 20:2	1958
w thou hast given us to inherit	2Chr 20:11	834
w were come against Judah	2Chr 20:22	
jewels, *w* they stripped off for	2Chr 20:25	

doing that *w* was right in the	2Chr 20:32	
he wrought that *w* was evil in the	2Chr 21:6	
the Edomites *w* compassed him in	2Chr 21:9	
w were better than thyself	2Chr 21:13	
wounds *w* were given him at Ramah	2Chr 22:6	834
w were in the house of God	2Chr 23:9	834
that none *w* was unclean in any	2Chr 23:19	
Joash did that *w* was right in the	2Chr 24:2	
w stood above the people, and said	2Chr 24:20	
remembered not the kindness *w*	2Chr 24:22	834
he did that *w* was right in the	2Chr 25:2	
w I have given to the army of	2Chr 25:9	834
of the army *w* Amaziah sent back	2Chr 25:13	834
w said unto him, Why hast thou	2Chr 25:15	
w could not deliver their own	2Chr 25:15	834
w belongeth to Judah	2Chr 25:21	834
he did that *w* was right in the	2Chr 26:4	
burial *w* belonged to the kings	2Chr 26:23	834
he did that *w* was right in the	2Chr 27:2	
but he did not that *w* was right	2Chr 28:1	
one day, *w* were all valiant men	2Chr 28:6	
w ye have taken captive of your	2Chr 28:11	834
the men *w* were expressed by name	2Chr 28:15	834
the gods of Damascus, *w* smote him	2Chr 28:23	
he did that *w* was right in the	2Chr 29:2	
done that *w* was evil in the eyes	2Chr 29:6	
w king Ahaz in his reign did cast	2Chr 29:19	834
w the congregation brought, was	2Chr 29:32	834
w trespassed against the LORD God	2Chr 30:7	834
w he hath sanctified for ever	2Chr 30:8	834
w they received of the hand of	2Chr 30:16	
the tithe of holy things *w* were	2Chr 31:6	
that *w* is left is this great	2Chr 31:10	
over *w* Cononiah the Levite was	2Chr 31:12	
w were in the fields of the	2Chr 31:19	
Judah, and wrought that *w* was good	2Chr 31:20	
fountains *w* were without the city	2Chr 32:3	834
w were the work of the hands of	2Chr 32:19	
w cut off all the mighty men of	2Chr 32:21	
But did that *w* was evil in the	2Chr 33:2	
w Hezekiah his father had broken	2Chr 33:3	834
the idol *w* he had made, in the	2Chr 33:7	834
of *w* God had said to David and to	2Chr 33:7	834
w I have chosen before all the	2Chr 33:7	834
land *w* I have appointed for your	2Chr 33:8	834
w took Manasseh among the thorns,	2Chr 33:11	
But he did that *w* was evil in the	2Chr 33:22	
unto all the carved images *w*	2Chr 33:22	834
he did that *w* was right in the	2Chr 34:2	
w the Levites that kept the doors	2Chr 34:9	834
to floor the houses *w* the kings	2Chr 34:11	834
that are written in the book *w*	2Chr 34:24	834
the words *w* thou hast heard	2Chr 34:26	834
w are written in this book	2Chr 34:31	
w were holy unto the LORD, Put	2Chr 35:3	
w Solomon the son of David king	2Chr 35:3	834
according to that *w* was written	2Chr 35:26	
he did that *w* was evil in the	2Chr 36:5	
and his abominations *w* he did	2Chr 36:8	834
that *w* was found in him, behold,	2Chr 36:8	
he did that *w* was evil in the	2Chr 36:9	
he did that *w* was evil in the	2Chr 36:12	
w he had hallowed in Jerusalem	2Chr 36:14	834
house in Jerusalem, *w* is in Judah	2Chr 36:23	834
house at Jerusalem, *w* is in Judah	Ezr 1:2	834
w is in Judah, and build the house	Ezr 1:3	834
he is the God,) *w* is in Jerusalem	Ezr 1:3	834
of the LORD *w* is in Jerusalem	Ezr 1:5	834
w Nebuchadnezzar had brought	Ezr 1:7	834
of those *w* had been carried away,	Ezr 2:1	
W came with Zerubbabel	Ezr 2:2	834
these were they *w* went up from	Ezr 2:59	
w took a wife of the daughters of	Ezr 2:61	
of the LORD *w* is at Jerusalem	Ezr 2:68	834
of Assur, *w* brought us up hither	Ezr 4:2	
that the Jews *w* came up from thee	Ezr 4:12	1768
for *w* cause was this city	Ezr 4:15	1836
The letter *w* ye sent unto us hath	Ezr 4:18	1768
w have ruled over all countries	Ezr 4:20	
house of God *w* is at Jerusalem	Ezr 4:24	1768
house of God *w* is at Jerusalem	Ezr 5:2	1768
w were on this side the river,	Ezr 5:6	1768
w is builded with great stones,	Ezr 5:8	1931
w a great king of Israel builded	Ezr 5:11	
w Nebuchadnezzar took out of the	Ezr 5:14	1768
house of God *w* is in Jerusalem	Ezr 5:16	1768
w is there at Babylon, whether it	Ezr 5:17	1768
w Nebuchadnezzar took forth out	Ezr 6:5	1768
of the temple *w* is at Jerusalem	Ezr 6:5	834
unto the temple *w* is at Jerusalem	Ezr 6:5	1768
w are beyond the river, be ye far	Ezr 6:6	1768
that *w* they have need of, both	Ezr 6:9	
of the priests *w* are at Jerusalem	Ezr 6:9	1768
house of God *w* is at Jerusalem	Ezr 6:12	1768
according to that *w* Darius the	Ezr 6:13	1768
w was in the sixth year of the	Ezr 6:15	1768
service of God, *w* is at Jerusalem	Ezr 6:18	1768
Israel, *w* were come again out of	Ezr 6:21	
w the LORD God of Israel had	Ezr 7:6	834
w was in the seventh year of the	Ezr 7:8	1958
w are minded of their own	Ezr 7:13	1768
law of thy God *w* is in thine hand	Ezr 7:14	1768
w the king and his counsellors	Ezr 7:15	1768
of their God *w* is in Jerusalem	Ezr 7:16	1768
of your God *w* is in Jerusalem	Ezr 7:17	1768
w thou shalt have occasion to	Ezr 7:20	1768
treasurers *w* are beyond the river	Ezr 7:21	1768
w may judge all the people that	Ezr 7:25	1768
w hath put such a thing as this	Ezr 7:27	834
of the LORD *w* is in Jerusalem	Ezr 7:27	834
w the king, and his counsellors,	Ezr 8:25	
w were come out of the captivity,	Ezr 8:35	
W thou hast commanded by thy	Ezr 9:11	834
unto *w* ye go to possess it, is an	Ezr 9:11	834
w have filled it from one end to	Ezr 9:11	834
let all them *w* have taken strange	Ezr 10:14	
w were left of the captivity, and	Neh 1:2	834
w I pray before thee now, day and	Neh 1:6	834
w we have sinned against thee	Neh 1:6	834
w thou commandedst thy servant	Neh 1:7	834
palace *w* appertained to the house	Neh 2:8	834
w were broken down, and the gates	Neh 2:13	834
hand of my God *w* was good upon me	Neh 2:18	834
the tower *w* lieth out from the	Neh 3:25	
heaps of the rubbish *w* are burned	Neh 4:2	1992
Even that *w* they build, if a fox	Neh 4:3	834
the Jews *w* dwelt by them came	Neh 4:12	
w is great and terrible, and fight	Neh 4:14	
They *w* builded on the wall, and	Neh 4:17	
men of the guard *w* followed me	Neh 4:23	834
w were sold unto the heathen	Neh 5:8	
Now that *w* was prepared for me	Neh 5:18	834
for *w* cause thou buildest the	Neh 6:6	3651
of them *w* came up at the first	Neh 7:5	
these were they *w* went up also	Neh 7:61	
w took one of the daughters of	Neh 7:63	834
that *w* the rest of the people	Neh 7:72	834
w the LORD had commanded to	Neh 8:1	834
w they had made for the purpose	Neh 8:4	834
w is the Tirshatha, and Ezra the	Neh 8:9	1931
they found written in the law *w*	Neh 8:14	834
w is exalted above all blessing	Neh 9:5	
go in to possess the land *w* thou	Neh 9:15	834
concerning *w* thou hadst promised	Neh 9:23	834
slew thy prophets *w* testified	Neh 9:26	834
(*w* if a man do, he shall live in	Neh 9:29	834
fat land *w* thou gavest before	Neh 9:35	834
w was given by Moses the servant	Neh 10:29	834
w was over the thanksgiving, he	Neh 12:8	
w was over against them, they	Neh 12:37	
w was commanded to be given to	Neh 13:5	
w they brought into Jerusalem on	Neh 13:15	
w brought fish, and all manner of	Neh 13:16	
(this is Ahasuerus *w* reigned from	Est 1:1	
w was in Shushan the palace,	Est 1:2	834
w belonged to king Ahasuerus	Est 1:9	
w knew the times, (for so was the	Est 1:13	
w saw the king's face	Est 1:14	
w sat the first in the kingdom	Est 1:14	
w have heard of the deed of the	Est 1:18	834
decree *w* he shall make shall be	Est 1:20	834
let the maiden *w* pleaseth the	Est 2:4	834
w had been carried away with	Est 2:6	834
w were meet to be given her, out	Est 2:9	
w kept the concubines	Est 2:14	
w is the month Tebeth, in the	Est 2:16	
of those *w* kept the door, were	Est 2:21	
w were in the king's gate, said	Est 3:3	834
w is the month Adar, and to take	Est 3:13	1931
w was before the king's gate	Est 4:6	834
w is not according to the law	Est 4:16	834
brought *w* the king useth to wear	Est 6:8	834
the crown royal *w* is set upon his	Est 6:8	834
w Haman had made for Mordecai,	Est 7:9	834
w he had taken from Haman, and	Est 8:2	834
w he wrote to destroy the Jews	Est 8:5	834
he wrote to destroy the Jews *w*	Est 8:5	834
for the writing *w* is written in	Est 8:8	834
rulers of the provinces *w* are	Est 8:9	834
the king granted the Jews *w* were	Est 8:11	834
month, *w* is the month Adar	Est 8:12	1931
let it be granted to the Jews *w*	Est 9:13	834
the month *w* was turned unto them	Est 9:22	834
w he devised against the Jews,	Est 9:25	834
and of that *w* they had seen	Est 9:26	4100
matter, and *w* had come unto them	Est 9:26	4100
and the night in *w* it was said	Job 3:3	
w built desolate places for	Job 3:14	
as infants *w* never saw light	Job 3:16	
W long for death, but it cometh	Job 3:21	
W rejoice exceedingly, and are	Job 3:22	
For the thing *w* I greatly feared	Job 3:25	
that *w* I was afraid of is come	Job 3:25	834
w made all my bones to shake	Job 4:14	
w are crushed before the moth	Job 4:19	
excellency *w* is in them go away	Job 4:21	
to *w* of the saints wilt thou turn	Job 5:1	4310
W doeth great things and	Job 5:9	
that those *w* mourn may be exalted	Job 5:11	
Can that *w* is unsavoury be eaten	Job 6:6	
W are blackish by reason of the	Job 6:16	
that is desperate, *w* are as wind	Job 6:26	
W removeth the mountains, and they	Job 9:5	
w overturneth them in his anger	Job 9:5	834
W shaketh the earth out of her	Job 9:6	
W commandeth the sun, and it	Job 9:7	
W alone spreadeth out the heavens	Job 9:8	
W maketh Arcturus, Orion, and	Job 9:9	
W doeth great things past finding	Job 9:10	
that they are double to that *w* is	Job 11:6	
w grow out of the dust of the	Job 14:19	
thou, *w* is not in us	Job 15:9	1931
he *w* is born of a woman, that he	Job 15:14	
w drinketh iniquity like water	Job 15:16	
that *w* I have seen I will declare	Job 15:17	
W wise men have told from their	Job 15:18	834
in houses *w* no man inhabiteth,	Job 15:28	
w are ready to become heaps	Job 15:28	834
w is a witness against me	Job 16:8	
they *w* have seen him shall say,	Job 20:7	
The eye also *w* saw him shall see	Job 20:9	
w shall lie down with him in the	Job 20:11	
That *w* he laboured for shall he	Job 20:18	
away an house *w* he builded not	Job 20:19	
not save of that *w* he desired	Job 20:20	
the devices *w* ye wrongfully	Job 21:27	
old way *w* wicked men have trodden	Job 22:15	834
W were cut down out of time,	Job 22:16	834
W said unto God, Depart from us	Job 22:17	
the words *w* he would answer me	Job 23:5	
W make oil within their walls, and	Job 24:11	
w they had marked for themselves	Job 24:16	
the grave those *w* have sinned	Job 24:19	
and the son of man, *w* is a worm	Job 25:6	
that *w* is with the Almighty will	Job 27:11	834
w they shall receive of the	Job 27:13	
There is a path *w* no fowl knoweth	Job 28:7	
w the vulture's eye hath not seen	Job 28:7	
the cause *w* I knew not I searched	Job 29:16	
belly is as wine *w* hath no vent	Job 32:19	
and perverted that *w* was right	Job 33:27	
W goeth in company with the	Job 34:8	
That *w* I see not teach thou me	Job 34:32	
behold the clouds *w* are higher	Job 35:5	834
that *w* should be set on thy table	Job 36:16	
magnify his work, *w* men behold	Job 36:24	834
W the clouds do drop and distil	Job 36:28	834
doeth he, *w* we cannot comprehend	Job 37:5	
of him *w* is perfect in knowledge	Job 37:16	
w is strong, and as a molten	Job 37:18	
bright light *w* is in the clouds	Job 37:21	1931
W I have reserved against the	Job 38:23	834
w scattereth the east wind upon	Job 38:24	
W leaveth her eggs in the earth,	Job 39:14	3588
now behemoth, *w* I made with thee	Job 40:15	834
with a cord *w* thou lettest down	Job 41:1	
wonderful for me, *w* I knew not	Job 42:3	
spoken of me the thing *w* is right	Job 42:8	
the chaff *w* the wind driveth away	Ps 1:4	834
Many there be *w* say of my soul,	Ps 3:2	
David, *w* he sang unto the LORD,	Ps 7:t	834
w saveth the upright in heart	Ps 7:10	
fallen into the ditch *w* he made	Ps 7:15	
the stars, *w* thou hast ordained	Ps 8:3	834
to the LORD, *w* dwelleth in Zion	Ps 9:11	
consider my trouble *w* I suffer of	Ps 9:13	
in the net *w* they hid is their	Ps 9:15	2098
by the judgment *w* he executeth	Ps 9:16	
w put their trust in thee from	Ps 17:7	
from the wicked, *w* is thy sword	Ps 17:13	
From men *w* are thy hand, O LORD,	Ps 17:14	
w have their portion in this life	Ps 17:14	
enemy, and from them *w* hated me	Ps 18:17	
W is as a bridegroom coming out	Ps 19:5	
w they are not able to perform	Ps 21:11	
let them be ashamed *w* transgress	Ps 25:3	
w speak peace to their neighbours	Ps 28:3	
w speak grievous things proudly	Ps 31:18	
w thou hast laid up for them that	Ps 31:19	834
w thou hast wrought for them that	Ps 31:19	
thee in the way *w* thou shalt go	Ps 32:8	2098
the mule, *w* have no understanding	Ps 32:9	
w without cause they have digged	Ps 35:7	
w deliverest the poor from him	Ps 35:10	
w hath pleasure in the prosperity	Ps 35:27	
wonderful works *w* thou hast done	Ps 40:5	
thy thoughts *w* are to us-ward	Ps 40:5	
w did eat of my bread, hath	Ps 41:9	
and they *w* hate us spoil for	Ps 44:10	
I speak of the things *w* I have	Ps 45:1	
that the bones *w* thou hast broken	Ps 51:8	
W will not hearken to the voice	Ps 58:5	834
away as waters *w* run continually	Ps 58:7	
As a snail *w* melteth, let every	Ps 58:8	
for cursing and lying *w* they speak	Ps 59:12	
thou, O God, *w* hadst cast us off	Ps 60:10	
w didst not go out with our	Ps 60:10	
and truth, *w* may preserve him	Ps 61:7	
W by his strength setteth fast	Ps 65:6	
W stilleth the noise of the seas,	Ps 65:7	
river of God, *w* is full of water	Ps 65:9	
W holdeth our soul in life, and	Ps 66:9	
W my lips have uttered, and my	Ps 66:14	834
w hath not turned away my prayer,	Ps 66:20	834
out those *w* are bound with chains	Ps 68:6	
this is the hill *w* God desireth	Ps 68:16	
that *w* thou hast wrought for us	Ps 68:28	2098
heavens of heavens, *w* were of old	Ps 68:33	
I restored that *w* I took not away	Ps 69:4	834
that *w* should have been for their	Ps 69:22	
w hast shewed me great and sore	Ps 71:20	834
and my soul, *w* thou hast redeemed	Ps 71:23	834
w thou hast purchased of old	Ps 74:2	
inheritance, *w* thou hast redeemed	Ps 74:2	
W we have heard and known, and our	Ps 78:3	834
w he commanded our fathers, that	Ps 78:5	834
the children *w* should be born	Ps 78:6	
flies among them, *w* devoured them	Ps 78:45	
and frogs, *w* destroyed them	Ps 78:45	
w his right hand had purchased	Ps 78:54	
the tent *w* he placed among men	Ps 78:60	
Judah, the mount Zion *w* he loved	Ps 78:68	834
palaces, like the earth *w* he hath	Ps 78:69	
blood of thy servants *w* is shed	Ps 79:10	
so that all they *w* pass by the	Ps 80:12	
the vineyard *w* thy right hand	Ps 80:15	834
w brought thee out of the land of	Ps 81:10	
W perished at En-dor	Ps 83:10	
LORD shall give that *w* is good	Ps 85:12	
that they *w* hate me may see it,	Ps 86:17	
w thou swarest unto David in thy	Ps 89:49	
they are like grass *w* groweth up	Ps 90:5	
w is my refuge, even the most	Ps 91:9	
w frameth mischief by a law	Ps 94:20	
the people *w* shall be created	Ps 102:18	
w thou hast founded for them	Ps 104:8	2088
valleys, *w* run among the hills	Ps 104:10	
w sing among the branches	Ps 104:12	
bread *w* strengtheneth man's heart	Ps 104:15	
of Lebanon, *w* he hath planted	Ps 104:16	834
the word *w* he commanded to a	Ps 105:8	
W covenant he made with Abraham,	Ps 105:9	834

w had done great things in Egypt Ps 106:21
w were a snare unto them Ps 106:36
w lifteth up the waves thereof Ps 107:25
w may yield fruits of increase Ps 107:37
him as the garment *w* covereth him Ps 109:19
W turned the rock into a standing Ps 114:8
blessed of the LORD *w* made heaven Ps 115:15
into *w* the righteous shall enter Ps 118:20
The stone *w* the builders refused Ps 118:22
This is the day *w* the LORD hath Ps 118:24
the LORD, *w* hath shewed us light Ps 118:27
w do err from thy commandments Ps 119:21
Turn away my reproach *w* I fear Ps 119:39 834
thy commandments, *w* I have loved Ps 119:47 834
thy commandments, *w* I have loved Ps 119:48 834
upon *w* thou hast caused me to Ps 119:49 834
for me, *w* are not after thy law Ps 119:85 834
peace have they *w* love thy law Ps 119:165
the LORD, *w* made heaven and earth Ps 121:2
w cannot be removed, but abideth Ps 125:1
w withereth afore it groweth up Ps 129:6
Neither do they *w* go by say Ps 129:8
w by night stand in the house of Ps 134:1
of Zion, *w* dwelleth at Jerusalem Ps 135:21
To him *w* divided the Red sea into Ps 136:13
To him *w* led his people through Ps 136:16
To him *w* smote great kings Ps 136:17
will perfect that *w* concerneth me Ps 138:8
w in continuance were fashioned, Ps 139:16
W imagine mischiefs in their Ps 140:2 834
w shall not break my head Ps 141:5
snares *w* they have laid for me Ps 141:9
W teacheth my hands to war, and my Ps 144:1
W made heaven, and earth, the sea, Ps 146:6
w keepeth truth for ever Ps 146:6
W executeth judgment for the Ps 146:7
w giveth food to the hungry Ps 146:7
and to the young ravens *w* cry Ps 147:9 834
made a decree *w* shall not pass Ps 148:6
w taketh away the life of the Prov 1:19
woman, even from the stranger *w* Prov 2:16
W forsaketh the guide of her Prov 2:17
W having no guide, overseer, or Prov 6:7 834
from the stranger *w* flattereth Prov 7:5
of the wine *w* I have mingled Prov 9:5
so is a fair woman *w* is without Prov 11:22
not that *w* he took in hunting Prov 12:27
There is a way *w* seemeth right Prov 14:12
but that *w* is in the midst of Prov 14:33
that *w* he hath given will he pay Prov 19:17
man who devoureth that *w* is holy Prov 20:25
landmark, *w* thy fathers have set Prov 22:28 834
set thine eyes upon that *w* is not Prov 23:5
The morsel *w* thou hast eaten Prov 23:8
w is sweet to thy taste Prov 24:13
w the men of Hezekiah king of Prov 25:1 834
right hand, *w* bewrayeth itself Prov 27:16
a sweeping rain *w* leaveth no food Prov 28:3
There be three things *w* are too Prov 30:18
for me, yea, four *w* I know not Prov 30:18 834
for four *w* it cannot bear Prov 30:21
There be four things *w* are little Prov 30:24
There be three things *w* go well Prov 30:29
A lion *w* is strongest among Prov 30:30
ways to that *w* destroyeth kings Prov 31:3
labour *w* he taketh under the sun Eccl 1:3
hath been, it is that *w* shall be Eccl 1:9
that *w* is done Eccl 1:9
is that *w* shall be done Eccl 1:9
of old time, *w* was before us Eccl 1:10 834
That *w* is crooked cannot be made Eccl 1:15
that *w* is wanting cannot be Eccl 1:15
w they should do under the heaven Eccl 2:3 834
even that *w* hath been already Eccl 2:12 834
seeing that *w* now is in the days Eccl 2:16
I hated all my labour *w* I had Eccl 2:18
the labour *w* I took under the sun Eccl 2:20
to pluck up that *w* is planted Eccl 3:2
w God hath given to the sons of Eccl 3:10 834
That *w* hath been is now Eccl 3:15
that *w* is to be hath already been Eccl 3:15 834
and God requireth that *w* is past Eccl 3:15
For that *w* befalleth the sons of Eccl 3:19
Wherefore I praised the dead *w* Eccl 4:2
than the living *w* are yet alive Eccl 4:2 834
w hath not yet been, who hath not Eccl 4:3 834
the living *w* walk under the sun Eccl 4:15
pay that *w* thou hast vowed Eccl 5:4 834
There is a sore evil *w* I have Eccl 5:13
w he may carry away in his hand Eccl 5:15
Behold that *w* I have seen Eccl 5:18 834
of his life, *w* God giveth him Eccl 5:18 834
There is an evil *w* I have seen Eccl 6:1 834
That *w* hath been is named already Eccl 6:10 834
life *w* he spendeth as a shadow Eccl 6:12
straight, *w* he hath made crooked Eccl 7:13 834
ten mighty men *w* are in the city Eccl 7:19 834
That *w* is far off, and exceeding Eccl 7:24 4100
W yet my soul seeketh, but I find Eccl 7:28 834
he knoweth not that *w* shall be Eccl 8:7 4100
that fear God, *w* fear before him Eccl 8:12 834
his days, *w* are as a shadow Eccl 8:13
There is a vanity *w* is done upon Eccl 8:14 834
w God giveth him under the sun Eccl 8:15 834
w he hath given thee under the Eccl 9:9 834
in thy labour *w* thou takest under Eccl 9:9
There is an evil *w* I have seen Eccl 10:5
as an error *w* proceedeth from the Eccl 10:5
that *w* hath wings shall tell the Eccl 10:20
shall be afraid of that *w* is high Eccl 12:5
that *w* was written was upright, Eccl 12:10
w are given from one shepherd Eccl 12:11
The song of songs, *w* is Solomon's Song 1:1 834
Behold his bed, *w* is Solomon's Song 3:7

w came up from the washing Song 4:2
twins, *w* feed among the lilies Song 4:5
of sheep *w* go up from the washing Song 6:6
goblet, *w* wanteth not liquor Song 7:2
Lebanon *w* looketh toward Damascus Song 7:4
w I have laid up for thee, O my Song 7:13
w hath a most vehement flame Song 8:6
vineyard, *w* is mine, is before me Song 8:12
w he saw concerning Judah and Is 1:1 834
of the oaks *w* ye have desired Is 1:29 834
that *w* their own fingers have Is 2:8 834
w they made each one for himself Is 2:20 834
they *w* lead thee cause thee to Is 3:12
W justify the wicked for reward, Is 5:23
w he had taken with the tongs Is 6:6
hosts, *w* dwelleth in mount Zion Is 8:18
w they have prescribed Is 10:1
in the desolation *w* shall come Is 10:3
w shall stand for an ensign of Is 11:10 834
w shall be left, from Assyria, and Is 11:11 834
w shall be left, from Assyria Is 11:16 834
w Isaiah the son of Amoz did see Is 13:1 834
w shall not regard silver Is 13:17 834
w didst weaken the nations Is 14:12
that *w* they have laid up, shall Is 15:7
w shall lie down, and none shall Is 17:2
that *w* his fingers have made Is 17:8 834
w they left because of the Is 17:9 834
w make a noise like the noise of Is 17:12
w is beyond the rivers of Is 18:1 834
w the head or tail, branch or Is 19:15
of hosts, *w* he shaketh over it Is 19:16 834
w he hath determined against it Is 19:17 834
that *w* I have heard of the LORD Is 21:10 834
together, *w* have fled from far Is 22:3
w is over the house, and say, Is 22:15 834
that the righteous nation *w* Is 26:2
they shall come *w* were ready to Is 27:13
w are on the head of the fat Is 28:1 834
w as a tempest of hail and a Is 28:2
w is on the head of the fat Is 28:4 834
w when he that looketh upon it Is 28:4 834
this people *w* is in Jerusalem Is 28:14 834
w is wonderful in counsel, and Is 28:29
w men deliver to one that is Is 29:11 834
W say to the seers, See not Is 30:10 834
w hath been winnowed with the Is 30:24 834
beaten down, *w* smote with a rod Is 30:31
w the LORD shall lay upon him, it Is 30:32 834
w your own hands have made unto Is 31:7 834
w was over the house, and Shebna Is 36:3 834
will reprove the words *w* the LORD Is 37:4 834
them *w* my fathers have destroyed Is 37:12 834
of Eden *w* were in Telassar Is 37:12 834
w hath sent to reproach the Is 37:17 834
This is the word *w* the LORD hath Is 37:22 834
back by the way by *w* thou camest Is 37:29 834
the second year that *w* springeth Is 37:30
have done that *w* is good in thy Is 38:3
w is gone down in the sun dial of Is 38:8 834
by *w* degrees it was gone down Is 38:8
that *w* thy fathers have laid up Is 39:6 834
w thou shalt beget, shall they Is 39:7 834
of the LORD *w* thou hast spoken Is 39:8 834
earth, and that *w* cometh out of it Is 42:5
w maketh a way in the sea, and a Is 43:16
W bringeth forth the chariot and Is 43:17
from the womb, *w* will help thee Is 44:2
w he strengtheneth for himself Is 44:14
w call thee by thy name, am the Is 45:3
w are borne by me from the belly, Is 46:3
w are carried from the womb Is 46:3
suddenly, *w* thou shalt not know Is 47:11
w are called by the name of Is 48:1
w swear by the name of the LORD, Is 48:1
w among them hath declared these Is 48:14 4310
I am the LORD thy God *w* teacheth Is 48:17
w leadeth thee by the way that Is 48:17
The children *w* thou shalt have, Is 49:20
or *w* of my creditors is it to Is 50:1 4310
Art thou not it *w* hath dried the Is 51:10
of the son of man *w* shall be made Is 51:12
w hast drunk at the hand of the Is 51:17 834
w have said to thy soul, Bow down Is 51:23 834
for that *w* had not been told them Is 52:15 834
that *w* they had not heard shall Is 52:15 834
money for that *w* is not bread Is 55:2 834
labour for that *w* satisfieth not Is 55:2 834
unto me, and eat ye that *w* is good Is 55:2 834
shall accomplish that *w* I please Is 55:11 834
The Lord GOD *w* gathereth the Is 56:8
they are greedy dogs *w* can never Is 56:11
me, and the souls *w* I have made Is 57:16
that *w* is crushed breaketh out Is 59:5
my words *w* I have put in thy Is 59:21 834
the seed *w* the LORD hath blessed Is 61:9 834
w the mouth of the LORD shall Is 62:2 834
w shall never hold their peace Is 62:6
for the *w* thou hast laboured Is 62:8 834
w he hath bestowed on them Is 63:7 834
things *w* we looked not for Is 64:3
w walketh in a way that was not Is 65:2
W remain among the graves, and Is 65:4
w eat swine's flesh, and broth of Is 65:4
W say, Stand by thyself, come not Is 65:5 834
w have burned incense upon the Is 65:7 834
for ever in that *w* I create Is 65:18 834
chose that in *w* I delighted not Is 66:4 834
w I will make, shall remain Is 66:22 834
their gods, *w* are yet no gods Jer 2:11 1992
glory for that *w* doth not profit Jer 2:11 1992
Hast thou seen that *w* backsliding Jer 3:6 834
w shall feed you with knowledge Jer 3:15
w thy sons and thy daughters Jer 5:17

w have eyes, and see not Jer 5:21
w have ears, and hear not Jer 5:21
w have placed the sand for the Jer 5:22 834
w is called by my name, and say, Jer 7:10 834
w is called by my name, become a Jer 7:11 834
now unto my place *w* was in Shiloh Jer 7:12 834
w is called by my name, wherein Jer 7:14 834
and unto the place *w* I gave to you Jer 7:14 834
the house *w* is called by my name Jer 7:30 834
w is in the valley of the son of Jer 7:31 834
w I commanded them not, neither Jer 7:31 834
w remain in all the places Jer 8:3
w will not be charmed, and they Jer 8:17 834
my law *w* I set before them Jer 9:13 834
w their fathers taught them Jer 9:14 834
that I am the LORD *w* exercise Jer 9:24
them *w* are circumcised with the Jer 9:25
Hear ye the word *w* the LORD Jer 10:1 834
W I commanded your fathers in the Jer 11:4 834
according to all *w* I command you Jer 11:4 834
That I may perform the oath *w* I Jer 11:5 834
w I commanded them to do Jer 11:8 834
w refused to hear my words Jer 11:10 834
w I made with their fathers Jer 11:10 834
w they shall not be able to Jer 11:11 834
Judah, *w* they have done against Jer 11:17 834
that touch the inheritance *w* I Jer 12:14 834
w is upon thy loins, and arise, go Jer 13:4 834
w I commanded thee to hide there Jer 13:6 834
w refuse to hear my words Jer 13:10
w walk in the imagination of Jer 13:10
girdle, *w* is good for nothing Jer 13:10 834
for that *w* he did in Jerusalem Jer 15:4 834
into a land *w* thou knowest not Jer 15:14
mine anger, *w* shall burn upon you Jer 15:14
w refuseth to be healed Jer 15:18
in the land *w* thou knowest not Jer 17:4 834
mine anger, *w* shall burn for ever Jer 17:4
that *w* came out of my lips was Jer 17:16
by the *w* they go out, and in all Jer 17:19 834
The word *w* came to Jeremiah from Jer 18:1 834
w cometh from the rock of the Jer 18:14
w is by the entry of the east Jer 19:2 834
the *w* whosoever heareth, his ears Jer 19:3 834
w I commanded not, nor spake it, Jer 19:5 834
w was by the house of the LORD Jer 20:2 834
w shall spoil them, and take them, Jer 20:5
the cities *w* the LORD overthrew Jer 20:16 834
The word *w* came unto Jeremiah Jer 21:1 834
w besiege you without the walls, Jer 21:4
w say, Who shall come down Jer 21:13
cities *w* are not inhabited Jer 22:6
w reigned instead of Josiah his Jer 22:11
w went forth out of this place Jer 22:11 834
cast into a land *w* they know not Jer 22:28 834
over them *w* shall feed them Jer 23:4
w brought up the children of Jer 23:7 834
w brought up and *w* led the Jer 23:8 834
W think to cause my people to Jer 23:27
w they tell every man to his Jer 23:27 834
shame, *w* shall not be forgotten Jer 23:40 834
w could not be eaten, they were Jer 24:2 834
w cannot be eaten, they are so Jer 24:8 834
The *w* Jeremiah the prophet spake Jer 25:2 834
upon that land all my words *w* I Jer 25:13 834
w Jeremiah hath prophesied Jer 25:13 834
of the isles *w* are beyond the sea Jer 25:22 834
w are upon the face of the earth Jer 25:26 834
because of the sword *w* I will Jer 25:27 834
the city *w* is called by my name Jer 25:29 834
w come to worship in the LORD'S Jer 26:2
w I purpose to do unto them Jer 26:3 834
my law, *w* I have set before you, Jer 26:4 834
LORD repented him of the evil *w* Jer 26:19 834
by the hand of the messengers *w* Jer 27:3
kingdom *w* will not serve the same Jer 27:8 834
w speak unto you, saying, Ye Jer 27:9 834
that the vessels *w* are left in Jer 27:18
W Nebuchadnezzar king of Babylon Jer 27:20 834
w was of Gibeon, spake unto me in Jer 28:1 834
thy words *w* thou hast prophesied Jer 28:6 834
The prophet *w* prophesieth of Jer 28:9 834
w were carried away captives Jer 29:1
dreams *w* ye cause to be dreamed Jer 29:8 834
w I sent unto them by my servants Jer 29:19 834
w prophesy a lie unto you in my Jer 29:21
of Judah *w* are in Babylon Jer 29:22 834
w I have not commanded them Jer 29:23 834
w maketh himself a prophet to you Jer 29:27
The people *w* were left of the Jer 31:2
even the way *w* thou wentest Jer 31:21
w my covenant they brake, Jer 31:32 834
w giveth the sun for a light by Jer 31:35
w divideth the sea when the waves Jer 31:35
w was the eighteenth year of Jer 32:1 1958
w was in the king of Judah's Jer 32:2 834
w is in the country of Benjamin Jer 32:8 834
both that *w* was sealed according Jer 32:11
law and custom, and that *w* was open Jer 32:11
both *w* is sealed, and this Jer 32:14
and this evidence *w* is open Jer 32:14
W hast set signs and wonders in Jer 32:20 834
w thou didst swear to their Jer 32:22 834
w they have done to provoke me to Jer 32:32 834
w is called by my name, to defile Jer 32:34 834
w are in the valley of the son of Jer 32:35 834
w I commanded them not, neither Jer 32:35 834
mighty things, *w* thou knowest not Jer 33:3
w are thrown down by the mounts, Jer 33:4
w shall hear all the good that I Jer 33:9 834
w ye say shall be desolate Jer 33:10 834
w is desolate without man and Jer 33:12
w I have promised unto the house Jer 33:14 834
The two families *w* the LORD hath Jer 33:24 834

The word *w* came unto Jeremiah.......... Jer 34:1 834
former kings *w* were before thee.......... Jer 34:5 834
the people *w* were at Jerusalem.......... Jer 34:8 834
w had entered into the covenant,.......... Jer 34:10 834
w hath been sold unto thee.......... Jer 34:14 834
the house *w* is called by my name.......... Jer 34:15 834
w have not performed the words of.......... Jer 34:18 834
w they had made before me.......... Jer 34:18 834
w passed between the parts of the.......... Jer 34:19
army, *w* are gone up from you.......... Jer 34:21
The word *w* came unto Jeremiah.......... Jer 35:1 834
w was by the chamber of the.......... Jer 35:4 834
w was above the chamber of.......... Jer 35:4 834
in the land *w* I have given to you.......... Jer 35:15 834
their father, *w* he commanded them.......... Jer 35:16 834
evil *w* I purpose to do unto them.......... Jer 36:3 834
w he had spoken unto him, upon a.......... Jer 36:4 834
w thou hast written from my mouth.......... Jer 36:6 834
princes *w* stood beside the king.......... Jer 36:21
the words *w* Baruch wrote at the.......... Jer 36:27 834
w Jehoiakim the king of Judah.......... Jer 36:28 834
all the words of the book *w*.......... Jer 36:32 834
w he spake by the prophet.......... Jer 37:2 834
w is come forth to help you,.......... Jer 37:7
prophets *w* prophesied unto you.......... Jer 37:19 834
Babylon's army, *w* shall take it.......... Jer 38:3
one of the eunuchs *w* was in the.......... Jer 38:7 1931
of the LORD, *w* I speak unto thee.......... Jer 38:20 834
w had nothing, in the land of.......... Jer 39:10 834
w were carried away captive unto.......... Jer 40:1
the chains *w* were upon thine hand.......... Jer 40:4 834
the forces *w* were in the fields.......... Jer 40:7 834
Chaldeans, *w* will come unto us.......... Jer 40:10 834
that all the Jews *w* are gathered.......... Jer 40:15
was it *w* Asa the king had made.......... Jer 41:9 834
that when all the people *w* were.......... Jer 41:13 834
w is by Bethlehem, to go to enter.......... Jer 41:17 834
the *w* the LORD thy God shall send.......... Jer 42:5 834
of the forces *w* were with him.......... Jer 42:8 834
w ye feared, shall overtake you.......... Jer 42:16 834
nor any thing for the *w* he hath.......... Jer 42:21 834
for *w* the LORD their God had sent.......... Jer 43:1 834
w is at the entry of Pharaoh's.......... Jer 43:9 834
concerning all the Jews *w* dwell.......... Jer 44:1
Egypt, *w* dwell at Migdol, and at.......... Jer 44:1
Because of their wickedness *w*.......... Jer 44:3 834
w they have committed in the land.......... Jer 44:9 834
w are gone into the land of Egypt.......... Jer 44:14
to the *w* they have a desire to.......... Jer 44:14 834
Then all the men *w* knew that.......... Jer 44:15
to all the people *w* had given him.......... Jer 44:20
abominations *w* ye have committed.......... Jer 44:22 834
that *w* I have built will I break.......... Jer 45:4 834
that *w* I have planted I will.......... Jer 45:4 834
The word of the LORD *w* came to.......... Jer 46:1 834
w was by the river Euphrates in.......... Jer 46:2 834
w Nebuchadrezzar king of Babylon.......... Jer 46:2 834
w Nebuchadrezzar king of Babylon.......... Jer 49:28 834
w have neither gates nor bars,.......... Jer 49:31
gates nor bars, *w* dwell alone.......... Jer 49:31
w shall make her land desolate,.......... Jer 50:3 1931
done that *w* he spake against the.......... Jer 51:12 834
w destroyest all the earth.......... Jer 51:25
mouth that *w* he hath swallowed up.......... Jer 51:44
The word *w* Jeremiah the prophet.......... Jer 51:59 834
he did that *w* was evil in the.......... Jer 52:2
w was by the king's garden.......... Jer 52:7 834
w was the nineteenth year of.......... Jer 52:12 1958
w served the king of Babylon,.......... Jer 52:12
that *w* was of gold in gold, and.......... Jer 52:19 834
that *w* was of silver in silver,.......... Jer 52:19 834
w king Solomon had made in the.......... Jer 52:20 834
w had the charge of the men of.......... Jer 52:25 834
person, *w* were found in the city.......... Jer 52:25 834
w is done unto me, wherewith the.......... Lam 1:12 834
fire, *w* devoureth round about.......... Lam 2:3
hath done that *w* he had devised.......... Lam 2:17 834
w is desolate, the foxes walk.......... Lam 5:18
w was the fifth year of king.......... Eze 1:2 1958
w covered on this side, and every.......... Eze 1:23
w covered on that side, their.......... Eze 1:23
his righteousness *w* he hath done.......... Eze 3:20 834
as the glory *w* I saw by the river.......... Eze 3:23 834
thy meat *w* thou shalt eat shall.......... Eze 4:10 834
eaten of that *w* dieth of itself.......... Eze 4:14
do in thee that *w* I have not done.......... Eze 5:9 834
w shall be for their destruction,.......... Eze 5:16 834
w I will send to destroy you.......... Eze 5:16 834
w hath departed from me, and with.......... Eze 6:9 834
w go a whoring after their idols.......... Eze 6:9 834
w they have committed in all.......... Eze 6:9 834
not return to that *w* is sold.......... Eze 7:13
thereof, *w* shall not return.......... Eze 7:13
jealousy, *w* provoketh to jealousy.......... Eze 8:3
house *w* was toward the north.......... Eze 8:14 834
abominations *w* they commit here.......... Eze 8:17 834
w lieth toward the north, and.......... Eze 9:2 834
w had the writer's inkhorn by his.......... Eze 9:3 834
men *w* were before the house.......... Eze 9:6 834
w had the inkhorn by his side,.......... Eze 9:11 834
w I saw by the river of Chebar.......... Eze 10:22 834
LORD's house, *w* looketh eastward.......... Eze 11:1
W say, It is not near.......... Eze 11:3
stood upon the mountain *w* is on.......... Eze 11:23 834
w have eyes to see, and see not.......... Eze 12:2 834
but the word *w* I have spoken.......... Eze 12:28 834
Say unto them *w* daub it with.......... Eze 13:11 834
the prophets of Israel *w* prophesy.......... Eze 13:16
w see visions of peace for her,.......... Eze 13:16
w prophesy out of their own heart.......... Eze 13:17
w separateth himself from me, and.......... Eze 14:7
or than a branch *w* is among the.......... Eze 15:2 834
w I have given to the fire for.......... Eze 15:6 834
w I had put upon thee, saith the.......... Eze 16:14 834

w I had given thee, and madest to.......... Eze 16:17 834
My meat also *w* I gave thee.......... Eze 16:19 834
w are ashamed of thy lewd way.......... Eze 16:27
w taketh strangers instead of her.......... Eze 16:32
w thou didst give unto them.......... Eze 16:36 834
w lothed their husbands and their.......... Eze 16:45 834
abominations *w* thou hast done.......... Eze 16:51 834
w hast judged thy sisters, bear.......... Eze 16:52 834
w despise thee round about.......... Eze 16:57
w hast despised the oath in.......... Eze 16:59 834
w had divers colours, came unto.......... Eze 17:3 834
do that *w* is lawful and right,.......... Eze 18:5
his father's sins *w* he hath done.......... Eze 18:14 834
did that *w* is not good among his.......... Eze 18:18 834
son hath done that *w* is lawful.......... Eze 18:19
do that *w* is lawful and right, he.......... Eze 18:21
and doeth that *w* is lawful.......... Eze 18:27
w hath devoured her fruit, so.......... Eze 19:14
w is the glory of all lands.......... Eze 20:6 1958
w if a man do, he shall even live.......... Eze 20:11 834
w if a man do, he shall even live.......... Eze 20:13 834
into the land *w* I had given them.......... Eze 20:15 834
w is the glory of all lands.......... Eze 20:15 1958
w if a man do, he shall even live.......... Eze 20:21 834
for the *w* I lifted up mine hand.......... Eze 20:28 834
that *w* cometh into your mind.......... Eze 20:32
into the country for the *w* I.......... Eze 20:42 834
w entereth into their privy.......... Eze 21:14
in thine idols *w* thou hast made.......... Eze 22:4 834
w art infamous and much vexed.......... Eze 22:5
dishonest gain *w* thou hast made.......... Eze 22:13 834
at thy blood *w* hath been in the.......... Eze 22:13 834
W were clothed with blue,.......... Eze 23:6
w shall set against thee buckler.......... Eze 23:24
w put bracelets upon their hands,.......... Eze 23:42
eyes, and that *w* your soul pitieth.......... Eze 24:21
be opened to him *w* is escaped.......... Eze 24:27
from his cities *w* are on his.......... Eze 25:9
her daughters *w* are in the field.......... Eze 26:6 834
w wast strong in the sea, she and.......... Eze 26:17 834
w cause their terror to be on all.......... Eze 26:17 834
w art a merchant of the people.......... Eze 27:3
work from Egypt was that *w* thou.......... Eze 27:7
Elishah was that *w* covered thee.......... Eze 27:7
in all thy company *w* is in the.......... Eze 27:27 834
w hath said, My river is mine own.......... Eze 29:3
w bringeth their iniquity to.......... Eze 29:16
the strong, and that *w* was broken.......... Eze 30:22
into the countries *w* thou hast.......... Eze 32:9 834
w caused terror in the land of.......... Eze 32:23 834
w are gone down uncircumcised.......... Eze 32:24 834
w caused their terror in the land.......... Eze 32:24 834
w are gone down to hell with.......... Eze 32:27 834
w with their might are laid by.......... Eze 32:29 834
w are gone down with the slain.......... Eze 32:30 834
do that *w* is lawful and right.......... Eze 33:14
he hath done that *w* is lawful.......... Eze 33:16
do that *w* is lawful and right, he.......... Eze 33:19 834
w they have committed.......... Eze 33:29 834
have ye healed that *w* was sick.......... Eze 34:4
ye bound up that *w* was broken.......... Eze 34:4
again that *w* was driven away.......... Eze 34:4
have ye sought that *w* was lost.......... Eze 34:4
I will seek that *w* was lost.......... Eze 34:16
again that *w* was driven away.......... Eze 34:16
and will bind up that *w* was broken.......... Eze 34:16
will strengthen that *w* was sick.......... Eze 34:16
they eat that *w* ye have trodden.......... Eze 34:19
they drink that *w* ye have fouled.......... Eze 34:19
according to thine envy *w* thou.......... Eze 35:11 834
w thou hast spoken against the.......... Eze 35:12 834
w became a prey and derision to.......... Eze 36:4 834
w have appointed my land into.......... Eze 36:5 834
w the house of Israel had.......... Eze 36:21 834
w ye have profaned among the.......... Eze 36:22 834
w was profaned among the heathen,.......... Eze 36:23
w ye have profaned in the midst.......... Eze 36:23 834
of the valley *w* was full of bones.......... Eze 37:1 1958
w is in the hand of Ephraim, and.......... Eze 37:19 834
Israel, *w* have been always waste.......... Eze 38:8 834
w have gotten cattle and goods,.......... Eze 38:12
w prophesied in those days many.......... Eze 38:17
drunken, of my sacrifice *w* I have.......... Eze 39:19 834
w caused them to be led into.......... Eze 39:28
by *w* was as the frame of a city.......... Eze 40:2
gate *w* looketh toward the east.......... Eze 40:6 834
of the gate, *w* was one reed broad.......... Eze 40:6
of the gate, *w* was one reed broad.......... Eze 40:6
w was at the porch of the gate,.......... Eze 40:40 834
w was at the side of the north.......... Eze 40:44 834
w come near to the LORD to.......... Eze 40:46
side, *w* was the breadth of the.......... Eze 41:1
they entered into the wall *w* was.......... Eze 41:6 834
w was for the side chamber.......... Eze 41:9 834
that *w* was left was the place of.......... Eze 41:9
separate place *w* was behind it.......... Eze 41:15 834
w was before the building toward.......... Eze 42:1 834
cubits *w* were for the inner court.......... Eze 42:3 834
w was for the utter court.......... Eze 42:3 834
chambers *w* were toward the north.......... Eze 42:11 834
w are before the separate place,.......... Eze 42:13 834
those things *w* are for the people.......... Eze 42:14 834
appearance of the vision *w* I saw.......... Eze 43:3 834
w approach unto me, to minister.......... Eze 43:19
w looketh toward the east.......... Eze 44:1
w went astray away from me after.......... Eze 44:10 834
their abominations *w* they have.......... Eze 44:13 834
w shall come near to minister.......... Eze 45:4
w is an homer of ten baths.......... Eze 45:14 4480
w was at the side of the gate,.......... Eze 46:19 834
w looked toward the north.......... Eze 46:19
w being brought forth into the.......... Eze 47:8
w moveth, whithersoever the.......... Eze 47:9 834
concerning the *w* I lifted up mine.......... Eze 47:14 834

w is between the border of.......... Eze 47:16 834
w is by the coast of Hauran.......... Eze 47:16 834
w shall beget children among you.......... Eze 47:22 834
shall be the offering *w* ye shall.......... Eze 48:8 834
w have kept my charge.......... Eze 48:11 834
w went not astray when the.......... Eze 48:11 834
midst of that *w* is the prince's.......... Eze 48:22 834
This is the land *w* ye shall.......... Eze 48:29 834
w he carried into the land of.......... Dan 1:2
meat, and of the wine *w* he drank.......... Dan 1:5
nor with the wine *w* he drank.......... Dan 1:8
the children *w* are of your sort.......... Dan 1:10 834
w did eat the portion of the.......... Dan 1:15
w was gone forth to slay the wise.......... Dan 2:14 1768
unto me the dream *w* I have seen.......... Dan 2:26 1768
The secret *w* the king hath.......... Dan 2:27 1768
w smote the image upon his feet.......... Dan 2:34
w shall bear rule over all the.......... Dan 2:39 1768
w shall never be destroyed.......... Dan 2:44 1768
to the dedication of the image *w*.......... Dan 3:2 1768
golden image *w* thou hast set up.......... Dan 3:12 1768
the golden image *w* I have set up.......... Dan 3:14 1768
worship the image *w* I have made.......... Dan 3:15 1768
golden image *w* thou hast set up.......... Dan 3:18 1768
w speak any thing amiss against.......... Dan 3:29 1768
I saw a dream *w* made me afraid,.......... Dan 4:5
w grew, and was strong, whose.......... Dan 4:20 1768
under *w* the beasts of the field.......... Dan 4:21
w is come upon my lord the king.......... Dan 4:24 1768
silver vessels *w* his father.......... Dan 5:2 1768
of the temple *w* was in Jerusalem.......... Dan 5:2 1768
house of God *w* was at Jerusalem.......... Dan 5:3 1768
w art of the children of the.......... Dan 5:13 1768
w see not, nor hear, nor know.......... Dan 5:23 1768
w should be over the whole.......... Dan 6:1 1768
Medes and Persians, *w* altereth not.......... Dan 6:8 1768
Medes and Persians, *w* altereth not.......... Dan 6:12 1768
w is of the children of the.......... Dan 6:13 1768
That no decree nor statute *w* the.......... Dan 6:15 1768
those men *w* had accused Daniel.......... Dan 6:24 1768
his kingdom that *w* shall not be.......... Dan 6:26 1768
w had upon the back of it four.......... Dan 7:6 1768
the great words *w* the horn spake.......... Dan 7:11 1768
w shall not pass away, and his.......... Dan 7:14 1768
his kingdom that *w* shall not be.......... Dan 7:14 1768
w are four, are four kings.......... Dan 7:17 1768
w shall arise out of the earth.......... Dan 7:17
w was diverse from all the others.......... Dan 7:19 1768
w devoured, brake in pieces, and.......... Dan 7:19
head, and of the other *w* came up.......... Dan 7:20 1768
w shall be diverse from all.......... Dan 7:23 1768
after that *w* appeared unto me at.......... Dan 8:1
w is in the province of Elam.......... Dan 8:2 834
the river a ram *w* had two horns.......... Dan 8:3
w I had seen standing before the.......... Dan 8:6 834
w waxed exceeding great, toward.......... Dan 8:9
unto that certain saint *w* spake.......... Dan 8:13
w called, and said, Gabriel, make.......... Dan 8:16
The ram *w* thou sawest having two.......... Dan 8:20 834
the morning *w* was told is true.......... Dan 8:26 834
w was made king over the realm of.......... Dan 9:1 834
w spake in thy name to our kings,.......... Dan 9:6 834
w he set before us by his.......... Dan 9:10 834
w he spake against us, and against.......... Dan 9:12 834
in all his works *w* he doeth.......... Dan 9:14 834
the city *w* is called by thy name.......... Dan 9:18 834
of the great river, *w* is Hiddekel.......... Dan 10:4 1931
w set me upon my knees and upon.......... Dan 10:10
But I will shew thee that *w* is.......... Dan 10:21
to his dominion *w* he ruled.......... Dan 11:4 834
w shall come with an army, and.......... Dan 11:7
w by his hand shall be consumed.......... Dan 11:16
he shall do that *w* his fathers.......... Dan 11:24 834
the great prince *w* standeth for.......... Dan 12:1
w was upon the waters of the.......... Dan 12:6 834
w was upon the waters of the.......... Dan 12:7 834
w conceived, and bare him a son.......... Hos 1:3
w cannot be measured nor numbered.......... Hos 1:10 834
and gold, *w* they prepared for Baal.......... Hos 2:8
say to them *w* were not my people.......... Hos 2:23
made known that *w* shall surely be.......... Hos 5:9
That *w* the palmerworm hath left.......... Joel 1:4
that *w* the locust hath left hath.......... Joel 1:4
that *w* the cankerworm hath left.......... Joel 1:4
my great army *w* I sent among you.......... Joel 2:25 834
w he saw concerning Israel in the.......... Amos 1:1 834
w shall devour the palaces of.......... Amos 1:4
w shall devour the palaces.......... Amos 1:7
w shall devour the palaces.......... Amos 1:10
w shall devour the palaces of.......... Amos 1:12
after the *w* their fathers have.......... Amos 2:4 834
against the whole family *w* I.......... Amos 3:1 834
w oppress the poor, *w* crush.......... Amos 4:1
w say to their masters, Bring, and.......... Amos 4:1
every cow at that *w* is before her.......... Amos 4:3
Hear ye this word *w* I take up.......... Amos 5:1 834
that *w* went forth by an hundred.......... Amos 5:3
your god, *w* ye made to yourselves.......... Amos 5:26 834
w are named chief of the nations,.......... Amos 6:1
Ye *w* rejoice in a thing of nought.......... Amos 6:13
w say, Have we not taken to us.......... Amos 6:13
w say, The evil shall not.......... Amos 9:10
w are called by my name, saith.......... Amos 9:12 834
of their land *w* I have given them.......... Amos 9:15 834
w is in Sepharad, shall possess.......... Obad 20 834
w hath made the sea and the dry.......... Jonah 1:9 834
for the *w* thou hast not laboured,.......... Jonah 4:10 834
w came up in a night, and perished.......... Jonah 4:10
w he saw concerning Samaria and.......... Mic 1:1 834
from *w* ye shall not remove your.......... Mic 2:3 834
until the time that she *w*.......... Mic 5:3
that *w* thou deliverest will I.......... Mic 6:14 834
shall cover her *w* said unto me.......... Mic 7:10
w dwell solitarily in the wood,.......... Mic 7:14

w thou hast sworn unto our	Mic 7:20	834
w camp in the hedges in the cold	Nah 3:17	
The burden *w* Habakkuk the prophet	Hab 1:1	834
w ye will not believe, though it	Hab 1:5	
w shall march through the breadth	Hab 1:6	
his soul *w* is lifted up is not	Hab 2:4	
that increaseth that *w* is not his	Hab 2:6	
w made them afraid, because of	Hab 2:17	
The word of the LORD *w* came unto	Zeph 1:1	834
w fill their masters' houses with	Zeph 1:9	
w have wrought his judgment	Zeph 2:3	834
upon that *w* the ground bringeth	Hag 1:11	834
that *w* they offer there is	Hag 2:14	834
w I commanded my servants the	Zec 1:6	834
w is the month Sebat, in the	Zec 1:7	1931
of Judah, against *w* thou hast had	Zec 1:12	834
These are the horns *w* have	Zec 1:19	834
These are the horns *w* have	Zec 1:21	834
w lifted up their horn over the	Zec 1:21	
me unto the nations *w* spoiled you	Zec 2:8	
w are upon the top thereof	Zec 4:2	
w run to and fro through the whole	Zec 4:10	
be these two olive branches *w*	Zec 4:12	834
w go forth from standing before	Zec 6:5	
The black horses *w* are therein go	Zec 6:6	834
w are come from Babylon, and come	Zec 6:10	834
to speak unto the priests *w* were	Zec 7:3	834
w the LORD hath cried by the	Zec 7:7	834
the words *w* the LORD of hosts	Zec 7:12	834
w were in the day that the	Zec 8:9	834
w tread down their enemies in the	Zec 10:5	
w I had made with all the people	Zec 11:10	834
w shall not visit those that be	Zec 11:16	
w stretcheth forth the heavens,	Zec 12:1	
Those with *w* I was wounded in the	Zec 13:6	834
w is before Jerusalem on the east	Zec 14:4	834
But it shall be one day *w* shall	Zec 14:7	1931
w came against Jerusalem shall	Zec 14:16	
and ye brought that *w* was torn	Mal 1:13	
w hath in his flock a male, and	Mal 1:14	3426
holiness of the LORD *w* he loved	Mal 2:11	834
w I commanded unto him in Horeb	Mal 4:4	834
for that *w* is conceived in her is	Mt 1:20	
that it might be fulfilled *w* was	Mt 1:22	*3588*
w being interpreted is, God with	Mt 1:23	*3739*
w they saw in the east, went	Mt 2:9	*3739*
that it might be fulfilled *w* was	Mt 2:15	*3588*
according to the time *w* he had	Mt 2:16	*3739*
Then was fulfilled that *w* was	Mt 2:17	*3588*
for they are dead *w* sought the	Mt 2:20	*3588*
w was spoken by the prophets	Mt 2:23	*3588*
therefore every tree *w* bringeth	Mt 3:10	
w is upon the sea coast, in the	Mt 4:13	*3588*
w was spoken by Esaias the	Mt 4:14	*3588*
The people *w* sat in darkness saw	Mt 4:16	*3588*
to them *w* sat in the region and	Mt 4:16	*3588*
those *w* were possessed with	Mt 4:24	
those *w* were lunatick, and those	Mt 4:24	
Blessed are they *w* do hunger	Mt 5:6	*3588*
Blessed are they *w* are persecuted	Mt 5:10	
the prophets *w* were before you	Mt 5:12	*3588*
your Father *w* is in heaven	Mt 5:16	*3588*
pray for them *w* despitefully use	Mt 5:44	*3588*
of your Father *w* is in heaven	Mt 5:45	*3588*
For if ye love them *w* love you	Mt 5:46	*3588*
even as your Father *w* is in	Mt 5:48	*3588*
of your Father *w* is in heaven	Mt 6:1	*3588*
thy Father *w* seeth in secret	Mt 6:4	*3588*
pray to thy Father *w* is in secret	Mt 6:6	*3588*
thy Father *w* seeth in secret	Mt 6:6	*3588*
Our Father *w* art in heaven,	Mt 6:9	*3588*
unto thy Father *w* is in secret	Mt 6:18	*3588*
w seeth in secret, shall reward	Mt 6:18	*3588*
W of you by taking thought can	Mt 6:27	*5101*
w to day is, and to morrow is cast	Mt 6:30	
Give not that *w* is holy unto the	Mt 7:6	*3588*
w is in heaven give good things	Mt 7:11	*3588*
and many there be *w* go in thereat	Mt 7:13	*3588*
w leadeth unto life, and few there	Mt 7:14	*3588*
w come to you in sheep's clothing	Mt 7:15	*3748*
will of my Father *w* is in heaven	Mt 7:21	*3588*
w built his house upon a rock	Mt 7:24	*3748*
w built his house upon the sand	Mt 7:26	*3748*
w was spoken by Esaias the	Mt 8:17	*3588*
w had given such power unto men	Mt 9:8	*3588*
for that *w* is put in to fill it	Mt 9:16	
w was diseased with an issue of	Mt 9:20	
of your Father *w* speaketh in you	Mt 10:20	*3588*
And fear not them *w* kill the body	Mt 10:28	*3588*
but rather fear him *w* is able to	Mt 10:28	*3588*
before my Father *w* is in heaven	Mt 10:32	*3588*
before my Father *w* is in heaven	Mt 10:33	*3588*
again those things *w* ye do hear	Mt 11:4	*3739*
w shall prepare thy way before	Mt 11:10	*3739*
this is Elias, *w* was for to come	Mt 11:14	*3588*
w were done in you, had been done	Mt 11:21	*3588*
w art exalted unto heaven, shalt	Mt 11:23	*3588*
w have been done in thee, had	Mt 11:23	*3588*
thy disciples do that *w* is not	Mt 12:2	*3739*
w was not lawful for him to eat,	Mt 12:4	*3739*
neither for them *w* were with him	Mt 12:4	
there was a man *w* had his hand	Mt 12:10	
w was spoken by Esaias the	Mt 12:17	*3588*
will of my Father *w* is in heaven	Mt 12:50	*3588*
w saith, By hearing ye shall hear	Mt 13:14	*3588*
to see those things *w* ye see	Mt 13:17	*3739*
and to hear those things *w* ye hear	Mt 13:17	*3739*
catcheth away that *w* was sown in	Mt 13:19	*3588*
This is he *w* received seed by the	Mt 13:19	*3588*
w also beareth fruit, and bringeth	Mt 13:23	*3739*
w sowed good seed in his field	Mt 13:24	
w a man took, and sowed in his	Mt 13:31	*3739*
W indeed is the least of all	Mt 13:32	*3739*
w a woman took, and hid in three	Mt 13:33	*3739*
w was spoken by the prophet	Mt 13:35	*3588*
I will utter things *w* have been	Mt 13:35	
offend, and them *w* do iniquity	Mt 13:41	
the *w* when a man hath found, he	Mt 13:44	*3739*
W, when it was full, they drew to	Mt 13:48	*3739*
Therefore every scribe *w* is	Mt 13:52	
w bringeth forth out of his	Mt 13:52	*3748*
them *w* sat with him at meat, he	Mt 14:9	
w were of Jerusalem, saying,	Mt 15:1	*3588*
Not that *w* goeth into the mouth	Mt 15:11	
but that *w* cometh out of the	Mt 15:11	
w my heavenly Father hath not	Mt 15:13	*3739*
But those things *w* proceed out of	Mt 15:18	*3588*
are the things *w* defile a man	Mt 15:20	*3588*
w fall from their masters' table	Mt 15:27	*3588*
W when Jesus perceived, he said	Mt 16:8	
but my Father *w* is in heaven	Mt 16:17	*3588*
w shall not taste of death, till	Mt 16:28	*3748*
w said, This is my beloved Son,	Mt 17:5	
these little ones *w* believe in me	Mt 18:6	*3588*
face of my Father *w* is in heaven	Mt 18:10	*3588*
is come to save that *w* was lost	Mt 18:11	*3588*
seeketh that *w* is gone astray	Mt 18:12	*3588*
ninety and nine *w* went not astray	Mt 18:13	*3588*
of your Father *w* is in heaven	Mt 18:14	*3588*
them of my Father *w* is in heaven	Mt 18:19	*3588*
w would take account of his	Mt 18:23	*3739*
w owed him ten thousand talents	Mt 18:24	
w owed him an hundred pence	Mt 18:28	*3739*
that he *w* made them at the	Mt 19:4	*3588*
whoso marrieth her *w* is put away	Mt 19:9	*3588*
w were so born from their	Mt 19:12	*3748*
w were made eunuchs of men	Mt 19:12	*3748*
w have made themselves eunuchs	Mt 19:12	*3748*
He saith unto him, *W*	Mt 19:18	*4169*
That ye *w* have followed me, in	Mt 19:28	*3588*
w went out early in the morning	Mt 20:1	*3748*
w have borne the burden and heat	Mt 20:12	*3588*
w was spoken by the prophet	Mt 21:4	*3588*
do this *w* is done to the fig tree	Mt 21:21	
w if ye tell me, I in like wise	Mt 21:24	*3739*
w planted a vineyard, and hedged	Mt 21:33	*3748*
w shall render him the fruits in	Mt 21:41	*3748*
The stone *w* the builders rejected	Mt 21:42	*3739*
w made a marriage for his son,	Mt 22:2	*3748*
Tell them *w* are bidden, Behold, I	Mt 22:4	
but they *w* were bidden were not	Mt 22:8	
he saw there a man *w* had not on a	Mt 22:11	
Caesar the things *w* are Caesar's	Mt 22:21	
Sadducees, *w* say that there is no	Mt 22:23	*3588*
have ye not read that *w* was	Mt 22:31	*3588*
w was a lawyer, asked him a	Mt 22:35	
w is the great commandment in the	Mt 22:36	*4169*
is your Father, *w* is in heaven	Mt 23:9	*3588*
w say, Whosoever shall swear by	Mt 23:16	*3588*
w strain at a gnat, and swallow a	Mt 23:24	*3588*
first that *w* is within the cup	Mt 23:26	*3588*
w indeed appear beautiful outward	Mt 23:27	*3748*
of them *w* killed the prophets	Mt 23:31	*3588*
stonest them *w* are sent unto thee	Mt 23:37	*3588*
Then let them *w* be in Judaea flee	Mt 24:16	*3588*
Let him *w* is on the housetop not	Mt 24:17	
Neither let him *w* is in the field	Mt 24:18	
w took their lamps, and went forth	Mt 25:1	*3748*
Then he *w* had received the one	Mt 25:24	
it unto him *w* hath ten talents	Mt 25:28	
be taken away even that *w* he hath	Mt 25:29	
w betrayed him, answered and said,	Mt 26:25	*3588*
w is shed for many for the	Mt 26:28	*3588*
one of them *w* were with Jesus	Mt 26:51	
what is it *w* these witness	Mt 26:62	
w said unto him, Before the cock	Mt 26:75	*3588*
w had betrayed him, when he saw	Mt 27:3	*3588*
Then was fulfilled that *w* was	Mt 27:9	*3588*
or Jesus *w* is called Christ	Mt 27:17	*3588*
with Jesus *w* is called Christ	Mt 27:22	*3588*
w was spoken by the prophet	Mt 27:35	*3588*
w were crucified with him, cast	Mt 27:44	*3588*
of the saints *w* slept arose	Mt 27:52	*3588*
w followed Jesus from Galilee,	Mt 27:55	*3748*
Among *w* was Mary Magdalene, and	Mt 27:56	*3739*
w he had hewn out in the rock	Mt 27:60	*3588*
ye seek Jesus, *w* was crucified	Mt 28:5	*3588*
w shall prepare thy way before	Mk 1:2	*3739*
those things *w* Moses commanded	Mk 1:44	*3739*
of the palsy, *w* was borne of four	Mk 2:3	
sabbath day that *w* is not lawful	Mk 2:24	*3739*
w is not lawful to eat but for	Mk 2:26	*3739*
gave also to them *w* were with him	Mk 2:26	
a man there *w* had a withered hand	Mk 3:1	
the man *w* had the withered hand	Mk 3:3	
w is, The sons of thunder	Mk 3:17	*3739*
Iscariot, *w* also betrayed him	Mk 3:19	*2076*
the scribes *w* came down from	Mk 3:22	*3588*
about on them *w* sat about him	Mk 3:34	*3588*
these are they likewise *w* are	Mk 4:16	
these are they *w* are sown among	Mk 4:18	
these are they *w* are sown on good	Mk 4:20	
w shall not be manifested	Mk 4:22	*3739*
be taken even that *w* he hath	Mk 4:25	*3588*
like a grain of mustard seed, *w*	Mk 4:31	*3739*
w had an issue of blood twelve	Mk 5:25	
synagogue's house certain *w* said	Mk 5:35	
w is, being interpreted, Damsel,	Mk 5:41	*3739*
is this *w* is given unto him	Mk 6:2	
and for their sakes *w* sat with him	Mk 6:26	*3588*
scribes, *w* came from Jerusalem	Mk 7:1	
w they have received to hold, as	Mk 7:4	*3739*
tradition, *w* ye have delivered	Mk 7:13	*3739*
but the things *w* come out of him,	Mk 7:15	
That *w* cometh out of the man,	Mk 7:20	
w shall not taste of death, till	Mk 9:1	*3748*
thee my son, *w* hath a dumb spirit	Mk 9:17	
for there is no man *w* shall do a	Mk 9:39	*3739*
Ye know that they *w* are accounted	Mk 10:42	
the fig tree *w* thou cursedst is	Mk 11:21	*3739*
w he saith shall come to pass	Mk 11:23	*3739*
that your Father also *w* is in	Mk 11:25	*3588*
neither will your Father *w* is in	Mk 11:26	*3588*
The stone *w* the builders rejected	Mk 12:10	*3739*
w say there is no resurrection	Mk 12:18	*3748*
are as the angels *w* are in heaven	Mk 12:25	*3588*
W is the first commandment of all	Mk 12:28	*4169*
w love to go in long clothing, and	Mk 12:38	*3588*
W devour widows' houses, and for a	Mk 12:40	*3739*
in two mites, *w* make a farthing	Mk 12:42	*2076*
than all they *w* have cast into	Mk 12:43	
w God created unto this time	Mk 13:19	*3739*
not the angels *w* are in heaven	Mk 13:32	*3588*
One of you *w* eateth with me shall	Mk 14:18	*3588*
new testament, *w* is shed for many	Mk 14:24	*3588*
to a place *w* was named Gethsemane	Mk 14:32	*3588*
what is it *w* these witness	Mk 14:60	
w lay bound with them that had	Mk 15:7	
w is, being interpreted, The	Mk 15:22	*3739*
w saith, And he was numbered with	Mk 15:28	*3588*
w is, being interpreted, My God,	Mk 15:34	*3739*
w stood over against him, saw	Mk 15:39	*3588*
many other women *w* came up with	Mk 15:41	*3588*
w also waited for the kingdom of	Mk 15:43	
w was hewn out of a rock, and	Mk 15:46	*3739*
of Nazareth, *w* was crucified	Mk 16:6	*3588*
because they believed not them *w*	Mk 16:14	
a declaration of those things *w*	Lk 1:1	
w from the beginning were	Lk 1:2	*3588*
w shall be fulfilled in their	Lk 1:20	*3748*
w shall be born of thee shall be	Lk 1:35	
w were told her from the Lord	Lk 1:45	
w have been since the world began	Lk 1:70	*3588*
The oath *w* he sware to our father	Lk 1:73	*3739*
of David, *w* is called Bethlehem	Lk 2:4	*3748*
joy, *w* shall be to all people	Lk 2:10	*3748*
a Saviour, *w* is Christ the Lord	Lk 2:11	*3739*
see this thing *w* is come to pass,	Lk 2:15	*3588*
w the Lord hath made known unto	Lk 2:15	*3588*
made known abroad the saying *w*	Lk 2:17	*3588*
it wondered at those things *w*	Lk 2:18	*3588*
w was so named of the angel	Lk 2:21	*3588*
a sacrifice according to that *w*	Lk 2:24	
W thou hast prepared before the	Lk 2:31	*3739*
those things *w* were spoken of him	Lk 2:33	
for a sign *w* shall be spoken	Lk 2:34	
w departed not from the temple,	Lk 2:37	*3739*
the saying *w* he spake unto them	Lk 2:50	*3739*
every tree therefore *w* bringeth	Lk 3:9	
more than that *w* is appointed you	Lk 3:13	
all the evils *w* Herod had done	Lk 3:19	*3739*
w said, Thou art my beloved Son	Lk 3:22	
of Joseph, *w* was the son of Heli,	Lk 3:23	
W was the son of Matthat	Lk 3:24	
w was the son of Levi, *w* was	Lk 3:24	
w was the son of Melchi	Lk 3:24	
w was the son of Janna	Lk 3:24	
w was the son of Joseph	Lk 3:24	
W was the son of Mattathias	Lk 3:25	
w was the son of Amos	Lk 3:25	
w was the son of Naum	Lk 3:25	
w was the son of Esli	Lk 3:25	
w was the son of Nagge	Lk 3:25	
W was the son of Maath	Lk 3:26	
w was the son of Mattathias	Lk 3:26	
w was the son of Semei	Lk 3:26	
w was the son of Joseph	Lk 3:26	
w was the son of Juda	Lk 3:26	
W was the son of Joanna	Lk 3:27	
w was the son of Rhesa	Lk 3:27	
w was the son of Zorobabel	Lk 3:27	
w was the son of Salathiel	Lk 3:27	
w was the son of Neri	Lk 3:27	
W was the son of Melchi	Lk 3:28	
w was the son of Addi	Lk 3:28	
w was the son of Cosam	Lk 3:28	
w was the son of Elmodam	Lk 3:28	
w was the son of Er	Lk 3:28	
W was the son of Jose	Lk 3:29	
w was the son of Eliezer	Lk 3:29	
w was the son of Jorim	Lk 3:29	
w was the son of Matthat	Lk 3:29	
w was the son of Levi	Lk 3:29	
W was the son of Simeon	Lk 3:30	
w was the son of Juda	Lk 3:30	
w was the son of Joseph	Lk 3:30	
w was the son of Jonan	Lk 3:30	
w was the son of Eliakim	Lk 3:30	
W was the son of Melea	Lk 3:31	
w was the son of Menan	Lk 3:31	
w was the son of Mattatha	Lk 3:31	
w was the son of Nathan	Lk 3:31	
w was the son of David	Lk 3:31	
W was the son of Jesse	Lk 3:32	
w was the son of Obed	Lk 3:32	
w was the son of Booz	Lk 3:32	
w was the son of Salmon	Lk 3:32	
w was the son of Naasson	Lk 3:32	
W was the son of Aminadab	Lk 3:33	
w was the son of Aram	Lk 3:33	
w was the son of Esrom	Lk 3:33	
w was the son of Phares	Lk 3:33	
w was the son of Juda	Lk 3:33	
W was the son of Jacob	Lk 3:34	
w was the son of Isaac	Lk 3:34	
w was the son of Abraham	Lk 3:34	
w was the son of Thara	Lk 3:34	
w was the son of Nachor	Lk 3:34	
W was the son of Saruch	Lk 3:35	
w was the son of Ragau	Lk 3:35	
w was the son of Phalec	Lk 3:35	
w was the son of Heber	Lk 3:35	

Context	Reference	Strong's
w was the son of Sala	Lk 3:35	
W was the son of Cainan	Lk 3:36	
w was the son of Arphaxad	Lk 3:36	
w was the son of Sem	Lk 3:36	
w was the son of Noe	Lk 3:36	
w was the son of Lamech	Lk 3:36	
W was the son of Mathusala	Lk 3:37	
w was the son of Enoch	Lk 3:37	
w was the son of Jared	Lk 3:37	
w was the son of Maleleel	Lk 3:37	
w was the son of Cainan	Lk 3:37	
W was the son of Enos	Lk 3:38	
w was the son of Seth	Lk 3:38	
w was the son of Adam	Lk 3:38	
w was the son of God	Lk 3:38	
w proceeded out of his mouth	Lk 4:22	*3588*
w had a spirit of an unclean	Lk 4:33	
w was Simon's, and prayed him that	Lk 5:3	*3739*
w were in the other ship, that	Lk 5:7	*3588*
of the fishes *w* they had taken	Lk 5:9	*3739*
w were partners with Simon	Lk 5:10	*3739*
w were come out of every town of	Lk 5:17	*3739*
a man *w* was taken with a palsy	Lk 5:18	*3739*
saying, Who is this *w* speaketh	Lk 5:21	*3739*
Why do ye that *w* is not lawful to	Lk 6:2	*3739*
hungred, and they *w* were with him	Lk 6:3	*3739*
w it is not lawful to eat but for	Lk 6:4	
said to the man *w* had the	Lk 6:8	*3739*
Iscariot, *w* also was the traitor	Lk 6:16	*3739*
w came to hear him, and to be	Lk 6:17	*3739*
But I say unto you *w* hear	Lk 6:27	
do good to them *w* hate you	Lk 6:27	*3588*
pray for them *w* despitefully use	Lk 6:28	
For if ye love them *w* love you	Lk 6:32	
do good to them *w* do good to you	Lk 6:33	
bringeth forth that *w* is good	Lk 6:45	
bringeth forth that *w* is evil	Lk 6:45	
and do not the things *w* I say	Lk 6:46	*3739*
He is like a man *w* built an house	Lk 6:48	*3739*
against *w* the stream did beat	Lk 6:49	*3739*
they *w* are gorgeously apparelled,	Lk 7:25	
w shall prepare thy way before	Lk 7:27	*3739*
w was a sinner, when she knew	Lk 7:37	*3748*
Pharisee *w* had bidden him saw it	Lk 7:39	*3588*
creditor *w* had two debtors	Lk 7:41	
w of them will love him most	Lk 7:42	*5101*
sins, *w* are many, are forgiven	Lk 7:47	*3588*
w had been healed of evil spirits	Lk 8:2	*3739*
w ministered unto him of their	Lk 8:3	*3748*
They on the rock are they, *w*	Lk 8:13	*3739*
w for a while believe, and in time	Lk 8:13	*3739*
that *w* fell among thorns	Lk 8:14	
w, when they have heard	Lk 8:14	
w in an honest and good heart,	Lk 8:15	*3748*
that they *w* enter in may see the	Lk 8:16	
even that *w* he seemeth to have	Lk 8:18	*3739*
it was told him by certain *w* said	Lk 8:20	
are these *w* hear the word of God	Lk 8:21	*3588*
w is over against Galilee	Lk 8:26	*3748*
w had devils long time, and ware	Lk 8:27	*3739*
They also *w* saw it told them by	Lk 8:36	
w had spent all her living upon	Lk 8:43	*3748*
w shall not taste of death, till	Lk 9:27	*3739*
two men, *w* were Moses and Elias	Lk 9:30	*3748*
spake of his decease *w* he should	Lk 9:31	*3739*
of those things *w* they had seen	Lk 9:36	*3739*
one at all things *w* Jesus did	Lk 9:43	*3739*
w of them should be greatest	Lk 9:46	*5101*
w are at home at my house	Lk 9:61	
w cleaveth on us, we do wipe off	Lk 10:11	*3588*
w have been done in you, they had	Lk 10:13	*3739*
w art exalted to heaven, shalt be	Lk 10:15	*3588*
Blessed are the eyes *w* see the	Lk 10:23	*3588*
to see those things *w* ye see	Lk 10:24	*3739*
and to hear those things *w* ye hear	Lk 10:24	*3739*
w stripped him of his raiment, and	Lk 10:30	*3739*
W now of these three, thinkest	Lk 10:36	*5101*
w also sat at Jesus' feet, and	Lk 10:39	
w shall not be taken away from	Lk 10:42	*3748*
Our Father *w* art in heaven,	Lk 11:2	*3588*
W of you shall have a friend, and	Lk 11:5	*5101*
the paps *w* thou hast sucked	Lk 11:27	*3739*
that they *w* come in may see the	Lk 11:33	*3588*
w is in thee be not darkness	Lk 11:35	*3588*
did not he that made that *w* is	Lk 11:40	*3588*
make that *w* is within also	Lk 11:40	
for ye are as graves *w* appear not	Lk 11:44	*3588*
w was shed from the foundation of	Lk 11:50	*3588*
w perished between the altar and	Lk 11:51	*3588*
of the Pharisees, *w* is hypocrisy	Lk 12:1	*3748*
that *w* ye have spoken in the ear	Lk 12:3	*3739*
w after he hath killed hath power	Lk 12:5	
of the things *w* he possesseth	Lk 12:15	
things be, *w* thou hast provided	Lk 12:20	*3739*
w neither have storehouse nor	Lk 12:24	*3739*
w of you with taking thought can	Lk 12:25	*5101*
able to do that thing *w* is least	Lk 12:26	
w is to day in the field, and to	Lk 12:28	
yourselves bags *w* wax not old	Lk 12:33	
w knew his lord's will, and	Lk 12:47	*3588*
there was a woman *w* had a spirit	Lk 13:11	
six days in *w* men ought to work	Lk 13:14	*3739*
w a man took, and cast into his	Lk 13:19	*3739*
w a woman took and hid in three	Lk 13:21	*3739*
there are last *w* shall be first	Lk 13:30	*3739*
there are first *w* shall be last	Lk 13:30	*3739*
w killest the prophets, and	Lk 13:34	*3588*
man before him *w* had the dropsy	Lk 14:2	
W of you shall have an ass or an	Lk 14:5	*5101*
a parable to those *w* were bidden	Lk 14:7	
That none of those men *w* were	Lk 14:24	*3588*
For *w* of you, intending to build	Lk 14:28	*5101*
and go after that *w* is lost	Lk 15:4	
I have found my sheep *w* was lost	Lk 15:6	*3588*
persons, *w* need no repentance	Lk 15:7	*3748*
have found the piece *w* I had lost	Lk 15:9	*3739*
w hath devoured thy living with	Lk 15:30	*3588*
certain rich man, *w* had a steward	Lk 16:1	*3739*
He that is faithful in that *w* is	Lk 16:10	
in that *w* is another man's	Lk 16:12	
shall give you that *w* is your own	Lk 16:12	
Ye are they *w* justify yourselves	Lk 16:15	*3588*
for that *w* is highly esteemed	Lk 16:15	*3588*
w was clothed in purple and fine	Lk 16:19	*2532*
w was laid at his gate, full of	Lk 16:20	*3739*
to be fed with the crumbs *w* fell	Lk 16:21	*3588*
so that they *w* would pass from	Lk 16:26	
But *w* of you, having a servant	Lk 17:7	*5101*
those things *w* are commanded you	Lk 17:10	
we have done that *w* was our duty	Lk 17:10	*3739*
were lepers, *w* stood afar off	Lk 17:12	*3739*
he *w* shall be upon the housetop,	Lk 17:31	*3739*
w feared not God, neither	Lk 18:2	
w cry day and night unto him,	Lk 18:7	*3588*
w trusted in themselves that they	Lk 18:9	*3588*
The things *w* are impossible with	Lk 18:27	
they the things *w* were spoken	Lk 18:34	
they *w* went before rebuked him,	Lk 18:39	
w was the chief among the	Lk 19:2	
seek and to save that *w* was lost	Lk 19:10	
w I have kept laid up in a napkin	Lk 19:20	*3739*
every one *w* hath shall be given	Lk 19:26	*3588*
w would not that I should reign	Lk 19:27	*3588*
in the *w* at your entering ye	Lk 19:30	*3739*
the things *w* belong unto thy	Lk 19:42	
The stone *w* the builders rejected	Lk 20:17	*3739*
w should feign themselves just	Lk 20:20	
Caesar the things *w* be Caesar's	Lk 20:25	
and unto God the things *w* be God's	Lk 20:25	
w deny that there is any	Lk 20:27	*3588*
But they *w* shall be accounted	Lk 20:35	
w desire to walk in long robes,	Lk 20:46	*3588*
W devour widows' houses, and for a	Lk 20:47	*3739*
As for these things *w* ye behold	Lk 21:6	*3739*
in the *w* there shall not be left	Lk 21:6	*3739*
w all your adversaries shall not	Lk 21:15	*3739*
Then let them *w* are in Judaea	Lk 21:21	
let them *w* are in the midst of it	Lk 21:21	
that all things *w* are written may	Lk 21:22	*3588*
things *w* are coming on the earth	Lk 21:26	
nigh, *w* is called the Passover	Lk 22:1	
This is my body *w* is given for	Lk 22:19	*3588*
in my blood, *w* is shed for you	Lk 22:20	*3588*
w of them it was that should do	Lk 22:23	*5101*
w of them should be accounted the	Lk 22:24	*5101*
Ye are they *w* have continued with	Lk 22:28	
When they *w* were about him saw	Lk 22:49	
w were come to him, Be ye come	Lk 22:52	
w also bewailed and lamented him	Lk 23:27	*3739*
in the *w* they shall say, Blessed	Lk 23:29	*3739*
the paps *w* never gave suck	Lk 23:29	*3739*
w is called Calvary, there they	Lk 23:33	*3588*
one of the malefactors *w* were	Lk 23:39	
beholding the things *w* were done	Lk 23:48	
w came with him from Galilee,	Lk 23:55	*3748*
the spices *w* they had prepared	Lk 24:1	*3739*
w told these things unto the	Lk 24:10	*3739*
at that *w* was come to pass	Lk 24:12	
w was from Jerusalem about	Lk 24:13	
all these things *w* had happened	Lk 24:14	
hast not known the things *w* are	Lk 24:18	
w was a prophet mighty in deed and	Lk 24:19	*3739*
he *w* should have redeemed Israel	Lk 24:21	
w were early at the sepulchre	Lk 24:22	
angels, *w* said that he was alive	Lk 24:23	*3739*
certain of them *w* were with us	Lk 24:24	
are the words *w* I spake unto you	Lk 24:44	*3739*
w were written in the law of	Lk 24:44	*3588*
w lighteth every man that cometh	Jn 1:9	*3739*
W were born, not of blood, nor of	Jn 1:13	*3739*
w is in the bosom of the Father,	Jn 1:18	*3588*
they *w* were sent were of the	Jn 1:24	*3588*
w taketh away the sin of the	Jn 1:29	*3588*
After me cometh a man *w* is	Jn 1:30	*3739*
the same is he *w* baptizeth with	Jn 1:33	
(*w* is to say, being interpreted,	Jn 1:38	*3739*
One of the two *w* heard John speak	Jn 1:40	*3588*
w is, being interpreted, the	Jn 1:41	*3739*
w is by interpretation, A stone	Jn 1:42	*3739*
(but the servants *w* drew the	Jn 2:9	*3588*
well drunk, then that *w* is worse	Jn 2:10	
the word *w* Jesus had said	Jn 2:22	*3739*
they saw the miracles *w* he did	Jn 2:23	*3739*
That *w* is born of the flesh is	Jn 3:6	
that *w* is born of the Spirit is	Jn 3:6	
the Son of man *w* is in heaven	Jn 3:13	*3588*
w standeth and heareth him,	Jn 3:29	*3588*
w is called Sychar, near to the	Jn 4:5	
of me, *w* am a woman of Samaria	Jn 4:9	
w gave us the well, and drank	Jn 4:12	*3739*
cometh, *w* is called Christ	Jn 4:25	*3588*
w told me all things that ever I	Jn 4:29	*3739*
w testified, He told me all that	Jn 4:39	
in the *w* Jesus said unto him, Thy	Jn 4:53	*3739*
w is called in the Hebrew tongue	Jn 5:2	*3588*
w had an infirmity thirty and	Jn 5:5	
What man is that *w* said unto thee	Jn 5:12	*3588*
was Jesus, *w* had made him whole	Jn 5:15	*3588*
not the Father *w* hath sent him	Jn 5:23	*3588*
in the *w* all that are in the	Jn 5:28	*3739*
will of the Father *w* hath sent me	Jn 5:30	*3739*
I know that the witness *w* he	Jn 5:32	*3739*
for the works *w* the Father hath	Jn 5:36	*3739*
w hath sent me, hath borne	Jn 5:37	
and they are they *w* testify of me	Jn 5:39	
w receive honour one of another,	Jn 5:44	
Galilee, *w* is the sea of Tiberias	Jn 6:1	
w he did on them that were	Jn 6:2	*3739*
w hath five barley loaves, and two	Jn 6:9	*3739*
w remained over and above unto	Jn 6:13	*3739*
when the people *w* stood on the	Jn 6:22	*3588*
not for the meat *w* perisheth	Jn 6:27	*3588*
but for that meat *w* endureth unto	Jn 6:27	*3588*
w the Son of man shall give unto	Jn 6:27	*3739*
is he *w* cometh down from heaven	Jn 6:33	*3588*
the Father's will *w* hath sent me	Jn 6:39	*3588*
that of all *w* he hath given me I	Jn 6:39	
that every one *w* seeth the Son	Jn 6:40	*3588*
I am the bread *w* came down from	Jn 6:41	*3588*
except the Father *w* hath sent me	Jn 6:44	*3588*
save he *w* is of God, he hath seen	Jn 6:46	*3588*
This is the bread *w* cometh down	Jn 6:50	*3588*
bread *w* came down from heaven	Jn 6:51	*3588*
w I will give for the life of the	Jn 6:51	*3739*
This is that bread *w* came down	Jn 6:58	*3588*
than these *w* this man hath done	Jn 7:31	*3739*
w they that believe on him should	Jn 7:39	*3739*
they *w* heard it, being convicted	Jn 8:9	
things *w* I have heard of him	Jn 8:26	*3739*
to those Jews *w* believed on him	Jn 8:31	*3588*
I speak that *w* I have seen with	Jn 8:38	*3739*
ye do that *w* ye have seen with	Jn 8:38	*3739*
the truth, *w* I have heard of God	Jn 8:40	*3739*
W of you convinceth me of sin	Jn 8:46	*5101*
our father Abraham, *w* is dead	Jn 8:53	*3748*
he saw a man *w* was blind from his	Jn 9:1	
(*w* is by interpretation, Sent	Jn 9:7	*3739*
they *w* before had seen him that	Jn 9:8	
that they *w* see not might see	Jn 9:39	
that they *w* see might be made	Jn 9:39	
some of the Pharisees *w* were with	Jn 9:40	*3588*
they were he *w* spake unto them	Jn 10:6	*3739*
I have, *w* are not of this fold	Jn 10:16	*3739*
w gave them me, is greater than	Jn 10:29	*3739*
for *w* of those works do ye stone	Jn 10:32	*4169*
(It was that Mary *w* anointed the	Jn 11:2	*3588*
w is called Didymus, unto his	Jn 11:16	*3588*
w should come into the world	Jn 11:27	*3588*
The Jews then *w* were with her in	Jn 11:31	*3588*
Jews also weeping *w* came with her	Jn 11:33	
w opened the eyes of the blind,	Jn 11:37	*3588*
the people *w* stand by I said it	Jn 11:42	*3588*
many of the Jews *w* came to Mary	Jn 11:45	*3588*
had seen the things *w* Jesus did	Jn 11:45	*3739*
where Lazarus was *w* had been dead	Jn 12:1	*3588*
Simon's son, *w* should betray him,	Jn 12:4	*3588*
w was of Bethsaida of Galilee, and	Jn 12:21	
w he spake, Lord, who hath	Jn 12:38	*3739*
but the Father *w* sent me, he gave	Jn 12:49	*3588*
loved his own *w* were in the world	Jn 13:1	*3588*
the word *w* ye hear is not mine,	Jn 14:24	*3739*
but the Father's *w* sent me	Jn 14:24	*3588*
w is the Holy Ghost, whom the	Jn 14:26	
the word *w* I have spoken unto you	Jn 15:3	*3739*
the works *w* none other man did	Jn 15:24	*3739*
w proceedeth from the Father, he	Jn 15:26	*3739*
the work *w* thou gavest me to do	Jn 17:4	*3739*
w I had with thee before the	Jn 17:5	*3739*
thy name unto the men *w* thou	Jn 17:6	*3739*
them the words *w* thou gavest me	Jn 17:8	*3739*
but for them *w* thou hast given me	Jn 17:9	*3739*
but for them also *w* shall believe	Jn 17:20	
the glory *w* thou gavest me I have	Jn 17:22	*3739*
my glory, *w* thou hast given me	Jn 17:24	*3739*
into the *w* he entered, and his	Jn 18:1	*3739*
w betrayed him, knew the place	Jn 18:2	*3588*
w betrayed him, stood with them	Jn 18:5	*3588*
w he spake, Of them *w* thou	Jn 18:9	*3739*
the cup *w* my Father hath given me	Jn 18:11	*3739*
w was the high priest that same	Jn 18:13	*3588*
w gave counsel to the Jews, that	Jn 18:14	*3588*
w was known unto the high priest,	Jn 18:16	*3739*
ask them *w* heard me, what I have	Jn 18:21	
one of the officers *w* stood by	Jn 18:22	
w he spake, signifying what death	Jn 18:32	*3739*
w is called in the Hebrew	Jn 19:17	*3739*
w saith, They parted my raiment	Jn 19:24	*3588*
of the other *w* was crucified with	Jn 19:32	*3588*
w at the first came to Jesus by	Jn 19:39	*3588*
w came first to the sepulchre, and	Jn 20:8	*3588*
w is to say, Master	Jn 20:16	*3739*
w are not written in this book	Jn 20:30	*3739*
Bring of the fish *w* ye have now	Jn 21:10	*3739*
w also leaned on his breast at	Jn 21:20	*3739*
w is he that betrayeth thee	Jn 21:20	*5101*
This is the disciple *w* testifieth	Jn 21:24	*3588*
many other things *w* Jesus did	Jn 21:25	*3745*
the *w*, if they should	Jn 21:25	*3748*
the day in *w* he was taken up	Acts 1:2	*3739*
for the promise of the Father, *w*	Acts 1:4	*3739*
w the Father hath put in his own	Acts 1:7	*3739*
W also said, Ye men of Galilee,	Acts 1:11	*3739*
w is taken up from you into	Acts 1:11	*3588*
w is from Jerusalem a sabbath	Acts 1:12	*3739*
w the Holy Ghost by the mouth of	Acts 1:16	*3739*
w was guide to them that took	Acts 1:16	*3588*
Wherefore of these men *w* have	Acts 1:21	
w knowest the hearts of all men,	Acts 1:24	
from *w* Judas by transgression	Acts 1:25	*3739*
not all these *w* speak Galilaeans	Acts 2:7	*3588*
But this is that *w* was spoken by	Acts 2:16	
w God did by him in the midst of	Acts 2:22	*3739*
forth this, *w* ye now see and hear	Acts 2:33	*3739*
the temple *w* is called Beautiful	Acts 3:2	*3588*
they knew that it was he *w* sat	Acts 3:10	*3588*
amazement at that *w* had happened	Acts 3:10	
as the lame man *w* was healed held	Acts 3:11	
the faith *w* is by him hath given	Acts 3:16	
w God before had shewed by the	Acts 3:18	*3739*
w before was preached unto you	Acts 3:20	
w God hath spoken by the mouth of	Acts 3:21	*3739*
w will not hear that prophet,	Acts 3:23	

of the covenant *w* God made with........ Acts 3:25 3739
Howbeit many of them *w* heard the..... Acts 4:4
This is the stone *w* was set at............. Acts 4:11 3588
w is become the head of the................. Acts 4:11 3588
beholding the man *w* was healed........ Acts 4:14
speak the things *w* we have seen........ Acts 4:20 3739
glorified God for that *w* was done........ Acts 4:21
w hast made heaven, and earth, and..... Acts 4:24 3588
things *w* he possessed was his own..... Acts 4:32
(*w* is, being interpreted, The son.......... Acts 4:36 3739
the feet of them *w* have buried.......... Acts 5:9
them *w* were vexed with unclean......... Acts 5:16
(*w* is the sect of the Sadducees,).......... Acts 5:17 3588
w is called the synagogue of the.......... Acts 6:9 3588
and the spirit by *w* he spake................ Acts 6:10 3739
w said, We have heard him speak......... Acts 6:11
w said, This man ceaseth not to........... Acts 6:13
the customs *w* Moses delivered us........ Acts 6:14 3739
into the land *w* I shall shew thee......... Acts 7:3 3739
w God had sworn to Abraham, the....... Acts 7:17 3739
king arose, *w* knew not Joseph............ Acts 7:18 3739
In *w* time Moses was born, and was.... Acts 7:20 3739
of my people *w* is in Egypt.................. Acts 7:34 3588
by the hand of the angel *w*................. Acts 7:35 3558
w said unto the children of................. Acts 7:37 3558
the wilderness with the angel *w*.......... Acts 7:38 3558
w brought us out of the land of........... Acts 7:40 3739
figures *w* ye made to worship them..... Acts 7:43 3739
W also our fathers that came.............. Acts 7:45 3739
W of the prophets have not your.......... Acts 7:52 5101
they have slain them *w* shewed............ Acts 7:52 3558
the church *w* was at Jerusalem............ Acts 8:1 3558
unto those things *w* Philip spake......... Acts 8:6
and seeing the miracles *w* he did......... Acts 8:6
w beforetime in the same city.............. Acts 8:9
the miracles and signs *w* were done..... Acts 8:13
Now when the apostles *w* were at........ Acts 8:14 3558
that none of these things *w* ye............. Acts 8:24 3739
Jerusalem unto Gaza, *w* is desert.......... Acts 8:26 3778
the scripture *w* he read was this.......... Acts 8:32
the men *w* journeyed with him............. Acts 9:7 3588
the street *w* is called Straight............. Acts 9:11 3588
the disciples *w* were at Damascus........ Acts 9:19
them *w* called on this name in............. Acts 9:21 3588
the Jews *w* dwelt at Damascus............. Acts 9:22 3588
W when the brethren knew, they.......... Acts 9:30
to the saints *w* dwelt at Lydda............ Acts 9:32 3588
w had kept his bed eight years,............ Acts 9:33
w by interpretation is called................ Acts 9:36 3739
good works and almsdeeds *w* she did... Acts 9:36 3739
garments *w* Dorcas made, while she.... Acts 9:39 3745
w gave much alms to the people,.......... Acts 10:2
when the angel *w* spake unto............... Acts 10:7 3588
vision *w* he had seen should mean....... Acts 10:17 3739
behold, the men *w* were sent from....... Acts 10:17 3588
w was surnamed Peter, were lodged.... Acts 10:18 3588
the men *w* were sent unto him from..... Acts 10:21 3588
The word *w* God sent unto the............ Acts 10:36 3739
w was published throughout all............ Acts 10:37
after the baptism *w* John preached...... Acts 10:37 3739
w he did both in the land of the........... Acts 10:39 3739
to testify that it is he *w* was.............. Acts 10:42 3588
fell on all them *w* heard the word........ Acts 10:44
w believed were astonished.................. Acts 10:45
w have received the Holy Ghost as...... Acts 10:47 3748
Upon the *w* when I had fastened.......... Acts 11:6 3739
w stood and said unto him, Send......... Acts 11:13
Now they *w* were scattered abroad...... Acts 11:19
were men of Cyprus and Cyrene, *w*..... Acts 11:20 3748
of the church *w* was in Jerusalem........ Acts 11:22 3588
w came to pass in the days of............ Acts 11:28 3748
the brethren *w* dwelt in Judaea............ Acts 11:29
W also they did, and sent it to............ Acts 11:30 3739
was true *w* was done by the angel....... Acts 12:9 3588
w opened to them of his own............... Acts 12:10 3748
w had been brought up with Herod...... Acts 13:1
W was with the deputy of the.............. Acts 13:7 3739
w shall fulfil all my will..................... Acts 13:22 3588
w are read every sabbath day............. Acts 13:27 3588
w came up with him from Galilee........ Acts 13:31
how that the promise *w* was made....... Acts 13:32
from *w* ye could not be justified.......... Acts 13:39 3739
w is spoken of in the prophets............ Acts 13:40
a work *w* ye shall in no wise............... Acts 13:41
things *w* were spoken by Paul............. Acts 13:45
w gave testimony unto the word of...... Acts 14:3 3588
w was before their city, brought......... Acts 14:13 3588
W when the apostles, Barnabas and..... Acts 14:14
w made heaven, and earth, and the...... Acts 14:15 3739
God for the work *w* they fulfilled........ Acts 14:26 3739
certain men *w* came down from........... Acts 15:1
sect of the Pharisees *w* believed......... Acts 15:5
w knoweth the hearts, bare them........ Acts 15:8
w neither our fathers nor we were...... Acts 15:10 3739
of David, *w* is fallen down.................. Acts 15:16 3588
w from among the Gentiles are........... Acts 15:19 3588
w are of the Gentiles in Antioch.......... Acts 15:23 3588
that certain *w* went out from us.......... Acts 15:24
from *w* if ye keep yourselves, ye.......... Acts 15:29 3739
W when they had read, they................ Acts 15:31
w was a Jewess, and believed.............. Acts 16:1
W was well reported of by the............. Acts 16:2 3739
the Jews *w* were in those quarters....... Acts 16:3 3588
elders *w* were at Jerusalem................. Acts 16:4 3588
w is the chief city of that part............ Acts 16:12 3748
unto the women *w* resorted thither...... Acts 16:13
w worshipped God, heard us............... Acts 16:14
the things *w* were spoken of Paul......... Acts 16:14
w brought her masters much gain....... Acts 16:16 3748
w shew unto us the way of.................. Acts 16:17 3748
w are not lawful for us to.................... Acts 16:21 3588
But the Jews *w* believed not............... Acts 17:5
of honourable women *w* were Greeks.. Acts 17:12 3588
strangers *w* were there spent.............. Acts 17:21 3588

in the *w* he will judge the world........... Acts 17:31 3739
among the *w* was Dionysius the........... Acts 17:34 3739
helped them much *w* had believed........ Acts 18:27
on him *w* should come after him.......... Acts 19:4
so that all they *w* dwelt in Asia........... Acts 19:10
upon them to call over them *w* had..... Acts 19:13
and chief of the priests, *w* did so.......... Acts 19:14
Many of them also *w* used curious........ Acts 19:19
w made silver shrines for Diana,.......... Acts 19:24
be no gods, *w* are made with hands..... Acts 19:26 3588
w were his friends, sent unto him........ Acts 19:31
of the image *w* fell down from.............. Acts 19:35
w are neither robbers of churches....... Acts 19:37
and the craftsmen *w* are with him........ Acts 19:38
w befell me by the lying in wait........... Acts 20:19 3588
w I have received of the Lord.............. Acts 20:24 3739
over the *w* the Holy Ghost hath............ Acts 20:28 3739
w he hath purchased with his own....... Acts 20:28 3739
w is able to build you up, and to......... Acts 20:32 3588
among all them *w* are sanctified........... Acts 20:32
of all for the words *w* he spake........... Acts 20:38 3739
w was one of the seven....................... Acts 21:8
virgins, *w* did prophesy....................... Acts 21:9
of Jews there are *w* believe................ Acts 21:20 3588
Jews *w* are among the Gentiles to........ Acts 21:21
We have four men *w* have a vow on...... Acts 21:23
touching the Gentiles *w* believe........... Acts 21:25
the Jews *w* were of Asia, when............ Acts 21:27
w before these days madest an........... Acts 21:38
I am a man *w* am a Jew of Tarsus,........ Acts 21:39
hear ye my defence *w* I make now......... Acts 22:1
I am verily a man *w* am a Jew.............. Acts 22:3
to bring them *w* were there bound........ Acts 22:5
be told thee of all things *w* are............ Acts 22:10 3739
of all the Jews *w* dwelt there.............. Acts 22:12
they departed from him *w* should......... Acts 22:29 3588
forty *w* had made this conspiracy......... Acts 23:13 3588
w have bound themselves with an........ Acts 23:21 3748
after the way *w* they call heresy.......... Acts 24:14 3739
believing all things *w* are................... Acts 24:14 3588
w they themselves also allow,.............. Acts 24:15 3739
w was a Jewess, he sent for Paul,........ Acts 24:24
w among you are able, go down........... Acts 25:5
the Jews *w* came down from................ Acts 25:7
Paul, *w* they could not prove.............. Acts 25:7 3588
before that he *w* is accused have......... Acts 25:16
w was dead, whom Paul affirmed to..... Acts 25:19
all men *w* are here present with.......... Acts 25:24 3588
questions *w* are among the Jews........... Acts 26:3
w was at the first among mine own...... Acts 26:4 3588
W knew me from the beginning, if........ Acts 26:5
Unto *w* promise our twelve tribes,........ Acts 26:7 3739
For *w* hope's sake, king Agrippa,.......... Acts 26:7 3739
W thing I also did in Jerusalem........... Acts 26:10 3739
me and them *w* journeyed with me........ Acts 26:13
of these things *w* thou hast seen.......... Acts 26:16 3739
of those things in the *w* I will............. Acts 26:16 3739
inheritance among them *w* are.............. Acts 26:18
things than those *w* the prophets......... Acts 26:22 3588
came unto a place *w* is called The........ Acts 27:8
things *w* were spoken by Paul............... Acts 27:11
w is an haven of Crete, and lieth.......... Acts 27:12
certain island *w* is called Clauda........... Acts 27:16
W when they had taken up, they.......... Acts 27:17 3739
into the *w* they were minded, if............ Acts 27:39 3739
commanded that they *w* could swim..... Acts 27:43
w had diseases in the island,................ Acts 28:9 3588
w had wintered in the isle, whose........ Acts 28:11
believed the things *w* were spoken....... Acts 28:24
teaching those things *w* concern.......... Acts 28:31
(*W* he had promised afore by his.......... Rom 1:2 3739
w was made of the seed of David.......... Rom 1:3 3588
Because that *w* may be known of......... Rom 1:19
use into that *w* is against nature.......... Rom 1:26
men working that *w* is unseemly........... Rom 1:27
of their error *w* was meet.................... Rom 1:27 3739
those things *w* are not convenient........ Rom 1:28
that they *w* commit such things............ Rom 1:32
against them *w* commit such things...... Rom 2:2
judgest them *w* do such things............. Rom 2:3
w have not the law, do by nature......... Rom 2:14 3588
W shew the work of the law................ Rom 2:15 3748
a light of them *w* are in darkness.......... Rom 2:19
w hast the form of knowledge and....... Rom 2:20
Thou therefore *w* teachest another....... Rom 2:21 3588
not uncircumcision *w* is by nature......... Rom 2:27
is not a Jew, *w* is one outwardly.......... Rom 2:28
w is outward in the flesh.................... Rom 2:28
he is a Jew, *w* is one inwardly.............. Rom 2:29
God *w* is by faith of Jesus Christ.......... Rom 3:22
of him *w* believeth in Jesus................. Rom 3:26
w shall justify the circumcision........... Rom 3:30 3739
w he had yet being uncircumcised........ Rom 4:11 3588
w he had being yet uncircumcised........ Rom 4:12
For if they *w* are of the law be............. Rom 4:14
not to that only *w* is of the law............ Rom 4:16
but to that also *w* is of the.................. Rom 4:16
calleth those things *w* be not as.......... Rom 4:17
according to that *w* was spoken........... Rom 4:18
the Holy Ghost *w* is given unto us........ Rom 5:5 3588
w is by one man, Jesus Christ,............. Rom 5:15 3588
much more they *w* receive................... Rom 5:17
of doctrine *w* was delivered you........... Rom 6:17 3739
For the woman *w* hath an husband...... Rom 7:2
w were by the law, did work in............ Rom 7:5 3588
w was ordained to life, I found............ Rom 7:10 3588
Was then that *w* is good made............. Rom 7:13
death in me by that *w* is good.............. Rom 7:13
For that *w* I do I allow not.................. Rom 7:15 3739
If then I do that *w* I would not............ Rom 7:16 3739
perform that *w* is good I find not.......... Rom 7:18
but the evil *w* I would not................... Rom 7:19 3739
the law of sin *w* is in my members......... Rom 7:23 3588
to them *w* are in Christ Jesus.............. Rom 8:1

glory *w* shall be revealed in us.............. Rom 8:18
w have the firstfruits of the................. Rom 8:23
groanings *w* cannot be uttered.............. Rom 8:26
w is in Christ Jesus our Lord................ Rom 8:39 3588
not all Israel, *w* are of Israel................ Rom 9:6 3588
They *w* are the children of the.............. Rom 9:8
w he had afore prepared unto............... Rom 9:23 3739
my people, *w* were not my people......... Rom 9:25
and her beloved, *w* was not beloved..... Rom 9:25
Gentiles, *w* followed not after.............. Rom 9:30 3588
the righteousness *w* is of faith.............. Rom 9:30 3588
w followed after the law of................. Rom 9:31
the righteousness *w* is of the law......... Rom 10:5 3588
That the man *w* doeth those things...... Rom 10:5
But the righteousness *w* is of............... Rom 10:6
the word of faith, *w* we preach............ Rom 10:8 3588
away his people *w* he foreknew............ Rom 11:2 3739
obtained that *w* he seeketh for............ Rom 11:7 3739
to emulation them *w* are my flesh........ Rom 11:14
on them *w* fell, severity...................... Rom 11:22
olive tree *w* is wild by nature............... Rom 11:24
w be the natural branches, be............. Rom 11:24
w is your reasonable service................ Rom 12:1
Abhor that *w* is evil............................. Rom 12:9
cleave to that *w* is good....................... Rom 12:9
Bless them *w* persecute you................. Rom 12:14
do that *w* is good, and thou shalt.......... Rom 13:3
But if thou do that *w* is evil................. Rom 13:4
let not him *w* eateth not judge.............. Rom 14:3
after the things *w* make for peace........ Rom 14:19
in that thing *w* he alloweth................. Rom 14:22 3739
in those things *w* pertain to God.......... Rom 15:17
w Christ hath not wrought by me......... Rom 15:18 3739
For *w* cause also I have been much...... Rom 15:22 1352
poor saints *w* are at Jerusalem............ Rom 15:26 3588
that my service *w* I have for................ Rom 15:31 3588
w is a servant of the church................. Rom 16:1
of the church *w* is at Cenchrea............. Rom 16:1 3588
Salute them *w* are of Aristobulus'.......... Rom 16:10
of Narcissus, *w* are in the Lord............. Rom 16:11 3588
w laboured much in the Lord.............. Rom 16:12 3748
the brethren *w* are with them............... Rom 16:14
and all the saints *w* are with them....... Rom 16:15
mark them *w* cause divisions and........ Rom 16:17
to the doctrine *w* ye have learned........ Rom 16:17 3739
have you wise unto that *w* is good......... Rom 16:19
w was kept secret since the world........ Rom 16:25
the church of God *w* is at Corinth........ 1Cor 1:2 3588
for the grace of God *w* is given............ 1Cor 1:4 3588
by them *w* are of the house of............. 1Cor 1:11
but unto us *w* are saved it is the.......... 1Cor 1:18
But unto them *w* are called.................. 1Cor 1:24 3588
confound the things *w* are mighty......... 1Cor 1:27
things *w* are despised, hath God........... 1Cor 1:28
things *w* are not, to bring to................ 1Cor 1:28 3588
w God ordained before the world......... 1Cor 2:7 3739
W none of the princes of this............. 1Cor 2:8 3739
the things *w* God hath prepared........... 1Cor 2:9 3739
the spirit of man *w* is in him.............. 1Cor 2:11 3588
world, but the spirit *w* is of God.......... 1Cor 2:12 3588
W things also we speak...................... 1Cor 2:13 3739
not in the words *w* man's wisdom......... 1Cor 2:13
but *w* the Holy Ghost teacheth............ 1Cor 2:13
grace of God *w* is given unto me.......... 1Cor 3:10 3588
that is laid, *w* is Jesus Christ.............. 1Cor 3:11 3739
abide *w* he hath built thereupon.......... 1Cor 3:14 3739
of God is holy, *w* temple ye are............ 1Cor 3:17 3748
of men above that *w* is written............. 1Cor 4:6 3739
of my ways *w* be in Christ.................... 1Cor 4:17 3588
speech of them *w* are puffed up............ 1Cor 4:19
know ye not that he *w* is joined........... 1Cor 6:16
of the Holy Ghost *w* is in you............... 1Cor 6:19
w ye have of God, and ye are not.......... 1Cor 6:19 3739
and in your spirit, *w* are God's............. 1Cor 6:20 3748
the woman *w* hath an husband that..... 1Cor 7:13 3748
you, but for that *w* is comely.............. 1Cor 7:35
For if any man see thee *w* hast............. 1Cor 8:10 3588
w is weak be emboldened to eat........... 1Cor 8:10
things *w* are offered to idols................ 1Cor 8:10
Do ye not know that they *w*................ 1Cor 9:13
they *w* wait at the altar are................. 1Cor 9:13
the Lord ordained that they *w*............. 1Cor 9:14
that they *w* run in a race run all.......... 1Cor 9:24
The cup of blessing *w* we bless............. 1Cor 10:16 3739
The bread *w* we break, is it not............ 1Cor 10:16 3739
are not they *w* eat of the................... 1Cor 10:18
or that *w* is offered in sacrifice............ 1Cor 10:19
that the things *w* the Gentiles............. 1Cor 10:20 3739
of for that for *w* I give thanks.............. 1Cor 10:30 3739
that they *w* are approved may be......... 1Cor 11:19
that *w* also I delivered unto you........... 1Cor 11:23 3739
in *w* he was betrayed took bread.......... 1Cor 11:23 3739
is my body, *w* is broken for you........... 1Cor 11:24 3588
the same God *w* worketh all in all......... 1Cor 12:6 3588
w seem to be more feeble, are............ 1Cor 12:22
w we think to be less honourable,......... 1Cor 12:23 3739
honour to that part *w* lacked.............. 1Cor 12:24
But when that *w* is perfect is............... 1Cor 13:10
then that *w* is in part shall be............. 1Cor 13:10
not, but for them *w* believe................ 1Cor 14:22
the gospel *w* I preached unto you......... 1Cor 15:1 3739
w also ye have received, and............... 1Cor 15:1 3739
By *w* also ye are saved, if ye............... 1Cor 15:2 3739
of all that *w* I also received................ 1Cor 15:3 3739
his grace *w* was bestowed upon me....... 1Cor 15:10
the grace of God *w* was with me........... 1Cor 15:10 3588
Then they also *w* are fallen.................. 1Cor 15:18
w did put all things under him............ 1Cor 15:27
Else what shall they do *w* are.............. 1Cor 15:29
I protest by your rejoicing *w* I.............. 1Cor 15:31 3739
that *w* thou sowest is not.................... 1Cor 15:36 3739
that *w* thou sowest, thou sowest.......... 1Cor 15:37 3739
that was not first *w* is spiritual............ 1Cor 15:46
spiritual, but that *w* is natural.............. 1Cor 15:46

and afterward that *w* is spiritual 1Cor 15:46
w giveth us the victory through 1Cor 15:57 *3588*
for that *w* was lacking on your 1Cor 16:17
the church of God *w* is at Corinth 2Cor 1:1 *3588*
the saints *w* are in all Achaia 2Cor 1:1 *3588*
comfort them *w* are in any trouble 2Cor 1:4
w is effectual in the enduring of 2Cor 1:6 *3588*
same sufferings *w* we also suffer 2Cor 1:6 *3588*
our trouble *w* came to us in Asia 2Cor 1:8 *3588*
but in God *w* raiseth the dead 2Cor 1:9 *3588*
Now he *w* stablisheth us with you 2Cor 1:21
but the same *w* is made sorry by 2Cor 2:2
w I have more abundantly unto you 2Cor 2:4 *3739*
w was inflicted of many 2Cor 2:6 *3588*
w always causeth us to triumph in 2Cor 2:14
w corrupt the word of God 2Cor 2:17
w glory was to be done away 2Cor 3:7 *3588*
For even that *w* was made glorious 2Cor 3:10
For if that *w* is done away was 2Cor 3:11
much more that *w* remaineth is 2Cor 3:11
w put a vail over his face, that 2Cor 3:13
to the end of that *w* is abolished 2Cor 3:13
w vail is done away in Christ 2Cor 3:14 *3748*
the minds of them *w* believe not 2Cor 4:4
For we *w* live are alway delivered 2Cor 4:11 *3588*
Knowing that he *w* raised up the 2Cor 4:14
For *w* cause we faint not 2Cor 4:16 *1352*
w is but for a moment, worketh 2Cor 4:17 *3588*
look not at the things *w* are seen 2Cor 4:18
but at the things *w* are not seen 2Cor 4:18
for the things *w* are seen are 2Cor 4:18
but the things *w* are not seen are 2Cor 4:18
with our house *w* is from heaven 2Cor 5:2 *3588*
answer them *w* glory in appearance 2Cor 5:12
that they *w* live should not 2Cor 5:15
but unto him *w* died for them, and 2Cor 5:15
w I made before Titus, is found a 2Cor 7:14 *3588*
also out of that *w* ye have 2Cor 8:11
w put the same earnest care into 2Cor 8:16 *3588*
w is administered by us to the 2Cor 8:19 *3588*
abundance *w* is administered by us 2Cor 8:20 *3588*
great confidence *w* I have in you 2Cor 8:22 *3588*
for *w* I boast of you to them of 2Cor 9:2 *3739*
He *w* soweth sparingly shall reap 2Cor 9:6
he *w* soweth bountifully shall 2Cor 9:6 *3588*
w causeth through us thanksgiving 2Cor 9:11 *3748*
for you, *w* long after you for the 2Cor 9:14
w think of us as if we walked 2Cor 10:2 *3588*
w the Lord hath given us for 2Cor 10:8 *3739*
rule *w* God hath distributed to us 2Cor 10:13 *3739*
w ye have not received, or 2Cor 11:4 *3739*
w ye have not accepted, ye might 2Cor 11:4
for that *w* was lacking to me the 2Cor 11:9
w came from Macedonia supplied 2Cor 11:9
from them *w* desire occasion 2Cor 11:12
That *w* I speak, I speak it not 2Cor 11:17 *3739*
that *w* cometh upon me daily, the 2Cor 11:28 *3588*
things *w* concern mine infirmities 2Cor 11:30
w is blessed for evermore, 2Cor 11:31 *3588*
w it is not lawful for a man to 2Cor 12:4 *3739*
me above that *w* he seeth me to be 2Cor 12:6 *3739*
bewail many *w* have sinned already 2Cor 12:21 *3588*
lasciviousness *w* they have 2Cor 12:21 *3739*
to them *w* heretofore have sinned 2Cor 13:2
w to you-ward is not weak, but is 2Cor 13:3 *3739*
ye should do that *w* is honest 2Cor 13:7
according to the power *w* the Lord 2Cor 13:10 *3739*
And all the brethren *w* are with me Gal 1:2
W is not another Gal 1:7 *3739*
that *w* we have preached unto you Gal 1:8 *3739*
that the gospel *w* was preached of Gal 1:11 *3588*
to them *w* were apostles before me Gal 1:17
Now the things *w* I write unto you Gal 1:20 *3739*
of Judaea *w* were in Christ Gal 1:22 *3588*
That he *w* persecuted us in times Gal 1:23
the faith *w* once he destroyed Gal 1:23 *3739*
unto them that gospel *w* I preach Gal 2:2 *3739*
to them *w* were of reputation Gal 2:2
liberty *w* we have in Christ Jesus Gal 2:4 *3739*
the same *w* I also was forward to Gal 2:10 *3739*
fearing them *w* were of the Gal 2:12
again the things *w* I destroyed Gal 2:18 *3739*
the life *w* I now live in the Gal 2:20 *3739*
that they *w* are of faith, the Gal 3:7
So then they *w* be of faith are Gal 3:9
continueth not in all things *w* Gal 3:10 *3588*
one, And to thy seed, *w* is Christ Gal 3:16 *3739*
w was four hundred and thirty Gal 3:17
law given *w* could have given life Gal 3:21 *3588*
shut up unto the faith *w* should Gal 3:23 *3588*
unto them *w* by nature are no gods Gal 4:8
my temptation *w* was in my flesh Gal 4:14
W things are an allegory Gal 4:24 *3748*
w gendereth to bondage Gal 4:24
bondage, *w* is Agar Gal 4:24 *3748*
answereth to Jerusalem *w* now is Gal 4:25 *3588*
But Jerusalem *w* is above is free, Gal 4:26
w is the mother of us all Gal 4:26 *3748*
than she *w* hath a husband Gal 4:27
but faith *w* worketh by love Gal 5:6
were even cut off *w* trouble you Gal 5:12
flesh are manifest, *w* are these Gal 5:19 *3748*
of the *w* I tell you before, as I Gal 5:21 *3739*
that they *w* do such things shall Gal 5:21
ye *w* are spiritual, restore such Gal 6:1 *3588*
to the saints *w* are at Ephesus, Eph 1:1 *3588*
w he hath purposed in himself Eph 1:9 *3739*
both *w* are in heaven Eph 1:10 *3588*
and *w* are on earth Eph 1:10 *3588*
W is the earnest of our Eph 1:14 *3739*
W he wrought in Christ, when he Eph 1:20 *3739*
but also in that *w* is to come Eph 1:21
W is his body, the fulness of him Eph 1:23 *3748*
w God hath before ordained that Eph 2:10 *3739*
w is called the Circumcision in Eph 2:11 *3588*
peace to you *w* were afar off Eph 2:17 *3588*
of the grace of God *w* is given me Eph 3:2 *3588*
W in other ages was not made Eph 3:5 *3739*
w from the beginning of the world Eph 3:9 *3588*
to the eternal purpose *w* he Eph 3:11 *3739*
for you, *w* is your glory Eph 3:13 *3748*
w passeth knowledge, that ye Eph 3:19
w is the head, even Christ Eph 4:15 *3739*
compacted by that *w* every joint Eph 4:16
w is corrupt according to the Eph 4:22 *3588*
w after God is created in Eph 4:24 *3588*
his hands the thing *w* is good Eph 4:28
but that *w* is good to the use of Eph 4:29 *1536*
nor jesting, *w* are not convenient Eph 5:4 *3588*
w are done of them in secret Eph 5:12
w is the first commandment with Eph 6:2 *3748*
the Spirit, *w* is the word of God Eph 6:17 *3739*
For *w* I am an ambassador in bonds Eph 6:20 *3739*
in Christ Jesus *w* are at Philippi Phil 1:1 *3588*
that he *w* hath begun a good work Phil 1:6
w are by Jesus Christ, unto the Phil 1:11 *3588*
that the things *w* happened unto Phil 1:12
w is far better Phil 1:23
w is to them an evident token of Phil 1:28 *3748*
the same conflict *w* ye saw in me Phil 1:30 *3634*
w was also in Christ Jesus Phil 2:5 *3739*
given him a name *w* is above every Phil 2:9 *3588*
For it is God *w* worketh in you Phil 2:13 *3588*
not the things *w* are Jesus Phil 2:21
w worship God in the spirit, and Phil 3:3 *3588*
the righteousness *w* is in the law Phil 3:6 *3588*
w is of the law Phil 3:9 *3588*
but that *w* is through the faith Phil 3:9 *3588*
the righteousness *w* is of God by Phil 3:9 *3588*
that I may apprehend that for *w* Phil 3:12 *3739*
those things *w* are behind Phil 3:13
unto those things *w* are before Phil 3:13
mark them *w* walk so as ye have us Phil 3:17
help those women *w* laboured with Phil 4:3 *3748*
w passeth all understanding, Phil 4:7 *3588*
w ye have both learned, and Phil 4:9 *3739*
through Christ *w* strengtheneth me Phil 4:13 *3588*
the things *w* were sent from you Phil 4:18
The brethren *w* are with me greet Phil 4:21
in Christ *w* are at Colosse Col 1:2
of the love *w* ye have to all the Col 1:4 *3588*
For the hope *w* is laid up for you Col 1:5 *3588*
W is come unto you, as it is in Col 1:6 *3588*
w hath made us meet to be Col 1:12 *3588*
w ye have heard Col 1:23
w was preached to every creature Col 1:23 *3558*
every creature *w* is under heaven Col 1:23
fill up that *w* is behind of the Col 1:24
his body's sake, *w* is the church Col 1:24 *3739*
of God *w* is given to me for you Col 1:25 *3588*
Even the mystery *w* hath been hid Col 1:26 *3588*
w is Christ in you, the hope of Col 1:27 *3739*
working, *w* worketh in me mightily Col 1:29 *3588*
w is the head of all principality Col 2:10 *3739*
w was contrary to us, and took it Col 2:14 *3739*
W are a shadow of things to come Col 2:17 *3739*
those things *w* he hath not seen Col 2:18 *3739*
from *w* all the body by joints and Col 2:19 *3739*
W all are to perish with the Col 2:22 *3739*
W things have indeed a shew of Col 2:23 *3748*
seek those things *w* are above Col 3:1
your members *w* are upon the earth Col 3:5 *3588*
and covetousness, *w* is idolatry Col 3:5 *3748*
For *w* things' sake the wrath of Col 3:6 *3739*
In the *w* ye also walked some time Col 3:7 *3739*
w is renewed in knowledge after Col 3:10 *3588*
w is the bond of perfectness Col 3:14 *3748*
to the *w* also ye are called in Col 3:15 *3739*
for the wrong *w* he hath done Col 3:25 *3739*
unto your servants that *w* is just Col 4:1
Christ, for *w* I am also in bonds Col 4:3 *3739*
you all things *w* are done here Col 4:9 *3588*
w is called Justus, who are of Col 4:11 *3588*
w have been a comfort unto me Col 4:11 *3748*
the brethren *w* are in Laodicea Col 4:15
the church *w* is in his house Col 4:15 *3588*
Take heed to the ministry *w* thou Col 4:17 *3739*
w is in God the Father and in the 1Th 1:1
w delivered us from the wrath to 1Th 1:10 *3588*
men, but God, *w* trieth our hearts 1Th 2:4
the word of God *w* ye heard of us 1Th 2:13
w effectually worketh also in you 1Th 2:13 *3739*
of the churches of God *w* in 1Th 2:14 *3588*
might perfect that *w* is lacking 1Th 3:10
as the Gentiles *w* know not God 1Th 4:5 *3588*
brethren *w* are in all Macedonia 1Th 4:10 *3588*
concerning them *w* are asleep 1Th 4:13
even as others *w* have no hope 1Th 4:13 *3588*
even so them also *w* sleep in 1Th 4:14
that we *w* are alive and remain 1Th 4:15 *3588*
not prevent them *w* are asleep 1Th 4:15 *3588*
Then we *w* are alive and remain 1Th 4:17 *3588*
to know them *w* labour among you, 1Th 5:12 *3588*
but ever follow that *w* is good 1Th 5:15 *3588*
hold fast that *w* is good 1Th 5:21 *3588*
W is a manifest token of the 2Th 1:5
of God, for *w* ye also suffer 2Th 1:5 *3739*
traditions *w* ye have been taught 2Th 2:15 *3739*
w hath loved us, and hath given us 2Th 2:16 *3588*
do the things *w* we command you 2Th 3:4 *3739*
the tradition *w* he received of us 2Th 3:6 *3739*
some *w* walk among you disorderly 2Th 3:11 *3588*
w is the token in every epistle 2Th 3:17 *3739*
Lord Jesus Christ, *w* is our hope 1Ti 1:1 *3588*
w minister questions, rather than 1Ti 1:4 *3748*
than godly edifying *w* is in faith 1Ti 1:4 *3588*
From *w* some having swerved have 1Ti 1:6 *3739*
w was committed to my trust 1Ti 1:11 *3739*
love *w* is in Christ Jesus 1Ti 1:14 *3588*
for a pattern to them *w* should 1Ti 1:16
prophecies *w* went before on thee 1Ti 1:18
w some having put away concerning 1Ti 1:19 *3739*
But (*w* becometh women professing 1Ti 2:10 *3739*
good report of them *w* are without 1Ti 3:7
in the faith *w* is in Christ Jesus 1Ti 3:13 *3588*
w is the church of the living God 1Ti 3:15 *3748*
w God hath created to be received 1Ti 4:3 *3739*
thanksgiving of them *w* believe 1Ti 4:3
now is, and of that *w* is to come 1Ti 4:8
w was given thee by prophecy, 1Ti 4:14 *3739*
speaking things *w* they ought not 1Ti 5:13 *3588*
to the doctrine *w* is according to 1Ti 6:3
w drown men in destruction and 1Ti 6:9 *3748*
w while some coveted after, they 1Ti 6:10 *3739*
W in his times he shall shew, who 1Ti 6:15 *3739*
dwelling in the light *w* no man 1Ti 6:16 *3739*
keep that *w* is committed to thy 1Ti 6:20
W some professing have erred 1Ti 6:21 *3588*
was written from Laodicea *w* is 1Ti *s* *3748*
of life *w* is in Christ Jesus 2Ti 1:1 *3588*
w dwelt first in thy grandmother 2Ti 1:5 *3748*
w is in thee by the putting on of 2Ti 1:6 *3739*
w was given us in Christ Jesus 2Ti 1:9 *3588*
For the *w* cause I also suffer 2Ti 1:12 *3739*
that *w* I have committed unto him 2Ti 1:12
w thou hast heard of me, in faith 2Ti 1:13 *3739*
love *w* is in Christ Jesus 2Ti 1:13 *3588*
That good thing *w* was committed 2Ti 1:14
the Holy Ghost *w* dwelleth in us 2Ti 1:14 *3588*
that all they *w* are in Asia be 2Ti 1:15
may also obtain the salvation *w* 2Ti 2:10 *3588*
sort are they *w* creep into houses 2Ti 3:6
w came unto me at Antioch, at 2Ti 3:11 *3634*
in the things *w* thou hast learned 2Ti 3:14 *3739*
w are able to make thee wise unto 2Ti 3:15 *3588*
faith *w* is in Christ Jesus 2Ti 3:15 *3588*
w the Lord, the righteous judge, 2Ti 4:8 *3739*
of the truth *w* is after godliness Titus 1:1 *3588*
w God, that cannot lie, promised Titus 1:2 *3739*
w is committed unto me according Titus 1:3 *3739*
teaching things *w* they ought not Titus 1:11 *3739*
things *w* become sound doctrine Titus 2:1 *3739*
of righteousness *w* we have done Titus 3:5 *3739*
W he shed on us abundantly Titus 3:6 *3739*
that they *w* have believed in God Titus 3:8
w thou hast toward the Lord Jesus Philem 5 *3739*
of every good thing *w* is in you Philem 6 *3588*
enjoin thee that *w* is convenient Philem 8
W in time past was to thee Philem 11 *3588*
For unto *w* of the angels said he Heb 1:5 *5101*
But to *w* of the angels said he at Heb 1:13 *5101*
to the things *w* we have heard Heb 2:1
w at the first began to be spoken Heb 2:3 *3748*
for *w* cause he is not ashamed to Heb 2:11 *3739*
the children *w* God hath given me Heb 2:13 *3739*
things *w* were to be spoken after Heb 3:5
For we *w* have believed do enter Heb 4:3 *3588*
w cannot be touched with the Heb 4:15
by the things *w* he suffered Heb 5:8 *3739*
need that one teach you again *w* Heb 5:12 *5101*
For the earth *w* drinketh in the Heb 6:7 *3588*
But that *w* beareth thorns and Heb 6:8
w ye have shewed toward his name, Heb 6:10 *3739*
in *w* it was impossible for God to Heb 6:18 *3739*
W hope we have as an anchor of Heb 6:19 *3739*
w entereth into that within the Heb 6:19
of Salem, *w* is, King of peace Heb 7:2 *3739*
of *w* no man gave attendance at Heb 7:13 *3739*
of *w* tribe Moses spake nothing Heb 7:14 *3739*
by the *w* we draw nigh unto God Heb 7:19 *3739*
men high priests *w* have infirmity Heb 7:28
w was since the law, maketh the Heb 7:28 *3588*
Now of the things *w* we have Heb 8:1
w the Lord pitched, and not man Heb 8:2 *3739*
w was established upon better Heb 8:6 *3748*
Now that *w* decayeth and waxeth old Heb 8:13
w is called the sanctuary Heb 9:2 *3748*
the tabernacle *w* is called the Heb 9:3 *3588*
W had the golden censer, and the Heb 9:4
of *w* we cannot now speak Heb 9:5 *3739*
w he offered for himself, and for Heb 9:7 *3588*
W was a figure for the time then Heb 9:9 *3748*
in *w* were offered both gifts and Heb 9:9 *3739*
W stood only in meats and drinks, Heb 9:10
they *w* are called might receive Heb 9:15
w God hath enjoined unto you Heb 9:20 *3739*
w are the figures of the true Heb 9:24
w they offered year by year Heb 10:1 *3739*
w are offered by the law Heb 10:8 *3748*
By the *w* will we are sanctified Heb 10:10 *3739*
w can never take away sins Heb 10:11 *3748*
w he hath consecrated for us, Heb 10:20 *3739*
w shall devour the adversaries Heb 10:27
remembrance the former days, in *w* Heb 10:32 *3739*
w hath great recompence of reward Heb 10:35 *3748*
so that things *w* are seen were Heb 11:3 *3588*
not made of things *w* do appear Heb 11:3
by *w* he obtained witness that he Heb 11:4 *3739*
by the *w* he condemned the world, Heb 11:7 *3739*
the righteousness *w* is by faith Heb 11:7
called to go out into a place *w* Heb 11:8 *3739*
for a city *w* hath foundations Heb 11:10
as the sand *w* is by the sea shore Heb 11:12 *3588*
w the Egyptians assaying to do Heb 11:29 *3739*
the sin *w* doth so easily beset us Heb 12:1
w speaketh unto you as unto Heb 12:5 *3748*
of our flesh *w* corrected us Heb 12:9
unto them *w* are exercised thereby Heb 12:11
lift up the hands *w* hang down Heb 12:12
lest that *w* is lame be turned out Heb 12:13
without *w* no man shall see the Heb 12:14 *3739*
w voice they that heard intreated Heb 12:19 *3739*

not endure that *w* was commanded	Heb 12:20	
w are written in heaven, and to	Heb 12:23	
that those things *w* cannot be	Heb 12:27	
a kingdom *w* cannot be moved	Heb 12:28	
them *w* suffer adversity, as being	Heb 13:3	
Remember them *w* have the rule	Heb 13:7	
w have not profited them that	Heb 13:9	3739
to eat *w* serve the tabernacle	Heb 13:10	
will, working in you that *w* is	Heb 13:21	
tribes *w* are scattered abroad	Jas 1:1	3739
w the Lord hath promised to them	Jas 1:12	3739
w is able to save your souls	Jas 1:21	3588
heirs of the kingdom *w* he hath	Jas 2:5	3735
name by the *w* ye are called	Jas 2:7	3588
things *w* are needful to the body	Jas 2:16	
scripture was fulfilled *w* saith	Jas 2:23	3588
w though they be so great, and are	Jas 3:4	
w are made after the similitude	Jas 3:9	3588
w is of you kept back by fraud,	Jas 5:4	3588
the cries of them *w* have reaped	Jas 5:4	
we count them happy *w* endure	Jas 5:11	
that he *w* converteth the sinner	Jas 5:20	
w according to his abundant mercy	1Pet 1:3	3588
Of *w* salvation the prophets have	1Pet 1:10	3739
Christ *w* was in them did signify	1Pet 1:11	3588
w are now reported unto you by	1Pet 1:12	3739
w things the angels desire to	1Pet 1:12	3739
But as he *w* hath called you is	1Pet 1:15	
w liveth and abideth for ever	1Pet 1:23	
this is the word *w* by the gospel	1Pet 1:25	3588
Unto you therefore *w* believe he	1Pet 2:7	3588
but unto them *w* be disobedient,	1Pet 2:7	
the stone *w* the builders	1Pet 2:7	
even to them *w* stumble at the	1Pet 2:8	3739
W in time past were not a people,	1Pet 2:10	3588
w had not obtained mercy, but now	1Pet 2:10	3588
lusts, *w* war against the soul	1Pet 2:11	3748
w they shall behold, glorify God	1Pet 2:12	
in that *w* is not corruptible,	1Pet 3:4	
w is in the sight of God of great	1Pet 3:4	3739
ye be followers of that *w* is good	1Pet 3:13	
By *w* also he went and preached	1Pet 3:19	3739
W sometime were disobedient, when	1Pet 3:20	
it as of the ability *w* God giveth	1Pet 4:11	3739
the fiery trial *w* is to try you	1Pet 4:12	
The elders *w* are among you I	1Pet 5:1	
the flock of God *w* is among you	1Pet 5:2	
this voice *w* came from heaven we	2Pet 1:18	
w are greater in power and might,	2Pet 2:11	
W have forsaken the right way, and	2Pet 2:15	
in both *w* I stir up your pure	2Pet 3:1	3739
w were spoken before by the holy	2Pet 3:2	
w are now, by the same word are	2Pet 3:7	
in the *w* the heavens shall pass	2Pet 3:10	3739
in *w* are some things hard to be	2Pet 3:16	3739
w they that are unlearned and	2Pet 3:16	3739
That *w* was from the beginning,	1Jn 1:1	3739
w we have heard	1Jn 1:1	3739
w we have seen with our eyes,	1Jn 1:1	3739
w we have looked upon, and our	1Jn 1:1	3739
w was with the Father, and was	1Jn 1:2	3748
That *w* we have seen and heard	1Jn 1:3	3739
message *w* we have heard of him	1Jn 1:5	3739
but an old commandment *w* ye had	1Jn 2:7	3739
the word *w* ye have heard from the	1Jn 2:7	3739
w thing is true in him and in you	1Jn 2:8	3739
in you, *w* ye have heard from the	1Jn 2:24	3739
If that *w* ye have heard from the	1Jn 2:24	3739
But the anointing *w* ye have	1Jn 2:27	3739
by the Spirit *w* he hath given us	1Jn 3:24	3739
w he hath testified of his Son	1Jn 5:9	3739
sin a sin *w* is not unto death	1Jn 5:16	
w dwelleth in us, and shall be	2Jn 2	3588
but that *w* we had from the	2Jn 5	3739
those things *w* we have wrought	2Jn 8	3739
W have borne witness of thy	3Jn 6	3739
remember his deeds *w* he doeth	3Jn 10	3739
follow not that *w* is evil	3Jn 11	
but that *w* is good	3Jn 11	
w was once delivered unto the	Jude 3	
the angels *w* kept not their first	Jude 6	
of those things *w* they know not	Jude 10	3745
w they have ungodly committed	Jude 15	3739
of all their hard speeches *w*	Jude 15	3739
remember ye the words *w* were	Jude 17	3588
w God gave unto him, to shew unto	Rev 1:1	3739
w must shortly come to pass	Rev 1:1	3739
keep those things *w* are written	Rev 1:3	
the seven churches *w* are in Asia	Rev 1:4	3588
and peace, from him *w*	Rev 1:4	3588
w was, and *w* is to come	Rev 1:4	3588
Spirits *w* are before his throne	Rev 1:4	3739
him, and they also *w* pierced him	Rev 1:7	3748
w is, and *w* was	Rev 1:8	3588
w was, and *w* is to come, the	Rev 1:8	3588
w is to come, the Almighty	Rev 1:8	3588
the seven churches *w* are in Asia	Rev 1:11	3588
Write the things *w* thou hast seen	Rev 1:19	3739
and the things *w* are	Rev 1:19	3739
the things *w* shall be hereafter	Rev 1:19	3739
w thou sawest in my right hand	Rev 1:20	3739
the seven candlesticks *w* thou	Rev 1:20	3739
canst not bear them *w* are evil	Rev 2:2	
thou hast tried them *w* say they	Rev 2:2	
the Nicolaitanes, *w* I also hate	Rev 2:6	3739
w is in the midst of the paradise	Rev 2:7	3739
the last, *w* was dead, and is alive	Rev 2:8	3739
of them *w* say they are Jews	Rev 2:9	3588
those things *w* thou shalt suffer	Rev 2:10	3739
These things saith he *w* hath the	Rev 2:12	
the Nicolaitanes, *w* thing I hate	Rev 2:15	3739
w no man knoweth saving he that	Rev 2:17	3739
w calleth herself a prophetess,	Rev 2:20	3588
I am he *w* searcheth the reins	Rev 2:23	3739

w have not known the depths of	Rev 2:24	3748
But that *w* ye have already hold	Rev 2:25	
and strengthen the things *w* remain	Rev 3:2	
w have not defiled their garments	Rev 3:4	3739
w say they are Jews, and are not,	Rev 3:9	3588
w shall come upon all the world,	Rev 3:10	3588
hold that fast *w* thou hast	Rev 3:11	3739
w is new Jerusalem	Rev 3:12	3588
w cometh down out of heaven from	Rev 3:12	3588
the first voice *w* I heard was as	Rev 4:1	3739
w said, Come up hither, and I will	Rev 4:1	
thee things *w* must be hereafter	Rev 4:1	3739
w are the seven Spirits of God	Rev 4:5	3739
w was, and is, and is to come	Rev 4:8	3588
w are the seven Spirits of God	Rev 5:6	3739
w are the prayers of saints	Rev 5:8	3739
And every creature *w* is in heaven	Rev 5:13	3739
and for the testimony *w* they held	Rev 6:9	3739
the number of them *w* were sealed	Rev 7:4	
w no man could number, of all	Rev 7:9	3739
Salvation to our God *w* sitteth	Rev 7:10	3588
What are these *w* are arrayed in	Rev 7:13	3588
These are they *w* came out of	Rev 7:14	
For the Lamb *w* is in the midst of	Rev 7:17	3588
seven angels *w* stood before God	Rev 8:2	3739
altar *w* was before the throne	Rev 8:3	3588
w came with the prayers of the	Rev 8:4	
the seven angels *w* had the seven	Rev 8:6	3588
the creatures *w* were in the sea	Rev 8:9	3588
three angels, *w* are yet to sound	Rev 8:13	3588
but only those men *w* have not the	Rev 9:4	3748
w is the angel of the bottomless	Rev 9:11	
the golden altar *w* is before God	Rev 9:13	3588
the sixth angel *w* had the trumpet	Rev 9:14	3739
Loose the four angels *w* are bound	Rev 9:14	3588
w were prepared for an hour, and a	Rev 9:15	3588
w issued out of their mouths	Rev 9:18	3588
the rest of the men *w* were not	Rev 9:20	3739
w neither can see, nor hear, nor	Rev 9:20	3739
Seal up those things *w* the seven	Rev 10:4	3739
the angel *w* I saw stand upon the	Rev 10:5	3739
the things *w* are therein, that	Rev 10:6	
the voice *w* I heard from heaven	Rev 10:8	3739
take the little book *w* is open in	Rev 10:8	3588
the angel *w* standeth upon the sea	Rev 10:8	3588
But the court *w* is without the	Rev 11:2	3588
w spiritually is called Sodom and	Rev 11:8	3748
fear fell upon them *w* saw them	Rev 11:11	
w sat before God on their seats,	Rev 11:16	3588
w art, and wast, and art to come	Rev 11:17	3588
destroy them *w* destroy the earth	Rev 11:18	
woman *w* was ready to be delivered	Rev 12:4	3588
w deceiveth the whole world	Rev 12:9	3588
w accused them before our God day	Rev 12:10	3588
he persecuted the woman *w* brought	Rev 12:13	3748
swallowed up the flood *w* the	Rev 12:16	3739
w keep the commandments of God,	Rev 12:17	3588
the beast *w* I saw was like unto a	Rev 13:2	3739
w gave power unto the beast	Rev 13:4	3739
them *w* dwell therein to worship	Rev 13:12	
by the means of those miracles *w*	Rev 13:14	3739
w had the wound by a sword, and	Rev 13:14	3739
w were redeemed from the earth	Rev 14:3	3588
These are they *w* were not defiled	Rev 14:4	3739
These are they *w* follow the Lamb	Rev 14:4	3588
w is poured out without mixture	Rev 14:10	3588
Blessed are the dead *w* die in the	Rev 14:13	3588
out of the temple *w* is in heaven	Rev 14:17	3588
the altar, *w* had power over fire	Rev 14:18	
men *w* had the mark of the beast	Rev 16:2	3588
upon them *w* worshipped his image	Rev 16:2	
w art, and wast, and shalt be,	Rev 16:5	3588
w hath power over these plagues	Rev 16:9	3588
w go forth unto the kings of the	Rev 16:14	
angels *w* had the seven vials	Rev 17:1	3588
w hath the seven heads and ten	Rev 17:7	3588
And here is the mind *w* hath wisdom	Rev 17:9	3588
mountains, on *w* the woman sitteth	Rev 17:9	
the ten horns *w* thou sawest are	Rev 17:12	3739
w have received no kingdom as yet	Rev 17:12	3748
The waters *w* thou sawest, where	Rev 17:15	3739
the ten horns *w* thou sawest upon	Rev 17:16	3739
the woman *w* thou sawest is that	Rev 17:18	3739
w reigneth over the kings of the	Rev 17:18	3588
in the cup *w* she hath filled fill	Rev 18:6	3739
all things *w* were dainty and	Rev 18:14	3588
w were made rich by her, shall	Rev 18:15	3739
w did corrupt the earth with her	Rev 19:2	3748
Blessed are they *w* are called	Rev 19:9	
the armies *w* were in heaven	Rev 19:14	3588
with *w* he deceived them that had	Rev 19:20	3739
w sword proceeded out of his	Rev 19:21	3588
w is the Devil, and Satan, and	Rev 20:2	3739
w had not worshipped the beast,	Rev 20:4	3748
go out to deceive the nations *w*	Rev 20:8	3588
was opened, *w* is the book of life	Rev 20:12	3739
w were written in the books	Rev 20:12	
sea gave up the dead *w* were in it	Rev 20:13	3588
up the dead *w* were in them	Rev 20:13	3588
in the lake *w* burneth with fire	Rev 21:8	3739
w is the second death	Rev 21:8	3739
w had the seven vials full of the	Rev 21:9	3588
w are the names of the twelve	Rev 21:12	3739
the nations of them *w* are saved	Rev 21:24	
but they *w* are written in the	Rev 21:27	
w bare twelve manner of fruits,	Rev 22:2	
the things *w* must shortly be done	Rev 22:6	3588
angel *w* shewed me these things	Rev 22:8	3588
of them *w* keep the sayings of	Rev 22:9	
he *w* is filthy, let him be filthy	Rev 22:11	
from the things *w* are written in	Rev 22:19	
He *w* testifieth these things	Rev 22:20	

WHILE

W the earth remaineth, seedtime	Gen 8:22	5750
w he lingered, the men laid hold	Gen 19:16	
w he yet lived, eastward, unto	Gen 25:6	
w he yet spake with them, Rachel	Gen 29:9	
w Joseph made himself known unto	Gen 45:1	
and wept on his neck a good *w*	Gen 46:29	5750
w my glory passeth by, that I	Ex 33:22	5704
thee with my hand *w* I pass by	Ex 33:22	5704
face shone *w* he talked with him	Ex 34:29	
w he doeth somewhat against any	Lev 4:27	
the *w* that it is shut up shall be	Lev 14:46	
w she lieth desolate without them	Lev 26:43	
w the flesh was yet between their	Num 11:33	
w the children of Israel were in	Num 15:32	
w I meet the LORD yonder	Num 23:15	
w he was zealous for my sake	Num 25:11	
w his heart is hot, and overtake	Deut 19:6	3588
w I am yet alive with you this	Deut 31:27	
w the children of Israel wandered	Josh 14:10	834
And Ehud escaped *w* they tarried	Judg 3:26	5704
W Israel dwelt in Heshbon and her	Judg 11:26	
seven days, *w* their feast lasted	Judg 14:17	
it came to pass within a *w* after	Judg 15:1	
that beheld *w* Samson made sport	Judg 16:27	
w the flesh was in seething, with	1Sa 2:13	
w the ark abode in Kirjath-jearim	1Sa 7:2	3117
on,) but stand thou still a *w*	1Sa 9:27	3117
w Saul talked unto the priest,	1Sa 14:19	5704
thou shalt not only *w* yet I live	1Sa 20:14	518
the *w* that David was in the hold	1Sa 22:4	3117
all the *w* they were in Carmel	1Sa 25:7	3117
all the *w* we were with them	1Sa 25:16	3117
w he dwelleth in the country of	1Sa 27:11	3117
w there was war between the house	2Sa 3:6	
to eat meat *w* it was yet day	2Sa 3:35	
house for a great *w* to come	2Sa 7:19	7350
w the child was yet alive, we	2Sa 12:18	
for the child, *w* it was alive	2Sa 12:21	
W the child was yet alive, I	2Sa 12:22	
w they were in the way, that	2Sa 13:30	
vow *w* I abode at Geshur in Syria	2Sa 15:8	
Giloh, *w* he offered sacrifices	2Sa 15:12	
will come upon him *w* he is weary	2Sa 17:2	
w he was yet alive in the midst	2Sa 18:14	5750
sustenance *w* he lay at Mahanaim	2Sa 19:32	
thine enemies, *w* they pursue thee	2Sa 24:13	
w thou yet talkest there with the	1Kin 1:14	
w she yet talked with the king,	1Kin 1:22	
w he yet spake, behold, Jonathan	1Kin 1:42	
w thine handmaid slept, and laid	1Kin 3:20	
the house, *w* it was in building	1Kin 6:7	
Solomon his father *w* he yet lived	1Kin 12:6	
And it came to pass after a *w*	1Kin 17:7	3117
And it came to pass in the mean *w*	1Kin 18:45	3541
w he yet talked with them, behold	2Kin 6:33	
w he yet kept himself close	1Chr 12:1	
house for a great *w* to come	1Chr 17:17	
w that the sword of thine enemies	1Chr 21:12	*2193*
Solomon his father *w* he yet lived	2Chr 10:6	
w the land is yet before us	2Chr 14:7	
is with you, *w* ye be with him	2Chr 15:2	
w he was wroth with the priests,	2Chr 26:19	
w he was yet young, he began to	2Chr 34:3	
w they stand by, let them shut	Neh 7:3	5704
w Mordecai sat in the king's gate	Est 2:21	
w they were yet talking with him,	Est 6:14	
W he was yet speaking, there came	Job 1:16	
W he was yet speaking, there came	Job 1:17	
W he was yet speaking, there came	Job 1:18	
rain it upon him *w* he is eating	Job 20:23	
They are exalted for a little *w*	Job 24:24	
All the *w* my breath is in me, and	Job 27:3	5750
w there is none to deliver	Ps 7:2	
w they took counsel together	Ps 31:13	
For yet a little *w*, and the wicked	Ps 37:10	
w the wicked is before me	Ps 39:1	5750
w I was musing the fire burned	Ps 39:3	
w they continually say unto me,	Ps 42:3	
w they say daily unto me, Where	Ps 42:10	
Though *w* he lived he blessed his	Ps 49:18	
Thus will I bless thee *w* I live	Ps 63:4	
mine eyes fail *w* I wait for my	Ps 69:3	
but *w* their meat was yet in their	Ps 78:30	
w I suffer thy terrors I am	Ps 88:15	
to my God *w* I have my being	Ps 104:33	5750
W I live will I praise the LORD	Ps 146:2	
unto my God *w* I have any being	Ps 146:2	5750
W as yet he had not made the	Prov 8:26	
Chasten thy son *w* there is hope	Prov 19:18	3588
She riseth also *w* it is yet night	Prov 31:15	
is in their heart *w* they live	Eccl 9:3	
w the evil days come not, nor the	Eccl 12:1	5704
W the sun, or the light, or the	Eccl 12:2	5704
W the king sitteth at his table,	Song 1:12	5704
For yet a very little *w*, and the	Is 10:25	
w it is yet in his hand he eateth	Is 28:4	
Is it not yet a very little *w*	Is 29:17	
ye the LORD *w* he may be found	Is 55:6	
call ye upon him *w* he is near	Is 55:6	
have possessed it but a little *w*	Is 63:18	4705
w they are yet speaking, I will	Is 65:24	
w ye look for light, he turn it	Jer 13:16	
sun is gone down *w* it was yet day	Jer 15:9	
w he was yet shut up in the court	Jer 33:1	
w he was shut up in the court of	Jer 39:15	
Now *w* he was not yet gone back,	Jer 40:5	
yet a little *w*, and the time of	Jer 51:33	
w they sought their meat to	Lam 1:19	3588
w they were slaying them, and I	Eze 9:8	
W the word was in the king's	Dan 4:31	5751
for yet a little *w*, and I will	Hos 1:4	
For *w* they be folden together as	Nah 1:10	5704
w they are drunken as drunkards,	Nah 1:10	

Yet once, it is a little *w* Hag 2:6
away *w* they stand upon their feet Zec 14:12
But *w* he thought on these things, Mt 1:20
W he spake these things unto them Mt 9:18
W he yet talked to the people, Mt 12:46
in himself, but dureth for a *w* Mt 13:21 *4340*
But *w* men slept, his enemy came Mt 13:25
lest *w* ye gather up the tares, ye Mt 13:29
w he sent the multitudes away Mt 14:22 *2193*
W he yet spake, behold, a bright Mt 17:5
w they abode in Galilee, Jesus Mt 17:22
W the Pharisees were gathered Mt 22:41
W the bridegroom tarried, they Mt 25:5
And *w* they went to buy, the Mt 25:10
ye here, *w* I go and pray yonder Mt 26:36 *2193*
w he yet spake, lo, Judas, one of Mt 26:47
after a *w* came unto him they that Mt 26:73 *3397*
w he was yet alive, After three Mt 27:63
and stole him away *w* we slept Mt 28:13
rising up a great *w* before day Mk 1:35
w the bridegroom is with them Mk 2:19
W he yet spake, there came from Mk 5:35
into a desert place, and rest a *w* Mk 6:31 *3641*
w he sent away the people Mk 6:45 *2193*
w he taught in the temple, How Mk 12:35
Sit ye here, *w* I shall pray Mk 14:32 *2193*
w he yet spake, cometh Judas, one Mk 14:43
whether he had been any *w* dead Mk 15:44 *3819*
that *w* he executed the priest's Lk 1:8
w they were there, the days were Lk 2:6
w the bridegroom is with them Lk 5:34
no root, which for a *w* believe Lk 8:13 *2540*
W he yet spake, there cometh one Lk 8:49
W he thus spake, there came a Lk 9:34
But *w* they wondered every one at Lk 9:43
they had a great *w* ago repented Lk 10:13
w the other is yet a great way Lk 14:32
And he would not for a *w* Lk 18:4 *5550*
And *w* he yet spake, behold a Lk 22:47
after a little *w* another saw him, Lk 22:58
w he yet spake, the cock crew Lk 22:60
w they communed together and Lk 24:15
w he talked with us by the way, Lk 24:32 *5613*
w he opened to us the scriptures Lk 24:32 *5613*
w they yet believed not for joy, Lk 24:41
w I was yet with you, that all Lk 24:44
w he blessed them, he was parted Lk 24:51
In the mean *w* his disciples Jn 4:31
but *w* I am coming, another Jn 5:7
Yet a little *w* am I with you, and Jn 7:33 *5550*
of him that sent me, *w* it is day Jn 9:4 *2193*
Yet a little *w* is the light with Jn 12:35 *5550*
Walk *w* ye have the light, lest Jn 12:35 *2193*
W ye have light, believe in the Jn 12:36 *2193*
yet a little *w* I am with you Jn 13:33
Yet a little *w*, and the world Jn 14:19
A little *w*, and ye shall not see Jn 16:16
and again, a little *w*, and ye shall Jn 16:16
that he saith unto us, A little *w* Jn 16:17
and again, a little *w*, and ye shall Jn 16:17
is this that he saith, A little *w* Jn 16:18
of that I said, A little *w* Jn 16:19
and again, a little *w*, and ye shall Jn 16:19
W I was with them in the world, I Jn 17:12 *3153*
w they beheld, he was taken up Acts 1:9
w they looked stedfastly toward Acts 1:10 *5613*
Dorcas made, *w* she was with them Acts 9:39
but *w* they made ready, he fell Acts 10:10
Now *w* Peter doubted in himself Acts 10:17 *5613*
W Peter thought on the vision, Acts 10:19
W Peter yet spake these words, Acts 10:44
ye know how that a good *w* ago God Acts 15:7 *2250*
Now *w* Paul waited for them at Acts 17:16
this tarried there yet a good *w* Acts 18:18 *2250*
w Apollos was at Corinth, Paul Acts 19:1
and eaten, and talked a long *w* Acts 20:11
even *w* I prayed in the temple, I Acts 22:17
w I stood before the council, Acts 24:20
W he answered for himself, Acts 25:8
w the day was coming on, Paul Acts 27:33
after they had looked a great *w* Acts 28:6
their thoughts the mean *w* Rom 2:15
w we were yet sinners, Christ Rom 5:8
w her husband liveth, she be Rom 7:3
For *w* one saith, I am of Paul 1Cor 3:4 *3752*
eat no flesh *w* the world standeth 1Cor 8:13
but I trust to tarry a *w* with you 1Cor 16:7
W we look not at the things which 2Cor 4:18
W we seek to be justified by Gal 2:17
in pleasure is dead *w* she liveth 1Ti 5:6
which *w* some coveted after, they 1Ti 6:10
daily, *w* it is called To day Heb 3:13
W it is said, To day if ye will Heb 3:15
w as the first tabernacle was yet Heb 9:8
at all *w* the testator liveth Heb 9:17 *3753*
For yet a little *w*, and he that Heb 10:37 *3397*
W they behold your chaste 1Pet 3:2
w the ark was a preparing, 1Pet 3:20
after that ye have suffered a *w* 1Pet 5:10 *3641*
deceivings *w* they feast with you 2Pet 2:13
W they promise them liberty, they 2Pet 2:19

WHILES

W they see vanity unto thee, Eze 21:29
w they divine a lie unto thee, to Eze 21:29
w they minister in the gates of Eze 44:17
w he tasted the wine, commanded Dan 5:2
w I was speaking, and praying, and Dan 9:20 5750
w I was speaking in prayer, even Dan 9:21
like an oven, *w* they lie in wait Hos 7:6
w thou art in the way with him Mt 5:25
W it remained, was it not thine Acts 5:4
W by the experiment of this 2Cor 9:13

WHILST

put to death *w* it is yet morning Judg 6:31 5704
w I leave it, and come down to you Neh 6:3 834
W it is yet in his greenness, and Job 8:12 5704
w ye searched out what to say Job 32:11 5704
own nets, *w* that I withal escape Ps 141:10 5704
W their children remember their Jer 17:2
w we are at home in the body, we 2Cor 5:6
w he remembereth the obedience of 2Cor 7:15
w ye were made a gazingstock both Heb 10:33
w ye became companions of them Heb 10:33

WHIP

A *w* for the horse, a bridle for Prov 26:3 7752
The noise of a *w*, and the noise of Nah 3:2 7752

WHIPS

father hath chastised you with *w* 1Kin 12:11 7752
father also chastised you with *w* 1Kin 12:14 7752
my father chastised you with *w* 2Chr 10:11 7752
my father chastised you with *w* 2Chr 10:14 7752

WHIRLETH

it *w* about continually, and the Eccl 1:6 1980

WHIRLWIND

take up Elijah into heaven by a *w* 2Kin 2:1 5591
Elijah went up by a *w* into heaven 2Kin 2:11 5591
Out of the south cometh the *w* Job 37:9 5492
LORD answered Job out of the *w* Job 38:1 5591
the LORD unto Job out of the *w* Job 40:6 5591
shall take them away as with a *w* Ps 58:9 8175
and your destruction cometh as a *w* Prov 1:27 5492
As the *w* passeth, so is the Prov 10:25
flint, and their wheels like a *w* Is 5:28
like a rolling thing before the *w* Is 17:13
the *w* shall take them away as Is 40:24 5591
away, and the *w* shall scatter them Is 41:16 5591
and with his chariots like a *w* Is 66:15 5492
and his chariots shall be as a *w* Jer 4:13 5492
a *w* of the LORD is gone forth in Jer 23:19 5591
forth in fury, even a grievous *w* Jer 23:19 5591
a great *w* shall be raised up from Jer 25:32 5591
the *w* of the LORD goeth forth Jer 30:23 5591
forth with fury, a continuing *w* Jer 30:23 5591
a *w* came out of the north, a Eze 1:4
shall come against him like a *w* Dan 11:40 8175
wind, and they shall reap the *w* Hos 8:7 5492
with the *w* out of the floor Hos 13:3 5590
a tempest in the day of the *w* Amos 1:14 5492
the LORD hath his way in the *w* Nah 1:3 5492
came out as a *w* to scatter me Hab 3:14 5590
But I scattered them with a *w* Zec 7:14 5590

WHIRLWINDS

As *w* in the south pass through Is 21:1 5492
and shall go with *w* of the south Zec 9:14 5591

WHISPER

All that hate me *w* together Ps 41:7 3907
speech shall *w* out of the dust Is 29:4 6850

WHISPERED

David saw that his servants *w* 2Sa 12:19 3907

WHISPERER

a *w* separateth chief friends Prov 16:28 5372

WHISPERERS

deceit, malignity; *w*, Rom 1:29 *5588*

WHISPERINGS

wraths, strifes, backbitings, *w* 2Cor 12:20 *5587*

WHIT

and all the spoil thereof every *w* Deut 13:16 3632
And Samuel told him every *w* 1Sa 3:18 1697
every *w* whole on the sabbath day Jn 7:23 *3650*
his feet, but is clean every *w* Jn 13:10 *3650*
not a *w* behind the very chiefest 2Cor 11:5 *3367*

WHITE

every one that had some *w* in it Gen 30:35 3836
pilled *w* strakes in them Gen 30:37 3836
made the *w* appear which was in Gen 30:37 3836
I had three *w* baskets on my head Gen 40:16 2751
wine, and his teeth *w* with milk Gen 49:12 3836
and it was like coriander seed, *w* Ex 16:31 3836
hair in the plague is turned *w* Lev 13:3 3836
If the bright spot be *w* in the Lev 13:4 3836
the hair thereof be not turned *w* Lev 13:4 3836
if the rising be *w* in the skin Lev 13:10 3836
and it have turned the hair *w* Lev 13:10 3836
it is all turned *w* Lev 13:13 3836
turn again, and be changed unto *w* Lev 13:16 3836
if the plague be turned into *w* Lev 13:17 3836
of the boil there be a *w* rising Lev 13:19 3836
or a bright spot, *w* Lev 13:19 3836
and the hair thereof be turned *w* Lev 13:20 3836
there be no *w* hairs therein, and Lev 13:21 3836
that burneth have a *w* bright spot Lev 13:24 3836
somewhat reddish, or *w* Lev 13:24 3836
in the bright spot be turned *w* Lev 13:25 3836
there be no *w* hair in the bright Lev 13:26 3836
bright spots, even *w* bright spots Lev 13:38 3836
skin of their flesh be darkish *w* Lev 13:39 3836
bald forehead, a *w* reddish sore Lev 13:42 3836
be *w* reddish in his bald head Lev 13:43 3836
Miriam became leprous, *w* as snow Num 12:10
Speak, ye that ride on *w* asses Judg 5:10 6715
his presence a leper as *w* as snow 2Kin 5:27
being arrayed in *w* linen 2Chr 5:12
Where were *w*, green, and blue, Est 1:6 2353
a pavement of red, and blue, and *w* Est 1:6 1858
in royal apparel of blue and *w* Est 8:15 2353
any taste in the *w* of an egg Job 6:6 7388
it was *w* as snow in Salmon Ps 68:14
Let thy garments be always *w* Eccl 9:8 3836
My beloved is *w* and ruddy, the Song 5:10 6703
they shall be as *w* as snow Is 1:18 3835
in the wine of Helbon, and *w* wool Eze 27:18 6713
sit, whose garment was *w* as snow Dan 7:9
and to purge, and to make them *w* Dan 11:35 3835
Many shall be purified, and made *w* Dan 12:10 3835
the branches thereof are made *w* Joel 1:7 3835
there red horses, speckled, and *w* Zec 1:8 3836
And in the third chariot *w* horses Zec 6:3 3836
the *w* go forth after them Zec 6:6 3836
not make one hair *w* or black Mt 5:36 *3022*
and his raiment was *w* as the light Mt 17:2 *3022*
and his raiment *w* as snow Mt 28:3 *3022*
shining, exceeding *w* as snow Mk 9:3 *3022*
as no fuller on earth can *w* them Mk 9:3 *3021*
side, clothed in a long *w* garment Mk 16:5 *3022*
was altered, and his raiment was *w* Lk 9:29 *3022*
for they are *w* already to harvest Jn 4:35 *3022*
And seeth two angels in *w* sitting Jn 20:12 *3022*
men stood by them in *w* apparel Acts 1:10 *3022*
w like wool, as *w* as snow Rev 1:14 *3022*
manna, and will give him a *w* stone Rev 2:17 *3022*
and they shall walk with me in *w* Rev 3:4 *3022*
shall be clothed in *w* raiment Rev 3:5 *3022*
w raiment, that thou mayest be Rev 3:18 *3022*
sitting, clothed in *w* raiment Rev 4:4 *3022*
And I saw, and behold a *w* horse Rev 6:2 *3022*
w robes were given unto every one Rev 6:11 *3022*
the Lamb, clothed with *w* robes Rev 7:9 *3022*
which are arrayed in *w* robes Rev 7:13 *3022*
made them *w* in the blood of the Rev 7:14 *3021*
And I looked, and behold a *w* cloud Rev 14:14 *3022*
w linen, and having their breasts Rev 15:6 *2986*
arrayed in fine linen, clean and *w* Rev 19:8 *2986*
opened, and behold a *w* horse Rev 19:11 *3022*
heaven followed him upon *w* horses Rev 19:14 *3022*
clothed in fine linen, *w* Rev 19:14 *3022*
And I saw a great *w* throne Rev 20:11 *3022*

WHITED

for ye are like unto *w* sepulchres Mt 23:27 *2867*
God shall smite thee, thou *w* wall Acts 23:3 *2867*

WHITER

me, and I shall be *w* than snow Ps 51:7 3835
than snow, they were *w* than milk Lam 4:7 6705

WHITHER

and *w* wilt thou go Gen 16:8 575
at every place *w* we shall come Gen 20:13
thee in all places *w* thou goest Gen 28:15 834
and *w* goest thou Gen 32:17 575
and I, *w* shall I go Gen 37:30 575
thee a place *w* he shall flee Ex 21:13
of the land *w* thou goest, lest it Ex 34:12
w I bring you, shall ye not do Lev 18:3
w I bring you to dwell therein, Lev 20:22
unto the land *w* thou sentest us Num 13:27 834
come into the land *w* I bring you Num 15:18
city of his refuge, *w* he was fled Num 35:25
city of his refuge, *w* he was fled Num 35:26
W shall we go up Deut 1:28 575
all the kingdoms *w* thou passest Deut 3:21
in the land *w* ye go to possess it Deut 4:5
land *w* ye go over to possess it Deut 4:14
w the LORD shall lead you Deut 4:27
in the land *w* ye go to possess it Deut 6:1
land *w* thou goest to possess it Deut 7:1
the land, *w* ye go to possess it Deut 11:8
w thou goest in to possess it, is Deut 11:10
w ye go to possess it, is a land Deut 11:11
land *w* thou goest to possess it Deut 11:29
w thou goest to possess them, and Deut 12:29
thou shalt let her go *w* she will Deut 21:14
w thou shalt go forth abroad Deut 23:12 8033
land *w* thou goest to possess it Deut 23:20
w thou goest to possess it Deut 28:21
among all nations *w* the LORD Deut 28:37
land *w* thou goest to possess it Deut 28:63
w the LORD thy God hath driven Deut 30:1
w the LORD thy God hath scattered Deut 30:3
land *w* thou goest to possess it Deut 30:16
w thou passest over Jordan to go Deut 30:18
as long as ye live in the land *w* Deut 31:13
w they go to be among them, and Deut 31:16
w ye go over Jordan to possess it Deut 32:47
die in the mount *w* thou goest up Deut 32:50
w the men went I wot not Josh 2:5 575
and the old man said, *W* goest thou Judg 19:17 575
for *w* thou goest, I will go Ruth 1:16
him and to his servant, *W* went ye 1Sa 10:14 575
W have ye made a road to day 1Sa 27:10 413
And David said, *W* shall I go up 2Sa 2:1 575
w shall I cause my shame to go 2Sa 13:13 575
seeing I go *w* I may, return thou, 2Sa 15:20
w they went down 2Sa 17:18 8033
and go not forth thence any *w* 1Kin 2:36 575
out, and walkest abroad any *w* 1Kin 2:42 575
land *w* they were carried captives 1Kin 8:47
w my lord hath not sent to seek 1Kin 18:10
shall carry thee *w* I know not 1Kin 18:12
w he is gone down to possess it 1Kin 21:18
And he said, Thy servant went no *w* 2Kin 5:25 575
land *w* they are carried captive 2Chr 6:37
w they have carried them captives 2Chr 6:38 834
w he had fled from the presence 2Chr 10:2 834
And the rulers knew not *w* I went Neh 2:16 575
W the tribes go up, the tribes of Ps 122:4 8033
W shall I go from thy spirit Ps 139:7 575
or *w* shall I flee from thy Ps 139:7 575
in the grave, *w* thou goest Eccl 9:10
W is thy beloved gone, O thou Song 6:1 575
w is thy beloved turned aside Song 6:1 575
w we flee for help to be Is 20:6
the places *w* I have driven them Jer 8:3
unto thee, *W* shall we go forth Jer 15:2 575
the lands *w* he had driven them Jer 16:15

w the LORD had sent him to Jer 19:14 834
place *w* they have led him captive Jer 22:12
countries *w* I have driven them Jer 23:3
all countries *w* I had driven them Jer 23:8
in all places *w* I shall drive Jer 24:9
seek the peace of the city *w* I Jer 29:7
the places *w* I have driven you Jer 29:14
the nations *w* I have driven them Jer 29:18
nations *w* I have scattered thee Jer 30:11
w I have driven them in mine Jer 32:37
w it seemeth good and convenient Jer 40:4 413
of all places *w* they were driven Jer 40:12
in the place *w* ye desire to go and Jer 42:22
w they had been driven, to dwell Jer 43:5
w ye be gone to dwell, that ye Jer 44:8
a prey in all places *w* thou goest Jer 45:5
the nations *w* I have driven thee Jer 46:28
there shall be no nation *w* the Jer 49:36
w the spirit was to go, they went Eze 1:12
the Gentiles, *w* I will drive them Eze 4:13
remember me among the nations *w* Eze 6:9
but to the place *w* the head Eze 10:11 834
among the heathen *w* they come Eze 12:16
the people *w* they were scattered Eze 29:13
w they went, they profaned my Eze 36:20
among the heathen, *w* they went Eze 36:21
among the heathen, *w* ye went Eze 36:22
w they be gone, and will gather Eze 37:21
shall live *w* the river cometh Eze 47:9
countries *w* thou hast driven them Dan 9:7
of the place *w* ye have sold them Joel 3:7
Then said I, *W* goest thou Zec 2:2 575
W do these bear the ephah Zec 5:10 575
and place, *w* he himself would come Lk 10:1 3757
unto the village, *w* they went Lk 24:28 3757
whence it cometh, and *w* it goeth Jn 3:8 *4226*
ship was at the land *w* they went Jn 6:21
W will he go, that we shall not Jn 7:35 *4226*
I know whence I came, and *w* I go Jn 8:14 *4226*
tell whence I come, and *w* I go Jn 8:14 *4226*
w I go, ye cannot come Jn 8:21 *3699*
he saith, *W* I go, ye cannot come Jn 8:22 *3699*
darkness knoweth not *w* he goeth Jn 12:35 *4226*
the Jews, *W* I go, ye cannot come Jn 13:33 *3699*
said unto him, Lord, *w* goest thou Jn 13:36 *4226*
W I go, thou canst not follow me Jn 13:36 *3699*
w I go ye know, and the way ye Jn 14:4 *3699*
Lord, we know not *w* thou goest Jn 14:5 *4226*
of you asketh me, *W* goest thou Jn 16:5 *4226*
temple, *w* the Jews always resort Jn 18:20 *3699*
and walkedst *w* thou wouldest Jn 21:18 *3699*
carry thee *w* thou wouldest not Jn 21:18 *3699*
W the forerunner is for us Heb 6:20 *3699*
went out, not knowing *w* he went Heb 11:8 *4226*
and knoweth not *w* he goeth 1Jn 2:11 *4226*

WHITHERSOEVER

thou mayest prosper *w* thou goest Josh 1:7
thy God is with thee *w* thou goest Josh 1:9
w thou sendest us, we will go Josh 1:16
W they went out, the hand of the Judg 2:15
w he turned himself, he vexed 1Sa 14:47
And David went out *w* Saul sent him 1Sa 18:5
Keilah, and went *w* they could go 1Sa 23:13 834
And I was with thee *w* thou wentest 2Sa 7:9
LORD preserved David *w* he went 2Sa 8:6
LORD preserved David *w* he went 2Sa 8:14
doest, and *w* thou turnest thyself 1Kin 2:3
w thou shalt send them, and shall 1Kin 8:44
he prospered *w* he went forth 2Kin 18:7
been with thee *w* thou hast walked 1Chr 17:8
LORD preserved David *w* he went 1Chr 18:6
LORD preserved David *w* he went 1Chr 18:13
w the king's commandment and his Est 4:3
w the king's commandment and his Est 8:17
w it turneth, it prospereth Prov 17:8
he turneth it *w* he will Prov 21:1
W the spirit was to go, they went Eze 1:20
or on the left, *w* thy face is set Eze 21:16 575
w the rivers shall come, shall Eze 47:9
I will follow thee *w* thou goest Mt 8:19
w he entered, into villages, or Mk 6:56
I will follow thee *w* thou goest Lk 9:57
may bring me on my journey *w* I go 1Cor 16:6
helm, *w* the governor listeth Jas 3:4
which follow the Lamb *w* he goeth Rev 14:4

WHO

W told thee that thou wast naked Gen 3:11 4310
the LORD, *w* appeared unto him Gen 12:7 4310
w dwelt in Sodom, and his goods, Gen 14:12 1931
W would have said unto Abraham, Gen 21:7 4310
I wot not *w* hath done this thing Gen 21:26 4310
w was born to Bethuel, son of Gen 24:15 834
w hath not left destitute my Gen 24:27 4310
w art thou, my son Gen 27:18 4310
father said unto him, *W* art thou Gen 27:32 4310
very exceedingly, and said, *W* Gen 27:33 4310
w hath withheld from thee the Gen 30:2 834
and said, *W* are those with thee Gen 33:5 4310
w answered me in the day of my Gen 35:3
generations of Esau, *w* is Edom Gen 36:1 1931
w is Edom, and these are their Gen 36:19
the Horite, *w* inhabited the land Gen 36:20
w smote Midian in the field of Gen 36:35
w is the lord of the land, spake Gen 42:30
we cannot tell *w* put our money in Gen 43:22 4310
sons, and said, *W* are these Gen 48:8 4310
w was the younger, and his left Gen 48:14 1931
w shall rouse him up Gen 49:9 4310
of thy father, *w* shall help thee Gen 49:25
w shall bless thee with blessings Gen 49:25
W made thee a prince and a judge Ex 2:14 4310
W am I, that I should go unto Ex 3:11 4310
unto him, *W* hath made man's mouth Ex 4:11 4310
or *w* maketh the dumb, or deaf, or Ex 4:11 4310
words of the LORD *w* had sent him Ex 4:28 834
W is the LORD, that I should obey Ex 5:2 4310
w stood in the way, as they came Ex 5:20 4310
w am of uncircumcised lips Ex 6:12 589
but *w* are they that shall go Ex 10:8 4310
w passed over the houses of the Ex 12:27 4310
w dwelt in Egypt, was four Ex 12:40 834
W is like unto thee, O LORD, Ex 15:11 4310
W is like thee, glorious in Ex 15:11 4310
w hath delivered you out of the Ex 18:10 834
w hath delivered the people from Ex 18:10 834
w hath betrothed her to himself, Ex 21:8 834
and said, *W* is on the LORD's side Ex 32:26 4310
w shall offer that which is for Lev 5:8
W shall offer it before the LORD, Lev 12:7
w art the priest, so shall it be Lev 27:12
law of the Nazarite *w* hath vowed Num 6:21 834
w were the princes of the tribes, Num 7:2 1992
w were defiled by the dead body Num 9:6 834
W shall give us flesh to eat Num 11:4 4310
W shall give us flesh to eat Num 11:18 4310
w is faithful in all mine house Num 12:7 1931
w returned, and made all the Num 14:36
shew *w* are his, and *w* is holy Num 16:5 4310
w had fought against the former Num 21:26 1931
W can count the dust of Jacob, and Num 23:10 4310
w shall stir him up Num 24:9 4310
w shall live when God doeth this Num 24:23 4310
w were weeping before the door of Num 25:6 1992
w strove against Moses and against Num 26:9 834
w were fifty and three thousand and Num 26:47
w numbered the children of Israel Num 26:63 834
w shall ask counsel for him after Num 27:21
w went out to battle, and between Num 31:27
W went in the way before you, to Deut 1:33
w shall hear report of thee, and Deut 2:25 834
w hath God so nigh unto them, as Deut 4:7 834
w dwelt at Heshbon Deut 4:46 834
w are all of us here alive this Deut 5:3 428
For *w* is there of all flesh, that Deut 5:26 4310
W led thee through that great and Deut 8:15
w brought thee forth water out of Deut 8:15
W fed thee in the wilderness with Deut 8:16
W can stand before the children Deut 9:2 4310
it be not known *w* hath slain him Deut 21:1 4310
W shall go up for us to heaven, Deut 30:12 4310
W shall go over the sea for us, Deut 30:13 4310
W said unto his father and to his Deut 33:9
w rideth upon the heaven in thy Deut 33:26
w is like unto thee, O people Deut 33:29 4310
w is the sword of thy excellency Deut 33:29 834
Joshua said unto them, *W* are ye Josh 9:8 4310
w smote them, and chased them unto Josh 11:8
w dwelt in Heshbon, and ruled from Josh 12:2
w remained of the remnant of the Josh 13:12 1931
W answered, Give me a blessing Josh 15:19
both they *w* are of Beth-shean and Josh 17:16 834
they *w* are of the valley of Josh 17:16 834
w were of the children of Levi, Josh 21:10
W shall go up for us against the Judg 1:1 4310
w had seen all the great works of Judg 2:7 834
w delivered them, even Othniel Judg 3:9
w said, Keep silence Judg 3:19
another, *W* hath done this thing Judg 6:29 4310
w also was gathered after him Judg 6:35
w is Gideon, and all the people Judg 7:1 4310
w had delivered them out of the Judg 8:34
W is Abimelech Judg 9:28 4310
w is Shechem, that we should Judg 9:28 4310
W is Abimelech, that we should Judg 9:38 4310
w did with her according to his Judg 11:39
said, *W* hath done this Judg 15:6 4310
w made thereof a graven image and Judg 17:4
of his sons, *w* became his priest Judg 17:5
w was a Levite, and he sojourned Judg 17:7 1931
w when they came to mount Ephraim Judg 18:2
unto him, *W* brought thee hither Judg 18:3 4310
father, *w* was born unto Israel Judg 18:29 834
w took to him a concubine out of Judg 19:1
W is there among all the tribes Judg 21:5 4310
w was of the kindred of Elimelech Ruth 2:3 834
w hath not left off his kindness Ruth 2:20 834
And he said, *W* art thou Ruth 3:9 4310
she said, *W* art thou, my daughter Ruth 3:16 4310
the LORD, *w* shall intreat for him 1Sa 2:25 4310
w shall deliver us out of the 1Sa 4:8 4310
W is able to stand before this 1Sa 6:20 4310
and said, But *w* is their father 1Sa 10:12 4310
w himself saved you out of all 1Sa 10:19 834
W is he that said, Shall Saul 1Sa 11:12 4310
now, and see *w* is gone from us 1Sa 14:17 4310
w hath wrought this great 1Sa 14:45 834
w is a cunning player on an harp 1Sa 16:16
be, that the man *w* killeth him 1Sa 17:25 834
for *w* is this uncircumcised 1Sa 17:26 4310
And David said unto Saul, *W* am I 1Sa 18:18 4310
to Jonathan, *W* shall tell me 1Sa 20:10 4310
w is so faithful among all thy 1Sa 22:14 4310
is, and *w* hath seen him there 1Sa 23:22 4310
servants, and said, *W* is David 1Sa 25:10 4310
and *w* is the son of Jesse 1Sa 25:10 4310
W will go down with me to Saul to 1Sa 26:6 4310
for *w* can stretch forth his hand 1Sa 26:9 4310
W art thou that criest to the 1Sa 26:14 4310
w is like to thee in Israel 1Sa 26:15 4310
w hath preserved us, and delivered 1Sa 30:23
For *w* will hearken unto you in 1Sa 30:24 4310
And he said unto me, *W* art thou 2Sa 1:8 4310
w clothed you in scarlet, with 2Sa 1:24 4310
w put on ornaments of gold upon 2Sa 1:24 4310
w lay on a bed at noon 2Sa 4:5 4310
w hath redeemed my soul out of 2Sa 4:9 834
w thought that I would have given 2Sa 4:10 834
Israel today, *w* uncovered himself 2Sa 6:20 834
and he said, *W* am I, O Lord GOD 2Sa 7:18 4310
of their host, *w* died there 2Sa 10:18
W smote Abimelech the son of 2Sa 11:21 4310
W can tell whether GOD will be 2Sa 12:22 4310
W shall then say, Wherefore hast 2Sa 16:10 4310
w is worthy to be praised 2Sa 22:4
For *w* is God, save the LORD 2Sa 22:32 4310
w is a rock, save our God 2Sa 22:32
the man *w* was raised up on high, 2Sa 23:1
w had done many acts, he slew two 2Sa 23:20
w shall sit on the throne of my 1Kin 1:20 4310
w should sit on the throne of my 1Kin 1:27 4310
w hath made me an house, as he 1Kin 2:24 834
head, *w* fell upon two men more 1Kin 2:32 4310
for *w* is able to judge this thy 1Kin 3:9 4310
w keepest covenant and mercy with 1Kin 8:23
W hast kept with thy servant 1Kin 8:24 834
them *w* carried them captive 1Kin 8:50
w brought forth their fathers out 1Kin 9:9 834
w was yet in Egypt 1Kin 12:2 1931
w have spoken to me, saying, Make 1Kin 12:9 834
Adoram, *w* was over the tribute 1Kin 12:18 834
w was disobedient unto the word 1Kin 13:26 834
w kept my commandments 1Kin 14:8 834
w followed me with all his heart, 1Kin 14:8 834
w shall cut off the house of 1Kin 14:14 834
w did sin 1Kin 14:16 834
and *w* made Israel to sin 1Kin 14:16 834
w was of the inhabitants of 1Kin 17:1
w was plowing with twelve yoke of 1Kin 19:19 1931
he said, *W* shall order the battle 1Kin 20:14 4310
the nobles *w* were the inhabitants 1Kin 21:11 834
W shall persuade Ahab, that he 1Kin 22:20 4310
of Nebat, *w* made Israel to sin 1Kin 22:52 834
w brought the vessels to her 2Kin 4:5 1992
w spake when the king came down 2Kin 7:17 834
w said to him, What said Elisha 2Kin 8:14 4310
Zimri peace, *w* slew his master 2Kin 9:31
W is on my side? *w* 2Kin 9:32 4310
but *w* slew all these 2Kin 10:9 4310
king of Judah, and said, *W* are ye 2Kin 10:13 4310
w made Israel to sin, Jehu 2Kin 10:29 834
w made Israel sin, but walked 2Kin 13:6 834
son of Nebat, *w* made Israel sin 2Kin 13:11 834
of Nebat, *w* made Israel to sin 2Kin 14:24 834
of Nebat, *w* made Israel to sin 2Kin 15:9 834
of Nebat, *w* made Israel to sin 2Kin 15:18 834
of Nebat, *w* made Israel to sin 2Kin 15:24 834
of Nebat, *w* made Israel to sin 2Kin 15:28 834
w brought you up out of the land 2Kin 17:36 834
W are they among all the gods of 2Kin 18:35 4310
w made Israel to sin, had made, 2Kin 23:15 834
w proclaimed these words 2Kin 23:16 834
w transgressed in the thing 1Chr 2:7 834
w had three and twenty cities in 1Chr 2:22
w had the dominion in Moab, and 1Chr 4:22 4310
w dwelt in Aroer, even unto Nebo 1Chr 5:8 1931
Hagarites, *w* fell by their hand 1Chr 5:10
w stood on his right hand, even 1Chr 6:39
w built Beth-horon the nether, and 1Chr 7:24
w is the father of Birzavith 1Chr 7:31 1931
w built Ono, and Lod, with the 1Chr 8:12 4310
w were heads of the fathers of 1Chr 8:13 1992
w drove away the inhabitants of 1Chr 8:13 1992
w were carried away to Babylon 1Chr 9:1
W hitherto waited in the king's 1Chr 9:18
w was the firstborn of Shallum 1Chr 9:31 1931
w remaining in the chambers were 1Chr 9:33
w strengthened themselves with 1Chr 11:10
w was one of the three mighties 1Chr 11:12 1931
of Kabzeel, *w* had done many acts 1Chr 11:22
w was chief of the captains, and 1Chr 12:18
w were expressed by name, to give 1Chr 16:41 834
W am I, O LORD God, and what is 1Chr 17:16 4310
w came and pitched before Medeba 1Chr 19:7
w were clothed in sackcloth, fell 1Chr 21:16
to thee, *w* shall be a man of rest 1Chr 22:9 1931
Mahli came Eleazar, *w* had no sons 1Chr 24:28
w should prophesy with harps, 1Chr 25:1
w prophesied with a harp, to give 1Chr 25:3
w with his brethren and sons were 1Chr 25:9 1931
w was mighty among the thirty, and 1Chr 27:6
w then is willing to consecrate 1Chr 29:5 4310
But *w* am I, and what is my people, 1Chr 29:14 4310
for *w* can judge this thy people, 2Chr 1:10 4310
But *w* is able to build him an 2Chr 2:6 4310
w am I then, that I should build 2Chr 2:6 4310
w hath given to David the king a 2Chr 2:12 834
w hath with his hands fulfilled 2Chr 6:4
w were left after them in the 2Chr 8:8 834
w was in Egypt, whither he had 2Chr 10:2 1931
w willingly offered himself unto 2Chr 17:16
W shall entice Ahab king of 2Chr 18:19 4310
w is with you in the judgment 2Chr 19:6
w didst drive out the inhabitants 2Chr 20:7
w is mentioned in the book of the 2Chr 20:34 834
of Israel, *w* did very wickedly 2Chr 20:35 1931
w sought the LORD with all his 2Chr 22:9 834
w was sixteen years old, and made 2Chr 26:1 1931
w had understanding in the 2Chr 26:5
Israel, *w* smote him with a great 2Chr 28:5
w therefore gave them up to 2Chr 30:7
w stopped all the fountains, and 2Chr 32:4
W was there among all the gods of 2Chr 32:14 4310
w sent unto him to enquire of the 2Chr 32:31
w sent you to enquire of the LORD 2Chr 34:26
w is with me, that he destroy 2Chr 35:21 834
w had made him swear by God 2Chr 36:13 834
w slew their young men with the 2Chr 36:17
W is there among you of all his 2Chr 36:23 4310
W is there among you of all his Ezr 1:3 4310
w were ancient men, that had seen Ezr 3:12
W hath commanded you to build Ezr 5:3 4479

W

W hath ears to hear, let him hear	Mt 13:9	3588
W hath ears to hear, let him hear	Mt 13:43	3588
W, when he had found one pearl of	Mt 13:46	3739
W is the greatest in the kingdom	Mt 18:1	5101
saying, W then can be saved	Mt 19:25	5101
city was moved, saying, W is this	Mt 21:10	5101
w gave thee this authority	Mt 21:23	5101
W then is a faithful and wise	Mt 24:45	5101
w called his own servants, and	Mt 25:14	
priest, w was called Caiaphas,	Mt 26:3	3588
Christ, W is he that smote thee	Mt 26:68	5101
w also himself was Jesus'	Mt 27:57	3739
w also were in the ship mending	Mk 1:19	841
I know thee w thou art, the Holy	Mk 1:24	5101
w can forgive sins but God only	Mk 2:7	5101
W is my mother, or my brethren	Mk 3:33	5101
w, when they have heard the word,	Mk 4:16	3739
W had his dwelling among the	Mk 5:3	3739
and said, W touched my clothes	Mk 5:30	5101
and sayest thou, W touched me	Mk 5:31	5101
w should be the greatest	Mk 9:34	5101
themselves, W then can be saved	Mk 10:26	5101
w gave thee this authority to do	Mk 11:28	5101
w left his house, and gave	Mk 13:34	
w had committed murder in the	Mk 15:7	3748
w passed by, coming out of the	Mk 15:21	
(W also, when he was in Galilee,	Mk 15:41	3739
W shall roll us away the stone	Mk 16:3	5101
with her, w was called barren	Lk 1:36	3588
w hath warned you to flee from	Lk 3:7	5101
I know thee w thou art	Lk 4:34	5101
w seeing Jesus fell on his face,	Lk 5:12	2532
saying, W is this which speaketh	Lk 5:21	5101
W can forgive sins, but God alone	Lk 5:21	5101
w was dear unto him, was sick, and	Lk 7:2	3739
a prophet, would have known w	Lk 7:39	5101
W is this that forgiveth sins	Lk 7:49	5101
And Jesus said, W touched me	Lk 8:45	5101
and sayest thou, W touched me	Lk 8:45	5101
but w is this, of whom I hear	Lk 9:9	5101
W appeared in glory, and spake of	Lk 9:31	3739
and no man knoweth w the Son is	Lk 10:22	5101
w the Father is, but the Son, and	Lk 10:22	5101
unto Jesus, And w is my neighbour	Lk 10:29	5101
w made me a judge or a divider	Lk 12:14	5101
W then is that faithful and wise	Lk 12:42	5101
w will commit to your trust the	Lk 16:11	5101
w shall give you that which is	Lk 16:12	5101
w were covetous, heard all these	Lk 16:14	
it said, W then can be saved	Lk 18:26	5101
W shall not receive manifold more	Lk 18:30	3739
he sought to see Jesus w he was	Lk 19:3	5101
or w is he that gave thee this	Lk 20:2	5101
Prophesy, w is it that smote thee	Lk 22:64	5101
w himself also was at Jerusalem	Lk 23:7	
(W for a certain sedition made in	Lk 23:19	3748
w also himself waited for the	Lk 23:51	3739
Jerusalem to ask him, W art thou	Jn 1:19	5101
said they unto him, W art thou	Jn 1:22	5101
w coming after me is preferred	Jn 1:27	3588
w it is that saith to thee, Give	Jn 4:10	5101
that was healed wist not w it was	Jn 5:13	5101
w can hear it	Jn 6:60	5101
w they were that believed not	Jn 6:64	5101
and w should betray him	Jn 6:64	5101
w goeth about to kill thee	Jn 7:20	5101
But this people w knoweth not the	Jn 7:49	3588
said they unto him, W art thou	Jn 8:25	5101
w did sin, this man, or his	Jn 9:2	5101
your son, w ye say was born blind	Jn 9:19	3739
or w hath opened his eyes, we	Jn 9:21	5101
W is he, Lord, that I might	Jn 9:36	5101
w is this Son of man	Jn 12:34	5101
w hath believed our report	Jn 12:38	5101
For he knew w should betray him	Jn 13:11	3588
that he should ask w it should be	Jn 13:24	5101
saith unto him, Lord, w is it	Jn 13:25	5101
w had made a fire of coals	Jn 18:18	
durst ask him, W art thou	Jn 21:12	5101
w was surnamed Justus, and	Acts 1:23	3739
W seeing Peter and John about to	Acts 3:3	3739
W by the mouth of thy servant	Acts 4:25	3588
w by the apostles was surnamed	Acts 4:36	3588
w was slain;	Acts 5:36	3739
W made thee a ruler and a judge	Acts 7:27	5101
W made thee a ruler and a judge	Acts 7:35	5101
w received the lively oracles to	Acts 7:38	3739
W found favour before God, and	Acts 7:46	3739
W have received the law by the	Acts 7:53	3748
W, when they were come down,	Acts 8:15	3748
w had the charge of all her	Acts 8:27	3739
w shall declare his generation	Acts 8:33	5101
And he said, W art thou, Lord	Acts 9:5	5101
w, when he cometh, shall speak	Acts 10:32	3739
w went about doing good, and	Acts 10:38	3739
w did eat and drink with him after	Acts 10:41	3748
W shall tell thee words, whereby	Acts 11:14	3749
w believed on the Lord Jesus	Acts 11:17	
W, when he came, and had seen the	Acts 11:23	3739
w called for Barnabas and Saul, and	Acts 13:7	3778
(w also is called Paul,) filled	Acts 13:9	3739
w are his witnesses unto the	Acts 13:31	3748
w, speaking to them, persuaded	Acts 13:43	3748
mother's womb, w never had walked	Acts 14:8	3739
w stedfastly beholding him, and	Acts 14:9	3739
W in times past suffered all	Acts 14:16	3739
w persuaded the people, and,	Acts 14:19	2532
Lord, w doeth all these things	Acts 15:17	3588
w shall also tell you the same	Acts 15:27	846
w departed from them from	Acts 15:38	3588
W, having received such a charge,	Acts 16:24	3739
w coming thither went into the	Acts 17:10	3748
w, when he was come, helped them	Acts 18:27	3739
but w are ye?	Acts 19:15	5101
w said to Paul through the Spirit	Acts 21:4	3748
W immediately took soldiers and	Acts 21:32	3739
and demanded w he was, and what he	Acts 21:33	5101
W said, Canst thou speak Greek	Acts 21:37	3588
And I answered, W art thou, Lord	Acts 22:8	5101
w hath something to say unto thee	Acts 23:18	
W, when they came to Caesarea, and	Acts 23:33	3748
w informed the governor against	Acts 24:1	3748
W also hath gone about to profane	Acts 24:6	3739
W ought to have been here before	Acts 24:19	3739
And I said, W art thou, Lord	Acts 26:15	5101
w received us, and lodged us three	Acts 28:7	3739
W also honoured us with many	Acts 28:10	3739
W, when they had examined me,	Acts 28:18	3748
of men, w hold the truth in	Rom 1:18	3588
W changed the truth of God into a	Rom 1:25	3748
Creator, w is blessed for ever	Rom 1:25	3739
W knowing the judgment of God,	Rom 1:32	3748
W will render to every man	Rom 2:6	3739
To them w by patient continuance	Rom 2:7	
w by the letter and circumcision	Rom 2:27	3588
unrighteous w taketh vengeance	Rom 3:5	3588
it saith to them w are under the	Rom 3:19	
w are not of the circumcision	Rom 4:12	3588
but w also walk in the steps of	Rom 4:12	3588
w is the father of us all,	Rom 4:16	3739
w quickeneth the dead, and calleth	Rom 4:17	3588
W against hope believed in hope,	Rom 4:18	3739
W was delivered for our offences,	Rom 4:25	3739
w is the figure of him that was	Rom 5:14	3739
even to him w is raised from the	Rom 7:4	
w shall deliver me from the body	Rom 7:24	5101
w walk not after the flesh, but	Rom 8:1	
w walk not after the flesh, but	Rom 8:4	
but by reason of him w hath	Rom 8:20	
God, to them w are the called	Rom 8:28	
be for us, w can be against us	Rom 8:31	5101
W shall lay any thing to the	Rom 8:33	5101
W is he that condemneth	Rom 8:34	5101
w is even at the right hand of	Rom 8:34	3739
w also maketh intercession for us	Rom 8:34	3739
W shall separate us from the love	Rom 8:35	5101
W are Israelites	Rom 9:4	3748
w is over all, God blessed for	Rom 9:5	3588
For w hath resisted his will	Rom 9:19	5101
w art thou that repliest against	Rom 9:20	5101
W shall ascend into heaven	Rom 10:6	5101
W shall descend into the deep	Rom 10:7	5101
w hath believed our report	Rom 10:16	5101
w have not bowed the knee to the	Rom 11:4	3748
For w hath known the mind of the	Rom 11:34	5101
or w hath been his counsellor	Rom 11:34	5101
Or w hath first given to him, and	Rom 11:35	5101
another, w is weak, eateth herbs	Rom 14:2	3588
W art thou that judgest another	Rom 14:4	5101
that man w eateth with offence	Rom 14:20	3588
W have for my life laid down	Rom 16:4	3748
w is the firstfruits of Achaia	Rom 16:5	3739
w bestowed much labour on us	Rom 16:6	3748
w are of note among the apostles,	Rom 16:7	3748
w also were in Christ before me	Rom 16:7	3739
and Tryphosa, w labour in the Lord	Rom 16:12	3588
w wrote this epistle, salute you	Rom 16:22	3588
W shall also confirm you unto the	1Cor 1:8	3739
w of God is made unto us wisdom,	1Cor 1:30	3739
For w hath known the mind of the	1Cor 2:16	5101
W then is Paul, and	1Cor 3:5	5101
w is Apollos, but ministers by	1Cor 3:5	5101
w both will bring to light the	1Cor 4:5	3739
For w maketh thee to differ from	1Cor 4:7	5101
w is my beloved son, and faithful	1Cor 4:17	3739
the Lord, w shall bring you into	1Cor 4:17	3739
set them to judge w are least	1Cor 6:4	
W goeth a warfare any time at his	1Cor 9:7	5100
w planteth a vineyard, and eateth	1Cor 9:7	5100
or w feedeth a flock, and eateth	1Cor 9:7	5100
w will not suffer you to be	1Cor 10:13	3739
w shall prepare himself to the	1Cor 14:8	5101
W comforteth us in all our	2Cor 1:4	3588
W delivered us from so great a	2Cor 1:10	5101
w was preached among you by us,	2Cor 1:19	3588
W hath also sealed us, and given	2Cor 1:22	3588
w is he then that maketh me glad,	2Cor 2:2	5101
w is sufficient for these things	2Cor 2:16	5101
W also hath made us able	2Cor 3:6	3739
w is the image of God, should	2Cor 4:4	3739
w commanded the light to shine	2Cor 4:6	3588
w also hath given unto us the	2Cor 5:5	3588
w hath reconciled us to himself	2Cor 5:18	3588
to be sin for us, w knew no sin	2Cor 5:21	
w have begun before, not only to	2Cor 8:10	3748
but w was also chosen of the	2Cor 8:19	
w in presence am base among you,	2Cor 10:1	3739
W is weak, and I am not weak	2Cor 11:29	5101
w is offended, and I burn not	2Cor 11:29	5101
w raised him from the dead	Gal 1:1	3588
W gave himself for our sins, that	Gal 1:4	3588
w separated me from my mother's	Gal 1:15	3588
w was with me, being a Greek, was	Gal 2:3	3588
w came in privily to spy out our	Gal 2:4	3748
But of these w seemed to be	Gal 2:6	
for they w seemed to be somewhat	Gal 2:6	
w seemed to be pillars, perceived	Gal 2:9	3588
We w are Jews by nature, and not	Gal 2:15	
w loved me, and gave himself for	Gal 2:20	3588
w hath bewitched you, that ye	Gal 3:1	5101
But he w was of the bondwoman was	Gal 4:23	
w did hinder you that ye should	Gal 5:7	5101
especially unto them w are of the	Gal 6:10	
For neither they themselves w are	Gal 6:13	
w hath blessed us with all	Eph 1:3	3588
w worketh all things after the	Eph 1:11	
w first trusted in Christ	Eph 1:12	3588
of his power to us-ward w believe	Eph 1:19	3588
w were dead in trespasses and sins	Eph 2:1	
w is rich in mercy, for his great	Eph 2:4	
w are called Uncircumcision by	Eph 2:11	3588
But now in Christ Jesus ye w	Eph 2:13	3739
w hath made both one, and hath	Eph 2:14	3739
w am less than the least of all	Eph 3:8	
w created all things by Jesus	Eph 3:9	3588
w is above all, and through all,	Eph 4:6	3588
W being past feeling have given	Eph 4:19	3748
w is an idolater, hath any	Eph 5:5	3739
W, being in the form of God,	Phil 2:6	
w will naturally care for your	Phil 2:20	3748
shame, w mind earthly things	Phil 3:19	3588
W shall change our vile body,	Phil 3:21	5101
w is for you a faithful minister	Col 1:7	5101
W also declared unto us your love	Col 1:8	3588
W hath delivered us from the	Col 1:13	3739
W is the image of the invisible	Col 1:15	3739
w is the beginning, the firstborn	Col 1:18	3739
W now rejoice in my sufferings	Col 1:24	
w hath raised him from the dead	Col 2:12	3588
w is our life, shall appear, then	Col 3:4	
w is a beloved brother, and a	Col 4:7	
beloved brother, w is one of you	Col 4:9	3739
w are of the circumcision	Col 4:11	3588
w is one of you, a servant of	Col 4:12	3588
w hath called you unto his	1Th 2:12	5101
W both killed the Lord Jesus, and	1Th 2:15	3588
w hath also given unto us his	1Th 4:8	5101
w are of the day, be sober,	1Th 5:8	
W died for us, that, whether we	1Th 5:10	3588
calleth you, w also will do it	1Th 5:24	3739
to you w are troubled rest with	2Th 1:7	
W shall be punished with	2Th 1:9	3748
W opposeth and exalteth himself	2Th 2:4	3588
only he w now letteth will let,	2Th 2:7	
damned w believed not the truth	2Th 2:12	3588
w shall stablish you, and keep you	2Th 3:3	3739
w hath enabled me, for that he	1Ti 1:12	3588
W was before a blasphemer, and a	1Ti 1:13	3588
W will have all men to be saved,	1Ti 2:4	3739
W gave himself a ransom for all,	1Ti 2:6	3588
w is the Saviour of all men,	1Ti 4:10	3739
especially they w labour in the	1Ti 5:17	
w quickeneth all things, and	1Ti 6:13	3588
w before Pontius Pilate witnessed	1Ti 6:13	3588
shew, w is the blessed and only	1Ti 6:15	3588
W only hath immortality, dwelling	1Ti 6:16	3588
w giveth us richly all things to	1Ti 6:17	3588
W hath saved us, and called us	2Ti 1:9	3588
w hath abolished death, and hath	2Ti 1:10	
w shall be able to teach others	2Ti 2:2	3748
that he may please him w hath	2Ti 2:4	
W concerning the truth have erred	2Ti 2:18	3748
w are taken captive by him at his	2Ti 2:26	
w shall judge the quick and the	2Ti 4:1	3588
w subvert whole houses, teaching	Titus 1:11	3748
W gave himself for us, that he	Titus 2:14	3739
w at sundry times and in divers	Heb 1:1	
W being the brightness of his	Heb 1:3	
W maketh his angels spirits, and	Heb 1:7	3739
w shall be heirs of salvation	Heb 1:14	
w was made a little lower than	Heb 2:9	3588
they w are sanctified are all of	Heb 2:11	
deliver them w through fear of	Heb 2:15	3745
W was faithful to him that	Heb 3:2	
inasmuch as he w hath builded the	Heb 3:3	
W can have compassion on the	Heb 5:2	
W in the days of his flesh, when	Heb 5:7	3739
even those w by reason of use	Heb 5:14	
for those w were once enlightened	Heb 6:4	
followers of them w through faith	Heb 6:12	
w have fled for refuge to lay	Heb 6:18	3588
w met Abraham returning from the	Heb 7:1	3588
w receive the office of the	Heb 7:5	3588
w receiveth tithes, payed tithes	Heb 7:9	3588
W is made, not after the law of a	Heb 7:16	3739
w is holy, harmless, undefiled,	Heb 7:26	
W needeth not daily, as those	Heb 7:27	3739
w is consecrated for evermore	Heb 7:28	
w is set on the right hand of the	Heb 8:1	3739
W serve unto the example and	Heb 8:5	3748
w through the eternal Spirit	Heb 9:14	3739
w hath trodden under foot the Son	Heb 10:29	3588
But we are not of them w draw	Heb 10:39	
him faithful w had promised	Heb 11:11	
as seeing him w is invisible	Heb 11:27	
W through faith subdued kingdoms,	Heb 11:33	3739
w for the joy that was set before	Heb 12:2	3739
w for one morsel of meat sold his	Heb 12:16	3739
For if they escaped not w refused	Heb 12:25	
w have spoken unto you the word	Heb 13:7	3748
W is a wise man and endued with	Jas 3:13	5101
w is able to save and to destroy	Jas 4:12	3588
w art thou that judgest another	Jas 4:12	5101
the hire of the labourers w have	Jas 5:4	3588
w have spoken in the name of the	Jas 5:10	3739
W are kept by the power of God	1Pet 1:5	3588
w prophesied of the grace that	1Pet 1:10	3588
w without respect of persons	1Pet 1:17	3588
W verily was foreordained before	1Pet 1:20	
W by him do believe in God, that	1Pet 1:21	3588
shew forth the praises of him w	1Pet 2:9	
W did no sin, neither was guile	1Pet 2:22	3739
W, when he was reviled, reviled	1Pet 2:23	3739
W his own self bare our sins in	1Pet 2:24	3739
w trusted in God, adorned	1Pet 3:5	3588
w is he that will harm you, if ye	1Pet 3:13	5101
W is gone into heaven, and is on	1Pet 3:22	3739
W shall give account to him that	1Pet 4:5	3739
w am also an elder, and a witness	1Pet 5:1	3588
w hath called us unto his eternal	1Pet 5:10	3588
w privily shall bring in damnable	2Pet 2:1	3748
of Bosor, w loved the wages of	2Pet 2:15	3739

escaped from them *w* live in error	2Pet 2:18	
W is a liar but he that denieth	1Jn 2:22	*5101*
w was of that wicked one, and slew	1Jn 3:12	
That he *w* loveth God love his	1Jn 4:21	
W is he that overcometh the world	1Jn 5:5	*5101*
w confess not that Jesus Christ	2Jn 7	*3588*
w loveth to have the preeminence	3Jn 9	*3588*
w were before of old ordained to	Jude 4	*3588*
w should walk after their own	Jude 18	
These be they *w* separate	Jude 19	
W bare record of the word of God,	Rev 1:2	*3739*
w is the faithful witness, and the	Rev 1:5	
w also am your brother, and	Rev 1:9	*3588*
w walketh in the midst of the	Rev 2:1	*3588*
w was slain among you, where	Rev 2:13	*3739*
Balaam, *w* taught Balac to cast a	Rev 2:14	*3739*
w hath his eyes like unto a flame	Rev 2:18	*3588*
w liveth for ever and ever,	Rev 4:9	*3588*
W is worthy to open the book, and	Rev 5:2	*5101*
and *w* shall be able to stand	Rev 6:17	*5101*
w created heaven, and the things	Rev 10:6	*3739*
w was to rule all nations with a	Rev 12:5	*3739*
saying, *W* is like unto the beast	Rev 13:4	*5101*
w is able to make war with him	Rev 13:4	*5101*
w worship the beast and his image,	Rev 14:11	*3588*
W shall not fear thee, O Lord, and	Rev 15:4	*5101*
w liveth for ever and ever	Rev 15:7	*3588*
is the Lord God *w* judgeth her	Rev 18:8	*3588*
w have committed fornication and	Rev 18:9	*3588*

WHOLE

watered the *w* face of the ground	Gen 2:6	
compasseth the *w* land of Havilah	Gen 2:11	
compasseth the *w* land of Ethiopia	Gen 2:13	
that were under the *w* heaven	Gen 7:19	3605
were on the face of the *w* earth	Gen 8:9	3605
and of them was the *w* earth	Gen 9:19	3605
the *w* earth was of one language,	Gen 11:1	3605
upon the face of the *w* earth	Gen 11:4	3605
Is not the *w* land before thee	Gen 13:9	3605
so the *w* age of Jacob was an	Gen 47:28	
covered the face of the *w* earth	Ex 10:15	3605
and the *w* assembly of the	Ex 12:6	3605
the *w* congregation of the	Ex 16:2	3605
to kill this *w* assembly with	Ex 16:3	
as Aaron spake unto the *w*	Ex 16:10	3605
the *w* mount quaked greatly	Ex 19:18	3605
burn the *w* ram upon the altar	Ex 29:18	
the *w* rump, it shall he take off	Lev 3:9	8549
Even the *w* bullock shall he carry	Lev 4:12	
if the *w* congregation of Israel	Lev 4:13	3605
he shall offer one out of the *w*	Lev 7:14	3605
Moses burnt the *w* ram upon the	Lev 8:21	
the *w* house of Israel, bewail the	Lev 10:6	3605
within a *w* year after it is sold	Lev 25:29	8552
the charge of the *w* congregation	Num 3:7	3605
thou shalt gather the *w* assembly	Num 8:9	
of a *w* piece shalt thou make them	Num 10:2	4749
But even a *w* month, until it come	Num 11:20	3117
that they may eat a *w* month	Num 11:21	3117
the *w* congregation said unto them	Num 14:2	3605
you, according to your *w* number	Num 14:29	3605
even the *w* congregation, into the	Num 20:1	3605
Israel, even the *w* congregation,	Num 20:22	3605
that are under the *w* heaven	Deut 2:25	3605
all nations under the *w* heaven	Deut 4:19	3605
of the LORD thy God of *w* stones	Deut 27:6	8003
that the *w* land thereof is	Deut 29:23	3605
w burnt sacrifice upon thine	Deut 33:10	3632
in the camp, till they were *w*	Josh 5:8	2421
of Moses, an altar of *w* stones	Josh 8:31	8003
not to go down about a *w* day	Josh 10:13	8549
So Joshua took the *w* land	Josh 11:23	
the *w* congregation of the	Josh 18:1	3605
the *w* congregation of the	Josh 22:12	3605
Thus saith the *w* congregation of	Josh 22:16	3605
with the *w* congregation of Israel	Josh 22:18	3605
and was there four *w* months	Judg 19:2	3117
the *w* congregation sent some to	Judg 21:13	3605
because my life is yet *w* in me	2Sa 1:9	3605
good to the *w* house of Benjamin	2Sa 3:19	3605
even among the *w* multitude of	2Sa 6:19	3605
the *w* family is risen against	2Sa 14:7	3605
the *w* house he overlaid with gold	1Kin 6:22	3605
also the *w* altar that was by the	1Kin 6:22	3605
the *w* kingdom out of his hand	1Kin 11:34	
For the *w* house of Ahab shall	2Kin 9:8	3605
blessed the *w* congregation of	2Chr 6:3	
and sought him with their *w* desire	2Chr 15:15	3605
to and fro throughout the *w* earth	2Chr 16:9	3605
The *w* number of the chief of the	2Chr 26:12	3605
the *w* assembly took counsel to	2Chr 30:23	3605
them, according to the *w* law	2Chr 33:8	3605
The *w* congregation together was	Ezr 2:64	3605
The *w* congregation together was	Neh 7:66	3605
the *w* kingdom of Ahasuerus	Est 3:6	3605
he woundeth, and his hands make *w*	Job 5:18	7495
and seeth under the *w* heaven	Job 28:24	3605
Or who hath disposed the *w* world	Job 34:13	3605
directeth it under the *w* heaven	Job 37:3	3605
is under the *w* heaven is mine	Job 41:11	3605
thee, O LORD, with my *w* heart	Ps 9:1	3605
situation, the joy of the *w* earth	Ps 48:2	3605
offering and *w* burnt offering	Ps 51:19	3632
let the *w* earth be filled with	Ps 72:19	
of the LORD of the *w* earth	Ps 97:5	3605
he brake the *w* staff of bread	Ps 105:16	3605
praise the LORD with my *w* heart	Ps 111:1	3605
and that seek him with the *w* heart	Ps 119:2	3605
With my *w* heart have I sought	Ps 119:10	3605
shall observe it with my *w* heart	Ps 119:34	3605
thy favour with my *w* heart	Ps 119:58	3605
keep thy precepts with my *w* heart	Ps 119:69	3605
I cried with my *w* heart	Ps 119:145	
will praise thee with my *w* heart	Ps 138:1	3605
and *w*, as those that go down into	Prov 1:12	8549
but the *w* disposing thereof is of	Prov 16:33	3605
shewed before the *w* congregation	Prov 26:26	
the conclusion of the *w* matter	Eccl 12:13	3605
for this is the *w* duty of man	Eccl 12:13	3605
the *w* head is sick	Is 1:5	3605
and the *w* heart faint	Is 1:5	3605
the *w* stay of bread	Is 3:1	3605
and the *w* stay of water	Is 3:1	3605
the *w* earth is full of his glory	Is 6:3	3605
his *w* work upon mount Zion	Is 10:12	
to destroy the *w* land	Is 13:5	3605
The *w* earth is at rest, and is	Is 14:7	3605
that is purposed upon the *w* earth	Is 14:26	3605
w Palestina, because the rod of	Is 14:29	3605
w Palestina, art dissolved	Is 14:31	3605
and I am set in my ward *w* nights	Is 21:8	3605
even determined upon the *w* earth	Is 28:22	3605
The God of the *w* earth shall he	Is 54:5	3605
brasen walls against the *w* land	Jer 1:18	3605
turned unto me with her *w* heart	Jer 3:10	3605
for the *w* land is spoiled	Jer 4:20	3605
The *w* land shall be desolate	Jer 4:27	3605
The *w* city shall flee for the	Jer 4:29	3605
even the *w* seed of Ephraim	Jer 7:15	3605
the *w* land trembled at the sound	Jer 8:16	3605
the *w* land is made desolate,	Jer 12:11	3605
unto me the *w* house of Israel	Jer 13:11	3605
the *w* house of Judah, saith the	Jer 13:11	3605
man of contention to the *w* earth	Jer 15:10	3605
that cannot be made *w* again	Jer 19:11	7495
return unto me with their *w* heart	Jer 24:7	3605
this *w* land shall be a desolation	Jer 25:11	3605
the *w* valley of the dead bodies,	Jer 31:40	3605
my *w* heart and with my *w* soul	Jer 32:41	3605
the *w* house of the Rechabites	Jer 35:3	3605
the *w* army of the Chaldeans that	Jer 37:10	3605
I will pluck up, even this *w* land	Jer 45:4	3605
of the *w* earth cut in asunder	Jer 50:23	3605
praise of the *w* earth surprised	Jer 51:41	3605
her *w* land shall be confounded,	Jer 51:47	3605
of beauty, The joy of the *w* earth	Lam 2:15	3605
the *w* remnant of thee will I	Eze 5:10	3605
touching the *w* multitude thereof	Eze 7:13	3605
And their *w* body, and their backs,	Eze 10:12	3605
Behold, when it was *w*, it was	Eze 15:5	8549
beasts of the *w* earth with thee	Eze 32:4	3605
When the *w* earth rejoiceth, I	Eze 35:14	3605
bones are the *w* house of Israel	Eze 37:11	3605
mercy upon the *w* house of Israel	Eze 39:25	3605
they may keep the *w* form thereof	Eze 43:11	3605
the top of the mountain the *w*	Eze 43:12	3605
be for the *w* house of Israel	Eze 45:6	3605
mountain, and filled the *w* earth	Dan 2:35	3606
over the *w* province of Babylon	Dan 2:48	3606
should be over the *w* kingdom	Dan 6:1	3606
to set him over the *w* realm	Dan 6:3	3606
and shall devour the *w* earth	Dan 7:23	3606
of the kingdom under the *w* heaven	Dan 7:27	3606
west on the face of the *w* earth	Dan 8:5	3605
for under the *w* heaven hath not	Dan 9:12	3605
till three *w* weeks were fulfilled	Dan 10:3	3117
the strength of his *w* kingdom	Dan 11:17	3605
away captive the *w* captivity	Amos 1:6	8003
up the *w* captivity to Edom	Amos 1:9	8003
against the *w* family which I	Amos 3:1	3605
unto the Lord of the *w* earth	Mic 4:13	3605
but the *w* land shall be devoured	Zeph 1:18	3605
run to and fro through the *w* earth	Zec 4:10	3605
stand by the Lord of the *w* earth	Zec 4:14	3605
over the face of the *w* earth	Zec 5:3	3605
robbed me, even this *w* nation	Mal 3:9	3605
not that thy *w* body should be	Mt 5:29	*3650*
not that thy *w* body should be	Mt 5:30	*3650*
thy *w* body shall be full of light	Mt 6:22	*3650*
thy *w* body shall be full of	Mt 6:23	*3650*
the *w* herd of swine ran violently	Mt 8:32	*3956*
the *w* city came out to meet Jesus	Mt 8:34	*3956*
They that be *w* need not a	Mt 9:12	*2480*
touch his garment, I shall be *w*	Mt 9:21	*4982*
thy faith hath made thee *w*	Mt 9:22	*4982*
woman was made *w* from that hour	Mt 9:22	*4982*
and it was restored *w*, like as the	Mt 12:13	*5199*
the *w* multitude stood on the	Mt 13:2	*3956*
of meal, till the *w* was leavened	Mt 13:33	*3650*
as touched were made perfectly *w*	Mt 14:36	*1295*
was made *w* from that very hour	Mt 15:28	*2390*
dumb to speak, the maimed to be *w*	Mt 15:31	*5199*
if he shall gain the *w* world	Mt 16:26	*3650*
shall be preached in the *w* world	Mt 26:13	*3650*
unto him the *w* band of soldiers	Mt 27:27	*3650*
They that are *w* have no need of	Mk 2:17	*2480*
hand was restored *w* as the other	Mk 3:5	*5199*
the *w* multitude was by the sea on	Mk 4:1	*3956*
but his clothes, I shall be *w*	Mk 5:28	*4982*
thy faith hath made thee *w*	Mk 5:34	*4982*
in peace, and be *w* of thy plague	Mk 5:34	*5199*
ran through that *w* region round	Mk 6:55	*3650*
many as touched him were made *w*	Mk 6:56	*4982*
man, if he shall gain the *w* world	Mk 8:36	*3650*
thy faith hath made thee *w*	Mk 10:52	*4982*
more than all *w* burnt offerings	Mk 12:33	*3646*
preached throughout the *w* world	Mk 14:9	*3650*
the *w* council, and bound Jesus, and	Mk 15:1	*3650*
and they call together the *w* band	Mk 15:16	*3650*
the *w* land until the ninth hour	Mk 15:33	*3650*
the *w* multitude of the people	Lk 1:10	*3956*
They that are *w* need not a	Lk 5:31	*5198*
hand was restored *w* as the other	Lk 6:10	*5199*
the *w* multitude sought to touch	Lk 6:19	*3956*
found the servant *w* that had been	Lk 7:10	*5198*
Then the *w* multitude of the	Lk 8:37	*537*
published throughout the *w* city	Lk 8:39	*3650*
thy faith hath made thee *w*	Lk 8:48	*4982*
only, and she shall be made *w*	Lk 8:50	*4982*
if he gain the *w* world, and lose	Lk 9:25	*3650*
thy *w* body also is full of light	Lk 11:34	*3650*
If thy *w* body therefore be full	Lk 11:36	*3650*
the *w* shall be full of light, as	Lk 11:36	*3650*
of meal, till the *w* was leavened	Lk 13:21	*3650*
thy faith hath made thee *w*	Lk 17:19	*4982*
the *w* multitude of the disciples	Lk 19:37	*537*
dwell on the face of the *w* earth	Lk 21:35	*3956*
the *w* multitude of them arose, and	Lk 23:1	*537*
himself believed, and his *w* house	Jn 4:53	*3650*
w of whatsoever disease he had	Jn 5:4	*5199*
unto him, Wilt thou be made *w*	Jn 5:6	*5199*
the man was made *w*	Jn 5:9	*5199*
answered them, He that made me *w*	Jn 5:11	*5199*
unto him, Behold, thou art made *w*	Jn 5:14	*5199*
was Jesus, which had made him *w*	Jn 5:15	*5199*
every whit *w* on the sabbath day	Jn 7:23	*5199*
that the *w* nation perish not	Jn 11:50	*3650*
man, by what means he is made *w*	Acts 4:9	*4982*
this man stand here before you *w*	Acts 4:10	*5199*
saying pleased the *w* multitude	Acts 6:5	*3956*
Jesus Christ maketh thee *w*	Acts 9:34	*2390*
that a *w* year they assembled	Acts 11:26	*3650*
sabbath day came almost the *w*	Acts 13:44	*3956*
and elders, with the *w* church	Acts 15:22	*3650*
the *w* city was filled with	Acts 19:29	*3650*
Paul dwelt two *w* years in his own	Acts 28:30	*3650*
spoken of throughout the *w* world	Rom 1:8	*3650*
know that the *w* creation groaneth	Rom 8:22	*3956*
mine host, and of the *w* church	Rom 16:23	*3650*
leaven leaveneth the *w* lump	1Cor 5:6	*3650*
If the *w* body were an eye, where	1Cor 12:17	*3650*
If the *w* were hearing, where were	1Cor 12:17	*3650*
If therefore the *w* church be come	1Cor 14:23	*3650*
he is a debtor to do the *w* law	Gal 5:3	*3650*
leaven leaveneth the *w* lump	Gal 5:9	*3650*
Of whom the *w* family in heaven and	Eph 3:15	*3956*
From whom the *w* body fitly joined	Eph 4:16	*3956*
Put on the *w* armour of God, that	Eph 6:11	
take unto you the *w* armour of God	Eph 6:13	
and I pray God your *w* spirit	1Th 5:23	*3648*
be stopped, who subvert *w* houses	Titus 1:11	*3650*
whosoever shall keep the *w* law	Jas 2:10	*3650*
and able also to bridle the *w* body	Jas 3:2	*3650*
and we turn about their *w* body	Jas 3:3	*3650*
that it defileth the *w* body	Jas 3:6	*3650*
also for the sins of the *w* world	1Jn 2:2	*3650*
the *w* world lieth in wickedness	1Jn 5:19	*3650*
which deceiveth the *w* world	Rev 12:9	*3650*
of the earth and of the *w* world	Rev 16:14	*3650*

WHOLESOME

A *w* tongue is a tree of life	Prov 15:4	4832
and consent not to *w* words	1Ti 6:3	*5198*

WHOLLY

it shall be *w* burnt	Lev 6:22	3632
for the priest shall be *w* burnt	Lev 6:23	3632
thou shalt not *w* reap the corners	Lev 19:9	3615
they are *w* given unto him out of	Num 3:9	
spread over it a cloth *w* of blue	Num 4:6	3632
For they are *w* given unto me from	Num 8:16	
they have not *w* followed me	Num 32:11	4390
for they have *w* followed the LORD	Num 32:12	4390
because he hath *w* followed the	Deut 1:36	4390
but I *w* followed the LORD my God	Josh 14:8	4390
because thou hast *w* followed the	Josh 14:9	4390
because that he *w* followed the	Josh 14:14	4390
I had *w* dedicated the silver unto	Judg 17:3	6942
a burnt offering *w* unto the LORD	1Sa 7:9	3632
will be *w* at thy commandment	1Chr 28:21	3605
being *w* at ease and quiet	Job 21:23	3605
that thou art *w* gone up to the	Is 22:1	3605
thee a noble vine, *w* a right seed	Jer 2:21	3605
she is *w* oppression in the midst	Jer 6:6	3605
it shall be *w* carried away	Jer 13:19	7965
If ye *w* set your faces to enter	Jer 42:15	7760
I not leave thee *w* unpunished	Jer 46:28	5352
but it shall be *w* desolate	Jer 50:13	3605
and all the house of Israel *w*	Eze 11:15	3605
and it shall rise up *w* as a flood	Amos 8:8	3605
it shall rise up *w* like a flood	Amos 9:5	3605
saw the city *w* given to idolatry	Acts 17:16	
very God of peace sanctify you *w*	1Th 5:23	*3651*
give thyself *w* to them	1Ti 4:15	

WHOM

he put the man *w* he had formed	Gen 2:8	834
The woman *w* thou gavest to be	Gen 3:12	834
seed instead of Abel, *w* Cain slew	Gen 4:25	3588
I will destroy man *w* I have	Gen 6:7	834
(out of *w* came Philistim,) and	Gen 10:14	834
w they shall serve, will I judge	Gen 15:14	834
w Sarah bare to him, Isaac	Gen 21:3	834
w thou lovest, and get thee into	Gen 22:2	834
the Canaanites, among *w* I dwell	Gen 24:3	834
that the damsel to *w* I shall say	Gen 24:14	834
me, The LORD, before *w* I walk	Gen 24:40	834
let the same be the woman *w* the	Gen 24:44	834
son, *w* Milcah bare unto him	Gen 24:47	834
w Hagar the Egyptian, Sarah's	Gen 25:12	834
for *w* I have served thee, and let	Gen 30:26	834
a man in *w* the Spirit of God is	Gen 41:38	834
well, the old man of *w* ye spake	Gen 43:27	834
brother, of *w* ye spake unto me	Gen 43:29	834
he with *w* it is found shall be my	Gen 44:10	834
he also with *w* the cup is found	Gen 44:16	834
brother, *w* ye sold into Egypt	Gen 45:4	834
w Laban gave to Leah his daughter	Gen 46:18	834
w God hath given me in this place	Gen 48:9	834
before *w* my fathers Abraham and	Gen 48:15	834
thou art he *w* thy brethren shall	Gen 49:8	
the hand of him *w* thou wilt send	Ex 4:13	

w the Egyptians keep in bondage	Ex 6:5	834
to *w* the LORD said, Bring out the	Ex 6:26	834
for the Egyptians *w* ye have seen	Ex 14:13	834
w he had delivered out of the	Ex 18:9	834
w the judges shall condemn, he	Ex 22:9	834
the people to *w* thou shalt come	Ex 23:27	834
w I have filled with the spirit	Ex 28:3	834
to *w* thou swarest by thine own	Ex 32:13	834
me know *w* thou wilt send with me	Ex 33:12	
gracious to *w* I will be gracious	Ex 33:19	
shew mercy on *w* I will shew mercy	Ex 33:19	
every one *w* his spirit made	Ex 35:21	834
with *w* was found blue, and purple,	Ex 35:23	834
with *w* was found shittim wood for	Ex 35:24	834
in *w* the LORD put wisdom and	Ex 36:1	
it unto him to *w* it appertaineth	Lev 6:5	834
the leper in *w* the plague is, his	Lev 13:45	834
him in *w* is the plague of leprosy	Lev 14:32	834
The woman also with *w* man shall	Lev 15:18	834
w he shall anoint	Lev 16:32	834
w he shall consecrate to minister	Lev 16:32	834
after *w* they have gone a whoring	Lev 17:7	
or a man of *w* he may take	Lev 22:5	834
unto the man to *w* he sold it	Lev 25:27	834
they are my servants *w* I brought	Lev 25:55	
w I brought forth out of the land	Lev 26:45	
unto him of *w* it was bought	Lev 27:24	
even to him to *w* the possession	Lev 27:24	834
w he consecrated to minister in	Num 3:3	834
w Moses and Aaron did number	Num 4:41	834
w Moses and Aaron numbered	Num 4:45	834
w Moses and Aaron and the chief of	Num 4:46	834
him against *w* he hath trespassed	Num 5:7	834
w thou knowest to be the elders	Num 11:16	834
said, The people, among *w* I am	Num 11:21	834
Ethiopian woman *w* he had married	Num 12:1	834
of *w* the flesh is half consumed	Num 12:12	
even him *w* he hath chosen will he	Num 16:5	834
the man *w* the LORD doth choose	Num 16:7	834
w I shall choose, shall blossom	Num 17:5	834
for I wot that he *w* thou blessest	Num 22:6	834
he *w* thou cursest is cursed	Num 22:6	834
I curse, *w* God hath not cursed	Num 23:8	
w the LORD hath not defied	Num 23:8	
of *w* cometh the family of the	Num 26:5	
w her mother bare to Levi in	Num 26:59	
was not a man of them *w* Moses	Num 26:64	
a man in *w* is the spirit, and lay	Num 27:18	834
These are they *w* the LORD	Num 34:29	834
them marry to *w* they think best	Num 36:6	
w Moses and the children of Israel	Deut 4:46	834
the people of *w* thou art afraid	Deut 7:19	
w thou knowest, and of *w* thou	Deut 9:2	834
w the LORD thy God shall choose	Deut 17:15	834
w he hated not in time past	Deut 19:4	
between *w* the controversy is,	Deut 19:17	
w thou hast redeemed, and lay not	Deut 21:8	834
the man to *w* thou dost lend shall	Deut 24:11	834
of his children *w* he shall eat	Deut 28:55	834
gods *w* they knew not	Deut 29:26	834
w he had not given unto them	Deut 29:26	834
the land of them, *w* he destroyed	Deut 31:4	
to gods *w* they knew not, to new	Deut 32:17	
w your fathers feared not	Deut 32:17	
children in *w* is no faith	Deut 32:20	
their rock in *w* they trusted	Deut 32:37	
w thou didst prove at Massah, and	Deut 33:8	834
with *w* thou didst strive at the	Deut 33:8	
w the LORD knew face to face,	Deut 34:10	834
and Og, *w* ye utterly destroyed	Josh 2:10	
w he had prepared of the children	Josh 4:4	834
unto *w* the LORD sware that he	Josh 5:6	
w he raised up in their stead,	Josh 5:7	
w the children of Israel slew	Josh 10:11	834
your enemies against *w* ye fight	Josh 10:25	
With *w* the Reubenites and the	Josh 13:8	5973
w Moses smote with the princes of	Josh 13:21	834
you this day *w* ye will serve	Josh 24:15	4310
the people through *w* we passed	Josh 24:17	834
shew thee the man *w* thou seekest	Judg 4:22	834
that of *w* I say unto thee, This	Judg 7:4	834
with *w* ye did upbraid me, saying,	Judg 8:15	834
men were they *w* ye slew at Tabor	Judg 8:18	834
w he sent abroad, and took in	Judg 12:9	
w he had used as his friend	Judg 14:20	834
them that danced, *w* they caught	Judg 21:23	834
in law with *w* she had wrought	Ruth 2:19	
The man's name with *w* I wrought	Ruth 2:19	
the kinsman of *w* Boaz spake came	Ruth 4:1	834
unto *w* he said, Ho, such a one	Ruth 4:1	
w Tamar bare unto Judah, of the	Ruth 4:12	834
w I shall not cut off from mine	1Sa 2:33	
to *w* shall he go up from us	1Sa 6:20	4310
Behold the man *w* I spake to thee	1Sa 9:17	834
on *w* is all the desire of Israel	1Sa 9:20	4310
See ye him *w* the LORD hath chosen	1Sa 10:24	834
or *w* have I defrauded	1Sa 12:3	4310
w have I oppressed	1Sa 12:3	
behold the king *w* ye have chosen	1Sa 12:13	4310
and *w* ye have desired	1Sa 12:13	4310
unto me him *w* I name unto thee	1Sa 16:3	834
with *w* hast thou left those few	1Sa 17:28	4310
of Israel, *w* thou hast defied	1Sa 17:45	834
w thou slewest in the valley of	1Sa 21:9	834
After *w* is the king of Israel	1Sa 24:14	4310
after *w* dost thou pursue	1Sa 24:14	4310
w I know not whence they be	1Sa 25:11	834
men of my lord, *w* thou didst send	1Sa 25:25	834
him up, *w* I shall name unto thee	1Sa 28:8	
W shall I bring up unto thee	1Sa 28:11	
of *w* they sang one to another in	1Sa 29:5	834
unto him, To *w* belongest thou	1Sa 30:13	4310
w they had made also to abide at	1Sa 30:21	
w I commanded to feed my people	2Sa 7:7	834
Saul, *w* I put away before thee	2Sa 7:15	834
w God went to redeem for a people	2Sa 7:23	834
the life of his brother *w* he slew	2Sa 14:7	834
Unto *w* David said, If thou	2Sa 15:33	
but *w* the LORD, and this people,	2Sa 16:18	834
And again, *w* should I serve	2Sa 16:19	4310
the man *w* thou seekest is as if	2Sa 17:3	834
w we anointed over us, is dead in	2Sa 19:10	834
w he had left to keep the house,	2Sa 20:3	834
of Saul, *w* the LORD did choose	2Sa 21:6	
w she bare unto Saul, Armoni and	2Sa 21:8	834
w she brought up for Adriel the	2Sa 21:8	
of the mighty men *w* David had	2Sa 23:8	834
hundred, *w* he slew at one time	2Sa 23:8	
w he slew, and shed the blood of	1Kin 2:5	
w I will set upon thy throne in	1Kin 5:5	834
w he had taken to wife, like unto	1Kin 7:8	834
w the children of Israel also	1Kin 9:21	
w he bestowed in the cities for	1Kin 10:26	
w Tahpenes weaned in Pharaoh's	1Kin 11:20	
w I chose, because he kept my	1Kin 11:34	834
for the prophet *w* he had brought	1Kin 13:23	834
before *w* I stand, there shall not	1Kin 17:1	834
upon the widow with *w* I sojourn	1Kin 17:20	834
before *w* I stand, I will surely	1Kin 18:15	834
unto *w* the word of the LORD came,	1Kin 18:31	834
And Ahab said, By *w*	1Kin 20:14	4310
hand a man *w* I appointed to utter	1Kin 20:42	
w Jezebel his wife stirred up	1Kin 21:25	834
w the LORD cast out before the	1Kin 21:26	834
by *w* we may enquire of the LORD	1Kin 22:8	
before *w* I stand, surely, were it	2Kin 3:14	834
before *w* I stand, I will receive	2Kin 5:16	834
bring you to the man *w* ye seek	2Kin 6:19	834
wouldest thou smite those *w* thou	2Kin 6:22	834
w Elisha restored to life	2Kin 8:5	834
If any of the men *w* I have	2Kin 10:24	834
w the LORD cast out from before	2Kin 16:3	834
w the LORD cast out from before	2Kin 17:8	834
as did the heathen *w* the LORD	2Kin 17:11	834
concerning *w* the LORD had charged	2Kin 17:15	834
priests *w* ye brought from thence	2Kin 17:27	834
Then one of the priests *w* they	2Kin 17:28	834
w they carried away from thence	2Kin 17:33	834
of Jacob, *w* he named Israel	2Kin 17:34	834
With *w* the LORD had made a	2Kin 17:35	
Now on *w* dost thou trust, that	2Kin 18:20	4310
w the king of Assyria his master	2Kin 19:4	834
Let not thy God in *w* thou	2Kin 19:10	834
W hast thou reproached and	2Kin 19:22	
against *w* hast thou exalted thy	2Kin 19:22	4310
w the LORD cast out before the	2Kin 21:2	834
w the LORD destroyed before the	2Kin 21:9	834
w the kings of Judah had ordained	2Kin 23:5	834
w Nebuchadnezzar king of Babylon	2Kin 25:22	834
(of *w* came the Philistines,) and	1Chr 1:12	834
Gilead, *w* he married when he was	1Chr 2:21	
w Tilgath-pilneser king of	1Chr 5:6	834
w God destroyed before them	1Chr 5:25	834
these are they *w* David set over	1Chr 6:31	834
Ashriel, *w* she bare	1Chr 7:14	834
w the men of Gath that were born	1Chr 7:21	
w David and Samuel the seer did	1Chr 9:22	
of the mighty men *w* David had	1Chr 11:10	834
of the mighty men *w* David had	1Chr 11:11	834
w I commanded to feed my people,	1Chr 17:6	834
w God went to redeem to be his	1Chr 17:21	834
w thou hast redeemed out of Egypt	1Chr 17:21	834
w king David made rulers over the	1Chr 26:32	834
w alone God hath chosen, is yet	1Chr 29:1	
they with *w* precious stones were	1Chr 29:8	834
over *w* I have made thee king	2Chr 1:11	
w David my father did provide	2Chr 2:7	834
w the children of Israel consumed	2Chr 8:8	834
w he bestowed in the chariot	2Chr 9:25	
beside those *w* the king put in	2Chr 17:19	834
by *w* we may enquire of the LORD	2Chr 18:7	
w thou wouldest not let Israel	2Chr 20:10	834
w the LORD had anointed to cut	2Chr 22:7	834
w David had distributed in the	2Chr 23:18	834
w the LORD had cast out before	2Chr 28:3	834
w the LORD had cast out before	2Chr 33:2	834
w the LORD had destroyed before	2Chr 33:9	834
w Nebuchadnezzar the king of	Ezr 2:1	834
of *w* there were seven thousand	Ezr 2:65	428
rest of the nations *w* the great	Ezr 4:10	1768
w he had made governor	Ezr 5:14	1768
w David and the princes had	Ezr 8:20	
had wives by *w* they had children	Ezr 10:44	
w thou hast redeemed by thy great	Neh 1:10	834
w Nebuchadnezzar the king of	Neh 7:6	834
of *w* there were seven thousand	Neh 7:67	428
them for *w* nothing is prepared	Neh 8:10	
much increase unto the kings *w*	Neh 9:37	834
w Nebuchadnezzar the king of	Est 2:6	834
w Mordecai, when her father and	Est 2:7	
w he had appointed to attend upon	Est 4:5	834
except such to *w* the king shall	Est 4:11	834
w the king delighteth to honour	Est 6:6	
To *w* would the king delight to do	Est 6:6	
For the man *w* the king delighteth	Est 6:7	4310
w the king delighteth to honour	Est 6:9	834
shall it be done to the man *w* the	Est 6:9	834
w the king delighteth to honour	Est 6:11	834
before *w* thou hast begun to fall,	Est 6:13	834
is hid, and *w* God hath hedged in	Job 3:23	
happy is the man *w* God correcteth	Job 5:17	
W, though I were righteous, yet	Job 9:15	834
Unto *w* alone the earth was given,	Job 15:19	1992
they *w* I loved are turned against	Job 19:19	
W I shall see for myself, and mine	Job 19:27	834
upon *w* doth not his light arise	Job 25:3	4310
To *w* hast thou uttered words	Job 26:4	4310
in *w* old age was perished	Job 30:2	5921
covetous, *w* the LORD abhorreth	Ps 10:3	
excellent, in *w* is all my delight	Ps 16:3	
my strength, in *w* I will trust	Ps 18:2	
a people *w* I have not known shall	Ps 18:43	
w shall I fear	Ps 27:1	4310
of *w* shall I be afraid	Ps 27:1	4310
Blessed is the man unto *w* the	Ps 32:2	
the people *w* he hath chosen for	Ps 33:12	
in *w* I trusted, which did eat of	Ps 41:9	834
w thou mayest make princes in all	Ps 45:16	
excellency of Jacob *w* he loved	Ps 47:4	834
is the man *w* thou choosest	Ps 65:4	
persecute him *w* thou hast smitten	Ps 69:26	834
of those *w* thou hast wounded	Ps 69:26	
W have I in heaven but thee	Ps 73:25	4310
upon the son of man *w* thou madest	Ps 80:17	
All nations *w* thou hast made	Ps 86:9	834
w thou rememberest no more	Ps 88:5	834
With *w* my hand shall be	Ps 89:21	834
God, to *w* vengeance belongeth	Ps 94:1	
to *w* vengeance belongeth, shew	Ps 94:1	
is the man *w* thou chastenest	Ps 94:12	834
Unto *w* I sware in my wrath that	Ps 95:11	834
w thou hast made to play therein	Ps 104:26	
and Aaron *w* he had chosen	Ps 105:26	834
concerning *w* the LORD commanded	Ps 106:34	834
w they sacrificed unto the idols	Ps 106:38	834
w he hath redeemed from the hand	Ps 107:2	834
my shield, and he in *w* I trust	Ps 144:2	
son of man, in *w* there is no help	Ps 146:3	
For *w* the LORD loveth he	Prov 3:12	
father the son in *w* he delighteth	Prov 3:12	
not good from them to *w* it is due	Prov 3:27	
the prince *w* thine eyes have seen	Prov 25:7	834
against *w* there is no rising up	Prov 30:31	5973
For *w* do I labour, and bereave my	Eccl 4:8	4310
Every man also to *w* God hath	Eccl 5:19	834
A man to *w* God hath given riches,	Eccl 6:2	834
unto *w* it happeneth according to	Eccl 8:14	
to *w* it happeneth according to	Eccl 8:14	413
Live joyfully with the wife *w*	Eccl 9:9	834
O thou *w* my soul loveth, where	Song 1:7	
bed I sought him *w* my soul loveth	Song 3:1	
I will seek him *w* my soul loveth	Song 3:2	
to *w* I said	Song 3:3	
Saw ye him *w* my soul loveth	Song 3:3	853
but I found him *w* my soul loveth	Song 3:4	
W shall I send, and who will go	Is 6:8	
to all them to *w* this people	Is 8:12	834
the children *w* the LORD hath	Is 8:18	834
to *w* will ye flee for help	Is 10:3	4310
W the LORD of hosts shall bless,	Is 19:25	834
w hast thou here, that thou hast	Is 22:16	4310
thou *w* the merchants of Zidon,	Is 23:2	
W shall he teach knowledge	Is 28:9	
w shall he make to understand	Is 28:9	
To *w* he said, This is the rest	Is 28:12	
Turn ye unto him from *w* the	Is 31:6	834
now on *w* dost thou trust, that	Is 36:5	4310
w the king of Assyria his master	Is 37:4	834
in *w* thou trustest, deceive thee,	Is 37:10	834
W hast thou reproached and	Is 37:23	
against *w* hast thou exalted thy	Is 37:23	4310
With *w* took he counsel, and who	Is 40:14	4310
To *w* then will ye liken God	Is 40:18	4310
To *w* then will ye liken me, or	Is 40:25	4310
Jacob *w* I have chosen, the seed	Is 41:8	834
Thou *w* I have taken from the ends	Is 41:9	834
Behold my servant, *w* I uphold	Is 42:1	
elect, in *w* my soul delighteth	Is 42:1	
he against *w* we have sinned	Is 42:24	2098
my servant *w* I have chosen	Is 43:10	834
and Israel, *w* I have chosen	Is 44:1	
and thou, Jesurun, *w* I have chosen	Is 44:2	
To *w* will ye liken me, and make me	Is 46:5	4310
thee with *w* thou hast laboured	Is 47:15	834
Israel, in *w* I will be glorified	Is 49:3	834
to him *w* man despiseth	Is 49:7	
to him *w* the nation abhorreth, to	Is 49:7	
divorcement, *w* I have put away	Is 50:1	834
is it to *w* I have sold you	Is 50:1	834
the sons *w* she hath brought forth	Is 51:18	
by *w* shall I comfort thee	Is 51:19	4310
to *w* is the arm of the LORD	Is 53:1	4310
Against *w* do ye sport yourselves	Is 57:4	4310
against *w* make ye a wide mouth,	Is 57:4	4310
of *w* hast thou been afraid or	Is 57:11	4310
As one *w* his mother comforteth,	Is 66:13	834
To *w* the word of the LORD came in	Jer 1:2	834
To *w* shall I speak, and give	Jer 6:10	4310
after other gods *w* ye know not	Jer 7:9	834
w they have loved	Jer 8:2	834
w they have served	Jer 8:2	834
after *w* they have walked	Jer 8:2	834
and *w* they have sought	Jer 8:2	
and *w* they have worshipped	Jer 8:2	834
who is he to *w* the mouth of the	Jer 9:12	834
w neither they nor their fathers	Jer 9:16	834
gods unto *w* they offer incense	Jer 11:12	
the people to *w* they prophesy	Jer 14:16	
against *w* I have pronounced, turn	Jer 18:8	834
w neither they nor their fathers	Jer 19:4	834
to *w* thou hast prophesied lies	Jer 20:6	
like a man *w* wine hath overcome,	Jer 23:9	
w I have sent out of this place	Jer 24:5	834
to *w* I send thee, to drink it	Jer 25:15	
unto *w* the LORD had sent me	Jer 25:17	
w I sent unto you, both rising up	Jer 26:5	834
have given it unto *w* it seemed	Jer 27:5	834
prophets, and to all the people *w*	Jer 29:1	834
(*w* Zedekiah king of Judah sent	Jer 29:3	834
w I have caused to be carried	Jer 29:4	834
w I have sent from Jerusalem to	Jer 29:20	834
w the king of Babylon roasted in	Jer 29:22	834

w I will raise up unto them	Jer 30:9	834
is Zion, w no man seeketh after	Jer 30:17	
w I have slain in mine anger and	Jer 33:5	834
w they had let go free, to return	Jer 34:11	834
w he had set at liberty at their	Jer 34:16	834
w Nebuchadrezzar king of Babylon	Jer 37:1	834
w they have cast into the dungeon	Jer 38:9	
of the men of w thou art afraid	Jer 39:17	
w the king of Babylon hath made	Jer 40:5	834
w the king of Babylon had made	Jer 41:2	834
w he had slain because of	Jer 41:9	834
w Nebuzar-adan the captain of the	Jer 41:10	834
w he had recovered from Ishmael	Jer 41:16	834
w he had brought again from	Jer 41:16	834
w the king of Babylon made	Jer 41:18	834
LORD our God, to w we send thee	Jer 42:6	
unto w ye sent me to present your	Jer 42:9	
of Babylon, of w ye are afraid	Jer 42:11	
w they knew not, neither they, ye	Jer 44:3	834
I will pardon them w I reserve	Jer 50:20	834
This is the people w	Jer 52:28	834
w thou didst command that they	Lam 1:10	834
from w I am not able to rise up	Lam 1:14	
consider to w thou hast done this	Lam 2:20	4310
of w we said, Under his shadow we	Lam 4:20	834
near any man upon w is the mark	Eze 9:6	834
among w I saw Jaazaniah the son	Eze 11:1	
Your slain w ye have laid in the	Eze 11:7	834
are they unto w the inhabitants	Eze 11:15	834
sad, w I have not made sad	Eze 13:22	
w thou hast borne unto me, and	Eze 16:20	834
with w thou hast taken pleasure,	Eze 16:37	834
among w they were, in whose sight	Eze 20:9	834
and with all on w she doted	Eze 23:7	834
the Assyrians, upon w she doted	Eze 23:9	834
from w thy mind is alienated, and	Eze 23:22	
the hand of them w thou hatest	Eze 23:28	834
them from w thy mind is alienated	Eze 23:28	834
w they bare unto me, to pass for	Eze 23:37	834
unto w a messenger was sent	Eze 23:40	
for w thou didst wash thyself,	Eze 23:40	834
your daughters w ye have left	Eze 24:21	834
people among w they are scattered	Eze 28:25	834
W art thou like in thy greatness	Eze 31:2	
To w art thou thus like in glory	Eze 31:18	4310
W dost thou pass in beauty	Eze 32:19	4310
Art thou he of w I have spoken in	Eze 38:17	834
Children in w was no blemish, but	Dan 1:4	
w they might teach the learning	Dan 1:4	
Unto w the prince of the eunuchs	Dan 1:7	1992
w the prince of the eunuchs had	Dan 1:11	834
w the king had ordained to	Dan 2:24	1768
There are certain Jews w thou	Dan 3:12	3487
our God w we serve is able to	Dan 3:17	1768
in w is the spirit of the holy	Dan 4:8	1768
in w is the spirit of the holy	Dan 5:11	1768
w the king Nebuchadnezzar thy	Dan 5:11	
w the king named Belteshazzar	Dan 5:12	1768
w the king my father brought out	Dan 5:13	1768
w he would he slew	Dan 5:19	1768
and w he would he kept alive	Dan 5:19	1768
and w he would he set up	Dan 5:19	1768
and w he would he put down	Dan 5:19	
of w Daniel was first	Dan 6:2	
Daniel, Thy God w thou servest	Dan 6:16	1768
w thou servest continually, able	Dan 6:20	1768
before w there were three of the	Dan 7:8	
came up, and before w three fell	Dan 7:20	4479
w I had seen in the vision at the	Dan 9:21	834
to w they shall not give the	Dan 11:21	5921
a god w his fathers knew not	Dan 11:38	834
w he shall acknowledge and	Dan 11:39	834
and thy judges of w thou saidst	Hos 13:10	834
in the remnant w the LORD shall	Joel 2:32	834
w they have scattered among the	Joel 3:2	834
to w the house of Israel came	Amos 6:1	1992
by w shall Jacob arise	Amos 7:2	4310
by w shall Jacob arise	Amos 7:5	4310
for upon w hath not thy	Nah 3:19	4310
to w the reproach of it was a	Zeph 3:18	5921
unto w the former prophets have	Zec 1:4	
These are they w the LORD hath	Zec 1:10	834
all the nations w they knew not	Zec 7:14	834
look upon me w they have pierced	Zec 12:10	
The people against w the LORD	Mal 1:4	834
against w thou hast dealt	Mal 2:14	834
w ye seek, shall suddenly come to	Mal 3:1	834
of the covenant, w ye delight in	Mal 3:1	834
of w was born Jesus, who is	Mt 1:16	3739
Son, in w I am well pleased	Mt 3:17	3739
w if his son ask bread, will he	Mt 7:9	3739
of w it is written, Behold, I	Mt 11:10	3739
my servant, w I have chosen	Mt 12:18	3739
in w my soul is well pleased	Mt 12:18	3739
by w do your children cast them	Mt 12:27	5101
W do men say that I the Son of	Mt 16:13	5101
unto them, But w say ye that I am	Mt 16:15	5101
Son, in w I am well pleased	Mt 17:5	3939
of w do the kings of the earth	Mt 17:25	5101
that man by w the offence cometh	Mt 18:7	3739
save they to w it is given	Mt 19:11	3739
for w it is prepared of my Father	Mt 20:23	3739
w ye slew between the temple and	Mt 23:35	3739
w his lord hath made ruler over	Mt 24:45	3739
w his lord when he cometh shall	Mt 24:46	3739
but woe unto that man by w the	Mt 26:24	3739
w they of the children of Israel	Mt 27:9	3739
people a prisoner, w they would	Mt 27:15	3739
W will ye that I release unto you	Mt 27:17	5101
Son, in w I am well pleased	Mk 1:11	3739
and calleth unto him w he would	Mk 3:13	3739
he said, It is John, w I beheaded	Mk 6:16	3739
unto them, W do men say that I am	Mk 8:27	5101
unto them, But w say ye that I am	Mk 8:29	5101
to them for w it is prepared	Mk 10:40	3739
w he hath chosen, he hath	Mk 13:20	3739
but woe to that man by w the Son	Mk 14:21	3739
I know not this man of w ye speak	Mk 14:71	3739
w ye call the King of the Jews	Mk 15:12	3739
among w was Mary Magdalene, and	Mk 15:40	3739
out of w he had cast seven devils	Mk 16:9	3739
twelve, w also he named apostles	Lk 6:13	3739
(w he also named Peter,) and	Lk 6:14	3739
to them of w ye hope to receive	Lk 6:34	3739
I will shew you to w he is like	Lk 6:47	5101
worthy for w he should do this	Lk 7:4	3739
of w it is written, Behold, I	Lk 7:27	3739
that he, to w he forgave most	Lk 7:43	3739
but to w little is forgiven, the	Lk 7:47	3739
out of w went seven devils,	Lk 8:2	3739
out of w the devils were departed	Lk 8:35	3739
Now the man out of w the devils	Lk 8:38	3739
is this, of w I hear such things	Lk 9:9	3739
W say the people that I am	Lk 9:18	5101
unto them, But w say ye that I am	Lk 9:20	5101
he to w the Son will reveal him	Lk 10:22	3739
by w do your sons cast them out	Lk 11:19	5101
will forewarn you w ye shall fear	Lk 12:5	5101
w the lord when he cometh shall	Lk 12:37	3739
w his lord shall make ruler over	Lk 12:42	3739
w his lord when he cometh shall	Lk 12:43	3739
to w men have committed much, of	Lk 12:48	3739
upon w the tower in Siloam fell,	Lk 13:4	3739
w Satan hath bound, lo, these	Lk 13:16	3739
woe unto him, through w they come	Lk 17:1	3739
to w he had given the money, that	Lk 19:15	3739
unto that man by w he is betrayed	Lk 22:22	3739
into prison, w they had desired	Lk 23:25	3739
saying, This was he of w I spake	Jn 1:15	3739
one among you, w ye know not	Jn 1:26	3739
This is he of w I said, After me	Jn 1:30	3739
Upon w thou shalt see the Spirit	Jn 1:33	3739
of w Moses in the law, and the	Jn 1:45	3739
indeed, in w is no guile	Jn 1:47	3739
to w thou barest witness, behold,	Jn 3:26	3739
For he w God hath sent speaketh	Jn 3:34	3739
he w thou now hast is not thy	Jn 4:18	3739
so the Son quickeneth w he will	Jn 5:21	3739
for w he hath sent, him ye	Jn 5:38	3739
you, even Moses, in w ye trust	Jn 5:45	3739
ye believe on him w he hath sent	Jn 6:29	3739
him, Lord, to w shall we go	Jn 6:68	5101
not this he, w they seek to kill	Jn 7:25	3739
sent me is true, w ye know not	Jn 7:28	3739
w makest thou thyself	Jn 8:53	5101
of w ye say, that he is your God	Jn 8:54	3739
unto w the word of God came, and	Jn 10:35	3739
w the Father hath sanctified, and	Jn 10:36	3739
behold, he w thou lovest is sick	Jn 11:3	3739
w he raised from the dead	Jn 12:1	3739
w he had raised from the dead	Jn 12:9	3739
to w hath the arm of the Lord	Jn 12:38	5101
I know w I have chosen	Jn 13:18	3739
another, doubting of w he spake	Jn 13:22	5101
of his disciples, w Jesus loved	Jn 13:23	3739
who it should be of w he spake	Jn 13:24	5101
to w I shall give a sop, when I	Jn 13:26	3739
w the world cannot receive,	Jn 14:17	3739
w the Father will send in my name	Jn 14:26	3739
w I will send unto you from the	Jn 15:26	3739
and Jesus Christ, w thou hast sent	Jn 17:3	3739
name those w thou hast given me	Jn 17:11	3739
w thou hast given me, be with me	Jn 17:24	3739
and said unto them, W seek ye	Jn 18:4	5101
asked he them again, W seek ye	Jn 18:7	5101
w he loved, he saith unto his	Jn 19:26	3739
shall look on him w they pierced	Jn 19:37	3739
w Jesus loved, and saith unto them	Jn 20:2	3739
w seekest thou	Jn 20:15	5101
Therefore that disciple w Jesus	Jn 21:7	3739
seeth the disciple w Jesus loved	Jn 21:20	3739
unto the apostles w he had chosen	Acts 1:2	3739
To w also he shewed himself alive	Acts 1:3	3739
W God hath raised up, having	Acts 2:24	3739
w ye have crucified, both Lord and	Acts 2:36	3739
w they laid daily at the gate of	Acts 3:2	3739
w ye delivered up, and denied him	Acts 3:13	3739
w God hath raised from the dead	Acts 3:15	3739
this man strong, w ye see and know	Acts 3:16	3739
W the heaven must receive until	Acts 3:21	3739
w ye crucified, w God raised	Acts 4:10	3739
on w this miracle of healing was	Acts 4:22	3739
w thou hast anointed, both Herod,	Acts 4:27	3739
the men w ye put in prison are	Acts 5:25	3739
w ye slew and hanged on a tree	Acts 5:30	3739
w God hath given to them that	Acts 5:32	3739
to w a number of men, about four	Acts 5:36	3739
w we may appoint over this	Acts 6:3	3739
W they set before the apostles	Acts 6:6	3739
the nation to w they shall be in	Acts 7:7	3739
This Moses w they refused, saying	Acts 7:35	3739
To w our fathers would not obey,	Acts 7:39	3739
w God drave out before the face	Acts 7:45	3739
of w ye have been now the	Acts 7:52	3739
To w they all gave heed, from the	Acts 8:10	3739
of w speaketh the prophet this	Acts 8:34	5101
I am Jesus w thou persecutest	Acts 9:5	3739
w when they had washed, they laid	Acts 9:37	
said, Behold, I am he w ye seek	Acts 10:21	3739
w they slew and hanged on a tree	Acts 10:39	3739
to w also he gave testimony, and	Acts 13:22	3739
he said, W think ye that I am	Acts 13:25	5101
w God raised again, saw no	Acts 13:37	3739
to the Lord, on w they believed	Acts 14:23	3739
upon w my name is called, saith	Acts 15:17	3739
to w we gave no such commandment	Acts 15:24	3739
w I preach unto you, is Christ	Acts 17:3	3739
W Jason hath received	Acts 17:7	3739
W therefore ye ignorantly worship	Acts 17:23	3739
by that man w he hath ordained	Acts 17:31	3739
w when Aquila and Priscilla had	Acts 18:26	846
you by Jesus w Paul preacheth	Acts 19:13	3739
the man in w the evil spirit was	Acts 19:16	3739
W he called together with the	Acts 19:25	3739
w all Asia and the world	Acts 19:27	3739
among w I have gone preaching the	Acts 20:25	3739
disciple, with w we should lodge	Acts 21:16	3739
w they supposed that Paul had	Acts 21:29	3739
from w also I received letters	Acts 22:5	3739
of Nazareth, w thou persecutest	Acts 22:8	3739
W I perceived to be accused of	Acts 23:29	3739
w we took, and would have judged	Acts 24:6	3739
by examining of w thyself mayest	Acts 24:8	3739
About w, when I was at Jerusalem,	Acts 25:15	3739
To w I answered, It is not the	Acts 25:16	3739
Against w when the accusers stood	Acts 25:18	3739
w Paul affirmed to be alive	Acts 25:19	3739
about w all the multitude of the	Acts 25:24	3739
Of w I have no certain thing to	Acts 25:26	3739
I am Jesus w thou persecutest	Acts 26:15	3739
Gentiles, unto w now I send thee,	Acts 26:17	3739
before w also I speak freely	Acts 26:26	3739
of God, whose I am, and w I serve,	Acts 27:23	3739
doubt this man is a murderer, w	Acts 28:4	3739
to w Paul entered in, and prayed,	Acts 28:8	3739
w when Paul saw, he thanked God,	Acts 28:15	3739
to w he expounded and testified	Acts 28:23	3739
By w we have received grace and	Rom 1:5	3739
Among w are ye also the called of	Rom 1:6	3739
w I serve with my spirit in the	Rom 1:9	3739
W God hath set forth to be a	Rom 3:25	3739
unto w God imputeth righteousness	Rom 4:6	3739
Blessed is the man to w the Lord	Rom 4:8	3739
before him w he believed	Rom 4:17	3739
to w it shall be imputed, if we	Rom 4:24	3739
By w also we have access by faith	Rom 5:2	3739
by w we have now received the	Rom 5:11	3739
that to w ye yield yourselves	Rom 6:16	3739
his servants ye are to w ye obey	Rom 6:16	3739
For w he did foreknow, he also	Rom 8:29	3739
Moreover w he did predestinate,	Rom 8:30	3739
w he called, them he also	Rom 8:30	3739
w he justified, them he also	Rom 8:30	3739
to w pertaineth the adoption, and	Rom 9:4	3739
of w as concerning the flesh	Rom 9:5	3739
have mercy on w I will have mercy	Rom 9:15	3739
on w I will have compassion	Rom 9:15	3739
he mercy on w he will have mercy	Rom 9:18	3739
and w he will he hardeneth	Rom 9:18	3739
w he hath called, not of the Jews	Rom 9:24	3739
him in w they have not believed	Rom 10:14	3739
in him of w they have not heard	Rom 10:14	3739
to w be glory for ever	Rom 11:36	846
tribute to w tribute is due	Rom 13:7	3588
custom to w custom	Rom 13:7	3588
fear to w fear	Rom 13:7	3588
honour to w honour	Rom 13:7	3588
with thy meat, for w Christ died	Rom 14:15	3739
To w he was not spoken of, they	Rom 15:21	3739
unto w not only I give thanks,	Rom 16:4	3739
by w ye were called unto the	1Cor 1:9	3739
but ministers by w ye believed	1Cor 3:5	3739
to be married to w she will	1Cor 7:39	3739
of w are all things, and we in him	1Cor 8:6	3739
by w are all things, and we by him	1Cor 8:6	3739
brother perish, for w Christ died	1Cor 8:11	3739
upon w the ends of the world are	1Cor 10:11	3739
of w the greater part remain unto	1Cor 15:6	3739
w he raised not up, if so be that	1Cor 15:15	3739
In w we trust that he will yet	2Cor 1:10	3739
from them of w I ought to rejoice	2Cor 2:3	3739
To w ye forgive any thing, I	2Cor 2:10	3739
to w I forgave it, for your sakes	2Cor 2:10	3739
In w the god of this world hath	2Cor 4:4	3739
w we have oftentimes proved	2Cor 8:22	3739
but w the Lord commendeth	2Cor 10:18	3739
w we have not preached, or if ye	2Cor 11:4	3739
by any of them w I sent unto you	2Cor 12:17	3739
To w be glory for ever and ever	Gal 1:5	3739
To w we gave place by subjection,	Gal 2:5	3739
come to w the promise was made	Gal 3:19	3739
of w I travail in birth again	Gal 4:19	3739
by w the world is crucified unto	Gal 6:14	3739
In w we have redemption through	Eph 1:7	3739
In w also we have obtained an	Eph 1:11	3739
In w ye also trusted, after that	Eph 1:13	3739
in w also after that ye believed,	Eph 1:13	3739
Among w also we all had our	Eph 2:3	3739
In w all the building fitly	Eph 2:21	3739
In w ye also are builded together	Eph 2:22	3739
In w we have boldness and access	Eph 3:12	3739
Of w the whole family in heaven	Eph 3:15	3739
From w the whole body fitly	Eph 4:16	3739
W I have sent unto you for the	Eph 6:22	3739
among w ye shine as lights in the	Phil 2:15	3739
for w I have suffered the loss of	Phil 3:8	3739
of w I have told you often, and	Phil 3:18	3739
In w we have redemption through	Col 1:14	3739
To w God would make known what is	Col 1:27	3739
W we preach, warning every man,	Col 1:28	3739
In w are hid all the treasures of	Col 2:3	3739
In w also ye are circumcised with	Col 2:11	3739
W I have sent unto you for the	Col 4:8	3739
Barnabas, (touching w ye received	Col 4:10	3739
w he raised from the dead, even	1Th 1:10	3739
w the Lord shall consume with the	2Th 2:8	3739
of w I am chief	1Ti 1:15	3739
Of w is Hymenaeus and Alexander	1Ti 1:20	3739
w I have delivered unto Satan,	1Ti 1:20	3739
w no man hath seen, nor can see	1Ti 6:16	3739
to w be honour and power	1Ti 6:16	3739
w I serve from my forefathers	2Ti 1:3	3739

for I know *w* I have believed, and 2Ti 1:12 3739
of *w* are Phygellus and Hermogenes 2Ti 1:15 3739
of *w* is Hymenaeus and Philetus 2Ti 2:17 3739
knowing of *w* thou hast learned 2Ti 3:14 5101
Of *w* be thou ware also 2Ti 4:15 3739
to *w* be glory for ever and ever 2Ti 4:18 3739
w I have begotten in my bonds Philem 10 3739
W I have sent again Philem 12 3739
W I would have retained with me, Philem 13 3739
w he hath appointed heir of all Heb 1:2 3739
by *w* also he made the worlds Heb 1:2 3739
for *w* are all things Heb 2:10 3739
by *w* are all things, in bringing Heb 2:10 3739
But with *w* was he grieved forty Heb 3:17 5101
to *w* sware he that they should Heb 3:18 5101
they to *w* it was first preached Heb 4:6
eyes of him with *w* we have to do Heb 4:13 3739
Of *w* we have many things to say, Heb 5:11 3739
meet for them by *w* it is dressed Heb 6:7 3739
To *w* also Abraham gave a tenth Heb 7:2 3739
unto *w* even the patriarch Abraham Heb 7:4 3739
of *w* it is witnessed that he Heb 7:8
For he of *w* these things are Heb 7:13 3739
Of *w* it was said, That in Isaac Heb 11:18 3739
(Of *w* the world was not worthy Heb 11:38 3739
For *w* the Lord loveth he Heb 12:6 3739
every son *w* he receiveth Heb 12:6 3739
for what son is he *w* the father Heb 12:7 3739
to *w* be glory for ever and ever Heb 13:21 3739
with *w*, if he come shortly, I Heb 13:23 3739
with *w* is no variableness, Jas 1:17 3739
W having not seen, ye love 1Pet 1:8 3739
in *w*, though now ye see him not, 1Pet 1:8
Unto *w* it was revealed, that not 1Pet 1:12 3739
To *w* coming, as unto a living 1Pet 2:4 3739
to *w* be praise and dominion for 1Pet 4:11 3739
about, seeking *w* he may devour 1Pet 5:8 5101
W resist stedfast in the faith, 1Pet 5:9 3739
Son, in *w* I am well pleased 2Pet 1:17 3739
by reason of *w* the way of truth 2Pet 2:2 3739
to *w* the mist of darkness is 2Pet 2:17 3739
for of *w* a man is overcome, of 2Pet 2:19 3739
not his brother *w* he hath seen 1Jn 4:20 3739
he love God *w* he hath not seen 1Jn 4:20 3739
children, *w* I love in the truth 2Jn 1 3739
Gaius, *w* I love in the truth 3Jn 1 3739
w if thou bring forward on their 3Jn 6 3739
to *w* is reserved the blackness of Jude 13 3739
to *w* it was given to hurt the Rev 7:2 3739
With *w* the kings of the earth Rev 17:2 3739
the number of *w* is as the sand of Rev 20:8 3739

WHOMSOEVER
With *w* thou findest thy gods, let Gen 31:32 834
With *w* of thy servants it be Gen 44:9 834
w he toucheth that hath the issue Lev 15:11
of *w* I say unto thee, This shall Judg 7:4 834
So *w* the LORD our God shall drive Judg 11:24
of men, and giveth it to *w* he will Dan 4:17 4479
of men, and giveth it to *w* he will Dan 4:25 4479
of men, and giveth it to *w* he will Dan 4:32 4479
he appointeth over it *w* he will Dan 5:21
he to *w* the Son will reveal him Mt 11:27
but on *w* it shall fall, it will Mt 21:44
W I shall kiss, that same is he Mt 26:48
W I shall kiss, that same is he Mk 14:44
them one prisoner, *w* they desired Mk 15:6 3746
and to *w* I will I give it Lk 4:6
For unto *w* much is given, of him Lk 12:48
but on *w* it shall fall, it will Lk 20:18
He that receiveth *w* I send Jn 13:20
that on *w* I lay hands, he may Acts 8:19
w ye shall approve by your 1Cor 16:3

WHORE
daughter, to cause her to be a *w* Lev 19:29 2181
shall not take a wife that is a *w* Lev 21:7 2181
profane herself by playing the *w* Lev 21:9 2181
to play the *w* in her father's Deut 22:21 2181
There shall be no *w* of the Deut 23:17 6948
shalt not bring the hire of a *w* Deut 23:18 2181
played the *w* against him, and went Judg 19:2 2181
For a *w* is a deep ditch Prov 23:27 2181
seed of the adulterer and the *w* Is 57:3 2181
Thou hast played the *w* also with Eze 16:28 2181
w that sitteth upon many waters Rev 17:1 4204
thou sawest, where the *w* sitteth Rev 17:15 4204
the beast, these shall hate the *w* Rev 17:16 4204
for he hath judged the great *w* Rev 19:2 4204

WHOREDOM
behold, she is with child by *w* Gen 38:24 2183
lest the land fall to *w*, and the Lev 19:29 2181
to commit *w* with Molech, from Lev 20:5 2181
w with the daughters of Moab Num 25:1 2181
through the lightness of her *w* Jer 3:9 2184
neighings, the lewdness of thy *w* Jer 13:27 2184
men, and didst commit *w* with them Eze 16:17 2181
unto thee on every side for thy *w* Eze 16:33 8457
and commit ye *w* after their Eze 20:30 2181
and poured their *w* upon her Eze 23:8 8457
and they defiled her with their *w* Eze 23:17 8457
thy *w* brought from the land of Eze 23:27 2184
they, nor their kings, by their *w* Eze 43:7 2184
Now let them put away their *w* Eze 43:9 2184
the land hath committed great *w* Hos 1:2 2181
they shall commit *w*, and shall not Hos 4:10 2181
W and wine and new wine take away Hos 4:11 2184
your daughters shall commit *w* Hos 4:13 2181
your daughters when they commit *w* Hos 4:14 2181
they have committed *w* continually Hos 4:18 2181
now, O Ephraim, thou committest *w* Hos 5:3 2181
there is the *w* of Ephraim Hos 6:10 2184

WHOREDOMS
forty years, and bear your *w* Num 14:33 2184
so long as the *w* of thy mother 2Kin 9:22 2183
like to the *w* of the house of 2Chr 21:13 2181
hast polluted the land with thy *w* Jer 3:2 2184
Is this of thy *w* a small matter Eze 16:20 8457
thy *w* thou hast not remembered Eze 16:22 8457
passed by, and multiplied thy *w* Eze 16:25 8457
and hast increased thy *w*, to Eze 16:26 8457
in thee from other women in thy *w* Eze 16:34 8457
none followeth thee to commit *w* Eze 16:34 2181
through thy *w* with thy lovers Eze 16:36 8457
And they committed *w* in Egypt Eze 23:3
they committed *w* in their youth Eze 23:3
she committed her *w* with them Eze 23:7 8457
left she her *w* brought from Egypt Eze 23:8 8457
in her *w* more than her sister in Eze 23:11 8457
more than her sister in her *w* Eze 23:11 2183
And that she increased her *w* Eze 23:14 8457
So she discovered her *w*, and Eze 23:18 8457
Yet she multiplied her *w*, in Eze 23:19 8457
of thy *w* shall be discovered Eze 23:29 2183
both thy lewdness and thy *w* Eze 23:29 8457
thou also thy lewdness and thy *w* Eze 23:35 8457
Will they now commit *w* with her Eze 23:43 8457
Go, take unto thee a wife of *w* Hos 1:2 2183
and children of *w* Hos 1:2 2183
put away her *w* out of her sight Hos 2:2 2183
for they be the children of *w* Hos 2:4 2183
for the spirit of *w* hath caused Hos 4:12 2183
for the spirit of *w* is in the Hos 5:4 2183
the *w* of the wellfavoured harlot Nah 3:4 2183
selleth nations through her *w* Nah 3:4 2183

WHOREMONGER
For this ye know, that no *w* Eph 5:5 4205

WHOREMONGERS
For *w*, for them that defile 1Ti 1:10 4205
but *w* and adulterers God will Heb 13:4 4205
abominable, and murderers, and *w* Rev 21:8 4205
are dogs, and sorcerers, and *w* Rev 22:15 4205

WHORE'S
and thou hadst a *w* forehead Jer 3:3 2181

WHORES
They give gifts to all *w* Eze 16:33 2181
themselves are separated with *w* Hos 4:14 2181

WHORING
they go a *w* after their gods, and Ex 34:15 2181
daughters go a *w* after their gods Ex 34:16 2181
thy sons go a *w* after their gods Ex 34:16 2181
after whom they have gone a *w* Lev 17:7 2181
off, and all that go a *w* after him Lev 20:5 2181
to go a *w* after them, I will even Lev 20:6 2181
after which ye use to go a *w* Num 15:39 2181
go a *w* after the gods of the Deut 31:16 2181
but they went a *w* after other Judg 2:17 2181
Israel went thither a *w* after it Judg 8:27 2181
went a *w* after Baalim, and made Judg 8:33 2181
went a *w* after the gods of the 1Chr 5:25 2181
of Jerusalem to go a *w*, like to 2Chr 21:13 2181
all them that go a *w* from thee Ps 73:27 2181
works, and went a *w* with their own Ps 106:39 2181
which go a *w* after their idols Eze 6:9 2181
hast gone a *w* after the heathen Eze 23:30 2181
they have gone a *w* from under Hos 4:12 2181
thou hast gone a *w* from thy God Hos 9:1 2181

WHORISH
For by means of a *w* woman a man Prov 6:26 2181
I am broken with their *w* heart Eze 6:9 2181
the work of an imperious *w* woman Eze 16:30 2181

WHOSE
w seed is in itself, upon the Gen 1:11 834
w seed was in itself, after his Gen 1:12 834
All in *w* nostrils was the breath Gen 7:22 834
w top may reach unto heaven Gen 11:4
an Egyptian, *w* name was Hagar Gen 16:1
the uncircumcised man child *w* Gen 17:14 834
w name was Reumah, she bare also Gen 22:24
And said, *W* daughter art thou Gen 24:23 4310
the Canaanites, in *w* land I dwell Gen 24:37
her, and said, *W* daughter art thou Gen 24:47
asketh thee, saying, *W* art thou Gen 32:17 4310
and *w* are these before thee Gen 32:17 4310
Adullamite, *w* name was Hirah Gen 38:1
Canaanite, *w* name was Shuah Gen 38:2
his firstborn, *w* name was Tamar Gen 38:6
w these are, am I with child Gen 38:25 834
w are these, the signet, and Gen 38:25 834
but the man in *w* hand the cup is Gen 44:17
w branches run over the wall Gen 49:22
w name is Jealous, is a jealous Ex 34:14
every one *w* heart stirred him up, Ex 35:21 834
all the women *w* heart stirred Ex 35:26 834
w heart made them willing to Ex 35:29 834
in *w* heart the LORD had put Ex 36:2 834
even every one *w* heart stirred Ex 36:2 834
the man *w* hair is fallen off his Lev 13:40 3588
w hand is not able to get that Lev 14:32 834
of him *w* seed goeth from him, and Lev 15:32 834
w blood was brought in to make Lev 16:27 834
upon *w* head the anointing oil was Lev 21:10 834
or a man *w* seed goeth from him Lev 22:4 834
w father was an Egyptian, went Lev 24:10
the man *w* eyes are open hath said Num 24:3
the man *w* eyes are open hath said Num 24:15
a land *w* stones are iron Deut 8:9 834
out of *w* hills thou mayest dig Deut 8:9
w land the LORD thy God giveth Deut 19:1 834
a nation *w* tongue thou shalt not Deut 28:49 834
w heart turneth away this day Deut 29:18 834
the Amorites, in *w* land ye dwell Josh 24:15 834
the captain of *w* host was Sisera, Judg 4:2
the Amorites, in *w* land ye dwell Judg 6:10 834
w name he called Abimelech Judg 8:31 853
of the Danites, *w* name was Manoah Judg 13:2
of Sorek, *w* name was Delilah Judg 16:4
mount Ephraim, *w* name was Micah Judg 17:1
him in *w* sight I shall find grace Ruth 2:2 834
the reapers, *W* damsel is this Ruth 2:5 4310
under *w* wings thou art come to Ruth 2:12 834
kindred, with *w* maidens thou wast Ruth 3:2 834
w name was Kish, the son of Abiel 1Sa 9:1
w name was Saul, a choice young 1Sa 9:2
of men, *w* hearts God had touched 1Sa 10:26 834
w ox have I taken 1Sa 12:3 4310
or *w* ass have I taken 1Sa 12:3 4310
or of *w* hand have I received any 1Sa 12:3 4310
w height was six cubits and a span 1Sa 17:4
w name was Jesse 1Sa 17:12
host, Abner, *w* son is this youth 1Sa 17:55 4310
Enquire thou *w* son the stripling 1Sa 17:56 4310
W son art thou, thou young man 1Sa 17:58 4310
w possessions were in Carmel 1Sa 25:2
w name was Rizpah, the daughter 2Sa 3:7
his behalf, saying, *W* is the land 2Sa 3:12 4310
w name is called by the name of 2Sa 6:2 834
of Saul a servant *w* name was Ziba 2Sa 9:2
had a young son, *w* name was Micha 2Sa 9:12
a fair sister, *w* name was Tamar 2Sa 13:1
w name was Jonadab, the son of 2Sa 13:3
and one daughter, *w* name was Tamar 2Sa 14:27
w name was Shimei, the son of 2Sa 16:5
in *w* stead thou hast reigned 2Sa 16:8 834
w heart is as the heart of a lion 2Sa 17:10 834
w name was Ithra an Israelite, 2Sa 17:25
w name was Sheba, the son of 2Sa 20:1
the weight of *w* spear weighed 2Sa 21:16
the staff of *w* spear was like a 2Sa 21:19
Then spake the woman *w* the living 1Kin 3:26 834
to his ways, *w* heart thou knowest 1Kin 8:39 834
w mother's name was Zeruah, a 1Kin 11:26
Then a lord on *w* hand the king 2Kin 7:2 834
on *w* hand he leaned to have the 2Kin 7:17 834
w son he had restored to life, 2Kin 8:1 834
w son he had restored to life, 2Kin 8:5 834
into *w* hand they delivered the 2Kin 12:15 834
w high places and *w* altars 2Kin 18:22
W sisters were Zeruiah, and 1Chr 2:16
another wife, *w* name was Atarah 1Chr 2:26
an Egyptian, *w* name was Jarha 1Chr 2:34
w number was in the days of David 1Chr 7:2
w sister's name was Maachah 1Chr 7:15
w wife's name was Maachah 1Chr 8:29
w names are these, Azrikam, 1Chr 8:38
w wife's name was Maachah 1Chr 9:35
w names are these, Azrikam, 1Chr 9:44
w faces were like the faces of 1Chr 12:8
cherubims, *w* name is called on it 1Chr 13:6
w spear staff was like a weaver's 1Chr 20:5
w fingers and toes were four and 1Chr 20:6
w brethren were strong men, Elihu 1Chr 26:7
his ways, *w* heart thou knowest 2Chr 6:30
w heart is perfect toward him 2Chr 16:9
LORD was there, *w* name was Oded 2Chr 28:9
with all them *w* spirit God had Ezr 1:5 853
w name was Sheshbazzar, whom he Ezr 5:14
w habitation is in Jerusalem, Ezr 7:15 1768
w names are these, Eliphelet, Ezr 8:13
w name was Mordecai, the son of Est 2:5
in the land of Uz, *w* name was Job Job 1:1
light given to a man *w* way is hid Job 3:23 834
w foundation is in the dust, Job 4:19 834
W harvest the hungry eateth up, Job 5:5 834
W hope shall be cut off Job 8:14 834
w trust shall be a spider's web Job 8:14
into *w* hand God bringeth Job 12:6 834
In *w* hand is the soul of every Job 12:10 834
w foundation was overflown with a Job 22:16
and *w* spirit came from thee Job 26:4 4310
w fathers I would have disdained Job 30:1 834
Out of *w* womb came the ice Job 38:29 4310
W house I have made the Job 39:6 834
In *w* eyes a vile person is Ps 15:4
w belly thou fillest with thy hid Ps 17:14
In *w* hands is mischief, and their Ps 26:10 834
Blessed is he *w* transgression is Ps 32:1
is forgiven, *w* sin is covered Ps 32:1
in *w* spirit there is no guile Ps 32:2
w mouth must be held in with bit Ps 32:9
is the nation *w* God is the LORD Ps 33:12 834
in *w* mouth are no reproofs Ps 38:14
w teeth are spears and arrows, and Ps 57:4
w spirit was not stedfast with Ps 78:8
w name alone is JEHOVAH, art the Ps 83:18
Blessed is the man *w* strength is Ps 84:5
in *w* heart are the ways of them Ps 84:5
W feet they hurt with fetters Ps 105:18
W mouth speaketh vanity, and their Ps 144:8 834
w mouth speaketh vanity, and their Ps 144:11 834
is that people, *w* God is the LORD Ps 144:15
w hope is in the LORD his God Ps 146:5
W ways are crooked, and they Prov 2:15 834
W hatred is covered by deceit, Prov 26:26
w teeth are as swords, and their Prov 30:14
For there is a man *w* labour is in Eccl 2:21
w heart is snares and nets, and her Eccl 7:26
shall be as an oak *w* leaf fadeth Is 1:30
w breath is in his nostrils Is 2:22 834
W arrows are sharp, and all their Is 5:28 834
w substance is in them, when they Is 6:13 834
w graven images did excel them of Is 10:10
captives, *w* captives they were Is 14:2
w land the rivers have spoiled Is 18:2 834
w land the rivers have spoiled, Is 18:7 834
w antiquity is of ancient days Is 23:7

W

w merchants are princes ... Is 23:8 834
w traffickers are the honourable ... Is 23:8
peace, *w* mind is stayed on thee ... Is 26:3
w glorious beauty is a fading ... Is 28:1
w breaking cometh suddenly at an ... Is 30:13 834
w fire is in Zion, and his furnace ... Is 31:9 834
w high places and *w* altars ... Is 36:7
Chaldeans, *w* cry is in the ships ... Is 43:14
w right hand I have holden, to ... Is 45:1 834
the people in *w* heart is my law ... Is 51:7
divided the sea, *w* waves roared ... Is 51:15
eternity, *w* name is Holy ... Is 57:15
w waters cast up mire and dirt ... Is 57:20
of water, *w* waters fail not ... Is 58:11 834
a nation *w* language thou knowest ... Jer 5:15
w heart departeth from the LORD ... Jer 17:5
the LORD, and *w* hope the LORD is ... Jer 17:7
w roofs they have burned incense ... Jer 19:13 834
hand of them *w* face thou fearest ... Jer 22:25
upon *w* roofs they have offered ... Jer 32:29 834
for all *w* wickedness I have hid ... Jer 33:5 834
w name was Irijah, the son of ... Jer 37:13
shall know *w* words shall stand, ... Jer 44:28 4310
w waters are moved as the rivers ... Jer 46:7
w name is the LORD of hosts, ... Jer 46:18
w name is the LORD of hosts ... Jer 48:15
they *w* judgment was not to drink ... Jer 49:12 834
w name is the LORD of hosts ... Jer 51:57
w words thou canst not understand ... Eze 3:6 834
But as for them *w* heart walketh ... Eze 11:21
w branches turned toward him, and ... Eze 17:6
w oath he despised ... Eze 17:16
w covenant he brake, even with ... Eze 17:16 853
in *w* sight I made myself known ... Eze 20:9 853
in *w* sight I brought them out ... Eze 20:14 834
in *w* sight I brought them forth ... Eze 20:22 834
w day is come, when iniquity ... Eze 21:25 834
more, until he come *w* right it is ... Eze 21:27 834
w day is come, when their ... Eze 21:29 834
w flesh is as the flesh of asses, ... Eze 23:20
w issue is like the issue of ... Eze 23:20
to the pot *w* scum is therein, and ... Eze 24:6 834
w scum is not gone out of it ... Eze 24:6
W graves are set in the sides of ... Eze 32:23 834
w appearance was like the ... Eze 40:3
w prospect is toward the south, ... Eze 40:45 834
the chamber *w* prospect is toward ... Eze 40:46 834
me forth toward the gate *w* ... Eze 42:15 834
w prospect is toward the east ... Eze 43:4 834
w leaf shall not fade, neither ... Eze 47:12
w dwelling is not with flesh ... Dan 2:11 1768
w name was Belteshazzar, Art thou ... Dan 2:26 1768
w brightness was excellent, stood ... Dan 2:31
w height was threescore cubits, ... Dan 3:1 1768
upon *w* bodies the fire had no ... Dan 3:27 1768
me, *w* name was Belteshazzar, ... Dan 4:8 1768
w name was Belteshazzar, was ... Dan 4:19 1768
w height reached unto the heaven, ... Dan 4:20
W leaves were fair, and the fruit ... Dan 4:21
upon *w* branches the fowls of the ... Dan 4:21
w dominion is an everlasting ... Dan 4:34 1768
all *w* works are truth, and his ... Dan 4:37
the God in *w* hand thy breath is, ... Dan 5:23 1768
w are all thy ways, hast thou not ... Dan 5:23
w garment was white as snow, and ... Dan 7:9
w teeth were of iron, and his ... Dan 7:19 1768
w look was more stout than his ... Dan 7:20
w kingdom is an everlasting ... Dan 7:27
w name was called Belteshazzar ... Dan 10:1 834
w loins were girded with fine ... Dan 10:5
w teeth are the teeth of a lion, ... Joel 1:6
w height was like the height of ... Amos 2:9 834
w name is The God of hosts ... Amos 5:27
of the rock, *w* habitation is high ... Obad 3
that we may know for *w* cause this ... Jonah 1:7 4310
for *w* cause this evil is upon us ... Jonah 1:8
w goings forth have been from of ... Mic 5:2
w rampart was the sea, and her ... Nah 3:8 834
Behold the man *w* name is The ... Zec 6:12
W possessors slay them, and hold ... Zec 11:5 834
w shoes I am not worthy to bear ... Mt 3:11 *3739*
W fan is in his hand, and he will ... Mt 3:12 *3739*
Lebbaeus, *w* surname was Thaddaeus .. Mt 10:3 *3588*
W is this image and superscription ... Mt 22:20 *5101*
Therefore in the resurrection *w* ... Mt 22:28 *5101*
w son is he? ... Mt 22:42 *5101*
the latchet of *w* shoes I am not ... Mk 1:7 *3739*
w young daughter had an unclean ... Mk 7:25 *3739*
W is this image and superscription ... Mk 12:16 *5101*
w wife shall she be of them ... Mk 12:23 *5101*
to a man *w* name was Joseph ... Lk 1:27 *3739*
in Jerusalem, *w* name was Simeon ... Lk 2:25 *3739*
the latchet of *w* shoes I am not ... Lk 3:16 *3739*
W fan is in his hand, and he will ... Lk 3:17 *3739*
there was a man *w* right hand was ... Lk 6:6
then *w* shall those things be, ... Lk 12:20 *1501*
w blood Pilate had mingled with ... Lk 13:1 *3739*
W image and superscription hath it ... Lk 20:24 *5100*
w wife of them is she ... Lk 20:33 *5100*
w name was Cleopas, answering ... Lk 24:18 *3739*
sent from God, *w* name was John ... Jn 1:6 *846*
w shoe's latchet I am not worthy ... Jn 1:27 *3739*
w son was sick at Capernaum ... Jn 4:46 *3739*
w father and mother we know ... Jn 6:42 *3739*
w own the sheep are not, seeth ... Jn 10:12 *3739*
w brother Lazarus was sick ... Jn 11:2 *3739*
his kinsman *w* ear Peter cut off ... Jn 18:26 *3739*
cast lots for it, *w* it shall be ... Jn 19:24 *5101*
W soever sins ye remit, they are ... Jn 20:23 *5100*
w soever sins ye retain, they are ... Jn 20:23 *5100*
young man's feet, *w* name was Saul ... Acts 7:58
for one Simon, *w* surname is Peter ... Acts 10:5 *3739*
w house is by the sea side ... Acts 10:6 *3739*
hither Simon, *w* surname is Peter ... Acts 10:32 *3739*
for Simon, *w* surname is Peter ... Acts 11:13 *3588*
of John, *w* surname was Mark ... Acts 12:12 *3588*
them John, *w* surname was Mark ... Acts 12:25 *3588*
a Jew, *w* name was Bar-jesus ... Acts 13:6
w shoes of his feet I am not ... Acts 13:25 *3739*
them John, *w* surname was Mark ... Acts 15:37 *3588*
w heart the Lord opened, that she ... Acts 16:14 *3739*
w house joined hard to the ... Acts 18:7 *3739*
of God, *w* I am, and whom I serve, ... Acts 27:23 *3739*
of the island, *w* name was Publius ... Acts 28:7
w sign was Castor and Pollux ... Acts 28:11
w praise is not of men, but of ... Rom 2:29 *3739*
w damnation is just ... Rom 3:8 *3739*
W mouth is full of cursing and ... Rom 3:14 *3739*
Blessed are they *w* iniquities are ... Rom 4:7 *3739*
forgiven, and *w* sins are covered ... Rom 4:7 *3739*
W are the fathers, and of whom as ... Rom 9:5 *3739*
w praise is in the gospel ... 2Cor 8:18 *3739*
w end shall be according to their ... 2Cor 11:15 *3739*
before *w* eyes Jesus Christ hath ... Gal 3:1 *3739*
W end is destruction ... Phil 3:19 *3739*
w God is their belly ... Phil 3:19 *3739*
w glory is in their shame, who ... Phil 3:19 *3588*
w names are in the book of life ... Phil 4:3 *3739*
w coming is after the working of ... 2Th 2:9 *3739*
W mouths must be stopped, who ... Titus 1:11 *3739*
w house are we, if we hold fast ... Heb 3:6 *3739*
w carcases fell in the wilderness ... Heb 3:17 *3739*
w end is to be burned ... Heb 6:8 *3739*
But he *w* descent is not counted ... Heb 7:6
w builder and maker is God ... Heb 11:10 *3739*
W voice then shook the earth ... Heb 12:26 *3739*
w faith follow, considering the ... Heb 13:7 *3739*
w blood is brought into the ... Heb 13:11 *3739*
by *w* stripes ye were healed ... 1Pet 2:24 *3739*
W adorning let it not be that ... 1Pet 3:3 *3739*
w daughters ye are, as long as ye ... 1Pet 3:6 *3739*
w judgment now of a long time ... 2Pet 2:3 *3739*
trees *w* fruit withereth, without ... Jude 12
w name in the Hebrew tongue is ... Rev 9:11
w names are not written in the ... Rev 13:8 *3739*
w deadly wound was healed ... Rev 13:12 *3739*
w names were not written in the ... Rev 17:8 *3739*
from *w* face the earth and the ... Rev 20:11 *3739*

WHOSO

W sheddeth man's blood, by man ... Gen 9:6
w toucheth their carcase shall be ... Lev 11:27 3605
w toucheth any thing that is ... Lev 22:4
W killeth any person, the ... Num 35:30 3605
W killeth his neighbour ... Deut 19:4 834
w followeth her, let him be slain ... 2Chr 23:14
W offereth praise glorifieth me ... Ps 50:23
W privily slandereth his ... Ps 101:5
W is wise, and will observe these ... Ps 107:43 4310
But *w* hearkeneth unto me shall ... Prov 1:33
But *w* committeth adultery with a ... Prov 6:32
For *w* findeth me findeth life, and ... Prov 8:35
W is simple, let him turn in ... Prov 9:4 4310
W is simple, let him turn in ... Prov 9:16 4310
W loveth instruction loveth ... Prov 12:1
W despiseth the word shall be ... Prov 13:13
w trusteth in the LORD, happy is ... Prov 16:20
W mocketh the poor reproacheth ... Prov 17:5
W rewardeth evil for good, evil ... Prov 17:13
W findeth a wife findeth a good ... Prov 18:22
w provoketh him to anger sinneth ... Prov 20:2
W curseth his father or his ... Prov 20:20
W stoppeth his ears at the cry of ... Prov 21:13
W keepeth his mouth and his tongue .. Prov 21:23
W boasteth himself of a false ... Prov 25:14
W diggeth a pit shall fall ... Prov 26:27
W keepeth the fig tree shall eat ... Prov 27:18
W keepeth the law is a wise son ... Prov 28:7
W causeth the righteous to go ... Prov 28:10
but *w* confesseth and forsaketh ... Prov 28:13
W walketh uprightly shall be ... Prov 28:18
W robbeth his father or his ... Prov 28:24
but *w* walketh wisely, he shall be ... Prov 28:26
W loveth wisdom rejoiceth his ... Prov 29:3
W is partner with a thief hateth ... Prov 29:24
but *w* putteth his trust in the ... Prov 29:25
w pleaseth God shall escape from ... Eccl 7:26
W keepeth the commandment shall ... Eccl 8:5
w breaketh an hedge, a serpent ... Eccl 10:8
W removeth stones shall be hurt ... Eccl 10:9
w falleth not down and worshippeth ... Dan 3:6
w falleth not down and worshippeth ... Dan 3:11
that *w* will not come up of all ... Zec 14:17 834
w shall receive one such little ... Mt 18:5
But *w* shall offend one of these ... Mt 18:6
w marrieth her which is put away ... Mt 19:9 *3588*
W therefore shall swear by the ... Mt 23:20 *3588*
w shall swear by the temple, ... Mt 23:21 *3588*
(*w* readeth, let him understand ... Mt 24:15 *3588*
W curseth father or mother, let ... Mk 7:10 *3588*
W eateth my flesh, and drinketh my ... Jn 6:54 *3588*
But *w* looketh into the perfect ... Jas 1:25 *3588*
But *w* keepeth his word, in him ... 1Jn 2:5
But *w* hath this world's good, and ... 1Jn 3:17

WHOSOEVER

Therefore *w* slayeth Cain, ... Gen 4:15 3605
for *w* eateth leavened bread from ... Ex 12:15
for *w* eateth that which is ... Ex 12:19
w toucheth the mount shall be ... Ex 19:12 3605
W lieth with a beast shall surely ... Ex 22:19 3605
W compoundeth any like it ... Ex 30:33 376
or *w* putteth any of it upon a ... Ex 30:33 834
W shall make like unto that, to ... Ex 30:38 834
for *w* doeth any work therein, ... Ex 31:14
w doeth any work in the sabbath ... Ex 31:15 3605
W hath any gold, let them break ... Ex 32:24 4310
W hath sinned against me, him ... Ex 32:33
w doeth work therein shall be put ... Ex 35:2 3605
w is of a willing heart, let him ... Ex 35:5 3605
For *w* eateth the fat of the beast ... Lev 7:25 3605
w toucheth the carcase of them ... Lev 11:24 3605
w beareth ought of the carcase of ... Lev 11:25 3605
w doth touch them, when they be ... Lev 11:31 3605
w toucheth his bed shall wash his ... Lev 15:5
w toucheth any thing that was ... Lev 15:10 3605
w toucheth her shall be unclean ... Lev 15:19 3605
w toucheth her bed shall wash his ... Lev 15:21 3605
w toucheth any thing that she sat ... Lev 15:22 3605
w toucheth those things shall be ... Lev 15:27 3605
w eateth it shall be cut off ... Lev 17:14 3605
For *w* shall commit any of these ... Lev 18:29
w lieth carnally with a woman, ... Lev 19:20
W he be of the children of Israel ... Lev 20:2 376
W he be of thy seed in their ... Lev 21:17
W he be of all your seed among ... Lev 22:3
Or *w* toucheth any creeping thing, ... Lev 22:5
w offereth a sacrifice of peace ... Lev 22:21
W curseth his God shall bear his ... Lev 24:15
and *w* is defiled by the dead ... Num 5:2 3605
or *w* be among you in your ... Num 15:14 834
W cometh any thing near unto the ... Num 17:13 3605
W toucheth the dead body of any ... Num 19:13 3605
w toucheth one that is slain with ... Num 19:16
w hath killed any person, and ... Num 31:19 3605
w hath touched any slain, purify ... Num 31:19 3605
that *w* will not hearken unto my ... Deut 18:19
W he be that doth rebel against ... Josh 1:18
that *w* shall go out of the doors ... Josh 2:19
w shall be with thee in the house ... Josh 2:19
that *w* killeth any person at ... Josh 20:9 3605
W is fearful and afraid, let him ... Judg 7:3 4310
W cometh not forth after Saul and ... 1Sa 11:7 834
W getteth up to the gutter, and ... 2Sa 5:8
W saith ought unto thee, bring ... 2Sa 14:10
that *w* heareth it will say, There ... 2Sa 17:9
w would, he consecrated him, and ... 1Kin 13:33
w shall be wanting, he shall not ... 2Kin 10:19
that *w* heareth of it, both his ... 2Kin 21:12
W smiteth the Jebusites first ... 1Chr 11:6 3605
w had dedicated any thing, it was ... 1Chr 26:28 3605
so that *w* cometh to consecrate ... 2Chr 13:9 3605
That *w* would not seek the LORD ... 2Chr 15:13 3605
w else cometh into the house, he ... 2Chr 23:7
w remaineth in any place where he ... Ezr 1:4 3605
that *w* shall alter this word, let ... Ezr 6:11 3605
w will not do the law of thy God, ... Ezr 7:26 3605
that *w* would not come within ... Ezr 10:8 3605
king's provinces, do know, that *w* ... Est 4:11 834
w toucheth her shall not be ... Prov 6:29 3605
w is deceived thereby is not wise ... Prov 20:1 3605
W hideth her hideth the wind, and ... Prov 27:16
w shall gather together against ... Is 54:15 4310
w goeth therein shall not know ... Is 59:8 3605
this place, the which *w* heareth ... Jer 19:3 3605
Then *w* heareth the sound of the ... Eze 33:4
W shall read this writing, and ... Dan 5:7 3605
that *w* shall ask a petition of ... Dan 6:7 3605
that *w* shall call on the name of ... Joel 2:32 834
W therefore shall break one of ... Mt 5:19
but *w* shall do and teach them, the ... Mt 5:19
w shall kill shall be in danger ... Mt 5:21
That *w* is angry with his brother ... Mt 5:22
w shall say to his brother, Raca, ... Mt 5:22
but *w* shall say, Thou fool, shall ... Mt 5:22
That *w* looketh on a woman to lust ... Mt 5:28
W shall put away his wife, let ... Mt 5:31
That *w* shall put away his wife, ... Mt 5:32
w shall marry her that is ... Mt 5:32
but *w* shall smite thee on thy ... Mt 5:39 *3748*
w shall compel thee to go a mile, ... Mt 5:41
Therefore *w* heareth these sayings ... Mt 7:24
w shall not receive you, nor hear ... Mt 10:14
W therefore shall confess me ... Mt 10:32
But *w* shall deny me before men, ... Mt 10:33
w shall give to drink unto one of ... Mt 10:42
w shall not be offended in me ... Mt 11:6
w speaketh a word against the Son ... Mt 12:32
but *w* speaketh against the Holy ... Mt 12:32
For *w* shall do the will of my ... Mt 12:50
For *w* hath, to him shall be given ... Mt 13:12
but *w* hath not, from him shall be ... Mt 13:12
W shall say to his father or his ... Mt 15:5
For *w* will save his life shall ... Mt 16:25
w will lose his life for my sake ... Mt 16:25
W therefore shall humble himself ... Mt 18:4
W shall put away his wife, except ... Mt 19:9
but *w* will be great among you, ... Mt 20:26
w will be chief among you, let ... Mt 20:27
w shall fall on this stone shall ... Mt 21:44 *3588*
w shall exalt himself shall be ... Mt 23:12 *3748*
W shall swear by the temple, it ... Mt 23:16
but *w* shall swear by the gold of ... Mt 23:16
W shall swear by the altar, it is ... Mt 23:18
but *w* sweareth by the gift that ... Mt 23:18
For *w* shall do the will of God, ... Mk 3:35
w shall not receive you, nor hear ... Mk 6:11
W will come after me, let him ... Mk 8:34 *3748*
For *w* will save his life shall ... Mk 8:35
but *w* shall lose his life for my ... Mk 8:35
W therefore shall be ashamed of ... Mk 8:38
W shall receive one of such ... Mk 9:37
w shall receive me, receiveth not ... Mk 9:37
For *w* shall give you a cup of ... Mk 9:41
w shall offend one of these ... Mk 9:42
W shall put away his wife, and ... Mk 10:11
W shall not receive the kingdom ... Mk 10:15
but *w* will be great among you, ... Mk 10:43
w of you will be the chiefest, ... Mk 10:44
That *w* shall say unto this ... Mk 11:23
W cometh to me, and heareth my ... Lk 6:47
w shall not be offended in me ... Lk 7:23
for *w* hath, to him shall be given ... Lk 8:18

w hath not, from him shall be	Lk 8:18	
w will not receive you, when ye	Lk 9:5	
For *w* will save his life shall	Lk 9:24	
but *w* will lose his life for my	Lk 9:24	
For *w* shall be ashamed of me and	Lk 9:26	
W shall receive this child in my	Lk 9:48	
w shall receive me receiveth him	Lk 9:48	
W shall confess me before men,	Lk 12:8	
w shall speak a word against the	Lk 12:10	
For *w* exalteth himself shall be	Lk 14:11	
w doth not bear his cross, and	Lk 14:27	3748
w he be of you that forsaketh not	Lk 14:33	3956
W putteth away his wife, and	Lk 16:18	
w marrieth her that is put away	Lk 16:18	
W shall seek to save his life	Lk 17:33	
w shall lose his life shall	Lk 17:33	
W shall not receive the kingdom	Lk 18:17	
W shall fall upon that stone	Lk 20:18	
That *w* believeth in him should	Jn 3:15	
that *w* believeth in him should	Jn 3:16	
W drinketh of this water shall	Jn 4:13	
But *w* drinketh of the water that	Jn 4:14	
w then first after the troubling	Jn 5:4	
W committeth sin is the servant	Jn 8:34	
w liveth and believeth in me shall	Jn 11:26	
that *w* believeth on me should not	Jn 12:46	
that *w* killeth you will think	Jn 16:2	
w maketh himself a king speaketh	Jn 19:12	
that *w* shall call on the name of	Acts 2:21	
that through his name *w* believeth	Acts 10:43	
w among you feareth God, to you	Acts 13:26	3588
O man, *w* thou art that judgest	Rom 2:1	
w believeth on him shall not be	Rom 9:33	
W believeth on him shall not be	Rom 10:11	
For *w* shall call upon the name of	Rom 10:13	
W therefore resisteth the power,	Rom 13:2	3588
Wherefore *w* shall eat this bread,	1Cor 11:27	
w of you are justified by the law	Gal 5:4	3748
shall bear his judgment, *w* he be	Gal 5:10	
For *w* shall keep the whole law,	Jas 2:10	3748
w therefore will be a friend of	Jas 4:4	
W denieth the Son, the same hath	1Jn 2:23	
W committeth sin transgresseth	1Jn 3:4	
W abideth in him sinneth not	1Jn 3:6	
w sinneth hath not seen him,	1Jn 3:6	
W is born of God doth not commit	1Jn 3:9	
w doeth not righteousness is not	1Jn 3:10	
W hateth his brother is a	1Jn 3:15	
W shall confess that Jesus is the	1Jn 4:15	
W believeth that Jesus is the	1Jn 5:1	
We know that *w* is born of God	1Jn 5:18	
W transgresseth, and abideth not	2Jn 9	
w receiveth the mark of his name	Rev 14:11	1536
w was not found written in the	Rev 20:15	1536
and *w* loveth and maketh a lie	Rev 22:15	
w will, let him take the water of	Rev 22:17	3588

WHY

said unto Cain, *W* art thou wroth	Gen 4:6	4100
w is thy countenance fallen	Gen 4:6	4100
w didst thou not tell me that she	Gen 12:18	4100
W saidst thou, She is my sister	Gen 12:19	4100
said, If it be so, *w* am I thus	Gen 25:22	4100
w should I be deprived also of	Gen 27:45	4100
W do ye look one upon another	Gen 42:1	4100
for *w* should we die in thy	Gen 47:15	4100
W have ye done this thing, and	Ex 1:18	4069
w is it that ye have left the man	Ex 2:20	4100
sight, *w* the bush is not burnt	Ex 3:3	4069
w is it that thou hast sent me	Ex 5:22	4100
W have we done this, that we have	Ex 14:5	4100
unto them, *W* chide ye with me	Ex 17:2	4100
w sittest thou thyself alone, and	Ex 18:14	4069
w doth thy wrath wax hot against	Ex 32:11	4100
W came we forth out of Egypt	Num 11:20	4100
And *w* have ye brought up the	Num 20:4	4100
W should the name of our father	Num 27:4	4100
Now therefore *w* should we die	Deut 5:25	4100
this is the cause *w* Joshua did	Josh 5:4	
said, *W* hast thou troubled us	Josh 7:25	4100
W hast thou given me but one lot	Josh 17:14	4069
w have ye done this	Judg 2:2	4100
W abodest thou among the	Judg 5:16	4100
w did Dan remain in ships	Judg 5:17	4100
W is his chariot so long in	Judg 5:28	4069
W tarry the wheels of his	Judg 5:28	4069
w then is all this befallen us	Judg 6:13	4100
W hast thou served us thus, that	Judg 8:1	4100
for *w* should we serve him	Judg 9:28	4100
w are ye come unto me now when ye	Judg 11:7	4069
w therefore did ye not recover	Judg 11:26	4069
W askest thou thus after my name,	Judg 13:18	4100
W are ye come up against us	Judg 15:10	4100
w is this come to pass in Israel,	Judg 21:3	4100
w will ye go with me	Ruth 1:11	4100
w then call ye me Naomi, seeing	Ruth 1:21	4100
W have I found grace in thine	Ruth 2:10	4069
to her, Hannah, *w* weepest thou	1Sa 1:8	4100
and *w* eatest thou not	1Sa 1:8	4100
and *w* is thy heart grieved	1Sa 1:8	4100
unto them, *W* do ye such things	1Sa 2:23	4100
it shall be known to you *w* his	1Sa 6:3	4100
W are ye come out to set your	1Sa 17:8	4100
W camest thou down hither	1Sa 17:28	4100
W hast thou deceived me so, and	1Sa 19:17	4100
w should I kill thee	1Sa 19:17	4100
w should my father hide this	1Sa 20:2	4060
for *w* shouldest thou bring me to	1Sa 20:8	4100
W art thou alone, and no man with	1Sa 21:1	4069
W have ye conspired against me,	1Sa 22:13	4100
for *w* should thy servant dwell in	1Sa 27:5	4100
saying, *W* hast thou deceived me	1Sa 28:12	4100
W hast thou disquieted me, to	1Sa 28:15	4100
w is it that thou hast sent him	2Sa 3:24	4100
W build ye not me an house of	2Sa 7:7	4100
w then didst thou not go down	2Sa 11:10	4069
w went ye nigh the wall	2Sa 11:21	4100
W art thou, being the king's son,	2Sa 13:4	4069
him, *W* should he go with thee	2Sa 13:26	4100
W should this dead dog curse my	2Sa 16:9	4100
W wentest thou not with thy	2Sa 16:17	4100
w didst thou not smite him there	2Sa 18:11	4069
Now therefore *w* speak ye not a	2Sa 19:10	4100
W are ye the last to bring the	2Sa 19:11	4100
W speakest thou any more of thy	2Sa 19:29	4100
w should the king recompense it	2Sa 19:36	4100
W have our brethren the men of	2Sa 19:41	4069
w then did ye despise us, that	2Sa 19:43	4069
w wilt thou swallow up the	2Sa 20:19	4100
but *w* doth my lord the king	2Sa 24:3	4100
in saying, *W* hast thou done so	1Kin 1:6	4069
w then doth Adonijah reign	1Kin 1:13	4069
w dost thou ask Abishag the	1Kin 2:22	4100
W then hast thou not kept the	1Kin 2:43	4100
W hath the LORD done thus unto	1Kin 9:8	
w feignest thou thyself to be	1Kin 14:6	4100
W is thy spirit so sad, that thou	1Kin 21:5	4100
them, *W* are ye now turned back	2Kin 1:5	4100
W sit we here until we die	2Kin 7:3	4100
And Hazael said, *W* weepeth my lord	2Kin 8:12	4069
W repair ye not the breaches of	2Kin 12:7	4069
for *w* shouldest thou meddle to	2Kin 14:10	
W have ye not built me an house	1Chr 17:6	4100
w then doth my lord require this	1Chr 21:3	4100
w will he be a cause of trespass	1Chr 21:3	
W hath the LORD done thus unto	2Chr 7:21	4100
W hast thou not required of the	2Chr 24:6	4069
W transgress ye the commandments	2Chr 24:20	4100
W hast thou sought after the gods	2Chr 25:15	4100
w shouldest thou be smitten	2Chr 25:16	4100
w shouldest thou meddle to thine	2Chr 25:19	4100
W should the kings of Assyria	2Chr 32:4	4100
w should damage grow to the hurt	Ezr 4:22	4101
for *w* should there be wrath	Ezr 7:23	4101
W is thy countenance sad, seeing	Neh 2:2	4069
w should not my countenance be	Neh 2:3	4069
w should the work cease, whilst I	Neh 6:3	4100
W is the house of God forsaken	Neh 13:11	4069
W lodge ye about the wall	Neh 13:21	4069
W transgressest thou the king's	Est 3:3	4069
to know what it was, and *w* it was	Est 4:5	4100
W died I not from the womb	Job 3:11	4100
w did I not give up the ghost	Job 3:11	
W did the knees prevent me	Job 3:12	4069
or *w* the breasts that I should	Job 3:12	4069
W is light given to a man whose	Job 3:23	
w hast thou set me as a mark	Job 7:20	4100
w dost thou not pardon my	Job 7:21	4100
wicked, *w* then labour I in vain	Job 9:29	4100
W doth thine heart carry thee	Job 15:12	4100
W do ye persecute me as God, and	Job 19:22	4100
W persecute we him, seeing the	Job 19:28	4100
w should not my spirit be	Job 21:4	4069
W, seeing times are not hidden	Job 24:1	4069
w then are ye thus altogether	Job 27:12	4100
w then should I think upon a maid	Job 31:1	4100
W dost thou strive against him	Job 33:13	4069
W do the heathen rage, and the	Ps 2:1	4100
W standest thou afar off, O LORD	Ps 10:1	4100
w hidest thou thyself in times of	Ps 10:1	
my God, *w* hast thou forsaken me	Ps 22:1	4100
w art thou so far from helping me	Ps 22:1	
W art thou cast down, O my soul	Ps 42:5	
w art thou disquieted in me	Ps 42:5	
my rock, *W* hast thou forgotten me	Ps 42:9	4100
w go I mourning because of the	Ps 42:9	4100
W art thou cast down, O my soul	Ps 42:11	4100
w art thou disquieted within me	Ps 42:11	4100
w dost thou cast me off	Ps 43:2	4100
W go I mourning because of the	Ps 43:2	4100
W art thou cast down, O my soul	Ps 43:5	4100
w art thou disquieted within me	Ps 43:5	4100
Awake, *w* sleepest thou, O Lord	Ps 44:23	4100
W boastest thou thyself in	Ps 52:1	4100
W leap ye, ye high hills	Ps 68:16	4100
w hast thou cast us off for ever	Ps 74:1	4100
w doth thine anger smoke against	Ps 74:1	
W withdrawest thou thy hand, even	Ps 74:11	4100
W hast thou then broken down her	Ps 80:12	4100
w castest thou off my soul	Ps 88:14	4100
w hidest thou thy face from me	Ps 88:14	
w wilt thou, my son, be ravished	Prov 5:20	
w should he take away thy bed	Prov 22:27	4100
and *w* was I then more wise	Eccl 2:15	4100
w shouldest thou destroy thyself	Eccl 7:16	4100
w shouldest thou die before thy	Eccl 7:17	4100
for *w* should I be as one that	Song 1:7	4100
W should ye be stricken any more	Is 1:5	
W sayest thou, O Jacob, and	Is 40:27	4100
w hast thou made us to err from	Is 63:17	4100
w is he spoiled	Jer 2:14	4069
W trimmest thou thy way to seek	Jer 2:33	4100
W gaddest thou about so much to	Jer 2:36	4100
W then is this people of	Jer 8:5	4069
W do we sit still	Jer 8:14	
W have they provoked me to anger	Jer 8:19	4069
w then is not the health of the	Jer 8:22	4069
w shouldest thou be as a stranger	Jer 14:8	4100
W shouldest thou be as a man	Jer 14:9	4100
w hast thou smitten us, and there	Jer 14:19	4069
W is my pain perpetual, and my	Jer 15:18	4100
W hast thou prophesied in the	Jer 26:9	4069
W will ye die, thou and thy people	Jer 27:13	4100
Now therefore *w* hast thou not	Jer 29:27	4100
W criest thou for thine	Jer 30:15	4100
W hast thou written therein,	Jer 36:29	4069
W are thy valiant men swept away	Jer 46:15	4069
w then doth their king inherit	Jer 49:1	4069
Yet say ye, *W*	Eze 18:19	4069
for *w* will ye die, O house of	Eze 18:31	4100
for *w* will ye die, O house of	Eze 33:11	4100
for *w* should he see your faces	Dan 1:10	4100
W is the decree so hasty from the	Dan 2:15	
unto him, *W* hast thou done this	Jonah 1:10	4100
Now *w* dost thou cry out aloud	Mic 4:9	4100
W dost thou shew me iniquity, and	Hab 1:3	4100
W? saith the LORD	Hag 1:9	
w do we deal treacherously every	Mal 2:10	4069
w take ye thought for raiment	Mt 6:28	5101
w beholdest thou the mote that is	Mt 7:3	5101
W are ye fearful, O ye of little	Mt 8:26	5101
W eateth your Master with	Mt 9:11	1302
W do we and the Pharisees fast oft	Mt 9:14	1302
W speakest thou unto them in	Mt 13:10	1302
W do thy disciples transgress the	Mt 15:2	1302
W do ye also transgress the	Mt 15:3	1302
w reason ye among yourselves,	Mt 16:8	5101
W then say the scribes that Elias	Mt 17:10	5101
W could not we cast him out	Mt 17:19	1302
W did Moses then command to give	Mt 19:7	5101
unto him, *W* callest thou me good	Mt 19:17	5101
W stand ye here all the day idle	Mt 20:6	5101
W did ye not then believe him	Mt 21:25	1302
W tempt ye me, ye hypocrites	Mt 22:18	5101
unto them, *W* trouble ye the woman	Mt 26:10	5101
And the governor said, *W*, what	Mt 27:23	1063
my God, *w* hast thou forsaken me	Mt 27:46	2444
W doth this man thus speak	Mk 2:7	5101
W reason ye these things in your	Mk 2:8	5101
W do the disciples of John and of	Mk 2:18	1302
w do they on the sabbath day that	Mk 2:24	5101
unto them, *W* are ye so fearful	Mk 4:40	5101
w troublest thou the Master any	Mk 5:35	5101
W make ye this ado, and weep	Mk 5:39	5101
him, *W* walk not thy disciples	Mk 7:5	1302
W doth this generation seek after	Mk 8:12	5101
W reason ye, because ye have no	Mk 8:17	5101
W say the scribes that Elias must	Mk 9:11	3754
W could not we cast him out	Mk 9:28	3754
unto him, *W* callest thou me good	Mk 10:18	5101
man say unto you, *W* do ye this	Mk 11:3	5101
W then did ye not believe him	Mk 11:31	1302
said unto them, *W* tempt ye me	Mk 12:15	5101
W was this waste of the ointment	Mk 14:4	
w trouble ye her	Mk 14:6	5101
Then Pilate said unto them, *W*	Mk 15:14	1063
my God, *w* hast thou forsaken me	Mk 15:34	
w hast thou thus dealt with us	Lk 2:48	5101
W do ye eat and drink with	Lk 5:30	1302
W do the disciples of John fast	Lk 5:33	1302
W do ye that which is not lawful	Lk 6:2	5101
w beholdest thou the mote that is	Lk 6:41	5101
W call ye me, Lord, Lord, and do	Lk 6:46	5101
w take ye thought for the rest	Lk 12:26	5101
w even of yourselves judge ye not	Lk 12:57	5101
w cumbereth it the ground	Lk 13:7	2444
unto him, *W* callest thou me good	Lk 18:19	5101
man ask you, *W* do ye loose him	Lk 19:31	1302
unto them, *W* loose ye the colt	Lk 19:33	5101
W then believed ye him not	Lk 20:5	1302
and said unto them, *W* tempt ye me	Lk 20:23	5101
And said unto them, *W* sleep ye	Lk 22:46	5101
said unto them the third time, *W*	Lk 23:22	1063
W seek ye the living among the	Lk 24:5	5101
said unto them, *W* are ye troubled	Lk 24:38	5101
w do thoughts arise in your	Lk 24:38	1302
W baptizest thou then, if thou be	Jn 1:25	5101
or, *W* talkest thou with her	Jn 4:27	5101
W go ye about to kill me	Jn 7:19	5101
W have ye not brought him	Jn 7:45	1302
W do ye not understand my speech	Jn 8:43	1302
the truth, *w* do ye not believe me	Jn 8:46	1302
W herein is a marvellous thing,	Jn 9:30	1063
w hear ye him	Jn 10:20	5101
W was not this ointment sold for	Jn 12:5	1302
w cannot I follow thee now	Jn 13:37	1302
W askest thou me	Jn 18:21	5101
but if well, *w* smitest thou me	Jn 18:23	5101
unto her, Woman, *w* weepest thou	Jn 20:13	5101
unto her, Woman, *w* weepest thou	Jn 20:15	5101
w stand ye gazing up into heaven	Acts 1:11	5101
of Israel, *w* marvel ye at this	Acts 3:12	5101
or *w* look ye so earnestly on us,	Acts 3:12	5101
W did the heathen rage, and the	Acts 4:25	2444
w hath Satan filled thine heart	Acts 5:3	1302
w hast thou conceived this thing	Acts 5:4	5101
w do ye wrong one to another	Acts 7:26	2444
Saul, Saul, *w* persecutest thou me	Acts 9:4	5101
Sirs, *w* do ye these things	Acts 14:15	5101
Now therefore *w* tempt ye God	Acts 15:10	5101
Saul, Saul, *w* persecutest thou me	Acts 22:7	5101
And now *w* tarriest thou	Acts 22:16	5101
W should it be thought a thing	Acts 26:8	5101
Saul, Saul, *w* persecutest thou me	Acts 26:14	5101
w yet am I also judged as a	Rom 3:7	5101
man seeth, *w* doth he yet hope for	Rom 8:24	5101
unto me, *W* doth he yet find fault	Rom 9:19	5101
it, *W* hast thou made me thus	Rom 9:20	5101
But *w* dost thou judge thy brother	Rom 14:10	5101
or *w* dost thou set at nought thy	Rom 14:10	5101
w dost thou glory, as if thou	1Cor 4:7	5101
W do ye not rather take wrong	1Cor 6:7	1302
w do ye not rather suffer	1Cor 6:7	1302
for *w* is my liberty judged of	1Cor 10:29	
w am I evil spoken of for that	1Cor 10:30	5101
w are they then baptized for the	1Cor 15:29	5101
w stand we in jeopardy every hour	1Cor 15:30	5101
w compellest thou the Gentiles to	Gal 2:14	5101
w do I yet suffer persecution	Gal 5:11	5101
the rudiments of the world, *w*	Col 2:20	5101

WICKED

But the men of Sodom were *w*	Gen 13:13	7451
destroy the righteous with the *w*	Gen 18:23	7563
to slay the righteous with the *w*	Gen 18:25	7563
the righteous should be as the *w*	Gen 18:25	7563
was *w* in the sight of the LORD	Gen 38:7	7451
and I and my people are *w*	Ex 9:27	7563
put not thine hand with the *w* to	Ex 23:1	7563
for I will not justify the *w*	Ex 23:7	7563
it is a *w* thing	Lev 20:17	2617
from the tents of these *w* men	Num 16:26	7563
be not a thought in thy *w* heart	Deut 15:9	1100
which have committed that *w* thing	Deut 17:5	7451
then keep thee from every *w* thing	Deut 23:9	7451
the righteous, and condemn the *w*	Deut 25:1	7563
if the *w* man be worthy to be	Deut 25:2	7563
the *w* shall be silent in darkness	1Sa 2:9	7563
Wickedness proceedeth from the *w*	1Sa 24:13	7563
Then answered all the *w* men	1Sa 30:22	7451
as a man falleth before *w* men	2Sa 3:34	5766
when *w* men have slain a righteous	2Sa 4:11	7563
thy servants, condemning the *w*	1Kin 8:32	7563
wrought *w* things to provoke the	2Kin 17:11	7451
thy servants, by requiting the *w*	2Chr 6:23	7563
face, and turn from their *w* ways	2Chr 7:14	7451
that *w* woman, had broken up the	2Chr 24:7	4849
turned they from their *w* works	Neh 9:35	7451
and enemy is this *w* Haman	Est 7:6	7451
by letters that his *w* device	Est 9:25	7451
There the *w* cease from troubling	Job 3:17	7563
of the *w* shall come to nought	Job 8:22	7563
destroyeth the perfect and the *w*	Job 9:22	7563
is given into the hand of the *w*	Job 9:24	7563
If I be *w*, why then labour I in	Job 9:29	7561
shine upon the counsel of the *w*	Job 10:3	7563
Thou knowest that I am not *w*	Job 10:7	7561
If I be *w*, woe unto me	Job 10:15	7561
But the eyes of the *w* shall fail	Job 11:20	7563
The *w* man travaileth with pain	Job 15:20	7563
me over into the hands of the *w*	Job 16:11	7563
light of the *w* shall be put out	Job 18:5	7563
such are the dwellings of the *w*	Job 18:21	5767
the triumphing of the *w* is short	Job 20:5	7563
every hand of the *w* shall come	Job 20:22	6001
the portion of a *w* man from God	Job 20:29	7563
Wherefore do the *w* live, become	Job 21:7	7563
counsel of the *w* is far from me	Job 21:16	7563
is the candle of the *w* put out	Job 21:17	7563
are the dwelling places of the *w*	Job 21:28	7563
That the *w* is reserved to the day	Job 21:30	7451
old way which *w* men have trodden	Job 22:15	205
counsel of the *w* is far from me	Job 22:18	7563
they gather the vintage of the *w*	Job 24:6	7563
Let mine enemy be as the *w*	Job 27:7	7563
the portion of a *w* man with God	Job 27:13	7563
And I brake the jaws of the *w*	Job 29:17	5767
Is not destruction to the *w*	Job 31:3	5767
iniquity, and walketh with *w* men	Job 34:8	7562
fit to say to a king, Thou art *w*	Job 34:18	1100
He striketh them as *w* men in the	Job 34:26	7563
because of his answers for *w* men	Job 34:36	205
preserveth not the life of the *w*	Job 36:6	7563
fulfilled the judgment of the *w*	Job 36:17	7563
that the *w* might be shaken out of	Job 38:13	7563
from the *w* their light is	Job 38:15	7563
tread down the *w* in their place	Job 40:12	7563
of the *w* come to an end	Ps 7:9	7563
God is angry with the *w* every day	Ps 7:11	
thou hast destroyed the *w*	Ps 9:5	7563
the *w* is snared in the work of	Ps 9:16	7563
The *w* shall be turned into hell,	Ps 9:17	7563
The *w* in his pride doth persecute	Ps 10:2	7563
For the *w* boasteth of his heart's	Ps 10:3	7563
The *w*, through the pride of his	Ps 10:4	7563
Wherefore doth the *w* contemn God	Ps 10:13	7563
Break thou the arm of the *w*	Ps 10:15	7563
the *w* bend their bow, they make	Ps 11:2	7563
but the *w* and him that loveth	Ps 11:5	7563
Upon the *w* he shall rain snares,	Ps 11:6	7563
The *w* walk on every side, when	Ps 12:8	7563
From the *w* that oppress me, from	Ps 17:9	7563
deliver my soul from the *w*	Ps 17:13	7563
of the *w* have inclosed me	Ps 22:16	7489
and will not sit with the *w*	Ps 26:5	7563
When the *w*, even mine enemies and	Ps 27:2	7489
Draw me not away with the *w*	Ps 28:3	7563
let the *w* be ashamed, and let them	Ps 31:17	7563
Many sorrows shall be to the *w*	Ps 32:10	7563
Evil shall slay the *w*	Ps 34:21	7563
of the *w* saith within my heart	Ps 36:1	7563
not the hand of the *w* remove me	Ps 36:11	7563
who bringeth *w* devices to pass	Ps 37:7	4209
while, and the *w* shall not be	Ps 37:10	7563
The *w* plotteth against the just,	Ps 37:12	7563
The *w* have drawn out the sword,	Ps 37:14	7563
better than the riches of many *w*	Ps 37:16	7563
the arms of the *w* shall be broken	Ps 37:17	7563
But the *w* shall perish, and the	Ps 37:20	7563
The *w* borroweth, and payeth not	Ps 37:21	7563
seed of the *w* shall be cut off	Ps 37:28	7563
The *w* watcheth the righteous, and	Ps 37:32	7563
when the *w* are cut off, thou	Ps 37:34	7563
I have seen the *w* in great power	Ps 37:35	7563
the end of the *w* shall be cut off	Ps 37:38	7563
he shall deliver them from the *w*	Ps 37:40	7563
bridle, while the *w* is before me	Ps 39:1	7563
But unto the *w* God saith, What	Ps 50:16	7563
of the oppression of the *w*	Ps 55:3	7563
The *w* are estranged from the womb	Ps 58:3	7563
his feet in the blood of the *w*	Ps 58:10	7563
merciful to any *w* transgressors	Ps 59:5	205
from the secret counsel of the *w*	Ps 64:2	7489
so let the *w* perish at the	Ps 68:2	7563
my God, out of the hand of the *w*	Ps 71:4	7563
I saw the prosperity of the *w*	Ps 73:3	7563
unto the multitude of the *w*	Ps 74:19	
and to the *w*, Lift not up the horn	Ps 75:4	7563
all the *w* of the earth shall	Ps 75:8	7563
of the *w* also will I cut off	Ps 75:10	7563
and accept the persons of the *w*	Ps 82:2	7563
rid them out of the hand of the *w*	Ps 82:4	7563
behold and see the reward of the *w*	Ps 91:8	7563
When the *w* spring as the grass,	Ps 92:7	7563
of the *w* that rise up against me	Ps 92:11	7489
LORD, how long shall the *w*	Ps 94:3	7563
how long shall the *w* triumph	Ps 94:3	7563
until the pit be digged for the *w*	Ps 94:13	7563
them out of the hand of the *w*	Ps 97:10	7563
I will set no *w* thing before mine	Ps 101:3	1100
I will not know a *w* person	Ps 101:4	7451
destroy all the *w* of the land	Ps 101:8	7563
that I may cut off all *w* doers	Ps 101:8	205
earth, and let the *w* be no more	Ps 104:35	7563
the flame burned up the *w*	Ps 106:18	7563
For the mouth of the *w* and the	Ps 109:2	7563
Set thou a *w* man over him	Ps 109:6	7563
The *w* shall see it, and be grieved	Ps 112:10	7563
the desire of the *w* shall perish	Ps 112:10	7563
of the *w* that forsake thy law	Ps 119:53	7563
The bands of the *w* have robbed me	Ps 119:61	7563
The *w* have waited for me to	Ps 119:95	7563
The *w* have laid a snare for me	Ps 119:110	7563
all the *w* of the earth like dross	Ps 119:119	7563
Salvation is far from the *w*	Ps 119:155	7563
For the rod of the *w* shall not	Ps 125:3	7562
cut asunder the cords of the *w*	Ps 129:4	7563
Surely thou wilt slay the *w*	Ps 139:19	7563
see if there be any *w* way in me	Ps 139:24	6090
O LORD, from the hands of the *w*	Ps 140:4	7563
not, O LORD, the desires of the *w*	Ps 140:8	7563
further not his *w* device	Ps 140:8	2162
to practise *w* works with men that	Ps 141:4	7562
Let the *w* fall into their own	Ps 141:10	7563
but all the *w* will he destroy	Ps 145:20	7563
but the way of the *w* he turneth	Ps 146:9	7563
he casteth the *w* down to the	Ps 147:6	7563
in the frowardness of the *w*	Prov 2:14	7451
But the *w* shall be cut off from	Prov 2:22	7563
of the desolation of the *w*	Prov 3:25	7563
the LORD is in the house of the *w*	Prov 3:33	7563
Enter not into the path of the *w*	Prov 4:14	7563
The way of the *w* is as darkness	Prov 4:19	7563
shall take the *w* himself, and he	Prov 5:22	7563
a *w* man, walketh with a froward	Prov 6:12	205
that deviseth *w* imaginations	Prov 6:18	205
he that rebuketh a *w* man getteth	Prov 9:7	7563
away the substance of the *w*	Prov 10:3	7563
covereth the mouth of the *w*	Prov 10:6	7563
but the name of the *w* shall rot	Prov 10:7	7563
covereth the mouth of the *w*	Prov 10:11	7563
the fruit of the *w* to sin	Prov 10:16	7563
heart of the *w* is little worth	Prov 10:20	7563
The fear of the *w*, it shall come	Prov 10:24	7563
passeth, so is the *w* no more	Prov 10:25	7563
years of the *w* shall be shortened	Prov 10:27	7563
expectation of the *w* shall perish	Prov 10:28	7563
but the *w* shall not inhabit the	Prov 10:30	7563
of the *w* speaketh frowardness	Prov 10:32	7563
but the *w* shall fall by his own	Prov 11:5	7563
When a *w* man dieth, his	Prov 11:7	7563
the *w* cometh in his stead	Prov 11:8	7563
and when the *w* perish, there is	Prov 11:10	7563
overthrown by the mouth of the *w*	Prov 11:11	7563
The *w* worketh a deceitful work	Prov 11:18	7563
the *w* shall not be unpunished	Prov 11:21	7451
the expectation of the *w* is wrath	Prov 11:23	7563
much more the *w* and the sinner	Prov 11:31	7563
but a man of *w* devices will he	Prov 12:2	4209
the counsels of the *w* are deceit	Prov 12:5	7563
The words of the *w* are to lie in	Prov 12:6	7563
The *w* are overthrown, and are not	Prov 12:7	7563
tender mercies of the *w* are cruel	Prov 12:10	7563
The *w* desireth the net of evil	Prov 12:12	7563
The *w* is snared by the	Prov 12:13	7451
but the *w* shall be filled with	Prov 12:21	7563
the way of the *w* seduceth them	Prov 12:26	7563
but a *w* man is loathsome, and	Prov 13:5	7563
lamp of the *w* shall be put out	Prov 13:9	7563
A *w* messenger falleth into	Prov 13:17	7563
but the belly of the *w* shall want	Prov 13:25	7563
The house of the *w* shall be	Prov 14:11	7563
a man of *w* devices is hated	Prov 14:17	4209
the *w* at the gates of the	Prov 14:19	7563
The *w* is driven away in his	Prov 14:32	7563
the revenues of the *w* is trouble	Prov 15:6	7563
The sacrifice of the *w* is an	Prov 15:8	7563
The way of the *w* is an	Prov 15:9	7563
The thoughts of the *w* are an	Prov 15:26	7451
but the mouth of the *w* poureth	Prov 15:28	7563
The LORD is far from the *w*	Prov 15:29	7563
even the *w* for the day of evil	Prov 16:4	7563
A *w* doer giveth heed to false	Prov 17:4	7489
He that justifieth the *w*, and he	Prov 17:15	7563
A *w* man taketh a gift out of the	Prov 17:23	7563
When the *w* cometh, then cometh	Prov 18:3	7563
to accept the person of the *w*	Prov 18:5	7563
the mouth of the *w* devoureth	Prov 19:28	7563
A wise king scattereth the *w*	Prov 20:26	7563
heart, and the plowing of the *w*	Prov 21:4	7563
of the *w* shall destroy them	Prov 21:7	7563
The soul of the *w* desireth evil	Prov 21:10	7563
considereth the house of the *w*	Prov 21:12	7563
the *w* for their wickedness	Prov 21:12	7563
The *w* shall be a ransom for the	Prov 21:18	7563
sacrifice of the *w* is abomination	Prov 21:27	7563
when he bringeth it with a *w* mind	Prov 21:27	2154
A *w* man hardeneth his face	Prov 21:29	7563
O *w* man, against the dwelling of	Prov 24:15	7563
but the *w* shall fall into	Prov 24:16	7563
neither be thou envious at the *w*	Prov 24:19	7563
candle of the *w* shall be put out	Prov 24:20	7563
He that saith unto the *w*, Thou	Prov 24:24	7563
Take away the *w* from before the	Prov 25:5	7563
the *w* is as a troubled fountain	Prov 25:26	7563
a *w* heart are like a potsherd	Prov 26:23	7451
The *w* flee when no man pursueth	Prov 28:1	7563
that forsake the law praise the *w*	Prov 28:4	7563
but when the *w* rise, a man is	Prov 28:12	7563
so is a *w* ruler over the poor	Prov 28:15	7563
When the *w* rise, men hide	Prov 28:28	7563
but when the *w* beareth rule	Prov 29:2	7563
but the *w* regardeth not to know	Prov 29:7	7563
to lies, all his servants are *w*	Prov 29:12	7563
When the *w* are multiplied,	Prov 29:16	7563
the way is abomination to the *w*	Prov 29:27	7563
judge the righteous and the *w*	Eccl 3:17	7563
there is a *w* man that prolongeth	Eccl 7:15	7563
Be not over much *w*, neither be	Eccl 7:17	7561
And so I saw the *w* buried, who had	Eccl 8:10	7563
it shall not be well with the *w*	Eccl 8:13	7563
according to the work of the *w*	Eccl 8:14	7563
again, there be *w* men, to whom it	Eccl 8:14	7563
to the righteous, and to the *w*	Eccl 9:2	7563
Woe unto the *w*	Is 3:11	7563
Which justify the *w* for reward	Is 5:23	7563
of his lips shall he slay the *w*	Is 11:4	7563
evil, and the *w* for their iniquity	Is 13:11	7563
hath broken the staff of the *w*	Is 14:5	7563
Let favour be shewed to the *w*	Is 26:10	7563
he deviseth *w* devices to destroy	Is 32:7	2154
peace, saith the LORD, unto the *w*	Is 48:22	7563
And he made his grave with the *w*	Is 53:9	7563
Let the *w* forsake his way, and the	Is 55:7	7563
But the *w* are like the troubled	Is 57:20	7563
no peace, saith my God, to the *w*	Is 57:21	7563
also taught the *w* ones thy ways	Jer 2:33	7451
among my people are found *w* men	Jer 5:26	7563
they overpass the deeds of the *w*	Jer 5:28	7451
for the *w* are not plucked away	Jer 6:29	7451
doth the way of the *w* prosper	Jer 12:1	7563
thee out of the hand of the *w*	Jer 15:21	7451
all things, and desperately *w*	Jer 17:9	605
grievously upon the head of the *w*	Jer 23:19	7563
give them that are *w* to the sword	Jer 25:31	7563
with pain upon the head of the *w*	Jer 30:23	7563
When I say unto the *w*, Thou shalt	Eze 3:18	7563
to warn the *w* from his *w* way	Eze 3:18	7563
the same *w* man shall die in his	Eze 3:18	7563
Yet if thou warn the *w*, and he	Eze 3:19	7563
wickedness, nor from his *w* way	Eze 3:19	7563
to the *w* of the earth for a spoil	Eze 7:21	7563
behold the *w* abominations that	Eze 8:9	7451
give *w* counsel in this city	Eze 11:2	7451
strengthened the hands of the *w*	Eze 13:22	7451
should not return from his *w* way	Eze 13:22	7563
of the *w* shall be upon him	Eze 18:20	7563
But if the *w* will turn from all	Eze 18:21	7563
at all that the *w* should die	Eze 18:23	7563
abominations that the *w* man doeth	Eze 18:24	7563
when the *w* man turneth away from	Eze 18:27	7563
not according to your *w* ways	Eze 20:44	7451
from thee the righteous and the *w*	Eze 21:3	7563
from thee the righteous and the *w*	Eze 21:4	7563
profane *w* prince of Israel, whose	Eze 21:25	7563
of them that are slain, of the *w*	Eze 21:29	7563
the land into the hand of the *w*	Eze 30:12	7451
When I say unto the *w*	Eze 33:8	7563
O *w* man, thou shalt surely die	Eze 33:8	7563
speak to warn the *w* from his way	Eze 33:8	7563
that *w* man shall die in his	Eze 33:8	7563
if thou warn the *w* of his way to	Eze 33:9	7563
no pleasure in the death of the *w*	Eze 33:11	7563
but that the *w* turn from his way	Eze 33:11	7563
as for the wickedness of the *w*	Eze 33:12	7563
Again, when I say unto the *w*	Eze 33:14	7563
If the *w* restore the pledge, give	Eze 33:15	7563
But if the *w* turn from his	Eze 33:19	7563
but the *w* shall do wickedly	Dan 12:10	7563
none of the *w* shall understand	Dan 12:10	7563
wickedness in the house of the *w*	Mic 6:10	7563
them pure with the *w* balances	Mic 6:11	7562
and will not at all acquit the *w*	Nah 1:3	7563
against the LORD, a *w* counsellor	Nah 1:11	1100
for the *w* shall no more pass	Nah 1:15	1100
for the *w* doth compass about the	Hab 1:4	7563
holdest thy tongue when the *w*	Hab 1:13	7563
head out of the house of the *w*	Hab 3:13	7563
and the stumblingblocks with the *w*	Zeph 1:3	7563
between the righteous and the *w*	Mal 3:18	7563
And ye shall tread down the *w*	Mal 4:3	7563
other spirits more *w* than himself	Mt 12:45	*4191*
it be also unto this *w* generation	Mt 12:45	*4190*
it not, then cometh the *w* one	Mt 13:19	*4190*
are the children of the *w* one	Mt 13:38	*4190*
sever the *w* from among the just,	Mt 13:49	*4190*
A *w* and adulterous generation	Mt 16:4	*4190*
O thou *w* servant, I forgave thee	Mt 18:32	*4190*
miserably destroy those *w* men	Mt 21:41	*2556*
answered and said unto him, Thou *w*	Mt 25:26	*4190*
other spirits more *w* than himself	Lk 11:26	*4191*
will I judge thee, thou *w* servant	Lk 19:22	*4190*
by *w* hands have crucified and	Acts 2:23	*459*
a matter of wrong or *w* lewdness	Acts 18:14	*4190*
among yourselves that *w* person	1Cor 5:13	*4190*
all the fiery darts of the *w*	Eph 6:16	*4190*
enemies in your mind by *w* works	Col 1:21	*4190*
And then shall that *W* be revealed	2Th 2:8	*459*
from unreasonable and *w* men	2Th 3:2	*4190*
the filthy conversation of the *w*	2Pet 2:7	*113*
led away with the error of the *w*	2Pet 3:17	*113*
ye have overcome the *w* one	1Jn 2:13	*4190*
and ye have overcome the *w* one	1Jn 2:14	*4190*

as Cain, who was of that *w* one	1Jn 3:12	*4190*
that *w* one toucheth him not	1Jn 5:18	*4190*

WICKEDLY

I pray you, brethren, do not so *w*	Gen 19:7	7489
in doing *w* in the sight of the	Deut 9:18	7561
nay, I pray you, do not so *w*	Judg 19:23	7489
But if ye shall still do *w*	1Sa 12:25	7489
have not *w* departed from my God	2Sa 22:22	7561
I have sinned, and I have done *w*	2Sa 24:17	5753
hath done *w* above all that the	2Kin 21:11	7489
have done amiss, and have dealt *w*	2Chr 6:37	7561
king of Israel, who did very *w*	2Chr 20:35	7561
mother was his counsellor to do *w*	2Chr 22:3	7561
done right, but we have done *w*	Neh 9:33	7561
Will ye speak *w* for God	Job 13:7	5766
Yea, surely God will not do *w*	Job 34:12	7561
have not *w* departed from my God	Ps 18:21	7561
speak *w* concerning oppression	Ps 73:8	7451
hath done *w* in the sanctuary	Ps 74:3	7489
iniquity, we have done *w*	Ps 106:6	7561
For they speak against thee *w*	Ps 139:20	4209
iniquity, and have done *w*, and have	Dan 9:5	7561
we have sinned, we have done *w*	Dan 9:15	7561
such as do *w* against the covenant	Dan 11:32	7561
but the wicked shall do *w*	Dan 12:10	7561
the proud, yea, and all that do *w*	Mal 4:1	7564

WICKEDNESS

God saw that the *w* of man was	Gen 6:5	7451
how then can I do this great *w*	Gen 39:9	7451
it is *w*	Lev 18:17	2154
and the land become full of *w*	Lev 19:29	2154
a wife and her mother, it is *w*	Lev 20:14	2154
that there be no *w* among you	Lev 20:14	2154
but for the *w* of these nations	Deut 9:4	7564
but for the *w* of these nations	Deut 9:5	7564
of this people, nor to their *w*	Deut 9:27	7562
any such *w* as this is among you	Deut 13:11	7451
that hath wrought *w* in the sight	Deut 17:2	7451
because of the *w* of thy doings	Deut 28:20	7455
God rendered the *w* of Abimelech	Judg 9:56	7451
Israel, Tell us, how was this *w*	Judg 20:3	7451
What *w* is this that is done among	Judg 20:12	7451
and see that your *w* is great	1Sa 12:17	7451
ye have done all this *w*	1Sa 12:20	7451
W proceedeth from the wicked	1Sa 24:13	7562
the *w* of Nabal upon his own head	1Sa 25:39	7451
doer of evil according to his *w*	2Sa 3:39	7451
of *w* afflict them any more	2Sa 7:10	5766
but if *w* shall be found in him,	1Kin 1:52	7451
Thou knowest all the *w* which	1Kin 2:44	7451
return thy *w* upon thine own head	1Kin 2:44	7451
perversely, we have committed *w*	1Kin 8:47	7561
work *w* in the sight of the LORD	1Kin 21:25	7451
he wrought much *w* in the sight of	2Kin 21:6	7451
children of *w* waste them any more	1Chr 17:9	5766
they that plow iniquity, and sow *w*	Job 4:8	5999
he seeth *w* also	Job 11:11	205
away, and let not *w* dwell in thy	Job 11:14	5766
Though *w* be sweet in his mouth,	Job 20:12	7451
Is not thy *w* great	Job 22:5	7451
w shall be broken as a tree	Job 24:20	5766
My lips shall not speak *w*	Job 27:4	5766
it from God, that he should do *w*	Job 34:10	7562
Thy *w* may hurt a man as thou art	Job 35:8	7562
not a God that hath pleasure in *w*	Ps 5:4	7562
their inward part is very *w*	Ps 5:9	1942
Oh let the *w* of the wicked come	Ps 7:9	7451
seek out his *w* till thou find	Ps 10:15	7562
according to the *w* of their	Ps 28:4	7455
lovest righteousness, and hatest *w*	Ps 45:7	7562
and strengthened himself in his *w*	Ps 52:7	1942
W is in the midst thereof	Ps 55:11	1942
for *w* is in their dwellings, and	Ps 55:15	7451
Yea, in heart ye work *w*	Ps 58:2	5766
than to dwell in the tents of *w*	Ps 84:10	7562
nor the son of *w* afflict him	Ps 89:22	5766
shall cut them off in their own *w*	Ps 94:23	7451
for the *w* of them that dwell	Ps 107:34	7451
For they eat the bread of *w*	Prov 4:17	7562
w is an abomination to my lips	Prov 8:7	7562
Treasures of *w* profit nothing	Prov 10:2	7562
wicked shall fall by his own *w*	Prov 11:5	7564
man shall not be established by *w*	Prov 12:3	7562
but *w* overthroweth the sinner	Prov 13:6	7564
wicked is driven away in his *w*	Prov 14:32	7451
abomination to kings to commit *w*	Prov 16:12	7562
the wicked for their *w*	Prov 21:12	7451
his *w* shall be shewed before the	Prov 26:26	7451
mouth, and saith, I have done no *w*	Prov 30:20	205
of judgment, that *w* was there	Eccl 3:16	7562
that prolongeth his life in his *w*	Eccl 7:15	7451
things, and to know the *w* of folly	Eccl 7:25	7562
neither shall *w* deliver those	Eccl 8:8	7562
For *w* burneth as the fire	Is 9:18	7564
For thou hast trusted in thy *w*	Is 47:10	7451
and to smite with the fist of *w*	Is 58:4	7562
to loose the bands of *w*, to undo	Is 58:6	7562
against them touching all their *w*	Jer 1:16	7451
Thine own *w* shall correct thee,	Jer 2:19	7451
with thy whoredoms and with thy *w*	Jer 3:2	7451
wash thine heart from *w*, that	Jer 4:14	7451
this is thy *w*, because it is	Jer 4:18	7451
waters, so she casteth out her *w*	Jer 6:7	7451
it for the *w* of my people Israel	Jer 7:12	7451
no man repented him of his *w*	Jer 8:6	7451
for the *w* of them that dwell	Jer 12:4	7451
for I will pour their *w* upon them	Jer 14:16	7451
We acknowledge, O LORD, our *w*	Jer 14:20	7562
and confounded for all thy *w*	Jer 22:22	7451
in my house have I found their *w*	Jer 23:11	7451
that none doth return from his *w*	Jer 23:14	7451
for all whose *w* I have hid my	Jer 33:5	7451
Because of their *w* which they	Jer 44:3	7451
their ear to turn from their *w*	Jer 44:5	7451
forgotten the *w* of your fathers	Jer 44:9	7451
the *w* of the kings of Judah, and	Jer 44:9	7451
the *w* of their wives, and your own	Jer 44:9	7451
of their wives, and your own *w*	Jer 44:9	7451
the *w* of your wives, which they	Jer 44:9	7451
Let all their *w* come before thee	Lam 1:22	7451
wicked, and he turn not from his *w*	Eze 3:19	7562
into *w* more than the nations	Eze 5:6	7564
is risen up into a rod of *w*	Eze 7:11	7562
it came to pass after all thy *w*	Eze 16:23	7451
Before thy *w* was discovered, as	Eze 16:57	7451
the *w* of the wicked shall be upon	Eze 18:20	7564
from his *w* that he hath committed	Eze 18:27	7564
I have driven him out for his *w*	Eze 31:11	7562
as for the *w* of the wicked, he	Eze 33:12	7564
day that he turneth from his *w*	Eze 33:12	7562
But if the wicked turn from his *w*	Eze 33:19	7564
discovered, and the *w* of Samaria	Hos 7:1	7451
that I remember all their *w*	Hos 7:2	7451
make the king glad with their *w*	Hos 7:3	7451
All their *w* is in Gilgal	Hos 9:15	7451
for the *w* of their doings I will	Hos 9:15	7455
Ye have plowed *w*, ye have reaped	Hos 10:13	7562
unto you because of your great *w*	Hos 10:15	7451
for their *w* is great	Joel 3:13	7451
for their *w* is come up before me	Jonah 1:2	7451
of *w* in the house of the wicked	Mic 6:10	7562
hath not thy *w* passed continually	Nah 3:19	7451
And he said, This is *w*	Zec 5:8	7564
shall call them, The border of *w*	Mal 1:4	7564
yea, they that work *w* are set up	Mal 3:15	7564
But Jesus perceived their *w*	Mt 22:18	*4189*
Thefts, covetousness, *w*, deceit,	Mk 7:22	*4189*
part is full of ravening and *w*	Lk 11:39	*4189*
Repent therefore of this thy *w*	Acts 8:22	*2549*
man, if there be any *w* in him	Acts 25:5	
unrighteousness, fornication, *w*	Rom 1:29	*4189*
with the leaven of malice and *w*	1Cor 5:8	*4189*
spiritual *w* in high places	Eph 6:12	*4189*
and the whole world lieth in *w*	1Jn 5:19	*4190*

WIDE

shalt open thine hand *w* unto him	Deut 15:8	6605
thine hand *w* unto thy brother	Deut 15:11	6605
and good, and the land was *w*	1Chr 4:40	
mouth *w* as for the latter rain	Job 29:23	
me as a *w* breaking in of waters	Job 30:14	7342
opened their mouth *w* against me	Ps 35:21	7337
open thy mouth *w*, and I will fill	Ps 81:10	7337
w sea, wherein are things	Ps 104:25	
but he that openeth *w* his lips	Prov 13:3	
a brawling woman and in a *w* house	Prov 21:9	2267
a brawling woman and in a *w* house	Prov 25:24	2267
against whom make ye a *w* mouth	Is 57:4	7337
saith, I will build me a *w* house	Jer 22:14	4060
be set *w* open unto thine enemies	Nah 3:13	6605
for *w* is the gate, and broad is	Mt 7:13	*4116*

WIDENESS

w of twenty cubits round about	Eze 41:10	7341

WIDOW

Remain a *w* at thy father's house,	Gen 38:11	490
Ye shall not afflict any *w*	Ex 22:22	490
A *w*, or a divorced woman, or	Lev 21:14	490
if the priest's daughter be a *w*	Lev 22:13	490
But every vow of a *w*, and of her	Num 30:9	490
judgment of the fatherless and *w*	Deut 10:18	490
and the fatherless, and the *w*	Deut 14:29	490
and the fatherless, and the *w*	Deut 16:11	490
and the fatherless, and the *w*	Deut 16:14	490
for the fatherless, and for the *w*	Deut 24:19	490
for the fatherless, and for the *w*	Deut 24:20	490
for the fatherless, and for the *w*	Deut 24:21	490
the fatherless, and the *w*	Deut 26:12	490
to the fatherless, and to the *w*	Deut 26:13	490
of the stranger, fatherless, and *w*	Deut 27:19	490
answered, I am indeed a *w* woman	2Sa 14:5	490
a *w* woman, even he lifted up his	1Kin 11:26	490
I have commanded a *w* woman there	1Kin 17:9	490
the *w* woman was there gathering	1Kin 17:10	490
upon the *w* with whom I sojourn	1Kin 17:20	490
and doeth not good to the *w*	Job 24:21	490
caused the eyes of the *w* to fail	Job 31:16	490
They slay the *w* and the stranger,	Ps 94:6	490
be fatherless, and his wife a *w*	Ps 109:9	490
he relieveth the fatherless and *w*	Ps 146:9	490
establish the border of the *w*	Prov 15:25	490
the fatherless, plead for the *w*	Is 1:17	490
the cause of the *w* come unto them	Is 1:23	490
I shall not sit as a *w*, neither	Is 47:8	490
the fatherless, and the *w*	Jer 7:6	490
the fatherless, nor the *w*	Jer 22:3	490
how is she become as a *w*	Lam 1:1	490
vexed the fatherless and the *w*	Eze 22:7	490
they take for their wives a *w*	Eze 44:22	490
or a *w* that had a priest before	Eze 44:22	490
And oppress not the *w*, nor the	Zec 7:10	490
the hireling in his wages, the *w*	Mal 3:5	490
And there came a certain poor *w*	Mk 12:42	*5503*
That this poor *w* hath cast more	Mk 12:43	*5503*
she was a *w* of about fourscore and	Lk 2:37	*5503*
Sidon, unto a woman that was a *w*	Lk 4:26	*5503*
son of his mother, and she was a *w*	Lk 7:12	*5503*
there was a *w* in that city	Lk 18:3	*5503*
Yet because this *w* troubleth me	Lk 18:5	*5503*
he saw also a certain poor *w*	Lk 21:2	*5503*
that this poor *w* hath cast in	Lk 21:3	*5503*
But if any *w* have children or	1Ti 5:4	*5503*
Now she that is a *w* indeed	1Ti 5:5	*5503*
Let not a *w* be taken into the	1Ti 5:9	*5503*
heart, I sit a queen, and am no *w*	Rev 18:7	*5503*

WIDOWHOOD

and put on the garments of her *w*	Gen 38:19	491
day of their death, living in *w*	2Sa 20:3	491
day, the loss of children, and *w*	Is 47:9	489
the reproach of thy *w* any more	Is 54:4	491

WIDOW'S

she put her *w* garments off from	Gen 38:14	491
nor take a *w* raiment to pledge	Deut 24:17	490
He was a *w* son of the tribe of	1Kin 7:14	490
they take the *w* ox for a pledge	Job 24:3	490
I caused the *w* heart to sing for	Job 29:13	490

WIDOWS

and your wives shall be *w*, and your	Ex 22:24	490
Thou hast sent *w* away empty	Job 22:9	490
and his *w* shall not weep	Job 27:15	490
fatherless, and a judge of the *w*	Ps 68:5	490
their *w* made no lamentation	Ps 78:64	490
mercy on their fatherless and *w*	Is 9:17	490
that *w* may be their prey, and that	Is 10:2	490
Their *w* are increased to me above	Jer 15:8	490
of their children, and be *w*	Jer 18:21	490
and let thy *w* trust in me	Jer 49:11	490
fatherless, our mothers are as *w*	Lam 5:3	490
her many *w* in the midst thereof	Eze 22:25	490
many *w* were in Israel in the days	Lk 4:25	*5503*
because their *w* were neglected in	Acts 6:1	*5503*
all the *w* stood by him weeping,	Acts 9:39	*5503*
he had called the saints and *w*	Acts 9:41	*5503*
therefore to the unmarried and *w*	1Cor 7:8	*5503*
Honour *w* that are *w* indeed	1Ti 5:3	*5503*
But the younger *w* refuse	1Ti 5:11	*5503*
or woman that believeth have *w*	1Ti 5:16	*5503*
relieve them that are *w* indeed	1Ti 5:16	*5503*
w in their affliction, and to keep	Jas 1:27	*5503*

WIDOWS'

for ye devour *w* houses, and for a	Mt 23:14	*5503*
Which devour *w* houses, and for a	Mk 12:40	*5503*
Which devour *w* houses, and for a	Lk 20:47	*5503*

WIFE

and shall cleave unto his *w*	Gen 2:24	802
were both naked, the man and his *w*	Gen 2:25	802
his *w* hid themselves from the	Gen 3:8	802
hearkened unto the voice of thy *w*	Gen 3:17	802
to his *w* did the LORD God make	Gen 3:21	802
And Adam knew Eve his *w*	Gen 4:1	802
And Cain knew his *w*	Gen 4:17	802
And Adam knew his *w* again	Gen 4:25	802
ark, thou, and thy sons, and thy *w*	Gen 6:18	802
went in, and his sons, and his *w*	Gen 7:7	802
the sons of Noah, and Noah's *w*	Gen 7:13	802
forth of the ark, thou, and thy *w*	Gen 8:16	802
went forth, and his sons, and his *w*	Gen 8:18	802
the name of Abram's *w* was Sarai	Gen 11:29	802
and the name of Nahor's *w*, Milcah,	Gen 11:29	802
in law, his son Abram's *w*	Gen 11:31	802
And Abram took Sarai his *w*	Gen 12:5	802
that he said unto Sarai his *w*	Gen 12:11	802
they shall say, This is his *w*	Gen 12:12	802
because of Sarai Abram's *w*	Gen 12:17	802
not tell me that she was thy *w*	Gen 12:18	802
I might have taken her to me to *w*	Gen 12:19	802
now therefore behold thy *w*	Gen 12:19	802
and they sent him away, and his *w*	Gen 12:20	802
up out of Egypt, he, and his *w*	Gen 13:1	802
Now Sarai Abram's *w* bare him no	Gen 16:1	802
Sarai Abram's *w* took Hagar her	Gen 16:3	802
to her husband Abram to be his *w*	Gen 16:3	802
unto Abraham, As for Sarai thy *w*	Gen 17:15	802
Sarah thy *w* shall bear thee a son	Gen 17:19	802
unto him, Where is Sarah thy *w*	Gen 18:9	802
Sarah thy *w* shall have a son	Gen 18:10	802
Lot, saying, Arise, take thy *w*	Gen 19:15	802
hand, and upon the hand of his *w*	Gen 19:16	802
But his *w* looked back from behind	Gen 19:26	802
And Abraham said of Sarah his *w*	Gen 20:2	802
for she is a man's *w*	Gen 20:3	1166
therefore restore the man his *w*	Gen 20:7	802
and she became my *w*	Gen 20:12	802
and restored him Sarah his *w*	Gen 20:14	802
and God healed Abimelech, and his *w*	Gen 20:17	802
because of Sarah Abraham's *w*	Gen 20:18	802
his mother took him a *w* out of	Gen 21:21	802
Abraham buried Sarah his *w* in the	Gen 23:19	802
that thou shalt not take a *w* unto	Gen 24:3	802
take a *w* unto my son Isaac	Gen 24:4	802
thou shalt take a *w* unto my son	Gen 24:7	802
the *w* of Nahor, Abraham's brother	Gen 24:15	802
Sarah my master's *w* bare a son to	Gen 24:36	802
Thou shalt not take a *w* to my son	Gen 24:37	802
kindred, and take a *w* unto my son	Gen 24:38	802
thou shalt take a *w* for my son of	Gen 24:40	802
let her be thy master's son's *w*	Gen 24:51	802
took Rebekah, and she became his *w*	Gen 24:67	802
Then again Abraham took a *w*	Gen 25:1	802
Abraham buried, and Sarah his *w*	Gen 25:10	802
old when he took Rebekah to *w*	Gen 25:20	802
intreated the LORD for his *w*	Gen 25:21	802
him, and Rebekah his *w* conceived	Gen 25:21	802
of the place asked him of his *w*	Gen 26:7	802
for he feared to say, She is my *w*	Gen 26:7	802
was sporting with Rebekah his *w*	Gen 26:8	802
Behold, of a surety she is thy *w*	Gen 26:9	802
lightly have lien with thy *w*	Gen 26:10	802
w shall surely be put to death	Gen 26:11	802
to *w* Judith the daughter of Beeri	Gen 26:34	802
if Jacob take a *w* of the	Gen 27:46	802
Thou shalt not take a *w* of the	Gen 28:1	802
take thee a *w* from thence of the	Gen 28:2	802
to take him a *w* from thence	Gen 28:6	802
Thou shalt not take a *w* of the	Gen 28:6	802
sister of Nebajoth, to be his *w*	Gen 28:9	802
said unto Laban, Give me my *w*	Gen 29:21	802

W

him Rachel his daughter to *w* also Gen 29:28 802
gave him Bilhah her handmaid to *w* Gen 30:4 802
her maid, and gave her Jacob to *w* Gen 30:9 802
saying, Get me this damsel to *w* Gen 34:4 802
I pray you give her him to *w* Gen 34:8 802
but give me the damsel to *w* Gen 34:12 802
the son of Adah the *w* of Esau Gen 36:10 802
son of Bashemath the *w* of Esau Gen 36:10 802
were the sons of Adah Esau's *w* Gen 36:12 802
the sons of Bashemath Esau's *w* Gen 36:13 802
the daughter of Zibeon, Esau's *w* Gen 36:14 802
the sons of Bashemath Esau's *w* Gen 36:17 802
the sons of Aholibamah Esau's *w* Gen 36:18 802
the daughter of Anah, Esau's *w* Gen 36:18 802
Judah took a *w* for Er his Gen 38:6 802
Onan, Go in unto thy brother's *w* Gen 38:8 802
he went in unto his brother's *w* Gen 38:9 802
daughter of Shuah Judah's *w* died Gen 38:12 802
she was not given unto him to *w* Gen 38:14 802
that his master's *w* cast her eyes Gen 39:7 802
and said unto his master's *w* Gen 39:8 802
but thee, because thou art his *w* Gen 39:9 802
master heard the words of his *w* Gen 39:19 802
he gave him to *w* Asenath the Gen 41:45 802
Ye know that my *w* bare me two Gen 44:27 802
The sons of Rachel Jacob's *w* Gen 46:19 802
buried Abraham and Sarah his *w* Gen 49:31 802
buried Isaac and Rebekah his *w* Gen 49:31 802
took to *w* a daughter of Levi Ex 2:1
And Moses took his *w* and his sons, Ex 4:20 802
Jochebed his father's sister to *w* Ex 6:20 802
sister of Naashon, to *w* Ex 6:23 802
of the daughters of Putiel to *w* Ex 6:25 802
in law, took Zipporah, Moses' *w* Ex 18:2 802
his *w* unto Moses into the Ex 18:5 802
am come unto thee, and thy *w* Ex 18:6 802
shalt not covet thy neighbour's *w* Ex 20:17 802
then his *w* shall go out with him Ex 21:3 802
If his master have given him a *w* Ex 21:4 802
the *w* and her children shall be Ex 21:4 802
say, I love my master, my *w* Ex 21:5 802
If he take him another *w* Ex 21:10
surely endow her to be his *w* Ex 22:16 802
father's *w* shalt thou not uncover Lev 18:8 802
thou shalt not approach to his *w* Lev 18:14 802
she is thy son's *w* Lev 18:15 802
the nakedness of thy brother's *w* Lev 18:16 802
shalt thou take a *w* to her sister Lev 18:18 802
carnally with thy neighbour's *w* Lev 18:20 802
adultery with another man's *w* Lev 20:10 802
adultery with his neighbour's *w* Lev 20:10 802
w hath uncovered his father's Lev 20:11 802
And if a man take a *w* and her Lev 20:14 802
man shall lie with his uncle's *w* Lev 20:20 1753
a man shall take his brother's *w* Lev 20:21 802
not take a *w* that is a whore Lev 21:7 802
And he shall take a *w* in her Lev 21:13 802
a virgin of his own people to *w* Lev 21:14 802
them, If any man's *w* go aside Num 5:12 802
him, and he be jealous of his *w* Num 5:14 802
him, and he be jealous of his *w* Num 5:14 802
man bring his *w* unto the priest Num 5:15 802
when a *w* goeth aside to another Num 5:29 802
him, and he be jealous over his *w* Num 5:30 802
name of Amram's *w* was Jochebed Num 26:59 802
Moses, between a man and his *w* Num 30:16 802
shall be *w* unto one of the family Num 36:8 802
thou desire thy neighbour's *w* Deut 5:21 802
or the *w* of thy bosom, or thy Deut 13:6 802
is there that hath betrothed a *w* Deut 20:7 802
thou wouldest have her to thy *w* Deut 21:11 802
husband, and she shall be thy *w* Deut 21:13 802
If any man take a *w*, and go in Deut 22:13 802
my daughter unto this man to *w* Deut 22:16 802
and she shall be his *w* Deut 22:19 802
he hath humbled his neighbour's *w* Deut 22:24 802
of silver, and she shall be his *w* Deut 22:29 802
man shall not take his father's *w* Deut 22:30 802
When a man hath taken a *w* Deut 24:1 802
she may go and be another man's *w* Deut 24:2
die, which took her to be his *w* Deut 24:3 802
not take her again to be his *w* Deut 24:4 802
When a man hath taken a new *w* Deut 24:5 802
shall cheer up his *w* which he Deut 24:5 802
the *w* of the dead shall not marry Deut 25:5 802
unto her, and take her to him to *w* Deut 25:5 802
like not to take his brother's *w* Deut 25:7 2994
then let his brother's *w* go up to Deut 25:7 2994
Then shall his brother's *w* come Deut 25:9 2994
the *w* of the one draweth near for Deut 25:11 802
he that lieth with his father's *w* Deut 27:20 802
Thou shalt betroth a *w*, and Deut 28:30 802
toward the *w* of his bosom, and Deut 28:54 802
I give Achsah my daughter to *w* Josh 15:16 802
gave him Achsah his daughter to *w* Josh 15:17 802
I give Achsah my daughter to *w* Judg 1:12 802
gave him Achsah his daughter to *w* Judg 1:13 802
the *w* of Lapidoth, she judged Judg 4:4 802
of Jael the *w* of Heber the Kenite Judg 4:17 802
Then Jael Heber's *w* took a nail Judg 4:21 802
Jael the *w* of Heber the Kenite be Judg 5:24 802
And Gilead's *w* bare him sons Judg 11:2 802
his *w* was barren, and bare not Judg 13:2 802
Manoah arose, and went after his *w* Judg 13:11 802
and Manoah and his *w* looked on Judg 13:19 802
his *w* looked on it, and fell on Judg 13:20 802
more appear to Manoah and to his *w* Judg 13:21 802
And Manoah said unto his *w* Judg 13:22 802
But his *w* said unto him, If the Judg 13:23 802
now therefore get her for me to *w* Judg 14:2 802
to take a *w* of the uncircumcised Judg 14:3 802
that they said unto Samson's *w* Judg 14:15 802
Samson's *w* wept before him, and Judg 14:16 802
But Samson's *w* was given to his Judg 14:20 802
Samson visited his *w* with a kid Judg 15:1 802
go in to my *w* into the chamber Judg 15:1 802
because he had taken his *w* Judg 15:6 802
his daughter unto Benjamin to *w* Judg 21:1 802
be he that giveth a *w* to Benjamin Judg 21:18 802
catch you every man his *w* of the Judg 21:21 802
not to each man his *w* in the war Judg 21:22 802
the country of Moab, he, and his *w* Ruth 1:1 802
and the name of his *w* Naomi Ruth 1:2 802
the *w* of the dead, to raise up Ruth 4:5 802
the *w* of Mahlon, have I purchased Ruth 4:10 802
have I purchased to be my *w* Ruth 4:10 802
Boaz took Ruth, and she was his *w* Ruth 4:13 802
he gave to Peninnah his *w* 1Sa 1:4 802
and Elkanah knew Hannah his *w* 1Sa 1:19 802
And Eli blessed Elkanah and his *w* 1Sa 2:20 802
his daughter in law, Phinehas' *w* 1Sa 4:19 802
the name of Saul's *w* was Ahinoam 1Sa 14:50 802
Merab, her will I give thee to *w* 1Sa 18:17 802
unto Adriel the Meholathite to *w* 1Sa 18:19 802
gave him Michal his daughter to *w* 1Sa 18:27 802
and Michal David's *w* told him 1Sa 19:11 802
and the name of his *w* Abigail 1Sa 25:3 802
young men told Abigail, Nabal's *w* 1Sa 25:14 802
his *w* had told him these things, 1Sa 25:37 802
Abigail, to take her to him to *w* 1Sa 25:39 802
thee, to take thee to him to *w* 1Sa 25:40 802
of David, and became his *w* 1Sa 25:42 802
Michal his daughter, David's *w* 1Sa 25:44 802
the Carmelitess, Nabal's *w* 1Sa 27:3 802
Abigail the *w* of Nabal the 1Sa 30:5 802
save to every man his *w* and his 1Sa 30:22 802
Abigail Nabal's *w* the Carmelite 2Sa 2:2 802
of Abigail the *w* of Nabal the 2Sa 3:3 802
Ithream, by Eglah David's *w* 2Sa 3:5 802
saying, Deliver me my *w* Michal 2Sa 3:14 802
the *w* of Uriah the Hittite 2Sa 11:3 802
and to drink, and to lie with my *w* 2Sa 11:11 802
when the *w* of Uriah heard that 2Sa 11:26 802
to his house, and she became his *w* 2Sa 11:27 802
hast taken his *w* to be thy *w* 2Sa 12:9 802
hast taken the *w* of Uriah the 2Sa 12:10 802
of Uriah the Hittite to be thy *w* 2Sa 12:10 802
that Uriah's *w* bare unto David 2Sa 12:15 802
David comforted Bath-sheba his *w* 2Sa 12:24 802
me Abishag the Shunammite to *w* 1Kin 2:17 802
to Adonijah thy brother to *w* 1Kin 2:21 802
the daughter of Solomon to *w* 1Kin 4:11 802
the daughter of Solomon to *w* 1Kin 4:15 802
daughter, whom he had taken to *w* 1Kin 7:8
unto his daughter, Solomon's *w* 1Kin 9:16 802
so that he gave him to *w* the 1Kin 11:19 802
the sister of his own *w* 1Kin 11:19 802
And Jeroboam said to his *w* 1Kin 14:2 802
not known to be the *w* of Jeroboam 1Kin 14:2 802
And Jeroboam's *w* did so, and arose, 1Kin 14:4 802
the *w* of Jeroboam cometh to ask a 1Kin 14:5 802
said, Come in, thou *w* of Jeroboam 1Kin 14:6 802
And Jeroboam's *w* arose, and 1Kin 14:17 802
that he took to *w* Jezebel the 1Kin 16:31 802
But Jezebel his *w* came to him 1Kin 21:5 802
Jezebel his *w* said unto him, Dost 1Kin 21:7 802
whom Jezebel his *w* stirred up 1Kin 21:25 802
and she waited on Naaman's *w* 2Kin 5:2 802
the daughter of Ahab was his *w* 2Kin 8:18 802
Give thy daughter to my son to *w* 2Kin 14:9 802
the *w* of Shallum the son of 2Kin 22:14 802
begat children of Azubah his *w* 1Chr 2:18 802
then Abiah Hezron's *w* bare him 1Chr 2:24 802
Jerahmeel had also another *w* 1Chr 2:26 802
the name of the *w* of Abishur was 1Chr 2:29 802
to Jarha his servant to *w* 1Chr 2:35 802
the sixth, Ithream by Eglah his *w* 1Chr 3:3 802
his *w* Jehudijah bare Jered the 1Chr 4:18 802
the sons of his *w* Hodiah the 1Chr 4:19 802
Machir took to *w* the sister of 1Chr 7:15 802
Maachah the *w* of Machir bare a 1Chr 7:16 802
And when he went in to his *w* 1Chr 7:23 802
And he begat of Hodesh his *w* 1Chr 8:9 802
My *w* shall not dwell in the house 2Chr 8:11 802
of Jerimoth the son of David to *w* 2Chr 11:18 802
he had the daughter of Ahab to *w* 2Chr 21:6 802
the *w* of Jehoiada the priest, 2Chr 22:11 802
Give thy daughter to my son to *w* 2Chr 25:18 802
the *w* of Shallum the son of 2Chr 34:22 802
which took a *w* of the daughters Ezr 2:61 802
of Barzillai the Gileadite to *w* Neh 7:63 802
for his friends, and Zeresh his *w* Est 5:10 802
Then said Zeresh his *w* and all his Est 5:14 802
And Haman told Zeresh his *w* Est 6:13 802
wise men and Zeresh his *w* unto him Est 6:13 802
Then said his *w* unto him, Dost Job 2:9 802
My breath is strange to my *w* Job 19:17 802
Then let my *w* grind unto another, Job 31:10 802
be fatherless, and his *w* a widow Ps 109:9 802
Thy *w* shall be as a fruitful vine Ps 128:3 802
rejoice with the *w* of thy youth Prov 5:18 802
goeth in to his neighbour's *w* Prov 6:29 802
Whoso findeth a *w* findeth a good Prov 18:22 802
the contentions of a *w* are a Prov 19:13 802
a prudent *w* is from the LORD Prov 19:14
Live joyfully with the *w* whom Eccl 9:9
the children of the married *w* Is 54:1
a *w* of youth, when thou wast Is 54:6 802
They say, If a man put away his *w* Jer 3:1 802
Surely as a *w* treacherously Jer 3:20 802
neighed after his neighbour's *w* Jer 5:8 802
husband with the *w* shall be taken Jer 6:11 802
Thou shalt not take thee a *w* Jer 16:2 802
But as a *w* that committeth Eze 16:32 802
hath defiled his neighbour's *w* Eze 18:6 802
and defiled his neighbour's *w* Eze 18:11 802
not defiled his neighbour's *w* Eze 18:15 802
with his neighbour's *w* Eze 22:11 802
and at even my *w* died Eze 24:18 802
every one his neighbour's *w* Eze 33:26 802
take unto thee a *w* of whoredoms Hos 1:2 802
for she is not my *w*, neither am I Hos 2:2 802
Syria, and Israel served for a *w* Hos 12:12 802
and for a *w* he kept sheep Hos 12:12 802
Thy *w* shall be an harlot in the Amos 7:17 802
the *w* of thy youth, against whom Mal 2:14 802
and the *w* of thy covenant Mal 2:14 802
against the *w* of his youth Mal 2:15 802
her that had been the *w* of Urias Mt 1:6
not to take unto thee Mary thy *w* Mt 1:20 *1135*
him, and took unto him his *w* Mt 1:24 *1135*
Whosoever shall put away his *w* Mt 5:31 *1135*
whosoever shall put away his *w* Mt 5:32 *1135*
sake, his brother Philip's *w* Mt 14:3 *1135*
him to be sold, and his *w*, and Mt 18:25 *1135*
to put away his *w* for every cause Mt 19:3 *1135*
mother, and shall cleave to his *w* Mt 19:5 *1135*
Whosoever shall put away his *w* Mt 19:9 *1135*
case of the man be so with his *w* Mt 19:10 *1135*
or father, or mother, or *w* Mt 19:29 *1135*
his brother shall marry his *w* Mt 22:24 *1135*
first, when he had married a *w* Mt 22:25
left his *w* unto his brother Mt 22:25 *1135*
whose *w* shall she be of the seven Mt 22:28 *1135*
his *w* sent unto him, saying, Have Mt 27:19 *1135*
sake, his brother Philip's *w* Mk 6:17 *1135*
for thee to have thy brother's *w* Mk 6:18 *1135*
for a man to put away his *w* Mk 10:2 *1135*
and mother, and cleave to his *w* Mk 10:7 *1135*
Whosoever shall put away his *w* Mk 10:11 *1135*
or father, or mother, or *w* Mk 10:29 *1135*
leave his *w* behind him, and leave Mk 12:19 *1135*
his brother should take his *w* Mk 12:19 *1135*
and the first took a *w*, and dying Mk 12:20 *1135*
whose *w* shall she be of them Mk 12:23 *1135*
for the seven had her to *w* Mk 12:23 *1135*
his *w* was of the daughters of Lk 1:5 *1135*
thy *w* Elisabeth shall bear thee a Lk 1:13 *1135*
my *w* well stricken in years Lk 1:18 *1135*
days his *w* Elisabeth conceived Lk 1:24 *1135*
be taxed with Mary his espoused *w* Lk 2:5 *1135*
Herodias his brother Philip's *w* Lk 3:19 *1135*
Joanna the *w* of Chuza Herod's Lk 8:3 *1135*
another said, I have married a *w* Lk 14:20 *1135*
not his father, and mother, and *w* Lk 14:26 *1135*
Whosoever putteth away his *w* Lk 16:18 *1135*
Remember Lot's *w* Lk 17:32 *1135*
or parents, or brethren, or *w* Lk 18:29 *1135*
any man's brother die, having a *w* Lk 20:28 *1135*
his brother should take his *w* Lk 20:28 *1135*
and the first took a *w*, and died Lk 20:29 *1135*
And the second took her to *w* Lk 20:30 *1135*
whose *w* of them is she Lk 20:33 *1135*
for seven had her to *w* Lk 20:33 *1135*
Mary the *w* of Cleophas, and Mary Jn 19:25
Ananias, with Sapphira his *w* Acts 5:1 *1135*
his *w* also being privy to it, and Acts 5:2 *1135*
of three hours after, when his *w* Acts 5:7 *1135*
from Italy, with his *w* Priscilla Acts 18:2 *1135*
Felix came with his *w* Drusilla Acts 24:24 *1135*
one should have his father's *w* 1Cor 5:1 *1135*
let every man have his own *w* 1Cor 7:2 *1135*
render unto the *w* due benevolence 1Cor 7:3 *1135*
also the *w* unto the husband 1Cor 7:3 *1135*
The *w* hath not power of her own 1Cor 7:4 *1135*
power of his own body, but the *w* 1Cor 7:4 *1135*
Let not the *w* depart from her 1Cor 7:10 *1135*
not the husband put away his *w* 1Cor 7:11 *1135*
hath a *w* that believeth not 1Cor 7:12 *1135*
husband is sanctified by the *w* 1Cor 7:14 *1135*
the unbelieving *w* is sanctified 1Cor 7:14 *1135*
For what knowest thou, O *w* 1Cor 7:16 *1135*
whether thou shalt save thy *w* 1Cor 7:16 *1135*
Art thou bound unto a *w* 1Cor 7:27 *1135*
Art thou loosed from a *w* 1Cor 7:27 *1135*
seek not a *w* 1Cor 7:27 *1135*
world, how he may please his *w* 1Cor 7:33 *1135*
is difference also between a *w* 1Cor 7:34 *1135*
The *w* is bound by the law as long 1Cor 7:39 *1135*
power to lead about a sister, a *w* 1Cor 9:5 *1135*
the husband is the head of the *w* Eph 5:23 *1135*
that loveth his *w* loveth himself Eph 5:28 *1135*
and shall be joined unto his *w* Eph 5:31 *1135*
so love his *w* even as himself Eph 5:33 *1135*
the *w* see that she reverence her Eph 5:33 *1135*
blameless, the husband of one *w* 1Ti 3:2 *1135*
deacons be the husbands of one *w* 1Ti 3:12 *1135*
old, having been the *w* of one man 1Ti 5:9 *1135*
blameless, the husband of one *w* Titus 1:6 *1135*
giving honour unto the *w* 1Pet 3:7 *1134*
his *w* hath made herself ready Rev 19:7 *1135*
shew thee the bride, the Lamb's *w* Rev 21:9 *1135*

WIFE'S

And Adam called his *w* name Eve Gen 3:20 802
they will slay me for my *w* sake Gen 20:11 802
his *w* name was Mehetabel, the Gen 36:39 802
of thy father's *w* daughter Lev 18:11 802
his *w* sons grew up, and they Judg 11:2 802
his *w* name was Mehetabel, the 1Chr 1:50 802
whose *w* name was Maachah 1Chr 8:29 802
Jehiel, whose *w* name was Maachah 1Chr 9:35 802
he saw his *w* mother laid, and sick Mt 8:14 *3994*
But Simon's *w* mother lay sick of Mk 1:30 *3994*
Simon's *w* mother was taken with a Lk 4:38 *3994*

WILD

And he will be a *w* man Gen 16:12 6501
will also send *w* beasts among you Lev 26:22 7704
the *w* goat, and the pygarg Deut 14:5 689
the pygarg, and the *w* ox Deut 14:5 8377
to the *w* beasts of the earth 1Sa 17:46 2416
men upon the rocks of the *w* goats 1Sa 24:2 3277

was as light of foot as a *w* roe 2Sa 2:18 7704
gather herbs, and found a *w* vine 2Kin 4:39 7704
gathered thereof *w* gourds his lap 2Kin 4:39 7704
there passed by a *w* beast that 2Kin 14:9 7704
there passed by a *w* beast that 2Chr 25:18 7704
Doth the *w* ass bray when he hath Job 6:5 6501
man be born like a *w* ass's colt Job 11:12 6501
as *w* asses in the desert, go they Job 24:5 6501
w goats of the rock bring forth Job 39:1 3277
Who hath sent out the *w* ass free Job 39:5 6501
loosed the bands of the *w* ass Job 39:5 6171
or that the *w* beast may break Job 39:15 7704
the *w* beasts of the field are Ps 50:11 2123
the *w* beast of the field doth Ps 80:13 2123
the *w* asses quench their thirst Ps 104:11 6501
are a refuge for the *w* goats Ps 104:18 3277
and it brought forth *w* grapes Is 5:2 891
grapes, brought it forth *w* grapes Is 5:4 891
But *w* beasts of the desert shall Is 13:21 6728
the *w* beasts of the islands shall Is 13:22 338
dens for ever, a joy of *w* asses Is 32:14 6501
The *w* beasts of the desert shall Is 34:14 6728
with the *w* beasts of the island Is 34:14 338
the streets, as a *w* bull in a net Is 51:20 8377
A *w* ass used to the wilderness, Jer 2:24 6501
the *w* asses did stand in the high Jer 14:6 6501
Therefore the *w* beasts of the Jer 50:39 6728
the *w* beasts of the islands shall Jer 50:39 338
his dwelling was with the *w* asses Dan 5:21 6167
Assyria, a *w* ass alone by himself Hos 8:9 6501
the *w* beast shall tear them Hos 13:8 7704
his meat was locusts and *w* honey Mt 3:4 *66*
and he did eat locusts and *w* honey Mk 1:6 *66*
and was with the *w* beasts Mk 1:13 *2342*
w beasts, and creeping things, and Acts 10:12 *2342*
w beasts, and creeping things, and Acts 11:6 *2342*
being a *w* olive tree, wert Rom 11:17 *65*
olive tree which is *w* by nature Rom 11:24 *65*

WILDERNESS

unto El-paran, which is by the *w* Gen 14:6 4057
by a fountain of water in the *w* Gen 16:7 4057
wandered in the *w* of Beer-sheba Gen 21:14 4057
and he grew, and dwelt in the *w* Gen 21:20 4057
And he dwelt in the *w* of Paran Gen 21:21 4057
that found the mules in the *w* Gen 36:24 4057
into this pit that is in the *w* Gen 37:22 4057
three days' journey into the *w* Ex 3:18 4057
Go into the *w* to meet Moses Ex 4:27 4057
may hold a feast unto me in the *w* Ex 5:1 4057
that they may serve me in the *w* Ex 7:16 4057
go three days' journey into the *w* Ex 8:27 4057
to the LORD your God in the *w* Ex 8:28 4057
the way of the *w* of the Red sea Ex 13:18 4057
in Etham, in the edge of the *w* Ex 13:20 4057
the land, the *w* hath shut them in Ex 14:3 4057
taken us away to die in the *w* Ex 14:11 4057
than that we should die in the *w* Ex 14:12 4057
they went out into the *w* of Shur Ex 15:22 4057
and they went three days in the *w* Ex 15:22 4057
of Israel came unto the *w* of Sin Ex 16:1 4057
against Moses and Aaron in the *w* Ex 16:2 4057
have brought us forth into this *w* Ex 16:3 4057
that they looked toward the *w* Ex 16:10 4057
upon the face of the *w* there lay Ex 16:14 4057
wherewith I have fed you in the *w* Ex 16:32 4057
journeyed from the *w* of Sin Ex 17:1 4057
and his wife unto Moses into the *w* Ex 18:5 4057
day came they into the *w* of Sinai Ex 19:1 4057
of Sinai, and had pitched in the *w* Ex 19:2 4057
unto the LORD, in the *w* of Sinai Lev 7:38 4057
him go for a scapegoat into the *w* Lev 16:10 4057
the hand of a fit man into the *w* Lev 16:21 4057
he shall let go the goat in the *w* Lev 16:22 4057
unto Moses in the *w* of Sinai Num 1:1 4057
numbered them in the *w* of Sinai Num 1:19 4057
in the *w* of Sinai, and they had no Num 3:4 4057
unto Moses in the *w* of Sinai Num 3:14 4057
unto Moses in the *w* of Sinai Num 9:1 4057
month at even in the *w* of Sinai Num 9:5 4057
journeys out of the *w* of Sinai Num 10:12 4057
cloud rested in the *w* of Paran Num 10:12 4057
how we are to encamp in the *w* Num 10:31 4057
and pitched in the *w* of Paran Num 12:16 4057
sent them from the *w* of Paran Num 13:3 4057
land from the *w* of Zin unto Rehob Num 13:21 4057
of Israel, unto the *w* of Paran Num 13:26 4057
would God we had died in this *w* Num 14:2 4057
he hath slain them in the *w* Num 14:16 4057
which I did in Egypt and in the *w* Num 14:22 4057
get you into the *w* by the way of Num 14:25 4057
carcases shall fall in this *w* Num 14:29 4057
they shall fall in this *w* Num 14:32 4057
shall wander in the *w* forty years Num 14:33 4057
your carcases be wasted in the *w* Num 14:33 4057
in this *w* they shall be consumed, Num 14:35 4057
children of Israel were in the *w* Num 15:32 4057
and honey, to kill us in the *w* Num 16:13 4057
of the LORD into this *w*, that we Num 20:4 4057
up out of Egypt to die in the *w* Num 21:5 4057
in the *w* which is before Moab, Num 21:11 4057
which is in the *w* that cometh out Num 21:13 4057
from the *w* they went to Mattanah Num 21:18 4057
out against Israel into the *w* Num 21:23 4057
but he set his face toward the *w* Num 24:1 4057
of Israel in the *w* of Sinai Num 26:64 4057
They shall surely die in the *w* Num 26:65 4057
Our father died in the *w*, and he Num 27:3 4057
Meribah in Kadesh in the *w* of Zin Num 27:14 4057
them wander in the *w* forty years Num 32:13 4057
yet again leave them in the *w* Num 32:15 4057
which is in the edge of the *w* Num 33:6 4057
the midst of the sea into the *w* Num 33:8 4057
days' journey in the *w* of Etham Num 33:8 4057
sea, and encamped in the *w* of Sin Num 33:11 4057
their journey out of the *w* of Sin Num 33:12 4057
and pitched in the *w* of Sinai Num 33:15 4057
and pitched in the *w* of Zin Num 33:36 4057
w of Zin along by the coast of Num 34:3 4057
on this side Jordan in the *w* Deut 1:1 4057
all that great and terrible *w* Deut 1:19 4057
And in the *w*, where thou hast seen Deut 1:31 4057
the *w* by the way of the Red sea Deut 1:40 4057
the *w* by the way of the Red sea Deut 2:1 4057
thy walking through this great *w* Deut 2:7 4057
by the way of the *w* of Moab Deut 2:8 4057
I sent messengers out of the *w* of Deut 2:26 4057
Namely, Bezer in the *w*, in the Deut 4:43 4057
thee these forty years in the *w* Deut 8:2 4057
through that great and terrible *w* Deut 8:15 4057
Who fed thee in the *w* with manna Deut 8:16 4057
LORD thy God to wrath in the *w* Deut 9:7 4057
them out to slay them in the *w* Deut 9:28 4057
And what he did unto you in the *w* Deut 11:5 4057
from the *w* and Lebanon, from the Deut 11:24 4057
have led you forty years in the *w* Deut 29:5 4057
land, and in the waste howling *w* Deut 32:10 3452
Meribah-kadesh, in the *w* of Zin Deut 32:51 4057
From the *w* and this Lebanon even Josh 1:4 4057
of war, died in the *w* by the way Josh 5:4 4057
people that were born in the *w* by Josh 5:5 4057
walked forty years in the *w* Josh 5:6 4057
them, and fled by the way of the *w* Josh 8:15 4057
the people that fled to the *w* Josh 8:20 4057
in the *w* wherein they chased them Josh 8:24 4057
and in the springs, and in the *w* Josh 12:8 4057
of Israel wandered in the *w* Josh 14:10 4057
the *w* of Zin southward was the Josh 15:1 4057
In the *w*, Beth-arabah, Middin, and Josh 15:61 4057
to the *w* that goeth up from Josh 16:1 4057
were at the *w* of Beth-aven Josh 18:12 4057
they assigned Bezer in the *w* upon Josh 20:8 4057
ye dwelt in the *w* a long season Josh 24:7 4057
of Judah into the *w* of Judah Judg 1:16 4057
flesh with the thorns of the *w* Judg 8:7 4057
of the city, and thorns of the *w* Judg 8:16 4057
through the *w* unto the Red sea Judg 11:16 4057
they went along through the *w* Judg 11:18 4057
from the *w* even unto Jordan Judg 11:22 4057
of Israel unto the way of the *w* Judg 20:42 4057
fled toward the *w* unto the rock Judg 20:45 4057
fled to the *w* unto the rock Judg 20:47 4057
with all the plagues in the *w* 1Sa 4:8 4057
the valley of Zeboim toward the *w* 1Sa 13:18 4057
left those few sheep in the *w* 1Sa 17:28 4057
abode in the *w* in strong holds 1Sa 23:14 4057
in a mountain in the *w* of Ziph 1Sa 23:14 4057
David was in the *w* of Ziph in a 1Sa 23:15 4057
and his men were in the *w* of Maon 1Sa 23:24 4057
a rock, and abode in the *w* of Maon 1Sa 23:25 4057
after David in the *w* of Maon 1Sa 23:25 4057
David is in the *w* of En-gedi 1Sa 24:1 4057
and went down to the *w* of Paran 1Sa 25:1 4057
David heard in the *w* that Nabal 1Sa 25:4 4057
out of the *w* to salute our master 1Sa 25:14 4057
that this fellow hath in the *w* 1Sa 25:21 4057
and went down to the *w* of Ziph 1Sa 26:2 4057
to seek David in the *w* of Ziph 1Sa 26:2 4057
But David abode in the *w*, and he 1Sa 26:3 4057
Saul came after him into the *w* 1Sa 26:3 4057
by the way of the *w* of Gibeon 2Sa 2:24 4057
over, toward the way of the *w* 2Sa 15:23 4057
will tarry in the plain of the *w* 2Sa 15:28 4057
as be faint in the *w* may drink 2Sa 16:2 4057
this night in the plains of the *w* 2Sa 17:16 4057
and weary, and thirsty, in the *w* 2Sa 17:29 4057
buried in his own house in the *w* 1Kin 2:34 4057
And Baalath, and Tadmor in the *w* 1Kin 9:18 4057
went a day's journey into the *w* 1Kin 19:4 4057
on thy way to the *w* of Damascus 1Kin 19:15 4057
The way through the *w* of Edom 2Kin 3:8 4057
of the *w* from the river Euphrates 1Chr 5:9 4057
Bezer in the *w* with her suburbs, 1Chr 6:78 4057
the hold to the *w* men of might 1Chr 12:8 4057
LORD, which Moses made in the *w* 1Chr 21:29 4057
of the LORD had made in the *w* 2Chr 1:3 4057
And he built Tadmor in the *w* 2Chr 8:4 4057
the brook, before the *w* of Jeruel 2Chr 20:16 4057
and went forth into the *w* of Tekoa 2Chr 20:20 4057
toward the watch tower in the *w* 2Chr 20:24 4057
of God laid upon Israel in the *w* 2Chr 24:9 4057
forsookest them not in the *w* Neh 9:19 4057
didst thou sustain them in the *w* Neh 9:21 4057
came a great wind from the *w* Job 1:19 4057
in a *w* where there is no way Job 12:24 8414
the *w* yieldeth food for them and Job 24:5 6160
fleeing into the *w* in former time Job 30:3 6723
on the *w*, wherein there is no man Job 38:26 4057
Whose house I have made the *w* Job 39:6 6160
voice of the LORD shaketh the *w* Ps 29:8 4057
the LORD shaketh the *w* of Kadesh Ps 29:8 4057
far off, and remain in the *w* Ps 55:7 4057
when he was in the *w* of Judah Ps 63:*t* 4057
drop upon the pastures of the *w* Ps 65:12 4057
thou didst march through the *w* Ps 68:7 3452
in the *w* shall bow before him Ps 72:9 6728
to the people inhabiting the *w* Ps 74:14 6728
He clave the rocks in the *w* Ps 78:15 4057
provoking the most High in the *w* Ps 78:17 6723
Can God furnish a table in the *w* Ps 78:19 4057
oft did they provoke him in the *w* Ps 78:40 4057
guided them in the *w* like a flock Ps 78:52 4057
in the day of temptation in the *w* Ps 95:8 4057
I am like a pelican of the *w* Ps 102:6 4057
the depths, as through the *w* Ps 106:9 4057
But lusted exceedingly in the *w* Ps 106:14 4057
them, to overthrow them in the *w* Ps 106:26 4057
in the *w* in a solitary way Ps 107:4 4057
He turneth rivers into a *w* Ps 107:33 4057
He turneth the *w* into a standing Ps 107:35 4057
causeth them to wander in the *w* Ps 107:40 8414
led his people through the *w* Ps 136:16 4057
It is better to dwell in the *w* Prov 21:19 4057
of the *w* like pillars of smoke Song 3:6 4057
is this that cometh up from the *w* Song 8:5 4057
That made the world as a *w* Is 14:17 4057
of the land from Sela to the *w* Is 16:1 4057
they wandered through the *w* Is 16:8 4057
it for them that dwell in the *w* Is 23:13 6728
forsaken, and left like a *w* Is 27:10 4057
the *w* be a fruitful field, and the Is 32:15 4057
judgment shall dwell in the *w* Is 32:16 4057
Sharon is like a *w* Is 33:9 6160
The *w* and the solitary place shall Is 35:1 4057
for in the *w* shall waters break Is 35:6 4057
voice of him that crieth in the *w* Is 40:3 4057
I will make the *w* a pool of water Is 41:18 4057
I will plant in the *w* the cedar Is 41:19 4057
Let the *w* and the cities thereof Is 42:11 4057
I will even make a way in the *w* Is 43:19 4057
because I give waters in the *w* Is 43:20 4057
up the sea, I make the rivers a *w* Is 50:2 4057
and he will make her *w* like Eden Is 51:3 4057
the deep, as an horse in the *w* Is 63:13 4057
are a *w*, Zion is a *w* Is 64:10 4057
thou wentest after me in the *w* Jer 2:2 4057
Egypt, that led us through the *w* Jer 2:6 4057
A wild ass used to the *w*, that Jer 2:24 4057
Have I been a *w* unto Israel Jer 2:31 4057
for them, as the Arabian in the *w* Jer 3:2 4057
the *w* toward the daughter of my Jer 4:11 4057
lo, the fruitful place was a *w* Jer 4:26 4057
Oh that I had in the *w* a lodging Jer 9:2 4057
of the *w* a lamentation, because Jer 9:10 4057
and is burned up like a *w*, that Jer 9:12 4057
corners, that dwell in the *w* Jer 9:26 4057
my pleasant portion a desolate *w* Jer 12:10 4057
all high places through the *w* Jer 12:12 4057
passeth away by the wind of the *w* Jer 13:24 4057
the parched places in the *w* Jer 17:6 4057
yet surely I will make thee a *w* Jer 22:6 4057
places of the *w* are dried up Jer 23:10 4057
of the sword found grace in the *w* Jer 31:2 4057
and be like the heath in the *w* Jer 48:6 4057
of the nations shall be a *w* Jer 50:12 4057
a desolation, a dry land, and a *w* Jer 51:43 6160
like the ostriches in the *w* Lam 4:3 4057
they laid wait for us in the *w* Lam 4:19 4057
because of the sword of the *w* Lam 5:9 4057
than the *w* toward Diblath Eze 6:14 4057
And now she is planted in the *w* Eze 19:13 4057
Egypt, and brought them into the *w* Eze 20:10 4057
rebelled against me in the *w* Eze 20:13 4057
out my fury upon them in the *w* Eze 20:13 4057
up my hand unto them in the *w* Eze 20:15 4057
I make an end of them in the *w* Eze 20:17 4057
said unto their children in the *w* Eze 20:18 4057
my anger against them in the *w* Eze 20:21 4057
mine hand unto them also in the *w* Eze 20:23 4057
you into the *w* of the people Eze 20:35 4057
in the *w* of the land of Egypt Eze 20:36 4057
were brought Sabeans from the *w* Eze 23:42 4057
will leave thee thrown into the *w* Eze 29:5 4057
they shall dwell safely in the *w* Eze 34:25 4057
she was born, and make her as a *w* Hos 2:3 4057
her, and bring her into the *w* Hos 2:14 4057
found Israel like grapes in the *w* Hos 9:10 4057
I did know thee in the *w*, in the Hos 13:5 4057
the LORD shall come up from the *w* Hos 13:15 4057
devoured the pastures of the *w* Joel 1:19 4057
devoured the pastures of the *w* Joel 1:20 4057
them, and behind them a desolate *w* Joel 2:3 4057
the pastures of the *w* do spring Joel 2:22 4057
and Edom shall be a desolate *w* Joel 3:19 4057
led you forty years through the *w* Amos 2:10 4057
and offerings in the *w* forty years Amos 5:25 4057
of Hemath unto the river of the *w* Amos 6:14 6166
a desolation, and dry like a *w* Zeph 2:13 4057
waste for the dragons of the *w* Mal 1:3 4057
preaching in the *w* of Judaea Mt 3:1 *2048*
The voice of one crying in the *w* Mt 3:3 *2048*
the *w* to be tempted of the devil Mt 4:1 *2048*
went ye out into the *w* to see Mt 11:7 *2048*
we have so much bread in the *w* Mt 15:33 *2047*
The voice of one crying in the *w* Mk 1:3 *2048*
John did baptize in the *w* Mk 1:4 *2048*
the spirit driveth him into the *w* Mk 1:12 *2048*
he was there in the *w* forty days Mk 1:13 *2048*
men with bread here in the *w* Mk 8:4 *2047*
the son of Zacharias in the *w* Lk 3:2 *2048*
The voice of one crying in the *w* Lk 3:4 *2048*
was led by the Spirit into the *w* Lk 4:1 *2048*
And he withdrew himself into the *w* Lk 5:16 *2048*
went ye out into the *w* for to see Lk 7:24 *2048*
driven of the devil into the *w* Lk 8:29 *2048*
leave the ninety and nine in the *w* Lk 15:4 *2048*
the voice of one crying in the *w* Jn 1:23 *2048*
lifted up the serpent in the *w* Jn 3:14 *2048*
fathers did eat manna in the *w* Jn 6:49 *2048*
unto a country near to the *w* Jn 11:54 *2048*
there appeared to him in the *w* of Acts 7:30 *2048*
Red sea, and in the *w* forty years Acts 7:36 *2048*
w with the angel which spake to Acts 7:38 *2048*
the space of forty years in the *w* Acts 7:42 *2048*
tabernacle of witness in the *w* Acts 7:44 *2048*
he their manners in the *w* Acts 13:18 *2048*
leddest out into the *w* four Acts 21:38 *2048*
for they were overthrown in the *w* 1Cor 10:5 *2048*
in the city, in perils in the *w* 2Cor 11:26 *2047*
in the day of temptation in the *w* Heb 3:8 *2048*
whose carcases fell in the *w* Heb 3:17 *2048*
And the woman fled into the *w* Rev 12:6 *2048*

W

that she might fly into the *w* Rev 12:14 *2048*
me away in the spirit into the *w* Rev 17:3 *2048*

WILES
For they vex you with their *w* Num 25:18 5231
stand against the *w* of the devil Eph 6:11 *3180*

WILFULLY
For if we sin *w* after that we Heb 10:26 *1596*

WILILY
They did work *w*, and went and made. Josh 9:4 6195

WILL
I *w* make him an help meet for him Gen 2:18
I *w* put enmity between thee and Gen 3:15
I *w* greatly multiply thy sorrow Gen 3:16
I *w* destroy man whom I have Gen 6:7
I *w* destroy them with the earth Gen 6:13
But with thee *w* I establish my Gen 6:18
I *w* cause it to rain upon the Gen 7:4
substance that I have made *w* I Gen 7:4
I *w* not again curse the ground Gen 8:21
neither *w* I again smite any more Gen 8:21
blood of your lives *w* I require Gen 9:5
of every beast *w* I require it Gen 9:5
w I require the life of man Gen 9:5
I *w* establish my covenant with Gen 9:11
I *w* remember my covenant, which Gen 9:15
I *w* look upon it, that I may Gen 9:16
now nothing *w* be restrained from Gen 11:6
unto a land that I *w* shew thee Gen 12:1
I *w* make of thee a great nation, Gen 12:2
I *w* bless thee, and make thy name Gen 12:2
I *w* bless them that bless thee, Gen 12:3
Unto thy seed *w* I give this land Gen 12:7
they *w* kill me, but they *w* Gen 12:12
hand, then I *w* go to the right Gen 13:9
hand, then I *w* go to the left Gen 13:9
to thee *w* I give it, and to thy Gen 13:15
I *w* make thy seed as the dust of Gen 13:16
for I *w* give it unto thee Gen 13:17
That I *w* not take from a thread Gen 14:23
that I *w* not take any thing that Gen 14:23
whom they shall serve, *w* I judge Gen 15:14
I *w* multiply thy seed exceedingly Gen 16:10
And he *w* be a wild man Gen 16:12
his hand *w* be against every man, Gen 16:12
I *w* make my covenant between me Gen 17:2
w multiply thee exceedingly Gen 17:2
I *w* make thee exceeding fruitful, Gen 17:6
I *w* make nations of thee, and Gen 17:6
I *w* establish my covenant between Gen 17:7
I *w* give unto thee, and to thy Gen 17:8
and I *w* be their God Gen 17:8
I *w* bless her, and give thee a son Gen 17:16
I *w* bless her, and she shall be a Gen 17:16
I *w* establish my covenant with Gen 17:19
w make him fruitful Gen 17:20
w multiply him exceedingly Gen 17:20
I *w* make him a great nation Gen 17:20
But my covenant *w* I establish Gen 17:21
I *w* fetch a morsel of bread, and Gen 18:5
I *w* certainly return unto thee Gen 18:10
appointed I *w* return unto thee Gen 18:14
that he *w* command his children and Gen 18:19
I *w* go down now, and see whether Gen 18:21
and if not, I *w* know Gen 18:21
then I *w* spare all the place for Gen 18:26
forty and five, I *w* not destroy it Gen 18:28
I *w* not do it for forty's sake Gen 18:29
the LORD be angry, and I *w* speak Gen 18:30
I *w* not do it, if I find thirty Gen 18:30
I *w* not destroy it for twenty's Gen 18:31
I *w* speak yet but this once Gen 18:32
I *w* not destroy it for ten's sake Gen 18:32
but we *w* abide in the street all Gen 19:2
sojourn, and he *w* needs be a judge Gen 19:9
now *w* we deal worse with thee, Gen 19:9
For we *w* destroy this place, Gen 19:13
for the LORD *w* destroy this city Gen 19:14
that I *w* not overthrow this city, Gen 19:21
we *w* lie with him, that we may Gen 19:32
they *w* slay me for my wife's sake Gen 20:11
all that hear *w* laugh with me Gen 21:6
the bondwoman *w* I make a nation Gen 21:13
for I *w* make him a great nation Gen 21:18
And Abraham said, I *w* swear Gen 21:24
mountains which I *w* tell thee of Gen 22:2
the lad *w* go yonder and worship, Gen 22:5
God *w* provide himself a lamb for Gen 22:8
That in blessing I *w* bless thee Gen 22:17
in multiplying I *w* multiply thy Gen 22:17
I *w* give thee money for the field Gen 23:13
of me, and I *w* bury my dead there Gen 23:13
I *w* make thee swear by the LORD, Gen 24:3
Peradventure the woman *w* not be Gen 24:5
Unto thy seed *w* I give this land Gen 24:7
if the woman *w* not be willing to Gen 24:8
I *w* give thy camels drink also Gen 24:14
I *w* draw water for thy camels Gen 24:19
I *w* not eat, until I have told Gen 24:33
the woman *w* not follow me Gen 24:39
w send his angel with thee, and Gen 24:40
I *w* also draw for thy camels Gen 24:44
I *w* give thy camels drink also Gen 24:46
now if ye *w* deal kindly and truly Gen 24:49
We *w* call the damsel, and enquire Gen 24:57
And she said, I *w* go Gen 24:58
I *w* be with thee Gen 26:3
and *w* bless thee Gen 26:3
I *w* give all these countries, and Gen 26:3
I *w* perform the oath which I Gen 26:3
I *w* make thy seed to multiply as Gen 26:4
w give unto thy seed all these Gen 26:4
w bless thee, and multiply thy Gen 26:24
I *w* make them savoury meat for Gen 27:9
My father peradventure *w* feel me Gen 27:12
I *w* eat of my son's venison, that Gen 27:25
then *w* I slay my brother Jacob Gen 27:41
then I *w* send, and fetch thee from Gen 27:45
to thee *w* I give it, and to thy Gen 28:13
w keep thee in all places whither Gen 28:15
w bring thee again into this land Gen 28:15
for I *w* not leave thee, until I Gen 28:15
If God *w* be with me Gen 28:20
w keep me in this way that I go, Gen 28:20
w give me bread to eat, and Gen 28:20
all that thou shalt give me I *w* Gen 28:22
I *w* serve thee seven years for Gen 29:18
we *w* give thee this also for the Gen 29:27
therefore my husband *w* love me Gen 29:32
Now this time *w* my husband be Gen 29:34
she said, Now *w* I praise the LORD Gen 29:35
the daughters *w* call me blessed Gen 30:13
now *w* my husband dwell with me, Gen 30:20
me thy wages, and I *w* give it Gen 30:28
I *w* again feed and keep thy flock Gen 30:31
I *w* pass through all thy flock to Gen 30:32
and I *w* be with thee Gen 31:3
that I *w* not pass over this heap Gen 31:52
and I *w* deal well with thee Gen 32:9
for I fear him, lest he *w* come Gen 32:11
I *w* surely do thee good, and make Gen 32:12
I *w* appease him with the present Gen 32:20
afterward I *w* see his face Gen 32:20
peradventure he *w* accept of me Gen 32:20
I *w* not let thee go, except thou Gen 32:26
let us go, and I *w* go before thee Gen 33:12
them one day, all the flock *w* die Gen 33:13
I *w* lead on softly, according as Gen 33:14
ye shall say unto me I *w* give Gen 34:11
I *w* give according as ye shall Gen 34:12
But in this *w* we consent unto you Gen 34:15
If ye *w* be as we be, that every Gen 34:15
Then *w* we give our daughters unto Gen 34:16
we *w* take your daughters to us, Gen 34:16
we *w* dwell with you Gen 34:16
and we *w* become one people Gen 34:16
But if ye *w* not hearken unto us, Gen 34:17
then *w* we take our daughter, and Gen 34:17
our daughter, and we *w* be gone Gen 34:17
Only herein *w* the men consent Gen 34:22
them, and they *w* dwell with us Gen 34:23
I *w* make there an altar unto God, Gen 35:3
and Isaac, to thee I *w* give it Gen 35:12
seed after thee *w* I give the land Gen 35:12
come, and I *w* send thee unto them Gen 37:13
we *w* say, Some evil beast hath Gen 37:20
we shall see what *w* become of his Gen 37:20
For I *w* go down into the grave Gen 37:35
I *w* send thee a kid from the Gen 38:17
God *w* shortly bring it to pass Gen 41:32
only in the throne *w* I be greater Gen 41:40
so *w* I deliver you your brother, Gen 42:34
not, and ye *w* take Benjamin away Gen 42:36
I *w* bring him to thee again Gen 42:37
we *w* go down and buy thee food Gen 43:4
not send him, we *w* not go down Gen 43:5
lad with me, and we *w* arise and go Gen 43:8
I *w* be surety for him Gen 43:9
we also *w* be my lord's bondmen Gen 44:9
be with us, then *w* we go down Gen 44:26
lad is not with us, that he *w* die Gen 44:31
And there *w* I nourish thee Gen 45:11
I *w* give you the good of the land Gen 45:18
I *w* go and see him before I die Gen 45:28
for I *w* there make of thee a Gen 46:3
I *w* go down with thee into Egypt Gen 46:4
I *w* also surely bring thee up Gen 46:4
I *w* go up, and shew Pharaoh, and Gen 46:31
I *w* give you for your cattle, if Gen 47:16
We *w* not hide it from my lord, Gen 47:18
our land *w* be servants unto Gen 47:19
we *w* be Pharaoh's servants Gen 47:25
But I *w* lie with my fathers, and Gen 47:30
he said, I *w* do as thou hast said Gen 47:30
I *w* make thee fruitful, and Gen 48:4
I *w* make of thee a multitude of Gen 48:4
w give this land to thy seed Gen 48:4
thee, unto me, and I *w* bless them Gen 48:9
I *w* divide them in Jacob, and Gen 49:7
bury my father, and I *w* come again Gen 50:5
Joseph *w* peradventure hate us, and Gen 50:15
w certainly requite us all the Gen 50:15
I *w* nourish you, and your little Gen 50:21
God *w* surely visit you, and bring Gen 50:24
God *w* surely visit you, and ye Gen 50:25
me, and I *w* give thee thy wages Ex 2:9
I *w* now turn aside, and see this Ex 3:3
I *w* send thee unto Pharaoh, that Ex 3:10
Certainly I *w* be with thee Ex 3:12
I *w* bring you up out of the Ex 3:17
king of Egypt *w* not let you go Ex 3:19
I *w* stretch out my hand, and smite Ex 3:20
which I *w* do in the midst thereof Ex 3:20
and after that he *w* let you go Ex 3:20
I *w* give this people favour in Ex 3:21
they *w* not believe me, nor Ex 4:1
for they *w* say, The LORD hath not Ex 4:1
if they *w* not believe thee, Ex 4:8
that they *w* believe the voice of Ex 4:8
if they *w* not believe also these Ex 4:9
I *w* be with thy mouth, and teach Ex 4:12
he *w* be glad in his heart Ex 4:14
I *w* be with thy mouth, and with Ex 4:15
w teach you what ye shall do Ex 4:15
but I *w* harden his heart, that he Ex 4:21
I *w* slay thy son, even thy Ex 4:23
neither *w* I let Israel go Ex 5:2
Pharaoh, I *w* not give you straw Ex 5:10
thou see what I *w* do to Pharaoh Ex 6:1
I *w* bring you out from under the Ex 6:6
I *w* rid you out of their bondage, Ex 6:6
I *w* redeem you with a stretched Ex 6:6
I *w* take you to me for a people, Ex 6:7
and I *w* be to you a God Ex 6:7
I *w* bring you in unto the land, Ex 6:8
I *w* give it you for an heritage Ex 6:8
I *w* harden Pharaoh's heart, and Ex 7:3
I *w* smite with the rod that is in Ex 7:17
I *w* smite all thy borders with Ex 8:2
I *w* let the people go, that they Ex 8:8
I *w* send swarms of flies upon Ex 8:21
I *w* sever in that day the land of Ex 8:22
I *w* put a division between my Ex 8:23
eyes, and *w* they not stone us Ex 8:26
We *w* go three days' journey into Ex 8:27
I *w* let you go, that ye may Ex 8:28
I *w* intreat the LORD that the Ex 8:29
For I *w* at this time send all my Ex 9:14
For now I *w* stretch out my hand, Ex 9:15
time I *w* cause it to rain a very Ex 9:18
I *w* let you go, and ye shall stay Ex 9:28 7522
I *w* spread abroad my hands unto Ex 9:29
I know that ye *w* not yet fear the Ex 9:30
to morrow *w* I bring the locusts Ex 10:4
We *w* go with our young and with Ex 10:9
flocks and with our herds *w* we go Ex 10:9
as I *w* let you go, and your little Ex 10:10
I *w* see thy face again no more Ex 10:29
Yet *w* I bring one plague more Ex 11:1
afterwards he *w* let you go hence Ex 11:1
About midnight *w* I go out into Ex 11:4
and after that I *w* go out Ex 11:8
For I *w* pass through the land of Ex 12:12
w smite all the firstborn in the Ex 12:12
of Egypt I *w* execute judgment Ex 12:12
I *w* pass over you, and the plague Ex 12:13
For the LORD *w* pass through to Ex 12:23
the LORD *w* pass over the door, and Ex 12:23
w not suffer the destroyer to Ex 12:23
land which the LORD *w* give you Ex 12:25
w keep the passover to the LORD, Ex 12:48
saying, God *w* surely visit you Ex 13:19
For Pharaoh *w* say of the children Ex 14:3
I *w* harden Pharaoh's heart, that Ex 14:4
I *w* be honoured upon Pharaoh, and Ex 14:4
which he *w* shew to you to day Ex 14:13
I *w* harden the hearts of the Ex 14:17
I *w* get me honour upon Pharaoh, Ex 14:17
I *w* sing unto the LORD, for he Ex 15:1
I *w* prepare him an habitation Ex 15:2
my father's God, and I *w* exalt him Ex 15:2
I *w* pursue, I *w* overtake, I Ex 15:9
overtake, I *w* divide the spoil Ex 15:9
I *w* draw my sword, my hand shall Ex 15:9
I *w* put none of these diseases Ex 15:26
I *w* rain bread from heaven for Ex 16:4
whether they *w* walk in my law, or Ex 16:4
bake that which ye *w* bake to day Ex 16:23
and seethe that ye *w* seethe Ex 16:23
I *w* stand before thee there upon Ex 17:6
to morrow I *w* stand on the top of Ex 17:9
for I *w* utterly put out the Ex 17:14
LORD *w* have war with Amalek from Ex 17:16
I *w* give thee counsel, and God Ex 18:19
if ye *w* obey my voice indeed, and Ex 19:5
that the LORD hath spoken we *w* do Ex 19:8
for the third day the LORD *w* come Ex 19:11
for the LORD *w* not hold him Ex 20:7
Speak thou with us, and we *w* hear Ex 20:19
record my name I *w* come unto thee Ex 20:24
come unto thee, and I *w* bless thee Ex 20:24
I *w* not go out free Ex 21:5
then I *w* appoint thee a place Ex 21:13
woman's husband *w* lay upon him Ex 21:22
I *w* surely hear their cry Ex 22:23
I *w* kill you with the sword Ex 22:24
he crieth unto me, that I *w* hear Ex 22:27
for I *w* not justify the wicked Ex 23:7
for he *w* not pardon your Ex 23:21
then I *w* be an enemy unto thine Ex 23:22
and I *w* cut them off Ex 23:23
I *w* take sickness away from the Ex 23:25
the number of thy days I *w* fulfil Ex 23:26
I *w* send my fear before thee, and Ex 23:27
w destroy all the people to whom Ex 23:27
I *w* make all thine enemies turn Ex 23:27
I *w* send hornets before thee, Ex 23:28
I *w* not drive them out from Ex 23:29
little I *w* drive them out from Ex 23:30
I *w* set thy bounds from the Red Ex 23:31
for I *w* deliver the inhabitants Ex 23:31
it *w* surely be a snare unto thee Ex 23:33
which the LORD hath said *w* we do Ex 24:3
that the LORD hath said *w* we do Ex 24:7
I *w* give thee tables of stone, and Ex 24:12
there I *w* meet with thee, and I Ex 25:22
I *w* commune with thee from above Ex 25:22
of all things which I *w* give thee Ex 25:22
where I *w* meet you, to speak Ex 29:42
there I *w* meet with the children Ex 29:43
I *w* sanctify the tabernacle of Ex 29:44
I *w* sanctify also both Aaron and Ex 29:44
I *w* dwell among the children of Ex 29:45
of Israel, and *w* be their God Ex 29:45
where I *w* meet with thee Ex 30:6
where I *w* meet with thee Ex 30:36
I *w* make of thee a great nation Ex 32:10
I *w* multiply your seed as the Ex 32:13
spoken of *w* I give unto your seed Ex 32:13
now I *w* go up unto the LORD Ex 32:30
him *w* I blot out of my book Ex 32:33

I *w* visit their sin upon them...... Ex 32:34
saying, Unto thy seed *w* I give it...... Ex 33:1
I *w* send an angel before thee...... Ex 33:2
I *w* drive out the Canaanite, the...... Ex 33:2
for I *w* not go up in the midst of...... Ex 33:3
I *w* come up into the midst of...... Ex 33:5
with thee, and I *w* give thee rest...... Ex 33:14
I *w* do this thing also that thou...... Ex 33:17
I *w* make all my goodness pass...... Ex 33:19
I *w* proclaim the name of the LORD...... Ex 33:19
w be gracious to whom...... Ex 33:19
gracious to whom I *w* be gracious...... Ex 33:19
w shew mercy on whom...... Ex 33:19
on whom I *w* shew mercy...... Ex 33:19
that I *w* put thee in a clift of...... Ex 33:22
w cover thee with my hand while I...... Ex 33:22
I *w* take away mine hand, and thou...... Ex 33:23
I *w* write upon these tables the...... Ex 34:1
that *w* by no means clear the...... Ex 34:7
all thy people I *w* do marvels...... Ex 34:10
thing that I *w* do with thee...... Ex 34:10
For I *w* cast out the nations...... Ex 34:24
w at the door of the tabernacle...... Lev 1:3 7522
when any *w* offer a meat offering...... Lev 2:1
to day the LORD *w* appear unto you...... Lev 9:4
I *w* be sanctified in them that...... Lev 10:3
all the people I *w* be glorified...... Lev 10:3
for I *w* appear in the cloud upon...... Lev 16:2
I *w* even set my face against that...... Lev 17:10
w cut him off from among his...... Lev 17:10
ye shall offer it at your own *w*...... Lev 19:5 7522
I *w* set my face against that man,...... Lev 20:3
w cut him off from among his...... Lev 20:3
Then I *w* set my face against that...... Lev 20:5
w cut him off, and all that go a...... Lev 20:5
I *w* even set my face against that...... Lev 20:6
w cut him off from among his...... Lev 20:6
I *w* give it unto you to possess...... Lev 20:24
that *w* offer his oblation for all...... Lev 22:18
which they *w* offer unto the LORD...... Lev 22:18
your own *w* a male without blemish...... Lev 22:19 7522
when ye *w* offer a sacrifice of...... Lev 22:29
the LORD, offer it at your own *w*...... Lev 22:29 7522
but I *w* be hallowed among the...... Lev 22:32
the same soul *w* I destroy from...... Lev 23:30
Then I *w* command my blessing upon...... Lev 25:21
Then I *w* give you rain in due...... Lev 26:4
I *w* give peace in the land, and ye...... Lev 26:6
I *w* rid evil beasts out of the...... Lev 26:6
For I *w* have respect unto you, and...... Lev 26:9
I *w* set my tabernacle among you...... Lev 26:11
I *w* walk among you...... Lev 26:12
w be your God, and ye shall be my...... Lev 26:12
But if ye *w* not hearken unto me,...... Lev 26:14
w not do all these commandments...... Lev 26:14
so that ye *w* not do all my...... Lev 26:15
I also *w* do this unto you...... Lev 26:16
I *w* even appoint over you terror,...... Lev 26:16
I *w* set my face against you, and...... Lev 26:17
if ye *w* not yet for all this...... Lev 26:18
then I *w* punish you seven times...... Lev 26:18
I *w* break the pride of your power...... Lev 26:19
I *w* make your heaven as iron, and...... Lev 26:19
unto me, and *w* not hearken unto me...... Lev 26:21 14
I *w* bring seven times more...... Lev 26:21
I *w* also send wild beasts among...... Lev 26:22
if ye *w* not be reformed by me by...... Lev 26:23
but *w* walk contrary unto me...... Lev 26:23
Then *w* I also walk contrary unto...... Lev 26:24
w punish you yet seven times for...... Lev 26:24
I *w* bring a sword upon you, that...... Lev 26:25
I *w* send the pestilence among you...... Lev 26:25
if ye *w* not for all this hearken...... Lev 26:27
Then I *w* walk contrary unto you...... Lev 26:28
w chastise you seven times for...... Lev 26:28
I *w* destroy your high places, and...... Lev 26:30
I *w* make your cities waste, and...... Lev 26:31
I *w* not smell the savour of your...... Lev 26:31
And I *w* bring the land into...... Lev 26:32
I *w* scatter you among the heathen...... Lev 26:33
w draw out a sword after you...... Lev 26:33
I *w* send a faintness into their...... Lev 26:36
Then *w* I remember my covenant...... Lev 26:42
with Abraham *w* I remember...... Lev 26:42
and I *w* remember the land...... Lev 26:42
I *w* not cast them away...... Lev 26:44
neither *w* I abhor them, to...... Lev 26:44
But I *w* for their sakes remember...... Lev 26:45
But if he *w* at all redeem it,...... Lev 27:13 7522
sanctified it *w* redeem his house...... Lev 27:15
the field *w* in any wise redeem it...... Lev 27:19
if he *w* not redeem the field, or...... Lev 27:20
if a man *w* at all redeem ought of...... Lev 27:31
and I *w* bless them...... Num 6:27
I *w* hear what the LORD...... Num 9:8
the LORD *w* command concerning you...... Num 9:8
w keep the passover unto the LORD...... Num 9:14
the LORD said, I *w* give it you...... Num 10:29
with us, and we *w* do thee good...... Num 10:29
And he said unto him, I *w* not go...... Num 10:30
but I *w* depart to mine own land,...... Num 10:30
the same *w* we do unto thee...... Num 10:32
I *w* come down and talk with thee...... Num 11:17
I *w* take of the spirit which is...... Num 11:17
upon thee, and *w* put it upon them...... Num 11:17
the LORD *w* give you flesh...... Num 11:18
I *w* give them flesh, that they...... Num 11:21
I the LORD *w* make myself known...... Num 12:6
w speak unto him in a dream...... Num 12:6
With him *w* I speak mouth to mouth...... Num 12:8
then he *w* bring us into this land...... Num 14:8
How long *w* this people provoke me...... Num 14:11
how long *w* it be ere they believe...... Num 14:11
I *w* smite them with the...... Num 14:12

w make of thee a greater nation...... Num 14:12
they *w* tell it to the inhabitants...... Num 14:14
heard the fame of thee *w* speak...... Num 14:15
him *w* I bring into the land...... Num 14:24
in mine ears, so *w* I do to you...... Num 14:28
them *w* I bring in, and they shall...... Num 14:31
I *w* surely do it unto all this...... Num 14:35
w go up unto the place which the...... Num 14:40
the LORD *w* not be with you...... Num 14:43
w make an offering by fire unto...... Num 15:3
w offer an offering made by fire,...... Num 15:14
the LORD *w* shew who are his...... Num 16:5
w cause him to come near unto him...... Num 16:5
even him whom he hath chosen *w* he...... Num 16:5
which said, We *w* not come up...... Num 16:12
we *w* not come up...... Num 16:14
where I *w* meet with you...... Num 17:4
I *w* make to cease from me the...... Num 17:5
we *w* not pass through the fields,...... Num 20:17
neither *w* we drink of the water...... Num 20:17
we *w* go by the king's high way,...... Num 20:17
we *w* not turn to the right hand...... Num 20:17
unto him, We *w* go by the high way...... Num 20:19
of thy water, then I *w* pay for it...... Num 20:19
I *w* only, without doing any thing...... Num 20:19
then I *w* utterly destroy their...... Num 21:2
together, and I *w* give them water...... Num 21:16
we *w* not turn into the fields, or...... Num 21:22
we *w* not drink of the waters of...... Num 21:22
but we *w* go along by the king's...... Num 21:22
I *w* bring you word again, as the...... Num 22:8
For I *w* promote thee unto very...... Num 22:17
I *w* do whatsoever thou sayest...... Num 22:17
what the LORD *w* say unto me more...... Num 22:19
thee, I *w* get me back again...... Num 22:34
by thy burnt offering, and I *w* go...... Num 23:3
the LORD *w* come to meet me...... Num 23:3
he sheweth me I *w* tell thee...... Num 23:3
I *w* bring thee unto another place...... Num 23:27
peradventure it *w* please God that...... Num 23:27
the LORD saith, that *w* I speak...... Num 24:13
I *w* advertise thee what this...... Num 24:14
he *w* yet again leave them in the...... Num 32:15
We *w* build sheepfolds here for...... Num 32:16
But we ourselves *w* go ready armed...... Num 32:17
We *w* not return unto our houses,...... Num 32:18
For we *w* not inherit with them on...... Num 32:19
If ye *w* do this thing...... Num 32:20
if ye *w* go armed before the LORD...... Num 32:20
w go all of you armed over Jordan...... Num 32:21
But if ye *w* not do so, behold, ye...... Num 32:23
be sure your sin *w* find you out...... Num 32:23
Thy servants *w* do as my lord...... Num 32:25
But thy servants *w* pass over...... Num 32:27
the children of Reuben *w* pass...... Num 32:29
But if they *w* not pass over with...... Num 32:30
unto thy servants, so *w* we do...... Num 32:31
We *w* pass over armed before the...... Num 32:32
But if ye *w* not drive out the...... Num 33:55
I *w* make them rulers over you...... Deut 1:13
bring it unto me, and I *w* hear it...... Deut 1:17
We *w* send men before us, and they...... Deut 1:22
to him *w* I give the land that he...... Deut 1:36
thither, and unto them *w* I give it...... Deut 1:39
we *w* go up and fight, according to...... Deut 1:41
for I *w* not give you of their...... Deut 2:5
for I *w* not give thee of their...... Deut 2:9
for I *w* not give thee of the land...... Deut 2:19
This day *w* I begin to put the...... Deut 2:25
I *w* go along by the high way...... Deut 2:27
I *w* neither turn unto the right...... Deut 2:27
only I *w* pass through on my feet...... Deut 2:28
for I *w* deliver him, and all his...... Deut 3:2
I *w* make them hear my words, that...... Deut 4:10
he *w* not forsake thee...... Deut 4:31
for the LORD *w* not hold him...... Deut 5:11
for this great fire *w* consume us...... Deut 5:25
and we *w* hear it, and do it...... Deut 5:27
I *w* speak unto thee all the...... Deut 5:31
For they *w* turn away thy son from...... Deut 7:4
so *w* the anger of the LORD be...... Deut 7:4
he *w* not be slack to him that...... Deut 7:10
he *w* repay him to his face...... Deut 7:10
he *w* love thee, and bless thee, and...... Deut 7:13
he *w* also bless the fruit of thy...... Deut 7:13
the LORD *w* take away from thee...... Deut 7:15
w put none of the evil diseases...... Deut 7:15
but *w* lay them upon all them that...... Deut 7:15
for that *w* be a snare unto thee...... Deut 7:16
Moreover the LORD thy God *w* send...... Deut 7:20
the LORD thy God *w* put out those...... Deut 7:22
I *w* make of thee a nation...... Deut 9:14
I *w* write on the tables the words...... Deut 10:2
That I *w* give you the rain of...... Deut 11:14
I *w* send grass in thy fields for...... Deut 11:15
Then *w* the LORD drive out all...... Deut 11:23
if ye *w* not obey the commandments...... Deut 11:28
I *w* eat flesh, because thy soul...... Deut 12:20
even so *w* I do likewise...... Deut 12:30
I *w* not go away from thee...... Deut 15:16
the man that *w* do presumptuously,...... Deut 17:12
w not hearken unto the priest...... Deut 17:12
I *w* set a king over me, like as...... Deut 17:14
The LORD thy God *w* raise up unto...... Deut 18:15
I *w* raise them up a Prophet from...... Deut 18:18
w put my words in his mouth...... Deut 18:18
that whosoever *w* not hearken unto...... Deut 18:19
in my name, I *w* require it of him...... Deut 18:19
if it *w* make no peace with thee,...... Deut 20:12
but *w* make war against thee, then...... Deut 20:12
shalt let her go whither she *w*...... Deut 21:14 5315
which *w* not obey the voice of his...... Deut 21:18
him, *w* not hearken unto them...... Deut 21:18
he *w* not obey our voice...... Deut 21:20

for the LORD thy God *w* surely...... Deut 23:21
he *w* not perform the duty of my...... Deut 25:7 14
that *w* not build up his brother's...... Deut 25:9
that the LORD thy God *w* set thee...... Deut 28:1
The LORD *w* smite thee with the...... Deut 28:27
So that he *w* not give to any of...... Deut 28:55
Then the LORD *w* make thy plagues...... Deut 28:59
Moreover he *w* bring upon thee all...... Deut 28:60
them *w* the LORD bring upon thee,...... Deut 28:61
so the LORD *w* rejoice over you to...... Deut 28:63
The LORD *w* not spare him, but...... Deut 29:20
LORD thy God *w* turn thy captivity...... Deut 30:3
w return and gather thee from all...... Deut 30:3
from thence *w* the LORD thy God...... Deut 30:4
from thence *w* he fetch thee...... Deut 30:4
the LORD thy God *w* bring thee...... Deut 30:5
he *w* do thee good, and multiply...... Deut 30:5
the LORD thy God *w* circumcise...... Deut 30:6
the LORD thy God *w* put all these...... Deut 30:7
the LORD thy God *w* make thee...... Deut 30:9
for the LORD *w* again rejoice over...... Deut 30:9
he *w* go over before thee, and he...... Deut 31:3
he *w* destroy these nations from...... Deut 31:3
he *w* not fail thee, nor forsake...... Deut 31:6
he *w* be with thee...... Deut 31:8
he *w* not fail thee, neither...... Deut 31:8
and this people *w* rise up, and go a...... Deut 31:16
w forsake me, and break my...... Deut 31:16
I *w* forsake them...... Deut 31:17
I *w* hide my face from them, and...... Deut 31:17
so that they *w* say in that day,...... Deut 31:17
I *w* surely hide my face in that...... Deut 31:18
then *w* they turn unto other gods,...... Deut 31:20
and I *w* be with thee...... Deut 31:23
ye *w* utterly corrupt yourselves...... Deut 31:29
evil *w* befall you in the latter...... Deut 31:29
because ye *w* do evil in the sight...... Deut 31:29
ear, O ye heavens, and I *w* speak...... Deut 32:1
Because I *w* publish the name of...... Deut 32:3
ask thy father, and he *w* shew thee...... Deut 32:7
thy elders, and they *w* tell thee...... Deut 32:7
I *w* hide my face from them...... Deut 32:20
I *w* see what their end shall be...... Deut 32:20
I *w* move them to jealousy with...... Deut 32:21
I *w* provoke them to anger with a...... Deut 32:21
I *w* heap mischiefs upon them...... Deut 32:23
I *w* spend mine arrows upon them...... Deut 32:23
I *w* also send the teeth of beasts...... Deut 32:24
I *w* render vengeance to mine...... Deut 32:41
w reward them that hate me...... Deut 32:41
I *w* make mine arrows drunk with...... Deut 32:42
for he *w* avenge the blood of his...... Deut 32:43
w render vengeance to his...... Deut 32:43
w be merciful unto his land, and...... Deut 32:43
for the good *w* of him that dwelt...... Deut 33:16 7522
I *w* give it unto thy seed...... Deut 34:4
with Moses, so I *w* be with thee...... Josh 1:5
I *w* not fail thee, nor forsake...... Josh 1:5
that thou commandest us we *w* do...... Josh 1:16
thou sendest us, we *w* go...... Josh 1:16
so *w* we hearken unto thee...... Josh 1:17
w not hearken unto thy words in...... Josh 1:18
that ye *w* also shew kindness unto...... Josh 2:12
that ye *w* save alive my father,...... Josh 2:13
that we *w* deal kindly and truly...... Josh 2:14
We *w* be blameless of this thine...... Josh 2:17
his head, and we *w* be guiltless...... Josh 2:19
then we *w* be quit of thine oath...... Josh 2:20
the LORD *w* do wonders among you...... Josh 3:5
This day *w* I begin to magnify...... Josh 3:7
with Moses, so I *w* be with thee...... Josh 3:7
that he *w* without fail drive out...... Josh 3:10
neither *w* I be with you any more,...... Josh 7:12
with me, *w* approach unto the city...... Josh 8:5
that we *w* flee before them,...... Josh 8:5
(For they *w* come out after us)...... Josh 8:6
for they *w* say, They flee before...... Josh 8:6
therefore we *w* flee before them...... Josh 8:6
for the LORD your God *w* deliver...... Josh 8:7
for I *w* give it into thine hand...... Josh 8:18
This we *w* do to them...... Josh 9:20
we *w* even let them live, lest...... Josh 9:20
w I deliver them up all slain...... Josh 11:6
them *w* I drive out from before...... Josh 13:6
if so be the LORD *w* be with me...... Josh 14:12
to him *w* I give Achsah my...... Josh 15:16
I *w* send them, and they shall rise...... Josh 18:4
and it *w* be, seeing ye rebel to...... Josh 22:18
that to morrow he *w* be wroth with...... Josh 22:18
that the LORD your God *w* no more...... Josh 23:13
you this day whom ye *w* serve...... Josh 24:15
and my house, we *w* serve the LORD...... Josh 24:15
therefore *w* we also serve the...... Josh 24:18
he *w* not forgive your...... Josh 24:19
strange gods, then he *w* turn...... Josh 24:20
but we *w* serve the LORD...... Josh 24:21
The LORD our God *w* we serve...... Josh 24:24
we serve, and his voice *w* we obey...... Josh 24:24
I likewise *w* go with thee into...... Judg 1:3
to him *w* I give Achsah my...... Judg 1:12
the city, and we *w* shew thee mercy...... Judg 1:24
I *w* never break my covenant with...... Judg 2:1
I *w* not drive them out from...... Judg 2:3
I also *w* not henceforth drive out...... Judg 2:21
whether they *w* keep the way of...... Judg 2:22
I *w* draw unto thee to the river...... Judg 4:7
I *w* deliver him into thine hand...... Judg 4:7
thou wilt go with me, then I *w* go...... Judg 4:8
not go with me, then I *w* not go...... Judg 4:8
she said, I *w* surely go with thee...... Judg 4:9
I *w* shew thee the man whom thou...... Judg 4:22
I, even I, *w* sing unto the LORD...... Judg 5:3
I *w* sing praise to the LORD God...... Judg 5:3
Surely I *w* be with thee, and thou...... Judg 6:16

I *w* tarry until thou come again Judg 6:18
against him, *W* ye plead for Baal Judg 6:31
w ye save him Judg 6:31
he that *w* plead for him, let him Judg 6:31
I *w* put a fleece of wool in the Judg 6:37
me, and I *w* speak but this once Judg 6:39
I *w* try them for thee there Judg 7:4
men that lapped *w* I save you Judg 7:7
then I *w* tear your flesh with the Judg 8:7
I *w* break down this tower Judg 8:9
I *w* not rule over you, neither Judg 8:23
We *w* willingly give them Judg 8:25
wherefore I *w* deliver you no more Judg 10:13
What man is he that *w* begin to Judg 10:18
from before us, them *w* we possess Judg 11:24
I *w* offer it up for a burnt Judg 11:31
we *w* burn thine house upon thee Judg 12:1
me, I *w* not eat of thy bread Judg 13:16
I *w* now put forth a riddle unto Judg 14:12
then I *w* give you thirty sheets Judg 14:12
I *w* go in to my wife into the Judg 15:1
yet *w* I be avenged of you, and Judg 15:7
of you, and after that I *w* cease Judg 15:7
that ye *w* not fall upon me Judg 15:12
but we *w* bind thee fast, and Judg 15:13
but surely we *w* not kill thee Judg 15:13
we *w* give thee every one of us Judg 16:5
then my strength *w* go from me Judg 16:17
I *w* go out as at other times Judg 16:20
now therefore I *w* restore it unto Judg 17:3
I *w* give thee ten shekels of Judg 17:10
know I that the LORD *w* do me good Judg 17:13
We *w* not turn aside hither into Judg 19:12
we *w* pass over to Gibeah Judg 19:12
them I *w* bring out now, and humble Judg 19:24
We *w* not any of us go to his tent Judg 20:8
neither *w* we any of us turn into Judg 20:8
the thing which we *w* do to Gibeah Judg 20:9
we *w* go up by lot against it Judg 20:9
we *w* take ten men of an hundred Judg 20:10
for to morrow I *w* deliver them Judg 20:28
w not give them of our daughters Judg 21:7
that we *w* say unto them, Be Judg 21:22
Surely we *w* return with thee unto Ruth 1:10
why *w* ye go with me Ruth 1:11
for whither thou goest, I *w* go Ruth 1:16
and where thou lodgest, I *w* lodge Ruth 1:16
w I die, and there *w* I be Ruth 1:17
he *w* tell thee what thou shalt do Ruth 3:4
that thou sayest unto me I *w* do Ruth 3:5
I *w* do to thee all that thou Ruth 3:11
that if he *w* perform unto thee Ruth 3:13
but if he *w* not do the part of a Ruth 3:13 2654
then *w* I do the part of a kinsman Ruth 3:13
thou know how the matter *w* fall Ruth 3:18
for the man *w* not be in rest, Ruth 3:18
And he said, I *w* redeem it Ruth 4:4
then I *w* give him unto the LORD 1Sa 1:11
I *w* not go up until the child be 1Sa 1:22
then I *w* bring him, that he may 1Sa 1:22
He *w* keep the feet of his saints, 1Sa 2:9
for he *w* not have sodden flesh of 1Sa 2:15
and if not, I *w* take it by force 1Sa 2:16
them that honour me I *w* honour 1Sa 2:30
that I *w* cut off thine arm, and 1Sa 2:31
I *w* raise me up a faithful priest 1Sa 2:35
I *w* build him a sure house 1Sa 2:35
I *w* do a thing in Israel, at 1Sa 3:11
In that day I *w* perform against 1Sa 3:12
I begin, I *w* also make an end 1Sa 3:12
For I have told him that I *w* 1Sa 3:13
peradventure he *w* lighten his 1Sa 6:5
he *w* deliver you out of the hand 1Sa 7:3
I *w* pray for you unto the LORD 1Sa 7:5
that he *w* save us out of the hand 1Sa 7:8
This *w* be the manner of the king 1Sa 8:11
He *w* take your sons, and appoint 1Sa 8:11
he *w* appoint him captains over 1Sa 8:12
w set them to ear his ground, and 1Sa 8:12
he *w* take your daughters to be 1Sa 8:13
he *w* take your fields, and your 1Sa 8:14
he *w* take the tenth of your seed, 1Sa 8:15
he *w* take your menservants, and 1Sa 8:16
He *w* take the tenth of your sheep 1Sa 8:17
the LORD *w* not hear you in that 1Sa 8:18
but we *w* have a king over us 1Sa 8:19
that *w* I give to the man of God, 1Sa 9:8
for the people *w* not eat until he 1Sa 9:13
To morrow about this time I *w* 1Sa 9:16
day, and to morrow I *w* let thee go 1Sa 9:19
w tell thee all that is in thine 1Sa 9:19
they *w* say unto thee, The asses 1Sa 10:2
they *w* salute thee, and give thee 1Sa 10:4
of the LORD *w* come upon thee 1Sa 10:6
I *w* come down unto thee, to offer 1Sa 10:8
with us, and we *w* serve thee 1Sa 11:1
On this condition *w* I make a 1Sa 11:2
to save us, we *w* come out to thee 1Sa 11:3
To morrow we *w* come out unto you, 1Sa 11:10
and I *w* restore it you 1Sa 12:3
our enemies, and we *w* serve thee 1Sa 12:10
If ye *w* fear the LORD, and serve 1Sa 12:14
But if ye *w* not obey the voice of 1Sa 12:15
which the LORD *w* do before your 1Sa 12:16
I *w* call unto the LORD, and he 1Sa 12:17
For the LORD *w* not forsake his 1Sa 12:22
but I *w* teach you the good and the 1Sa 12:23
The Philistines *w* come down now 1Sa 13:12
be that the LORD *w* work for us 1Sa 14:6
we *w* pass over unto these men, and 1Sa 14:8
we *w* discover ourselves unto them 1Sa 14:8
then we *w* stand still in our 1Sa 14:9
place, and *w* not go up unto them 1Sa 14:9
then we *w* go up 1Sa 14:10
to us, and we *w* shew you a thing 1Sa 14:12
Jonathan my son *w* be on the other 1Sa 14:40
I *w* tell thee what the LORD hath 1Sa 15:16
Saul, I *w* not return with thee 1Sa 15:26
of Israel *w* not lie nor repent 1Sa 15:29
I *w* send thee to Jesse the 1Sa 16:1
if Saul hear it, he *w* kill me 1Sa 16:2
I *w* shew thee what thou shalt do 1Sa 16:3
for we *w* not sit down till he 1Sa 16:11
then *w* we be your servants 1Sa 17:9
the king *w* enrich him with great 1Sa 17:25
w give him his daughter, and make 1Sa 17:25
thy servant *w* go and fight with 1Sa 17:32
he *w* deliver me out of the hand 1Sa 17:37
I *w* give thy flesh unto the fowls 1Sa 17:44
This day *w* the LORD deliver thee 1Sa 17:46
I *w* smite thee, and take thine 1Sa 17:46
I *w* give the carcases of the host 1Sa 17:46
he *w* give you into our hands 1Sa 17:47
I *w* smite David even to the wall 1Sa 18:11
her *w* I give thee to wife 1Sa 18:17
I *w* give him her, that she may be 1Sa 18:21
I *w* go out and stand beside my 1Sa 19:3
I *w* commune with my father of 1Sa 19:3
and what I see, that I *w* tell thee 1Sa 19:3
my father *w* do nothing either 1Sa 20:2
small, but that he *w* shew it me 1Sa 20:2
desireth, I *w* even do it for thee 1Sa 20:4
then I *w* shew it thee, and send 1Sa 20:13
because thy seat *w* be empty 1Sa 20:18
I *w* shoot three arrows on the 1Sa 20:20
I *w* send a lad, saying, Go, find 1Sa 20:21
till I know what God *w* do for me 1Sa 22:3
w the son of Jesse give every one 1Sa 22:7
for I *w* deliver the Philistines 1Sa 23:4
W the men of Keilah deliver me up 1Sa 23:11
w Saul come down, as thy servant 1Sa 23:11
And the LORD said, He *w* come down 1Sa 23:11
W the men of Keilah deliver me and 1Sa 23:12
LORD said, They *w* deliver thee up 1Sa 23:12
the certainty, and I *w* go with you 1Sa 23:23
the land, that I *w* search him out 1Sa 23:23
I *w* deliver thine enemy into 1Sa 24:4
I *w* not put forth mine hand 1Sa 24:10
w he let him go well away 1Sa 24:19
young men, and they *w* shew thee 1Sa 25:8
for the LORD *w* certainly make my 1Sa 25:28
Who *w* go down with me to Saul to 1Sa 26:6
said, I *w* go down with thee 1Sa 26:6
I *w* not smite him the second time 1Sa 26:8
for I *w* no more do thee harm, 1Sa 26:21
so *w* be his manner all the while 1Sa 27:11
Therefore *w* I make thee keeper of 1Sa 28:2
Moreover the LORD *w* also deliver 1Sa 28:19
he refused, and said, I *w* not eat 1Sa 28:23
I *w* bring thee down to this 1Sa 30:15
we *w* not give them ought of the 1Sa 30:22
For who *w* hearken unto you in 1Sa 30:24
I also *w* requite you this 2Sa 2:6
knowest thou not that it *w* be 2Sa 2:26
I *w* make a league with thee 2Sa 3:13
I *w* save my people Israel out of 2Sa 3:18
I *w* arise and go 2Sa 3:21
w gather all Israel unto my lord 2Sa 3:21
for I *w* doubtless deliver the 2Sa 5:19
therefore *w* I play before the 2Sa 6:21
I *w* yet be more vile than thus, 2Sa 6:22
w be base in mine own sight 2Sa 6:22
Moreover I *w* appoint a place for 2Sa 7:10
w plant them, that they may dwell 2Sa 7:10
thee that he *w* make thee an house 2Sa 7:11
I *w* set up thy seed after thee, 2Sa 7:12
I *w* establish his kingdom 2Sa 7:12
I *w* stablish the throne of his 2Sa 7:13
I *w* be his father, and he shall be 2Sa 7:14
I *w* chasten him with the rod of 2Sa 7:14
saying, I *w* build thee an house 2Sa 7:27
for I *w* surely shew thee kindness 2Sa 9:7
w restore thee all the land of 2Sa 9:7
I *w* shew kindness unto Hanun the 2Sa 10:2
strong for thee, then I *w* come 2Sa 10:11
liveth, I *w* not do this thing 2Sa 11:11
to morrow I *w* let thee depart 2Sa 11:12
I *w* raise up evil against thee 2Sa 12:11
I *w* take thy wives before thine 2Sa 12:11
but I *w* do this thing before all 2Sa 12:12
how *w* he then vex himself, if we 2Sa 12:18
whether GOD *w* be gracious to me 2Sa 12:22
for he *w* not withhold me from 2Sa 13:13
we *w* destroy the heir also 2Sa 14:7
I *w* give charge concerning thee 2Sa 14:8
I *w* now speak unto the king 2Sa 14:15
it may be that the king *w* perform 2Sa 14:15
For the king *w* hear, to deliver 2Sa 14:16
the LORD thy God *w* be with thee 2Sa 14:17
then I *w* serve the LORD 2Sa 15:8
even there also *w* thy servant be 2Sa 15:21
he *w* bring me again, and shew me 2Sa 15:25
I *w* tarry in the plain of the 2Sa 15:28
I *w* be thy servant, O king 2Sa 15:34
so *w* I now also be thy servant 2Sa 15:34
LORD *w* look on mine affliction 2Sa 16:12
that the LORD *w* requite me good 2Sa 16:12
his *w* I be 2Sa 16:18
and with him *w* I abide 2Sa 16:18
so *w* I be in thy presence 2Sa 16:19
I *w* arise and pursue after David 2Sa 17:1
I *w* come upon him while he is 2Sa 17:2
weak handed, and *w* make him afraid 2Sa 17:2
and I *w* smite the king only 2Sa 17:2
I *w* bring back all the people 2Sa 17:3
w not lodge with the people 2Sa 17:8
it *w* come to pass, when some of 2Sa 17:9
that whosoever heareth it *w* say 2Sa 17:9
we *w* light upon him as the dew 2Sa 17:12
we *w* draw it into the river, 2Sa 17:13
I *w* surely go forth with you 2Sa 18:2
flee away, they *w* not care for us 2Sa 18:3
of us die, *w* they care for us 2Sa 18:3
What seemeth you best I *w* do 2Sa 18:4
there *w* not tarry one with thee 2Sa 19:7
that *w* be worse unto thee than 2Sa 19:7
I *w* saddle me an ass, that I may 2Sa 19:26
me, and I *w* feed thee with me in 2Sa 19:33
Thy servant *w* go a little way 2Sa 19:36
I *w* do to him that which shall 2Sa 19:38
of me, that *w* I do for thee 2Sa 19:38
only, and I *w* depart from the city 2Sa 20:21
We *w* have no silver nor gold of 2Sa 21:4
ye shall say, that *w* I do for you 2Sa 21:4
we *w* hang them up unto the LORD 2Sa 21:6
And the king said, I *w* give them 2Sa 21:6
in him *w* I trust 2Sa 22:3
I *w* call on the LORD, who is 2Sa 22:4
the LORD *w* lighten my darkness 2Sa 22:29
Therefore I *w* give thanks unto 2Sa 22:50
but I *w* surely buy it of thee at 2Sa 24:24
neither *w* I offer burnt offerings 2Sa 24:24
himself, saying, I *w* be king 1Kin 1:5
I also *w* come in after thee, and 1Kin 1:14
even so *w* I certainly do this day 1Kin 1:30
swear unto me to day that he *w* 1Kin 1:51
If he *w* shew himself a worthy man 1Kin 1:52
I *w* not put thee to death with 1Kin 2:8
(for he *w* not say thee nay,) that 1Kin 2:17
I *w* speak for thee unto the king 1Kin 2:18
for I *w* not say thee nay 1Kin 2:20
but I *w* not at this time put thee 1Kin 2:26
but I *w* die here 1Kin 2:30
hath said, so *w* thy servant do 1Kin 2:38
then I *w* lengthen thy days 1Kin 3:14
whom I *w* set upon thy throne in 1Kin 5:5
unto thee *w* I give hire for thy 1Kin 5:6
I *w* do all thy desire concerning 1Kin 5:8
I *w* convey them by sea in floats 1Kin 5:9
w cause them to be discharged 1Kin 5:9
then *w* I perform my word with 1Kin 6:12
I *w* dwell among the children of 1Kin 6:13
w not forsake my people Israel 1Kin 6:13
But *w* God indeed dwell on the 1Kin 8:27
Then I *w* establish the throne of 1Kin 9:5
w not keep my commandments 1Kin 9:6
Then *w* I cut off Israel out of 1Kin 9:7
my name, *w* I cast out of my sight 1Kin 9:7
for surely they *w* turn away your 1Kin 11:2
I *w* surely rend the kingdom from 1Kin 11:11
thee, and *w* give it to thy servant 1Kin 11:11
days I *w* not do it for David thy 1Kin 11:12
but I *w* rend it out of the hand 1Kin 11:12
Howbeit I *w* not rend away all the 1Kin 11:13
but *w* give one tribe to thy son 1Kin 11:13
I *w* rend the kingdom out of the 1Kin 11:31
w give ten tribes to thee 1Kin 11:31
Howbeit I *w* not take the whole 1Kin 11:34
But I *w* make him prince all the 1Kin 11:34
But I *w* take the kingdom out of 1Kin 11:35
w give it unto thee, even ten 1Kin 11:35
unto his son *w* I give one tribe, 1Kin 11:36
I *w* take thee, and thou shalt 1Kin 11:37
that I *w* be with thee, and build 1Kin 11:38
David, and *w* give Israel unto thee 1Kin 11:38
I *w* for this afflict the seed of 1Kin 11:39
us, lighter, and we *w* serve thee 1Kin 12:4
then they *w* be thy servants for 1Kin 12:7
heavy yoke, I *w* add to your yoke 1Kin 12:11
but I *w* chastise you with 1Kin 12:11
heavy, and I *w* add to your yoke 1Kin 12:14
but I *w* chastise you with 1Kin 12:14
and I *w* give thee a reward 1Kin 13:7
I *w* not go in with thee 1Kin 13:8
neither *w* I eat bread nor drink 1Kin 13:8
neither *w* I eat bread nor drink 1Kin 13:16
I *w* bring evil upon the house of 1Kin 14:10
w cut off from Jeroboam him that 1Kin 14:10
w take away the remnant of the 1Kin 14:10
I *w* take away the posterity of 1Kin 16:3
w make thy house like the house 1Kin 16:3
I *w* send rain upon the earth 1Kin 18:1
I *w* surely shew myself unto him 1Kin 18:15
I *w* dress the other bullock, and 1Kin 18:23
I *w* call on the name of the LORD 1Kin 18:24
mother, and then I *w* follow thee 1Kin 19:20
Yet I *w* send my servants unto 1Kin 20:6
thy servant at the first I *w* do 1Kin 20:9
I *w* deliver it into thine hand 1Kin 20:13
of Syria *w* come up against thee 1Kin 20:22
we *w* fight against them in the 1Kin 20:25
therefore *w* I deliver all this 1Kin 20:28
peradventure he *w* save thy life 1Kin 20:31
took from thy father, I *w* restore 1Kin 20:34
I *w* send thee away with this 1Kin 20:34
I *w* give thee for it a better 1Kin 21:2
I *w* give thee the worth of it in 1Kin 21:2
I *w* not give thee the inheritance 1Kin 21:4
I *w* give thee another vineyard 1Kin 21:6
I *w* not give thee my vineyard 1Kin 21:6
I *w* give thee the vineyard of 1Kin 21:7
I *w* bring evil upon thee 1Kin 21:21
w take away thy posterity, and 1Kin 21:21
w cut off from Ahab him that 1Kin 21:21
w make thine house like the house 1Kin 21:22
I *w* not bring the evil in his 1Kin 21:29
but in his son's days *w* I bring 1Kin 21:29
saith unto me, that *w* I speak 1Kin 22:14
LORD, and said, I *w* persuade him 1Kin 22:21
I *w* go forth 1Kin 22:22
I *w* be a lying spirit in the 1Kin 22:22
I *w* disguise myself, and enter 1Kin 22:30

soul liveth, I *w* not leave thee 2Kin 2:2
Knowest thou that the LORD *w* take 2Kin 2:3
soul liveth, I *w* not leave thee 2Kin 2:4
Knowest thou that the LORD *w* take 2Kin 2:5
soul liveth, I *w* not leave thee 2Kin 2:6
And he said, I *w* go up 2Kin 3:7
he *w* deliver the Moabites also 2Kin 3:18
soul liveth, I *w* not leave thee 2Kin 4:30
I *w* send a letter unto the king 2Kin 5:5
He *w* surely come out to me, and 2Kin 5:11
whom I stand, I *w* receive none 2Kin 5:16
for thy servant *w* henceforth 2Kin 5:17
I *w* run after him, and take 2Kin 5:20
And he answered, I *w* go 2Kin 6:3
W ye not shew me which of us is 2Kin 6:11
I *w* bring you to the man whom ye 2Kin 6:19
we *w* eat my son to morrow 2Kin 6:28
We *w* enter into the city, then 2Kin 7:4
some mischief *w* come upon us 2Kin 7:9
I *w* now shew you what the Syrians 2Kin 7:12
I *w* cut off from Ahab him that 2Kin 9:8
I *w* make the house of Ahab like 2Kin 9:9
I *w* requite thee in this plat, 2Kin 9:26
w do all that thou shalt bid us 2Kin 10:5
we *w* not make any king 2Kin 10:5
if ye *w* hearken unto my voice, 2Kin 10:6
which thou puttest on me *w* I bear 2Kin 18:14
it *w* go into his hand, and pierce 2Kin 18:21
I *w* deliver thee two thousand 2Kin 18:23
The LORD *w* surely deliver us, and 2Kin 18:30
saying, The LORD *w* deliver us 2Kin 18:32
thy God *w* hear all the words of 2Kin 19:4
w reprove the words which the 2Kin 19:4
I *w* send a blast upon him, and he 2Kin 19:7
I *w* cause him to fall by the 2Kin 19:7
w cut down the tall cedar trees 2Kin 19:23
I *w* enter into the lodgings of 2Kin 19:23
therefore I *w* put my hook in thy 2Kin 19:28
I *w* turn thee back by the way by 2Kin 19:28
For I *w* defend this city, to save 2Kin 19:34
behold, I *w* heal thee 2Kin 20:5
I *w* add unto thy days fifteen 2Kin 20:6
I *w* deliver thee and this city out 2Kin 20:6
I *w* defend this city for mine own 2Kin 20:6
the sign that the LORD *w* heal me 2Kin 20:8
that the LORD *w* do the thing that 2Kin 20:9
In Jerusalem *w* I put my name 2Kin 21:4
Israel, *w* I put my name for ever 2Kin 21:7
Neither *w* I make the feet of 2Kin 21:8
only if they *w* observe to do 2Kin 21:8
I *w* stretch over Jerusalem the 2Kin 21:13
I *w* wipe Jerusalem as a man 2Kin 21:13
I *w* forsake the remnant of mine 2Kin 21:14
I *w* bring evil upon this place, 2Kin 22:16
I *w* gather thee unto thy fathers, 2Kin 22:20
which I *w* bring upon this place 2Kin 22:20
I *w* remove Judah also out of my 2Kin 23:27
w cast off this city Jerusalem 2Kin 23:27
He *w* fall to his master Saul to 1Chr 12:19
for I *w* deliver them into thine 1Chr 14:10
Unto thee *w* I give the land of 1Chr 16:18
Also I *w* ordain a place for my 1Chr 17:9
w plant them, and they shall dwell 1Chr 17:9
Moreover I *w* subdue all thine 1Chr 17:10
the LORD *w* build thee an house 1Chr 17:10
that I *w* raise up thy seed after 1Chr 17:11
I *w* establish his kingdom 1Chr 17:11
I *w* stablish his throne for ever 1Chr 17:12
I *w* be his father, and he shall be 1Chr 17:13
I *w* not take my mercy away from 1Chr 17:13
But I *w* settle him in mine house 1Chr 17:14
I *w* shew kindness unto Hanun the 1Chr 19:2
for thee, then I *w* help thee 1Chr 19:12
why *w* he be a cause of trespass 1Chr 21:3
but I *w* verily buy it for the 1Chr 21:24
for I *w* not take that which is 1Chr 21:24
I *w* therefore now make 1Chr 22:5
I *w* give him rest from all his 1Chr 22:9
I *w* give peace and quietness unto 1Chr 22:9
be my son, and I *w* be his father 1Chr 22:10
I *w* establish the throne of his 1Chr 22:10
be my son, and I *w* be his father 1Chr 28:6
Moreover I *w* establish his 1Chr 28:7
seek him, he *w* be found of thee 1Chr 28:9
he *w* cast thee off for ever 1Chr 28:9
God, even my God, *w* be with thee 1Chr 28:20
he *w* not fail thee, nor forsake 1Chr 28:20
all the people *w* be wholly at thy 1Chr 28:21
I *w* give thee riches, and wealth, 2Chr 1:12
I *w* give to thy servants, the 2Chr 2:10
we *w* cut wood out of Lebanon, as 2Chr 2:16
we *w* bring it to thee in flotes 2Chr 2:16
But *w* God in very deed dwell with 2Chr 6:18
then *w* I hear from heaven, and 2Chr 7:14
w forgive their sin 2Chr 7:14
and *w* heal their land 2Chr 7:14
Then *w* I stablish the throne of 2Chr 7:18
Then *w* I pluck them up by the 2Chr 7:20
w I cast out of my sight 2Chr 7:20
w make it to be a proverb and a 2Chr 7:20
put upon us, and we *w* serve thee 2Chr 10:4
they *w* be thy servants for ever 2Chr 10:7
I *w* put more to your yoke 2Chr 10:11
but I *w* chastise you with 2Chr 10:11
yoke heavy, but I *w* add thereto 2Chr 10:14
but I *w* chastise you with 2Chr 10:14
therefore I *w* not destroy them, 2Chr 12:7
but I *w* grant them some 2Chr 12:7
ye seek him, he *w* be found of you 2Chr 15:2
ye forsake him, he *w* forsake you 2Chr 15:2
we *w* be with thee in the war 2Chr 18:3
for God *w* deliver it into the 2Chr 18:5
what my God saith, that *w* I speak 2Chr 18:13
the LORD, and said, I *w* entice him 2Chr 18:20

I *w* go out, and be a lying spirit 2Chr 18:21
I *w* disguise myself 2Chr 18:29
and *w* go to the battle 2Chr 18:29
for the LORD *w* be with you 2Chr 20:17
with a great plague *w* the LORD 2Chr 21:14
therefore *w* I sacrifice to them, 2Chr 28:23
he *w* return to the remnant of you 2Chr 30:6
w not turn away his face from you 2Chr 30:9
Israel, *w* I put my name for ever 2Chr 33:7
Neither *w* I any more remove the 2Chr 33:8
so that they *w* take heed to do 2Chr 33:8
I *w* bring evil upon this place, 2Chr 34:24
I *w* gather thee to thy fathers, 2Chr 34:28
that I *w* bring upon this place 2Chr 34:28
but we ourselves together *w* build Ezr 4:3
then *w* they not pay toll, tribute Ezr 4:13
that do after the *w* of your God Ezr 7:18 7470
whosoever *w* not do the law of thy Ezr 7:26
we also *w* be with thee Ezr 10:4
I *w* scatter you abroad among the Neh 1:8
yet *w* I gather them from thence, Neh 1:9
w bring them unto the place that Neh 1:9
w ye rebel against the king Neh 2:19
God of heaven, he *w* prosper us Neh 2:20
therefore we his servants *w* arise Neh 2:20
w they fortify themselves Neh 4:2
w they sacrifice Neh 4:2
w they make an end in a day Neh 4:2
w they revive the stones out of Neh 4:2
return unto us they *w* be upon you Neh 4:12
w ye even sell your brethren Neh 5:8
We *w* restore them Neh 5:12
w require nothing of them Neh 5:12
so *w* we do as thou sayest Neh 5:12
for they *w* come to slay thee Neh 6:10
in the night *w* they come to slay Neh 6:10
I *w* not go in Neh 6:11
we *w* not forsake the house of our Neh 10:39
do so again, I *w* lay hands on you Neh 13:21
I *w* pay ten thousand talents of Est 3:9
my maidens *w* fast likewise Est 4:16
so *w* I go in unto the king, which Est 4:16
I *w* do to morrow as the king hath Est 5:8
W he force the queen also before Est 7:8
he *w* curse thee to thy face Job 1:11
all that a man hath *w* he give for Job 2:4
he *w* curse thee to thy face Job 2:5
there be any that *w* answer thee Job 5:1
Teach me, and I *w* hold my tongue Job 6:24
Therefore I *w* not refrain my Job 7:11
I *w* speak in the anguish of my Job 7:11
I *w* complain in the bitterness of Job 7:11
God *w* not cast away a perfect man Job 8:20
neither *w* he help the evil doers Job 8:20
If he *w* contend with him, he Job 9:3
who *w* say unto him, What doest Job 9:12
If God *w* not withdraw his anger, Job 9:13
He *w* not suffer me to take my Job 9:18
he *w* laugh at the trial of the Job 9:23
I *w* forget my complaint Job 9:27
I *w* leave off my heaviness, and Job 9:27
I *w* leave my complaint upon Job 10:1
I *w* speak in the bitterness of my Job 10:1
I *w* say unto God, Do not condemn Job 10:2
yet *w* I not lift up my head Job 10:15
w he not then consider it Job 11:11
W ye speak wickedly for God Job 13:7
W ye accept his person Job 13:8
w ye contend for God Job 13:8
He *w* surely reprove you, if ye do Job 13:10
speak, and let come on me what *w* Job 13:13
he slay me, yet *w* I trust in him Job 13:15
but I *w* maintain mine own ways Job 13:15
Who is he that *w* plead with me Job 13:19
then I *w* not hide myself from Job 13:20
Then call thou, and I *w* answer Job 13:22
that it *w* sprout again, and that Job 14:7
tender branch thereof *w* not cease Job 14:7
the scent of water it *w* bud Job 14:9
of my appointed time *w* I wait Job 14:14
shalt call, and I *w* answer thee Job 14:15
I *w* shew thee, hear me Job 15:17
which I have seen I *w* declare Job 15:17
who is he that *w* strike hands Job 17:3
How long *w* it be ere ye make an Job 18:2
mark, and afterwards we *w* speak Job 18:2
How long *w* ye vex my soul, and Job 19:2
If indeed ye *w* magnify yourselves Job 19:5
W he reprove thee for fear of Job 22:4
w he enter with thee into Job 22:4
W he plead against me with his Job 23:6
who *w* make me a liar, and make my Job 24:25
till I die I *w* not remove mine Job 27:5
I hold fast, and *w* not let it go Job 27:6
W God hear his cry when trouble Job 27:9
W he delight himself in the Job 27:10
w he always call upon God Job 27:10
I *w* teach you by the hand of God Job 27:11
with the Almighty *w* I not conceal Job 27:11
Howbeit he *w* not stretch out his Job 30:24
I also *w* shew mine opinion Job 32:10
neither *w* I answer him with your Job 32:14
I *w* answer also my part Job 32:17
I also *w* shew mine opinion Job 32:17
I *w* speak, that I may be Job 32:20
I *w* open my lips and answer Job 32:20
I *w* answer thee, that God is Job 33:12
he *w* be favourable unto him Job 33:26
for he *w* render unto man his Job 33:26
He *w* deliver his soul from going Job 33:28
hold thy peace, and I *w* speak Job 33:31
surely God *w* not do wickedly, Job 34:12
neither *w* the Almighty pervert Job 34:12
For he *w* not lay upon man more Job 34:23

I *w* not offend any more Job 34:31
done iniquity, I *w* do no more Job 34:32
he *w* recompense it, whether thou Job 34:33
What advantage *w* it be unto thee Job 35:3
I *w* answer thee, and thy Job 35:4
Surely God *w* not hear vanity, Job 35:13
neither *w* the Almighty regard it Job 35:13
I *w* shew thee that I have yet to Job 36:2
I *w* fetch my knowledge from afar, Job 36:3
w ascribe righteousness to my Job 36:3
W he esteem thy riches Job 36:19
he *w* not stay them when his voice Job 37:4
he *w* not afflict Job 37:23
for I *w* demand of thee, and answer Job 38:3
W the unicorn be willing to serve Job 39:9
or *w* he harrow the valleys after Job 39:10
that he *w* bring home thy seed, and Job 39:12
I *w* lay mine hand upon my mouth Job 40:4
but I *w* not answer Job 40:5
but I *w* proceed no further Job 40:5
I *w* demand of thee, and declare Job 40:7
Then *w* I also confess unto thee Job 40:14
W he make many supplications unto Job 41:3
w he speak soft words unto thee Job 41:3
W he make a covenant with thee Job 41:4
I *w* not conceal his parts, nor Job 41:12
I beseech thee, and I *w* speak Job 42:4
I *w* demand of thee, and declare Job 42:4
for him *w* I accept Job 42:8
I *w* declare the decree Ps 2:7
I *w* not be afraid of ten Ps 3:6
how long *w* ye turn my glory into Ps 4:2
how long *w* ye love vanity, and Ps 4:2
the LORD *w* hear when I call unto Ps 4:3
that say, Who *w* shew us any good Ps 4:6
I *w* both lay me down in peace, and Ps 4:8
for unto thee *w* I pray Ps 5:2
in the morning *w* I direct my Ps 5:3
my prayer unto thee, and *w* look up Ps 5:3
the LORD *w* abhor the bloody and Ps 5:6
I *w* come into thy house in the Ps 5:7
in thy fear *w* I worship toward Ps 5:7
the LORD *w* receive my prayer Ps 6:9
he turn not, he *w* whet his sword Ps 7:12
I *w* praise the LORD according to Ps 7:17
w sing praise to the name of the Ps 7:17
I *w* praise thee, O LORD, with my Ps 9:1
I *w* shew forth all thy marvellous Ps 9:1
I *w* be glad and rejoice in thee Ps 9:2
I *w* sing praise to thy name, O Ps 9:2
The LORD also *w* be a refuge for Ps 9:9
name *w* put their trust in thee Ps 9:10
I *w* rejoice in thy salvation Ps 9:14
countenance, *w* not seek after God Ps 10:4
he *w* never see it Ps 10:11
With our tongue *w* we prevail Ps 12:4
now *w* I arise, saith the LORD Ps 12:5
I *w* set him in safety from him Ps 12:5
I *w* sing unto the LORD, because Ps 13:6
offerings of blood *w* I not offer Ps 16:4
I *w* bless the LORD, who hath Ps 16:7
As for me, I *w* behold thy face in Ps 17:15
I *w* love thee, O LORD, my Ps 18:1
my strength, in whom I *w* trust Ps 18:2
I *w* call upon the LORD, who is Ps 18:3
the LORD my God *w* enlighten my Ps 18:28
Therefore *w* I give thanks unto Ps 18:49
We *w* rejoice in thy salvation, and Ps 20:5
our God we *w* set up our banners Ps 20:5
he *w* hear him from his holy Ps 20:6
but we *w* remember the name of the Ps 20:7
so *w* we sing and praise thy power Ps 21:13
I *w* declare thy name unto my Ps 22:22
the congregation *w* I praise thee Ps 22:22
I *w* pay my vows before them that Ps 22:25
shadow of death, I *w* fear no evil Ps 23:4
I *w* dwell in the house of the Ps 23:6
therefore *w* he teach sinners in Ps 25:8
The meek *w* he guide in judgment Ps 25:9
the meek *w* he teach his way Ps 25:9
he *w* shew them his covenant Ps 25:14
persons, neither *w* I go in with Ps 26:4
w not sit with the wicked Ps 26:5
I *w* wash mine hands in innocency Ps 26:6
so *w* I compass thine altar, O Ps 26:6
I *w* walk in mine integrity Ps 26:11
congregations *w* I bless the LORD Ps 26:12
me, in this *w* I be confident Ps 27:3
of the LORD, that *w* I seek after Ps 27:4
therefore *w* I offer in his Ps 27:6
I *w* sing, yea, I *w* sing Ps 27:6
thee, Thy face, LORD, *w* I seek Ps 27:8
me, then the LORD *w* take me up Ps 27:10
over unto the *w* of mine enemies Ps 27:12 5315
Unto thee *w* I cry, O LORD my rock Ps 28:1
and with my song *w* I praise him Ps 28:7
The LORD *w* give strength unto his Ps 29:11
the LORD *w* bless his people with Ps 29:11
I *w* extol thee, O LORD Ps 30:1
I *w* give thanks unto thee for Ps 30:12
I *w* be glad and rejoice in thy Ps 31:7
I *w* confess my transgressions Ps 32:5
I *w* instruct thee and teach thee Ps 32:8
I *w* guide thee with mine eye Ps 32:8
I *w* bless the LORD at all times Ps 34:1
I *w* teach you the fear of the Ps 34:11
I *w* give thee thanks in the great Ps 35:18
I *w* praise thee among much people Ps 35:18
The LORD *w* not leave him in his Ps 37:33
For I *w* declare mine iniquity Ps 38:18
I *w* be sorry for my sin Ps 38:18
I *w* take heed to my ways, that I Ps 39:1
I *w* keep my mouth with a bridle, Ps 39:1
I delight to do thy *w*, O my God Ps 40:8 7522

the LORD *w* deliver him in time of Ps 41:1
The LORD *w* preserve him, and keep Ps 41:2
him unto the *w* of his enemies Ps 41:2 5315
The LORD *w* strengthen him upon Ps 41:3
therefore *w* I remember thee from Ps 42:6
Yet the LORD *w* command his Ps 42:8
I *w* say unto God my rock, Why Ps 42:9
Then *w* I go unto the altar of God Ps 43:4
upon the harp *w* I praise thee Ps 43:4
Through thee *w* we push down our Ps 44:5
through thy name *w* we tread them Ps 44:5
For I *w* not trust in my bow, Ps 44:6
I *w* make thy name to be Ps 45:17
Therefore *w* not we fear, though Ps 46:2
I *w* be exalted among the heathen, Ps 46:10
I *w* be exalted in the earth Ps 46:10
God *w* establish it for ever Ps 48:8
he *w* be our guide even unto death Ps 48:14
I *w* incline mine ear to a parable Ps 49:4
I *w* open my dark saying upon the Ps 49:4
But God *w* redeem my soul from the Ps 49:15
men *w* praise thee, when thou Ps 49:18
Hear, O my people, and I *w* speak Ps 50:7
and I *w* testify against thee Ps 50:7
I *w* not reprove thee for thy Ps 50:8
I *w* take no bullock out of thy Ps 50:9
W I eat the flesh of bulls, or Ps 50:13
I *w* deliver thee, and thou shalt Ps 50:15
but I *w* reprove thee, and set them Ps 50:21
his conversation aright *w* I shew Ps 50:23
Then *w* I teach transgressors thy Ps 51:13
I *w* praise thee for ever, because Ps 52:9
and I *w* wait on thy name Ps 52:9
I *w* freely sacrifice unto thee Ps 54:6
I *w* praise thy name, O LORD Ps 54:6
As for me, I *w* call upon God Ps 55:16
at noon, *w* I pray, and cry aloud Ps 55:17
but I *w* trust in thee Ps 55:23
I am afraid, I *w* trust in thee Ps 56:3
In God I *w* praise his word, in Ps 56:4
I *w* not fear what flesh can do Ps 56:4
In God *w* I praise his word Ps 56:10
in the LORD *w* I praise his word Ps 56:10
I *w* not be afraid what man can do Ps 56:11
I *w* render praises unto thee Ps 56:12
of thy wings *w* I make my refuge Ps 57:1
I *w* cry unto God most high Ps 57:2
I *w* sing and give praise Ps 57:7
I myself *w* awake early Ps 57:8
I *w* praise thee, O Lord, among Ps 57:9
I *w* sing unto thee among the Ps 57:9
Which *w* not hearken to the voice Ps 58:5
his strength *w* I wait upon thee Ps 59:9
But I *w* sing of thy power Ps 59:16
I *w* sing aloud of thy mercy in Ps 59:16
thee, O my strength, *w* I sing Ps 59:17
I *w* rejoice, I *w* divide Ps 60:6
over Edom *w* I cast out my shoe Ps 60:8
Who *w* bring me into the strong Ps 60:9
who *w* lead me into Edom Ps 60:9
of the earth *w* I cry unto thee Ps 61:2
I *w* abide in thy tabernacle for Ps 61:4
I *w* trust in the covert of thy Ps 61:4
So *w* I sing praise unto thy name Ps 61:8
How long *w* ye imagine mischief Ps 62:3
early *w* I seek thee Ps 63:1
Thus *w* I bless thee while I live Ps 63:4
I *w* lift up my hands in thy name Ps 63:4
shadow of thy wings *w* I rejoice Ps 63:7
I *w* go into thy house with burnt Ps 66:13
I *w* pay thee my vows, Ps 66:13
I *w* offer unto thee burnt Ps 66:15
I *w* offer bullocks with goats Ps 66:15
I *w* declare what he hath done for Ps 66:16
my heart, the Lord *w* not hear me Ps 66:18
the LORD *w* dwell in it for ever Ps 68:16
I *w* bring again from Bashan Ps 68:22
I *w* bring my people again from Ps 68:22
I *w* praise the name of God with a Ps 69:30
w magnify him with thanksgiving Ps 69:30
For God *w* save Zion Ps 69:35
w build the cities of Judah Ps 69:35
But I *w* hope continually Ps 71:14
w yet praise thee more and more Ps 71:14
I *w* go in the strength of the Ps 71:16
I *w* make mention of thy Ps 71:16
I *w* also praise thee with the Ps 71:22
unto thee *w* I sing with the harp, Ps 71:22
If I say, I *w* speak thus Ps 73:15
congregation I *w* judge uprightly Ps 75:2
But I *w* declare for ever Ps 75:9
I *w* sing praises to the God of Ps 75:9
of the wicked also *w* I cut off Ps 75:10
W the Lord cast off for ever Ps 77:7
w he be favourable no more Ps 77:7
but I *w* remember the years of the Ps 77:10
I *w* remember the works of the Ps 77:11
surely I *w* remember thy wonders Ps 77:11
I *w* meditate also of all thy work Ps 77:12
I *w* open my mouth in a parable Ps 78:2
I *w* utter dark sayings of old Ps 78:2
We *w* not hide them from their Ps 78:4
sheep of thy pasture *w* give thee Ps 79:13
we *w* shew forth thy praise to all Ps 79:13
So *w* not we go back from thee Ps 80:18
us, and we *w* call upon thy name Ps 80:18
people, and I *w* testify unto thee Ps 81:8
thy mouth wide, and I *w* fill it Ps 81:10
How long *w* ye judge unjustly, and Ps 82:2
neither *w* they understand Ps 82:5
they *w* be still praising thee Ps 84:4
the LORD *w* give grace and glory Ps 84:11
no good thing *w* he withhold from Ps 84:11
I *w* hear what God the Ps 85:8

God the LORD *w* speak Ps 85:8
for he *w* speak peace unto his Ps 85:8
of my trouble I *w* call upon thee Ps 86:7
I *w* walk in thy truth Ps 86:11
I *w* praise thee, O Lord my God, Ps 86:12
I *w* glorify thy name for evermore Ps 86:12
I *w* make mention of Rahab and Ps 87:4
I *w* sing of the mercies of the Ps 89:1
with my mouth *w* I make known thy Ps 89:1
Thy seed *w* I establish for ever, Ps 89:4
I *w* beat down his foes before his Ps 89:23
I *w* set his hand also in the sea, Ps 89:25
Also I *w* make him my firstborn, Ps 89:27
My mercy *w* I keep for him for Ps 89:28
His seed also *w* I make to endure Ps 89:29
Then *w* I visit their Ps 89:32
w I not utterly take from him Ps 89:33
My covenant *w* I not break Ps 89:34
that I *w* not lie unto David Ps 89:35
I *w* say of the LORD, He is my Ps 91:2
in him *w* I trust Ps 91:2
therefore *w* I deliver him Ps 91:14
I *w* set him on high, because he Ps 91:14
call upon me, and I *w* answer him Ps 91:15
I *w* be with him in trouble Ps 91:15
I *w* deliver him, and honour him Ps 91:15
With long life *w* I satisfy him Ps 91:16
I *w* triumph in the works of thy Ps 92:4
and ye fools, when *w* ye be wise Ps 94:8
For the LORD *w* not cast off his Ps 94:14
people, neither *w* he forsake his Ps 94:14
Who *w* rise up for me against the Ps 94:16
or who *w* stand up for me against Ps 94:16
To day if ye *w* hear his voice, Ps 95:7
I *w* sing of mercy and judgment Ps 101:1
unto thee, O LORD, *w* I sing Ps 101:1
I *w* behave myself wisely in a Ps 101:2
I *w* walk within my house with a Ps 101:2
I *w* set no wicked thing before Ps 101:3
I *w* not know a wicked person Ps 101:4
his neighbour, him *w* I cut off Ps 101:5
and a proud heart *w* not I suffer Ps 101:5
I *w* early destroy all the wicked Ps 101:8
He *w* regard the prayer of the Ps 102:17
He *w* not always chide Ps 103:9
neither *w* he keep his anger for Ps 103:9
I *w* sing unto the LORD as long as Ps 104:33
I *w* sing praise to my God while I Ps 104:33
I *w* be glad in the LORD Ps 104:34
Unto thee *w* I give the land of Ps 105:11
w observe these things, even they Ps 107:43
I *w* sing and give praise, even Ps 108:1
I myself *w* awake early Ps 108:2
I *w* praise thee, O LORD, among Ps 108:3
I *w* sing praises unto thee among Ps 108:3
I *w* rejoice, I *w* divide Ps 108:7
over Edom *w* I cast out my shoe Ps 108:9
over Philistia *w* I triumph Ps 108:9
Who *w* bring me into the strong Ps 108:10
who *w* lead me into Edom Ps 108:10
I *w* greatly praise the LORD with Ps 109:30
yea, I *w* praise him among the Ps 109:30
w not repent, Thou art a priest Ps 110:4
I *w* praise the LORD with my whole Ps 111:1
he *w* ever be mindful of his Ps 111:5
he *w* guide his affairs with Ps 112:5
he *w* bless us Ps 115:12
he *w* bless the house of Israel Ps 115:12
he *w* bless the house of Aaron Ps 115:12
He *w* bless them that fear the Ps 115:13
But we *w* bless the LORD from this Ps 115:18
therefore *w* I call upon him as Ps 116:2
I *w* walk before the LORD in the Ps 116:9
I *w* take the cup of salvation, and Ps 116:13
I *w* pay my vows unto the LORD now Ps 116:14
I *w* offer to thee the sacrifice Ps 116:17
w call upon the name of the LORD Ps 116:17
I *w* pay my vows unto the LORD now Ps 116:18
I *w* not fear Ps 118:6
name of the LORD *w* I destroy them Ps 118:10
name of the LORD I *w* destroy them Ps 118:11
name of the LORD I *w* destroy them Ps 118:12
I *w* go into them Ps 118:19
I *w* praise the LORD Ps 118:19
I *w* praise thee Ps 118:21
we *w* rejoice and be glad in it Ps 118:24
art my God, and I *w* praise thee Ps 118:28
thou art my God, I *w* exalt thee Ps 118:28
I *w* praise thee with uprightness Ps 119:7
I *w* keep thy statutes Ps 119:8
I *w* meditate in thy precepts, and Ps 119:15
I *w* delight myself in thy Ps 119:16
I *w* not forget thy word Ps 119:16
I *w* run the way of thy Ps 119:32
And I *w* walk at liberty Ps 119:45
I *w* speak of thy testimonies also Ps 119:46
before kings, and *w* not be ashamed Ps 119:46
I *w* delight myself in thy Ps 119:47
My hands also *w* I lift up unto Ps 119:48
I *w* meditate in thy statutes Ps 119:48
At midnight I *w* rise to give Ps 119:62
but I *w* keep thy precepts with my Ps 119:69
They that fear thee *w* be glad Ps 119:74
but I *w* meditate in thy precepts Ps 119:78
I *w* never forget thy precepts Ps 119:93
but I *w* consider thy testimonies Ps 119:95
I *w* perform it Ps 119:106
that I *w* keep thy righteous Ps 119:106
for I *w* keep the commandments of Ps 119:115
I *w* have respect unto thy Ps 119:117
so *w* I keep thy precepts Ps 119:134
I *w* keep thy statutes Ps 119:145
I *w* lift up mine eyes unto the Ps 121:1
He *w* not suffer thy foot to be Ps 121:3

that keepeth thee *w* not slumber Ps 121:3
I *w* now say, Peace be within thee Ps 122:8
LORD our God I *w* seek thy good Ps 122:9
Surely I *w* not come into the Ps 132:3
I *w* not give sleep to mine eyes, Ps 132:4
We *w* go into his tabernacles Ps 132:7
we *w* worship at his footstool Ps 132:7
he *w* not turn from it Ps 132:11
thy body *w* I set upon thy throne Ps 132:11
If thy children *w* keep my Ps 132:12
here *w* I dwell Ps 132:14
I *w* abundantly bless her Ps 132:15
I *w* satisfy her poor with bread Ps 132:15
I *w* also clothe her priests with Ps 132:16
There *w* I make the horn of David Ps 132:17
His enemies *w* I clothe with shame Ps 132:18
For the LORD *w* judge his people, Ps 135:14
he *w* repent himself concerning Ps 135:14
I *w* praise thee with my whole Ps 138:1
before the gods *w* I sing praise Ps 138:1
I *w* worship toward thy holy Ps 138:2
The LORD *w* perfect that which Ps 138:8
I *w* praise thee Ps 139:14
I know that the LORD *w* maintain Ps 140:12
Teach me to do thy *w* Ps 143:10 7522
I *w* sing a new song unto thee, O Ps 144:9
w I sing praises unto thee Ps 144:9
I *w* extol thee, my God, O king Ps 145:1
I *w* bless thy name for ever and Ps 145:1
Every day *w* I bless thee Ps 145:2
I *w* praise thy name for ever and Ps 145:2
I *w* speak of the glorious honour Ps 145:5
I *w* declare thy greatness Ps 145:6
He *w* fulfil the desire of them Ps 145:19
he also *w* hear their cry Ps 145:19
and *w* save them Ps 145:19
but all the wicked *w* he destroy Ps 145:20
While I live *w* I praise the LORD Ps 146:2
I *w* sing praises unto my God Ps 146:2
he *w* beautify the meek with Ps 149:4
A wise man *w* hear Prov 1:5
and *w* increase learning Prov 1:5
simple ones, *w* ye love simplicity Prov 1:22
I *w* pour out my spirit unto you, Prov 1:23
I *w* make known my words unto you Prov 1:23
I also *w* laugh at your calamity Prov 1:26
I *w* mock when your fear cometh Prov 1:26
call upon me, but I *w* not answer Prov 1:28
come again, and to morrow I *w* give Prov 3:28
the adulteress *w* hunt for the Prov 6:26
therefore he *w* not spare in the Prov 6:34
He *w* not regard any ransom Prov 6:35
neither *w* he rest content, though Prov 6:35
w come home at the day appointed Prov 7:20
for I *w* speak of excellent things Prov 8:6
and I *w* fill their treasures Prov 8:21
a wise man, and he *w* love thee Prov 9:8
a wise man, and he *w* be yet wiser Prov 9:9
he *w* increase in learning Prov 9:9
The LORD *w* not suffer the soul of Prov 10:3
The wise in heart *w* receive Prov 10:8
of wicked devices *w* he condemn Prov 12:2
A faithful witness *w* not lie Prov 14:5
but a false witness *w* utter lies Prov 14:5
neither *w* he go unto the wise Prov 15:12
The LORD *w* destroy the house of Prov 15:25
but he *w* establish the border of Prov 15:25
but a wise man *w* pacify it Prov 16:14
The spirit of a man *w* sustain his Prov 18:14
Many *w* intreat the favour of the Prov 19:6
he hath given *w* he pay him again Prov 19:17
w not so much as bring it to his Prov 19:24
a scorner, and the simple *w* beware Prov 19:25
he *w* understand knowledge Prov 19:25
but every fool *w* be meddling Prov 20:3
The sluggard *w* not plow by reason Prov 20:4
of understanding *w* draw it out Prov 20:5
Most men *w* proclaim every one his Prov 20:6
Say not thou, I *w* recompense evil Prov 20:22
he turneth it whithersoever he *w* Prov 21:1 2654
is old, he *w* not depart from it Prov 22:6
For the LORD *w* plead their cause, Prov 22:23
for he *w* despise the wisdom of Prov 23:9
I *w* seek it yet again Prov 23:35
I *w* do so to him as he hath done Prov 24:29
I *w* render to the man according Prov 24:29
a stone, it *w* return upon him Prov 26:27
yet *w* not his foolishness depart Prov 27:22
it for him that *w* pity the poor Prov 28:8
of bread that man *w* transgress Prov 28:21
A servant *w* not be corrected by Prov 29:19
he understand he *w* not answer Prov 29:19
She *w* do him good and not evil all Prov 31:12
I *w* prove thee with mirth, Eccl 2:1
the one *w* lift up his fellow Eccl 4:10
who *w* no more be admonished Eccl 4:13 3045
rich *w* not suffer him to sleep Eccl 5:12
the living *w* lay it to his heart Eccl 7:2
I said, I *w* be wise Eccl 7:23
Surely the serpent *w* bite without Eccl 10:11
of a fool *w* swallow up himself Eccl 10:12
God *w* bring thee into judgment Eccl 11:9
Draw me, we *w* run after thee Song 1:4
we *w* be glad and rejoice in thee, Song 1:4
we *w* remember thy love more than Song 1:4
We *w* make thee borders of gold Song 1:11
I *w* rise now, and go about the Song 3:2
in the broad ways I *w* seek him Song 3:2
I *w* get me to the mountain of Song 4:6
What *w* ye see in the Shulamite Song 6:13
I *w* go up to the palm tree Song 7:8
I *w* take hold of the boughs Song 7:8
there *w* I give thee my loves Song 7:12
we *w* build upon her a palace of Song 8:9

we *w* inclose her with boards of ... Song 8:9
ye *w* revolt more and more ... Is 1:5
I *w* hide mine eyes from you ... Is 1:15
make many prayers, I *w* not hear ... Is 1:15
I *w* ease me of mine adversaries, ... Is 1:24
I *w* turn my hand upon thee, and ... Is 1:25
I *w* restore thy judges as at the ... Is 1:26
he *w* teach us of his ways ... Is 2:3
and we *w* walk in his paths ... Is 2:3
I *w* give children to be their ... Is 3:4
saying, I *w* not be an healer ... Is 3:7
The LORD *w* enter into judgment ... Is 3:14
Therefore the Lord *w* smite with a ... Is 3:17
the LORD *w* discover their secret ... Is 3:17
In that day the Lord *w* take away ... Is 3:18
We *w* eat our own bread, and wear ... Is 4:1
the LORD *w* create upon every ... Is 4:5
Now *w* I sing to my wellbeloved a ... Is 5:1
I *w* tell you what I *w* do to my ... Is 5:5
I *w* take away the hedge thereof, ... Is 5:5
And I *w* lay it waste ... Is 5:6
I *w* also command the clouds that ... Is 5:6
he *w* lift up an ensign to the ... Is 5:26
w hiss unto them from the end of ... Is 5:26
shall I send, and who *w* go for us ... Is 6:8
If ye *w* not believe, surely ye ... Is 7:9
I *w* not ask, neither *w* I tempt ... Is 7:12
but *w* ye weary my God also ... Is 7:13
I *w* wait upon the LORD, that ... Is 8:17
of Jacob, and I *w* look for him ... Is 8:17
the LORD of hosts *w* perform this ... Is 9:7
but we *w* build with hewn stones ... Is 9:10
but we *w* change them into cedars ... Is 9:10
Therefore the LORD *w* cut off from ... Is 9:14
what *w* ye do in the day of ... Is 10:3
to whom *w* ye flee for help ... Is 10:3
where *w* ye leave your glory ... Is 10:3
I *w* send him against an ... Is 10:6
of my wrath *w* I give him a charge ... Is 10:6
I *w* punish the fruit of the stout ... Is 10:12
say, O LORD, I *w* praise thee ... Is 12:1
I *w* trust, and not be afraid ... Is 12:2
I *w* punish the world for their ... Is 13:11
I *w* cause the arrogancy of the ... Is 13:11
w lay low the haughtiness of the ... Is 13:11
I *w* make a man more precious than ... Is 13:12
Therefore I *w* shake the heavens, ... Is 13:13
I *w* stir up the Medes against ... Is 13:17
For the LORD *w* have mercy on ... Is 14:1
w yet choose Israel, and set them ... Is 14:1
I *w* ascend into heaven ... Is 14:13
I *w* exalt my throne above the ... Is 14:13
I *w* sit also upon the mount of ... Is 14:13
I *w* ascend above the heights of ... Is 14:14
I *w* be like the most High ... Is 14:14
For I *w* rise up against them, ... Is 14:22
I *w* also make it a possession for ... Is 14:23
I *w* sweep it with the besom of ... Is 14:23
That I *w* break the Assyrian in my ... Is 14:25
I *w* kill thy root with famine, and ... Is 14:30
for I *w* bring more upon Dimon, ... Is 15:9
Therefore I *w* bewail with the ... Is 16:9
I *w* water thee with my tears, O ... Is 16:9
I *w* take my rest ... Is 18:4
I *w* consider in my dwelling place ... Is 18:4
I *w* set the Egyptians against the ... Is 19:2
I *w* destroy the counsel thereof ... Is 19:3
the Egyptians *w* I give over into ... Is 19:4
if ye *w* enquire, enquire ye ... Is 21:12
I *w* weep bitterly, labour not to ... Is 22:4
the LORD *w* carry thee away with a ... Is 22:17
captivity, and *w* surely cover thee ... Is 22:17
He *w* surely violently turn and ... Is 22:18
I *w* drive thee from thy station, ... Is 22:19
that I *w* call my servant Eliakim ... Is 22:20
I *w* clothe him with thy robe, and ... Is 22:21
I *w* commit thy government into ... Is 22:21
David *w* I lay upon his shoulder ... Is 22:22
I *w* fasten him as a nail in a ... Is 22:23
years, that the LORD *w* visit Tyre ... Is 23:17
I *w* exalt thee, I *w* praise thy ... Is 25:1
he *w* destroy in this mountain the ... Is 25:7
He *w* swallow up death in victory ... Is 25:8
the Lord GOD *w* wipe away tears ... Is 25:8
waited for him, and he *w* save us ... Is 25:9
we *w* be glad and rejoice in his ... Is 25:9
salvation *w* God appoint for walls ... Is 26:1
within me *w* I seek thee early ... Is 26:9
the world *w* learn righteousness ... Is 26:9
yet *w* he not learn righteousness ... Is 26:10
of uprightness *w* he deal unjustly ... Is 26:10
w not behold the majesty of the ... Is 26:10
hand is lifted up, they *w* not see ... Is 26:11
but by thee only *w* we make ... Is 26:13
I *w* water it every moment ... Is 27:3
hurt it, I *w* keep it night and day ... Is 27:3
them *w* not have mercy on them ... Is 27:11
formed them *w* shew them no favour ... Is 27:11
another tongue *w* he speak to this ... Is 28:11
Judgment also *w* I lay to the line ... Is 28:17
because he *w* not ever be ... Is 28:28
Yet I *w* distress Ariel, and there ... Is 29:2
I *w* camp against thee round about ... Is 29:3
w lay siege against thee with a ... Is 29:3
I *w* raise forts against thee ... Is 29:3
I *w* proceed to do a marvellous ... Is 29:14
they *w* carry their riches upon ... Is 30:6
children that *w* not hear the law ... Is 30:9
for we *w* flee upon horses ... Is 30:16
and, We *w* ride upon the swift ... Is 30:16
therefore *w* the LORD wait, that ... Is 30:18
therefore *w* he be exalted, that ... Is 30:18
he *w* be very gracious unto thee ... Is 30:19
shall hear it, he *w* answer thee ... Is 30:19

of shaking *w* he fight with it ... Is 30:32
w bring evil, and *w* not call ... Is 31:2
but *w* arise against the house of ... Is 31:2
he *w* not be afraid of their voice ... Is 31:4
so *w* the LORD of hosts defend ... Is 31:5
defending also he *w* deliver it ... Is 31:5
and passing over he *w* preserve it ... Is 31:5
the vile person *w* speak villany ... Is 32:6
his heart *w* work iniquity, to ... Is 32:6
he *w* cause the drink of the ... Is 32:6
Now *w* I rise, saith the LORD ... Is 33:10
now *w* I be exalted ... Is 33:10
now *w* I lift up myself ... Is 33:10
w be unto us a place of broad ... Is 33:21
he *w* save us ... Is 33:22
your God *w* come with vengeance, ... Is 35:4
he *w* come and save you ... Is 35:4
it *w* go into his hand, and pierce ... Is 36:6
I *w* give thee two thousand horses ... Is 36:8
The LORD *w* surely deliver us ... Is 36:15
saying, The LORD *w* deliver us ... Is 36:18
It may be the LORD thy God *w* hear ... Is 37:4
w reprove the words which the ... Is 37:4
I *w* send a blast upon him, and he ... Is 37:7
I *w* cause him to fall by the ... Is 37:7
I *w* cut down the tall cedars ... Is 37:24
I *w* enter into the height of his ... Is 37:24
therefore *w* I put my hook in thy ... Is 37:29
I *w* turn thee back by the way by ... Is 37:29
For I *w* defend this city to save ... Is 37:35
I *w* add unto thy days fifteen ... Is 38:5
I *w* deliver thee and this city out ... Is 38:6
and I *w* defend this city ... Is 38:6
that the LORD *w* do this thing ... Is 38:7
I *w* bring again the shadow of the ... Is 38:8
he *w* cut me off with pining ... Is 38:12
so *w* he break all my bones ... Is 38:13
therefore we *w* sing my songs to ... Is 38:20
the Lord GOD *w* come with strong ... Is 40:10
To whom then *w* ye liken God ... Is 40:18
or what likeness *w* ye compare ... Is 40:18
chooseth a tree that *w* not rot ... Is 40:20
To whom then *w* ye liken me ... Is 40:25
I *w* strengthen thee ... Is 41:10
yea, I *w* help thee ... Is 41:10
I *w* uphold thee with the right ... Is 41:10
thy God *w* hold thy right hand ... Is 41:13
I *w* help thee ... Is 41:13
I *w* help thee, saith the LORD, and ... Is 41:14
I *w* make thee a new sharp ... Is 41:15
thirst, I the LORD *w* hear them ... Is 41:17
God of Israel *w* not forsake them ... Is 41:17
I *w* open rivers in high places, ... Is 41:18
I *w* make the wilderness a pool of ... Is 41:18
I *w* plant in the wilderness the ... Is 41:19
I *w* set in the desert the fir ... Is 41:19
I *w* give to Jerusalem one that ... Is 41:27
w hold thine hand ... Is 42:6
w keep thee, and give thee for a ... Is 42:6
my glory *w* I not give to another, ... Is 42:8
now *w* I cry like a travailing ... Is 42:14
I *w* destroy and devour at once ... Is 42:14
I *w* make waste mountains and hills ... Is 42:15
I *w* make the rivers islands ... Is 42:15
and I *w* dry up the pools ... Is 42:15
I *w* bring the blind by a way that ... Is 42:16
I *w* lead them in paths that they ... Is 42:16
I *w* make darkness light before ... Is 42:16
These things *w* I do unto them, and ... Is 42:16
he *w* magnify the law, and make it ... Is 42:21
Who among you *w* give ear to this ... Is 42:23
who *w* hearken and hear for the ... Is 42:23
the waters, I *w* be with thee ... Is 43:2
therefore *w* I give men for thee, ... Is 43:4
I *w* bring thy seed from the east, ... Is 43:5
I *w* say to the north, Give up ... Is 43:6
I *w* work, and who shall let it ... Is 43:13
Behold, I *w* do a new thing ... Is 43:19
I *w* even make a way in the ... Is 43:19
sake, and *w* not remember thy sins ... Is 43:25
from the womb, which *w* help thee ... Is 44:2
For I *w* pour water upon him that ... Is 44:3
I *w* pour my spirit upon thy seed, ... Is 44:3
for he *w* take thereof, and warm ... Is 44:15
I *w* raise up the decayed places ... Is 44:26
Be dry, and I *w* dry up thy rivers ... Is 44:27
I *w* loose the loins of kings, to ... Is 45:1
I *w* go before thee, and make the ... Is 45:2
I *w* break in pieces the gates of ... Is 45:2
I *w* give thee the treasures of ... Is 45:3
and I *w* direct all his ways ... Is 45:13
even to hoar hairs *w* I carry you ... Is 46:4
I have made, and I *w* bear ... Is 46:4
I *w* carry, and *w* deliver you ... Is 46:4
To whom *w* ye liken me ... Is 46:5
stand, and I *w* do all my pleasure ... Is 46:10
I *w* also bring it to pass ... Is 46:11
have purposed it, I *w* also do it ... Is 46:11
I *w* place salvation in Zion for ... Is 46:13
I *w* take vengeance ... Is 47:3
I *w* not meet thee as a man ... Is 47:3
and *w* not ye declare it ... Is 48:6
name's sake *w* I defer mine anger ... Is 48:9
for my praise *w* I refrain for ... Is 48:9
even for mine own sake, *w* I do it ... Is 48:11
I *w* not give my glory unto ... Is 48:11
he *w* do his pleasure on Babylon, ... Is 48:14
Israel, in whom I *w* be glorified ... Is 49:3
I *w* also give thee for a light to ... Is 49:6
I *w* preserve thee, and give thee ... Is 49:8
I *w* make all my mountains a way, ... Is 49:11
w have mercy upon his afflicted ... Is 49:13
forget, yet *w* I not forget thee ... Is 49:15
I *w* lift up mine hand to the ... Is 49:22

for I *w* contend with him that ... Is 49:25
thee, and I *w* save thy children ... Is 49:25
I *w* feed them that oppress thee ... Is 49:26
For the Lord GOD *w* help me ... Is 50:7
who *w* contend with me ... Is 50:8
Behold, the Lord GOD *w* help me ... Is 50:9
he *w* comfort all her waste places ... Is 51:3
he *w* make her wilderness like ... Is 51:3
I *w* make my judgment to rest for ... Is 51:4
But I *w* put it into the hand of ... Is 51:23
for the LORD *w* go before you ... Is 52:12
God of Israel *w* be your rereward ... Is 52:12
Therefore *w* I divide him a ... Is 53:12
great mercies *w* I gather thee ... Is 54:7
kindness *w* I have mercy on thee ... Is 54:8
I *w* lay thy stones with fair ... Is 54:11
I *w* make thy windows of agates, ... Is 54:12
I *w* make an everlasting covenant ... Is 55:3
LORD, and he *w* have mercy upon him ... Is 55:7
for he *w* abundantly pardon ... Is 55:7
Even unto them *w* I give in mine ... Is 56:5
I *w* give them an everlasting name ... Is 56:5
Even them *w* I bring to my holy ... Is 56:7
Yet *w* I gather others to him, ... Is 56:8
I *w* fetch wine ... Is 56:12
we *w* fill ourselves with strong ... Is 56:12
I *w* declare thy righteousness, and ... Is 57:12
For I *w* not contend for ever, ... Is 57:16
neither *w* I be always wroth ... Is 57:16
have seen his ways, and *w* heal him ... Is 57:18
I *w* lead him also, and restore ... Is 57:18
and I *w* heal him ... Is 57:19
I *w* cause thee to ride upon the ... Is 58:14
face from you, that he *w* not hear ... Is 59:2
deeds, accordingly he *w* repay ... Is 59:18
the islands he *w* repay recompence ... Is 59:18
I *w* glorify the house of my glory ... Is 60:7
kingdom that *w* not serve thee ... Is 60:12
I *w* make the place of my feet ... Is 60:13
thee, I *w* make thee an eternal ... Is 60:15
For brass I *w* bring gold, and for ... Is 60:17
for iron I *w* bring silver, and for ... Is 60:17
I *w* also make thy officers peace, ... Is 60:17
I the LORD *w* hasten it in his ... Is 60:22
I *w* direct their work in truth, ... Is 61:8
I *w* make an everlasting covenant ... Is 61:8
I *w* greatly rejoice in the LORD, ... Is 61:10
so the Lord GOD *w* cause ... Is 61:11
For Zion's sake *w* I not hold my ... Is 62:1
for Jerusalem's sake I *w* not rest ... Is 62:1
Surely I *w* no more give thy corn ... Is 62:8
for I *w* tread them in mine anger, ... Is 63:3
and I *w* stain all my raiment ... Is 63:3
I *w* tread down the people in mine ... Is 63:6
I *w* bring down their strength to ... Is 63:6
I *w* mention the lovingkindnesses ... Is 63:7
people, children that *w* not lie ... Is 63:8
I *w* not keep silence ... Is 65:6
but *w* recompense, even recompense ... Is 65:6
therefore *w* I measure their ... Is 65:7
so *w* I do for my servants' sakes, ... Is 65:8
I *w* bring forth a seed out of ... Is 65:9
Therefore *w* I number you to the ... Is 65:12
I *w* rejoice in Jerusalem, and joy ... Is 65:19
that before they call, I *w* answer ... Is 65:24
they are yet speaking, I *w* hear ... Is 65:24
but to this man *w* I look, even to ... Is 66:2
I also *w* choose their delusions, ... Is 66:4
w bring their fears upon them ... Is 66:4
I *w* extend peace to her like a ... Is 66:12
comforteth, so *w* I comfort you ... Is 66:13
the LORD *w* come with fire, and ... Is 66:15
by his sword *w* the LORD plead ... Is 66:16
that I *w* gather all nations and ... Is 66:18
I *w* set a sign among them ... Is 66:19
I *w* send those that escape of ... Is 66:19
I *w* also take of them for priests ... Is 66:21
and the new earth, which I *w* make ... Is 66:22
for I *w* hasten my word to perform ... Jer 1:12
I *w* call all the families of the ... Jer 1:15
I *w* utter my judgments against ... Jer 1:16
Wherefore I *w* yet plead with you, ... Jer 2:9
children's children *w* I plead ... Jer 2:9
thou saidst, I *w* not transgress ... Jer 2:20
seek her *w* not weary themselves ... Jer 2:24
strangers, and after them *w* I go ... Jer 2:25
time of their trouble they *w* say ... Jer 2:27
Wherefore *w* ye plead with me ... Jer 2:29
we *w* come no more unto thee ... Jer 2:31
I *w* plead with thee, because thou ... Jer 2:35
W he reserve his anger for ever ... Jer 3:5
w he keep it to the end ... Jer 3:5
I *w* not cause mine anger to fall ... Jer 3:12
I *w* not keep anger for ever ... Jer 3:12
I *w* take you one of a city, and ... Jer 3:14
family, and I *w* bring you to Zion ... Jer 3:14
I *w* give you pastors according to ... Jer 3:15
I *w* heal your backslidings ... Jer 3:22
for I *w* bring evil from the north ... Jer 4:6
now also *w* I give sentence ... Jer 4:12
yet *w* I not make a full end ... Jer 4:27
w not repent ... Jer 4:28
neither *w* I turn back from it ... Jer 4:28
thy lovers *w* despise thee, they ... Jer 4:30
thee, they *w* seek thy life ... Jer 4:30
and I *w* pardon it ... Jer 5:1
I *w* get me unto the great ... Jer 5:5
and *w* speak unto them ... Jer 5:5
I *w* make my words in thy mouth ... Jer 5:14
I *w* bring a nation upon you from ... Jer 5:15
I *w* not make a full end with you ... Jer 5:18
w ye not tremble at my presence, ... Jer 5:22
what *w* ye do in the end thereof ... Jer 5:31
I *w* pour it out upon the children ... Jer 6:11

for I *w* stretch out my hand upon Jer 6:12
they said, We *w* not walk therein Jer 6:16
But they said, We *w* not hearken Jer 6:17
I *w* bring evil upon this people, Jer 6:19
I *w* lay stumblingblocks before Jer 6:21
I *w* cause you to dwell in this Jer 7:3
Then *w* I cause you to dwell in Jer 7:7
W ye steal, murder, and commit Jer 7:9
Therefore *w* I do unto this house, Jer 7:14
I *w* cast you out of my sight, as Jer 7:15
for I *w* not hear thee Jer 7:16
I *w* be your God, and ye shall be Jer 7:23
but they *w* not hearken to thee Jer 7:27
but they *w* not answer thee Jer 7:27
Then *w* I cause to cease from the Jer 7:34
Therefore *w* I give their wives Jer 8:10
I *w* surely consume them, saith Jer 8:13
I *w* send serpents, cockatrices, Jer 8:17
which *w* not be charmed, and they Jer 8:17
every brother *w* utterly supplant Jer 9:4
every neighbour *w* walk with Jer 9:4
they *w* deceive every one his Jer 9:5
and *w* not speak the truth Jer 9:5
I *w* melt them, and try them Jer 9:7
For the mountains *w* I take up a Jer 9:10
I *w* make Jerusalem heaps, and a Jer 9:11
I *w* make the cities of Judah Jer 9:11
I *w* feed them, even this people, Jer 9:15
I *w* scatter them also among the Jer 9:16
I *w* send a sword after them, till Jer 9:16
that I *w* punish all them which Jer 9:25
I *w* sling out the inhabitants of Jer 10:18
w distress them, that they may Jer 10:18
be my people, and I *w* be your God Jer 11:4
therefore I *w* bring upon them all Jer 11:8
I *w* bring evil upon them, which Jer 11:11
I *w* not hearken unto them Jer 11:11
for I *w* not hear them in the time Jer 11:14
of hosts, Behold, I *w* punish them Jer 11:22
for I *w* bring evil upon the men Jer 11:23
I *w* pluck them out of their land, Jer 12:14
have plucked them out I *w* return Jer 12:15
w bring them again, every man to Jer 12:15
if they *w* diligently learn the Jer 12:16
But if they *w* not obey Jer 12:17
I *w* utterly pluck up and destroy Jer 12:17
After this manner *w* I mar the Jer 13:9
I *w* fill all the inhabitants of Jer 13:13
I *w* dash them one against another Jer 13:14
I *w* not pity, nor spare, nor have Jer 13:14
But if ye *w* not hear it, my soul Jer 13:17
Therefore *w* I scatter them as the Jer 13:24
Therefore *w* I discover thy skirts Jer 13:26
he *w* now remember their iniquity, Jer 14:10
they fast, I *w* not hear their cry Jer 14:12
an oblation, I *w* not accept them Jer 14:12
but I *w* consume them by the sword Jer 14:12
but I *w* give you assured peace in Jer 14:13
for I *w* pour their wickedness Jer 14:16
therefore we *w* wait upon thee Jer 14:22
I *w* appoint over them four kinds, Jer 15:3
I *w* cause them to be removed into Jer 15:4
therefore *w* I stretch out my hand Jer 15:6
I *w* fan them with a fan in the Jer 15:7
I *w* bereave them of children Jer 15:7
I *w* destroy my people, since they Jer 15:7
the residue of them *w* I deliver Jer 15:9
verily I *w* cause the enemy to Jer 15:11
thy treasures *w* I give to the Jer 15:13
I *w* make thee to pass with thine Jer 15:14
then *w* I bring thee again, and Jer 15:19
I *w* make thee unto this people a Jer 15:20
I *w* deliver thee out of the hand Jer 15:21
I *w* redeem thee out of the hand Jer 15:21
I *w* cause to cease out of this Jer 16:9
Therefore *w* I cast you out of Jer 16:13
where I *w* not shew you favour Jer 16:13
I *w* bring them again into their Jer 16:15
I *w* send for many fishers, saith Jer 16:16
after *w* I send for many hunters, Jer 16:16
first I *w* recompense their Jer 16:18
I *w* this once cause them to know, Jer 16:21
I *w* cause them to know mine hand Jer 16:21
I *w* give thy substance and all thy Jer 17:3
I *w* cause thee to serve thine Jer 17:4
But if ye *w* not hearken unto me Jer 17:27
then *w* I kindle a fire in the Jer 17:27
there I *w* cause thee to hear my Jer 18:2
I *w* repent of the evil that I Jer 18:8
then I *w* repent of the good, Jer 18:10
but we *w* walk after our own Jer 18:12
we *w* every one do the imagination Jer 18:12
W a man leave the snow of Lebanon Jer 18:14
I *w* scatter them as with an east Jer 18:17
I *w* shew them the back, and not Jer 18:17
I *w* bring evil upon this place, Jer 19:3
I *w* make void the counsel of Jer 19:7
I *w* cause them to fall by the Jer 19:7
their carcases *w* I give to be Jer 19:7
I *w* make this city desolate, and Jer 19:8
I *w* cause them to eat the flesh Jer 19:9
Even so *w* I break this people and Jer 19:11
Thus *w* I do unto this place, Jer 19:12
I *w* bring upon this city and upon Jer 19:15
I *w* make thee a terror to thyself Jer 20:4
I *w* give all Judah into the hand Jer 20:4
Moreover I *w* deliver all the Jer 20:5
w I give into the hand of their Jer 20:5
I *w* not make mention of him, nor Jer 20:9
say they, and we *w* report it Jer 20:10
Peradventure he *w* be enticed Jer 20:10
if so be that the LORD *w* deal Jer 21:2
I *w* turn back the weapons of war Jer 21:4
I *w* assemble them into the midst Jer 21:4

I myself *w* fight against you with Jer 21:5
I *w* smite the inhabitants of this Jer 21:6
I *w* deliver Zedekiah king of Jer 21:7
But I *w* punish you according to Jer 21:14
I *w* kindle a fire in the forest Jer 21:14
But if ye *w* not hear these words, Jer 22:5
yet surely I *w* make thee a Jer 22:6
I *w* prepare destroyers against Jer 22:7
I *w* build me a wide house and Jer 22:14
but thou saidst, I *w* not hear Jer 22:21
I *w* give thee into the hand of Jer 22:25
I *w* cast thee out, and thy mother Jer 22:26
I *w* visit upon you the evil of Jer 23:2
I *w* gather the remnant of my Jer 23:3
w bring them again to their folds Jer 23:3
I *w* set up shepherds over them Jer 23:4
that I *w* raise unto David a Jer 23:5
for I *w* bring evil upon them, Jer 23:12
I *w* feed them with wormwood, and Jer 23:15
I *w* even forsake you, saith the Jer 23:33
I *w* even punish that man and his Jer 23:34
w utterly forget you Jer 23:39
I *w* forsake you, and the city that Jer 23:39
I *w* bring an everlasting reproach Jer 23:40
so *w* I acknowledge them that are Jer 24:5
For I *w* set mine eyes upon them Jer 24:6
I *w* bring them again to this land Jer 24:6
I *w* build them, and not pull them Jer 24:6
I *w* plant them, and not pluck them Jer 24:6
I *w* give them an heart to know me Jer 24:7
be my people, and I *w* be their God Jer 24:7
So *w* I give Zedekiah the king of Jer 24:8
I *w* deliver them to be removed Jer 24:9
I *w* send the sword, the famine, Jer 24:10
and I *w* do you no hurt Jer 25:6
I *w* send and take all the families Jer 25:9
w bring them against this land, Jer 25:9
w utterly destroy them, and make Jer 25:9
Moreover I *w* take from them the Jer 25:10
that I *w* punish the king of Jer 25:12
w make it perpetual desolations Jer 25:12
I *w* bring upon that land all my Jer 25:13
I *w* recompense them according to Jer 25:14
sword that I *w* send among them Jer 25:16
sword which I *w* send among you Jer 25:27
for I *w* call for a sword upon all Jer 25:29
he *w* plead with all flesh Jer 25:31
he *w* give them that are wicked to Jer 25:31
If so be they *w* hearken, and turn Jer 26:3
If ye *w* not hearken to me, to Jer 26:4
Then *w* I make this house like Jer 26:6
w make this city a curse to all Jer 26:6
the LORD *w* repent him of the evil Jer 26:13
kingdom which *w* not serve the Jer 27:8
that *w* not put their neck under Jer 27:8
Babylon, that nation *w* I punish Jer 27:8
those *w* I let remain still in Jer 27:11
Why *w* ye die, thou and thy people, Jer 27:13
w not serve the king of Babylon Jer 27:13
then *w* I bring them up, and Jer 27:22
Within two full years *w* I bring Jer 28:3
I *w* bring again to this place Jer 28:4
for I *w* break the yoke of the Jer 28:4
Even so *w* I break the yoke of Jer 28:11
I *w* cast thee from off the face Jer 28:16
at Babylon I *w* visit you, and Jer 29:10
unto me, and I *w* hearken unto you Jer 29:12
I *w* be found of you, saith the Jer 29:14
I *w* turn away your captivity, and Jer 29:14
I *w* gather you from all the Jer 29:14
I *w* bring you again into the Jer 29:14
I *w* send upon them the sword, the Jer 29:17
w make them like vile figs, that Jer 29:17
I *w* persecute them with the sword Jer 29:18
w deliver them to be removed to Jer 29:18
I *w* deliver them into the hand of Jer 29:21
Behold, I *w* punish Shemaiah the Jer 29:32
good that I *w* do for my people Jer 29:32
LORD, that I *w* bring again the Jer 30:3
I *w* cause them to return to the Jer 30:3
that I *w* break his yoke from off Jer 30:8
w burst thy bonds, and strangers Jer 30:8
whom I *w* raise up unto them Jer 30:9
I *w* save thee from afar, and thy Jer 30:10
yet *w* I not make a full end of Jer 30:11
but I *w* correct thee in measure, Jer 30:11
w not leave thee altogether Jer 30:11
upon thee *w* I give for a prey Jer 30:16
For I *w* restore health unto thee, Jer 30:17
I *w* heal thee of thy wounds, Jer 30:17
I *w* bring again the captivity of Jer 30:18
I *w* multiply them, and they shall Jer 30:19
I *w* also glorify them, and they Jer 30:19
I *w* punish all that oppress them Jer 30:20
I *w* cause him to draw near, and he Jer 30:21
be my people, and I *w* be your God Jer 30:22
w I be the God of all the Jer 31:1
Again I *w* build thee, and thou Jer 31:4
I *w* bring them from the north Jer 31:8
with supplications *w* I lead them Jer 31:9
I *w* cause them to walk by the Jer 31:9
scattered Israel *w* gather him Jer 31:10
for I *w* turn their mourning into Jer 31:13
w comfort them, and make them Jer 31:13
I *w* satiate the soul of the Jer 31:14
I *w* surely have mercy upon him, Jer 31:20
that I *w* sow the house of Israel Jer 31:27
so *w* I watch over them, to build, Jer 31:28
that I *w* make a new covenant with Jer 31:31
shall be the covenant that I *w* Jer 31:33
I *w* put my law in their inward Jer 31:33
w be their God, and they shall be Jer 31:33
for I *w* forgive their iniquity, Jer 31:34
I *w* remember their sin no more Jer 31:34

I *w* also cast off all the seed of Jer 31:37
I *w* give this city into the hand Jer 32:3
I *w* give this city into the hand Jer 32:28
I *w* gather them out of all Jer 32:37
I *w* bring them again unto this Jer 32:37
I *w* cause them to dwell safely Jer 32:37
be my people, and I *w* be their God Jer 32:38
I *w* give them one heart, and one Jer 32:39
I *w* make an everlasting covenant Jer 32:40
that I *w* not turn away from them, Jer 32:40
but I *w* put my fear in their Jer 32:40
I *w* rejoice over them to do them Jer 32:41
I *w* plant them in this land Jer 32:41
so *w* I bring upon them all the Jer 32:42
for I *w* cause their captivity to Jer 32:44 7522
I *w* answer thee, and shew thee Jer 33:3
I *w* bring it health and cure Jer 33:6
I *w* cure them, and *w* reveal Jer 33:6
I *w* cause the captivity of Judah Jer 33:7
w build them, as at the first Jer 33:7
I *w* cleanse them from all their Jer 33:8
I *w* pardon all their iniquities, Jer 33:8
For I *w* cause to return the Jer 33:11
that I *w* perform that good thing Jer 33:14
time, *w* I cause the Branch of Jer 33:15
so *w* I multiply the seed of David Jer 33:22
Then *w* I cast away the seed of Jer 33:26
so that I *w* not take any of his Jer 33:26
for I *w* cause their captivity to Jer 33:26
I *w* give this city into the hand Jer 34:2
they *w* lament thee, saying, Ah Jer 34:5
I *w* make you to be removed into Jer 34:17
I *w* give the men that have Jer 34:18
I *w* even give them into the hand Jer 34:20
his princes *w* I give into the Jer 34:21
I *w* command, saith the LORD, and Jer 34:22
I *w* make the cities of Judah a Jer 34:22
But they said, We *w* drink no wine Jer 35:6
W ye not receive instruction to Jer 35:13
I *w* bring upon Judah and upon all Jer 35:17
Judah *w* hear all the evil which I Jer 36:3
It may be they *w* present their Jer 36:7
w return every one from his evil Jer 36:7
We *w* surely tell the king of all Jer 36:16
I *w* punish him and his seed and his Jer 36:31
I *w* bring upon them, and upon the Jer 36:31
Jeremiah, I *w* ask thee a thing Jer 38:14
I *w* not put thee to death, Jer 38:16
neither *w* I give thee into the Jer 38:16
we *w* not put thee to death Jer 38:25
I *w* bring my words upon this city Jer 39:16
But I *w* deliver thee in that day, Jer 39:17
For I *w* surely deliver thee, and Jer 39:18
and I *w* look well unto thee Jer 40:4
I *w* dwell at Mizpah to serve the Jer 40:10
Chaldeans, which *w* come unto us Jer 40:10
I *w* slay Ishmael the son of Jer 40:15
I *w* pray unto the LORD your God Jer 42:4
you, I *w* declare it unto you Jer 42:4
I *w* keep nothing back from you Jer 42:4
we *w* obey the voice of the LORD Jer 42:6
If ye *w* still abide in this land, Jer 42:10
then *w* I build you, and not pull Jer 42:10
I *w* plant you, and not pluck you Jer 42:10
I *w* shew mercies unto you, that Jer 42:12
We *w* not dwell in this land, Jer 42:13
but we *w* go into the land of Jer 42:14
and there *w* we dwell Jer 42:14
the evil that I *w* bring upon them Jer 42:17
so declare unto us, and we *w* do it Jer 42:20
I *w* send and take Nebuchadrezzar Jer 43:10
w set his throne upon these Jer 43:10
I *w* kindle a fire in the houses Jer 43:12
I *w* set my face against you for Jer 44:11
I *w* take the remnant of Judah, Jer 44:12
For I *w* punish them that dwell in Jer 44:13
we *w* not hearken unto thee Jer 44:16
But we *w* certainly do whatsoever Jer 44:17
We *w* surely perform our vows that Jer 44:25
ye *w* surely accomplish your vows, Jer 44:25
I *w* watch over them for evil, and Jer 44:27
that I *w* punish you in this place Jer 44:29
I *w* give Pharaoh-hophra king of Jer 44:30
which I have built *w* I break down Jer 45:4
which I have planted I *w* pluck up Jer 45:4
I *w* bring evil upon all flesh, Jer 45:5
but thy life *w* I give unto thee Jer 45:5
I *w* go up, and *w* cover the Jer 46:8
I *w* destroy the city and the Jer 46:8
I *w* punish the multitude of No, Jer 46:25
I *w* deliver them into the hand of Jer 46:26
I *w* save thee from afar off, and Jer 46:27
for I *w* make a full end of all Jer 46:28
but I *w* not make a full end of Jer 46:28
yet *w* I not leave thee wholly Jer 46:28
for the LORD *w* spoil the Jer 47:4
how long *w* it be ere thou be Jer 47:6
that I *w* send unto him wanderers, Jer 48:12
Therefore *w* I howl for Moab Jer 48:31
I *w* cry out for all Moab Jer 48:31
I *w* weep for thee with the Jer 48:32
Moreover I *w* cause to cease in Jer 48:35
for I *w* bring upon it, even upon Jer 48:44
Yet *w* I bring again the captivity Jer 48:47
that I *w* cause an alarm of war to Jer 49:2
I *w* bring a fear upon thee, saith Jer 49:5
afterward I *w* bring again the Jer 49:6
for I *w* bring the calamity of Jer 49:8
him, the time that I *w* visit him Jer 49:8
they *w* destroy till they have Jer 49:9
children, I *w* preserve them alive Jer 49:11
I *w* make thee small among the Jer 49:15
I *w* bring thee down from thence, Jer 49:16
but I *w* suddenly make him run Jer 49:19

who *w* appoint me the time Jer 49:19
shepherd that *w* stand before me Jer 49:19
I *w* kindle a fire in the wall of Jer 49:27
I *w* scatter into all winds them Jer 49:32
I *w* bring their calamity from all Jer 49:32
I *w* break the bow of Elam, the Jer 49:35
upon Elam *w* I bring the four Jer 49:36
w scatter them toward all those Jer 49:36
For I *w* cause Elam to be dismayed Jer 49:37
I *w* bring evil upon them, even my Jer 49:37
I *w* send the sword after them, Jer 49:37
I *w* set my throne in Elam, and Jer 49:38
w destroy from thence the king and Jer 49:38
days, that I *w* bring again the Jer 49:39
I *w* raise and cause to come up Jer 50:9
I *w* punish the king of Babylon and Jer 50:18
I *w* bring Israel again to his Jer 50:19
for I *w* pardon them whom I Jer 50:20
the time that I *w* visit thee Jer 50:31
I *w* kindle a fire in his cities, Jer 50:32
are cruel, and *w* not shew mercy Jer 50:42
but I *w* make them suddenly run Jer 50:44
who *w* appoint me the time Jer 50:44
shepherd that *w* stand before me Jer 50:44
I *w* raise up against Babylon, and Jer 51:1
w send unto Babylon fanners, that Jer 51:2
he *w* render unto her a recompence Jer 51:6
Surely I *w* fill thee with men, as Jer 51:14
for with thee *w* I break in pieces Jer 51:20
with thee *w* I destroy kingdoms Jer 51:20
with thee *w* I break in pieces the Jer 51:21
with thee *w* I break in pieces the Jer 51:21
With thee also *w* I break in Jer 51:22
with thee *w* I break in pieces old Jer 51:22
with thee *w* I break in pieces the Jer 51:22
I *w* also break in pieces with Jer 51:23
with thee *w* I break in pieces the Jer 51:23
with thee *w* I break in pieces Jer 51:23
I *w* render unto Babylon and to all Jer 51:24
I *w* stretch out mine hand upon Jer 51:25
w make thee a burnt mountain Jer 51:25
I *w* plead thy cause, and take Jer 51:36
I *w* dry up her sea, and make her Jer 51:36
In their heat I *w* make their Jer 51:39
I *w* make them drunken, that they Jer 51:39
I *w* bring them down like lambs to Jer 51:40
I *w* punish Bel in Babylon Jer 51:44
I *w* bring forth out of his mouth Jer 51:44
that I *w* do judgment upon the Jer 51:47
that I *w* do judgment upon her Jer 51:52
I *w* make drunk her princes, and Jer 51:57
the evil that I *w* bring upon her Jer 51:64
therefore *w* I hope in him Lam 3:24
For the Lord *w* not cast off for Lam 3:31
grief, yet *w* he have compassion Lam 3:32
he *w* no more regard them Lam 4:16
he *w* no more carry thee away into Lam 4:22
he *w* visit thine iniquity, O Lam 4:22
he *w* discover thy sins Lam 4:22
thy feet, and I *w* speak unto thee Eze 2:1
And they, whether they *w* hear Eze 2:5
or whether they *w* forbear Eze 2:5
unto them, whether they *w* hear Eze 2:7
or whether they *w* forbear Eze 2:7
of Israel *w* not hearken unto thee Eze 3:7 14
for they *w* not hearken unto me Eze 3:7 14
whether they *w* hear Eze 3:11
or whether they *w* forbear Eze 3:11
but his blood *w* I require at Eze 3:18
but his blood *w* I require at Eze 3:20
and I *w* there talk with thee Eze 3:22
I *w* make thy tongue cleave to the Eze 3:26
I *w* open thy mouth, and thou shalt Eze 3:27
I *w* lay bands upon thee, and thou Eze 4:8
Gentiles, whither I *w* drive them Eze 4:13
I *w* break the staff of bread in Eze 4:16
I *w* draw out a sword after them Eze 5:2
w execute judgments in the midst Eze 5:8
I *w* do in thee that which I have Eze 5:9
whereunto I *w* not do any more the Eze 5:9
I *w* execute judgments in thee, and Eze 5:10
the whole remnant of thee *w* I Eze 5:10
therefore *w* I also diminish thee Eze 5:11
neither *w* I have any pity Eze 5:11
I *w* scatter a third part into all Eze 5:12
I *w* draw out a sword after them Eze 5:12
I *w* cause my fury to rest upon Eze 5:13
upon them, and I *w* be comforted Eze 5:13
Moreover I *w* make thee waste, and Eze 5:14
which I *w* send to destroy you Eze 5:16
I *w* increase the famine upon you, Eze 5:16
w break your staff of bread Eze 5:16
So *w* I send upon you famine and Eze 5:17
I *w* bring the sword upon thee Eze 5:17
w bring a sword upon you Eze 6:3
I *w* destroy your high places Eze 6:3
I *w* cast down your slain men Eze 6:4
I *w* lay the dead carcases of the Eze 6:5
I *w* scatter your bones round Eze 6:5
Yet *w* I leave a remnant, that ye Eze 6:8
thus *w* I accomplish my fury upon Eze 6:12
So *w* I stretch out my hand upon Eze 6:14
I *w* send mine anger upon thee, and Eze 7:3
w judge thee according to thy Eze 7:3
w recompense upon thee all thine Eze 7:3
spare thee, neither *w* I have pity Eze 7:4
but I *w* recompense thy ways upon Eze 7:4
Now *w* I shortly pour out my fury Eze 7:8
I *w* judge thee according to thy Eze 7:8
w recompense thee for all thine Eze 7:8
not spare, neither *w* I have pity Eze 7:9
I *w* recompense thee according to Eze 7:9
I *w* give it into the hands of the Eze 7:21
My face *w* I turn also from them, Eze 7:22
Wherefore I *w* bring the worst of Eze 7:24
I *w* also make the pomp of the Eze 7:24
I *w* do unto them after their way, Eze 7:27
to their deserts *w* I judge them Eze 7:27
Therefore *w* I also deal in fury Eze 8:18
not spare, neither *w* I have pity Eze 8:18
loud voice, yet *w* I not hear them Eze 8:18
neither *w* I have pity Eze 9:10
but I *w* recompense their way upon Eze 9:10
but I *w* bring you forth out of Eze 11:7
I *w* bring a sword upon you, saith Eze 11:8
I *w* bring you out of the midst Eze 11:9
w execute judgments among you Eze 11:9
I *w* judge you in the border of Eze 11:10
but I *w* judge you in the border Eze 11:11
yet *w* I be to them as a little Eze 11:16
I *w* even gather you from the Eze 11:17
I *w* give you the land of Israel Eze 11:17
I *w* give them one heart Eze 11:19
I *w* put a new spirit within you Eze 11:19
I *w* take the stony heart out of Eze 11:19
w give them an heart of flesh Eze 11:19
be my people, and I *w* be their God Eze 11:20
I *w* recompense their way upon Eze 11:21
it may be they *w* consider Eze 12:3
My net also *w* I spread upon him, Eze 12:13
I *w* bring him to Babylon to the Eze 12:13
I *w* scatter toward every wind all Eze 12:14
I *w* draw out the sword after them Eze 12:14
But I *w* leave a few men of them Eze 12:16
I *w* make this proverb to cease, Eze 12:23
I *w* speak, and the word that I Eze 12:25
w I say the word Eze 12:25
w perform it, saith the Lord GOD Eze 12:25
I *w* even rend it with a stormy Eze 13:13
So *w* I break down the wall that Eze 13:14
Thus *w* I accomplish my wrath upon Eze 13:15
w say unto you, The wall is no Eze 13:15
W ye hunt the souls of my people, Eze 13:18
w ye save the souls alive that Eze 13:18
w ye pollute me among my people Eze 13:19
I *w* tear them from your arms, and Eze 13:20
w let the souls go, even the Eze 13:20
Your kerchiefs also *w* I tear Eze 13:21
for I *w* deliver my people out of Eze 13:23
I the LORD *w* answer him that Eze 14:4
I the LORD *w* answer him by myself Eze 14:7
I *w* set my face against that man, Eze 14:8
w make him a sign and a proverb, Eze 14:8
I *w* cut him off from the midst of Eze 14:8
I *w* stretch out my hand upon him, Eze 14:9
w destroy him from the midst of Eze 14:9
then *w* I stretch out mine hand Eze 14:13
w break the staff of the bread Eze 14:13
w send famine upon it Eze 14:13
w cut off man and beast from it Eze 14:13
or *w* men take a pin of it to hang Eze 15:3
so *w* I give the inhabitants of Eze 15:6
I *w* set my face against them Eze 15:7
I *w* make the land desolate, Eze 15:8
unto the *w* of them that hate thee Eze 16:27 5314
therefore I *w* gather all thy Eze 16:37
I *w* even gather them round about Eze 16:37
w discover thy nakedness unto Eze 16:37
I *w* judge thee, as women that Eze 16:38
I *w* give thee blood in fury and Eze 16:38
I *w* also give thee into their Eze 16:39
I *w* cause thee to cease from Eze 16:41
So *w* I make my fury toward thee Eze 16:42
I *w* be quiet Eze 16:42
and *w* be no more angry Eze 16:42
therefore I also *w* recompense thy Eze 16:43
then *w* I bring again the Eze 16:53
I *w* even deal with thee as thou Eze 16:59
Nevertheless I *w* remember my Eze 16:60
I *w* establish unto thee an Eze 16:60
I *w* give them unto thee for Eze 16:61
I *w* establish my covenant with Eze 16:62
even it *w* I recompense upon his Eze 17:19
I *w* spread my net upon him, and he Eze 17:20
I *w* bring him to Babylon Eze 17:20
w plead with him there for his Eze 17:20
I *w* also take of the highest Eze 17:22
of the high cedar, and *w* set it Eze 17:22
I *w* crop off from the top of his Eze 17:22
w plant it upon an high mountain Eze 17:22
the height of Israel *w* I plant it Eze 17:23
But if the wicked *w* turn from all Eze 18:21
Therefore I *w* judge you, O house Eze 18:30
for why *w* ye die, O house of Eze 18:31
I *w* not be enquired of by you Eze 20:3
I *w* pour out my fury upon them, Eze 20:8
I *w* not be enquired of by you Eze 20:31
We *w* be as the heathen, as the Eze 20:32
poured out, *w* I rule over you Eze 20:33
I *w* bring you out from the people Eze 20:34
w gather you out of the countries Eze 20:34
I *w* bring you into the wilderness Eze 20:35
there *w* I plead with you face to Eze 20:35
so *w* I plead with you, saith the Eze 20:36
I *w* cause you to pass under the Eze 20:37
I *w* bring you into the bond of Eze 20:37
I *w* purge out from among you the Eze 20:38
I *w* bring them forth out of the Eze 20:38
if ye *w* not hearken unto me Eze 20:39
there *w* I accept them Eze 20:40
there *w* I require your offerings, Eze 20:40
I *w* accept you with your sweet Eze 20:41
I *w* be sanctified in you before Eze 20:41
I *w* kindle a fire in thee, and it Eze 20:47
w draw forth my sword out of his Eze 21:3
w cut off from thee the righteous Eze 21:3
Seeing then that I *w* cut off from Eze 21:4
I *w* also smite mine hands Eze 21:17
I *w* cause my fury to rest Eze 21:17
but he *w* call to remembrance the Eze 21:23
I *w* overturn, overturn, overturn, Eze 21:27
and I *w* give it him Eze 21:27
I *w* judge thee in the place where Eze 21:30
I *w* pour out mine indignation Eze 21:31
I *w* blow against thee in the fire Eze 21:31
LORD have spoken it, and *w* do it Eze 22:14
I *w* scatter thee among the Eze 22:15
w consume thy filthiness out of Eze 22:15
therefore I *w* gather you into the Eze 22:19
so *w* I gather you in mine anger Eze 22:20
I *w* leave you there, and melt you Eze 22:20
I *w* gather you, and blow upon you Eze 22:21
I *w* raise up thy lovers against Eze 23:22
I *w* bring them against thee on Eze 23:22
I *w* set judgment before them, and Eze 23:24
I *w* set my jealousy against thee, Eze 23:25
Thus *w* I make thy lewdness to Eze 23:27
I *w* deliver thee into the hand of Eze 23:28
I *w* do these things unto thee, Eze 23:30
therefore *w* I give her cup into Eze 23:31
W they now commit whoredoms with Eze 23:43
I *w* bring up a company upon them, Eze 23:46
w give them to be removed and Eze 23:46
Thus *w* I cause lewdness to cease Eze 23:48
I *w* even make the pile for fire Eze 24:9
shall come to pass, and I *w* do it Eze 24:14
I *w* not go back Eze 24:14
not go back, neither *w* I spare Eze 24:14
w I spare, neither *w* I repent Eze 24:14
I *w* profane my sanctuary, the Eze 24:21
therefore I *w* deliver thee to the Eze 25:4
I *w* make Rabbah a stable for Eze 25:5
therefore I *w* stretch out mine Eze 25:7
w deliver thee for a spoil to the Eze 25:7
I *w* cut thee off from the people, Eze 25:7
I *w* cause thee to perish out of Eze 25:7
I *w* destroy thee Eze 25:7
I *w* open the side of Moab from Eze 25:9
w give them in possession, that Eze 25:10
I *w* execute judgments upon Moab Eze 25:11
I *w* also stretch out mine hand Eze 25:13
w cut off man and beast from it Eze 25:13
I *w* make it desolate from Teman Eze 25:13
I *w* lay my vengeance upon Edom by Eze 25:14
I *w* stretch out mine hand upon Eze 25:16
I *w* cut off the Cherethims, and Eze 25:16
I *w* execute great vengeance upon Eze 25:17
w cause many nations to come up Eze 26:3
I *w* also scrape her dust from her Eze 26:4
Behold, I *w* bring upon Tyrus Eze 26:7
I *w* cause the noise of thy songs Eze 26:13
I *w* make thee like the top of a Eze 26:14
I *w* make thee a terror, and thou Eze 26:21
therefore I *w* bring strangers Eze 28:7
therefore I *w* cast thee as Eze 28:16
I *w* destroy thee, O covering Eze 28:16
I *w* cast thee to the ground Eze 28:17
I *w* lay thee before kings, that Eze 28:17
therefore *w* I bring forth a fire Eze 28:18
I *w* bring thee to ashes upon the Eze 28:18
I *w* be glorified in the midst of Eze 28:22
For I *w* send into her pestilence, Eze 28:23
But I *w* put hooks in thy jaws, and Eze 29:4
I *w* cause the fish of thy rivers Eze 29:4
I *w* bring thee up out of the Eze 29:4
I *w* leave thee thrown into the Eze 29:5
I *w* bring a sword upon thee, and Eze 29:8
I *w* make the land of Egypt Eze 29:10
I *w* make the land of Egypt Eze 29:12
I *w* scatter the Egyptians among Eze 29:12
w disperse them through the Eze 29:12
At the end of forty years *w* I Eze 29:13
I *w* bring again the captivity of Eze 29:14
w cause them to return into the Eze 29:14
for I *w* diminish them, that they Eze 29:15
I *w* give the land of Egypt unto Eze 29:19
In that day *w* I cause the horn of Eze 29:21
I *w* give thee the opening of the Eze 29:21
I *w* also make the multitude of Eze 30:10
I *w* make the rivers dry, and sell Eze 30:12
I *w* make the land waste, and all Eze 30:12
I *w* also destroy the idols Eze 30:13
I *w* cause their images to cease Eze 30:13
I *w* put a fear in the land of Eze 30:13
I *w* make Pathros desolate, and Eze 30:14
w set fire in Zoan Eze 30:14
w execute judgments in No Eze 30:14
I *w* pour my fury upon Sin, the Eze 30:15
I *w* cut off the multitude of No Eze 30:15
And I *w* set fire in Egypt Eze 30:16
Thus *w* I execute judgments in Eze 30:19
w break his arms, the strong, and Eze 30:22
I *w* cause the sword to fall out Eze 30:22
I *w* scatter the Egyptians among Eze 30:23
w disperse them through the Eze 30:23
I *w* strengthen the arms of the Eze 30:24
but I *w* break Pharaoh's arms, and Eze 30:24
But I *w* strengthen the arms of Eze 30:25
I *w* scatter the Egyptians among Eze 30:26
I *w* therefore spread out my net Eze 32:3
Then *w* I leave thee upon the land Eze 32:4
I *w* cast thee forth upon the open Eze 32:4
w cause all the fowls of the Eze 32:4
I *w* fill the beasts of the whole Eze 32:4
I *w* lay thy flesh upon the Eze 32:5
I *w* also water with thy blood the Eze 32:6
I *w* cover the heaven, and make the Eze 32:7
I *w* cover the sun with a cloud, Eze 32:7
of heaven *w* I make dark over thee Eze 32:8
I *w* also vex the hearts of many Eze 32:9
I *w* make many people amazed at Eze 32:10
By the swords of the mighty *w* I Eze 32:12

I *w* destroy also all the beasts.... Eze 32:13
Then *w* I make their waters deep,.... Eze 32:14
but his blood *w* I require at the.... Eze 33:6
but his blood *w* I require at.... Eze 33:8
for why *w* ye die, O house of.... Eze 33:11
I *w* judge you every one after his.... Eze 33:20
w I give to the beasts to be.... Eze 33:27
For I *w* lay the land most.... Eze 33:28
thy words, but they *w* not do them.... Eze 33:31
it *w* come,) then shall they know.... Eze 33:33
I *w* require my flock at their.... Eze 34:10
for I *w* deliver my flock from.... Eze 34:10
w both search my sheep, and seek.... Eze 34:11
so *w* I seek out my sheep.... Eze 34:12
w deliver them out of all places.... Eze 34:12
I *w* bring them out from the.... Eze 34:13
w bring them to their own land,.... Eze 34:13
I *w* feed them in a good pasture,.... Eze 34:14
I *w* feed my flock.... Eze 34:15
I *w* cause them to lie down, saith.... Eze 34:15
I *w* seek that which was lost, and.... Eze 34:16
w bind up that which was broken,.... Eze 34:16
w strengthen that which was sick.... Eze 34:16
but I *w* destroy the fat and the.... Eze 34:16
I *w* feed them with judgment.... Eze 34:16
w judge between the fat cattle and.... Eze 34:20
Therefore *w* I save my flock, and.... Eze 34:22
I *w* judge between cattle and.... Eze 34:22
I *w* set up one shepherd over them.... Eze 34:23
I the LORD *w* be their God, and my.... Eze 34:24
I *w* make with them a covenant of.... Eze 34:25
w cause the evil beasts to cease.... Eze 34:25
I *w* make them and the places round.... Eze 34:26
I *w* cause the shower to come down.... Eze 34:26
I *w* raise up for them a plant of.... Eze 34:29
I *w* stretch out mine hand against.... Eze 35:3
I *w* make thee most desolate.... Eze 35:3
I *w* lay thy cities waste, and thou.... Eze 35:4
I *w* prepare thee unto blood, and.... Eze 35:6
Thus *w* I make mount Seir most.... Eze 35:7
I *w* fill his mountains with his.... Eze 35:8
I *w* make thee perpetual.... Eze 35:9
shall be mine, and we *w* possess it.... Eze 35:10
I *w* even do according to thine.... Eze 35:11
I *w* make myself known among them,.. Eze 35:11
rejoiceth, I *w* make thee desolate.... Eze 35:14
was desolate, so *w* I do unto thee.... Eze 35:15
I *w* turn unto you, and ye shall be.... Eze 36:9
I *w* multiply men upon you, all.... Eze 36:10
I *w* multiply upon you man and.... Eze 36:11
I *w* settle you after your old.... Eze 36:11
w do better unto you than at your.... Eze 36:11
I *w* cause men to walk upon you,.... Eze 36:12
Neither *w* I cause men to hear in.... Eze 36:15
I *w* sanctify my great name, which.... Eze 36:23
For I *w* take you from among the.... Eze 36:24
w bring you into your own land.... Eze 36:24
Then *w* I sprinkle clean water.... Eze 36:25
all your idols, *w* I cleanse you.... Eze 36:25
A new heart also *w* I give you.... Eze 36:26
a new spirit *w* I put within you.... Eze 36:26
I *w* take away the stony heart out.... Eze 36:26
I *w* give you an heart of flesh.... Eze 36:26
I *w* put my spirit within you, and.... Eze 36:27
be my people, and I *w* be your God.... Eze 36:28
I *w* also save you from all your.... Eze 36:29
I *w* call for the corn.... Eze 36:29
w increase it, and lay no famine.... Eze 36:29
I *w* multiply the fruit of the.... Eze 36:30
w also cause you to dwell in the.... Eze 36:33
LORD have spoken it, and I *w* do it.... Eze 36:36
I *w* yet for this be enquired of.... Eze 36:37
I *w* increase them with men like a.... Eze 36:37
I *w* cause breath to enter into.... Eze 37:5
I *w* lay sinews upon you.... Eze 37:6
w bring up flesh upon you, and.... Eze 37:6
I *w* open your graves, and cause.... Eze 37:12
I *w* take the stick of Joseph,.... Eze 37:19
w put them with him, even with.... Eze 37:19
I *w* take the children of Israel.... Eze 37:21
w gather them on every side, and.... Eze 37:21
I *w* make them one nation in the.... Eze 37:22
but I *w* save them out of all.... Eze 37:23
have sinned, and *w* cleanse them.... Eze 37:23
be my people, and I *w* be their God.... Eze 37:23
Moreover I *w* make a covenant of.... Eze 37:26
I *w* place them, and multiply them,.... Eze 37:26
w set my sanctuary in the midst.... Eze 37:26
I *w* be their God, and they shall.... Eze 37:27
I *w* turn thee back, and put hooks.... Eze 38:4
I *w* bring thee forth, and all.... Eze 38:4
I *w* go up to the land of unwalled.... Eze 38:11
I *w* go to them that are at rest,.... Eze 38:11
I *w* bring thee against my land,.... Eze 38:16
I *w* call for a sword against him.... Eze 38:21
I *w* plead against him with.... Eze 38:22
I *w* rain upon him, and upon his.... Eze 38:22
Thus *w* I magnify myself, and.... Eze 38:23
I *w* be known in the eyes of many.... Eze 38:23
I *w* turn thee back, and leave but.... Eze 39:2
w cause thee to come up from the.... Eze 39:2
w bring thee upon the mountains.... Eze 39:2
I *w* smite thy bow out of thy left.... Eze 39:3
w cause thine arrows to fall out.... Eze 39:3
I *w* give thee unto the ravenous.... Eze 39:4
I *w* send a fire on Magog, and.... Eze 39:6
So *w* I make my holy name known in. Eze 39:7
I *w* not let them pollute my holy.... Eze 39:7
that I *w* give unto Gog a place.... Eze 39:11
I *w* set my glory among the.... Eze 39:21
Now *w* I bring again the captivity.... Eze 39:25
w be jealous for my holy name.... Eze 39:25
Neither *w* I hide my face any more.... Eze 39:29
where I *w* dwell in the midst of.... Eze 43:7

I *w* dwell in the midst of them.... Eze 43:9
I *w* accept you, saith the Lord.... Eze 43:27
But I *w* make them keepers of the.... Eze 44:14
we *w* shew the interpretation.... Dan 2:4
if ye *w* not make known unto me.... Dan 2:5
we *w* shew the interpretation of.... Dan 2:7
But if ye *w* not make known unto.... Dan 2:9
I *w* shew unto the king the.... Dan 2:24
that *w* make known unto the king.... Dan 2:25
we *w* tell the interpretation.... Dan 2:36
he *w* deliver us out of thine hand.... Dan 3:17
that we *w* not serve thy gods, nor.... Dan 3:18
and giveth it to whomsoever he *w*.... Dan 4:17 6634
and giveth it to whomsoever he *w*.... Dan 4:25 6634
and giveth it to whomsoever he *w*.... Dan 4:32 6634
to his *w* in the army of heaven.... Dan 4:35 6634
he *w* shew the interpretation.... Dan 5:12
yet I *w* read the writing unto the.... Dan 5:17
over it whomsoever he *w*.... Dan 5:21 6634
continually, he *w* deliver thee.... Dan 6:16
but he did according to his *w*.... Dan 8:4 7522
I *w* make thee know what shall be.... Dan 8:19
now *w* I return to fight with the.... Dan 10:20
But I *w* shew thee that which is.... Dan 10:21
now *w* I shew thee the truth.... Dan 11:2
and do according to his *w*.... Dan 11:3 7522
shall do according to his own *w*.... Dan 11:16 7522
king shall do according to his *w*.... Dan 11:36 7522
I *w* avenge the blood of Jezreel.... Hos 1:4
w cause to cease the kingdom of.... Hos 1:4
that I *w* break the bow of Israel.... Hos 1:5
for I *w* no more have mercy upon.... Hos 1:6
but I *w* utterly take them away.... Hos 1:6
But I *w* have mercy upon the house.... Hos 1:7
w save them by the LORD their God.... Hos 1:7
w not save them by bow, nor by.... Hos 1:7
my people, and I *w* not be your God.... Hos 1:9
I *w* not have mercy upon her.... Hos 2:4
I *w* go after my lovers, that give.... Hos 2:5
I *w* hedge up thy way with thorns,.... Hos 2:6
I *w* go and return to my first.... Hos 2:7
Therefore *w* I return, and take.... Hos 2:9
w recover my wool and my flax.... Hos 2:9
now *w* I discover her lewdness in.... Hos 2:10
I *w* also cause all her mirth to.... Hos 2:11
I *w* destroy her vines and her fig.... Hos 2:12
I *w* make them a forest, and the.... Hos 2:12
I *w* visit upon her the days of.... Hos 2:13
I *w* allure her, and bring her into.... Hos 2:14
I *w* give her her vineyards from.... Hos 2:15
For I *w* take away the names of.... Hos 2:17
in that day *w* I make a covenant.... Hos 2:18
I *w* break the bow and the sword and. Hos 2:18
w make them to lie down safely.... Hos 2:18
I *w* betroth thee unto me for ever.... Hos 2:19
I *w* betroth thee unto me in.... Hos 2:19
I *w* even betroth thee unto me in.... Hos 2:20
I *w* hear, saith the LORD.... Hos 2:21
I *w* hear the heavens, and they.... Hos 2:21
I *w* sow her unto me in the earth.... Hos 2:23
I *w* have mercy upon her that had.... Hos 2:23
I *w* say to them which were not my.... Hos 2:23
so *w* I also be for thee.... Hos 3:3
night, and I *w* destroy thy mother.... Hos 4:5
I *w* also reject thee, that thou.... Hos 4:6
I *w* also forget thy children.... Hos 4:6
therefore *w* I change their glory.... Hos 4:7
I *w* punish them for their ways,.... Hos 4:9
I *w* not punish your daughters.... Hos 4:14
now the LORD *w* feed them as a.... Hos 4:16
They *w* not frame their doings to.... Hos 5:4
therefore I *w* pour out my wrath.... Hos 5:10
Therefore *w* I be unto Ephraim as.... Hos 5:12
For I *w* be unto Ephraim as a lion.... Hos 5:14
I, even I, *w* tear and go away.... Hos 5:14
I *w* take away, and none shall.... Hos 5:14
I *w* go and return to my place,.... Hos 5:15
affliction they *w* seek me early.... Hos 5:15
for he hath torn, and he *w* heal us.... Hos 6:1
hath smitten, and he *w* bind us up.... Hos 6:1
After two days *w* he revive us.... Hos 6:2
in the third day he *w* raise us up.... Hos 6:2
I *w* spread my net upon them.... Hos 7:12
I *w* bring them down as the fowls.... Hos 7:12
I *w* chastise them, as their.... Hos 7:12
how long *w* it be ere they attain.... Hos 8:5
now *w* I gather them, and they.... Hos 8:10
now *w* he remember their iniquity,.... Hos 8:13
but I *w* send a fire upon his.... Hos 8:14
What *w* ye do in the solemn day,.... Hos 9:5
therefore he *w* remember their.... Hos 9:9
iniquity, he *w* visit their sins.... Hos 9:9
yet *w* I bereave them, that there.... Hos 9:12
I *w* drive them out of mine house.... Hos 9:15
I *w* love them no more.... Hos 9:15
yet *w* I slay even the beloved.... Hos 9:16
My God *w* cast them away, because.... Hos 9:17
I *w* make Ephraim to ride.... Hos 10:11
I *w* not execute the fierceness of.... Hos 11:9
I *w* not return to destroy Ephraim.... Hos 11:9
I *w* not enter into the city.... Hos 11:9
I *w* place them in their houses,.... Hos 11:11
w punish Jacob according to his.... Hos 12:2
to his doings *w* he recompense him.... Hos 12:2
Egypt *w* yet make thee to dwell in.... Hos 12:9
Therefore I *w* be unto them as a.... Hos 13:7
by the way *w* I observe them.... Hos 13:7
I *w* meet them as a bear that is.... Hos 13:8
w rend the caul of their heart,.... Hos 13:8
there *w* I devour them like a lion.... Hos 13:8
I *w* be thy king.... Hos 13:10 165
I *w* ransom them from the power of.... Hos 13:14
I *w* redeem them from death.... Hos 13:14
O death, I *w* be thy plagues.... Hos 13:14 165

O grave, I *w* be thy destruction.... Hos 13:14 165
so *w* we render the calves of our.... Hos 14:2
we *w* not ride upon horses.... Hos 14:3
neither *w* we say any more to the.... Hos 14:3
I *w* heal their backsliding.... Hos 14:4
I *w* love them freely.... Hos 14:4
I *w* be as the dew unto Israel.... Hos 14:5
O LORD, to thee *w* I cry.... Joel 1:19
Who knoweth if he *w* return.... Joel 2:14
Then *w* the LORD be jealous for.... Joel 2:18
Yea, the LORD *w* answer and say.... Joel 2:19
I *w* send you corn, and wine, and.... Joel 2:19
I *w* no more make you a reproach.... Joel 2:19
But I *w* remove far off from you.... Joel 2:20
w drive him into a land barren and.... Joel 2:20
for the LORD *w* do great things.... Joel 2:21
he *w* cause to come down for you.... Joel 2:23
I *w* restore to you the years that.... Joel 2:25
that I *w* pour out my spirit upon.... Joel 2:28
those days *w* I pour out my spirit.... Joel 2:29
I *w* shew wonders in the heavens.... Joel 2:30
I *w* also gather all nations, and.... Joel 3:2
w bring them down into the valley.... Joel 3:2
w plead with them there for my.... Joel 3:2
w ye render me a recompence.... Joel 3:4
and speedily *w* I return your.... Joel 3:4
I *w* raise them out of the place.... Joel 3:7
w return your recompence upon.... Joel 3:7
I *w* sell your sons and your.... Joel 3:8
for there *w* I sit to judge all.... Joel 3:12
but the LORD *w* be the hope of his.... Joel 3:16
For I *w* cleanse their blood that.... Joel 3:21
The LORD *w* roar from Zion, and.... Amos 1:2
I *w* not turn away the punishment.... Amos 1:3
But I *w* send a fire into the.... Amos 1:4
I *w* break also the bar of.... Amos 1:5
I *w* not turn away the punishment.... Amos 1:6
But I *w* send a fire on the wall.... Amos 1:7
I *w* cut off the inhabitant from.... Amos 1:8
I *w* turn mine hand against Ekron.... Amos 1:8
I *w* not turn away the punishment.... Amos 1:9
But I *w* send a fire on the wall.... Amos 1:10
I *w* not turn away the punishment.... Amos 1:11
But I *w* send a fire upon Teman,.... Amos 1:12
I *w* not turn away the punishment.... Amos 1:13
But I *w* kindle a fire in the wall.... Amos 1:14
I *w* not turn away the punishment.... Amos 2:1
But I *w* send a fire upon Moab, and.... Amos 2:2
I *w* cut off the judge from the.... Amos 2:3
w slay all the princes thereof.... Amos 2:3
I *w* not turn away the punishment.... Amos 2:4
But I *w* send a fire upon Judah,.... Amos 2:5
I *w* not turn away the punishment.... Amos 2:6
his father *w* go in unto the same.... Amos 2:7
therefore I *w* punish you for all.... Amos 3:2
W a lion roar in the forest, when.... Amos 3:4
w a young lion cry out of his den.... Amos 3:4
Surely the Lord GOD *w* do nothing.... Amos 3:7
lion hath roared, who *w* not fear.... Amos 3:8
of Israel upon him I *w* also visit.... Amos 3:14
I *w* smite the winter house with.... Amos 3:15
that he *w* take you away with.... Amos 4:2
Therefore thus *w* I do unto thee.... Amos 4:12
because I *w* do this unto thee,.... Amos 4:12
be that the LORD God of hosts *w*.... Amos 5:15
for I *w* pass through thee, saith.... Amos 5:17
I *w* not smell in your solemn.... Amos 5:21
offerings, I *w* not accept them.... Amos 5:22
neither *w* I regard the peace.... Amos 5:22
for I *w* not hear the melody of.... Amos 5:23
Therefore *w* I cause you to go.... Amos 5:27
therefore *w* I deliver up the city.... Amos 6:8
he *w* smite the great house with.... Amos 6:11
w one plow there with oxen.... Amos 6:12
I *w* raise up against you a nation.... Amos 6:14
I *w* set a plumbline in the midst.... Amos 7:8
I *w* not again pass by them any.... Amos 7:8
I *w* rise against the house of.... Amos 7:9
I *w* not again pass by them any.... Amos 8:2
When *w* the new moon be gone, that.. Amos 8:5
Surely I *w* never forget any of.... Amos 8:7
that I *w* cause the sun to go down.... Amos 8:9
I *w* darken the earth in the clear.... Amos 8:9
I *w* turn your feasts into.... Amos 8:10
I *w* bring up sackcloth upon all.... Amos 8:10
I *w* make it as the mourning of an.... Amos 8:10
that I *w* send a famine in the.... Amos 8:11
I *w* slay the last of them with.... Amos 9:1
thence *w* I bring them down.... Amos 9:2
I *w* search and take them out.... Amos 9:3
thence *w* I command the serpent,.... Amos 9:3
thence *w* I command the sword, and.... Amos 9:4
I *w* set mine eyes upon them for.... Amos 9:4
I *w* destroy it from off the face.... Amos 9:8
saving that I *w* not utterly.... Amos 9:8
I *w* command.... Amos 9:9
I *w* sift the house of Israel.... Amos 9:9
In that day *w* I raise up the.... Amos 9:11
I *w* raise up his ruins, and I *w*.... Amos 9:11
I *w* build it as in the days of.... Amos 9:11
I *w* bring again the captivity of.... Amos 9:14
I *w* plant them upon their land,.... Amos 9:15
thence *w* I bring thee down, saith.... Obad 4
if so be that God *w* think upon us.... Jonah 1:6
yet I *w* look again toward thy.... Jonah 2:4
But I *w* sacrifice unto thee with.... Jonah 2:9
I *w* pay that that I have vowed.... Jonah 2:9
Who can tell if God *w* turn.... Jonah 3:9
w come down, and tread upon the.... Mic 1:3
Therefore I *w* make Samaria as an.... Mic 1:6
I *w* pour down the stones thereof.... Mic 1:6
I *w* discover the foundations.... Mic 1:6
idols thereof *w* I lay desolate.... Mic 1:7
I *w* wail and howl.... Mic 1:8

I *w* go stripped and naked — Mic 1:8
I *w* make a wailing like the — Mic 1:8
Yet *w* I bring an heir unto thee, — Mic 1:15
I *w* prophesy unto thee of wine and — Mic 2:11
I *w* surely assemble, O Jacob, all — Mic 2:12
I *w* surely gather the remnant of — Mic 2:12
I *w* put them together as the — Mic 2:12
the LORD, but he *w* not hear them — Mic 3:4
he *w* even hide his face from them — Mic 3:4
yet *w* they lean upon the LORD, and — Mic 3:11
he *w* teach us of his ways — Mic 4:2
and we *w* walk in his paths — Mic 4:2
For all people *w* walk every one — Mic 4:5
we *w* walk in the name of the LORD — Mic 4:5
w I assemble her that halteth, and — Mic 4:6
I *w* gather her that is driven out — Mic 4:6
I *w* make her that halted a — Mic 4:7
I *w* make thine horn iron — Mic 4:13
and I *w* make thy hoofs brass — Mic 4:13
I *w* consecrate their gain unto — Mic 4:13
Therefore *w* he give them up, — Mic 5:3
that I *w* cut off thy horses out — Mic 5:10
thee, and I *w* destroy thy chariots — Mic 5:10
I *w* cut off the cities of thy — Mic 5:11
I *w* cut off witchcrafts out of — Mic 5:12
graven images also *w* I cut off — Mic 5:13
I *w* pluck up thy groves out of — Mic 5:14
so *w* I destroy thy cities — Mic 5:14
I *w* execute vengeance in anger and — Mic 5:15
people, and he *w* plead with Israel — Mic 6:2
W the LORD be pleased with — Mic 6:7
Therefore also *w* I make thee sick — Mic 6:13
w I give up to the sword — Mic 6:14
Therefore I *w* look unto the LORD — Mic 7:7
I *w* wait for the God of my — Mic 7:7
my God *w* hear me — Mic 7:7
I *w* bear the indignation of the — Mic 7:9
he *w* bring me forth to the light, — Mic 7:9
w I shew unto him marvellous — Mic 7:15
He *w* turn again — Mic 7:19
he *w* have compassion upon us — Mic 7:19
he *w* subdue our iniquities — Mic 7:19
the LORD *w* take vengeance on his — Nah 1:2
w not at all acquit the wicked — Nah 1:3
with an overrunning flood he *w* — Nah 1:8
he *w* make an utter end — Nah 1:9
thee, I *w* afflict thee no more — Nah 1:12
For now *w* I break his yoke from — Nah 1:13
w burst thy bonds in sunder — Nah 1:13
gods *w* I cut off the graven image — Nah 1:14
I *w* make thy grave — Nah 1:14
I *w* burn her chariots in the — Nah 2:13
I *w* cut off thy prey from the — Nah 2:13
I *w* discover thy skirts upon thy — Nah 3:5
face, and I *w* shew the nations thy — Nah 3:5
I *w* cast abominable filth upon — Nah 3:6
w set thee as a gazingstock — Nah 3:6
who *w* bemoan her — Nah 3:7
for I *w* work a work in your days, — Hab 1:5
which ye *w* not believe, though it — Hab 1:5
I *w* stand upon my watch, and set — Hab 2:1
w watch to see what — Hab 2:1
to see what he *w* say unto me — Hab 2:1
because it *w* surely come — Hab 2:3
it *w* not tarry — Hab 2:3
he *w* invade them with his troops — Hab 3:16
Yet I *w* rejoice in the LORD — Hab 3:18
I *w* joy in the God — Hab 3:18
he *w* make my feet like hinds' — Hab 3:19
he *w* make me to walk upon mine — Hab 3:19
I *w* utterly consume all things — Zeph 1:2
I *w* consume man and beast — Zeph 1:3
I *w* consume the fowls of the — Zeph 1:3
I *w* cut off man from off the land — Zeph 1:3
I *w* also stretch out mine hand — Zeph 1:4
I *w* cut off the remnant of Baal — Zeph 1:4
that I *w* punish the princes, and — Zeph 1:8
In the same day also *w* I punish — Zeph 1:9
that I *w* search Jerusalem with — Zeph 1:12
LORD *w* not do good — Zeph 1:12
neither *w* he do evil — Zeph 1:12
I *w* bring distress upon men, that — Zeph 1:17
I *w* even destroy thee, that there — Zeph 2:5
The LORD *w* be terrible unto them — Zeph 2:11
for he *w* famish all the gods of — Zeph 2:11
he *w* stretch out his hand against — Zeph 2:13
w make Nineveh a desolation, and — Zeph 2:13
he *w* not do iniquity — Zeph 3:5
For then *w* I turn to the people a — Zeph 3:9
for then I *w* take away out of the — Zeph 3:11
I *w* also leave in the midst of — Zeph 3:12
he *w* save, he *w* rejoice over — Zeph 3:17
he *w* rejoice over thee with joy — Zeph 3:17
he *w* rest in his love — Zeph 3:17
he *w* joy over thee with singing — Zeph 3:17
I *w* gather them that are — Zeph 3:18
at that time I *w* undo all that — Zeph 3:19
I *w* save her that halteth, and — Zeph 3:19
I *w* get them praise and fame in — Zeph 3:19
At that time *w* I bring you again, — Zeph 3:20
for I *w* make you a name and a — Zeph 3:20
I *w* take pleasure in it — Hag 1:8
I *w* be glorified, saith the LORD — Hag 1:8
I *w* shake the heavens, and the — Hag 2:6
I *w* shake all nations, and the — Hag 2:7
I *w* fill this house with glory, — Hag 2:7
and in this place *w* I give peace — Hag 2:9
from this day *w* I bless you — Hag 2:19
I *w* shake the heavens and the — Hag 2:21
I *w* overthrow the throne of — Hag 2:22
I *w* destroy the strength of the — Hag 2:22
I *w* overthrow the chariots, and — Hag 2:22
w I take thee, O Zerubbabel, my — Hag 2:23
LORD, and *w* make thee as a signet — Hag 2:23

I *w* turn unto you, saith the LORD — Zec 1:3
I *w* shew thee what these be — Zec 1:9
w be unto her a wall of fire — Zec 2:5
w be the glory in the midst of — Zec 2:5
I *w* shake mine hand upon them, and — Zec 2:9
I *w* dwell in the midst of thee, — Zec 2:10
I *w* dwell in the midst of thee, — Zec 2:11
I *w* clothe thee with change of — Zec 3:4
I *w* give thee places to walk — Zec 3:7
I *w* bring forth my servant the — Zec 3:8
I *w* engrave the graving thereof, — Zec 3:9
I *w* remove the iniquity of that — Zec 3:9
I *w* bring it forth, saith the — Zec 5:4
if ye *w* diligently obey the voice — Zec 6:15
w dwell in the midst of Jerusalem — Zec 8:3
I *w* save my people from the east — Zec 8:7
I *w* bring them, and they shall — Zec 8:8
I *w* be their God, in truth and in — Zec 8:8
But now I *w* not be unto the — Zec 8:11
I *w* cause the remnant of this — Zec 8:12
so *w* I save you, and ye shall be a — Zec 8:13
I *w* go also — Zec 8:21
a Jew, saying, We *w* go with you — Zec 8:23
the Lord *w* cast her out — Zec 9:4
he *w* smite her power in the sea — Zec 9:4
I *w* cut off the pride of the — Zec 9:6
I *w* take away his blood out of — Zec 9:7
I *w* encamp about mine house — Zec 9:8
I *w* cut off the chariot from — Zec 9:10
that I *w* render double unto thee — Zec 9:12
I *w* strengthen the house of Judah — Zec 10:6
I *w* save the house of Joseph, and — Zec 10:6
I *w* bring them again to place — Zec 10:6
LORD their God, and *w* hear them — Zec 10:6
I *w* hiss for them, and gather them — Zec 10:8
I *w* sow them among the people — Zec 10:9
I *w* bring them again also out of — Zec 10:10
I *w* bring them into the land of — Zec 10:10
I *w* strengthen them in the LORD — Zec 10:12
For I *w* no more pity the — Zec 11:6
I *w* deliver the men every one — Zec 11:6
their hand I *w* not deliver them — Zec 11:6
I *w* feed the flock of slaughter, — Zec 11:7
Then said I, I *w* not feed you — Zec 11:9
I *w* raise up a shepherd in the — Zec 11:16
I *w* make Jerusalem a cup of — Zec 12:2
in that day *w* I make Jerusalem a — Zec 12:3
I *w* smite every horse with — Zec 12:4
I *w* open mine eyes upon the house — Zec 12:4
w smite every horse of the people — Zec 12:4
In that day *w* I make the — Zec 12:6
that I *w* seek to destroy all the — Zec 12:9
I *w* pour upon the house of David, — Zec 12:10
that I *w* cut off the names of the — Zec 13:2
also I *w* cause the prophets and — Zec 13:2
I *w* turn mine hand upon the — Zec 13:7
I *w* bring the third part through — Zec 13:9
w refine them as silver is — Zec 13:9
w try them as gold is tried — Zec 13:9
call on my name, and I *w* hear them — Zec 13:9
I *w* say, It is my people — Zec 13:9
For I *w* gather all nations — Zec 14:2
the plague wherewith the LORD *w* — Zec 14:12
that whoso *w* not come up of all — Zec 14:17
wherewith the LORD *w* smite the — Zec 14:18
are impoverished, but we *w* return — Mal 1:4
shall build, but I *w* throw down — Mal 1:4
The LORD *w* be magnified from the — Mal 1:5
w he be pleased with thee, or — Mal 1:8
God that he *w* be gracious unto us — Mal 1:9
w he regard your persons — Mal 1:9
neither *w* I accept an offering at — Mal 1:10
If ye *w* not hear — Mal 2:2
if ye *w* not lay it to heart, to — Mal 2:2
I *w* even send a curse upon you, — Mal 2:2
and I *w* curse your blessings — Mal 2:2
I *w* corrupt your seed, and spread — Mal 2:3
The LORD *w* cut off the man that — Mal 2:12
it with good *w* at your hand — Mal 2:13 — 7522
I *w* send my messenger, and he — Mal 3:1
I *w* come near to you to judgment — Mal 3:5
I *w* be a swift witness against — Mal 3:5
I *w* return unto you, saith the — Mal 3:7
W a man rob God — Mal 3:8
if I *w* not open you the windows — Mal 3:10
I *w* rebuke the devourer for your — Mal 3:11
I *w* spare them, as a man spareth — Mal 3:17
I *w* send you Elijah the prophet — Mal 4:5
for Herod *w* seek the young child — Mt 2:13 — *3195*
he *w* throughly purge his floor, — Mt 3:12
but he *w* burn up the chaff with — Mt 3:12
All these things *w* I give thee — Mt 4:9
I *w* make you fishers of men — Mt 4:19
if any man *w* sue thee at the law, — Mt 5:40 — *2309*
Thy *w* be done in earth, as it is — Mt 6:10 — *2307*
Father *w* also forgive you — Mt 6:14
neither *w* your Father forgive — Mt 6:15
there *w* your heart be also — Mt 6:21
for either he *w* hate the one — Mt 6:24
or else he *w* hold to the one, and — Mt 6:24
ask bread, *w* he give him a stone — Mt 7:9
a fish, *w* he give him a serpent — Mt 7:10
but he that doeth the *w* of my — Mt 7:21 — *2307*
Many *w* say to me in that day, — Mt 7:22
then *w* I profess unto them, I — Mt 7:23
I *w* liken him unto a wise man, — Mt 7:24
hand, and touched him, saying, I *w* — Mt 8:3 — *2309*
unto him, I *w* come and heal him — Mt 8:7
I *w* follow thee whithersoever — Mt 8:19
I *w* have mercy, and not sacrifice — Mt 9:13 — *2309*
but the days *w* come, when the — Mt 9:15
that he *w* send forth labourers — Mt 9:38
for they *w* deliver you up to the — Mt 10:17
they *w* scourge you in their — Mt 10:17

him *w* I confess also before my — Mt 10:32
him *w* I also deny before my — Mt 10:33
if ye *w* receive it, this is Elias — Mt 11:14 — *2309*
whomsoever the Son *w* reveal him — Mt 11:27 — *1014*
heavy laden, and I *w* give you rest — Mt 11:28
I *w* have mercy, and not sacrifice, — Mt 12:7 — *2309*
w he not lay hold on it, and lift — Mt 12:11
I *w* put my Spirit upon him, and he — Mt 12:18
then he *w* spoil his house — Mt 12:29
I *w* return into my house from — Mt 12:44
For whosoever shall do the *w* of — Mt 12:50 — *2307*
of harvest I *w* say to the reapers — Mt 13:30
I *w* open my mouth in parables — Mt 13:35
I *w* utter things which have been — Mt 13:35
I *w* not send them away fasting, — Mt 15:32 — *2309*
ye say, It *w* be fair weather — Mt 16:2
It *w* be foul weather to day — Mt 16:3
this rock I *w* build my church — Mt 16:18
I *w* give unto thee the keys of — Mt 16:19
If any man *w* come after me, let — Mt 16:24 — *2309*
For whosoever *w* save his life — Mt 16:25 — *2309*
whosoever *w* lose his life for my — Mt 16:25
Even so it is not the *w* of your — Mt 18:14 — *2307*
But if he *w* not hear thee, then — Mt 18:16
with me, and I *w* pay thee all — Mt 18:26
with me, and I *w* pay thee all — Mt 18:29
whatsoever is right I *w* give you — Mt 20:4
I *w* give unto this last, even as — Mt 20:14 — *2309*
me to do what I *w* with mine own — Mt 20:15 — *2309*
but whosoever *w* be great among — Mt 20:26 — *2309*
whosoever *w* be chief among you, — Mt 20:27 — *2309*
What *w* ye that I shall do unto — Mt 20:32 — *2309*
and straightway he *w* send them — Mt 21:3
I also *w* ask you one thing, which — Mt 21:24
I in like wise *w* tell you by what — Mt 21:24
he *w* say unto us, Why did ye not — Mt 21:25
He answered and said, I *w* not — Mt 21:29 — *2309*
twain did the *w* of his father — Mt 21:31 — *2307*
saying, They *w* reverence my son — Mt 21:37
cometh, what *w* he do unto those — Mt 21:40
He *w* miserably destroy those — Mt 21:41
w let out his vineyard unto other — Mt 21:41
fall, it *w* grind him to powder — Mt 21:44
but they themselves *w* not move — Mt 23:4 — *2309*
there *w* the eagles be gathered — Mt 24:28
I *w* make thee ruler over many — Mt 25:21
I *w* make thee ruler over many — Mt 25:23
What *w* ye give me — Mt 26:15 — *2309*
and I *w* deliver him unto you — Mt 26:15
I *w* keep the passover at thy — Mt 26:18
I *w* not drink henceforth of this — Mt 26:29
I *w* smite the shepherd, and the — Mt 26:31
I *w* go before you into Galilee — Mt 26:32
yet *w* I never be offended — Mt 26:33
with thee, yet *w* I not deny thee — Mt 26:35
nevertheless not as I *w*, but as — Mt 26:39 — *2309*
except I drink it, thy *w* be done — Mt 26:42 — *2307*
Whom *w* ye that I release unto you — Mt 27:17 — *2309*
Whether of the twain *w* ye that I — Mt 27:21 — *2309*
the cross, and we *w* believe him — Mt 27:42
deliver him now, if he *w* have him — Mt 27:43 — *2309*
whether Elias *w* come to save him — Mt 27:49
After three days I *w* rise again — Mt 27:63
we *w* persuade him, and secure you — Mt 28:14
I *w* make you to become fishers of — Mk 1:17
him, and saith unto him, I *w* — Mk 1:41 — *2309*
But the days *w* come, when the — Mk 2:20
and the bottles *w* be marred — Mk 2:22
except he *w* first bind the strong — Mk 3:27
then he *w* spoil his house — Mk 3:27
whosoever shall do the *w* of God — Mk 3:35 — *2307*
how then *w* ye know all parables — Mk 4:13
thou wilt, and I *w* give it thee — Mk 6:22
I *w* give it thee, unto the half — Mk 6:23
I *w* that thou give me by and by in — Mk 6:25 — *2309*
houses, they *w* faint by the way — Mk 8:3
Whosoever *w* come after me, let — Mk 8:34 — *2309*
For whosoever *w* save his life — Mk 8:35 — *2309*
wherewith *w* ye season it — Mk 9:50
but whosoever *w* be great among — Mk 10:43 — *2309*
of you *w* be the chiefest, shall — Mk 10:44 — *2309*
straightway he *w* send him hither — Mk 11:3
neither *w* your Father which is in — Mk 11:26
I *w* also ask of you one question, — Mk 11:29
I *w* tell you by what authority I — Mk 11:29
he *w* say, Why then did ye not — Mk 11:31
saying, They *w* reverence my son — Mk 12:6
he *w* come and destroy the — Mk 12:9
w give the vineyard unto others — Mk 12:9
whensoever ye *w* ye may do them — Mk 14:7 — *2309*
he *w* shew you a large upper room — Mk 14:15
I *w* drink no more of the fruit of — Mk 14:25
I *w* smite the shepherd, and the — Mk 14:27
I *w* go before you into Galilee — Mk 14:28
shall be offended, yet *w* not I — Mk 14:29
I *w* not deny thee in any wise — Mk 14:31
nevertheless not what I *w* — Mk 14:36 — *2309*
I *w* destroy this temple that is — Mk 14:58
within three days I *w* build — Mk 14:58
W ye that I release unto you the — Mk 15:9 — *2309*
What *w* ye then that I shall do — Mk 15:12 — *2309*
Elias *w* come to take him down — Mk 15:36
on earth peace, good *w* toward men — Lk 2:14 — *2107*
he *w* throughly purge his floor, — Lk 3:17
w gather the wheat into his — Lk 3:17
but the chaff he *w* burn with fire — Lk 3:17
him, All this power *w* I give thee — Lk 4:6
and to whomsoever I *w* I give it — Lk 4:6 — *2309*
Ye *w* surely say unto me this — Lk 4:23
at thy word I *w* let down the net — Lk 5:5
hand, and touched him, saying, I *w* — Lk 5:13 — *2309*
But the days *w* come, when the — Lk 5:35
the new wine *w* burst the bottles — Lk 5:37
unto them, I *w* ask you one thing — Lk 6:9

I *w* shew you to whom he is like	Lk 6:47	
which of them *w* love him most	Lk 7:42	
whosoever *w* not receive you, when	Lk 9:5	
If any man *w* come after me, let	Lk 9:23	*2309*
For whosoever *w* save his life	Lk 9:24	*2309*
but whosoever *w* lose his life for	Lk 9:24	
I *w* follow thee whithersoever	Lk 9:57	
also said, Lord, I *w* follow thee	Lk 9:61	
he to whom the Son *w* reveal him	Lk 10:22	*1014*
when I come again, I *w* repay thee	Lk 10:35	
Thy *w* be done, as in heaven, so	Lk 11:2	*2307*
unto you, Though he *w* not rise	Lk 11:8	
of his importunity he *w* rise	Lk 11:8	
a father, *w* he give him a stone	Lk 11:11	
w he for a fish give him a	Lk 11:11	
w he offer him a scorpion	Lk 11:12	
I *w* return unto my house whence I	Lk 11:24	
I *w* send them prophets and	Lk 11:49	
But I *w* forewarn you whom ye	Lk 12:5	
And he said, This *w* I do	Lk 12:18	
I *w* pull down my barns, and build	Lk 12:18	
there *w* I bestow all my fruits and	Lk 12:18	
I *w* say to my soul, Soul, thou	Lk 12:19	
how much more *w* he clothe you	Lk 12:28	
there *w* your heart be also	Lk 12:34	
when he *w* return from the wedding	Lk 12:36	
w come forth and serve them	Lk 12:37	
that he *w* make him ruler over all	Lk 12:44	
The lord of that servant *w* come	Lk 12:46	
w cut him in sunder	Lk 12:46	
w appoint him his portion with	Lk 12:46	
servant, which knew his lord's *w*	Lk 12:47	*2307*
neither did according to his *w*	Lk 12:47	*2307*
of him they *w* ask the more	Lk 12:48	
and what *w* I, if it be already	Lk 12:49	*2309*
blow, ye say, There *w* be heat	Lk 12:55	
w seek to enter in, and shall not	Lk 13:24	
for Herod *w* kill thee	Lk 13:31	*2309*
w not straightway pull him out on	Lk 14:5	
I *w* arise and go to my father, and	Lk 15:18	
w say unto him, Father, I have	Lk 15:18	
who *w* commit to your trust the	Lk 16:11	
for either he *w* hate the one	Lk 16:13	
or else he *w* hold to the one, and	Lk 16:13	
them from the dead, they *w* repent	Lk 16:30	
neither *w* they be persuaded,	Lk 16:31	
but that offences *w* come	Lk 17:1	
w say unto him by and by, when he	Lk 17:7	
w not rather say unto him, Make	Lk 17:8	
the disciples, The days *w* come	Lk 17:22	
thither *w* the eagles be gathered	Lk 17:37	
I *w* avenge her, lest by her	Lk 18:5	
I tell you that he *w* avenge them	Lk 18:8	
We *w* not have this man to reign	Lk 19:14	*2309*
of thine own mouth *w* I judge thee	Lk 19:22	
I *w* also ask you one thing	Lk 20:3	
he *w* say, Why then believed ye	Lk 20:5	
all the people *w* stone us	Lk 20:6	
I *w* send my beloved son	Lk 20:13	
it may be they *w* reverence him	Lk 20:13	
fall, it *w* grind him to powder	Lk 20:18	
which ye behold, the days *w* come	Lk 21:6	
what sign *w* there be when these	Lk 21:7	
For I *w* give you a mouth and	Lk 21:15	
I *w* not any more eat thereof,	Lk 22:16	
I *w* not drink of the fruit of the	Lk 22:18	
nevertheless not my *w*, but thine,	Lk 22:42	*2307*
If I tell you, ye *w* not believe	Lk 22:67	
ye *w* not answer me, nor let me go	Lk 22:68	
I *w* therefore chastise him, and	Lk 23:16	
I *w* therefore chastise him, and	Lk 23:22	
but he delivered Jesus to their *w*	Lk 23:25	*2307*
nor of the *w* of the flesh	Jn 1:13	*2307*
nor of the *w* of man	Jn 1:13	*2307*
and in three days I *w* raise it up	Jn 2:19	
is come, he *w* tell us all things	Jn 4:25	
to do the *w* of him that sent me	Jn 4:34	*2307*
and wonders, ye *w* not believe	Jn 4:48	
he *w* shew him greater works than	Jn 5:20	
so the Son quickeneth whom he *w*	Jn 5:21	*2309*
because I seek not mine own *w*	Jn 5:30	*2307*
but the *w* of the Father which	Jn 5:30	*2307*
ye *w* not come to me, that ye	Jn 5:40	*2309*
in his own name, him ye *w* receive	Jn 5:43	
Do not think that I *w* accuse you	Jn 5:45	
to me I *w* in no wise cast out	Jn 6:37	
from heaven, not to do mine own *w*	Jn 6:38	*2307*
but the *w* of him that sent me	Jn 6:38	*2307*
the Father's *w* which hath sent me	Jn 6:39	*2307*
this is the *w* of him that sent me	Jn 6:40	*2307*
I *w* raise him up at the last day	Jn 6:40	
I *w* raise him up at the last day	Jn 6:44	
bread that I *w* give is my flesh	Jn 6:51	
which I *w* give for the life of	Jn 6:51	
I *w* raise him up at the last day	Jn 6:54	
the twelve, *W* ye also go away	Jn 6:67	*2309*
If any man *w* do his	Jn 7:17	*2309*
do his *w*, he shall	Jn 7:17	*2307*
w he do more miracles than these	Jn 7:31	
among themselves, Whither *w* he go	Jn 7:35	*3195*
w he go unto the dispersed among	Jn 7:35	*3195*
said the Jews, *W* he kill himself	Jn 8:22	
the lusts of your father ye *w* do	Jn 8:44	*2309*
w ye also be his disciples	Jn 9:27	*2309*
worshipper of God, and doeth his *w*	Jn 9:31	*2307*
a stranger *w* they not follow	Jn 10:5	
but *w* flee from him	Jn 10:5	
ask of God, God *w* give it thee	Jn 11:22	
alone, all men *w* believe on him	Jn 11:48	
that he *w* not come to the feast	Jn 11:56	
serve me, him *w* my Father honour	Jn 12:26	
it, and *w* glorify it again	Jn 12:28	
the earth, *w* draw all men unto me	Jn 12:32	
I *w* lay down my life for thy sake	Jn 13:37	
I *w* come again, and receive you	Jn 14:3	
shall ask in my name, that *w* I do	Jn 14:13	
any thing in my name, I *w* do it	Jn 14:14	
I *w* pray the Father, and he shall	Jn 14:16	
I *w* not leave you comfortless	Jn 14:18	
I *w* come to you	Jn 14:18	
I *w* love him	Jn 14:21	
and *w* manifest myself to him	Jn 14:21	
a man love me, he *w* keep my words	Jn 14:23	
and my Father *w* love him	Jn 14:23	
we *w* come unto him, and make our	Jn 14:23	
whom the Father *w* send in my name	Jn 14:26	
Hereafter I *w* not talk much with	Jn 14:30	
in you, ye shall ask what ye *w*	Jn 15:7	*2309*
they *w* also persecute you	Jn 15:20	
my saying, they *w* keep yours also	Jn 15:20	
But all these things *w* they do	Jn 15:21	
whom I *w* send unto you from the	Jn 15:26	
that whosoever killeth you *w*	Jn 16:2	
these things *w* they do unto you,	Jn 16:3	
the Comforter *w* not come unto you	Jn 16:7	
I depart, I *w* send him unto you	Jn 16:7	
he *w* reprove the world of sin, and	Jn 16:8	
he *w* guide you into all truth	Jn 16:13	
he *w* shew you things to come	Jn 16:13	
but I *w* see you again, and your	Jn 16:22	
in my name, he *w* give it you	Jn 16:23	
that I *w* pray the Father for you	Jn 16:26	
I *w* that they also, whom thou	Jn 17:24	*2309*
them thy name, and *w* declare it	Jn 17:26	
w ye therefore that I release	Jn 18:39	*1014*
laid him, and I *w* take him away	Jn 20:15	
into his side, I *w* not believe	Jn 20:25	
If I *w* that he tarry till I come,	Jn 21:22	*2309*
If I *w* that he tarry till I come,	Jn 21:23	*2309*
I *w* pour out of my Spirit upon	Acts 2:17	
on my handmaidens I *w* pour out in	Acts 2:18	
I *w* shew wonders in heaven above,	Acts 2:19	
which *w* not hear that prophet,	Acts 3:23	
be of men, it *w* come to nought	Acts 5:38	
But we *w* give ourselves	Acts 6:4	
shall be in bondage *w* I judge	Acts 7:7	
come, I *w* send thee into Egypt	Acts 7:34	
I *w* carry you away beyond Babylon	Acts 7:43	
what house *w* ye build me	Acts 7:49	
For I *w* shew him how great things	Acts 9:16	
which shall fulfil all my *w*	Acts 13:22	*2307*
I *w* give you the sure mercies of	Acts 13:34	
own generation by the *w* of God	Acts 13:36	*1012*
After this I *w* return	Acts 15:16	
w build again the tabernacle of	Acts 15:16	
I *w* build again the ruins thereof	Acts 15:16	
ruins thereof, and I *w* set it up	Acts 15:16	
said, What *w* this babbler say	Acts 17:18	*2309*
in the which he *w* judge the world	Acts 17:31	*3195*
We *w* hear thee again of this	Acts 17:32	
from henceforth I *w* go unto the	Acts 18:6	
for I *w* be no judge of such	Acts 18:15	*1014*
I *w* return again unto you	Acts 18:21	
return again unto you, if God *w*	Acts 18:21	*2309*
The *w* of the Lord be done	Acts 21:14	*2307*
for they *w* hear that thou art	Acts 21:22	
that thou shouldest know his *w*	Acts 22:14	*2307*
for they *w* not receive thy	Acts 22:18	
for I *w* send thee far hence unto	Acts 22:21	
that we *w* eat nothing until we	Acts 23:14	
that they *w* neither eat nor drink	Acts 23:21	
I *w* hear thee, said he, when	Acts 23:35	
I *w* know the uttermost of your	Acts 24:22	
season, I *w* call for thee	Acts 24:25	
in the which I *w* appear unto thee	Acts 26:16	
that this voyage *w* be with hurt	Acts 27:10	*3195*
Gentiles, and that they *w* hear it	Acts 28:28	
by the *w* of God to come unto you	Rom 1:10	*2307*
Who *w* render to every man	Rom 2:6	
And knowest his *w*, and approvest	Rom 2:18	*2307*
to whom the Lord *w* not impute sin	Rom 4:8	
for a righteous man *w* one die	Rom 5:7	
for to *w* is present with me	Rom 7:18	*2309*
saints according to the *w* of God	Rom 8:27	
of promise, At this time *w* I come	Rom 9:9	
I *w* have mercy on whom	Rom 9:15	
on whom I *w* have mercy	Rom 9:15	
I *w* have compassion on whom I	Rom 9:15	
on whom I *w* have compassion	Rom 9:15	
he mercy on whom he *w* have mercy	Rom 9:18	*2309*
and whom he *w* he hardeneth	Rom 9:18	*2309*
For who hath resisted his *w*	Rom 9:19	*1013*
I *w* call them my people, which	Rom 9:25	
For he *w* finish the work, and cut	Rom 9:28	
because a short work *w* the Lord	Rom 9:28	
I *w* provoke you to jealousy by	Rom 10:19	
by a foolish nation I *w* anger you	Rom 10:19	
acceptable, and perfect, *w* of God	Rom 12:2	*2307*
I *w* repay, saith the Lord	Rom 12:19	
For this cause I *w* confess to	Rom 15:9	
For I *w* not dare to speak of any	Rom 15:18	
into Spain, I *w* come to you	Rom 15:24	
I *w* come by you into Spain	Rom 15:28	
unto you with joy by the *w* of God	Rom 15:32	*2307*
Jesus Christ through the *w* of God	1Cor 1:1	*2307*
I *w* destroy the wisdom of the	1Cor 1:19	
wise, and *w* bring to nothing the	1Cor 1:19	
who both *w* bring to light the	1Cor 4:5	
w make manifest the counsels of	1Cor 4:5	
I *w* come to you shortly	1Cor 4:19	
to you shortly, if the Lord *w*	1Cor 4:19	*2309*
w know, not the speech of them	1Cor 4:19	
What *w* ye	1Cor 4:21	*2309*
but I *w* not be brought under the	1Cor 6:12	
w also raise up us by his own	1Cor 6:14	
so require, let him do what he *w*	1Cor 7:36	*2309*
but hath power over his own *w*	1Cor 7:37	*2307*
heart that he *w* keep his virgin	1Cor 7:37	
to be married to whom she *w*	1Cor 7:39	*2309*
I *w* eat no flesh while the world	1Cor 8:13	
but if against my *w*, a	1Cor 9:17	*210*
who *w* not suffer you to be	1Cor 10:13	
but *w* with the temptation also	1Cor 10:13	
the rest *w* I set in order when I	1Cor 11:34	
to every man severally as he *w*	1Cor 12:11	*1014*
I *w* pray with the spirit	1Cor 14:15	
I *w* pray with the understanding	1Cor 14:15	
I *w* sing with the spirit	1Cor 14:15	
I *w* sing with the understanding	1Cor 14:15	
other lips *w* I speak unto this	1Cor 14:21	
for all that *w* they not hear me	1Cor 14:21	
w they not say that ye are mad	1Cor 14:23	
down on his face he *w* worship God	1Cor 14:25	
if they *w* learn any thing, let	1Cor 14:35	*2309*
But some man *w* say, How are the	1Cor 15:35	
them *w* I send to bring your	1Cor 16:3	
Now I *w* come unto you, when I	1Cor 16:5	
And it may be that I *w* abide	1Cor 16:6	
For I *w* not see you now by the	1Cor 16:7	*2309*
But I *w* tarry at Ephesus until	1Cor 16:8	
but his *w* was not at all to come	1Cor 16:12	*2307*
but he *w* come when he shall have	1Cor 16:12	
of Jesus Christ by the *w* of God	2Cor 1:1	*2307*
we trust that he *w* yet deliver us	2Cor 1:10	
I *w* dwell in them, and walk in	2Cor 6:16	
I *w* be their God, and they shall	2Cor 6:16	
and I *w* receive you,	2Cor 6:17	
w be a Father unto you, and ye	2Cor 6:18	
Lord, and unto us by the *w* of God	2Cor 8:5	*2307*
as there was a readiness to *w*	2Cor 8:11	*2309*
such *w* we be also in deed when we	2Cor 10:11	
But we *w* not boast of things	2Cor 10:13	
unto you, and so *w* I keep myself	2Cor 11:9	
But what I do, that I *w* do	2Cor 11:12	
after the flesh, I *w* glory also	2Cor 11:18	
I *w* glory of the things which	2Cor 11:30	
I *w* come to visions and	2Cor 12:1	
Of such an one *w* I glory	2Cor 12:5	
yet of myself I *w* not glory	2Cor 12:5	
for I *w* say the truth	2Cor 12:6	
therefore *w* I rather glory in my	2Cor 12:9	
I *w* not be burdensome to you	2Cor 12:14	
I *w* very gladly spend and be spent	2Cor 12:15	
God *w* humble me among you	2Cor 12:21	
if I come again, I *w* not spare	2Cor 13:2	
world, according to the *w* of God	Gal 1:4	*2307*
that ye *w* be none otherwise	Gal 5:10	
of Jesus Christ by the *w* of God	Eph 1:1	*2307*
to the good pleasure of his *w*	Eph 1:5	*2307*
unto us the mystery of his *w*	Eph 1:9	*2307*
after the counsel of his own *w*	Eph 1:11	*2307*
what the *w* of the Lord is	Eph 5:17	*2307*
doing the *w* of God from the heart	Eph 6:6	*2307*
With good *w* doing service, as to	Eph 6:7	*2133*
you *w* perform it until the day of	Phil 1:6	
and some also of good *w*	Phil 1:15	*2107*
do rejoice, yea, and *w* rejoice	Phil 1:18	
which worketh in you both to *w*	Phil 2:13	*2309*
who *w* naturally care for your	Phil 2:20	
I shall see how it *w* go with me	Phil 2:23	
of Jesus Christ by the *w* of God	Col 1:1	*2307*
knowledge of his *w* in all wisdom	Col 1:9	*2307*
a shew of wisdom in *w* worship	Col 2:23	*1479*
and complete in all the *w* of God	Col 4:12	*2307*
For this is the *w* of God, even	1Th 4:3	*2307*
in Jesus *w* God bring with him	1Th 4:14	
for this is the *w* of God in	1Th 5:18	*2307*
calleth you, who also *w* do it	1Th 5:24	
only he who now letteth *w* let	2Th 2:7	
w do the things which we command	2Th 3:4	
Who *w* have all men to be saved,	1Ti 2:4	*2309*
I *w* therefore that men pray every	1Ti 2:8	*1014*
against Christ, they *w* marry	1Ti 5:11	*2309*
I *w* therefore that the younger	1Ti 5:14	*1014*
But they that *w* be rich fall into	1Ti 6:9	*1014*
of Jesus Christ by the *w* of God	2Ti 1:1	*2307*
if we deny him, he also *w* deny us	2Ti 2:12	
for they *w* increase unto more	2Ti 2:16	
their word *w* eat as doth a canker	2Ti 2:17	
if God peradventure *w* give them	2Ti 2:25	
are taken captive by him at his *w*	2Ti 2:26	*2307*
all that *w* live godly in Christ	2Ti 3:12	*2309*
For the time *w* come when they	2Ti 4:3	
they *w* not endure sound doctrine	2Ti 4:3	
w preserve me unto his heavenly	2Ti 4:18	
these things I *w* that thou affirm	Titus 3:8	*1014*
with mine own hand, I *w* repay it	Philem 19	
I *w* be to him a Father, and he	Heb 1:5	
Ghost, according to his own *w*	Heb 2:4	*2308*
I *w* declare thy name unto my	Heb 2:12	
church *w* I sing praise unto thee	Heb 2:12	
And again, I *w* put my trust in him	Heb 2:13	
To day if ye *w* hear his voice,	Heb 3:7	
To day if ye *w* hear his voice	Heb 3:15	
To day if ye *w* hear his voice,	Heb 4:7	
this *w* we do, if God permit	Heb 6:3	
Surely blessing I *w* bless thee	Heb 6:14	
and multiplying I *w* multiply thee	Heb 6:14	
w not repent, Thou art a priest	Heb 7:21	
when I *w* make a new covenant with	Heb 8:8	
I *w* make with the house of Israel	Heb 8:10	
I *w* put my laws into their mind,	Heb 8:10	
I *w* be to them a God, and they	Heb 8:10	
For I *w* be merciful to their	Heb 8:12	
their iniquities *w* I remember no	Heb 8:12	
it is written of me,) to do thy *w*	Heb 10:7	*2307*
said he, Lo, I come to do thy *w*	Heb 10:9	*2307*
By the which *w* we are sanctified	Heb 10:10	*2307*
This is the covenant that I *w*	Heb 10:16	
I *w* put my laws into their hearts	Heb 10:16	
and in their minds *w* I write them	Heb 10:16	
iniquities *w* I remember no more	Heb 10:17	

I *w* recompense, saith the Lord	Heb 10:30	
after ye have done the *w* of God	Heb 10:36	*2307*
and he that shall come *w* come	Heb 10:37	
w come, and *w* not tarry	Heb 10:37	
and adulterers God *w* judge	Heb 13:4	
I *w* never leave thee, nor forsake	Heb 13:5	
I *w* not fear what man shall do	Heb 13:6	
in every good work to do his *w*	Heb 13:21	*2307*
if he come shortly, I *w* see you	Heb 13:23	
Of his own *w* begat he us with the	Jas 1:18	*1014*
I *w* shew thee my faith by my	Jas 2:18	
whosoever therefore *w* be a friend	Jas 4:4	*1014*
the devil, and he *w* flee from you	Jas 4:7	
to God, and he *w* draw nigh to you	Jas 4:8	
morrow we *w* go into such a city	Jas 4:13	
ye ought to say, If the Lord *w*	Jas 4:15	*2309*
For so is the *w* of God, that with	1Pet 2:15	*2307*
For he that *w* love life, and see	1Pet 3:10	*2309*
And who is he that *w* harm you	1Pet 3:13	
if the *w* of God be so, that ye	1Pet 3:17	*2307*
lusts of men, but to the *w* of God	1Pet 4:2	*2307*
wrought the *w* of the Gentiles	1Pet 4:3	*2307*
w of God commit the keeping of	1Pet 4:19	*2307*
Wherefore I *w* not be negligent to	2Pet 1:12	
Moreover I *w* endeavour that ye	2Pet 1:15	
not in old time by the *w* of man	2Pet 1:21	*2307*
But the day of the Lord *w* come as	2Pet 3:10	
but he that doeth the *w* of God	1Jn 2:17	*2307*
ask any thing according to his *w*	1Jn 5:14	*2307*
I *w* remember his deeds which he	3Jn 10	
but I *w* not with ink and pen write	3Jn 13	*2309*
I *w* therefore put you in	Jude 5	*1014*
or else I *w* come unto thee	Rev 2:5	
w remove thy candlestick out of	Rev 2:5	
To him that overcometh *w* I give	Rev 2:7	
I *w* give thee a crown of life	Rev 2:10	
or else I *w* come unto thee	Rev 2:16	
w fight against them with the	Rev 2:16	
To him that overcometh *w* I give	Rev 2:17	
w give him a white stone, and in	Rev 2:17	
I *w* cast her into a bed, and them	Rev 2:22	
I *w* kill her children with death	Rev 2:23	
I *w* give unto every one of you	Rev 2:23	
I *w* put upon you none other	Rev 2:24	
to him *w* I give power over the	Rev 2:26	
I *w* give him the morning star	Rev 2:28	
I *w* come on thee as a thief, and	Rev 3:3	
know what hour I *w* come upon thee	Rev 3:3	
I *w* not blot out his name out of	Rev 3:5	
but I *w* confess his name before	Rev 3:5	
I *w* make them of the synagogue of	Rev 3:9	
I *w* make them to come and worship	Rev 3:9	
I also *w* keep thee from the hour	Rev 3:10	
Him that overcometh *w* I make a	Rev 3:12	
I *w* write upon him the name of my	Rev 3:12	
I *w* write upon him my new name	Rev 3:12	
I *w* spue thee out of my mouth	Rev 3:16	*3195*
I *w* come in to him	Rev 3:20	
w sup with him, and he with me	Rev 3:20	
To him that overcometh *w* I grant	Rev 3:21	
I *w* shew thee things which must	Rev 4:1	
I *w* give power unto my two	Rev 11:3	
And if any man *w* hurt them	Rev 11:5	*2309*
and if any man *w* hurt them	Rev 11:5	*2309*
all plagues, as often as they *w*	Rev 11:6	*2309*
I *w* shew unto thee the judgment	Rev 17:1	
I *w* tell thee the mystery of the	Rev 17:7	
in their hearts to fulfil his *w*	Rev 17:17	*1106*
he *w* dwell with them, and they	Rev 21:3	
I *w* give unto him that is athirst	Rev 21:6	
I *w* be his God, and he shall be my	Rev 21:7	
I *w* shew thee the bride, the	Rev 21:9	
And whosoever *w*, let him take the	Rev 22:17	*2309*

WILLETH

So then it is not of him that *w*	Rom 9:16	*2309*

WILLING

the woman will not be *w* to follow	Gen 24:5	14
will not be *w* to follow thee	Gen 24:8	14
whosoever is of a *w* heart	Ex 35:5	5081
every one whom his spirit made *w*	Ex 35:21	5068
women, as many as were *w* hearted	Ex 35:22	5081
a *w* offering unto the LORD	Ex 35:29	5071
whose heart made them *w* to bring	Ex 35:29	5068
a perfect heart and with a *w* mind	1Chr 28:9	2655
workmanship every *w* skilful man	1Chr 28:21	5081
who then is *w* to consecrate his	1Chr 29:5	5068
the unicorn be *w* to serve thee	Job 39:9	14
Thy people shall be *w* in the day	Ps 110:3	5071
If ye be *w* and obedient, ye shall	Is 1:19	14
not *w* to make her a publick	Mt 1:19	*2309*
the spirit indeed is *w*, but the	Mt 26:41	*4289*
w to content the people, released	Mk 15:15	*1014*
w to justify himself, said unto	Lk 10:29	*2309*
Saying, Father, if thou be *w*	Lk 22:42	*1014*
w to release Jesus, spake again	Lk 23:20	*2309*
ye were *w* for a season to rejoice	Jn 5:35	*2309*
w to shew the Jews a pleasure,	Acts 24:27	*2309*
w to do the Jews a pleasure,	Acts 25:9	*2309*
w to save Paul, kept them from	Acts 27:43	*1014*
w to shew his wrath, and to make	Rom 9:22	*2309*
w rather to be absent from the	2Cor 5:8	*2106*
power they were *w* of themselves	2Cor 8:3	*830*
For if there be first a *w* mind	2Cor 8:12	*4288*
we were *w* to have imparted unto	1Th 2:8	*2106*
to distribute, *w* to communicate	1Ti 6:18	*2843*
w more abundantly to shew unto	Heb 6:17	*1014*
in all things *w* to live honestly	Heb 13:18	*2309*
not *w* that any should perish, but	2Pet 3:9	*1014*

WILLINGLY

of every man that giveth it *w*	Ex 25:2	5068
when the people *w* offered	Judg 5:2	5068
themselves *w* among the people	Judg 5:9	5068
answered, We will *w* give them	Judg 8:25	5414
of the king's work, offered *w*	1Chr 29:6	5068
rejoiced, for that they offered *w*	1Chr 29:9	5068
heart they offered *w* to the LORD	1Chr 29:9	5068
to offer so *w* after this sort	1Chr 29:14	5068
of mine heart I have *w* offered	1Chr 29:17	5068
here, to offer *w* unto thee	1Chr 29:17	5068
who *w* offered himself unto the	2Chr 17:16	5068
princes gave *w* unto the people	2Chr 35:8	5071
beside all that was *w* offered	Ezr 1:6	5068
of every one that *w* offered a	Ezr 3:5	5068
offering *w* for the house of their	Ezr 7:16	5068
that *w* offered themselves to	Neh 11:2	
flax, and worketh *w* with her hands	Prov 31:13	2656
For he doth not afflict *w* nor	Lam 3:33	3820
because he *w* walked after the	Hos 5:11	2974
Then they *w* received him into the	Jn 6:21	*2309*
was made subject to vanity, not *w*	Rom 8:20	*1635*
For if I do this thing *w*, I have	1Cor 9:17	*1635*
be as it were of necessity, but *w*	Philem 14	
thereof, not by constraint, but *w*	1Pet 5:2	*1596*
For this they *w* are ignorant of,	2Pet 3:5	*2309*

WILLOW

waters, and set it as a *w* tree	Eze 17:5	6851

WILLOWS

of thick trees, and *w* of the brook	Lev 23:40	6155
the *w* of the brook compass him	Job 40:22	6155
upon the *w* in the midst thereof	Ps 137:2	6155
carry away to the brook of the *w*	Is 15:7	6155
as *w* by the water courses	Is 44:4	6155

WILT

if thou *w* take the left hand,	Gen 13:9
what *w* thou give me, seeing I go	Gen 15:2
and whither *w* thou go	Gen 16:8
W thou also destroy the righteous	Gen 18:23
w thou also destroy and not spare	Gen 18:24
w thou destroy all the city for	Gen 18:28
w thou slay also a righteous	Gen 20:4
thou *w* not deal falsely with me	Gen 21:23
saying, But if thou *w* give it	Gen 23:13
unto her, *W* thou go with this man	Gen 24:58
That thou *w* do us no hurt, as we	Gen 26:29
if thou *w* do this thing for me, I	Gen 30:31
What *w* thou give me, that thou	Gen 38:16
W thou give me a pledge, till	Gen 38:17
If thou *w* send our brother with	Gen 43:4
But if thou *w* not send him, we	Gen 43:5
the hand of him whom thou *w* send	Ex 4:13
if thou *w* not let my people go,	Ex 8:21
them go, and *w* hold them still,	Ex 9:2
that thou *w* not let them go	Ex 9:17
How long *w* thou refuse to humble	Ex 10:3
if thou *w* not redeem it, then	Ex 13:13
If thou *w* diligently hearken to	Ex 15:26
w do that which is right in his	Ex 15:26
w give ear to his commandments,	Ex 15:26
Thou *w* surely wear away, both	Ex 18:18
if thou *w* make me an altar of	Ex 20:25
if thou *w* forgive their sin	Ex 32:32
me know whom thou *w* send with me.	Ex 33:12
w thou put out the eyes of these	Num 16:14
w thou be wroth with all the	Num 16:22
If thou *w* indeed deliver this	Num 21:2
when thou *w* ease thyself abroad,	Deut 23:13
if thou *w* not hearken unto the	Deut 28:15
If thou *w* not observe to do all	Deut 28:58
away, so that thou *w* not hear	Deut 30:17
what *w* thou do unto thy great	Josh 7:9
Caleb said unto her, What *w* thou	Judg 1:14
If thou *w* go with me, then I will	Judg 4:8
but if thou *w* not go with me,	Judg 4:8
If thou *w* save Israel by mine	Judg 6:36
thou *w* save Israel by mine hand	Judg 6:37
W not thou possess that which	Judg 11:24
if thou *w* offer a burnt offering,	Judg 13:16
If thou *w* redeem it, redeem it	Ruth 4:4
but if thou *w* not redeem it, then	Ruth 4:4
if thou *w* indeed look on the	1Sa 1:11
but *w* give unto thine handmaid a	1Sa 1:11
How long *w* thou be drunken	1Sa 1:14
w thou deliver them into the hand	1Sa 14:37
How long *w* thou mourn for Saul,	1Sa 16:1
wherefore then *w* thou sin against	1Sa 19:5
if thou *w* take that, take it	1Sa 21:9
that thou *w* not cut off my seed	1Sa 24:21
that thou *w* not destroy my name	1Sa 24:21
know and consider what thou *w* do	1Sa 25:17
that thou *w* neither kill me, nor	1Sa 30:15
w thou deliver them into mine	2Sa 5:19
w thou not tell me	2Sa 13:4
Joab said, Wherefore *w* thou run	2Sa 18:22
why *w* thou swallow up the	2Sa 20:19
thou *w* shew thyself merciful	2Sa 22:26
man thou *w* shew thyself upright	2Sa 22:26
the pure thou *w* shew thyself pure	2Sa 22:27
with the froward thou *w* shew	2Sa 22:27
the afflicted people thou *w* save	2Sa 22:28
or *w* thou flee three months	2Sa 24:13
if thou *w* walk in my ways, to	1Kin 3:14
if thou *w* walk in my statutes, and	1Kin 6:12
if thou *w* walk before me, as	1Kin 9:4
thee, and *w* keep my statutes and my	1Kin 9:4
if thou *w* hearken unto all that I	1Kin 11:38
w walk in my ways, and do that is	1Kin 11:38
If thou *w* be a servant unto this	1Kin 12:7
w serve them, and answer them, and	1Kin 12:7
If thou *w* give me half thine	1Kin 13:8
W thou go with me to battle to	1Kin 22:4
w thou go with me against Moab to	2Kin 3:7
Wherefore *w* thou go to him to day	2Kin 4:23
I know the evil that thou *w* do	2Kin 8:12
strong holds *w* thou set on fire	2Kin 8:12
their young men *w* thou slay with	2Kin 8:12
w dash their children, and rip up	2Kin 8:12
How then *w* thou turn away the	2Kin 18:24
w thou deliver them into mine	1Chr 14:10
that thou *w* build him an house	1Chr 17:25
if thou *w* walk before me, as	2Chr 7:17
of Judah, *W* thou go with me to	2Chr 18:3
our affliction, then thou *w* hear	2Chr 20:9
O our God, *w* thou not judge them	2Chr 20:12
But if thou *w* go, do it, be	2Chr 25:8
and when *w* thou return	Neh 2:6
the king unto her, What *w* thou	Est 5:3
with thee, *w* thou be grieved	Job 4:2
which of the saints *w* thou turn	Job 5:1
How long *w* thou not depart from	Job 7:19
How long *w* thou speak these	Job 8:2
I know that thou *w* not hold me	Job 9:28
w thou bring me into dust again	Job 10:9
thou *w* not acquit me from mine	Job 10:14
W thou break a leaf driven to and	Job 13:25
w thou pursue the dry stubble	Job 13:25
thou *w* have a desire to the work	Job 14:15
that thou *w* bring me to death	Job 30:23
w thou condemn him that is most	Job 34:17
W thou hunt the prey for the lion	Job 38:39
W thou trust him, because his	Job 39:11
or *w* thou leave thy labour to him	Job 39:11
W thou believe him, that he will	Job 39:12
W thou also disannul my judgment	Job 40:8
w thou condemn me, that thou	Job 40:8
w thou take him for a servant for	Job 41:4
W thou play with him as with a	Job 41:5
or *w* thou bind him for thy	Job 41:5
thou, LORD, *w* bless the righteous	Ps 5:12
with favour *w* thou compass him as	Ps 5:12
his heart, Thou *w* not require it	Ps 10:13
thou *w* prepare their heart	Ps 10:17
thou *w* cause thine ear to hear	Ps 10:17
How long *w* thou forget me, O LORD	Ps 13:1
how long *w* thou hide thy face	Ps 13:1
For thou *w* not leave my soul in	Ps 16:10
neither *w* thou suffer thine Holy	Ps 16:10
Thou *w* shew me the path of life	Ps 16:11
upon thee, for thou *w* hear me	Ps 17:6
thou *w* shew thyself merciful	Ps 18:25
man thou *w* shew thyself upright	Ps 18:25
the pure thou *w* shew thyself pure	Ps 18:26
thou *w* shew thyself froward	Ps 18:26
For thou *w* save the afflicted	Ps 18:27
but *w* bring down high looks	Ps 18:27
For thou *w* light my candle	Ps 18:28
LORD, how long *w* thou look on	Ps 35:17
thou *w* hear, O Lord my God	Ps 38:15
thou *w* not deliver him unto the	Ps 41:2
thou *w* make all his bed in his	Ps 41:3
heart, O God, thou *w* not despise	Ps 51:17
w not thou deliver my feet from	Ps 56:13
W not thou, O God, which hadst	Ps 60:10
Thou *w* prolong the king's life	Ps 61:6
in righteousness *w* thou answer us	Ps 65:5
w thou be angry for ever	Ps 79:5
how long *w* thou be angry against	Ps 80:4
if thou *w* hearken unto me	Ps 81:8
W thou be angry with us for ever	Ps 85:5
w thou draw out thine anger to	Ps 85:5
W thou not revive us again	Ps 85:6
for thou *w* answer me	Ps 86:7
W thou shew wonders to the dead	Ps 88:10
w thou hide thyself for ever	Ps 89:46
O when *w* thou come unto me	Ps 101:2
W not thou, O God, who hast cast	Ps 108:11
w not thou, O God, go forth with	Ps 108:11
saying, When *w* thou comfort me	Ps 119:82
when *w* thou execute judgment on	Ps 119:84
of trouble, thou *w* revive me	Ps 138:7
Surely thou *w* slay the wicked, O	Ps 139:19
if thou *w* receive my words, and	Prov 2:1
why *w* thou, my son, be ravished	Prov 5:20
How long *w* thou sleep, O sluggard	Prov 6:9
when *w* thou arise out of thy	Prov 6:9
W thou set thine eyes upon that	Prov 23:5
Thou *w* keep him in perfect peace,	Is 26:3
thou *w* ordain peace for us	Is 26:12
forth, thou *w* debate with it	Is 27:8
How then *w* thou turn away the	Is 36:9
to night *w* thou make an end of me	Is 38:12
to night *w* thou make an end of me	Is 38:13
so *w* thou recover me, and make me	Is 38:16
w thou call this a fast, and an	Is 58:5
W thou refrain thyself for these	Is 64:12
w thou hold thy peace, and afflict	Is 64:12
W thou not from this time cry	Jer 3:4
If thou *w* return, O Israel, saith	Jer 4:1
and if thou *w* put away thine	Jer 4:1
thou art spoiled, what *w* thou do	Jer 4:30
then how *w* thou do in the	Jer 12:5
What *w* thou say when he shall	Jer 13:21
w thou not be made clean	Jer 13:27
w thou be altogether unto me as a	Jer 15:18
How long *w* thou go about, O thou	Jer 31:22
w thou not surely put me to death	Jer 38:15
w thou not hearken unto me	Jer 38:15
If thou *w* assuredly go forth unto	Jer 38:17
But if thou *w* not go forth to the	Jer 38:18
how long *w* thou cut thyself	Jer 47:5
thou *w* bring the day that thou	Lam 1:21
w thou destroy all the residue of	Eze 9:8
w thou make a full end of the	Eze 11:13
W thou judge them, son of man,	Eze 20:4
son of man, *w* thou judge them	Eze 20:4
w thou judge, *w* thou judge the	Eze 22:2
w thou judge Aholah and Aholibah	Eze 23:36
W thou not tell us what these	Eze 24:19
W thou yet say before him that	Eze 28:9

W thou not shew us what thou Eze 37:18
what *w* thou give Hos 9:14
thou *w* cast all their sins into Mic 7:19
Thou *w* perform the truth to Jacob Mic 7:20
shall I cry, and thou *w* not hear Hab 1:2
of violence, and thou *w* not save Hab 1:2
I said, Surely thou *w* fear me Zeph 3:7
thou *w* receive instruction Zeph 3:7
how long *w* thou not have mercy on Zec 1:12
If thou *w* walk in my ways Zec 3:7
if thou *w* keep my charge, then Zec 3:7
if thou *w* fall down and worship me Mt 4:9
Or how *w* thou say to thy brother, Mt 7:4
him, saying, Lord, if thou *w* Mt 8:2 *2309*
W thou then that we go and gather Mt 13:28 *2309*
be it unto thee even as thou *w* Mt 15:28 *2309*
if thou *w*, let us make here three Mt 17:4 *2309*
but if thou *w* enter into life, Mt 19:17 *2309*
If thou *w* be perfect, go and sell Mt 19:21 *2309*
And he said unto her, What *w* thou Mt 20:21 *2309*
Where *w* thou that we prepare for Mt 26:17 *2309*
not as I will, but as thou *w* Mt 26:39
and saying unto him, If thou *w* Mk 1:40 *2309*
Ask of me whatsoever thou *w* Mk 6:22 *2309*
What *w* thou that I should do unto Mk 10:51 *2309*
Where *w* thou that we go and Mk 14:12 *2309*
not what I will, but what thou *w* Mk 14:36 *2309*
If thou therefore *w* worship me Lk 4:7
him, saying, Lord, if thou *w* Lk 5:12 *2309*
w thou that we command fire to Lk 9:54 *2309*
What *w* thou that I shall do unto Lk 18:41
Where *w* thou that we prepare Lk 22:9 *2309*
w thou rear it up in three days Jn 2:20
unto him, *W* thou be made whole Jn 5:6 *2309*
now, whatsoever thou *w* ask of God Jn 11:22
W thou lay down thy life for my Jn 13:38
how is it that thou *w* manifest Jn 14:22
w thou at this time restore again Acts 1:6
Because thou *w* not leave my soul Acts 2:27
neither *w* thou suffer thine Holy Acts 2:27
W thou kill me, as thou diddest Acts 7:28 *2309*
what *w* thou have me to do Acts 9:6 *2309*
w thou not cease to pervert the Acts 13:10
W thou go up to Jerusalem, and Acts 25:9
Thou *w* say then unto me, Why doth Rom 9:19
Thou *w* say then, The branches Rom 11:19
W thou then not be afraid of the Rom 13:3 *2309*
knowing that thou *w* also do more Philem 21
But *w* thou know, O vain man, that Jas 2:20 *2309*

WIMPLES
apparel, and the mantles, and the *w* Is 3:22 4304

WIN
thought to *w* them for himself 2Chr 32:1 1234
but dung, that I may *w* Christ Phil 3:8 *2770*

WIND
God made a *w* to pass over the Gen 8:1 7307
the east *w* sprung up after them Gen 41:6
thin, and blasted with the east *w* Gen 41:23
ears blasted with the east *w* Gen 41:27
the LORD brought an east *w* upon Ex 10:13 7307
the east *w* brought the locusts Ex 10:13 7307
turned a mighty strong west *w* Ex 10:19 7307
by a strong east *w* all that night Ex 14:21 7307
Thou didst blow with thy *w* Ex 15:10 7307
went forth a *w* from the LORD Num 11:31 7307
was seen upon the wings of the *w* 2Sa 22:11 7307
heaven was black with clouds and *w* 1Kin 18:45 7307
strong *w* rent the mountains, and 1Kin 19:11 7307
but the LORD was not in the *w* 1Kin 19:11 7307
after the *w* an earthquake 1Kin 19:11 7307
the LORD, Ye shall not see *w* 2Kin 3:17 7307
there came a great *w* from the Job 1:19 7307
that is desperate, which are as *w* Job 6:26 7307
O remember that my life is *w* Job 7:7 7307
of thy mouth be like a strong *w* Job 8:2 7307
and fill his belly with the east *w* Job 15:2 7307
They are as stubble before the *w* Job 21:18 7307
The east *w* carrieth him away, and Job 27:21
they pursue my soul as the *w* Job 30:15 7307
Thou liftest me up to the *w* Job 30:22 7307
quieteth the earth by the south *w* Job 37:17
but the *w* passeth, and cleanseth Job 37:21 7307
the east *w* upon the earth Job 38:24
chaff which the *w* driveth away Ps 1:4 7307
did fly upon the wings of the *w* Ps 18:10 7307
small as the dust before the *w* Ps 18:42 7307
Let them be as chaff before the *w* Ps 35:5 7307
ships of Tarshish with an east *w* Ps 48:7 7307
He caused an east *w* to blow in Ps 78:26
power he brought in the south *w* Ps 78:26
a *w* that passeth away, and cometh Ps 78:39 7307
as the stubble before the *w* Ps 83:13 7307
For the *w* passeth over it, and it Ps 103:16 7307
walketh upon the wings of the *w* Ps 104:3 7307
and raiseth the stormy *w*, which Ps 107:25 7307
he bringeth the *w* out of his Ps 135:7 7307
he causeth his *w* to blow, and the Ps 147:18 7307
stormy *w* fulfilling his word Ps 148:8 7307
his own house shall inherit the *w* Prov 11:29 7307
is like clouds and *w* without rain Prov 25:14 7307
The north *w* driveth away rain Prov 25:23 7307
Whosoever hideth her hideth the *w* Prov 27:16 7307
hath gathered the *w* in his fists Prov 30:4 7307
The *w* goeth toward the south, and Eccl 1:6 7307
the *w* returneth again according Eccl 1:6 7307
he that hath laboured for the *w* Eccl 5:16 7307
observeth the *w* shall not sow Eccl 11:4 7307
Awake, O north *w* Song 4:16
of the wood are moved with the *w* Is 7:2 7307
with his mighty *w* shall he shake Is 11:15 7307
of the mountains before the *w* Is 17:13 7307
have as it were brought forth *w* Is 26:18 7307
he stayeth his rough *w* in the day Is 27:8 7307
the day of the east *w* Is 27:8
be as an hiding place from the *w* Is 32:2 7307
the *w* shall carry them away, and Is 41:16 7307
their molten images are *w* Is 41:29 7307
but the *w* shall carry them all Is 57:13 7307
and our iniquities, like the *w* Is 64:6 7307
snuffeth up the *w* at her pleasure Jer 2:24 7307
A dry *w* of the high places in the Jer 4:11 7307
Even a full *w* from those places Jer 4:12 7307
And the prophets shall become *w* Jer 5:13 7307
bringeth forth the *w* out of his Jer 10:13 7307
away by the *w* of the wilderness Jer 13:24 7307
snuffed up the *w* like dragons Jer 14:6 7307
with an east *w* before the enemy Jer 18:17 7307
The *w* shall eat up all thy Jer 22:22 7307
up against me, a destroying *w* Jer 51:1 7307
bringeth forth the *w* out of his Jer 51:16 7307
part thou shalt scatter in the *w* Eze 5:2 7307
I will scatter toward every *w* all Eze 12:14 7307
and a stormy *w* shall rend it Eze 13:11 7307
it with a stormy *w* in my fury Eze 13:13 7307
when the east *w* toucheth it Eze 17:10 7307
the east *w* dried up her fruit Eze 19:12 7307
the east *w* hath broken thee in Eze 27:26 7307
he unto me, Prophesy unto the *w* Eze 37:9 7307
son of man, and say to the *w* Eze 37:9 7307
the *w* carried them away, that no Dan 2:35 7308
The *w* hath bound her up in her Hos 4:19 7307
For they have sown the *w*, and they Hos 8:7 7307
Ephraim feedeth on *w* Hos 12:1 7307
and followeth after the east *w* Hos 12:1
an east *w* shall come Hos 13:15
the *w* of the LORD shall come up Hos 13:15 7307
the mountains, and createth the *w* Amos 4:13 7307
sent out a great *w* into the sea Jonah 1:4 7307
God prepared a vehement east *w* Jonah 4:8 7307
faces shall sup up as the east *w* Hab 1:9
and the *w* was in their wings Zec 5:9 7307
A reed shaken with the *w* Mt 11:7 *417*
for the *w* was contrary Mt 14:24 *417*
But when he saw the *w* boisterous Mt 14:30 *417*
come into the ship, the *w* ceased Mt 14:32 *417*
And there arose a great storm of *w* Mk 4:37 *417*
And he arose, and rebuked the *w* Mk 4:39 *417*
the *w* ceased, and there was a Mk 4:39 *417*
of man is this, that even the *w* Mk 4:41 *417*
for the *w* was contrary unto them Mk 6:48 *417*
and the *w* ceased Mk 6:51 *417*
A reed shaken with the *w* Lk 7:24 *417*
down a storm of *w* on the lake Lk 8:23 *417*
Then he arose, and rebuked the *w* Lk 8:24 *417*
And when ye see the south *w* blow Lk 12:55
The *w* bloweth where it listeth, Jn 3:8 *4151*
by reason of a great *w* that blew Jn 6:18 *417*
heaven as of a rushing mighty *w* Acts 2:2 *4157*
the *w* not suffering us, we sailed Acts 27:7 *417*
And when the south *w* blew softly Acts 27:13
arose against it a tempestuous *w* Acts 27:14 *417*
and could not bear up into the *w* Acts 27:15 *417*
hoised up the mainsail to the *w* Acts 27:40 *4154*
and after one day the south *w* blew Acts 28:13
about with every *w* of doctrine Eph 4:14 *417*
wave of the sea driven with the *w* Jas 1:6 *416*
when she is shaken of a mighty *w* Rev 6:13 *417*
that the *w* should not blow on the Rev 7:1 *417*

WINDING
they went up with *w* stairs into 1Kin 6:8 3583
a *w* about still upward to the Eze 41:7 5437
for the *w* about of the house went Eze 41:7 4141

WINDOW
A *w* shalt thou make to the ark, Gen 6:16 6672
that Noah opened the *w* of the ark Gen 8:6 2474
the Philistines looked out at a *w* Gen 26:8 2474
them down by a cord through the *w* Josh 2:15 2474
line of scarlet thread in the *w* Josh 2:18 2474
bound the scarlet line in the *w* Josh 2:21 2474
of Sisera looked out at a *w* Judg 5:28 2474
Michal let David down through a *w* 1Sa 19:12 2474
daughter looked through a *w* 2Sa 6:16 2474
her head, and looked out at a *w* 2Kin 9:30 2474
And he lifted up his face to the *w* 2Kin 9:32 2474
And he said, Open the *w* eastward 2Kin 13:17 2474
out at a *w* saw king David dancing 1Chr 15:29 2474
For at the *w* of my house I looked Prov 7:6 2474
there sat in a *w* a certain young Acts 20:9 *2376*
through a *w* in a basket was I let 2Cor 11:33 *2376*

WINDOWS
the *w* of heaven were opened Gen 7:11 699
the *w* of heaven were stopped, and Gen 8:2 699
house he made *w* of narrow lights 1Kin 6:4 2474
there were *w* in three rows, and 1Kin 7:4 8261
and posts were square, with the *w* 1Kin 7:5 8260
the LORD would make *w* in heaven 2Kin 7:2 699
the LORD should make *w* in heaven 2Kin 7:19 699
look out of the *w* be darkened Eccl 12:3 699
wall, he looketh forth at the *w* Song 2:9 2474
for the *w* from on high are open, Is 24:18 699
And I will make thy *w* of agates Is 54:12 8121
cloud, and as the doves to their *w* Is 60:8 699
For death is come up into our *w* Jer 9:21 2474
chambers, and cutteth him out *w* Jer 22:14 2474
there were narrow *w* to the little Eze 40:16 2474
w were round about inward Eze 40:16 2474
And their *w*, and their arches, and Eze 40:22 2474
And there were *w* in it and in the Eze 40:25 2474
thereof round about, like those *w* Eze 40:25 2474
and there were *w* in it and in the Eze 40:29 2474
and there were *w* therein and in the Eze 40:33 2474
and the *w* to it round about Eze 40:36 2474
The door posts, and the narrow *w* Eze 41:16 2474
and from the ground up to the *w* Eze 41:16 2474
and the *w* were covered Eze 41:16 2474
And there were narrow *w* and palm Eze 41:26 2474
his *w* being open in his chamber Dan 6:10 3551
enter in at the *w* like a thief Joel 2:9 2474
their voice shall sing in the *w* Zeph 2:14 2474
will not open you the *w* of heaven Mal 3:10 699

WINDS
To make the weight for the *w* Job 28:25 7307
I will scatter into all *w* them Jer 49:32 7307
four *w* from the four quarters of Jer 49:36 7307
scatter them toward all those *w* Jer 49:36 7307
will I scatter into all the *w* Eze 5:10 7307
a third part into all the *w* Eze 5:12 7307
shall be scattered toward all *w* Eze 17:21 7307
Come from the four *w*, O breath, Eze 37:9 7307
the four *w* of the heaven strove Dan 7:2 7308
ones toward the four *w* of heaven Dan 8:8 7307
toward the four *w* of heaven Dan 11:4 7307
as the four *w* of the heaven Zec 2:6 7307
the *w* blew, and beat upon that Mt 7:25 *417*
the *w* blew, and beat upon that Mt 7:27 *417*
Then he arose, and rebuked the *w* Mt 8:26 *417*
of man is this, that even the *w* Mt 8:27 *417*
his elect from the four *w* Mt 24:31 *417*
his elect from the four *w* Mk 13:27 *417*
for he commandeth even the *w* Lk 8:25 *417*
because the *w* were contrary Acts 27:4 *417*
great, and are driven of fierce *w* Jas 3:4 *417*
without water, carried about of *w* Jude 12 *417*
holding the four *w* of the earth Rev 7:1 *417*

WINDY
hasten my escape from the *w* storm Ps 55:8 7307

WINE
And he drank of the *w*, and was Gen 9:21 3196
Noah awoke from his *w* Gen 9:24 3196
of Salem brought forth bread and *w* Gen 14:18 3196
let us make our father drink *w* Gen 19:32 3196
their father drink *w* that night Gen 19:33 3196
make him drink *w* this night also Gen 19:34 3196
father drink *w* that night also Gen 19:35 3196
and he brought him *w*, and he drank Gen 27:25 3196
the earth, and plenty of corn and *w* Gen 27:28 8492
corn and *w* have I sustained him Gen 27:37 8492
he washed his garments in *w* Gen 49:11 3196
His eyes shall be red with *w* Gen 49:12 3196
an hin of *w* for a drink offering Ex 29:40 3196
Do not drink *w* nor strong drink, Lev 10:9 3196
offering thereof shall be of *w* Lev 23:13 3196
He shall separate himself from *w* Num 6:3 3196
and shall drink no vinegar of *w* Num 6:3 3196
that the Nazarite may drink *w* Num 6:20 3196
the fourth part of an hin of *w* Num 15:5 3196
the third part of an hin of *w* Num 15:7 3196
a drink offering half an hin of *w* Num 15:10 3196
the oil, and all the best of the *w* Num 18:12 8492
shalt thou cause the strong *w* to Num 28:7 7491
half an hin of *w* unto a bullock Num 28:14 3196
of thy land, thy corn, and thy *w* Deut 7:13 8492
gather in thy corn, and thy *w* Deut 11:14 8492
tithe of thy corn, or of thy *w* Deut 12:17 8492
the tithe of thy corn, of thy *w* Deut 14:23 8492
for oxen, or for sheep, or for *w* Deut 14:26 3196
gathered in thy corn and thy *w* Deut 16:13 3342
also of thy corn, of thy *w* Deut 18:4 8492
but shalt neither drink of the *w* Deut 28:39 3196
not leave thee either corn, *w* Deut 28:51 8492
have ye drunk *w* or strong drink Deut 29:6 3196
Their *w* is the poison of dragons, Deut 32:33 3196
drank the *w* of their drink Deut 32:38 3196
shall be upon a land of corn and *w* Deut 33:28 8492
w bottles, old, and rent, and bound Josh 9:4 3196
And these bottles of *w*, which we Josh 9:13 3196
unto them, Should I leave my *w* Judg 9:13 8492
drink not *w* nor strong drink, and Judg 13:4 3196
now drink no *w* nor strong drink, Judg 13:7 3196
let her drink *w* or strong drink Judg 13:14 3196
w also for me, and for thy Judg 19:19 3196
put away thy *w* from thee 1Sa 1:14 3196
neither *w* nor strong drink 1Sa 1:15 3196
ephah of flour, and a bottle of *w* 1Sa 1:24 3196
and another carrying a bottle of *w* 1Sa 10:3 3196
with bread, and a bottle of *w* 1Sa 16:20 3196
loaves, and two bottles of *w* 1Sa 25:18 3196
when the *w* was gone out of Nabal, 1Sa 25:37 3196
piece of flesh, and a flagon of *w* 2Sa 6:19
Amnon's heart is merry with *w* 2Sa 13:28 3196
summer fruits, and a bottle of *w* 2Sa 16:1 3196
and the *w*, that such as be faint 2Sa 16:2 3196
own land, a land of corn and *w* 2Kin 18:32 8492
and the fine flour, and the *w* 1Chr 9:29 3196
figs, and bunches of raisins, and *w* 1Chr 12:40 3196
piece of flesh, and a flagon of *w* 1Chr 16:3
of the vineyards for the *w* 1Chr 27:27 3196
and twenty thousand baths of *w* 2Chr 2:10 3196
and the barley, the oil, and the *w* 2Chr 2:15 3196
store of victual, and of oil and *w* 2Chr 11:11 3196
the firstfruits of corn, *w* 2Chr 31:5 8492
for the increase of corn, and *w* 2Chr 32:28 8492
the God of heaven, wheat, salt, *w* Ezr 6:9 2562
and to an hundred baths of *w* Ezr 7:22 2562
the king, that *w* was before him Neh 2:1 3196
and I took up the *w*, and gave it Neh 2:1 3196
the money, and of the corn, the *w* Neh 5:11 8492
and had taken of them bread and *w* Neh 5:15 3196
ten days store of all sorts of *w* Neh 5:18 3196
of all manner of trees, of *w* Neh 10:37 8492
of the corn, of the new *w* Neh 10:39 8492
the tithes of the corn, the new *w* Neh 13:5 8492
tithe of the corn and the new *w* Neh 13:12 8492
as also *w*, grapes, and figs, and Neh 13:15 3196
royal *w* in abundance, according Est 1:7 3196
of the king was merry with *w* Est 1:10 3196

unto Esther at the banquet of *w* Est 5:6 3196
second day at the banquet of *w* Est 7:2 3196
of *w* in his wrath went into the Est 7:7 3196
the place of the banquet of *w* Est 7:8 3196
drinking *w* in their eldest Job 1:13 3196
drinking *w* in their eldest Job 1:18 3196
my belly is as *w* which hath no Job 32:19 3196
their corn and their *w* increased Ps 4:7 8492
us to drink the *w* of astonishment Ps 60:3 3196
there is a cup, and the *w* is red Ps 75:8 3196
man that shouteth by reason of *w* Ps 78:65 3196
w that maketh glad the heart of Ps 104:15 3196
shall burst out with new *w* Prov 3:10 8492
and drink the *w* of violence Prov 4:17 3196
she hath mingled her *w* Prov 9:2 3196
drink of the *w* which I have Prov 9:5 3196
W is a mocker, strong drink is Prov 20:1 3196
he that loveth *w* and oil shall not Prov 21:17 3196
They that tarry long at the *w* Prov 23:30 3196
they that go to seek mixed *w* Prov 23:30 4469
thou upon the *w* when it is red Prov 23:31 3196
it is not for kings to drink *w* Prov 31:4 3196
w unto those that be of heavy Prov 31:6 3196
mine heart to give myself unto *w* Eccl 2:3 3196
drink thy *w* with a merry heart Eccl 9:7 3196
for laughter, and *w* maketh merry Eccl 10:19 3196
for thy love is better than *w* Song 1:2 3196
remember thy love more than *w* Song 1:4 3196
much better is thy love than *w* Song 4:10 3196
I have drunk my *w* with my milk Song 5:1 3196
like the best *w* for my beloved Song 7:9 3196
cause thee to drink of spiced *w* Song 8:2 3196
dross, thy *w* mixed with water Is 1:22 5435
until night, till *w* inflame them Is 5:11 3196
viol, the tabret, and pipe, and *w* Is 5:12 3196
them that are mighty to drink *w* Is 5:22 3196
tread out no *w* in their presses Is 16:10 3196
eating flesh, and drinking *w* Is 22:13 3196
The new *w* mourneth, the vine Is 24:7 8492
shall not drink *w* with a song Is 24:9 3196
is a crying for *w* in the streets Is 24:11 3196
ye unto her, A vineyard of red *w* Is 27:2 2561
of them that are overcome with *w* Is 28:1 3196
they also have erred through *w* Is 28:7 3196
drink, they are swallowed up of *w* Is 28:7 3196
they are drunken, but not with *w* Is 29:9 3196
own land, a land of corn and *w* Is 36:17 8492
their own blood, as with sweet *w* Is 49:26 6071
and drunken, but not with *w* Is 51:21 3196
yea, come, buy *w* and milk without Is 55:1 3196
Come ye, say they, I will fetch *w* Is 56:12 3196
stranger shall not drink thy *w* Is 62:8 8492
As the new *w* is found in the Is 65:8 8492
bottle shall be filled with *w* Jer 13:12 3196
bottle shall be filled with *w* Jer 13:12 3196
like a man whom *w* hath overcome Jer 23:9 3196
Take the *w* cup of this fury at my Jer 25:15 3196
of the LORD, for wheat, and for *w* Jer 31:12 8492
chambers, and give them *w* to drink Jer 35:2 3196
of the Rechabites pots full of *w* Jer 35:5 3196
and I said unto them, Drink ye *w* Jer 35:5 3196
But they said, We will drink no *w* Jer 35:6 3196
us, saying, Ye shall drink no *w* Jer 35:6 3196
to drink no *w* all our days, we, Jer 35:8 3196
commanded his sons not to drink *w* Jer 35:14 3196
but ye, gather ye *w*, and summer Jer 40:10 3196
unto Mizpah, and gathered *w* Jer 40:12 3196
I have caused *w* to fail from the Jer 48:33 3196
the nations have drunken of her *w* Jer 51:7 3196
their mothers, Where is corn and *w* Lam 2:12 3196
in the *w* of Helbon, and white wool Eze 27:18 3196
Neither shall any priest drink *w* Eze 44:21 3196
meat, and of the *w* which he drank Dan 1:5 3196
nor with the *w* which he drank Dan 1:8 3196
the *w* that they should drink Dan 1:16 3196
drank *w* before the thousand Dan 5:1 2562
whiles he tasted the *w*, Dan 5:2 2562
They drank *w*, and praised the gods Dan 5:4 2562
concubines, have drunk *w* in them Dan 5:23 2562
came flesh nor *w* in my mouth Dan 10:3 3196
know that I gave her corn, and *w* Hos 2:8 8492
my *w* in the season thereof, and Hos 2:9 8492
shall hear the corn, and the *w* Hos 2:22 8492
other gods, and love flagons of *w* Hos 3:1 6025
Whoredom and *w* and new Hos 4:11 3196
new *w* take away the heart Hos 4:11 8492
made him sick with bottles of *w* Hos 7:5 3196
assemble themselves for corn and *w* Hos 7:14 8492
the new *w* shall fail in her Hos 9:2 8492
They shall not offer *w* offerings Hos 9:4 3196
shall be as the *w* of Lebanon Hos 14:7 3196
and howl, all ye drinkers of *w* Joel 1:5 3196
because of the new *w* Joel 1:5 6071
the new *w* is dried up, the oil Joel 1:10 8492
I will send you corn, and *w* Joel 2:19 8492
and the fats shall overflow with *w* Joel 2:24 8492
an harlot, and sold a girl for *w* Joel 3:3 3196
mountains shall drop down new *w* Joel 3:18 6071
they drink the *w* of the condemned Amos 2:8 3196
ye gave the Nazarites *w* to drink Amos 2:12 3196
but ye shall not drink *w* of them Amos 5:11 3196
That drink *w* in bowls, and anoint Amos 6:6 3196
the mountains shall drop sweet *w* Amos 9:13 6071
vineyards, and drink the *w* thereof Amos 9:14 3196
I will prophesy unto thee of *w* Mic 2:11 3196
with oil; and sweet *w* Mic 6:15 8492
but shalt not drink *w* Mic 6:15 3196
because he transgresseth by *w* Hab 2:5 3196
but not drink the *w* thereof Zeph 1:13 3196
upon the corn, and upon the new *w* Hag 1:11 8492
do touch bread, or pottage, or *w* Hag 2:12 3196
and make a noise as through *w* Zec 9:15 3196
men cheerful, and new *w* the maids Zec 9:17 8492
heart shall rejoice as through *w* Zec 10:7 3196

do men put new *w* into old bottles Mt 9:17 *3631*
the *w* runneth out, and the bottles Mt 9:17 *3631*
they put new *w* into new bottles Mt 9:17 *3631*
putteth new *w* into old bottles Mk 2:22 *3631*
else the new *w* doth burst the Mk 2:22 *3631*
the *w* is spilled, and the bottles Mk 2:22 *3631*
but new *w* must be put into new Mk 2:22 *3631*
him to drink *w* mingled with myrrh Mk 15:23 *3631*
drink neither *w* nor strong drink Lk 1:15 *3631*
putteth new *w* into old bottles Lk 5:37 *3631*
else the new *w* will burst the Lk 5:37 *3631*
But new *w* must be put into new Lk 5:38 *3631*
old *w* straightway desireth new Lk 5:39
eating bread nor drinking *w* Lk 7:33 *3631*
his wounds, pouring in oil and *w* Lk 10:34 *3631*
And when they wanted *w*, the mother Jn 2:3 *3631*
saith unto him, They have no *w* Jn 2:3 *3631*
tasted the water that was made *w* Jn 2:9 *3631*
beginning doth set forth good *w* Jn 2:10 *3631*
hast kept the good *w* until now Jn 2:10 *3631*
where he made the water *w* Jn 4:46 *3631*
said, These men are full of new *w* Acts 2:13 *1098*
to eat flesh, nor to drink *w* Rom 14:21 *3631*
And be not drunk with *w*, wherein Eph 5:18 *3631*
Not given to *w*, no striker, not 1Ti 3:3 *3943*
not given to much *w*, not greedy 1Ti 3:8 *3631*
but use a little *w* for thy 1Ti 5:23 *3631*
not soon angry, not given to *w* Titus 1:7 *3943*
accusers, not given to much *w* Titus 2:3 *3631*
lusts, excess of *w*, revellings, 1Pet 4:3 *3632*
thou hurt not the oil and the *w* Rev 6:6 *3631*
made all nations drink of the *w* Rev 14:8 *3631*
of the *w* of the wrath of God Rev 14:10 *3631*
w of the fierceness of his wrath Rev 16:19 *3631*
with the *w* of her fornication Rev 17:2 *3631*
all nations have drunk of the *w* Rev 18:3 *3631*
ointments, and frankincense, and *w* Rev 18:13 *3631*

WINEBIBBER
Behold a man gluttonous, and a *w* Mt 11:19 *3630*
Behold a gluttonous man, and a *w* Lk 7:34

WINEBIBBERS
Be not among *w* Prov 23:20

WINEFAT
like him that treadeth in the *w* Is 63:2 1660
it, and digged a place for the *w* Mk 12:1 *5276*

WINEPRESS
and as the fulness of the *w* Num 18:27 3342
and as the increase of the *w* Num 18:30 3342
out of thy floor, and out of thy *w* Deut 15:14 3342
Gideon threshed wheat by the *w* Judg 6:11 1660
Zeeb they slew at the *w* of Zeeb Judg 7:25 3342
of the barnfloor, or out of the *w* 2Kin 6:27 3342
of it, and also made a *w* therein Is 5:2 3342
I have trodden the *w* alone Is 63:3 6333
the daughter of Judah, as in a *w* Lam 1:15 1660
the *w* shall not feed them, and the Hos 9:2 3342
round about, and digged a *w* in it Mt 21:33 *3025*
the great *w* of the wrath of God Rev 14:19 *3025*
the *w* was trodden without the Rev 14:20 *3025*
city, and blood came out of the *w* Rev 14:20 *3025*
and he treadeth the *w* of the Rev 19:15

WINEPRESSES
some treading *w* on the sabbath Neh 13:15 1660
their walls, and tread their *w* Job 24:11 3342
caused wine to fail from the *w* Jer 48:33 3342
of Hananeel unto the king's *w* Zec 14:10 3342

WINES
a feast of *w* on the lees, of fat Is 25:6 8105
of *w* on the lees well refined Is 25:6 8105

WING
was the one *w* of the cherub 1Kin 6:24 3671
cubits the other *w* of the cherub 1Kin 6:24 3671
the uttermost part of the one *w* 1Kin 6:24 3671
so that the *w* of the one touched 1Kin 6:27 3671
the *w* of the other cherub touched 1Kin 6:27 3671
one *w* of the one cherub was five 2Chr 3:11 3671
the other *w* was likewise five 2Chr 3:11 3671
reaching to the *w* of the other 2Chr 3:11 3671
one *w* of the other cherub was 2Chr 3:12 3671
the other *w* was five cubits also, 2Chr 3:12 3671
joining to the *w* of the other 2Chr 3:12 3671
there was none that moved the *w* Is 10:14 3671
shall dwell all fowl of every *w* Eze 17:23 3671

WINGED
every *w* fowl after his kind Gen 1:21 3671
the likeness of any *w* fowl that Deut 4:17 3671

WINGS
and how I bare you on eagles' *w* Ex 19:4 3671
stretch forth their *w* on high Ex 25:20 3671
the mercy seat with their *w* Ex 25:20 3671
spread out their *w* on high Ex 37:9 3671
covered with their *w* over the Ex 37:9 3671
cleave it with the *w* thereof Lev 1:17 3671
her young, spreadeth abroad her *w* Deut 32:11 3671
them, beareth them on her *w* Deut 32:11 84
under whose *w* thou art come to Ruth 2:12 3671
was seen upon the *w* of the wind 2Sa 22:11 3671
forth the *w* of the cherubims 1Kin 6:27 3671
their *w* touched one another in 1Kin 6:27 3671
even under the *w* of the cherubims 1Kin 8:6 3671
spread forth their two *w* over the 1Kin 8:7 3671
that spread out their *w*, and 1Chr 28:18
the *w* of the cherubims were 2Chr 3:11 3671
The *w* of these cherubims spread 2Chr 3:13 3671
even under the *w* of the cherubims 2Chr 5:7 3671
their *w* over the place of the ark 2Chr 5:8 3671
the goodly *w* unto the peacocks Job 39:13 3671
or *w* and feathers unto the ostrich Job 39:13 34
stretch her *w* toward the south Job 39:26 3671

hide me under the shadow of thy *w* Ps 17:8 3671
he did fly upon the *w* of the wind Ps 18:10 3671
trust under the shadow of thy *w* Ps 36:7 3671
said, Oh that I had *w* like a dove Ps 55:6 83
in the shadow of thy *w* will I Ps 57:1 3671
will trust in the covert of thy *w* Ps 61:4 3671
shadow of thy *w* will I rejoice Ps 63:7 3671
yet shall ye be as the *w* of a Ps 68:13 3671
under his *w* shalt thou trust Ps 91:4 3671
walketh upon the *w* of the wind Ps 104:3 3671
If I take the *w* of the morning, Ps 139:9 3671
certainly make themselves *w* Prov 23:5 3671
that which hath *w* shall tell the Eccl 10:20 3671
each one had six *w* Is 6:2 3671
the stretching out of his *w* shall Is 8:8 3671
Woe to the land shadowing with *w* Is 18:1 3671
shall mount up with *w* as eagles Is 40:31 83
Give *w* unto Moab, that it may Jer 48:9 6731
and shall spread his *w* over Moab Jer 48:40 3671
and spread his *w* over Bozrah Jer 49:22 3671
faces, and every one had four *w* Eze 1:6 3671
under their *w* on their four sides Eze 1:8 3671
four had their faces and their *w* Eze 1:8 3671
Their *w* were joined one to Eze 1:9 3671
their *w* were stretched upward Eze 1:11 3671
two *w* of every one were joined Eze 1:11
firmament were their *w* straight Eze 1:23 3671
I heard the noise of their *w* Eze 1:24 3671
they stood, they let down their *w* Eze 1:24 3671
stood, and had let down their *w* Eze 1:25 3671
w of the living creatures that Eze 3:13 3671
w was heard even to the outer Eze 10:5 3671
of a man's hand under their *w* Eze 10:8 3671
backs, and their hands, and their *w* Eze 10:12 3671
w to mount up from the earth Eze 10:16 3671
the cherubims lifted up their *w* Eze 10:19 3671
faces apiece, and every one four *w* Eze 10:21 3671
hands of a man was under their *w* Eze 10:21 3671
did the cherubims lift up their *w* Eze 11:22 3671
A great eagle with great *w* Eze 17:3 3671
another great eagle with great *w* Eze 17:7 3671
was like a lion, and had eagle's *w* Dan 7:4 1611
I beheld till the *w* thereof were Dan 7:4 1611
the back of it four *w* of a fowl Dan 7:6 1611
wind hath bound her up in her *w* Hos 4:19 3671
women, and the wind was in their *w* Zec 5:9 3671
had *w* like the *w* of a stork Zec 5:9 3671
arise with healing in his *w* Mal 4:2 3671
her chickens under her *w*, and ye Mt 23:37 *4420*
doth gather her brood under her *w* Lk 13:34 *4420*
had each of them six *w* about him Rev 4:8 *4420*
the sound of their *w* was as the Rev 9:9 *4420*
were given two *w* of a great eagle Rev 12:14 *4420*

WINK
and what do thy eyes *w* at, Job 15:12 7335
neither let them *w* with the eye Ps 35:19 7169

WINKED
times of this ignorance God *w* at Acts 17:30 *5237*

WINKETH
He *w* with his eyes, he speaketh Prov 6:13 7169
He that *w* with the eye causeth Prov 10:10 7169

WINNETH
and he that *w* souls is wise Prov 11:30 3947

WINNOWED
which hath been *w* with the shovel Is 30:24 2219

WINNOWETH
he *w* barley to night in the Ruth 3:2 2219

WINTER
and cold and heat, and summer and *w* Gen 8:22 2779
thou hast made summer and *w* Ps 74:17 2779
the *w* is past, the rain is over Song 2:11 5638
of the earth shall *w* upon them Is 18:6 2778
I will smite the *w* house with the Amos 3:15 2779
in summer and in *w* shall it be Zec 14:8 2778
that your flight be not in the *w* Mt 24:20 *5494*
that your flight be not in the *w* Mk 13:18 *5494*
of the dedication, and it was *w* Jn 10:22 *5494*
haven was not commodious to *w* in Acts 27:12 *3915*
attain to Phenice, and there to *w* Acts 27:12 *3914*
w with you, that ye may bring me 1Cor 16:6 *3914*
Do thy diligence to come before *w* 2Ti 4:21 *5494*
for I have determined there to *w* Titus 3:12 *3914*

WINTERED
which had *w* in the isle, whose Acts 28:11 *3916*

WINTERHOUSE
sat in the *w* in the ninth month Jer 36:22 2779

WIPE
I will *w* Jerusalem as a man 2Kin 21:13 4229
w not out my good deeds that I Neh 13:14 4229
the Lord GOD will *w* away tears Is 25:8 4229
did *w* them with the hairs of her Lk 7:38 *1591*
on us, we do *w* off against you Lk 10:11 *631*
feet, and to *w* them with the towel Jn 13:5 *1591*
God shall *w* away all tears from Rev 7:17 *1813*
God shall *w* away all tears from Rev 21:4 *1813*

WIPED
his reproach shall not be *w* away Prov 6:33 4229
w them with the hairs of her head Lk 7:44 *1591*
w his feet with her hair, whose Jn 11:2 *1591*
and *w* his feet with her hair Jn 12:3 *1591*

WIPETH
wipe Jerusalem as a man *w* a dish 2Kin 21:13 4229
w her mouth, and saith, I have Prov 30:20 4229

WIPING
w it, and turning it upside down 2Kin 21:13 4229

WIRES
thin plates, and cut it into *w* Ex 39:3 6616

WISDOM
have filled with the spirit of *w* Ex 28:3 2451
him with the spirit of God, in *w* Ex 31:3 2451
are wise hearted I have put *w* Ex 31:6 2451
them up in *w* spun goats' hair Ex 35:26 2451
him with the spirit of God, in *w* Ex 35:31 2451
hath he filled with *w* of heart Ex 35:35 2451
man, in whom the LORD put *w* Ex 36:1 2451
in whose heart the LORD had put *w* Ex 36:2 2451
for this is your *w* and your Deut 4:6 2451
Nun was full of the spirit of *w* Deut 34:9 2451
according to the *w* of an angel of 2Sa 14:20 2451
went unto all the people in her *w* 2Sa 20:22 2451
Do therefore according to thy *w* 1Kin 2:6 2451
saw that the *w* of God was in him 1Kin 3:28 2451
And God gave Solomon *w* and 1Kin 4:29 2451
Solomon's *w* excelled the *w* 1Kin 4:30 2451
country, and all the *w* of Egypt 1Kin 4:30 2451
people to hear the *w* of Solomon 1Kin 4:34 2451
earth, which had heard of his *w* 1Kin 4:34 2451
And the LORD gave Solomon *w* 1Kin 5:12 2451
and he was filled with *w*, and 1Kin 7:14 2451
of Sheba had seen all Solomon's *w* 1Kin 10:4 2451
own land of thy acts and of thy *w* 1Kin 10:6 2451
thy *w* and prosperity exceedeth the 1Kin 10:7 2451
before thee, and that hear thy *w* 1Kin 10:8 2451
of the earth for riches and for *w* 1Kin 10:23 2451
sought to Solomon, to hear his *w* 1Kin 10:24 2451
and all that he did, and his *w* 1Kin 11:41 2451
Only the LORD give thee *w* 1Chr 22:12 7922
Give me now *w* and knowledge, that 2Chr 1:10 2451
but hast asked *w* and knowledge for 2Chr 1:11 2451
W and knowledge is granted unto 2Chr 1:12 2451
Sheba had seen the *w* of Solomon 2Chr 9:3 2451
land of thine acts, and of thy *w* 2Chr 9:5 2451
of thy *w* was not told me 2Chr 9:6 2451
before thee, and hear thy *w* 2Chr 9:7 2451
kings of the earth in riches and *w* 2Chr 9:22 2451
of Solomon, to hear his *w* 2Chr 9:23 2451
after the *w* of thy God, that is Ezr 7:25 2452
they die, even without *w* Job 4:21 2451
is *w* driven quite from me Job 6:13 8454
would shew thee the secrets of *w* Job 11:6 2451
people, and *w* shall die with you Job 12:2 2451
With the ancient is *w* Job 12:12 2451
With him is *w* and strength, he Job 12:13 2451
With him is strength and *w* Job 12:16 8454
and it should be your *w* Job 13:5 2451
dost thou restrain *w* to thyself Job 15:8 2451
thou counseled him that hath no *w* Job 26:3 2451
But where shall *w* be found Job 28:12 2451
the price of *w* is above rubies Job 28:18 2451
Whence then cometh *w* Job 28:20 2451
the fear of the LORD, that is *w* Job 28:28 2451
multitude of years should teach *w* Job 32:7 2451
should say, We have found out *w* Job 32:13 2451
peace, and I shall teach thee *w* Job 33:33 2451
and his words were without *w* Job 34:35 7919
he is mighty in strength and *w* Job 36:5 3820
Who hath put *w* in the inward Job 38:36 2451
Who can number the clouds in *w* Job 38:37 2451
God hath deprived her of *w* Job 39:17 2451
Doth the hawk fly by thy *w* Job 39:26 998
mouth of the righteous speaketh *w* Ps 37:30 2451
My mouth shall speak of *w* Ps 49:3 2454
part thou shalt make me to know *w* Ps 51:6 2451
we may apply our hearts unto *w* Ps 90:12 2451
In *w* hast thou made them all Ps 104:24 2451
and teach his senators *w* Ps 105:22 2449
of the LORD is the beginning of *w* Ps 111:10 2451
To him that by *w* made the heavens Ps 136:5 8394
To know *w* and instruction Prov 1:2 2451
To receive the instruction of *w* Prov 1:3 7919
but fools despise *w* and Prov 1:7 2451
W crieth without Prov 1:20 2454
thou incline thine ear unto *w* Prov 2:2 2451
For the LORD giveth *w* Prov 2:6 2451
up sound *w* for the righteous Prov 2:7 8454
When *w* entereth into thine heart, Prov 2:10 2451
Happy is the man that findeth *w* Prov 3:13 2451
The LORD by *w* hath founded the Prov 3:19 2451
keep sound *w* and discretion Prov 3:21 8454
Get *w*, get understanding Prov 4:5 2451
W is the principal thing Prov 4:7 2451
therefore get *w* Prov 4:7 2451
have taught thee in the way of *w* Prov 4:11 2451
My son, attend unto my *w*, and bow Prov 5:1 2451
Say unto *w*, Thou art my sister Prov 7:4 2451
Doth not *w* cry Prov 8:1 2451
O ye simple, understand *w* Prov 8:5 6195
For *w* is better than rubies Prov 8:11 2451
I *w* dwell with prudence, and find Prov 8:12 2451
Counsel is mine, and sound *w* Prov 8:14 8454
W hath builded her house, she Prov 9:1 2454
of the LORD is the beginning of *w* Prov 9:10 2451
hath understanding *w* is found Prov 10:13 2451
but fools die for want of *w* Prov 10:21 3820
but a man of understanding hath *w* Prov 10:23 2451
of the just bringeth forth *w* Prov 10:31 2451
but with the lowly is *w* Prov 11:2 2451
He that is void of *w* despiseth Prov 11:12 3820
be commended according to his *w* Prov 12:8 7922
but with the well advised is *w* Prov 13:10 2451
A scorner seeketh *w*, and findeth Prov 14:6 2451
The *w* of the prudent is to Prov 14:8 2451
W resteth in the heart of him Prov 14:33 2451
joy to him that is destitute of *w* Prov 15:21 3820
the LORD is the instruction of *w* Prov 15:33 2451
better is it to get *w* than gold Prov 16:16 2451
in the hand of a fool to get *w* Prov 17:16 2451
W is before him that hath Prov 17:24 2451
and intermeddleth with all *w* Prov 18:1 8454
the wellspring of *w* as a flowing Prov 18:4 2451
He that getteth *w* loveth his own Prov 19:8 3820
There is no *w* nor understanding Prov 21:30 2451
cease from thine own *w* Prov 23:4 998
will despise the *w* of thy words Prov 23:9 7922
also *w*, and instruction, and Prov 23:23 2451
Through *w* is an house builded Prov 24:3 2451
W is too high for a fool Prov 24:7 2454
knowledge of *w* be unto thy soul Prov 24:14 2451
Whoso loveth *w* rejoiceth his Prov 29:3 2451
The rod and reproof give *w* Prov 29:15 2451
I neither learned *w*, nor have the Prov 30:3 2451
She openeth her mouth with *w* Prov 31:26 2451
search out by *w* concerning all Eccl 1:13 2451
have gotten more *w* than all they Eccl 1:16 2451
heart had great experience of *w* Eccl 1:16 2451
And I gave my heart to know *w* Eccl 1:17 2451
For in much *w* is much grief Eccl 1:18 2451
yet acquainting mine heart with *w* Eccl 2:3 2451
also my *w* remained with me Eccl 2:9 2451
And I turned myself to behold *w* Eccl 2:12 2451
Then I saw that *w* excelleth folly Eccl 2:13 2451
is a man whose labour is in *w* Eccl 2:21 2451
a man that is good in his sight *w* Eccl 2:26 2451
W is good with an inheritance Eccl 7:11 2451
For *w* is a defence, and money is a Eccl 7:12 2451
that *w* giveth life to them that Eccl 7:12 2451
W strengtheneth the wise more Eccl 7:19 2451
All this have I proved by *w* Eccl 7:23 2451
and to search, and to seek out *w* Eccl 7:25 2451
a man's *w* maketh his face to Eccl 8:1 2451
I applied mine heart to know *w* Eccl 8:16 2451
nor device, nor knowledge, nor *w* Eccl 9:10 2451
This *w* have I seen also under the Eccl 9:13 2451
he by his *w* delivered the city Eccl 9:15 2451
W is better than strength Eccl 9:16 2451
the poor man's *w* is despised Eccl 9:16 2451
W is better than weapons of war Eccl 9:18 2451
him that is in reputation for *w* Eccl 10:1 2451
his *w* faileth him, and he saith to Eccl 10:3 3820
but *w* is profitable to direct Eccl 10:10 2451
hand I have done it, and by my *w* Is 10:13 2451
rest upon him, the spirit of *w* Is 11:2 2451
for the *w* of their wise men shall Is 29:14 2451
And *w* and knowledge shall be the Is 33:6 2451
Thy *w* and thy knowledge, it hath Is 47:10 2451
and what *w* is in them Jer 8:9 2451
not the wise man glory in his *w* Jer 9:23 2451
established the world by his *w* Jer 10:12 2451
Is *w* no more in Teman Jer 49:7 2451
is their *w* vanished Jer 49:7 2451
established the world by his *w* Jer 51:15 2451
With thy *w* and with thine Eze 28:4 2451
By thy great *w* and by thy traffick Eze 28:5 2451
against the beauty of thy *w* Eze 28:7 2451
sealest up the sum, full of *w* Eze 28:12 2451
thou hast corrupted thy *w* by Eze 28:17 2451
favoured, and skilful in all *w* Dan 1:4 2451
and skill in all learning and *w* Dan 1:17 2451
And in all matters of *w* and Dan 1:20 2451
w to Arioch the captain of the Dan 2:14 2942
for *w* and might are his Dan 2:20 2452
he giveth *w* unto the wise, and Dan 2:21 2452
my fathers, who hast given me *w* Dan 2:23 2452
any *w* that I have more than any Dan 2:30 2452
light and understanding and *w* Dan 5:11 2452
like the *w* of the gods, was found Dan 5:11 2452
excellent *w* is found in thee Dan 5:14 2452
the man of *w* shall see thy name Mic 6:9 8454
But *w* is justified of her Mt 11:19 4678
earth to hear the *w* of Solomon Mt 12:42 4678
said, Whence hath this man this *w* Mt 13:54 4678
what *w* is this which is given Mk 6:2 4678
disobedient to the *w* of the just Lk 1:17 5428
strong in spirit, filled with *w* Lk 2:40 4678
And Jesus increased in *w* Lk 2:52 4678
But *w* is justified of all her Lk 7:35 4678
earth to hear the *w* of Solomon Lk 11:31 4678
Therefore also said the *w* of God Lk 11:49 4678
For I will give you a mouth and *w* Lk 21:15 4678
full of the Holy Ghost and *w* Acts 6:3 4678
were not able to resist the *w* Acts 6:10 4678
w in the sight of Pharaoh king of Acts 7:10 4678
in all the *w* of the Egyptians Acts 7:22 4678
depth of the riches both of the *w* Rom 11:33 4678
not with *w* of words, lest the 1Cor 1:17 4678
I will destroy the *w* of the wise 1Cor 1:19 4678
made foolish the *w* of this world 1Cor 1:20 4678
For after that in the *w* of God 1Cor 1:21 4678
God the world by *w* knew not God 1Cor 1:21 4678
sign, and the Greeks seek after *w* 1Cor 1:22 4678
the power of God, and the *w* of God 1Cor 1:24 4678
who of God is made unto us *w* 1Cor 1:30 4678
with excellency of speech or of *w* 1Cor 2:1 4678
with enticing words of man's *w* 1Cor 2:4 4678
should not stand in the *w* of men 1Cor 2:5 4678
Howbeit we speak *w* among them 1Cor 2:6 4678
yet not the *w* of this world, nor 1Cor 2:6 4678
But we speak the *w* of God in a 1Cor 2:7 4678
in a mystery, even the hidden *w* 1Cor 2:7
the words which man's *w* teacheth 1Cor 2:13 4678
For the *w* of this world is 1Cor 3:19 4678
given by the Spirit the word of *w* 1Cor 12:8 4678
sincerity, not with fleshly *w* 2Cor 1:12 4678
hath abounded toward us in all *w* Eph 1:8 4678
may give unto you the spirit of *w* Eph 1:17 4678
the church the manifold *w* of God Eph 3:10 4678
knowledge of his will in all *w* Col 1:9 4678
and teaching every man in all *w* Col 1:28 4678
are hid all the treasures of *w* Col 2:3 4678
a shew of *w* in will worship Col 2:23 4678
dwell in you richly in all *w* Col 3:16 4678
Walk in *w* toward them that are Col 4:5 4678
If any of you lack *w*, let him ask Jas 1:5 4678
his works with meekness of *w* Jas 3:13 4678
This *w* descendeth not from above, Jas 3:15 4678
But the *w* that is from above is Jas 3:17 4678
Paul also according to the *w* 2Pet 3:15 4678
to receive power, and riches, and *w* Rev 5:12 4678
Blessing, and glory, and *w*, and Rev 7:12 4678
Here is *w* Rev 13:18 4678
And here is the mind which hath *w* Rev 17:9 4678

WISE
tree to be desired to make one *w* Gen 3:6 7919
Egypt, and all the *w* men thereof Gen 41:8 2450
look out a man discreet and *w* Gen 41:33 2450
none so discreet and *w* as thou art Gen 41:39 2450
Pharaoh also called the *w* men Ex 7:11 2450
If thou afflict them in any *w* Ex 22:23 6031
for the gift blindeth the *w* Ex 23:8 6493
speak unto all that are *w* hearted Ex 28:3 2450
are *w* hearted I have put wisdom Ex 31:6 2450
every *w* hearted among you shall Ex 35:10 2450
all the women that were *w* hearted Ex 35:25 2450
every *w* hearted man, in whom the Ex 36:1 2450
every *w* hearted man, in whose Ex 36:2 2450
And all the *w* men, that wrought Ex 36:4 2450
every *w* hearted man among them Ex 36:8 2450
but ye shall in no *w* eat of it Lev 7:24
thou shalt in any *w* rebuke thy Lev 19:17 3198
the field will in any *w* redeem it Lev 27:19
On this *w* ye shall bless the Num 6:23
Take you *w* men, and understanding, Deut 1:13 2450
w men, and known, and made them Deut 1:15 2450
Surely this great nation is a *w* Deut 4:6 2450
gift doth blind the eyes of the *w* Deut 16:19 2450
Thou shalt in any *w* set him king Deut 17:15
shalt in any *w* bury him that day Deut 21:23
shalt in any *w* let the dam go Deut 22:7
O that they were *w*, that they Deut 32:29 2449
in any *w* keep yourselves from the Josh 6:18
Else if ye do in any *w* go back Josh 23:12
Her *w* ladies answered her, yea, Judg 5:29 2450
but in any *w* return him a 1Sa 6:3
and fetched thence a *w* woman 2Sa 14:2 2450
and my lord is *w*, according to the 2Sa 14:20 2450
Then cried a *w* woman out of the 2Sa 20:16 2450
for thou art a *w* man, and knowest 1Kin 2:9 2450
lo, I have given thee a *w* 1Kin 3:12 2450
living child, and in no *w* slay it 1Kin 3:26
living child, and in no *w* slay it 1Kin 3:27
a *w* son over this great people 1Kin 5:7 2450
howbeit let me go in any *w* 1Kin 11:22
a *w* counsellor, they cast lots 1Chr 26:14 7922
counsellor, a *w* man, and a scribe 1Chr 27:32 995
given to David the king a *w* son 2Chr 2:12 2450
Then the king said to the *w* men Est 1:13 2450
Then said his *w* men and Zeresh his Est 6:13 2450
He taketh the *w* in their own Job 5:13 2450
He is *w* in heart, and mighty in Job 9:4 2450
For vain man would be *w*, though Job 11:12 3823
Should a *w* man utter vain Job 15:2 2450
Which *w* men have told from their Job 15:18 2450
I cannot find one *w* man among you Job 17:10 2450
as he that is *w* may be profitable Job 22:2 7919
Great men are not always *w* Job 32:9 2449
Hear my words, O ye *w* men Job 34:2 2450
let a *w* man hearken unto me Job 34:34 2450
not any that are *w* of heart Job 37:24 2450
Be *w* now therefore, O ye kings Ps 2:10 7919
LORD is sure, making *w* the simple Ps 19:7 2449
he hath left off to be *w*, and to Ps 36:3 7919
not thyself in any *w* to do evil Ps 37:8
For he seeth that *w* men die Ps 49:10 2450
and ye fools, when will ye be *w* Ps 94:8 7919
Whoso is *w*, and will observe these Ps 107:43 2450
A *w* man will hear, and will Prov 1:5 2450
shall attain unto *w* counsels Prov 1:5
the words of the *w*, and their dark Prov 1:6 2450
Be not *w* in thine own eyes Prov 3:7 2450
The *w* shall inherit glory Prov 3:35 2450
consider her ways, and be *w* Prov 6:6 2449
Hear instruction, and be *w* Prov 8:33 2449
rebuke a *w* man, and he will love Prov 9:8 2450
Give instruction to a *w* man Prov 9:9 2450
If thou be *w*, thou shalt Prov 9:12 2449
thou shalt be *w* for thyself Prov 9:12 2449
A *w* son maketh a glad father Prov 10:1 2450
gathereth in summer is a *w* son Prov 10:5 7919
The *w* in heart will receive Prov 10:8 2450
W men lay up knowledge Prov 10:14 2450
he that refraineth his lips is *w* Prov 10:19 7919
be servant to the *w* of heart Prov 11:29 2450
and he that winneth souls is *w* Prov 11:30 2450
that hearkeneth unto counsel is *w* Prov 12:15 2450
but the tongue of the *w* is health Prov 12:18 2450
A *w* son heareth his father's Prov 13:1 2450
The law of the *w* is a fountain of Prov 13:14 2450
walketh with *w* men shall Prov 13:20 2450
men shall be *w* Prov 13:20 2449
Every *w* woman buildeth her house Prov 14:1 2454
lips of the *w* shall preserve them Prov 14:3 2450
A *w* man feareth, and departeth Prov 14:16 2450
crown of the *w* is their riches Prov 14:24 2450
favour is toward a *w* servant Prov 14:35 7919
The tongue of the *w* useth Prov 15:2 2450
The lips of the *w* disperse Prov 15:7 2450
neither will he go unto the *w* Prov 15:12 2450
A *w* son maketh a glad father Prov 15:20 2450
The way of life is above to the *w* Prov 15:24 7919
of life abideth among the *w* Prov 15:31 2450
but a *w* man will pacify it Prov 16:14 2450
The *w* in heart shall be called Prov 16:21 2450
The heart of the *w* teacheth his Prov 16:23 2450

A *w* servant shall have rule over ... Prov 17:2 7919
a *w* man than an hundred stripes ... Prov 17:10 995
holdeth his peace, is counted *w* ... Prov 17:28 2450
and the ear of the *w* seeketh ... Prov 18:15 2450
mayest be *w* in thy latter end ... Prov 19:20 2449
is deceived thereby is not *w* ... Prov 20:1 2449
A *w* king scattereth the wicked, ... Prov 20:26 2450
is punished, the simple is made *w* ... Prov 21:11 2449
when the *w* is instructed, he ... Prov 21:11 2450
and oil in the dwelling of the *w* ... Prov 21:20 2450
A *w* man scaleth the city of the ... Prov 21:22 2450
ear, and hear the words of the *w* ... Prov 22:17 2450
My son, if thine heart be *w* ... Prov 23:15 2449
Hear thou, my son, and be *w* ... Prov 23:19 2449
he that begetteth a *w* child shall ... Prov 23:24 2450
A *w* man is strong ... Prov 24:5 2450
For by *w* counsel thou shalt make ... Prov 24:6
These things also belong to the *w* ... Prov 24:23 2450
so is a *w* reprover upon an ... Prov 25:12 2450
lest he be *w* in his own conceit ... Prov 26:5 2450
Seest thou a man *w* in his own ... Prov 26:12 2450
My son, be *w*, and make my heart ... Prov 27:11 2449
Whoso keepeth the law is a *w* son ... Prov 28:7 995
The rich man is *w* in his own ... Prov 28:11 2450
but *w* men turn away wrath ... Prov 29:8 2450
If a *w* man contendeth with a ... Prov 29:9 2450
but a *w* man keepeth it in till ... Prov 29:11 2450
earth, but they are exceeding *w* ... Prov 30:24 2450
The *w* man's eyes are in his head ... Eccl 2:14 2450
and why was I then more *w* ... Eccl 2:15 2449
w more than of the fool for ever ... Eccl 2:16 2450
And how dieth the *w* man ... Eccl 2:16 2450
he shall be a *w* man or a fool ... Eccl 2:19 2450
shewed myself *w* under the sun ... Eccl 2:19 2449
a *w* child than an old and foolish ... Eccl 4:13 2450
For what hath the *w* more than the ... Eccl 6:8 2450
The heart of the *w* is in the ... Eccl 7:4 2450
to hear the rebuke of the *w* ... Eccl 7:5 2450
oppression maketh a *w* man mad ... Eccl 7:7 2450
neither make thyself over *w* ... Eccl 7:16 2449
Wisdom strengtheneth the *w* more ... Eccl 7:19 2450
I said, I will be *w* ... Eccl 7:23 2449
Who is as the *w* man ... Eccl 8:1 2450
a *w* man's heart discerneth both ... Eccl 8:5 2450
though a *w* man think to know it, ... Eccl 8:17 2450
that the righteous, and the *w* ... Eccl 9:1 2450
neither yet bread to the *w* ... Eccl 9:11 2450
was found in it a poor *w* man ... Eccl 9:15 2450
The words of *w* men are heard in ... Eccl 9:17 2450
A *w* man's heart is at his right ... Eccl 10:2 2450
The words of a *w* man's mouth are ... Eccl 10:12 2450
because the preacher was *w* ... Eccl 12:9 2450
The words of the *w* are as goads ... Eccl 12:11 2450
them that are *w* in their own eyes ... Is 5:21 2450
the counsel of the *w* counsellors ... Is 19:11 2450
Pharaoh, I am the son of the *w* ... Is 19:11 2450
where are thy *w* men ... Is 19:12 2450
of their *w* men shall perish ... Is 29:14 2450
Yet he also is *w*, and will bring ... Is 31:2 2450
that turneth *w* men backward ... Is 44:25 2450
they are *w* to do evil, but to do ... Jer 4:22 2450
How do ye say, We are *w*, and the ... Jer 8:8 2450
The *w* men are ashamed, they are ... Jer 8:9 2450
Who is the *w* man, that may ... Jer 9:12 2450
Let not the *w* man glory in his ... Jer 9:23 2450
all the *w* men of the nations ... Jer 10:7 2450
priest, nor counsel from the *w* ... Jer 18:18 2450
her princes, and upon her *w* men ... Jer 50:35 2450
drunk her princes, and her *w* men ... Jer 51:57 2450
thy *w* men, O Tyrus, that were in ... Eze 27:8 2450
the *w* men thereof were in thee ... Eze 27:9 2450
destroy all the *w* men of Babylon ... Dan 2:12 2445
that the *w* men should be slain ... Dan 2:13 2445
to slay the *w* men of Babylon ... Dan 2:14 2445
the rest of the *w* men of Babylon ... Dan 2:18 2445
he giveth wisdom unto the *w* ... Dan 2:21 2445
to destroy the *w* men of Babylon ... Dan 2:24 2445
Destroy not the *w* men of Babylon ... Dan 2:24 2445
hath demanded cannot the *w* men ... Dan 2:27 2445
over all the *w* men of Babylon ... Dan 2:48 2445
the *w* men of Babylon before me ... Dan 4:6 2445
forasmuch as all the *w* men of my ... Dan 4:18 2445
said to the *w* men of Babylon, ... Dan 5:7 2445
Then came in all the king's *w* men ... Dan 5:8 2445
And now the *w* men, the astrologers ... Dan 5:15 2445
they that be *w* shall shine as the ... Dan 12:3 7919
but the *w* shall understand ... Dan 12:10 7919
Who is *w*, and he shall understand ... Hos 14:9 2450
destroy the *w* men out of Edom ... Obad 8 2450
and Zidon, though it be very *w* ... Zec 9:2 2449
of Jesus Christ was on this *w* ... Mt 1:18 *3779*
there came *w* men from the east to ... Mt 2:1 *3097*
he had privily called the *w* men ... Mt 2:7 *3097*
that he was mocked of the *w* men ... Mt 2:16 *3097*
diligently enquired of the *w* men ... Mt 2:16 *3097*
shall in no *w* pass from the law ... Mt 5:18 *3364*
I will liken him unto a *w* man ... Mt 7:24 *5429*
be ye therefore *w* as serpents ... Mt 10:16 *5429*
he shall in no *w* lose his reward ... Mt 10:42
hast hid these things from the *w* ... Mt 11:25 *4680*
I in like *w* will tell you by what ... Mt 21:24
prophets, and *w* men, and scribes ... Mt 23:34 *4680*
w servant, whom his lord hath ... Mt 24:45 *5429*
And five of them were *w*, and five ... Mt 25:2 *5429*
But the *w* took oil in their ... Mt 25:4 *5429*
And the foolish said unto the *w* ... Mt 25:8 *5429*
But the *w* answered, saying, Not ... Mt 25:9 *5429*
I will not deny thee in any *w* ... Mk 14:31
hast hid these things from the *w* ... Lk 10:21 *4680*
w steward, whom his lord shall ... Lk 12:42 *5429*
could in no *w* lift up herself ... Lk 13:11
child shall in no *w* enter therein ... Lk 18:17
to me I will in no *w* cast out ... Jn 6:37
on this *w* shewed he himself ... Jn 21:1 *3779*
And God spake on this *w*, That his ... Acts 7:6 *3779*
to corruption, he said on this *w* ... Acts 13:34 *3779*
which ye shall in no *w* believe ... Acts 13:41
both to the *w*, and to the unwise ... Rom 1:14 *4680*
Professing themselves to be *w* ... Rom 1:22 *4680*
No, in no *w*: ... Rom 3:9 *3843*
is of faith speaketh on this *w* ... Rom 10:6 *3779*
lest ye should be *w* in your own ... Rom 11:25 *5429*
Be not *w* in your own conceits ... Rom 12:16 *5429*
you *w* unto that which is good ... Rom 16:19 *4680*
To God only *w*, be glory through ... Rom 16:27 *4680*
will destroy the wisdom of the *w* ... 1Cor 1:19 *4680*
Where is the *w* ... 1Cor 1:20 *4680*
how that not many *w* men after the ... 1Cor 1:26 *4680*
of the world to confound the *w* ... 1Cor 1:27 *4680*
as a *w* masterbuilder, I have laid ... 1Cor 3:10 *4680*
you seemeth to be *w* in this world ... 1Cor 3:18 *4680*
become a fool, that he may be *w* ... 1Cor 3:18 *4680*
He taketh the *w* in their own ... 1Cor 3:19 *4680*
knoweth the thoughts of the *w* ... 1Cor 3:20 *4680*
sake, but ye are *w* in Christ ... 1Cor 4:10 *5429*
there is not a *w* man among you ... 1Cor 6:5 *4680*
I speak as to *w* men ... 1Cor 10:15 *5429*
among themselves, are not *w* ... 2Cor 10:12 *4920*
seeing ye yourselves are *w* ... 2Cor 11:19 *5429*
not as fools, but as *w*, ... Eph 5:15 *4680*
invisible, the only *w* God ... 1Ti 1:17 *4680*
which are able to make thee *w* ... 2Ti 3:15 *4679*
of the seventh day on this *w* ... Heb 4:4 *3779*
Who is a *w* man and endued with ... Jas 3:13 *4680*
To the only *w* God our Saviour, be ... Jude 25 *4680*
there shall in no *w* enter into it ... Rev 21:27

WISELY
Come on, let us deal *w* with them ... Ex 1:10 2449
sent him, and behaved himself *w* ... 1Sa 18:5 7919
behaved himself *w* in all his ways ... 1Sa 18:14 7919
that he behaved himself very *w* ... 1Sa 18:15 7919
w than all the servants of Saul ... 1Sa 18:30 7919
And he dealt *w*, and dispersed of ... 2Chr 11:23 995
of charmers, charming never so *w* ... Ps 58:5 2449
for they shall *w* consider of his ... Ps 64:9 7919
behave myself *w* in a perfect way ... Ps 101:2 7919
a matter *w* shall find good ... Prov 16:20 7919
The righteous man *w* considereth ... Prov 21:12 7919
but whoso walketh *w*, he shall be ... Prov 28:26 2451
not enquire *w* concerning this ... Eccl 7:10 2451
steward, because he had done *w* ... Lk 16:8 *5430*

WISER
For he was *w* than all men ... 1Kin 4:31 2449
maketh us *w* than the fowls of ... Job 35:11 2449
hast made me *w* than mine enemies ... Ps 119:98 2449
a wise man, and he will be yet *w* ... Prov 9:9 2449
The sluggard is *w* in his own ... Prov 26:16 2450
Behold, thou art *w* than Daniel ... Eze 28:3 2450
w than the children of light ... Lk 16:8 *5429*
foolishness of God is *w* than men ... 1Cor 1:25 *4680*

WISH
according to thy *w* in God's stead ... Job 33:6 6310
and put to shame that *w* me evil ... Ps 40:14 2655
they have more than heart could *w* ... Ps 73:7 4906
For I could *w* that myself were ... Rom 9:3 *2172*
and this also we *w*, even your ... 2Cor 13:9 *2172*
I *w* above all things that thou ... 3Jn 2 *2172*

WISHED
w in himself to die, and said, It ... Jonah 4:8 7592
of the stern, and *w* for the day ... Acts 27:29 *2172*

WISHING
to sin by *w* a curse to his soul ... Job 31:30 7592

WIST
for they *w* not what it was ... Ex 16:15 3045
that Moses *w* not that the skin of ... Ex 34:29 3045
though he *w* it not, yet is he ... Lev 5:17 3045
w it not, and it shall be forgiven ... Lev 5:18 3045
but I *w* not whence they were ... Josh 2:4 3045
but he *w* not that there were ... Josh 8:14 3045
he *w* not that the LORD was ... Judg 16:20 3045
For he *w* not what to say ... Mk 9:6 *1492*
neither *w* they what to answer ... Mk 14:40 *1492*
w ye not that I must be about my ... Lk 2:49 *1492*
that was healed *w* not who it was ... Jn 5:13 *1492*
w not that it was true which was ... Acts 12:9 *1492*
I *w* not, brethren, that he was ... Acts 23:5 *1492*

WIT
to *w* whether the LORD had made ... Gen 24:21 3045
to *w* what would be done to him ... Ex 2:4 3045
to *w*, for Machir the firstborn of ... Josh 17:1
David not knowing thereof, to *w* ... 1Kin 2:32
for the doors of the house, to *w* ... 1Kin 7:50
he saddled for him the ass, to *w* ... 1Kin 13:23
not from after them, to *w* ... 2Kin 10:29
of their father's house, to *w* ... 1Chr 7:2
Israel after their number, to *w* ... 1Chr 27:1
To *w*, the two pillars, and the ... 2Chr 4:12
the LORD is not with Israel, to *w* ... 2Chr 25:7
Then Amaziah separated them, to *w* ... 2Chr 25:10
for the burnt offerings, to *w* ... 2Chr 31:3
possession in their cities, to *w* ... Neh 11:3
purifications accomplished, to *w* ... Est 2:12
To *w*, Jerusalem, and the cities of ... Jer 25:18
serve himself of them, to *w* ... Jer 34:9
To *w*, the prophets of Israel ... Eze 13:16
waiting for the adoption, to *w* ... Rom 8:23
To *w*, that God was in Christ, ... 2Cor 5:19 *5613*
we do you to *w* of the grace of ... 2Cor 8:1 *1107*

WITCH
Thou shalt not suffer a *w* to live ... Ex 22:18 3784
of times, or an enchanter, or a *w* ... Deut 18:10 3784

WITCHCRAFT
For rebellion is as the sin of *w* ... 1Sa 15:23 7081
and used enchantments, and used *w* ... 2Chr 33:6 3784
Idolatry, *w*, hatred, variance, ... Gal 5:20 *5331*

WITCHCRAFTS
Jezebel and her *w* are so many ... 2Kin 9:22 3785
I will cut off *w* out of thine ... Mic 5:12 3785
harlot, the mistress of *w* ... Nah 3:4 3785
and families through her *w* ... Nah 3:4 3785

WITH See PREFACE.

WITHAL
and bowls thereof, to cover *w* ... Ex 25:29 2004
for the staves to bear it *w* ... Ex 30:4 1992
his foot also of brass, to wash *w* ... Ex 30:18
of the sanctuary, to make it *w* ... Ex 36:3
bowls, and his covers to cover *w* ... Ex 37:16 2004
for the staves to bear it *w* ... Ex 37:27
sides of the altar, to bear it *w* ... Ex 38:7
and put water there, to wash *w* ... Ex 40:30
be that a man shall be defiled *w* ... Lev 5:3
to reconcile *w* in the holy place ... Lev 6:30
feet, to leap *w* upon the earth ... Lev 11:21 2004
be holy to praise the LORD *w* ... Lev 19:24
the bowls, and covers to cover *w* ... Num 4:7
in their right hands to blow *w* ... Judg 7:20
w of a beautiful countenance, and ... 1Sa 16:12 5973
w how he had slain all the ... 1Kin 19:1
that Manasseh had provoked him *w* ... 2Kin 23:26
overlay the walls of the houses *w* ... 1Chr 29:4
to minister, and to offer *w* ... 2Chr 24:14
to shoot arrows and great stones *w* ... 2Chr 26:15
man *w* whom the king delighteth to ... Est 6:9
a potsherd to scrape himself *w* ... Job 2:8
own nets, whilst that I *w* escape ... Ps 141:10 3162
they shall *w* be fitted in thy ... Prov 22:18 3162
or to take water *w* out of the pit ... Is 30:14
that thou shalt sow the ground *w* ... Is 30:23
baptized *w* shall ye be baptized ... Mk 10:39
w it shall be measured to you ... Lk 6:38
not *w* to signify the crimes laid ... Acts 25:27
is given to every man to profit *w* ... 1Cor 12:7
W praying also for us, that God ... Col 4:3 *260*
And *w* they learn to be idle, ... 1Ti 5:13 *260*
But *w* prepare me also a lodging ... Philem 22 *260*

WITHDRAW
unto the priest, *W* thine hand ... 1Sa 14:19 622
If God will not *w* his anger ... Job 9:13 7725
W thine hand far from me ... Job 13:21 7368
That he may *w* man from his ... Job 33:17 5493
W thy foot from thy neighbour's ... Prov 25:17 3365
also from this *w* not thine hand ... Eccl 7:18 3240
neither shall thy moon *w* itself ... Is 60:20 622
the stars shall *w* their shining ... Joel 2:10 622
the stars shall *w* their shining ... Joel 3:15 622
that ye *w* yourselves from every ... 2Th 3:6 *4724*
from such *w* thyself ... 1Ti 6:5 *868*

WITHDRAWEST
Why *w* thou thy hand, even thy ... Ps 74:11 7725

WITHDRAWETH
He *w* not his eyes from the ... Job 36:7 1639

WITHDRAWN
have *w* the inhabitants of their ... Deut 13:13 5080
but my beloved had *w* himself ... Song 5:6 2559
he hath not *w* his hand from ... Lam 2:8 7725
that hath *w* his hand from ... Eze 18:8 7725
he hath *w* himself from them ... Hos 5:6 2502
he was *w* from them about a ... Lk 22:41 *645*

WITHDREW
w the shoulder, and hardened their ... Neh 9:29
Nevertheless I *w* mine hand ... Eze 20:22 7725
knew it, he *w* himself from thence ... Mt 12:15 *402*
But Jesus *w* himself with his ... Mk 3:7 *402*
he *w* himself into the wilderness, ... Lk 5:16 *5298*
but when they were come, he *w* ... Gal 2:12 *5288*

WITHER
his leaf also shall not *w* ... Ps 1:3 5034
the grass, and *w* as the green herb ... Ps 37:2 5034
the reeds and flags shall *w* ... Is 19:6 7060
thing sown by the brooks, shall *w* ... Is 19:7 3001
blow upon them, and they shall *w* ... Is 40:24 3001
and the herbs of every field *w* ... Jer 12:4 3001
off the fruit thereof, that it *w* ... Eze 17:9 3001
it shall *w* in all the leaves of ... Eze 17:9 3001
shall it not utterly *w*, when the ... Eze 17:10 3001
it shall *w* in the furrows where ... Eze 17:10 3001
and the top of Carmel shall *w* ... Amos 1:2 3001

WITHERED
And, behold, seven ears, *w* ... Gen 41:23 6798
heart is smitten, and *w* like grass ... Ps 102:4 3001
and I am *w* like grass ... Ps 102:11 3001
for the hay is *w* away, the grass ... Is 15:6 3001
When the boughs thereof are *w* ... Is 27:11 3001
it is *w*, it is become like a ... Lam 4:8 3001
her strong rods were broken and *w* ... Eze 19:12 3001
all the trees of the field, are *w* ... Joel 1:12 3001
because joy is *w* away from the ... Joel 1:12 3001
for the corn is *w* ... Joel 1:17 3001
piece whereupon it rained not *w* ... Amos 4:7 3001
and it smote the gourd that it *w* ... Jonah 4:7 3001
was a man which had his hand *w* ... Mt 12:10 *3584*
they had no root, they *w* away ... Mt 13:6 *3583*
And presently the fig tree *w* away ... Mt 21:19 *3583*
How soon is the fig tree *w* away ... Mt 21:20 *3583*
a man there which had a *w* hand ... Mk 3:1 *3583*
unto the man which had the *w* hand ... Mk 3:3 *3583*
because it had no root, it *w* away ... Mk 4:6 *3583*
which thou cursedst is *w* away ... Mk 11:21 *3583*
was a man whose right hand was *w* ... Lk 6:6 *3584*
to the man which had the *w* hand ... Lk 6:8 *3584*

it *w* away, because it lacked Lk 8:6 *3583*
impotent folk, of blind, halt, *w* Jn 5:3 *3584*
cast forth as a branch, and is *w* Jn 15:6 *3583*

WITHERETH
it *w* before any other herb Job 8:12 3001
the evening it is cut down, and *w* Ps 90:6 3001
which *w* afore it groweth up Ps 129:6 3001
The grass *w*, the flower fadeth Is 40:7 3001
The grass *w*, the flower fadeth Is 40:8 3001
but it *w* the grass, and the flower Jas 1:11 *3583*
The grass *w*, and the flower 1Pet 1:24 *3583*
trees whose fruit *w*, without Jude 12 *5352*

WITHHELD
for I also *w* thee from sinning Gen 20:6 2820
seeing thou hast not *w* thy son Gen 22:12 2820
this thing, and hast not *w* thy son Gen 22:16 2820
who hath *w* from thee the fruit of Gen 30:2 4513
If I have *w* the poor from their Job 31:16 4513
I *w* not my heart from any joy Eccl 2:10 4513

WITHHELDEST
w not thy manna from their mouth, Neh 9:20 4513

WITHHOLD
none of us shall *w* from thee his Gen 23:6 3607
for he will not *w* me from thee 2Sa 13:13 4513
but who can *w* himself from Job 4:2 6113
W not thou thy tender mercies Ps 40:11 3607
no good thing will he *w* from them Ps 84:11 4513
W not good from them to whom it Prov 3:27 4513
W not correction from the child Prov 23:13 4513
in the evening *w* not thine hand Eccl 11:6 3240
W thy foot from being unshod, and Jer 2:25 4513

WITHHOLDEN
seeing the LORD hath *w* thee from 1Sa 25:26 4513
thou hast *w* bread from the hungry Job 22:7 4513
from the wicked their light is *w* Job 38:15 4513
no thought can be *w* from thee Job 42:2 1219
hast not *w* the request of his Ps 21:2 4513
Therefore the showers have been *w* Jer 3:3 4513
your sins have *w* good things from Jer 5:25 4513
hath not *w* the pledge, neither Eze 18:16 2254
the drink offering is *w* from the Joel 1:13 4513
also I have *w* the rain from you, Amos 4:7 4513

WITHHOLDETH
he *w* the waters, and they dry up Job 12:15 6113
there is that *w* more than is meet Prov 11:24 2820
He that *w* corn, the people shall Prov 11:26 4513
now ye know what *w* that he might 2Th 2:6 *2722*

WITHIN
in the ark, and shalt pitch it *w* Gen 6:14 1004
and he was uncovered *w* his tent Gen 9:21 8432
Therefore Sarah laughed *w* herself Gen 18:12 7130
be fifty righteous *w* the city Gen 18:24 8432
Sodom fifty righteous *w* the city Gen 18:26 8432
children struggled together *w* her Gen 25:22 7130
of the men of the house there *w* Gen 39:11 1004
Yet *w* three days shall Pharaoh Gen 40:13
Yet *w* three days shall Pharaoh Gen 40:19
thy stranger that is *w* thy gates Ex 20:10
overlay it with pure gold, *w* Ex 25:11 1004
thither *w* the vail the ark of the Ex 26:33 1004
he overlaid it with pure gold *w* Ex 37:2 1004
not brought in *w* the holy place Lev 10:18 6441
whether it be bare *w* or without Lev 13:55 7146
house to be scraped *w* round about Lev 14:41 1004
all times into the holy place *w* Lev 16:2 1004
small, and bring it *w* the vail Lev 16:12 1004
and bring his blood *w* the vail Lev 16:15 1004
then he may redeem it *w* a whole Lev 25:29 5704
w a full year may he redeem it Lev 25:29 8537
if it be not redeemed *w* the space Lev 25:30 5704
gathered together *w* your cities Lev 26:25 413
all the vessels thereof *w* a Num 4:10 413
thing of the altar, and *w* the vail Num 18:7 1004
thy stranger that is *w* thy gates Deut 5:14
the Levite that is *w* your gates Deut 12:12
Thou mayest not eat *w* thy gates Deut 12:17
and the Levite that is *w* thy gates Deut 12:18
And the Levite that is *w* thy gates Deut 14:27
and shalt lay it up *w* thy gates Deut 14:28
the widow, which are *w* thy gates Deut 14:29
w any of thy gates in thy land Deut 15:7
Thou shalt eat it *w* thy gates Deut 15:22
the passover *w* any of thy gates Deut 16:5
and the Levite that is *w* thy gates Deut 16:11
the widow, that are *w* thy gates Deut 16:14
w any of thy gates which the LORD Deut 17:2
of controversy *w* thy gates Deut 17:8
he shall not come *w* the camp Deut 23:10 8432
that are in thy land *w* thy gates Deut 24:14
that they may eat *w* thy gates Deut 26:12
The stranger that is *w* thee shall Deut 28:43 7130
thy stranger that is *w* thy gates Deut 31:12
The sword without, and terror *w* Deut 32:25 2315
for *w* three days ye shall pass Josh 1:11 5750
their inheritance was *w* the Josh 19:1 8432
w the inheritance of them Josh 19:9 8432
All the cities of the Levites *w* Josh 21:41 8432
pitchers, and lamps *w* the pitchers Judg 7:16 8432
was a strong tower *w* the city Judg 9:51 8432
but came not *w* the border of Moab Judg 11:18
ye not recover them *w* that time Judg 11:26
me *w* the seven days of the feast Judg 14:12
it came to pass *w* a while after Judg 15:1
camest not *w* the days appointed 1Sa 13:11
w as it were an half acre of land 1Sa 14:14
Nabal's heart was merry *w* him for 1Sa 25:36 5921
things, that his heart died *w* him 1Sa 25:37 7130
Saul lay sleeping *w* the trench 1Sa 26:7
ark of God dwelleth *w* curtains 2Sa 7:2 8432
me the men of Judah *w* three days 2Sa 20:4
the house *w* with boards of cedar 1Kin 6:15 1004
he even built them for it *w* 1Kin 6:16 1004
the house *w* was carved with knops 1Kin 6:18 6441
oracle he prepared in the house *w* 1Kin 6:19 6441
the house *w* with pure gold 1Kin 6:21 6441
And *w* the oracle he made two 1Kin 6:23
the cherubims *w* the inner house 1Kin 6:27 8432
and palm trees and open flowers, *w* 1Kin 6:29 6441
house he overlaid with gold, *w* 1Kin 6:30 6441
had another court *w* the porch 1Kin 7:8 1004
hewed stones, sawed with saws, *w* 1Kin 7:9 1004
And the mouth of it *w* the chapiter 1Kin 7:31 1004
for her soul is vexed *w* her 2Kin 4:27
he had sackcloth *w* upon his flesh 2Kin 6:30 1004
told it to the king's house *w* 2Kin 7:11 6441
and he that cometh *w* the ranges 2Kin 11:8
he overlaid it *w* with pure gold 2Chr 3:4 6441
sedition *w* the same of old time Ezr 4:15 4481
would not come *w* three days Ezr 10:8
unto Jerusalem *w* three days Ezr 10:9
his servant lodge *w* Jerusalem Neh 4:22 8432
w the temple, and let us shut the Neh 6:10 8432
arrows of the Almighty are *w* me Job 6:4 5978
his soul *w* him shall mourn Job 14:22 5921
though my reins be consumed *w* me Job 19:27 2436
but keep it still *w* his mouth Job 20:13 8432
it is the gall of asps *w* him Job 20:14 7130
Which make oil *w* their walls Job 24:11 996
the spirit *w* me constraineth me Job 32:18 990
of the wicked saith *w* my heart Ps 36:1 7130
My heart was hot *w* me Ps 39:3 7130
yea, thy law is *w* my heart Ps 40:8 8432
hid thy righteousness *w* my heart Ps 40:10 8432
my God, my soul is cast down *w* me Ps 42:6 5921
and why art thou disquieted *w* me Ps 42:11 5921
and why art thou disquieted *w* me Ps 43:5 5921
king's daughter is all glorious *w* Ps 45:13 6441
and renew a right spirit *w* me Ps 51:10 7130
My heart is sore pained *w* me Ps 55:4 7130
w me thy comforts delight my soul Ps 94:19 7130
I will walk *w* my house with a Ps 101:2 7130
deceit shall not dwell *w* my house Ps 101:7 7130
and all that is *w* me, bless his Ps 103:1 7130
and my heart is wounded *w* me Ps 109:22 7130
Our feet shall stand *w* thy gates Ps 122:2
Peace be *w* thy walls Ps 122:7
and prosperity *w* thy palaces Ps 122:7
I will now say, Peace be *w* thee Ps 122:8
my spirit was overwhelmed *w* me Ps 142:3 5921
is my spirit overwhelmed *w* me Ps 143:4 5921
my heart *w* me is desolate Ps 143:4 8432
hath blessed thy children *w* thee Ps 147:13 7130
thing if thou keep them *w* thee Prov 22:18 990
lips, and layeth up deceit *w* him Prov 26:24 7130
a little city, and few men *w* it Eccl 9:14
thou hast doves' eyes *w* thy locks Song 4:1 1157
of a pomegranate *w* thy locks Song 4:3 1157
are thy temples *w* thy locks Song 6:7 1157
w threescore and five years shall Is 7:8
W three years, as the years of an Is 16:14
W a year, according to the years Is 21:16 5750
with my spirit *w* me will I seek Is 26:9 7130
w my walls a place and a name Is 56:5
nor destruction *w* thy borders Is 60:18
he that put his holy Spirit *w* him Is 63:11 7130
thy vain thoughts lodge *w* thee Jer 4:14 7130
Mine heart *w* me is broken because Jer 23:9 7130
W two full years will I bring Jer 28:3 5750
w the space of two full years Jer 28:11 5750
mine heart is turned *w* me Lam 1:20 7130
of fire round about *w* it, from Eze 1:27 1004
and it was written *w* and without Eze 2:10 6440
Go, shut thyself *w* thine house Eze 3:24 8432
and the pestilence and the famine *w* Eze 7:15 1004
and I will put a new spirit *w* you Eze 11:19 7130
divination *w* the house of Israel Eze 12:24 8432
and a new spirit will I put *w* you Eze 36:26 7130
And I will put my spirit *w* you Eze 36:27 7130
porch of the gate *w* was one reed Eze 40:7 1004
also the porch of the gate *w* Eze 40:8 1004
to their posts *w* the gate round Eze 40:16 6441
w were hooks, an hand broad, Eze 40:43 1004
of the side chambers that were *w* Eze 41:9 1004
and by all the wall round about *w* Eze 41:17 6442
gates of the inner court, and *w* Eze 44:17 1004
of any God or man *w* thirty days Dan 6:12 5705
but *w* few days he shall be Dan 11:20
mine heart is turned *w* me Hos 11:8
When my soul fainted *w* me I Jonah 2:7 5921
pot, and as flesh *w* the caldron Mic 3:3 8432
and when he treadeth *w* our borders Mic 5:6
Her princes *w* her are roaring Zeph 3:3 7130
formeth the spirit of man *w* him Zec 12:1 7130
And think not to say *w* yourselves Mt 3:9 *1722*
of the scribes said *w* themselves Mt 9:3 *1722*
For she said *w* herself, If I may Mt 9:21 *1722*
but *w* they are full of extortion Mt 23:25 *2081*
first that which is *w* the cup Mt 23:26 *1787*
but are *w* full of dead men's Mt 23:27 *2081*
but *w* ye are full of hypocrisy and Mt 23:28 *2081*
they so reasoned *w* themselves Mk 2:8 *1722*
For from *w*, out of the heart of Mk 7:21 *2081*
All these evil things come from *w* Mk 7:23 *2081*
that had indignation *w* themselves Mk 14:4 *4314*
w three days I will build another Mk 14:58 *1223*
and begin not to say *w* yourselves Lk 3:8 *1722*
him saw it, he spake *w* himself Lk 7:39 *1722*
him began to say *w* themselves Lk 7:49 *1722*
he from *w* shall answer and say, Lk 11:7 *2081*
without make that which is *w* also. Lk 11:40 *2081*
And he thought *w* himself, saying, Lk 12:17 *1722*
Then the steward said *w* himself Lk 16:3 *1722*
the kingdom of God is *w* you Lk 17:21 *1737*
but afterward he said *w* himself Lk 18:4 *1722*
ground, and thy children *w* thee Lk 19:44 *1722*
Did not our heart burn *w* us Lk 24:32 *1722*
days again his disciples were *w* Jn 20:26 *2080*
we had opened, we found no man *w* Acts 5:23 *2080*
we ourselves groan *w* ourselves Rom 8:23 *1722*
do not ye judge them that are *w* 1Cor 5:12 *2080*
were fightings, *w* were fears 2Cor 7:5 *2081*
entereth into that *w* the veil Heb 6:19 *2082*
and they were full of eyes *w* Rev 4:8 *2081*
on the throne a book written *w* Rev 5:1 *2081*

WITHOUT
And the earth was *w* form, and void Gen 1:2 8414
pitch it within and *w* with pitch Gen 6:14 2351
and told his two brethren *w* Gen 9:22 2351
him forth, and set him *w* the city Gen 19:16 2351
made his camels to kneel down *w* Gen 24:11 2351
wherefore standest thou *w* Gen 24:31 2351
Joseph is *w* doubt rent in pieces Gen 37:33 2963
w thee shall no man lift up his Gen 41:44 1107
for it was *w* number Gen 41:49 369
Your lamb shall be *w* blemish Ex 12:5 8549
shall she go out free *w* money Ex 21:11
w shalt thou overlay it, and shalt Ex 25:11 2351
shalt set the table *w* the vail Ex 26:35 2351
of the congregation *w* the vail Ex 27:21 2351
bullock, and two rams *w* blemish Ex 29:1 8549
thou burn with fire *w* the camp Ex 29:14 2351
and pitched it *w* the camp Ex 33:7 2351
which was *w* the camp Ex 33:7 2351
it with pure gold within and *w* Ex 37:2 2351
tabernacle northward, *w* the vail Ex 40:22 2351
let him offer a male *w* blemish Lev 1:3 8549
shall bring it a male *w* blemish Lev 1:10 8549
he shall offer it *w* blemish Lev 3:1 8549
he shall offer it *w* blemish Lev 3:6 8549
a young bullock *w* blemish unto Lev 4:3 8549
w the camp unto a clean place Lev 4:12 2351
forth the bullock *w* the camp Lev 4:21 2351
of the goats, a male *w* blemish Lev 4:23 8549
of the goats, a female *w* blemish Lev 4:28 8549
shall bring it a female *w* blemish Lev 4:32 8549
a ram *w* blemish out of the flocks Lev 5:15 8549
he shall bring a ram *w* blemish Lev 5:18 8549
a ram *w* blemish out of the flock, Lev 6:6 8549
carry forth the ashes *w* the camp Lev 6:11 2351
he burnt with fire *w* the camp Lev 8:17 2351
w blemish, and offer them before Lev 9:2 8549
w blemish, for a burnt offering Lev 9:3 8549
he burnt with fire *w* the camp Lev 9:11 2351
eat it *w* leaven beside the altar Lev 10:12 4682
w the camp shall his habitation Lev 13:46 2351
whether it be bare within or *w* Lev 13:55 1372
shall take two he lambs *w* blemish Lev 14:10 8549
lamb of the first year *w* blemish Lev 14:10 8549
into an unclean place *w* the city Lev 14:40 2351
the dust that they scrape off *w* Lev 14:41 2351
shall one carry forth *w* the camp Lev 16:27 2351
at your own will a male *w* blemish Lev 22:19 8549
ye wave the sheaf an he lamb *w* Lev 23:12 8549
lambs *w* blemish of the first year Lev 23:18 8549
W the vail of the testimony, in Lev 24:3 2351
him that hath cursed *w* the camp Lev 24:14 2351
while she lieth desolate *w* them Lev 26:43
w the camp shall ye put them Num 5:3 2351
so, and put them out *w* the camp Num 5:4 2351
w blemish for a burnt offering Num 6:14 8549
year *w* blemish for a sin offering Num 6:14 8549
one ram *w* blemish for peace Num 6:14 8549
ignorance *w* the knowledge of the Num 15:24
stone him with stones *w* the camp Num 15:35 2351
brought him *w* the camp, and stoned Num 15:36 2351
bring thee a red heifer *w* spot Num 19:2 8549
he may bring her forth *w* the camp Num 19:3 2351
lay them up *w* the camp in a clean Num 19:9 2351
w doing any thing else, go Num 20:19 369
the first year *w* spot day by day Num 28:3 8549
lambs of the first year *w* spot Num 28:9 8549
lambs of the first year *w* spot Num 28:11 8549
they shall be unto you *w* blemish Num 28:19 8549
they shall be unto you *w* blemish) Num 28:31 8549
lambs of the first year *w* blemish Num 29:2 8549
they shall be unto you *w* blemish Num 29:8 8549
they shall be *w* blemish Num 29:13 8549
lambs of the first year *w* spot Num 29:17 8549
lambs of the first year *w* blemish Num 29:20 8549
lambs of the first year *w* blemish Num 29:23 8549
lambs of the first year *w* spot Num 29:26 8549
lambs of the first year *w* blemish Num 29:29 8549
lambs of the first year *w* blemish Num 29:32 8549
lambs of the first year *w* blemish Num 29:36 8549
forth to meet them *w* the camp Num 31:13 2351
do ye abide *w* the camp seven days Num 31:19 2351
ye shall measure from *w* the city Num 35:5 2351
he thrust him suddenly *w* enmity Num 35:22 3808
him any thing *w* laying of wait Num 35:22 3808
w the border of the city of his Num 35:26
w the borders of the city of his Num 35:27 2351
thou shalt eat bread *w* scarceness Deut 8:9 3808
have a place also *w* the camp Deut 23:12 2351
shall not marry *w* unto a stranger Deut 25:5 2351
w iniquity, just and right is he Deut 32:4 369
The sword *w*, and terror within, Deut 32:25 2351
that he will *w* fail drive out Josh 3:10
left them *w* the camp of Israel Josh 6:23 2351
w driving them out hastily Judg 2:23 1115
and their camels were *w* number Judg 6:5 369
and their camels were *w* number Judg 7:12 369
If thou shalt *w* fail deliver the Judg 11:30
left thee this day *w* a kinsman Ruth 4:14
blood, to slay David *w* a cause 1Sa 19:5 2600
them, and *w* fail recover all 1Sa 30:8
riseth, even a morning *w* clouds 2Sa 23:4 3808
for *w* in the wall of the house he 1Kin 6:6 2351

and open flowers, within and *w* 1Kin 6:29 2435
overlaid with gold, within and *w* 1Kin 6:30 2435
sawed with saws, within and *w* 1Kin 7:9 2351
oracle, and they were not seen *w* 1Kin 8:8 2351
three years *w* war between Syria 1Kin 22:1
Jehu appointed fourscore men *w* 2Kin 10:24 2351
them, Have her forth *w* the ranges 2Kin 11:15
the house, and the king's entry *w* 2Kin 16:18 2435
Am I now come up *w* the LORD 2Kin 18:25 1107
he burned them *w* Jerusalem in the 2Kin 23:4 2351
w Jerusalem, unto the brook 2Kin 23:6 2351
of all these vessels was *w* weight 2Kin 25:16 3808
but Seled died *w* children 1Chr 2:30 3808
and Jether died *w* children 1Chr 2:32 3808
nor offer burnt offerings *w* cost 1Chr 21:24 2600
and brass in abundance *w* weight 1Chr 22:3
and of brass and iron *w* weight 1Chr 22:14 369
but they were not seen *w* 2Chr 5:9 2351
the people were *w* number that 2Chr 12:3 369
Israel hath been *w* the true God 2Chr 15:3 3808
w a teaching priest 2Chr 15:3 3808
a teaching priest, and *w* law 2Chr 15:3 3808
and departed *w* being desired 2Chr 21:20 3808
set it *w* at the gate of the house 2Chr 24:8 2351
fountains which were *w* the city 2Chr 32:3 2351
to the towers, and another wall *w* 2Chr 32:5 2351
built a wall *w* the city of David 2Chr 33:14 2435
be given them day by day *w* fail Ezr 6:9
salt *w* prescribing how much Ezr 7:22 3809
and we are not able to stand *w* Ezr 10:13 2351
lodged *w* Jerusalem once or twice Neh 13:20 2351
him, to destroy him *w* cause Job 2:3 2600
for ever *w* any regarding it Job 4:20
they die, even *w* wisdom Job 4:21 3808
marvellous things *w* number Job 5:9
is unsavoury be eaten *w* salt Job 6:6 1097
shuttle, and are spent *w* hope Job 7:6 657
Can the rush grow up *w* mire Job 8:11 3808
can the flag grow *w* water Job 8:11 1097
yea, and wonders *w* number Job 9:10
and multiplieth my wounds *w* cause Job 9:17 2600
w any order, and where the light Job 10:22 3808
thou lift up thy face *w* spot Job 11:15
They grope in the dark *w* light Job 12:25 3808
the naked to lodge *w* clothing Job 24:7 1097
cause him to go naked *w* clothing Job 24:10 1097
thou helped him that is *w* power Job 26:2 3808
I went mourning *w* the sun Job 30:28 3808
clothing, or any poor *w* covering Job 31:19 369
eaten the fruits thereof *w* money Job 31:39 1097
I am clean *w* transgression, I am Job 33:9 1097
is incurable *w* transgression Job 34:6 1097
mighty shall be taken away *w* hand Job 34:20 3808
in pieces mighty men *w* number Job 34:24 3808
Job hath spoken *w* knowledge Job 34:35 3808
and his words were *w* wisdom Job 34:35 3808
he multiplieth words *w* knowledge Job 35:16 1097
and they shall die *w* knowledge Job 36:12 1097
counsel by words *w* knowledge Job 38:2 1097
her labour is in vain *w* fear Job 39:16 1097
not his like, who is made *w* fear Job 41:33 1097
that hideth counsel *w* knowledge Job 42:3 1097
him that *w* cause is mine enemy Ps 7:4 7387
ashamed which transgress *w* cause Ps 25:3 7387
that did see me *w* fled from me Ps 31:11 2351
For *w* cause have they hid for me Ps 35:7 2600
which *w* cause they have digged Ps 35:7 2600
the eye that hate me *w* a cause Ps 35:19 2600
and prepare themselves *w* my fault Ps 59:4
They that hate me *w* a cause are Ps 69:4 2600
caterpillers, and that *w* number, Ps 105:34 369
and fought against me *w* a cause Ps 109:3 2600
perversely with me *w* a cause Ps 119:78 8267
have persecuted me *w* a cause Ps 119:161 2600
privily for the innocent *w* cause Prov 1:11 2600
Wisdom crieth *w* Prov 1:20 2351
Strive not with a man *w* cause Prov 3:30 2600
He shall die *w* instruction Prov 5:23 369
shall he be broken *w* remedy Prov 6:15 369
Now is she *w*, now in the streets, Prov 7:12 2351
fair woman which is *w* discretion Prov 11:22 5493
W counsel purposes are Prov 15:22 369
than great revenues *w* right Prov 16:8 3808
that the soul be *w* knowledge Prov 19:2 3808
man saith, There is a lion *w* Prov 22:13 2351
who hath wounds *w* cause Prov 23:29 2600
Prepare thy work *w*, and make it Prov 24:27 2351
against thy neighbour *w* cause Prov 24:28 2600
is like clouds and wind *w* rain Prov 25:14 369
that is broken down, and *w* walls Prov 25:28 369
be destroyed, and that *w* remedy Prov 29:1 369
serpent will bite *w* enchantment Eccl 10:11 3808
concubines, and virgins *w* number Song 6:8 369
when I should find thee *w* Song 8:1 2351
even great and fair, *w* inhabitant Is 5:9 369
and opened her mouth *w* measure Is 5:14 1097
the cities be wasted *w* inhabitant Is 6:11 369
and the houses *w* man Is 6:11 369
W me they shall bow down under Is 10:4 1115
their valiant ones shall cry *w* Is 33:7 2351
am I now come up *w* the LORD Is 36:10 1107
nor confounded world *w* end Is 45:17
and ye shall be redeemed *w* money Is 52:3 3808
Assyrian oppressed them *w* cause Is 52:4 657
milk *w* money and *w* price Is 55:1 3808
cities are burned *w* inhabitant Jer 2:15 1097
have forgotten me days *w* number Jer 2:32 369
be laid waste, *w* an inhabitant Jer 4:7 369
the earth, and, lo, it was *w* form Jer 4:23 8414
people, and *w* understanding Jer 5:21 369
Judah desolate, *w* an inhabitant Jer 9:11 1097
to cut off the children from *w* Jer 9:21 2351
will I give to the spoil *w* price Jer 15:13
which besiege you *w* the walls Jer 21:4 2351
his neighbour's service *w* wages Jer 22:13 2600
shall be desolate *w* an inhabitant Jer 26:9 369
It is desolate *w* man or beast Jer 32:43 369
ye say shall be desolate *w* man Jer 33:10 369
w beast, even in the cities of Jer 33:10 369
that are desolate, *w* man Jer 33:10 369
w inhabitant, and *w* beast, Jer 33:10 369
place, which is desolate *w* man Jer 33:12
w beast, and in all the cities Jer 33:12
a desolation *w* an inhabitant Jer 34:22 369
offerings unto her, *w* our men Jer 44:19 1107
w an inhabitant, as at this day Jer 44:22 369
waste and desolate *w* an inhabitant Jer 46:19 369
desolate, *w* any to dwell therein Jer 48:9 369
nation, that dwelleth *w* care Jer 49:31
a desolation *w* an inhabitant Jer 51:29 369
and an hissing, *w* an inhabitant Jer 51:37 369
of all these vessels was *w* weight Jer 52:20 3808
they are gone *w* strength before Lam 1:6 3808
ceaseth not, *w* any intermission, Lam 3:49 369
me sore, like a bird, *w* cause Lam 3:52 2600
and it was written within and *w* Eze 2:10 268
The sword is *w*, and the pestilence Eze 7:15 2351
w cause all that I have done in Eze 14:23 2600
even *w* great power or many people Eze 17:9 3808
of life, *w* committing iniquity Eze 33:15 1115
all of them dwelling *w* walls Eze 38:11 369
forefront of the inner court *w* Eze 40:19 2351
And at the side *w*, as one goeth up Eze 40:40 2351
w the inner gate were the Eze 40:44 2351
which was for the side chamber *w* Eze 41:9 2351
even unto the inner house, and *w* Eze 41:17 2351
the wall round about within and *w* Eze 41:17 2435
upon the face of the porch *w* Eze 41:25 2351
the wall that was *w* over against Eze 42:7 2351
of the house, *w* the sanctuary Eze 43:21 2351
w blemish for a sin offering Eze 43:22 8549
offer a young bullock *w* blemish Eze 43:23 8549
a ram out of the flock *w* blemish Eze 43:23 8549
a ram out of the flock, *w* blemish Eze 43:25 8549
take a young bullock *w* blemish Eze 45:18 8549
seven rams *w* blemish daily the Eze 45:23 8549
way of the porch of that gate *w* Eze 46:2 2351
day shall be six lambs *w* blemish Eze 46:4 8549
blemish, and a ram *w* blemish Eze 46:4 8549
be a young bullock *w* blemish Eze 46:6 8549
they shall be *w* blemish Eze 46:6 8549
lamb of the first year *w* blemish Eze 46:13 8549
led me about the way *w* unto the Eze 47:2 2351
that a stone was cut out *w* hands Dan 2:34
cut out of the mountain *w* hands Dan 2:45
but he shall be broken *w* hand Dan 8:25 657
w his own reproach he shall cause Dan 11:18 1115
shall abide many days *w* a king Hos 3:4 369
and *w* a prince Hos 3:4 369
w a sacrifice Hos 3:4 369
w an image, and *w* an ephod, Hos 3:4 369
and *w* teraphim Hos 3:4
the troop of robbers spoileth *w* Hos 7:1 2351
also is like a silly dove *w* heart Hos 7:11 369
w number, whose teeth are the Joel 1:6 369
shall be inhabited as towns *w* Zec 2:4
is angry with his brother *w* a Mt 5:22 1500
fall on the ground *w* your Father Mt 10:29 427
mother and his brethren stood *w* Mt 12:46 1854
mother and thy brethren stand *w* Mt 12:47 1854
w a parable spake he not unto Mt 13:34 5565
them, A prophet is not *w* honour Mt 13:57 820
Are ye also yet *w* understanding Mt 15:16 801
Now Peter sat *w* in the palace Mt 26:69 1854
but was *w* in desert places Mk 1:45 1854
and his mother, and, standing *w* Mk 3:31 1854
thy brethren *w* seek for thee Mk 3:32 1854
but unto them that are *w*, all Mk 4:11 1854
But *w* a parable spake he not unto Mk 4:34 5565
them, A prophet is not *w* honour Mk 6:4 820
There is nothing from *w* a man Mk 7:15 1855
Are ye so *w* understanding also Mk 7:18 801
from *w* entereth into the man Mk 7:18 1855
w in a place where two ways met Mk 11:4 1854
I will build another made *w* hands Mk 14:58 886
praying *w* at the time of incense Lk 1:10 1854
enemies might serve him *w* fear Lk 1:74 870
is like a man that *w* a foundation Lk 6:49 5565
mother and thy brethren stand *w* Lk 8:20 1854
w make that which is within also Lk 11:40 1855
the door, and ye begin to stand *w* Lk 13:25 1854
he die *w* children, that his Lk 20:28 815
took a wife, and died *w* children Lk 20:29 815
them, When I sent you *w* purse Lk 22:35 817
w him was not any thing made that Jn 1:3 5565
He that is *w* sin among you, let Jn 8:7 361
for *w* me ye can do nothing Jn 15:5 5565
law, They hated me *w* a cause Jn 15:25 1432
But Peter stood at the door *w* Jn 18:16 1854
now the coat was *w* seam, woven Jn 19:23 729
But Mary stood *w* at the sepulchre Jn 20:11 1854
standing *w* before the doors Acts 5:23 1854
and brought them *w* violence Acts 5:26
And he was three days *w* sight Acts 9:9 3361
came I unto you *w* gainsaying Acts 10:29 369
but prayer was made *w* ceasing of Acts 12:5 1618
he left not himself *w* witness Acts 14:17 267
w any delay on the morrow I sat Acts 25:17
that *w* ceasing I make mention of Rom 1:9 89
so that they are *w* excuse Rom 1:20 379
W understanding, covenantbreakers Rom 1:31 801
w natural affection, implacable, Rom 1:31 794
For as many as have sinned *w* law Rom 2:12 460
law shall also perish *w* law Rom 2:12 460
make the faith of God *w* effect Rom 3:3 2673
of God *w* the law is manifested Rom 3:21 5565
by faith *w* the deeds of the law Rom 3:28 5565
imputeth righteousness *w* works Rom 4:6 5565
For when we were yet *w* strength Rom 5:6 772
For *w* the law sin was dead Rom 7:8 5565
For I was alive *w* the law once Rom 7:9 5565
how shall they hear *w* a preacher Rom 10:14 5565
calling of God are *w* repentance Rom 11:29 278
Let love be *w* dissimulation Rom 12:9 505
ye have reigned as kings *w* us 1Cor 4:8 5565
do to judge them also that are *w* 1Cor 5:12 1854
But them that are *w* God judgeth 1Cor 5:13 1854
that a man doeth is *w* the body 1Cor 6:18 1622
I would have you *w* carefulness 1Cor 7:32 275
upon the Lord *w* distraction 1Cor 7:35 563
the gospel of Christ *w* charge 1Cor 9:18 77
To them that are *w* law 1Cor 9:21 459
as *w* law 1Cor 9:21 459
being not *w* law to God 1Cor 9:21 459
I might gain them that are *w* law 1Cor 9:21 459
neither is the man *w* the woman 1Cor 11:11 5565
neither the woman *w* the man 1Cor 11:11 5565
even things *w* life giving sound, 1Cor 14:7 895
none of them is *w* signification 1Cor 14:10 880
that he may be with you *w* fear 1Cor 16:10 870
w were fightings, within were 2Cor 7:5 1855
not boast of things *w* our measure 2Cor 10:13 280
boasting of things *w* our measure 2Cor 10:15 280
Beside those things that are *w* 2Cor 11:28 3924
w blame before him in love Eph 1:4 299
at that time ye were *w* Christ Eph 2:12 5565
no hope, and *w* God in the world Eph 2:12 112
throughout all ages, world *w* end Eph 3:21
it should be holy and *w* blemish Eph 5:27 299
w offence till the day of Christ Phil 1:10 677
bold to speak the word *w* fear Phil 1:14 870
Do all things *w* murmurings Phil 2:14 5565
w rebuke, in the midst of a Phil 2:15 298
the circumcision made *w* hands Col 2:11 886
in wisdom toward them that are *w* Col 4:5 1854
Remembering *w* ceasing your work 1Th 1:3 89
cause also thank we God *w* ceasing 1Th 2:13 89
honestly toward them that are *w* 1Th 4:12 1854
Pray *w* ceasing 1Th 5:17 89
holy hands, *w* wrath and doubting 1Ti 2:8 5565
a good report of them which are *w* 1Ti 3:7 1855
w controversy great is the 1Ti 3:16 3672
w preferring one before another 1Ti 5:21 5565
thou keep this commandment *w* spot 1Ti 6:14 784
that *w* ceasing I have remembrance 2Ti 1:3 88
W natural affection, 2Ti 3:3 794
But *w* thy mind would I do nothing Philem 14 5565
tempted like as we are, yet *w* sin Heb 4:15 5565
W father Heb 7:3 540
w mother, *w* descent, having Heb 7:3 282
w descent Heb 7:3 35
w all contradiction the less is Heb 7:7 5565
inasmuch as not *w* an oath he was Heb 7:20 5565
those priests were made *w* an oath Heb 7:21 5565
not *w* blood, which he offered for Heb 9:7 5565
offered himself *w* spot to God Heb 9:14 299
testament was dedicated *w* blood Heb 9:18 5565
w shedding of blood is no Heb 9:22 5565
second time *w* sin unto salvation Heb 9:28 5565
of our faith *w* wavering Heb 10:23 186
died *w* mercy under two or three Heb 10:28 5565
But *w* faith it is impossible to Heb 11:6 5565
that they *w* us should not be made Heb 11:40 5565
But if ye be *w* chastisement Heb 12:8 5565
w which no man shall see the Lord Heb 12:14 5565
conversation be *w* covetousness Heb 13:5 866
for sin, are burned *w* the camp Heb 13:11 1854
own blood, suffered *w* the gate Heb 13:12 1854
therefore unto him *w* the camp Heb 13:13 1854
he shall have judgment *w* mercy Jas 2:13 448
shew me thy faith *w* thy works Jas 2:18 5565
that faith *w* works is dead Jas 2:20 5565
For as the body *w* the spirit is Jas 2:26 5565
so faith *w* works is dead also Jas 2:26 5565
fruits, *w* partiality Jas 3:17 87
partiality, and *w* hypocrisy Jas 3:17 505
who *w* respect of persons judgeth 1Pet 1:17 678
of Christ, as of a lamb *w* blemish 1Pet 1:19 299
blemish and *w* spot 1Pet 1:19 784
they also may *w* the word be won 1Pet 3:1 427
one to another *w* grudging 1Pet 4:9 427
These are wells *w* water, clouds 2Pet 2:17 504
in peace, *w* spot, and blameless 2Pet 3:14 784
you, feeding themselves *w* fear Jude 12 870
clouds they are *w* water, carried Jude 12 504
w fruit, twice dead, plucked up Jude 12 175
which is *w* the temple leave out Rev 11:2 1855
for they are *w* fault before the Rev 14:5 299
which is poured out *w* mixture Rev 14:10 194
winepress was trodden *w* the city Rev 14:20 1854
For *w* are dogs, and sorcerers, and Rev 22:15 1854

WITHS

green *w* that were never dried Judg 16:7 3499
green *w* which had not been dried Judg 16:8 3499
And he brake the *w*, as a thread of Judg 16:9 3499

WITHSTAND

behold, I went out to *w* thee Num 22:32 7854
and could not *w* them 2Chr 13:7 2388
now ye think to *w* the kingdom of 2Chr 13:8 2388
so that none is able to *w* thee 2Chr 20:6 3320
and no man could *w* them Est 9:2 5975
against him, two shall *w* him Eccl 4:12 5975
the arms of the south shall not *w* Dan 11:15 5975
shall there be any strength to *w* Dan 11:15 5975
what was I, that I could *w* God Acts 11:17 2967
may be able to *w* in the evil day Eph 6:13 436

WITHSTOOD

they *w* Uzziah the king, and said 2Chr 26:18 5975
of the kingdom of Persia *w* me one Dan 10:13 5975
name by interpretation) *w* them Acts 13:8 436

I *w* him to the face, because he Gal 2:11 *436*
Now as Jannes and Jambres *w* Moses 2Ti 3:8 *436*
for he hath greatly *w* our words 2Ti 4:15 *436*

WITNESS

that they may be a *w* unto me Gen 21:30 5713
and let it be for a *w* between me Gen 31:44 5707
said, This heap is a *w* between me Gen 31:48 5707
God is *w* betwixt me and thee Gen 31:50 5707
This heap be *w* Gen 31:52 5707
and this pillar be *w* Gen 31:52 5711
false *w* against thy neighbour Ex 20:16 5707
then let him bring it for *w* Ex 22:13 5707
the wicked to be an unrighteous *w* Ex 23:1 5707
the voice of swearing, and is a *w* Lev 5:1 5707
and there be no *w* against her Num 5:13 5707
the LORD in the tabernacle of *w* Num 17:7 5715
went into the tabernacle of *w* Num 17:8 5715
before the tabernacle of *w* Num 18:2 5715
but one *w* shall not testify Num 35:30 5707
earth to *w* against you this day, Deut 4:26 5749
false *w* against thy neighbour Deut 5:20 5707
but at the mouth of one *w* he Deut 17:6 5707
One *w* shall not rise up against a Deut 19:15 5707
If a false *w* rise up against any Deut 19:16 5707
if the *w* be a false *w* Deut 19:18 5707
that this song may be a *w* for me Deut 31:19 5707
shall testify against them as a *w* Deut 31:21 5707
may be there for a *w* against thee Deut 31:26 5707
But that it may be a *w* between us Josh 22:27 5707
but it is a *w* between us and you Josh 22:28 5707
for it shall be a *w* between us Josh 22:34 5707
this stone shall be a *w* unto us Josh 24:27 5713
shall be therefore a *w* unto you Josh 24:27 5713
The LORD be *w* between us Judg 11:10 8085
w against me before the LORD, and 1Sa 12:3 6030
them, The LORD is *w* against you 1Sa 12:5 5707
and his anointed is *w* this day 1Sa 12:5 5707
And they answered, He is *w* 1Sa 12:5 5707
to bear *w* against him, saying, 1Kin 21:10 5749
Israel, for the tabernacle of *w* 2Chr 24:6 5715
wrinkles, which is a *w* against me Job 16:8 5707
up in me beareth *w* to my face Job 16:8 6030
my *w* is in heaven, and my record Job 16:19 5707
the eye saw me, it gave *w* to me Job 29:11 5749
and as a faithful *w* in heaven Ps 89:37 5707
A false *w* that speaketh lies, and Prov 6:19 5707
but a false *w* deceit Prov 12:17 5707
A faithful *w* will not lie Prov 14:5 5707
but a false *w* will utter lies Prov 14:5 5707
A true *w* delivereth souls Prov 14:25 5707
but a deceitful *w* speaketh lies Prov 14:25
A false *w* shall not be unpunished Prov 19:5 5707
A false *w* shall not be unpunished Prov 19:9 5707
An ungodly *w* scorneth judgment Prov 19:28 5707
A false *w* shall perish Prov 21:28 5707
Be not a *w* against thy neighbour Prov 24:28 5707
A man that beareth false *w* Prov 25:18 5707
countenance doth *w* against them Is 3:9 5707
for a *w* unto the LORD of hosts in Is 19:20 5707
given him for a *w* to the people Is 55:4 5707
even I know, and am a *w*, saith the Jer 29:23 5707
faithful *w* between us, if we do Jer 42:5 5707
thing shall I take to *w* for thee Lam 2:13 5749
let the Lord GOD be *w* against you Mic 1:2 5707
the LORD hath been *w* between thee Mal 2:14 5749
I will be a swift *w* against the Mal 3:5 5707
fornications, thefts, false *w* Mt 15:19 *5577*
Thou shalt not bear false *w* Mt 19:18 *5576*
world for a *w* unto all nations Mt 24:14 *3142*
sought false *w* against Jesus, to Mt 26:59 *5577*
is it which these *w* against thee Mt 26:62 *2649*
many things they *w* against thee Mt 27:13 *2649*
Do not steal, Do not bear false *w* Mk 10:19 *5576*
all the council sought for *w* Mk 14:55 *3141*
For many bare false *w* against him Mk 14:56 *5576*
but their *w* agreed not together Mk 14:56 *3141*
bare false *w* against him, saying, Mk 14:57 *5576*
so did their *w* agree together Mk 14:59 *3141*
is it which these *w* against thee Mk 14:60 *2649*
many things they *w* against thee Mk 15:4 *2649*
And all bare him *w*, and wondered at Lk 4:22 *3140*
Truly ye bear *w* that ye allow the Lk 11:48 *3140*
Do not steal, Do not bear false *w* Lk 18:20 *5576*
said, What need we any further *w* Lk 22:71 *3141*
The same came for a *w* Jn 1:7 *3141*
to bear *w* of the Light, that all Jn 1:7 *3140*
was sent to bear *w* of that Light Jn 1:8 *3140*
John bare *w* of him, and cried, Jn 1:15 *3140*
and ye receive not our *w* Jn 3:11 *3141*
Jordan, to whom thou barest *w* Jn 3:26 *3140*
Ye yourselves bear me *w*, that I Jn 3:28 *3140*
If I bear *w* of myself Jn 5:31 *3140*
of myself, my *w* is not true Jn 5:31 *3141*
is another that beareth *w* of me Jn 5:32 *3140*
I know that the *w* which he Jn 5:32 *3141*
John, and he bare *w* unto the truth Jn 5:33 *3140*
have greater *w* than that of John Jn 5:36 *3141*
bear *w* of me, that the Father Jn 5:36 *3140*
hath sent me, hath borne *w* of me Jn 5:37 *3140*
I am one that bear *w* of myself Jn 8:18 *3140*
that sent me beareth *w* of me Jn 8:18 *3140*
Father's name, they bear *w* of me Jn 10:25 *3140*
And ye also shall bear *w*, because Jn 15:27 *3140*
spoken evil, bear *w* of the evil Jn 18:23 *3140*
I should bear *w* unto the truth Jn 18:37 *3140*
a *w* with us of his resurrection Acts 1:22 *3144*
great power gave the apostles *w* Acts 4:33 *3142*
tabernacle of *w* in the wilderness Acts 7:44 *3142*
To him give all the prophets *w* Acts 10:43 *3140*
he left not himself without *w* Acts 14:17 *267*
knoweth the hearts, bare them *w* Acts 15:8 *3140*
the high priest doth bear me *w* Acts 22:5 *3140*
For thou shalt be his *w* unto all Acts 22:15 *3144*
so must thou bear *w* also at Rome Acts 23:11 *3140*
a *w* both of these things which Acts 26:16 *3144*
For God is my *w*, whom I serve Rom 1:9 *3144*
their conscience also bearing *w* Rom 2:15 *4828*
itself beareth *w* with our spirit Rom 8:16 *4828*
bearing me *w* in the Holy Ghost Rom 9:1 *4828*
Thou shalt not bear false *w* Rom 13:9 *5576*
God is *w* 1Th 2:5 *3144*
This *w* is true Titus 1:13 *3141*
God also bearing them *w*, both Heb 2:4 *4901*
the Holy Ghost also is a *w* to us Heb 10:15 *3140*
by which he obtained *w* that he Heb 11:4 *3140*
of them shall be a *w* against you Jas 5:3 *3142*
a *w* of the sufferings of Christ, 1Pet 5:1 *3144*
and we have seen it, and bear *w* 1Jn 1:2 *3140*
it is the Spirit that beareth *w* 1Jn 5:6 *3140*
are three that bear *w* in earth 1Jn 5:8 *3140*
If we receive the *w* of men 1Jn 5:9 *3141*
the *w* of God is greater 1Jn 5:9 *3141*
for this is the *w* of God which he 1Jn 5:9 *3141*
Son of God hath the *w* in himself 1Jn 5:10 *3141*
Which have borne *w* of thy charity 3Jn 6 *3140*
Christ, who is the faithful *w* Rev 1:5 *3144*
the Amen, the faithful and true *w* Rev 3:14 *3144*
were beheaded for the *w* of Jesus Rev 20:4 *3141*

WITNESSED

the men of Belial *w* against him 1Kin 21:13 5749
being *w* by the law and the Rom 3:21 *3140*
Pilate *w* a good confession 1Ti 6:13 *3140*
of whom it is *w* that he liveth Heb 7:8 *3140*

WITNESSES

be put to death by the mouth of *w* Num 35:30 5707
of two *w*, or three *w* Deut 17:6 5707
The hands of the *w* shall be first Deut 17:7 5707
at the mouth of two *w* Deut 19:15 5707
or at the mouth of three *w* Deut 19:15 5707
Ye are *w* against yourselves that Josh 24:22 5707
And they said, We are *w* Josh 24:22 5707
Ye are *w* this day, that I have Ruth 4:9 5707
ye are *w* this day Ruth 4:10 5707
and the elders, said, We are *w* Ruth 4:11 5707
Thou renewest thy *w* against me Job 10:17 5707
for false *w* are risen up against Ps 27:12 5707
False *w* did rise up Ps 35:11 5707
took unto me faithful *w* to record Is 8:2 5707
let them bring forth their *w* Is 43:9 5707
Ye are my *w*, saith the LORD, and Is 43:10 5707
therefore ye are my *w*, saith the Is 43:12 5707
ye are even my *w* Is 44:8 5707
and they are their own *w* Is 44:9 5707
evidence, and sealed it, and took *w* Jer 32:10 5707
in the presence of the *w* that Jer 32:12 5707
the field for money, and take *w* Jer 32:25 5707
take *w* in the land of Benjamin, Jer 32:44 5707
in the mouth of two or three *w* Mt 18:16 *3144*
Wherefore ye be *w* unto yourselves Mt 23:31 *3140*
yea, though many false *w* came Mt 26:60 *5575*
At the last came two false *w* Mt 26:60 *5575*
what further need have we of *w* Mt 26:65 *3144*
saith, What need we any further *w* Mk 14:63 *3144*
And ye are *w* of these things Lk 24:48 *3144*
ye shall be *w* unto me both in Acts 1:8 *3144*
raised up, whereof we all are *w* Acts 2:32 *3144*
whereof we are *w* Acts 3:15 *3144*
we are his *w* of these things Acts 5:32 *3144*
And set up false *w*, which said, Acts 6:13 *3144*
the *w* laid down their clothes at Acts 7:58 *3144*
we are *w* of all things which he Acts 10:39 *3144*
but unto *w* chosen before of God, Acts 10:41 *3144*
who are his *w* unto the people Acts 13:31 *3144*
and we are found false *w* of God 1Cor 15:15 *5575*
In the mouth of two or three *w* 2Cor 13:1 *3144*
Ye are *w*, and God also, how holily 1Th 2:10 *3144*
but before two or three *w* 1Ti 5:19 *3144*
a good profession before many *w* 1Ti 6:12 *3144*
hast heard of me among many *w* 2Ti 2:2 *3144*
mercy under two or three *w* Heb 10:28 *3144*
about with so great a cloud of *w* Heb 12:1 *3144*
I will give power unto my two *w* Rev 11:3 *3144*

WITNESSETH

witness which he *w* of me is true Jn 5:32 *3140*
the Holy Ghost *w* in every city Acts 20:23 *1263*

WITNESSING

w both to small and great, saying Acts 26:22 *3140*

WIT'S

man, and are at their *w* end Ps 107:27 2451

WITTINGLY

head, guiding his hands *w* Gen 48:14 7919

WITTY

out knowledge of *w* inventions Prov 8:12

WIVES

And Lamech took unto him two *w* Gen 4:19 802
And Lamech said unto his *w* Gen 4:23 802
ye *w* of Lamech, hearken unto my Gen 4:23 802
they took them *w* of all which Gen 6:2 802
wife, and thy sons' *w* with thee Gen 6:18 802
his wife, and his sons' *w* with him Gen 7:7 802
the three *w* of his sons with them Gen 7:13 802
sons, and thy sons' *w* with thee Gen 8:16 802
his wife, and his sons' *w* with him Gen 8:18 802
And Abram and Nahor took them *w* Gen 11:29 802
took unto the *w* which he had Gen 28:9 802
Give me my *w* and my children, for Gen 30:26 802
set his sons and his *w* upon camels Gen 31:17 802
take other *w* beside my daughters Gen 31:50 802
up that night, and took his two *w* Gen 32:22 802
take their daughters to us for *w* Gen 34:21 802
their *w* took they captive, and Gen 34:29 802
Esau took his *w* of the daughters Gen 36:2 802
And Esau took his *w*, and his sons, Gen 36:6 802
sons of Zilpah, his father's *w* Gen 37:2 802
your little ones, and for your *w* Gen 45:19 802
and their little ones, and their *w* Gen 46:5 802
loins, besides Jacob's sons' *w* Gen 46:26 802
come not at your *w* Ex 19:15 802
your *w* shall be widows, and your Ex 22:24 802
which are in the ears of your *w* Ex 32:2 802
to fall by the sword, that our *w* Num 14:3 802
door of their tents, and their *w* Num 16:27 802
Our little ones, our *w*, our Num 32:26 802
But your *w*, and your little ones, Deut 3:19 802
shall he multiply *w* to himself Deut 17:17 802
If a man have two *w*, one beloved, Deut 21:15 802
Your little ones, your *w*, and thy Deut 29:11 802
Your *w*, your little ones, and your Josh 1:14 802
their daughters to be their *w* Judg 3:6 802
for he had many *w* Judg 8:30 802
How shall we do for *w* for them Judg 21:7 802
give them of our daughters to *w* Judg 21:7 802
they gave them *w* which they had Judg 21:14 802
How shall we do for *w* for them Judg 21:16 802
not give them *w* of our daughters Judg 21:18 802
Benjamin did so, and took them *w* Judg 21:23 802
they took them *w* of the women of Ruth 1:4 802
And he had two *w* 1Sa 1:2 802
they were also both of them his *w* 1Sa 25:43 802
even David with his two *w* 1Sa 27:3 802
and their *w*, and their sons, and 1Sa 30:3 802
David's two *w* were taken captives 1Sa 30:5 802
and David rescued his two *w* 1Sa 30:18 802
up thither, and his two *w* also 2Sa 2:2 802
w out of Jerusalem, after he was 2Sa 5:13 802
thy master's *w* into thy bosom, and 2Sa 12:8 802
I will take thy *w* before thine 2Sa 12:11 802
he shall lie with thy *w* in the 2Sa 12:11 802
daughters, and the lives of thy *w* 2Sa 19:5 802
And he had seven hundred *w* 1Kin 11:3 802
his *w* turned away his heart 1Kin 11:3 802
that his *w* turned away his heart 1Kin 11:4 802
did he for all his strange *w* 1Kin 11:8 802
thy *w* also and thy children, even 1Kin 20:3 802
thy silver, and thy gold, and thy *w* 1Kin 20:5 802
for he sent unto me for my *w* 1Kin 20:7 802
the *w* of the sons of the prophets 2Kin 4:1 802
king's mother, and the king's *w* 2Kin 24:15 802
the father of Tekoa had two *w* 1Chr 4:5 802
for they had many *w* and sons 1Chr 7:4 802
Hushim and Baara were his *w* 1Chr 8:8 802
And David took more *w* at Jerusalem 1Chr 14:3 802
of Absalom above all his *w* 2Chr 11:21 802
(for he took eighteen *w*, and 2Chr 11:21 802
And he desired many *w* 2Chr 11:23 802
mighty, and married fourteen *w* 2Chr 13:21 802
with their little ones, their *w* 2Chr 20:13 802
people, and thy children, and thy *w* 2Chr 21:14 802
house, and his sons also, and his *w* 2Chr 21:17 802
And Jehoiada took for him two *w* 2Chr 24:3 802
our *w* are in captivity for this 2Chr 29:9 802
of all their little ones, their *w* 2Chr 31:18 802
have taken strange *w* of the Ezr 10:2 802
our God to put away all the *w* Ezr 10:3 802
and have taken strange *w*, to Ezr 10:10 802
the land, and from the strange *w* Ezr 10:11 802
them which have taken strange *w* Ezr 10:14 802
w by the first day of the first Ezr 10:17 802
found that had taken strange *w* Ezr 10:18 802
that they would put away their *w* Ezr 10:19 802
All these had taken strange *w* Ezr 10:44 802
some of them had *w* by whom they Ezr 10:44 802
sons, and your daughters, your *w* Neh 4:14 802
of their *w* against their brethren Neh 5:1 802
unto the law of God, their *w* Neh 10:28 802
the *w* also and the children Neh 12:43 802
Jews that had married *w* of Ashdod Neh 13:23 802
our God in marrying strange *w* Neh 13:27 802
all the *w* shall give to their Est 1:20 802
be spoiled, and their *w* ravished Is 13:16 802
with their fields and *w* together Jer 6:12 802
will I give their *w* unto others Jer 8:10 802
none to bury them, them, their *w* Jer 14:16 802
let their *w* be bereaved of their Jer 18:21 802
Take ye *w*, and beget sons and Jer 29:6 802
take *w* for your sons, and give Jer 29:6 802
adultery with their neighbours' *w* Jer 29:23 802
no wine all our days, we, our *w* Jer 35:8 802
So they shall bring out all thy *w* Jer 38:23 802
and the wickedness of their *w* Jer 44:9 802
and the wickedness of your *w* Jer 44:9 802
w had burned incense unto other Jer 44:15 802
your *w* have both spoken with your Jer 44:25 802
they take for their *w* a widow Eze 44:22 802
the king, and his princes, his *w* Dan 5:2 7695
the king, and his princes, his *w* Dan 5:3 7695
and thou, and thy lords, thy *w* Dan 5:23 7695
them, their children, and their *w* Dan 6:24 5389
of David apart, and their *w* apart Zec 12:12 802
of Nathan apart, and their *w* apart Zec 12:12 802
of Levi apart, and their *w* apart Zec 12:13 802
of Shimei apart, and their *w* apart Zec 12:13 802
family apart, and their *w* apart Zec 12:14 802
suffered you to put away your *w* Mt 19:8 *1135*
eat, they drank, they married *w* Lk 17:27 *1135*
all brought us on our way, with *w* Acts 21:5 *1135*
that both they that have *w* be as 1Cor 7:29 *1135*
W, submit yourselves unto your Eph 5:22 *1135*
so let the *w* be to their own Eph 5:24 *1135*
Husbands, love your *w*, even as Eph 5:25 *1135*
love their *w* as their own bodies Eph 5:28 *1135*
W, submit yourselves unto your Col 3:18 *1135*
Husbands, love your *w*, and be not Col 3:19 *1135*
Even so must their *w* be grave 1Ti 3:11 *1135*
Likewise, ye *w*, be in subjection 1Pet 3:1 *1135*
won by the conversation of the *w* 1Pet 3:1 *1135*

WIVES'
old *w* fables, and exercise thyself	1Ti 4:7	*1126*

WIZARD
a familiar spirit, or that is a *w*	Lev 20:27	3049
with familiar spirits, or a *w*	Deut 18:11	3049

WIZARDS
spirits, neither seek after *w*	Lev 19:31	3049
have familiar spirits, and after *w*	Lev 20:6	3049
had familiar spirits, and the *w*	1Sa 28:3	3049
have familiar spirits, and the *w*	1Sa 28:9	3049
dealt with familiar spirits and *w*	2Kin 21:6	3049
with familiar spirits, and the *w*	2Kin 23:24	3049
with a familiar spirit, and with *w*	2Chr 33:6	3049
unto *w* that peep, and that mutter	Is 8:19	3049
familiar spirits, and to the *w*	Is 19:3	3049

WOE
W to thee, Moab	Num 21:29	188
And they said, *W* unto us	1Sa 4:7	188
W unto us	1Sa 4:8	188
If I be wicked, *w* unto me	Job 10:15	480
W is me, that I sojourn in Mesech	Ps 120:5	190
Who hath *w*	Prov 23:29	188
but *w* to him that is alone when	Eccl 4:10	337
W to thee, O land, when thy king	Eccl 10:16	337
W unto their soul	Is 3:9	188
W unto the wicked	Is 3:11	188
W unto them that join house to	Is 5:8	1945
W unto them that rise up early in	Is 5:11	1945
W unto them that draw iniquity	Is 5:18	1945
W unto them that call evil good,	Is 5:20	1945
W unto them that are wise in	Is 5:21	1945
W unto them that are mighty to	Is 5:22	1945
Then said I, *W* is me	Is 6:5	188
W unto them that decree	Is 10:1	1945
W to the multitude of many people	Is 17:12	1945
W to the land shadowing with	Is 18:1	1945
leanness, my leanness, *w* unto me	Is 24:16	188
W to the crown of pride, to the	Is 28:1	1945
W to Ariel, to Ariel, the city	Is 29:1	1945
W unto them that seek deep to	Is 29:15	1945
W to the rebellious children,	Is 30:1	1945
W to them that go down to Egypt	Is 31:1	1945
W to thee that spoilest, and thou	Is 33:1	1945
W unto him that striveth with his	Is 45:9	1945
W unto him that saith unto his	Is 45:10	1945
W unto us	Jer 4:13	188
her hands, saying, *W* is me now	Jer 4:31	188
W unto us	Jer 6:4	188
W is me for my hurt	Jer 10:19	188
W unto thee, O Jerusalem	Jer 13:27	188
W is me, my mother, that thou	Jer 15:10	188
W unto him that buildeth his	Jer 22:13	1945
W be unto the pastors that	Jer 23:1	1945
Thou didst say, *W* is me now	Jer 45:3	188
W unto Nebo	Jer 48:1	1945
W be unto thee, O Moab	Jer 48:46	188
w unto them	Jer 50:27	1945
w unto us, that we have sinned	Lam 5:16	188
lamentations, and mourning, and *w*	Eze 2:10	1958
W unto the foolish prophets, that	Eze 13:3	1945
W to the women that sew pillows	Eze 13:18	1945
w, *w* unto thee	Eze 16:23	188
W to the bloody city, to the pot	Eze 24:6	188
W to the bloody city	Eze 24:9	188
Howl ye, *W* worth the day	Eze 30:2	1929
W be to the shepherds of Israel	Eze 34:2	1945
W unto them	Hos 7:13	188
w also to them when I depart from	Hos 9:12	188
W unto you that desire the day of	Amos 5:18	1945
W to them that are at ease in	Amos 6:1	1945
W to them that devise iniquity,	Mic 2:1	1945
W is me	Mic 7:1	480
W to the bloody city	Nah 3:1	1945
W to him that increaseth that	Hab 2:6	1945
W to him that coveteth an evil	Hab 2:9	1945
W to him that buildeth a town	Hab 2:12	1945
W unto him that giveth his	Hab 2:15	1945
W unto him that saith to the wood	Hab 2:19	1945
W unto the inhabitants of the sea	Zeph 2:5	1945
W to her that is filthy and	Zeph 3:1	1945
W to the idol shepherd that	Zec 11:17	1945
W unto thee, Chorazin	Mt 11:21	*3759*
w unto thee, Bethsaida	Mt 11:21	*3759*
W unto the world because of	Mt 18:7	*3759*
but *w* to that man by whom the	Mt 18:7	*3759*
But *w* unto you, scribes and	Mt 23:13	*3759*
W unto you, scribes and Pharisees,	Mt 23:14	*3759*
W unto you, scribes and Pharisees,	Mt 23:15	*3759*
W unto you, ye blind guides,	Mt 23:16	*3759*
W unto you, scribes and Pharisees,	Mt 23:23	*3759*
W unto you, scribes and Pharisees,	Mt 23:25	*3759*
W unto you, scribes and Pharisees,	Mt 23:27	*3759*
W unto you, scribes and Pharisees,	Mt 23:29	*3759*
w unto them that are with child,	Mt 24:19	*3759*
but *w* unto that man by whom the	Mt 26:24	*3759*
But *w* to them that are with child	Mk 13:17	*3759*
but *w* to that man by whom the Son	Mk 14:21	*3759*
But *w* unto you that are rich	Lk 6:24	*3759*
W unto you that are full	Lk 6:25	*3759*
W unto you that laugh now	Lk 6:25	*3759*
W unto you, when all men shall	Lk 6:26	*3759*
W unto thee, Chorazin	Lk 10:13	*3759*
w unto thee, Bethsaida	Lk 10:13	*3759*
But *w* unto you, Pharisees	Lk 11:42	*3759*
W unto you, Pharisees	Lk 11:43	*3759*
W unto you, scribes and Pharisees,	Lk 11:44	*3759*
W unto you also, ye lawyers	Lk 11:46	*3759*
W unto you for ye build the	Lk 11:47	*3759*
W unto you, lawyers	Lk 11:52	*3759*
but *w* unto him, through whom they	Lk 17:1	*3759*
But *w* unto them that are with	Lk 21:23	*3759*
but *w* unto that man by whom he is	Lk 22:22	*3759*
w is unto me, if I preach not the	1Cor 9:16	*3759*
W unto them	Jude 11	*3759*
saying with a loud voice, *W*, *w*	Rev 8:13	*3759*
with a loud voice, *W*, *w*, *w*	Rev 8:13	*3759*
One *w* is past	Rev 9:12	*3759*
The second *w* is past	Rev 11:14	*3759*
the third *w* cometh quickly	Rev 11:14	*3759*
W to the inhabiters of the earth	Rev 12:12	*3759*

WOEFUL
neither have I desired the *w* day	Jer 17:16	605

WOES
there come two *w* more hereafter	Rev 9:12	*3759*

WOLF
Benjamin shall ravin as a *w*	Gen 49:27	2061
The *w* also shall dwell with the	Is 11:6	2061
The *w* and the lamb shall feed	Is 65:25	2061
a *w* of the evenings shall spoil	Jer 5:6	2061
sheep are not, seeth the *w* coming	Jn 10:12	*3074*
and the *w* catcheth them, and	Jn 10:12	*3074*

WOLVES
are like *w* ravening the prey	Eze 22:27	2061
more fierce than the evening *w*	Hab 1:8	2061
her judges are evening *w*	Zeph 3:3	2061
but inwardly they are ravening *w*	Mt 7:15	*3074*
forth as sheep in the midst of *w*	Mt 10:16	*3074*
I send you forth as lambs among *w*	Lk 10:3	*3074*
grievous *w* enter in among you	Acts 20:29	*3074*

WOMAN
had taken from man, made he a *w*	Gen 2:22	802
she shall be called *W*, because	Gen 2:23	802
And he said unto the *w*, Yea, hath	Gen 3:1	802
the *w* said unto the serpent, We	Gen 3:2	802
And the serpent said unto the *w*	Gen 3:4	802
when the *w* saw that the tree was	Gen 3:6	802
The *w* whom thou gavest to be with	Gen 3:12	802
And the LORD God said unto the *w*	Gen 3:13	802
the *w* said, The serpent beguiled	Gen 3:13	802
put enmity between thee and the *w*	Gen 3:15	802
Unto the *w* he said, I will	Gen 3:16	802
thou art a fair *w* to look upon	Gen 12:11	802
the *w* that she was very fair	Gen 12:14	802
the *w* was taken into Pharaoh's	Gen 12:15	802
for the *w* which thou hast taken	Gen 20:3	802
Peradventure the *w* will not be	Gen 24:5	802
if the *w* will not be willing to	Gen 24:8	802
Peradventure the *w* will not	Gen 24:39	802
let the same be the *w* whom the	Gen 24:44	802
Shaul the son of a Canaanitish *w*	Gen 46:10	
the *w* conceived, and bare a son	Ex 2:2	802
the *w* took the child, and nursed	Ex 2:9	802
But every *w* shall borrow of her	Ex 3:22	802
Shaul the son of a Canaanitish *w*	Ex 6:15	
every *w* of her neighbour, jewels	Ex 11:2	802
hurt a *w* with child, so that her	Ex 21:22	802
If an ox gore a man or a *w*	Ex 21:28	802
that he hath killed a man or a *w*	Ex 21:29	802
unto the LORD, every man and *w*	Ex 35:29	802
Let neither man nor *w* make any	Ex 36:6	802
If a *w* have conceived seed, and	Lev 12:2	802
If a man or *w* have a plague upon	Lev 13:29	802
If a man also or a *w* have in the	Lev 13:38	802
The *w* also with whom man shall	Lev 15:18	802
if a *w* have an issue, and her	Lev 15:19	802
if a *w* have an issue of her blood	Lev 15:25	802
an issue, of the man, and of the *w*	Lev 15:33	5347
not uncover the nakedness of a *w*	Lev 18:17	802
unto a *w* to uncover her nakedness	Lev 18:19	802
neither shall any *w* stand before	Lev 18:23	802
whosoever lieth carnally with a *w*	Lev 19:20	802
mankind, as he lieth with a *w*	Lev 20:13	802
if a *w* approach unto any beast,	Lev 20:16	802
thereto, thou shalt kill the *w*	Lev 20:16	802
lie with a *w* having her sickness	Lev 20:18	802
A man also or *w* that hath a	Lev 20:27	802
a *w* put away from her husband	Lev 21:7	802
A widow, or a divorced *w*, or	Lev 21:14	
And the son of an Israelitish *w*	Lev 24:10	802
and this son of the Israelitish *w*	Lev 24:10	
When a man or *w* shall commit any	Num 5:6	802
shall set the *w* before the LORD	Num 5:18	802
her by an oath, and say unto the *w*	Num 5:19	802
the *w* with an oath of cursing	Num 5:21	802
the priest shall say unto the *w*	Num 5:21	802
the *w* shall say, Amen, amen	Num 5:22	802
he shall cause the *w* to drink the	Num 5:24	802
cause the *w* to drink the water	Num 5:26	802
the *w* shall be a curse among her	Num 5:27	802
if the *w* be not defiled, but be	Num 5:28	802
shall set the *w* before the LORD,	Num 5:30	802
this *w* shall bear her iniquity	Num 5:31	802
When either man or *w* shall	Num 6:2	802
Ethiopian *w* whom he had married	Num 12:1	802
for he had married an Ethiopian *w*	Num 12:1	802
w in the sight of Moses, and in	Num 25:6	
and the *w* through her belly	Num 25:8	802
was slain with the Midianitish *w*	Num 25:14	
w that was slain was Cozbi	Num 25:15	802
If a *w* also vow a vow unto the	Num 30:3	802
kill every *w* that hath known man	Num 31:17	802
an Hebrew man, or an Hebrew *w*	Deut 15:12	
thy God giveth thee, man or *w*	Deut 17:2	802
bring forth that man or that *w*	Deut 17:5	802
gates, even that man or that *w*	Deut 17:5	802
among the captives a beautiful *w*	Deut 21:11	802
The *w* shall not wear that which	Deut 22:5	802
upon her, and say, I took this *w*	Deut 22:14	802
with a *w* married to an husband	Deut 22:22	802
that lay with the *w*, and the *w*	Deut 22:22	802
delicate *w* among you, which would	Deut 28:56	
should be among you man, or *w*	Deut 29:18	802
the *w* took the two men, and hid	Josh 2:4	802
was in the city, both man and *w*	Josh 6:21	802
house, and bring out thence the *w*	Josh 6:22	802
sell Sisera into the hand of a *w*	Judg 4:9	802
a certain *w* cast a piece of a	Judg 9:53	802
men say not of me, A *w* slew him	Judg 9:54	802
thou art the son of a strange *w*	Judg 11:2	802
of the LORD appeared unto the *w*	Judg 13:3	802
Then the *w* came and told her	Judg 13:6	802
the *w* as she sat in the field	Judg 13:9	802
the *w* made haste, and ran, and	Judg 13:10	802
the man that spakest unto the *w*	Judg 13:11	802
I said unto the *w* let her beware	Judg 13:13	802
the *w* bare a son, and called his	Judg 13:24	802
saw a *w* in Timnath of the	Judg 14:1	802
I have seen a *w* in Timnath of the	Judg 14:2	802
Is there never a *w* among the	Judg 14:3	802
went down, and talked with the *w*	Judg 14:7	802
his father went down unto the *w*	Judg 14:10	802
that he loved a *w* in the valley	Judg 16:4	802
Then came the *w* in the dawning of	Judg 19:26	802
the *w* his concubine was fallen	Judg 19:27	802
husband of the *w* that was slain	Judg 20:4	802
every *w* that hath lain by man	Judg 21:11	802
the *w* was left of her two sons and	Ruth 1:5	802
and, behold, a *w* lay at his feet	Ruth 3:8	802
know that thou art a virtuous *w*	Ruth 3:11	802
that a *w* came into the floor	Ruth 3:14	802
The LORD make the *w* that is come	Ruth 4:11	802
shall give thee of this young *w*	Ruth 4:12	5291
I am a *w* of a sorrowful spirit	1Sa 1:15	802
So the *w* went her way, and did eat	1Sa 1:18	802
So the *w* abode, and gave her son	1Sa 1:23	802
I am the *w* that stood by thee	1Sa 1:26	802
w for the loan which is lent to	1Sa 2:20	802
but slay both man and *w*, infant and	1Sa 15:3	802
son of the perverse rebellious *w*	1Sa 20:30	
she was a *w* of good understanding	1Sa 25:3	802
and left neither man nor *w* alive	1Sa 27:9	802
saved neither man nor *w* alive	1Sa 27:11	802
Seek me a *w* that hath a familiar	1Sa 28:7	802
there is a *w* that hath a familiar	1Sa 28:7	802
and they came to the *w* by night	1Sa 28:8	802
the *w* said unto him, Behold, thou	1Sa 28:9	802
Then said the *w*, Whom shall I	1Sa 28:11	802
when the *w* saw Samuel, she cried	1Sa 28:12	802
the *w* spake to Saul, saying, Why	1Sa 28:12	802
the *w* said unto Saul, I saw gods	1Sa 28:13	802
the *w* came unto Saul, and saw that	1Sa 28:21	802
his servants, together with the *w*	1Sa 28:23	802
the *w* had a fat calf in the house	1Sa 28:24	802
with a fault concerning this *w*	2Sa 3:8	802
roof he saw a *w* washing herself	2Sa 11:2	802
the *w* was very beautiful to look	2Sa 11:2	802
sent and enquired after the *w*	2Sa 11:3	802
the *w* conceived, and sent and told	2Sa 11:5	802
did not a *w* cast a piece of a	2Sa 11:21	802
said, Put now this *w* out from me	2Sa 13:17	
and fetched thence a wise *w*	2Sa 14:2	802
but be as a *w* that had a long	2Sa 14:2	802
when the *w* of Tekoah spake to the	2Sa 14:4	802
answered, I am indeed a widow *w*	2Sa 14:5	802
And the king said unto the *w*	2Sa 14:8	802
the *w* of Tekoah said unto the	2Sa 14:9	802
Then the *w* said, Let thine	2Sa 14:12	802
the *w* said, Wherefore then hast	2Sa 14:13	802
king answered and said unto the *w*	2Sa 14:18	802
the *w* said, Let my lord the king	2Sa 14:18	802
the *w* answered and said, As thy	2Sa 14:19	802
she was a *w* of a fair countenance	2Sa 14:27	802
the *w* took and spread a covering	2Sa 17:19	802
came to the *w* to the house	2Sa 17:20	802
the *w* said unto them, They be	2Sa 17:20	802
cried a wise *w* out of the city	2Sa 20:16	802
the *w* said, Art thou Joab	2Sa 20:17	802
the *w* said unto Joab, Behold, his	2Sa 20:21	802
Then the *w* went unto all the	2Sa 20:22	802
And the one *w* said, O my lord, I	1Kin 3:17	802
this *w* dwell in one house	1Kin 3:17	802
that this *w* was delivered also	1Kin 3:18	802
And the other *w* said, Nay	1Kin 3:22	802
Then spake the *w* whose the living	1Kin 3:26	802
name was Zeruah, a widow *w*	1Kin 11:26	802
feign herself to be another *w*	1Kin 14:5	
a widow *w* there to sustain thee	1Kin 17:9	802
the widow *w* was there gathering	1Kin 17:10	802
things, that the son of the *w*	1Kin 17:17	802
the *w* said to Elijah, Now by this	1Kin 17:24	802
Now there cried a certain *w* of	2Kin 4:1	802
to Shunem, where was a great *w*	2Kin 4:8	802
the *w* conceived, and bare a son at	2Kin 4:17	802
wall, there cried a *w* unto him	2Kin 6:26	802
This *w* said unto me, Give thy son	2Kin 6:28	802
the king heard the words of the *w*	2Kin 6:30	802
Then spake Elisha unto the *w*	2Kin 8:1	802
the *w* arose, and did after the	2Kin 8:2	802
that the *w* returned out of the	2Kin 8:3	802
body to life, that, behold, the *w*	2Kin 8:5	802
My lord, O king, this is the *w*	2Kin 8:5	802
And when the king asked the *w*	2Kin 8:6	802
said, Go, see now this cursed *w*	2Kin 9:34	
one of Israel, both man and *w*	1Chr 16:3	802
The son of a *w* of the daughters	2Chr 2:14	802
small or great, whether man or *w*	2Chr 15:13	802
sons of Athaliah, that wicked *w*	2Chr 24:7	
that whosoever, whether man or *w*	Est 4:11	802
is born of a *w* is of few days	Job 14:1	802
and he which is born of a *w*	Job 15:14	802
he be clean that is born of a *w*	Job 25:4	802
heart have been deceived by a *w*	Job 31:9	802
and pain, as of a *w* in travail	Ps 48:6	
like the untimely birth of a *w*	Ps 58:8	802
maketh the barren *w* to keep house	Ps 113:9	
deliver thee from the strange *w*	Prov 2:16	802
a strange *w* drop as an honeycomb	Prov 5:3	

son, be ravished with a strange *w* Prov 5:20
To keep thee from the evil *w* Prov 6:24 802
of the tongue of a strange *w* Prov 6:24
For by means of a whorish *w* a man Prov 6:26 802
with a *w* lacketh understanding Prov 6:32 802
may keep thee from the strange *w* Prov 7:5 802
there met him a *w* with the attire Prov 7:10 802
A foolish *w* is clamorous Prov 9:13 802
A gracious *w* retaineth honour Prov 11:16 802
so is a fair *w* which is without Prov 11:22 802
A virtuous *w* is a crown to her Prov 12:4 802
Every wise *w* buildeth her house Prov 14:1 802
a pledge of him for a strange *w* Prov 20:16
housetop, than with a brawling *w* Prov 21:9 802
with a contentious and an angry *w* Prov 21:19 802
a strange *w* is a narrow pit Prov 23:27
housetop, than with a brawling *w* Prov 25:24 802
a pledge of him for a strange *w* Prov 27:13
day and a contentious *w* are alike Prov 27:15 802
is the way of an adulterous *w* Prov 30:20 802
For an odious *w* when she is Prov 30:23
Who can find a virtuous *w* Prov 31:10 802
but a *w* that feareth the LORD, Prov 31:30 802
find more bitter than death the *w* Eccl 7:26 802
but a *w* among all those have I Eccl 7:28 802
be in pain as a *w* that travaileth Is 13:8
the pangs of a *w* that travaileth Is 21:3
Like as a *w* with child, that Is 26:17
will I cry like a travailing *w* Is 42:14
or to the *w*, What hast thou Is 45:10 802
Can a *w* forget her sucking child, Is 49:15 802
hath called thee as a *w* forsaken Is 54:6 802
a voice as of a *w* in travail Jer 4:31
of Zion to a comely and delicate *w* Jer 6:2
us, and pain, as of a *w* in travail Jer 6:24
take thee, as a *w* in travail Jer 13:21 802
the pain as of a *w* in travail Jer 22:23
as a *w* in travail, and all faces Jer 30:6
the *w* with child and her that Jer 31:8
earth, A *w* shall compass a man Jer 31:22 5347
to cut off from you man and *w* Jer 44:7 802
as the heart of a *w* in her pangs Jer 48:41 802
as the heart of a *w* in her pangs Jer 49:22 802
have taken her, as a *w* in travail Jer 49:24
and pangs as of a *w* in travail Jer 50:43
will I break in pieces man and *w* Jer 51:22 802
is as a menstruous *w* among them Lam 1:17
work of an imperious whorish *w* Eze 16:30 802
hath come near to a menstruous *w* Eze 18:6 802
as they go in unto a *w* that Eze 23:44 802
as the uncleanness of a removed *w* Eze 36:17
love a *w* beloved of her friend, Hos 3:1 802
travailing *w* shall come upon him Hos 13:13
have taken thee as a *w* in travail Mic 4:9
of Zion, like a *w* in travail Mic 4:10
this is a *w* that sitteth in the Zec 5:7 802
on a *w* to lust after her hath Mt 5:28 *1135*
And, behold, a *w*, which was Mt 9:20 *1135*
the *w* was made whole from that Mt 9:22 *1135*
like unto leaven, which a *w* took Mt 13:33 *1135*
a *w* of Canaan came out of the Mt 15:22 *1135*
answered and said unto her, O *w* Mt 15:28 *1135*
And last of all the *w* died also Mt 22:27 *1135*
There came unto him a *w* having an Mt 26:7 *1135*
unto them, Why trouble ye the *w* Mt 26:10 *1135*
also this, that this *w* hath done Mt 26:13
And a certain *w*, which had an Mk 5:25 *1135*
But the *w* fearing and trembling, Mk 5:33 *1135*
For a certain *w*, whose young Mk 7:25 *1135*
The *w* was a Greek, a Mk 7:26 *1135*
if a *w* shall put away her husband Mk 10:12 *1135*
last of all the *w* died also Mk 12:22 *1135*
at meat, there came a *w* having an Mk 14:3 *1135*
unto a *w* that was a widow Lk 4:26 *1135*
a *w* in the city, which was a Lk 7:37 *1135*
what manner of *w* this is that Lk 7:39 *1135*
And he turned to the *w*, and said Lk 7:44 *1135*
unto Simon, Seest thou this *w* Lk 7:44
but this *w* since the time I came Lk 7:45
but this *w* hath anointed my feet Lk 7:46
And he said to the *w*, Thy faith Lk 7:50 *1135*
a *w* having an issue of blood Lk 8:43 *1135*
when the *w* saw that she was not Lk 8:47 *1135*
a certain *w* named Martha received Lk 10:38 *1135*
a certain *w* of the company lifted Lk 11:27 *1135*
there was a *w* which had a spirit Lk 13:11 *1135*
her to him, and said unto her, *W* Lk 13:12 *1135*
And ought not this *w*, being a Lk 13:16
It is like leaven, which a *w* took Lk 13:21 *1135*
Either what *w* having ten pieces Lk 15:8 *1135*
Last of all the *w* died also Lk 20:32 *1135*
And he denied him, saying, *W* Lk 22:57 *1135*
Jesus saith unto her, *W*, what Jn 2:4 *1135*
There cometh a *w* of Samaria to Jn 4:7 *1135*
Then saith the *w* of Samaria unto Jn 4:9 *1135*
of me, which am a *w* of Samaria Jn 4:9 *1135*
The *w* saith unto him, Sir, thou Jn 4:11 *1135*
The *w* saith unto him, Sir, give Jn 4:15 *1135*
The *w* answered and said, I have no Jn 4:17 *1135*
The *w* saith unto him, Sir, I Jn 4:19 *1135*
Jesus saith unto her, *W*, believe Jn 4:21 *1135*
The *w* saith unto him, I know that Jn 4:25 *1135*
that he talked with the *w* Jn 4:27 *1135*
The *w* then left her waterpot, and Jn 4:28 *1135*
on him for the saying of the *w* Jn 4:39 *1135*
And said unto the *w*, Now we Jn 4:42 *1135*
unto him a *w* taken in adultery Jn 8:3 *1135*
this *w* was taken in adultery, in Jn 8:4 *1135*
the *w* standing in the midst Jn 8:9 *1135*
up himself, and saw none but the *w* Jn 8:10 *1135*
he said unto her, *W* Jn 8:10 *1135*
A *w* when she is in travail hath Jn 16:21 *1135*
he saith unto his mother, *W*, Jn 19:26 *1135*
And they say unto her, *W*, why Jn 20:13 *1135*
Jesus saith unto her, *W*, why Jn 20:15 *1135*
this *w* was full of good works and Acts 9:36
Timotheus, the son of a certain *w* Acts 16:1 *1135*
a certain *w* named Lydia, a seller Acts 16:14 *1135*
a *w* named Damaris, and others with Acts 17:34 *1135*
leaving the natural use of the *w* Rom 1:27 *2338*
For the *w* which hath an husband Rom 7:2 *1135*
good for a man not to touch a *w* 1Cor 7:1 *1135*
let every *w* have her own husband 1Cor 7:2
the *w* which hath an husband that 1Cor 7:13 *1135*
The unmarried *w* careth for the 1Cor 7:34 *1135*
and the head of the *w* is the man 1Cor 11:3 *1135*
But every *w* that prayeth or 1Cor 11:5 *1135*
For if the *w* be not covered, let 1Cor 11:6 *1135*
for a *w* to be shorn or shaven 1Cor 11:6 *1135*
but the *w* is the glory of the man 1Cor 11:7 *1135*
For the man is not of the *w* 1Cor 11:8 *1135*
but the *w* of the man 1Cor 11:8 *1135*
was the man created for the *w* 1Cor 11:9 *1135*
but the *w* for the man 1Cor 11:9 *1135*
For this cause ought the *w* to 1Cor 11:10 *1135*
neither is the man without the *w* 1Cor 11:11 *1135*
neither the *w* without the man, in 1Cor 11:11 *1135*
For as the *w* is of the man 1Cor 11:12 *1135*
even so is the man also by the *w* 1Cor 11:12 *1135*
is it comely that a *w* pray unto 1Cor 11:13 *1135*
But if a *w* have long hair, it is 1Cor 11:15 *1135*
sent forth his Son, made of a *w* Gal 4:4 *1135*
heir with the son of the free *w* Gal 4:30 *1658*
as travail upon a *w* with child 1Th 5:3
Let the *w* learn in silence with 1Ti 2:11 *1135*
But I suffer not a *w* to teach 1Ti 2:12 *1135*
but the *w* being deceived was in 1Ti 2:14 *1135*
If any man or *w* that believeth 1Ti 5:16
thou sufferest that *w* Jezebel Rev 2:20 *1135*
a *w* clothed with the sun, and the Rev 12:1 *1135*
the dragon stood before the *w* Rev 12:4 *1135*
the *w* fled into the wilderness, Rev 12:6 *1135*
he persecuted the *w* which brought Rev 12:13 *1135*
to the *w* were given two wings of Rev 12:14 *1135*
water as a flood after the *w* Rev 12:15 *1135*
And the earth helped the *w* Rev 12:16 *1135*
the dragon was wroth with the *w* Rev 12:17 *1135*
I saw a *w* sit upon a scarlet Rev 17:3 *1135*
the *w* was arrayed in purple and Rev 17:4 *1135*
I saw the *w* drunken with the Rev 17:6 *1135*
tell thee the mystery of the *w* Rev 17:7 *1135*
mountains, on which the *w* sitteth Rev 17:9 *1135*
the *w* which thou sawest is that Rev 17:18 *1135*

WOMANKIND

not lie with mankind, as with *w* Lev 18:22 802

WOMAN'S

his pledge from the *w* hand Gen 38:20 802
according as the *w* husband will Ex 21:22 802
the Israelitish *w* son blasphemed Lev 24:11 802
the LORD, and uncover the *w* head Num 5:18 802
offering out of the *w* hand Num 5:25 802
shall a man put on a *w* garment Deut 22:5 802
this *w* child died in the night 1Kin 3:19 802

WOMB

her, Two nations are in thy *w* Gen 25:23 990
behold, there were twins in her *w* Gen 25:24 990
Leah was hated, he opened her *w* Gen 29:31 7358
from thee the fruit of the *w* Gen 30:2 990
hearkened to her, and opened her *w* Gen 30:22 7358
that, behold, twins were in her *w* Gen 38:27 990
of the breasts, and of the *w* Gen 49:25 7356
whatsoever openeth the *w* among Ex 13:2 7358
instead of such as open every *w* Num 8:16 7358
he cometh out of his mother's *w* Num 12:12 7358
also bless the fruit of thy *w* Deut 7:13 990
be a Nazarite unto God from the *w* Judg 13:5 990
the *w* to the day of his death Judg 13:7 990
unto God from my mother's *w* Judg 16:17 990
there yet any more sons in my *w* Ruth 1:11 4578
but the LORD had shut up her *w* 1Sa 1:5 7358
the LORD had shut up her *w* 1Sa 1:6 7358
Naked came I out of my mother's *w* Job 1:21 990
not up the doors of my mother's *w* Job 3:10 990
Why died I not from the *w* Job 3:11 7358
brought me forth out of the *w* Job 10:18 7358
carried from the *w* to the grave Job 10:19 990
The *w* shall forget him Job 24:20 7358
he that made me in the *w* make him Job 31:15 990
did not one fashion us in the *w* Job 31:15 7358
guided her from my mother's *w* Job 31:18 990
as if it had issued out of the *w* Job 38:8 7358
Out of whose *w* came the ice Job 38:29 990
art he that took me out of the *w* Ps 22:9 990
I was cast upon thee from the *w* Ps 22:10 7358
wicked are estranged from the *w* Ps 58:3 7358
have I been holden up from the *w* Ps 71:6 990
from the *w* of the morning Ps 110:3 7358
the fruit of the *w* is his reward Ps 127:3 990
hast covered me in my mother's *w* Ps 139:13 990
and the barren *w* Prov 30:16 7356
and what, the son of my *w* Prov 31:2 990
he came forth of his mother's *w* Eccl 5:15 990
the *w* of her that is with child Eccl 11:5 990
no pity on the fruit of the *w* Is 13:18 990
thee, and formed thee from the *w* Is 44:2 990
and he that formed thee from the *w* Is 44:24 990
which are carried from the *w* Is 46:3 7356
called a transgressor from the *w* Is 48:8 990
LORD hath called me from the *w* Is 49:1 990
me from the *w* to be his servant Is 49:5 990
compassion on the son of her *w* Is 49:15 990
to bring forth, and shut the *w* Is 66:9
out of the *w* I sanctified thee Jer 1:5 7358
Because he slew me not from the *w* Jer 20:17 7358
her *w* to be always great with me Jer 20:17 7358
forth out of the *w* to see labour Jer 20:18 7358
the fire all that openeth the *w* Eze 20:26 7356
from the birth, and from the *w* Hos 9:11 990
give them a miscarrying *w* Hos 9:14 7358
even the beloved fruit of their *w* Hos 9:16 990
his brother by the heel in the *w* Hos 12:3 990
so born from their mother's *w* Mt 19:12 *2836*
Ghost, even from his mother's *w* Lk 1:15 *2836*
thou shalt conceive in thy *w* Lk 1:31 *1064*
of Mary, the babe leaped in her *w* Lk 1:41 *2836*
and blessed is the fruit of thy *w* Lk 1:42 *2836*
the babe leaped in my *w* for joy Lk 1:44 *2836*
before he was conceived in the *w* Lk 2:21 *2836*
the *w* shall be called holy to the Lk 2:23 *3388*
Blessed is the *w* that bare thee Lk 11:27 *2836*
second time into his mother's *w* Jn 3:4 *2836*
from his mother's *w* was carried Acts 3:2 *2836*
a cripple from his mother's *w* Acts 14:8 *2836*
yet the deadness of Sarah's *w* Rom 4:19 *3388*
separated me from my mother's *w* Gal 1:15 *2836*

WOMBS

the *w* of the house of Abimelech Gen 20:18 7358
the *w* that never bare, and the Lk 23:29 *2836*

WOMEN

the *w* also, and the people Gen 14:16 802
with Sarah after the manner of *w* Gen 18:11 802
even the time that *w* go out to Gen 24:11
for the custom of *w* is upon me Gen 31:35 802
lifted up his eyes, and saw the *w* Gen 33:5 802
of a midwife to the Hebrew *w* Ex 1:16
Because the Hebrew *w* are not as Ex 1:19 802
not as the Egyptian *w* Ex 1:19 802
to thee a nurse of the Hebrew *w* Ex 2:7
all the *w* went out after her with Ex 15:20 802
And they came, both men and *w* Ex 35:22 802
all the *w* that were wise hearted Ex 35:25 802
all the *w* whose heart stirred Ex 35:26 802
of the *w* assembling, which Ex 38:8
ten *w* shall bake your bread in Lev 26:26 802
took all the *w* of Midian captives Num 31:9 802
Have ye saved all the *w* alive Num 31:15 5347
But all the *w* children, that have Num 31:18 802
of *w* that had not known man by Num 31:35 802
destroyed the men, and the *w* Deut 2:34 802
utterly destroying the men, *w* Deut 3:6 802
But the *w*, and the little ones, and Deut 20:14 802
the people together, men, and *w* Deut 31:12 802
fell that day, both of men and *w* Josh 8:25 802
of Israel, with the *w*, and the Josh 8:35 802
Blessed above *w* shall Jael the Judg 5:24 802
shall she be above *w* in the tent Judg 5:24 802
also, about a thousand men and *w* Judg 9:49 802
and thither fled all the men and *w* Judg 9:51 802
the house was full of men and *w* Judg 16:27 802
about three thousand men and *w* Judg 16:27 802
the edge of the sword, with the *w* Judg 21:10 802
alive of the *w* of Jabesh-gilead Judg 21:14 802
seeing the *w* are destroyed out of Judg 21:16 802
took them wives of the *w* of Moab Ruth 1:4 802
the *w* said unto Naomi, Blessed be Ruth 4:14 802
the *w* her neighbours gave it a Ruth 4:17
how they lay with the *w* that 1Sa 2:22 802
w that stood by her said unto her 1Sa 4:20
thy sword hath made *w* childless 1Sa 15:33 802
thy mother be childless among *w* 1Sa 15:33 802
that the *w* came out of all cities 1Sa 18:6 802
the *w* answered one another as 1Sa 18:7 802
kept themselves at least from *w* 1Sa 21:4 802
Of a truth *w* have been kept from 1Sa 21:5 802
edge of the sword, both men and *w* 1Sa 22:19 802
And had taken the *w* captives 1Sa 30:2 802
wonderful, passing the love of *w* 2Sa 1:26 802
Israel, as well to the *w* as men 2Sa 6:19 802
And the king left ten *w*, which 2Sa 15:16 802
voice of singing men and singing *w* 2Sa 19:35
took the ten *w* his concubines 2Sa 20:3 802
Then came there two *w*, that were 1Kin 3:16 802
king Solomon loved many strange *w* 1Kin 11:1 802
w of the Moabites, Ammonites, 1Kin 11:1
and rip up their *w* with child 2Kin 8:12
all the *w* therein that were with 2Kin 15:16
where the *w* wove hangings for the 2Kin 23:7 802
brethren two hundred thousand, *w* 2Chr 28:8 802
the singing *w* spake of Josiah in 2Chr 35:25
hundred singing men and singing *w* Ezr 2:65
great congregation of men and *w* Ezr 10:1 802
and five singing men and singing *w* Neh 7:67
the congregation both of men and *w* Neh 8:2 802
midday, before the men and the *w* Neh 8:3 802
him did outlandish *w* cause to sin Neh 13:26 802
the *w* in the royal house which Est 1:9 802
shall come abroad unto all *w* Est 1:17 802
the palace, to the house of the *w* Est 2:3 802
chamberlain, keeper of the *w* Est 2:3 802
custody of Hegai, keeper of the *w* Est 2:8 802
best place of the house of the *w* Est 2:9 802
according to the manner of the *w* Est 2:12 802
things for the purifying of the *w* Est 2:12 802
of the *w* unto the king's house Est 2:13 802
into the second house of the *w* Est 2:14 802
chamberlain, the keeper of the *w* Est 2:15 802
king loved Esther above all the *w* Est 2:17 802
and old, little children and *w* Est 3:13 802
them, both little ones and *w* Est 8:11 802
as one of the foolish *w* speaketh Job 2:10
in all the land were no *w* found Job 42:15 802
were among thy honourable *w* Ps 45:9
mouth of strange *w* is a deep pit Prov 22:14
Thine eyes shall behold strange *w* Prov 23:33
Give not thy strength unto *w* Prov 31:3 802
w singers, and the delights of the Eccl 2:8
know not, O thou fairest among *w* Song 1:8 802
beloved, O thou fairest among *w* Song 5:9 802
gone, O thou fairest among *w* Song 6:1 802

oppressors, and *w* rule over them ... Is 3:12 802
in that day seven *w* shall take ... Is 4:1 802
day shall Egypt be like unto *w* ... Is 19:16 802
the *w* come, and set them on fire ... Is 27:11 802
Rise up, ye *w* that are at ease ... Is 32:9 802
ye be troubled, ye careless *w* ... Is 32:10
Tremble, ye *w* that are at ease ... Is 32:11
the *w* knead their dough, to make ... Jer 7:18 802
ye, and call for the mourning *w* ... Jer 9:17
and send for cunning *w*, that they ... Jer 9:17
hear the word of the LORD, O ye *w* ... Jer 9:20 802
all the *w* that are left in the ... Jer 38:22 802
those *w* shall say, Thy friends ... Jer 38:22
had committed unto him men, and *w* .. Jer 40:7 802
even mighty men of war, and the *w* ... Jer 41:16 802
Even men, and *w*, and children, and ... Jer 43:6 802
all the *w* that stood by, a great ... Jer 44:15 802
people, to the men, and to the *w* ... Jer 44:20 802
all the people, and to all the *w* ... Jer 44:24 802
and they shall become as *w* ... Jer 50:37 802
they became as *w* ... Jer 51:30 802
Shall the *w* eat their fruit, and ... Lam 2:20 802
The hands of the pitiful *w* have ... Lam 4:10 802
They ravished the *w* in Zion ... Lam 5:11 802
there sat *w* weeping for Tammuz ... Eze 8:14 802
maids, and little children, and *w* ... Eze 9:6 802
Woe to the *w* that sew pillows to ... Eze 13:18
from other *w* in thy whoredoms ... Eze 16:34 802
as *w* that break wedlock and shed ... Eze 16:38
upon thee in the sight of many *w* ... Eze 16:41 802
Son of man, there were two *w* ... Eze 23:2 802
and she became famous among *w* ... Eze 23:10 802
and unto Aholibah, the lewd *w* ... Eze 23:44 802
the manner of *w* that shed blood ... Eze 23:45
that all *w* may be taught not to ... Eze 23:48 802
shall give him the daughter of *w* ... Dan 11:17 802
his fathers, nor the desire of *w* ... Dan 11:37 802
their *w* with child shall be ... Hos 13:16
up the *w* with child of Gilead ... Amos 1:13
The *w* of my people have ye cast ... Mic 2:9 802
people in the midst of thee are *w* ... Nah 3:13 802
and, behold, there came out two *w* ... Zec 5:9 802
old *w* dwell in the streets of ... Zec 8:4
houses rifled, and the *w* ravished ... Zec 14:2 802
Among them that are born of *w* ... Mt 11:11 *1135*
about five thousand men, beside *w* ... Mt 14:21 *1135*
were four thousand men, beside *w* ... Mt 15:38 *1135*
Two *w* shall be grinding at the ... Mt 24:41 *1135*
many *w* were there beholding afar ... Mt 27:55 *1135*
angel answered and said unto the *w* ... Mt 28:5 *1135*
There were also *w* looking on afar ... Mk 15:40 *1135*
many other *w* which came up with ... Mk 15:41 *1135*
blessed art thou among *w* ... Lk 1:28 *1135*
and said, Blessed art thou among *w* ... Lk 1:42 *1135*
Among those that are born of *w* ... Lk 7:28 *1135*
And certain *w*, which had been ... Lk 8:2 *1135*
Two *w* shall be grinding together ... Lk 17:35 *1135*
great company of people, and of *w* ... Lk 23:27 *1135*
the *w* that followed him from ... Lk 23:49 *1135*
the *w* also, which came with him ... Lk 23:55 *1135*
other *w* that were with them, ... Lk 24:10 *1135*
certain *w* also of our company ... Lk 24:22 *1135*
it even so as the *w* had said ... Lk 24:24 *1135*
and supplication, with the *w* ... Acts 1:14 *1135*
Lord, multitudes both of men and *w* ... Acts 5:14 *1135*
w committed them to prison ... Acts 8:3 *1135*
they were baptized, both men and *w* ... Acts 8:12 *1135*
way, whether they were men or *w* ... Acts 9:2 *1135*
up the devout and honourable *w* ... Acts 13:50 *1135*
spake unto the *w* which resorted ... Acts 16:13 *1135*
and of the chief *w* not a few ... Acts 17:4 *1135*
of honourable *w* which were Greeks ... Acts 17:12 *1135*
into prisons both men and *w* ... Acts 22:4 *1135*
for even their *w* did change the ... Rom 1:26 *2338*
Let your *w* keep silence in the ... 1Cor 14:34 *1135*
for it is a shame for *w* to speak ... 1Cor 14:35 *1135*
help those *w* which laboured with ... Phil 4:3
that *w* adorn themselves in modest ... 1Ti 2:9 *1135*
But (which becometh *w* professing ... 1Ti 2:10 *1135*
The elder *w* as mothers ... 1Ti 5:2
that the younger *w* marry, bear ... 1Ti 5:14
captive silly *w* laden with sins ... 2Ti 3:6 *1133*
The aged *w* likewise, that they be ... Titus 2:3 *4247*
may teach the young *w* to be sober ... Titus 2:4
W received their dead raised to ... Heb 11:35 *1135*
in the old time the holy *w* also ... 1Pet 3:5 *1135*
And they had hair as the hair of *w* ... Rev 9:8 *1135*
which were not defiled with *w* ... Rev 14:4 *1135*

WOMEN'S

before the court of the *w* house ... Est 2:11 802

WOMENSERVANTS

and oxen, and menservants, and *w* ... Gen 20:14 8198
flocks, and menservants, and *w* ... Gen 32:5 8198
took his two wives, and his two *w* ... Gen 32:22 8198

WON

Out of the spoils *w* in battles ... 1Chr 26:27
harder to be *w* than a strong city ... Prov 18:19
be *w* by the conversation of the ... 1Pet 3:1 *2770*

WONDER

and giveth thee a sign or a *w* ... Deut 13:1 4159
And the sign or the *w* come to pass ... Deut 13:2 4159
upon thee for a sign and for a *w* ... Deut 28:46 4159
the *w* that was done in the land ... 2Chr 32:31 4159
I am as a *w* unto many ... Ps 71:7 4159
w upon Egypt and upon Ethiopia ... Is 20:3 4159
Stay yourselves, and *w* ... Is 29:9 8539
even a marvellous work and a *w* ... Is 29:14 6382
and the prophets shall *w* ... Jer 4:9 8539
and regard, and *w* marvellously ... Hab 1:5 8539
and they were filled with *w* ... Acts 3:10 *2285*
Behold, ye despisers, and *w* ... Acts 13:41 *2296*
appeared a great *w* in heaven ... Rev 12:1 *4592*
appeared another *w* in heaven ... Rev 12:3 *4592*
that dwell on the earth shall *w* ... Rev 17:8 *2296*

WONDERED

w that there was no intercessor ... Is 59:16 8074
I *w* that there was none to uphold ... Is 63:5 8074
for they are men *w* at ... Zec 3:8 4159
Insomuch that the multitude *w* ... Mt 15:31 *2296*
themselves beyond measure, and *w* ... Mk 6:51 *2296*
all they that heard it *w* at those ... Lk 2:18 *2296*
w at the gracious words which ... Lk 4:22 *2296*
And they being afraid *w*, saying ... Lk 8:25 *2296*
But while they *w* every one at all ... Lk 9:43 *2296*
and the people *w* ... Lk 11:14 *2296*
yet believed not for joy, and *w* ... Lk 24:41 *2296*
Moses saw it, he *w* at the sight ... Acts 7:31 *2296*
he continued with Philip, and *w* ... Acts 8:13 *1839*
all the world *w* after the beast ... Rev 13:3 *2296*
I *w* with great admiration ... Rev 17:6 *2296*

WONDERFUL

the LORD will make thy plagues *w* ... Deut 28:59 6381
thy love to me was *w*, passing the ... 2Sa 1:26 6381
about to build shall be *w* great ... 2Chr 2:9 6381
things too *w* for me, which I knew ... Job 42:3 6381
are thy *w* works which thou hast ... Ps 40:5 6381
his *w* works that he hath done ... Ps 78:4 6381
for his *w* works to the children ... Ps 107:8 6381
for his *w* works to the children ... Ps 107:15 6381
for his *w* works to the children ... Ps 107:21 6381
for his *w* works to the children ... Ps 107:31 6381
He hath made his *w* works to be ... Ps 111:4 6381
Thy testimonies are *w* ... Ps 119:129 6382
Such knowledge is too *w* for me ... Ps 139:6 6383
things which are too *w* for me ... Prov 30:18 6381
and his name shall be called W ... Is 9:6 6382
for thou hast done *w* things ... Is 25:1 6382
which is *w* in counsel, and ... Is 28:29 6381
A *w* and horrible thing is ... Jer 5:30 8047
and in thy name done many *w* works .. Mt 7:22 *1411*
scribes saw the *w* things that he ... Mt 21:15 *2297*
in our tongues the *w* works of God ... Acts 2:11 *3167*

WONDERFULLY

when he had wrought *w* among them . 1Sa 6:6 5953
for I am fearfully and *w* made ... Ps 139:14 6395
therefore she came down *w* ... Lam 1:9 6382
and he shall destroy *w*, and shall ... Dan 8:24 6381

WONDERING

the man *w* at her held his peace, ... Gen 24:21 7583
w in himself at that which was ... Lk 24:12 *2296*
is called Solomon's, greatly *w* ... Acts 3:11 *1569*

WONDEROUSLY

and the angel did *w* ... Judg 13:19 6381

WONDERS

smite Egypt with all my *w* which I ... Ex 3:20 6381
do all those *w* before Pharaoh ... Ex 4:21 4159
my *w* in the land of Egypt ... Ex 7:3 4159
that my *w* may be multiplied in ... Ex 11:9 4159
did all these *w* before Pharaoh ... Ex 11:10 4159
fearful in praises, doing *w* ... Ex 15:11 6382
by temptations, by signs, and by *w* ... Deut 4:34 4159
And the LORD shewed signs and *w* ... Deut 6:22 4159
eyes saw, and the signs, and the *w* ... Deut 7:19 4159
and with signs, and with *w* ... Deut 26:8 4159
In all the signs and the *w* ... Deut 34:11 4159
the LORD will do *w* among you ... Josh 3:5 6381
works that he hath done, his *w* ... 1Chr 16:12 4159
w upon Pharaoh, and on all his ... Neh 9:10 4159
thy *w* that thou didst among them ... Neh 9:17 6381
yea, and *w* without number ... Job 9:10 6381
I will remember thy *w* of old ... Ps 77:11 6382
Thou art the God that doest *w* ... Ps 77:14 6382
his *w* that he had shewed them ... Ps 78:11 6381
his *w* in the field of Zoan ... Ps 78:43 4159
Wilt thou shew *w* to the dead ... Ps 88:10 6382
Shall thy *w* be known in the dark ... Ps 88:12 6382
And the heavens shall praise thy *w* ... Ps 89:5 6382
heathen, his *w* among all people ... Ps 96:3 6381
his *w*, and the judgments of his ... Ps 105:5 4159
them, and *w* in the land of Ham ... Ps 105:27 4159
understood not thy *w* in Egypt ... Ps 106:7 6381
of the LORD, and his *w* in the deep ... Ps 107:24 6381
w into the midst of thee, O Egypt ... Ps 135:9 4159
To him who alone doeth great *w* ... Ps 136:4 6381
for *w* in Israel from the LORD of ... Is 8:18 4159
w in the land of Egypt, even unto ... Jer 32:20 4159
of Egypt with signs, and with *w* ... Jer 32:21 4159
w that the high God hath wrought ... Dan 4:2 8540
and how mighty are his *w* ... Dan 4:3 8540
w in heaven and in earth, who hath ... Dan 6:27 8540
shall it be to the end of these *w* ... Dan 12:6 6382
I will shew *w* in the heavens and ... Joel 2:30 4159
and shall shew great signs and *w* ... Mt 24:24 *5059*
rise, and shall shew signs and *w* ... Mk 13:22 *5059*
him, Except ye see signs and *w* ... Jn 4:48 *5059*
I will shew *w* in heaven above, and ... Acts 2:19 *5059*
of God among you by miracles and *w* . Acts 2:22 *5059*
and many *w* and signs were done by ... Acts 2:43 *5059*
w may be done by the name of thy ... Acts 4:30 *5059*
w wrought among the people ... Acts 5:12 *5059*
of faith and power, did great *w* ... Acts 6:8 *5059*
out, after that he had shewed *w* ... Acts 7:36 *5059*
w to be done by their hands ... Acts 14:3 *5059*
w God had wrought among the ... Acts 15:12 *5059*
Through mighty signs and *w* ... Rom 15:19 *5059*
in all patience, in signs, and *w* ... 2Cor 12:12 *5059*
all power and signs and lying *w* ... 2Th 2:9 *5059*
witness, both with signs and *w* ... Heb 2:4 *5059*
And he doeth great *w*, so that he ... Rev 13:13 *4592*

WONDROUS

him, talk ye of all his *w* works ... 1Chr 16:9 6381
and consider the *w* works of God ... Job 37:14 6381
the *w* works of him which is ... Job 37:16 4652
and tell of all thy *w* works ... Ps 26:7 6381
have I declared thy *w* works ... Ps 71:17 6381
Israel, who only doeth *w* things ... Ps 72:18 6381
name is near thy *w* works declare ... Ps 75:1 6381
and believed not for his *w* works ... Ps 78:32 6381
thou art great, and doest *w* things ... Ps 86:10 6381
talk ye of all his *w* works ... Ps 105:2 6381
W works in the land of Ham, and ... Ps 106:22 6381
that I may behold *w* things out of ... Ps 119:18 6381
so shall I talk of thy *w* works ... Ps 119:27 6381
of thy majesty, and of thy *w* works ... Ps 145:5 6381
us according to all his *w* works ... Jer 21:2 6381

WONDROUSLY

God, that hath dealt *w* with you ... Joel 2:26 6381

WONT

But if the ox were *w* to push with ... Ex 21:29 5056
was I ever *w* to do so unto thee ... Num 22:30 5532
and his men were *w* to haunt ... 1Sa 30:31 1980
They were *w* to speak in old time, ... 2Sa 20:18 1696
more than it was *w* to be heated ... Dan 3:19 2370
w to release unto the people a ... Mt 27:15 *1486*
and, as he was *w*, he taught them ... Mk 10:1 *1486*
he came out, and went, as he was *w* ... Lk 22:39
where prayer was *w* to be made ... Acts 16:13 *3543*

WOOD

Make thee an ark of gopher *w* ... Gen 6:14 6086
clave the *w* for the burnt ... Gen 22:3 6086
Abraham took the *w* of the burnt ... Gen 22:6 6086
he said, Behold the fire and the *w* ... Gen 22:7 6086
there, and laid the *w* in order ... Gen 22:9 6086
laid him on the altar upon the *w* ... Gen 22:9 6086
of Egypt, both in vessels of *w* ... Ex 7:19 6086
and badgers' skins, and shittim *w* ... Ex 25:5 6086
shall make an ark of shittim *w* ... Ex 25:10 6086
shalt make staves of shittim *w* ... Ex 25:13 6086
also make a table of shittim *w* ... Ex 25:23 6086
make the staves of shittim *w* ... Ex 25:28 6086
of shittim *w* standing up ... Ex 26:15 6086
thou shalt make bars of shittim *w* ... Ex 26:26 6086
of shittim *w* overlaid with gold ... Ex 26:32
hanging five pillars of shittim *w* ... Ex 26:37
shalt make an altar of shittim *w* ... Ex 27:1 6086
the altar, staves of shittim *w* ... Ex 27:6 6086
of shittim *w* shalt thou make it ... Ex 30:1 6086
make the staves of shittim *w* ... Ex 30:5 6086
and badgers' skins, and shittim *w* ... Ex 35:7 6086
w for any work of the service ... Ex 35:24 6086
to set them, and in carving of *w* ... Ex 35:33 6086
for the tabernacle of shittim *w* ... Ex 36:20 6086
And he made bars of shittim *w* ... Ex 36:31 6086
four pillars of shittim *w* ... Ex 36:36
made the ark of shittim *w* ... Ex 37:1 6086
And he made staves of shittim *w* ... Ex 37:4 6086
And he made the table of shittim *w* ... Ex 37:10 6086
he made the staves of shittim *w* ... Ex 37:15 6086
the incense altar of shittim *w* ... Ex 37:25 6086
he made the staves of shittim *w* ... Ex 37:28 6086
of burnt offering of shittim *w* ... Ex 38:1 6086
he made the staves of shittim *w* ... Ex 38:6 6086
lay the *w* in order upon the fire ... Lev 1:7 6086
in order upon the *w* that is on ... Lev 1:8 6086
w that is on the fire which is ... Lev 1:12 6086
upon the *w* that is upon the fire ... Lev 1:17 6086
which is upon the *w* that is on ... Lev 3:5 6086
and burn him on the *w* with fire ... Lev 4:12 6086
shall burn *w* on it every morning ... Lev 6:12 6086
whether it be any vessel of *w* ... Lev 11:32 6086
birds alive and clean, and cedar *w* ... Lev 14:4 6086
he shall take it, and the cedar *w* ... Lev 14:6 6086
the house two birds, and cedar *w* ... Lev 14:49 6086
And he shall take the cedar *w* ... Lev 14:51 6086
living bird, and with the cedar *w* ... Lev 14:52 6086
every vessel of *w* shall be rinsed ... Lev 15:12 6086
lean, whether there be *w* therein ... Num 13:20 6086
And the priest shall take cedar *w* ... Num 19:6 6086
hair, and all things made of *w* ... Num 31:20 6086
him with an hand weapon of *w* ... Num 35:18 6086
gods, the work of men's hands, *w* ... Deut 4:28 6086
mount, and make thee an ark of *w* ... Deut 10:1 6086
And I made an ark of shittim *w* ... Deut 10:3 6086
As when a man goeth into the *w* ... Deut 19:5 3293
his neighbour to hew *w* ... Deut 19:5 6086
shalt thou serve other gods, *w* ... Deut 28:36 6086
thy fathers have known, even *w* ... Deut 28:64 6086
from the hewer of thy *w* unto the ... Deut 29:11 6086
abominations, and their idols, *w* ... Deut 29:17 6086
but let them be hewers of *w* ... Josh 9:21 6086
being bondmen, and hewers of *w* ... Josh 9:23 6086
made them that day hewers of *w* ... Josh 9:27 6086
then get thee up to the *w* country ... Josh 17:15 3293
for it is a *w*, and thou shalt cut ... Josh 17:18 3293
a burnt sacrifice with the *w* of ... Judg 6:26 6086
and they clave the *w* of the cart ... 1Sa 6:14 6086
all they of the land came to a *w* ... 1Sa 14:25 3293
the people were come into the *w* ... 1Sa 14:26 3293
in the wilderness of Ziph in a *w* ... 1Sa 23:15 2793
and went to David into the *w* ... 1Sa 23:16 2793
and David abode in the *w*, and ... 1Sa 23:18 2793
with us in strong holds in the *w* ... 1Sa 23:19 2793
of instruments made of fir *w* ... 2Sa 6:5 6086
battle was in the *w* of Ephraim ... 2Sa 18:6 3293
the *w* devoured more people that ... 2Sa 18:8 3293
him into a great pit in the *w* ... 2Sa 18:17 3293
instruments of the oxen for *w* ... 2Sa 24:22 6086
covered them on the inside with *w* ... 1Kin 6:15 6086
cut it in pieces, and lay it on *w* ... 1Kin 18:23 6086
the other bullock, and lay it on *w* ... 1Kin 18:23 6086
And he put the *w* in order, and cut ... 1Kin 18:33 6086
in pieces, and laid him on the *w* ... 1Kin 18:33 6086
the burnt sacrifice, and on the *w* ... 1Kin 18:33 6086
the burnt sacrifice, and the *w* ... 1Kin 18:38 6086

W

forth two she bears out of the *w*	2Kin 2:24	3293
came to Jordan, they cut down *w*	2Kin 6:4	6086
but the work of men's hands, *w*	2Kin 19:18	6086
Then shall the trees of the *w*	1Chr 16:33	3293
the threshing instruments for *w*	1Chr 21:23	6086
brought much cedar *w* to David	1Chr 22:4	6086
of iron, and *w* for things of *w*	1Chr 29:2	6086
we will cut *w* out of Lebanon, as	2Chr 2:16	6086
scribe stood upon a pulpit of *w*	Neh 8:4	6086
for the *w* offering, to bring it	Neh 10:34	6086
for the *w* offering, at times	Neh 13:31	6086
as straw, and brass as rotten *w*	Job 41:27	6086
boar out of the *w* doth waste it	Ps 80:13	3293
As the fire burneth a *w*, and as	Ps 83:14	3293
all the trees of the *w* rejoice	Ps 96:12	3293
found it in the fields of the *w*	Ps 132:6	3293
cleaveth *w* upon the earth	Ps 141:7	
Where no *w* is, there the fire	Prov 26:20	6086
to burning coals, and *w* to fire	Prov 26:21	6086
to water therewith the *w* that	Eccl 2:6	3293
he that cleaveth *w* shall be	Eccl 10:9	6086
tree among the trees of the *w*	Song 2:3	3293
a chariot of the *w* of Lebanon	Song 3:9	6086
as the trees of the *w* are moved	Is 7:2	3293
up itself, as if it were no *w*	Is 10:15	6086
pile thereof is fire and much *w*	Is 30:33	6086
but the work of men's hands, *w*	Is 37:19	6086
up the *w* of their graven image	Is 45:20	6086
for *w* brass, and for stones iron	Is 60:17	6086
thy mouth fire, and this people *w*	Jer 5:14	6086
The children gather *w*, and the	Jer 7:18	6086
Thou hast broken the yokes of *w*	Jer 28:13	6086
her with axes, as hewers of *w*	Jer 46:22	6086
our *w* is sold unto us	Lam 5:4	6086
and the children fell under the *w*	Lam 5:13	6086
Shall *w* be taken thereof to do	Eze 15:3	6086
of the countries, to serve *w*	Eze 20:32	6086
Heap on *w*, kindle the fire,	Eze 24:10	6086
shall take no *w* out of the field	Eze 39:10	6086
door, cieled with *w* round about	Eze 41:16	6086
The altar of *w* was three cubits	Eze 41:22	6086
and the walls thereof, were of *w*	Eze 41:22	6086
silver, of brass, of iron, of *w*	Dan 5:4	636
and gold, of brass, iron, *w*	Dan 5:23	636
which dwell solitarily in the *w*	Mic 7:14	3293
Woe unto him that saith to the *w*	Hab 2:19	6086
Go up to the mountain, and bring *w*	Hag 1:8	6086
an hearth of fire among the *w*	Zec 12:6	6086
gold, silver, precious stones, *w*	1Cor 3:12	*3586*
gold and of silver, but also of *w*	2Ti 2:20	*3585*
and brass, and stone, and of *w*	Rev 9:20	*3585*
silk, and scarlet, and all thyine *w*	Rev 18:12	*3586*
manner vessels of most precious *w*	Rev 18:12	*3586*

WOODS

the wilderness, and sleep in the *w*	Eze 34:25	3264

WOOF

Whether it be in the warp, or *w*	Lev 13:48	6154
either in the warp, or in the *w*	Lev 13:49	6154
either in the warp, or in the *w*	Lev 13:51	6154
that garment, whether warp or *w*	Lev 13:52	6154
either in the warp, or in the *w*	Lev 13:53	6154
out of the warp, or out of the *w*	Lev 13:56	6154
either in the warp, or in the *w*	Lev 13:57	6154
And the garment, either warp, or *w*	Lev 13:58	6154
linen, either in the warp, or *w*	Lev 13:59	6154

WOOL

put a fleece of *w* in the floor	Judg 6:37	6785
hundred thousand rams, with the *w*	2Kin 3:4	6785
He giveth snow like *w*	Ps 147:16	6785
She seeketh *w*, and flax, and	Prov 31:13	6785
like crimson, they shall be as *w*	Is 1:18	6785
and the worm shall eat them like *w*	Is 51:8	6785
in the wine of Helbon, and white *w*	Eze 27:18	6785
fat, and ye clothe you with the *w*	Eze 34:3	6785
no *w* shall come upon them, whiles	Eze 44:17	6785
hair of his head like the pure *w*	Dan 7:9	6015
me my bread and my water, my *w*	Hos 2:5	6785
thereof, and will recover my *w*	Hos 2:9	6785
goats, with water, and scarlet *w*	Heb 9:19	*2053*
and his hairs were white like *w*	Rev 1:14	*2053*

WOOLLEN

is in, whether it be a *w* garment	Lev 13:47	6785
of linen, or of *w*	Lev 13:48	6785
in *w* or in linen, or any thing of	Lev 13:52	6785
in a garment of *w* or linen	Lev 13:59	6785
of linen and *w* come upon thee	Lev 19:19	8162
garment of divers sorts, as of *w*	Deut 22:11	6785

WORD

After these things the *w* of the	Gen 15:1	1697
the *w* of the LORD came unto him,	Gen 15:4	1697
it might be according to thy *w*	Gen 30:34	1697
and bring me *w* again	Gen 37:14	1697
according unto thy *w* shall all my	Gen 41:40	6310
to the *w* that Joseph had spoken	Gen 44:2	1697
speak a *w* in my lord's ears, and	Gen 44:18	1697
he said, Be it according to thy *w*	Ex 8:10	1697
did according to the *w* of Moses	Ex 8:13	1697
did according to the *w* of Moses	Ex 8:31	1697
He that feared the *w* of the LORD	Ex 9:20	1697
he that regarded not the *w* of the	Ex 9:21	1697
did according to the *w* of Moses	Ex 12:35	1697
Is not this the *w* that we did	Ex 14:12	1697
did according to the *w* of Moses	Ex 32:28	1697
did according to the *w* of Moses	Lev 10:7	1697
according to the *w* of the LORD	Num 3:16	6310
according to the *w* of the LORD	Num 3:51	6310
the *w* of the LORD by the hand of	Num 4:45	6310
thou shalt see now whether my *w*	Num 11:23	1697
and brought back *w* unto them	Num 13:26	1697
have pardoned according to thy *w*	Num 14:20	1697
hath despised the *w* of the LORD	Num 15:31	1697
my *w* at the water of Meribah	Num 20:24	6310
and I will bring you *w* again	Num 22:8	1697
beyond the *w* of the LORD my God	Num 22:18	6310
but yet the *w* which I shall say	Num 22:20	1697
but only the *w* that I shalt speak	Num 22:35	1697
the *w* that God putteth in my	Num 22:38	1697
the LORD put a *w* in Balaam's	Num 23:5	1697
put a *w* in his mouth, and said, Go	Num 23:16	1697
at his *w* shall they go out	Num 27:21	6310
at his *w* they shall come in, both	Num 27:21	6310
he shall not break his *w*, he	Num 30:2	1697
according to the *w* of the LORD	Num 36:5	6310
bring us *w* again by what way we	Deut 1:22	1697
unto us, and brought us *w* again	Deut 1:25	1697
unto the *w* which I command you	Deut 4:2	1697
to shew you the *w* of the LORD	Deut 5:5	1697
but by every *w* that proceedeth	Deut 8:3	
that he may perform the *w* which	Deut 9:5	1697
presume to speak a *w* in my name	Deut 18:20	1697
How shall we know the *w* which the	Deut 18:21	1697
and by their *w* shall every	Deut 21:5	6310
But the *w* is very nigh unto thee,	Deut 30:14	1697
for they have observed thy *w*	Deut 33:9	565
according to the *w* of the LORD	Deut 34:5	6310
Remember the *w* which Moses the	Josh 1:13	1697
neither shall any *w* proceed out	Josh 6:10	1697
according unto the *w* of the LORD	Josh 8:27	1697
There was not a *w* of all that	Josh 8:35	1697
I brought him *w* again as it was	Josh 14:7	1697
the LORD spake this *w* unto Moses	Josh 14:10	1697
According to the *w* of the LORD	Josh 19:50	6310
according to the *w* of the LORD by	Josh 22:9	6310
Israel, and brought them *w* again	Josh 22:32	1697
only the LORD establish his *w*	1Sa 1:23	1697
the *w* of the LORD was precious in	1Sa 3:1	1697
neither was the *w* of the LORD yet	1Sa 3:7	1697
in Shiloh by the *w* of the LORD	1Sa 3:21	1697
the *w* of Samuel came to all	1Sa 4:1	1697
that I may shew thee the *w* of God	1Sa 9:27	1697
Then came the *w* of the LORD unto	1Sa 15:10	1697
hast rejected the *w* of the LORD	1Sa 15:23	1697
hast rejected the *w* of the LORD	1Sa 15:26	1697
could not answer Abner a *w* again	2Sa 3:11	1697
that the *w* of the LORD came unto	2Sa 7:4	1697
I a *w* with any of the tribes of	2Sa 7:7	1697
the *w* that thou hast spoken	2Sa 7:25	1697
speak one *w* unto my lord the king	2Sa 14:12	1697
The *w* of my lord the king shall	2Sa 14:17	1697
until there come *w* from you to	2Sa 15:28	1697
not a *w* of bringing the king back	2Sa 19:10	
they sent this *w* unto the king	2Sa 19:14	
the *w* of the LORD is tried	2Sa 22:31	565
by me, and his *w* was in my tongue	2Sa 23:2	4405
king's *w* prevailed against Joab	2Sa 24:4	1697
the *w* of the LORD came unto the	2Sa 24:11	1697
w which he spake concerning me	1Kin 2:4	1697
this *w* against his own life	1Kin 2:23	1697
he might fulfil the *w* of the LORD	1Kin 2:27	1697
Benaiah brought the king *w* again	1Kin 2:30	1697
The *w* that I have heard is good	1Kin 2:42	1697
the *w* of the LORD came to Solomon	1Kin 6:11	1697
will I perform my *w* with thee	1Kin 6:12	1697
performed his *w* that he spake	1Kin 8:20	1697
now, O God of Israel, let thy *w*	1Kin 8:26	1697
one *w* of all his good promise	1Kin 8:56	1697
But the *w* of God came unto	1Kin 12:22	1697
therefore to the *w* of the LORD	1Kin 12:24	1697
according to the *w* of the LORD	1Kin 12:24	1697
by the *w* of the LORD unto Beth-el	1Kin 13:1	1697
the altar in the *w* of the LORD	1Kin 13:2	1697
had given by the *w* of the LORD	1Kin 13:5	1697
charged me by the *w* of the LORD	1Kin 13:9	1697
said to me by the *w* of the LORD	1Kin 13:17	1697
unto me by the *w* of the LORD	1Kin 13:18	1697
that the *w* of the LORD came unto	1Kin 13:20	1697
unto the *w* of the LORD	1Kin 13:26	6310
according to the *w* of the LORD	1Kin 13:26	1697
saying which he cried by the *w* of	1Kin 13:32	1697
according to the *w* of the LORD	1Kin 14:18	1697
Then the *w* of the LORD came to	1Kin 16:1	1697
the *w* of the LORD against Baasha	1Kin 16:7	1697
according to the *w* of the LORD	1Kin 16:12	1697
according to the *w* of the LORD	1Kin 16:34	1697
years, but according to my *w*	1Kin 17:1	1697
the *w* of the LORD came unto him,	1Kin 17:2	1697
according unto the *w* of the LORD	1Kin 17:5	1697
the *w* of the LORD came unto him,	1Kin 17:8	1697
according to the *w* of the LORD	1Kin 17:16	1697
that the *w* of the LORD in thy	1Kin 17:24	1697
that the *w* of the LORD came to	1Kin 18:1	1697
the people answered him not a *w*	1Kin 18:21	1697
unto whom the *w* of the LORD came,	1Kin 18:31	1697
done all these things at thy *w*	1Kin 18:36	1697
the *w* of the LORD came to him, and	1Kin 19:9	1697
departed, and brought him *w* again	1Kin 20:9	1697
neighbour in the *w* of the LORD	1Kin 20:35	1697
displeased because of the *w* which	1Kin 21:4	1697
the *w* of the LORD came to Elijah	1Kin 21:17	1697
the *w* of the LORD came to Elijah	1Kin 21:28	1697
at the *w* of the LORD to day	1Kin 22:5	1697
let thy *w*, I pray thee	1Kin 22:13	1697
be like the *w* of one of them, and	1Kin 22:13	1697
thou therefore the *w* of the LORD	1Kin 22:19	1697
according unto the *w* of the LORD	1Kin 22:38	1697
God in Israel to enquire of his *w*	2Kin 1:16	1697
So he died according to the *w* of	2Kin 1:17	1697
The *w* of the LORD is with him	2Kin 3:12	1697
according to the *w* of the LORD	2Kin 4:44	1697
according to the *w* of Elisha	2Kin 6:18	1697
said, Hear ye the *w* of the LORD	2Kin 7:1	1697
according to the *w* of the LORD	2Kin 7:16	1697
according to the *w* of the LORD	2Kin 9:26	1697
said, This is the *w* of the LORD	2Kin 9:36	1697
nothing of the *w* of the LORD	2Kin 10:10	1697
according to the *w* of the LORD	2Kin 14:25	1697
This was the *w* of the LORD which	2Kin 15:12	1697
Hear the *w* of the great king, the	2Kin 18:28	1697
peace, and answered him not a *w*	2Kin 18:36	1697
This is the *w* that the LORD hath	2Kin 19:21	1697
that the *w* of the LORD came to	2Kin 20:4	1697
Hezekiah, Hear the *w* of the LORD	2Kin 20:16	1697
Good is the *w* of the LORD which	2Kin 20:19	1697
king, and brought the king *w* again	2Kin 22:9	1697
And they brought the king *w* again	2Kin 22:20	1697
according to the *w* of the LORD	2Kin 23:16	1697
according to the *w* of the LORD	2Kin 24:2	1697
even against the *w* of the LORD	1Chr 10:13	1697
according to the *w* of the LORD by	1Chr 11:3	1697
according to the *w* of the LORD	1Chr 11:10	1697
according to the *w* of the LORD	1Chr 12:23	6310
according to the *w* of the LORD	1Chr 15:15	1697
the *w* which he commanded to a	1Chr 16:15	1697
that the *w* of God came to Nathan,	1Chr 17:3	1697
spake I a *w* to any of the judges	1Chr 17:6	1697
king's *w* prevailed against Joab	1Chr 21:4	1697
for the king's *w* was abominable	1Chr 21:6	1697
therefore advise thyself what *w* I	1Chr 21:12	1697
But the *w* of the LORD came to me,	1Chr 22:8	1697
his *w* that he hath spoken	2Chr 6:10	1697
let thy *w* be verified, which thou	2Chr 6:17	1697
that the LORD might perform his *w*	2Chr 10:15	1697
But the *w* of the LORD came to	2Chr 11:2	1697
the *w* of the LORD came to	2Chr 12:7	1697
at the *w* of the LORD to day	2Chr 18:4	1697
let thy *w* therefore, I pray thee,	2Chr 18:12	1697
Therefore hear the *w* of the LORD	2Chr 18:18	1697
the princes, by the *w* of the LORD	2Chr 30:12	1697
and brought the king *w* back again	2Chr 34:16	1697
have not kept the *w* of the LORD	2Chr 34:21	1697
So they brought the king *w* again	2Chr 34:28	1697
the *w* of the LORD by the hand of	2Chr 35:6	1697
To fulfil the *w* of the LORD by	2Chr 36:21	1697
that the *w* of the LORD spoken by	2Chr 36:22	1697
that the *w* of the LORD by the	Ezr 1:1	1697
that whosoever shall alter this *w*	Ezr 6:11	6600
should do according to this *w*	Ezr 10:5	1697
the *w* that thou commandedst thy	Neh 1:8	1697
did according to the *w* of Memucan	Est 1:21	1697
As the *w* went out of the king's	Est 7:8	1697
and none spake a *w* unto him	Job 2:13	1697
by the *w* of thy lips I have kept	Ps 17:4	1697
the *w* of the LORD is tried	Ps 18:30	565
For the *w* of the LORD is right	Ps 33:4	1697
By the *w* of the LORD were the	Ps 33:6	1697
In God I will praise his *w*	Ps 56:4	1697
In God will I praise his *w*	Ps 56:10	1697
in the LORD will I praise his *w*	Ps 56:10	1697
The Lord gave the *w*	Ps 68:11	562
unto the voice of his *w*	Ps 103:20	1697
the *w* which he commanded to a	Ps 105:8	1697
Until the time that his *w* came	Ps 105:19	1697
the *w* of the LORD tried him	Ps 105:19	565
they rebelled not against his *w*	Ps 105:28	1697
land, they believed not his *w*	Ps 106:24	1697
He sent his *w*, and healed them, and	Ps 107:20	1697
heed thereto according to thy *w*	Ps 119:9	1697
Thy *w* have I hid in mine heart,	Ps 119:11	565
I will not forget thy *w*	Ps 119:16	1697
that I may live, and keep thy *w*	Ps 119:17	1697
thou me according to thy *w*	Ps 119:25	1697
thou me according unto thy *w*	Ps 119:28	1697
Stablish thy *w* unto thy servant,	Ps 119:38	565
thy salvation, according to thy *w*	Ps 119:41	565
for I trust in thy *w*	Ps 119:42	1697
take not the *w* of truth utterly	Ps 119:43	1697
Remember the *w* unto thy servant,	Ps 119:49	1697
for thy *w* hath quickened me	Ps 119:50	565
unto me according to thy *w*	Ps 119:58	565
O LORD, according unto thy *w*	Ps 119:65	1697
but now have I kept thy *w*	Ps 119:67	565
because I have hoped in thy *w*	Ps 119:74	1697
to thy *w* unto thy servant	Ps 119:76	565
but I hope in thy *w*	Ps 119:81	1697
Mine eyes fail for thy *w*, saying,	Ps 119:82	565
thy *w* is settled in heaven	Ps 119:89	1697
evil way, that I might keep thy *w*	Ps 119:101	1697
Thy *w* is a lamp unto my feet, and	Ps 119:105	1697
me, O LORD, according unto thy *w*	Ps 119:107	1697
I hope in thy *w*	Ps 119:114	1697
Uphold me according unto thy *w*	Ps 119:116	565
for the *w* of thy righteousness	Ps 119:123	565
Order my steps in thy *w*	Ps 119:133	565
Thy *w* is very pure	Ps 119:140	565
I hoped in thy *w*	Ps 119:147	1697
that I might meditate in thy *w*	Ps 119:148	565
quicken me according to thy *w*	Ps 119:154	565
because they kept not thy *w*	Ps 119:158	565
Thy *w* is true from the beginning	Ps 119:160	1697
my heart standeth in awe of thy *w*	Ps 119:161	1697
I rejoice at thy *w*, as one that	Ps 119:162	565
understanding according to thy *w*	Ps 119:169	1697
deliver me according to thy *w*	Ps 119:170	565
My tongue shall speak of thy *w*	Ps 119:172	565
doth wait, and in his *w* do I hope	Ps 130:5	1697
thy *w* above all thy name	Ps 138:2	565
For there is not a *w* in my tongue	Ps 139:4	4405
his *w* runneth very swiftly	Ps 147:15	1697
He sendeth out his *w*, and melteth	Ps 147:18	1697
He sheweth his *w* unto Jacob	Ps 147:19	1697
stormy wind fulfilling his *w*	Ps 148:8	1697
but a good *w* maketh it glad	Prov 12:25	1697
the *w* shall be destroyed	Prov 13:13	1697
The simple believeth every *w*	Prov 14:15	1697
a *w* spoken in due season, how	Prov 15:23	1697
A *w* fitly spoken is like apples	Prov 25:11	1697
Every *w* of God is pure	Prov 30:5	565
Where the *w* of a king is, there	Eccl 8:4	1697
Hear the *w* of the LORD, ye rulers	Is 1:10	1697

The *w* that Isaiah the son of Amoz	Is 2:1	1697
the *w* of the LORD from Jerusalem	Is 2:3	1697
despised the *w* of the Holy One of	Is 5:24	565
speak the *w*, and it shall not	Is 8:10	1697
speak not according to this *w*	Is 8:20	1697
The Lord sent a *w* into Jacob	Is 9:8	1697
This is the *w* that the LORD hath	Is 16:13	1697
for the LORD hath spoken this *w*	Is 24:3	1697
But the *w* of the LORD was unto	Is 28:13	1697
Wherefore hear the *w* of the LORD	Is 28:14	1697
make a man an offender for a *w*	Is 29:21	1697
Israel, Because ye despise this *w*	Is 30:12	1697
ears shall hear a *w* behind thee	Is 30:21	1697
peace, and answered him not a *w*	Is 36:21	1697
This is the *w* which the LORD hath	Is 37:22	1697
Then came the *w* of the LORD to	Is 38:4	1697
Hear the *w* of the LORD of hosts	Is 39:5	1697
Good is the *w* of the LORD which	Is 39:8	1697
but the *w* of our God shall stand	Is 40:8	1697
I asked of them, could answer a *w*	Is 41:28	1697
confirmeth the *w* of his servant	Is 44:26	1697
the *w* is gone out of my mouth in	Is 45:23	1697
I should know how to speak a *w* in	Is 50:4	1697
So shall my *w* be that goeth forth	Is 55:11	1697
spirit, and trembleth at my *w*	Is 66:2	1697
Hear the *w* of the LORD	Is 66:5	1697
ye that tremble at his *w*	Is 66:5	1697
To whom the *w* of the LORD came in	Jer 1:2	1697
Then the *w* of the LORD came unto	Jer 1:4	1697
Moreover the *w* of the LORD came	Jer 1:11	1697
I will hasten my *w* to perform it	Jer 1:12	1697
the *w* of the LORD came unto me	Jer 1:13	1697
Moreover the *w* of the LORD came	Jer 2:1	1697
Hear ye the *w* of the LORD	Jer 2:4	1697
see ye the *w* of the LORD	Jer 2:31	1697
wind, and the *w* is not in them	Jer 5:13	1699
of hosts, Because ye speak this *w*	Jer 5:14	1697
the *w* of the LORD is unto them a	Jer 6:10	1697
The *w* that came to Jeremiah from	Jer 7:1	1697
house, and proclaim there this *w*	Jer 7:2	1697
Hear the *w* of the LORD, all ye of	Jer 7:2	1697
have rejected the *w* of the LORD	Jer 8:9	1697
Yet hear the *w* of the LORD	Jer 9:20	1697
ear receive the *w* of his mouth	Jer 9:20	1697
Hear ye the *w* which the LORD	Jer 10:1	1697
The *w* that came to Jeremiah from	Jer 11:1	1697
according to the *w* of the LORD	Jer 13:2	1697
the *w* of the LORD came unto me	Jer 13:3	1697
Then the *w* of the LORD came unto	Jer 13:8	1697
thou shalt speak unto them this *w*	Jer 13:12	1697
The *w* of the LORD that came to	Jer 14:1	1697
thou shalt say this *w* unto them	Jer 14:17	1697
thy *w* was unto me the joy and	Jer 15:16	1697
The *w* of the LORD came also unto	Jer 16:1	1697
me, Where is the *w* of the LORD	Jer 17:15	1697
them, Hear ye the *w* of the LORD	Jer 17:20	1697
The *w* which came to Jeremiah from	Jer 18:1	1697
Then the *w* of the LORD came to me	Jer 18:5	1697
nor the *w* from the prophet	Jer 18:18	1697
And say, Hear ye the *w* of the LORD	Jer 19:3	1697
because the *w* of the LORD was	Jer 20:8	1697
But his *w* was in mine heart as a	Jer 20:9	1697
The *w* which came unto Jeremiah	Jer 21:1	1697
say, Hear ye the *w* of the LORD	Jer 21:11	1697
of Judah, and speak there this *w*	Jer 22:1	1697
Hear the *w* of the LORD, O king of	Jer 22:2	1697
earth, hear the *w* of the LORD	Jer 22:29	1697
and hath perceived and heard his *w*	Jer 23:18	1697
who hath marked his *w*, and heard	Jer 23:18	1697
and he that hath my *w*	Jer 23:28	1697
let him speak my *w* faithfully	Jer 23:28	1697
Is not my *w* like as a fire	Jer 23:29	1697
for every man's *w* shall be his	Jer 23:36	1697
Because ye say this *w*, The burden	Jer 23:38	1697
Again the *w* of the LORD came unto	Jer 24:4	1697
The *w* that came to Jeremiah	Jer 25:1	1697
the *w* of the LORD hath come unto	Jer 25:3	1697
Judah came this *w* from the LORD	Jer 26:1	1697
diminish not a *w*	Jer 26:2	1697
w unto Jeremiah from the LORD	Jer 27:1	1697
if the *w* of the LORD be with them	Jer 27:18	1697
this *w* that I speak in thine ears	Jer 28:7	1697
when the *w* of the prophet shall	Jer 28:9	1697
Then the *w* of the LORD came unto	Jer 28:12	1697
and perform my good *w* toward you	Jer 29:10	1697
ye therefore the *w* of the LORD	Jer 29:20	1697
Then came the *w* of the LORD unto	Jer 29:30	1697
The *w* that came to Jeremiah from	Jer 30:1	1697
Hear the *w* of the LORD, O ye	Jer 31:10	1697
The *w* that came to Jeremiah from	Jer 32:1	1697
The *w* of the LORD came unto me,	Jer 32:6	1697
according to the *w* of the LORD	Jer 32:8	1697
that this was the *w* of the LORD	Jer 32:8	1697
Then came the *w* of the LORD unto	Jer 32:26	1697
Moreover the *w* of the LORD came	Jer 33:1	1697
the *w* of the LORD came unto	Jer 33:19	1697
Moreover the *w* of the LORD came	Jer 33:23	1697
The *w* which came unto Jeremiah	Jer 34:1	1697
Yet hear the *w* of the LORD	Jer 34:4	1697
for I have pronounced the *w*	Jer 34:5	1697
This is the *w* that came unto	Jer 34:8	1697
Therefore the *w* of the LORD came	Jer 34:12	1697
The *w* which came unto Jeremiah	Jer 35:1	1697
Then came the *w* of the LORD unto	Jer 35:12	1697
that this *w* came unto Jeremiah	Jer 36:1	1697
Then the *w* of the LORD came to	Jer 36:27	1697
Then came the *w* of the LORD unto	Jer 37:6	1697
Is there any *w* from the LORD	Jer 37:17	1697
this is the *w* that the LORD hath	Jer 38:21	1697
Now the *w* of the LORD came unto	Jer 39:15	1697
The *w* that came to Jeremiah from	Jer 40:1	1697
that the *w* of the LORD came unto	Jer 42:7	1697
therefore hear the *w* of the LORD	Jer 42:15	1697
Then came the *w* of the LORD unto	Jer 43:8	1697
The *w* that came to Jeremiah	Jer 44:1	1697
As for the *w* that thou hast	Jer 44:16	1697
Hear the *w* of the LORD, all Judah	Jer 44:24	1697
hear ye the *w* of the LORD	Jer 44:26	1697
The *w* that Jeremiah the prophet	Jer 45:1	1697
The *w* of the LORD which came to	Jer 46:1	1697
The *w* that the LORD spake to	Jer 46:13	1697
The *w* of the LORD that came to	Jer 47:1	1697
The *w* of the LORD that came to	Jer 49:34	1697
The *w* that the LORD spake against	Jer 50:1	1697
The *w* which Jeremiah the prophet	Jer 51:59	1697
he hath fulfilled his *w* that he	Lam 2:17	565
The *w* of the LORD came expressly	Eze 1:3	1697
that the *w* of the LORD came unto	Eze 3:16	1697
therefore hear the *w* at my mouth	Eze 3:17	1697
the *w* of the LORD came unto me,	Eze 6:1	1697
hear the *w* of the Lord GOD	Eze 6:3	1697
Moreover the *w* of the LORD came	Eze 7:1	1697
Again the *w* of the LORD came unto	Eze 11:14	1697
The *w* of the LORD also came unto	Eze 12:1	1697
came the *w* of the LORD unto me	Eze 12:8	1697
Moreover the *w* of the LORD came	Eze 12:17	1697
the *w* of the LORD came unto me,	Eze 12:21	1697
the *w* that I shall speak shall	Eze 12:25	1697
house, will I say the *w*, and will	Eze 12:25	1697
Again the *w* of the LORD came to	Eze 12:26	1697
but the *w* which I have spoken	Eze 12:28	1697
the *w* of the LORD came unto me,	Eze 13:1	1697
hearts, Hear ye the *w* of the LORD	Eze 13:2	1697
that they would confirm the *w*	Eze 13:6	1697
the *w* of the LORD came unto me,	Eze 14:2	1697
The *w* of the LORD came again to	Eze 14:12	1697
the *w* of the LORD came unto me,	Eze 15:1	1697
Again the *w* of the LORD came unto	Eze 16:1	1697
O harlot, hear the *w* of the LORD	Eze 16:35	1697
the *w* of the LORD came unto me,	Eze 17:1	1697
Moreover the *w* of the LORD came	Eze 17:11	1697
The *w* of the LORD came unto me	Eze 18:1	1697
Then came the *w* of the LORD unto	Eze 20:2	1697
Moreover the *w* of the LORD came	Eze 20:45	1697
drop thy *w* toward the south, and	Eze 20:46	
the south, Hear the *w* of the LORD	Eze 20:47	1697
the *w* of the LORD came unto me,	Eze 21:1	1697
drop thy *w* toward the holy places	Eze 21:2	
Again the *w* of the LORD came unto	Eze 21:8	1697
The *w* of the LORD came unto me	Eze 21:18	1697
Moreover the *w* of the LORD came	Eze 22:1	1697
the *w* of the LORD came unto me,	Eze 22:17	1697
the *w* of the LORD came unto me,	Eze 22:23	1697
The *w* of the LORD came again unto	Eze 23:1	1697
the *w* of the LORD came unto me,	Eze 24:1	1697
Also the *w* of the LORD came unto	Eze 24:15	1697
The *w* of the LORD came unto me,	Eze 24:20	1697
The *w* of the LORD came again unto	Eze 25:1	1697
Hear the *w* of the Lord GOD	Eze 25:3	1697
that the *w* of the LORD came unto	Eze 26:1	1697
The *w* of the LORD came again unto	Eze 27:1	1697
The *w* of the LORD came again unto	Eze 28:1	1697
Moreover the *w* of the LORD came	Eze 28:11	1697
Again the *w* of the LORD came unto	Eze 28:20	1697
the *w* of the LORD came unto me,	Eze 29:1	1697
the *w* of the LORD came unto me,	Eze 29:17	1697
The *w* of the LORD came again unto	Eze 30:1	1697
that the *w* of the LORD came unto	Eze 30:20	1697
that the *w* of the LORD came unto	Eze 31:1	1697
that the *w* of the LORD came unto	Eze 32:1	1697
that the *w* of the LORD came unto	Eze 32:17	1697
Again the *w* of the LORD came unto	Eze 33:1	1697
thou shalt hear the *w* at my mouth	Eze 33:7	1697
Then the *w* of the LORD came unto	Eze 33:23	1697
hear what is the *w* that cometh	Eze 33:30	1697
the *w* of the Lord came unto me,	Eze 34:1	1697
shepherds, hear the *w* of the LORD	Eze 34:7	1697
shepherds, hear the *w* of the LORD	Eze 34:9	1697
Moreover the *w* of the LORD came	Eze 35:1	1697
of Israel, hear the *w* of the LORD	Eze 36:1	1697
hear the *w* of the Lord GOD	Eze 36:4	1697
Moreover the *w* of the LORD came	Eze 36:16	1697
dry bones, hear the *w* of the LORD	Eze 37:4	1697
The *w* of the LORD came again unto	Eze 37:15	1697
the *w* of the LORD came unto me,	Eze 38:1	1697
him, and have changed the king's *w*	Dan 3:28	4406
demand by the *w* of the holy ones	Dan 4:17	3983
While the *w* was in the king's	Dan 4:31	4406
whereof the *w* of the LORD came to	Dan 9:2	1697
when he had spoken this *w* unto me	Dan 10:11	1697
The *w* of the LORD that came unto	Hos 1:1	1697
of the *w* of the LORD by Hosea	Hos 1:2	1699
Hear the *w* of the LORD, ye	Hos 4:1	1697
The *w* of the LORD that came to	Joel 1:1	1697
he is strong that executeth his *w*	Joel 2:11	1697
Hear this *w* that the LORD hath	Amos 3:1	1697
Hear this *w*, ye kine of Bashan,	Amos 4:1	1697
Hear ye this *w* which I take up	Amos 5:1	1697
hear thou the *w* of the LORD	Amos 7:16	1697
drop not thy *w* against the house	Amos 7:16	
and fro to seek the *w* of the LORD	Amos 8:12	1697
Now the *w* of the LORD came unto	Jonah 1:1	1697
the *w* of the LORD came unto Jonah	Jonah 3:1	1697
according to the *w* of the LORD	Jonah 3:3	1697
For *w* came unto the king of	Jonah 3:6	1697
The *w* of the LORD that came to	Mic 1:1	1697
the *w* of the LORD from Jerusalem	Mic 4:2	1697
oaths of the tribes, even thy *w*	Hab 3:9	562
The *w* of the LORD which came unto	Zeph 1:1	1697
the *w* of the LORD is against you	Zeph 2:5	1697
came the *w* of the LORD by Haggai	Hag 1:1	1697
Then came the *w* of the LORD by	Hag 1:3	1697
came the *w* of the LORD by the	Hag 2:1	1697
According to the *w* that I	Hag 2:5	1697
came the *w* of the LORD by Haggai	Hag 2:10	1697
again the *w* of the LORD came unto	Hag 2:20	1697
came the *w* of the LORD unto	Zec 1:1	1697
came the *w* of the LORD unto	Zec 1:7	1697
This is the *w* of the LORD unto	Zec 4:6	1697
Moreover the *w* of the LORD came	Zec 4:8	1697
the *w* of the LORD came unto me,	Zec 6:9	1697
that the *w* of the LORD came unto	Zec 7:1	1697
Then came the *w* of the LORD of	Zec 7:4	1697
the *w* of the LORD came unto	Zec 7:8	1697
Again the *w* of the LORD of hosts	Zec 8:1	1697
the *w* of the LORD of hosts came	Zec 8:18	1697
The burden of the *w* of the LORD	Zec 9:1	1697
that it was the *w* of the LORD	Zec 11:11	1697
The burden of the *w* of the LORD	Zec 12:1	1697
The burden of the *w* of the LORD	Mal 1:1	1697
have found him, bring me *w* again	Mt 2:8	*518*
thou there until I bring thee *w*	Mt 2:13	*2036*
but by every *w* that proceedeth	Mt 4:4	*4487*
but speak the *w* only, and my	Mt 8:8	*3056*
cast out the spirits with his *w*	Mt 8:16	*3056*
whosoever speaketh a *w* against	Mt 12:32	*3056*
That every idle *w* that men shall	Mt 12:36	*4487*
one heareth the *w* of the kingdom	Mt 13:19	*3056*
the same is he that heareth the *w*	Mt 13:20	*3056*
ariseth because of the *w*, by and	Mt 13:21	*3056*
thorns is he that heareth the *w*	Mt 13:22	*3056*
of riches, choke the *w*, and he	Mt 13:22	*3056*
ground is he that heareth the *w*	Mt 13:23	*3056*
But he answered her not a *w*	Mt 15:23	*3056*
every *w* may be established	Mt 18:16	*4487*
no man was able to answer him a *w*	Mt 22:46	*3056*
Peter remembered the *w* of Jesus	Mt 26:75	*4487*
And he answered him to never a *w*	Mt 27:14	*4487*
did run to bring his disciples *w*	Mt 28:8	*518*
and he preached the *w* unto them	Mk 2:2	*3056*
The sower soweth the *w*	Mk 4:14	*3056*
the way side, where the *w* is sown	Mk 4:15	*3056*
taketh away the *w* that was sown	Mk 4:15	*3056*
who, when they have heard the *w*	Mk 4:16	*3056*
such as hear the *w*,	Mk 4:18	*3056*
things entering in, choke the *w*	Mk 4:19	*3056*
such as hear the *w*, and receive it	Mk 4:20	*3056*
parables spake he the *w* unto them	Mk 4:33	*3056*
Jesus heard the *w* that was spoken	Mk 5:36	*3056*
Making the *w* of God of none	Mk 7:13	*3056*
the *w* that Jesus said unto him	Mk 14:72	*4487*
confirming the *w* with signs	Mk 16:20	*3056*
and ministers of the *w*	Lk 1:2	*3056*
be it unto me according to thy *w*	Lk 1:38	*4487*
in peace, according to thy *w*	Lk 2:29	*4487*
the *w* of God came unto John the	Lk 3:2	*4487*
alone, but by every *w* of God	Lk 4:4	*4487*
for his *w* was with power	Lk 4:32	*3056*
saying, What a *w* is this	Lk 4:36	*3056*
upon him to hear the *w* of God	Lk 5:1	*3056*
nevertheless at thy *w* I will let	Lk 5:5	*4487*
but say in a *w*, and my servant	Lk 7:7	*3056*
The seed is the *w* of God	Lk 8:11	*3056*
taketh away the *w* out of their	Lk 8:12	*3056*
they hear, receive the *w* with joy	Lk 8:13	*3056*
and good heart, having heard the *w*	Lk 8:15	*3056*
are these which hear the *w* of God	Lk 8:21	*3056*
at Jesus' feet, and heard his *w*	Lk 10:39	*3056*
are they that hear the *w* of God	Lk 11:28	*3056*
speak a *w* against the Son of man	Lk 12:10	*3056*
remembered the *w* of the Lord	Lk 22:61	*3056*
w before God and all the people	Lk 24:19	*3056*
In the beginning was the *W*	Jn 1:1	*3056*
the *W* was with God	Jn 1:1	*3056*
and the *W* was God	Jn 1:1	*3056*
the *W* was made flesh, and dwelt	Jn 1:14	*3056*
the *w* which Jesus had said	Jn 2:22	*3056*
believed because of his own *w*	Jn 4:41	*3056*
the man believed the *w* that Jesus	Jn 4:50	*3056*
unto you, He that heareth my *w*	Jn 5:24	*3056*
ye have not his *w* abiding in you	Jn 5:38	*3056*
on him, If ye continue in my *w*	Jn 8:31	*3056*
because my *w* hath no place in you	Jn 8:37	*3056*
even because ye cannot hear my *w*	Jn 8:43	*3056*
gods, unto whom the *w* of God came	Jn 10:35	*3056*
the *w* that I have spoken, the	Jn 12:48	*3056*
the *w* which ye hear is not mine,	Jn 14:24	*3056*
w which I have spoken unto you	Jn 15:3	*3056*
Remember the *w* that I said unto	Jn 15:20	*3056*
that the *w* might be fulfilled	Jn 15:25	*3056*
and they have kept thy *w*	Jn 17:6	*3056*
I have given them thy *w*	Jn 17:14	*3056*
thy *w* is truth	Jn 17:17	*3056*
believe on me through their *w*	Jn 17:20	*3056*
received his *w* were baptized	Acts 2:41	*3056*
them which heard the *w* believed	Acts 4:4	*3056*
all boldness they may speak thy *w*	Acts 4:29	*3056*
they spake the *w* of God with	Acts 4:31	*3056*
that we should leave the *w* of God	Acts 6:2	*3056*
and to the ministry of the *w*	Acts 6:4	*3056*
And the *w* of God increased	Acts 6:7	*3056*
went every where preaching the *w*	Acts 8:4	*3056*
Samaria had received the *w* of God	Acts 8:14	*3056*
and preached the *w* of the Lord	Acts 8:25	*3056*
The *w* which God sent unto the	Acts 10:36	*3056*
That *w*, I say, ye know, which was	Acts 10:37	*4487*
on all them which heard the *w*	Acts 10:44	*3056*
had also received the *w* of God	Acts 11:1	*3056*
remembered I the *w* of the Lord	Acts 11:16	*4487*
preaching the *w* to none but unto	Acts 11:19	*3056*
But the *w* of God grew and	Acts 12:24	*3056*
they preached the *w* of God in the	Acts 13:5	*3056*
and desired to hear the *w* of God	Acts 13:7	*3056*
if ye have any *w* of exhortation	Acts 13:15	*3056*
to you is the *w* of this salvation	Acts 13:26	*3056*
together to hear the *w* of God	Acts 13:44	*3056*
It was necessary that the *w* of	Acts 13:46	*3056*
and glorified the *w* of the Lord	Acts 13:48	*3056*
the *w* of the Lord was published	Acts 13:49	*3056*
testimony unto the *w* of his grace	Acts 14:3	*3056*
they had preached the *w* in Perga	Acts 14:25	*3056*
should hear the *w* of the gospel	Acts 15:7	*3056*

and preaching the *w* of the Lord.......... Acts 15:35 *3056*
have preached the *w* of the Lord......... Acts 15:36 *3056*
Ghost to preach the *w* in Asia.............. Acts 16:6 *3056*
spake unto him the *w* of the Lord......... Acts 16:32 *3056*
in that they received the *w* with.......... Acts 17:11 *3056*
had knowledge that the *w* of God........ Acts 17:13 *3056*
teaching the *w* of God among them..... Acts 18:11 *3056*
heard the *w* of the Lord Jesus.............. Acts 19:10 *3056*
So mightily grew the *w* of God............. Acts 19:20 *3056*
to the *w* of his grace, which is.............. Acts 20:32 *3056*
gave him audience unto this *w*............. Acts 22:22 *3056*
after that Paul had spoken one *w*......... Acts 28:25 *4487*
Not as though the *w* of God hath.......... Rom 9:6 *3056*
For this is the *w* of promise.................. Rom 9:9 *3056*
The *w* is nigh thee, even in thy............ Rom 10:8 *4487*
the *w* of faith, which we preach............ Rom 10:8 *4487*
and hearing by the *w* of God................. Rom 10:17 *4487*
make the Gentiles obedient, by *w*......... Rom 15:18 *3056*
the kingdom of God is not in *w*............. 1Cor 4:20 *3056*
by the Spirit the *w* of wisdom............... 1Cor 12:8 *3056*
to another the *w* of knowledge by......... 1Cor 12:8 *3056*
came the *w* of God out from you........... 1Cor 14:36 *3056*
our *w* toward you was not yea and........ 2Cor 1:18 *3056*
many, which corrupt the *w* of God........ 2Cor 2:17 *3056*
nor handling the *w* of God..................... 2Cor 4:2 *3056*
unto us the *w* of reconciliation.............. 2Cor 5:19 *3056*
By the *w* of truth, by the power............ 2Cor 6:7 *3056*
such as we are in *w* by letters.............. 2Cor 10:11 *3056*
shall every *w* be established.................. 2Cor 13:1 *4487*
all the law is fulfilled in one *w*............. Gal 5:14 *3056*
the *w* communicate unto him that......... Gal 6:6 *3056*
that ye heard the *w* of truth.................. Eph 1:13 *3056*
the washing of water by the *w*.............. Eph 5:26 *4487*
the Spirit, which is the *w* of God.......... Eph 6:17 *4487*
bold to speak the *w* without fear.......... Phil 1:14 *3056*
Holding forth the *w* of life..................... Phil 2:16 *3056*
the *w* of the truth of the gospel............ Col 1:5 *3056*
for you, to fulfil the *w* of God............... Col 1:25 *3056*
Let the *w* of Christ dwell in you............ Col 3:16 *3056*
And whatsoever ye do in *w* or deed..... Col 3:17 *3056*
came not unto you in *w* only................. 1Th 1:5 *3056*
received the *w* in much affliction.......... 1Th 1:6 *3056*
out the *w* of the Lord not only in.......... 1Th 1:8 *3056*
when ye received the *w* of God............. 1Th 2:13 *3056*
received it not as the *w* of men............ 1Th 2:13 *3056*
the *w* of God, which effectually............. 1Th 2:13 *3056*
say unto you by the *w* of the Lord....... 1Th 4:15 *3056*
neither by spirit, nor by *w*..................... 2Th 2:2 *3056*
ye have been taught, whether by *w*...... 2Th 2:15 *3056*
and stablish you in every good *w*......... 2Th 2:17 *3056*
that the *w* of the Lord may have.......... 2Th 3:1 *3056*
obey not our *w* by this epistle............... 2Th 3:14 *3056*
it is sanctified by the *w* of God.............. 1Ti 4:5 *3056*
an example of the believers, in *w*.......... 1Ti 4:12 *3056*
they who labour in the *w* and............... 1Ti 5:17 *3056*
but the *w* of God is not bound.............. 2Ti 2:9 *3056*
rightly dividing the *w* of truth.............. 2Ti 2:15 *3056*
their *w* will eat as doth a canker........... 2Ti 2:17 *3056*
Preach the *w*... 2Ti 4:2 *3056*
his *w* through preaching, which is......... Titus 1:3 *3056*
faithful *w* as he hath been taught......... Titus 1:9 *3056*
that the *w* of God be not...................... Titus 2:5 *3056*
all things by the *w* of his power............ Heb 1:3 *4487*
For if the *w* spoken by angels was......... Heb 2:2 *3056*
but the *w* preached did not profit.......... Heb 4:2 *3056*
For the *w* of God is quick, and.............. Heb 4:12 *3056*
in the *w* of righteousness..................... Heb 5:13 *3056*
And have tasted the good *w* of God...... Heb 6:5 *4487*
but the *w* of the oath, which was......... Heb 7:28 *3056*
were framed by the *w* of God................ Heb 11:3 *4487*
w should not be spoken to them........... Heb 12:19 *3056*
And this *w*, Yet once more,.................... Heb 12:27
have spoken unto you the *w* of God...... Heb 13:7 *3056*
suffer the *w* of exhortation.................... Heb 13:22 *3056*
begat he us with the *w* of truth............ Jas 1:18 *3056*
with meekness the engrafted *w*............. Jas 1:21 *3056*
But be ye doers of the *w*, and not......... Jas 1:22 *3056*
For if any be a hearer of the *w*............. Jas 1:23 *3056*
If any man offend not in *w*.................... Jas 3:2 *3056*
of incorruptible, by the *w* of God.......... 1Pet 1:23 *3056*
But the *w* of the Lord endureth............. 1Pet 1:25 *4487*
this is the *w* which by the gospel.......... 1Pet 1:25 *4487*
desire the sincere milk of the *w*............ 1Pet 2:2 *3050*
to them which stumble at the *w*............ 1Pet 2:8 *3056*
that, if any obey not the *w*................... 1Pet 3:1 *3056*
they also may without the *w* be............. 1Pet 3:1 *3056*
also a more sure *w* of prophecy............ 2Pet 1:19 *3056*
that by the *w* of God the heavens.......... 2Pet 3:5 *3056*
by the same *w* are kept in store,........... 2Pet 3:7 *3056*
have handled, of the *W* of life............... 1Jn 1:1 *3056*
him a liar, and his *w* is not in us.......... 1Jn 1:10 *3056*
But whoso keepeth his *w*, in him........... 1Jn 2:5 *3056*
The old commandment is the *w*............. 1Jn 2:7 *3056*
the *w* of God abideth in you, and.......... 1Jn 2:14 *3056*
children, let us not love in *w*................ 1Jn 3:18 *3056*
in heaven, the Father, the *W*................ 1Jn 5:7 *3056*
Who bare record of the *w* of God.......... Rev 1:2 *3056*
called Patmos, for the *w* of God............ Rev 1:9 *3056*
strength, and hast kept my *w*.............. Rev 3:8 *3056*
hast kept the *w* of my patience............ Rev 3:10 *3056*
that were slain for the *w* of God........... Rev 6:9 *3056*
by the *w* of their testimony.................. Rev 12:11 *3056*
his name is called The *W* of God.......... Rev 19:13 *3056*
of Jesus, and for the *w* of God............. Rev 20:4 *3056*

WORD'S

For thy *w* sake, and according to.......... 2Sa 7:21 1697
ariseth for the *w* sake,.......................... Mk 4:17 *3056*

WORDS

when he heard the *w* of Rebekah.......... Gen 24:30 1697
Abraham's servant heard their *w*......... Gen 24:52 1697
Esau heard the *w* of his father.............. Gen 27:34 1697
these *w* of Esau her elder son............... Gen 27:42 1697
he heard the *w* of Laban's sons,............ Gen 31:1 1697
their *w* pleased Hamor, and Shechem.. Gen 34:18 1697
more for his dreams, and for his *w*....... Gen 37:8 1697
unto him according to these *w*............. Gen 39:17 1697
master heard the *w* of his wife.............. Gen 39:19 1697
that your *w* may be proved,.................... Gen 42:16 1697
so shall your *w* be verified..................... Gen 42:20 1697
according to the tenor of these *w*........ Gen 43:7 1697
he spake unto them these same *w*........ Gen 44:6 1697
Wherefore saith my lord these *w*......... Gen 44:7 1697
let it be according unto your *w*............ Gen 44:10 1697
we told him the *w* of my lord................ Gen 44:24 1697
they told him all the *w* of Joseph......... Gen 45:27 1697
he giveth goodly *w*.................................. Gen 49:21 561
unto him, and put *w* in his mouth........ Ex 4:15 1697
Moses told Aaron all the *w* of the......... Ex 4:28 1697
Aaron spake all the *w* which the........... Ex 4:30 1697
and let them not regard vain *w*............. Ex 5:9 1697
These are the *w* which thou shalt......... Ex 19:6 1697
w which the LORD commanded him...... Ex 19:7 1697
Moses returned the *w* of the.................. Ex 19:8 1697
Moses told the *w* of the people............. Ex 19:9 1697
And God spake all these *w*, saying,....... Ex 20:1 1697
perverteth the *w* of the righteous.......... Ex 23:8 1697
the people all the *w* of the LORD........... Ex 24:3 1697
All the *w* which the LORD hath............... Ex 24:3 1697
Moses wrote all the *w* of the LORD........ Ex 24:4 1697
with you concerning all these *w*............ Ex 24:8 1697
write upon these tables the *w*.............. Ex 34:1 1697
unto Moses, Write thou these *w*............ Ex 34:27 1697
w I have made a covenant with............ Ex 34:27 1697
the tables the *w* of the covenant.......... Ex 34:28 1697
These are the *w* which the LORD........... Ex 35:1 1697
told the people the *w* of the LORD......... Num 11:24 1697
And he said, Hear now my *w*................ Num 12:6 1697
an end of speaking all these *w*............. Num 16:31 1697
and spake unto him the *w* of Balak...... Num 22:7 1697
said, which heard the *w* of God............. Num 24:4 561
said, which heard the *w* of God............. Num 24:16 561
These be the *w* which Moses spake...... Deut 1:1 1697
LORD heard the voice of your *w*........... Deut 1:34 1697
king of Heshbon with *w* of peace.......... Deut 2:26 1697
and I will make them hear my *w*........... Deut 4:10 1697
ye heard the voice of the *w*.................. Deut 4:12 1697
thou heardest his *w* out of the.............. Deut 4:36 1697
These *w* the LORD spake unto all.......... Deut 5:22 1697
LORD heard the voice of your *w*........... Deut 5:28 1697
the voice of the *w* of this people.......... Deut 5:28 1697
And these *w*, which I command thee... Deut 6:6 1697
written according to all the *w*.............. Deut 9:10 1697
w that were in the first tables.............. Deut 10:2 1697
lay up these my *w* in your heart.......... Deut 11:18 1697
hear all these *w* which I command....... Deut 12:28 1697
unto the *w* of that prophet.................... Deut 13:3 1697
pervert the *w* of the righteous.............. Deut 16:19 1697
to keep all the *w* of this law................. Deut 17:19 1697
will put my *w* in his mouth.................. Deut 18:18 1697
will not hearken unto my *w* which........ Deut 18:19 1697
upon them all the *w* of this law............ Deut 27:3 1697
the *w* of this law very plainly................ Deut 27:8 1697
all the *w* of this law to do them.......... Deut 27:26 1697
not go aside from any of the *w*............. Deut 28:14 1697
wilt not observe to do all the *w*........... Deut 28:58 1697
These are the *w* of the covenant,.......... Deut 29:1 1697
therefore the *w* of this covenant........... Deut 29:9 1697
he heareth the *w* of this curse............. Deut 29:19 1697
we may do all the *w* of this law............ Deut 29:29 1697
spake these *w* unto all Israel................ Deut 31:1 1697
to do all the *w* of this law.................... Deut 31:12 1697
the *w* of this law in a book................... Deut 31:24 1697
I may speak these *w* in their ears........ Deut 31:28 1697
of Israel the *w* of this song.................. Deut 31:30 1697
hear, O earth, the *w* of my mouth........ Deut 32:1 561
spake all the *w* of this song in.............. Deut 32:44 1697
all these *w* to all Israel........................ Deut 32:45 1697
Set your hearts unto all the *w*.............. Deut 32:46 1697
to do, all the *w* of this law.................... Deut 32:46 1697
every one shall receive of thy *w*........... Deut 33:3 1703
will not hearken unto thy *w* in.............. Josh 1:18 1697
she said, According unto your *w*.......... Josh 2:21 1697
hear the *w* of the LORD your God......... Josh 3:9 1697
he read all the *w* of the law.................. Josh 8:34 1697
heard the *w* that the children of.......... Josh 22:30 1697
Joshua wrote these *w* in the book......... Josh 24:26 1697
for it hath heard all the *w* of............... Josh 24:27 561
angel of the LORD spake these *w*.......... Judg 2:4 1697
the men of Shechem all these *w*........... Judg 9:3 1697
the *w* of Gaal the son of Ebed.............. Judg 9:30 1697
we do not so according to thy *w*........... Judg 11:10 1697
Jephthah uttered all his *w* before........ Judg 11:11 1697
w of Jephthah which he sent him......... Judg 11:28 1697
Now let thy *w* come to pass.................. Judg 13:12 1697
she pressed him daily with her *w*......... Judg 16:16 1697
none of his *w* fall to the ground........... 1Sa 3:19 1697
Samuel told all the *w* of the LORD........ 1Sa 8:10 1697
heard all the *w* of the people................ 1Sa 8:21 1697
the voice of the *w* of the LORD............. 1Sa 15:1 1697
of the LORD, and thy *w*.......................... 1Sa 15:24 1697
heard those *w* of the Philistine............. 1Sa 17:11 1697
and spake according to the same *w*...... 1Sa 17:23 1697
when the *w* were heard which David.... 1Sa 17:31 1697
those *w* in the ears of David................. 1Sa 18:23 1697
his servants told David these *w*.......... 1Sa 18:26 1697
laid up these *w* in his heart................. 1Sa 21:12 1697
stayed his servants with these *w*......... 1Sa 24:7 1697
Wherefore hearest thou men's *w*......... 1Sa 24:9 1697
end of speaking these *w* unto Saul....... 1Sa 24:16 1697
all those *w* in the name of David.......... 1Sa 25:9 1697
hear the *w* of thine handmaid................ 1Sa 25:24 1697
king hear the *w* of his servant............... 1Sa 26:19 1697
because of the *w* of Samuel................... 1Sa 28:20 1697
have hearkened unto thy *w* which........ 1Sa 28:21 1697
wroth for the *w* of Ish-bosheth............. 2Sa 3:8 1697
According to all these *w*, and................ 2Sa 7:17 1697
thy *w* be true, and thou hast................. 2Sa 7:28 1697
So Joab put the *w* in her mouth............ 2Sa 14:3 1697
he put all these *w* in the mouth........... 2Sa 14:19 1697
the *w* of the men of Judah were............ 2Sa 19:43 1697
than the *w* of the men of Israel............ 2Sa 19:43 1697
Hear the *w* of thine handmaid............... 2Sa 20:17 1697
unto the LORD the *w* of this song.......... 2Sa 22:1 1697
Now these be the last *w* of David.......... 2Sa 23:1 1697
in after thee, and confirm thy *w*........... 1Kin 1:14 1697
I have done according to thy *w*............ 1Kin 3:12 1697
when Hiram heard the *w* of Solomon.. 1Kin 5:7 1697
And let these my *w*, wherewith I.......... 1Kin 8:59 1697
Howbeit I believed not the *w*.............. 1Kin 10:7 1697
them, and speak good *w* to them........... 1Kin 12:7 1697
the *w* which he had spoken unto........... 1Kin 13:11 1697
to pass, when Ahab heard those *w*....... 1Kin 21:27 1697
the *w* of the prophets declare............... 1Kin 22:13 1697
to meet you, and told you these *w*....... 2Kin 1:7 1697
the *w* that thou speakest in thy........... 2Kin 6:12 1697
the king heard the *w* of the woman...... 2Kin 6:30 1697
sayest, (but they are but vain *w*........... 2Kin 18:20 1697
and to thee, to speak these *w*.............. 2Kin 18:27 1697
told him the *w* of Rab-shakeh.............. 2Kin 18:37 1697
will hear all the *w* of Rab-shakeh......... 2Kin 19:4 1697
will reprove the *w* which the LORD....... 2Kin 19:4 1697
Be not afraid of the *w* which thou........ 2Kin 19:6 1697
hear the *w* of Sennacherib, which......... 2Kin 19:16 1697
the *w* of the book of the law................. 2Kin 22:11 1697
concerning the *w* of this book.............. 2Kin 22:13 1697
hearkened unto the *w* of this book....... 2Kin 22:13 1697
even all the *w* of the book which.......... 2Kin 22:16 1697
As touching the *w* which thou hast....... 2Kin 22:18 1697
the *w* of the book of the covenant....... 2Kin 23:2 1697
to perform the *w* of this covenant........ 2Kin 23:3 1697
who proclaimed these *w*........................ 2Kin 23:16 1697
that he might perform the *w* of............. 2Kin 23:24 1697
According to all these *w*, and.............. 1Chr 17:15 1697
For by the last *w* of David the............... 1Chr 23:27 1697
the king's seer in the *w* of God............ 1Chr 25:5 1697
Howbeit I believed not their *w*............ 2Chr 9:6 1697
them, and speak good *w* to them.......... 2Chr 10:7 1697
And they obeyed the *w* of the LORD..... 2Chr 11:4 1697
And when Asa heard these *w*............... 2Chr 15:8 1697
the *w* of the prophets declare............... 2Chr 18:12 1697
by the *w* of the LORD, to cleanse......... 2Chr 29:15 1697
unto the LORD with the *w* of David....... 2Chr 29:30 1697
the *w* of Hezekiah king of Judah.......... 2Chr 32:8 1697
the *w* of the seers that spake to........... 2Chr 33:18 1697
king had heard the *w* of the law.......... 2Chr 34:19 1697
concerning the *w* of the book that....... 2Chr 34:21 1697
the *w* which thou hast heard............... 2Chr 34:26 1697
heardest his *w* against this place......... 2Chr 34:27 1697
the *w* of the book of the covenant........ 2Chr 34:30 1697
to perform the *w* of the covenant......... 2Chr 34:31 1697
hearkened not unto the *w* of Necho...... 2Chr 35:22 1697
of God, and despised his *w*.................. 2Chr 36:16 1697
even a scribe of the *w* of the................. Ezr 7:11 1697
at the *w* of the God of Israel................. Ezr 9:4 1697
The *w* of Nehemiah the son of.............. Neh 1:1 1697
to pass, when I heard these *w*............. Neh 1:4 1697
as also the king's *w* that he had.......... Neh 2:18 1697
when I heard their cry and these *w*..... Neh 5:6 1697
their king, according to these *w*........... Neh 6:6 1697
to the king according to these *w*......... Neh 6:7 1697
before me, and uttered my *w* to him..... Neh 6:19 1697
when they heard the *w* of the law......... Neh 8:9 1697
w that were declared unto them........... Neh 8:12 1697
to understand the *w* of the law............ Neh 8:13 1697
his seed, and hast performed thy *w*...... Neh 9:8 1697
and told Esther the *w* of Mordecai....... Est 4:9 1697
they told to Mordecai Esther's *w*......... Est 4:12 1697
for all the *w* of this letter.................... Est 9:26 1697
with *w* of peace and truth,.................... Est 9:30 1697
Thy *w* have upholden him that was...... Job 4:4 4405
therefore my *w* are swallowed up.......... Job 6:3 1697
concealed the *w* of the Holy One.......... Job 6:10 561
How forcible are right *w*...................... Job 6:25 561
Do ye imagine to reprove *w*................. Job 6:26 4405
how long shall the *w* of thy mouth....... Job 8:2 561
utter *w* out of their heart.................... Job 8:10 4405
choose out my *w* to reason with........... Job 9:14 1697
the multitude of *w* be answered............ Job 11:2 1697
Doth not the ear try *w*......................... Job 12:11 4405
lettest such *w* go out of thy................. Job 15:13 4405
Shall vain *w* have an end..................... Job 16:3 1697
I could heap up *w* against you............. Job 16:4 4405
it be ere ye make an end of *w*.............. Job 18:2 4405
and break me in pieces with *w*............. Job 19:2 4405
Oh that my *w* were now written........... Job 19:23 4405
lay up his *w* in thine heart.................. Job 22:22 561
I would know the *w* which he would... Job 23:5 4405
I have esteemed the *w* of his.............. Job 23:12 561
To whom hast thou uttered *w*.............. Job 26:4 4405
After my *w* they spake not again.......... Job 29:22 1697
The *w* of Job are ended........................ Job 31:40 1697
Behold, I waited for your *w*................. Job 32:11 1697
Job, or that answered his *w*................. Job 32:12 561
not directed his *w* against me.............. Job 32:14 4405
speeches, and hearken to all my *w*...... Job 33:1 1697
My *w* shall be of the uprightness.......... Job 33:3 561
set thy *w* in order before me,............... Job 33:5
I have heard the voice of thy *w*........... Job 33:8 4405
Hear my *w*, O ye wise men.................. Job 34:2 4405
For the ear trieth *w*, as the.................. Job 34:3 4405
hearken to the voice of my *w*............... Job 34:16 4405
his *w* were without wisdom.................. Job 34:35 1697
and multiplieth his *w* against God........ Job 34:37 561
he multiplieth *w* without...................... Job 35:16 4405
For truly my *w* shall not be false.......... Job 36:4 4405
counsel by *w* without knowledge.......... Job 38:2 4405
will he speak soft *w* unto thee.............. Job 41:3
LORD had spoken these *w* unto Job...... Job 42:7 1697
Give ear to my *w*, O LORD..................... Ps 5:1 561
concerning the *w* of Cush the............... Ps 7:*t* 1697
The *w* of the LORD.................................. Ps 12:6 565

the LORD are pure *w*	Ps 12:6	565
Concerning the *w* of men, by the	Ps 17:4	
who spake unto the LORD the *w* of	Ps 18:t	1697
their *w* to the end of the world	Ps 19:4	4405
Let the *w* of my mouth, and the	Ps 19:14	561
me, and from the *w* of my roaring	Ps 22:1	1697
The *w* of his mouth are iniquity	Ps 36:3	1697
and castest my *w* behind thee	Ps 50:17	1697
Thou lovest all devouring *w*	Ps 52:4	1697
give ear to the *w* of my mouth	Ps 54:2	561
The *w* of his mouth were smoother	Ps 55:21	
his *w* were softer than oil, yet	Ps 55:21	1697
Every day they wrest my *w*	Ps 56:5	1697
the *w* of their lips let them even	Ps 59:12	1697
shoot their arrows, even bitter *w*	Ps 64:3	1697
your ears to the *w* of my mouth	Ps 78:1	561
Then believed they his *w*	Ps 106:12	1697
rebelled against the *w* of God	Ps 107:11	561
me about also with *w* of hatred	Ps 109:3	1697
have said that I would keep thy *w*	Ps 119:57	1697
How sweet are thy *w* unto my taste	Ps 119:103	565
entrance of thy *w* giveth light	Ps 119:130	1697
mine enemies have forgotten thy *w*	Ps 119:139	1697
when they hear the *w* of thy mouth	Ps 138:4	561
places, they shall hear my *w*	Ps 141:6	561
to perceive the *w* of	Prov 1:2	561
the *w* of the wise, and their dark	Prov 1:6	1697
in the city she uttereth her *w*	Prov 1:21	561
I will make known my *w* unto you	Prov 1:23	1697
My son, if thou wilt receive my *w*	Prov 2:1	561
which flattereth with her *w*	Prov 2:16	561
me, Let thine heart retain my *w*	Prov 4:4	1697
decline from the *w* of my mouth	Prov 4:5	561
My son, attend to my *w*	Prov 4:20	1697
depart not from the *w* of my mouth	Prov 5:7	561
snared with the *w* of thy mouth	Prov 6:2	561
art taken with the *w* of thy mouth	Prov 6:2	561
My son, keep my *w*, and lay up my	Prov 7:1	561
which flattereth with her *w*	Prov 7:5	561
and attend to the *w* of my mouth	Prov 7:24	561
All the *w* of my mouth are in	Prov 8:8	561
In the multitude of *w* there	Prov 10:19	1697
The *w* of the wicked are to lie in	Prov 12:6	1697
but grievous *w* stir up anger	Prov 15:1	1697
but the *w* of the pure are	Prov 15:26	
the pure are pleasant *w*	Prov 15:26	
Pleasant *w* are as an honeycomb	Prov 16:24	561
that hath knowledge spareth his *w*	Prov 17:27	561
The *w* of a man's mouth are as	Prov 18:4	1697
The *w* of a talebearer are as	Prov 18:8	1697
he pursueth them with *w*, yet they	Prov 19:7	561
to err from the *w* of knowledge	Prov 19:27	561
the *w* of the transgressor	Prov 22:12	1697
hear the *w* of the wise, and apply	Prov 22:17	1697
the certainty of the *w* of truth	Prov 22:21	561
that thou mightest answer the *w*	Prov 22:21	561
vomit up, and lose thy sweet *w*	Prov 23:8	1697
will despise the wisdom of thy *w*	Prov 23:9	4405
thine ears to the *w* of knowledge	Prov 23:12	561
The *w* of a talebearer are as	Prov 26:22	1697
will not be corrected by *w*	Prov 29:19	1697
thou a man that is hasty in his *w*	Prov 29:20	1697
The *w* of Agur the son of Jakeh,	Prov 30:1	1697
Add thou not unto his *w*, lest he	Prov 30:6	1697
The *w* of king Lemuel, the	Prov 31:1	1697
The *w* of the Preacher, the son of	Eccl 1:1	1697
therefore let thy *w* be few	Eccl 5:2	1697
voice is known by multitude of *w*	Eccl 5:3	1697
many *w* there are also divers	Eccl 5:7	1697
heed unto all *w* that are spoken	Eccl 7:21	1697
despised, and his *w* are not heard	Eccl 9:16	1697
The *w* of wise men are heard in	Eccl 9:17	1697
The *w* of a wise man's mouth are	Eccl 10:12	1697
The beginning of the *w* of his	Eccl 10:13	1697
A fool also is full of *w*	Eccl 10:14	1697
sought to find out acceptable *w*	Eccl 12:10	1697
was upright, even *w* of truth	Eccl 12:10	1697
The *w* of the wise are as goads,	Eccl 12:11	1697
as the *w* of a book that is sealed	Is 29:11	1697
the deaf hear the *w* of the book	Is 29:18	1697
evil, and will not call back his *w*	Is 31:2	1697
to destroy the poor with lying *w*	Is 32:7	561
are but vain *w*) I have counsel	Is 36:5	1697
and to thee to speak these *w*	Is 36:12	1697
Hear ye the *w* of the great king,	Is 36:13	1697
and told him the *w* of Rabshakeh	Is 36:22	1697
God will hear the *w* of Rabshakeh	Is 37:4	1697
will reprove the *w* which the LORD	Is 37:4	1697
of the *w* that thou hast heard	Is 37:6	1697
hear all the *w* of Sennacherib,	Is 37:17	1697
there is none that heareth your *w*	Is 41:26	561
And I have put my *w* in thy mouth	Is 51:16	1697
nor speaking thine own *w*	Is 58:13	1697
from the heart *w* of falsehood	Is 59:13	1697
my *w* which I have put in thy	Is 59:21	1697
The *w* of Jeremiah the son of	Jer 1:1	1697
I have put my *w* in thy mouth	Jer 1:9	1697
proclaim these *w* toward the north	Jer 3:12	1697
I will make my *w* in thy mouth	Jer 5:14	1697
they have not hearkened unto my *w*	Jer 6:19	1697
Trust ye not in lying *w*, saying,	Jer 7:4	1697
Behold, ye trust in lying *w*	Jer 7:8	1697
shalt speak all these *w* unto them	Jer 7:27	1697
Hear ye the *w* of this covenant,	Jer 11:2	1697
not the *w* of this covenant	Jer 11:3	1697
Proclaim all these *w* in the	Jer 11:6	1697
Hear ye the *w* of this covenant,	Jer 11:6	1697
them all the *w* of this covenant	Jer 11:8	1697
which refused to hear my *w*	Jer 11:10	1697
they speak fair *w* unto thee	Jer 12:6	
people, which refuse to hear my *w*	Jer 13:10	1697
Thy *w* were found, and I did eat	Jer 15:16	1697
shew this people all these *w*	Jer 16:10	1697
I will cause thee to hear my *w*	Jer 18:2	1697
us not give heed to any of his *w*	Jer 18:18	1697
proclaim there the *w* that I shall	Jer 19:2	1697
that they might not hear my *w*	Jer 19:15	1697
But if ye will not hear these *w*	Jer 22:5	1697
because of the *w* of his holiness	Jer 23:9	1697
Hearken not unto the *w* of the	Jer 23:16	1697
had caused my people to hear my *w*	Jer 23:22	1697
that steal my *w* every one from	Jer 23:30	1697
perverted the *w* of the living God	Jer 23:36	1697
Because ye have not heard my *w*	Jer 25:8	1697
bring upon that land all my *w*	Jer 25:13	1697
thou against them all these *w*	Jer 25:30	1697
all the *w* that I command thee to	Jer 26:2	1697
To hearken to the *w* of my	Jer 26:5	1697
these *w* in the house of the LORD	Jer 26:7	1697
city all the *w* that ye have heard	Jer 26:12	1697
to speak all these *w* in your ears	Jer 26:15	1697
to all the *w* of Jeremiah	Jer 26:20	1697
and all the princes, heard his *w*	Jer 26:21	1697
of Judah according to all these *w*	Jer 27:12	1697
Therefore hearken not unto the *w*	Jer 27:14	1697
Hearken not to the *w* of your	Jer 27:16	1697
the LORD perform thy *w* which thou	Jer 28:6	1697
Now these are the *w* of the letter	Jer 29:1	1697
they have not hearkened to my *w*	Jer 29:19	1697
and have spoken lying *w* in my name	Jer 29:23	1697
Write thee all the *w* that I have	Jer 30:2	1697
these are the *w* that the LORD	Jer 30:4	1697
the prophet spake all these *w*	Jer 34:6	1697
which have not performed the *w* of	Jer 34:18	1697
instruction to hearken to my *w*	Jer 35:13	1697
The *w* of Jonadab the son of	Jer 35:14	1697
write therein all the *w* that I	Jer 36:2	1697
of Jeremiah all the *w* of the LORD	Jer 36:4	1697
the *w* of the LORD in the ears of	Jer 36:6	1697
reading in the book the *w* of the	Jer 36:8	1697
read Baruch in the book the *w* of	Jer 36:10	1697
of the book all the *w* of the LORD	Jer 36:11	1697
them all the *w* that he had heard	Jer 36:13	1697
when they had heard all the *w*	Jer 36:16	1697
tell the king of all these *w*	Jer 36:16	1697
write all these *w* at his mouth	Jer 36:17	1697
these *w* unto me with his mouth	Jer 36:18	1697
told all the *w* in the ears of the	Jer 36:20	1697
servants that heard all these *w*	Jer 36:24	1697
the *w* which Baruch wrote at the	Jer 36:27	1697
write in it all the former *w* that	Jer 36:28	1697
the *w* of the book which Jehoiakim	Jer 36:32	1697
besides unto them many like *w*	Jer 36:32	1697
hearken unto the *w* of the LORD	Jer 37:2	1697
heard the *w* that Jeremiah had	Jer 38:1	1697
in speaking such *w* unto them	Jer 38:4	1697
Let no man know of these *w*	Jer 38:24	1697
w that the king had commanded	Jer 38:27	1697
I will bring my *w* upon this city	Jer 39:16	1697
LORD your God according to your *w*	Jer 42:4	1697
all the *w* of the LORD their God	Jer 43:1	1697
him to them, even all these *w*	Jer 43:1	1697
shall know whose *w* shall stand	Jer 44:28	1697
that ye may know that my *w* shall	Jer 44:29	1697
these *w* in a book at the mouth of	Jer 45:1	1697
even all these *w* that are written	Jer 51:60	1697
see, and shalt read all these *w*	Jer 51:61	1697
Thus far are the *w* of Jeremiah	Jer 51:64	1697
neither be afraid of their *w*	Eze 2:6	1697
be not afraid of their *w*, nor be	Eze 2:6	1697
thou shalt speak my *w* unto them	Eze 2:7	1697
and speak with my *w* unto them	Eze 3:4	1697
whose *w* thou canst not understand	Eze 3:6	1697
all my *w* that I shall speak unto	Eze 3:10	1697
of my *w* be prolonged any more	Eze 12:28	1697
as my people, and they hear thy *w*	Eze 33:31	1697
for they hear thy *w*, but they do	Eze 33:32	1697
have multiplied your *w* against me	Eze 35:13	1697
corrupt *w* to speak before me,	Dan 2:9	4406
by reason of the *w* of the king	Dan 5:10	4406
the king, when he heard these *w*	Dan 6:14	4406
the great *w* which the horn spake	Dan 7:11	4406
he shall speak great *w* against	Dan 7:25	4406
And he hath confirmed his *w*	Dan 9:12	1697
the voice of his *w* like the voice	Dan 10:6	1697
Yet heard I the voice of his *w*	Dan 10:9	1697
when I heard the voice of his *w*	Dan 10:9	1697
understand the *w* that I speak	Dan 10:11	1697
thy *w* were heard	Dan 10:12	1697
and I am come for thy *w*	Dan 10:12	1697
when he had spoken such *w* unto me	Dan 10:15	1697
But thou, O Daniel, shut up the *w*	Dan 12:4	1697
for the *w* are closed up and sealed	Dan 12:9	1697
slain them by the *w* of my mouth	Hos 6:5	561
They have spoken *w*, swearing	Hos 10:4	1697
Take with you *w*, and turn to the	Hos 14:2	1697
The *w* of Amos, who was among the	Amos 1:1	1697
is not able to bear all his *w*	Amos 7:10	1697
but of hearing the *w* of the LORD	Amos 8:11	1697
do not my *w* do good to him that	Mic 2:7	1697
the *w* of Haggai the prophet, as	Hag 1:12	1697
But my *w* and my statutes, which I	Zec 1:6	1697
that talked with me with good *w*	Zec 1:13	1697
and comfortable *w*	Zec 1:13	1697
Should ye not hear the *w* which	Zec 7:7	1697
the *w* which the LORD of hosts	Zec 7:12	1697
w by the mouth of the prophets	Zec 8:9	1697
have wearied the LORD with your *w*	Mal 2:17	1697
Your *w* have been stout against me	Mal 3:13	1697
not receive you, nor hear your *w*	Mt 10:14	*3056*
For by thy *w* thou shalt be	Mt 12:37	*3056*
by thy *w* thou shalt be condemned	Mt 12:37	*3056*
When they had heard these *w*	Mt 22:22	
but my *w* shall not pass away	Mt 24:35	*3056*
the third time, saying the same *w*	Mt 26:44	*3056*
of my *w* in this adulterous and	Mk 8:38	*3056*
were astonished at his *w*	Mk 10:24	*3056*
Herodians, to catch him in his *w*	Mk 12:13	*3056*
but my *w* shall not pass away	Mk 13:31	*3056*
and prayed, and spake the same *w*	Mk 14:39	*3056*
because thou believest not my *w*	Lk 1:20	*3056*
of the *w* of Esaias the prophet	Lk 3:4	*3056*
wondered at the gracious *w* which	Lk 4:22	*3056*
shall be ashamed of me and of my *w*	Lk 9:26	*3056*
they might take hold of his *w*	Lk 20:20	*3056*
hold of his *w* before the people	Lk 20:26	4487
but my *w* shall not pass away	Lk 21:33	*3056*
he questioned with him in many *w*	Lk 23:9	*3056*
And they remembered his *w*	Lk 24:8	4487
their *w* seemed to them as idle	Lk 24:11	4487
These are the *w* which I spake	Lk 24:44	*3056*
hath sent speaketh the *w* of God	Jn 3:34	4487
how shall ye believe my *w*	Jn 5:47	4487
the *w* that I speak unto you, they	Jn 6:63	4487
thou hast the *w* of eternal life	Jn 6:68	4487
he had said these *w* unto them	Jn 7:9	
These *w* spake Jesus in the	Jn 8:20	4487
As he spake these *w*, many	Jn 8:30	
He that is of God heareth God's *w*	Jn 8:47	4487
These *w* spake his parents,	Jn 9:22	
which were with him heard these *w*	Jn 9:40	
These are not the *w* of him that	Jn 10:21	4487
And if any man hear my *w*, and	Jn 12:47	4487
me, and receiveth not my *w*	Jn 12:48	4487
the *w* that I speak unto you I	Jn 14:10	4487
a man love me, he will keep my *w*	Jn 14:23	*3056*
my *w* abide in you, ye shall ask	Jn 15:7	4487
These *w* spake Jesus, and lifted up	Jn 17:1	
them the *w* which thou gavest me	Jn 17:8	4487
When Jesus had spoken these *w*	Jn 18:1	
unto you, and hearken to my *w*	Acts 2:14	4487
Ye men of Israel, hear these *w*	Acts 2:22	*3056*
with many other *w* did he testify	Acts 2:40	*3056*
Ananias hearing these *w* fell down	Acts 5:5	*3056*
the people all the *w* of this life	Acts 5:20	4487
speak blasphemous *w* against Moses	Acts 6:11	4487
w against this holy place	Acts 6:13	4487
the Egyptians, and was mighty in *w*	Acts 7:22	*3056*
his house, and to hear *w* of thee	Acts 10:22	4487
While Peter yet spake these *w*	Acts 10:44	4487
Who shall tell thee *w*, whereby	Acts 11:14	4487
Gentiles besought that these *w*	Acts 13:42	4487
this agree the *w* of the prophets	Acts 15:15	*3056*
from us have troubled you with *w*	Acts 15:24	*3056*
exhorted the brethren with many *w*	Acts 15:32	*3056*
told these *w* unto the magistrates	Acts 16:38	4487
But if it be a question of *w*	Acts 18:15	*3056*
to remember the *w* of the Lord	Acts 20:35	*3056*
of all for the *w* which he spake	Acts 20:38	*3056*
hear us of thy clemency a few *w*	Acts 24:4	
but speak forth the *w* of truth	Acts 26:25	4487
And when he had said these *w*	Acts 28:29	
their *w* unto the ends of the	Rom 10:18	4487
and by good *w* and fair speeches	Rom 16:18	5542
not with wisdom of *w*, lest the	1Cor 1:17	*3056*
with enticing *w* of man's wisdom	1Cor 2:4	*3056*
not in the *w* which man's wisdom	1Cor 2:13	*3056*
tongue *w* easy to be understood	1Cor 14:9	*3056*
five *w* with my understanding	1Cor 14:19	*3056*
than ten thousand *w* in an unknown	1Cor 14:19	*3056*
paradise, and heard unspeakable *w*	2Cor 12:4	4487
(as I wrote afore in few *w*	Eph 3:3	
no man deceive you with vain *w*	Eph 5:6	*3056*
beguile you with enticing *w*	Col 2:4	4086
at any time used we flattering *w*	1Th 2:5	*3056*
comfort one another with these *w*	1Th 4:18	*3056*
nourished up in the *w* of faith	1Ti 4:6	*3056*
and consent not to wholesome *w*	1Ti 6:3	*3056*
even the *w* of our Lord Jesus	1Ti 6:3	
about questions and strifes of *w*	1Ti 6:4	3055
Hold fast the form of sound *w*	2Ti 1:13	*3056*
strive not about *w* to no profit	2Ti 2:14	*3054*
he hath greatly withstood our *w*	2Ti 4:15	*3056*
of a trumpet, and the voice of *w*	Heb 12:19	4487
a letter unto you in few *w*	Heb 13:22	
feigned *w* make merchandise of you	2Pet 2:3	*3056*
speak great swelling *w* of vanity	2Pet 2:18	
That ye may be mindful of the *w*	2Pet 3:2	4487
against us with malicious *w*	3Jn 10	*3056*
mouth speaketh great swelling *w*	Jude 16	
remember ye the *w* which were	Jude 17	4487
that hear the *w* of this prophecy	Rev 1:3	*3056*
until the *w* of God shall be	Rev 17:17	4487
for these *w* are true and faithful	Rev 21:5	*3056*
w of the prophecy of this book	Rev 22:18	*3056*
w of the book of this prophecy	Rev 22:19	*3056*

WORK

God ended his *w* which he had made	Gen 2:2	4399
from all his *w* which he had made	Gen 2:2	4399
from all his *w* which God created	Gen 2:3	4399
shall comfort us concerning our *w*	Gen 5:29	4639
Let there more *w* be laid upon the	Ex 5:9	5656
of your *w* shall be diminished	Ex 5:11	5656
Go therefore now, and *w*	Ex 5:18	5647
no manner of *w* shall be done in	Ex 12:16	4399
Israel saw that great *w* which the	Ex 14:31	3027
walk, and the *w* that they must do	Ex 18:20	4640
thou labour, and do all thy *w*	Ex 20:9	4399
in it thou shalt not do any *w*	Ex 20:10	4399
Six days thou shalt do thy *w*	Ex 23:12	4639
a paved *w* of a sapphire stone	Ex 24:10	4639
of beaten *w* shalt thou make them,	Ex 25:18	4749
of beaten *w* shall the candlestick	Ex 25:31	4749
be one beaten *w* of pure gold	Ex 25:36	4749
of cunning *w* shalt thou make them	Ex 26:1	4639
and fine twined linen of cunning *w*	Ex 26:31	4639
fine twined linen, with cunning *w*	Ex 28:6	4639
same, according to the *w* thereof	Ex 28:8	4639
With the *w* of an engraver in	Ex 28:11	4639
of wreathen *w* shalt thou make	Ex 28:14	4639
of judgment with cunning *w*	Ex 28:15	4639

after the *w* of the ephod thou ... Ex 28:15 4639
ends of wreathen *w* of pure gold ... Ex 28:22 4639
w round about the hole of it ... Ex 28:32 4639
to *w* in gold, and in silver, and in ... Ex 31:4 6213
to *w* in all manner of workmanship ... Ex 31:5 6213
for whosoever doeth any *w* therein ... Ex 31:14 4399
Six days may *w* be done ... Ex 31:15 4399
doeth any *w* in the sabbath day ... Ex 31:15 4399
And the tables were the *w* of God ... Ex 32:16 4639
art shall see the *w* of the LORD ... Ex 34:10 4639
Six days thou shalt *w*, but on the ... Ex 34:21 5627
Six days shall *w* be done, but on ... Ex 35:2 4399
whosoever doeth *w* therein shall ... Ex 35:2 4399
to the *w* of the tabernacle of the ... Ex 35:21 4399
wood for any *w* of the service ... Ex 35:24 4399
to bring for all manner of *w* ... Ex 35:29 4399
to *w* in gold, and in silver, and in ... Ex 35:32 6213
to make any manner of cunning *w* ... Ex 35:33 4399
to *w* all manner of ... Ex 35:35 6213
all manner of *w* ... Ex 35:35 4399
even of them that do any *w* ... Ex 35:35 4399
and of those that devise cunning *w* ... Ex 35:35
to *w* all manner of ... Ex 36:1 6213
of *w* for the service of the ... Ex 36:1 4399
up to come unto the *w* to do it ... Ex 36:2 4399
of Israel had brought for the *w* ... Ex 36:3 4399
all the *w* of the sanctuary ... Ex 36:4 4399
man from his *w* which they made ... Ex 36:4 4399
enough for the service of the *w* ... Ex 36:5 4399
more *w* for the offering of the ... Ex 36:6 4399
for all the *w* to make it, and too ... Ex 36:7 4399
the *w* of the tabernacle made ten ... Ex 36:8 4399
of cunning *w* made he them ... Ex 36:8 4639
cherubims made he it of cunning *w* ... Ex 36:35 4639
of beaten *w* made he the ... Ex 37:17 4749
it was one beaten *w* of pure gold ... Ex 37:22 4749
according to the *w* of the ... Ex 37:29 4639
the *w* in all the *w* of the holy ... Ex 38:24 4399
to *w* it in the blue, and in the ... Ex 39:3 6213
in the fine linen, with cunning *w* ... Ex 39:3 4639
same, according to the *w* thereof ... Ex 39:5 4639
made the breastplate of cunning *w* ... Ex 39:8 4639
like the *w* of the ephod ... Ex 39:8 4639
of wreathen *w* of pure gold ... Ex 39:15 4639
the robe of the ephod of woven *w* ... Ex 39:22 4639
fine linen of woven *w* for Aaron ... Ex 39:27 4639
Thus was all the *w* of the ... Ex 39:32 5656
children of Israel made all the *w* ... Ex 39:42 5656
And Moses did look upon all the *w* ... Ex 39:43 4399
So Moses finished the *w* ... Ex 40:33 4399
it be, wherein any *w* is done ... Lev 11:32 4399
or in any *w* that is made of skin ... Lev 13:51 4399
do no *w* at all, whether it be one ... Lev 16:29 4399
Six days shall *w* be done ... Lev 23:3 4399
ye shall do no *w* therein ... Lev 23:3 4399
ye shall do no servile *w* therein ... Lev 23:7 4399
ye shall do no servile *w* therein ... Lev 23:8 4399
ye shall do no servile *w* therein ... Lev 23:21 4399
Ye shall do no servile *w* therein ... Lev 23:25 4399
ye shall do no *w* in that same day ... Lev 23:28 4399
that doeth any *w* in that same day ... Lev 23:30 4399
Ye shall do no manner of *w* ... Lev 23:31 4399
ye shall do no servile *w* therein ... Lev 23:35 4399
ye shall do no servile *w* therein ... Lev 23:36 4399
to do the *w* in the tabernacle of ... Num 4:3 4399
to do the *w* in the tabernacle of ... Num 4:23 5656
to do the *w* of the tabernacle of ... Num 4:30 5656
for the *w* in the tabernacle of ... Num 4:35 5656
for the *w* in the tabernacle of ... Num 4:39 5656
for the *w* in the tabernacle of ... Num 4:43 5656
this *w* of the candlestick was of ... Num 8:4 4639
the flowers thereof, was beaten *w* ... Num 8:4
do no manner of servile *w* therein ... Num 28:18 4399
ye shall do no servile *w* ... Num 28:25 4399
ye shall do no servile *w* ... Num 28:26 4399
ye shall do no servile *w* ... Num 29:1 4399
ye shall not do any *w* therein ... Num 29:7 4399
ye shall do no servile *w*, and ye ... Num 29:12 4399
ye shall do no servile *w* therein ... Num 29:35 4399
all *w* of goats' hair, and all ... Num 31:20 4639
the *w* of men's hands, wood and ... Deut 4:28 4639
shalt labour, and do all thy *w* ... Deut 5:13 4399
in it thou shalt not do any *w* ... Deut 5:14 4399
God may bless thee in all the *w* ... Deut 14:29 4639
thou shalt do no *w* with the ... Deut 15:19 5647
thou shalt do no *w* therein ... Deut 16:8 4399
thee in all the *w* of thine hands ... Deut 24:19 4639
the *w* of the hands of the ... Deut 27:15 4639
to bless all the *w* of thine hand ... Deut 28:12 4639
in every *w* of thine hand, in the ... Deut 30:9 4639
anger through the *w* of your hands ... Deut 31:29 4639
He is the Rock, his *w* is perfect ... Deut 32:4 6467
accept the *w* of his hands ... Deut 33:11 6467
They did *w* wilily, and went and ... Josh 9:4 6213
his *w* out of the field at even ... Judg 19:16 4639
The LORD recompense thy *w* ... Ruth 2:12 6467
your asses, and put them to his *w* ... 1Sa 8:16 4399
be that the LORD will *w* for us ... 1Sa 14:6 6213
officers which were over the *w* ... 1Kin 5:16 4399
the people that wrought in the *w* ... 1Kin 5:16 4399
gold fitted upon the carved *w* ... 1Kin 6:35
porch, which was of the like *w* ... 1Kin 7:8 4649
cunning to *w* all works in brass ... 1Kin 7:14 6213
Solomon, and wrought all his *w* ... 1Kin 7:14 4399
And nets of checker *w* ... 1Kin 7:17 4639
and wreaths of chain *w* ... 1Kin 7:17 4639
were of lily *w* in the porch ... 1Kin 7:19 4639
the top of the pillars was lily *w* ... 1Kin 7:22 4639
so was the *w* of the pillars ... 1Kin 7:22 4399
the *w* of the bases was on this ... 1Kin 7:28 4639
certain additions made of thin *w* ... 1Kin 7:29 4639
was round after the *w* of the base ... 1Kin 7:31 4639
the *w* of the wheels was like the ... 1Kin 7:33 4639
was like the *w* of a chariot wheel ... 1Kin 7:33 4639

made an end of doing all the *w* ... 1Kin 7:40 4399
So was ended all the *w* that king ... 1Kin 7:51 4399
that were over Solomon's *w* ... 1Kin 9:23 4399
the people that wrought in the *w* ... 1Kin 9:23 4399
to anger with the *w* of his hands ... 1Kin 16:7 4639
thou hast sold thyself to *w* evil ... 1Kin 21:20 6213
which did sell himself to *w* ... 1Kin 21:25 6213
the hands of them that did the *w* ... 2Kin 12:11 4399
but the *w* of men's hands, wood and ... 2Kin 19:18 4639
the hand of the doers of the *w* ... 2Kin 22:5 4399
give it to the doers of the *w* ... 2Kin 22:5 4399
the hand of them that do the *w* ... 2Kin 22:9 4399
and the wreathen *w*, and ... 2Kin 25:17 7639
the second pillar with wreathen *w* ... 2Kin 25:17 7639
dwelt with the king for his *w* ... 1Chr 4:23 4399
all the *w* of the place most holy ... 1Chr 6:49 4399
very able men for the *w* of the ... 1Chr 9:13 4399
were over the *w* of the service ... 1Chr 9:19 4399
they were employed in that *w* day ... 1Chr 9:33 4399
as every day's *w* required ... 1Chr 16:37 1697
cunning men for every manner of *w* ... 1Chr 22:15 4399
were to set forward the *w* of the ... 1Chr 23:4 4399
that did the *w* for the service of ... 1Chr 23:24 4399
the *w* of the service of the house ... 1Chr 23:28 4639
over them that did the *w* of the ... 1Chr 27:26 4399
for all the *w* of the service of ... 1Chr 28:13 4399
thou hast finished all the *w* for ... 1Chr 28:20 4399
and tender, and the *w* is great ... 1Chr 29:1 4399
for all manner of *w* to be made by ... 1Chr 29:5 4399
with the rulers of the king's *w* ... 1Chr 29:6 4399
a man cunning to *w* in gold ... 2Chr 2:7 6213
man of Tyre, skilful to *w* in gold ... 2Chr 2:14 6213
overseers to set the people a *w* ... 2Chr 2:18 5647
he made two cherubims of image *w* ... 2Chr 3:10 4639
like the *w* of the brim of a cup ... 2Chr 4:5 4639
Huram finished the *w* that he was ... 2Chr 4:11 4399
Thus all the *w* that Solomon made ... 2Chr 5:1 4399
make no servants for his *w* ... 2Chr 8:9 4399
Now all the *w* of Solomon was ... 2Chr 8:16 4399
for your *w* shall be rewarded ... 2Chr 15:7 6468
of Ramah, and let his *w* cease ... 2Chr 16:5 4399
gave it to such as did the *w* of ... 2Chr 24:12 4399
the *w* was perfected by them, and ... 2Chr 24:13 4399
till the *w* was ended, and until ... 2Chr 29:34 4399
in every *w* that he began in the ... 2Chr 31:21 4639
which were the *w* of the hands of ... 2Chr 32:19 4639
And the men did the *w* faithfully ... 2Chr 34:12 4399
of all that wrought the *w* in any ... 2Chr 34:13 4399
the treasure of the *w* threescore ... Ezr 2:69 4399
to set forward the *w* of the house ... Ezr 3:8 4399
Then ceased the *w* of the house of ... Ezr 4:24 5673
and this *w* goeth fast on, and ... Ezr 5:8 5673
Let the *w* of this house of God ... Ezr 6:7 5673
in the *w* of the house of God ... Ezr 6:22 4399
is this a *w* of one day or two ... Ezr 10:13 4399
nor to the rest that did the *w* ... Neh 2:16 4399
their hands for this good *w* ... Neh 2:18
necks to the *w* of their Lord ... Neh 3:5 5656
for the people had a mind to *w* ... Neh 4:6 6213
them, and cause the *w* to cease ... Neh 4:11 4399
to the wall, every one unto his *w* ... Neh 4:15 4399
of my servants wrought in the *w* ... Neh 4:16 4399
one of his hands wrought in the *w* ... Neh 4:17 4399
The *w* is great and large, and we ... Neh 4:19 4399
So we laboured in the *w* ... Neh 4:21 4399
I continued in the *w* of this wall ... Neh 5:16 4399
were gathered thither unto the *w* ... Neh 5:16 4399
saying, I am doing a great *w* ... Neh 6:3 4399
why should the *w* cease, whilst I ... Neh 6:3 4399
shall be weakened from the *w* ... Neh 6:9 4399
this *w* was wrought of our God ... Neh 6:16 4399
of the fathers gave unto the *w* ... Neh 7:70 4399
gave to the treasure of the *w* ... Neh 7:71 4399
for all the *w* of the house of our ... Neh 10:33 4399
their brethren that did the *w* of ... Neh 11:12 4399
and the singers, that did the *w* ... Neh 13:10 4399
hast blessed the *w* of his hands ... Job 1:10 4639
looketh for the reward of his *w* ... Job 7:2 6467
despise the *w* of thine hands ... Job 10:3 3018
a desire to the *w* of thine hands ... Job 14:15 4639
On the left hand, where he doth *w* ... Job 23:9 6213
desert, go they forth to their *w* ... Job 24:5 6467
For the *w* of a man shall he ... Job 34:11 6467
they all are the *w* of his hands ... Job 34:19 4639
Then he sheweth them their *w* ... Job 36:9 6467
Remember that thou magnify his *w* ... Job 36:24 6467
that all men may know his *w* ... Job 37:7 4639
the *w* of thy fingers, the moon and ... Ps 8:3 4639
snared in the *w* of his own hands ... Ps 9:16 6467
them after the *w* of their hands ... Ps 28:4 4639
what *w* thou didst in their days ... Ps 44:1 6467
Yea, in heart ye *w* wickedness ... Ps 58:2 6466
to every man according to his *w* ... Ps 62:12 4639
and shall declare the *w* of God ... Ps 64:9 6467
w thereof at once with axes ... Ps 74:6 6603
I will meditate also of all thy *w* ... Ps 77:12 6467
Let thy *w* appear unto thy ... Ps 90:16 6467
establish thou the *w* of our hands ... Ps 90:17 4639
the *w* of our hands establish thou ... Ps 90:17 4639
hast made me glad through thy *w* ... Ps 92:4 6467
me, proved me, and saw my *w* ... Ps 95:9 6467
I hate the *w* of them that turn ... Ps 101:3 6213
heavens are the *w* of thy hands ... Ps 102:25 4639
Man goeth forth unto his *w* ... Ps 104:23 6467
His *w* is honourable and glorious ... Ps 111:3 6467
and gold, the *w* of men's hands ... Ps 115:4 4639
It is time for thee, LORD, to *w* ... Ps 119:126 6213
and gold, the *w* of men's hands ... Ps 135:15 4639
works with men that *w* iniquity ... Ps 141:4 5950
I muse on the *w* of thy hands ... Ps 143:5 4639
The wicked worketh a deceitful *w* ... Prov 11:18 6468
the weights of the bag are his *w* ... Prov 16:11 4639
his *w* is brother to him that is a ... Prov 18:9 4399
his doings, whether his *w* be pure ... Prov 20:11 6467

as for the pure, his *w* is right ... Prov 21:8 6467
Prepare thy *w* without, and make it ... Prov 24:27 4399
to the man according to his *w* ... Prov 24:29 6467
because the *w* that is wrought ... Eccl 2:17 4639
the *w* that God maketh from the ... Eccl 3:11 4639
for every purpose and for every *w* ... Eccl 3:17 4639
evil *w* that is done under the sun ... Eccl 4:3 4639
all travail, and every right *w* ... Eccl 4:4 4639
destroy the *w* of thine hands ... Eccl 5:6 4639
Consider the *w* of God ... Eccl 7:13 4639
w that is done under the sun ... Eccl 8:9 4639
evil *w* is not executed speedily ... Eccl 8:11 4639
according to the *w* of the wicked ... Eccl 8:14 4639
to the *w* of the righteous ... Eccl 8:14 4639
Then I beheld all the *w* of God ... Eccl 8:17 4639
the *w* that is done under the sun ... Eccl 8:17 4639
for there is no *w*, nor device ... Eccl 9:10 4639
shall bring every *w* into judgment ... Eccl 12:14 4639
the *w* of the hands of a cunning ... Song 7:1 4639
they worship the *w* of their own ... Is 2:8 4639
they regard not the *w* of the LORD ... Is 5:12 6467
him make speed, and hasten his *w* ... Is 5:19 4639
his whole *w* upon mount Zion ... Is 10:12 4639
the *w* of his hands, neither shall ... Is 17:8 4639
Moreover they that *w* in fine flax ... Is 19:9 5647
Egypt to err in every *w* thereof ... Is 19:14 4639
shall there be any *w* for Egypt ... Is 19:15 4639
and Assyria the *w* of my hands ... Is 19:25 4639
he may do his *w*, his strange *w* ... Is 28:21 4639
a marvellous *w* among this people ... Is 29:14 6381
this people, even a marvellous *w* ... Is 29:14 6381
for shall the *w* say of him that ... Is 29:16 4639
the *w* of mine hands, in the midst ... Is 29:23 4639
the help of them that *w* iniquity ... Is 31:2 6213
and his heart will *w* iniquity ... Is 32:6 6213
the *w* of righteousness shall be ... Is 32:17 4639
but the *w* of men's hands, wood and ... Is 37:19 4639
is with him, and his *w* before him ... Is 40:10 6468
of nothing, and your *w* of nought ... Is 41:24 6467
I will *w*, and who shall let it ... Is 43:13 6466
or thy *w*, He hath no hands ... Is 45:9 6467
concerning the *w* of my hands ... Is 45:11 6467
the LORD, and my *w* with my God ... Is 49:4 6468
forth an instrument for his *w* ... Is 54:16 4639
the *w* of my hands, that I may be ... Is 60:21 4639
and I will direct their *w* in truth ... Is 61:8 6468
is with him, and his *w* before him ... Is 62:11 6468
and we all are the *w* of thy hand ... Is 64:8 4639
their former *w* into their bosom ... Is 65:7 6468
long enjoy the *w* of their hands ... Is 65:22 4639
the *w* of the hands of the workman ... Jer 10:3 4639
the *w* of the workman, and of the ... Jer 10:9 4639
they are all the *w* of cunning men ... Jer 10:9 4639
are vanity, and the *w* of errors ... Jer 10:15 4639
sabbath day, neither do ye any *w* ... Jer 17:22 4399
sabbath day, to do no *w* therein ... Jer 17:24 4399
he wrought a *w* on the wheels ... Jer 18:3 4399
and giveth him not for his *w* ... Jer 22:13 6467
for thy *w* shall be rewarded ... Jer 31:16 6468
Great in counsel, and mighty in *w* ... Jer 32:19 5950
anger with the *w* of their hands ... Jer 32:30 4639
the *w* of the LORD deceitfully ... Jer 48:10 4399
for this is the *w* of the Lord GOD ... Jer 50:25 4399
recompense her according to her *w* ... Jer 50:29 6467
in Zion the *w* of the LORD our God ... Jer 51:10 4639
They are vanity, the *w* of errors ... Jer 51:18 4639
according to the *w* of their hands ... Lam 3:64 4639
the *w* of the hands of the potter ... Lam 4:2 4639
their *w* was like unto the colour ... Eze 1:16 4639
their *w* was as it were a wheel in ... Eze 1:16 4639
wood be taken thereof to do any *w* ... Eze 15:3 4399
Is it meet for any *w* ... Eze 15:4 4399
was whole, it was meet for no *w* ... Eze 15:5 4399
shall it be meet yet for any *w* ... Eze 15:5 4399
thee also with broidered *w* ... Eze 16:10 7553
linen, and silk, and broidered *w* ... Eze 16:13 7553
the *w* of an imperious whorish ... Eze 16:30 4639
Fine linen with broidered *w* from ... Eze 27:7 7553
emeralds, purple, and broidered *w* ... Eze 27:16 7553
in blue clothes, and broidered *w* ... Eze 27:24 7553
ye *w* abomination, and ye defile ... Eze 33:26 6213
with him he shall *w* deceitfully ... Dan 11:23 6213
is a city of them that *w* iniquity ... Hos 6:8 6466
all of it the *w* of the craftsmen ... Hos 13:2 4639
any more to the *w* of our hands ... Hos 14:3 4639
and *w* evil upon their beds ... Mic 2:1 6466
more worship the *w* of thine hands ... Mic 5:13 4639
for I will *w* a ... Hab 1:5 6466
a *w* in your days ... Hab 1:5 6467
maker of his *w* trusteth therein ... Hab 2:18 3336
revive thy *w* in the midst of the ... Hab 3:2 6467
for he shall uncover the cedar *w* ... Zeph 2:14 731
did *w* in the house of the LORD of ... Hag 1:14 4399
of the land, saith the LORD, and *w* ... Hag 2:4 6213
so is every *w* of their hands ... Hag 2:14 4639
they that *w* wickedness are set up ... Mal 3:15 6213
from me, ye that *w* iniquity ... Mt 7:23 *2038*
go *w* to day in my vineyard ... Mt 21:28 *2038*
she hath wrought a good *w* upon me ... Mt 26:10 *2041*
And he could there do no mighty *w* ... Mk 6:5 *1411*
servants, and to every man his *w* ... Mk 13:34 *2041*
she hath wrought a good *w* on me ... Mk 14:6 *2041*
six days in which men ought to *w* ... Lk 13:14 *2038*
that sent me, and to finish his *w* ... Jn 4:34 *2041*
Father worketh hitherto, and I *w* ... Jn 5:17 *2038*
that we might *w* the works of God ... Jn 6:28 *2038*
unto them, This is the *w* of God ... Jn 6:29 *2041*
what dost thou *w* ... Jn 6:30 *2038*
said unto them, I have done one *w* ... Jn 7:21 *2041*
I must *w* the works of him that ... Jn 9:4 *2038*
night cometh, when no man can *w* ... Jn 9:4 *2038*
For a good *w* we stone thee not ... Jn 10:33 *2041*
I have finished the *w* which thou ... Jn 17:4 *2041*
this counsel or this *w* be of men ... Acts 5:38 *2041*

Saul for the *w* whereunto I have ... Acts 13:2 *2041*
for I *w* a ... Acts 13:41 *2038*
a *w* in your days ... Acts 13:41 *2040*
a *w* which ye shall in no wise ... Acts 13:41 *2041*
for the *w* which they fulfilled ... Acts 14:26 *2041*
and went not with them to the *w* ... Acts 15:38 *2041*
we had much *w* to come by the boat ... Acts 27:16
Which shew the *w* of the law ... Rom 2:15 *2041*
did *w* in our members to bring ... Rom 7:5 *1754*
we know that all things *w* ... Rom 8:28 *4903*
For he will finish the *w*, and cut ... Rom 9:28 *3056*
because a short *w* will the Lord ... Rom 9:28 *3056*
otherwise *w* is no more *w* ... Rom 11:6 *2041*
For meat destroy not the *w* of God ... Rom 14:20 *2041*
Every man's *w* shall be made ... 1Cor 3:13 *2041*
every man's *w* of what sort it is ... 1Cor 3:13 *2041*
If any man's *w* abide which he ... 1Cor 3:14 *2041*
If any man's *w* shall be burned, ... 1Cor 3:15 *2041*
are not ye my *w* in the Lord ... 1Cor 9:1 *2041*
abounding in the *w* of the Lord ... 1Cor 15:58 *2041*
for he worketh the *w* of the Lord ... 1Cor 16:10 *2041*
may abound to every good *w* ... 2Cor 9:8 *2041*
But let every man prove his own *w* ... Gal 6:4 *2041*
for the *w* of the ministry, for ... Eph 4:12 *2041*
to *w* all uncleanness with ... Eph 4:19 *2039*
w in you will perform it until ... Phil 1:6 *2041*
w out your own salvation with ... Phil 2:12 *2716*
Because for the *w* of Christ he ... Phil 2:30 *2041*
being fruitful in every good *w* ... Col 1:10 *2041*
without ceasing your *w* of faith ... 1Th 1:3 *2041*
to *w* with your own hands, as we ... 1Th 4:11 *2038*
the *w* of faith with power ... 2Th 1:11 *2041*
of iniquity doth already *w* ... 2Th 2:7 *1754*
you in every good word and *w* ... 2Th 2:17 *2041*
you, that if any would not *w* ... 2Th 3:10 *2038*
that with quietness they *w* ... 2Th 3:12 *2038*
of a bishop, he desireth a good *w* ... 1Ti 3:1 *2041*
diligently followed every good *w* ... 1Ti 5:10 *2041*
and prepared unto every good *w* ... 2Ti 2:21 *2041*
do the *w* of an evangelist, make ... 2Ti 4:5 *2041*
deliver me from every evil *w* ... 2Ti 4:18 *2041*
and unto every good *w* reprobate ... Titus 1:16 *2041*
to be ready to every good *w* ... Titus 3:1 *2041*
not unrighteous to forget your *w* ... Heb 6:10 *2041*
in every good *w* to do his will ... Heb 13:21 *2041*
let patience have her perfect *w* ... Jas 1:4 *2041*
hearer, but a doer of the *w* ... Jas 1:25 *2041*
is confusion and every evil *w* ... Jas 3:16 *4229*
according to every man's *w* ... 1Pet 1:17 *2041*
man according as his *w* shall be ... Rev 22:12 *2041*

WORKER

was a man of Tyre, a *w* in brass ... 1Kin 7:14 2790

WORKERS

Moreover the *w* with familiar ... 2Kin 23:24
w of stone and timber, and all ... 1Chr 22:15 2796
punishment to the *w* of iniquity ... Job 31:3 6466
in company with the *w* of iniquity ... Job 34:8 6466
where the *w* of iniquity may hide ... Job 34:22 6466
thou hatest all *w* of iniquity ... Ps 5:5 6466
from me, all ye *w* of iniquity ... Ps 6:8 6466
Have all the *w* of iniquity no ... Ps 14:4 6466
with the *w* of iniquity, which ... Ps 28:3 6466
There are the *w* of iniquity ... Ps 36:12 6466
envious against the *w* of iniquity ... Ps 37:1 6213
Have the *w* of iniquity no ... Ps 53:4 6466
Deliver me from the *w* of iniquity ... Ps 59:2 6466
insurrection of the *w* of iniquity ... Ps 64:2 6466
when all the *w* of iniquity do ... Ps 92:7 6466
all the *w* of iniquity shall be ... Ps 92:9 6466
all the *w* of iniquity boast ... Ps 94:4 6466
for me against the *w* of iniquity ... Ps 94:16 6466
them forth with the *w* of iniquity ... Ps 125:5 6466
and the gins of the *w* of iniquity ... Ps 141:9 6466
shall be to the *w* of iniquity ... Prov 10:29 6466
shall be to the *w* of iniquity ... Prov 21:15 6466
from me, all ye *w* of iniquity ... Lk 13:27 *2040*
are all *w* of miracles ... 1Cor 12:29 *1411*
as *w* together with him, beseech ... 2Cor 6:1 *4903*
are false apostles, deceitful *w* ... 2Cor 11:13 *2040*
Beware of dogs, beware of evil *w* ... Phil 3:2 *2040*
fellow *w* unto the kingdom of God ... Col 4:11

WORKETH

all these things *w* God oftentimes ... Job 33:29 6466
w righteousness, and speaketh the ... Ps 15:2 6466
He that *w* deceit shall not dwell ... Ps 101:7 6213
The wicked *w* a deceitful work ... Prov 11:18 6213
and a flattering mouth *w* ruin ... Prov 26:28 6213
w willingly with her hands ... Prov 31:13 6213
What profit hath he that *w* in ... Eccl 3:9 6213
the tongs both *w* in the coals ... Is 44:12 6466
w it with the strength of his ... Is 44:12 6466
w righteousness, those that ... Is 64:5 6213
he *w* signs and wonders in heaven ... Dan 6:27 5648
them, My Father *w* hitherto ... Jn 5:17 *2038*
w righteousness, is accepted with ... Acts 10:35 *2038*
peace, to every man that *w* good ... Rom 2:10 *2038*
Now to him that *w* is the reward ... Rom 4:4 *2038*
But to him that *w* not, but ... Rom 4:5 *2038*
Because the law *w* wrath ... Rom 4:15 *2716*
that tribulation *w* patience ... Rom 5:3 *2716*
Love *w* no ill to his neighbour ... Rom 13:10 *2038*
the same God which *w* all in all ... 1Cor 12:6 *1754*
But all these *w* that one and the ... 1Cor 12:11 *1754*
for he *w* the work of the Lord, as ... 1Cor 16:10 *2038*
So then death *w* in us, but life ... 2Cor 4:12 *1754*
w for us a far more exceeding and ... 2Cor 4:17 *2716*
For godly sorrow *w* repentance to ... 2Cor 7:10 *2716*
the sorrow of the world *w* death ... 2Cor 7:10 *2716*
w miracles among you, doeth he it ... Gal 3:5 *1754*
but faith which *w* by love ... Gal 5:6 *1754*
to the purpose of him who *w* all ... Eph 1:11 *1754*
the spirit that now *w* in the ... Eph 2:2 *1754*
to the power that *w* in us ... Eph 3:20 *1754*
God which *w* in you both to will ... Phil 2:13 *1754*
working, which *w* in me mightily ... Col 1:29 *1754*
which effectually *w* also in you ... 1Th 2:13 *1754*
trying of your faith *w* patience ... Jas 1:3 *2716*
For the wrath of man *w* not the ... Jas 1:20 *2716*
neither whatsoever *w* abomination ... Rev 21:27 *4160*

WORKFELLOW

Timotheus my *w*, and Lucius, and ... Rom 16:21 *4904*

WORKING

like a sharp rasor, *w* deceitfully ... Ps 52:2 6213
w salvation in the midst of the ... Ps 74:12 6466
in counsel, and excellent in *w* ... Is 28:29 8454
east shall be shut the six *w* days ... Eze 46:1 4639
where, the Lord *w* with them, and ... Mk 16:20 *4903*
men with men *w* that which is ... Rom 1:27 *2716*
w death in me by that which is ... Rom 7:13 *2716*
And labour, *w* with our own hands ... 1Cor 4:12 *2038*
have not we power to forbear *w* ... 1Cor 9:6 *2038*
To another the *w* of miracles ... 1Cor 12:10 *1755*
according to the *w* of his mighty ... Eph 1:19 *1753*
by the effectual *w* of his power ... Eph 3:7 *1753*
according to the effectual *w* in ... Eph 4:16 *1753*
w with his hands the thing which ... Eph 4:28 *2038*
according to the *w* whereby he is ... Phil 3:21 *1753*
striving according to his *w* ... Col 1:29 *1753*
the *w* of Satan with all power ... 2Th 2:9 *1753*
w not at all, but are busybodies ... 2Th 3:11 *2038*
his will, *w* in you that which is ... Heb 13:21 *4160*
w miracles, which go forth unto ... Rev 16:14 *4160*

WORKMAN

the engraver, and of the cunning *w* ... Ex 35:35 2803
Dan, an engraver, and a cunning *w* ... Ex 38:23 2803
work of the hands of a cunning *w* ... Song 7:1 542
The *w* melteth a graven image, and ... Is 40:19 2796
w to prepare a graven image ... Is 40:20 2796
the work of the hands of the *w* ... Jer 10:3 2796
from Uphaz, the work of the *w* ... Jer 10:9 2796
the *w* made it ... Hos 8:6 2796
for the *w* is worthy of his meat ... Mt 10:10 *2040*
a *w* that needeth not to be ... 2Ti 2:15 *2040*

WORKMANSHIP

knowledge, and in all manner of *w* ... Ex 31:3 4399
to work in all manner of *w* ... Ex 31:5 4399
knowledge, and in all manner of *w* ... Ex 35:31 4399
according to all the *w* thereof ... 2Kin 16:10 4639
of *w* every willing skilful man ... 1Chr 28:21 4399
the *w* of thy tabrets and of thy ... Eze 28:13 4399
For we are his *w*, created in ... Eph 2:10 *4161*

WORKMEN

But they gave that to the *w* ... 2Kin 12:14
the money to be bestowed on the *w* ... 2Kin 12:15
Moreover there are *w* with thee in ... 1Chr 22:15
the number of the *w* according to ... 1Chr 25:1
So the *w* wrought, and the work was ... 2Chr 24:13
w that had the oversight of the ... 2Chr 34:10
they gave it to the *w* that ... 2Chr 34:10
and to the hand of the *w* ... 2Chr 34:17
to set forward the *w* in the house ... Ezr 3:9
and the *w*, they are of men ... Is 44:11 2796
with the *w* of like occupation ... Acts 19:25 *2040*

WORKMEN'S

and her right hand to the *w* hammer ... Judg 5:26 6001

WORK'S

highly in love for their *w* sake ... 1Th 5:13 *2041*

WORKS

let the people from their *w* ... Ex 5:4 4639
them, saying, Fulfil your *w* ... Ex 5:13 4639
serve them, nor do after their *w* ... Ex 23:24 4639
To devise cunning *w*, to work in ... Ex 31:4
And to devise curious *w*, to work ... Ex 35:32
hath sent me to do all these *w* ... Num 16:28 4639
thee in all the *w* of thy hand ... Deut 2:7 4639
that can do according to thy *w* ... Deut 3:24 4639
God shall bless thee in all thy *w* ... Deut 15:10 4639
in all the *w* of thine hands, ... Deut 16:15 4639
had known all the *w* of the LORD ... Josh 24:31 4639
seen all the great *w* of the LORD ... Judg 2:7 4639
nor yet the *w* which he had done ... Judg 2:10 4639
According to all the *w* which they ... 1Sa 8:8 4639
because his *w* have been to ... 1Sa 19:4 4639
and cunning to work all *w* in brass ... 1Kin 7:14 4399
told him all the *w* that the man ... 1Kin 13:11 4639
with all the *w* of their hands ... 2Kin 22:17 4639
talk ye of all his wondrous *w* ... 1Chr 16:9
marvellous *w* that he hath done ... 1Chr 16:12
his marvellous *w* among all ... 1Chr 16:24
even all the *w* of this pattern ... 1Chr 28:19 4399
the LORD hath broken thy *w* ... 2Chr 20:37 4639
Hezekiah prospered in all his *w* ... 2Chr 32:30 4639
with all the *w* of their hands ... 2Chr 34:25 4639
according to these their *w* ... Neh 6:14 4639
turned they from their wicked *w* ... Neh 9:35 4611
Therefore he knoweth their *w* ... Job 34:25 4566
and consider the wondrous *w* of God ... Job 37:14
the wondrous *w* of him which is ... Job 37:16
dominion over the *w* of thy hands ... Ps 8:6 4639
shew forth all thy marvellous *w* ... Ps 9:1
they have done abominable *w* ... Ps 14:1 5949
and tell of all thy wondrous *w* ... Ps 26:7
they regard not the *w* of the LORD ... Ps 28:5 6468
all his *w* are done in truth ... Ps 33:4 4640
he considereth all their *w* ... Ps 33:15 4640
are thy wonderful *w* which thou ... Ps 40:5
behold the *w* of the LORD, what ... Ps 46:8 4659
How terrible art thou in thy *w* ... Ps 66:3 4639
Come and see the *w* of God ... Ps 66:5 4659
have I declared thy wondrous *w* ... Ps 71:17
GOD, that I may declare all thy *w* ... Ps 73:28 4399
is near thy wondrous *w* declare ... Ps 75:1
I will remember the *w* of the LORD ... Ps 77:11 4611
his wonderful *w* that he hath done ... Ps 78:4
God, and not forget the *w* of God ... Ps 78:7 4611
And forgat his *w*, and his wonders ... Ps 78:11 5949
believed not for his wondrous *w* ... Ps 78:32
there any *w* like unto thy *w* ... Ps 86:8 4639
triumph in the *w* of thy hands ... Ps 92:4 4639
O LORD, how great are thy *w* ... Ps 92:5 4639
all his *w* in all places of his ... Ps 103:22 4639
satisfied with the fruit of thy *w* ... Ps 104:13 4639
O LORD, how manifold are thy *w* ... Ps 104:24 4639
the LORD shall rejoice in his *w* ... Ps 104:31 4639
talk ye of all his wondrous *w* ... Ps 105:2
marvellous *w* that he hath done ... Ps 105:5
They soon forgat his *w* ... Ps 106:13 4639
Wondrous *w* in the land of Ham, and ... Ps 106:22
the heathen, and learned their *w* ... Ps 106:35 4639
they defiled with their own *w* ... Ps 106:39 4639
for his wonderful *w* to the ... Ps 107:8
for his wonderful *w* to the ... Ps 107:15
for his wonderful *w* to the ... Ps 107:21
declare his *w* with rejoicing ... Ps 107:22 4639
These see the *w* of the LORD ... Ps 107:24 4639
for his wonderful *w* to the ... Ps 107:31
The *w* of the LORD are great, ... Ps 111:2 4639
his wonderful *w* to be remembered ... Ps 111:4
his people the power of his *w* ... Ps 111:6 4639
The *w* of his hands are verity and ... Ps 111:7 4639
and declare the *w* of the LORD ... Ps 118:17 4639
so shall I talk of thy wondrous *w* ... Ps 119:27
forsake not the *w* of thine own ... Ps 138:8 4639
marvellous are thy *w* ... Ps 139:14 4639
to practise wicked *w* with men ... Ps 141:4 5949
I meditate on all thy *w* ... Ps 143:5 6467
shall praise thy *w* to another ... Ps 145:4 4639
thy majesty, and of thy wondrous *w* ... Ps 145:5 1697
tender mercies are over all his *w* ... Ps 145:9 4639
All thy *w* shall praise thee, O ... Ps 145:10 4639
his ways, and holy in all his *w* ... Ps 145:17 4639
of tapestry, with carved *w* ... Prov 7:16
of his way, before his *w* of old ... Prov 8:22 4659
Commit thy *w* unto the LORD, and ... Prov 16:3 4639
to every man according to his *w* ... Prov 24:12 6467
let her own *w* praise her in the ... Prov 31:31 4639
I have seen all the *w* that are ... Eccl 1:14 4639
I made me great *w* ... Eccl 2:4 4639
Then I looked on all the *w* that ... Eccl 2:11 4639
a man should rejoice in his own *w* ... Eccl 3:22 4639
and the wise, and their *w*, are in ... Eccl 9:1 5652
for God now accepteth thy *w* ... Eccl 9:7 4639
not the *w* of God who maketh all ... Eccl 11:5 4639
also hast wrought all our *w* in us ... Is 26:12 4639
their *w* are in the dark, and they ... Is 29:15 4639
their *w* are nothing ... Is 41:29 4639
thy righteousness, and thy *w* ... Is 57:12 4639
cover themselves with their *w* ... Is 59:6 4639
their *w* are *w* of iniquity ... Is 59:6 4639
For I know their *w* and their ... Is 66:18 4639
worshipped the *w* of their own ... Jer 1:16 4639
because ye have done all these *w* ... Jer 7:13 4639
according to all his wondrous *w* ... Jer 21:2
to anger with the *w* of your hands ... Jer 25:6 4639
provoke me to anger with the *w* of ... Jer 25:7 4639
according to the *w* of their own ... Jer 25:14 4639
wrath with the *w* of your hands ... Jer 44:8 4639
thou hast trusted in thy *w* ... Jer 48:7 4639
down, and your *w* may be abolished ... Eze 6:6 4639
of heaven, all whose *w* are truth ... Dan 4:37 4567
in all his *w* which he doeth ... Dan 9:14 4639
will never forget any of their *w* ... Amos 8:7 4639
And God saw their *w*, that they ... Jonah 3:10 4639
all the *w* of the house of Ahab, ... Mic 6:16 4639
that they may see your good *w* ... Mt 5:16 *2041*
in thy name done many wonderful *w* ... Mt 7:22
in the prison the *w* of Christ ... Mt 11:2 *2041*
most of his mighty *w* were done ... Mt 11:20
for if the mighty *w*, which were ... Mt 11:21
for if the mighty *w*, which have ... Mt 11:23
this wisdom, and these mighty *w* ... Mt 13:54
he did not many mighty *w* there ... Mt 13:58
therefore mighty *w* do shew forth ... Mt 14:2
every man according to his *w* ... Mt 16:27 *4234*
but do not ye after their *w* ... Mt 23:3 *2041*
But all their *w* they do for to be ... Mt 23:5 *2041*
that even such mighty *w* are ... Mk 6:2
therefore mighty *w* do shew forth ... Mk 6:14
for if the mighty *w* had been done ... Lk 10:13
the mighty *w* that they had seen ... Lk 19:37
shew him greater *w* than these ... Jn 5:20 *2041*
for the *w* which the Father hath ... Jn 5:36 *2041*
the same *w* that I do, bear ... Jn 5:36 *2041*
that we might work the *w* of God ... Jn 6:28 *2041*
may see the *w* that thou doest ... Jn 7:3 *2041*
that the *w* thereof are evil ... Jn 7:7 *2041*
ye would do the *w* of Abraham ... Jn 8:39 *2041*
but that the *w* of God should be ... Jn 9:3 *2041*
I must work the *w* of him that ... Jn 9:4 *2041*
the *w* that I do in my Father's ... Jn 10:25 *2041*
Many good *w* have I shewed you ... Jn 10:32 *2041*
which of those *w* do ye stone me ... Jn 10:32 *2041*
If I do not the *w* of my Father ... Jn 10:37 *2041*
ye believe not me, believe the *w* ... Jn 10:38 *2041*
dwelleth in me, he doeth the *w* ... Jn 14:10 *2041*
the *w* that I do shall he do also ... Jn 14:12 *2041*
greater *w* than these shall he do ... Jn 14:12 *2041*
the *w* which none other man did ... Jn 15:24 *2041*
tongues the wonderful *w* of God ... Acts 2:11
rejoiced in the *w* of their own ... Acts 7:41 *2041*
this woman was full of good *w* ... Acts 9:36 *2041*
Known unto God are all his *w* from ... Acts 15:18 *2041*
God, and do *w* meet for repentance ... Acts 26:20 *2041*
what law? of *w*? ... Rom 3:27 *2041*
if Abraham were justified by *w* ... Rom 4:2 *2041*
imputeth righteousness without *w* ... Rom 4:6 *2041*

W

to election might stand, not of *w*	Rom 9:11	*2041*
as it were by the *w* of the law	Rom 9:32	*2041*
by grace, then is it no more of *w*	Rom 11:6	*2041*
But if it be of *w*, then is it no	Rom 11:6	*2041*
rulers are not a terror to good *w*	Rom 13:3	*2041*
cast off the *w* of darkness	Rom 13:12	*2041*
end shall be according to their *w*	2Cor 11:15	*2041*
not justified by the *w* of the law	Gal 2:16	*2041*
and not by the *w* of the law	Gal 2:16	*2041*
for by the *w* of the law shall no	Gal 2:16	*2041*
ye the Spirit by the *w* of the law	Gal 3:2	*2041*
doeth he it by the *w* of the law	Gal 3:5	*2041*
For as many as are of the *w* of	Gal 3:10	*2041*
Now the *w* of the flesh are	Gal 5:19	*2041*
Not of *w*, lest any man should	Eph 2:9	*2041*
in Christ Jesus unto good *w*	Eph 2:10	*2041*
with the unfruitful *w* of darkness	Eph 5:11	*2041*
enemies in your mind by wicked *w*	Col 1:21	*2041*
professing godliness) with good *w*	1Ti 2:10	*2041*
Well reported of for good *w*	1Ti 5:10	*2041*
Likewise also the good *w* of some	1Ti 5:25	*2041*
good, that they be rich in good *w*	1Ti 6:18	*2041*
calling, not according to our *w*	2Ti 1:9	*2041*
furnished unto all good *w*	2Ti 3:17	*2041*
reward him according to his *w*	2Ti 4:14	*2041*
but in *w* they deny him, being	Titus 1:16	*2041*
thyself a pattern of good *w*	Titus 2:7	*2041*
people, zealous of good *w*	Titus 2:14	*2041*
Not by *w* of righteousness which	Titus 3:5	*2041*
be careful to maintain good *w*	Titus 3:8	*2041*
good *w* for necessary uses	Titus 3:14	*2041*
heavens are the *w* of thine hands	Heb 1:10	*2041*
set him over the *w* of thy hands	Heb 2:7	*2041*
me, and saw my *w* forty years	Heb 3:9	*2041*
although the *w* were finished from	Heb 4:3	*2041*
the seventh day from all his *w*	Heb 4:4	*2041*
also hath ceased from his own *w*	Heb 4:10	*2041*
of repentance from dead *w*	Heb 6:1	*2041*
dead *w* to serve the living God	Heb 9:14	*2041*
to provoke unto love and to good *w*	Heb 10:24	*2041*
say he hath faith, and have not *w*	Jas 2:14	*2041*
Even so faith, if it hath not *w*	Jas 2:17	*2041*
say, Thou hast faith, and I have *w*	Jas 2:18	*2041*
shew me thy faith without thy *w*	Jas 2:18	*2041*
I will shew thee my faith by my *w*	Jas 2:18	*2041*
man, that faith without *w* is dead	Jas 2:20	*2041*
Abraham our father justified by *w*	Jas 2:21	*2041*
thou how faith wrought with his *w*	Jas 2:22	*2041*
by *w* was faith made perfect	Jas 2:22	*2041*
how that by *w* a man is justified	Jas 2:24	*2041*
Rahab the harlot justified by *w*	Jas 2:25	*2041*
so faith without *w* is dead also	Jas 2:26	*2041*
his *w* with meekness of wisdom	Jas 3:13	*2041*
they may by your good *w*, which	1Pet 2:12	*2041*
the *w* that are therein shall be	2Pet 3:10	*2041*
might destroy the *w* of the devil	1Jn 3:8	*2041*
Because his own *w* were evil	1Jn 3:12	*2041*
I know thy *w*, and thy labour, and	Rev 2:2	*2041*
and repent, and do the first *w*	Rev 2:5	*2041*
I know thy *w*, and tribulation, and	Rev 2:9	*2041*
I know thy *w*, and where thou	Rev 2:13	*2041*
I know thy *w*, and charity, and	Rev 2:19	*2041*
faith, and thy patience, and thy *w*	Rev 2:19	*2041*
one of you according to your *w*	Rev 2:23	*2041*
keepeth my *w* unto the end, to him	Rev 2:26	*2041*
I know thy *w*, that thou hast a	Rev 3:1	*2041*
found thy *w* perfect before God	Rev 3:2	*2041*
I know thy *w*	Rev 3:8	*2041*
I know thy *w*, that thou art	Rev 3:15	*2041*
not of the *w* of their hands	Rev 9:20	*2041*
and their *w* do follow them	Rev 14:13	*2041*
Great and marvellous are thy *w*	Rev 15:3	*2041*
her double according to her *w*	Rev 18:6	*2041*
the books, according to their *w*	Rev 20:12	*2041*
every man according to their *w*	Rev 20:13	*2041*

WORKS'

believe me for the very *w* sake	Jn 14:11	*2041*

WORLD

and he hath set the *w* upon them	1Sa 2:8	8398
of the *w* were discovered, at the	2Sa 22:16	8398
the *w* also shall be stable, that	1Chr 16:30	8398
darkness, and chased out of the *w*	Job 18:18	8398
Or who hath disposed the whole *w*	Job 34:13	8398
the face of the *w* in the earth	Job 37:12	8398
judge the *w* in righteousness	Ps 9:8	8398
hand, O LORD, from men of the *w*	Ps 17:14	2465
the foundations of the *w* were	Ps 18:15	8398
their words to the end of the *w*	Ps 19:4	8398
the ends of the *w* shall remember	Ps 22:27	776
the *w*, and they that dwell therein	Ps 24:1	8398
of the *w* stand in awe of him	Ps 33:8	8398
ear, all ye inhabitants of the *w*	Ps 49:1	2465
for the *w* is mine, and the fulness	Ps 50:12	8398
the ungodly, who prosper in the *w*	Ps 73:12	5769
the lightnings lightened the *w*	Ps 77:18	8398
as for the *w* and the fulness	Ps 89:11	8398
hadst formed the earth and the *w*	Ps 90:2	8398
the *w* also is stablished, that it	Ps 93:1	8398
the *w* also shall be established	Ps 96:10	8398
judge the *w* with righteousness	Ps 96:13	8398
His lightnings enlightened the *w*	Ps 97:4	8398
the *w*, and they that dwell therein	Ps 98:7	8398
shall he judge the *w*, and the	Ps 98:9	8398
highest part of the dust of the *w*	Prov 8:26	8398
he hath set the *w* in their heart	Eccl 3:11	5769
will punish the *w* for their evil	Is 13:11	8398
That made the *w* as a wilderness,	Is 14:17	8398
the face of the *w* with cities	Is 14:21	8398
All ye inhabitants of the *w*	Is 18:3	8398
the *w* upon the face of the earth	Is 23:17	776
the *w* languisheth and fadeth away,	Is 24:4	8398
the inhabitants of the *w* will	Is 26:9	8398
the inhabitants of the *w* fallen	Is 26:18	8398
fill the face of the *w* with fruit	Is 27:6	8398
the *w*, and all things that come	Is 34:1	8398
with the inhabitants of the *w*	Is 38:11	2309
nor confounded *w* without end	Is 45:17	5769
proclaimed unto the end of the *w*	Is 62:11	776
of the *w* men have not heard	Is 64:4	5769
established the *w* by his wisdom	Jer 10:12	8398
and all the kingdoms of the *w*	Jer 25:26	776
established the *w* by his wisdom	Jer 51:15	8398
and all the inhabitants of the *w*	Lam 4:12	8398
at his presence, yea, the *w*	Nah 1:5	8398
him all the kingdoms of the *w*	Mt 4:8	*2889*
Ye are the light of the *w*	Mt 5:14	*2889*
forgiven him, neither in this *w*	Mt 12:32	*165*
neither in the *w* to come	Mt 12:32	
and the care of this *w*, and the	Mt 13:22	*165*
from the foundation of the *w*	Mt 13:35	*2889*
The field is the *w*	Mt 13:38	*2889*
the harvest is the end of the *w*	Mt 13:39	*165*
shall it be in the end of this *w*	Mt 13:40	*165*
shall it be at the end of the *w*	Mt 13:49	*165*
if he shall gain the whole *w*	Mt 16:26	*2889*
Woe unto the *w* because of	Mt 18:7	*2889*
coming, and of the end of the *w*	Mt 24:3	*165*
shall be preached in all the *w*	Mt 24:14	*3625*
beginning of the *w* to this time	Mt 24:21	*2889*
you from the foundation of the *w*	Mt 25:34	*2889*
shall be preached in the whole *w*	Mt 26:13	*2889*
alway, even unto the end of the *w*	Mt 28:20	*165*
And the cares of this *w*, and the	Mk 4:19	*165*
man, if he shall gain the whole *w*	Mk 8:36	*2889*
in the *w* to come eternal life	Mk 10:30	*165*
preached throughout the whole *w*	Mk 14:9	*2889*
unto them, Go ye into all the *w*	Mk 16:15	*2889*
which have been since the *w* began	Lk 1:70	*165*
that all the *w* should be taxed	Lk 2:1	*3625*
of the *w* in a moment of time	Lk 4:5	*3625*
if he gain the whole *w*, and lose	Lk 9:25	*2889*
shed from the foundation of the *w*	Lk 11:50	*2889*
the nations of the *w* seek after	Lk 12:30	*2889*
for the children of this *w* are in	Lk 16:8	*165*
in the *w* to come life everlasting	Lk 18:30	*165*
The children of this *w* marry	Lk 20:34	*165*
accounted worthy to obtain that *w*	Lk 20:35	*165*
every man that cometh into the *w*	Jn 1:9	*2889*
He was in the *w*	Jn 1:10	*2889*
the *w* was made by him, and the	Jn 1:10	*2889*
by him, and the *w* knew him not	Jn 1:10	*2889*
taketh away the sin of the *w*	Jn 1:29	*2889*
For God so loved the *w*, that he	Jn 3:16	*2889*
into the *w* to condemn the *w*	Jn 3:17	*2889*
but that the *w* through him might	Jn 3:17	*2889*
that light is come into the *w*	Jn 3:19	*2889*
the Christ, the Saviour of the *w*	Jn 4:42	*2889*
that should come into the *w*	Jn 6:14	*2889*
heaven, and giveth life unto the *w*	Jn 6:33	*2889*
I will give for the life of the *w*	Jn 6:51	*2889*
things, shew thyself to the *w*	Jn 7:4	*2889*
The *w* cannot hate you	Jn 7:7	*2889*
saying, I am the light of the *w*	Jn 8:12	*2889*
ye are of this *w*	Jn 8:23	*2889*
I am not of this *w*	Jn 8:23	*2889*
I speak to the *w* those things	Jn 8:26	*2889*
As long as I am in the *w*	Jn 9:5	*2889*
I am the light of the *w*	Jn 9:5	*2889*
Since the *w* began was it not	Jn 9:32	*165*
judgment I am come into this *w*	Jn 9:39	*2889*
sanctified, and sent into the *w*	Jn 10:36	*2889*
he seeth the light of this *w*	Jn 11:9	*2889*
God, which should come into the *w*	Jn 11:27	*2889*
behold, the *w* is gone after him	Jn 12:19	*2889*
w shall keep it unto life eternal	Jn 12:25	*2889*
Now is the judgment of this *w*	Jn 12:31	*2889*
the prince of this *w* be cast out	Jn 12:31	*2889*
I am come a light into the *w*	Jn 12:46	*2889*
for I came not to judge the *w*	Jn 12:47	*2889*
but to save the *w*	Jn 12:47	*2889*
out of this *w* unto the Father	Jn 13:1	*2889*
loved his own which were in the *w*	Jn 13:1	*2889*
whom the *w* cannot receive,	Jn 14:17	*2889*
while, and the *w* seeth me no more	Jn 14:19	
unto us, and not unto the *w*	Jn 14:22	*2889*
not as the *w* giveth, give I unto	Jn 14:27	*2889*
for the prince of this *w* cometh	Jn 14:30	*2889*
But that the *w* may know that I	Jn 14:31	*2889*
If the *w* hate you, ye know that	Jn 15:18	*2889*
If ye were of the *w*	Jn 15:19	*2889*
the *w* would love his own	Jn 15:19	*2889*
but because ye are not of the *w*	Jn 15:19	*2889*
I have chosen you out of the *w*	Jn 15:19	*2889*
therefore the *w* hateth you	Jn 15:19	*2889*
he will reprove the *w* of sin	Jn 16:8	*2889*
the prince of this *w* is judged	Jn 16:11	*2889*
lament, but the *w* shall rejoice	Jn 16:20	*2889*
joy that a man is born into the *w*	Jn 16:21	*2889*
the Father, and am come into the *w*	Jn 16:28	*2889*
again, I leave the *w*, and go to	Jn 16:28	*2889*
In the *w* ye shall have	Jn 16:33	*2889*
I have overcome the *w*	Jn 16:33	*2889*
I had with thee before the *w* was	Jn 17:5	*2889*
which thou gavest me out of the *w*	Jn 17:6	*2889*
I pray not for the *w*, but for	Jn 17:9	*2889*
And now I am no more in the *w*	Jn 17:11	*2889*
but these are in the *w*	Jn 17:11	*2889*
While I was with them in the *w*	Jn 17:12	*2889*
and these things I speak in the *w*	Jn 17:13	*2889*
the *w* hath hated them	Jn 17:14	*2889*
because they are not of the *w*	Jn 17:14	*2889*
even as I am not of the *w*	Jn 17:14	*2889*
shouldest take them out of the *w*	Jn 17:15	*2889*
They are not of the *w*	Jn 17:16	*2889*
even as I am not of the *w*	Jn 17:16	*2889*
As thou hast sent me into the *w*	Jn 17:18	*2889*
have I also sent them into the *w*	Jn 17:18	*2889*
that the *w* may believe that thou	Jn 17:21	*2889*
that the *w* may know that thou	Jn 17:23	*2889*
me before the foundation of the *w*	Jn 17:24	*2889*
the *w* hath not known thee	Jn 17:25	*2889*
him, I spake openly to the *w*	Jn 18:20	*2889*
My kingdom is not of this *w*	Jn 18:36	*2889*
if my kingdom were of this *w*	Jn 18:36	*2889*
for this cause came I into the *w*	Jn 18:37	*2889*
I suppose that even the *w* itself	Jn 21:25	*2889*
holy prophets since the *w* began	Acts 3:21	*165*
great dearth throughout all the *w*	Acts 11:28	*3625*
works from the beginning of the *w*	Acts 15:18	*165*
These that have turned the *w*	Acts 17:6	*3625*
God that made the *w* and all things	Acts 17:24	*2889*
w in righteousness by that man	Acts 17:31	*3625*
all Asia and the *w* worshippeth	Acts 19:27	*3625*
all the Jews throughout the *w*	Acts 24:5	*3625*
spoken of throughout the whole *w*	Rom 1:8	*2889*
of the *w* are clearly seen	Rom 1:20	*2889*
then how shall God judge the *w*	Rom 3:6	*2889*
all the *w* may become guilty	Rom 3:19	*2889*
he should be the heir of the *w*	Rom 4:13	*2889*
by one man sin entered into the *w*	Rom 5:12	*2889*
until the law sin was in the *w*	Rom 5:13	*2889*
words unto the ends of the *w*	Rom 10:18	*3625*
of them be the riches of the *w*	Rom 11:12	*2889*
them be the reconciling of the *w*	Rom 11:15	*2889*
And be not conformed to this *w*	Rom 12:2	*165*
was kept secret since the *w* began	Rom 16:25	*166*
where is the disputer of this *w*	1Cor 1:20	*165*
made foolish the wisdom of this *w*	1Cor 1:20	*2889*
God the *w* by wisdom knew not God	1Cor 1:21	*2889*
of the *w* to confound the wise	1Cor 1:27	*2889*
w to confound the things which	1Cor 1:27	*2889*
And base things of the *w*, and	1Cor 1:28	*2889*
yet not the wisdom of this *w*	1Cor 2:6	*165*
nor of the princes of this *w*	1Cor 2:6	*165*
before the *w* unto our glory	1Cor 2:7	*165*
of the princes of this *w* knew	1Cor 2:8	*165*
received, not the spirit of the *w*	1Cor 2:12	*2889*
you seemeth to be wise in this *w*	1Cor 3:18	*165*
For the wisdom of this *w* is	1Cor 3:19	*2889*
or Apollos, or Cephas, or the *w*	1Cor 3:22	*2889*
are made a spectacle unto the *w*	1Cor 4:9	*2889*
we are made as the filth of the *w*	1Cor 4:13	*2889*
with the fornicators of this *w*	1Cor 5:10	*2889*
must ye needs go out of the *w*	1Cor 5:10	*2889*
that the saints shall judge the *w*	1Cor 6:2	*2889*
if the *w* shall be judged by you,	1Cor 6:2	*2889*
And they that use this *w*, as not	1Cor 7:31	*2889*
fashion of this *w* passeth away	1Cor 7:31	*2889*
for the things that are of the *w*	1Cor 7:33	*2889*
careth for the things of the *w*	1Cor 7:34	*2889*
that an idol is nothing in the *w*	1Cor 8:4	*2889*
eat no flesh while the *w* standeth	1Cor 8:13	*165*
whom the ends of the *w* are come	1Cor 10:11	*165*
not be condemned with the *w*	1Cor 11:32	*2889*
so many kinds of voices in the *w*	1Cor 14:10	*2889*
had our conversation in the *w*	2Cor 1:12	*2889*
In whom the god of this *w* hath	2Cor 4:4	*165*
reconciling the *w* unto himself	2Cor 5:19	*2889*
the sorrow of the *w* worketh death	2Cor 7:10	*2889*
us from this present evil *w*	Gal 1:4	*165*
under the elements of the *w*	Gal 4:3	*2889*
by whom the *w* is crucified unto	Gal 6:14	*2889*
unto me, and I unto the *w*	Gal 6:14	*2889*
before the foundation of the *w*	Eph 1:4	*2889*
that is named, not only in this *w*	Eph 1:21	*165*
according to the course of this *w*	Eph 2:2	*2889*
no hope, and without God in the *w*	Eph 2:12	*2889*
of the *w* hath been hid in God	Eph 3:9	*165*
all ages, *w* without end	Eph 3:21	*165*
rulers of the darkness of this *w*	Eph 6:12	*165*
whom ye shine as lights in the *w*	Phil 2:15	*2889*
unto you, as it is in all the *w*	Col 1:6	*2889*
men, after the rudiments of the *w*	Col 2:8	*2889*
from the rudiments of the *w*	Col 2:20	*2889*
why, as though living in the *w*	Col 2:20	*2889*
came into the *w* to save sinners	1Ti 1:15	*2889*
Gentiles, believed on in the *w*	1Ti 3:16	*2889*
we brought nothing into this *w*	1Ti 6:7	*2889*
them that are rich in this *w*	1Ti 6:17	*165*
Christ Jesus before the *w* began	2Ti 1:9	*166*
me, having loved this present *w*	2Ti 4:10	*165*
lie, promised before the *w* began	Titus 1:2	*166*
and godly, in this present *w*	Titus 2:12	*165*
in the firstbegotten into the *w*	Heb 1:6	*3625*
put in subjection the *w* to come	Heb 2:5	*3625*
from the foundation of the *w*	Heb 4:3	*2889*
and the powers of the *w* to come	Heb 6:5	*165*
since the foundation of the *w*	Heb 9:26	*2889*
w hath he appeared to put away	Heb 9:26	*165*
when he cometh into the *w*	Heb 10:5	*2889*
by the which he condemned the *w*	Heb 11:7	*2889*
(Of whom the *w* was not worthy	Heb 11:38	*2889*
keep himself unspotted from the *w*	Jas 1:27	*2889*
the poor of this *w* rich in faith	Jas 2:5	*2889*
tongue is a fire, a *w* of iniquity	Jas 3:6	*2889*
of the *w* is enmity with God	Jas 4:4	*2889*
of the *w* is the enemy of God	Jas 4:4	*2889*
before the foundation of the *w*	1Pet 1:20	*2889*
your brethren that are in the *w*	1Pet 5:9	*2889*
that is in the *w* through lust	2Pet 1:4	*2889*
And spared not the old *w*, but	2Pet 2:5	*2889*
flood upon the *w* of the ungodly	2Pet 2:5	*2889*
w through the knowledge of the	2Pet 2:20	*2889*
Whereby the *w* that then was,	2Pet 3:6	*2889*
also for the sins of the whole *w*	1Jn 2:2	*2889*
Love not the *w*, neither the	1Jn 2:15	*2889*
the things that are in the *w*	1Jn 2:15	*2889*
If any man love the *w*, the love	1Jn 2:15	*2889*
For all that is in the *w*, the	1Jn 2:16	*2889*
of the Father, but is of the *w*	1Jn 2:16	*2889*
the *w* passeth away, and the lust	1Jn 2:17	*2889*

therefore the *w* knoweth us not, 1Jn 3:1 *2889*
my brethren, if the *w* hate you 1Jn 3:13 *2889*
prophets are gone out into the *w* 1Jn 4:1 *2889*
even now already is it in the *w* 1Jn 4:3 *2889*
in you, than he that is in the *w* 1Jn 4:4 *2889*
They are of the *w* 1Jn 4:5 *2889*
therefore speak they of the *w* 1Jn 4:5 *2889*
and the *w* heareth them 1Jn 4:5 *2889*
his only begotten Son into the *w* 1Jn 4:9 *2889*
Son to be the Saviour of the *w* 1Jn 4:14 *2889*
as he is, so are we in this *w* 1Jn 4:17 *2889*
is born of God overcometh the *w* 1Jn 5:4 *2889*
the victory that overcometh the *w* 1Jn 5:4 *2889*
Who is he that overcometh the *w* 1Jn 5:5 *2889*
the whole *w* lieth in wickedness 1Jn 5:19 *2889*
deceivers are entered into the *w* 2Jn 7 *2889*
which shall come upon all the *w* Rev 3:10 *3625*
The kingdoms of this *w* are become Rev 11:15 *2889*
which deceiveth the whole *w* Rev 12:9 *3625*
all the *w* wondered after the Rev 13:3 *1093*
from the foundation of the *w* Rev 13:8 *2889*
of the earth and of the whole *w* Rev 16:14 *3625*
life from the foundation of the *w* Rev 17:8 *2889*

WORLDLY
w lusts, we should live soberly, Titus 2:12 *2886*
divine service, and a *w* sanctuary Heb 9:1 *2886*

WORLD'S
But whoso hath this *w* good 1Jn 3:17 *2889*

WORLDS
by whom also he made the *w* Heb 1:2 *165*
faith we understand that the *w* Heb 11:3 *165*

WORM
neither was there any *w* therein Ex 16:24 7415
to the *w*, Thou art my mother, and Job 17:14 7415
the *w* shall feed sweetly on him Job 24:20 7415
How much less man, that is a *w* Job 25:6 7415
and the son of man, which is a *w* Job 25:6 8438
But I am a *w*, and no man Ps 22:6 8438
the *w* is spread under thee, and Is 14:11 7415
thou *w* Jacob, and ye men of Israel Is 41:14 8438
the *w* shall eat them like wool Is 51:8 5580
for their *w* shall not die, Is 66:24 8438
But God prepared a *w* when the Jonah 4:7 8438
Where their *w* dieth not, and the Mk 9:44 *4663*
Where their *w* dieth not, and the Mk 9:46 *4663*
Where their *w* dieth not, and the Mk 9:48 *4663*

WORMS
until the morning, and it bred *w* Ex 16:20 8438
for the *w* shall eat them Deut 28:39 8438
My flesh is clothed with *w* Job 7:5 7415
after my skin *w* destroy this body Job 19:26
dust, and the *w* shall cover them Job 21:26 7415
under thee, and the *w* cover thee Is 14:11 8438
their holes like *w* of the earth Mic 7:17 2119
and he was eaten of *w*, and gave up Acts 12:23 *4662*

WORMWOOD
you a root that beareth gall and *w* Deut 29:18 3939
But her end is bitter as *w* Prov 5:4 3939
them, even this people, with *w* Jer 9:15 3939
Behold, I will feed them with *w* Jer 23:15 3939
he hath made me drunken with *w* Lam 3:15 3939
affliction and my misery, the *w* Lam 3:19 3939
Ye who turn judgment to *w* Amos 5:7 3939
the name of the star is called W Rev 8:11 *894*
third part of the waters became *w* Rev 8:11 *894*

WORSE
now will we deal *w* with thee Gen 19:9 7489
that will be *w* unto thee than all 2Sa 19:7 7489
did *w* than all that were before 1Kin 16:25 7489
was put to the *w* before Israel 2Kin 14:12 5062
were put to the *w* before Israel 1Chr 19:16 5062
were put to the *w* before Israel 1Chr 19:19 5062
be put to the *w* before the enemy 2Chr 6:24 5062
was put to the *w* before Israel 2Chr 25:22 5062
to do *w* than the heathen, whom 2Chr 33:9 7451
they did *w* than their fathers Jer 7:26 7489
ye have done *w* than your fathers Jer 16:12 7489
why should he see your faces *w* Dan 1:10 2196
garment, and the rent is made *w* Mt 9:16 *5501*
of that man is *w* than the first Mt 12:45 *5501*
error shall be *w* than the first Mt 27:64 *5501*
the old, and the rent is made *w* Mk 2:21 *5501*
bettered, but rather grew *w* Mk 5:26 *5501*
of that man is *w* than the first Lk 11:26 *5501*
well drunk, then that which is *w* Jn 2:10 *1640*
lest a *w* thing come unto thee Jn 5:14 *5501*
if we eat not, are we the *w* 1Cor 8:8 *5302*
not for the better, but for the *w* 1Cor 11:17 *2276*
faith, and is *w* than an infidel 1Ti 5:8 *5501*
and seducers shall wax *w* and *w* 2Ti 3:13 *5501*
the latter end is *w* with them 2Pet 2:20 *5501*

WORSHIP
I and the lad will go yonder and *w* Gen 22:5 7812
and *w* ye afar off Ex 24:1 7812
For thou shalt *w* no other god Ex 34:14 7812
shouldest be driven to *w* them Deut 4:19 7812
w them, I testify against you Deut 8:19 7812
and serve other gods, and *w* them Deut 11:16 7812
w before the LORD thy God Deut 26:10 7812
w other gods, and serve them Deut 30:17 7812
his face to the earth, and did *w* Josh 5:14 7812
up out of his city yearly to *w* 1Sa 1:3 7812
with me, that I may *w* the LORD 1Sa 15:25 7812
that I may *w* the LORD thy God 1Sa 15:30 7812
go and serve other gods, and *w* them 1Kin 9:6 7812
people went to *w* before the one 1Kin 12:30
the house of Rimmon to *w* there 2Kin 5:18 7812
shall ye fear, and him shall ye *w* 2Kin 17:36 7812
Ye shall *w* before this altar in 2Kin 18:22 7812
w the LORD in the beauty of 1Chr 16:29 7812
go and serve other gods, and *w* them 2Chr 7:19 7812
Ye shall *w* before one altar, and 2Chr 32:12 7812
in thy fear will I *w* toward thy Ps 5:7 7812
the nations shall *w* before thee Ps 22:27 7812
be fat upon earth shall eat and *w* Ps 22:29 7812
w the LORD in the beauty of Ps 29:2 7812
and *w* thou him Ps 45:11 7812
All the earth shall *w* thee Ps 66:4 7812
shalt thou *w* any strange god Ps 81:9 7812
come and *w* before thee, O Lord Ps 86:9 7812
O come, let us *w* and bow down Ps 95:6 7812
O *w* the LORD in the beauty of Ps 96:9 7812
w him, all ye gods Ps 97:7 7812
our God, and *w* at his footstool Ps 99:5 7812
our God, and *w* at his holy hill Ps 99:9 7812
we will *w* at his footstool Ps 132:7 7812
I will *w* toward thy holy temple, Ps 138:2 7812
they *w* the work of their own Is 2:8 7812
made each one for himself to *w* Is 2:20 7812
shall *w* the LORD in the holy Is 27:13 7812
Ye shall *w* before this altar Is 36:7 7812
they fall down, yea, they *w* Is 46:6 7812
and arise, princes also shall *w* Is 49:7 7812
all flesh come to *w* before me Is 66:23 7812
in at these gates to *w* the LORD Jer 7:2 7812
to *w* them, shall even be as this Jer 13:10 7812
to *w* them, and provoke me not to Jer 25:6 7812
which come to *w* in the LORD's Jer 26:2 7812
did we make her cakes to *w* her Jer 44:19 6087
he shall *w* at the threshold of Eze 46:2 7812
the people of the land shall *w* at Eze 46:3 7812
w shall go out by the way of the Eze 46:9 7812
down and *w* the golden image that Dan 3:5 5457
fall down and *w* the golden image Dan 3:10 5457
nor *w* the golden image which thou Dan 3:12 5457
nor *w* the golden image which I Dan 3:14 5457
w the image which I have made Dan 3:15 5457
but if ye *w* not, ye shall be cast Dan 3:15 5457
nor *w* the golden image which thou Dan 3:18 5457
might not serve nor *w* any god Dan 3:28 5457
thou shalt no more *w* the work of Mic 5:13 7812
them that *w* the host of heaven Zeph 1:5 7812
and them that *w* and that swear by Zeph 1:5 7812
and men shall *w* him, every one Zeph 2:11 7812
from year to year to *w* the King Zec 14:16 7812
unto Jerusalem to *w* the King Zec 14:17 7812
in the east, and are come to *w* him Mt 2:2 *4352*
that I may come and *w* him also Mt 2:8 *4352*
if thou wilt fall down and *w* me Mt 4:9 *4352*
Thou shalt *w* the Lord thy God, and Mt 4:10 *4352*
But in vain they do *w* me, Mt 15:9 *4576*
Howbeit in vain do they *w* me Mk 7:7 *4576*
If thou therefore wilt *w* me Lk 4:7 *1799*
Thou shalt *w* the Lord thy God, and Lk 4:8 *4352*
then shalt thou have *w* in the Lk 14:10 *1391*
is the place where men ought to *w* Jn 4:20 *4352*
yet at Jerusalem, *w* the Father Jn 4:21 *4352*
Ye *w* ye know not what Jn 4:22 *4352*
we know what we *w* Jn 4:22 *4352*
shall *w* the Father in spirit Jn 4:23 *4352*
the Father seeketh such to *w* him Jn 4:23 *4352*
they that *w* him must Jn 4:24 *4352*
must *w* him in spirit Jn 4:24 *4352*
that came up to *w* at the feast Jn 12:20 *4352*
gave them up to *w* the host of Acts 7:42 *3000*
figures which ye made to *w* them Acts 7:43 *4352*
and had come to Jerusalem for to *w* Acts 8:27 *4352*
Whom therefore ye ignorantly *w* Acts 17:23 *2151*
men to *w* God contrary to the law Acts 18:13 *4576*
I went up to Jerusalem for to *w* Acts 24:11 *4352*
so *w* I the God of my fathers, Acts 24:14 *3000*
down on his face he will *w* God 1Cor 14:25 *4352*
which *w* God in the spirit, and Phil 3:3 *3000*
indeed a shew of wisdom in will *w* Col 2:23 *1479*
let all the angels of God *w* him Heb 1:6 *4352*
w before thy feet, and to know Rev 3:9 *4352*
w him that liveth for ever and Rev 4:10 *4352*
that they should not *w* devils Rev 9:20 *4352*
the altar, and them that *w* therein Rev 11:1 *4352*
dwell upon the earth shall *w* him Rev 13:8 *4352*
therein to *w* the first beast Rev 13:12 *4352*
w the image of the beast should Rev 13:15 *4352*
w him that made heaven, and earth, Rev 14:7 *4352*
voice, If any man *w* the beast Rev 14:9 *4352*
who *w* the beast and his image, and Rev 14:11 *4352*
shall come and *w* before thee Rev 15:4 *4352*
And I fell at his feet to *w* him Rev 19:10 *4352*
w God Rev 19:10 *4352*
I fell down to *w* before the feet Rev 22:8 *4352*
w God Rev 22:9 *4352*

WORSHIPPED
down his head, and *w* the LORD Gen 24:26 7812
w the LORD, and blessed the LORD Gen 24:48 7812
he *w* the LORD, bowing himself to Gen 24:52 7812
then they bowed their heads and *w* Ex 4:31 7812
And the people bowed the head and *w* Ex 12:27 7812
them a molten calf, and have *w* it Ex 32:8 7812
and all the people rose up and *w* Ex 33:10 7812
his head toward the earth, and *w* Ex 34:8 7812
w them, either the sun, or moon, Deut 17:3 7812
w them, gods whom they knew not, Deut 29:26 7812
interpretation thereof, that he *w* Judg 7:15 7812
w before the LORD, and returned, 1Sa 1:19 7812
And he *w* the LORD there 1Sa 1:28 7812
and Saul *w* the LORD 1Sa 15:31 7812
into the house of the LORD, and *w* 2Sa 12:20 7812
top of the mount, where he *w* God 2Sa 15:32 7812
upon other gods, and have *w* them 1Kin 9:9 7812
have *w* Ashtoreth the goddess of 1Kin 11:33 7812
and went and served Baal, and *w* him 1Kin 16:31 7812
w him, and provoked to anger the 1Kin 22:53 7812
w all the host of heaven, and 2Kin 17:16 7812
w all the host of heaven, and 2Kin 21:3 7812
that his father served, and *w* them 2Kin 21:21 7812
heads, and *w* the LORD, and the king 1Chr 29:20 7812
ground upon the pavement, and *w* 2Chr 7:3 7812
gods, and *w* them, and served them 2Chr 7:22 7812
And all the congregation *w* 2Chr 29:28 7812
with him bowed themselves, and *w* 2Chr 29:29 7812
and they bowed their heads and *w* 2Chr 29:30 7812
w all the host of heaven, and 2Chr 33:3 7812
w the LORD with their faces to Neh 8:6 7812
and *w* the LORD their God Neh 9:3 7812
fell down upon the ground, and *w* Job 1:20 7812
in Horeb, and *w* the molten image Ps 106:19 7812
w the works of their own hands Jer 1:16 7812
have sought, and whom they have *w* Jer 8:2 7812
have served them, and have *w* them Jer 16:11 7812
w other gods, and served them Jer 22:9 7812
they *w* the sun toward the east Eze 8:16 7812
w Daniel, and commanded that they Dan 2:46 5457
down and *w* the golden image that Dan 3:7 5457
mother, and fell down, and *w* him Mt 2:11 *4352*
w him, saying, Lord, if thou wilt Mt 8:2 *4352*
w him, saying, My daughter is Mt 9:18 *4352*
w him, saying, Of a truth thou Mt 14:33 *4352*
w him, saying, Lord, help me Mt 15:25 *4352*
w him, saying, Lord, have Mt 18:26 *4352*
and held him by the feet, and *w* him Mt 28:9 *4352*
And when they saw him, they *w* him Mt 28:17 *4352*
Jesus afar off, he ran and *w* him, Mk 5:6 *4352*
him, and bowing their knees *w* him Mk 15:19 *4352*
And they *w* him, and returned to Lk 24:52 *4352*
Our fathers *w* in this mountain Jn 4:20 *4352*
And he *w* him Jn 9:38 *4352*
fell down at his feet, and *w* him Acts 10:25 *4352*
the city of Thyatira, which *w* God Acts 16:14 *4576*
Neither is *w* with men's hands, as Acts 17:25 *2323*
named Justus, one that *w* God Acts 18:7 *4576*
the truth of God into a lie, and *w* Rom 1:25 *4573*
that is called God, or that is *w* 2Th 2:4 *4574*
and *w*, leaning upon the top of his Heb 11:21 *4352*
w him that liveth for ever and Rev 5:14 *4352*
throne on their faces, and *w* God, Rev 7:11 *4352*
fell upon their faces, and *w* God, Rev 11:16 *4352*
they *w* the dragon which gave Rev 13:4 *4352*
they *w* the beast, saying, Who is Rev 13:4 *4352*
and upon them which *w* his image Rev 16:2 *4352*
w God that sat on the throne, Rev 19:4 *4352*
beast, and them that *w* his image Rev 19:20 *4352*
God, and which had not *w* the beast Rev 20:4 *4352*

WORSHIPPER
but if any man be a *w* of God Jn 9:31 *2318*
is a *w* of the great goddess Diana Acts 19:35 *3511*

WORSHIPPERS
he might destroy the *w* of Baal 2Kin 10:19 5647
all the *w* of Baal came, so that 2Kin 10:21 5647
vestments for all the *w* of Baal 2Kin 10:22 5647
Baal, and said unto the *w* of Baal 2Kin 10:23 5647
the LORD, but the *w* of Baal only 2Kin 10:23 5647
when the true *w* shall worship the Jn 4:23 *4353*
because that the *w* once purged Heb 10:2 *3000*

WORSHIPPETH
and the host of heaven *w* thee Neh 9:6 7812
yea, he maketh a god, and *w* it Is 44:15 7812
w it, and prayeth unto it, and Is 44:17 7812
w shall the same hour be cast Dan 3:6 5457
And whoso falleth not down and *w* Dan 3:11 5457
whom all Asia and the world *w* Acts 19:27 *4576*

WORSHIPPING
as he was *w* in the house of 2Kin 19:37 7812
fell before the LORD, *w* the LORD 2Chr 20:18 7812
as he was *w* in the house of Is 37:38 7812
w him, and desiring a certain Mt 20:20 *4352*
w of angels, intruding into those Col 2:18 *2356*

WORST
I will bring the *w* of the heathen Eze 7:24 7451

WORTH
it is *w* he shall give it me for a Gen 23:9 4392
the land is *w* four hundred Gen 23:15
unto him the *w* of thy estimation Lev 27:23 4373
for he hath been *w* a double hired Deut 15:18 7939
but now thou art *w* ten thousand 2Sa 18:3 3644
give thee the *w* of it in money 1Kin 21:2 4242
liar, and make my speech nothing *w* Job 24:25
heart of the wicked is little *w* Prov 10:20
Howl ye, Woe *w* the day Eze 30:2

WORTHIES
He shall recount his *w* Nah 2:5 117

WORTHILY
do thou *w* in Ephratah, and be Ruth 4:11 2428

WORTHY
I am not *w* of the least of all Gen 32:10 6994
shall he that is *w* of death be Deut 17:6
whereas he was not *w* of death Deut 19:6
have committed a sin *w* of death Deut 21:22
in the damsel no sin *w* of death Deut 22:26
the wicked man be *w* to be beaten Deut 25:2 1121
unto Hannah he gave a *w* portion 1Sa 1:5 639
the LORD liveth, ye are *w* to die 1Sa 26:16 1121
the LORD, who is *w* to be praised 2Sa 22:4
If he will shew himself a *w* man 1Kin 1:52 2428
for thou art *w* of death 1Kin 2:26 376
the LORD, who is *w* to be praised Ps 18:3
saying, This man is *w* to die Jer 26:11
This man is not *w* to die Jer 26:16
I, whose shoes I am not *w* to bear Mt 3:11 *2425*
I am not *w* that thou shouldest Mt 8:8 *2425*
for the workman is *w* of his meat Mt 10:10 *514*
enter, enquire who in it is *w* Mt 10:11 *514*
And if the house be *w*, let your Mt 10:13 *514*
but if it be not *w*, let your Mt 10:13 *514*

W

more than me is not *w* of me Mt 10:37 *514*
more than me is not *w* of me Mt 10:37 *514*
after me, is not *w* of me Mt 10:38 *514*
they which were bidden were not *w* Mt 22:8 *514*
shoes I am not *w* to stoop down Mk 1:7 *2425*
therefore fruits *w* of repentance Lk 3:8 *514*
whose shoes I am not *w* to unloose Lk 3:16 *2425*
That he was *w* for whom he should Lk 7:4 *514*
for I am not *w* that thou Lk 7:6 *2425*
I myself *w* to come unto thee Lk 7:7 *515*
for the labourer is *w* of his hire Lk 10:7 *514*
and did commit things *w* of stripes Lk 12:48 *514*
am no more *w* to be called thy son Lk 15:19 *514*
am no more *w* to be called thy son Lk 15:21 *514*
accounted *w* to obtain that world Lk 20:35 *2661*
that ye may be accounted *w* to Lk 21:36 *2661*
nothing *w* of death is done unto Lk 23:15 *514*
latchet I am not *w* to unloose Jn 1:27 *514*
that they were counted *w* to Acts 5:41 *2661*
of his feet I am not *w* to loose Acts 13:25 *514*
his charge *w* of death or of bonds Acts 23:29 *514*
that very *w* deeds are done unto Acts 24:2 *2735*
committed any thing *w* of death Acts 25:11 *514*
had committed nothing *w* of death Acts 25:25 *514*
nothing *w* of death or of bonds Acts 26:31 *514*
commit such things are *w* of death Rom 1:32 *514*
of this present time are not *w* to Rom 8:18 *514*
beseech you that ye walk *w* of the Eph 4:1 *516*
That ye might walk *w* of the Lord Col 1:10 *516*
That ye would walk *w* of God 1Th 2:12 *516*
counted *w* of the kingdom of God 2Th 1:5 *2661*
would count you *w* of this calling 2Th 1:11 *515*
w of all acceptation, that Christ 1Ti 1:15 *514*
saying and *w* of all acceptation 1Ti 4:9 *514*
be counted *w* of double honour 1Ti 5:17 *515*
The labourer is *w* of his reward 1Ti 5:18 *514*
their own masters *w* of all honour 1Ti 6:1 *514*
w of more glory than Moses Heb 3:3 *515*
suppose ye, shall he be thought *w* Heb 10:29 *515*
(Of whom the world was not *w* Heb 11:38 *514*
Do not they blaspheme that *w* name Jas 2:7 *2570*
for they are *w* Rev 3:4 *514*
Thou art *w*, O Lord, to receive Rev 4:11 *514*
Who is *w* to open the book, and to Rev 5:2 *514*
no man was found *w* to open Rev 5:4 *514*
Thou art *w* to take the book, and Rev 5:9 *514*
W is the Lamb that was slain to Rev 5:12 *514*
for they are *w* Rev 16:6 *514*

WOT

I *w* not who hath done this thing Gen 21:26 3045
w ye not that such a man as I can Gen 44:15 3045
we *w* not what is become of him Ex 32:1 3045
we *w* not what is become of him Ex 32:23 3045
for I *w* that he whom thou Num 22:6 3045
whither the men went I *w* not Josh 2:5 3045
I *w* that through ignorance ye did Acts 3:17 *1492*
we *w* not what is become of him Acts 7:40 *1492*
W ye not what the scripture saith Rom 11:2 *1492*
yet what I shall choose I *w* not Phil 1:22 *1107*

WOTTETH

my master *w* not what is with me Gen 39:8 3045

WOULD

Adam to see what he *w* call them Gen 2:19
Who *w* have said unto Abraham, Gen 21:7
I *w* it might be according to thy Gen 30:34 3863
he besought us, and we *w* not hear Gen 42:21
and ye *w* not hear Gen 42:22
we certainly know that he *w* say Gen 43:7
his father, his father *w* die Gen 44:22
to wit what *w* be done to him Ex 2:4
neither *w* he let the people go Ex 8:32
neither *w* he let the children of Ex 9:35
so that he *w* not let the children Ex 10:20
heart, and he *w* not let them go Ex 10:27 14
so that he *w* not let the children Ex 11:10
when Pharaoh *w* hardly let us go, Ex 13:15
W to God we had died by the hand Ex 16:3
w God that all the LORD's people Num 11:29
that the LORD *w* put his spirit Num 11:29
W God that we had died in the Num 14:2 3863
or *w* God we had died in this Num 14:2 3863
W God that we had died when our Num 20:3 3863
Sihon *w* not suffer Israel to pass Num 21:23
If Balak *w* give me his house full Num 22:18
I *w* there were a sword in mine Num 22:29 3863
mine hand, for now *w* I kill thee Num 22:29
If Balak *w* give me his house full Num 24:13
Notwithstanding ye *w* not go up Deut 1:26 14
ye *w* not hear, but rebelled Deut 1:43
but the LORD *w* not hearken to Deut 1:45
Heshbon *w* not let us pass by him Deut 2:30 14
for your sakes, and *w* not hear me Deut 3:26
in them, that they *w* fear me Deut 5:29
because he *w* keep the oath which Deut 7:8
because ye *w* not be obedient unto Deut 8:20
LORD had said he *w* destroy you Deut 9:25
the LORD *w* not destroy thee Deut 10:10 14
thy God *w* not hearken unto Balaam Deut 23:5 14
and it *w* be sin in thee Deut 23:21
which *w* not adventure to set the Deut 28:56
shalt say, *W* God it were even Deut 28:67
shalt say, *W* God it were morning Deut 28:67
I *w* scatter them into corners Deut 32:26
I *w* make the remembrance of them Deut 32:26
that they *w* consider their latter Deut 32:29
that he *w* not shew them the land Josh 5:6
their fathers that he *w* give us Josh 5:6
w to God we had been content, and Josh 7:7 3863
Canaanites *w* dwell in that land Josh 17:12 2974
But I *w* not hearken unto Balaam Josh 24:10 14
Canaanites *w* dwell in that land Judg 1:27 2974
for they *w* not suffer them to Judg 1:34
But the Amorites *w* dwell in mount Judg 1:35 2974
yet they *w* not hearken unto their Judg 2:17
to know whether they *w* hearken Judg 3:4
them alive, I *w* not slay you Judg 8:19
I *w* desire a request of you Judg 8:24
that ye *w* give me every man the Judg 8:24
w to God this people were under Judg 9:29
then *w* I remove Abimelech Judg 9:29
of Edom *w* not hearken thereto Judg 11:17
but he *w* not consent Judg 11:17 14
he *w* not have received a burnt Judg 13:23
neither *w* he have shewed us all Judg 13:23
nor *w* as at this time have told Judg 13:23
rent him as he *w* have rent a kid Judg 14:6
But her father *w* not suffer him Judg 15:1
But the man *w* not tarry that Judg 19:10 14
But the men *w* not hearken to him Judg 19:25 14
w not hearken to the voice of Judg 20:13 14
W ye tarry for them till they Ruth 1:13
w ye stay for them from having Ruth 1:13
then he *w* answer him, Nay 1Sa 2:16
because the LORD *w* slay them 1Sa 2:25 2654
for now *w* the LORD have 1Sa 13:13
w not utterly destroy them 1Sa 15:9 14
w let him go no more home to his 1Sa 18:2
then *w* not I tell it thee 1Sa 20:9
w not put forth their hand to 1Sa 22:17 14
that he *w* surely tell Saul 1Sa 22:22
but I *w* not stretch forth mine 1Sa 26:23 14
But his armourbearer *w* not 1Sa 31:4 14
But Asahel *w* not turn aside from 2Sa 2:21 14
as though they *w* have fetched 2Sa 4:6
who thought that I *w* have given 2Sa 4:10
So David *w* not remove the ark of 2Sa 6:10 14
that they *w* shoot from the wall 2Sa 11:20
I *w* moreover have given unto thee 2Sa 12:8
but he *w* not, neither did he eat 2Sa 12:17 14
he *w* not hearken unto our voice 2Sa 12:18
Howbeit he *w* not hearken unto her 2Sa 13:14 14
But he *w* not hearken unto her 2Sa 13:16 14
howbeit he *w* not go, but blessed 2Sa 13:25 14
hand of the man that *w* destroy me 2Sa 14:16
but he *w* not come to him 2Sa 14:29 14
the second time, he *w* not come 2Sa 14:29 14
unto me, and I *w* do him justice 2Sa 15:4
I *w* have given thee ten shekels 2Sa 18:11
yet *w* I not put forth mine hand 2Sa 18:12
w God I had died for thee, O 2Sa 18:33
Oh that one *w* give me drink of 2Sa 23:15
nevertheless he *w* not drink 2Sa 23:16 14
therefore he *w* not drink it 2Sa 23:17 14
The LORD said that he *w* dwell in 1Kin 8:12
whosoever *w*, he consecrated him, 1Kin 13:33 2655
as great as *w* contain two 1Kin 18:32
whether any thing *w* come from him 1Kin 20:33
away his face, and *w* eat no bread 1Kin 21:4
Did I not tell thee that he *w* 1Kin 22:18
But Jehoshaphat *w* not 1Kin 22:49 14
when the LORD *w* take up Elijah 2Kin 2:1
I *w* not look toward thee, nor see 2Kin 3:14
W God my lord were with the 2Kin 5:3 305
for he *w* recover him of his 2Kin 5:3
if the LORD *w* make windows in 2Kin 7:2
Yet the LORD *w* not destroy Judah 2Kin 8:19 14
w not destroy them, neither cast 2Kin 13:23 14
But Amaziah *w* not hear 2Kin 14:11
the LORD said not that he *w* blot 2Kin 14:27
Notwithstanding they *w* not hear 2Kin 17:14
w not hear them, nor do them 2Kin 18:12
which the LORD *w* not pardon 2Kin 24:4 14
But his armourbearer *w* not 1Chr 10:4 14
Oh that one *w* give me drink of 1Chr 11:17
but David *w* not drink of it, but 1Chr 11:18 14
Therefore he *w* not drink it 1Chr 11:19 14
said that they *w* do so 1Chr 13:4
neither *w* the Syrians help the 1Chr 19:19 14
he *w* increase Israel like to the 1Chr 27:23
The LORD hath said that he *w* 2Chr 6:1
the king *w* not hearken unto them 2Chr 10:16
that he *w* not destroy him 2Chr 12:12
That whosoever *w* not seek the 2Chr 15:13
he *w* not prophesy good unto me 2Chr 18:17
Howbeit the LORD *w* not destroy 2Chr 21:7 14
but they *w* not give ear 2Chr 24:19
But Amaziah *w* not hear 2Chr 25:20
but they *w* not hearken 2Chr 33:10
Nevertheless Josiah *w* not turn 2Chr 35:22
that whosoever *w* not come within Ezr 10:8
that they *w* put away their wives Ezr 10:19
w go into the temple to save his Neh 6:11
that *w* have put me in fear Neh 6:14
they might do with them as they *w* Neh 9:24
their neck, and *w* not hear Neh 9:29
yet *w* they not give ear Neh 9:30
that we *w* not give our daughters Neh 10:30
that we *w* not buy it of them on Neh 10:31
that we *w* leave the seventh year, Neh 10:31
Mordecai's matters *w* stand Est 3:4
To whom *w* the king delight to do Est 6:6
and province that *w* assault them Est 8:11
did what they *w* unto those that Est 9:5
that they *w* keep these two days Est 9:27
I *w* seek unto God, and unto God Job 5:8
unto God *w* I commit my cause Job 5:8
For now it *w* be heavier than the Job 6:3
that God *w* grant me the thing Job 6:8
Even that it *w* please God to Job 6:9
that he *w* let loose his hand, and Job 6:9
I *w* harden myself in sorrow Job 6:10
I *w* not live alway Job 7:16
surely now he *w* awake for thee, Job 8:6
yet *w* I not answer Job 9:15
but I *w* make supplication to my Job 9:15
yet *w* I not believe that he had Job 9:16
perfect, yet *w* I not know my soul Job 9:21
I *w* despise my life Job 9:21
Then *w* I speak, and not fear him Job 9:35
But oh that God *w* speak, and open Job 11:5
that he *w* shew thee the secrets Job 11:6
For vain man *w* be wise, though Job 11:12
Surely I *w* speak to the Almighty, Job 13:3
Oh that ye *w* altogether hold your Job 13:5
But I *w* strengthen you with my Job 16:5
I *w* order my cause before him, and Job 23:4
I *w* know the words which Job 23:5
the words which he *w* answer me Job 23:5
understand what he *w* say unto me Job 23:5
but he *w* put strength in me Job 23:6
he *w* fain flee out of his hand Job 27:22
whose fathers I *w* have disdained Job 30:1
w root out all mine increase Job 31:12
Oh that one *w* hear me Job 31:35
is, that the Almighty *w* answer me Job 31:35
Surely I *w* take it upon my Job 31:36
I *w* declare unto him the number Job 31:37
as a prince *w* I go near unto him Job 31:37
my maker *w* soon take me away Job 32:22
w not consider any of his ways Job 34:27
Even so *w* he have removed thee Job 36:16
one *w* think the deep to be hoary Job 41:32
on the LORD that he *w* deliver him Ps 22:8
their hearts, Ah, so *w* we have it Ps 35:25 5315
if I *w* declare and speak of them, Ps 40:5
I were hungry, I *w* not tell thee Ps 50:12
else *w* I give it Ps 51:16
for then *w* I fly away, and be at Ps 55:6
then *w* I wander far off, and Ps 55:7
I *w* hasten my escape from the Ps 55:8
then I *w* have hid myself from him Ps 55:12
for man *w* swallow me up Ps 56:1
Mine enemies *w* daily swallow me Ps 56:2
of him that *w* swallow me up Ps 57:3
they that *w* destroy me, being Ps 69:4
But my people *w* not hearken to my Ps 81:11
and Israel *w* none of me Ps 81:11 14
he said that he *w* destroy them Ps 106:23
Oh that men *w* praise the LORD for Ps 107:8
Oh that men *w* praise the LORD for Ps 107:15
Oh that men *w* praise the LORD for Ps 107:21
Oh that men *w* praise the LORD for Ps 107:31
have said that I *w* keep thy words Ps 119:57
there was no man that *w* know me Ps 142:4
counsel, and *w* none of my reproof Prov 1:25 14
They *w* none of my counsel Prov 1:30 14
w not let him go, until I had Song 3:4
find thee without, I *w* kiss thee Song 8:1
I *w* lead thee, and bring thee into Song 8:2
mother's house, who *w* instruct me Song 8:2
I *w* cause thee to drink of spiced Song 8:2
if a man *w* give all the substance Song 8:7
it *w* utterly be contemned Song 8:7
who *w* set the briers and thorns Is 27:4
I *w* go through them Is 27:4
I *w* burn them together Is 27:4
yet they *w* not hear Is 28:12 14
and ye *w* not Is 30:15 14
for they *w* not walk in his ways, Is 42:24 14
that I *w* not be wroth with thee Is 54:9
When I *w* comfort myself against Jer 8:18
Who *w* not fear thee, O King of Jer 10:7
but they *w* not hear Jer 13:11
wherewith I said I *w* benefit them Jer 18:10
yet *w* I pluck thee thence Jer 22:24
but ye *w* not hear, saith the LORD Jer 29:19
king that he *w* not burn the roll Jer 36:25
but he *w* not hear them Jer 36:25
that he *w* not cause me to return Jer 38:26
w they not leave some gleaning Jer 49:9
We *w* have healed Babylon, but she Jer 51:9
w not have believed that the Lam 4:12
they *w* have hearkened unto thee Eze 3:6
that I *w* do this evil unto them Eze 6:10
hope that they *w* confirm the word Eze 13:6
me, and *w* not hearken unto me Eze 20:8 14
I *w* pour out my fury upon them in Eze 20:13
that I *w* not bring them into the Eze 20:15
I *w* pour out my fury upon them, Eze 20:21
that I *w* scatter them among the Eze 20:23
that I *w* bring thee against them Eze 38:17
he *w* not defile himself with the Dan 1:8
certainty that ye *w* gain the time Dan 2:8
the king that he *w* give him time Dan 2:16
that he *w* shew the king the Dan 2:16
That they *w* desire mercies of the Dan 2:18
whom he *w* he slew Dan 5:19 6634
and whom he *w* he kept alive Dan 5:19 6634
and whom he *w* he set up Dan 5:19 6634
and whom he *w* he put down Dan 5:19 6634
Then I *w* know the truth of the Dan 7:19 6634
that he *w* accomplish seventy Dan 9:2
When I *w* have healed Israel, then Hos 7:1
High, none at all *w* exalt him Hos 11:7
w they not have stolen till they Obad 5
w they not leave some grapes Obad 5 14
had said that he *w* do unto them Jonah 3:10
see what *w* become of the city Jonah 4:5
as he cried, and they *w* not hear Zec 7:13
I *w* not hear, saith the LORD of Zec 7:13
that *w* shut the doors for nought Mal 1:10
w not be comforted, because they Mt 2:18 *2309*
from him that *w* borrow of thee Mt 5:42 *2309*
all things whatsoever ye *w* that Mt 7:12 *2309*
they besought him that he *w* Mt 8:34
they *w* have repented long ago in Mt 11:21
it *w* have remained until this day Mt 11:23
ye *w* not have condemned the Mt 12:7
we *w* see a sign from thee Mt 12:38 *2309*
when he *w* have put him to death, Mt 14:5 *2309*

to give her whatsoever she *w* ask Mt 14:7
he *w* shew them a sign from heaven Mt 16:1
which *w* take account of his Mt 18:23 2309
And he *w* not Mt 18:30 2309
and they *w* not come Mt 22:3 2309
we *w* not have been partakers with Mt 23:30
how often *w* I have gathered thy Mt 23:37 2309
under her wings, and ye *w* not Mt 23:37 2309
in what watch the thief *w* come Mt 24:43
he *w* have watched Mt 24:43
w not have suffered his house to Mt 24:43
people a prisoner, whom they *w* Mt 27:15 2309
tasted thereof, he *w* not drink Mt 27:34 2309
whether he *w* heal him on the Mk 3:2
and calleth unto him whom he *w* Mk 3:13 2309
he besought him much that he *w* Mk 5:10
against him, and *w* have killed him Mk 6:19 2309
sat with him, he *w* not reject her Mk 6:26 2309
the sea, and *w* have passed by them Mk 6:48 2309
house, and *w* have no man know it Mk 7:24 2309
she besought him that he *w* cast Mk 7:26
he *w* not that any man should know Mk 9:30 2309
we *w* that thou shouldest do for Mk 10:35 2309
What *w* ye that I should do for Mk 10:36 2309
w not suffer that any man should Mk 11:16
father, how he *w* have him called Lk 1:62 2309
That he *w* grant unto us, that we, Lk 1:74
prayed him that he *w* thrust out a Lk 5:3
whether he *w* heal on the sabbath Lk 6:7
as ye *w* that men should do to you Lk 6:31 2309
beseeching him that he *w* come Lk 7:3
him that he *w* eat with him Lk 7:36
w have known who and what manner Lk 7:39
they besought him that he *w* not Lk 8:31
they besought him that he *w* Lk 8:32
him that he *w* come into his house Lk 8:41
as though he *w* go to Jerusalem Lk 9:53
place, whither he himself *w* come Lk 10:1 3195
that he *w* send forth labourers Lk 10:2
known what hour the thief *w* come Lk 12:39
he *w* have watched, and not have Lk 12:39
how often *w* I have gathered thy Lk 13:34 2309
under her wings, and ye *w* not Lk 13:34 2309
he *w* fain have filled his belly Lk 15:16
And he was angry, and *w* not go in Lk 15:28 2309
so that they which *w* pass from Lk 16:26 2309
to us, that *w* come from thence Lk 16:26
And he *w* not for a while Lk 18:4 2309
w not lift up so much as his eyes Lk 18:13 2309
infants, that he *w* touch them Lk 18:15
which *w* not that I should reign Lk 19:27 2309
the stones *w* immediately cry out Lk 19:40
were about him saw what *w* follow Lk 22:49
as though he *w* have gone further Lk 24:28
Jesus *w* go forth into Galilee Jn 1:43 2309
he *w* have given thee living water Jn 4:10
him that he *w* tarry with them Jn 4:40
besought him that he *w* come down Jn 4:47
Moses, ye *w* have believed me Jn 5:46
for he himself knew what he *w* do Jn 6:6 3195
of the fishes as much as they *w* Jn 6:11 2309
perceived that they *w* come Jn 6:15 3195
for he *w* not walk in Jewry, Jn 7:1 2309
some of them *w* have taken him Jn 7:44 2309
ye *w* do the works of Abraham Jn 8:39
were your Father, ye *w* love me Jn 8:42
wherefore *w* ye hear it again Jn 9:27 2309
him, saying, Sir, we *w* see Jesus Jn 12:21 2309
it were not so, I *w* have told you Jn 14:2
ye *w* rejoice, because I said, I Jn 14:28
world, the world *w* love his own Jn 15:19
we *w* not have delivered him up Jn 18:30
then *w* my servants fight, that I Jn 18:36
he *w* raise up Christ to sit on Acts 2:30
of them whereunto this *w* grow Acts 5:24
yet he promised that he *w* give it Acts 7:5
For he supposed his brethren *w* Acts 7:25
God by his hand *w* deliver them Acts 7:25
w have set them at one again, Acts 7:26
To whom our fathers *w* not obey Acts 7:39 2309
desired Philip that he *w* come up Acts 8:31
desiring him that he *w* not delay Acts 9:38
very hungry, and *w* have eaten Acts 10:10 2309
heart they *w* cleave unto the Lord Acts 11:23
when Herod *w* have brought him Acts 12:6 3195
w have done sacrifice with the Acts 14:13 2309
Him *w* Paul have to go forth with Acts 16:3 2309
w have killed himself, supposing Acts 16:27 3195
we *w* know therefore what these Acts 17:20
reason *w* that I should bear with Acts 18:14
when Paul *w* have entered in unto Acts 19:30
desiring him that he *w* not Acts 19:31
w have made his defence unto the Acts 19:33 2309
because he *w* not spend the time Acts 20:16 1096
when he *w* not be persuaded, we Acts 21:14
because he *w* have known the Acts 22:30
saying that ye *w* neither eat Acts 23:12
as though ye *w* enquire something Acts 23:15 3195
as though they *w* enquire somewhat Acts 23:20 3195
when I *w* have known the cause Acts 23:28
w have judged according to our Acts 24:6 2309
that he *w* send for him to Acts 25:3
that he himself *w* depart shortly Acts 25:4 3195
him whether he *w* go to Jerusalem Acts 25:20
I *w* also hear the man myself Acts 25:22
the beginning, if they *w* testify Acts 26:5 2309
I *w* to God, that not only thou, Acts 26:29 2172
under colour as though they *w* Acts 27:30 3195
w have let me go, because there Acts 28:18
Now I *w* not have you ignorant, Rom 1:13 2309
good man some *w* even dare to die Rom 5:7
for what I *w*, that do I not Rom 7:15 2309
If then I do that which I *w* not Rom 7:16 2309
For the good that I *w* I do not Rom 7:19 2309
but the evil which I *w* not Rom 7:19 2309
Now if I do that I *w* not, it is Rom 7:20 2309
when I *w* do good, evil is present Rom 7:21 2309
For I *w* not, brethren, that ye Rom 11:25 2309
but yet I *w* have you wise unto Rom 16:19 2309
they *w* not have crucified the 1Cor 2:8
I *w* to God ye did reign, that we 1Cor 4:8 3785
as though I *w* not come to you 1Cor 4:18
For I *w* that all men were even as 1Cor 7:7 2309
But I *w* have you without 1Cor 7:32 2309
I *w* not that ye should be 1Cor 10:1 2309
I *w* not that ye should have 1Cor 10:20 2309
But I *w* have you know, that the 1Cor 11:3 2309
For if we *w* judge ourselves, we 1Cor 11:31
I *w* not have you ignorant 1Cor 12:1 2309
I *w* that ye all spake with 1Cor 14:5 2309
For we *w* not, brethren, have you 2Cor 1:8 2309
that I *w* not come again to you in 2Cor 2:1
ye *w* confirm your love toward him 2Cor 2:8
not for that we *w* be unclothed 2Cor 5:4 2309
that we *w* receive the gift 2Cor 8:4
so he *w* also finish in you the 2Cor 8:6
that they *w* go before unto you, 2Cor 9:5
as if I *w* terrify you by letters 2Cor 10:9
W to God ye could bear with me a 2Cor 11:1 3785
For though I *w* desire to glory, I 2Cor 12:6
I shall not find you such as I *w* 2Cor 12:20 2309
found unto you such as ye *w* not 2Cor 12:20 2309
w pervert the gospel of Christ Gal 1:7
Only they *w* that we should Gal 2:10
This only *w* I learn of you, Gal 3:2 2309
foreseeing that God *w* justify the Gal 3:8
ye *w* have plucked out your own Gal 4:15
they *w* exclude you, that ye might Gal 4:17 2309
I *w* they were even cut off which Gal 5:12 3785
ye cannot do the things that ye *w* Gal 5:17 2309
That he *w* grant you, according to Eph 3:16
But I *w* ye should understand, Phil 1:12
To whom God *w* make known what is Col 1:27 2309
For I *w* that ye knew what great Col 2:1 2309
that God *w* open unto us a door of Col 4:3
because we *w* not be chargeable 1Th 2:9
That ye *w* walk worthy of God, who 1Th 2:12
Wherefore we *w* have come unto you 1Th 2:18 2309
so ye *w* abound more and more 1Th 4:1
But I *w* not have you to be 1Th 4:13 2309
that our God *w* count you worthy 2Th 1:11
you, that if any *w* not work 2Th 3:10 2309
Whom I *w* have retained with me, Philem 13
without thy mind *w* I do nothing Philem 14 2309
then *w* he not afterward have Heb 4:8
For then *w* they not have ceased Heb 10:2
for the time *w* fail me to tell of Heb 11:32
when he *w* have inherited the Heb 12:17 2309
they *w* no doubt have continued 1Jn 2:19
I *w* not write with paper and ink 2Jn 12
and forbiddeth them that *w* 3Jn 10
I *w* thou wert cold or hot Rev 3:15 3785
cause that as many as *w* not Rev 13:15

WOULDEST
w thou take away my son's Gen 30:15
though thou *w* needs be gone, Gen 31:30
Peradventure thou *w* take by force Gen 31:31
behold, hitherto thou *w* not hear Ex 7:16
w forbear to help him, thou shalt Ex 23:5
heart, whether thou *w* keep his Deut 8:2
that thou *w* have her to thy wife Deut 21:11
because thou *w* not obey the voice Deut 28:62
Caleb said unto her, What *w* thou Josh 15:18
that thou *w* not suffer the 2Sa 14:11
thou thyself *w* have set thyself 2Sa 18:13
And the king said, What *w* thou 1Kin 1:16
that thou *w* deliver thy servant 1Kin 18:9
w thou be spoken for to the king, 2Kin 4:13 3426
thing, *w* thou not have done it 2Kin 5:13
w thou smite those whom thou hast 2Kin 6:22
Oh that thou *w* bless me indeed, 1Chr 4:10
that thou *w* keep me from evil, 1Chr 4:10
that thou *w* put thy name there 2Chr 6:20
whom thou *w* not let Israel invade 2Chr 20:10
w not thou be angry with us till Ezr 9:14
that thou *w* send me unto Judah, Neh 2:5
If thou *w* seek unto God betimes, Job 8:5
Oh that thou *w* hide me in the Job 14:13
that thou *w* keep me secret, until Job 14:13
that thou *w* appoint me a set time Job 14:13
for I knew that thou *w* deal very Is 48:8
Oh that thou *w* rend the heavens, Is 64:1
that thou *w* come down Is 64:1
that thou *w* send him to my Lk 16:27
thou *w* have asked of him, and he Jn 4:10
thee, that, if thou *w* believe Jn 11:40
and walkedst whither thou *w* Jn 21:18 2309
and carry thee whither thou *w* not Jn 21:18 2309
w bring down Paul to morrow into Acts 23:20
I pray thee that thou *w* hear us Acts 24:4
Sacrifice and offering thou *w* not Heb 10:5 2309
and offering for sin thou *w* not Heb 10:8 2309

WOUND
w for *w*, stripe for stripe Ex 21:25 6482
I *w*, and I heal Deut 32:39 4272
the blood ran out of the *w* into 1Kin 22:35 4347
my *w* is incurable without Job 34:6 2671
But God shall *w* the head of his Ps 68:21 4272
he shall *w* the heads over many Ps 110:6 4272
A *w* and dishonour shall he get Prov 6:33 5061
The blueness of a *w* cleanseth Prov 20:30 6482
and healeth the stroke of their *w* Is 30:26 4347
my *w* is grievous Jer 10:19 4347
my *w* incurable, which refuseth to Jer 15:18 4347
incurable, and thy *w* is grievous Jer 30:12 4347
thee with the *w* of an enemy Jer 30:14 4347
his sickness, and Judah saw his *w* Hos 5:13 4205
heal you, nor cure you of your *w* Hos 5:13 4205
bread have laid a *w* under thee Obad 7 4204
For her *w* is incurable Mic 1:9 4347
thy *w* is grievous Nah 3:19 4347
w it in linen clothes with the Jn 19:40 1210
w him up, and carried him out, and Acts 5:6 4958
w their weak conscience, ye sin 1Cor 8:12 5180
and his deadly *w* was healed Rev 13:3 4127
beast, whose deadly *w* was healed Rev 13:12 4127
beast, which had the *w* by a sword Rev 13:14 4127

WOUNDED
He that is *w* in the stones, or Deut 23:1 1795
many were overthrown and *w* Judg 9:40 2491
the *w* of the Philistines fell 1Sa 17:52 2491
he was sore *w* of the archers 1Sa 31:3 2342
w them, that they could not arise 2Sa 22:39 4272
him, so that in smiting he *w* him 1Kin 20:37 6481
for I am *w* 1Kin 22:34 2470
and the Syrians *w* Joram 2Kin 8:28 5221
him, and he was *w* of the archers 1Chr 10:3 2342
for I am *w* 2Chr 18:33 2470
for I am sore *w* 2Chr 35:23 2470
and the soul of the *w* crieth out Job 24:12 2491
I have *w* them that they were not Ps 18:38 4272
suddenly shall they be *w* Ps 64:7 4347
grief of those whom thou hast *w* Ps 69:26 2491
needy, and my heart is *w* within me Ps 109:22 2490
For she hath cast down many *w* Prov 7:26 2491
but a *w* spirit who can bear Prov 18:14 5218
me, they smote me, they *w* me Song 5:7 6481
hath cut Rahab, and *w* the dragon Is 51:9 2490
But he was *w* for our Is 53:5 2490
for I have *w* thee with the wound Jer 30:14 5221
remained but *w* men among them Jer 37:10 1856
all her land the *w* shall groan Jer 51:52 2491
when they swooned as the *w* in the Lam 2:12 2491
sound of thy fall, when the *w* cry Eze 26:15 2491
the *w* shall be judged in the Eze 28:23 2491
the groanings of a deadly *w* man Eze 30:24 2491
the sword, they shall not be *w* Joel 2:8 1214
Those with which I was *w* in the Zec 13:6 5221
w him in the head, and sent him Mk 12:4
w him, and departed, leaving him Lk 10:30
they *w* him also, and cast him out Lk 20:12 5135
fled out of that house naked and *w* Acts 19:16 5135
his heads as it were *w* to death Rev 13:3 4969

WOUNDEDST
thou *w* the head out of the house Hab 3:13 4272

WOUNDETH
he *w*, and his hands make whole Job 5:18 4272

WOUNDING
for I have slain a man to my *w* Gen 4:23 6482

WOUNDS
to be healed in Jezreel of the *w* 2Kin 8:29 4347
to be healed in Jezreel of the *w* 2Kin 9:15 4347
in Jezreel because of the *w* which 2Chr 22:6 4347
and multiplieth my *w* without cause Job 9:17 6482
My *w* stink and are corrupt because Ps 38:5 2250
in heart, and bindeth up their *w* Ps 147:3 6094
words of a talebearer are as *w* Prov 18:8 3859
who hath *w* without cause Prov 23:29 6482
words of a talebearer are as *w* Prov 26:22 3859
Faithful are the *w* of a friend Prov 27:6 6482
but *w*, and bruises, and putrifying Is 1:6 6482
me continually is grief and *w* Jer 6:7 4347
and I will heal thee of thy *w* Jer 30:17 4347
What are these *w* in thine hands Zec 13:6 4347
And went to him, and bound up his *w* Lk 10:34 5134

WOVE
where the women *w* hangings for 2Kin 23:7 707

WOVEN
it shall have a binding of *w* work Ex 28:32 707
the robe of the ephod of *w* work Ex 39:22 707
of fine linen of *w* work for Aaron Ex 39:27 707
w from the top throughout Jn 19:23 5307

WRAP
than that he can *w* himself in it Is 28:20 3664
so they *w* it up Mic 7:3 5686

WRAPPED
w herself, and sat in an open Gen 38:14 5968
it is here *w* in a cloth behind 1Sa 21:9 3874
that he *w* his face in his mantle, 1Kin 19:13 3874
w it together, and smote the 2Kin 2:8 1563
His roots are *w* about the heap, Job 8:17 5440
of his stones are *w* together Job 40:17 8276
it is *w* up for the slaughter Eze 21:15 4593
the weeds were *w* about my head Jonah 2:5 2280
he *w* it in a clean linen cloth, Mt 27:59 1794
w him in the linen, and laid him Mk 15:46 1750
w him in swaddling clothes, and Lk 2:7 4683
the babe *w* in swaddling clothes Lk 2:12 4683
w it in linen, and laid it in a Lk 23:53 1794
but *w* together in a place by Jn 20:7 1794

WRATH
that his *w* was kindled Gen 39:19 639
and their *w*, for it was cruel Gen 49:7 5678
thou sentest forth thy *w*, which Ex 15:7 2740
my *w* shall wax hot, and I will Ex 22:24 639
that my *w* may wax hot against Ex 32:10 639
why doth thy *w* wax hot against Ex 32:11 639
Turn from thy fierce *w*, and repent Ex 32:12 639
lest *w* come upon all the people Lev 10:6 7107
that there be no *w* upon the Num 1:53 7110
the *w* of the LORD was kindled Num 11:33 639
for there is *w* gone out from the Num 16:46 7110
that there be no *w* any more upon Num 18:5 7110
hath turned my *w* away from the Num 25:11 2534
thy God to *w* in the wilderness Deut 9:7 7107
Horeb ye provoked the LORD to *w* Deut 9:8 7107

ye provoked the LORD to *w* Deut 9:22 7107
then the LORD's *w* be kindled Deut 11:17 639
in his anger, and in his *w* Deut 29:23 2534
of their land in anger, and in *w* Deut 29:28 2534
that I feared the *w* of the enemy Deut 32:27 3708
lest *w* be upon us, because of the Josh 9:20 7110
w fell on all the congregation of Josh 22:20 7110
his fierce *w* upon Amalek, 1Sa 28:18 639
if so be that the king's *w* arise 2Sa 11:20 2534
for great is the *w* of the LORD 2Kin 22:13 2534
therefore my *w* shall be kindled 2Kin 22:17 2534
the fierceness of his great *w* 2Kin 23:26 639
because there fell *w* for it 1Chr 27:24 7110
my *w* shall not be poured out upon 2Chr 12:7 2534
the *w* of the LORD turned from him 2Chr 12:12 639
therefore is *w* upon thee from 2Chr 19:2 7110
so *w* come upon you, and upon your 2Chr 19:10 7110
w came upon Judah and Jerusalem 2Chr 24:18 7110
for the fierce *w* of the LORD is 2Chr 28:11 639
there is fierce *w* against Israel 2Chr 28:13 639
Wherefore the *w* of the LORD was 2Chr 29:8 7110
that his fierce *w* may turn away 2Chr 29:10 639
of his *w* may turn away from you 2Chr 30:8 639
therefore there was *w* upon him 2Chr 32:25 7110
so that the *w* of the LORD came 2Chr 32:26 7110
for great is the *w* of the LORD 2Chr 34:21 2534
therefore my *w* shall be poured 2Chr 34:25 2534
until the *w* of the LORD arose 2Chr 36:16 2534
provoked the God of heaven unto *w* Ezr 5:12 7265
for why should there be *w* against Ezr 7:23 7109
his *w* is against all them that Ezr 8:22 639
until the fierce *w* of our God for Ezr 10:14 639
yet ye bring more *w* upon Israel Neh 13:18 2740
arise too much contempt and *w* Est 1:18 7110
when the *w* of king Ahasuerus was Est 2:1 2534
then was Haman full of *w* Est 3:5 2534
his *w* went into the palace garden Est 7:7 2534
Then was the king's *w* pacified Est 7:10 2534
For *w* killeth the foolish man, and Job 5:2 3708
me secret, until thy *w* be past Job 14:13 639
He teareth me in his *w*, who Job 16:9 639
also kindled his *w* against me Job 19:11 639
for *w* bringeth the punishments of Job 19:29 2534
cast the fury of his *w* upon him Job 20:23 639
flow away in the day of his *w* Job 20:28 639
drink of the *w* of the Almighty Job 21:20 2534
be brought forth to the day of *w* Job 21:30 5678
Then was kindled the *w* of Elihu Job 32:2 639
against Job was his *w* kindled Job 32:2 639
three friends was his *w* kindled Job 32:3 639
three men, then his *w* was kindled Job 32:5 639
the hypocrites in heart heap up *w* Job 36:13 639
Because there is *w*, beware lest Job 36:18 2534
Cast abroad the rage of thy *w* Job 40:11 639
My *w* is kindled against thee, and Job 42:7 639
shall he speak unto them in his *w* Ps 2:5 639
when his *w* is kindled but a Ps 2:12 639
shall swallow them up in his *w* Ps 21:9 639
Cease from anger, and forsake *w* Ps 37:8 2534
O LORD, rebuke me not in thy *w* Ps 38:1 7110
upon me, and in *w* they hate me Ps 55:3 639
both living, and in his *w* Ps 58:9 2740
Consume them in *w*, consume them, Ps 59:13 2534
Surely the *w* of man shall praise Ps 76:10 2534
the remainder of *w* shalt thou Ps 76:10 2534
The *w* of God came upon them, and Ps 78:31 639
and did not stir up all his *w* Ps 78:38 2534
the fierceness of his anger, *w* Ps 78:49 5678
Pour out thy *w* upon the heathen Ps 79:6 2534
Thou hast taken away all thy *w* Ps 85:3 5678
Thy *w* lieth hard upon me, and thou Ps 88:7 2534
Thy fierce *w* goeth over me Ps 88:16 2740
shall thy *w* burn like fire Ps 89:46 2534
and by thy *w* are we troubled Ps 90:7 2534
our days are passed away in thy *w* Ps 90:9 5678
to thy fear, so is thy *w* Ps 90:11 5678
Unto whom I sware in my *w* that Ps 95:11 639
of thine indignation and thy *w* Ps 102:10 7110
in the breach, to turn away his *w* Ps 106:23 2534
Therefore was the *w* of the LORD Ps 106:40 639
through kings in the day of his *w* Ps 110:5 639
when their *w* was kindled against Ps 124:3 639
against the *w* of mine enemies Ps 138:7 639
Riches profit not in the day of *w* Prov 11:4 5678
expectation of the wicked is *w* Prov 11:23 5678
A fool's *w* is presently known Prov 12:16 3708
He that is slow to *w* is of great Prov 14:29 639
but his *w* is against him that Prov 14:35 5678
A soft answer turneth away *w* Prov 15:1 2534
The *w* of a king is as messengers Prov 16:14 2534
The king's *w* is as the roaring of Prov 19:12 2197
A man of great *w* shall suffer Prov 19:19 2534
and a reward in the bosom strong *w* Prov 21:14 2534
his name, who dealeth in proud *w* Prov 21:24 5678
and he turn away his *w* from him Prov 24:18 639
but a fool's *w* is heavier than Prov 27:3 3708
W is cruel, and anger is Prov 27:4 2534
but wise men turn away *w* Prov 29:8 639
so the forcing of *w* bringeth Prov 30:33 639
sorrow and *w* with his sickness Eccl 5:17 7110
Through the *w* of the LORD of Is 9:19 5678
of my *w* will I give him a charge Is 10:6 5678
LORD cometh, cruel both with *w* Is 13:9 5678
in the *w* of the LORD of hosts, and Is 13:13 5678
in *w* with a continual stroke Is 14:6 5678
and his pride, and his *w* Is 16:6 5678
In a little *w* I hid my face from Is 54:8 7110
for in my *w* I smote thee, but in Is 60:10 7110
forsaken the generation of his *w* Jer 7:29 5678
at his *w* the earth shall tremble, Jer 10:10 7110
and to turn away thy *w* from them Jer 18:20 2534
anger, and in fury, and in great *w* Jer 21:5 7110
and in my fury, and in great *w* Jer 32:37 7110
In that ye provoke me unto *w* with Jer 44:8 3707
I know his *w*, saith the LORD Jer 48:30 5678
Because of the *w* of the LORD it Jer 50:13 7110
in his *w* the strong holds of the Lam 2:2 5678
affliction by the rod of his *w* Lam 3:1 5678
for *w* is upon all the multitude Eze 7:12 2740
for my *w* is upon all the Eze 7:14 2740
in the day of the *w* of the LORD Eze 7:19 5678
I accomplish my *w* upon the wall Eze 13:15 2534
against thee in the fire of my *w* Eze 21:31 5678
blow upon you in the fire of my *w* Eze 22:21 5678
them with the fire of my *w* Eze 22:31 5678
in the fire of my *w* have I spoken Eze 38:19 5678
out my *w* upon them like water Hos 5:10 5678
anger, and took him away in my *w* Hos 13:11 5678
and he kept his *w* for ever Amos 1:11 5678
he reserveth *w* for his enemies Nah 1:2
in *w* remember mercy Hab 3:2 7267
was thy *w* against the sea, that Hab 3:8 5678
That day is a day of *w*, a day of Zeph 1:15 5678
them in the day of the LORD's *w* Zeph 1:18 5678
a great *w* from the LORD of hosts Zec 7:12 7110
your fathers provoked me to *w* Zec 8:14 7107
you to flee from the *w* to come Mt 3:7 *3709*
you to flee from the *w* to come Lk 3:7 *3709*
these things, were filled with *w* Lk 4:28 *2372*
the land, and *w* upon this people Lk 21:23 *3709*
but the *w* of God abideth on him Jn 3:36 *3709*
sayings, they were full of *w* Acts 19:28 *2372*
For the *w* of God is revealed from Rom 1:18 *3709*
w against the day of *w* Rom 2:5 *3709*
w against the day of *w* Rom 2:5 *3709*
unrighteousness, indignation and *w* Rom 2:8 *3709*
Because the law worketh *w* Rom 4:15 *3709*
shall be saved from *w* through him Rom 5:9 *3709*
if God, willing to shew his *w* Rom 9:22 *3709*
of *w* fitted to destruction Rom 9:22 *3709*
but rather give place unto *w* Rom 12:19 *3709*
a revenger to execute *w* upon him Rom 13:4 *3709*
needs be subject, not only for *w* Rom 13:5 *3709*
hatred, variance, emulations, *w* Gal 5:20 *2372*
were by nature the children of *w* Eph 2:3 *3709*
not the sun go down upon your *w* Eph 4:26 *3950*
Let all bitterness, and *w*, and Eph 4:31 *2372*
of these things cometh the *w* of Eph 5:6 *3709*
provoke not your children to *w* Eph 6:4 *3949*
For which things' sake the *w* of Col 3:6 *3709*
anger, *w*, malice, blasphemy, Col 3:8 *2372*
delivered us from the *w* to come 1Th 1:10 *3709*
for the *w* is come upon them to 1Th 2:16 *3709*
God hath not appointed us to *w* 1Th 5:9 *3709*
lifting up holy hands, without *w* 1Ti 2:8 *3709*
So I sware in my *w*, They shall Heb 3:11 *3709*
he said, As I have sworn in my *w* Heb 4:3 *3709*
not fearing the *w* of the king Heb 11:27 *2372*
to hear, slow to speak, slow to *w* Jas 1:19 *3709*
For the *w* of man worketh not the Jas 1:20 *3709*
throne, and from the *w* of the Lamb Rev 6:16 *3709*
the great day of his *w* is come Rev 6:17 *3709*
thy *w* is come, and the time of the Rev 11:18 *3709*
down unto you, having great *w* Rev 12:12 *2372*
wine of the *w* of her fornication Rev 14:8 *2372*
drink of the wine of the *w* of God Rev 14:10 *2372*
great winepress of the *w* of God Rev 14:19 *2372*
in them is filled up the *w* of God Rev 15:1 *2372*
golden vials full of the *w* of God Rev 15:7 *2372*
of the *w* of God upon the earth Rev 16:1 *2372*
wine of the fierceness of his *w* Rev 16:19 *3709*
wine of the *w* of her fornication Rev 18:3 *2372*
fierceness and *w* of Almighty God Rev 19:15 *3709*

WRATHFUL
let thy *w* anger take hold of them Ps 69:24 2740
A *w* man stirreth up strife Prov 15:18 2534

WRATHS
there be debates, envyings, *w* 2Cor 12:20 *2372*

WREATH
rows of pomegranates on each *w* 2Chr 4:13 7639

WREATHED
they are *w*, and come up upon my Lam 1:14 8276

WREATHEN
of *w* work shalt thou make them, Ex 28:14 5688
fasten the *w* chains to the ouches Ex 28:14 5688
the ends of *w* work of pure gold Ex 28:22 5688
thou shalt put the two *w* chains Ex 28:24 5688
the other two ends of the two *w* Ex 28:25 5688
the ends, of *w* work of pure gold Ex 39:15 5688
they put the two *w* chains of gold Ex 39:17 5688
the two ends of the two *w* chains Ex 39:18 5688
the *w* work, and pomegranates upon 2Kin 25:17 7639
had the second pillar with *w* work 2Kin 25:17 7639

WREATHS
work, and *w* of chain work, for the 1Kin 7:17 1434
the two *w* to cover the two 2Chr 4:12 7639
hundred pomegranates on the two *w* 2Chr 4:13 7639

WREST
decline after many to *w* judgment Ex 23:2 5186
Thou shalt not *w* the judgment of Ex 23:6 5186
Thou shalt not *w* judgment Deut 16:19 5186
Every day they *w* my words Ps 56:5 6087
that are unlearned and unstable *w* 2Pet 3:16 *4761*

WRESTLE
For we *w* not against flesh and Eph 6:12

WRESTLED
have I *w* with my sister, and I Gen 30:8 6617
there *w* a man with him until the Gen 32:24 79
out of joint, as he *w* with him Gen 32:25 79

WRESTLINGS
With great *w* have I wrestled with Gen 30:8 5319

WRETCHED
O *w* man that I am Rom 7:24 *5005*
and knowest not that thou art *w* Rev 3:17 *5005*

WRETCHEDNESS
and let me not see my *w* Num 11:15 7451

WRING
w off his head, and burn it on the Lev 1:15 4454
w off his head from his neck, but Lev 5:8 4454
of the earth shall *w* them out Ps 75:8 4680

WRINGED
w the dew out of the fleece, a Judg 6:38 4680

WRINGING
the *w* of the nose bringeth forth Prov 30:33 4330

WRINKLE
church, not having spot, or *w* Eph 5:27 *4512*

WRINKLES
And thou hast filled me with *w* Job 16:8 7059

WRITE
W this for a memorial in a book, Ex 17:14 3789
I will *w* upon these tables the Ex 34:1 3789
unto Moses, *W* thou these words Ex 34:27 3789
the priest shall *w* these curses Num 5:23 3789
w thou every man's name upon his Num 17:2 3789
thou shalt *w* Aaron's name upon Num 17:3 3789
thou shalt *w* them upon the posts Deut 6:9 3789
I will *w* on the tables the words Deut 10:2 3789
thou shalt *w* them upon the door Deut 11:20 3789
that he shall *w* him a copy of Deut 17:18 3789
then let him *w* her a bill of Deut 24:1 3789
w her a bill of divorcement, and Deut 24:3 3789
thou shalt *w* upon them all the Deut 27:3 3789
thou shalt *w* upon the stones all Deut 27:8 3789
Now therefore *w* ye this song for Deut 31:19 3789
the prophet, the son of Amoz, *w* 2Chr 26:22 3789
that we might *w* the names of the Ezr 5:10 3790
we make a sure covenant, and *w* it Neh 9:38 3789
W ye also for the Jews, as it Est 8:8 3789
w them upon the table of thine Prov 3:3 3789
w them upon the table of thine Prov 7:3 3789
roll, and *w* in it with a man's pen Is 8:1 3789
that *w* grievousness which they Is 10:1 3789
be few, that a child may *w* them Is 10:19 3789
w it before them in a table, and Is 30:8 3789
W ye this man childless, a man Jer 22:30 3789
W thee all the words that I have Jer 30:2 3789
parts, and *w* it in their hearts Jer 31:33 3789
w therein all the words that I Jer 36:2 3789
How didst thou *w* all these words Jer 36:17 3789
w in it all the former words that Jer 36:28 3789
w thee the name of the day, even Eze 24:2 3789
w upon it, For Judah, and for the Eze 37:16 3789
w upon it, For Joseph, the stick Eze 37:16 3789
w it in their sight, that they Eze 43:11 3789
W the vision, and make it plain Hab 2:2 3789
Moses suffered to *w* a bill of Mk 10:4 *1125*
to *w* unto thee in order, most Lk 1:3 *1125*
and sit down quickly, and *w* fifty Lk 16:6 *1125*
Take thy bill, and *w* fourscore Lk 16:7 *1125*
the law, and the prophets, did *w* Jn 1:45 *1125*
W not, The King of the Jews Jn 19:21 *1125*
But that we *w* unto them, that Acts 15:20 *1989*
certain thing to *w* unto my lord Acts 25:26 *1125*
had, I might have somewhat to *w* Acts 25:26 *1125*
I *w* not these things to shame you 1Cor 4:14 *1125*
that the things that I *w* unto you 1Cor 14:37 *1125*
For we *w* none other things unto 2Cor 1:13 *1125*
For to this end also did I *w* 2Cor 2:9 *1125*
is superfluous for me to *w* to you 2Cor 9:1 *1125*
being absent now I *w* to them 2Cor 13:2 *1125*
Therefore I *w* these things being 2Cor 13:10 *1125*
Now the things which I *w* unto you Gal 1:20 *1125*
To *w* the same things to you, to Phil 3:1 *1125*
ye need not that I *w* unto you 1Th 4:9 *1125*
ye have no need that I *w* unto you 1Th 5:1 *1125*
so I *w* 2Th 3:17 *1125*
These things *w* I unto thee 1Ti 3:14 *1125*
mind, and *w* them in their hearts Heb 8:10 *1924*
and in their minds will I *w* them Heb 10:16 *1924*
beloved, I now *w* unto you 2Pet 3:1 *1125*
And these things *w* we unto you 1Jn 1:4 *1125*
these things *w* I unto you 1Jn 2:1 *1125*
I *w* no new commandment unto you, 1Jn 2:7 *1125*
a new commandment I *w* unto you 1Jn 2:8 *1125*
I *w* unto you, little children, 1Jn 2:12 *1125*
I *w* unto you, fathers, because ye 1Jn 2:13 *1125*
I *w* unto you, young men, because 1Jn 2:13 *1125*
I *w* unto you, little children, 1Jn 2:13 *1125*
Having many things to *w* unto you 2Jn 12 *1125*
I would not *w* with paper 2Jn 12
I had many things to *w*, but I 3Jn 13 *1125*
not with ink and pen *w* unto thee 3Jn 13 *1125*
to *w* unto you of the common Jude 3 *1125*
was needful for me to *w* unto you Jude 3 *1125*
w in a book, and send it unto the Rev 1:11 *1125*
W the things which thou hast seen Rev 1:19 *1125*
angel of the church of Ephesus *w* Rev 2:1 *1125*
angel of the church in Smyrna *w* Rev 2:8 *1125*
angel of the church in Pergamos *w* Rev 2:12 *1125*
angel of the church in Thyatira *w* Rev 2:18 *1125*
angel of the church in Sardis *w* Rev 3:1 *1125*
of the church in Philadelphia *w* Rev 3:7 *1125*
I will *w* upon him the name of my Rev 3:12 *1125*
I will *w* upon him my new name Rev 3:12
of the church of the Laodiceans *w* Rev 3:14 *1125*
their voices, I was about to *w* Rev 10:4 *1125*
thunders uttered, and *w* them not Rev 10:4 *1125*
from heaven saying unto me, *W* Rev 14:13 *1125*
And he saith unto me, *W*, Blessed Rev 19:9 *1125*

And he said unto me, W Rev 21:5 1125

WRITER

they that handle the pen of the w Judg 5:14 5608
my tongue is the pen of a ready w Ps 45:1 5608

WRITER'S

with a w inkhorn by his side Eze 9:2 5608
which had the w inkhorn by his Eze 9:3 5608

WRITEST

For thou w bitter things against Job 13:26 3789
the sticks whereon thou w shall Eze 37:20 3789

WRITETH

when he w up the people, that Ps 87:6 3789

WRITING

the w was the w of God, Ex 32:16 4385
pure gold, and wrote upon it a w Ex 39:30 4385
tables, according to the first w Deut 10:4 4385
when Moses had made an end of w Deut 31:24 3789
in w by his hand upon me, even 1Chr 28:19 3791
the king of Tyre answered in w 2Chr 2:11 3791
there came a w to him from Elijah 2Chr 21:12 4385
according to the w of David king 2Chr 35:4 3791
according to the w of Solomon his 2Chr 35:4 4385
his kingdom, and put it also in w 2Chr 36:22 4385
his kingdom, and put it also in w Ezr 1:1 4385
the w of the letter was written Ezr 4:7 3791
according to the w thereof Est 1:22 3791
according to the w thereof Est 3:12 3791
The copy of the w for a Est 3:14 3791
he gave him the copy of the w of Est 4:8 3791
for the w which is written in the Est 8:8 3791
according to the w thereof Est 8:9 3791
to the Jews according to their w Est 8:9 3791
The copy of the w for a Est 8:13 3791
two days according to their w Est 9:27 3791
The w of Hezekiah king of Judah, Is 38:9 4385
in the w of the house of Israel Eze 13:9 3791
Whosoever shall read this w Dan 5:7 3792
but they could not read the w Dan 5:8 3792
me, that they should read this w Dan 5:15 3792
now if thou canst read the w Dan 5:16 3792
I will read the w unto the king Dan 5:17 3792
and this w was written Dan 5:24 3792
this is the w that was written, Dan 5:25 3792
the decree, and sign the w Dan 6:8 3792
king Darius signed the w and the Dan 6:9 3792
Daniel knew that the w was signed Dan 6:10 3792
him give her a w of divorcement Mt 5:31
to give a w of divorcement Mt 19:7 975
And he asked for a w table Lk 1:63 4093
the w was, JESUS OF Jn 19:19 1125

WRITINGS

But if ye believe not his w Jn 5:47 1121

WRITTEN

and commandments which I have w Ex 24:12 3789
stone, w with the finger of God Ex 31:18 3789
the tables were w on both their Ex 32:15 3789
side and on the other were they w Ex 32:15 3789
out of thy book which thou hast w Ex 32:32 3789
and they were of them that were w Num 11:26 3789
of stone w with the finger of God Deut 9:10 3789
on them was w according to all Deut 9:10
this law that are w in this book Deut 28:58 3789
which is not w in the book of Deut 28:61 3789
all the curses that are w in this Deut 29:20 3789
are w in this book of the law Deut 29:21 3789
curses that are w in this book Deut 29:27 3789
his statutes which are w in this Deut 30:10 3789
to all that is w therein Josh 1:8 3789
as it is w in the book of the law Josh 8:31 3789
that is w in the book of the law Josh 8:34 3789
Is not this w in the book of Josh 10:13 3789
to do all that is w in the book Josh 23:6 3789
it is w in the book of Jasher 2Sa 1:18 3789
as it is w in the law of Moses, 1Kin 2:3 3789
are they not w in the book of the 1Kin 11:41 3789
they are w in the book of the 1Kin 14:19 3789
are they not w in the book of the 1Kin 14:29 3789
are they not w in the book of the 1Kin 15:7 3789
are they not w in the book of the 1Kin 15:23 3789
are they not w in the book of the 1Kin 15:31 3789
are they not w in the book of the 1Kin 16:5 3789
are they not w in the book of the 1Kin 16:14 3789
are they not w in the book of the 1Kin 16:20 3789
are they not w in the book of the 1Kin 16:27 3789
as it was w in the letters which 1Kin 21:11 3789
are they not w in the book of the 1Kin 22:39 3789
are they not w in the book of the 1Kin 22:45 3789
are they not w in the book of the 2Kin 1:18 3789
are they not w in the book of the 2Kin 8:23 3789
are they not w in the book of the 2Kin 10:34 3789
are they not w in the book of the 2Kin 12:19 3789
are they not w in the book of the 2Kin 13:8 3789
are they not w in the book of the 2Kin 13:12 3789
according unto that which is w in 2Kin 14:6 3789
are they not w in the book of the 2Kin 14:15 3789
are they not w in the book of the 2Kin 14:18 3789
are they not w in the book of the 2Kin 14:28 3789
are they not w in the book of the 2Kin 15:6 3789
they are w in the book of the 2Kin 15:11 3789
they are w in the book of the 2Kin 15:15 3789
are they not w in the book of the 2Kin 15:21 3789
they are w in the book of the 2Kin 15:26 3789
they are w in the book of the 2Kin 15:31 3789
are they not w in the book of the 2Kin 15:36 3789
are they not w in the book of the 2Kin 16:19 3789
are they not w in the book of the 2Kin 20:20 3789
are they not w in the book of the 2Kin 21:17 3789
are they are not w in the book of 2Kin 21:25 3789
all that which is w concerning us 2Kin 22:13 3789
covenant that were w in this book 2Kin 23:3 3789
as it is w in the book of this 2Kin 23:21 3789
w in the book that Hilkiah the 2Kin 23:24 3789
are they not w in the book of the 2Kin 23:28 3789
are they not w in the book of the 2Kin 24:5 3789
these w by name came in the days 1Chr 4:41 3789
they were w in the book of the 1Chr 9:1 3789
that is w in the law of the LORD 1Chr 16:40 3789
they are w in the book of Samuel 1Chr 29:29 3789
are they not w in the book of 2Chr 9:29 3789
are they not w in the book of 2Chr 12:15 3789
are w in the story of the prophet 2Chr 13:22 3789
they are w in the book of the 2Chr 16:11 3789
they are w in the book of Jehu 2Chr 20:34 3789
as it is w in the law of Moses, 2Chr 23:18 3789
they are w in the story of the 2Chr 24:27 3789
but did as it is w in the law in 2Chr 25:4 3789
are they not w in the book of the 2Chr 25:26 3789
they are w in the book of the 2Chr 27:7 3789
they are w in the book of the 2Chr 28:26 3789
time in such sort as it was w 2Chr 30:5 3789
passover otherwise than it was w 2Chr 30:18 3789
as it is w in the law of the LORD 2Chr 31:3 3789
they are w in the vision of 2Chr 32:32 3789
they are w in the book of the 2Chr 33:18
they are w among the sayings of 2Chr 33:19 3789
after all that is w in this book 2Chr 34:21 3789
are w in the book which they have 2Chr 34:24 3789
covenant which are w in this book 2Chr 34:31 3789
as it is w in the book of Moses 2Chr 35:12 3789
they are w in the lamentations 2Chr 35:25 3789
was w in the law of the LORD 2Chr 35:26 3789
they are w in the book of the 2Chr 35:27 3789
they are w in the book of the 2Chr 36:8 3789
as it is w in the law of Moses Ezr 3:2 3789
feast of tabernacles, as it is w Ezr 3:4 3789
letter was w in the Syrian tongue Ezr 4:7 3789
unto him, wherein was w thus Ezr 5:7 3790
and therein was a record thus w Ezr 6:2 3790
as it is w in the book of Moses Ezr 6:18 3792
all the weight was w at that time Ezr 8:34 3789
Wherein was w, It is reported Neh 6:6 3789
at the first, and found w therein, Neh 7:5 3789
they found w in the law which the Neh 8:14 3789
trees, to make booths, as it is w Neh 8:15 3789
our God, as it is w in the law Neh 10:34 3789
as it is w in the law, and the Neh 10:36 3789
were w in the book of the Neh 12:23 3789
and therein was found w, that the Neh 13:1 3789
let it be w among the laws of the Est 1:19 3789
it was w in the book of the Est 2:23 3789
let it be w that they may be Est 3:9 3789
there was w according to all that Est 3:12 3789
name of king Ahasuerus was it w Est 3:12 3789
And it was found w, that Mordecai Est 6:2 3789
let it be w to reverse the Est 8:5 3789
which is w in the king's name Est 8:8 3789
it was w according to all that Est 8:9 3789
and as Mordecai had w unto them Est 9:23 3789
and it was w in the book Est 9:32 3789
are they not w in the book of the Est 10:2 3789
Oh that my words were now w Job 19:23 3789
that mine adversary had w a book Job 31:35 3789
volume of the book it is w of me Ps 40:7 3789
not be w with the righteous Ps 69:28 3789
This shall be w for the Ps 102:18 3789
in thy book all my members were w Ps 139:16 3789
execute upon them the judgment w Ps 149:9 3789
Have not I w to thee excellent Prov 22:20 3789
and that which was w was upright Eccl 12:10 3789
even every one that is w among Is 4:3 3789
Behold, it is w before me Is 65:6 3789
of Judah is w with a pen of iron Jer 17:1 3789
from me shall be w in the earth Jer 17:13 3789
even all that is w in this book Jer 25:13 3789
which thou hast w from my mouth Jer 36:6 3789
saying, Why hast thou w therein Jer 36:29 3789
when he had w these words in a Jer 45:1 3789
words that are w against Babylon Jer 51:60 3789
and it was w within and without Eze 2:10 3789
there was w therein lamentations, Eze 2:10 3789
neither shall they be w in the Eze 13:9 3789
and this writing was w Dan 5:24 7560
And this is the writing that was w Dan 5:25 7560
the oath that is w in the law of Dan 9:11 3789
As it is w in the law of Moses, Dan 9:13 3789
that shall be found w in the book Dan 12:1 3789
I have w to him the great things Hos 8:12 3789
a book of remembrance was w Mal 3:16 3789
for thus it is w by the prophet Mt 2:5 1125
But he answered and said, It is w Mt 4:4 1125
for it is w, He shall give his Mt 4:6 1125
said unto him, It is w again Mt 4:7 1125
for it is w, Thou shalt worship Mt 4:10 1125
For this is he, of whom it is w Mt 11:10 1125
And said unto them, It is w Mt 21:13 1125
of man goeth as it is w of him Mt 26:24 1125
for it is w, I will smite the Mt 26:31 1125
up over his head his accusation w Mt 27:37 1125
As it is w in the prophets, Mk 1:2 1125
of you hypocrites, as it is w Mk 7:6 1125
how it is w of the Son of man, Mk 9:12 1125
they listed, as it is w of him Mk 9:13 1125
saying unto them, Is it not w Mk 11:17 1125
indeed goeth, as it is w of him Mk 14:21 1125
for it is w, I will smite the Mk 14:27 1125
of his accusation was w over Mk 15:26 1924
(As it is w in the law of the Lk 2:23 1125
As it is w in the book of the Lk 3:4 1125
answered him, saying, It is w Lk 4:4 1125
for it is w, Thou shalt worship Lk 4:8 1125
For it is w, He shall give his Lk 4:10 1125
he found the place where it was w Lk 4:17 1125
This is he, of whom it is w Lk 7:27 1125
your names are w in heaven Lk 10:20 1125
unto him, What is w in the law Lk 10:26 1125
all things that are w by the Lk 18:31 1125
Saying unto them, It is w Lk 19:46 1125
said, What is this then that is w Lk 20:17 1125
which are w may be fulfilled Lk 21:22 1125
that this that is w must yet be Lk 22:37 1125
a superscription also was w over Lk 23:38 1125
which were w in the law of Moses, Lk 24:44 1125
And said unto them, Thus it is w Lk 24:46 1125
remembered that it was w, The Jn 2:17 1125
as it is w, He gave them bread Jn 6:31 1125
It is w in the prophets, And they Jn 6:45 1125
It is also w in your law, that Jn 8:17 1125
Is it not w in your law, I said, Jn 10:34 1125
as it is w, Jn 12:14 1125
that these things were w of him Jn 12:16 1125
fulfilled that is w in their law Jn 15:25 1125
it was w in Hebrew, and Greek, and Jn 19:20 1125
What I have w I have w Jn 19:22 1125
which are not w in this book Jn 20:30 1125
But these are w, that ye might Jn 20:31 1125
if they should be w every one Jn 21:25 1125
the books that should be w Jn 21:25 1125
For it is w in the book of Psalms Acts 1:20 1125
as it is w in the book of the Acts 7:42 1125
fulfilled all that was w of him Acts 13:29 1125
as it is also w in the second Acts 13:33 1125
as it is w, Acts 15:15 1125
Gentiles which believe, we have w Acts 21:25 1989
for it is w, Thou shalt not speak Acts 23:5 1125
all things which are w in the law Acts 24:14 1125
as it is w, The just shall live Rom 1:17 1125
work of the law w in their hearts Rom 2:15 1123
Gentiles through you, as it is w Rom 2:24 1125
as it is w, That thou mightest be Rom 3:4 1125
As it is w, There is none Rom 3:10 1125
(As it is w, I have made thee a Rom 4:17 1125
Now it was not w for his sake Rom 4:23 1125
As it is w, For thy sake we are Rom 8:36 1125
As it is w, Jacob have I loved, Rom 9:13 1125
As it is w, Behold, I lay in Sion Rom 9:33 1125
as it is w, How beautiful are the Rom 10:15 1125
(According as it is w, God hath Rom 11:8 1125
as it is w, There shall come out Rom 11:26 1125
for it is w, Vengeance is mine Rom 12:19 1125
For it is w, As I live, saith the Rom 14:11 1125
but, as it is w, The reproaches Rom 15:3 1125
For whatsoever things were w Rom 15:4 4270
aforetime were w for our learning Rom 15:4 4270
as it is w, For this cause I will Rom 15:9 1125
I have w the more boldly unto you Rom 15:15 1125
But as it is w, To whom he was Rom 15:21 1125
W to the Romans from Corinthus, Rom s 1125
For it is w, I will destroy the 1Cor 1:19 1125
That, according as it is w 1Cor 1:31 1125
But as it is w, Eye hath not seen 1Cor 2:9 1125
For it is w, He taketh the wise 1Cor 3:19 1125
of men above that which is w 1Cor 4:6 1125
But now I have w unto you not to 1Cor 5:11 1125
For it is w in the law of Moses, 1Cor 9:9 1125
our sakes, no doubt, this is w 1Cor 9:10 1125
neither have I w these things 1Cor 9:15 1125
as it is w, The people sat down 1Cor 10:7 1125
they are w for our admonition, 1Cor 10:11 1125
In the law it is w, With men of 1Cor 14:21 1125
And so it is w, The first man Adam 1Cor 15:45 1125
to pass the saying that is w 1Cor 15:54 1125
was w from Philippi by Stephanus 1Cor s 1125
are our epistle w in our hearts 2Cor 3:2 1449
w not with ink, but with the 2Cor 3:3 1449
if the ministration of death, w 2Cor 3:7
of faith, according as it is w 2Cor 4:13 1125
As it is w, He that had gathered 2Cor 8:15 1125
(As it is w, He hath dispersed 2Cor 9:9 1125
Corinthians was w from Philippi 2Cor s 1125
for it is w, Cursed is every one Gal 3:10 1125
not in all things which are w in Gal 3:10 1125
for it is w, Cursed is every one Gal 3:13 1125
For it is w, that Abraham had two Gal 4:22 1125
For it is w, Rejoice, thou barren Gal 4:27 1125
w unto you with mine own hand Gal 6:11 1125
Unto the Galatians w from Rome Gal s 1125
W from Rome unto the Ephesians by Eph s 1125
It was w to the Philippians from Phil s 1125
W from Rome to the Colossians by Col s 1125
Thessalonians was w from Athens 1Th s 1125
Thessalonians was w from Athens 2Th s 1125
The first to Timothy was w from 1Ti s 1125
was w from Rome, when Paul was 2Ti s 1125
It was w to Titus, ordained the Titus s 1125
I Paul have w it with mine own Philem 19 1125
W from Rome to Philemon, by Philem s 1125
volume of the book it is w of me Heb 10:7 1125
firstborn, which are w in heaven Heb 12:23 583
for I have w a letter unto you in Heb 13:22 1989
W to the Hebrews from Italy by Heb s 1125
Because it is w, Be ye holy 1Pet 1:16 1125
I have w briefly, exhorting, and 1Pet 5:12 1125
given unto him hath w unto you 2Pet 3:15 1125
I have w unto you, fathers, 1Jn 2:14 1125
I have w unto you, young men, 1Jn 2:14 1125
I have not w unto you because ye 1Jn 2:21 1125
These things have I w unto you 1Jn 2:26 1125
These things have I w unto you 1Jn 5:13 1125
those things which are w therein Rev 1:3 1125
and in the stone a new name w Rev 2:17 1125
sat on the throne a book w within Rev 5:1 1125
whose names are not w in the book Rev 13:8 1125
name w in their foreheads Rev 14:1 1125
And upon her forehead was a name w Rev 17:5 1125
whose names were not w in the Rev 17:8 1125
and he had a name w, that no man Rev 19:12 1125
vesture and on his thigh a name w Rev 19:16 1125
things which were w in the books Rev 20:12 1125

whosoever was not found *w* in the....... Rev 20:15 *1125*
names *w* thereon, which are the .... Rev 21:12 *1924*
but they which are *w* in the.................. Rev 21:27 *1125*
plagues that are *w* in this book .... Rev 22:18 *1125*
things which are *w* in this book .... Rev 22:19 *1125*

WRONG
unto Abram, My *w* be upon thee .... Gen 16:5 2555
and he said to him that did the *w* .... Ex 2:13 7563
against him that which is *w* .... Deut 19:16 5627
thou doest me *w* to war against me ..... Judg 11:27 7451
there is no *w* in mine hands 1Chr 12:17 2555
He suffered no man to do them *w* 1Chr 16:21 6231
hath not done *w* to the king only .... Est 1:16 5753
Behold, I cry out of *w*, but I am............ Job 19:7 2555
He suffered no man to do them *w* .... Ps 105:14 6231
and do no *w*, do no violence to the ...... Jer 22:3 3238
and his chambers by *w* .... Jer 22:13
O LORD, thou hast seen my *w* .... Lam 3:59 5792
therefore *w* judgment proceedeth .... Hab 1:4 6127
and said, Friend, I do thee no *w* .... Mt 20:13 *91*
And seeing one of them suffer *w* .... Acts 7:24 *91*
why do ye *w* one to another .... Acts 7:26 *91*
his neighbour *w* thrust him away .... Acts 7:27 *91*
a matter of *w* or wicked lewdness .... Acts 18:14 *92*
to the Jews have I done no *w* .... Acts 25:10 *91*
Why do ye not rather take *w* 1Cor 6:7 *91*
Nay, ye do *w*, and defraud, and that 1Cor 6:8 *91*
for his cause that had done the *w* 2Cor 7:12 *91*
nor for his cause that suffered *w* 2Cor 7:12 *91*
forgive me this *w* 2Cor 12:13 *93*
But he that doeth *w* shall receive .... Col 3:25 *91*
for the *w* which he hath done .... Col 3:25 *91*

WRONGED
we have *w* no man, we have 2Cor 7:2 *91*
If he hath *w* thee, or oweth thee .... Philem 18 *91*

WRONGETH
sinneth against me *w* his own soul .... Prov 8:36 2554

WRONGFULLY
which ye *w* imagine against me .... Job 21:27 2554
mine enemies *w* rejoice over me .... Ps 35:19 8267
that hate me *w* are multiplied................ Ps 38:19 8267
destroy me, being mine enemies *w* .... Ps 69:4 8267
they persecute me *w* .... Ps 119:86 8267
have oppressed the stranger *w* .... Eze 22:29
God endure grief, suffering *w* 1Pet 2:19 *95*

WROTE
Moses *w* all the words of the LORD .... Ex 24:4 3789
he *w* upon the tables the words of .... Ex 34:28 3789
w upon it a writing, like to the .... Ex 39:30 3789
And Moses *w* their goings out .... Num 33:2 3789
he *w* them upon two tables of .... Deut 4:13 3789
he *w* them in two tables of stone, ... Deut 5:22 3789
he *w* on the tables, according to .... Deut 10:4 3789
Moses *w* this law, and delivered it .... Deut 31:9 3789
Moses therefore *w* this song the .... Deut 31:22 3789
he *w* there upon the stones a copy .... Josh 8:32 3789
which he *w* in the presence of the .... Josh 8:32 3789
Joshua *w* these words in the book .... Josh 24:26 3789
w it in a book, and laid it up 1Sa 10:25 3789
that David *w* a letter to Joab, and 2Sa 11:14 3789
he *w* in the letter, saying, Set 2Sa 11:15 3789
So she *w* letters in Ahab's name, ... 1Kin 21:8 3789
she *w* in the letters, saying, ... 1Kin 21:9 3789
Jehu *w* letters, and sent to 2Kin 10:1 3789
Then he *w* a letter the second 2Kin 10:6 3789
commandment, which he *w* for you 2Kin 17:37 3789
w them before the king, and the 1Chr 24:6 3789
w letters also to Ephraim and 2Chr 30:1 3789
He *w* also letters to rail on the 2Chr 32:17 3789
they *w* unto him an accusation .... Ezr 4:6 3789
the days of Artaxerxes *w* Bishlam .... Ezr 4:7 3789
Shimshai the scribe *w* a letter .... Ezr 4:8 3790
Then *w* Rehum the chancellor, and .... Ezr 4:9
which he *w* to destroy the Jews .... Est 8:5 3789
he *w* in the king Ahasuerus' name, ... Est 8:10 3789
Mordecai *w* these things, and sent .... Est 9:20 3789
w with all authority, to confirm .... Est 9:29 3789
Baruch *w* from the mouth of .... Jer 36:4 3789
I *w* them with ink in the book .... Jer 36:18 3789
the words which Baruch *w* at the .... Jer 36:27 3789
who *w* therein from the mouth of .... Jer 36:32 3789
So Jeremiah *w* in a book all the .... Jer 51:60 3789
w over against the candlestick .... Dan 5:5 3790
saw the part of the hand that *w* .... Dan 5:5 3790
king Darius *w* unto all people .... Dan 6:25 3790
then he *w* the dream, and told the .... Dan 7:1 3790
your heart he *w* you this precept .... Mk 10:5 *1125*
Moses *w* unto us, If a man's .... Mk 12:19 *1125*
asked for a writing table, and *w* .... Lk 1:63 *1125*
Moses *w* unto us, If any man's .... Lk 20:28 *1125*
for he *w* of me .... Jn 5:46 *1125*
with his finger *w* on the ground .... Jn 8:6 *1125*
stooped down, and *w* on the ground .... Jn 8:8 *1125*
Pilate *w* a title, and put it on .... Jn 19:19 *1125*
these things, and *w* these things .... Jn 21:24 *1125*
they *w* letters by them after this .... Acts 15:23 *1125*
pass into Achaia, the brethren *w* .... Acts 18:27 *1125*
he *w* a letter after this manner .... Acts 23:25 *1125*
who *w* this epistle, salute you in .... Rom 16:22 *1125*
I *w* unto you in an epistle not to 1Cor 5:9 *1125*
the things whereof ye *w* unto me 1Cor 7:1 *1125*
I *w* this same unto you, lest, ... 2Cor 2:3 *1125*
anguish of heart I *w* unto you 2Cor 2:4 *1125*
Wherefore, though I *w* unto you 2Cor 7:12 *1125*
(as I *w* afore in few words, ... Eph 3:3 *4270*
in thy obedience I *w* unto thee .... Philem 21 *1125*
lady, not as though I *w* a new 2Jn 5 *1125*
I *w* unto the church 3Jn 9 *1125*

WROTH
And Cain was very *w*, and his .... Gen 4:5 2734
said unto Cain, Why art thou *w* .... Gen 4:6 2734
And Jacob was *w*, and chode with .... Gen 31:36 2734
were grieved, and they were very *w* .... Gen 34:7 2734
Pharaoh was *w* against two of his .... Gen 40:2 7107
Pharaoh was *w* with his servants, ... Gen 41:10 7107
and Moses was *w* with them .... Ex 16:20 7107
And Moses was very *w*, and said unto ..... Num 16:15 2734
wilt thou be *w* with all the .... Num 16:22 7107
Moses was *w* with the officers of .... Num 31:14 7107
the voice of your words, and was *w* .... Deut 1:34 7107
But the LORD was *w* with me for .... Deut 3:26 5674
wherewith the LORD was *w* against .... Deut 9:19 7107
that to morrow he will be *w* with .... Josh 22:18 7107
And Saul was very *w*, and the saying 1Sa 18:8 2734
but if he be very *w*, then be sure 1Sa 20:7 2734
the Philistines were *w* with him 1Sa 29:4 7107
Then was Abner very *w* for the 2Sa 3:8 2734
all these things, he was very *w* 2Sa 13:21 2734
moved and shook, because he was *w* 2Sa 22:8 2734
But Naaman was *w*, and went away, ... 2Kin 5:11 7107
And the man of God was *w* with him 2Kin 13:19 7107
Then Asa was *w* with the seer, and 2Chr 16:10 3707
Then Uzziah was *w*, and had a 2Chr 26:19 2196
while he was *w* with the priests, ... 2Chr 26:19 2196
of your fathers was *w* with Judah 2Chr 28:9 2534
we builded the wall, he was *w* .... Neh 4:1 2734
be stopped, then they were very *w* .... Neh 4:7 2734
therefore was the king very *w* .... Est 1:12 7107
those which kept the door, were *w* .... Est 2:21 7107
and were shaken, because he was *w* .... Ps 18:7 2734
the LORD heard this, and was *w* .... Ps 78:21 5674
When God heard this, he was *w* .... Ps 78:59 5674
was *w* with his inheritance .... Ps 78:62 5674
thou hast been *w* with thine .... Ps 89:38 5674
he shall be *w* as in the valley of .... Is 28:21 7264
I was *w* with my people, I have .... Is 47:6 7107
that I would not be *w* with thee .... Is 54:9 7107
ever, neither will I be always *w* .... Is 57:16 7107
of his covetousness was I *w* .... Is 57:17 7107
I hid me, and was *w*, and he went on ...... Is 57:17 7107
behold, thou art *w* .... Is 64:5 7107
Be not *w* very sore, O LORD, ... Is 64:9 7107
the princes were *w* with Jeremiah .... Jer 37:15 7107
thou art very *w* against us .... Lam 5:22 7107
of the wise men, was exceeding *w* .... Mt 2:16 *2373*
And his lord was *w*, and delivered .... Mt 18:34 *3710*
the king heard thereof, he was *w* .... Mt 22:7 *3710*
the dragon was *w* with the woman .... Rev 12:17 *3710*

WROUGHT
because he had *w* folly in Israel .... Gen 34:7 6213
what things I have *w* in Egypt .... Ex 10:2 5953
twined linen, *w* with needlework .... Ex 26:36 4639
twined linen, *w* with needlework .... Ex 27:16
Then *w* Bezaleel and Aholiab, and .... Ex 36:1 6213
that *w* all the work of the .... Ex 36:4 6213
hearted man among them that *w* the .... Ex 36:8 6213
they *w* onyx stones inclosed in .... Ex 39:6 6213
they have *w* confusion .... Lev 20:12 6213
and of Israel, What hath God *w* .... Num 23:23 6466
gold of them, even all *w* jewels .... Num 31:51 4639
such abomination is *w* among you .... Deut 13:14 6213
that hath *w* wickedness in the .... Deut 17:2 6213
such abomination is *w* in Israel .... Deut 17:4 6213
which hath not been *w* with .... Deut 21:3 5647
she hath *w* folly in Israel .... Deut 22:21 6213
the evils which they shall have *w* .... Deut 31:18 6213
because he hath *w* folly in Israel .... Josh 7:15 6213
folly that they have *w* in Israel .... Judg 20:10 6213
mother in law with whom she had *w* .... Ruth 2:19 6213
name with whom I *w* to day is Boaz .... Ruth 2:19 6213
when he had *w* wonderfully among 1Sa 6:6 5953
LORD hath *w* salvation in Israel 1Sa 11:13 6213
who hath *w* this great salvation 1Sa 14:45 6213
for he hath *w* with God this day 1Sa 14:45 6213
the LORD *w* a great salvation for 1Sa 19:5 6213
Otherwise I should have *w* 2Sa 18:13 6213
the LORD *w* a great victory that 2Sa 23:10 6213
the LORD *w* a great victory 2Sa 23:12 6213
the people that *w* in the work 1Kin 5:16 6213
king Solomon, and *w* all his work 1Kin 7:14 6213
the brim thereof was *w* like the 1Kin 7:26 4639
the people that *w* in the work 1Kin 9:23 6213
Zimri, and his treason that he *w* 1Kin 16:20 7194
But Omri *w* evil in the eyes of 1Kin 16:25 6213
he *w* evil in the sight of the 2Kin 3:2 6213
that *w* upon the house of the LORD 2Kin 12:11 6213
w wicked things to provoke the 2Kin 17:11 6213
he *w* much wickedness in the sight 2Kin 21:6 6213
house of them that *w* fine linen 1Chr 4:21 5656
he set masons to hew *w* stones to 1Chr 22:2 1496
linen, and *w* cherubims thereon 2Chr 3:14 5927
he *w* that which was evil in the 2Chr 21:6 6213
the LORD, and also such as *w* iron 2Chr 24:12 2790
So the workmen *w*, and the work was 2Chr 24:13 6213
w that which was good and right and 2Chr 31:20 6213
he *w* much evil in the sight of 2Chr 33:6 6213
that *w* in the house of the LORD 2Chr 34:10 6213
that *w* the work in any manner of 2Chr 34:13 6213
half of my servants *w* in the work .... Neh 4:16 6213
one of his hands *w* in the work .... Neh 4:17 6213
that this work was *w* of our God .... Neh 6:16 6213
and had *w* great provocations .... Neh 9:18 6213
they *w* great provocations .... Neh 9:26 6213
the hand of the LORD hath *w* this .... Job 12:9 6213
who can say, Thou hast *w* iniquity .... Job 36:23 6466
which thou hast *w* for them that .... Ps 31:19 6466
her clothing is of *w* gold .... Ps 45:13 4865
that which thou hast *w* for us .... Ps 68:28 6466
How he had *w* his signs in Egypt, ... Ps 78:43 7760
curiously *w* in the lowest parts .... Ps 139:15 7551
all the works that my hands had *w* .... Eccl 2:11 6213
because the work that is *w* under .... Eccl 2:17 6213
for thou also hast *w* all our .... Is 26:12 6466
we have not *w* any deliverance in .... Is 26:18 6213
Who hath *w* and done it, calling .... Is 41:4 6466
seeing she hath *w* lewdness with .... Jer 11:15 6213
he *w* a work on the wheels .... Jer 18:3 6213
But I *w* for my name's sake, that .... Eze 20:9 6213
But I *w* for my name's sake, that .... Eze 20:14 6213
w for my name's sake, that it .... Eze 20:22 6213
when I have *w* with you for my .... Eze 20:44 6213
against it, because they *w* for me .... Eze 29:20 6213
the high God hath *w* toward me .... Dan 4:2 5648
for the sea *w*, and was tempestuous .... Jonah 1:11 1980
for the sea *w*, and was tempestuous .... Jonah 1:13 1980
which have *w* his judgment .... Zeph 2:3 6466
These last have *w* but one hour .... Mt 20:12 *4160*
for she hath *w* a good work upon .... Mt 26:10 *2038*
mighty works are *w* by his hands .... Mk 6:2 *1096*
she hath *w* a good work on me .... Mk 14:6 *2038*
manifest, that they are *w* in God .... Jn 3:21 *2038*
wonders *w* among the people .... Acts 5:12 *1096*
wonders God had *w* among the .... Acts 15:12 *4160*
craft, he abode with them, and *w* .... Acts 18:3 *2038*
God *w* special miracles by the .... Acts 19:11 *4160*
what things God had *w* among the .... Acts 21:19 *4160*
w in me all manner of .... Rom 7:8 *2716*
which Christ hath not *w* by me .... Rom 15:18 *2716*
Now he that hath *w* us for the 2Cor 5:5 *2716*
what carefulness it *w* in you 2Cor 7:11 *2716*
were *w* among you in all patience 2Cor 12:12 *2716*
(For he that *w* effectually in .... Gal 2:8 *1754*
Which he *w* in Christ, when he .... Eph 1:20 *1754*
but *w* with labour and travail 2Th 3:8 *2038*
w righteousness, obtained .... Heb 11:33 *2038*
thou how faith *w* with his works .... Jas 2:22 *4903*
have *w* the will of the Gentiles 1Pet 4:3 *2716*
not those things which we have *w* 2Jn 8 *2038*
that *w* miracles before him .... Rev 19:20 *4160*

WROUGHTEST
and where *w* thou .... Ruth 2:19 6213

WRUNG
the blood thereof shall be *w* out .... Lev 1:15 4680
w out at the bottom of the altar .... Lev 5:9 4680
of a full cup are *w* out to them .... Ps 73:10 4680
cup of trembling, and *w* them out .... Is 51:17 4680

XERXES See AHASUERUS.

XERXES' See AHASUERUS'.

Y

YAH See JAH.

YARN
brought out of Egypt, and linen y 1Kin 10:28 4723
received the linen y at a price 1Kin 10:28 4723
brought out of Egypt, and linen y 2Chr 1:16 4723
received the linen y at a price 2Chr 1:16 4723

YE See PREFACE.

YEA
And he said unto the woman, Y Gen 3:1
y, I will bless her, and she shall Gen 17:16
God said unto him in a dream, Y Gen 20:6 1571
y, and he shall be blessed Gen 27:33 1571
y, though he be a stranger, or a Lev 25:35
shall be, if thou go with us, y Num 10:32
Y, he loved the people Deut 33:3 637
Her wise ladies answered her, y Judg 5:29 637
And Saul said unto Samuel, Y 1Sa 15:20 834
bread is in a manner common, y 1Sa 21:5 637
Moreover, my father, see, y 1Sa 24:11 637
said unto the king, Y, let him 2Sa 19:30 637
y, they are fallen under my feet 2Sa 22:39
And he said, Y, I know it 2Kin 2:3 1571
And he answered, Y, I know it 2Kin 2:5 1571
the way of the kings of Israel, y 2Kin 16:3 1571
y, he reproved kings for their 1Chr 16:21
y, himself hasted also to go out, 2Chr 26:20
y, the hand of the princes and Ezr 9:2
y, even their servants bare rule Neh 5:15 1571
Y, also I continued in the work Neh 5:16 1571
y, in the night will they come to Neh 6:10
Y, when they had made them a Neh 9:18 637
Y, forty years didst thou sustain Neh 9:21
Haman said moreover, Y, Esther Est 5:12
y, they have slain the servants Job 1:15
and have carried them away, y Job 1:17
LORD, and said, Skin for skin, y Job 2:4
y, in seven there shall no evil Job 5:19
y, I would harden myself in Job 6:10
Y, ye overwhelm the fatherless, Job 6:27 637
y, return again, my righteousness Job 6:29
y, and wonders without number Job 9:10
y, thou shalt be stedfast, and Job 11:15
y, thou shalt dig about thee, and Job 11:18
y, many shall make suit unto thee Job 11:19
y, who knoweth not such things as Job 12:3
y, man giveth up the ghost, and Job 14:10
Y, thou castest off fear, and Job 15:4 637
y, thine own lips testify against Job 15:6
y, the heavens are not clean in Job 15:15
Y, the light of the wicked shall Job 18:5 1571
Y, young children despised me Job 19:18 1571
y, he shall be chased away as a Job 20:8
y, the glittering sword cometh Job 20:25
do the wicked live, become old, y Job 21:7 1571
Y, the Almighty shall be thy Job 22:25
y, the stars are not pure in his Job 25:5
he prepared it, y, and searched it Job 28:27 1571
Y, whereto might the strength of Job 30:2 1571
They were children of fools, y Job 30:8 1571
And now am I their song, y Job 30:9
y, let my offspring be rooted out Job 31:8
y, it is an iniquity to be Job 31:11
Y, I attended unto you, and, Job 32:12
y twice, yet man perceiveth it Job 33:14
Y, his soul draweth near unto the Job 33:22
Y, surely God will not do Job 34:12 637
y, he doth establish them for Job 36:7
y, twice Job 40:5
y, as hard as a piece of the Job 41:24
(y, I have delivered him that Ps 7:4
y, let him tread down my life Ps 7:5
All sheep and oxen, y, and the Ps 8:7 1571
y, I have a goodly heritage Ps 16:6 637
y, he did fly upon the wings of Ps 18:10
Y, he sent out his arrows, and Ps 18:14
y, thou liftest me up above those Ps 18:48 637
be desired are they than gold, y Ps 19:10
Y, though I walk through the Ps 23:4 1571
Y, let none that wait on thee be Ps 25:3 1571
I will sing, y, I will sing Ps 27:6
y, the LORD breaketh the cedars Ps 29:5
y, the LORD sitteth King for ever Ps 29:10
eye is consumed with grief, y Ps 31:9
him that is too strong for him, y Ps 35:10
y, the abjects gathered Ps 35:15
Y, they opened their mouth wide Ps 35:21
y, let them say continually, Let Ps 35:27
y, thou shalt diligently consider Ps 37:10
y, I sought him, but he could not Ps 37:36
y, thy law is within my heart Ps 40:8
Y, mine own familiar friend, in Ps 41:9 1571
y, upon the harp will I praise Ps 43:4
Y, for thy sake are we killed all Ps 44:22 3588
y, in the shadow of thy wings Ps 57:1
Y, in heart ye work wickedness Ps 58:2 637
y, I will sing aloud of thy mercy Ps 59:16
y, let them exceedingly rejoice Ps 68:3
y, the LORD will dwell in it for Ps 68:16 637
y, for the rebellious also, that Ps 68:18 637
Y, all kings shall fall down Ps 72:11
Y, they spake against God Ps 78:19
y, many a time turned he his Ps 78:38
Y, they turned back and tempted Ps 78:41
y, all their princes as Zebah, and Ps 83:11
y, let them be put to shame, and Ps 83:17
My soul longeth, y, even fainteth Ps 84:2 1571
y, the sparrow hath found an Ps 84:3 1571
Y, the LORD shall give that which Ps 85:12 1571
y, the work of our hands Ps 90:17
than the noise of many waters, y Ps 93:4
y, the LORD our God shall cut Ps 94:23
for the time to favour her, y Ps 102:13 3588
y, all of them shall wax old like Ps 102:26
y, very few, and strangers in it Ps 105:12
y, he reproved kings for their Ps 105:14
Y, they despised the pleasant Ps 106:24
Y, they sacrificed their sons and Ps 106:37
y, I will praise him among the Ps 109:30
y, our God is merciful Ps 116:5
y, they compassed me about Ps 118:11 1571
y, I shall observe it with my Ps 119:34
y, sweeter than honey to my mouth Ps 119:103
y, above fine gold Ps 119:127
Y, thou shalt see thy children's Ps 128:6
of Babylon, there we sat down, y Ps 137:1 1571
Y, they shall sing in the ways of Ps 138:5
Y, the darkness hideth not from Ps 139:12 1571
y, happy is that people, whose Ps 144:15
Y, if thou criest after knowledge Prov 2:3 3588
y, every good path Prov 2:9
y, thou shalt lie down, and thy Prov 3:24
y, seven are an abomination unto Prov 6:16
y, many strong men have been Prov 7:26
y, durable riches and Prov 8:18
My fruit is better than gold, y Prov 8:19
y, even the wicked for the day of Prov 16:4 1571
y, strife and reproach shall cease Prov 22:10
Y, my reins shall rejoice, when Prov 23:16
Y, thou shalt be as he that lieth Prov 23:34
y, a man of knowledge increaseth Prov 24:5
y, he shall give delight unto thy Prov 29:17
that are never satisfied, y Prov 30:15
which are too wonderful for me, y Prov 30:18
be three things which go well, y Prov 30:29
y, she reacheth forth her hands Prov 31:20
y, my heart had great experience Eccl 1:16
Y, I hated all my labour which I Eccl 2:18
y, his heart taketh not rest in Eccl 2:23 1571
y, they have all one breath Eccl 3:19
Y, better is he than both they, Eccl 4:3
y, he hath neither child nor Eccl 4:8 1571
This is also vanity, y, it is a Eccl 4:8
Y, though he live a thousand Eccl 6:6 432
y, also from this withdraw not Eccl 7:18 1571
not find it; y further Eccl 8:17 1571
y, also the heart of the sons of Eccl 9:3 1571
Y also, when he that is a fool Eccl 10:3 1571
y, he gave good heed, and sought Eccl 12:9
thou art fair, my beloved, y Song 1:16 637
drink, y, drink abundantly, O Song 5:1
y, he is altogether lovely Song 5:16
y, the queens and the concubines, Song 6:9
y, I should not be despised Song 8:1 1571
y, when ye make many prayers, I Is 1:15 1571
Y, ten acres of vineyard shall Is 5:10 3588
y, they shall roar, and lay hold Is 5:29
Y, the fir trees rejoice at thee, Is 14:8 1571
y, they shall vow a vow unto the Is 19:21
y, the treacherous dealers have Is 24:16
Y, in the way of thy judgments, O Is 26:8 637
y, with my spirit within me will Is 26:9 637
y, the fire of thine enemies Is 26:11 637
y, it shall be at an instant Is 29:5
y, for the king it is prepared Is 30:33 1571
y, upon all the houses of joy in Is 32:13 3588
Y, they shall not be planted Is 40:24 637
y, they shall not be sown Is 40:24 637
y, their stock shall not take Is 40:24 637
y, I will help thee Is 41:10 637
y, I will uphold thee with the Is 41:10 637
y, do good, or do evil, that we Is 41:23 637
y, there is none that sheweth, Is 41:26 637
there is none that sheweth, y Is 41:26 637
there is none that declareth, y Is 41:26 637
he shall cry, y, roar Is 42:13 637
y, I have made him Is 43:7 637
Y, before the day was I am he Is 43:13 1571
y, there is no God Is 44:8
y, he is hungry, and his strength Is 44:12 1571
y, he kindleth it, and baketh Is 44:15 637
y, he maketh a god, and Is 44:15 637
y, he warmeth himself, and saith, Is 44:16 637
y, also I have baked bread upon Is 44:19 637
y, let them take counsel together Is 45:21 637
they fall down, y, they worship Is 46:6 637
y, one shall cry unto him, yet Is 46:7 637
y, I have spoken it, I will also Is 46:11 637
nakedness shall be uncovered, y Is 47:3 1571
Y, thou heardest not Is 48:8 1571
y, thou knewest not Is 48:8 1571
y, from that time that thine ear Is 48:8 1571
y, I have called him Is 48:15 637
y, they may forget, yet will I Is 49:15 1571
y, come, buy wine and milk without Is 55:1
of the field, come to devour, y Is 56:9
Y, they are greedy dogs which can Is 56:11
Y, truth faileth Is 59:15
y, those nations shall be utterly Is 60:12
Y, they have chosen their own Is 66:3 1571
Y, thou shalt go forth from him, Jer 2:37 1571
y, they overpass the deeds of the Jer 5:28 1571
Y, the stork in the heaven Jer 8:7 1571
Thou hast planted them, y Jer 12:2 1571
they grow, y, they bring forth Jer 12:2 1571
y, they have called a multitude Jer 12:6 1571
Y, the hind also calved in the Jer 14:5
y, both the prophet and the priest Jer 14:18
y, in my house have I found their Jer 23:11 1571
y, they are prophets of the Jer 23:26
Y, thus saith the LORD of hosts, Jer 27:21 3588
of old unto me, saying, Y Jer 31:3
I was ashamed, y, even confounded Jer 31:19 1571
Y, I will rejoice over them to do Jer 32:41
He made many to fall, y, one fell Jer 46:16
y, the wall of Babylon shall fall Jer 51:44 1571
y, she sigheth, and turneth Lam 1:8 1571
and make the land desolate, y Eze 6:14
y, I said unto thee when thou Eze 16:6
y, I sware unto thee, and entered Eze 16:8
y, I throughly washed away thy Eze 16:9
y, thou hast played the harlot Eze 16:28
y, be thou confounded also, and Eze 16:52 1571
Y, behold, being planted, shall Eze 17:10
y, thou shalt shew her all her Eze 22:2
Y, I will gather you, and blow Eze 22:21
y, they have oppressed the Eze 22:29
y, declare unto them their Eze 23:36
y, the isles that are in the sea Eze 26:18
y, they shall dwell with Eze 28:26
Y, I will make many people amazed Eze 32:10
Y, thou shalt be broken in the Eze 32:28
y, my flock was scattered upon Eze 34:6
Y, I will cause men to walk upon Eze 36:12
y, I will be their God, and they Eze 37:27
Y, all the people of the land Eze 39:13
Y, he magnified himself even to Dan 8:11
Y, all Israel have transgressed Dan 9:11
Y, whiles I was speaking in Dan 9:21
peace be unto thee, be strong, y Dan 10:19
y, also the prince of the Dan 11:22 1571
y, and he shall forecast his Dan 11:24
Y, they that feed of the portion Dan 11:26
y, I will betroth thee unto me in Hos 2:19
y, the fishes of the sea also Hos 4:3 1571
y, gray hairs are here and there Hos 7:9 1571
Y, though they have hired among Hos 8:10 1571
y, woe also to them when I depart Hos 9:12 3588
y, though they bring forth, yet Hos 9:16 1571
Y, he had power over the angel, Hos 12:4
y, their altars are as heaps in Hos 12:11 1571
meat cut off before our eyes, y Joel 1:16
y, the flocks of sheep are made Joel 1:18 1571
y, and nothing shall escape them Joel 2:3 1571
Y, the LORD will answer and say Joel 2:19
Y, and what have ye to do with me, Joel 3:4 1571
y, and sell the refuse of the Amos 8:6
y, thou shouldest not have looked Obad 13 1571
the heathen drink continually, y Obad 16
y, let them turn every one from Jonah 3:8
y, they shall all cover their Mic 3:7
is burned at his presence, y Nah 1:5
Y also, because he transgresseth Hab 2:5 637
Gather yourselves together, y Zeph 2:1
y, as yet the vine, and the fig Hag 2:19
Y, they made their hearts as an Zec 7:12
Y, many people and strong nations Zec 8:22
y, their children shall see it, Zec 10:7
y, ye shall flee, like as ye fled Zec 14:5
Y, every pot in Jerusalem and in Zec 14:21
y, I have cursed them already, Mal 2:2 1571
y, they that work wickedness are Mal 3:15 1571
y, they that tempt God are even Mal 3:15 1571
and all the proud, y, and all that Mal 4:1
But let your communication be, Y Mt 5:37 *3483*
let your communication be, Y, y Mt 5:37 *3483*
They said unto him, Y, Lord Mt 9:28 *3483*
y, I say unto you, and more than a Mt 11:9 *3483*
They say unto him, Y, Lord Mt 13:51 *3483*
And Jesus saith unto them, Y Mt 21:16 *3483*
y, though many false witnesses Mt 26:60 *2532*
(Y, a sword shall pierce through Lk 2:35 *1161*
Y, I say unto you, and much more Lk 7:26 *3483*
Y rather, blessed are they that Lk 11:28 *3304*
y, I say unto you, Fear him Lk 12:5 *3483*
Y, and why even of yourselves Lk 12:57
and brethren, and sisters, y Lk 14:26 *2089*
Y, and certain women also of our Lk 24:22 *235*
She saith unto him, Y, Lord Jn 11:27 *3483*
y, the time cometh, that Jn 16:2 *235*
Behold, the hour cometh, y Jn 16:32 *2532*
He saith unto him, Y, Lord Jn 21:15 *3483*
He saith unto him, Y, Lord Jn 21:16 *3483*
y, the faith which is by him hath Acts 3:16 *2532*
Y, and all the prophets from Acts 3:24 *1161*
And she said, Y, for so much Acts 5:8 *3483*
Y, ye took up the tabernacle of Acts 7:43 *2532*
Y, ye yourselves know, that these Acts 20:34 *1161*
He said, Y Acts 22:27 *3483*
y, let God be true, but every man Rom 3:4 *1161*
y, we establish the law Rom 3:31 *235*
y rather, that is risen again, Rom 8:34 *1161*
Y, he shall be holden up Rom 14:4 *235*
Y, so have I strived to preach Rom 15:20 *235*
are despised, hath God chosen, y 1Cor 1:28
Spirit searcheth all things, y 1Cor 2:10 *2532*
y, I judge not mine own self 1Cor 4:3 *235*
y, woe is unto me, if I preach 1Cor 9:16 *1161*
Y, and we are found false 1Cor 15:15 *1161*
And it may be that I will abide, y 1Cor 16:6 *2228*
with me there should be y y 2Cor 1:17 *3483*
with me there should be y y 2Cor 1:17 *3483*

our word toward you was not y 2Cor 1:18 *3483*
Silvanus and Timotheus, was not y 2Cor 1:19 *3483*
not y and nay, but in him was y 2Cor 1:19 *3483*
the promises of God in him are y 2Cor 1:20 *3483*
y, though we have known Christ 2Cor 5:16 *1161*
carefulness it wrought in you, y 2Cor 7:11 *235*
what clearing of yourselves, y 2Cor 7:11 *235*
indignation, y, what fear, y 2Cor 7:11 *235*
desire, y, what zeal, y 2Cor 7:11 *235*
y, and exceedingly the more joyed 2Cor 7:13
to their power, I bear record, y 2Cor 8:3
y, they would exclude you, that Gal 4:17 *235*
and I therein do rejoice, y Phil 1:18 *235*
Y, and if I be offered upon the Phil 2:17 *235*
Y doubtless, and I count all Phil 3:8 *235*
Y, and all that will live godly in 2Ti 3:12 *1161*
Y, brother, let me have joy of Philem 20 *3483*
cruel mockings and scourgings, y Heb 11:36 *1161*
Y, a man may say, Thou hast faith Jas 2:18 *235*
but let your y be y Jas 5:12 *3483*
Y, all of you be subject one to 1Pet 5:5 *1161*
Y, I think it meet, as long as I 2Pet 1:13 *1161*
y, and we also bear record 3Jn 12 *1161*
Y, saith the Spirit, that they Rev 14:13 *3483*

YEAR

six hundredth y of Noah's life Gen 7:11 8141
in the six hundredth and first y Gen 8:13 8141
in the thirteenth y they rebelled Gen 14:4 8141
fourteenth y came Chedorlaomer Gen 14:5 8141
at this set time in the next y Gen 17:21 8141
in the same y an hundredfold Gen 26:12 8141
for all their cattle for that y Gen 47:17 8141
When that y was ended, they came Gen 47:18 8141
they came unto him the second y Gen 47:18 8141
the first month of the y to you Ex 12:2 8141
blemish, a male of the first y Ex 12:5 8141
in his season from y to y Ex 13:10 3117
in his season from y to y Ex 13:10 3117
But the seventh y thou shalt let Ex 23:11
keep a feast unto me in the y Ex 23:14 8141
which is in the end of the y Ex 23:16 8141
Three times in the y all thy Ex 23:17 8141
out from before thee in one y Ex 23:29 8141
first y day by day continually Ex 29:38 8141
in a y with the blood of the sin Ex 30:10 8141
once in the y shall he make Ex 30:10 8141
Thrice in the y shall all your Ex 34:23 8141
the LORD thy God thrice in the y Ex 34:24 8141
the first month in the second y Ex 40:17 8141
and a lamb, both of the first y Lev 9:3 8141
the first y for a burnt offering Lev 12:6 8141
of the first y without blemish Lev 14:10 8141
for all their sins once a y Lev 16:34 8141
But in the fourth y all the fruit Lev 19:24 8141
in the fifth y shall ye eat of Lev 19:25 8141
without blemish of the first y Lev 23:12 8141
without blemish of the first y Lev 23:18 8141
two lambs of the first y for a Lev 23:19 8141
unto the LORD seven days in the y Lev 23:41 8141
But in the seventh y shall be a Lev 25:4 8141
for it is a y of rest unto the Lev 25:5 8141
And ye shall hallow the fiftieth y Lev 25:10 8141
shall that fiftieth y be unto you Lev 25:11 8141
In the y of this jubile ye shall Lev 25:13 8141
What shall we eat the seventh y Lev 25:20 8141
blessing upon you in the sixth y Lev 25:21 8141
And ye shall sow the eighth y Lev 25:22 8141
of old fruit until the ninth y Lev 25:22 8141
bought it until the y of jubile Lev 25:28 8141
within a whole y after it is sold Lev 25:29 8141
within a full y may he redeem it Lev 25:29 3117
within the space of a full y Lev 25:30 8141
shall go out in the y of jubile Lev 25:33
serve thee unto the y of jubile Lev 25:40 8141
y that he was sold to him unto Lev 25:50 8141
sold to him unto the y of jubile Lev 25:50 8141
few years unto the y of jubile Lev 25:52 8141
shall go out in the y of jubile Lev 25:54 8141
his field from the y of jubile Lev 27:17 8141
even unto the y of the jubile Lev 27:18 8141
even unto the y of the jubile Lev 27:23 8141
In the y of the jubile the field Lev 27:24 8141
in the second y after they were Num 1:1 8141
first y for a trespass offering Num 6:12 8141
one he lamb of the first y Num 6:14 8141
first y without blemish for a sin Num 6:14 8141
one ram, one lamb of the first y Num 7:15 8141
goats, five lambs of the first y Num 7:17 8141
one ram, one lamb of the first y Num 7:21 8141
goats, five lambs of the first y Num 7:23 8141
one ram, one lamb of the first y Num 7:27 8141
goats, five lambs of the first y Num 7:29 8141
one ram, one lamb of the first y Num 7:33 8141
goats, five lambs of the first y Num 7:35 8141
one ram, one lamb of the first y Num 7:39 8141
goats, five lambs of the first y Num 7:41 8141
one ram, one lamb of the first y Num 7:45 8141
goats, five lambs of the first y Num 7:47 8141
one ram, one lamb of the first y Num 7:51 8141
goats, five lambs of the first y Num 7:53 8141
one ram, one lamb of the first y Num 7:57 8141
goats, five lambs of the first y Num 7:59 8141
one ram, one lamb of the first y Num 7:63 8141
goats, five lambs of the first y Num 7:65 8141
one ram, one lamb of the first y Num 7:69 8141
goats, five lambs of the first y Num 7:71 8141
one ram, one lamb of the first y Num 7:75 8141
goats, five lambs of the first y Num 7:77 8141
one ram, one lamb of the first y Num 7:81 8141
goats, five lambs of the first y Num 7:83 8141
the lambs of the first y twelve Num 7:87 8141
the lambs of the first y sixty Num 7:88 8141
the first month of the second y Num 9:1 8141
were two days, or a month, or a y Num 9:22 3117
the second month, in the second y Num 10:11 8141
even forty days, each day for a y Num 14:34 8141
of the first y for a sin offering Num 15:27 8141
two lambs of the first y without Num 28:3 8141
lambs of the first y without spot Num 28:9 8141
lambs of the first y without spot Num 28:11 8141
throughout the months of the y Num 28:14 8141
and seven lambs of the first y Num 28:19 8141
ram, seven lambs of the first y Num 28:27 8141
of the first y without blemish Num 29:2 8141
and seven lambs of the first y Num 29:8 8141
and fourteen lambs of the first y Num 29:13 8141
lambs of the first y without spot Num 29:17 8141
of the first y without blemish Num 29:20 8141
of the first y without blemish Num 29:23 8141
lambs of the first y without spot Num 29:26 8141
of the first y without blemish Num 29:29 8141
of the first y without blemish Num 29:32 8141
of the first y without blemish Num 29:36 8141
in the fortieth y after the Num 33:38 8141
it came to pass in the fortieth y Deut 1:3 8141
from the beginning of the y even Deut 11:12 8141
y even unto the end of the y Deut 11:12 8141
field bringeth forth y by y Deut 14:22 8141
field bringeth forth y by y Deut 14:22 8141
of thine increase the same y Deut 14:28 8141
heart, saying, The seventh y Deut 15:9 8141
the y of release, is at hand Deut 15:9 8141
then in the seventh y thou shalt Deut 15:12 8141
y by y in the place which the Deut 15:20 8141
by y in the place which the LORD Deut 15:20 8141
Three times in a y shall all thy Deut 16:16 8141
he shall be free at home one y Deut 24:5 8141
of thine increase the third y Deut 26:12 8141
which is the y of tithing Deut 26:12 8141
the solemnity of the y of release Deut 31:10 8141
of the land of Canaan that y Josh 5:12 8141
that y they vexed and oppressed Judg 10:8 8141
the Gileadite four days in a y Judg 11:40 8141
ten shekels of silver by the y Judg 17:10 3117
And as he did so y by y 1Sa 1:7 8141
brought it to him from y to y 1Sa 2:19 3117
he went from y to y in circuit 1Sa 7:16 8141
Saul reigned one y 1Sa 13:1 8141
of the Philistines was a full y 1Sa 27:7
after the y was expired, at the 2Sa 11:1 8141
David three years, y after y 2Sa 21:1 8141
his month in a y made provision 1Kin 4:7 8141
gave Solomon to Hiram y by y 1Kin 5:11 8141
eightieth y after the children of 1Kin 6:1 8141
in the fourth y of Solomon's 1Kin 6:1 8141
In the fourth y was the 1Kin 6:37 8141
And in the eleventh y, in the 1Kin 6:38 8141
three times in a y did Solomon 1Kin 9:25 8141
one y was six hundred threescore 1Kin 10:14 8141
and mules, a rate y by y 1Kin 10:25 8141
in the fifth y of king Rehoboam 1Kin 14:25 8141
Now in the eighteenth y of king 1Kin 15:1 8141
in the twentieth y of Jeroboam 1Kin 15:9 8141
the second y of Asa king of Judah 1Kin 15:25 8141
Even in the third y of Asa king 1Kin 15:28 8141
In the third y of Asa king of 1Kin 15:33 8141
sixth y of Asa king of Judah 1Kin 16:8 8141
seventh y of Asa king of Judah, 1Kin 16:10 8141
seventh y of Asa king of Judah 1Kin 16:15 8141
first y of Asa king of Judah 1Kin 16:23 8141
eighth y of Asa king of Judah 1Kin 16:29 8141
came to Elijah in the third y 1Kin 18:1 8141
for at the return of the y the 1Kin 20:22 8141
to pass at the return of the y 1Kin 20:26 8141
And it came to pass in the third y 1Kin 22:2 8141
fourth y of Ahab king of Israel 1Kin 22:41 8141
in Samaria the seventeenth y of 1Kin 22:51 8141
second y of Jehoram the son of 2Kin 1:17 8141
in Samaria the eighteenth y of 2Kin 3:1 8141
in the fifth y of Joram the son 2Kin 8:16 8141
In the twelfth y of Joram the son 2Kin 8:25 8141
and he reigned one y in Jerusalem 2Kin 8:26 8141
in the eleventh y of Joram the 2Kin 9:29 8141
the seventh y Jehoiada sent and 2Kin 11:4 8141
In the seventh y of Jehu Jehoash 2Kin 12:1 8141
twentieth y of king Jehoash the 2Kin 12:6 8141
twentieth y of Joash the son of 2Kin 13:1 8141
seventh y of Joash king of Judah 2Kin 13:10 8141
land at the coming in of the y 2Kin 13:20 8141
In the second y of Joash son of 2Kin 14:1 8141
In the fifteenth y of Amaziah the 2Kin 14:23 8141
seventh y of Jeroboam king of 2Kin 15:1 8141
eighth y of Azariah king of Judah 2Kin 15:8 8141
thirtieth y of Uzziah king of 2Kin 15:13 8141
thirtieth y of Azariah king of 2Kin 15:17 8141
In the fiftieth y of Azariah king 2Kin 15:23 8141
fiftieth y of Azariah king of 2Kin 15:27 8141
in the twentieth y of Jotham the 2Kin 15:30 8141
In the second y of Pekah the son 2Kin 15:32 8141
In the seventeenth y of Pekah the 2Kin 16:1 8141
In the twelfth y of Ahaz king of 2Kin 17:1 8141
Assyria, as he had done y by y 2Kin 17:4 8141
In the ninth y of Hoshea the king 2Kin 17:6 8141
it came to pass in the third y of 2Kin 18:1 8141
in the fourth y of king Hezekiah 2Kin 18:9 8141
which was the seventh y of Hoshea 2Kin 18:9 8141
even in the sixth y of Hezekiah 2Kin 18:10 8141
that is the ninth y of Hoshea 2Kin 18:10 8141
fourteenth y of king Hezekiah did 2Kin 18:13 8141
Ye shall eat this y such things 2Kin 19:29 8141
in the second y that which 2Kin 19:29 8141
and in the third y sow ye, and reap 2Kin 19:29 8141
the eighteenth y of king Josiah 2Kin 22:3 8141
the eighteenth y of king Josiah 2Kin 23:23 8141
him in the eighth y of his reign 2Kin 24:12 8141
pass in the ninth y of his reign 2Kin 25:1 8141
the eleventh y of king Zedekiah 2Kin 25:2 8141
which is the nineteenth y of king 2Kin 25:8 8141
thirtieth y of the captivity of 2Kin 25:27 8141
king of Babylon in the y that he 2Kin 25:27 8141
that after the y was expired 1Chr 20:1 8141
In the fortieth y of the reign of 1Chr 26:31 8141
all the months of the y, of every 1Chr 27:1 8141
in the fourth y of his reign 2Chr 3:2 8141
feasts, three times in the y 2Chr 8:13 8141
Solomon in one y was six hundred 2Chr 9:13 8141
and mules, a rate y by y 2Chr 9:24 8141
that in the fifth y of king 2Chr 12:2 8141
Now in the eighteenth y of king 2Chr 13:1 8141
in the fifteenth y of the reign 2Chr 15:10 8141
thirtieth y of the reign of Asa 2Chr 15:19 8141
thirtieth y of the reign of Asa 2Chr 16:1 8141
ninth y of his reign was diseased 2Chr 16:12 8141
one and fortieth y of his reign 2Chr 16:13 8141
Also in the third y of his reign 2Chr 17:7 8141
and he reigned one y in Jerusalem 2Chr 22:2 8141
in the seventh y Jehoiada 2Chr 23:1 8141
house of your God from y to y 2Chr 24:5 8141
came to pass at the end of the y 2Chr 24:23 8141
of Ammon gave him the same y an 2Chr 27:5 8141
pay unto him, both the second y 2Chr 27:5 8141
He in the first y of his reign 2Chr 29:3 8141
For in the eighth y of his reign 2Chr 34:3 8141
in the twelfth y he began to 2Chr 34:3 8141
in the eighteenth y of his reign 2Chr 34:8 8141
In the eighteenth y of the reign 2Chr 35:19 8141
when the y was expired, king 2Chr 36:10 8141
Now in the first y of Cyrus king 2Chr 36:22 8141
Now in the first y of Cyrus king Ezr 1:1 8141
Now in the second y of their Ezr 3:8 8141
So it ceased unto the second y of Ezr 4:24 8140
But in the first y of Cyrus the Ezr 5:13 8140
In the first y of Cyrus the king Ezr 6:3 8140
which was in the sixth y of the Ezr 6:15 8140
in the seventh y of Artaxerxes Ezr 7:7 8141
was in the seventh y of the king Ezr 7:8 8141
month Chisleu, in the twentieth y Neh 1:1 8141
in the twentieth y of Artaxerxes Neh 2:1 8141
the twentieth y even unto the two Neh 5:14 8141
thirtieth y of Artaxerxes the Neh 5:14 8141
that we would leave the seventh y Neh 10:31 8141
at times appointed y by y Neh 10:34 8141
at times appointed y by y Neh 10:34 8141
all fruit of all trees, y by y Neh 10:35 8141
thirtieth y of Artaxerxes king of Neh 13:6 8141
In the third y of his reign Est 1:3 8141
in the seventh y of his reign Est 2:16 8141
Nisan, in the twelfth y of king Est 3:7 8141
to their appointed time every y Est 9:27 8141
be joined unto the days of the y Job 3:6 8141
crownest the y with thy goodness Ps 65:11 8141
In the y that king Uzziah died I Is 6:1 8141
In the y that king Ahaz died was Is 14:28 8141
In the y that Tartan came unto Is 20:1 8141
the Lord said unto me, Within a y Is 21:16 8141
add ye y to y Is 29:1 8141
the y of recompences for the Is 34:8 8141
the fourteenth y of king Hezekiah Is 36:1 8141
Ye shall eat this y such as Is 37:30 8141
the second y that which springeth Is 37:30 8141
and in the third y sow ye, and reap Is 37:30 8141
the acceptable y of the LORD Is 61:2 8141
the y of my redeemed is come Is 63:4 8141
in the thirteenth y of his reign Jer 1:2 8141
unto the end of the eleventh y of Jer 1:3 8141
even the y of their visitation Jer 11:23 8141
be careful in the y of drought Jer 17:8 8141
even the y of their visitation Jer 23:12 8141
people of Judah in the fourth y Jer 25:1 8141
of Judah, that was the first y of Jer 25:1 8141
From the thirteenth y of Josiah Jer 25:3 8141
that is the three and twentieth y Jer 25:3 8141
And it came to pass the same y Jer 28:1 8141
king of Judah, in the fourth y Jer 28:1 8141
this y thou shalt die, because Jer 28:16 8141
the same y in the seventh month Jer 28:17 8141
tenth y of Zedekiah king of Judah Jer 32:1 8141
eighteenth y of Nebuchadrezzar Jer 32:1 8141
it came to pass in the fourth y Jer 36:1 8141
it came to pass in the fifth y of Jer 36:9 8141
In the ninth y of Zedekiah king Jer 39:1 8141
And in the eleventh y of Zedekiah Jer 39:2 8141
in the fourth y of Jehoiakim the Jer 45:1 8141
y of Jehoiakim the son of Josiah Jer 46:2 8141
the y of their visitation, saith Jer 48:44 8141
a rumour shall both come one y Jer 51:46 8141
in another y shall come a rumour Jer 51:46 8141
in the fourth y of his reign Jer 51:59 8141
pass in the ninth y of his reign Jer 52:4 8141
the eleventh y of king Zedekiah Jer 52:5 8141
which was the nineteenth y of Jer 52:12 8141
in the seventh y three thousand Jer 52:28 8141
In the eighteenth y of Jer 52:29 8141
twentieth y of Nebuchadrezzar Jer 52:30 8141
thirtieth y of the captivity of Jer 52:31 8141
king of Babylon in the first y of Jer 52:31 8141
came to pass in the thirtieth y Eze 1:1 8141
which was the fifth y of king Eze 1:2 8141
appointed thee each day for a y Eze 4:6 8141
And it came to pass in the sixth y Eze 8:1 8141
it came to pass in the seventh y Eze 20:1 8141
Again in the ninth y, in the Eze 24:1 8141
it came to pass in the eleventh y Eze 26:1 8141
In the tenth y, in the tenth Eze 29:1 8141
pass in the seven and twentieth y Eze 29:17 8141
it came to pass in the eleventh y Eze 30:20 8141
it came to pass in the eleventh y Eze 31:1 8141
it came to pass in the twelfth y Eze 32:1 8141
to pass also in the twelfth y Eze 32:17 8141
in the twelfth y of our captivity Eze 33:21 8141
twentieth y of our captivity, in Eze 40:1 8141

in the beginning of the y ... Eze 40:1 8141
in the fourteenth y after that ... Eze 40:1 8141
of the first y without blemish ... Eze 46:13 8141
shall be his to the y of liberty ... Eze 46:17 8141
In the third y of the reign of ... Dan 1:1 8141
unto the first y of king Cyrus ... Dan 1:21 8141
in the second y of the reign of ... Dan 2:1 8141
In the first y of Belshazzar king ... Dan 7:1 8140
In the third y of the reign of ... Dan 8:1 8141
In the first y of Darius the son ... Dan 9:1 8141
In the first y of his reign I ... Dan 9:2 8141
In the third y of Cyrus king of ... Dan 10:1 8141
in the first y of Darius the Mede ... Dan 11:1 8141
offerings, with calves of a y old ... Mic 6:6 8141
In the second y of Darius the ... Hag 1:1 8141
in the second y of Darius the ... Hag 1:15 8141
month, in the second y of Darius ... Hag 2:10 8141
month, in the second y of Darius ... Zec 1:1 8141
Sebat, in the second y of Darius ... Zec 1:7 8141
in the fourth y of king Darius ... Zec 7:1 8141
y to y to worship the King ... Zec 14:16 8141
y at the feast of the passover ... Lk 2:41 *2094*
Now in the fifteenth y of the ... Lk 3:1 *2094*
the acceptable y of the Lord ... Lk 4:19 *1763*
Lord, let it alone this y also ... Lk 13:8 *2094*
being the high priest that same y ... Jn 11:49 *1763*
but being high priest that y ... Jn 11:51 *1763*
was the high priest that same y ... Jn 18:13 *1763*
that a whole y they assembled ... Acts 11:26 *1763*
And he continued there a y ... Acts 18:11 *1763*
but also to be forward a y ago ... 2Cor 8:10 *4070*
that Achaia was ready a y ago ... 2Cor 9:2 *4070*
high priest alone once every y ... Heb 9:7 *1763*
every y with blood of others ... Heb 9:25 *1763*
y by y continually make the ... Heb 10:1 *1763*
which they offered y by y ... Heb 10:1 *1763*
again made of sins every y ... Heb 10:3 *1763*
a city, and continue there a y ... Jas 4:13 *1763*
and a day, and a month, and a y ... Rev 9:15 *1763*

YEARLY

as a y hired servant shall he be ... Lev 25:53 8141
went y to lament the daughter of ... Judg 11:40 3117
y in a place which is on the ... Judg 21:19 3117
up out of his city y to worship ... 1Sa 1:3 3117
unto the LORD the y sacrifice ... 1Sa 1:21 3117
husband to offer the y sacrifice ... 1Sa 2:19 3117
for there is a y sacrifice there ... 1Sa 20:6 3117
to charge ourselves y with the ... Neh 10:32 8141
the fifteenth day of the same, y ... Est 9:21 8141

YEARN

his bowels did y upon his brother ... Gen 43:30 3648

YEARNED

for her bowels y upon her son ... 1Kin 3:26 3648

YEAR'S

feast of ingathering at the y end ... Ex 34:22 8141
(for it was at every y end that ... 2Sa 14:26 3117

YEARS

and for seasons, and for days, and y ... Gen 1:14 8141
Adam lived an hundred and thirty y ... Gen 5:3 8141
Seth were eight hundred y ... Gen 5:4 8141
were nine hundred and thirty y ... Gen 5:5 8141
Seth lived an hundred and five y ... Gen 5:6 8141
Enos eight hundred and seven y ... Gen 5:7 8141
were nine hundred and twelve y ... Gen 5:8 8141
And Enos lived ninety y, and begat ... Gen 5:9 8141
Cainan eight hundred and fifteen y ... Gen 5:10 8141
Enos were nine hundred and five y ... Gen 5:11 8141
And Cainan lived seventy y ... Gen 5:12 8141
eight hundred and forty y, and ... Gen 5:13 8141
Cainan were nine hundred and ten y ... Gen 5:14 8141
Mahalaleel lived sixty and five y ... Gen 5:15 8141
Jared eight hundred and thirty y ... Gen 5:16 8141
eight hundred ninety and five y ... Gen 5:17 8141
lived an hundred sixty and two y ... Gen 5:18 8141
he begat Enoch eight hundred y ... Gen 5:19 8141
were nine hundred sixty and two y ... Gen 5:20 8141
And Enoch lived sixty and five y ... Gen 5:21 8141
begat Methuselah three hundred y ... Gen 5:22 8141
three hundred sixty and five y ... Gen 5:23 8141
an hundred eighty and seven y ... Gen 5:25 8141
seven hundred eighty and two y ... Gen 5:26 8141
were nine hundred sixty and nine y ... Gen 5:27 8141
lived an hundred eighty and two y ... Gen 5:28 8141
five hundred ninety and five y ... Gen 5:30 8141
seven hundred seventy and seven y ... Gen 5:31 8141
And Noah was five hundred y old ... Gen 5:32 8141
shall be an hundred and twenty y ... Gen 6:3 8141
Noah was six hundred y old when ... Gen 7:6 8141
flood three hundred and fifty y ... Gen 9:28 8141
Noah were nine hundred and fifty y ... Gen 9:29 8141
Shem was an hundred y old ... Gen 11:10 8141
Arphaxad two y after the flood ... Gen 11:10 8141
he begat Arphaxad five hundred y ... Gen 11:11 8141
Arphaxad lived five and thirty y ... Gen 11:12 8141
Salah four hundred and three y ... Gen 11:13 8141
And Salah lived thirty y, and begat ... Gen 11:14 8141
Eber four hundred and three y ... Gen 11:15 8141
And Eber lived four and thirty y ... Gen 11:16 8141
Peleg four hundred and thirty y ... Gen 11:17 8141
And Peleg lived thirty y, and begat ... Gen 11:18 8141
begat Reu two hundred and nine y ... Gen 11:19 8141
And Reu lived two and thirty y ... Gen 11:20 8141
Serug two hundred and seven y ... Gen 11:21 8141
And Serug lived thirty y, and begat ... Gen 11:22 8141
he begat Nahor two hundred y ... Gen 11:23 8141
And Nahor lived nine and twenty y ... Gen 11:24 8141
Terah an hundred and nineteen y ... Gen 11:25 8141
And Terah lived seventy y, and ... Gen 11:26 8141
Terah were two hundred and five y ... Gen 11:32 8141
five y old when he departed out ... Gen 12:4 8141
Twelve y they served Chedorlaomer ... Gen 14:4 8141
Take me an heifer of three y old ... Gen 15:9 8027
old, and a she goat of three y old ... Gen 15:9 8027
old, and a ram of three y old ... Gen 15:9 3027
shall afflict them four hundred y ... Gen 15:13 8141
dwelt ten y in the land of Canaan ... Gen 16:3 8141
Abram was fourscore and six y old ... Gen 16:16 8141
And when Abram was ninety y old ... Gen 17:1 8141
unto him that is an hundred y old ... Gen 17:17 8141
shall Sarah, that is ninety y old ... Gen 17:17 8141
And Abraham was ninety y old ... Gen 17:24 8141
his son was thirteen y old ... Gen 17:25 8141
And Abraham was an hundred y old ... Gen 21:5 8141
hundred and seven and twenty y old ... Gen 23:1 8141
these were the y of the life of ... Gen 23:1 8141
these are the days of the y of ... Gen 25:7 8141
hundred threescore and fifteen y ... Gen 25:7 8141
old age, an old man, and full of y ... Gen 25:8
these are the y of the life of ... Gen 25:17 8141
an hundred and thirty and seven y ... Gen 25:17 8141
Isaac was forty y old when he ... Gen 25:20 8141
Isaac was threescore y old when ... Gen 25:26 8141
Esau was forty y old when he took ... Gen 26:34 8141
I will serve thee seven y for ... Gen 29:18 8141
Jacob served seven y for Rachel ... Gen 29:20 8141
serve with me yet seven other y ... Gen 29:27 8141
served with him yet seven other y ... Gen 29:30 8141
This twenty y have I been with ... Gen 31:38 8141
have I been twenty y in thy house ... Gen 31:41 8141
fourteen y for thy two daughters ... Gen 31:41 8141
and six y for thy cattle ... Gen 31:41 8141
were an hundred and fourscore y ... Gen 35:28 8141
Joseph, being seventeen y old ... Gen 37:2 8141
to pass at the end of two full y ... Gen 41:1 8141
The seven good kine are seven y ... Gen 41:26 8141
the seven good ears are seven y ... Gen 41:26 8141
came up after them are seven y ... Gen 41:27 8141
wind shall be seven y of famine ... Gen 41:27 8141
there come seven y of great ... Gen 41:29 8141
after them seven y of famine ... Gen 41:30 8141
of Egypt in the seven plenteous y ... Gen 41:34 8141
food of those good y that come ... Gen 41:35 8141
against the seven y of famine ... Gen 41:36 8141
Joseph was thirty y old when he ... Gen 41:46 8141
in the seven plenteous y the ... Gen 41:47 8141
up all the food of the seven y ... Gen 41:48 8141
sons before the y of famine came ... Gen 41:50 8141
the seven y of plenteousness, ... Gen 41:53 8141
the seven y of dearth began to ... Gen 41:54 8141
For these two y hath the famine ... Gen 45:6 8141
and yet there are five y, in the ... Gen 45:6 8141
yet there are five y of famine ... Gen 45:11 8141
Pharaoh, The days of the y of my ... Gen 47:9 8141
are an hundred and thirty y ... Gen 47:9 8141
the days of the y of my life been ... Gen 47:9 8141
y of the life of my fathers in ... Gen 47:9 8141
in the land of Egypt seventeen y ... Gen 47:28 8141
was an hundred forty and seven y ... Gen 47:28 8141
Joseph lived an hundred and ten y ... Gen 50:22 8141
being an hundred and ten y old ... Gen 50:26 8141
the y of the life of Levi were an ... Ex 6:16 8141
were an hundred thirty and seven y ... Ex 6:16 8141
the y of the life of Kohath were ... Ex 6:18 8141
were an hundred thirty and three y ... Ex 6:18 8141
the y of the life of Amram were ... Ex 6:20 8141
an hundred and thirty and seven y ... Ex 6:20 8141
And Moses was fourscore y old ... Ex 7:7 8141
and Aaron fourscore and three y old ... Ex 7:7 8141
was four hundred and thirty y ... Ex 12:40 8141
of the four hundred and thirty y ... Ex 12:41 8141
of Israel did eat manna forty y ... Ex 16:35 8141
servant, six y he shall serve ... Ex 21:2 8141
six y thou shalt sow thy land, and ... Ex 23:10 8141
are numbered, from twenty y old ... Ex 30:14 8141
to be numbered, from twenty y old ... Ex 38:26 8141
three y shall it be as ... Lev 19:23 8141
Six y thou shalt sow thy field, ... Lev 25:3 8141
six y thou shalt prune thy ... Lev 25:3 8141
seven sabbaths of y unto thee ... Lev 25:8 8141
unto thee, seven times seven y ... Lev 25:8 8141
of y shall be unto thee forty ... Lev 25:8 8141
be unto thee forty and nine y ... Lev 25:8 8141
According to the number of y ... Lev 25:15 8141
of y of the fruits he shall sell ... Lev 25:15 8141
y thou shalt increase the price ... Lev 25:16 8141
according to the fewness of y ... Lev 25:16 8141
according to the number of the y ... Lev 25:16 8141
bring forth fruit for three y ... Lev 25:21 8141
count the y of the sale thereof ... Lev 25:27 8141
be according unto the number of y ... Lev 25:50 8141
If there be yet many y behind ... Lev 25:51 8141
but few y unto the year of jubile ... Lev 25:52 8141
according unto his y shall he ... Lev 25:52 8141
if he be not redeemed in these y ... Lev 25:54 8141
be of the male from twenty y old ... Lev 27:3 8141
even unto sixty y old ... Lev 27:3 8141
if it be from five y old even ... Lev 27:5 8141
y old even unto twenty y old ... Lev 27:5 8141
a month old even unto five y old ... Lev 27:6 8141
And if it be from sixty y old ... Lev 27:7 8141
according to the y that remain ... Lev 27:18 8141
From twenty y old and upward, all ... Num 1:3 8141
of the names, from twenty y old ... Num 1:18 8141
every male from twenty y old ... Num 1:20 8141
every male from twenty y old ... Num 1:22 8141
of the names, from twenty y old ... Num 1:24 8141
of the names, from twenty y old ... Num 1:26 8141
of the names, from twenty y old ... Num 1:28 8141
of the names, from twenty y old ... Num 1:30 8141
of the names, from twenty y old ... Num 1:32 8141
of the names, from twenty y old ... Num 1:34 8141
of the names, from twenty y old ... Num 1:36 8141
of the names, from twenty y old ... Num 1:38 8141
of the names, from twenty y old ... Num 1:40 8141
of the names, from twenty y old ... Num 1:42 8141
their fathers, from twenty y old ... Num 1:45 8141
From thirty y old and upward even ... Num 4:3 8141
and upward even until fifty y old ... Num 4:3 8141
From thirty y old and upward until ... Num 4:23 8141
upward until fifty y old shalt ... Num 4:23 8141
From thirty y old and upward even ... Num 4:30 8141
upward even unto fifty y old ... Num 4:30 8141
From thirty y old and upward even ... Num 4:35 8141
and upward even unto fifty y old ... Num 4:35 8141
From thirty y old and upward even ... Num 4:39 8141
and upward even unto fifty y old ... Num 4:39 8141
From thirty y old and upward even ... Num 4:43 8141
and upward even unto fifty y old ... Num 4:43 8141
From thirty y old and upward even ... Num 4:47 8141
and upward even unto fifty y old ... Num 4:47 8141
from twenty and five y old ... Num 8:24 8141
from the age of fifty y they ... Num 8:25 8141
seven y before Zoan in Egypt ... Num 13:22 8141
whole number, from twenty y old ... Num 14:29 8141
wander in the wilderness forty y ... Num 14:33 8141
your iniquities, even forty y ... Num 14:34 8141
of Israel, from twenty y old ... Num 26:2 8141
of the people, from twenty y old ... Num 26:4 8141
out of Egypt, from twenty y old ... Num 32:11 8141
wander in the wilderness forty y ... Num 32:13 8141
three y old when he died in mount ... Num 33:39 8141
these forty y the LORD thy God ... Deut 2:7 8141
Zered, was thirty and eight y ... Deut 2:14 8141
these forty y in the wilderness ... Deut 8:2 8141
did thy foot swell, these forty y ... Deut 8:4 8141
At the end of three y thou shalt ... Deut 14:28 8141
seven y thou shalt make a release ... Deut 15:1 8141
unto thee, and serve thee six y ... Deut 15:12 8141
to thee, in serving thee six y ... Deut 15:18 8141
led you forty y in the wilderness ... Deut 29:5 8141
hundred and twenty y old this day ... Deut 31:2 8141
At the end of every seven y ... Deut 31:10 8141
of old, consider the y of many ... Deut 32:7 8141
twenty y old when he died ... Deut 34:7 8141
walked forty y in the wilderness ... Josh 5:6 8141
Joshua was old and stricken in y ... Josh 13:1 8141
Thou art old and stricken in y ... Josh 13:1 8141
Forty y old was I when Moses the ... Josh 14:7 8141
as he said, these forty and five y ... Josh 14:10 8141
this day fourscore and five y old ... Josh 14:10 8141
being an hundred and ten y old ... Josh 24:29 8141
being an hundred and ten y old ... Judg 2:8 8141
served Chushan-rishathaim eight y ... Judg 3:8 8141
And the land had rest forty y ... Judg 3:11 8141
Eglon the king of Moab eighteen y ... Judg 3:14 8141
And the land had rest fourscore y ... Judg 3:30 8141
twenty y he mightily oppressed ... Judg 4:3 8141
And the land had rest forty y ... Judg 5:31 8141
into the hand of Midian seven y ... Judg 6:1 8141
the second bullock of seven y old ... Judg 6:25 8141
forty y in the days of Gideon ... Judg 8:28 8141
had reigned three y over Israel ... Judg 9:22 8141
judged Israel twenty and three y ... Judg 10:2 8141
and judged Israel twenty and two y ... Judg 10:3 8141
eighteen y, all the children of ... Judg 10:8 8141
coasts of Arnon, three hundred y ... Judg 11:26 8141
And Jephthah judged Israel six y ... Judg 12:7 8141
And he judged Israel seven y ... Judg 12:9 8141
and he judged Israel ten y ... Judg 12:11 8141
and he judged Israel eight y ... Judg 12:14 8141
hand of the Philistines forty y ... Judg 13:1 8141
days of the Philistines twenty y ... Judg 15:20 8141
And he judged Israel twenty y ... Judg 16:31 8141
and they dwelled there about ten y ... Ruth 1:4 8141
Now Eli was ninety and eight y old ... 1Sa 4:15 8141
And he had judged Israel forty y ... 1Sa 4:18 8141
for it was twenty y ... 1Sa 7:2 8141
he had reigned two y over Israel ... 1Sa 13:1 8141
with me these days, or these y ... 1Sa 29:3 8141
Saul's son was forty y old when ... 2Sa 2:10 8141
over Israel, and reigned two y ... 2Sa 2:10 8141
the house of Judah was seven y ... 2Sa 2:11 8141
He was five y old when the ... 2Sa 4:4 8141
David was thirty y old when he ... 2Sa 5:4 8141
to reign, and he reigned forty y ... 2Sa 5:4 8141
he reigned over Judah seven y ... 2Sa 5:5 8141
three y over all Israel and Judah ... 2Sa 5:5 8141
it came to pass after two full y ... 2Sa 13:23 8141
to Geshur, and was there three y ... 2Sa 13:38 8141
dwelt two full y in Jerusalem ... 2Sa 14:28 8141
And it came to pass after forty y ... 2Sa 15:7 8141
aged man, even fourscore y old ... 2Sa 19:32 8141
I am this day fourscore y old ... 2Sa 19:35 8141
in the days of David three y ... 2Sa 21:1 8141
Shall seven y of famine come unto ... 2Sa 24:13 8141
David was old and stricken in y ... 1Kin 1:1 3117
reigned over Israel were forty y ... 1Kin 2:11 8141
seven y reigned he in Hebron, and ... 1Kin 2:11 8141
three y reigned he in Jerusalem ... 1Kin 2:11 8141
to pass at the end of three y ... 1Kin 2:39 8141
So was he seven y in building it ... 1Kin 6:38 8141
building his own house thirteen y ... 1Kin 7:1 8141
to pass at the end of twenty y ... 1Kin 9:10 8141
once in three y came the navy of ... 1Kin 10:22 8141
over all Israel was forty y ... 1Kin 11:42 8141
reigned were two and twenty y ... 1Kin 14:20 8141
one y old when he began to reign, ... 1Kin 14:21 8141
reigned seventeen y in Jerusalem ... 1Kin 14:21 8141
Three y reigned he in Jerusalem ... 1Kin 15:2 8141
one y reigned he in Jerusalem ... 1Kin 15:10 8141
and reigned over Israel two y ... 1Kin 15:25 8141
in Tirzah, twenty and four y ... 1Kin 15:33 8141
over Israel in Tirzah, two y ... 1Kin 16:8 8141
to reign over Israel, twelve y ... 1Kin 16:23 8141
six y reigned he in Tirzah ... 1Kin 16:23 8141
Israel in Samaria twenty and two y ... 1Kin 16:29 8141
shall not be dew nor rain these y ... 1Kin 17:1 8141
they continued three y without ... 1Kin 22:1 8141
five y old when he began to reign ... 1Kin 22:42 8141

twenty and five y in Jerusalem 1Kin 22:42 8141
and reigned two y over Israel 1Kin 22:51 8141
of Judah, and reigned twelve y 2Kin 3:1 8141
also come upon the land seven y 2Kin 8:1 8141
land of the Philistines seven y 2Kin 8:2 8141
two y old was he when he began to 2Kin 8:17 8141
he reigned eight y in Jerusalem 2Kin 8:17 8141
twenty y old was Ahaziah when he 2Kin 8:26 8141
in Samaria was twenty and eight y 2Kin 10:36 8141
in the house of the LORD six y 2Kin 11:3 8141
Seven y old was Jehoash when he 2Kin 11:21 8141
forty y reigned he in Jerusalem 2Kin 12:1 8141
Samaria, and reigned seventeen y 2Kin 13:1 8141
in Samaria, and reigned sixteen y 2Kin 13:10 8141
five y old when he began to reign 2Kin 14:2 8141
twenty and nine y in Jerusalem 2Kin 14:2 8141
Jehoahaz king of Israel fifteen y 2Kin 14:17 8141
Azariah, which was sixteen y old 2Kin 14:21 8141
and reigned forty and one y 2Kin 14:23 8141
Sixteen y old was he when he 2Kin 15:2 8141
two and fifty y in Jerusalem 2Kin 15:2 8141
and reigned ten y in Samaria 2Kin 15:17 8141
in Samaria, and reigned two y 2Kin 15:23 8141
in Samaria, and reigned twenty y 2Kin 15:27 8141
twenty y old was he when he began 2Kin 15:33 8141
he reigned sixteen y in Jerusalem 2Kin 15:33 8141
Twenty y old was Ahaz when he 2Kin 16:2 8141
and reigned sixteen y in Jerusalem 2Kin 16:2 8141
in Samaria over Israel nine y 2Kin 17:1 8141
Samaria, and besieged it three y 2Kin 17:5 8141
five y old was he when he began 2Kin 18:2 8141
twenty and nine y in Jerusalem 2Kin 18:2 8141
the end of three y they took it 2Kin 18:10 8141
will add unto thy days fifteen y 2Kin 20:6 8141
Manasseh was twelve y old when he 2Kin 21:1 8141
fifty and five y in Jerusalem 2Kin 21:1 8141
two y old when he began to reign, 2Kin 21:19 8141
and he reigned two y in Jerusalem 2Kin 21:19 8141
Josiah was eight y old when he 2Kin 22:1 8141
thirty and one y in Jerusalem 2Kin 22:1 8141
three y old when he began to 2Kin 23:31 8141
five y old when he began to reign 2Kin 23:36 8141
he reigned eleven y in Jerusalem 2Kin 23:36 8141
became his servant three y 2Kin 24:1 8141
Jehoiachin was eighteen y old 2Kin 24:8 8141
one y old when he began to reign, 2Kin 24:18 8141
he reigned eleven y in Jerusalem 2Kin 24:18 8141
when he was threescore y old 1Chr 2:21 8141
and there he reigned seven y 1Chr 3:4 8141
he reigned thirty and three y 1Chr 3:4 8141
numbered from the age of thirty y 1Chr 23:3 8141
LORD, from the age of twenty y 1Chr 23:24 8141
were numbered from twenty y old 1Chr 23:27 8141
number of them from twenty y old 1Chr 27:23 8141
reigned over Israel was forty y 1Chr 29:27 8141
seven y reigned he in Hebron, and 1Chr 29:27 8141
three y reigned he in Jerusalem 1Chr 29:27 8141
to pass at the end of twenty y 2Chr 8:1 8141
every three y once came the ships 2Chr 9:21 8141
Jerusalem over all Israel forty y 2Chr 9:30 8141
son of Solomon strong, three y 2Chr 11:17 8141
for three y they walked in the 2Chr 11:17 8141
forty y old when he began to 2Chr 12:13 8141
reigned seventeen y in Jerusalem 2Chr 12:13 8141
He reigned three y in Jerusalem 2Chr 13:2 8141
his days the land was quiet ten y 2Chr 14:1 8141
rest, and he had no war in those y 2Chr 14:6 8141
after certain y he went down to 2Chr 18:2 8141
five y old when he began to reign 2Chr 20:31 8141
twenty and five y in Jerusalem 2Chr 20:31 8141
two y old when he began to reign, 2Chr 21:5 8141
he reigned eight y in Jerusalem 2Chr 21:5 8141
of time, after the end of two y 2Chr 21:19 3117
two y old was he when he began to 2Chr 21:20
he reigned in Jerusalem eight y 2Chr 21:20 8141
two y old was Ahaziah when he 2Chr 22:2 8141
hid in the house of God six y 2Chr 22:12 8141
Joash was seven y old when he 2Chr 24:1 8141
he reigned forty y in Jerusalem 2Chr 24:1 8141
thirty y old was he when he died 2Chr 24:15 8141
five y old when he began to reign 2Chr 25:1 8141
twenty and nine y in Jerusalem 2Chr 25:1 8141
numbered them from twenty y old 2Chr 25:5 8141
Jehoahaz king of Israel fifteen y 2Chr 25:25 8141
Uzziah, who was sixteen y old 2Chr 26:1 8141
Sixteen y old was Uzziah when he 2Chr 26:3 8141
fifty and two y in Jerusalem 2Chr 26:3 8141
five y old when he began to reign 2Chr 27:1 8141
he reigned sixteen y in Jerusalem 2Chr 27:1 8141
twenty y old when he began to 2Chr 27:8 8141
and reigned sixteen y in Jerusalem 2Chr 27:8 8141
Ahaz was twenty y old when he 2Chr 28:1 8141
he reigned sixteen y in Jerusalem 2Chr 28:1 8141
when he was five and twenty y old 2Chr 29:1 8141
nine and twenty y in Jerusalem 2Chr 29:1 8141
of males, from three y old 2Chr 31:16 8141
and the Levites from twenty y old 2Chr 31:17 8141
Manasseh was twelve y old when he 2Chr 33:1 8141
fifty and five y in Jerusalem 2Chr 33:1 8141
twenty y old when he began to 2Chr 33:21 8141
reigned two y in Jerusalem 2Chr 33:21 8141
Josiah was eight y old when he 2Chr 34:1 8141
in Jerusalem one and thirty y 2Chr 34:1 8141
three y old when he began to 2Chr 36:2 8141
five y old when he began to reign 2Chr 36:5 8141
he reigned eleven y in Jerusalem 2Chr 36:5 8141
Jehoiachin was eight y old when 2Chr 36:9 8141
twenty y old when he began to 2Chr 36:11 8141
and reigned eleven y in Jerusalem 2Chr 36:11 8141
to fulfil threescore and ten y 2Chr 36:21 8141
the Levites, from twenty y old Ezr 3:8 8141
that was builded these many y ago Ezr 5:11 8140
the king, that is, twelve y Neh 5:14 8141
forty y didst thou sustain them Neh 9:21 8141
Yet many y didst thou forbear Neh 9:30 8141
are thy y as man's days, Job 10:5 8141
the number of y is hidden to the Job 15:20 8141
When a few y are come, then I Job 16:22 8141
multitude of y should teach Job 32:7 8141
and their y in pleasures Job 36:11 8141
number of his y be searched out Job 36:26 8141
lived Job an hundred and forty y Job 42:16 8141
with grief, and my y with sighing Ps 31:10 8141
his y as many generations Ps 61:6 8141
of old, the y of ancient times Ps 77:5 8141
but I will remember the y of the Ps 77:10 8141
in vanity, and their y in trouble Ps 78:33 8141
For a thousand y in thy sight are Ps 90:4 8141
we spend our y as a tale that is Ps 90:9 8141
of our y are threescore Ps 90:10 8141
of strength they be fourscore y Ps 90:10 8141
the y wherein we have seen evil Ps 90:15 8141
Forty y long was I grieved with Ps 95:10 8141
thy y are throughout all Ps 102:24 8141
same, and thy y shall have no end Ps 102:27 8141
the y of thy life shall be many Prov 4:10 8141
others, and thy y unto the cruel Prov 5:9 8141
the y of thy life shall be Prov 9:11 8141
but the y of the wicked shall be Prov 10:27 8141
hundred children, and live many y Eccl 6:3 8141
so that the days of his y be many Eccl 6:3 8141
he live a thousand y twice told Eccl 6:6 8141
But if a man live many y, and Eccl 11:8 8141
nor the y draw nigh, when thou Eccl 12:1 8141
five y shall Ephraim be broken, Is 7:8 8141
Zoar, an heifer of three y old Is 15:5
spoken, saying, Within three y Is 16:14 8141
as the y of an hireling, and the Is 16:14 8141
and barefoot three y for a sign Is 20:3 8141
according to the y of an hireling Is 21:16 8141
Tyre shall be forgotten seventy y Is 23:15 8141
after the end of seventy y shall Is 23:15 8141
pass after the end of seventy y Is 23:17 8141
y shall ye be troubled, ye Is 32:10 8141
will add unto thy days fifteen y Is 38:5 8141
deprived of the residue of my y Is 38:10 8141
I shall go softly all my y in the Is 38:15 8141
child shall die an hundred y old Is 65:20 8141
hundred y old shall be accursed Is 65:20 8141
the king of Babylon seventy y Jer 25:11 8141
when seventy y are accomplished, Jer 25:12 8141
Within two full y will I bring Jer 28:3 8141
within the space of two full y Jer 28:11 8141
the LORD, That after seventy y be Jer 29:10 8141
At the end of seven y let ye go Jer 34:14 8141
and when he hath served thee six y Jer 34:14 8141
as an heifer of three y old Jer 48:34
twenty y old when he began to Jer 52:1 8141
he reigned eleven y in Jerusalem Jer 52:1 8141
upon thee the y of their iniquity Eze 4:5 8141
near, and art come even unto thy y Eze 22:4 8141
shall it be inhabited forty y Eze 29:11 8141
waste shall be desolate forty y Eze 29:12 8141
At the end of forty y will I Eze 29:13 8141
in the latter y thou shalt come Eze 38:8 8141
prophesied in those days many y Eze 38:17 8141
shall burn them with fire seven y Eze 39:9 8141
so nourishing them three y Dan 1:5 8141
about threescore and two y old Dan 5:31 8140
by books the number of the y Dan 9:2 8141
he would accomplish seventy y in Dan 9:2 8141
in the end of y they shall join Dan 11:6 8141
he shall continue more y than the Dan 11:8 8141
after certain y with a great army Dan 11:13 8141
even to the y of many generations Joel 2:2 8141
I will restore to you the y that Joel 2:25 8141
two y before the earthquake Amos 1:1 8141
led you forty y through the Amos 2:10 8141
and your tithes after three y Amos 4:4 3117
in the wilderness forty y Amos 5:25 8141
thy work in the midst of the y Hab 3:2 8141
in the midst of the y make known Hab 3:2 8141
these threescore and ten y Zec 1:12 8141
as I have done these so many y Zec 7:3 8141
month, even those seventy y Zec 7:5 8141
days of old, and as in former y Mal 3:4 8141
coasts thereof, from two y old Mt 2:16 *1332*
with an issue of blood twelve y Mt 9:20 *2094*
had an issue of blood twelve y Mk 5:25 *2094*
she was of the age of twelve y Mk 5:42 *2094*
both were now well stricken in y Lk 1:7 *2250*
and my wife well stricken in y Lk 1:18 *2250*
seven y from her virginity Lk 2:36 *2094*
of about fourscore and four y Lk 2:37 *2094*
And when he was twelve y old Lk 2:42 *2094*
began to be about thirty y of age Lk 3:23 *2094*
the heaven was shut up three y Lk 4:25 *2094*
daughter, about twelve y of age Lk 8:42 *2094*
having an issue of blood twelve y Lk 8:43 *2094*
much goods laid up for many y Lk 12:19 *2094*
these three y I come seeking Lk 13:7 *2094*
a spirit of infirmity eighteen y Lk 13:11 *2094*
hath bound, lo, these eighteen y Lk 13:16 *2094*
these many y do I serve thee, Lk 15:29 *2094*
six y was this temple in building Jn 2:20 *2094*
an infirmity thirty and eight y Jn 5:5 *2094*
him, Thou art not yet fifty y old Jn 8:57 *2094*
For the man was above forty y old Acts 4:22 *2094*
entreat them evil four hundred y Acts 7:6 *2094*
And when he was full forty y old Acts 7:23 *5063*
when forty y were expired, there Acts 7:30 *2094*
sea, and in the wilderness forty y Acts 7:36 *2094*
of forty y in the wilderness Acts 7:42 *2094*
which had kept his bed eight y Acts 9:33 *2094*
about the time of forty y Acts 13:18 *5063*
space of four hundred and fifty y Acts 13:20 *2094*
Benjamin, by the space of forty y Acts 13:21 *2094*
continued by the space of two y Acts 19:10 *2094*
that by the space of three y I Acts 20:31 *5148*
many y a judge unto this nation Acts 24:10 *2094*
Now after many y I came to bring Acts 24:17 *2094*
But after two y Porcius Festus Acts 24:27 *1333*
Paul dwelt two whole y in his own Acts 28:30 *1333*
he was about an hundred y old Rom 4:19 *1541*
these many y to come unto you Rom 15:23 *2094*
in Christ above fourteen y ago 2Cor 12:2 *2094*
Then after three y I went up to Gal 1:18 *2094*
Then fourteen y after I went up Gal 2:1 *2094*
four hundred and thirty y after Gal 3:17 *2094*
days, and months, and times, and y Gal 4:10 *1763*
the number under threescore y old 1Ti 5:9 *2094*
the same, and thy y shall not fail Heb 1:12 *2094*
me, and saw my works forty y Heb 3:9 *2094*
with whom was he grieved forty y Heb 3:17 *2094*
Moses, when he was come to y Heb 11:24
the earth by the space of three y Jas 5:17 *1763*
is with the Lord as a thousand y 2Pet 3:8 *2094*
and a thousand y as one day 2Pet 3:8 *2094*
Satan, and bound him a thousand y Rev 20:2 *2094*
till the thousand y should be Rev 20:3 *2094*
reigned with Christ a thousand y Rev 20:4 *2094*
the thousand y were finished Rev 20:5 *2094*
shall reign with him a thousand y Rev 20:6 *2094*
when the thousand y are expired Rev 20:7 *2094*

YEARS'
came to pass at the seven y end 2Kin 8:3 8141
Either three y famine 1Chr 21:12 8141

YELL
they shall y as lions' whelps Jer 51:38 5286

YELLED
young lions roared upon him, and y Jer 2:15

YELLOW
and there be in it a y thin hair Lev 13:30 6669
not, and there be in it no y hair Lev 13:32 6669
priest shall not seek for y hair Lev 13:36 6669
and her feathers with y gold Ps 68:13 3422

YES
He saith, Y Mt 17:25 *3483*
she answered and said unto him, Y Mk 7:28 *3483*
Y, of the Gentiles also Rom 3:29 *3483*
Y verily, their sound went into Rom 10:18 *3304*

YESTERDAY
your task in making brick both y Ex 5:14 8543
son of Jesse to meat, neither y 1Sa 20:27 8543
Whereas thou camest but y 2Sa 15:20 8543
Surely I have seen y the blood of 2Kin 9:26 570
(For we are but of y, and know Job 8:9 8543
are but as y when it is past Ps 90:4 865
Y at the seventh hour the fever Jn 4:52 *5504*
as thou diddest the Egyptian y Acts 7:28 *5504*
Jesus Christ the same y, and to Heb 13:8 *5504*

YESTERNIGHT
Behold, I lay y with my father Gen 19:34 570
of your father spake unto me y Gen 31:29 570
of my hands, and rebuked thee y Gen 31:42 570

YET
y his days shall be an hundred and Gen 6:3
For y seven days, and I will cause Gen 7:4 5750
he stayed y other seven days Gen 8:10
he stayed y other seven days Gen 8:12
of the Amorites is not y full Gen 15:16
Abraham stood y before the LORD Gen 18:22 5750
And he spake unto him y again Gen 18:29 5750
I will speak y but this once Gen 18:32 389
y indeed she is my sister Gen 20:12 1571
neither y heard I of it, but to Gen 21:26 1571
Isaac his son, while he y lived Gen 25:6
Jacob was y scarce gone out from Gen 27:30 389
it is y high day, neither is it Gen 29:7 5750
while he y spake with them, Gen 29:9 5750
serve with me y seven other years Gen 29:27 5750
served with him y seven other Gen 29:30 5750
Is there y any portion or Gen 31:14 5750
y wherefore hast thou stolen my Gen 31:30
and they hated him y the more Gen 37:5 5750
they hated him y the more for his Gen 37:8 5750
he dreamed y another dream, and Gen 37:9 5750
she y again conceived, and bare a Gen 38:5 5750
Y within three days shall Pharaoh Gen 40:13 5750
Y within three days shall Pharaoh Gen 40:19 5750
Y did not the chief butler Gen 40:23
man whether ye had y a brother Gen 43:6 5750
saying, Is your father y alive Gen 43:7 5750
Is he y alive Gen 43:27 5750
is in good health, he is y alive Gen 43:28 5750
not y far off, Joseph said unto Gen 44:4
for he was y there Gen 44:14 5750
doth my father y live Gen 45:3 5750
y there are five years, in the Gen 45:6 5750
for y there are five years of Gen 45:11 5750
him, saying, Joseph is y alive Gen 45:26 5750
Joseph my son is y alive Gen 45:28 5750
face, because thou art y alive Gen 46:30 5750
when y there was but a little way Gen 48:7 5750
and see whether they be y alive Ex 4:18 5750
y not ought of your work shall be Ex 5:11 3588
y shall ye deliver the tale of Ex 5:18
As y exaltest thou thyself Ex 9:17 5750
ye will not y fear the LORD God Ex 9:30 2962
were ceased, he sinned y more Ex 9:34
knowest thou not y that Egypt is Ex 10:7 2962
Y will I bring one plague more Ex 11:1 5750
from her, and y no mischief follow Ex 21:22
Y now, if thou wilt forgive their Ex 32:32
Y thou hast said, I know thee by Ex 33:12 5750
they brought y unto him free Ex 36:3 5750
y is he guilty, and shall bear his Lev 5:17
y he cheweth not the cud Lev 11:7

Y these may ye eat of every ... Lev 11:21 389
y is he clean ... Lev 13:40
y is he clean ... Lev 13:41
eat y of old fruit until the ... Lev 25:22
If there be y many years behind, ... Lev 25:51 5750
if ye will not y for all this ... Lev 26:18 5704
will punish you y seven times for ... Lev 26:24
y for all that, when they be in ... Lev 26:44 637
y he shall keep the passover unto ... Num 9:10
flesh was y between their teeth ... Num 11:33 5750
his uncleanness is y upon him ... Num 19:13 5750
Balak sent y again princes, more, ... Num 22:15 5750
but y the word which I shall say ... Num 22:20 389
being y in her youth in her ... Num 30:16
to augment y the fierce anger of ... Num 32:14 5750
he will y again leave them in the ... Num 32:15 5750
Y in this thing ye did not ... Deut 1:32
Y they are thy people and thine ... Deut 9:29
ye are not as y come to the rest ... Deut 12:9
y cheweth not the cud, it is ... Deut 14:8
and hath not y eaten of it ... Deut 20:6
y these are the tokens of my ... Deut 22:17
Y the LORD hath not given you an ... Deut 29:4
while I am y alive with you this ... Deut 31:27 5750
Y thou shalt see the land before ... Deut 32:52 3588
Y there shall be a space between ... Josh 3:4 389
there remaineth y very much land ... Josh 13:1
This is the land that y remaineth ... Josh 13:2
As y I am as strong this day as I ... Josh 14:11 5750
Y the children of Manasseh could ... Josh 17:12
Y it came to pass, when the ... Josh 17:13
which had not y received their ... Josh 18:2
y the hand of the house of Joseph ... Judg 1:35
nor y the works which he had done ... Judg 2:10 1571
y they would not hearken unto ... Judg 2:17 1571
unto this day it is y in Ophrah ... Judg 6:24 5750
to death whilst it is y morning ... Judg 6:31
Gideon, The people are y too many ... Judg 7:4 5750
with him, faint, y pursuing them ... Judg 8:4
feared, because he was y a youth ... Judg 8:20 5750
notwithstanding y Jotham the ... Judg 9:5
Y ye have forsaken me, and served ... Judg 10:13
y will I be avenged of you, and ... Judg 15:7
Y he restored the money unto his ... Judg 17:4
Y there is both straw and ... Judg 19:19 1571
Shall I y again go out to battle ... Judg 20:28 5750
y so they sufficed them not ... Judg 21:14
are there y any more sons in my ... Ruth 1:11 5750
And the LORD called y again ... 1Sa 3:6 5750
Samuel did not y know the LORD ... 1Sa 3:7 2962
of the LORD y revealed unto him ... 1Sa 3:7 2962
howbeit y protest solemnly unto ... 1Sa 8:9 3588
if the man should y come thither ... 1Sa 10:22 5750
y turn not aside from following ... 1Sa 12:20 389
he was y in Gilgal, and all the ... 1Sa 13:7 5750
Y they had a file for the ... 1Sa 13:21
y honour me now, I pray thee, ... 1Sa 15:30
There remaineth y the youngest ... 1Sa 16:11 5750
Saul was y the more afraid of ... 1Sa 18:29
thou shalt not only while y I ... 1Sa 20:14 5750
enquired of the LORD y again ... 1Sa 23:4 5750
Go, I pray you, prepare y ... 1Sa 23:22
y thou huntest my soul to take it ... 1Sa 24:11
Y a man is risen to pursue thee, ... 1Sa 25:29
because my life is y whole in me ... 2Sa 1:9 5750
to eat meat while it was y day ... 2Sa 3:35 5750
and there were y sons and daughters ... 2Sa 5:13 5750
the Philistines came up y again ... 2Sa 5:22 5750
I will y be more vile than thus, ... 2Sa 6:22 5750
this was y a small thing in thy ... 2Sa 7:19 5750
Is there y any that is left of ... 2Sa 9:1 5750
is there not y any of the house ... 2Sa 9:3 5750
the king, Jonathan hath y a son ... 2Sa 9:3 5750
while the child was y alive ... 2Sa 12:18
said, While the child was y alive ... 2Sa 12:22 5750
y doth he devise means, that his ... 2Sa 14:14
y would I not put forth mine hand ... 2Sa 18:12
while he was y alive in the midst ... 2Sa 18:14
the son of Zadok y again to Joab ... 2Sa 18:22 5750
y didst thou set thy servant ... 2Sa 19:28
What right therefore have I y to ... 2Sa 19:28
then should thy servant be y a ... 2Sa 19:35 5750
had y war again with Israel ... 2Sa 21:15 5750
there was y a battle in Gath, ... 2Sa 21:20 5750
y he hath made with me an ... 2Sa 23:5 3588
while thou y talkest there with ... 1Kin 1:14 5750
while she y talked with the king, ... 1Kin 1:22 5750
And while he y spake, behold, ... 1Kin 1:42 5750
Y have thou respect unto the ... 1Kin 8:28
Y if they shall bethink ... 1Kin 8:47
Hadad being y a little child ... 1Kin 11:17
who was y in Egypt, heard of it, ... 1Kin 12:2 5750
Depart y for three days, then ... 1Kin 12:5 5750
his father while he y lived ... 1Kin 12:6
y thou hast not been as my ... 1Kin 14:8
Y I have left me seven thousand ... 1Kin 19:18
Y I will send my servants unto ... 1Kin 20:6 3588
And he said, Is he y alive ... 1Kin 20:32 3588
Jehoshaphat, There is y one man ... 1Kin 22:8 3588
burnt incense y in the high ... 1Kin 22:43 3588
y that valley shall be filled ... 2Kin 3:17
unto her son, Bring me y a vessel ... 2Kin 4:6
while he y talked with them, ... 2Kin 6:33 5750
Y the LORD would not destroy ... 2Kin 8:19
Y Edom revolted from under the ... 2Kin 8:22
he them from his presence as y ... 2Kin 13:23
y not like David his father ... 2Kin 14:3 7535
as y the people did sacrifice and ... 2Kin 14:4 5750
Y the LORD testified against ... 2Kin 17:13
shall y again take root downward ... 2Kin 19:30
while he y kept himself close ... 1Chr 12:1 5750
the Philistines y again spread ... 1Chr 14:13 5750
y this was a small thing in thine ... 1Chr 17:17
y again there was war at Gath, ... 1Chr 20:6 5750

y his father made him the chief ... 1Chr 26:10
is y young and tender, and the work ... 1Chr 29:1
neither y hast asked long life ... 2Chr 1:11 1571
y so that thy children take heed ... 2Chr 6:16 7535
y if they pray toward this place, ... 2Chr 6:26
Y if they bethink themselves in ... 2Chr 6:37
his father while he y lived ... 2Chr 10:6
Y Jeroboam the son of Nebat, the ... 2Chr 13:6
while the land is y before us ... 2Chr 14:7 5750
y, because thou didst rely on the ... 2Chr 16:8
y in his disease he sought not to ... 2Chr 16:12 1571
Jehoshaphat, There is y one man ... 2Chr 18:7 5750
for as y the people had not ... 2Chr 20:33 5750
Y he sent prophets to them, to ... 2Chr 24:19
And the people did y corruptly ... 2Chr 27:2 5750
trespass y more against the LORD ... 2Chr 28:22
y did they eat the passover ... 2Chr 30:18 3588
manner, neither y believe him ... 2Chr 32:15
his servants spake y more against ... 2Chr 32:16 5750
y unto the LORD their God only ... 2Chr 33:17
his reign, while he was y young ... 2Chr 34:3 5750
temple of the LORD was not y laid ... Ezr 3:6
building, and y it is not finished ... Ezr 5:16
y our God hath not forsaken us in ... Ezr 9:9
for we remain y escaped, as it is ... Ezr 9:15
y now there is hope in Israel ... Ezr 10:2
y will I gather them from thence, ... Neh 1:9
neither had I as y told it to the ... Neh 2:16
Y now our flesh is as the flesh ... Neh 5:5
y for all this required not I the ... Neh 5:18
Y they sent unto me four times ... Neh 6:4
Y thou in thy manifold mercies ... Neh 9:19
y when they returned, and cried ... Neh 9:28
y they dealt proudly, and ... Neh 9:29
Y many years didst thou forbear ... Neh 9:30
y would they not give ear ... Neh 9:30
y ye bring more wrath upon Israel ... Neh 13:18
y among many nations was there no ... Neh 13:26
Esther had not y shewed her ... Est 2:20
Y all this availeth me nothing, ... Est 5:13
while they were y talking with ... Est 6:14 5750
Esther spake y again before the ... Est 8:3
While he was y speaking, there ... Job 1:16
While he was y speaking, there ... Job 1:17
While he was y speaking, there ... Job 1:18
y trouble came ... Job 3:26
Y man is born unto trouble, as ... Job 5:7 3588
Then should I y have comfort ... Job 6:10 5750
y thy latter end should greatly ... Job 8:7
Whilst it is y in his greenness, ... Job 8:12 5750
y would I not answer, but I would ... Job 9:15
y would I not believe that he had ... Job 9:16
y would I not know my soul ... Job 9:21
Y shalt thou plunge me in the ... Job 9:31 227
y thou dost destroy me ... Job 10:8
y will I not lift up my head ... Job 10:15
he slay me, y will I trust in him ... Job 13:15
Y through the scent of water it ... Job 14:9
y in my flesh shall I see God ... Job 19:26
Y he shall perish for ever like ... Job 20:7
Y his meat in his bowels is ... Job 20:14
Y shall he be brought to the ... Job 21:32
Y he filled their houses with ... Job 22:18
y God layeth not folly to them ... Job 24:12
y his eyes are upon their ways ... Job 24:23
When the Almighty was y with me ... Job 29:5 5750
no answer, and y had condemned Job ... Job 32:3
twice, y man perceiveth it not ... Job 33:14
see him, y judgment is before him ... Job 35:14
y he knoweth it not in great ... Job 35:15
I have y to speak on God's behalf ... Job 36:2 5750
Y have I set my king upon my holy ... Ps 2:6
For y a little while, and the ... Ps 37:10 5750
y have I not seen the righteous ... Ps 37:25
Y he passed away, and, lo, he was ... Ps 37:36
y the Lord thinketh upon me ... Ps 40:17
for I shall y praise him for the ... Ps 42:5 5750
Y the LORD will command his ... Ps 42:8
for I shall y praise him, who is ... Ps 42:11 5750
for I shall y praise him, who is ... Ps 43:5 5750
y have we not forgotten thee, ... Ps 44:17
y their posterity approve their ... Ps 49:13
oil, y were they drawn swords ... Ps 55:21
y shall ye be as the wings of a ... Ps 68:13
will y praise thee more and more ... Ps 71:14
they sinned y more against him by ... Ps 78:17 5750
their meat was y in their mouths ... Ps 78:30 5750
Y they tempted and provoked the ... Ps 78:56
y is their strength labour and ... Ps 90:10
Y they say, The LORD shall not ... Ps 94:7
Y setteth he the poor on high ... Ps 107:41
y have I not declined from thy ... Ps 119:51
y do I not forget thy statutes ... Ps 119:83
y do I not forget thy law ... Ps 119:109
y I erred not from thy precepts ... Ps 119:110
y do not I forget thy precepts ... Ps 119:141
y thy commandments are my ... Ps 119:143
y do I not decline from thy ... Ps 119:157
y they have not prevailed against ... Ps 129:2 1571
y hath he respect unto the lowly ... Ps 138:6
my substance, y being unperfect ... Ps 139:16
when as y there was none of them ... Ps 139:16
for y my prayer also shall be in ... Ps 141:5 5750
Y a little sleep, a little ... Prov 6:10
While as y he had not made the ... Prov 8:26 5704
a wise man, and he will be y wiser ... Prov 9:9 5750
that scattereth, and y increaseth ... Prov 11:24 5750
himself rich, y hath nothing ... Prov 13:7
himself poor, y hath great riches ... Prov 13:7
y they are wanting to him ... Prov 19:7
him, y thou must do it again ... Prov 19:19 5750
I will seek it y again ... Prov 23:35
Y a little sleep, a little ... Prov 24:33
y will not his foolishness depart ... Prov 27:22

y is not washed from their ... Prov 30:12
y they prepare their meat in the ... Prov 30:25
y make they their houses in the ... Prov 30:26
y go they forth all of them by ... Prov 30:27
riseth also while it is y night ... Prov 31:15 5750
y the sea is not full ... Eccl 1:7
y acquainting mine heart with ... Eccl 2:3
y shall he have rule over all my ... Eccl 2:19
y to a man that hath not laboured ... Eccl 2:21
than the living which are y alive ... Eccl 4:2 5728
both they, which hath not y been ... Eccl 4:3 5728
y is there no end of all his ... Eccl 4:8
y God giveth him not power to eat ... Eccl 6:2
told, y hath he seen no good ... Eccl 6:6
y the appetite is not filled ... Eccl 6:7 1571
Which y my soul seeketh, but I ... Eccl 7:28 5750
y surely I know that it shall be ... Eccl 8:12 3588
it out, y he shall not find it ... Eccl 8:17
y shall he not be able to find it ... Eccl 8:17
neither y bread to the wise, nor ... Eccl 9:11 1571
the wise, nor y riches to men of ... Eccl 9:11 1571
nor y favour to men of skill ... Eccl 9:11 1571
y no man remembered that same ... Eccl 9:15
y let him remember the days of ... Eccl 11:8
But y in it shall be a tenth, and ... Is 6:13 5750
y a remnant of them shall return ... Is 10:22
For y a very little while, and the ... Is 10:25 5750
As y shall he remain at Nob that ... Is 10:32 5750
will y choose Israel, and set them ... Is 14:1 5750
Y thou shalt be brought down to ... Is 14:15 389
Y gleaning grapes shall be left ... Is 17:6
y will he not learn righteousness ... Is 26:10
Y the defenced city shall be ... Is 27:10
while it is y in his hand he ... Is 28:4 5750
y they would not hear ... Is 28:12
Y I will distress Ariel, and there ... Is 29:2
Is it not y a very little while, ... Is 29:17 5750
y shall not thy teachers be ... Is 30:20
Y he also is wise, and will bring ... Is 31:2
fire round about, y he knew not ... Is 42:25
y he laid it not to heart ... Is 42:25
Y now hear, O Jacob my servant ... Is 44:1
y they shall fear, and they shall ... Is 44:11
y can he not answer, nor save him ... Is 46:7
the things that are not y done ... Is 46:10
y surely my judgment is with the ... Is 49:4
y shall I be glorious in the eyes ... Is 49:5
forget, y will I not forget thee ... Is 49:15
y we did esteem him stricken, ... Is 53:4
y he opened not his mouth ... Is 53:7
Y it pleased the LORD to bruise ... Is 53:10
Y will I gather others to him, ... Is 56:8 5750
y saidst thou not, There is no ... Is 57:10
Y they seek me daily, and delight ... Is 58:2
and while they are y speaking ... Is 65:24 5750
Wherefore I will y plead with you ... Jer 2:9 5750
their gods, which are y no gods ... Jer 2:11
Y I had planted thee a noble vine ... Jer 2:21
y thine iniquity is marked before ... Jer 2:22
y my people have forgotten me ... Jer 2:32
Y thou sayest, Because I am ... Jer 2:35
y return again to me, saith the ... Jer 3:1
y her treacherous sister Judah ... Jer 3:8
y for all this her treacherous ... Jer 3:10
y will I not make a full end ... Jer 4:27
y can they not prevail ... Jer 5:22
y can they not pass over it ... Jer 5:22
of the fatherless, y they prosper ... Jer 5:28
Y they hearkened not unto me, nor ... Jer 7:26
Y hear the word of the LORD, O ye ... Jer 9:20 3588
Y they obeyed not, nor inclined ... Jer 11:8
y let me talk with thee of thy ... Jer 12:1 389
y thou, O LORD, art in the midst ... Jer 14:9
y they say, Sword and famine shall ... Jer 14:15
y my mind could not be toward ... Jer 15:1
is gone down while it was y day ... Jer 15:9 5750
y every one of them doth curse me ... Jer 15:10
Y, LORD, thou knowest all their ... Jer 18:23
y surely I will make thee a ... Jer 22:6
y would I pluck thee thence ... Jer 22:24 3588
sent these prophets, y they ran ... Jer 23:21
spoken to them, y they prophesied ... Jer 23:21
y I sent them not, nor commanded ... Jer 23:32
Y ye have not hearkened unto me, ... Jer 25:7
y they prophesy a lie in my name ... Jer 27:15
y will I not make a full end of ... Jer 30:11 389
Thou shalt y plant vines upon the ... Jer 31:5 5750
As y they shall use this speech ... Jer 31:23 5750
the measuring line shall y go ... Jer 31:39 5750
y they have not hearkened to ... Jer 32:33
while he was y shut up in the ... Jer 33:1 5750
Y hear the word of the LORD, O ... Jer 34:4 389
Y they were not afraid, nor rent ... Jer 36:24
y should they rise up every man ... Jer 37:10
Now while he was not y gone back ... Jer 40:5 5750
Y a small number that escape the ... Jer 44:28
y will I not leave thee wholly ... Jer 46:28
Y will I bring again the ... Jer 48:47
y a little while, and the time of ... Jer 51:33 5750
y from me shall spoilers come ... Jer 51:53
y will he have compassion ... Lam 3:32
our eyes as y failed for our vain ... Lam 4:17 5750
y shall know that there hath ... Eze 2:5
Y if thou warn the wicked, and he ... Eze 3:19
Y will I leave a remnant, that ye ... Eze 6:8
sold, although they were y alive ... Eze 7:13 5750
but turn thee y again, and thou ... Eze 8:6 5750
also unto me, Turn thee y again ... Eze 8:13 5750
turn thee y again, and thou shalt ... Eze 8:15 5750
voice, y will I not hear them ... Eze 8:18
y will I be to them as a little ... Eze 11:16
y shall he not see it, though he ... Eze 12:13
Y, behold, therein shall be left ... Eze 14:22
shall it be meet y for any work ... Eze 15:5

y couldest not be satisfied	Eze 16:28	
y thou wast not satisfied	Eze 16:29	1571
Y hast thou not walked after	Eze 16:47	
Y say ye, Why	Eze 18:19	
Y ye say, The way of the Lord is	Eze 18:25	
Y saith the house of Israel, The	Eze 18:29	
Y also I lifted up my hand unto	Eze 20:15	
Y in this your fathers have	Eze 20:27	5750
Y she multiplied her whoredoms,	Eze 23:19	
Y they went in unto her, as they	Eze 23:44	
y neither shalt thou mourn nor	Eze 24:16	
y shalt thou never be found again	Eze 26:21	
y thou art a man, and not God,	Eze 28:2	
Wilt thou y say before him that	Eze 28:9	559
Y thus saith the Lord GOD	Eze 29:13	3588
Y had he no wages, nor his army,	Eze 29:18	
y shalt thou be brought down with	Eze 31:18	
y have they borne their shame	Eze 32:24	
y have they borne their shame	Eze 32:25	
Y the children of thy people say,	Eze 33:17	
Y ye say, The way of the Lord is	Eze 33:20	
I will y for this be enquired of	Eze 36:37	5750
Y they shall be ministers in my	Eze 44:11	
y leave the stump of the roots	Dan 4:23	1297
y I will read the writing unto	Dan 5:17	1297
y their lives were prolonged for	Dan 7:12	
y made we not our prayer before	Dan 9:13	
Y heard I the voice of his words	Dan 10:9	
for y the vision is for many days	Dan 10:14	5750
there shall stand up y three	Dan 11:2	5750
for y the end shall be at the	Dan 11:27	5750
y they shall fall by the sword,	Dan 11:33	
because it is y for a time	Dan 11:35	5750
y he shall come to his end, and	Dan 11:45	
for y a little while, and I will	Hos 1:4	5750
Y the number of the children of	Hos 1:10	
Then said the LORD unto me, Go y	Hos 3:1	5750
y an adulteress, according to the	Hos 3:1	
Y let no man strive, nor reprove	Hos 4:4	389
harlot, y let not Judah offend	Hos 4:15	
y could he not heal you, nor cure	Hos 5:13	
there upon him, y he knoweth not	Hos 7:9	
y they have spoken lies against	Hos 7:13	
y do they imagine mischief	Hos 7:15	
y will I bereave them, that there	Hos 9:12	
y will I slay even the beloved	Hos 9:16	
but Judah y ruleth with God, and	Hos 11:12	5750
Y I am become rich, I have found	Hos 12:8	389
will y make thee to dwell in	Hos 12:9	5750
Y I am the LORD thy God from the	Hos 13:4	
Y destroyed I the Amorite before	Amos 2:9	
y I destroyed his fruit from	Amos 2:9	
y have ye not returned unto me,	Amos 4:6	
when there were y three months to	Amos 4:7	5750
y have ye not returned unto me,	Amos 4:8	
y have ye not returned unto me,	Amos 4:9	
y have ye not returned unto me,	Amos 4:10	
y have ye not returned unto me,	Amos 4:11	
house, Is there y any with thee	Amos 6:10	
y shall not the least grain fall	Amos 9:9	
y I will look again toward thy	Jonah 2:4	389
y hast thou brought up my life	Jonah 2:6	
Y forty days, and Nineveh shall be	Jonah 3:4	5750
when I was y in my country	Jonah 4:2	5704
Y will I bring an heir unto thee,	Mic 1:15	5750
y will they lean upon the LORD,	Mic 3:11	
y out of thee shall he come forth	Mic 5:2	
Are there y the treasures of	Mic 6:10	5750
y thus shall they be cut down,	Nah 1:12	
y they shall flee away	Nah 2:8	
Y was she carried away, she went	Nah 3:10	1571
For the vision is y for an	Hab 2:3	5750
Y I will rejoice in the LORD, I	Hab 3:18	
Y now be strong, O Zerubbabel,	Hag 2:4	
Y once, it is a little while, and	Hag 2:6	5750
y ye turned not to me, saith the	Hag 2:17	
Is the seed y in the barn	Hag 2:19	5750
as y the vine, and the fig tree,	Hag 2:19	5704
Cry y, saying, Thus saith the	Zec 1:17	5750
shall y be spread abroad	Zec 1:17	5750
and the LORD shall y comfort Zion	Zec 1:17	5750
Zion, and shall y choose Jerusalem	Zec 1:17	5750
There shall y old men and old	Zec 8:4	5750
It shall y come to pass, that	Zec 8:20	5750
Take unto thee y the instruments	Zec 11:15	5750
that when any shall y prophesy	Zec 13:3	5750
Y ye say, Wherein hast thou loved	Mal 1:2	
y I loved Jacob,	Mal 1:2	
Y ye say, Wherefore	Mal 2:14	
y is she thy companion, and the	Mal 2:14	
Y had he the residue of the	Mal 2:15	
Y ye say, Wherein have we wearied	Mal 2:17	
Y ye have robbed me	Mal 3:8	
Y ye say, What have we spoken so	Mal 3:13	
nor y for your body, what ye	Mt 6:25	
y your heavenly Father feedeth	Mt 6:26	
y I say unto you, That even	Mt 6:29	
neither shoes, nor y staves	Mt 10:10	
While he y talked to the people,	Mt 12:46	*2089*
Y hath he not root in himself,	Mt 13:21	*1161*
Jesus said, Are ye also y without	Mt 15:16	*188*
Do not ye y understand, that	Mt 15:17	*3768*
y the dogs eat of the crumbs	Mt 15:27	*1063*
Do ye not y understand, neither	Mt 16:9	*3768*
While he y spake, behold, a	Mt 17:5	*2089*
what lack I y	Mt 19:20	*2089*
to pass, but the end is not y	Mt 24:6	*3768*
When his branch is y tender	Mt 24:32	*2236*
y will I never be offended	Mt 26:33	
with thee, y will I not deny thee	Mt 26:35	*3364*
And while he y spake, lo, Judas,	Mt 26:47	*2089*
witnesses came, y found they none	Mt 26:60	
said, while he was y alive	Mt 27:63	*2089*
While he y spake, there came from	Mk 5:35	*2089*
y for his oath's sake, and for	Mk 6:26	
y the dogs under the table eat of	Mk 7:28	*1063*
perceive ye not y, neither	Mk 8:17	*3768*
have ye your heart y hardened	Mk 8:17	*2089*
for the time of figs was not y	Mk 11:13	
Having y therefore one son, his	Mk 12:6	*2089*
but the end shall not be y	Mk 13:7	*3768*
When her branch is y tender	Mk 13:28	*2236*
shall be offended, y will not I	Mk 14:29	*235*
And immediately, while he y spake	Mk 14:43	*2089*
But Jesus y answered nothing	Mk 15:5	*3765*
Added y this above all, that he	Lk 3:20	*2596*
While he y spake, there cometh	Lk 8:49	*2089*
And as he was y a coming, the	Lk 9:42	*2089*
y because of his importunity he	Lk 11:8	*1065*
y I say unto you, that Solomon in	Lk 12:27	
commanded, and y there is room	Lk 14:22	*2089*
the other is y a great way off	Lk 14:32	*2089*
the land, nor y for the dunghill	Lk 14:35	
But when he was y a great way off	Lk 15:20	*2089*
y thou never gavest me a kid,	Lk 15:29	
Y because this widow troubleth me	Lk 18:5	*1065*
him, Y lackest thou one thing	Lk 18:22	*2089*
tied, whereon y never man sat	Lk 19:30	
must y be accomplished in me	Lk 22:37	*2089*
And while he y spake, behold a	Lk 22:47	*2089*
And immediately, while he y spake	Lk 22:60	*2089*
No, nor y Herod	Lk 23:15	
unto you when he was y in Galilee	Lk 24:6	*2089*
while they y believed not for joy	Lk 24:41	*2089*
unto you, while I was y with you	Lk 24:44	*2089*
mine hour is not y come	Jn 2:4	*3768*
John was not y cast into prison	Jn 3:24	*3768*
nor y at Jerusalem, worship the	Jn 4:21	
y no man said, What seekest thou	Jn 4:27	*3305*
There are y four months, and then	Jn 4:35	*2089*
unto them, My time is not y come	Jn 7:6	*3768*
I go not up y unto this feast	Jn 7:8	*3768*
for my time is not y full come	Jn 7:8	*3768*
y none of you keepeth the law	Jn 7:19	
because his hour was not y come	Jn 7:30	*3768*
Y a little while am I with you,	Jn 7:33	*2089*
the Holy Ghost was not y given	Jn 7:39	*3768*
that Jesus was not y glorified	Jn 7:39	*3764*
of myself, y my record is true	Jn 8:14	
y if I judge, my judgment is true	Jn 8:16	
for his hour was not y come	Jn 8:20	*3768*
Y ye have not known him	Jn 8:55	
Thou art not y fifty years old,	Jn 8:57	*2532*
y he hath opened mine eyes	Jn 9:30	
he were dead, y shall he live	Jn 11:25	
Now Jesus was not y come into the	Jn 11:30	*3768*
Y a little while is the light	Jn 12:35	*2089*
y they believed not on him	Jn 12:37	
y a little while I am with you	Jn 13:33	*2089*
y hast thou not known me, Philip	Jn 14:9	
Y a little while, and the world	Jn 14:19	*2089*
you, being y present with you	Jn 14:25	
I have y many things to say unto	Jn 16:12	*2089*
y I am not alone, because the	Jn 16:32	
wherein was never man y laid	Jn 19:41	*3764*
early, when it was y dark	Jn 20:1	*2089*
y went he not in	Jn 20:5	*3305*
For as y they knew not the	Jn 20:9	*3764*
for I am not y ascended to my	Jn 20:17	*3768*
have not seen, and y have believed	Jn 20:29	
so many, y was not the net broken	Jn 21:11	
y Jesus said not unto him, He	Jn 21:23	*2532*
y he promised that he would give	Acts 7:5	*2532*
when as y he had no child	Acts 7:5	*2532*
(For as y he was fallen upon none	Acts 8:16	*3768*
y breathing out threatenings and	Acts 9:1	*2089*
While Peter y spake these words,	Acts 10:44	*2089*
nor y the voices of the prophets	Acts 13:27	
y desired they Pilate that he	Acts 13:28	
this tarried there y a good while	Acts 18:18	*2089*
nor y blasphemers of your goddess	Acts 19:37	
y brought up in this city at the	Acts 22:3	
that there are y but twelve days	Acts 24:11	
nor y against Caesar, have I	Acts 25:8	
y vengeance suffereth not to live	Acts 28:4	
y was I delivered prisoner from	Acts 28:17	
why y am I also judged as a	Rom 3:7	*2089*
he had y being uncircumcised	Rom 4:11	
he had being y uncircumcised	Rom 4:12	
neither y the deadness of Sarah's	Rom 4:19	
when we were y without strength	Rom 5:6	*2089*
y peradventure for a good man	Rom 5:7	*1063*
in that, while we were y sinners	Rom 5:8	*2089*
man seeth, why doth he y hope for	Rom 8:24	
For the children being not y born	Rom 9:11	*3380*
unto me, Why doth he y find fault	Rom 9:19	*2089*
y have now obtained mercy through	Rom 11:30	
but y I would have you wise unto	Rom 16:19	*1161*
y not the wisdom of this world,	1Cor 2:6	*1161*
y he himself is judged of no man	1Cor 2:15	*1161*
neither y now are ye able	1Cor 3:2	*2089*
For ye are y carnal	1Cor 3:3	*2089*
y so as by fire	1Cor 3:15	*1161*
y am I not hereby justified	1Cor 4:4	*235*
y have ye not many fathers	1Cor 4:15	*235*
Y not altogether with the	1Cor 5:10	*2532*
y not I, but the Lord, Let not	1Cor 7:10	
y I give my judgment, as one that	1Cor 7:25	*1161*
he knoweth nothing y as he ought	1Cor 8:2	*3764*
others, y doubtless I am to you	1Cor 9:2	*235*
y have I made myself servant unto	1Cor 9:19	
they many members, y but one body	1Cor 12:20	*1161*
and y shew I unto you a more	1Cor 12:31	*2089*
Y in the church I had rather	1Cor 14:19	*235*
y for all that will they not hear	1Cor 14:21	
y not I, but the grace of God	1Cor 15:10	*1161*
ye are y in your sins	1Cor 15:17	*2089*
trust that he will y deliver us	2Cor 1:10	*2089*
you I came not as y unto Corinth	2Cor 1:23	*3765*
on every side, y not distressed	2Cor 4:8	*235*
y the inward man is renewed day	2Cor 4:16	*235*
y now henceforth know we him no	2Cor 5:16	*235*
as deceivers, and y true	2Cor 6:8	
As unknown, and y well known	2Cor 6:9	
As sorrowful, y alway rejoicing	2Cor 6:10	*1161*
as poor, y making many rich	2Cor 6:10	*1161*
and y possessing all things	2Cor 6:10	
y for your sakes he became poor,	2Cor 8:9	
Y have I sent the brethren, lest	2Cor 9:3	*1161*
in speech, y not in knowledge	2Cor 11:6	*235*
y as a fool receive me, that I	2Cor 11:16	*2579*
y of myself I will not glory, but	2Cor 12:5	*1161*
y he liveth by the power of God	2Cor 13:4	*235*
for if I y pleased men, I should	Gal 1:10	*2089*
y not I, but Christ liveth in me	Gal 2:20	*3765*
if it be y in vain	Gal 3:4	*2596*
y if it be confirmed, no man	Gal 3:15	
if I y preach circumcision, why	Gal 5:11	*2089*
why do I y suffer persecution	Gal 5:11	*2089*
For no man ever y hated his own	Eph 5:29	
that your love may abound y more	Phil 1:9	*2089*
y what I shall choose I wot not	Phil 1:22	*2532*
Y I supposed it necessary to send	Phil 2:25	*1161*
works, y now hath he reconciled	Col 1:21	*1161*
y am I with you in the spirit,	Col 2:5	*235*
nor y of others, when we might	1Th 2:6	
not, that, when I was y with you	2Th 2:5	*2089*
Y count him not as an enemy, but	2Th 3:15	*2532*
y is he not crowned, except he	2Ti 2:5	
not, y he abideth faithful	2Ti 2:13	
Y for love's sake I rather	Philem 9	
But now we see not y all things	Heb 2:8	*3768*
like as we are, y without sin	Heb 4:15	
y learned he obedience by the	Heb 5:8	
For he was y in the loins of his	Heb 7:10	*2089*
And it is y far more evident	Heb 7:15	*2089*
of all was not y made manifest	Heb 9:8	*2089*
first tabernacle was y standing	Heb 9:8	*2089*
Nor y that he should offer	Heb 9:25	
For y a little while, and he that	Heb 10:37	*2089*
and by it he being dead y speaketh	Heb 11:4	*2089*
of God of things not seen as y	Heb 11:7	*3369*
Ye have not y resisted unto blood	Heb 12:4	*3768*
Y once more I shake not the earth	Heb 12:26	*2089*
Y once more, signifieth the	Heb 12:27	*2089*
y offend in one point, he is	Jas 2:10	
y if thou kill, thou art become a	Jas 2:11	*1161*
y are they turned about with a	Jas 3:4	
y ye have not, because ye ask not	Jas 4:2	*1161*
y believing, ye rejoice with joy	1Pet 1:8	*1161*
Y if any man suffer as a	1Pet 4:16	*1161*
it doth not y appear what we	1Jn 3:2	*3768*
Y Michael the archangel, when	Jude 9	*1161*
should rest y for a little season	Rev 6:11	*2089*
angels, which are y to sound	Rev 8:13	*3195*
not killed by these plagues y	Rev 9:20	
that was, and is not, and y is	Rev 17:8	*2539*
is, and the other is not y come	Rev 17:10	*3768*
have received no kingdom as y	Rev 17:12	*3768*

YIELD

y unto thee her strength	Gen 4:12	5414
he shall y royal dainties	Gen 49:20	5414
that it may y unto you the	Lev 19:25	3254
And the land shall y her fruit	Lev 25:19	5414
and the land shall y her increase	Lev 26:4	5414
of the field shall y their fruit	Lev 26:4	5414
land shall not y her increase	Lev 26:20	5414
trees of the land y their fruits	Lev 26:20	5414
and that the land y not her fruit	Deut 11:17	5414
but y yourselves unto the LORD,	2Chr 30:8	
shall the earth y her increase	Ps 67:6	5414
and our land shall y her increase	Ps 85:12	5414
which may y fruits of increase	Ps 107:37	6213
fair speech she caused him to y	Prov 7:21	5186
of vineyard shall y one bath	Is 5:10	6213
seed of an homer shall y an ephah	Is 5:10	6213
of the field shall y her fruit	Eze 34:27	5414
and the earth shall y her increase	Eze 34:27	5414
y your fruit to my people of	Eze 36:8	5375
the bud shall y no meal	Hos 8:7	6213
if so be it y, the strangers	Hos 8:7	6213
the vine do y their strength	Joel 2:22	5414
and the fields shall y no meat	Hab 3:17	6213
did y fruit that sprang up and	Mk 4:8	*1325*
But do not thou y unto them	Acts 23:21	*3982*
Neither y ye your members as	Rom 6:13	*3936*
but y yourselves unto God, as	Rom 6:13	*3936*
that to whom ye y yourselves	Rom 6:16	*3936*
even so now y your members	Rom 6:19	*3936*
can no fountain both y salt water	Jas 3:12	*4160*

YIELDED

y up the ghost, and was gathered	Gen 49:33	1478
and bloomed blossoms, and y almonds	Num 17:8	1580
y their bodies, that they might	Dan 3:28	3052
with a loud voice, y up the ghost	Mt 27:50	*863*
and choked it, and it y no fruit	Mk 4:7	*1325*
at his feet, and y up the ghost	Acts 5:10	*1634*
for as ye have y your members	Rom 6:19	*3936*
and y her fruit every month	Rev 22:2	*591*

YIELDETH

it y much increase unto the kings	Neh 9:37	7235
the wilderness y food for them	Job 24:5	
the root of the righteous y fruit	Prov 12:12	5414
it y the peaceable fruit of	Heb 12:11	*591*

YIELDING

forth grass, the herb y seed	Gen 1:11	2232
the fruit tree y fruit after his	Gen 1:11	6213
herb y seed after his kind, and	Gen 1:12	2232
his kind, and the tree y fruit	Gen 1:12	6213
is the fruit of a tree y seed	Gen 1:29	2232

for y pacifieth great offences	Eccl 10:4	4832
neither shall cease from y fruit	Jer 17:8	6213

YIRON See IRON.

YOKE

break his y from off thy neck	Gen 27:40	5923
I have broken the bands of your y	Lev 26:13	5923
and upon which never came y	Num 19:2	5923
and which hath not drawn in the y	Deut 21:3	5923
he shall put a y of iron upon thy	Deut 28:48	5923
on which there hath come no y	1Sa 6:7	5923
And he took a y of oxen, and hewed	1Sa 11:7	6776
which a y of oxen might plow	1Sa 14:14	6776
Thy father made our y grievous	1Kin 12:4	5923
his heavy y which he put upon us,	1Kin 12:4	5923
Make the y which thy father did	1Kin 12:9	5923
Thy father made our y heavy	1Kin 12:10	5923
heavy y, I will add to your y	1Kin 12:11	5923
My father made your y heavy	1Kin 12:14	5923
and I will add to your y	1Kin 12:14	5923
with twelve y of oxen before him	1Kin 19:19	6776
took a y of oxen, and slew them,	1Kin 19:21	6776
Thy father made our y grievous	2Chr 10:4	5923
his heavy y that he put upon us,	2Chr 10:4	5923
Ease somewhat the y that thy	2Chr 10:9	5923
Thy father made our y heavy	2Chr 10:10	5923
my father put a heavy y upon you	2Chr 10:11	5923
you, I will put more to your y	2Chr 10:11	5923
My father made your y heavy	2Chr 10:14	5923
camels, and five hundred y of oxen	Job 1:3	6776
camels, and a thousand y of oxen	Job 42:12	6776
hast broken the y of his burden	Is 9:4	5923
his y from off thy neck, and the	Is 10:27	5923
the y shall be destroyed because	Is 10:27	5923
then shall his y depart from off	Is 14:25	5923
hast thou very heavily laid thy y	Is 47:6	5923
go free, and that ye break every y	Is 58:6	4133
away from the midst of thee the y	Is 58:9	4133
of old time I have broken thy y	Jer 2:20	5923
have altogether broken the y	Jer 5:5	5923
the y of the king of Babylon	Jer 27:8	5923
the y of the king of Babylon	Jer 27:11	5923
the y of the king of Babylon	Jer 27:12	5923
I have broken the y of the king	Jer 28:2	5923
for I will break the y of the	Jer 28:4	5923
Hananiah the prophet took the y	Jer 28:10	4133
Even so will I break the y of	Jer 28:11	5923
the y from off the neck of the	Jer 28:12	4133
I have put a y of iron upon the	Jer 28:14	5923
break his y from off thy neck	Jer 30:8	5923
a bullock unaccustomed to the y	Jer 31:18	
the husbandman and his y of oxen	Jer 51:23	6776
The y of my transgressions is	Lam 1:14	5923
that he bear the y in his youth	Lam 3:27	5923
have broken the bands of their y	Eze 34:27	5923
that take off the y on their jaws	Hos 11:4	5923
will I break his y from off thee	Nah 1:13	4132
Take my y upon you, and learn of	Mt 11:29	*2218*
For my y is easy, and my burden is	Mt 11:30	*2218*
I have bought five y of oxen	Lk 14:19	*2201*
to put a y upon the neck of the	Acts 15:10	*2218*
again with the y of bondage	Gal 5:1	*2218*
y count their own masters worthy	1Ti 6:1	*2218*

YOKED

Be ye not unequally y together	2Cor 6:14	*2086*

YOKEFELLOW

And I intreat thee also, true y	Phil 4:3	*4805*

YOKES

Make thee bonds and y, and put them	Jer 27:2	4133
Thou hast broken the y of wood	Jer 28:13	4133
shalt make for them y of iron	Jer 28:13	4133
shall break there the y of Egypt	Eze 30:18	4133

YONDER

and I and the lad will go y	Gen 22:5	3541
and scatter thou the fire y	Num 16:37	1973
offering, while I meet the LORD y	Num 23:15	3541
with them on y side Jordan	Num 32:19	5676
Behold, y is that Shunammite	2Kin 4:25	
mountain, Remove hence to y place	Mt 17:20	*1563*
Sit ye here, while I go and pray y	Mt 26:36	*1563*

YOU See PREFACE.

YOUNG

wounding, and a y man to my hurt	Gen 4:23	3206
that which the y men have eaten	Gen 14:24	5288
and a turtledove, and a y pigeon	Gen 15:9	1469
and good, and gave it unto a y man	Gen 18:7	5288
the house round, both old and y	Gen 19:4	5288
and took two of his y men with him	Gen 22:3	5288
And Abraham said unto his y men	Gen 22:5	5288
Abraham returned unto his y men	Gen 22:19	5288
she goats have not cast their y	Gen 31:38	
and herds with y are with me	Gen 33:13	5763
the y man deferred not to do the	Gen 34:19	5288
there was there with us a y man	Gen 41:12	5288
Moses said, We will go with our y	Ex 10:9	5288
There shall nothing cast their y	Ex 23:26	
he sent y men of the children of	Ex 24:5	5288
Take one y bullock, and two rams	Ex 29:1	
a y man, departed not out of the	Ex 33:11	5288
of turtledoves, or of y pigeons	Lev 1:14	1121
a y bullock without blemish unto	Lev 4:3	
offer a y bullock for the sin	Lev 4:14	
or two y pigeons, unto the LORD	Lev 5:7	1121
or two y pigeons, then he that	Lev 5:11	1121
Take thee a y calf for a sin	Lev 9:2	
a y pigeon, or a turtledove, for	Lev 12:6	1121
two turtles, or two y pigeons	Lev 12:8	1121
or two y pigeons, such as he is	Lev 14:22	1121
turtledoves, or of the y pigeons	Lev 14:30	1121
or two y pigeons, and come before	Lev 15:14	1121
or two y pigeons, and bring them	Lev 15:29	1121
with a y bullock for a sin	Lev 16:3	
kill it and her y both in one day	Lev 22:28	1121
one y bullock, and two rams	Lev 23:18	
or two y pigeons, to the priest,	Num 6:10	1121
One y bullock, one ram, one lamb	Num 7:15	
One y bullock, one ram, one lamb	Num 7:21	
One y bullock, one ram, one lamb	Num 7:27	
One y bullock, one ram, one lamb	Num 7:33	
One y bullock, one ram, one lamb	Num 7:39	
One y bullock, one ram, one lamb	Num 7:45	
One y bullock, one ram, one lamb	Num 7:51	
One y bullock, one ram, one lamb	Num 7:57	
One y bullock, one ram, one lamb	Num 7:63	
One y bullock, one ram, one lamb	Num 7:69	
One y bullock, one ram, one lamb	Num 7:75	
One y bullock, one ram, one lamb	Num 7:81	
Then let them take a y bullock	Num 8:8	
another y bullock shalt thou take	Num 8:8	
And there ran a y man, and told	Num 11:27	5288
of Moses, one of his y men	Num 11:28	979
y bullock for a burnt offering	Num 15:24	
and lift up himself as a y lion	Num 23:24	
two y bullocks, and one ram, seven	Num 28:11	
two y bullocks, and one ram, and	Num 28:19	
two y bullocks, one ram, seven	Num 28:27	
one y bullock, one ram, and seven	Num 29:2	
one y bullock, one ram, and seven	Num 29:8	
thirteen y bullocks, two rams, and	Num 29:13	
ye shall offer twelve y bullocks	Num 29:17	
ground, whether they be y ones	Deut 22:6	667
and the dam sitting upon the y	Deut 22:6	667
shalt not take the dam with the y	Deut 22:6	1121
the dam go, and take the y to thee	Deut 22:7	1121
the old, nor shew favour to the y	Deut 28:50	5288
toward her y one that cometh out	Deut 28:57	7988
her nest, fluttereth over her y	Deut 32:11	1469
shall destroy both the y man	Deut 32:25	970
in the city, both man and woman, y	Josh 6:21	5288
the y men that were spies went in	Josh 6:23	5288
him, Take thy father's y bullock	Judg 6:25	6499
caught a y man of the men of	Judg 8:14	5288
unto the y man his armourbearer	Judg 9:54	5288
his y man thrust him through, and	Judg 9:54	5288
a y lion roared against him	Judg 14:5	3715
for so used the y men to do	Judg 14:10	970
And there was a y man out of	Judg 17:7	5288
the y man was unto him as one of	Judg 17:11	5288
the y man became his priest, and	Judg 17:12	5288
the voice of the y man the Levite	Judg 18:3	5288
the house of the y man the Levite	Judg 18:15	5288
for the y man which is with thy	Judg 19:19	5288
four hundred y virgins, that had	Judg 21:12	5291
have I not charged the y men that	Ruth 2:9	5288
that which the y men have drawn	Ruth 2:9	5288
glean, Boaz commanded his y men	Ruth 2:15	5288
Thou shalt keep fast by my y men	Ruth 2:21	5288
as thou followedst not y men	Ruth 3:10	970
shall give thee of this y woman	Ruth 4:12	5291
and the child was y	1Sa 1:24	5288
Wherefore the sin of the y men	1Sa 2:17	5288
and your goodliest y men, and your	1Sa 8:16	970
name was Saul, a choice y man	1Sa 9:2	970
they found y maidens going out to	1Sa 9:11	5291
the y man that bare his armour	1Sa 14:1	5288
Jonathan said to the y man that	1Sa 14:6	5288
Whose son art thou, thou y man	1Sa 17:58	5288
But if I say thus unto the y man	1Sa 20:22	5958
if the y men have kept themselves	1Sa 21:4	5288
the vessels of the y men are holy	1Sa 21:5	5288
And David sent out ten y men	1Sa 25:5	5288
men, and David said unto the y men	1Sa 25:5	5288
Ask thy y men, and they will shew	1Sa 25:8	5288
Wherefore let the y men find	1Sa 25:8	5288
And when David's y men came	1Sa 25:9	5288
So David's y men turned their way	1Sa 25:12	5288
But one of the y men told Abigail	1Sa 25:14	5288
saw not the y men of my lord	1Sa 25:25	5288
the y men that follow my lord	1Sa 25:27	5288
and let one of the y men come over	1Sa 26:22	5288
I am a y man of Egypt, servant to	1Sa 30:13	5288
of them, save four hundred y men	1Sa 30:17	5288
said unto the y man that told him	2Sa 1:5	5288
the y man that told him said, As	2Sa 1:6	5288
said unto the y man that told him	2Sa 1:13	5288
And David called one of the y men	2Sa 1:15	5288
Let the y men now arise, and play	2Sa 2:14	5288
lay thee hold on one of the y men	2Sa 2:21	5288
And David commanded his y men	2Sa 4:12	5288
And Mephibosheth had a y son	2Sa 9:12	6996
all the y men the king's sons	2Sa 13:32	5288
the y man that kept the watch	2Sa 13:34	5288
bring the y man Absalom again	2Sa 14:21	5288
summer fruit for the y men to eat	2Sa 16:2	5288
gently for my sake with the y man	2Sa 18:5	5288
that none touch the y man Absalom	2Sa 18:12	5288
ten y men that bare Joab's armour	2Sa 18:15	5288
Is the y man Absalom safe	2Sa 18:29	5288
Is the y man Absalom safe	2Sa 18:32	5288
do thee hurt, be as that y man is	2Sa 18:32	5288
for my lord the king a y virgin	1Kin 1:2	5291
Solomon seeing the y man that he	1Kin 11:28	5288
consulted with the y men that	1Kin 12:8	3206
the y men that were grown up with	1Kin 12:10	3206
after the counsel of the y men	1Kin 12:14	3206
Even by the y men of the princes	1Kin 20:14	5288
Then he numbered the y men of the	1Kin 20:15	5288
the y men of the princes of the	1Kin 20:17	5288
So these y men of the princes of	1Kin 20:19	5288
me, I pray thee, one of the y men	2Kin 4:22	5288
to me from mount Ephraim two y	2Kin 5:22	5288
LORD opened the eyes of the y man	2Kin 6:17	5288
their y men wilt thou slay with	2Kin 8:12	970
So the y man, even the y man	2Kin 9:4	5288
even the y man the prophet, went	2Kin 9:4	5288
a y man mighty of valour, and of	1Chr 12:28	5288
David said, Solomon my son is y	1Chr 22:5	5288
alone God hath chosen, is yet y	1Chr 29:1	5288
took counsel with the y men that	2Chr 10:8	3206
the y men that were brought up	2Chr 10:10	3206
after the advice of the y men	2Chr 10:14	3206
of Solomon, when Rehoboam was y	2Chr 13:7	5288
himself with a y bullock and seven	2Chr 13:9	
of his reign, while he was yet y	2Chr 34:3	5288
who slew their y men with the	2Chr 36:17	970
compassion upon y man or maiden	2Chr 36:17	970
both y bullocks, and rams, and	Ezr 6:9	1123
Let there be fair y virgins	Est 2:2	5291
gather together all the fair y	Est 2:3	5291
cause to perish, all Jews, both y	Est 3:13	5288
mules, camels, and y dromedaries	Est 8:10	1121
house, and it fell upon the y men	Job 1:19	5288
lion, and the teeth of the y lions	Job 4:10	3715
Yea, y children despised me	Job 19:18	
The y men saw me, and hid	Job 29:8	5288
Buzite answered and said, I am y	Job 32:6	
fill the appetite of the y lions	Job 38:39	3715
when his y ones cry unto God,	Job 38:41	3206
they bring forth their y ones	Job 39:3	3206
Their y ones are in good liking,	Job 39:4	1121
is hardened against her y ones	Job 39:16	1121
Her y ones also suck up blood	Job 39:30	667
as it were a y lion lurking in	Ps 17:12	3715
and Sirion like a y unicorn	Ps 29:6	1121
The y lions do lack, and suffer	Ps 34:10	3715
I have been y, and now am old	Ps 37:25	5288
the great teeth of the y lions	Ps 58:6	3715
The fire consumed their y men	Ps 78:63	970
y he brought him to feed Jacob	Ps 78:71	5763
herself, where she may lay her y	Ps 84:3	667
the y lion and the dragon shalt	Ps 91:13	3715
The y lions roar after their prey	Ps 104:21	3715
shall a y man cleanse his way	Ps 119:9	5288
to the y ravens which cry	Ps 147:9	1121
Both y men, and maidens	Ps 148:12	970
to the y man knowledge and	Prov 1:4	5288
a y man void of understanding,	Prov 7:7	5288
The glory of y men is their	Prov 20:29	970
the y eagles shall eat it	Prov 30:17	1121
Rejoice, O y man, in thy youth	Eccl 11:9	970
beloved is like a roe or a y hart	Song 2:9	6082
be thou like a roe or a y hart	Song 2:17	6082
like two y roes that are twins	Song 4:5	6082
like two y roes that are twins	Song 7:3	6082
to a y hart upon the mountains of	Song 8:14	6082
they shall roar like y lions	Is 5:29	3715
that a man shall nourish a y cow	Is 7:21	1241
shall have no joy in their y men	Is 9:17	970
the y lion and the fatling	Is 11:6	3715
their y ones shall lie down	Is 11:7	3206
shall dash the y men to pieces	Is 13:18	5288
and the Ethiopians captives, y	Is 20:4	5288
neither do I nourish up y men	Is 23:4	970
anguish, from whence come the y	Is 30:6	3833
upon the shoulders of y asses	Is 30:6	
the y asses that ear the ground	Is 30:24	
the y lion roaring on his prey,	Is 31:4	3715
his y men shall be discomfited	Is 31:8	970
gently lead those that are with y	Is 40:11	5763
the y men shall utterly fall	Is 40:30	
For as a y man marrieth a virgin,	Is 62:5	970
The y lions roared upon him, and	Jer 2:15	3715
the assembly of y men together	Jer 6:11	970
the y men from the streets	Jer 9:21	970
the y men shall die by the sword	Jer 11:22	970
of the y men a spoiler at noonday	Jer 15:8	970
let their y men be slain by the	Jer 18:21	970
for the y of the flock and of the	Jer 31:12	1121
rejoice in the dance, both y men	Jer 31:13	970
his chosen y men are gone down to	Jer 48:15	970
Therefore her y men shall fall in	Jer 49:26	970
Therefore shall her y men fall in	Jer 50:30	970
and spare ye not her y men	Jer 51:3	970
will I break in pieces old and y	Jer 51:22	5288
will I break in pieces the y man	Jer 51:22	970
against me to crush my y men	Lam 1:15	970
my y men are gone into captivity	Lam 1:18	970
for the life of thy y children	Lam 2:19	
The y and the old lie on the	Lam 2:21	5288
my y men are fallen by the sword	Lam 2:21	970
they give suck to their y ones	Lam 4:3	1482
the y children ask bread, and no	Lam 4:4	
They took the y men to grind	Lam 5:13	970
the y men from their musick	Lam 5:14	970
Slay utterly old and y, both maids	Eze 9:6	970
off the top of his y twigs	Eze 17:4	3242
top of his y twigs a tender one	Eze 17:22	3127
her whelps among y lions	Eze 19:2	3715
it became a y lion, and it learned	Eze 19:3	3715
her whelps, and made him a y lion	Eze 19:5	3715
the lions, he became a y lion	Eze 19:6	3715
all of them desirable y men	Eze 23:6	970
all of them desirable y men	Eze 23:12	970
all of them desirable y men	Eze 23:23	970
The y men of Aven and of Pi-beseth	Eze 30:17	970
of the field bring forth their y	Eze 31:6	
Thou art like a y lion of the	Eze 32:2	3715
with all the y lions thereof,	Eze 38:13	3715
the face of a y lion toward the	Eze 41:19	3715
a y bullock for a sin offering	Eze 43:19	
thou shalt offer a y bullock	Eze 43:23	
shall also prepare a y bullock	Eze 43:25	
thou shalt take a y bullock	Eze 45:18	
be a y bullock without blemish	Eze 46:6	
as a y lion to the house of Judah	Hos 5:14	3715
your y men shall see visions	Joel 2:28	970
of your y men for Nazarites	Amos 2:11	970
will a y lion cry out of his den,	Amos 3:4	3715
your y men have I slain with the	Amos 4:10	970

virgins and y men faint for thirst	Amos 8:13	970
as a y lion among the flocks of	Mic 5:8	3715
the feeding place of the y lions	Nah 2:11	3715
sword shall devour thy y lions	Nah 2:13	3715
her y children also were dashed	Nah 3:10	
him, Run, speak to this y man	Zec 2:4	5288
shall make the y men cheerful	Zec 9:17	970
a voice of the roaring of y lions	Zec 11:3	3715
off, neither shall seek the y one	Zec 11:16	5288
search diligently for the y child	Mt 2:8	3813
stood over where the y child was	Mt 2:9	3813
they saw the y child with Mary	Mt 2:11	3813
Arise, and take the y child	Mt 2:13	3813
seek the y child to destroy him	Mt 2:13	3813
he arose, he took the y child	Mt 2:14	3813
Arise, and take the y child	Mt 2:20	3813
which sought the y child's life	Mt 2:20	3813
And he arose, and took the y child	Mt 2:21	3813
The y man saith unto him, All	Mt 19:20	3495
But when the y man heard that	Mt 19:22	3495
whose y daughter had an unclean	Mk 7:25	2365
they brought y children to him,	Mk 10:13	3813
followed him a certain y man	Mk 14:51	3495
the y men laid hold on him	Mk 14:51	3495
they saw a y man sitting on the	Mk 16:5	3495
of turtledoves, or two y pigeons	Lk 2:24	3502
Y man, I say unto thee, Arise	Lk 7:14	3495
Jesus, when he had found a y ass	Jn 12:14	3678
I say unto thee, When thou wast y	Jn 21:18	3501
your y men shall see visions, and	Acts 2:17	3495
the y men arose, wound him up, and	Acts 5:6	3501
the y men came in, and found her	Acts 5:10	3495
they cast out their y children	Acts 7:19	1025
their clothes at a y man's feet	Acts 7:58	3494
a certain y man named Eutychus	Acts 20:9	3494
And they brought the y man alive	Acts 20:12	3816
Bring this y man unto the chief	Acts 23:17	3494
me to bring this y man unto thee	Acts 23:18	3494
captain then let the y man depart	Acts 23:22	3494
may teach the y women to be sober	Titus 2:4	3501
Y men likewise exhort to be sober	Titus 2:6	3501
y men, because ye have overcome	1Jn 2:13	3495
y men, because ye are strong, and	1Jn 2:14	3495

YOUNGER

knew what his y son had done unto	Gen 9:24	6996
And the firstborn said unto the y	Gen 19:31	6810
the firstborn said unto the y	Gen 19:34	6810
the y arose, and lay with him	Gen 19:35	6810
And the y, she also bare a son, and	Gen 19:38	6810
and the elder shall serve the y	Gen 25:23	6810
and put them upon Jacob her y son	Gen 27:15	6996
sent and called Jacob her y son	Gen 27:42	6996
and the name of the y was Rachel	Gen 29:16	6996
years for Rachel thy y daughter	Gen 29:18	6996
country, to give the y before the	Gen 29:26	6810
and said, Is this your y brother	Gen 43:29	6996
Ephraim's head, who was the y	Gen 48:14	6810
but truly his y brother shall be	Gen 48:19	6996
son of Kenaz, Caleb's y brother	Judg 1:13	6996
son of Kenaz, Caleb's y brother	Judg 3:9	6996
is not her y sister fairer than	Judg 15:2	6996
and the name of the y Michal	1Sa 14:49	6996
over against their y brethren	1Chr 24:31	6996
But now they that are y than I	Job 30:1	
thy y sister, that dwelleth at	Eze 16:46	6996
thy sisters, thine elder and thy y	Eze 16:61	6996
the y of them said to his father,	Lk 15:12	3501
not many days after the y son	Lk 15:13	3501
among you, let him be as the y	Lk 22:26	3501
her, The elder shall serve the y	Rom 9:12	1640
and the y men as brethren	1Ti 5:1	3501
the y as sisters, with all purity	1Ti 5:2	3501
But the y widows refuse	1Ti 5:11	3501
therefore that the y women marry	1Ti 5:14	3501
Likewise, ye y, submit yourselves	1Pet 5:5	3501

YOUNGEST

the y is this day with our father	Gen 42:13	6996
except your y brother come hither	Gen 42:15	6996
But bring your y brother unto me	Gen 42:20	6996
the y is this day with our father	Gen 42:32	6996
bring your y brother unto me	Gen 42:34	6996
the y according to his youth	Gen 43:33	6810
cup, in the sack's mouth of the y	Gen 44:2	6996
at the eldest, and left at the y	Gen 44:12	6996
Except your y brother come down	Gen 44:23	6996
if our y brother be with us, then	Gen 44:26	6996
except our y brother be with us	Gen 44:26	6996
in his y son shall he set up the	Josh 6:26	6810
the y son of Jerubbaal was left	Judg 9:5	6996
said, There remaineth yet the y	1Sa 16:11	6996
And David was the y	1Sa 17:14	6996
gates thereof in his y son Segub	1Kin 16:34	6810
save Jehoahaz, the y of his sons	2Chr 21:17	6996
his y son king in his stead	2Chr 22:1	6996

YOUR

then y eyes shall be opened, and	Gen 3:5
into y hand are they delivered	Gen 9:2
surely y blood of y lives will	Gen 9:5
you, and with y seed after you	Gen 9:9
the flesh of y foreskin	Gen 17:11
every man child in y generations	Gen 17:12
my covenant shall be in y flesh	Gen 17:13
you, be fetched, and wash y feet	Gen 18:4
of bread, and comfort ye y hearts	Gen 18:5
are ye come to y servant	Gen 18:5
into y servant's house, and tarry	Gen 19:2
tarry all night, and wash y feet	Gen 19:2
rise up early, and go on y ways	Gen 19:2
ye to them as is good in y eyes	Gen 19:8
If it be y mind that I should	Gen 23:8
I see y father's countenance,	Gen 31:5
my power I have served y father	Gen 31:6
y father hath deceived me, and	Gen 31:7
taken away the cattle of y father	Gen 31:9
but the God of y father spake	Gen 31:29
Shechem longeth for y daughter	Gen 34:8
give y daughters unto us, and take	Gen 34:9
Let me find grace in y eyes	Gen 34:11
we will take y daughters to us,	Gen 34:16
and be clean, and change y garments	Gen 35:2
y sheaves stood round about, and	Gen 37:7
except y youngest brother come	Gen 42:15
you, and let him fetch y brother	Gen 42:16
that y words may be proved,	Gen 42:16
let one of y brethren be bound in	Gen 42:19
be bound in the house of y prison	Gen 42:19
corn for the famine of y houses	Gen 42:19
But bring y youngest brother unto	Gen 42:20
so shall y words be verified, and	Gen 42:20
leave one of y brethren here with	Gen 42:33
for the famine of y households	Gen 42:33
bring y youngest brother unto me	Gen 42:34
so will I deliver you y brother	Gen 42:34
except y brother be with you	Gen 43:3
except y brother be with you	Gen 43:5
saying, Is y father yet alive	Gen 43:7
would say, Bring y brother down	Gen 43:7
fruits in the land in y vessels	Gen 43:11
And take double money in y hand	Gen 43:12
again in the mouth of y sacks	Gen 43:12
carry it again in y hand	Gen 43:12
Take also y brother, and arise, go	Gen 43:13
he may send away y other brother	Gen 43:14
y God, and the God of y father,	Gen 43:23
given you treasure in y sacks	Gen 43:23
I had y money	Gen 43:23
Is y father well, the old man of	Gen 43:27
Is this y younger brother, of	Gen 43:29
let it be according unto y words	Gen 44:10
get you up in peace unto y father	Gen 44:17
Except y youngest brother come	Gen 44:23
And he said, I am Joseph y brother	Gen 45:4
to save y lives by a great	Gen 45:7
y eyes see, and the eyes of my	Gen 45:12
lade y beasts, and go, get you	Gen 45:17
take y father and y households,	Gen 45:18
land of Egypt for y little ones	Gen 45:19
for y wives, and bring y father	Gen 45:19
Also regard not y stuff	Gen 45:20
shall say, What is y occupation	Gen 46:33
brethren, What is y occupation	Gen 47:3
And Joseph said, Give y cattle	Gen 47:16
and I will give you for y cattle	Gen 47:16
this day and y land for Pharaoh	Gen 47:23
and four parts shall be y own	Gen 47:24
for y food, and for them of y	Gen 47:24
and for food for y little ones	Gen 47:24
again unto the land of y fathers	Gen 48:21
and hearken unto Israel y father	Gen 49:2
now I have found grace in y eyes	Gen 50:4
nourish you, and y little ones	Gen 50:21
The God of y fathers hath sent me	Ex 3:13
Israel, The LORD God of y fathers	Ex 3:15
them, The LORD God of y fathers	Ex 3:16
and ye shall put them upon y sons	Ex 3:22
y sons, and upon y daughters	Ex 3:22
get you unto y burdens	Ex 5:4
yet not ought of y work shall be	Ex 5:11
them, saying, Fulfil y works	Ex 5:13
y daily tasks, as when there was	Ex 5:13
y task in making brick both	Ex 5:14
from y bricks of y daily task	Ex 5:19
know that I am the LORD y God	Ex 6:7
sacrifice to y God in the land	Ex 8:25
the LORD y God in the wilderness	Ex 8:28
them, Go, serve the LORD y God	Ex 10:8
will let you go, and y little ones	Ex 10:10
sinned against the LORD y God	Ex 10:16
once, and intreat the LORD y God	Ex 10:17
only let y flocks and y herds	Ex 10:24
let y little ones also go with	Ex 10:24
shall make y count for the lamb	Ex 12:4
Y lamb shall be without blemish,	Ex 12:5
with y loins girded, y shoes	Ex 12:11
girded, y shoes on y feet	Ex 12:11
feet, and y staff in y hand	Ex 12:11
the LORD throughout y generations	Ex 12:14
put away leaven out of y houses	Ex 12:15
selfsame day have I brought y	Ex 12:17
shall ye observe this day in y	Ex 12:17
be no leaven found in y houses	Ex 12:19
in all y habitations shall ye eat	Ex 12:20
a lamb according to y families	Ex 12:21
in unto y houses to smite you	Ex 12:23
when y children shall say unto	Ex 12:26
Also take y flocks and y herds,	Ex 12:32
for you, and ye shall hold y peace	Ex 14:14
for that he heareth y murmurings	Ex 16:7
for that the LORD heareth y	Ex 16:8
y murmurings are not against us,	Ex 16:8
for he hath heard y murmurings	Ex 16:9
know that I am the LORD y God	Ex 16:12
to the number of y persons	Ex 16:16
it to be kept for y generations	Ex 16:32
to be kept for y generations	Ex 16:33
come not at y wives	Ex 19:15
his fear may be before y faces	Ex 20:20
y wives shall be widows, and y	Ex 22:24
widows, and y children fatherless	Ex 22:24
will not pardon y transgressions	Ex 23:21
And ye shall serve the LORD y God	Ex 23:25
of the land into y hand	Ex 23:31
burnt offering throughout y	Ex 29:42
the LORD throughout y generations	Ex 30:8
upon it throughout y generations	Ex 30:10
to make an atonement for y souls	Ex 30:15
to make an atonement for y souls	Ex 30:16
unto me throughout y generations	Ex 30:31
and you throughout y generations	Ex 31:13
which are in the ears of y wives	Ex 32:2
of y sons, and of y daughters,	Ex 32:2
I will multiply y seed as the	Ex 32:13
spoken of will I give unto y seed	Ex 32:13
shall make an atonement for y sin	Ex 32:30
Thrice in the year shall all y	Ex 34:23
y habitations upon the sabbath	Ex 35:3
ye shall bring y offering of the	Lev 1:2
be a perpetual statute for y	Lev 3:17
throughout all y dwellings	Lev 3:17
in y generations concerning the	Lev 6:18
of beast, in any of y dwellings	Lev 7:26
sacrifices of y peace offerings	Lev 7:32
until the days of y consecration	Lev 8:33
carry y brethren from before the	Lev 10:4
his sons, Uncover not y heads	Lev 10:6
heads, neither rend y clothes	Lev 10:6
but let y brethren, the whole	Lev 10:6
for ever throughout y generations	Lev 10:9
For I am the LORD y God	Lev 11:44
of the land of Egypt, to be y God	Lev 11:45
house of the land of y possession	Lev 14:34
month, ye shall afflict y souls	Lev 16:29
it be one of y own country	Lev 16:29
from all y sins before the LORD	Lev 16:30
you, and ye shall afflict y souls	Lev 16:31
to make an atonement for y souls	Lev 17:11
it be one of y own country	Lev 17:15
unto them, I am the LORD y God	Lev 18:2
I am the LORD y God	Lev 18:4
neither any of y own nation	Lev 18:26
I am the LORD y God	Lev 18:30
for I the LORD y God am holy	Lev 19:2
I am the LORD y God	Lev 19:3
I am the LORD y God	Lev 19:4
ye shall offer it at y own will	Lev 19:5
ye reap the harvest of y land	Lev 19:9
I am the LORD y God	Lev 19:10
I am the LORD y God	Lev 19:25
not round the corners of y heads	Lev 19:27
cuttings in y flesh for the dead	Lev 19:28
I am the LORD y God	Lev 19:31
sojourn with thee in y land	Lev 19:33
I am the LORD y God	Lev 19:34
I am the LORD y God, which	Lev 19:36
for I am the LORD y God	Lev 20:7
I am the LORD y God, which have	Lev 20:24
ye shall not make y souls	Lev 20:25
all y seed among y generations	Lev 22:3
Ye shall offer at y own will a	Lev 22:19
any offering thereof in y land	Lev 22:24
bread of y God of any of these	Lev 22:25
the LORD, offer it at y own will	Lev 22:29
of the land of Egypt, to be y God	Lev 22:33
of the LORD in all y dwellings	Lev 23:3
of y harvest unto the priest	Lev 23:10
brought an offering unto y God	Lev 23:14
y generations in all y	Lev 23:14
Ye shall bring out of y	Lev 23:17
all y dwellings throughout y	Lev 23:21
ye reap the harvest of y land	Lev 23:22
I am the LORD y God	Lev 23:22
and ye shall afflict y souls	Lev 23:27
for you before the LORD y God	Lev 23:28
y generations in all y	Lev 23:31
rest, and ye shall afflict y souls	Lev 23:32
shall ye celebrate y sabbath	Lev 23:32
y gifts, and beside all y vows	Lev 23:38
beside all y freewill offerings,	Lev 23:38
before the LORD y God seven days	Lev 23:40
statute for ever in y generations	Lev 23:41
That y generations may know that	Lev 23:43
I am the LORD y God	Lev 23:43
statute for ever in y generations	Lev 24:3
as for one of y own country	Lev 24:22
for I am the LORD y God	Lev 24:22
sound throughout all y land	Lev 25:9
for I am the LORD y God	Lev 25:17
her fruit, and ye shall eat y fill	Lev 25:19
in all the land of y possession	Lev 25:24
I am the LORD y God, which	Lev 25:38
land of Canaan, and to be y God	Lev 25:38
you, which they begat in y land	Lev 25:45
and they shall be y possession	Lev 25:45
for y children after you, to	Lev 25:46
they shall be y bondmen for ever	Lev 25:46
but over y brethren the children	Lev 25:46
I am the LORD y God	Lev 25:55
up any image of stone in y land	Lev 26:1
for I am the LORD y God	Lev 26:1
y threshing shall reach unto the	Lev 26:5
ye shall eat y bread to the full,	Lev 26:5
full, and dwell in y land safely	Lev 26:5
shall the sword go through y land	Lev 26:6
And ye shall chase y enemies	Lev 26:7
y enemies shall fall before you	Lev 26:8
walk among you, and will be y God	Lev 26:12
I am the LORD y God, which	Lev 26:13
I have broken the bands of y yoke	Lev 26:13
or if y soul abhor my judgments,	Lev 26:15
and ye shall sow y seed in vain	Lev 26:16
for y enemies shall eat it	Lev 26:16
shall be slain before y enemies	Lev 26:17
you seven times more for y sins	Lev 26:18
I will break the pride of y power	Lev 26:19
I will make y heaven as iron, and	Lev 26:19
as iron, and y earth as brass	Lev 26:19
y strength shall be spent in vain	Lev 26:20
for y land shall not yield her	Lev 26:20
upon you according to y sins	Lev 26:21
which shall rob you of y children	Lev 26:22

and destroy y cattle Lev 26:22
y high ways shall be desolate Lev 26:22
you yet seven times for y sins Lev 26:24
gathered together within y cities Lev 26:25
have broken the staff of y bread Lev 26:26
shall bake y bread in one oven Lev 26:26
you y bread again by weight Lev 26:26
you seven times for y sins Lev 26:28
ye shall eat the flesh of y sons Lev 26:29
the flesh of y daughters shall ye Lev 26:29
And I will destroy y high places Lev 26:30
high places, and cut down y images Lev 26:30
cast y carcases upon the carcases Lev 26:30
upon the carcases of y idols Lev 26:30
I will make y cities waste, and Lev 26:31
and bring y sanctuaries unto Lev 26:31
the savour of y sweet odours Lev 26:31
y enemies which dwell therein Lev 26:32
y land shall be desolate Lev 26:33
be desolate, and y cities waste Lev 26:33
and ye be in y enemies' land Lev 26:34
it did not rest in y sabbaths Lev 26:35
power to stand before y enemies Lev 26:37
the land of y enemies shall eat Lev 26:38
iniquity in y enemies' lands Lev 26:39
If any man of you or of y Num 9:10
for ever throughout y generations Num 10:8
if ye go to war in y land against Num 10:9
remembered before the LORD y God Num 10:9
ye shall be saved from y enemies Num 10:9
Also in the day of y gladness Num 10:10
in y solemn days, and in the Num 10:10
and in the beginnings of y months Num 10:10
trumpets over y burnt offerings Num 10:10
sacrifices of y peace offerings Num 10:10
you for a memorial before y God Num 10:10
I am the LORD y God Num 10:10
until it come out at y nostrils Num 11:20
Y carcases shall fall in this Num 14:29
you, according to y whole number Num 14:29
But y little ones, which ye said Num 14:31
y carcases, they shall fall in Num 14:32
y children shall wander in the Num 14:33
bear y whoredoms, Num 14:33
until y carcases be wasted in the Num 14:33
year, shall ye bear y iniquities Num 14:34
be not smitten before y enemies Num 14:42
into the land of y habitations Num 15:2
or in y solemn feasts, to make a Num 15:3
be among you in y generations Num 15:14
for ever in y generations Num 15:15
of y dough for an heave offering Num 15:20
Of the first of y dough ye shall Num 15:21
heave offering in y generations Num 15:21
henceforward among y generations Num 15:23
ye seek not after y own heart Num 15:39
y own eyes, after which ye use to Num 15:39
and be holy unto y God Num 15:40
I am the LORD y God, which Num 15:41
of the land of Egypt, to be y God Num 15:41
I am the LORD y God Num 15:41
bear the iniquity of y priesthood Num 18:1
I have taken y brethren the Num 18:6
thy sons with thee shall keep y Num 18:7
I have given y priest's office Num 18:7
for ever throughout y generations Num 18:23
you from them for y inheritance Num 18:26
this y heave offering shall be Num 18:27
unto the LORD of all y tithes Num 18:28
Out of all y gifts ye shall offer Num 18:29
every place, ye and y households Num 18:31
for it is y reward for y Num 18:31
of Balak, Get you into y land Num 22:13
in the beginnings of y months ye Num 28:11
after y weeks be out, ye shall Num 28:26
and ye shall afflict y souls Num 29:7
in y set feasts, beside y vows Num 29:39
y freewill offerings, for y Num 29:39
for y meat offerings, and for y Num 29:39
and for y peace offerings Num 29:39
y captives on the third day, and Num 31:19
And purify all y raiment, and all Num 31:20
ye shall wash y clothes on the Num 31:24
Shall y brethren go to war, and Num 32:6
Thus did y fathers, when I sent Num 32:8
are risen up in y fathers' stead Num 32:14
this land shall be y possession Num 32:22
be sure y sin will find you out Num 32:23
you cities for y little ones Num 32:24
little ones, and folds for y sheep Num 32:24
hath proceeded out of y mouth Num 32:24
an inheritance among y families Num 33:54
of y fathers ye shall inherit Num 33:54
y eyes, and thorns in y sides Num 33:55
Then y south quarter shall be Num 34:3
y south border shall be the Num 34:3
y border shall turn from the Num 34:4
this shall be y west border Num 34:6
And this shall be y north border Num 34:7
out y border unto the entrance of Num 34:8
this shall be y north border Num 34:9
ye shall point out y east border Num 34:10
this shall be y land with the Num 34:12
y generations in all y Num 35:29
take y journey, and go to the Deut 1:7
the LORD sware unto y fathers Deut 1:8
The LORD y God hath multiplied Deut 1:10
(The LORD God of y fathers make Deut 1:11
I myself alone bear y cumbrance Deut 1:12
and y burden, and y strife Deut 1:12
and known among y tribes, and I Deut 1:13
So I took the chief of y tribes Deut 1:15
tens, and officers among y tribes Deut 1:15
I charged y judges at that time, Deut 1:16
the causes between y brethren Deut 1:16
the commandment of the LORD y God. Deut 1:26
And ye murmured in y tents Deut 1:27
The LORD y God which goeth before Deut 1:30
for you in Egypt before y eyes Deut 1:30
ye did not believe the LORD y God Deut 1:32
out a place to pitch y tents in Deut 1:33
LORD heard the voice of y words Deut 1:34
I sware to give unto y fathers Deut 1:35
was angry with me for y sakes Deut 1:37
Moreover y little ones, which ye Deut 1:39
y children, which in that day had Deut 1:39
you, and take y journey into the Deut 1:40
ye be smitten before y enemies Deut 1:42
LORD would not hearken to y voice Deut 1:45
to pass through the coast of y Deut 2:4
take y journey, and pass over the Deut 2:24
The LORD y God hath given you Deut 3:18
y brethren the children of Israel Deut 3:18
But y wives, and y little ones, Deut 3:19
y cattle, (for I know that ye Deut 3:19
shall abide in y cities which I Deut 3:19
have given rest unto y brethren Deut 3:20
LORD y God hath given them beyond Deut 3:20
have seen all that the LORD y God Deut 3:21
for the LORD y God he shall fight Deut 3:22
was wroth with me for y sakes Deut 3:26
LORD God of y fathers giveth you Deut 4:1
LORD y God which I command you Deut 4:2
Y eyes have seen what the LORD Deut 4:3
that did cleave unto the LORD y Deut 4:4
for this is y wisdom and y Deut 4:6
was angry with me for y sakes Deut 4:21
the covenant of the LORD y God Deut 4:23
shall not prolong y days upon it Deut 4:26
according to all that the LORD y Deut 4:34
for you in Egypt before y eyes Deut 4:34
which I speak in y ears this day Deut 5:1
y assembly in the mount out of Deut 5:22
even all the heads of y tribes Deut 5:23
heads of y tribes, and y elders Deut 5:23
LORD heard the voice of y words Deut 5:28
them, Get you into y tents again Deut 5:30
the LORD y God hath commanded you Deut 5:32
the LORD y God hath commanded you Deut 5:33
that ye may prolong y days in the Deut 5:33
which the LORD y God commanded to. Deut 6:1
Ye shall not tempt the LORD y God Deut 6:16
commandments of the LORD y God Deut 6:17
which he had sworn unto y fathers Deut 7:8
among you, or among y cattle Deut 7:14
the LORD sware unto y fathers Deut 8:1
the LORD destroyeth before y face Deut 8:20
unto the voice of the LORD y God Deut 8:20
had sinned against the LORD y God Deut 9:16
and brake them before y eyes Deut 9:17
because of all y sins which ye Deut 9:18
And I took y sin, the calf which Deut 9:21
the commandment of the LORD y God. Deut 9:23
therefore the foreskin of y heart Deut 10:16
For the LORD y God is God of gods Deut 10:17
for I speak not with y children Deut 11:2
chastisement of the LORD y God Deut 11:2
But y eyes have seen all the Deut 11:7
ye may prolong y days in the land Deut 11:9
unto y fathers to give unto them Deut 11:9
this day, to love the LORD y God Deut 11:13
all y heart and with all y soul Deut 11:13
rain of y land in his due season Deut 11:14
that y heart be not deceived, and Deut 11:16
lay up these my words in y heart Deut 11:18
in y soul, and bind them for a Deut 11:18
bind them for a sign upon y hand Deut 11:18
be as frontlets between y eyes Deut 11:18
And ye shall teach them y children Deut 11:19
That y days may be multiplied, and Deut 11:21
and the days of y children Deut 11:21
sware unto y fathers to give them Deut 11:21
do them, to love the LORD y God Deut 11:22
place whereon the soles of y feet Deut 11:24
uttermost sea shall y coast be Deut 11:24
for the LORD y God shall lay the Deut 11:25
commandments of the LORD y God Deut 11:27
commandments of the LORD y God Deut 11:28
which the LORD y God giveth you Deut 11:31
not do so unto the LORD y God Deut 12:4
y God shall choose out of all Deut 12:5
God shall choose out of all y Deut 12:5
ye shall bring y burnt offerings Deut 12:6
y sacrifices, and y tithes, and Deut 12:6
and heave offerings of y hand Deut 12:6
hand, and y vows, and y freewill Deut 12:6
of y herds and of y flocks Deut 12:6
shall eat before the LORD y God Deut 12:7
in all that ye put y hand unto Deut 12:7
y households, wherein the LORD Deut 12:7
which the LORD y God giveth you Deut 12:9
LORD y God giveth you to inherit Deut 12:10
from all y enemies round about Deut 12:10
y God shall choose to cause his Deut 12:11
y burnt offerings, and y Deut 12:11
y tithes, and the heave offering Deut 12:11
and the heave offering of y hand Deut 12:11
all y choice vows which ye vow Deut 12:11
rejoice before the LORD y God Deut 12:12
y sons, and y daughters, and Deut 12:12
and y menservants, and y Deut 12:12
the Levite that is within y gates Deut 12:12
for the LORD y God proveth you, Deut 13:3
LORD y God with all y heart Deut 13:3
and with all y soul Deut 13:3
shall walk after the LORD y God Deut 13:4
turn you away from the LORD y God Deut 13:5
the children of the LORD y God Deut 14:1
between y eyes for the dead Deut 14:1
day unto battle against y enemies Deut 20:3
let not y hearts faint, fear not, Deut 20:3
For the LORD y God is he that Deut 20:4
fight for you against y enemies Deut 20:4
ye sin against the LORD y God Deut 20:18
sold unto y enemies for bondmen Deut 28:68
all that the LORD did before y Deut 29:2
y clothes are not waxen old upon Deut 29:5
know that I am the LORD y God Deut 29:6
all of you before the LORD y God Deut 29:10
y captains of y tribes Deut 29:10
y elders, and y officers, with Deut 29:10
Y little ones, y wives, and thy Deut 29:11
of y children that shall rise up Deut 29:22
not prolong y days upon the land Deut 30:18
shall give them up before y face Deut 31:5
may learn, and fear the LORD y God Deut 31:12
and learn to fear the LORD y God Deut 31:13
of the covenant of the LORD y God Deut 31:26
me all the elders of y tribes Deut 31:28
y officers, that I may speak Deut 31:28
anger through the work of y hands Deut 31:29
whom y fathers feared not Deut 32:17
and help you, and be y protection Deut 32:38
Set y hearts unto all the words Deut 32:46
which ye shall command y children Deut 32:46
because it is y life Deut 32:47
shall prolong y days in the land Deut 32:47
sole of y foot shall tread upon Josh 1:3
down of the sun, shall be y coast Josh 1:4
which the LORD y God giveth you Josh 1:11
The LORD y God hath given you Josh 1:13
Y wives, y little ones, and Josh 1:14
y cattle, shall remain in the Josh 1:14
pass before y brethren armed Josh 1:14
LORD have given y brethren rest Josh 1:15
which the LORD y God giveth them Josh 1:15
unto the land of y possession Josh 1:15
that y terror is fallen upon us, Josh 2:9
for the LORD y God, he is God in Josh 2:11
and afterward may ye go y way Josh 2:16
she said, According unto y words Josh 2:21
of the covenant of the LORD y God Josh 3:3
then ye shall remove from y place Josh 3:3
hear the words of the LORD y God Josh 3:9
y God into the midst of Jordan Josh 4:5
that when y children ask their Josh 4:6
When y children shall ask their Josh 4:21
Then ye shall let y children know Josh 4:22
For the LORD y God dried up the Josh 4:23
as the LORD y God did to the Red Josh 4:23
fear the LORD y God for ever Josh 4:24
nor make any noise with y voice Josh 6:10
any word proceed out of y mouth Josh 6:10
be brought according to y tribes Josh 7:14
for the LORD y God will deliver Josh 8:7
God will deliver it into y hand Josh 8:7
say unto them, We are y servants Josh 9:11
not, but pursue after y enemies Josh 10:19
for the LORD y God hath delivered Josh 10:19
hath delivered them into y hand Josh 10:19
put y feet upon the necks of Josh 10:24
y enemies against whom ye fight Josh 10:25
this shall be y south coast Josh 15:4
which the LORD God of y fathers Josh 18:3
they shall be y refuge from the Josh 20:3
Ye have not left y brethren these Josh 22:3
the commandment of the LORD y God. Josh 22:3
now the LORD y God hath given Josh 22:4
hath given rest unto y brethren Josh 22:4
ye, and get you unto y tents Josh 22:4
and unto the land of y possession Josh 22:4
you, to love the LORD y God Josh 22:5
all y heart and with all y soul Josh 22:5
with much riches unto y tents Josh 22:8
divide the spoil of y enemies Josh 22:8
of y enemies with y brethren Josh 22:8
if the land of y possession be Josh 22:19
In time to come y children might Josh 22:24
so shall y children make our Josh 22:25
that y children may not say to Josh 22:27
y God hath done unto all these Josh 23:3
for the LORD y God is he that Josh 23:3
to be an inheritance for y tribes Josh 23:4
And the LORD y God, he shall expel Josh 23:5
and drive them from out of y sight Josh 23:5
as the LORD y God hath promised Josh 23:5
But cleave unto the LORD y God Josh 23:8
for the LORD y God, he it is that Josh 23:10
that ye love the LORD y God Josh 23:11
for a certainty that the LORD y Josh 23:13
y sides, and thorns in y eyes Josh 23:13
the LORD y God hath given you Josh 23:13
all y hearts and in all y souls Josh 23:14
LORD y God spake concerning you Josh 23:14
which the LORD y God promised you Josh 23:15
the LORD y God hath given you Josh 23:15
the covenant of the LORD y God Josh 23:16
Y fathers dwelt on the other side Josh 24:2
I took y father Abraham from the Josh 24:3
I brought y fathers out of Egypt Josh 24:6
after y fathers with chariots Josh 24:6
y eyes have seen what I have done Josh 24:7
and I gave them into y hand Josh 24:8
and I delivered them into y hand Josh 24:11
put away the gods which y fathers Josh 24:14
whether the gods which y fathers Josh 24:15
y transgressions nor y sins Josh 24:19
incline y heart unto the LORD God Josh 24:23
unto you, lest ye deny y God Josh 24:27
land which I sware unto y fathers Judg 2:1
shall be as thorns in y sides Judg 2:3
for the LORD hath delivered y Judg 3:28

enemies the Moabites into y hand .... Judg 3:28
unto you, I am the LORD y God .... Judg 6:10
into y hand the host of Midian .... Judg 7:15
God hath delivered into y hands .... Judg 8:3
then I will tear y flesh with the .... Judg 8:7
that I am y bone and y flesh .... Judg 9:2
come and put y trust in my shadow .... Judg 9:15
Shechem, because he is y brother .... Judg 9:18
you in the time of y tribulation .... Judg 10:14
them before me, shall I be y head .... Judg 11:9
the LORD is y way wherein ye go .... Judg 18:6
God hath given it into y hands .... Judg 18:10
of bread, and afterward go y way .... Judg 19:5
to morrow get you early on y way .... Judg 19:9
it, take advice, and speak y minds .... Judg 19:30
give here y advice and counsel .... Judg 20:7
womb, that they may be y husbands .... Ruth 1:11
again, my daughters, go y way .... Ruth 1:12
for it grieveth me much for y .... Ruth 1:13
not arrogancy come out of y mouth 1Sa 2:3
for I hear of y evil dealings by 1Sa 2:23
was on you all, and on y lords 1Sa 6:4
ye shall make images of y emerods 1Sa 6:5
images of y mice that mar the 1Sa 6:5
off y gods, and from off y land 1Sa 6:5
then do ye harden y hearts 1Sa 6:6
unto the LORD with all y hearts 1Sa 7:3
prepare y hearts unto the LORD, ... 1Sa 7:3
He will take y sons, and appoint 1Sa 8:11
he will take y daughters to be 1Sa 8:13
And he will take y fields, and y 1Sa 8:14
y oliveyards, even the best of 1Sa 8:14
he will take the tenth of y seed 1Sa 8:15
of y vineyards, and give to his 1Sa 8:15
And he will take y menservants 1Sa 8:16
y maidservants, and y goodliest 1Sa 8:16
y asses, and put them to his work 1Sa 8:16
He will take the tenth of y sheep 1Sa 8:17
cry out in that day because of y 1Sa 8:18
ye have this day rejected y God 1Sa 10:19
you out of all y adversities 1Sa 10:19
adversities and y tribulations 1Sa 10:19
before the LORD by y tribes 1Sa 10:19
by y tribes, and by y thousands 1Sa 10:19
I may thrust out all y right eyes 1Sa 11:2
I have hearkened unto y voice in 1Sa 12:1
that brought y fathers up out of 1Sa 12:6
he did to you and to y fathers 1Sa 12:7
y fathers cried unto the LORD, ... 1Sa 12:8
which brought forth y fathers out 1Sa 12:8
hand of y enemies on every side 1Sa 12:11
when the LORD y God was y king 1Sa 12:12
continue following the LORD y God 1Sa 12:14
you, as it was against y fathers 1Sa 12:15
the LORD will do before y eyes 1Sa 12:16
see that y wickedness is great, ... 1Sa 12:17
serve the LORD with all y heart 1Sa 12:20
him in truth with all y heart 1Sa 12:24
be consumed, both ye and y king 1Sa 12:25
come out to set y battle in array 1Sa 17:8
me, then will we be y servants 1Sa 17:9
because ye have not kept y master 1Sa 26:16
ornaments of gold upon y apparel 2Sa 1:24
shewed this kindness unto y lord 2Sa 2:5
Therefore now let y hands be 2Sa 2:7
for y master Saul is dead, and 2Sa 2:7
Rend y clothes, and gird you with 2Sa 3:31
now require his blood of y hand 2Sa 4:11
Jericho until y beards be grown 2Sa 10:5
y two sons with you, Ahimaaz thy 2Sa 15:27
with you the servants of y lord 1Kin 1:33
Let y heart therefore be perfect 1Kin 8:61
ye or y children, and will not 1Kin 9:6
away y heart after their gods 1Kin 11:2
heavy yoke, I will add to y yoke 1Kin 12:11
My father made y yoke heavy 1Kin 12:14
heavy, and I will add to y yoke 1Kin 12:14
to y tents, O Israel 1Kin 12:16
nor fight against y brethren the 1Kin 12:24
And call ye on the name of y gods 1Kin 18:24
and call on the name of y gods 1Kin 18:25
hold ye y peace 2Kin 2:3
ye, and y cattle, and y beasts 2Kin 3:17
the Moabites also into y hand 2Kin 3:18
And Jehu said, If it be y minds 2Kin 9:15
seeing y master's sons are with 2Kin 10:2
meetest of y master's sons, and 2Kin 10:3
fight for y master's house 2Kin 10:3
heads of the men y master's sons 2Kin 10:6
have brought into y hands escape 2Kin 10:24
no more money of y acquaintance 2Kin 12:7
saying, Turn ye from y evil ways 2Kin 17:13
law which I commanded y fathers 2Kin 17:13
But the LORD y God ye shall fear 2Kin 17:39
out of the hand of all y enemies 2Kin 17:39
away to a land like y own land 2Kin 18:32
Thus shall ye say to y master 2Kin 19:6
the passover unto the LORD y God 2Kin 23:21
y brethren, that ye may bring up 1Chr 15:12
Canaan, the lot of y inheritance 1Chr 16:18
Jericho until y beards be grown 1Chr 19:5
Is not the LORD y God with you 1Chr 22:18
Now set y heart and 1Chr 22:19
y soul to seek the LORD y God 1Chr 22:19
y soul to seek the LORD y God 1Chr 22:19
commandments of the LORD y God 1Chr 28:8
for y children after you for ever 1Chr 28:8
Now bless the LORD y God 1Chr 29:20
you, I will put more to y yoke 2Chr 10:11
My father made y yoke heavy 2Chr 10:14
every man to y tents, O Israel, ... 2Chr 10:16
up, nor fight against y brethren 2Chr 11:4
against the LORD God of y fathers 2Chr 13:12
and let not y hands be weak 2Chr 15:7
for y work shall be rewarded 2Chr 15:7
shall be delivered into y hand 2Chr 18:14
soever shall come to you of y 2Chr 19:10
come upon you, and upon y brethren 2Chr 19:10
Believe in the LORD y God 2Chr 20:20
house of y God from year to year 2Chr 24:5
because the LORD God of y fathers 2Chr 28:9
hath delivered them into y hand 2Chr 28:9
you, sins against the LORD y God 2Chr 28:10
have taken captive of y brethren 2Chr 28:11
of the LORD God of y fathers 2Chr 29:5
to hissing, as ye see with y eyes 2Chr 29:8
And be not ye like y fathers 2Chr 30:7
like y brethren, which trespassed 2Chr 30:7
as y fathers were, but yield 2Chr 30:8
and serve the LORD y God, that the 2Chr 30:8
y brethren and y children shall 2Chr 30:9
for the LORD y God is gracious and 2Chr 30:9
that y God should be able to 2Chr 32:14
how much less shall y God deliver 2Chr 32:15
I have appointed for y fathers 2Chr 33:8
not be a burden upon y shoulders 2Chr 35:3
serve now the LORD y God, and his 2Chr 35:3
by the houses of y fathers 2Chr 35:4
after y courses, according to the 2Chr 35:4
fathers of y brethren the people 2Chr 35:5
prepare y brethren, that they may 2Chr 35:6
for we seek y God, as ye do .... Ezr 4:2
y companions the Apharsachites, ... Ezr 6:6
of y God which is in Jerusalem .... Ezr 7:17
that do after the will of y God .... Ezr 7:18
unto the LORD God of y fathers .... Ezr 8:28
Now therefore give not y .... Ezr 9:12
take their daughters unto y sons .... Ezr 9:12
to y children for ever .... Ezr 9:12
unto the LORD God of y fathers .... Ezr 10:11
terrible, and fight for y brethren .... Neh 4:14
y sons, and y daughters .... Neh 4:14
y wives, and y houses .... Neh 4:14
and will ye even sell y brethren .... Neh 5:8
day is holy unto the LORD y God .... Neh 8:9
Go y way, eat the fat, and drink .... Neh 8:10
the joy of the LORD is y strength .... Neh 8:10
Hold y peace, for the day is holy .... Neh 8:11
and bless the LORD y God for ever .... Neh 9:5
Did not y fathers thus, and did .... Neh 13:18
Ye shall not give y daughters .... Neh 13:25
take their daughters unto y sons .... Neh 13:25
a reward for me of y substance .... Job 6:22
but what doth y arguing reprove .... Job 6:25
and ye dig a pit for y friend .... Job 6:27
ye would altogether hold y peace .... Job 13:5
and it should be y wisdom .... Job 13:5
Y remembrances are like unto .... Job 13:12
y bodies to bodies of clay .... Job 13:12
Hold y peace, let me alone, that .... Job 13:13
and my declaration with y ears .... Job 13:17
if y soul were in my soul's stead .... Job 16:4
of my lips should asswage y grief .... Job 16:5
and reputed vile in y sight .... Job 18:3
let this be y consolations .... Job 21:2
lay y hand upon y mouth .... Job 21:5
and lay y hand upon y mouth .... Job 21:5
I know y thoughts, and the devices .... Job 21:27
seeing in y answers there .... Job 21:34
Behold, I waited for y words .... Job 32:11
I gave ear to y reasons, whilst .... Job 32:11
will I answer him with y speeches .... Job 32:14
I deal with you after y folly .... Job 42:8
with y own heart upon y bed .... Ps 4:4
and put y trust in the LORD .... Ps 4:5
Flee as a bird to y mountain .... Ps 11:1
y heart shall live for ever .... Ps 22:26
Lift up y heads, O ye gates .... Ps 24:7
Lift up y heads, O ye gates .... Ps 24:9
and he shall strengthen y heart .... Ps 31:24
O clap y hands, all ye people .... Ps 47:1
violence of y hands in the earth .... Ps 58:2
Before y pots can feel the thorns .... Ps 58:9
pour out y heart before him .... Ps 62:8
set not y heart upon them .... Ps 62:10
y heart shall live that seek God .... Ps 69:32
Lift not up y horn on high .... Ps 75:5
Vow, and pay unto the LORD y God .... Ps 76:11
incline y ears to the words of my .... Ps 78:1
Harden not y heart, as in the .... Ps 95:8
When y fathers tempted me, proved .... Ps 95:9
Canaan, the lot of y inheritance .... Ps 105:11
more and more, you and y children .... Ps 115:14
Lift up y hands in the sanctuary, ... Ps 134:2
Put not y trust in princes, nor .... Ps 146:3
I also will laugh at y calamity .... Prov 1:26
I will mock when y fear cometh .... Prov 1:26
When y fear cometh as desolation, ... Prov 1:27
y destruction cometh as a .... Prov 1:27
Y country is desolate .... Is 1:7
y cities are burned with fire .... Is 1:7
y land, strangers devour it in .... Is 1:7
strangers devour it in y presence .... Is 1:7
multitude of y sacrifices unto me .... Is 1:11
who hath required this at y hand .... Is 1:12
Y new moons and y appointed .... Is 1:14
And when ye spread forth y hands .... Is 1:15
y hands are full of blood .... Is 1:15
put away the evil of y doings .... Is 1:16
though y sins be as scarlet, they .... Is 1:18
spoil of the poor is in y houses .... Is 3:14
and let him be y fear, and let him .... Is 8:13
y fear, and let him be y dread .... Is 8:13
and where will ye leave y glory .... Is 10:3
Is this y joyous city, whose .... Is 23:7
for y strength is laid waste .... Is 23:14
y covenant with death shall be .... Is 28:18
y agreement with hell shall not .... Is 28:18
lest y bands be made strong .... Is 28:22
deep sleep, and hath closed y eyes .... Is 29:10
y rulers, the seers hath he .... Is 29:10
Surely y turning of things upside .... Is 29:16
strength of Pharaoh be y shame .... Is 30:3
the shadow of Egypt y confusion .... Is 30:3
in confidence shall be y strength .... Is 30:15
which y own hands have made unto .... Is 31:7
and gird sackcloth upon y loins .... Is 32:11
y spoil shall be gathered like .... Is 33:4
y breath, as fire, shall devour .... Is 33:11
y God will come with vengeance, ... Is 35:4
away to a land like y own land .... Is 36:17
Thus shall ye say unto y master .... Is 37:6
comfort ye my people, saith y God .... Is 40:1
the cities of Judah, Behold y God .... Is 40:9
Lift up y eyes on high, and behold .... Is 40:26
Produce y cause, saith the LORD .... Is 41:21
bring forth y strong reasons, ... Is 41:21
of nothing, and y work of nought .... Is 41:24
is none that heareth y words .... Is 41:26
y redeemer, the Holy One of .... Is 43:14
For y sake I have sent to Babylon .... Is 43:14
y Holy One, the creator of Israel .... Is 43:15
the creator of Israel, y King .... Is 43:15
y carriages were heavy loaden .... Is 46:1
even to y old age I am he .... Is 46:4
bill of y mother's divorcement .... Is 50:1
for y iniquities have ye sold .... Is 50:1
for y transgressions is y .... Is 50:1
walk in the light of y fire .... Is 50:11
Look unto Abraham y father .... Is 51:2
Lift up y eyes to the heavens, and .... Is 51:6
God of Israel will be y rereward .... Is 52:12
and y labour for that which .... Is 55:2
let y soul delight itself in .... Is 55:2
Incline y ear, and come unto me .... Is 55:3
hear, and y soul shall live .... Is 55:3
my thoughts are not y thoughts .... Is 55:8
neither are y ways my ways, saith .... Is 55:8
so are my ways higher than y ways .... Is 55:9
and my thoughts than y thoughts .... Is 55:9
in the day of y fast ye find .... Is 58:3
pleasure, and exact all y labours .... Is 58:3
to make y voice to be heard on .... Is 58:4
But y iniquities have separated .... Is 59:2
y God, and y sins have hid his .... Is 59:2
For y hands are defiled with .... Is 59:3
blood, and y fingers with iniquity .... Is 59:3
y lips have spoken lies .... Is 59:3
lies, y tongue hath muttered .... Is 59:3
feed y flocks, and the sons of the .... Is 61:5
be y plowmen and y vinedressers .... Is 61:5
For y shame ye shall have double .... Is 61:7
Y iniquities, and the iniquities .... Is 65:7
iniquities of y fathers together .... Is 65:7
ye shall leave y name for a curse .... Is 65:15
Y brethren that hated you, that .... Is 66:5
but he shall appear to y joy .... Is 66:5
y heart shall rejoice .... Is 66:14
y bones shall flourish like an .... Is 66:14
they shall bring all y brethren .... Is 66:20
shall y seed and y name remain .... Is 66:22
What iniquity have y fathers .... Jer 2:5
with y children's children will I .... Jer 2:9
In vain have I smitten y children .... Jer 2:30
y own sword hath devoured y .... Jer 2:30
for an inheritance unto y fathers .... Jer 3:18
I will heal y backslidings .... Jer 3:22
Break up y fallow ground, and sow .... Jer 4:3
away the foreskins of y heart .... Jer 4:4
because of the evil of y doings .... Jer 4:4
and served strange gods in y land .... Jer 5:19
Y iniquities have turned away .... Jer 5:25
y sins have withholden good .... Jer 5:25
and ye shall find rest for y souls .... Jer 6:16
y burnt offerings are not .... Jer 6:20
nor y sacrifices sweet unto me .... Jer 6:20
the God of Israel, Amend y ways .... Jer 7:3
y doings, and I will cause you to .... Jer 7:3
amend y ways and y doings .... Jer 7:5
walk after other gods to y hurt .... Jer 7:6
the land that I gave to y fathers .... Jer 7:7
become a den of robbers in y eyes .... Jer 7:11
to y fathers, as I have done to .... Jer 7:14
as I have cast out all y brethren .... Jer 7:15
Put y burnt offerings unto y .... Jer 7:21
For I spake not unto y fathers .... Jer 7:22
Obey my voice, and I will be y God .... Jer 7:23
Since the day that y fathers came .... Jer 7:25
let y ear receive the word of his .... Jer 9:20
teach y daughters wailing, and .... Jer 9:20
Which I commanded y fathers in .... Jer 11:4
be my people, and I will be y God .... Jer 11:4
which I have sworn unto y fathers .... Jer 11:5
unto y fathers in the day that I .... Jer 11:7
they shall be ashamed of y .... Jer 12:13
Give glory to the LORD y God .... Jer 13:16
before y feet stumble upon the .... Jer 13:16
weep in secret places for y pride .... Jer 13:17
for y principalities shall come .... Jer 13:18
down, even the crown of y glory .... Jer 13:18
Lift up y eyes, and behold them .... Jer 13:20
cease out of this place in y eyes .... Jer 16:9
in y days, the voice of mirth, and .... Jer 16:9
Because y fathers have forsaken .... Jer 16:11
ye have done worse than y fathers .... Jer 16:12
not, neither ye nor y fathers .... Jer 16:13
and upon the horns of y altars .... Jer 17:1
of y houses on the sabbath day .... Jer 17:22
day, as I commanded y fathers .... Jer 17:22
make y ways and y doings good .... Jer 18:11
of war that are in y hands .... Jer 21:4
because of the evil of y doings .... Jer 21:12

to the fruit of y doings, saith Jer 21:14
upon you the evil of y doings Jer 23:2
y fathers, and cast you out of my Jer 23:39
nor inclined y ear to hear Jer 25:4
way, and from the evil of y doings Jer 25:5
to y fathers for ever and ever Jer 25:5
anger with the works of y hands Jer 25:6
works of y hands to y own hurt Jer 25:7
for the days of y slaughter Jer 25:34
of y dispersions are accomplished Jer 25:34
as ye have heard with y ears Jer 26:11
Therefore now amend y ways Jer 26:13
y doings, and obey the voice of Jer 26:13
obey the voice of the LORD y God Jer 26:13
As for me, behold, I am in y hand Jer 26:14
speak all these words in y ears Jer 26:15
Thus shall ye say unto y masters Jer 27:4
hearken not ye to y prophets Jer 27:9
nor to y diviners Jer 27:9
nor to y dreamers Jer 27:9
nor to y enchanters Jer 27:9
nor to y sorcerers Jer 27:9
to remove you far from y land Jer 27:10
Bring y necks under the yoke of Jer 27:12
Hearken not to the words of y Jer 27:16
and take wives for y sons, and give Jer 29:6
give y daughters to husbands, Jer 29:6
Let not y prophets and y Jer 29:8
neither hearken to y dreams which Jer 29:8
search for me with all y heart Jer 29:13
and I will turn away y captivity Jer 29:14
of y brethren that are not gone Jer 29:16
he shall slay them before y eyes Jer 29:21
be my people, and I will be y God Jer 30:22
I made a covenant with y fathers Jer 34:13
but y fathers hearkened not unto Jer 34:14
neither ye, nor y sons for ever Jer 35:6
but all y days ye shall dwell in Jer 35:7
amend y doings, and go not after Jer 35:15
have given to you and to y fathers Jer 35:15
but ye have not inclined y ear Jer 35:15
commandment of Jonadab y father Jer 35:18
Where are now y prophets which Jer 37:19
said, Behold, he is in y hand Jer 38:5
and oil, and put them in y vessels Jer 40:10
dwell in y cities that ye have Jer 40:10
y God according to y words Jer 42:4
present y supplication before him Jer 42:9
cause you to return to y own land Jer 42:12
obey the voice of the LORD y God Jer 42:13
If ye wholly set y faces to enter Jer 42:15
For ye dissembled in y hearts Jer 42:20
ye sent me unto the LORD y God Jer 42:20
the voice of the LORD y God Jer 42:21
neither they, ye, nor y fathers Jer 44:3
this great evil against y souls Jer 44:7
wrath with the works of y hands Jer 44:8
the wickedness of y fathers Jer 44:9
and y own wickedness, and the Jer 44:9
and the wickedness of y wives Jer 44:9
before you and before y fathers Jer 44:10
y fathers, y kings, and y Jer 44:21
because of the evil of y doings Jer 44:22
therefore is y land a desolation, Jer 44:22
y wives have both spoken with Jer 44:25
have both spoken with y mouths Jer 44:25
mouths, and fulfilled with y hand Jer 44:25
ye will surely accomplish y vows Jer 44:25
and surely perform y vows Jer 44:25
and stand forth with y helmets Jer 46:4
save y lives, and be like the Jer 48:6
Y mother shall be sore confounded Jer 50:12
they have done in Zion in y sight Jer 51:24
lest y heart faint, and ye fear Jer 51:46
and let Jerusalem come into y mind Jer 51:50
will break y staff of bread Eze 5:16
and I will destroy y high places Eze 6:3
y altars shall be desolate, and Eze 6:4
and y images shall be broken Eze 6:4
I will cast down y slain men Eze 6:4
y slain men before y idols Eze 6:4
y bones round about y altars Eze 6:5
In all y dwellingplaces the Eze 6:6
that y altars may be laid waste Eze 6:6
y idols may be broken and cease, Eze 6:6
y images may be cut down, and y Eze 6:6
let not y eye spare, neither have Eze 9:5
the things that come into y mind Eze 11:5
multiplied y slain in this city Eze 11:6
Y slain whom ye have laid in the Eze 11:7
This city shall not be y caldron Eze 11:11
Say, I am y sign Eze 12:11
for in y days, O rebellious house Eze 12:25
by y lying to my people that hear Eze 13:19
to my people that hear y lies Eze 13:19
Behold, I am against y pillows Eze 13:20
and I will tear them from y arms Eze 13:20
Y kerchiefs also will I tear, and Eze 13:21
deliver my people out of y hand Eze 13:21
be no more in y hand to be hunted Eze 13:21
deliver my people out of y hand Eze 13:23
and turn yourselves from y idols Eze 14:6
turn away y faces from all y Eze 14:6
y mother was an Hittite Eze 16:45
Hittite, and y father an Amorite Eze 16:45
shall return to y former estate Eze 16:55
are not y ways unequal Eze 18:25
are not y ways unequal Eze 18:29
from all y transgressions Eze 18:30
so iniquity shall not be y ruin Eze 18:30
from you all y transgressions Eze 18:31
them, saying, I am the LORD y God Eze 20:5
I am the LORD y God Eze 20:7
not in the statutes of y fathers Eze 20:18

I am the LORD y God Eze 20:19
may know that I am the LORD y God Eze 20:20
Yet in this y fathers have Eze 20:27
after the manner of y fathers Eze 20:30
For when ye offer y gifts Eze 20:31
when ye make y sons to pass Eze 20:31
yourselves with all y idols Eze 20:31
that which cometh into y mind Eze 20:32
Like as I pleaded with y fathers Eze 20:36
my holy name no more with y gifts Eze 20:39
with y gifts, and with y idols Eze 20:39
there will I require y offerings Eze 20:40
and the firstfruits of y oblations Eze 20:40
oblations, with all y holy things Eze 20:40
accept you with y sweet savour Eze 20:41
mine hand to give it to y fathers Eze 20:42
And there shall ye remember y ways Eze 20:43
all y doings, wherein ye have Eze 20:43
in y own sight for all y evils Eze 20:43
not according to y wicked ways Eze 20:44
nor according to y corrupt doings Eze 20:44
Because ye have made y iniquity Eze 21:24
in that y transgressions are Eze 21:24
all y doings y sins do appear Eze 21:24
taught not to do after y lewdness Eze 23:48
recompense y lewdness upon you Eze 23:49
ye shall bear the sins of y idols Eze 23:49
the excellency of y strength Eze 24:21
strength, the desire of y eyes Eze 24:21
that which y soul pitieth Eze 24:21
y sons and y daughters whom ye Eze 24:21
ye shall not cover y lips Eze 24:22
y tires shall be upon y heads, Eze 24:23
heads, and y shoes upon y feet Eze 24:23
shall pine away for y iniquities Eze 24:23
turn ye, turn ye from y evil ways Eze 33:11
lift up y eyes toward y idols, Eze 33:25
Ye stand upon y sword, ye work Eze 33:26
with y feet the residue of y Eze 34:18
must foul the residue with y feet Eze 34:18
which ye have trodden with y feet Eze 34:19
which ye have fouled with y feet Eze 34:19
all the diseased with y horns Eze 34:21
pasture, are men, and I am y God Eze 34:31
Thus with y mouth ye have boasted Eze 35:13
have multiplied y words against Eze 35:13
ye shall shoot forth y branches Eze 36:8
yield y fruit to my people of Eze 36:8
settle you after y old estates Eze 36:11
unto you than at y beginnings Eze 36:11
I do not this for y sakes Eze 36:22
and will bring you into y own land Eze 36:24
from all y filthiness, and from Eze 36:25
filthiness, and from all y idols Eze 36:25
the stony heart out of y flesh Eze 36:26
the land that I gave to y fathers Eze 36:28
be my people, and I will be y God Eze 36:28
save you from all y uncleannesses Eze 36:29
shall ye remember y own evil ways Eze 36:31
y doings that were not good, and Eze 36:31
y own sight for y iniquities Eze 36:31
iniquities and for y abominations Eze 36:31
Not for y sakes do I this, saith Eze 36:32
and confounded for y own ways Eze 36:32
have cleansed you from all y Eze 36:33
O my people, I will open y graves Eze 37:12
you to come up out of y graves Eze 37:12
LORD, when I have opened y graves Eze 37:13
and brought you up out of y graves Eze 37:13
I shall place you in y own land Eze 37:14
wherein y fathers have dwelt Eze 37:25
the priests shall make y burnt Eze 43:27
the altar, and y peace offerings Eze 43:27
suffice you of all y abominations Eze 44:6
because of all y abominations Eze 44:7
all, of every sort of y oblations Eze 44:30
the priest the first of y dough Eze 44:30
take away y exactions from my Eze 45:9
fifteen shekels, shall be y maneh Eze 45:12
hand to give it unto y fathers Eze 47:14
appointed y meat and y drink Dan 1:10
for why should he see y faces Dan 1:10
the children which are of y sort Dan 1:10
y houses shall be made a dunghill Dan 2:5
that y God is a God of gods, and a Dan 2:47
things, but Michael y prince Dan 10:21
my people, and I will not be y God Hos 1:9
Say ye unto y brethren, Ammi Hos 2:1
and to y sisters, Ruhamah Hos 2:1
Plead with y mother, plead Hos 2:2
therefore y daughters shall Hos 4:13
y spouses shall commit adultery Hos 4:13
I will not punish y daughters Hos 4:14
nor y spouses when they commit Hos 4:14
heal you, nor cure you of y wound Hos 5:13
for y goodness is as a morning Hos 6:4
I saw y fathers as the firstripe Hos 9:10
break up y fallow ground Hos 10:12
you because of y great wickedness Hos 10:15
Hath this been in y days, or even Joel 1:2
or even in the days of y fathers Joel 1:2
Tell ye y children of it, and let Joel 1:3
let y children tell their Joel 1:3
for it is cut off from y mouth Joel 1:5
from the house of y God Joel 1:13
into the house of the LORD y God Joel 1:14
ye even to me with all y heart Joel 2:12
rend y heart, and not y Joel 2:13
and turn unto the LORD y God Joel 2:13
offering unto the LORD y God Joel 2:14
and rejoice in the LORD y God Joel 2:23
praise the name of the LORD y God Joel 2:26
and that I am the LORD y God Joel 2:27
y sons and y daughters shall Joel 2:28

y old men shall dream dreams, Joel 2:28
y young men shall see visions Joel 2:28
y recompence upon y own head Joel 3:4
have carried into y temples my Joel 3:5
y recompence upon y own head Joel 3:7
And I will sell y sons and y Joel 3:8
Beat y plowshares into swords, and Joel 3:10
y pruninghooks into spears Joel 3:10
the LORD y God dwelling in Zion Joel 3:17
I raised up of y sons for Amos 2:11
of y young men for Nazarites Amos 2:11
punish you for all y iniquities Amos 3:2
y posterity with fishhooks Amos 4:2
bring y sacrifices every morning, Amos 4:4
y tithes after three years Amos 4:4
of teeth in all y cities, and want Amos 4:6
and want of bread in all y places Amos 4:6
when y gardens and y vineyards Amos 4:9
y fig trees and y olive trees Amos 4:9
y young men have I slain with the Amos 4:10
and have taken away y horses Amos 4:10
I have made the stink of y camps Amos 4:10
camps to come up unto y nostrils Amos 4:10
Forasmuch therefore as y treading Amos 5:11
For I know y manifold Amos 5:12
transgressions and y mighty sins Amos 5:12
I despise y feast days, and I will Amos 5:21
not smell in y solemn assemblies Amos 5:21
y meat offerings, I will not Amos 5:22
peace offerings of y fat beasts Amos 5:22
borne the tabernacle of y Moloch Amos 5:26
y images, the star of y god Amos 5:26
border greater than y border Amos 6:2
I will turn y feasts into Amos 8:10
all y songs into lamentation Amos 8:10
which ye shall not remove y necks Mic 2:3
for this is not y rest Mic 2:10
Therefore shall Zion for y sake Mic 3:12
for I will work a work in y days Hab 1:5
back y captivity before y eyes Zeph 3:20
to dwell in y cieled houses, and Hag 1:4
Consider y ways Hag 1:5
Consider y ways Hag 1:7 5315
is it not in y eyes in comparison Hag 2:3
in all the labours of y hands Hag 2:17
sore displeased with y fathers Zec 1:2
Be ye not as y fathers, unto whom Zec 1:4
Turn ye now from y evil ways Zec 1:4
evil ways, and from y evil doings Zec 1:4
Y fathers, where are they Zec 1:5
they not take hold of y fathers Zec 1:6
obey the voice of the LORD y God Zec 6:15
against his brother in y heart Zec 7:10
Let y hands be strong, ye that Zec 8:9
but let y hands be strong Zec 8:13
when y fathers provoked me to Zec 8:14
of truth and peace in y gates Zec 8:16
in y hearts against his neighbour Zec 8:17
y eyes shall see, and ye shall say Mal 1:5
this hath been by y means Mal 1:9
will he regard y persons Mal 1:9
I accept an offering at y hand Mal 1:10
should I accept this of y hand Mal 1:13
you, and I will curse y blessings Mal 2:2
Behold, I will corrupt y seed Mal 2:3
seed, and spread dung upon y faces Mal 2:3
even the dung of y solemn feasts Mal 2:3
it with good will at y hand Mal 2:13
Therefore take heed to y spirit Mal 2:15
therefore take heed to y spirit Mal 2:16
wearied the LORD with y words Mal 2:17
Even from the days of y fathers Mal 3:7
rebuke the devourer for y sakes Mal 3:11
destroy the fruits of y ground Mal 3:11
neither shall y vine cast her Mal 3:11
Y words have been stout against Mal 3:13
be ashes under the soles of y Mal 4:3
for great is y reward in heaven Mt 5:12 *5216*
Let y light so shine before men, Mt 5:16 *5216*
that they may see y good works Mt 5:16 *5216*
glorify y Father which is in Mt 5:16 *5216*
That except y righteousness shall Mt 5:20 *5216*
But let y communication be, Yea, Mt 5:37 *5216*
Love y enemies, bless them that Mt 5:44 *5216*
of y Father which is in heaven Mt 5:45 *5216*
if ye salute y brethren only, Mt 5:47 *5216*
even as y Father which is in Mt 5:48 *5216*
that ye do not y alms before men Mt 6:1 *5216*
of y Father which is in heaven Mt 6:1 *5216*
for y Father knoweth what things Mt 6:8 *5216*
y heavenly Father will also Mt 6:14 *5216*
y Father forgive y trespasses Mt 6:15 *5216*
For where y treasure is, there Mt 6:21 *5216*
there will y heart be also Mt 6:21 *5216*
you, Take no thought for y life Mt 6:25 *5216*
nor yet for y body, what ye shall Mt 6:25 *5216*
yet y heavenly Father feedeth Mt 6:26 *5216*
for y heavenly Father knoweth Mt 6:32 *5216*
neither cast ye y pearls before Mt 7:6 *5216*
give good gifts unto y children Mt 7:11 *5216*
how much more shall y Father Mt 7:11 *5216*
think ye evil in y hearts Mt 9:4 *5216*
Why eateth y Master with Mt 9:11 *5216*
According to y faith be it unto Mt 9:29 *5216*
nor silver, nor brass in y purses Mt 10:9 *5216*
Nor scrip for y journey, neither Mt 10:10
worthy, let y peace come upon it Mt 10:13 *5216*
let y peace return to you Mt 10:13 *5216*
not receive you, nor hear y words Mt 10:14 *5216*
shake off the dust of y feet Mt 10:14 *5216*
but the Spirit of y Father which Mt 10:20 *5216*
on the ground without y Father Mt 10:29 *5216*
hairs of y head are all numbered Mt 10:30 *5216*
ye shall find rest unto y souls Mt 11:29 *5216*

by whom do y children cast them	Mt 12:27	*5216*
therefore they shall be y judges	Mt 12:27	*5216*
But blessed are y eyes, for they	Mt 13:16	*5216*
and y ears, for they hear	Mt 13:16	*5216*
commandment of God by y tradition	Mt 15:3	*5216*
God of none effect by y tradition	Mt 15:6	*5216*
unto them, Because of y unbelief	Mt 17:20	*5216*
Doth not y master pay tribute	Mt 17:24	*5216*
of y Father which is in heaven	Mt 18:14	*5216*
if ye from y hearts forgive not	Mt 18:35	*5216*
because of the hardness of y	Mt 19:8	*5216*
suffered you to put away y wives	Mt 19:8	*5216*
among you, let him be y minister	Mt 20:26	*5216*
among you, let him be y servant	Mt 20:27	*5216*
for one is y Master, even Christ	Mt 23:8	*5216*
call no man y father upon the	Mt 23:9	*5216*
for one is y Father, which is in	Mt 23:9	*5216*
for one is y Master, even Christ	Mt 23:10	*5216*
among you shall be y servant	Mt 23:11	*5216*
up then the measure of y fathers	Mt 23:32	*5216*
shall ye scourge in y synagogues	Mt 23:34	*5216*
y house is left unto you desolate	Mt 23:38	*5216*
But pray ye that y flight be not	Mt 24:20	*5216*
not what hour y Lord doth come	Mt 24:42	*5216*
unto the wise, Give us of y oil	Mt 25:8	*5216*
Sleep on now, and take y rest	Mt 26:45	
go y way, make it as sure as ye	Mt 27:65	
ye these things in y hearts	Mk 2:8	*5216*
shake off the dust under y feet	Mk 6:11	*5216*
that ye may keep y own tradition	Mk 7:9	*5216*
none effect through y tradition	Mk 7:13	*5216*
have ye y heart yet hardened	Mk 8:17	*5216*
For the hardness of y heart he	Mk 10:5	*5216*
among you, shall be y minister	Mk 10:43	*5216*
Go y way into the village over	Mk 11:2	
that y Father also which is in	Mk 11:25	*5216*
may forgive you y trespasses	Mk 11:25	*5216*
neither will y Father which is in	Mk 11:26	*5216*
is in heaven forgive y trespasses	Mk 11:26	*5216*
pray ye that y flight be not in	Mk 13:18	*5216*
Sleep on now, and take y rest	Mk 14:41	
But go y way, tell his disciples	Mk 16:7	
and be content with y wages	Lk 3:14	*5216*
scripture fulfilled in y ears	Lk 4:21	*5216*
let down y nets for a draught	Lk 5:4	*5216*
them, What reason ye in y hearts	Lk 5:22	*5216*
cast out y name as evil, for the	Lk 6:22	*5216*
y reward is great in heaven	Lk 6:23	*5216*
ye have received y consolation	Lk 6:24	*5216*
Love y enemies, do good to them	Lk 6:27	*5216*
But love ye y enemies, and do good	Lk 6:35	*5216*
y reward shall be great, and ye	Lk 6:35	*5216*
as y Father also is merciful	Lk 6:36	*5216*
over, shall men give into y bosom	Lk 6:38	*5216*
Go y way, and tell John what	Lk 7:22	
said unto them, Where is y faith	Lk 8:25	*5216*
them, Take nothing for y journey	Lk 9:3	*3588*
y feet for a testimony against	Lk 9:5	*5216*
sayings sink down into y ears	Lk 9:44	*5216*
Go y ways	Lk 10:3	
y peace shall rest upon it	Lk 10:6	*5216*
go y ways out into the streets of	Lk 10:10	
Even the very dust of y city	Lk 10:11	*5216*
because y names are written in	Lk 10:20	*5216*
give good gifts unto y children	Lk 11:13	*5216*
how much more shall y heavenly	Lk 11:13	*3588*
by whom do y sons cast them out	Lk 11:19	*5216*
therefore shall they be y judges	Lk 11:19	*5216*
but y inward part is full of	Lk 11:39	*5216*
the burdens with one of y fingers	Lk 11:46	*5216*
and y fathers killed them	Lk 11:47	*5216*
ye allow the deeds of y fathers	Lk 11:48	*5216*
hairs of y head are all numbered	Lk 12:7	*5216*
you, Take no thought for y life	Lk 12:22	*5216*
y Father knoweth that ye have	Lk 12:30	*5216*
for it is y Father's good	Lk 12:32	*5216*
For where y treasure is, there	Lk 12:34	*5216*
there will y heart be also	Lk 12:34	*5216*
Let y loins be girded about, and	Lk 12:35	*5216*
girded about, and y lights burning	Lk 12:35	*3588*
y house is left unto you desolate	Lk 13:35	*5216*
who will commit to y trust the	Lk 16:11	*5213*
give you that which is y own	Lk 16:12	*5212*
but God knoweth y hearts	Lk 16:15	*5216*
in the which at y entering ye	Lk 19:30	
Settle it therefore in y hearts	Lk 21:14	*5216*
which all y adversaries shall not	Lk 21:15	*5213*
not an hair of y head perish	Lk 21:18	*5216*
y patience possess ye y souls	Lk 21:19	*5216*
then look up, and lift up y heads	Lk 21:28	*5216*
for y redemption draweth nigh	Lk 21:28	*5216*
know of y own selves that summer	Lk 21:30	*1438*
lest at any time y hearts be	Lk 21:34	*5216*
but this is y hour, and the power	Lk 22:53	*5216*
for yourselves, and for y children	Lk 23:28	*5216*
why do thoughts arise in y hearts	Lk 24:38	*5216*
I say unto you, Lift up y eyes	Jn 4:35	*5216*
Y fathers did eat manna in the	Jn 6:49	*5216*
not as y fathers did eat manna,	Jn 6:58	*5216*
but y time is alway ready	Jn 7:6	*5212*
It is also written in y law	Jn 8:17	*5212*
seek me, and shall die in y sins	Jn 8:21	*5216*
you, that ye shall die in y sins	Jn 8:24	*5216*
I am he, ye shall die in y sins	Jn 8:24	*5216*
which ye have seen with y father	Jn 8:38	*5216*
Ye do the deeds of y father	Jn 8:41	*5216*
unto them, If God were y Father	Jn 8:42	*5216*
Ye are of y father the devil, and	Jn 8:44	
the lusts of y father ye will do	Jn 8:44	*5216*
of whom ye say, that he is y God	Jn 8:54	*5216*
Y father Abraham rejoiced to see	Jn 8:56	*5216*
asked them, saying, Is this y son	Jn 9:19	*5216*
therefore y sin remaineth	Jn 9:41	*5216*
them, Is it not written in y law	Jn 10:34	*5216*

I am glad for y sakes that I was	Jn 11:15	*5209*
because of me, but for y sakes	Jn 12:30	*5209*
y Lord and Master, have washed	Jn 13:14	*3588*
and Master, have washed y feet	Jn 13:14	*5216*
Let not y heart be troubled	Jn 14:1	*5216*
bring all things to y remembrance	Jn 14:26	*5209*
Let not y heart be troubled,	Jn 14:27	*5216*
you, and that y joy might be full	Jn 15:11	*5216*
that y fruit should remain	Jn 15:16	*5216*
you, sorrow hath filled y heart	Jn 16:6	*5216*
but y sorrow shall be turned into	Jn 16:20	*5216*
y heart shall rejoice, and y	Jn 16:22	*5216*
receive, that y joy may be full	Jn 16:24	*5216*
and judge him according to y law	Jn 18:31	*5216*
unto the Jews, Behold y King	Jn 19:14	*5216*
unto them, Shall I crucify y King	Jn 19:15	*5216*
unto my Father, and y Father	Jn 20:17	*5216*
and to my God, and y God	Jn 20:17	*5216*
y sons and y daughters shall	Acts 2:17	*5216*
y young men shall see visions, and	Acts 2:17	*5216*
y old men shall dream dreams	Acts 2:17	*5216*
to y children, and to all that are	Acts 2:39	*5216*
ye did it, as did also y rulers	Acts 3:17	*5216*
that y sins may be blotted out,	Acts 3:19	*5216*
A prophet shall the Lord y God	Acts 3:22	*5216*
raise up unto you of y brethren	Acts 3:22	*5216*
filled Jerusalem with y doctrine	Acts 5:28	*5216*
A prophet shall the Lord y God	Acts 7:37	*5216*
raise up unto you of y brethren	Acts 7:37	*5216*
and the star of y god Remphan	Acts 7:43	*5216*
as y fathers did, so do ye	Acts 7:51	*5216*
have not y fathers persecuted	Acts 7:52	*5216*
for I work a work in y days	Acts 13:41	*5216*
with words, subverting y souls	Acts 15:24	*5216*
beheld y devotions, I found an	Acts 17:23	*5216*
as certain also of y own poets	Acts 17:28	
Y blood be upon y own heads	Acts 18:6	*546*
names, and of y law, look ye to it	Acts 18:15	
nor yet blasphemers of y goddess	Acts 19:37	*5216*
Also of y own selves shall men	Acts 20:30	*5216*
know the uttermost of y matter	Acts 24:22	
for this is for y health	Acts 27:34	*5212*
that y faith is spoken of	Rom 1:8	*5216*
therefore reign in y mortal body	Rom 6:12	*5216*
Neither yield ye y members as	Rom 6:13	*5216*
y members as instruments of	Rom 6:13	*5216*
of the infirmity of y flesh	Rom 6:19	*5216*
for as ye have yielded y members	Rom 6:19	*5216*
even so now yield y members	Rom 6:19	*5216*
ye have y fruit unto holiness, and	Rom 6:22	*5216*
y mortal bodies by his Spirit	Rom 8:11	*5216*
should be wise in y own conceits	Rom 11:25	
they are enemies for y sakes	Rom 11:28	*5209*
that through y mercy they also	Rom 11:31	*5212*
that ye present y bodies a living	Rom 12:1	*5216*
which is y reasonable service	Rom 12:1	*5216*
by the renewing of y mind	Rom 12:2	*5216*
Be not wise in y own conceits	Rom 12:16	*5216*
Let not then y good be evil	Rom 14:16	*5216*
be somewhat filled with y company	Rom 15:24	*5216*
me in y prayers to God for me	Rom 15:30	*3588*
For y obedience is come abroad	Rom 16:19	*5216*
I am glad therefore on y behalf	Rom 16:19	*5213*
bruise Satan under y feet shortly	Rom 16:20	*5216*
I thank my God always on y behalf	1Cor 1:4	*5216*
For ye see y calling, brethren,	1Cor 1:26	*5216*
That y faith should not stand in	1Cor 2:5	*5216*
myself and to Apollos for y sakes	1Cor 4:6	*5209*
Y glorying is not good	1Cor 5:6	*5216*
I speak to y shame	1Cor 6:5	*5213*
and defraud, and that y brethren	1Cor 6:8	
Know ye not that y bodies are the	1Cor 6:15	*5216*
know ye not that y body is the	1Cor 6:19	*1438*
have of God, and ye are not y own	1Cor 6:19	*5216*
therefore glorify God in y body	1Cor 6:20	*5216*
in y spirit, which are God's	1Cor 6:20	*5216*
tempt you not for y incontinency	1Cor 7:5	*5216*
else were y children unclean	1Cor 7:14	*5216*
And this I speak for y own profit	1Cor 7:35	*5216*
if we shall reap y carnal things	1Cor 9:11	*5216*
Let y women keep silence in the	1Cor 14:34	*5216*
vain, and y faith is also vain	1Cor 15:14	*5216*
be not raised, y faith is vain	1Cor 15:17	*5216*
ye are yet in y sins	1Cor 15:17	*5216*
I protest by y rejoicing which I	1Cor 15:31	*5212*
I speak this to y shame	1Cor 15:34	*5213*
forasmuch as ye know that y	1Cor 15:58	*5216*
ye shall approve by y letters	1Cor 16:3	
bring y liberality unto Jerusalem	1Cor 16:3	*5216*
Let all y things be done with	1Cor 16:14	*5216*
on y part they have supplied	1Cor 16:17	*5216*
it is for y consolation and	2Cor 1:6	*5216*
it is for y consolation and	2Cor 1:6	*5216*
in part, that we are y rejoicing	2Cor 1:14	*5216*
we have dominion over y faith	2Cor 1:24	*5216*
faith, but are helpers of y joy	2Cor 1:24	*5216*
would confirm y love toward him	2Cor 2:8	
for y sakes forgave I it in the	2Cor 2:10	*5209*
ourselves y servants for Jesus'	2Cor 4:5	*5216*
For all things are for y sakes	2Cor 4:15	*5209*
made manifest in y consciences	2Cor 5:11	*5216*
we be sober, it is for y cause	2Cor 5:13	*5213*
ye are straitened in y own bowels	2Cor 6:12	*5216*
when he told us y earnest desire	2Cor 7:7	*5216*
y mourning, y fervent mind	2Cor 7:7	*5216*
we were comforted in y comfort	2Cor 7:13	*5213*
in y love to us, see that ye	2Cor 8:7	*5209*
to prove the sincerity of y love	2Cor 8:8	*5212*
yet for y sakes he became poor,	2Cor 8:9	*5216*
that now at this time y abundance	2Cor 8:14	*5216*
also may be a supply for y want	2Cor 8:14	*5216*
and declaration of y ready mind	2Cor 8:19	*5216*
the churches, the proof of y love	2Cor 8:24	*5216*
and of our boasting on y behalf	2Cor 8:24	*5216*

I know the forwardness of y mind	2Cor 9:2	*5216*
y zeal hath provoked very many	2Cor 9:2	*5216*
and make up beforehand y bounty	2Cor 9:5	*5216*
both minister bread for y food	2Cor 9:10	
multiply y seed sown, and increase	2Cor 9:10	*5216*
the fruits of y righteousness	2Cor 9:10	*5216*
they glorify God for y professed	2Cor 9:13	*5216*
for y liberal distribution unto	2Cor 9:13	*3588*
when y obedience is fulfilled	2Cor 10:6	*5216*
not for y destruction, I should	2Cor 10:8	*5216*
when y faith is increased, that	2Cor 10:15	*5216*
so y minds should be corrupted	2Cor 11:3	*5216*
dearly beloved, for y edifying	2Cor 12:19	*5216*
prove y own selves	2Cor 13:5	*1438*
Know ye not y own selves, how	2Cor 13:5	*1438*
also we wish, even y perfection	2Cor 13:9	*5216*
Spirit of his Son into y hearts	Gal 4:6	*5216*
would have plucked out y own eyes	Gal 4:15	*5216*
Am I therefore become y enemy	Gal 4:16	*5216*
that they may glory in y flesh	Gal 6:13	*5212*
Jesus Christ be with y spirit	Gal 6:18	*5212*
truth, the gospel of y salvation	Eph 1:13	*5216*
after I heard of y faith in the	Eph 1:15	*5209*
The eyes of y understanding being	Eph 1:18	*5216*
for you, which is y glory	Eph 3:13	
may dwell in y hearts by faith	Eph 3:17	*5216*
called in one hope of y calling	Eph 4:4	*5216*
renewed in the spirit of y mind	Eph 4:23	*5216*
not the sun go down upon y wrath	Eph 4:26	*5216*
proceed out of y mouth, but that	Eph 4:29	*5216*
making melody in y heart to the	Eph 5:19	*5216*
yourselves unto y own husbands	Eph 5:22	*3588*
love y wives, even as Christ also	Eph 5:25	*1438*
obey y parents in the Lord	Eph 6:1	*5216*
provoke not y children to wrath	Eph 6:4	*5216*
be obedient to them that are y	Eph 6:5	
in singleness of y heart	Eph 6:5	*5216*
knowing that y Master also is in	Eph 6:9	*5216*
having y loins girt about with	Eph 6:14	*5216*
y feet shod with the preparation	Eph 6:15	*3588*
and that he might comfort y hearts	Eph 6:22	*5216*
For y fellowship in the gospel	Phil 1:5	*5216*
that y love may abound yet more	Phil 1:9	*5216*
to my salvation through y prayer	Phil 1:19	*5216*
with you all for y furtherance	Phil 1:25	*5216*
That y rejoicing may be more	Phil 1:26	*5216*
Only let y conversation be as it	Phil 1:27	
absent, I may hear of y affairs	Phil 1:27	*5216*
terrified by y adversaries	Phil 1:28	*3588*
work out y own salvation with	Phil 2:12	*1438*
sacrifice and service of y faith	Phil 2:17	*5216*
good comfort, when I know y state	Phil 2:19	*5216*
will naturally care for y state	Phil 2:20	*5216*
but y messenger, and he that	Phil 2:25	*5216*
to supply y lack of service	Phil 2:30	*5216*
Let y moderation be known unto	Phil 4:5	*5216*
with thanksgiving let y requests	Phil 4:6	*5216*
shall keep y hearts and minds	Phil 4:7	*5216*
that now at the last y care of me	Phil 4:10	*3588*
that may abound to y account	Phil 4:17	*5216*
But my God shall supply all y	Phil 4:19	*5216*
Since we heard of y faith in	Col 1:4	*5216*
unto us y love in the Spirit	Col 1:8	*5216*
enemies in y mind by wicked works	Col 1:21	*3588*
joying and beholding y order	Col 2:5	*5216*
stedfastness of y faith in Christ	Col 2:5	*5216*
And you, being dead in y sins	Col 2:13	*5216*
and the uncircumcision of y flesh	Col 2:13	*5216*
Let no man beguile you of y	Col 2:18	
Set y affection on things above,	Col 3:2	
y life is hid with Christ in God	Col 3:3	*5216*
Mortify therefore y members which	Col 3:5	*5216*
communication out of y mouth	Col 3:8	*5216*
the peace of God rule in y hearts	Col 3:15	*5216*
grace in y hearts to the Lord	Col 3:16	*5216*
yourselves unto y own husbands	Col 3:18	*2398*
love y wives, and be not bitter	Col 3:19	*3588*
obey y parents in all things	Col 3:20	*3588*
provoke not y children to anger,	Col 3:21	*5216*
obey in all things y masters	Col 3:22	*3588*
give unto y servants that which	Col 4:1	*3588*
Let y speech be alway with grace,	Col 4:6	*5216*
y estate, and comfort y hearts	Col 4:8	*5216*
without ceasing y work of faith	1Th 1:3	*5209*
beloved, y election of God	1Th 1:4	*5216*
men we were among you for y sake	1Th 1:5	*5209*
but also in every place y faith	1Th 1:8	*5216*
like things of y own countrymen	1Th 2:14	*2398*
to see y face with great desire	1Th 2:17	*5216*
to comfort you concerning y faith	1Th 3:2	*5216*
forbear, I sent to know y faith	1Th 3:5	*5216*
us good tidings of y faith	1Th 3:6	*5216*
affliction and distress by y faith	1Th 3:7	*5216*
we joy for y sakes before our God	1Th 3:9	*5209*
that we might see y face, and	1Th 3:10	*5216*
that which is lacking in y faith	1Th 3:10	*5216*
To the end he may stablish y	1Th 3:13	*5216*
even y sanctification, that ye	1Th 4:3	*5216*
to do y own business, and to work	1Th 4:11	*2398*
and to work with y own hands	1Th 4:11	*2398*
I pray God y whole spirit and soul	1Th 5:23	*3588*
because that y faith groweth	2Th 1:3	*5216*
churches of God for y patience	2Th 1:4	*5216*
and faith in all y persecutions	2Th 1:4	*5216*
Comfort y hearts, and stablish you	2Th 2:17	*5216*
the Lord direct y hearts into the	2Th 3:5	*5216*
for I trust that through y	Philem 22	*5216*
Jesus Christ be with y spirit	Philem 25	*5216*
Harden not y hearts, as in the	Heb 3:8	*5216*
When y fathers tempted me, proved	Heb 3:9	*5216*
his voice, harden not y hearts	Heb 3:15	*5216*
his voice, harden not y hearts	Heb 4:7	*5216*
not unrighteous to forget y work	Heb 6:10	*5216*
purge y conscience from dead	Heb 9:14	*5216*

joyfully the spoiling of y goods	Heb 10:34	5216
not away therefore y confidence	Heb 10:35	5216
ye be wearied and faint in y minds	Heb 12:3	5216
And make straight paths for y feet	Heb 12:13	5216
Let y conversation be without	Heb 13:5	3588
for they watch for y souls	Heb 13:17	5216
that the trying of y faith	Jas 1:3	5216
which is able to save y souls	Jas 1:21	5216
only, deceiving y own selves	Jas 1:22	1438
For if there come unto y assembly	Jas 2:2	5216
envying and strife in y hearts	Jas 3:14	5216
y lusts that war in y members	Jas 4:1	5216
ye may consume it upon y lusts	Jas 4:3	5216
Cleanse y hands, ye sinners	Jas 4:8	
and purify y hearts, ye double	Jas 4:8	
let y laughter be turned to	Jas 4:9	5216
mourning, and y joy to heaviness	Jas 4:9	3588
For what is y life	Jas 4:14	5216
But now ye rejoice in y boastings	Jas 4:16	5216
howl for y miseries that shall	Jas 5:1	5216
Y riches are corrupted, and y	Jas 5:2	5216
Y gold and silver is cankered	Jas 5:3	5216
shall eat y flesh as it were fire	Jas 5:3	5216
who have reaped down y fields	Jas 5:4	5216
ye have nourished y hearts	Jas 5:5	5216
stablish y hearts	Jas 5:8	5216
but let y yea be yea	Jas 5:12	5216
and y nay, nay	Jas 5:12	3588
Confess y faults one to another,	Jas 5:16	3588
That the trial of y faith	1Pet 1:7	5216
Receiving the end of y faith	1Pet 1:9	5216
even the salvation of y souls	1Pet 1:9	
gird up the loins of y mind	1Pet 1:13	5216
the former lusts in y ignorance	1Pet 1:14	5216
pass the time of y sojourning	1Pet 1:17	5216
from y vain conversation received	1Pet 1:18	5216
by tradition from y fathers	1Pet 1:18	5216
that y faith and hope might be in	1Pet 1:21	5216
Seeing ye have purified y souls	1Pet 1:22	5216
Having y conversation honest	1Pet 2:12	5216
they may by y good works	1Pet 2:12	3588
not using y liberty for a cloke	1Pet 2:16	3588
be subject to y masters with all	1Pet 2:18	3588
when ye be buffeted for y faults	1Pet 2:20	
the Shepherd and Bishop of y souls	1Pet 2:25	5216
in subjection to y own husbands	1Pet 3:1	3588
While they behold y chaste	1Pet 3:2	5216
that y prayers be not hindered	1Pet 3:7	5216
sanctify the Lord God in y hearts	1Pet 3:15	5216
y good conversation in Christ	1Pet 3:16	5216
but on y part he is glorified	1Pet 4:14	5209
Casting all y care upon him	1Pet 5:7	5216
because y adversary the devil, as	1Pet 5:8	5216
y brethren that are in the world	1Pet 5:9	5216
diligence, add to y faith virtue	2Pet 1:5	5216
give diligence to make y calling	2Pet 1:10	5216
and the day star arise in y hearts	2Pet 1:19	5216
I stir up y pure minds by way of	2Pet 3:1	5216
fall from y own stedfastness	2Pet 3:17	3588
unto you, that y joy may be full	1Jn 1:4	5216
because y sins are forgiven you	1Jn 2:12	3588
receive him not into y house	2Jn 10	
are spots in y feasts of charity	Jude 12	5216
yourselves on y most holy faith	Jude 20	5216
I John, who also am y brother	Rev 1:9	5216
one of you according to y works	Rev 2:23	5216
Go y ways, and pour out the vials	Rev 16:1	

YOURS

of all the land of Egypt is y	Gen 45:20	
your feet shall tread shall be y	Deut 11:24	
men answered her, Our life for y	Josh 2:14	
for the battle is not y, but	2Chr 20:15	
strangers in a land that is not y	Jer 5:19	
for y is the kingdom of God	Lk 6:20	5212
my saying, they will keep y also	Jn 15:20	5212
For all things are y	1Cor 3:21	5216
all are y	1Cor 3:22	5216
by any means this liberty of y	1Cor 8:9	5216
have refreshed my spirit and y	1Cor 16:18	5216
for I seek not y, but you	2Cor 12:14	5216

YOURSELVES

feet, and rest y under the tree	Gen 18:4	
be not grieved, nor angry with y	Gen 45:5	5869
Gather y together, that I may	Gen 49:1	
Gather y together, and hear, ye	Gen 49:2	
about, saying, Take heed to y	Ex 19:12	
ye shall not make to y according	Ex 30:37	
Consecrate y to day to the LORD,	Ex 32:29	3027
Ye shall not make y abominable	Lev 11:43	5315
shall ye make y unclean with them	Lev 11:43	5315
ye shall therefore sanctify y	Lev 11:44	5315
neither shall ye defile y with	Lev 11:44	5315
Defile not ye y in any of these	Lev 18:24	
and that ye defile not y therein	Lev 18:30	
idols, nor make to y molten gods	Lev 19:4	
Sanctify y therefore, and be ye	Lev 20:7	
Sanctify y against to morrow, and	Num 11:18	
wherefore then lift ye up y above	Num 16:3	
Separate y from among this	Num 16:21	
Arm some of y unto the war, and	Num 31:3	853
lying with him, keep alive for y	Num 31:18	
touched any slain, purify both y	Num 31:19	
ye good heed unto y therefore	Deut 2:4	
ye therefore good heed unto y	Deut 4:15	5315
Lest ye corrupt y, and make you a	Deut 4:16	
Take heed unto y, lest ye forget	Deut 4:23	
in the land, and shall corrupt y	Deut 4:25	
Take heed to y, that your heart	Deut 11:16	
nations and mightier than y	Deut 11:23	
ye shall not cut y, nor make any	Deut 14:1	
present y in the tabernacle of	Deut 31:14	
death ye will utterly corrupt y	Deut 31:29	
hide y there three days, until	Josh 2:16	
said unto the people, Sanctify y	Josh 3:5	
in any wise keep y from the	Josh 6:18	
thing, lest ye make y accursed	Josh 6:18	
Sanctify y against to morrow	Josh 7:13	
shall ye take for a prey unto y	Josh 8:2	
serve them, nor bow y unto them	Josh 23:7	
Take good heed therefore unto y	Josh 23:11	5315
other gods, and bowed y to them	Josh 23:16	
Ye are witnesses against y that	Josh 24:22	
that ye will not fall upon me y	Judg 15:12	859
to make y fat with the chiefest	1Sa 2:29	
quit y like men, O ye Philistines	1Sa 4:9	
quit y like men, and fight	1Sa 4:9	
Now therefore present y before	1Sa 10:19	
Disperse y among the people, and	1Sa 14:34	
sanctify y, and come with me to	1Sa 16:5	
Choose you one bullock for y	1Kin 18:25	
unto his servants, Set y in array	1Kin 20:12	
other gods, nor bow y to them	2Kin 17:35	
sanctify y, both ye and your	1Chr 15:12	
set y, stand ye still, and see the	2Chr 20:17	
me, ye Levites, sanctify now y	2Chr 29:5	
have consecrated y unto the LORD	2Chr 29:31	3027
but yield y unto the LORD, and	2Chr 30:8	3027
to give over y to die by famine	2Chr 32:11	
prepare y by the houses of your	2Chr 35:4	
kill the passover, and sanctify y	2Chr 35:6	
separate y from the people of the	Ezr 10:11	
unto your sons, or for y	Neh 13:25	
that ye make y strange to me	Job 19:3	
ye will magnify y against me	Job 19:5	
Behold, all ye y have seen it	Job 27:12	
offer up for y a burnt offering	Job 42:8	
Associate y, O ye people, and ye	Is 8:9	
gird y, and ye shall be broken in	Is 8:9	
gird y, and ye shall be broken in	Is 8:9	
Stay y, and wonder	Is 29:9	
Assemble y and come	Is 45:20	
Remember this, and shew y men	Is 46:8	
All ye, assemble y, and hear	Is 48:14	
them that are in darkness, Shew y	Is 49:9	
your iniquities have ye sold y	Is 50:1	
that compass y about with sparks	Is 50:11	
LORD, Ye have sold y for nought	Is 52:3	
Against whom do ye sport y	Is 57:4	
Enflaming y with idols under	Is 57:5	
in their glory shall ye boast y	Is 61:6	
Circumcise y to the LORD, and take	Jer 4:4	
together, and say, Assemble y	Jer 4:5	
gather y to flee out of the midst	Jer 6:1	
assemble y, and let us enter into	Jer 8:14	
king and to the queen, Humble y	Jer 13:18	
Take heed to y, and bear no burden	Jer 17:21	5315
wallow y in the ashes, ye	Jer 25:34	
bring innocent blood upon y	Jer 26:15	
Deceive not y, saying, The	Jer 37:9	5315
to dwell, that ye might cut y off	Jer 44:8	
Put y in array against Babylon	Jer 50:14	
Repent, and turn y from your idols	Eze 14:6	
Repent, and turn y from all your	Eze 18:30	
wherefore turn y, and live ye	Eze 18:32	
defile not y with the idols of	Eze 20:7	
nor defile y with their idols	Eze 20:18	
ye pollute y with all your idols,	Eze 20:31	
ye shall lothe y in your own	Eze 20:43	
shall lothe y in your own sight	Eze 36:31	
beast of the field, Assemble y	Eze 39:17	
gather y on every side to my	Eze 39:17	
my charge in my sanctuary for y	Eze 44:8	
Sow to y in righteousness, reap	Hos 10:12	
Gird y, and lament, ye priests	Joel 1:13	
Assemble y, and come, all ye	Joel 3:11	
gather y together round about	Joel 3:11	
Assemble y upon the mountains of	Amos 3:9	
of your god, which ye made to y	Amos 5:26	
Gather y together, yea, gather	Zeph 2:1	
did drink, did not ye eat for y	Zec 7:6	
for y, and drink for y	Zec 7:6	
And think not to say within y	Mt 3:9	1438
Lay not up for y treasures upon	Mt 6:19	5213
But lay up for y treasures in	Mt 6:20	5213
faith, why reason ye among y	Mt 16:8	1438
for ye neither go in y, neither	Mt 23:13	
more the child of hell than y	Mt 23:15	5216
Wherefore ye be witnesses unto y	Mt 23:31	1438
to them that sell, and buy for y	Mt 25:9	1438
Come ye y apart into a desert	Mk 6:31	
ye disputed among y by the way	Mk 9:33	1438
Have salt in y, and have peace one	Mk 9:50	1438
But take heed to y	Mk 13:9	1438
and begin not to say within y	Lk 3:8	1438
ye y touch not the burdens with	Lk 11:46	846
ye entered not in y, and them that	Lk 11:52	846
provide y bags which wax not old,	Lk 12:33	1438
ye y like unto men that wait for	Lk 12:36	
why even of y judge ye not what	Lk 12:57	1438
of God, and you y thrust out	Lk 13:28	
Make to y friends of the mammon	Lk 16:9	1438
they which justify y before men	Lk 16:15	1438
Take heed to y	Lk 17:3	1438
Go shew y unto the priests	Lk 17:14	1438
And take heed to y, lest at any	Lk 21:34	1438
Take this, and divide it among y	Lk 22:17	1438
weep not for me, but weep for y	Lk 23:28	1438
Ye y bear me witness, that I said	Jn 3:28	
unto them, Murmur not among y	Jn 6:43	240
ye enquire among y of that I said	Jn 16:19	240
midst of you, as ye y also know	Acts 2:22	846
Save y from this untoward	Acts 2:40	
take heed to y what ye intend to	Acts 5:35	1438
judge y unworthy of everlasting	Acts 13:46	1438
from which if ye keep y, ye shall	Acts 15:29	1438
embracing him said, Trouble not y	Acts 20:10	
Take heed therefore unto y	Acts 20:28	1438
ye y know, that these hands have	Acts 20:34	846
Likewise reckon ye also y to be	Rom 6:11	1438
but yield y unto God, as those	Rom 6:13	1438
whom ye yield y servants to obey	Rom 6:16	1438
Dearly beloved, avenge not y	Rom 12:19	1438
from among y that wicked person	1Cor 5:13	
rather suffer y to be defrauded	1Cor 6:7	
that ye may give y to fasting	1Cor 7:5	
Judge in y	1Cor 11:13	
That ye submit y unto such	1Cor 16:16	
in you, yea, what clearing of y	2Cor 7:11	
y to be clear in this matter	2Cor 7:11	1438
gladly, seeing ye y are wise	2Cor 11:19	
Examine y, whether ye be in the	2Cor 13:5	1438
and that not of y	Eph 2:8	5216
Speaking to y in psalms and hymns	Eph 5:19	1438
Submitting y one to another in	Eph 5:21	
submit y unto your own husbands,	Eph 5:22	
submit y unto your own husbands,	Col 3:18	
For y, brethren, know our	1Th 2:1	846
for y know that we are appointed	1Th 3:3	846
for ye y are taught of God to	1Th 4:9	846
For y know perfectly that the day	1Th 5:2	846
Wherefore comfort y together	1Th 5:11	240
And be at peace among y	1Th 5:13	1438
that which is good, both among y	1Th 5:15	1438
that ye withdraw y from every	2Th 3:6	
For y know how ye ought to follow	2Th 3:7	846
knowing in y that ye have in	Heb 10:34	1438
as being y also in the body	Heb 13:3	846
the rule over you, and submit y	Heb 13:17	5216
Are ye not then partial in y	Jas 2:4	1438
Submit y therefore to God	Jas 4:7	
Humble y in the sight of the Lord	Jas 4:10	
not fashioning y according to the	1Pet 1:14	
Submit y to every ordinance of	1Pet 2:13	
arm y likewise with the same mind	1Pet 4:1	
have fervent charity among y	1Pet 4:8	1438
younger, submit y unto the elder	1Pet 5:5	
Humble y therefore under the	1Pet 5:6	
children, keep y from idols	1Jn 5:21	1438
Look to y, that we lose not those	2Jn 8	1438
building up y on your most holy	Jude 20	1438
Keep y in the love of God,	Jude 21	1438
gather y together unto the supper	Rev 19:17	

YOUTH

of man's heart is evil from his y	Gen 8:21	5271
the youngest according to his y	Gen 43:33	6812
cattle from our y even until now	Gen 46:34	5271
her father's house, as in her y	Lev 22:13	5271
in her father's house in her y	Num 30:3	5271
being yet in her y in her	Num 30:16	5271
But the y drew not his sword	Judg 8:20	5288
he feared, because he was yet a y	Judg 8:20	5288
for thou art but a y, and he a man	1Sa 17:33	5288
and he a man of war from his y	1Sa 17:33	5271
for he was but a y, and ruddy, and	1Sa 17:42	5288
host, Abner, whose son is this y	1Sa 17:55	5288
befell thee from thy y until now	2Sa 19:7	5271
servant fear the LORD from my y	1Kin 18:12	5271
to possess the iniquities of my y	Job 13:26	5271
are full of the sin of his y	Job 20:11	5934
As I was in the days of my y	Job 29:4	2779
Upon my right hand rise the y	Job 30:12	6526
(For from my y he was brought up	Job 31:18	5271
shall return to the days of his y	Job 33:25	5934
They die in y, and their life is	Job 36:14	5290
Remember not the sins of my y	Ps 25:7	5271
thou art my trust from my y	Ps 71:5	5271
thou hast taught me from my y	Ps 71:17	5271
and ready to die from my y up	Ps 88:15	5290
The days of his y hast thou	Ps 89:45	5934
so that thy y is renewed like the	Ps 103:5	5271
thou hast the dew of thy y	Ps 110:3	3208
so are children of the y	Ps 127:4	5271
have they afflicted me from my y	Ps 129:1	5271
have they afflicted me from my y	Ps 129:2	5271
be as plants grown up in their y	Ps 144:12	5271
forsaketh the guide of her y	Prov 2:17	5271
and rejoice with the wife of thy y	Prov 5:18	5271
Rejoice, O young man, in thy y	Eccl 11:9	3208
cheer thee in the days of thy y	Eccl 11:9	979
for childhood and y are vanity	Eccl 11:10	7839
thy Creator in the days of thy y	Eccl 12:1	979
thou hast laboured from thy y	Is 47:12	5271
even thy merchants, from thy y	Is 47:15	5271
shalt forget the shame of thy y	Is 54:4	5934
grieved in spirit, and a wife of y	Is 54:6	5271
thee, the kindness of thy y	Jer 2:2	5271
thou art the guide of my y	Jer 3:4	5271
labour of our fathers from our y	Jer 3:24	5271
from our y even unto this day, and	Jer 3:25	5271
hath been thy manner from thy y	Jer 22:21	5271
I did bear the reproach of my y	Jer 31:19	5271
done evil before me from their y	Jer 32:30	5271
Moab hath been at ease from his y	Jer 48:11	5271
that he bear the yoke in his y	Lam 3:27	5271
for from my y up even till now	Eze 4:14	5271
not remembered the days of thy y	Eze 16:22	5271
not remembered the days of thy y	Eze 16:43	5271
with thee in the days of thy y	Eze 16:60	5271
committed whoredoms in their y	Eze 23:3	5271
for in her y they lay with her,	Eze 23:8	5271
to remembrance the days of her y	Eze 23:19	5271
remembrance the lewdness of thy y	Eze 23:21	5271
Egyptians for the paps of thy y	Eze 23:21	5271
there, as in the days of her y	Hos 2:15	5271
for the husband of her y	Joel 1:8	5271
me to keep cattle from my y	Zec 13:5	5271
between thee and the wife of thy y	Mal 2:14	5271
against the wife of his y	Mal 2:15	5271
things have I kept from my y up	Mt 19:20	3503
these have I observed from my y	Mk 10:20	3503
these have I kept from my y up	Lk 18:21	3503

My manner of life from my y........ Acts 26:4 *3503*
Let no man despise thy y........ 1Ti 4:12 *3503*

YOUTHFUL
Flee also y lusts........ 2Ti 2:22 *3512*

YOUTHS
ones, I discerned among the y........ Prov 7:7 1121
Even the y shall faint and be........ Is 40:30 5288

YOU-WARD
world, and more abundantly to y........ 2Cor 1:12
which to y is not weak, but is........ 2Cor 13:3
of God which is given me to y........ Eph 3:2

Z

ZAANAIM (*za-an-a'-im*) See Zaanannim. *A plain in Naphtali.*
his tent unto the plain of Z........ Judg 4:11 6815

ZAANAN (*za'-an-an*) See Zenan. *A city of Judah.*
the inhabitant of Z came not........ Mic 1:11 6630

ZA-ANANNIM See Zaanaim.

ZAANANNIM (*za-an-an'-nim*) *Same as Zaanaim.*
was from Heleph, from Allon to Z........ Josh 19:33 6815

ZAAVAN (*za'-av-an*) See Zavan. *A son of Ezer.*
Bilhan, and Z, and Akan........ Gen 36:27 2190

ZABAD (*za'-bad*) See Josabad, Jozachar.
1. A son of Nathan.
begat Nathan, and Nathan begat Z........ 1Chr 2:36 2066
Z begat Ephlal, and Ephlal begat........ 1Chr 2:37 2066
2. Son of Tahath.
Z his son, and Shuthelah his son,........ 1Chr 7:21 2066
3. A "mighty man" of David.
the Hittite, Z the son of Ahlai,........ 1Chr 11:41 2066
4. A son of Shimeath.
Z the son of Shimeath an........ 2Chr 24:26 2066
5. A son of Zatta.
Mattaniah, and Jeremoth, and Z........ Ezr 10:27 2066
6. A son of Hasham.
Mattenai, Mattathah, Z, Eliphelet........ Ezr 10:33 2066
7. A son of Nebo.
Jeiel, Mattithiah, Z, Zebina,........ Ezr 10:43 2066

ZABBAI (*zab'-bahee*) See Zaccai.
1. Married a foreigner in exile.
Jehohanan, Hananiah, Z, and Athlai........ Ezr 10:28 2079
2. Father of Baruch.
After him Baruch the son of Z........ Neh 3:20 2079

ZABBUD (*zab'-bud*) See Zaccur. *An exile with Ezra.*
Uthai, and Z, and with them seventy........ Ezr 8:14 2072

ZABDI (*zab'-di*) See Zacchur, Zichri.
1. Father of Carmi.
the son of Carmi, the son of Z........ Josh 7:1 2067
and Z was taken........ Josh 7:17 2067
the son of Carmi, the son of Z........ Josh 7:18 2067
2. Son of Shimhi.
And Jakim, and Zichri, and Z........ 1Chr 8:19 2067
3. A storekeeper in David's court.
wine cellars was Z the Shiphmite........ 1Chr 27:27 2067
4. A Levite.
the son of Micha, the son of Z........ Neh 11:17 2067

ZABDIEL (*zab'-de-el*)
1. Father of Jashobeam.
month was Jashobeam the son of Z........ 1Chr 27:2 2068
2. An overseer of priests.
and their overseer was Z, the son........ Neh 11:14 2068

ZABUD (*za'-bud*) *A family of exiles.*
Z the son of Nathan was principal........ 1Kin 4:5 2071

ZABULON (*zab'-u-lon*) See Zebulun. *Greek form of Zebulon.*
sea coast, in the borders of Z........ Mt 4:13 *2194*
The land of Z, and the land of........ Mt 4:15 *2194*
Of the tribe of Z were sealed........ Rev 7:8 *2194*

ZACCAI (*zac'-cahee*) See Zabbai. *A family of exiles.*
The children of Z, seven hundred........ Ezr 2:9 2140
The children of Z, seven hundred........ Neh 7:14 2140

ZACCHAEUS (*zak-ke'-us*) *A tax collector visited by Jesus.*
behold, there was a man named Z........ Lk 19:2 *2195*
and saw him, and said unto him, Z........ Lk 19:5 *2195*
Z stood, and said unto the Lord........ Lk 19:8 *2195*

ZACCHUR (*zac'-cur*) See Zaccur. *Father of Shimei.*
Z his son, Shimei his son........ 1Chr 4:26 2139

ZACCUR (*zac'-cur*) See Zabbud, Zabdi, Zacchur, Zichri.
1. Father of Shammua.
of Reuben, Shammua the son of Z........ Num 13:4 2139
2. A sanctuary servant.
Beno, and Shoham, and Z, and Ibri........ 1Chr 24:27 2139
3. A son of Asaph.
Z, and Joseph, and Nethaniah, and........ 1Chr 25:2 2139
The third to Z, he, his sons, and........ 1Chr 25:10 2139
the son of Michaiah, the son of Z........ Neh 12:35 2139
4. A rebuilder of Jerusalem's wall.
to them builded Z the son of Imri........ Neh 3:2 2139
5. A Levite who renewed the covenant.
Z, Sherebiah, Shebaniah,........ Neh 10:12 2139
6. Father of Hanan.
to them was Hanan the son of Z........ Neh 13:13 2139

ZACHARIAH (*zak-a-ri'-ah*) See Zechariah.
1. A king of Israel.
Z his son reigned in his stead........ 2Kin 14:29 2148
of Azariah king of Judah did Z........ 2Kin 15:8 2148
And the rest of the acts of Z........ 2Kin 15:11 2148
2. Father of Abi.
also was Abi, the daughter of Z........ 2Kin 18:2 2148

ZACHARIAS (*zak'-a-ri'-as*) See Zechariah.
1. Son of Barachias.
the blood of Z son of Barachias........ Mt 23:35 *2197*
blood of Abel unto the blood of Z........ Lk 11:51 *2197*
2. Father of John the Baptist.
Judaea, a certain priest named Z........ Lk 1:5 *2197*
when Z saw him, he was troubled,........ Lk 1:12 *2197*
angel said unto him, Fear not, Z........ Lk 1:13 *2197*
Z said unto the angel, Whereby........ Lk 1:18 *2197*
And the people waited for Z........ Lk 1:21 *2197*
And entered into the house of Z........ Lk 1:40 *2197*
and they called him Z, after the........ Lk 1:59 *2197*
his father Z was filled with the........ Lk 1:67 *2197*
the son of Z in the wilderness........ Lk 3:2 *2197*

ZACHER (*za'-kur*) See Zechariah. *Father of Gibeon.*
And Gedor, and Ahio, and Z........ 1Chr 8:31 2144

ZADOK (*za'-dok*) See Zadok's.
1. A priest in David's time.
Z the son of Ahitub, and Ahimelech........ 2Sa 8:17 6659
lo Z also, and all the Levites........ 2Sa 15:24 6659
And the king said unto Z, Carry........ 2Sa 15:25 6659
king said also unto Z the priest........ 2Sa 15:27 6659
Z therefore and Abiathar carried........ 2Sa 15:29 6659
hast thou not there with thee Z........ 2Sa 15:35 6659
house, thou shalt tell it to Z........ 2Sa 15:35 6659
Then said Hushai unto Z and to........ 2Sa 17:15 6659
Then said Ahimaaz the son of Z........ 2Sa 18:19 6659
the son of Z yet again to Joab........ 2Sa 18:22 6659
running of Ahimaaz the son of Z........ 2Sa 18:27 6659
And king David sent to Z and to........ 2Sa 19:11 6659
and Z and Abiathar were the priests........ 2Sa 20:25 6659
But Z the priest, and Benaiah the........ 1Kin 1:8 6659
Z the priest, and Benaiah the son........ 1Kin 1:26 6659
Call me Z the priest, and Nathan........ 1Kin 1:32 6659
let Z the priest and Nathan the........ 1Kin 1:34 6659
So Z the priest, and Nathan the........ 1Kin 1:38 6659
Z the priest took an horn of oil........ 1Kin 1:39 6659
hath sent with him Z the priest........ 1Kin 1:44 6659
Z the priest and Nathan the........ 1Kin 1:45 6659
Z the priest did the king put in........ 1Kin 2:35 6659
Azariah the son of Z the priest........ 1Kin 4:2 6659
and Z and Abiathar were the priests........ 1Kin 4:4 6659
And Ahitub begat Z........ 1Chr 6:8 6659
and Z begat Ahimaaz........ 1Chr 6:8 6659
Z his son, Ahimaaz his son........ 1Chr 6:53 6659
And David called for Z and Abiathar........ 1Chr 15:11 6659
Z the priest, and his brethren the........ 1Chr 16:39 6659
Z the son of Ahitub, and Abimelech........ 1Chr 18:16 6659
both Z of the sons of Eleazar, and........ 1Chr 24:3 6659
Z the priest, and Ahimelech the........ 1Chr 24:6 6659
presence of David the king, and Z........ 1Chr 24:31 6659
of the Aaronites, Z........ 1Chr 27:17 6659
chief governor, and Z to be priest........ 1Chr 29:22 6659
of the house of Z answered him........ 2Chr 31:10 6659
The son of Shallum, the son of Z........ Ezr 7:2 6659
these are the sons of Z among the........ Eze 40:46 6659
Levites that be of the seed of Z........ Eze 43:19 6659
the Levites, the sons of Z........ Eze 44:15 6659
are sanctified of the sons of Z........ Eze 48:11 6659
2. Father of Jerusha.
was Jerusha, the daughter of Z........ 2Kin 15:33 6659
was Jerushah, the daughter of Z........ 2Chr 27:1 6659
3. Son of Ahitub.
And Ahitub begat Z, and Zadok begat........ 1Chr 6:12 6659
begat Zadok, and Z begat Shallum,........ 1Chr 6:12 6659
son of Meshullam, the son of Z........ 1Chr 9:11 6659
4. A warrior in David's army.
And Z, a young man mighty of........ 1Chr 12:28 6659
5. The son of Baana.
them repaired Z the son of Baana........ Neh 3:4 6659
6. A priest who rebuilt the wall.
After them repaired Z the son of........ Neh 3:29 6659
7. A renewer of the covenant.
Meshezabeel, Z, Jaddua,........ Neh 10:21 6659
8. A son of Meraioth.
son of Meshullam, the son of Z........ Neh 11:11 6659
9. A Temple servant.
Z the scribe, and of the Levites,........ Neh 13:13 6659

ZADOKITES See Zadok's.

ZADOK'S (*za'-doks*) *Refers to Zadok 1.*
their two sons, Ahimaaz Z son........ 2Sa 15:36 6659

ZAHAM (*za'-ham*) *A son of Rehoboam.*
Jeush, and Shamariah, and Z........ 2Chr 11:19 2093

ZAIR (*za'-ur*) *A city in Edom.*
So Joram went over to Z, and all........ 2Kin 8:21 6811

ZALAPH (*za'-laf*) *Father of Hanun.*
and Hanun the sixth son of Z........ Neh 3:30 6764

ZALMON (*zal'-mon*) See Ilai, Salmon.
1. A hill in Ephraim.
Abimelech gat him up to mount Z........ Judg 9:48 6756
2. A "mighty man" of David.
Z the Ahohite, Maharai the........ 2Sa 23:28 6756

ZALMONAH (*zal'-mo-nah*) *An Israelite encampment in the wilderness.*
from mount Hor, and pitched in Z........ Num 33:41 6758
And they departed from Z, and........ Num 33:42 6758

ZALMUNNA (*zal-mun'-nah*) *A Midianite king.*
and I am pursuing after Zebah and Z........ Judg 8:5 6759
Z now in thine hand, that we........ Judg 8:6 6759
Z into mine hand, then I will........ Judg 8:7 6759
Z were in Karkor, and their hosts........ Judg 8:10 6759
Z fled, he pursued after them, and........ Judg 8:12 6759
two kings of Midian, Zebah and Z........ Judg 8:12 6759
and said, Behold Zebah and Z........ Judg 8:15 6759
Z now in thine hand, that we........ Judg 8:15 6759
Then said he unto Zebah and Z........ Judg 8:18 6759
Z said, Rise thou, and fall upon........ Judg 8:21 6759
Gideon arose, and slew Zebah and Z........ Judg 8:21 6759
their princes as Zebah, and as Z........ Ps 83:11 6759

ZAMZUMMIMS (*zam-zum'-mims*) See Zuzims. *A tribe in Canaan.*
and the Ammonites call them Z........ Deut 2:20 2157

ZAMZUMMITES See Zamzummims.

ZANOAH (*za-no'-ah*)
1. A city on the plain of Judah.
And Z, and En-gannim, Tappuah, and........ Josh 15:34 2182
Hanun, and the inhabitants of Z........ Neh 3:13 2182
Z, Adullam, and in their villages,........ Neh 11:30 2182
2. A city in the hills of Judah.
And Jezreel, and Jokdeam, and Z........ Josh 15:56 2182
3. A descendant of Caleb.
and Jekuthiel the father of Z........ 1Chr 4:18 2182

ZAPHENATH-PANEAH See Zaphnath-paaneah.

ZAPHNATH-PAANEAH (*zaf''-nath-pa-a-ne'-ah*) *Name given to Joseph by Pharaoh.*
And Pharaoh called Joseph's name Z........ Gen 41:45 6847

ZAPHON (*za'-fon*) *A city in Gad.*
and Beth-nimrah, and Succoth, and Z........ Josh 13:27 6829

ZARA (*za'-rah*) See Zarah, Zerah. *Greek form of Zarah; an ancestor of Jesus.*
Judas begat Phares and Z of Thamar........ Mt 1:3 *2196*

ZARAH (*za'-rah*) See Zara, Zerah. *A son of Judah.*
and his name was called Z........ Gen 38:30 2226
Onan, and Shelah, and Pharez, and Z........ Gen 46:12 2226

ZAREAH (*za'-re-ah*) See Zareathites, Zorah. *A city in Judah.*
And at En-rimmon, and at Z, and at........ Neh 11:29 6881

ZAREATHITES (*za'-re-ath-ites*) See Zorathites. *Descendants of Shobal.*
of them came the Z, and the........ 1Chr 2:53 6882

ZARED (*za'-red*) See Zered. *A brook near the Dead Sea.*
and pitched in the valley of Z........ Num 21:12 2218

ZAREPHATH (*zar'-e-fath*) See Sarepta. *A city in Phoenicia.*
Arise, get thee to Z, which........ 1Kin 17:9 6886
So he arose and went to Z........ 1Kin 17:10 6886
of the Canaanites, even unto Z........ Obad 20 6886

ZARETAN (*zar'-e-tan*) See Zartanah, Zeredathah. *A city in Ephraim.*
the city Adam, that is beside Z........ Josh 3:16 6891

ZARETHAN See Zarthan.

ZARETH-SHAHAR (*za''-reth-sha'-har*) *A city in Reuben.*
Z in the mount of the valley,........ Josh 13:19 6890

ZARHITES (*zar'-hites*)
1. Descendants of Zerah, the Simeonite.
Of Zerah, the family of the Z........ Num 26:13 2227
and he took the family of the Z........ Josh 7:17 2227
the family of the Z man by man........ Josh 7:17 2227
Sibbecai the Hushathite, of the Z........ 1Chr 27:11 2227
the Netophathite, of the Z........ 1Chr 27:13 2227
2. Descendants of Zerah, son of Judah.
of Zerah, the family of the Z........ Num 26:20 2227

ZARTANAH (*zar'-ta-nah*) See Zaretan, Zarthan. *Same as Zaretan.*
which is by Z beneath Jezreel,........ 1Kin 4:12 6891

ZARTHAN (*zar'-than*) See Zaretan, Zartanah. *Same as Zaretan.*
clay ground between Succoth and Z........ 1Kin 7:46 6891

ZATTHU (*zath'-u*) See Zattu. *A renewer of the covenant.*
Parosh, Pahath-moab, Elam, Z........ Neh 10:14 2240

ZATTU (*zat'-tu*) See Zatthu. *A family of exiles.*
The children of Z, nine hundred........ Ezr 2:8 2240
And of the sons of Z........ Ezr 10:27 2240
The children of Z, eight hundred........ Neh 7:13 2240

ZAVAN (*za'-van*) See ZAAVAN. *Son of Ezer.*
Bilhan, and Z, and Jakan 1Chr 1:42 2190

ZAZA (*za'-zah*) *A son of Jonathan.*
Peleth, and Z 1Chr 2:33 2117

ZEAL
his *z* to the children of Israel 2Sa 21:2 7065
with me, and see my *z* for the LORD 2Kin 10:16 7068
the *z* of the LORD of hosts shall 2Kin 19:31 7068
For the *z* of thine house hath Ps 69:9 7068
My *z* hath consumed me, because Ps 119:139 7068
The *z* of the LORD of hosts will Is 9:7 7068
the *z* of the LORD of hosts shall Is 37:32 7068
and was clad with *z* as a cloke Is 59:17 7068
where is thy *z* and thy strength, Is 63:15 7068
I the LORD have spoken it in my *z* Eze 5:13 7068
The *z* of thine house hath eaten Jn 2:17 *2205*
record that they have a *z* of God Rom 10:2 *2205*
what vehement desire, yea, what *z* 2Cor 7:11 *2205*
your *z* hath provoked very many 2Cor 9:2 *2205*
Concerning *z*, persecuting the Phil 3:6 *2205*
that he hath a great *z* for you Col 4:13 *2205*

ZEALOT See ZELOTES.

ZEALOUS
while he was *z* for my sake among Num 25:11 7065
because he was *z* for his God Num 25:13 7065
and they are all *z* of the law Acts 21:20 *2207*
was *z* toward God, as ye all are Acts 22:3 *2207*
as ye are *z* of spiritual gifts 1Cor 14:12 *2207*
being more exceedingly *z* of the Gal 1:14 *2207*
peculiar people, *z* of good works Titus 2:14 *2207*
be *z* therefore, and repent Rev 3:19 *2206*

ZEALOUSLY
They *z* affect you, but not well Gal 4:17 *2206*
But it is good to be *z* affected Gal 4:18 *2206*

ZEBADIAH (*zeb-ad-i'-ah*)
1. Grandson of Elpael.
And Z, and Arad, and Ader, 1Chr 8:15 2069
2. A son of Elpael.
And Z, and Meshullam 1Chr 8:17 2069
3. A warrior in David's army.
And Joelah, and Z, the sons of 1Chr 12:7 2069
4. A Levite gatekeeper.
Z the third, Jathniel the fourth, 1Chr 26:2 2069
5. A son of Asahel.
of Joab, and Z his son after him 1Chr 27:7 2069
6. A messenger for King Jehoshaphat.
even Shemaiah, and Nethaniah, and Z. 2Chr 17:8 2069
7. Son of Ishmael.
Z the son of Ishmael, the ruler 2Chr 19:11 2069
8. A family of exiles.
Z the son of Michael, and with him Ezr 8:8 2069
9. Married a foreigner in exile.
Hanani, and Z Ezr 10:20 2069

ZEBAH (*ze'-bah*) *A king of Midian.*
faint, and I am pursuing after Z Judg 8:5 2078
Succoth said, Are the hands of Z Judg 8:6 2078
when the LORD hath delivered Z Judg 8:7 2078
Now Z and Zalmunna were in Karkor, Judg 8:10 2078
And when Z and Zalmunna fled, he Judg 8:12 2078
took the two kings of Midian, Z Judg 8:12 2078
men of Succoth, and said, Behold Z Judg 8:15 2078
me, saying, Are the hands of Z Judg 8:15 2078
Then said he unto Z and Zalmunna, Judg 8:18 2078
Then Z and Zalmunna said, Rise Judg 8:21 2078
And Gideon arose, and slew Z Judg 8:21 2078
yea, all their princes as Z Ps 83:11 2078

ZEBAIM (*ze-ba'-im*) *Residence of some exiles in Babylonia.*
the children of Pochereth of Z Ezr 2:57 6380
the children of Pochereth of Z Neh 7:59 6380

ZEBEDEE (*zeb'-e-dee*) See ZEBEDEE'S. *Father of James and John.*
two brethren, James the son of Z Mt 4:21 *2199*
in a ship with Z their father Mt 4:21 *2199*
James the son of Z, and John his Mt 10:2 *2199*
him Peter and the two sons of Z Mt 26:37 *2199*
thence, he saw James the son of Z Mk 1:19 *2199*
they left their father Z in the Mk 1:20 *2199*
And James the son of Z, and John Mk 3:17 *2199*
And James and John, the sons of Z Mk 10:35 *2199*
James, and John, the sons of Z Lk 5:10 *2199*
Cana in Galilee, and the sons of Z Jn 21:2 *2199*

ZEBEDEE'S (*zeb'-e-dees*)
of Z children with her sons Mt 20:20 *2199*
and the mother of Z children Mt 27:56 *2199*

ZEBIDAH See ZEBUDAH.

ZEBINA (*ze-bi'-nah*) *Married a foreigner in exile.*
Jeiel, Mattithiah, Zabad, Z Ezr 10:43 2081

ZEBOIIM (*ze-boy'-im*) See ZEBOIM. *City destroyed with Sodom and Gomorrah.*
of Admah, and Shemeber king of Z Gen 14:2 6636
king of Admah, and the king of Z Gen 14:8 6636

ZEBOIM (*ze-bo'-im*) See ZEBOIIM.
1. Same as Zeboiim.
and Gomorrah, and Admah, and Z Gen 10:19 6636
Sodom, and Gomorrah, Admah, and Z. Deut 29:23 6636
how shall I set thee as Z Hos 11:8 6636
2. A city in Benjamin.
valley of Z toward the wilderness 1Sa 13:18 6650
Hadid, Z, Neballat, Neh 11:34 6650

ZEBUDAH (*ze-bu'-dah*) *Mother of King Jehoshaphat.*
And his mother's name was Z 2Kin 23:36 2081

ZEBUL (*ze'-bul*) *A ruler of Shechem.*
and Z his officer Judg 9:28 2083
when Z the ruler of the city Judg 9:30 2083
Gaal saw the people, he said to Z Judg 9:36 2083
Z said unto him, Thou seest the Judg 9:36 2083
Then said Z unto him, Where is Judg 9:38 2083
Z thrust out Gaal and his brethren Judg 9:41 2083

ZEBULONITE (*zeb'-u-lon-ite*) See ZEBULONITES. *A descendant of Zebulun 1.*
And after him Elon, a Z, judged Judg 12:11 2075
And Elon the Z died, and was buried Judg 12:12 2075

ZEBULUN (*zeb'-u-lun*) See ZABULON, ZEBULONITE, ZEBULUNITES.
1. A son of Jacob.
and she called his name Z Gen 30:20 2074
Levi, and Judah, and Issachar, and Z Gen 35:23 2074
And the sons of Z Gen 46:14 2074
Z shall dwell at the haven of the Gen 49:13 2074
Issachar, Z, and Benjamin, Ex 1:3 2074
Levi, and Judah, Issachar, and Z 1Chr 2:1 2074
2. Descendants of Zebulun.
Of Z; Eliab the Num 1:9 2074
Of the children of Z, by their Num 1:30 2074
of them, even of the tribe of Z Num 1:31 2074
Then the tribe of Z Num 2:7 2074
be captain of the children of Z Num 2:7 2074
prince of the children of Z Num 7:24 2074
of Z was Eliab the son of Helon Num 10:16 2074
Of the tribe of Z, Gaddiel the Num 13:10 2074
Of the sons of Z after their Num 26:26 2074
of the tribe of the children of Z Num 34:25 2074
Reuben, Gad, and Asher, and Z Deut 27:13 2074
And of Zebulun he said, Rejoice, Z Deut 33:18 2074
of Z according to their families Josh 19:10 2074
of Z according to their families Josh 19:16 2074
to Beth-dagon, and reacheth to Z Josh 19:27 2074
reacheth to Z on the south side, Josh 19:34 2074
of Gad, and out of the tribe of Z Josh 21:7 2074
Levites, out of the tribe of Z Josh 21:34 2074
Neither did Z drive out the Judg 1:30 2074
Naphtali and of the children of Z Judg 4:6 2074
And Barak called Z and Naphtali to Judg 4:10 2074
out of Z they that handle the pen Judg 5:14 2074
Z and Naphtali were a people that Judg 5:18 2074
messengers unto Asher, and unto Z Judg 6:35 2074
in Aijalon in the country of Z Judg 12:12 2074
of Gad, and out of the tribe of Z 1Chr 6:63 2074
were given out of the tribe of Z 1Chr 6:77 2074
Of Z, such as went forth to 1Chr 12:33 2074
them, even unto Issachar and Z 1Chr 12:40 2074
Of Z, Ishmaiah the son of Obadiah 1Chr 27:19 2074
Ephraim and Manasseh even unto Z 2Chr 30:10 2074
of Z humbled themselves, and came 2Chr 30:11 2074
and Manasseh, Issachar, and Z 2Chr 30:18 2074
their council, the princes of Z Ps 68:27 2074
lightly afflicted the land of Z Is 9:1 2074
unto the west side, Z a portion Eze 48:26 2074
And by the border of Z, from the Eze 48:27 2074
gate of Issachar, one gate of Z Eze 48:33 2074

ZEBULUNITES (*zeb'-u-lun-ites*) *Descendants of Zebulun.*
Z according to those that were Num 26:27 2075

ZECHARIAH (*zek-a-ri'-ah*) See ZACCUR, ZACHARIAH, ZACHARIAS, ZACHER.
1. A chief Reubenite.
were the chief, Jeiel, and Z 1Chr 5:7 2148
2. A Levite gatekeeper.
Z the son of Meshelemiah was 1Chr 9:21 2148
Z the firstborn, Jediael the 1Chr 26:2 2148
Then for Z his son, a wise 1Chr 26:14 2148
was Abijah, the daughter of Z 2Chr 29:1 2148
3. A Benjamite.
And Gedor, and Ahio, and Z, and 1Chr 9:37 2148
4. A Levite musician.
brethren of the second degree, Z 1Chr 15:18 2148
And Z, and Aziel, and Shemiramoth, 1Chr 15:20 2148
Asaph the chief, and next to him Z 1Chr 16:5 2148
5. A Tabernacle priest.
and Nethaneel, and Amasai, and Z 1Chr 15:24 2148
6. A son of Isshiah.
sons of Isshiah; Z 1Chr 24:25 2148
7. Son of Hosah.
Tebaliah the third, Z the fourth 1Chr 26:11 2148
8. A chief of Manasseh.
in Gilead, Iddo the son of Z 1Chr 27:21 2148
9. A messenger of King Jehoshaphat.
Ben-hail, and to Obadiah, and to Z 2Chr 17:7 2148
10. Father of Jehaziel.
Then upon Jahaziel the son of Z 2Chr 20:14 2148
11. A son of Jehoshaphat.
Azariah, and Jehiel, and Z 2Chr 21:2 2148
12. Son of Jehoida.
the Spirit of God came upon Z the 2Chr 24:20 2148
13. A prophet in King Uzziah's time.
And he sought God in the days of Z 2Chr 26:5 2148
14. A Levite who cleansed the Temple.
Z, and Mattaniah 2Chr 29:13 2148
15. An overseer of the Temple repairs.
and Z and Meshullam, of the sons of 2Chr 34:12 2148
16. A prince of Judah.
Hilkiah and Z and Jehiel, rulers of 2Chr 35:8 2148
17. A prophet in Judah.
Z the son of Iddo, prophesied Ezr 5:1 2148
the prophet and Z the son of Iddo Ezr 6:14 2148
came the word of the LORD unto Z Zec 1:1 2148
came the word of the LORD unto Z Zec 1:7 2148
Z in the fourth day of the ninth Zec 7:1 2148
the word of the LORD came unto Z Zec 7:8 2148
18. A son of Pharosh.
sons of Pharosh; Z Ezr 8:3 2148
19. A son of Bebai.
Z the son of Bebai, and with him Ezr 8:11 2148
Elnathan, and for Nathan, and for Z Ezr 8:16 2148
20. Married a foreigner in exile.
Mattaniah, Z, and Jehiel, and Abdi, Ezr 10:26 2148
21. A prince who aided Ezra.
and Hashum, and Hashbadana, Z Neh 8:4 2148
22. A descendant of Pharez.
the son of Uzziah, the son of Z Neh 11:4 2148
23. A son of Shiloni.
the son of Joiarib, the son of Z Neh 11:5 2148
24. Father of a resettler in Jerusalem.
the son of Amzi, the son of Z Neh 11:12 2148
25. A priest in Joiakim's time.
Of Iddo, Z Neh 12:16 2148
26. A priest who dedicated the wall.
Z the son of Jonathan, the son of Neh 12:35 2148
Miniamin, Michaiah, Elioenai, Z Neh 12:41 2148
27. Son of Jeber.
and Z the son of Jeberechiah Is 8:2 2148

ZECHER See ZACHER.

ZEDAD (*ze'-dad*) *A place near Hamath.*
forth of the border shall be to Z Num 34:8 6657
way of Hethlon, as men go to Z Eze 47:15 6657

ZEDEKIAH (*zed-e-ki'-ah*) See MATTANIAH, ZEDEKIAH'S, ZIDKIJAH.
1. A false prophet.
Z the son of Chenaanah made him 1Kin 22:11 6667
But Z the son of Chenaanah went 1Kin 22:24 6667
Z the son of Chenaanah had made 2Chr 18:10 6667
Then Z the son of Chenaanah came 2Chr 18:23 6667
2. Name given to Mattaniah by Nebuchadnezzar.
stead, and changed his name to Z 2Kin 24:17 6667
Z was twenty and one years old 2Kin 24:18 6667
that Z rebelled against the king 2Kin 24:20 6667
unto the eleventh year of king Z 2Kin 25:2 6667
the sons of Z before his eyes 2Kin 25:7 6667
eyes, and put out the eyes of Z 2Kin 25:7 6667
the second Jehoiakim, the third Z 1Chr 3:15 6667
made Z his brother king over 2Chr 36:10 6667
Z was one and twenty years old 2Chr 36:11 6667
Z the son of Josiah king of Judah Jer 1:3 6667
when king Z sent unto him Pashur Jer 21:1 6667
unto them, Thus shall ye say to Z Jer 21:3 6667
I will deliver Z king of Judah Jer 21:7 6667
So will I give Z the king of Jer 24:8 6667
to Jerusalem unto Z king of Judah Jer 27:3 6667
I spake also to Z king of Judah Jer 27:12 6667
of the reign of Z king of Judah Jer 28:1 6667
(whom Z king of Judah sent unto Jer 29:3 6667
the tenth year of Z king of Judah Jer 32:1 6667
For Z king of Judah had shut him Jer 32:3 6667
Z king of Judah shall not escape Jer 32:4 6667
And he shall lead Z to Babylon Jer 32:5 6667
speak to Z king of Judah, and tell Jer 34:2 6667
of the LORD, O Z king of Judah Jer 34:4 6667
unto Z king of Judah in Jerusalem Jer 34:6 6667
after that the king Z had made a Jer 34:8 6667
Z king of Judah and his princes Jer 34:21 6667
king Z the son of Josiah reigned Jer 37:1 6667
Z the king sent Jehucal the son Jer 37:3 6667
Then Z the king sent, and took him Jer 37:17 6667
Jeremiah said unto king Z Jer 37:18 6667
Then Z the king commanded that Jer 37:21 6667
Then Z the king said, Behold, he Jer 38:5 6667
Then Z the king sent, and took Jer 38:14 6667
Then Jeremiah said unto Z Jer 38:15 6667
So Z the king sware secretly unto Jer 38:16 6667
Then said Jeremiah unto Z Jer 38:17 6667
Z the king said unto Jeremiah, I Jer 38:19 6667
Then said Z unto Jeremiah, Let no Jer 38:24 6667
the ninth year of Z king of Judah Jer 39:1 6667
And in the eleventh year of Z Jer 39:2 6667
that when Z the king of Judah saw Jer 39:4 6667
overtook Z in the plains of Jer 39:5 6667
of Z in Riblah before his eyes Jer 39:6 6667
as I gave Z king of Judah into Jer 44:30 6667
of the reign of Z king of Judah Jer 49:34 6667
when he went with Z the king of Jer 51:59 6667
Z was one and twenty years old Jer 52:1 6667
that Z rebelled against the king Jer 52:3 6667
unto the eleventh year of king Z Jer 52:5 6667
overtook Z in the plains of Jer 52:8 6667
the sons of Z before his eyes Jer 52:10 6667
Then he put out the eyes of Z Jer 52:11 6667
3. Grandson of Jehoiakim.
Jeconiah his son, Z his son 1Chr 3:16 6667
4. A false prophet denounced by Jeremiah.
of Z the son of Maaseiah, which Jer 29:21 6667
saying, The LORD make thee like Z Jer 29:22 6667
5. A prince of Judah.
Z the son of Hananiah, and all the Jer 36:12 6667

ZEDEKIAH'S (*zed-e-ki'-ahs*) *Refers to Zedekiah 2.*
Moreover he put out Z eyes Jer 39:7 6667

ZEEB (*ze'-eb*) *A Midianite prince.*
of the Midianites, Oreb and Z Judg 7:25 2062
Z they slew at the winepress of Judg 7:25 2062
they slew at the winepress of Z Judg 7:25 2062
Z to Gideon on the other side Judg 7:25 2062
the princes of Midian, Oreb and Z Judg 8:3 2062
their nobles like Oreb, and like Z Ps 83:11 2062

ZELA See ZELAH.

ZELAH (*ze'-lah*) *A city in Benjamin.*
And Z, Eleph, and Jebusi, which is Josh 18:28 6762
in the country of Benjamin in Z 2Sa 21:14 6762

ZELEK (*ze'-lek*) *A "mighty man" of David.*
Z the Ammonite, Nahari the 2Sa 23:37 6768
Z the Ammonite, Naharai the 1Chr 11:39 6768

ZELOPHEHAD (*ze-lo'-fe-had*) *Son of Hepher.*
Z the son of Hepher had no sons, ... Num 26:33 6765
of the daughters of Z were Mahlah ... Num 26:33 6765
Then came the daughters of Z ... Num 27:1 6765
The daughters of Z speak right ... Num 27:7 6765
Z our brother unto his daughters ... Num 36:2 6765
concerning the daughters of Z ... Num 36:6 6765
Moses, so did the daughters of Z ... Num 36:10 6765
and Noah, the daughters of Z ... Num 36:11 6765
But Z, the son of Hepher, the son ... Josh 17:3 6765
and the name of the second was Z ... 1Chr 7:15 6765
and Z had daughters ... 1Chr 7:15 6765

ZELOTES (*ze-lo'-teze*) See CANAANITE, SIMON. *Surname of Simon, disciple of Jesus.*
of Alphaeus, and Simon called Z ... Lk 6:15 *2208*
the son of Alphaeus, and Simon Z ... Acts 1:13 *2208*

ZELZAH (*zel'-zah*) *A city in Benjamin.*
in the border of Benjamin at Z ... 1Sa 10:2 6766

ZEMARAIM (*zem-a-ra'-im*) See ZEMARITE.
1. A city in Benjamin.
And Beth-arabah, and Z, and Beth-el, .. Josh 18:22 6787
2. A mountain in Ephraim.
And Abijah stood up upon mount Z ... 2Chr 13:4 6787

ZEMARITE *A descendant of Canaan.*
And the Arvadite, and the Z ... Gen 10:18 6786
And the Arvadite, and the Z ... 1Chr 1:16 6786

ZEMIRA (*ze-mi'-rah*) *A son of Becher.*
Z, and Joash, and Eliezer, and ... 1Chr 7:8 2160

ZEMIRAH See ZEMIRA.

ZENAN (*ze'-nan*) See ZAANAN. *A city in Judah.*
Z, and Hadashah, and Migdal-gad, ... Josh 15:37 6799

ZENAS (*ze'-nas*) *A Christian lawyer.*
Bring Z the lawyer and Apollos on ... Titus 3:13 *2211*

ZEPHANIAH (*zef-a-ni'-ah*)
1. A priest in exile.
Z the second priest, and the three ... 2Kin 25:18 6846
Z the son of Maaseiah the priest, ... Jer 21:1 6846
to Z the son of Maaseiah the ... Jer 29:25 6846
Z the priest read this letter in ... Jer 29:29 6846
Z the son of Maaseiah the priest ... Jer 37:3 6846
Z the second priest, and the three ... Jer 52:24 6846
2. An ancestor of Samuel.
the son of Azariah, the son of Z ... 1Chr 6:36 6846
3. A prophet.
came unto Z the son of Cushi ... Zeph 1:1 6846
4. Son of Josiah the priest.
the house of Josiah the son of Z ... Zec 6:10 6846
Jedaiah, and to Hen the son of Z ... Zec 6:14 6846

ZEPHATH (*ze'-fath*) See HORMAH. *A city in Simeon.*
the Canaanites that inhabited Z ... Judg 1:17 6857

ZEPHATHAH (*zef'-a-thah*) *A valley in Judah.*
in the valley of Z at Mareshah ... 2Chr 14:10 6859

ZEPHI (*ze'-fi*) See ZEPHO. *Son of Eliphaz.*
Teman, and Omar, Z, and Gatam, ... 1Chr 1:36 6825

ZEPHO (*ze'-fo*) See ZEPHI. *Same as Zephi.*
of Eliphaz were Teman, Omar, Z ... Gen 36:11 6825
duke Teman, duke Omar, duke Z ... Gen 36:15 6825

ZEPHON (*ze'-fon*) See ZEPHONITES, ZIPHION. *A son of Gad.*
of Z, the family of the ... Num 26:15 6827

ZEPHONITES (*zef'-on-ites*) *Descendants of Zephon.*
of Zephon, the family of the Z ... Num 26:15 6831

ZER (*zur*) *A city in Naphtali.*
the fenced cities are Ziddim, Z ... Josh 19:35 6863

ZERAH (*ze'-rah*) See EZRAHITE, ZARAH, ZARHITES, ZOHAR.
1. A son of Reuel.
Nahath, and Z, Shammah, and Mizzah Gen 36:13 2226
duke Nahath, duke Z, duke Shammah. Gen 36:17 2226
Nahath, Z, Shammah, and Mizzah ... 1Chr 1:37 2226
2. Father of Jobab.
Jobab the son of Z of Bozrah ... Gen 36:33 2226
Jobab the son of Z of Bozrah ... 1Chr 1:44 2226
3. Son of Judah.
of Z, the family of the Zarhites ... Num 26:20 2226
the son of Zabdi, the son of Z ... Josh 7:1 2226
the son of Zabdi, the son of Z ... Josh 7:18 2226
with him, took Achan the son of Z ... Josh 7:24 2226
son of Z commit a trespass in the ... Josh 22:20 2226
in law bare him Pharez and Z ... 1Chr 2:4 2226
And the sons of Z ... 1Chr 2:6 2226
And of the sons of Z ... 1Chr 9:6 2226
children of Z the son of Judah ... Neh 11:24 2226
4. A son of Simeon.
Of Z, the family of the Zarhites ... Num 26:13 2226
were, Nemuel, and Jamin, Jarib, Z ... 1Chr 4:24 2226
5. Son of Iddo.
Z his son, Jeaterai his son ... 1Chr 6:21 2226
6. Father of Ethni.
The son of Ethni, the son of Z ... 1Chr 6:41 2226
7. An Ethiopian king.
there came out against them Z the ... 2Chr 14:9 2226

ZERAHIAH (*zer-a-hi'-ah*)
1. An ancestor of Ezra.
And Uzzi begat Z, and Z ... 1Chr 6:6 2228
Z, and Z begat Meraioth, ... 1Chr 6:6 2228
his son, Uzzi his son, Z his son, ... 1Chr 6:51 2228
The son of Z, the son of Uzzi, ... Ezr 7:4 2228
2. Father of Elihoenai.
Elihoenai the son of Z, and with ... Ezr 8:4 2228

ZERAHITE See ZARHITES.

ZERED (*ze'-red*) See ZARED. *Same as Zared.*
I, and get you over the brook Z ... Deut 2:13 2218
And we went over the brook Z ... Deut 2:13 2218
we were come over the brook Z ... Deut 2:14 2218

ZEREDA (*zer'-e-dah*) *A city north of Mt. Ephraim.*
son of Nebat, an Ephrathite of Z ... 1Kin 11:26 6868

ZEREDAH See ZEREDATHAH.

ZEREDATHAH (*ze-red'-a-thah*) See ZARTHAN, ZERERATH. *A city in Manasseh.*
clay ground between Succoth and Z ... 2Chr 4:17 6868

ZERERAH See ZERERATH.

ZERERATH (*zer'-e-rath*) See ZARTHAN, ZEREDATHAH. *A district in Manasseh.*
host fled to Beth-shittah in Z ... Judg 7:22 6888

ZERESH (*ze'-resh*) *Wife of Haman.*
for his friends, and Z his wife ... Est 5:10 2238
Then said Z his wife and all his ... Est 5:14 2238
And Haman told Z his wife and all ... Est 6:13 2238
Z his wife unto him, If Mordecai ... Est 6:13 2238

ZERETH (*ze'-reth*) *A descendant of Judah.*
And the sons of Helah were, Z ... 1Chr 4:7 6889

ZERETH-SHAHAR See ZERETH.

ZERI (*ze'-ri*) See IZRI. *Son of Jeduthun.*
Gedaliah, and Z, and Jeshaiah, ... 1Chr 25:3 6874

ZEROR (*ze'-ror*) *Ancestor of King Saul.*
the son of Abiel, the son of Z ... 1Sa 9:1 6872

ZERUAH (*ze-ru'-ah*) *Mother of Jeroboam I.*
whose mother's name was Z ... 1Kin 11:26 6871

ZERUBBABEL (*ze-rub'-ba-bel*) See SHESHBAZZAR, ZOROBABEL. *A leader of a group of exiles.*
And the sons of Pedaiah were, Z ... 1Chr 3:19 2216
and the sons of Z ... 1Chr 3:19 2216
Which came with Z ... Ezr 2:2 2216
Z the son of Shealtiel, and his ... Ezr 3:2 2216
began Z the son of Shealtiel, and ... Ezr 3:8 2216
Then they came to Z, and to the ... Ezr 4:2 2216
But Z, and Jeshua, and the rest of ... Ezr 4:3 2216
Then rose up Z the son of ... Ezr 5:2 2217
Who came with Z, Jeshua, Nehemiah .. Neh 7:7 2216
up with Z the son of Shealtiel ... Neh 12:1 2216
And all Israel in the days of Z ... Neh 12:47 2216
unto Z the son of Shealtiel ... Hag 1:1 2216
Then Z the son of Shealtiel, and ... Hag 1:12 2216
spirit of Z the son of Shealtiel ... Hag 1:14 2216
Speak now to Z the son of ... Hag 2:2 2216
Yet now be strong, O Z, saith the ... Hag 2:4 2216
Speak to Z, governor of Judah, ... Hag 2:21 2216
of hosts, will I take thee, O Z ... Hag 2:23 2216
is the word of the LORD unto Z ... Zec 4:6 2216
before Z thou shalt become a ... Zec 4:7 2216
The hands of Z have laid the ... Zec 4:9 2216
in the hand of Z with those seven ... Zec 4:10 2216

ZERUIAH (*ze-ru-i'-ah*) *Sister of David.*
and to Abishai the son of Z ... 1Sa 26:6 6870
And Joab the son of Z, and the ... 2Sa 2:13 6870
there were three sons of Z there ... 2Sa 2:18 6870
the sons of Z be too hard for me ... 2Sa 3:39 6870
Joab the son of Z was over the ... 2Sa 8:16 6870
Now Joab the son of Z perceived ... 2Sa 14:1 6870
the son of Z unto the king ... 2Sa 16:9 6870
I to do with you, ye sons of Z ... 2Sa 16:10 6870
sister to Z Joab's mother ... 2Sa 17:25 6870
the hand of Abishai the son of Z ... 2Sa 18:2 6870
But Abishai the son of Z answered ... 2Sa 19:21 6870
I to do with you, ye sons of Z ... 2Sa 19:22 6870
the son of Z succoured him ... 2Sa 21:17 6870
the brother of Joab, the son of Z ... 2Sa 23:18 6870
armourbearer to Joab the son of Z ... 2Sa 23:37 6870
conferred with Joab the son of Z ... 1Kin 1:7 6870
what Joab the son of Z did to me ... 1Kin 2:5 6870
priest, and for Joab the son of Z ... 1Kin 2:22 6870
Whose sisters were Z, and Abigail ... 1Chr 2:16 6870
And the sons of Z ... 1Chr 2:16 6870
Joab the son of Z went first up ... 1Chr 11:6 6870
armourbearer of Joab the son of Z ... 1Chr 11:39 6870
Abishai the son Z slew of the ... 1Chr 18:12 6870
Joab the son of Z was over the ... 1Chr 18:15 6870
son of Ner, and Joab the son of Z ... 1Chr 26:28 6870
Joab the son of Z began to number ... 1Chr 27:24 6870

ZETHAM (*ze'-tham*) *A descendant of Laadan.*
the chief was Jehiel, and Z ... 1Chr 23:8 2241
Z, and Joel his brother, which ... 1Chr 26:22 2241

ZETHAN (*ze'-than*) *A son of Bilhan.*
and Ehud, and Chenaanah, and Z ... 1Chr 7:10 2133

ZETHAR (*ze'-thar*) *A servant of King Ahasuerus.*
Harbona, Bigtha, and Abagtha, Z ... Est 1:10 2242

ZEUS See MERCURIUS.

ZIA (*zi'-ah*) *A Gadite in Bashan.*
Sheba, and Jorai, and Jachan, and Z ... 1Chr 5:13 2127

ZIBA (*zi'-bah*) *A servant of King Saul.*
Saul a servant whose name was Z ... 2Sa 9:2 6717
king said unto him, Art thou Z ... 2Sa 9:2 6717
Z said unto the king, Jonathan ... 2Sa 9:3 6717
Z said unto the king, Behold, he ... 2Sa 9:4 6717
Then the king called to Z ... 2Sa 9:9 6717
Now Z had fifteen sons and twenty ... 2Sa 9:10 6717
Then said Z unto the king, ... 2Sa 9:11 6717
all that dwelt in the house of Z ... 2Sa 9:12 6717
Z the servant of Mephibosheth met ... 2Sa 16:1 6717
And the king said unto Z, What ... 2Sa 16:2 6717
Z said, The asses be for the ... 2Sa 16:2 6717
Z said unto the king, Behold, he ... 2Sa 16:3 6717
Then said the king to Z, Behold, ... 2Sa 16:4 6717
Z said, I humbly beseech thee ... 2Sa 16:4 6717
Z the servant of the house of ... 2Sa 19:17 6717
said, Thou and Z divide the land ... 2Sa 19:29 6717

ZIBEON (*zib'-e-un*)
1. Grandfather of Adah.
Anah the daughter of Z the Hivite ... Gen 36:2 6649
of Anah the daughter of Z ... Gen 36:14 6649
2. A son of Seir.
Lotan, and Shobal, and Z, and Anah, ... Gen 36:20 6649
And these are the children of Z ... Gen 36:24 6649
he fed the asses of Z his father ... Gen 36:24 6649
duke Lotan, duke Shobal, duke Z ... Gen 36:29 6649
Lotan, and Shobal, and Z, and Anah, ... 1Chr 1:38 6649
And the sons of Z ... 1Chr 1:40 6649

ZIBIA (*zib'-e-ah*) *Son of Hodesh.*
of Hodesh his wife, Jobab, and Z ... 1Chr 8:9 6644

ZIBIAH (*zib'-e-ah*) *Mother of King Jehoash.*
mother's name was Z of Beer-sheba ... 2Kin 12:1 6645
name also was Z of Beer-sheba ... 2Chr 24:1 6645

ZICHRI (*zik'-ri*) See ZITHRI.
1. A son of Izhar.
Korah, and Nepheg, and Z ... Ex 6:21 2147
2. A Benjamite.
And Jakim, and Z, and Zabdi, ... 1Chr 8:19 2147
3. Son of Shishak.
And Abdon, and Z, and Hanan, ... 1Chr 8:23 2147
4. Son of Jeroham.
And Jaresiah, and Eliah, and Z ... 1Chr 8:27 2147
5. Son of Asaph.
the son of Micah, the son of Z ... 1Chr 9:15 2147
6. Descendant of Eliezer.
Z his son, and Shelomith his son ... 1Chr 26:25 2147
7. Father of Eliezer.
was Eliezer the son of Z ... 1Chr 27:16 2147
8. Father of Amasiah.
next him was Amasiah the son of Z ... 2Chr 17:16 2147
9. Father of Elishaphat.
and Elishaphat the son of Z ... 2Chr 23:1 2147
10. A "mighty man" of Ephraim.
And Z, a mighty man of Ephraim, ... 2Chr 28:7 2147
11. Father of Joel.
Joel the son of Z was their ... Neh 11:9 2147
12. A priest with Zerubbabel.
Of Abijah, Z ... Neh 12:17 2147

ZICRI See ZICHRI.

ZIDDIM (*zid'-dim*) *A city in Naphtali.*
And the fenced cities are Z ... Josh 19:35 6661

ZIDKIJAH (*zid-ki'-jah*) See ZEDEKIAH. *A clan leader who renewed the covenant.*
the son of Hachaliah, and Z ... Neh 10:1 6667

ZIDON (*zi'-don*)
1. A city in Asher.
and his border shall be unto Z ... Gen 49:13 6721
them, and chased them unto great Z ... Josh 11:8 6721
and Kanah, even unto great Z ... Josh 19:28 6721
Accho, nor the inhabitants of Z ... Judg 1:31 6721
gods of Syria, and the gods of Z ... Judg 10:6 6721
because it was far from Z ... Judg 18:28 6721
came to Dan-jaan, and about to Z ... 2Sa 24:6 6721
Zarephath, which belongeth to Z ... 1Kin 17:9 6721
and drink, and oil, unto them of Z ... Ezr 3:7 6722
thou whom the merchants of Z ... Is 23:2 6721
Be thou ashamed, O Z ... Is 23:4 6721
oppressed virgin, daughter of Z ... Is 23:12 6721
of Tyrus, and all the kings of Z ... Jer 25:22 6721
of Tyrus, and to the king of Z ... Jer 27:3 6721
Z every helper that remaineth ... Jer 47:4 6721
The inhabitants of Z and Arvad ... Eze 27:8 6721
of man, set thy face against Z ... Eze 28:21 6721
Behold, I am against thee, O Z ... Eze 28:22 6721
ye to do with me, O Tyre, and Z ... Joel 3:4 6721
Tyrus, and Z, though it be very ... Zec 9:2 6721
2. A son of Canaan.
Canaan begat Z his firstborn, and ... 1Chr 1:13 6721

ZIDONIANS (*zi-do'-ne-uns*) See SIDONIANS. *Inhabitants of Zidon.*
The Z also, and the Amalekites, and ... Judg 10:12 6722
after the manner of the Z ... Judg 18:7 6722
and they were far from the Z ... Judg 18:7 6722
Moabites, Ammonites, Edomites, Z ... 1Kin 11:1 6722
Ashtoreth the goddess of the Z ... 1Kin 11:5 6722
Ashtoreth the goddess of the Z ... 1Kin 11:33 6722
daughter of Ethbaal king of the Z ... 1Kin 16:31 6722
the abomination of the Z, and for ... 2Kin 23:13 6722
for the Z and they of Tyre brought ... 1Chr 22:4 6722
north, all of them, and all the Z ... Eze 32:30 6722

ZIF (*zif*) *Second month of the Hebrew year.*
reign over Israel, in the month Z ... 1Kin 6:1 2099
of the LORD laid, in the month Z ... 1Kin 6:37 2099

ZIHA (*zi'-hah*)
1. A family of exiles.
the children of Z, the children ... Ezr 2:43 6727
the children of Z, the children ... Neh 7:46 6727
2. An overseer of Temple servants.
and Z and Gispa were over the ... Neh 11:21 6727

ZIKLAG (*zik'-lag*) *A city in Judah.*
And Z, and Madmannah ... Josh 15:31 6860
And Z, and Beth-marcaboth, and ... Josh 19:5 6860
Then Achish gave him Z that day ... 1Sa 27:6 6860
wherefore Z pertaineth unto the ... 1Sa 27:6 6860
were come to Z on the third day ... 1Sa 30:1 6860
south, and Z, and smitten Z ... 1Sa 30:1 6860
and we burned Z with fire ... 1Sa 30:14 6860
And when David came to Z, he sent ... 1Sa 30:26 6860
and David had abode two days in Z ... 2Sa 1:1 6860
hold of him, and slew him in Z ... 2Sa 4:10 6860

at Bethuel, and at Hormah, and at Z.... 1Chr 4:30 6860
are they that came to David to Z.......... 1Chr 12:1 6860
As he went to Z, there fell to................ 1Chr 12:20 6860
And at Z, and at Mekonah, and in the. Neh 11:28 6860

ZILLAH (*zil'-lah*) *A wife of Lamech.*
Adah, and the name of the other Z...... Gen 4:19 6741
And Z, she also bare Tubal-cain,........... Gen 4:22 6741
said unto his wives, Adah and Z............ Gen 4:23 6741

ZILLETHAI See Zilthai.

ZILPAH (*zil'-pah*) *Handmaid of Leah.*
Leah Z his maid for an handmaid......... Gen 29:24 2153
left bearing, she took Z her maid.......... Gen 30:9 2153
Z Leah's maid bare Jacob a son............. Gen 30:10 2153
Z Leah's maid bare Jacob a second......... Gen 30:12 2153
And the sons of Z, Leah's handmaid.... Gen 35:26 2153
of Bilhah, and with the sons of Z.......... Gen 37:2 2153
These are the sons of Z, whom............. Gen 46:18 2153

ZILTHAI (*zil'-thahee*)
1. Son of Shimhi.
And Elienai, and Z, and Eliel,............... 1Chr 8:20 6769
2. A warrior in David's army.
and Jozabad, and Elihu, and Z............. 1Chr 12:20 6769

ZIMMAH (*zim'-mah*)
1. A son of Jahath.
son, Jahath his son, Z his son,.............. 1Chr 6:20 2155
2. A Gershonite.
The son of Ethan, the son of Z.............. 1Chr 6:42 2155
3. Father of Joah.
Joah the son of Z, and Eden the............ 2Chr 29:12 2155

ZIMRAN (*zim'-ran*) *A son of Abraham.*
And she bare him Z, and Jokshan, and Gen 25:2 2175
she bare Z, and Jokshan, and Medan,.. 1Chr 1:32 2175

ZIMRI (*zim'-ri*)
1. A Simeonite.
with the Midianitish woman, was Z...... Num 25:14 2174
2. A king of Israel.
And his servant Z, captain of half......... 1Kin 16:9 2174
Z went in and smote him, and killed.... 1Kin 16:10 2174
Thus did Z destroy all the house........... 1Kin 16:12 2174
did Z reign seven days in Tirzah........... 1Kin 16:15 2174
Z hath conspired, and hath also............ 1Kin 16:16 2174
when Z saw that the city was............... 1Kin 16:18 2174
Now the rest of the acts of Z................ 1Kin 16:20 2174
Had Z peace, who slew his master........ 2Kin 9:31 2174
3. A son of Zerah.
Z, and Ethan, and Heman, and Calcol,. 1Chr 2:6 2174
4. Son of Jehoadah.
begat Alemeth, and Azmaveth, and Z.. 1Chr 8:36 2174
and Z begat Moza,................................ 1Chr 8:36 2174
begat Alemeth, and Azmaveth, and Z.. 1Chr 9:42 2174
and Z begat Moza.................................. 1Chr 9:42 2174
5. An unspecified place.
And all the kings of Z, and all the........ Jer 25:25 2174

ZIN (*zin*) *A wilderness south of Judah.*
the wilderness of Z unto Rehob............ Num 13:21 6790
desert of Z in the first month................ Num 20:1 6790
my commandment in the desert of Z... Num 27:14 6790
in Kadesh in the wilderness of Z.......... Num 27:14 6790
and pitched in the wilderness of Z........ Num 33:36 6790
of Z along by the coast of Edom........... Num 34:3 6790
of Akrabbim, and pass on to Z.............. Num 34:4 6790
in the wilderness of Z........................... Deut 32:51 6790
of Edom the wilderness of Z................. Josh 15:1 6790
and passed along to Z, and.................. Josh 15:3 6790

ZINA (*zi'-nah*) *A son of Shimei.*
sons of Shimei were, Jahath, Z............. 1Chr 23:10 2126

ZION (*zi'-un*) See Sion, Zion's. *A term for Jerusalem.*
David took the strong hold of Z............ 2Sa 5:7 6726
of the city of David, which is Z............ 1Kin 8:1 6726
daughter of Z hath despised thee......... 2Kin 19:21 6726
they that escape out of mount Z........... 2Kin 19:31 6726
David took the castle of Z.................... 1Chr 11:5 6726
of the city of David, which is Z............ 2Chr 5:2 6726
my king upon my holy hill of Z.............. Ps 2:6 6726
to the Lord, which dwelleth in Z.......... Ps 9:11 6726
in the gates of the daughter of Z.......... Ps 9:14 6726
of Israel were come out of Z................ Ps 14:7 6726
and strengthen thee out of Z................. Ps 20:2 6726
of the whole earth, is mount Z.............. Ps 48:2 6726
Let mount Z rejoice, let the.................. Ps 48:11 6726
Walk about Z, and go round about......... Ps 48:12 6726
Out of Z, the perfection of.................... Ps 50:2 6726
good in thy good pleasure unto Z......... Ps 51:18 6726
of Israel were come out of Z................ Ps 53:6 6726
For God will save Z, and will................ Ps 69:35 6726
this mount Z, wherein thou hast........... Ps 74:2 6726
and his dwelling place in Z.................. Ps 76:2 6726
the mount Z which he loved.................. Ps 78:68 6726
of them in Z appeareth before God........ Ps 84:7 6726
The Lord loveth the gates of Z............. Ps 87:2 6726
of Z it shall be said, This and............. Ps 87:5 6726
Z heard, and was glad......................... Ps 97:8 6726
The Lord is great in Z......................... Ps 99:2 6726
shalt arise, and have mercy upon Z...... Ps 102:13 6726
When the Lord shall build up Z............ Ps 102:16 6726
declare the name of the Lord in Z........ Ps 102:21 6726
the rod of thy strength out of Z........... Ps 110:2 6726
in the Lord shall be as mount Z........... Ps 125:1 6726
turned again the captivity of Z............. Ps 126:1 6726
Lord shall bless thee out of Z............. Ps 128:5 6726
and turned back that hate Z................ Ps 129:5 6726
For the Lord hath chosen Z................. Ps 132:13 6726
descended upon the mountains of Z..... Ps 133:3 6726
and earth bless thee out of Z.............. Ps 134:3 6726
Blessed be the Lord out of Z............... Ps 135:21 6726
we wept, when we remembered Z.......... Ps 137:1 6726
Sing us one of the songs of Z.............. Ps 137:3 6726
reign for ever, even thy God, O Z......... Ps 146:10 6726
praise thy God, O Z.............................. Ps 147:12 6726
let the children of Z be joyful.............. Ps 149:2 6726
Go forth, O ye daughters of Z.............. Song 3:11 6726
the daughter of Z is left as a............... Is 1:8 6726
Z shall be redeemed with judgment...... Is 1:27 6726
for out of Z shall go forth the.............. Is 2:3 6726
the daughters of Z are haughty............ Is 3:16 6726
of the head of the daughters of Z......... Is 3:17 6726
pass, that he that is left in Z............... Is 4:3 6726
the filth of the daughters of Z............. Is 4:4 6726
every dwelling place of mount Z........... Is 4:5 6726
hosts, which dwelleth in mount Z......... Is 8:18 6726
his whole work upon mount Z............... Is 10:12 6726
O my people that dwellest in Z............. Is 10:24 6726
the mount of the daughter of Z............ Is 10:32 6726
and shout, thou inhabitant of Z........... Is 12:6 6726
That the Lord hath founded Z.............. Is 14:32 6726
the mount of the daughter of Z............ Is 16:1 6726
of the Lord of hosts, the mount Z........ Is 18:7 6726
of hosts shall reign in mount Z........... Is 24:23 6726
I lay in Z for a foundation a................ Is 28:16 6726
be, that fight against mount Z............ Is 29:8 6726
shall dwell in Z at Jerusalem............... Is 30:19 6726
come down to fight for mount Z.......... Is 31:4 6726
the Lord, whose fire is in Z................ Is 31:9 6726
he hath filled Z with judgment............. Is 33:5 6726
The sinners in Z are afraid.................. Is 33:14 6726
Look upon Z, the city of our................. Is 33:20 6726
for the controversy of Z...................... Is 34:8 6726
and come to Z with songs and.............. Is 35:10 6726
The virgin, the daughter of Z............... Is 37:22 6726
they that escape out of mount Z.......... Is 37:32 6726
O Z, that bringest good tidings,.......... Is 40:9 6726
The first shall say to Z, Behold,.......... Is 41:27 6726
in Z for Israel my glory....................... Is 46:13 6726
But Z said, The Lord hath................... Is 49:14 6726
For the Lord shall comfort Z............... Is 51:3 6726
and come with singing unto Z.............. Is 51:11 6726
of the earth, and say unto Z............... Is 51:16 6726
put on thy strength, O Z..................... Is 52:1 6726
thy neck, O captive daughter of Z........ Is 52:2 6726
that saith unto Z, Thy God.................. Is 52:7 6726
when the Lord shall bring again Z........ Is 52:8 6726
And the Redeemer shall come to Z........ Is 59:20 6726
The Z of the Holy One of Israel........... Is 60:14 6726
appoint unto them that mourn in Z....... Is 61:3 6726
Say ye to the daughter of Z................. Is 62:11 6726
Z is a wilderness, Jerusalem a............ Is 64:10 6726
for as soon as Z travailed................... Is 66:8 6726
family, and I will bring you to Z.......... Jer 3:14 6726
Set up the standard toward Z.............. Jer 4:6 6726
the voice of the daughter of Z............. Jer 4:31 6726
the daughter of Z to a comely.............. Jer 6:2 6726
war against thee, O daughter of Z........ Jer 6:23 6726
Is not the Lord in Z........................... Jer 8:19 6726
of wailing is heard out of Z................. Jer 9:19 6726
hath thy soul lothed Z......................... Jer 14:19 6726
Z shall be plowed like a field,.............. Jer 26:18 6726
an Outcast, saying, This is Z............... Jer 30:17 6726
let us go up to Z unto the Lord........... Jer 31:6 6726
come and sing in the height of Z......... Jer 31:12 6726
They shall ask the way to Z with.......... Jer 50:5 6726
to declare in Z the vengeance of.......... Jer 50:28 6726
let us declare in Z the work of............. Jer 51:10 6726
they have done in Z in your sight......... Jer 51:24 6726
shall the inhabitant of Z say................ Jer 51:35 6726
The ways of Z do mourn, because......... Lam 1:4 6726
from the daughter of Z all her............. Lam 1:6 6726
Z spreadeth forth her hands, and......... Lam 1:17 6726
of Z with a cloud in his anger............. Lam 2:1 6726
tabernacle of the daughter of Z........... Lam 2:4 6726
and sabbaths to be forgotten in Z........ Lam 2:6 6726
the wall of the daughter of Z.............. Lam 2:8 6726
daughter of Z sit upon the ground........ Lam 2:10 6726
thee, O virgin daughter of Z............... Lam 2:13 6726
Lord, O wall of the daughter of Z......... Lam 2:18 6726
The precious sons of Z,....................... Lam 4:2 6726
and hath kindled a fire in Z................. Lam 4:11 6726
is accomplished, O daughter of Z......... Lam 4:22 6726
They ravished the women in Z.............. Lam 5:11 6726
Because of the mountain of Z............... Lam 5:18 6726
Blow ye the trumpet in Z, and............. Joel 2:1 6726
Blow the trumpet in Z, sanctify a......... Joel 2:15 6726
Be glad then, ye children of Z............ Joel 2:23 6726
for in mount Z and in Jerusalem........... Joel 2:32 6726
The Lord also shall roar out of Z......... Joel 3:16 6726
the Lord your God dwelling in Z.......... Joel 3:17 6726
for the Lord dwelleth in Z.................. Joel 3:21 6726
said, The Lord will roar from Z............ Amos 1:2 6726
Woe to them that are at ease in Z........ Amos 6:1 6726
But upon mount Z shall be.................. Obad 17 6726
Z to judge the mount of Esau.............. Obad 21 6726
of the sin to the daughter of Z........... Mic 1:13 6726
They build up Z with blood.................. Mic 3:10 6726
Therefore shall Z for your sake............ Mic 3:12 6726
for the law shall go forth of Z............. Mic 4:2 6726
them in mount Z from henceforth......... Mic 4:7 6726
strong hold of the daughter of Z......... Mic 4:8 6726
to bring forth, O daughter of Z........... Mic 4:10 6726
and let our eye look upon Z................ Mic 4:11 6726
Arise and thresh, O daughter of Z....... Mic 4:13 6726
Sing, O daughter of Z......................... Zeph 3:14 6726
and to Z, Let not thine hands be......... Zeph 3:16 6726
for Z with a great jealousy.................. Zec 1:14 6726
and the Lord shall yet comfort Z......... Zec 1:17 6726
Deliver thyself, O Z, that.................... Zec 2:7 6726
Sing and rejoice, O daughter of Z....... Zec 2:10 6726
I was jealous for Z with great............. Zec 8:2 6726
I am returned unto Z, and will............ Zec 8:3 6726
Rejoice greatly, O daughter of Z......... Zec 9:9 6726
and raised up thy sons, O Z............... Zec 9:13 6726

ZION'S (*zi'-uns*)
For Z sake will I not hold my............... Is 62:1 6726

ZIOR (*zi'-or*) *A city in Judah.*
which is Hebron, and Z....................... Josh 15:54 6730

ZIPH (*zif*) See Ziphites.
1. A city in southeast Judah.
Z, and Telem, and Bealoth,.................. Josh 15:24 2128
a mountain in the wilderness of Z........ 1Sa 23:14 2128
in the wilderness of Z in a wood.......... 1Sa 23:15 2128
arose, and went to Z before Saul.......... 1Sa 23:24 2128
went down to the wilderness of Z......... 1Sa 26:2 2128
seek David in the wilderness of Z........ 1Sa 26:2 2128
And Gath, and Mareshah, and Z.......... 2Chr 11:8 2128
2. A city in Judah near Carmel.
Maon, Carmel, and Z, and Juttah,......... Josh 15:55 2128
3. A descendant of Caleb.
which was the father of Z..................... 1Chr 2:42 2128
4. A son of Jehalaleel.
Z, and Ziphah, Tiria, and Asareel......... 1Chr 4:16 2128

ZIPHAH (*zi'-fah*) *A son of Jehalaleel.*
Ziph, and Z, Tiria, and Asareel............ 1Chr 4:16 2129

ZIPHIMS (*zif'-ims*) See Ziphites. *Same as Ziphites.*
A Psalm of David, when the Z came.... Ps 54:t 2130

ZIPHION (*zif'-e-on*) See Zephon. *A son of Gad.*
Z, and Haggi, Shuni, and Ezbon, Eri....... Gen 46:16 6837

ZIPHITES (*zif'-ites*) See Ziphims. *Inhabitants of Ziph.*
Then came up the Z to Saul to.............. 1Sa 23:19 2130
the Z came unto Saul to Gibeah,........... 1Sa 26:1 2130

ZIPHRON (*zif'-ron*) *A place in northern Palestine.*
And the border shall go on to Z............ Num 34:9 2202

ZIPPOR (*zip'-por*) *Father of Balak.*
Balak the son of Z saw all that............. Num 22:2 6834
Balak the son of Z was king of............. Num 22:4 6834
said unto God, Balak the son of Z......... Num 22:10 6834
Thus saith Balak the son of Z............... Num 22:16 6834
hearken unto me, thou son of Z........... Num 23:18 6834
Then Balak the son of Z, king of.......... Josh 24:9 6834
better than Balak the son of Z............. Judg 11:25 6834

ZIPPORAH (*zip-po'-rah*) *Wife of Moses.*
and he gave Moses Z his daughter........ Ex 2:21 6855
Then Z took a sharp stone, and cut...... Ex 4:25 6855
Moses' father in law, took Z............... Ex 18:2 6855

ZITHRI (*zith'-ri*) See Zichri. *A son of Uzziel.*
Mishael, and Elzaphan, and Z.............. Ex 6:22 5644

ZIV See Zif.

ZIZ (*ziz*) *A place in Judah.*
they come up by the cliff of Z............... 2Chr 20:16 6732

ZIZA (*zi'-zah*) See Zizah.
1. Son of Ziphi.
Z the son of Shiphi, the son of.............. 1Chr 4:37 2124
2. A son of Rehoboam.
bare him Abijah, and Attai, and Z......... 2Chr 11:20 2124

ZIZAH (*zi'-zah*) See Zina, Ziza. *Son of Shimei.*
was the chief, and Z the second.......... 1Chr 23:11 2125

ZOAN (*zo'-an*) *An Egyptian city.*
seven years before Z in Egypt............... Num 13:22 6814
land of Egypt, in the field of Z............. Ps 78:12 6814
and his wonders in the field of Z.......... Ps 78:43 6814
Surely the princes of Z are fools........... Is 19:11 6814
The princes of Z are become fools........ Is 19:13 6814
For his princes were at Z.................... Is 30:4 6814
desolate, and will set fire in Z............. Eze 30:14 6814

ZOAR (*zo'-ar*) *A Canaanite city.*
of Egypt, as thou comest unto Z........... Gen 13:10 6820
and the king of Bela, which is Z........... Gen 14:2 6820
the king of Bela (the same is Z............ Gen 14:8 6820
the name of the city was called Z......... Gen 19:22 6820
the earth when Lot entered into Z........ Gen 19:23 6820
And Lot went up out of Z, and dwelt... Gen 19:30 6820
for he feared to dwell in Z.................. Gen 19:30 6820
the city of palm trees, unto Z.............. Deut 34:3 6820
his fugitives shall flee unto Z.............. Is 15:5 6820
from Z even unto Horonaim, as an........ Jer 48:34 6820

ZOBA (*zo'-bah*) See Zobah. *A district in northern Syria.*
Beth-rehob, and the Syrians of Z.......... 2Sa 10:6 6678
and the Syrians of Z, and of Rehob,...... 2Sa 10:8 6678

ZOBAH (*zo'-bah*) See Zoba. *Same as Zoba.*
Edom, and against the kings of Z.......... 1Sa 14:47 6678
the son of Rehob, king of Z.................. 2Sa 8:3 6678
to succour Hadadezer king of Z............. 2Sa 8:5 6678
son of Rehob, king of Z....................... 2Sa 8:12 6678
Igal the son of Nathan of Z.................. 2Sa 23:36 6678
from his lord Hadadezer king of Z......... 1Kin 11:23 6678
a band, when David slew them of Z....... 1Kin 11:24 6678
Hadarezer king of Z unto Hamath......... 1Chr 18:3 6678
came to help Hadarezer king of Z......... 1Chr 18:5 6678
the host of Hadarezer king of Z............ 1Chr 18:9 6678
out of Syria-maachah, and out of Z....... 1Chr 19:6 6678

ZOBEBAH (*zo-be'-bah*) *A daughter of Coz.*
And Coz begat Anub, and Z, and the... 1Chr 4:8 6637

ZOHAR (*zo'-har*) See Zerah, Zeror.
1. Father of Ephron.
for me to Ephron the son of Z.............. Gen 23:8 6714
Ephron the son of Z the Hittite............ Gen 25:9 6714
2. Son of Simeon.
Jamin, and Ohad, and Jachin, and Z...... Gen 46:10 6714
Jamin, and Ohad, and Jachin, and Z...... Ex 6:15 6714

ZOHELETH (*zo'-he-leth*) *A stone near En-rogel.*
and fat cattle by the stone of *Z* 1Kin 1:9 2120

ZOHETH (*zo'heth*) *Son of Ishi.*
And the sons of Ishi were, *Z* 1Chr 4:20 2105

ZOPHAH (*zo'-fah*) *Son of Helem.*
Z, and Imna, and Shelesh, and Amal.... 1Chr 7:35 6690
The sons of *Z*.. 1Chr 7:36 6690

ZOPHAI (*zo'-fahee*) See Zuph. *Brother of Samuel.*
Z his son, and Nahath his son,.............. 1Chr 6:26 6689

ZOPHAR (*zo'-far*) *A friend of Job.*
the Shuhite, and *Z* the Naamathite....... Job 2:11 6691
Then answered *Z* the Naamathite,........ Job 11:1 6691
Then answered *Z* the Naamathite,........ Job 20:1 6691
Z the Naamathite went, and did.......... Job 42:9 6691

ZOPHIM (*zo'-fim*) *A peak on Mt. Pisgah.*
brought him into the field of *Z* .... Num 23:14 6839

ZORAH (*zo'-rah*) See Zareah, Zorathites, Zoreah, Zorites. *A city in Judah.*
coast of their inheritance was *Z*.......... Josh 19:41 6681
And there was a certain man of *Z* .... Judg 13:2 6681
in the camp of Dan between *Z*............... Judg 13:25 6681
him up, and buried him between *Z*...... Judg 16:31 6681
coasts, men of valour, from *Z*................ Judg 18:2 6681
came unto their brethren to *Z*................ Judg 18:8 6681
family of the Danites, out of *Z*............... Judg 18:11 6681
And *Z*, and Aijalon, and Hebron,........... 2Chr 11:10 6681

ZORATHITES (*zo'-rath-ites*) *Descendants of Shobal.*
These are the families of the *Z* 1Chr 4:2 6882

ZOREAH (*zo'-re-ah*) *Same as Zorah.*
And in the valley, Eshtaol, and *Z*......... Josh 15:33 6881

ZORITES (*zo'-rites*) See Zareathites, Zorathites. *Descendants of Salma.*
half of the Manahethites, the *Z* 1Chr 2:54 6882

ZOROBABEL (*zo-rob'-a-bel*) See Zerubbabel. *Father of Abiud; ancestor of Jesus.*
and Salathiel begat *Z*............................. Mt 1:12 *2216*
And *Z* begat Abiud.................................... Mt 1:13 *2216*
of Rhesa, which was the son of *Z*.......... Lk 3:27 *2216*

ZUAR (*zu'-ar*) *Father of Nethaneel.*
Nethaneel the son of *Z*.......................... Num 1:8 6686
Nethaneel the son of *Z* shall be .... Num 2:5 6686
second day Nethaneel the son of *Z*....... Num 7:18 6686
of Nethaneel the son of *Z*....................... Num 7:23 6686
was Nethaneel the son of *Z*................... Num 10:15 6686

ZUPH (*zuf*)
1. An ancestor of Samuel.
the son of Tohu, the son of *Z*................ 1Sa 1:1 6689
The son of *Z*, the son of Elkanah,......... 1Chr 6:35 6689
2. A district in Jerusalem.
they were come to the land of *Z* 1Sa 9:5 6689

ZUPHITE See Zuph.

ZUR (*zur*)
1. Father of Cozbi.
was Cozbi, the daughter of *Z*................ Num 25:15 6698
namely, Evi, and Rekem, and *Z*............ Num 31:8 6698
of Midian, Evi, and Rekem, and *Z*......... Josh 13:21 6698
2. Son of Jeiel.
And his firstborn son Abdon, and *Z*...... 1Chr 8:30 6698
his firstborn son Abdon, then *Z*............ 1Chr 9:36 6698

ZURIEL (*zu'-re-el*) *Son of Abihail.*
Merari was *Z* the son of Abihail............. Num 3:35 6700

ZURISHADDAI (*zu-re-shad'-da-i*) *Father of Shelumiel.*
Shelumiel the son of *Z*........................... Num 1:6 6701
shall be Shelumiel the son of *Z*............. Num 2:12 6701
fifth day Shelumiel the son of *Z* .... Num 7:36 6701
of Shelumiel the son of *Z*....................... Num 7:41 6701
Simeon was Shelumiel the son of *Z*...... Num 10:19 6701

ZUZIMS (*zu'-zims*) See Zamzummims. *A tribe in the land of Ham.*
the *Z* in Ham, and the Emims in .... Gen 14:5 2104

APPENDIX TO THE MAIN CONCORDANCE

Misc.

EXPLANATION

The Appendix to the Main Concordance is a listing, by chapter and verse only, of forty-seven words that appear in the Bible so frequently that they would not be used to search for specific texts. Indeed, if the concordance were to quote in full the passages where these words appear, it would be necessary to reprint the entire Bible under each entry!

By resetting this information in the new format, considerable space has been saved, thus reducing the cost of the book. Because this resetting was done solely by computer, the errors found in all other editions of *Strong's* have been corrected.

NOTE: The small "superior" figures (for example, 2, 3, 4, etc.) that appear following some verse numbers indicate the number of times the word appears in that verse.

The forty-seven words include in this appendix are:

a	as	for	him	is	not	out	that	them	to	us	with
an	be	from	his	it	O	shall	the	they	unto	was	ye
and	but	he	I	me	of	shalt	thee	thou	up	we	you
are	by	her	in	my	our	she	their	thy	upon	were	

Appendix to the Main Concordance

APPENDIX TO THE MAIN CONCORDANCE

A (Also see AN)

GENESIS

1:6, 29
2:5, 6, 7, 8, 10, 21, 22, 24
3:6, 24
4:1, 2^2, 12^2, 14^2, 15, 17, 23^2, 25, 26
5:3, 28
6:9, 16^2, 17
8:1, 7, 8, 21
9:11^2, 13^2, 14, 15, 20, 23, 25
10:8, 9, 12, 30
11:2, 4^3
12:1, 2^2, 8, 10, 11
13:7, 16
14:23^2
15:1, 9^4, 12, 13^3, 15, 17^2, 18
16:7, 11, 12, 15
17:4, 5, 7, 8, 11, 16^2, 17, 19, 20
18:4, 5, 7^2, 10, 13^2, 14, 18
19:3, 9, 20^2, 26, 28, 30, 31, 37, 38
20:3^3, 4, 6, 7, 9, 16^2
21:2, 7, 8, 13, 14, 16^2, 18, 19, 21, 25, 27, 30, 32, 33
22:2, 6, 7, 8^2, 13^3
23:4^4, 6, 9^2, 18, 20^2
24:3, 4, 7, 11, 16, 17, 22^2, 29, 36, 37, 38, 40, 43, 55, 65
25:1, 8, 27^3
26:1, 8^2, 9, 19, 25, 28, 30, 35
27:11^2, 12^3, 27, 34, 36, 44, 46
28:1, 2, 3, 4, 6^3, 11, 12, 18, 20, 22
29:2^2, 14, 20, 22, 32, 33, 34, 35
30:5, 6, 7, 10, 11, 12, 15, 20, 21, 23, 30
31:10, 11, 13, 24, 44^2, 45^2, 48
32:13, 16, 18, 24, 28
33:18, 19^2
34:14
35:11^2, 14^3, 16, 20
37:1, 3, 5, 9, 15, 24, 25, 31
38:1, 2^2, 3, 4, 5, 6, 11, 14, 17^2, 28
39:2, 6, 14, 20
40:4, 5, 8, 9, 19, 20
41:2, 7, 11, 12, 15^2, 18, 33, 38^2, 42
43:2, 6, 11^3
44:15, 18, 19^2, 20^3, 25, 33
45:7^2, 8^2
46:3, 10, 29
47:11, 22, 26
48:4, 7, 16, 19^2
49:6^2, 9^2, 10, 14, 15, 17, 19, 21, 22^3, 27, 30^2
50:9, 10^2, 11, 13^2, 16, 26

EXODUS

1:8, 16^3
2:1^2, 2^2, 7, 14^2, 15, 22^3
3:2^2, 8^3, 12, 17, 19
4:2, 3, 4, 10, 16, 25^2, 26
5:1, 21
6:1^2, 6, 7^2, 13, 15
7:1, 9^2, 10, 15
8:23, 24
9:3, 5, 9, 10, 18, 24
10:7, 9, 19, 22
11:6, 7^2, 8
12:3^2, 5, 13, 14^3, 19, 21, 22, 30^2, 38, 42, 45, 46, 48
13:5, 6, 9^3, 12, 13, 16, 21^3
14:20, 21, 22, 29
15:3, 5, 16, 20, 25^2
16:4, 14, 25, 33, 35
17:12, 14^2
18:3, 12, 16
19:5, 6, 9, 16, 18^2, 19
20:5
21:4, 7^2, 8, 12, 13^2, 14, 16, 18, 20^2, 21, 22, 26, 28^2, 29^2, 30, 31^2, 32^2, 33^4
22:1^3, 2, 5^2, 7, 10^2, 14, 16^2, 18, 19, 21, 25
23:1, 2^2, 3, 7, 9^2, 14, 19, 33
24:10^2, 12, 15
25:8, 10^5, 11, 17^4, 23^4, 24, 25^2, 31, 33^4, 35^3, 39
26:7, 13^2, 14^2, 16^3, 31
27:4, 21
28:4^5, 11, 12, 16^2, 17^3, 18^2, 19, 20^2, 21, 28, 29, 32, 34^4, 36^2, 37, 43
29:9, 10, 14, 18^2, 22, 24, 25^2, 26, 28, 33, 36^2, 40^2, 41, 42
30:2^2, 3, 8, 10, 12, 13^2, 15, 16, 18, 21, 33, 34, 35^2
31:13, 16, 17
32:4^2, 5, 8, 9, 10, 11, 17, 21, 29, 30, 31
33:3^2, 5^2, 11^2, 21^2, 22
34:9, 10^2, 12^2, 14, 15^2, 16^2, 20, 26, 27, 33
35:2, 5, 29
36:19^2, 21^3, 35
37:1^5, 2, 6^2, 10^3, 11, 12^2, 19^4, 21^3, 24, 25^2, 26
38:4, 23, 25, 26^2, 27^2
39:7, 9^2, 10^3, 11^2, 12, 13^2, 14, 21, 23, 26^4, 28, 29, 30^2, 31
40:34

LEVITICUS

1:3^2, 9^2, 10^2, 13^2, 17^2
2:1, 2, 3, 4, 5^2, 6, 7, 9^2, 10, 12, 14, 15
3:1^2, 5, 6, 7, 12, 16, 17
4:2, 3^2, 12, 14, 20, 21, 22, 23^2, 24, 28^2, 31, 32^3, 33
5:1^2, 2^3, 3, 4^2, 6^4, 7^3, 9, 10, 11^2, 12^2, 13, 15^4, 17, 18^2, 19
6:2^3, 3, 6^2, 11, 15, 18, 20, 21^2, 22, 28
7:5, 12, 16^2, 30, 34, 36
8:2^2, 21^2, 26, 27, 28, 29
9:2^4, 3^5, 4^3, 18, 21, 24
10:9, 14, 15^2
11:36, 47
12:2^2, 5, 6^7, 7^2, 8^2
13:2^3, 3, 5, 6, 8, 9, 12, 15, 18, 19^2, 20, 22, 23, 24^2, 25, 28, 29^2, 30^3, 37, 38^2, 39, 42^2, 44, 45, 47^2, 48, 49, 51^2, 52, 57, 59
14:10, 12^2, 21^3, 22^2, 24, 31^2, 34^2, 35, 44, 55^2, 56^3
15:2, 15^2, 19, 25, 30^2
16:3^4, 4, 5^2, 9, 10, 12, 21, 22, 29^2, 31^2, 34
17:6, 7^2, 8, 15
18:5, 17, 18, 19, 23
19:5, 14, 16, 19^2, 20^2, 21^2, 29, 33, 36^2
20:5, 6, 12, 13^2, 14^2, 15^2, 16, 17^2, 18^2, 20, 21, 24, 27^3
21:3, 4, 7^3, 13, 14^3, 18^4, 19, 20^2, 21^2, 23
22:4^3, 5, 10, 12, 13, 14, 18, 19, 20, 21^2, 22, 23^4, 25, 27^3, 29
23:10, 12, 13^2, 14, 16, 18, 19^2, 20, 21, 24^2, 27, 28, 31, 32, 36, 37^3, 39^3, 41^2
24:3, 6, 7, 9, 10, 18, 19^2, 20^2, 21^2
25:2, 4^2, 5, 10, 11, 24, 29^8, 30, 33, 35^2, 39, 40, 46, 47, 53
26:1, 25, 33, 36^3, 37
27:2^2, 4, 6, 7, 9, 10^4, 11, 13, 14, 16^3, 21, 22^2, 23, 27, 28, 31

NUMBERS

1:4
3:15, 22, 28, 34, 39, 40, 43, 50
4:6, 7, 8^2, 9, 10^2, 11^2, 12^3, 13, 14
5:6^2, 12, 13, 21, 23, 27, 29
6:2^3, 11^2, 12^2, 14^2, 15, 17, 20
7:3, 13, 15, 16, 17, 19, 21, 22, 23, 25, 27, 28, 29, 31, 33, 34, 35, 37, 39, 40, 41, 43^2, 45, 46, 47, 49, 51, 52, 53, 55, 57, 58, 59, 61, 63, 64, 65, 67, 69, 70, 71, 73, 75, 76, 77, 79, 81, 82, 83
8:8^2, 12^2, 19
9:6, 7, 10^2, 13, 14, 20, 22^2
10:2, 10, 33
11:4, 8, 12, 20, 21, 25, 27, 31^3, 33
12:6^3
13:2^2, 23^2, 32^2
14:3, 4, 8, 12, 14^3, 31, 34, 36
15:3^5, 4^2, 5, 6^2, 7^2, 8^4, 9^2, 10^2, 11^2, 13, 14^2, 20, 24^3, 25, 27^2, 30, 32, 38, 39^2
16:9, 13^3, 14, 21, 30, 35, 38^2, 39, 40, 45, 46
17:2, 6, 10
18:4, 6, 7, 11, 16, 17^4, 19^2, 23, 26
19:2, 9^4, 10, 14^2, 16^5, 17, 18^3, 21
20:15, 16, 20
21:2, 8^2, 9^3, 28^2
22:5, 11, 24^3, 26, 27, 29, 36
23:2^2, 4^2, 5, 14^2, 16, 19, 21, 22, 24^2, 30^2
24:4, 8, 9^2, 16, 17^2, 18^2, 21
25:6, 7, 14^2, 15^2, 18
26:10, 51, 62, 64, 65
27:4, 7, 8, 11, 16, 18, 19, 23
28:2, 3, 5^2, 6^3, 7, 8^2, 9, 11, 12^2, 13^5, 14^4, 15, 19^2, 20^2, 21, 22, 23, 24, 26, 27, 29
29:1, 2^2, 3^2, 5, 6^2, 8^2, 9, 10, 11, 12, 13^3, 15, 16, 19, 22, 25, 28, 31, 34, 35, 36^3, 38
30:2^3, 3^3, 9, 10, 16
31:4, 5, 6, 16, 18, 28, 54
32:1^2, 4, 5, 29
34:5, 6
35:4, 15, 16, 17^2, 18, 21, 23, 29, 31

DEUTERONOMY

1:11, 23, 25, 31, 33^2, 39
2:5^2, 9^2, 10, 19, 20, 21, 35
3:4, 5, 7, 11^2
4:6, 12, 16, 20, 23, 24^2, 25, 31, 34^3
5:2, 9, 15^3, 22
6:8, 15, 21
7:6, 8, 9, 16, 21, 23, 26^2
8:5, 7^2, 8^2, 9^2
9:2, 3, 6, 12, 13, 14, 16, 26
10:7, 15, 17^3
11:9, 10, 11, 12, 18, 26^2, 27, 28
12:11
13:1^4
14:2, 21
15:1, 3, 7, 9, 15, 18
16:8, 10^2, 12, 15, 16, 19^2, 21
17:8, 14, 15, 18^2
18:3, 6, 10, 11^4, 15, 18, 20, 22
19:3, 5^2, 15, 16, 18
20:1, 5, 6, 7, 10, 19^2
21:4, 11^2, 13, 15, 17, 18^2, 20^2, 22^3
22:5^3, 6, 8^2, 11, 13, 14, 17, 19, 22^2, 23^3, 25^2, 26, 28^3, 30
23:2, 5, 7, 12, 13, 17, 18^2, 20, 21, 23, 25
24:1^3, 3, 5^2, 6, 7, 17, 18, 19, 22
25:1, 2, 5, 7, 13^2, 14^2, 15^2
26:2, 5^3, 8, 9, 15
27:3, 14, 15
28:22^2, 30^2, 33, 35, 36, 37^2, 46^2, 48, 49^2, 50, 65
29:13^2, 18, 22
31:6, 7, 14, 15^2, 16, 19, 21, 23^2, 24, 26
32:4, 5, 10, 20, 21^2, 22, 28, 30, 47, 49
33:2, 4, 20, 21, 22, 28
34:6, 10

JOSHUA

1:6, 9, 18
2:12, 15
3:4, 12
4:2, 4, 5, 6, 7
5:6, 13
6:5^2, 18, 20
7:1, 21^2, 26
8:2, 11, 14, 17, 27, 28, 29^2, 32, 35
9:6^2, 7, 9, 11, 15, 16
10:2, 8, 10, 13, 14, 16, 17, 20
11:14, 18, 19
12:6, 7
14:15
15:3, 13, 18, 19^2
17:1^2, 2, 14, 15, 17, 18
18:9, 14
20:4
21:13, 21, 27, 32, 38, 44
22:10, 14, 17, 20, 25, 26, 27, 28, 34
23:1, 10, 13
24:7, 13, 19, 25^2, 26, 27^2, 32, 33

JUDGES

1:14, 15^2, 24, 26
2:3, 17
3:9, 15^4, 16^2, 17, 19, 20^2, 25, 27, 28, 29
4:4, 9, 16, 18, 19^2, 21
5:7, 8, 12, 14, 18, 25, 28, 30^3
6:8, 17, 19^3, 26, 31, 34, 37, 38
7:5, 13^5, 14, 16, 18
8:14, 18, 20, 24, 25, 26, 27^2, 31, 32, 33
9:8^2, 48, 49, 51, 53^3, 54
10:1, 3
11:1, 2, 30, 31, 33, 39, 40
12:11, 13
13:2, 3, 5^2, 6, 7^2, 15, 16, 19^3, 23^2, 24
14:1, 2, 3^2, 5, 6, 8^2, 10, 12, 16, 18
15:1^2, 3, 4, 8, 15^2, 16
16:4, 9, 12, 17^2, 19, 23
17:1, 3^2, 4^2, 7^2, 8, 9^2, 10^3, 13
18:10^3, 14^2, 19^6, 22, 23, 27, 28
19:1^2, 3, 5, 12, 15, 17, 24^2, 29
20:10^2, 38, 40
21:5, 15, 17, 18, 19^2

RUTH

1:1^2
2:1^2, 3, 7, 10, 11, 12
3:8, 9, 11, 12, 13^3, 14
4:1, 3, 7^2, 13, 14, 15^2, 17^2

1 SAMUEL

1:1, 5, 9^2, 11^2, 15^2, 16, 20, 24, 25
2:3, 13, 18^2, 19, 25, 27, 34, 35^2, 36^3
3:11, 20
4:5, 7, 10, 12, 13, 17, 20
5:9, 11
6:3, 7, 8^2, 9, 14^3, 17, 19
7:9^2, 10, 12
8:5, 6, 10, 19, 22
9:1^3, 2^4, 6, 7, 8, 9^3, 12, 15, 16, 21, 27
10:1, 2, 3, 5^3, 10, 12, 19, 25, 26
11:1, 2^3, 7, 11
12:1, 12, 13, 17, 19
13:2, 4, 6, 9, 12, 14, 21
14:1, 2, 4^3, 10, 12, 14, 15, 20, 25, 29, 30, 33, 36, 39, 41, 43
15:5, 12, 18, 28, 29
16:1, 12, 16^2, 17, 18^4, 20^2
17:3^3, 4^2, 5, 6, 7^2, 8^2, 10, 20, 29, 33^2, 34^3, 38, 40^2, 42^2, 43, 45^3, 46, 49, 50^2
18:3, 10, 13, 21, 23^3
19:2, 5^2, 8, 12, 13^2, 16, 22
20:3, 6, 8, 16, 20, 21, 25, 29, 33, 35, 41
21:2^2, 5^2, 7, 9
22:2, 6, 8, 13, 18
23:5, 7, 14, 15, 18, 25, 27
24:3, 14^2, 19
25:2^2, 3^2, 8, 10, 16, 17^2, 28, 29^2, 36^2, 37, 41
26:12, 13, 15, 20^2
27:5, 7, 10
28:7^4, 9, 12, 14, 22, 24
29:1
30:12^2, 13, 17, 25, 26
31:4, 13

2 SAMUEL

1:2, 13
2:17, 18, 28
3:7, 8^2, 11, 13, 20, 21, 22^2, 29^2, 33, 34, 38^2
4:2, 4, 5, 10, 11
5:2, 3, 23, 24
6:3, 8, 14, 16, 19^3
7:6^2, 7, 9, 10^2, 19^2, 23^2, 24
8:2, 4, 13
9:2, 3, 8, 12
10:6
11:2, 8, 14, 16, 21^3, 27
12:3, 4, 24, 30
13:1, 2, 3^2, 6, 9, 18
14:2^4, 5, 13, 27^2
15:2, 8, 13, 17, 19, 23, 27, 33
16:1^3, 5, 8, 22, 23
17:8^2, 9, 10^2, 13, 17, 18^3, 19, 25
18:2^3, 7, 9^2, 10, 11, 12, 17^2, 18, 24, 27, 29
19:4, 10, 16, 17, 18, 32^2, 35, 36^2
20:1^3, 8^2, 12, 15, 16, 19^2, 21, 22, 26
21:1, 16, 18, 19^3, 20^2
22:9, 11, 20, 30^2, 31, 32, 35, 44
23:4, 7, 10, 11^2, 12, 20^3, 21^3, 29
24:14, 15, 23, 24

1 KINGS

1:2, 3^2, 6, 42, 52
2:2, 4, 8^2, 9, 19, 42
3:4, 5, 6, 7, 8, 9, 12, 15^2, 17, 24^2
4:7, 32
5:1, 7, 12, 13, 14^2
6:21, 31, 33, 36
7:3, 6, 7, 12, 14^3, 15, 23^2, 24, 26, 29, 31^2, 32^3, 33, 35^2
8:9, 13, 21, 25, 41^2, 55, 63, 65^2
9:5, 7^2, 16, 21, 25, 26
10:2, 6, 18, 22, 25, 26, 28, 29
11:17, 24, 26, 28, 29, 36, 38
12:7, 11, 30, 32, 33
13:1, 2, 3, 7, 18, 24
14:3, 5, 10, 14, 15
15:4, 13, 19^2, 22
16:11, 31, 33
17:7, 9, 10^2, 11, 12^4, 13, 19, 24
18:2, 4, 13, 21, 22, 27^2, 32, 41, 44^2, 45
19:2, 4^2, 5, 6^2, 9, 11, 12^2, 13, 21
20:13, 21, 28, 30, 34, 35, 36^2, 39^3, 42
21:1, 2^2, 9, 12
22:7, 10, 17, 21, 22, 23, 34^3, 36, 47

2 KINGS

1:2, 3, 6^2, 8, 9, 10, 12, 13
2:1, 9, 10, 11^2, 20
3:4, 9, 11, 15, 18, 27
4:1, 2, 3, 6^2, 8^2, 10^5, 11, 16, 17, 18, 19, 28, 29, 38, 39, 42
5:1^3, 2, 5, 7^2, 8, 10, 12, 14, 15, 19, 22, 26, 27
6:2^2, 5, 6, 8, 9, 14, 25^2, 26, 32^2
7:1^3, 2, 6^3, 9, 16^3, 18^3, 19
8:1, 5, 6, 8, 9, 13, 15, 19, 20
9:16, 17^2, 19, 24, 28, 30, 34
10:2, 6, 8, 18, 19, 20, 21, 27
11:4, 5, 6^2, 14, 17
12:9^2, 20
13:5, 21^2
14:9, 19
15:5^2, 13, 19, 25, 30
16:8, 17
17:16, 21, 35, 36
18:17, 21, 28, 31, 32^4, 36
19:3, 7^2, 17, 29, 31, 32
20:3, 7, 10, 12, 14, 20^2
21:3, 7, 13^2, 14
22:10, 12, 19^2
23:3^2, 8, 22, 30, 33^2
24:16
25:8, 23, 30^2

1 CHRONICLES

2:34
5:25
6:33
7:16, 23
9:13
10:4, 13
11:3, 11, 13, 14, 20, 22^4, 23^4, 42
12:2, 4, 14, 22, 28, 34, 38
13:7, 11
14:12, 15
15:1^2, 13, 27, 28, 29
16:3^3, 5, 15, 17, 19, 42
17:6, 8, 9, 17^3, 21, 24
18:4
19:6
20:2, 5, 6
21:3, 5, 13, 16
22:9^2, 14
25:3
26:14, 17^2, 30
27:5, 32^3
28:3, 9^2
29:15, 19, 21^3, 28

2 CHRONICLES

1:4, 6, 9, 14, 16, 17
2:7, 12, 13, 14^2, 18
4:2^3, 3, 5
5:10, 13
6:2, 5, 13, 16, 22, 32, 36
7:5, 8, 9, 18, 20^2
8:13
9:1, 5, 17, 18, 24
10:11
13:5, 8, 9^2, 15, 17
14:9
15:3^2, 12, 14, 16
16:3, 8, 10^2, 14
17:17
18:6, 9, 20, 21, 22, 33^3
19:9
20:2, 3, 8, 14, 19
21:7, 8, 12, 13, 14, 17
22:11
23:3, 4, 5^2, 16
24:8, 9, 24^2, 26
25:2, 7, 15, 18, 27
26:19, 21^3, 23
28:5^2, 7, 9^2, 21
29:10, 21, 31, 36
30:5^2, 13, 18, 24^3
32:18, 24
33:6, 7, 14^2
34:14, 18, 20, 31
35:1, 3, 18
36:3, 22

EZRA

1:1, 9, 10^2
2:7, 12, 31, 37, 38, 39, 61, 63
3:5, 11, 12, 13
4:8, 10, 11, 15, 17
5:7, 11, 13, 17
6:1, 2^3, 3, 4, 8, 11^2, 12, 17
7:6, 11, 12^2, 13, 21, 27
8:18, 21^2, 22, 27, 28, 35^2
9:7^2, 8^4, 9^2
10:1, 3, 12, 13^2, 19

NEHEMIAH

2:6, 8, 10, 17
3:13
4:2, 3, 4, 6, 9, 17, 22
5:1, 7
6:3, 7, 11
7:2, 5, 12, 34, 40, 41, 42, 65, 70
8:4, 18
9:4, 8, 10, 11, 12^2, 17^2, 18, 25, 29, 31, 38
10:29, 32
11:23
13:2, 5, 7

ESTHER

1:3, 5, 6, 9, 19
2:5^2, 18^2, 23
3:4, 8, 13, 14
4:1^2, 5, 14
5:9, 14
8:11, 13, 15^2, 17^2
9:17, 18, 19^2, 22
10:1

JOB

1:1, 3, 6, 8, 13, 14, 19
2:1, 3, 4, 8, 13
3:3, 5, 23
4:12^3, 15, 16, 17
5:26^2
6:15, 22, 27
7:1, 2^3, 6, 12^3, 20^2
8:2, 9, 14, 20
9:2, 3, 17, 19, 25, 32
10:16, 20, 22
11:2, 12
12:5, 14, 18, 24, 25
13:25, 27, 28^2
14:1, 2^2, 4, 7, 9, 13, 14, 15, 17
15:2, 14, 21, 24
16:8, 14, 21^2, 22
17:3, 6^2, 7
18:8^2, 10
19:10, 15, 23, 29
20:5, 8^2, 26, 29
21:11, 13
22:2, 6, 14, 16, 28
24:3, 5, 8, 9, 14, 20, 24, 25
25:4, 6^2
26:14
27:13, 18^2, 20, 21
28:1^2, 7, 26^2
29:14^2, 16, 25
30:5, 14, 15, 29^2
31:1^2, 3, 9, 12, 18, 23, 30, 34, 35, 36, 37
32:8
33:15^2, 23^2, 24, 25
34:9, 11, 13, 18, 20, 29^2, 34
35:8
36:2, 16, 18
37:4, 18, 20
38:3, 9, 14, 25^2, 28, 30
39:20
40:7, 9, 17, 23
41:1, 2, 4^2, 5, 6, 15, 18, 20, 21, 24^2, 29, 31^2, 32, 34
42:8, 11, 12^2

PSALMS

1:3
2:1, 9^2, 12
3:t, 3
4:t
5:t, 4, 12
6:t
7:2, 15
8:t, 5
9:t, 6, 9^2
10:9
11:t, 1
12:t, 2, 6
13:t
14:t
15:t, 3, 4
16:6
17:t, 12^2
18:t, 8, 10, 19, 29^2, 30, 31, 34, 43
19:t, 4, 5^3
20:t
21:t, 3, 9, 11
22:t, 6^2, 13^2, 15, 30^2, 31
23:t, 5
24:t, 4
25:t
26:t
27:t, 5, 11
28:t
29:t, 6^2
30:t, 5^2
31:t, 8, 11^2, 12^2, 20, 21
32:t^2, 6
33:3^2, 16, 17
34:t, 18^2
35:t, 7, 19
36:t, 4, 6
37:t, 10, 16^2, 23, 35
38:t, 7, 13^2, 14
39:t, 1, 6, 11, 12^2
40:t, 2, 3, 15
41:t
42:4, 10
44:3, 13^3, 14^2, 20
45:t^3, 1^2, 6, 12
46:t, 1, 4
47:t, 2, 5^2
48:t, 3, 6
49:t, 4, 7
50:t, 3, 5, 10, 18
51:t, 10^2, 17^3
52:t, 2, 8
53:t
54:t
55:t, 2, 6, 13
56:t
57:4, 6^2
58:4, 8^2, 9, 11^3
59:6^2, 14^2
60:4
61:t, 3^2
62:t, 3^3, 8, 9
63:t, 1, 10
64:t, 3, 6
65:t
66:t, 1, 12
67:t
68:t, 5^2, 6, 9, 13, 33
69:t, 4, 8, 11, 22^2, 30
70:t, 3
71:7
72:t
73:t, 1, 6^2, 10, 19, 20, 22, 27
74:5
75:t, 5, 8
76:t, 6
77:t, 13, 17, 20
78:2, 5^2, 8^2, 14^2, 19, 21, 38, 39, 50, 52, 57, 65, 66
79:t, 4^2
80:t, 1, 6, 8
81:t, 1, 2, 4^2, 5^2
82:t
83:t, 2, 4, 13, 14
84:t, 3, 6, 10^3, 11
85:t
86:t, 15, 17
87:t
88:t, 4
89:3, 8, 13, 37, 41
90:t, 4^2, 5^2, 9
91:7, 12

PSALMS

92:t, 1, 3, 6^2, 12
94:2, 20
95:1, 2, 3^2, 10
96:1
97:3
98:t, 1, 4^2, 5, 6
99:8
100:t, 1
101:t, 2^2, 4^2, 5, 6
102:t, 6, 7, 11, 26^2
103:t, 13, 15
104:2^2, 4, 6, 9, 18
105:8, 10, 12, 16, 17^2, 39^2, 41
106:18, 19, 36, 39
107:4, 7, 27, 29, 33, 34, 35, 36, 41
108:t
109:t, 2, 3, 6, 9, 19, 25, 29
110:t, 4
111:10
112:5
113:9
114:1, 8^2
118:5
119:9, 19, 63, 69, 78, 83, 105^2, 110, 161, 164, 176
120:t, 2
121:t
122:t, 3
123:t, 2
124:t, 6, 7
125:t
126:t
127:t, 4
128:t, 3
129:t, 1, 2
130:t
131:t, 2^2
132:t, 5, 17
133:t
134:t
136:12^2
137:3, 4
138:t
139:t, 4
140:t, 3, 5^2
141:t, 3, 5
142:t, 3
143:t, 6
144:t, 4, 8, 9^2, 11, 12, 15
147:10
148:6, 14
149:1, 6

PROVERBS

1:5^2, 6, 27
2:7
3:12, 18, 30
4:1, 9, 24
5:3, 4, 10, 20^2
6:1, 5^2, 10^3, 12^3, 17^2, 19, 23, 24, 26^3, 27, 30, 32, 33, 34
7:7, 10, 19, 20, 22, 23^2
8:27
9:7^3, 8^2, 9^2, 13, 14
10:1^3, 4, 5^2, 8, 10, 11^2, 13, 18^2, 23^2
11:1^2, 7, 12, 13^2, 15, 16, 18^2, 20, 22^3, 28, 30
12:2^2, 3, 4^2, 8^2, 9, 10, 14^2, 15, 16^2, 17, 18, 19^2, 23, 25, 27
13:1^2, 2, 5^2, 8, 12, 14, 16, 17^2, 20, 22
14:3, 5^2, 6, 7, 9, 10, 12^2, 14, 16, 17, 25^2, 26, 27, 30, 34^2, 35
15:1, 4^3, 5, 12, 13^2, 15^2, 17^2, 18, 20^3, 21, 23^2, 30
16:2, 7, 8, 9, 10, 11, 14^2, 15, 18, 20, 22, 25^2, 27, 28^2, 29, 31, 32
17:1, 2^2, 4^3, 7^2, 8^2, 9^2, 10^3, 11, 12^3, 16^2, 17^2, 18, 20^2, 21^2, 22^3, 23^2, 24, 25^2, 27, 28^2
18:1, 2, 4^2, 6, 7, 8, 9, 10, 13, 14^2, 16, 19^3, 20, 22^2, 24^3
19:1, 5, 6, 9, 10^2, 11^2, 12, 13^3, 14, 15, 19, 21, 22^3, 24, 25, 26
20:1, 2^3, 3, 5, 6, 8, 11, 15^2, 16^3, 17, 19, 23, 24, 25, 26, 30
21:2, 4, 6^2, 9^3, 14^2, 17, 18, 19, 20, 22, 27, 28, 29
22:1, 3, 6, 9, 13, 14, 15, 18, 24, 25, 29
23:1, 2^3, 9, 21, 24, 27^4, 28, 32, 34
24:5^2, 7, 8, 14, 16, 25, 26, 28, 33^3
25:2^2, 4, 9, 11, 12, 13, 14, 15^2, 18^4, 19^2, 20, 23, 24^2, 25^2, 26^3, 28
26:1, 3^3, 4, 5, 6^2, 7, 8^3, 9^3, 11^2, 12^3, 13^2, 16, 17, 18, 21, 22, 23^2, 27^2, 28^2
27:1, 2, 3^2, 6, 8^2, 9, 10^2, 12, 13^3, 14^2, 15^3, 17, 21, 22^3
28:1, 2^2, 3^2, 7^2, 12, 15^3, 16, 17, 20, 21, 23, 24, 25, 26, 27
29:5^2, 6, 8^2, 9^2, 11^2, 12, 15, 19, 20^2, 21, 22, 23, 24, 25
30:2, 4, 5, 6, 10, 11, 12, 13, 14, 19^5, 22^2, 25, 26, 30, 31^2
31:10, 15, 16^2, 30

ECCLESIASTES

1:3
2:19^2, 21^3, 24, 26
3:1^2, 2^4, 3^4, 4^4, 5^4, 6^4, 7^4, 8^4, 12, 17, 19^2, 22
4:4, 8^2, 9, 12, 13^2
5:3^2, 4, 8, 12, 13, 14, 16
6:2^2, 3, 6, 12^2
7:1, 5, 6, 7^2, 8, 12^2, 15^2, 20, 28^2

ECCLESIASTES

8:1^2, 4, 5, 9, 12, 13, 14, 15, 17^3
9:4^2, 5, 6, 7, 14^2, 15
10:1^2, 2^2, 3^2, 8^2, 11, 12^2, 14^2, 16, 19, 20
11:2, 7, 8
12:5, 12

SONG OF SOLOMON

1:9, 13, 14
2:9^2, 13, 17^2
3:4, 9
4:1, 2, 3^3, 4, 12^3, 15^2
5:11, 13
6:5, 6, 7^2
7:1, 2, 4, 7, 13
8:6^3, 7, 8, 9^3, 10, 11^2, 12, 14^2

ISAIAH

1:4^2, 8^5, 9, 14, 30, 31
2:20
3:6, 7, 16, 17, 24^4
4:5^3, 6^4
5:1^3, 2^2, 7, 9, 18, 28, 29
6:1, 5^2, 6, 12, 13^2
7:6^2, 8, 11, 13, 14^3, 20, 21^2, 23^2
8:1^2, 3, 11, 12^2, 14^5, 19
9:2, 6^2, 8
10:6, 7, 13, 14, 16^2, 17^2, 18, 19, 22, 23, 24, 25, 26, 34
11:1^2, 6, 10
13:2, 4^3, 5, 6, 8, 12^2, 14
14:6, 17, 19^2, 23, 29^2, 31
15:5
16:2, 4
17:1^2, 7, 9, 11, 12^2, 13
18:2^3, 3, 4^2, 7^3
19:1, 4^2, 14^2, 17, 19, 20^4, 21, 23, 24
20:3
21:1, 2, 3, 6, 7^4, 8, 9^2, 16
22:2^2, 5, 11, 16^2, 17, 18^2, 21, 23^3
23:3, 10, 11
24:9, 11, 20^2
25:2^4, 4^5, 5^2, 6^2
26:1, 16, 17, 20
27:2, 10, 11
28:1, 2^4, 4, 5^2, 6, 10^2, 13^2, 15, 16^5, 19, 20, 22, 27^4
29:3, 4, 7^2, 8, 11, 14^3, 17^3, 21^4
30:1, 5^3, 6, 8^2, 9, 13^2, 14, 17^2, 18, 20, 21, 22, 27, 28, 29^3, 30, 31, 33
31:4, 7, 8^2
32:1, 2^5, 14^2, 15^2, 18, 19
33:9, 19^4, 20^2, 21, 23
34:4^2, 6^2, 13, 14
35:4^2, 7, 8
36:2, 6, 13, 16, 17^3, 21
37:3, 7^2, 18, 30, 32, 33
38:3, 7, 12^2, 13, 14^3, 21^2
39:1, 3
40:3, 11, 12^2, 15^3, 16, 19, 20^3, 22^2
41:12, 15, 18, 28
42:3, 6^2, 10, 13^2, 14, 16, 22^3, 24
43:16^2, 19^2
44:8, 9, 10^2, 13^3, 15^3, 17, 19, 20^2, 22^2
45:15, 19, 20, 21^2
46:1, 6^2, 11^2
47:3, 7, 8, 9, 14
48:8, 18, 20
49:2^2, 6^2, 7, 8^2, 11, 15, 18, 21
50:2, 4, 7, 9, 11
51:4^2, 6, 8, 10, 12, 20^2
53:2^3, 3, 7^2, 12
54:6^2, 7, 8^2
55:4^2, 5, 13
56:3, 5^2
57:4^2, 6^2, 7, 8, 15
58:1, 2, 5^8, 11^2, 13
59:5, 15, 17^2, 19^2
60:8, 15, 22^4
61:10^2
62:1, 2, 3^2, 5^2, 7, 10, 12
63:14^2, 18
64:6, 10^3
65:1, 2^2, 3, 5^2, 8, 9, 10^2, 11, 15, 17, 18^2, 22
66:2, 3^3, 6^3, 7, 8^2, 12^2, 15, 19, 20

JEREMIAH

1:5, 6, 7, 11, 13, 18
2:2, 6^3, 7, 10, 11, 14^2, 21^3, 23, 24, 27^2, 30, 31^2, 32^2
3:1, 3, 8, 14^2, 19^2, 20, 21
4:6, 11, 12, 13, 15, 16, 17, 19, 20, 26, 27, 29, 31^2
5:1, 3, 6^3, 9, 10, 15^3, 18, 19, 22, 23^2, 26, 27, 29, 30
6:1, 2, 6, 7, 8, 9^2, 10, 20, 22^2, 24, 27^2
7:5, 11, 28, 29
8:5, 15, 19
9:1, 2, 9, 10^2, 11, 12, 16, 18, 19
10:3, 8, 13, 19, 22^2
11:5, 9, 14, 16^2, 19
12:6, 8, 9, 10
13:1, 2, 4, 11^5, 21
14:8^3, 9^2, 14^2, 17^2, 18
15:7, 8, 10^2, 14^2, 18, 20
16:2, 13, 20
17:1^2, 4, 6, 8, 11, 12, 16, 17, 22, 27^2
18:3, 7^2, 9^2, 11, 13, 14, 15, 16, 20, 22^3
19:1, 11
20:4, 8^2, 9, 11, 15
21:5, 6, 9, 14
22:5, 6, 14, 23, 28^3, 30

JEREMIAH

23:5^2, 9^2, 16, 19^2, 23^2, 28^2, 29^2, 33, 40
24:9^4
25:11, 18^2, 29, 30, 31^2, 32, 34, 36
26:2, 6, 15, 18^2, 20
27:10, 14, 15, 16
28:14, 15
29:18^2, 21, 22, 23, 26, 27, 31, 32
30:2, 5, 6^2, 11^2, 14, 16^2, 23
31:6, 8, 9^2, 10, 12, 15, 18, 20, 22^3, 29, 31, 35^2, 36
32:20, 21^2, 22, 31
33:9^2, 17, 18, 21, 24
34:8, 9, 13, 15, 17, 22
35:4, 19
36:2^2, 4^2, 9, 22
37:13, 21
38:2, 14
39:18
40:5, 8, 11
42:2, 5, 18^2
43:12^2
44:2, 8^2, 12^2, 14, 15, 22^2, 28, 29
45:1, 5
46:7, 8, 10^2, 17, 20, 22, 28^2
47:7
48:2, 3, 4, 5, 27, 38, 39^2, 41, 42, 45^2
49:2, 5, 13^4, 14, 17, 18, 19^2, 22, 24, 27, 30, 32^2, 33^2
50:2, 3, 5, 9, 10, 12^3, 17, 22, 23, 24, 32, 35, 36^2, 37^2, 38, 41^2, 42, 43, 44^2
51:1, 6, 7, 14, 16, 25, 26^3, 27^2, 29, 33^2, 34, 37, 39, 43^4, 46^2, 54^2, 55, 57, 59, 60, 63
52:21, 22, 23, 34^2

LAMENTATIONS

1:1, 13, 15, 17
2:1, 3, 6, 7^2, 8, 18, 20, 22
3:10^2, 12, 14, 26, 27, 35, 36, 39^2, 44, 47, 52, 53, 64
4:6, 8^2, 11, 17

EZEKIEL

1:4^4, 5, 7, 8, 10^2, 14, 16^3, 25, 26^3, 28
2:3, 5^2, 6, 9^2
3:5^2, 6, 9, 12^2, 13^2, 17, 20^2, 26^2, 27
4:1, 2^3, 3^2, 6, 10
5:1^2, 2^5, 3, 4, 12^4, 14, 15^2
6:3, 8, 9
7:11, 21^2, 23, 26
8:2, 3, 7, 8, 11, 17, 18
9:1, 2^2, 4
10:1^2, 8, 9, 10^2, 14^3, 21
11:8, 13^2, 16, 19, 24
12:2^3, 3, 6, 16, 23
13:7^2, 10, 11, 13
14:7, 8^2, 9, 17, 19, 22
15:2, 3, 8
16:8, 11, 12^3, 13, 19, 20, 32, 34, 40, 47, 54
17:2^3, 3, 4^2, 5^2, 6^2, 8^2, 13, 22, 23
18:5, 6, 7, 10^3, 14, 16, 26, 31^2
19:1, 2, 3, 5, 6, 10, 13, 14^4
20:6, 11, 12, 13, 20, 21, 27, 33^2, 34^2, 47
21:9^2, 10, 13, 19, 20, 22^2, 23, 29
22:4^2, 25^2, 30
23:30, 40, 41^2, 42^2, 44, 46
24:3^2, 7, 8, 16, 24, 27
25:4, 5^2, 7, 15
26:4, 5^2, 7, 8^2, 10^2, 12^2, 14^2, 17, 19, 21
27:2, 3, 15, 32, 36
28:2^2, 9, 12, 18, 19, 24
29:6, 7, 8, 14, 18
30:3, 8, 13^2, 18, 21, 24
31:3^2, 15
32:2^3, 3, 7, 25
33:2^2, 7, 32^2, 33
34:8, 12, 14^3, 18, 22, 24, 25, 26, 28, 29
35:5
36:3, 4, 5, 17, 26^2, 37
37:7^2, 26
38:4, 7, 9^2, 12^2, 13^3, 15^2, 16, 19, 21
39:6, 11, 13, 15^2, 17
40:2^2, 3^3, 5^2, 17, 24, 27, 42^2
41:7, 8, 18^3, 19^2
42:4^2, 12, 20^2
43:2, 13^4, 17^2, 19^2, 22^2, 23^2, 24, 25^4
44:13, 22^3
45:4, 5, 7, 10^2, 14, 15^2, 18, 21, 22^2, 23^3, 24^3
46:4, 5, 6^2, 7^3, 11^2, 12, 13^2, 14^3, 15, 16, 17, 19, 21, 23
47:3, 4^2, 5^3, 9, 10, 20
48:1, 2, 3, 4, 5, 6, 7, 12, 15, 23, 24, 25, 26, 27

DANIEL

1:5
2:3, 5, 10, 11, 19, 25, 28, 31, 34, 35, 37^2, 44, 47^4, 48
3:6, 10, 11, 15, 29^2
4:5, 6, 10, 13, 15, 16, 23^2, 27, 31
5:1^2, 5, 7, 11, 16, 18, 29^2
6:7^3, 10, 12^2, 13, 17, 20, 26
7:1, 4^3, 5^2, 6^2, 7, 8, 10, 12, 14, 20, 25
8:1, 2^2, 3, 5, 9, 15, 16, 18, 23
9:12, 15, 16, 26
10:1, 5, 6, 7, 9, 11, 18

DANIEL

11:3, 5, 7, 10, 11, 13^2, 15, 18, 20, 21, 22, 23, 24, 25^2, 34, 35, 38, 39, 40
12:1^2, 7, 11

HOSEA

1:2, 3, 4, 6, 8
2:3^2, 6, 12, 15, 18
3:1, 4^3
4:1, 12, 16^3
5:1^2, 2, 7, 12, 14^2
6:4, 8, 9
7:6, 8, 11, 16
8:8, 9, 10, 12, 14
9:1^2, 7, 8^2, 11, 12, 13, 14
10:3, 4, 6, 14, 15
11:1, 4, 10, 11^2
12:1, 2, 7, 12^2, 13^2
13:7^3, 8^2, 10, 11, 13
14:8

JOEL

1:6^3, 8, 14^2, 15
2:2^4, 3^3, 5^2, 9, 14^3, 15^2, 19, 20
3:3^2, 4, 8, 18, 19^2

AMOS

1:4, 7, 10, 12, 14^2
2:2, 5, 6, 7, 13
3:4^2, 5^3, 6^2, 12^3
4:5, 11
5:1, 3, 12, 19^4, 24
6:10, 13, 14
7:4, 7^3, 8^2, 14, 17
8:1, 2, 6, 8, 10, 11^3
9:5, 9

OBADIAH

1, 7, 12, 18^2

JONAH

1:3, 4^2, 16, 17
3:4, 5
4:2, 5, 6^2, 7, 8, 10^2

MICAH

1:4, 6, 8, 14
2:2^2, 4^2, 5, 10, 11
3:6, 12
4:3, 7^2, 9, 10
5:1, 7, 8^2
6:2, 6, 16
7:2, 3, 4^2, 5^2, 6, 8, 17, 18

NAHUM

1:7, 11, 14
2:8
3:2, 3^2, 6

HABAKKUK

1:5, 10
2:5, 6^2, 12^2, 18
3:1, 14

ZEPHANIAH

1:7, 10^2, 13^2, 15^5, 16, 18
2:4, 9, 13^2, 15^2
3:9, 13, 18, 20^2

HAGGAI

1:6, 11
2:6, 13, 15^2, 23

ZECHARIAH

1:8^2, 14, 15, 16
2:1^2, 5, 9
3:2, 5^2
4:1, 2^3, 7
5:1, 2, 7^2, 9
6:13, 14
7:12, 14
8:3, 13^2, 23
9:3, 6, 7^2, 9, 13, 15, 16
10:2^3, 7
11:3^2, 13, 15, 16
12:2, 3, 6^2, 11
13:1, 4
14:4, 10, 13

MALACHI

1:6^4, 11, 13, 14^3
2:2, 11, 15
3:2, 3, 5, 8, 9, 10, 12, 16, 17
4:6

MATTHEW

1:19^2, 20, 21, 23^2
2:6, 12, 13, 18, 19, 22, 23^2
3:4, 16, 17
4:5, 6, 18, 21
5:1, 14, 15^3, 22, 28, 31, 38^2, 41
6:2, 16
7:4, 9, 10^2, 17, 18^2, 24^2, 25, 26
8:2, 4, 5, 9, 14, 19, 23, 24, 26, 30, 32
9:1, 2^2, 9, 12, 16, 18, 20, 23, 32^2
10:18, 29, 34, 35, 36, 41^6, 42^2
11:7, 8, 9^2, 11, 18, 19^3
12:10, 11, 12^2, 14, 20, 22, 29, 32, 35, 38, 39, 41, 42, 43
13:2, 3, 21, 24, 31^2, 32, 33, 34, 42, 44^2, 45, 47, 52, 57
14:5, 8, 11, 13, 14, 15, 22, 23, 26, 33
15:5, 11^2, 20^2, 22^2, 23, 29, 33, 34
16:1, 4^2, 26^2
17:5^2, 14, 20, 27
18:2, 6, 12, 17, 23
19:3, 5, 7, 23, 24^3
20:1, 2^2, 9, 10, 13, 20, 28, 29
21:2, 5, 8, 13, 19, 26, 28, 33^3, 43, 46

MATTHEW

22:2^2, 11^2, 12, 19, 24, 25, 35^2, 46
23:14, 16, 24^2, 37
24:14, 31^2, 32, 45, 50
25:6, 14^2, 19, 21, 23, 32, 35, 38, 43, 44
26:7, 10, 13, 18, 36, 39, 47, 48, 51, 55, 69, 73
27:14, 15, 16, 19, 24, 28, 29^2, 32, 33^3, 46, 48^2, 50, 57, 59, 60, 65, 66
28:2, 16

MARK

1:6^2, 10, 11, 16, 19, 23, 26, 30, 35^2, 40, 44
2:21
3:1^2, 7, 8, 9, 13, 24, 25, 27
4:1^2, 3, 17, 21^4, 26, 31, 34, 37, 38, 39
5:2, 7, 11, 13, 25, 42
6:4, 5, 8, 10, 11, 15, 19, 20, 21^2, 25, 28, 29, 31^2, 32, 34, 35, 46, 49
7:11^2, 15, 25, 26^2, 36
8:4, 7, 10, 11, 12, 22, 36, 37
9:7^2, 14, 17, 21, 36, 39, 41, 42
10:2, 4, 7, 12, 15, 25^3, 45, 46, 48
11:2, 4, 13, 17, 32
12:1^5, 2, 15, 19, 20, 40, 42^2
13:9, 28, 34^2
14:3, 6, 9, 13^2, 15, 32, 35, 43, 44, 47^2, 48, 51^2, 69, 70^2
15:1, 17, 19, 21, 22, 34, 36^2, 37, 46^3
16:5^2

LUKE

1:1, 5, 13, 17, 22, 26, 27^2, 31, 34, 36, 39, 42, 45, 57, 63
2:1, 7, 11, 12^2, 13, 16, 24^2, 25, 32, 34, 35, 36^2, 37, 44
3:22^3
4:5, 9, 11, 13, 14, 25, 26^3, 31, 33^3, 36, 38, 42
5:3, 4, 6, 8, 12^2, 14, 15, 17, 18^3, 27, 29^2, 31, 36^4
6:6, 12, 17, 39, 43^2, 44, 45, 48^3, 49^2
7:2, 5, 7, 8, 11, 12^2, 16^2, 24, 25, 26^2, 28, 33, 34^3, 37^2, 39^2, 41
8:4, 5, 6, 13, 16^4, 22^2, 23, 24, 27, 28, 33, 41^2, 42, 43
9:5, 10, 12, 14, 25, 27, 28, 34, 35, 38, 39, 42, 46, 47, 52, 57
10:13, 25, 30, 31, 32, 33, 38^2, 39
11:1, 5, 6, 11^6, 12, 14, 16, 17^2, 21, 22, 24, 27, 29, 30, 31, 32, 33^4, 36, 37
12:10, 14^2, 15, 16^2, 33, 44, 46, 50, 54^2
13:6^2, 11^2, 16, 19^3, 21, 33, 34
14:2, 5, 7, 8^2, 12^3, 13, 16^2, 18, 20, 28, 32
15:8, 11, 13, 14, 15, 20, 22, 29
16:1^2, 19, 20, 26
17:2, 4^2, 6, 7, 12, 15, 16
18:1, 2^2, 3, 4, 10^2, 13, 17, 18, 25^3, 35
19:2, 4, 7^2, 9, 11, 12^3, 14, 17, 20, 30, 37, 43, 46
20:6, 9^4, 10, 12, 24, 28, 29, 38, 47
21:2, 3, 13, 15, 27, 29, 35
22:10^2, 12, 24, 29, 36, 41, 47, 48, 52, 55, 56, 58, 59^2
23:2, 6, 8, 11, 19, 26, 27, 31, 38, 44, 46, 47, 50^4, 51, 53
24:13, 18, 19, 23, 37, 39, 42^2

JOHN

1:6, 7, 30, 32, 42
2:1, 15
3:1^2, 2, 3, 4, 5, 10, 25, 27
4:5, 7, 9^2, 14, 19, 24, 29, 44, 46
5:1, 2, 3, 4, 5, 6, 13, 14, 35^3
6:2, 3, 4, 5, 7, 9, 14, 15^2, 17, 18, 50, 70
7:12, 20, 22, 23^2, 33, 40, 43
8:3, 7, 40, 44^3, 48^2, 49, 51, 52^2, 55
9:1, 11, 16^3, 17, 24, 25, 30, 31
10:1^2, 5, 19, 20, 21^2, 33^2
11:1, 10, 38^2, 43, 44, 47, 54^2, 57
12:2, 3, 6, 14, 24, 28, 35, 46, 49
13:4, 5, 26, 33, 34
14:2, 3, 19, 23
15:6^2, 13, 25
16:16^2, 17^2, 18, 19^2, 21^2
18:1, 3, 10, 18, 30, 35, 37^2, 39, 40
19:2^2, 7, 12, 13, 17^2, 19, 23, 29^2, 34, 36, 38, 39, 41^2
20:7
21:3^2, 8, 9

THE ACTS

1:9, 12, 18, 22
2:2^2, 22, 30
3:2, 14, 22
4:16, 27, 36
5:1^2, 2, 16, 30, 31^2, 34^3, 36
6:1, 5^2, 7
7:5, 6, 11, 16, 27^2, 29, 30^2, 35^4, 37, 41, 46, 57, 58, 60
8:1, 9, 27, 32^2, 36
9:3, 4, 7, 10^2, 12^2, 15, 25, 26, 33, 36, 43
10:1^2, 2, 3, 4, 6, 7, 10, 11^2, 13, 22, 26, 28^2, 30, 32, 34, 39
11:5^4, 7, 21, 24, 26
12:7, 9, 11, 13, 21, 22^3

THE ACTS

13:6^3, 7, 11^3, 21^2, 22, 23, 29, 41^3, 47
14:1, 8^2, 10
15:7, 10, 14, 33
16:1^4, 3, 9^2, 11, 12, 13, 14^2, 16^2, 24, 26, 28, 29
17:1, 4^2, 5, 12, 15, 18, 31, 34
18:2, 7, 9, 11, 14, 15, 18^2, 24
19:14, 22, 24^2, 34, 35, 38, 39
20:9^3, 11, 12
21:1, 2, 10, 23, 39^4, 40
22:3^3, 6, 7, 12^2, 17, 22, 25^2, 26, 27, 28, 29
23:6^2, 7, 9^2, 10, 12, 14, 17, 21, 25, 27
24:1, 4, 5^3, 10, 15, 16, 23, 24, 25, 27
25:9, 14, 27
26:5, 8, 13, 14, 16^2, 24, 26, 28
27:1, 2^2, 5, 6, 8, 14, 16, 18, 26, 28, 39^2, 41
28:2, 3^2, 4, 6^2, 8^2, 11, 13, 16, 23

ROMANS

1:1, 10, 25, 28
2:14, 17, 19^2, 20, 21, 22, 25, 28, 29
3:4, 5, 7, 25, 28
4:11, 17
5:7^2
7:1, 21
8:24
9:9, 27, 28, 29, 33
10:2, 14, 19, 21
11:5, 9^4, 17, 24
12:1
13:3, 4
14:13
15:8, 12, 23, 26
16:1, 2, 23

1 CORINTHIANS

1:22, 23
2:7, 11
3:10, 14, 18
4:1, 2, 3, 6, 9, 21
5:5, 6, 7, 11^4
6:1, 5, 7, 18, 20
7:1^2, 5, 12, 15^2, 21, 22, 23, 26, 27^3, 28, 34^2, 35
8:7, 9
9:5^2, 7^3, 8, 11, 17^2, 20, 24, 25, 27
10:13, 27, 30
11:6^2, 7, 13, 14^2, 15^3, 28
12:31
13:1, 11^5, 12
14:7, 11^2, 22, 25, 26^4, 35, 37
15:38, 44^4, 45^2, 51, 52
16:7, 9

2 CORINTHIANS

1:10, 15, 23
2:6, 7, 12, 15
3:13, 18
4:17^2
5:1, 17
6:2, 13, 18
7:8^2, 9, 11, 14
8:2, 10, 11^2, 12^2, 14^2
9:2, 5, 7
10:6, 13
11:1, 2, 5, 16^3, 20^5, 23, 25^2, 32, 33^2
12:2, 3, 4, 6, 7, 11, 17, 18^2
13:3
S

GALATIANS

2:3, 14, 16, 18
3:13^2, 15, 19, 20^2, 21, 25
4:1^2, 4, 7^3, 18, 22^2, 27
5:3, 9
6:1^2, 3, 7, 11, 12, 15

EPHESIANS

3:7
4:13
5:2^2, 12, 27, 31, 32
6:21

PHILIPPIANS

1:6, 23^2
2:7, 8, 9, 15, 22
3:5
4:17, 18^2

COLOSSIANS

1:7, 23, 25
2:15, 17, 18, 23
3:13
4:1, 3, 7^2, 9, 11, 12, 13

1 THESSALONIANS

2:5, 7, 11, 17
4:16
5:2, 3, 4

2 THESSALONIANS

1:5, 6
2:3, 11
3:15

1 TIMOTHY

1:5^2, 8, 9, 13^2, 15, 16, 18, 19
2:2, 6, 7^2, 12
3:1^4, 2, 3, 5, 6, 7, 9, 10, 13^2
4:2, 6, 9
5:1, 5, 9, 23
6:9, 12, 13, 19

2 TIMOTHY
1:7, 11^{2}
2:3, 4, 5, 11, 15, 17, 20, 21^{2}, 22
3:5, 15
4:7, 8

TITUS
1:1, 7, 8^{2}, 12
2:7, 14
3:8, 10

PHILEMON
1, 9, 15, 16^{3}, 17, 22
S

HEBREWS
1:4, 5^{2}, 7, 8, 11, 12
2:2, 6, 7, 9, 17
3:5^{2}, 6
4:1, 4, 7^{2}, 9, 12, 14
5:6, 8, 13
6:18
7:2, 3, 5, 12, 16, 17, 18, 19, 21, 22^{2}
8:2, 4, 6^{2}, 8, 10^{2}, 13
9:1, 2, 9, 11, 16, 17
10:1, 3, 5, 15, 20, 22, 27, 31, 32, 33, 34, 37
11:2, 4, 6, 8, 9, 10, 11, 14, 16^{2}, 19, 21, 23, 25, 35, 39
12:1, 10, 19, 20^{2}, 28, 29
13:9, 18, 22

JAMES
1:1, 6, 8, 11, 18, 23^{4}, 25^{2}
2:2^{3}, 3, 11, 14, 15, 18, 24
3:2, 4, 5^{3}, 6^{2}, 11, 12, 13^{2}
4:4, 11^{2}, 13^{2}, 14^{2}
5:3, 5, 16, 17, 20^{2}

1 PETER
1:3, 6, 19, 22
2:4, 5, 6, 8^{2}, 9^{3}, 10, 16, 19
3:4, 9, 15, 16, 20, 21
4:15^{3}, 16, 19
5:1^{2}, 2, 4, 8, 10, 12, 14

2 PETER
1:1, 17, 19^{3}
2:3, 5, 17, 19
3:8^{2}, 10^{2}, 13

1 JOHN
1:10
2:4, 8, 22
3:15
4:20^{2}
5:10, 16^{2}, 17

2 JOHN
4, 5, 7, 8

3 JOHN
6

JUDE
9, 22

REVELATION
1:10^{2}, 11, 13^{2}, 14, 15, 16
2:10, 14^{2}, 17^{2}, 18, 20^{2}, 22, 27^{2}
3:1, 3, 4, 8, 12
4:1^{2}, 2, 3^{3}, 6, 7^{5}
5:1, 2^{2}, 6, 9, 12
6:2^{3}, 4, 5^{2}, 6^{4}, 8, 10, 11, 12, 13^{2}, 14
7:2, 9, 10
8:3, 8, 10^{2}, 12, 13
9:1, 2^{2}, 5^{2}, 11, 13, 15^{3}
10:1^{2}, 2, 3^{2}, 4
11:1^{2}, 3, 12^{2}, 13
12:1^{3}, 3, 5^{2}, 6^{2}, 10, 12, 14^{3}, 15
13:1, 2^{3}, 5, 11^{2}, 14, 16, 18
14:1, 2^{2}, 3, 7, 9, 13, 14^{3}, 15, 17, 18, 20
15:2
16:1, 2, 3, 15, 16, 17, 18, 21^{2}
17:3^{2}, 4, 5, 10
18:2^{2}, 7, 21^{3}, 22, 23
19:1, 5, 6, 11, 12^{2}, 13, 15^{2}, 16, 17, 20
20:1, 2, 3^{2}, 4, 6, 11
21:1^{2}, 2, 3, 10, 11^{2}, 12, 15, 17, 19, 20^{3}, 27
22:1, 15

AN (Also see A)

GENESIS
2:18, 20
4:3, 22
5:3, 6, 18, 25, 28
6:3, 14
7:24
8:11, 20
9:20
11:10, 25
12:7, 8
13:18
15:9, 12
16:1^{2}
17:7, 8, 13, 17, 19
21:5, 20
22:9
23:1
25:7, 8, 17, 25
26:12, 25, 28
27:30
29:24
31:46
33:17, 19, 20
34:31
35:1, 3, 7, 8, 28
37:33, 36
38:14, 15
39:1^{2}, 14
41:12, 16
42:23
43:12, 32
44:20
46:34
47:9, 28
48:4
49:9, 13, 17, 33
50:22, 25, 26

EXODUS
2:3, 11^{2}, 19
4:20
6:8, 16, 18, 20
10:13, 26
12:3, 14, 16^{2}, 17, 24, 45
13:13
14:8
15:2, 8, 25
16:16, 18, 32, 33, 36^{2}
17:15
18:3
19:6, 13
20:24, 25
21:2, 6, 28, 33^{2}
22:1^{2}, 10^{2}, 11, 15
23:1, 20, 22^{2}
24:4
25:2, 10, 25
26:36
27:1, 9, 11, 16, 18
28:4, 11, 18, 19^{2}, 20, 32^{2}
29:18, 25, 28^{2}, 36, 37^{2}, 40^{2}, 41
30:1, 10, 13, 14, 15^{2}, 16, 24, 25^{3}, 31
31:18
32:5, 30
33:2
34:20
35:2, 5^{2}, 22, 24
36:37
37:12
38:9, 11, 23^{2}, 25, 27
39:11, 12^{2}, 13, 23^{2}
40:10, 15

LEVITICUS
1:2, 9, 13, 17
2:2, 4, 9, 16
3:3, 5, 9, 14
4:20, 26, 31, 35
5:2, 4, 6, 10, 11, 13, 16, 18
6:7, 20
7:5, 14, 18, 25, 32
8:21, 28, 33, 34
9:7^{2}, 17
11:10, 11, 12, 13, 20, 23, 41, 42
12:7, 8
13:11, 28
14:5, 18, 19, 20, 21, 29, 31, 40, 41, 45, 50, 53
15:13, 15, 19, 25, 30, 32, 33
16:6, 10, 11, 16, 17^{2}, 18, 20, 24, 30, 33^{3}, 34^{2}
17:3, 4, 11^{2}
19:20, 22
20:13, 21
21:14
22:10, 12, 22, 27
23:3, 7, 8^{2}, 12, 13, 14, 18, 21, 24, 25, 27^{2}, 28, 35, 36^{3}, 37
24:7, 8, 10^{2}
25:40, 46, 50
26:8^{2}
27:9, 27

NUMBERS
2:9, 16, 24^{2}, 31
4:15
5:2, 8, 15^{3}, 17, 19, 21^{2}, 26
6:11
7:3, 13, 19, 25, 31, 37, 43, 49, 55, 61, 67, 73, 79, 85, 86
8:11, 12, 13, 15, 19, 21^{2}
9:7
10:5, 6^{2}, 7, 8, 9
12:1
13:32
14:7
15:3, 4, 5, 6, 7, 9, 10^{2}, 13, 14, 15, 19, 20, 21, 25, 28^{2}
16:31, 46, 47
18:8, 17, 21, 24, 26, 28
19:17
20:16
22:22
23:3, 22
24:8
25:13^{2}
26:53
27:7
28:5^{2}, 7, 14^{3}, 18, 22, 25, 26, 30
29:1, 5, 7, 12
30:2, 6, 10
31:29, 50^{2}
32:14
33:3, 39, 54
34:2
35:16, 18
36:2, 8

DEUTERONOMY
4:21, 38
5:29
7:6, 25, 26
10:1, 3
13:16
14:2, 21^{2}
15:4, 12^{2}, 17
17:1
18:10^{2}, 12
19:10
20:9, 16, 19
21:3, 23
22:10^{2}, 14, 19^{2}, 22, 23
23:3, 7^{2}
24:4, 14
25:5, 16, 19
26:1, 8, 12, 19
27:5^{2}, 15, 25
28:9, 22^{2}, 30, 37
29:4, 8
31:2, 24
32:11, 45
33:7
34:7

JOSHUA
1:6
2:1
3:13, 16
7:13
8:2, 24, 28, 30, 31
10:20
11:23
13:6, 7
14:3, 13
17:4^{2}, 6
19:49^{2}, 51^{2}
22:10, 11, 14, 16, 19, 23, 26, 29
23:4
24:19, 25, 26, 29, 32

JUDGES
2:1, 8
3:18, 31
4:21
6:11^{2}, 19, 22^{2}, 24, 26
8:10, 27
9:23, 46, 48
11:1
12:5
13:6, 16, 21
14:4
15:15, 16^{2}, 17, 19
16:1, 3
17:5^{2}
18:1, 14
19:9, 16, 28
20:10^{2}, 16, 35, 38
21:4, 17

RUTH
1:12^{2}
2:17

1 SAMUEL
1:1
2:28, 31, 32^{2}
3:12
4:18
7:17
9:6
10:13
13:10
14:3, 14, 27, 28, 35, 48
16:2, 14, 15, 16, 20, 23
17:5, 12, 17, 38
18:1, 25
19:13, 16
20:36
21:7
23:6
24:16
25:18, 42
26:13, 19
28:14
29:4, 9
30:11, 13, 14, 25

2 SAMUEL
1:8, 13
2:25
3:14, 29
5:11
6:18
7:2, 5, 7, 11, 13, 27
8:4
11:2, 19
13:36
14:17, 20
15:19
16:1^{2}
17:25
18:10
19:26, 27
23:5, 14, 21, 38^{2}
24:3, 18, 21, 25

1 KINGS
1:39, 41^{2}, 52
2:24, 36
3:1, 9, 12
4:23
5:3, 5^{2}
7:2, 8, 26, 31, 40
8:13, 16, 17, 18, 20, 31, 36, 54, 63
10:10, 29^{2}
11:7, 14, 18, 25, 26
12:21, 31
13:11, 14, 18
14:21, 31
15:13
16:32
17:12
18:4, 10, 13, 32
19:5, 11
20:20, 25, 29, 30
22:9, 25

2 KINGS
1:8, 9
3:4^{2}
4:9, 24, 43
6:15, 25
9:2, 5, 17
10:25
11:4
16:10, 11
18:31
19:32, 35
23:33
25:19

1 CHRONICLES
2:34
5:21
6:49
8:40
11:23
12:14, 37
14:1
15:5, 7, 10, 27
16:2, 17, 29
17:1, 4, 5, 6, 10, 12, 25
18:4
21:3, 5, 15, 18, 22, 26
22:6, 7, 8, 10, 14
27:4
28:2, 3, 8, 10
29:16

2 CHRONICLES
1:17^{2}
2:1^{2}, 3, 4^{2}, 6^{2}, 12^{2}, 17
3:4, 16
4:1, 5, 8
5:12
6:2, 5, 7, 8, 22, 27
7:1, 5, 12, 21
9:9
11:1
12:13
13:3, 13
14:8, 9
15:16
17:18
18:24
20:23
21:18
24:10, 15, 26
25:6^{2}
26:11, 13
27:5
28:6
29:17, 24, 29, 32
32:8, 21
35:25
36:3, 23

EZRA
1:2
2:3, 18, 21, 23, 27, 30, 41, 42
4:3, 6, 17
6:17
7:22^{4}
8:3, 10, 12, 26^{2}
9:11, 12
10:17

NEHEMIAH
4:2
5:12, 17
6:5, 13
7:8, 24, 26, 27, 31, 32, 44, 45
10:29, 33
11:14, 19

ESTHER
1:1, 4
8:9

JOB
1:8, 10
2:3, 11
3:16
4:16
6:6
7:1
13:16
14:3, 4, 6
16:3
18:2
19:15, 24
20:19
26:10
28:3
31:6, 11^{2}, 28
33:23
40:9, 15
41:1, 2
42:11, 16

PSALMS
5:9
7:9
11:6
18:25
26:12
27:3
31:2
33:2, 7, 16, 17
38:4
39:5
40:2
41:8
43:1
48:7
50:21
55:12
64:5, 7
68:15, 21
69:8, 13, 31
72:16
78:13, 26, 55
84:3
88:8
92:3, 10
96:8
101:5
102:3, 6
105:10
106:20
119:96, 111, 142
127:3
132:5
135:12^{2}
136:21, 22
140:11
141:5
144:9
145:13

PROVERBS
1:9
4:9
5:3
6:11, 16, 18
7:10, 13, 22
8:5, 7
10:25
11:9
13:22
15:8, 9, 19, 26
16:5, 12, 18, 19, 24, 27
17:1, 10, 11, 27
18:11
19:15, 28
20:3, 21, 23
21:4, 19
22:24
23:5, 6, 18, 32
24:3, 9, 34
25:12^{3}, 19, 20, 23
27:6, 7
28:10, 22
29:6, 22, 27^{2}
30:19, 20, 23^{2}, 31

ECCLESIASTES
4:6, 13
5:6
6:1, 2, 3^{2}
7:11
8:3, 11, 12
9:2, 3, 12^{2}
10:5^{2}, 8

SONG OF SOLOMON
4:4, 13
6:4, 10
7:2

ISAIAH
1:13, 21, 30
3:7
5:10^{2}, 26
6:13
9:17^{2}
10:6
11:10, 12, 16
14:19
15:5
16:4, 11, 14
17:6, 9
18:3
19:19
21:16
22:16^{2}
23:15, 16
24:13
25:2
29:5, 8, 21
30:5, 13, 17^{2}, 28
32:2
33:1
34:13
35:6, 8
36:16
37:33, 36
38:12, 13
41:24
43:23
44:14, 19
45:17
48:4
49:8, 18
53:10
54:16
55:3, 13
56:5, 7
58:5
59:17
60:15, 19
61:8
63:12, 13
64:6
65:9, 20^{4}
66:3^{3}, 14, 20^{2}, 24

JEREMIAH
1:11, 14, 18
2:7, 19
3:18
4:7
5:15, 16
6:26
9:2, 8, 11
10:10
11:19
14:12
18:17
19:8
21:5
22:19
23:14, 40
24:7
25:9^{2}, 11, 18^{2}, 36
26:8, 9
29:11, 18^{2}
30:14, 17
31:3, 32
32:14, 40
33:9, 12
34:9^{2}, 14, 22
42:18^{2}
43:1
44:12^{2}, 22^{2}, 27
46:19, 22
47:2
48:34, 40
49:2, 14
50:9
51:29, 34, 37^{3}, 41, 63
52:23, 25

LAMENTATIONS
1:15
2:4^{2}, 5
5:10

EZEKIEL
1:10^{2}, 24
2:9
3:5, 6, 9
4:3, 11
5:15^{2}
7:2, 5^{2}, 6
8:3
10:14
11:19
13:11, 13
16:3^{2}, 24^{2}, 30, 31, 45^{2}, 60
17:13, 22
20:17
21:25, 29
23:24
31:3
33:32
35:5
36:3, 26
37:10, 26
38:10, 22
40:5, 19, 23, 27, 42^{2}, 43, 47^{2}
41:7, 13^{2}, 14, 15
42:2, 8, 15
43:13, 23
44:28
45:1^{2}, 4, 11^{2}, 13^{4}, 14^{2}, 24^{4}
46:5^{3}, 7^{4}, 11^{4}, 14^{2}
47:22

DANIEL
2:46
3:1, 4, 27
4:3, 13, 23, 34
5:12
6:1, 3
7:14, 27
8:5, 12
9:24
10:10
11:6, 7
12:7

HOSEA
3:1, 2^{2}, 4^{2}
6:10, 11
7:4, 6, 7
8:1
10:1, 11
13:13, 15

JOEL

2:1
3:3

AMOS

3:11, 12, 15
5:3[2], 13
7:2, 14[2], 17
8:10

OBADIAH

1

JONAH

1:9
3:3

MICAH

1:6, 7[2], 15
2:3, 8
6:16

NAHUM

1:8[2], 9

HABAKKUK

2:3, 9

ZEPHANIAH

1:10
3:12

HAGGAI

2:16

ZECHARIAH

5:6, 11
7:12
9:9[2], 16
12:6
13:5

MALACHI

1:10, 13
2:11, 12
3:3
4:1

MATTHEW

2:19
4:2, 8
5:14, 38[2]
8:30
9:16, 20
10:12
11:1
12:1, 3, 35, 39
13:8, 23, 28, 52
14:7
16:23
17:1, 27
18:12, 17, 28
19:29
20:1
21:2, 5[2]
24:44, 50
25:24, 35, 37, 42, 44
26:5, 7, 30, 72

MARK

1:23
2:21, 25
3:19, 26, 30
4:8, 20
5:2, 25
6:20, 27
7:22, 24, 25, 32
9:2
10:30
12:1
14:2, 3, 26
15:43

LUKE

1:11, 18, 69
2:36
4:5, 33
5:36

LUKE

6:3, 7, 45, 48, 49
7:37
8:8, 15, 32, 43
9:28
10:34
11:12, 29
12:1, 40, 46
14:5[2], 32
15:4
16:2, 6, 7
19:21, 22
21:18
22:37, 43, 44
24:42

JOHN

1:22, 47
2:16
5:4, 5
6:60
10:12, 13
12:15, 29
13:15
19:31, 39
21:11

THE ACTS

1:13, 15
2:30
3:3
6:15
7:30, 47
8:27
9:37
10:3, 22, 28
11:13
12:21
13:17
14:5
17:5, 23
18:24
19:40
20:32

THE ACTS

21:16, 26, 29, 31, 38
23:9, 21, 27
25:11
27:12, 34

ROMANS

1:1, 23
2:20
3:13
4:19
7:2, 3
11:1
14:13
16:16

1 CORINTHIANS

1:1
5:9, 11[3]
6:15, 16
7:13
8:4, 7
9:1, 2, 25
12:17
14:2, 4, 8, 13, 14, 19, 26, 27
15:9, 52
16:20

2 CORINTHIANS

1:1
2:11
5:1
6:15
8:14
10:11
11:7, 14
12:2, 5, 12
13:12

GALATIANS

1:1, 8
2:5
4:7, 14, 24
5:13
6:1

EPHESIANS

1:1, 11
2:21, 22
5:2, 5
6:20

PHILIPPIANS

1:28
3:5, 17
4:18

COLOSSIANS

1:1
2:16

1 THESSALONIANS

5:8, 26

2 THESSALONIANS

3:9, 15

1 TIMOTHY

1:1
2:7
4:12
5:1, 8, 19[2]

2 TIMOTHY

1:1, 9, 11
2:9
4:5

TITUS

1:1
3:10

PHILEMON

9

HEBREWS

3:12
4:15
5:5, 10
6:6, 16[2], 17, 19, 20
7:16, 20, 21[2], 24, 26
8:1

HEBREWS

9:11, 13
10:21, 22, 29, 34
11:7, 8, 16
12:22
13:10

JAMES

3:8
5:10

1 PETER

1:1, 4
2:5, 9, 21
3:15
4:15
5:1

2 PETER

1:1, 11
2:6[2], 14

1 JOHN

2:1, 7, 20
5:20

2 JOHN

7

JUDE

7

REVELATION

2:7, 11, 17, 29
3:6, 8, 13, 22
4:3
7:4
8:1, 5, 13
9:15
11:9, 11, 19
13:9, 14
14:1
16:18
19:17
20:1
21:17, 19, 20

AND 2532

GENESIS

1:1, 2[4], 3[2], 4[2], 5[4], 6[2], 7[3], 8[3], 9[3], 10[3], 11[3], 12[4], 13[2], 14[5], 15[2], 16[2], 17, 18[4], 19[2], 20[2], 21[4], 22[4], 23[2], 24[4], 25[4], 26[6], 27, 28[8], 29[2], 30[4], 31[4]
2:1[2], 2[2], 3[3], 4[2], 5[3], 6, 7[3], 8[2], 9[4], 10[3], 12[2], 13, 14[2], 15[3], 16, 17, 18, 19[4], 20[3], 21[4], 22[2], 23[2], 24[3], 25[3]
3:1, 2, 4, 5[2], 6[6], 7[4], 8[3], 9[2], 10[3], 11, 12[2], 13[3], 14[3], 15[5], 16[3], 17[2], 18[2], 19, 20, 21[2], 22[6], 24[2]
4:1[4], 2[2], 3, 4[4], 5[3], 6[2], 7[3], 8[3], 9[2], 10, 11, 12, 13, 14[4], 15[2], 16[2], 17[5], 18[4], 19[2], 20[2], 21[2], 22[3], 23[3], 24, 25[3], 26[2]
5:2[3], 3[4], 4[3], 5[3], 6[3], 7[4], 8[3], 9[2], 10[4], 11[3], 12[2], 13[4], 14[3], 15[3], 16[4], 17[3], 18[3], 19[3], 20[3], 21[3], 22[3], 23[2], 24[2], 25[3], 26[4], 27[3], 28[3], 29[2], 30[4], 31[3], 32[3]
6:1[2], 2, 3[2], 4[2], 5[2], 6[2], 7[4], 9[2], 10[2], 11, 12[2], 13[2], 14[2], 15[2], 16[3], 17[2], 18[4], 19[2], 20, 21[4]
7:1[2], 2[3], 3, 4[3], 5, 6, 7[4], 8[3], 9[2], 10, 11, 12[2], 13[5], 14[4], 15[2], 16[3], 17[4], 18[3], 19[2], 20, 21[5], 23[7], 24[2]
8:1[5], 2[2], 3[3], 4, 5, 6, 7[2], 9[3], 10[2], 11[2], 12[2], 13[5], 14[2], 15, 16[3], 17[4], 18[4], 19[2], 20[4], 21[2], 22[7]
9:1[5], 2[4], 5[2], 7[3], 8[2], 9[2], 10[2], 11, 12[3], 13[2], 14, 15[4], 16[3], 17[2], 18[4], 19, 20[2], 21[3], 22[2], 23[7], 24[2], 25, 26[2], 27[2], 28[2], 29[3]
10:1[2], 2[6], 3[3], 4[3], 6[4], 7[7], 8, 10[4], 11[3], 12[2], 13[4], 14[3], 15[2], 16[3], 17[3], 18[4], 19[4], 20, 22[4], 23[4], 24[2], 25[2], 26[4], 27[3], 28[3], 29[3], 30, 32
11:1[2], 2[2], 3[4], 4[3], 5[2], 6[4], 7, 8, 9, 10, 11[3], 12[3], 13[4], 14[2], 15[4], 16[3], 17[4], 18[2], 19[4], 20[3], 21[4], 22[2], 23[3], 24[3], 25[4], 26[3], 27[2], 28, 29[4], 31[6], 32[3]
12:1[2], 2[4], 3[3], 4[3], 5[6], 6[2], 7[3], 8[5], 9, 10[2], 11, 12, 13, 14, 15[2], 16[8], 17[2], 18[2], 19, 20[4]
13:1[4], 2[2], 3[2], 4, 5[3], 6, 7[4], 8[4], 10[3], 11[2], 12[2], 13, 14[5], 15, 16, 17, 18[3]
14:1[2], 2[3], 4, 5[5], 6, 7[4], 8[6], 9[3], 10[5], 11[4], 12[3], 13[4], 14[3], 15[4], 16[5], 17[2], 18[3], 19[3], 20[2], 21[2], 22[2], 23, 24[2]
15:1, 2[2], 3[2], 4, 5[4], 6[2], 7, 8, 9[5], 10[3], 11, 12[2], 13[3], 14[2], 15, 17[3], 19[2], 20[3], 21[4]
16:1, 2[2], 3[2], 4[3], 5[3], 6, 7, 8[3], 9[2], 10, 11[3], 12[3], 13, 14, 15[2], 16[2]
17:1[4], 2[3], 3[2], 4, 6[3], 7[4], 8[3], 9[2], 10[2], 11[3], 12, 13[2], 14, 15, 16[3], 17[3], 18, 19[4], 20[4], 22[2], 23[4], 24[2], 25, 26, 27[2]
18:1[2], 2[5], 3, 4[2], 5[3], 6[3], 7[5], 8[6], 9[2], 10[3], 11[3], 13, 14, 15, 16[3], 17, 18[2], 19[3], 20[3], 21[2], 22[2], 23[2], 24, 25, 26, 27[3], 28[2], 29[3], 30[3], 31[2], 32[3], 33[2]
19:1[4], 2[6], 3[6], 4, 5[2], 6[2], 7, 8, 9[5], 10[2], 11[2], 12[4], 13, 14[3], 15[2], 16[5], 17, 18, 19[3], 20[2], 21, 24[2], 25[4], 26, 27, 28[5], 29[2], 30[5], 31[2], 32, 33[4], 34[3], 35[4], 37[2], 38[2]
20:1[4], 2[3], 3, 4, 5[2], 6, 7[4], 8[3], 9[3], 10, 11[2], 12[2], 13, 14[6], 15, 16[2], 17[4]
21:1[2], 2, 3, 4, 5, 6, 7, 8[3], 9, 10, 11, 12[2], 13, 14[8], 15[2], 16[5], 17[3], 18, 19[5], 20[4], 21[2], 22[2], 23, 24, 25, 26, 27[4], 28, 29, 30, 32[2], 33[2], 34
22:1[3], 2[3], 3[7], 4, 5[5], 6[5], 7[5], 8, 9[5], 10[2], 11[3], 12, 13[6], 14, 15, 16[2], 17[3], 18, 19[3], 20, 21[2], 22[5], 23, 24[4]
23:1[3], 2[3], 3[2], 4, 5, 7[2], 8[2], 10[2], 11, 12, 13[2], 14, 15, 16[2], 17[3], 19, 20[2]
24:1[3], 2, 3[2], 4[2], 5, 6, 7[4], 8, 9[2], 10[4], 11, 12[2], 13, 14[4], 15, 16[4], 17[2], 18[4], 19, 20[4], 21, 22[2], 23, 24, 25[2], 26[2], 27[2], 28[2], 29[3], 30[4], 31[2], 32[6], 33[2], 34, 35[10], 36[2], 37, 38[2], 39, 40[4], 41, 42[2], 43[2], 44[2], 45[4], 46[5], 47[5], 48[3], 49[3], 50[2], 51[2], 52, 53[5], 54[6], 55[2], 56, 57[2], 58[3], 59[4], 60[3], 61[6], 62, 63[4], 64[2], 65[2], 66, 67[5]
25:1, 2[6], 3[5], 4[5], 5, 6, 7[2], 8[3], 9[2], 10, 11[2], 13[4], 14[3], 15[2], 16[2], 17[6], 18[2], 19, 20, 21[3], 22[3], 23[4], 24, 25[2], 26[4], 27[3], 28, 29[3], 30, 31, 32[2], 33[3], 34[5]
26:1[2], 2[2], 3[4], 4[3], 5[2], 6, 7[2], 8[3], 9[4], 10[2], 11, 12[2], 13[3], 14[3], 15, 16, 17[3], 18[2], 19[2], 20[2], 21[3], 22[6], 23, 24[4], 25[4], 26[2], 27[2], 28[4], 29[2], 30[3], 31[4], 32[3], 33, 34[2], 35
27:1[4], 2, 3[3], 4[2], 5[3], 6, 7[2], 9[2], 10[2], 11[2], 12[3], 13[2], 14[4], 15[2], 16[2], 17[2], 18[3], 19[2], 20[2], 21, 22[3], 23, 24[2], 25[6], 26[2], 27[5], 28[3], 29[3], 30[2], 31[4], 32[2], 33[6], 34[3], 35[2], 36[3], 37[6], 38[3], 39[3], 40[3], 41[2], 42[4], 43, 44, 45[2], 46
28:1[4], 2, 3[3], 4[2], 5[3], 6[2], 7[3], 8, 9, 10[2], 11[5], 12[5], 13[4], 14[7], 15[3], 16[3], 17[3], 18[4], 19, 20[4], 22[2]
29:1, 2[4], 3[4], 4[2], 5[2], 6[3], 7[3], 8[2], 9, 10[4], 11[3], 12[4], 13[5], 14[3], 15, 16[2], 17, 18[2], 19, 20[2], 21, 22[2], 23[3], 24, 25[2], 26, 27, 28[3], 29, 30[3], 31, 32[3], 33[4], 34[3], 35[4]
30:1[2], 2[2], 3[2], 4[2], 5[2], 6[3], 7[2], 8[3], 9, 10, 11[2], 12, 13[2], 14[3], 15[3], 16[4], 17[3], 18[2], 19[2], 20[2], 21[2], 22[3], 23[3], 24[2], 25[2], 26[2], 27, 28[2], 29[2], 30[3], 31[3], 32[5], 33[2], 34, 35[7], 36[3], 37[5], 38, 39[3], 40[5], 41, 42, 43[6]
31:1[2], 2[2], 3[3], 4[3], 5, 6, 7[2], 8, 9, 10[4], 11[2], 12[3], 13[2], 14[3], 15, 16, 17[2], 18[2], 19[2], 20, 21[3], 22, 23[3], 24[2], 25, 26[2], 27[4], 28[2], 30, 31[2], 32, 33[4], 34[3], 35[2], 36[4], 37, 38[2], 40[2], 41[2], 42[3], 43[6], 44[3], 45[2], 46[4], 47, 48[2], 49[2], 50, 51[3], 52[3], 53[2], 54[3], 55[6]
32:1[2], 2[2], 3, 4[2], 5[5], 6[3], 7[5], 8[2], 9[4], 10[2], 11[2], 12[2], 13[2], 14[2], 15[2], 16[4], 17[4], 18, 19[3], 20[2], 21, 22[5], 23[3], 24[2], 25[2], 26[2], 27[2], 28[3], 29[4], 30[2], 31[2]
33:1[7], 2[6], 3[2], 4[5], 5[5], 6[2], 7[5], 8[2], 9, 10[2], 11[3], 12[3], 13[4], 14[2], 15[2], 17[3], 18[2], 19, 20[2]
34:1, 2[3], 3[3], 4, 5[2], 6, 7[3], 8, 9[3], 10[4], 11[3], 12[2], 13[3], 14, 16[3], 17, 18[2], 19[2], 20[3], 21[2], 23[3], 24[3], 25[4], 26[4], 27, 28[4], 29[4], 30[7], 31
35:1[3], 2[3], 3[4], 4[3], 5[3], 6, 7[2], 8[2], 9[2], 10[2], 11[4], 12[3], 13, 14[3], 15, 16[4], 17, 18, 19[2], 20, 21[2], 22[3], 23[5], 24, 25[2], 26[2], 27[2], 28[2], 29[6]
36:2, 3, 4[2], 5[3], 6[8], 7, 9, 11[3], 12[2], 13[3], 14[4], 16, 17, 18, 19, 20[3], 21[3], 22[3], 23[4], 24[2], 25[2], 26[4], 27[2], 28, 31, 32[2], 33[2], 34[2], 35[3], 36[2], 37[2], 38[2], 39[4], 40
37:1, 2[3], 3, 4[2], 5[3], 6, 7[4], 8[3], 9[6], 10[6], 11, 12, 13[3], 14[4], 15[3], 16, 17[3], 18, 19, 20[4], 21[3], 22[2], 23, 24[3], 25[6], 26[2], 27[4], 28[4], 29[3], 30[3], 31[3], 32[3], 33[2], 34[3], 35[3], 36[2]
38:1[2], 2[3], 3[3], 4[3], 5[4], 6, 7[2], 8[2], 9[2], 10, 11[2], 12[4], 13, 14[5], 16[3], 17[2], 18[7], 19[4], 20, 21, 22[3], 23[2], 24[4], 25[3], 26[3], 27, 28[3], 29[2], 30[2]
39:1[2], 2[3], 3[2], 4[4], 5[4], 6[4], 7[2], 8[2], 9, 10, 11[2], 12[4], 13[2], 14[2], 15[4], 16, 17, 18[3], 19, 20[3], 21[2], 22[2], 23
40:1[2], 2[2], 3, 4[3], 5[2], 6[3], 7, 8[3], 9[2], 10[4], 11[4], 12, 13[2], 14[3], 15, 16, 17[2], 18[2], 19[2], 20[3], 21[2]
41:1[2], 2[3], 3[3], 4[3], 5[4], 6[2], 7[4], 8[5], 10[2], 11[2], 12[3], 13[2], 14[5], 15[3], 16, 17, 18[3], 19[3], 20[2], 21, 22[3], 23[2], 24[2], 25, 26, 27[3], 30[3], 31, 32[2], 33[2], 34[2], 35[3], 36, 37[2], 38, 39[2], 40, 41, 42[4], 43[3], 44[2], 45[3], 46[3], 47, 48[2], 49, 50, 51[2], 52, 53, 54[2], 55[2], 56[4], 57
42:2[3], 3, 5, 6[4], 7[5], 8, 9[2], 10, 12, 13[3], 14, 16[2], 17, 18[2], 20[2], 21[2], 22[2], 23, 24[6], 25[3], 26[2], 27, 28[4], 29[2], 30, 31, 32, 33[3], 34[2], 35[3], 36[3], 37[2], 38[2]
43:1, 2, 3, 4, 6, 7[3], 8[6], 9, 11[5], 12[2], 13, 14[2], 15[6], 16[3], 17[2], 18[5], 19[2], 20, 21[3], 22, 23[3], 24[4], 25, 26[2], 27[2], 28[3], 29[4], 30[4], 31[4], 32[3], 33[3], 34[4]
44:1[2], 2[3], 3, 4[3], 5, 6[2], 7, 9, 10[2], 11, 12[4], 13[2], 14[3], 15, 16[2], 17[2], 18[2], 20[5], 21, 22, 23, 24, 25[2], 26, 27, 28[3], 29[2], 30, 31, 33, 34
45:1[2], 2[3], 3[2], 4[3], 6, 7[2], 8[3], 9[2], 10[7], 11[3], 12[2], 13[4], 14[3], 15[2], 16[3], 17[2], 18[5], 19[3], 21[3], 22, 23[4], 24[2], 25[2], 26[3], 27[2], 28[2]
46:1[3], 2[3], 3, 4[2], 5[4], 6[4], 7[3], 8[2], 9[4], 10[6], 11[2], 12[8], 13[4], 14[3], 15[2], 16[5], 17[7], 18, 19, 20[2], 21[7], 23, 24[4], 25, 26, 27[2], 28[2], 29[5], 30, 31[5], 32[4], 33[2], 34
47:1[7], 2[2], 3[3], 5[2], 6[2], 7[3], 8, 9[4], 10[2], 11[3], 12[3], 13[2], 14[3], 15[3], 16[2], 17[6], 18[2], 19[6], 20, 21, 22, 23[2], 24[5], 25[2], 26, 27[4], 28[2], 29[5], 30[3], 31[3]
48:1[3], 2[4], 3[2], 4[4], 5[3], 6[2], 7[2], 8[2], 9[3], 10[3], 11[2], 12[2], 13[3], 14[3], 15[3], 16[4], 17[2], 18, 19[4], 20[3], 21[2], 22
49:1[2], 2[2], 3[2], 5, 6, 7[2], 9, 10, 11[2], 12, 13[2], 15[4], 20, 23[2], 24, 25[2], 26, 27, 28[2], 29[2], 31[3], 32, 33[3]
50:1[3], 2[2], 3[3], 4, 5[2], 6[2], 7[3], 8[5], 9[3], 10[4], 11, 12, 13, 14[3], 15[2], 16, 17[3], 18[3], 19, 21[3], 22[4], 23, 24[4], 25[2], 26[3]

EXODUS

1:1, 2, 3, 4[2], 5, 6[3], 7[5], 9[2], 10[3], 11[2], 12[2], 13, 14[3], 15[2], 16[2], 17, 18[3], 19[2], 20[2], 21, 22[2]
2:1[2], 2[3], 3[5], 4, 5[3], 6[4], 7, 8[3], 9[5], 10[5], 11[3], 12[4], 13[2], 14[4], 15[2], 16[3], 17[4], 18, 19[3], 20[2], 21[2], 22[2], 23[4], 24[3], 25[2]
3:1[2], 2[4], 3[2], 4[3], 5, 6[2], 7[2], 8[9], 9, 10, 11[2], 12[2], 13[3], 14[2], 15[3], 16[4], 17[7], 18[5], 19, 20[3], 21[2], 22[6]
4:1[2], 2[2], 3[4], 4[5], 5, 6[3], 7[4], 8, 9[3], 10[2], 11, 12[2], 13, 14[4], 15[5], 16[3], 17, 18[4], 19, 20[5], 21, 22, 23[2], 24[2], 25[3], 27[4], 28[2], 29[3], 30[2], 31[4]
5:1[3], 2, 3[2], 4[2], 5[2], 6[2], 7, 8[2], 9, 10[3], 13, 14[3], 15, 16[2], 17, 18, 19, 20[2], 21[3], 22[2]
6:1, 2[2], 3[2], 4, 5[2], 6[4], 7[3], 8[3], 9[2], 10, 12, 13[4], 14[2], 15[6], 16[5], 17, 18[6], 19[2], 20[6], 21[3], 22[3], 23[4], 24[3], 25[2], 26, 27, 28, 30[2]
7:1[2], 2, 3[3], 4[2], 5[2], 6[2], 7[3], 8[2], 9[2], 10[6], 11, 12, 13, 14, 15[2], 16[2], 17, 18[3], 19[6], 20[6], 21[4], 22[2], 23[2], 24, 25
8:1[2], 2, 3[8], 4[3], 5[3], 6[3], 7[2], 8[4], 9[4], 10[2], 11[4], 12[3], 13[3], 14[2], 15, 16[2], 17[4], 18[2], 19[2], 20[3], 21[5], 22, 23[2], 24[4], 25[3], 26[2], 27, 28, 29[3], 30[2], 31[3], 32
9:1, 2, 3, 4[3], 5, 6[2], 7[4], 8[3], 9[3], 10[5], 11[2], 12[2], 13[3], 14[2], 15[2], 16[2], 19[5], 20, 21[2], 22[3], 23[5], 24, 25[4], 27[6], 28[3], 29[2], 30, 31[3], 32, 33[5], 34[5], 35
10:1[2], 2[3], 3[3], 5[3], 6[5], 7, 8[3], 9[4], 10[2], 11[2], 12[2], 13[4], 14[2], 15[3], 16[3], 17, 18[2], 19[2], 21, 22[2], 24[3], 25[2], 26, 27, 28, 29
11:1[2], 2[3], 3[2], 4, 5[2], 6, 7, 8[5], 9, 10[3]
12:1[2], 4[2], 6[2], 7[3], 8[3], 9, 10[2], 11[3], 12[3], 13[3], 14[2], 16[2], 17, 18, 21[3], 22[5], 23[3], 24[2], 25, 26, 27[3], 28[3], 29[2], 30[4], 31[6], 32[3], 33, 34, 35[4], 36[2], 37, 38[3], 39[2], 40, 41[2], 43[2], 45, 48[5], 49, 50, 51
13:1, 2, 3, 5[6], 6, 7, 8, 9[2], 11[3], 12, 13[3], 14, 15[2], 16[2], 17[2], 18, 19[2], 20[2], 21[3]
14:1, 2[2], 4[4], 5[4], 6[2], 7[3], 8[3], 9[4], 10[4], 11, 13[2], 14, 15, 16[3], 17[5], 18[2], 19[4], 20[4], 21[4], 22[3], 23[3], 24[3], 25, 26[2], 27[4], 28[4], 29[2], 30, 31[4]
15:1[3], 2[4], 4, 7, 8[2], 14, 16, 17, 18, 19[2], 20[3], 21[2], 22[3], 23, 24, 25[4], 26[4], 27[4]
16:1[3], 2[2], 3[2], 4[2], 5[2], 6[2], 7[2], 8[3], 9, 10[2], 11, 12[2], 13[3], 14, 15[2], 17[2], 18[2], 19, 20[3], 21[2], 22[3], 23[3], 24[2], 25, 27[2], 28[2], 31[3], 32, 33[3], 35
17:1[3], 2[2], 3[5], 4, 5[4], 6[3], 7[3], 8, 9[2], 10[3], 11[2], 12[7], 13[2], 14[2], 15[2]
18:1[2], 3, 4[2], 5[2], 6[3], 7[5], 8[4], 9, 10[2], 12[4], 13[2], 14[2], 15, 16[4], 17, 18, 19, 20[4], 21[3], 22[3], 23[2], 24, 25[3], 26, 27[2]
19:2[3], 3[3], 4[2], 5, 6[2], 7[3], 8[3], 9[3], 10[4], 11, 12, 14[3], 15, 16[4], 17[2], 18[3], 19[4], 20[3], 21[2], 22, 23[2], 24[4], 25
20:1, 5, 6[2], 9, 11[4], 12, 18[6], 19[2], 20[2], 21[2], 22, 24[4], 25
21:2, 4[3], 5[2], 6[2], 7, 9, 10, 11, 13, 15, 16[2], 17, 18[3], 19[2], 20[2], 22[3], 23, 26, 27, 28, 29[3], 32, 33[3], 34[2], 35[3], 36[2]
22:1[2], 2, 5[3], 6, 7, 9, 10, 11[2], 12, 13, 14[2], 16[2], 23, 24[4], 27, 29, 30, 31
23:5, 7[2], 8[2], 10[2], 11[3], 12[4], 13[2], 15, 16[2], 20, 21, 22[2], 23[6], 24, 25[4], 27[2], 28[2], 29, 30[2], 31[3]
24:1[5], 2, 3[5], 4[4], 5[2], 6[3], 7[4], 8[3], 9[3], 10[3], 11[3], 12[5], 13[3], 14[3], 15[2], 16[3], 17, 18[4]
25:1, 3[3], 4[5], 5[3], 6, 7[2], 8, 9, 10[6], 11[3], 12[4], 13[2], 14, 16, 17[4], 18, 19[2], 20[2], 21[2], 22[2], 23[3], 24[2], 25[2], 26[2], 28[2], 29[4], 30, 31[3], 32[2], 33[3], 34[2], 35[3], 36, 37[2], 38[2], 40
26:1[3], 2[3], 3, 4[2], 5, 6[3], 7, 8[2], 9[3], 10[2], 11[3], 12, 13[3], 14[2], 15, 16[2], 18, 19[2], 20, 21[2], 22, 23, 24[2], 25[3], 26, 27[2], 28, 29[3], 30, 31[4], 32, 33[3], 34, 35[3], 36[4], 37[4]
27:1[3], 2[2], 3[5], 4[2], 5, 6[2], 7[2], 9, 10[3], 11[4], 12[2], 13, 14, 15[2], 16[6], 17, 18[3], 19[2], 20, 21
28:1[4], 2[2], 3, 4[7], 5[5], 6[3], 7, 8[4], 9[2], 10, 12[2], 13, 14[2], 15[4], 16, 17[2], 18[2], 19[2], 20[3], 21, 22, 23[2], 24, 25[2], 26[2], 27[2], 28[2], 29, 30[4], 31, 32, 33[4], 34[2], 35[3], 36[2], 37, 38[2], 39[3], 40[4], 41[5], 42, 43[4]
29:1[2], 2[3], 3[3], 4[3], 5[6], 6[2], 7[2], 8[2], 9[6], 10[3], 11, 12[3], 13[5], 14[2], 15[2], 16[3], 17[5], 18, 19[3], 20[6], 21[10], 22[6], 23[3], 24[3], 25[2], 26[3], 27[4], 28[3], 29[2], 30, 31[2], 32[3], 33[2], 34, 35[2], 36[3], 37[2], 39, 40[2], 41[3], 43[2], 44[3], 45[2], 46
30:1, 2[2], 3[4], 4[2], 5[2], 6, 7, 8, 10, 11, 14, 15, 16[2], 17, 18[4], 19[2], 21[3], 23[4], 24[2], 25, 26[2], 27[5], 28[3], 29, 30[3], 31, 32, 34[3], 35[2], 36[2], 37
31:1, 3[4], 4[2], 5[2], 6[2], 7[3], 8[4], 9[3], 10[3], 11[2], 12, 13, 17[4], 18
32:1[2], 2[3], 3[2], 4[3], 5[3], 6[6], 7, 8[3], 9[2], 10[2], 11[3], 12[3], 13[4], 14, 15[4], 16[2], 17, 18, 19[5], 20[5], 21, 22, 24[2], 25, 26[2], 27[6], 28[2], 29, 30[2], 31[3], 32, 33, 35
33:1[4], 2[5], 3, 4[2], 5, 6, 7[4], 8[3], 9[3], 10[3], 11[2], 12[3], 13, 14[2], 15, 16[2], 17[2], 18, 19[4], 20[2], 21[2], 22[2], 23[2]
34:1[2], 2[3], 3, 4[4], 5[3], 6[5], 7[5], 8[3], 9[4], 10[2], 11[5], 13, 15[4], 16[3], 19, 20[2], 21, 22[2], 24, 27[2], 28[3], 29, 30[3], 31[4], 32[2], 33, 34[2], 35[2]
35:1[2], 4, 5[2], 6[5], 7[3], 8[3], 9[3], 10[2], 11[3], 12[2], 13[3], 14[2], 15[5], 16[2], 17[2], 18[2], 19, 20, 21[5], 22[7], 23[7], 24[2], 25[5], 26, 27[3], 28[4], 29, 30, 31[3], 32[3], 33[2], 34[2], 35[6]
36:1[3], 2[3], 3[2], 4, 5, 6[2], 7, 8[4], 9[2], 10[2], 11, 12, 13[2], 14, 15, 16[2], 17[2], 18, 19[2], 20, 21[2], 23, 24[2], 25, 26[2], 27, 28, 29[2], 30[2], 31, 32[2], 33, 34[3], 35[4], 36[3], 37[4], 38[3]
37:1[6], 2[3], 3[2], 4[2], 5, 6[4], 7, 8, 9[2], 10[4], 11[2], 12, 13[2], 15[2], 16[4], 17[3], 18[2], 19[3], 20[2], 21[3], 22, 23[3], 24, 25[3], 26[3], 27, 28[2], 29[2]
38:1[3], 2[2], 3[5], 4, 5, 6[2], 7, 8[2], 9, 10[2], 11[3], 12[3], 13, 14, 15[3], 17[4], 18[6], 19[4], 20[2], 22, 23[6], 24[3], 25[4], 26[4], 27[2], 28[4], 29[3], 30[4], 31[4]
39:1[4], 2[4], 3[5], 5[4], 6, 7, 8[4], 9, 10[2], 11[2], 12[2], 13[2], 14, 15, 16[3], 17, 18[4], 19[4], 20[4], 21[2], 22, 23, 24[4], 25[2], 26[2], 27[2], 28[3], 29[4], 30[2], 31, 32, 33[4], 34[3], 35[2], 36[2], 37[2], 38[4], 39[3], 40[4], 41[2], 43[3]
40:1, 3[2], 4[4], 5[2], 6, 7[3], 8[2], 9[6], 10[4], 11[3], 12[3], 13[3], 14[2], 15, 17, 18[5], 19[2], 20[4], 21[3], 22, 23, 24, 25, 26, 27, 28, 29[3], 30[3], 31[4], 32, 33[3], 34, 35[2], 36, 38

LEVITICUS

1:1[2], 2[2], 4[2], 5[3], 6[2], 7[2], 8[2], 9[2], 10, 11[2], 12[3], 13[3], 14, 15[4], 16[2], 17[2]
2:1[3], 2[4], 3[2], 4, 5, 6, 7, 8[2], 9[2], 10[2], 13, 14, 15[2], 16[2]
3:1, 2[3], 3[2], 4[3], 5, 6, 8[3], 9[4], 10[3], 11, 12, 13[3], 14[2], 15[3], 16
4:1, 2, 4[3], 5[2], 6[2], 7[2], 8[2], 9[3], 10, 11[5], 12, 13[4], 14, 15[2], 16, 17[2], 18[2], 19[2], 20[3], 21[2], 22[2], 24[2], 25[3], 26[3], 27[2], 29[2], 30[3], 31[4], 32, 33[2], 34[3], 35[4]
5:1[3], 2[2], 3, 4, 5, 6[2], 7[2], 8[2], 9[2], 10[3], 12[2], 13[3], 14, 15, 16[5], 17[3], 18[4]
6:1, 2[2], 3[2], 4, 5[2], 6, 7[2], 8, 9[2], 10[4], 11[3], 12[4], 14, 15[4], 16[2], 17, 19, 20[2], 21[2], 22, 24, 25, 27, 28[2], 30
7:2, 3[2], 4[3], 5, 8, 9[3], 10[2], 11, 12[2], 14[2], 15, 16, 18[2], 19[2], 21, 22, 24[2], 28, 31[2], 32, 33, 34[3], 35, 37[4]
8:1, 2[6], 3, 4[2], 5, 6[3], 7[6], 8[2], 9, 10[4], 11[4], 12[2], 13[4], 14[3], 15[6], 16[5], 17[2], 18[3], 19[2], 20[4], 21[4], 22[3], 23[5], 24[5], 25[7], 26[5], 27[3], 28[2], 29[2], 30[10], 31[4], 32[2], 33, 35[2], 36
9:1[3], 2[3], 3[3], 4[2], 5[3], 6[2], 7[7], 8, 9[4], 10[2], 11[2], 12[2], 13[3], 14[3], 15[4], 16[2], 17[3], 18[2], 19[5], 20[2], 21[2], 22[5], 23[5], 24[4]
10:1[5], 2[3], 3[2], 4[4], 5, 6[4], 7[2], 8, 10[4], 11, 12[4], 13[2], 14[5], 15[3], 16[4], 17, 19[4], 20
11:1[2], 3[2], 5, 6, 7[2], 8, 9[2], 10[4], 13[3], 14[2], 16[4], 17[3], 18[3], 19[3], 22[3], 24, 25[2], 26, 27, 28[2], 29[2], 30[5], 32[2],

LEVITICUS

33[2], 34, 35[2], 37, 38, 39, 40[3], 41, 42, 44, 46[3], 47[3]
12:1, 2, 3, 4[2], 5[2], 6[2], 7[2], 8[4]
13:1[2], 2, 3[5], 4[2], 5[3], 6[5], 8, 10[4], 11[2], 12[2], 13, 15[2], 16, 17[2], 18, 19[3], 20[2], 21[2], 22, 23[2], 24, 25[2], 26[2], 27[2], 28[3], 30[2], 31[3], 32[4], 33, 34[4], 36, 37[2], 39, 40, 41, 42, 43, 45[4], 49[2], 50[2], 51, 53[2], 54, 55[3], 56[2], 57, 58[2]
14:1, 3[3], 4[4], 5, 6[5], 7[3], 8[5], 9[4], 10[4], 11[2], 12[4], 13[2], 14[4], 15[2], 16[2], 17[3], 18[2], 19[3], 20[4], 21[4], 22[3], 23, 24[3], 25[5], 26, 27, 28[3], 29, 30, 31[2], 32[2], 34, 35[2], 36, 37[2], 38, 39[3], 40, 41[2], 42[4], 43[4], 44[2], 45[4], 47[2], 48[3], 49[4], 50, 51[7], 52[6], 53[2], 54, 55[2], 56[3], 57
15:1[2], 2, 3, 4, 5[3], 6[3], 7[3], 8[3], 9, 10[4], 11[4], 12[2], 13[4], 14[3], 15[3], 16[2], 17[3], 18, 19[3], 20, 21[3], 22[3], 23, 24[3], 25, 26, 27[4], 28, 29[2], 30[3], 32[2], 33[4]
16:1[2], 2, 3, 4[4], 5[2], 6[3], 7[2], 8[2], 9[2], 10, 11[4], 12[3], 13, 14[3], 15[4], 16[3], 17[4], 18[5], 19[3], 20[3], 21[4], 22[2], 23[3], 24[7], 25, 26[3], 27[5], 28[3], 29[2], 31, 32[3], 33[5], 34[2]
17:1, 2[3], 4[2], 5, 6[2], 7, 8, 9, 10[2], 11, 13[3], 15[3]
18:1, 2, 3, 4, 5, 17, 21, 25[2], 26[2], 27, 30
19:1, 2, 3[2], 5, 6[2], 7, 8, 9, 10[2], 12, 16, 17, 19, 20[2], 21, 22[2], 23[2], 25, 29, 30, 32[2], 33, 34, 36, 37[2]
20:1, 3[3], 4[2], 5[3], 6[3], 7, 8[2], 10[2], 11, 12, 14[3], 15[2], 16[3], 17[4], 18[4], 19, 20, 21, 22[2], 23[2], 24[2], 25[4], 26[2]
21:1[2], 2[4], 3, 6[2], 9, 10[2], 13, 16, 22, 24[3]
22:1, 2[2], 4, 6, 7[2], 9, 11, 13[2], 14[2], 15, 17, 18[4], 21, 25, 26, 27[2], 28[2], 29, 31
23:1, 2, 6, 9, 10[2], 11, 12, 13[2], 14, 15, 16, 18[4], 19, 20, 21, 22[2], 23, 26, 27[2], 28, 30, 32, 33, 36[2], 37[2], 38[3], 39, 40[4], 41, 44
24:1, 5[2], 6, 7, 9[3], 10[3], 11[4], 12, 13, 14[2], 15, 16[2], 17, 18, 19, 21[2], 23[3]
25:1, 2, 3[2], 6[5], 7[2], 8[3], 10[4], 14, 15, 16, 18[3], 19[3], 20, 21, 22[2], 23, 24, 25[2], 26[2], 27, 28[2], 29, 30, 31, 32, 33[2], 35[2], 38, 39[2], 40[2], 41[4], 44[2], 45[2], 46, 47[3], 50[2], 52[2], 53[2], 54[2]
26:2, 3[2], 4[2], 5[4], 6[4], 7[2], 8[3], 9[3], 10[2], 11[2], 12[3], 13[2], 14, 15, 16[3], 17[3], 18, 19[3], 20, 21[2], 22[3], 23, 24, 25[3], 26[4], 27, 28, 29[2], 30[4], 31[3], 32[2], 33[4], 34[2], 36[4], 37[2], 38[2], 39[2], 40[2], 41[3], 42[3], 43[3], 44[2], 46[3]
27:1, 2, 3, 4, 5[2], 6[2], 7[3], 8, 9, 10[2], 11, 12, 14, 15[2], 16, 18, 19[2], 20, 22, 23, 25, 27[2], 28[2], 30, 31, 32, 33[2]

NUMBERS

1:1, 3[2], 4, 5, 17[2], 18[3], 20[2], 21[2], 22, 23[2], 24, 25[2], 26, 27[2], 28, 29[2], 30, 31[2], 32, 33, 34, 35[2], 36, 37[2], 38, 39[2], 40, 41[2], 42, 43[2], 44[2], 45, 46[3], 50[5], 51[3], 52[2], 53, 54
2:1[2], 3[2], 4[4], 5[2], 6[4], 7, 8[4], 9[3], 10, 11[4], 12[2], 13[4], 14, 15[5], 16[5], 18, 19[3], 20[2], 21[4], 22, 23[4], 24[3], 25, 26[4], 27[2], 28[4], 29, 30[4], 31[3], 32[3], 34[2]
3:1, 2[3], 4[5], 5, 6, 7[2], 8[2], 9[2], 10[4], 11, 12, 13, 14, 15, 16, 17[3], 18[2], 19[3], 20[2], 21, 22[2], 24, 25[3], 26[4], 27[4], 28[2], 30, 31[7], 32[2], 33, 34[3], 35, 36[7], 37[4], 38[3], 39[3], 40[3], 41[2], 42, 43[5], 44, 45[2], 46[3], 48[2], 49[2], 50[2], 51[2]
4:1[2], 3, 5[4], 6[3], 7[6], 8[3], 9[6], 10[3], 11[3], 12[4], 13[2], 14[5], 15[3], 16[7], 17[2], 19[4], 21, 23, 24, 25[4], 26[6], 27[3], 28, 30, 31[4], 32[6], 34[4], 35, 36[2], 37, 38[2], 39, 40[2], 41, 42, 43, 44, 45, 46[3], 47[2], 48[2], 49
5:1, 2[2], 3, 4[2], 5, 6, 7[3], 9, 10, 11, 12[2], 13[5], 14[5], 15, 16[2], 17[3], 18[4], 19[3], 20[2], 21[3], 22[3], 23[2], 24[3], 25[2], 26[3], 27[6], 28[2], 29, 30[3], 31
6:1, 2, 3[2], 5, 9[2], 10, 11[4], 12[2], 13, 14[3], 15[4], 16[3], 17[2], 18[3], 19[4], 20[3], 21, 22, 23, 24, 25, 26, 27[2]
7:1[7], 2, 3[4], 4, 5, 6[3], 7, 8[2], 10, 11, 12, 13[2], 17, 19, 23, 25, 29, 31, 35, 37, 41, 43, 47, 49, 53, 55, 59, 61, 65, 67, 71, 73, 77, 79, 83, 85[2], 86, 87, 88[2], 89[2]
8:1, 2, 3, 4, 5, 6, 7[4], 8, 9[2], 10[2], 11, 12[3], 13[3], 14, 15[3], 17, 18, 19[3], 20[3], 21[4], 22[2], 23, 24[2], 25[2], 26
9:1, 3, 4, 5, 6[3], 7, 8[2], 9, 11[2], 13[2], 14[4], 15[2], 16, 17[2], 18, 19[2], 20[2], 21[2], 22, 23
10:1, 2, 3, 4, 8[2], 9[3], 10[3], 11, 12[2], 13, 14, 15, 16, 17[3], 18[2], 19, 20, 21[2], 22[2], 23, 24, 25[2], 26, 27, 29[2], 30[2], 31[2], 32, 33[2], 34, 35[3], 36
11:1[5], 2[2], 3, 4[3], 5[4], 7[2], 8[6], 9, 10, 11[2], 15[2], 16[3], 17[5], 18[3], 20[2], 21[2], 22, 23, 24[4], 25[6], 26[4], 27[4], 28[2], 29[2], 30[2], 31[5], 32[5], 33[2], 34, 35[2]
12:1[2], 2[2], 4[4], 5[5], 6[2], 8[2], 9[2], 10[4], 11[2], 13, 14[2], 15[2], 16[2]
13:1, 3, 4, 16, 17[3], 18[2], 19[2], 20[3], 21, 22[3], 23[5], 25, 26[7], 27[5], 28[3], 29[5], 30[3], 32[2], 33[3]
14:1[3], 2[3], 3[2], 4[2], 5, 6[2], 7, 8[2], 9, 10, 11[2], 12[3], 13, 14[4], 17, 18[4], 19, 20, 22[4], 24[2], 25[2], 26[2], 29[2], 30, 31, 33[2], 34, 35, 36[2], 38, 39[2], 40[3], 41, 43[2], 44, 45[3]
15:1, 2, 3, 5, 7, 8, 10, 14[2], 15, 16[2], 17, 18, 22[2], 23, 24[2], 25[4], 26[2], 27, 28[2], 29, 30, 31, 32, 33[3], 34, 35, 36[3], 37, 38[2], 39[5], 40[2]
16:1[3], 2[2], 3[4], 4, 5[4], 6, 7[3], 8, 9, 10[3], 11[2], 12[2], 13, 14[2], 15[2], 16[4], 17[5], 18[5], 19[2], 20[2], 22[3], 23, 24, 25[4], 26[2], 27[7], 28, 30[3], 31, 32[5], 33[3], 34, 35[3], 36, 37, 38, 39[2], 40, 41, 42[4], 43[2], 44, 45, 46[5], 47[5], 48[3], 49, 50[2]
17:1, 2, 3, 4, 5[2], 6[3], 7, 8[5], 9[3], 10[2], 11, 12
18:1[5], 2[3], 3[3], 4[3], 5[2], 6, 7[4], 8[2], 9[3], 11[3], 12[2], 13, 15, 16, 17, 18[2], 19[3], 20[2], 21, 22, 23, 25, 26, 27[2], 28, 30, 31[2], 32
19:1[2], 2, 3[2], 4[2], 5[3], 6[4], 7[3], 8[3], 9[3], 10[4], 12, 13[2], 14, 15, 16, 17[2], 18[6], 19[6], 20, 21[2], 22[2]
20:1[3], 2[3], 3[2], 4[2], 5, 6[4], 7, 8[6], 9, 10[3], 11[5], 12[2], 13, 14, 15[3], 16[4], 18, 19[3], 20[3], 22[2], 23[2], 25[2], 26[4], 27[2], 28[5], 29
21:1[2], 2[2], 3[5], 4[2], 5[3], 6[3], 7[3], 8[3], 9[3], 10[2], 11[2], 12, 13[2], 14, 15[2], 16[2], 18, 19[2], 20, 21, 23[4], 24[2], 25[3], 26, 27, 28, 29, 30, 32[3], 33[4], 34[4], 35[3]
22:1[2], 2, 3[2], 4[2], 5, 6[2], 7[4], 8[3], 9[2], 10, 11, 12, 13[2], 14[3], 15[2], 16[2], 17, 18[3], 20[3], 21[3], 22[3], 23[5], 24, 25[3], 26[2], 27[3], 28[2], 29, 30[2], 31[4], 32, 33[3], 34, 35, 36, 37, 38, 39[2], 40[4], 41[2]
23:1[3], 2[4], 3[4], 4[4], 5[3], 6[3], 7[3], 9[2], 10[2], 11[2], 12[2], 13[3], 14[4], 15, 16[4], 17[3], 18[3], 19[2], 20[2], 21, 23, 24[2], 25, 26, 27, 28, 29[3], 30[3]
24:1, 2[3], 3[3], 5, 6, 7[3], 8[2], 9[2], 10[4], 12, 13, 14[2], 15[3], 16, 17[3], 18[2], 19, 20[2], 21[4], 23[2], 24[4], 25[4]
25:1[2], 2[3], 3[2], 4[2], 5, 6[3], 7[2], 8[3], 9[2], 10, 13[3], 15[2], 16, 17, 18
26:1[2], 2, 3[2], 4[2], 7[4], 8, 9[5], 10[4], 14[2], 18, 19[3], 20, 21, 22[2], 25[2], 27, 28, 29, 31[2], 32[2], 33[4], 34[3], 36, 37[2], 40[3], 41[3], 43[2], 46, 47[2], 50[3], 51[2], 52, 54, 56, 57, 58, 59[4], 60[3], 61[2], 62[3], 63, 64, 65[2]
27:1[4], 2[4], 3[2], 5, 6, 7, 8[2], 9, 10, 11[3], 12[2], 13, 15, 17[3], 18[2], 19[3], 20, 21[3], 22[4], 23[2]
28:1, 2[2], 3, 4, 5, 7, 8[2], 9[3], 10, 11[2], 12[2], 13, 14[3], 15[2], 16, 17, 19[2], 20[2], 22, 24, 25, 28, 30, 31[2]
29:1, 2[2], 3[2], 4, 5, 6[4], 7[2], 8, 9[2], 11[3], 12[2], 13[2], 14, 15, 16[2], 17, 18[3], 19[3], 20, 21[3], 22[3], 23[2], 24[2], 25[2], 26[2], 27[3], 28[3], 29[2], 30[3], 31[2], 32[2], 33[3], 34[2], 37[2], 38[3], 39[4], 40
30:1, 3, 4[4], 5, 6, 7[3], 8[2], 9, 10, 11[4], 12, 13, 16[2]
31:1, 3[3], 6[3], 7[2], 8[5], 9[5], 10[2], 11[3], 12[5], 13[3], 14[2], 15, 16, 17, 19[4], 20[4], 21, 22[2], 23[2], 24[3], 25, 26[3], 27[2], 28[4], 29, 30[3], 31[2], 32[3], 33[2], 34[2], 35[2], 36[4], 37[3], 38[3], 39[3], 40[2], 41, 42, 43[3], 44[2], 45[2], 46, 47[2], 48[2], 49[2], 50[2], 51[2], 52[3], 54[4]
32:1[3], 2[4], 3[8], 4, 5, 6[3], 7, 9, 10[2], 11[2], 12, 13[2], 14, 15, 16[3], 17, 20, 21, 22[4], 23, 24[2], 25[2], 26, 28[2], 29[3], 31[2], 33[4], 34[3], 35[3], 36[3], 37[3], 38[4], 39[3], 40[2], 41[3], 42[4]
33:1, 2[2], 3, 5[2], 6[2], 7[3], 8[4], 9[6], 10[2], 11[2], 12[2], 13[2], 14[2], 15[2], 16[2], 17[2], 18[2], 19[2], 20[2], 21[2], 22[2], 23[2], 24[2], 25[2], 26[2], 27[2], 28[2], 29[2], 30[2], 31[2], 32[2], 33[2], 34[2], 35[2], 36[2], 37[2], 38[2], 39[3], 40, 41[2], 42[2], 43[2], 44[2], 45[2], 46[2], 47[2], 48[2], 49, 50, 51, 52[3], 53[2], 54[3], 55[2]
34:1, 2, 3, 4[5], 5[2], 6, 7, 8, 9[2], 10, 11[3], 12[2], 13[2], 14[2], 15, 16, 17, 18, 19, 20, 22, 24, 25, 26, 27, 28
35:1, 2, 3[4], 4[2], 5[5], 6[3], 7, 8, 9, 10, 12, 13, 14, 15[2], 16, 17[2], 18, 23[2], 24, 25[3], 27[2], 32, 33
36:1[3], 2[2], 3[2], 4, 5, 8, 11[3], 12[2], 13

DEUTERONOMY

1:1[4], 3, 4, 7[7], 8[3], 9, 10, 11, 12[2], 13[3], 14[2], 15[6], 16[4], 17[2], 18, 19[3], 20, 21, 22[5], 23[2], 24[4], 25[4], 27[2], 28[3], 31, 33, 34[3], 36[2], 39[4], 40, 41[3], 42, 43[2], 44[3], 45[2]
2:1[2], 2, 4[2], 6, 8[3], 9, 10[2], 12, 13[2], 14[2], 16, 19, 20, 21[4], 22[2], 23[2], 24[3], 25[3], 26, 28, 29, 30, 31[2], 32, 33[4], 34[4], 35, 36
3:1[3], 2[4], 3[2], 4, 5, 6[2], 7, 8, 9, 10[3], 11, 12[4], 13[2], 14[2], 15, 16[3], 17[2], 18, 19[2], 20[2], 21, 23, 24[2], 25[2], 26[2], 27[5], 28[3]
4:1[3], 5, 6[4], 8[2], 9[3], 10[2], 11[4], 12, 13[2], 14[2], 16, 19[5], 20, 21[2], 22, 23, 25[5], 26, 27[2], 28[2], 29, 30[2], 32, 33, 34[6], 36[2], 37[2], 38, 39[2], 40[3], 42[2], 43[2], 44, 45[2], 46, 47[2], 49
5:1[5], 5[2], 9, 10[2], 13, 14, 15[3], 16[2], 22[4], 23[2], 24[4], 26, 27[4], 28[2], 29[2], 31[3], 33[2]
6:1, 2[4], 3[3], 5[3], 6, 7[5], 8[2], 9[2], 10[3], 11[4], 13[2], 15, 17[2], 18[4], 20[3], 21, 22[4], 23, 24, 25
7:1[8], 2[2], 4, 5[3], 8[2], 9[2], 10, 11[2], 12[3], 13[7], 15[2], 16, 18, 19[4], 20, 21, 22[2], 23, 24[2], 26
8:1[3], 2[2], 3[3], 6, 7[2], 8[5], 9, 10, 11[2], 12[3], 13[5], 14, 15[3], 16, 17[2], 19[4]
9:1[2], 2[2], 3[2], 5[2], 7, 9, 10[2], 11[2], 12, 13, 14[3], 15[3], 16[3], 17[3], 18[2], 19, 20[2], 21[5], 22[3], 23[2], 25, 26[2], 27, 28, 29[2]
10:1[2], 2[2], 3[3], 4[2], 5[4], 6[3], 7, 8, 10[4], 11[2], 12[4], 13, 14, 15, 16, 17[2], 18[3], 20[2], 21[2], 22[2]
11:1[4], 2[3], 3[3], 4[3], 5, 6[6], 8[2], 9[3], 10, 11[2], 13[3], 14[3], 15[2], 16[3], 17[4], 18[2], 19[3], 20[2], 21, 22, 23[2], 24, 25, 26, 28, 29[2], 31[2], 32[2]
12:1, 2[2], 3[5], 5, 6[8], 7[3], 9, 10[2], 11[3], 12[6], 14, 15[3], 18[6], 20, 21[2], 22[2], 23, 25, 26[2], 27[4], 28[3], 29[2], 30, 31
13:1, 2[2], 3, 4[5], 5[2], 6, 9, 10, 11[3], 13[2], 14[4], 15[2], 16[4], 17[4]
14:2, 4, 5[6], 6[3], 7[2], 8, 9, 10[2], 12[2], 13[3], 14, 15[4], 16[2], 17[3], 18[4], 19, 23[4], 24, 25[2], 26[4], 27, 28, 29[6]
15:2, 6[2], 8, 9[4], 10[2], 11, 12[2], 13, 14[2], 15[2], 16[2], 17[3], 18, 19, 20, 21, 22[2]
16:1, 2, 4, 7[4], 8, 10, 11[9], 12[3], 13, 14[8], 15, 16[3], 18[2], 19, 20
17:3[3], 4[5], 5, 7, 8[5], 9[4], 10[2], 11, 12[3], 13[3], 14[3], 17, 18, 19[3], 20[2]
18:1[2], 3[4], 4[2], 5, 6[2], 12, 14, 17, 18[2], 19, 21
19:1[3], 3, 4, 5[4], 6[2], 8[2], 9, 10, 11[4], 12[2], 17, 18[3], 20[3], 21
20:1[3], 2[2], 3[2], 5[4], 6[4], 7[4], 8[4], 9, 11[3], 12, 13, 14[4], 17[3], 19, 20[2]
21:1, 2[2], 3[2], 4[2], 5[4], 6, 7[2], 8[2], 10[2], 11[2], 12[2], 13[7], 14, 15[4], 18[2], 19[3], 20[3], 21[3], 22[3]
22:1, 2[3], 3[3], 4, 6, 7[2], 9, 10, 11, 13[2], 14[4], 15[2], 16[2], 17[3], 18[2], 19[3], 20, 21, 22, 23[2], 24[2], 25[2], 26, 27[2], 28[3], 29
23:4[2], 11, 13[4], 14[2], 21, 23
24:1[4], 2[2], 3[4], 4, 5, 7[2], 8, 11, 12, 13[2], 14, 15[2], 18, 19[2], 20, 21, 22
25:1[2], 2[2], 3[2], 5[4], 6, 7[2], 8[3], 9[4], 10, 11[3], 13, 14, 15[2], 16, 18[3]
26:1[3], 2[2], 3[2], 4[2], 5[6], 6[3], 7[4], 8[5], 9[3], 10[3], 11[4], 12[3], 13[3], 14, 15[3], 16[3], 17[5], 18[2], 19[4]
27:1, 2[2], 3[2], 4, 5, 6, 7[3], 8, 9[3], 10[2], 11, 12[5], 13[4], 14[2], 15[3], 16, 17, 18, 19[2], 20, 21, 22, 23, 24, 25, 26
28:1[2], 2[2], 3, 4[3], 5, 6, 7, 8[2], 9, 10[2], 11[3], 12[3], 13[5], 14, 15[2], 16, 17, 18[2], 19, 20[2], 22[7], 23[2], 24, 25[2], 26[3], 27[3], 28[2], 29[5], 30[3], 31[3], 32[4], 33[3], 35, 36[3], 37[2], 38, 39, 41, 42, 43, 44[2], 45[3], 46[3], 47, 48[4], 51[2], 52[3], 53[3], 54[3], 55, 56[4], 57[3], 58, 59[4], 60, 61, 62, 63[4], 64[3], 65[3], 66[4], 67[2], 68[4]
29:2[4], 3, 4[2], 5[2], 7[3], 8[4], 9, 10, 11, 12, 13[3], 14, 15, 16, 17[4], 18[2], 19, 20[3], 21, 22[2], 23[6], 26[3], 27, 28[4], 29
30:1[3], 2[4], 3[3], 4, 5[4], 6[3], 7[2], 8[3], 9[3], 10[3], 12[2], 13[2], 14, 15[3], 16[5], 17[2], 18, 19[4], 20[4]
31:1[2], 2[3], 3[3], 4[3], 5, 6, 7[4], 8, 9[3], 10, 12[6], 13[2], 14[5], 15[2], 16[5], 17[5], 18, 19, 20[7], 21[2], 22, 23[4], 24, 26, 27[2], 28[3], 29[2], 30
32:1[2], 2, 4[2], 5, 6[2], 7[2], 10, 12, 13[2], 14[4], 15[2], 18, 19[2], 20, 21, 22[3], 24[2], 25[2], 27[2], 30[2], 32, 33, 34, 35[2], 36[2], 37, 38[3], 39[3], 40, 41[2], 42[3], 43[3], 44[3], 45, 46, 47, 48, 49, 50[3]
33:1, 2[3], 3, 5[2], 6[2], 7[4], 8[3], 9[2], 10[2], 11[2], 12[3], 13[2], 14[2], 15[2], 16[4], 17[3], 18[2], 19, 20[2], 21[3], 22, 23[3], 24[2], 25[2], 26, 27[3], 28, 29[3]
34:1[2], 2[4], 3[2], 4[2], 6, 7[2], 8[2], 9[3], 10, 11[3], 12[2]

JOSHUA

1:2, 4[2], 6, 7, 8[2], 9, 11, 12[3], 13, 14[2], 15[2], 16[2], 18[2]
2:1[4], 2, 3, 4[3], 5, 6, 7[2], 8, 9[3], 10[2], 11[2], 12, 13[6], 14[3], 15, 16[3], 17, 18[4], 19[3], 20, 21[4], 22[4], 23[4], 24
3:1[5], 2, 3[3], 4, 5, 6[4], 7, 8, 9[2], 10[8], 13[2], 14[2], 15[2], 16[4], 17[2]
4:1, 3[3], 5[2], 7, 8[4], 9[2], 10[2], 11[2], 12[3], 14, 15, 18[3], 19[2], 20, 21
5:1[2], 2, 3[2], 4, 6, 7, 8, 9, 10[2], 11[2], 12, 13[5], 14[4], 15[2]
6:1, 2[3], 3[2], 4[3], 5[4], 6[3], 7[3], 8[3], 9[3], 10, 11[2], 12[2], 13[4], 14[2], 15[2], 16, 17[3], 18[3], 19[3], 20[3], 21[6], 22[2], 23[8], 24[5], 25[4], 26[3], 27
7:1, 2[5], 3[4], 4, 5[4], 6[4], 7[2], 9[4], 10, 11[4], 13, 14[3], 15[3], 16[2], 17[4], 18[2], 19[3], 20[4], 21[5], 22[3], 23[4], 24[13], 25[3], 26
8:1[5], 2[4], 3[3], 4, 5[3], 7, 8, 9[3], 10[4], 11[5], 12[3], 13[2], 14[4], 15[3], 16[3], 17[3], 18[2], 19[6], 20[4], 21[4], 22[3], 23[2], 24[3], 25[2], 27, 28[2], 29[4], 31[2], 32, 33[6], 34[2], 35[2]
9:1[5], 2, 3[2], 4[6], 5[5], 6[3], 7[2], 8[3], 9[2], 10[2], 11[3], 12, 13[4], 14[2], 15[3], 16[2], 17[5], 18[2], 21[2], 22[2], 23[3], 24[4], 25[2], 26[2], 27[3]
10:1[5], 2[2], 3[3], 4[2], 5[4], 6[3], 7[2], 8, 9, 10[5], 11[3], 12[2], 13[3], 14, 15[2], 16, 17, 18[2], 19[2], 20[2], 21, 22, 23[3], 24[4], 25[2], 26[4], 27[4], 28[5], 29[2], 30[4], 31[4], 32[3], 33[2], 34[4], 35[3], 36[3], 37[6], 38[3], 39[7], 40[4], 41[2], 42[2], 43[2]
11:1[3], 2[4], 3[7], 4[3], 5[2], 6[2], 7[2], 8[5], 9[2], 10[3], 11[2], 12[4], 14[2], 15, 16[6], 17[3], 20, 21[4], 22, 23[2]
12:1[2], 2[3], 3[3], 4[2], 5[5], 6[4], 7[2], 8[7], 24
13:1[4], 2, 3[2], 4, 5[2], 6, 7, 8, 9[2], 10, 11[5], 12[2], 13, 15, 16[3], 17[3], 18[3], 19[3], 20[3], 21[6], 23[3], 24, 25[3], 26[3], 27[5], 28, 29[2], 30[2], 31[3]
14:1[3], 2, 3, 4[2], 5, 6[2], 7, 9[2], 10[4], 11, 12[2], 13[2], 15[2]
15:2, 3[6], 4[2], 5[2], 6[3], 7[4], 8[2], 9[3], 10[4], 11[5], 12[2], 13, 14[3], 15[2], 16[2], 17[2], 18[3], 19[2], 21[3], 22[3], 23[3], 24[2], 25[3], 26[2], 27[3], 28[3], 29[2], 30[3], 31[3], 32[5], 33[3], 34[3], 35[2], 36[4], 37[2], 38[3], 39[2], 40[3], 41[3], 42[2], 43[3], 44[3], 45, 47[4], 48[3], 49[2], 50[3], 51[3], 52[2], 53[3], 54[3], 55[2], 56[3], 57, 58, 59[3], 60, 61, 62[3]
16:1, 2[2], 3[3], 4, 5, 6[3], 7[4], 8, 9, 10[2]
17:1, 2[5], 3[3], 4[3], 5[2], 6, 7[2], 9[2], 10[4], 11[13], 14[2], 15[3], 16[4], 17[3], 18[3]
18:1[3], 2, 3, 4[5], 5[2], 6, 7[3], 8[6], 9[4], 10[2], 11[3], 12[4], 13[2], 14[3], 15[3], 16[4], 17[4], 18[2], 19[2], 20, 21[2], 22[3], 23[3], 24[3], 25[2], 26[3], 27[3], 28[3]
19:1[2], 2[2], 3[3], 4[3], 5[3], 6[3], 7[3], 8, 10[2], 11[4], 12[3], 13[2], 14[2], 15[5], 17, 18[3], 19[3], 20[3], 21[4], 22[4], 23, 24, 25[4], 26[5], 27[5], 28[4], 29[4], 30[3], 33[4], 34[5], 35[3], 36[3], 37[3], 38[4], 39, 40, 41[3], 42[3], 43[3], 44[3], 45[3], 46[2], 47[6], 50[2], 51[2]
20:3[2], 4[3], 5[2], 6[4], 7[3], 8[3], 9[2]
21:1[2], 2, 3[2], 4[4], 5[3], 6[4], 7[2], 8, 9[2], 11, 12, 13, 14[2], 15[2], 16[3], 17, 18, 20, 21, 22[2], 23, 25[2], 27[2], 28, 30, 31, 32[3], 34[2], 36[2], 37, 38[2], 41, 43[3], 44[2]
22:1[2], 2[2], 4[3], 5[6], 6[2], 7, 8[6], 9[4], 10[3], 11[3], 12, 13[3], 14[2], 15[4], 18, 19, 20[2], 21[3], 22, 24, 25[2], 27[4], 28, 29, 30[5], 31[3], 32[4], 33[4], 34[2]
23:1[2], 2[7], 3, 5[3], 6, 9, 12[4], 13[3], 14[4], 16[4]
24:1[6], 2[3], 3[4], 4[4], 5[3], 6[4], 7[6], 8[4], 9[3], 11[9], 12, 13[4], 14[5], 15[2], 16[2], 17[4], 18, 19, 20[3], 21, 22[2], 23, 24[2], 25[2], 26[3], 27, 29[2], 30, 31[3], 32[2], 33[2]

JUDGES

1:2, 3[2], 4[4], 5[4], 6[4], 7[5], 8[3], 9[3], 10[4], 11[2], 12[2], 13[2], 14[3], 15[3], 16[3], 17[4], 18[2], 19[2], 20[2], 21, 22[2], 23, 24[3], 25[2], 26[3], 27[5], 28[2], 30, 33, 34, 35, 36[2]
2:1[4], 2, 3, 4[2], 5[2], 6, 7[2], 8[2], 9, 10[2], 11[2], 12[4], 13[3], 14[3], 15[2], 17[2], 18[3], 19[3], 20[3]
3:3[3], 4, 5[5], 6[3], 7[4], 8[2], 9, 10[5], 11[2], 12[2], 13[5], 15, 16, 17[2], 18, 19[2], 20[4], 21[3], 22[3], 23[2], 24, 25[4], 26[3], 27[3], 28[4], 29[3], 30, 31[2]
4:1, 2, 3[2], 4, 5[3], 6[6], 7[3], 8, 9[3], 10[4], 11, 12, 13[2], 14[2], 15[4], 16[3], 17, 18[3], 19[4], 20[3], 21[5], 22[5], 24[2]
5:1, 4, 6, 10, 12, 14, 15[2], 17[2], 18, 19, 25, 26[3], 28, 31
6:1[2], 2[4], 3[3], 4[3], 5[4], 6[2], 7, 8, 9[4], 10, 11[3], 12[2], 13[3], 14[3], 15[2], 16[2], 17, 18[3], 19[6], 20[5], 21[5], 22, 23, 24, 25[3], 26[3], 27[3], 28[3], 29[3], 30, 31, 33[4], 34[2], 35[5], 36, 37[2], 38[3], 39[3], 40[2]
7:1[2], 2, 3[5], 4[4], 5, 6, 7[3], 8[4], 9, 11[2], 12[4], 13[6], 14[3], 15[4], 16[3], 17[3], 18[3], 19[4], 20[6], 21[4], 22[4], 23[4], 24[5], 25[7]
8:1[2], 2, 3[2], 4[3], 5[3], 6[2], 7[3], 8[3], 9, 10[3], 11[3], 12[5], 13, 14[5], 15[4], 16[4], 17[2], 18[2], 19, 20[2], 21[6], 22[2], 23, 24, 25[3], 26[5], 27[4], 28, 29[2], 30[2], 31, 32[2], 33[3], 34
9:1[3], 2[2], 3[2], 4[3], 5[3], 6[4], 7[5], 8, 9[2], 10[2], 11[2], 12, 13[3], 14, 15[4], 16[4], 17[2], 18[4], 19[3], 20[5], 21[4], 23[2], 24[3], 25[3], 26[3], 27[8], 28[3], 29[3], 30, 31[3], 32[2], 33[4], 34[3], 35[4], 36[2], 37[3], 38, 39[2], 40[4], 41[3], 42[2], 43[7], 44[5], 45[5], 46, 47, 48[8], 49[5], 50[2], 51[5], 52[3], 53[2], 54[4], 55, 57[2]
10:1[2], 2[4], 3[3], 4[2], 5[2], 6[10], 7[3], 8[2], 9[2], 10[2], 11[3], 12[4], 13, 14, 15, 16[3], 17[3], 18[2]
11:1[2], 2[4], 3[3], 4, 5, 6[2], 7[3], 8[3], 9[2], 10, 11[3], 12, 13[2], 14, 15, 16[2], 17[2], 18[4], 19[2], 20[2], 21[3], 22[2], 23, 25, 26[4], 27, 29[4], 30[2], 31, 32, 33[2], 34[4], 35[4], 36, 37[4], 38[4], 39[3]
12:1[4], 2[3], 3[3], 4[3], 5[2], 6[4], 7[2], 8, 9[4], 10, 11[2], 12[2], 13, 14[4], 15[2]
13:1[2], 2[3], 3[4], 4[2], 5[3], 6[2], 7[2], 8[2], 9[2], 10[4], 11[5], 12[2], 13, 15, 16[2], 17, 18, 19[4], 20[3], 21, 22, 23, 24[4], 25[2]
14:1[2], 2[4], 3[2], 4, 5[4], 6[3], 7[3], 8[4], 9[6], 10, 11, 12[3], 13[2], 14[3], 15[2], 16[6], 17[3], 18[3], 19[7]
15:1, 2, 3, 4[5], 5[4], 6[5], 7[2], 8[4], 9[2], 10[2], 11[2], 12[2], 13[4], 14[4], 15[4], 16, 17[2], 18[5], 19[3], 20
16:1[2], 2[4], 3[8], 4, 5[5], 6[2], 7[2], 8, 9[2], 10[2], 11[2], 12[4], 13[3], 14[5], 15[2], 16[2], 17[3], 18[3], 19[5], 20[5], 21[4], 23, 24[2], 25[4], 26, 27[4], 28[3], 29[3], 30[4], 31[6]
17:1, 2[3], 3[2], 4[4], 5[4], 7[2], 8[2], 9[3], 10[6], 11[2], 12[3]
18:1, 2[4], 3[4], 4[4], 5, 6, 7[6], 8[3], 9[4], 10, 11[2], 12[2], 13[2], 14[4], 15[3], 16, 17[7], 18[4], 19[5], 20[5], 21[4], 22[2], 23[3], 24[5], 25[2], 26[3], 27[6], 28[5], 29, 30[3], 31
19:1, 2[3], 3[6], 4[4], 5[3], 6[5], 7, 8[4], 9[4], 10[3], 11[4], 12, 13[2], 14[3], 15[3], 16[2], 17[3], 18[3], 19[5], 20, 21[4], 22[2], 23[2], 24[3], 25[4], 26, 27[5], 28[4], 29[4], 30[2]
20:1, 2, 4[3], 5[4], 6[4], 7, 8, 10[3], 12, 13, 15[2], 16, 17, 18[5], 19[2], 20[2], 21[3], 22[2], 23[4], 24, 25[2], 26[7], 27, 28[2], 29, 30[2], 31[5], 32[2], 33[3], 34[2], 35[4], 37[4], 38, 39[2], 40, 41, 42, 43[2], 44, 45[5], 46, 47[2], 48[3]
21:2[4], 3, 4[4], 5, 6[2], 8[2], 9, 10[4], 11[2], 12[2], 13[2], 14[3], 15, 17, 19, 20, 21[4], 22, 23[6], 24[3]

RUTH

1:1[3], 2[6], 3[3], 4[3], 5[4], 7[2], 8[2], 9[2], 10, 11, 12, 14[3], 15[2], 16[3], 17[3], 19[2], 20, 21[2], 22[2]
2:1[2], 2[3], 3[4], 4[3], 6[2], 7[3], 9[3], 10[2], 11[6], 12, 13, 14[8], 15[2], 16[3], 17[2], 18[5], 19[4], 20[3], 21, 22, 23[2]
3:2, 3[4], 4[5], 5, 6[2], 7[6], 8[3], 9[2], 10, 11, 12, 13, 14[3], 15[4], 16[2], 17
4:1[4], 2[3], 3, 4[4], 6, 7[3], 9[4], 10, 11[5], 12, 13[3], 14, 15[2], 16[3], 17[2], 19[2], 20[2], 21[2], 22[2]

1 SAMUEL

1:1, 2[3], 3[4], 4[3], 6, 7[2], 8[2], 9, 10[3], 11[5], 12, 14, 15[2], 16, 17[2], 18[3], 19[6], 20, 21[3], 22[2], 23[2], 24[5], 25[2], 26, 27, 28
2:1[2], 3, 4, 5[2], 6[2], 7[2], 8[3], 9, 10[2], 11[2], 13, 14, 15, 16[3], 19, 20[4], 21[4], 22[2], 23, 26[3], 27[2], 28[2], 29[2], 30[2], 31, 32[2], 33[3], 34[2], 35[4], 36[4]
3:1[2], 2[2], 3[2], 4, 5[5], 6[5], 8[5], 9[2], 10[3], 11, 13, 14, 15[3], 16[2], 17[2], 18[3], 19[3], 20, 21
4:1[3], 2[3], 3, 4[2], 5, 6[2], 7[2], 9[2], 10[4], 11[3], 12[3], 13[3], 14[3], 15[2], 16[3], 17[6], 18[5], 19[5], 20, 21[3], 22
5:1[2], 2, 3[3], 4[3], 6[3], 7[2], 8[4], 9[4], 10[2], 11[4], 12[2]
6:1, 2[2], 3[2], 4[2], 5[4], 6[2], 7[3], 8[4], 9, 10[4], 11[3], 12[4], 13[4], 14[4], 15[5], 16, 17, 18[2], 19[4], 20[2], 21[2]
7:1[4], 2[2], 3[5], 4[2], 5[2], 6[6], 7[2], 8, 9[4], 10[3], 11[3], 12[3], 13[2], 14[4], 15, 16[4], 17[3]
8:1, 2, 3[3], 4, 5[2], 6, 7, 8, 9, 10, 11[4], 12[6], 13[3], 14[4], 15[4], 16[5], 17, 18[2], 19, 20[3], 21[2], 22[3]
9:2[4], 3[3], 4[4], 5[3], 6[2], 7, 8[2], 9, 11[2], 12[2], 13, 14[2], 16, 17, 18, 19[4], 20[3], 21[3], 22[4], 23, 24[5], 25, 26[5], 27[2]
10:1[3], 2[3], 3[4], 4[2], 5[5], 6[3], 7, 8[4], 9[2], 10[3], 11, 12[2], 13, 14[4], 15, 16, 17, 18[4], 19[4], 20, 21[2], 22, 23[4], 24[3], 25[3], 26[2], 27[2]
11:1[3], 2[2], 3[2], 4[3], 5[3], 6[2], 7[6], 8[2], 9[4], 10, 11[4], 12, 13, 14[2], 15[5]
12:1[2], 2[5], 3[2], 4, 5[3], 6[3], 7, 8[3], 9[4], 10[5], 11[6], 12, 13[2], 14[4], 16, 17[3], 18[4], 19, 20, 21, 23, 24, 25
13:1, 2[3], 3[3], 4[3], 5[5], 6[4], 7[3], 8[2], 9[3], 10[2], 11[4], 12[2], 13, 14, 15[3], 16[3], 17, 18[2], 20[3], 21[4], 22[2], 23
14:1, 2[2], 3[2], 4[4], 5, 6[2], 7, 8, 9, 10, 11[2], 12[5], 13[5], 14[2], 15[4], 16[3], 17[3], 18, 19[3], 20[5], 21, 23, 24, 25[2], 26, 27[3], 28[2], 31[2], 32[6], 33, 34[8], 35, 36[4], 37, 38[3], 40[3], 41[2], 42[3], 43[3], 44[2], 45, 46, 47[6], 48[3], 49[4], 50[2], 51[2], 52[2]
15:3[7], 4[3], 5[2], 6, 7, 8[2], 9[8], 11[3], 12[5], 13[2], 14[2], 15[3], 16[2], 17[2], 18[4], 19, 20[4], 21, 22[3], 23[2], 24[3], 25, 26[2], 27[2], 28[2], 29, 30[2], 31, 32[2], 33[2], 34, 35[2]
16:1[2], 2[3], 3[3], 4[4], 5[5], 6[2], 8[2], 9, 10, 11[5], 12[5], 13[3], 14, 15, 16[2], 17[2], 18[6], 19, 20[4], 21[4], 22, 23[4]
17:1[3], 2[4], 3[3], 4[2], 5[3], 6[2], 7[3], 8[5], 9[3], 10, 11[2], 12[2], 13[5], 14[2], 15, 16[3], 17[3], 18[3], 19[2], 20[6], 21, 22[4], 23[3], 24[2], 25[4], 26[2], 27, 28[5], 29, 30[3], 31[2], 32[2], 33[2], 34[4], 35[6], 36[2], 37[3], 38[2], 39[4], 40[5], 41[3], 42[4], 43[2], 44[3], 45[2], 46[4], 47[3], 48[4], 49[5], 50[3], 51[6], 52[7], 53[2], 54[2], 55[2], 56, 57[2], 58[2]
18:1[2], 2[2], 3, 4[5], 5[5], 6[3], 7[3], 8[5], 9[2], 10[4], 11[2], 12[2], 13[3], 14[2], 16[2], 17[2], 18[2], 20[3], 21[2], 22[3], 23[3], 24, 25, 26[2], 27[6], 28[3], 29[2], 30
19:1[2], 2[3], 3[4], 4[3], 5[3], 6[2], 7[4], 8[5], 9[2], 10[4], 11[2], 12[3], 13[4], 14, 15, 16, 17[3], 18[6], 19, 20[4], 21[4], 22[5], 23[4], 24[4]
20:1[4], 2[2], 3[5], 5[2], 9, 11[3], 12[4], 13[3], 14, 17, 18, 19[3], 20, 21[2], 23[3], 24, 25[4], 27[2], 28, 29[4], 30[2], 31, 32[2], 33, 34, 35[2], 36[2], 37[2], 38[3], 39, 40[2], 41[5], 42[7]
21:1[3], 2[5], 4[2], 5[4], 7, 8[2], 9[2], 10[3], 11[2], 12[2], 13[4]
22:1[3], 2[5], 3[4], 4[2], 5[3], 6[2], 7[3], 8[2], 9, 10[3], 11[2], 12[2], 13[4], 14[4], 16[2], 17[4], 18[6], 19[6], 20[2], 21, 22
23:1, 2[4], 3, 4[2], 5[4], 6, 7[3], 8[2], 9[2], 11, 12[2], 13[5], 14[3], 15[2], 16[3], 17[4], 18[3], 20, 21, 22[3], 23[4], 24[3], 25[4], 26[6], 27, 28, 29[2]
24:1, 2[2], 3[4], 4[2], 5, 6, 7[2], 8[4], 9, 10[2], 11[3], 12[2], 15[5], 16[3], 17, 18, 20[2], 21, 22[3]
25:1[6], 2[5], 3[5], 4, 5[4], 6[3], 7, 8[2], 9[2], 10[3], 11[3], 12[3], 13[5], 14, 15, 16, 17[2], 18[7], 19, 20[4], 21, 22, 23[4], 24[4], 25, 26[3], 27, 28, 29[2], 30[2], 32, 33[3], 34, 35[2], 36[3], 37[2], 38, 39[4], 40, 41[3], 42[5], 43
26:1, 2, 3[2], 4, 5[6], 6[3], 7[4], 8, 9[2], 10, 11[2], 12[3], 13, 14[3], 15[2], 16[2], 17[3], 18, 21, 22[4], 23, 24[2], 25[2]
27:1[2], 2[2], 3[3], 4[2], 5, 7[2], 8[5], 9[9], 10[4], 11[2], 12
28:1[3], 2[2], 3[4], 4[5], 5[2], 6, 7[2], 8[7], 9[2], 10, 11, 12[2], 13[2], 14[6], 15[4], 16, 17[2], 19[2], 20[2], 21[5], 22[2], 23[3], 24[6], 25[4]
29:1, 2[3], 3[2], 4[3], 5, 6[3], 7, 8[2], 9[2], 10[2], 11[2]
30:1[5], 2[2], 3[5], 4[2], 5[2], 6[2], 7[2], 8[3], 9[2], 10, 11[5], 12[4], 13[4], 14[3], 15[3], 16[4], 17[3], 18[2], 19, 20[3], 21[4], 22[4], 23, 25[2], 26, 27[2], 28[3], 29[3], 30[3], 31[3]
31:1[2], 2[5], 3[3], 4[4], 5[2], 6[3], 7[7], 8[2], 9[4], 10[2], 11, 12[5], 13[3]

2 SAMUEL

1:1, 2[3], 3[2], 4[6], 5[2], 6[3], 7[3], 8[2], 9, 10[4], 11[2], 12[6], 13[2], 14, 15[4], 16, 17[2], 22, 23[3], 27
2:1[4], 2[2], 3[2], 4[3], 5[3], 6[3], 7[2], 8, 9[6], 10, 11[2], 12[2], 13[5], 14[3], 15[2], 16[2], 17[3], 18[4], 19[2], 20[2], 21[3], 22, 23[4], 24[2], 25[3], 26, 27, 28[2], 29[5], 30[3], 31[2], 32[5]
3:1[4], 2[2], 3[2], 4[2], 5, 6[2], 7[2], 8[3], 9, 10[2], 11, 12[2], 13, 14, 15[2], 16[2], 17, 18, 19[3], 20[3], 21[6], 22[4], 23[3], 24[2], 25[3], 26, 27[2], 28[2], 29[2], 30, 31[5], 32[4], 33[2], 34, 35[2], 36[2], 37, 38[2], 39[2]
4:1[2], 2[2], 3[2], 4[7], 5[3], 6[4], 7[5], 8[4], 9[3], 10, 11, 12[6]
5:1[2], 2[3], 3[2], 4, 5[4], 6[3], 8[6], 9[3], 10[3], 11[5], 12[2], 13[4], 14[4], 15[3], 16[3], 17[2], 18, 19[2], 20[3], 21[3], 22[2], 23[2], 24, 25[2]
6:2[2], 3[4], 4[2], 5[6], 6[2], 7[3], 8[2], 9[2], 11[3], 12[3], 13[2], 14[2], 15[2], 16[4], 17[4], 18[2], 19[3], 20[2], 21[2], 22[3]
7:1[2], 3, 4, 5, 6, 9[3], 10[2], 11[2], 12[3], 13, 14[2], 16[2], 17, 18[3], 19[2], 20, 21, 23[5], 24, 25[3], 26[2], 28[3], 29
8:1[3], 2[5], 4[4], 5[2], 6[3], 7[2], 8[2], 10[5], 11, 12[5], 13, 14[3], 15[3], 16[2], 17[3], 18[3]
9:1, 2[3], 3[2], 4[2], 5, 6[3], 7[3], 8[2], 9[2], 10[4], 12[2], 13
10:1[2], 2[2], 3[3], 4[3], 5[2], 6[5], 7[2], 8[6], 9[2], 10, 11[2], 12[3], 13[3], 14[3], 15, 16[4], 17[5], 18[4], 19[2]
11:1[5], 2[4], 3[3], 4[5], 5[4], 6[2], 7[3], 8[4], 9, 10, 11[8], 12[3], 13[4], 14[2], 15[3], 16, 17[4], 18, 19, 20[2], 22[2], 23[3], 24[3], 25[2], 26, 27[4]
12:1[4], 2, 3[6], 4[4], 5[2], 6[2], 7[2], 8[6], 9[2], 10, 11[3], 12, 13[2], 15[3], 16[3], 17[2], 18[3], 19, 20[7], 21[2], 22[2], 24[6], 25[2], 26[2], 27[3], 28[3], 29[4], 30[3], 31[7]
13:1[2], 2[2], 3, 4[2], 5[6], 6[3], 7, 8[5], 9[4], 10[3], 11[2], 12, 13[2], 14, 15, 16, 17[2], 18[2], 19[4], 20, 22, 23[2], 24[3], 25[2], 26, 27, 28[2], 29[3], 30[2], 31[3], 32[2], 34[3], 35, 36[5], 37[2], 38[2], 39
14:2[5], 3[2], 4[3], 5[3], 6[4], 7[5], 8[2], 9[4], 10[2], 11, 12, 13, 14, 15, 16, 17, 18[2], 19[4], 20, 21, 22[4], 23[2], 24[3], 26, 27[2], 28, 29, 30[3], 31[2], 32[2], 33[4]
15:1[3], 2[5], 3[2], 4, 5[3], 6, 7[2], 9[2], 11[3], 12[2], 13, 14[4], 15, 16[3], 17[3], 18[4], 19[2], 20[3], 21[3], 22[5], 23[3], 24[4], 25[3], 27[2], 29[2], 30[6], 31[2], 32[2], 34, 35[3], 36[2], 37
16:1[5], 2[5], 3[3], 4, 5[2], 6[5], 7[2], 8[2], 9, 10, 11[3], 12, 13[5], 14[3], 15[3], 16, 17, 18[4], 19, 21[2], 22, 23[2]
17:1[2], 2[5], 3, 4[2], 5, 6, 7, 8[4], 9, 10[2], 11, 12[3], 13, 14[2], 15[5], 16[2], 17[5], 18[2], 19[4], 20[5], 21[5], 22[2], 23[7], 24[2], 25, 26, 27[3], 28[9], 29[7]
18:1[3], 2[4], 4[4], 5[4], 6, 7, 8, 9[7], 10[3], 11[5], 12[3], 13, 14[2], 15[3], 16[2], 17[4], 18[3], 19, 20, 21[2], 22, 23[2], 24[5], 25[5], 26[4], 27[3], 28[4], 29[3], 30[4], 31[2], 32[3], 33[4]
19:1[2], 2, 3, 4, 5[6], 6[2], 7[2], 8[3], 9[3], 10, 11[2], 12, 13[3], 14[2], 15[2], 16[2], 17[5], 18[3], 19, 21, 22, 23, 24[2], 25, 26[2], 27, 29[2], 30, 31[2], 32, 33[2], 34, 35[3], 36, 37[3], 38[3], 39[4], 40[3], 41[5], 42, 43[4]
20:1[3], 2, 3[4], 4, 6[3], 7[5], 8[3], 9[2], 10[4], 11[3], 12[3], 14[5], 15[5], 17[3], 18, 19[2], 20[2], 21[2], 22[5], 23[2], 24[2], 25[3], 26
21:1[3], 2[5], 3, 4[2], 5[2], 6[2], 7, 8[2], 9[4], 10[3], 11, 12[3], 13[3], 14[4], 15[4], 16, 17[2], 18, 19, 20[4], 21, 22[2]

2 SAMUEL

1 KINGS

2 KINGS

1 CHRONICLES

2 CHRONICLES

EZRA

NEHEMIAH

ESTHER

JOB

PSALMS

PSALMS

40:1[2], 2[2], 3[3], 4, 5[2], 6[2], 10[2], 11, 14[2], 16, 17[2]
41:2[3], 5, 6, 8, 10, 12[2], 13[2]
42:2, 3, 4, 5, 6, 7, 8[2], 11[2]
43:1[2], 3[2], 5[2]
44:2[2], 3[2], 7, 8, 9[2], 10, 11, 12, 13, 15, 16[2], 19, 24[2], 26
45:3, 4[4], 6, 7, 8[2], 10[3], 11, 12, 15, 17
46:1, 2, 3, 5, 9, 10
47:3
48:t, 1, 5[2], 6, 12, 14
49:2[2], 3, 6, 8, 9, 10[2], 11, 14[2], 18, 20
50:1, 3[2], 4, 6, 7[2], 10, 11, 12, 14, 15[2], 17, 18, 19, 20, 21[2], 22, 23
51:2, 3, 4[2], 5, 6, 7[2], 8, 9, 10, 11, 12, 13, 14, 15, 17, 19
52:t[2], 3, 5[2], 6[2], 7, 8, 9
53:1, 6
54:t, 1, 3, 7
55:1, 2[2], 3, 4, 5[2], 6[2], 7, 8, 9[2], 10[2], 11, 13, 14, 15[2], 16, 17[4], 19, 22, 23
57:3[2], 4[3], 7, 8, 10
58:9
59:t, 2, 4[2], 6, 11, 12[3], 13, 14[3], 15[2], 16, 17
60:t[2], 5, 6, 7, 10
61:3, 6, 7
62:2, 3, 6, 7[2], 9, 10
63:1, 2, 5[2], 6
64:3, 4, 6, 9[2], 10[2]
65:t, 1, 4, 5, 7, 8, 9, 11, 12
66:4, 5, 8, 9, 12, 14, 16[2], 17
67:1[2], 4[2], 6, 7
68:4, 5, 12, 13, 20, 21, 23, 27[2], 33, 34, 35
69:5, 8, 9, 10, 11, 12, 14[2], 15, 17, 18, 19[2], 20[3], 21, 22, 23, 24, 25, 26, 27, 28, 29, 30, 31, 32[2], 33, 34[2], 35[2], 36
70:2[2], 4[2], 5[2]
71:2[2], 3, 4, 8, 10, 11, 13[2], 14[2], 15, 17, 18[2], 20[2], 21, 23
72:1, 2, 3, 4, 5, 7, 8, 9, 10[2], 12, 13[2], 14[2], 15[3], 16, 17, 19[3]
73:8, 9, 10, 11[2], 13, 14, 21, 22, 24, 25, 26[2]
74:6, 14, 15, 16, 17, 18, 21
75:3, 4, 7, 8[3]
76:2, 3[2], 4, 5, 6, 7, 8, 11
77:1, 2, 3[2], 6, 7, 10, 12, 15, 18, 19[2], 20
78:3[2], 4[2], 5, 6, 7, 8[3], 9, 10, 11[2], 13[2], 14, 15, 16, 17, 18, 20, 21[2], 22, 23, 24[2], 26, 27, 28, 29, 31[2], 32, 33, 34[2], 35[2], 36, 38[2], 39, 40, 41[2], 43, 44[2], 45, 46, 47, 48, 49[2], 51, 52, 53, 54, 55[2], 56[2], 57, 58, 59, 61[2], 62, 63, 64, 65, 66, 67, 69, 70, 71, 72
79:3, 4, 6, 7, 9[2], 12, 13
80:2[4], 3[2], 5, 6, 7[2], 8, 9[2], 10, 11, 13, 14[2], 15[2], 18, 19
81:2, 4, 7, 8, 10, 11, 12, 13, 14, 16
82:2, 3[2], 4, 6, 7
83:1, 2, 3, 4, 6[2], 7[2], 11[2], 14, 15, 17[2]
84:2, 3[2], 9, 11[2]
85:4, 7, 8, 10[2], 11, 12, 13
86:1, 5[2], 6, 9[2], 10, 12, 13, 14[2], 15[3], 16[2], 17[2]
87:4[2], 5[3]
88:1, 3, 5, 7, 8, 10, 12, 13, 15, 18[2]
89:4, 5, 7, 11, 12[2], 13, 14[2], 16, 17, 18, 19, 23[2], 24[2], 25, 26, 28, 29, 30, 31, 32, 36, 37, 38, 43, 44, 48, 52
90:2, 3, 4, 6[2], 7, 10[4], 13, 14, 15, 16, 17[2]
91:2, 3, 4[2], 7, 8, 13[2], 15[2], 16
92:1, 2, 3, 5, 7, 11, 14, 15
94:4[2], 5, 6[2], 8, 12, 15, 21, 22, 23[2]
95:2, 3, 5[2], 6, 7[2], 8, 9, 10[2]
96:4, 6[2], 7, 8, 11[2], 12, 13
97:2[2], 3, 4, 6, 8[2], 11, 12
98:1, 3, 4[2], 5, 6, 7[2], 9
99:2, 3, 4, 5, 6[3], 7, 9
100:3[2], 4[2], 5
101:1, 5
102:t, 1, 3, 4, 7, 8, 9, 10[2], 11, 12, 13, 14, 15, 17, 18, 21, 22, 25, 26, 27, 28
103:1, 2, 4, 6, 8[2], 16[2], 17, 18, 19
104:1, 14, 15[3], 18, 20, 21, 22, 23, 25[2], 29, 30, 32[2], 35
105:4, 5, 9, 10[2], 12, 15, 20[2], 21, 22, 23, 24[2], 26, 27, 28[2], 29, 31[2], 32, 33[2], 34[3], 35[2], 37[2], 39, 40[2], 41, 42, 43[2], 44[2], 45
106:3, 9, 10[2], 11, 14, 15, 16, 17[2], 18, 19, 22, 25, 27, 28, 29, 30[2], 31, 35, 36, 37, 38[3], 39, 41[2], 42, 43, 45[2], 47[2], 48
107:3[3], 5, 6, 7, 8, 9, 10[2], 11, 12, 13, 14[2], 15, 16, 17, 18, 19, 20[2], 21, 22[2], 24, 25, 27[3], 28, 31, 32, 33, 35, 36, 37[2], 38, 39[2], 40, 41, 42[2], 43
108:1, 2, 3, 4, 5, 6, 7, 11
109:2, 3, 5[2], 6, 7, 8, 9, 10, 11, 13, 14, 16, 18, 19, 20, 22[2], 23, 24, 29
110:4
111:1, 3[2], 4, 7, 8[3], 9
112:3[2], 4[2], 5, 10[2]

PSALMS

113:2, 4, 6, 7, 9
114:2, 3, 4, 6
115:1, 4, 9, 10, 11, 13, 14[2], 15, 18
116:1, 3[2], 5, 6, 8, 13, 16, 17
117:2
118:5, 14[2], 15, 17, 19, 21, 24, 28
119:2, 15, 17, 22, 23, 24, 26, 29, 33, 34, 36, 37, 43, 44, 45, 46, 47, 48, 52, 55, 59, 60, 63, 66, 68, 72, 73, 75, 79, 90, 105, 106, 108, 114, 116, 117[2], 120, 121, 123, 124, 128, 131, 132, 133, 135, 137, 138, 141, 142, 143, 144, 146, 147, 151, 153, 154, 157, 158, 160, 163, 165, 166, 167, 168, 174, 175[2]
120:1, 2
121:2, 8[2]
122:7, 8
123:2, 4
124:7, 8
125:4
126:2, 6
127:3
128:2, 5, 6
129:5
130:5, 7, 8
131:2, 3
132:1, 2, 8, 9, 12, 16
133:1, 3
134:2, 3
135:4, 5, 6[2], 8, 9[2], 10, 11[2], 12, 13, 14, 15
136:9, 11, 12, 14, 15, 18, 20, 21, 24
137:3, 9
138:2[2], 3, 7
139:1, 2, 3[2], 5[2], 9, 10, 12, 14[2], 15, 16, 20, 21, 23[2], 24[2]
140:5, 12
141:2, 4, 5, 7, 9
142:4, 5
143:1, 2, 12[2]
144:1, 2[3], 5[2], 6[2], 7, 8, 9, 11[2], 13
145:1[2], 2[2], 3[2], 4, 5, 6[2], 7, 8[2], 9, 10, 11, 12, 13, 14, 15, 16, 17, 19, 21[2]
146:6[2], 9
147:1, 3, 5, 9, 14, 18[2], 19, 20
148:3, 4, 5, 6, 7, 8[2], 9[2], 10[2], 11[2], 12[2], 13
149:1, 3, 6, 7, 8
150:3, 4[2]

PROVERBS

1:2, 3[2], 4, 5[2], 6[2], 7, 8, 9, 12, 16, 18, 22[2], 24[2], 25, 27[2], 29, 31, 32, 33
2:1, 2, 3, 4, 5, 6, 8, 9[2], 10, 14, 15, 17, 18, 20, 21, 22
3:2[2], 3, 4[2], 5, 6, 7, 8, 9, 10, 13, 14, 15, 16[2], 17, 18, 20, 21, 22, 23, 24, 26, 28[2], 31
4:1, 3, 4[2], 6[2], 7, 8, 10[2], 12, 14, 15, 16, 17, 18, 22, 24, 25, 26
5:1, 2, 3, 7, 8, 9, 10, 11[2], 12[2], 13, 14, 15, 16, 17, 18, 19[2], 20[2], 21, 22, 23
6:3[2], 5, 6, 8, 11, 17, 19, 20, 21, 22, 23[2], 26, 27, 28, 33[2]
7:1, 2[2], 4, 7, 8, 9, 10[2], 11, 12, 13[2], 15, 17, 20, 23, 24
8:1, 4, 5, 6, 7, 9, 10[2], 11, 12, 13[3], 14, 15, 16, 17, 18[2], 19, 21, 30, 31, 33[2], 35
9:5, 6[2], 7, 8, 9[2], 10, 11, 13, 16, 17, 18
10:18, 22, 26
11:7, 8, 10, 15, 16, 24[2], 25, 29, 30, 31
12:7, 9[2], 14, 28
13:4, 5, 18, 22
14:6, 10, 13, 14, 16[2], 17, 19, 22, 26
15:3, 10, 11, 16, 17, 23, 30, 33
16:1, 3, 6[2], 11, 13, 15, 16, 18, 20, 21, 23, 24, 27, 28, 29, 32
17:1, 2, 3, 4, 5, 6, 15, 17, 18, 19, 20, 21, 25, 27, 28
18:1, 3, 4, 6, 7, 8, 10, 11, 12, 13, 15, 16, 17, 18, 19, 20, 21[2], 22, 24
19:1, 2, 3, 5, 6, 9, 11, 13, 14[2], 15, 17, 18, 20, 22, 23, 24, 25[3], 26[2], 28, 29
20:1, 4, 10, 11, 12, 13, 15, 16, 18, 22, 23, 25, 26, 28[2], 29
21:3, 4[2], 6, 8, 9, 11, 14, 17, 18, 19, 20, 21[2], 22, 23, 24, 26
22:1[2], 2, 3[2], 4[3], 5, 6, 7, 8, 10[2], 12, 16, 17[2], 20, 23, 24, 25
23:2, 7, 8, 10, 12, 14, 18, 19[2], 21[2], 22, 23[3], 24, 25[2], 26, 27, 28, 32, 33, 35[2]
24:2, 3, 4[2], 6, 9, 11, 12[2], 13, 14, 16, 17, 18[2], 21[2], 22, 25, 27[2], 28, 30, 31[3], 32[2], 34
25:3[2], 4, 5, 6, 9, 10, 12, 14, 15, 16, 17, 18[2], 19, 20, 21, 22, 24, 26, 28
26:1, 3, 6, 10, 17, 18, 19, 21, 22, 23, 24, 27, 28
27:2[2], 3, 4, 9, 10, 11, 12[2], 13, 15, 16, 20, 21, 23, 24, 25[2], 26, 27[2]
28:2, 8, 13, 15, 22, 24
29:1, 6, 13, 15, 17, 22, 24, 27
30:1, 2, 4, 6, 8, 9[4], 10, 11, 12, 13, 14[2], 16[2], 17[2], 19, 20[2], 21, 22, 23, 28, 30, 31, 33

PROVERBS

31:2[2], 5[2], 6, 7[2], 9[2], 12, 13[2], 15[2], 16, 17, 19, 22, 24[2], 25[2], 26, 27, 28[2], 30, 31

ECCLESIASTES

1:4, 5[2], 6[2], 9[2], 13[2], 14[2], 15, 16[2], 17[3], 18
2:1, 2, 3, 5[2], 7[3], 8[6], 9, 10[2], 11[4], 12[3], 14, 15, 16, 17, 19[2], 21[3], 22, 23, 24[2], 26[4]
3:1, 2[2], 3[2], 4[2], 5[2], 6[2], 7[2], 8[2], 12, 13[3], 14, 15[2], 16[2], 17[2], 18, 20, 21
4:1[4], 4[2], 5, 6, 7, 8[2], 12[2], 13[2], 16
5:1, 2[2], 3, 5, 6, 7, 8[3], 11, 14[2], 15, 16[2], 17[2], 18[3], 19[4]
6:1, 2[2], 3[3], 4[2], 7, 9, 10
7:1, 2, 7, 8, 11, 12, 15, 20, 24, 25[5], 26[3]
8:1[2], 2, 4, 5[2], 6, 8, 9, 10[3], 12, 15[2], 16
9:1[2], 2[5], 3[2], 6[2], 7, 8, 9, 11[2], 12, 13, 14[4], 15, 16
10:1, 3, 6, 7, 8, 9, 10, 11, 13, 14, 16, 17[2], 18, 19, 20[2]
11:2, 3, 4, 6, 7, 8, 9[3], 10[2]
12:3[3], 4[3], 5[5], 7, 9[3], 10, 11, 12[2], 13

SONG OF SOLOMON

1:4, 8, 17
2:1, 3, 4, 6, 7, 10[2], 11, 12, 13[2], 14, 16, 17[2]
3:2[2], 4[2], 5, 6, 11[2]
4:2, 3, 6[2], 8, 10, 11[2], 14[3], 15, 16[2]
5:2, 4, 5[2], 6, 10, 11, 12, 16
6:2, 3, 6, 8[2], 9[3], 10, 11[2]
7:5, 6, 7, 8, 9, 10, 12, 13[2]
8:2, 3, 8, 9, 10, 12, 14

ISAIAH

1:1[2], 2[3], 3, 5[2], 6[2], 7, 8, 9, 11[2], 13, 14, 15, 18, 19, 20, 23[2], 24, 25[3], 26[2], 27, 28[3], 29, 30, 31[4]
2:1, 2[3], 3[6], 4[4], 5, 6[2], 7, 9[2], 10[2], 11[2], 12[3], 13[3], 14[2], 15[2], 16[2], 17[3], 18, 19[3], 20[2], 21[2]
3:1[3], 2[4], 3[4], 4[2], 5[3], 6, 8[2], 9, 12[2], 13, 14, 15, 16[4], 17, 18[2], 19[2], 20[4], 21, 22[3], 23[3], 24[5], 25, 26[3]
4:1[2], 2[3], 3[2], 4[2], 5[4], 6[4]
5:2[7], 3[3], 5[4], 6[2], 7[2], 9, 10, 12[4], 13[2], 14[5], 15[3], 16, 17, 18, 19[3], 20[3], 21, 22, 23, 24[3], 25[4], 26[3], 28[2], 29[3], 30[4]
6:1[2], 2[2], 3[2], 4[2], 5, 7[4], 8, 9[3], 10[6], 11[3], 12[2], 13[3]
7:1[2], 2[3], 3, 4[3], 5, 6[3], 8[3], 9[2], 13, 14[2], 15[2], 16, 17[2], 18[2], 19[5], 20[2], 21[2], 22[2], 23[2], 24[2], 25[3]
8:1, 2[2], 3[3], 4[2], 6[2], 7[4], 8[3], 9[4], 10[2], 11, 13[2], 14[3], 15[5], 17[2], 18[2], 19[3], 20, 21[6], 22[4]
9:1[2], 3[2], 4, 5[2], 6[2], 7[4], 8, 9[3], 11, 12[2], 14[2], 15[2], 16, 17[3], 18[3], 19, 20[4], 21[2]
10:1, 2[2], 3[3], 4, 5, 6[3], 7, 10[2], 11[2], 12[2], 13[4], 14[3], 16, 17[5], 18[4], 19, 20[2], 24, 25[2], 26[2], 27[3], 33[2], 34[2]
11:1[2], 2[4], 3[2], 4[3], 5[2], 6[5], 7[3], 8[2], 10[2], 11[8], 12[3], 13[2], 14[2], 15[4], 16
12:1[2], 2[2], 4, 6
13:5, 7, 8[2], 9[2], 10[2], 11[4], 13[2], 14[3], 15, 16, 17, 18, 19[2], 21[3], 22[4]
14:1[4], 2[6], 3[3], 4, 5, 6, 7, 8, 10, 11[2], 16, 17, 19, 20, 22[4], 23[2], 24, 25[2], 26, 27[3], 29, 30[4], 31, 32
15:1[2], 2[3], 3, 4[2], 7, 8, 9
16:5[4], 6[2], 8, 9[2], 10[3], 11, 12, 14[3]
17:1, 2, 3[2], 4[2], 5[3], 7, 8, 9[2], 10[2], 11[2], 12, 13[3], 14[3]
18:2[2], 3[2], 4[2], 5[3], 6[3], 7[3]
19:1[3], 2[4], 3[6], 4[2], 5[3], 6[4], 7[2], 8[2], 9, 10[2], 12[2], 14, 16[2], 17, 18, 19, 20[5], 21[5], 22[5], 23[3], 24, 25[2]
20:1[2], 2[4], 3[4], 4[3], 5[3], 6[2]
21:2, 5, 7[3], 8[2], 9[4], 10, 12, 15[2], 16, 17
22:5[3], 6[3], 7[2], 8[2], 9, 10[2], 12[4], 13[5], 14, 15, 16[2], 17, 18[2], 19[2], 20, 21[5], 22[4], 23[2], 24[2], 25[3]
23:3[2], 9, 12, 13, 15, 17[3], 18[3]
24:1[3], 2, 3, 4[2], 6[2], 12, 13, 17[2], 18[3], 20[5], 21[2], 22[3], 23[3]
25:1, 6, 7[2], 8[2], 9[3], 10, 11[2], 12[2]
26:1, 6, 8, 10, 11, 14[2], 17, 19[2], 20, 21
27:1[3], 3, 4, 5, 6[2], 9[2], 10[4], 11[2], 12[2], 13[4]
28:2[2], 4[2], 5, 6[2], 7[2], 8, 9[2], 10, 11, 12, 13[5], 15[2], 17[3], 18[2], 19[2], 20, 21, 23[2], 24, 25[4], 26, 27, 29
29:2[3], 3[3], 4[5], 5, 6[4], 7[3], 8[5], 9[2], 10[2], 11[2], 12[2], 13[2], 14[2], 15[3], 17[2], 18[3], 19, 20[2], 21[2], 23[2], 24
30:1, 2[2], 3, 4, 5, 6[4], 7, 8[2], 10, 12[3], 14, 15[3], 16, 17, 18[2], 20[2], 21[2], 22, 23[3], 24[2], 25[3], 26[2], 27[2], 28[2], 29, 30[5], 32[3], 33[2]
31:1[3], 2[3], 3[5], 4[2], 5, 7, 8[2], 9[3]
32:1, 2[2], 3[2], 4, 6[3], 8, 10, 11[2], 13, 14, 15[2], 16, 17[3], 18[3], 19, 20
33:1[4], 4[2], 5, 6[3], 9[4], 12, 13, 15[2], 21, 24
34:1[3], 2, 3[2], 4[4], 5, 6[3], 7[4], 8, 9[3], 10, 11[4], 12, 13[4], 14[2], 15[3], 16[2], 17[2]
35:1[3], 2[4], 3, 4, 5, 6[2], 7[3], 8[3], 10[6]
36:1, 2[2], 3[2], 4, 5, 6, 7[3], 8, 9[2], 10[2], 11[3], 12[2], 13[2], 16[4], 17[3], 19[2], 21, 22[3]

ISAIAH

37:1[3], 2[3], 3[4], 4, 6, 7[3], 8, 9[2], 11, 12[3], 13[3], 14[4], 15, 16, 17[3], 18, 19[2], 22, 23[3], 24[5], 25[2], 26, 27[3], 28[3], 29[3], 30[6], 31[2], 32, 34, 35, 36[4], 37[3], 38[4]
38:1[3], 2, 3[4], 5, 6[3], 7, 9, 12, 15, 16[2], 21[2]
39:1[2], 2[7], 3[3], 4, 6, 7[2], 8
40:2, 4[4], 5[2], 6[2], 10[2], 11[2], 12[4], 14[4], 15, 16, 17[2], 19[2], 22[2], 24[3], 26, 27[2], 29, 30[2], 31[3]
41:1, 2[2], 3, 4[2], 5[2], 6, 7[2], 9[3], 11[2], 12[2], 14[2], 15[2], 16[4], 17[3], 18[2], 19[4], 20[4], 22[2], 23, 24, 25[3], 26, 27, 28[2], 29
42:3, 4, 5[3], 6[3], 7, 8, 9, 10[3], 11, 12, 14[2], 15[4], 16[3], 18, 19, 21, 22[4], 23, 24, 25[3]
43:1, 2, 3, 4[2], 5, 6[2], 8, 9[3], 10[3], 11, 12[2], 13[2], 14[2], 16, 17[2], 19, 20[2], 25, 27, 28[2]
44:1, 2[2], 3[2], 4, 5[3], 6[3], 7[5], 8, 9[2], 11[2], 12[4], 13[2], 14[3], 15[4], 16[2], 17[4], 18, 19[3], 21, 22, 23[2], 24, 25[2], 26[3], 27, 28[2]
45:1[2], 2[2], 3[2], 4, 5, 6[2], 7[2], 8[3], 11[2], 12[2], 13[2], 14[5], 16, 18[2], 20[2], 21[3], 22[2], 23, 24[2], 25
46:1, 3, 4[4], 5[2], 6[3], 7[2], 8, 9[2], 10[2], 13[2]
47:1[2], 2, 3, 5, 6, 7, 8, 9[2], 10[3], 11[2], 12, 13
48:1[2], 2, 3[3], 4[2], 5[2], 6[2], 7, 8, 9, 11, 12, 13, 14[2], 15, 16[2], 18, 19, 21[2]
49:1, 2[2], 3, 4[2], 5[2], 6[2], 7[4], 8[3], 9, 11[2], 12[3], 13[3], 14, 17, 18[3], 19[3], 21[4], 22[3], 23[4], 25[2], 26[4]
50:1, 2, 3, 5, 6[2], 7, 10[2], 11
51:1, 2[3], 3[4], 4[2], 5[2], 6[4], 8[2], 9, 11[5], 12, 13[4], 14, 16[4], 17, 19[3], 21, 22, 23[2]
52:1, 2, 3, 4, 5, 10, 12, 13[2], 14, 15
53:1, 2[2], 3[4], 4[2], 5, 6, 7[2], 8[2], 9[2], 10, 11, 12[4]
54:1, 2[2], 3[3], 4, 5, 6[2], 10, 11[2], 12[3], 13[2], 14, 16[2], 17[2]
55:1[4], 2[3], 3[3], 4, 5[2], 7[4], 9, 10[5], 11, 12[3], 13[2]
56:1[2], 2[2], 4[2], 5[3], 6[2], 7[2], 11, 12[3]
57:1[2], 3, 4, 7, 8[3], 9[4], 11[3], 12, 13, 14, 15[4], 16, 17[3], 18[3], 19[2], 20
58:1[2], 2[2], 3[3], 4[2], 5[3], 6[2], 7[2], 8[2], 9[3], 10[3], 11[5], 12[2], 13[2], 14[2]
59:2[2], 3, 4[2], 5[2], 6, 7[2], 8, 10, 11, 12[2], 13[4], 14[3], 15[3], 16[3], 17[3], 19, 20[2], 21[2]
60:1, 2[2], 3[2], 4[2], 5[3], 6[3], 7, 8, 9[3], 10[2], 11, 12, 13[2], 14[2], 15, 16[3], 17[4], 18, 19, 20, 22
61:1, 2, 4[2], 5[4], 6, 7, 8[2], 9[2], 10, 11[2]
62:1[2], 2[3], 3, 4[2], 5, 7[2], 8[2], 9[2], 11, 12[2]
63:2, 3[4], 4, 5[4], 6[3], 7[3], 9[4], 10[2], 11, 15[4], 16, 17
64:5[2], 6[3], 7[2], 8[2], 11[2], 12
65:3, 4[2], 7[2], 8, 9[4], 10[2], 11, 12[2], 14, 15[2], 16[2], 17[2], 18[2], 19[3], 21[4], 22[3], 23, 24[2], 25[3]
66:1[2], 2[3], 3, 4[2], 5, 9[2], 10, 11[2], 12[2], 13, 14[4], 15[2], 16[2], 17[3], 18[4], 19[5], 20[5], 21[2], 22[2], 23[2], 24[3]

JEREMIAH

1:5[2], 7, 9[2], 10[5], 11, 13[3], 15[4], 16[3], 17[2], 18[3], 19
2:2, 3, 4, 5[2], 6[3], 7[3], 8[3], 9, 10[4], 12, 13, 15[2], 16, 18, 19[4], 20[3], 22, 25[2], 26[2], 27[3], 37[2]
3:1[2], 2[3], 3[2], 5, 6[2], 7[2], 8[3], 9[3], 10, 11, 12[4], 13[2], 14[3], 15[2], 16[2], 17, 18, 19[3], 21[2], 22, 23, 24[2], 25[3]
4:1, 2[4], 3[2], 4[3], 5[4], 6, 7[2], 8, 9[4], 10, 11, 13, 15, 16, 18, 20, 21, 22, 23[4], 24[2], 25[2], 26[3], 28[2], 29[3], 30, 31
5:1[5], 2, 5[3], 6[2], 7[2], 9, 10, 11, 12, 13[2], 14[2], 17[5], 19[2], 20, 21[3], 22, 23[2], 24, 25, 27, 28, 30, 31[3]
6:1[3], 2, 4, 5[2], 6, 7[2], 10[2], 11, 12[2], 13, 16[4], 18, 20, 21[3], 22, 23[3], 24, 25, 26, 27[2], 28
7:2[2], 3[2], 5[2], 6[2], 7, 9[4], 10[3], 12, 13[4], 14[2], 15, 17, 18[3], 20[6], 21, 23[3], 24[3], 25, 28, 29[3], 31[2], 33[3], 34[3]
8:1[4], 2[7], 3, 4[2], 6, 7[3], 8, 9[2], 10, 13[2], 14[3], 15[2], 16[3], 17, 19, 20
9:1[2], 2, 3[2], 4[2], 5[3], 7, 10[3], 11[3], 12[2], 13[2], 14, 15, 16, 17[2], 18[3], 20[3], 21[2], 22[2], 24[2], 26[6]
10:2, 4[2], 6, 7, 8, 9[3], 10[2], 11[2], 12, 13[2], 14, 15, 16, 18, 19, 20[3], 21[2], 22[2], 25[4]
11:2[2], 3, 4[2], 5[2], 6[2], 7, 9[2], 10[2], 11, 12[2], 13, 15, 16[2], 17, 18[2], 19[2], 20, 22, 23
12:2, 3[2], 4[2], 5[2], 6, 11, 13, 14, 15[4], 16, 17
13:1[3], 2, 3, 4[2], 5, 6[2], 7[3], 9, 10[2], 11[4], 12, 13[3], 14[2], 15, 16[3], 17[2], 18, 19, 20, 21, 22[2], 25, 27[2]
14:2[2], 3[4], 5, 6, 8, 9, 10, 12[4], 14[3], 15[3], 16[3], 17[2], 18[2], 19[4], 20
15:1[2], 2[4], 3[5], 4, 6, 7, 8, 9[2], 10, 11, 12, 13[2], 14, 15[2], 16[3], 18[2], 19[2], 20[3], 21[2]
16:3[3], 4[4], 5, 6, 8, 9[3], 10[2], 11[5], 12, 13[2], 15[2], 16[5], 18[3], 19[4], 20, 21[2]

JEREMIAH

17:1[2], 2, 3[2], 4[2], 5[2], 6[2], 7, 8[3], 9, 10, 11[3], 13, 14[2], 18, 19[3], 20[3], 21, 24, 25[5], 26[10], 27[3]
18:2[2], 3, 4, 7[3], 9[3], 11[4], 12[2], 15, 16[2], 17, 18[3], 19, 20, 21[4], 22
19:1[3], 2[2], 3[2], 4[3], 7[6], 8[3], 9[5], 11[3], 12[2], 13[3], 14[2], 15
20:2, 3, 4[6], 5[5], 6[6], 7[2], 8[2], 9[2], 10[3], 11, 12[2], 16[4], 17, 18
21:1, 4[2], 5[4], 6[2], 7[8], 8[2], 9[4], 10[2], 11, 12[2], 13, 14[2]
22:1, 2[3], 3[3], 4[3], 6[2], 7[3], 8[2], 9[2], 12, 13[2], 14[4], 15[4], 16, 17[4], 19, 20[3], 22[2], 25[3], 26[3], 28[2], 30
23:1, 2[2], 3[4], 4[2], 5[4], 6[2], 8[3], 9[2], 10[2], 11, 12, 13[2], 14[2], 15, 16, 17, 18[3], 20, 22[2], 23, 24, 28, 29, 31, 32[3], 33, 34[4], 35[2], 36, 37, 38, 39[4], 40[2]
24:1[4], 2, 3[2], 6[5], 7[3], 8[4], 9[3], 10[3]
25:2, 3[3], 4[2], 5[4], 6[4], 9[9], 10[3], 11[3], 12[4], 13, 14[3], 15, 16[3], 17, 18[4], 19[3], 20[7], 21[2], 22[3], 23[3], 24[2], 25[3], 26[4], 27[4], 28, 29, 30[2], 32, 33, 34[4], 35, 36, 37, 38
26:2, 3, 4, 5, 6, 7[2], 8[2], 9[2], 10, 11[2], 12[2], 13[3], 14, 15[2], 16[2], 17, 18[3], 19[3], 20[2], 21[4], 22[2], 23[3]
27:2[2], 3[5], 4, 5[3], 6[2], 7[5], 8[5], 10[2], 11[3], 12[3], 13[2], 15[2], 16, 17, 18[3], 19[3], 20[2], 21[2], 22[2]
28:1[3], 3, 4, 5, 6, 7, 8[4], 10, 11[2], 13, 14[2]
29:1[3], 2[5], 3, 5[3], 6[6], 7[2], 8, 10, 11, 12[3], 13[2], 14[5], 16[2], 17[2], 18[6], 19, 21[2], 22[2], 23[3], 25[2], 26[2], 28[3], 29, 31[2], 32
30:3[3], 4[2], 5, 6[2], 8[2], 9, 10[5], 11, 12, 16[3], 17, 18[3], 19[5], 20[2], 21[4], 22[2], 24
31:1, 4[2], 5, 6, 7[2], 8[4], 9[2], 10[3], 11, 12[8], 13[3], 14[2], 15, 16[2], 17, 18[2], 19, 23[2], 24[3], 25, 26[2], 27[2], 28[6], 29, 31, 33[3], 34[3], 35[2], 37, 39[2], 40[3]
32:2, 3[2], 4[3], 5[2], 6, 8[2], 9[2], 10[4], 11[2], 12[2], 13, 14[2], 15[2], 17[3], 18, 19[2], 20[4], 21[5], 22[2], 23[2], 24[5], 25[2], 28[2], 29[4], 30, 31, 32[4], 33[3], 35[2], 36[3], 37[4], 38[2], 39[3], 40, 41[2], 43, 44[8]
33:3[3], 4[2], 5[2], 6[4], 7[3], 8[3], 9[5], 10[4], 11[3], 12[2], 13[4], 14, 15[3], 16[2], 18[2], 19, 20[3], 21, 22, 25[3], 26[3]
34:1[4], 2[3], 3[5], 5[2], 7[2], 9, 10[3], 11[4], 14, 15[3], 16[5], 17[3], 18[2], 19[3], 20[3], 21[4], 22[6]
35:2[3], 3[3], 4, 5[3], 10[2], 11[2], 13[2], 14, 15[5], 17[2], 18[3]
36:1, 2[3], 3, 4, 5, 6[2], 7[2], 8, 9[2], 12[6], 14[2], 15[2], 16[2], 17, 18, 19[2], 20[2], 21[3], 22, 23[2], 25[2], 26[3], 27, 28, 29[4], 30[2], 31[6], 32[2]
37:1, 3[2], 4, 5, 8[4], 10[2], 11, 13[2], 14, 15[2], 16[2], 17[4], 21
38:1[3], 2[2], 4, 6[3], 8, 9, 10, 11[4], 12[3], 13[2], 14[2], 15, 17[3], 18[2], 19[2], 20, 22[4], 23[3], 24, 25[3], 27[2], 28
39:1[2], 2, 3[2], 4[4], 5[2], 7, 8[3], 9, 10[2], 12[2], 13[3], 14[2], 16[3], 17, 18
40:1, 2[2], 3[2], 4[3], 5[3], 6, 7[5], 8[6], 9[4], 10[4], 11[4], 12[3], 13, 14, 15[3]
41:1[2], 2[3], 3[2], 4[2], 5[4], 6[2], 7[3], 8[4], 9, 10[3], 11, 12[2], 13, 14[2], 15, 16[4], 17[2]
42:1[3], 2[2], 3, 4, 5, 7, 8[2], 9, 10[3], 11, 12[2], 14, 15[2], 16[2], 17[2], 18[6], 20[2], 21, 22[2]
43:1, 2[2], 3, 4[2], 5, 6[6], 9, 10[4], 11[4], 12[5], 13
44:1[3], 2[3], 3, 4, 6[5], 7[2], 8[2], 9[5], 10, 11, 12[9], 13, 15, 17[6], 18[3], 19[3], 20[2], 21[5], 22[3], 23[2], 24, 25[4], 27[3], 28, 29, 30[2]
45:3, 4, 5
46:3[2], 4[3], 5[4], 6, 8[4], 9[5], 10[3], 11, 12[2], 13, 14[4], 16[3], 18, 19, 21[2], 22, 23, 25[4], 26[4], 27[6]
47:2[5], 3, 4[2], 6, 7
48:1[2], 2, 3, 6, 7[3], 8[3], 9, 10, 11[3], 12[2], 13, 14, 15[2], 16, 17[2], 18[2], 19[3], 20, 21[3], 22[3], 23[3], 24[3], 25, 26, 28[2], 29[3], 31, 32, 33[4], 34, 35, 36, 37[2], 38, 39, 40, 41[2], 42, 43[2], 44, 45[3], 46
49:1, 2[2], 3[4], 5[2], 6, 10[4], 11, 12, 13[2], 14[3], 15, 16, 17, 18[2], 19[3], 20, 22[3], 23, 24[3], 26, 27[2], 28[2], 29[4], 30, 32[4], 33[2], 36[3], 37[3], 38[3]
50:1, 2[3], 3[2], 4[4], 5, 7, 8[2], 9[2], 10, 11, 12, 13, 16[2], 17, 18, 19[5], 20[4], 21[3], 22, 23, 24[3], 25, 26, 28, 30, 32[5], 33[2], 34, 35[3], 36[2], 37[4], 38[2], 39[2], 40[2], 41[2], 42[3], 43[2], 44[3], 45, 46
51:1, 2[2], 3[2], 4, 6, 8, 9[2], 10, 12, 13, 14, 15, 16[2], 17, 19, 20[2], 21[4], 22[5], 23[5], 24[2], 25[3], 26, 27, 28[2], 29[2], 31, 32[3], 33, 35[2], 36[3], 37[2], 39[3], 41, 43, 44[3], 45, 46[4], 47[2], 48[2], 50, 52, 53, 54, 55, 56, 57[6], 58[4], 59, 61[3], 63[2], 64[3]
52:1[3], 2, 3, 4[4], 6, 7[3], 8[2], 9, 10, 11[3], 13[4], 14, 15[3], 16, 17[3], 18[5], 19[8], 20, 21[3], 22[4], 23[3], 24[3], 25[3], 26, 27[2], 28[2], 29, 30[3], 31[4], 32[2], 33[2], 34

LAMENTATIONS

1:1, 2, 3, 4, 6[2], 7[3], 8, 11, 12, 13[2], 14, 17, 18[2], 19, 21, 22[2]

LAMENTATIONS

2:1[2], 2[2], 3, 4, 5[2], 6[4], 8, 9[2], 10, 11, 12, 14[3], 15, 16, 17[2], 18, 20[3], 21[3], 22
3:2, 4, 5[2], 8, 10, 11, 12, 14, 17, 18[2], 19[2], 20, 26, 28, 37, 38, 40[2], 42, 43, 45, 47[2], 49, 50, 53, 60, 61, 62, 63, 66
4:4, 6, 11[2], 12[2], 13, 15, 21[2]
5:1, 3, 5, 6, 7[2], 11, 13, 20, 21

EZEKIEL

1:1, 3, 4[5], 5, 6[2], 7[3], 8[3], 10[2], 11[2], 12[2], 13[4], 14[2], 16[4], 17, 18, 19[2], 20, 21[2], 22, 23[2], 24, 25[2], 26[2], 27[3], 28[2]
2:1[2], 2[2], 3[2], 4[2], 5, 6[3], 7, 8, 9[2], 10[6]
3:1, 2, 3[3], 4[2], 5, 6, 7, 8, 10, 11[3], 12, 13[2], 14[2], 15[2], 16, 17, 18, 19, 20[3], 21, 22[3], 23[3], 24[3], 25[2], 26[2], 27[2]
4:1[2], 2[4], 3[5], 4, 5, 6[2], 7[2], 8[2], 9[8], 10, 12[2], 13, 15, 16[4], 17[3]
5:1[4], 2[4], 3, 4[2], 5, 6[3], 7, 8, 9[2], 10[3], 11, 12[4], 13[3], 14, 15[4], 16[3], 17[5]
6:1, 2, 3[4], 4[3], 5[2], 6[6], 7[2], 9[3], 10[2], 11[3], 12[3], 13[2], 14[2]
7:3[3], 4[3], 7, 8[3], 9[3], 15[4], 16, 17, 18[3], 19[2], 20, 21[3], 22[2], 23, 24[2], 25[2], 26[2], 27[4]
8:1[2], 2[2], 3[5], 4, 5, 6, 7[2], 8, 9[2], 10[4], 11[3], 13, 14, 15, 16[6], 17[2], 18
9:2[5], 3[2], 4[3], 5[2], 6[4], 7[4], 8[4], 9[4], 10, 11
10:1, 2[5], 3, 4[3], 5, 6[2], 7[4], 8, 9[3], 10, 12[5], 14[4], 15, 16[2], 17, 18, 19[4], 20, 21[2], 22[2]
11:1[4], 2, 3, 5[2], 6, 7, 8, 9[3], 10, 12, 13[3], 15, 16, 17[2], 18[3], 19[4], 20[4], 21, 22[2], 23[2], 24
12:2[2], 3[2], 4, 5, 6, 7[3], 8, 10, 11, 12[2], 13[2], 14[3], 15[2], 16[2], 18[2], 19[3], 20[3], 21, 22, 23[2], 25[2], 27
13:1, 2, 3, 6[3], 7, 8, 9[3], 10[3], 11[2], 13[2], 14[4], 15[2], 16[2], 17, 18[3], 19[3], 20[2], 21[3], 22, 23
14:1, 2, 3, 4[3], 6[2], 7[3], 8[5], 9[3], 10, 11, 13[4], 14, 15, 17[2], 19[2], 20, 21[4], 22[4], 23[3]
15:1, 4, 5, 7[3], 8
16:3[3], 4, 6[2], 7[5], 8[5], 9, 10[3], 11[2], 12[3], 13[8], 14, 15[2], 16[3], 17[3], 18[4], 19[3], 20[2], 21, 22[4], 23, 24, 25[3], 26, 27[2], 28, 29, 31[2], 33, 34[3], 36[3], 37[2], 38[4], 39[6], 40[2], 41[4], 42[3], 43, 45[4], 46[4], 48, 49[3], 50[2], 51, 52, 53[3], 54, 55[4], 57, 58, 60, 61[3], 62[2], 63[2]
17:1, 2, 3[2], 4, 5[2], 6[5], 7[3], 8, 9, 12[3], 13[3], 15[2], 16, 17[2], 18, 19, 20[4], 21[3], 22[3], 23[4], 24[3]
18:2, 5[2], 6, 7[2], 8, 9, 10, 11[2], 12[2], 13, 14[2], 16, 18, 19[3], 20, 21[3], 23[2], 24[3], 26[2], 27[2], 28, 30, 31[2], 32
19:2, 3[2], 4, 5[2], 6[4], 7[4], 8, 9[2], 10, 11[3], 12[2], 13[2], 14[2]
20:1[2], 3, 5[3], 6, 7, 8, 10, 11[2], 12, 13[2], 15, 16, 19[2], 20[3], 22, 23, 24[2], 25, 26, 27, 28[4], 29, 30, 31, 32[2], 33[2], 34[4], 35[2], 37[2], 38[4], 39[2], 40[2], 41[2], 42, 43[3], 44, 46[2], 47[4], 48
21:1, 2[2], 3[4], 4, 6, 7[6], 9[2], 11[2], 12, 13, 14[2], 15, 17, 19, 20, 22, 23, 25, 26[2], 27[2], 28[3], 31[3]
22:3, 4[4], 5[2], 7[2], 8, 9, 11[3], 12[3], 13, 14, 15[3], 16[2], 17, 18[3], 20[7], 21[2], 22, 23, 25, 26[5], 27, 28[2], 29[3], 30[2]
23:3[2], 4[6], 5[2], 6, 7, 8[2], 10[3], 11[2], 12, 14, 16[2], 17[4], 18, 20, 22, 23[6], 24[7], 25[6], 26, 27, 29[6], 30, 32[2], 33[2], 34[3], 35[2], 36, 37[3], 38, 39, 40[3], 41[3], 42[3], 43, 44, 45[3], 46[2], 47[4], 49[3]
24:3[3], 4, 5[3], 6, 10[2], 11[2], 12, 13, 14[2], 17[3], 18[2], 19, 21[3], 22, 23[3], 24, 25[2], 27[4]
25:2, 3[3], 4[3], 5[3], 6[2], 7[4], 8, 9, 10, 11[2], 12[2], 13[4], 14[4], 15, 16[2], 17[2]
26:1, 3, 4[3], 5, 6[2], 7[4], 8[3], 9[2], 10[2], 11, 12[7], 13[2], 14, 16[4], 17[3], 19, 20[2], 21
27:3, 7, 8, 9, 10[3], 11, 12, 13[2], 14[2], 15, 16[4], 17[5], 18, 19[3], 21[3], 22[3], 23[3], 24[3], 25[2], 27[5], 29[2], 30[3], 31[4], 32[2], 33, 34, 35, 36
28:2[2], 4[3], 5[2], 7[2], 8, 9, 12[2], 13[5], 14[2], 16[2], 18, 19, 21, 22[4], 23[3], 24[2], 25, 26[4]
29:2[2], 3[2], 4[3], 5[3], 6, 7[3], 8[2], 9[4], 10[3], 12[4], 14[3], 16, 17[2], 18, 19[4], 21[2]
30:2, 4[4], 5[5], 6, 7[2], 8[2], 9, 11[3], 12[4], 13[3], 14[3], 15[2], 16[3], 17[2], 18[2], 19, 20, 21, 22[3], 23[2], 24[3], 25[3], 26[3]
31:1, 2, 3[3], 4, 5[2], 6[2], 8, 10[2], 12[6], 13, 15[4], 16[2], 17, 18[2]
32:1, 2[5], 3, 4[2], 5[2], 6, 7[3], 8, 10[2], 12[2], 14, 15, 16, 18[2], 19, 20, 22, 23, 24, 26, 27[2], 28, 29[2], 30[3], 31[2], 32[2]
33:2[2], 3, 4[2], 5, 6[3], 7, 10[2], 11, 13, 14[2], 16, 18, 19[2], 21, 22[3], 24, 25[3], 26[2], 27[3], 28[2], 30[3], 31[3], 32[2], 33
34:1, 2, 3, 4, 5[2], 6[2], 8[2], 10[2], 11, 12[2], 13[5], 14[2], 15, 16[4], 17[3], 18, 19[2], 20, 21[2], 22[3], 23[3], 24[2], 25[4], 26[3], 27[5], 28[2], 29[2], 30, 31[2]

EZEKIEL

35:2, 3[3], 4[2], 5, 6, 7[2], 8[3], 9[2], 10[2], 11[2], 12[2], 13, 15[2]

36:1, 3[4], 4[4], 5, 6[4], 8, 9[3], 10[3], 11[7], 12[3], 13, 17, 18, 19[3], 20[2], 23[2], 24[2], 25[2], 26[3], 27[4], 28[3], 29[3], 30[2], 31[3], 32, 33, 34, 35[5], 36[2], 38

37:1[2], 2[3], 3[2], 4, 5, 6[6], 7[3], 8[3], 9[2], 10[3], 11, 12[3], 13[2], 14[4], 16[4], 17[2], 18, 19[4], 20, 21[3], 22[3], 23[2], 24[4], 25[5], 26[3], 27, 28

38:1, 2[2], 3[2], 4[6], 5[2], 6[3], 7[3], 8[2], 9[3], 10, 11[2], 12[3], 13[4], 14, 15[3], 16[2], 18, 19, 20[7], 21, 22[8], 23[3]

39:1[2], 2[4], 3[2], 4[3], 6[3], 7[2], 8, 9[8], 10[2], 11[5], 12, 13, 14, 15, 16, 17[4], 18[2], 19[2], 20[2], 21[3], 22, 23[2], 24[2], 25[2], 26[2], 27[2], 28

40:1[2], 2, 3[4], 4[3], 5[4], 6[3], 7[4], 9[2], 10[4], 11[2], 12[3], 13, 15, 16[5], 17[2], 18, 19, 20[2], 21[6], 22[5], 23[3], 24[3], 25[4], 26[4], 27[2], 28[2], 29[7], 30[3], 31[3], 32[2], 33[7], 34[4], 35[2], 36[4], 37[4], 38[2], 39[4], 40[2], 41, 42[6], 43[2], 44[2], 45, 46, 47[2], 48[5], 49[4]

41:1[2], 2[5], 3[3], 4[2], 5, 6[3], 7[3], 9, 10, 11[3], 12[2], 13[2], 14, 15[4], 16[4], 17[3], 18[4], 19, 20[2], 21, 22[5], 23[2], 24[2], 25[3], 26[5]

42:1[2], 2, 3, 4[2], 5, 6, 7, 8, 9, 10, 11[4], 12, 13[4], 14[2], 15, 19, 20[2]

43:2[3], 3[3], 4, 5[2], 6[2], 7[3], 8[3], 9[2], 10, 11[11], 13[5], 14[4], 15[2], 16, 17[5], 18[2], 19, 20[5], 21, 22[2], 23, 24[3], 25, 26[2], 27[4]

44:1, 2, 3, 4[3], 5[5], 6, 7[3], 8, 10, 11[3], 12[2], 13[2], 14, 15[2], 16[2], 17[3], 18, 19[4], 23[4], 24[5], 25, 26, 27, 28[2], 29[3], 30[2]

45:1[2], 2, 3[5], 4[2], 5[3], 6[3], 7[6], 8[2], 9[3], 10[2], 11[2], 12[2], 13, 15[3], 17[8], 18, 19[4], 20[2], 22[2], 23[3], 24[3], 25[2]

46:1, 2[5], 3, 4[2], 5[3], 6[3], 7[4], 8[2], 9, 10[2], 11[5], 12[3], 14[2], 15[2], 19, 20, 21[2], 22, 23[2]

47:1[2], 2[2], 3[2], 4[2], 5, 6[2], 7, 8[2], 9[3], 10, 11, 12[4], 14[2], 15, 16, 17[4], 18[5], 19[2], 22[3], 23

48:1, 2, 3, 4, 5, 6, 7, 8[4], 9[2], 10[7], 12, 13[5], 14, 15[4], 16[8], 17[8], 18[4], 19, 20[2], 21[8], 22[2], 24, 25, 26, 27, 28[2], 29, 30[2], 31, 32[4], 33[3], 34, 35

DANIEL

1:1, 2[2], 3[3], 4[6], 5[2], 6, 7[3], 9, 10[2], 11, 12[2], 13[2], 14, 15[2], 16[2], 17[4], 19[3], 20[3], 21

2:1[2], 2[4], 3[2], 4, 5[2], 6[4], 7[2], 8, 9[2], 10, 11[2], 12[2], 13[3], 14, 15, 16[2], 17[2], 18, 20[3], 21[4], 22[2], 23[3], 24[2], 25, 26[2], 27, 28[2], 29, 30, 31[2], 32[2], 33, 34[2], 35[5], 36, 37[2], 38[3], 39[2], 40[4], 41[3], 42[3], 43, 44[4], 45[4], 46[3], 47[3], 48[3], 49[2]

3:1, 2[2], 3[3], 4, 5[2], 6[2], 7[3], 8, 9, 10[3], 11[2], 12, 13[2], 14[2], 15[4], 16[2], 17, 19[3], 20[3], 21[3], 22[2], 23[2], 24[4], 25[3], 26[5], 27[3], 28[5], 29[3], 30

4:1, 2, 3[2], 4, 5[2], 7[2], 8[2], 9[2], 10[2], 11[3], 12[4], 13[2], 14[4], 15[3], 16[2], 17[3], 19[4], 20[2], 21[3], 22[3], 23[7], 24, 25[5], 26, 27[2], 30[2], 32[4], 33[4], 34[6], 35[4], 36[6], 37[4]

5:1, 2[3], 3[2], 4[2], 5[2], 6[2], 7[6], 9[2], 10[3], 11[4], 12[5], 13[2], 14[3], 15[2], 16[5], 17[3], 18[3], 19[6], 20[2], 21[5], 22, 23[9], 24, 25, 26, 27, 28[2], 29[3], 31[2]

6:1, 2[2], 3[2], 4, 6[2], 7[3], 8[2], 9, 10[3], 11[2], 12[3], 13, 14[2], 15[2], 16[3], 17[4], 18[2], 19, 20[3], 22[2], 23[2], 24[6], 25, 26[4], 27[4], 28

7:1[2], 2[2], 3, 4[4], 5[4], 6[2], 7[8], 8[3], 9[3], 10[3], 11[2], 12, 13[3], 14[5], 15, 16[2], 18[2], 19[2], 20[4], 21[2], 22[2], 23[3], 24[4], 25[7], 26[2], 27[5], 28

8:2[4], 3[4], 4[3], 5[3], 6[2], 7[7], 8[2], 9[3], 10[4], 11[2], 12[4], 13[3], 14[2], 15[2], 16[2], 17[2], 18, 19, 20, 21[2], 23[2], 24[6], 25[3], 26[2], 27[4]

9:3[4], 4[6], 5[4], 6[2], 7[3], 8, 9, 11, 12[2], 13, 14, 15[2], 16[3], 17[2], 18[3], 19[2], 20[5], 22[4], 23[2], 24[7], 25[5], 26[6], 27[5]

10:1[3], 4[2], 5[2], 6[5], 7, 8[3], 9[2], 10[2], 11[3], 12[2], 13[2], 15[2], 16[4], 18[2], 19[3], 20[2], 21

11:1, 2[3], 3[2], 4[3], 5[4], 6[4], 7[3], 8[4], 9, 10[5], 11[4], 12[2], 13[3], 14, 15[3], 16[2], 17[2], 18, 19[2], 21[2], 22[2], 23[2], 24[4], 25[4], 26[2], 27[2], 28[3], 29, 30[3], 31[4], 32[2], 33[3], 35[3], 36[5], 38[4], 39[3], 40[7], 41[3], 42, 43[4], 44[2], 45[2]

12:1[3], 2[3], 3[3], 4[3], 5[2], 6, 7[5], 8, 9[2], 10[3], 11[3], 12[3], 13

HOSEA

1:1[2], 2[2], 3[2], 4[3], 5, 6[3], 7[2], 8, 9, 10, 11[3]

2:1, 2, 3[4], 4, 5[3], 6, 7[3], 8[4], 9[4], 10[2], 11[2], 12[4], 13[5], 14[2], 15[4], 16[2], 17, 18[7], 19[4], 20, 21[2], 22[4], 23[4]

3:1, 2[2], 3[2], 4[5], 5[4]

4:2[5], 3[2], 5[2], 8, 9[3], 10[2], 11[2], 12[2], 13[4], 14, 15, 19

5:1[3], 2, 3[2], 4, 5[2], 6, 8, 11, 12, 13[2], 14[3], 15[2]

6:1[3], 2, 3[2], 4, 5, 6[2], 8, 9

7:1[3], 2, 3, 7, 9[2], 10[2], 14[3], 15

8:1, 4[2], 7, 10, 13[2], 14[3]

9:2[2], 3, 5, 7, 8, 10[2], 11[2], 14, 17

10:5, 6, 8[3], 10, 11[3], 12, 14

11:1, 2, 4[2], 6[3], 7, 9[2], 11[2], 12[2]

HOSEA

12:1[4], 2, 3, 4[3], 6[2], 8, 9, 10[2], 12[3], 13[2], 14

13:2[4], 3[2], 4, 6, 8[2], 10[2], 11, 15[2], 16

14:2[2], 5, 6[2], 7, 8, 9[3]

JOEL

1:2, 3[2], 4[2], 5[2], 6[2], 7[2], 9, 11, 12[2], 13[2], 14[2], 15, 16, 19, 20

2:1, 2[3], 3[3], 4, 7[2], 8, 9, 10[2], 11[3], 12[3], 13[6], 14[3], 16[2], 17[3], 18, 19[5], 20[5], 21, 22, 23[3], 24[3], 25[3], 26[4], 27[4], 28[3], 29[2], 30[4], 31[2], 32[3]

3:1[2], 2[4], 3[3], 4[5], 5[2], 6, 7, 8[3], 10, 11[2], 12, 15[2], 16[4], 17, 18[5], 19, 20

AMOS

1:1, 2[4], 3, 5[3], 6, 8[4], 9[2], 11[4], 13, 14, 15[2]

2:1, 2[3], 3[2], 4[3], 5, 6[2], 7[3], 8[2], 9[2], 10, 11[2], 12, 14, 15, 16

3:5, 6[2], 9[4], 10, 11[2], 12, 13, 14[2], 15[3]

4:1, 2, 3[2], 4[3], 5[3], 6[2], 7[4], 9[4], 10[2], 11[2], 12, 13[3]

5:3, 4, 5[2], 6[3], 7, 8[4], 10, 11, 12[2], 14[2], 15[2], 16[3], 17, 18, 19[3], 20[2], 21, 22, 24, 25, 26

6:1, 2[2], 3, 4[3], 5, 6, 7, 8, 9, 10[4], 11[2], 12, 14

7:1[2], 2, 4[3], 7, 8[2], 9[3], 11, 12[2], 13, 14[2], 15[2], 16, 17[5]

8:1, 2[2], 3, 5[3], 6[2], 8[4], 9[2], 10[6], 12[4], 13, 14[3]

9:1[4], 3[4], 4[4], 5[5], 6[2], 7[2], 8, 9, 11[3], 12, 13[3], 14[6], 15[2]

OBADIAH

1[2], 4, 7, 8, 9, 10, 11[2], 16[2], 17[2], 18[6], 19[5], 20[2], 21[2]

JONAH

1:2, 3[3], 4, 5[4], 6, 7[3], 8[2], 9[3], 10, 11, 12[2], 13, 14[2], 15[2], 16[2], 17[2]

2:2[3], 3[2], 7, 10[2]

3:1, 2, 3, 4[4], 5[2], 6[4], 7[3], 8[3], 9[2], 10[3]

4:1, 2[5], 5[3], 6[2], 7, 8[4], 9[2], 10, 11[3]

MICAH

1:1[2], 2[2], 3[2], 4[3], 5[2], 6[3], 7[4], 8[3], 16

2:1, 2[6], 4[2], 10, 11[2], 13[4]

3:1[2], 2[2], 3[4], 5[2], 6[3], 7, 8[3], 9[2], 10, 11[3], 12[2]

4:1[2], 2[7], 3[4], 4[2], 5[2], 6[2], 7[3], 8, 10[3], 11, 13[5]

5:4[3], 5[3], 6[3], 7, 8[3], 9, 10[2], 11[2], 12[2], 13[2], 14, 15[2]

6:1, 2[2], 3, 4[3], 5, 6, 8[3], 9[2], 10, 11, 12[2], 14[3], 15, 16[3]

7:2, 3[2], 4, 9[2], 10, 12[4], 14, 16, 17, 18, 19, 20

NAHUM

1:2[3], 3[4], 4[4], 5[3], 6[2], 7, 8, 10, 12, 13, 14[2]

2:2, 3, 5, 6, 7[2], 9, 10[6], 11[3], 12[3], 13[4]

3:1, 2[3], 3[4], 4, 5[3], 6[3], 7[2], 8, 9[3], 10[2], 14, 16, 17[2], 18

HABAKKUK

1:2[2], 3[4], 4, 5[2], 6, 7[2], 8[3], 9, 10[3], 11[2], 12, 13[2], 14, 15[2], 16[2], 17

2:1[3], 2[3], 3, 5[3], 6[3], 7[4], 8[4], 10, 11, 12, 13, 15, 16[2], 17[3], 18, 19[2]

3:2, 3[2], 4[2], 5, 6[3], 7, 8, 10[2], 11[2], 16, 17[2], 19[2]

ZEPHANIAH

1:3[4], 4[3], 5[4], 6[2], 8[3], 9, 10[3], 12[2], 13[2], 14, 15[4], 16[2], 17[3]

2:4[2], 6[3], 7[2], 8[2], 9[4], 10, 11, 13[4], 14[2], 15[2]

3:1, 4, 7, 11, 12[2], 13[2], 14, 16, 19[4], 20

HAGGAI

1:1, 4, 6[2], 8[4], 9[3], 10, 11[9], 12[3], 14[5], 15

2:1, 2[2], 3, 4[3], 6[4], 7[3], 8, 9, 10, 12[3], 13[2], 14[4], 15[2], 17[2], 18[2], 19[3], 20[2], 21, 22[6], 23

ZECHARIAH

1:3, 4, 5, 6[4], 7, 8[4], 9, 10[3], 11[5], 12[3], 13[2], 14, 15[2], 16, 17[2], 18[2], 19[3], 20, 21

2:1[2], 2[2], 3[2], 4[2], 5, 6, 9[2], 10[2], 11[4], 12[2]

3:1[2], 2, 3, 4[4], 5[3], 6, 7[3], 8, 9, 10

4:1[2], 2[5], 3[2], 4, 5[2], 6, 7, 9, 10[2], 11[2], 12[2], 13[3]

5:1[3], 2[3], 3, 4[5], 5[2], 6[2], 7[2], 8[3], 9[5], 11[3]

6:1[5], 2, 3[3], 4, 5[2], 6[2], 7[6], 8, 9, 10[3], 11[3], 12[3], 13[5], 14[4], 15[4]

7:1, 2[2], 3[2], 5[3], 6[3], 7[3], 8, 9[2], 10[2], 11[2], 12, 13[2]

8:2, 3[3], 4[2], 5[2], 7, 8[5], 12[3], 13[3], 14, 15, 16, 17[2], 18, 19[6], 20, 21[2], 22[2]

9:1, 2[2], 3[3], 4[2], 5[5], 6[2], 7[4], 8[3], 9[3], 10[6], 13[2], 14[4], 15[6], 16, 17[2]

10:1, 2[2], 3[2], 5[3], 6[5], 7[3], 8[2], 9[4], 10[4], 11[5], 12[3]

11:5[3], 6[3], 7[4], 8[2], 9[2], 10[2], 11[2], 12[2], 13[3], 14, 15, 16, 17[2]

12:1[2], 2, 3, 4[3], 5, 6[4], 7, 8[2], 9, 10[6], 12[3], 13[2], 14

13:1[2], 2[4], 3[4], 4, 6, 7[3], 8[2], 9[5]

ZECHARIAH

14:1, 2[5], 3, 4[6], 5[3], 6, 8[3], 9[2], 10[3], 11[2], 12[3], 13[3], 14[4], 15[3], 16[2], 17, 18[2], 19, 20, 21[5]

MALACHI

1:3[3], 4[3], 5[2], 6[3], 7, 8[3], 9, 11[2], 12, 13[4], 14[3]

2:1, 2[2], 3[2], 4, 5[3], 6[3], 7, 9, 11[3], 12[2], 13[2], 14[2], 15[3], 17

3:1[2], 2[2], 3[5], 4[2], 5[8], 7[2], 8, 10[2], 11[2], 12, 14[2], 15, 16[4], 17[2], 18[3]

4:1[3], 2[2], 3, 4, 5, 6[3]

MATTHEW

1:2[3], 3[4], 4[3], 5[3], 6[2], 7[3], 8[3], 9[3], 10[3], 11[2], 12[2], 13[3], 14[3], 15[3], 16, 17[2], 19, 21[2], 23[2], 24, 25[2]

2:2, 3, 4[2], 5, 6, 8[5], 9[2], 11[6], 12, 13[5], 14[2], 15, 16[4], 18[3], 20[3], 21[4], 23[2]

3:2, 4[4], 5[2], 6, 7, 9, 10[2], 11, 12[2], 14, 15, 16[4], 17

4:2[2], 3, 4, 5, 6[2], 8[2], 9[2], 10, 11[2], 13[3], 15, 16[2], 17, 18[2], 19[2], 20[2], 21[3], 22[3], 23[4], 24[7], 25[5]

5:1[2], 2[2], 6, 11[2], 12, 13, 15[2], 16, 18, 19[2], 20, 21, 22, 23, 24[3], 25[2], 29[3], 30[3], 32, 38, 40[2], 41, 42, 43, 44[2], 45[3], 47

6:2, 4, 5[2], 6[2], 12, 13[3], 17, 18, 19[3], 20, 24[3], 25, 28, 29, 30, 33[2]

7:2, 3, 4, 5, 6[2], 7[3], 8[2], 12, 13[2], 14[2], 19, 22[2], 23, 24, 25[5], 26[2], 27[6], 28, 29

8:2[2], 3[3], 4[2], 5, 6, 7[2], 8[2], 9[6], 10, 11[5], 12, 13[3], 14[2], 15[4], 16[2], 17, 19[2], 20[2], 21[2], 22, 23, 24, 25[2], 26[4], 27, 28, 29, 30, 32[4], 33[4], 34[2]

9:1[3], 2[2], 3, 4, 5, 6, 7[2], 8, 9[4], 10[4], 11[2], 13[2], 14, 15[2], 16, 17[3], 18[3], 19[3], 20[2], 22[2], 23[3], 24, 25[2], 26, 27[2], 28[2], 30[2], 33[2], 35[5], 36

10:1[3], 2[2], 3[3], 4, 5[2], 7, 11[2], 12, 13, 14, 15, 16, 17, 18[3], 21[4], 22, 25, 26, 27, 28[2], 29, 35[2], 36, 37, 38[2], 39, 40, 41, 42

11:1[2], 3, 4[3], 5[3], 6, 7, 9, 12[2], 13, 14, 16, 17[3], 18, 19[4], 21[2], 22, 23, 25[4], 27[2], 28[2], 29[3], 30

12:1[3], 3, 4, 5, 7, 9, 10[2], 11[3], 13[2], 14, 15[2], 16, 18, 20, 21, 22[4], 23[2], 25[3], 26, 27, 29[2], 30, 31, 32, 33[2], 35, 37, 38, 39[3], 40[2], 41[2], 42[2], 43, 44[2], 45[4], 46, 47, 48[2], 49[3], 50[2]

13:1, 2[3], 3, 4[3], 5, 6[2], 7[3], 8, 10[2], 11, 12, 13, 14[4], 15[6], 16, 17[4], 19[2], 20, 21, 22[3], 23[2], 25[2], 26, 27, 28, 30[2], 31, 32[2], 33, 34, 36[2], 37, 39, 40, 41[2], 42[2], 44[3], 46[2], 47, 48[2], 49, 50[2], 52, 53, 54[3], 55[4], 56, 57[2], 58

14:2[2], 3[2], 5, 6, 8, 9[2], 10[2], 11[3], 12[5], 13, 14[4], 15[3], 17[2], 19[7], 20[3], 21[2], 22[2], 23[2], 25, 26[2], 28[2], 29[2], 30, 31[3], 32, 33, 34, 35[2], 36[2]

15:1, 3, 4[2], 6, 8, 10[3], 12, 13, 14, 15, 16, 17, 18, 21[2], 22[2], 23[2], 24, 25, 26[2], 27, 28[2], 29[4], 30[4], 31[2], 32[3], 33, 34[3], 35, 36[6], 37[3], 38[2], 39[3]

16:1, 2, 3[2], 4[4], 5, 6[2], 7, 9, 10, 11, 13, 14[3], 16[2], 17[3], 18[3], 19[3], 21[5], 22, 23, 24[2], 25, 26, 27

17:1[3], 2[3], 3[2], 4[3], 5, 6[2], 7[4], 8, 9, 10, 11[3], 12, 14[2], 15[2], 16[2], 17[2], 18[3], 19, 20[3], 21, 22, 23[3], 24[2], 25, 27[5]

18:2[2], 3[2], 5, 6, 8, 9[2], 12[4], 13[2], 15[2], 17[2], 18, 21[2], 24, 25[4], 26[2], 27[2], 28[3], 29[3], 30[2], 31[2], 34[2]

19:1[2], 2[2], 3, 4[3], 5[4], 7, 9[3], 12[2], 13[2], 14, 15[2], 16[2], 17, 19[2], 21[5], 24, 26, 27[2], 28, 29[2], 30

20:2, 3[2], 4[3], 5[2], 6[3], 7, 8, 9, 10, 11, 12[2], 13, 14, 16, 17[2], 18[3], 19[4], 20, 21[2], 22[2], 23[3], 24, 25[2], 27, 28, 29, 30, 31, 32[3], 34[3]

21:1[2], 2[3], 3[2], 5[2], 6[2], 7[4], 8[2], 9[2], 10, 11, 12[5], 13, 14[3], 15[4], 16[3], 17[3], 19[4], 20, 21[3], 22, 23[4], 24[2], 25, 27[3], 28[2], 29[2], 30[5], 31, 32[3], 33[5], 34, 35[4], 36, 38, 39[3], 41, 42, 43, 44, 45[2]

22:1[3], 3[2], 4[2], 5, 6[3], 7[3], 9, 10[3], 11, 12[2], 13[4], 15, 16[2], 18, 19, 20[2], 21, 22[2], 23, 24, 25[2], 26, 27, 29, 32[2], 33, 35, 37[2], 38, 39, 40, 46

23:1, 2, 3[2], 4[2], 5, 6[2], 7[2], 8, 9, 12[2], 13, 14[2], 15[3], 17, 18, 19, 20, 21[2], 22[2], 23[6], 24, 25[3], 26, 27[2], 28, 29[2], 30, 34[6], 35, 37[2]

24:1[3], 2, 3[3], 4[2], 5, 6[2], 7[4], 9[2], 10[3], 11[2], 12, 14[2], 19[2], 22, 24[3], 27, 29[3], 30[4], 31[2], 32, 35, 36, 38[2], 39[2], 40, 41, 43, 45, 48, 49[3], 50, 51[3]

25:1, 2[2], 3, 5, 6, 7, 8, 9[2], 10[3], 12, 14, 15[3], 16[2], 17, 18[2], 19, 20[2], 21, 22, 23, 24[2], 25[3], 26[3], 27, 28, 29, 30[2], 31, 32[2], 33, 35[3], 36[3], 37[2], 38[2], 39, 40[2], 41, 42[2], 43[4], 44, 46

26:1, 2, 3[2], 4[2], 7, 9, 15[3], 16, 18[2], 19[2], 21, 22[2], 23[2], 25, 26[5], 27[3], 30, 31, 33, 36[2], 37[4], 38, 39[3], 40[3], 41, 42, 43[2], 44[3], 45[3], 47[4], 49[3], 50[3], 51[4], 53, 55[2], 56, 57[2], 58[2], 59[2], 61[2], 62[2], 63[2], 64, 66, 67[2], 69, 71[2], 72, 73[2], 74[2], 75[3]

27:1, 2[2], 3[2], 4, 5[4], 6[2], 7[2], 9, 10, 11[3], 12[2], 14, 16, 20[2], 21, 23, 24, 25[2], 26, 27, 28[2], 29[4], 30[3], 31[3], 32, 33, 34, 35[3], 36, 37, 38, 39, 40[2], 41, 42, 46, 48[5], 51[3], 52[2], 53[3], 54[2], 55, 56[3], 58, 59, 60[3], 61[2], 62, 64[2], 66[2]

28:1, 2[4], 3, 4[2], 5[2], 7[3], 8[3], 9[4], 10, 11, 12[2], 13, 14[2], 15[2], 17, 18[3], 19[3], 20

MARK

1:4, 5[3], 6[4], 7[2], 9[2], 10[2], 11, 12, 13[3], 15[3], 16, 17[2], 18[2], 19[2], 20[3], 21[3], 22[2], 23[2], 25[2], 26[2], 27[2], 28, 29[2], 30, 31[5], 32[2], 33, 34[3], 35[3], 36[2], 37, 38, 39[2], 40[3], 41[3], 42[2], 43[2], 44[2], 45[3]

2:1[2], 2[2], 3, 4[2], 6, 8, 9[2], 11[2], 12[3], 13[3], 14[4], 15[4], 16[5], 18[5], 19, 20, 21, 22[3], 23[2], 24, 25[3], 26[2], 27[2]

3:1[2], 2, 3, 4, 5[3], 6[2], 7[2], 8[5], 9, 11[2], 12, 13[3], 14[2], 15[2], 16, 17[3], 18[8], 19[2], 20, 21, 22[2], 23[2], 24, 25, 26[2], 27[2], 28, 31[2], 32[3], 33, 34[3], 35[2]

4:1[4], 2[2], 4[3], 5[2], 6, 7[4], 8[6], 9, 10, 11, 12[4], 13[2], 15[2], 16, 17[2], 18, 19[4], 20[4], 21[2], 24[2], 25, 26, 27[5], 30, 32[2], 33, 34, 35, 36[2], 37[2], 38[3], 39[5], 40, 41[3]

5:1, 2, 3, 4[3], 5[4], 6, 7[2], 9[2], 10, 12, 13[5], 14[4], 15[6], 16[2], 17, 18, 19[2], 20[3], 21[2], 22[2], 23[3], 24[3], 25, 26[3], 27, 29[2], 30[2], 31[2], 32, 33[3], 34[2], 37[3], 38[4], 39[2], 40[4], 41[2], 42[3], 43[2]

6:1[3], 2[3], 3[5], 4[2], 5[2], 6[2], 7[4], 8, 9, 10, 11[2], 12[2], 13[3], 14[3], 15, 17[2], 19, 20[4], 21[2], 22[5], 23, 24[3], 25[3], 26[2], 27[4], 28[3], 29[3], 30[3], 31[4], 32, 33[5], 34[3], 35[3], 36[2], 37[4], 38[3], 39, 40[2], 41[6], 42[2], 43[2], 44, 45[2], 46, 47[2], 48[3], 49, 50[3], 51[4], 53[2], 54, 55[2], 56[3]

7:1, 2, 3, 4[4], 5, 6, 8[2], 9, 10[2], 12, 13, 14[2], 17, 18, 19, 20, 23, 24[5], 25[2], 26, 27, 28[2], 29, 30[2], 31[2], 32[3], 33[4], 34[2], 35[3], 36, 37[2]

8:1[2], 2, 3, 4, 5[2], 6[6], 7[3], 8[2], 9[2], 10[2], 11[2], 12[2], 13[2], 15[2], 16, 17, 18[2], 20[2], 21, 22[3], 23[4], 24[2], 25[3], 26, 27[3], 28[2], 29[3], 30, 31[6], 32[3], 33, 34[3], 35, 36, 38[2]

9:1, 2[5], 3, 4[2], 5[5], 7[2], 8, 9, 10, 11, 12[5], 13, 14[2], 15[2], 16, 17[2], 18[6], 19, 20[4], 21[2], 22[3], 24[2], 25[2], 26[4], 27[2], 28, 29[2], 30[3], 31[3], 32, 33[2], 35[4], 36[3], 37, 38[3], 42[2], 43, 44, 45, 46, 47, 48, 49, 50

10:1[4], 2[2], 3[2], 4[2], 5[2], 6, 7[2], 8, 10, 11[2], 12[2], 13[2], 14[2], 16[2], 17[3], 18, 19, 20[2], 21[5], 22[2], 23[2], 24[2], 26, 27, 28, 29[3], 30[6], 31, 32[6], 33[4], 34[5], 35[2], 36, 37, 38, 39[3], 40, 41[2], 42[2], 44, 45, 46[3], 47[2], 48, 49[3], 50[2], 51[2], 52[3]

11:1[2], 2[3], 3[2], 4[3], 5, 6[2], 7[3], 8[3], 9[2], 11[4], 12, 13[2], 14[3], 15[6], 16, 17, 18[3], 19, 20, 21, 22, 23[2], 24, 25, 27[4], 28[2], 29[4], 31, 33[3]

12:1[6], 2, 3[3], 4[4], 5[4], 7, 8[3], 9[2], 10, 11, 12[3], 13[2], 14[2], 16[4], 17[3], 18, 19[3], 20[2], 21[3], 22[2], 24, 26[3], 28[3], 29, 30[4], 31, 32[2], 33[6], 34[2], 35[2], 37[4], 38[4], 39[6], 40, 41[3], 42[2], 43[2]

13:1[2], 2, 3[4], 4, 5, 6, 7[2], 8[4], 9[3], 10, 11, 12[3], 13, 15, 16, 17, 18, 20, 21, 22[3], 24, 25[2], 26[2], 27[2], 28, 31, 32, 33, 34[3], 37

14:1[4], 3[3], 4[2], 5[2], 6, 7, 10, 11[3], 12[2], 13[3], 14, 15[2], 16[4], 17, 18[2], 19[3], 20[2], 22[5], 23[3], 24, 26, 27[2], 30, 32[2], 33[5], 34[2], 35[3], 36, 37[3], 38, 39[3], 40, 41[3], 43[5], 44[2], 45[3], 46[2], 47[3], 48[3], 49, 50[2], 51[2], 52[2], 53[4], 54[3], 55[3], 57[2], 58, 60[2], 61[2], 62[3], 63, 64, 65[5], 66, 67[3], 68[2], 69[2], 70[3], 71, 72[3]

15:1[6], 2[2], 3, 4, 7, 8, 12[2], 13, 14, 15[2], 16[2], 17[3], 18, 19[3], 20[3], 21[2], 22, 23, 24, 25[2], 26, 27[2], 28[2], 29[3], 30, 32[2], 33, 34, 35, 36[4], 37[2], 38, 39[2], 40[3], 41[2], 42, 43[2], 44[2], 45, 46[5], 47[2]

16:1[4], 2, 3, 4, 5[2], 6, 7, 8[3], 10[3], 11[2], 12, 13[2], 14[2], 15[2], 16, 17, 18[2], 19, 20[3]

LUKE

1:2, 5[2], 6[2], 7[2], 8, 10, 11, 12[2], 13[2], 14[3], 15[2], 16, 17[3], 18[2], 19[3], 20[2], 21[2], 22[3], 23, 24[2], 26, 27, 28[2], 29[2], 30, 31[3], 32[2], 33[2], 35[3], 36[2], 38[2], 39[2], 40[2], 41[2], 42[3], 43, 45, 46, 47, 49, 50, 52, 53, 55, 56[2], 57, 58[3], 59[2], 60[2], 61, 62, 63[3], 64[4], 65[2], 66[2], 67[2], 68, 69, 71, 72, 75, 76, 79, 80[3]

2:1, 2, 3, 4[2], 6, 7[3], 8, 9[3], 10, 12, 13[2], 14, 15[2], 16[4], 17, 18, 19, 20[3], 21, 22, 24, 25[4], 26, 27[2], 28[2], 32, 33[2], 34[4], 36[2], 37[4], 38[2], 39, 40[3], 42, 43[3], 44[2], 45, 46[2], 47[2], 48[3], 49, 50, 51[3], 52[4]

3:1[4], 2, 3, 5[4], 6, 8, 9[2], 10, 11[2], 12, 13, 14[4], 15[2], 16, 17[2], 18, 19, 21, 22[2], 23

4:1[2], 2[2], 3, 4, 5, 6[3], 8[3], 9[3], 11, 12, 13, 14[2], 15, 16[3], 17[2], 18, 20[4], 21, 22[3], 23, 24, 25, 27[2], 28, 29[3], 31[2], 32, 33[2], 35[4], 36[4], 37, 38[4], 39[5], 40[2], 41[3], 42[5], 43, 44

5:1, 2[2], 3[4], 4, 5[2], 6[2], 7[4], 9, 10[3], 11[2], 12[2], 13[3], 14[3], 15[2], 16[2], 17[5], 18[3], 19[2], 20, 21[2], 23, 24[2], 25[3], 26[3], 27[3], 28[2], 29[3], 30[3], 31, 33[4], 34, 35, 36[2], 37[3], 38

6:1[3], 2, 3[2], 4[3], 5, 6[3], 7[2], 8[4], 10[3], 11[2], 12[2], 13[2], 14[3], 15[2], 16[2], 17[8], 18[2], 19[2], 20[2], 22[3], 23, 25, 28, 29[2], 30, 31, 33, 34, 35[5], 37[3], 38[3], 39, 41, 42, 45, 46[2], 47[2], 48[4], 49[3]

7:2[2], 3[2], 4, 5, 6, 7, 8[6], 9[2], 10, 11[3], 12[2], 13[2], 14[4], 15[3], 16[3], 17[2], 18, 19, 21[4], 22[2], 23, 24, 25, 26, 29[2], 30, 31[2], 32[4], 33, 34[4], 36[3], 37, 38[5], 39, 40[2], 41, 42, 43[2], 44[3], 48, 49, 50

8:1[4], 2[2], 3[3], 4[2], 5[3], 6[2], 7[3], 8[4], 9, 10[2], 12[2], 13[2], 14[5], 15[2], 17, 18, 19[2], 20[2], 21[4], 22[2], 23[3], 24[6], 25[4], 26, 27[2], 28[2], 29[4], 30[2], 31, 32[3], 33[3], 34[3], 35[4], 37[2], 39[3], 40, 41[4], 42, 43, 44[2], 45[4], 46, 47[3], 48, 50, 51[5], 52[2], 53, 54[3], 55[3], 56

9:1[3], 2[2], 3, 4[2], 5, 6[3], 7, 8[2], 9[2], 10[3], 11[4], 12[5], 13[3], 14, 15[2], 16[4], 17[3], 18[2], 19, 21[2], 22[5], 23[3], 25, 26[3], 28[4], 29[3], 30[2], 31, 32[3], 33[4], 34[2], 35, 36[3], 37, 38, 39[4], 40[2], 41[3], 42[5], 43, 45[2], 47[2], 48[2], 49[3], 50, 51, 52[3], 53, 54[3], 55[2], 56, 57, 58[2], 59[2], 60, 61, 62[2]

10:1[3], 4, 5, 6, 7[2], 8[2], 9[2], 10[2], 13[2], 14, 15, 16[2], 17, 18, 19[3], 21[4], 22[3], 23[2], 24[4], 25[2], 27[5], 28[2], 29, 30[4], 31[2], 32[3], 33, 34[6], 35[4], 37[2], 38, 39[2], 40[2], 41[3], 42

11:1, 2, 4[2], 5[3], 6, 7[4], 8[2], 9[4], 10[2], 14[4], 16, 17, 19, 22[2], 23, 24, 25[2], 26[4], 27[3], 28, 29[2], 31[2], 32[2], 37[3], 38, 39[3], 41, 42[5], 43, 44[2], 45, 46[2], 47, 48, 49[3], 51, 52, 53[3], 54

12:3, 4[2], 6, 10, 11[3], 13, 14, 15[2], 16, 17, 18[4], 19[2], 21, 22, 23, 24, 25, 27, 28, 29, 30, 31, 33, 35, 36[2], 37[3], 38[2], 39[2], 42[2], 45[6], 46[3], 47[2], 48[2], 49, 50, 52, 53[3], 54[2], 55[2], 56, 57, 58[2]

13:2, 4, 6[3], 7, 8[2], 9[2], 10, 11[3], 12[2], 13[3], 14[4], 15[2], 16, 17[2], 18, 19[4], 20, 21, 22[3], 23, 24, 25[5], 26[2], 28[5], 29[5], 30[2], 31, 32[5], 33[2], 34[2], 35

14:1, 2, 3[2], 4[4], 5[2], 6, 7, 9[4], 10, 11, 12, 14, 15, 16, 17, 18[3], 19[2], 20[2], 21[6], 22[2], 23[3], 25[3], 26[7], 27[2], 28, 29, 30, 31, 32

15:1, 2[3], 3, 4[2], 5, 6[2], 7, 8[2], 9[2], 11, 12[2], 13[3], 14[2], 15[3], 16[2], 17[3], 18[3], 19, 20[6], 21[3], 22[3], 23[4], 24[3], 25[3], 26[2], 27[3], 28[3], 29[2], 31[2], 32[4]

16:1[2], 2[2], 5, 6[4], 7[4], 8, 9, 10, 12, 13[3], 14[2], 15, 16[2], 17[2], 18[2], 19[2], 20, 21[2], 22[3], 23[3], 24[4], 25[2], 26[2], 29, 30, 31[2]

17:2, 3, 4[2], 5, 6[3], 7[2], 8[6], 11[2], 12, 13[2], 14[2], 15[2], 16[2], 17, 19, 20[2], 22[2], 23, 25, 26, 27[2], 29[2], 31[2], 33, 34, 35, 36, 37[3]

18:1[2], 3[2], 4, 6, 7[2], 9[2], 10, 11, 13, 14, 15, 16[2], 18, 19, 20, 21, 22[3], 23, 24, 26, 27, 28, 29, 30, 31[2], 32[3], 33[3], 34[2], 35, 36, 37, 38, 39, 40[3], 41, 42, 43[3]

19:1[2], 2[2], 3[2], 4[2], 5[4], 6[3], 7, 8[3], 9, 10, 11[3], 12, 13[3], 14, 15, 17, 18, 19, 20, 21, 22[2], 24[2], 25, 26, 27, 28, 29[2], 30, 31, 32[2], 33, 34, 35[3], 36, 37[2], 38, 39, 40[2], 41[2], 43[2], 44[3], 45[3], 47[3], 48

20:1[3], 2, 3[3], 5, 6, 7, 8, 9[2], 10[2], 11[4], 12[3], 15, 16[3], 17[2], 19[3], 20[3], 21[2], 23, 24[2], 25[2], 26[3], 27, 28[2], 29[2], 30[2], 31[4], 34[2], 35, 36, 37[2], 40, 41, 42, 46[3], 47

21:1[2], 2, 3, 5[2], 7[2], 8[2], 9[2], 10, 11[5], 12[3], 13, 15, 16[5], 17, 20, 21[2], 23[2], 24[3], 25[5], 26, 27[2], 28[2], 29[2], 30, 33, 34[4], 36[2], 37[3], 38

22:2[2], 4[3], 5[2], 6[2], 8[3], 9, 10, 11, 12, 13[3], 14[2], 15, 17[4], 19[4], 22, 23, 24, 25[2], 26, 29, 30[2], 31, 32, 33[2], 34, 35[4], 36[3], 37, 38[2], 39[3], 40, 41[3], 43, 44[2], 45[2], 46[2], 47[3], 50[2], 51[4], 52[3], 53, 54[3], 55[2], 56[2], 57, 58[3], 59, 60[2], 61[3], 62[2], 63[2], 64[2], 65, 66[4], 67, 68, 70, 71

23:1[2], 2[2], 3[3], 4, 5, 7, 8[2], 10[3], 11[4], 12[2], 13[3], 14, 15, 16, 18[2], 19, 22[2], 23[3], 24, 25[2], 26[2], 27[3], 28, 29[2], 30, 32, 33[3], 34[2], 35[2], 36[2], 37, 38[3], 39[2], 41, 42, 43, 44[2], 45[2], 46[2], 48[2], 49[2], 50[3], 51, 52, 53[3], 54[2], 55[3], 56[4]

24:1, 2, 3[2], 4, 5[2], 7[2], 8, 9[3], 10[3], 11[2], 12[3], 13, 14, 15[3], 17[2], 18[2], 19[4], 20[3], 21, 22, 23, 24[2], 25, 26, 27[2], 28[2], 29[2], 30[4], 31[3], 32[2], 33[4], 34, 35[2], 36[2], 37[2], 38[2], 39[3], 40[2], 41[2], 42[2], 43[2], 44[3], 46[3], 47[2], 48, 49, 50[3], 51[2], 52[2], 53[2]

JOHN

1:1[2], 3, 4, 5[2], 10[2], 11, 14[4], 15, 16[2], 17, 19[2], 20[2], 21[3], 24, 25[2], 29, 31, 32[2], 33[2], 34[2], 35, 36, 37[2], 38[2], 39[3], 40, 41, 42[2], 43[2], 44, 45[2], 46[2], 47, 48, 49, 50, 51[3]

2:1[2], 2[2], 3, 6, 7, 8[3], 9, 10[2], 11[2], 12[4], 13[2], 14[4], 15[5], 16, 17, 18, 19[2], 20[2], 22[2], 25

3:2, 3, 4, 5, 6, 8[2], 9, 10[2], 11[2], 12, 13, 14, 19[2], 22[3], 23[3], 25, 26[3], 27, 29, 31, 32[3], 35, 36

4:1, 3, 4, 6, 10[3], 11, 12[3], 13, 16, 17, 18, 20, 23[2], 24[2], 27[2], 28[2], 30, 34, 35[2], 36[3], 37[2], 38, 39, 40, 41, 42[2], 43, 46, 47[2], 48, 50[2], 51[2], 52, 53[2]

5:1, 4, 5[2], 6, 8, 9[4], 11, 12, 13, 14, 15, 16[2], 17, 19, 20[2], 21, 24[2], 25[2], 27, 29[2], 30, 32, 33, 35[2], 37, 38, 39, 40, 43, 44

6:2, 3[2], 4, 5, 6, 9, 10, 11[4], 13[2], 15, 16, 17[4], 18, 19[3], 21, 22, 24, 25, 26[2], 29, 30, 33, 35[2], 36, 37, 39, 40[3], 42[2], 43, 44, 45[2], 49, 50, 51, 53, 54[2], 55, 56[2], 57, 58, 62, 63, 64, 65, 66, 69[2], 70

7:3, 4, 11, 12, 14, 15, 16, 18, 19, 20, 21[2], 22, 26, 28[2], 29, 31[2], 32[2], 33, 34[2], 35, 36[2], 37[2], 42, 44, 45[2], 51, 52[2], 53

8:1[2], 2[4], 3[3], 6, 7, 8[2], 9[3], 10, 11[2], 14[3], 16[2], 18, 20, 21[2], 23, 25, 26[2], 28, 29, 32[2], 33, 35, 38, 39, 42, 44[3], 45, 46, 48[2], 49, 50[2], 52[2], 53, 55[2], 56[2], 57, 59[2]

9:1, 2, 6[2], 7[3], 8[2], 11[7], 14[2], 15[2], 16, 18, 19, 20[2], 24, 25, 27, 28, 30[2], 31, 34[3], 35, 36, 37[2], 38[2], 39[2], 40[2]

10:1, 3[3], 4[2], 5, 8, 9[3], 10[3], 12[5], 13, 14[2], 15, 16[4], 18, 20[2], 22[2], 23, 24, 25, 27[2], 28[2], 29, 30, 33, 35, 36, 38[2], 40[2], 41[2], 42

11:1, 2, 5[2], 8, 11, 15, 19[2], 20, 25, 26[2], 28[3], 29, 31[2], 32, 33[2], 34[2], 37, 38, 41[2], 42, 43, 44[4], 45, 46, 47[2], 48[3], 49, 50, 51, 52, 54, 55[2], 56, 57

12:2, 3[3], 5, 6[2], 9, 11, 13[2], 14, 16, 17, 20, 21, 22[3], 23, 24, 25, 26, 27, 28, 29, 30, 32, 34, 36[2], 38, 40[3], 41, 44, 45, 47[2], 48, 49, 50

13:2, 3[2], 4[3], 5[2], 6, 7, 9, 10, 12[2], 13[2], 14, 20, 21[2], 26, 27, 30, 31, 32, 33

14:3[3], 4[2], 5, 6, 7[2], 8, 9[2], 10, 11, 12, 13, 16[2], 17, 19, 20[2], 21[4], 22, 23[4], 24, 26, 28, 29, 30, 31

15:1, 2, 4, 5, 6[4], 7[2], 10, 11, 16[3], 22, 24[2], 27

16:3, 4, 5, 8[3], 10, 13, 14, 15, 16[3], 17[4], 19[4], 20[2], 22[3], 23, 24, 26, 27, 28[2], 29, 30, 32[2]

17:1[2], 3[2], 5, 6[2], 8[3], 10[3], 11[2], 12, 13[2], 14, 19, 21, 22, 23[3], 25, 26[3]

18:1, 2, 3[4], 4, 5, 6, 7, 10[2], 12[3], 13, 15[3], 16[2], 18[5], 19, 20[2], 22, 25[3], 27, 28[2], 29, 30, 31, 33[2], 35, 37, 38[2]

19:1, 2[3], 3[2], 4, 5[2], 6[2], 7, 9[2], 10, 12, 13, 14[3], 16[2], 17, 18[2], 19[3], 20[3], 23[2], 24, 25[2], 26, 27, 29[3], 30[2], 31, 32[2], 33, 34[2], 35[3], 37, 38[3], 39[3], 40, 41

20:1, 2[4], 3[2], 4[2], 5[2], 6[2], 7, 8[2], 11[2], 12[2], 13[2], 14[3], 15, 16, 17[4], 18[2], 19[2], 20[2], 22[2], 23, 25[2], 26[4], 27[4], 28[3], 29, 30, 31

21:1, 2[4], 3[2], 6[3], 7, 8, 9[2], 11[4], 12[2], 13[3], 17, 18[3], 19, 20, 21, 24[2], 25

THE ACTS

1:1, 3, 4, 7, 8[4], 9[2], 10, 13[8], 14[3], 15[3], 16, 17, 18[2], 19, 20[2], 21, 23[2], 24[2], 25, 26[3]

2:1, 2[2], 3[2], 4[2], 5, 6, 7[2], 8, 9[6], 10[4], 11, 12[2], 14[3], 17[5], 18[3], 19[4], 20[2], 21, 22[2], 23[3], 26, 29[3], 30, 33[2], 36, 37[3], 38[2], 39[2], 40[2], 41, 42[4], 43[3], 44[2], 45[3], 46[3], 47[2]

3:1, 2, 3, 4, 5, 6[2], 7[4], 8[5], 9[2], 10[3], 11[2], 12, 13[3], 14[2], 15, 16[2], 17, 19, 20, 23, 24[2], 25[2]

4:1[3], 2, 3[2], 4, 5[3], 6[5], 7, 8, 10, 13[4], 14, 16, 18[2], 19[2], 20, 23[3], 24[5], 25, 26[2], 27[2], 28, 29[2], 30[2], 31[3], 32[2], 33[2], 34, 35[2], 36[2], 37[2]

5:2[3], 3, 4, 5[3], 6[3], 7, 8[2], 9, 10[4], 11[2], 12[3], 13, 14[2], 15[2], 16[2], 17[2], 18[2], 19[2], 20, 21[6], 22[2], 23, 24[2], 25[2], 26, 27[2], 28[2], 29[2], 30, 31[2], 32[2], 33, 34, 35, 36[2], 37[2], 38[2], 40[4], 41, 42[3]

6:1, 2[2], 3, 4, 5[9], 6, 7[3], 8[3], 9[4], 10[2], 11, 12[6], 13[2], 14, 15

7:2[2], 3[3], 4[2], 5[2], 6[3], 7[3], 8[5], 9, 10[5], 11[3], 13[2], 14[3], 15[2], 16[2], 17, 19, 20[2], 21[2], 22[3], 23, 24[3], 26[2], 27, 29, 30, 31, 32[3], 34[3], 35[2], 36[3], 38, 39, 41[3], 42[2], 43[2], 46, 49, 51[2], 52[2], 53, 54, 55[2], 56[2], 57[2], 58[3], 59[2], 60[3]

8:1[4], 2[2], 3[2], 5, 6[2], 7[2], 8, 9, 11, 12[2], 13[3], 14, 17, 18, 22, 23, 24, 25[3], 26[2], 27[4], 28, 29, 30[3], 31[3], 32, 33, 34[2], 35[2], 36[2], 37[3], 38[4], 39[2], 40

9:1[2], 2, 3[2], 4[2], 5[2], 6[5], 7, 8[3], 9[2], 10[3], 11[3], 12[2], 14, 15[2], 17[4], 18[4], 19, 20, 21[2], 22, 23, 24[2], 25, 26[2], 27[4], 28[2], 29[2], 30, 31[5], 32,

THE ACTS

33[2], 34[3], 35[3], 36, 37[2], 38[2], 39[4], 40[5], 41[4], 42[2], 43
10:2[2], 3, 4[4], 5[2], 7[2], 8, 9, 10[2], 11[3], 12[3], 13[2], 15, 16, 17, 18[3], 20[2], 21, 22[4], 23[3], 24[4], 25[3], 27[2], 28, 30[3], 31[2], 32, 33, 34, 35, 37, 38[2], 39[3], 40, 41, 42[3], 45, 46, 48
11:1[2], 2, 3, 4, 5[2], 6[4], 7[2], 10[2], 11, 12[2], 13[3], 14, 15, 18, 19[2], 20[2], 21[3], 22, 23[2], 24[3], 26[4], 27, 28[2], 30[2]
12:2, 3, 4[2], 6[2], 7[3], 8[5], 9[3], 10[4], 11[3], 12, 13, 14[2], 15, 16[3], 17[4], 19[5], 20[3], 21[2], 22[2], 23[3], 24, 25[3]
13:1[5], 2[2], 3[3], 4, 5[2], 6, 7[2], 10[2], 11[5], 13[2], 14[2], 15[3], 16[2], 17[2], 18, 19, 20[2], 21[2], 22[2], 25, 26[2], 27, 28, 29[2], 31, 32, 34, 36[2], 38, 39, 41[2], 42, 43[2], 44, 45[2], 46[3], 48[3], 49, 50[5], 51, 52[2]
14:1[3], 2, 3[2], 4[2], 5[3], 6[3], 7, 8, 9, 10[2], 11, 12[3], 13[2], 14[2], 15[5], 17[3], 18, 19[3], 20[2], 21[4], 22[2], 23[2], 24, 25, 26, 27[3], 28
15:1[2], 2[5], 3[3], 4[4], 5, 6[2], 7[4], 8, 9[2], 12[3], 13[2], 15, 16[3], 17, 20[3], 22[3], 23[5], 24, 25, 27, 28, 29[3], 30, 32[3], 33, 35[2], 36[3], 37, 38, 39[3], 40[2], 41[2]
16:1[3], 2, 3[2], 4[2], 5[2], 6[2], 8, 9[3], 10, 11, 12[3], 13[3], 14, 15[4], 16, 17[2], 18[3], 19[3], 20, 21, 22[3], 23, 24, 25[4], 26[3], 27[3], 29[4], 30[2], 31[3], 32[2], 33[4], 34[2], 35, 36[2], 37[3], 38[2], 39[4], 40[4]
17:1, 2[2], 3[3], 4[5], 5[4], 6[2], 7, 8[2], 9[2], 10[2], 11, 12, 13, 14[2], 15[3], 17[2], 18[3], 19[2], 21, 22, 23, 24[2], 25[2], 26[3], 27, 28[2], 29, 30, 32[2], 34[3]
18:1, 2[2], 3[2], 4[3], 5[3], 6[3], 7[2], 8[3], 9, 10, 11[2], 12[2], 14, 15[2], 16, 17[2], 18[5], 19[3], 21, 22[3], 23[3], 24[2], 25[2], 26[3], 27, 28
19:1[2], 2, 3[2], 6[3], 7, 8[3], 9[2], 10[2], 11, 12[2], 14[2], 15[3], 16[4], 17[4], 18[3], 19[3], 20, 21, 22, 25, 26[2], 27[2], 28[2], 29[3], 30, 31, 32[2], 33[3], 35[2], 36, 38[2], 41
20:1[3], 2[2], 3[2], 4[7], 6[2], 7[2], 8, 9[4], 10[3], 11[3], 12[2], 13[2], 14[2], 15[5], 17[2], 18, 19[2], 20[3], 21[2], 22, 23, 24, 25, 28, 31[2], 32[3], 34, 35, 36[2], 37[3], 38
21:1[4], 2[2], 3[2], 4, 5[6], 6[2], 7[3], 8[4], 9, 10, 11[5], 12[2], 13, 14, 15[2], 16, 17, 18[2], 19, 20[3], 21, 24[4], 25[4], 26, 27[2], 28[4], 30[5], 31, 32[4], 33[4], 34[2], 35, 37, 38, 39, 40[3]
22:1, 2[2], 3[2], 4[3], 5[2], 6[2], 7[2], 8[2], 9[2], 10[4], 11, 12, 13[3], 14[3], 15, 16[3], 17, 18[2], 19[2], 20[3], 21, 22[3], 23[3], 24, 25[2], 26, 27, 28[2], 29[2], 30[4]
23:1[2], 2, 3, 4, 6[3], 7[3], 9[3], 10[3], 11[2], 12[2], 13, 14[3], 15, 16[3], 17, 18[3], 19[2], 20, 21, 22, 23[4], 24[2], 25, 27[2], 28, 30[2], 31, 32, 33, 34[2], 35

THE ACTS

24:1[2], 2[2], 3, 5[2], 6, 7, 9, 12, 14, 15[2], 16[2], 17, 19, 22[2], 23[3], 24[2], 25[3], 26, 27
25:2[2], 3, 4, 5, 6[2], 7[3], 9[2], 13[2], 14, 15, 16, 17, 19, 20[2], 23[4], 24[3], 25, 26, 27
26:1, 3, 6[2], 7, 10[2], 11[3], 12, 13, 14[2], 15[2], 16[3], 17, 18[3], 20[5], 21, 22[3], 23[3], 24, 25, 29[2], 30[4], 31
27:1[2], 2, 3[3], 4, 5[2], 6[2], 7[2], 8, 9, 10[3], 11, 12[4], 13, 15[2], 16, 17[2], 18, 19, 20[2], 21[4], 22, 23, 24, 27, 28[4], 29, 30, 31, 32, 33[2], 35[3], 36, 37[2], 38[2], 39, 40[4], 41[3], 42[3], 44[3]
28:1, 2[3], 3[3], 4, 5[2], 6[2], 7, 8[5], 9, 10, 11[2], 12, 13[4], 14[2], 15[3], 16, 17[3], 20, 21, 23[3], 24[2], 25, 26[4], 27[6], 28, 29[2], 30[2], 31

ROMANS

1:4, 5, 7[2], 12, 14[2], 16, 18, 20, 21, 23[4], 25[2], 27[2], 28
2:3[2], 4[2], 5[2], 7[2], 8[2], 9[2], 10[2], 12, 15, 17[2], 18[2], 19, 20, 27[2], 29[2]
3:4, 8[2], 9, 14, 16, 17, 19, 21, 22, 23, 26, 30
4:3, 7, 11, 12, 14, 17, 19, 21, 22, 25
5:2, 3, 4[2], 5, 11, 12[2], 15, 16, 17
6:13, 19, 22[2]
7:6, 9, 10, 11, 12[3], 23
8:2, 3, 6, 10, 17[2], 22, 23, 27, 28, 30[2]
9:2, 4[5], 5, 9, 10, 15, 17, 18, 21, 22, 23, 25, 26, 28, 29[2], 33[2]
10:1, 3, 8, 9, 10, 12, 14[2], 15[2], 17, 18, 19, 20, 21
11:3[3], 6, 7, 8, 9[4], 10, 12, 14, 16, 17[4], 20, 22, 23, 24, 26[2], 29, 33[2], 35, 36[2]
12:2[3], 4, 5, 14, 15
13:2, 3, 9, 11, 12, 13[3], 14
14:3, 6[3], 7, 8, 9[3], 11, 14, 17[3], 18, 19, 23
15:1, 4, 5, 6, 9[2], 10, 11[2], 12[2], 13, 14, 18, 19[2], 21, 23, 24, 26, 27, 28, 29, 30, 31, 32
16:2[2], 3, 7[2], 9, 12, 13[2], 14, 15[4], 17[2], 18[2], 19, 20, 21[3], 23[2], 25, 26
S

1 CORINTHIANS

1:1, 2, 3[2], 5, 10[2], 12[3], 14, 16, 19, 22, 23, 24[2], 25, 27, 28[3], 30[3]
2:1, 2, 3[3], 4[3]
3:1, 2, 3, 4, 5, 8[2], 10, 13, 16, 20, 23[2]
4:1, 5[2], 6[2], 7, 8, 9[2], 11[4], 12, 13, 17, 19, 21
5:1, 2[2], 4, 8[2]
6:1, 2, 6, 8[2], 11[2], 13[3], 14[2], 15, 19, 20
7:2, 3, 4, 5[2], 6, 7, 8, 10, 11[2], 12, 13[2], 14, 17, 19, 28[2], 30[3], 31, 34[2], 35[2], 36, 37, 40
8:2, 4, 5, 6[3], 7, 11, 12

1 CORINTHIANS

9:4, 5[2], 6, 7[2], 10, 13, 20, 23, 25, 27
10:1, 2[2], 3, 4[2], 7[2], 8[2], 9, 10, 11, 17, 20[2], 21[2], 26, 27, 28[2]
11:2, 3[2], 7, 18, 21[2], 22[2], 24[2], 26, 27[2], 28[2], 29[2], 30[2], 34[2]
12:3, 5, 6, 11, 12[2], 13, 16, 19, 21, 23[2], 26, 27, 28, 31
13:1[2], 2[3], 3[3], 4, 9, 13
14:1, 3[2], 7, 10, 11, 15[2], 21[2], 23[2], 24, 25[3], 27[2], 28[2], 29, 31, 32, 35, 39, 40
15:1, 4[2], 5, 8, 10, 11, 14[2], 15, 17, 20, 24[2], 28, 30, 32, 34, 35, 37, 38, 39, 40[2], 41[2], 44, 45, 46, 48, 49, 50, 52[3], 53, 54, 56
16:3, 4, 6[2], 9[2], 15, 16[2], 17[2], 18, 19
S[3]

2 CORINTHIANS

1:1, 2[2], 3, 6[3], 7, 10, 12[2], 13, 15, 16[3], 17, 18, 19[3], 20, 21, 22
2:3, 4, 7, 12, 14, 15, 16[2]
3:2, 4, 7, 13, 17
4:5, 7, 13[2], 14, 17
5:8[2], 11, 12, 15[2], 18[2], 19
6:2, 7, 8[3], 9[3], 10, 14, 15, 16[4], 17[3], 18[3]
7:1, 3, 7, 13, 15[2]
8:2, 3, 4, 5[2], 7[4], 8, 10, 12, 13, 15, 18, 19[2], 22, 23, 24[2]
9:2, 4, 5[2], 6, 8, 10[2], 13[2], 14
10:1, 5[2], 6, 8, 10[2], 12, 16
11:1, 9[4], 14, 25, 27[3], 29[2], 31, 33[2]
12:1, 3, 4, 7, 9, 12[2], 14, 15[2], 18, 20, 21[5]
13:2[3], 9[2], 10, 11[2], 14[2]
S

GALATIANS

1:1, 2, 3[2], 4, 5, 7, 13, 14, 15, 16, 17, 18, 21, 22, 24
2:1, 2[2], 4, 9[4], 12, 13, 14, 15, 16, 20[2]
3:5, 6, 8, 12, 16[3], 17[2], 19, 29[2]
4:2, 6, 7, 9, 10[3], 14, 15, 18, 20, 25[2], 27, 30
5:1, 11, 15, 16, 17[2], 21, 24[2]
6:2, 4[2], 9, 14, 16[3]

EPHESIANS

1:1, 2[3], 3, 4, 8, 10, 15, 17, 18, 19, 20, 21[4], 22[2]
2:1[2], 3[2], 6[2], 8, 12[2], 14, 16, 17[3], 19[2], 20[2]
3:5, 6[2], 9, 10, 12, 15, 17, 18[3], 19
4:2, 4, 6[3], 8, 11[5], 13, 14[3], 16, 17, 21, 23, 24[2], 26, 30, 31[4], 32
5:2[3], 3, 5, 9[2], 11, 14[2], 18, 19[3], 20, 23, 25, 26, 27, 29, 30, 31[3], 32, 33
6:2, 3, 4[2], 5, 7, 9, 10, 12, 13, 14, 15, 17[2], 18[3], 19, 21[2], 22, 23[2]

PHILIPPIANS

1:1[2], 2[2], 7[2], 9[3], 10, 11, 13, 14, 15[2], 18[2], 19, 20, 21, 23, 25[3], 27, 28[2], 30

PHILIPPIANS

2:1, 7[2], 8[2], 9, 10[2], 11, 12, 13, 14, 15[2], 17[3], 18, 25[3], 26, 27, 28, 29
3:3[2], 8[2], 9, 10[2], 13, 15, 17, 18, 19
4:1[2], 2, 3[2], 4, 6, 7[2], 8, 9[4], 12[4], 15, 16, 18, 20[2]

COLOSSIANS

1:1, 2[3], 3, 4, 6[2], 9[2], 10, 11, 13, 16[3], 17[2], 18, 20, 21[2], 22[2], 23[3], 24, 26, 28
2:1[2], 2[3], 3, 4, 5[2], 7[2], 8[2], 10[2], 13[2], 14, 15[2], 18, 19[3], 22, 23[2]
3:3, 5, 10, 11, 12, 13, 14, 15[2], 16[3], 17[2], 19, 23[2], 25
4:1, 2, 7[2], 8, 9, 10, 11, 12, 13[2], 14, 15[2], 16[2], 17
S

1 THESSALONIANS

1:1[5], 3[3], 5[2], 6[2], 7, 8, 9[2], 10
2:2, 9[2], 10[3], 11[2], 12, 15[4], 18, 20
3:2[4], 4, 5, 6[3], 7, 10[2], 11[2], 12[3]
4:1[3], 4, 6[2], 10[2], 11[3], 12, 14, 15, 16[2], 17[2]
5:1, 3[2], 5, 6, 7, 8[2], 11, 12[3], 13[2], 15, 23[4]

2 THESSALONIANS

1:1[3], 2[2], 3, 4[2], 7, 8, 9, 10, 11[2], 12[2]
2:1, 3, 4, 6, 8[2], 9[2], 10, 11, 13, 15, 16[3], 17[2]
3:1, 2[2], 3, 4[2], 5[2], 6, 8[2], 12[2], 14[2]

1 TIMOTHY

1:1, 2[2], 4, 5[2], 9[4], 10, 12, 13[2], 14[2], 15, 17[2], 19, 20
2:1, 2[3], 3, 4, 5[2], 7[3], 8, 9, 14, 15[2]
3:7, 10, 12, 13, 15, 16
4:1, 3[2], 4, 5, 6, 7[2], 8, 9, 10, 11, 16[2]
5:1, 4[2], 5[4], 7, 8[2], 13[3], 16, 17, 18, 21[2], 23, 24, 25
6:1, 2[3], 3[2], 4, 5, 7, 8[2], 9[4], 10, 11, 12, 13, 15[2], 16, 20[2]

2 TIMOTHY

1:2[2], 3, 5[2], 7[2], 9[2], 10[2], 11[2], 12, 13, 15, 16, 17, 18
2:2, 5, 7, 16, 17[2], 18, 19, 20[4], 21[2], 23, 24, 26
3:6, 7, 8, 12, 13[3], 14, 15, 16
4:1[3], 2, 4[2], 6, 8, 10, 11, 12, 13, 17[3], 18[3], 19[2], 21[4]

TITUS

1:1[2], 4[2], 5, 9, 10[2], 14, 15[2], 16[2]
2:9, 12[2], 13[2], 14, 15[2]
3:1, 3[3], 4, 5, 8[2], 9[4], 10, 11, 13, 14

PHILEMON

1[2], 2[3], 3[2], 5[2], 7, 9, 11, 16

HEBREWS

1:1, 3[2], 5[2], 6[2], 7[2], 8, 9, 10[2], 11, 12[3]

PHILEMON

2:2[2], 3, 4[3], 7[2], 9, 10, 11, 13[3], 14, 15, 17
3:1, 5, 6, 9, 10[2], 18
4:4, 5, 6, 12[7], 13, 16
5:1, 2, 3, 4, 7[3], 9, 11, 12[2], 14
6:1, 2[3], 3, 4[2], 5[2], 6, 7, 8[2], 9, 10[2], 11, 12, 14, 15, 16, 19[2]
7:1, 2, 5, 6, 7, 8, 9, 11, 15, 18, 20, 21, 23, 26, 27
8:2[2], 3, 5, 8, 9, 10[3], 11[2], 12[2], 13
9:1, 2[2], 3, 4[3], 5, 7, 9, 10[3], 11, 12, 13[2], 15, 19[5], 21, 22[2], 27, 28
10:1, 4, 5, 6, 8[3], 11[2], 16, 17[2], 20, 21, 22, 24[2], 25, 27, 29[2], 30, 33[2], 34[2], 37[2]
11:4, 5, 6, 7, 8, 9, 10, 11, 12[3], 13[4], 15, 17, 20, 21, 22, 23, 28, 32[6], 35, 36[3], 37, 38[3], 39
12:1[2], 2[3], 3, 5, 6, 8, 9[2], 12, 13, 14, 15, 18[3], 19[2], 20, 21[2], 22[2], 23[3], 24[2], 27, 28
13:3, 4[2], 5, 6, 8[2], 9, 16, 17[2], 21, 22, 24

JAMES

1:1, 4, 5[2], 6, 11[2], 14, 15, 17[2], 21[2], 22, 23, 24[2], 25, 26, 27[4]
2:2, 3[3], 4, 5, 6, 9, 10, 12, 13, 14, 15, 16[2], 18[2], 19, 22, 23[3], 24, 25
3:2, 3, 4, 5, 6[3], 7[4], 9, 10, 11, 12, 13, 14[2], 16[2], 17[3], 18
4:1, 2[4], 3, 4, 7, 8[2], 9[3], 10, 11[2], 12, 13[4], 14, 15, 17
5:1, 2, 3[3], 4, 5, 6[2], 7[2], 10, 11[2], 12, 14, 15[3], 16, 17[3], 18[3], 19, 20

1 PETER

1:1, 2[2], 3, 4[2], 7[2], 8, 10, 11, 13, 17, 18, 19, 21[2], 23, 24[2], 25
2:1[4], 4, 6, 8[2], 11, 14, 16, 18, 20, 25
3:3, 4, 6, 7, 10[2], 11[2], 12, 13, 14[2], 15[2], 19, 22[3]
4:3, 5, 7, 8, 11[2], 14, 17, 18[2]
5:1[2], 4, 5[2], 11[2], 12, 13

2 PETER

1:1[2], 2[2], 3[2], 4, 5[2], 6[3], 7[2], 8, 9[2], 10, 11, 12, 16, 17, 18, 19
2:1, 2, 3[2], 4, 5, 6[2], 7, 8, 9, 10, 11, 12[3], 13[2], 14, 15, 20[2], 22
3:2[2], 4, 5[2], 7[2], 8, 10[2], 11, 12[2], 13, 14, 15, 16, 18[3]

1 JOHN

1:1, 2[4], 3[3], 4, 5[2], 6[2], 7, 8, 9[2], 10
2:1, 2[2], 3, 4[2], 8[2], 9, 10, 11[2], 14[2], 16[2], 17[2], 18, 20, 21, 22, 24, 25, 27[4], 28[2]
3:2, 3, 5[2], 9, 10, 12[3], 15, 16, 17[2], 18, 19[2], 20, 22[2], 23[2], 24[3]
4:3[3], 4, 5, 6, 7[2], 10, 12, 13, 14[2], 15, 16[4], 20, 21
5:1, 2, 3, 4, 6[3], 7[2], 8[4], 11[2], 12, 13, 14, 15, 16, 17, 18, 19[2], 20[4]

2 JOHN

1[2], 2, 3[3], 5, 6, 7, 9[2], 10, 12[2]

3 JOHN

2, 3, 5, 10[3], 12[3], 13, 14

JUDE

1[3], 2[2], 3, 4[2], 6, 7[3], 8, 11[2], 14, 15[2], 16, 22, 23, 24, 25[3]

REVELATION

1:1[2], 2[2], 3[2], 4[4], 5[4], 6[5], 7[3], 8[4], 9[4], 10, 11[10], 12[2], 13[2], 14[2], 15[2], 16[3], 17[3], 18[4], 19[2], 20[2]
2:2[6], 3[4], 5[3], 8[3], 9[4], 10[2], 12, 13[3], 14, 16, 17[2], 18[2], 19[6], 20[2], 21[2], 22, 23[4], 24[2], 26[2], 27, 28
3:1[3], 2, 3[4], 4, 5[2], 7[4], 8[3], 9[3], 12[4], 14[2], 16, 17[7], 18[3], 19[2], 20[4], 21
4:1[3], 2[3], 3[3], 4[5], 5[4], 6[4], 7[4], 8[6], 9[4], 10[4], 11[4]
5:1[2], 2[2], 3, 4[2], 5[2], 6[5], 7[2], 8[4], 9[6], 10[3], 11[6], 12[6], 13[10], 14[5]
6:1[3], 2[6], 3[2], 4[4], 5[6], 6[4], 7[2], 8[2], 9[2], 10[3], 11[3], 12[4], 13, 14[3], 15[8], 16[4], 17
7:1, 2[3], 4[4], 9[6], 10[2], 11[5], 12[7], 13[2], 14[4], 15[3], 17[2]
8:1, 2[2], 3[3], 4, 5[7], 6, 7[5], 8[3], 9[3], 10[4], 11[3], 12[6], 13[2]
9:1[3], 2[4], 3[2], 4, 5[2], 6[4], 7[3], 8[2], 9[2], 10[3], 11, 12, 13[2], 15[4], 16[2], 17[8], 18[2], 19[3], 20[6]
10:1[4], 2[3], 3[2], 4[3], 5[2], 6[7], 8[4], 9[5], 10[4], 11[4]
11:1[5], 2[3], 3[3], 4, 5[3], 6[2], 7[3], 8[2], 9[6], 10[3], 11[4], 12[3], 13[5], 14, 15[6], 16[3], 17[3], 18[8], 19[7]
12:1[3], 2[2], 3[4], 4[3], 5[3], 6[2], 7[4], 8, 9[3], 10[5], 11[3], 12[2], 13, 14[3], 15, 16[3], 17[3]
13:1[5], 2[6], 3[3], 4[2], 5[4], 6[3], 7[5], 8, 10, 11[3], 12[3], 13, 14[2], 15[2], 16[4], 17, 18[2]
14:1[4], 2[3], 3[6], 4, 5, 6[5], 7[5], 8, 9[3], 10[3], 11[5], 12, 13[2], 14[4], 15[2], 16[2], 17, 18[3], 19[3], 20[3]
15:1[2], 2[5], 3[4], 4[2], 5[2], 6[3], 7[2], 8[3]
16:1[2], 2[5], 3[2], 4[3], 5[3], 6[2], 7[2], 8[2], 9[3], 10[3], 11[3], 12[3], 13, 14, 15[2], 16, 17[2], 18[5], 19[3], 20[2], 21[2]
17:1[2], 2, 3[2], 4[6], 5[2], 6[3], 7[3], 8[6], 9, 10[4], 11[4], 12, 13[2], 14[5], 15[4], 16[5], 17[2], 18
18:1[2], 2[5], 3[2], 4[2], 5, 6, 7[4], 8[3], 9[3], 11[2], 12[13], 13[14], 14[4], 15, 16[6], 17[4], 18, 19[3], 20[2], 21[3], 22[6], 23[3], 24[3]
19:1[4], 2[2], 3[3], 4[4], 5[3], 6[3], 7[2], 8[2], 9[2], 10[3], 11[6], 12[2], 13[2], 14[2], 15[4], 16[3], 17[3], 18[7], 19[4], 20[3], 21[2]
20:1[2], 2[3], 3[4], 4[8], 6[3], 7[2], 8[2], 9[6], 10[6], 11[4], 12[5], 13[4], 14[2], 15
21:1[4], 2, 3[5], 4[2], 5[3], 6[3], 7[2], 8[8], 9[2], 10[3], 11, 12[5], 13, 14[2], 15[3], 16[5], 17[3], 18[2], 19, 21[2], 22[2], 23[2], 24[3], 25, 26[2], 27
22:1[2], 2[3], 3[3], 4[2], 5[4], 6[3], 8[4], 9[2], 10, 11[3], 12[2], 13[3], 14, 15[6], 16[3], 17[5], 19[3]

ARE

1526

GENESIS

2:4
6:9
7:2, 8
9:2, 19
10:1, 20, 31, 32
11:10, 27
18:5, 24
19:5, 15
20:7, 16
25:7, 12, 13, 16[2], 17, 19, 23
27:22, 41, 46
29:4, 21
31:12, 15, 43[3], 49
32:17
33:5, 8, 13[2], 15
34:21, 22
35:2, 26
36:1, 5, 9, 10, 13, 16, 17[3], 18, 19[2], 20, 21, 24, 26, 27, 28, 29, 30, 31, 40
37:2, 17
38:25[2]
40:12, 18
41:26[2], 27
42:9[2], 10, 11[3], 12, 13, 14, 16, 21, 31[2], 33, 34[2], 36
43:18
44:16
45:6, 11, 16
46:8, 18, 22, 25, 31, 32
47:1[2], 3, 4, 5, 9
48:5, 8, 9
49:5[2], 28
50:3[2]

EXODUS

1:1, 9, 19[3]
2:18
3:7
4:18, 19
5:5, 16, 17[2]
6:15, 16, 19, 24, 25, 26, 27[2]
7:17
8:21
9:27

EXODUS

10:8, 11
12:13
14:3
15:4
16:7, 8[2], 16
19:6
21:1
24:14
25:22, 26
28:3, 4, 24
29:33
30:13, 14
31:6
32:2, 22
33:5, 16
35:1
39:6
40:4

LEVITICUS

4:12[2], 13
5:17
10:14
11:2[2], 8, 9, 13[2], 26, 27, 28, 31, 32, 35, 42
12:6
14:37
16:4
18:17, 24
23:2, 4, 17, 37, 42
25:7, 23, 33, 42, 44, 45, 55[2]
26:25, 36, 39, 46
27:34

NUMBERS

1:3, 5, 17, 44
2:32
3:1, 2, 3, 9, 13, 18, 20, 21, 27, 33, 46[2]
4:15, 20, 41
6:13
8:16, 17
9:7[2]
10:4, 29, 31
11:21
13:16, 28, 30, 31, 32

NUMBERS

14:9, 35, 43[2]
15:13, 15
16:3, 5, 11, 37, 38
18:6, 16, 17, 18
20:16
22:4, 6, 9, 12
24:3, 5, 6, 15
26:2, 7, 14, 18, 22, 25, 27, 30, 34, 35, 36, 37[2], 41, 42[2], 47, 50, 57, 58, 63
27:1
30:14, 16
31:12, 49
32:14
33:1, 2, 51
34:17, 19, 29
35:33
36:3, 4, 13

DEUTERONOMY

1:2, 10, 11, 20, 28
2:4, 25
3:18
4:4, 20, 30, 32, 45
5:3
6:1, 14
7:6, 17, 20
8:9
9:12, 29
11:12, 30
12:1, 9
13:7, 13
14:1, 2, 4, 7, 9, 12, 29
16:11, 14
17:14
18:12
20:2, 15[2]
21:2, 6
22:5, 17
23:8, 18
24:14
25:16
27:12
28:58
29:1, 5, 20, 21, 27, 29
30:1, 10

DEUTERONOMY

31:17, 18, 21
32:4, 5, 20, 21, 28, 32[2], 37
33:3, 17[3], 27

JOSHUA

2:3[2]
3:8
4:9
6:17[2], 19
7:3, 21
8:5
9:8[2], 9, 11, 13, 22, 23, 25
10:6, 17
12:1, 7
13:14, 17, 30, 32
14:1
15:32
16:3
17:3, 9, 16[2]
18:3
19:14, 29, 35, 51
21:9
22:10, 17
23:14, 15
24:22[2], 23

JUDGES

3:1
5:11
6:2
7:2[2], 4, 18
8:6, 15[2]
9:2, 18
10:4[2]
11:7[2]
12:3, 4
15:10[2], 11, 12
18:9, 24
19:18
20:7, 13, 32, 39
21:16

RUTH

1:11
4:9, 10, 11, 18

1 SAMUEL

2:3, 4[2], 8
4:8, 17
6:17
9:20
10:2, 7
12:2, 21
16:11, 16
17:8
19:22
20:21, 22
21:5
26:16
29:10

2 SAMUEL

1:4[3], 19, 25, 27
3:28
5:1, 8
7:9
11:11
13:33
14:14, 20
15:3, 13, 15
16:4, 21
17:2, 10, 12, 16
19:11, 12[3]
20:19
22:28, 39
24:14

1 KINGS

1:20, 45
4:8, 13
8:8
9:13
10:8[2], 27
11:41
13:3, 32
14:19, 29
15:7, 23, 31
16:5, 14, 20, 27
18:22, 25
20:3, 17, 23, 31
22:39, 45

2 KINGS

1:5, 18
3:23
5:12
6:9, 16
7:12, 13[5]
8:23
9:22
10:2[2], 5, 13[2], 34
12:19
13:8, 12
14:15, 18, 28
15:6, 11, 15, 21, 26, 31, 36
16:19
18:20, 26, 34[2], 35
19:3, 4
20:14, 15, 20
21:17, 25[2]
23:28
24:5

1 CHRONICLES

1:29, 31, 33, 43, 54
2:1, 18, 55
4:2, 4, 12, 18, 22
5:14
6:19, 31, 33, 50, 54, 65
7:8, 33
8:6[2], 38, 40
9:33, 44
11:1, 10
12:1, 15, 18, 23
13:2[2]
14:4
15:12
16:14, 26, 27[2]
17:8
19:3
21:3, 13
22:15
24:1
26:19
29:15[2], 17, 29

2 CHRONICLES

1:15
2:7

2 CHRONICLES
3:3
6:37
7:14
8:11
9:7^{2}, 27, 29
11:10
12:15
13:7, 8, 9, 10, 22
16:11
17:14
19:3
20:12, 34
23:6
24:26, 27
25:26
26:18
27:7
28:10, 26
29:9, 19
30:6
32:32
33:18, 19
34:21, 24, 31
35:25, 27
36:8

EZRA
2:1
4:10, 12
5:4, 11
6:6, 9
7:13, 19, 21, 25
8:1, 13, 28^{3}
9:6, 15
10:3, 13^{3}

NEHEMIAH
1:3^{3}, 10
2:3, 17^{2}
4:2, 4, 10, 19
5:2, 5, 17
6:8
7:6
9:6, 36^{2}, 37
10:39
11:3, 7
12:1

ESTHER
1:16
3:8
4:16
7:4
8:5, 9
9:13
10:2

JOB
1:19
3:8, 19, 22, 24
4:9, 10, 11, 19, 20
5:4^{2}
6:3, 4, 7, 16, 17, 18, 21^{2}, 25, 26
7:1, 3, 6^{2}, 8, 16
8:9^{2}, 13, 17
9:25, 26
10:5^{2}, 17, 20
11:6
12:2, 6, 16
13:4^{2}, 12, 23
14:5^{2}, 21
15:10, 11, 15, 28
16:2, 22
17:1^{2}, 2, 7, 11^{2}
18:3, 21
19:3, 13, 19, 22
20:11, 25
21:7, 9, 18, 22, 24^{2}, 28, 33
22:10, 12, 14, 19, 29
23:14
24:1, 8, 13, 17, 23, 24^{3}
25:2, 5
26:5, 11, 14
27:12
28:4^{2}, 6
30:1, 15, 17, 30
31:40
32:6, 9
34:18, 19, 21, 25
35:5
36:7^{2}, 20
37:17, 24
38:6, 30, 35
39:4, 30
40:17, 18^{2}
41:14, 15, 17, 18, 23^{2}, 25, 28, 29, 30

PSALMS
1:4^{2}
2:12
3:1^{2}
6:2
9:3, 6, 15
10:5^{2}, 8, 16
12:4, 6, 8
14:1, 3^{2}
16:3, 6, 11
17:2, 10, 14^{2}
18:38
19:8, 9, 10
20:8^{2}
21:11
22:14
25:10, 15, 17, 19
27:12
31:10, 15
32:11
33:4
34:15^{2}, 18, 19
35:19, 20
36:3, 6, 12^{2}
37:23, 28, 34
38:4^{2}, 5, 7, 14, 19^{3}, 20
39:6
40:5^{3}, 12
42:7
44:13, 22^{2}
45:5
47:9
49:14
50:11
51:17
53:1, 3
54:3
55:4, 5, 10
56:5, 8, 12
57:4^{2}, 6
58:3, 4
59:3, 7
62:9^{3}
65:5, 8, 13^{2}
68:6, 17
69:1, 4^{2}, 5, 9, 19
71:13, 24^{2}
72:20
73:1, 4, 5^{2}, 8, 10, 12, 19^{2}, 27
74:20
75:3
76:5, 6
77:19
79:1, 4^{2}, 8, 11
82:5, 6^{2}
83:5
84:1, 4, 5
85:10
86:8, 14
87:3, 7
88:5
89:7, 11, 14, 49
90:4, 5^{2}, 7^{2}, 9, 10
92:5^{2}
93:5
94:11
95:4, 7
96:5, 6^{2}
97:2^{2}
100:3
102:3^{2}, 8^{2}, 11, 20, 22, 24, 25
103:6, 14, 15
104:16, 17, 18, 24, 25, 28, 29, 30
105:7
106:3
107:17, 27, 29, 30, 38, 39
109:2, 4, 24
111:2, 7^{2}, 8
113:6
115:4, 8, 15, 16
116:11
118:12
119:1, 2, 21, 24, 39, 75, 84, 85, 86, 91, 98, 99, 103, 111, 129, 137, 138, 143, 150, 151, 156, 157, 168, 172
120:7
122:5
123:3, 4
124:7
125:2, 4
126:3
127:3, 4^{2}
135:15, 18
139:12, 14, 17, 18
140:2
141:6, 7, 8
142:6
144:4
145:9
146:8

PROVERBS
1:19
2:15
3:15, 17^{2}, 20
4:22, 23
5:6, 11, 21
6:16, 23
8:8, 9, 11, 18, 32
9:17, 18^{2}
10:6
11:20^{4}
12:5^{2}, 6, 7^{2}, 10, 22^{2}
13:8
14:4, 12, 18
15:3, 11, 15, 22^{2}, 26^{2}
16:2, 11^{2}, 13, 24, 25
17:6^{2}, 15, 24
18:4, 7, 8, 19, 21
19:7, 13, 14, 21, 29
20:7, 10, 15, 23, 24
22:3, 4, 5, 26
23:3
24:11^{2}, 21
25:1
26:7, 21, 22, 23, 25, 28
27:6^{2}, 12, 15, 20^{2}, 24, 25, 26^{2}
28:1, 2
29:2, 12, 16
30:12, 13^{2}, 14, 15^{2}, 18, 24^{2}, 25, 26, 29
31:8, 21, 25

ECCLESIASTES
1:8, 11, 13, 14
2:14, 23
3:18, 20
4:1, 2^{2}, 9
5:7, 11
7:19, 21
8:8, 13
9:1, 3, 12^{3}, 16, 17
10:12
11:10
12:3, 11^{2}

SONG OF SOLOMON
1:10, 17
3:7
4:2^{2}, 3^{2}, 5^{2}, 11, 13
5:11, 12, 13, 14, 15
6:6, 7, 8
7:1^{2}, 3^{2}, 9, 13
8:6

ISAIAH
1:4^{2}, 7, 14, 15, 23
2:6, 13, 14
3:8, 12, 16
4:2
5:12, 13^{2}, 21, 22, 28
7:2
8:18
9:10^{2}, 16^{2}
10:8, 14, 20, 29
14:19
16:4, 7, 8^{3}
17:2
19:11, 12^{2}, 13^{3}
21:3
22:2, 3^{4}, 9
23:8^{2}
24:6^{2}, 17, 18, 21, 22
25:1
26:9, 14^{2}
27:7, 9, 11
28:1^{2}, 7^{3}, 8, 9, 15, 27^{2}
29:9, 15, 20
30:18, 27
31:1^{2}, 3
32:7, 9, 11, 20
33:13^{2}, 14, 23
35:4
36:5, 11, 19^{2}, 20
37:3
39:3
40:11, 15^{2}, 17^{2}, 22
41:23^{2}, 24, 29^{3}
42:9, 17, 22^{3}
43:10, 12, 17^{2}
44:7, 8, 9^{2}, 11
45:16, 19, 20, 24
46:1, 2, 3^{2}, 10, 12
48:1^{2}, 7
49:9, 16
51:1^{2}, 19, 20
52:7
53:5
54:1
55:8^{2}, 9^{2}
56:8, 10^{3}, 11^{2}
57:1, 4, 6, 20
58:7
59:3, 6, 7^{2}, 10, 12^{2}
60:8
61:1, 9, 11
63:8, 15, 19
64:6^{2}, 8^{2}, 9, 10, 11
65:5, 11, 16^{2}, 22, 23, 24

JEREMIAH
2:5^{2}, 11, 15, 28^{2}, 31
4:13^{2}, 17, 20, 22^{2}
5:3, 4^{2}, 6^{2}, 7, 10, 16, 23, 26, 27^{2}, 28
6:4, 20, 23, 28^{3}, 29^{2}
7:4, 10
8:8, 9^{2}, 16, 20
[illegible], 10, 10, 25, 26
10:2, 3, 5, 8, 9, 15, 20^{3}, 21
11:10, 16
12:1, 4, 9, 12
13:22, 23
14:2, 7, 9, 18, 22
15:2^{4}, 8
16:3, 17^{2}, 20
18:6
21:4, 7
22:6, 17, 20, 28^{2}
23:10, 11, 14, 26
24:2, 3, 5, 8
25:12, 22, 23, 26, 31, 34, 37
27:5, 18
29:1, 4, 16, 17, 22, 25
30:4, 6
31:20, 29
32:19, 24, 35
33:4, 10
34:21
35:14
37:19
38:19, 22^{3}
40:15
41:12
42:2, 11
43:11^{3}
44:2, 6, 10, 14, 24, 27, 28
46:5^{2}, 7, 8, 12, 15, 21^{3}, 23^{2}
48:14, 15, 17, 32, 36, 41, 46
49:23, 32
50:2^{2}, 11, 15^{2}, 37, 38, 42
51:4, 7, 18, 30, 32^{2}, 43, 51^{2}, 56, 60, 64

LAMENTATIONS
1:2^{2}, 4^{2}, 5^{2}, 6^{2}, 14, 16, 18, 20, 21, 22
2:9^{2}, 11, 21
3:22, 23
4:1, 2, 5, 8, 9, 18, 19
5:3^{2}, 5, 7, 12, 17

EZEKIEL
2:4, 5, 7
3:7, 26, 27
5:2, 5, 6, 7^{2}, 14, 15
7:9
11:2, 7, 12, 15
12:2, 10, 14, 20, 22, 23, 27
13:4
14:5
16:7, 27, 38, 52, 57
18:2, 4, 25, 29^{2}
20:3, 30, 34
21:14, 24^{2}, 29
22:9, 18^{2}, 19, 27
23:45
24:19
25:9
26:6, 18, 19
27:4, 27
28:8, 24, 25
29:12^{2}
30:7^{2}
31:12^{3}, 14
32:20, 21, 22, 23, 24, 25, 26, 27^{2}, 28, 29, 30^{2}, 32
33:24, 27, 30
34:3, 12, 30, 31
35:8, 12^{2}
36:2, 3^{2}, 4^{2}, 7, 8, 20^{2}, 35^{2}, 36
37:11^{3}
38:7, 11, 12^{2}, 20, 22
40:46
42:13, 14^{2}
43:13, 18, 27
44:10
45:14
46:24
48:1^{2}, 11, 15, 29, 30

DANIEL
1:10
2:20, 28
3:12, 16
4:3^{2}, 18, 35, 37
5:23
7:17^{2}, 24
8:20, 23
9:7^{2}, 16^{2}, 19, 24, 26
10:16
12:9

HOSEA
1:9, 10^{2}
2:12
4:4, 6, 14
5:2
6:5
7:2, 4, 7^{2}, 9, 16
8:9
9:6, 7^{2}, 15
11:7, 8
12:7, 11^{2}
14:3, 9

JOEL
1:6, 7, 12, 17^{2}, 18^{2}, 20

AMOS
4:1
5:16
6:1^{2}, 6
9:7, 8, 12

OBADIAH
6^{2}

JONAH
4:11

MICAH
1:4, 5^{2}, 16
2:7, 13
4:11
6:10, 12, 16
7:6, 11

NAHUM
1:3, 6, 10
2:3
3:13, 17^{2}

HABAKKUK
1:3^{2}, 6, 7, 8^{2}, 15
3:6

ZEPHANIAH
1:6, 8, 11^{2}, 12
3:3^{2}, 4, 6^{2}, 18^{2}

HAGGAI
1:6

ZECHARIAH
1:5, 9, 10, 15, 19, 21^{2}
3:8
4:2, 4, 10, 11, 14
6:4, 5, 6, 10, 15
8:16, 17
11:2
13:6

MALACHI
1:4
2:8
3:6, 7, 9, 15^{2}

MATTHEW
1:17^{3}
2:2, 18, 20
5:3, 4, 5, 6, 7, 8, 9, 10^{2}, 11, 13, 14, 15
6:5, 26
7:15
8:26
9:12, 17, 37
10:2, 28, 29, 30, 31
11:5^{2}, 8, 11, 27, 28
12:5, 48
13:15, 16, 38^{2}, 39, 40, 56
15:16, 20
17:26
18:20
19:6, 12^{2}, 26, 30
20:22^{2}, 25
22:4^{3}, 14^{2}, 21^{2}, 30^{2}
23:8, 13, 25, 27^{2}, 28, 31, 37
24:8, 19
25:8
26:55

MARK
2:17^{2}
4:11^{2}, 15, 16^{2}, 17, 18^{2}, 20^{2}, 40
5:9
6:2, 3
7:15, 18
9:23
10:8, 27, 31, 42
12:17^{2}, 25^{3}
13:1, 8, 17, 25, 32
14:36, 48

LUKE
1:1
4:18
5:20, 31^{2}, 38
6:21^{2}, 22, 24, 25
7:22^{2}, 25^{2}, 28, 31, 32, 47^{2}, 48
8:12, 13, 14^{2}, 15, 21
9:12, 55, 61
10:2, 8, 9, 17, 20^{2}, 22, 23
11:7, 21, 28, 41, 44^{2}
12:6, 7^{2}, 24, 37, 38
13:14, 23, 25, 27, 30^{2}, 34
14:17
16:8, 15
17:10^{2}, 17, 18
18:11, 27^{2}, 31
19:42
20:34, 35, 36^{2}, 37
21:21^{3}, 22, 23, 26
22:10, 25, 28, 38
23:29^{2}
24:17^{2}, 18, 38, 44, 48

JOHN
3:21
4:35^{2}, 38
5:28, 39
6:9, 49, 58, 63^{2}, 64, 69
7:7, 23, 47, 49
8:10, 23^{2}, 31, 37, 44, 47, 53
9:28, 40
10:8, 12, 16, 21, 26, 30, 34
11:9
13:10, 11, 17, 35
14:2
15:3, 5, 6, 14, 19
16:15, 30
17:7, 9, 10^{2}, 11^{2}, 14, 16, 22
20:23^{2}, 29, 30, 31
21:25

THE ACTS
2:7, 13, 15, 32, 39
3:15, 25
5:9, 25, 32
7:1, 26
[illegible]
13:27, 31, 39
14:11, 15^{2}
15:18, 19, 23
16:17, 21, 28
17:6, 22, 28, 29
19:15, 26, 37, 38^{2}, 40
20:32
21:20^{2}, 21^{2}, 24
22:3, 10
23:15, 21, 35
24:2, 11, 14
25:5, 24
26:3, 18, 26
28:27

ROMANS
1:6, 15, 20^{3}, 28, 32
2:2, 8, 13, 14, 18, 19
3:9^{2}, 12^{2}, 15, 16, 19, 25
4:7^{3}, 12, 14
6:2, 4, 13, 14, 15, 16, 21
7:4, 6
8:1, 5^{2}, 8, 9, 12, 14^{2}, 16, 18, 24, 28, 36^{2}, 37
9:4, 5, 6^{2}, 7^{2}, 8^{3}, 26
10:15, 19
11:14, 16, 28^{2}, 29, 33, 36
12:5
13:1, 3, 6
14:8, 20
15:1, 14, 26, 27
16:7, 10, 11, 14, 15, 18

1 CORINTHIANS
1:2, 5, 11^{2}, 18, 24, 26, 27, 28^{3}, 30
2:6, 12, 14^{2}
3:2, 3^{2}, 4, 8, 9^{3}, 16, 17, 20, 21, 22, 23
4:8^{2}, 9, 10^{6}, 11^{2}, 13^{2}, 18, 19
5:2, 4, 7, 12^{2}, 13
6:2, 4, 11^{3}, 12^{3}, 15, 19, 20^{2}
7:14, 23, 33
8:4, 5, 6^{2}, 8^{2}, 9, 10
9:1, 2, 12, 13, 20^{2}, 21^{2}
10:11^{2}, 13, 17^{2}, 18, 22, 23^{3}
11:19, 30, 32^{2}
12:4, 5, 6, 12, 13, 20, 22, 27, 29^{4}
14:10, 12, 22, 23^{2}, 25, 32, 34, 37
15:2, 6, 15, 17, 18^{2}, 19, 23, 27, 29^{2}, 35, 40, 48^{4}
16:9, 18

2 CORINTHIANS
1:1, 4^{2}, 7, 14^{2}, 20, 24
2:11, 15^{2}, 16, 17
3:2, 3, 5, 18
4:3, 8^{2}, 11, 15, 18^{6}
5:4, 6^{3}, 8, 11^{2}, 17^{2}, 18, 20
6:12^{2}, 16
7:3, 6
8:23
10:4, 7, 10, 11^{3}, 12, 14
11:13, 19, 22^{3}, 23, 28
13:4, 6, 9^{3}

GALATIANS
1:2, 6
2:15, 17
3:3^{2}, 7^{2}, 9, 10^{3}, 25, 26, 28, 29
4:6, 8, 9, 12, 24^{2}, 28, 31
5:4^{2}, 17, 18, 19^{2}, 24
6:1, 10, 13

EPHESIANS
1:1, 10^{2}
2:5, 8, 10, 11, 13, 19, 20, 22
4:1, 4, 25, 30
5:4, 8, 12, 13^{2}, 16, 30
6:5

PHILIPPIANS
1:1, 7, 10, 11, 13, 14
2:21
3:3, 13^{2}, 18
4:3, 8^{6}, 21, 22

COLOSSIANS
1:2, 16^{2}
2:3, 10, 11, 12, 17, 20, 22
3:1, 3, 5, 15
4:5, 9, 11^{2}, 13, 15

1 THESSALONIANS
2:10, 14, 15, 19, 20
3:3
4:9, 10, 12, 13, 15^{2}, 17
5:4, 5^{2}, 7, 8, 12, 14

2 THESSALONIANS
1:3, 7
2:13
3:11^{2}, 12

1 TIMOTHY
2:2
3:7
5:3, 15, 16, 24, 25^{2}
6:1, 2^{2}, 17

2 TIMOTHY
1:15^{2}
2:19, 20, 26
3:3, 6, 15

TITUS
1:5, 10, 12, 15^{2}
3:8, 9, 15

PHILEMON
7

HEBREWS
1:10, 14
2:10^{2}, 11^{2}, 14, 18
3:6, 14
4:13, 15
5:2, 11, 12, 14
6:9
7:5, 13
8:4
9:15, 17, 22, 24
10:8, 10, 14, 39
11:3
12:1, 8^{2}, 11, 18, 22, 23, 27^{2}
13:3, 11

JAMES
1:1
2:4^{2}, 7, 9, 16
3:4^{2}, 9
5:2^{2}, 4, 17

1 PETER
1:5, 6, 12
2:5, 9, 10, 14, 25
3:6^{2}, 9, 12^{2}, 14
4:6, 13, 14
5:1, 9^{2}, 14

2 PETER
1:4
2:10^{2}, 11, 13, 15, 17^{2}, 19, 20
3:5, 7^{2}, 10, 16^{2}

1 JOHN
2:5, 12, 14, 15, 18
3:2, 10, 19, 22
4:1^{2}, 4, 5, 6, 17
5:3, 7^{2}, 8, 19, 20

2 JOHN
7

JUDE

1, 4, 7, 12^2, 15, 16

REVELATION

1:3, 4^2, 11, 19, 20^2
2:2^3, 9^3, 18
3:2, 4, 9^2
4:5, 11
5:6, 8, 13^2
7:13^2, 14, 15
8:13
9:14
10:6^3
11:4, 15
13:8
14:4^3, 5, 12, 13, 18
15:3^2, 4
16:6, 7, 14
17:9, 10^2, 12, 14^2, 15
18:3, 14^2
19:2, 9^3
20:7, 8, 10
21:4, 5, 12, 16, 22, 24, 27
22:6, 14, 15, 18, 19

AS *5613*

GENESIS

3:5, 22
4:20^2, 21
7:9, 16
8:21
9:3
10:9, 19^2, 30
11:2
12:4
13:10^2, 16
16:6
17:4, 15, 20, 23
18:5, 25, 33^2
19:8, 14, 28
21:1^2, 4, 16
22:14, 17^2
23:9^2
24:22, 51
25:18
26:4, 29^2
27:4, 9, 12, 14, 19, 23, 27, 30^2, 42, 46
28:6, 14
31:2, 5, 26
32:12, 25, 28, 31
33:10, 14
34:12, 15, 22, 31
35:18
36:24
38:11, 29
39:10, 18
40:10, 22
41:13, 19, 21, 38, 39^2, 49, 54
42:27, 35
43:6, 17, 34
44:1^2, 3^2, 15, 17, 18
47:11, 21, 30
48:5, 7, 20^2
49:4, 9^2, 16, 27
50:6, 12, 20^2

EXODUS

1:17, 19
2:14
4:6, 7
5:7, 13, 14, 20
7:6, 10, 13, 20, 22
8:15, 19, 27
9:12, 17, 18, 24, 29^2, 30, 35
10:10, 14
11:6
12:25, 28, 31, 32, 36, 48, 50
13:11
14:28
15:5, 7, 8, 10, 16^2
16:5^2, 10, 14^2, 22, 24, 34
17:10
18:21
19:18
21:7, 22^2
22:25
23:15
24:10^2
27:8
28:32
30:37
32:1, 13, 17, 19^2, 23
33:9, 11
34:4, 10, 18
35:22^2
38:21
39:1, 5, 6, 7, 21, 23, 26, 29, 31, 43
40:15, 19, 21, 23, 25, 27, 29, 32

LEVITICUS

2:12
4:10, 20, 21, 26^2, 31, 35
5:13^2
6:17^2
7:7, 10^2, 19, 21
8:4, 9, 13, 17, 21, 29, 31, 34
9:7, 10, 15, 21
10:5, 15, 18
11:4
12:5
13:43
14:6, 13, 22, 30, 31, 35
15:25, 26^2
16:15, 34
18:19^2, 22, 28
19:16, 18, 23^2, 34^2
20:6, 13, 25
22:13
24:16^2, 19, 20, 22^2, 23
25:31, 39, 40^2, 42, 46, 53
26:19^2, 34^2, 35^2, 36, 37
27:12, 14, 21, 23

NUMBERS

1:19
2:17, 33
3:16, 42, 51
4:15, 29, 49
5:4
8:3, 16, 19, 21, 22
9:15, 18^2
10:31
11:7^2, 8, 12, 31^3
12:10, 12
13:21, 33
14:15, 17, 19, 21^2, 28^3, 32
15:14, 15, 20, 36
16:31, 40^3, 45, 47
17:11
18:6, 7, 18^2, 24, 27^2, 30^2
20:9, 27
21:34
22:4, 8
23:2, 22, 24^2, 30
24:1, 6^4, 8, 9^2
26:4
27:11, 13, 17, 22, 23
28:8^2
31:7, 31, 41, 47
32:25, 27, 31
33:56
34:6
36:10

DEUTERONOMY

1:10, 11^2, 17^2, 19, 21, 31, 40, 44
2:1, 5, 10, 11, 12, 14, 21, 22, 29, 30
3:2, 6, 20^2
4:5, 7, 8, 20, 32, 33, 38
5:12, 14^2, 16, 26, 31, 32
6:3, 8, 16, 19, 24, 25
8:5, 18, 20
9:3^2, 18, 21^2, 25
10:5, 9, 15, 22
11:4, 10^2, 18, 21, 25
12:9, 12, 15^2, 16, 19^2, 20, 21, 22, 24
13:6, 11, 17
14:7
15:6, 21, 22^2, 23
16:9, 10, 17
17:14, 16
18:2, 7, 14
19:5, 6, 8, 19
20:8^2, 17
22:11, 26
23:23
24:8
26:15, 18, 19
27:3
28:9, 29, 49^2, 62, 63
29:13^2, 28
30:9
31:3, 4, 13^2, 21
32:2^4, 10, 11, 31, 50
33:20, 25
34:9

JOSHUA

1:3, 5, 15, 17^2
2:7^2, 11^2
3:7, 13^2, 15
4:8^2, 12, 14, 18, 23
5:5, 14
6:22
7:5
8:2, 5, 6, 15, 19^2, 29^2, 31^2, 33^3
9:4, 21, 25
10:1, 2, 11, 28, 30, 39^2, 40
11:4, 9, 12, 13, 15, 20
13:6, 8, 14, 33
14:2, 5, 7, 10, 11^4, 12
15:18, 63
17:14
21:8
22:4
23:5, 8, 9, 10, 15
24:15

JUDGES

1:7, 20
2:3, 15^2, 22
3:1^2, 2
4:22
5:31
6:5, 16, 27, 36, 37
7:5, 12, 17
8:8, 18, 19, 21, 33^2
9:33^3, 36, 48
11:36
13:9, 23^2
14:6, 20
15:10, 11, 14
16:7, 9, 11, 20
17:8, 11
19:22
20:1, 8, 11, 30, 31, 32, 39, 48^2

RUTH

1:8
3:10, 13

1 SAMUEL

1:7, 12, 26, 28^2
2:2, 16^2
3:10
4:9
5:10
6:6, 12
7:10
9:11, 13^2, 20, 27
10:7
12:15, 23
13:5, 7, 10^2
14:14, 39, 45
15:22^3, 23^2, 27, 33
16:7
17:20^2, 23, 36, 55, 57
18:1, 3, 6, 7, 10
19:6, 7, 9, 20
20:3^2, 13, 17, 20, 21, 23, 25, 31^2, 36, 41^2, 42
22:8, 13, 14
23:11
24:4, 13, 18
25:15^2, 20, 25, 26^3, 29, 34, 37
26:10, 16, 20, 24
27:8
28:10, 17
29:6, 8, 9, 10^2
30:24

2 SAMUEL

1:6, 21
2:18^2, 23^2, 27
3:9, 33, 34, 36
4:4, 6, 9
5:20, 25
6:16, 18^2, 19^2, 20
7:10, 11, 15, 25
8:3
9:8, 11^2
10:2
11:11^2, 25^2
12:3, 5
13:13^2, 29, 35, 36^2
14:2, 11, 13, 14, 17, 19, 25
15:10^2, 21^2, 26, 30^2, 34
16:2, 5, 13^2, 19, 23
17:3, 8, 10, 11, 12^2
18:32, 33
19:3, 14, 18, 27, 30
20:8
22:23, 31, 43^3, 45^2
23:4^2, 6
24:19, 23

1 KINGS

1:29, 30, 37, 41
2:3, 24^2, 31, 38
3:6^2, 14
4:20, 29
5:5, 12
8:20, 24, 25, 43, 53, 57, 59, 61
9:2, 4, 5
10:10, 27^2
11:4, 6, 11, 33, 38^2
12:12, 17
13:6, 18, 20, 21
14:6, 7, 8, 10, 15
15:3, 11
16:2, 9, 11^2, 31
17:1, 11, 12, 13
18:7, 10, 12^2, 15, 32^2
19:2, 5
20:11, 12, 34, 36^4, 39, 40
21:11^2, 26
22:4^3, 14, 17

2 KINGS

1:16
2:2^2, 4^2, 6^2, 11, 19, 23
3:7^3, 14, 22^2
4:8^2, 30^2, 40
5:16, 20, 27^2
6:5, 26
7:7, 10, 13^2, 17, 18
8:5, 18, 19, 27
9:17, 22, 31, 37
10:2^2, 12, 15, 25^2
11:8^2, 14
12:9
13:5, 21, 23
14:3, 4, 5^2
15:9
17:2, 4, 11, 23, 41
19:12, 26^4, 29, 37
21:3, 13, 20
22:18
23:16, 21, 27
24:13
25:15, 22

1 CHRONICLES

5:1
6:26
12:8^2, 20, 33, 36
14:16
15:15, 29
16:37
17:1, 9, 13, 23
18:3
21:3, 15, 17, 21
22:7, 11
23:24
24:19
25:8^3
26:13^2, 21
28:2, 7
29:11, 15^2, 17, 23, 25

2 CHRONICLES

1:12, 15^3
2:3, 16^2
3:16
4:6
5:13^2
6:8, 10, 15, 16, 31, 33
7:17^2, 18
8:7, 14
9:9, 27^2
10:12, 17
11:16
13:10, 15
16:3
18:3^2, 13, 16
20:9, 20, 21, 33
21:6, 7
23:3, 13, 18^2
24:12^2
25:4, 16
26:5^2
29:8, 31^2
30:5, 7, 8
31:3, 5^2, 15^2
32:17, 19
33:22, 23
34:26
35:12, 18
36:21^2

EZRA

2:62
3:1, 2, 4^2
4:2, 3
6:18, 21
7:14, 25, 27, 28
8:27, 31
9:7, 13, 15
10:3, 12

NEHEMIAH

1:1
2:16, 18
5:5^2, 12
6:8, 11^2
7:64
8:1, 15
9:10, 11, 23, 24
10:34, 36
13:15

ESTHER

2:9, 20^2
3:11
4:14
5:5, 8, 13
6:10
7:8
8:8
9:2, 22, 23^2, 27^2, 31^2

JOB

2:10
3:6, 16^2
4:8
5:7, 14, 25, 26
6:7, 15^2, 26
7:2^2, 9, 20
9:26^2, 32
10:4, 5^2, 9, 10, 16, 19, 22^2
11:8^2, 16, 17, 20
12:3^3, 4, 5
13:9, 28^2
14:2, 6, 11
15:24, 33^2
16:4, 21
17:6, 7, 10, 15
18:3, 20
19:11, 22
20:8^2
21:4, 18^2, 33
22:2, 8, 24^2
23:10
24:5, 14, 17, 18, 20, 24^2
26:3
27:2, 6, 7^2, 16^2, 18^2, 20, 21
28:5^2
29:2^2, 4, 14, 18, 23^2, 25^2
30:5, 14, 15^2, 18
31:18, 33, 36, 37
32:19
34:3, 26
35:8
37:18
38:8, 14^2, 19, 30
39:16, 20
40:15, 18
41:5, 15, 20, 24^4, 27^2, 29
42:7, 9, 10^2, 15

PSALMS

5:7, 12
10:5, 9
11:1
12:6
14:4
17:8, 12^2, 15
18:30, 42^2, 44^2
19:5^2
21:9
22:13
25:10
26:11
27:12
31:12
32:9^2
33:7, 22
34:18
35:5, 13, 14^2
37:2, 6^2, 14, 20, 22
38:4, 10, 13^2, 14
39:5^2, 12
40:4, 16
41:12
42:1, 10
44:22
48:6, 8
50:21
53:4
55:16, 20
58:3^2, 7^2, 8, 9
61:6
62:3^2
63:2, 5
65:3
66:10
68:2^2, 13, 14, 15^2, 17, 21
69:13
70:4
71:7
72:5^2, 6, 7, 17^2
73:1, 2, 5, 6^2, 19, 20, 22
74:5
77:13
78:8, 13, 15, 27^2, 65
83:9^3, 10, 11^2, 13, 14^2
87:7^2
88:4
89:10, 11, 29, 36, 37^2
90:4^2, 5^2, 9
92:7
95:8^2
102:3, 7, 26
103:11, 12^2, 13, 15^3, 18
104:2, 6, 17, 33^2
106:9
107:10
109:17^2, 18^2, 19, 23, 29
116:2^2
118:12
119:14^2, 70^2, 111, 132, 162
122:3
123:2^2
124:6, 7
125:1, 2, 5^2
126:4
127:4
128:3
129:6
131:2^2
133:3^2
137:8
139:12, 16
140:9
141:2^2, 7
143:3, 6
144:4, 12^2
147:20

PROVERBS

1:12^2, 27^2
2:4^2
3:12
4:18, 19
5:3, 4^2, 19
6:5^2, 11^2
7:2, 22^2, 23
8:26, 30
9:4, 16
10:20, 23, 25, 26^2
11:19, 20, 22, 28
12:4
15:19
16:14, 15, 24, 27
17:8, 14
18:4^2, 8, 11
19:12^2, 24
20:2, 19
21:1, 8, 29
23:5, 7, 28, 34^2
24:29, 34^2
25:12, 13, 16, 20^2, 25, 26
26:1^2, 2^2, 8, 9, 11, 14, 18, 21, 22
27:8, 19, 21
28:1, 4, 15
30:14^2
31:8

ECCLESIASTES

2:8, 13^2, 15, 16
3:19
4:1
5:15^2, 16
6:12
7:6, 26
8:1, 13
9:2^2, 12^2
10:5, 7
11:5
12:7, 11^2

SONG OF SOLOMON

1:3, 5^2, 7, 14
2:2, 3
4:1, 11
5:11^2, 12, 13^2, 14^2, 15^3
6:4^3, 5, 6, 7, 10^4, 13
7:4^2, 8
8:1, 6^4, 10

ISAIAH

1:7, 8^3, 9, 18^4, 26^2, 30^2, 31^2
3:9, 12, 16
5:18, 24^3
6:13^2
7:2
8:6
9:1, 3, 4, 18, 19
10:9^3, 10, 11, 14^2, 15^3, 18, 20, 22, 26, 32
11:9, 16
13:4, 6, 8^2, 14^2, 17, 19
14:10, 17, 19^2, 24^2
16:2, 3, 14
17:3, 5^2, 6, 9, 13
19:14
20:3
21:1, 3
22:16, 23
23:5, 10, 15
24:2^6, 13^2, 22
25:4, 5, 10, 11
26:17, 18, 19, 20
27:7, 9
28:2^2, 4, 21^2
29:2, 4, 5, 7, 8^2, 11, 13, 16, 17
30:13, 14, 17^2, 22, 26^2, 27, 28, 29^2
31:4, 5
32:2^3
33:4, 11, 12^2
34:4^3
35:1, 6
37:12, 27^4, 30, 38
38:12, 13, 14, 19
40:6, 15^3, 17, 22^3, 23, 24, 31
41:2^2, 11, 12^2, 15, 25^2
42:13, 19^3
43:17
44:4^2, 7, 22^2
47:3, 4, 8, 14
48:18^2, 19
49:18^3, 26
50:4, 9
51:9, 12, 13, 20, 23^2
52:14
53:2^2, 3, 7^2
54:6, 9^2
55:9, 10
56:12
58:2, 4, 5, 8, 10
59:10^3, 12, 17^2, 21
60:8^2
61:10^2, 11^2
62:1^2, 5^2
63:13, 14
64:2, 6^3
65:8, 22
66:3^4, 8^2, 13, 20, 22

JEREMIAH

2:26, 36
3:2, 5, 20
4:13^2, 17, 31^2
5:8, 9, 16, 19, 26, 27, 29
6:7, 9^2, 23, 24, 26
7:14, 15
8:6
9:8, 9, 22^2
10:5, 6, 7
11:5
12:8, 9, 16
13:5, 10, 11, 21^2, 24
14:8^2, 9^2
15:2^4, 18^2, 19
16:4
17:8, 11, 16, 22
18:4, 6^2, 17
19:11, 12, 13
20:9, 11, 16
21:7
22:23, 24
23:12, 14^2, 27, 29, 34
24:8
25:18, 30, 38
26:11, 14^2, 18
27:13
30:6, 20
31:5, 10, 12, 18, 23, 28
32:20, 31, 42
33:7, 11, 22
38:16
39:12
40:3, 10
41:6^2
42:2, 18
43:11^3, 12
44:6, 13, 14, 16, 17, 22, 23, 30
46:7^2, 18^3, 22, 26
48:8, 13, 34, 40, 41
49:16^2, 18, 22^2, 24
50:8, 9, 11^2, 15, 18, 26, 37, 40, 43
51:14, 27, 30, 38, 49

LAMENTATIONS

1:1, 15, 17, 20, 22
2:4, 5, 6, 7, 12, 22

LAMENTATIONS

3:6, 10[2], 12, 45
4:2, 6, 14, 17[2]
5:3, 21

EZEKIEL

1:1, 4, 10, 13, 14, 15, 16, 18, 22, 24[2], 26[2], 27[3], 28
3:3, 9, 23
4:12
5:11
7:17, 20
8:1, 2[3]
9:10, 11
10:1[2], 5, 9, 10[2], 11[2], 13
11:16, 21
12:4[2], 7[2], 11, 23
14:10, 16, 18, 20
15:6
16:4, 7, 31, 32, 38, 44, 47, 48[2], 50, 57, 59
17:5, 16, 19
18:3, 4, 18
20:3, 31, 32[2], 33, 36, 39
21:7, 10, 23
22:20, 22
23:16[2], 18, 20, 44
24:18, 22
26:3, 10
28:2, 6, 16
30:9, 18
32:2
33:11, 12, 17, 27, 31[2], 32
34:8, 12, 17, 19
35:6, 11, 15
36:17, 38[2]
37:7[2], 10
38:16
40:2, 40
41:21, 25
42:6, 9, 11[4], 12
43:22
46:5, 7, 11, 12
47:10, 14[2], 15, 22
48:1, 8, 11, 23

DANIEL

1:4, 13, 17
2:29, 30, 40[3], 41, 42, 43, 45
4:18, 25, 32, 33, 35
5:12
6:4, 10, 22
7:4, 9[2], 12, 28
8:5, 15, 18
9:7, 12, 13, 15
10:4, 6[2], 17
11:29[2], 32
12:1, 3[2]

HOSEA

1:10
2:3[2], 15[2]
4:4, 7, 16[2]
5:12[2], 14[2]
6:3[3], 4[2], 5, 9
7:4, 6, 7, 12[2]
8:1, 8, 12
9:1, 4, 9, 10[2], 11, 13
10:4, 7[2], 11, 14
11:2, 4, 8[2], 11[2]
12:9, 11
13:3[4], 7[2], 8
14:5[3], 6[2], 7[3]

JOEL

1:15
2:2, 3, 4[2], 5, 32

AMOS

2:9, 13
3:12
4:11[2]
5:11, 14, 16, 19, 24[2]
7:15
8:8[2], 10[2]
9:5, 7, 9, 11

OBADIAH

4, 11, 15, 16[2]

JONAH

1:14

MICAH

1:4[2], 6[2], 8, 16
2:8[2], 12[2]
3:3[2], 4, 12[2]
4:9, 12
5:7[2], 8[2], 15
7:1[2], 4, 10, 14

NAHUM

1:10[3]
2:2, 7
3:6, 15[2], 17[2]

HABAKKUK

1:8, 9[2], 14[2]
2:5[2], 14
3:4, 14[2]

ZEPHANIAH

1:8, 17[2]
2:2, 9[3]

HAGGAI

1:12
2:3, 19, 23

ZECHARIAH

1:4, 6
2:4, 6
4:1
5:3[2]
7:3, 12, 13
8:11, 13, 14
9:1, 3[2], 7[2], 11, 13, 14, 15[2], 16[3]
10:2, 3, 5, 6, 7, 8
12:8[3], 10[2], 11
13:9[2]
14:3, 5, 10, 15

MALACHI

2:9
3:3[2], 4[2], 17
4:1, 2

MATTHEW

1:18, 24
5:48
6:2, 5, 7, 10, 12, 16
7:29[2]
8:13
9:9, 10, 15[2], 32, 36
10:7, 16[3], 25[2]
11:7
12:13, 40
13:40, 43
14:5, 36[2]
15:28, 33

MATTHEW

17:2[2], 9, 20
18:3, 4, 17, 19, 25, 33
19:19
20:14, 28, 29
21:6, 18, 23, 26
22:9[2], 10[2], 30, 31, 39
23:37
24:3, 21, 27, 37, 38, 44
25:14, 32, 40, 45
26:7, 19, 21, 24, 26, 39[2], 55
27:10, 32, 65[2]
28:1, 3, 4, 6, 9, 15

MARK

1:2, 16, 22[2], 42[2]
2:2, 14, 15, 19[2], 23
3:5, 10[2], 20
4:4, 18, 20, 26, 33, 36
5:36[2]
6:15, 31, 34, 56[2]
7:4, 6, 8
8:24
9:3[2], 9, 13, 26
10:1, 15, 32, 46
11:2[2], 6, 20, 27
12:25, 26, 31, 33
13:1, 3, 19, 34
14:3, 16, 18, 21, 22, 45[2], 48, 66
15:8
16:7, 10, 12, 14

LUKE

1:1, 2, 23[2], 44[2], 55, 70
2:15, 20, 23, 43
3:4, 15, 23
4:16
5:1, 14, 17
6:3, 10, 22, 31, 34, 36, 40
8:5, 6[2], 23, 42
9:18, 29, 33, 34, 42, 53, 54, 57
10:3, 7, 8, 18, 27, 33, 38
11:1[2], 2, 8[2], 27, 30, 36, 37, 41, 44, 53
12:58
13:34
14:1, 22
15:19, 25, 30[2]
17:6, 11, 12, 14, 24, 26, 28
18:11[2], 13, 17, 35
19:9, 11, 32, 33, 36
20:1
21:5, 6, 35
22:13, 22, 26[2], 27, 29, 31, 39, 44, 52, 56, 66[2]
23:7[2], 14, 24, 26
24:4, 5, 11, 17, 24, 28, 30, 36, 39, 50[2]

JOHN

1:12[2], 14, 23, 36
3:14
4:51
5:21, 23, 26, 30
6:11[2], 31, 57, 58, 59
7:10, 28, 38
8:6, 20, 28, 30
9:1, 5[2], 29
10:15, 26
11:20[2], 29[2], 56
12:14, 50
13:15, 33, 34
14:27, 31

JOHN

15:4, 6, 9, 10, 12
16:21[2]
17:2[3], 11, 14, 16, 18, 21, 22, 23
18:6[2]
19:40
20:9, 11, 21
21:8, 9[2]

THE ACTS

1:10, 11, 19
2:2, 3, 4, 15, 22, 39[2], 45, 47
3:6, 11, 12, 17, 24[2]
4:1, 6[2], 34[2], 35
5:11[2], 35, 36[2], 37[2]
6:15
7:5[2], 26, 28, 31, 40, 42, 44, 48, 51
8:3, 16, 32, 36
9:3, 17, 18, 32, 38
10:9, 11, 25, 27, 29[2], 45[2], 47[2]
11:5, 15[2], 17[2], 19[2], 22[2]
12:13, 18[2]
13:1, 2, 17, 25, 33, 34, 48[2]
14:20
15:8, 11, 15, 24
16:4, 16
17:2, 14, 23, 25, 28, 29
19:2
20:3, 9
21:10, 25, 31, 37
22:3, 5, 6, 23, 25
23:11, 15, 20, 31
24:10, 25
25:10, 18
26:12, 24, 29
27:25, 27, 30[2]
28:10, 15[2], 22

ROMANS

1:13, 15[2], 17, 21, 28
2:12[4], 24
3:4, 5, 7, 8[2], 10
4:1, 6, 17[2]
5:12, 15, 16, 18, 19, 21
6:3, 4, 13[3], 19
7:1[2], 2
8:14[2], 26, 36[2]
9:5, 6, 13, 25, 27, 29[2], 32, 33
10:15
11:8, 13, 26, 28[2], 30
12:3, 4, 18[2]
13:9, 13
14:11
15:3, 7, 9, 15, 21
16:2

1 CORINTHIANS

1:6, 31
2:9
3:1[3], 3, 5, 10, 15
4:1, 7, 8, 9, 13, 14, 17, 18
5:1[2], 3[2], 7
7:7, 8, 17[2], 25, 29, 30[3], 31, 39[2]
8:1, 2, 4, 5, 7
9:5[3], 8, 20[2], 21, 22, 26[2]
10:6, 7[2], 8, 9, 10, 13, 15, 33
11:1, 2, 5, 7, 12, 25[2], 26[2]
12:2, 11, 12, 18
13:1, 11[3], 12
14:12, 33, 34
15:8, 22, 38, 48[2], 49, 58
16:1, 2, 10, 12

2 CORINTHIANS

1:5, 7, 14[2], 18, 23
2:17[3]
3:1, 3, 5, 13, 18[2]
4:1, 13
5:20
6:1, 4, 8, 9[3], 10[3], 13, 16
7:14
8:5, 6, 7, 11, 15
9:1, 3, 5[2], 7, 9
10:2, 7, 9, 11, 14[3]
11:2, 3, 10, 12, 15, 16, 17, 21[2], 23
12:20[2]
13:2, 7

GALATIANS

1:9
2:7, 14[2]
3:6, 10[2], 16[2], 27[2]
4:1[2], 12[2], 14[2], 28, 29
5:14, 21
6:10, 12[2], 16[2]

EPHESIANS

1:4
2:3
3:3, 5
4:4, 17, 21, 32
5:1, 2, 3, 8, 15[2], 22, 23, 24, 25, 28, 29, 33
6:5, 6[2], 7, 20

PHILIPPIANS

1:7[2], 20, 27
2:8, 12[2], 15, 22, 23
3:5, 12, 15[2], 17
4:15

COLOSSIANS

1:6[2], 7
2:1[2], 6, 7, 20
3:12, 13, 18, 22, 23
4:4

1 THESSALONIANS

1:5
2:2, 4[2], 5, 6, 7, 11[2], 13[2], 14
3:4, 6, 12
4:1, 5, 6, 9, 11, 13
5:2, 3, 4, 6, 11

2 THESSALONIANS

1:3
2:2[2], 4
3:1, 15[2]

1 TIMOTHY

1:3
5:1[2], 2[2]
6:1[2]

2 TIMOTHY

2:3, 9, 17
3:8, 9

TITUS

1:5, 7, 9
2:3

PHILEMON

9, 14, 16, 17

HEBREWS

1:4, 11, 12
2:14
3:2, 3, 5, 6, 7, 8, 15
4:2[2], 3[2], 7, 10, 15
5:3, 4, 6, 12
6:19
7:9, 20, 27
8:5
9:8, 9, 25, 27
10:25[2]
11:7, 9, 12[4], 27, 29
12:5, 7, 16, 20, 27
13:3[2], 5, 17

JAMES

1:10
2:8, 9, 12, 26
5:3, 5, 17

1 PETER

1:14, 15, 18[2], 19, 24[2]
2:2, 4, 5, 11, 12, 13, 14, 16[2], 25
3:6[3], 7[2], 8, 16
4:1, 10[2], 11[2], 12, 13, 15[4], 16, 19
5:3, 8, 12

2 PETER

1:3, 13[2], 14, 19, 21
2:1, 12, 13
3:4, 8[2], 9, 10, 15, 16[2]

1 JOHN

1:7
2:6, 18, 27[2]
3:2, 3, 7, 12, 23
4:17

2 JOHN

4, 5, 6

3 JOHN

2, 3

JUDE

7, 10

REVELATION

1:10, 14[3], 15[2], 16, 17
2:24[3], 27[2]
3:3, 19[2], 21
4:1, 7
5:6, 13
6:1, 11, 12[2], 13, 14
8:8, 10, 12
9:2, 3, 5, 7[2], 8[2], 9[2], 17
10:1[2], 3, 7, 9, 10[3]
11:6[2]
12:4[2], 15
13:2[2], 3, 11, 15[2]
14:2[2], 3
15:2
16:3, 15, 18
17:12[2]
18:6, 17[2]
19:6[3], 12
20:8
21:2, 11, 16[2], 21
22:1, 12

BE

1961, *1510*

GENESIS

1:3, 6, 9, 14[2], 15, 22, 28, 29
2:18, 23, 24
3:5[2], 6, 12, 16
4:7[2], 12, 14[2], 15, 24
6:3, 15, 19, 21
8:17
9:1, 2, 3, 6, 7, 11[2], 13, 14, 16, 20, 25[2], 26[2], 27
10:8
11:4, 6
12:2, 3, 13
13:8[2], 16
14:19, 20
15:4[2], 5[2], 13, 15
16:2, 3, 5, 10, 12[2]
17:1, 4, 5[2], 7, 8, 10, 11, 12, 13[2], 14, 15, 16[2], 17
18:4, 11, 18, 24, 25[3], 29, 30[2], 31, 32[2]
19:9, 15, 17, 22
20:9
21:10, 12[2], 30
22:14, 18
23:8
24:5, 8[2], 14, 27, 41[2], 44, 51, 60
25:22, 23[2], 24
26:3, 4, 11, 22, 28
27:13, 21, 29[3], 33, 39, 45
28:3, 9, 14[2], 20, 21, 22
29:4, 7, 8, 15, 26, 29, 34
30:32, 33, 34
31:3, 8[2], 30, 44, 52[2]
32:12, 18, 28
33:14
34:7, 10, 15[3], 17[2], 22[2], 23, 30
35:2, 10[2], 11[2]
36:43
37:14, 27, 32, 35
38:9, 11, 15, 23, 24, 29
39:10
40:14
41:21, 27, 30, 31[2], 36[2], 40[3], 52

GENESIS

42:15, 16[3], 19[2], 20, 32, 33
43:3, 5, 9, 11, 14, 23, 29
44:9[2], 10[3], 17, 26[2], 30, 34
45:5, 6, 10
46:15
47:19[2], 24, 25
48:5, 6[2], 16, 19[2], 21
49:6, 7, 8, 10, 12, 13[2], 17, 20, 26, 29
50:18

EXODUS

1:16[2]
2:4
3:12[2]
4:12, 14, 15, 16[4], 18
5:8, 9, 11, 18, 21
6:7, 14[2]
7:1, 17, 19
8:10, 21, 22, 23
9:3, 9, 15, 16, 19[2], 22, 28, 29
10:5, 7, 10, 14, 21[2], 24, 26
11:6[2], 9
12:2[2], 4, 5, 13[2], 14, 15, 16[4], 19[3], 25, 32, 33, 42[2], 46, 48[2], 49
13:3, 5, 6, 7[3], 9[2], 11, 12, 14, 16
14:4
15:9, 14, 15, 16
16:5, 8, 12, 23, 26, 32, 33, 34
17:4
18:10, 19[2], 21, 22[2], 23
19:5, 6, 11, 12, 13[2], 15
20:12, 20, 26
21:4, 7, 8, 12, 15, 16[2], 17, 19[2], 20, 21, 22, 28[3], 29[2], 30, 31, 32, 34, 36[2]
22:2[3], 3[3], 4[2], 5, 6, 7[2], 8[2], 9[2], 10, 11, 12, 13, 14, 15[2], 16, 19, 20, 24, 25, 30, 31
23:1, 12, 13[2], 22, 26, 30, 33
24:7, 12
25:7, 10, 12, 14, 15[2], 17, 20, 23, 27, 28, 31[2], 34, 35, 36[2], 38

EXODUS

26:2, 3[2], 6, 7, 8[2], 11, 16[2], 17, 20, 24[4], 25, 31, 32, 37
27:1[2], 2, 5, 7[2], 9, 10[2], 11, 12, 13, 14, 15, 16[2], 17[2], 18, 19, 21
28:7, 8, 11, 16[3], 17[2], 18, 20, 21[2], 28[2], 30, 32[2], 35[2], 37[2], 38[3], 43[2]
29:9, 10, 21, 26, 28[2], 29[3], 34, 37[2], 42, 43, 45
30:2[4], 4, 12, 13, 16, 21, 25, 29[2], 31, 32[2], 33, 34, 36, 37, 38
31:14[2], 15[2]
32:4, 8
33:16[2], 19[2], 23
34:2, 3, 12, 25
35:2[3], 9, 27, 29
36:6, 18, 34
37:3, 27
38:5, 26
39:7, 21[2], 37
40:4, 9, 10, 15

LEVITICUS

1:3, 4, 9, 10, 14, 15
2:1, 2, 3, 4, 5[2], 7[2], 10, 11, 12, 13
3:1[2], 6, 12, 17
4:2, 12, 13[2], 15, 20, 22, 26, 27[2], 31, 35
5:2[3], 3[4], 4[3], 5[2], 7, 9, 10, 11, 13[2], 16, 17, 18
6:4, 7, 9, 12[2], 13, 16, 17, 18[2], 21, 22, 23[2], 25, 26, 27, 28[3], 30[2]
7:6, 9, 14, 15, 16[3], 17, 18[4], 19[3], 20, 21, 24, 25, 26, 27[2], 30, 31, 36
8:5, 33
10:3[2], 9, 14, 15
11:7, 10, 11, 12, 13, 20, 23, 24[2], 25, 26, 27, 28, 29, 31[2], 32[6], 33, 34[4], 35[4], 36[2], 37[2], 38[2], 39, 40[2], 41[2], 43, 44, 45[2], 47[2]
12:2[2], 3, 4, 5, 7, 8[2]
13:2[2], 3, 4[3], 5, 6[2], 7, 9, 10[2], 14,

LEVITICUS

15, 16, 17, 19[2], 20[2], 21[3], 24, 25[2], 26[3], 27, 28, 30[2], 31, 32[2], 33, 34[3], 36, 37, 39, 42, 43, 45, 46[3], 47, 48, 49[2], 51, 52, 53, 55[2], 56, 58[4]
14:2[2], 3, 4, 5, 7, 8[2], 9[2], 11, 14, 17, 18, 19, 20, 21[2], 22, 25, 28, 29, 31, 34, 36, 37, 39, 41, 44, 46, 53
15:3[2], 4, 5, 6, 7, 8, 9, 10[2], 11, 12[2], 13, 16, 17[2], 18, 19[3], 20[2], 21, 22, 23[2], 24[3], 25[2], 26[2], 27[2], 28[2]
16:4[2], 10[2], 17, 29[2], 30, 31, 34
17:3, 4[2], 7, 8, 9, 10, 13[2], 14, 15[3]
18:9, 29
19:2, 6[2], 7[2], 8, 20[2], 22, 23[2], 24, 29, 31, 34
20:2[2], 7, 9[2], 10, 11[2], 12[2], 13[2], 14[2], 15, 16[2], 17, 18, 21, 26[2], 27[2]
21:1, 3, 6[2], 8, 9, 17, 18, 20
22:3[2], 4, 5, 6, 7, 12, 13, 18, 20, 21[3], 23, 25[2], 27[2], 28, 30, 32, 33
23:2, 3, 10, 11, 13[2], 14, 15, 17[2], 18, 20, 21[2], 27[2], 29[3], 30, 31, 32, 34, 35, 36, 37, 39[2], 41
24:3, 5, 7, 9, 12, 16[2], 17, 19, 20, 21
25:4, 6, 7, 8, 10, 11, 12, 23, 25, 26, 28, 30[2], 31[2], 34, 35[2], 38, 39[2], 40, 42, 44, 45, 46, 48, 49, 50[2], 51, 53, 54
26:12[2], 13, 17, 20, 22, 23, 25, 26, 32, 33, 34, 41, 43, 44, 45
27:2, 3[2], 4[2], 5[2], 6[3], 7[3], 8, 9[2], 10, 11, 12[2], 14[2], 15, 16[2], 18, 19, 20, 21[2], 25[2], 26[2], 27[3], 28, 29[3], 32, 33[3]

NUMBERS

1:4, 51[2], 53
2:3, 5[2], 7, 10[2], 12[2], 14, 18[2], 20[2], 22, 25[2], 27[2], 29
3:10, 12, 13, 24, 25, 30, 31, 32, 36, 38[2], 45, 46, 48
4:4, 7, 27, 28, 45
5:6, 8[2], 9, 10[2], 13[5], 14[4], 19, 20, 27[2], 28[3], 30, 31
6:5[2], 12, 13, 25
7:5
8:14, 19
9:10[2], 13
10:7, 8, 9[2], 10, 31, 32[2], 35
11:16, 20, 22[2]
12:6, 12, 14[3]
13:18, 19[2], 20[3], 28, 31
14:3, 11, 17, 21, 31, 33, 35, 40, 42, 43
15:2, 11, 14, 15[2], 16, 19, 24[2], 25, 26, 28, 30[2], 31[2], 34, 35, 39, 40, 41
16:7[2], 16, 22, 26, 29, 38, 40[2]
17:3, 10, 13
18:2, 4, 5, 7, 9[2], 10, 13, 14, 15[2], 16, 18, 23, 27, 30
19:7, 8, 9, 10[2], 11, 12[2], 13[2], 14, 16, 17, 19, 20[2], 21[2], 22[2]
20:24, 26
21:22, 27
22:11
23:9, 10, 23
24:7[3], 18[2], 20, 22
25:4
26:53, 54, 55, 56
27:4, 11, 13, 17, 20
28:7[2], 14, 15, 17, 18, 19, 20, 24, 26, 31
29:3, 8, 9, 13, 14, 18, 21, 24, 27, 30, 33, 37
31:2, 23[2], 24
32:5, 22[3], 23, 26, 29, 32
33:54, 55

NUMBERS

34:3[2], 4, 5, 6, 7, 8, 9[2], 12[2]
35:3, 5[2], 6, 7, 8, 10, 11, 12, 14, 15, 16, 17, 18, 21, 27, 29, 30, 31, 33
36:3[4], 4[3], 8

DEUTERONOMY

1:1, 17, 21, 29, 39, 42
2:4, 25
4:19, 20, 26, 27, 30
5:16, 29, 33
6:2, 3, 6, 8, 10, 11, 15, 18, 25
7:4, 6, 10, 14[2], 16, 18, 20, 21, 23, 24, 25, 26
8:14, 19, 20
10:5, 16
11:8, 15, 16, 17[2], 18, 21, 24[2], 25
12:11, 21, 23, 27, 30[2]
13:5, 9, 14, 16[2]
14:2, 19, 24[2], 29
15:4, 7, 9[3], 10, 12, 16, 17, 21[2]
16:4, 8
17:2, 4[2], 6[2], 7, 9, 18, 19, 20
18:3[2], 10, 13, 22
19:10[2], 15, 17, 18
20:1, 2, 3, 9, 11[3], 20[2]
21:1[2], 3, 5, 8[2], 13[2], 14, 15, 16, 22[2], 23
22:2[2], 6[2], 7, 9, 19, 20[2], 22, 23, 28, 29
23:10, 11, 13, 14, 17, 21, 22
24:2, 3, 4, 5[2], 7, 12, 13, 14, 15, 16[3], 19, 20, 21
25:1, 2[4], 6[2], 9, 10, 15, 19
26:1, 3, 12, 17, 18, 19
27:2, 4[2], 15, 16, 17, 18, 19, 20, 21, 22, 23, 24, 25, 26
28:3[2], 4, 5, 6[2], 7, 10, 13[2], 16[2], 17, 18, 19[2], 20, 23[2], 24, 25[2], 26, 27, 29, 31[4], 32[2], 33, 34, 35, 44[2], 45, 46, 51, 54, 56, 61, 62, 63, 68
29:13, 18[2]

DEUTERONOMY

30:4, 17
31:6[2], 7, 8[2], 16, 17[2], 19, 21, 23[2], 26
32:20, 24, 38, 43, 50
33:6, 7[2], 8, 13, 20, 24[2], 25[2], 28, 29

JOSHUA

1:4, 5[2], 6, 7, 9[3], 17, 18[3]
2:3, 14, 16, 17, 19[6], 20, 21
3:4, 7, 13
4:6, 7
6:17, 26
7:12, 14[2], 15[2]
8:1, 4, 8
9:6, 13, 20, 21, 23
10:25[2]
11:6
13:1
14:9, 12[3]
15:4
17:15[2], 18[3]
20:3, 6
21:13, 21, 27, 32, 38
22:18[2], 19, 22, 27, 28, 34
23:4, 6, 13, 16
24:27[2]

JUDGES

2:3[2]
3:6
4:9, 20
5:24[2], 31
6:13[2], 16, 23, 31[2], 37[2], 39[3]
7:4, 11, 17
8:5
9:9, 11, 13, 24, 31, 33
10:18
11:6, 8, 9, 10, 26, 27, 31[2], 37
13:5, 7, 8
14:11
15:3, 7
16:6, 7[2], 9, 10, 11[2], 12, 13, 14, 17[2], 20, 28
17:2, 10
18:5, 9, 19[3], 25
19:6[2], 9, 20, 28
20:9
21:3, 5, 17[3], 18, 22[3]

RUTH

1:11, 16, 17
2:4, 9, 12, 13, 19, 20
3:1, 4, 10, 13, 14, 18
4:10[2], 11, 12, 14[2], 15

1 SAMUEL

1:14, 22, 28
2:9, 10, 28, 30[2], 31, 32, 33, 34
3:9, 14, 20
4:9[2], 19
5:8
6:3[2], 4
8:11[2], 13[3], 17, 20
9:13[2], 16
10:1, 6, 7, 21
11:3, 7, 9, 13
12:15, 25
13:14
14:6, 10, 21, 24[2], 28, 39, 40[2]
15:1, 11, 13, 18, 33
16:16
17:9[3], 25, 26, 27, 36, 37
18:17[3], 18, 21[3], 22, 23, 25, 26, 27
19:6, 11, 22
20:3, 7[2], 8, 9, 12, 13, 18[2], 23, 29, 31, 32, 42
22:3, 15, 23
23:3, 17[2], 20, 21, 23
24:12, 13, 15, 20[2]
25:6[3], 10, 11, 24, 26, 27, 29, 31, 32, 33[2], 39, 41
26:9, 19[2], 24, 25
27:11, 12
28:13, 19
29:4[2], 10
30:24

2 SAMUEL

1:5, 16, 21[2]
2:5, 7[2], 26[2]
3:12, 17, 35, 39
5:2, 8, 14, 24
6:22[3]
7:8, 11, 12, 14[2], 16[2], 24, 26[2], 28, 29
10:5, 11[2], 12
11:15, 20, 24
12:9, 10, 22, 28
13:12, 13, 15, 25, 28[2]
14:2[2], 9[2], 14[2], 15, 17[2], 25, 32
15:20, 21[2], 33, 34[2], 35
16:2[2], 12, 18, 19, 21
17:3, 8[2], 9, 10, 11, 12[2], 13[2], 16, 17, 20
18:25, 28, 32
19:7, 13, 21, 22[2], 35, 37, 42, 43
20:1, 4, 20[2], 21
21:5, 6
22:4[2], 44, 45, 46, 47[2]
23:1, 3, 4, 5, 6[2], 7[2], 8, 17
24:3, 13, 17, 21, 22

1 KINGS

1:2, 5, 21, 35[2], 37, 48, 52
2:2, 7, 19, 21, 24, 33, 37[2], 39, 45[2]
3:8, 13, 26
5:6, 7, 9
6:6
8:5, 15, 16[2], 26, 29[2], 31, 33, 37[4], 38, 46, 51, 52, 53, 56, 57, 59, 61

1 KINGS

9:3, 7, 8
10:9, 27[2]
11:37, 38[2]
12:7[2], 10
13:2[2], 3[2], 6
14:2[3], 5[2], 6, 10
17:1, 4
18:21, 24, 27, 31, 36
19:15, 16[2]
20:6, 18[2], 23, 25, 39[2], 40
21:7
22:3, 13, 22

2 KINGS

1:10, 12, 13, 14, 15
2:9[2], 10[2], 16, 21
3:17
4:1, 10, 13[2], 14, 23
5:10, 12, 13, 17, 22, 23
6:3, 8, 16[2]
7:1, 2, 12, 18, 19
8:13, 29
9:10, 15[2], 37
10:6, 9, 15, 19[2], 23, 24
11:5, 6[2], 8[2], 15, 17
12:5, 15
14:6[3]
15:19
16:15
18:23, 29, 30
19:4, 6, 10, 11, 25, 26, 29
20:8, 17[2], 18, 19
22:17[2], 20
23:27
25:12, 24[2]

1 CHRONICLES

1:10
4:10
5:1
6:17
9:22
11:2, 6
12:17[3], 18[2]
13:2
14:15
15:16
16:15, 25[2], 30[2], 31, 36, 38
17:7, 9, 10, 11[3], 13[2], 14, 21, 23, 24[3], 27[2]
19:5, 12[2], 13
21:3[2], 12, 17[3], 22
22:5[2], 9[3], 10[2], 11, 13[2], 16[2], 19
28:4[2], 6[2], 7, 9, 10, 20[3], 21[3]
29:2[2], 5, 10, 14, 22[2]

2 CHRONICLES

1:9
2:8, 9, 12, 14, 18[2]
4:18
5:6, 13
6:4, 5[2], 6[2], 17, 20, 22, 24, 28[4], 29, 36, 40[2], 41
7:13, 15, 16[2], 18, 20, 21, 22
9:8[2]
10:7[2], 10
11:22
12:7, 8
13:8, 9
15:2[2], 7[3], 13
18:3, 10, 12, 14, 21
19:7, 11[2]
20:2, 15, 17[2], 20
22:6
23:4, 5[2], 7[2], 14, 16
25:8, 14, 16
26:15, 18
29:11, 24
30:7, 8, 19
31:4
32:7[3], 14
33:4
34:25[2], 28
35:3
36:22, 23

EZRA

1:1, 3
4:12, 13[2], 15, 16, 21[2]
5:8, 15, 17[2]
6:3[2], 4, 5, 6, 8[2], 9, 11[3], 12
7:20, 21, 23[2], 24, 26[2], 27
9:12, 14[2]
10:3, 4[2], 8, 14

NEHEMIAH

1:6, 11
2:3, 6, 7, 17
4:5, 7, 12, 14, 22
5:5, 8, 13, 14
6:6, 7, 9[2], 13
7:3[3], 5
8:10, 11
9:5
10:38
11:23
13:5, 19[4]

ESTHER

1:17[2], 19[2], 20, 22
2:2, 3, 4, 9
3:9[2], 14[2]
4:14
5:3, 6[2], 14[3]
6:6, 8, 9[2], 11, 13
7:2[2], 3, 4[2]
8:5[2], 13[2]
9:1, 12[2], 13[2], 14, 25, 28

JOB

1:5, 21
3:4, 6, 7, 9, 17

JOB

4:2, 17[2]
5:1, 11[2], 21[2], 22, 23[2], 24, 25
6:3, 6, 14, 28, 29
7:4, 21
8:2, 14[2], 22
9:2, 29
10:15[2]
11:2[2], 12[2], 14, 15, 17[2], 18, 20
12:14[2]
13:5, 16, 18
14:7, 12[2], 13
15:14[2], 29, 31, 32[2], 34
17:8, 9
18:2, 4[2], 5, 6[2], 7, 12[2], 14, 15, 16[2], 18, 20
19:4, 27, 29
20:8[2], 12, 18, 21, 22, 26
21:2, 4, 5, 30, 32, 33
22:2[2], 21, 23, 25, 28
23:7
24:20[2], 23[2], 25
25:4[2]
27:7, 14[2], 15, 19
28:12, 15[2], 16, 17, 18, 19
31:6, 8, 11, 22, 28, 31
32:20
33:3, 7, 21, 23, 25, 26, 30
34:10, 20[2], 29, 30, 31, 33, 36
35:2, 3[2], 6, 7
36:4, 8[2], 16[2], 26
37:6, 20[2]
38:11, 13, 15
39:9
40:8
41:9, 17, 23, 32
42:2

PSALMS

1:3
2:10[2], 12
3:2, 6
4:4, 6
5:11
6:10[2]
7:3
9:2, 9, 17, 18, 19, 20
10:2, 6[2]
11:3, 6
13:2
14:7
15:5
16:4, 8
17:15
18:3[2], 45, 46[2]
19:10, 13[2], 14
21:7, 13
22:11, 19, 25, 26, 29, 30, 31
24:7
25:2, 3[2], 20
26:11
27:1, 3, 6, 14
28:1[2], 6
30:6, 10, 12
31:1, 2, 7, 17[3], 18, 21, 24
32:6, 9[2], 10, 11
33:22
34:1, 2, 18, 21, 22
35:4[2], 5, 6, 9, 22, 26[2], 27[2]
36:2[2], 3, 8, 12
37:1, 2, 3, 9, 10[2], 14, 15, 17, 18, 19[2], 20, 22[3], 24, 28, 36, 38[2]
38:18, 21
39:13
40:5[2], 13, 14[2], 15, 16[2]
41:2, 4, 10, 13
42:8
45:12, 14[2], 15, 16, 17
46:2[2], 3, 5, 10[3]
48:1, 11, 14
49:3, 16
50:3, 22
51:4[2], 7[2], 13, 19
53:6
55:6, 20, 22
56:1, 2, 11
57:1[3], 5[2], 11[2]
58:3, 7
59:5, 12, 13, 15
60:4, 5
62:2, 3[2], 6, 9
63:5, 10, 11
64:7, 10
65:1, 4
66:8, 9, 20
67:1, 2, 4
68:1, 3, 13, 19, 23, 35
69:6[2], 14, 23, 25, 28[2], 32
70:2[2], 3, 4[2]
71:1, 3, 6, 8, 12, 13[2]
72:14, 15[3], 16, 17[2], 18, 19[2]
74:14
75:10
76:7, 8, 11[2]
77:2, 7, 9
78:6, 8
79:2, 5, 10
80:3, 4, 7, 17, 19
81:9
83:1, 4, 17[2]
84:4, 10
85:5
86:3, 17
87:5, 7
88:11, 12
89:2, 6[2], 7[2], 16, 17, 21, 24[2], 37, 52
90:10, 14, 17
91:4, 5, 15
92:7, 9, 10, 13, 14
93:1
94:8, 13
96:4[2], 10[2], 11, 12

PSALMS

97:1, 7
98:8
99:1
100:4
101:6
102:18[2], 26, 28
104:5, 34[2], 35[2]
106:8, 46, 48
107:30
108:5, 6
109:7[2], 8, 9, 10, 12[2], 13[2], 14[2], 15, 17, 19, 20, 28, 29
110:3
111:4, 5
112:2[2], 3, 6[2], 7, 8, 9, 10
113:2, 3, 9
118:24, 26
119:6, 46, 58, 74, 76, 78, 80[2], 116, 117, 122, 128, 132
120:3[2]
121:3
122:7, 8
124:6
125:1[2], 4, 5
127:5
128:2[2], 3, 4
129:5, 6, 8
130:2, 4
132:9
135:21
137:8[2], 9
138:6
139:11, 24
140:10, 11
141:2, 5[3]
143:2, 7
144:1, 12[2], 13, 14[3]
145:3, 14
148:4
149:2, 5, 6

PROVERBS

1:9, 31, 33
2:22[2]
3:7, 8, 10, 11, 15, 22, 24[2], 25, 26, 35
4:10, 12, 26
5:10[2], 16, 17, 18, 19[2], 20, 22
6:1, 6, 15, 18, 27, 28, 29, 31, 33
8:5, 6, 11[2], 33
9:9, 11[2], 12[2]
10:9, 24, 27, 28, 29, 30, 31
11:6, 9, 18, 21[2], 25[2], 26, 29, 31
12:3[2], 8[2], 11, 14[2], 19, 21, 24
13:4, 9, 11, 13[2], 18[2], 20[2], 21
14:11, 14[2], 22
16:3, 5, 7, 16, 19, 21, 31
17:5, 11, 14
18:19, 20[2]
19:2, 5, 9, 20, 23
20:3, 11[2], 13, 17, 20, 21[2]
21:13, 15, 17[2], 18, 20
22:1, 5, 9, 11, 13, 18, 19, 26
23:2, 3, 4, 15, 17, 18, 19, 20, 25, 34
24:1[2], 4, 8, 11, 14[3], 17, 19, 20[2], 25, 28
25:5, 7[2], 16, 17, 21[2]
26:4, 5, 26
27:11, 14, 18, 23
28:2, 6, 9, 18, 20[2], 22, 25, 26
29:1, 14, 19, 25
30:6, 9[2], 10, 18, 24, 29
31:6, 30

ECCLESIASTES

1:9[2], 10, 11, 13, 15[2]
2:16, 18, 19
3:2, 10, 14[2], 15, 22
4:11, 13
5:1, 2[3], 6, 8, 10
6:3[2], 4, 11, 12
7:9[2], 14, 16, 17[2], 23, 26
8:1, 3, 7[2], 12[2], 13, 14[2], 15, 17
9:8
10:9[2], 10, 14[2]
11:2, 3[2], 6, 8
12:2, 3, 4[2], 5[3], 6[3], 12, 14[2]

SONG OF SOLOMON

1:4, 7
2:17
7:8
8:1, 3, 7, 8, 9[2], 14

ISAIAH

1:5, 18[4], 19, 20, 26, 27, 28[2], 29[2], 30, 31
2:2[2], 6, 11[3], 12[2], 17[3], 22
3:4, 5, 6[2], 7, 10, 11[2], 24
4:1, 2[2], 3, 5, 6
5:5[2], 6, 8[2], 9, 15[3], 16[2], 24, 27[3], 28, 29
6:10, 11[2], 12, 13[3]
7:4[2], 8[2], 9, 16, 23[2], 25[2]
8:4, 9[3], 12, 13[2], 14, 15[3], 21, 22
9:1, 5, 6[2], 7, 19, 20[2], 21
10:2, 17, 18, 19, 22, 24, 27[2], 30, 33[2]
11:5, 9, 10[2], 11, 13, 16[2]
12:2
13:7, 8[4], 10, 14, 15, 16[2], 19, 20[2], 21, 22
14:1, 14, 15, 20[2], 29, 31
15:2, 4[2], 6, 9
16:2[2], 4, 5, 6, 10[2], 14[2]
17:1, 2, 3, 4, 5[2], 6, 9[2], 11, 13
18:6, 7
19:1, 5, 6, 7[2], 9, 10, 15, 16[2], 17[2], 18, 19, 20, 21, 22, 23, 24, 25
20:5, 6
21:17

ISAIAH

22:7, 14, 18, 21, 23, 25[3]
23:2, 4, 5, 15, 16, 18[3]
24:2, 3, 9, 13[2], 18, 20[2], 22[3], 23
25:2[2], 5, 9[2], 10
26:1, 10, 11, 20
27:9, 10, 11, 12, 13
28:3, 4, 5, 10, 13, 18[2], 19, 21, 22[2], 28
29:2[2], 4[3], 5[3], 6, 7, 8[2], 14, 16, 17[2], 22
30:3, 5, 8, 13, 14, 15[2], 16, 17, 18[2], 19, 20, 23, 25, 26[2], 28, 30, 31, 32
31:4, 8, 9
32:2, 3, 4, 5[2], 10, 11, 14[3], 15[3], 17, 19
33:1, 2[2], 4, 6, 10, 12[2], 16[3], 20[3], 21, 24
34:3[2], 4[2], 5, 7, 9, 10, 12[2], 13, 15
35:1, 2, 4, 5[2], 7, 8[3], 9[2]
36:8, 14, 15
37:4, 6, 10, 11, 26, 27, 30
38:7
39:6[2], 7, 8
40:4[3], 5, 9, 20, 24[2], 25, 30, 31
41:6, 7, 10, 11[2], 12, 22, 23
42:2, 4, 17[2]
43:2[2], 9[3], 10, 26
44:8, 9, 11[3], 15, 21, 26[2], 27, 28[2]
45:1, 14, 16, 17[2], 18, 22, 24, 25
46:5, 13
47:1, 3[2], 5, 7, 11, 12[3], 14[2], 15
48:11, 14
49:3, 5[4], 6[2], 9, 11, 13, 19[2], 22, 23[2], 24, 25[2], 26
50:7[2]
51:3, 6[2], 7, 8, 11, 12[2], 14, 19
52:3, 11, 12, 13[2]
53:11
54:3, 4[3], 5, 9, 10[2], 13[2], 14[2]
55:6, 11, 12, 13[2]
56:1, 5, 6, 7[2], 12
57:16
58:4, 8, 10, 11, 12[2]
60:2, 4, 5[2], 7, 11[3], 12, 18, 19[2], 20[2], 21[2]
61:3[2], 5, 6, 7, 9, 10
62:2, 3, 4[4], 8, 12
63:3, 10, 16
64:5, 9
65:10, 13[3], 17, 18, 19, 20[2], 25
66:5[2], 8[2], 10, 11[2], 12[2], 13, 14, 16, 17, 24[2]

JEREMIAH

1:8, 17
2:10, 12[3], 36
3:1, 3, 16[2], 17
4:7, 9, 11, 13, 14, 27, 28, 29
5:1, 6, 9, 13, 29
6:6, 8, 11, 12, 15, 22
7:20[2], 23[3], 32[2], 33, 34
8:2[3], 3, 12, 13, 14, 17
9:2, 9
10:2, 5[2], 10, 21
11:3, 4[2], 5, 11, 19, 23
12:13, 16
13:10, 11, 12[2], 15, 19[3], 21, 27[2]
14:8, 9, 15[2], 16
15:1, 4, 11, 18[2], 19
16:4[5], 6, 14
17:5, 6, 8[3], 11, 13[2], 14[2], 17, 18[4], 27
18:14, 16, 20, 21[4], 22, 23
19:6, 7, 8, 11[2], 13
20:6, 10, 11[2], 14[2], 15, 16, 17, 18
21:2, 9, 10
22:19, 22, 23
23:1, 3, 4[2], 6[2], 12[2], 26, 36, 40
24:2, 3, 7[2], 8, 9[2], 10
25:11, 16[2], 27, 28, 29[2], 32, 33[3], 36
26:3, 9[2], 18
27:16, 17, 18[2], 22[2]
28:9
29:4, 6, 7, 8[2], 10, 14[2], 17, 18[2], 22, 26
30:7, 10[3], 13, 16[2], 18, 19[2], 20[2], 21, 22[2]
31:1[2], 4[2], 6, 12, 14, 15, 16, 18, 30, 33[3], 37, 38, 40[2]
32:4, 5, 15, 36, 38[2], 43
33:9, 10[2], 12, 16[2], 20, 21, 22, 24, 25, 26
34:3, 16, 17, 20
35:7
36:3, 7, 19, 30
37:17, 20
38:3, 4, 17, 18, 20, 22, 23[2]
39:16, 17, 18
40:9, 15
42:2, 5, 6[3], 11[2], 17, 18[2]
44:8[2], 12[3], 26, 27[2], 29
46:10, 11, 19, 23, 24[2], 26, 27[2]
47:2, 6[3], 7
48:2[2], 3, 4, 6, 7, 8, 9, 10[2], 13, 26, 28, 30, 33, 34, 37[2], 38, 39, 41, 42, 43, 44, 46
49:2[4], 5[2], 10, 13, 17[2], 22, 23, 26, 32, 33, 36, 37
50:5, 8, 9[2], 10[2], 12[3], 13[3], 19, 20[3], 26, 30, 36, 37, 38, 39[2], 41
51:2, 6, 8[2], 26, 29, 35, 46, 47, 58[3], 62, 63, 64

LAMENTATIONS

1:12, 17, 21
2:6, 20
3:6, 29[2]
4:9[2], 21[2]
5:6, 21

EZEKIEL

2:6[6], 8
3:9[2], 12, 20, 26[2]
4:3[2], 7, 10, 17
5:12, 13[2], 15, 16
6:4[2], 6[6], 8, 9, 13
7:4, 11, 16, 17[2], 18, 19[2], 24, 25, 26, 27[2]
9:4
11:3, 11[2], 16, 20[2]
12:3[2], 11, 13, 19, 20[2], 24, 25, 28[2]
13:9[3], 11, 12, 13, 14[2], 21[2]
14:3, 9, 10, 11[3], 15, 16[2], 18, 22[3]
15:3, 5
16:16, 20, 25, 28, 42[2], 52, 54, 61, 63
17:8, 14, 15, 20, 21, 23
18:5, 13, 20[2], 22, 24, 30
19:9, 14[2]
20:3, 9, 12, 14, 20, 22, 31[2], 32[2], 41, 47[2], 48
21:7[4], 11[2], 12[3], 13, 14, 15, 23[2], 24[2], 26, 27, 32[3]
22:5[2], 14, 21, 22
23:25, 29, 32, 33, 46, 48
24:8, 10, 11[3], 12, 13, 23, 25, 27[3]
25:10
26:2, 5, 6, 13, 14[2], 16, 17, 18, 20, 21[3]
27:7, 30, 34, 35[3], 36[2]
28:9, 19[3], 22[2], 23, 24, 25
29:5, 7, 9, 11, 12, 14, 15, 16, 19
30:3, 4[2], 7[2], 8, 11, 13, 16, 18, 21[2]
31:13, 16, 17, 18[2]
32:6, 10, 12, 15, 19, 25, 27, 28, 30[2], 31, 32
33:4, 5, 6, 10, 12, 13, 16, 27[2], 28
34:2, 10, 14, 22, 23, 24, 26, 27, 28, 29
35:4, 10, 15
36:3, 9, 10[2], 12, 23, 25, 28[2], 32[2], 33, 34, 37, 38
37:19, 20, 21, 22[3], 23[2], 24, 25, 26, 27[3], 28
38:7[2], 8, 9, 16[2], 19, 20, 21, 23
39:4, 12, 13[2], 16, 19[2], 20, 25, 28
42:13
43:10, 11, 12, 13[3], 14[2], 15[2], 16, 17[3], 19, 27
44:2[3], 7, 11, 14, 17, 28, 29, 30, 31
45:1[3], 2, 3, 4[2], 6, 7[2], 8, 11[2], 12[2], 17, 21
46:1[3], 2, 4, 5[2], 6[2], 11, 16[2], 17[2], 18
47:5, 8, 9[2], 10[2], 11[2], 12[2], 13, 15, 17, 20, 22
48:8[2], 9, 10[2], 11, 12, 13, 15[2], 16, 17, 18[3], 20, 21[3], 22, 28, 31, 35

DANIEL

1:13
2:5[2], 9, 13[2], 20, 28, 40, 41[2], 42, 44[2]
3:6, 11, 15[2], 17, 18, 19, 28, 29[2]
4:1, 15[2], 16[2], 19, 23[2], 25, 26, 27[2], 32
5:7[2], 10, 12, 16[2], 17, 29
6:1, 7, 8, 12, 15, 17, 25, 26[2]
7:14, 23[2], 24, 25, 27
8:13[2], 14, 17, 19[2], 24, 25, 26
9:16, 25[2], 26[2], 27
10:19[3]
11:2, 4[3], 5[3], 6, 10[2], 11[2], 12[2], 15, 16, 17, 19, 20, 22[2], 25, 27[2], 28, 29, 30, 32, 34, 36[2], 41, 43
12:1[3], 3, 4, 6, 7[2], 8, 10, 11[2], 13

HOSEA

1:9, 10[3], 11[2]
2:4, 16, 17
3:3[2]
4:3, 6, 9, 19
5:9[2], 12, 14
7:4, 16
8:4, 5, 6, 7, 8, 11
9:4[3], 6, 12, 17
10:2, 6[2], 8, 10, 14, 15
11:5
13:3, 7, 10, 14[3], 15[2], 16[2]
14:5, 6, 7

JOEL

1:11
2:2, 6, 8, 10, 18, 19, 21, 22, 23, 24, 26[2], 27, 31, 32[2]
3:12, 15, 16, 17, 19[2]

AMOS

3:3, 6[3], 11[2], 12, 14
5:6, 14, 15[2], 16, 17, 20
6:2, 7
7:3, 6, 9[2], 11, 17[2]
8:3[2], 5, 8
9:1, 3, 5, 15

OBADIAH

9[2], 10, 15, 16, 17[2], 18[2], 21

JONAH

1:4, 6, 11, 12
3:4, 7, 8
4:4, 6, 9[2]

MICAH

1:2, 4[2], 7[2], 14
2:4, 11
3:6[3], 7, 12
4:1[2], 10[2], 11
5:2[2], 4, 5, 7, 8, 9[2]
6:7, 14[2]
7:4, 8, 10, 11[2], 13, 16[2], 17

NAHUM

1:10^{2}, 12^{2}, 14
2:3^{2}, 5, 6^{2}, 7^{2}, 13
3:11^{2}, 12^{2}, 13

HABAKKUK

1:5, 10
2:5, 7, 9, 14, 16^{3}
3:17^{3}

ZEPHANIAH

1:10, 17, 18^{2}
2:3^{2}, 4^{2}, 5, 6, 7, 9, 11, 12, 14
3:7, 8, 11^{2}, 13, 14, 16^{2}

HAGGAI

1:2, 8
2:4^{3}, 9, 12, 13^{2}

ZECHARIAH

1:4, 9, 16^{2}, 17, 19
2:4, 5^{2}, 9, 11^{2}, 13
3:9
4:5, 12, 13
5:3^{2}, 11
6:13^{2}, 14
8:3, 5, 6^{2}, 8^{2}, 9^{2}, 11, 12, 13^{2}, 19
9:1^{2}, 2, 4, 5^{3}, 7^{2}, 10^{2}, 14, 15, 16
10:5^{2}, 6, 7^{2}, 10, 11
11:5, 9^{2}, 16, 17^{3}
12:2, 3^{2}, 5, 6, 8^{2}, 10, 11
13:1, 2, 4, 7, 8^{2}
14:1, 2^{2}, 4, 6, 7^{3}, 8^{2}, 9^{2}, 10^{2}, 11^{2}, 12, 13, 14, 15^{2}, 17^{2}, 18, 19, 20^{2}, 21^{2}

MALACHI

1:5, 6^{2}, 8, 9, 11^{3}, 14
2:4
3:4, 5, 10^{2}, 12, 17
4:1, 3

MATTHEW

1:22, 23
2:4, 13, 15, 18, 23^{2}
3:13, 14, 15
4:1, 3^{2}, 6, 14
5:4, 6, 9, 12, 13^{3}, 14, 18, 19^{2}, 21, 22^{3}, 24, 25, 29, 30, 37, 45, 48
6:1, 4, 5^{2}, 7, 8, 9, 10, 16, 21, 22^{2}, 23^{3}, 31, 33
7:1, 2^{2}, 7^{2}, 8, 13, 14, 26
8:3, 8, 12^{2}, 13, 17
9:2^{2}, 5, 12, 15, 21, 22, 29
10:13^{2}, 15, 16, 18, 19, 21, 22^{2}, 23, 25, 26^{2}, 36
11:6, 22, 23, 24
12:11, 17, 27, 31^{2}, 32^{2}, 37^{2}, 39, 40, 45
13:12^{2}, 15, 35, 40, 42, 49, 50
14:9, 27^{2}, 28
15:5, 6, 13, 14, 28, 31
16:2, 3, 4, 19^{2}, 21^{2}, 22^{2}, 23^{2}, 28
17:4, 7, 9, 17, 20, 22, 23

MATTHEW

18:3, 7, 8, 9, 12, 13, 16, 17, 18^{2}, 19, 25^{2}
19:5, 9, 10, 12, 21, 25, 30^{2}
20:16^{2}, 18, 22, 23^{2}, 26^{3}, 27^{2}, 28, 33
21:4, 13, 21^{3}, 43, 44
22:13, 28
23:4, 5, 7, 8, 10, 11, 12^{2}, 26, 31
24:2^{2}, 3^{2}, 6, 7, 9^{2}, 10, 13, 14, 16, 20, 21^{2}, 22^{3}, 27, 28, 29^{2}, 34, 37, 39, 40^{2}, 41^{2}, 43, 44, 51
25:1, 9, 29^{2}, 30, 32
26:2, 5, 13^{2}, 31^{2}, 33^{2}, 37, 39, 42, 46, 54^{2}, 56, 63
27:22, 23, 25, 26, 35, 40, 42, 49, 58, 64^{2}
28:10

MARK

1:41
2:5, 9, 20, 22^{2}
3:14, 24, 25, 26, 28
4:12^{2}, 21^{2}, 22, 24^{2}, 25^{2}, 31, 39
5:18, 23, 28, 34, 36, 43
6:9, 11, 27, 50^{2}
7:4, 11^{2}, 24, 27, 34
8:12, 31^{2}, 33^{2}, 38^{2}
9:1, 5, 12, 19, 34, 35^{2}, 43, 45^{2}, 47, 49^{2}
10:8, 12, 26, 31, 33, 38, 39, 40, 41, 43^{3}, 44^{2}, 45, 49^{2}
11:2, 10, 17, 23^{2}
12:7, 23
13:2^{2}, 4^{3}, 7^{3}, 8^{2}, 9^{2}, 10, 11, 12, 13^{2}, 14, 18, 19^{2}, 20, 24, 25, 30
14:2, 9^{2}, 19, 27^{2}, 29, 33^{2}, 49, 64
15:15
16:6, 16^{2}

LUKE

1:15^{2}, 20^{3}, 29, 32^{2}, 33, 34, 35^{2}, 37, 38, 45, 57, 60, 66, 68, 71, 76
2:1, 3, 5, 6, 10, 12, 23, 34, 35, 49
3:5^{4}, 7, 12, 14, 23
4:3^{2}, 7, 9
5:13, 15, 23, 35, 37, 38
6:17, 20, 21, 35^{2}, 36, 37^{3}, 38^{2}, 40
7:7, 23
8:9, 12, 17^{2}, 18^{2}, 38, 43, 48, 50
9:22^{3}, 25, 26^{2}, 27, 33, 41, 44, 46, 48, 51
10:5, 6, 11, 12, 14, 15, 42
11:2^{2}, 9^{2}, 10, 18, 19, 29, 30, 35, 36^{2}, 46, 50, 51
12:2^{2}, 3^{2}, 4, 9, 10^{2}, 19, 20^{2}, 26, 29, 31, 34, 35, 39, 40, 45, 47, 48^{2}, 49, 50^{2}, 52, 53, 55, 58
13:14, 16, 23, 24, 28, 30^{2}, 32, 33
14:8, 11^{2}, 12, 14^{2}, 23, 26, 27, 31, 33^{2}, 34
15:7, 14, 19, 21, 23, 24, 32

LUKE

16:2, 21, 31
17:6^{2}, 24, 25, 26, 30, 31, 34^{3}, 35^{2}, 36^{2}, 37
18:13, 14^{2}, 26, 31, 32^{2}, 40
19:7, 15, 19, 26^{2}, 38
20:6, 13, 14, 18, 25^{2}, 35
21:6^{2}, 7^{2}, 8, 9, 11^{2}, 15, 16^{2}, 17, 22^{2}, 23, 24^{3}, 25, 26, 32, 34, 36
22:7, 16, 24, 26^{2}, 37, 42^{2}, 52
23:23, 24, 31, 32, 35, 37, 39, 43
24:7^{2}, 20, 36, 44, 47, 49

JOHN

1:25, 31, 42
3:2, 3, 4^{2}, 5, 7, 9, 14, 17, 20, 21, 27
4:14
5:6, 34
6:12, 20, 45
7:4, 17, 23
8:5, 33^{2}, 36, 41, 55
9:3, 22, 25, 27, 31, 39
10:9, 16, 24, 35
11:4
12:23, 26, 31, 32, 34, 36, 38, 40, 42
13:18, 24, 32
14:1, 3, 13, 17, 21, 27^{2}
15:7, 8, 11, 25
16:1, 20^{2}, 24, 32, 33
17:11, 12, 19, 21^{2}, 22, 23, 24, 26
18:9, 28, 32, 36
19:16, 24^{2}, 28, 31^{2}, 36^{2}
20:15, 19, 21, 26, 27
21:18, 25^{2}

THE ACTS

1:5, 8, 20, 22^{2}
2:14, 20, 21, 24, 25, 38, 47
3:14, 19^{2}, 23, 25
4:9, 10, 12, 19, 28, 30
5:31, 36, 38, 39^{2}
7:7, 35
8:20, 22, 36
9:6, 17
10:42, 47, 48
11:14, 16, 28
12:19
13:11, 22, 28, 38, 39, 42, 47^{2}
14:3, 9
15:1^{2}, 11, 24
16:13, 15, 30, 31
17:18, 27
18:6, 9, 15^{2}
19:2, 26, 27^{3}, 36^{2}, 39, 40
20:16
21:13, 14^{2}, 24, 26, 33, 34, 37
22:5, 10, 15, 16, 24^{2}
23:3, 11, 29, 35
24:4, 15, 21
25:4, 5, 6, 9, 10, 11^{2}, 17, 19, 20, 21^{2}
26:3, 8, 23, 28

THE ACTS

27:10, 20, 22^{2}, 24, 25^{2}, 26, 31
28:27, 28

ROMANS

1:1, 4, 7^{2}, 11, 12, 19, 22
2:12, 13, 25, 26
3:4^{2}, 8, 19, 20, 25, 26
4:11^{3}, 13, 14, 16^{2}, 17, 18, 24
5:9, 10, 15, 19
6:5, 6, 8, 11, 17
7:2, 3^{4}, 4, 10
8:4, 6^{2}, 7, 9, 10, 17^{2}, 18^{2}, 21, 26, 29^{2}, 31^{2}, 39
9:7, 17, 26, 27^{2}, 33
10:1, 9, 11, 13, 15
11:6, 9, 10, 12, 15^{2}, 16^{2}, 17, 19, 20, 22, 23, 24^{2}, 25^{3}, 26, 35, 36
12:2^{2}, 9, 10, 16^{2}, 18, 21
13:1^{2}, 3, 4, 5, 9
14:4, 5, 9, 14, 15, 16
15:5, 12, 16^{2}, 24^{2}, 31^{2}, 32, 33
16:11, 20, 24, 27

1 CORINTHIANS

1:1, 2, 3, 8, 10^{2}, 17
3:13^{2}, 15^{2}, 18^{2}
4:2, 3, 6, 16, 17
5:2, 5, 7, 11
6:2, 5, 7, 9, 12, 16
7:5, 11, 12, 13, 18, 21, 23, 25, 26, 27, 29, 34, 39^{2}
8:5^{2}, 10
9:2, 10, 12, 15, 19, 23, 27
10:1, 7, 13^{2}, 21, 27, 30, 33
11:1, 6^{5}, 16, 18, 19^{2}, 27, 31, 32
12:13^{2}, 22, 23, 25, 26
13:3, 8^{3}, 10
14:7, 9^{2}, 10, 11^{2}, 20^{3}, 23, 26, 27, 28, 30, 31, 34, 37, 38^{2}, 40
15:9, 12, 13, 14, 15, 17, 22, 26, 28^{3}, 33, 37, 51, 52^{2}, 54, 57, 58
16:2, 4, 6, 10, 13, 14, 22, 23, 24

2 CORINTHIANS

1:2, 3, 4, 6^{2}, 7, 11, 16, 17
2:4, 7, 9, 14
3:3, 7, 8, 9, 16
4:3, 7, 10, 11
5:2, 3^{2}, 4^{2}, 8^{2}, 9, 10, 13^{2}, 17, 20, 21^{2}
6:3, 13, 14, 16^{2}, 17, 18^{2}
7:10, 11
8:9, 10, 11, 12, 13, 14^{3}, 16, 23
9:3^{2}, 4, 5, 15
10:2^{2}, 8, 11, 15
11:3, 6, 7, 12, 15^{2}
12:6^{2}, 7^{2}, 11, 13, 14, 15^{2}, 16, 20^{2}
13:1, 5^{2}, 7, 11^{4}, 14

GALATIANS

1:3, 5, 7, 8, 9, 10
2:3, 6^{2}, 9, 11, 16^{2}, 17
3:4, 8, 9, 15^{2}, 18, 22, 23, 24, 29
4:1, 9, 12, 18, 19, 20, 21, 30

GALATIANS

5:1, 2, 10^{2}, 15, 18, 26
6:1^{2}, 3, 7, 9, 12, 16, 18

EPHESIANS

1:2, 3, 4, 12, 22
3:6, 10, 16, 18, 19, 21
4:14, 21, 23, 26, 31, 32
5:1, 3, 7, 17, 18^{2}, 24, 27, 31^{2}
6:3, 5, 8, 10, 11, 13, 16, 19, 23, 24

PHILIPPIANS

1:2, 10, 20^{3}, 23, 26, 27^{2}, 30
2:1, 2, 3, 5, 6, 15, 17, 19, 28
3:9, 15^{3}, 17, 21
4:2, 5, 6^{2}, 8^{2}, 9, 11, 12^{3}, 20, 23

COLOSSIANS

1:2, 9, 12, 16, 20, 23
2:2, 5, 20
3:1, 15, 19, 21
4:6, 16, 18

1 THESSALONIANS

1:1
2:4, 9, 16
3:1, 3, 5
4:11, 13, 17^{2}
5:6, 7, 8, 13, 14, 23, 27, 28

2 THESSALONIANS

1:5, 7, 9, 10^{2}, 12
2:2^{2}, 3, 6, 7, 8, 10, 12
3:1, 2, 8, 13, 14, 16, 18

1 TIMOTHY

1:7, 10, 17
2:1, 4, 6, 12, 15
3:2, 8, 10, 11, 12
4:3, 4^{2}, 6, 12
5:7, 9, 13, 16, 17, 22, 25
6:1, 8, 9, 16, 17, 18, 21

2 TIMOTHY

1:4, 8^{2}, 15
2:1, 2, 4, 6, 11, 15, 21, 24
3:2, 9, 17
4:2, 4, 6, 15, 16, 17, 18, 22^{2}

TITUS

1:6, 7, 9, 11, 13
2:2, 3, 4, 5^{2}, 6, 8^{2}, 9
3:1^{2}, 2, 7, 8, 12, 13, 14, 15

PHILEMON

8, 14, 22, 25

HEBREWS

1:5^{2}, 12, 14
2:3, 17^{2}
3:5, 12, 13
4:15
5:5, 11, 12^{2}
6:8, 12
7:11
8:4, 10^{2}, 12

HEBREWS

9:16, 23
10:2, 13, 29
11:16, 18, 24, 40
12:3, 8, 9, 10, 11, 13^{2}, 15, 16, 18, 19, 20, 27, 28
13:2, 5^{2}, 9^{2}, 19, 21, 25

JAMES

1:4, 5, 13, 18, 19, 22, 23, 25, 26
2:12, 15, 16
3:1, 4, 10, 17
4:4, 9^{2}, 14
5:3, 7, 8, 9, 12, 15, 16

1 PETER

1:2, 3, 5, 6, 7^{2}, 13^{2}, 15, 16, 21
2:3, 6, 7, 13, 18, 20
3:1^{2}, 3, 4, 7, 8^{3}, 13, 14^{2}, 15, 16, 17
4:6, 7, 11^{2}, 13^{2}, 14, 16, 17, 18
5:1, 5^{2}, 8^{2}, 11, 14

2 PETER

1:2, 4, 8^{2}, 11, 12^{2}, 15
2:1, 2, 4, 9, 12
3:2, 8, 10, 11^{2}, 12, 14^{2}, 16, 18

1 JOHN

1:4
2:19, 28
3:1, 2^{2}
4:10, 14

2 JOHN

2, 3, 12

3 JOHN

2, 8, 14

JUDE

2, 18, 19, 25

REVELATION

1:4, 6, 19
2:10^{2}, 11, 19, 27
3:2, 5, 18^{2}, 19
4:1
5:13
6:11^{2}, 17
7:12
9:5
10:6, 7, 9
11:5, 9, 18
12:2, 4, 15
13:10, 15
14:10
16:5, 12
17:17
18:4, 8, 21^{2}, 22^{4}, 23
19:7, 8
20:3^{2}, 6, 7, 10
21:3^{3}, 4^{2}, 7^{2}, 25^{2}
22:3^{2}, 4, 5, 6, 11^{4}, 12, 21

BUT

235

GENESIS

2:6, 17, 20
3:3
4:2, 5
6:8, 18
8:9
9:4
11:30
12:12
13:13
15:4, 10, 16
16:6
17:5, 15, 21
18:15, 22, 27, 32
19:2, 4, 10, 14, 26
20:3^{2}, 4, 12
21:23, 26
22:7
23:6, 13
24:4, 33, 38
25:6, 28
26:29
27:22, 38
28:17, 19
29:17, 20, 31
30:42
31:5, 7, 29, 33, 34, 35, 47
32:28
34:12, 15, 17
35:8, 10, 16, 18
37:11, 22, 35
38:20
39:8, 9, 21
40:14, 22, 23
41:8, 21, 24, 54
42:4, 7, 8, 10, 12, 20, 34
43:5, 34
44:17
45:8, 22
46:12
47:18, 30
48:7, 19, 21
49:19, 24
50:20^{2}

EXODUS

1:12, 16, 17^{2}
2:15, 17
3:22
4:1, 10, 21
5:16, 17
6:3, 9

EXODUS

7:4, 12
8:15, 18, 29
9:6, 30, 32
10:8, 20, 23, 27
11:7
12:9, 44
13:15, 18
14:9, 16, 20, 29
15:19
16:8, 20, 26
17:12
18:22, 26
19:13, 24
20:10, 19
21:13, 14, 18, 28, 29^{2}
22:15
23:11, 22, 24
24:2
29:14, 33
31:15
32:18
33:11, 23
34:13, 20, 21, 34
35:2
36:38
40:37

LEVITICUS

1:9, 13, 17
2:12
5:8, 11
6:28
7:16, 17, 20, 24, 31
8:17
9:10
10:6
11:4, 5, 6, 11, 23, 36, 38
12:5
13:6, 7, 14, 21^{2}, 23, 26^{2}, 28, 33, 35, 37
14:9, 53
15:28
16:10
17:16
19:14, 15, 18, 24, 34
20:24
21:2, 4, 14
22:11, 13^{2}, 20, 23, 32
23:3, 8, 25

LEVITICUS

25:4, 17, 28, 31, 34, 36, 40, 43, 46, 52
26:14, 15, 23, 27, 45
27:8, 13, 18, 21, 29

NUMBERS

1:47, 50, 53
2:33
3:38
4:15, 19, 20
5:8, 20, 28
6:12
7:9
8:26
9:13, 22
10:4, 7^{2}, 30
11:6, 20, 26^{2}
12:14
13:31
14:10, 21, 24, 31, 32, 38, 41, 44
15:30
16:9, 30, 41
18:2, 17, 23, 24
19:12, 20
21:22, 23
22:20, 24, 35
23:13, 26
24:1, 4, 11, 13, 16, 17^{2}, 20
26:33, 64
27:3
28:19, 27
29:8, 36
30:5, 8, 9, 12, 14, 15
31:18
32:17, 23, 27, 30
33:55
35:8, 20, 22, 26, 28, 30, 31, 33
36:9

DEUTERONOMY

1:17, 26, 38, 40, 43, 45
2:11, 12, 21, 30
3:7, 19, 26, 28
4:4, 9, 12, 20, 22^{2}, 26, 29
5:3, 14, 31
7:5, 8, 15, 18, 23, 26
8:3, 18
9:4, 5, 19
10:12
11:7, 11, 28
12:5, 10, 14, 18

DEUTERONOMY

13:9
14:7, 12, 20
15:3, 6^{2}, 8
16:6
17:6, 16
18:14, 20, 22
19:11, 13, 21
20:12, 14, 16, 17
21:14, 17, 23
22:7, 20, 25, 26
23:5, 11, 20, 22, 24, 25
24:5, 18
25:15
26:14
28:15, 38, 39, 40, 41, 65
29:15, 20, 29
30:14, 17^{2}
32:15, 52
34:4, 6

JOSHUA

1:8, 14
2:4, 6, 22
5:5, 12, 14
6:13, 19, 22
7:1, 3^{2}, 12
8:4, 9, 14
9:12, 19, 21
10:16, 19, 30, 37, 40
11:13, 14, 20
13:13, 33
14:3, 8
15:63
16:10
17:3^{2}, 8, 12, 13, 14, 18
18:7
21:12
22:3, 5, 7, 18, 19, 27, 28
23:8, 9, 13
24:4, 10, 12, 15, 21

JUDGES

1:6, 19, 21, 25, 27, 29, 30, 32, 33, 35
2:2, 3, 17^{2}
3:15, 16, 19
4:8, 16
5:31
6:10, 13, 34, 39^{2}
7:6, 10, 19

JUDGES

8:20
9:9, 11, 20, 51
11:16, 17^{2}, 18, 20^{2}, 27
13:3, 6, 7, 9, 21, 23
14:4, 6, 9, 13, 16, 20
15:1, 13^{2}, 19
16:21
17:6
19:10^{2}, 16, 18, 24, 25, 28
20:9, 13, 14, 32, 34, 40, 42, 47

RUTH

1:14, 17
2:8
3:3, 13
4:4

1 SAMUEL

1:2, 5^{2}, 11, 13, 15, 22
2:15, 16, 18, 25, 30
4:20
5:6
6:3, 9
7:10
8:3, 6, 7, 19
9:4^{2}, 7, 27
10:12, 16, 19, 27^{2}
12:10, 12, 15^{2}, 20, 23, 25
13:8, 14, 16, 20, 22
14:1, 10, 26, 27, 37, 39, 41, 43
15:3, 9^{2}, 19, 21
16:7^{2}, 14
17:9, 15, 33, 42, 45, 50, 54
18:8^{2}, 16, 17, 19, 25^{2}
19:2, 10
20:2, 3^{2}, 5, 7, 13, 15, 22, 39
21:4, 6
22:17, 23
23:14, 24, 27
24:7, 10, 12, 13, 22
25:3, 14, 15, 19, 25, 29, 31, 37, 44
26:3, 7, 11, 19, 23
28:23^{2}
29:2, 8
30:2, 6, 10, 24
31:4

2 SAMUEL

2:8, 10, 21, 31
3:1, 13, 22, 26

2 SAMUEL

4:12
5:17, 23
6:10
7:2, 6, 15, 19
8:4
9:10
10:11
11:1, 9, 13, 27
12:3, 4, 12, 17, 19, 21, 23^{2}
13:3, 9, 14, 16, 20, 21, 25, 27, 34, 37
14:2, 6, 25, 29
15:3, 10, 20, 26, 34
16:18
17:16, 18
18:3^{2}, 20^{2}, 22, 23, 29
19:4, 21, 27, 28, 37
20:2, 3, 5, 10, 21
21:2, 7, 8, 17
22:19, 28, 42^{2}
23:6, 7, 12, 16, 21, 23
24:3, 17, 24

1 KINGS

1:1, 4, 8, 10, 19, 26, 52
2:7, 8, 9, 26, 30, 33
3:7, 11, 21, 22^{2}, 23, 26^{2}
5:4
7:1, 31
8:16, 19, 27, 41
9:6^{2}, 22^{2}, 24
11:1, 10, 12, 13, 22, 32, 34, 35, 39
12:8, 10, 11, 14, 17, 20, 22
13:18, 22, 33
14:4, 9, 14
15:14
16:22, 25
17:1, 12, 13
18:12, 18, 21, 22, 25, 26
19:4, 11^{2}, 12
20:9, 16, 23, 27, 28, 30
21:5, 15, 25, 29
22:8^{2}, 16, 18, 24, 30, 31, 48, 49

2 KINGS

1:3, 4, 6, 16
2:10, 17, 19
3:2, 5, 11, 15, 18, 24, 26
4:27, 31, 41

2 KINGS

5:1, 11, 15, 16^{2}, 17, 20^{2}, 25
6:5, 12, 19, 32^{2}
7:2, 4, 10, 19
8:13
9:15, 18, 27, 35
10:4, 9, 18, 19, 23, 31
11:2, 15
12:3, 6, 7, 9, 14
13:6, 7, 11, 19, 22
14:6^{2}, 11, 19, 27
15:25
16:3, 5
17:2, 14, 18, 19, 36, 39, 40
18:6, 12, 20^{2}, 22, 27, 36
19:18, 27
20:10
21:9
22:18
23:9, 23, 35
25:12, 25

1 CHRONICLES

2:30, 34
4:27
5:1, 2
6:49, 56
7:14
10:4
11:18^{2}, 25
12:17, 19
13:13
15:2
16:5, 19, 26
17:1, 5, 14
18:4
19:3, 12, 18
20:1, 7
21:3, 6, 8, 13, 17^{2}, 24, 30
22:8
23:11, 17, 22
24:2
27:23, 24
28:3, 9
29:1, 14

2 CHRONICLES

1:4, 11
2:6
4:6
5:9
6:2, 6, 8, 9, 18, 32,
7:19
8:8, 9^{2}
10:8, 10, 11, 14^{2}, 17, 18
11:2
12:7
13:10, 11, 13, 21
15:2, 4, 5, 17
16:12
17:4
18:6, 7^{2}, 15, 17, 29, 31
19:6
20:10, 12, 15
21:3, 13, 20
22:10, 11
23:6^{2}, 7
24:15, 19, 22, 25
25:2, 4^{3}, 7, 8, 9, 13, 20, 27
26:16, 18
28:1, 9, 10, 20, 21, 23, 27
29:34
30:8, 10, 18
32:8, 9, 25
33:2, 10, 22, 23, 25
35:13, 21^{2}, 22
36:13, 16

EZRA

2:59, 62
3:6, 12
4:3^{2}
5:5, 12, 13
8:22
9:9
10:13

NEHEMIAH

1:9
2:2, 14, 19, 20
3:3, 5, 14, 15
4:1, 7
5:15^{2}
6:2, 8, 12
7:4, 61, 64
9:16, 17^{2}, 28, 29, 33
11:3, 21
13:2, 6, 24

ESTHER

1:12, 16, 17
2:15
3:2, 15
4:4, 11, 14
5:9, 12
6:12, 13
7:4
9:10, 15, 16^{2}, 18, 25

JOB

1:11
2:5, 6, 10
3:9, 21
4:2, 5, 16
5:3, 15
6:1, 14, 25
7:21
8:9, 15^{2}
9:2, 11, 15, 18, 35
11:5, 20
12:2, 3, 7
13:4, 15
14:10, 21, 22
16:5, 7, 12, 20
17:10
19:7^{2}, 28
20:5, 13
21:1
22:8, 18, 20
23:6, 8^{2}, 9, 10, 13
24:24
26:1, 14^{2}
27:17, 19
28:12
30:1
31:32
32:8, 16
35:10, 12, 15
36:6, 7, 12, 13, 17
37:21
38:11
40:5^{2}
42:5

PSALMS

1:2, 4, 6
2:12
3:3
4:3
5:7, 11
6:3
7:9
9:7, 20
11:5
13:5
15:4
16:3
18:18, 27, 41^{2}
20:7, 8
22:2, 3, 6, 9, 19, 24
26:11
28:3
30:5^{2}
31:6, 11, 14
32:10
34:10, 19
35:13, 15, 20
37:9, 11, 17, 20, 21, 28, 36, 38, 39
38:13, 19
40:17
41:10
44:3, 7, 9
49:15
50:16, 21
52:7, 8
55:13, 21, 23^{2}
59:8, 16
62:4
63:9, 11^{2}
64:7
66:12, 19
68:3, 6, 21
69:13, 20^{2}, 29
70:5
71:7, 14
73:2, 4, 25, 26, 28
74:6
75:7, 8, 9, 10
77:10
78:7, 30, 38, 39, 50, 52, 53, 57, 68
81:11, 15
82:7
85:8
86:15
88:13
89:24, 38
90:4
91:7
92:8, 10
94:15, 22
96:5
102:12, 26, 27
103:17
105:12
106:7, 14, 15, 25, 35, 43
109:4, 16, 21, 28^{2}
115:1, 3, 5^{2}, 6^{2}, 7^{2}, 16, 18
118:10, 11, 13, 17, 18
119:23, 61, 67, 69, 70, 78, 81, 87, 95, 96, 113, 161, 163
120:7
125:1, 5
127:1, 5
130:4
132:18
135:16^{2}, 17
136:15
138:6
139:4, 12
141:8
142:4
145:20
146:9

PROVERBS

1:7, 25, 28^{2}, 33
2:22
3:1, 32, 33, 34, 35
4:18
5:4
6:31, 32
8:36
9:12, 18
10:1, 2, 3, 4, 5, 6, 7, 8, 9, 10, 11, 12, 13, 14, 17, 19, 21, 23, 24, 25, 27, 28, 29, 30, 31, 32
11:1, 2, 3, 4, 5, 6, 9, 11, 12, 13, 14, 17, 18, 20, 21, 23, 24, 26, 27, 28
12:1, 2, 3, 4, 5, 6, 7, 8, 10, 11, 12, 13, 15, 16, 17, 18, 19^{2}, 20, 21, 22, 23, 24, 25, 26, 27
13:1, 2, 3, 4, 5, 6, 8, 9, 10, 11,

PROVERBS

12, 13, 15, 16, 17, 18, 19, 20, 21, 23, 24, 25
14:1, 2, 3, 4, 5, 6, 8, 9, 11, 12, 15, 16, 18, 20, 21, 22, 23, 24, 25, 28, 29, 30, 31, 32, 33, 34, 35
15:1, 2, 4, 5, 6, 7, 8, 9, 13, 14, 15, 18, 19, 20, 21, 22, 25, 26, 27, 28, 29, 32
16:2, 9, 14, 22, 25, 33
17:3, 9, 22, 24
18:2, 14, 17, 23
19:4, 12, 16
20:3, 5, 6, 14, 15, 17, 21, 22
21:2, 5, 8, 12, 13, 15, 20, 26, 28, 29, 31
22:3, 15
23:7, 17
24:16, 25
25:2
27:3, 4, 6, 7, 12
28:1, 2, 4, 5, 7, 10, 11, 12, 13, 14, 16, 18, 19, 20, 25, 26, 27, 28
29:2, 3, 4, 6, 7, 8, 10, 11, 15, 16, 18, 23, 25, 26
30:24, 26
31:29, 30

ECCLESIASTES

1:4
2:14, 26
3:12
4:1, 10, 11
5:7, 12, 14
6:2
7:4, 12, 14, 23, 26, 28^{2}, 29
8:13
9:5, 11, 18
10:2, 10, 12, 19
11:8, 9

SONG OF SOLOMON

1:5, 6
3:1, 2, 4^{2}
5:2, 6^{3}
6:9

ISAIAH

1:3, 6, 20, 21
5:6, 7^{2}, 12, 16, 25
6:9^{2}, 13
7:1, 12, 13, 25
8:14
9:5, 10^{2}, 12, 17, 21
10:4, 7, 20
11:4, 14
13:21
14:19
16:6, 12, 14
17:11, 13
22:11
24:16
26:11, 13
28:7, 13, 27
29:8^{2}, 9^{2}, 13, 23
30:1^{2}, 5, 16, 20
31:1, 2, 8
32:8
33:21
34:11, 12
35:8, 9
36:5^{2}, 7, 12, 21
37:19, 28
38:17
40:8, 31
41:8
42:19, 20^{2}, 22
43:1, 22^{2}, 24
45:17
46:2
47:9
48:1, 10
49:14, 25
51:6, 8, 15, 21, 23
53:5
54:7, 8, 10, 15
55:10, 11
57:3, 13^{2}, 20
59:2, 9^{2}, 11^{2}
60:2, 10, 18, 19
61:6
62:4, 9
63:10, 18
64:6, 8
65:6, 11, 12, 13^{3}, 14, 18, 20
66:2, 4, 5

JEREMIAH

1:7, 19
2:7, 11, 25, 27, 28, 34
3:1, 7, 8, 10, 19
4:22
5:3^{2}, 5, 10, 23
6:16, 17, 19
7:12, 13^{2}, 23, 24^{2}, 26, 27^{2}, 28, 32
8:6, 7, 15
9:3, 8, 14, 24
10:5, 8, 10, 19, 24
11:8^{2}, 12, 19, 20
12:3, 13^{2}, 17
13:11, 14, 17
14:12, 13
15:19, 20
16:4, 15
17:6, 8, 18^{2}, 22, 23^{2}, 24, 27
18:12, 23
19:6
20:3, 9, 11, 12
21:9, 14
22:5, 10, 12, 17^{2}, 21, 27

JEREMIAH

23:8, 22, 38
25:3, 4
26:5, 15, 21
27:11, 18
28:13, 15
29:19
30:7, 9, 11
31:30, 33
32:4, 23, 34, 40
33:5
34:3, 5, 11, 14, 16
35:6, 7, 10, 11, 14^{2}, 15, 16, 17^{2}
36:20, 25, 26^{2}, 31
37:2, 10, 14
38:2, 4, 6, 18, 20, 21, 23, 25
39:5, 10, 12, 17, 18
40:4, 10, 14, 16
41:8, 11, 15
42:2, 13, 14, 21
43:3, 5
44:5, 14, 17, 18
45:5
46:17, 20, 27, 28^{2}
48:30, 45
49:10, 12, 19, 39
50:13, 44
51:9, 26, 62
52:8, 16

LAMENTATIONS

1:19
2:14
3:2, 32
5:22

EZEKIEL

2:8
3:5, 7, 14, 18, 19, 20, 25, 27
7:4, 14, 16, 20, 26
8:6
9:6, 10
10:11
11:7, 11, 12, 21
12:16, 23, 28
14:11, 14, 16, 18, 20
16:5, 15, 32, 33, 43, 47, 51, 61
17:14, 15
18:5, 7, 11, 16, 21, 24
19:12
20:8, 9, 13, 14, 16, 18, 24, 39
21:23
22:30
24:23
28:9
29:4, 16
30:24, 25
32:27
33:5, 6^{2}, 8, 9, 11, 13, 17, 19, 24, 31^{2}, 32
34:3, 4, 8, 16, 18^{2}, 28
36:8, 21, 22
37:8, 23
38:8
39:2, 28
41:6
42:6, 14
44:8, 13, 14, 15, 22, 25
46:1, 2, 9^{2}, 17^{2}, 18
47:11

DANIEL

1:4, 8
2:6, 9^{2}, 28, 30^{2}, 41, 43, 44, 49
3:15, 18
4:7, 8, 18
5:8, 15, 20, 23
6:4, 13
7:18, 26, 28
8:3, 4, 7, 17, 18, 22, 24, 25, 27
9:7, 18, 26
10:1, 7, 13^{2}, 21^{2}
11:6^{2}, 7, 10, 11, 12, 14, 16, 17, 18, 19, 20, 21, 25, 27, 29, 32, 34, 38, 41, 43, 44
12:4, 8, 10^{2}, 13

HOSEA

1:6, 7
2:7^{2}
5:6
6:7
7:16
8:4, 6, 12, 13, 14
9:3, 8, 10, 13
10:11
11:3, 5, 12
13:1, 4, 9
14:9

JOEL

2:20
3:16, 20

AMOS

1:4, 7, 10, 12, 14
2:2, 5, 12
3:7, 8
4:8
5:5, 11^{2}, 24, 26
6:6, 14
7:13, 14
8:11

OBADIAH

12, 17

JONAH

1:3, 4, 5, 13
2:9
3:8
4:1, 7

MICAH

1:12
3:4, 8
4:1, 4, 12
5:2
6:8, 14^{2}, 15^{3}

NAHUM

1:8
2:8^{2}
3:17

HABAKKUK

2:3, 4, 5, 20

ZEPHANIAH

1:13^{2}, 18
3:5, 7

HAGGAI

1:6^{3}
2:16^{2}

ZECHARIAH

1:4, 6, 15, 21
4:6
7:11, 14
8:11, 13
9:7
11:6, 16
13:5, 8
14:7^{2}, 11

MALACHI

1:4^{2}, 12, 14
2:8, 9
3:2, 7, 8
4:2

MATTHEW

1:20
2:19, 22
3:7, 11, 12, 14
4:4^{2}
5:13^{2}, 15, 17, 19, 22^{2}, 28, 32, 33, 34, 37, 39^{2}, 44
6:3, 6, 7, 13, 15, 17, 18, 20, 23, 33
7:3, 15, 17, 21
8:4, 8, 12, 20, 22, 24, 27
9:6, 8, 12^{2}, 13^{2}, 14, 15, 17, 18, 21, 22, 24, 25, 31, 34, 36, 37
10:6, 13, 17, 19, 20, 22, 23, 28^{2}, 30, 33, 34
11:8, 9, 16, 19, 22, 24, 27
12:2, 3, 4, 6, 7, 15, 24^{2}, 28, 31, 32, 36, 39^{2}, 48
13:8, 11, 12, 16, 20, 21, 23, 25, 26, 29, 30, 32, 38, 48, 57
14:6, 16, 17, 24, 27, 30
15:3, 5, 8, 9, 11, 13, 18, 20, 23, 24^{2}, 26
16:3, 4, 12, 15, 17, 23^{2}
17:12^{2}, 21
18:6, 7, 16, 17, 22, 25, 28, 30
19:6, 8, 11, 14, 17^{2}, 22, 26^{2}, 30
20:10, 12, 13, 16, 22, 23^{2}, 25, 26^{2}, 28, 31
21:13, 19, 21, 26, 28, 29, 32, 37, 38, 44, 46
22:5, 7, 8, 14, 18, 30, 31, 32, 34
23:3, 4, 5, 8, 11, 13, 16, 18, 25, 27, 28
24:6, 13, 20, 22, 35, 36^{2}, 37, 43, 48
25:4, 9^{2}, 12, 18, 29, 33, 46
26:5, 8, 11, 24, 29, 32, 39, 41, 54, 56, 58, 60, 63, 70
27:20, 23, 24
28:17

MARK

1:8, 30, 44, 45^{2}
2:6, 7, 10, 17^{2}, 18, 20, 22, 26
3:4, 7, 26, 29^{2}
4:6, 11, 15, 17, 22, 29, 32, 34
5:6, 19, 26, 28, 33, 39, 40
6:4^{2}, 9, 16, 19, 49, 56
7:5, 6, 11, 15, 19, 24, 27, 36
8:28, 29, 33^{2}, 35
9:13, 22, 27, 29, 32, 34, 37, 39, 50
10:6, 8, 14, 18, 24, 27, 30, 31, 38, 40^{2}, 42, 43^{2}, 45, 48
11:13, 17, 23, 26, 32
12:7, 12, 14, 15, 25, 27, 32, 44
13:7, 9, 11^{3}, 13, 14, 17, 20, 23, 24, 31, 32^{2}
14:2, 7, 21, 28, 29, 31, 36, 38, 49, 56, 59, 61, 68, 71
15:3, 5, 9, 11, 23
16:7, 16

LUKE

1:13, 60
2:19, 37, 44, 51
3:16, 17, 19
4:4, 25, 26, 30
5:2, 14, 15, 21, 22, 24, 30, 31, 32, 33, 35, 38
6:4, 8, 24, 27, 35, 40, 41, 49
7:7, 25, 26, 28, 30, 35, 44, 45, 46, 47
8:10, 15, 16, 23, 27, 38, 42, 50, 52^{2}, 56
9:9, 13^{2}, 19, 20, 24, 27, 32, 43, 45, 55, 56, 58, 59, 60, 61
10:2, 10, 12, 14, 20, 22^{2}, 29, 33, 40, 42
11:4, 15, 17, 20, 22, 28, 29, 33, 34, 39, 41, 42
12:5, 7, 9, 10, 20, 31, 45, 48, 50, 51, 56
13:3, 5, 27

LUKE

14:10, 13, 34, 35
15:20, 22, 30
16:15, 25^{2}, 30
17:1^{2}, 7, 17, 25, 29
18:4, 13, 15, 16, 39
19:14, 27, 42, 46, 47
20:6, 10, 14, 18, 21, 23, 35, 38
21:4, 7, 9^{2}, 12, 18, 23, 33
22:21, 22, 26^{2}, 27, 32, 36, 42, 48, 53, 56
23:9, 21, 25, 28^{2}, 40, 41
24:6, 16, 21, 24, 29, 37, 49

JOHN

1:8, 12, 13, 17, 20, 26, 31, 33
2:9, 10, 21, 24
3:8, 13, 15, 16, 17, 18, 21, 28, 29, 30, 36
4:2, 14^{2}, 23, 32
5:7, 17, 18, 19, 22, 24, 30, 34^{2}, 36, 42, 47
6:9, 20, 22, 26, 27, 32, 36, 38, 39, 64
7:6, 7, 10^{2}, 12, 16, 18, 22, 24, 26, 27, 28, 29, 30, 39, 41, 44, 49
8:5, 6, 10, 12, 14, 16, 26, 28, 35, 37, 40, 42, 49, 55^{2}, 59
9:3, 9, 18, 21, 28, 31, 41
10:1, 2, 5, 6, 8, 10, 12, 18, 26, 33, 38, 39, 41
11:4, 10, 11, 13, 20, 22, 30, 42, 46, 51, 52, 54
12:2, 6, 8, 9, 10, 16, 24, 27, 30, 37, 42, 44, 47, 49
13:7, 9, 10^{2}, 18, 36
14:6, 10, 17, 19, 24, 26, 31
15:15, 16, 19^{2}, 21, 22, 24, 25, 26
16:4, 5, 6, 7, 12, 13, 20^{2}, 21, 22, 25^{2}, 33
17:9, 11, 12, 15, 20, 25
18:16, 23, 28, 36, 39, 40
19:9, 12, 13, 15^{2}, 21, 24, 33, 34, 38
20:7, 11, 17, 24, 25, 27, 31
21:4^{2}, 8, 18, 23

THE ACTS

1:4, 5, 8
2:14, 15, 16, 34
3:6, 14, 18
4:15, 17, 19, 20, 32
5:1, 3, 4, 13, 19, 21, 22, 23, 39
6:4
7:9, 12, 17, 25, 27, 39, 47, 55
8:9, 12, 20, 40
9:7, 8, 15, 21, 22, 24, 26, 27, 29, 40
10:10, 14, 26, 28, 35, 41
11:4, 8, 9, 16, 19
12:5, 9, 14, 15, 16, 17, 20, 24
13:8, 14, 25, 30, 37, 45, 46, 50, 51
14:2, 4
15:5, 11, 20, 38
16:1, 7, 18, 28, 37^{2}
17:5, 13, 14, 21, 30
18:9, 15, 19, 21^{2}
19:9^{2}, 15, 22, 26, 27, 34, 39
20:20, 24
21:13, 24, 39
22:9, 28
23:6, 8, 9, 21, 29
24:7, 11, 14, 27
25:4, 9, 11, 19, 21, 25
26:16, 20, 25^{2}, 29
27:10, 14, 21, 22, 27, 39, 41, 43
28:6, 16, 19, 22

ROMANS

1:13, 21, 32
2:2, 5, 8^{2}, 10, 13, 25, 29^{2}
3:4, 5, 21, 27
4:2, 4, 5^{2}, 10, 12, 13, 16, 20, 24
5:3, 8, 11, 13, 15, 16, 20
6:10, 11, 13, 14, 15, 17^{2}, 22, 23
7:2, 3, 6, 7, 8, 9, 13, 14, 15, 17, 18, 19, 20, 23, 25
8:1, 4, 5, 6, 9^{2}, 10, 11, 13, 15, 20, 23, 24, 25, 26, 32
9:7, 8, 10, 11, 13, 16, 20, 24, 31, 32
10:2, 6, 8, 16, 18, 19, 20, 21
11:4, 6, 7, 11, 15, 18^{2}, 20, 22, 28
12:2, 3, 16, 19, 21
13:1, 3, 4, 5, 8, 14
14:1, 10, 13, 14, 15, 17, 20
15:3, 21, 23, 25
16:4, 18, 19, 26

1 CORINTHIANS

1:10, 14, 17, 18, 23, 24, 27, 30
2:4, 5, 7, 9, 10, 11, 12, 13, 14, 15, 16
3:1, 5, 6, 7, 10, 15
4:3, 4, 10^{3}, 14, 19^{2}, 20
5:3, 8, 11, 13
6:6, 11^{3}, 12^{2}, 13^{2}, 17, 18
7:4^{2}, 6, 7, 9, 10, 11, 12, 14, 15^{2}, 17, 19, 21, 28^{2}, 29, 32, 33, 34, 35, 36, 37, 38, 39, 40
8:1, 3, 4, 6^{2}, 8, 9, 12
9:12, 15, 17, 21, 24, 25, 27
10:5, 13^{3}, 20, 23^{2}, 24, 28, 29, 33
11:3, 5, 6, 7, 8, 9, 12, 15, 16, 17, 28, 32
12:3, 4, 5, 6, 7, 11, 14, 18, 20^{2}, 24, 25, 31
13:6, 8, 10, 11, 12^{2}, 13
14:1, 2, 3, 4, 5, 14, 17, 20, 22^{3}, 24, 28, 33, 34, 38

1 CORINTHIANS
15:6, 10^{3}, 13, 20, 23, 27, 35, 37, 38, 39, 40, 46, 51, 57
16:7, 8, 11, 12^{2}

2 CORINTHIANS
1:9^{2}, 12, 18, 19, 24
2:1, 2, 4, 5^{2}, 13, 17^{2}
3:3^{2}, 5, 6^{2}, 7, 14, 15, 18
4:2^{2}, 3, 5, 7, 8, 9^{2}, 12, 16, 17, 18^{2}
5:4, 11, 12, 15
6:4, 12
7:5, 7, 8, 9, 10, 12, 14
8:5, 8, 10, 14, 16, 17, 19, 21, 22
9:6, 12
10:1, 2, 4, 10, 12, 13^{2}, 15, 17, 18
11:3, 6^{2}, 12, 17
12:5, 6, 14^{2}, 16, 19
13:3, 4, 6, 7, 8

GALATIANS
1:1, 7, 8, 11, 12, 15, 17, 19, 23
2:2, 3, 6, 7, 11, 12, 14, 16, 17, 20
3:11, 12, 15, 16, 18, 20, 22, 23, 25
4:2, 4, 7, 9, 14, 17, 18, 23^{2}, 26, 29, 31
5:6, 10, 13, 15, 18, 22
6:4, 8, 13, 14, 15

EPHESIANS
1:21
2:4, 13, 19
4:7, 9, 15, 20, 28, 29
5:3, 4, 8, 11, 13, 15, 17, 18, 27, 29, 32
6:4, 6, 12, 21

PHILIPPIANS
1:12, 17, 20, 22, 28, 29
2:3, 4, 7, 12, 19, 22, 24, 25, 27^{2}
3:1, 7, 8^{2}, 9, 12, 13
4:6, 10^{2}, 15, 17, 18, 19

COLOSSIANS
1:26
2:17
3:8, 11, 22, 25

1 THESSALONIANS
1:5, 8
2:2, 4^{2}, 7, 8, 13, 17, 18
3:6
4:7, 8, 9, 10, 13
5:1, 4, 6, 8, 9, 15

2 THESSALONIANS
2:12, 13
3:3, 8, 9, 11, 13, 15

1 TIMOTHY
1:8, 9, 13
2:10, 12^{2}, 14
3:3, 15
4:7, 8, 12
5:1, 4, 6, 8, 11, 13, 19, 23
6:2, 4, 6, 9, 11, 17

2 TIMOTHY
1:7, 8, 9, 10, 17
2:9, 14, 16, 20^{2}, 22, 23, 24
3:5, 9, 10, 11, 13, 14
4:3, 5, 8, 13, 16, 20

TITUS
1:3, 8, 15^{2}, 16
2:1, 10
3:2, 4, 5, 9

PHILEMON
11, 14^{2}, 16^{2}, 22

HEBREWS
1:8, 11, 12, 13
2:6, 8, 9, 16
3:4, 6, 13, 17, 18
4:2, 13, 15
5:4, 5, 14
6:8, 9, 12
7:3, 6, 8, 16, 19, 21, 24, 28
8:6
9:7, 11, 12, 23, 24, 26, 27
10:3, 5, 12, 25, 27, 32, 38, 39^{2}
11:6, 13, 16
12:8, 10, 11, 13, 22, 26^{2}
13:4, 14, 16, 19

JAMES
1:4, 6, 10, 11, 14, 22, 25^{2}, 26
2:6, 9, 20
3:8, 14, 15, 17
4:6^{2}, 11^{2}, 16
5:12^{2}

1 PETER
1:12, 15, 19, 20, 23, 25
2:4, 7, 9, 10^{2}, 16, 18, 20, 23, 25
3:4, 9, 12, 14, 15, 18, 21
4:2, 6, 7, 13, 14, 15, 16
5:2^{2}, 3, 10

2 PETER
1:9, 16, 21
2:1, 4, 5, 10, 12, 16, 22
3:7, 8, 9^{2}, 10, 18

1 JOHN
1:7
2:2, 5, 7, 11, 16, 17, 19^{2}, 20, 21, 22, 23, 27^{2}
3:2, 17, 18
4:1, 10, 18
5:5, 6, 18

2 JOHN
1, 5, 8, 12

3 JOHN
9, 11^{2}, 13, 14

JUDE
6, 9, 10^{2}, 17, 20

REVELATION
2:6, 9^{2}, 14, 24, 25
3:5, 9
9:4, 5, 11
10:7, 9
11:2
12:12
14:3
17:12
19:12
20:5, 6
21:8, 27
22:3

BY

GENESIS
7:2^{2}, 3
9:6, 11
10:5, 32
14:6, 15
16:2, 7^{2}
18:2, 8
19:36
20:3
21:23, 28, 29
22:13, 16
23:20
24:3, 11, 13, 30, 43
25:11, 13, 16^{2}
26:18
27:40
29:2
30:3, 27, 40
31:24, 31, 39^{2}, 40, 53
32:16
33:8
35:4
36:37, 40
37:28
38:14, 16, 18, 19, 20, 21, 24, 25
39:10^{2}, 12, 16
41:1, 3, 31, 32, 47
42:15, 16, 23, 38
43:32^{3}
45:1, 7, 23, 24
47:13
48:7
49:17, 22, 24, 25^{2}

EXODUS
2:3, 5, 15, 23^{2}
3:7, 19
4:4, 13, 24
6:3^{2}
7:4, 15
8:24
9:35
12:14, 17, 26, 31, 51
13:3, 14, 16, 21^{3}, 22^{4}
14:2, 9, 20, 21
15:16, 27
16:3^{2}
18:8, 13, 14
19:19
20:26
21:3^{2}, 4
22:25, 26
23:30
25:14
26:9^{2}
28:28
29:11, 18, 25, 28, 32, 38, 41, 43
30:4, 6, 20
31:2
32:13, 27
33:6, 12, 17, 21, 22^{2}
34:6, 7
35:29, 30
36:16^{2}
37:3, 5, 27
38:21
39:4, 21
40:29, 38^{2}

LEVITICUS
1:5, 9, 13, 16, 17
2:2, 3, 9, 10, 11, 14, 16
3:3, 4, 5, 9^{2}, 10, 11, 14, 15, 16
4:9, 35
5:12, 15, 17
6:2, 17, 18
7:4, 5, 25, 30, 34, 35, 36
8:21, 28, 36
10:11, 12, 13, 15^{2}
16:21, 31
19:12, 31
20:25^{3}
21:6, 9, 21
22:4, 22, 27
23:8, 13, 18, 25, 27, 36^{2}, 37
24:7, 8, 9^{2}
25:39, 47^{3}
26:7, 8, 23^{2}, 26, 46
27:2

NUMBERS
1:2^{2}, 3, 17, 18^{2}, 20^{3}, 22^{3}, 24^{2}, 26^{2}, 28^{2}, 30^{2}, 32^{2}, 34^{2}, 36^{2}, 38^{2}, 40^{2}, 42, 45, 52^{2}
2:2, 12, 17, 20, 25, 27, 32, 34
3:15, 17, 18, 19, 20, 26^{2}, 43, 47, 49
4:2, 22, 26^{2}, 29, 32, 36, 37, 38, 40, 42, 45, 49
5:2, 19
6:9, 11
7:84
9:6, 7, 10, 16^{2}, 21^{2}, 23
10:13, 34
11:31
12:2^{2}
13:3, 22, 29^{2}
14:3, 14^{2}, 18, 25, 36, 37, 43
15:3, 10, 13, 14, 23, 24, 25, 28
16:40
18:8^{2}, 11, 17, 19, 32
20:17, 18, 19, 23
21:1, 4, 18, 22, 33
22:1, 5
23:3, 6, 15, 17
24:6
26:3, 55, 63^{2}
27:2, 23
28:2, 3^{2}, 6, 8, 13, 19, 24
29:6, 13, 36
30:3, 10
31:12, 17, 18, 35
33:2, 10, 48, 49, 50, 54
34:3, 13, 18
35:1, 20, 30, 33
36:2^{2}, 13^{2}

DEUTERONOMY
1:2, 7, 19, 22, 33^{3}, 40
2:1, 8^{2}, 27, 30, 36^{2}
3:12
4:34^{7}, 48
5:5, 15, 31
6:7, 13
7:22
8:3
9:29^{2}
10:20
11:19, 30
12:30
14:22
15:20
16:1
18:1
20:19
21:5, 17
22:4
23:10^{2}
24:9
25:2, 11, 17, 18
27:16
28:10, 68
29:16
33:12, 14^{2}, 29

JOSHUA
2:12, 15, 18
3:4^{2}
4:6
5:1, 4, 5, 7, 13
7:14^{2}, 16, 17, 18
8:3, 15
9:13, 18, 19
10:18
11:7, 23
13:6, 14, 16, 22, 29, 31, 32
14:2^{2}
15:1, 6, 8
16:1, 6, 8
17:2^{2}
18:9, 20
19:49, 51
20:2, 8, 9
21:2, 4, 5, 6, 7, 8^{2}, 9, 40^{2}
22:9, 10
23:4, 7
24:26

JUDGES
2:18
3:1, 4^{2}, 15, 19^{2}
4:11
5:10, 19, 22
6:11, 25, 27^{2}, 28, 30, 36, 37
7:1, 5, 7, 12
8:11
9:6, 9, 25, 32, 34, 37^{2}
11:18, 26
16:5, 26
17:10
18:3, 16, 28
19:11, 14
20:5, 9
21:7, 11, 12

RUTH
2:8, 21, 23
4:1

1 SAMUEL
1:7, 9, 26
2:3, 9, 16, 23, 28
3:21
4:13, 18, 20
5:2
6:8, 9
9:23
10:2, 19^{2}, 21
11:7, 9
14:4, 6^{2}, 36
16:9, 20
17:2, 23, 26, 35, 43, 52
18:25, 30
20:7, 9, 19, 25^{2}
23:7
24:3, 21
25:13, 16, 20, 22, 34
26:3, 7, 24^{2}
27:1
28:6^{3}, 8^{2}, 10, 15^{2}, 17
29:1, 2^{2}
30:15, 24

2 SAMUEL
1:6, 12
2:13, 15, 16, 24
3:5, 18
6:2, 7
10:2, 8
11:14
12:14, 25
13:31, 32, 34
15:30, 36
16:2, 13
17:11, 17, 22
18:4^{3}, 23
19:3, 7, 37
20:9, 11, 12, 21
21:10^{2}, 22^{2}
22:9, 30^{2}, 35
23:2, 4, 15, 16
24:16

1 KINGS
1:9^{2}, 17, 27, 30
2:8, 23, 25, 29, 42
3:5
4:12, 20
5:9, 11, 14
6:21, 22
7:20
8:38^{2}, 43, 53, 56
9:8
10:5, 25, 29
12:15
13:1^{2}, 2, 5, 9^{2}, 10, 17^{2}, 18, 24^{3}, 25^{2}, 28, 32
14:4, 18
15:13, 29, 30
16:7, 12, 13^{2}, 34
17:3, 5, 16, 20, 24
18:4, 6^{2}, 13, 24
19:2, 11, 19
20:14^{2}, 38, 39^{2}
21:1, 23
22:8, 19, 28

2 KINGS
2:1, 7, 11, 13, 23
3:11, 20
4:8, 9, 27
5:1, 2
6:14, 26, 30
8:8, 21
9:27^{2}, 36
10:6, 10, 33
11:11, 14^{2}, 16^{2}, 19
13:7, 25
14:7, 9, 25, 27
16:15
17:4, 6, 13^{3}, 23
18:11, 17, 31
19:7, 11, 23, 28^{2}, 33^{2}
20:11
21:10
23:3, 7, 11
24:2
25:4^{3}

1 CHRONICLES
1:48
3:3
4:38, 41
5:7, 10, 17
6:15, 61, 63, 65^{2}, 78
7:4, 5, 7, 9, 11, 29
8:28
9:1, 22, 23, 28
11:3, 11, 14, 18
12:22, 31
14:11
15:16
16:41
17:21
18:3
19:4, 9
20:8^{2}
21:15, 25, 26
23:3^{2}, 24^{2}, 27, 31
24:5, 27
26:16, 25
27:1
28:1, 12, 14^{2}, 15^{2}, 16, 17^{2}, 18, 19
29:5, 8

2 CHRONICLES
1:17
2:16
3:3
5:11, 14
6:23^{4}, 33, 34
7:6, 12, 14, 20, 21
8:14, 18
9:4, 18, 24
10:15
12:7
13:5
16:14
18:7, 27
19:5
20:15, 16
21:9, 15^{3}, 19
22:7
23:10^{2}, 13, 15, 18^{2}
24:11^{2}, 13
25:18
26:11^{2}, 15
28:15
29:9, 15, 25, 27
30:12, 21
31:6, 15, 17^{2}, 19^{2}
32:11^{2}
33:8
34:14
35:4, 6, 20
36:13, 15, 21, 22

EZRA
1:1, 8
2:62
3:4, 11
4:16, 23
5:5
6:9
7:23
8:3, 18, 20, 31, 33, 34^{2}
9:11
10:16, 17, 44

NEHEMIAH
1:10^{2}
2:6, 13^{2}, 15^{2}
3:15, 23, 25
4:3, 12, 18^{2}
7:3, 5, 64
8:14, 18
9:9, 12^{2}, 14, 19^{2}, 30
10:29, 34, 35
12:37
13:18, 25, 26

ESTHER
1:12, 15
2:14
3:13, 15
7:7
8:5, 10, 14
9:25

JOB
4:9^{2}
6:16
9:11
11:7
15:30
16:12
17:7
18:8, 9
20:29
21:29
22:30
26:12, 13
27:11
28:8, 9, 25
29:3, 19
30:4, 18
31:9, 11, 23, 28, 30, 33
33:18
35:9^{2}
36:12, 22, 31, 32
37:10, 11, 12, 17, 19
38:2, 24
39:9, 26
41:18, 25
42:5

PSALMS
1:3
5:10
9:16
10:10
17:4, 7
18:8, 29^{2}, 34
19:11
30:7
33:6^{2}, 16^{2}, 17
37:23
38:8
39:10
41:11
44:3, 12, 16
48:4
49:7
50:5
54:1^{2}
56:7
59:11
63:10, 11
65:5, 6
66:7
68:4
71:6
72:3
73:23
74:7, 13
77:20
78:17, 18, 26, 49, 55, 64, 65, 72
79:10
80:12
88:9
89:35, 39, 41
90:7^{2}, 10
91:5^{2}
94:20
102:5
104:8^{2}, 12
106:22
107:7
119:9
121:6^{2}
128:3
129:8
134:1
136:5, 8, 9
137:1
140:5
147:4

PROVERBS
3:19^{2}, 20, 28, 29
4:15
6:26
7:26
8:2, 15, 16, 30
9:11
11:5, 11^{2}
12:3, 13, 14
13:2, 10, 11^{2}
14:4
15:13, 23
16:6^{2}, 12
20:4, 11, 18, 28
21:6
22:4
24:3, 4, 6, 30^{2}
25:15
26:2^{2}, 6, 17^{2}, 26, 28
27:9
28:2, 8
29:4, 19
30:27
31:18

ECCLESIASTES
1:13
5:3, 9, 14
7:3, 11, 23, 26, 27
9:1, 15
10:3, 18
12:11, 12

SONG OF SOLOMON
1:7, 8
2:7^{2}
3:1, 5^{2}
5:4, 12
7:4

ISAIAH
1:7
3:5^{2}, 25
4:1, 4^{2}, 5^{2}
7:20^{2}
9:1
10:13^{2}, 34
13:15
15:5
18:2
19:7^{3}
20:2
22:3, 5, 14
23:3
26:13
27:7, 9, 12
28:18, 19^{3}
29:13
32:8
34:17
36:2, 16
37:7, 11, 24^{2}, 29^{2}, 34^{2}
38:8, 16
40:26^{3}
41:3
42:16
43:1, 7
44:4, 5^{2}, 24
45:3, 4, 23
46:3
48:1^{2}, 17
49:10, 19
50:4
51:18, 19
52:12
53:11
54:15
60:19
62:2, 8^{2}
63:12, 19
64:4
65:1, 5, 15, 16
66:16^{2}

JEREMIAH
2:8, 17, 34
4:26

JEREMIAH
5:7^{2}, 22, 31
6:5, 25
7:10, 11, 14, 30
8:3, 5
10:12^{3}, 14
11:21, 22^{2}
12:16^{2}
13:5, 24
14:9, 12^{3}, 15
15:16
16:4^{2}
17:2, 8^{2}, 11, 19, 20, 21
18:21^{2}
19:2, 7^{2}
20:2, 4
21:9^{3}
22:2, 4, 5, 8, 13^{2}
23:27, 32^{2}
25:29
27:3, 5^{2}, 8, 13^{3}
29:3, 19, 22
31:9, 32, 35^{2}
32:17, 34, 36^{3}
33:4^{2}
34:4, 15
35:4
37:2
38:2^{3}, 11, 23
39:4^{3}, 18
41:12, 17
42:17^{3}, 22^{3}
44:12^{4}, 13^{3}, 15, 18^{2}, 26, 27^{2}
46:2, 6, 10, 18
48:19
49:3, 9, 13, 17
50:1, 13
51:14, 15^{3}, 17^{2}
52:7^{5}

LAMENTATIONS
1:12, 14
2:15, 21
3:1
5:12

EZEKIEL
1:1, 3, 15, 19
3:15, 23
4:10, 11, 16^{2}
5:12, 14
6:11^{3}, 12^{2}
8:3
9:2, 3, 11
10:9^{3}, 15, 16, 20, 22
11:10, 24
12:3, 4, 7
13:19, 22
14:3, 7, 13, 14, 20
16:6, 8, 15, 25, 36, 56, 61
17:5, 7, 8, 9, 14, 17, 18, 21
18:7, 12, 16, 18
19:7, 10^{2}
20:3, 31^{2}
21:12
22:7^{2}, 12
23:21, 25^{2}
24:6, 21
25:12, 13, 14, 15
26:6, 10, 11
27:12, 16, 34
28:5^{2}, 10, 16, 17, 18^{2}, 23

EZEKIEL
29:7
30:5, 6, 10, 12, 17
31:7, 9, 12, 14, 18
32:12, 20, 21, 22, 23, 24, 25, 26, 29^{2}, 30, 31
33:27, 30
34:13
35:5
36:17^{2}, 34, 37
37:2, 18
38:17
39:15, 23
40:2, 5, 7, 18, 22, 28, 38, 41, 49^{2}
41:7, 17^{2}
42:20
43:3, 4, 6, 7^{2}, 8^{3}, 13
44:2^{3}, 3^{2}
45:1
46:2^{2}, 8^{2}, 9^{6}, 14, 16, 18, 21
47:2, 12, 16, 18, 22
48:2, 3, 4, 5, 6, 7, 8, 12, 20, 24, 25, 26, 27, 28, 29

DANIEL
4:17^{2}, 27^{2}, 30
5:10
7:2, 8, 16
8:2, 11, 12, 24, 25
9:2, 3, 5, 10, 11, 12, 18, 19
10:4, 16
11:2, 12, 16, 18, 21, 32, 33^{4}
12:7

HOSEA
1:2, 7^{6}
2:17
4:2
6:5^{2}, 9
7:4, 16
8:4, 9
11:3
12:3^{2}, 10^{2}, 13^{2}
13:7, 16
14:1

AMOS
2:8
4:2
5:3^{2}
6:8, 10, 13
7:2, 4, 5, 7, 8, 11, 17^{2}
8:2, 5, 7, 8, 14
9:5, 10, 12

OBADIAH
5, 9

JONAH
2:2
3:7

MICAH
2:2, 5, 8, 12, 13
3:8
7:18

NAHUM
1:6

HABAKKUK
1:16
2:4, 5, 10, 12
3:10, 13

ZEPHANIAH
1:5^{2}, 18
2:12, 15
3:6

HAGGAI
1:1, 3
2:1, 10, 13, 22

ZECHARIAH
1:8
3:5, 7
4:3, 6^{3}, 14
5:4
7:7, 12
8:9
9:8, 11

MALACHI
1:1, 9
2:10

MATTHEW
1:22
2:5, 14, 15, 17, 23
3:3
4:4^{2}, 14, 15, 18
5:21, 26, 27, 33, 34, 35^{2}, 36
6:27
7:16, 20
8:17, 28
9:25
11:12
12:17, 24, 27^{2}, 28, 33, 37^{2}
13:1, 4, 14, 19, 21^{2}, 35
14:13
15:3, 5^{2}, 6
17:21
18:7, 28
20:30^{2}
21:4, 23, 24, 27
22:1, 31
23:16^{2}, 18^{2}, 20^{3}, 21^{3}, 22^{3}
24:15
26:4, 24, 63, 73
27:9, 32, 35, 39, 64
28:9, 13

MARK
1:16, 31
2:13, 14
3:22
4:1^{2}, 2, 4, 15
5:4, 7, 21, 22, 41
6:2, 7, 25^{2}, 32, 39, 40^{2}, 48
7:11^{2}, 26
8:3, 23, 27
9:2, 27, 29^{2}, 33, 34
10:1, 46
11:4, 20, 28, 29, 33
12:1, 36
13:14
14:1, 19, 21, 47, 69, 70
15:21, 29, 35

LUKE
1:61, 70, 77
2:8, 18, 26, 27
3:19
4:1, 4^{2}
5:1, 2, 15, 17, 19
6:44
8:4, 5, 12, 20, 36, 54
9:7, 14, 47

LUKE
10:4, 19, 31^{2}, 32
11:3, 19^{2}
13:17
16:22
17:6, 7^{2}
18:5, 31, 35, 36, 37
19:8, 15, 24
20:2, 8
21:9^{2}, 16, 24
22:22, 56
23:8
24:4, 12, 32

JOHN
1:3, 10, 17^{2}, 42
3:2, 34
5:2
6:15, 18, 57^{2}
7:50
8:9^{2}, 59
9:1, 7, 21
10:1, 2, 3, 9
11:39, 42
12:11, 29
13:35
14:6
16:30
18:22
19:7, 25, 26, 39
20:7
21:19

THE ACTS
1:3, 10, 16, 25
2:16, 22^{2}, 23^{2}, 33, 43
3:7, 12, 16, 18, 21
4:7^{2}, 9, 10^{2}, 16, 25, 30^{2}, 36
5:10, 12, 15, 19
6:10
7:25, 35, 42, 53
9:8, 13, 25^{2}, 36, 39
10:6, 22, 32, 36
11:4, 5, 28, 30
12:9, 20
13:4, 8, 11, 19, 21, 36, 39^{2}, 45
14:3
15:3, 7, 9, 12, 23, 27, 40
16:2, 8, 13, 16
17:10, 23, 29, 31
18:3, 9, 21, 28
19:10, 11, 13, 25
20:16, 19, 31
21:19
22:11, 20, 24, 25
23:2, 4, 10, 11, 19, 31
24:2^{2}, 8, 21
25:14
26:18
27:2, 11, 12, 13, 16, 23
28:16, 25

ROMANS
1:2, 4, 5, 10^{2}, 12, 17, 20
2:7, 12, 14, 16, 27^{2}
3:20^{2}, 21, 22, 24, 27^{2}, 28, 30
4:2, 16
5:1, 2^{2}, 5, 9, 10^{2}, 11, 12^{2}, 15^{2}, 16^{2}, 17^{3}, 18^{2}, 19^{2}, 21
6:4^{2}
7:2, 4, 5, 7, 8, 11^{2}, 13^{2}
8:11, 14, 20, 24
9:10^{2}, 32^{2}
10:5, 17^{2}, 19^{2}

ROMANS
11:6, 14, 20, 24
12:1, 2
14:14
15:16, 18^{2}, 19, 24, 28, 32
16:18, 26
S

1 CORINTHIANS
1:4, 5, 9, 10, 11, 21^{2}
2:10
3:5, 13, 15
4:4
6:2, 11, 14
7:6, 14^{2}, 39
8:6^{2}, 9
9:22, 27
10:30
11:12
12:3^{2}, 8^{2}, 9^{2}, 13
14:6^{4}, 9, 19, 27^{3}, 30, 31
15:2, 10, 21^{2}, 31
16:2, 3, 7
S

2 CORINTHIANS
1:1, 4, 5, 11^{3}, 12, 16, 19^{2}, 20, 24
2:2, 14
3:3, 10, 18
4:2, 14, 16
5:7^{2}, 18, 20
6:6^{8}, 7^{3}, 8^{2}
7:6, 7^{2}, 9, 13
8:5, 8^{2}, 14, 19, 20
9:12, 13, 14
10:1, 9, 11, 12, 15
11:3, 26^{2}, 33
12:17
13:4^{2}
S

GALATIANS
1:1^{2}, 12, 15, 22
2:2^{2}, 5, 15, 16^{5}, 17, 20, 21
3:2^{2}, 3, 5^{2}, 11^{2}, 18, 19, 21, 22, 24, 26
4:8, 22^{2}, 23
5:4, 5, 6, 13
6:14

EPHESIANS
1:1, 5
2:3, 5, 8, 11^{2}, 13, 16, 18
3:3, 5, 6, 7, 9, 10, 12, 16, 17, 21
4:14, 16, 21
5:13, 26
S

PHILIPPIANS
1:11, 14, 20^{2}, 26, 28
3:9, 11, 16
4:6, 19
S

COLOSSIANS
1:1, 16^{2}, 17, 20^{2}, 21
2:11, 18, 19
3:17
4:18
S

1 THESSALONIANS
3:3, 5, 7
4:1, 2, 15
5:9, 27

2 THESSALONIANS
2:1^{2}, 2^{3}, 3, 14, 15
3:12, 14, 16

1 TIMOTHY
1:1, 18
4:5, 14
5:21

2 TIMOTHY
1:1, 6, 10, 14
2:26
3:16
4:17

TITUS
1:9
3:5^{2}, 7

PHILEMON
6, 7
S

HEBREWS
1:1, 2^{2}, 3^{2}, 4
2:2, 3^{2}, 9, 10
3:4, 16
5:3, 8, 14
6:7, 13^{2}, 16, 17, 18
7:2, 11, 19, 21, 22, 23, 25
8:6, 9
9:11, 12^{2}, 15, 22, 26
10:1, 8, 10, 14, 19, 20, 33, 38
11:2, 3, 4^{3}, 5, 7^{3}, 8, 9, 12, 17, 20, 21, 22, 23, 24, 27, 29^{2}, 30, 31
13:11, 15
S

JAMES
2:7, 12, 18, 21, 22, 24^{2}, 25
5:4, 12^{3}, 17

1 PETER
1:3, 5, 12, 18, 21, 23, 25
2:5, 12, 14, 24
3:1, 18, 19, 20, 21
5:2, 10, 12

2 PETER
1:4, 13, 21^{2}
2:2
3:1, 2, 5, 7

1 JOHN
3:24
5:2, 6^{3}

3 JOHN
14

JUDE
1, 12, 23

REVELATION
1:1
5:9
8:13
9:2, 18^{4}, 20
10:6
12:11^{2}
13:14^{2}
14:20
18:15, 17, 19, 23
21:25

FOR 3588, *1063*

GENESIS
1:14^{3}, 15, 29, 30
2:5, 9, 17, 18, 20^{2}
3:5, 6, 17, 19^{2}, 22
4:23, 25
5:24
6:3, 7, 12, 13, 21^{3}
7:1, 4
8:9^{2}, 21^{2}
9:3, 6, 12, 13
10:25
11:3^{2}
12:10, 13, 16
13:6, 8, 15^{2}, 17
14:13
15:6, 16
16:10, 13
17:4, 5, 7, 8, 13, 15, 19, 20
18:5, 14, 15, 19, 24, 26, 28, 29, 31, 32
19:8, 13, 14, 17, 21, 22, 30
20:3^{2}, 6, 7^{2}, 11, 18
21:2, 7, 10, 12, 16, 17, 18, 30
22:2, 3, 7, 8, 12, 13, 16
23:2^{2}, 8, 9^{2}, 13, 18, 20
24:10, 14, 19, 20, 22, 23, 31^{2}, 32, 40, 44^{2}, 62, 65
25:21, 30
26:3, 7^{2}, 9, 14, 15, 16, 18, 21, 22^{3}, 24^{2}
27:5, 9, 36^{2}, 37, 41
28:11, 15, 18^{2}, 22
29:2, 9, 15, 18, 20^{2}, 21, 24, 25, 27, 32
30:13, 15, 16, 26^{2}, 27^{2}, 30^{2}, 31, 33^{2}
31:12, 14, 15, 16, 18, 31, 32, 35, 41^{2}, 44, 45, 49, 52
32:10, 11, 12, 13, 20, 26, 28, 30
33:10, 17, 19
34:8, 14, 21^{3}, 22
35:18
36:7

GENESIS
37:7, 8^{2}, 17, 27, 28, 34, 35^{2}
38:6, 11, 14, 16
39:5
40:15, 17
41:8, 19, 31, 32, 36, 49, 51, 52, 55, 57
42:2, 4, 5, 18, 19, 23, 25, 27, 30, 33, 38
43:5, 9^{2}, 10, 16, 18, 25, 30, 32^{4}
44:4, 14, 17, 18, 22, 26, 32^{3}, 34
45:3, 5, 6, 11, 19^{2}, 20, 21, 23, 26
46:3, 32, 34
47:4^{4}, 13, 14, 15^{2}, 16, 17^{6}, 19, 20^{2}, 21, 22, 23^{2}, 24^{5}
48:4, 7, 10, 14, 18
49:6, 7^{2}, 13, 18, 30
50:3^{3}, 5, 10, 13^{2}, 17, 19, 20

EXODUS
1:5, 11, 18, 19
2:3, 7, 9, 19, 22
3:5, 6, 7, 15
4:1, 19
5:7, 8, 18, 23
6:1, 7, 8, 9^{2}
7:9, 12, 24^{2}
8:8, 9^{3}, 17, 25^{2}, 26, 28
9:2, 11, 14, 15, 16^{2}, 19, 27, 28, 30, 31, 32
10:1, 5, 9, 10, 11, 12, 15, 16, 23, 26, 28
12:3, 4^{2}, 12, 13, 14^{2}, 15, 17^{2}, 19, 21, 23, 24^{2}, 30, 31, 33, 39^{2}, 42, 44, 48
13:3, 9^{3}, 16^{3}, 17, 19
14:3, 12^{2}, 13^{2}, 14, 25^{2}
15:1, 17, 18, 19, 21, 23, 25, 26
16:3, 4, 7, 8, 9, 15, 16^{2}, 22, 23, 25, 27, 29, 32, 33
17:1, 3, 14^{2}, 16
18:1^{2}, 3, 4, 8, 9, 11, 12, 18^{2}, 19, 22

EXODUS
19:2, 5, 7, 9, 11, 23
20:5, 7, 11, 20, 25
21:2, 6, 19, 21, 23, 24^{4}, 25^{3}, 26, 27, 30, 36
22:1^{2}, 2, 3^{3}, 9^{6}, 13, 15, 21, 27^{3}
23:7, 8, 9, 15, 21^{2}, 23, 31, 33
24:14
25:6^{3}, 12, 26, 27
26:14, 15, 17, 18, 19^{2}, 20, 22, 23, 24^{2}, 26, 27^{3}, 29^{2}, 36, 37^{2}
27:4, 6, 9^{3}, 11, 12, 16, 20, 21
28:2^{3}, 4, 12^{2}, 29, 40^{5}, 43
29:9, 22, 24, 25^{2}, 26, 27^{2}, 28^{2}, 36^{3}, 37, 40, 41
30:4^{2}, 12, 15, 16^{2}, 19, 21, 37^{2}
31:10, 11, 13, 14^{2}, 16, 17^{2}
32:1^{2}, 7, 12, 13, 18^{2}, 23^{3}, 25, 29, 30
33:3^{2}, 5, 16, 17, 20
34:7, 9^{2}, 10, 12, 14^{2}, 18, 24, 27
35:8^{3}, 9^{2}, 14^{2}, 15, 17, 19, 21^{2}, 24, 27^{2}, 28^{3}, 29
36:1, 3, 5, 6, 7^{2}, 14, 19, 20, 22, 23^{2}, 24^{2}, 25, 27, 28, 31, 32^{3}, 34, 36, 37
37:3, 12, 13, 14, 27^{2}
38:4, 5^{2}, 11, 12, 13, 15, 17, 18, 21, 24, 26^{3}, 27, 28, 30
39:1, 4, 7, 27^{2}, 37, 38, 40^{2}, 41
40:5, 15, 38

LEVITICUS
1:4^{2}, 10, 14
2:11, 12^{2}, 14
3:6, 7, 16, 17
4:3^{2}, 8, 14, 20^{2}, 21, 26, 28, 31^{2}, 32, 33, 35
5:6^{3}, 7^{3}, 8, 10^{3}, 11^{3}, 13, 15^{2}, 16^{2}, 18^{2}
6:6, 7^{2}, 15, 17, 18, 20, 21, 22, 23^{2}, 26

LEVITICUS
7:5, 7, 12, 13, 14, 15, 19, 25, 30, 32, 33, 34^{2}, 36
8:2, 14^{2}, 18, 21, 27, 28, 29^{2}, 33, 34, 35
9:2^{2}, 3^{2}, 4^{2}, 7^{3}, 8, 15^{2}, 18^{2}, 21
10:7, 9, 12, 13, 14, 15^{2}, 17
11:24, 35^{2}, 42, 44^{2}, 45^{2}
12:2, 6^{4}, 7^{2}, 8^{3}
13:7, 11, 15, 28, 36, 52
14:4, 6, 10, 12^{2}, 13, 18, 19, 20, 21^{3}, 23, 24, 29, 31^{3}, 34, 53, 54, 55, 56^{3}
15:13, 15^{4}, 30^{4}
16:2, 3^{2}, 5^{2}, 6^{3}, 8^{2}, 9, 10, 11^{4}, 15, 16^{2}, 17^{3}, 18, 24^{2}, 26, 27^{2}, 29, 30^{2}, 31, 33^{5}, 34^{2}
17:5, 6, 7, 11^{4}, 14^{3}
18:10, 13, 17, 19, 24, 27, 29
19:2, 10, 21, 22^{2}, 23, 28, 34
20:7, 9, 19, 23, 26
21:1, 2^{6}, 3^{2}, 6, 7, 8^{2}, 11^{2}, 12, 15, 18, 23
22:9, 16, 18^{3}, 20^{2}, 23^{2}, 25, 27
23:11, 12, 13, 14, 18, 19^{2}, 20^{2}, 21, 28^{2}, 29, 31, 34, 41
24:2, 3, 7, 9, 18, 20^{3}, 22^{3}
25:4, 5, 6^{8}, 7^{2}, 12, 16, 17, 21, 23^{3}, 24, 30, 33, 34, 37, 42, 46^{3}, 51, 55
26:1, 9, 16, 18^{2}, 20, 24, 27, 28, 44^{2}, 45
27:2, 5, 6, 7, 10^{3}, 34

NUMBERS
1:44, 48
3:13, 25, 26^{2}, 38, 41, 46
4:16, 24, 25, 26^{2}, 29, 35, 39, 43
5:8, 15^{2}
6:7^{4}, 11^{4}, 12, 14^{3}, 17, 20^{2}, 21
7:3^{2}, 10, 11, 13, 15, 16, 17, 19^{2}, 21, 22, 23, 25, 27, 28, 29, 31,

NUMBERS
33, 34, 35, 37, 39, 40, 41, 43, 45, 46, 47, 49, 51, 52, 53, 55, 57, 58, 59, 61, 63, 64, 65, 67, 69, 70, 71, 73, 75, 76, 77, 79, 81, 82, 83, 87^{2}, 88
8:8, 11, 12^{3}, 13, 15, 16, 17^{2}, 18, 19, 21
9:14^{2}
10:2^{2}, 6, 8^{2}, 10, 29, 33
11:13, 14, 18^{2}, 22^{2}, 29, 32
12:1
13:30, 31
14:3, 9^{2}, 11, 13, 14, 32, 34, 40, 42, 43
15:5^{2}, 6^{2}, 7^{2}, 8^{2}, 10^{2}, 11^{3}, 15^{3}, 16^{2}, 20, 24^{3}, 25^{3}, 27, 28^{2}, 29^{3}, 39
16:11, 28, 34, 37, 38^{2}, 39, 46^{2}, 47
17:3^{2}, 6, 8, 10
18:4, 6, 7, 8, 9^{2}, 11, 16, 17^{2}, 19^{2}, 21^{2}, 23, 26^{2}, 31^{2}
19:9^{3}, 10^{2}, 17^{2}
20:2, 19, 24, 29
21:5, 7^{2}, 13, 24, 26, 28, 34
22:6^{3}, 12, 13, 17, 22, 29, 34
23:9
24:1, 18, 20, 24
25:11, 13^{2}, 18^{2}
26:53, 62, 65
27:14, 21
28:2^{2}, 3, 5, 6, 7^{2}, 9, 12^{4}, 13^{2}, 15, 19, 20^{2}, 21, 22^{2}, 23, 27, 30
29:2, 3^{2}, 4, 5^{2}, 6, 8, 10, 11, 16, 18^{3}, 19, 21^{3}, 22, 24^{3}, 25, 27^{3}, 28, 30^{3}, 31, 33^{3}, 34, 37^{3}, 38, 39^{4}
31:5, 18, 29, 50^{2}, 53^{2}, 54^{2}
32:1, 4, 5, 9, 12, 15, 16^{2}, 19, 24^{2}, 27, 29
33:4, 14, 53, 54

NUMBERS
34:2, 6^{2}, 7, 14, 23
35:2, 3^{3}, 6^{2}, 11, 12, 13, 15^{3}, 21, 29, 31, 32, 33, 34
36:2, 7, 11

DEUTERONOMY
1:10, 14, 17^{2}, 30^{2}, 37, 38, 40, 42
2:5^{2}, 6^{2}, 7, 9^{3}, 15, 19^{2}, 28^{2}, 30, 35, 36
3:2, 7, 11, 18, 19, 22^{2}, 24, 26, 27, 28
4:1, 3, 6, 7^{2}, 15, 21^{2}, 24, 31, 32, 34, 38, 40
5:5, 9, 11, 23, 25, 26, 29, 31
6:8, 15, 24
7:4, 6, 7, 16, 21, 25, 26
8:7, 10, 18
9:4^{2}, 5^{3}, 6^{2}, 12, 19, 20
10:13, 17, 19, 21, 22
11:2, 10, 12, 15, 18, 22, 25, 31
12:9, 23, 28, 31^{2}
13:3, 16^{2}
14:1, 2, 7, 21, 24, 26^{6}, 27
15:4^{2}, 6, 8, 10, 11, 17, 18
16:1, 3, 19
17:1, 8
18:5^{2}, 12, 14^{2}
19:2, 7, 9, 10, 11, 15^{2}, 21^{5}
20:1, 4^{2}, 16, 19^{2}, 20
21:5, 14, 17^{2}, 23^{2}
22:5, 8, 20, 26, 27
23:3, 6, 7, 14, 18^{2}, 21
24:4^{2}, 6, 15, 16^{3}, 19^{3}, 20^{3}, 21^{3}
25:11, 16, 19
26:1, 3, 14^{2}
28:20, 32, 34, 38, 39, 40, 41, 46^{3}, 47, 56, 57^{2}, 62, 67^{2}, 68
29:8, 13, 16, 26, 29
30:9^{3}, 11, 12, 13, 20
31:6, 7, 18, 19^{2}, 20, 21^{2}, 23, 26, 27, 29

DEUTERONOMY
32:4, 9, 20, 22, 28, 31, 32, 35, 36[2], 40[2], 43, 47[2], 49
33:2, 7, 9, 13[3], 14[2], 15[2], 16[2], 19, 21
34:8[2], 9

JOSHUA
1:6[2], 8, 9, 11
2:3, 5, 10[2], 11, 14, 15, 24
3:4, 5, 15
4:7[2], 10, 13, 23, 24
5:6, 7, 13[2], 15
6:16
7:1, 3, 5, 9, 11, 13
8:2[2], 6[2], 7, 18, 26, 27, 28
9:9, 11, 12, 22, 23, 27[2]
10:4, 6, 8, 14[2], 18, 19, 24, 25, 42
11:6, 10, 13, 14, 20, 23
12:6, 7
13:6, 7, 12, 32
14:1, 2[2], 3, 4[3], 9, 11, 12, 13
15:19, 63
16:9
17:1[3], 2[7], 15[2], 16, 18[2]
18:4, 6, 7, 8, 10
19:1, 9[2], 10, 17, 24, 32, 40, 47, 49, 51
20:2, 6, 9[2]
21:2, 4, 10, 12, 13, 21[2], 26, 27, 32, 38, 40
22:17, 24, 25, 26[2], 28[2], 29[3], 34
23:2[5], 3[2], 4, 9[2], 10[2], 13
24:1[4], 13, 15, 17, 18, 19, 27, 31, 32

JUDGES
1:1, 15, 32, 34
2:7, 10, 15, 18
3:20, 28
4:3, 5, 9[2], 14, 17, 19, 21
5:2, 15, 16, 30
6:4, 5[3], 22, 31[3], 38, 40
7:2, 4, 9, 12[2], 14, 15
8:5, 10, 11, 20, 21, 22, 24, 30
9:2, 3, 5, 17[2], 21, 25, 28
10:16
11:2, 18, 31, 35, 36, 37, 38
12:6, 9
13:5[2], 7, 15, 16, 20
14:2, 3[2], 4, 10
15:18
16:2, 17, 18[2], 19, 23[2], 24, 25[2], 28
17:3
18:1, 9, 10, 19, 26
19:6, 15, 19[4]
20:6, 10, 27, 28, 36, 39, 41
21:5, 6, 7[2], 9, 15, 16[2], 17, 18, 22[2]

RUTH
1:6, 12, 13[4], 16, 20
2:13[2], 16
3:1, 9, 10, 11, 17, 18
4:4, 6[2], 7, 8, 15

1 SAMUEL
1:5, 6, 16[2], 22[2], 27
2:2, 3, 5, 8, 9, 14, 15[2], 17, 20, 23, 24, 25, 30[2], 32, 35, 36
3:5, 6, 8, 9, 10, 13[3], 14, 21
4:7[2], 10, 13[2], 18, 19, 20, 22
5:7, 11
6:2, 4, 8, 17[6]
7:2, 5, 8, 9[2], 17
8:7, 11[2]
9:5[2], 7, 9, 12[3], 13[2], 14, 16, 19, 20[2], 24[2]
10:2[2], 7
11:2, 13
12:19[2], 21[2], 22[3], 23[2], 24[2]
13:6, 7, 13[2], 19, 21[4]
14:6[2], 10, 12, 18, 24, 26, 30, 39, 44, 45
15:2, 6, 11, 15, 23, 24, 26, 29, 35
16:1[2], 7[2], 11, 12, 22
17:8, 12, 17, 20, 21, 26, 28, 31, 33, 39[2], 42, 47
18:11, 17[2]
19:5[2], 13, 16
20:4, 6[2], 8[2], 9, 15, 17, 21, 22, 23, 26, 29, 31[2], 34[2], 42
21:6, 8, 9, 10
22:3, 8, 10, 13, 15[2], 23
23:4, 7, 10, 17, 21, 22, 26[2], 27
24:10, 11, 17, 19[2]
25:8, 11, 17[2], 21, 25, 28, 34, 36, 39
26:9, 12, 15, 18, 19, 20, 21, 23
27:1, 4, 5, 8, 12
28:1, 2, 9, 10, 12, 13, 15, 17, 20
29:4, 6
30:6[3], 8, 10, 12, 24, 25, 26
31:4

2 SAMUEL
1:9, 12[4], 16, 21, 26
2:7, 26
3:6, 8, 14, 17, 18, 22, 27, 28, 37, 39
4:2, 7, 10
5:12, 19, 24
6:6, 7, 17
7:5, 10, 13[2], 16[2], 19, 20, 21, 22, 23[3], 24[2], 25, 26, 27, 29[3]
8:4, 10
9:1, 7[2], 10, 11, 13
10:2, 11[2], 12[2]
11:4, 22, 25, 26
12:4[2], 12, 16, 18, 21, 22
13:2[3], 12, 13[2], 18, 22, 32[3], 33, 37, 39

2 SAMUEL
14:2, 7, 13, 14, 16, 17, 19, 25, 26, 29, 32, 33
15:2, 6, 8, 12[2], 14, 19, 34
16:2[3], 3, 11, 12
17:8, 10, 11, 14, 17, 21, 29[3]
18:3[3], 5, 8, 12, 13, 16, 18[2], 31, 33
19:1, 2[2], 6[2], 7, 8, 9, 20, 21, 22, 26, 28, 32, 38, 42
20:11
21:1[2], 3, 4[2], 8, 10, 14
22:18[2], 22, 23[2], 29, 30, 31, 32, 40, 51[2]
23:5
24:2, 10, 11, 14, 22[2], 24, 25

1 KINGS
1:2, 3, 25, 31, 35, 42, 51
2:7, 9, 15, 17, 18, 19[2], 20, 22[6], 26, 28, 33[2], 36, 37[2], 42[3], 45
3:4, 6, 8, 9, 11[3], 26, 28
4:7, 22, 24, 26, 27[2], 28, 31
5:1[2], 3, 6[2], 8, 9, 11
6:2, 4, 6, 8, 16[3], 31, 33
7:7, 8, 12[2], 15, 17[3], 18, 36, 40, 42[2], 45, 50[2], 51
8:5, 7, 11, 13[2], 17, 20, 21, 36, 39, 41, 42, 43, 44, 46, 48, 51, 52, 53, 64, 66[3]
9:3, 5, 7, 15, 16[2], 19[2], 24
10:9, 12[3], 22, 23[2], 26, 27, 29[4]
11:2, 4, 5, 7[2], 8, 12, 13[2], 15, 16, 31, 32[2], 34, 38, 39[2]
12:1, 2, 5, 7, 15, 17, 24, 28, 30
13:6, 9, 12, 17, 23[2], 32
14:4, 5[3], 6, 9, 11, 13[2], 15, 18, 23
15:4, 27
16:7, 13, 19, 24, 26, 31, 32
17:5, 12, 13[2], 14
18:4, 23, 25[2], 27, 41
19:3, 4[2], 7, 10[2], 14, 20
20:7[5], 9, 10[2], 18[2], 22, 25[2], 34, 38, 39, 42[2]
21:2[2], 4, 6[2], 15[2], 22
22:6, 8, 12, 15, 34, 43, 48[2], 53

2 KINGS
2:2, 4, 6, 9, 18
3:2, 9[2], 13, 17, 26, 27
4:2, 10, 13[3], 14, 24, 27, 38, 39, 40, 41, 43
5:3, 17, 27
6:1, 5, 9, 11[2], 16, 23, 25[2], 33
7:1[2], 6, 7, 16[2], 18[2], 20
8:1[2], 3[2], 5[2], 18, 19, 27
9:8, 16, 20, 25, 34
10:3, 10, 16, 19, 20, 22, 24, 31
11:15
12:7[2], 12[2], 13, 15, 21
13:4, 7, 17
14:6[3], 10, 26[3], 28
15:14
16:8, 9, 15, 18[2]
17:4, 7, 12, 21, 22, 32, 37[2]
18:4, 6, 20, 24[2], 26, 29, 31, 36
19:3, 4, 8, 18, 31, 34[3]
20:1, 6[2], 10, 12
21:3[2], 5, 7
22:13[4]
23:4[3], 7, 13[3]
24:3, 4[2], 7, 16, 20
25:3, 16, 22, 26, 30

1 CHRONICLES
4:14, 23, 39, 40, 41, 42
5:1, 2, 20, 22
6:26, 49[2], 54, 70
7:4[2], 11
9:1, 13, 26, 33
10:4, 13[2]
11:9, 19, 20, 21
12:8, 18, 19, 21, 22, 25, 29, 37, 39[2], 40
13:3, 4, 9
14:2, 10, 15
15:1[2], 2[2], 3, 11[3], 12, 13[2], 22, 23, 24
16:1, 17[2], 21, 25, 26, 34[3], 36, 41, 42
17:2, 5, 9, 12, 14[2], 17[2], 18[2], 19, 22[2], 23, 24, 25, 27[3]
18:10
19:3, 5, 12[2], 13[2]
21:6, 8, 13, 17, 22, 23[3], 24[3], 25, 29, 30
22:1, 3[3], 4, 5[2], 6[2], 7, 9, 10[2], 14[2], 15, 18
23:13[2], 24, 25[2], 26, 27, 28, 29[7]
24:5, 6[2]
25:6[2], 9
26:5, 6, 8[2], 10, 13, 14, 29[2], 31, 32
27:2, 3, 5, 7, 8, 9, 10, 11, 12, 13, 14, 15, 24, 26, 27
28:2[4], 3, 4[2], 5, 6, 7, 8[4], 9[2], 10[2], 13[3], 14[4], 15[7], 16[3], 17[4], 18[2], 20[2], 21[3]
29:1[3], 2[6], 3, 5[3], 7, 9, 10, 11, 14, 15, 16, 17, 18, 19, 21

2 CHRONICLES
1:3, 4[3], 9, 10, 11, 15, 17[4]
2:1[2], 4[3], 5, 8, 9, 12[2]
3:3, 6
4:6[3], 9, 11[2], 16, 18, 19, 22
5:1, 6, 8, 11, 13[3], 14
6:2[3], 7, 8, 9, 10[2], 13, 27, 30, 32, 33, 34, 36, 38
7:3[3], 6, 7, 9, 10, 12, 16[2], 17, 20
8:7, 9, 11[2], 14
9:6, 8[2], 11, 21, 25
10:1, 7, 10, 11, 15, 17

2 CHRONICLES
11:4, 5, 14[2], 15[3], 17, 21, 22
12:13
13:5, 8, 10, 11, 12[2]
14:3, 6, 11, 13, 14[2]
15:3, 6, 7, 9, 15
16:9, 10, 14[2]
17:18
18:2[2], 5, 7, 8, 11, 32, 33
19:6[3], 7, 8[2], 11
20:7, 8, 9, 12, 15, 17, 21[2], 23, 25, 26, 27, 30, 33
21:6, 7, 19
22:1, 3, 4, 7, 9, 11
23:6, 8, 14
24:3, 6[2], 7, 14, 18, 24, 25[2]
25:4[3], 6, 7, 8[2], 9, 20
26:8, 10[2], 14, 15, 16, 18[2], 21, 23
28:2[2], 6, 10, 11, 13[2], 17, 19[2], 21, 23
29:6, 9[2], 11, 21[4], 23, 24[3], 25, 32, 34, 35, 36
30:2, 3, 5, 8, 9[2], 14, 17[2], 18[2], 24, 26
31:2[2], 3[5], 10, 16, 18
32:1, 7[3], 15, 20, 25, 26, 27[6], 28[3], 29
33:3[2], 4, 5, 7, 8, 22
34:3, 11, 21[3], 26
35:7[2], 8, 9, 14[4], 15[2], 21, 23, 24, 25
36:17, 21

EZRA
1:4
2:68
3:3, 11[2], 12, 13
4:2, 14, 15
6:8, 9, 10, 11, 17[2], 18, 20[4], 22
7:9, 10, 16, 19, 20, 23[2]
8:16[11], 17, 20, 21[3], 22[2], 23, 35[2]
9:2[3], 6, 7, 8, 9, 10, 12[3], 13[2], 15[2]
10:1, 4, 6, 9, 13, 14, 19

NEHEMIAH
1:5, 6, 11
2:3, 4, 6, 8[3], 14, 18
4:2, 5, 6, 14, 18, 20, 23
5:2[2], 4, 5, 18[3], 19[2]
6:6, 9, 10, 12, 13, 16, 18
7:2
8:4, 5, 9, 10[3], 11, 17
9:5, 8, 10, 15[3], 20, 31[2], 33, 35, 36
10:30, 32[2], 33[8], 34, 39
11:23[3], 25
12:29, 43, 44[8], 46
13:1, 5, 6, 7, 10, 13, 14[2], 25, 31[3]

ESTHER
1:8, 9, 11, 13, 17, 20, 22
2:2, 3, 7[2], 9, 10, 12[2], 15, 20
3:2, 4, 6, 8, 13, 14
4:2, 5, 7, 8, 14[2], 16
5:4, 8, 9, 10
6:3[2], 4, 7
7:4[2], 7[2], 9[2], 10
8:1, 6, 8[2], 11[2], 13, 17
9:2, 4[2], 15, 16, 26, 31[2]
10:3

JOB
1:4, 5, 9
2:4[2], 11, 13
3:6, 9, 13, 14, 21[3], 24, 25
4:11, 20
5:2, 18, 23, 27
6:3, 4, 8, 10, 19, 21, 22, 27, 28
7:2, 16, 21
8:4, 6, 8, 9
9:17, 32
10:16
11:4, 11, 12, 15
13:7[2], 8, 16, 19, 24, 26
14:7, 16, 20
15:5, 22, 23, 25, 31, 34
16:12, 17, 21[2]
17:1, 4, 10[2], 15
18:4, 8, 10[2]
19:15, 17, 21, 24, 25, 27, 29
20:2, 5, 7, 18, 21
21:4, 14, 19, 21, 28
22:4, 6[2], 8, 17, 26
23:7, 14[2], 16
24:3, 5[3], 8, 15, 16, 17, 24
27:8, 14, 22
28:1[2], 5, 15[2], 17, 18, 24, 25, 26[2]
29:13, 23[3]
30:3, 4, 23[2], 25[2], 26[2]
31:2, 11, 12, 18, 19, 23, 28
32:11, 16, 18, 22
33:10, 13, 14, 26, 32
34:3, 5, 9, 11, 19, 21, 23, 36, 37
35:3
36:4, 7, 21, 27, 31
37:6, 13[3], 19
38:3, 7, 9, 10, 19, 25[2], 39, 41[2]
41:4[2], 5
42:3, 7, 8[3], 10, 12

PSALMS
1:6
2:8[2]
3:2, 3, 5, 7
4:3, 8
5:2, 4, 7, 9, 10, 11, 12
6:2[2], 4, 5, 8
7:6, 7, 9, 13
8:5
9:4, 5, 7[2], 9, 10, 12, 18[2]
10:3, 5, 6, 14, 16
11:2, 7
12:1[2], 5[2], 7

PSALMS
13:1
14:5
16:1, 10, 11
17:6, 15
18:17[2], 21, 22, 27, 28, 29, 30, 31, 39, 50
19:4, 9
21:3, 4, 6[2], 7, 11
22:11[2], 16, 21, 24, 26, 28, 30
23:3, 4, 6
24:2
25:5, 6, 7, 11[2], 15, 16, 19, 20, 21
26:1, 3, 11
27:5, 12
28:9
29:10
30:1, 5[2], 11, 12
31:2, 3[2], 4[2], 7, 9, 10, 13, 16, 17, 19[2], 21, 22, 23
32:4, 6, 11
33:1[2], 4, 9, 11, 12, 17, 20, 21
34:9
35:2, 7[3], 10, 12, 13, 14, 20, 27
36:2, 9
37:2, 7, 9, 10, 13, 17, 18, 22, 24, 27, 28[2], 29, 37
38:2, 4[2], 7, 10, 12, 15, 16, 17, 18[2], 20
39:7, 11, 12
40:1, 12, 15
41:4, 12[2]
42:t, 2[2], 4, 5[2], 11
43:2, 5
44:t, 3, 4, 6, 8, 10, 11, 12, 16, 21, 22[2], 23, 25, 26[2]
45:t, 2, 6, 11, 17
46:t
47:t, 2, 4, 7, 9
48:t, 2, 3, 4, 8, 14[2]
49:t, 7, 8[2], 9, 10, 11, 15, 17
50:6, 8, 10, 12
51:3, 16
52:5, 8, 9[2]
53:5
54:3, 6, 7
55:3, 6, 9, 12, 15, 16, 18
56:1, 2, 5, 6, 9[2], 13
57:1, 2, 6, 10
58:11
59:3[4], 7, 9, 12[2], 15, 16, 17
60:2, 11, 12
61:3[2], 4, 5, 7, 8
62:5, 8, 12
63:1[2], 10
64:9
65:1, 3, 9, 13
66:7, 10, 16
67:4[2]
68:10, 16, 18[2], 28
69:1, 3, 6[2], 7, 9, 13, 16, 17, 20[2], 21, 22, 26, 33, 35
70:3
71:3, 5, 10[2], 11, 12, 15, 24[2]
72:t, 12, 15, 17, 19
73:2, 3, 4, 14, 16, 26, 27, 28
74:1, 4, 10, 12, 19, 20
75:1, 6, 8, 9
77:7, 8[2]
78:5, 18, 20, 29, 32[2], 37, 39, 58, 69
79:5, 7, 8, 9[2], 13
80:15, 17
81:4[2], 5, 15
82:8
83:2, 5, 10, 17
84:t, 2[2], 3, 10, 11
85:t, 5, 8
86:1, 2, 3, 4, 5, 7, 10, 12, 13, 17
87:t
88:t, 3
89:1, 2[2], 4, 6, 11, 17, 18, 28[2], 29, 36, 37, 46, 52
90:4, 7, 9, 10
91:5[2], 6[2], 11
92:t, 4, 7, 8, 9[2]
93:5
94:13, 14, 16[2]
95:3, 7
96:4, 5, 13[2]
97:9, 11[2]
98:1, 9
99:3, 5, 9
100:5
102:3, 9, 10, 12, 13, 14, 18, 19
103:6, 9, 11, 14, 15, 16
104:5, 8, 14[2], 17, 18[2], 19, 31
105:8, 10[2], 14, 16, 17, 32, 38, 39, 42
106:1[3], 8, 13, 31[2], 32, 43, 45
107:1[3], 8[2], 9, 15[2], 16, 21[2], 25, 31[2], 34, 36
108:4, 12, 13
109:2, 4, 5[2], 19, 21[2], 22, 31
110:4
111:3, 8, 9, 10
112:3, 6, 9
113:2
115:1[2], 18
116:7, 8, 12
117:2[2]
118:1[2], 2, 3, 4, 12, 21, 29[3]
119:20, 22, 28, 35, 39, 42, 43, 44, 45, 50, 66, 71, 76, 77, 78, 81, 82, 83, 85, 89, 91, 93, 94, 95, 98, 99, 102, 110, 111[2], 115, 118, 120, 122[2], 123[2], 126[2], 131[2], 152, 153, 155, 160, 166, 168, 172, 173, 174, 176
120:7[2]
121:8
122:5, 6, 8
123:3

PSALMS
125:1, 2, 3, 5
126:2, 3
127:t, 2[2]
128:2
130:5, 6[3], 7
131:1, 3
132:5[2], 9, 10, 12, 13[2], 14[2], 16, 17
133:1, 3[2]
135:3[2], 4[2], 5, 7, 12, 13, 14
136:1[3], 2[2], 3[2], 4[2], 5[2], 6[2], 7[2], 8[2], 9[2], 10[2], 11[2], 12[2], 13[2], 14[2], 15[2], 16[2], 17[2], 18[2], 19[2], 20[2], 21[3], 22[2], 23[2], 24[2], 25[2], 26[2]
137:3
138:2[3], 5, 8
139:4, 6, 13, 14, 20
140:2, 5[2], 9
141:5, 6, 9
142:3, 4, 6[2], 7
143:2, 3, 8[2], 10, 11[2], 12
145:1, 2, 21
146:5, 6, 10
147:1[2], 8, 13, 20
148:5, 6, 13
149:4
150:2

PROVERBS
1:9, 11[2], 16, 18[2], 29, 32
2:3, 4[2], 6, 7, 18, 21
3:2, 12, 14, 26, 32
4:2, 3, 13, 16, 17, 22, 23
5:3, 21
6:1, 23, 26[2], 34
7:6, 19, 23, 26
8:6, 7, 11, 32, 35
9:4, 11, 12, 14, 16
10:13, 21
11:15[2]
12:6, 19[2]
13:22, 23
16:4[2], 12, 26[2]
17:3[2], 13, 17, 26
18:6, 16
19:10[2], 18, 19, 29[2]
20:3, 16[2]
21:8, 12, 18[2], 25, 29
22:9, 11, 18, 23, 26
23:3, 5, 7, 9, 11, 13, 18, 21, 27, 28
24:2, 6, 7, 16, 20, 22, 27
25:3[2], 4, 7, 13, 16, 22, 27
26:1, 3[2], 25
27:1, 10, 13[2], 21[2], 24[2], 26, 27[4]
28:2, 8, 21[2]
29:5, 14, 19
30:8, 18, 21[2], 22, 23, 30
31:4[3], 8, 10, 21[2]

ECCLESIASTES
1:4, 18
2:3, 10, 12, 16[2], 17, 21[2], 22, 23, 24, 25, 26
3:12, 14, 17[3], 19[2], 22[2]
4:4, 8, 9, 10[2], 14
5:1, 2, 3, 4, 7, 8, 9, 13, 16, 18[2], 20
6:2, 4, 7, 8, 12[3]
7:2, 3, 5, 6, 9, 10, 12, 13, 18, 20, 22
8:3, 7[2], 15, 16
9:1, 4[2], 5[2], 6, 7, 9, 10, 12
10:1, 4, 17[2], 19, 20
11:1, 2, 6, 7, 8, 9, 10
12:13, 14

SONG OF SOLOMON
1:2, 7
2:5, 11, 14, 15
3:10
4:4
5:2, 4
6:5
7:6, 9, 13
8:6, 7, 8[2], 11

ISAIAH
1:2, 17, 20, 29[2], 30
2:3, 10[2], 12, 19[2], 20, 21[2], 22
3:1, 7, 8, 9, 10, 11, 12, 14
4:2, 5, 6[3]
5:7[3], 20[4], 23, 25
6:5[2], 8
7:4[2], 6, 8, 13, 16, 18[2], 22[2], 23, 25[2]
8:4, 10, 11, 14[5], 17, 18[2], 19
9:4, 5, 6, 7, 12, 13, 16, 17[2], 18, 21
10:3, 4, 8, 13[2], 17[2], 22, 23, 25, 26
11:4, 9, 10, 12, 16
12:2, 5, 6
13:3, 6, 10, 11[2], 17
14:1, 2, 9[2], 13, 21[2], 22, 23, 27, 29, 31
15:5[3], 6[2], 8, 9[2]
16:2, 4, 7[2], 8, 9[3], 11[2]
17:2
18:4, 5
19:10, 15, 20[3]
20:3, 6
21:6, 15, 16, 17
22:5, 11, 13, 16, 23, 25
23:1, 4, 13, 14, 18[3]
24:3, 11, 14, 18
25:1, 2, 4, 8, 9[2], 10[2]
26:1, 4[2], 5, 8, 9, 11, 12[2], 19, 20, 21[2]
27:11
28:5[2], 6[2], 8, 10, 11, 15, 16, 19, 20, 21, 22, 26, 27

ISAIAH
29:10, 11, 14, 16, 20[2], 21[3]
30:4, 7, 8[2], 15, 16, 18[2], 19, 31, 33[2]
31:1, 4[4], 7[2], 9
32:6, 10, 12[3], 14[2], 15, 17
33:2, 5, 22
34:2, 5, 6, 8[2], 10[2], 13, 14, 16, 17[2]
35:1, 6, 8
36:5, 9[2], 11, 14, 16, 21
37:3, 4, 8, 19, 32, 35[3]
38:1, 14, 17[2], 18[2], 21[2]
39:1, 8
40:2[2], 3, 5, 8, 10, 16, 26
41:7, 10[2], 13, 17, 22, 28
42:4, 6[2], 21, 22[2], 23, 24[2]
43:1, 3[3], 4[2], 5, 7[2], 14, 21, 25
44:3, 7, 10, 14, 15[2], 17, 18, 21, 22, 23[2]
45:4, 13, 18, 22
46:9, 13
47:1, 4, 5, 7, 9[2], 10
48:2, 8, 9[3], 11[3], 21
49:4, 6, 8, 10, 13, 19, 20, 23[2], 25
50:1[2], 2, 7
51:2, 3, 4[2], 6[2], 8[2], 10, 19
52:1, 3[2], 4, 5, 8, 9, 12[2], 15
53:2, 5, 8[2], 10, 11, 12
54:1, 3, 4[3], 5, 6, 7, 8, 9[2], 10, 14[2], 15, 16
55:2[2], 4, 5[2], 7, 8, 9, 10, 12, 13[2]
56:1, 4, 7[2], 11
57:8, 12, 15, 16[3], 17
58:4, 5, 14
59:3, 4[2], 9[2], 10, 11[2], 12[3], 14, 17[2], 21[2]
60:1, 2, 9, 10, 12, 17[4], 19, 20, 21
61:3[3], 7[2], 8[2], 10, 11
62:1[2], 4, 5, 8[2], 10
63:3, 4, 8, 17
64:3, 4[3], 5, 7, 9, 12
65:1, 5, 8[2], 10[2], 11, 14[3], 15[2], 17, 18[2], 20, 22, 23[2]
66:2, 5, 8, 10[2], 12, 15, 16, 18, 20, 21[2], 22, 24

JEREMIAH
1:6, 7, 8, 12, 15, 18, 19
2:10, 11, 13, 20, 22, 25, 27, 28, 37
3:2, 5, 8, 10, 12[2], 14, 18, 21, 22, 23, 24, 25
4:3, 6, 8[2], 13, 15, 20, 22, 27, 28, 29, 31[2]
5:4, 5, 7, 9, 10, 11, 22, 26, 29
6:1, 4[2], 6, 11, 12, 13, 16[2], 23, 25, 26[2], 27, 29
7:5, 7, 12, 16[3], 22, 29, 30, 32, 33[2], 34
8:2, 10, 11, 14, 15[2], 16, 17, 21
9:1, 2, 3[3], 4, 7[2], 9, 10[2], 12, 17[2], 18, 19, 21, 24, 26
10:2, 3[2], 5, 7, 14, 16, 18, 19, 21, 25
11:7, 13, 14[4], 17[2], 20, 23
12:3[2], 4, 6, 12
13:7, 10, 11[5], 15, 16, 17, 18, 21, 22
14:4, 7[2], 8, 11[2], 16, 17, 19[3], 20, 21, 22
15:2[4], 4, 5, 13, 14, 15, 16, 17, 20
16:3, 4[2], 5[2], 6[2], 7[4], 9, 12, 16[2], 17
17:3, 4[2], 6, 8, 14, 16, 25
18:18, 20[4], 22[2]
19:5, 7[2]
20:4, 8, 10[2], 11, 12, 13
21:2[2], 9, 10[3]
22:4, 6, 10[3], 11, 13, 17[4], 18[2], 20, 22, 30
23:10[2], 11, 12, 15, 18, 27, 34, 36[2]
24:5, 6[2], 7, 9
25:5, 12, 14, 15, 29[3], 31, 34, 36, 38
26:11, 14, 15[2], 16
27:10, 14, 15, 16, 19
28:4, 13, 14
29:6, 7[2], 8, 9, 10, 11, 13, 26, 28, 32
30:3, 5, 7, 8, 10, 11, 12, 14[2], 15[2], 16, 17, 21
31:6, 7[2], 9, 11, 12[4], 13, 15[2], 16, 18, 20[2], 22, 25, 30, 34[2], 35[2], 36, 37, 40
32:2, 3, 7, 8[2], 15, 17, 19, 25[2], 27, 30[2], 31, 39[2], 42, 44[2]
33:4, 5, 9[2], 11[4], 17, 26
34:5[2], 7, 11[2], 16[2], 17, 20
35:6[2], 9, 11[2], 14, 19
36:7, 31
37:3, 4, 9, 10, 11, 15, 17
38:2[2], 4[2], 5, 9[2], 27
39:16[2], 18[2]
40:4, 10, 16
41:8, 9, 18
42:2[3], 5, 10, 11, 18, 20[2], 21
43:1, 3, 7, 11[3]
44:11, 13, 14, 16, 17, 27[2], 29
45:3, 5[3]
46:5, 10[2], 11, 12, 14, 19, 21, 22, 27, 28[2]
47:3, 4
48:1, 5[2], 7, 9, 14, 18, 20, 26, 27[3], 31[3], 32, 34, 36[2], 37, 38, 40, 44, 46
49:3[2], 8, 12, 13, 15, 19, 23, 30, 33[2], 37
50:3, 9, 14, 15, 16, 20[2], 24, 25, 27, 29, 31, 33, 39, 44
51:2, 5, 6, 8[2], 9, 11, 12, 17, 19, 20, 26[3], 29, 33, 36, 37, 46, 48[2], 51, 56, 62
52:3, 6, 16[2], 34

FROM

Misc.

NAHUM
1:13
2:13
3:7, 8

HABAKKUK
1:8, 12
2:9
3:3[2], 17

ZEPHANIAH
1:2, 3, 4, 6, 10[3]
2:11
3:10

HAGGAI
1:10[2]
2:15[2], 18[3], 19

ZECHARIAH
1:4[2]
2:6
3:4[2]
6:1, 5, 10
7:12
8:7[2]
9:5, 7, 10[4]
13:5
14:2, 5, 8, 10[3], 13, 16

MALACHI
1:5, 11
2:6
3:5, 7[2]

MATTHEW
1:17[3], 21, 24
2:1, 16
3:7, 13, 17
4:17, 21, 25[5]
5:18, 29, 30, 42
6:13
7:23
8:1, 11, 30
9:9, 15, 16, 22
11:12, 25
12:15, 38, 42, 44
13:12, 27, 35, 49
14:2
15:8, 18, 27, 28, 29
16:1, 21, 22
17:9[2], 18
18:8, 9, 35
19:1, 8, 12, 20
20:8, 29
21:8, 25[2], 43
22:46
23:34, 35
24:1, 29, 31[2]
25:28, 29, 32[2], 34, 41
26:16, 39, 42, 47
27:31, 40, 42, 45, 51, 55, 64
28:2[2], 7, 8

MARK
1:9, 11, 42, 45
2:20, 21
3:7[2], 8[3], 22
4:25
5:35
6:1, 2, 10, 14, 16
7:1, 4, 6, 15, 17, 18, 21, 23, 24, 31, 33
8:3, 4, 11
9:9[2], 10
10:1, 6, 20
11:12, 20, 30, 31
12:2, 25, 34
13:19, 27[2]
14:35, 36, 43, 52
15:20, 30, 32, 38
16:3, 8

LUKE
1:2, 3, 15, 26, 38, 45, 48, 50, 52, 71[2], 78
2:1, 4, 15, 36, 37
3:7, 22
4:1, 9, 13, 42
5:3, 8, 10, 13, 35
6:17, 22
7:6
8:18, 37, 49
9:5, 7, 33, 37, 39, 45, 54
10:7, 18, 21, 30, 42
11:4, 7, 16, 22, 31, 50, 51
12:36, 52, 58
13:12, 15, 16, 27, 29[4]
16:3, 18, 21, 26[2], 30, 31
17:7, 29
18:21, 34
19:8, 24, 26[2], 39, 42
20:4, 5, 35
21:11
22:41, 42, 43, 45
23:5, 49, 55
24:2, 9, 13, 46, 49, 51

JOHN
1:6, 19, 32
2:22
3:2, 13, 27, 31[2]
4:11
5:24, 34, 41, 44
6:23, 31, 32[2], 33, 38, 41, 42, 50, 51, 58, 64, 66
7:29
8:23[2], 25, 42, 44
9:1, 29, 30
10:5, 18, 32
11:41, 53
12:1, 9, 17, 27, 28, 32, 36
13:3, 4
14:7
15:26[2], 27
16:22, 27, 28, 30
17:8, 15
18:3, 28, 36
19:11, 12, 23, 27
20:1, 9
21:8, 14

THE ACTS
1:4, 11, 12[2], 22[2], 25
2:2, 40, 46
3:2, 15, 19, 23, 24, 26
4:2, 10
5:38, 41
7:3, 4, 33, 39
8:10, 26, 33
9:3, 8, 14, 18
10:17, 21, 22, 23, 37, 41
11:4, 5, 9, 11, 27
12:7, 10, 11, 19, 25
13:4, 8, 13[2], 14, 29, 30, 31, 34, 39[2], 46
14:8, 15, 17, 19, 26
15:1, 18, 19, 20[4], 24, 29[5], 33, 38[2], 39
16:11, 12
17:3, 27, 31, 33
18:1, 2[2], 5, 6, 16, 21
19:9, 12[2], 35
20:6, 9, 17, 18, 20, 26
21:1[2], 7, 10, 25[4]
22:5, 6, 22, 29, 30
23:10, 21
24:18
25:1, 7
26:4, 5, 10, 12, 13, 17[2], 18[2], 23, 26
27:4, 21, 34, 43
28:13, 15, 17, 23

ROMANS
1:4, 7, 17, 18, 20
4:24
5:9, 14
6:4, 7, 9, 13, 17, 18, 20, 22
7:2, 3, 4, 6, 24
8:2, 11[2], 21, 35, 39
9:3
10:6, 7, 9
11:15, 26
15:19, 22, 31
S

1 CORINTHIANS
1:3[2]
4:7
5:2, 13
7:10, 27
9:19
10:14
14:36
15:12, 20, 41, 47
S

2 CORINTHIANS
1:2[2], 10
2:3, 13
3:1, 18
5:2, 6, 8
6:17
7:1
11:3, 9[2], 12
12:8
S

GALATIANS
1:1, 3[2], 4, 6, 8, 15
2:12
3:13
4:1, 24
5:4
6:17
S

EPHESIANS
1:2[2], 20
2:12[2]
3:9
4:16, 18, 31
5:14
6:6, 23
S

PHILIPPIANS
1:2[2], 5
3:20
4:15, 18
S

COLOSSIANS
1:2, 13, 18, 23, 26[2]
2:12, 19, 20
4:16
S

1 THESSALONIANS
1:1, 8, 9, 10[3]
2:17
3:6
4:3, 16
5:22
S

2 THESSALONIANS
1:2, 7, 9[2]
2:2, 13
3:2, 3, 6
S

1 TIMOTHY
1:2, 6
4:1, 3
5:13
6:5, 10
S

2 TIMOTHY
1:2, 3, 15
2:8, 19, 21
3:5, 15
4:4, 18
S

TITUS
1:4, 14
2:14
S

PHILEMON
3
S

HEBREWS
3:12
4:3, 4, 10[2]
5:1, 7
6:1, 7
7:1, 6, 26
8:11
9:14
10:13, 22
11:15, 19[2]
12:25[2]
13:20
S

JAMES
1:17[2], 27
3:15, 17
4:1, 7
5:19, 20[2]

1 PETER
1:3, 12, 18[2], 21
2:11
3:10
4:1

2 PETER
1:9, 17[2], 18
2:8, 14, 18, 21
3:4, 17

1 JOHN
1:1, 7, 9
2:7[2], 13, 14, 19, 20, 24[2]
3:8, 11, 14, 17
4:21
5:21

2 JOHN
3[2], 4, 5, 6

JUDE
14, 24

REVELATION
1:4[2], 5[2]
2:5
3:10, 12
6:4, 16[2]
7:2, 17
8:10
9:1, 6, 13
10:1, 4, 8
11:11, 12
12:14
13:8, 13
14:2, 3, 4, 13[3], 18
15:8[2]
16:17
17:8
18:1, 4, 14[2]
20:1, 9, 11
21:2, 4, 10
22:19[2]

HE

1931, *846*

GENESIS
1:5, 10, 16, 27[2], 31
2:2[3], 3, 8[2], 19, 21[2], 22
3:1, 6, 10, 11, 16[2], 17, 22, 23, 24[2]
4:4, 5, 9, 10, 17, 20, 21, 26
5:1, 2, 4[2], 5, 7, 8, 10, 11, 13, 14, 16, 17, 18, 19, 20, 22, 24, 26, 27, 29, 30, 31
6:3, 6, 22
8:6, 7, 8, 9, 10[2], 12
9:6, 20, 21[2], 25[2], 26, 27, 29
10:8, 9
11:11, 13, 15, 17, 19, 21, 23, 25
12:4, 7, 8[2], 11[2], 16[3], 20
13:1[2], 3, 4
14:13, 14, 15[2], 16, 18, 19, 20
15:4, 5[2], 6[2], 7, 8, 9, 10[2], 13
16:4, 8, 12[2]
17:12[2], 13[2], 14, 20, 22, 24, 25
18:1, 2[3], 7, 8[3], 9, 10, 15, 19[2], 28, 29[2], 30[2], 31[2], 32[2], 33
19:1, 2, 3[2], 9, 14, 16, 17, 21, 25, 27, 28, 29, 30[3], 33, 35
20:4, 5[2], 7[2], 13, 16[2]
21:1[2], 13, 17, 20, 21, 30, 31
22:1, 2, 6, 7[2], 11, 12
23:8, 9[3], 13, 16
24:2, 7, 10, 11, 12, 15, 27, 30[4], 31, 32, 33[2], 34, 35[2], 36[2], 40, 52, 53, 54[2], 56, 62, 63, 66, 67
25:5, 6, 7, 17, 18, 20, 28, 29, 33[2], 34
26:7[3], 8, 11, 13, 14, 18, 20, 21, 22[3], 23, 25, 30, 33, 34
27:1[3], 2, 9, 10[2], 14, 18[2], 20, 22, 23[2], 24[2], 25[5], 27[2], 29, 31, 32, 33[2], 34, 35, 36[6], 45
28:5, 6[2], 9, 11[2], 12, 16, 17, 18, 19
29:2, 5, 6[3], 7, 9, 12[2], 13[2], 14, 20, 23[2], 25, 28, 30[2], 31, 33
30:2, 15, 16, 28, 29, 31, 35[2], 36, 38[2], 40, 42
31:1[2], 8[2], 12, 15, 18[3], 20[2], 21[3], 23, 33[2], 35, 49
32:2[2], 4, 6, 7, 11, 13, 14, 16, 17, 18, 19, 20[2], 22, 23[2], 25[4], 26[2], 27[2], 28, 29[2], 31[2], 32
33:1, 2, 3[2], 5[2], 8[2], 11[2], 12, 13, 15, 18, 19[2], 20
34:2, 3, 5, 7, 13, 19[2], 31
35:6, 7[2], 9, 10, 13, 14[3]
36:6, 24, 43
37:3[2], 5, 6, 9, 10, 13, 14[3], 15, 16, 18, 21, 22, 27, 29, 30, 33, 35[2]
38:2, 3, 5, 9[3], 10[2], 11[2], 12, 15, 16[2], 17, 18[2], 20, 21, 22, 26, 29
39:2[2], 3, 4[4], 5[3], 6[5], 8[3], 9, 10, 12, 13, 14[2], 15[2], 18, 20, 22, 23
40:3, 4, 7, 16, 20[2], 21[2], 22
41:1, 5, 8, 11, 12[2], 13[3], 14, 25, 28, 43[3], 45, 46, 48[2], 49, 51, 52, 55
42:2, 4, 6, 7[2], 9, 12, 17, 21, 23, 24, 25, 27, 28, 38[2]
43:7, 14, 16, 18, 23[2], 24, 27[2], 28, 29[2], 30[2], 31, 34
44:1, 2, 5, 6[2], 10[2], 12, 14, 16, 17[2], 20, 22, 28, 31[2]
45:1, 2, 4, 8, 14, 15, 22[2], 23, 24[2], 26[2], 27[2]
46:1, 2, 3, 7, 28, 29
47:2, 17, 21, 22, 29, 30, 31[2]
48:1, 9, 10[3], 12, 15, 17, 19[3], 20[2]
49:4, 8, 9[2], 11, 13, 15, 19, 20, 21, 27[2], 28, 29, 33
50:6, 10, 12, 14[2], 16, 21, 22, 24, 26

EXODUS
1:9, 16, 21
2:2, 10, 11[2], 12[3], 13[2], 14, 15[2], 18, 20[3], 21, 22[2]
3:1, 2, 4[2], 5, 6[2], 12, 14, 20
4:2, 3[2], 4, 6[2], 7[2], 13, 14[5], 16[3], 20, 21, 23, 26, 27, 28, 31
5:3, 17, 23
6:1[2], 11
7:2, 13[2], 14, 15[2], 20, 22, 23
8:8, 10[2], 12, 15, 19, 20, 27, 31, 32
9:7, 12, 20, 21, 34[2], 35
10:6, 8, 10, 16, 17, 18, 20, 27
11:1[3], 8, 10
12:19, 23, 25, 27, 30, 31, 44, 48
13:5, 11, 19, 22
14:4, 6, 7, 8, 13
15:1[2], 2[2], 4, 21[2], 25[4]
16:7, 9, 18[2], 23, 29
17:7, 11, 12, 16
18:2, 3, 4, 5, 6, 9, 11, 14[2], 24, 27
19:13, 15, 24
21:2[2], 3[3], 4, 6[2], 8[3], 9[2], 10[2], 11, 12[2], 13, 14, 15, 16[3], 17, 18, 19[3], 20[2], 21[3], 22[2], 26, 27[2], 29[2], 30, 31, 32, 35, 36
22:1, 2, 3[3], 4, 5, 6, 8, 9, 11[2], 12, 13, 14, 15, 16, 17, 20[2], 27[2]
23:21, 25
24:1, 5, 6, 7, 11, 14, 16
25:39
28:1, 3, 4, 29, 30, 35[3]
29:21, 30
30:7[2], 8, 10
31:15, 17, 18[2]
32:4[2], 5, 12, 14, 17, 18, 19[3], 20, 27, 29
33:8, 11, 14, 15, 18, 19, 20
34:4, 9, 10, 28[3], 29[2], 32, 33, 34[4], 35
35:31, 34[3], 35
36:8, 10[2], 11[2], 12[2], 13, 14[2], 16, 17[2], 18, 19, 20, 22, 23, 24, 25, 27, 28, 29, 31, 33, 34, 35[2], 36[2], 37, 38
37:2, 3, 4, 5, 6, 7[2], 8, 10, 11, 12, 13, 15, 16, 17[2], 23, 24, 25, 26[2], 27, 28, 29
38:1, 2[2], 3[2], 4, 5, 6, 7[2], 8, 9, 28, 30
39:2, 7, 8, 22
40:13, 16, 19, 20, 21, 22, 23, 24, 25, 26, 27, 28, 29, 30, 33

LEVITICUS
1:3, 4, 5, 6, 9, 10, 11, 12, 13, 14, 16, 17
2:1, 2[2], 8
3:1[2], 2, 3, 4, 6, 7[2], 8, 9[2], 10, 12, 13, 14, 15
4:3, 4, 8, 9, 12[2], 18, 19, 20[3], 21[2], 23[2], 24, 26, 27, 28[3], 29, 31, 32[2], 33, 35[2]
5:1[3], 2, 3[3], 4[2], 5[3], 6[2], 7[3], 8, 9, 10[2], 11[4], 12, 13, 15, 16[2], 17[2], 18[2], 19
6:4[5], 5[2], 6, 7, 10[2], 11, 12, 15, 20
7:2, 3, 4, 8, 11, 12[2], 13, 14, 15, 16, 29, 30, 33, 35, 36, 38
8:7[2], 8[2], 9[2], 11, 12, 14, 15, 16, 17, 18, 19, 20, 21, 22, 23, 24, 25, 26, 27, 33, 34
9:2, 9, 10, 11, 12[2], 13, 14, 15, 16, 17, 18[2], 20
10:1, 16, 20
11:4[2], 5[2], 6[2], 7[3], 28, 39, 40[2]
13:2, 6, 7[2], 9, 11, 13[2], 14, 16, 17, 33[2], 34, 36, 37, 39, 40[2], 41[3], 44[2], 45, 46[3], 51, 52, 54, 56
14:2, 6, 7, 8[3], 9[5], 10[2], 12, 13[2], 18, 19, 20, 21[2], 22, 23, 25, 29, 30[2], 31, 35, 37, 41, 42, 43[2], 45[2], 46, 47[2], 49, 50, 51, 52, 53
15:2, 4[2], 6[2], 7, 8[2], 9, 10, 11[2], 12, 13[2], 14, 16, 23[2], 24[2]
16:2[2], 4[4], 5, 7, 12, 13[2], 14[2], 15[2], 16[2], 17[2], 18, 19, 20[2], 22, 23[2], 24, 25, 26, 28[2], 32[2], 33[3], 34
17:4, 13, 15[2], 16[2]
18:5
19:8, 21, 22[2]
20:2[2], 3, 4, 9, 10, 13, 14, 15, 17[2], 18, 19, 20, 21
21:3, 4, 7, 8[2], 10, 11, 12, 13, 14[2], 15, 17, 18[3], 21[2], 22, 23[3]
22:3, 4[2], 5[3], 6, 7, 8, 11[2], 14, 18
23:11, 12, 29
24:4, 8, 16[4], 17, 18, 19, 20, 21[4]
25:15, 16, 25, 27[2], 28[2], 29[2], 35[2], 40, 41[3], 48[2], 49[2], 50[2], 51[2], 52[2], 53, 54[3]
27:8[2], 10[2], 11, 13[2], 15[2], 17, 18, 19[2], 20[2], 22, 23, 27, 28, 31, 33[3]

NUMBERS
1:19
3:3, 16, 50
5:7[2], 14[2], 15[2], 23, 24, 27, 30
6:3[2], 4, 5[2], 6[2], 7, 8, 9[3], 10, 11, 12, 13, 14[2], 17, 21[2]
7:7, 8, 9, 12, 17, 19, 23, 29, 35, 41, 47, 53, 59, 65, 71, 77, 83, 88, 89[2]
8:3, 4
9:10, 13, 14
10:30, 31, 36
11:3, 30, 32, 34
12:1[2], 2, 6, 8, 9, 12
14:8, 16[2], 24[2]
15:4, 9, 14, 27, 28, 30, 31, 36
16:4, 5[3], 7, 10, 26, 31, 37, 40, 47, 48
17:11
19:3, 5, 7[2], 8, 10, 11, 12[4], 13, 19, 20[2], 21[2]
20:9, 10, 11, 13, 16, 20, 24
21:1, 3, 7, 8, 9[2], 14, 23, 29, 33
22:5, 6[2], 8, 22[2], 25, 27, 30, 31[2], 36, 41
23:3[2], 4, 6[3], 7, 12, 14, 15, 17[2], 18, 19[6], 20, 21[2], 22, 24[2]
24:1[2], 2, 3, 4, 7, 8[2], 9[4], 10, 15, 16, 19, 20[3], 21, 23, 24
25:7, 8, 11, 13[2], 15
27:3, 4, 9, 10, 11, 21[2], 22, 23
30:2[2], 5, 7, 8[2], 12, 14[4], 15[3]
32:10, 13, 15, 21, 40
33:39
35:6, 8, 12, 16[3], 17[4], 18[4], 19[2], 20[2], 21[4], 22, 23, 25[2], 26, 27, 28, 31, 32

DEUTERONOMY
1:4, 11, 27, 30[2], 36[3], 38[2]
2:7, 22[2], 30, 32
3:1, 22, 28[2]
4:13[3], 23, 31[2], 35, 36[3], 37[2], 39, 42
5:22[2], 24
6:10, 17, 23[3], 24, 25
7:8[2], 9, 10[2], 12, 13[3], 24
8:3[2], 10, 16[2], 18[3]
9:3[3], 5, 25, 28[3]
10:4, 6, 15, 18, 21[2]
11:3, 4[2], 5, 6, 7, 17, 25
12:10, 12, 15, 20, 31
13:2, 5, 10[2], 17
14:21, 23, 27, 29
15:2, 6, 8, 9, 16[3], 17, 18
16:16, 17[2]
17:6[2], 16[2], 17[2], 18[2], 19[2], 20[3]
18:2, 6, 7, 18, 19
19:4[2], 5[2], 6[2], 8[2], 11, 12, 15, 19
20:4, 5, 6[2], 7
21:16[3], 17[3], 20[2], 21, 22, 23
22:3, 16, 17, 19[2], 24, 27, 29[2]
23:1, 2, 7, 10[2], 11[2], 14, 16[2]
24:1, 5[4], 6, 13, 14, 15[2]
25:3[2], 4, 7, 8, 18[2]
26:5, 9, 18, 19[2]
27:16, 17, 18, 19, 20[2], 21, 22, 23, 24, 25, 26
28:8, 9, 21, 44[2], 45, 48[2], 51[2], 52[2], 54, 55[3], 60
29:1, 13[4], 19[2], 25[2], 26
30:4, 5, 9, 20
31:2, 3[3], 4[2], 6[2], 8[3], 11, 23
32:4[2], 6[2], 7, 8[2], 10[4], 13[3], 15, 19, 20, 36, 37, 39, 43, 44, 46
33:2[3], 3, 5, 7, 8, 9, 12[2], 13, 17, 18, 20[3], 21[4], 22[2], 23, 24, 27
34:6, 7

JOSHUA
1:15, 17, 18[2]
2:11
3:1, 10
4:4, 21, 23
5:6[2], 7, 13, 14
6:7, 26[2]
7:6, 15[5], 17[3], 18, 24
8:4, 10, 12, 14[2], 18, 19, 26[2], 27, 29, 32[2], 33, 34
9:9, 10, 22, 26, 27
10:1[2], 7, 12, 28[4], 30[3], 32, 33, 35[2], 37[2], 39[5], 40
11:1, 9, 11, 12, 15, 17, 20[2]
13:14[2], 33
14:3, 10, 14
15:13, 15, 16, 17, 19
17:1[3], 4
19:50[2]
20:4[2], 5, 6[3], 9
21:43, 44
22:4, 7, 8, 18, 22[2]
23:3, 5, 10[2], 15, 16[2]
24:7, 10, 17, 18, 19[3], 20[2], 23, 27, 31

JUDGES
1:7, 11, 12, 13, 19, 20, 25, 33
2:7, 10, 14[2], 20, 21, 23
3:4, 8, 10, 13, 16, 17, 18[2], 19, 20[3], 22, 24[2], 25, 27[3], 28, 31
4:3[2], 10, 18, 19, 20, 21[2], 22
5:13, 15, 25, 27[7], 31
6:15, 17, 18, 19[2], 20, 22, 27[3], 30[3], 31[2], 32[2], 34, 35[2], 38
7:5, 8, 11, 15, 16[2], 17
8:2, 3, 4, 5, 8, 9, 12, 14, 15, 16[2], 17, 18, 19, 20[3], 26, 30, 31, 35
9:3, 5[2], 7, 18, 28, 29, 31, 33, 36, 40, 43[2], 45, 48, 54[2], 56
10:1, 2, 4, 7, 18[2]
11:1, 17, 25[2], 28, 29[2], 33, 34, 35[2], 38[2], 39
12:5, 6[2], 9[3], 11, 14[2]
13:5, 6[2], 7, 11, 16, 21, 23[2]
14:2, 4, 6[5], 7, 8[2], 9[3], 14, 15, 16, 17, 18, 19[2], 20
15:1, 5[2], 6, 8[2], 10, 11, 14, 15, 17[2], 18, 19[3], 20
16:4, 9, 11, 12, 13, 14, 17, 18[2], 20[2], 21, 22, 25[2], 30[3], 31
17:2, 3, 4, 7, 8[3], 9
18:4, 20, 24, 26, 27, 30, 31
19:3, 4, 5, 7, 8, 9, 10, 13, 15[2], 16, 17[2], 18, 21, 28, 29[2]
21:5, 18

RUTH
1:1
2:14, 19, 20, 21
3:2, 3, 4[3], 7, 9, 10, 13[2], 14, 15[2], 17[2], 18
4:1[2], 2, 3, 4, 8, 13, 15, 17

1 SAMUEL
1:2, 4, 5[2], 7, 22, 28[3]
2:6, 7, 8[2], 9, 10[2], 14, 15, 16, 23, 35
3:2, 4, 5[3], 6, 8, 9, 13[2], 16, 17[2], 18
4:13, 14, 15, 16[2], 18[5]
5:6, 9
6:5, 6, 9, 19[2], 20
7:3, 8, 16, 17[2]
8:1, 11[2], 12, 13, 14, 15, 16, 17, 21
9:2[3], 4[2], 6[4], 9[2], 12[3], 13[3], 16, 26, 27
10:9, 10, 11, 13[2], 14, 16[2], 21[2], 22, 23[2], 27
11:6, 7, 8, 12
12:5[2], 7, 9, 17, 24
13:1, 2, 7, 8, 9, 10[2], 13
14:1, 27, 33, 35, 37, 39, 40, 45[2], 47[2], 48, 52
15:2[2], 8, 11[2], 12, 16, 23, 27, 29[2], 30, 35
16:2, 5[2], 6, 8, 9, 11[3], 12[3], 16, 21[2], 22
17:5[2], 6, 8, 9, 12, 20, 23, 25, 26, 28[2], 30, 31, 33, 35, 36, 37, 38[2], 39[2], 40[3], 42[2], 47, 49, 54, 55
18:1, 3, 5, 8[2], 10, 11, 13, 15[2], 16, 27[2]
19:4, 5, 6, 7, 9, 10[2], 12, 14, 17[2], 18, 21, 22[2], 23[3], 24
20:1, 2[2], 3[2], 6, 7[2], 13, 17[3], 26[3], 29[3], 30, 31, 32[2], 34, 36[2], 42

1 SAMUEL

21:13
22:2, 3, 4, 10, 12, 13, 17, 18, 19, 22, 23
23:6, 7, 9, 11, 13, 17, 22, 23[2], 25[2]
24:3, 5, 6[2], 10, 17, 19
25:2[2], 3, 14, 17, 21, 25, 29, 30, 36[2], 37, 38, 39
26:3, 10, 18
27:2, 3, 4, 11, 12[2]
28:5, 8[2], 9, 11, 14[4], 17, 20, 21, 23[3]
29:3, 4[3], 9
30:8, 9, 10, 11, 12[2], 13, 15, 16, 21, 25, 26
31:3, 4, 5

2 SAMUEL

1:2[2], 3, 4, 7[2], 8, 9, 10[2], 13, 15[2], 18, 21
2:1, 10, 19, 20, 23[2], 30
3:11[2], 13, 16, 21, 22[2], 23[2], 24, 25, 26, 27, 28, 30
4:4[2], 7
5:2, 4[2], 5[2], 8, 12, 13, 20, 23
6:7, 8, 13, 18, 19
7:11, 13, 14[2], 18
8:2[2], 3, 6, 10, 11[2], 13, 14[3]
9:2[2], 4[2], 6[2], 8, 11, 13
10:3, 5, 7, 9, 10[2], 11, 17
11:2, 4, 13[3], 15[2], 16[2], 20, 21
12:1, 3, 4, 5, 6[3], 11, 17[2], 18[2], 19, 20[3], 22, 23[2], 24, 25[2], 30[2], 31[2]
13:2, 4, 8, 9, 11, 13, 14, 15[2], 16, 17, 20, 21, 22, 25[2], 26, 27, 32, 36, 39[2]
14:7, 10, 11, 12, 14, 19[2], 26[4], 29[3], 30[2], 33[2]
15:2, 5, 9, 12, 14, 25, 26, 30[2], 32
16:3[2], 5[2], 6, 7, 13, 21, 23
17:2, 5, 9, 10, 12, 13, 23, 24
18:9, 14[2], 18[2], 23[2], 25[2], 26, 27, 28, 30, 33[2]
19:9[2], 14, 18[2], 21, 24, 25, 26, 27, 32[3], 39, 42
20:1, 3, 5[2], 6, 8[2], 10[2], 11[2], 12[2], 13, 14, 17[4], 22
21:1, 4, 9, 13, 16, 20, 21
22:2, 3, 7, 8, 10, 11[2], 12, 15, 17[3], 18, 20[3], 21, 31, 33, 34, 35, 42, 51
23:3, 4, 5[2], 8[2], 10, 12, 16, 17[2], 18, 19[3], 20[2], 21[2], 23[2]
24:1, 10, 17

1 KINGS

1:1, 5, 6, 7, 10, 13, 17, 19[2], 23[2], 24, 25, 26, 30, 35[2], 37, 41, 42, 51[2], 52[2], 53
2:1[2], 4[2], 5[2], 8, 11[2], 13, 14, 15, 17[3], 22, 24, 25[2], 27[2], 28, 29, 30[2], 31, 32, 34, 46
3:1, 3, 6, 15
4:2, 15, 19, 24[2], 31, 32, 33[2]
5:1, 5, 7, 12, 14
6:1, 4, 5[2], 6, 9, 10, 15[2], 16[2], 19, 20, 21[2], 22[3], 23, 27, 28, 29, 30, 31, 32, 33, 35, 36, 38
7:1, 2, 6, 7[2], 8[2], 14[3], 15, 16, 18[2], 21[3], 23, 27, 36, 37, 38, 39[2], 40, 51
8:12, 15, 19, 20, 21[2], 23, 42, 54, 55, 56[2], 57, 58[2], 59, 63, 64, 66
9:1, 2, 13[2], 24, 25[3]
10:3, 4, 5, 9, 15, 17, 26[2], 27
11:3, 8, 10[2], 14, 15, 16, 17, 19, 22, 24, 25[2], 26, 27, 28[2], 29, 31, 32, 34, 41
12:2, 4, 5, 6, 8, 9, 15, 18, 21, 29[2], 31, 32[5], 33[4]
13:2[2], 3, 4[3], 10[2], 11, 12, 13[2], 14[2], 15, 16, 18[3], 19, 21, 23[4], 24, 26[2], 27, 28, 30, 31[2], 32, 33[2]
14:3, 5, 6, 13, 15[2], 16, 18, 19[2], 20, 21[2], 26[3], 29
15:2, 3[2], 5, 7, 10, 12, 13, 15, 17, 19, 20, 21, 23[3], 26[2], 29[5], 30[3], 31, 34[2]
16:5, 7[2], 9, 11[4], 12, 14, 18, 19[2], 20, 23, 24[2], 26[2], 27[2], 31, 32[2], 34[2]
17:5[2], 6, 10[3], 11, 15, 16, 19[3], 20, 21, 22
18:7, 8, 9, 10[2], 12[2], 14, 17, 18, 27[5], 30, 32[2], 33, 34[2], 35, 39[2], 42, 43[2], 44[2], 46
19:1, 3[2], 4[3], 5, 6[2], 8, 9[2], 10, 11, 13, 14, 19[2], 20[2], 21[2]
20:1, 2, 7, 9, 11, 12[3], 14[3], 15[2], 16, 18, 25, 28, 31, 32[3], 33[2], 34, 36[2], 37[2], 39[3], 40, 41[2], 42
21:4[2], 6[2], 10, 13, 15, 18[2], 20, 26, 27, 29
22:4, 8, 11, 15[2], 17, 18, 19, 20, 22[2], 28, 34, 38, 39[3], 42[2], 43[2], 45[2], 46, 52, 53

2 KINGS

1:2, 5, 7[2], 8[2], 9[3], 11[2], 13, 15, 16, 17[2], 18
2:3, 4, 5, 6, 10, 12[3], 13, 14[2], 16, 17[2], 18[2], 20, 21, 22, 23[2], 24, 25[2]
3:2[2], 3[2], 7[2], 8[2], 16, 18, 26, 27
4:3, 6, 7, 8[2], 10[2], 11[2], 12[2], 13, 14, 15[2], 16, 18, 19[2], 20[2], 23, 25, 29, 30, 31, 33, 34[2], 35, 36[3], 38, 41[3], 42, 43, 44
5:1[2], 3, 5, 6, 7[2], 8[2], 11, 12, 13, 14[2], 15[3], 16[3], 18, 19[2], 20, 21, 22, 23, 24[3], 25[2], 26, 27
6:2, 3, 4, 5, 6[2], 7[2], 11, 13[3], 14, 16, 17[2], 18, 19, 21, 22, 23[2], 27, 30[3], 31, 32, 33[2]
7:2, 11, 17[2], 19, 20
8:1, 5[3], 10, 11[2], 12, 13, 14[3], 15[2], 17[3], 18[2], 19, 21, 23, 26[2], 27[2], 28, 29[2]
9:5[3], 6[2], 10, 11, 12[2], 14, 15, 17[2], 18, 19, 20[2], 22[2], 24, 27[2], 32, 33[2], 34[2], 36[2]
10:5[2], 6, 8, 9, 10, 11, 12[2], 14[2], 15[5], 16, 17[4], 19[2], 22[2], 24, 25, 31, 34
11:2, 3, 5, 8[3], 12, 19[2], 21
12:1, 18, 19, 21
13:2[2], 3, 4, 7, 8, 11[3], 12[2], 14, 15, 16[2], 17[4], 18[4], 21, 23, 25
14:2[2], 3[2], 5, 6, 7, 11, 14, 15[2], 19, 20, 22, 24[2], 25[2], 27[2], 28[3]
15:2[3], 3, 5, 6, 9[2], 12, 13, 15, 16[2], 18[2], 21, 24[2], 25, 26, 28[2], 31, 33[3], 34[2], 35, 36
16:2, 3, 4, 13, 14, 18, 19
17:2, 4[2], 15[2], 20, 21, 22, 23, 26, 34, 37, 39
18:2[3], 3, 4[2], 5, 6, 7[3], 8, 22, 27, 29, 32
19:1, 2, 7, 8[2], 9[3], 32, 33[2], 37
20:2, 7, 9, 11, 12, 15, 19, 20
21:1, 2, 3[2], 4, 5, 6[2], 7[2], 16[2], 17[2], 19[2], 20, 21, 22, 25, 26
22:1[2], 2, 4, 8, 11
23:2, 4, 5, 6, 7, 8, 10, 11, 14, 15, 16, 17, 18, 19, 20, 24, 28, 29[2], 31[2], 32, 33, 34, 35[2], 36[2], 37
24:1, 2, 3, 4[2], 5, 8[2], 9, 12, 13, 14, 15[2], 18[2], 19, 20
25:1, 9[2], 19, 22, 25, 27, 28, 29

1 CHRONICLES

1:10
2:3, 21[2], 23
3:4[2]
4:10
5:1[2], 6, 9, 20, 26
6:10
7:23[2]
8:7, 8, 9, 11
10:3, 4, 5, 13[2], 14
11:2, 8, 11, 13, 19, 20[2], 21[3], 22[2], 23[2], 25
12:1, 18, 19[2], 20
13:10[3], 14
14:4
15:3, 22[2]
16:2, 3, 4, 12, 14, 15, 16, 21[2], 25, 33, 34, 37, 40
17:12, 13
18:2, 3, 6, 10[2], 11, 13[2]
19:3, 5, 8, 10, 11, 12, 17
20:2, 3, 6, 7
21:3, 6, 7, 15[2], 19, 26, 27, 28, 30
22:2, 6, 10[2], 11, 18[2]
23:1, 2, 13[2]
25:10, 11, 12, 13, 14, 15, 16, 17, 18, 19, 20, 21, 22, 23, 24, 25, 26, 27, 28, 29, 30, 31
26:10
27:23, 24
28:4[2], 5, 6[2], 7, 9[2], 12, 14, 16, 17, 20
29:27[3], 28

2 CHRONICLES

1:4, 5, 14[2], 15
2:11[4], 18
3:2, 4, 5[2], 6, 7, 8[2], 9, 10, 14, 15, 16, 17
4:1, 2, 6, 7, 8[2], 9, 10, 11, 14[2], 21
5:1, 13
6:1, 4[2], 9, 10, 11, 12, 13
7:3, 7, 10, 11, 21, 22
8:4[2], 5, 11[2], 12, 14
9:2, 3, 4, 8, 16, 25, 26, 27, 31
10:2, 4, 5, 6, 8, 9, 15, 18
11:1[2], 6, 11, 12, 15[2], 20, 21, 22, 23[3]
12:1, 4, 9[2], 12[2], 13[2], 14[2]
13:2, 20
14:3, 5, 6[2], 7[2]
15:2[3], 4, 8[2], 9, 15, 16, 18[2]
16:1, 3, 5, 6, 8, 10, 12, 14
17:2, 3, 5, 6, 7, 8, 11, 12, 13
18:2[2], 3, 7, 14[2], 16, 17, 18, 19, 21, 27, 33, 34
19:4, 5, 9
20:15, 21[2], 31[3], 32, 36
21:2, 3[2], 4, 5[2], 6[3], 7[2], 9, 10, 11, 19, 20[3]
22:2[2], 3, 4, 5, 6[3], 7[2], 8, 9[3], 12
23:3, 7[3], 10, 19, 20
24:1[2], 3, 5, 15[3], 16, 19, 20, 22[2], 25
25:1[2], 2, 3, 4, 5, 6, 14, 15, 16, 20, 21, 24, 27
26:2, 3[2], 4, 5[2], 6, 8, 10[3], 15[3], 16[2], 19, 20, 21, 23
27:1[2], 2[2], 3[2], 4[2], 5, 6, 8[2]
28:1[3], 2, 3, 4, 5, 9[2], 19, 21, 22, 23[2], 24, 25
29:1[2], 2, 3, 4, 8, 21[2], 23, 25
30:6, 8, 19
31:3, 4, 21[2]
32:2, 3, 5, 6, 9, 17, 21[2], 23, 24[2], 26, 27, 29, 31
33:1[2], 3[2], 4, 5, 6[3], 7[2], 12[2], 13[2], 14, 15[2], 16, 19[2], 21, 22
34:1[2], 2, 3[3], 4[2], 5, 6, 7[2], 8[2], 19, 30, 32
35:2, 21[2], 22, 24[2]
36:2[2], 5[3], 8, 9[3], 11, 12, 13[2], 14, 15, 17[2], 18, 20, 22, 23

EZRA

1:1, 2, 3, 4
3:11
5:12, 14
6:17
7:6, 8, 9[2]
8:23, 31, 35
10:1, 6[3]

NEHEMIAH

1:2
2:8, 18, 20
3:12, 14, 15
4:1, 2, 3[2], 18
5:13
6:10, 12, 13, 18
7:2
8:3, 5[2], 10, 18
9:29
12:8
13:2, 5

ESTHER

1:3, 4, 10, 20, 22
2:1, 4, 7, 9[2], 17, 18
3:4[3], 6
4:4, 5, 8, 11
5:5, 9[2], 10[2], 11, 14
6:1, 4
7:5[2], 7, 8, 10
8:1, 2, 3, 5, 7, 10
9:25[3], 30

JOB

1:10, 11[2], 12, 16, 17, 18
2:3, 4, 5, 6, 8[2], 10
4:18[2]
5:12, 13, 15, 18[2], 19, 20
6:5, 9, 14
7:9, 10
8:4, 6, 15[2], 16, 18, 20, 21
9:3[2], 4, 11[2], 12, 16[2], 17, 18, 19, 22, 23, 24[2], 32
11:6, 10, 11[3]
12:4, 5, 13, 14[2], 15[2], 17, 18, 19, 20, 21, 22, 23[2], 24, 25
13:9, 10, 15, 16, 19, 28
14:2[2], 5, 6[2], 10, 14, 20, 21[2]
15:3[2], 14[3], 15, 22[3], 23[2], 25, 26, 27, 28, 29[2], 30[2], 33
16:7, 9[2], 12[2], 13[2], 14[2]
17:3, 5, 6, 9
18:4, 8[2], 17, 18, 19
19:8[2], 9, 10[2], 11[2], 13, 16, 25
20:7[2], 8[2], 12, 13, 15[2], 16, 17, 18[3], 19[3], 20[3], 22, 23[2], 24
21:19[2], 20, 21, 22, 31, 32
22:2, 4[2], 8, 13, 14[2], 18, 27, 29, 30
23:5[2], 6[2], 8, 9[2], 10[2], 13[2], 14, 17
24:18[2], 20, 21, 22[2], 23
25:2, 4
26:7, 8, 9, 10, 12[2], 13
27:7, 8, 10[2], 16, 17, 18, 19[3], 21, 22
28:3, 9[2], 10, 11[2], 23, 24, 25, 26, 27[2], 28
30:11, 19, 24
31:4, 14, 15, 18, 20
32:1, 2, 4, 14
33:10[2], 11[2], 13, 16, 17, 18, 19, 24, 25, 26[4], 27, 28
34:9[2], 10[2], 11, 14[2], 17, 21, 23[2], 24, 25[2], 26, 28, 29[2], 33, 37[2]
35:7, 15[2], 16
36:4, 5, 6, 7[2], 9, 10, 13, 15, 16, 18, 19, 27, 30, 31[2], 33
37:3, 4[2], 5, 6, 7, 11[2], 12, 13, 17, 20, 23[2], 24
39:7[2], 8, 10, 12, 17, 21[2], 22[2], 24[2], 25[2]
40:2[2], 15, 17, 19[2], 21, 23[3], 24
41:3[2], 4, 25, 27, 29, 30, 31[2], 32, 34[2]
42:3, 10[2], 12, 13, 14

PSALMS

1:2, 3[2]
2:4, 5, 12
3:t, 4
7:t, 2, 12[3], 13[2], 14, 15[2]
9:7, 8[2], 12[3], 16
10:5, 6, 8[2], 9[4], 10, 11[3], 13
11:6
13:6
15:2, 3, 4[2], 5[2]
16:8
18:t, 6, 7, 9, 10[2], 11, 14[2], 16[3], 17, 19[3], 20, 30, 33, 34, 41, 48, 50
19:4
20:6
21:1, 4, 7
22:8[3], 9, 24[4], 28, 31
23:2[2], 3[2]
24:2, 4, 5, 10
25:8, 9[2], 12[3], 14, 15
27:5[3], 14
28:5, 6, 8
29:6
31:21, 24
32:1, 10
33:5, 7[2], 9[2], 10, 12, 13, 14, 15[2], 17, 20
34:t[2], 4, 12[2], 20
35:8, 14
36:2, 3, 4[3]
37:4, 5, 6, 13, 23, 24[2], 26, 33, 34, 36[3], 39, 40
39:6
40:1, 2, 3
41:1, 2, 5, 6[4], 8[2]
44:21

PSALMS

45:11
46:6, 8, 9[3]
47:2, 3, 4[2], 9
48:14
49:9, 10, 12, 15, 17[2], 18[2], 19
50:4[2], 9
51:t
52:5
54:5, 7
55:12, 17, 18, 19, 20[2], 22[2]
56:1
57:t, 3
58:7, 9, 10[2], 11
60:t, 12
61:7
62:2[2], 6[2]
63:t
65:4
66:5, 6, 7, 16, 17, 19
68:6, 20, 33, 35
71:6
72:2, 4[2], 6, 8, 12[2], 13, 14, 15[2]
74:5
75:7, 8
76:3, 12[2]
77:1, 7, 9
78:4, 5[2], 11, 12, 13[2], 14, 15, 16, 20[3], 23, 25, 26[2], 27, 28, 29, 33, 34, 38[2], 39, 42, 43, 45, 46, 47, 48, 49, 50[2], 53, 54, 55, 59, 60[2], 62, 66[2], 67, 68, 69[2], 70, 71, 72
81:5[2], 16
82:1
84:11
85:8
87:6
89:26, 41, 48[2]
91:1, 2, 3, 4, 11, 14[2], 15
92:12, 15
93:1[2]
94:9[4], 10[4], 14, 23
95:5, 7
96:4, 10, 13[3]
97:10[2]
98:1, 2, 3, 9[2]
99:1, 2, 5, 6, 7[2]
100:3[2]
101:6[2], 7[2]
102:t, 16, 17, 19, 23[2]
103:7, 9[2], 10, 12, 14[2], 15
104:10, 13, 14[2], 16, 19, 32[2]
105:5, 7, 8[2], 9, 14[2], 16[2], 17, 18, 21, 24, 25, 26[2], 28, 29, 31, 32, 33, 34, 36, 37, 39, 40, 41, 42, 43
106:1, 3, 8[2], 9[2], 10, 15, 23[3], 26, 33, 40, 41, 43, 44[2], 45, 46
107:1, 2, 6, 7, 9, 12, 13, 14, 16, 19, 20, 25, 28, 29, 30, 33, 35, 36, 38, 40, 41
108:13
109:7, 11, 15, 16[2], 17[2], 18, 19, 31
110:6[3], 7[2]
111:4, 5[2], 6[2], 9[2]
112:4, 5, 6, 7, 8[2], 9[2], 10
113:7, 8, 9
115:3[2], 9, 10, 11, 12[3], 13, 16
116:1, 2, 6
118:1, 18, 26, 29
120:1
121:3[2], 4, 7
123:2
126:6
127:2
129:4, 7
130:8
132:2, 11, 13
135:6, 7[3], 14
136:1
137:8, 9
138:6[2]
142:t
143:3[2]
144:2, 10
145:19[2], 20
146:4, 5, 9[2]
147:2, 3, 4[2], 6, 9, 10[2], 13[2], 14, 15, 16[2], 17, 18[2], 19, 20
148:5, 6[2], 14
149:4

PROVERBS

2:7[2], 8
3:6, 12[2], 19, 29, 30, 33, 34[2]
4:4
5:21, 22, 23[2]
6:13[3], 14[2], 15, 19, 29, 30[2], 31[3], 32, 33, 34, 35[2]
7:8, 19, 20, 22
8:26, 27[2], 28[2], 29[2], 36
9:7[2], 8[2], 9[2], 18
10:3, 4, 5[2], 9[2], 10, 17[2], 18[2], 19, 22
11:12, 13, 15[2], 17, 19, 25, 26, 27[2], 28, 29, 30
12:1, 2, 8, 9[2], 11[2], 15, 17, 27
13:3[2], 11, 13, 18, 20, 24[2]
14:2[2], 17, 21[3], 29[2], 31[2]
15:5, 9, 10, 12, 15, 18, 24, 25, 27[2], 29, 32[2]
16:5, 7, 17, 20[2], 26, 30[2], 32[3]
17:5, 9[2], 15[2], 16, 19[2], 20[2], 21, 27, 28[2]
18:9, 13[2], 17, 20
19:1, 2, 5, 7, 8[2], 9, 16[2], 17[3], 23[2], 25, 26
20:4, 14[2], 19, 22
21:1[2], 11, 13, 17[2], 21, 26, 27, 29
22:5, 6[3], 8, 9[2], 11, 12, 14, 16[2], 22, 27, 29[2]

PROVERBS

23:7[3], 9, 11, 13, 24, 34[2]
24:7, 8, 12[4], 17, 18, 24, 29
25:10, 13, 17, 20[2], 21, 28
26:5, 6, 8[2], 17, 24, 25, 27
27:14, 18
28:6[2], 7, 8[2], 9, 10, 13, 14, 16, 18, 19[2], 20, 22, 23[2], 25[2], 26[2], 27[2]
29:1, 3, 4, 9, 17[2], 18[2], 19[2], 21, 24, 27
30:5, 6, 10, 22[2], 31
31:11, 23, 28

ECCLESIASTES

1:3, 5, 18
2:19[2], 21, 22, 24[2], 26[2]
3:9[2], 11[2]
4:3, 8[2], 10[2], 14[2]
5:4, 8, 10[2], 12, 14, 15[4], 16[3], 17[2], 18, 20
6:2[2], 3[2], 4, 5, 6[2], 10[2], 12
7:13, 18
8:3, 7, 8, 13[2], 17[2]
9:2[2], 9, 15
10:3[3], 8, 9, 10[2], 15
11:4[2]
12:4, 9[2]

SONG OF SOLOMON

1:13
2:4, 7, 8, 9[2], 16
3:5, 10
5:6[2], 16
6:3
8:4, 11

ISAIAH

1:1, 11
2:3, 4, 12, 18, 19, 21, 22
3:7
4:3[2]
5:2[2], 7, 14, 25, 26
6:2[3], 6, 7, 9, 11
7:13, 15[2], 22
8:7, 8[3], 14
9:1, 15[2], 20[2]
10:7, 8, 13, 16, 24, 26, 28[3], 32[2], 34
11:3, 4[3], 12, 15, 16
12:2, 5
13:9
14:6[2], 30
15:2
16:5, 6, 12[2]
17:5, 8, 14
18:3[2], 5
19:16, 17, 20[2], 22[2]
20:2
21:4, 6, 7[2], 8, 9[2], 11
22:8, 16, 18, 19, 21, 22[2], 23
23:11[2], 12, 13
24:18[2]
25:7, 8[2], 9, 11[3], 12
26:3, 5[4], 10[2]
27:1, 5[2], 6, 7[3], 8, 9, 10, 11[2]
28:4[2], 9[2], 11, 12, 16, 20, 21[2], 24, 25[2], 28
29:8[5], 10, 11, 12, 16[2], 23
30:14[2], 18[3], 19[3], 23, 32, 33
31:2, 3[2], 4, 5[2], 8, 9
32:6, 7, 8
33:4, 5[2], 8[3], 15[2], 16, 18, 22
34:2[2], 11, 17
35:4
36:2, 7, 12, 14
37:1, 2, 7, 8[2], 9[4], 33, 34[2], 38
38:7, 9, 12, 13, 15, 19, 21
39:1[2], 4, 8
40:6, 11[2], 14, 15, 20[3], 22, 23, 24, 26[2], 29[2]
41:2, 3[2], 4, 7[2], 24, 25[3], 26
42:1, 2, 3[3], 4[2], 5[3], 13[3], 19, 20, 21, 24, 25[3]
43:1, 10, 13, 25
44:12[2], 13[3], 14[3], 15[4], 16[4], 17[2], 18, 20[2], 24, 28
45:9, 13[2], 18[3]
46:4, 6, 7[3]
48:12, 14, 15, 21[3]
49:1, 2[3], 6, 7, 10[2]
50:4[2], 8, 9
51:3[2], 12, 13, 14[2]
52:6, 9, 13, 15
53:2[2], 3[2], 4, 5[2], 7[5], 8[3], 9[2], 10[3], 11[2], 12[4]
54:5
55:1, 5, 6[2], 7[2]
57:2, 13, 17
58:9
59:2, 5, 15, 16, 17[2], 18[2]
60:9
61:1, 3, 10[2]
62:7[2]
63:7, 8[2], 9[3], 10[2], 11[3]
64:4
65:16[2]
66:3[8], 5

JEREMIAH

2:14[2], 17, 26
3:1, 5[2]
4:7, 13
5:12, 24, 26
8:4, 8
9:8, 12[2], 24
10:10, 12[2], 13[3], 16
11:16
12:4
13:16[2], 21
14:10, 22
15:4
16:15

JEREMIAH

17:6, 8, 11
18:3, 4[2]
19:14
20:4, 10, 13, 17
21:2, 7[2], 9[3], 10
22:4, 10, 11, 12, 16, 19, 28[2]
23:6, 20[2], 28, 31
25:30[2], 31[2], 38
26:11, 13, 16, 19[2], 21
27:20
29:21, 28, 31, 32[3]
30:7, 21, 24[2]
31:10, 11, 20
32:3, 5[2], 28
33:1, 15, 21, 24
34:2, 3, 14, 16
35:8, 14, 16, 18
36:4, 12, 13, 18, 21, 23, 25[2], 30
37:2[2], 13[2], 14, 17
38:2[3], 4, 5[2], 9[2], 10, 26, 27, 28
39:4, 5, 7, 12, 14[2], 15
40:1, 3, 5[2], 11, 15
41:4, 6[3], 7, 8, 9, 16[3]
42:8, 12, 21
43:10, 11[2], 12[3], 13[2]
45:1
46:8, 10, 16, 17, 18
47:7
48:10[2], 11[2], 18, 26[2], 27, 29, 36, 40, 42, 44[2]
49:1, 10[2], 12, 19, 20[3], 22
50:8, 19, 34[2], 44, 45[3]
51:6, 12, 15[2], 16[3], 19, 34[5], 40, 44, 59
52:1[2], 2, 3, 4, 9, 10, 11, 13, 25, 29, 33

LAMENTATIONS

1:13[4], 14, 15
2:2[3], 3[3], 4[3], 5[3], 6[2], 7[2], 8[3], 9, 17[6]
3:2, 3[2], 4[2], 5, 6, 7[2], 8, 9[2], 10, 11[2], 12, 13, 15[2], 16[2], 27, 28[2], 29, 30[2], 32[2], 33, 37
4:11, 16, 22[3]

EZEKIEL

2:1, 2, 3, 10
3:1, 2, 3, 4, 10, 19[2], 20[3], 21[3], 22, 27[2]
4:15, 16
6:12[3]
7:15[2], 20
8:3, 5, 6, 7, 8, 9, 12, 13, 14, 15, 16, 17
9:1, 3[2], 5, 7, 9
10:2[2], 5, 6[2]
11:2
12:12[2], 13[3], 27[2]
13:22
14:9
17:4[2], 5[2], 7, 9, 13, 15[4], 16[3], 18[3], 19[2], 20[2]
18:8, 9[2], 10, 13[4], 14[2], 17[2], 18[2], 19, 21[3], 22[3], 23, 24[5], 26[2], 27[2], 28[4]
19:4, 6[2], 7[2], 8
20:11, 13, 21, 49
21:11, 21[3], 23, 27
24:24, 26
26:8[2], 9[2], 10, 11[2]
29:9, 18[2], 19, 20
30:11, 24, 25
31:5, 7, 10, 11, 15
32:25, 32
33:3[2], 5[2], 6, 9[2], 12[3], 13[4], 14, 15[3], 16[3], 18, 19, 22[2], 24
34:12, 17, 23[6]
37:3, 4, 9, 10, 11
38:17
39:15
40:2, 3[2], 5, 6, 8, 9, 11, 13, 14, 17, 19, 20, 23, 24[2], 27, 28[2], 32[2], 35, 45, 47, 48, 49
41:1, 2, 3, 4[2], 5, 13, 15, 22
42:1[2], 13, 15[2], 16, 17, 18, 19, 20
43:1, 7, 18, 21
44:1, 3[2], 4, 26, 27[2], 30
45:17, 23, 24, 25
46:2[2], 5, 7, 8[2], 9[4], 11, 12[3], 17, 18, 19, 20, 21, 24
47:1, 2, 3[2], 4[2], 5, 6[2], 8

DANIEL

1:2[2], 3, 5, 7, 8[4], 10, 14, 18, 20
2:15, 16[2], 21[3], 22[2], 24, 29, 38, 49
3:1, 11, 17, 19, 20, 25
4:14, 17, 25, 29, 32, 33, 35, 37
5:2, 12, 19[9], 20, 21[4], 29
6:4, 7, 10[3], 14[2], 16, 20[2], 23, 26, 27[2]
7:1, 16, 23, 24[2], 25
8:4, 5, 6, 7[2], 8[2], 11, 14, 17[3], 18[2], 19, 24, 25[4]
9:2, 10, 12[2], 14, 22, 27[3]
10:1, 11[2], 12, 15, 18, 19, 20
11:2, 4[2], 5, 6[3], 8, 10, 11, 12[3], 16[2], 17[3], 18[2], 19[2], 20, 21, 23[2], 24[4], 25[2], 28[2], 29, 30[3], 32, 36, 37[2], 38[2], 39[3], 40, 41, 42, 43, 44, 45[2]
12:7[2], 9, 12

HOSEA

1:3
5:6, 11, 13
6:1[4], 2[2], 3, 11
7:4, 5, 8, 9[2]
8:1, 13
9:9[2]
10:1[2], 2[2], 12
11:5, 10[2]

HOSEA
12:1, 2, 3[2], 4[4], 7[2], 12, 13, 14
13:1[3], 13[2], 15[2]
14:5, 9[2]

JOEL
1:6, 7[2]
2:11, 13, 14, 20, 23[2]

AMOS
1:1, 2, 11[2], 15
2:1, 9, 15[3], 16
3:4[2], 7, 11
4:2, 13
5:6
6:10[3], 11
7:1, 2, 5, 7
8:2
9:1[3], 3, 5, 6[2]

OBADIAH
12

JONAH
1:3[2], 5, 9, 10[2], 12
2:2
3:4, 6[2], 7, 10[3]
4:1, 2, 5, 8, 9

MICAH
1:1, 9, 11, 15
2:4[3], 11
3:4[2], 5
4:2, 3, 12
5:1, 2, 3, 4[2], 5, 6[3], 8
6:2, 8
7:3, 9[2], 12, 18[2], 19[3]

NAHUM
1:2, 4, 7, 8, 9, 12, 15
2:1, 5

HABAKKUK
1:11, 13
2:1, 2, 5[2], 9[2]
3:4, 6[2], 16[2], 19[2]

ZEPHANIAH
1:7, 12, 18
2:11, 13, 14
3:5[3], 15, 17[4]

HAGGAI
1:6

ZECHARIAH
1:6, 8, 19, 21
2:2, 8[2], 13
3:1, 4[2]
4:6, 7, 13, 14
5:2, 3, 6[2], 8[3], 11
6:7, 8, 12[2], 13[3]
7:13
9:4, 7[3], 9, 10
10:11
11:16
12:8
13:3, 4, 5, 6
14:3

MALACHI
1:8, 9[2]
2:5, 6, 7, 11, 13, 15[3], 16, 17
3:1[2], 2[2], 3[2], 11
4:6

MATTHEW
1:20, 21, 25
2:2, 3, 4[2], 7, 8, 14[2], 16[3], 21, 22[3], 23[2]
3:3, 7[2], 11[2], 12[2], 15, 16[2]
4:2[3], 3, 4, 6, 12, 13, 19, 21[2], 24
5:1[2], 2, 19, 45
6:24[2], 30
7:8, 9, 10[2], 21, 29
8:1, 9[3], 10, 14, 15, 16, 18, 23, 24, 26[2], 28, 32, 34
9:1, 6, 7, 9[3], 12, 18, 22[2], 24, 25, 28, 29, 34, 36[2], 37, 38
10:1[2], 22, 25, 37[2], 38, 39[2], 40[2], 41[2], 42
11:1, 2, 3, 6, 10, 11[2], 15, 18, 20, 27
12:3[2], 4, 9[2], 11[2], 13[2], 15[2], 18, 19, 20[3], 22, 26, 29[2], 30[2], 39, 43, 44[3], 45, 46, 48, 49
13:2, 3, 4, 11, 12[3], 19, 20[2], 21[2], 22[3], 23[2], 24, 28, 29, 31, 33, 34, 37[2], 44[2], 46[2], 52, 53, 54[2], 58
14:2, 5[2], 7, 9, 10, 13, 14, 18, 19[2], 22, 23[3], 29[2], 30[3]
15:3, 4, 6, 10, 13, 23, 24, 26, 30, 35, 36, 39
16:1, 2, 4, 8, 12, 13, 15, 20[2], 21, 23, 26, 27
17:5, 13, 15[2], 18, 23, 25[2]
18:6, 12, 13[2], 15, 16, 17[2], 24, 25[2], 28, 30[2], 32, 34
19:1, 2, 4[2], 8, 11, 12, 13, 15, 17, 18, 22[2]
20:2[2], 3, 5, 6, 7, 13, 19, 21, 23
21:3, 9, 10, 14, 15, 17[2], 18[2], 19[2], 23[2], 25, 27, 28, 29[2], 30[2], 34, 36, 37, 40, 41, 45
22:4, 7[2], 8, 11, 12[2], 20, 21, 25, 34, 42, 43, 45
23:11, 12, 15, 16, 18, 22, 39
24:3, 13, 26[2], 31, 43, 46, 47, 50[2]
25:12, 15, 16, 17[2], 18, 20, 22, 24, 29[2], 31, 32, 33, 41, 45
26:1, 7, 10, 16, 18, 20, 21, 23[2], 24, 25, 27, 37, 38, 39, 40, 42, 43, 44, 45, 46, 47, 48[2], 49, 53, 65, 66, 68, 70, 71, 72, 74, 75
27:3[2], 5, 12[2], 14, 18, 19, 23, 24[2], 26[3], 34[2], 42[3], 43[2], 50, 58, 59, 60[2], 63, 64
28:6[3], 7[2]

MARK
1:6, 8, 10, 13, 16[2], 19[2], 20, 21, 22, 23, 26, 27, 31, 34, 35, 38, 39, 42[3], 43, 45
2:1[2], 2, 4, 5, 8, 10, 12, 13[2], 14[3], 16, 17, 23, 25[3], 26, 27
3:1, 2, 3, 4, 5[3], 8, 9, 10, 12, 13[2], 14[2], 16, 17, 21, 22[2], 23, 26, 27[2], 29, 30, 33, 34
4:1[2], 2, 4, 9[2], 10, 11, 13, 21, 24, 25[3], 26, 27, 29, 30, 33, 34[2], 35, 36, 38, 39, 40
5:2, 4, 5, 6[2], 8, 9[2], 10[2], 18[3], 20, 21, 22[2], 32, 34, 35, 36, 37, 38, 39[2], 40[2], 41, 43
6:1, 2, 5[2], 6[2], 7, 10, 14, 16[2], 17, 20[3], 23, 26, 27, 31, 34[2], 37, 38, 39, 41[3], 45[2], 46[2], 47, 48[2], 50, 51, 55, 56
7:6, 9, 11, 14[2], 17, 18, 20, 24[2], 26, 29, 31, 33[2], 34, 35, 36[2], 37[2]
8:5, 6[2], 7, 9, 10, 12, 13, 15, 17, 21, 22, 23[4], 24, 25[2], 26, 27, 29, 30, 31, 32, 33[2], 34[2], 36, 38
9:1, 2, 6, 9, 12[2], 14[2], 16, 18[3], 19, 20[2], 21[2], 25, 26[2], 27, 28, 29, 30, 31[3], 33[2], 35, 36[3], 38[2], 40, 41, 42
10:1[3], 3, 5, 11, 13, 14, 15, 16, 17, 20, 22[2], 30, 32, 34, 36, 46, 47[2], 48[2], 49, 50, 52
11:1, 3, 7, 9, 11[2], 12, 13[4], 17, 19, 23[3], 27, 31, 32
12:1, 2[2], 4, 5, 6, 9, 12, 15, 16, 21, 27, 28, 32, 34[2], 35, 37, 38, 43
13:1, 3, 13, 20[2], 21, 27, 36
14:3, 11[2], 13, 14, 15, 16, 17, 20, 21, 23[3], 24, 31, 32, 33, 35, 36, 37, 39, 40[2], 41, 42, 43, 44[2], 45[2], 52, 54, 61, 68[2], 70, 71, 72[2]
15:2, 3, 6, 8, 10, 11, 14, 15, 23, 28, 31[2], 35, 39[2], 41, 44[3], 45[2], 46, 47
16:6[3], 7[2], 9[2], 11, 12, 14[2], 15, 16[2], 19

LUKE
1:8, 9, 12, 15[2], 16, 17, 21, 22[4], 23, 25, 32, 33, 48, 49, 51[2], 52, 53[2], 54, 55, 60, 62, 63, 64, 68, 70, 73, 74
2:4, 21, 26[2], 27, 28, 42, 49, 50, 51
3:3, 7, 11[3], 13, 14, 15, 16, 17[2], 18, 20
4:2[2], 9, 10, 13, 15, 16[3], 17[2], 18[2], 20[2], 21, 23, 24, 30, 35, 36, 38, 39, 40, 41[2], 42[3], 43, 44
5:1, 3[3], 4[2], 8, 9, 12, 13, 14, 16, 17, 20[2], 22, 24, 25[2], 27[2], 28, 34, 36, 39
6:1, 4, 5, 6, 7, 8[2], 10[2], 12, 13[3], 14, 17, 20, 35, 39, 47, 48, 49
7:1[2], 3[3], 4[2], 5[2], 6, 8[3], 9, 11, 12, 13, 14[2], 15[2], 19, 20, 21[2], 23, 24, 27, 28[2], 33, 36[2], 39[2], 40, 42, 43[3], 44, 48, 50
8:1, 4, 5, 8[3], 10, 16, 18, 21, 22[2], 23, 24, 25[2], 27, 28[2], 29[3], 30, 31, 32[2], 36, 37, 38, 39, 41[3], 42[2], 48, 49, 50, 51[2], 52, 54, 55, 56
9:1, 2, 3, 7, 9, 10, 11, 13, 14, 16[2], 18[2], 20, 21, 23, 25, 26, 28, 29, 31, 33, 34, 38, 39[2], 42, 43, 48, 49, 50, 51[2], 53, 55, 59[2]
10:1, 2[2], 16[3], 18, 22, 23, 26, 27, 28, 29, 31[2], 32, 33[4], 35[2], 37[2], 38
11:1[2], 2, 5, 7, 8[4], 10, 11[3], 12[2], 14, 15, 17, 22[3], 23[2], 24[2], 25[2], 26, 27, 28, 29, 33, 37[2], 38[2], 40, 46, 53
12:1, 5, 9, 13, 14, 15[2], 16, 17, 18, 21, 22, 28, 36[2], 37[2], 38, 39, 43, 44[2], 46[2], 48, 54, 58
13:6[2], 7, 8, 10, 12, 13, 17, 18, 20, 22, 23, 25, 27, 32, 35
14:1, 4, 7[2], 9, 10[2], 11, 12, 15[2], 16, 25, 26, 28, 29, 31, 32, 33[3], 35
15:3, 4[2], 5[2], 6[2], 11, 12, 14[2], 15[2], 16, 17[2], 20[2], 24, 25[2], 26, 27[2], 28, 29, 31
16:1[2], 2, 5, 6[2], 7[3], 8, 10[2], 13[2], 15, 23, 24[2], 25, 27, 28, 30, 31
17:1, 2[2], 3, 4, 7, 9[2], 11[2], 12, 14[2], 15[2], 16, 19, 20[2], 22, 25, 31[2], 37
18:1, 4[2], 7, 8[2], 9, 14, 15, 21, 22, 23[3], 24[2], 27, 29, 31, 32, 33, 35, 36, 38, 39[2], 40[2], 41, 43
19:2, 3[3], 4[2], 5, 6, 7, 9, 11[2], 12, 13, 15[4], 17, 19, 22, 24, 25, 26, 28[2], 29[2], 32, 36, 37, 40, 41[2], 45, 47
20:1, 2, 3, 5, 9, 10, 11, 12, 16, 17, 19, 23, 25, 28, 30, 37, 38, 41, 44, 45
21:1, 2, 3, 5, 8, 10, 29, 37[2]
22:4[2], 6, 8, 10[2], 12, 13, 14, 15, 17, 19, 22, 25, 26[3], 27[4], 31, 33, 34, 35, 36[3], 37, 38, 39[2], 40[2], 41, 44, 45[2], 47[2], 51, 56, 57, 59, 60, 61, 67, 70
23:2, 3, 5, 6, 7[3], 8[4], 9[2], 13, 17, 22[2], 23, 25[2], 26, 35[2], 42, 46[2], 47, 50, 51, 53
24:6[3], 12, 17, 19, 21, 23, 25, 27, 28[2], 29, 30[2], 31, 32[2], 35, 38, 40[2], 41, 43, 44, 45, 50[2], 51[2]

JOHN
1:8, 10, 11, 12, 15[3], 18, 20, 21[2], 23, 27, 30[2], 31, 33[2], 36[2], 39[2], 41, 42[2], 51
2:5, 8, 12[2], 15[2], 21, 22[2], 23[2], 24, 25
3:3, 4[2], 5, 13, 16, 18[3], 21, 22, 26, 29, 30, 31[3], 32[2], 33, 34, 36[2]
4:3, 4, 5, 10, 18, 25[2], 26, 27, 32, 36[3], 39, 40[2], 43, 45[2], 46, 47[4], 50, 51, 52[2], 54
5:4, 6[2], 11[2], 13, 16, 18, 19[2], 20, 21, 23, 24, 26, 27, 32, 33, 35, 38, 46
6:2, 3, 5, 6[3], 11[2], 12, 15, 20, 29, 31, 33, 35[2], 39, 41, 42, 44[2], 46, 47, 51, 56, 57[2], 58, 59[2], 61, 62, 65, 71[2]
7:1, 4, 9[2], 10, 11, 12[2], 17, 18[2], 25, 26, 27[2], 28[2], 29, 31, 35[2], 36, 38, 39, 50, 51
8:1, 2[2], 6, 7[2], 8, 10, 12, 20, 22[2], 23, 24, 26, 27, 28, 29, 30, 42, 44[4], 47, 51, 52, 54, 56
9:1, 2, 6[3], 7, 8[2], 9[4], 11, 12[2], 15[3], 16, 17[3], 18, 19, 20, 21[3], 22[2], 23, 25[2], 26[2], 27, 29, 30[2], 31, 33, 35[2], 36[2], 37, 38[2]
10:1, 2, 3, 4[2], 6, 9, 12, 13, 20, 35, 39, 40
11:3, 4, 6[4], 7, 9[2], 10, 11[2], 12[2], 13, 17[2], 24, 25[3], 33, 36, 39[2], 43[2], 44, 51[2], 52, 56, 57[2]
12:1, 6[3], 9[2], 14, 17, 18, 25[2], 33[2], 35[2], 37, 38, 40, 41, 44, 45, 48, 49
13:1[2], 3, 4, 5[2], 6, 10, 11[2], 12[2], 16[2], 18, 19, 20[2], 21, 22, 24[2], 25, 26[3], 28, 29, 30, 31
14:9, 10, 12[3], 16[2], 17, 21[3], 23, 24, 26
15:2[2], 5, 6, 16, 23, 26
16:2, 8[2], 13[6], 14[2], 15, 17, 18[2], 23
17:2
18:1[2], 5, 6[2], 7, 8, 9, 13, 14, 17, 22, 25, 30, 32[2], 38[2]
19:7[2], 8, 11, 13, 14, 16, 17, 21, 26[2], 27, 30[2], 33, 35[3], 38[2], 41
20:5[2], 8, 9, 18, 20[2], 22[2], 25, 27
21:1, 6, 7[2], 14, 15[2], 16[3], 17[3], 19[4], 20, 22, 23[2]

THE ACTS
1:2[3], 3, 4, 7, 9[2], 10, 17, 18, 22, 25[2], 26
2:24, 25, 29, 30, 31, 33, 34, 40
3:5, 7, 8, 10, 12, 13, 18, 20, 22
4:9, 32, 35
5:37
6:10
7:2[3], 4[2], 5[4], 8, 10, 12, 15, 21, 23, 24, 25, 26, 27, 29, 31[2], 36[2], 38, 44[3], 55, 60[3]
8:3, 6, 11, 13[2], 16, 18, 19, 27, 31[3], 32[3], 37, 38[2], 39, 40[2]
9:2[2], 3[2], 4, 5, 6, 8, 9, 10, 11, 12, 13, 14, 15, 16, 18, 19[2], 20[2], 21[2], 26[2], 27[3], 28, 29, 32, 33, 34, 38, 39, 41[2], 43
10:3, 4[3], 6[2], 7, 8[2], 10[2], 17, 21, 23, 27[2], 28, 32[2], 35, 36, 39, 41, 42[2], 48
11:13[2], 16, 17, 22, 23, 24, 26[2]
12:2, 3[2], 4[2], 7, 8[2], 9[2], 11, 12[2], 17[3], 19[2], 23[2]
13:11, 12, 17, 18, 19[2], 20, 22[3], 25[2], 28, 31, 33, 34[2], 35, 36, 37
14:9, 10, 12, 17[2], 19, 20[2], 27
15:8, 41
16:1, 10, 18, 27, 29, 33[2], 34[2]
17:16, 17, 18[2], 24, 25[2], 27, 31[5]
18:3[2], 4, 6, 7, 11, 16, 18, 19[2], 20, 21, 22[2], 23[2], 25, 26, 27[2], 28
19:2, 3, 8, 9, 21, 22[2], 25, 31, 34, 35, 41[2]
20:2[2], 3[2], 9, 11[2], 13, 14, 16[2], 17, 18, 28, 35, 36[2], 38
21:4, 11[2], 14, 19[2], 33[2], 34[2], 35[2], 37, 40[2]
22:2[2], 8, 14, 21, 22, 24[2], 26, 27, 29[3], 30[3]
23:5, 6, 7, 15[2], 16, 17, 18, 20, 23, 25, 27, 34[4], 35[2]
24:2, 22, 23[2], 24, 25, 26[3]
25:1, 3, 4, 5, 6[2], 7, 8, 12, 16, 20, 22, 24, 25[2]
26:15, 23, 24, 25, 30, 32
27:6, 35[4]
28:4, 5, 6[2], 15, 17, 23, 29

ROMANS
1:2
2:28, 29
3:26, 29[2]
4:2, 10, 11[3], 12, 13, 17, 18, 19[2], 20, 21[2]
6:7, 10[4]
7:1, 2
8:9, 11, 24, 27[2], 29[3], 30[6], 32[2], 34
9:15, 18[4], 19, 23[2], 24, 25, 28
10:21
11:2[2], 7, 21, 32
12:3, 7, 8[4], 20
13:4[3], 8
14:2, 4[2], 6[7], 9, 18, 22[2], 23[3]
15:10, 12, 21

1 CORINTHIANS
1:31
2:14, 15[2], 16
3:7[2], 8[2], 10, 14[2], 15[2], 18, 19
4:4
5:2
6:16[2], 17, 18
7:13, 20, 22[2], 24, 32[2], 33[2], 36[3], 37[2], 38[2]
8:2[3]
9:10[3]
10:12[2], 22
11:7, 23, 24[2], 25[2], 26, 29
12:11
14:2[2], 3, 4[2], 5[3], 11, 13, 16[2], 24[2], 25
15:4[2], 5, 6, 7, 8, 12, 15[2], 24[2], 25[2], 27[3]
16:10[2], 11, 12[2]

2 CORINTHIANS
1:10, 21
2:2, 5
4:14
5:5, 10, 15, 17, 21
6:2, 15
7:7[2], 15
8:6[2], 9[2], 12, 15[2], 17[2], 23
9:6[2], 7, 9[2], 10
10:7[2], 17, 18
11:4
12:4, 6[2], 9
13:4[2]

GALATIANS
1:4, 23[2]
2:8, 11, 12[2]
3:5[2], 16
4:1[2], 23[2], 29
5:3, 10[2]
6:3[2], 4, 7, 8[2]

EPHESIANS
1:4, 6, 8, 9, 10, 20[2]
2:1, 4, 7, 14, 16
3:3, 11, 16
4:8[3], 9[2], 10[2], 11, 28
5:14, 23, 26, 27, 28
6:8[2], 22

PHILIPPIANS
1:6
2:8, 22, 25, 26[2], 27, 30
3:4[2], 21

COLOSSIANS
1:17, 18[2], 21
2:13, 15, 18
3:25[2]
4:8, 10, 13

1 THESSALONIANS
1:10
3:13
4:8
5:24

2 THESSALONIANS
1:10
2:4[2], 6, 7[2], 14
3:6, 10, 14

1 TIMOTHY
1:12
3:1, 5, 6, 7[2]
5:8
6:4, 15

2 TIMOTHY
1:12, 16, 17[2], 18[2]
2:4, 5[2], 12, 13[2], 21
4:11, 15

TITUS
1:9[2]
2:8, 14
3:5, 6, 11

PHILEMON
13, 15, 18

HEBREWS
1:2[2], 3, 4, 5[2], 6[2], 7, 8, 13
2:5, 8[2], 9, 11[2], 14[2], 16[2], 17, 18[2]
3:3, 4, 17, 18
4:3, 4, 7, 8, 10[2]
5:1, 2, 3, 4, 5, 6, 7[2], 8[3], 9, 13
6:13[2], 15[2]
7:6, 8[2], 10, 13, 17, 20, 24, 25[2], 27[2]
8:4[2], 5[2], 6[2], 8, 13[2]
9:7, 12, 15, 19, 21, 25, 26[2], 28
10:5[2], 8, 9[3], 12, 14, 15, 20, 23, 28, 29[2], 37
11:4[3], 5[3], 6[3], 7, 8[4], 9, 10, 16, 17[2], 19, 21, 22, 23[2], 24, 26, 27[2], 28[2]
12:6[2], 7, 10, 17[4], 26
13:5, 12, 23

JAMES
1:6, 7, 9, 10[2], 12[2], 13[2], 14, 18, 23, 24[2], 25
2:5, 10, 11, 13, 14, 21, 23
4:6[2], 7, 8, 10, 11
5:6, 7, 15, 17, 18, 20

1 PETER
1:15
2:6, 7, 23[3]
3:10, 13, 18, 19
4:1, 2, 14[2]
5:6, 7, 8

2 PETER
1:9[2], 17
2:19

1 JOHN
1:7, 9
2:2, 4, 6[3], 9[2], 10, 11[2], 17, 22[2], 23, 25, 28, 29
3:2[2], 3, 5, 7[2], 8[2], 9[2], 10, 12, 14, 16, 23, 24[4]
4:4[2], 6[2], 8, 10, 13[2], 15, 16, 17, 18, 19, 20[5], 21
5:5[2], 6, 9, 10[3], 12[2], 14, 15, 16[3], 18

2 JOHN
9[2], 11

3 JOHN
10[2], 11[2]

JUDE
6, 9

REVELATION
1:1, 2, 3, 7, 16, 17, 18
2:1, 7, 11[2], 12, 17[2], 23, 26, 27, 29
3:1, 5, 6, 7[4], 12, 13, 20, 22
4:3
5:7, 8
6:2[2], 3, 5[2], 7, 9, 12
7:2, 14, 15
8:1, 3
9:2, 5
10:2[3], 3, 7[2], 9, 11
11:5, 15
12:9, 12[2], 13[2], 15
13:6, 10[2], 11[2], 12, 13[2], 14, 15, 16, 17
14:4, 10, 16, 17
16:15[2], 16
17:3, 10[2], 11, 14, 15
18:2, 22
19:2, 9[2], 10, 11[2], 12[2], 13, 15[3], 16, 17, 20
20:2, 3[2], 6
21:3, 5[2], 6, 7[2], 10, 15, 16, 17
22:1, 6, 7, 9, 10, 11[4], 20

HER

846

GENESIS
2:22
3:6[2], 15
4:11, 12
8:9[3], 11
12:15[2], 16, 19[2]
16:2, 3[3], 4[2], 5, 6[3], 7, 9[2], 10, 11, 13
17:15[2], 16[4]
19:33
20:4, 6, 7, 13
21:10, 12, 14[2], 16[2], 17, 19
23:2
24:15[2], 16[2], 17, 18[2], 20, 21, 22, 28, 43, 45[3], 46[2], 47[3], 51[2], 53[2], 55[2], 57, 58, 59, 60, 61, 64, 67[3]
25:1, 22, 23, 24[2]
26:9
27:6, 15[3], 17, 42[2]
29:9, 12[2], 19[2], 20, 21, 23[2], 27, 28, 29, 31
30:1, 3[2], 4[2], 9[2], 15, 16, 21, 22[2]
31:19, 35
33:2, 7
34:2[4], 8, 11[2]
35:17, 18, 20
38:2[2], 8, 11, 14[3], 15[3], 16, 18[2], 19[3], 20, 22, 23[3], 24[2], 25, 26[2], 27[2]
39:7, 10[3], 12, 13, 14, 16
40:10
48:7

EXODUS
2:5[2], 8, 9, 10
3:22[3]
4:25
11:2
15:20[2]
18:2, 3, 6[2]
21:4[2], 8[5], 9[2], 10[3], 11, 22[2]
22:16[2], 17[2]

LEVITICUS
11:19
12:2, 4[2], 5[2], 6, 7[3], 8
15:19[3], 20, 21, 23, 24[2], 25[5], 26[4], 28, 29, 30[2], 33[3]
18:7, 11, 15, 17[5], 18[4], 19[2], 20, 25
19:20, 29
20:14, 17, 18[4]
21:3, 7, 9, 13
22:13[3], 28
25:19, 22
26:4, 20, 34[2], 43

NUMBERS
5:13[3], 15[2], 16[2], 18, 19, 24, 27[6], 29, 30, 31
12:12, 13, 14[4]
16:30, 32
19:3[3], 4[2], 5[4], 8
22:23, 25, 33
25:8
26:10, 59
30:3[2], 4[8], 5[8], 6[2], 7[5], 8[6], 9[2], 10[2], 11[5], 12[6], 13[2], 14[6], 15, 16[2]
36:8

DEUTERONOMY
11:6, 17
14:18
20:7[2]
21:11[2], 12[3], 13[6], 14[5]
22:13[2], 14[4], 15, 16, 17, 19, 21[4], 23[2], 25[3], 27[2], 28[2], 29[3]
24:1[5], 3[5], 4[3]
25:5[4], 8, 11[2], 12[2]
28:30, 56[5], 57[3]
32:11[4], 22

JOSHUA
2:14, 15, 17
6:17, 22, 23[4], 25
8:2[3]
10:1[2], 39
13:17
15:18[3], 19, 45[2], 47[4]
17:11[6], 16
21:13[2], 14[2], 15[2], 16[3], 17[2], 18[2], 21[2], 22[2], 23[2], 24[2], 25[2], 27[2], 28[2], 29[2], 30[2], 31[2], 32[3], 34[2], 35[2], 36[2], 37[2], 38[2], 39[2]

JUDGES
1:14[3], 15, 27[5]
4:5, 8, 18, 19, 20, 21, 22
5:26[2], 27[2], 29[2]
11:26[2], 34, 35, 37, 38[3], 39[2]
13:3, 6, 9[2], 10, 13, 14[3]
14:2, 3, 8, 16, 17[2]
15:1, 2[6], 6[3]
16:1, 5[2], 7, 8, 9, 11, 13, 16, 17[2], 18[2], 19
19:2, 3[5], 25[4], 26, 27[2], 28[2], 29[3]
20:6[2]

RUTH
1:3, 5[2], 6, 7[2], 8[2], 9, 10, 14[2], 15[2], 18[2], 22[2]
2:1, 2, 3, 10, 11, 14[2], 15[2], 16[2], 18[2], 19[3], 20[2], 22, 23
3:1[2], 5, 6[2], 7, 15, 16[3]
4:13[2], 16, 17

1 SAMUEL
1:4[2], 5, 6[4], 7, 8[2], 12, 13[3], 14, 18[2], 19, 22, 23[3], 24
2:19
4:19[4], 20[3], 21[2]
18:17, 21
25:19[2], 20, 23, 35[2], 39, 40, 41, 42
28:7[2], 10, 13, 14

2 SAMUEL
3:15[2], 16[3]
6:16, 23
11:4[4], 26[2], 27
12:24[2]
13:1, 2, 5, 6, 8, 10, 11[2], 14[3], 15[4], 16, 17, 18[3], 19[5], 20[3]
14:2, 3, 4, 5
17:8
20:17, 22
21:10

1 KINGS
1:2[3], 3, 4, 31
2:19[2], 20
3:1, 17, 20[2], 26[3], 27
9:24[2]
10:2, 3[3], 5, 13[4]

1 KINGS
14:5^2, 6
15:13^2
17:10, 11, 13, 15, 19^2, 20
21:6

2 KINGS
4:2, 5^3, 6^2, 9, 12, 13, 14^2, 15^2, 17, 20, 22, 24, 25, 26^2, 27^4, 30, 36, 37
5:3
6:28, 29^2
8:2, 3^2, 5^3, 6
9:10, 22, 30^2, 33^4, 34, 35^3
11:1, 3, 14, 15^3, 16
19:21
22:14

1 CHRONICLES
2:18
5:16
6:57, 58^2, 59^2, 60^3, 67^2, 68^2, 69^2, 70^2, 71^2, 72^2, 73^2, 74^2, 75^2, 76^3, 77^2, 78^2, 79^2, 80^2, 81^2
7:29^4
15:29
18:1

2 CHRONICLES
8:11
9:1, 2^3, 4, 12^3
11:20
15:16^2
22:10
23:13, 14^3, 15^2
34:22
36:21

ESTHER
1:11, 19
2:1, 7, 9^6, 10^3, 11, 13^2, 14, 15^2, 17^2, 20^3
4:4^2, 5, 8^3
5:1, 3, 12
8:1

JOB
2:10
5:16
9:6
21:10
31:10, 18
39:14, 16^2, 17^2, 26, 27, 29, 30

PSALMS
34:2
45:13, 14^2
46:5^2
48:3, 12, 13^2
55:11

PSALMS
58:4
67:6
68:13, 31
69:15
80:11^2, 12^2
84:3
85:12
87:5^2
102:13, 14
104:17
107:42
123:2
132:15^2, 16^2
137:5

PROVERBS
1:20, 21
2:4^2, 16, 17^2, 18^2, 19
3:15, 16^2, 17^2, 18^2
4:6^2, 8^2, 13^2
5:3, 4, 5^2, 6, 8^2, 19^3
6:6, 8^2, 25^3, 29
7:5, 8^2, 11^2, 21^2, 22, 25^2, 26, 27
8:1
9:1^2, 2^3, 3, 14, 18
12:4
14:1^2
17:12, 25
27:8, 16
30:20, 23, 28
31:10, 11^2, 12, 13, 14, 15^2, 16, 17^2, 18^2, 19^2, 20^2, 21^2, 22, 23, 25, 26^2, 27, 28^4, 31^4

ECCLESIASTES
7:26^3
11:5

SONG OF SOLOMON
2:13
3:4
6:9^6
8:5, 9^2

ISAIAH
1:27
3:26
4:5
5:14
7:16
9:1^2
10:11^2
13:10, 13, 22^2
16:8
21:9
23:3, 7^2, 17, 18^3
24:2
26:17^2, 21^2
27:2

ISAIAH
29:7^3
34:12, 13, 15^3, 16
37:22
40:2^4
49:15^2
51:3^3, 18^2
52:11
53:7
61:10, 11
65:18, 19
66:7, 8, 10^4, 11^2, 12^3

JEREMIAH
2:23, 24^6, 32^2
3:1, 7, 8^3, 9, 10^2, 20
4:17, 31^3
5:10^2
6:3^2, 4, 5, 6, 7^3
8:7, 19^2
9:20
12:7, 9
15:9
17:8^2
19:15
20:17
30:18
31:8, 15^2
44:17, 18, 19^4, 25
46:21^2, 22, 23
48:4, 15, 19, 28, 41
49:2, 4, 14, 19^2, 22, 24^2, 26^2
50:2^2, 3^2, 9, 10, 13, 14, 15^6, 26^5, 27, 29^3, 30^2, 35^2, 36, 37^2, 38, 44^2
51:2^3, 3^2, 4, 6^2, 7, 8^2, 9^2, 27^3, 28, 30^2, 33^2, 36^2, 43, 45, 47^3, 48, 52^2, 53^2, 55^2, 56^2, 57^5, 58, 64

LAMENTATIONS
1:2^7, 3^2, 4^3, 5^5, 6^2, 7^7, 8^3, 9^3, 10^2, 11, 17^2
2:5, 7, 9^5, 16
4:6, 7, 13^3

EZEKIEL
5:5, 6
12:19
13:16
16:2, 32, 44, 45^2, 46^2, 48, 49^2, 53^2, 55^2, 57
17:7^3, 9
19:2, 3, 5^2, 11^3, 12^2, 14^2
22:2^2, 3, 10, 24, 25^2, 26, 27, 28
23:4, 5^2, 7, 8^5, 9^2, 10^5, 11^5, 12, 14, 16, 17^3, 18^4, 19^2, 31, 42, 43^2, 44
24:7^2, 8, 12^3
26:4^4, 6, 17
28:22^2, 23^4

EZEKIEL
29:12, 19^3
30:4^2, 6, 7, 8, 18^5
31:4^2
32:7, 16^4, 18, 20^2, 22, 23^2, 24^2, 25^3, 26^2, 29^2
33:28
34:27^2
36:38
44:22

DANIEL
11:6^3, 7, 17

HOSEA
1:6
2:2^6, 3^5, 4, 6, 7, 8^2, 9, 10^3, 11^5, 12^2, 13^4, 14^3, 15^3, 17, 23^2
3:1, 2, 3
4:18, 19^2
9:2, 10
10:7, 11, 14
13:8, 16

JOEL
1:8
2:16, 22
3:17

AMOS
4:3
5:2^2

OBADIAH
1

JONAH
1:15
2:6

MICAH
1:9
4:6^3, 7^2, 11
7:5, 6^2, 10^2

NAHUM
2:7^2, 13
3:4^2, 7, 8, 9, 10^3

ZEPHANIAH
2:14, 15^2
3:1, 2, 3^3, 4^2, 19^2

HAGGAI
1:10
2:3

ZECHARIAH
2:5^2
5:11

ZECHARIAH
7:7
8:2, 12^2
9:4^2, 5
12:6
14:10

MALACHI
3:11

MATTHEW
1:6, 19^3, 20, 25^2
2:18
5:28^2, 31, 32^2
8:15^2
9:18, 22, 25
10:35^2
11:19
14:4, 7, 8, 9, 11
15:23^2, 28^2
19:7, 9
20:20, 21
21:2
22:28
23:37^2
24:29
26:13

MARK
1:30, 31^3
5:23, 29^2, 32, 33, 34, 41, 43
6:17, 23, 24, 26, 28
7:26, 27, 29, 30^2
10:4, 11, 12
12:21, 22, 23, 44^2
13:24, 28
14:5, 6^2, 9
16:11

LUKE
1:5, 28, 29, 30, 35, 36^2, 38, 41, 45, 56^2, 58^4, 61
2:7, 19, 22, 36, 51
4:38, 39^2
7:12, 13^3, 35, 38, 44, 47, 48
8:43, 44, 48, 52, 54, 55^2, 56
10:38, 40, 41, 42
11:27
12:53^2
13:12^3, 13, 34^2
15:9^2
16:18^2
18:5^2
20:30, 31, 33
21:4

JOHN
2:4
4:7, 10, 13, 16, 17, 21, 26, 27, 28^2

JOHN
8:3, 7, 10, 11
11:1, 2, 5, 23, 25, 28^2, 31^3, 33^2, 40
12:3, 7
16:21
18:16
19:27
20:13, 15, 16, 17, 18

THE ACTS
5:8, 9, 10^4
7:21
8:27
9:37, 40, 41^3
12:15
16:15, 16, 18, 19
19:27
21:3
27:15, 32

ROMANS
7:2^2, 3^2
9:12, 25
16:2^2

1 CORINTHIANS
7:2, 4, 10, 11^2, 12, 13^2, 34, 36, 38^2, 39^2
11:5^2, 6^2, 10, 15^3
13:5

GALATIANS
4:25, 30

EPHESIANS
5:33

1 THESSALONIANS
2:7

JAMES
1:4
5:18

2 PETER
2:22

2 JOHN
1

REVELATION
2:21^2, 22^2, 23
6:13
12:1^2, 4, 5, 6, 14, 15, 16, 17
14:8, 18
16:19
17:2, 4^2, 5, 6, 7, 16^3
18:3^3, 4^3, 5^2, 6^4, 7^2, 8^2, 9^4, 10, 11, 15^2, 18, 19, 20^2, 24
19:2^2, 3, 8
21:2, 11
22:2

HIM

846

GENESIS
1:27
2:15, 18^2, 20
3:9, 23
4:7, 8, 15^4, 19, 26
5:1, 24
6:6, 22
7:5, 7, 16^2, 23
8:1, 8, 9^2, 11, 12, 18
9:8, 24
10:21
12:3, 4^2, 7, 20^2
13:1, 11, 14
14:5, 17^2, 19, 20
15:4, 5^2, 6, 7, 9, 10, 12
16:1, 12, 13
17:1, 3, 17, 19^2, 20^4, 22, 23, 27
18:1, 2, 9, 10, 18, 19^3, 29, 30
19:3, 5, 6, 16^3, 21, 26, 30, 32, 34^2, 35
20:3, 6, 9, 14
21:2, 3^2, 4, 5, 7, 16^2, 18^2, 21
22:1, 2, 3^2, 9^2, 11, 12, 13^2
23:5, 14
24:5, 6, 9, 18, 19, 24, 25, 32, 33, 35, 36, 47, 54
25:2, 9, 21, 33
26:2, 7, 9, 12, 14, 20, 24, 26, 31, 32^2
27:1^2, 12, 13, 22, 23^2, 25^2, 26, 27^2, 32, 33, 37^3, 39, 41, 42, 44, 45
28:1^3, 6^4
29:5, 13^4, 14^2, 20, 23, 28, 30, 34
30:4, 16, 20, 27, 29, 37
31:2, 7, 14, 15, 20, 23^3, 24, 32
32:1, 3, 6, 7, 11, 19, 20, 21, 24, 25^2, 27, 29^2, 31
33:1, 4^3, 11, 13, 17
34:6, 8
35:2, 6, 7, 9, 10, 11, 13^2, 14, 15, 18, 26, 29
36:5
37:3, 4^3, 5, 8^2, 10^2, 11, 13, 14^2, 15^2, 18^3, 20^3, 21^2, 22^4, 23, 24^2, 27^2, 33, 35^2, 36
38:5, 7, 10, 14, 18
39:1^2, 3, 4^2, 5, 12^2, 15, 17, 19, 20^2, 21^2, 23
40:7, 8, 9, 12, 23
41:12, 13, 14, 33, 34, 42, 43^3, 45, 50
42:4, 6, 8, 10, 16, 24, 29, 31, 37^3, 38
43:3, 5, 7, 9^4, 19, 26^2, 32^2, 33, 34^2

GENESIS
44:7, 9, 14, 18, 20, 21^2, 24, 28, 29, 32
45:1^2, 3, 9, 15, 26, 27^2, 28
46:5, 6, 7^2, 20, 27, 28, 29, 31
47:7, 18^2, 29, 31
48:1, 10, 13, 17
49:9, 10, 19, 23^3, 26
50:1^2, 3^2, 7, 9, 12, 13^2, 14, 15, 17, 26

EXODUS
1:16
2:2^2, 3^2, 4, 6, 10^2, 12, 13, 20, 22
3:2, 4, 18
4:2, 6, 11, 13, 15, 16, 18, 23, 24^2, 26, 27^2, 28^2
6:2, 20^2, 23^2, 25^2
7:16
8:1, 20
9:1, 13, 29
10:1, 3, 7, 28
12:4, 44, 48, 49
13:14, 19
14:6
15:2^2, 25
16:8
17:10, 12
18:7, 17
19:3, 7, 19, 24
20:7
21:3, 4^2, 6^3, 10, 13, 14^2, 16, 19^2, 22, 26, 27, 29, 30^2, 31, 36
22:2, 3^2, 7, 12, 13, 17, 21, 25^2, 26
23:4, 5^3, 21^3
24:2, 14, 18
28:1, 3, 41, 43^2
29:5, 7, 17, 21^2, 29
30:21
31:3, 6, 18
32:1^2, 23, 26^2, 33
33:4, 15
34:4, 5, 6, 20, 29, 30, 31, 32, 34, 35
35:5, 21, 31
36:2, 3
38:23
40:13^2, 16

LEVITICUS
1:1, 3, 4^2
4:3, 12, 14, 19, 21, 26^2, 31^2, 35
5:2, 3, 4, 6, 10^2, 13^2, 16^2, 18^2
6:2, 4, 5, 7^2

LEVITICUS
7:18, 20
8:2, 4, 7^6, 8, 12^2, 30^2
9:9, 12, 13, 18
13:3^2, 4, 5^2, 6^2, 8, 10, 11^2, 12, 13, 14, 15, 17^2, 20, 21, 22, 23, 25, 26, 27^2, 28, 30, 31, 33, 34, 36, 37, 44, 46
14:4, 7^2, 11, 12, 14, 17, 18^2, 19, 20, 21, 25, 28, 29^2, 31, 32
15:7, 8, 10, 14, 15, 16, 24, 32^3, 33^2
16:9, 10^2, 21^2, 22
17:10
18:6
19:13^2, 17, 22^2, 33, 34
20:2, 3, 4, 5^2, 6, 9
21:2, 3, 8, 12, 15, 17
22:3, 4
24:9, 11, 12, 14^3, 16, 19, 20, 23^2
25:27, 28^2, 30, 35, 36, 37^2, 39, 41, 43, 47, 48, 49^3, 50^4, 52^2, 53^2, 54
26:46
27:8^2, 18, 19, 23, 24^2

NUMBERS
2:5, 12, 20, 27
3:6, 9, 42
4:49
5:7, 8, 12, 14^2, 30
6:9, 11
7:89^3
8:2
9:7, 14
10:30
11:20, 25^2, 29, 30
12:6^2, 8
13:27, 31
14:24^2, 36
15:28^2, 29^2, 31, 33^2, 34^2, 35, 36^2
16:5^4, 10, 11, 25, 40
17:6, 11
19:13^2, 18, 20
20:9, 18, 19, 20, 21
21:24, 34^3, 35^2
22:5, 7, 16, 20, 22^2, 32, 36, 40, 41
23:4, 6, 9^2, 13, 14, 17^3, 21
24:2, 8, 9, 17^2, 19
25:12, 13
26:54
27:11, 18, 19^2, 20, 21^2, 22^2, 23^2
31:17, 18, 35
32:15, 16, 21

NUMBERS
35:16, 17, 18, 19^2, 20^2, 21^3, 22^2, 23^2, 25, 27, 30, 32, 33

DEUTERONOMY
1:3, 16, 36, 38
2:24, 30^2, 33^2
3:2^3, 3^2, 28^2
4:7, 20, 25, 29^2, 34, 35, 42
5:11
6:13, 16
7:9, 10^4
8:6
9:18, 20, 23
10:8, 9, 12, 18, 20^2
11:13, 22
13:4^3, 8^4, 9^3, 10
14:27
15:8^2, 9, 10^2, 12, 13^2, 14^2, 18
17:7^2, 15, 18, 19
18:4, 5^2, 15, 18, 19, 20, 22
19:6^3, 11^3, 12^2, 13, 16, 19
20:5, 6, 7, 8
21:1, 2, 5, 15, 17, 18, 19^2, 21, 22, 23
22:2^2, 4, 18, 19, 26
23:10, 16^2
24:1, 7^2, 13, 15
25:2, 3^2, 5, 8^2, 9, 10, 11^3
26:3
28:44, 55
29:15^2, 20^2, 21
30:20
31:7, 14, 29
32:10^4, 12^2, 13^2, 15, 16^2
33:7^3, 9, 11^2, 12^2, 16^2, 24^2
34:1, 4, 6, 9^2, 11

JOSHUA
1:18
2:19, 23
4:14
5:3, 13^3, 14
6:5, 7, 20
7:3, 19, 24, 25, 26
8:11, 14, 23
9:6, 9^2
10:7, 15, 23, 24, 29, 31, 33^2, 34, 36, 38, 43
11:7, 9
13:1
14:6, 7, 13
15:16, 17, 18^2
19:50
20:4^2, 5^2

JOSHUA
22:5^2, 14, 27, 30
24:3^2, 14, 22, 30, 33^2

JUDGES
1:3, 5, 6^2, 7, 12, 13, 14^2, 15, 24
2:9
3:10, 13, 15, 16, 19^2, 20, 23, 27, 28, 31
4:6, 7, 10, 13, 14, 18^2, 19^2, 21, 22^2
5:13, 25, 31
6:12^2, 13, 14, 15, 16, 17, 19, 20, 23, 25, 27, 31^5, 32^2, 34, 35
7:1, 3, 5, 8, 9, 19
8:1^2, 3, 4, 8^2, 14^2, 31
9:3, 4^2, 16, 19, 24, 25, 26, 28^2, 33, 34, 35, 36, 38^2, 40^2, 44, 48^3, 54^3
10:3, 6
11:2^2, 3, 11, 15, 19, 28, 34, 36
12:5, 6^3, 8, 11, 13
13:6, 10, 11, 12, 18, 23, 24, 25
14:3, 5, 6^2, 11^2, 13, 16, 17^2, 18, 19
15:1, 10, 12, 13^3, 14^2
16:2^3, 5^4, 8, 9, 12^2, 14, 15, 16^2, 19^4, 20, 21^3, 24, 25, 26, 31^3
17:9^2, 10, 11
18:3, 5, 15, 19, 25, 26
19:1, 2^2, 3^4, 4^2, 7, 9, 10^2, 12, 15, 18, 21, 22, 25, 28
20:23
21:5

RUTH
2:2, 4, 10
3:13
4:1, 15

1 SAMUEL
1:11, 17, 20, 22, 23^2, 24^3, 27, 28
2:3, 16^2, 19^2, 25^2, 27, 28, 35, 36
3:7, 13, 18^4, 19
5:3, 4
6:3, 4, 8
7:3, 9
8:5, 10, 12
9:5, 6, 13^2, 16, 17
10:1, 9, 10^2, 11, 14, 16, 19, 21, 23, 24^2, 26, 27^2
11:3, 5
12:14, 24
13:2, 7, 8, 10^2, 14^2, 15^2
14:2, 7, 13^2, 17, 20, 34, 37, 39, 43, 52^2

1 SAMUEL
15:2, 12, 13, 16, 28, 32
16:1, 3, 6, 7, 8, 11, 12^2, 13, 14, 15, 17, 18, 21^2, 23
17:7, 8, 9^2, 13, 20, 24, 25^3, 26, 27^2, 30^2, 31, 32, 33, 35^5, 38, 39, 40, 41, 42, 50, 51, 57^2, 58
18:1, 2^2, 3, 4, 5^2, 8, 12, 13^3, 14, 15, 17^2, 20, 21^3, 24, 27, 28
19:4, 7, 8, 11^3, 15^2, 18^2, 23
20:2, 7, 17^2, 24, 26, 30, 31, 32, 33^2, 34, 35, 36, 40
21:1, 5, 6, 11^2, 14
22:1, 2^2, 4, 6^2, 7, 10^3, 13^3, 15, 17
23:3, 4, 7, 9, 14^2, 17, 20, 22, 23, 25
24:1, 4^2, 5, 6, 8, 19
25:1^2, 5, 6, 12, 17, 21, 22, 25, 35, 36^2, 37^2, 39, 40
26:2, 3, 5, 7, 8^2, 9, 10, 19, 24
27:2, 4, 6, 12
28:3^2, 6, 7, 8^2, 9, 17, 20, 21, 23
29:3, 4^4, 6
30:4, 6, 8, 9, 11^3, 12^2, 13, 15, 16, 21
31:3, 5

2 SAMUEL
1:3^2, 4, 5, 6^2, 7, 8, 10^2, 11, 13, 14, 15^2, 16
2:1, 3, 5, 8, 9, 20, 21^2, 23^2, 32
3:9, 11, 16, 20^2, 22, 23^2, 24, 26, 27^3, 31, 34
4:4, 6, 7^3, 10^3
5:10, 12, 13, 14, 25
6:2, 7, 10, 12, 16
7:1, 14, 15, 23
8:4, 10^4, 13
9:1, 2^2, 3, 4, 5, 7, 9, 10
10:2, 9, 12, 13^2, 17
11:1, 4, 7^2, 8, 13^3, 15, 21, 22, 25, 27
12:1^2, 3^2, 4^2, 9, 17^2, 18^3, 20, 21, 23^2, 24
13:2, 4^2, 5^2, 6, 7, 9^2, 11, 12, 16, 17, 25^2, 26, 27^2, 28, 29, 34
14:3, 6, 7^2, 10, 14, 24^2, 25, 26, 29^2, 31, 32, 33
15:1^2, 2, 3, 4, 5^4, 9, 14, 16, 17, 18^2, 22, 24, 26^2, 30, 32
16:1, 10^2, 11^3, 13^2, 14, 15, 18
17:2^3, 6, 10, 12^4, 16, 22, 23, 24, 29
18:1, 9, 11^3, 15, 17^2, 19, 20, 23, 30

2 SAMUEL

19:17[2], 23, 25, 29, 30, 31, 37[2], 38, 39, 40, 41
20:5, 6[2], 7, 8, 9, 10[2], 11[2], 12[2], 14, 15, 17, 21
21:4, 15, 17[3], 21
22:1, 3, 12, 13, 24, 31
23:9, 10, 11, 21[2], 23
24:2, 10, 13[3], 16, 18, 20, 22

1 KINGS

1:1, 2[2], 4, 5[2], 6[2], 7, 13, 17, 20, 25, 27, 33, 34, 35[2], 38, 40, 41, 42, 44[2], 45, 52[2], 53[2]
2:8, 9[2], 16, 19, 22[2], 25, 29, 30, 31[3], 34[2], 36, 42, 46
3:6[2], 11, 16, 28
4:10, 12, 13[2], 24
5:1, 3, 12
8:5[2], 24, 25, 31[2], 32, 57, 58, 62, 65
9:2, 3, 12[2]
10:1, 2
11:9, 10, 17, 18[3], 19, 20, 22, 23, 24, 28, 29, 30, 34
12:1, 3, 7, 8[3], 10[2], 13, 18[2], 20[2]
13:4[3], 6, 11, 13, 14[2], 15, 18[3], 19, 20, 23, 24[2], 26[5], 27, 29, 30, 31, 33
14:3, 10[2], 11[2], 13[3], 14, 18[2], 22
15:3, 4[2], 5, 8, 27[2], 28, 29
16:4[2], 7[2], 9, 10[2], 11, 17, 18, 21, 25, 30, 31[2], 33
17:2, 6, 8, 17, 19[3], 21, 22, 23[2]
18:7[2], 8, 15, 16, 17, 21[3], 24, 30, 33
19:5[2], 6, 7, 9[2], 13, 15, 17[2], 18, 19[3], 20, 21[2]
20:1, 2, 7, 8[2], 9, 10, 11[2], 16, 17, 22, 23, 31, 33[4], 34[3], 35, 36[4], 37[2], 40, 41, 42
21:4[2], 5[2], 6, 7, 10[4], 13[4], 19[2], 21[2], 24[2]
22:7, 8, 11, 13, 15[2], 16, 19, 21, 22[2], 26, 27, 32, 33, 53

2 KINGS

1:5, 6[2], 8, 9[3], 10, 11[2], 12, 13[2], 15[3], 16
2:2, 3, 4, 5, 6, 12, 13, 14, 15[3], 16[3], 17[2], 18, 20, 23[2]
3:11, 12[2], 13, 15, 26[2], 27[2]
4:1, 5, 8, 10, 12, 13, 19, 20[2], 21[2], 23, 27, 29[2], 31[2], 35, 36, 38
5:1, 3, 5, 6, 8, 10, 13, 15, 16, 19[2], 20[2], 21[3], 23[2], 25, 26
6:6, 10[2], 13[2], 15, 18, 26, 28, 29[2], 31, 32[5], 33
7:17[2], 20[2]
8:6, 7, 8, 9[3], 10[2], 14, 19[2], 21[2], 29
9:1, 2[2], 6, 8[2], 11, 13, 15, 17, 18, 21, 25[2], 26, 27[2], 28[2], 32, 36
10:3, 4, 7, 8, 9, 11, 15[6], 16, 17, 18, 22, 24[2], 35
11:2[3], 4, 8, 12[4], 15
12:2, 21[2]
13:4, 9, 14, 15[2], 19, 20, 25
14:19[3], 20, 21
15:7, 10[3], 14, 16, 19, 25[4], 30[2]
16:5, 9
17:2, 3[2], 4[2], 17, 27, 36[3]
18:5[3], 6, 7[2], 15, 21, 36[2], 37
19:3, 7[2], 16, 21, 37
20:1[2], 4, 14
21:6, 11, 23
22:18
23:1, 2, 17, 18, 25[4], 26, 29[3], 30[5], 33
24:1, 2, 12
25:5[2], 6[2], 7[2], 25[2], 28[2], 29, 30

1 CHRONICLES

2:3[2], 4, 9, 19[2], 21, 24, 29, 35
3:1, 4, 5
4:6, 9, 10
5:2, 20
7:22
9:20
10:3, 9, 14
11:9, 10[2], 11, 12, 23[2], 25, 42
12:19, 20, 22, 23, 27
13:10
14:1, 2, 10, 14, 16, 17
15:1, 2, 13, 27, 29
16:5, 9[2], 29, 30
17:13[2], 14, 25
18:4, 10[3]
19:2[3], 10, 14[2], 17
20:7
21:11, 12, 15, 20, 26, 28
22:6, 9
23:13
24:19
26:5, 10
27:7
28:6, 9[3]
29:22, 23, 25[2], 30

2 CHRONICLES

1:1[2], 3, 7
2:3[2], 4[2], 6[4], 14, 15
5:6
6:15, 16, 22[2], 23
7:8, 12
8:18
9:1
10:1, 3, 7, 8[3], 10[2], 18[2]
11:13, 15, 18, 19, 20, 22
12:1, 3, 12[2]
13:3, 5, 7, 10, 11, 19, 20
14:1, 5, 6, 7, 10, 13
15:2[4], 4, 5[2], 9[2], 15
16:7, 9, 10[2], 14[3]
17:11, 14, 15[2], 16[2], 17, 18[2]
18:2[4], 3, 6, 7, 10, 12, 14, 15, 20[2], 21, 25, 26, 30, 31[3], 32
19:2
20:30, 36
21:7, 9[2], 12, 17, 18, 19, 20
22:6, 9[4], 11[4]
23:1, 11[4], 14, 16
24:3, 6, 16, 21[2], 22, 23, 25[6], 26, 27
25:3, 7, 10, 13, 15[2], 16[2], 23, 27[3], 28[2]
26:1, 5, 7, 17[2], 18, 20[3], 23
27:5[2], 9
28:5[3], 16, 20[3], 21, 23[2], 24, 27[2]
29:6, 11[3], 29
30:9
31:10, 15
32:3, 6, 7[2], 9, 15, 17, 21, 24[2], 25[2], 29[2], 31[3], 33[2]
33:6, 11[2], 13[3], 18, 19, 20, 24[2]
34:26
35:20, 21, 22[2], 24[3]
36:1, 3, 4, 6[3], 8, 10, 13, 17, 20, 23[3]

EZRA

1:2, 3[2], 4
4:2, 6, 11
5:7, 15
6:11
7:6[2], 9, 26
8:3, 4, 5, 6, 7, 8, 9, 10, 11, 12, 19, 21, 22[2], 33
10:1

NEHEMIAH

1:5, 11
2:1, 6[2]
3:2, 8[2], 10, 12, 16, 17[2], 18, 19, 20, 21, 22, 23[2], 24, 25, 29, 30[2], 31
4:3
6:8, 12[2], 18, 19
8:4
9:7[3], 8
11:8
13:5, 7, 26[3], 28

ESTHER

1:3, 12, 14, 17, 19
2:2, 9[2], 20
3:1[2], 2[3], 4, 5, 6
4:4, 5, 7[2], 8[3], 10, 11, 17
5:4, 9, 11[2], 14
6:3[2], 4, 5[2], 6, 9[2], 11[2], 13[4], 14
7:7, 9
8:3, 7
10:2

JOB

1:2, 8, 10
2:3[3], 8, 9, 11[3], 12, 13[2]
3:20
4:4
6:10, 14
7:8, 10, 17[2], 18[2]
8:4, 18[2]
9:3[2], 4, 11[2], 12[2], 13, 14[2], 32, 34, 35
11:10, 13
12:4, 5, 13, 16
13:7, 9, 15[2], 16
14:6, 20[2], 22[2]
15:21, 24[2], 26, 31
18:6, 7, 9[2], 10[2], 11[2], 14, 20, 21
19:11, 16, 28
20:7, 9[3], 11, 14, 16, 22, 23[2], 24, 25, 26[2], 27, 29
21:15[2], 19, 21, 31, 33[3]
22:3, 14, 21, 27
23:3, 4, 7, 8, 9[2], 13, 14, 15
24:1, 10, 20[2], 23
25:2
26:2, 3, 6, 14
27:9, 15, 20[2], 21[2], 22, 23[2]
29:12[2], 13
30:25
31:14, 15, 29[2], 37[2]
32:13, 14
33:13, 23, 24[2], 26
34:11, 13, 17, 19, 27, 28, 29
35:6[2], 7, 14[3]
36:11, 22, 23, 26
37:16, 18, 19, 20, 23, 24
39:11[2], 12, 20, 23
40:2[2], 9, 11, 12, 19[2], 20, 22[2]
41:4, 5[2], 6[2], 8, 9[2], 10, 11, 13, 22, 26[2], 28[2], 30, 32
42:8, 11[6]

PSALMS

2:12
3:2
4:3[2]
5:12
7:4[2], 5, 13
8:4[2], 5[2], 6
10:9
11:5
12:5[3]
13:4
17:13[2]
18:t, 6, 11, 12, 23, 30
20:6
21:2, 3, 4, 5, 6[2]
22:8[4], 23[3], 24[2], 25, 26, 29, 30
24:6
25:12, 14
28:7[2]
32:6, 10
33:2, 3, 8, 18, 21
34:t, 5, 6[2], 7, 8, 9, 19, 22
35:8[2], 10[4], 25
37:5, 7[2], 12, 13, 22[2], 24, 32, 33[2], 36, 40
41:1, 2[3], 3, 8
42:5, 11
43:5
44:16
45:11
49:7, 17
50:3[2], 18, 23
51:t
52:t, 6
53:5
55:12, 20
56:t
57:3
59:t
61:7
62:1, 4, 5, 8[2]
63:11
64:4, 10
66:6, 17
67:7
68:1[2], 4[2], 33
69:26, 30, 34
71:11[3]
72:9, 11[2], 12, 15[2], 17[2]
74:14
76:11[2]
78:17, 34, 36[2], 37, 40[2], 58[2], 70, 71
79:10
81:15
85:9, 13
89:7, 20, 21, 22[2], 23, 24, 27, 28[2], 33, 41, 43, 45
91:2, 14[2], 15[4], 16[2]
92:15
94:12, 13
95:2
96:6, 9
97:2, 3, 7
98:1
100:4
101:5[2]
103:11, 13, 17
104:34
105:2[2], 19, 20[2], 21
106:7, 10, 23, 29, 31, 32, 43
107:32[2], 41
109:6, 7, 12, 17[2], 19[2], 30, 31
111:5
113:8
116:2
117:1
119:2, 42
120:6
126:6
130:7
135:1
136:4, 5, 6, 7, 10, 13, 16, 17
140:11
141:5
142:2[2]
144:3[2]
145:18[2], 19, 20
147:11
148:1, 2[2], 3[2], 4, 14
149:2[2], 3
150:1, 2[2], 3[2], 4[2], 5[2]

PROVERBS

3:6
6:16
7:10, 13[3], 20, 21[2]
8:9, 30[3]
9:4[3], 16[3]
10:13[2], 24, 26
11:18, 26[2], 27
12:14
13:6, 18, 24[2]
14:2, 6, 7, 31, 33, 35
15:9, 10, 12, 14, 21
16:7, 13, 22, 26, 29
17:8, 11, 24, 25
18:9, 13, 16[2], 17
19:6, 7[3], 17, 19
20:2, 7, 16, 19
21:25
22:15
23:6, 13, 14, 24
24:18[2], 24[2], 25, 29
25:13, 21[2]
26:4, 12, 15, 17, 24, 25, 27
27:11, 13, 14, 22
28:8, 11, 17, 22
29:20, 21, 23
30:5
31:1, 6, 7, 12

ECCLESIASTES

2:26
3:14, 22[2]
4:10[2], 12[2], 16
5:12, 18, 19, 20
6:2, 10, 12
7:14
8:3, 4, 6, 7, 12, 15[2]
9:2[2], 4, 17
10:1, 3, 8, 14[2]
11:8

SONG OF SOLOMON

1:2
3:1[3], 2[3], 3, 4[4], 11
5:4, 6[3], 8
6:1

ISAIAH

3:10, 11[2]
5:19, 23
6:4
7:4
8:13[2], 17
9:11, 13
10:6[2], 15[2], 20, 26
11:2, 3
14:25, 29
15:4, 9
16:3
20:1
21:6, 14[2]
22:11, 16, 21[2], 23, 24
24:2
25:9[2], 10
26:3
27:5, 7[3]
28:6, 26[2]
29:12, 16[2], 21, 23
30:18, 32
31:4, 6, 8
33:16
36:3, 6, 21[2], 22
37:3, 7[2], 22, 38
38:1[2]
39:3
40:3, 10[3], 13, 14[4], 17[2], 18, 20
41:2[3], 7
42:1, 25[3]
43:7[3]
44:3, 14, 20
45:1[2], 9[2], 10, 13, 24[2]
46:7[3]
48:14, 15[2]
49:5, 7[2], 25
50:4, 8, 10
51:2[3]
52:7, 15
53:2[3], 3[2], 4, 5, 6, 10[2], 12
55:4, 6, 7[2]
56:6, 8[2]
57:15, 17, 18[3], 19[3]
58:5, 7, 13
59:15, 16[2], 19
62:7, 11[2]
63:2, 11, 14
64:4[2], 5
66:2

JEREMIAH

2:3, 15, 37
3:1
4:2[2]
6:11
8:6
9:24
10:25[2]
11:19
15:8
18:18
19:14
20:2, 3, 9, 10[2], 15, 16
21:1, 9, 12
22:10[2], 12, 13[2], 14, 15, 16, 18[2]
23:24, 28[2]
26:8[2], 13, 19[2], 21, 22, 23[2], 24[2]
27:6, 7[2], 11, 12
28:9, 14[2]
29:26, 31
30:8, 10, 21
31:2, 10[2], 11[2], 20[4]
32:3, 4, 5, 9, 10
33:13
34:2, 14
36:4, 8, 15, 22, 31
37:4, 14[2], 15[2], 17[2], 21
38:6, 11, 13, 14, 27[2]
39:5[3], 7[2], 9, 12[4], 14[2]
40:1[2], 2, 5[3], 6, 7, 14
41:1, 2[2], 3, 7, 11, 12, 13, 16
42:8, 9, 11
43:1
44:20
45:4
46:10, 25, 27
48:11, 12[3], 17[2], 19, 26, 27, 35[2], 39
49:5, 8[2], 19
50:16, 17[2], 32[2], 43
51:3[2], 44
52:8, 9[2], 11[3], 31, 32[2], 33, 34

LAMENTATIONS

1:17
2:19
3:24, 25[2], 28, 30[2]

EZEKIEL

1:3
2:2
3:18, 20[2], 27[2]
7:15
9:4, 5
10:7
12:13[2], 14[2]
13:22
14:4, 7[2], 8[2], 9[2], 10[2]
17:6[2], 7[2], 12, 13[2], 15[2], 16[2], 17, 20[3]
18:13, 20[2], 22, 32
19:4[2], 5, 8[2], 9[3]
21:26[2], 27
24:27
28:9[2], 12
29:2, 20
30:11, 24
31:4[2], 8[2], 9[2], 11[3], 12[3], 15[3], 16, 17
32:2, 21[2], 22, 25, 26
33:2, 4, 5, 12, 16, 27
35:7[2]
37:19
38:2, 21, 22[3]
40:46
43:6
44:26
45:20
46:12
47:23

DANIEL

2:1, 16, 22, 24, 25, 46, 48[2]
3:28
4:8, 16[2], 19, 23, 34, 35
5:6, 9, 11, 17, 19[2], 20, 21, 24, 29
6:3[2], 4, 5, 6, 14[2], 16, 18[2], 22, 23[2]
7:10[3], 13[2], 14[2], 16, 27
8:4, 6, 7[5], 11, 12
9:4, 9, 11
10:16
11:1, 5, 11, 16[2], 17[3], 18[2], 22, 23, 25, 26, 30, 40[2], 44, 45
12:7

HOSEA

1:3, 4, 6
4:17
5:6, 14
7:5, 9, 10
8:3, 11, 12
9:4, 17
11:1, 7
12:2, 4[2], 14[3]
13:11, 13
14:2, 4, 8[2]

JOEL

2:13, 14, 20

AMOS

1:5, 8
2:3
3:5, 14
5:8, 10[2], 11, 19[2]
6:10[3]
9:13

OBADIAH

7

JONAH

1:6[2], 8, 10, 11, 15
3:6[2]
4:5, 6

MICAH

1:4
2:7
3:5
5:5
6:5, 6
7:9, 15

NAHUM

1:5, 6, 7, 15

HABAKKUK

2:4, 5[2], 6[4], 9, 12, 15[3], 19, 20
3:5

ZEPHANIAH

1:6
2:11
3:9

HAGGAI

1:12

ZECHARIAH

1:8
2:3, 4
3:1, 4[3], 5
4:11, 12
5:4
6:12
8:10, 23
9:8[2]
10:4[4]
12:1, 10[2]
13:3[4], 6

MALACHI

2:5[2], 12, 17
3:16, 17, 18[3]
4:4

MATTHEW

1:20, 24[2]
2:2, 3, 5, 8[2], 11[2], 13
3:5, 6, 13, 14, 15[2], 16[2]
4:3, 5[2], 6, 7, 8[2], 9, 10[2], 11[2], 20, 22, 24, 25
5:1, 25, 31, 39, 40, 41, 42[2]
6:8
7:8, 9, 10, 11, 24
8:1, 2, 3, 4, 5[2], 7[2], 16, 18, 19, 20, 21, 22, 23, 25[2], 27, 28, 31, 34[2]
9:2, 9[2], 10, 14, 18, 19, 20, 22, 24, 27, 28[2], 32
10:1, 4, 28, 32, 33, 40
11:3, 15, 27
12:2, 3, 4[2], 10[2], 14[2], 15, 16, 18, 22[2], 32[2], 46, 47, 48[2]
13:2, 9, 10, 12[2], 27, 28, 36, 43, 51, 57
14:2, 3[2], 4, 5[2], 9, 13, 15, 17, 22, 26, 28, 31[2], 33, 35[2], 36
15:4, 12, 15, 22, 23, 25, 30, 32, 33
16:1, 17, 22[2], 24
17:3, 5, 10, 12[2], 14[2], 16[2], 17, 18, 19, 23, 25, 26[2]
18:2[2], 6, 15[2], 17, 21[2], 22, 24[2], 25, 26, 27[2], 28[3], 29, 30, 32[2], 34[2]
19:2, 3[3], 7, 10, 12, 13, 16, 17, 18, 20, 21, 27
20:7, 18, 19[2], 20[3], 21, 22, 25, 26, 27, 29, 33, 34
21:7, 14, 16, 23, 25, 31, 32[3], 38, 39[3], 41[2], 44, 46[2]
22:12, 13[3], 15, 16, 19, 21, 22, 23[2], 35[2], 37, 42, 43, 45, 46[2]
23:15, 21, 22
24:1[2], 3, 15, 17, 18, 47, 50, 51[2]
25:6, 10, 21, 23, 26, 28[2], 29, 31, 32, 37, 44
26:4, 7, 15[2], 16, 17, 18, 22, 24, 25[2], 33, 34, 35, 37, 47, 48[2], 49, 50[2], 52, 56, 57, 58, 59, 62, 63, 64, 67[2], 69, 71, 73, 75
27:1, 2[3], 3, 9, 11[2], 13, 14, 18, 19[2], 22[2], 23, 26, 27, 28[2], 29[2], 30[2], 31[5], 32, 34, 35, 36, 38, 39, 41, 42[2], 43[3], 44, 48, 49, 54, 55, 64
28:4, 7, 9[2], 13, 14, 17[2]

MARK

1:5[2], 10, 12, 13, 18, 20, 25[2], 26[2], 27, 30, 32, 34, 36[2], 37[2], 40[4], 41[2], 42, 43[2], 44, 45
2:3, 4, 13, 14[2], 15, 16, 18, 24, 25, 26
3:2[3], 6[2], 7, 8, 9[2], 10[2], 11[2], 12, 13[2], 14, 19, 21, 23, 31[2], 32[2], 34
4:1, 9, 10[2], 23, 25[2], 36[2], 38[2], 41
5:2, 3, 4[2], 6, 8, 9, 10, 12, 15, 16, 17, 18[2], 19[2], 20, 21, 22, 23, 24[3], 30[2], 31, 33[2], 37, 40[2]
6:1, 2[3], 3, 7, 14[2], 17, 19[2], 20[3], 22, 26, 27, 30, 33[2], 35, 37, 49, 50, 54, 56[2]
7:1, 5, 10, 12, 14, 15[3], 16, 17, 18, 25, 26, 28, 32[3], 33, 34
8:1, 4, 11[3], 19, 22[3], 23[3], 25, 26, 29, 30, 32[2], 34[2], 38
9:2, 7, 11, 13[2], 15[3], 18[3], 19[2], 20[4], 21, 22[2], 23[2], 25[3], 26[2], 27[2], 28[2], 31, 32, 36[2], 37, 38[2], 39, 42
10:1, 2[3], 10, 13, 17[2], 18, 20, 21[3], 28, 32, 33[2], 34[4], 35, 37, 39, 42, 48, 49[2], 51[2], 52
11:2[2], 3[2], 4, 7[2], 18[2], 21, 27, 28, 31
12:3[3], 4[3], 5, 6, 7, 8[3], 12[2], 13[2], 14, 16, 17, 18[2], 19, 26, 28, 29, 32, 33, 34[2], 37[2], 43
13:1, 2, 3, 14, 15, 16, 21
14:1[2], 10, 11[2], 12, 13, 19, 21, 29, 30, 33, 35, 40, 43, 44[3], 45[2], 46[2], 50, 51[2], 53, 54, 55, 56, 57, 58, 61[2], 64, 65[4], 67, 69, 72
15:1[2], 2[2], 3, 4, 7, 8, 10, 12, 13, 14, 15, 16, 17, 18, 19[3], 20[3], 22, 23, 24, 25, 27, 29, 32[2], 36[2], 39, 41[3], 44[2], 46[3]
16:1, 6, 7, 10, 14

LUKE

1:11, 12[2], 13, 17, 19, 29, 32, 50, 59, 62, 66, 74, 75
2:7[2], 22[2], 25, 26, 27, 28, 33, 38, 40, 44[2], 45[2], 46, 47, 48[2]
3:7, 10, 11[3], 12, 14, 19, 22
4:3, 4, 5[2], 6, 8[2], 9[3], 12, 13, 14, 17, 20, 22, 29[3], 35[5], 37, 38, 40, 42[3]
5:1, 3, 5, 9, 11, 12, 13[2], 14, 15[2], 18[3], 19[2], 20, 27, 28, 29, 33
6:3, 4, 7[2], 13, 17, 19[2], 29[2], 30
7:2, 3[2], 4, 6[2], 9[3], 11, 14, 15, 17, 18, 19, 20, 29, 30, 36[2], 38, 39[2], 40, 42, 43, 49
8:1, 3, 4, 8, 9, 18[2], 19[2], 20, 24[2], 25, 27, 28, 29, 30[2], 31, 32, 37, 38[3], 39, 40[2], 41, 42, 44, 45, 47[3], 49, 50, 53
9:7, 9, 10, 11, 12, 18, 23, 26, 30, 32[2], 33, 35, 37, 39[4], 40, 42[3], 45, 47[2], 48, 49, 50[2], 52, 53, 57, 58, 60, 62
10:16, 22, 23, 25, 26, 28, 30[3], 31, 32, 33[2], 34[4], 35[2], 36, 37[2], 38, 40
11:1, 5[2], 6, 8[2], 10, 11[2], 12, 13, 16[2], 22[3], 26, 27, 37[2], 39, 45, 53[2], 54[2]
12:5[2], 8, 10[2], 13, 14, 20, 36, 41, 44, 46[3], 48[2], 58
13:1, 8, 12, 15[2], 17, 23, 31
14:1, 2, 4[3], 5, 6, 8, 9, 12[2], 15[2], 16, 18, 25, 29, 31[2], 35
15:1[2], 15, 16, 18, 20[2], 21, 22, 27[2], 28, 30, 31
16:1, 2[2], 5, 6, 7, 14, 27, 29, 31
17:1, 2, 3[2], 4, 7, 8, 9, 12, 16, 19, 31[2], 37
18:3, 7, 15, 16, 18, 19, 22, 31, 33[2], 37, 39, 40[3], 42, 43
19:4, 5[2], 6, 8, 9, 14[2], 15, 17, 19, 22, 24[2], 25, 26[2], 30[2], 31[3], 34, 35, 39, 47, 48
20:1, 2, 5, 10[3], 11[3], 12[2], 13[2], 14[2], 15[2], 18, 19, 20[2], 21, 27[2], 38, 40, 44
21:7, 38[2]
22:2, 4, 5, 6, 9, 10, 14, 21, 26, 33, 36[2], 39, 43[2], 47, 48, 49[2], 51, 52, 54[3], 56[3], 57[2], 58, 59, 61, 63[2], 64[3], 65, 66
23:1, 2, 3[2], 7, 8[3], 9[2], 10, 11[4], 14[2], 15[2], 16[2], 21[2], 22[3], 25, 26[2], 27[2], 32, 33, 35[2], 36[3], 38, 39, 40, 43, 49, 55

LUKE
24:16, 18, 19, 20[2], 24, 29, 31, 42, 52

JOHN
1:3[2], 4, 7, 10[2], 11, 12, 15, 18, 19, 21, 22, 25[2], 29, 31, 32, 33[2], 37, 38, 39, 40, 41, 42[2], 43, 45[2], 46[2], 47[2], 48[2], 49, 50, 51
2:3, 10, 11, 18
3:2[2], 3, 4, 9, 10, 15, 16, 17, 18, 26[2], 27, 28, 29, 34, 36
4:9, 10, 11, 14[3], 15, 19, 23, 24[2], 25, 30, 31, 33, 34, 39, 40[2], 42, 45, 47[2], 48, 49, 50[2], 51[2], 52[2], 53
5:6[2], 7, 8, 10, 12, 14[2], 15, 16, 18, 20[2], 23, 24, 27, 38, 43
6:2, 5, 6, 7, 8, 15[2], 21, 25[2], 27, 28, 29, 30, 34, 37, 38, 40[3], 41, 44[2], 54, 56, 64, 65, 66, 68, 71
7:1, 3, 5, 11, 12, 13, 18[2], 26, 29[2], 30[2], 31, 32[2], 33, 35, 37, 39, 43, 44[2], 45, 48, 51, 52
8:2, 3, 4, 6[2], 7[2], 13, 19, 20, 25, 26, 29, 30, 31, 33, 39, 41, 44, 48, 52, 55[4], 57, 59
9:2, 3, 4, 7, 8, 9, 10, 12, 13, 15, 17, 18[2], 21, 23, 24, 26, 28, 31, 34[2], 35[3], 36, 37[2], 38, 40[2]
10:3, 4, 5, 20, 21, 24[2], 31, 33, 36, 38, 39, 41, 42
11:3, 8, 10, 11, 15, 16, 20, 24, 27, 29, 30, 32[2], 34[2], 36, 39[2], 44[2], 45, 48[2], 53, 57
12:2[2], 4, 11, 13, 16[2], 17[2], 18, 19, 21, 26[2], 29, 34, 37, 41, 42[2], 44, 45, 47, 48[2]
13:2, 6, 7, 8[2], 9, 10, 11, 16, 20, 24, 25, 27[2], 28, 29, 31, 32[3], 36[2], 37, 38
14:5, 6, 7[2], 8, 9, 17[3], 21[2], 22, 23[4]
15:5, 21
16:5, 7, 19, 29

JOHN
17:2[2]
18:2, 4, 5[2], 12, 13, 20, 23, 24, 25, 26, 30[2], 31[3], 33, 34, 37, 38[2]
19:1, 2, 3, 4[2], 6[6], 7, 9, 10, 12, 15[3], 16[2], 18[2], 32, 36, 37, 38
20:2, 6, 13, 15[5], 16, 25, 28, 29
21:3, 5, 7, 12, 15[2], 16[3], 17[4], 19, 21, 22, 23

THE ACTS
1:6, 9, 11
2:22, 23, 25, 30
3:4, 7[2], 9, 10, 13[2], 16[2], 22, 26
4:10
5:6[3], 17, 21, 31, 32, 36, 37[2], 40
6:11, 12[3], 14, 15
7:3, 4, 5[3], 8[2], 9, 10[3], 14, 21[2], 24[2], 27, 30, 31, 33, 35, 37, 38, 39, 40, 47, 54, 57, 58[2]
8:2, 11, 20, 30[2], 31, 35, 38, 39
9:2, 3, 4, 6, 7, 8[2], 10, 11, 12, 15, 16, 17, 21, 23, 24, 25[2], 26, 27[3], 29, 30[2], 34, 35, 38[2], 39[2], 40
10:3[2], 4[2], 7, 11, 13, 15, 19, 21, 23, 25[2], 26, 27, 35[2], 38, 40[2], 41, 43[2], 48
11:2, 13, 26[2]
12:4[5], 5, 6, 7[2], 8[2], 9, 10, 16, 17, 19[2], 20, 23
13:9, 11[2], 22, 27[2], 28, 29[3], 30, 31, 34, 39
14:9, 19, 20
15:21, 38
16:3[3], 9, 32
17:15[2], 16, 17, 18, 19[2], 23, 27[2], 28, 31, 34
18:12, 17, 18, 20, 26[2], 27
19:2, 4[2], 22, 30, 31[2], 33, 38
20:1, 3, 4, 10[3], 14, 16, 18, 37, 38
21:8, 11, 12, 20, 27[2], 29, 30, 31, 33[2], 34, 36, 40

THE ACTS
22:9, 13, 18, 20, 22, 24[2], 25, 27, 29[3], 30[2]
23:2[2], 3, 9, 10[2], 11, 15[3], 17[2], 18[3], 19[3], 20, 21[2], 22, 23, 24, 27, 28[2], 30, 31, 32, 33, 35
24:2, 7, 8, 10, 23[2], 24, 26[4]
25:2[2], 3[3], 5, 15, 16, 19, 20, 21[2], 22, 25, 26, 27
26:26
27:3
28:6, 8[2], 16, 21, 23[2], 30, 31

ROMANS
1:20, 21
3:26
4:3, 4, 5[2], 17, 22, 23, 24
5:9, 14
6:4, 6, 8, 9
7:4
8:11, 17, 20, 32[2], 37
9:11, 16[2], 20, 33
10:9, 11, 12, 14[2]
11:4, 35[2], 36[3]
12:8, 20[2]
13:4
14:1, 3[5], 4, 14[2], 15
15:11, 12
16:25

1 CORINTHIANS
1:5, 30, 31
2:2, 9, 11, 14, 16
3:17, 18
5:3
7:12[2], 13, 15, 17, 18[2], 36
8:3, 6[2], 10
10:12
11:14, 28, 34
12:18
14:2, 11, 13, 28[2], 37, 38
15:27[2], 28[3], 38
16:2[2], 11[3], 12, 22

2 CORINTHIANS
1:19, 20[2]
2:7[2], 8
5:9, 15, 16, 21[2]
6:1
7:14, 15
8:18
9:7
10:7, 17
11:4
12:18
13:4[2]

GALATIANS
1:1, 6, 8, 9, 16, 18
2:11, 13
3:6
4:29
5:8
6:6[2]

EPHESIANS
1:4[2], 10, 11, 17, 20[2], 22, 23
2:18
3:12, 20, 21
4:15, 21[2], 28[3]
6:9

PHILIPPIANS
1:29
2:7, 9[2], 22, 23, 27[2], 28[2], 29
3:9, 10

COLOSSIANS
1:16[3], 17, 19, 20[2]
2:6, 7, 9, 10, 12[3], 13
3:4, 10[2], 17
4:10, 13

1 THESSALONIANS
4:14
5:10

2 THESSALONIANS
1:12
2:1, 9
3:14, 15[2]

1 TIMOTHY
1:16
5:1

2 TIMOTHY
1:12, 18
2:4[2], 11[2], 12[2], 26
4:11, 14

TITUS
1:16

PHILEMON
12, 15, 17

HEBREWS
1:5, 6
2:3, 6[2], 7[3], 8[3], 10, 13, 14, 16[2], 17
3:2[2]
4:13
5:5, 7[2], 9
6:6
7:1, 6, 10, 21[2], 25
9:9, 28
10:30, 38
11:5, 6[2], 9, 11, 12, 19[2], 27
12:2, 3, 5, 25[3]
13:13, 15

JAMES
1:5[2], 6, 12
2:3[2], 5, 14, 23
3:13
4:17[2]
5:13[2], 14[3], 15[2], 19, 20

1 PETER
1:8, 21[3]
2:6, 9, 14, 23

1 PETER
3:6, 10, 11[2], 22
4:5, 11[2], 16[2], 19
5:7, 11

2 PETER
1:3, 17, 18
3:14, 15, 18

1 JOHN
1:5[2], 6, 10
2:3, 4[2], 5[2], 6, 8, 10, 13, 14, 15, 27[2], 28[2], 29
3:1, 2[2], 3, 5, 6[3], 9, 12, 15, 17[2], 19, 22, 24[2]
4:9, 13, 15, 16, 19, 21
5:1[3], 10, 14, 15, 16, 18, 20[2]

2 JOHN
10[2], 11

JUDE
9, 15, 24

REVELATION
1:1, 4, 5, 6, 7[3], 17
2:7[2], 11, 17[3], 26, 28, 29
3:6, 12[3], 13, 20[2], 21, 22
4:8, 9, 10[2]
5:1, 7, 13, 14
6:2[2], 4[2], 5, 8[2], 16
7:14, 15
8:3
9:1
10:6, 9
12:9, 11
13:2, 4, 5[2], 7[2], 8, 9, 12, 18
14:1, 7[2], 15, 18
16:8, 9
17:14
19:5, 7, 10, 11, 14, 19, 20[2], 21
20:2, 3[3], 6, 11
21:6
22:3, 11[4], 17[3], 18

HIS

848

GENESIS
1:11, 12[2], 21, 24[2], 25[2], 27
2:2[2], 3, 7, 21, 24[3], 25
3:8, 15, 20, 21, 22
4:1, 2, 4[2], 5[2], 7, 8[2], 17[2], 21, 23, 25[2], 26
5:3[3], 29
6:3, 5, 6, 9, 12, 20
7:2[2], 7[3], 13, 14[3]
8:9, 18[3], 21[2]
9:1, 6, 8, 21, 22[2], 24[2], 25, 26, 27
10:5, 10, 15, 25[2]
11:28[2], 31[4]
12:5[2], 8, 11, 12, 17, 20[2]
13:1, 3[2], 10, 12, 18
14:12, 14[3], 15, 16[2], 17
16:3, 11, 12[2], 15
17:3, 14[2], 17[2], 19[2], 23[3], 24, 25[2], 26, 27
18:2, 19[2], 33[2]
19:1, 3, 14[3], 16[3], 26, 30[2], 37, 38
20:2, 7, 8, 14, 17[2]
21:2, 3, 4, 5, 7, 11, 21, 22, 32
22:3[3], 4, 5, 6[2], 7, 9, 10[2], 13[3], 17, 19, 21[2], 24
23:3, 6, 9, 10, [illegible]
24:2[2], 7, 9[2], 10[3], 11, 20, 21[2], 26, 27[2], 29, 30[2], 32[2], 40, 48, 59, 61, 63, 67[3]
25:6, 8, 9, 10, 11, 17, 18, 21[2], 25, 26[3], 28, 30, 33, 34[2]
26:7, 8, 11[2], 15[2], 17, 18[2], 25, 26[2]
27:1[2], 5, 10, 11, 13, 14[3], 16[2], 18, 19, 20, 22, 23[2], 26, 27, 30[3], 31[3], 32, 34[2], 37, 38[2], 39, 40, 41[2]
28:7[2], 8, 9, 11, 16, 18
29:1, 3, 6, 10[3], 11, 13[2], 23, 24[2], 28, 29[2], 32, 33, 34, 35
30:6, 8, 11, 13, 14, 18, 20, 24, 35, 40
31:4, 17[2], 18[4], 19, 21, 23, 25[2], 46, 53, 54, 55[3]
32:1, 3, 13[2], 16[2], 20, 22[3], 25, 31
33:1, 3, 4, 5, 14, 16, 17, 18, 19
34:3, 4, 5[4], 13, 19, 20, 24[3], 25, 26
35:2, 7, 10, 18[2], 21, 22, 27, 29[2]
36:2, 6[8], 24, 32, 33, 34, 35[2], 36, 37, 38, 39[3]
37:1, 2[3], 3[2], 4[2], 5, 8[3], 9, 10[3], 11[2], 12, 17, 20, 22, 23[3], 26[2], 27, 29, 30, 34[3], 35[3]
38:1, 3, 4, 5, 6, 9[3], 11[2], 12[2], 13, 16, 20[2], 28[2], 29[3], 30[3]
39:2, 3[2], 4[3], 5, 7, 8, 9, 11, 12[2], 13, 15, 16[2], 18, 19[3], 23
40:1, 2, 5[2], 7, 9, 13[2], 20[2], 21
41:8[2], 10, 11, 12, 14, 37, 38, 42[3], 44
42:1, 4, 7, 8, 21, 22, 25, 27[4], 28, 35, 37, 38
43:8, 16, 21, 29[3], 30[3], 31, 33[2]
44:1[2], 2, 4, 11[2], 13, 14, 19, 20[4], 22[3], 30, 33
45:1, 3[3], 4, 8, 14[2], 15[2], 16, 23[2], 24
46:1[2], 4, 6, 7[5], 8, 15[3], 18, 25, 26, 28, 29[4], 31[2]
47:2, 3, 7, 11[2], 12[3], 20, 29
48:1, 9, 12[2], 13[2], 14[3], 17[3], 18[2], 19[3]

GENESIS
49:1, 10, 11[4], 12[2], 13, 15, 16, 17, 20, 24[2], 26, 28, 31[2], 33[3]
50:1, 2[2], 4, 7[2], 8[2], 10, 12, 13, 14[3], 18[2], 22, 24

EXODUS
1:1, 6, 9, 22
2:4, 7, 10, 11[2], 20, 21, 22, 24
3:1, 6, 13
4:4[2], 6[3], 7[4], 14, 15[2], 18, 20[3], 21, 25
5:2, 21
6:1, 11, 20
7:2, 10[2], 12, 20, 23[2]
8:6, 15, 17[2], 24, 29[2], 31[2], 32
9:20[2], 21[2], 23, 33, 34[2]
10:1[2], 13, 22, 23
11:2, 5, 7, 10
12:4[3], 9[2], 22, 29, 30, 48
13:10, 13
14:4, 5, 6[2], 9[2], 17[3], 18[2], 21, 23[2], 27[2], 31
15:1, 3, 4[2], 19[2], 21, 26[3]
16:16[2], 18, 21, 29[2]
17:11[2], 12[2], 13
18:1, 5[2], 7, 8, 15, 16, 24, 27[3]
20:7, 17[4], 20
21:3, 4, 6[3], 7, 9, 13, 14, 15[2], 16, 17[2], 18[2], 19[2], 20[3], 21, 26[3], 27[3], 28, 29[3], 30, 34, 36[2]
22:3, 4, 5[3], 7, 8[2], 9[2], 10, 11[2], 14, 15, 16, 27[3], 30
23:3, 4, 5, 6, 19, 21, 22
24:10[2], 11, 13
25:2, 31[5]
26:19[2]
27:2, 3[6], 11, 21
28:1, 4, 12, 21, 29, 30, 35, 38, 41, 43[2]
29:4, 6, 7, 8, 9[2], 10, 14[2], 15, 16, 17[3], 19, 20[2], 21[6], 24, 27, 28, 29, 30, 31, 32, 35, 44
30:12, 18, 19, 21, 27[2], 28[2], 30, 33, 38
31:8[2], 9[2], 10, 14
32:11, 14, 15, 19, 27[5], 29[2]
33:4, 8, 10, 11[2]
34:4, 8, 15, 20, 26, 29, 30, 33, 35
35:11[7], 13[2], 14[2], 15, 16[4], 17, 19, 21[2], 34
36:4, 24[2]
37:16[4], 17[5], 20[2], 23[3]
39:5, 14, 21, 27, 33[6], 39[4], 40[4], 41
40:10, 11, 12, 14, 18[2], 31

LEVITICUS
1:3[2], 4, 6, 9[2], 10, 11, 12[3], 14[2], 15, 16[2]
2:1, 2, 3, 10
3:1, 2[2], 6, 7, 8[2], 12, 13, 14
4:3, 4, 6, 11[5], 17, 19, 22, 23[3], 24, 25[2], 26[2], 28[4], 29, 30, 33, 34, 35
5:1, 4, 6[3], 7, 8[2], 10, 11, 12, 13, 15, 17, 18
6:2[2], 5, 6, 9, 10[3], 11, 15, 16, 20, 22[2], 25
7:13[2], 15, 16[2], 18[2], 20[2], 21, 25, 27, 29[3], 30, 31, 33, 34, 35

LEVITICUS
8:2, 6, 9[2], 11[2], 14, 15, 17[3], 18, 22, 23[2], 27, 30[6], 31[2], 36
9:1, 9, 22
10:1, 3, 6, 12
11:14, 15, 16, 22[4], 25, 27, 28, 29, 40[2]
12:3
13:2[3], 3, 4, 5, 6, 7, 11, 12[2], 13, 23, 28, 34, 35, 37, 40, 41[3], 42[2], 43[2], 44[2], 45[3], 46, 55
14:2, 8[3], 9[7], 14[2], 15, 16[3], 17[3], 19, 23, 25[2], 26, 27[2], 28[3], 32, 47[2]
15:2[2], 3[7], 5[2], 6, 7, 8, 10, 11[2], 13[4], 15, 16, 21, 22, 27
16:4[2], 6[2], 11, 12, 14[2], 15, 17, 19, 21, 24[3], 26[2], 28[2], 32
17:2, 4, 9, 10, 15, 16[2]
18:14
19:3[2], 8[2], 21, 22
20:2, 3[2], 4, 5, 6, 9[5], 10, 11[2], 12, 17[6], 19, 20[2], 21[2]
21:1, 2[6], 3, 4, 7, 10[3], 11[2], 12[2], 14, 15[2], 17, 20[2], 21, 22, 24
22:2, 3, 6, 7, 11[3], 18[4], 21, 23
23:29, 30, 37
24:9, 11, 14, 15[2], 19
25:10[2], 13, 25[3], 27, 28, 30, 33, 41[3], 48, 49[3], 50, 51, 52[2], 54
27:8, 14, 15[2], 16, 17, 18, 22, 28, 31

NUMBERS
1:4, 44, 52[2]
2:2, 4, 6, 8, 11, 13, 15, 17, 19, 21, 23, 26, 28, 30
3:7, 9, 10, 38, 48, 51
4:5, 9[3], 15, 19[3], 25, 27, 49[2]
5:7, 9, 10[2], 14[2], 15, 18, 30
6:4, 5[3], 7[6], 8, 9[3], 11, 12[2], 13, 14, 16[2], 17[2], 18[2], 19, 21[4], 23, 25, 26
7:5, 11, 12, 13, 19, 25, 31, 37, 43, 49, 55, 61, 67, 73, 79
8:8, 13, 19, 22
9:2, 3, 7, 13[3]
10:14, 18, 22, 25
11:1, 10, 28, 29
12:12
14:24
15:4, 24[2], 30, 31[2]
16:4, 5[2], 6, 17[3], 18, 40
17:2, 9
19:3, 4, 5, 7[2], 8[2], 10, 13, 19, 21
20:8, 11[2], 21, 24, 25, 26[3], 28[2]
21:23[2], 24, 26[2], 29[2], 33, 34[2], 35[3]
22:5, 18, 21, 22[2], 23[2], 31[4]
23:6, 7, 10, 16, 17, 18, 21
24:1, 2[2], 3, 4, 7[4], 8[2], 10, 13, 15, 16, 18, 20[2], 21, 23, 25[2]
25:5, 6, 7, 13[2]
26:54
27:1, 3, 4, 8[2], 9[2], 10[2], 11[4], 21[2], 23
28:10, 15, 24, 31
29:6[2], 16[2], 22[2], 25[2], 28[2], 31[2], 34[2], 38[2]
30:2[3], 4, 7, 11, 14[2], 16[2]
31:6
32:18, 21, 42
33:54

NUMBERS
35:8[2], 21, 23[2], 25, 26, 27, 28[2], 32
36:2, 7, 8, 9

DEUTERONOMY
1:16, 31, 36, 41
2:12, 24, 30[2], 31[2], 32, 33[2], 34
3:1, 2[2], 3, 4, 11, 14, 20
4:13, 30, 36[3], 37[2], 40[2], 42, 47
5:11, 21[5], 24[3]
6:2[2], 13, 17[2], 22
7:3[2], 7, 9, 10
8:2, 5, 6, 11[3], 18
9:23
10:6[2], 8, 9[2], 12, 13, 20
11:1[4], 2[3], 3[3], 14, 22
12:5[2], 8, 11, 21
13:4[2], 17, 18
14:13, 14, 15, 21, 23, 24
15:2[3], 8, 17
16:2, 6, 11
17:2, 17, 18, 19[2], 20[5]
18:1, 5, 6, 7[2], 8, 10[2], 18
19:4, 5[3], 6, 9, 11, 12, 18, 19
20:5, 6, 7, 8[3]
21:16, 17[2], 18[2], 19[4], 20, 21, 23
22:1, 3[2], 4, 19[2], 24, 26, 29[2], 30[2]
23:1, 2, 7, 15[2]
24:1[2], 2, 3[2], 4, 5, 7, 10[2], 12, 13, 15[3], 16
25:2[2], 6[2], 7[3], 8, 9[5], 10[2]
26:2, 17[5], 18[2]
27:10[2], 16[2], 17, 20[2], 22[3], 23, 24
28:1, 9, 12[2], 15[2], 40, 45[2], 54[4], 55
29:2[2], 12, 19, 20[2], 23[2]
30:2, 8, 10[2], 16[4], 20
32:4[2], 5, 9[2], 10, 15, 19[2], 36[2], 43[5], 50
33:1, 2, 3, 6, 7[3], 9[4], 11[2], 12, 13, 16, 17[3], 21, 24[2], 26, 28
34:6, 7[2], 9, 11[2]

JOSHUA
2:19[3]
3:15
4:5, 14, 18
5:13[3], 14[2]
6:26[2], 27
7:6[2], 18, 22, 24[6], 26
8:1[3], 14, 18, 19, 26, 29
9:24
10:21, 33
11:15
13:27
15:17
17:3, 6, 10
20:4, 5[2], 6[2]
21:12
22:5[2], 20, 29
24:3, 4, 10, 24, 28, 30, 33

JUDGES
1:2, 3, 6[2], 13, 17, 25
2:6, 9
3:10[2], 16[2], 20, 21[3], 22, 24[3]
4:7[2], 10, 11, 13, 15[4], 17, 21, 22
5:11, 17, 26[2], 28[2], 31
6:11, 13, 21[2], 27[2], 31, 32
7:5[2], 7, 8, 11, 13, 14[2], 21, 22
8:20[2], 21, 24, 25, 27[2], 29, 30, 31, 32

JUDGES
9:1[2], 3, 5[2], 7, 16[2], 17, 18[2], 19, 21, 24, 26, 28, 30, 31, 41, 48[2], 49, 53, 54[2], 55, 56[2]
10:16
11:2, 3, 11, 20[2], 21, 23, 32, 34[3], 35, 39
12:9
13:2, 5, 6[2], 7, 11, 19, 20, 21, 22, 23, 24
14:2[2], 3[3], 4[2], 5[2], 6[3], 9[2], 10, 19[2], 20[2]
15:1, 6[2], 14[3], 15, 17, 19
16:3, 5, 9, 12, 14, 16, 17, 18[2], 19[2], 20, 21, 22, 29[2], 30[3], 31[3]
17:2[2], 3[2], 4[2], 5[2], 6, 11, 12
18:4, 26, 30
19:2, 3, 4, 5, 7, 9[3], 10, 11, 12, 13, 15, 16, 17, 21, 24, 25, 27[2], 28, 29[2]
20:8[2]
21:1, 21, 22, 24[3], 25

RUTH
1:1[2], 2[2], 6
2:1, 5, 15, 20, 22
3:4, 7[2], 8, 14
4:5, 7[2], 8, 10[3], 13, 14, 17

1 SAMUEL
1:1, 3, 4, 11[2], 19, 20, 21[2], 23
2:9, 10[2], 11, 13, 19, 20, 22
3:2[2], 9, 12, 13[2], 19
4:10, 12[2], 13, 15, 18, 19
5:3[2], 4[2], 7, 11
6:2, 3, 5, 9[2]
7:1, 15, 17[2]
8:1, 2[2], 3[2], 11[3], 12[4], 14, 15[2], 16, 17, 22
9:2, 3, 5, 7, 10, 15, 22
10:1[2], 9, 14, 16, 23, 25, 27
11:6, 7
12:3, 5, 14, 22[3]
13:2, 14[2], 16, 20[4], 22
14:1[2], 6, 7, 12[2], 13[4], 14, 17, 20, 26[2], 27[5], 34[3], 45, 47, 49, 50
15:1, 27, 34, 35
16:1, 4, 5, 7[2], 10, 13, 16, 17, 20, 21, 23
17:5, 6[2], 7[2], 13, 15, 17, 22[2], 25[2], 28, 33, 34, 35[2], 38[2], 39[2], 40[4], 43, 49[5], 51[2], 54[2], 57
18:1, 2, 3, 4[4], 7[2], 10, 11, 13, 14, 22[2], 26, 27[2], 30
19:1[2], 4[3], 5[2], 7, 9[4], 13, 16, 24
20:6, 17, 25, 27, 32, 33, 34, 36, 38, 40[2], 41
21:7, 11[2], 12, 13[3], 14
22:1[2], 6[3], 7, 11, 15
23:5, 6, 8, 11, 13, 14, 15, 16, 18, 22[2], 24, 25, 26[3]
24:2, 3[2], 6, 7[2], 8, 16, 19, 22
25:1, 2, 3[2], 4, 10, 13[4], 17, 20, 24, 25[2], 36, 37[2], 39[2], 42, 43, 44
26:5, 7[2], 9, 10, 11, 16, 18, 19, 23[2], 25[2]
27:1[2], 3[3], 8, 11, 12
28:3, 5, 7[2], 14, 18, 23, 25
29:2, 4[2], 5[2], 11

1 SAMUEL
30:1, 3, 6[3], 12, 18, 22[2], 24[2], 26, 31
31:2, 4[2], 5[2], 6[3], 7, 8, 9[2], 10[2], 12

2 SAMUEL
1:2[2], 4, 5, 6, 10[2], 11, 12, 17
2:2, 3[2], 16[3], 21, 27, 29, 32[2]
3:2, 3, 8[2], 12, 27, 29, 30, 32, 38, 39
4:1, 4[3], 6, 7[3], 8, 9, 10, 11[3], 12
5:6, 12[2], 21
6:6, 7, 11, 14, 17, 19, 20[2], 21
7:1[2], 12, 13, 14, 25, 27
8:3, 10, 15
9:3, 6, 9, 11, 13
10:1[2], 2[3], 3, 10
11:1, 2, 9[2], 10, 13[3], 27[2]
12:3[4], 4[2], 9[2], 15, 17, 19[2], 20[2], 21, 24[2], 25, 30
13:2, 8, 17, 18, 22[2], 24, 28, 29, 31[2], 32, 33, 34, 36, 37
14:7[2], 9, 13, 14, 15, 16, 22[2], 24[2], 25[3], 26[2], 30, 31, 33
15:5, 12, 14, 16, 18, 22, 25, 30[2], 32[2]
16:6[2], 9, 11, 12, 13, 18, 19, 22
17:6, 8, 18, 23[6]
18:9, 14, 17, 18[2], 19, 24, 25, 28
19:2, 4, 8, 11[2], 17[2], 19, 24[3], 30, 39, 41
20:1, 3[2], 8, 10[2], 21[2], 22
21:1, 2, 4, 6, 12, 13, 14[2], 15, 22
22:1, 7[2], 9[2], 10, 14, 16, 23[2], 25, 31, 51[3]
23:2, 8, 10[2], 18, 21[2], 23
24:14, 16, 20[2], 21

1 KINGS
1:2, 6[2], 9, 10, 21, 23, 37, 47, 49, 51
2:1, 3[5], 4, 5[4], 6, 9, 10, 12[2], 15, 19[2], 22, 23, 32[2], 33[4], 34, 35, 40[3]
3:1, 3, 6, 15
4:7[2], 21, 25[2], 26, 27, 28, 31, 32, 34
5:1[2], 3[2], 10, 11
7:1[2], 8, 14[2], 23, 51
8:6, 14, 15[2], 20, 22, 28, 31, 32[3], 38[2], 39, 54[2], 56[3], 58[4], 59[2], 61[2], 66[2]
9:11, 15, 16, 19[3], 22[5], 27
10:5[5], 13, 24[2], 25
11:3[2], 4[5], 6, 8, 9, 17, 19, 20, 21, 23, 26, 27[2], 33, 34[2], 35, 36, 41, 43[4]
12:4, 6, 15, 18, 24, 26, 33
13:4[2], 11, 12, 13, 19, 24, 27, 28, 30[2], 31[2], 33
14:2, 4[2], 8, 18, 20[3], 21[2], 31[5]
15:2, 3[4], 4[2], 5, 6, 8[3], 10, 11, 12, 13, 14, 15, 18, 23[3], 24[5], 26[2], 28, 29, 30, 34
16:3, 4, 5, 6[3], 7[2], 9[3], 10, 11[3], 13, 19[2], 20, 26, 27, 28[3], 34[3]
17:17, 19, 23
18:3, 7, 42[2], 43, 46
19:3[2], 6, 13[2], 19
20:1, 11, 12, 20, 24, 31, 35, 38, 39, 41, 42[2], 43
21:4[3], 5, 7, 8[2], 11[2], 25, 27[2], 29[3]

1 KINGS

22:3, 10, 17, 19[3], 22, 31[2], 34, 35, 36[2], 38[2], 40[3], 42, 43, 45, 46, 50[5], 52[2], 53

2 KINGS

1:2, 8, 9, 10, 11, 12, 13[2], 16, 17
2:8, 12
3:2[3], 25, 27[2]
4:12, 18, 19[2], 20, 25, 32, 34[6], 35, 37, 38, 39, 43
5:1, 3, 4, 6, 7[2], 8, 9[2], 11[2], 13, 14, 15, 20, 23, 25, 26, 27
6:7, 8, 11, 12, 15, 17, 24, 30[2], 32[2]
7:12, 13
8:11, 14, 15[2], 18, 19[2], 20, 24[4], 26
9:2, 3, 6, 11[2], 13, 21[2], 23, 24[4], 25[2], 26, 28[3], 31, 32, 36
10:3, 10, 11[3], 15, 16, 19[2], 24, 31, 34, 35[3]
11:2, 8[2], 9, 11[2], 18[2]
12:1, 2, 5, 17, 18[2], 20, 21[4]
13:8, 9[3], 12, 13[2], 14[2], 16[2], 21, 23[2], 24[2], 25
14:2, 3[2], 5[3], 6, 15, 16[3], 20, 21, 22, 25, 28, 29[3]
15:2, 3, 5, 7[4], 9, 10, 14, 15, 18, 19[2], 22[3], 25[2], 30, 33, 34, 38[5]
16:2[2], 3, 13[4], 15, 20[4]
17:3, 15[3], 18, 20, 23[2]
18:2, 3, 6, 12, 21, 29, 31[3], 33
19:1, 4, 7[2], 19, 23[2], 37[4]
20:2, 13[5], 20, 21[3]
21:1, 3, 6, 7, 10, 11, 12, 16, 17, 18[4], 19, 20, 21[2], 22, 23, 24[2], 26[3]
22:1, 2, 11
23:3[3], 10[2], 18[2], 25[3], 26[2], 29, 30[3], 31, 32, 34[2], 35, 36, 37
24:1[2], 2, 3, 6[3], 7, 8, 9, 11, 12[5], 15, 17[3], 18, 20
25:1[2], 5, 7, 28, 29[2], 30[2]

1 CHRONICLES

1:13, 19[2], 43, 44, 45, 46[2], 47, 48, 49, 50[3]
2:4, 13, 18, 35[2], 42
3:3, 10[3], 11[3], 12[3], 13[3], 14[2], 16[2], 17
4:9[3], 18, 19, 23, 25[3], 26[3], 27
5:1[2], 2, 4[3], 5[3], 6, 7
6:20[3], 21[4], 22[3], 23[3], 24[4], 26[2], 27[3], 29[3], 30[3], 39[2], 49, 50[3], 51[3], 52[3], 53[2]
7:14, 16[3], 18, 20[4], 21[2], 22, 23[3], 24, 25[3], 26[3], 27[2], 35
8:1, 8, 9, 10, 30, 37[3], 39[2]
9:5, 19[2], 36, 43[3]
10:2, 4[2], 5, 6[2], 7, 8, 9[2], 10[2], 12, 13
11:10, 11, 20, 23, 25, 45
12:15, 19, 28
13:9, 10, 14
14:2[2], 4
15:3, 5, 6, 7, 8, 9, 10, 17
16:7, 8[2], 9, 10, 11[2], 12[3], 13[2], 14, 15, 16, 23, 24[2], 27[2], 29, 34, 37, 39, 41, 43[2]
17:1, 11, 12, 13, 14, 21, 23, 25
18:3, 10[2], 14
19:1[2], 2[2], 3, 7, 11, 13, 15, 19
20:2, 8
21:3, 13, 16[2], 20, 21, 23, 27
22:5, 6, 9[3], 10[2], 17, 18
23:1, 13[2], 14, 25
25:9, 10[2], 11[2], 12[2], 13[2], 14[2], 15[2], 16[2], 17[2], 18[2], 19[2], 20[2], 21[2], 22[2], 23[2], 24[2], 25[2], 26[2], 27[2], 28[2], 29[2], 30[2], 31[2]
26:6, 10, 14[2], 15, 22, 25[6], 26, 28, 29, 30, 31, 32
27:2, 4[2], 5, 6[2], 7[2], 8, 9, 10, 11, 12, 13, 14, 15
28:1, 2, 6, 7, 11, 19, 20
29:5, 23, 28[2], 30[2]

2 CHRONICLES

1:1[2], 8, 13
2:1, 11, 12, 14, 15, 17
3:1, 2
4:16
5:1, 7, 13
6:3, 4[2], 10, 12, 13[2], 19, 22, 23[3], 29[3], 30
7:3, 6, 10, 11
8:1, 6, 9[3], 14, 18
9:4[5], 8, 23[2], 24, 31[4]
10:4, 6, 15, 18
11:4, 12, 14, 21[2], 22, 23
12:8, 13[2], 14, 16[3]
13:2, 5, 6, 12, 17, 22[2]
14:1[4], 2, 11, 13
15:9, 17, 18
16:4, 5, 12[4], 13[2], 14
17:1[2], 2, 3, 4[2], 5, 6, 7[2]
18:8, 9, 16, 18[3], 21, 33, 34
19:1
20:18[2], 20, 21, 25, 30, 31, 32
21:1[4], 4[2], 7, 8, 9[2], 10[2], 17[3], 18, 19[4]
22:1[2], 2, 3[2], 4[3], 9, 11
23:7[2], 8, 10[2], 11, 13, 17[2]
24:1, 11, 13, 16, 22[2], 25[2], 27[3]
25:1, 3[2], 4, 11, 14, 22, 28
26:1, 2, 3, 4, 8, 15, 16[3], 19[2], 20, 21[2], 23[4]
27:1, 2, 6[2], 7[2], 9[3]
28:1, 3, 5, 22, 25, 26[2], 27[3]
29:1, 2, 3, 10, 19[2], 25
30:2, 6, 8[2], 9, 19[2], 27
31:1, 2, 3, 8, 10, 12, 13, 16, 20, 21[2]

2 CHRONICLES

32:3[2], 8, 9[2], 12[2], 14, 15, 16[2], 17, 21[3], 25, 26, 30, 31, 32, 33[4]
33:3, 6, 7, 10, 12[2], 13[2], 18[2], 19[3], 20[4], 22[2], 23, 24[2], 25[2]
34:2, 3[2], 4, 8[2], 19, 27, 31[6], 33
35:3, 4, 8, 9, 22, 23, 24[2], 26, 27
36:1, 4[3], 5, 7, 8[3], 10, 11, 13[2], 15[3], 16[3], 17, 18, 20, 22, 23[2]

EZRA

1:1, 3[2], 4, 7
2:1, 68
3:2[2], 3, 9[3], 11
4:6
5:6, 15, 17
6:5, 7, 10, 11[2], 12
7:6[2], 9, 10, 11, 13, 14, 15, 23, 28
8:17, 18[2], 19, 22[2], 25[2]
9:8
10:8, 11, 18

NEHEMIAH

1:5
2:1, 20
3:1, 10, 12, 17, 23, 28, 29, 30
4:2, 15, 17, 18[2], 22
5:7, 13[2]
6:5[2], 11, 18, 19
7:3[2], 6
8:4[2], 16
9:8[2], 10[2]
10:29[2]
11:3, 13, 17, 20
12:8, 36, 45, 47
13:10, 26, 30

ESTHER

1:2, 3[3], 4[2], 8, 12[2], 20, 22
2:3, 7[2], 8, 15, 16[2], 17, 18[2]
3:1, 10[2]
4:1, 3, 4, 11, 17
5:1, 2[2], 10[2], 11[2], 14[2]
6:6, 8, 12[2], 13[4]
7:5, 7[2]
8:2, 3[2], 5[2], 7, 17
9:1, 4, 25[3]
10:2[2], 3[3]

JOB

1:3, 4[2], 10[3], 13[2], 20[2]
2:3, 4, 5[2], 6, 7[2], 9, 10, 11, 12, 13
3:1[2], 19
4:9, 17, 18[2]
5:3, 4, 18, 26
6:5, 9, 14
7:1, 2, 10[2]
8:12, 15, 16[2], 17, 18, 19
9:5, 13, 33, 34[2]
11:5
12:4, 5, 11, 16
13:8, 11[2]
14:5[3], 6, 18, 20, 21, 22[2]
15:2, 15[2], 20, 21, 23, 25, 26[2], 27[3], 29, 30[2], 31, 32[2], 33[2]
16:9[3], 12, 13, 21
17:5[2], 9
18:4[2], 5, 6[2], 7[2], 8, 11, 12[3], 13[2], 14[2], 15[3], 16[2], 17, 19[2], 20
19:6, 11[2], 12
20:6[2], 7, 9, 10[2], 11[2], 12[2], 13, 14[2], 15, 18, 20, 21[2], 22, 23[2], 25, 26[2], 27, 28[3]
21:17, 19[2], 20[2], 21[2], 23, 24[2], 25, 31[2]
22:22[2]
23:3, 6, 11[2], 12[2], 13, 15
24:1, 6, 15, 22, 23
25:2, 3[2], 5
26:8, 9[2], 11, 12[2], 13[2], 14[2]
27:1, 8, 9, 14[2], 15, 18, 19, 21, 22, 23
28:9, 10
29:1, 3[2], 17
30:24[2]
31:20, 23, 30, 31
32:1, 2, 3[2], 5, 12, 14
33:10, 13, 17, 18[2], 19[2], 20[2], 21[2], 22[2], 23, 25[2], 26[2], 28[2], 30
34:11, 14[3], 19, 21[2], 27, 29, 35, 36, 37[3]
35:15, 16
36:7, 15, 18, 22, 23, 24, 26, 29, 30
37:1, 2[2], 3, 4[2], 5, 6, 7, 11, 12, 13, 15
38:12, 32[2], 41[2]
39:6, 8, 10, 11, 18, 19, 20, 21
40:16[4], 17[2], 18[2], 19, 23, 24[2]
41:1, 2[2], 7[2], 12[3], 13[2], 14[2], 15[2], 18[2], 19, 20, 21[2], 22, 23, 24, 33
42:10, 11[4], 12, 16[2]

PSALMS

1:2[2], 3[3]
2:2, 5[2], 12
3:t, 4
7:12[2], 13, 16[4], 17
8:6
9:7, 11, 16
10:2, 3, 4[2], 5[3], 6, 7[2], 8, 9[2], 10, 11[2], 13, 15, 16
11:4[3], 5, 7
12:2
14:1, 6, 7
15:2, 3[3], 4, 5
17:12
18:t, 6[2], 8[2], 9, 11[2], 12, 13, 14, 22[2], 24, 30, 50[3]
19:1, 5[2], 6[2], 12
20:6[3]
21:2[2], 3, 5, 9
22:24, 29, 31
23:3

PSALMS

24:3, 4, 5
25:9, 10[2], 13[2], 14, 22
27:4, 5[2], 6
28:5, 8
29:2, 9[2], 11[2]
30:4[2], 5[2]
31:21, 23
33:4, 6, 11, 12, 14, 17, 18, 21
34:t, 1, 3, 6, 9, 15, 20, 22
35:8, 9, 14, 27
36:1, 2[2], 3, 4
37:7, 10, 12, 13, 23, 24, 25, 26, 28, 30, 31[3], 33, 34
38:13
39:5, 11
40:4
41:2, 3[2], 5, 6, 9
42:5, 8[2]
46:6
47:8
48:1
49:7, 16, 17, 18, 19
50:4, 6, 23
52:7[3]
53:1, 6
54:7
55:20[2], 21[3]
56:4, 10[2]
57:3[2]
58:7[2], 9, 10
59:9
60:6
61:6
62:4, 12
64:9
65:6
66:2[2], 5, 7[2], 8, 20
67:1
68:1, 4[2], 5, 21[2], 33, 34[2], 35
69:33, 36[2]
72:7, 9, 14, 17[2], 19[2]
73:10
76:1, 2[2]
77:8[2], 9
78:4[2], 7, 10, 11[2], 20, 22, 26, 32, 37, 38[2], 42, 43[2], 49, 50, 52, 54[2], 56, 61[2], 62[2], 66, 69, 70, 71[2], 72[2]
79:7
81:6[2]
85:8[2], 9, 13
87:1
89:23[2], 24, 25[2], 29[2], 30, 36[2], 39, 40[2], 41, 42[2], 43, 44[2], 45, 48
91:4[3], 11, 14
94:14[2]
95:2, 4[2], 5[2], 7[3]
96:2[2], 3[2], 6, 8[2], 13
97:2, 3, 4, 6[2], 10, 12
98:1[2], 2[2], 3[2]
99:5, 6[2], 7, 9
100:2, 3[2], 4[3], 5[2]
101:5
102:t, 16, 19, 21
103:1, 2, 7[2], 9, 11, 13, 15, 17, 18[2], 19[2], 20[3], 21[3], 22[2]
104:3[2], 4[2], 13, 15, 19, 23[2], 31
105:1[2], 2, 3, 4[2], 5[3], 6[2], 7, 8, 9, 19, 21[2], 22[3], 24, 25[2], 26, 27, 28, 42[2], 43[2], 45[2]
106:1, 2, 8[2], 12[2], 13[2], 23[2], 24, 26, 33[2], 40[2], 45[2]
107:1, 8[2], 15[2], 20, 21[2], 22, 24, 31[2]
108:7
109:6, 7, 8[2], 9[2], 10, 11, 12, 13, 14[2], 18[3], 31
110:5
111:3[2], 4, 5, 6[2], 7[2], 9[3], 10[2]
112:1, 2, 3[2], 5, 7, 8[3], 9[2], 10
113:4, 8
114:2[2]
116:2, 12, 14, 15, 18
117:2
118:1, 2, 3, 4, 29
119:2, 3, 9
125:2
126:6
127:2, 3, 5
128:1
129:7[2]
130:5, 8
131:2
132:1, 7[2], 13, 18[2]
133:2
135:3, 4, 7, 9, 12, 14[2]
136:1, 2, 3, 4, 5, 6, 7, 8, 9, 10, 11, 12, 13, 14, 15[2], 16[2], 17, 18, 19, 20, 21, 22[2], 23, 24, 25, 26
140:8
144:4, 10
145:3, 9[2], 12[2], 17[2], 21
146:4[3], 5[2]
147:5, 9, 11, 15[2], 17[2], 18[2], 19[3], 20
148:2[2], 8, 13[2], 14[2]
149:1, 3, 4, 9
150:1[2], 2[2]

PROVERBS

2:6, 8
3:11, 20, 31, 32
5:21, 22[2], 23
6:13[3], 14, 15, 27[2], 28, 29, 30, 31, 32, 33
7:23[2]
8:22[2], 29[2], 30, 31, 36
10:1, 9, 15, 19
11:1, 5[2], 7, 8, 9[2], 12[2], 17[2], 19, 20, 28, 29

PROVERBS

12:4, 8, 10, 11, 13, 14, 15, 22, 26
13:1, 2, 3[3], 8, 16, 22, 24[2], 25
14:2[2], 8, 10[2], 14, 15, 20, 21, 26, 31, 32[2], 35
15:5, 8, 20, 23, 27, 32
16:2, 7, 9[2], 10, 11, 15, 17[2], 23[2], 26, 27, 29, 30[2], 32
17:5, 12, 13, 18, 19, 21, 25, 27, 28[2]
18:2, 6, 7[3], 9, 11[2], 14, 17[2], 20[2]
19:1[2], 2, 3[2], 4, 7, 8, 11[2], 12, 13, 16[2], 18, 22, 24[3], 26[2]
20:2, 6, 7[2], 8, 11[2], 14, 16, 17, 19, 20[3], 24, 28
21:2, 8, 10[2], 13, 23[3], 24, 25, 29[2]
22:5, 8, 9, 11[2], 16, 25, 29
23:3, 6, 7[2], 14, 31
24:7, 12, 15, 18, 26, 29
25:5, 13, 18, 22, 28
26:4, 5[2], 11[2], 12, 14[2], 15[3], 16, 19, 24, 25, 26
27:8, 13, 14, 16, 17, 18, 21, 22
28:6[2], 7, 8, 9[2], 10, 11, 13, 14, 16, 18, 19, 24[2], 25, 26, 27
29:1, 3[2], 5[2], 10, 11, 12, 14, 15, 20, 21[2], 24, 25
30:4[3], 6, 10, 17[2]
31:1, 7[2]

ECCLESIASTES

1:3, 5, 6
2:14, 21, 22[2], 23[3], 24[2], 26
3:11, 12, 13, 22[2]
4:4, 5[2], 8[2], 10, 14, 15
5:14, 15[3], 17[2], 18[3], 19[2], 20[2]
6:2, 3[2], 4, 7, 12
7:2, 15[3]
8:1[2], 3, 9, 12, 13, 15[2], 16
9:12, 15, 16
10:2[2], 3, 13[2]
12:5, 13

SONG OF SOLOMON

1:2, 4, 12
2:3[2], 4, 6[2], 16
3:7, 8[2], 11[3]
4:16[2]
5:4, 11[2], 12, 13[2], 14[2], 15[2], 16
6:2
7:10
8:3[2], 7, 10

ISAIAH

1:3[2]
2:3[2], 10, 19, 20[2], 21, 22
3:5, 6[2], 8, 11, 14
5:1, 7, 12, 19, 25[4]
6:1, 2[2], 3, 6
7:2[2], 14
8:3, 7[3], 8, 17
9:4[3], 6[2], 7[2], 11, 12[2], 17[2], 19, 20, 21[2]
10:4[2], 7[2], 12[2], 16[2], 17[3], 18[2], 19, 24, 26, 27[2], 28, 32
11:1, 3[2], 4[2], 5[2], 8, 10, 11[2], 15[2], 16
12:4[3]
13:5, 10, 13, 14[2]
14:17, 18, 21, 25[2], 27, 29, 31, 32
15:4, 5
16:6[4], 12
17:4, 5, 7[2], 8[2], 9
19:1, 2[2], 14
22:21, 22, 23, 24
23:11
24:2, 23
25:4, 8, 9, 11[2]
26:21
27:1, 8, 9
28:4, 5, 21[4], 24, 26, 28[2]
29:8[2], 22, 23
30:4[2], 26, 27[3], 28, 30[3]
31:2, 3, 4, 7[2], 8, 9[3]
32:6
33:6, 15[3], 16[2], 17
34:2, 14, 16, 17
36:6, 16[3], 18
37:1, 4, 7[2], 20, 24[2], 38[4]
38:2, 9
39:2[5]
40:10[3], 11[3], 12, 13, 26, 28
41:2[3], 3, 6[2]
42:2, 4, 10, 12, 13, 21, 24[2], 25
44:5, 6, 11, 12[2], 13, 17, 19, 20, 26[2]
45:1, 9, 10, 11, 13
46:7[3]
47:4, 15
48:2, 14[2], 15, 16, 19, 20
49:2[2], 5, 7, 13[2]
50:10[2]
51:14, 15, 17, 22
52:9, 10, 14[2]
53:5, 6, 7[2], 8, 9[3], 10[4], 11[2], 12
54:5, 16
55:7[2]
56:2, 3, 6, 10, 11[2]
57:2, 13, 17[2], 18[2]
58:5[2]
59:1, 2, 16[2], 17, 18[2], 19
60:2, 22
62:8[2], 11[2]
63:1[2], 7[2], 9[3], 10, 11[3], 12
65:15, 20
66:5, 6, 13, 14[3], 15[3], 16

JEREMIAH

1:2, 9, 15
2:3, 15[2], 35
3:1, 5
4:7[3], 13[2], 26

JEREMIAH

5:8, 24
6:3, 21
7:5, 29
8:1, 6[2], 16[2]
9:4, 5, 8[3], 20, 23[3]
10:10[2], 12[3], 13[2], 14[2], 16[2], 23, 25
11:19
12:15[2]
13:23[2]
16:12
17:5, 10[2], 11[2]
18:11, 12, 16, 18
19:3, 9
20:9[2]
21:2, 7, 9
22:4[2], 7, 8, 10, 11, 13[4], 18, 28, 30[2]
23:6[2], 9, 14, 17, 18[2], 20, 27, 30, 34, 35[2], 36
24:8
25:4, 5, 19[3], 30[3], 38[2]
26:3, 21[2], 23
27:7[3], 8, 12
28:11
29:32
30:6[2], 8, 18, 21, 24
31:10, 30[2], 34[2], 35
32:4[2], 18, 19[2]
33:2, 11, 21, 26
34:1[2], 3[2], 9[3], 10[2], 14, 15, 16[2], 17[2], 21
35:3[2], 14, 15, 18
36:3, 7, 14, 17, 18, 24, 30, 31[2]
37:2, 10, 17
38:2
39:1, 6
40:3
42:11
43:10[2], 12
44:21, 23[3], 30[4]
46:8, 10, 26
47:3[3]
48:7[2], 10, 11[4], 12, 15, 16, 17, 25, 26, 29[4], 30[2], 35, 40
49:1[2], 2, 3[2], 10[4], 20, 22
50:16[2], 17, 18, 19[2], 25[2], 28, 32, 34, 43, 45
51:3[2], 5, 6, 9, 11[2], 15[3], 16[2], 17[2], 19[2], 21[2], 23[2], 28, 31, 34, 44, 45, 59
52:1, 3, 4[2], 8, 10, 11, 27, 31, 32, 33[2], 34[3]

LAMENTATIONS

1:10, 12, 14, 17, 18
2:1[3], 2, 3[2], 4[3], 5, 6[3], 7[2], 8, 17
3:1, 3, 12, 13, 22, 27, 29, 30, 32, 34, 36, 39
4:4, 11[2], 20

EZEKIEL

1:15, 27[2]
3:12, 18[4], 19[3], 20[4]
7:13, 16, 20
8:2[2], 11[2], 12
9:1[2], 2[2], 3, 11
10:7
12:12[3], 14
13:22
14:4[5], 7[4]
16:15
17:4, 14, 15, 17, 18, 19, 20, 21[2], 22
18:6[2], 7[2], 8, 11, 12, 13, 14, 15[2], 16, 17[2], 18[4], 21, 22[2], 23, 24[4], 26[2], 27[2], 28, 30
19:7, 9
20:7, 39
21:3, 4, 5, 21, 22, 30
22:11[4]
25:9[2]
26:3, 9, 10, 11
29:3, 18[2], 19, 20
30:11, 22[2], 24
31:2, 3, 4, 5[3], 6[3], 7[3], 8[3], 9, 10[3], 11, 12[3], 13[2], 16, 17[2], 18
32:10, 22, 31[2], 32
33:4[2], 5[2], 6[2], 8[3], 9[3], 11, 12[3], 13[3], 14, 16, 18, 19, 20, 26, 30
34:12[2], 26
35:8[2]
36:20
37:7, 16[2], 19
38:6[2], 21, 22
39:11
40:3
43:2[2], 17
44:27
45:8
46:2[2], 7, 12[3], 16[2], 17[3], 18[3]
47:3, 12, 23
48:1

DANIEL

1:2[3], 3, 8, 20
2:1[2], 2, 7, 13, 17[2], 18, 20, 32[4], 33[2], 34, 46
3:13, 19, 20, 24, 28[2]
4:3[4], 14[4], 15[2], 16, 19, 23, 33[3], 34, 35[2], 37
5:1, 2[4], 3[3], 6[3], 7, 9[2], 10, 20[4], 21[3], 22, 23, 29
6:5, 10[5], 11, 13, 14, 17[2], 18[2], 22, 23, 26[2]
7:1[2], 9[3], 11, 14[2], 19[2], 20[2], 25, 26
8:4[2], 5, 6, 7[2], 11, 21, 22, 24[2], 25[3]
9:2, 4, 10[2], 12, 14[2], 17
10:6[8], 9[2]
11:2[2], 3, 4[4], 5[2], 6, 7, 9[2], 10[2], 11, 12, 15, 16[2], 17[3], 18[3], 19[2], 20,

DANIEL

21, 24[3], 25[2], 26[2], 28[3], 31, 36, 37, 38[2], 41, 42, 43, 45[2]
12:7[2]

HOSEA

1:4, 9
3:5
5:5, 13[2]
6:2, 3
7:5, 9, 10
8:14[2]
9:8[2], 13
10:1[2], 6, 11
11:5, 6[2]
12:2[3], 3[2], 5, 7, 14[3]
13:12, 15[3]
14:5, 6[3], 7

JOEL

2:7, 8, 11[4], 16, 18[2], 19, 20[4]
3:16[2]

AMOS

1:2, 11[3], 15
2:4, 7, 9[2], 14
3:4, 7[2]
4:2, 13[2]
5:8, 19
6:8
7:7, 10, 17
9:6[3], 11

OBADIAH

3, 6, 11[2], 14[2]

JONAH

1:5, 7
2:1
3:6[2], 7, 8, 9
4:6[2]

MICAH

1:2, 3, 11
2:2[2], 7
3:4, 8[2]
4:2[2], 4[2], 5, 12
5:3, 4
6:2
7:2, 3, 6, 9, 18[2]

NAHUM

1:2[2], 3[2], 5, 6[3], 8, 13
2:3[2], 5, 12[4]

HABAKKUK

1:11[3]
2:4[2], 5, 6, 9[2], 15, 18, 20
3:3[2], 4[3], 5, 6, 10[2], 14[2], 16

ZEPHANIAH

1:7, 18
2:3, 11, 13, 15
3:5, 17

HAGGAI

1:9
2:12[2], 22

ZECHARIAH

1:21
2:1, 8, 12, 13
3:1, 5[2], 10
4:1, 2, 9
5:4
6:12, 13[2]
7:9, 10, 12
8:4[2], 10, 16, 17
9:7[4], 10, 14, 16[2], 17[2]
10:3[2], 12
11:6[2], 17[4]
12:4, 10[2]
13:3[4], 4
14:4, 9, 13[3]

MALACHI

1:3[2], 6[2], 12, 14
2:6[2], 7, 10, 15, 16
3:1, 2, 5[2], 14, 16, 17
4:2

MATTHEW

1:2, 11, 18, 21[2], 23, 24, 25
2:2, 11, 13, 14, 20, 21, 22
3:3, 4[3], 7, 12[3]
4:6, 18, 21, 24
5:1, 2, 13, 22[2], 28, 31, 32, 35, 45
6:27, 29, 33
7:9, 24, 26, 28
8:3[2], 13, 14, 16, 20, 21, 23, 25
9:1, 7, 10, 11, 19, 20, 21, 31, 37, 38
10:1, 2[2], 10, 24[2], 25[3], 35, 36, 38, 39[2], 42
11:1, 2, 20
12:1, 10, 19, 21, 26, 29[2], 33[3], 46[2], 49[2]
13:19, 24, 25[2], 31, 36, 41[2], 52, 54, 55[2], 56, 57[2]
14:2, 3, 11, 12, 15, 19, 22, 31, 36
15:5[2], 6[2], 12, 23, 32, 33, 36
16:5, 13, 20, 21, 24[2], 25[2], 26[2], 27[3], 28
17:1, 2[2], 10, 27
18:6, 15, 23, 25[2], 28, 29[2], 31, 32, 34, 35
19:3, 5, 9, 10[2], 13, 15, 23, 25, 28
20:1, 2, 8, 28
21:31, 34, 35, 37, 38, 41, 45
22:2, 3, 5[2], 6, 7, 8, 15, 24[3], 25[2], 33, 45
23:1
24:1, 17, 18, 31[2], 32, 43, 45[2], 46, 47, 48[2], 49, 51

MATTHEW
25:14[2], 15[2], 18, 21, 23, 26, 31[2], 32, 33, 34, 41
26:1, 7, 8, 23, 39, 45, 51[3], 52, 63, 65[2], 67
27:19, 24, 25, 29[2], 31, 32, 35, 37[2], 44, 53, 60, 64
28:3[2], 7, 8, 9, 13

MARK
1:3, 6, 16, 19, 22, 28, 41
2:8, 15[2], 16, 23
3:5, 7, 9, 21, 27[2], 31[2]
4:2, 34
5:3, 15, 22, 27, 28, 31
6:1[2], 2, 3, 4[3], 5, 14, 17, 21[2], 26, 27, 28, 29[2], 35, 41, 45, 56
7:2, 11, 12[2], 17, 19, 25, 32[2], 33[3], 35[2]
8:1, 4, 6, 10, 12, 23[2], 25[2], 26, 27[2], 33, 34[2], 35[2], 36, 37, 38
9:3, 14, 18, 21, 28, 31, 36, 41, 42, 50
10:2, 7[2], 10, 11, 13, 16[2], 23, 24, 45, 46, 48, 50, 52
11:1, 14, 18, 23
12:6, 13, 19[4], 33, 37, 38, 43
13:1, 15, 16, 27[2], 34[3]
14:3, 12, 13, 16, 32, 47, 51, 61, 63, 65
15:17, 20, 21, 24, 26, 27[2]
16:7

LUKE
1:5, 8, 9, 13, 14, 15, 23[2], 24, 29, 31, 32, 33, 48, 49, 50, 51, 54[2], 55, 59, 60, 62, 63, 64[2], 67, 68, 69, 70, 72, 76, 77, 80
2:3, 5, 21, 28, 33, 34, 41, 43, 47, 48, 51
3:1, 4, 17[3], 18, 19
4:10, 16, 22, 24, 30, 32[2], 40
5:12, 13, 19, 25, 29, 30
6:1, 10, 13, 14, 17, 20[2], 40[2], 44, 45[3]
7:1, 3, 11, 12, 15, 16, 19, 38[3]
8:5, 9, 19[2], 22, 35, 39, 41, 44
9:1, 14, 18, 23, 24[2], 26[2], 29[2], 31, 32, 42, 43, 51, 52, 53, 54, 58, 62
10:1, 2, 7, 23, 30, 34[2], 39
11:1[2], 6, 8[2], 18, 21[2], 22[2], 54
12:1, 22, 25, 27, 39, 42[2], 43, 45[2], 46, 47[2]
13:6, 7, 13, 15[2], 17, 19
14:17, 21[2], 26[2], 27, 34
15:5, 6, 12[2], 13[2], 15, 16, 20[3], 22[3], 25, 28, 29
16:1[2], 5, 18, 20, 21, 23[2], 24
17:2, 16[2], 24, 31, 33[2]
18:7, 13[2], 14, 15, 39, 43
19:13, 14, 29
20:20, 26[2], 28[3], 44, 45
22:4, 36[2], 39, 44, 45, 50, 51, 71
23:11, 34, 49, 55
24:8, 23, 26, 40[2], 47, 50

JOHN
1:11[2], 12, 14, 16, 35, 41
2:2, 5, 11[2], 12[3], 17, 21, 22, 23
3:4, 16, 17, 20, 21, 22, 32, 33[2], 35
4:2, 5, 6, 8, 12[2], 27, 31, 34, 41, 44, 47, 50, 51, 53
5:9, 18, 28, 35, 37[2], 38, 43, 47
6:2, 3, 5, 8, 12, 16, 22[3], 24, 52, 53, 60, 61, 66
7:3, 5, 10, 16, 17, 18[2], 30, 38, 53
8:6, 20, 44, 55
9:1, 2[2], 3, 7, 14, 15, 18[2], 20, 21, 22, 23, 27, 28, 31
10:3[2], 4[2], 11
11:2, 3, 7, 8, 12, 13, 16, 32, 41, 44, 54
12:3, 4, 16, 17, 25[2], 41, 50
13:1[2], 3, 4, 10, 12, 16, 18, 23
15:10, 13[2], 15, 19, 20
16:17, 29, 32
17:1
18:1[2], 2, 10, 19[2], 22, 25, 26
19:2, 17, 23[2], 25[2], 26[2], 27, 29, 30, 33, 34, 35
20:7, 20[2], 25[2], 26, 30, 31
21:2, 7, 14, 20, 24

THE ACTS
1:3, 7, 14, 18, 20[2], 22, 25
2:6, 14, 29, 30[2], 31[2], 41
3:2, 4, 7, 13, 16[2], 18, 21, 26[2]
4:26, 32
5:1, 2, 7, 10, 31, 32, 41
6:15
7:4, 5[2], 6, 10[2], 13, 14[2], 20, 23[2], 25[2], 27
8:1, 2, 28, 32[2], 33[4], 35, 39
9:8, 12[2], 17[2], 18, 33, 41
10:2, 7, 22, 24, 25, 34, 43
11:13, 29
12:1, 7[2], 10, 11, 15, 21
13:8, 9, 13, 16, 23, 24, 25[2], 31, 36[2]
14:3, 8[2]
15:14, 18
16:1, 3, 27[2], 32, 33, 34[2]
17:2, 16, 28
18:2, 6, 8, 14, 18[2]
19:6, 12, 31, 33
20:7, 10, 28, 32, 38
21:11, 19
22:14[2], 15, 20, 30
23:29, 30
24:8, 23, 24
27:3
28:3, 4, 8, 23, 30

ROMANS
1:2, 3, 5, 9, 20
2:4, 6, 18, 26
3:7, 20, 24, 25[2], 26
4:5, 13, 19, 23
5:8, 9, 10[2]
6:3, 5[2], 16
8:3, 9, 11, 28, 29, 32
9:19, 22[2], 23
11:1, 2, 22, 33[2], 34
12:20
13:10
14:4, 5, 13
15:2[2], 9, 10
16:13, 15

1 CORINTHIANS
1:9, 29
2:10
3:8[2]
5:1
6:5, 14, 18
7:2, 4, 7, 11, 33, 36, 37[4]
9:7, 10
10:24, 28
11:4[2], 7, 21
14:25[2], 30
15:10, 23[2], 25, 27, 38
16:12

2 CORINTHIANS
2:11, 14
3:7, 13
5:10
7:7, 12[2], 13, 15
8:9, 17
9:7, 9, 15
10:10[3]
11:3, 15, 33

GALATIANS
1:15, 16
3:16
4:4, 6
5:10
6:4, 5, 8

EPHESIANS
1:5, 6, 7[2], 9[2], 11, 12, 14, 18[2], 19[2], 20, 22, 23
2:4, 7[2], 10, 15
3:5, 6, 7, 16[2]
4:25, 28
5:28, 29, 30[3], 31[2], 33
6:10

PHILIPPIANS
1:29
2:4, 13, 30
3:10[3], 21
4:19

COLOSSIANS
1:9, 11, 13, 14, 20, 22[2], 24, 26, 29
2:14, 18
3:9
4:15

1 THESSALONIANS
1:10
2:11, 12, 19
3:13
4:4, 6, 8

2 THESSALONIANS
1:7, 9, 10, 11
2:6, 8[2]

1 TIMOTHY
3:4[2], 5
5:8[2], 18
6:1, 15

2 TIMOTHY
1:8, 9
2:19, 26
4:1[2], 8, 14, 18

TITUS
1:3
3:5, 7

HEBREWS
1:2, 3[3], 7[2]
2:4, 8, 17
3:2, 5, 6, 7, 15, 18
4:1, 4, 7, 10[3], 13
5:7
6:10, 17
7:10, 27
8:11[2]
9:12
10:13[2], 20, 30
11:4, 5, 7, 17, 21, 22, 23
12:10, 16
13:12, 13, 15, 21[2]

JAMES
1:8, 11, 14, 18[2], 23, 24, 25, 26[2]
2:21, 22
3:13
4:11[2]
5:20

1 PETER
1:3
2:9, 21, 22, 24[2]
3:10[2], 12
4:2, 13
5:10

2 PETER
1:3, 9, 16
2:8, 16, 22
3:4, 9, 13, 16

1 JOHN
1:3, 7, 10
2:3, 4, 5, 9, 10, 11[2], 12, 28
3:9, 10, 12[3], 14, 15, 16, 17[2], 22[2], 23[2], 24
4:9, 10, 12, 13, 20[2], 21
5:2, 3[2], 9, 10, 11, 14, 16, 20

2 JOHN
6, 11

3 JOHN
7, 10

JUDE
14, 24

REVELATION
1:1[3], 4, 5, 6, 14[3], 15[2], 16[4], 17[2]
2:1, 5, 18[2]
3:5[3], 21
6:5, 8, 17
7:15
9:11
10:1[3], 2[3], 5, 7
11:15, 19[2]
12:3, 4, 5, 7[2], 9, 10, 15, 16
13:1[2], 2[4], 3[2], 6[3], 17, 18
14:1, 7, 9[4], 10, 11[2], 14[2], 16, 19
15:2[3], 8
16:2[2], 3, 4, 8, 10[2], 12, 15[2], 17, 19
17:17
18:1
19:2[2], 5, 7, 10, 12[2], 13, 15, 16[2], 19, 20, 21
20:1, 4[2], 7
21:3, 7
22:3, 4[2], 6[2], 12, 14, 19

I

589, *1473*

GENESIS
1:29, 30
2:18
3:10[4], 11, 12, 13, 15, 16, 17
4:1, 9[2], 13, 14[2], 23
6:7[3], 13, 17[2], 18
7:1, 4[3]
8:21[3]
9:3, 5[3], 9[2], 11, 12, 13, 14, 15, 16[2], 17
12:1, 2[2], 3, 7, 11, 13, 19
13:8, 9[3], 15, 16, 17
14:22, 23[3]
15:1, 2, 7, 8[2], 14, 18
16:2[2], 5[2], 8, 10, 13
17:1, 2, 5, 6[2], 7, 8[2], 16[2], 19, 20[3], 21
18:3[2], 4, 5, 10, 12[2], 13, 14, 15, 17[2], 19, 21[2], 26[2], 27, 28[2], 29, 30[3], 31[2], 32[2]
19:2, 7, 8[2], 19[2], 21[2], 22, 34
20:5, 6[2], 9, 11, 13, 16
21:7, 13, 18, 23, 24, 26[2], 30
22:1, 2, 5, 7, 11, 12, 16, 17[2]
23:4[2], 8, 11[3], 13[3]
24:2, 3[2], 5, 7, 12, 13, 14[5], 17, 19, 23, 24, 27, 31, 33[2], 34, 37, 39, 40, 42[2], 43[3], 44, 45[3], 46[2], 47[2], 48, 49, 56, 58
25:22, 30[2], 32
26:2, 3[4], 4, 9[2], 24[2]
27:1, 2[2], 3, 4[3], 6, 7, 8, 9, 11, 12[2], 18, 19[3], 21[2], 24, 25, 32, 33, 37[4], 41, 45[2], 46
28:13[2], 15[4], 16, 20, 21, 22[2]
29:18, 19[2], 21, 25, 33, 34, 35
30:1, 2, 3, 8[2], 13, 14, 16, 18, 20, 25, 26[2], 27[3], 28, 29, 30[2], 31[2], 32, 34
31:3, 5, 6, 10, 11[2], 12, 13, 27, 31[2], 35, 38[2], 39[2], 40, 41[2], 43, 44, 51, 52
32:4, 5[3], 9, 10[3], 11[2], 12, 20[2], 26, 29, 30
33:8, 9, 10[4], 11[2], 12, 14[3]
34:8, 11, 12, 30[3]
35:3[2], 11, 12[3]
37:6[2], 9, 10, 13[2], 14, 16[2], 17, 30[2], 35
38:16, 17, 18, 22, 23, 25[2], 26[2]
39:9[2], 14, 15, 18
40:8, 11[2], 14, 15[2], 16[2]
41:9, 11, 15[2], 17, 19, 21, 22, 24, 28, 40, 41, 44
42:2, 14, 18, 22, 33, 34[2], 37[2]
43:9[2], 14[2], 23
44:15, 17, 18, 21, 28[2], 30, 32[2], 33, 34[2]
45:3, 4[2], 11, 18, 28[2]
46:2, 3[2], 4[2], 30, 31
47:16, 23, 29[3], 30[2]
48:4[2], 5, 7[2], 9[2], 11, 19[2], 21, 22[2]
49:1, 7, 18, 29, 31
50:4[2], 5[4], 17, 19, 21, 24

EXODUS
2:7, 9, 10, 22
3:3, 4, 6, 7[2], 8, 9, 10, 11[3], 12[2], 13[2], 14[3], 16, 17[2], 19, 20[2], 21
4:10[2], 11, 12, 13, 14, 15, 18, 21[2], 23[2]
5:2[3], 10, 23
6:1, 2, 3[2], 4, 5[2], 6[4], 7[3], 8[4], 29[2], 30
7:1, 2, 3, 4, 5[2], 17[2]
8:2, 8, 9, 21, 22[2], 23, 28, 29[2]
9:14, 15[2], 16, 18, 27[2], 28, 29[2], 30
10:1[2], 2[3], 4, 10, 16, 17, 29
11:1, 4, 8
12:12[3], 13[3], 17
13:8, 15[2]
14:4[3], 17[3], 18[2]
15:1, 2[2], 9[4], 26[3]
16:4[2], 12[2], 32[2]
17:4, 6, 9, 14
18:3, 6, 11, 16[2], 19
19:4[2], 9[2]
20:2, 5, 22, 24[2]
21:5[2], 13
22:23, 24, 27[2]
23:7, 13, 15, 20[2], 22[2], 23, 25, 26, 27[2], 28, 29, 30, 31[2]
24:12[2]
25:8, 9, 16, 21, 22[3]
28:3
29:35, 42, 43, 44[2], 45, 46[3]
30:6, 36
31:2, 3, 6[4], 11, 13
32:8, 9, 10[2], 13[3], 18, 24[2], 30[2], 32, 33, 34[3]
33:1[2], 2[2], 3[2], 5[2], 12, 13[4], 14, 16[2], 17[2], 18, 19[4], 22[2], 23
34:1, 9[2], 10[3], 11[2], 18, 24, 27

LEVITICUS
6:17
7:34
8:31, 35
10:3[2], 13, 18, 19
11:44[2], 45[2]
14:34[2]
16:2
17:10, 11, 12, 14
18:2, 3, 4, 5, 6, 21, 24, 25, 30
19:2, 3, 4, 10, 12, 14, 16, 18, 25, 28, 30, 31, 32, 34, 36, 37
20:3, 5, 6, 7, 8, 22, 23[2], 24[3], 25, 26
21:8, 12, 15, 23
22:2, 3, 8, 9, 16, 30, 31, 32[2], 33
23:10, 22, 30, 43[3]
24:22
25:2, 17, 21, 38, 42, 55[2]
26:1, 2, 4, 6[2], 9, 11, 12, 13[2], 16[2], 17, 18, 19[2], 21, 22, 24, 25[2], 26, 28[3], 30, 31[2], 32, 33, 36, 41, 42[3], 44[3], 45[4]

NUMBERS
3:12[2], 13[3], 41, 45
5:3
6:27
8:16, 17[2], 18, 19
9:8
10:10, 29, 30[2], 31
11:11, 12[2], 13, 14, 15[2], 17[2], 21[2]
12:6, 8, 11, 13
13:2
14:11, 12, 17, 19, 20, 21, 22, 23, 24, 27[2], 28[2], 30, 31, 35[2]
15:2, 18, 41[2]
16:8, 15[2], 21, 26, 28, 45
17:4, 5[2]
18:6[2], 7, 8[2], 11, 12, 19, 20, 21, 24[2], 26
20:12, 17, 18, 19[3], 24
21:2, 16, 34
22:6[4], 8, 11, 16, 17[3], 18, 19[2], 20, 28, 29[2], 30[3], 32, 33, 34[3], 35, 37[2], 38[3]
23:3[2], 4[2], 8[2], 9[2], 11, 12, 13, 15, 20[2], 26[2], 27[2]
24:10, 11, 12, 13[2], 14[2], 17[2]
25:11, 12
27:12
32:8, 11
33:53, 56[2]
35:34[2]

DEUTERONOMY
1:8, 9[2], 12, 13, 15, 16, 17, 18, 20, 23, 29, 35, 36, 39, 42, 43
2:5[2], 9[2], 13, 19[2], 24, 25, 26, 27[2], 28[3], 29, 31
3:2, 12, 13, 15, 16, 18, 19[2], 20, 21, 23, 25
4:1, 2[2], 5, 8, 10, 21[2], 22[2], 26, 40
5:1, 5, 6, 9, 28, 31[2]
6:2, 6
7:11, 17[2]
8:1, 11, 19
9:9[3], 12, 13, 14[2], 15, 16, 17, 18[2], 19, 20, 21[2], 23, 24, 25[2], 26
10:2, 3, 5[2], 10, 11, 13
11:2, 8, 13, 14, 15, 22, 26, 27, 28, 32
12:11, 14, 20, 21, 28, 30, 32
13:18
15:5, 11, 15, 16
17:3, 14
18:16, 18[2], 19, 20
19:7, 9
22:14[3], 16, 17
24:8, 18, 22
25:8
26:3[2], 10, 13[3], 14[3]
27:1, 4, 10
28:1, 13, 14, 15, 68
29:5, 6, 14, 19[2]
30:1, 2, 8, 11, 15, 16, 18, 19[2]
31:2[2], 5, 14, 16, 17[2], 18, 20[2], 21[3], 23[2], 27[2], 28, 29[2]
32:1, 3, 20[2], 21[2], 23[2], 24, 26[3], 27, 39[6], 40[2], 41[2], 42, 46, 49, 52
33:9
34:4[3]

JOSHUA
1:2, 3[2], 5[3], 6, 9
2:4, 5, 9, 12[2]
3:7[3]
5:9, 14
6:2, 10
7:8, 11, 12, 19, 20[2], 21[2]
8:1, 5, 8, 18
10:8
11:6
13:6[2]
14:7[2], 8, 10, 11[2], 12
15:16
17:14
18:4, 6, 8
20:2
22:2
23:2, 4[2], 14
24:3, 4[2], 5[4], 6, 7, 8[3], 10[2], 11, 12, 13

JUDGES
1:2, 3, 7, 12
2:1[4], 3[2], 20, 21, 22
3:19, 20
4:7[2], 8[2], 9, 19[2], 22
5:3[3], 7[2]
6:8, 9, 10[2], 14, 15[2], 16, 17, 18[3], 22, 37[2], 39[2]
7:4[3], 7, 9, 13, 17[2], 18[2]
8:2, 3, 5[2], 7, 9[2], 19, 23, 24
9:2[2], 9, 11, 13, 29, 38, 48
10:11, 12, 13
11:9, 17, 27, 31[2], 35[2], 37[2]
12:2[2], 3[2]
13:4, 6, 11, 13, 14, 15, 16
14:2, 12[2], 16[2]
15:1, 2[3], 3[2], 7[2], 11, 16, 18
16:6, 7, 10, 11, 15, 17[3], 20, 26[2], 28[3]
17:2, 3[2], 9[3], 10, 13[2]
18:4, 24[2]
19:6, 8, 9, 11, 18[3], 23, 24
20:4[2], 6, 23, 28[3]

RUTH
1:12[4], 16[2], 17[2], 21
2:2, 7, 9, 10[2], 13, 19
3:1, 5, 9, 11, 12[2], 13
4:4[4], 6[3], 9, 10

1 SAMUEL
1:8, 11, 15[2], 16, 20, 22[2], 26, 27[2], 28
2:1, 16, 23, 24, 27, 28[2], 29, 30[2], 31, 33, 35[2], 36[2]
3:4, 5[2], 6[2], 8, 11, 12[4], 13[2], 14, 16, 17
4:16[2]
7:5
8:7, 8
9:8[2], 16[2], 17, 18, 19[2], 21, 23[2], 24[2], 26, 27
10:2, 8[2], 15, 18
11:2[2]
12:1, 2[2], 3[7], 7, 17, 23[2]
13:11, 12[3]
14:7, 24, 29[2], 37, 40, 43[2]
15:2, 6, 11, 13, 14, 16, 20, 24[3], 25[2], 26, 30[3]
16:1[3], 2[2], 3[2], 5, 7, 18, 22
17:8, 9, 10, 28, 29, 35[2], 39[2], 43, 44, 45, 46[2], 55, 58
18:11, 17, 18[2], 21, 23
19:2, 3[4], 15, 17
20:1, 3, 4, 5[2], 9[2], 12[2], 13, 14[2], 20[2], 21[2], 22, 23, 29[3], 30, 36
21:2[3], 5, 8, 15
22:3[2], 9, 12, 15, 22[2]
23:2, 4, 11, 17, 22, 23[2]
24:4, 6, 10[2], 11[2], 17[2], 20
25:7, 8, 11[3], 19, 21, 22, 24, 25[2], 28, 35
26:6, 8[2], 11[2], 18, 19, 21[3], 23
27:1[3], 5[2]
28:2, 7, 8[2], 11, 13, 15[3], 21, 22, 23
29:3, 6, 8[3], 9
30:7, 8[2], 13[2], 15

2 SAMUEL
1:3, 4, 6, 7[2], 8[2], 9, 10[3], 13, 16, 26
2:1[2], 6, 20, 22[2]
3:8, 9, 13[2], 14, 18, 21, 28, 35, 39
4:10[2], 11
5:19[2]
6:21, 22[2]
7:2, 6[2], 7[3], 8, 9, 10, 11, 12[2], 13, 14[2], 15[2], 18, 27
9:1, 3, 7, 8, 9
10:2, 11
11:5, 11[2], 12
12:7[2], 8[2], 11[2], 12, 13, 22[2], 23[3], 27, 28
13:4, 5[2], 6[2], 10, 13[3], 24, 26, 28[2]
14:2, 5, 8, 11, 12, 15[2], 18[2], 21, 22, 32[3]
15:4[2], 7[2], 8[2], 20[3], 25, 26[2], 28, 31, 34[3]
16:4[2], 9, 10, 18[2], 19[4]
17:1, 2[2], 3, 11, 15
18:2, 4, 10, 11, 12[2], 13, 14, 18, 22, 29[2], 33
19:6, 7, 20[2], 22[3], 26[2], 28, 29, 33, 34[2], 35[5], 37[2], 38[2]
20:16[2], 17[2], 19, 20, 21
21:3[2], 4, 6
22:3, 4[2], 7, 22, 23, 24, 30[2], 38[2], 39, 41, 43[2], 44, 50[2]
23:17
24:2, 10[4], 12[2], 13, 14, 17[3], 24[2]

1 KINGS
1:5, 12, 14, 21, 30[2], 35
2:2, 7, 8[3], 14, 15, 16, 17, 18, 20[3], 26, 30, 42[2], 43
3:5, 7[2], 9, 12[2], 13, 14, 17[2], 18, 21[3]
5:5[2], 6, 8[2], 9
6:12[2], 13
8:13, 16[3], 20, 21, 26, 27, 43, 44, 48, 59
9:3[2], 4, 5[2], 6, 7[4]
10:6, 7[3]
11:11[2], 12[2], 13[2], 21, 31, 32, 34[3], 35, 36[2], 37, 38[3], 39
12:6, 11[2], 14[2]
13:7, 8[2], 14, 16[2], 18, 31
14:2[2], 6, 7, 10
15:19
16:2, 3
17:1, 4, 9, 10[2], 11, 12[3], 18, 20, 21, 24
18:1, 8, 9, 12[4], 13[2], 15[2], 18, 22[2], 23, 24, 36[2]
19:2, 4, 10[3], 14[3], 18, 20[3]
20:4[2], 5, 6, 7[2], 9[2], 13[2], 28[2], 31, 32, 34[2], 35, 37, 42
21:2[3], 3, 4, 6[3], 7, 20, 21, 29[2]
22:4, 5, 6[2], 8, 13, 14, 16, 17, 18, 19, 21, 22[2], 27, 30, 34

2 KINGS
1:2, 10, 12, 13
2:2[2], 3, 4[2], 5, 6[2], 9[3], 10, 18, 19, 21
3:7[2], 13, 14[3]
4:2, 9, 10, 13, 22[2], 24, 26, 28[2], 30, 43
5:5, 6, 7[2], 11, 12, 15[2], 16[2], 17, 18[2], 20, 22
6:3[2], 13, 17, 18, 19, 21[2], 27, 29, 33
7:12, 13[2]
8:4, 8, 9, 12
9:3, 5, 6, 7, 8, 9, 12, 17, 25, 26[2]
10:9, 19, 24
16:7
17:13[2], 38
18:14[2], 20, 23[2], 25, 26, 32
19:7[2], 19, 20, 23[2], 24[2], 25[3], 27, 28[2], 34
20:3[2], 5[3], 6[3], 8, 15
21:4, 7[2], 8[3], 12, 13[2], 14
22:8, 16, 19[2], 20[2]
23:17, 27[4]

1 CHRONICLES
4:9
5:3
11:19[2]
13:12
14:10[2]
15:12
16:18
17:1, 5[2], 6[3], 7, 8, 9, 10[3], 11[2], 12, 13[3], 14, 16
19:2, 12
21:2, 8[4], 10[2], 12, 13, 17[3], 22, 23[2], 24[2]
22:5, 9[2], 10[2], 14[2]
23:5
28:2, 6[2], 7
29:2, 3[4], 14, 17[3], 19

2 CHRONICLES
1:7, 10, 11, 12
2:4, 5, 6[2], 8, 9, 10, 13
6:2, 5[3], 6, 10, 11, 18, 33, 34, 38, 40

2 CHRONICLES

7:12, 13[3], 14, 16, 17, 18[2], 19, 20[4]
9:5, 6[3]
10:11[2], 14[2]
12:5, 7[2]
16:3
18:3, 4, 5, 7, 12, 13, 14, 15, 16, 17, 18, 20, 21, 26, 29, 33
20:11
25:9, 16
28:23
32:13
33:7[2], 8[3]
34:15, 24, 27, 28[2]
35:21[3], 23

EZRA

4:19
6:8, 11, 12
7:13, 21[2], 28[2]
8:15[2], 16, 17[2], 21, 22, 24, 26, 28
9:3[2], 4, 5[2], 6

NEHEMIAH

1:1, 2, 4[2], 5, 6[2], 8[2], 9[2], 11[3]
2:1[2], 2, 4, 5[2], 6, 7[2], 8, 9, 11, 12[4], 13, 14, 15, 16[3], 17, 18, 20
4:13[2], 14, 19, 22, 23
5:6[2], 7[3], 8, 9, 10[2], 11, 12, 13, 14[2], 15, 16, 18, 19
6:1[2], 3[4], 4, 8, 10, 11[4], 12, 13
7:1, 2, 3, 5, 7
9:8
12:31, 38, 40
13:6[3], 7, 8, 9[2], 10, 11[2], 13, 14, 15[2], 17, 19[2], 21[2], 22, 23, 25, 28, 30

ESTHER

3:9
4:11, 16[4]
5:4, 8[3], 12, 13
7:3, 4[2]
8:5[2], 6[2], 7

JOB

1:15, 16, 17, 19, 21[2]
3:3, 11[3], 12, 13[3], 16, 24, 25[2], 26[3]
4:7, 8, 16[2]
5:3[2], 8[2]
6:8[2], 10[3], 11[2], 22, 24[2], 28, 29
7:3, 4[4], 8, 11[3], 12, 13, 16[2], 19, 20[3], 21[2]
8:8, 18
9:2, 11[2], 14, 15[3], 16[2], 19, 20[3], 21[3], 22, 27[3], 28[2], 29[2], 30, 32[2], 35
10:1[2], 2, 7, 9, 13, 14, 15[4], 18, 19[3], 20, 21[2]
11:4
12:3[2], 4
13:2[2], 3[2], 13, 14, 15[2], 18[3], 19[2], 20, 22
14:14, 15
15:6, 17[3]
16:2, 4[2], 5, 6[3], 12, 15, 22[2]
17:6, 10, 13[2], 14
19:4, 7[3], 8, 10, 15, 16[2], 17, 18, 19, 20, 25, 26, 27
20:2, 3
21:3[2], 6[2], 27
22:22
23:3[3], 4, 5, 7, 8[2], 9[2], 10[2], 11, 12[2], 15[3], 17
27:5[3], 6[2], 11[2]
29:2, 3, 4, 6, 7[2], 12, 13, 14, 15[2], 16[3], 17, 18[3], 24, 25
30:1[2], 9[2], 19, 20[2], 23, 25, 26[2], 28[3], 29
31:1[2], 5, 9, 13, 14[2], 16, 18, 19, 21[2], 23, 24, 25, 26, 28, 29, 30, 32, 33, 34[2], 36, 37[2], 39
32:6[2], 7, 10[2], 11[2], 12, 14, 16, 17[3], 18, 20[3], 21, 22
33:1, 2, 6[2], 8, 9[2], 12, 24, 27, 31, 32, 33
34:5, 6, 31[2], 32[3], 33
35:3[2], 4
36:2[2], 3
37:20
38:3, 4, 9, 23
39:6
40:4[3], 5[3], 7, 14, 15
41:11, 12
42:2, 3[3], 4[3], 5, 6, 8[2]

PSALMS

2:6, 7[2], 8
3:4, 5[2], 6
4:1[2], 3, 8
5:2, 3, 7[2]
6:2, 6[3]
7:1, 3, 4[2], 17
8:3
9:1[2], 2[2], 13, 14[2]
10:6[2]
11:1
12:5[2]
13:2, 3, 4[2], 5, 6
16:1, 4, 6, 7, 8[2]
17:3, 4, 6, 15[3]
18:1, 2, 3[2], 6, 21, 22, 23[2], 29[2], 37[2], 38, 40, 42[2], 43, 49
19:13[2]
20:6
22:2, 6, 9, 10, 14, 17, 22[2], 25
23:1, 4[2], 6
25:1, 2, 5, 16, 20, 21
26:1[3], 3, 4[2], 5, 6[2], 7, 8, 11, 12
27:1[2], 3, 4[3], 6[3], 7, 8, 13[2], 14
28:1[2], 2[2], 7[2]
30:1, 2, 3, 6[2], 7, 8[2], 9, 12

PSALMS

31:1, 5, 6[2], 7, 9, 11, 12[2], 13, 14[2], 17, 22[3]
32:3, 5[4], 8[2]
34:1, 4, 11
35:3, 11, 13, 14[2], 15, 18[2]
37:25[2], 35, 36
38:6[3], 8[2], 13[2], 14, 15, 16, 17, 18[2], 20
39:1[4], 2[2], 3[2], 4[2], 7, 9[2], 10, 12, 13[2]
40:1, 5, 7[2], 8, 9[2], 10[3], 12, 17
41:4[2], 9, 10, 11
42:2, 4[4], 5, 6, 9[2], 11
43:2, 4[2], 5
44:6
45:1[2], 17
46:10[3]
49:4[2], 5
50:7[3], 8, 9, 11, 12[2], 13, 15, 21[3], 22, 23
51:3, 4, 5, 7[2], 13, 16
52:8[2], 9[2]
54:6[2]
55:2, 6[3], 7, 8, 9, 12[2], 16, 17, 23
56:3[2], 4[3], 9[2], 10[2], 11[2], 12, 13
57:1, 2, 4, 7, 8, 9[2]
59:9, 16[2], 17
60:6[2], 8
61:2[2], 4[2], 8[2]
62:2, 6, 11
63:1, 2, 4[3], 6, 7
66:13[2], 14, 15[2], 16, 17, 18
68:22[2]
69:2[2], 3[2], 4[2], 7, 8, 10, 11[2], 12, 17, 20[3], 29, 30
70:5
71:1, 3, 6, 7, 14, 15, 16[2], 17, 18[2], 22[2], 23
73:3[2], 13, 14, 15[3], 16, 17[2], 21, 22[2], 23, 25[2], 28[2]
75:2[2], 3, 4, 9[2], 10
77:1, 2, 3[2], 4[2], 5, 6[2], 10[2], 11[2], 12
78:2[2]
81:5[2], 6, 7[3], 8, 10[2], 12, 14, 16
82:6
84:10
85:8
86:1, 2, 3, 4, 7, 11, 12[2]
87:4
88:1, 4[2], 8[2], 9[2], 13, 15[3]
89:1[2], 2, 3[2], 4, 19[2], 20[2], 23, 25, 27, 28, 29, 32, 33, 34, 35[2], 50
91:2[2], 14[2], 15[3], 16
92:4, 10
94:18
95:10, 11
101:1[2], 2[2], 3[2], 4, 5[2], 8[2]
102:2[2], 4, 6[2], 7, 9, 11, 24
104:33[4], 34
105:11
106:5[3]
108:1, 2, 3[2], 7[2], 9[2]
109:4, 22, 23[2], 25, 30[2]
110:1
111:1
116:1, 2[2], 3, 4[2], 6, 9, 10[3], 11, 12, 13, 14, 16[2], 17, 18
118:5, 6, 7, 10, 11, 12, 13, 17, 19[2], 21, 25[2], 28[2]
119:6[2], 7[2], 8, 10, 11[2], 13, 14, 15, 16[2], 17, 18, 19, 22, 26, 27, 30[2], 31, 32, 33, 34[2], 35, 39, 40, 42[2], 43, 44, 45[2], 46, 47[2], 48[3], 51, 52, 55, 56[2], 57[2], 58, 59, 60, 61, 62, 63, 66, 67[3], 69, 70, 71[2], 73, 74, 75, 76, 77, 78, 80, 81, 83[2], 87, 88, 92, 93, 94[2], 95, 96, 97, 99, 100[2], 101[2], 102, 104[2], 106[3], 107, 108, 109, 110, 111, 112, 113[2], 114, 115, 116, 117[2], 119, 120, 121, 125[2], 127, 128[2], 131[2], 134, 141[2], 144, 145[2], 146[2], 147[2], 148, 152, 153, 157, 158, 159, 162, 163[2], 164, 166, 167, 168, 173, 174, 176[2]
120:1, 5[2], 7[2]
121:1
122:1, 8, 9
123:1
130:1, 5[2], 6
131:1, 2
132:3, 4, 5, 11, 12, 14[2], 15[2], 16, 17[2], 18
135:5
137:5, 6[2]
138:1[2], 2, 3, 7
139:6, 7[2], 8[2], 9, 11, 14[2], 15, 18[3], 21[2], 22[2]
140:6, 12
141:1[2], 10
142:1[2], 2[2], 3, 4, 5[2], 6[2], 7
143:5[3], 6, 7, 8[3], 9, 12
144:2, 9[2]
145:1[2], 2[2], 5, 6
146:2[4]

PROVERBS

1:23[2], 24[2], 26[2], 28
3:28
4:2, 3, 11[2]
5:12, 14
7:6, 7, 14[2], 15[2], 16, 17
8:4, 6, 12, 13, 14[2], 17, 20, 21[2], 23, 24, 25, 27, 30[2]
9:5
20:9[2], 22
22:13, 19, 20, 21
23:35[4]
24:29[2], 30, 32[2]
26:19

PROVERBS

27:11
30:2, 3, 7[2], 9[2], 18, 20

ECCLESIASTES

1:12, 13, 14, 16[2], 17[2]
2:1[2], 2, 3[2], 4[3], 5[2], 6, 7[2], 8[2], 9, 10[2], 11[2], 12, 13, 14, 15[3], 17, 18[3], 19[2], 20[2], 24, 25
3:10, 12, 14, 16, 17, 18, 22
4:1, 2, 4, 7[2], 8, 15
5:13, 18
6:1, 3
7:15, 23[3], 25, 26, 27, 28[3], 29
8:2, 9, 10, 12, 14, 15, 16, 17
9:1, 11, 13, 16
10:5, 7
12:1

SONG OF SOLOMON

1:5, 6[2], 7, 9
2:1, 3, 5, 7, 16
3:1[3], 2[4], 3, 4[4], 5
4:6
5:1[4], 2, 3[4], 5, 6[4], 8[2]
6:3, 11, 12
7:8[3], 10, 12, 13
8:1[3], 2[2], 4, 5, 10[2]

ISAIAH

1:2, 11[2], 13, 14, 15[2], 24, 25, 26
3:4, 7
5:1, 3, 4[2], 5[3], 6[2]
6:1, 5[4], 8[4], 11
7:12[2]
8:2, 3, 11, 17[2], 18
10:6[2], 11[2], 12, 13[4], 14
12:1, 2
13:3[2], 11[2], 12, 13, 17
14:13[3], 14[2], 22, 23[2], 24[2], 25, 30
15:9
16:9[2], 10
18:4[2]
19:2, 3, 4, 11
21:2, 3[2], 8[2], 10[2]
22:4[2], 19, 20, 21[2], 22, 23
23:4[2]
24:16
25:1[2]
26:9[2]
27:3[3], 4[2]
28:16, 17, 22
29:2, 3[2], 11[2], 12[2], 14
30:7
33:10[3], 13, 24
36:5[2], 8[2], 10, 11, 17
37:7[2], 24[3], 25[2], 26[3], 28, 29[2], 35
38:3[2], 5[3], 6[2], 8, 10[3], 11[3], 12, 13, 14[3], 15[2], 17, 19, 22
39:4
40:6, 25
41:4[2], 8, 9[2], 10[5], 13[2], 14, 15, 17[2], 18[2], 19[2], 25, 27, 28[2]
42:1[2], 6, 8[2], 9[2], 14[4], 15[3], 16[4], 19
43:1[2], 2, 3[2], 4[2], 5[2], 6, 7[3], 10[2], 11[2], 12[3], 13[2], 14, 15, 19[2], 20, 21, 23, 25[2], 28
44:1, 2, 3[2], 5, 6[2], 7[2], 8[2], 16[2], 19[5], 21, 22[2], 24, 26, 27
45:1[2], 2[2], 3[2], 4[2], 5[2], 6, 7[3], 8, 12[3], 13[2], 18, 19[4], 21, 22, 23, 24
46:4[5], 9[2], 10, 11[4], 13[2]
47:3[2], 6[2], 7, 8[3], 10
48:3[3], 4, 5[2], 6, 7, 8, 9[3], 10[2], 11[2], 12[3], 13, 15[4], 16[2], 17
49:3, 4[3], 5, 6, 8[3], 11, 15, 16, 18, 20, 21[2], 22, 23, 25[2], 26[2]
50:1[2], 2[5], 3[2], 4, 5, 6[2], 7[4]
51:2, 4, 12[2], 15, 16[3], 19, 22, 23
52:5, 6[2]
53:12
54:7[2], 8[2], 9[3], 11, 12, 16[2]
55:3, 4, 11[2]
56:3, 5[2], 7, 8, 12
57:6, 11, 12, 15, 16[3], 17[2], 18[2], 19[2]
58:5, 6, 9, 14
59:21
60:7, 10[2], 13, 15, 16, 17[3], 21, 22
61:8[4], 10
62:1[2], 6, 8
63:1, 3[3], 5[2], 6[2], 7
65:1[3], 2, 5, 6, 7, 8[2], 9, 12[4], 17, 18[2], 19, 24[2]
66:2, 4[4], 9[2], 12, 13, 18[2], 19[2], 21, 22

JEREMIAH

1:5[4], 6[3], 7[3], 8, 9, 10, 11[2], 12, 13[2], 15, 16, 17[2], 18, 19
2:2, 7, 9[2], 20[2], 21, 23[2], 25[2], 30, 31, 34, 35[3]
3:7, 8[2], 12[3], 14[3], 15, 18, 19[3], 22
4:6, 10, 12, 19[2], 21, 23, 24, 25, 26, 27, 28[3], 31
5:1, 4, 5, 7[2], 9, 14, 15, 18, 29
6:2, 8, 10, 11[3], 12, 15, 17, 19, 21, 27
7:3, 7[2], 11, 12[2], 13[2], 14[3], 15[2], 16, 22[2], 23[3], 25, 31, 34
8:3, 6[2], 10, 13[2], 17, 18, 21[2]
9:1, 2[2], 7[2], 9, 10, 11[2], 13, 15, 16[3], 24[2], 25
10:18, 19[2], 23
11:4[4], 5[3], 7[2], 8[2], 10, 11[2], 14, 18, 19[2], 20, 22, 23
12:1, 7[3], 8, 14[2], 15[2], 17
13:2, 5, 6, 7[2], 9, 11, 13, 14[2], 24, 26, 27
14:12[3], 13[2], 14[2], 15, 16, 18[2]
15:3, 4, 6[2], 7[3], 8[2], 9, 10, 11, 13, 14, 15, 16[2], 17[2], 19, 20[2], 21[2]

JEREMIAH

16:5, 9, 13[2], 15[2], 16[2], 18, 21[2]
17:3, 4[2], 10[2], 14[2], 16[2], 22, 27
18:2, 3, 6, 7, 8[3], 9, 10[3], 11, 17[2], 20
19:2, 3, 5, 7[3], 8, 9, 11, 12, 15[2]
20:4[2], 5[2], 7[3], 8[3], 9[4], 10, 12, 14, 18
21:2, 4[2], 5, 6, 7, 8, 10, 13, 14[2]
22:5, 6, 7, 14, 21[2], 24[2], 25, 26
23:2, 3[2], 4, 5, 8, 9, 11, 12, 13, 14, 15, 21[2], 23, 24[2], 25[3], 30, 31, 32[2], 33, 34, 38, 39[4], 40
24:3, 5[2], 6[4], 7[3], 8, 9[2], 10[2]
25:3, 6, 9, 10, 12, 13[2], 14, 15, 16, 17, 27, 29[2]
26:2, 3[2], 4, 5, 6, 14
27:5, 6[2], 8[2], 10, 11, 12, 15[2], 16, 22[2]
28:2, 3, 4[2], 7, 11, 14[2], 16
29:4, 7, 9, 10, 11[2], 12, 14[6], 17, 18[2], 19, 20, 21, 23[2], 31, 32[2]
30:2, 3[3], 6, 8, 9, 10, 11[5], 14, 15, 16, 17[2], 18, 19[2], 20, 21, 22
31:1, 2, 3[2], 4, 8, 9[3], 13, 14, 18[3], 19[6], 20[3], 23, 25[2], 26, 27, 28[2], 31, 32[3], 33[2], 34[2], 37
32:3, 5, 8[2], 9, 10, 11, 12, 13, 16[2], 27, 28, 31, 33, 35, 37[4], 38, 39, 40[3], 41[2], 42[3], 44
33:3, 5[2], 6[2], 7, 8[2], 9[2], 11, 14[2], 15, 22, 25, 26[3]
34:2, 5, 13[2], 17[2], 18, 20, 21, 22[2]
35:3, 4, 5[2], 14, 15[2], 17[4]
36:2[2], 3[2], 5[2], 18, 31[3]
37:14, 18, 20[3]
38:14, 15[2], 16[2], 19, 20[2], 25, 26
39:16, 17, 18
40:4[2], 10, 15[2]
42:4[4], 10[4], 11, 12, 17, 19, 21
43:10[2], 12
44:2, 4[2], 10, 11, 12, 13[2], 26, 27, 29, 30[2]
45:3[2], 4[4], 5[2]
46:5, 8[2], 18, 25, 26, 27, 28[5]
48:12, 30, 31[2], 32, 33, 35, 38, 44, 47
49:2, 5, 6, 8[2], 10[2], 11, 13, 14, 15, 16, 19[2], 27, 32[2], 35, 36, 37[4], 38, 39
50:9, 18[2], 19, 20[2], 21, 24, 31[2], 32, 44[2]
51:1, 14, 20[2], 21[2], 22[3], 23[3], 24, 25[2], 36[2], 39[2], 40, 44[2], 47, 52, 57, 64

LAMENTATIONS

1:11, 14, 16, 18[2], 19, 20[2], 21
2:13[4], 22
3:1, 7, 8, 14, 17, 18, 21[2], 24, 54[2], 55, 57, 63

EZEKIEL

1:1[2], 4, 15, 24, 27[2], 28[3]
2:1, 2, 3, 4, 8[2], 9
3:2, 3[2], 6, 8, 9, 10, 12, 13, 14, 15[2], 17, 18[2], 20[2], 22, 23[3], 26, 27[2]
4:5, 6, 8, 13, 14[2], 15, 16
5:2, 5, 8[2], 9[3], 10[2], 11[3], 12[2], 13[4], 14, 15[2], 16[3], 17[3]
6:3[3], 4, 5[2], 7, 8, 9, 10[3], 12, 13, 14[2]
7:3, 4[3], 8[2], 9[3], 20, 21, 22, 24[2], 27[3]
8:1, 2, 4, 5, 6, 7, 8, 10, 18[3]
9:8[2], 10[2], 11
10:1, 9, 15, 20[2], 22
11:1, 5, 7, 8, 9, 10[2], 11, 12, 13[2], 16[3], 17[2], 19[3], 20, 21, 24, 25
12:6, 7[6], 11[2], 13[2], 14[2], 15[2], 16[2], 20, 23, 25[4], 28
13:7, 8, 9, 13, 14[2], 15, 20[2], 21[2], 22, 23[2]
14:3, 4, 5, 7, 8[3], 9[2], 11, 13, 15, 16, 17[2], 18, 19, 20, 21, 22[2], 23[2]
15:6[2], 7[3], 8
16:6[3], 7, 8[3], 9[3], 10[3], 11[2], 12, 14, 17, 19[2], 27, 37[2], 38[2], 39, 41, 42[2], 43, 48, 50[2], 53[2], 59, 60[2], 61, 62[2], 63
17:16, 19[2], 20[2], 21, 22[2], 23, 24[2]
18:3, 23, 30, 32
20:3[2], 5[3], 6[2], 7[2], 8[2], 9[2], 10, 11, 12[2], 13[2], 14[2], 15[3], 17, 18, 19, 20, 21[2], 22[2], 23[2], 25, 26[3], 28[2], 29, 31[3], 33[2], 34, 35[2], 36[2], 37[2], 38[3], 40[2], 41[3], 42[3], 44[2], 47, 48, 49
21:3, 4, 5, 15, 17[3], 24, 27[2], 30[2], 31[2], 32
22:4, 13, 14[2], 15, 16, 19, 20[2], 21, 22, 26, 30[3], 31[3]
23:9, 13, 22[2], 24, 25, 27, 28, 30, 31, 34, 43, 46, 48, 49
24:8, 9, 13[2], 14[5], 16, 18[3], 20, 21, 22, 24, 25, 27
25:4, 5[2], 7[5], 9, 11[2], 13[2], 14, 16[2], 17[3]
26:2, 3, 4, 5, 6, 7, 13, 14[2], 19[2], 20[2], 21
27:3
28:2[2], 7, 9, 10, 14, 16[2], 17[2], 18[2], 22[4], 23[2], 24, 25[2], 26[2]
29:3[2], 4[3], 5[2], 6, 8, 9[2], 10[2], 12[2], 13, 14, 15, 16, 19, 20, 21[3]
30:8[2], 10, 12[3], 13[3], 14, 15[2], 16, 18, 19[2], 21, 22[2], 23, 24[2], 25[3], 26[2]
31:9, 11[2], 15[4], 16[2]

EZEKIEL

32:3, 4[3], 5, 6, 7[3], 8, 9[2], 10[2], 12, 13, 14, 15[3], 32
33:2, 6, 7, 8[2], 11[2], 13, 14, 20, 22, 27[2], 28, 29[2], 30
34:8, 10[3], 11[2], 12, 13, 14, 15[2], 16[3], 17, 20[2], 22[2], 23, 24[2], 25, 26[2], 27[2], 29, 30, 31
35:3[3], 4[2], 6[2], 7, 8, 9[2], 11[4], 12[2], 13, 14, 15[2]
36:5, 6, 7, 9[2], 10, 11[3], 12, 15, 18, 19[2], 21, 22, 23[3], 24, 25[2], 26[4], 27, 28[2], 29[2], 30, 32, 33[2], 36[3], 37[2], 38
37:3, 5, 6[2], 7[3], 8, 10, 12, 13[2], 14[2], 19, 21, 22, 23[2], 25, 26[2], 27, 28
38:3, 4[2], 11[2], 16[2], 17[2], 19, 21, 22[2], 23[3]
39:1, 2, 3, 4, 5, 6[2], 7[3], 8, 11, 13, 17, 19, 21[3], 22, 23, 24, 25, 27, 28[2], 29[2]
40:4[2]
41:8
43:3[5], 6, 7, 8, 9, 27
44:4[2], 5, 12, 14, 28[2]
47:5, 7, 14

DANIEL

1:10, 12
2:3, 8, 9, 23, 24, 25, 26, 30
3:14, 15, 25, 29
4:2, 4, 5, 6, 7, 8, 9[2], 10, 13, 18, 30, 34[3], 36, 37
5:11, 14, 16, 17
6:22, 26
7:2, 4, 6, 7, 8, 9, 11[2], 13, 15, 16, 19, 21, 28
8:2[5], 3, 4, 5, 6, 7, 13, 15[2], 16, 17[2], 18, 19, 27[3]
9:2, 3, 4, 16, 20, 21[2], 22, 23
10:2, 3[2], 4, 5, 7, 8[2], 9[3], 11[3], 12, 13, 14, 15[2], 16[2], 19, 20[3], 21
11:1[2], 2
12:5, 7, 8[3]

HOSEA

1:4, 5, 6[2], 7, 9
2:2, 3, 4, 5, 6, 7, 8, 9, 10, 11, 12[2], 13, 14, 15, 17, 18[2], 19[2], 20, 21[2], 23[3]
3:2, 3[2]
4:5, 6[2], 7, 9, 14
5:2, 3, 9, 10, 12, 14[4], 15
6:4[2], 5[2], 6, 10, 11
7:1, 2, 12[3], 13, 15
8:4, 10, 12, 14
9:10[2], 12[2], 13, 15[3], 16
10:10, 11[2]
11:1, 3[2], 4[3], 8[4], 9[4], 11
12:8[2], 9, 10[2]
13:4, 5, 7[2], 8[2], 10, 11, 14[4]
14:4[2], 5, 8[3]

JOEL

1:19
2:19[2], 20, 25[2], 27[2], 28, 29, 30
3:1, 2, 4, 7, 8, 10, 12, 17, 21[2]

AMOS

1:3, 4, 5, 6, 7, 8[2], 9, 10, 11, 12, 13, 14
2:1, 2, 3, 4, 5, 6, 9[2], 10, 11, 13
3:1, 2[2], 14[2], 15
4:6, 7[2], 9, 10[3], 11, 12[2]
5:1, 12, 17, 21[3], 22[2], 23, 27
6:8[2], 14
7:2[2], 5[2], 8[3], 9, 14[3], 15
8:2[2], 7, 9[2], 10[3], 11
9:1[2], 2, 3[2], 4[2], 7, 8[2], 9[2], 11[3], 14, 15[2]

OBADIAH

2, 4, 8

JONAH

1:9[2], 12
2:2[2], 4[3], 6, 7, 9[3]
3:2
4:2[4], 3, 9, 11

MICAH

1:6[3], 7, 8[3], 15
2:3, 11, 12[3]
3:1[2], 8, 9
4:6[3], 7, 13[3]
5:10[2], 11, 12, 13, 14[2], 15
6:3[2], 4[2], 6[2], 7, 11, 13, 14, 16
7:1, 7[2], 8[3], 9[3], 15

NAHUM

1:12[2], 13, 14[2]
2:13[3]
3:5[3], 6, 7

HABAKKUK

1:2, 5, 6
2:1[3]
3:2, 7, 16[3], 18[2]

ZEPHANIAH

1:2, 3[3], 4[2], 8, 9, 12, 17
2:5, 8, 9, 15
3:6[2], 7[2], 8[2], 9, 11, 12, 18, 19[3], 20[4]

HAGGAI

1:8[2], 9, 11, 13
2:4, 5, 6, 7[2], 9, 15, 17, 19, 21, 22[3], 23[2]

ZECHARIAH

1:3, 6, 8, 9[2], 14, 15[2], 16, 18, 19, 21

ZECHARIAH

2:1, 2, 5, 6, 9, 10[2], 11
3:4[2], 5, 7, 8, 9[3]
4:2[2], 4, 5, 11, 12, 13
5:1, 2[2], 4, 6, 9, 10
6:1, 4
7:3[2], 13, 14
8:2[2], 3, 7, 8[2], 10, 11, 12, 13, 14[2], 15, 17, 21
9:6, 7, 8[2], 10, 11, 12[2], 13
10:3, 6[6], 8[2], 9, 10[2], 12
11:5, 6[3], 7[5], 8, 9[2], 10[3], 12, 13[2], 14[2], 16
12:2, 3, 4[2], 6, 9, 10
13:2[2], 5[2], 6, 7, 9[3]
14:2

MALACHI

1:2[2], 3, 4, 6[2], 9, 10[2], 13, 14
2:2[3], 3, 4, 5, 9
3:1, 5[2], 6[2], 7, 10, 11, 17[2]
4:3, 4, 5, 6

MATTHEW

2:8, 13, 15
3:9, 11[3], 14, 17
4:9, 19
5:17[2], 18, 20, 22, 26, 28, 32, 34, 39, 44
6:2, 5, 16, 25, 29
7:23[2], 24
8:3, 7, 8, 9[2], 10[2], 11, 19
9:13[2], 21[2], 28
10:15, 16, 23, 27, 32, 33, 34[2], 35, 42
11:9, 10, 11, 16, 22, 24, 25, 28, 29
12:6, 7, 18[2], 27, 28, 31, 36, 44[2]
13:13, 15, 17, 30, 35[2]
14:27
15:24, 32[2]
16:11, 13, 15, 18[2], 19, 28
17:5, 12, 16, 17[2], 20
18:3, 10, 13, 18, 19, 20, 21, 22, 26, 29, 32, 33
19:9, 16[2], 20[2], 23, 24, 28
20:4, 13, 14, 15[2], 22[2], 23, 32
21:21, 24[3], 27[2], 29, 30, 31, 43
22:4, 32, 44
23:34, 36, 37, 39
24:2, 5, 25, 34, 47
25:12[2], 20, 21, 22, 23, 24, 25, 26[3], 27, 35[3], 36[2], 40, 42[2], 43, 45
26:13, 15, 18, 21, 22, 25, 29[3], 31, 32[2], 33, 34, 35[2], 36, 39, 42, 48, 53, 55, 61, 63, 64, 70, 72, 74
27:4[2], 17, 19, 21, 22, 24, 43, 63
28:5, 7, 20[2]

MARK

1:2, 7[2], 8, 11, 17, 24, 38[2], 41
2:11, 17
3:28
5:7[2], 23, 28[2], 41
6:11, 16, 22, 23, 24, 25, 50
8:2, 3, 12, 19, 24, 27, 29
9:1, 13, 17, 18, 19[2], 24, 25, 41
10:15, 17[2], 20, 29, 36, 38[2], 39[2], 51[2]
11:23, 24, 29[3], 33[2]
12:15, 26, 36, 43
13:6, 23, 30, 37[2]
14:9, 14, 18, 19[2], 25[3], 27, 28[2], 29, 30, 31[2], 32, 36, 44, 49, 58[2], 62, 68[2], 71
15:9, 12

LUKE

1:18[2], 19, 34
2:10, 48, 49
3:8, 16[3], 22
4:6[3], 24, 25, 34, 43[2]
5:5, 8, 13, 24, 32
6:9, 27, 46, 47
7:6, 7, 8[2], 9[2], 14, 26, 27, 28, 31, 40, 43, 44, 45, 47
8:28[2], 46
9:9[2], 18, 20, 27, 38, 40, 41, 57, 61
10:3, 12, 18, 19, 21, 24, 25, 35[2]
11:6, 7, 8, 9, 18, 19, 20, 24[2], 49, 51
12:4, 5[2], 8, 17[2], 18[3], 19, 22, 27, 37, 44, 49[2], 50[2], 51[2], 59
13:3, 5, 7, 8, 18, 20, 24, 25, 27[2], 32[3], 33, 34, 35
14:18[3], 19[3], 20[2], 24
15:6, 7, 9[2], 10, 17, 18[2], 21, 29[3], 31
16:2, 3[3], 4[2], 9, 24, 27, 28
17:4, 8[2], 9, 34
18:4, 5, 8, 11[2], 12[3], 14, 17, 18, 21, 29, 41[2]
19:5, 8[3], 13, 20, 21, 22[4], 23, 26, 27, 40
20:3, 8[2], 13[2], 43
21:3, 8, 15, 32
22:11, 15[2], 16[2], 18[2], 27, 29, 32, 33, 34, 35, 37, 53, 57, 58, 60, 67, 68, 70
23:4, 14, 15, 16, 22[2], 43, 46
24:39, 44[2], 49

JOHN

1:15, 20, 21, 23, 26, 27, 30, 31[2], 32, 33, 34, 48, 50[2], 51
2:4, 19
3:3, 5, 7, 11, 12[2], 28[3], 30
4:14[2], 15, 17[2], 19, 25, 26, 29, 32, 35, 38, 39
5:7[2], 17, 19, 24, 25, 30[4], 31, 32, 34[2], 36[2], 41, 42, 43, 45

In

JOHN

6:20, 26, 32, 35, 36, 37, 38, 39, 40, 41, 42, 44, 47, 48, 51[3], 53, 54, 56, 57, 63, 65, 70
7:7, 8, 17, 21, 23, 28[2], 29[2], 33[2], 34, 36
8:11, 12, 14[6], 15, 16[3], 18, 21[2], 22, 23[2], 24[2], 25, 26[3], 28[3], 29, 34, 37, 38[2], 40, 42[2], 45, 46, 49[2], 50, 51, 54, 55[5], 58[2]
9:4, 5[2], 9, 11[2], 12, 15, 25[4], 27, 36, 38, 39
10:1, 7[2], 9, 10, 11, 14, 15[2], 16[2], 17[2], 18[4], 25[2], 26, 27, 28, 30, 32, 34, 36[2], 37, 38[2]
11:11[2], 15[2], 22, 24, 25, 27, 40, 41, 42[2]
12:24, 26, 27[2], 28, 32[2], 40, 46, 47[2], 48, 49[3], 50[3]
13:7, 8, 12, 13, 14, 15[2], 16, 18[3], 19[2], 20[2], 21, 26[2], 33[4], 34[2], 36, 37[2], 38
14:2[2], 3[3], 4, 6, 9, 10[3], 11, 12[3], 13, 14, 16, 18[2], 19, 20[2], 21, 25, 26, 27[3], 28[5], 29, 30, 31[2]
15:1, 3, 4, 5[2], 9, 10, 11, 12, 14, 15[4], 16, 17, 19, 20, 22, 24, 26
16:1, 4[4], 5, 6, 7[5], 10, 12, 15, 16, 17, 19, 20, 22, 23, 25[3], 26[2], 27, 28[2], 32, 33[2]
17:4[2], 5, 6, 8[2], 9[2], 10, 11[2], 12[3], 13[2], 14[2], 15, 16, 18, 19, 20, 21, 22, 23, 24[2], 25, 26[2]
18:5, 6, 8[2], 9, 11, 17, 20[3], 21[2], 23, 25, 26, 35, 36, 37[4], 38, 39[2]
19:4[2], 6, 10, 15, 21, 22[2], 28
20:13, 15, 17[2], 21, 25[2]
21:3, 15, 16, 17, 18, 22[2], 23[2], 25

THE ACTS

1:1
2:17, 18, 19, 25[2], 35
3:6[3], 17
5:38
7:3, 7, 32, 34[4], 43, 56
8:19, 23, 31, 34, 37
9:5, 10, 13, 16
10:14, 20, 21, 26, 28, 29[3], 30[2], 33, 34, 37
11:5[2], 6[2], 7, 8, 11, 15, 16, 17[2]
12:11
13:2, 22, 25[3], 33, 34, 41, 47
15:16[3]
16:18, 30
17:3, 22, 23[3]
18:6[2], 10[2], 14, 15, 21[2]
19:15[2], 21[2]
20:18[2], 20, 22, 24[3], 25[2], 26[2], 27, 29, 31, 32, 33, 35
21:13, 37, 39[2]
22:1, 3, 4, 5, 6, 7, 8[2], 10[2], 11[2], 13, 17[3], 19[2], 20, 21, 28[2]
23:1, 5, 6[2], 27, 28[2], 29, 30, 35
24:4[2], 10[2], 11, 14[2], 16, 17, 20, 21[2], 22, 25[2]
25:8, 10[3], 11[3], 15, 16, 17, 18, 20[2], 21[2], 22, 25[2], 26[3]
26:2[3], 3[2], 5, 6, 7, 9[2], 10[3], 11[2], 12, 13, 14, 15[2], 16[2], 17, 19, 22, 25, 26[2], 27, 29[2]
27:10, 22, 23[2], 25, 34
28:17[2], 19[2], 20[2], 27

ROMANS

1:8, 9[2], 10, 11[2], 12, 13[3], 14, 15, 16
3:5, 7, 26
4:17
6:19
7:1, 7[2], 9[2], 10, 14, 15[6], 16[3], 17, 18[2], 19[4], 20[3], 21[2], 22, 23, 24, 25[2]
8:18, 38
9:1[2], 2, 3, 9, 13[2], 15[4], 17[2], 25, 33
10:2, 18, 19[3], 20[2], 21
11:1[2], 3, 4, 11, 13[3], 14, 19, 25, 27
12:1, 3, 19
14:11, 14
15:8, 9, 14, 15, 16, 17[2], 18, 19, 20[2], 22, 24[4], 25, 28[2], 29[3], 30, 31[2], 32
16:1, 4, 17, 19[2], 22

1 CORINTHIANS

1:4, 10, 12[5], 14[2], 15, 16[3], 19
2:1[2], 2, 3
3:1, 2, 4[2], 6, 10
4:3[2], 4[2], 6, 8, 9, 14[2], 15, 16, 17[2], 18, 19, 21
5:3[2], 9, 11, 12
6:5, 12, 15
7:6, 7[2], 8[2], 10[2], 12, 17, 25[2], 26[2], 28, 29, 32, 35[2], 40[2]
8:13[2]
9:1[3], 2[2], 6, 8, 15[2], 16[3], 17[2], 18[3], 19[3], 20[3], 21, 22[4], 23[2], 26[2], 27[3]
10:1, 15[2], 19, 20[2], 29, 30[3], 33
11:1, 2[2], 3, 17[2], 18[2], 22[3], 23[2], 34[2]
12:1, 3, 15[2], 16[2], 21[2], 31
13:1[2], 2[4], 3[2], 11[6], 12[3]
14:5, 6[3], 11[2], 14, 15[4], 18[2], 19[2], 21, 37
15:1[2], 2, 3[2], 9[2], 10[4], 11, 31[3], 32, 34, 50, 51
16:1, 2, 3[2], 4, 5[3], 6[2], 7[2], 8, 10, 11, 12, 15, 17

2 CORINTHIANS

1:13, 15, 17[4], 23[2]
2:1[2], 2, 3[4], 4[2], 5, 8, 9[2], 10[4], 12, 13[3]
4:13[2]
5:8, 11
6:2[2], 13, 16[2], 17
7:3[2], 4[2], 7, 8[4], 9, 12[2], 14[3], 16[2]
8:3, 8, 10, 13, 22
9:2[2], 3[2], 5, 6
10:1, 2[4], 8[2], 9[2]
11:2[3], 3, 5[2], 6, 7[2], 8, 9[4], 11, 12[3], 16[2], 17[2], 18, 21[3], 22[3], 23[2], 24, 25[4], 29[2], 30[2], 31, 33
12:1, 2[3], 3[2], 5[2], 6[4], 7[2], 8, 9, 10[3], 11[4], 13, 14[3], 15[3], 16[2], 17[2], 18[2], 20[5], 21[2]
13:1, 2[5], 6, 7, 10[2]

GALATIANS

1:6, 9, 10[4], 11, 12[2], 13, 16[2], 17[2], 18, 19, 20[2], 21
2:1, 2[3], 10, 11, 14[2], 18[3], 19[2], 20[5], 21
3:2, 15, 17
4:1, 11[2], 12[3], 13, 15, 16[2], 18, 19, 20[2]
5:2, 3, 10, 11[3], 12, 16, 21[2]
6:11, 14[2], 17

EPHESIANS

1:15[2]
3:1, 3, 7, 8, 13, 14
4:1, 17
5:32
6:19, 20[3], 21, 22

PHILIPPIANS

1:3, 7, 8, 9, 12, 17, 18, 19, 20, 22[3], 23, 25[2], 27[2]
2:16[2], 17[2], 19[3], 20, 23[2], 24[2], 25, 27, 28[2]
3:4[2], 7, 8[3], 10, 11, 12[4], 13[2], 14, 18
4:2, 3, 4, 10, 11[3], 12[3], 13, 15, 17[2], 18[2]

COLOSSIANS

1:20, 23, 25, 29
2:1[2], 4, 5[2]
4:3, 4[2], 8, 13

1 THESSALONIANS

2:18
3:5[2]
4:9, 13
5:1, 23, 27

2 THESSALONIANS

2:5[2]
3:17

1 TIMOTHY

1:3[2], 12, 13[2], 15, 16, 18, 20
2:1, 7[2], 8, 12
3:14, 15
4:13
5:14, 21
6:13

2 TIMOTHY

1:3[3], 4, 5[2], 6, 11, 12[5]
2:7, 9, 10
3:11
4:1, 6, 7[3], 12, 13, 16, 17, 20

TITUS

1:5[2]
3:8, 12[2]

PHILEMON

4, 8, 9, 10[2], 12, 13, 14, 19[3], 21[2], 22[2]

HEBREWS

1:5[2], 13
2:12[2], 13[2]
3:10, 11
4:3
5:5
6:14[2]
7:9
8:8, 9[3], 10[3], 12[2]
10:7[2], 9, 16[3], 17, 30
11:32
12:21, 26
13:5, 6, 19[2], 22[2], 23

JAMES

1:13
2:18[2]

1 PETER

1:16
2:6, 11
5:1, 12[2]

2 PETER

1:12, 13[2], 14, 15, 17
3:1[2]

1 JOHN

2:1, 4, 7, 8, 12, 13[3], 14[2], 21, 26
4:20
5:13, 16

2 JOHN

1[2], 4[2], 5[2], 12[2]

3 JOHN

1, 2, 3, 4, 9, 10[2], 13[2], 14[2]

JUDE

3, 5

REVELATION

1:8, 9, 10, 11, 12[2], 17[3], 18[2]
2:2, 4, 5, 6, 7, 9[2], 10, 13, 14, 15, 16, 17, 19, 20, 21, 22, 23[3], 24[2], 25, 26, 27, 28
3:1, 2, 3[2], 5[2], 8[2], 9[3], 10, 11, 12[3], 15[2], 16, 17, 18, 19[2], 20[2], 21[2]
4:1[3], 2, 4
5:1, 2, 4, 6, 11[2], 13
6:1[2], 2, 3, 5[2], 6, 7, 8, 9, 12
7:1, 2, 4, 9, 14
8:2, 13
9:1, 13, 16, 17
10:1, 4[2], 5, 8, 9, 10[2]
11:3
12:10
13:1, 2, 3, 11
14:1, 2[2], 6, 13, 14
15:1, 2, 5
16:1, 5, 7, 13, 15
17:1, 3, 6[3], 7
18:1, 4, 7
19:1, 6, 10[2], 11, 17, 19
20:1, 4[2], 11, 12
21:1, 2, 3, 5, 6[2], 7, 9, 22
22:7, 8[3], 9, 12, 13, 16[2], 18, 20

IN

1722

GENESIS

1:1, 6, 11, 12, 14, 15, 17, 20, 22[2], 26, 27[2], 29
2:3, 4, 5, 8, 9, 17
3:3, 5, 8[2], 10, 16, 17, 19
4:3, 8, 12, 14, 16, 20, 22
5:1[2], 2, 3
6:4[3], 5, 8, 9, 14, 16[2], 17
7:1, 7, 9, 11[2], 13, 15, 16[3], 22[2], 23
8:1, 4, 5, 9, 11[3], 13[2], 14, 17, 21
9:6, 7, 13, 14, 16, 27
10:5[2], 8, 10, 20[2], 25, 31, 32[2]
11:2, 28[2], 31, 32
12:3, 5, 6, 10[2]
13:2[3], 7, 12[2], 17[2], 18[2]
14:1, 3, 4, 5[4], 6, 7, 8, 12, 13, 14
15:1, 3, 6, 10, 13, 15[2], 16, 18
16:2, 3, 4[2], 5, 6, 7[2], 12
17:7, 9, 12[2], 13[2], 17, 21, 23[2], 24, 25, 26, 27
18:1[3], 3, 9, 10, 11, 18, 26
19:1, 2[2], 3, 5, 8, 9, 12[2], 14[2], 15, 17, 19[2], 27, 29, 30[3], 31[2], 33, 34
20:1, 3, 5, 6[2], 8[2], 11
21:2, 7, 11, 12[3], 14[2], 15, 18, 20, 21, 22, 33, 34
22:3, 6, 9, 13[2], 14, 17[2], 18
23:2[2], 6, 9, 10[2], 11, 13, 16, 17[3], 18[2], 19[2]
24:1[2], 10, 23[2], 25, 27, 31, 37, 45, 48, 54, 62, 63, 65
25:8, 9[2], 18, 23, 24, 27
26:1[2], 2, 3, 4, 6, 12[2], 15, 17, 18, 19, 22, 29, 31[2]
27:15, 30, 41, 45
28:11, 14[2], 15, 16, 18, 20, 21
29:2, 3, 21, 23[2], 25, 26, 30
30:2, 3, 4, 14[2], 16[2], 27, 33, 35, 37[2], 38[2], 40, 41, 42
31:10, 11, 14, 18[2], 20, 23, 24, 25[2], 28, 29, 34, 40, 41, 54, 55
32:5, 21, 32
33:8, 10, 15, 18
34:5, 7[2], 11, 15, 19, 21, 28[2], 29, 30
35:3[2], 4[2], 6, 13, 14, 17, 18, 19, 22, 26
36:5, 6, 8, 9, 16, 17, 21, 24, 30, 31, 32, 33, 34, 35[2], 36, 37, 38, 39, 43
37:1[2], 7, 12, 13, 15, 17, 22, 24, 29, 31, 33
38:1, 2, 7, 8, 9, 11[2], 12, 13, 14, 16[3], 18[2], 21, 22, 24, 25, 27[2]
39:2, 3, 4, 5[3], 6, 8, 9, 12, 13, 14[2], 17, 20, 21, 22
40:3[2], 4, 5[2], 6[2], 7, 9, 10, 11, 16, 17
41:2, 8, 10[2], 11, 14, 16, 17, 18, 19, 22[2], 30, 31, 34, 35, 36, 37[2], 38, 40, 42, 43, 44, 47, 48[3], 52, 53, 54[2], 56, 57
42:1, 2, 3, 5, 13, 16[2], 19, 21, 27[2], 28, 32, 34, 35, 38
43:1, 11[2], 12[3], 15, 18[2], 21[3], 22[2], 23, 26, 28
44:1, 2, 5[2], 8, 12, 17[2], 18, 28, 30
45:6[2], 7, 10, 13, 16
46:2, 5, 6, 12, 15, 20, 27, 31, 34
47:1, 4[3], 6[2], 7, 9, 11[3], 13, 14[2], 15[3], 17, 18, 24, 25, 27[2], 28, 29[2], 30
48:3, 5, 6, 7[3], 9, 13[2], 16, 20
49:1, 5, 6[2], 7[2], 8, 11[2], 17, 24, 27, 29[2], 30[3]
50:4[2], 5[2], 8, 11, 13, 19, 22, 26[2]

EXODUS

1:5, 14[4], 19
2:3, 11, 12, 15, 22, 23
3:1, 2, 7, 16, 20, 21, 22
4:2, 4, 14, 15, 17, 18[3], 19, 20, 21, 24, 27, 30
5:1[2], 14, 16, 19, 20, 21[3], 23
6:5, 8, 11, 28
7:3, 10, 11, 15[2], 16, 17[3], 18, 19[2], 20[4], 21
8:9, 11, 17[2], 20, 22[3], 25, 28, 29
9:1, 3, 5, 8, 9, 13, 14, 16[2], 18, 19[2], 21, 22, 24, 25, 26, 31
10:1, 2[2], 3, 14, 15[2], 16, 19, 22, 23, 28
11:2, 3[4], 5, 8, 9
12:1, 3, 6, 8, 11[2], 12, 16[3], 17[2], 18, 19[2], 20, 22[3], 23, 27, 29[2], 30[2], 33, 34, 36, 40, 42, 46, 48
13:3, 4, 5, 6, 7, 8, 9, 10, 14, 15, 20[2], 21[2]
14:3[2], 11[2], 12[2], 23, 24, 27, 29
15:4, 6[2], 7, 8, 10, 11[2], 13[2], 17[5], 19[2], 20, 22, 26
16:2, 3, 4, 5, 7, 8[2], 10, 12, 13, 16, 25, 26, 29, 32
17:1, 5, 6[2], 8, 9, 14[2]
18:1, 2, 3, 5, 6, 7, 8, 11, 12[2], 14, 15, 17, 23, 24, 27
19:1, 2, 9, 11, 16[2], 18
20:4[3], 7[2], 10, 11[2], 24
21:2, 3, 13, 16, 29[2], 36[2]
22:4, 5[2], 6, 13, 21, 23, 31
23:2, 3, 6, 9, 10, 11, 13, 14, 15[2], 16[3], 17, 19, 20, 21, 23, 26, 29, 33
24:4, 6, 7, 10, 17, 18
25:7[2], 12[3], 15, 18, 21, 22, 26, 33[3], 34, 40
26:4[3], 5[3], 9, 10[2], 13, 17[2], 23, 28, 30, 33, 34
27:4, 8, 11, 19, 21
28:1, 3, 4, 11[2], 17, 20[2], 24, 25, 26[2], 29[2], 30[2], 32[2], 35, 38, 41, 43[2]
29:1, 3, 17, 24[2], 29, 30[2], 31, 32, 39, 44
30:10[2], 30, 36
31:3[4], 4[3], 5[3], 6, 10, 15[2], 17
32:2, 3, 12, 15, 17, 20, 26, 27, 34
33:3[2], 5, 10, 12, 13[2], 16[2], 17, 22
34:1, 2[3], 4[2], 5, 6, 9, 10[2], 12, 18[2], 21[2], 23, 24, 26, 29, 32[2], 34, 35
35:15, 19[2], 26, 31[4], 32[3], 33[2], 34, 35[4]
36:1, 2, 11[3], 12[3], 17, 28, 29
37:13, 19[2], 20
38:18, 23[3], 24
39:1, 3[4], 6, 10, 13[2], 16, 17, 18, 23, 26, 37, 41[2]
40:4[4], 13, 15, 17[2], 18, 22, 23, 24, 26, 36, 38

LEVITICUS

1:7, 8, 9, 12
2:4, 5, 6, 7, 11
4:6, 7, 17, 18, 24, 29, 33
5:4, 5[2], 13, 15, 16
6:2[3], 3, 5[2], 7, 9, 12[2], 16[2], 18, 20[2], 21[2], 22, 25, 26[2], 27, 28[2], 30[2]
7:2, 6, 9[3], 24[2], 26, 35[2], 36, 38[3]
8:8, 21, 31, 33
9:9
10:3, 5, 13, 14, 17, 18[2], 19
11:9[4], 10[4], 11, 12, 13, 33, 34, 46
12:3, 4, 5[2]
13:2[2], 3[3], 4[2], 5[2], 6, 7, 8, 9, 10[2], 11, 12, 14, 18[2], 19, 20, 22, 23, 24, 25[2], 26, 27, 28[2], 30[2], 31[2], 32[3], 34[3], 35, 36, 37, 38, 39[2], 42[2], 43[3], 44, 45, 46, 47, 48[3], 49[5], 51[5], 52[3], 53[4], 55, 57[4], 59[2]
14:2, 3, 5, 6, 8, 9, 13[2], 16[2], 17, 18, 27, 28, 29, 32, 34, 35, 36[illegible], 37[2], 39, 40, 42, 43, 44[2], 47[2], 48[2], 50, 51[2]
15:3, 5, 6, 7, 8, 10, 11[2], 12, 13, 16, 18, 19, 20, 21, 22, 27, 31
16:2, 4, 16[2], 17[3], 21, 22, 24, 26, 27[3], 28, 29, 32[2]
17:3, 5, 11, 15
18:3, 5, 15, 18, 24[2]
19:6, 15[2], 17[2], 24, 25, 28, 33, 34, 35[4]
20:2, 12, 17, 23
21:5, 11, 13, 17, 20, 23
22:2, 11, 13, 18, 21, 23, 24, 25[2], 28
23:3, 4, 5, 7, 8, 14, 21, 24[2], 28, 29, 30, 31, 32, 39[2], 41[3], 42[2], 43
24:3[2], 5, 6, 8, 9, 10, 12, 16, 19, 20
25:1, 3, 4, 7, 9, 11[2], 13, 18[2], 19, 20, 21, 22, 24, 28[2], 29, 30[2], 31, 33, 35, 45, 53, 54[2]
26:1, 3, 4, 5, 6, 16, 20, 22, 26, 28, 34, 35, 36, 39[3], 44, 45, 46
27:19, 21, 23, 24, 34

NUMBERS

1:1[3], 3, 16, 19, 45
2:9, 16[2], 17[2], 24, 31
3:1[2], 3, 4[3], 13[2], 14, 25, 28
4:3, 4, 6, 8, 12[2], 15, 16[2], 19, 20, 23[2], 27[3], 28, 31, 33, 35, 37, 39, 41, 43, 47
5:3, 17[2], 18[2], 23
6:5, 9, 18
7:10, 84
8:15, 17, 19, 22[2], 24, 26
9:1[2], 3[2], 5, 7, 10, 13[2], 14, 17, 18, 20, 21, 22, 23
10:9, 10[3], 11, 12, 14, 29, 31, 33
11:1, 5, 8[3], 9, 10, 11, 12, 15, 18[2], 25, 26[2], 27
12:5[2], 6[2], 7, 8, 14[2], 15, 16
13:19[4], 22, 28, 29[2], 32, 33[2]
14:2[2], 8, 10, 13, 14[2], 16, 22[2], 25, 28, 29, 31, 32, 33[2], 34, 35, 40, 45
15:3[3], 8, 13, 14, 15, 21, 26, 30, 32, 34, 38
16:2, 7, 13, 17, 18[2], 21, 26, 27, 45, 49
17:4, 7
18:10, 11, 13[2], 14, 15, 20, 21, 31[2]
19:5, 7, 8[2], 9, 14[2], 16, 17, 18, 19
20:1[2], 5, 12, 13, 15, 16[2], 23, 27, 28
21:1, 5, 10, 11, 12, 13, 14[3], 20[2], 25[3], 27, 31
22:1, 7, 13, 21, 22, 23[2], 24, 26, 29, 31[2], 34, 36[2], 38
23:5, 12, 16, 21[2]
24:2, 7, 14, 21
25:1, 6[2], 7, 9, 11, 15, 18[3]
26:2, 3, 9[2], 19, 59, 63, 64, 65
27:3[4], 14[4], 17[2], 18, 19, 21
28:2, 4, 6, 7, 11, 16, 17, 18, 23, 26
29:1, 39
30:3[2], 5, 7, 10, 14, 16[2]
31:6, 16, 35, 36
32:5, 13[2], 14, 15, 17, 26, 30, 33, 39
33:3[2], 5, 6[2], 8[2], 9, 11, 12, 13, 15, 18, 20, 22, 23, 24, 25, 28, 29, 31, 33, 36, 37[2], 38[2], 39, 40[2], 41, 42, 43, 44[2], 45, 46, 47, 48, 49, 50, 54, 55[3]
34:29
35:1, 2, 3, 5, 12, 14, 21, 25, 28, 29, 32
36:8, 12, 13

DEUTERONOMY

1:1[2], 3[3], 4[2], 5, 6[2], 7[4], 8, 17, 25, 27, 30, 31[2], 32, 33[4], 37, 38, 39[2], 44[2], 46
2:4, 7, 8, 9, 10, 12[2], 14, 20, 21, 22[2], 23[2], 24, 25, 29[2], 37
3:4, 10, 11, 19, 24[2], 29
4:1, 5, 6, 7, 10, 14, 15, 17, 18, 21, 22, 25[2], 27, 30[2], 34, 37, 38, 39[2], 42, 43[4], 46[2]
5:1, 2, 4, 8[3], 11[2], 14, 15, 16, 22[2], 29, 31, 33[2]
6:1, 3, 6, 7, 16, 18[2], 20, 21, 23
7:7, 13, 17
8:1, 2[2], 5, 6, 9, 11, 16, 17
9:1, 4[2], 7, 8, 9, 10[2], 15, 18[2], 28
10:2[2], 3, 4[2], 5, 6[2], 8, 10, 11, 12, 15, 18, 19
11:3, 5, 6[2], 8, 9, 10, 14[2], 15, 18[2], 19, 21, 22, 29, 30[2], 31
12:1, 7, 8, 10[2], 13, 14[2], 15, 18[2], 21, 25, 28, 29, 31
13:5, 12, 18
14:9, 21[2], 23, 25, 29
15:4, 7, 8, 9, 10[2], 11, 12, 15, 18[2], 20
16:1, 2, 3, 4, 6, 7[2], 11, 12, 13, 14, 15[3], 16[5], 18
17:2[2], 4, 8, 9, 15, 18, 20[2]
18:5, 7, 16[2], 18, 19, 20[2], 21, 22
19:1[2], 2, 4, 6, 9, 10, 11, 14[2], 15, 17
20:5, 6, 7, 14, 19[2]
21:1[2], 3, 4, 5, 6, 9, 13[2], 14, 23
22:1, 3, 6[2], 7, 13, 15, 19, 21[2], 23, 24, 25, 26, 27
23:1, 4, 7, 8, 14[2], 16[2], 20[2], 21, 22, 24
24:1[3], 3, 8, 13[2], 14, 18, 19[3], 22
25:5, 6, 7, 9[2], 10, 13, 14, 15, 19
26:1, 2, 3, 11, 14, 17, 19[3]
27:3, 4, 15, 23
28:3[2], 6, 8[3], 9, 11[5], 12, 16[2], 19, 20, 29[2], 32, 35[2], 38, 48[4], 52[2], 53[2], 55[3], 57[2], 58, 61, 62, 66, 67
29:1[2], 2, 5, 9, 11, 16, 19[2], 20, 21, 23[2], 27, 28[3]
30:9[4], 10, 12, 14[2], 16[3], 20
31:2, 7, 10[2], 11[2], 13, 14[2], 15[2], 17[2], 18[2], 19, 24, 26, 28, 29[2], 30
32:10[2], 20, 22, 28, 34, 35, 37, 44, 47, 49, 50[2], 51[2]
33:3, 5, 12, 16, 18[2], 19, 21, 24, 26[illegible], 28
34:5, 6[2], 8, 10, 11[2], 12[3]

JOSHUA

1:11, 14, 17, 18
2:2, 6, 11[3], 18, 19, 21
3:1, 7, 8, 13, 15, 17
4:3, 6, 9[2], 10, 11, 14, 19[2], 20, 21
5:1, 4, 5, 6, 7, 8[2], 10[2], 11, 13
6:1, 11, 12, 17, 18, 21, 23, 25, 26[2]
7:1, 5, 13, 14, 15, 16, 21[2], 22
8:4, 9, 10, 12, 13, 14, 16, 17, 18[2], 22, 24[2], 30, 31, 32, 34
9:1[3], 9, 25, 27
10:6, 11, 12[3], 13[2], 16, 17, 21, 27, 30
11:2[2], 3[2], 4, 13, 17, 19, 20, 22[4]
12:2, 5[3], 7, 8[6], 23
13:1[2], 9, 10, 12[3], 16, 17, 19, 21[2], 27, 30, 31, 32
14:1, 4[2], 6[2], 7, 10, 11[2], 12[2]
15:5, 33, 48, 61
16:10
17:10[2], 11[2], 12, 15, 16
18:5[2], 8, 9, 10, 16
19:2, 14, 50, 51
20:4, 6[2], 7[4], 8[3]
21:2[2], 6, 11, 21, 27, 32, 38, 39
22:2, 5, 7, 9, 10, 11, 16, 17, 19, 20[2], 22[2], 24, 25, 27[2], 28, 33
23:1, 2, 6, 12[2], 13[2], 14[2]
24:2, 7[2], 13, 14[3], 15, 17[2], 18, 25, 26, 30[3], 32[2], 33[2]

JUDGES

1:4, 5, 9[3], 10, 16[2], 21, 27, 29[2], 35[3]
2:3, 9[3], 11, 17, 19
3:3[2], 7, 12[2], 20, 22, 24, 27
4:1, 2[2], 5, 11, 14, 18[3], 20, 21, 22
5:6[2], 7[2], 8[2], 10, 11[2], 17[2], 18, 19, 20, 24, 25, 28, 31
6:1, 2, 10, 11, 14, 15[2], 17, 19[3], 21, 24, 26, 28, 33, 37
7:1, 3, 8[2], 11, 12, 16, 19[2], 20[2], 21, 22
8:2, 3, 6, 9, 10, 11, 15, 27[2], 28[2], 29, 31, 32[3]
9:2, 3, 6, 7, 15[2], 16, 19[2], 24, 25[2], 26, 32[2], 33, 34, 35[2], 41, 43, 44[2], 48, 56
10:1[2], 2, 4, 5, 6, 8[2], 14, 17[2]
11:2, 3, 4, 7, 11, 12, 17[2], 20, 26[3], 31, 39, 40
12:3, 7, 9, 12[2], 15[3]
13:1, 9, 20, 25
14:1, 2, 6, 8, 9, 14
15:1[3], 4, 6, 8, 9[2], 19[2], 20
16:1, 2[3], 4, 9[2], 12[2], 18, 21, 30, 31
17:2, 4, 6[3], 10, 12
18:1[4], 3[2], 6, 7[2], 10, 12[2], 14, 17[2], 19, 20, 22, 28, 31
19:1[2], 4, 5[2], 7, 8, 9, 11[2], 13[2], 15[4], 16, 17, 20, 26, 27
20:1, 2, 6[2], 10, 13, 19, 20, 22[3], 27, 28, 29, 30, 31[2], 33[2], 36, 37[2], 38, 39[2], 42, 45, 47
21:1, 3[2], 12, 13, 15, 19[2], 20[2], 21, 22, 23, 25[3]

RUTH

1:1[3], 6[3], 7, 8, 9, 11, 14, 15[2], 22[2]
2:2, 3, 7, 8, 10, 11, 13, 14, 17, 18, 19[2], 20, 22[2], 23
3:1, 2, 4, 6, 10, 13, 16, 17, 18
4:7[3], 11[3], 13, 14, 15, 16

1 SAMUEL

1:3, 9, 10, 13, 17, 18, 19, 24
2:1[3], 9, 13[2], 14, 26, 27[2], 29, 31, 32[3], 33, 34, 35[2], 36
3:1, 2, 3, 9, 11, 12, 21[2]
4:1, 2[2], 6, 8, 14, 19[2], 21
5:3, 5, 9
6:1, 3, 8, 13, 18
7:1, 2, 6, 16[2]
8:2, 3, 5, 7, 18[2], 21
9:6, 7, 9, 12, 15, 18, 19, 22
10:2, 25
11:4, 7, 8, 11[2], 13, 15
12:1, 5, 8, 17[2], 23, 24
13:2[3], 3, 4, 5[2], 6[6], 7, 16[2], 17, 22[2]
14:2[2], 3, 7, 9, 15[2], 16, 19, 22[2], 27[2], 33, 34, 39, 43, 45
15:2, 4, 5, 12, 14, 17, 19, 21, 22[2], 33[2]
16:12, 13, 18[2], 22
17:1, 2, 8, 12, 19, 20, 21, 22, 25, 28, 40[4], 45, 46, 49[2], 50, 54, 57
18:5[2], 10[2], 13, 14, 16, 18[2], 21[2], 22[2], 23[2], 26, 27[2]
19:2[2], 3, 5, 7[2], 9[2], 11, 13, 15, 16[2], 18, 19, 22[2], 23[2], 24
20:1, 3, 5, 8, 13, 19, 24, 29[2], 34, 35, 42[2]
21:3, 5[2], 6, 9[2], 11, 12, 13, 15
22:2[2], 4, 5, 6[3], 8, 11, 13[2], 14[2], 23
23:3, 6, 7, 14[4], 15[2], 16, 18, 19[3], 23, 24[2], 25[2], 29
24:1, 3[2], 10, 11[3], 20
25:1, 2[3], 3, 4, 5, 6, 7, 8[2], 9, 15, 21[2], 24, 28, 29, 34, 35, 36, 37

1 SAMUEL

26:1, 2, 3[2], 4, 5, 7, 15[2], 18, 19, 20, 21, 24[2]
27:1[2], 5[4], 7, 11
28:1, 3[2], 4[2], 20, 21, 24
29:1, 2, 3, 4, 5, 6[4], 7, 8, 9, 10[2], 11
30:6, 11, 24, 27[3], 28[3], 29[3], 30[3], 31
31:1, 7, 8, 9, 10

2 SAMUEL

1:1, 9, 18, 20[2], 23[2], 24, 25[2]
2:3, 11, 16[2], 19, 23, 26, 27, 32[2]
3:2, 5, 7, 17, 19[3], 21, 22[3], 23, 25, 27, 30, 32, 38
4:1, 7, 10, 11, 12[3]
5:2[2], 3, 5[2], 6[2], 9, 14, 18, 22, 24
6:3, 11, 16, 17[3], 18, 20, 22[2]
7:1, 2, 3, 5, 6[3], 7, 9, 10, 18, 19, 23, 27
8:6, 13, 14
9:4[2], 10, 12, 13
10:1, 4, 8[3], 9, 10, 17
11:2, 4, 11[2], 12, 14, 15[2], 21
12:1, 3, 9, 11, 16, 24, 30
13:5, 6, 8, 12, 13, 16, 20, 23, 30
14:3, 6, 13, 19[2], 20, 22[2], 25[2], 28, 32
15:4, 7, 8, 9, 10, 11, 17, 21[2], 25, 26, 27, 28
16:2, 4, 8[2], 19[3], 21, 22[2], 23
17:3, 8[2], 9[2], 11, 12, 16, 18[2], 23[2], 25, 26, 29
18:6, 10, 12[2], 14[2], 17, 18[3], 25
19:3, 6, 8[2], 10, 13, 22, 24, 27, 30, 33, 37, 43[3]
20:1[2], 3[3], 8[2], 9, 10[2], 12[2], 15[2], 18, 19[2], 22
21:1, 2, 4, 5, 6, 9[4], 12, 14[3], 16, 19, 20[2], 22
22:1, 3, 7, 19, 20, 25, 31
23:2, 3, 5, 7, 8, 12, 13[2], 14[2], 17, 20[2], 21, 39
24:3, 5[2], 9, 10, 11, 13[2], 14, 18

1 KINGS

1:1, 2, 6, 13, 14, 15, 19, 22, 23, 25, 30, 35, 41, 42, 45, 52
2:3[3], 4, 5[2], 6, 8, 10, 11[2], 26, 27, 34[2], 35[2], 36, 38, 39, 46
3:2, 3[2], 5[2], 6[3], 7, 8, 14, 17[2], 18[2], 19, 20[2], 21[2], 25, 26, 27, 28
4:7, 8, 9[2], 10, 11, 13[3], 15, 16[2], 17, 18, 19[3], 20, 27, 31, 33
5:1, 5, 9[2], 14, 15, 16
6:1[3], 6[2], 7[3], 8, 12[3], 19, 20[4], 27, 37[2], 38[3]
7:3, 4[2], 5, 14[2], 19, 20, 21, 24[2], 35, 46[2], 51
8:1, 2, 4, 6, 8, 9, 12, 13[2], 17, 18[2], 20, 22, 23, 25, 30, 31, 32, 33, 34, 36, 37[2], 39, 40, 43, 45, 47[2], 48, 49, 52, 58, 61, 65
9:4[2], 11, 16, 18[2], 19[3], 21, 23, 25, 26[2], 27
10:2, 5, 6, 9, 11, 14, 17, 20, 21, 22, 24, 26, 27[2]
11:2[3], 6, 7, 12, 14, 15[2], 16, 19, 20[2], 21, 22, 24, 29[2], 30, 33[2], 36, 38[2], 40, 41, 42, 43[2]
12:2[2], 16[2], 17, 25, 26, 27, 29[2], 32[4], 33[2]
13:2, 4[2], 8[2], 11[2], 16[2], 19, 22, 24, 25[2], 28, 30, 31, 32[2]
14:5, 6[2], 8, 10, 11[2], 13[2], 15, 19, 20, 21[2], 22, 24, 25, 27, 29, 31[2]
15:1, 2, 3, 4, 5[2], 7, 8[2], 9, 10, 11, 13, 15, 17, 18, 21, 23[3], 24[2], 25, 26[3], 28[2], 31, 33[2], 34[3]
16:2, 4[2], 5, 6[2], 7[3], 8[2], 9[3], 10[3], 13, 14, 15[2], 16, 19[5], 20, 23[2], 25, 26[2], 27, 28[2], 29[2], 30, 31, 32[2], 34[3]
17:6[2], 7, 10, 11, 12[3], 17, 24
18:1, 2, 4, 7, 13, 18, 23, 27, 32, 33[2], 36, 38, 45
19:8, 11[3], 12, 13[3], 16, 18
20:6[2], 12[3], 16, 23, 24, 25, 29[2], 34[2], 35, 37
21:1, 2, 8[2], 9, 11[2], 13[2], 18[2], 19, 20, 21, 24[2], 25, 26, 27, 29[2]
22:2, 3, 10[2], 16, 17, 22, 23, 25, 27[2], 28, 35, 37, 38, 39, 40, 41, 42, 43[3], 45, 46, 47, 49, 50[2], 51, 52[4]

2 KINGS

1:2[2], 3, 6, 13, 14, 16, 17[2], 18
2:12, 21, 24
3:1, 2, 18, 20, 21, 22, 24, 25, 27
4:2[2], 4, 8, 10, 15, 29, 33, 35, 36, 37, 38, 40, 41, 42
5:1, 3, 4, 8, 10, 12[2], 14, 15[2], 18[4], 19, 20, 23, 24, 25
6:6, 8, 12[2], 13, 20, 25, 32
7:1, 2, 3, 4, 5, 7, 12[2], 13[2], 15, 17, 18, 19, 20
8:2, 8, 15[2], 16, 17, 18[2], 20, 23, 24[2], 25, 26, 27[3], 28, 29[2]
9:1, 2, 8, 10, 15[2], 16, 17, 21[2], 24, 25, 26, 27, 28[3], 29, 31, 34, 36, 37
10:1, 5, 7, 8[2], 9, 11, 12, 16, 17, 19, 24, 25, 29[2], 30[3], 31, 32[2], 34, 35[2], 36
11:2, 3, 4, 5, 8[2], 9, 10, 11, 15, 18, 20
12:1[2], 2, 3, 6, 9, 10[3], 18[2], 19, 20, 21[2]
13:1[2], 2, 5, 6, 8, 9[2], 10[2], 11, 12, 13, 17, 20, 24
14:1, 2, 3, 5, 6, 7, 8, 9[3], 11, 14[2], 15, 16[2], 18, 19, 20, 23[2], 24, 28, 29
15:1, 2, 3, 5, 6, 7[2], 8[2], 9, 10, 11, 13[2], 14[2], 15, 17[2], 18, 19, 20, 21, 22, 23[2], 24, 25[3], 26, 27[2], 28, 29, 30[2], 31, 32, 33, 34, 35, 36, 37, 38[2]
16:1, 2[2], 3, 4, 8[2], 18, 19, 20[2]
17:1[2], 2, 4[2], 6[4], 8, 9, 10, 11, 14, 17, 19, 22, 24[2], 26, 28, 29[2], 31, 32
18:1, 2, 3, 4, 5, 9, 10, 11[3], 13, 15[2], 17, 22[2], 26[3], 28, 30
19:7, 10, 12, 27, 28[2], 29[2], 35[2], 37[2]
20:1[2], 3[2], 11, 13[3], 15[2], 17[2], 18, 19, 20, 21
21:1, 2, 4[2], 5, 6, 7[3], 15, 16[2], 17, 18[3], 19, 20, 21[2], 22, 23, 24, 25, 26[3]
22:1, 2[2], 3, 5, 8, 9, 14[2], 20
23:2[2], 3, 4, 5[3], 8[2], 9, 10, 11[2], 12, 14, 16, 19[2], 21, 22, 23[2], 24[4], 28, 29, 30[3], 31, 32, 33[3], 34, 36, 37
24:1, 5, 6, 8, 9, 12, 13[2], 17, 18, 19, 20
25:1[3], 3, 5, 8, 11, 13[3], 15[2], 19[3], 21, 22, 24, 25, 27[3], 28

1 CHRONICLES

1:19, 43, 44, 45, 46[2], 47, 48, 49, 50
2:3, 4, 6, 7, 21, 22, 24
3:1, 4[2], 5
4:22, 38, 41[2]
5:8, 9[2], 10[2], 11, 12, 16[4], 17[2], 18, 20[2], 22, 23
6:10[2], 31, 32, 54, 55, 62, 67, 71, 76, 78, 80
7:2[2], 5, 21, 23, 29
8:8, 28, 32
9:1, 2[2], 3, 9, 16, 18[2], 20, 22[3], 24, 25, 26, 28, 31, 33[2], 35
10:1, 7[2], 8, 10[2], 12
11:2[2], 3, 7, 10, 14, 15, 16, 19, 22[2], 23
12:2, 15, 17, 21, 33, 35, 36, 40
13:2[2], 3, 4, 7, 14
14:4, 9, 11, 13, 15
15:1, 29
16:1, 2, 10, 14, 19, 27[2], 29, 35, 39, 40
17:1[2], 2, 4, 5, 8, 9, 14[2], 17, 19, 21, 25
18:6, 12, 13
19:1, 4, 9[2], 10, 11, 13, 17[2], 18
20:2, 3, 8
21:12, 13, 16[2], 18, 19, 23, 28, 29[2]
22:2, 3[2], 4, 7, 8, 9, 14[2], 15
23:11, 13, 25, 28[3], 29, 31[2], 32
24:3, 19, 31
25:5, 6, 7
26:12, 27, 30[2], 31
27:1[2], 2, 4, 5, 6, 7, 8, 9, 10, 11, 12, 13, 14, 15, 21, 24, 25[4], 28, 29[2]
28:2, 8[2], 13, 19
29:2, 11[2], 12[2], 17[2], 18, 21, 25[2], 27[2], 28[2], 29[3]

2 CHRONICLES

1:1, 2, 3, 7, 8, 9, 10, 11, 14, 15
2:2, 7[7], 8, 9, 11, 14[10], 16, 17, 18
3:1[3], 2[2], 4, 10, 16
4:2, 3, 6[3], 7, 8, 17[2], 18
5:1, 3[2], 5, 7, 10, 12, 13
6:1, 5, 7, 8[3], 10, 11, 12, 13, 14[2], 16[2], 18, 22, 24, 28[2], 29, 31[2], 32, 37[2], 38, 40, 41
7:8, 9, 10, 11[2], 15, 18
8:4[2], 6[2], 8, 11, 13[4], 17
9:1[2], 4, 5, 8, 11, 13, 16, 19, 20, 22, 23, 25, 27[3], 29[3], 30, 31[2]
10:2, 16[2], 17
11:3, 5[2], 10[2], 11, 12, 13, 17, 23
12:2, 5, 12, 13[2], 15, 16[2]
13:1, 2, 3[2], 4, 8, 11, 20, 22
14:1[3], 2, 6[2], 10[2], 11, 14, 15
15:4, 5[2], 9, 10[2], 16
16:1[2], 9, 10[2], 11, 12[3], 13, 14[3]
17:1, 2[3], 3, 4, 5[2], 6, 7[2], 9, 12, 13[2], 19
18:1, 2, 3, 9[3], 15, 16, 21, 22, 26[2], 27, 34
19:1, 3[2], 5, 6, 8, 9, 10, 11
20:2, 5[2], 6[2], 9[3], 14, 17, 20[2], 24, 25[2], 26, 27, 31, 32[2], 34[2], 36
21:1[2], 3, 5, 6[2], 8, 9, 11, 12[2], 13, 17, 18, 19, 20[3]
22:1, 2, 3, 4, 6, 9, 11, 12
23:1, 2, 3, 5, 6, 7[2], 8, 9, 10, 13, 14, 17, 18[2], 19[2]
24:1, 2, 6, 9[2], 10, 11, 13, 14, 16[2], 21, 25[3], 27[2]
25:1, 2, 4[2], 10, 12, 17, 18[3], 21, 24, 26, 27, 28
26:1, 3, 4, 5[2], 7, 8, 9, 10[5], 15, 17, 19[3], 20, 21, 23[2]
27:1, 2, 4[2], 7, 8, 9[2]
28:1[2], 2, 3[2], 4, 6[2], 9, 13, 22, 24[2], 25, 26, 27[3]
29:1, 2, 3[2], 4, 6, 7, 9, 10, 16, 17[2], 18, 19[2], 25, 31, 34, 35[2]
30:2[2], 5, 12, 13, 14, 15, 16, 17, 25, 26[2]
31:1[2], 2, 3, 4[2], 5[2], 6[2], 7[2], 11, 12, 15[2], 16, 17, 18[2], 19[2], 21[4]
32:5[2], 6, 10[2], 18, 21, 23, 24, 26, 29, 30, 31[3], 32[2], 33[2]
33:1, 2, 4[2], 5, 6[2], 7[3], 12, 14[3], 15[2], 17, 18[2], 20[2], 21, 22, 24, 25
34:1, 2[2], 3[2], 4[2], 6, 8, 10[2], 13, 15, 17, 21[3], 22[2], 24, 28, 30[2], 31[2], 32, 33
35:1, 2, 3, 5, 10[2], 12, 13[3], 14, 15, 18, 19, 22, 24[2], 25[3], 26, 27
36:1[2], 2, 3, 5[2], 6, 7, 8[3], 9[2], 11, 12, 14, 17, 22[2], 23[2]

EZRA

1:1[2], 2, 3[2], 4[2], 5, 7
2:42, 68, 70[2]
3:1, 2, 8[2], 9, 10, 11
4:4, 6[2], 7[3], 8, 10, 15[2], 17, 23
5:1[2], 8[2], 13, 14, 15[2], 16[2], 17
6:1[2], 2[2], 3, 5, 7, 15, 18[3], 22
7:1, 6, 7, 8[2], 10, 13, 14, 15, 16[2], 17, 25, 27[2]
8:1, 15, 22, 29, 31, 33
9:2, 7, 8[2], 9[4], 14, 15
10:2, 9, 13, 14, 16

NEHEMIAH

1:1[3], 3[2], 11
2:1[3], 5, 12[2], 15, 17, 20
3:17, 26
4:2, 4, 11, 13, 16, 17, 20, 21, 22
5:5, 9, 14, 16, 18
6:2[2], 5[2], 7, 10[2], 11, 14, 15[2], 16, 17, 18[2], 19
7:3, 73[2]
8:5, 7, 8[2], 14[3], 15[2], 16[4], 18
9:1, 3[2], 9, 12[3], 15, 17, 19[3], 21, 23, 24, 25[2], 27, 28, 29, 30, 33, 35[3], 36, 37
10:29, 34, 36[2], 37
11:1[2], 3[4], 17, 18, 20[2], 21, 24, 25[3], 27, 28, 30[2], 31, 36[2]
12:7, 9, 12, 22, 23, 26[2], 39, 40, 46, 47[2]
13:1[2], 6[2], 7[2], 11, 15[4], 16, 19, 23, 24[2], 27, 28, 30

ESTHER

1:1, 2[2], 3, 5[2], 7[2], 9, 10, 12, 14, 16, 17[2], 22
2:3, 5, 12, 14[3], 15[2], 16[2], 17, 19, 21[2], 22, 23
3:2, 3, 7[2], 8, 12, 13, 14, 15
4:3[2], 8, 11, 13, 16[2]
5:1[2], 2[3], 8, 9, 12, 14
6:4, 5[2], 6[2]
7:3, 5, 7, 8, 9
8:5[3], 8[2], 9, 10, 11, 12, 13, 15, 17[2]
9:1[3], 2, 4, 6, 11, 12[2], 13, 15, 16, 19, 20, 31, 32
10:2

JOB

1:1, 4, 5[2], 7[2], 8, 10, 12, 13, 18, 22
2:2[2], 3, 6, 10
3:3, 20[2], 23, 26
4:13, 18, 19[3], 21
5:4, 13, 14[3], 19[2], 20[2], 23, 24, 26[3]
6:2, 4, 6, 10, 13, 29, 30
7:11[2], 21[2]
8:12, 16
9:4[2], 5, 29, 31, 32
10:1, 13
11:4, 14[2], 18
12:5, 9, 10, 12, 24, 25
13:14[2], 15, 27
14:8[2], 13, 17
15:9, 15[2], 21[2], 28[2], 31
16:4, 8, 9, 15, 17, 19
17:2, 3, 13, 16
18:3, 4, 6, 10[2], 15, 17, 19
19:2, 8, 15[2], 23, 24, 26, 28
20:11, 12, 14, 20, 22[2], 26[2], 28
21:7, 8, 13[2], 16, 17, 21[2], 23, 25, 26, 32, 34[2]
22:8, 12, 14, 22, 26
23:6, 13
24:5, 6, 7, 13, 14, 16[2], 17, 18, 23
25:2, 5
26:8
27:3[2], 10, 15, 20
28:13, 14
29:2[2], 4, 7, 18, 20[2], 25
30:1, 2, 3, 6[3], 10, 14[2], 17[2], 24, 25, 28
31:6, 15[2], 21, 26, 32, 33
32:1, 5, 8, 22
33:2, 5, 6, 8, 9, 11, 12, 15[3]
34:8, 20, 24[2], 25, 26
35:10, 14, 15[2], 16
36:4, 5, 8[2], 11[2], 13, 14, 15[2], 20, 31
37:8, 12, 16, 21, 23[3]
38:16, 32, 33, 36, 37, 40[3]
39:4, 10, 14[2], 16, 21[2]
40:12, 13[2], 16[2], 21
41:9, 22, 23
42:6, 8, 11, 15

PSALMS

1:1[3], 2[2], 3, 5[2]
2:4[2], 5[2], 9, 12
3:2
4:1, 4, 5, 7[2], 8[2]
5:3[2], 4, 5, 7[2], 8, 9, 10, 11[2]
6:1[2], 5[2]
7:1, 2, 3, 5, 6, 8, 10
8:1, 9
9:2, 4, 8[2], 9, 10, 11, 14[2], 15[2], 16, 19, 20
10:1, 2[2], 4, 6[2], 8[2], 9[3], 11, 13
11:1, 2, 4[2]
12:5, 6
13:2[2], 5[2]
14:1, 5[2]
15:1[2], 2, 4
16:1, 3[2], 6, 7, 9, 10, 11
17:3, 5, 7, 10, 11, 12, 14, 15
18:t, 2, 6, 13, 18, 19, 24, 30, 42
19:4, 11, 14
20:1, 5[2], 7[2]
21:1[2], 5, 7, 9[2], 13
22:2[2], 4, 5, 8, 14, 22, 25
23:2, 3, 5, 6
24:3, 7, 8, 9
25:2, 5, 8, 9, 12, 20
26:1[2], 3, 4, 6, 10, 11, 12[2]
27:3, 4[2], 5[3], 6, 9, 11, 13
28:3, 7
29:2, 9
30:5[2], 6, 9
31:1[2], 6, 7[2], 8, 9, 14, 15, 17, 19, 20[2], 21, 22, 24
32:2, 6[2], 8, 9, 10, 11[2]
33:1, 4, 7, 8, 18, 19, 21[2], 22
34:1, 2, 8, 22
35:7, 9[2], 15, 16, 18, 20, 25, 27
36:2, 4, 5, 9, 10
37:3[2], 4, 5, 7[2], 8, 11, 19[2], 23, 31, 33, 35, 39, 40
38:1[2], 2, 3[2], 7, 14, 15
39:6[2], 7
40:3[2], 5, 7, 9, 16
41:1, 3, 9, 12
42:4, 5[2], 8[2], 10, 11
43:5
44:1[2], 3, 6, 8, 17, 19
45:4, 5, 9, 14, 16, 17
46:1, 5, 8, 9[2], 10
48:1[2], 3, 6, 8[2], 9
49:5, 6[2], 12, 14[3], 20
50:15, 16, 21, 22
51:t, 4, 5[2], 6[2], 10, 16, 18
52:1, 7[2], 8[2]
53:1, 5
54:5
55:2, 3, 7, 9, 10, 11, 14, 15, 18, 21, 23
56:t, 3, 4[2], 7, 8, 10[2], 11, 13
57:t, 1[2]
58:2[2], 6, 7, 9, 10, 11
59:3, 7, 8, 12, 13[2], 16[2]
60:t, 6
61:4[2]
62:4, 7[2], 8, 9, 10[2]
63:t, 1, 2, 4, 6, 7, 11
64:1, 4, 5, 10[3]
65:1, 4, 5, 8
66:3, 5, 6, 9, 14, 18
68:5, 6[2], 14[2], 16[2], 17[2], 21, 23[2], 24, 26, 30, 34
69:1, 2, 12, 13[3], 17, 21, 25, 35
70:4
71:1, 2, 9, 16
72:4, 7, 9, 14, 16, 17
73:4, 5, 11, 12[2], 13[2], 18, 19, 21, 25, 28
74:3, 4, 8[2], 12, 13, 14
75:8
76:1[2], 2[2], 7
77:2[2], 6, 9, 13, 18, 19[2]
78:2, 5[2], 7, 9, 10, 12[3], 14, 15, 17, 18, 19, 22[2], 26[2], 28, 30, 33[2], 37, 40[2], 43[2], 51[2], 52, 55, 66
79:10
80:5
81:3[2], 5, 7[2], 9, 12, 13
82:1, 5
83:4, 12
84:4, 5[2], 7, 10[3], 12
85:6, 9, 13
86:2, 5, 7, 11, 15
87:1, 5, 7
88:5, 6[3], 11[2], 12[2], 13
89:2, 5, 6, 7[2], 10, 12, 15, 16[2], 17, 19, 24, 25[2], 30, 37, 43, 47, 49, 50
90:1, 4[2], 5, 6[2], 8, 9
91:1, 2, 6, 11, 12, 15
92:2, 4, 12, 13[2], 14, 15
94:5, 15, 17, 19, 23
95:4, 8[3], 10, 11
96:6, 9
97:11, 12
98:2
99:2, 4, 7
101:2, 6, 7
102:2[3], 14, 16, 21[2], 23, 24
103:8, 19, 20, 22
104:3, 22, 24, 27, 31, 34
105:3, 7, 12[2], 18, 23, 27, 30[2], 31, 32, 35, 36, 39, 41
106:5, 7, 14[2], 16, 18, 19, 21, 22, 23, 25, 26, 27, 29, 47
107:4[3], 5, 6, 10[3], 13, 14, 16, 19, 23[2], 24, 28, 32[2], 40
108:7
109:13, 16, 17
110:2, 3[2], 5, 7
111:1[2], 8
112:1, 3, 4, 6, 7
113:6[2]
115:3, 8, 9, 10, 11
116:9, 11, 14, 15, 18, 19[2]
118:5[2], 8[2], 9[2], 10, 11, 12, 15, 23, 24, 26
119:1[2], 3, 11, 14[2], 15, 16, 19, 23, 35, 37, 40, 42, 43, 47, 48, 50, 51, 54, 55, 70, 74, 75, 78, 80, 81, 83, 89, 92, 109, 114, 133, 147, 148, 161
120:1, 5[2]
121:8
123:1
124:8
125:1, 4
126:4, 5[2]
127:1[2], 4, 5
128:1
129:8
130:5, 7
131:1[2], 3
132:6, 11
133:1
134:1, 2
135:2[2], 6[3], 17, 18
136:10, 15, 23
137:2, 4, 7
138:3[2], 5, 7
139:4, 8, 9, 13, 15[2], 16[2], 18, 20, 24[2]
140:2, 7, 11, 13
141:5, 6, 8
142:t, 3, 5
143:1[2], 2, 3, 8[2]
144:2, 12, 13, 14[2], 15
145:15, 17[2], 18
146:3[3], 4, 5
147:3, 10[2], 11[3], 14
148:1
149:1, 2[2], 3, 4, 5, 6[2]
150:1[2]

PROVERBS

1:14, 15, 17[2], 20, 21[3], 22
2:13, 14, 15, 20, 21[2]
3:4, 5, 6, 7, 12, 16[2], 23, 27, 33
4:3, 11[2], 14, 21
5:10, 14[2], 16, 23
6:8[2], 14, 18, 25, 27, 29, 34
7:9[3], 11, 12[2], 25
8:2[2], 3, 8[2], 20[2], 22, 31
9:4, 6, 9, 14, 16, 17, 18
10:5[2], 8, 13, 17, 19
11:4, 6, 8, 14, 20, 21, 22, 28, 31
12:4, 6, 15, 20, 25, 27, 28[2]
13:6, 23
14:2[2], 3, 7, 13, 14, 23, 26, 28[2], 32[2], 33[2]
15:3, 4, 6[2], 22, 23
16:1, 2, 5[2], 10[2], 15, 20, 21, 27, 31
17:8, 12, 16, 18, 24
18:2, 5, 9, 11, 17, 21
19:1[2], 20, 21, 24
20:4, 5, 7, 8, 20
21:1, 2, 9[2], 10, 14[2], 16, 19, 20, 24
22:5, 6, 13, 15, 18, 19, 20, 22, 29
23:7, 9, 17, 19, 28, 31, 34
24:6, 7, 10, 23, 27
25:5, 6[2], 7, 8, 11, 13, 19[2], 20, 24[2]
26:1[2], 5, 7, 8, 9, 12, 13[2], 15, 16, 19, 25
27:10, 14, 15, 19, 22
28:6[2], 10[2], 11, 18, 25, 26
29:2, 6, 11, 20, 22, 23, 25, 27
30:4[2], 5, 9, 12, 19[2], 25, 26, 28, 29, 32
31:8, 11, 23, 25, 26, 31

ECCLESIASTES

1:1, 12, 16, 18
2:1, 3, 5, 7[2], 9, 10, 14[2], 15[2], 16, 21[3], 23, 24, 26
3:9, 10, 11[2], 12[2], 17, 18, 22
4:14, 15, 16
5:2, 4, 7, 8, 14, 15, 16, 17, 19, 20
6:4[2], 12
7:4[2], 8[2], 9[2], 14[2], 15[3], 19
8:2, 3, 8[2], 10, 11
9:1[2], 3, 6, 9[2], 10, 12[3], 15, 17
10:1, 6[2], 16, 17, 20[2]
11:3, 5, 6[2], 8, 9[4]
12:1[2], 3, 4, 5, 9

SONG OF SOLOMON

1:4, 9, 14
2:12, 14[2]
3:2[2], 8[2], 11[2]
4:7
5:4
6:2, 13
7:4, 5, 11
8:8, 10, 13

ISAIAH

1:1, 6, 7, 8[2], 11, 21
2:2[2], 3, 5, 6, 10, 11, 17, 20, 22
3:7[2], 14, 18, 25
4:1, 2, 3[3], 6
5:1, 2, 4, 8, 9, 11, 12, 16[2], 21[2], 25, 30[2]
6:1, 5, 6, 12, 13[2]
7:1, 3, 6, 11[2], 18[3], 19[2], 20, 21, 22, 23
8:1, 6, 9[3], 11, 18[2], 20
9:1[2], 2[2], 3, 4, 5, 9, 14, 17, 18
10:3[2], 5, 7, 17, 20[2], 23, 24, 25, 27
11:3, 9, 10, 11, 15, 16
12:1, 4, 5, 6
13:3, 4, 8, 10, 13[2], 17, 20, 22[2]
14:1, 2, 3, 6[2], 13[2], 18[2], 20, 25, 28, 30, 31, 32
15:1[2], 3[2], 5
16:3, 5[3], 10[2]
17:4, 5, 6[3], 9, 11[3]
18:2, 4[2], 5, 7
19:1, 3, 9, 10, 14[3], 16, 17, 18[2], 19[2], 20, 21, 23, 24[2]
20:1, 6
21:1, 5, 8[2], 13[2]
22:2, 3, 5, 7, 8, 12, 14, 16, 20, 23, 25[2]
23:1, 13, 15
24:10, 11, 12, 13, 15[2], 18, 21, 22[2], 23[2]
25:4, 5, 6, 7, 8, 9[2], 10, 11
26:1[2], 2, 3[2], 4[2], 8, 9[2], 10, 12, 16, 17[3], 18[2], 19
27:1[2], 2, 4[2], 8[2], 9, 12, 13[4]
28:4, 5, 6, 7[2], 14, 16, 20, 21[2], 25[2], 29[2]
29:15, 18, 19[2], 21, 23, 24
30:2[2], 3, 7, 8[2], 12, 13, 14[2], 15[3], 19, 21, 23[2], 25, 26, 28, 29, 32[2]
31:1[2], 7, 9[2]
32:1[2], 2[2], 13, 16[2], 18[3], 19
33:2, 12, 14, 17
34:5, 6[2], 11, 13[2]
35:6[2], 7
36:1, 2, 6[2], 7, 11[3], 13, 15
37:7, 10, 12, 28, 29[2], 30, 36[2], 38[2]
38:1[2], 3[2], 8, 10, 11, 15, 16, 17, 20
39:2[3], 4[2], 6[2], 7, 8
40:3[2], 11, 12[4], 14, 22, 24, 26
41:16[2], 18[2], 19[2]
42:1, 2, 4, 6, 7, 12, 16, 17, 22[2], 24
43:4, 14, 16[2], 19[2], 20[2], 26
44:7, 12, 13, 16, 19[2], 20, 23
45:2[2], 13, 14[2], 17, 18, 19[3], 23, 24, 25
46:6, 7, 13
47:1, 8, 9[3], 10[2], 13
48:1[2], 10, 16
49:2[2], 3, 4[2], 5, 8[2], 9[3], 20, 21, 22
50:4, 10[2], 11[3]
51:6, 7, 9[2], 14, 16[2], 20
52:6, 10
53:9[2], 10
54:6, 8, 14, 16, 17
55:2, 11
56:5, 7, 9
57:2[2], 5, 6, 10, 13, 15, 17
58:2, 3, 10, 11, 12, 14
59:4, 6, 7, 8, 9, 10[2], 13, 14, 19, 20, 21
60:10[2], 18, 22
61:3, 6, 7[2], 8, 10[2], 11
62:3[2], 4, 7, 9
63:1[3], 2[2], 3[2], 4, 6[2], 9[3], 13
64:5[2]
65:2, 3, 4[2], 5, 8[2], 10, 16[3], 18, 19[3], 23, 25
66:3, 4, 8, 13, 17[2], 20[3]

JEREMIAH

1:1[2], 2[2], 3[2], 5, 9
2:2[3], 5, 17, 18[2], 19, 23, 24[2], 27, 28, 30, 34, 37
3:2[2], 6, 16[2], 18, 23[2], 25
4:2[5], 5[3], 11, 19, 20, 30, 31
5:1, 6, 7, 8, 13, 14, 18, 19[2], 20[2], 24[2], 30, 31
6:1[2], 3, 6, 7, 10, 11, 16, 23, 24, 26, 29
7:2[2], 3, 4, 6, 7[2], 8, 10, 11, 12, 17[2], 22, 23, 24[2], 30[2], 31[2], 32
8:3, 7, 8[2], 9, 12, 16, 18, 19[3], 22
9:2, 4, 6, 8, 23[3], 24[3], 26[3]
10:5, 6, 7, 13, 14[2], 15, 23[2], 24
11:4, 6[2], 7, 8, 12, 14, 15, 17, 21
12:2, 5[2], 8, 16
13:1, 4, 10, 17, 21, 22, 25, 27
14:4, 5, 6, 8[2], 9, 13, 14, 15[2], 16
15:4, 7, 11[2], 13, 14, 15, 17
16:2, 3[2], 6, 7, 9[2], 19
17:3, 4[2], 5, 6[3], 7, 8, 11, 13, 17, 19[3], 20, 21, 24, 25, 27[2]
18:4, 6[2], 10, 15[3], 17, 21, 23
19:4, 7, 9, 10, 11, 14
20:1, 2[2], 6, 7, 9[3], 16
21:4, 5[3], 7, 9, 12, 14
22:2, 3, 4[2], 12, 15, 20, 21, 23[2], 30[2]
23:5, 6, 8, 11, 12, 13[2], 14[2], 18, 19, 20, 22, 24, 25, 26, 29
24:8[2], 9
25:1, 5, 13, 23, 24, 34
26:1, 2[2], 4, 7, 9[2], 10, 14, 15, 16, 18, 20
27:1, 11, 15, 18[2], 19, 21[2]
28:1[5], 5[3], 7[2], 11, 15, 17
29:5, 7, 8, 9, 10, 15, 16, 21, 22[2], 23[2], 25, 26[4], 28[2], 29, 31
30:2, 6, 8, 10, 11, 24
31:2, 4, 9, 10, 12, 13, 15, 17, 22, 23[2], 24[2], 29, 32, 33[2]
32:1, 2[2], 7, 8[3], 9, 10, 12[3], 14, 15, 19[2], 20[2], 23[2], 34, 35, 37[3], 40, 41, 43, 44[6]
33:1, 5[2], 10[3], 12[2], 13[6], 15[2], 16, 20
34:5, 6, 13, 15[3], 17, 18
35:1, 7[2], 8, 9, 10, 15
36:1, 6[4], 8[2], 9[3], 10[5], 13, 14[3], 15[2], 18, 20[3], 21[2], 22[2], 23, 28[2], 30[2], 32
37:1, 4, 10, 12, 13, 15[2], 17, 18, 21[2]
38:2, 4[2], 5, 6[3], 7[3], 9[3], 13, 14, 22[2], 28
39:1[2], 2[2], 3[2], 5[2], 6, 9, 10, 15, 16, 17, 18
40:1, 6, 7[2], 9, 10[2], 11[3], 13, 15[2]
41:1[2], 5, 8, 10[2], 12, 17, 18
42:10, 13, 16[2], 20, 22
43:4, 5, 8, 9[5], 12[2], 13
44:1[2], 3, 6[2], 8[2], 9[2], 10[2], 12, 13, 15[2], 16, 17[2], 21[2], 23[3], 24, 26[3], 27, 29

JEREMIAH

45:1[2], 3, 5
46:2[2], 10, 11, 14[4], 19, 21, 25, 26, 27, 28
48:2, 5[2], 6, 7[2], 11, 18, 20, 26[2], 28[3], 35[2], 38, 41[2], 44, 47
49:1, 2, 4[2], 7, 11, 16, 18[2], 21, 22, 24, 26[2], 27, 32, 33, 34, 38, 39
50:2[2], 4[2], 5, 9[2], 14, 16, 20[2], 22, 23, 25, 28, 30[2], 32, 37, 39, 42, 43
51:1, 2, 3, 4[2], 6, 7, 10, 13, 16, 17, 18, 20, 21[2], 22[3], 23[3], 24[2], 27, 30, 39, 44, 46[3], 47, 58[2], 59, 60, 62
52:1, 2, 3, 4[3], 6[3], 8, 9, 10, 11[2], 12[2], 15, 17[2], 19[2], 20, 25[2], 27[2], 28, 29, 30, 31[4], 32

LAMENTATIONS

1:2, 4, 7[2], 9, 12, 15[2], 19, 20
2:1[2], 2, 3, 4, 5, 6[2], 7[2], 11, 12, 17, 19[3], 20, 21[2], 22[2]
3:6, 10[2], 11, 20[2], 24, 27, 29, 36, 41, 45, 53, 57, 66
4:1, 3, 5[2], 6, 7, 8, 10, 11, 13, 14, 17, 18, 19, 20, 21
5:11[2]

EZEKIEL

1:1[3], 2, 3, 16, 20, 21, 28[2]
3:3, 10, 14[2], 18, 19, 20
4:9, 12, 14, 16
5:2[2], 3[2], 4, 5, 6, 7, 8[2], 9, 10[2], 12, 13[2], 14, 15[4]
6:6, 7, 9, 10, 13, 14
7:4, 7, 9, 13, 15[2], 19[2], 20
8:1[4], 3, 4, 5, 7, 8[2], 9, 10, 11[2], 12[2], 18[2]
9:1[2], 2[2], 4, 5, 7, 8
10:1, 2[3], 3, 6, 8, 10, 13, 17, 19
11:2, 6, 7, 10, 11[2], 12, 15, 16, 20, 24
12:2, 3[2], 4[2], 5, 6[2], 7[3], 8, 10, 12, 13, 15, 22, 23, 25
13:4, 5[2], 9[2], 13[3], 14, 21
14:3, 4, 5, 7[2], 14, 16, 18, 19, 20, 23
16:4[2], 5[2], 6[3], 12, 15, 22[2], 24, 29, 31[4], 34[3], 38, 41, 43, 47, 49[2], 51, 52, 53, 54[2], 56, 59, 60
17:4, 5, 8, 9, 10, 15, 16[2], 17, 20, 23[2]
18:3, 9, 17, 18, 22, 24[3], 26, 32
19:4, 8, 9[2], 10, 11, 12, 13[2]
20:1[2], 5[2], 6, 8, 9[2], 11, 13[4], 14, 15, 16, 17, 18[2], 19, 21[3], 22[2], 23, 26[2], 27[2], 36, 40[3], 41, 43, 47[2]
21:20, 21, 22, 23, 24[2], 30[2], 31, 32
22:3, 4[2], 6, 7[3], 9[3], 10[2], 11[2], 12, 13, 14, 15, 16[2], 18, 20[2], 21[2], 22[2], 24, 25[2], 27, 30
23:3[2], 8, 11[3], 15, 19[2], 21, 31, 32, 37, 38, 39, 43, 44[3], 45
24:1[3], 7, 11, 12, 13, 18[2], 25, 26, 27
25:4[2], 6, 10, 14
26:1[2], 5, 6, 8, 12, 15, 17, 18[2], 20[3]
27:4, 8, 9[2], 10[2], 11, 12, 13, 14, 16, 17, 18[2], 19[2], 20, 21[2], 22, 24[3], 25[2], 26, 27[4], 30, 32[2], 34[3], 35
28:2[2], 8, 9, 12, 13[3], 14, 15[2], 18, 22[3], 23, 25[3]
29:1[3], 3, 4, 12, 17[3], 21[2]
30:4[2], 5, 6, 7[2], 8, 9[3], 13, 14[2], 16, 18, 19, 20[3], 24
31:1[3], 2, 3, 6, 7[2], 8[3], 9, 10[2], 12, 14[2], 15, 16, 17, 18[3]
32:1[3], 2, 3, 10, 17[2], 19, 20, 23[2], 24, 25[3], 26, 27, 28, 32[2]
33:6, 8, 9, 10, 11, 12[3], 15, 21[3], 22[2], 27[4], 30
34:12[2], 13, 14[3], 25[2], 26, 27, 29
35:5[2], 8[3]
36:2, 3, 5, 6[2], 15, 17, 23[2], 27, 28, 31, 33[2], 34, 38
37:1[2], 2, 6, 8, 14[2], 17, 19[2], 20, 22, 24, 25, 26, 28
38:8, 12, 14, 16[2], 17[2], 18, 19[4], 23
39:6, 7[2], 9, 11[2], 15, 26, 27[2]
40:1[5], 2, 3[2], 5, 25[2], 27, 29[2], 33, 39, 44
41:6[2]
42:3, 6, 8, 10, 12
43:7[2], 8[2], 9, 11[2], 16, 17, 18, 21
44:2[2], 3, 5, 7[4], 8, 9[2], 11, 13, 17[2], 19, 24[3], 27[2], 28, 29, 30
45:1, 2[2], 3, 8[2], 16, 17[4], 18[2], 21[2], 25[3]
46:1, 3[2], 4, 6, 8, 9[3], 10[3], 11[2], 21, 22, 23
47:3, 5, 19, 22, 23
48:8[3], 9[2], 10[5], 13[2], 15[2], 18, 21, 22, 28

DANIEL

1:1, 4[5], 8, 14, 15, 17[2], 18[2], 20[2]
2:1, 4, 5, 16, 19, 22, 24[2], 25[2], 27, 28[2], 40[2], 41, 44[2], 45, 49
3:1[2], 13, 16, 20, 21, 24, 25, 28, 29, 30
4:1, 4[2], 6, 7, 8[2], 9, 10[2], 12[2], 13, 15[3], 17, 18, 21, 23[2], 25, 29, 31, 32, 35, 36, 37
5:2, 3, 5, 7[2], 8, 9, 11[4], 12, 13, 14[2], 15, 16, 20, 21, 23[2], 27, 29, 30
6:3, 4, 10, 19[2], 22, 23, 24, 25, 26, 27[2], 28[2]
7:1, 2, 5, 7[2], 8, 13, 15[2], 19, 20, 23, 28[2]
8:1, 2[4], 6, 7, 18, 19, 22, 23, 25[2]
9:1, 2[2], 6, 10, 11, 13, 14, 21[2], 24, 25, 27
10:1, 2, 3, 4, 5, 6, 8[2], 9, 14, 17[2], 21[2]
11:1, 2, 6[2], 7, 14, 16, 20[4], 21[2], 38, 39, 45
12:1, 2, 6, 7, 13

HOSEA

1:1[2], 5, 10
2:3, 9[2], 10, 15[2], 18, 19[4], 20, 21, 23
3:5
4:1, 5[2], 16, 19
5:4, 5, 8[2], 9, 11, 15
6:2[2], 9, 10
7:1, 2, 5, 6[2], 16
8:6
9:2, 3[2], 5[2], 6, 8[2], 9, 10[2], 13, 15
10:4[2], 9, 10[2], 12[2], 13[2], 14[2], 15
11:9, 11
12:3, 4, 7, 8[2], 9[2], 11[3]
13:1[2], 5[2], 9, 10, 11[2], 13, 16
14:3, 9

JOEL

1:2[2], 13
2:1[2], 5, 8, 9[2], 15, 23[2], 26, 27, 29, 30[2], 32[3]
3:1[2], 13, 14[2], 17, 18, 19, 21

AMOS

1:1[2], 14[3]
2:7, 8, 16
3:4, 5, 6[2], 9[5], 10, 12[4], 13, 14
4:1, 6[2]
5:6[2], 7, 10, 11, 12, 13, 15, 16[2], 17, 20, 21, 25
6:1[2], 6, 9, 13, 14
7:1, 7, 8, 10, 17[2]
8:3[2], 9[2], 11, 13
9:1, 3[2], 6[2], 9, 11[2]

OBADIAH

1, 3[2], 7, 8, 11[2], 12[3], 13[3], 14[2], 18, 20

JONAH

1:4, 5, 17
2:3, 7
3:6, 8
4:2, 5, 8, 10[2]

MICAH

1:1, 10[2], 11, 13
2:1, 4, 5, 11, 12
3:3, 4
4:1[4], 2, 5[4], 6, 7, 8[6], 10[7], 13
5:1, 2, 4[2], 5, 6, 7, 8[2], 10, 15
6:10, 12, 13[2], 14, 16
7:2, 5[3], 6[2], 8, 11[2], 12, 14[4], 18

NAHUM

1:3[3], 6, 7[2], 13
2:1, 3[2], 4[2], 5, 10, 12, 13
3:10[2], 13, 17[2], 18

HABAKKUK

1:5, 15[2]
2:4, 13, 19, 20
3:2[3], 7, 11, 12[2], 16[2], 17[2], 18[2]

ZEPHANIAH

1:1, 8, 9, 10, 12, 18[2]
2:3, 7[2], 14[4], 15[2]
3:2, 5, 11[2], 12[2], 13, 15, 16, 17[2], 19, 20

HAGGAI

1:1[3], 4, 6, 8, 13, 14, 15[2]
2:1[2], 3[3], 9, 10[2], 12, 15, 17, 19, 20, 22, 23

ZECHARIAH

1:1[2], 7, 8, 16
2:1, 5, 10, 11[2], 12
3:7, 9, 10
4:10
5:4, 7, 9, 11
6:2[2], 3[2], 8, 14, 15
7:1[3], 3[2], 5, 7, 10, 12
8:3, 4[2], 5, 6[3], 8[3], 9[2], 10, 11, 15, 16, 17, 22, 23
9:1, 4, 6, 7, 16
10:1[2], 2, 3, 5[2], 7, 9, 11, 12[2]

ZECHARIAH

11:8, 11, 13, 16[2]
12:2, 3[2], 4, 5[2], 6[4], 8, 9, 10[2], 11[3]
13:1, 2, 3, 4, 6[2], 8
14:1, 3, 4[2], 5, 6, 8[3], 9, 10, 11, 12[2], 13, 14, 15, 20[2], 21[4]

MALACHI

1:7, 10, 11, 12, 14
2:6[3], 9, 11[2], 17[2]
3:1, 3, 4[2], 5, 8, 10, 11, 17
4:2, 3, 4

MATTHEW

1:20[2]
2:1[2], 2, 5, 6, 9, 12, 13, 16[2], 18, 19[2], 22[3], 23
3:1[2], 3, 6, 12, 17
4:6, 13[2], 16[2], 21, 23
5:3, 8, 12, 15, 16, 18, 19[2], 20, 21, 22[3], 25, 28, 45, 48
6:1, 2[2], 4[2], 5[2], 6[2], 9, 10[2], 18[2], 20, 23, 29
7:3[2], 4, 11, 13[2], 15, 21, 22[4]
8:10, 11, 13, 24, 32
9:4, 10, 16, 25, 31, 33, 35
10:9, 11, 15, 16, 17, 19, 20, 23, 27[3], 28, 32, 33, 35[2], 41[2], 42[2]
11:1, 2, 6, 8[2], 11, 16, 21[3], 23[2], 24, 26, 29
12:5[2], 6, 18, 19, 21, 32[2], 36, 40[2], 41, 42, 45, 50
13:3, 10, 13, 14, 19, 21, 24, 27, 30[2], 31, 32, 33, 34, 35, 40[2], 43, 44, 54, 57[3]
14:2, 3, 8, 10, 11, 24, 25, 33
15:9, 17, 32, 33
16:3, 17, 19[2], 26, 27, 28
17:5, 22
18:1, 2, 4, 5, 6[2], 10[2], 14, 16, 18[2], 19, 20[2]
19:21, 28[2]
20:1, 3, 17, 21
21:8[2], 9[2], 12, 14, 15, 18, 19, 22, 24, 28, 32, 33, 41, 42[2]
22:11, 12, 15, 16, 28, 30[3], 36, 43
23:2, 6, 7, 9, 13[2], 30[2], 34, 39
24:5, 7, 14, 15, 16, 18, 19, 20, 26[2], 30[2], 38[2], 40, 43, 44, 45, 48, 50[2]
25:4, 10, 18, 25, 31, 35, 36, 38, 39, 43[2], 44
26:6[2], 12, 13, 23, 29, 55[2], 58, 61, 64, 67, 69
27:4, 5, 7, 19, 29, 40, 43, 44, 51, 59, 60[2]
28:1, 18[2], 19

MARK

1:2, 3, 4, 5, 9[2], 11, 13, 14, 19, 20, 23, 35, 39, 45
2:1, 6, 8[2], 15, 20, 26
3:23, 29
4:1, 2, 11, 15, 17, 19, 28, 29, 31[2], 36, 38
5:4, 5[2], 13, 14[2], 15, 20, 27, 29, 30[2], 33, 34, 39, 40
6:2, 4[2], 8, 10, 11, 14, 17, 22, 25[2], 27, 28, 29, 40, 47, 48, 51, 55, 56
7:7, 32
8:1, 4, 12, 14, 26, 37, 38[2]
9:33, 36[2], 37, 38, 39, 41, 42, 50
10:10, 16, 21, 24, 30[2], 32, 37, 52
11:4, 8[2], 9, 10[2], 15, 20, 22, 23, 25, 26, 27
12:4, 11, 13, 14, 23, 25[2], 26[2], 35, 38[3], 39, 41, 42, 43, 44[2]
13:6, 8, 9, 11, 14, 16, 17, 18, 19, 24, 25, 26, 29, 32, 35
14:3[2], 14, 17, 20, 25, 30, 31, 49, 60, 62, 66
15:1, 7, 29, 38, 41, 43, 46[2]
16:2, 5, 12, 17

LUKE

1:1[2], 3, 5, 6, 7, 8, 15, 17, 18, 19, 20, 21, 22, 25, 26, 28, 29, 31, 36, 39, 41, 44[2], 47, 51, 54, 66, 69, 75, 79[2], 80[2]
2:1, 7[3], 8[2], 11, 12[2], 14, 16, 19, 21, 23, 24, 25, 27, 28, 29, 34, 38[2], 40, 43, 44, 46[2], 51, 52[2]
3:1, 2, 4[2], 15[2], 17, 18, 20, 22[2]
4:2, 5, 11, 14, 15, 20, 21, 23[2], 24, 25[2], 27[2], 28, 33, 35, 44
5:7, 12, 18[2], 19, 22, 29, 35
6:1, 8, 12[2], 17, 23[3], 41[2], 42[3]
7:1, 7, 9, 21, 23, 25[2], 28, 32, 37[2], 45, 50
8:10, 13, 15, 16, 23, 27[2], 29, 34[2], 35, 48, 51
9:12, 14, 26[2], 31, 36, 48, 49, 57
10:7, 12, 13[3], 20[2], 21[3], 26, 34
11:1, 2[3], 6, 7, 21, 26, 31, 32, 33[2], 35, 37, 43[2], 52[2]
12:1, 3[4], 12, 15, 27, 28, 33, 38[2], 42, 45, 46[2], 52, 53[4], 58
13:4[2], 6, 10, 11, 14[2], 19, 21, 24[2], 26[2], 28, 29, 35
14:8, 10[2], 15, 21, 23
15:4, 7, 10, 14[2], 21, 25, 28

LUKE

16:8, 10[4], 11, 12, 15, 19, 23[3], 24[2], 25
17:4[2], 6, 24, 26[2], 27, 28, 30, 31[3], 34[2], 36
18:2, 3, 9, 12, 17, 22, 30[2]
19:17, 20, 30, 36, 38[3], 42, 43, 44, 47
20:1, 31, 33, 34, 35, 42, 45, 46[3]
21:2, 3, 4[2], 6, 8, 11, 14, 19, 21[3], 23[2], 25[3], 27, 37[3], 38[2]
22:6, 10, 16, 19, 20, 28, 30, 37, 44, 53, 55
23:4, 9, 11, 14, 19, 22, 29, 31[2], 38, 40, 43, 45, 53[3]
24:1, 3, 4, 6, 12, 18[2], 19, 27, 29, 35[2], 36, 38, 44[3], 47, 49, 53

JOHN

1:1, 2, 4, 5, 10, 18, 23, 28, 45, 47
2:1, 11, 14, 19, 20[2], 23[3], 25
3:13, 14, 15, 16, 18, 21, 23
4:14, 18, 20[2], 21, 23[2], 24[2], 31, 44, 53
5:2, 3, 4, 6, 13, 14, 26[2], 28[2], 35, 38, 39, 42, 43[2], 45
6:10[2], 31, 37, 45, 49, 53, 56[2], 59[2], 61
7:1[2], 4, 5, 9, 10, 18, 28, 37
8:1, 2, 3[2], 4[2], 5, 9, 12, 17, 20[2], 21, 24[2], 31, 33, 35, 37, 44[2]
9:3, 5, 7, 34
10:2, 9[2], 23[2], 25, 34, 38[2]
11:6, 9[2], 10[2], 13, 17, 20, 24, 25, 26, 30, 31, 33, 38, 52, 56
12:13, 25, 35, 36, 46, 48
13:1, 21, 31, 32[2]
14:1[2], 2, 10[3], 11[2], 13[2], 14, 17, 20[3], 26, 30
15:2, 4[4], 5[2], 6, 7[2], 9, 10[2], 11, 16, 25
16:21, 23[2], 24, 25[2], 26, 33[2]
17:10, 11[2], 12[2], 13[2], 21[3], 23[3], 26[2]
18:13, 15, 16, 20[3], 26, 38
19:4, 6, 13[3], 17, 18, 20, 40, 41[2]
20:5[2], 7, 8, 12, 19, 25, 26, 30[2]
21:2, 8

THE ACTS

1:2, 7, 8[3], 10, 11, 13, 14, 15[2], 18, 19, 20, 21
2:1, 6, 8, 9[3], 10[2], 11, 12, 17, 18, 19[2], 22, 26, 27, 31, 37, 38, 42[3], 46
3:6, 11, 13, 16[2], 22, 25, 26
4:3, 7, 12, 16, 17, 18, 19, 24
5:4[2], 7, 10, 12, 18, 20, 21, 22, 25[2], 28, 34[2], 37, 40, 42[2]
6:1[2], 7, 15
7:2[2], 4, 5, 6, 7[2], 10, 12, 16, 17, 20[2], 22[3], 29, 30[3], 34, 35, 36[3], 38[3], 39, 41[2], 42[2], 44, 45, 48, 51
8:8, 9, 16, 21[2], 23[2], 25, 28, 33, 40
9:10, 11, 12[2], 17, 20, 21, 22, 25, 27[2], 28, 29, 31[2], 37[2], 42, 43
10:1, 3[2], 17, 23, 25, 27, 30[2], 31[2], 32, 35, 39[2], 43, 48
11:1, 3, 5[2], 13, 22, 26, 27, 28, 29
12:4, 5, 7, 14, 21
13:1, 5, 13, 14, 17, 18, 19, 27, 28, 29, 33[2], 35, 40, 41[2], 43
14:1, 2, 8, 11[2], 14, 16[2], 17, 22, 23, 25
15:21[2], 23, 33, 35, 36, 39
16:3, 5[2], 6, 9, 12, 18, 24, 29, 32, 34, 36
17:2, 11[2], 16, 17[2], 21, 22[2], 24, 28, 31[3]
18:2, 4, 5, 9, 10, 18, 21, 23, 24, 25[2], 26
19:5, 9, 10, 16, 21, 22, 27, 29, 30, 39, 40[2]
20:6, 8, 9, 10, 13, 14, 16, 19, 22, 23, 29
21:18, 27, 29, 31, 39, 40
22:2, 3[3], 17[2], 19
23:1, 6[2], 9, 10, 11, 16, 21, 35
24:3, 12[3], 14[2], 18, 20, 21, 24
25:3, 5, 14
26:3, 10[2], 11, 13, 14, 16, 18, 21, 26
27:12, 20, 21, 27, 31, 35, 37[2], 39
28:7, 8, 9, 11[2], 18, 30[2]

ROMANS

1:2, 7, 9[2], 15, 18, 19, 21, 27[2], 28, 32
2:7, 12, 14, 15, 16, 17, 19, 20, 28, 29[2]
3:4, 9, 16, 20, 24, 25, 26
4:10[4], 12, 18, 19, 20
5:2, 3, 5, 6, 8, 11, 13, 17
6:1, 4, 5[2], 10[2], 12[2], 21
7:5[2], 6[2], 8, 13, 17, 18[2], 20, 22, 23[2]
8:1, 2, 3[3], 4, 8, 9[3], 10, 11[2], 18, 20, 22, 37, 39
9:1[2], 2, 7, 17, 25, 26, 28, 33

ROMANS

10:6, 8[2], 9, 14[2]
11:17, 19, 22, 23[3], 25[3], 30, 32
12:4, 5, 10, 11[2], 12[3], 16, 17, 18, 20
13:4, 9, 13[4]
14:1, 5, 13, 17, 18, 22
15:12, 13[2], 15[2], 17, 23, 24, 27, 29, 30, 31
16:2[2], 3, 5, 7, 8, 9, 10, 11, 12[2], 13, 22

1 CORINTHIANS

1:2[2], 5[3], 6, 7, 8, 10[2], 13, 15, 21, 29, 30, 31
2:3[3], 4, 5[2], 7, 11, 13
3:1, 16, 18, 19, 21
4:2, 6[2], 10, 15[2], 17[3], 20[2], 21[2]
5:3[2], 4, 5, 9
6:4, 11, 19, 20[2]
7:15, 17, 18, 20, 22, 28, 34[2], 37[2], 38[2], 39
8:4[2], 5[2], 6, 7, 10
9:1, 2, 9, 10[2], 18, 24, 25
10:2[2], 5, 8, 19, 25, 28, 33
11:2, 11, 13, 17, 18, 21, 22[2], 23, 24, 25[2], 34
12:6, 18, 25, 27, 28
13:6[2], 9[2], 10, 12
14:2[2], 4, 7, 10, 13, 14, 19[2], 20[3], 21, 23, 24, 25, 27, 28, 33, 34, 35, 40
15:2[2], 10, 17, 18, 19[2], 22[2], 23, 28, 30, 31, 41, 42[2], 43[4], 52[2], 54, 58[3]
16:2, 11, 13, 19[2], 24

2 CORINTHIANS

1:1, 4[2], 5, 6, 8, 9[3], 10, 12[2], 14[2], 15, 19, 20[2], 21, 22
2:1, 3, 5, 9, 10, 13, 14[2], 15[2], 17[2]
3:2, 3[2], 7, 9, 10, 14[2], 18
4:2[2], 4, 6[2], 7, 8, 10[2], 11, 12[2]
5:1, 2, 4, 6, 10, 11, 12[2], 17, 19, 20, 21
6:1, 2[2], 3, 4[5], 5[6], 12[2], 13, 16[2]
7:1, 3, 4, 7, 9, 11[3], 12, 13, 14, 16[2]
8:2, 6, 7[5], 18, 20, 21[2], 22[2]
9:3[2], 4, 7, 8, 11, 14
10:1, 3, 6, 11[2], 14, 16[2], 17
11:1, 3, 6[3], 7, 9, 10[2], 17, 23[4], 25, 26[12], 27[5], 32, 33
12:2[2], 3, 5, 7, 9[2], 10[5], 11[2], 12[2], 18[2], 19
13:1, 3[2], 4, 5[2], 11

GALATIANS

1:13[2], 14[2], 16, 22, 23, 24
2:2, 4[3], 6, 8[2], 16, 20[2], 21
3:3, 4[2], 8, 10[2], 11, 12, 17, 19, 26, 28
4:3, 9, 11, 14, 18, 19[2], 20, 25[2]
5:1, 6, 10, 14[2], 16, 21, 25[2]
6:1[2], 4[2], 6[2], 9[2], 12, 13, 14, 15, 17

EPHESIANS

1:1, 3[2], 4[2], 6, 7, 8, 9, 10[5], 11, 12, 13[2], 15, 16, 17, 18, 20[2], 21[2], 23
2:1, 2[2], 3[2], 4, 5, 6[2], 7[2], 10[2], 11[3], 12, 13, 15[3], 16, 21[2], 22
3:3, 4, 5, 6, 9, 10, 11, 12, 15, 16, 17[2], 20, 21
4:2, 3, 4, 6, 13, 14, 15[2], 16[2], 17[2], 18, 21, 23, 24
5:2, 3, 8, 9, 12, 13[4], 20, 21, 31, 33
6:1, 4, 5, 9, 10[2], 12, 13, 18, 20, 21, 24

PHILIPPIANS

1:1, 4, 5, 6, 7[3], 8, 9[2], 13[3], 14, 18[2], 20[2], 22, 23, 24, 26, 27, 28, 29, 30[2]
2:1, 3, 5[2], 6, 7, 8, 10[2], 12[2], 13, 15[2], 16[3], 19, 22, 24, 25, 29[2]
3:1, 3[3], 4[2], 6, 9, 14, 15, 19, 20
4:1, 2, 3[2], 4, 6, 9, 10, 11[2], 12, 15, 16, 19, 21

COLOSSIANS

1:2, 4, 5[2], 6[3], 8, 9, 10[2], 12, 14, 16[2], 18, 19, 20[2], 21, 22[2], 23, 24[2], 27, 28[2], 29
2:1, 2, 3, 5[3], 6, 7[2], 9, 10, 11[2], 12, 13, 15, 16[3], 18, 20, 23[2]
3:3, 4, 7[2], 10, 11, 15[2], 16[4], 17[2], 18, 20, 22[2]
4:1, 2[2], 3, 5, 7, 12[2], 13[2], 15[2], 16, 17

1 THESSALONIANS

1:1[2], 2, 3[2], 5[4], 6, 7, 8[2], 9
2:1[2], 2, 3, 4, 13[2], 14[2], 17[2], 19
3:2, 5, 7, 8, 10, 12, 13
4:4, 5, 6, 10, 14, 16, 17[2]
5:2, 4, 7[2], 12, 13, 18[2]

2 THESSALONIANS

1:1, 4[3], 8, 10[3], 12[2]
2:2, 4, 6, 10, 12, 17
3:4, 6, 13, 17

1 TIMOTHY

1:2, 4, 13, 14, 16
2:2[2], 3, 6, 7[2], 9[2], 11, 12, 14, 15[2]
3:4, 9, 11, 13[2], 15, 16[3]
4:1, 2, 6[2], 10, 12[6], 14, 16[2]
5:5[2], 6, 7, 17
6:9, 13, 15, 16, 17[3], 18, 19

2 TIMOTHY

1:1, 3, 5[3], 6[2], 9, 13[2], 14, 15, 17, 18[2]
2:1[2], 7, 10, 14, 20, 25
3:1, 12, 14, 15, 16
4:2, 5

TITUS

1:2, 3, 5[3], 13, 16
2:2[3], 3, 7[2], 9, 10, 12
3:1, 3, 8, 15

PHILEMON

2, 4, 6[2], 7, 8, 10, 11, 13[2], 16[2], 20[2], 21, 23

HEBREWS

1:1[2], 2, 6, 10
2:5, 6, 8[3], 10, 12, 13, 17[2], 18
3:2, 5, 8[3], 10, 11, 12[2], 15, 17, 19
4:2, 3, 4, 5, 6, 7, 13, 15, 16
5:1, 6, 7[2], 13
6:7, 10, 18
7:9, 10, 19
8:1, 5, 9[2], 10, 13
9:9, 10, 12, 23, 24, 26
10:3, 6, 7, 16, 22, 32, 34[3], 38
11:9[3], 12, 13, 18, 19, 26, 34, 37, 38[3]
12:3, 9, 23
13:3[2], 4, 18, 21[3], 22

JAMES

1:6, 8, 9, 10, 11, 23, 25, 27
2:2[3], 3, 4, 5, 10, 16
3:2[2], 3, 7, 14, 18
4:1, 5[2], 10, 16
5:5[2], 10, 14

1 PETER

1:4, 5, 6, 8, 11, 14, 15, 17, 20, 21[2], 22
2:6[2], 10, 12, 22, 24
3:1, 4[2], 5[3], 15[2], 16, 18, 19, 20
4:1[2], 2, 3, 6[2], 11, 15, 19
5:6, 9[3], 14

2 PETER

1:4, 8[2], 12[2], 13[2], 15, 17, 18, 19[2], 21
2:1, 5, 8, 10, 11, 12, 13, 18, 19, 22
3:1, 3, 5, 7, 10[2], 11, 14, 16[3], 18[2]

1 JOHN

1:5, 6, 7[2], 8, 10
2:4, 5[2], 6, 8[2], 9[2], 10[2], 11[2], 14, 15[2], 16, 24[4], 27[2], 28
3:3, 5, 6, 9, 10, 14, 15, 17, 18[4], 22, 24[3]
4:2, 3[2], 4[2], 9, 12[2], 13[2], 15[2], 16[3], 17[2], 18[2]
5:7, 8[2], 10, 11, 14, 19, 20[2]

2 JOHN

1, 2, 3, 4, 6, 7, 9[2]

3 JOHN

1, 2, 3[2], 4

JUDE

1, 4, 5, 6, 7, 10, 11[2], 12, 16, 18, 20, 21

REVELATION

1:4, 5, 9[3], 10, 11[2], 13, 15, 16[2], 20
2:1[2], 7, 8, 12, 13, 17, 18, 24
3:1, 4[2], 5, 7, 12, 18, 20, 21[2]
4:1, 2[2], 3, 4, 6
5:1, 3[2], 6[2], 13[3]
6:5, 6, 15[2]
7:3, 9, 13, 14, 15, 17
8:1, 9
9:4, 6, 10, 11[2], 14, 17, 19[2]
10:2, 7, 8, 9, 10
11:3, 5, 6, 8, 9, 12, 13, 15, 19[2]
12:1, 2, 3, 7, 8, 10, 12
13:6[2], 8, 13, 14, 16[2]
14:1, 5, 6, 9[2], 10[2], 13, 14, 15, 16, 17, 18, 19
15:1[2], 5, 6
16:3, 16, 19
17:3, 4[2], 8, 17
18:6, 7, 8, 10, 16, 17[2], 19[2], 22[3], 23[2], 24
19:1, 8, 11, 13, 14[2], 17[2]
20:1, 4, 6, 8, 12, 13[2], 15
21:8, 10, 14, 23, 24, 27[2]
22:2, 3, 4, 14, 16, 18, 19

IS

1961, *2076*

GENESIS
1:11, 29^2, 30
2:9, 11^3, 12^2, 13^2, 14^3, 18, 23
3:3, 13, 17, 22
4:6, 9, 13
5:1
6:3, 13^2, 15, 17^2, 21
7:15
8:17, 21
9:4, 10, 12^2, 15, 16, 17^2, 18
10:9, 12
11:6, 9
12:12, 18, 19
13:9, 18
14:2, 3, 6, 7, 8, 15, 17, 23
15:2, 3, 13, 16
16:6, 14
17:4, 10, 12^3, 13^2, 14, 17^2
18:9, 14, 20^2, 21
19:8, 13, 20^3, 31^2, 37, 38
20:2, 3, 5^2, 7, 11, 12^2, 13^2, 15, 16
21:13, 17, 22
22:7, 14, 17
23:2, 9^2, 11, 15^2, 19, 20
24:23, 35, 51, 65^2
25:9, 18
26:7^2, 9^2, 10, 20, 33
27:11, 20, 22, 27, 33, 36
28:16, 17^3
29:6^2, 7^2, 19, 25
30:15, 30, 33
31:5, 14, 16, 29, 32, 35, 36^2, 43, 48, 50^2
32:2, 8, 18^2, 20, 27, 29, 30, 32
33:11, 17, 18
34:14, 21
35:6^2, 10, 19, 20, 27
36:1, 8, 19, 43
37:10, 22, 26, 27, 30, 33^2
38:14, 18, 21, 24
39:8, 9
40:8, 12, 18
41:15, 16, 25^2, 26, 28^2, 32^2, 38^2, 39
42:2, 13^2, 14, 21, 22, 28^3, 30, 32^2, 36^2, 38^2
43:7, 27^2, 28^2, 29, 32
44:5, 10, 15, 16, 17, 20^2, 28, 30, 31
45:12, 20, 26^2, 28^2
46:33, 34
47:3, 4, 6, 18^2, 23
48:1, 7, 18
49:9, 14, 21, 22, 24, 28, 29, 30^2, 32
50:10, 11^2, 20

EXODUS
1:22
2:6, 14, 18, 20^2
3:3, 5, 9, 13, 15^2, 16
4:2, 14, 22
5:2, 16^2, 22
7:14, 17, 18
8:10, 19, 26
9:3^2, 4, 14, 27, 28, 29
10:5, 7, 10
11:5
12:11, 19, 22^2, 27, 42^2, 43, 44, 48, 49
13:2, 8, 14
14:12
15:2^3, 3^2, 6, 11^2, 26
16:1, 15^2, 16, 23^2, 25, 26, 32, 36
17:3, 7
18:11, 14, 17, 18^2
19:5
20:4^3, 10^2, 11, 17, 20
21:21, 30
22:16, 25, 27^2, 31
23:16, 21
25:3
26:5, 10
27:21
28:8, 26
29:1, 13^2, 14, 18^2, 21, 22^2, 23, 25, 27^4, 28, 30, 32, 34, 38
30:6^2, 10, 13, 32
31:7, 13, 14, 15, 17
32:1, 5, 9, 17, 18^2, 23, 26
33:13, 16, 21
34:9, 10, 14^2, 19^2
35:4, 5
36:25
38:21, 26
40:9

LEVITICUS
1:5, 8^2, 12^2, 13, 17^2
2:3, 6, 8^2, 9, 10^2, 15, 16
3:3, 4^2, 5^3, 9, 10^2, 11, 14, 15^2, 16^2
4:3, 5, 7^2, 8, 9^2, 14, 16, 18^3, 21, 22, 24, 31, 35
5:1, 8, 9, 11, 12, 17, 19
6:4, 9^2, 14, 15, 17^2, 20^2, 21, 22^2, 25^3, 27, 28, 29, 30
7:1^2, 4^3, 5, 6, 7^3, 9^2, 11, 15, 24, 35, 37
8:5, 28, 31
9:6
10:3, 7, 12, 13, 17
11:3, 4, 5, 6, 7, 10, 26, 32, 33, 36, 37, 46
12:7
13:3^2, 6, 8, 9, 11^2, 13^2, 15^2, 17, 18, 20, 22, 23, 24, 25^2, 27, 28^2, 30, 31, 36, 37^3, 39^2, 40^3, 41^2, 42, 44^3, 45, 46, 47, 49, 51^3, 52^2, 54, 55^3, 57^2, 59
14:4, 7, 8, 11, 13^3, 14, 16, 17^2, 18^2, 19, 22, 25, 27, 28^2, 29^2, 31^2, 32^3, 35, 36, 40, 43, 44^2, 46, 48, 54, 57^3
15:2, 3, 4, 8, 13, 17, 31, 32^2, 33^2
16:2, 6, 11^2, 13, 15, 18
17:2, 11^2, 14^3
18:6, 7, 8, 10, 11, 12, 13, 14, 15, 16, 17, 19, 22, 23, 25, 27
19:7, 13, 20
20:14, 17, 21, 27
21:2^3, 3, 7^2, 10^2, 12, 19
22:4^2, 7^2, 8, 11, 13, 24, 25, 27
23:3^2, 5, 6, 8, 28, 36
24:9, 16
25:5, 12, 23, 28, 29, 30, 34, 48, 49
27:22, 26, 28, 30^2

NUMBERS
1:51
3:26, 47, 48
4:15, 16, 24, 25, 26^2, 28, 31, 33
5:2, 15, 17, 18, 29^2
6:4, 7, 8, 13, 18, 19, 20, 21
8:24
9:13^2
10:7
11:6^2, 14, 17, 20, 23
12:7^2, 12
13:18, 19, 20, 27, 32
14:7, 9^2, 18, 42
15:25, 29
16:3, 5, 11, 13, 40, 46^2
18:11^2, 13^2, 16, 19, 31
19:2^2, 9^2, 13^2, 14^2, 15, 16, 20
20:5^2, 13
21:5^2, 8, 11, 13^2, 14, 16, 20, 28, 30
22:5^2, 6^2, 11, 32, 36^2
23:19, 21^2, 23^2
24:9^2, 21
26:9
27:11, 14, 18
28:3, 6, 10, 14, 16, 17, 23
29:1
30:1, 9
31:20, 21
32:4, 19
33:6, 7, 36
34:2, 13
35:16, 17, 18, 21, 31, 32, 33
36:6

DEUTERONOMY
1:14, 16, 17^2, 25, 28
2:36^2
3:11, 12, 16, 24, 25
4:6^2, 7^2, 8, 17, 18, 24, 31, 32, 35^2, 38, 39^2, 44, 48^2
5:8^3, 14^2, 21, 26
6:4, 15, 18, 24
7:9, 21, 25^2, 26
8:13^2, 18^2
9:3, 13
10:9, 14^2, 15, 17, 21^2
11:10, 11
12:8, 12, 18, 22, 23, 25, 28
13:6, 11, 14, 15, 18
14:8, 10, 19, 21, 27
15:2^2, 3, 9, 16
16:11, 17, 20
17:1^2, 4, 6, 15, 18
18:2, 22
19:4, 6^2, 16, 17
20:1, 4, 5, 6, 7, 8^2, 11, 14, 19
21:2, 3, 4, 6, 9, 16, 17^2, 20^2, 23^2
22:23, 26^2, 28^2
23:1, 7, 10, 11, 15, 19, 23
24:2, 4^2, 14, 15
25:6
26:11, 12
28:23^2, 43, 54, 61
29:5, 11, 15, 23^2, 28
30:11^2, 12, 13, 14, 20
31:6, 8, 11, 12, 17
32:4^3, 5, 6, 9^2, 20, 21, 22, 27, 28, 31, 32, 33, 34, 35, 36^2, 39^2, 47^2, 49^2
33:1, 7, 17, 22, 26, 27, 29^2
34:1, 4

JOSHUA
1:2, 8, 9
2:9, 11
3:10, 16
4:24
5:4, 9, 15
6:7
7:2, 13, 15
8:18, 31, 34
9:12^2
10:13
11:4
12:2^2, 9
13:2, 3^2, 4, 9^2, 16^2, 25, 28
14:11
15:7^2, 8^2, 9, 10, 12, 13, 20, 25, 49, 54, 60
16:8
17:10, 16, 18
18:7, 13, 14, 16, 17, 28^2
19:8, 11, 16, 23, 31, 39, 48
20:7
21:11
22:9, 16, 17, 28, 29, 31, 34
23:3, 6, 10
24:17, 18, 19^2, 30

JUDGES
1:26
4:11, 14^2, 20
5:9, 28
6:12, 13, 15, 24, 25, 31
7:1, 3, 14
8:2, 21^2
9:2, 3, 18, 28^3, 32, 33^2, 38^3
10:8, 18
13:17, 18
14:3, 15, 18^2
15:2, 11, 19
16:2^3, 3, 9, 15
17:2
18:6, 9, 10^2, 12, 14, 19, 24
19:10, 12, 18, 19^4, 23, 24
20:5, 12^2
21:3, 5, 6, 8, 11, 12, 19^2

RUTH
1:13, 15, 19
2:5, 6, 19, 20, 22
3:2, 12^2
4:3, 4, 11, 15, 17^2

1 SAMUEL
1:8
2:1^2, 2^3, 3, 5, 20, 24, 35, 36
3:17, 18
4:7, 16, 17^2, 21, 22^2
5:7
6:3, 9, 20
9:6^2, 7^2, 9, 11, 12^3, 16, 18, 19, 20^2, 24
10:1, 5, 7, 11^3, 12^2, 24
11:12
12:5^3, 6, 17^2
13:5
14:1, 2, 6, 7, 17
15:7, 11, 12, 22, 23^2, 28, 29, 32
16:6, 12, 16^2, 18^2, 19
17:25^2, 26, 29, 46, 47, 55, 56
18:18
19:14, 17, 19, 22, 24
20:1^2, 2, 3, 5, 6, 7^2, 18, 21, 26^2, 37
21:3^2, 4^2, 5, 8, 9^3, 11, 14
22:8^3, 14^3, 17
23:7, 19, 22^2
24:1, 6, 10, 11, 14, 16
25:10^2, 17^2, 25^4, 29
26:1, 3, 11, 15, 16^2, 17^2, 18, 20
27:1
28:7, 14^2, 15, 16^2
29:1, 3, 5, 6
30:20, 24

2 SAMUEL
1:9^2, 18, 19, 21
2:7, 16
3:12, 13, 23, 24^2, 29, 38
4:10
5:7
6:2
7:3^2, 18, 19, 22^2, 23, 26
9:1^2, 2, 3^2, 4^2, 8
11:3, 21, 24
12:14, 18, 19^2, 21, 23
13:16^2, 20, 23, 28, 30, 32, 33, 35
14:5, 7^2, 13, 15, 17, 19, 20, 30
15:2, 3, 31
16:3, 17
17:2, 3, 7, 8, 9^2, 10^3, 11, 14, 20, 29
18:3, 13, 18^2, 20, 25, 27^2, 28, 29, 32^2
19:9, 10, 11, 26, 27^2, 30, 42
20:8, 11, 21
21:1
22:2, 3, 4, 31^3, 32^2, 33, 35, 48, 51
23:5, 15, 17
24:16, 21

1 KINGS
1:9, 25, 27, 41, 45
2:3, 15^2, 22, 29, 38, 42, 44
3:6, 8, 9, 22^4, 23^4, 27
4:12^2, 13, 20, 29, 33
5:4, 6
6:1, 17, 38
8:1, 2, 21, 23, 24, 35^2, 41, 43, 46, 60^2
9:8, 15, 26
11:7, 11, 33, 38
12:24, 28, 32
13:3, 26, 31
14:2, 5, 10, 13, 15
15:19
17:3, 5, 24
18:8, 10^2, 11, 14, 24, 27^4, 39^2, 41, 43
19:4, 7
20:3, 6, 28^2, 32^2
21:2, 5, 14^2, 15, 18^3, 21
22:3, 7, 8, 13, 16, 32

2 KINGS
1:3^2, 6^2, 8, 16^2
2:14, 19^2
3:11^2, 12, 18, 23
4:1^2, 4, 6, 9, 13, 14^2, 23, 25, 26^4, 27, 31, 40
5:3, 4, 6, 8, 15, 21, 22, 26
6:1, 11, 12, 13^2, 19^2, 32, 33
7:4, 9
8:5^2, 7, 13
9:8, 11, 12, 13, 17, 18, 19, 20, 22, 23, 27, 32, 34, 36, 37
10:5, 15^3, 30, 33
11:5
12:4^2
14:6
18:10, 17, 19, 21, 22
19:3^2, 9, 13, 21, 28, 30
20:3, 10, 15, 17, 19^2
22:4, 5, 13^4
23:10, 17^2, 21
25:4, 8

1 CHRONICLES
1:27
5:1
6:10
7:31
11:4, 5, 11, 17
12:17
13:6^2, 11
14:15
16:14, 25^2, 32, 34, 40
17:2^2, 16, 20^2, 21, 24
19:13
21:15, 17^2, 23, 24
22:1^2, 5^2, 14, 16, 18^2, 19
23:29^2
27:6
29:1^3, 5, 11^4, 12^2, 14, 15, 16

2 CHRONICLES
1:10, 12
2:4, 5^2, 6
5:2, 9, 13
6:11, 14, 15, 26^2, 32^2, 33, 36, 40
7:3, 15, 21
11:4
12:6
13:4, 6, 10, 12
14:7, 11
15:2
16:3, 7, 9
18:6, 7^2, 31
19:2, 6, 7, 11
20:2, 6^2, 9, 15, 34
22:9
23:4, 18
25:4, 7, 9
26:23
28:11, 13^2, 22
29:10
30:9
31:3, 10^2
32:7, 8^2
34:21^4
35:12, 21
36:23^2

EZRA
1:2, 3^4, 4, 5, 9
2:68
3:2, 4, 11
4:11, 15, 19, 24
5:2, 8^2, 15, 16^2, 17
6:2, 5^2, 12, 18^2
7:11, 14, 15, 16, 17, 23, 25, 27
8:1, 22^2
9:6, 7, 11, 13, 15
10:2, 13^2, 23

NEHEMIAH
1:3
2:2^2, 19
4:10^2, 14, 19
5:5^2, 9, 14
6:6, 7, 11
8:9^2, 10^3, 11, 15
9:5, 6, 10, 18, 33
10:34, 36
13:11, 17

ESTHER
1:1, 19, 20
2:7, 16
3:7^3, 8^2, 11, 13
4:11^2, 16
5:3, 6^2, 7
6:3, 4, 8
7:2^2, 5^2, 6
8:8, 9, 12
9:1, 12^2, 24

JOB
1:8, 10, 12, 16
2:3, 6
3:3, 19, 20^2, 23^2, 25^2
4:5, 6, 19, 21
5:4, 7, 13, 17, 27
6:6^2, 11^2, 12^2, 13^2, 14, 16, 17, 26, 28, 29, 30
7:1, 5^2, 7, 9, 17
8:12, 16, 19
9:2, 4, 19, 22, 24^2, 32, 33, 35
10:1, 3, 7, 13, 22
11:4, 6, 8, 9, 18
12:4, 5^3, 10, 12, 13, 16, 24
13:9, 19, 28
14:1^2, 2, 7, 10, 17, 18
15:9, 11, 14^2, 16, 20, 21, 22, 23^2, 31
16:6, 8, 16^2, 17, 19^2
17:1, 3, 7, 12, 13, 15, 16
18:8, 10, 15, 21
19:7, 17, 28, 29
20:5, 7, 14^2, 23^2, 25, 26, 29
21:4, 8, 9, 15, 16^2, 17, 21, 28, 30
22:2, 3^2, 5, 12, 18, 20, 29, 30
23:2^2, 8, 13, 14
24:14, 17, 18^2, 22
25:3, 4, 6^2
26:2, 3, 6, 8, 14
27:3^2, 8, 11, 13, 14, 19
28:1, 2^2, 5, 7, 11, 12, 13, 14^2, 18, 20, 21, 28^2
30:16, 18, 30, 31
31:2, 3, 11^2, 12, 28, 35
32:8, 19^2
33:9, 12, 19, 21, 24
34:4, 6, 7, 17, 18, 22, 31, 36
35:2, 10, 14, 15
36:4^2, 5^2, 14, 16, 18, 26
37:1, 4, 10^2, 12, 16, 18, 21, 22, 23
38:2, 14, 15, 19^2, 21, 24, 26^2, 30
39:8, 11, 16^2, 20, 22, 24, 30
40:11, 12, 16^2, 19
41:9, 10^2, 11^2, 16, 22, 24, 33^2, 34
42:3, 7^2, 8

PSALMS
1:1, 2
2:12
3:2, 8
4:3
5:9^3
6:3, 5, 7
7:2, 4, 8, 10, 11, 15
8:1, 4, 9
9:6, 15, 16^2
10:4, 7^2, 16
11:4^2
12:4
14:1^2, 3, 5, 6
15:4
16:3, 5, 8, 9, 11
17:12, 13
18:2, 3, 30^3, 31^2, 32, 34, 47
19:3^2, 4, 5, 6^2, 7^2, 8, 9, 11^2
21:5
22:11^2, 14^2, 15, 28^2
23:1
24:1, 6, 8, 10^2
25:8, 11, 12, 14
26:3, 10^2
27:1^2
28:3, 7, 8^2
29:3^2, 4^2
30:5, 9
31:9, 10, 19
32:1^3, 2^3, 4, 6
33:1, 4, 5, 12^2, 16^2, 17, 18, 20
34:8^2, 9, 12, 16, 18, 20
35:10^2
36:1, 4, 5, 6, 7, 9
37:13, 16, 26^2, 31, 33, 37, 39^2
38:3^2, 7, 9^2, 10, 17, 20
39:1, 4, 5^2, 7, 11
40:4, 7, 8
41:1
42:3, 6, 10, 11
43:5
44:15, 17, 18, 25
45:1^2, 2, 6^2, 11, 13^2
46:1, 4, 5, 7^2, 11^2
47:2^2, 5, 7, 9
48:1, 2, 3, 10^2, 14
49:8, 11, 12, 13, 16^2, 20^2
50:6, 10, 12
51:3
52:t, 7, 9
53:1^2, 3^2
54:4^2, 6
55:4, 11, 15
56:9
57:4, 6, 7^2, 10
58:4, 11^2
59:9, 17
60:7^4, 8, 11, 12
61:2^2
62:2^2, 5, 6^2, 7^2, 8
63:1, 3
64:6
65:4, 9
66:5, 10
68:2, 5, 15, 16, 17, 20^2, 27, 34^2, 35
69:2, 3, 13, 16
71:11, 18, 19^2
73:1, 4, 11, 25, 26, 28
74:9^2, 12, 16^2
75:1, 7, 8^3
76:1^2, 2, 12
77:8, 10, 13^2, 19
79:10^2
80:16^2
83:8, 18
84:5^2, 10, 11, 12
85:9, 12
86:8, 13
87:1
88:3
89:7, 8, 10, 11, 13^2, 15, 18^2, 19, 34, 41, 47, 48
90:4, 6, 9, 10^2, 11
91:2, 9
92:1, 7, 15^3
93:1^3, 2, 4
94:12, 22^2
95:3, 4, 5, 7, 10
96:4^2, 12
97:11
99:2^2, 3, 5, 9
100:3^2, 5^2
102:t, 4, 13
103:1, 5, 8, 11^2, 12, 16, 17
104:13, 20, 24, 25, 26
105:7
106:1
107:1, 26, 40, 43
108:1, 4, 8^4, 9, 12, 13
109:19, 21, 22, 27
111:3, 4, 9, 10
112:1, 4, 7, 8
113:3, 4, 5
115:2, 3, 8, 9, 10, 11
116:5^2, 15
117:2
118:1, 6, 8, 9, 14^2, 15, 16, 22, 23^2, 24, 27, 29
119:38, 50, 64, 70, 71, 72, 77, 89, 90, 96, 97, 105, 109, 118, 126, 140, 142^2, 144, 155, 160, 174
120:5
121:5^2
122:3^2
123:4
124:7^2, 8
125:2
127:2, 3, 5
128:1
129:4
130:4, 7^2
131:1, 2^2
132:14
133:1, 2
135:3^2, 5^2, 17, 18
136:1
138:5
139:4, 6^2, 17
140:3
141:8
143:4^2, 10
144:3, 4, 8, 10, 11, 15^4
145:3^2, 8, 9, 13, 17, 18
146:3, 5^2, 6
147:1^3, 5^2
148:13^2

PROVERBS
1:7, 17, 19
2:7, 10
3:13, 14, 15, 16, 18^2, 27^2, 32^2, 33
4:7, 13, 16, 18, 19
5:3, 4
6:14, 23^2, 26, 30, 34
7:11, 12, 19^2, 23, 27
8:4, 7, 8, 11, 13, 14, 19, 34
9:4, 10^2, 13^2, 16, 17
10:1, 5^2, 7, 11, 13^3, 14, 15^2, 17, 18, 19, 20^2, 23, 25^2, 26, 29, 32
11:1^2, 2, 8, 10, 11^2, 12, 13, 14^2, 15^2, 17, 22^2, 23^2, 24^3, 30^2
12:1, 4^2, 8, 9^2, 11, 13, 15^2, 16, 18^2, 19, 20^2, 26, 27, 28^2
13:5, 6, 7^2, 10, 12, 14, 15, 17, 19^2, 22, 23^3
14:2, 3, 4^2, 6, 8^2, 9, 12, 13^2, 16, 17^2, 20, 21, 23, 24^2, 26, 27, 28^2, 29^3, 30, 32, 33^2, 34, 35^2
15:4^2, 5, 6^2, 8^2, 9, 10, 13, 15, 16, 17^2, 18, 19^2, 21^2, 23, 24, 27, 29, 33^2
16:1, 5^2, 6, 8, 10, 12^2, 14, 15^2, 16, 17, 19, 20, 22^2, 25, 27, 29, 31, 32^2, 33^2
17:1, 3, 5, 8, 14, 16, 17, 24, 25, 26, 27, 28^2
18:5, 7, 9^3, 10^2, 11, 12^2, 13, 17, 19, 24
19:1^3, 2, 4, 6, 10, 11, 12^2, 13, 14, 18, 22^2, 26
20:1^4, 2, 3, 5, 11, 14^3, 15, 16, 17, 18, 23, 25^2, 27, 28, 29^2
21:1, 2, 3, 4, 5, 6, 8^2, 9, 11^3, 15, 19, 20, 24, 27, 30, 31^2
22:1, 2, 6, 7, 13, 14^2, 15, 18, 22
23:1, 5, 7^2, 11, 18, 22, 27^2, 31
24:3^2, 5, 6, 7, 9^2, 10, 13^2, 23
25:2^2, 3, 7, 11, 12, 13, 14, 15, 16, 18, 19, 20, 24, 25, 26, 27^2, 28^2
26:1, 7, 8, 9, 12, 13^2, 16, 17, 19, 20^2, 21, 26
27:3^2, 4^3, 5, 7, 8, 10^2, 13, 21
28:3, 6^2, 7^2, 11, 12^2, 14, 15, 16, 18, 21, 24^2, 25, 26
29:6, 9, 18^2, 20^2, 24, 27^3
30:4^2, 5^2, 9, 11, 12^2, 13, 14, 15, 16^2, 20, 21, 22, 23^2, 28, 30, 31
31:4^2, 6, 10, 14, 15, 18, 21, 22, 23, 26, 30^2

ECCLESIASTES
1:2, 7, 8, 9^4, 10^2, 11, 14, 15^2, 17, 18
2:1, 2, 15, 16^2, 17^3, 19, 21^3, 23, 24, 26^3

ECCLESIASTES

3:1, 2, 12, 13, 15^{3}, 17, 19, 22^{2}
4:3^{2}, 4^{2}, 6, 8^{6}, 10, 12, 13, 14, 16^{2}
5:2, 3, 5, 8, 9^{2}, 10, 11, 12, 13, 14, 16, 18^{2}, 19
6:1^{2}, 2^{3}, 3, 7^{2}, 9^{2}, 10^{4}, 11, 12
7:1, 2^{2}, 3^{2}, 4^{2}, 5, 6^{2}, 8^{2}, 10, 11^{2}, 12^{3}, 15^{2}, 18, 20, 24, 26
8:1, 4^{2}, 6^{2}, 8^{2}, 9^{2}, 10, 11^{2}, 14^{3}, 16^{2}, 17
9:1, 2^{3}, 3^{4}, 4^{3}, 5, 6^{2}, 9, 10, 11, 16^{2}, 18
10:1, 2, 3^{2}, 5, 6, 10, 11, 13^{2}, 14, 16, 17, 19
11:5^{2}, 7^{2}, 8
12:4, 5, 8, 12^{2}, 13

SONG OF SOLOMON

1:1, 2, 3, 13, 14, 16
2:2, 3, 6, 9, 11^{2}, 12^{2}, 14^{2}, 16
3:6, 7
4:1, 2, 3, 4, 7, 10^{2}, 11, 12
5:2^{3}, 9^{2}, 10, 11, 14, 15, 16^{4}
6:1^{2}, 2, 3, 5, 6, 9^{3}, 10
7:2^{2}, 4^{2}, 5^{2}, 7, 10
8:5, 6^{2}, 12^{2}

ISAIAH

1:5, 6, 7^{2}, 8, 11, 13^{2}, 21, 22
2:7^{4}, 8, 12^{2}, 22^{2}
3:7, 8^{2}, 14
4:3^{2}
5:7, 16, 25^{3}, 30
6:3^{2}, 5, 7, 13
7:2, 8^{2}, 9^{3}, 13, 18^{2}, 20, 22
8:10, 20^{2}
9:5, 6^{2}, 12^{2}, 15^{2}, 17^{3}, 19, 21^{2}
10:4^{2}, 5, 7, 9^{3}, 28^{2}, 29^{2}, 31
12:1, 2^{3}, 4, 5, 6
13:6, 15^{2}, 22
14:6, 7^{2}, 8, 9, 11^{2}, 16, 26^{4}, 27, 29
15:1^{2}, 2, 6^{2}, 8
16:4, 6, 9, 10, 12^{2}, 13
17:1, 14^{2}
18:1, 5^{2}
19:11
20:6
21:2, 9^{2}
22:5, 15, 25
23:1^{3}, 3^{2}, 7^{2}, 10, 14
24:5, 10^{2}, 11^{3}, 12^{2}, 13, 19^{3}
25:4, 7, 9^{2}, 10
26:3, 4, 7, 8, 11, 17, 19
27:1, 4, 7, 9, 11
28:1, 4^{2}, 8, 12^{2}, 14, 20, 27, 28, 29
29:8^{2}, 11^{4}, 12^{2}, 13, 17, 20^{2}
30:7, 9, 14, 18, 21, 27, 29, 33^{3}
31:2, 3, 4, 9
33:5, 6, 9^{2}, 17, 18^{3}, 22^{3}, 23
34:1, 2, 6^{2}, 8
36:4, 6, 7
37:3^{2}, 4, 9, 13, 22, 29, 31
38:3, 8, 12^{2}, 16, 22
39:4^{2}, 6, 8
40:2^{2}, 6^{2}, 7, 10, 16, 20, 22, 26, 27^{2}, 28^{2}
41:7, 17, 24, 26^{4}
42:8, 10, 19^{3}, 21, 22
43:7, 9, 11, 13, 14
44:3, 6, 8^{2}, 10, 12^{2}, 16, 19, 20, 28
45:5^{2}, 6^{2}, 14^{3}, 18, 21^{2}, 22, 23
46:9^{2}
47:1, 4
48:2, 4, 22
49:4, 6, 7, 20
50:1^{3}, 2^{2}, 4, 8^{2}, 9, 10
51:5^{2}, 7, 13, 15, 18^{2}
52:5^{2}, 6
53:1, 2, 3, 7^{2}
54:5^{2}, 9, 17^{3}
55:2^{2}, 6
56:1, 2
57:1, 6, 10, 15^{2}, 19^{2}, 21
58:5^{2}, 6, 7
59:1, 5, 6, 8, 9, 11^{2}, 14^{2}, 21^{2}
60:1^{2}
61:1
62:11
63:1^{2}, 4^{2}, 11^{2}, 15, 16
64:5, 7, 10, 11
65:4, 6, 8^{2}
66:1^{4}, 2, 3

JEREMIAH

1:13
2:6, 8, 14^{3}, 19^{2}, 22, 25, 26^{3}, 34
3:6, 23^{2}
4:7^{3}, 8, 18^{2}, 20^{2}, 22, 31^{2}
5:12, 13, 15^{2}, 16, 19, 27, 30
6:6^{2}, 7^{2}, 10^{2}, 11, 13, 14, 16, 18, 25, 29
7:10, 11^{2}, 14, 28^{3}, 30, 31
8:5, 8^{2}, 9, 10, 11, 16, 18, 19^{2}, 20^{2}, 22^{3}
9:6, 8, 12^{3}, 19, 21^{2}
10:5, 6^{2}, 7, 8, 9^{2}, 10^{2}, 13, 14^{4}, 16^{4}, 19^{3}, 20^{2}, 22, 23^{2}
11:5, 9, 15, 19
12:8, 9, 11
13:4, 10, 17, 20, 25
14:2, 4, 17, 19^{2}
15:9, 10, 14, 18
16:10^{2}, 17, 19, 21
17:1^{2}, 7^{2}, 9, 12, 15
18:6, 12

JEREMIAH

19:2
20:11, 15
21:12
22:14, 28^{3}
23:6, 9, 10^{3}, 15, 19, 28, 29, 33
25:3, 13, 18, 29, 38
26:11, 16
28:6
29:26, 28
30:7^{3}, 12^{2}, 13, 15, 17, 21
31:9, 17, 20^{2}, 35
32:7^{2}, 8^{4}, 14^{2}, 17, 18, 24^{2}, 25, 27, 34, 43^{2}
33:2, 5, 11, 12, 16
34:8, 15
36:7
37:7, 14, 17^{2}
38:5^{2}, 9^{3}, 14, 21
40:3, 4
41:17
43:9, 13
44:22, 23
45:3
46:7, 10, 17, 18^{2}, 20
47:2, 5^{2}
48:1^{3}, 4, 11, 15^{2}, 16, 17, 19, 20^{3}, 21, 25^{2}, 29, 32, 33, 38, 39, 41, 47
49:3, 7^{3}, 10^{2}, 14, 19^{3}, 21, 23^{2}, 24, 25, 29
50:2^{3}, 15, 17, 22, 23^{2}, 25, 27, 31, 34^{2}, 35, 36^{2}, 37^{2}, 38^{2}, 44^{3}, 46^{2}
51:6, 8, 9^{2}, 11^{2}, 13, 16, 17^{4}, 19^{4}, 31, 33^{2}, 41^{3}, 42^{2}, 48, 55, 56^{2}, 57
52:28

LAMENTATIONS

1:1^{2}, 3, 4, 6, 8, 9, 12^{2}, 14, 16, 17^{2}, 18, 20^{2}, 21, 22
2:9, 11, 12, 13, 15, 16
3:3, 18, 20, 22, 23, 24, 25, 26, 27, 30, 37, 47
4:1^{2}, 3, 6, 8^{3}, 15, 18^{2}, 22
5:1, 2, 4, 8, 15^{2}, 16, 17, 18

EZEKIEL

1:28
3:21
4:14
5:5
6:12^{3}
7:2, 3, 5, 6^{3}, 7^{3}, 10^{2}, 11, 12^{2}, 13^{2}, 14, 15^{3}, 19, 23^{2}
8:17
9:6, 9^{2}
10:15, 20
11:3^{2}, 7, 15, 23
12:12, 19, 22, 27
13:12^{3}, 15, 16
15:2^{2}, 4^{3}, 5
16:3, 7, 20, 30, 34^{2}, 44^{2}, 46^{2}
17:12
18:4, 5, 9, 10, 18, 19, 21, 25^{2}, 27, 29
19:2, 10, 13, 14^{2}
20:6, 15, 29^{2}
21:9, 10^{2}, 11^{2}, 13, 14, 15^{2}, 16, 25, 26^{2}, 27, 28^{2}, 29
22:18, 22, 24, 25
23:4, 20^{2}, 22, 28, 37, 45
24:6^{2}, 7, 13, 24, 27
25:8
26:2^{3}, 10, 15
27:27, 32
28:2, 3, 5
29:3, 9
30:3^{2}, 5, 12
31:10, 18
32:16, 20, 22, 23, 24, 25, 26, 29
33:6, 14, 16, 17^{2}, 19, 20, 21, 24, 27, 30
34:5, 12
36:35
37:11, 19
38:8^{3}
39:4, 8^{3}
40:45^{2}, 46^{2}
41:4, 22^{2}
42:13, 15
43:4, 12^{2}, 13
44:3, 9, 22, 26, 31
45:13, 14, 20
46:11, 20
47:16^{2}, 17, 18, 19, 20
48:12, 14, 22, 29, 35

DANIEL

2:5, 8, 9, 10^{2}, 11^{3}, 15, 22, 28, 30, 36, 43, 45, 47^{2}
3:4, 14, 15, 17, 25, 29
4:3^{2}, 8, 9, 17, 18, 22^{2}, 24^{3}, 30, 31^{2}, 34^{2}, 37
5:11^{2}, 14^{2}, 23, 25, 26, 28
6:12, 13, 15, 20, 26
7:14, 27, 28
8:2, 21^{3}, 26
9:11^{2}, 13^{2}, 14, 17, 18
10:4, 14, 17, 21^{2}
11:35, 36
12:12

HOSEA

2:2
4:1, 13, 17, 18
5:1, 3^{2}, 4, 11
6:3, 4, 8^{2}, 10^{2}

HOSEA

7:7, 8, 11
8:3, 5, 6, 8^{2}
9:7^{2}, 8, 13, 15, 16^{2}
10:1, 2, 5, 7, 10, 11^{2}, 12
11:8, 12
12:1, 5, 7, 11
13:3, 4, 8, 9, 10, 12^{2}, 13
14:4, 8, 9

JOEL

1:5, 6, 9, 10^{3}, 11, 12^{2}, 13, 15, 16, 17^{2}
2:1, 3, 4, 11^{3}, 13, 17
3:13^{3}, 14

AMOS

2:11, 13^{2}, 15, 16
3:5
4:3, 13^{2}
5:2^{3}, 8, 11, 13, 18^{2}, 27
6:8, 10^{2}
7:2, 5, 10, 13^{2}
8:2
9:5, 6^{2}, 9, 11

OBADIAH

1, 3, 7, 15, 20

JONAH

1:2, 7, 8^{3}, 12
2:9
3:8
4:3, 8

MICAH

1:2, 5^{3}, 9^{3}, 13
2:1^{2}, 3, 7, 8, 10^{2}, 13
3:1, 7, 11
4:6, 9^{2}
5:2
6:8, 10, 12
7:1^{2}, 2^{2}, 4^{2}, 10^{2}, 18

NAHUM

1:2^{2}, 3, 5, 6, 7, 11, 15
2:1, 3, 8, 9, 10^{2}, 11
3:1, 3^{2}, 7, 17, 18, 19^{2}

HABAKKUK

1:4, 13, 16
2:3, 4^{2}, 5^{2}, 6, 13, 19^{2}, 20
3:19

ZEPHANIAH

1:7, 14^{2}, 15
2:5, 15^{3}
3:1, 5, 6^{2}, 8, 15, 17

HAGGAI

1:2, 4, 6, 9, 10^{2}
2:3^{2}, 6, 8^{2}, 13, 14^{4}, 19

ZECHARIAH

1:7, 11
2:2^{2}, 13
3:2
4:1, 6
5:2, 3, 5, 6^{3}, 7, 8
6:12
7:13
8:23^{2}
9:9, 11, 17^{2}
10:5
11:2^{2}, 3^{3}, 9, 16
12:8, 10
13:7, 9^{4}
14:4, 16

MALACHI

1:6^{2}, 7, 8^{2}, 10, 12^{2}, 13, 14
2:1, 7, 11, 14, 17^{2}
3:2, 14^{2}

MATTHEW

1:16, 20^{2}, 23
2:2^{2}, 5
3:2, 3, 9, 10^{2}, 11, 12, 17
4:4, 6, 7, 10, 13, 16, 17
5:3, 10, 12, 13, 14, 16, 22, 29, 30, 32, 34, 35^{2}, 37, 45, 48^{2}
6:1, 6, 10, 13, 18, 21, 22, 23^{2}, 25, 30^{2}, 34
7:3^{2}, 4, 6, 9, 11, 12, 13^{2}, 14^{2}, 19, 21
8:27
9:5, 15, 16^{2}, 18, 24, 37
10:2, 7, 10, 11, 20, 24, 25, 26, 28, 32, 33, 37^{2}, 38
11:6, 10^{2}, 11^{2}, 14, 16, 19, 30^{2}
12:2, 6, 8, 10, 12^{2}, 18, 23, 25, 26, 28, 30^{2}, 33, 41, 42, 43, 44, 45, 48, 50^{2}
13:11^{2}, 14, 15, 19, 20, 21, 22, 23, 24, 31, 32^{3}, 33, 37, 38, 39^{2}, 44, 45, 47, 52^{3}, 55^{2}, 57
14:2^{2}, 4, 15^{2}, 26, 27
15:5, 8, 17, 22, 26, 28
16:2^{2}, 3, 7, 11, 17, 26
17:4, 5, 12, 15
18:1, 4, 8, 9, 10, 11, 12, 14^{2}, 19, 23
19:3, 9, 10, 11, 12, 14, 17^{2}, 24, 26
20:1^{2}, 4, 7, 14, 15^{2}, 23^{2}
21:9, 10, 11, 13, 20, 21, 38, 42^{3}
22:2, 8, 17, 20, 23, 32, 36, 38, 39, 42, 45
23:8, 9^{2}, 10, 11, 15, 16^{2}, 17, 18^{3}, 19, 26, 38, 39

MATTHEW

24:6, 17, 18, 23, 26^{2}, 28, 32^{2}, 33, 45, 46, 50
25:14, 25
26:2^{2}, 8, 18, 22, 24^{2}, 25, 26, 28^{2}, 31, 38, 41^{2}, 45^{2}, 46, 48, 62, 66, 68
27:4, 6^{2}, 17, 22, 33, 37, 46, 64
28:6^{2}, 7, 15, 18

MARK

1:2, 15^{2}, 27^{2}
2:9, 16, 19, 21, 22, 24, 26, 28
3:4, 17, 21, 29, 33, 35
4:11, 15, 21, 22, 26, 29^{2}, 31^{3}, 32, 40, 41
5:9^{2}, 35, 39, 41
6:2^{2}, 3, 4, 15^{2}, 16^{2}, 18, 35^{2}, 50
7:2, 6^{2}, 11^{2}, 15, 27, 29, 34
8:16, 21
9:5, 7, 12, 13^{2}, 21, 26, 31^{2}, 39, 40^{2}, 42, 43, 44, 45, 46, 47, 48, 50
10:2, 14, 18^{2}, 24, 25, 27, 29, 40^{2}
11:9, 17, 21, 25, 26
12:7, 10, 11, 14, 16, 18, 27, 28, 29^{2}, 30, 31^{2}, 32^{2}, 33, 35, 37
13:11, 15, 16, 21^{2}, 28^{2}, 29, 33, 34
14:8, 14, 19^{2}, 20, 21^{2}, 22, 24^{2}, 27, 34, 38^{2}, 41^{3}, 42, 44, 58, 60, 69
15:22, 34, 42
16:6^{2}, 16

LUKE

1:13, 28, 36, 42, 43, 45, 49^{2}, 50, 61^{2}, 63
2:4, 11^{2}, 15, 23, 24, 34, 49
3:4, 8, 9^{2}, 13, 17
4:4, 6, 8, 10, 12, 18, 21, 22, 24, 36
5:21, 23, 34, 39
6:2, 4, 5, 9, 20, 23, 35, 36, 40^{2}, 41^{2}, 42^{3}, 44, 45^{2}, 47, 48, 49
7:16, 22, 23, 27^{2}, 28^{3}, 34, 35, 39^{2}, 47, 49
8:10, 11^{2}, 17, 25^{2}, 26, 30, 46, 49, 52
9:9, 19, 25, 33, 35, 38, 48, 50^{2}, 56, 62
10:2, 7, 9, 11, 22^{2}, 26, 29, 42
11:4, 6, 7, 8, 11, 17, 20, 23^{2}, 24, 26, 27, 29, 31, 32, 34^{5}, 35, 39, 40^{2}
12:1, 2, 6, 21^{2}, 23^{2}, 26, 28^{2}, 32, 34, 42, 43, 46, 48, 54, 56, 57
13:18, 19, 21, 25, 35^{2}
14:3, 15, 22^{2}, 29, 32, 34, 35
15:4, 10, 24^{2}, 27, 31, 32^{2}
16:2, 10^{5}, 12^{2}, 15^{2}, 16, 17, 18, 25, 26
17:1, 7, 21, 30, 31, 37
18:16, 19^{2}, 25, 29
19:7, 9^{2}, 10, 20, 46^{2}
20:2, 14, 17^{3}, 22, 27, 33, 38, 41, 44
21:9, 20, 30, 31, 37
22:1, 11, 19^{2}, 20^{2}, 21, 22, 26^{2}, 27^{2}, 37, 38, 53, 59, 64
23:2, 15, 33, 38
24:6^{2}, 21, 29^{2}, 34, 39, 46

JOHN

1:15, 18, 19, 27^{2}, 30^{2}, 33, 34, 38, 41, 42, 47
2:4, 10
3:4, 6^{4}, 8^{2}, 13, 18^{2}, 19^{2}, 29^{2}, 31^{4}, 33
4:5, 9, 10, 11, 18, 20, 22, 23, 24, 25^{2}, 29, 34, 37, 42, 54
5:2^{2}, 7, 10^{2}, 12, 24, 25^{2}, 27, 28, 30, 31, 32^{2}, 45
6:1, 7, 9, 14, 20, 29, 31, 33, 39, 40, 42^{2}, 45, 46, 50, 51, 55^{2}, 58, 60, 63, 70
7:4, 6^{2}, 8, 11, 12, 16, 18^{2}, 22, 25, 26, 27^{2}, 28, 36, 40, 41
8:7, 13, 14, 16, 17^{2}, 19, 26, 29, 34, 39, 44^{2}, 47, 50, 52, 53, 54^{3}
9:4, 7, 8, 9^{2}, 11, 12, 16^{2}, 17, 19, 20, 21, 23, 24, 29, 30^{2}, 36, 37
10:1, 2, 12, 13, 20, 29^{2}, 34, 38
11:3, 4, 10, 14, 16, 28, 50
12:13, 14, 19, 23, 27, 31, 34, 35, 50
13:10^{2}, 16^{2}, 19, 25, 26, 31^{2}
14:21, 22, 24, 26, 28, 29
15:1, 6^{2}, 8, 12, 20, 25, 26
16:7, 8, 11, 13, 17, 18, 21^{4}, 32^{2}
17:1, 3, 12, 17
18:31, 36^{2}, 37, 38
19:13, 17, 30, 35, 40
20:16, 31
21:7, 14, 20, 22, 23, 24^{2}

THE ACTS

1:7, 8, 11, 12, 19^{2}, 20
2:15, 16, 25, 29^{2}, 34, 39
3:2, 11, 16
4:9, 11^{2}, 12^{2}, 16, 24, 36
5:9, 17, 32
6:2, 9
7:33, 34, 37, 38, 40, 42, 49^{3}
8:10, 21, 26, 33, 36, 37
9:5, 11, 15, 20, 21, 22, 36
10:4, 5, 6, 14, 21, 28^{2}, 31, 32^{2}, 34, 35, 36, 42

THE ACTS

11:13
12:15, 22
13:8, 9, 11, 26, 33, 38, 40
15:15, 16, 17, 19
16:12
17:3, 7, 19, 24, 25, 29
19:4, 27, 28, 34, 35^{2}, 38
20:10, 32, 35
21:22, 28
22:22, 25^{2}, 26
23:5, 8, 19
25:14, 16^{2}
26:14, 18
27:8, 12, 16, 33, 34
28:4, 22, 27, 28

ROMANS

1:8, 9, 12, 15, 16, 17^{2}, 18, 19, 25, 26, 27
2:2, 11, 24^{2}, 25, 27, 28^{4}, 29^{4}
3:1, 4, 5, 8, 10^{2}, 11^{2}, 12, 13^{2}, 14, 18, 20, 21, 22^{2}, 24, 27^{2}, 28, 29^{2}, 30
4:4, 5, 8, 14, 15^{2}, 16^{4}, 17
5:5^{2}, 13^{2}, 14, 15^{2}, 16^{2}
6:6, 7^{2}, 21, 23^{2}
7:2^{2}, 3^{2}, 4, 7, 12, 13^{2}, 14, 16, 17, 18^{3}, 20, 21, 23
8:1, 6^{2}, 7^{2}, 9, 10^{2}, 24^{2}, 27, 33, 34^{4}, 36, 39
9:5, 8, 9, 13, 14, 16, 30, 33
10:1, 4, 5, 6^{2}, 7, 8^{2}, 10, 12^{2}, 15, 20
11:5, 6^{4}, 8, 11, 16, 23, 24, 25, 26, 27
12:1, 2, 3, 6, 9^{2}, 19^{2}
13:1, 3, 4^{3}, 7, 9, 10, 11^{2}, 12^{2}
14:1, 2, 4, 11, 14^{2}, 17, 18, 20, 21^{3}, 22, 23^{3}
15:3, 9, 15, 21, 27
16:1^{2}, 5^{2}, 19^{2}, 25, 26

1 CORINTHIANS

1:2, 4, 9, 13, 18^{2}, 19, 20^{3}, 25^{2}, 30, 31
2:9, 11, 12, 15^{2}
3:3, 5^{2}, 7, 10, 11^{2}, 13, 17, 19^{2}, 23
4:2, 3, 4, 6, 17, 20
5:1^{3}, 6, 7, 11
6:5^{2}, 7, 13, 16^{2}, 17^{2}, 18, 19^{2}
7:1, 8, 9, 14^{2}, 15, 18^{2}, 19^{2}, 22^{4}, 24, 26^{2}, 29, 32, 33, 34^{2}, 35, 39^{2}, 40
8:3, 4^{2}, 6, 7^{2}, 10
9:3, 9, 10, 11, 16^{2}, 17, 18, 25
10:7, 13^{2}, 16^{2}, 19^{3}, 25, 26, 27, 28^{2}, 29
11:3^{3}, 5, 7^{2}, 8, 11, 12^{2}, 13, 14, 15^{2}, 20, 21^{2}, 24^{2}, 25
12:3, 6, 7, 8, 12^{2}, 14, 15, 16
13:4^{2}, 5, 10^{3}, 13
14:5, 7, 9, 10, 14, 15, 17, 21, 24^{2}, 25, 26, 33, 34, 35
15:12, 13, 14^{2}, 16, 17, 20, 26, 27^{2}, 36, 39^{2}, 40^{2}, 41, 42^{3}, 43^{4}, 44^{4}, 45, 46^{3}, 47^{2}, 48^{2}, 54^{2}, 55^{2}, 56^{2}, 58
16:9, 15, 19

2 CORINTHIANS

1:1, 6^{3}, 7, 12, 18, 21
2:2^{2}, 3, 6, 16
3:5, 11^{2}, 13, 14, 15^{2}, 17^{3}
4:3, 4, 13, 16, 17
5:2, 5, 13^{2}, 17
6:2^{2}, 11^{2}
7:1^{2}, 14, 15
8:10, 12, 15, 18, 19, 20, 23
9:1, 8, 9, 12
10:6, 7^{2}, 10, 15^{2}, 18
11:3, 10, 14, 15, 21, 29^{2}, 31
12:1, 4, 9^{2}, 13
13:1, 3^{2}, 5, 7

GALATIANS

1:7, 11
2:16, 17, 21
3:10^{2}, 11^{2}, 12, 13^{2}, 16, 18, 20^{2}, 21, 25, 28^{3}
4:1, 2, 15, 18, 22, 24, 25^{3}, 26^{3}, 27, 29
5:3^{2}, 4, 11, 14, 22, 23
6:3, 6, 7, 14

EPHESIANS

1:14, 18, 19, 21^{2}, 23
2:4, 8, 11, 14
3:2, 5, 8, 9, 13, 15, 18, 20
4:4, 6, 7, 9, 10, 15, 18, 21, 22, 24, 28, 29
5:5, 9, 10, 12, 13, 17, 18, 23^{3}, 24, 32
6:1, 2, 9^{2}, 17

PHILIPPIANS

1:7, 8, 18, 21^{2}, 22, 23, 24, 28, 29
2:9, 11, 13
3:1^{2}, 6, 9^{3}, 19^{3}, 20, 21
4:5

COLOSSIANS

1:5, 6^{2}, 7, 15, 17, 18^{2}, 23, 24^{2}, 25, 26, 27^{2}
2:10, 17
3:3, 4, 5, 10, 11^{2}, 14, 18, 20, 25
4:1, 7, 9, 11, 12, 15, 16

1 THESSALONIANS

1:1, 8
2:5, 13, 16, 19
3:10
4:3, 6
5:15, 18, 21, 24

2 THESSALONIANS

1:3, 5, 6
2:2, 4^{3}, 9
3:1, 3, 17

1 TIMOTHY

1:1, 4, 5, 8, 9, 10, 14, 15, 20
2:3, 5
3:1, 13, 15, 16
4:4, 5, 8^{3}, 9, 10, 14
5:4, 5, 6, 8, 18
6:3, 4, 5, 6, 7, 10, 15, 20
S

2 TIMOTHY

1:1, 5, 6, 10, 12, 13
2:1, 5, 9, 10, 11, 17, 18
3:15, 16^{2}
4:6, 8, 10, 11^{2}

TITUS

1:1, 3, 13, 15^{2}
2:8
3:8, 10, 11^{2}

PHILEMON

6, 8, 12

HEBREWS

1:8^{2}
2:6, 8, 11, 14, 18
3:4^{2}, 13, 15
4:7, 10, 12^{2}, 13^{2}, 14
5:1, 2, 4, 13^{2}
6:4, 7, 8^{3}, 10, 16, 20
7:2, 5, 6, 7, 8, 12, 14, 15, 16, 18, 25, 26, 28
8:1^{2}, 3^{2}, 6, 10, 13
9:2, 3, 11, 15, 16, 17^{2}, 20, 22, 24, 27
10:3, 4, 7, 15, 16, 18^{2}, 20, 23, 25, 31
11:1, 6^{3}, 7, 10, 12, 16^{2}, 27
12:1, 2, 7, 13, 29
13:4, 6, 9, 11, 15, 16, 17, 21, 23

JAMES

1:6, 8, 9, 10, 11, 12^{2}, 13, 14^{2}, 15, 17^{2}, 21, 23, 26, 27
2:10, 17, 19, 20, 24, 26^{2}
3:2, 5, 6^{3}, 7, 8, 13, 15, 16^{2}, 17^{2}, 18
4:4^{2}, 12^{2}, 14^{2}, 16, 17
5:3, 4, 11, 13^{2}, 14

1 PETER

1:13, 15, 16, 24, 25^{2}
2:3, 6, 7^{2}, 15, 19, 20^{2}
3:4^{2}, 10, 12, 13^{2}, 15, 17, 20, 22^{2}
4:5, 7, 12, 14^{2}, 17
5:2, 12, 13

2 PETER

1:4, 9, 17, 20
2:17, 19^{2}, 20, 22^{2}
3:4, 8, 9^{2}, 15

1 JOHN

1:3, 5^{3}, 7, 8, 9, 10
2:2, 4^{2}, 5, 7, 8^{2}, 9^{2}, 10, 11, 13, 14, 15, 16^{3}, 18^{2}, 21, 22^{3}, 25, 27^{2}, 29^{2}
3:2, 3, 4, 5, 7^{4}, 8, 9^{4}, 10, 11, 16, 20, 23
4:2^{2}, 3^{4}, 4^{3}, 6, 7^{2}, 8, 10, 12, 15, 16, 17^{2}, 18^{2}, 20
5:1^{3}, 3, 4^{2}, 5^{2}, 6^{3}, 9^{2}, 11^{2}, 14, 16^{2}, 17^{2}, 18^{2}, 20^{4}

2 JOHN

6^{2}, 7^{2}, 11

3 JOHN

3, 11^{3}, 12

JUDE

13, 24

REVELATION

1:3^{2}, 4^{2}, 5, 8^{2}, 9
2:7, 8, 13
3:7^{2}, 12
4:8^{2}
5:2, 12, 13
6:13, 14, 17
7:17
8:11
9:11^{2}, 12, 13, 19
10:8
11:2^{2}, 8, 14, 18
12:10^{2}, 12, 14
13:4^{2}, 10, 18^{3}
14:7, 8^{2}, 10, 12, 15^{2}, 17
15:1
16:15, 17
17:8^{3}, 9, 10^{2}, 11^{3}, 14, 18
18:2^{3}, 8, 10, 17, 18, 19
19:7, 8, 10, 13
20:2, 5, 6, 8, 12, 14
21:3, 6^{2}, 8, 16, 17, 23
22:7, 10, 11^{4}, 12, 17

IT

GENESIS

1:4, 6, 7, 9, 10, 11, 12, 15, 18, 21, 24, 25, 28, 29, 30, 31
2:3[2], 5[3], 10, 11, 13, 14, 15[2], 17, 18
3:3[2], 6, 15, 17[2], 18, 19
4:3, 8, 12, 14
6:1, 6[2], 7, 12, 14, 15[3], 16[2], 21[2]
7:4, 10, 17
8:6, 13
9:5, 13, 14, 16, 23
10:9
11:2, 9
12:11, 12, 13, 14
13:10, 15, 17[3]
14:1
15:6, 7, 8, 17[2]
16:2, 6, 10, 14
17:11
18:6, 7[2], 8, 10, 11, 21, 28, 29, 30, 31, 32
19:13, 17, 20[2], 29, 34
20:13, 15
21:12, 14[2], 16, 22, 26
22:1, 6, 14[2], 20[2]
23:8, 9[2], 11[2], 13[2]
24:14, 15, 22, 30, 43, 52, 65
25:11, 22
26:8, 21, 22, 32, 33
27:1, 4, 5, 10, 20[3], 25[2], 30, 31, 33, 40
28:12[2], 13[2], 16, 18[2]
29:2, 7[2], 10, 13, 19, 23, 25[2], 26
30:15, 25, 28, 30[2], 33, 34, 35, 41
31:2, 5, 10, 22, 29, 32, 35, 37, 39[2], 44, 45, 47[2], 48
32:8, 18, 29
33:11, 15, 20
34:7, 21, 25
35:8, 12, 17, 18, 22[2]
37:5, 9, 10, 14, 21, 23, 24, 25, 26, 32[2], 33[2]
38:1, 9[2], 13, 17, 18, 23, 24[2], 27, 28, 29
39:5, 7, 10, 11, 13, 15, 18, 19, 22, 23
40:1, 8, 10[2], 12, 14, 20
41:1, 7, 8, 13[2], 15[2], 16, 21, 24, 31, 32[2], 42, 49
42:6, 14, 27, 28, 35
43:2, 11, 12[2], 21[2]
44:5, 9, 10[2], 24, 31
45:8, 12, 16, 28
46:33
47:18, 24, 26
48:1, 14, 17[2], 19[2]
49:4, 7[2], 15, 28
50:9, 11, 20[2]

EXODUS

1:10, 16[2], 21
2:3[2], 5, 6, 9[2], 11, 18, 20, 23
3:21
4:3[4], 4[3], 6, 7[2], 8, 9[2], 24, 25
5:11, 19, 22
6:8[2], 28
7:9[2], 10
8:10, 16, 17, 26
9:8, 9, 10[2], 18, 24[2], 28
10:10, 13
11:6[2]
12:2, 4, 5, 6[2], 7[2], 8, 9, 10[2], 11[3], 14[2], 22, 25, 26, 27, 29, 34, 39, 41[2], 42, 46, 47, 48, 51
13:2, 5, 9, 11[2], 13, 14, 15, 16, 17
14:2, 5, 12, 16, 20[3], 24, 27
15:23
16:5[2], 10, 13, 15[3], 16, 18, 19, 20[2], 21[2], 22, 24[2], 25, 26[2], 27, 31[2], 32, 33, 34
17:6, 11, 12, 14, 15
18:13, 18, 22[2]
19:12, 13[3], 16, 18, 23
20:8, 10, 11, 18, 25[3]
21:26, 29, 31, 33, 34, 35, 36
22:1[2], 4, 7, 9, 10[2], 11[2], 12, 13[2], 14[3], 15[4], 26, 27[2], 30[2], 31
23:4, 11, 13, 15, 33
24:6, 8, 10[2], 16
25:2, 9, 11[3], 12[3], 15, 24, 25, 26, 32, 36, 37, 39
26:6, 11, 13[2], 24[2], 31, 32
27:2[2], 4, 5, 7, 8[3], 21[2]
28:7[2], 8, 15[2], 16, 17, 25, 28, 32[5], 33, 35, 36, 37[3], 38[2], 43
29:7, 12, 14, 16, 18[2], 20, 21, 22, 25, 26[2], 28[3], 34[2], 36[3], 37[2]
30:1, 2, 3[2], 4[5], 6, 7, 8, 10[3], 16[2], 18, 21, 25[2], 32[5], 33[2], 35, 36[3], 37
31:13, 14[2], 17
32:4[2], 5[2], 8, 9, 13, 18[2], 19, 20[4], 24[3], 30
33:1, 7[3], 8, 9, 16[2], 22
34:9, 10, 12, 29
35:5, 24
36:2, 3, 6, 7, 13, 18, 35, 38
37:1[3], 2[2], 3[4], 11, 13, 21, 22, 24, 25[4], 26[4], 27[3]
38:1, 2[2], 4, 7, 8, 21, 30
39:3[2], 4[3], 5, 9, 10, 18, 19, 20, 21, 23, 30, 31[2], 43[2]
40:4, 9[2], 10, 11, 17, 19, 23, 29, 37, 38

LEVITICUS

1:3, 4, 6, 10, 11, 12, 13[3], 15[2], 16, 17[4]
2:1, 2[2], 3, 4, 5, 6[2], 7, 8[2], 9[2], 10, 15[2], 16[2]
3:1[3], 2, 4, 5[2], 6, 7, 8, 9, 10, 11[2], 12, 13[2], 15, 16, 17
4:5, 8, 9, 10, 14, 17, 19, 20, 21, 24[2], 25, 26, 30, 31[2], 32, 33, 34, 35
5:1[2], 2[2], 3[3], 4[3], 5, 8, 9, 10, 11[2], 12[4], 13, 16[2], 17, 18[2], 19
6:3, 4, 5[3], 7, 9[2], 12[4], 13, 14, 15[3], 16[2], 17[3], 18[2], 20, 21[3], 22[3], 23, 25, 26[3], 27, 28[3], 29, 30
7:1, 3, 4, 5, 6[2], 7, 9, 12, 14[2], 15[2], 16[2], 18[5], 19, 24, 25, 26, 27, 30
8:7, 15[4], 16, 19, 21, 23[3], 28, 29[2], 30, 31[2]
9:1, 9, 15[2], 16, 17
10:3, 9, 12[2], 13[2], 15[2], 16, 17[2], 18[2], 19
11:32[6], 33[2], 35, 37, 38, 40[2], 41
12:7
13:2, 3, 6, 8, 10, 11, 13, 15, 19, 20[3], 21[2], 22[2], 23, 25[4], 26[2], 27[2], 28[3], 30[3], 31[2], 32, 39, 42, 43, 47, 48, 49, 50, 51, 52[2], 54, 55[5], 56[2], 57[2], 58[2], 59[2]
14:6, 9, 13, 14, 15, 25, 35[2], 36, 43, 44[2], 45, 46, 48, 53, 57[2]
15:3, 23[2], 25
16:12, 14, 15, 18[2], 19[3], 29, 31
17:3, 4, 9[2], 11[2], 13, 14[3], 15
18:8, 16, 17, 22, 23, 25, 28[2]
19:5, 6[3], 7[3], 8, 23[2], 25
20:14, 17, 21, 24[2]
21:24
22:7, 9[2], 11, 14[2], 20, 21, 23, 27[2], 28[2], 29, 30[2]
23:3, 11, 14, 21[2], 27, 28, 29, 30, 31, 32, 36, 41[3]
24:3[2], 7, 8, 9[3], 18, 19, 20, 21
25:5, 10, 11[2], 12[2], 16, 21, 25, 26[2], 27, 28[3], 29[3], 30[3], 34, 50
26:1, 16, 32, 34, 35[4], 37
27:4, 5, 6, 7[2], 9, 10[3], 11, 12[4], 13, 14[4], 15[3], 17, 18, 19[3], 20, 21, 24, 26[3], 27[5], 30, 33[5]

NUMBERS

1:50[2], 51[2]
3:26
4:5, 6, 9, 10[2], 11, 14[4], 15, 25
5:7[2], 10, 13, 15[2], 17, 25, 26, 27
6:9, 18
7:1[3], 5, 10, 84, 88
8:24
9:3[3], 11[2], 12[3], 15, 16[2], 20, 21[2], 22[2]
10:11, 29, 32[2], 35, 36
11:1[2], 8[6], 9, 14, 17[2], 18, 20[2], 25[2], 31[3], 33
12:2
13:18, 19, 20, 23, 27[2], 30[2], 32[2]
14:3, 7, 8, 11, 13, 14, 23, 24, 35, 41
15:11, 19, 20, 24, 25[2], 26, 28, 34, 39[2]
16:4, 7, 9, 13, 31, 42[2]
17:5, 8
18:10[3], 11, 13, 15, 19, 23, 26, 27, 29, 30[2], 31[2], 32[3]
19:6, 9[2], 10, 12, 15, 18[2], 21, 22
20:5, 8, 19
21:8[3], 9[2], 14, 17, 18, 28
22:34, 41
23:19[2], 20, 22, 23, 27
24:1, 8
25:7, 13
26:1
27:11[2], 13
28:6, 8, 24
29:1, 11
30:7[2], 8, 11, 13[2]
31:23[3], 29[2], 54
32:39[2], 42
33:53, 55, 56
34:5, 9, 12
35:23, 25, 33[2]
36:3

DEUTERONOMY

1:3, 17[2], 21, 24, 25[2], 36, 38, 39[2]
2:16, 19, 24
3:9, 11[2], 18, 26, 27
4:2, 5, 14, 26[2], 32, 35, 38, 39, 40
5:12, 14, 16, 23, 27[2], 29, 31, 33
6:1, 3[2], 10, 18, 24, 25
7:1, 12, 25[2], 26[4]
8:9, 18[2], 19
9:6, 11, 13, 21[4]
10:15
11:8, 10[2], 11, 12, 13, 29[2], 31
12:1, 16, 24[2], 25[2], 28, 32[2]
13:14, 15, 16[3]
14:8[2], 10, 21[3], 24, 25, 28
15:2[3], 3, 4, 9, 16, 17, 18, 20, 21[2], 22[2], 23
16:3, 7
17:4[3], 14, 18, 19
18:3, 19[2], 22
19:2, 13, 14
20:2, 5[2], 6[2], 9, 10[2], 11[3], 12[2], 13, 19[2], 20
21:1[2], 3, 7, 14, 16
22:2[4], 7
23:11, 13, 16, 20, 21[3], 22
24:1[2], 3, 13, 15[3], 19[2], 20, 21[2]
25:2, 6, 8, 9, 19[3]

DEUTERONOMY

26:1[2], 2, 4, 10, 12
27:2, 4, 15
28:1, 15, 21, 24, 38, 63[2], 67[2], 68
29:8, 19, 22, 23, 27, 28
30:1, 5, 11[2], 12[4], 13[4], 14, 16, 18
31:6, 7, 8, 9, 13, 19[2], 21[2], 22, 24, 26[2]
32:19, 27, 47[3]
34:4[2]

JOSHUA

1:1, 7, 11, 15
2:2, 5[2], 14, 19, 21
3:2, 3[2], 4[2], 13, 14
4:1, 7, 11, 18, 24
5:1, 8, 13
6:5, 8, 11, 15, 16, 17, 18, 20, 26
7:9, 11, 14, 15, 19, 21, 22[2]
8:2, 5, 7, 8, 14[2], 18, 19, 24[2], 25, 28, 29, 31
9:1, 12[2], 16, 24, 25
10:1[2], 2, 4, 5, 11, 14[2], 17, 18, 20, 24, 27, 28, 30[3], 31[2], 32[2], 34[2], 35[2], 36, 37[3], 38, 39
11:1, 20, 23
12:6
13:6
14:7
15:3, 4, 16, 17, 18
16:6, 7
17:9, 10[2], 13, 18[3]
18:4, 5, 8, 9, 20
19:14, 47[3]
21:11, 43
22:12, 18, 22, 23, 24, 27, 28[2], 30, 34
23:1, 10, 15
24:4, 15, 17, 26, 27[2], 29, 32

JUDGES

1:1, 8[2], 12, 13, 14, 17, 28
2:4, 18, 19, 22
3:16, 21, 27
4:20, 21
6:3, 5, 7, 11, 18, 19[2], 24[2], 25[2], 27[3], 28, 30, 31, 37, 38, 39, 40
7:4, 9[2], 13[3], 15, 17
8:27[2], 33
9:7, 25, 33, 42, 45, 47, 48[2], 50, 51, 52[2]
11:4, 5, 23, 31[2], 35, 39[2]
12:5, 6
13:16, 18, 19, 20[2]
14:4, 11, 12[2], 13[2], 15[2], 16[3], 17
15:1, 15, 17
16:2[2], 4, 9, 14, 16, 25, 29
17:2, 3
18:2, 9, 10, 12, 19, 28[2]
19:1, 5, 11, 26, 30[3]
20:9, 28
21:4, 22

RUTH

1:1, 13, 19
2:6, 11, 17, 18, 22
3:1, 4, 8, 12, 13, 14, 15[3]
4:4[6], 5, 6[2], 7, 8, 16[2], 17

1 SAMUEL

1:12, 20
2:14, 16[2], 19, 24, 30, 36
3:2, 9, 11, 17, 18
4:3[2], 13, 18, 20
5:1, 2[2], 7, 9[2], 10, 11[2]
6:2, 3[2], 8[3], 9[3], 13, 15, 16, 21
7:1, 2[2], 6, 7, 9, 12[2]
8:1
9:20, 23, 24[4], 26
10:1[2], 5, 7, 9, 11, 12, 25[2]
11:2, 7, 9, 11[2]
12:3, 6, 15, 17, 22
13:3, 10, 22
14:1, 6, 14, 15, 19, 27, 39
15:11[2], 12, 27, 28
16:2, 6, 16, 23
17:25, 27, 35, 39, 48, 49, 51, 54
18:1, 4, 6, 10, 11, 19, 23, 26, 30
19:5, 13[2], 19, 21
20:2[2], 4, 7, 9[2], 12, 13[2], 16, 27, 33, 35
21:5, 6, 9[3]
22:1, 15, 17, 22
23:6, 7, 13, 22, 23
24:1[2], 4, 5, 11, 16
25:11, 20, 27, 30, 37, 38
26:12[2], 17, 22
27:4
28:1, 14, 17, 24[2], 25
29:4
30:1[2], 3, 25[2]
31:4, 8, 9

2 SAMUEL

1:1, 2[2], 18, 20[2]
2:1, 23, 26[2]
3:6, 18, 24, 26, 28, 29, 35, 36[2], 37
4:4, 12
5:9, 17, 24
6:3, 4, 6[2], 10, 12, 13, 17[2], 21
7:1, 4, 15, 25, 29[3]
8:1
10:1, 3[2], 5, 7, 17
11:1, 2, 14[2], 16, 25

2 SAMUEL

12:3[2], 4, 12, 15, 18, 21, 28[2], 29[2], 30
13:1, 2, 5[2], 8, 23, 30, 35, 36
14:15[2], 26[3], 30, 32
15:1, 2, 5, 7, 25, 32, 35[2]
16:11, 12, 16
17:9[2], 13, 21, 27
18:3, 10, 18, 29
19:1, 6, 19, 25, 36
20:8[2], 15[2], 20[2], 22
21:1, 10, 11, 18
22:9, 48
23:5, 12, 16[3], 17[2]
24:3, 12, 16[2], 24

1 KINGS

1:11, 18, 21, 27, 41, 48, 51
2:3, 15, 29, 37, 39, 41
3:6, 15, 18, 19, 20, 21[3], 26[3], 27
5:7
6:1, 7[3], 9, 14, 16, 17, 20, 21, 26, 38[2]
7:3, 7, 23[2], 24[3], 25, 26[2], 27, 31[2]
8:10, 15, 17, 18[2], 24[2], 54
9:1, 8, 10, 16[2], 28
10:6, 7, 18, 21
11:4, 11, 12[2], 15, 29, 30, 35, 38
12:2[2], 10, 20, 28
13:3, 4[2], 6, 9, 17, 20, 23, 24, 25, 26, 29[2], 31, 34[2]
14:5, 6, 8, 10, 11, 25, 28
15:13, 21, 29
16:11, 18, 31[2]
17:4, 7, 11, 12[2], 13, 17
18:1, 4, 6, 12, 13, 17, 23[3], 24, 25, 26, 27, 29, 33, 34[4], 36[2], 39, 44, 45
19:4, 10, 13[2], 14, 17
20:1, 6[3], 11, 12, 13, 26, 29, 33, 40
21:1, 2[6], 3, 6[2], 11, 15, 16[2], 18, 27
22:2, 3, 6, 12, 15, 32[2], 33[2], 43

2 KINGS

1:3, 6, 8, 16
2:1, 3, 5, 8, 9, 10[2], 11, 12, 20
3:5, 14, 15, 20, 25[3]
4:6, 8[2], 10, 11, 18, 23[2], 25, 26[4], 27, 40, 41, 44
5:7, 8, 13, 16, 26
6:5, 6[2], 7[2], 13, 20, 24, 25, 30
7:2, 7, 8[2], 11, 13, 18, 19, 20
8:1, 3, 5, 7, 15[3]
9:3, 12, 13, 15[2], 17, 18, 19, 22[2], 30
10:7, 9, 15[2], 19, 20, 25, 27
11:6, 18
12:5, 6, 7, 9[2], 10, 11, 12, 16, 17, 18
13:16, 17, 19, 21
14:5, 7, 22, 26
15:12, 16
16:8, 9[2], 10, 11, 14, 15, 17[2]
17:5, 7, 25
18:1, 4[2], 9[2], 10, 16, 21[2], 25[2], 26
19:1[2], 4, 14[2], 25[3], 26, 32[2], 34, 35, 37
20:4, 7, 10, 11, 19
21:12, 13[2]
22:3, 5[2], 8, 9, 10, 11
23:6[2], 15, 16, 17, 21, 35
24:2, 11, 20
25:1[3], 17, 24, 25, 27

1 CHRONICLES

4:10
6:10, 55
7:23
9:32
10:4, 8, 13
11:7, 14, 18[4], 19[3]
12:15, 17, 22
13:2[2], 3, 6, 13
14:8, 15
15:1, 3, 12, 13, 26, 29
16:1[2], 19, 30
17:1, 3, 11, 13, 24, 27[3]
18:1
19:1, 8, 17
20:1[2], 2[3], 3, 4
21:2, 10, 15[2], 17[2], 22, 23[2], 24, 30
22:5, 7, 14
23:26
26:28
27:24
28:8, 10, 20
29:12

2 CHRONICLES

1:4[2], 5, 6
2:4, 16[2]
3:4[2], 8
4:2, 3[3], 4, 5[3], 15
5:9, 11, 13
6:7, 8[2], 11, 13[2], 15[2]
7:20, 21, 22
8:1, 3, 16
9:5, 6, 17, 20
10:2[2], 10
12:1, 2
13:15
14:11
15:16[2]
16:5[2]
18:5, 11, 31[2], 32[2]

2 CHRONICLES

19:7
20:1, 7, 25, 32
21:17, 19
22:8
23:17, 18[2]
24:4, 5, 8, 11[3], 12, 13, 14, 22[2], 23
25:3, 4, 8, 14, 16, 20
26:2, 18[2]
28:21
29:10, 16[3], 22
30:3, 5[2], 18
31:3, 21
32:5, 12, 30
33:14
34:4, 10[2], 11, 12, 16, 17, 18, 19, 32
35:3, 12
36:22

EZRA

1:1
2:68
3:2, 4
4:12, 13, 14, 19, 24
5:8, 16[2], 17[2]
6:9, 12, 14, 18
7:10, 20, 21, 23, 24, 26
9:7, 11[2], 12, 15
10:3, 4, 9, 13

NEHEMIAH

1:1, 4
2:1[2], 5[2], 6, 7, 10[2], 16, 19
3:1[3], 13, 14, 15[2]
4:1, 7, 8, 12, 15[2], 16
5:5, 9
6:1, 3, 6[2], 7, 9, 16
7:1, 64
8:5, 15
9:8, 10, 23, 36, 37, 38[2]
10:31, 34[2], 36
11:23
13:3, 8, 19

ESTHER

1:1, 17, 19[3], 20, 22
2:8, 10, 22, 23[2]
3:4, 8, 9[3], 10, 11, 12
4:4[2], 5[2], 8[2]
5:1, 2, 3, 4, 6[2], 8
6:2, 9, 11
7:2[2], 3
8:2, 5[2], 8[2], 9, 10
9:1, 12[2], 13[2], 14, 17, 18, 27, 32

JOB

1:5[2], 7, 19
2:2
3:3, 4[2], 5[3], 6[3], 8, 9[2], 10, 21[2]
4:5[2], 16, 20
5:5, 21, 27[4]
6:3, 9, 17, 28, 29[2]
7:16
8:12[2], 15[3], 18
9:2, 7, 20, 22, 35
10:3, 16
11:8, 11, 14, 16
12:8, 14
13:1, 5, 9
14:7[2], 9, 21[2]
15:18, 23, 32
17:15
18:2, 13, 14, 15[2]
19:4
20:12, 13[3], 14, 18, 23, 25, 26
21:4, 19
22:3[2], 8, 19, 28, 30
24:23, 25
25:5
26:3, 9
27:6, 12, 14, 17[2]
28:1, 5[3], 6[2], 8[2], 13, 14[2], 15, 16, 17[2], 19[2], 21, 27[4]
29:11[2], 14, 24
30:18, 22
31:11, 12, 26, 36[2]
32:19
33:14, 21, 27
34:9, 10, 18, 29, 31, 33[2]
35:3, 13, 15[2]
36:25[2], 30, 32, 33
37:3, 4, 12, 13, 20
38:5, 8[2], 9, 10, 13[2], 14, 18, 20, 21, 26, 29
39:12, 24
40:2, 24
42:7

PSALMS

6:7
7:2, 5, 12, 15
10:11, 13, 14[2]
17:12
18:8, 32, 47
19:6
21:4
22:14, 30
24:2[2]
25:11
30:9
33:9[2]
34:14
35:9, 15, 21, 25
37:5, 10, 34
38:10
39:4, 9

PSALMS

40:3, 7, 14
41:6
48:5, 8, 13
49:8
50:3
51:16
52:9[2]
54:6
55:10[2], 12[3], 13
60:2[2], 4, 12
63:9
65:9[3], 10
68:9, 11, 14[2], 16
69:18, 22, 35, 36
73:16, 28
74:11
75:3, 8
78:28
80:8, 9[3], 10, 13[2], 16[2]
81:10
84:6
86:17
87:5
89:37, 39
90:4, 6[2], 10, 13, 17
91:7
92:1, 7
93:1
94:7, 15
95:5, 10
96:10
99:3
100:3
101:3
103:16[3]
104:5, 6, 20, 32
105:12, 28
106:9, 32
107:42
108:13
109:17[2], 18, 19, 23, 27
112:10
114:3
118:8, 9, 23, 24
119:20, 33, 34, 71, 90, 97, 106, 126, 130, 140, 175
124:1, 2
127:1, 2
128:2
129:6
132:6[2], 11, 13, 14
133:1, 2
135:3
136:14
137:7[2]
139:4, 6[2]
141:5[2]
144:10
147:1[2]

PROVERBS

2:21, 22
3:8, 14, 25, 27[3], 28
4:5, 15[3], 23
6:22[3], 32
7:23
8:11, 33
9:12
10:22[2], 23, 24
11:10, 11, 15, 19, 24, 26, 27
12:25[2]
13:12, 19
14:1, 6
15:23
16:12, 14, 16, 19, 22, 26, 31
17:8[3], 14, 16, 21
18:5, 10, 13[2], 21
19:2, 11, 19, 23, 24
20:3, 5, 11, 14[2], 25
21:1, 9, 15, 19, 20, 27
22:6, 15, 18
23:23, 31[3], 32, 35[2]
24:3, 12[3], 13, 14, 18[2], 23, 27, 31, 32[2]
25:2, 7[2], 10, 16, 24, 27
26:15[2], 27, 28
27:14
28:8, 24
29:4, 7, 11, 24
30:15, 16, 17[2], 21
31:4[2], 15, 16, 24

ECCLESIASTES

1:6, 8, 9, 10[2]
2:2[2], 15[2], 18, 21, 24
3:10, 13, 14[4]
4:8
5:4, 5, 6, 18[2]
6:1, 2[2], 10[2]
7:2[2], 5, 11, 12, 18, 23, 24
8:7, 8, 12, 13, 14[2], 17[4]
9:10, 12, 13, 14[4], 15
10:8
11:1, 3, 7
12:7[2], 14[2]

SONG OF SOLOMON

3:4, 7, 10
5:2, 3
6:13
8:7[2], 13

ISAIAH

1:6, 7[2], 13, 20, 21[2], 31
2:2[2]
3:9, 10, 11, 24
4:3

ISAIAH

5:2[5], 4[3], 5[2], 6[3], 14, 18, 19[2], 29[2]
6:2, 7, 13[2]
7:1[3], 2, 6[2], 7[2], 8, 11, 13, 18, 20, 21, 22, 23[2], 25
8:1, 10[2], 20, 21[2]
9:7[2], 8, 18
10:7, 12, 13, 15[3], 17, 20, 26, 27, 30
11:10, 11, 15, 16
13:6, 9, 14, 17, 20[2]
14:3, 9[2], 23[2], 24[2], 27[2], 32
15:5
16:2, 5, 12[2]
17:1, 4, 5[2], 6, 10
19:1, 16[2], 17, 20, 21, 22
20:1
21:1, 3[2], 17
22:5, 7, 11, 14, 20, 25[2]
23:1[2], 9, 13[2], 15, 17, 18
24:1[2], 2, 9, 13, 18, 20[2], 21
25:2, 8, 9
26:5[3], 6, 15, 18, 20
27:3[4], 8[2], 11, 12, 13
28:4[3], 15, 18, 19[4], 20[2], 28[3]
29:2, 5, 8, 11, 16[2], 17
30:8[3], 14[2], 19, 21, 22, 23, 32[2], 33[3]
31:5[2]
32:19
34:1, 5, 6, 8, 10[3], 11[3], 13, 16[2], 17[2]
35:2[2], 8[3], 9
36:1, 6[2], 7, 10[2], 11
37:1[2], 4, 9, 14[2], 26[3], 27, 33[2], 35, 38
38:8, 15, 17, 21
40:5[2], 7, 9, 19, 21, 22
41:4, 5, 7[3], 20, 23
42:5[2], 21, 25[3]
43:9, 13, 19[2]
44:7[2], 8, 12[2], 13[5], 14, 15[4], 17[3], 19[2], 23
45:8, 9, 12, 18[4], 21
46:6, 8, 11[4], 13
47:7, 10, 11, 14
48:5[3], 6, 11, 16, 20
49:6
50:1, 2
51:9, 10, 22, 23
52:6
53:3, 10
54:14
55:10[2], 11[4], 13
56:2[2], 6
57:1, 8, 11, 20
58:5[2], 7, 14
59:1[2], 11, 15[2], 16
60:22
61:11
62:9[4]
63:5, 18
65:6, 8[2], 9, 24
66:18, 23

JEREMIAH

1:3, 12
2:19, 34
3:5, 7, 9, 16[4], 17
4:4, 9, 11, 18[2], 23, 28[3]
5:1, 12, 13, 14, 15[2], 19, 20, 22[3], 31
6:10, 11, 19
7:11, 12, 20, 23, 29, 30, 31, 32
8:8, 10
9:8, 12
10:4[3], 5, 7, 18, 19, 23
11:5[2], 16[2], 18[2]
12:8[2], 11[3], 15, 16
13:1[2], 2, 4, 5, 6, 7[2], 16[2], 17, 19[2], 27
14:5, 7
15:2, 8, 9, 11
16:10, 14
17:1, 9, 15, 21, 24, 27[2]
18:4[2], 7, 9, 10[2]
19:4, 5[2], 15
20:3, 4, 10
21:10[2], 12, 14[2]
22:14, 15, 16, 17
23:18, 19, 20
25:12[2], 13, 15, 18, 28
26:8, 21
27:5[2], 8, 11
28:1, 10
29:7
30:3, 7[3], 8, 23, 24[2]
31:10, 28, 33, 39, 40

JEREMIAH

32:3, 7, 8, 10, 23, 24[3], 28, 29, 31[2], 34, 35, 36, 43[2]
33:2[2], 5, 6, 9[2]
34:2, 22[3]
35:11
36:1, 3, 7, 9, 15[2], 16, 21[2], 23[3], 28, 32
37:8[2], 11, 14
38:3, 15, 18, 20, 25
39:1, 4
40:3, 4[3], 5, 9, 15
41:1, 4[2], 6, 7, 9[2], 13
42:4[2], 6[3], 7, 16, 17, 20, 21
43:1
44:21
46:10, 20, 23, 26
47:6, 7[3]
48:1, 2[2], 9, 20[2], 30[2], 39, 44
49:2, 12, 17, 18, 23, 27, 33, 39
50:13[2], 15, 21, 29, 32, 38, 39[2]
51:11[2], 33, 62[3], 63[3]
52:3, 4[3], 21[2], 22, 31

LAMENTATIONS

1:12, 13, 21
2:6, 16
3:22, 26, 27, 28, 37[2]
4:4, 8[2], 11, 15
5:18

EZEKIEL

1:1, 4, 13, 16, 26, 27[3], 28
2:10[2]
3:3[2], 16
4:1[2], 2[5], 3[4], 4[2], 7, 10, 12[2]
5:1, 2, 5, 13, 15[2], 17
7:6[2], 10, 19, 20[2], 21[2], 22[2]
8:1, 17
9:8
10:1, 6, 7[2], 11, 13
11:3, 7[2], 13
12:3, 6[2], 7[2], 11, 13, 23, 25[2]
13:7, 10, 11[3], 12[2], 13[2], 14[2], 15[2]
14:13[3], 14, 15[2], 16, 17, 18, 19[2], 20, 21, 22, 23
15:3, 4[4], 5[5]
16:14, 15, 16, 19[2], 23
17:4[2], 5[3], 6[2], 7, 8[4], 9[4], 10[5], 14[2], 19, 21, 22[2], 23[3], 24
18:4, 20
19:3[3]
20:1, 9, 14, 22, 28, 42, 47, 48[2]
21:5, 7[3], 10[4], 11[4], 12[2], 13[2], 14, 15[2], 17, 19, 23, 27[4], 28, 30, 32
22:3, 14[2], 20[2], 30
23:32, 34[3], 39, 41
24:3[2], 4[2], 5[3], 6[3], 7[3], 8[2], 10, 11[5], 14[3], 25, 26
25:3[2], 13[2], 15
26:1, 5[3], 14, 17
28:10, 18, 21
29:3, 9, 11[3], 15[2], 16, 17, 18, 19, 20
30:3, 6, 9, 12, 20, 21[3], 25
31:1
32:1, 15, 17
33:9, 13, 21, 33
34:18, 24
35:2, 3, 7, 10, 15[2]
36:5, 10, 17, 18, 29, 32, 34, 36[2], 37
37:14[2], 16[2], 26
38:8, 10, 14, 16, 18
39:5, 8[2], 11[3], 13, 14, 15[2]
40:22, 25, 26[2], 29[2], 31, 33, 34, 35, 36, 37, 40
41:15, 18, 19
42:15, 20[2]
43:3, 11, 17, 18, 20[3], 21, 22, 23, 26, 27
44:1, 2[4], 3[2], 6, 7, 17, 24, 28, 31
45:3, 4, 6, 9, 17, 19
46:1[2], 6, 9, 13, 14, 16, 17[2], 23
47:5, 9, 10[2], 12, 14[2], 22[2], 23
48:8, 11, 14[2], 18, 19, 21, 35

DANIEL

1:1
2:7, 11[2], 40, 41, 44[2], 45, 47
3:1, 4, 14, 17, 18, 19
4:2, 12[3], 14, 15, 17[2], 21, 22, 23[2], 25, 27, 31, 32
5:21, 26
6:1, 5, 8, 17
7:4[2], 5[5], 6[2], 7[6], 23[2], 26
8:2, 8, 10[2], 12[2], 15, 22, 26, 27
9:13, 14, 27
11:12, 18, 27, 29, 35
12:6, 7

HOSEA

1:5, 10[3]
2:7, 16, 21
6:4
7:4, 6, 9
8:4, 5, 6[3], 7[3], 13, 14
9:7
10:5[4], 6, 10, 12
13:2

JOEL

1:3, 5, 7[2], 15
2:1, 2, 11, 28, 32
3:8, 18

AMOS

1:14
2:2, 5, 11
3:6
4:7[3]
5:6[2], 13, 15, 18, 20
6:9
7:1, 2, 3, 4, 13[2]
8:8[2], 9, 10, 12
9:4, 5[2], 6, 8, 11

OBADIAH

15, 18

JONAH

1:2, 3, 5, 13, 14
2:10
3:2, 7, 10
4:1, 3, 5, 6[2], 7[2], 8[2], 10

MICAH

1:5, 7, 9, 10
2:1[2], 4, 10[2], 13
3:1, 6
4:1[3], 4, 8
5:10
6:9
7:3, 10

NAHUM

1:4
3:1, 7, 8, 9, 15

HABAKKUK

1:5, 10
2:2[2], 3[5], 11, 13, 18, 19[3]

ZEPHANIAH

1:8, 10, 12, 14
2:3, 14
3:16, 18

HAGGAI

1:4, 6, 8, 9[3]
2:3[3], 6, 12, 13[2], 18

ZECHARIAH

1:16, 21
4:2, 3, 7, 9
5:3[2], 4[4], 6, 8, 11[2]
7:1, 13
8:6[2], 13, 20, 23
9:2, 5[2]
10:7
11:9[2], 10, 11[2], 13
12:3[2], 9
13:2, 3, 4, 8, 9
14:4, 6, 7[3], 8[2], 10, 11, 13, 16, 17

MALACHI

1:8[3], 12, 13[2]
2:2[4], 5, 10
3:10, 14[2], 16
4:1

MATTHEW

1:22
2:5, 9, 15, 23
3:15[2]
4:4, 6, 7, 10, 14
5:13[2], 15[2], 21, 27, 29[3], 30[3], 31, 33, 34, 35[2], 38, 43
6:10
7:2, 7[2], 8, 14, 25[2], 27[2], 28
8:9, 10, 13, 17
9:8, 10, 11, 16, 29, 30, 33
10:11, 12, 13[2], 15, 19, 20, 25, 39[2]
11:1, 10, 12, 14, 16, 22, 23, 24, 26
12:2, 10, 11[3], 12, 13[2], 15, 17, 24, 32[2], 39, 41, 42, 44, 45
13:11[2], 19, 20, 23, 27, 32[2], 35, 40, 46, 48, 49, 53

MATTHEW

14:4, 9, 11, 12, 13, 15, 26, 27, 28
15:5, 26[2], 28
16:2[2], 3, 4, 7, 11[2], 17, 18, 22, 25[2]
17:4, 6, 20
18:6, 7, 8, 9[3], 13, 14, 17, 19
19:1, 3, 8, 9, 10, 11, 12[2], 24, 25
20:11, 15, 23[2], 24, 26
21:4, 13[2], 19[2], 20, 21, 25, 32, 33[3], 34, 42, 44[2]
22:5, 17, 39
23:16, 18[2], 20, 21
24:23, 24, 26, 33
25:28, 40[2], 45[2]
26:1, 7, 8, 10, 12, 22, 24[2], 25, 26[3], 27[2], 29, 31, 39, 42, 54, 61, 62
27:6[2], 24, 29, 35, 40, 48[2], 59, 60, 65
28:1, 2

MARK

1:2, 9, 45
2:1, 4, 9, 12, 15, 16, 17, 21, 23
3:4, 5, 21
4:4[2], 5[3], 6[3], 7[2], 11, 16, 19, 20, 22, 24, 30, 31[2], 32[3], 33, 37, 40
5:14[2], 16[2], 43
6:11, 15[2], 16, 18, 22, 23, 28[2], 29[2], 49, 50, 56
7:6, 11, 18, 19, 24, 27[2], 36
8:16, 17, 21, 26, 35[2], 36
9:5, 12, 13, 21, 22, 30, 33, 42, 43[2], 45[2], 47[2], 50
10:2, 14, 24, 25, 27, 40[2], 41, 43, 47
11:2, 13, 14[2], 17[2], 18, 30
12:1[2], 11, 14, 15, 16
13:11, 14, 22, 29
14:3, 5, 11, 19[2], 20, 21[2], 22, 23[2], 25, 27, 35, 41, 60, 70
15:2, 17, 23, 25, 29, 35, 36, 42, 45
16:4, 13, 18

LUKE

1:3, 8, 23, 38, 41, 59
2:1, 6, 15, 17, 18, 20, 23, 26, 43, 46, 49
3:4, 21
4:3, 4, 6, 8, 10, 12, 17, 20, 39, 42
5:1, 8, 12, 17
6:1, 4, 6, 9[2], 12, 13, 38[2], 48[2], 49
7:8, 11, 27, 39
8:1, 5[2], 6[3], 7[2], 10, 15, 16[3], 20, 21, 22, 29, 34, 36, 40, 50
9:7, 11, 18, 24[2], 28, 33[2], 36, 37, 39, 45[2], 51, 57
10:6[2], 12, 14, 21, 38
11:1, 9[2], 10, 14[2], 25, 27, 28, 29, 32, 33, 38, 51
12:10[2], 32, 49, 50, 54, 55, 56
13:7[2], 8[3], 9[2], 18, 19[3], 21, 33
14:1, 3, 18, 22, 28, 29[2], 34, 35[2]
15:4, 5[2], 8, 9, 22, 23, 32
16:2, 16, 17, 22
17:1, 2, 6, 11, 14, 22, 26[2], 28, 29, 30, 31, 33[2]
18:15, 25, 26, 35, 36, 43
19:7, 15, 24, 29, 41, 46[2]
20:1, 4, 7, 9, 13, 16, 18[2], 22, 24
21:5, 13, 14, 21, 35
22:16, 17, 19, 22, 23, 36, 38, 44, 64, 66
23:3, 24, 26, 44, 53[3]
24:4, 10, 15, 21, 24, 29, 30[2], 39, 43, 46[2], 51

JOHN

1:5, 27, 32, 39
2:5, 8, 9, 17, 19, 20
3:8[3], 27
4:6, 9, 10, 53
5:10[2], 13, 15
6:17, 20, 31, 39, 42, 45, 60, 61, 63, 65, 71
7:7[2], 10, 17, 22, 51
8:9, 17, 44, 54, 56
9:4, 14, 27, 32, 37
10:10, 17, 18[4], 22[2], 34
11:2, 22, 38[2], 42, 50, 57
12:14, 24[3], 25[2], 28[2], 29[2]
13:19[2], 24, 25, 26[3], 30
14:2, 8, 14, 17, 21, 22, 27, 29[2]
15:2[2], 4, 7, 16, 18[2]
16:7, 14, 15, 23
17:26

JOHN

18:10, 11, 14, 18, 25, 28, 31, 34
19:2, 11, 14, 19, 20, 24[3], 29[2], 30, 31, 35, 40
20:1, 14, 27
21:4, 6, 7[2], 8, 12

THE ACTS

1:7, 19, 20
2:2, 3, 15, 17, 21, 24[2]
3:10, 12, 17, 23
4:3, 5, 10, 14, 16, 17, 19, 37[2]
5:2[2], 4[4], 7, 9, 38, 39[2]
6:2, 15
7:5[2], 23, 31[2], 42, 44, 53
9:5, 6, 18, 32, 37, 42, 43
10:4, 11, 28, 42
11:4, 5[2], 26, 30
12:3, 9, 15[2], 18, 22
13:17, 33, 38, 41, 46[2]
14:1, 6
15:5, 15, 16, 22, 25, 28, 34
16:16, 35
17:14
18:14, 15[2]
19:1, 19, 39
20:16, 35
21:1, 3, 20, 22, 35
22:6, 10, 17, 22, 25
23:5, 12, 30, 31
24:3, 21
25:16, 27
26:8, 14
27:1, 8, 14, 25[2], 28[2], 35, 39[2], 44
28:8, 17, 19, 22, 28[2]

ROMANS

1:16, 17, 19
2:24, 27
3:4, 10, 19, 27, 30
4:3, 10, 16[2], 17, 22, 23[2], 24
5:16
6:12
7:11, 13, 16, 17[2], 20[2]
8:3, 7, 25, 33, 34, 36
9:12, 13, 16, 20, 26[2], 28, 32[2], 33
10:8, 15
11:6[3], 7, 8, 26, 35
12:8, 18, 19
13:9, 11
14:6[2], 11, 14, 20, 21, 22
15:3, 9, 21, 26, 27

1 CORINTHIANS

1:11, 18, 19, 21, 31
2:8, 9
3:2, 13[3], 19
4:2, 3, 7[2], 9, 12
5:1
6:5, 13
7:1, 5, 8, 9, 21[2], 26, 29, 31
8:7
9:9, 10, 11, 15[2], 25, 27
10:7, 13, 16[2], 28
11:6, 13, 14, 15, 18, 24, 25
12:6, 15, 16, 18, 26[2]
13:3, 8
14:7, 9, 10, 15, 21, 26, 27, 34, 35, 36
15:11, 27, 32, 36, 37, 38[2], 42[2], 43[4], 44[2], 45
16:4, 6, 15

2 CORINTHIANS

1:6[2]
2:10[2]
3:16
4:3, 13
5:10, 13[2]
7:8, 11, 12
8:11, 12, 15
9:1, 5, 9
11:15, 17[2]
12:1, 4, 8, 13[2], 16

GALATIANS

1:12[2], 13, 15
2:6
3:4, 5, 6, 10, 11, 13, 15[2], 17, 18[2], 19[2]
4:15, 18, 22, 27, 29

EPHESIANS

2:8
3:5
4:9, 29
5:3, 12, 25, 26, 27[2], 29
6:3

PHILIPPIANS

1:6, 7, 20, 27, 29

PHILIPPIANS

2:6, 13, 23, 25
3:1, 21
S

COLOSSIANS

1:6[3], 9, 19
2:14[2], 15
3:18, 23
4:4, 16, 17

1 THESSALONIANS

2:1, 13[2]
3:1, 4
4:10
5:24

2 THESSALONIANS

1:3, 6
3:1

1 TIMOTHY

1:8, 13
4:4, 5
5:16
6:7

2 TIMOTHY

2:11
4:16

TITUS

S

PHILEMON

14, 19[2]

HEBREWS

2:10, 17
3:13, 15, 17
4:1, 2, 6[2], 7
6:4, 7[2], 17, 18
7:8, 11, 14, 15
8:3
9:5, 17, 23, 27
10:4, 7, 31
11:2, 4, 6, 18
12:11, 13, 17, 20
13:9, 17

JAMES

1:2, 5, 11[2], 15[2]
2:14, 16, 17, 23
3:6[2], 8
4:3, 14, 17[2]
5:3, 7, 17[2]

1 PETER

1:7, 11, 12, 16
2:6, 13, 20[4]
3:3, 4, 11, 17
4:4, 11, 12, 17

2 PETER

1:13
2:13, 21[2], 22

1 JOHN

1:2
2:18[2], 21, 27
3:1, 2
4:3[2]
5:6, 16

2 JOHN

6

JUDE

3

REVELATION

1:1, 11
2:17
3:8
4:1
5:6
6:1, 11, 14
7:2
8:3, 5[2], 8, 10[2], 12
9:4, 5, 6, 7, 9
10:1, 9[4], 10[3]
11:2[2], 6
12:4
13:3, 7, 18
14:3, 19
15:2
16:3, 17
18:21
19:6, 10, 15
20:11, 13
21:6, 16, 18, 21, 22, 23[2], 24[2], 25, 26, 27
22:2, 3, 9

ME

1691 or 3165

GENESIS

3:12[2], 13
4:10, 14[3], 25
6:7, 13
7:1
9:12, 13, 15, 17
12:12, 13, 18[2], 19
13:8, 9
14:21, 24
15:2, 3, 9
16:2, 5, 13[2]
17:1, 2, 4, 7, 10, 11
18:21, 27, 31
19:8, 19[2], 20
20:5, 6, 9[2], 11, 13[3]
21:6[2], 16, 23[3], 26, 30
22:12
23:4, 8[2], 9[2], 11, 13[2], 15[2]
24:5, 7[3], 12, 17, 23, 27, 30, 37, 39, 40, 43, 44, 45, 48, 49[2], 54, 56[2]
25:30, 31, 32, 33
26:7, 27[3]
27:3, 4[2], 7[2], 9, 12[2], 13[2], 19[2], 20, 25, 26, 31, 33, 34[2], 36[2], 38[2], 46
28:20[3], 22
29:15[2], 19, 21, 25[2], 27, 32, 33, 34
30:1, 6[2], 13, 14, 16, 18, 20[2], 24, 25, 26[2], 27, 28, 29, 31[2], 33[2]
31:5[2], 7[2], 9, 11, 13, 26, 27[2], 28, 29, 31, 32, 35, 36, 40, 42[2], 44, 48, 49, 50, 51, 52
32:9, 11[2], 16, 20[2], 26[2], 29
33:10, 11, 13, 14, 15[3]
34:4, 11[2], 12[3], 30[4]
35:3[2]
37:9, 14, 16
38:16[3], 17
39:7, 8, 9, 12, 14[2], 15, 17[2], 18, 19
40:8, 9, 14[4], 15
41:10[2], 13, 16, 24, 51, 52
42:20, 33, 34, 36[2]
43:6, 8, 9, 16, 29
44:21, 27, 28, 29, 34
45:1, 4, 5[2], 7, 8[2], 9[2], 10, 18
46:30, 31
47:29[2], 30[2], 31
48:3[2], 4, 7[2], 9[2], 11, 15, 16
49:29
50:5[4], 20

EXODUS

2:9, 14
3:9, 13[2], 14, 15, 16
4:1, 18, 23, 25
5:1, 22
6:7, 12[2], 30
7:16[2]
8:1, 8, 9, 20, 28
9:1, 13, 14
10:3[2], 17, 28
11:8[2]
12:32
13:2, 8
14:15, 17, 18
17:2, 4
18:4, 15, 16
19:5, 6
20:3, 5, 6, 23, 24, 25
22:23, 27, 29, 30, 31
23:14, 15, 33
24:12
25:2, 8, 30
28:1, 3, 4, 41
29:1, 44
30:30, 31
31:13, 17
32:2, 10, 23, 24, 26, 32, 33
33:12[3], 13, 15, 18, 20, 21
34:2, 20
40:13, 15

LEVITICUS

10:3, 19
14:35
20:26
22:2
25:23, 55
26:14, 18, 21[2], 23[2], 27[2], 40[2]

NUMBERS
3:13, 41
8:16[2]
11:11, 12, 13, 14, 15[3], 16
14:11[2], 22, 23, 24, 27[2], 29, 35
16:28, 29
17:5, 10
18:9
20:12[2], 18
21:22
22:5, 6[2], 8, 10, 11, 13, 16, 17[2], 18, 19, 28, 29, 32, 33[3], 34[2], 37
23:1[2], 3[2], 7[2], 10, 11, 13[2], 18, 27, 29[2]
24:12, 13
27:14
28:2[2]
32:11

DEUTERONOMY
1:14, 17, 22, 23, 37, 41, 42
2:1, 2, 9, 17, 27, 28[2], 29, 31
3:2, 25, 26[4]
4:5, 10[3], 14, 21
5:7, 9, 10, 22, 23, 28[2], 29, 31
7:4
8:17
9:4, 10, 11, 12, 13, 14, 19
10:1[2], 4, 5, 10, 11
17:14[2]
18:15, 16[2], 17
26:10, 13, 14
28:20
31:2, 16, 19, 20, 28
32:21[2], 34, 35, 39, 41, 51[2]

JOSHUA
2:4, 12[2]
7:19[2]
8:5
10:4[2], 22
14:6, 7, 8, 10, 11, 12[2]
15:19[3]
17:14[2]
18:4, 6, 8
24:15

JUDGES
1:3, 7, 15[3]
3:28
4:8[2], 18, 19
5:13
6:17[2], 39[2]
7:2[3], 17, 18
8:5, 15, 24
9:7, 9, 15, 48, 54[2]
10:12, 13
11:7[3], 9[2], 12[2], 17, 27[2], 31, 35[2], 36, 37[2]
12:2, 3[3], 5
13:6[2], 7, 10[2], 16
14:2, 3[2], 12, 13[2], 16[3]
15:11, 12[2]
16:6, 7, 10[3], 11, 13[3], 15[3], 17, 18, 26, 28[2], 30
17:2, 10[2], 13
18:4[2], 24
19:18, 19, 20
20:5[3]

RUTH
1:8, 11, 13[2], 16, 17[2], 20[3], 21[4]
2:2, 7, 10, 11, 13[2], 21
3:5, 17[2]
4:4

1 SAMUEL
1:11, 27
2:16, 28, 29, 30[4], 35, 36
3:5, 6, 8, 17[2]
8:7, 8
9:16, 18, 19[2], 21
10:2, 8, 15
12:1, 3, 12, 23
13:9, 11, 12
14:12, 33, 34, 42, 43
15:1, 11[2], 16, 20, 25, 30[2], 32
16:1, 2, 3, 5, 17[2], 19, 22
17:8, 9[2], 10, 35, 37[2], 43, 44, 45
18:8, 17
19:15, 17[3]
20:2[2], 3, 5, 6[2], 8[3], 10, 14, 23, 28, 29[3], 31, 42
21:2[2], 3, 8, 9, 14
22:3, 8[5], 13[2], 15, 17, 23[2]
23:11, 12, 21, 22, 23
24:10, 12[2], 15[2], 17, 18[3], 19, 21[2]
25:19, 21, 24[2], 32, 33, 34[2]
26:6, 8, 19[2], 24
27:1[3], 5
28:1, 7, 8[2], 9, 11, 12, 15[6], 16, 17, 19, 21, 22
29:3[2], 6[2]
30:7, 13, 15[4]
31:4[3]

2 SAMUEL
1:4, 7[2], 8, 9[8], 26[2]
2:7, 22
3:8, 12, 14[2], 35, 39
4:10
5:20
6:9, 21[2]
7:5[2], 7, 18
10:2, 11[2]
11:6
12:10, 22, 23
13:4, 5, 6, 9, 11, 12, 13, 16[2], 17
14:9, 10, 15, 16, 18, 19, 32[4]
15:4, 7, 8, 25[2], 26, 28, 33[2], 34, 36
16:3, 9, 12
17:1

2 SAMUEL
18:13, 19, 22, 23, 27, 29
19:13[2], 19, 22, 25, 26[2], 33[2], 36, 38[2]
20:4, 20
22:3, 5[2], 6[2], 17[2], 18[3], 19, 20[3], 21[2], 23, 25, 34, 36[2], 37, 40[3], 41[2], 44[3], 45[2], 48[2], 49[4]
23:2, 3, 5, 15, 17
24:13, 14, 17, 24

1 KINGS
1:12, 13, 17, 24, 26[2], 28, 30, 32, 51
2:4[2], 5, 7, 8[2], 15, 16, 17, 20, 23, 24[3], 30, 31, 42
3:20, 24
5:4, 6, 8, 9
8:25[2]
9:3, 4, 6, 13
10:7
11:21, 22[2], 33, 36[2]
12:5, 9, 12, 24, 27
13:6[2], 7, 8, 9, 13, 15, 17, 18, 27, 31
14:2, 8, 9[2]
15:19[2]
16:2
17:10, 11, 12, 13[2], 18, 19
18:9, 12, 14, 19, 30, 37[2]
19:2, 18, 20
20:5, 7, 10[2], 32, 35, 36, 37, 39
21:2, 3, 6, 20, 22, 29[2]
22:4, 8, 14, 16, 18, 24, 28, 34

2 KINGS
2:2, 4, 6, 9, 10, 20
3:7[2], 15
4:2, 6, 22, 24, 27[2], 28
5:7[2], 8, 11, 22[2]
6:11, 19, 28, 31
8:4, 9, 10, 13, 14
9:12, 18, 19
10:6, 15, 16, 19
16:7[2], 15
18:14[2], 20, 22, 25, 27[2], 31[2]
19:6, 20, 27, 28
20:8
21:15
22:10, 13, 15, 17[2], 19

1 CHRONICLES
4:10[4]
10:4[2]
11:17, 19
12:17[3]
13:12
17:4, 6, 12, 16, 17
19:2, 12[2]
21:2, 12, 13[2], 17, 22[2]
22:7, 8
28:2[2], 3, 4[3], 5, 6, 19[2]
29:17

2 CHRONICLES
1:8, 9, 10
2:3, 7[2], 8, 9
6:16
7:17
9:6
10:5, 6, 9, 12
11:4
12:5
13:4
15:2
16:3[2]
18:3, 7, 15, 17, 23, 27, 33
20:20
28:11, 23
29:5
34:18, 21, 23, 25[2], 27[2]
35:21[2], 23
36:23[2]

EZRA
1:2[2]
4:18, 21
7:28[3]
8:1
9:1, 4

NEHEMIAH
1:3, 9
2:2, 4, 5, 6[2], 7[2], 8[3], 9, 12[2], 14, 18[2]
4:18, 23
5:15, 18[2], 19
6:2[2], 4, 5, 12, 13, 14, 19[2]
12:40
13:8, 14, 22[2], 28, 31

ESTHER
4:16
5:13
7:3, 8

JOB
2:3
3:12, 25[2]
4:12, 14
6:4[2], 8, 9[2], 13[2], 22[2], 23[2], 24[2], 28
7:3, 8[3], 12, 13, 14[2], 16, 19[2], 20, 21
9:11, 16, 17, 18[2], 19, 20[2], 28, 31[2], 34[2], 35
10:2[3], 8[3], 9[2], 10[2], 11[2], 12, 14[2], 15, 16[2], 17[3], 18[2], 20
13:13[2], 15, 19, 20, 21[2], 22[2], 23, 24, 26[2]
14:3, 13[4]
15:17
16:7, 8[3], 9[4], 10[3], 11[2], 12[4], 13, 14[2], 20
17:1, 2, 3[2], 6

JOB
19:2, 3[2], 5[2], 6[2], 9, 10, 11[2], 12, 13[2], 14, 15, 16, 18[2], 19[2], 21[3], 22, 27, 28
20:2, 3
21:3, 4, 5, 16, 27, 34
22:18
23:5[2], 6[2], 10, 14, 16
24:15, 25
27:3, 5, 6, 7
28:14[2]
29:2, 5[2], 6, 8, 11[4], 13, 14, 20, 21, 23
30:1, 2, 10[2], 11[2], 12, 14[2], 15, 16[2], 17, 18, 19, 20[2], 21[2], 22[2], 23, 26, 27, 30
31:6, 8, 13, 15, 18, 20, 23, 29, 34, 35[2], 36, 38
32:10, 14, 18[2], 21[2], 22
33:4[2], 5[2], 9, 10[2], 27, 31, 32, 33
34:2, 10, 32, 34[2]
36:2
38:3
40:7, 8
41:10, 11
42:3, 4, 7, 8

PSALMS
2:7, 8
3:1[2], 3, 4, 5[2], 6, 7
4:1[3], 8[2]
5:7, 8
6:1[2], 2[2], 4, 8
7:1[3], 4, 6, 8[2]
9:13[3]
13:1[2], 2, 3, 4, 6
16:1, 6, 7[2], 8, 11
17:3[2], 4, 6[2], 8[2], 9[2], 15
18:4[2], 5[2], 16[2], 17[3], 18, 19[3], 20[2], 22[2], 24, 32, 33, 35[3], 36, 39[3], 40[2], 43[3], 44[3], 47[2], 48[4]
19:12, 13
22:1[2], 7[2], 9[2], 11, 12[2], 13, 15, 16[2], 17, 19[2], 21[2]
23:2[2], 3, 4[2], 5, 6
25:2[2], 4[2], 5[2], 7, 16[2], 17, 19, 20[2], 21
26:1, 2[2], 11[3]
27:2, 3[2], 5[3], 6, 7[2], 9[3], 10[2], 11[2], 12[2]
28:1[2], 3
30:1[2], 2, 3, 10, 11[2]
31:1[2], 2[3], 3[2], 4[2], 5, 8, 9, 11[2], 13, 15[2], 16, 17, 21
32:4, 7[2]
34:3, 4[2], 11
35:1[2], 3, 7, 12, 13, 15[2], 16, 19[2], 21, 22, 24[2], 26
36:11[2]
38:1[2], 2[2], 4, 10[2], 12, 16[3], 17, 19, 21[2], 22
39:1, 3, 4, 8[2], 10, 13
40:1, 2, 7, 11[2], 12[3], 13[2], 14, 15, 17
41:4, 5, 6, 7[3], 9, 10[2], 11[2], 12[3]
42:3, 4, 5, 6, 7, 8, 9, 10[2], 11
43:1[2], 2, 3[2], 5
44:6, 15[2]
49:5, 15
50:5[2], 8, 15[2], 23
51:1, 2[2], 3, 5, 6, 7[2], 8, 10[2], 11[2], 12[2], 14
54:1[2], 3, 7
55:2[2], 3[2], 4[2], 5[2], 12[3], 16[2], 18[2]
56:1[3], 2[2], 4, 5, 9, 11, 12
57:1[2], 2, 3[2], 6
59:1[3], 2[2], 3, 4, 10[2]
60:5, 8, 9[2]
61:2, 3, 5
63:8
64:2
65:3
66:18, 19, 20
69:1, 2, 4[2], 9[2], 12, 13[2], 14[4], 15[3], 16[2], 17, 18, 21[2], 29
70:1[2], 5
71:1, 2[4], 3, 4, 6, 9[2], 10, 12, 17, 18, 20[3], 21
73:2, 16, 23, 24[2], 28
77:1
81:8, 11, 13
86:1, 3, 7, 11, 13, 14, 16[2], 17[4]
87:4
88:6, 7[2], 8[2], 14, 16[2], 17[2], 18
89:26, 36
91:14, 15
92:4, 11
94:16[2], 18, 19
95:9[2]
101:2, 3, 4, 6[2]
102:2[3], 8[3], 10[2], 24
103:1
106:4[2]
108:6, 10[2]
109:2[3], 3[2], 5, 21[2], 22, 25, 26[2]
116:2, 3[2], 6, 12
118:5[2], 6, 7[2], 10, 11[2], 12, 13[2], 18[2], 19, 21
119:8, 10, 12, 19, 22, 23, 25, 26[2], 27, 28, 29[2], 30, 31, 33, 34, 35, 37, 40, 41, 42, 49, 50, 51, 53, 58, 61, 64, 66, 68, 69, 71, 72, 73[3], 74, 75, 77, 78, 79, 82, 84, 85, 86[2], 87, 88, 93, 94, 95[2], 98[2], 102, 107, 108, 110, 115, 116[2], 117, 121, 122, 124, 125, 132[2], 133, 134, 135, 139, 143, 144, 145, 146, 149, 153, 154[2], 156, 159, 161, 169, 170, 171, 173, 175
120:1, 5
122:1
129:1, 2[2]

PSALMS
131:1
138:3[2], 7[2], 8
139:1[2], 5[2], 6, 10[2], 11[2], 13, 17, 19, 23[2], 24[2]
140:1[2], 4[2], 5[2], 9
141:1, 4, 5[2], 9[2]
142:3[2], 4[2], 6, 7[2]
143:1, 3, 4[2], 7[2], 8[2], 9[2], 10[2], 11
144:2, 7[2], 11[2]

PROVERBS
1:28[3], 33
4:4[2]
5:7, 13
7:14, 24
8:15, 16, 17[3], 18, 21, 22, 32, 34, 35, 36[2]
9:11
23:26, 35[2]
24:29
27:11
30:7, 8[4], 18

ECCLESIASTES
1:16
2:4[3], 5, 6, 7[2], 8[2], 9[2], 15, 17, 18
7:23
9:13

SONG OF SOLOMON
1:2, 4[2], 6[4], 7, 13, 14
2:4[2], 5[2], 6, 10, 14[2]
3:3, 4
4:6, 8[2]
5:2, 6, 7[4]
6:5[2], 12
7:10
8:2, 3, 6, 12, 13

ISAIAH
1:2, 11, 12, 13, 14, 24[2]
3:7
5:3
6:5, 6, 8
8:1, 2, 3, 5, 11[2], 18
10:4
12:1[2]
18:4
21:2, 3, 4[2], 6, 11, 16
22:4[2]
24:16
26:9
27:4[2], 5[2]
29:2, 13[4], 16
30:1
31:4
36:5, 7, 10, 12[2], 16[2]
37:6, 21, 28, 29
38:12[3], 13, 14, 15, 16[2], 20
39:3
40:25
41:1
43:10[3], 11, 20, 22[2], 23[2], 24[4], 26, 27
44:6, 7, 8, 17, 21, 22
45:4, 5[2], 6, 11[2], 19, 21[2], 22, 23
46:3[2], 5[3], 9, 12
47:8, 10[2]
48:12, 16[2], 19
49:1[2], 2[3], 3, 5, 14[2], 16, 20[2], 21, 23
50:4, 7, 8[3], 9[2]
51:1, 4[3], 5, 7
54:9, 15, 17
55:2, 3, 11
56:3, 4
57:8, 11[2], 13, 16, 17
58:2[2]
59:21
60:9
61:1[3], 10[2]
63:3, 5[2], 15
65:1[4], 3, 5, 6, 7, 10
66:1, 22, 23, 24

JEREMIAH
1:4, 7, 9, 11, 12, 13, 14, 16
2:1, 2, 5[2], 8[2], 13, 21, 22, 27[2], 29[2], 32, 35
3:1, 4, 6, 7, 10, 11, 19[2], 20
4:1, 12, 17, 19, 22, 31
5:5, 7, 11, 19, 22
6:7, 20[2]
7:10, 16, 18, 19, 26
8:18, 19, 21
9:3, 6, 24
10:19, 20, 24[2]
11:6, 9, 11, 14, 17, 18[2], 19, 20
12:1, 3[2], 8[2], 9, 11
13:1, 3, 5, 6, 8, 11[2], 22, 25[2]
14:11, 14
15:1[2], 6, 8, 10[4], 15[4], 16, 17, 18, 19
16:1, 11[2], 12
17:13, 14[2], 15, 16, 17, 18[3], 19, 24, 27
18:5, 15, 19[2], 22, 23[2]
19:4
20:7[2], 8, 11, 12, 14, 17[2]
22:6, 14, 16
23:9, 14, 17
24:1, 3, 4, 7[2]
25:3, 6, 7[2], 15, 17
26:3, 4, 12, 14[2], 15[2]
27:2, 5
28:1, 8
29:12[2], 13[3]
30:20, 21[2]
31:3, 18[2], 26, 34, 36[2]
32:6, 8[2], 25, 27, 29, 30[2], 31, 32, 33, 39, 40
33:3, 8[2], 9, 18, 22

JEREMIAH
34:14, 15, 17, 18
35:14, 15, 16, 19
36:18
37:7[2], 18, 20
38:14, 15[2], 19[2], 21, 26
39:18
40:4[2], 10, 15
42:9, 10, 20, 21
44:3, 8
45:3
49:4, 11, 19[3]
50:44[3]
51:1, 34[5], 35, 53

LAMENTATIONS
1:12[2], 13[2], 14, 15[2], 16, 19, 20, 21[2], 22
3:2[2], 3[2], 5[2], 6, 7, 10, 11[2], 12, 15[2], 16, 20, 52, 53, 60, 61, 62[2]

EZEKIEL
2:1, 2[4], 3[3], 9, 10
3:1, 2, 3, 4, 7, 10, 12[2], 14[3], 16, 17, 22[2], 24[4]
4:15, 16
6:1, 9[2]
7:1
8:1[2], 3[3], 5, 6, 7, 8, 9, 12, 13, 14, 15, 16, 17[2]
9:9, 10, 11
11:1[2], 2, 5[2], 14, 24[3], 25
12:1, 8, 17, 21, 26
13:1, 19
14:1[2], 2, 5, 7[2], 11, 12, 13
15:1
16:1, 20, 26, 43, 50
17:1, 11, 20
18:1
20:1, 2, 3, 8[2], 12, 13, 20, 21, 27[2], 38, 39, 40, 45, 49
21:1, 8, 18
22:1, 12, 17, 18, 23, 30
23:1, 35[2], 36, 37, 38
24:1, 15, 19, 20
25:1
26:1, 2
27:1
28:1, 11, 20
29:1, 17, 20
30:1, 9, 20
31:1
32:1, 17
33:1, 7, 21, 22[2], 23
34:1
35:1, 13[2]
36:16, 17
37:1[3], 2, 3, 4, 9, 10, 11, 15
38:1, 16
39:23, 26
40:1[2], 2[3], 3, 4, 17, 24, 28, 32, 35, 45, 48, 49
41:1, 4, 22
42:1[2], 13, 15
43:1, 5[2], 6[2], 7, 8, 9, 18, 19[2]
44:1, 2, 4, 5, 10[2], 13[2], 15[5], 16
46:19, 20, 21[2], 24
47:1, 2[2], 3, 4[2], 6[3], 8

DANIEL
1:10
2:5[2], 6[2], 8, 9[4], 23[2], 24, 26, 30[2]
4:2, 5[2], 6[2], 7, 8, 9, 18, 34, 36[4]
5:7, 15[2], 16
6:22[2]
7:15, 16[2], 28[3]
8:1[3], 14, 15, 17, 18[3]
9:21, 22[2]
10:7, 8[2], 10[2], 11[2], 12, 13[2], 15, 16[2], 17[3], 18[2], 19[2], 21

HOSEA
2:5, 7, 12, 13, 16[2], 19[2], 20, 23
3:1, 2, 3
4:6, 7
5:3, 15
6:7
7:7, 13[3], 14[2], 15
8:2, 4
11:7, 8, 12
12:8[2]
13:4[2], 6, 9, 10
14:8

JOEL
2:12
3:4[3]

AMOS
4:6, 8, 9, 10, 11
5:4, 22, 23, 25
7:1, 4, 7, 8, 15[2]
8:1, 2
9:7

OBADIAH
3

JONAH
1:2, 12[2]
2:2, 3[3], 5[2], 6, 7
4:3[2], 8

MICAH
2:4
5:2
6:3
7:1, 7, 8[2], 9[2], 10

HABAKKUK
1:3[3]
2:1[2], 2
3:14, 19

ZEPHANIAH
2:15
3:7, 8, 11

HAGGAI
2:14, 17

ZECHARIAH
1:3, 4, 9[2], 13, 14[2], 19[2], 20
2:2, 3, 8, 9, 11
3:1
4:1[2], 2, 4, 5[2], 6, 8, 9, 13
5:2, 3, 5[2], 10, 11
6:4, 5, 8[2], 9, 15
7:4, 5[2]
8:1, 14, 18
9:13
10:9
11:7, 8, 11, 12, 13, 15
12:10
13:5

MALACHI
2:5, 6
3:1, 5, 7, 8, 9, 10, 13

MATTHEW
2:8
3:11, 14
4:9, 19
7:4, 21, 22, 23
8:2, 9, 21, 22
9:9
10:32, 33, 37[4], 38[2], 40[3]
11:6, 27, 28, 29
12:30[3]
14:8, 18, 28, 30
15:5, 8[3], 9, 22, 25, 32
16:23[2], 24[2]
17:17, 27
18:5, 6, 21, 26, 28, 29, 32
19:14, 17, 21, 28
20:13, 15
21:2, 24
22:18, 19
23:39
25:20, 22, 35[3], 36[3], 40, 41, 42[2], 43[3], 45
26:10, 11, 15, 21, 23[2], 31, 34, 38, 39, 40, 42, 46, 53, 55[2], 75
27:10, 46
28:10, 18

MARK
1:7, 17, 40
2:14
5:7, 31
6:22, 23, 25
7:6[2], 7, 11, 14
8:2, 33, 34[2], 38
9:19, 37[4], 39, 42
10:14, 18, 21, 47, 48
11:29, 30
12:15[2]
14:6, 7, 18[2], 20, 27, 30, 36, 42, 48, 49, 72
15:34

LUKE
1:3, 25[2], 38, 43[2], 48, 49
2:49
4:6, 7, 8, 18[3], 23
5:8, 12, 27
6:42, 46, 47
7:8, 23, 42, 44, 45
8:28, 45[2], 46[2]
9:23[2], 26, 48[3], 59[2], 61
10:16[4], 22, 40[2]
11:5, 6, 7[2], 23[3]
12:8, 9, 13, 14
13:27, 35
14:18, 19, 26, 27
15:6, 9, 12[2], 19, 29, 31
16:3, 4, 24
17:8
18:3, 5[2], 13, 16, 19, 22, 38, 39
19:27
20:3, 23, 24
22:19, 21[2], 28, 29, 34, 37[2], 42, 53, 61, 68[2]
23:14, 28, 42, 43
24:39[2], 44

JOHN
1:15[3], 27[2], 30[3], 33[2], 43, 48
2:17
3:28
4:7, 9, 10, 15, 21, 29, 34, 39
5:7[2], 11[2], 24, 30, 32[2], 36[3], 37[2], 39, 40, 43, 46[2]
6:26, 35[2], 36, 37[3], 38, 39[2], 40, 44[2], 45, 47, 56, 57[3], 65
7:7, 16, 19, 23, 28[2], 29, 33, 34[2], 36[2], 37, 38
8:12, 16, 18[2], 19[2], 21, 26, 28, 29[3], 37, 40, 42[2], 45, 46[2], 49, 54
9:4, 11
10:8, 9, 15, 17, 18, 25, 27, 29, 32, 37, 38[2]
11:25, 26, 41, 42[2]
12:8, 26[3], 27, 30, 32, 44[3], 45[2], 46, 48, 49[2], 50
13:8, 13, 18[2], 20[3], 21, 33, 36[2], 38
14:1, 6, 7, 9[2], 10[2], 11[3], 12, 15, 19[2], 20, 21[2], 23, 24[2], 28, 30, 31
15:2, 4[2], 5[2], 6, 7, 9, 16, 18, 20, 21, 23, 24, 25, 26, 27
16:3, 5[2], 9, 10, 14, 16[2], 17[2], 19[2], 23, 27, 32[2], 33
17:4, 5, 6[2], 7, 8[2], 9, 11, 12, 18, 20, 21[2], 22, 23[2], 24[4], 25, 26

JOHN

18:8, 9, 11, 21[2], 23, 34, 35
19:10, 11[2]
20:15, 17, 21, 29
21:15, 16, 17[2], 19, 22

THE ACTS

1:4, 8
2:28[2], 29
3:22
5:8
7:7, 28, 37, 42, 49
8:19, 24[2], 31, 36
9:4, 6, 15, 17
10:28, 29, 30
11:5, 7, 9, 11, 12[2]
12:8, 11
13:2, 25
15:13
16:15
20:19, 22, 23, 24, 34
21:39
22:5, 6, 7[2], 8, 9[2], 10, 11, 13[2], 18[2], 21, 27
23:3[2], 11, 18[2], 19, 22, 30
24:12, 13, 18, 19, 20
25:5, 9, 11[2], 15, 24, 27
26:3, 5, 13[2], 14[2], 18, 21[2], 28, 29
27:21, 23, 25
28:18[3]

ROMANS

1:12, 15
7:8, 11[2], 13[2], 17, 18[2], 20, 21, 23, 24
8:2
9:1, 19, 20
10:20[2]
12:3
14:11
15:3, 15, 18, 30[2]
16:7

1 CORINTHIANS

1:11, 17
3:10
4:3, 4, 16
6:12[2]
7:1
9:3, 15[2], 16[2], 17
10:23[2]
11:1, 2, 24, 25
13:3
14:11, 21
15:8, 10[2], 32
16:4, 6, 9, 11, 21

2 CORINTHIANS

1:17, 19
2:2[2], 5, 12
7:7
9:1, 4
11:1[2], 9, 10[2], 16[2], 28, 32
12:1, 6[3], 7[2], 8, 9[2], 11, 13, 21
13:3, 10

GALATIANS

1:2, 11, 15[2], 16, 17, 24
2:1, 3, 6[2], 7, 8, 9[2], 20[3]
4:12, 14, 15, 21
6:14, 17

EPHESIANS

3:2, 3, 7, 8
6:19[2]

PHILIPPIANS

1:7, 12, 21, 26, 30[2]
2:18, 22, 23, 27, 30
3:1, 7, 17
4:3, 9, 10, 13, 15, 21

COLOSSIANS

1:25, 29
4:11, 18

1 TIMOTHY

1:12[3], 16

2 TIMOTHY

1:8, 13, 15, 16, 17[2], 18
2:2
3:11[2]
4:8[3], 9, 10, 11[2], 14, 16[2], 17[3], 18[2]

TITUS

1:3
3:12, 15

PHILEMON

11, 13[2], 16, 17, 19, 20, 22

HEBREWS

1:5
2:13
3:9[2]
8:10, 11
10:5, 7, 30, 34
11:32
13:6

JAMES

2:18

2 PETER

1:14

JUDE

3

REVELATION

1:10, 12, 17[2]
3:4, 18, 20, 21
4:1
5:5
7:13, 14
10:4, 8, 9[2], 11
11:1
14:13
17:1[2], 3, 7, 15
19:9[2], 10
21:5, 6, 9[2], 10[2], 15
22:1, 6, 8, 9, 10, 12

MY

1700 or 3450

GENESIS

2:23[2]
4:9, 13, 23[4]
6:3, 18
9:9, 11, 13, 15
12:13[2], 19
13:8
15:2, 3
16:2, 5[2], 8
17:2, 4, 7, 9, 10, 13, 14, 19, 21
18:3, 12
19:2, 8, 18, 19, 20, 34
20:2, 5[4], 9, 11, 12[4], 13[2], 15
21:10, 23[2], 30
22:7[2], 8, 18
23:4[2], 6, 8[2], 11[2], 13, 15
24:2, 3, 4[3], 6, 7[3], 8[2], 12[2], 14, 18, 27[3], 35, 36[2], 37[2], 38[3], 39, 40[3], 41[3], 42[2], 44, 48[3], 49, 54, 56[2], 65
26:5[5], 7[2], 9, 24
27:1, 2, 4, 7, 8[2], 11, 12, 13[2], 18[2], 19, 20, 21[2], 24, 25[2], 26, 27, 31, 34, 36[2], 37, 38[2], 41[2], 43[3], 46[2]
28:21[2]
29:4, 14[2], 15, 21[2], 32[2], 34
30:3[2], 6, 8, 15[2], 16, 18[3], 20, 23, 25, 26[3], 30, 32, 33[2]
31:5, 6, 7, 26, 28[2], 29, 30, 35, 36[2], 37[2], 39, 40, 41, 42[2], 43[4], 50[2]
32:4, 5, 9[2], 10, 11, 17, 18, 29, 30
33:8, 9, 10[2], 11, 13, 14[2], 15
34:8, 30
35:3
37:7[2], 16, 33, 35
38:11, 26
39:8[2], 15, 18
40:9, 11, 16[2], 17
41:9, 17, 22, 40[2], 51[2], 52
42:10, 28[2], 36, 37[2], 38[2]
43:3, 5, 9, 14, 29
44:2, 5, 7, 9, 10, 16[2], 17, 18[2], 19, 20, 22, 23, 24[2], 27[2], 29, 30, 32[2], 33, 34[2]
45:3, 9, 12[2], 13[3], 28
46:31[2]
47:1[2], 6, 9[3], 18[3], 25, 29, 30
48:9, 15[2], 16[2], 18, 19, 22[2]
49:3[3], 4, 6, 9, 26, 29[2]
50:5[3], 25

EXODUS

3:7, 10, 15[2], 20[2]
4:1, 10, 13, 18, 22[2], 23
5:1
6:3, 4, 5
7:3[2], 4[2], 16
8:1, 8, 20, 21, 22, 23
9:1, 13, 14, 15, 16[2], 17, 27, 29
10:1, 2, 3, 4, 17, 28[2]
11:9
12:31
13:15, 19
15:2[4], 9[3]
16:4, 28[2]
18:4, 19
19:5[2]
20:6, 24
21:5[3]
22:24, 25
23:18[2], 21, 27
25:2
29:43
31:13
32:10, 22, 33
33:12, 14, 17, 19, 20, 22[2], 23[2]
34:9, 25

LEVITICUS

6:17
15:31
17:10
18:4, 5[2], 26[2]
19:3, 12, 19, 30[2], 37[2]
20:3[3], 5, 6, 8, 22[2]
21:23
22:2, 3, 31, 32
23:2
25:18[2], 21, 42, 55
26:2[2], 3[2], 9, 11[2], 12, 15[4], 17, 25, 30, 42[3], 43[2], 44

NUMBERS

6:27
10:30
11:15, 23, 28, 29
12:6, 7, 8, 11
14:17, 22[3], 24, 34
15:40
20:19[2], 24
21:2
22:18, 38
23:10, 12
24:14
25:11[3], 12
27:14
28:2[3]
32:25, 27
36:2[2]

DEUTERONOMY

2:28
4:5, 10
5:10, 29
8:17
9:4, 15, 17
11:13, 18
18:16, 18, 19[2], 20
22:16, 17
25:7[2]
26:5, 14[2]
31:16, 17[2], 18, 20, 27, 29
32:1, 2[2], 20, 34, 39, 40, 41, 42

JOSHUA

1:2, 7
2:12, 13[4]
5:14
7:11, 19, 21
9:23
14:8[2], 9, 11[2]
15:16
22:2
24:15

JUDGES

1:3, 7, 12
2:1, 2, 20[2]
4:18
5:9, 21
6:10, 13, 15[3], 18
8:19[2], 23
9:9, 11[2], 13, 15, 17, 18, 29
11:7, 12, 13, 19, 31, 35[2], 36, 37[2]
12:2, 3[3]
13:8, 18
14:3, 16[3], 18[2]
15:1
16:13, 17[2], 28
17:2, 3[2], 13
18:24
19:23, 24
20:4, 5, 6, 23, 28

RUTH

1:11[2], 12, 13, 16[2]
2:2, 8[2], 13, 21[2], 22
3:1, 10, 11[2], 16, 18
4:4, 6, 10

1 SAMUEL

1:15[2], 16, 26[2], 27
2:1[2], 24, 28, 29[3], 32, 35
3:6, 16
4:16
9:5, 16[3], 17, 21
10:2
12:2[2], 5
14:29, 39, 40, 42
15:11, 25, 30
16:22
18:17, 18[2], 21
19:2, 3[2]
20:1[2], 2[2], 9, 12, 13[2], 15, 29[2], 42
21:2, 8[2], 15[2]
22:3[2], 8[3], 12, 15, 23
23:10, 12, 17[2]
24:6, 8, 10, 11[3], 15, 16, 21[3]
25:5, 11[4], 24, 25[2], 26[2], 27[2], 28[2], 29, 30, 31[3], 39, 41
26:17[3], 18, 19, 20, 21[2], 23, 24, 25
27:12
28:9, 21[2]
29:6, 8, 9
30:13, 15, 23

2 SAMUEL

1:9, 10, 26
2:22
3:7, 12, 13[2], 14, 18[2], 21, 28
4:8, 9
5:2
7:5, 7, 8[2], 10, 11, 13, 14, 15, 18
9:7, 10, 11[2]
11:11[3]
12:28
13:4, 5[2], 6[2], 11, 12, 13, 20, 25, 26, 32, 33
14:7[2], 9[2], 11, 12, 15, 16, 17[2], 18, 19[2], 20, 22, 24, 31
15:7, 15, 21[2]
16:3, 4, 9, 11[3]
18:5, 18, 22, 28, 31, 32, 33[5]
19:4[3], 12[3], 13[2], 19[2], 20, 26[2], 27[2], 28[2], 30, 35, 37[3]
20:9
22:2[3], 3[6], 7[4], 18, 19[2], 21[2], 22, 25[2], 29[2], 30, 33[2], 34[2], 35, 37[2], 39, 44, 47[2]
23:2, 5[3]
24:3[2], 17, 21, 22, 24

1 KINGS

1:2[2], 13[2], 17[2], 18, 20[2], 21[2], 24[2], 27[2], 29, 30[2], 31, 33, 35[2], 36, 37[2], 48
2:15, 20, 24, 26[2], 31, 32, 38, 44
3:6, 7[2], 14[3], 17, 20[2], 21[2], 22[2], 23[2], 26
5:3, 4, 5[3], 6, 9[3]
6:12[4], 13
8:15, 16[3], 17, 18[2], 19, 20, 24, 25[2], 26, 28, 29, 59
9:3, 4[2], 6[2], 7[2], 13
11:11[2], 13, 32, 33[3], 34[3], 36[2], 38[5]
12:10[2], 11[2], 14[2]
13:6, 30, 31
14:7, 8[2]
15:19
16:2[2]
17:1, 12, 18[2], 20, 21
18:7, 10, 12, 13
19:4[2], 10, 14, 20[2]
20:4, 6, 7[4], 9, 32, 34[2]
21:2, 3, 4, 6
22:4[2], 49

2 KINGS

1:13, 14
2:12[2], 19
3:7[2]
4:1[2], 16, 19[2], 28, 29[2]
5:3, 6, 13, 18[2], 20, 22
6:8, 12, 15, 21, 26, 28, 29
8:5, 12
9:7, 32
10:6, 9, 15, 16
13:14[2]
14:9
17:13[3]
18:23, 24, 27
19:12, 23, 24, 28[2], 34
20:5, 6, 15, 19
21:4, 7, 8, 15
22:17
23:27[2]

1 CHRONICLES

4:10
11:2[2], 19
16:22
17:4, 6, 7[2], 9, 10, 13[2], 14, 25
21:3[3], 17[2], 23
22:5, 7[3], 8[2], 10[2], 11, 14
28:2[2], 3, 4[3], 5[2], 6[3], 7[2], 9, 20
29:1, 2[2], 3[3], 14, 17, 19

2 CHRONICLES

1:8, 9, 11
2:3, 4, 7, 8, 13, 14, 15
6:4, 5[3], 6[2], 7, 8[2], 9, 10, 15, 16[3], 19, 40
7:13, 14[3], 16, 17[2], 19[2], 20[3]
8:11
10:10[2], 11[2], 14[2]
12:7, 8
16:3
18:3, 13
25:16, 18
29:11
32:13, 14, 15
33:4, 7
34:25

EZRA

7:13, 28
9:3[4], 5[6], 6[3]
10:3

NEHEMIAH

1:2, 6, 9[2]
2:3[2], 5, 8, 12[2], 18
4:16, 23[2]
5:10[2], 13, 14, 16, 17, 19
6:9, 14, 19
7:2, 5
13:14[3], 19, 22, 29, 31

ESTHER

4:16
5:7[2], 8[2]
7:3[4], 4[2]
8:6[2]

JOB

1:5, 8, 21
2:3
3:10, 24[2]
4:14, 15[2]
5:8
6:2[2], 3, 4, 7[2], 8, 11[2], 12[2], 13, 15, 21, 24, 29, 30[2]
7:5[2], 6, 7, 11[3], 13[3], 15[2], 16, 19, 21
9:14, 15, 16, 17, 18, 21[2], 25, 27[2], 28, 30
10:1[4], 6, 12, 15, 20
11:4
13:6[2], 14[3], 16, 17[2], 18, 19, 23[2], 26, 27[3]
14:14[2], 16[2], 17
16:4, 5[2], 6, 7, 8[2], 12, 13[2], 15[2], 16[2], 17, 18[2], 19[2], 20
17:1[2], 7, 11[3], 13, 14[3], 15[2]
19:2, 5, 8[2], 9[2], 12, 13, 14[2], 15, 16[2], 17[2], 19, 20[4], 21, 22, 23, 25, 26[2], 27
20:2, 3[2]
21:2, 4[2], 6
23:2[3], 4[2], 7, 11, 12, 16, 17
24:25
27:2[2], 3[2], 4[2], 6[2]
29:3, 4[2], 5, 6, 7, 14, 18[2], 19[2], 20[3], 21, 22[2], 24
30:1, 10, 11, 12[2], 13[2], 15[2], 16, 17[2], 18[3], 22, 25, 27, 30[2], 31[2]
31:4[2], 5, 7, 8, 9, 10, 13[2], 17, 18[2], 20, 21[2], 22, 24[2], 25, 27[3], 30, 31, 32, 33[2], 35, 36, 37, 38
32:17, 19, 20, 22
33:1[2], 2[3], 3[3], 7[2], 11[2]
34:2, 5, 6[2], 16, 36
35:2, 3, 10
36:3[2], 4
37:1
38:10
40:4, 8
42:7[2], 8[3]

PSALMS

2:6[2], 7
3:2, 3, 4, 7
4:1[2], 2, 7
5:1[2], 2[3], 3[2], 8
6:2, 3, 4, 6[4], 8, 9[2]
7:1[2], 2, 3[2], 5[2], 8, 10
9:1, 4[2], 13
11:1[2]
13:2[2], 3, 5
14:4
16:1, 2[3], 3, 4, 5[2], 7, 8, 9[3], 10
17:1[2], 2, 3, 5[2], 6, 9, 13
18:1, 2[8], 6[4], 17, 18[2], 20[2], 21, 24[2], 28[3], 29, 32, 33[2], 34, 36[2], 38, 46[2]
19:14[4]
22:1[3], 2, 9, 10[2], 14[3], 15[3], 16[2], 17, 18[2], 19, 20[2], 22, 25[2]
23:1, 3, 5[2], 6
25:1, 2, 5, 7[2], 15, 17[2], 18[2], 20[2]
26:2[2], 9[2], 12
27:1[3], 2[2], 3, 4, 7, 8[2], 9[2], 10[2]
28:1, 2[2], 6, 7[5]
30:1, 2, 3, 6, 7, 9, 10, 11[2], 12[2]
31:1, 2, 3[2], 4, 5, 7[2], 8, 9[2], 10[4], 11, 13, 14, 15, 22[2]
32:3[2], 4, 5[3], 7
34:1, 2, 4
35:1, 3, 4[2], 7, 9, 10, 11, 12, 13[3], 14, 17[2], 23[4], 24, 27, 28
36:1
38:3[3], 5[2], 7[2], 8, 9[2], 10[2], 11[4], 12[2], 15, 16, 17, 18, 21, 22
39:1[3], 2[2], 3[2], 4, 5, 7, 8, 9, 12[4]
40:1, 2[2], 3, 5, 8[2], 9, 10, 12, 14, 17[3]
41:4, 7, 9
42:1, 2, 3[2], 4, 5, 6[2], 8[2], 9, 10, 11[3]
43:1, 2, 4[2], 5[3]
44:4, 6[2], 15[2]
45:1[2]
49:3[2], 4, 5, 15
50:5, 7, 16[2], 17
51:1, 2, 3[2], 5, 9, 14[2], 15[2]
53:4
54:2[2], 3, 4
55:1[2], 2, 4, 8, 13, 17, 18
56:4, 5, 6[2], 8[2], 11, 13[2]
57:1[2], 4, 6[2], 7[2], 8
59:1, 3[3], 4, 9, 10[2], 11, 16[2], 17[3]
60:7, 8[2]
61:1[2], 2, 5, 8
62:1[2], 2[3], 5[2], 6[3], 7[4]
63:1[3], 3, 4, 5[2], 6, 7, 8, 9
64:1[3]
66:13, 14[2], 16, 17[2], 18, 19, 20
68:22, 24[2]
69:1, 3[3], 5[2], 6[2], 7, 8[2], 10[2], 11, 13, 18, 19[3], 20, 21[2]
70:2[2], 5[2]
71:1, 3[3], 4, 5[3], 6[2], 7, 8, 9, 10, 12[2], 13[2], 15, 17, 21, 22, 23[2], 24[2]
73:2[2], 13[2], 21[2], 23, 26[4], 28
74:12
77:1[2], 2[3], 3, 6[2], 10
78:1[3], 2
81:8, 11[2], 13[2], 14
83:13
84:2[3], 3[2], 8, 10
86:2[2], 4, 6[2], 7, 11, 12[2], 13, 14
87:7
88:1, 2[2], 3[2], 9, 13, 14, 15
89:1, 3[2], 20[2], 21, 24[3], 26[3], 27, 28[2], 30[2], 31[2], 33[2], 34[2], 35, 47, 50
91:2[3], 9, 14, 16
92:10, 11[2], 15
94:17[2], 18, 19[2], 22[3]
95:9, 10, 11[2]
101:2, 7[2]
102:1[2], 3[2], 4[2], 5[3], 9, 11, 23[2], 24[2]
103:1, 2, 22
104:1[2], 33[2], 34, 35
105:15
108:1[2], 8, 9[2]
109:1, 4[2], 5, 20, 22, 24[2], 26, 30
110:1[2]
111:1
116:1[2], 4, 7, 8[2], 11, 14, 16, 18
118:6, 7[2], 14[2], 21, 28[2]
119:5, 10, 13, 20, 24[2], 25, 26, 28, 32, 34, 36, 39, 43, 48, 50[2], 54[2], 57, 58, 59[2], 69, 76, 77, 80, 81, 92, 97, 99[2], 101, 103[2], 105[2], 108, 109[2], 111, 114[2], 115, 116, 120, 129, 131, 133, 139, 143, 145, 149, 154, 157, 161, 167, 168, 169, 170, 171, 172, 174, 175
120:1, 2, 6
121:1, 2
122:8
129:1, 2, 3
130:2[2], 5, 6
131:1, 2
132:3[2], 12[2], 14
137:5, 6[3]
138:1, 3
139:2[2], 3[3], 4, 8, 13[2], 14, 15, 16[2], 23[2]
140:4, 6[2], 7[2]
141:1, 2[2], 3[2], 4, 5[2], 6, 8[2]
142:1[3], 2[2], 3[2], 4[2], 5[2], 6[2], 7
143:1[2], 3[2], 4[2], 6[2], 7, 8, 10, 11, 12
144:1[3], 2[6]
145:1, 21
146:1, 2

PROVERBS

1:8, 10, 15, 23[3], 24, 25[2], 30[2]
2:1[3]
3:1[3], 11, 21
4:2, 3[2], 4[2], 5, 10[2], 20[3]
5:1[3], 7, 12, 13, 20
6:1, 3, 20
7:1[3], 2[2], 4, 6[2], 14, 16, 17, 24
8:4, 6, 7[2], 8, 10, 19[2], 31, 32, 34[2]
9:5
19:27
20:9[2]
22:17
23:15[2], 16, 19, 26[2]
24:13, 21
27:11[2]
30:9
31:2[3]

ECCLESIASTES

1:13, 16, 17
2:7, 9, 10[5], 11, 15[2], 18, 19, 20
4:8
7:15, 28
8:9
9:1
12:12

SONG OF SOLOMON

1:6, 7, 9, 12, 13[2], 14, 15, 16
2:2, 3[2], 6, 7, 8, 9, 10[3], 13[2], 14, 16, 17
3:1[2], 2, 3, 4[2], 5
4:1, 7, 8, 9[4], 10[2], 11, 12[2], 16[2]
5:1[9], 2[8], 3[2], 4[2], 5[3], 6[3], 7, 8, 10, 16[2]
6:2, 3[2], 4, 9[2], 12
7:9, 10, 11, 12, 13
8:1[2], 2[2], 3, 4, 10, 12, 14

ISAIAH

1:3, 12, 14, 25
3:7, 12[2], 15
5:1[3], 3, 4, 5, 13
6:7
7:13
8:4[4], 10
10:2, 6, 8, 10, 13[2], 14, 24
11:9
12:2[4]
13:3[3]
14:13, 25[2]
15:5
16:9, 11
18:4[2]
19:25[2]
20:3
21:3, 4[2], 8[2], 10[2]
22:4, 20
24:16[2]
25:1
26:9[2], 19, 20
27:5
28:23[2]
29:23
30:1, 2
32:9[2], 13, 18
33:13
34:5[2], 16
36:8, 9, 12, 19, 20[2]
37:12, 24, 25, 29[2], 35
38:10[2], 12, 13, 15[2], 16, 17[2], 20
39:4, 8
40:1, 27[3]
41:8[2], 9, 10, 25
42:1[3], 8[3], 14, 19[2]
43:4, 6[2], 7[2], 10[2], 12, 13, 20[2], 21
44:1, 2, 3[2], 8, 17, 20, 21[2], 28[2]
45:4, 11[2], 12, 13[2], 23
46:10[2], 11, 13[3]
47:6
48:3, 5[2], 9[2], 11[2], 12, 13, 18
49:1[2], 2, 3, 4[4], 5[2], 6[2], 11[2], 14, 16, 21, 22
50:1, 2[2], 6[3], 7
51:4[3], 5[2], 6[2], 7, 8[2], 16[2], 22
52:4, 5[2], 6[2], 13
53:8, 11
54:8, 10[2]
55:8[2], 9[2], 11[2]
56:1[2], 4[2], 5, 6, 7[2]

ISAIAH
57:11, 13, 14, 21
58:1, 2, 13
59:21^3
60:7, 10^2, 13^2, 21^2
61:10^2
62:1, 9
63:3^3, 4, 5, 6, 8
65:1, 2, 3, 5, 8, 9^2, 10, 11, 13^3, 14, 15, 19, 22, 25
66:1^3, 2, 5, 18, 19^3, 20

JEREMIAH
1:9^2, 12, 16
2:7, 11, 13, 19, 27, 31, 32
3:4^2, 13, 19
4:1, 4, 11, 19^6, 20^2, 22, 31
5:9, 14, 22, 26, 29, 31
6:8, 12, 14, 19^2, 26, 27
7:10, 11, 12^3, 14, 15, 20, 23^2, 25, 30^2, 31
8:7, 11, 18, 19, 21, 22
9:1^2, 2, 7, 9, 13^2
10:19^2, 20^5
11:4^2, 7, 10^2, 15, 20
12:7, 10^3, 14, 16^4
13:2, 10, 17
14:14, 15, 17
15:1^2, 6, 7, 10, 15, 18^2, 19
16:5, 11, 17, 18, 19^3, 21^2
17:3, 14, 16, 17
18:2, 10^2, 15, 20, 22
19:5, 15
20:9, 10^2, 11, 12, 14, 15, 17^2, 18
21:10, 12
22:18, 21, 24
23:1, 2^2, 3, 9, 11, 13, 22^3, 25, 27^3, 28^2, 29, 30, 32, 39
24:7
25:8, 9, 13, 15, 29
26:4, 5
27:5^2, 6, 15
29:9, 10, 19^2, 21, 23, 32
30:3, 10, 22
31:1, 9, 14^2, 18, 19^2, 20^2, 26, 32, 33^2
32:7, 8, 9, 31^2, 34, 35, 37, 38, 40, 41^2
33:5^2, 20^2, 21^3, 22, 24, 25, 26
34:15^2, 16, 18
35:13, 15
36:6
37:20^2
38:9, 26
39:16
42:18^2
43:10
44:4, 6, 10^2, 11, 26^2, 29
45:3^2
46:27, 28
49:25, 37, 38
50:6
51:20, 34, 35^2, 45

LAMENTATIONS
1:9, 12, 13^2, 14^3, 15^2, 16^2, 18^3, 19^2, 20, 21, 22^3
2:11^3, 21^2, 22
3:4^3, 7, 8, 9^2, 11, 13, 14, 16, 17, 18^2, 19, 20, 21, 24^2, 48, 51, 53, 56^3, 58^2, 59^2
4:3, 6, 10

EZEKIEL
1:28
2:2, 7
3:2, 3, 4, 10, 14, 17, 23, 24
4:14^3
5:6^4, 7^2, 11, 13^3
6:12, 14
7:8, 14, 22^2
8:6
9:6, 8
10:2, 13, 19
11:12^2, 13, 20^2
12:7^2, 13^2, 28
13:9, 10, 13^2, 15, 18, 19^2, 21, 23
14:8^2, 9^2, 11, 19, 21
15:7^2
16:8, 14, 17^2, 19, 21, 27, 42^2, 60, 62
17:19, 20^2
18:9^2, 17^2, 19, 21, 25, 29
20:8^2, 9, 11^2, 12, 13^4, 14, 15, 16^3, 19^2, 20, 21^5, 22, 24^3, 39, 44
21:3, 4, 5, 10, 12^2, 17, 31
22:8, 20, 21, 22, 26^2, 31
23:18^2, 25, 38^2, 39
24:13, 18, 21
25:3, 14^4, 17
28:25
29:3
30:15, 24, 25
32:3^2, 10, 32
33:7, 22^2, 31
34:6^2, 8^5, 10^2, 11, 12, 15, 17, 19, 22, 23, 24, 26, 30, 31^2
36:5^2, 6^2, 8, 12, 18, 20, 23, 27^3, 28
37:12, 13, 14, 23, 24^3, 25^2, 26, 27^2, 28
38:14, 16^2, 17, 18^2, 19^2, 20, 21
39:7^3, 17, 19, 20, 21^3, 23, 24, 25, 29^2
43:3, 7^3, 8^3
44:4, 7^5, 8^2, 9, 11, 13, 15, 16^3, 23, 24^4
45:8^2, 9
46:18
48:11

DANIEL
1:10^2
2:3, 23
3:14, 15
4:4, 5^2, 8, 9, 10, 13^2, 18, 19, 24, 27, 30^2, 36^3
5:13
6:22, 26
7:2, 15^3, 28^3
8:17, 18
9:3, 4^2, 18, 19, 20^5
10:3, 8, 9^2, 10^2, 15, 16^4, 17^2, 19
12:8

HOSEA
1:9, 10
2:2, 5^6, 7, 9^4, 12^2, 23^3
4:6, 8, 12
5:10, 15^2
6:5, 11
7:2, 12
8:1^2, 2, 12
9:8, 17
10:10
11:1, 7, 8
12:8
13:11

JOEL
1:6, 7^2, 13
2:1, 25, 26, 27, 28, 29
3:2^3, 3, 5^3, 17

AMOS
2:7
7:8, 15
8:2
9:3, 10, 12, 14

OBADIAH
13, 16

JONAH
1:12
2:2, 5, 6^2, 7^2
4:2^3, 3

MICAH
1:9
2:4, 7, 8, 9^2
3:3, 5
6:3, 5, 7^4, 16
7:1, 7^2, 9

HABAKKUK
1:12
2:1
3:16^3, 18, 19^3

ZEPHANIAH
2:8, 9^2, 12
3:8^3, 10^2, 11

HAGGAI
2:5, 23

ZECHARIAH
1:6^3, 9, 16, 17
2:11
3:7^4, 8
4:4, 5, 6, 13
5:4
6:4, 8
8:7, 8
11:4, 8, 10^2, 12^2
12:5
13:5, 6, 7^2, 9^3
14:5

MALACHI
1:6^2, 11^3, 14
2:2, 4, 5^2, 9
3:1, 17
4:2, 4

MATTHEW
2:6, 15
3:17
5:11
7:21
8:6, 8^2, 9, 21
9:18
10:18, 22, 32, 33, 39
11:10, 27, 29, 30^2
12:18^4, 44, 48^2, 49^2, 50^2
13:30, 35
15:13, 22
16:17, 18, 25
17:5, 15
18:5, 10, 19, 20, 21, 35
19:20, 29
20:21, 23^4
21:13, 28, 37
22:4^3, 44^2
24:5, 9, 35, 36, 48
25:27^2, 34, 40
26:12^2, 18^2, 26, 28, 29, 38, 39, 42, 53
27:35^2, 46^2
28:10

MARK
1:2, 11
3:33^2, 34^2, 35^2
5:9, 23, 30
6:23
8:35, 38
9:7, 17, 37, 39, 41
10:20, 29, 40^2, 51
11:17
12:6, 36^2
13:6, 9, 13, 31
14:8, 14, 22, 24, 34
15:34^2
16:17

LUKE
1:18, 20, 25, 43, 44, 46, 47^2
2:49
3:22
6:47
7:6, 7, 8, 27, 44^2, 45, 46^2
8:21^2
9:24, 26, 35, 38, 48, 59, 61
10:22, 29, 40
11:7, 24
12:4, 13, 17, 18^3, 19, 45
14:23, 24, 26, 27, 33
15:6, 17, 18, 24, 29
16:3, 5, 24, 27
18:21, 41
19:8, 23^2, 46
20:13, 42^2
21:8, 12, 17, 33
22:11, 19, 20, 28, 29, 30^2, 42
23:46
24:39^2, 49

JOHN
2:16
3:29
4:34, 49
5:17, 24, 30, 31, 43, 47
6:32, 51, 54^2, 55^2, 56^2, 65
7:6, 8, 16
8:14, 16, 19^2, 21, 28, 31^2, 37, 38, 43^2, 49, 51, 52, 54^2, 56
10:14, 15, 16, 17^2, 18, 25, 26, 27^2, 28, 29^2, 30, 32, 37
11:21, 32
12:7, 26^2, 27, 47, 48
13:6, 8, 9^3, 35, 37, 38
14:2, 7, 12, 13, 14, 15, 20, 21^2, 23^2, 24, 26, 27, 28
15:1, 7, 8^2, 9, 10^3, 11, 12, 14, 15, 16, 20, 21, 23, 24
16:5, 10, 23, 24, 26
17:13, 24
18:11, 36^4, 37
19:24^2
20:13, 17^4, 21, 25^2, 27^2, 28^2
21:15, 16, 17

THE ACTS
2:14, 17, 18^3, 25^2, 26^3, 27, 34^2
7:34, 49^3, 50, 59
9:15, 16
10:30
11:8
13:22, 33
15:7, 17, 19
16:15
20:24^2, 25, 29, 34
22:1, 6
24:14, 17
25:26
26:4^2, 10
28:19

ROMANS
1:8, 9^3
2:16
3:7
7:4, 18, 23^3
9:1, 2, 3^2, 17^2, 25^2, 26
10:1, 21
11:3, 14, 27
15:14, 24^3, 31
16:3, 4, 5, 7^2, 8, 9, 11, 21^2, 25

1 CORINTHIANS
1:4, 11
2:4^2
4:14, 17^2
5:4
7:25, 40
8:13^2
9:1, 15, 17, 18^2, 27
10:14, 29
11:24, 25, 33
13:3^2
14:14^2, 18, 19^2
15:58
16:6, 18, 24

2 CORINTHIANS
1:16, 23
2:3, 13^3
6:13, 16, 18
7:4^2
8:10, 23
11:1
12:9^3, 21

GALATIANS
1:13, 14^2, 15
4:14^2, 19, 20
6:17

EPHESIANS
1:16
3:4, 13, 14
6:10, 19, 21

PHILIPPIANS
1:3, 7^3, 8, 13, 14, 16, 19, 20^3, 22, 26
2:2, 12^3, 25^2
3:1, 8
4:1^3, 3, 14, 16, 19

COLOSSIANS
1:24^2
2:1
4:7, 10, 11, 18

1 TIMOTHY
1:2, 11

2 TIMOTHY
1:2, 3^2, 6, 16
2:1, 8
3:10
4:6, 7, 16

PHILEMON
4^2, 10^2, 20, 23, 24

HEBREWS
1:5, 13
2:12, 13
3:9, 10, 11^2
4:3^2, 5
5:5
8:9, 10
10:16, 34, 38
12:5
13:6

JAMES
1:2, 16, 19
2:1, 3, 5, 14, 18^2
3:1, 10, 12
5:10, 12

1 PETER
5:13

2 PETER
1:14, 15, 17

1 JOHN
2:1
3:13, 18

3 JOHN
4

REVELATION
1:20
2:3, 13^3, 16, 20, 26, 27
3:5, 8^2, 10, 12^5, 16, 20, 21^2
10:10^2
11:3
18:4
21:7
22:12

NOT 3808, *3756*

GENESIS
2:5^2, 17, 18, 20, 25
3:1, 3, 4, 11, 17
4:5, 7^2, 9, 12
5:24
6:3
7:2, 8
8:12, 21, 22
9:4, 23
11:7
12:18
13:6^2, 9
14:23^2
15:1, 4, 10, 13, 16
16:10
17:12, 14, 15
18:3, 15, 21, 24, 25, 28, 29, 30^2, 31, 32^2
19:7, 8, 17, 18, 20, 21, 31, 33, 35
20:4, 5, 6, 7, 9, 11, 12
21:10, 12, 16, 17, 23, 26
22:12^2, 16
24:3, 5, 6, 8^2, 21, 27, 33, 37, 39, 41, 49, 56
26:2, 22, 24, 29
27:1, 2, 12, 21, 23, 36^2
28:1, 6, 8, 15, 16
29:25, 26
30:31, 33, 40, 42
31:2, 5, 7, 15, 20, 24, 27, 28, 29, 32^2, 33, 34, 35^2, 38^2, 39, 52^2
32:10, 25, 26, 32
34:7, 17, 19, 23
35:5, 10, 17
36:7
37:4, 13, 21, 27, 29, 30
38:9, 14, 16, 20, 23, 26
39:6, 8, 10, 23
40:8, 23
41:16, 21, 31, 36
42:2, 4, 8, 13, 15, 20, 21, 22^3, 23, 32, 36^2, 37, 38
43:3, 5^3, 8, 9, 23, 32
44:4, 5, 15, 18, 26, 28, 30, 31, 32, 34
45:1, 3, 5, 8, 9, 20, 24, 26
46:3
47:9, 18^2, 19^2, 22^2, 26, 29
48:10, 11, 18
49:4, 6^2, 10
50:19, 21

EXODUS
1:8, 17, 19
2:3
3:2, 3, 5, 19^2, 21
4:1^2, 8, 9, 10, 11, 14, 21
5:2, 8, 9, 10, 11, 14, 19
6:3, 9, 12
7:4, 13, 16, 21, 24
8:15, 18, 19, 21, 26^2, 28, 29^2, 31
9:6, 7^2, 11, 12, 17, 18, 19, 21, 30, 32^2, 33
10:7, 11, 15, 19, 20, 23, 26^2, 27
11:7, 9, 10
12:9, 13, 23, 30^2, 39^2, 45, 46
13:13, 17, 22
14:12, 13, 20, 28
15:23
16:8, 15, 20, 24, 25
17:7
18:17, 18
19:12, 13^2, 15, 24
20:4, 5, 7^2, 10, 13, 14, 15, 16, 17^2, 19, 20^2, 23, 25, 26
21:5, 7, 8, 10, 11, 13, 18, 21, 28, 29, 33, 36
22:8, 11^2, 13, 14, 15, 16, 18, 22, 25, 28, 29
23:1^2, 2, 6, 7^2, 9, 18, 19, 21^2, 24, 29, 33
24:2, 11
25:15
28:28, 32, 35, 43
29:33, 34
30:15^2, 20, 21, 32, 37
32:1, 18, 22, 23, 32
33:3, 11, 12, 15^2, 16, 20, 23
34:10, 20, 25, 26, 29
39:21, 23
40:35, 37^2

LEVITICUS
1:17
2:12
4:2, 13, 22, 27
5:1, 7, 8, 11, 17, 18
6:12, 17, 23
7:15, 18, 19
8:33, 35
10:1, 6, 7, 9, 17, 18
11:4^2, 5, 6, 7, 8^2, 10, 11, 13, 26, 41, 42, 43, 47
12:8
13:4^2, 5, 6, 11, 21, 23, 28, 31, 32^2, 33, 34, 36, 53, 55^2
14:32, 36, 48
15:11, 31
16:2^2, 13, 22
17:4, 9, 16
18:3^2, 7^2, 8, 9, 10, 11, 12, 13, 14^2, 15^2, 16, 17, 19, 20, 21, 22, 24, 26, 28, 30^2
19:4, 7, 9, 10, 11, 12, 13^2, 14, 15, 16, 17^2, 18, 19^2, 20^3, 23, 26, 27, 28, 29, 31, 33
20:4, 19, 22, 23, 25
21:4, 5, 6, 7, 10, 14, 17, 18, 21, 23^2
22:2, 4, 6, 8, 10, 12, 15, 20^2, 22, 23, 24, 25, 28
23:22, 29
25:5, 11, 14, 17, 20, 23, 28, 30^2, 34, 37, 39, 42, 43, 46, 53, 54
26:11, 13, 14^2, 15, 18, 20, 21, 23, 26, 27, 31, 35, 44
27:10, 11, 20^2, 22, 27, 33^2

NUMBERS
1:47, 49
2:33
4:15, 18, 19, 20
5:3, 14, 19, 28
6:7
9:6, 7, 13^2, 19, 22
10:7, 30, 31
11:11, 14, 15, 17, 19, 23, 25, 26
12:2, 7, 8^2, 11, 12, 14, 15
13:20, 31
14:3, 9^2, 16, 22, 23, 30, 41, 42^3, 43, 44
15:22, 34, 39
16:12, 14^2, 15^2, 28, 29, 40^2
17:10
18:3, 4, 17
19:12^2, 13^2, 20^2
20:12^2, 17^2, 18, 20, 24
21:22^2, 23, 34
22:12^2, 30, 34, 37^3
23:8^2, 9, 12, 13, 19^3, 21, 24, 26
24:1, 12, 17^2
25:11
26:11, 62, 64, 65
27:3, 17
29:7
30:2, 5, 11, 12
31:18, 23, 35, 49
32:5, 9, 11, 18, 19, 23, 30
33:55
35:12, 23^2, 27, 30, 33, 34
36:7

DEUTERONOMY
1:9, 17^2, 21, 26, 29, 32, 35, 37, 42^2, 43, 45
2:5^3, 9^2, 19^2, 30, 36, 37
3:2, 4^2, 11, 22, 26, 27
4:2, 21^2, 22, 26, 31, 42
5:3, 5, 8, 9, 11^2, 14, 17, 32
6:10, 11^3, 14, 16
7:3, 7, 10, 14, 18, 21, 22, 25
8:3^2, 4, 9, 11^2, 16, 20
9:4, 5, 6, 7, 23, 26, 27, 28
10:10, 17
11:2^3, 10, 16, 17, 28^2, 30
12:4, 8, 9, 13, 16, 17, 19, 23^2, 24, 25, 30^2, 31, 32
13:2, 3, 6, 8, 13, 16
14:1, 3, 7^2, 8^2, 10^2, 12, 19, 21^2, 24, 27
15:2, 6^2, 7, 9, 10, 13, 16, 18, 21, 23
16:5, 16, 19^2, 21
17:1, 3, 6, 11, 12, 15^2, 16, 17, 20^2
18:9, 10, 14, 16^2, 19, 20, 21, 22^3
19:4, 6^2, 10, 13, 14, 15, 21
20:1, 3^3, 5, 6, 7, 15, 18, 19^2, 20
21:1, 3^2, 7, 8, 14^2, 16, 18^2, 20, 23^2
22:1, 2^2, 3, 4, 5, 6, 8, 9, 10, 11, 14, 17, 19, 20, 24, 28, 29, 30
23:1, 2^2, 3^2, 4, 5, 6, 7^2, 10^2, 15, 16, 18, 19, 20, 21, 24, 25
24:4^2, 5, 10, 12, 14, 16, 17, 19, 20, 21
25:3, 4, 5, 6, 7^2, 8, 9, 12, 13, 14, 18, 19
26:13, 14
27:5, 26
28:12, 13^2, 14, 15, 27, 29, 30^2, 31^2, 33, 40, 41, 44, 45, 47, 49, 50, 51, 55, 56, 58, 61, 62
29:4, 5^2, 6, 15, 20, 23, 26^2
30:11, 12, 17, 18
31:2, 6^2, 8^2, 13, 17^2, 21
32:5, 6^2, 17^3, 21^2, 27^2, 31, 34, 47, 51, 52
33:6^2, 9, 11
34:4, 7, 10

JOSHUA
1:5^2, 7, 8, 9^2, 18
2:4, 5, 14, 22
3:4^2
5:5, 6^2, 7
6:10
7:3^2, 12, 13, 19
8:1, 4, 14, 17^2, 26, 35^2
9:14, 18, 19, 26
10:6, 8^2, 13^2, 19^2, 25
11:6, 11, 19
13:13, 33
15:63
16:10
17:12, 13, 16, 17
18:2
20:5^2, 9
21:44, 45
22:3, 17, 19, 20^2, 22, 24, 26, 27, 28, 31, 33
23:6, 7, 14^2
24:10, 12, 13^3, 19

JUDGES
1:19, 21, 28, 32, 34
2:2, 3, 10, 14, 17^2, 19, 20, 21, 22
3:1, 22, 25, 28, 29
4:6, 8^2, 9, 14, 16, 18
5:23, 30^2
6:10^2, 13, 14, 18, 23^2, 27, 39
7:4^2
8:1, 2, 19, 20, 23, 34
9:15, 20, 28, 38, 41, 54
10:6, 11
11:2, 7, 10, 15, 17^2, 18, 20, 24, 26, 27, 28
12:1, 2, 3, 6
13:2, 3, 4^2, 6, 9, 14, 16^2, 23
14:4, 6, 9, 14, 15, 16^3, 18^2
15:1, 2, 11, 12, 13
16:8, 9, 15^2, 17, 20
18:1, 9, 25
19:10, 12^2, 20, 23^2, 24, 25
20:8, 13, 16, 34
21:1, 5^2, 7, 8, 14, 17, 18, 22^2

RUTH
1:16, 20
2:8^2, 9^2, 11, 13, 15, 16, 20, 22
3:1, 2, 3, 10, 11, 13, 14, 17, 18
4:4, 10, 14

1 SAMUEL
1:7, 8^2, 11, 13, 16, 22^2
2:3, 12, 15, 16^2, 25, 31, 32, 33
3:2, 5, 6, 7, 13, 14, 17
4:7, 9, 15, 20^2
5:7, 11, 12
6:3^2, 6, 9^2, 12
7:8
8:3, 5, 7^2, 18
9:2, 4^3, 7, 13, 20^2, 21
10:1, 16, 21
11:7, 11, 13
12:4, 5, 14, 15, 17, 19, 20^2, 21, 22
13:8, 11, 12, 13, 14^2
14:1, 3, 9, 17, 27, 30, 34, 36, 37, 39, 45^2
15:3, 9, 11, 17, 19, 26, 29^2
16:7^2, 10, 11
17:8, 29, 33, 39^2, 47
18:17, 25, 26
19:4^2, 6, 11
20:2^2, 3, 5, 9, 12, 14^2, 15^2, 26^3, 27, 29, 30, 31, 37, 38, 39
21:8, 11^2
22:5, 15, 17^2, 23
23:14, 17^2, 19
24:7, 10, 11^2, 12, 13, 18, 21^2
25:7, 11, 15, 19, 25^2, 28, 34
26:1, 8, 9, 14, 15^2, 16^2, 20, 23
28:6, 13, 18, 23
29:3, 4^2, 5, 6^2, 7, 8, 9
30:2, 10, 17, 21, 22^2, 23
31:4

2 SAMUEL
1:10, 14, 20^2, 21, 22^2, 23
2:19, 21, 26
3:8, 11, 13, 22, 26, 29, 34, 37, 38
4:11
5:6, 8, 23
6:10
7:6, 7, 15
9:3, 7
10:3
11:3, 9, 10^3, 11, 13, 20, 21, 25
12:13, 17, 18, 23
13:4, 12^2, 13, 14, 16, 20, 25^2, 26, 28^2, 30, 32, 33
14:2, 7, 10, 11^2, 13, 14, 18, 19, 24^2, 28, 29^2
15:11, 14, 27, 35
16:17, 19
17:6, 7, 8, 12, 13, 16, 17, 19, 20, 22^2, 23
18:3^2, 11, 12, 14, 20, 29
19:7^2, 10, 13^2, 19, 21, 22, 23, 25, 43
20:3, 10, 21
21:2, 17
22:22, 23, 37, 38, 39, 42, 44
23:5^2, 16, 17^2, 19^2, 23
24:14

1 KINGS
1:4, 6, 8, 10, 11^2, 13, 18, 19, 26, 27, 51, 52
2:4, 6, 8, 9, 16, 17, 20^2, 23, 26, 28, 32, 36, 42, 43
3:7, 11, 13^2, 21
5:3, 6
6:6, 13
7:31
8:5, 8, 11, 19, 25, 41, 46, 56, 57
9:5, 6, 12, 20, 21
10:[illegible]
11:2, 4, 6, 10^2, 11, 12, 13, 33, 34, 39, 41
12:15, 16, 24, 31
13:4, 8, 10, 16, 21, 22, 28, 33
14:2, 4, 8, 29
15:3, 5, 7, 14, 17, 23, 29, 31
16:5, 11, 14, 20, 27
17:1, 12, 13, 14, 16
18:5, 10^3, 12, 13, 18, 21, 40, 44
19:2, 4, 11^2, 12, 18^2
20:7, 8, 9, 11, 28, 36
21:4, 6, 15, 29
22:3, 7, 8^2, 17, 18, 28, 33, 39, 43^2, 45, 48, 49

2 KINGS
1:3^2, 4, 6^3, 15, 16^2, 18
2:2, 4, 6, 10^2, 16, 17, 18^2, 21
3:2, 3, 11, 14^2, 17, 26
4:2, 3, 6, 16, 24, 27, 28^2, 29^2, 30, 31, 39, 40
5:12^2, 13, 17, 20, 26
6:9, 10, 11, 16, 19, 22, 27, 32
7:2, 9, 19
8:19, 23
9:3, 18, 20, 37
10:4, 5, 19, 21^2, 29, 31, 34
11:2, 6, 15
12:3, 6, 7, 13, 15, 16, 19
13:2, 6, 8, 11, 12, 23
14:3, 4, 6^2, 11, 15, 18, 24, 26, 27, 28
15:4, 6, 9, 16, 18, 20, 21, 24, 28, 35, 36
16:2, 5, 19
17:2, 9, 12, 14^2, 15, 19, 22, 25, 26^2, 34, 35, 37, 38, 40
18:6, 7, 12^2, 22, 26, 27, 29^2, 30, 31, 32^2, 36^2
19:3, 6, 10^2, 25, 32, 33
20:1, 13, 15, 19, 20
21:9, 17, 22, 25
22:2, 13, 17, 20
23:9, 22, 26, 28, 33
24:4, 5, 7
25:24

1 CHRONICLES
4:10, 27
5:1
10:4, 13, 14
11:5, 18, 19, 21, 25
12:19, 33
13:3, 13
14:14
15:13^2
16:22, 30
17:4, 5, 6, 13
19:3
21:3, 6, 13, 17^2, 24, 30
22:8, 13, 18^2
23:11
26:10
27:23, 24
28:3, 20^2
29:1, 25

2 CHRONICLES
1:11
4:18
5:6, 9, 11, 14
6:9, 16, 32, 36, 42
7:2, 7, 18
8:7, 8, 11, 15
9:2, 6^2, 19, 20, 29
10:15, 16
11:4
12:7^2, 12, 14, 15
13:5, 7, 9, 10, 12^2
14:11, 13
15:7, 13, 17
16:7, 8, 12
17:3, 4
18:6, 7, 17^2, 27, 30, 32
19:6, 10^2
20:6^3, 7, 10^2, 12, 15^2, 17^2, 32, 33^2, 37
21:7, 12, 20
22:11
23:8, 14
24:5, 6, 19, 22, 25
25:2, 4^2, 7^2, 13, 15, 16, 20, 26
26:18
27:2
28:1, 10, 13, 20, 21, 27
29:7, 11, 34
30:3^2, 5, 7, 8, 9, 17^2, 18, 19, 26
32:7, 11, 12, 13, 15, 17^2, 25, 26
33:10, 23
34:21, 25, 33
35:3, 15, 21^2, 22^2
36:12

EZRA
2:59, 62, 63
3:6, 13
4:13, 14, 21, 22
5:5, 16
6:8
7:24, 25, 26
9:1, 9, 12, 14
10:8, 13

NEHEMIAH
1:7
2:1, 2, 3, 16
3:5
4:5^2, 10, 11, 14
5:9^2, 13, 14, 15, 18
6:1, 9, 11, 12
7:3, 4, 61, 64, 65
8:9, 17
9:16, 17, 19^2, 20, 21^2, 29^2, 30, 31, 32, 35
10:30, 31, 39
13:1, 2, 6, 10, 14, 18^2, 19, 24, 25, 26

ESTHER
1:15, 16, 17, 19
2:10^2, 20
3:2, 4, 5, 8
4:4, 11^2, 13, 16
5:9
6:1, 13
7:4
9:10, 15, 16, 27, 28
10:2

JOB
1:10, 12, 22
2:10^2, 12
3:4, 6^2, 10, 11^2, 16, 18, 21, 26
4:6, 16, 21
5:6, 17, 24
6:10^2, 13, 29
7:1^2, 8, 11, 16, 19, 21^2
8:10, 12, 15^2, 18, 20
9:5, 7, 11^2, 13, 15, 16, 18, 21, 24, 28, 32, 34, 35^2
10:2, 7, 10, 14, 15, 19, 20, 21
11:2, 11, 14, 15, 20
12:3^2, 9, 11
13:2, 11, 16, 20^2, 21
14:2, 4, 7, 12^2, 16, 21^2
15:6, 9^2, 15, 18, 22, 29, 30, 31, 32
16:6, 13, 17, 18, 22
17:2^2, 4
18:5, 21
19:3, 7, 22, 27
20:4, 8, 13, 17, 18^2, 19, 20^2, 26
21:4, 10^2, 14, 16, 29^2
22:5, 7, 11, 12, 14, 20
23:8, 11, 17
24:1^2, 12, 13, 16, 18, 21^2, 25
25:3, 5^2
26:8
27:4, 5, 6^2, 11, 14, 15, 19^2, 22

JOB
28:7, 8, 13, 14^2, 17, 19
29:16, 22, 24^2
30:10, 20^2, 24, 25^2, 27
31:3, 4, 15^2, 17, 20^2, 23, 31, 32, 34
32:6, 9, 13, 14, 16, 21, 22
33:7, 12, 13, 14, 21, 27, 33
34:12, 19, 23, 27, 30, 31, 32, 33
35:13, 14, 15^2
36:4, 5, 6, 7, 12, 13, 19, 20, 21, 26, 32
37:4, 21, 23, 24
39:4, 16, 22
40:5, 23
41:9, 12, 33
42:3^2, 7, 8

PSALMS
1:1, 3, 4, 5
3:6
4:4
5:4, 5
6:1
7:12
9:10, 12, 18^2, 19
10:4^2, 6, 12, 13
14:3, 4
15:3, 4, 5
16:2, 4, 8, 10
17:1, 3, 5
18:21, 22, 36, 38, 41, 43
19:3, 13
21:2, 7, 11
22:2^2, 5, 11, 19, 24
23:1
24:4
25:2^2, 7, 20
26:1, 4, 5, 9
27:3, 9^3, 12
28:1, 3, 5^2
30:1, 3, 12
31:8, 17
32:2, 5, 6, 9
33:16
34:5, 10, 20
35:11, 15^2, 19, 20, 22^2, 24, 25^2
36:4^2, 11^2, 12
37:1, 7, 8, 10^2, 19, 21, 24, 25, 28, 33, 36^2
38:1, 9, 13^2, 14, 21^2
39:1, 6, 8, 9, 12
40:4, 6^2, 9, 10^2, 11, 12
41:2, 11
44:3, 6, 9, 12, 17, 18, 21, 23
46:2, 5
49:9, 12, 16, 17, 20
50:3, 8, 12
51:11^2, 16^2, 17
52:7
53:3, 4
54:t, 3
55:1, 11, 12, 19, 23
56:4, 8, 11, 13
58:5, 8
59:3, 5, 11, 13, 15
60:10^2
62:2, 6, 10^3
64:4
66:7, 9, 18, 20
69:4, 5, 6^2, 14, 15^2, 17, 23, 27, 28, 33
71:9^2, 12, 15, 18
73:5
74:9, 19^2, 21, 23
75:4^2, 5^2
77:2, 19
78:4, 7, 8^3, 10, 22^2, 30, 32, 37, 38^2, 39, 42, 44, 50, 53, 56, 63, 67
79:6^2, 8
80:18
81:5, 11
82:5
83:1^3
85:6, 8
86:14
89:22, 30, 31, 33, 34, 35, 43, 48
91:5, 7
92:6
94:7, 9^2, 10^2, 14
95:8, 10, 11
96:10
100:3
101:3, 4, 5, 7^2
102:2, 17, 24
103:2, 9, 10
104:5, 9^2
105:15, 28, 37
106:7^2, 11, 13, 23, 24, 25, 34
107:38
108:11^2
109:1, 14, 16, 17
110:4
112:6, 7, 8
115:1^2, 5^2, 6^2, 7^2, 17
118:6, 17, 18
119:6, 8, 10, 11, 16, 19, 31, 36, 43, 46, 51, 60, 61, 80, 83, 85, 87, 102, 109, 110, 116, 121, 122, 133, 136, 141, 153, 155, 157, 158, 176
121:3^2, 6
124:1, 2, 6
125:3
127:5
129:2, 7
131:1
132:3, 4, 10, 11
135:16^2, 17
137:6^2
138:8
139:4, 12, 15, 21^2

PSALMS
140:8^2, 10, 11
141:4^2, 5, 8
143:2, 7
146:3
147:10^2, 20^2
148:6

PROVERBS
1:8, 10, 15, 28^2, 29
3:1, 3, 5, 7, 11, 15, 21, 23, 24, 25, 27, 28, 29, 30, 31
4:2, 5, 6, 12^2, 13, 14^2, 15, 16, 19, 21, 27
5:6, 7, 8, 13, 17
6:4, 20, 25, 27, 28, 29, 30, 33, 34, 35
7:11, 19, 23, 25^2
8:1, 10, 11, 26, 29, 33
9:8, 18
10:3, 19, 30
11:4, 21
12:3^2, 7, 27
13:1, 8
14:5, 6, 7, 10, 22
15:7, 12
16:5, 10, 29
17:5, 7, 13, 26
18:5
19:2, 5^2, 9, 10, 18, 23, 24
20:1, 4, 13, 19, 21, 22, 23
21:13, 17, 26
22:6, 20, 22, 24, 26, 28, 29
23:3, 4, 5, 6, 7, 9, 10^2, 13^2, 17, 18, 20, 22, 23, 31, 35^2
24:1, 7, 12^4, 14, 15^2, 17^2, 19, 21, 23, 28^2, 29
25:6^2, 8^2, 9, 10, 27^2
26:1, 2, 4, 7, 17, 19, 25
27:1^2, 2^2, 10, 22, 24
28:5, 13, 20, 21, 22, 27
29:7, 19^2, 24
30:2, 6, 7, 10, 11, 12, 15, 16^2, 18, 25, 30
31:3, 4^2, 12, 18, 21, 27

ECCLESIASTES
1:7, 8
2:10^2, 21, 23
4:3^2, 8, 10, 12, 16
5:1, 2^2, 4, 5^2, 6, 8, 10, 12, 20
6:2, 3, 5, 6, 7
7:9, 10^2, 16, 17, 18, 20^2, 28^2
8:3^2, 7, 11, 13^2, 17^2
9:2, 5, 11, 12, 16
10:4, 10, 15, 17, 20^3
11:2, 4^2, 5^2, 6^2
12:1, 2

SONG OF SOLOMON
1:6^2, 8
2:7
3:1, 2, 4, 5
5:6
6:6
7:2
8:1, 4

ISAIAH
1:3^2, 6, 11, 15, 23
2:4, 9
3:7^2, 9
5:4, 6, 12, 25
6:9^2
7:1, 4, 7, 8, 9^2, 12, 17, 25
8:10, 11, 12, 19, 20
9:1, 3, 12, 13, 17, 20, 21
10:1, 7^2, 8, 9^2, 11, 24
11:3, 9, 13^2
12:2
13:10^2, 17^2, 18, 22
14:17, 20, 21, 29
16:3, 6, 12
17:8, 10, 14
22:2, 4, 11, 14
23:4, 13, 18
24:9, 20
26:10^2, 11, 14^2, 18
27:4, 9, 11
28:12, 15, 16, 18, 22, 25, 27, 28
29:9^2, 12^2, 16, 17, 22
30:1^2, 2, 5, 6, 9, 10^2, 14^2, 15, 20
31:1, 2, 3^2, 4, 8^2
32:3, 10
33:1^2, 19^2, 20^2, 23^2, 24
34:10
35:4, 8^2, 9
36:7, 11, 12, 14^2, 15, 16, 21^2
37:3, 6, 10^2, 26, 33, 34
38:1, 11, 18
39:2, 4
40:9, 16, 20^2, 21^4, 24^3, 26, 28^3, 31^2
41:3, 7, 9, 10^2, 12, 13, 14, 17
42:2, 3^2, 4, 8, 16^3, 20^2, 24^2, 25^2
43:1, 2^2, 5, 6, 17, 18, 19, 22, 23^2, 25
44:2, 8^3, 9^2, 18, 20, 21
45:1, 4, 5, 13, 17, 18, 19^2, 21, 23
46:2, 7^2, 10, 13^2
47:3, 7, 8, 11^3, 14^2
48:1, 6^2, 7^2, 8^3, 9, 10, 11, 16, 19, 21
49:5, 10, 15^2, 23
50:5, 6, 7^2
51:6, 7, 9, 10, 14, 21
52:12, 15^2
53:3, 7^2
54:1^2, 2, 4^4, 9, 10, 11, 14^2, 15
55:2^2, 5^2, 8, 10, 11, 13
56:5
57:4, 10^2, 11^3, 12, 16
58:1, 2, 3, 4, 6, 7^2, 11, 13

ISAIAH
59:1, 2, 6, 8^2, 21
60:11, 12
62:1^2, 6, 8, 12
63:8, 13, 16, 19
64:3, 4, 9
65:1^3, 2, 5, 6, 8^2, 12^3, 17, 20, 22^2, 23, 25
66:4^2, 9, 19, 24

JEREMIAH
1:7, 8, 17, 19
2:2, 8^3, 11, 17, 19, 20, 23^2, 24, 27, 34, 35, 37
3:1, 2, 4, 7, 8, 10, 12^2, 13, 19, 25
4:1, 3, 6, 8, 11, 22, 27, 28, 29
5:3^2, 4, 9^2, 10^2, 12, 13, 15, 18, 19, 21^2, 22^4, 28^2, 29^2
6:8, 15, 16, 17, 19, 20, 25, 29
7:4, 6^2, 9, 13^2, 16^2, 17, 19, 20, 22, 24^2, 26, 27^2, 28, 31
8:2, 4^2, 6, 7, 12, 17, 19^2, 20, 22
9:3^2, 4, 5, 9^2, 13, 23^2
10:2^2, 4, 5^2, 7, 10, 11, 16, 20, 21^2, 23^2, 24, 25^2
11:3, 8^2, 11^2, 12, 14^2, 19, 21^2
12:4, 6, 13, 17
13:1, 11, 12, 14, 15, 17, 21, 27
14:9, 10^2, 11, 12^2, 13, 14, 15^2, 17, 18, 21^3, 22
15:1, 7, 14, 15, 17, 19, 20
16:2, 4, 5, 6, 8, 11, 12, 13^2, 17
17:4, 6^2, 8^2, 11^2, 16, 17, 18^2, 23^2, 27^3
18:10, 15, 17, 18^2, 23
19:5, 15
20:3, 9^2, 11^2, 14, 16, 17
21:7, 10
22:5, 6, 10, 11, 13, 15, 16, 17, 18^2, 21^2, 26, 27, 28, 30
23:2, 10, 16^2, 20, 21^2, 23, 24^2, 29, 32^2, 38, 40
24:2, 6^2
25:3, 4, 6^2, 7, 8, 29, 33
26:2, 4, 5, 16, 19, 24
27:8^2, 9^2, 13, 14^2, 15, 16, 17, 18, 20
28:15
29:6, 8, 9, 11, 16, 19^2, 23, 27, 31, 32
30:5, 10, 11^2, 14, 19^2, 24
31:9, 12, 15, 32, 40
32:4, 5, 23, 33^2, 35, 40^2
33:3, 20, 21, 24, 25^2, 26
34:3, 4, 14, 17, 18
35:13, 14^2, 15^2, 16, 17^2, 19
36:24, 25^2, 31
37:4, 9^2, 14^2, 19, 20
38:4, 5, 15^2, 16, 17, 18^2, 20, 23, 24, 25^2, 26, 27
39:16, 17, 18
40:3, 5, 7, 9, 14, 16
41:8^2
42:5, 10^2, 11^2, 13, 19, 21
43:2^2, 4, 7
44:3, 4, 5, 10, 16, 21^2, 23, 27
45:5
46:5, 6, 11, 15, 21, 27^2, 28^3
47:3
48:11^2, 27, 30^2
49:9, 10^2, 12^2, 25, 36
50:2, 5, 7, 13, 20, 24, 42
51:3, 5, 6, 9, 19, 26, 39, 44, 50, 57, 64

LAMENTATIONS
1:9, 10, 14
2:1, 2, 8, 14, 17, 18, 21
3:2, 22^2, 31, 33, 36, 37, 38, 42, 43, 44, 49, 56, 57
4:8, 12, 14, 15, 16^2, 17
5:7, 12

EZEKIEL
1:9, 12, 17
2:6^2, 8
3:5, 6^2, 7^2, 9, 18, 19, 20^2, 21^2, 25, 26
4:8, 14^2
5:6, 7, 9^2
6:10
7:4, 7, 9, 12, 13^2, 19^2
8:12, 18^2
9:5, 6, 9, 10
10:11^2, 16
11:3, 11, 12
12:2^2, 6, 9, 12, 13
13:5, 6, 7^3, 9, 12, 19^2, 22^2
14:23
16:4^2, 16, 22, 28, 29, 31, 43^2, 47, 48, 56, 61
17:9, 10, 12, 14, 18
18:3, 6, 7, 8, 11, 12, 13, 14, 15^2, 16, 17^2, 18, 19, 20, 21, 22, 23, 24, 25^3, 28, 29^3, 30
20:3, 7, 8^2, 9, 13, 14, 15, 16, 18, 21, 22, 24, 25^2, 31, 32, 38, 39, 44, 47, 48, 49
21:5, 26
22:24, 28, 30
23:27, 48
24:6, 7, 8, 12, 13^2, 14, 17^2, 19, 22, 23, 25
25:10
26:15, 19, 20
28:2
29:5
30:21
31:8^3
32:7, 9, 27
33:4, 5, 6^2, 8, 9, 12^2, 13, 15, 17^2, 20, 31, 32
34:2, 3, 4, 8, 10
35:6, 9

EZEKIEL
36:22, 31, 32
37:18
38:14
39:7
41:6
42:6, 14
44:2, 8, 13, 18, 19, 31
46:2, 9, 18^2, 20
47:5^2, 11, 12
48:11, 14

DANIEL
1:8^2
2:5, 9, 10, 11, 18, 24, 30, 43^2, 44
3:6, 11, 12^2, 14, 15, 16, 18^2, 24, 28
4:7, 18, 19, 30
5:8, 10, 15, 22, 23^2
6:5, 8^2, 12^2, 13, 17, 22, 26
7:14^2
8:5, 22, 24
9:11, 12, 13, 14, 18, 19, 26
10:7, 12, 19
11:4, 6, 12, 15, 17, 19, 21, 24, 25, 27, 29, 38, 42
12:8

HOSEA
1:7, 9^2, 10
2:2, 4, 6, 7^2, 8, 23^2
3:3^2
4:10^2, 14^2, 15^2
5:3, 4^2, 6, 13
6:6
7:2, 8, 9^2, 10, 14, 16
8:4^2, 6, 13
9:1, 2, 3, 4^2, 12, 17
10:3, 9
11:3, 5, 9^4
13:13
14:3^2

JOEL
1:16
2:2, 7, 8, 13, 17, 21, 22
3:21

AMOS
1:3, 6, 9^2, 11, 13
2:1, 4^2, 6, 11, 12, 14, 15
3:6^2, 8, 10
4:6, 7^2, 8^2, 9, 10, 11
5:5^2, 11^2, 14, 18, 20^2, 21, 22, 23
6:6, 10, 13
7:3, 6, 8, 10, 13, 16^2
8:2, 8, 11, 12
9:1^2, 4, 7^2, 8, 9, 10

OBADIAH
5^2, 8, 12, 13^2, 16, 18

JONAH
1:6, 13, 14^2
3:7, 9, 10
4:2, 10, 11

MICAH
1:5^2, 10^2, 11
2:3, 6^3, 7, 10
3:1, 4, 5, 6^2, 11
4:3, 12
5:7, 15
6:14^2, 15^3
7:5^2, 8, 18

NAHUM
1:3, 9
3:1, 17, 19

HABAKKUK
1:2^2, 5, 6, 12^2, 13, 17
2:3^2, 4, 6^2, 7, 13
3:17

ZEPHANIAH
1:6, 12, 13^2
2:1
3:2^4, 3, 5^2, 7, 11, 13, 15, 16^2

HAGGAI
1:2, 6^2
2:3, 5, 17, 19

ZECHARIAH
1:4^2, 6, 12
3:2
4:5, 6, 13
7:6, 7, 10, 11, 13^2, 14
8:11, 13, 14, 15
9:5
10:6, 10
11:5^2, 6, 9, 12, 16
12:7
13:3
14:2, 6, 7, 17, 18^3, 19

MALACHI
1:2, 8^2
2:2^3, 6, 9, 10^2, 13, 15, 16
3:5, 6^2, 7, 10^2, 11, 18

MATTHEW
1:19, 20, 25
2:6, 12, 18^2
3:9, 10, 11
4:4, 7
5:17^2, 21, 27, 29, 30, 33, 34, 36, 39, 42, 46, 47
6:1, 2, 3, 5, 7, 8, 13, 15, 16, 18, 19, 20, 25, 26^2, 28, 29, 30
7:1^2, 3, 6, 19, 21, 22, 25, 26, 29
8:8, 10^2, 20
9:12, 13^2, 14, 24
10:5^2, 13, 14, 20, 23, 24, 26^3, 28^2, 29^2, 31, 34^2, 37^2, 38^2
11:6, 11, 17^2, 20

MATTHEW
12:2, 3, 4, 5, 7[2], 11, 16, 19, 20[2], 23, 24, 25, 30[2], 31, 32
13:5, 11, 12, 13[2], 14[2], 17[2], 19, 21, 27, 34, 55[2], 56, 57, 58
14:4, 16, 27
15:2, 6, 11, 13, 17, 20, 23, 24, 26, 32
16:3, 9, 11[2], 12, 17, 18, 22, 23, 28
17:7, 12, 16, 19, 21, 24
18:3, 10, 12, 13, 14, 16, 22, 25, 30, 33, 35
19:4, 6, 8, 10, 14, 18[3]
20:13, 15, 22, 23, 26, 28
21:21[2], 25, 29, 30, 32[2]
22:3, 8, 11, 12, 16, 17, 29, 31, 32
23:3[2], 4, 8, 23, 30, 37, 39
24:2[3], 6[2], 17, 20, 21, 23, 26[2], 29, 34, 35, 36, 39, 42, 43, 44, 50[2]
25:9[2], 12, 24[2], 26[2], 29, 43[3], 44, 45[2]
26:5, 11, 24, 29, 35, 39, 40, 41, 42, 70, 72, 74
27:6, 13, 34
28:5, 6, 10

MARK
1:7, 22, 34
2:2, 4, 17, 18, 24, 26, 27
3:12, 20
4:5, 12[2], 13, 21, 22, 25, 27, 34, 38
5:3, 7, 10, 19, 36, 39
6:3[2], 4, 9, 11, 18, 19, 26, 34, 50, 52
7:3, 4, 5, 18, 19, 24, 27
8:17, 18[3], 21, 33
9:1, 6, 18, 28, 30, 32, 37, 38[2], 39, 40, 41, 44[2], 46[2], 48[2]
10:9, 14, 15[2], 19[6], 27, 38, 40, 43, 45
11:13, 16, 17, 23, 26, 31
12:10, 14[2], 15, 24[2], 26, 27, 34
13:2[2], 7[2], 11, 14, 15, 16, 18, 19, 21, 24, 30, 31, 32, 33, 35
14:2, 7, 29, 31, 36, 37, 49, 56, 68, 71
15:23
16:6[2], 11, 14, 16, 18

LUKE
1:13, 20[2], 22, 30, 34, 60
2:10, 26, 37, 43, 45, 49, 50
3:8, 9, 15, 16
4:4, 12, 22, 35, 41, 42
5:10, 19, 31, 32, 36
6:2, 3, 4, 29, 30, 37[4], 39, 40, 41, 42, 43, 44, 46, 48, 49
7:6[3], 9[2], 13, 23, 28, 30, 32[2], 45, 46
8:10[2], 17[2], 18, 19, 28, 31, 47, 49, 50, 52[2]
9:5, 27, 33, 40, 45[2], 49, 50[2], 53, 55, 56, 58
10:6, 7, 10, 20, 24[2], 40, 42
11:4, 7, 8, 23[2], 35, 38, 40, 42, 44[2], 46, 52
12:2[2], 4, 6[2], 7, 10, 15, 21, 26, 27[3], 29, 32, 33[2], 39, 40, 46[2], 47, 48, 56, 57, 59
13:9, 14, 15, 16, 24, 25, 27, 34, 35
14:5, 6, 8, 12, 26, 27, 28, 29, 30, 31, 33
15:4, 8, 13, 28
16:11, 12, 31
17:8, 9, 17, 18, 20, 22, 23, 31[2]
18:1, 2, 4[2], 7, 11, 13, 16, 17, 20[4], 30, 34
19:3, 14, 21[2], 22[2], 23, 26, 27, 44[2], 48
20:5, 7, 26, 38, 40
21:6[2], 8[2], 9[2], 14, 15, 18, 21, 32, 33
22:16, 18, 26, 27, 32, 34, 40, 42, 57, 58, 60, 67, 68
23:28, 34, 40, 51
24:3, 6, 11, 16, 18, 23, 24, 26, 32, 39, 41

JOHN
1:3, 5, 8, 10, 11, 13, 20[2], 21, 25, 26, 27, 31, 33
2:4, 9, 12, 16, 24, 25
3:7, 8, 10, 11, 12, 15, 16, 17, 18[3], 24, 28, 34, 36[2]
4:2, 15, 18, 22, 29, 32, 35, 42, 48
5:10, 13, 18, 23[2], 24, 28, 30, 31, 34, 38[2], 40, 41, 42, 43, 44, 45, 47
6:7, 17, 20, 22, 24, 26, 27, 32, 36, 38, 42, 43, 46, 50, 58, 64[2], 70
7:1, 6, 8[2], 10, 16, 19, 22, 23, 24, 25, 28[2], 30, 34, 35, 36, 39[2], 42, 45, 49
8:6, 12, 13, 16, 20, 23, 24, 27, 29, 35, 40, 41, 43, 44, 45, 46, 47[2], 48, 49, 50, 55[2], 57
9:8, 12, 16[2], 18, 21[2], 25, 27, 29, 30, 31, 32, 33, 39
10:1, 5[2], 6, 8, 10, 12[2], 13, 16, 21, 25, 26[2], 33, 34, 37[2], 38
11:4, 9[2], 15, 21, 30, 32, 37[2], 40, 50, 51, 52, 56
12:5, 6, 8, 9, 15, 16, 30, 35, 37, 39, 40, 42, 44, 46, 47[3], 48, 49
13:7, 8, 9, 10[2], 11, 16, 18, 36, 38
14:1, 2, 5, 9, 10[2], 17, 18, 22[2], 24[3], 27[2], 30
15:2, 6, 15[2], 16, 19, 20, 21, 22[2], 24[2]
16:1, 3, 4, 7[2], 9, 13, 16, 17, 19, 26, 30, 32
17:9, 14[2], 15, 16[2], 25
18:11, 17[2], 25[2], 26, 28, 30[2], 31, 36[3], 40
19:10[2], 12, 21, 24, 31, 33, 36
20:2, 5, 7, 9, 13, 14, 17[2], 24, 25, 27, 29, 30
21:4, 6, 8, 11, 18, 23[3], 25

THE ACTS
1:4, 5, 7
2:7, 15, 24, 25, 27, 31, 34
3:23
4:18
5:4[3], 7, 22, 28[2], 40, 42
6:2, 10, 13
7:5, 18, 19, 25, 32, 39, 40, 48, 50, 52, 53, 60
8:21, 32
9:21, 26, 38
10:14, 15, 28, 41, 47
11:8, 9
12:9, 14, 19, 22, 23
13:10, 11, 25[2], 27, 35, 39
14:17, 18
15:19, 38[2]
16:7, 21
17:4, 5, 6, 12, 24, 27, 29
18:9[2], 20
19:2, 9, 26, 27, 30, 31, 32, 35
20:10, 12, 16, 22, 27, 29, 31
21:4, 12, 13, 14, 21, 34, 38
22:9, 11, 18, 22
23:5[2], 9, 21
24:4
25:7, 11, 16, 24, 27
26:19, 25, 26, 29, 32
27:7, 10, 12, 14, 15, 21, 24, 34, 39
28:4, 19, 24, 25, 26[2]

ROMANS
1:13, 16, 21, 28[2], 32
2:4, 8, 13, 14[2], 21[2], 22, 26, 27, 28, 29[2]
3:3, 8, 10, 12, 17, 29
4:2, 4, 5, 8, 10, 11, 12, 13, 16, 17, 19[2], 20, 23
5:3, 5, 11, 13, 14, 15, 16
6:3, 6, 12, 14[2], 15, 16
7:1, 6, 7[3], 15[2], 16, 18, 19[2], 20
8:1, 3, 4, 7, 9[2], 12, 15, 18, 20, 23, 24, 25, 26, 32[2]
9:1, 6[2], 8, 10, 11[2], 16, 21, 24, 25[2], 26, 30, 31, 32, 33
10:2, 3, 6, 11, 14[2], 16, 18, 19, 20[2]
11:2[2], 4, 7, 8[2], 10, 18[2], 20, 21[2], 23, 25, 30, 31
12:2, 3, 4, 11, 14, 16[2], 19, 21
13:3[2], 4, 5, 9[5], 13[3], 14
14:1, 3[4], 6[4], 13, 15[2], 16, 17, 20, 22, 23[2]
15:1, 3, 18[2], 20, 21[2], 31
16:4, 18

1 CORINTHIANS
1:16, 17[2], 20, 21, 26[3], 28
2:1, 2, 4, 5, 6, 8, 9, 12, 13, 14
3:1, 2[2], 3, 4, 16
4:3, 4, 6, 7[2], 14, 15, 18, 19, 20
5:1, 2, 6[2], 8, 9, 10, 11[2], 12
6:1, 2, 3, 5[2], 7[2], 9[3], 12[2], 13, 15, 16, 19[2]
7:1, 4[2], 5[2], 6, 10[2], 11, 12[3], 13[2], 15, 18[2], 21, 23, 27[2], 28[2], 30[3], 31, 35, 36, 38
8:7, 8[2], 10
9:1[4], 2, 4, 5, 6, 7[2], 8, 9, 12[2], 13, 16, 18, 21, 24, 26[2]
10:1, 5, 6, 13, 16[2], 18, 20[2], 23[2], 27, 28, 29, 33
11:6, 7, 8, 14, 17[2], 20, 22[3], 29, 31, 32, 34
12:1, 14, 15[3], 16[3]
13:1, 2, 3, 4[3], 5[3], 6
14:2, 11, 16, 17, 20, 21, 22[4], 23, 24, 33, 34, 39
15:9, 10[2], 13, 14, 15[2], 16[2], 17, 29, 32, 33, 34[2], 36, 37, 39, 46, 51, 58
16:7, 12, 22

2 CORINTHIANS
1:8, 9, 12, 18, 19, 23, 24
2:1, 4, 5[2], 11, 13, 17
3:3[2], 5, 6, 7, 8, 13[2]
4:1, 2, 4, 5, 7, 8[3], 9[2], 16, 18[3]
5:1, 3, 4, 7, 12[2], 15, 19
6:1, 3, 9, 12, 14, 17
7:3, 7, 8, 9, 10, 12, 14
8:5, 8, 10, 12[2], 13, 19, 21
9:4, 5, 7, 12
10:2, 3, 4, 8[2], 9, 12[2], 13, 14[2], 15, 16, 18
11:4[3], 5, 6, 11, 17, 29[2], 31
12:1, 4, 5, 6, 13, 14[3], 16, 18[2], 20[2], 21
13:2, 3, 5, 6, 7, 10

GALATIANS
1:1, 7, 10, 11, 16, 20
2:5, 14[2], 15, 16[2], 20, 21
3:1, 10, 12, 16, 20
4:8, 12, 14, 17, 18, 21, 27[2], 30, 31
5:1, 7, 8, 13, 15, 16, 18, 21, 26
6:4, 7[2], 9[2]

EPHESIANS
1:16, 21
2:8, 9
3:5, 13
4:17, 20, 26[2], 30
5:3, 4, 7, 15, 17, 18, 27
6:4, 6, 7, 12

PHILIPPIANS
1:16, 22, 29
2:4, 6, 12, 16, 21, 27, 30
3:1, 9, 12, 13
4:11, 17

COLOSSIANS
1:9, 23
2:1, 8, 18, 19, 21[3], 23
3:2, 9, 19, 21, 22, 23

1 THESSALONIANS
1:5, 8[2]
2:1, 3, 4, 8, 9, 13, 15, 17, 19
4:5[2], 7, 8, 9, 13[2], 15
5:3, 4, 5, 6, 9, 19, 20

2 THESSALONIANS
1:8[2]
2:2, 3, 5, 10, 12
3:2, 6, 7, 8, 9[2], 10, 11, 13, 14, 15

1 TIMOTHY
1:9, 20
2:7, 9, 12, 14
3:3[4], 5, 6, 8[3], 11
4:14
5:1, 8, 9, 13[2], 16, 18, 19
6:1, 2, 3, 17

2 TIMOTHY
1:7, 8, 9, 12, 16
2:5, 9, 13, 14, 15, 20, 24
4:3, 8, 16

TITUS
1:6, 7[4], 11, 14
2:3[2], 5, 9, 10
3:5, 14

PHILEMON
14, 16, 19

HEBREWS
1:12, 14
2:5, 8[2], 11, 16
3:8, 10, 11, 15, 16, 17, 18[2], 19
4:2[2], 6, 7, 8, 13, 15
5:5, 12
6:1, 10, 12
7:6, 11, 16, 20, 21, 23, 27
8:2, 4, 9[3], 11
9:7, 8, 9, 11[2], 24
10:1, 2, 4, 5, 8, 25, 35, 37, 39
11:1, 3, 5[2], 7, 8, 13, 16, 23, 27, 31[2], 35, 38, 39, 40
12:4, 5, 7, 8, 9, 18, 19, 20, 25[3], 26
13:2, 6, 9[3], 16, 17

JAMES
1:5, 7, 16, 20, 22, 23, 25, 26
2:1, 4, 5, 6, 7, 11[2], 14, 16, 17, 21, 24, 25
3:1, 2, 10, 14[2], 15
4:1, 2[3], 3, 4, 11[2], 14, 17
5:6, 9, 12, 17[2]

1 PETER
1:4, 8[2], 12, 14, 18, 23
2:6, 10[2], 16, 18, 23[2]
3:1, 3, 4, 6, 7, 9, 14, 21
4:4, 12, 16, 17
5:2[2], 4

2 PETER
1:12, 16, 21
2:3[2], 4, 5, 10, 11, 12, 21
3:8, 9[2]

1 JOHN
1:6, 8, 10[2]
2:1, 2, 4[2], 11, 15[2], 16, 19[2], 21[2], 23, 27, 28
3:1[2], 2, 6[2], 9, 10[3], 12, 13, 14, 18, 21
4:1, 3[2], 6[2], 8[2], 10, 18, 20[2]
5:3, 6, 10[2], 12[2], 16[3], 17, 18[2]

2 JOHN
1, 5, 7, 8, 9[2], 10[2], 12

3 JOHN
9, 10, 11[2], 13

JUDE
5, 6, 9, 10, 19

REVELATION
1:17
2:2[2], 3, 9, 11, 13, 21, 24[2]
3:2, 3[2], 4, 5, 8, 9, 17, 18
4:8
5:5
6:6, 10
7:1, 3
8:12
9:4[2], 5, 6, 20[3]
10:4
11:2, 6, 9
12:8, 11
13:8, 15
14:4
15:4
16:9, 11, 18, 20
17:8[3], 10, 11
18:4[2]
19:10
20:4, 5, 15
21:25
22:9, 10

GENESIS
17:18
24:12, 42
27:34, 38
32:9
43:20
49:6, 18

EXODUS
4:10, 13
15:6[2], 11, 16, 17[2]
32:4, 8
34:9

NUMBERS
10:36
12:13
16:22
21:17, 29
24:5[2]

DEUTERONOMY
3:24
4:1
5:1, 29
6:3, 4
9:1, 26
20:3
21:8
26:10
27:9
32:1[2], 6, 29, 43
33:23, 29[2]

JOSHUA
7:7, 8, 13

JUDGES
3:19
5:3[2], 21, 31
6:22
13:8
16:28[2]
21:3

1 SAMUEL
1:11
4:9
17:55
20:12
23:10, 11, 20
26:17

2 SAMUEL
1:25
7:18, 19[2], 22, 25, 27, 28, 29
14:4, 9, 22
15:31, 34
16:4
18:33[2]
19:4[2], 26
20:1
22:29, 50
23:17
24:10

1 KINGS
1:13, 20, 24
3:7, 17, 26
8:26, 28, 53
12:16, 28
13:2
17:18, 20, 21
18:26, 37
19:4
20:4
21:20
22:28

2 KINGS
1:11, 13
4:40
6:12, 26
8:5
9:5[2], 23
13:14
19:15, 19
20:3

1 CHRONICLES
16:13, 34, 35
17:16, 17[2], 19, 20, 25, 27
21:17
29:11[2], 16, 18

2 CHRONICLES
1:9
6:14, 16, 17, 19, 41[2], 42
10:16
13:12
14:11[2]
20:6, 12, 17, 20
25:7

EZRA
9:6, 10, 15

NEHEMIAH
1:5, 11
4:4
6:9
13:14, 22, 29, 31

ESTHER
7:3

JOB
6:2
7:7, 20
13:5
16:18, 21
19:21
33:31
34:2
37:14

PSALMS
2:10
3:3, 7[2]
4:1, 2
5:1, 3, 8, 10
6:1, 2[3], 3, 4
7:1, 3, 6, 8
8:1, 9
9:1, 2, 6, 13, 19, 20
10:1, 12[2]
12:7
13:1, 3
16:1, 2
17:1, 6, 7, 13, 14
18:1, 15, 49
19:14
21:1
22:2, 3, 19[2]
24:6, 7, 9
25:1, 2, 4, 6, 7, 11, 17, 20, 22
26:1, 2, 6
27:7, 9, 11
28:1
29:1
30:1, 2, 3, 4, 8, 10, 12
31:1, 5, 9, 14, 17, 23
33:1, 22
34:3, 8, 9
35:1, 22[2], 24
36:5, 6, 7, 10
38:1, 15[2], 21[2], 22
39:12, 13
40:5, 8, 9, 11, 13[2], 17
41:10
42:1, 5, 6, 11
43:1[2], 3, 4, 5
44:1, 4, 23
45:3, 6, 10
47:1
48:9, 10
50:7[2]
51:1, 10, 14, 15, 17
52:1, 4
54:1, 2, 6
55:1, 9, 23
56:1, 2, 7, 12
57:1, 5, 7, 9, 11
58:1[2], 6[2]
59:1, 3, 5, 8, 11, 17
60:1[2], 10[2]
61:1, 5, 7
62:12
63:1
64:1
65:1, 2, 5
66:8, 10
67:3, 4, 5
68:7, 9, 10, 24, 28, 32, 35
69:1, 5, 6[2], 13[2], 16, 29
70:1[2], 5[2]
71:1, 4, 5, 12[2], 17, 18, 19[2], 22[2]
72:1
73:20
74:1, 10, 18, 19, 21, 22
75:1
76:6
77:13, 16
78:1
79:1, 8, 9, 12
80:1, 3, 4, 7, 14, 19
81:8[2]
82:8
83:1[2], 13, 16
84:1, 3, 8[2], 9, 12
85:4, 7
86:1, 2, 3, 4, 6, 8, 9, 11, 12, 14, 15, 16
87:3
88:1, 13
89:5, 8, 15, 51
90:13, 14
92:1, 5, 9

PSALMS
93:3, 5
94:1[2], 5, 12, 18
95:1, 6
96:1, 7, 9
97:8
98:1
99:8
101:1, 2
102:1, 12, 24
103:1, 2, 22
104:1[2], 24, 35
105:1, 6
106:1, 4[2], 47
107:1
108:1, 3, 5, 11[2]
109:1, 21, 26[2]
113:1
114:5
115:1, 9, 10
116:4, 7, 16, 19
117:1
118:1, 25[2], 29
119:5, 8, 10, 12, 31, 33, 41, 52, 55, 57, 64, 65, 75, 89, 97, 107, 108, 137, 145, 149, 151, 156, 159, 169, 174
120:2
122:2
123:1, 3
125:4
126:4
130:1, 3
132:8
135:1, 9, 13[2], 19[2], 20
136:1, 2, 3, 26
137:5, 7, 8
138:4, 8
139:1, 4, 17, 19, 21, 23
140:1, 4, 6, 7, 8
141:3, 8
142:5
143:1, 7, 9, 11
144:5, 9
145:1, 10
146:1, 10
147:12[2]

PROVERBS
4:10
5:7
6:9
7:24
8:4, 5, 32
24:15
30:13
31:4

ECCLESIASTES
10:16, 17
11:9

SONG OF SOLOMON
1:5, 7, 8, 9
2:7, 14
3:5, 11
4:11, 16
5:1[2], 8, 9, 16
6:1, 4, 13
7:1, 6, 13
8:1, 4, 12

ISAIAH
1:2[2]
2:5
3:12
5:3
7:13
8:8, 9
10:5, 24, 30[2]
12:1
14:12, 31[2]
16:9
21:2[2], 10, 13
23:4, 10, 12
24:17
25:1
26:8, 13, 15, 17
27:12
33:2
37:16, 17[2], 20
38:3, 14, 16
40:9[2], 27[2]
41:1
43:1[2], 22[2]
44:1, 2, 21[2], 23[2]
45:15
46:3, 8
47:1[2], 5
48:1, 12, 18
49:1, 3, 13[3]
51:4, 9, 17
52:1[2], 2[2]
54:1, 11

ISAIAH

62:6
63:16, 17
64:4, 8, 9, 12

JEREMIAH

2:4, 12, 28, 31
3:14, 20
4:1, 14, 19
5:3, 15, 21
6:1, 8, 18, 19, 23, 26
7:29
9:20
10:1, 6, 7, 17, 23, 24
11:5, 13, 20
12:1, 3
13:27
14:7, 8, 9, 20, 22
15:5, 15, 16
16:19
17:3, 13, 14
18:6[2], 19
19:3
20:7, 12
21:12, 13
22:2, 23, 29
30:10[2]
31:4, 7, 10, 21, 22, 23
32:25
34:4
37:20
42:19
45:2
46:11, 19, 27[2], 28
47:6
48:2, 19, 28, 32, 43, 46
49:3, 4, 8, 16, 30
50:11, 24, 31, 42
51:13, 25, 62

LAMENTATIONS

1:9, 11, 20
2:13[2], 18, 20
3:55, 58, 59, 61, 64
4:21, 22[2]
5:1, 19, 21

EZEKIEL

3:25
7:7
8:15, 17
10:13
11:4, 5
12:25
13:4, 11
16:35
18:25, 29, 30, 31
20:31, 39, 44
23:22
26:3
27:3[2], 8
28:16, 22
33:7, 8, 10, 11, 20
34:9, 17
35:3, 15
36:8, 22, 32
37:3, 4, 9, 12, 13
38:3, 16
39:1
44:6
45:9

DANIEL

2:4, 23, 29, 31, 37
3:4, 9, 10, 12, 14, 16, 17, 18, 24
4:9, 18, 22, 24, 27, 31
5:10, 18, 22
6:7, 8, 12, 13, 15, 20, 21, 22
8:17
9:4, 7, 8, 15, 16, 17, 18, 19[4], 22
10:11, 16, 19
12:4, 8

HOSEA

5:1[2], 3, 8
6:4[2], 11
8:5
9:1, 14
10:9
13:9, 14[2]
14:1

JOEL

1:11[2], 19
2:17, 21
3:4, 11

AMOS

2:11
3:1
4:5, 12[2]
5:1, 25
6:14
7:2, 5, 12
8:4, 14
9:7

OBADIAH

9

JONAH

1:6, 14[2]
2:6
4:2, 3

MICAH

1:2, 13, 15
2:7, 12
3:1
4:8, 10, 13
5:1
6:2, 3, 5, 8
7:8

NAHUM

1:15
3:18

HABAKKUK

1:2, 12[3]
3:2[2]

ZEPHANIAH

2:1, 5
3:14[3]

HAGGAI

1:4
2:4[2], 23

ZECHARIAH

1:9, 12
2:7, 10, 13
3:2, 8
4:7
8:13
9:9[2], 13[2]
11:1, 2, 7
13:7

MALACHI

1:6
2:1

MATTHEW

3:7
6:30
8:26
11:25
12:34
14:31
15:22, 28
16:3, 8
17:17
18:32
20:30, 31
23:37
26:39, 42

MARK

9:19
12:29

LUKE

3:7
5:8
9:41
10:21
12:28
13:34
24:25

JOHN

17:5, 25

THE ACTS

1:1
7:42
13:10
18:14
25:26
26:13, 19

ROMANS

2:1, 3
7:24
9:20
11:33

1 CORINTHIANS

7:16[2]
15:55[2]

2 CORINTHIANS

6:11

GALATIANS

3:1

1 TIMOTHY

6:11, 20

HEBREWS

1:8
10:7, 9

JAMES

2:20

REVELATION

4:11
6:10
11:17
15:4
16:5

OF

GENESIS

1:2[3], 6, 10, 14, 15, 17, 20, 24, 25, 26[2], 27, 28[2], 29[2], 30[2]
2:1, 4[2], 5[2], 6, 7[3], 9[5], 10, 11[2], 12, 13[2], 14[2], 15, 16[2], 17[4], 19[3], 20[2], 21, 23[3]
3:1[3], 2[3], 3[4], 6, 7, 8[4], 11, 12, 14[2], 17[6], 18, 19[2], 20, 21, 22[3], 23, 24[4]
4:2[2], 3[3], 4[3], 10, 14, 16[3], 17[2], 19[2], 20[2], 21, 22[2], 23, 25, 26
5:1[3], 4, 8, 11, 14, 17, 20, 23, 27, 29[2], 31
6:1, 2[3], 4[4], 5[3], 7[2], 8, 9, 13, 14, 15[4], 16, 17[2], 19[3], 20[5], 21
7:2[2], 3[3], 4, 6, 7[2], 8[4], 10, 11[4], 13[2], 14, 15[2], 16, 18, 21[4], 22[2], 23[2]
8:2[2], 3, 4[2], 5[2], 6[2], 8, 9[2], 10, 13[3], 14, 16, 17[4], 19, 20[2], 21
9:2[5], 5[5], 6, 10[6], 11, 12, 13, 15, 16, 17, 18[3], 19[2], 21, 22[2], 23, 25, 26, 27, 29
10:1[2], 2, 3, 4, 5, 6, 7[2], 10[2], 11, 14, 18, 19, 20, 21[3], 22, 23, 25, 29, 30, 31, 32[2]
11:1[2], 2, 4, 5, 8, 9[3], 10, 27, 28[2], 29[5], 31[3], 32
12:1, 2, 3, 4, 5[2], 6[2], 8[2], 13, 15, 17
13:1, 4[2], 7[2], 10[3], 11, 12[2], 13, 16[2], 17[2], 18
14:1[5], 2[5], 3, 7, 8[6], 9[4], 10[3], 11, 13[3], 15, 17[4], 18[2], 19[2], 20, 21, 22[2], 24
15:1, 2[2], 4[2], 7[2], 9[3], 12, 13, 16, 18
16:2, 3, 7[2], 8, 9, 10, 11, 12, 13
17:4, 5, 6[2], 8, 11[2], 12[2], 14, 16[4], 23[2], 24, 25, 27[2]
18:1[2], 5, 6, 10, 11, 13, 14, 18, 19[2], 20, 21, 25, 28[2]
19:1, 4[2], 8, 11, 12, 13[2], 14, 15, 16[2], 22, 24, 25, 26, 28[3], 29[3], 30, 31, 32, 34, 36, 37, 38[2]
20:2[2], 5[2], 6, 11, 12[2], 13, 16[2], 18[3]
21:2, 3, 9, 10, 11, 12[2], 13[2], 14[2], 15, 16, 17[4], 19, 21[3], 22, 25[2], 26, 27, 28, 30, 31, 32[2], 33
22:2[3], 3[2], 6[2], 8, 9, 11[2], 13, 14[2], 15[2], 17[2], 18, 21
23:1[2], 2, 3, 4[2], 5, 6[2], 7[2], 8[2], 9[3], 10[5], 11[2], 12, 13[3], 15, 16[3], 17, 18[3], 19[3], 20[2]
24:2, 3[4], 7[2], 9, 10[4], 11[2], 12, 13[3], 15[2], 17, 22[3], 24[2], 27[3], 28, 30, 31, 37[2], 40[2], 42, 43[2], 47, 48, 53[2], 60[3], 62
25:3, 4[2], 6, 7[2], 8, 9[3], 10[2], 11, 12, 13[3], 16, 17[2], 18, 19, 20[2], 21, 22, 23, 27, 28, 34
26:1[2], 2, 4[2], 7[3], 8, 9, 10, 14[3], 15, 17, 18[3], 19, 20[2], 21, 22, 24, 25, 26[2], 29, 33, 34[2], 35
27:2, 9, 15, 16[3], 17, 19, 22, 25, 27[3], 28[4], 30[2], 31, 33, 34, 39[3], 41[2], 42, 45, 46[7]
28:1[2], 2[3], 3, 4, 5[2], 6[2], 8, 9[2], 11[2], 12[2], 13[2], 14[2], 15, 16, 17[2], 18, 19[2], 22
29:1[2], 2[2], 4, 5, 10[3], 13, 14, 16[2], 22
30:2, 14[2], 16, 32, 35, 36, 37[2], 40[2], 41
31:1[2], 2, 3, 5, 9, 11, 13[2], 15, 18[2], 25, 29[2], 33, 35, 37, 38, 39[3], 42[4], 48, 53[4]
32:1, 2, 3[2], 9[2], 10[3], 11[2], 12, 13, 16, 20, 24, 25[3], 30, 32[4]
33:8, 10, 15[2], 17, 18[2], 19[4]
34:1[2], 2[2], 3, 6, 7[2], 8, 13, 15, 19, 20[2], 23, 24[4], 25[2], 26[2], 27, 30
35:1, 3, 5[2], 6, 7, 8, 9, 11[3], 14, 15, 20, 21, 22, 23, 24, 25, 26[2], 27, 28, 29
36:1, 2[5], 3, 5[2], 6[3], 7, 9[2], 10[5], 11, 12, 13[2], 14[3], 15[4], 16[3], 17[4], 18[3], 19, 20, 21[3], 22, 23, 24[2], 25[2], 26, 27, 28, 29, 30[2], 31[2], 32[2], 33[2], 34[2], 35[3], 36, 37, 38, 39[4], 40[2], 43[3]
37:1, 2[3], 3[2], 14[2], 20, 21, 22, 23[2], 25, 28[2], 31, 32, 36[2]
38:2, 7, 12[2], 19, 20, 21, 22, 27
39:1[4], 2, 5, 11[2], 14, 19, 21[2], 22[2], 23
40:1[3], 2[3], 3[2], 4, 5[4], 7, 8, 12, 14[2], 15[2], 17[3], 20[2]
41:1, 2, 3[2], 5, 8, 10, 11, 12, 14, 15, 16, 17, 18, 19, 25, 27, 29[2], 30[2], 31, 33, 34[2], 35[2], 36[2], 37[2], 38, 41, 42, 43, 44, 45[3], 46[3], 48[3], 49, 50[3], 51, 52[2], 53[2], 54[2], 55, 56[2]
42:5[2], 6, 7, 9[2], 12, 13[2], 15, 16[2], 19[3], 21, 27, 29, 30[2], 32[2], 33[3], 35[2], 36
43:2, 7[3], 9, 11, 12, 14, 16, 18, 19[2], 21, 23, 27[2], 29, 34
44:1, 2, 4, 8[3], 9, 16, 20[2], 24, 31, 33
45:2, 8[2], 9, 10, 11, 12, 13[2], 17, 18[3], 19[2], 20[2], 21[2], 22[4], 23, 25[2], 26, 27[2]
46:1, 2, 3[2], 5, 6, 8[2], 9, 10[2], 11, 12[3], 13, 14, 15[2], 16, 17[2], 18, 19, 20[3], 21, 22, 23, 24, 25, 26, 27[3], 28, 31, 34
47:1[3], 2, 4[2], 6[4], 9[8], 11[3], 13[3], 14[2], 15[2], 17, 18[2], 20, 21[2], 22[2], 24[2], 25, 26[2], 27[2], 28[2], 30
48:3, 4[2], 5, 6, 7[2], 10, 16[2], 17, 19, 21, 22[2]
49:2, 3[3], 5, 8, 10, 11, 13[2], 16[2], 20, 24[4], 25[5], 26[6], 28, 29, 30[4], 32[3], 33
50:3, 4[3], 5, 7[4], 8[2], 10, 11[3], 13[5], 17[4], 19, 23[3], 24, 25[2]

EXODUS

1:1[2], 5[2], 7, 9[2], 10, 12[2], 13, 14, 15[4], 16, 17, 18
2:1[3], 3, 5, 6, 7, 10, 11, 13, 15[2], 16, 19[2], 23[5], 25
3:1[4], 2[4], 4[2], 6[4], 7[2], 8[4], 9[2], 10[2], 11[2], 12, 13[2], 14, 15[5], 16[5], 17[3], 18[3], 19, 21, 22[4]
4:5[4], 7, 8[2], 9[3], 10[2], 13, 14, 16[2], 20[2], 25, 26, 27, 28, 29[2], 30, 31
5:1, 3, 4, 5, 6, 8, 10, 11, 12[2], 14[2], 15[2], 18, 19[3], 21[2]
6:1, 3, 4[2], 5[2], 6[3], 7, 9[2], 11[3], 12[2], 13[5], 14[4], 15[3], 16[4], 17, 18[3], 19[2], 20[2], 21, 22, 23[2], 24[2], 25[4], 26[2], 27[2], 28, 29, 30
7:2[2], 3, 4[3], 5, 11, 16, 18[2], 19[5], 20[2], 21[3], 22, 24[2]
8:3, 5, 6[2], 7, 12, 13[4], 16[2], 17[3], 19, 21[4], 22[3], 24[5], 26[2], 29, 31[2]
9:1, 3, 4[4], 6[4], 7[3], 8[3], 9[2], 10, 11, 12, 13, 20[2], 21, 22[3], 23, 24, 25[3], 26[2], 29, 33, 35[2]
10:1, 2[2], 3, 5[3], 6[2], 12[3], 13, 14[2], 15[5], 19, 20, 21, 22, 23
11:2[5], 3[4], 4, 5[4], 6, 7[2], 9, 10[2]
12:1, 2[2], 3[3], 4, 5, 6[3], 7[2], 9, 10[2], 12[3], 13, 15, 16[2], 17[3], 18[2], 19, 21, 22[3], 27[3], 28, 29[4], 31, 33, 35[5], 36, 37, 39[3], 40[2], 41[3], 42[4], 43, 46[2], 47, 50, 51[3]
13:2[3], 3[3], 5, 8[2], 9, 11, 12, 13[2], 14[2], 15[4], 16[2], 17[2], 18[5], 19[2], 20, 21[2], 22[2]
14:2, 3[2], 5[3], 7[2], 8[4], 9, 10[2], 11, 13, 15, 16[2], 17, 19[3], 20[2], 22[2], 23, 24[4], 25, 27, 28[2], 29[2], 30[2]
15:1, 3, 7, 8[2], 14, 15[3], 16, 17, 19[4], 20, 22, 23[3], 26[2], 27
16:1[6], 2[2], 3[3], 6[2], 7, 9[2], 10[3], 12[2], 14, 15, 16[2], 17, 19, 20[2], 22, 23, 27, 29[2], 31[2], 32[2], 33, 35[3], 36
17:1[4], 3, 5[2], 6[3], 7[4], 9[2], 10, 12, 13, 14[2], 15
18:1[3], 3[2], 4[3], 5, 7, 9[2], 10[5], 12, 15, 16, 21[6], 24, 25[5]
19:1[4], 2, 3[3], 6[2], 7, 8, 9, 11, 12, 16, 17[2], 18, 19, 20[2], 21
20:2[4], 4, 5[2], 6, 7, 10, 18, 22, 23[2], 24, 25[2]
21:9, 10, 19, 26[2], 28, 30[2], 32, 34[2], 35
22:5[4], 6, 7, 8, 9[3], 11[2], 14, 17, 21, 25, 28, 29[3], 31
23:5, 6, 8, 9[2], 11[2], 12, 13[3], 15[2], 16[5], 18[2], 19[3], 21, 25, 26, 29, 31[2]
24:1[2], 3, 4[2], 5[3], 6[2], 7[2], 8, 9[2], 10[3], 11[2], 12, 13, 16[3], 17[5], 18
25:2[2], 3, 9[2], 10, 11, 12[3], 13, 14, 15, 17, 18[3], 19, 20, 22[3], 23, 24, 25, 26, 27, 28, 29, 31[3], 32[6], 33, 35[4], 36[2], 38, 39[2]
26:1[2], 2[3], 4[4], 5[3], 6, 7, 8[3], 9, 10[2], 11, 12[3], 13[4], 14[2], 15, 16[2], 17, 19, 20, 21, 22, 23, 24, 25, 26[3], 27[4], 28, 29, 31[2], 32[3], 33, 34, 35, 36[2], 37[3]
27:1, 2[2], 3, 4[2], 5[2], 6, 7, 9[3], 10[3], 11[4], 12[2], 13, 14[2], 16[3], 17[2], 18[3], 19[3], 20, 21[3]
28:1, 3, 6[4], 8[4], 9[2], 10[2], 11[5], 12[3], 13, 14[2], 15[7], 17[2], 21[3], 22[2], 23[2], 24[2], 25[2], 26[3], 27[3], 28[3], 29[3], 30[3], 31[2], 32[4], 33[5], 34, 36[2], 37, 38[2], 39[3], 43
29:2, 4[2], 5[2], 10[2], 11[2], 12[4], 14, 15, 17, 19, 20[7], 21[3], 22[2], 23[4], 24[2], 25, 26[2], 27[6], 28[4], 29, 30, 31, 32[3], 34[3], 38, 40[5], 41, 42[2], 43, 44, 45, 46[2]
30:1, 2, 3, 4[2], 5, 6, 10[3], 12[2], 13[2], 16[5], 18[3], 20, 23[3], 24[3], 25[2], 26[2], 27, 28, 31, 32, 33, 34, 35, 36[3]
31:2[4], 3[2], 5[3], 6[4], 7[3], 8, 9, 10[2], 13, 15, 16, 17, 18[4]
32:1[4], 2[3], 4[2], 7[2], 8[3], 10, 11[2], 12[2], 13[2], 14, 15, 16[2], 17[2], 18[3], 19, 20[2], 22, 23[3], 26[2], 27, 28[3], 31, 32, 33, 34
33:1[2], 3, 5[2], 6[2], 7[2], 9, 11[2], 16, 19, 22
34:1, 2, 4[2], 5, 7, 10, 12[2], 15[2], 16, 18[2], 20[2], 22[4], 23, 25[3], 26[3], 27, 28, 29[2], 30[2], 31, 32, 34, 35[3]
35:1[2], 2, 4[2], 5[2], 12, 15, 16, 17[2], 18[2], 19[2], 20[3], 21[2], 22[2], 23, 24[2], 25[4], 29[3], 30[5], 31[2], 33[3], 34[3], 35[8]
36:1[2], 3[4], 4, 5, 6, 8[3], 9[3], 11[4], 12[2], 13, 14, 15[3], 17[2], 18, 19[2], 20, 21[2], 22, 24, 25, 26, 27, 28, 29, 30, 31[3], 32[3], 34, 35[2], 36[3], 37[2], 38[2]
37:1[4], 2, 3[4], 4, 5, 6, 7[3], 8, 9, 10, 11, 12[2], 13, 15, 16, 17[3], 18[5], 19[2], 21[4], 22[3], 23, 24[2], 25[5], 26[3], 27[2], 28, 29[2]
38:1[2], 2[2], 3[2], 4[2], 5[2], 6, 7, 8[7], 9[2], 10[2], 11[3], 12[3], 14[2], 15[2], 16[2], 17[6], 18[3], 19[4], 20[3], 21[6], 22[4], 23[3], 24[3], 25[3], 26, 27[5], 28, 29, 30[3], 31[4]
39:1[2], 2, 5[3], 6[3], 7[2], 8[3], 10, 13, 14[3], 15[2], 16[2], 17[2], 18[2], 19[4], 20[3], 21[3], 22[3], 23[2], 24[2], 25[2], 26, 27[2], 28[3], 29[2], 30[3], 31, 32[4], 34[3], 35, 39, 40[4], 41, 42
40:2[3], 3, 5[3], 6[4], 7, 10, 12[2], 17, 19, 21[2], 22[2], 24[2], 26, 28, 29[4], 30, 32, 33, 34[2], 35[2], 36, 38[3]

LEVITICUS

1:1[2], 2[5], 3[4], 4, 5[2], 7, 9, 10[3], 11, 13, 14[3], 15, 16, 17
2:1, 2[4], 3[3], 4[2], 5, 7, 8, 9, 10[3], 11, 12, 13[3], 14[4], 16[3]
3:1[2], 2[3], 3[2], 5, 6[2], 8[2], 9[2], 11, 13[3], 16
4:2[4], 3, 4[2], 5[2], 6[2], 7[9], 8, 10[3], 11, 13[4], 14, 15[2], 16[2], 17, 18[7], 22[2], 23, 24, 25[6], 26[2], 27[3], 28, 29[2], 30[4], 31, 33, 34[5], 35[2]
5:1[2], 2[3], 3[2], 4[2], 5, 6, 9[5], 11[2], 12, 13, 15[4], 16, 17[2], 18
6:3, 5, 6, 7, 9[3], 12, 14[2], 15[5], 16[2], 17, 18[3], 20[5], 21, 22, 25, 26[2], 27, 30[2]
7:1, 3, 8, 10, 11[2], 12[2], 13[2], 14[3], 15[3], 16[2], 17[2], 18[4], 20[3], 21[4], 23[5], 24[4], 25[2], 26[4], 27, 29[4], 30, 32[2], 33[2], 34[4], 35[6], 36[2], 37[7], 38[2]
8:2, 3[2], 4[2], 7, 12, 14, 15[2], 18, 22[2], 23[5], 24[4], 26[3], 29[2], 30[2], 31[3], 32[2], 33[4], 35[3], 36
9:1, 3[3], 5, 6, 7, 8, 9[3], 10, 17, 18, 19[2], 22, 23[2]
10:1[2], 4[3], 5, 6, 7[4], 9, 11[2], 12[2], 13[2], 14[4], 15, 16[2], 17, 18, 19
11:2, 4[2], 8, 9, 10[2], 11, 21, 22, 24, 25[2], 26, 27, 28, 32[2], 33, 34, 35, 36, 37, 38, 39, 40[3], 44, 45[2], 46[4]
12:2[2], 3, 4[2], 5, 6[4], 7
13:2[4], 3[3], 4, 7[2], 9, 11, 12, 19, 20[2], 25[2], 27, 28[2], 31[2], 38, 39, 41, 43[2], 47, 48[3], 49[2], 51, 52, 53, 56[5], 57, 58, 59[4]
14:2[2], 3[2], 5, 6, 8, 10[3], 11[2], 12, 14[6], 15[3], 16, 17[7], 18[2], 21[2], 23[2], 24[2], 25[7], 26[2], 27, 28[7], 29[2], 30[2], 32[2], 34[4], 37, 38[2], 39, 42, 45[3], 50, 51, 52, 53, 54[2], 55[2], 57
15:2[3], 7, 10, 12[2], 13, 14[2], 16, 17, 18, 25[7], 26[3], 28, 29[2], 30, 31, 32[2], 33[6]
16:1[2], 5[4], 6, 7[2], 11[2], 12[3], 13, 14[3], 15[2], 16[6], 17[2], 18[5], 19[3], 20[2], 21[5], 23, 24, 25, 29[2], 31, 33[2], 34
17:2, 3[3], 4[3], 5[3], 6[3], 8[3], 9[2], 10[4], 11, 12[2], 13[3], 14[6], 15[2]
18:2, 3[4], 6[2], 7[2], 8, 9[3], 10[2], 11[2], 12, 13, 14, 15, 16, 17, 21[2], 24, 26[2], 27, 29, 30
19:2[2], 5, 8, 9[3], 10, 12, 13, 15[2], 16, 18, 19, 21[2], 22, 23[2], 25, 27[2], 29, 32, 34, 36[2]
20:2[6], 3, 4[2], 11, 12, 13, 17, 18[2], 19[2], 23, 25
21:1, 5, 6[3], 8, 9, 12[4], 14, 17[2], 21[4], 22[3], 24
22:2[2], 3[2], 4[3], 5, 6, 7, 8, 10[3], 11[2], 12[2], 13, 14, 15[2], 16, 18[4], 19[3], 21, 22, 25[3], 29, 30, 32, 33[2]
23:2[2], 3[2], 4, 5, 6[2], 10[3], 12, 13[3], 15, 17[3], 18[2], 19[3], 20, 22[4], 24[4], 27[2], 28, 31, 32[2], 34[3], 37, 38, 39[2], 40[4], 43[3], 44[2]
24:2, 3[2], 8, 9[2], 10[4], 11[4], 12, 15, 16[2], 22[2], 23[3]
25:2, 4, 5[4], 6, 8[3], 9[3], 11[2], 12, 13, 14, 15[4], 16[5], 22[2], 24, 25[2], 27, 28[2], 30, 31[2], 32[3], 33[6], 34[2], 36, 38[3], 40, 41, 42[2], 44[2], 45[4], 46, 47, 48, 49[2], 50[4], 51[2], 52[2], 54, 55[3]
26:1, 4, 6, 8[2], 10, 13[3], 16, 19, 20, 22, 25[2], 26, 29[2], 30, 31, 36[3], 38, 39[2], 40, 41[3], 43[3], 44, 45[4], 46[2]
27:2, 3[3], 5, 6[3], 9, 11, 15[2], 16[4], 17, 18, 19[2], 22[2], 23[2], 24[3], 25, 26, 27[2], 28[4], 29, 30[5], 31, 32[3], 34

NUMBERS

1:1[5], 2[5], 4[3], 5[4], 6[2], 7[2], 8[2], 9[2], 10[6], 11[2], 12[2], 13[2], 14[2], 15[2], 16[4], 18[3], 19, 20[3], 21[3], 22[5], 23[3], 24[4], 25[3], 26[4], 27[3], 28[4], 29[3], 30[4], 31[3], 32[6], 33[3], 34[4], 35[3], 36[4], 37[3], 38[4], 39[3], 40[4], 41[3], 42[4], 43[3], 44[2], 45[3], 47, 49[3], 50, 52, 53[5], 54
2:2[4], 3[7], 4, 5[4], 7[4], 9, 10[5], 12[4], 13, 14[4], 15, 16, 17[3], 18[5], 19, 20[4], 21, 22[4], 23, 24[2], 25[5], 26, 27[4], 28, 29[4], 30, 31, 32[4], 33, 34[2]
3:1, 2[2], 3[2], 4[2], 6, 7[3], 8[5], 9[2], 12[3], 13, 14, 15[2], 16, 17, 18[2], 19, 20[3], 21[4], 22[3], 23, 24[4], 25[5], 26[3], 27[6], 28[2], 29[3], 30[5], 31, 32[4], 33[4], 34[2], 35[6], 36[3], 37, 38[4], 39[2], 40[4], 41[6], 42, 43[3], 45[4], 46[4], 47, 48, 49, 50[4], 51[2]
4:2[4], 3, 4[3], 5, 6[2], 7[2], 8[2], 9[2], 10, 11[2], 12[3], 14[3], 15[6], 16[4], 18[2], 22[3], 23, 24[2], 25[5], 26[4], 27[3], 28[6], 29[2], 30[2], 31[3], 32[3], 33[6], 34[3], 35, 36, 37[5], 38[3], 39, 40[2], 41[6], 42[4], 43, 44, 45[5], 46[3], 47[3], 48, 49[3]
5:2[2], 4[2], 6, 8, 9[3], 12, 13, 14[4], 15[4], 17[2], 18, 19, 20, 21, 25, 26, 29[2], 30
6:2[2], 3[3], 4[2], 5[4], 7, 8, 9[2], 10[2], 12[2], 13[4], 14[2], 15[3], 17[2], 18[6], 19[4], 21[3], 23, 27
7:2[4], 3, 5[3], 7, 8[3], 9[2], 10, 11, 12[3], 13[4], 14[3], 15, 16, 17[4], 18[2], 19[4], 20[3], 21, 22, 23[4], 24[3], 25[4], 26[2], 27, 28, 29[4], 30[3], 31[6], 32[2], 33, 34, 35[4], 36[3], 37[4], 38[2], 39, 40, 41[4], 42[3], 43[6], 44[2], 45, 46, 47[4], 48[3], 49[4], 50[2], 51, 52, 53[4], 54[3], 55[6], 56[2], 57, 58, 59[4], 60[3], 61[4], 62[2], 63, 64, 65[4], 66[3], 67[4], 68[2], 69, 70, 71[4], 72[3], 73[4], 74[2], 75, 76, 77[4], 78[3], 79[4], 80[2], 81, 82, 83[4], 84[4], 85[2], 86[3], 87[2], 88[3], 89[3]
8:4[2], 6, 7, 9[3], 10, 11[3], 12, 14, 15[2], 16[5], 17[3], 18[2], 19[7], 20[3], 22, 24[2], 25, 26
9:1[4], 2, 3[2], 4, 5[3], 6, 7[3], 10[4], 11, 12[3], 13, 14, 15[2], 16, 17[2], 18[3], 19[2], 20[2], 22, 23[5]
10:2[4], 3[2], 4[2], 8, 10[3], 11[2], 12[4], 13[2], 14[4], 15[4], 16[4], 17[2], 18[3], 19[4], 20[4], 22[4], 23[4], 24[4], 25[5], 26[4], 27[4], 28[2], 29[2], 31, 33[3], 34[2], 36
11:1[2], 3[2], 4, 7, 8[3], 10[2], 11, 15, 16[4], 17[2], 18, 20, 22, 24[3], 25, 26[4], 28[3], 30, 31, 33, 34
12:1, 3, 4, 5[2], 8, 9, 12[2], 16
13:2[4], 3[4], 4[3], 5[3], 6[3], 7[3], 8[3], 9[3], 10[3], 11[5], 12[3], 13[3], 14[3], 15[3], 16[2], 17, 20[4], 21, 22, 23[4], 24[3], 25, 26[4], 27, 28, 29[2], 32[3], 33[2]
14:2[2], 5[3], 6[3], 7[2], 9, 10[3], 12, 14[3], 15, 17, 18[2], 19[2], 21, 23, 25, 27[2], 29, 30[2], 34[2], 38[3], 39, 40, 41, 44[3]
15:2[2], 3[2], 4[4], 5[2], 6[3], 7[2], 9[3], 10[2], 13[2], 14, 15, 18, 19[2], 20[3], 21[2], 23, 24[2], 25[2], 26[2], 27, 29, 31, 32, 38[4], 39, 41[2]
16:1[6], 2[4], 3[2], 7, 8, 9[4], 10, 12, 13, 14[2], 15, 17, 18[2], 19[3], 22[2], 24, 25, 26[2], 27[2], 28, 29[2], 31, 34, 37[2], 38[3], 39, 40[4], 41[3], 42[2], 43, 47, 49, 50[2]
17:2[6], 3[3], 4, 5[2], 6[3], 7, 8[3], 9, 12, 13
18:1[2], 2[4], 3[2], 4[3], 5[3], 6[3], 7[2], 8[5], 9[5], 11[4], 12[4], 13, 15[3], 16[2], 17[3], 18, 19[3], 20, 21[3], 22[2], 23[3], 24[3], 26[4], 27[2], 28[3], 29[4], 30[2], 31, 32[4]
19:2[2], 4[3], 6[2], 9[4], 10[2], 11, 13[3], 16, 17[3], 20[2], 21[2]
20:1[2], 4, 5[5], 6[4], 8, 10, 12[2], 13[2], 14, 16[2], 17[2], 19[2], 22, 23[2], 24[2], 26, 27, 28[2], 29
21:1[2], 3[2], 4[4], 5, 6, 9[2], 10, 12, 13[4], 14[3], 15[3], 18[2], 20[2], 21, 22[2], 24[4], 25, 26[4], 27, 28[5], 29[2], 31, 33[2], 34
22:1[2], 2, 3[3], 4[4], 5[5], 6, 7[4], 8, 10[2], 11[2], 13, 14, 16, 18[3], 21, 22, 23[2], 24[2], 25, 26, 27, 28, 31[2], 32, 34, 35[2], 36[2], 41[2]
23:6, 7[3], 9, 10[4], 13, 14[2], 17, 18, 19, 21, 22[2], 23[2], 24[2], 28
24:2, 3, 4[2], 6, 7, 8[2], 13[3], 15, 16[3], 17[4], 19[2], 20, 24
25:1, 2, 3, 4[2], 5, 6[8], 7[2], 8[4], 11[4], 12, 13[2], 14[3], 15[3], 18[5]
26:1, 2[3], 3, 4[4], 5[6], 6[4], 7[2], 8, 9[2], 11, 12[7], 13[4], 14, 15[7], 16[4], 17[4], 18[3], 19[2], 20[7], 21[5], 22[2], 23[6], 24[4], 25[2], 26[8], 27[2], 28, 29[6], 30[5], 31[4], 32[4], 33[3], 34[2], 35[7], 36[3], 37[4], 38[7], 39[4], 40[5], 41[2], 42[4], 43[2], 44[8], 45[6], 46[2], 47[3], 48[6], 49[4], 50[2], 51[2], 53, 54, 55[2], 57[7], 58[6], 59[2], 62[3], 63[2], 64[3], 65[4]
27:1[9], 2[2], 3[2], 4[2], 7[3], 8, 11[3], 12, 14[4], 16[2], 17, 18, 20[3], 21[2], 23
28:2, 3, 5[4], 7, 8[2], 9[2], 10, 11[2], 12[2], 13[2], 14[5], 15, 16[2], 17, 18, 19, 20, 24[2], 26, 27, 28, 30
29:1[2], 2, 3, 5, 6, 7, 8, 9, 11[3], 12, 13[2], 14[3], 15, 16, 17, 19, 20, 23, 25, 26, 29, 32, 36[2], 40
30:1[2], 2, 5[2], 6, 8, 9[2], 12[2]
31:2[2], 3[2], 4[2], 5[3], 6[2], 8[4], 9[3], 11[2], 12[3], 13, 14, 16[4], 20[3], 21[2], 23, 26[4], 28[7], 29[2], 30[11], 32[2], 35, 36, 37, 38, 39, 40, 42[2], 47[7], 48[3], 49[3], 50[2], 51, 52[5], 53, 54[5]
32:1[5], 2[3], 4, 6[2], 7[2], 9[3], 11[2], 12[2], 13, 14[2], 17[3], 18, 21, 24, 25[2], 26, 28[4], 29[3], 30, 31[2], 32[2], 33[9], 34, 36, 37, 39[2], 40, 41
33:1[5], 2, 3[3], 5, 6, 8[2], 9, 11, 12[2], 15, 16, 36, 37[2], 38[5], 40[4], 44,

NUMBERS

47, 48[2], 49, 50, 51[2], 52, 53, 54, 55[2]
34:2[3], 3[3], 4, 5[2], 8[2], 9, 11[3], 12, 13, 14[7], 17[2], 18, 19[4], 20[4], 21[3], 22[4], 23[5], 24[4], 25[4], 26[4], 27[4], 28[4], 29[2]
35:1, 2[3], 3, 4[2], 5, 8[4], 10[2], 11, 13, 14[2], 15, 16, 18, 19, 20[2], 21, 22, 24, 25[5], 26[2], 27[5], 28[4], 29, 30, 31[2], 32[2], 33[2], 34
36:1[10], 2[2], 3[7], 4[5], 5[4], 6[3], 7[6], 8[7], 9[3], 10, 11, 12[5], 13[3]

DEUTERONOMY

1:2, 3[2], 4[2], 5, 7[2], 10, 11, 15, 17[2], 19[2], 20, 21, 22, 23[2], 24, 25[2], 26, 27[3], 28, 29, 34, 35[2], 36, 38, 40, 41, 43
2:1, 4[3], 5, 6[2], 7, 8[4], 9[2], 12[2], 14[2], 15, 16, 18, 19[5], 20, 22, 23, 24, 25[4], 26[4], 29, 30, 34, 35, 36[2], 37[3]
3:1, 2, 3, 4[2], 6[2], 7, 8[4], 10[3], 11[8], 13[5], 14[3], 16[2], 17, 18, 26, 27
4:1, 2, 3, 4, 6, 9, 11, 12[3], 13, 15[3], 16[2], 17[2], 18[2], 19, 20[3], 23[2], 25[2], 28, 31, 32[2], 33[3], 34, 36[3], 37, 42, 43[3], 44, 45[2], 46[4], 47[3], 48, 49[2]
5:3, 4[2], 5[2], 6[3], 8, 9[2], 10, 11, 14[2], 15, 22[5], 23[3], 24[2], 25, 26[4], 28[3]
6:2, 3, 7, 9, 11, 12[3], 14[2], 15[2], 17, 18, 21
7:4, 6, 7, 8[4], 13[4], 15[2], 18, 19, 22, 25
8:3[2], 6, 7[4], 8[2], 9, 14[3], 15[2], 17, 20
9:2[3], 4, 5[2], 7[2], 9[2], 10[5], 11[3], 12[2], 14, 15, 16, 17, 18[2], 19, 21, 23, 26, 27
10:1[2], 3[2], 4[3], 6[3], 7[2], 8[3], 12, 13, 14, 16, 17[2], 18, 19, 22
11:2, 3[2], 4[2], 6[3], 7, 10[2], 11[3], 12[3], 14, 19, 20, 21[2], 24, 25[2], 27, 28[2], 30[2]
12:1, 3[3], 5, 6[3], 11, 14, 15[3], 17[7], 21[2], 22, 25, 27[3], 28
13:1, 3[2], 5[7], 6[2], 7[4], 9, 10[3], 12, 13[2], 15[3], 16[2], 17[2], 18[2]
14:1, 7[2], 8, 9, 11, 12, 20, 21[2], 22, 23[5], 28[2], 29
15:1, 2[3], 3, 5, 7[3], 9, 11, 14[4], 15, 19[4]
16:1[3], 2, 3[6], 4, 5, 6[2], 10[3], 13, 15, 16[3], 17, 19[2], 21[2]
17:2[2], 3[2], 4, 6[3], 7[2], 8, 9, 10, 11, 18[3], 19[2], 20
18:1[2], 4[5], 5[2], 6[3], 7, 8[2], 9, 10, 12, 14, 15[2], 16[3], 19, 20, 22[2]
19:2, 3, 4, 5, 6[2], 11, 12[3], 13, 14, 15[2]
20:1[3], 3, 6[2], 9[2], 11, 13, 14, 15[2], 16[2], 19[2]
21:3, 4, 5[2], 6, 8, 9[2], 13, 14, 16[2], 17[4], 18[2], 19[2], 20, 21, 22, 23
22:3, 9[2], 11[2], 12, 14, 15[3], 17[3], 18, 19[3], 20, 21[2], 22, 24, 26, 29
23:1, 2[2], 3[2], 4[4], 8[2], 10[2], 14, 16, 17[4], 18[3], 19[3], 21, 23, 25
24:1[2], 2, 3[2], 7[4], 8, 9, 14[2], 17[2], 19, 21, 22
25:5[3], 6[2], 7, 8, 9, 10, 11[3], 17, 18, 19
26:2[4], 4[2], 7, 8, 10, 12[3], 13, 14
27:1, 3[2], 5, 6[2], 8, 9, 10, 14, 15[2], 18, 19, 21, 22[2], 26
28:1[2], 2, 4[5], 9, 10[3], 11[3], 12, 13, 14, 15, 18[4], 20[2], 24, 25, 26[2], 27, 28, 33, 34, 35[2], 39, 42, 45, 47[2], 48[2], 49, 50[2], 51[4], 53[3], 54[2], 55[3], 56[2], 57, 58, 59[3], 60[2], 61, 62[2], 64, 65[3], 66, 67[2]
29:1[3], 2, 7[2], 8, 9, 10[3], 11[2], 16, 18, 19[2], 20, 21[4], 22[2], 23, 24, 25[4], 27, 28, 29
30:4[2], 6, 8, 9[4], 10[2], 20
31:4[2], 6[2], 7[2], 9[4], 10[4], 12, 14[2], 15[3], 16[2], 19[2], 21[2], 22, 23[3], 24[2], 25[2], 26[4], 28, 29[2], 30[3]
32:1, 3, 4, 5, 7[2], 8[4], 9, 10, 13[4], 14[8], 15, 18, 19[3], 22, 24[3], 25, 26, 27, 28, 32[5], 33[2], 35, 38[2], 39, 42[3], 43, 44[3], 45, 46, 49[3], 51[5], 52
33:1[2], 2, 3, 4[2], 5[2], 7[2], 8[2], 11[3], 12[2], 13[3], 15[2], 16[5], 17[5], 18, 19[4], 20[2], 21[3], 22, 23[2], 24, 26, 28[2], 29[2]
34:1[4], 2[2], 3[3], 5[3], 6[2], 8[3], 9[4], 11, 12

JOSHUA

1:1[3], 2, 3, 4[2], 5, 6, 8[2], 9, 10, 12, 13, 14, 15, 18
2:1[2], 2[3], 3, 5[2], 6[2], 9[2], 10[3], 11, 17, 18, 19[2], 20, 23, 24[2]
3:1, 3[2], 6[2], 7, 8[3], 9[2], 11[3], 12[3], 13[6], 14, 15[3], 16, 17[3]
4:2[2], 3[3], 4[3], 5[6], 7[5], 8[6], 9[3], 10, 11[2], 12[4], 13, 14[2], 16[2], 17, 18[6], 19[3], 20, 21, 23, 24[2]
5:1[7], 2, 3[2], 4[3], 5, 6[4], 9[2], 10[3], 11[2], 12[6], 14[2], 15
6:1[2], 2, 3, 4, 5[2], 6[4], 7, 8[3], 10, 11, 12, 13[3], 15, 18[2], 19[2], 20, 21, 23, 24[4], 26
7:1[9], 2, 4[2], 5[3], 6[2], 7, 9[2], 11, 12, 13[2], 15, 16, 17[3], 18[5], 19, 20, 21[4], 23[3], 24[3], 26[4]
8:1[2], 3[2], 8, 9, 10, 11[2], 12, 13[3], 14[2], 15, 19, 20[2], 21[2], 22[3], 23, 24[4], 25[2], 26, 27[2], 29[4], 30, 31[5], 32[4], 33[6], 34[2], 35[2]
9:1, 3, 5, 6, 7, 9[3], 10[3], 11, 12, 13[2], 14[2], 15, 16, 17, 18[3], 19, 20, 21[2], 23[4], 24[3], 26[3], 27[3]
10:1[2], 2, 3[5], 4, 5[6], 6[2], 7[2], 8, 11, 12[3], 13[2], 14, 18, 19, 20[3], 21[2], 22[2], 23[6], 24[5], 25, 27[2], 28[3], 30[3], 32[2], 33, 35, 37, 39, 40[5], 41, 42
11:1[4], 2[4], 3, 5, 6, 7[2], 8[2], 10, 11, 12[4], 13, 14[3], 15, 16[3], 17, 19[2], 20, 21[2], 22[3]
12:1[3], 2[5], 3[2], 4[4], 5[3], 6[4], 7[4], 9[2], 10[2], 11[2], 12[2], 13[2], 14[2], 15[2], 16[2], 17[2], 18[2], 19[2], 20[2], 21[2], 22[3], 23[4], 24
13:2, 3[2], 4[2], 5, 6[2], 7, 8, 9[3], 10[4], 11, 12[3], 13, 14[3], 15[2], 16[2], 19, 21[5], 22[2], 23[4], 24[2], 25[3], 26, 27[5], 28[2], 29[4], 30[3], 31[6], 32, 33[2]
14:1[7], 2, 3, 4, 5, 6[3], 7, 8, 10, 13, 14[3], 15
15:1[6], 2, 4[2], 5[3], 6[3], 7[3], 8[7], 9[4], 10, 11[2], 12[2], 13[5], 14[2], 15[2], 17[2], 18, 19, 20[3], 21[4], 47, 62, 63[3]
16:1[3], 2, 3[2], 4, 5[3], 8[3], 9[3]
17:1[5], 2[10], 3[5], 4[3], 5, 6[3], 7[2], 8[3], 9[6], 11[4], 12[2], 13, 14, 15[2], 16[6], 17, 18
18:1[3], 2, 3[2], 4, 5, 7[3], 10, 11[6], 12[2], 13[2], 14[3], 15[3], 16[6], 17[3], 19[4], 20[3], 21[4], 28[2]
19:1[4], 8[4], 9[9], 10[2], 12, 14, 16[2], 17, 22, 23[3], 24[2], 27[2], 31[3], 32[2], 39[3], 40[2], 41, 47[5], 48[3], 49[3], 50, 51[8]
20:2[3], 3, 4[5], 5, 6, 7, 8[6], 9[3]
21:1[7], 2[2], 3[3], 4[9], 5[9], 6[10], 7[7], 8[2], 9[6], 10[5], 11[3], 12[2], 13[2], 16, 17[2], 19[2], 20[7], 21, 23[2], 25[2], 26[2], 27[6], 28[2], 30[2], 32[3], 33, 34[5], 36[2], 38[3], 40[3], 41[3], 44, 45[2]
22:1, 2, 3[2], 4[2], 5, 7[2], 8, 9[10], 10[5], 11[8], 12[4], 13[6], 14[5], 15[4], 16[2], 17[2], 18, 19[4], 20[2], 21[5], 22[2], 24[2], 25[2], 27, 28[2], 29, 30[6], 31[7], 32[7], 33[3], 34[2]
23:3, 5, 6[2], 7[2], 10, 12, 13, 14[2], 16[2]
24:1[2], 2[4], 3[2], 6, 8, 9[3], 10, 11, 12, 13, 14, 15[2], 17[3], 23, 26[3], 27, 29[2], 30[3], 31[3], 32[10], 33

JUDGES

1:1[2], 4, 8[2], 9, 10, 11[2], 13, 14, 15, 16[6], 17, 19[3], 20, 21[2], 22, 23[2], 24, 25, 26, 27[4], 30[2], 31[7], 32, 33[5], 34, 35[2], 36
2:1[2], 2, 4[2], 5, 6, 7[3], 8[2], 9[3], 11[2], 12[5], 14[3], 15, 16[2], 17[2], 18[5], 20, 21, 22, 23
3:1[2], 2[2], 3[2], 4[2], 5, 7[2], 8[4], 9[3], 10[2], 11, 12[4], 13[2], 14[2], 15[4], 16, 17, 20, 22, 23, 24, 25, 27[2], 28, 29[2], 30, 31[2]
4:1[2], 2[4], 3[3], 4, 5[2], 6[7], 7, 9, 11[4], 12, 13[3], 15, 16[3], 17[4], 19, 20[2], 21, 23[2], 24[4]
5:1, 2, 3, 4[3], 5, 6[3], 7, 9, 11[5], 12, 14[5], 15[3], 16[3], 18, 19[3], 21, 22[2], 23[3], 24, 28[2], 30[6]
6:1[3], 2[3], 3, 4, 6[2], 7[2], 8[4], 9[4], 10, 11, 12[2], 13[2], 14, 19[2], 20, 21[5], 22[2], 24, 25[2], 26[2], 27[2], 28[2], 29, 30[2], 33[2], 34, 37, 38[2]
7:1[4], 3[2], 4[2], 5, 6[2], 8[2], 11, 12, 13[2], 14[3], 15[3], 17, 18[3], 19[2], 20[2], 22, 23[4], 24, 25[3]
8:1, 2[4], 3[2], 5[3], 6[2], 7, 8[2], 9, 10[3], 11[2], 12, 13, 14[4], 15[2], 16[3], 17[2], 18[2], 19, 22[2], 24[2], 25, 26[3], 28[2], 29, 30, 32[3], 33, 34[3], 35
9:1[3], 2[3], 3[3], 4[3], 5[2], 6[3], 7[2], 15[2], 16, 17[2], 18[2], 20[4], 21, 23[2], 24[3], 25[2], 26[2], 27, 28[4], 30[3], 31, 35[3], 36[2], 37[2], 39, 40, 43, 44[2], 46[4], 47[2], 49[2], 51[2], 52, 53, 54, 55, 56, 57[4]
10:1[3], 4, 6[8], 7[4], 8[3], 9[2], 10, 11[2], 12, 14, 15, 16, 17[2], 18[3]
11:1[2], 2, 3, 4[2], 5[4], 6, 7[2], 8[3], 9[2], 10, 11, 12[2], 13[4], 14[2], 15[3], 17[3], 18[7], 19[2], 21[4], 22, 23, 25[2], 26, 27[2], 28[3], 29[4], 30, 31[3], 32, 33[3], 35, 36[4], 39, 40[2]
12:1[2], 2[2], 3, 4[3], 5[2], 6[2], 7[2], 8, 12, 13, 15[3]
13:1[3], 2[3], 3, 5[2], 6[3], 7, 8, 9[2], 13[2], 14[2], 15, 16[3], 17, 18, 20[2], 21[2], 25[2]
14:1[2], 2[2], 3[2], 4, 5, 6, 8[3], 9[2], 12[2], 13, 14[2], 16, 17, 18, 19[3]
15:1, 2, 5, 6, 7, 8, 10, 11[2], 12, 14, 15, 16[2], 17[2], 18[2], 20
16:2, 3[3], 4, 5[3], 8, 9, 13, 14[2], 18[2], 19, 20, 21, 22, 23, 24[2], 25, 27[2], 28, 29[3], 31[2]
17:1, 2[3], 3, 4[2], 5[2], 7[3], 8[2], 9, 10[2], 11, 12
18:1[2], 2[4], 3[2], 5, 7, 10, 11[5], 13, 14, 15[2], 16[4], 17[2], 19, 20, 22[2], 23, 25[2], 26, 27, 29[3], 30[6], 31
19:1[2], 3[2], 5, 6, 8, 11, 12[3], 13, 15, 16[3], 17, 18[2], 19, 22[3], 23, 26[2], 27[2], 29, 30[4]
20:1[2], 2[5], 3[3], 4, 5, 6[2], 7, 8[2], 10[5], 11, 12[2], 13[4], 14[3], 15[3], 17[2], 18[5], 19, 20[2], 21[3], 22, 23[3], 24[2], 25[3], 26[2], 27[4], 28[3], 30[2], 31[5], 32[2], 33[6], 34, 35[2], 36[2], 37, 38[2], 39[3], 40[3], 41[2], 42[4], 44[2], 45[3], 46[2], 48[4]
21:1[2], 2, 3, 5[2], 6, 7, 8[2], 9[2], 10[3], 12[2], 13, 14[2], 15, 16[2], 17[2], 18[2], 19[4], 20, 21[5], 23[2], 24

RUTH

1:1[2], 2[5], 4[4], 5[2], 6[2], 7[2], 9[2], 13, 22[3]
2:1[4], 2, 3[3], 6[2], 9, 10, 11[2], 12[2], 13, 14, 16[2], 17, 19, 20[3], 23[3]
3:2, 7[2], 10, 11, 13[3], 15, 17
4:1, 2[2], 3[3], 4, 5[5], 9[2], 10[4], 11, 12[3], 15[2], 17[2], 18

1 SAMUEL

1:1[6], 2[2], 3[4], 7, 9[2], 10, 11[3], 15, 16[3], 17[2], 20, 24[3], 27
2:3[2], 4, 8[3], 9, 10[4], 12[2], 13, 15, 17[2], 20, 22[2], 23, 25, 27[2], 28[5], 29[2], 30[2], 31, 33[3], 34, 36[4]
3:1, 3[3], 7, 11, 14[2], 15[2], 17, 19, 20, 21
4:1, 2, 3[6], 4[6], 5[2], 6[4], 8[2], 10, 11[2], 12[2], 13, 14[2], 16[2], 17, 18[3], 19, 20, 21[2], 22
5:1, 2[2], 3[2], 4[4], 5[2], 6[2], 7[3], 8[7], 9[2], 10[4], 11[4], 12
6:1[2], 2, 3[2], 4[2], 5[3], 8[2], 9, 11[3], 12[3], 13, 14[2], 15[3], 16, 18[7], 19[4], 20, 21[2]
7:1[4], 2, 3[3], 4, 6, 7[4], 8[3], 11[2], 12, 13[3], 14[2], 15
8:2[2], 4, 7, 8, 9, 10[2], 11, 12[2], 14, 15[2], 17, 18, 19, 21[2], 22
9:1[6], 2[2], 3[2], 4[3], 5, 6, 7, 8[3], 9, 10, 12, 16[4], 17, 20, 21[6], 23, 25, 26[3], 27[2]
10:1, 2[2], 3[3], 4[2], 5[3], 6, 8, 10[2], 11, 12, 13, 16[2], 18[8], 19, 20[2], 21[3], 22, 23, 25, 26, 27
11:1, 3[2], 4[2], 5[3], 6, 7[4], 8[2], 9[2], 10, 11[3], 15[2]
12:3, 4, 6[2], 7[2], 8, 9[6], 10[2], 11[2], 12[2], 14, 15[3], 17
13:2[3], 3[2], 4, 6, 7[2], 10, 13, 15, 16, 17[3], 18[2], 19, 22[3], 23[2]
14:1, 2, 3[3], 4[2], 5, 6, 11[3], 12[2], 14[2], 16[2], 18[3], 19, 22, 24[2], 25, 27, 28, 29, 30[2], 36, 37[2], 38, 41, 43, 45, 47[2], 48[2], 49[4], 50[5], 51[3], 52
15:1[2], 2, 4, 5, 6[2], 8[2], 9[3], 10, 13[2], 14[2], 15[2], 17[2], 19[2], 20[2], 21[2], 22[2], 23[2], 24, 26, 27, 28[2], 29, 30, 32[2], 34, 35
16:4, 7, 10, 12, 13[3], 14, 18[3], 20
17:2[2], 4[3], 5[4], 6[2], 7[2], 8, 10, 11, 12[3], 13[2], 17, 18, 19[2], 22[2], 23[3], 24, 25, 26, 28, 32, 33, 34, 35, 36[2], 37[6], 38[2], 40, 42, 44[2], 45[4], 46[4], 50, 51, 52[4], 53, 54, 55, 57[2], 58
18:1[3], 4, 5[3], 6[4], 10, 11, 12, 15, 17, 21[2], 23, 24, 25[3], 27, 29, 30[2]
19:3, 4, 6, 10, 13, 16, 20[3], 23
20:6, 8, 11, 12, 14, 15[2], 16[2], 21, 23, 27[2], 28, 30[3], 31, 33, 34, 37, 41, 42[2]
21:1, 2, 3, 5[2], 7[3], 9[2], 10[2], 11[3], 12[2], 13, 15
22:3[2], 4, 5[2], 7[4], 8[3], 9[3], 10[2], 11[2], 12, 13[2], 15[3], 17[3], 19[3], 20[3], 22[2]
23:2, 3, 4, 5, 6, 10, 11[2], 12[2], 13, 14, 15, 17, 19[2], 20, 21, 23[2], 24[2], 25[2], 26[3]
24:1, 2[2], 3, 4[3], 6, 7, 8, 11[2], 12, 13, 14, 15, 16, 20, 21
25:1, 3[6], 9, 10, 14[2], 17, 18[4], 20, 21, 22[2], 24, 25[2], 28[2], 29[5], 31, 32, 34, 35, 36, 37, 39[3], 40, 41[2], 42[2], 43[2], 44[2]
26:1, 2[3], 3, 5[2], 6, 11, 12, 13, 14, 15, 16, 19[3], 20[2], 22, 24[2]
27:1[5], 2[2], 6, 7, 8[3], 10[3], 11
28:2, 3, 5, 6, 7, 9, 13, 14, 16, 17, 18, 19[3], 20[2], 22[2]
29:2, 3[4], 4[3], 5, 6, 7, 8, 9[2], 11
30:5, 6[2], 12[3], 13, 14[2], 15, 16[5], 17[2], 22[3], 26[5], 29[2]
31:1, 3, 7[3], 9[2], 10[2], 11[2], 12[3]

2 SAMUEL

1:1[2], 2, 3[2], 4, 12[2], 13, 15, 18[3], 19, 20[3], 21[4], 22[4], 24[2], 25, 26, 27
2:1[3], 3, 4[3], 5[2], 7, 8[3], 10, 11, 12[3], 13[5], 15[4], 17[2], 18[2], 21[2], 23, 24[3], 25[2], 30, 31[3], 32[2]
3:1[3], 2, 3[5], 4[2], 6[3], 7, 8[3], 10[2], 13, 14, 15, 17, 18[6], 19[3], 22, 23, 25, 26, 27, 28[2], 29[2], 32, 36, 37[2], 39[2]
4:2[6], 4[3], 5[3], 6, 8[5], 9[2], 10, 11, 12[2]
5:1, 3, 6, 7[2], 8, 9, 10, 11, 13, 14, 17, 18, 19, 20[2], 22, 23, 24[3]
6:1, 2[4], 3[4], 4[3], 5[3], 6[2], 7[2], 8, 9[2], 10[3], 11[2], 12[6], 13, 15[3], 16[2], 17[2], 18[3], 19[4], 20[5], 21, 22[3], 23[2]
7:2[2], 4, 6[2], 7[4], 8, 9[2], 10[2], 12, 13, 14[3], 19[2], 26[2], 27[2], 29[2]
8:1[2], 3[2], 4, 5[3], 6, 7[2], 8, 9[2], 10[3], 11, 12[10], 13[2], 14, 16[2], 17[2], 18
9:1[2], 2[2], 3[3], 4[2], 5[3], 6[2], 7, 11, 12
10:1[2], 2[4], 3[2], 4, 6[6], 7[2], 8[4], 9[3], 10[3], 11, 12[2], 14[2], 16[2], 18[3], 19
11:1, 2, 3[2], 7, 8[2], 9[2], 11, 13, 14, 15, 17[4], 19[2], 21[2], 23, 24, 26
12:3[2], 4[2], 7[3], 8[2], 9[3], 10, 11[2], 14, 17, 18, 20, 25[2], 26[2], 27, 28, 30[2], 31[4]
13:1[2], 3, 6, 10, 11, 13, 18, 19, 21, 29, 30, 32[2], 34, 36, 37[2], 39
14:1, 4, 7, 9, 11[2], 13, 15[2], 16[4], 17[2], 19[2], 20[3], 22, 25[2], 26, 27
15:2[5], 3, 6[2], 10[2], 11, 13[2], 14, 23, 24[4], 25[2], 27, 28, 29, 30, 31, 32, 34, 35
16:1[7], 3[2], 5[4], 6, 7, 8[3], 9, 10, 11, 15, 18, 19, 21[2], 22[2], 23[3]
17:4, 8[2], 9, 10, 12[2], 14[4], 15, 16, 18, 20, 21, 22, 23, 24, 25[3], 26, 27[7], 29
18:1[2], 2[5], 3[3], 6, 7[3], 8, 9[3], 11, 12, 14[2], 17, 19[2], 22, 23, 27[3], 31, 32
19:5[5], 9[6], 10, 11[2], 13[4], 14[3], 16[3], 17[3], 18, 19, 20[2], 21, 22, 24, 27, 28, 29, 32, 35, 37[2], 38, 40[2], 41[2], 42[4], 43[6]
20:1[3], 2[3], 3, 4, 5, 6, 7[2], 10, 11, 12[2], 13[2], 14, 15, 16, 17, 19[2], 21[2], 22[2], 23[2], 24
21:1[2], 2[6], 3, 4[2], 5[2], 6[2], 7[4], 8[5], 9[3], 10[5], 11[2], 12[4], 13[3], 14[3], 16[4], 17[3], 18[2], 19[3], 20, 21[2], 22[2]
22:1[5], 3[2], 5[2], 6[2], 7, 8, 9[2], 11, 12, 13, 16[5], 17, 19, 21, 22, 31, 35, 36, 41, 43[2], 44[2], 46, 47[2], 51
23:1[5], 2, 3[3], 4[2], 6[2], 7, 8, 9[3], 11[3], 12, 13[4], 14, 15[3], 16[3], 17[2], 18[2], 19, 20[6], 21, 22, 24[4], 26, 29[5], 30[2], 32[2], 33, 34[3], 36[2], 37
24:1, 2[3], 3, 4[4], 5[3], 6, 7[4], 8, 9[3], 10, 11, 12, 13, 14[2], 15, 16[3], 18, 19, 21, 22, 24[3]

1 KINGS

1:3, 5, 7, 8, 9[2], 11[2], 12, 19[2], 20[2], 25, 26, 27, 29, 30, 32, 33, 36[2], 37, 38, 39[2], 40, 41[3], 42, 44, 46, 47, 48, 50[2], 51, 52
2:1, 2, 3[2], 4, 5[7], 7[3], 8[2], 10, 12, 13[2], 16, 20, 22, 24, 25[2], 26[2], 27[2], 28[2], 29[2], 30, 31, 32[6], 33[2], 34, 35[2], 39[5], 43, 45, 46[2]
3:1[5], 2, 3, 6, 7, 8, 11, 15[2], 17, 28[2]
4:2, 3[2], 4, 5[2], 6, 8, 9, 10[2], 11[3], 12, 13[4], 14, 15, 16, 17, 18, 19[6], 21[3], 22[2], 23, 25, 26, 29, 30[3], 31, 33[6], 34[4]
5:1[3], 3[2], 5, 6, 7, 8[2], 11[2], 13, 16, 17
6:1[5], 3[2], 4, 5[4], 6[2], 7[2], 8[2], 9, 10, 11, 13, 15[6], 16[2], 18, 19[2], 20, 21, 23, 24[4], 25, 26[2], 27[4], 29[2], 30, 31[3], 32[2], 33[3], 34[3], 36[2], 37[2], 38
7:2[3], 6, 7[2], 8, 9[2], 10[3], 11, 12[5], 13, 14[3], 15[4], 16[4], 17[3], 19[2], 21, 22[2], 23, 24, 26[2], 27[3], 28, 29, 30[2], 31[3], 32[2], 33[2], 34[2], 35[4], 36[2], 37, 38[2], 39[3], 40[2], 41[4], 42[2], 45[2], 46, 47, 48[3], 49[2], 50[5], 51[3]
8:1[9], 2, 3, 4[2], 5, 6[4], 7, 8, 9[4], 10[2], 11[3], 14[2], 15, 16[3], 17[3], 19, 20[4], 21[3], 22[3], 23, 25[2], 26, 27, 28, 29, 30[2], 34, 36[2], 37, 38, 39[2], 41[2], 42[3], 43, 46, 47, 48, 51[3], 52[2], 53[3], 54[2], 55, 56[2], 59[2], 60, 63[3], 64[4], 65[2], 66
9:1[2], 4, 5[2], 7[2], 9[2], 10[2], 11[2], 13, 14, 15[3], 16, 19[2], 20[3], 21[2], 22[4], 23, 24[2], 26[3], 27[2]
10:1[4], 2, 4, 5[4], 6[2], 9, 10[4], 11[2], 12[2], 13[2], 14[2], 15[7], 16[2], 17[4], 18, 19[2], 21[8], 22[3], 23, 25[2], 28, 29[4]
11:1[2], 2[2], 4, 5[2], 6, 7[3], 9, 11, 12[2], 14, 15, 17, 18[3], 19[3], 20[2], 21, 23[2], 24, 25, 26[2], 27[2], 28[3], 29, 31[3], 32[2], 33[4], 34[2], 35, 39, 40[2], 41[4], 43
12:2[3], 3, 4, 8, 14, 15, 16, 17[2], 19, 20[2], 21[4], 22[2], 23[4], 24[3], 26, 27[4], 28[3], 31[5], 32[2], 33[3]
13:1[3], 2[3], 4[2], 5[2], 6[3], 7, 8, 9, 11, 12, 14[2], 17, 18, 20, 21[2], 22[2], 26[3], 29[2], 31, 32[3], 33[5], 34[2]
14:1, 2, 3[2], 4[2], 5[2], 6[2], 7, 8, 10[3], 11[2], 13[3], 14, 15, 16[2], 17, 18[2], 19[5], 21[3], 22, 24[2], 25[2], 26[4], 27[3], 28, 29[5], 31
15:1[2], 2, 3[2], 5[3], 6, 7[5], 8, 9[2], 10, 11, 12, 15, 16, 17[2], 18[7], 19[2], 20[3], 21, 22[2], 23[6], 24, 25[3], 26[2], 27[3], 28[2], 29[2], 30[3], 31[5], 32, 33[3], 34[2]
16:1[2], 2[2], 3[4], 4[3], 5[5], 7[6], 8[3], 9[3], 10[2], 11[3], 12[2], 13[3], 14[5], 15[2], 16, 18, 19[2], 20[5], 21[3], 22, 23[2], 24[5], 25, 26[3], 27[5], 29[4], 30[2], 31[4], 32, 33[2], 34[2]
17:1[3], 2, 4, 5, 6, 8, 10[2], 11, 12, 14[3], 15, 16[3], 17[2], 18, 19, 22[2], 23, 24[2]
18:1, 3, 4, 5, 9, 10, 12, 13[2], 15, 18, 19[2], 20, 22, 24[2], 25[2], 26, 29[2], 30, 31[4], 32[2], 36[4], 38, 40[2], 41[2], 42, 44, 46[2]
19:2[2], 6, 7, 8[2], 9, 10[2], 13, 14[2], 15, 16[3], 17[2], 19[2], 21[2]
20:1, 2, 4, 6, 7[2], 9, 10, 11, 13, 14[2], 15[3], 17[3], 19[3], 20, 21, 22[3], 23[3], 24, 26, 27[3], 28[4], 29[2], 30, 31[3], 32, 35[3], 36, 39[2], 40, 41[2], 42, 43
21:1[2], 2[2], 3, 4[2], 7[2], 10, 11, 13[4], 15[2], 16[2], 17, 18[2], 19, 20, 22[4], 23[2], 24[2], 25, 26, 28
22:2[2], 3[4], 4, 5[2], 6[2], 7[2], 8[3], 9[2], 10[4], 11[2], 13[3], 15, 16, 18, 19[2], 22, 23, 24[2], 26[2], 27[2], 28, 29[2], 30[2], 31[2], 32[2], 33[2], 34[4], 35[2], 36, 38[2], 39[5], 41[3], 42, 43[2], 44, 45[5], 46[3], 48, 49, 50, 51[3], 52[5], 53

2 KINGS

1:1, 2[3], 3[5], 6[2], 7, 8, 9[3], 10[2], 11[2], 12[2], 13[4], 14, 15[2], 16[3], 17[4], 18[5]
2:3, 5, 7[2], 9, 11[2], 12[2], 13[2], 14[2], 15[2], 16, 19[2], 21, 22, 23, 24[3]
3:1[3], 2[2], 3[2], 4[2], 5[2], 6, 7[2], 8, 9[4], 10[2], 11[6], 12[3], 13[5], 14[3], 15, 16, 18, 19[2], 20, 24, 25[2], 26[2]
4:1[3], 2, 3, 7[2], 9, 13, 16[2], 17, 21[2], 22[3], 25[2], 27[2], 28, 29, 30, 31, 34, 38[2], 39, 40[2], 42[4], 44
5:1[3], 2[2], 3, 4[2], 5[5], 6[2], 7[2], 8[2], 9[2], 11, 12[2], 14[3], 15[2], 17, 18[3], 20[3], 22[4], 23[3], 27
6:1, 6, 8, 9[2], 10[3], 11[4], 12[2], 15[2], 17[3], 18, 20[2], 21, 23[2], 24, 25[4], 26, 27[2], 30, 31[2], 32[2], 33
7:1[4], 2, 3, 4, 5[3], 6[7], 8, 9, 10[3], 12[2], 13[4], 14, 15, 16[4], 17[2], 18[4], 19
8:2[3], 3[2], 4[2], 6, 7[2], 8[3], 9[4], 11, 12, 16[6], 18[5], 20, 21, 22, 23[5], 24, 25[5], 26[2], 27[6], 28[2], 29[5]
9:1[3], 2[2], 3, 5[2], 6[2], 7[5], 8, 9[5], 10, 11, 13, 14[4], 15[3], 16, 17, 20[2], 21[3], 22, 25[2], 26[4], 27[2], 28, 29[2], 30, 33, 35[2], 36[3], 37[3]
10:1, 3, 5, 6[2], 8[2], 10[3], 11[2], 13[5], 14[2], 15, 17, 19[2], 21[3], 22, 23[6], 24[2], 25[4], 26[2], 27[2], 28, 29[2], 30[3], 31[3], 32, 33, 34[5]
11:1, 2[3], 3, 4[3], 5[3], 6[2], 7[3], 10, 11[2], 13[3], 14, 15[3], 18[4], 19[5], 20
12:1[2], 2, 4[4], 5[2], 6[2], 7[3], 8[2], 9[3], 10, 11[4], 12[3], 13[6], 14, 16, 17, 18[5], 19[5], 20, 21[3]
13:1[4], 2[3], 3[5], 4[2], 5[2], 6[2], 7[2], 8[5], 10[3], 11[3], 12[6], 13, 14[3], 16, 17[2], 18, 19, 20[2], 21[3], 22[2], 23, 24, 25[7]
14:1[5], 2, 3, 6[3], 7[3], 8[3], 9[2], 10, 11[2], 13[6], 14[2], 15[6], 16, 17[5], 18[5], 20, 21[2], 23[5], 24[3], 25[8], 26, 27[3], 28[5], 29
15:1[4], 2, 3, 5[2], 6[5], 7, 8[3], 9[3], 10, 11[5], 12[2], 13[3], 14[2], 15[5], 17[3], 18[3], 19[2], 20[7], 21[5], 23[3], 24[3], 25[4], 26[5], 27[3], 28[3], 29[4], 30[4], 31[5], 32[5], 33, 34, 35[2], 36[5], 37[2], 38
16:1[4], 2, 3[4], 5[3], 6, 7[7], 8[3], 9[3], 10[3], 13, 14[3], 15[4], 17[2], 18[2], 19[5], 20
17:1[3], 2[2], 3, 4[4], 5, 6[4], 7[5], 8[4], 9[2], 14, 16[2], 17, 18[2], 19[2], 20[3], 21[2], 22[2], 23[2], 24[4], 25[2], 26[6], 27[4], 28, 29[2], 30[3], 31, 32[4], 33, 34, 36[2], 39[2]
18:1[5], 2, 3, 4, 5[2], 7, 8, 9[5], 10[4], 11[3], 12[2], 13[3], 14[6], 15[2], 16[4], 17[3], 18[2], 19, 21[2], 23, 24[3], 26[2], 28[2], 29, 30[2], 31[4], 32[4], 33[5], 34[4], 35[3], 37[3]
19:1, 2[2], 3[2], 4[2], 5, 6[3], 8, 9[2], 10[3], 11, 12[2], 13[5], 14[3], 15[3], 16, 17[2], 18, 19[2], 20[3], 21[2], 22, 23[5], 24[2], 25, 26[2], 29[2], 30[2], 31[4], 32, 35[2], 36, 37[2]
20:1, 4, 5[3], 6[3], 7, 8, 9, 11, 12[2], 13[2], 16, 18[3], 19, 20[5]
21:2[3], 3[2], 4[2], 5[3], 6, 7[4], 8[2], 9, 11, 12[2], 13[3], 14[2], 15, 16, 17[5], 18[2], 19[2], 20, 22[2], 23, 24[2], 25[5], 26
22:1[2], 2[2], 3[4], 4[3], 5[7], 7, 8[2], 9[3], 11[2], 12[3], 13[4], 14[4], 15, 16[2], 17, 18[3]
23:1[2], 2[6], 3, 4[7], 5[3], 6[3], 7[2], 8[7], 9[3], 10[2], 11[5], 12[6], 13[7], 14, 15, 16[3], 17[4], 18[2], 19[3], 20, 21, 22[5], 23, 24[3], 25, 26[2], 27[2], 28[5], 29[2], 30[2], 31[2], 32, 33[4], 34[2], 35[4], 36[2], 37
24:1, 2[6], 3[3], 5[5], 7[5], 8[2], 9, 10[2], 11, 12[4], 13[6], 14[3], 15, 16[2], 17, 18[2], 19, 20[2]
25:1[3], 2, 3[2], 4[2], 5[2], 6, 7[3], 8[6], 9[2], 10[3], 11[4], 12[3], 13[4], 14, 15[3], 16[2], 17[3], 18[2], 19[7], 20[2], 21[3], 22[4], 23[6], 24[2], 25[3], 26[2], 27[8], 28, 29, 30[2]

1 CHRONICLES

1:5, 6, 7, 8, 9[2], 12, 17, 19, 23, 28, 29, 31, 32[2], 33[2], 34, 35, 36, 37, 38, 39, 40[2], 41[2], 42[2], 43[4], 44[2], 45[2], 46[3], 47, 48, 49, 50[3], 51, 54
2:1, 3[5], 4, 5, 6[2], 7[2], 8, 9, 10[2], 16, 17, 18[3], 21[2], 22, 23[3], 24, 25[2], 26, 27[2], 28[2], 29[2], 30, 31[3], 32[2], 33[2], 42[5], 43, 44, 45[2], 47, 49[4], 50[4], 51[2], 52[2], 53[2], 54[3], 55[4]
3:1[3], 2[4], 3, 5[2], 9[2], 15, 16, 17, 19[2], 21[5], 22[2], 23, 24
4:1, 2[2], 3[3], 4[5], 5, 6, 7, 8[2], 10, 11[2], 12[2], 13[2], 14[2], 15[3], 16, 17[2], 18[5], 19[3], 20[2], 21[8], 22, 24, 26, 27, 31, 34, 35[3], 37[5], 38, 39[2], 40[2], 41[2], 42[4], 43
5:1[4], 2, 3[2], 4, 6[2], 7, 8[3], 9[2], 10[2], 11[2], 13[2], 14[8], 15[4], 16, 17[4], 18[3], 20, 21[4], 22, 23[2], 24[5], 25[3], 26[6]
6:1, 2, 3[2], 15, 16, 17[2], 18, 19[2], 20, 22, 25, 26, 28, 29, 31[2], 32[3], 33[4], 34[4], 35[4], 36[4], 37[4], 38[4], 39[2], 40[3], 41[3], 42[3], 43[3], 44[4], 45[3], 46[3], 47[4], 48[4], 49[4], 50, 54[4], 55, 56[2], 57[3], 60[2], 61[6], 62[9], 63[7], 64, 65[9], 66[6], 67[2], 70[5], 71[4], 72[2], 74[2], 76[2], 77[4], 78[3], 80[2]
7:1, 2[5], 3[3], 4[2], 5[2], 6, 7[4], 8[2], 9[4], 10[2], 11[3], 12[2], 13[2], 14[2], 15[2], 16[2], 17[4], 19, 20, 21, 29[4], 30, 31[2], 33[2], 34, 35, 36, 38, 39, 40[5]
8:3, 6[4], 8, 9, 10, 11, 12, 13[4], 16, 18, 21, 25, 27, 28, 29, 34, 35, 38, 39, 40[4]
9:1[2], 3[6], 4[7], 5, 6[2], 7[5], 8[6], 9[2], 10, 11[7], 12[8], 13[5], 14[6], 15[3], 16[6], 18[2], 19[10], 20, 21[4], 23[4], 26[2], 27, 28[2], 29[2], 30[3], 31[2], 32[3], 33[2], 34, 35, 40, 41, 44
10:1, 2, 3, 7, 9, 10[2], 12[2], 13[3], 14[2]
11:3[2], 4, 5[3], 6, 7, 8, 9, 10[2], 11[2], 12[2], 13[2], 14, 15[4], 17[3], 18[4], 19[2], 20[2], 21, 22[4], 23[2], 24, 26[4], 28, 30, 31[3], 32[2], 34[2], 35[2], 37, 38[2], 39[2], 41, 42[2], 43, 44, 45, 46
12:1[3], 2[3], 3[2], 7[2], 8[4], 14[4], 15, 16[2], 17, 18[3], 19[3], 20[3], 21[2], 22, 23[3], 24, 25[3], 26[2], 27, 28[2], 29[6], 30[4], 31[2], 32[4], 33[3], 34, 35, 36, 37[6], 38[3], 40[2]
13:1, 2[3], 3[2], 4, 5[3], 6, 7[3], 9, 10, 12[2], 13[2], 14[3]
14:1[2], 2, 4, 8, 9, 10, 11[2], 14, 15[3], 16, 17[2]
15:1[2], 2[2], 3, 4, 5[2], 6[2], 7[2], 8[2], 9[2], 10[2], 12[4], 14[2], 15[3], 16[2], 17[6], 18, 19, 22, 24, 25[5], 26[2], 27[3], 28[3], 29[4]
16:1[2], 2[2], 3[4], 4[3], 6[2], 7, 9, 10, 12, 13[2], 15, 16[2], 18[2], 26, 28, 29, 33[2], 35, 36, 37[2], 38, 39, 40[2], 42[2]
17:1[3], 3, 6[3], 7, 8, 9, 11, 17[3], 18, 21[2], 24[3], 27
18:1[2], 3, 4, 5[3], 7[2], 8[2], 9[3], 10[3], 11, 12[2], 15[2], 16[2], 17[2]
19:1[2], 2[4], 3[2], 6[6], 7[2], 8[2], 9[2], 10[2], 11[3], 12, 13[2], 15, 16[2], 18[2], 19[2]
20:1[3], 2[3], 3[3], 4[2], 5[2], 6[2], 7, 8[2]
21:2[2], 3, 5[3], 8, 10, 12[4], 13[2], 14, 15[3], 16[2], 18[2], 19[2], 21, 22, 25, 26, 28, 29[2], 30[4]
22:1[2], 2[2], 3, 4, 5[2], 6, 7, 8, 9, 10, 11[2], 12, 13, 14[4], 15[3], 16, 17, 18, 19[5]
23:1, 2, 3, 4[3], 6, 7, 8, 9[3], 10[2], 12, 13, 14[3], 15, 16[2], 17[2], 18[2], 19[2], 20[2], 21[2], 22, 23, 24[7], 25, 26, 27, 28[7], 29, 32[7]
24:1[3], 3[4], 4[9], 5[7], 6[5], 19[3], 20[6], 21[2], 22[3], 23, 24[4], 25[3], 26[2], 27, 28, 29, 30[3], 31[4]
25:1[6], 2[5], 3[3], 4[2], 5[2], 6[4], 7[2]
26:1[5], 2, 4, 6[2], 7, 8[3], 10[2], 11, 12[2], 13, 15, 16, 19[3], 20[4], 21[3], 22[3], 23, 24[3], 26[2], 27[2], 28[5], 29, 30[5], 31[5], 32[3]
27:1[5], 2, 3[4], 4[2], 5[2], 7, 9, 10[2], 11, 12, 13, 14[2], 15, 16[5], 17[3], 18[5], 19[4], 20[6], 21[5], 22[4], 23[2], 24[3], 25[2], 26[3], 27, 28, 29, 31, 32, 34[2]
28:1[5], 2[4], 3, 4[6], 5[3], 8[4], 9[3], 11[7], 12[10], 13[6], 14[7], 15[4], 16[2], 17, 18[5], 19, 20[3], 21[5]
29:2[8], 3[4], 4[5], 5[4], 6[6], 7[6], 8[3], 10, 12, 14[2], 16, 17, 18[5], 20, 22, 23[2], 24, 25, 26, 28, 29[4], 30

2 CHRONICLES

1:1, 2[3], 3[3], 4, 5[3], 6, 9, 11, 12, 13, 16, 17[4]
2:1, 3, 4[2], 6, 8, 10[4], 11, 12, 13, 14[6], 15, 16, 17, 18[2]
3:1[2], 2[2], 3[2], 4[3], 6, 8, 9[2], 10, 11[4], 12[3], 13, 14, 15[3], 16, 17[2]
4:1, 2[2], 3[2], 5[5], 7, 8, 9[2], 10, 11, 12[3], 13[2], 16[2], 17, 18, 19, 20, 21, 22[5]
5:1[3], 2[9], 3, 4, 5, 6, 7[4], 8, 9[2], 10[2], 11, 12[5], 13[2], 14[3]
6:2, 3[2], 4, 5[3], 7[3], 9, 10[4], 11[2], 12[3], 13[3], 14, 16[2], 17, 18, 19, 21[2], 25, 27[2], 28, 29[2], 30[2], 32, 33, 37, 38, 41, 42[2]
7:1[2], 2[2], 3[2], 5[2], 6[2], 7[3], 8[2], 9, 10, 11[2], 12, 18, 20[2], 22[3]
8:1[2], 2, 6[2], 7[2], 8[2], 9[5], 10, 11[6], 12, 13[4], 14[4], 15, 16[5], 17, 18[4]
9:1[4], 3[2], 4[4], 5[2], 6[2], 9[3], 10[2], 11[3], 12, 13[2], 14[2], 15[2], 16[4], 17, 18[2], 20[9], 21[2], 22, 23[2], 24[2], 26[2], 28[2], 29[6], 31
10:2[3], 4, 13, 14, 15[3], 16, 17[2], 18, 19
11:1[2], 2[2], 3[2], 4[2], 11[2], 13, 16[4], 17[3], 18[4], 20, 21, 22, 23[2]
12:1, 2[2], 3, 5[3], 6, 7[2], 8[2], 9[5], 10[5], 11, 12, 13[2], 15[3], 16
13:1, 2[2], 3[3], 5[2], 6[3], 7[2], 8[3], 9[5], 10, 11[2], 12[2], 15[2], 16, 17, 18[3], 20, 22[3]
14:1, 2, 3, 4, 5[2], 8[4], 9, 10, 14, 15
15:1[2], 2, 4[2], 5, 6[2], 8[6], 9[3], 10[2], 11, 12, 13, 15, 16, 17[2], 18, 19[2]
16:1[4], 2[5], 3, 4[3], 5, 6, 7[5], 9[2], 10[2], 11[3], 12, 13, 14[2]
17:2[3], 3, 4[2], 6[2], 7[2], 9[3], 10[2], 11, 12, 13[3], 14[5], 16[2], 17[2]
18:3[2], 4[2], 5[2], 6[2], 7[3], 8[3], 9[5], 10[2], 11, 12[2], 15, 17, 18[2], 19, 21, 22, 23[2], 25[2], 26[2], 28[2], 29[2], 30[3], 31[2], 32[2], 33[3], 34[2]
19:1, 2, 3, 4, 5, 7[3], 8[6], 9, 10, 11[4]
20:1[2], 4[3], 5[2], 6[2], 7[2], 10[3], 11, 14[8], 15[2], 16[3], 17, 18, 19[5], 20[2], 21, 22, 23[4], 25[2], 26[3], 27[2], 28, 29[3], 30, 31, 32[2], 33, 34[6], 35[2], 37[2]
21:1, 2[3], 3[3], 4[3], 6[5], 7[2], 8, 9, 10[2], 11[2], 12[4], 13[6], 15[2], 16[2], 17, 19[5], 20[2]
22:1[4], 2, 3[2], 4[3], 5[3], 6[5], 7[4], 8[4], 9[2], 10[3], 11[5], 12
23:1[6], 2[4], 3[3], 4[4], 5[3], 6[3], 9[2], 10[2],

Misc.

2 CHRONICLES

12[2], 13[2], 14[3], 15, 17[2], 18[6], 19[2], 20[5], 21
24:1, 2[2], 4, 5[3], 6[8], 7[4], 8[2], 9, 11, 12[5], 13, 14[5], 15, 16, 17[2], 18[2], 20[3], 21[3], 23[5], 24[3], 25[4], 26[2], 27[5]
25:1, 2, 4, 5, 6[3], 7[3], 9[3], 10, 11[3], 12[3], 13[3], 14[3], 15[3], 16, 17[4], 18[2], 20[3], 21[2], 23[6], 24[2], 25[5], 26[4], 28
26:1[2], 3, 4, 5[2], 6[3], 8, 9, 11[5], 12[4], 16[2], 17, 18[2], 19, 21[3], 22[3], 23
27:1, 2[2], 3[3], 4, 5[6], 7[4], 9
28:1, 2[2], 3[4], 5[5], 6[2], 7[2], 8[2], 9[2], 10, 11[2], 12[7], 15[2], 16, 18[3], 19[2], 20, 21[6], 22, 23[5], 24[7], 25[2], 26[4], 27[2]
29:1, 2, 3[3], 5[3], 6[2], 7[2], 8, 10, 12[11], 13[4], 14[4], 15[3], 16[5], 17[5], 18[2], 19, 20[2], 21[2], 25[4], 26, 27[2], 29, 30[2], 31[2], 32, 35[3]
30:1[2], 5[2], 6[7], 7, 8, 10, 11[2], 12[4], 13, 15[2], 16[4], 17[2], 18[2], 19[2], 21[2], 22[2], 24[2], 25[4], 26[3]
31:1[3], 2[3], 3[2], 4[2], 5[5], 6[4], 7, 10[3], 11, 13[4], 14[3], 15, 16[2], 17[2], 18, 19[4], 21[2]
32:1, 3, 4[2], 5, 6[3], 7, 8[3], 9[2], 10, 11[3], 13[4], 14[3], 15[5], 17[6], 18, 19[5], 20, 21[6], 22[4], 23[2], 26[4], 27, 28[2], 29, 30[3], 31[4], 32[6], 33[4]
33:2[3], 3, 4, 5[3], 6[3], 7[3], 8[3], 9[2], 11[3], 12, 13, 14[4], 15[5], 16[2], 18[7], 19[2], 22, 25[2]
34:2[2], 3[2], 4[3], 5, 6, 7, 8[5], 9[6], 10[4], 11, 12[8], 13[4], 14[3], 15[2], 17[3], 19, 20[3], 21[4], 22[4], 23, 24, 25, 26[3], 28, 29, 30[6], 31, 32[3], 33[3]
35:1, 2[2], 3[2], 4[4], 5[5], 6[2], 7[3], 8[2], 9, 12[3], 14[3], 15[2], 16[3], 17[2], 18[3], 19[2], 20, 21, 22[3], 24[3], 25, 26[3], 27[2]
36:1[2], 3[3], 4, 5, 6, 7[3], 8[4], 9, 10[2], 12[2], 13, 14[3], 15, 16[2], 17[2], 18[6], 19[2], 20[2], 21[2], 22[6], 23[4]

EZRA

1:1[6], 2[3], 3[3], 4[2], 5[3], 6, 7[4], 8[3], 9[3], 10[2], 11[3]
2:1[4], 2[3], 3, 4, 5, 6[3], 7, 8, 9, 10, 11, 12, 13, 14, 15, 16[2], 17, 18, 19, 20, 21, 22, 23, 24, 25, 26, 27, 28, 29, 30, 31, 32, 33, 34, 35, 36[3], 37, 38, 39, 40[3], 41, 42[7], 43[3], 44[3], 45[3], 46[3], 47[3], 48[3], 49[3], 50[3], 51[3], 52[3], 53[3], 54[2], 55[4], 56[3], 57[5], 58, 59, 60[3], 61[7], 63, 65, 68[4], 69[3], 70
3:1, 2[6], 3[2], 4[2], 5[4], 6[3], 7[5], 8[8], 9[3], 10[5], 11[2], 12[3], 13[4]
4:1[3], 2[3], 3[5], 4[3], 5[4], 6[3], 7[4], 9, 10[2], 11, 13, 15[4], 17, 19, 22, 23, 24[5]
5:1[3], 2[4], 4, 5[2], 6, 8[2], 10[2], 11[3], 12[3], 13[3], 14[7], 15, 16[2], 17[2]
6:1, 2, 3[2], 4[3], 5[4], 7[5], 8[5], 9[4], 10[4], 12, 14[7], 15[3], 16[5], 17[4], 18[2], 19[2], 20[2], 21[5], 22[6]
7:1[5], 2[3], 3[3], 4[3], 5[4], 6[3], 7[4], 8, 9[3], 10, 11[5], 12[4], 13[4], 14[3], 15, 16[4], 17[2], 18[2], 19[3], 20[2], 21[4], 22[4], 23[4], 24[3], 25[2], 26[3], 27[2], 28[2]
8:1[3], 2[6], 3[5], 4[3], 5[3], 6[3], 7[3], 8[3], 9[3], 10[3], 11[3], 12[3], 13[2], 14[2], 15[2], 16, 17, 18[6], 19[2], 20[3], 21[2], 22[3], 23, 24[3], 25[2], 26[2], 27[3], 28, 29[5], 30[2], 31[5], 33[6], 34, 35[3], 36
9:1[3], 2[3], 3[2], 4[4], 7[4], 9[3], 11[2], 12, 14, 15[7]
10:1[3], 2[5], 3[4], 4, 6[5], 7, 8[2], 9[5], 10, 11[2], 13[2], 14[3], 15[2], 16[5], 17, 18[4], 19, 20[2], 21[2], 22[2], 23, 24[2], 25[3], 26[2], 27[2], 28[2], 29[2], 30[2], 31[2], 33[2], 34[2], 43[2], 44

NEHEMIAH

1:1[2], 2[3], 3[2], 4, 5, 6[4], 9[2], 11[3]
2:1, 2, 3, 4, 5, 8[4], 9, 10[3], 13[2], 14, 15, 17, 18[2], 20
3:1[3], 2[2], 3, 4[5], 5, 6[2], 7[3], 8[4], 9[3], 10[2], 11[3], 12[3], 13, 14[3], 15[7], 16[5], 17[3], 18[3], 19[3], 20[4], 21[6], 22, 23[2], 24[3], 25[4], 27, 29[3], 30[3], 31[3], 32
4:2[3], 4, 7, 8, 9, 10[2], 14[2], 15, 16[3], 17, 19, 20, 21[2], 23[2]
5:1[2], 3, 5[2], 7, 9[3], 10, 11[3], 12[2], 14[3], 15[4], 16, 17, 18[3]
6:1, 2[2], 7, 8, 10[5], 14, 15, 16, 17[2], 18[4]
7:2, 3[3], 5[2], 6[4], 7[3], 8, 9, 10, 11[3], 12, 13, 14, 15, 16, 17, 18, 19, 20, 21[2], 22, 23, 24, 25, 26, 27, 28, 29, 30, 31, 32, 33, 34, 35, 36, 37, 38, 39[3], 40, 41, 42, 43[4], 44, 45[6], 46[3], 47[3], 48[3], 49[3], 50[3], 51[3], 52[3], 53[3], 54[3], 55[3], 56[2], 57[4], 58[3], 59[5], 60, 61, 62[3], 63[6], 65, 67, 70[3], 71[5], 72[3], 73[2]
8:1[2], 2[2], 3[2], 4, 5, 8, 9, 10, 13[3], 14[2], 15, 16[6], 17[5], 18[2]
9:1[2], 2[2], 3[3], 4, 6[2], 7[3], 8, 9, 10, 11, 12, 14, 15, 17[2], 18, 19[2], 22[5], 23, 24[2], 25, 27[4], 28, 30[2], 32[2], 37, 38
10:1, 9[3], 14, 28[3], 29[2], 30, 31[3], 32[3], 33[4], 34[3], 35[4], 36[6], 37[9], 38[3], 39[6]
11:1[3], 3[3], 4[13], 5[7], 6, 7[8], 9[2], 10[2], 11[7], 12[7], 13[5], 14[3], 15[5], 16[5], 17[6], 20[3], 22[9], 24[4], 25[2], 30, 31, 35, 36
12:1, 7[3], 12[4], 13[2], 14[2], 15[2], 16[2], 17[3], 18[2], 19[2], 20[2], 21[2], 22[3], 23[5], 24[4], 25, 26[5], 27[3], 28[3], 29[3], 31[2], 32[2], 35[7], 36[2], 37[4], 38[3], 39[3], 40[3], 43, 44[3], 45[4], 46[4], 47[4]

NEHEMIAH

13:1[3], 2, 4[3], 5[2], 6[3], 7[3], 8[2], 9[2], 10, 11, 12, 13[3], 14, 15, 16[3], 17, 19[2], 20[2], 22, 23[3], 24[2], 25, 26[2], 28[3], 29[2], 30

ESTHER

1:1, 2, 3[3], 4[2], 5[2], 6[4], 7[2], 8, 10[2], 14, 15, 16, 17, 18[3], 19, 21, 22
2:1, 3[4], 4, 5[3], 6[2], 8[3], 9[4], 11[2], 12[4], 13[2], 14[2], 15[5], 16, 17, 18, 20, 21[2], 23[2]
3:1, 5, 6[3], 7, 8, 9[3], 10, 12[4], 13[2], 14
4:1, 5, 6, 7[3], 8[2], 9, 11[2]
5:1[2], 2, 3, 6[2], 8, 9, 11[4], 14
6:1[2], 2[3], 4, 9[3], 10, 11, 13[2]
7:2[2], 7, 8[4], 9[2]
8:1, 2, 3, 5, 6, 7, 9, 11[2], 12[2], 13, 15[5], 17[3]
9:1[2], 2[2], 3[3], 5, 10[3], 11, 12[2], 15, 16, 17[3], 18[2], 19[4], 20, 21[2], 22[2], 24[2], 26[3], 28[2], 29[2], 30[3], 31[2], 32[2]
10:1, 2[7], 3[3]

JOB

1:1, 3[3], 5[2], 6, 10, 12, 15, 16, 17, 19, 21[2]
2:1, 7[2], 10[2], 11
3:5[2], 6[2], 9[2], 10, 11, 14, 18, 25
4:6, 9[2], 10[3], 11, 13, 15, 19
5:1, 5, 6[2], 12, 13, 15, 17, 20, 21[2], 22[2], 23[2], 25, 26
6:3, 4[2], 6, 10, 12[2], 14, 15, 16, 17, 18, 19[2], 22, 23, 26
7:1, 2, 3, 4[2], 5, 8, 11[2], 20
8:2, 6, 8[2], 9, 10, 13, 17, 19[2], 22
9:2, 3, 6, 8, 9, 19[2], 23, 24[2], 28
10:1[2], 3[2], 4, 5, 7, 15, 18, 21[2], 22[3]
11:2[2], 6[2], 20[2]
12:4, 5, 6, 7, 8, 9, 10[2], 12, 18, 20[2], 21, 22[2], 24[3]
13:4[2], 6, 12, 26, 27
14:1[3], 4, 5, 7, 9, 12, 14, 15, 18, 19[3], 21
15:5, 8, 11, 13, 14, 20, 22[2], 23, 26, 27, 30[2], 34[2]
16:5, 11, 16
17:5, 6, 7, 11, 12, 16
18:2, 4, 5[2], 7, 13[2], 14[2], 15, 18, 21[2]
19:7, 9, 11, 17, 20, 21, 28, 29[2]
20:3[2], 4, 5[2], 8, 11[2], 14, 15, 16, 17, 20, 21, 22[2], 23, 24, 25[2], 28[2], 29
21:9, 12, 14, 16, 17, 20[2], 21, 24, 25, 28[2], 30[2], 33
22:4, 6, 9, 11, 12[2], 14, 16, 18, 20, 24[2], 25, 30[2]
23:12[2], 15
24:3, 4[2], 6, 8[2], 9, 12[2], 13, 15, 17[3], 18, 22, 24[3]
25:3, 4, 6
26:9, 11, 14[3]
27:3, 8, 11, 13[3], 15, 21, 22, 23
28:2[2], 3[2], 4, 5, 6[3], 12, 13, 16, 17[2], 18[3], 19, 20, 21[2], 24, 26, 28
29:4[2], 6, 10, 13, 17[2], 24
30:1, 2, 6[2], 8[2], 12, 14, 16, 18[2], 27, 31
31:2[2], 3, 7, 13[2], 16, 19, 20, 23, 29, 31[2], 34[2], 37, 40[3]
32:2[4], 5, 6, 7, 8, 12, 18
33:3[2], 4[2], 6, 8, 13[2], 15, 16, 19, 25, 30
34:8, 10, 11, 16, 19[2], 21, 22[2], 26, 27, 28[2], 34, 36
35:7, 8, 9[4], 11[2], 12[2]
36:6, 8, 16[2], 17, 19, 26, 27, 29[2], 30
37:1, 2[2], 3, 4, 6, 7, 9[2], 10[2], 12, 14, 15, 16[2], 19, 22, 23, 24
38:1, 3, 4, 7, 8, 13[3], 16[2], 17[3], 18, 21, 22[2], 23[2], 25[2], 27, 28, 29[2], 30, 31[2], 33, 34, 37, 39, 41
39:1, 5, 7[2], 8, 17, 20, 24, 25, 28
40:6, 7, 11, 16, 17, 18[2], 19[2], 20, 21, 22
41:6, 9[2], 13, 14, 18, 19[2], 20[2], 21, 23, 24, 25, 26, 29, 31, 34
42:4, 5[2], 7, 8, 10, 11[3], 12[2], 14[3], 15, 17

PSALMS

1:1[3], 2, 3, 5, 6[2]
2:2, 6, 8[2], 9, 10
3:t, 2, 3, 4, 6[2], 7
4:t, 1, 2, 5, 6
5:t, 2, 5, 7, 8, 10
6:t, 5, 7[2], 8[2]
7:t[2], 6[2], 7, 9, 10, 13, 17
8:t, 2[3], 3, 4[2], 6, 7, 8[3]
9:t, 9, 12, 13[2], 14[2], 16, 18
10:1, 3, 4, 5, 7, 8, 14, 15, 16, 17, 18
11:t, 4, 6
12:t, 1, 5[2], 6[2]
13:t, 3
14:t, 2, 4, 5, 6, 7[3]
15:t
16:t, 4, 5[2], 11[2]
17:t, 1, 4[3], 8[2], 12, 14[3]
18:t[5], 2, 4[2], 5[2], 6, 7, 8[2], 10, 11, 12, 13, 15[4], 16, 18, 20, 21, 24, 30, 34, 35, 40, 43[2], 44, 45, 46
19:t, 1, 4, 5, 6[2], 7[2], 8[2], 9[2], 11, 14[2]
20:t, 1[3], 2, 5, 6, 7
21:t, 2, 3[2], 4[2], 7, 9, 10, 12
22:t, 1, 3, 6[2], 9, 12, 14[2], 15, 16, 20, 21, 22, 23[2], 24, 25, 27[2]
23:t, 3, 4[2], 5, 6[2]

PSALMS

24:t, 3, 5, 6, 7, 8, 9, 10[3]
25:t, 5, 6, 7, 10, 14, 15, 17[2], 22
26:t, 5, 7[2], 8, 10
27:t, 1[2], 4[4], 5[2], 6, 9, 11, 12, 13[2], 14
28:t, 2, 3, 4[2], 5[2], 6, 8
29:t, 2, 3[2], 4[3], 5[2], 7[2], 8[2], 9[2]
30:t[2], 4[2]
31:t, 2, 4, 5, 8, 10, 12, 13, 15, 19, 20[3], 22, 24
32:t, 4, 5, 6, 7
33:2, 4, 5[2], 6[3], 7, 8[2], 10[3], 11[2], 13, 14[2], 16, 18
34:t, 6, 7, 11, 15, 16[2], 17, 18[2], 19[2], 20, 22[2]
35:t, 2, 5, 6, 12, 27, 28[2]
36:t[2], 1[2], 3, 7[2], 8[3], 9, 11[2], 12
37:t, 1[2], 4, 7[2], 11, 14, 16, 17, 18, 19, 20[2], 22[2], 23, 28, 30[2], 31[2], 37, 38, 39[3]
38:t, 3[2], 5, 8[2], 10
39:t, 4, 8, 10
40:t, 2[2], 5, 7[2], 12, 15
41:t, 1, 2, 3, 5, 9, 13
42:t, 4[2], 5, 6[2], 7, 8, 9[2], 11
43:2[3], 4, 5
44:t, 1, 3, 14, 15, 16[2], 19[2], 20, 21
45:t[2], 1[2], 2, 4, 5, 6, 7, 8[2], 9, 12, 13, 14, 16
46:t, 2, 4[3], 5, 7[2], 8, 9, 11[2]
47:t, 1, 4, 5, 7, 8, 9[4]
48:t, 1[2], 2[3], 6, 7, 8[3], 9[2], 10[2], 11[2]
49:t, 1, 3[3], 5[2], 6, 7, 8, 15, 16, 19
50:t, 1, 2[2], 9[2], 10, 11[2], 13[2], 15, 23
51:t, 1, 12, 14[2], 17, 18, 19
52:t[2], 1, 5[3], 7, 8[2]
53:t, 2, 3, 4, 5, 6[3]
54:t, 2, 7
55:t, 3[4], 4, 10, 14, 19, 21, 23
56:t, 13
57:t, 1, 3, 4
58:t, 1, 2, 4, 5, 6, 8[2], 10
59:t, 2, 5[2], 9, 10, 12[2], 13, 16[3], 17
60:t[3], 3, 4, 6, 7, 8, 11
61:t, 2, 4, 5
62:t, 3, 7, 9[2]
63:t[2], 7, 9, 11
64:t, 1, 2[3], 5, 6[2], 9[2]
65:t, 4[2], 5[4], 7[3], 8, 9[2], 12
66:2, 3, 5[2], 8, 15[2], 19
67:7
68:t, 2, 5[2], 8[3], 10, 11, 12, 13, 15[3], 17[2], 19, 20, 21[2], 22, 23[2], 24, 26, 27[3], 29, 30[4], 31, 32, 33[2], 35[2]
69:t, 3, 4, 6[2], 9[2], 12, 13[2], 14[2], 16, 18, 20, 24, 26, 28[2], 30, 35, 36
70:t, 3
71:4[4], 6[2], 9, 16[3], 20, 22, 24
72:4[2], 7, 8, 10[3], 13, 15[2], 16[4], 18, 20[2]
73:t, 1, 3, 10, 15, 17, 26
74:t, 1, 2[2], 4, 7, 8, 11, 12[2], 13, 14, 17, 19[3], 20[3], 23[2]
75:t, 3, 8[4], 9, 10[2]
76:t, 3, 4, 5[2], 6, 9, 10[2], 12[2]
77:t, 2, 5[2], 10[2], 11[2], 12[2], 15, 18, 20
78:t, 1, 2, 4, 7, 9[2], 10, 12[3], 14, 15, 16, 23, 24[2], 27, 28, 31[3], 38, 41, 43, 45, 49, 51[2], 54, 55, 60, 65[2], 67[2], 68, 72[2]
79:t, 2[4], 9[2], 10[2], 11[2], 13
80:t, 1, 4[2], 5, 7, 8, 10, 13[2], 14, 16, 17[2], 19
81:t, 1, 4[2], 5, 7[2], 10[2], 11, 15, 16[2]
82:t, 1, 2, 4[2], 5[2], 6[2], 7
83:t, 4, 6[2], 7, 8, 9, 12
84:t, 1, 2, 3, 5, 6, 7, 8[2], 9, 10[2], 12
85:t, 1, 2, 3, 4, 11, 13
86:t, 4, 6, 7, 14, 15, 16
87:t, 2[2], 3[2], 4, 5
88:t[2], 1, 3, 9, 12
89:t, 1[2], 5, 6, 7[2], 8, 9, 14, 15, 17, 18, 19, 22, 26, 27, 29, 34, 39, 42, 43, 45, 48, 50[2], 51
90:t[2], 3, 8, 10[2], 11, 17[3]
91:1[2], 2, 3, 8
92:3, 4, 7, 9, 10, 11, 13[2]
93:2, 4[2]
94:2, 4, 7, 11, 12, 13, 16, 19, 20, 21, 22
95:1, 4[2], 7[2], 8
96:5, 7, 9, 12
97:1, 2, 5[3], 7, 8[2], 10[3], 12
98:2, 3[3], 5, 6
99:8
100:t, 3
101:t, 1, 3, 6, 8[2]
102:t, 5[2], 6[2], 10, 15[2], 17, 19, 20, 21, 24, 25[3], 26, 28
103:t, 7, 15, 17, 20, 21, 22
104:3[2], 5, 7, 11, 12, 13, 14[2], 15, 16[3], 20, 24, 30, 31, 34, 35
105:2, 3, 5, 6[2], 11[2], 16, 19, 20, 21[2], 23, 27, 30, 31, 33, 35, 36, 38, 40, 44[2]
106:2, 5[2], 7, 10[2], 11, 16, 17, 20, 22, 25, 28, 32, 38[3], 40, 41, 45, 46, 48
107:2[2], 3, 6, 7, 8, 10, 11[2], 13, 14[2], 15, 16[2], 17[2], 18[2], 19, 21, 22, 24, 26, 28, 31, 32[2], 34, 37, 43
108:t, 7, 8, 12
109:t, 1, 2[2], 3, 10, 14[2], 15, 20[2], 24, 31
110:t, 2[3], 3[4], 4, 5, 7

PSALMS

111:1, 2[2], 4, 5, 6[2], 7, 10[2]
112:2, 4, 7, 10
113:1[2], 2, 3[2], 7[2], 8, 9
114:1[3], 7[3], 8
115:4, 10, 12[3], 15, 16
116:3[2], 4, 9, 13[2], 14, 15[2], 16, 17[2], 18, 19[2]
117:2
118:3, 10, 11, 12[2], 15[3], 16[2], 17, 19, 20, 22, 26[3], 27
119:1, 7, 13, 14, 18, 27[2], 29, 30, 32, 33, 35, 43[2], 46, 52, 53, 54, 61, 62, 63[2], 64, 72[2], 84, 88, 96, 108, 111, 115, 116, 119, 120[2], 123, 130, 134, 136, 144, 147, 152, 160, 161, 164, 172
120:t, 4[2], 5
121:t
122:t[2], 1, 4[3], 5[3], 6, 9[2]
123:t, 2[4], 4[2]
124:t[2], 7[2], 8
125:t, 3[2], 5
126:t, 1
127:t, 2, 3[2], 4[2], 5
128:t, 2, 3, 5[3]
129:t, 4, 8[2]
130:t, 1, 2
131:t[2], 2
132:t, 2, 3, 5, 6[2], 8, 10, 11[2], 17
133:t[2], 2, 3[2]
134:t, 1[2], 3
135:1[2], 2[3], 7[2], 8[2], 9, 11[3], 15[2], 19[2], 20, 21
136:2, 3, 14, 19, 20, 26
137:1, 3[4], 6, 7[2], 8
138:t, 4[2], 5[2], 7[2], 8
139:t, 9[2], 15, 16, 17
140:t, 4, 6, 7[2], 8, 9[2], 12[2]
141:t, 2, 3, 4, 9[2]
142:t, 5, 7
143:t, 5[2], 10, 11, 12
144:t, 3[3], 7[2], 8, 9, 11[2], 12, 13
145:t, 5[3], 6[2], 7[2], 8[2], 11[3], 12[2], 15, 16, 19, 21
146:3, 5, 8, 9
147:2, 4, 5, 10[2], 13, 14
148:3, 4, 5, 11[2], 13, 14[4]
149:1, 2, 6, 8
150:1, 3

PROVERBS

1:1[3], 2, 3, 5, 6, 7[2], 8[2], 9, 17, 19[3], 21[2], 25, 29, 30, 31[2], 32[2], 33
2:5[2], 6, 8[2], 12, 13[2], 14, 17[2], 19[2], 20[2], 22
3:2, 3, 4, 9, 11[2], 14[2], 16, 17, 18, 25[3], 27, 31, 33[3], 35
4:1, 3, 5, 9[2], 10, 11, 13, 14[2], 17[2], 18, 19, 21, 23[2], 26
5:3, 6, 7, 8, 10, 13, 14, 15[2], 16, 18, 20, 21[2], 22, 23
6:2[2], 3, 5[2], 9, 10, 20, 23[2], 24[2], 26[2], 31, 34[2]
7:2, 3, 6, 7, 10[2], 16[2], 18, 20, 21, 22, 24, 27
8:2[2], 3, 4, 5, 6[2], 8, 12, 13, 16, 20[3], 22[2], 26[2], 27, 28, 29, 31[2], 34, 35
9:3, 5[2], 6, 10[3], 11, 14[2], 18
10:1[2], 2, 3[2], 4, 6[2], 7[2], 11[3], 13[3], 14, 15, 16[2], 17, 19, 20[2], 21[2], 22, 23, 24[2], 27[2], 28[2], 29[2], 31, 32[2]
11:3[2], 4, 5, 6, 7, 8, 11[2], 12[2], 13, 14, 20, 21, 22, 23[2], 26, 29, 30[2]
12:2[2], 3, 5[2], 6[2], 7, 8, 10[2], 11, 12[2], 13[2], 14[2], 15, 18[2], 19, 20[2], 23, 24, 25, 26, 27, 28
13:2[2], 4[2], 8, 9[2], 12, 14[3], 15, 20, 22, 23[2], 25[2]
14:3[3], 4, 7[2], 8[2], 11[2], 12, 13, 17, 19, 20, 23, 24[2], 26[2], 27[3], 28[3], 29[2], 30[2], 33[2]
15:2[2], 3, 4, 6[2], 7[2], 8[2], 9, 11[2], 13, 14[2], 15[2], 16, 17, 19[3], 21[2], 22, 23, 24, 25[2], 26[2], 27, 28[2], 29, 30, 31, 33[2]
16:1[2], 2, 4, 6, 10, 11, 13, 14[2], 15[2], 17, 19, 21, 22[2], 23, 25, 26, 31[2], 33
17:1, 2, 6[2], 8, 12, 14, 16, 18[2], 21, 23[2], 24[2], 27[2], 28
18:4[2], 5, 7, 8[2], 10, 12, 14, 15[2], 19, 20[2], 21, 22
19:3, 6, 7, 11, 12, 13[2], 14, 19, 21, 22, 23, 27, 28, 29
20:2[2], 4, 5[2], 8, 10, 12, 15[2], 16, 17, 24, 27[3], 29[2], 30[2]
21:1[2], 2, 4, 5[2], 6[2], 7, 8, 9, 10, 12, 13, 15, 16[3], 20, 22[2], 25, 27, 31[2]
22:2, 4, 5, 8, 9, 11[2], 12[2], 14[2], 15[2], 17, 21[3], 23, 26[2]
23:3, 6, 9[2], 10, 12, 17, 20, 24[2], 29, 34[2]
24:2, 5, 6, 9, 10, 14, 15, 19, 20, 22, 23, 30[3], 33
25:1[3], 2[2], 3, 6[2], 7, 11[2], 12[2], 13[3], 14, 17, 19[2], 22, 24
26:6, 7[2], 9[2], 12[2], 22[2]
27:1, 6[2], 9, 10, 13, 16, 17, 19, 20, 23, 25, 26, 27
28:2[2], 7, 17, 19, 21[2], 24, 25
29:6, 7, 20[2], 25
30:1[2], 2, 3, 4, 5, 7, 9, 17, 19[5], 20, 27, 33[3]
31:1, 2[2], 5[2], 6, 8, 9, 11[2], 12, 16, 21, 22, 23, 26, 27[2], 31[2]

ECCLESIASTES

1:1[2], 2[2], 3, 8, 10, 11[2], 13, 14, 16, 17

ECCLESIASTES

2:2[2], 3[2], 5[2], 6, 7, 8[5], 10, 11, 16[2], 17, 20, 22[3], 24, 26
3:8[2], 10, 13[2], 16[2], 18[2], 19, 20, 21[2]
4:1[2], 4[2], 6, 8[2], 14, 16[3]
5:1[2], 3[2], 6, 7, 8[2], 9, 11, 12[2], 15[2], 18[2], 19, 20[2]
6:2, 3, 7, 9[3], 12
7:1[2], 2[3], 3, 4[4], 5[2], 6[2], 8, 9, 12, 13, 14[2], 15, 18[2], 25[3]
8:1[2], 2[2], 3, 4, 6, 8, 10, 11[2], 14[2], 15[2], 17
9:1, 3[3], 5, 9[3], 11[2], 12, 17[2], 18
10:1, 4, 12[2], 13[3], 14, 15[2], 17, 18, 20
11:3, 5[3], 8, 9[3]
12:1, 3[2], 4[3], 5, 8, 10, 11[2], 12[2], 13[2]

SONG OF SOLOMON

1:1, 2, 3[2], 5[3], 6, 7, 8, 9, 10[2], 11[2], 13, 14[2], 17[2]
2:1[2], 3, 5, 7[2], 8, 12[3], 14[2], 17
3:4, 5[2], 6[3], 7[2], 8, 9[2], 10[5], 11[4]
4:1, 2, 3[2], 4[2], 6[2], 8[3], 9[2], 10, 11[2], 13, 14, 15[2]
5:2[2], 4, 5, 7, 8[2], 12[2], 13, 15[2], 16
6:2, 5, 6, 7, 9[2], 11[2], 12, 13
7:1[3], 2, 4[3], 5, 7, 8[3], 9[2], 13
8:1, 2[3], 4, 6, 7, 9[2], 11, 14

ISAIAH

1:1[4], 4[2], 6, 8[2], 9, 10[4], 11[7], 13, 15, 16, 19, 20, 21, 23[2], 24[4], 26, 28[2], 29, 31
2:1, 2[2], 3[6], 5[2], 6[2], 7[4], 8[2], 10[2], 11[2], 12[2], 13[2], 16, 17[2], 19[4], 20[2], 21[4], 22
3:1[3], 2, 3, 6[3], 7, 8, 9, 10, 11, 12, 14[2], 15[2], 16, 17[3], 18, 20, 22, 24[6]
4:1, 2[3], 4[5], 5[2], 6
5:1, 2, 3[2], 7[4], 8, 9[2], 10[2], 12[2], 15, 16, 17, 18, 19[2], 22, 23, 24[4], 25[2], 26, 27[2], 29, 30
6:3[2], 4[2], 5[4], 6, 8, 10, 12
7:1[7], 2[3], 3[3], 4[4], 5, 6[2], 8[2], 9[2], 11, 13, 16, 17, 18[3], 19[2], 20[2], 22, 25[3]
8:2, 4[3], 6, 7[2], 8[2], 9, 11, 13, 14[4], 17, 18, 22
9:1[4], 2[2], 4[4], 5[2], 6, 7[5], 9[2], 11, 13, 16[2], 18[2], 19[3], 20
10:2, 3, 5, 6[2], 10[3], 12[4], 13[2], 14, 16[2], 17, 18[2], 19[2], 20[4], 21, 22[2], 23[2], 24[3], 26[4], 27, 29, 30, 31, 32[3], 33[2], 34
11:1[3], 2[6], 3[4], 4[3], 5[2], 8, 9[2], 10[2], 11[2], 12[3], 13[2], 14[3], 15, 16[3]
12:3[2], 6[3]
13:1[2], 2, 4[6], 5[2], 6, 8, 9[2], 10, 11[2], 12, 13[4], 18, 19[2], 21[2], 22
14:1, 2[2], 4, 5[2], 8, 9[2], 11, 12, 13[3], 14, 15, 17, 18[2], 19[3], 20, 21[2], 22, 23[3], 24, 27, 29[2], 30, 32[2]
15:1[3], 3, 4, 5[4], 6, 7, 8, 9[4]
16:1[3], 2[3], 3, 4[2], 5, 6[3], 7, 8[3], 9[2], 10, 14[2]
17:1, 2, 3[4], 4[2], 5, 6[3], 7, 8, 9[2], 10[3], 11[2], 12[4], 13[2], 14[2]
18:1, 2, 3, 4[2], 6[3], 7[5]
19:1[4], 3, 4[2], 6, 7, 11[5], 12, 13[3], 16[4], 17[4], 18[4], 19[2], 20[3], 22, 23, 24, 25[2]
20:1, 2, 4[2], 5[4], 6[4]
21:1[2], 3[3], 4, 7[3], 9[3], 10[4], 11[4], 13, 14[2], 15, 16[2], 17[5]
22:1[2], 2, 4[3], 5[6], 6, 7, 8[3], 9[3], 10, 11, 12, 14[2], 15, 18[2], 20, 21[2], 22[2], 24[4], 25
23:1[3], 2[2], 3[3], 4, 5, 6, 7, 8, 9[3], 10, 12, 13, 14, 15[2], 17[3]
24:2[2], 4, 6, 8[3], 10, 11, 13[2], 14, 15[3], 16, 17, 18[4], 21[2], 23
25:1, 2[3], 3, 4, 5[3], 6[6], 7, 8, 10, 11[2], 12[2]
26:1, 6[2], 7[2], 8[3], 9, 10[2], 11, 13, 15, 17, 18, 19, 21[2]
27:2, 5, 6[2], 7, 8, 9[2], 11, 12[3], 13[2]
28:1[4], 2[2], 3[2], 4, 5[4], 6, 7[3], 8, 13, 14, 17, 21, 22, 24, 28, 29
29:4[5], 5[2], 6[3], 7[2], 8, 10, 11[2], 13, 14[2], 16[3], 18[4], 19, 21, 22, 23[4]
30:1[2], 2[2], 3[2], 5, 6[5], 9, 11[3], 12, 14[3], 15, 17[3], 18, 19, 20[2], 22[4], 23[3], 25[2], 26[6], 27[2], 28[3], 29[3], 30[3], 31, 32, 33[3]
31:1, 2[2], 4[4], 5, 6, 7[2], 8[2], 9
32:2[2], 3[2], 4[2], 6[2], 7, 13[2], 14[3], 17[2], 20
33:2, 3[2], 4[2], 6[3], 7, 12, 15[3], 16[2], 19[2], 20[3], 21, 23
34:1, 2, 3, 4, 5, 6[5], 8[3], 11[2], 13, 14[3], 16[3]
35:2[4], 4, 5[2], 6, 7[2], 8, 10
36:1[3], 2[3], 4, 6[2], 8, 9[3], 11, 13[2], 15[2], 16[4], 17[2], 18[5], 19[3], 20[3], 22[3]
37:1, 2[2], 3[3], 4[2], 5, 6[3], 8, 9, 10[3], 11, 12[2], 13[4], 14[2], 16[4], 17, 18[2], 19, 20, 21[3], 22[2], 23, 24[5], 25[2], 26, 27[2], 30[2], 31[2], 32[4], 33, 36[2], 37, 38[2]
38:1, 4, 5, 6[3], 8[2], 9[3], 10[4], 11[2], 12, 13, 15, 16, 17, 20[2], 21, 22
39:1[2], 2[3], 5[2], 7[3], 8
40:2, 3[2], 5[2], 6, 7, 8, 9, 12[2], 13, 14[2], 15[2], 21, 22, 23, 26, 28[3]
41:5, 6, 8, 9, 10, 12, 14[2], 16, 17, 18[3], 20[2], 21, 22, 24[2], 25, 28
42:5, 6[2], 7, 9, 10, 11[2], 13, 22, 25[2]

ISAIAH

43:3, 6, 13, 14, 15, 18, 20, 22, 23, 24, 28
44:5[2], 6[2], 9, 11, 12, 13[2], 14, 19[2], 21, 23, 25, 26[3], 28
45:1, 2[2], 3[3], 6, 9, 11[3], 13, 14[4], 15, 16[2], 19[2], 20[2], 22, 23, 25
46:3[3], 6, 7, 9
47:1[2], 4[2], 5[2], 7, 8, 9[3], 12, 13, 14
48:1[7], 2[3], 3, 10, 13, 17, 18, 19, 20[3], 21
49:1[2], 2, 5, 6[3], 7[4], 8[2], 10, 12, 15, 16, 17, 19[2], 23, 25[2], 26
50:1[2], 4, 10[2], 11[2]
51:1, 3[2], 4, 7[2], 9[2], 10[2], 11, 12[3], 13[4], 15, 16[2], 17[4], 18, 20[4], 22[5], 23
52:2[2], 7[2], 9, 10[3], 11[3], 12, 14
53:1, 2, 3[2], 4, 5, 6, 8[3], 10, 11[2], 12
54:1[2], 2[2], 4[2], 5[3], 6, 9[2], 10, 12[3], 13[2], 17[3]
55:3, 5[2], 11, 12, 13[2]
56:2, 3, 4, 5[2], 6[3], 7[2], 8, 9
57:3[2], 4[2], 5, 6, 10[2], 11[2], 14[2], 15[3], 17[2], 19
58:1, 2[3], 3, 4, 6, 8, 9[2], 11, 12[4], 13, 14[3]
59:5, 6[2], 7, 8, 13, 17[2], 19[3], 21[5]
60:1, 3, 5[2], 6[3], 7[3], 9[3], 10, 11, 13[3], 14[5], 15, 16[3], 20, 21[2]
61:1[2], 2[3], 3[5], 4, 5, 6[3], 10[2]
62:2, 3[3], 6, 8[2], 9, 10, 11[2], 12
63:1, 3, 4[2], 7[4], 9[2], 11[3], 12, 14, 15[4], 16, 17, 18
64:4, 7[2], 8
65:1[2], 3, 4, 7, 9[3], 10[2], 14[3], 16[2], 19[2], 20, 21, 22[3], 23[2]
66:1, 2, 5, 6[2], 7, 11[2], 12, 14, 15, 16, 19, 20[3], 21, 24

JEREMIAH

1:1[4], 2[5], 3[8], 4, 5, 8, 11[2], 13, 14[2], 15[5], 16, 18[2]
2:1, 2[3], 3, 4[4], 6[7], 10, 13, 16[2], 18[4], 19, 20, 21, 26, 27, 28[2], 31[2], 34[2], 36[2]
3:4, 6, 8, 9, 14[2], 16[2], 17[3], 18[4], 19[2], 20, 21[2], 23[2], 24, 25
4:1, 3, 4[5], 7, 8, 9[2], 11[2], 16, 17, 19[2], 21, 25, 26, 29, 30, 31[5]
5:1, 4[2], 5[2], 6[2], 11[2], 14, 15, 20, 22, 24, 27[2], 28[3]
6:1[5], 2, 4, 6[2], 9[2], 10, 11[4], 12, 13[2], 14[2], 17, 19, 22, 23, 24[2], 25, 26, 29
7:2[3], 3[2], 4[3], 11, 12, 15[2], 17[2], 18, 19, 20[2], 21[2], 22[2], 24, 25[2], 28, 29, 30, 31[3], 32[3], 33[3], 34[6]
8:1[8], 2[2], 3[3], 5, 6, 7[2], 8[2], 9, 11[2], 12, 14, 15, 16[3], 19[4], 21[2], 22[2]
9:1[3], 2[2], 4, 6, 7[2], 10[3], 11[2], 12, 14, 15[3], 17, 19[2], 20[2], 22, 26[2]
10:1, 2[2], 3[4], 5, 7[2], 8, 9[4], 13[3], 15[2], 16[4], 17[2], 18, 20, 22[4], 23
11:2[3], 3[2], 4[2], 6[3], 7[2], 8[2], 9[2], 10[3], 12[3], 13[3], 16[3], 17[5], 18, 19, 20, 21[3], 22, 23[3]
12:1[2], 3, 4[2], 5[2], 6, 7[2], 9, 12[3], 13[3], 14[2], 16[2]
13:2, 3, 4, 8, 9[2], 10, 11[3], 12, 13[2], 16, 18, 19[2], 22, 24, 25, 27
14:1, 2, 8[2], 9, 14[2], 16[2], 17, 19, 20, 21, 22
15:1, 3[2], 4[4], 7[2], 8[2], 9, 10[3], 11[2], 13, 16[4], 17[4], 21[1]
16:1, 4[4], 5, 7, 8, 9[7], 12, 13, 14[3], 15[2], 16[2], 18, 19[2]
17:1[5], 8, 10, 11, 12, 13[2], 15, 16, 17, 18, 19[4], 20[3], 21, 22, 24, 25[4], 26[4], 27[2]
18:4[2], 5, 6[2], 8, 10, 11[2], 12, 13, 14[2], 17, 18, 19, 21[2], 23
19:1[4], 2[3], 3[5], 4[2], 5, 6[3], 7[4], 8, 9[3], 10, 11, 13[6], 14, 15[2]
20:1[2], 2[2], 3, 4[3], 5[4], 8, 9, 10, 12, 13[2], 18
21:1[2], 2[2], 4[4], 6[2], 7[6], 8[2], 10[2], 11[3], 12[5], 13[2], 14
22:1[2], 2[3], 3[2], 4[2], 6[2], 9, 11[4], 16, 18[2], 19[2], 23[2], 24[2], 25[5], 29, 30[2]
23:1, 2[2], 3[2], 7[3], 8[3], 9[4], 10[3], 12, 13, 14[3], 15[3], 16[5], 17, 18, 19[2], 20[2], 22, 26[3], 33, 34, 36[4], 38[3], 39
24:1[6], 4, 5[4], 8[3], 9
25:1[6], 2[2], 3[4], 5, 6, 7, 8, 9[2], 10[6], 11, 12[2], 14[2], 15[2], 16, 18, 19, 20[5], 21, 22[3], 24[2], 25[3], 26[4], 27[3], 28, 29[2], 30, 31, 32[2], 33[3], 34[3], 35, 36[4], 37[2], 38[3]
26:1[4], 2[2], 3[3], 5, 6, 7, 8, 9[2], 10[4], 13[2], 15, 16, 17[3], 18[6], 19[2], 20[4], 22, 23[2], 24[3]
27:1[4], 3[7], 4[2], 6[3], 7[2], 8[3], 9, 11[2], 12[3], 13, 14[2], 16[2], 17, 18[5], 19[2], 20[4], 21[6]
28:1[8], 2[4], 3[2], 4[5], 5[3], 6, 7, 8[4], 9[2], 11[5], 12[2], 13[2], 14[6], 16
29:1[2], 2, 3[5], 4[2], 5, 7, 8[3], 11[2], 14, 16[4], 17, 18, 20[2], 21[8], 22[3], 25[3], 26[2], 27, 28, 29, 30, 31
30:2, 3, 5[3], 7[2], 8[2], 10, 11[2], 14[3], 15, 16, 17, 18, 19[2], 21[2], 23[2], 24[2]
31:1[2], 2, 3, 4[2], 5, 7[2], 8, 9, 10, 11, 12[4], 14, 16, 19, 21, 23[5], 27[4], 31[2], 32[2], 33, 34[2], 35[3], 36, 37[2], 38[2], 40[4]
32:1[3], 2[3], 3[3], 4[5], 6, 7[2], 8[5], 9[2], 11, 12[7], 14[3], 15[2], 16[2], 18[3], 19[3], 20, 21[2], 23, 24[4], 25, 26, 27, 28[3],

JEREMIAH

30[4], 31[2], 32[7], 35[3], 36[3], 37, 39[2], 43, 44[5]
33:1[2], 4[4], 5, 6, 7[2], 9[2], 10[2], 11[10], 12[2], 13[6], 14[2], 15, 17[2], 19, 20[2], 22[3], 23, 25, 26[3]
34:1[3], 2[4], 3[3], 4[3], 5, 6, 7[4], 9[2], 10, 12, 13[5], 14, 17, 18, 19[4], 20[4], 21[5], 22
35:1[3], 2[3], 3[3], 4[9], 5[3], 6, 8[2], 11[5], 12, 13[4], 14[2], 16[3], 17[3], 18[4], 19[3]
36:1[3], 2[2], 3, 4[4], 5, 6[4], 8[2], 9[4], 10[7], 11[4], 12[4], 13, 14[5], 16, 20[2], 21[3], 24, 26[3], 27[2], 28, 29[2], 30[3], 31[2], 32[4]
37:1[5], 2[2], 3[2], 5[2], 6, 7[3], 10, 11[2], 12[3], 13[4], 15, 17[2], 19, 20, 21[4]
38:1[4], 3[2], 4[4], 6[3], 7[2], 8, 10, 11, 13[2], 14, 16, 17[3], 18[3], 19, 20, 22[2], 23[3], 24, 28
39:1[3], 2[2], 3[5], 4[5], 5[3], 6[4], 8[2], 9[3], 10[4], 11[2], 13[2], 14[4], 15[2], 16[2], 17[2]
40:1[2], 2, 5[5], 6, 7[6], 8[5], 9[3], 11[4], 12[2], 13[2], 14[3], 15[2], 16[3]
41:1[5], 2[4], 3, 5, 6[2], 7[3], 8[4], 9[5], 10[4], 11[4], 12, 13[2], 14, 15, 16[6], 17, 18[5]
42:1[3], 2, 6[2], 7, 8[2], 9, 10, 11[4], 13, 14[3], 15[4], 16, 17, 18[3], 19, 21
43:1[2], 2[2], 3[2], 4[4], 5[4], 6[4], 7[2], 8, 9[3], 10[3], 11, 12[3], 13[4]
44:1[2], 2[3], 3, 6[2], 7[3], 8[3], 9[7], 11[2], 12[3], 13, 14[4], 15, 16, 17[5], 18, 19, 21[3], 22[3], 23, 24[2], 25[3], 26[5], 27[3], 28[5], 30[6]
45:1[5], 2
46:1, 2[6], 10[5], 11, 12, 13[2], 16, 17, 18, 20, 21[3], 22, 24[3], 25[3], 26[5], 27, 28[2]
47:1, 2[2], 3[6], 4[3], 5, 6
48:1[2], 2, 3, 5[3], 10, 13[3], 15[2], 16, 18, 19, 24[2], 25, 27, 28, 29[2], 31, 32[3], 33, 34[3], 36, 38, 41, 43, 44[2], 45[7], 46, 47[2]
49:2[2], 3, 5, 6[2], 7, 8[2], 12[2], 16[3], 18[2], 19[2], 20[3], 21, 22[3], 25[2], 26[2], 27[2], 28[3], 30[2], 32, 33, 34[4], 35[3], 36[2], 39
50:1, 3, 4[2], 7[2], 8[4], 9[2], 11, 12, 13[2], 15, 16[2], 17[2], 18[4], 20[2], 21[2], 22[2], 23, 25[4], 26, 27, 28[5], 29, 30, 31, 33[3], 34[2], 35, 37, 38, 39[2], 40, 41, 42, 43[4], 44[2], 45[3], 46[2]
51:1, 2, 4, 5[4], 6[3], 7, 10, 11[4], 12[2], 13, 14, 16[3], 18[2], 19[4], 20, 23, 24, 26, 27, 28[2], 29[2], 30, 31, 32, 33[4], 34, 35[2], 41, 42, 43, 44[2], 45[3], 47[2], 49[2], 51, 53, 54[2], 55[2], 56[2], 57, 58[2], 59[4], 63[2], 64
52:1[2], 2, 3[2], 4[3], 5, 6[2], 7[4], 8[2], 9[2], 10[3], 11[3], 12[5], 13[3], 14[3], 15[6], 16[3], 17[4], 18, 19[3], 20[2], 21[2], 22[3], 24[2], 25[9], 26[2], 27[3], 29, 30[3], 31[9], 32, 33, 34[4]

LAMENTATIONS

1:1, 3[2], 4, 5, 6, 7[4], 12, 14, 15[2], 21
2:1[3], 2[3], 3, 4[2], 5, 6[3], 7[4], 8[2], 10[3], 11[3], 12, 13[2], 14, 15[3], 17[2], 18[3], 19[4], 20[2], 21, 22
3:1, 6, 13, 22, 26, 32, 33, 34, 35[2], 38[2], 39, 45, 48[3], 51[2], 55, 58, 62, 64, 65, 66
4:1[2], 2[3], 3, 4[2], 6[5], 7, 9[2], 10[3], 12[3], 13[4], 16[2], 19, 20[3], 21[2], 22[3]
5:8, 9[3], 10, 11, 12, 15, 18[2], 21

EZEKIEL

1:1[3], 2[2], 3[4], 4[5], 5[3], 7[3], 8, 10[5], 11, 13[4], 14[2], 16[3], 18, 20, 21, 22[3], 24[5], 26[4], 27[5], 28[7]
2:1, 3[2], 6[4], 8, 9
3:1[2], 3, 4[2], 5[3], 6[2], 7[2], 10, 11[2], 12[2], 13[4], 14[2], 15[2], 16[2], 17[2], 22, 23[2], 25, 26
4:1, 3[2], 4[3], 5[4], 6[2], 7, 8, 9, 11, 12, 13, 14[2], 16[2]
5:1, 2[2], 4[3], 5, 7, 8[2], 9, 10[2], 12[2], 14, 16[2]
6:1, 2[2], 3[2], 5[2], 7, 9, 11[2], 12, 13
7:1, 2[3], 4, 7[2], 9, 11[5], 13, 16[3], 19[3], 20[3], 21[2], 23[2], 24[2], 26, 27[2]
8:1[3], 2[4], 3[6], 4[2], 5[3], 6[2], 7, 8, 10[3], 11[6], 12[4], 14[2], 15, 16[4], 17[2]
9:2, 3[3], 4[3], 8[2], 9[4]
10:1[3], 2, 3, 4[4], 5[2], 7, 8, 9[2], 10, 12, 14[4], 15, 17, 18[2], 19[4], 20[2], 21[2], 22[2]
11:1[5], 2, 4, 5[3], 7[3], 9[2], 10, 11, 12, 13[3], 14, 15[4], 17[2], 19[2], 21, 22[2], 23[3], 24[2], 25
12:1, 2[2], 3, 6, 8, 9[2], 10, 13, 16, 17, 18, 19[7], 21, 22[2], 23, 24, 26, 27[4], 28
13:1, 2[4], 5[2], 9[4], 16[2], 17[3], 18[2], 19[2], 21, 22[2], 23
14:1[2], 2, 3[3], 4[4], 5, 6, 7[5], 8, 9, 10[3], 11, 12, 13[2], 15
15:1, 2[2], 3, 4[2], 6[2]
16:1, 2, 3[2], 5[2], 7, 8, 13, 15, 16, 17[3], 20, 22, 25, 26, 27[3], 29, 30, 31, 32, 35, 36[2], 39, 41, 43, 45, 49[4], 51, 53[4], 56, 57[4], 60, 63
17:1, 2[2], 3[2], 4[3], 5[2], 6, 7, 9, 11, 12, 13[3], 14, 16, 22[3], 23[4], 24
18:1, 2, 4[2], 6[2], 10[2], 11, 15[2], 17, 19, 20[4], 25[2], 29[3], 30, 31, 32
19:1, 3, 4[2], 5, 7, 9[2], 10[2], 11[2], 14[2]
20:1[4], 2, 3[4], 4[2], 5[3], 6[3], 7[2], 8[4], 9[2], 10[2], 13, 15, 17, 18, 22, 27[2], 28, 30[2], 31[3], 32, 34, 35, 36[2], 37, 38[2], 39, 40[5], 41, 42, 44, 45, 46[2], 47[2], 49
21:1, 2[2], 3[2], 4, 5, 6[2], 8, 9, 10, 11, 12[3], 14[3], 15, 18, 19[5], 20, 21[3], 25, 28[2], 29[2], 30, 31[2], 32
22:1, 2, 3, 6, 7, 9, 12, 13, 15, 16, 17, 18[4], 19, 20, 21, 22, 23, 24[2], 25, 29, 31
23:1, 2[2], 3, 4, 6, 7, 8, 9[2], 12, 14, 15[4], 17, 19[2], 20[2], 21[2], 23[2], 24, 26, 27, 28[2], 29, 31, 32, 33[2], 36, 39, 42[2], 45[2], 48, 49
24:1[2], 2[4], 5[2], 6, 7[2], 8, 11[3], 12, 15, 16[2], 17[2], 20, 21[3], 22, 25[3]
25:1, 2, 3[3], 4, 6, 7, 8, 9[2], 10, 12, 13, 14, 16
26:1[2], 2[2], 4[2], 5[2], 7[2], 9, 10[5], 11, 12[3], 13[2], 14, 15[2], 16, 17, 18, 20[4]
27:1, 2, 3[3], 4, 5[2], 6[6], 7, 8, 9[2], 10[4], 11, 12[3], 13[2], 14[2], 15[3], 16[3], 17[2], 18[4], 21, 22[2], 23, 24[3], 25[3], 26, 27[5], 28[2], 29, 31, 32, 33[4], 34[2], 35
28:1, 2[5], 5, 6, 7[2], 8[2], 9, 10[2], 11, 12[3], 13[3], 14[3], 16[6], 17[2], 18[4], 20, 21, 22, 23, 24[2], 25[2]
29:1[2], 2[2], 3[2], 4[4], 5[3], 6[3], 7, 8, 9, 10[3], 11[2], 12[2], 13, 14[3], 15, 16[2], 17[2], 18[2], 19[2], 20, 21[4]
30:1, 2, 3[2], 5, 6[2], 7[2], 9, 10[3], 11, 12[2], 13[4], 15[2], 17[2], 18[2], 20[2], 21[3], 22[2], 24[3], 25[6]
31:1[2], 2[2], 3, 4, 5[3], 6[2], 7, 8[2], 9[3], 11[2], 12[3], 13[2], 14[4], 15, 16[4], 17, 18[4]
32:1[2], 2[3], 3, 4[2], 6, 8, 9, 10, 11[2], 12[4], 13[2], 15[2], 16, 17[2], 18[4], 20, 21[2], 22, 23[3], 24[3], 25[4], 26[2], 27[4], 28, 30[3], 32[2]
33:1, 2[4], 4, 5, 7[2], 9, 10[2], 11[2], 12[5], 15, 16, 17[2], 20[2], 21[3], 22, 23, 24[3], 27, 28[2], 29, 30[3], 32
34:1, 2[3], 5, 6, 7, 8, 9, 12, 13[2], 14[2], 18[2], 25[2], 26, 27[5], 28, 29[2], 30, 31
35:1, 2, 5[4], 11, 12, 15[3]
36:1[4], 3[3], 4[3], 5[3], 6[2], 8[2], 10[2], 12, 15[2], 16, 17[3], 20[2], 21, 22[2], 23, 24, 26[2], 30[3], 32, 34, 35, 37[2], 38[2]
37:1[4], 3, 4, 9, 11[2], 12[2], 13, 15, 16[4], 18, 19[4], 21, 22, 23[2], 26[2], 28
38:1, 2[3], 3, 4[3], 5, 6[2], 8[4], 11[2], 12[2], 13, 14[2], 15[2], 16, 17[2], 18, 19[2], 20[4], 23
39:1[2], 2[2], 3[2], 4[3], 7, 9, 10[2], 11[5], 12[2], 13, 14[3], 15, 16, 17[3], 18[9], 19, 20, 22, 23[2], 25[2], 27[2], 28, 29
40:1[4], 2[3], 3[2], 4[2], 5[3], 6[2], 7[2], 8, 9[2], 10[2], 11[3], 13[2], 14[2], 15[4], 18[2], 19[2], 20, 21, 22, 23, 38, 39, 40[2], 41, 42[2], 43, 44[3], 45[2], 46[4], 48[3], 49
41:1, 2[2], 3[2], 5[2], 6[2], 7[2], 8[3], 9[2], 10, 11[2], 12, 14[3], 15[2], 19[2], 20, 21[4], 22[2], 25[2], 26[2]
42:2, 4[2], 5, 6, 7, 8, 10[2], 11, 12[2], 14, 15
43:2[4], 3, 4[2], 5, 6, 7[8], 8, 9[2], 10[3], 11[2], 12[3], 13[2], 18[2], 19[2], 20[3], 21[2], 22, 23[2], 25
44:1[2], 2, 3[3], 4[3], 5[5], 6[3], 7, 8[2], 9[2], 11, 12, 13[2], 14[2], 15[3], 17[2], 22[3], 30[6], 31[2]
45:1[2], 2, 3[3], 4[2], 5[3], 6[3], 7[7], 8[2], 9, 11[3], 13[6], 14[5], 15[4], 16, 17[3], 18, 19[7], 20, 21[2], 22, 23[2], 24[2], 25[2]
46:1[2], 2[4], 3[2], 5, 6, 7, 8[2], 9[6], 10, 11, 13[2], 14[3], 16, 17[3], 18[3], 19[2], 21[2], 22[3], 23, 24[3]
47:1[5], 2[2], 6[2], 7, 9, 10, 12, 13, 15[2], 16[3], 17[2], 18, 19, 21, 22[2]
48:1[5], 2, 3, 4, 5, 6, 7, 8[4], 9[2], 10, 11[3], 12[2], 13, 14[2], 17, 18[2], 19[2], 20, 21[5], 22[5], 23, 24, 25, 26, 27, 28[2], 29, 30, 31[6], 32[3], 33[3], 34[3], 35

DANIEL

1:1[4], 2[7], 3[5], 4, 5[2], 6[2], 7[5], 8[3], 9, 10[2], 11, 13[3], 15[2], 16, 18[2], 20[2], 21
2:1[2], 6, 7, 8, 12, 14[2], 16, 18[4], 19, 20, 23[2], 24[2], 25[2], 27, 28, 30, 32[3], 33[3], 34, 35, 37[2], 38[4], 39, 41[4], 42[3], 43, 44[2], 45, 47[4], 48[3], 49[4]
3:1[3], 2[2], 3[2], 5[2], 6, 7[2], 10[2], 11, 12[2], 15[4], 17, 19[2], 21, 22, 23, 24, 25[3], 26[4], 27[2], 28, 29, 30
4:5, 6[2], 8[2], 9[3], 10[2], 11, 12[3], 13, 15[5], 17[4], 18[2], 21[2], 22, 23[5], 24, 25[3], 26, 27, 29[3], 30[3], 32[2], 33, 34, 35[3], 36, 37
5:1, 2, 3[3], 4[6], 5[4], 6, 7[2], 10[2], 11[4], 12[3], 13[4], 14[2], 15, 16[2], 21[3], 23[4], 24, 26, 29, 30
6:2, 5, 7[4], 8, 12[4], 13[3], 14, 15, 16, 17[2], 18, 19, 20, 23[3], 24[3], 26[2], 27, 28[2]
7:1[4], 2, 5[2], 6[2], 7, 8[2], 9[2], 11[2], 12, 13[3], 15[2], 16[3], 17, 18, 19[3], 20[3], 22[2], 24, 25[2], 27[3], 28
8:1[2], 2[2], 4, 5, 6, 7, 8, 9[2], 10[3], 11[2], 12, 13, 15, 16, 17[2], 19, 20, 21, 22, 23[2], 25, 26
9:1[5], 2[4], 6, 7[4], 8, 10, 11[2], 13, 15[2], 16, 17, 20[2], 21, 23, 24, 25, 26[2], 27[2]
10:1[3], 4[2], 5, 6[4], 9[2], 10, 13[4], 16[2], 17, 18, 20[2], 21
11:1, 2, 4, 5[2], 6[4], 7[4], 8[3], 9, 10, 11[2], 13, 14[2], 15[2], 17[2], 19, 20[2], 21, 22[2], 24, 25[2], 26[2], 30, 31, 35[3], 36, 37[2], 38, 40[3], 41[3], 42, 43[3], 44[2], 45
12:1[2], 2[2], 3, 4, 5[4], 6[2], 7[2], 8, 9, 10, 13

HOSEA

1:1[7], 2[4], 3, 4[4], 5[2], 6, 7, 10[4], 11[4]
2:2, 4, 10[2], 12, 13, 15[5], 17[2], 18[4]
3:1[4], 2[3], 4, 5
4:1[4], 3[3], 6[2], 8, 12, 13, 19
5:1[2], 2, 4[2], 5, 9[2], 10, 12, 13, 14
6:5, 6, 8, 9[2], 10[2], 11
7:1[3], 5[2], 10, 12, 16[2]
8:1, 4, 6, 10[2], 12, 13
9:4[2], 5[2], 6, 7[3], 8[3], 9, 15[2], 16
10:1[2], 4, 5[3], 6, 8[2], 9[2], 13[2], 14, 15[2]
11:1, 4[2], 5, 6, 9[2], 11[3], 12
12:5, 7, 9[2], 10, 11, 12, 13
13:2[4], 3[2], 4, 5, 8[2], 10, 12, 13[3], 14, 15[2]
14:2, 3, 7, 9

JOEL

1:1[2], 2[2], 3, 5[2], 6[2], 8, 9, 11, 12[2], 13[3], 14[2], 15, 16, 18[2], 19[2], 20[3]
2:1[2], 2[5], 3, 4[2], 5[4], 7, 11, 13[2], 16[2], 17, 22[2], 23, 24, 26, 27, 30, 31, 32
3:1, 2, 4, 6[2], 7, 8[2], 9, 12, 14[3], 16[4], 18[4], 19

AMOS

1:1[7], 2[2], 3[2], 4[2], 5[4], 6, 7, 8, 9, 10, 11, 12, 13[3], 14[3]
2:1[3], 2[2], 4[2], 5, 6[2], 7[3], 8[2], 9, 10[2], 11[3], 13, 15
3:1[2], 2[2], 4, 9[2], 12[5], 13[2], 14[3], 15
4:1[2], 5[2], 6[2], 10[2], 11[2], 13[2]
5:1, 2, 3, 4, 6, 8[3], 11[3], 14, 15[2], 16[2], 18[2], 20, 22, 23[2], 25, 26[2], 27
6:1[3], 2, 3, 4[4], 5[2], 6, 7, 8[2], 10[4], 12, 13, 14[4]
7:1[2], 2[2], 8, 9[3], 10[4], 11, 12, 14, 16[2], 17
8:1, 2[2], 3, 4, 6[2], 7[2], 8, 10, 11[3], 12, 14[2]
9:1[5], 3[2], 5[2], 6[2], 7[4], 8[3], 9, 10, 11[2], 12[2], 13, 14[3], 15

OBADIAH

1, 3[2], 6, 7, 8[3], 9[2], 11, 12[4], 13[4], 14[3], 15, 17, 18[5], 19[5], 20[6], 21

JONAH

1:1[2], 3[2], 5[2], 8, 9, 10, 17
2:1, 2[3], 3, 4, 6, 9[2]
3:1, 3[2], 5[3], 6, 7, 10
4:2[2], 5[3], 6, 8

MICAH

1:1[3], 3[2], 5[5], 6[2], 7[3], 9, 10, 11[4], 12[2], 13[4], 14[2], 15[2]
2:1, 4, 5, 7[2], 8, 9, 11[3], 12[6], 13
3:1[3], 3, 7, 8[4], 9[4], 12[2]
4:1[3], 2[6], 4[2], 5[2], 8[4], 10[3], 12, 13[2]
5:1[2], 2[3], 3[2], 4[4], 6[2], 7[3], 8[4], 10[2], 11, 12, 13[3], 14[2]
6:2, 4[4], 5[3], 6, 7[5], 8, 9, 10[2], 11, 12, 13, 14, 16[4]
7:1, 2, 4[2], 5, 6, 7, 9, 10, 13[2], 14[3], 15[3], 17[4], 18[2], 19, 20

NAHUM

1:1[3], 3, 4, 6, 7, 8, 11, 14[3], 15
2:2[2], 3[2], 6, 7, 8[2], 9[4], 10, 11[2], 13[2]
3:1, 2[5], 3[3], 4[4], 5, 10, 11, 12, 13[2], 16, 18, 19[2]

HABAKKUK

1:2, 6, 7, 13, 14, 15
2:8[5], 9, 11[2], 13[2], 14[2], 16, 17[6], 18[2], 19
3:1, 2[2], 3, 4[2], 7[3], 8, 9, 10, 11[2], 13[3], 14, 15, 16, 17, 18

ZEPHANIAH

1:1[8], 3[2], 4[3], 5, 7[2], 8, 10, 11, 14[3], 15[5], 16, 18[3]
2:2[2], 3[2], 5[4], 7[3], 8[3], 9[6], 10[2], 11[2], 14[3]
3:8, 9, 10[2], 11[3], 12[2], 13, 14[2], 15[2], 17, 18[2], 20

HAGGAI

1:1[6], 2, 3, 5, 7, 9[2], 11, 12[5], 14[9], 15[2]
2:1[2], 2[4], 3, 4[3], 5, 6, 7[2], 8, 9[4], 10[3], 11, 12, 13, 14, 15, 16[2], 17, 18[2], 20[2], 21, 22[4], 23[3]

ZECHARIAH

1:1[4], 3[3], 4, 6[2], 7[5], 11, 12[3], 14, 16, 17, 21[2]
2:4, 5[2], 6[2], 7, 8[2], 9, 10[2], 11[2], 13
3:1, 2, 4, 5, 6, 7, 9[2], 10
4:1, 2[2], 3, 6[2], 8, 9[3], 10[3], 11, 12, 14
5:3, 4[4], 7[2], 8[2], 9, 11
6:1, 5[2], 9, 10[7], 11[2], 12[3], 13[2], 14[2], 15[3]
7:1[3], 2, 3[2], 4[2], 5, 8, 9, 10, 12[2], 13
8:1[2], 2, 3[4], 4[2], 5[2], 6[4], 7, 8, 9[5], 10, 11[2], 12, 13[2], 14[2], 15, 16, 17, 18[2], 19[6], 20[2], 21[2], 22, 23[5]
9:1[6], 3, 6, 7, 8[3], 9[3], 10, 11[2], 12, 13, 14, 15[2], 16[2]
10:1[3], 3[2], 4[4], 5, 6[2], 7, 10[4], 11[3]
11:2[2], 3[5], 4, 6[3], 7[2], 9, 11[2], 12, 13[3], 15, 16
12:1[4], 2, 3, 4[2], 5[3], 6[3], 7[5], 8[3], 10[4], 11[2], 12[4], 13[3]
13:1[2], 2[4], 3, 4, 6, 7
14:1[2], 2[2], 3, 4[4], 5[4], 8[2], 10[3], 13[2], 14, 15[5], 16[3], 17[3], 18[2], 19[3], 20, 21[4]

MALACHI

1:1[2], 3, 4[2], 5, 6, 7, 8, 9, 10, 11[3], 12, 13[2], 14
2:2, 3, 4, 5, 6, 7[2], 8[3], 10, 11[2], 12[3], 13, 14[2], 15[2], 16[2], 17[2]
3:1[2], 2, 3[2], 4[2], 5, 6, 7[2], 10[2], 11[2], 12, 14, 16, 17
4:1, 2[2], 3[2], 4, 5[2], 6[2]

MATTHEW

1:1[4], 3, 5[2], 6[2], 16[2], 18[2], 20[3], 22, 24
2:1[2], 2, 4[2], 5, 6[3], 7, 12, 13, 15[3], 16[2], 19, 20, 21, 22[3]
3:1, 2, 3[3], 4, 6, 7[2], 9, 10, 13, 14, 16[2]
4:1[2], 3, 4[2], 5, 6, 8[2], 13, 15[4], 16, 17, 18, 19, 21, 23[3], 25
5:3, 9, 10, 11, 13[2], 14, 19[3], 20[2], 21[2], 22[3], 27, 29, 30, 31, 32, 33, 35, 37, 42, 45
6:1[2], 2, 5[2], 8, 16, 22[2], 23, 26, 27, 28, 29, 30[2], 32, 33, 34
7:4, 5[2], 9, 15, 16[2], 21[2], 24, 26, 27
8:6, 11, 12[2], 14, 20[2], 21, 26, 27, 28[2], 29, 30, 31, 32[2], 33, 34
9:2[3], 3, 6[2], 9, 14, 15, 16, 20[2], 22, 27, 34, 35, 38
10:1[2], 2[2], 3, 5[2], 6[2], 7, 10, 14[2], 15[2], 16, 17, 20, 22, 23[2], 25[2], 29, 30, 31, 36, 37[2], 38, 41[2], 42[3]
11:1, 2[2], 10, 11[2], 12[2], 19[3], 20, 22, 24[2], 25, 27, 29
12:1, 4, 8[2], 23, 24, 28[2], 31, 32, 34[3], 35[3], 36, 38[2], 39, 40[2], 41[2], 42[3], 43, 45, 50
13:1, 5, 11[2], 14, 15, 18, 19, 21, 22[2], 24, 27, 30, 31[2], 32[2], 33[2], 35, 36[2], 37, 38[2], 39, 40, 41[2], 42[2], 43, 44, 45, 46, 47[2], 49, 50[2], 52[2], 58
14:1[2], 6, 8, 13[2], 20, 24, 25, 27, 29, 31, 33[2], 34, 35[2], 36
15:1, 2, 3, 6[2], 7, 9, 11, 14, 18, 19, 21, 22[3], 24[2], 27, 29, 31, 37, 39
16:3[2], 4, 6[3], 8, 9, 10, 11[3], 12[5], 13[2], 14, 16, 18, 19[2], 21, 23[2], 27[2], 28[2]
17:5, 9, 12[2], 13, 18, 20[2], 22[2], 25[4], 26, 27
18:1, 2, 3, 4, 6[2], 7, 10[2], 11, 12, 13[2], 14[2], 16, 19[2], 20, 23[2], 27, 28
19:1, 7, 8[2], 10, 12[2], 14[2], 23, 24[2], 28[3]
20:1, 8, 11, 12, 13, 18, 20[2], 22[2], 23[2], 25, 28, 30, 31
21:1, 3, 5[2], 9[2], 11[2], 12[3], 13[2], 15, 16[2], 17, 23, 25[2], 26, 31[3], 32, 34[2], 37, 39, 40, 42, 43, 45
22:2, 5, 13, 16[2], 27, 28, 29, 30, 31, 32[5], 35, 42[2]
23:4, 5[2], 7, 13, 15, 16, 22, 23[2], 25[3], 26, 27[2], 28, 29[2], 30[2], 31, 32, 33[2], 34[2], 35[3], 39
24:1, 3[4], 6[2], 8, 9, 12, 14, 15[2], 17, 21, 27[3], 29[2], 30[5], 31[2], 32, 36[2], 37[3], 39[2], 43, 44, 50[2], 51
25:1, 2, 8, 13, 14, 19, 21, 23, 30, 31[2], 34[2], 40[2], 45[2]
26:2[2], 3[2], 6, 7, 13, 14, 15, 17[2], 21, 22, 24[3], 27, 28[2], 29[2], 30, 31[2], 33, 37, 45[2], 47[2], 51[2], 53, 56, 61, 63, 64[3], 65, 66, 67, 69, 71, 73, 75
27:1, 3, 5, 6, 8, 9[4], 11, 12, 19, 21, 24[2], 27[2], 29[2], 32, 33, 37, 40, 42, 43, 47, 48, 51, 52, 53, 54, 56[2], 57, 58, 60, 62
28:1[2], 2, 4, 11, 19[3], 20

MARK

1:1[3], 3[2], 4[2], 5[4], 6, 7, 9[2], 10, 13, 14[2], 15, 16, 17, 19, 24[2], 25, 26, 29[2], 30[2], 34
2:3[2], 4, 5, 6, 9, 10[2], 14[2], 17, 18[4], 19, 21, 23, 26[2], 28[2]
3:5, 9, 11, 17[3], 18, 21, 22, 28, 29, 35
4:4, 5, 10, 11[2], 19[3], 26, 28, 30, 31, 32[2], 37, 38, 41
5:1[2], 2[2], 7, 8, 10, 11, 17, 22[2], 23, 25, 26, 27, 29[2], 30, 34, 35, 36, 37, 38[2], 40, 42[2]
6:3[3], 6, 11, 14, 15, 21, 22[2], 23[2], 24, 25, 29, 33, 37, 43[2], 44, 47, 48, 50, 52, 53, 54, 56
7:1, 2, 3, 4[2], 5, 6, 7, 8[3], 9, 13[2], 14, 15, 20, 21[2], 24, 25, 26, 28, 29, 31[4], 35
8:3, 8, 10, 11, 15[4], 19, 20, 23, 27, 28, 30, 31[3], 33[2], 38[5]
9:1[3], 7, 9, 12[2], 13, 17, 21, 24, 25, 26, 31[2], 35[2], 36, 37, 39, 41, 42, 47
10:1[2], 4, 5, 6, 10, 14[2], 15, 23, 24, 25[2], 26, 33, 35, 38[2], 39[2], 44[2], 45, 46[3], 47[2], 48, 49
11:1[2], 3, 5, 9, 10[2], 13, 14, 15[2], 17[3], 19, 29, 30[2], 32
12:2[2], 8, 9, 10, 13[2], 14[2], 22, 23, 24, 26[4], 27[2], 28[2], 29, 34, 35, 38, 44[2]
13:1[3], 3, 7[2], 8, 13, 14[2], 15, 19, 25, 26, 27[2], 28, 32, 34, 35
14:1[2], 2, 3[3], 4, 9[2], 10, 12, 13[2], 14, 18, 20, 21[3], 23, 24, 25[3], 26, 27, 41[2], 43, 47[2], 54, 61, 62[3], 64, 65, 66[2], 67, 69, 70, 71
15:2, 3, 9, 12, 17, 18, 21[2], 22, 26[2], 32, 35, 36, 38, 39, 40[2], 43[3], 45, 46[2], 47
16:1, 2[2], 3, 6, 9[2], 11, 12, 14, 19

LUKE

1:1, 2, 3, 4, 5[6], 6, 8, 9[2], 10[2], 11[3], 15, 16[2], 17[3], 19, 23, 26, 27[2], 29, 32[2], 33[2], 35[3], 38, 39, 40, 41, 42, 43, 44, 45, 48, 51, 52, 54, 59, 61, 65, 66[2], 68, 69[2], 70, 71, 74[2], 75, 76[2], 77[2], 78, 79[2], 80
2:2, 4[5], 9[2], 10, 11, 13, 21[2], 22[2], 23, 24[2], 25, 27, 31, 32, 33, 34, 35, 36[4], 37, 38, 39, 40, 41, 42, 43, 46
3:1[8], 2[2], 3[2], 4[4], 6, 7[2], 8[2], 9, 14, 15, 16, 23[3], 24[5], 25[5], 26[5], 27[5], 28[5], 29[5], 30[5], 31[5], 32[5], 33[5], 34[5], 35[5], 36[5], 37[5], 38[4]
4:1, 2, 3, 4, 5[2], 6, 9[2], 14[2], 15, 17, 18[2], 19, 20, 22, 25[2], 26[2], 27[2], 29[2], 30, 31, 33, 34[2], 35[2], 37[2], 38, 40, 41[2], 43, 44
5:1[2], 2, 3[2], 6, 9, 10, 12, 15[2], 17[4], 19, 24[2], 27, 29[2], 33[2], 34, 36[2]
6:1, 2, 4, 5[2], 13, 15, 16, 17[5], 19, 20, 22, 26, 30[2], 34, 35, 42, 44[2], 45[6], 49
7:1, 3[2], 11, 12[3], 17, 18[2], 19, 21[2], 24, 27, 28[2], 29, 30[2], 31, 34[2], 35, 36, 37, 38, 39, 42, 44
8:1[2], 2[2], 3[2], 4, 5, 10[2], 11, 12, 13, 14, 21, 22, 23, 24, 25, 26, 27, 28, 29[2], 32, 33, 35[2], 36, 37[2], 38, 41, 42, 43[2], 44[2], 46, 48, 49, 51
9:2, 5, 7[2], 8[3], 9, 11[3], 17, 19, 20, 22[2], 26[5], 27[3], 29, 31, 35, 36, 38, 43, 44[2], 45, 46, 47, 52, 55[2], 56, 58[2], 60, 62
10:2, 6, 7, 9, 10, 11[3], 19, 21, 22, 30, 34, 35, 36
11:1, 5, 6, 8, 11[2], 15[2], 16, 20[2], 24, 26, 27, 28, 29, 30, 31[4], 32[2], 34[3], 36[3], 39[2], 41, 42[2], 44, 45, 46, 47, 48, 49[2], 50[3], 51[3], 52, 53, 54
12:1[4], 4, 6, 7[2], 8[2], 9, 10, 13, 15[2], 16, 20, 25, 27, 28, 29, 30[2], 31, 39, 40, 42, 44, 46, 48[3], 54, 56[2], 57
13:1, 7, 10, 11, 14, 15, 16, 18, 19[3], 20, 21, 25, 27, 28[2], 29, 31, 33, 35
14:1[2], 5, 8[2], 10, 14, 15[2], 18, 19, 21[2], 24[2], 28, 32, 33
15:4[2], 8, 10[2], 12[2], 15, 17, 19, 26
16:2[2], 4, 5, 6, 7, 8[2], 9[2], 15, 16, 17, 20, 24, 28
17:2, 6, 7, 11, 15, 20[3], 21, 22[3], 24[2], 25, 26[3], 28, 29, 30
18:3, 8, 12, 16[2], 17, 24, 25, 29, 31, 34, 37, 38, 39
19:3, 8, 9, 10, 11, 22, 29[2], 31, 34, 37[3], 38, 39, 44, 46[2], 47
20:1, 4[2], 6, 10[2], 13, 15[2], 17, 20[2], 21[2], 26, 27, 32, 33, 34, 36[2], 37[3], 38[2], 39, 42, 45, 46
21:3, 4[3], 5, 9, 16, 17, 18, 21, 22, 24[3], 25, 26, 27, 30, 31, 34, 35, 36, 37
22:1, 3[2], 6, 7, 10, 11, 16, 18[3], 19, 21, 22, 23, 24, 25, 30, 39, 44, 47, 48, 50[2], 52, 53, 55, 58, 59[2], 61, 66, 69[3], 70, 71
23:1, 3, 6, 8[2], 11, 15, 17, 22, 23[2], 26, 27[2], 28, 35, 37, 38[2], 39, 41, 45, 51[4], 52
24:1, 3, 7[2], 10, 13, 14, 17, 18, 19, 22, 23, 24, 25, 31, 35[2], 36, 42[2], 44, 47, 48, 49[2]

JOHN

1:4, 7, 8, 12, 13[6], 14[3], 15[2], 16, 18, 19, 22, 23[2], 24, 29[2], 30, 34, 35, 36, 40, 42, 44[2], 45[3], 46, 47, 49[2], 51[2]
2:1[2], 3, 6[3], 8, 9[2], 11[2], 14, 15[2], 16, 17, 21[2], 25
3:1[2], 3, 5[3], 6[2], 8, 10, 12, 13, 14, 18[2], 22, 25, 29[2], 31[2], 34, 36
4:5[2], 7, 9[3], 10[2], 13, 14[2], 22, 30, 32, 34, 39[3], 41, 42[2], 46, 47[2], 52, 54
5:1, 3[3], 4[2], 19, 25[2], 27, 29[2], 30[2], 31, 32[2], 36[2], 37, 39, 42, 44, 46
6:1[2], 4, 7[2], 8, 11, 13, 14, 18, 22, 25, 26, 27, 28, 29, 33, 35, 38, 39, 40, 42, 45[2], 46, 48, 51[2], 53[2], 58, 60, 62, 64, 65, 66, 68, 69, 70, 71[3]
7:2, 7, 13[2], 14, 17[3], 18, 19, 22[2], 23, 25[2], 28, 31, 36, 37, 38[2], 39, 40[2], 41, 42[4], 43, 44, 48[2], 50, 52[2]
8:1, 12[2], 13, 14, 17, 18[2], 23[2], 26[2], 27, 28[2], 34, 39, 40, 41[2], 42, 44[4], 46[2], 47[2], 52, 54, 59[2]
9:3, 4, 5, 6[2], 7, 11, 16[2], 17, 18, 21, 22, 23, 31, 32, 33, 35, 40
10:2, 5, 7, 14, 16, 18[2], 20, 21[2], 22, 25, 26, 28, 29, 32, 35, 36[2], 37, 39, 41
11:1[2], 4[2], 8, 9, 11, 13[3], 19, 22, 27, 37[2], 39, 40, 42, 45, 46, 49, 51, 52, 55
12:2, 3[4], 4, 7, 9, 11[2], 13[3], 15, 16, 17, 21[2], 23, 24, 30, 31[2], 34[3], 36, 38[2], 41, 42[2], 43[2], 49
13:1[2], 2, 18, 21, 22, 23, 24, 26, 29[2], 31
14:10, 17, 21, 30
15:4, 15, 16, 19[3], 26[2]
16:2, 4, 5, 8[3], 9, 10, 11[2], 13[2], 14, 15, 17, 19, 21, 25, 33
17:6, 7, 12[2], 14[2], 15, 16[2], 24
18:3, 5, 7, 9, 12, 15, 17, 18, 19[2], 22[2], 23, 25, 26[2], 28, 32, 33, 34[2], 36[2], 37, 39
19:2, 3, 5, 7, 14, 17, 19[2], 20, 21[3], 25[2], 29, 32[2], 34, 36, 38[5], 39, 40[2], 42
20:1, 2, 12, 19[2], 24, 25[2], 30, 31
21:1, 2[3], 6[2], 9, 10, 11, 12, 15, 16, 17, 24

THE ACTS

1:1, 3[3], 4[2], 6, 8, 9, 11, 13[2], 14, 15[2], 16, 17, 18, 19, 20, 21, 22[2], 24[2], 25
2:1, 2, 3[2], 5, 10[2], 11, 13, 14, 15, 17, 18, 19, 20, 21, 22[4], 23, 24[2], 28[2], 29, 30[2], 31[2], 33[3], 36, 37, 38[4], 42, 46
3:1, 2[2], 5, 6[2], 10, 12, 13[5], 15, 16, 18, 19[2], 21[3], 22, 24, 25[3], 26
4:1, 4[2], 6[2], 8[2], 9, 10[3], 11[2], 13[2], 15, 18, 19, 21, 22, 25, 26, 27[2], 30, 31, 32[5], 33[2], 34[2], 36[3]
5:2, 3[2], 7, 9[2], 12, 13, 14, 15[2], 16, 17, 19, 20, 21[2], 24[2], 30, 31, 32, 34, 35, 36, 37[2], 38, 39, 40, 41
6:1[2], 2[2], 3[2], 4, 5[3], 7[3], 8, 9[5], 14, 15
7:2, 3, 4[2], 8, 10[3], 11, 16[4], 17, 22, 23, 24, 29, 30[3], 31, 32[4], 34, 35, 36, 37[2], 40[3], 41, 42[4], 43[2], 44, 45[3], 46, 49, 52[4], 53, 55[3], 56[2], 58
8:1, 3, 5, 7, 9, 10, 11, 12[2], 14, 16[2], 18, 20, 21, 22[2], 23[2], 24, 25[2], 26, 27[4], 32, 34[3], 37, 39[2]
9:1, 2[2], 11[2], 13, 15, 20, 24, 26, 27, 29, 31[2], 33, 36
10:1, 3[2], 7[2], 12[3], 22[3], 28, 31, 32, 33, 34[2], 36[2], 38[2], 39[2], 41, 42[2], 43, 45[2], 48
11:1, 2, 5, 6[2], 16, 20[2], 21, 22[2], 23[2], 24[2], 28[2], 30
12:1, 2, 3, 4, 5, 7, 10, 11[5], 12[2], 13, 17, 18, 20, 22[2], 23[2], 24
13:1, 5[2], 7[2], 10[4], 11, 12, 15[3], 16, 17[4], 18, 19, 20, 21[4], 22, 23, 24[2], 25, 26[3], 27, 28, 29, 31, 34, 36, 38, 39, 40, 42, 43[2], 44, 46[2], 47[2], 48, 49, 50[2], 51
14:1[3], 3, 4, 5[2], 6[2], 11[2], 13, 14, 15, 19, 22[2], 26, 27
15:1, 2, 3, 4[2], 5[3], 6, 7, 10, 11, 14, 15, 16, 17, 18, 20, 21, 22, 23, 26, 35, 36, 40
16:1, 2, 3, 4, 6[2], 9, 12[2], 13, 14[4], 16, 17[2], 18[2], 19, 26, 27[2], 32, 33, 36, 39, 40[2]
17:1, 2, 4[3], 5[2], 6, 7, 8, 9[2], 10, 11, 12[3], 13[3], 18[3], 22[2], 24, 26[4], 27, 28, 29, 30, 32[3]
18:3, 8[2], 11, 12, 14, 15[3], 17[2], 18, 23, 25[3], 26
19:4, 5, 8[2], 9[2], 10[2], 11, 12, 13[2], 14[2], 16, 17, 19[3], 20, 22, 25, 27, 28[2], 29, 31[2], 33, 34[2], 35[4], 37[2], 40
20:4[4], 6, 7, 11, 16, 17, 19[2], 24[4], 25, 26, 27, 28, 30, 31, 32, 35, 38
21:5, 6, 8[3], 11, 12, 13, 14, 16[3], 20[2], 21, 26[3], 27, 28, 30, 31, 32, 35[2], 36, 39[2]
22:3[3], 5, 8, 9, 10, 11[2], 12, 14[2], 15, 16, 18, 20[2], 30
23:5[2], 6[3], 9, 10, 11[2], 12, 16, 17, 20, 21, 23, 27[2], 29[4], 34[2]
24:4, 5[3], 7, 8[2], 10, 14, 15[2], 16, 21, 22[2], 23, 25, 26
25:2, 8, 9, 11[2], 15, 16, 18, 19[2], 20[3], 21, 23[2], 24, 25, 26
26:2, 4, 5, 6[2], 7, 9[2], 10, 13, 16[2], 18[2], 20[2], 22, 25, 26[2], 31[2]
27:1, 2[3], 5[2], 6, 8, 10[2], 11, 12, 19, 21, 22[3], 23, 25, 29, 30[2], 32, 34[2], 35, 36, 41, 42, 44
28:2[2], 3[2], 7[2], 8[3], 11, 15, 16, 17[3], 18, 19, 20, 21[3], 22, 23[4], 27[2], 28, 31

ROMANS

1:1[2], 3[2], 4[2], 6, 7, 8, 9[2], 10, 12, 16[3], 17, 18[2], 19, 20[2], 23, 24, 25, 27[2], 29, 30[2], 32[2]
2:2, 3, 4[2], 5[3], 9[3], 11, 13[2], 15, 16, 17, 18, 19[2], 20[4], 23, 24, 25, 26, 29[3]
3:1, 2, 3, 5, 7, 12, 13, 14, 17, 18, 20[2], 21, 22[2], 23[2], 25[2], 26, 27[2], 28, 29[3]
4:4[2], 6, 11[4], 12[4], 13[2], 14[2], 16[5], 17, 18, 19, 20
5:2[2], 5, 10, 14[2], 15[2], 16, 17[3], 18[3], 19
6:3, 4[2], 5[2], 6, 13[2], 16[2], 17[2], 18, 19[3], 20, 21, 23[2]

Misc.

ROMANS

7:2, 4, 5, 6[2], 8, 22, 23[2], 24, 25[2]
8:2[3], 3, 4, 5[2], 7, 9[3], 10[2], 11, 13, 14[2], 15[2], 16, 17, 18, 19[3], 20, 21[3], 23[2], 27[2], 29, 33, 34, 35, 39
9:4[2], 5, 6[2], 7, 8[3], 9, 11[3], 16[3], 21, 22, 23[2], 24[2], 26, 27[3], 29, 30, 31[2], 32, 33
10:2, 3[2], 4, 5, 6, 8, 13, 14, 15[3], 17, 18, 20
11:14, 2, 4[2], 5, 6[2], 8, 12[4], 13, 14, 15[3], 17[3], 20, 22, 24, 25[2], 26, 29, 33[3], 34, 36
12:1, 2[2], 3[2], 5, 6, 13, 16[2], 17, 20, 21
13:1[2], 2, 3[2], 4[2], 10, 11, 12[2]
14:7, 9, 10, 12[2], 14, 16, 17, 18, 20, 23[2]
15:1, 2, 3, 4, 5, 6, 7, 8[2], 12, 13[2], 14[2], 15[2], 16[3], 18[2], 19[3], 21, 26, 27, 29[3], 30, 31, 32, 33
16:1, 2[3], 4, 5, 7, 10, 11[2], 16, 18, 20[2], 23[2], 24, 25[3], 26[3]
S

1 CORINTHIANS

1:1[2], 2[2], 4, 6, 7, 8, 9, 10, 11[3], 12[5], 13, 14, 16, 17[3], 18[2], 19[2], 20[2], 21[2], 24[2], 25[2], 27[2], 28, 30[2]
2:1[3], 4[3], 5[2], 6[3], 7, 8[3], 9, 10, 11[4], 12[3], 14[2], 15, 16[2]
3:4[2], 10, 13, 16[2], 17[2], 19, 20
4:1[5], 3[2], 5[3], 6[2], 13[2], 16, 17, 19, 20, 21
5:4[2], 5[2], 8[2], 10[2]
6:1, 4, 9[2], 10, 11[3], 12, 15[3], 19[2]
7:4[2], 6, 7, 19[2], 23, 25[2], 31, 33, 34[2], 36, 40
8:3, 4, 6, 7, 9, 10
9:2, 5, 7[3], 9[2], 10, 12[2], 13[2], 14, 15, 16, 17, 18
10:4, 5, 7, 8, 9[2], 10[2], 11, 16[5], 17, 18[2], 21[5], 27, 29[2], 30, 31, 32, 33
11:1[2], 3[3], 7[2], 8[2], 10, 12[2], 16, 18, 22, 23, 24, 25, 27[3], 28[2], 32
12:3, 4, 5, 6, 7, 8[2], 9, 10[4], 12, 15[2], 16[2], 18, 21[2], 22, 23, 27, 28[2], 29, 30
13:1[2], 2, 13
14:10[2], 11, 12[2], 16[2], 21, 24[2], 25[2], 26, 32, 33[3], 36, 37

1 CORINTHIANS

15:3, 5[2], 6[2], 7[2], 8[4], 9[2], 10[2], 12, 13, 15[3], 19, 20, 21, 32, 34, 37[2], 39[5], 40[2], 41[3], 42, 47, 49[2], 50, 52, 56[2], 58
16:1, 2[2], 10, 15[3], 17[2], 19, 21, 23

2 CORINTHIANS

1:1[3], 3[3], 4, 5, 6, 7[3], 8[3], 9, 11, 12[3], 14, 16[2], 19, 20[2], 22, 24
2:3[2], 4[2], 6, 9, 10, 11[2], 12, 13, 14, 15, 16[2], 17[4]
3:1[2], 2, 3[4], 5[3], 6[3], 7[4], 8, 9[2], 10, 12, 13[2], 14, 17, 18[2]
4:2[4], 4[5], 6[5], 7[3], 10[2], 11, 13, 15[2], 17
5:1[2], 4, 5, 9, 10, 11, 14, 18[2], 19, 21
6:1, 2[2], 4, 7[3], 16[2]
7:1[2], 4[2], 6, 10[2], 11, 12, 13, 14, 15
8:1[3], 2[3], 3, 4, 5, 8[3], 9, 11[2], 16, 17, 19[3], 21[2], 23[4], 24[2]
9:2[3], 3, 4, 5[2], 7, 10, 12[2], 13[2], 14
10:1, 2, 4[2], 5[2], 7, 8, 12, 13[2], 14, 15[2], 16
11:7, 8, 10[3], 13, 14, 15, 17, 20, 22, 23, 24, 26[2], 28, 30, 31, 32
12:1, 2, 3, 5[2], 6[2], 7[2], 9, 11, 12, 17[2], 18, 21
13:1, 3, 4[2], 11[3], 14[3]
S

GALATIANS

1:1, 2, 4, 6, 7, 10, 11, 12[2], 13[2], 14[2], 19, 21, 22
2:2, 4, 5, 6, 7[2], 8, 9, 12, 14[2], 15, 16[5], 17, 20[2], 21
3:2[3], 5[2], 7[2], 9, 10[3], 11, 12, 13, 14[2], 15, 16[2], 17[2], 18[2], 19[2], 20, 21, 22, 26, 27
4:1, 2, 3, 4[2], 5, 6, 7, 9, 11, 13, 14, 15, 19, 20, 23[2], 26, 28, 30[2], 31[2]
5:1, 4[2], 5, 8, 11, 15, 16, 18, 19, 21[2], 22, 26
6:1, 2, 8[2], 10[2], 12, 14, 16, 17, 18

EPHESIANS

1:1[2], 3, 4, 5[2], 6[2], 7[2], 9, 10[2], 11[2], 12, 13[3], 14[3], 15, 16, 17[4], 18[4], 19[2], 23
2:2[4], 3[4], 7, 8[2], 9, 12[2], 13, 14, 15[2], 19[2], 20, 22

EPHESIANS

3:1, 2[3], 4, 5, 6[2], 7[3], 8[2], 9[2], 10, 12, 14, 15, 16, 19[2]
4:1[2], 3[2], 4, 6, 7[3], 9, 12[4], 13[7], 14[2], 16[3], 17, 18[3], 23, 25, 29[2], 30[2]
5:1, 4, 5[2], 6[3], 8, 9, 11, 12[2], 17, 20, 21, 23[3], 26, 30[3], 33
6:4, 5, 6[2], 8, 9, 10, 11[2], 12[3], 13, 14, 15[2], 16[2], 17[3], 19

PHILIPPIANS

1:1, 3, 4, 6[2], 7[3], 8, 10, 11[2], 12, 14, 15[2], 16, 17[2], 19[2], 22, 25, 27[3], 28[3], 29
2:1[2], 2[2], 3, 4, 6, 7[3], 8, 10[2], 11, 13, 15[2], 16[2], 17, 19, 22, 26, 30[2]
3:2[3], 5[3], 8[3], 9[3], 10[2], 11, 12, 14[2], 17, 18[3]
4:2, 3, 7, 8, 9, 10, 11, 15, 18[2], 22, 23

COLOSSIANS

1:1[2], 3, 4[2], 5[2], 6[2], 7[2], 9, 10[2], 12[2], 13[2], 14, 15[2], 18, 20, 22, 23, 24[2], 25[2], 27[3]
2:2[6], 3, 5, 8[2], 9, 10, 11[3], 12[2], 13, 14[2], 15, 16[3], 17[2], 18[2], 19, 20, 22, 23[3]
3:1, 6[2], 8, 10, 12[3], 14, 15, 16, 17, 22, 24[2], 25
4:3[2], 9, 11[2], 12[3], 16, 18

1 THESSALONIANS

1:1, 2, 3[4], 4, 5, 6[3], 8, 9[2]
2:2, 3[2], 4, 5, 6[4], 8[2], 9[2], 11, 12, 13[4], 14[4], 19[2]
3:2[3], 6[2], 13
4:1, 3, 4, 5, 6, 9, 12, 15[2], 16[2]
5:1, 2, 5[4], 8[3], 18, 22, 23[2], 28

2 THESSALONIANS

1:1, 3[2], 4, 5[4], 8, 9[2], 11[3], 12[2]
2:1, 2, 3[2], 4, 7[2], 8[2], 9, 10[2], 13[3], 14[2]
3:1, 5, 6[2], 8, 16, 17, 18

1 TIMOTHY

1:1[2], 5[4], 7, 9[2], 11, 14, 15[2], 20
2:1[2], 3, 4, 7
3:1, 2[2], 3, 5[2], 6, 7[2], 8, 9, 10, 12, 13, 15[3], 16[2]
4:1, 3, 4, 5, 6[4], 8[2], 9, 10[2], 12, 14[2]

1 TIMOTHY

5:8, 9, 10, 17, 18, 22, 25
6:1[2], 2, 3, 4, 5[3], 10[2], 11, 12, 13, 14, 15[2], 20
S

2 TIMOTHY

1:1[3], 3, 4, 6[2], 7[4], 8[6], 10, 11, 13[2], 15, 16[2], 18
2:2, 3, 4, 6, 8[2], 9, 14[2], 15, 17, 18, 19[2], 20[4], 22, 24, 25, 26[2]
3:2, 3, 4[2], 5, 6, 7, 8, 10, 11, 14[2], 16, 17
4:2, 5[2], 6, 8, 15, 17[2], 19
S[2]

TITUS

1:1[4], 2, 3, 6[2], 7, 8[2], 10, 12[2], 14
2:3, 5, 7, 8[2], 10, 11, 13, 14
3:2, 4, 5[3], 7, 11
S[3]

PHILEMON

1, 4, 5, 6[2], 7, 9, 13, 14, 20, 25

HEBREWS

1:2, 3[4], 5, 6, 7[2], 8[2], 9, 10[2], 13, 14
2:2, 4, 6[2], 7, 9[2], 10, 11, 12, 14[3], 15, 16[2], 17
3:1[2], 3, 5, 6, 8, 12[2], 13[2], 14[2], 16, 19
4:1[3], 3, 4, 6, 8, 9, 11, 12[5], 13, 14, 15, 16[2]
5:2, 4, 6, 7, 9, 10[2], 11[2], 12[4], 13, 14[2]
6:1[4], 2[7], 4[2], 5[2], 6, 9, 10, 11[2], 12, 16, 17[2], 19, 20
7:1[3], 2[4], 3[3], 4, 5[7], 6, 7, 8, 10, 11[2], 12[2], 13[2], 14[2], 15, 16[2], 17, 18, 19, 21, 22, 23, 28
8:1[3], 2[2], 3, 5[2], 6, 8[2], 9[2], 10
9:1, 3, 4[2], 5[2], 6, 7, 8, 10, 11[2], 12, 13[4], 14, 15[4], 16[2], 17[2], 19[2], 20, 21, 22, 23, 24[2], 25, 26[3], 28
10:1[2], 2, 3, 4[2], 7[2], 10[2], 12, 18, 19, 21, 22, 23, 25[2], 26, 27, 29[4], 31, 32, 33, 34[2], 35, 36[2], 39[3]
11:1[2], 3[2], 4, 6, 7[4], 9[2], 11, 12[2], 13, 15, 18, 21[2], 22[3], 23[2], 24, 25[2], 26[2], 27, 28, 30, 32[6], 33, 34[4], 36[2], 38[2]

HEBREWS

12:1, 2[3], 3, 5[2], 9[2], 10, 11, 13, 15[3], 16, 17, 19[2], 22[2], 23[3], 24[3], 27[2]
13:7[2], 11, 15[2], 20[3], 22, 24

JAMES

1:1[2], 3, 5[2], 6, 7, 9, 10, 11[2], 12, 13, 14, 17[2], 18[4], 20[2], 21, 22, 23, 24, 25[2]
2:1[3], 4, 5[2], 9, 10, 11, 12, 15, 16, 23
3:4, 6[3], 7[5], 8, 9, 10, 13[2], 17, 18[2]
4:1, 4[3], 10, 11[4]
5:3, 4[5], 5, 7[2], 8, 10[3], 11[4], 14[2], 15, 16, 17, 19, 20[2]

1 PETER

1:1, 2[4], 3[2], 5, 7[3], 8, 9[2], 10[2], 11[3], 13[2], 15, 17[2], 19[2], 20, 22, 23[3], 24[2], 25
2:2, 4[2], 7, 8[2], 9[2], 10, 12, 13, 14[2], 15[2], 16[2], 25
3:1, 3[5], 4[4], 7[2], 8[2], 12[2], 13, 14, 15, 16[2], 17, 20[2], 21[4], 22
4:2[3], 3[3], 4[2], 7, 8, 10[2], 11[2], 13, 14[4], 15, 17[3], 19[2]
5:1[3], 2[2], 4, 5, 6, 10, 12, 14

2 PETER

1:1[2], 2[2], 3, 4, 8, 11, 12, 16[2], 19, 20[2], 21[2]
2:2[3], 3[2], 4, 5[2], 6, 7, 9[2], 10[2], 12, 13, 14, 15[3], 16, 17, 18[2], 19[3], 20[2], 21
3:1, 2[4], 4[2], 5[4], 7[2], 8, 10, 11, 12[2], 14, 15, 16, 17, 18

1 JOHN

1:1[2], 5, 7
2:2, 5, 10, 14, 15, 16[5], 17, 19[3], 21, 27[2], 29
3:1[2], 2, 4, 8[3], 9[2], 10[3], 12, 16, 17[2], 19, 22, 23
4:1, 2[2], 3[2], 4, 5[2], 6[4], 7[2], 9, 13, 14, 15, 17
5:1[2], 2, 3, 4, 5, 9[4], 10[2], 12, 13[4], 15, 18[2], 19, 20

2 JOHN

3, 4, 9[2], 11, 13

3 JOHN

3, 6, 7, 10, 11, 12[2]

JUDE

1[2], 3, 4[2], 5[2], 6, 7, 8, 9, 10, 11[3], 12[2], 13[2], 14[2], 15[2], 16, 17[2], 21[2], 22, 23, 24

REVELATION

1:1, 2[5], 3, 5[3], 7[2], 9[3], 10, 13[2], 14, 15, 16, 18[2], 20[2]
2:1[3], 5, 6, 7[4], 8, 9[2], 10[3], 11, 12, 14[2], 15, 16, 17, 18[3], 21, 22, 23, 24, 27[3]
3:1[2], 5[2], 7[2], 9[2], 10[2], 12[5], 14[4], 16, 17, 18[2]
4:1, 4, 5[3], 6[3], 8[2]
5:1, 5[4], 6[4], 7[2], 8[3], 9, 11[3]
6:1[3], 5, 6[3], 7, 8[2], 9[2], 11, 12, 13[2], 14, 15[2], 16[2], 17
7:1[2], 2, 3, 4[4], 5[6], 6[6], 7[6], 8[6], 9, 13, 14[2], 15, 17[2]
8:1, 3, 4[3], 5, 7, 8, 9[2], 10[2], 11[3], 12[5], 13[5]
9:1, 2[4], 3[2], 4[2], 5, 7[2], 8[2], 9[4], 11, 13, 15, 16[3], 17[5], 18[2], 20[5], 21[4]
10:1, 7[3], 8, 10
11:1, 4, 5, 6, 7, 8, 9, 11, 13[3], 15[3], 18, 19[2]
12:1, 4[2], 5, 6, 10[3], 11[2], 12[2], 14[2], 15[2], 16, 17[3]
13:1[3], 2[2], 3, 8[3], 10, 11, 12, 13, 14[2], 15[3], 17[2], 18[2]
14:2[3], 5, 6, 7[2], 8[3], 10[6], 11[2], 12[3], 14, 15[2], 17, 18[2], 19[3], 20[2]
15:1, 2[4], 3[4], 5[2], 6, 7[3], 8[2]
16:1[3], 2, 3, 4, 5, 6, 7, 9, 10[2], 11[3], 12[3], 13[6], 14[5], 17[2], 19[4], 21[4]
17:1[2], 2[3], 3[2], 4[2], 5[2], 6[3], 7[2], 8[3], 11, 14[2], 17, 18
18:2[3], 3[6], 4[3], 9[2], 10, 11, 12[5], 13, 15[2], 18, 19, 22[4], 23[4], 24[3]
19:1, 2, 5, 6[3], 7, 8, 9[2], 10[4], 12, 13, 15[4], 16[2], 17[2], 18[6], 19, 20[2], 21[2]
20:1, 4[3], 5, 6[2], 7, 8[3], 9[3], 10, 12[2], 14, 15[2]
21:2, 3[2], 6[3], 9[2], 10, 11, 12[3], 14[3], 16, 17[2], 18[3], 19[3], 21[2], 22, 23[3], 24[3], 25, 26, 27
22:1[5], 2[7], 3[2], 5, 6, 7[2], 8, 9[3], 10[2], 14, 16, 17, 18[2], 19[5], 21

OUR 2257

GENESIS

1:26[2]
5:29[2]
19:31, 32[2], 34
23:6
24:60
29:26
31:1[2], 14, 15, 16[2], 32
33:12
34:9, 14, 16, 17, 21, 31
37:26, 27[3]
41:12
42:13, 21, 32[2]
43:4, 7[2], 8, 18[2], 21[3], 22[3], 28
44:8, 25, 26[2], 31
[illegible]
47:3, 18[4], 19[3], 25

EXODUS

1:10
3:18
5:3, 8, 21
8:10, 26, 27
10:9[6], 25, 26[2]
12:27
17:3[2]
34:9[2]

LEVITICUS

25:20

NUMBERS

11:6[2]
13:33
14:3[2]
20:3, 4, 15[2], 16
21:5
27:3, 4[2]
31:49, 50
32:16[2], 17, 18, 19, 26[4], 32
36:2, 3[2], 4

DEUTERONOMY

1:6, 19, 20, 25, 28[2], 41
2:1, 8, 29, 33, 36, 37
3:3[2]
4:7
5:2, 3, 24, 25, 27[2]
6:4, 20, 22, 23, 24[2], 25[2]
21:7[3], 20[2]
26:3, 7[5], 15
29:15, 18, 29[2]
31:17
32:3, 27, 31[2]

JOSHUA

2:11, 13, 14[2], 19, 20, 24
5:13
7:9
9:11[2], 12[3], 13[2], 24
17:4
18:6
21:2
22:19, 24, 25, 27[5], 28[2], 29
24:17[3], 18, 24

JUDGES

6:13
9:3
10:10
11:2, 6, 8, 24
13:23
16:23[3], 24[4]
18:5
19:19
21:7, 18, 22

RUTH

2:20
3:2
4:3

1 SAMUEL

2:2
4:3
5:7, 10, 11
7:8
8:20[2]
9:6, 7, 8
12:10, 19
14:9, 10
16:16
17:9, 47
20:29
23:20
25:14, 17
30:23

2 SAMUEL

7:22
10:12[2]
12:18
18:12
19:9, 41, 43[2]
22:32

1 KINGS

1:11, 43, 47
8:21, 40, 53, 57[2], 58[2], 59, 61, 65
12:4, 10
20:31[2]

2 KINGS

7:9
18:22
19:19
22:13

1 CHRONICLES

12:17, 19
13:2[2], 3
15:13
16:14, 35
17:20
19:13[2]
28:2, 8
29:10, 13, 15[2], 16, 18

2 CHRONICLES

2:4, 5
6:31

2 CHRONICLES

10:4, 10
13:10, 11, 12
14:7, 11[2]
19:7
20:6, 7, 9, 12[2]
28:13[3]
29:6[2], 9[4]
32:8[2], 11
34:21

EZRA

4:3
5:12
7:27
8:17, 18, 21[3], 22, 23, 25, 30, 31, 33
9:6[3], 7[4], 8[4], 9[8], 10, 13[4], 15
10:2, 3[2], 14[3]

NEHEMIAH

4:4, 9[2], 11, 15, 20, 23
5:2[2], 3, 4, 5[8], 8[2], 9[2]
6:1, 16[2]
8:10
9:9, 16, 32[6], 34[4], 36, 37[3], 38
10:29, 30[2], 32, 33, 34[3], 35, 36[6], 37[5], 38, 39
13:2, 4, 18, 27

JOB

8:9
17:16
22:20
28:22
37:19

PSALMS

8:1, 9
12:4[3]
17:11
18:31
20:5[2], 7
22:4
33:20[3], 21
35:21
40:3
44:1[2], 5, 7, 9, 13, 18[2], 20[2], 24[2], 25[2], 26
46:1, 7, 11
47:3, 4, 6
48:1, 8, 14[2]
50:3
59:11
60:10, 12
65:3, 5
66:8, 9[2], 11, 12
67:6
68:19, 20
74:9
77:13
78:3, 5
79:4, 9[2], 10, 12
80:6[2]

PSALMS

81:1, 3
84:9
85:4, 9, 12
89:17, 18[2]
90:1, 8[2], 9[2], 10, 12[2], 14, 17[3]
92:13
94:23
95:1, 6, 7
98:3
99:5, 8, 9[2]
103:10[2], 12, 14
105:7
106:6, 7, 47
108:11, 13
113:5
115:3
116:5
118:23
122:2, 9
123:2[2], 4
124:1, 2, 4, 5, 7, 8
126:2[2], 4
135:2, 5
136:23, 24
137:2
141:7
144:12[2], 13[3], 14[2]
147:1, 5, 7

PROVERBS

1:13
7:18

SONG OF SOLOMON

1:16, 17[2]
2:9, 12, 15
7:13
8:8

ISAIAH

1:10
3:6
4:1[3]
20:6
25:9
26:8, 12, 13
28:15
33:2, 20, 22[3]
35:2
36:7
37:20
38:20
40:3, 8
42:17
47:4
52:10
53:1, 3, 4[2], 5[3]
55:7
58:3
59:12[4], 13
61:2, 6
63:16[3], 17, 18
64:6[2], 7, 8[2], 11[4]

JEREMIAH

3:22, 23, 24[2], 25[6]
5:19, 24
6:24
8:14
9:18[2], 19, 21[2]
11:21
12:4
14:7[2], 20[2], 22
16:10[3], 19
17:12
18:12
20:10
21:13
23:6, 36
26:16, 19
31:6
33:16
35:6, 8[5], 10
36:15
37:3
42:2, 6[2], 20[2]
43:2
44:17[4], 19, 25
46:16[2]
50:28
51:10[2], 51

LAMENTATIONS

3:40, 41[2], 44, 46
4:17[3], 18[5], 19, 20
5:1, 2[2], 3, 4[2], 5, 7, 9[2], 10, 15[2], 16, 17[2], 21

EZEKIEL

33:10[2], 21
37:11[3]
40:1

DANIEL

1:13
3:17
9:6[3], 8[3], 9, 10, 12, 13[3], 14, 15, 16[2], 17, 18[3]

HOSEA

7:5
14:2, 3[2]

JOEL

1:16[2]

AMOS

6:13

MICAH

2:4
4:5, 11
5:5[2], 6[2]
7:17, 19, 20

ZECHARIAH

1:6[2]
9:7

MALACHI

2:10

MATTHEW

3:9
6:9, 11, 12[2]
8:17[2]
20:33
21:42
23:30
25:8
27:25

MARK

9:40
11:10
12:11, 29

LUKE

1:55, 71, 72, 73, 74, 75, 78, 79
3:8
7:5
11:2, 3, 4
13:26
17:5, 10
23:41
24:20, 22, 32

JOHN

3:11
4:12, 20
6:31
7:51
8:39, 53
9:20
11:11, 48
12:38
14:23
19:7

THE ACTS

2:8, 11, 39
3:12, 13, 25
5:30
7:2, 11, 12, 15, 19[2], 38, 39, 44, 45[2]
13:17
14:17
15:10, 25, 26, 36
16:20
17:20, 28
19:25, 27
20:21
21:5[2], 6, 7, 15
22:14
24:6, 7
26:5, 6, 7
27:10, 19
28:17, 25

ROMANS

1:3, 7
3:5
4:1, 12, 24, 25[2]

ROMANS
5:1, 5, 11, 21
6:6, 11, 23
7:5, 25
8:16, 23, 26, 39
9:10
10:16
12:7
13:11
15:4, 6
16:1, 9, 18, 20, 24

1 CORINTHIANS
1:1, 2, 3, 7, 8, 9, 10
2:7
4:12
5:4[2], 7
6:11
9:1, 10[2]
10:1, 6, 11
12:23, 24
15:3, 14, 31, 57
16:12, 23

2 CORINTHIANS
1:1, 2, 3, 4, 5, 7, 8, 11, 12[3], 18, 22
3:2[2], 5
4:3, 6, 10, 11, 16, 17
5:1, 2, 12
6:11[2]
7:3, 4, 5, 12, 14
8:9, 22, 23, 24
9:3
10:4, 8, 13, 14, 15[2], 16
11:31

GALATIANS
1:3, 4[2]
2:4
3:24
6:14, 18

EPHESIANS
1:2, 3, 14, 17
2:3[2], 14
3:11, 14
5:20
6:22, 24

PHILIPPIANS
1:2
3:20, 21
4:20, 23

COLOSSIANS
1:1, 2, 3, 7
3:4

1 THESSALONIANS
1:1, 2, 3[2], 5
2:1, 2, 3, 4, 8, 9, 19[2], 20
3:2[2], 5, 7, 9, 11[3], 13[2]
5:9, 23, 28

2 THESSALONIANS
1:1, 2, 8, 10, 11, 12[2]
2:1[2], 14[2], 15, 16[2]
3:6, 12, 14, 18

1 TIMOTHY
1:1[2], 2[2], 12, 14
2:3
6:3, 14

2 TIMOTHY
1:2, 8, 9, 10
4:15

TITUS
1:3, 4
2:10, 13
3:4, 6

PHILEMON
1[2], 2[2], 3, 25

HEBREWS
1:3
3:1, 14
4:14, 15
7:14
10:22[2], 23
12:2, 9, 10, 29
13:15, 20, 23

JAMES
2:1, 21
3:6

1 PETER
1:3
2:24
4:3

2 PETER
1:1, 2, 8, 11, 14, 16
3:15[2], 18

1 JOHN
1:1[2], 3, 9[2]
2:2
3:5, 16, 19, 20[2], 21
4:10, 17
5:4

2 JOHN
12

3 JOHN
12, 14

JUDE
4[2], 17, 21, 25

REVELATION
1:5
5:10
6:10
7:3, 10, 12
11:8, 15
12:10[3]
19:1, 5
22:21

OUT — 4480, *1537*

GENESIS
2:9, 10, 19, 23
3:19, 24
4:14, 16
8:10, 19
9:10
10:11, 14
12:1, 4
13:1
14:8, 17
15:4, 7, 14
17:6
19:5, 6, 8, 12, 14[2], 24, 29, 30
21:10, 17, 21
22:11, 15
23:4, 8
24:11, 13, 15, 29, 44, 63
25:25, 26
26:8
27:3, 30
28:10, 16
29:2
30:16[2]
31:13, 33
32:25
34:1, 6, 7, 24[2], 26[2]
35:9, 11
37:14, 21, 22, 23, 28
38:28[2], 29, 30
39:12, 15, 18
40:14, 15, 17
41:2, 3, 14, 18, 33, 45, 46
43:2, 23, 31
44:4, 8[2], 16, 28
45:1, 19, 24, 25
46:26
47:1, 10, 30
48:12, 14, 22
49:20
50:24

EXODUS
1:5, 10[2]
2:10, 11, 13, 19
3:2, 4, 8[2], 10, 11, 12, 17, 20
4:6, 7, 9
5:10
6:1, 6[3], 7, 11, 13, 26, 27
7:2, 4, 5, 15, 19
8:6, 12, 13[3], 16, 17, 29, 30
9:15, 29, 33
10:5, 6, 11, 12, 18, 21
11:1, 4, 8[3], 10
12:5, 15, 17, 21, 22, 33, 39[2], 41, 42, 46, 51
13:3[3], 4, 8, 9, 14, 16, 18
14:8, 10, 11, 16, 21, 26, 30
15:12, 20, 22
16:1, 4, 6, 27, 29
17:3, 6, 9[2], 14
18:1, 7, 9, 10[2], 21, 25
19:1, 3, 17
20:2[2]
21:2, 3[2], 4, 5, 7, 11, 27
22:6, 7
23:13, 15, 16, 28, 29, 30, 31
24:16
25:32[3], 33, 35
28:35
29:23, 46
32:1[2], 4, 7, 8[2], 11, 12, 19, 23, 24, 27, 32, 33
33:1, 2, 7, 8, 11
34:11, 18, 24, 34[2]
37:7, 8, 9, 18[3], 19, 21

LEVITICUS
1:1, 15
2:14
4:12[2], 18, 25, 30, 34
5:9, 15, 18
6:6, 12, 13
7:14, 35
8:26, 33
9:9, 23, 24
10:2, 4, 5, 7, 14
11:45
13:12, 20, 25, 56[4]
14:3, 8, 38, 41, 43, 45, 53
15:2, 16, 25
16:17, 18
17:3, 13
18:24, 25, 28[2]
19:36
20:22, 23
21:12
22:33
23:17, 43
24:10, 23
25:12, 28, 30, 31, 33, 38, 42, 51, 54, 55
26:6, 13, 33, 45
27:21

NUMBERS
1:1
3:9
5:2, 3, 4, 23, 25
6:19
9:1
10:12, 33, 34
11:15, 20[2], 24, 26
12:4[2], 12, 14, 15
13:16, 17
14:44
15:41
16:13, 14, 27, 35, 37, 46
17:9
18:29[2]
20:5, 8, 10, 11, 16, 18, 20
21:5, 13, 23, 26, 28, 32[2], 33
22:5, 6, 11[2], 23, 32, 36
23:7, 22
24:7, 8, 17[2], 19
26:4
27:17[2], 21
28:26
30:2, 6, 12
31:5, 27, 28, 36
32:11, 21, 23, 24
33:1, 2[2], 3, 12, 38, 52, 55
34:5, 7, 8, 9, 10, 12
35:25

DEUTERONOMY
1:22, 24, 27, 33, 44
2:14, 23, 26, 32
3:1, 8
4:12, 15, 20[2], 33, 34, 36[2], 37[2], 38, 45, 46
5:4, 6, 15[2], 22, 23, 24, 26
6:12, 19, 21, 23
7:1, 8[2], 19[2], 22
8:3, 7, 9, 14, 15
9:3, 4[2], 5, 7, 10, 12[2], 14, 16, 17, 21, 26, 28[2], 29[2]
10:4
11:2, 10, 23, 28
12:3, 5, 27
13:5[3], 10, 13
15:11, 13, 14[3]
16:1, 3[2], 6
17:18
18:5, 6, 12
20:1[2]
21:19
22:21, 24
23:4, 10, 23
24:1, 2, 3, 5, 9, 11
25:4, 6, 11, 17, 19
26:4, 8, 13
27:18
28:6, 7, 19, 25, 38, 57
29:7, 20, 21, 25, 28
30:4
31:2, 21
32:13[2], 39
33:18, 27

JOSHUA
1:8
2:1, 2, 3, 5, 7, 10, 19
3:10, 12[2]
4:2[2], 3[2], 4, 8, 16, 17, 18, 19, 20
5:4[2], 5[2], 6
6:1, 10, 22[2], 23[2], 25
7:23[2]
8:3, 5, 6, 14, 17, 18[2], 19[2], 22, 26
9:12, 26
10:22[2], 23, 24
11:4
13:6, 12
14:7, 11, 12
15:3, 4[2], 7, 9, 11[3], 63
16:2, 3, 6, 7, 8[2], 10
17:12, 13, 18
18:4, 12, 14, 15[2]
19:9, 12, 13, 17, 24, 27, 32, 34, 40, 47
20:2, 8[3]
21:3, 4[4], 5[3], 6[4], 7[3], 9[2], 16, 17, 20, 23, 25, 27, 28, 30, 32, 34, 36, 38
22:9, 31, 32
23:5, 9, 13
24:5, 6, 10, 12, 17, 18, 32

JUDGES
1:16, 19[2], 21, 24, 27, 28, 29, 30, 31, 32, 33
2:1, 3, 12, 15, 16, 17, 18, 21, 23
3:10, 19, 20, 22[2], 24
4:6, 14, 18, 22
5:4[2], 14[3], 28
6:8, 9[3], 19, 20, 21[2], 30, 38
7:23[3]
8:34
9:4, 15, 17, 20[2], 27, 29, 33, 35, 38, 39, 41, 42, 43
10:12
11:2, 3, 5, 7, 13, 24, 34, 36
12:2
13:5
14:9, 12, 14[2], 18
15:17
16:14, 20[2], 21, 25
17:7, 8
18:2, 11[2], 14, 17
19:1, 16, 23, 24, 27, 30
20:1, 10, 14[2], 15, 20, 21, 25, 28, 31, 33[3], 34, 38, 40, 42
21:16, 17, 21[2], 24

RUTH
1:7, 13, 21, 22
2:6, 17, 22
4:3

1 SAMUEL
1:3, 15, 16
2:3, 5, 8, 10, 28
3:3
4:1, 3[2], 8, 12, 13, 16[2]
5:10
7:3, 6, 8, 11, 14
8:8, 18, 20
9:11, 14, 16[2], 26
10:18[3], 19
11:2, 3, 5, 7, 10
12:6, 8, 10, 11
13:10, 17, 23
14:11, 48
15:6
16:16
17:4[2], 8, 23, 34, 35[2], 37[3], 40, 51
18:5, 6, 11, 13, 16
19:3, 8, 10
20:11[2], 21, 35, 36, 41
21:5
23:13, 15, 23
24:2, 7, 8, 14, 15, 21
25:5, 14, 29[2], 37
26:4, 19, 20, 24
27:1
28:1, 3, 9, 13, 17
29:6
30:16[2]

2 SAMUEL
1:2, 3
2:12, 13, 23
3:18[2], 25, 26
4:4, 9
5:2, 13, 24
6:3, 4, 20
7:6, 9, 12
8:1
9:5
10:3, 8, 16
11:8, 13, 17, 23
12:7, 11
13:9[3], 17, 18
14:16[2]
15:11, 24, 35
16:5, 7[2]
17:1, 21
18:3, 4, 6
19:9[3], 19
20:7[2], 8, 10, 12, 13, 16, 22
21:10, 17
22:1[2], 7, 9[2], 15, 17, 46
23:4, 16[2], 21, 29
24:4, 7, 16, 20

1 KINGS
1:29, 39
2:27, 37, 42, 46
3:7
4:23, 33
5:6, 13
6:1, 8
7:13, 47
8:1, 8[2], 9, 10, 16[2], 19, 21, 41, 42, 44, 51, 53
9:7[2], 9, 12, 24
10:28, 29[2]
11:12, 18[2], 29, 31, 32, 34, 35
12:25, 28
13:1, 3, 5
14:15, 21, 24
15:12, 17
16:2
17:19, 23
18:28, 44
19:13
20:16, 17[3], 18[2], 19, 21, 24, 31, 39, 42
21:10, 13, 26
22:3, 32, 34, 35, 46

2 KINGS
2:23, 24
3:6
4:4, 5, 18, 21, 37, 39, 40[2], 41
5:2[2], 11, 27
6:7, 27[2]
7:12[2], 16, 20
8:3
9:2, 15, 19, 21[2], 24, 30, 32
10:3, 9, 25, 26, 28
11:8, 9
12:11, 12
13:5, 25[2]
14:27
16:3, 7[2]
17:7, 8, 18, 20, 23[2], 36[2], 39
18:18, 29, 31, 33, 34, 35[2]
19:9, 19, 27, 31[2], 35
20:4, 6
21:2, 7, 8, 15
23:4, 6, 8, 16, 18, 27
24:3, 7, 12, 13, 20
25:7, 19, 21, 27

1 CHRONICLES
5:18
6:60, 61[2], 62[4], 63[3], 65[3], 66, 70, 71, 72, 74, 76, 77, 78, 80
7:11
9:28
11:2, 18[2], 23
12:2, 17
13:7
14:8, 15, 17
15:25, 29
16:33
17:21[2]
18:1
19:3, 6[3], 9, 10
20:1, 2, 3
21:16, 21
26:14, 27
27:1
28:18

2 CHRONICLES
1:10, 16, 17[2]
2:2, 8, 14, 16
4:18
5:2, 9, 10, 11
6:5, 9, 32, 34
7:20[2], 22
8:11
9:28[2]
10:2
11:13, 16
12:3, 7, 13
13:9
14:5, 8[2], 9, 10
15:2, 5, 8[2], 9[3], 17
16:1, 2[2], 7
17:6
18:20, 21[2], 31, 33
19:2, 3, 4
20:4, 7, 10, 11, 17, 21
21:15, 19
22:7
23:2, 7, 8, 11, 14
24:5, 6[2]
25:6, 10, 15
26:11, 18, 20[2]
28:3, 9, 21[2]
29:5, 7, 16[2]
30:6, 25[2]
31:1[2]
32:11, 13, 14[2], 15[3], 17[2]
33:2, 8, 15[2]
34:14, 21, 25, 33
35:20, 24

EZRA
1:7
2:1
3:8
5:14[2]
6:4, 5, 21
7:20, 28
8:35
9:5
10:1

NEHEMIAH
1:9
2:13
3:25, 26, 27
4:2, 5
5:13[2]
6:8
7:6
8:17
9:7, 15, 18, 27
12:27, 28, 29, 44
13:8, 14

ESTHER
2:9, 13, 23
3:15
4:1, 11
5:2
7:8[2]
8:4, 14, 15
9:4

JOB
1:17, 21
3:11, 24
5:5, 6
6:17
8:10, 19
9:6, 8, 10, 14
10:7, 10, 18
11:7[2], 13
12:15, 22[2]
13:9
14:4, 12, 18, 19
15:13, 22, 25, 30
16:13, 20
18:4, 5, 6, 14, 18
19:7
20:15, 25[2]
21:17
22:16
24:4, 12[2], 24
26:7
27:21, 22, 23
28:2[2], 3, 4, 5, 10, 27
29:6, 7, 16, 17, 19, 25
30:16, 24
31:7, 8, 12, 34
32:11, 13
33:6, 21
35:9
36:16, 26
37:1, 2, 9[2], 18, 22, 23
38:1, 8, 13, 29
39:3, 5
40:6
41:1, 19[2], 20[2], 21

PSALMS
3:4
5:10
8:2
9:5
10:5, 15, 16
14:7
15:5
17:1
18:6, 8[2], 14[2], 16, 42, 45
19:4, 5
20:2
21:8[2]
22:7, 9, 14[2]
25:15, 17, 22
27:12
31:4, 12
34:6, 17, 19
35:3
37:14
40:2[2]
42:4
43:3
44:2[2], 20, 21
45:8
50:2, 9[2]
51:1, 9
52:5[2]
53:6
54:7
55:23
58:6
59:7
60:6, 8, 10
62:8
64:6
66:12
68:6, 31[2], 33, 35
69:14[2], 24, 28
71:4[2], 6
73:7, 10
74:11
75:8[2]
77:17[2]
78:15, 16, 20, 55, 65
79:6
80:8[2], 11, 13
81:5, 10, 16
82:4, 5
84:2
85:5, 11
88:9
89:19, 34
94:12
97:10
102:t
104:2, 14, 35
105:41
107:3, 6, 13, 14, 19, 28
108:7, 9
109:10, 13, 14
110:2
111:2
113:7[2]
114:1
118:26
119:18, 43
121:8
124:7
128:5
130:1
132:5
134:3
135:7, 21
136:6, 11, 12
142:2, 7
143:11
144:6, 7, 14
147:18

PROVERBS
1:23, 24
2:6, 22
3:10
4:23
5:15[2]
6:9
8:12
9:1
10:31
11:8
12:13
13:9
15:2, 28
17:14, 23
20:5, 20
21:16
22:10[2]
24:20

PROVERBS
25:1, 2, 19
26:20
28:11
30:17
31:18, 20

ECCLESIASTES
1:13
3:11
4:14
7:24, 25, 27, 29
8:3, 17[2]
12:3, 9, 10

SONG OF SOLOMON
3:6
4:16
8:11

ISAIAH
2:3
5:2, 25
8:8
9:12, 17, 21
10:4
11:1[2], 16
12:3, 6
13:9, 13
14:19, 26, 27, 29
15:4, 5
16:2, 4, 8, 10[2]
18:2, 7
19:23
21:11
22:16[2]
23:11
24:18
26:16, 17, 19, 21
28:7[2], 27
29:4[4], 9, 10, 18[2]
30:11[2], 13, 14
31:3
34:3[2], 11, 16
35:6
36:16, 18, 19, 20[2]
37:28, 32[2]
38:6
40:12, 22[2], 26
42:5[2], 7[2]
43:13, 25
44:13[3], 22
45:12, 23
46:6, 7
48:1, 3, 21[2]
51:17, 22
52:11[2], 12
53:2, 8, 12
55:11, 12
57:4, 14
58:7, 10
59:5, 21[3]
62:10, 12
63:11
65:2, 9[2]
66:5, 11, 20

JEREMIAH
1:5, 10, 14
2:6, 13
3:18
4:1, 16
5:6[2]
6:1[2], 4, 7[2], 11, 12
7:15[2], 18, 20, 22, 25
8:1[2]
9:8, 18, 19[2]
10:3, 12, 13, 17, 18, 22, 25
11:4, 7
12:3, 8, 14[2], 15
14:16
15:1, 6, 21[2]
16:9, 13, 14, 16
17:8, 16, 19, 22
18:21, 23
19:13
20:3, 8, 18
21:9, 12[2]
22:3, 11, 14, 26, 28
23:3, 7, 8, 16, 39
24:5
26:23
27:10, 15
30:7, 19
31:32, 37
32:4, 17, 21[2], 29, 37
34:3, 13[2]
36:6, 11, 21, 30
37:4, 5, 12, 17, 21
38:8, 10, 13, 18, 23[2]
39:4[2], 7, 14
40:12
44:7, 17[2], 18, 19[2], 25, 28
46:20
47:2
48:15, 31, 44, 45
49:5, 20
50:3, 8[2], 28, 45
51:6, 15, 16, 25, 34, 44, 45, 55
52:3, 7, 11, 25, 27, 31

LAMENTATIONS
1:10
2:4, 8, 12, 19[2]
3:7, 8, 38, 55
4:1, 3, 11
5:8

EZEKIEL
1:4[3], 5, 13
3:25
4:12
5:2, 12
6:14
7:8
9:8
10:7, 19
11:7, 9, 17, 19
12:5, 12, 14
13:2, 17, 21, 23
14:9, 13, 19
15:7
16:5, 15, 27, 36
19:14
20:8, 9, 10, 13, 14, 21, 28, 33[2], 34[4], 38[2], 41[2]
21:3, 4, 5, 19, 31
22:15, 22, 31
23:26, 34, 48
24:6[2], 12
25:7[2], 13, 16
27:6, 33
28:16
29:4, 8
30:13, 22, 25
31:4, 11
32:3, 7, 21
33:21
34:11, 12[3], 13, 25, 27
35:3, 7, 11
36:5, 20, 24, 26
37:1, 12, 13, 23
38:8[2], 12, 15
39:3[2], 10[2], 14, 27, 29
42:11, 14
43:6, 11, 23, 25
44:3
45:14, 15[3]
46:9, 18[2], 20
47:1, 2[2], 8, 12
48:19, 30

DANIEL
2:34, 45
3:15, 17
5:2, 3, 13
6:23[2]
7:17, 24, 25
8:4, 7, 9, 22
9:15
11:7, 41, 44[2]

HOSEA
1:11
2:2, 10, 15, 17, 18
4:2
5:10
7:5
9:15
10:11
11:1, 11[2]
12:8, 13
13:3[2]

JOEL
2:16, 28, 29
3:7, 16

AMOS
3:4, 12[2]
4:3, 11
5:3, 6, 8
6:4[2], 10[2]
7:11
8:8
9:3, 6, 7, 15

OBADIAH
6, 8[2]

JONAH
1:4
2:1, 2, 4, 10
4:5

MICAH
1:3
2:9, 13
4:6, 9, 10
5:2, 10, 12, 13, 14
6:4[2]
7:2, 15, 17

NAHUM
1:6, 11, 14
2:2, 9

HABAKKUK
1:2
2:11[2]
3:4, 13, 14

ZEPHANIAH
1:4, 17
2:4, 13
3:11, 15, 19

HAGGAI
2:5, 16[2]

ZECHARIAH
1:21
2:3, 13
3:2
4:1, 12
5:9
6:1, 12
8:10, 23
9:4, 7, 11
10:4[4], 10[2]
11:6
13:2[2]
14:8

MALACHI
2:8, 12, 13
3:10

MATTHEW
2:6, 15
3:5, 16
4:4
5:13, 26, 29
7:4[2], 5[4], 22
8:12, 16, 28, 29, 31, 32, 34[2]
9:17, 32, 33, 34
10:1, 8, 14
11:7, 8, 9
12:11, 14, 24, 26, 27[2], 28, 34, 35[2], 43, 44
13:1, 41, 52
14:13, 26, 29, 35
15:11, 17, 18, 19, 22
17:5, 18, 19, 21
18:9, 28
20:1, 3, 5, 6, 30
21:12, 16, 17, 33, 39, 41
22:10, 16
24:1, 17, 27
25:6, 8
26:30, 51, 55, 71, 75
27:23, 32, 53, 60

MARK
1:5, 10, 23, 25, 26, 29, 34, 35, 39, 45
3:5, 15, 21, 22, 23
4:3, 32
5:2[2], 8, 10, 13, 14, 17, 30, 40
6:1, 12, 13, 33, 34, 49, 54
7:15, 19, 20, 21, 26, 29, 30
8:23, 27
9:7, 18, 24, 25, 26, 28, 38, 47
10:26, 46, 47
11:11, 15, 19
12:1, 8
13:1, 15
14:26, 48, 68
15:13, 14, 20, 21, 39, 46
16:8, 9, 17

LUKE
1:22, 42, 74
2:1, 4
4:14, 22, 29, 33, 35[2], 36, 37, 38, 41[2]
5:2, 3[2], 4, 17, 36
6:12, 17, 19, 22, 42[4], 45[2]
7:12, 24, 25, 26
8:2, 4, 5, 12, 27, 28, 29, 31, 33, 35[2], 38, 46, 54
9:5, 35, 38, 39, 40, 49
10:10, 35
11:14[2], 15, 18, 19[2], 20, 24[2], 54
12:54
13:28, 31, 32, 33
14:5, 7, 21, 23, 35
15:28
16:4
17:21, 30
19:22, 40, 45
20:12, 15
21:21, 37
22:39, 52, 62
23:18, 26
24:31, 50

JOHN
1:46
2:8, 15[2]
4:30, 47, 54
6:37
7:38, 41, 42, 52
8:9, 59
9:22, 34, 35
10:3, 9, 28, 29, 39
11:11, 31, 55
12:17, 31, 34, 42
13:1, 30, 31
15:19
16:2, 27
17:6, 8, 15
18:16, 29, 38
19:6, 12, 15, 34
20:2

THE ACTS
1:9, 18, 21
2:5, 17, 18
3:19
4:15
5:6, 9, 16
6:3
7:3, 4, 10, 12, 19, 21, 36, 40, 45, 57, 58
8:7, 9, 39
9:1, 28
10:45
12:9, 10, 11, 17
13:17, 42, 50
14:14, 19
15:14, 24
16:13, 18[2], 27[2], 30, 37[2], 39[2], 40
17:2, 5
19:12, 16, 28, 33, 34
21:5, 28, 30, 38
22:18, 23
23:6
24:7
27:19, 29, 30[2], 38, 42
28:3, 21, 23[2]

ROMANS
2:18
3:12
11:24, 26, 33
13:11

1 CORINTHIANS
5:7, 10
9:9
14:36
15:8

2 CORINTHIANS
1:8, 16
2:4
4:6
6:17
8:11
12:2, 3

GALATIANS
2:4
4:15, 30

EPHESIANS
4:29

PHILIPPIANS
1:12
2:12

COLOSSIANS
2:14[2]
3:8

1 THESSALONIANS
1:8

2 THESSALONIANS
2:7

1 TIMOTHY
1:5
5:18
6:7

2 TIMOTHY
1:17
2:22, 26
3:11
4:2, 17

HEBREWS
3:16
5:2
7:5, 14
8:9
11:8[2], 15, 34
12:13

JAMES
2:25
3:10, 13

1 PETER
2:9

2 PETER
2:9
3:5

1 JOHN
2:19[2]
4:1, 18

3 JOHN
10

JUDE
5, 13, 23

REVELATION
1:16
2:5
3:5[2], 12[2], 16
4:5
5:7, 9
6:4, 14
7:14
8:4
9:2, 3, 17, 18
10:10
11:2, 5, 7
12:9[3], 15, 16
13:1, 11
14:10, 15, 17, 18, 20
15:6
16:1[2], 2, 3, 4, 7, 8, 10, 12, 13[3], 17[2], 21
17:8
18:4
19:5, 15, 21
20:7, 8, 9, 12
21:2, 3, 10
22:1, 19[2]

SHALL

GENESIS
1:29
2:23, 24[3]
3:1, 3[2], 4, 5[2], 15, 16[2], 18
4:7, 12, 14[4], 15, 24
5:29
6:3[2], 15, 17, 19, 20, 21
8:22
9:2, 3, 4, 6, 11[2], 13, 14[2], 15, 16, 25, 26, 27[3]
12:3, 12[3], 13
13:16
15:4[3], 5, 8[2], 13[3], 14[2], 16
16:10, 12
17:5[2], 6, 10[2], 11[2], 12, 13, 14, 15, 16[2], 17[2], 19, 20, 21
18:5, 10, 12, 13, 14, 17, 18[2], 19, 25, 28, 29, 30, 31, 32
19:2, 20
20:7, 13
21:10, 12
22:14, 17, 18
23:6, 9
24:7, 14[3], 43, 55
25:23[3], 32
26:2, 4, 11, 22
27:12[2], 33, 37, 39, 40, 46
28:14[2], 21, 22
29:15
30:3, 15, 24, 30, 31, 32, 33[3]
31:8[2]
32:4, 8, 19, 28
34:10[2], 11, 12, 23, 30[2]
35:10[2], 11[2]
37:10, 20, 30
38:18
40:13, 14, 19[3]
41:16, 27, 30[3], 31[2], 36[2], 40, 44
42:15[2], 16, 20[2], 33, 34[2], 38[2]
43:3, 5, 16
44:10[2], 16[3], 17, 23, 29, 31[2], 32, 34[2]
45:6, 13[2], 18
46:4, 33[3], 34
47:19, 23, 24[3]
48:5, 6[2], 19[4], 20, 21
49:1, 8[3], 9, 10[2], 12, 13[3], 16, 17[2], 19[2], 20[2], 25[2], 26, 27[3]
50:17, 25

EXODUS
1:16[2], 22[2]
2:7
3:12[2], 13[3], 18[2], 21[2], 22[3]
4:8, 9[2], 15, 16[3], 21
5:7, 8[2], 11, 18[2], 19
6:1[2], 7, 12, 30
7:1, 2, 4, 5, 9[2], 17, 18[3]
8:3[2], 4, 9, 11[2], 21, 22, 23, 26[2], 27, 28
9:3, 4[2], 5, 9[2], 19[4], 28, 29[2]
10:5[3], 6, 7, 8, 14, 26[2]
11:1[2], 5, 6[2], 7, 8, 9
12:2[2], 3, 4, 5[2], 6[2], 7[2], 8[2], 10[2], 11[2], 13[2], 14[3], 15[3], 16[3], 17[2], 18, 19[2], 20[2], 22[2], 24, 25[2], 26[2], 27, 43, 44, 45, 46[2], 47, 48[3], 49
13:3, 5[2], 6, 7[3], 9, 11[3], 12, 14, 16, 19
14:2, 4, 13, 14[2], 16, 17, 18
15:9[2], 14[2], 15[3], 16[2], 18, 24
16:4, 5[3], 6, 7, 8[2], 12[3], 25, 26[2]
17:4, 6
18:19, 22[5], 23
19:5, 6, 12, 13[4]
20:23[2]
21:2[2], 3[2], 4[2], 5, 6[4], 7, 8[2], 9, 10, 11, 12, 13, 15, 16, 17, 19[3], 20, 21, 22[2], 26, 27, 28[3], 29[2], 30, 31, 32[3], 33[2], 34[2], 35[2], 36[2]
22:1[2], 2, 3[2], 4, 5[4], 6, 7, 8, 9[3], 11[3], 12, 13, 14, 15, 16, 17, 19, 20, 22, 24[2], 27[2], 30, 31[3]
23:11, 15, 17, 18, 23, 25[2], 26, 28, 33
24:2[3]
25:2, 3, 9, 10[2], 12, 15[2], 16, 17, 19, 20[3], 21, 23, 27, 31[2], 32, 34, 35, 36[2], 37, 38, 39
26:2[2], 3[2], 6, 8[2], 12, 13, 16[2], 17, 20, 24[4], 25, 28, 31, 32, 33, 37
27:1[2], 2, 7[2], 8, 9, 10[2], 11, 12, 13, 14, 15, 16[2], 17[2], 18, 19, 21[2]
28:4[2], 5, 6, 7[2], 8, 12, 16[3], 17[2], 18, 20, 21[2], 28, 29, 30[2], 32[2], 35[2], 37, 38[3], 42, 43[2]
29:9, 10, 15, 19, 21, 26, 28[2], 29, 30, 32, 33[2], 34, 37[2], 42, 43, 46
30:2[4], 4, 7[2], 8, 9[2], 10[2], 12, 13[2], 14, 15[2], 19, 20, 21[2], 25, 29, 31, 32[3], 33, 34, 36, 37[2], 38[2]
31:11, 13, 14[3], 15, 16
32:1, 13, 23, 30, 34
33:14, 16[2], 20, 22, 23
34:3, 10, 13, 20, 23, 24, 25
35:2[3], 3, 10
40:9, 10, 15

LEVITICUS
1:2, 3, 4[2], 5[2], 6, 7, 8, 9[2], 10, 11[2], 12[2], 13[2], 14, 15[2], 16, 17[3]
2:1[2], 2[3], 3, 4, 5, 7, 8, 9[2], 10, 11[3], 12[2], 16
3:1, 2[2], 3, 4, 5, 6, 7, 8[2], 9[2], 10, 11, 12, 13[2], 14, 15, 16, 17
4:2[2], 4[2], 5, 6, 7[2], 8, 9, 10, 12[2], 14, 15[2], 16, 17, 18[2], 19, 20[4], 21, 23, 24, 25[2], 26[3], 28, 29, 30[2], 31[4], 32, 33, 34[2], 35[4]
5:1, 2, 3[2], 4[2], 5[3], 6[2], 7, 8[3], 9[2], 10[3], 11[3], 12[2], 13[3], 15, 16[4], 17, 18[3]
6:4[2], 5[2], 6, 7[2], 9, 10[3], 11, 12[4], 13[2], 14, 15[2], 16[3], 17, 18[3], 20, 21, 22[2], 23[2], 25, 26[2], 27[2], 28[2], 29, 30[2]
7:2[2], 3, 4, 5, 6[2], 7, 8, 9, 10, 11, 12, 13, 14[2], 15[2], 16[2], 17, 18[4], 19[3], 20, 21[2], 23, 24, 25, 26, 27, 29, 30[2], 31[2], 32, 33
8:31, 32, 33[2], 35
9:6
10:7, 9, 13, 14, 15[2]
11:2, 3, 4, 8[2], 9[2], 10, 11[3], 12, 13[2], 20, 23, 24[2], 25, 26, 27, 28, 29, 31, 32[3], 33[2], 34[2], 35[3], 36[2], 37, 38, 39, 40[2], 41[2], 42, 43[2], 44[3], 45
12:2[2], 3, 4[2], 5[2], 6, 7[2], 8[3]
13:2[2], 3[2], 4, 5[2], 6[3], 7, 8, 9, 10, 11[2], 13[2], 14, 15, 16, 17[2], 20, 21, 22, 23, 25[2], 26, 27[2], 28, 30[2], 31, 32, 33[3], 34[3], 36[2], 37, 39, 43, 44, 45[3], 46[4], 49, 50, 51, 52[2], 53, 54[2], 55, 56, 58[2]
14:2[2], 3[2], 4, 5, 6[2], 7[3], 8[3], 9[6], 10, 11, 12, 13[2], 14[2], 15, 16[2], 17, 18[2], 19[2], 20[3], 21, 22, 23, 24[2], 25[2], 26, 27, 28, 29, 30, 31, 35, 36[2], 37, 38, 39[2], 40[2], 41[2], 42[3], 44, 45[2], 46, 47[2], 48[2], 49, 50, 51, 52, 53[2]
15:3, 4, 5, 6, 7, 8, 9, 10[2], 11, 12[2], 13[2], 14, 15[2], 16, 17, 18[2], 19[2], 20[2], 21, 22, 23, 24[2], 25[2], 26[2], 27[2], 28[2], 29, 30[2], 31
16:3, 4[5], 5, 6, 7, 8, 9, 10, 11[3], 12, 13, 14[2], 15, 16[2], 17, 18[2], 19, 20, 21[2], 22[2], 23[3], 24, 25, 26, 27[2], 28[2], 29[2], 30, 31[2], 32[4], 33[3], 34
17:4[2], 6, 7[2], 9, 12[2], 13, 14[2], 15[2], 16
18:3[3], 4, 5[2], 6, 23, 26[2], 29[2], 30
19:2, 3, 5, 6[2], 7, 8[2], 11, 12, 13, 15, 19[2], 20[2], 21, 22[2], 23[5], 24, 25, 26[2], 27, 28, 30, 33, 34, 35, 36, 37
20:2[2], 8, 9[2], 10, 11[2], 12[2], 13[2], 14, 15[2], 16[2], 17[3], 18[3], 19, 20[3], 21[2], 22, 23, 24, 25[2], 26, 27[3]
21:1, 4, 5[2], 6[2], 7[2], 8, 9, 10, 11, 12, 13, 14[2], 15, 18, 21[2], 22, 23
22:3, 4, 6[2], 7[2], 8, 9, 10[2], 11[2], 13[2], 14[2], 15, 19, 20[2], 21[2], 22, 23, 24[2], 25[2], 27[2], 28, 30[2], 31, 32
23:2, 3[2], 4, 7[2], 8[2], 10[2], 11[2], 12, 13[2], 14[2], 15[2], 16[2], 17[3], 18[2], 19, 20[2], 21[3], 24, 25[2], 27[3], 28, 29[2], 31[2], 32[3], 34, 35[2], 36[4], 37, 39[3], 40[2], 41[3], 42[2]
24:3[2], 4, 5, 8, 9[2], 15, 16[3], 17, 18, 19, 20, 21[2], 22
25:2, 4, 6, 7, 8, 9, 10[4], 11[2], 12[2], 13, 14, 15, 17, 18[2], 19[2], 20[3], 21, 22[2], 23, 24, 25, 28[3], 30[2], 31[2], 33, 40[2], 41[3], 42, 44[2], 45[2], 46[3], 50[3], 51, 52[2], 53[2], 54
26:1[2], 2, 4[2], 5[3], 6[3], 7[2], 8[3], 10, 11, 12, 15, 16[3], 17[3], 20[3], 22[2], 25[2], 26[3], 29[2], 30, 32, 33, 34[2], 35, 36[3], 37[2], 38[2], 39[2], 40, 43[3]
27:2[2], 3[2], 4, 5, 6[2], 7, 8[3], 9, 10[3], 11, 12[2], 13, 14[4], 15[2], 16[3], 17, 18[2], 19[2], 20, 21[2], 23[2], 24, 25[2], 26, 27[3], 28[2], 29[3], 31, 32, 33[4]

NUMBERS
1:3, 4, 5, 50[3], 51[3], 52, 53[2]
2:2[2], 3[2], 5[2], 7, 9, 10[2], 12[2], 14, 16, 17[2], 18[2], 20[2], 22, 24, 25[2], 27[2], 29, 31
3:7, 8, 10[2], 12, 13, 23, 24, 25, 29, 30, 31, 32, 35, 36, 38[2], 45
4:4, 5[2], 6[3], 7[2], 8[2], 9, 10[2], 11[2], 12[2], 13, 14[2], 15[2], 19, 20, 25, 26, 27[2], 28, 32
5:3[2], 6, 7[2], 8, 9, 10[2], 15[3], 16, 17[2], 18[2], 19, 21[2], 22[2], 23[2], 24[2], 25[2], 26[2], 27[5], 28[2], 30[2], 31[2]
6:2, 3[3], 4, 5[3], 6, 7, 9[2], 10, 11[2], 12[3], 13, 14, 16[2], 17[2], 18[2], 19[2], 20, 21, 23, 27
7:11
8:2, 10, 11, 12, 14, 15, 24, 25[2], 26[2]
9:3[2], 10[2], 11, 12[2], 13[2], 14[3]
10:3[2], 4, 5, 6[2], 7[2], 8[2], 9[3], 10, 32[3]
11:4, 17, 18[3], 19, 22[2], 23
12:8
13:2
14:13, 21, 23[2], 24, 27, 29, 30, 31, 32, 33, 34[2], 35[2], 41, 43
15:4, 9, 11, 12[2], 13, 14, 15[2], 16, 19[2], 20[2], 21, 24[2], 25[3], 26, 27, 28[2], 29, 30, 31[2], 35[2], 39
16:7[2], 22, 28, 30, 38
17:3, 5[3], 13[2]
18:1[2], 2, 3[2], 4[2], 5, 7[3], 9[3], 10[2], 11, 12, 13[3], 14, 15, 18, 23[3], 24, 26, 27, 28[2], 29, 30, 31, 32[2]

NUMBERS

19:3[2], 4, 5[2], 6, 7[4], 8[2], 9[2], 10[2], 11, 12[3], 13[2], 14, 16, 17[2], 18, 19[3], 20[3], 21[3], 22[2]
20:8, 12, 24[2], 26[2]
21:8[2]
22:4, 6, 8, 11, 20, 35, 38
23:8[2], 9[2], 19[2], 23, 24[2]
24:7[4], 8[2], 9, 14, 17[5], 18[3], 19[3], 20, 22[2], 23, 24[4]
25:13
26:53, 54, 55[2], 56, 65
27:8, 9, 10, 11[3], 21[4]
28:2, 3, 7, 11, 14, 15, 17, 18[2], 19[2], 20[2], 23, 24[2], 25[2], 26[2], 27, 31[2]
29:1[2], 2, 3, 7[3], 8[2], 9, 12[3], 13[2], 14, 17, 18, 21, 24, 27, 30, 33, 35[2], 36, 37, 39
30:2[2], 4[3], 5[2], 7[2], 8[2], 9, 11[2], 12[2], 15[2]
31:4, 23[4], 24[3]
32:6[2], 11, 15, 17, 22[2], 26, 29[2], 30
33:52, 53, 54[5], 55[3], 56[2]
34:2, 3[2], 4[3], 5[2], 6[2], 7[2], 8[2], 9[3], 10, 11[3], 12[3], 13, 17, 18
35:2, 3[2], 4[2], 5[3], 6[4], 7[3], 8[5], 11, 12, 13[2], 14[3], 15, 16, 17, 18, 19[2], 21[2], 24, 25[3], 26, 27, 28, 29, 30[2], 31[2], 32, 33, 34
36:3[3], 4[3], 6, 7[2], 8, 9[2]

DEUTERONOMY

1:17[3], 22[2], 28, 30, 35, 36, 38[2], 39[2]
2:4, 6[2], 25[2], 29
3:18, 19, 20, 21, 22[2], 28[2]
4:2[2], 6, 10, 22, 25[3], 26[3], 27[3], 28
5:25, 27[2], 32[2], 33[2]
6:6, 8, 10[2], 14, 16, 17, 25
7:1, 2, 5[2], 12[2], 14, 16[2], 19, 23[2], 24[2], 25
8:1, 19[2], 20
9:3[2]
11:8, 13[2], 18, 19, 22, 23, 24[3], 25[3], 29, 31[2], 32
12:1, 2[2], 3[2], 4, 5[2], 6, 7[2], 8, 11[3], 12, 14, 16[2], 18, 20, 22, 26, 27, 29
13:4[2], 5, 8, 9, 11[2], 16[2], 17
14:1, 4, 6, 7, 8, 9[2], 11, 12, 19, 21, 23, 24, 25, 29[2]
15:2[2], 3, 4[2], 6, 10[2], 11, 16, 17, 18[2], 20, 22
16:2, 4[2], 6, 7, 8, 15[2], 16[3], 17, 18
17:6[2], 7, 8, 9[2], 10[2], 11[3], 12, 13, 15, 16[2], 17[2], 18[2], 19[2]
18:1[2], 2, 3[2], 6, 7, 8, 10, 15, 18[2], 19[2], 20[3], 21
19:4, 5, 12, 13, 15[2], 17[2], 18, 19, 20[2], 21[2]
20:2[2], 3, 5, 8[2], 9[2], 11[4]
21:2[2], 3[2], 4[2], 5[2], 6, 7, 8, 12, 13[3], 14, 16, 17, 19, 20, 21[2], 23
22:2, 5[2], 15, 16, 17, 18, 19[2], 21[2], 22, 24[2], 25, 29[2], 30
23:1, 2[2], 3[2], 8, 10[2], 11[3], 13, 14, 16[2], 17, 22
24:5[4], 6, 7, 8[2], 11, 13, 15, 16[3], 19, 20, 21
25:1, 2[2], 5[2], 6[2], 8, 9[3], 10, 12, 19
26:1, 2, 3, 4
27:2[2], 4[2], 12, 13, 14, 15, 16, 17, 18, 19, 20, 21, 22, 23, 24, 25, 26
28:1, 2, 4, 5, 7[2], 8[2], 9, 10[2], 11, 12, 13, 15[2], 17, 18, 20, 21, 22[2], 23[2], 24[2], 25, 26[2], 28, 29, 30, 31[4], 32[3], 33, 35, 36, 37, 38, 39, 40, 41, 42, 43, 44[2], 45[2], 46, 48[2], 49, 50, 51[2], 52[2], 53, 54[2], 55[2], 56, 57[3], 60, 62, 63[2], 64, 65[2], 66, 68[3]
29:19, 20[3], 21, 22[3], 24, 25
30:1, 12, 13, 16, 18[2]
31:3, 4, 5, 11, 17[3], 18, 20[2], 21[3]
32:2[2], 20, 22[2], 24, 25, 35[2], 36, 37, 42, 46, 47
33:3, 10[2], 12[3], 17, 19[3], 22, 25[2], 27[2], 28[3], 29

JOSHUA

1:3, 4, 5, 8, 11, 14[2], 15, 18
2:5, 14, 19[5]
3:3, 4, 8, 10, 13[4]
4:3[2], 7[2], 21, 22
6:3, 4[3], 5[4], 10[3], 17[2], 19, 26[2]
7:8, 9[2], 14[7], 15[2], 25
8:2, 4, 5, 7, 8[3]
9:7, 23
10:8, 25
14:9, 12
15:4
17:18[2]
18:4[2], 5[3], 6
20:3, 4[3], 5, 6[3]
22:22, 25, 28, 34
23:5[2], 10, 12, 13, 15[2], 16[2]
24:27[2]

JUDGES

1:1, 2
2:2[2], 3[2]
4:9[2], 20
5:11[2], 24[2]
6:15, 37
7:4[5], 11, 17[2]
8:23[2]
9:33
10:18
11:9, 24, 31[2]

JUDGES

13:5[3], 7, 8[2], 12[2], 15, 22
14:13, 16
15:3, 18
16:2, 7, 11, 17
18:5, 10
20:9, 18[2], 23, 28[2]
21:1, 5, 7, 11[2], 16, 22

RUTH

1:16
2:2, 9
3:1, 3, 4[2], 13
4:12, 15

1 SAMUEL

1:11, 28
2:9[2], 10[4], 25[2], 30, 31, 32[2], 33[3], 34[3], 35[2], 36[3]
3:9, 11, 14
4:8
5:7, 8
6:2[2], 3[2], 4[2], 5[2], 9, 20
8:9, 11[2], 17, 18[2]
9:7, 13[2], 17, 19
10:2, 3, 5[2], 27
11:7, 9[2], 10, 12, 13
12:12, 14, 15, 17, 25[2]
13:14
14:10, 37, 39, 45[2]
15:33
16:16[2]
17:9, 25, 26, 27, 36, 47
18:25
19:6
20:7, 10, 31, 32
21:15
23:2, 17[2], 20, 23
24:4, 12, 13, 20
25:6, 11, 29[2], 30[3], 31[2]
26:10[3]
27:1[3], 12
28:8, 10, 11, 15, 19
29:9
30:8[2], 23, 24[2]

2 SAMUEL

2:1[2], 26[2]
3:12, 39
4:11
5:8[2], 19, 24
6:9, 22
7:10, 12, 13, 14, 15, 16[2]
9:10[2], 11[2]
11:11
12:5, 6, 10, 11, 14, 23[2]
13:13
14:7[2], 10, 11, 17, 18
15:8, 10, 14, 15, 21, 25, 35, 36
16:3, 10, 20, 21[2]
17:2, 3, 6, 10, 12[3], 13
19:21, 22, 37, 38[2]
20:6, 18, 21
21:3[2], 4
22:4, 44, 45[2], 46[2]
23:4, 6, 7[2]
24:13[2]

1 KINGS

1:13[2], 17[2], 20, 21[3], 24[2], 30[2], 35[2], 52[3]
2:4, 24, 32, 33[2], 37[2], 44, 45[2]
3:5, 12, 13
5:5, 6, 9
8:19[2], 25, 29[2], 30, 33, 38, 42[2], 44, 47, 59
9:3, 5, 6, 7, 8[3], 9
11:2[2], 32, 38
12:10, 24, 26, 27[2]
13:2[3], 3[2], 22, 32
14:3[2], 5[2], 11[2], 12, 13[2], 14[2], 15[3], 16
16:4[2]
17:1, 4, 14[2]
18:12[3], 14, 31
19:17[3]
20:6[3], 10, 14, 23, 25, 28, 36, 39, 40, 42
21:19, 23, 24[2]
22:6[3], 12, 15[3], 16, 20

2 KINGS

1:2
2:9, 10[2], 16, 21
3:8, 17[3], 19[2]
4:2, 10[2], 23, 43[2]
5:8, 10, 17, 27
6:8, 15, 21[2], 27, 31
7:1, 4[3], 12, 18
8:1, 8, 9, 10
9:8, 10[2], 36, 37[2]
10:4, 10, 18, 19[2], 24, 30
11:5[2], 6[2], 7, 8
12:5
14:6[2]
15:12
16:15
17:12, 35, 36[3], 37[2], 38[2], 39[2]
18:22, 29, 30
19:6, 7[2], 10[2], 29[2], 30, 31[2], 32, 33[2]
20:8[2], 9, 17[2], 18[3]
21:12, 14
22:17[2], 18, 20
23:27
25:24

1 CHRONICLES

11:6, 19
12:17
13:12
14:10, 15
16:30, 33
17:9[3], 11[2], 12, 13, 14, 27

1 CHRONICLES

21:12
22:9[3], 10[2]
23:26
28:6, 21[2]

2 CHRONICLES

1:7, 12
2:8, 9, 14
6:9[2], 16, 21, 24, 29[3]
7:14, 15, 16, 18, 19, 21[2], 22
8:11
10:10
11:4
12:7, 8
13:12
15:7
18:5[2], 11, 14[3], 15, 19
19:9, 10[3], 11[2]
20:16, 17, 20[2]
23:3, 4[2], 5[2], 6[2], 7[2]
25:4[3], 8, 9
26:18
28:13
30:9[2]
32:11, 12, 15, 17
33:4
34:25[2], 26, 28
35:3

EZRA

4:21
6:8, 11, 12
7:18, 20, 21, 24
9:10

NEHEMIAH

2:6, 8
4:3, 11, 12, 20
5:8
6:7, 9
9:29
10:38[2], 39
13:25, 27

ESTHER

1:15, 17[3], 18[2], 20[3]
4:11[2], 14[2]
5:3, 6[2], 8
6:6, 9, 11
7:2[2]
8:6
9:12[2]

JOB

1:21
2:10[2]
4:17[2]
5:19[2], 20, 23, 24, 25
7:4, 7, 8, 9, 10[2], 13[2], 20, 21[2]
8:2, 10, 13, 14[2], 15[4], 18, 19, 22[2]
9:14, 19, 20[2], 31
10:21
11:3, 17, 19[2], 20[3]
12:2, 7[2], 8[2]
13:11, 16[2], 18, 19
14:6, 12, 14, 22[2]
15:21, 22, 24[2], 29[3], 30[3], 31, 32[2], 33[2], 34[2]
16:3, 22[2]
17:5, 8[2], 9[2], 15, 16
18:4[2], 5[2], 6[2], 7[2], 9[2], 11[2], 12[2], 13[2], 14[2], 15[2], 16[2], 17[2], 18, 19, 20
19:25, 26, 27[2]
20:7[2], 8[3], 9[2], 10[2], 11, 15[2], 16[2], 17, 18[4], 20[2], 21[2], 22[2], 23[2], 24[2], 26[3], 27[2], 28[2]
21:19, 20[2], 22, 26[2], 30, 31[2], 32[2], 33[2]
22:21, 25, 27, 28[2], 29, 30
23:10
24:15, 20[4]
27:4, 6, 13, 14, 15[2], 17[2], 19[2], 22, 23[2]
28:12, 15, 17, 18, 19[2]
29:18[2]
31:14[2]
33:3[2], 7[2], 25[2], 26[2], 28, 33
34:11, 15[2], 17, 20[3], 24
35:3
36:4, 11, 12[2]
37:19, 20[2]
38:11, 15
40:2, 4
41:6[2], 9
42:8

PSALMS

1:3[3], 5, 6
2:4[2], 5, 8
5:4, 5
6:5
7:7, 8, 16[2]
9:3, 7, 8[2], 17, 18[2]
10:6[2]
11:6[2]
12:3
13:2[2], 5
14:7[2]
15:1[2], 5
16:4, 8, 9
17:3, 15
18:3, 43, 44[2], 45
19:13[2]
21:1[2], 7, 8[2], 9[2]
22:25, 26[3], 27[2], 29[2], 30[2], 31[3]
23:1, 6
24:3[2], 5, 7, 9
25:12[2], 13[2], 15
26:1
27:1[2], 3, 5[3], 6, 14
28:5
30:6, 9[2]
31:24

PSALMS

32:6[2], 10[2]
33:17, 21
34:1, 2[2], 10, 21[2], 22
35:9[2], 10, 28
36:8, 9, 12
37:2, 4, 5, 6, 9[2], 10[2], 11[2], 13, 15[2], 17, 18, 19[2], 20[4], 22[2], 24, 28, 29, 31, 34, 38[2], 40[2]
39:6
40:3[2]
41:2, 5, 8
42:2, 5, 8, 11
43:5
44:6, 21
45:4, 11, 12[2], 14[2], 15[2], 16, 17
46:4, 5[2]
47:3, 4
49:3[2], 5, 11, 14[3], 15, 17[2], 19[2]
50:3[4], 4, 6
51:7[2], 13, 14, 15, 19
52:5[2], 6[2]
53:6[2]
54:5
55:16, 17, 19, 22[2], 23
56:7, 9
57:3[2]
58:9, 10[2], 11
59:10[2]
60:12[2]
61:7
62:2, 3[2], 6
63:3, 5[2], 9, 10[2], 11[3]
64:5, 7[2], 8[2], 9[3], 10[3]
65:1, 2, 4
66:3, 4[3]
67:6[2], 7[2]
68:13, 21, 29, 31[2]
69:31, 32[2], 36[2]
71:6, 15, 23, 24
72:2, 3, 4[3], 5, 6, 7, 8, 9[2], 10[2], 11[2], 12, 13[2], 14[2], 15[4], 16[3], 17[4]
73:27
74:10[2]
75:2, 8, 10
76:10, 12
79:5
80:3, 7, 19
81:9
82:7
85:11[2], 12[2], 13[2]
86:9[2]
87:5[2], 6, 7
88:10, 11, 12, 13
89:2, 5, 12, 14, 15, 16[2], 17, 21[2], 22, 24[2], 26, 28, 36, 37, 46, 48[2]
91:1, 3, 4[2], 7[2], 10[2], 11, 12, 15
92:7, 9[2], 10, 11[2], 12[2], 13, 14[2]
94:3[2], 4, 7[2], 9[2], 10[2], 15[2], 20, 23[3]
96:10[3], 12, 13
98:9
101:3, 4, 6[2], 7[2]
102:15, 16[2], 18[3], 26[3], 27, 28[2]
103:16
104:12, 31[2], 34
107:42[2], 43
108:13[2]
109:7, 31
110:2, 3, 5, 6[3], 7[2]
112:2[2], 3, 6[2], 7, 8, 9, 10[3]
115:14
116:12
118:7, 17, 20
119:6, 7, 9, 27, 33, 34[2], 42, 44, 88, 117, 144, 146, 165, 171, 172, 175
120:3[2]
121:4, 6, 7[2], 8
122:2, 6
125:1, 3, 5[2]
126:5, 6
127:5[2]
128:2, 3, 4, 5
130:3, 8
132:12[2], 16, 18
137:4, 8, 9
138:4, 5, 7
139:7[2], 10[2], 11[2]
140:11, 13[2]
141:5[4], 6
142:7
143:2
144:5
145:4[2], 6, 7[2], 10[2], 11, 21
146:10
148:6

PROVERBS

1:5, 9, 13[2], 28[3], 31, 32[2], 33[2]
2:11[2], 21[2], 22[2]
3:2, 6, 8, 10[2], 22, 23, 24, 26[2], 35[2]
4:6[2], 8[2], 9[2], 10, 12
5:22[2], 23[2]
6:11, 15[2], 22[3], 29, 31[2], 33[2]
8:6, 7, 17, 35
9:11[2]
10:7, 8, 9, 10, 24[2], 27, 28[2], 29, 30[2], 31
11:3[2], 5[2], 6[2], 7, 9, 15, 18, 21[2], 25[2], 26[2], 27, 28[2], 29[2], 31
12:3[2], 6, 7, 8[2], 11, 13, 14[2], 19, 21[2], 24[2]
13:2[2], 3, 4, 9, 11[2], 13[2], 18[2], 20[2], 21, 25
14:3, 11[2], 14[2], 22, 26
15:10, 27
16:3, 5, 20, 21
17:2[2], 5, 11, 13
18:20[2], 21
19:5[2], 8, 9[2], 15, 16, 19, 21, 23[2]
20:4, 17, 20, 21, 22
21:7, 13[2], 15, 16, 17[2], 18, 28

PROVERBS

22:5, 8[2], 9, 10[2], 11, 13, 14, 15, 16, 18, 29[2]
23:11, 13, 15, 16, 18, 21[2], 24[2], 25[2], 33[2], 35
24:4, 8, 12, 14[3], 16, 20[2], 22, 24[2], 25[2], 26, 34
25:4, 5, 22
26:2, 26, 27
27:14, 18[2]
28:2, 8, 9, 10[2], 13[2], 14, 16, 17, 18[2], 19[2], 20[2], 22, 23, 25, 26, 27[2]
29:1, 14, 16, 17[2], 21, 23[2], 25
30:17[2]
31:11, 25, 30

ECCLESIASTES

1:9[2], 11[2]
2:16, 18, 19[2], 21
3:14, 17, 22[2]
4:12, 15, 16
5:10, 15[2], 16, 20
6:4, 12
7:18, 26[2]
8:1, 5, 7[2], 8, 12, 13[2], 15, 17[2]
9:5
10:8[2], 9[2], 14[2], 20[2]
11:2, 3, 4[2], 6[2], 8
12:3[2], 4[3], 5[5], 7[2], 14

SONG OF SOLOMON

1:13
5:3[2]
7:8
8:8[2]

ISAIAH

1:18[2], 19, 20, 27, 28[2], 29[2], 30, 31[3]
2:2[4], 3[2], 4[5], 11[3], 12[2], 17[3], 18, 19, 20
3:4, 5[2], 6, 7, 10[2], 11[2], 24[2], 25, 26[2]
4:1, 2[2], 3[2], 4[2], 5, 6
5:5[2], 6[2], 9, 10[2], 14, 15[3], 16[2], 17[2], 24[2], 26, 27[3], 28, 29[5], 30
6:8, 13[4]
7:7[2], 8, 9, 14[3], 15, 16[2], 17, 18[2], 19[2], 20[2], 21[2], 22[4], 23[3], 24[2], 25[3]
8:4[2], 7, 8[4], 9[3], 10[2], 12, 14, 15, 19, 21[4], 22[2]
9:1, 5, 6[2], 7, 9, 11, 12, 17[2], 18[3], 19[2], 20[4], 21
10:3, 4[2], 11, 12, 15[2], 16[2], 17[2], 18[2], 19, 20[3], 21, 22[2], 23, 24[2], 25, 26[2], 27[3], 32[2], 33[3], 34[2]
11:1[2], 2, 3[2], 4[3], 5, 6[3], 7[3], 8[2], 9[2], 10[4], 11[3], 12[2], 13[4], 14[4], 15[3], 16[2]
12:3, 4
13:6, 7[2], 8[5], 9, 10[3], 13, 14[2], 15[2], 16[2], 17[2], 18[3], 19, 20[4], 21[4], 22[2]
14:1[2], 2[4], 3[2], 10, 16, 20, 24[2], 25, 27[2], 29[2], 30[3], 31[2], 32[2]
15:2[2], 3[2], 4[4], 5[4], 6, 7, 9
16:2[2], 5[2], 6, 7[3], 10[3], 11, 12[3], 14[2]
17:1, 2[3], 3[2], 4[3], 5[2], 6, 7[2], 8[2], 9[2], 11, 13[4]
18:5, 6[3], 7
19:1[3], 2, 3[2], 4, 5[2], 6[3], 7, 8[3], 9, 10, 15, 16[2], 17[2], 18[2], 19, 20[4], 21[4], 22[5], 23[3], 24, 25
20:4, 5, 6[2]
21:13, 16, 17
22:7[3], 13, 14, 18, 19, 20, 21, 22[4], 23, 24, 25[2]
23:5, 7, 15[3], 17[3], 18[3]
24:2, 3, 9[2], 13[2], 14[3], 18[3], 20[4], 21[2], 22[3], 23[2]
25:2, 3[2], 5, 6, 8, 9, 10[2], 11[2], 12
26:1, 6, 11[2], 14[2], 19[3], 21[2]
27:1[2], 5, 6[2], 9[2], 10[3], 11, 12[3], 13[4]
28:2, 3, 4, 5, 9[2], 15[2], 16, 17[2], 18[4], 19[3], 21[2]
29:2[2], 4[3], 5[3], 7, 8[2], 14[2], 16[3], 17[2], 18[2], 19[2], 22[2], 23[2], 24[2]
30:3, 6, 7, 13, 14[3], 15[2], 16[2], 17[2], 19[2], 20[2], 21, 22, 23[3], 24, 25, 26[2], 28[2], 29, 30[2], 31, 32[3]
31:3[4], 4, 7, 8[4], 9[2]
32:1[2], 2, 3[2], 4[2], 5, 8, 10[3], 12, 13, 14[3], 16, 17, 18, 19[2]
33:1, 4[2], 6, 7[2], 11[3], 12[2], 14[2], 16[4], 17[2], 18, 20[4], 21[2], 24[2]
34:3[3], 4[3], 5[2], 7[2], 9[2], 10[4], 11[3], 12[3], 13[2], 14[3], 15[2], 16[2], 17[2]
35:1[2], 2[3], 5[2], 6[2], 7[2], 8[5], 9[4], 10[3]
36:7, 14, 15
37:6, 7, 10[2], 30[2], 31, 32[2], 33, 34[2]
38:7, 10, 11[2], 15[2], 19[2], 21, 22
39:6[2], 7[3], 8
40:4[3], 5[2], 6, 8, 10, 11[3], 20, 24[6], 25, 30[2], 31[4]
41:11[3], 12, 16[2], 22, 25[3], 27
42:1, 2, 3[3], 4[2], 13[4], 17[2]
43:2[2], 10, 13, 17[2], 19[2], 20, 21
44:4, 5[3], 7[3], 9, 11[3], 15, 19[2], 26, 28[2]
45:1, 9, 13[2], 14[6], 16[2], 17[2], 23[3], 24[3], 25[2]
46:7[2], 10, 13[2]
47:3[2], 7, 8[2], 9[2], 11[3], 13, 14[4], 15[3]
48:14, 15
49:5[2], 7[3], 9[2], 10[4], 11, 12, 17[2], 19[2], 20, 22[2], 23[3], 24, 25[2], 26[2]
50:7[2], 9[3], 11[2]
51:3[2], 4, 5[3], 6[5], 8[3], 11[4], 12[2], 19[2]
52:1, 3, 6[2], 8[4], 10, 12, 13[2], 15[4]
53:2[2], 8, 10[3], 11[4], 12
54:3, 5, 10[3], 13[2], 14, 15[3], 17[2]
55:3, 5, 11[4], 12[3], 13[4]
56:5, 7[2], 12
57:2[2], 12, 13[4], 14

ISAIAH

58:4, 8[4], 9[2], 10, 11, 12[2]
59:6[2], 8, 19[3], 20, 21
60:2[3], 3, 4[2], 5[3], 6[4], 7[3], 9, 10[2], 11[2], 12[2], 13, 14[3], 18, 19[3], 20[4], 21[2], 22
61:4[3], 5[2], 6[4], 7[4], 9[2], 10
62:2[2], 4[2], 5[2], 6, 8, 9[2], 12
63:3
64:5
65:9[2], 10, 12, 13[6], 14[3], 15[2], 16[2], 17, 19, 20[3], 21[2], 22[3], 23, 24, 25[4]
66:5[2], 8[2], 9[2], 12[2], 13, 14[3], 16, 17, 18[2], 19, 20, 22[2], 23[2], 24[4]

JEREMIAH

1:7, 14, 15[2], 19[2]
2:3[2], 19[2], 24, 35
3:1[2], 15, 16[6], 17[3], 18[2], 19
4:2[2], 7, 9[4], 10, 11, 12, 13[2], 14, 21, 27, 28, 29[3]
5:6[4], 7, 9[2], 12[2], 13[2], 14, 17[4], 19[3], 29[2]
6:3[3], 9, 10, 11, 12, 15[2], 16, 21[2], 22, 23, 26, 30
7:20[3], 23, 32[2], 33[2], 34
8:1, 2[3], 3, 4[2], 10, 12[2], 13[3], 17
9:7, 9[2], 22[2]
10:10[2], 11[2], 15, 21[2]
11:4, 11[2], 12[2], 22[2], 23
12:4[2], 12[2], 13[3], 15, 16[2]
13:10, 12[3], 17[2], 18, 19[4], 21[2], 27
14:13[2], 15[2], 16[2]
15:2[2], 5[3], 11, 12, 14, 20[2]
16:4[6], 6[3], 7[2], 10[2], 13, 14, 16[2], 19[2], 20, 21
17:4, 6[3], 8[5], 11[2], 13[2], 14[2], 24, 25[2], 26, 27[2]
18:7, 9, 14, 16, 18, 20
19:2, 3, 6, 8, 9[2], 11, 13
20:4[4], 5, 6, 10[2], 11[5]
21:3, 6, 7[2], 9[3], 10[2], 13[2], 14
22:4, 5, 7, 8[2], 9, 10, 11, 12[2], 18[2], 19, 22[2], 26, 27, 30[2]
23:3, 4[3], 5[2], 6[3], 7, 8, 12[2], 17[2], 19, 20[2], 24, 26, 32, 33, 34, 35, 36[2], 38, 40
24:7[2], 9
25:11[2], 12, 14, 16, 26, 28[2], 29, 30[3], 31, 32[2], 33[3], 34, 35, 36
26:9[2], 15, 18[2]
27:4, 7[2], 8, 9, 11, 14, 16, 22[2]
28:9[2], 14
29:7, 12[2], 13[2], 21, 22, 32[2]
30:3, 7, 8[2], 9, 10[3], 16[3], 18[2], 19[3], 20[2], 21[3], 22, 23, 24[2]
31:1, 5[2], 6[2], 8, 9[2], 12[4], 13, 14, 16[2], 17, 18, 22, 23[2], 24, 28, 29, 30[2], 33[2], 34[2], 36, 38, 39[2], 40[2]
32:3, 4[4], 5[3], 7, 15, 28, 29, 36, 38, 40, 43, 44
33:9[3], 10[2], 11[2], 12, 13, 15, 16[3], 17, 18
34:2, 3[2], 5, 20, 22
35:6, 7[2], 15, 19
36:29[2], 30[2]
37:7[2], 8, 9[2], 19
38:2[4], 3[2], 17[2], 18[2], 20[3], 22[2], 23
39:12, 16, 18
40:9, 15
42:4[2], 5, 14, 16[4], 17[3], 18[4], 20, 22
43:10, 11, 12[3], 13[2]
44:12[4], 14[3], 26, 27, 28[3], 29[2]
46:6, 10[2], 14, 18, 19, 22[2], 23, 24[2], 26, 27[2]
47:2[4], 3
48:2[2], 3, 5, 7, 8[4], 9, 12[2], 13, 18[2], 26[2], 30[2], 31, 33[2], 34, 36[2], 37[2], 38, 39[2], 40[2], 41, 42, 43, 44[2], 45[2]
49:2[3], 3, 4, 5[2], 10, 12, 13[2], 17[3], 18[2], 19, 20[2], 22[2], 26[2], 27, 28, 29[3], 32, 33[2], 36[2], 39
50:3[4], 4[2], 5[2], 9[4], 10[2], 12[3], 13[3], 16[2], 19[2], 20[3], 30[2], 32[3], 34, 36[2], 37[2], 38, 39[4], 40[2], 41[2], 42[3], 44, 45[2]
51:2[3], 4, 14, 18, 26, 29[2], 31, 33, 35[2], 37, 38[2], 44[2], 46[3], 47[2], 48[2], 49, 52, 53, 56, 57, 58[4], 62[2], 63, 64[3]

LAMENTATIONS

1:21
2:13[3], 20[2]
4:15, 20, 21
5:21

EZEKIEL

2:5
3:10, 18, 19, 20[3], 21, 25[2]
4:3[2], 7, 10, 13, 16[2]
5:4, 10[2], 11, 12[3], 13[2], 15[2], 16[2], 17[2]
6:4[2], 6[2], 7[2], 8[2], 9[3], 10, 11, 12[3], 13[2], 14
7:4[3], 9[2], 11[2], 13[3], 15[2], 16[2], 17[2], 18[3], 19[4], 21, 22[2], 24[2], 25[2], 26[4], 27[4]
8:18
9:10
11:10[2], 11[2], 12, 16, 18[2], 20
12:11[2], 12[4], 13[3], 15[2], 16, 19, 20[3], 23, 24, 25[3], 28[2]
13:9[5], 11[4], 12, 13, 14[4], 21[2], 23[2]
14:8, 10[2], 16[3], 18[2], 20[2], 22[5], 23[2]
15:3, 5, 7[3]
16:16[2], 39[4], 40[2], 41, 42, 44, 53, 55[3]
17:9[3], 10[3], 15[3], 16, 17, 18, 20, 21[3], 23[3], 24

SHALT

1 SAMUEL
9:16
10:2, 3[2], 4, 5[2], 6[2], 8[3]
14:44
16:3[2], 16
18:21
19:11
20:2, 8, 14, 15, 18, 19[2], 31
22:16, 23
23:17
24:20
26:25[2]
28:1, 2, 19
30:8

2 SAMUEL
3:13
5:2[2], 6, 23, 24
7:5, 8, 12
9:7, 10
10:11
11:25
12:13
13:13
15:33, 35[2]
18:3, 20[3]
19:23, 38
21:4, 17

1 KINGS
2:37[2], 42
5:6, 9[3]
8:19, 44
11:37[2]
12:10[2]
13:17
14:5
17:4
19:16[2]
20:5, 13, 34, 39
21:19[2]
22:11, 22, 25[2]

2 KINGS
1:4[2], 6[2], 16[2]
4:4[3], 16
5:10
6:22
7:2[2], 19[2]
8:13
9:7
10:5
13:17, 19
19:11
20:1, 5, 9, 18
22:20

1 CHRONICLES
11:2[2], 5
14:15[2]
17:4, 7
19:12
21:22
22:8, 13
28:3

2 CHRONICLES
2:16[2]
6:9, 34
7:17
10:10[2]
16:9
18:10, 21[2], 24[2]
21:15
34:28

EZRA
4:13, 15, 16
7:20

ESTHER
4:13
6:13[2]

JOB
5:21[2], 22[2], 23, 24[3], 25, 26
7:21
9:31
11:15[3], 16, 17[2], 18[3], 19
14:15
17:4
22:23[2], 24, 25, 26[2], 27[2], 28, 29
35:14
38:11

PSALMS
2:9[2]
5:3, 6
12:7[2]
17:3
21:9, 10, 12[2]
31:20[2]
32:7[2], 8
36:8
37:3[2], 10, 34
50:15
51:6, 19
55:23
59:8[2]
65:3
67:4
71:20[2], 21
73:20, 24
76:10
81:9
82:8
89:2
91:4, 5, 8, 13[2]
92:10
102:12, 13, 26[2]
119:32
128:2[2], 5, 6
138:7
142:7

PROVERBS
2:5, 9
3:4, 23, 24[2]
4:12
9:12[2]
20:13
22:24
23:8, 14[2], 34, 35
24:6
25:22
27:27

ECCLESIASTES
11:1
12:1

ISAIAH
1:26
12:1
14:4, 15, 20
17:10[2], 11[2]
22:18
23:12[2]
25:5
29:4[2], 6
30:19, 22[2], 23
33:1[3], 19
37:11
38:1
39:7
41:12[2], 15[2], 16[3]
43:2
44:21, 26, 28
47:1, 5, 11[3], 12
49:18, 20, 21, 23
51:22
53:10
54:3, 4[4], 14[3], 17
55:5
58:9[2], 11, 12[2], 13, 14
60:5, 16[3], 18
62:2, 3, 4[2], 12

JEREMIAH
1:7[2]
2:36, 37[2]
3:19[2]
4:1, 2, 30
5:19
7:27[2], 28
8:4
13:12, 13
14:17
15:2, 19[2]
16:2[2], 8, 10, 11
17:4
18:22
19:10, 11
20:6[3]
21:8
22:15, 22, 23
23:33, 37
25:27, 28
26:4, 8
28:13, 16
29:24
31:4[3], 5
34:3[3], 4, 5, 14
36:6, 29
37:17
38:17, 18, 23[3], 24, 26
39:17, 18
40:16
45:4
46:11[2]
48:2, 7
49:12[2]
51:26, 61[2], 62, 63, 64

LAMENTATIONS
4:21[2]

EZEKIEL
2:4, 7
3:18, 25, 26[2], 27
4:3, 4[2], 5, 6, 7[2], 8, 9[2], 10[2], 11[2], 12[2], 15
5:2[3], 3
8:6, 13, 15
12:3, 4[2], 6[2]
16:41, 43, 61[2], 62
21:7, 32[2]
22:2, 16[2]
23:27, 32[2], 33, 34[2]
24:13, 16, 27[2]
25:7
26:14[2], 21[2]
27:34, 36[2]
28:8, 9, 10, 19[2]
29:5[2]
31:18[2]
32:28[2]
33:7, 8, 14
35:4[2], 12, 15
36:12[2], 14, 15[2]
38:8[2], 9[2], 10, 11, 14, 15, 16
39:4, 5
43:19, 20[2], 21, 22, 23, 24, 25
44:6
45:3, 18, 20
46:13[2], 14

DANIEL
4:26
5:16[2]
12:13

HOSEA
2:16[2], 20
3:3[3]
4:5, 6
13:4

AMOS
7:17

OBADIAH
10

MICAH
1:14
2:5
4:10[4], 13
5:12, 13
6:14[3], 15[5]

NAHUM
3:11[3]

HABAKKUK
2:7

ZEPHANIAH
3:11[2], 15

ZECHARIAH
2:11
3:7[2]
4:7, 9
13:3

MATTHEW
1:21
4:7, 10[2]
5:21, 26, 27, 33[2], 36, 43
6:5
7:5
11:23
12:37[2]
16:19[2]
17:27
19:18[4], 19, 21
22:37, 39
26:34, 75

MARK
6:23
10:21
12:30, 31
14:30, 72

LUKE
1:13, 14, 20, 31[2], 76[2]
4:8[2], 12
5:10
6:42
10:15, 27, 28
12:59
13:9
14:10, 14[2]
17:4, 8
18:22
22:34, 61
23:43

JOHN
1:33, 42, 50
13:7, 8, 36
21:18[2]

THE ACTS
2:28
13:11, 35
16:31
22:15
23:5
25:12, 22

ROMANS
2:3
7:7
10:9[3]
11:22
12:20
13:3, 9[6]

1 CORINTHIANS
7:16[2]
9:9
14:16

GALATIANS
5:14

1 TIMOTHY
4:6, 16
5:18

HEBREWS
1:12

JAMES
2:8

3 JOHN
6

REVELATION
2:10
3:3[2]
16:5
18:14

SHE 1931, *846*

GENESIS
2:23[2]
3:6, 12, 20
4:1, 2, 17, 22, 25[2]
8:9
11:30
12:14, 16, 18, 19
15:9
16:1, 4[3], 5[2], 6, 8, 13[2]
17:16
18:15
19:26, 33[2], 35[2], 38
20:2, 3, 5[3], 12[3], 16
21:7, 9, 10, 14, 15, 16[3], 19[2]
22:20, 24
24:14[2], 16, 18[2], 19[2], 20, 24[2], 25, 36, 44, 45, 46[2], 47, 55, 58, 64[2], 65[2], 67
25:2, 21, 22[2], 26
26:7[3], 9[2]
27:16, 17[2], 42
29:9, 12, 32[2], 33[2], 34, 35[3]
30:1, 3[2], 4, 6, 8, 9[2], 11, 13, 15, 17, 18, 20, 21, 23, 24, 35
31:35, 38
32:14, 15
34:1
35:8, 16, 17, 18[2]
36:12, 14
38:3, 4[2], 5[2], 14[3], 15, 16[2], 17, 18[2], 19, 24, 25[3], 26, 28, 29
39:7, 10, 12, 13, 14, 16, 17, 19
45:23
46:15, 18, 25

EXODUS
1:16
2:2[2], 3[3], 5[2], 6[3], 7, 10[3], 22
4:26
6:20, 23, 25
21:4, 7, 8, 11

LEVITICUS
12:2[2], 4[2], 5[3], 6, 7, 8[3]
15:19, 20[2], 22, 23, 25, 26[2], 28[3], 29
18:7, 9, 11, 12, 13, 14, 15, 19
19:20[2]
20:17, 18
21:9[3]
22:12, 13
26:43

NUMBERS
5:13[2], 14[2], 27, 28
12:10, 14
15:27
22:25, 27, 28, 33
26:59
30:4[2], 5, 6[3], 7, 8[3], 10, 11

DEUTERONOMY
21:12, 13[2], 14
22:19, 21[2], 24, 29
24:1, 2[2], 4
25:6
28:57[2]

JOSHUA
2:6[2], 8, 9, 15[2], 16, 21[3]
6:17[2], 22, 23, 25[3]
15:18[3]

JUDGES
1:14[3], 15
4:4, 5, 6, 9, 18, 19
5:24, 25[2], 26[4], 29
8:31
11:34, 36, 37, 38, 39[2]
13:9, 14
14:3, 7, 17[3]
15:2
16:8, 9, 14, 15, 16, 18, 19[4], 20
19:3
20:5

RUTH
1:3, 6[3], 7[2], 9, 15, 18[3], 20
2:2, 3, 7[3], 10, 13, 14[2], 15, 16, 17[2], 18[5], 19[2], 23
3:5, 6, 7, 9, 14[2], 15[2], 16[3], 17, 18
4:13[2]

1 SAMUEL
1:7[3], 10, 11, 12, 13[2], 18, 20, 22, 23, 24[2], 26
2:5, 19, 21
4:19[2], 20[2], 21, 22
18:19, 21
19:14
25:3, 19[2], 20[3], 23, 35, 36, 41, 42
28:12, 14, 24, 25

2 SAMUEL
4:4
6:16
11:4[3], 26, 27
12:24
13:2, 8, 9, 10, 11, 12, 14, 16, 18
14:4, 5, 11, 27
20:17, 18
21:8[2]

1 KINGS
1:17, 22, 28
2:13, 14, 16, 19, 20, 21
3:19, 20, 26, 27
10:1, 2[3], 6, 10, 13[3]
14:5[2], 6, 17
15:13
17:11, 12, 15[2], 18
21:8, 9, 11

2 KINGS
2:24
4:2, 5[2], 6, 7, 8, 9, 12, 13, 14, 15, 16, 21, 22, 23, 24, 25, 26, 27[2], 28, 36, 37
5:2, 3
6:28, 29
8:2, 3, 6[2]
9:30, 31, 34
11:1, 13, 14, 16[2]
22:14, 15

1 CHRONICLES
1:32
2:21, 26, 29, 35, 49
4:17
7:14, 16, 23
15:29

2 CHRONICLES
9:1[3], 5, 9, 12[4]
15:16
22:10, 11[2]
23:12, 13, 15
34:22, 23
36:21[2]

ESTHER
1:11, 15, 17, 19
2:1, 7, 9, 10, 12, 13, 14[4], 15, 17, 20
4:4, 8
5:2, 12

JOB
1:3
39:16, 18[2], 28, 29, 30
42:12

PSALMS
45:14
46:5
68:12
80:11
84:3

PROVERBS
1:20, 21[2]
3:15, 18
4:6[2], 8[2], 9[2], 13
7:11, 12, 13, 21[2], 26
8:2, 3
9:1, 2[3], 3[2], 4, 13, 14, 16
12:4
23:22, 25, 28
30:20, 23
31:12, 13, 14[2], 15, 16[2], 17, 18, 19, 20[2], 21, 22, 24, 25, 26, 27, 30

SONG OF SOLOMON
6:9[2], 10
8:5, 8[2], 9[2]

ISAIAH
3:26
8:3
23:3, 17
40:2
49:15
51:18[2]
66:7[3], 8

JEREMIAH
3:1, 6, 7[2], 9
4:17
6:6, 7
11:15
15:9[3]
33:16
46:24
50:9, 12, 14, 15[2], 29[2]
51:8, 9, 42, 53

LAMENTATIONS
1:1[3], 2[2], 3[2], 4, 7, 8[2], 9[3], 10

EZEKIEL
5:6
16:46, 48, 49
19:2[2], 3, 5[3], 10, 11[2], 12[2], 13, 14
23:5[2], 7[3], 8, 9, 10, 11[2], 12, 13, 14[2], 16[2], 17, 18, 19[2], 20, 43
24:7[2], 12
26:2[3], 17
32:20

DANIEL
11:6[2], 17

HOSEA
1:6, 8[2]
2:2, 3, 5[2], 6, 7[4], 8, 12, 13[3], 15[2]
13:16

AMOS
5:2[2]

MICAH
1:7, 13
5:3
7:10[2]

NAHUM
2:7, 10
3:10[2]

ZEPHANIAH
2:15
3:2[4]

ZECHARIAH
9:4

MALACHI
2:14

MATTHEW
1:18, 21, 25
8:15
9:18, 21
12:42
14:7, 8, 11
15:23, 25, 27
20:21
22:28
26:10, 12[2]

MARK
1:31
5:23[2], 26, 27, 28, 29[2], 42
6:19, 24[2], 25
7:26, 28, 30[2]
10:12
12:23, 42, 44[2]
14:3, 6, 8[3], 9, 67[2]
16:10

LUKE
1:29[2], 36, 42, 45, 57[2]
2:6, 7, 36, 37, 38
4:39
7:12, 37, 39, 44, 47
8:42, 47[5], 50, 52, 53, 55
10:39, 40
11:31
13:13
15:8[2], 9[2]
18:3, 5
20:33
21:4[2]

JOHN
8:11
11:20, 27, 28[2], 29[2], 31[2], 32
12:7
16:21[3]
20:2, 11[2], 13, 14[2], 15, 16, 18

THE ACTS
5:8, 10
9:36, 37, 39, 40[3]
12:14[2], 15
16:14, 15[3], 18

ROMANS
7:2, 3[5]
16:2[2]

1 CORINTHIANS
7:11, 12, 28, 34[3], 36, 39[2], 40[2]
11:5

GALATIANS
4:27

EPHESIANS
5:33

1 TIMOTHY
2:15
5:5, 6[2], 10[5]

HEBREWS
11:11[2], 31

JAMES
2:25

REVELATION
2:21
6:13
12:2, 5, 6, 14[2]
14:8
18:6[2], 7[2], 8, 19
19:8

THAT 834 or 2088 or 3588, *1565 or 3754*

GENESIS

1:4, 10, 12, 18, 20[2], 21[2], 25[2], 26, 28, 30, 31
2:3, 4, 9, 11, 12, 13, 14, 17, 18, 19
3:5, 6[2], 7, 11[2], 13
4:3, 8, 14[2]
5:1, 5
6:2[2], 3, 4, 5[2], 6, 7, 17, 21, 22
7:2, 4, 5, 8[2], 10, 14, 16, 19, 21[2], 22, 23
8:1, 6, 11, 17[3]
9:2, 3, 10[2], 12, 14, 16[2], 17, 18
10:11
11:2, 7
12:1, 3[2], 5[2], 11[2], 12, 13, 14[2], 18[2], 20
13:1, 6[2], 10, 14, 16
14:2, 5, 7, 10, 13, 14, 17, 23[3], 24
15:4, 7, 8, 13[2], 14, 17[2]
16:2, 4, 5, 10, 13[2]
17:12[2], 13[2], 14, 17[2], 18, 23[2]
18:5, 17, 18, 19[3], 24, 25[3]
19:5, 11[2], 14, 17, 21, 25, 29, 32, 33, 34[2], 35
20:6, 7[2], 9[2], 10, 13, 16
21:3, 6[2], 7, 8, 12, 22[3], 23[2], 30[2], 31
22:1, 12, 14, 17, 20
23:4, 6, 8, 9, 10, 11, 15, 17[2], 18, 20
24:2[2], 3, 6, 7, 9, 11, 14[4], 15, 22, 30, 32, 36, 43, 49, 52, 54, 55, 56, 65, 66
25:5, 11, 18, 26, 30
26:1, 5, 8, 11, 12, 21, 22, 28, 29, 32
27:1[2], 4[2], 7, 8, 10[2], 19, 20, 21, 25, 29[2], 30, 31, 33, 40, 45
28:3, 4, 6[2], 7, 8, 11[2], 15, 18, 19[2], 20, 21, 22
29:2, 7, 10, 12[2], 13, 19[2], 21, 23, 25, 31, 33
30:1, 3, 9, 15, 16, 25[2], 27, 33[2], 35[4], 38, 41[2]
31:1[2], 5, 6, 10[2], 12, 16, 19, 20[2], 21, 22, 24, 26, 27, 29, 32, 35, 36, 37, 39, 43, 52[2]
32:2, 5, 7, 13[2], 19, 20, 21, 22, 23, 25, 29, 32
33:9, 11, 13, 14, 15, 16
34:5, 14[2], 15, 24[2], 25, 28[2], 29
35:1, 2[2], 5, 6[2], 17, 18, 20, 22[2]
36:7, 16, 17, 18, 24[2], 29, 30, 31, 40
37:4, 10, 22[2], 23[2]
38:1[2], 9[3], 14, 16[2], 18, 21[2], 22, 24, 26, 27, 28, 29, 30
39:3[3], 4, 5[4], 6, 7, 8, 10, 11, 13, 14, 15[2], 18, 19, 22, 23[2]
40:1, 7, 15, 16, 20
41:1, 8[2], 15[2], 21, 24, 27, 31, 32, 35, 36[2], 53, 57
42:1, 2[2], 5, 6, 14[2], 16, 21, 23, 28, 29, 33, 34[2], 35
43:7, 8, 12, 14, 15, 18[2], 21, 25, 32
44:2, 7, 15[2], 17, 21, 27, 30, 31[2], 34
45:1, 5, 8, 10, 11, 12[2], 13, 15, 24
46:1, 26, 32, 34[2]
47:1, 13, 14, 17, 18[4], 19[4], 24, 30, 29
48:1, 10, 17, 20
49:1[2], 15[2], 17[2], 25, 26, 28, 29, 30, 32
50:14, 15

EXODUS

1:5, 6, 10, 21, 22
2:2, 7, 11, 12[2], 13, 18, 20[2], 23
3:4, 8, 10, 11[2], 12, 14, 16, 18, 19, 20, 21, 22
4:2, 5[2], 8, 9, 14, 21[2], 23, 24, 31[2]
5:1, 2, 9, 19, 22
6:7, 11, 26, 27, 29[2]
7:2[2], 4, 5, 13, 16, 17[2], 18, 19[2], 20[2], 21, 25
8:1, 8[2], 9, 10[2], 15, 16, 20, 22[3], 28, 29
9:1, 4, 6, 13, 14[2], 15, 16, 17, 19, 20, 21, 22, 25, 28, 29[2], 30, 34
10:1, 2[3], 3, 5[2], 6, 7[2], 8, 11[2], 12[2], 13[2], 15, 17, 20, 21, 25, 28
11:5[2], 7[2], 8[2], 9, 10
12:8, 10, 15, 16[2], 19[2], 22[2], 25, 27, 29[3], 33, 36, 37, 41, 42, 44, 48, 49[2], 51
13:5, 8[2], 9, 12[3], 14, 15[2], 17[2]
14:2, 4[3], 5[2], 12[3], 15, 18, 20, 21, 24, 25[2], 26, 28, 30, 31
15:7, 26[2]
16:4, 5[2], 6, 7[2], 8, 10, 12, 13, 14, 18[2], 22, 23[4], 25, 27, 29, 32
17:2, 3, 6, 11, 16
18:1[2], 8[2], 11, 13, 14[2], 17, 18, 19, 20, 22, 24
19:8, 9, 12, 16[3]
20:4[3], 5, 6, 7, 10, 11, 12, 17, 20[2], 22, 26
21:12[2], 14, 15, 16, 17, 19, 22, 26, 28, 29, 35, 36
22:2, 6[2], 11, 13, 16, 20, 25, 26, 27[2], 31
23:5, 11, 12, 13, 22
24:7, 12
25:2[2], 8, 9, 14, 21, 26, 28, 33, 35, 37, 40
26:5[2], 10, 11, 12[2], 13[2], 33
27:5, 20
28:1, 3[3], 4, 28[2], 32, 35, 37, 38[2], 41, 43
29:1, 13[3], 21, 22[2], 23, 27[2], 30[2], 32, 38, 46[3]
30:6[2], 12, 13[2], 14[2], 16, 20, 21, 29, 30, 38
31:6[3], 7, 11, 13[3], 14[2]
32:1[2], 10[2], 13, 18[3], 19, 21, 22, 23, 25, 28, 29, 30
33:5, 7, 8, 13[3], 16[3], 17, 22
34:1, 3, 7, 10, 11, 19[2], 29[2], 32, 34, 35
35:1, 10, 22, 24, 25[2], 34, 35[2]
36:1, 4, 8, 18, 19
37:8, 13
38:15, 22, 24, 25, 26[2]
39:5, 7, 21[2], 23, 32, 42
40:4, 9, 13, 15, 16, 17, 37

LEVITICUS

1:5, 8, 12, 17
2:8, 10
3:3[2], 4, 5, 9[2], 10, 14[2], 15, 17
4:3, 5, 8[2], 9, 16, 18, 35
5:3, 4, 5[3], 8, 11, 13, 16
6:2, 3[2], 4[3], 5, 7, 18, 22, 26, 27
7:3, 4[2], 7, 8, 9[3], 14, 15, 16, 18[2], 19[2], 20[3], 21[2], 24[2], 25, 27[2], 29, 30, 33, 36, 38
8:10, 16, 25, 26, 31, 32, 35
9:1, 5, 6, 19
10:3[2], 10, 11, 12[2], 20
11:2, 3, 4[2], 9, 10[2], 12, 20, 21, 26, 27, 28, 29, 31, 34[2], 36, 39, 40[2], 41, 42, 43[2], 44, 45, 46[2], 47[2]
12:7
13:4, 7, 8, 12, 13, 17, 24, 31[2], 33, 37, 39, 41, 47, 50, 51, 52, 54, 55, 57
14:4, 5, 6, 7, 8[3], 9, 11[2], 14, 16, 17[2], 18[2], 19, 25, 27, 28[2], 29[2], 31, 32, 35, 36[3], 40, 41, 43, 46[2], 47[2]
15:4, 6[2], 7[2], 8[2], 9, 10[2], 11, 12, 13, 20[2], 22, 28, 31[2], 32, 33[4]
16:2[2], 13[3], 15[2], 16, 18, 26, 28, 29[2], 30[2]
17:3[2], 4[2], 5[2], 8, 9, 10[4], 11, 12, 13[2], 15[3]
18:6, 26, 28[2], 29, 30[2]
19:8[2], 13, 20, 25, 31, 34
20:2[2], 3, 5[2], 6[2], 9, 10[2], 11, 14, 22, 24, 25, 26, 27[2]
21:2[2], 3, 7, 10[2], 17, 18[2], 19, 20, 21, 23
22:2[2], 3[2], 4, 8, 11, 18, 20, 23[2], 24, 33
23:12, 14, 15, 21, 28, 29[2], 30[2], 42, 43[2]
24:2, 7, 12, 14[2], 16[2], 17, 18, 21[2], 23[2]
25:5, 6, 7, 11[2], 25, 27, 28[2], 30[2], 33, 35, 36, 39, 44, 45[2], 47, 48, 49, 50[2], 51
26:13, 15[2], 16, 17, 25, 36, 39, 40, 41, 44, 45
27:8, 9, 15, 18, 19, 23, 28[2]

NUMBERS

1:3, 5, 20, 21, 22[2], 23, 24, 25, 26, 27, 28, 29, 30, 31, 32, 33, 34, 35, 36, 37, 38, 39, 40, 41, 42, 43, 44, 45[2], 46, 50, 51, 53, 54
2:4, 5, 6, 8, 9, 11, 13, 15, 16, 19, 21, 23, 24, 26, 27, 28, 30, 31, 32, 34
3:1, 6, 10, 12, 13, 22[2], 32, 34, 36, 38[2], 39, 43, 46, 49[2], 51
4:3, 15, 16, 19, 23, 25, 26, 30, 35, 36, 37[2], 38, 39, 40, 41[2], 42, 43, 44, 45, 46, 47, 48
5:2[2], 3, 6[2], 17, 18, 19, 22, 24[2], 27[3]
6:4, 6, 11[2], 12, 20, 21[2]
7:1, 2[2], 5, 9, 10, 12, 88, 89
8:11, 15, 17, 19, 20, 22, 24
9:4, 5, 6[3], 7, 13[2], 14, 15, 17, 21[2], 22
10:2, 5, 6, 9, 10, 11, 32, 35[2]
11:1, 4, 11, 12, 13, 16, 17, 20, 21, 25[2], 26, 29[2], 32[3], 34[2]
12:14
13:2, 18, 19[2], 28, 31, 32[2]
14:1, 2, 3, 6, 14[4], 23, 29, 35, 37, 38, 42, 45
15:4, 12, 13, 15, 16, 19, 23[2], 24, 26, 28, 29[3], 30[2], 31, 32, 33, 38[2], 39[2], 40
16:7, 9, 11, 13[2], 14, 21, 28, 30[2], 31[2], 32, 33, 34, 35, 37, 39, 40[2], 42, 45, 49[2]
17:5, 8, 10
18:2, 3, 5, 7, 11, 13, 15, 16, 23
19:2, 3, 8, 9, 10[2], 11, 13[2], 14[2], 16, 18[2], 20[2], 21[3], 22
20:3, 4, 14, 29
21:1, 7, 8[2], 9, 13, 15, 16, 20, 27, 29, 32
22:2, 4[2], 6[3], 19, 20, 24, 28, 34, 35[2], 36, 38[2], 40, 41[2]
23:12, 19[2], 26[2], 27, 28
24:1, 9[2], 13, 19[2], 20
25:4, 5, 9, 11, 14[2], 15
26:1, 2, 7, 9, 10, 18, 22, 25, 27, 34, 37, 41, 43, 47, 50, 54, 57, 62, 63
27:3, 11, 14, 17, 20
29:40
30:2, 5, 7, 8[2], 9, 14, 15
31:8, 17, 18, 20, 23[2], 26, 27, 35, 36, 42, 43, 52
32:1, 9, 11, 13, 24, 32
33:55, 56
34:2
35:2, 6, 8[2], 11, 12, 15[2], 16, 20, 21[2], 23, 32[2], 33[2]
36:8[2]

DEUTERONOMY

1:3[2], 9, 16[2], 17, 18, 19, 30, 31[2], 35, 36, 39, 41, 44, 46
2:6[2], 17, 20, 25, 28[2], 30, 31, 34, 36
3:4, 8[2], 12, 18[2], 19, 21[2], 23, 24, 25[2]
4:1, 2, 3, 4, 5, 7, 8, 10[4], 14[2], 15, 17[2], 18[2], 21[3], 22, 26, 32[2], 34, 35[2], 36, 39, 40[2], 42[2]
5:1, 5, 8[3], 9, 10, 11, 14[2], 15[2], 16[2], 21, 23, 24, 26, 27[2], 28, 29[3], 31, 33[3]
6:1, 2[2], 3[3], 18[3], 23, 24
7:4, 6, 9[2], 10[2], 12, 15, 16, 20, 25
8:1, 3[3], 5, 7, 11, 13, 15, 16[2], 18[2], 19
9:3, 4, 5, 6, 7, 8, 11, 14, 19, 21, 24
10:1, 2, 8, 10, 11, 14, 21
11:6, 8, 9[2], 14[2], 15, 16, 17[2], 18, 21, 25, 29
12:1, 3, 7, 8, 10, 11, 12, 13[2], 14, 18[2], 19, 23, 25[2], 28[2], 30[3]
13:3[2], 5[2], 10, 14, 15[2], 17, 18
14:2, 6[2], 7[2], 9[2], 19, 21[3], 22, 23, 24, 26, 27, 29
15:2, 3, 8, 9, 10[2], 14, 15, 18, 19
16:3, 6, 11[2], 12, 13, 14, 20[2]
17:1, 2, 4, 5[5], 6, 9, 10[2], 12[3], 14, 16[2], 17, 18[2], 19, 20[3]
18:3, 8, 10[2], 12, 16[2], 17, 18, 19, 20[2], 22
19:3, 4, 5, 10, 11, 12, 13, 14, 15, 16
20:2, 4, 5, 6, 7, 8, 9, 11[2], 14, 16, 18, 20[2]
21:2, 3[2], 4, 6[3], 9, 11, 13, 15, 16[2], 17, 18, 21, 23[3]
22:5[2], 7[2], 8, 18[2], 21, 22, 23, 24[2], 25, 28, 29
23:1, 8, 10[2], 13, 14, 16, 19, 20[2], 23
24:1, 4[2], 7, 8[2], 9, 13, 14[2], 18, 19, 22
25:1, 2, 6[2], 9[2], 10, 11, 15, 16[2], 18, 19
26:2[2], 3[2], 9, 11, 12, 14, 15, 18, 19
27:2, 3[2], 4, 15, 16, 17, 18, 19, 20, 21, 22, 23, 24, 25, 26
28:1, 7, 8, 10, 13, 15, 20, 23[2], 34, 35, 43, 54[2], 55, 57, 58[2], 63
29:2, 6[2], 9[2], 11, 12, 13[2], 15[2], 18, 19, 20[4], 21, 22[4], 23[4], 27, 30
30:2, 3, 6, 7, 12[2], 13[2], 14, 16[2], 17, 18[2], 19[2], 20[4]
31:5, 6, 8, 12[3], 13, 14[2], 17[3], 18[2], 19, 20, 21, 25, 26, 28, 29
32:6, 13, 17, 18[2], 21, 27, 29[3], 35, 36, 39[2], 41, 42, 48, 49
33:11[3], 13, 16[2], 20
34:1, 12

JOSHUA

1:1, 3[2], 7[2], 8[2], 16, 18[2]
2:3, 5, 9[3], 10, 12, 13[2], 14, 19, 23
3:2, 4, 7[2], 8, 10[2], 13[3], 15[2], 16[3], 17
4:1, 6[2], 7, 10[2], 11, 14, 16[2], 18[2], 24[3]
5:1[2], 2, 4[2], 5[2], 6[4], 8, 12, 13
6:5, 7, 8, 9, 15[2], 17[3], 20[2], 21, 22[2], 23[2], 24, 25, 26[2]
7:14, 15[3], 24, 26
8:5[2], 8, 9, 11, 13[2], 14[2], 16, 17, 18[2], 20[2], 21[2], 22[2], 24, 25[3], 27, 29[2], 33[3], 34, 35[2]
9:2, 9, 10[2], 16[3], 24, 26, 27
10:2, 4, 6, 10, 11, 14[2], 20, 24, 27, 28[2], 30, 32[2], 35[4], 37[3], 39, 40
11:1, 2, 4, 10, 11, 13[2], 15, 16, 17, 19, 20[4], 21, 23
12:4, 7
13:2, 4, 9[2], 16[2], 17, 22, 25
14:6, 8, 9, 11, 12[3], 14
15:2, 4, 7, 8, 16, 18, 46
16:1, 10
17:7, 12, 13, 16
18:6, 8[2], 13, 14, 16
19:8, 11
20:3[2], 4[3], 6[2], 9[2]
21:26, 44
22:2[2], 10, 16[3], 18[2], 20, 23, 27[3], 28[2], 29[2], 30, 31, 34
23:1[2], 3[2], 4[2], 6[2], 7[2], 10, 11, 12, 13, 14, 15
24:5, 8, 15, 16, 17, 20, 22, 25, 26, 29, 31[2], 33

JUDGES

1:1, 3, 9, 10, 12, 14, 17, 21, 27, 28, 29, 35
2:4, 5, 7[2], 10, 12, 14[2], 16, 18, 19, 20, 22
3:2, 3, 18, 19[2], 22, 24, 27, 29, 30
4:2, 4, 9, 12, 13, 15, 20, 23
5:1, 5, 7[2], 9, 10[2], 11, 13, 14, 18, 21, 30, 31
6:3, 8, 9, 11, 17, 21, 22, 25[3], 27[2], 28[2], 30[2], 31[2], 32, 37, 40
7:1[2], 2, 4, 5[2], 6, 7, 9, 11, 13[3], 15, 17, 18, 19[2]
8:1, 3, 4, 5, 6, 10[2], 11, 15[2], 21, 24, 26[3], 28, 31, 33
9:2[3], 6, 7, 16, 24, 25[2], 28, 32, 33[2], 34, 35, 38[2], 41, 42, 44[2], 45[2], 46, 47, 48[2], 49, 54, 55
10:4, 8[2], 9, 18
11:4, 5, 6, 8, 12, 21, 24, 26[2], 31, 35[2], 36, 37, 39, 40
12:3, 5[2], 6, 14
13:8, 10, 11, 13, 14[2], 16, 17, 20, 21
14:3, 4[3], 9, 11, 13, 15[3], 17
15:1, 2, 7, 11[2], 12[2], 14[2], 17[2], 19
16:3, 4, 5, 7, 11, 16, 17, 18, 20, 25[2], 26[3], 27, 28, 30
17:2, 6, 13
18:1, 5, 7[2], 9, 10, 12, 14[2], 17[2], 19, 22, 23, 24, 26, 27, 28, 31
19:1, 5, 9[2], 10, 12, 15, 18, 22[2], 23, 30[3]
20:2, 3, 4[2], 5, 10[2], 12, 13, 15[2], 17, 21, 26, 34, 35, 36, 38, 41, 46[3], 48[2]
21:3, 4, 5[2], 7[2], 8, 11[2], 12, 13, 14, 15, 16, 17[2], 18, 19, 22[2], 23, 24, 25

RUTH

1:1, 6[2], 9, 11, 13, 18, 19
2:5, 6[2], 7, 9[3], 10, 11, 13[2], 16, 17, 18, 19, 22[2]
3:1, 4, 5, 6, 8, 11[2], 12, 13, 14, 15, 16
4:3, 4, 9[3], 10, 11[2], 14

1 SAMUEL

1:4, 12, 17, 20, 22, 26
2:4, 5[4], 13, 14[2], 15, 21, 22[2], 24, 30[3], 31[2], 34, 35[2], 36[3]
3:2[2], 4, 8, 9, 11, 12, 13, 14, 17[2], 20
4:3, 4, 5, 6, 8, 9, 15, 16, 18, 19[2], 20
5:5, 7, 9, 10, 11, 12
6:5, 8, 9[3], 15
7:2, 6, 7, 8, 10
8:1, 7[2], 8, 9, 10, 11, 18[2], 20[2]
9:5, 6[2], 8, 9, 13, 16, 19, 20, 22, 24[3], 26[2], 27
10:5[2], 7, 9[2], 11[3], 14, 16, 18, 24
11:2, 3, 5, 9[2], 10, 11[3], 12[2]
12:1, 5, 6[2], 7, 12, 14, 17[2], 18, 19, 23
13:3, 4[2], 6, 8, 10[2], 11[3], 14, 15, 16, 17, 18, 22[2]
14:1[3], 2, 3, 6[2], 7, 14, 17, 18, 19[2], 20, 21[3], 22, 23, 24[3], 27, 28, 31, 33, 34, 36, 37, 38, 43, 45, 48
15:2, 3, 7, 9[3], 11, 25, 28, 29, 30, 35
16:4, 6, 13, 16, 17, 18, 23
17:10, 12, 13, 25[2], 26[3], 27, 28, 37, 41, 43, 46[2], 47, 48, 49
18:1, 2, 4, 6, 9, 10, 15, 18, 19, 21[2], 23, 27, 28[2], 30[2]
19:1, 3, 10, 15, 17, 18, 22, 24[2]
20:1, 2, 3, 5, 6, 7, 9, 13, 14, 26, 27, 30, 33, 35
21:6, 7[2], 9[3], 10, 15
22:2[3], 4, 6[2], 7, 8[5], 11, 13[2], 17, 18[2], 21, 22[2], 23
23:6, 7[2], 9, 10, 13, 15, 17, 22, 23, 25, 26, 28
24:1, 4, 5, 6, 10, 11[2], 16, 18, 19, 20[2], 21[2]
25:4, 6[2], 7, 10, 11, 17, 20, 21[3], 22[2], 26, 27, 30, 31[3], 34, 35, 37, 38[2], 39[2], 42
26:3, 4, 11[2], 14, 16[2]
27:1, 2, 4, 5, 6, 7
28:1[2], 3, 7[3], 9, 14, 15, 21, 22, 25
29:4, 7, 8, 9, 10
30:1, 2, 4, 9[2], 10, 15, 16, 18, 19, 21[2], 22[3], 23[2], 24[2], 25[2]
31:5, 6, 7[4], 8, 11

2 SAMUEL

1:2[2], 4, 5[2], 6, 10[4], 11, 13, 15
2:1, 3, 4[2], 5, 11, 16, 17, 23[2], 24, 26, 29, 31
3:6, 8, 13, 19[2], 20, 21[3], 23, 24, 25[2], 27, 29[5], 31, 37[2], 38
4:1, 2, 4[2], 10
5:2, 8[2], 12[2], 14, 17, 20, 24
6:2[2], 3, 9, 12, 13[2], 17
7:2, 3, 4[2], 6, 9, 10, 11[2], 18, 22, 25, 28, 29
8:1, 7, 9, 11
9:1[2], 3, 8, 9, 10, 11, 12
10:1, 3[2], 6, 9, 10, 12, 13, 14, 15, 16, 19[2]
11:1, 2, 12, 14, 15, 16[2], 20[2], 21, 22, 26, 27
12:4[2], 5, 8, 14, 15, 18[3], 19[2], 21, 22, 31
13:1, 2, 5, 6, 10, 15, 16, 17, 18, 19, 23, 27, 30, 32[2], 33, 34, 36
14:1, 2, 7[2], 11, 13, 14, 15[2], 16, 18, 19, 20, 22[2], 26, 32
15:1, 2[2], 4[2], 5, 6, 7, 11, 14, 17, 22, 30, 32, 35, 36
16:2, 4[2], 12[2], 14, 16, 21[2]
17:2, 7, 8, 9[2], 10[2], 11[3], 12, 13, 14, 16, 21, 22[2], 23, 25, 27, 29
18:1, 3, 7, 8, 9, 11, 12, 15, 19, 22, 28, 31, 32[2]
19:2[2], 3, 6[3], 7[2], 14, 19[3], 20, 22[2], 25, 26, 28, 34, 37, 38[2], 43
20:8, 10, 11[2], 12[3], 15, 16, 19, 20
21:3, 4, 5[3], 7, 13, 14[2], 17, 18, 20
22:1, 18, 28, 31, 35, 37, 39, 40, 41[2], 48[2], 49[2]
23:3, 7, 8, 9, 10, 15, 16, 17[2]
24:2, 3, 5, 9, 10[2], 12, 13[2], 16, 17, 18, 21, 24

1 KINGS

1:2, 11, 12, 20, 21, 29, 35, 40, 41, 45[2], 49, 51
2:1, 3[2], 4, 5[2], 7, 11, 15[3], 17, 25, 27, 29, 31, 37[2], 39, 41, 42[2], 43, 44, 46
3:4[2], 6, 8, 9, 10, 12, 13[2], 16, 18[2], 23, 28
4:12, 27, 29, 33[2]
5:1, 3, 4, 6[4], 7, 9, 15, 16
6:1, 6, 7, 17, 22, 27
7:3, 18, 19, 29, 40, 41, 42, 48, 51
8:1, 4, 5[2], 8, 10, 11, 12, 16[2], 18, 19, 20, 23, 24, 25[3], 27, 29[2], 36, 40[2], 41, 43[4], 44, 46[2], 47, 50[2], 52[2], 54, 56[2], 58, 59, 60[3], 64[2], 65, 66
9:2, 3, 4, 8, 11, 16, 19[2], 20, 21, 23[2], 25, 27
10:2[2], 4, 6, 8, 11, 13, 14, 15, 27
11:4, 7, 10[2], 17, 19, 21[3], 22, 25, 27, 28, 29[2], 30, 33[2], 36, 37, 38[3], 41, 42
12:3, 6[2], 8, 9, 10[2], 13, 15, 16, 18, 20[3], 32[2]
13:2, 3, 4[2], 6, 9, 10, 11[2], 14, 17, 18, 20[2], 21, 23, 26, 31
14:1, 2[2], 5, 6, 8, 9, 10[2], 11[2], 14, 22, 25, 28, 29
15:5[2], 7, 11, 12, 17, 18[2], 19, 21, 23, 29[2], 31
16:4[2], 7, 11[2], 14, 16[2], 18[2], 20, 22[2], 25, 27, 30, 31, 33
17:3, 4, 5, 7, 10, 12[2], 14, 17[2], 24[2]
18:1, 4, 5, 7, 9, 10, 12, 17[2], 18, 24, 26, 27, 29[2], 30, 36[4], 37[3], 38, 44[2], 45
19:1, 3, 4, 8, 13, 17[3]
20:4, 6, 9, 10, 11[2], 12, 13, 16, 25, 26, 28, 29, 30, 31, 37, 41
21:1, 2, 3, 5, 8, 10, 13, 15[2], 16[2], 21[2], 24[2], 27
22:2, 3, 7, 13[2], 14, 16[2], 17, 18, 20[2], 25, 31, 32, 33[2], 35, 39[2], 43, 45, 53

2 KINGS

1:2, 3, 4, 6[3], 16
2:1, 3[2], 5[2], 8, 9, 11, 13, 14
3:2, 5, 9, 10, 11, 14, 15, 17[2], 20, 21[2], 24, 26[2], 27
4:1, 4, 6, 8[2], 9, 10, 11, 17[2], 18, 22, 25[2], 40, 41, 42, 43
5:3, 4, 6, 7[2], 8[3], 15, 18, 20
6:9, 12[2], 13, 16[2], 17, 20[2], 22, 24, 28, 29, 30
7:9, 12, 13[3], 19
8:3, 4, 5, 6[2], 10, 12, 13[2], 14, 15[2], 23
9:7, 8[2], 22, 25, 37
10:1, 5[4], 7, 9, 10[2], 11, 17, 19, 21[2], 22, 23, 24, 25, 29[2], 30[2], 34, 36
11:1, 2, 5[2], 6, 7, 8, 9[3], 10, 15, 17
12:2, 4[4], 6, 9[2], 10[3], 11[3], 12, 13, 14, 18[2], 19
13:2, 5, 8, 11, 12, 21
14:3, 5, 6, 9[3], 10, 14, 22, 24, 26, 27, 28
15:3[2], 4, 5, 6, 9, 16[2], 18, 19, 21, 24, 26, 28, 31, 34[2], 36
16:2, 6, 8, 10, 11, 16, 17, 18
17:2[2], 7, 9, 14, 15[3], 25, 38
18:1, 3[2], 4, 5[2], 9, 10, 12, 14, 15, 16, 20, 21, 22, 26, 27, 32, 35[2]
19:1, 4, 8, 19[2], 20, 21, 25[2], 29, 30, 31, 33, 35[2], 37
20:3, 4, 8[2], 9[2], 12[2], 13[2], 15[2], 17[3], 18
21:2, 7, 8[2], 11, 12, 15, 16, 17[2], 20, 21[2], 24
22:2, 3, 4, 5, 7, 9[3], 11, 13[3], 15, 17, 19
23:3, 4, 5, 7, 8, 10, 11, 12, 13, 15[2], 16, 17[3], 18, 19[2], 20, 22, 24[3], 25, 26, 28, 32[2], 33, 37[2]
24:3, 4, 5, 7, 9[2], 10, 16, 19[2], 20
25:1, 10, 11[2], 13[2], 19[3], 22, 23, 25[3], 27[2], 28

1 CHRONICLES

1:43
2:9, 24, 55
4:10[5], 21, 23, 33, 41, 43
5:18, 20
6:10[2], 31, 33, 49, 61
7:21[2], 40
9:2, 16, 28, 31, 33
10:5, 7[3], 8, 11, 13
11:2, 14, 17[2], 18, 19[2], 31
12:1, 8, 15, 20, 22, 23, 24, 32, 38, 40
13:2[3], 4, 6[2], 11, 12, 14
14:2, 8, 11, 15
15:12[2], 13, 26[2], 27, 29
16:1, 7, 10, 12, 30, 32, 35, 39, 40, 41, 42
17:1, 2, 3, 5, 7, 8, 10[2], 11[2], 13, 16, 20, 23, 24, 25, 27
18:1, 7, 11
19:1, 3[2], 6, 9, 10, 13, 14, 15, 16[2], 19
20:1[2], 3, 4[2]
21:2, 5[2], 10, 12[2], 15, 17[3], 18, 22[2], 23, 24, 28[2], 29
22:2, 5, 12, 19
23:13, 24, 25, 29[2], 32
25:7[2]
26:6, 28
27:1, 6, 26, 28, 29[2]
28:1, 8, 12, 18
29:3, 9, 11, 14, 16, 17, 21, 22, 27, 30

2 CHRONICLES

1:3, 5, 7, 10[2], 11, 12, 13, 15
2:6, 7[2], 8, 10, 12[2], 17
3:1, 4, 15, 17[2]
4:11, 19, 20, 21
5:1[2], 5, 6, 9, 11, 13, 14
6:1, 4, 5[2], 6, 8, 10, 11, 14, 15, 16[2], 20[2], 31, 33[3], 34, 40
7:7, 10, 11, 13, 15, 16, 17, 21[2]
8:2, 6[2], 7, 10, 11, 18
9:1[2], 3, 6, 12, 13, 14, 23, 27
10:2, 4, 6, 8[2], 9[2], 10[2], 15, 16, 17, 18[2]
11:1, 13
12:2, 3, 5, 7, 8, 10, 12
13:5, 9[2], 15, 18
14:2, 8[2], 11, 13[2]
15:5[2], 8, 9, 13, 18[2]
16:1, 2, 3, 5, 7
17:10[2]
18:2, 6, 12, 13, 15, 16, 17, 19[2], 24, 30, 31, 32[2], 33, 34
19:2, 3, 10[2]
20:1, 2, 6, 12, 21, 29, 32, 37
21:6, 7, 16, 17[2], 19
22:1, 8[2], 10, 11[2]
23:4, 6, 8[3], 9, 14, 16, 19, 21
24:2, 4, 5, 7, 9, 11[2], 20, 23, 26
25:2, 3[2], 5, 10, 12, 13, 14[2], 16[2], 18[3], 19, 20, 24, 27
26:2, 4[2], 7, 11, 13, 17, 18
27:2[2]
28:1, 7, 9[2], 12, 15, 16, 22, 23
29:2[2], 6, 10, 11, 16, 24, 29, 34, 36
30:1, 3, 5, 6, 8, 9[2], 14, 17[2], 19, 21, 22, 25[3]
31:1, 4[2], 6, 10, 16, 19[2], 20, 21
32:2[4], 4, 5, 7, 8, 10, 11[2], 18[2], 21, 23, 26, 31[3]
33:2, 8[2], 13, 15, 18, 22, 25
34:2, 4[2], 9[2], 10[2], 12, 13, 14, 16, 17, 19, 21[4], 22[2], 23, 24, 25, 28, 30, 32, 33[2]
35:3, 6, 7, 12, 17[2], 18[2], 21, 22, 24[2], 26
36:5, 8, 9, 12, 17, 20, 22[2]

EZRA

1:1[2], 4, 6[2], 11
2:1, 62, 63
3:5[2], 7, 8, 12, 13
4:1, 10, 11, 12, 13, 15[3], 16, 17, 19[2], 21, 22
5:1, 4, 5, 6, 8, 10[2], 11, 12, 14, 15, 16, 17
6:2, 8[2], 9, 10, 11, 12[2], 13
7:11, 13, 16, 17, 18, 19, 21, 24, 25[3]
8:1, 17, 21, 22[2], 34, 35
9:2, 4[2], 8, 12, 13[2], 14
10:3, 5, 6, 7, 8[2], 13, 17, 18, 19

NEHEMIAH

1:2[2], 3, 4, 5[2], 6, 8, 9
2:1, 5[2], 7, 8[2], 10, 12, 14, 16, 17[2], 18, 19
3:15, 16, 25, 26, 27
4:1[2], 3, 7[3], 10, 12, 15[2], 16[2], 17[2], 18, 22, 23
5:2[2], 3[2], 4[2], 9, 11, 12, 13, 14[2], 15, 17[2], 18, 19
6:1[3], 2, 3, 6[2], 9, 11, 12[2], 13[3], 14, 16[3]
7:2, 5, 6[2], 64, 65, 72
8:1, 2, 3[2], 9, 12, 14, 15, 17[2]
9:6[2], 10, 11, 15, 17, 18, 21, 23, 24, 28, 29, 32, 33, 35, 36
10:1, 28, 30, 31[2], 36, 37[2], 39
11:2, 3, 6, 12, 19, 23
12:1, 31, 38, 40, 43[2], 44[2]
13:1[2], 2, 3, 7, 10[2], 14, 17, 19[4], 21, 22[2], 23

ESTHER

1:2, 5, 8, 10, 13, 16, 17, 19[3], 22[2]
2:2, 3, 7, 8, 10, 12, 14, 15, 17
3:1, 2, 4[2], 5, 6, 7[3], 9[2], 12[2], 14[2]
4:1, 7[2], 8[2], 11[2], 13, 16, 17
5:1, 2[2], 4, 5[2], 8, 9[2], 12, 14
6:1, 2, 3, 4, 8, 9, 10[2], 13, 14
7:5, 7, 10
8:1, 3, 6, 9[3], 11, 13[2], 14
9:1[4], 5, 11[2], 15, 16, 18, 19, 20, 21, 22, 24, 25[2], 26, 27, 28[2]

JOB

1:1[2], 3, 5[2], 8[2], 10, 11, 12
2:3[2], 4, 11, 13
3:4, 6, 7, 8, 12, 15, 20, 25
4:4, 8, 19
5:1, 11[2], 12, 24, 25
6:2, 6, 7, 8[3], 9[2], 11[2], 14, 26
7:7, 8, 9, 12, 15, 17[2], 18, 20
8:13, 22
9:16, 26, 28, 32, 33
10:3[2], 6, 7[2], 9, 13, 18, 20
11:5, 6[4], 16
12:5[2], 6, 9
13:5, 9, 13, 18, 19, 28
14:1, 5, 6, 7[2], 13[3]
15:7, 9, 13, 14[2], 17, 22, 23, 31
16:3, 21
17:3, 5, 9
18:20[2], 21
19:3, 4, 6, 8, 15, 23[2], 24, 25[2], 29
20:5, 18, 20, 26
21:3[2], 15, 18, 22, 29, 30
22:2, 3[2], 11, 14
23:3[2], 9, 10, 13, 14
24:1, 7, 13, 21
25:4, 6
26:2[2], 3
27:5, 7, 11, 15, 18
28:11, 28
29:2, 12[2], 13, 25
30:1, 23, 25, 31
31:6, 12, 15, 28, 29, 31, 34, 35[3], 38
32:5, 12[2], 20
33:12, 17, 20, 21[2], 27
34:2, 9, 10[2], 17[2], 19, 23, 25, 28, 30, 32, 36
35:2
36:2, 4, 9, 10, 16, 24, 32
37:2, 7, 12, 20, 24
38:2, 13[2], 20[2], 34, 35
39:2, 12, 15[2], 24
40:2[2], 8, 11, 12, 14, 19, 23
41:10, 11, 16, 17, 26
42:2[2], 3[2], 7[2], 8, 11[2]

PSALMS

1:1, 3
2:4, 12
3:1[2], 6
4:3[2], 6, 7
5:4, 6, 11[2]
7:1, 4[2], 6, 8
8:2, 4[2]
9:10[2], 13[2], 14, 15, 17, 20
10:2, 10, 18
11:2, 5
12:3, 5
13:4
14:1, 2, 3, 7
15:2, 3, 4[2], 5[2]
16:3, 4
17:1, 2, 3, 5, 7[2], 9, 12
18:t, 12, 30, 32, 34, 36, 38, 39, 40[2], 47, 48
20:6
21:8
22:3, 7, 8, 9, 23, 25, 26, 29[2], 31[2]
24:1, 4, 6[2]
25:3, 12[2], 14
26:7
27:4[2]
28:1
30:3, 12
31:4, 6, 11, 15, 19[2], 24
32:6, 10, 11
33:18[2]
34:7, 8[2], 9, 10, 12[2], 16, 18, 21, 22
35:1[2], 3, 4[2], 8[2], 10[2], 11, 14, 19[2], 20, 26[2], 27
36:1, 4, 10
37:9, 13, 16, 22, 37
38:12[2], 13, 14, 19, 20[2]
39:1, 4, 13
40:4[2], 12, 14[2], 15, 16
41:1, 7, 8, 10, 11
42:4
44:5, 7, 13, 16
45:14
46:5, 10
48:13
49:6, 9, 10, 11, 12, 20[2]
50:4, 5, 16, 21, 22, 23
51:4, 8
52:7
53:1, 2[2], 3, 5, 6
54:4
55:6, 12[3], 18, 19
56:2, 13
57:2, 3, 4
58:4, 8, 11[2]
59:1, 13[2]
60:4[2], 5, 12
61:2, 5, 8
62:11
63:9, 11[2]
64:4, 8
65:2, 4, 5, 8
66:16

PSALMS

67:2
68:1, 4, 11, 12, 18, 20, 23, 28, 30, 33[2], 35
69:4[3], 6[2], 9, 10, 12, 14, 22, 23, 31, 32, 34, 35, 36
70:2[2], 3, 4
71:6, 10, 13[2], 18, 24
72:6, 9, 12
73:25, 27[2], 28
74:3, 9, 18[2], 23
75:1
76:11[2]
77:4, 14
78:4, 5, 6, 7, 8, 11, 20, 35, 39[2], 44, 53, 60, 65
79:4, 6[2], 11
80:1[2], 12, 15
81:5, 13
83:2, 4, 16, 18[2]
84:4, 11, 12
85:6, 9[2], 12
86:2, 5, 17
87:4, 5, 6
88:4[2], 5
89:7, 10, 15, 19, 23, 34, 35, 41, 48
90:9, 12, 14
91:1, 5, 6[2]
92:7, 11, 13, 15
93:1
94:9[2], 10[2], 11, 13
95:10, 11
96:10[2], 12
97:7[2], 10
98:7
99:6, 7, 8
100:3[2]
101:3, 5, 6[2], 7[2], 8
102:4, 8, 11, 20
103:1, 5, 6, 11, 13, 14, 17, 18, 20[2], 21
104:5, 9[2], 14, 15, 26, 27, 28
105:3, 5, 19, 34, 45
106:3[2], 4, 5[3], 8, 10, 20, 23, 31, 32, 33, 40, 41, 46
107:7, 8, 15, 21, 23[2], 29, 31, 34, 36, 38
108:6, 13
109:11, 15, 16[2], 20, 27[3], 31
111:2, 5, 6, 10
112:1[2]
113:6, 8
114:5[2], 6
115:8[2], 11, 13, 17
118:2, 3, 4[2], 7[2], 13, 26
119:2[2], 5, 11, 17, 18, 20, 21, 42, 53, 57, 63[2], 71[2], 73, 74, 75[2], 77, 79[2], 80, 84, 101, 106, 116, 118, 125, 132, 138, 148, 150, 152, 162
120:5[2], 6
121:3, 4
122:3, 6
123:1, 2, 4
125:1, 4[2]
126:1, 5, 6
127:1, 5
128:1[2], 4[2]
129:5, 7
130:4, 6[2]
131:2
132:12
133:2[2], 3
134:3
135:2, 5[2], 6, 18[2], 20
136:5, 6, 7, 10
137:3[2], 8, 9
138:8
139:14, 21[2]
140:9, 10, 12
141:4, 10
142:4, 7
143:3, 7, 12
144:3[2], 4, 10, 12[2], 13[2], 14[3], 15[3]
145:14[2], 18[2], 19, 20
146:4, 5, 6, 8
147:11[2]
148:4
149:2
150:6

PROVERBS

1:12, 19, 29
2:2, 7, 12, 19, 20
3:13[2], 18[2]
4:18, 22
5:2[2], 6, 13
6:11, 17, 18[2], 19[2], 29, 32
7:5, 23
8:9[2], 11, 17[2], 21[2], 29, 32, 34, 36[2]
9:4, 7[2], 16, 18[2]
10:4, 5[2], 9[2], 10, 13[2], 17[2], 18[2], 19, 26
11:12, 13, 15[2], 17, 18, 19, 20, 24[2], 25, 26[2], 27[2], 28, 29, 30
12:1, 4, 8, 9[2], 11[2], 15, 17, 18, 20, 22, 27
13:3[2], 6, 7[2], 11, 13, 18[2], 20, 23, 24[2]
14:2[2], 6, 13, 17, 21[2], 22[2], 29[2], 31[2], 33[2], 35
15:5, 9, 10[2], 12, 14, 15, 18, 21, 24, 27[2], 31, 32[2]
16:5, 13, 17, 20, 22, 25, 26, 29, 32[3]
17:2, 5, 8, 9[2], 15[2], 19[2], 20[2], 21, 24, 25, 27, 28
18:2, 9[2], 13, 17, 21, 24[2]
19:1[2], 2[2], 5, 6, 8[2], 9, 16[2], 17[2], 20, 21, 23, 25, 26[2], 27
20:8, 16, 19[2], 25

PROVERBS

21:5, 6, 16, 17[2], 21, 28
22:5, 8, 9, 11, 14, 16[2], 19, 21[3], 23, 26[2]
23:5, 6, 22, 24, 25, 30[2], 34[2]
24:8, 11[2], 12[2], 21, 24, 25, 26, 34
25:7[2], 10, 13, 18, 20[2], 28[2]
26:6, 8[2], 10, 16, 17[2], 19, 24, 27, 28
27:8[2], 10, 11[2], 13, 14, 18
28:3, 4, 5, 6[2], 7, 8[2], 9, 11, 13, 14[2], 16[2], 17, 18, 19[2], 20, 21, 22[2], 23[2], 25[2], 26, 27[2]
29:1[2], 3, 4, 5, 14, 18, 20, 21, 27
30:5, 11, 12, 15, 16[2], 17, 23
31:1, 3, 6[2], 11, 18, 30

ECCLESIASTES

1:9[4], 11[2], 13, 14, 15[2], 16, 17, 18
2:3, 6, 7, 8, 9, 11[2], 12[2], 13, 14, 15, 16, 17, 18, 21, 24[3], 26[3]
3:2, 9[2], 11[2], 12, 13, 14[2], 15[3], 16[2], 18[3], 19[2], 21[2], 22[3]
4:1, 3, 4, 10, 14, 15, 16[2]
5:1, 4, 5[2], 6, 8, 10[2], 11, 16[2], 18[2]
6:2[3], 3[3], 8, 10[3], 11
7:2, 10, 11, 12[2], 13, 14, 15[2], 18[2], 20, 21, 22, 24, 29
8:2, 7, 8[3], 9, 12[2], 14[2], 15, 16[2], 17[2]
9:1[2], 2[4], 3[3], 4, 5, 6, 9, 11, 12[2], 15, 17
10:1, 3[2], 8, 9, 20
11:4[2], 5, 6, 8, 9
12:3, 5, 10

SONG OF SOLOMON

1:7
2:7, 14, 15
3:3, 4[2], 5, 6
4:1, 2, 5, 16
5:2, 7, 8[2], 9
6:1, 5, 9, 10, 13
7:3, 9[2]
8:1[2], 4, 5[2], 10, 12, 13

ISAIAH

1:4, 28, 29, 30
2:1, 2, 8, 11, 12[2], 13, 14, 17, 20
3:7, 10, 15, 18, 24
4:1, 2[2], 3[4]
5:2, 4[2], 6, 8[3], 11[3], 14, 16, 18, 19[3], 20[3], 21, 22, 30
6:1, 4
7:1, 8, 15, 16, 17[2], 18[4], 20, 21[2], 22[2], 23[2], 25
8:6, 11, 17, 19[3], 21
9:2[2], 9, 13, 15, 16
10:1[2], 2[2], 12, 14[2], 15[3], 19, 20[3], 24, 27[2], 32
11:10, 11[2], 16
12:1, 4[2]
13:2, 3, 8, 14, 15[2]
14:3, 4, 6, 16[3], 17[2], 19[2], 21, 25, 26[2], 28, 29, 32
15:7, 9
16:2, 3, 12[2], 13[2], 14
17:4[2], 5, 7, 8, 9, 12, 14[2]
18:2, 7
19:3, 8[2], 9[2], 10, 13, 16, 17, 18, 19, 21, 23, 24
20:1, 6
21:3, 10, 14[2]
22:1, 2, 3, 7, 8, 9, 11, 12, 16[3], 20[2], 25[3]
23:1, 2, 13, 15[2], 16[2], 17, 18
24:6, 8, 9, 10, 18[2], 21[3]
25:7, 9, 11
26:1, 2, 5, 17, 19
27:1[3], 2, 5, 6, 7[2], 9, 11[2], 12[2], 13[2]
28:1, 4, 5, 6[2], 8, 9, 13, 14, 16, 19, 20[2], 21
29:4, 5, 7[3], 8, 11[2], 12, 15, 16[2], 18, 20, 21[2], 24[2]
30:1[3], 2, 5, 6, 8, 9[2], 14[2], 16, 18[3], 23[2], 24, 26
31:1, 2, 3[2], 7
32:3[2], 9, 11, 20[2]
33:1, 13[2], 15[4], 17, 18, 19, 20, 24
34:1[2]
35:4
36:1, 5, 6, 11, 12[2], 20[2], 22
37:1, 4, 6, 8, 16, 20[2], 26[2], 30, 31, 32, 34, 38
38:3, 7[2], 13, 18, 22
39:1[2], 2[2], 4[2], 6[3], 7
40:2[2], 3, 9[2], 11, 20[4], 22[2], 23, 26[2], 28, 29, 31
41:3, 7[3], 11[2], 12[2], 20[2], 22, 23[4], 24, 26[5], 27, 28
42:5[4], 7, 8, 10[2], 11, 16[2], 17[2], 18, 19[2]
43:1[2], 7, 8[2], 9, 10[2], 12, 13, 25, 26
44:2, 3, 7, 8, 9[2], 10, 13, 18[2], 20, 24[4], 25[2], 26[2], 27, 28
45:3[2], 6[3], 9[2], 10, 15, 16, 18[2], 19, 20[3], 21, 23, 24
46:5, 10, 11, 12
47:7, 8[3], 13
48:4, 8[3], 9, 16, 17, 18
49:5, 6[2], 7, 9[2], 10, 15, 17, 19, 20, 23[2], 25, 26[2]
50:2, 4[2], 6, 7, 8, 9, 10[3], 11[3]
51:1[2], 2, 6, 7, 9, 10, 12[3], 13, 14[3], 15, 16, 18[2], 22, 23[3]
52:5[2], 6[3], 7[5], 11, 15[2]
53:2
54:1[2], 9[2], 10, 16[2], 17[2]
55:1[2], 2[3], 5[2], 10, 11[2], 13
56:2[3], 3, 4[2], 5, 6[2], 8, 11
57:1, 11, 13, 15[2], 19[2]
58:2, 5, 6[2], 7[4], 12

ISAIAH

59:1[2], 2, 5[2], 15[2], 16[2], 20, 21
60:8, 11[2], 12, 14[2], 15, 16, 21
61:1, 2, 3[3], 9[2], 11
62:1, 6, 9[2]
63:1[3], 2, 5, 7, 8, 11[2], 12, 13[2]
64:1[3], 2, 4, 5[2], 7[2]
65:1[3], 2, 3[2], 5, 8, 10, 11[6], 12, 16[2], 18, 20, 24
66:1, 2, 3[4], 4, 5[3], 6, 10[2], 11[2], 17, 18, 19[3], 23, 24

JEREMIAH

1:1, 7, 17
2:2, 3, 5, 6[3], 8[2], 11, 13, 17, 19[3], 24[2], 28
3:1, 6, 9, 13, 16, 17, 18
4:4, 9[2], 11, 14, 16, 31[3]
5:1[2], 6, 7, 19, 22, 24, 26
6:10, 11, 15[2], 27
7:1, 2, 7, 8, 18, 22, 23[2], 25, 28, 32
8:1, 3, 10, 12, 13, 16[2], 19
9:1[2], 2[2], 10, 12[3], 17[2], 18, 24[3], 25, 26[2]
10:4, 11, 18, 23[2], 25[2]
11:1, 3, 4, 5, 7, 13, 14, 17, 19[3], 20[2], 21[2]
12:1, 4, 14, 15, 17
13:4, 6, 11, 12, 13, 20[2], 23, 24, 26
14:1, 8, 9, 15, 18[2], 22
15:4, 9, 10, 13, 15, 18
16:3[3], 10, 12, 13, 14[2], 15[2], 21
17:4, 5, 7, 8, 11, 13[2], 16, 18, 20, 23
18:4, 8[2], 10, 14, 16, 19, 20
19:2, 6, 7, 8, 9, 10, 11, 15[2]
20:1, 2, 3, 6, 12, 16, 17, 18
21:2[2], 4, 7, 9[3], 12[2]
22:2[2], 5, 10, 13[2], 14, 21, 23, 25, 26, 30
23:1, 2, 5, 7, 14, 16, 17[2], 24, 25, 26, 28[2], 29, 30, 31, 32, 34[2], 39
24:1, 2, 3, 5, 7, 8[2], 10
25:1[2], 3, 5, 7, 12[2], 13[2], 16, 23, 24, 30, 31, 33
26:2, 3, 8[2], 12, 13, 15, 20, 24
27:5, 8[3], 10, 11, 13, 14, 15[3], 16, 18, 19, 21, 22
28:1, 3, 4, 5, 6, 7, 8, 9, 12, 14
29:1, 2, 4, 6[2], 8, 10, 11, 16[4], 17, 25, 26[3], 31, 32
30:1, 2, 3[2], 4, 7[2], 8[2], 13, 16[3], 19, 20, 21
31:4, 6, 8, 10, 11, 17, 19[2], 24, 27, 28, 30, 31, 32[2], 33, 37, 38
32:1, 7, 8[2], 9, 11[2], 12[2], 14, 23, 24, 29, 31[2], 35, 39, 40[2], 42
33:2, 9[2], 10, 11[2], 13, 14[2], 15, 20, 21, 22, 24, 26
34:7, 8[2], 9[2], 10[2], 13, 18, 20, 21
35:7, 8, 10, 11, 14, 17, 18
36:1, 2, 3[3], 6, 7, 8, 9[2], 13, 23[3], 24, 25, 27, 28, 31
37:5, 7, 10, 11, 15, 18, 20, 21[2]
38:1, 2[2], 4, 5, 6, 7, 9, 14, 16[2], 19, 21, 22, 25, 26, 27, 28
39:4, 9[4], 14, 16, 17
40:1[3], 6, 7[2], 10, 11[4], 13, 14, 15
41:1, 2, 3[2], 5, 7[2], 8, 9, 10[2], 11[2], 12, 13[2], 14, 16[2]
42:3[2], 4, 6, 7, 10, 12, 16, 17[2], 19, 20, 22
43:1, 3, 5, 6, 10, 13
44:1, 2, 3, 4, 8[3], 10, 12, 13, 14[2], 15[3], 16, 20, 21, 22, 24, 25, 26[2], 27, 28[2], 29[3], 30[2]
45:1, 4[2]
46:7, 9[2], 10, 13, 25, 26
47:1[2], 2[2], 4[2]
48:9, 10[2], 12[2], 17[2], 18, 19[2], 20, 28[2], 35[2], 36, 41, 44[2], 45
49:2[2], 4, 5[2], 8, 12, 13, 16[2], 17, 19[3], 20[2], 22, 26, 31, 32, 34, 37, 39
50:1, 4, 5, 7, 10, 12, 13, 14, 16, 20, 21, 28, 29[2], 30, 31, 33, 34, 37, 44[3], 45[2]
51:1[2], 2, 3[2], 4, 7, 12, 13, 24, 31, 32, 39, 44, 46[2], 47, 48, 50, 52, 60[2], 62[2], 63, 64
52:2[2], 3, 4, 6, 14, 15[3], 17[2], 19[2], 20, 25[2], 31, 32

LAMENTATIONS

1:1[2], 6, 7, 8, 10[2], 12, 16, 17, 21[3]
2:4, 13, 15[2], 16, 17[2], 19, 22[2]
3:1, 6, 7, 22, 25[2], 26, 27, 30, 37, 44, 57, 62
4:5[2], 6, 9[2], 12, 13, 14, 17, 18, 21
5:8, 16

EZEKIEL

1:1, 18, 23, 25, 26, 28[2]
2:2[2], 3, 5, 8[2]
3:1, 2, 3, 10, 13, 15, 16, 21, 26, 27
4:4, 9, 12, 14, 17
5:5, 6, 7[2], 9, 13, 14[2], 15
6:6, 7, 8[2], 9, 10[3], 12[3], 13, 14
7:4, 7, 9[3], 13, 15[2], 16, 27
8:1, 3, 4, 6[2], 9, 13, 17
9:1, 4[3], 8
10:1, 6, 7[2], 12, 15, 20[2]
11:2, 5, 10, 12[2], 13, 20, 24, 25
12:4, 6, 10, 12[2], 14, 15, 16[2], 19[3], 20[2], 22[2], 25, 27[2]
13:2[2], 3, 6, 9[3], 11, 14[3], 15[2], 18[2], 19[3], 20, 21, 22, 23
14:4[2], 5, 7, 8[2], 9, 10, 11[2], 15[2], 17[2], 19, 22[3], 23[2]
15:7

EZEKIEL

16:5, 15, 21, 24, 25, 27, 31[2], 32, 33, 34, 37[3], 38, 44, 45, 46[2], 47, 52[2], 54[3], 57, 62, 63[2]
17:7, 8[3], 9, 14[3], 15[2], 16, 19[2], 20, 21[2], 24
18:2, 4, 5, 8[2], 10[2], 11, 14, 15, 17[2], 18, 19, 20, 21[2], 22[2], 23[2], 24[4], 26, 27[2], 28, 32
19:5, 9, 11, 14
20:1, 6[2], 9, 12[3], 14, 15, 20[2], 22, 23, 25, 26[5], 27, 32[2], 38[2], 42, 43, 44, 48
21:4, 5[2], 7, 10, 11, 14, 15, 19, 20, 23[2], 24[3], 26[2], 29
22:3, 4, 5[2], 9, 10, 14, 16, 22, 24, 30[2]
23:7, 13[2], 14, 27, 37, 40, 43, 44, 45, 48, 49
24:8[2], 11[3], 19, 21, 24[2], 25, 26[3], 27[2]
25:5, 7, 8, 10, 11, 12, 17
26:1, 2[2], 6, 17[2], 18, 19, 20[3]
27:3, 7[2], 8, 27, 29
28:3, 8, 9[2], 13, 14, 15, 17, 18, 19, 22, 23, 24[3], 25, 26[2]
29:3, 6, 9, 12[2], 15, 16, 18, 21[2]
30:5, 6, 7[2], 8, 9, 12, 19, 20, 22, 25, 26
31:1, 9[2], 14[3], 16[2], 17[3], 18
32:1, 15[3], 17, 18, 20, 21, 24, 25[2], 27, 28, 29[2], 30[2], 32
33:5, 8, 11, 12[2], 13[2], 14, 15, 16[2], 19, 21[2], 22, 24, 27[3], 28, 29, 30, 32, 33
34:2, 3, 4[4], 10, 12[2], 16[4], 19[2], 27[2], 30[2]
35:4, 5, 7[2], 8, 9, 12[2], 15
36:3, 4[2], 7, 11, 18, 23, 28, 30, 31, 33, 34, 35, 36[4], 38
37:6, 9, 13, 14, 25, 28
38:7, 8, 10, 11[2], 12[3], 14, 16, 17, 18, 19, 20[3], 22, 23
39:4, 6[2], 7, 9, 10[3], 11[2], 12, 13, 14, 15, 17[2], 21[2], 22[2], 23, 26, 28
40:1, 4[3], 10[2], 12[2], 20, 21, 22, 24, 26, 34, 37, 39, 41, 47, 48[2], 49
41:6, 9[2], 11[2], 12, 17, 18, 19, 22
42:1, 7, 8, 12, 13
43:1, 3[2], 8, 10, 11[2], 19, 27
44:3, 5, 7, 9, 10, 14, 15, 17, 18, 22[2], 25, 27, 30, 31
45:11, 13, 20[2], 22
46:1, 2, 4, 8, 9[2], 12, 18, 20, 24
47:2, 3, 5[2], 9[2], 10, 12, 22[2], 23
48:9, 11, 12, 15, 18, 19, 22, 35

DANIEL

1:3, 5, 8[2], 13, 16, 18, 20[2]
2:8, 9, 10[2], 11[2], 13, 16[2], 18[2], 21, 25, 28, 29, 30[3], 34[2], 35[2], 40, 45[2], 46, 47
3:3[2], 5[2], 7[2], 8, 10[2], 11, 15[3], 18, 19, 20, 22, 28[2], 29[2]
4:1, 2, 6, 9[2], 17[2], 19, 20, 22, 25[2], 26[2], 30, 32, 34, 37
5:2, 3, 5, 6, 13, 14[2], 15, 16, 19, 21[2], 25, 29, 30
6:2, 7, 8, 10, 12[2], 13[2], 15[2], 17, 22, 23, 25, 26[2]
7:7, 14[2], 16, 20[4], 22, 24
8:1, 2, 4[2], 6, 7, 13, 21, 22
9:2, 4[2], 7, 11[2], 12, 13, 15, 16, 17, 25, 26, 27
10:7[2], 11, 12, 16, 21[2]
11:3, 6[3], 16, 24, 26, 30, 31, 32, 33, 36[2]
12:1[4], 2, 3[2], 5, 7[2], 11[2], 12

HOSEA

1:1, 5[2], 10
2:3, 5[2], 6, 8, 12, 16[2], 18, 21, 23
4:3, 4, 6, 14
5:9, 10
6:5, 8
7:2, 7
8:3, 4
9:4, 10, 12
10:5, 10, 11
11:3, 4
12:8, 9
13:2, 3[2], 8, 10
14:7

JOEL

1:1, 4[3]
2:5, 11, 16, 17, 25, 26, 27, 27[2], 28, 32
3:1, 3, 6, 17, 18[2], 21

AMOS

1:5, 8, 13
2:7, 13, 15[3], 16[2]
3:1, 12, 14[2]
4:1, 2[2], 3, 13[2]
5:3[2], 8[2], 9[2], 10[2], 13, 14, 15, 18
6:1, 3, 4, 5, 6, 7[2], 8, 9, 10[2]
7:2
8:3, 4, 5[2], 6, 8, 9[2], 11, 13, 14
9:1[3], 5[2], 6[2], 8, 11[2], 12[2], 13[2]

OBADIAH

3[2], 7[2], 8, 9, 11[2], 12, 14[2], 20

JONAH

1:2, 4, 5, 6[2], 7, 10, 11, 12
2:8, 9[2]
3:2[2], 8, 9, 10[3]
4:2, 6, 7, 8[2], 11[2]

MICAH

1:1, 2, 4
2:1, 4, 5, 6[2], 7[2], 8

MICAH

3:4, 5[3], 6[2], 9
4:1, 6[4], 7[2], 11
5:2, 3, 7, 10[2]
6:5, 10, 14, 16
7:3, 5, 10, 11[2], 12, 13, 18

NAHUM

1:5, 7, 11, 14, 15[2]
2:1
3:4, 7[2], 8[2], 19

HABAKKUK

1:3, 6[2], 8, 13[2], 14
2:2[2], 6[3], 7[2], 8, 9[3], 12, 13, 15[3], 17, 18[2], 19
3:8, 16

ZEPHANIAH

1:5[4], 6[2], 8, 9, 10[2], 11, 12[4], 15, 17, 18
2:5, 15[3]
3:1, 6[3], 8[2], 9, 11[2], 16, 18, 19[4], 20[2]

HAGGAI

1:2, 6, 9, 11
2:3, 5, 13, 14, 18, 22, 23

ZECHARIAH

1:8, 9, 10, 11, 13, 14, 15, 19, 21
2:3, 7, 8, 9, 11[2]
3:2, 4, 7, 8, 9[2], 10
4:1[2], 4, 5, 9, 14
5:3[4], 4, 5[2], 6, 7, 10
6:4, 7, 8, 15[2]
7:1, 11, 13, 14
8:9[3], 10, 13, 16, 17, 20, 23[3]
9:7, 8[2], 12, 16
11:1, 5, 9[4], 10, 11[3], 13, 14, 16[5], 17
12:3[2], 4, 6, 7, 8[3], 9[3], 10, 11, 14
13:1, 2[2], 3[3], 4[2], 7, 8
14:4, 6[2], 7, 8[2], 9, 12, 13[2], 15, 16[2], 17, 18[2], 19, 20, 21[2]

MALACHI

1:6, 7, 9, 10, 12, 13
2:4[2], 12[2], 13, 15, 16[2], 17
3:3, 5[2], 10[2], 14[2], 15[2], 16[3], 17[2], 18[2]
4:1[4], 2, 3

MATTHEW

1:6, 20, 22
2:2, 6, 8, 12, 15, 16[2], 17, 22, 23
3:3, 9, 11
4:3, 4, 12, 14, 17, 24[2]
5:4, 14, 15, 16, 17, 20, 21, 22, 23, 27, 28, 29[2], 30[2], 32[2], 33, 38, 39, 42[2], 43, 44[2], 45
6:1, 2, 4, 5, 7, 16, 18, 23[2], 29, 32
7:1, 3[2], 6, 8[3], 11, 12, 13, 14, 19, 21[2], 22, 23, 25, 26, 27
8:4, 8, 10, 11, 16[2], 17, 24, 27, 28[2], 33, 34
9:6[2], 12[3], 13, 16, 22, 26, 28, 30, 31, 38
10:14, 15, 19, 20, 22, 25, 26[2], 27[2], 34, 37[2], 38, 39[2], 40[3], 41[2]
11:3, 8, 11[2], 15, 24, 25, 28
12:1, 2, 3, 5, 6, 10, 11, 16, 17, 22, 30[2], 36[2], 45, 48
13:2, 12, 17, 19, 20[2], 22[2], 23[2], 28, 32, 35, 37, 39, 41, 44[2], 46, 47, 52, 53, 54
14:1, 15, 20, 21, 33, 35[3], 36
15:4, 11[2], 12, 17, 28, 30, 31, 37, 38
16:1, 11[3], 12, 13, 14, 15, 18, 20[2], 21[2], 23[2]
17:10, 12, 13, 18, 24, 27[2]
18:6[2], 7[2], 10[2], 11, 12, 13[2], 14, 16, 19[2], 25, 27, 28, 31, 32[2], 34
19:1, 4, 12, 13, 16, 17, 21, 22, 23, 28, 29, 30
20:1, 7, 9, 10, 14, 21, 22[2], 23, 25[2], 30, 32, 33
21:4, 9[3], 12[2], 15, 31, 32, 34, 45
22:3, 16, 21, 23, 31, 34, 46
23:3, 11, 12, 13, 17, 18, 19, 21, 22[2], 26[2], 31, 35, 37, 39
24:2, 4, 6, 13, 19[2], 20, 24, 32, 33, 36, 38[2], 43, 46, 47, 48, 50[2]
25:3, 9, 10, 16, 17, 18, 20, 22, 24, 25, 26, 29[3]
26:2, 4, 12, 13, 16, 17, 21, 23, 24[2], 29, 34, 41, 46, 48[2], 52, 53, 54, 55, 56, 57, 63, 68, 71, 73
27:3, 4[3], 8, 9[2], 14, 15, 17, 18, 19, 20, 21, 24[2], 31, 33, 35, 39, 40, 46, 47[2], 54[2], 62, 63[2], 64
28:5, 7, 10, 11

MARK

1:9, 14, 22, 27, 32[2], 34, 36, 38, 45
2:1, 2, 8, 10[2], 12, 15, 16, 17[2], 21, 23, 24, 25
3:2, 9, 10, 12, 14[2], 20, 24, 25, 29
4:1, 8, 9, 10, 11, 12, 15, 22, 24, 25[3], 28, 31, 32, 37, 38, 40, 41
5:4, 7, 10, 12, 14[2], 15, 16[2], 18[2], 23, 26, 29[2], 30, 32, 36, 38, 40, 43[2]
6:2, 5, 8, 10, 11, 12, 13, 14, 15[2], 20, 21, 22, 25, 36, 44, 55[2], 56
7:2, 9, 11, 15[2], 18, 20[2], 26, 32, 34, 36
8:8, 9, 21, 25, 27, 29, 30, 31, 32, 33[2]
9:1[2], 7, 9, 10, 11, 12, 13, 18, 23,

Misc.

MARK

25, 26, 30, 31, 32, 33, 37, 39, 40, 42[2], 43, 45
10:13[2], 17, 18, 22, 23, 24, 29, 31, 35, 36, 37, 38[2], 39[2], 42, 47, 48, 51[2]
11:3, 5, 9[3], 10, 15[2], 16, 23[2], 24, 25, 32
12:2, 12, 14, 15, 17[2], 19, 26, 28, 34[2], 35, 41, 43, 44
13:2, 11[3], 13, 14[2], 15, 16, 17[2], 18, 20, 24, 25, 28, 29, 30, 32[2]
14:4, 9, 12[2], 20, 21[2], 25[2], 28, 30, 35, 42, 44[2], 47, 58, 69, 70, 72
15:5, 6, 7, 9, 10, 11, 12, 29[2], 32[2], 35, 39, 42
16:1, 4, 7, 10, 11, 12, 16[2], 17

LUKE

1:4, 7, 8, 19, 20, 21, 22, 23, 28, 35, 41, 43, 45, 49, 50, 57, 59, 61, 65, 66, 71[2], 74[2], 79
2:1[2], 6[2], 18, 20, 23, 24, 26, 35, 38[2], 46, 47, 49[2]
3:7, 8, 11[3], 13, 20, 21
4:3, 4, 6, 18, 20, 26, 29, 40, 41, 42
5:1, 3, 7[2], 9, 17, 24[2], 25, 29, 31[2], 36
6:1, 2, 4, 5, 6, 7, 12, 18, 21[2], 23, 24, 25[2], 28, 29[2], 30[2], 31, 32, 38, 40, 41[2], 42[3], 45[2], 48, 49[3]
7:3, 4, 6, 9, 10[2], 11, 14, 15, 16[2], 19, 20, 21[2], 22, 28[2], 29, 36, 37, 39, 43, 49[2]
8:1, 8, 10, 12, 14, 15, 16, 17[2], 18, 22, 31, 32, 34, 36, 38, 40, 41, 45, 46, 47, 53, 56
9:5, 7[3], 8[2], 10, 11, 12, 17, 18, 19, 20, 21, 32[2], 37, 39, 45[2], 48[2], 50, 51, 54, 57
10:2, 9, 11, 12[3], 16[4], 20, 21[2], 23, 24, 31, 36, 37, 38, 40[2], 42
11:1, 4, 10[3], 11, 13, 18, 23[2], 26, 27, 28, 33, 35, 38, 40[3], 44, 48, 50, 52, 54
12:1, 2[2], 3, 4[3], 9, 10, 13, 21, 26, 27, 30, 33[2], 36[2], 37, 39, 42, 43, 44[2], 45, 46, 47, 48, 51, 56, 58
13:1[2], 2, 4[2], 9, 14, 17, 23, 32, 33, 34, 35
14:1, 9, 10[3], 11, 12, 15[2], 17, 21, 23, 24, 29, 31, 33[2], 35
15:4, 7[2], 10, 12, 14, 15, 16, 29, 31, 32
16:1, 2, 4, 9, 10[3], 12[2], 15, 16, 18, 22, 24, 25, 26[2], 27, 28
17:1, 2[2], 9[2], 10, 11, 12, 14, 15, 18, 24, 27, 29, 31[2], 34
18:1, 3, 8, 9, 11, 12, 14[2], 15, 19, 22, 24[2], 26, 29, 31, 35, 37, 39, 41[2]
19:4, 7[2], 10, 11, 15[2], 21[2], 22[3], 23, 24[2], 26[3], 27, 32, 37, 38, 40, 43, 45[2]
20:1, 2, 6, 7, 10, 14, 17, 18, 19, 20[2], 21, 27, 28, 35, 37, 40, 41
21:3, 4, 6, 8, 20, 21, 22, 23[2], 30, 31, 34, 35, 36[2], 37
22:8, 9, 21, 22, 23, 25, 26[3], 27[4], 30, 31, 32, 34[2], 36[2], 37[2], 40, 47, 63, 64, 70

LUKE

23:2, 7[2], 14, 23, 24, 25, 26, 29, 48[2], 49, 53, 54
24:10, 12, 13, 15, 16, 17, 21, 23[2], 25, 33, 37, 39, 44, 45, 47

JOHN

1:3, 7, 8[2], 9[2], 12, 15, 21, 22[2], 25[2], 31, 33, 34, 39, 48
2:9, 10, 14, 16, 17, 18, 22, 25
3:2[2], 6[2], 7, 8, 11[2], 13, 15, 16[2], 17, 18[2], 19, 20, 21[3], 26, 28[2], 29, 31[3], 32, 33[2], 36[2]
4:1, 5, 9, 10, 11, 14[2], 15, 18, 19, 20, 24, 25, 26, 27, 29, 32, 34, 36[4], 37, 38, 39[2], 40, 42, 44, 45, 47[2], 50, 53, 54
5:6[2], 10, 11, 12, 13[2], 15, 18, 20[2], 23[2], 24[2], 25, 28, 29[2], 32[2], 34, 36[3], 40, 42, 44, 45[2]
6:2, 5, 7, 11, 12[2], 13, 14[3], 15, 18, 22[4], 23, 24, 27, 28, 29, 30, 32, 35[2], 36, 37[2], 38, 39, 40[2], 42, 45, 46, 47, 48, 50, 51, 56, 57, 58[2], 61, 63[2], 64[2], 65, 66, 69[2], 71
7:3[2], 4, 7, 16, 18[3], 23, 26, 28, 32, 33, 35, 36, 37, 38, 39[2], 42, 50
8:5, 6, 7, 12, 16, 17, 18[2], 24[2], 25, 26, 27, 28[2], 29[2], 37, 38[2], 40, 47, 48, 50, 52, 54[2]
9:2, 3, 4, 8[2], 11, 13, 16, 17, 18[2], 20[2], 22[2], 24[2], 25, 29, 30, 31, 32[2], 35, 36, 37, 39[2]
10:1, 2, 8, 10[2], 12, 17, 21, 25, 33, 38[2], 41
11:2, 4[2], 6, 7, 11[2], 13, 15, 16, 17, 20, 22, 24, 25, 27, 29, 30, 31, 37, 39, 40, 41, 42[3], 44, 49, 50[3], 51[3], 52[3], 53, 56, 57[2]
12:2, 6, 9[2], 10, 11, 12[2], 13, 16[2], 17, 18[2], 20, 23, 25[2], 29[2], 34, 35, 36, 38, 39, 40, 44[2], 45[2], 46, 48[3], 50
13:1[2], 3[2], 5, 10, 15, 16[2], 18[2], 19[2], 20[3], 21, 24, 27, 29[3], 34[2], 35
14:3, 9, 10[3], 11, 12[2], 13[2], 16, 20[2], 21[3], 22, 24, 29, 31[2]
15:2[3], 5, 8, 11[2], 12, 13, 15, 16[3], 17, 18, 20, 21, 23, 25[2]
16:1, 2[2], 4[2], 5, 7, 13, 15[2], 17, 18, 19[2], 20, 21, 23, 24, 26[2], 27, 30[3], 32, 33
17:1, 2, 3, 7, 8[2], 11, 12[2], 13, 15[2], 19, 21[4], 22, 23[3], 24[2], 25, 26
18:4, 8, 9, 13, 14[2], 15, 16[2], 17, 28, 32, 36, 37[3], 39[2]
19:4[2], 8, 10, 11, 13[2], 21, 24, 27[2], 28[2], 31[4], 33, 35[3], 36, 38
20:3, 7, 8, 9, 14, 18[2], 29, 31[3]
21:3, 4, 7[2], 12, 14[2], 15, 16, 17, 20, 22[2], 23[4], 24, 25[2]

THE ACTS

1:1, 2, 4, 8, 16, 19[2], 21, 22[2], 25[2]
2:6, 14, 16, 20, 21, 24, 25, 29, 30[2], 31, 36[2], 39, 41, 44
3:2, 10[2], 11, 17, 18, 19, 23[2], 24
4:2, 5, 10, 13[2], 16[2], 17[2], 21, 23, 24[2], 29, 30, 32[2], 34[2]
5:5, 9, 15[2], 17, 21[2], 28, 32, 33, 40, 41

THE ACTS

6:2, 14, 15
7:5, 6[2], 7, 12, 16, 19, 24, 25, 27, 36, 37, 38, 44[2], 45
8:1, 4, 7[2], 8, 9, 11, 14, 15, 18, 19, 20, 23, 24, 26, 31, 37, 39
9:2, 12, 14, 17[2], 20, 21[4], 22, 23, 26, 27, 35, 37, 38[2], 43
10:2, 7, 14, 15, 22, 27, 28[3], 33[2], 34, 35, 37, 38, 42, 43, 45, 47
11:1[2], 2, 9, 16, 17, 19, 22, 23, 26, 28
12:1, 9, 10, 11, 15, 19
13:1[2], 16, 20, 25, 27, 28, 29, 32, 33, 34, 38, 39, 40, 42, 46, 47
14:1[2], 6, 9, 15[2], 17, 18, 21, 22, 27
15:2, 4, 5, 7[2], 11, 17, 19, 20[2], 21, 24, 26, 29, 39
16:2, 3, 4, 10, 12[2], 14, 19, 26, 27, 32, 38
17:3[2], 6, 7, 11, 13, 15, 17, 22, 24[2], 27, 29, 31[2]
18:2, 5, 7, 14, 21, 28[2]
19:1, 4[2], 9, 10, 12, 16[2], 18, 22, 23, 25, 26[2], 27[2], 31, 34, 35[2], 36
20:18, 20, 22, 23[2], 24, 25, 26, 29, 31, 34[2], 35, 38
21:1, 4, 8, 11, 12, 21[2], 22, 23, 24[3], 25[2], 26, 28, 29, 31, 35, 38[2]
22:2, 6, 9[2], 11[2], 14[2], 17, 19[2], 20, 22, 24[2], 25[2], 26, 29
23:2, 4, 5, 6, 8, 9, 12, 14, 15, 19, 20, 21, 22, 24, 27, 30, 34
24:2[2], 4[2], 9, 10[2], 11[2], 14, 15, 21, 22, 23, 26[2]
25:3, 4[2], 16, 24, 25[2], 26
26:5, 8, 9, 18[2], 20, 23[3], 26, 27, 29[2], 30
27:1, 10, 13, 20, 24, 25, 27, 33, 43, 44
28:1, 6, 8, 16, 17, 19, 20, 21, 22, 25, 28[2], 30

ROMANS

1:7, 8, 9, 11, 12[2], 13[2], 15, 16, 19, 20[2], 21, 26, 27[2], 32[2]
2:1[2], 2, 3[2], 4, 8, 9, 10, 18, 19, 21, 22[2], 23, 28, 29
3:2, 4, 8[2], 9, 11[2], 12, 19[2], 22, 24, 25, 26, 28
4:1, 4, 5[2], 9, 11[3], 12, 13, 16[3], 18[2], 21, 23, 24
5:3, 8, 12, 14[2], 16, 20, 21
6:1, 2, 3, 4, 6[3], 7, 8, 9, 10[2], 12, 13, 16, 17[2]
7:1[2], 3[2], 4[2], 6[2], 13[4], 14, 15[3], 16[2], 17[2], 18[3], 19[2], 20[3], 21, 24
8:3, 4, 5[2], 8, 9, 11[3], 16, 17[2], 18, 22, 24, 25, 27, 28[2], 29, 32, 33, 34[3], 37, 38
9:2, 3, 8, 11[2], 16[3], 17[2], 20[2], 23, 26, 30, 32
10:1, 2, 4, 5, 6, 7, 8, 9[2], 12, 15, 19, 20[2]
11:7, 8[2], 10, 11, 19, 25[2], 31, 32
12:1, 2[2], 3, 6, 7, 8[4], 9[2], 15[2]
13:1, 2, 3, 4[2], 8, 11[2]
14:1, 2, 3[3], 4, 6[4], 9, 13, 14[2], 18, 20, 22[2], 23

ROMANS

15:1, 3, 4, 6, 8, 9, 12, 13, 14, 15, 16[2], 19, 21, 29, 30, 31[3], 32
16:2[2], 5, 11, 18, 19, 25

1 CORINTHIANS

1:2[2], 5, 7, 8, 10[3], 11, 12, 14, 15, 18, 21[2], 26, 28, 29, 31[2]
2:5, 6[2], 9, 12[2], 15, 16
3:7[3], 8[2], 11, 16[2], 18, 20
4:2, 3, 4, 6[3], 7, 8, 9
5:1[2], 2[2], 3, 5, 6, 7, 11, 12[2], 13[2]
6:2, 3[2], 5[2], 6, 8, 9, 15, 16, 17, 18[2], 19
7:5[2], 7[2], 12, 13, 22[2], 25, 26[2], 29[2], 30[3], 31, 32[2], 33[2], 34[2], 35[3], 36, 37[2], 38[2], 40
8:1, 2, 4[3], 5, 7, 9
9:3, 9, 10[4], 13, 14, 15[2], 18[2], 19, 20[4], 21[3], 22[2], 23, 24[2], 25, 26, 27
10:1[2], 4[3], 12, 13[2], 17, 19[2], 20[2], 25, 27, 28, 30, 33
11:2, 3, 5[2], 13, 14, 17[2], 18, 19, 22, 23[2], 28[2], 29, 32, 34
12:2, 3[3], 11, 12, 24, 25[2], 28
13:2, 10[2]
14:1, 2, 3, 4[2], 5[5], 11[2], 12, 13[2], 16, 19, 21, 22[3], 23[2], 24, 25, 27, 30, 31, 37[2]
15:3[2], 4[2], 5, 6, 7, 9, 12[2], 15[2], 20, 23, 26, 27, 28[2], 36, 37[3], 46[3], 48[2], 50, 54, 58
16:2, 4, 6[2], 10, 11, 15[2], 16[2], 17, 18, 19

2 CORINTHIANS

1:4, 7, 8[2], 9, 10, 11, 12, 14, 15, 17[2], 23, 24
2:1, 2, 3, 4[2], 5, 7, 8, 9, 15[2]
3:5, 7, 10[2], 11[2], 12, 13[2], 17
4:3, 7, 10, 11, 14, 15
5:1, 3, 4[3], 5, 6, 9, 10[2], 12, 14, 15[2], 19, 21
6:1, 3, 15
7:3, 6[2], 7, 8, 9[3], 11, 12[3], 16
8:2, 4, 6[2], 7, 9[2], 11[2], 12[2], 13, 14[3], 15[2], 19, 20
9:2, 3, 4, 5[2], 8, 10
10:2[2], 5, 7[2], 9, 11, 12, 15[2], 17, 18
11:2, 3, 4, 7, 9, 12[3], 16, 17, 18, 28[2], 31
12:4, 6[2], 8, 9, 13, 19, 20, 21
13:2, 5, 6[2], 7[4]

GALATIANS

1:4, 6[2], 7, 8, 9, 11, 13, 16, 23
2:2, 4[2], 5, 7, 8, 9[2], 10, 12, 13, 14, 16[2], 19
3:1, 5, 7, 8, 10, 11, 12, 13, 14[2], 17[3], 22[2], 24, 25
4:1, 5[2], 9, 15, 17, 21, 22, 27[2], 29[2]
5:2, 3[2], 7, 8, 10[2], 15, 17[2], 21, 24
6:6[2], 7, 8[2], 13, 14

EPHESIANS

1:4, 10, 12, 13[3], 17, 18, 21[2], 23
2:2, 7, 8, 10, 11[2], 12[2], 16, 17
3:3, 6, 8, 10, 13, 16, 17[2], 19, 20[3]
4:1, 9[2], 10[3], 14, 16, 17, 18, 21, 22, 24, 28[3], 29[2]
5:5, 13, 14, 15, 26, 27[2], 28, 33

EPHESIANS

6:3, 5, 8, 9, 11, 13, 19[2], 20, 21, 22[2], 24

PHILIPPIANS

1:6, 9, 10[3], 12, 13, 17, 19, 20[2], 25, 26, 27[2], 28
2:2, 10, 11[2], 15, 16[2], 19, 22, 24, 25, 26[2], 28[2]
3:4, 8, 9, 10, 12[2], 18, 21
4:2, 10, 11, 14, 15, 17, 22

COLOSSIANS

1:9, 10, 16[2], 18, 19, 21, 24, 28
2:1, 2, 14
3:9, 10, 24, 25
4:1[2], 3, 4, 5, 6, 8, 12, 13[2], 16[2], 17

1 THESSALONIANS

1:7[2], 8
2:1, 2, 10, 12, 13, 16
3:3[2], 4, 6, 10[2]
4:1, 3, 4, 6[2], 8, 9, 10, 11, 12[3], 13, 14, 15
5:1, 2, 4[2], 7[2], 10, 14, 15[2], 21, 24, 27

2 THESSALONIANS

1:3, 4[2], 5, 6, 8[2], 10[2], 11, 12
2:2[2], 3[2], 4[4], 5, 6, 8, 10[2], 11, 12
3:1, 2, 4, 6[2], 8, 10, 11, 12[2], 14[2]

1 TIMOTHY

1:3[2], 8, 9, 10[2], 12, 15, 16, 18, 20
2:1, 2[2], 8, 9
3:4, 13, 15
4:1, 8[2], 10, 14, 15, 16
5:3, 4, 5, 6, 7, 14, 16[3], 17, 18, 20[2], 21, 25
6:1, 2, 5, 9, 14, 17[2], 18[2], 19, 20

2 TIMOTHY

1:3, 4, 5[2], 6, 12[3], 14, 15, 18[2]
2:1, 2, 4[2], 6, 8, 10, 14, 15, 18, 19[2], 22, 23, 25, 26
3:1, 3, 12, 15, 17
4:8[2], 13, 16, 17[2]

TITUS

1:2, 5[2], 9, 13, 14, 15, 16
2:2, 3, 4, 5, 8[3], 10, 11, 12, 13, 14
3:4, 7, 8[2], 10, 11[2], 13, 14, 15[2]

PHILEMON

6, 8, 12, 13, 14, 15, 18, 21, 22

HEBREWS

2:3, 6[2], 8[2], 9, 11, 14[3], 17, 18[2]
3:2, 4, 10, 16, 17, 18[2], 19
4:2, 6, 10, 11, 13, 14[2], 16
5:1, 2[2], 4, 5, 7[2], 9, 12, 13, 14
6:7, 8, 9, 10, 11, 12, 18, 19
7:2, 5[2], 6, 8[2], 11, 14, 15, 21, 25
8:3, 4[2], 5, 7, 9, 10, 13[2]
9:4[2], 8, 9[2], 11, 15[2], 23, 25, 28
10:2, 4, 9, 14, 15, 16, 20, 23, 26, 28, 30, 33, 34, 36, 37, 39
11:3[2], 4, 5[2], 6[4], 13, 14[2], 15, 16, 17, 18, 19, 28, 31, 35, 40
12:1, 2, 3, 10, 13, 17, 18[2], 19[2], 20, 21, 24[2], 25[4], 27[3]
13:3, 6, 9[2], 12, 15, 17[4], 19, 20[2], 21, 23, 24

JAMES

1:3, 4, 5, 6, 7[2], 9, 10, 12[2], 18
2:3, 5, 7, 11, 12, 13, 19, 20, 24
3:1, 3, 6, 17, 18
4:1, 3, 4, 5[2], 11, 12, 13, 14, 15[2], 17
5:1, 11, 16, 17, 20

1 PETER

1:4, 7[2], 10, 11, 12[2], 13, 18, 21[2], 22
2:2, 3, 6, 9, 12, 14[2], 15, 21, 23, 24
3:1, 3, 4, 7, 9[2], 10[2], 12, 13[2], 15[2], 16[2], 17, 18, 20
4:1, 2, 4, 5, 6[2], 11, 13, 17[2], 19
5:1, 4, 6, 9[2], 10, 12, 13, 14

2 PETER

1:1, 3[2], 4[2], 8, 9[2], 14, 15, 19[2], 20
2:1, 4, 6, 8, 10, 12, 13, 14, 17, 18, 22
3:2, 3, 5, 6, 8, 9[2], 10, 11, 14[2], 15, 16

1 JOHN

1:1, 2, 3[2], 4, 5, 6, 8, 10
2:1, 3, 4, 5, 6, 9, 10, 11[2], 13, 14, 15, 16, 17, 18[2], 19[2], 21, 22[3], 23, 24[2], 25, 26, 27, 28, 29[3]
3:1, 2, 3, 5, 7, 8[2], 10, 11[2], 12, 14[2], 15, 19, 22, 23, 24[2]
4:2[2], 3[4], 4[2], 6[2], 7, 8, 9[2], 10[2], 13, 14, 15, 16[2], 17, 18, 20, 21
5:1[4], 2, 3, 4, 5[3], 6[2], 7, 8, 10[3], 11, 12[2], 13[4], 14[2], 15[3], 16[2], 18[3], 19, 20[4]

2 JOHN

1, 4, 5[2], 6[2], 7, 8[2], 9, 11, 12

3 JOHN

2, 3, 4, 7, 8, 10, 11[4], 12

JUDE

1, 3, 5[2], 15, 18, 24

REVELATION

1:2, 3[2], 5, 9, 12, 18
2:1, 6, 7[2], 10, 11[2], 14, 15, 17[3], 20, 22, 23, 25, 26, 29
3:1[3], 2, 5, 6, 7[4], 9, 10, 11[2], 12, 13, 15, 17, 18[4], 21, 22
4:3, 9, 10[2]
5:1, 7, 12, 13[2], 14
6:2, 4[3], 5, 8, 9, 10, 11[2], 16
7:1, 15
8:3
9:4, 5[2], 17, 20
10:6[4]
11:1, 6, 7, 10[2], 18[3]
12:6, 9, 12[2], 13, 14, 15
13:6, 8, 10[2], 13, 14[3], 15[2], 17[2], 18
14:3, 6, 7, 8, 12, 13, 15, 16, 18
15:2, 5
16:12, 14, 15
17:1, 7, 8[3], 11, 14, 18
18:4[2], 10[2], 14, 16[2], 19[2], 21, 24
19:4, 5, 8, 10, 11, 12, 15, 17, 18[2], 19, 20[3], 21
20:2, 3[2], 4, 6, 10, 11
21:5, 6, 7, 10, 15, 17, 27
22:7, 11[3], 14[2], 17[2], 18[2]

THE 3588

GENESIS

1:1[3], 2[6], 4[3], 5[5], 6[4], 7[5], 8[4], 9[3], 10[3], 11[4], 12[2], 13[3], 14[4], 15[3], 16[5], 17[3], 18[4], 19[3], 20[4], 21, 22[3], 23[3], 24[3], 25[3], 26[7], 27, 28[6], 29[4], 30[3], 31[3]
2:1[3], 2[2], 3, 4[7], 5[6], 6[3], 7[4], 8[2], 9[7], 10, 11[3], 12[2], 13[4], 14[4], 15[3], 16[3], 17[3], 18[2], 19[5], 20[3], 21[2], 22[3], 25
3:1[5], 2[5], 3[4], 4[2], 5, 6[4], 7, 8[9], 9, 10, 11, 12[3], 13[4], 14[4], 15, 16, 17[4], 18[2], 19[2], 20, 21, 22[3], 23[3], 24[5]
4:1, 2, 3[3], 4[3], 6, 7, 8, 9, 10[2], 11, 12[2], 13, 14[3], 15[2], 16[4], 17[3], 19[4], 20, 21[2], 22, 26[2]
5:1[4], 2, 4, 5, 8, 11, 14, 17, 20, 23, 27, 29[2], 31
6:1[2], 2[2], 3, 4[4], 5[3], 6[2], 7[6], 8[2], 9, 11[2], 12[2], 13[3], 14, 15[5], 16[4], 17[3], 18, 19, 20
7:1[2], 2[2], 3[5], 4[3], 5, 6[2], 7[3], 8, 9[3], 10[3], 11[8], 12[2], 13[4], 14[2], 15[2], 16, 17[5], 18[5], 19[4], 20[2], 21[2], 22[2], 23[7], 24[2]
8:1[4], 2[4], 3[5], 4[5], 5[7], 6[3], 7[2], 8[3], 9[7], 10[2], 11[4], 12, 13[10], 14[4], 16, 17[3], 19[2], 20[2], 21[4], 22
9:1, 2[7], 3, 4[2], 5[4], 6, 7, 10[5], 11[2], 12[2], 13[2], 14[3], 15, 16[4], 17[3], 18[3], 19[2], 21, 22[2], 23, 26, 27, 28, 29
10:1[3], 2, 3, 4, 5[2], 6, 7[2], 8, 9[3], 10[2], 11, 12, 16[3], 17[3], 18[5], 19[2], 20, 21[4], 22, 23, 25[2], 29, 30, 31, 32[5]
11:1, 2[2], 4[2], 5[4], 6[2], 8[4], 9[7], 10[2], 27, 28[2], 29[5], 31[3], 32
12:1, 3, 4, 5[3], 6[5], 7[2], 8[6], 9, 10[3], 12, 14[2], 15[2], 17
13:1, 3[3], 4[5], 6, 7[5], 9[5], 10[5], 11[3], 12[3], 13[2], 14[2], 15, 16[4], 17[3], 18[2]
14:1, 2, 3[2], 4, 5[5], 6[2], 7[3], 8[7], 9, 10[3], 11, 13[3], 15, 16[3], 17[5], 18[2], 19, 20, 21[3], 22[4], 24[3]

GENESIS

15:1[2], 2, 4[2], 5, 6, 7[2], 10[2], 11[2], 12, 16[3], 17, 18[5], 19[3], 20[3], 21[4]
16:2[2], 3[2], 5, 7[5], 8, 9[2], 10[2], 11[3], 12, 13[2], 14
17:1[2], 8[2], 11[2], 12, 14, 21, 23[3], 24, 25, 26, 27[3]
18:1[5], 2[2], 4, 6[2], 7, 8[2], 9, 10[2], 11, 13, 14[3], 16[2], 17, 18[2], 19[3], 20[2], 21, 22[2], 23[2], 24[3], 25[6], 26[3], 27, 28[2], 30, 31, 32, 33
19:1[2], 2, 4[5], 5, 6[2], 8, 9[2], 10[3], 11[4], 12[2], 13[4], 14, 15[4], 16[5], 17[2], 19, 21, 22[2], 23[2], 24[2], 25[4], 27[3], 28[5], 29[6], 30, 31[5], 33, 34[3], 35, 36, 37[4], 38[4]
20:1, 3, 5, 6, 7, 8[2], 11, 12[2], 16, 18[3]
21:1[2], 2, 3, 8[2], 9[2], 10, 11, 12, 13[2], 14[3], 15[4], 16[2], 17[5], 18, 19[2], 20[2], 21[2], 22, 23[2], 28, 32[3], 33[3], 34
22:2[2], 3[4], 4[2], 5[2], 6[3], 7[3], 9[4], 10, 11[2], 12, 13[2], 14[3], 15[3], 16, 17[5], 18[2], 21
23:1[2], 2[2], 3, 5, 6, 7[3], 8, 9[2], 10[5], 11[4], 12[2], 13[4], 15, 16[4], 17[6], 18[3], 19[4], 20[3]
24:1, 3[6], 5[3], 7[2], 8, 9[2], 10[4], 11[4], 13[4], 14[2], 15, 16[2], 17, 20[2], 21[2], 22[2], 24[2], 26[2], 27[4], 28, 29[2], 30[6], 31[3], 32[4], 35, 37[2], 39, 40, 42, 43[2], 44[3], 45, 46, 47[3], 48[3], 49[2], 50[2], 51, 52[2], 53, 54[2], 55[2], 56, 57, 60[2], 61[3], 62[3], 63[3], 64, 65[3], 66
25:3, 4[2], 6[3], 7[2], 8, 9[4], 10[2], 11[2], 12[2], 13[3], 16, 17[3], 18, 19, 20[4], 21[2], 22[2], 23[5], 25, 27[2], 29, 32
26:1[4], 2[2], 3, 4[3], 7[4], 8, 10, 12[2], 13, 14, 15[3], 17, 18[5], 19, 20[4], 21, 22[3], 24[3], 25[2], 26, 28, 29[2], 31, 32[2], 33[2], 34[4]

GENESIS

27:2, 3, 5, 7, 9[2], 15, 16[4], 17[3], 20, 22[3], 27[4], 28[3], 30, 34, 39[3], 40, 41[2], 46[4]
28:1, 2[2], 4[2], 5[2], 6, 8, 9[3], 11[2], 12[3], 13[4], 14[8], 16, 17[2], 18[3], 19[3], 21, 22
29:1[3], 2[3], 3[6], 5, 6, 7[2], 8[4], 10[5], 13, 14, 16[4], 20, 22[2], 23, 25, 26[2], 27, 31, 32, 33, 35
30:2[2], 13, 14[2], 16[2], 17, 19, 24, 27, 30, 32[5], 33[2], 35[5], 36, 37[3], 38[5], 39[2], 40[6], 41[6], 42[3], 43
31:1, 2, 3[2], 4, 5, 8[4], 9, 10[4], 11, 12[2], 13[3], 16, 18[2], 19, 20, 21[2], 22, 23, 24, 25[2], 26, 29[2], 33, 34[3], 35[2], 38, 39, 40[3], 42[4], 46, 48, 49, 53[4], 54[2], 55
32:1, 2, 3[2], 6, 7[3], 8[2], 9, 10[3], 11[4], 12[2], 16, 17, 19[3], 20, 21[2], 22, 23, 24[2], 25[2], 26, 30[2], 31, 32[6]
33:1[2], 2, 3, 5[3], 6, 8, 10, 13[3], 14[2], 15[2], 17[2], 18[2], 19[2]
34:1[3], 2[3], 3[3], 5, 6, 7[3], 8, 10, 12, 13, 19[3], 20[2], 21[2], 22, 24[2], 25[4], 26[2], 27[3], 28[2], 29, 30[4]
35:1, 2, 3[2], 4[2], 5[3], 6[2], 7[2], 8, 12[2], 13, 14, 15[2], 17, 19, 20, 21, 22, 23, 24, 25, 26[2], 27, 28, 29
36:1, 2[6], 5[2], 6[4], 7, 9[3], 10[5], 11, 12, 13[2], 14[3], 15[3], 16[3], 17[4], 18[3], 19, 20[3], 21[4], 22, 23, 24[4], 25[2], 26, 27, 28, 29[2], 30[2], 31[3], 32[2], 33, 34, 35[3], 37, 38, 39[4], 40[2], 43[4]
37:1[2], 2[5], 3, 5, 7, 8, 9[3], 10, 11, 13, 14[2], 15[2], 17, 22, 24, 27, 28[2], 29[2], 30, 31[3], 32, 35, 36[2]
38:7[3], 9[2], 10[2], 12[2], 14, 16, 17, 19, 20[4], 21[3], 22[2], 24, 25[2], 27, 28[2], 30

GENESIS

39:1[3], 2[3], 3[2], 5[7], 6, 8, 11[3], 14, 17, 19, 20[3], 21[4], 22[5], 23[4]
40:1[3], 2[4], 3[5], 4[2], 5[5], 6, 7, 9, 10[2], 11[2], 12[2], 13, 15[3], 16[2], 17[3], 18[2], 19, 20[4], 21[2], 22, 23
41:1[2], 2, 3[4], 4[2], 5, 6, 7[2], 8[3], 9, 10[3], 11, 12[2], 14, 17[2], 18, 19, 20[3], 21, 23, 24[3], 25, 26[3], 27[3], 28, 29, 30[4], 31[2], 32[2], 33, 34[4], 35[3], 36[5], 37[3], 38, 40, 41, 43[3], 44, 45[2], 46[2], 47[2], 48[8], 49[2], 50[2], 51[2], 52[3], 53[2], 54[3], 55[3], 56[7], 57
42:5[3], 6[5], 7, 9[3], 12[2], 13[3], 15, 16, 18, 19[2], 21, 22, 25, 26, 27, 29, 30[4], 32[2], 33[4], 34, 35, 38[3]
43:1[2], 2, 3, 5, 6, 7[2], 8, 9, 11[3], 12[2], 13, 14, 15, 16, 17[3], 18[3], 19[3], 20, 21[2], 23, 24[2], 25, 26[3], 27, 32[4], 33[3]
44:1[2], 2[4], 3[2], 4[2], 8[2], 11, 12[3], 13, 14, 16[2], 17[2], 22, 24, 26, 28, 29, 30[2], 31[3], 32[2], 33[2], 34[2]
45:2[2], 6[3], 7, 8, 10, 12, 16, 17, 18[4], 19, 20[2], 21[3], 23[2], 24, 25, 26, 27[3]
46:1, 2[2], 3, 5[2], 6, 8[2], 9, 10[2], 11, 12[3], 13, 14, 15[2], 16, 17[2], 18, 19, 20[2], 21, 22[2], 23, 24, 25[2], 26[2], 27[3], 28, 31, 32, 34[2]
47:1[2], 4[4], 6[4], 9[8], 11[4], 13[5], 14[5], 15[4], 17[4], 18[2], 19, 20[4], 21[3], 22[3], 23[2], 24[3], 25, 26[4], 27[2], 28[2], 29, 31
48:2, 3, 5, 6, 7[4], 10, 12, 14[2], 15, 16[5], 17, 18, 21, 22[2]
49:1, 3[3], 8, 9, 10[3], 11[3], 13[2], 15, 16, 17[3], 19, 22, 23, 24[5], 25[5], 26[7], 27[3], 28, 29[3], 30[5], 32[4], 33[2]
50:2[2], 3[2], 4[3], 5, 7[4], 8[2], 10, 11[7], 13[5], 15, 17[4], 19, 23[3], 24, 25

EXODUS

1:1[2], 5[2], 7[2], 9[2], 10, 12[3], 13[2], 14, 15[6], 16[3], 17[3], 18[3], 19[4], 20[2], 21, 22
2:1, 2, 3[3], 5[5], 6[3], 7[2], 8[2], 9[2], 10[2], 12[2], 13[3], 14, 15[2], 16[2], 17, 19[3], 20, 21, 23[4], 25
3:1[6], 2[5], 3, 4[3], 5, 6[4], 7[2], 8[9], 9[4], 10, 11, 12, 13[2], 14, 15[5], 16[3], 17[8], 18[6], 19, 20, 21[2], 22
4:1, 2, 3[2], 4[2], 5[4], 6, 8[4], 9[6], 10, 11[5], 13, 14[3], 16, 19[2], 20[2], 21[2], 22, 24[3], 25, 26, 27[3], 28[3], 29[2], 30[5], 31[3]
5:1[2], 2[2], 3[5], 4[2], 5[2], 6[3], 7, 8[2], 9, 10[3], 12[2], 13, 14[2], 15[2], 16, 17, 18, 19[2], 20, 21[3], 22
6:1, 2, 3, 4[2], 5[3], 6[4], 7[3], 8[3], 9, 10, 11, 12[2], 13[4], 14[4], 15[3], 16[4], 17, 18[3], 19[2], 20[2], 21, 22, 24[3], 25[4], 26[3], 27, 28[3], 29[2], 30
7:1, 2, 3, 4[2], 5[3], 6, 8, 10, 11[3], 13, 14[2], 15[4], 16[3], 17[5], 18[6], 19[3], 20[8], 21[7], 22[2], 24[4], 25[2]
8:1[2], 3[2], 4, 5[5], 6[3], 7[2], 8[4], 9[2], 10, 11[2], 12[2], 13[6], 14, 15, 16[4], 17[5], 18, 19[3], 20[4], 21[3], 22[5], 24[5], 25, 26[5], 27[2], 28[2], 29[4], 30, 31[3], 32
9:1[3], 3[8], 4[4], 5[3], 6[5], 7[4], 8[4], 9[2], 10, 11[5], 12[3], 13[4], 14, 15, 16, 18, 19[3], 20[4], 21[3], 22[4], 23[5], 24[2], 25[6], 26[2], 27, 28, 29[5], 30, 31[5], 32[2], 33[5], 34[3], 35[3]
10:1[2], 2[2], 3[2], 4, 5[6], 6[5], 7[2], 8, 9, 10, 11, 12[6], 13[5], 14[3], 15[11], 16, 17, 18, 19[4], 20[2], 21[2], 22, 23, 24, 25, 26[2], 27
11:1, 2[2], 3[9], 4[2], 5[7], 6, 7[3], 8, 9[2], 10[2]
12:1[2], 2[3], 3[3], 4[5], 5[3], 6[5], 7[4], 8, 9, 10[2], 11, 12[5], 13[5], 14, 15[3], 16[2], 17[2], 18[5], 19[2], 21[2], 22[8], 23[8], 25[2], 27[7], 28[2], 29[8], 30[2], 31[2], 33[3], 34, 35[3], 36[5], 37, 39, 40[2], 41[6], 42[4], 43[3], 46[2], 47, 48[3], 49, 50[2], 51[4]
13:1, 2[3], 3[3], 4, 5[7], 6[2], 8, 9[2], 11[3], 12[4], 13, 14[2], 15[8], 16, 17[5], 18[6], 19[2], 20[2], 21[2], 22[4]
14:1, 2[3], 3[3], 4[2], 5[4], 7, 8[4], 9[3], 10[4], 11, 12[4], 13[4], 14, 15[2], 16[4], 17[2], 18[2], 19[4], 20[6], 21[5], 22[5], 23[3], 24[8], 25[4], 26[4], 27[8], 28[5], 29[4], 30[5], 31[5]
15:1[5], 2, 3[2], 4[2], 5[2], 6, 7, 8[6], 9[2], 10[2], 11, 12, 13, 14[2], 15[3], 16[2], 17[3], 18, 19[8], 20[3], 21[3], 22[3], 23[2], 24, 25[4], 26[4], 27
16:1[6], 2[3], 3[6], 4[2], 5, 6[3], 7[4], 8[6], 9[3], 10[6], 11, 12[4], 13[5], 14[5], 15[3], 16[3], 17, 19, 20, 21, 22[3], 23[5], 24, 25[2], 26[2], 27[2], 28, 29[5], 30[2], 31[3], 32[5], 33, 34[2], 35[3], 36
17:1[6], 2[2], 3[2], 4, 5[4], 6[5], 7[6], 9[3], 10[2], 12[6], 13[2], 14[3], 15, 16[2]
18:1[2], 3[2], 4[4], 5[2], 7, 8[5], 9[4], 10[7], 11[2], 12, 13[5], 14[3], 15, 16, 17, 19[2], 20[2], 21, 22[2], 24, 25, 26[2]
19:1[5], 2[3], 3[4], 4, 5, 6[2], 7[3], 8[5], 9[5], 10[2], 11[5], 12[4], 13[2], 14[3], 15[2], 16[7], 17[4], 18[4], 19[2], 20[6], 21[3], 22[3], 23[3], 24[4], 25
20:2[3], 4[3], 5[5], 7[3], 8, 10[3], 11[5], 12[2], 18[7], 20, 21[2], 22[2]
21:1, 2, 4, 5, 6[3], 7, 9, 19, 22[2], 26[2], 28[3], 29[2], 30, 32[2], 34[4], 35[3], 36[2]
22:3, 4, 5[2], 6[4], 7[2], 8[4], 9[3], 11[2], 12, 14, 15, 17, 20, 21, 24, 26, 28[2], 29[2], 30, 31[2]
23:1, 5, 6, 7[2], 8[4], 9[2], 10, 11[4], 12[3], 13, 14, 15[3], 16[7], 17[2], 18[3], 19[4], 20[2], 23[6], 25[2], 26, 27, 28[3], 29[3], 30, 31[7]
24:1[2], 2[2], 3[7], 4[5], 5[2], 6[3], 7[5], 8[5], 9,

EXODUS

10[2], 11[2], 12[2], 13, 14, 15[2], 16[6], 17[7], 18[4]
25:1, 2, 3, 6, 7[2], 9[4], 10[3], 12[3], 14[5], 15[3], 16[2], 17[2], 18[2], 19[6], 20[5], 21[4], 22[5], 23[3], 25, 26[3], 27[4], 28[2], 29, 30, 31[2], 32[5], 33[3], 34, 35[5], 36, 37[2], 38[2], 40
26:1, 2[3], 3, 4[7], 5[6], 6[2], 7, 8[3], 9[3], 10[6], 11[3], 12[6], 13[7], 14, 15, 16[2], 17[2], 18[3], 19, 20[3], 22[2], 23[3], 24[2], 26[3], 27[7], 28[3], 29[3], 30[3], 32, 33[8], 34[4], 35[9], 36[2], 37
27:1[2], 2[3], 3, 4[2], 5[5], 6, 7[5], 8, 9[4], 10[3], 11[3], 12[3], 13[3], 14[2], 15, 16[2], 17[2], 18[4], 19[6], 20[3], 21[7]
28:1[2], 3[2], 4[2], 6, 7[2], 8[4], 9[2], 10[3], 11[5], 12[5], 14[3], 15[3], 16[2], 17[2], 18, 19, 20, 21[5], 22[2], 23[4], 24[4], 25[5], 26[5], 27[6], 28[8], 29[5], 30[7], 31[2], 32[4], 33[2], 34[2], 35[2], 36[2], 37[3], 38[4], 39[3], 41, 42[2], 43[4]
29:1[2], 3[3], 4[3], 5[8], 6[3], 7, 9[2], 10[4], 11[5], 12[7], 13[7], 14[3], 15[2], 16[2], 17[2], 18[4], 19[3], 20[9], 21[4], 22[10], 23[3], 24[3], 25[3], 26[3], 27[6], 28[4], 29, 30[3], 31[3], 32[7], 33, 34[5], 36, 37[2], 38[2], 39[3], 40[3], 41[5], 42[4], 43[2], 44[4], 45, 46[3]
30:2[5], 3[3], 4[4], 5, 6[5], 7, 8[2], 10[5], 11, 12[3], 13[4], 14, 15[3], 16[7], 17, 18[3], 20[4], 22, 24[2], 25[2], 26[4], 27[3], 28[2], 30, 31, 32, 34, 35[2], 36[3], 37[3]
31:1, 2[3], 3, 6[3], 7[7], 8[3], 9[2], 10[5], 11[2], 12, 13[2], 14, 15[4], 16[3], 17[3], 18
32:1[5], 2[2], 3[2], 4, 5, 6[2], 7[2], 8[2], 9, 11[2], 12[4], 13, 14[2], 15[6], 16[5], 17[3], 18[3], 19[5], 20[4], 22[2], 23[2], 24, 25, 26[4], 27[2], 28[3], 29, 30[3], 31, 33, 34[3], 35[3]
33:1[4], 2[6], 3[2], 4, 5[3], 6[2], 7[9], 8[3], 9[5], 10[4], 11[4], 12, 16[3], 17, 19[2], 21, 22
34:1[4], 2[4], 3[2], 4[4], 5[4], 6[3], 7[7], 8, 10[4], 11[6], 12[3], 14, 15[2], 18[4], 19, 20[2], 21, 22[4], 23[3], 24[3], 25[5], 26[4], 27[2], 28[5], 29[3], 30[2], 31[2], 32[2], 34[3], 35[4]
35:1[4], 2[2], 3, 4[4], 5[2], 8[2], 9[2], 10, 11, 12[5], 13[2], 14[4], 15[7], 16[2], 17[5], 18[4], 19[6], 20[3], 21[5], 22, 24[2], 25, 26, 27[3], 28[3], 29[4], 30[5], 31, 33, 34[2], 35[4]
36:1[4], 2[2], 3[5], 4[3], 5[4], 6[4], 7[2], 8[2], 9[3], 10[2], 11[6], 12[5], 13[2], 14[2], 15[3], 17[6], 18, 19, 20, 21[2], 22[2], 23[2], 24, 25[3], 27[2], 28[3], 29[2], 31[3], 32[6], 33[4], 34[3], 37, 38
37:1[4], 3[3], 5[5], 6[3], 7[2], 8[5], 9[5], 10[4], 12, 13[3], 14[5], 15[2], 16[2], 17[3], 18[5], 19[3], 20, 21[4], 22, 24, 25[6], 26[3], 27[4], 28, 29[4]
38:1[4], 2[4], 3[8], 4[3], 5[3], 6, 7[5], 8[7], 9[4], 10[2], 11[4], 12[3], 13, 14[3], 15[2], 16[2], 17[7], 18[8], 19, 20[3], 21[8], 22[4], 23, 24[8], 25[4], 26[2], 27[6], 28[2], 29[2], 30[8], 31[8]
39:1[4], 2, 3[5], 4, 5[4], 6[2], 7[4], 8[3], 9[3], 10[2], 11, 12, 13, 14[5], 15[2], 16[3], 17[4], 18[5], 19[5], 20[6], 21[8], 22[2], 23[4], 24[2], 25[5], 26[3], 29, 30[4], 31[2], 32[6], 33[2], 34[4], 35[4], 36[3], 37[5], 38[5], 39[2], 40[9], 41[5], 42[3], 43[2]
40:1, 2[5], 3[4], 4[4], 5[7], 6[6], 7[4], 8[3], 9[3], 10[3], 11, 12[3], 13[2], 15, 16, 17[5], 18[3], 19[5], 20[6], 21[7], 22[6], 23[3], 24[6], 25[3], 26[4], 27, 28[3], 29[8], 30[4], 32[4], 33[6], 34[5], 35[6], 36[3], 37[2], 38[5]

LEVITICUS

1:1[3], 2[5], 3[5], 4[2], 5[9], 6, 7[5], 8[7], 9[3], 10[3], 11[5], 12[4], 13[5], 14[2], 15[6], 16[4], 17[6]
2:1, 2[8], 3[4], 4, 7, 8[4], 9[4], 10[3], 11[2], 12[4], 13[2], 14[3], 16[6]
3:1[2], 2[7], 3[7], 4[6], 5[5], 6[2], 7, 8[5], 9[10], 10[6], 11[5], 12, 13[6], 14[5], 15[6], 16[6]
4:1, 2[3], 3[4], 4[8], 5[4], 6[6], 7[15], 8[7], 9[6], 10[5], 11[2], 12[5], 13[6], 14[5], 15[7], 16[4], 17[4], 18[13], 19, 20[3], 21[4], 22[2], 23, 24[5], 25[7], 26[4], 27[3], 28, 29[5], 30[7], 31[7], 33[4], 34[8], 35[10]
5:1, 2, 3, 6[4], 7[2], 8[2], 9[8], 10[3], 11, 12[5], 13[3], 14, 15[6], 16[7], 17[2], 18[3], 19
6:1, 2, 4[2], 5[3], 6[3], 7[2], 8, 9[8], 10[6], 11[2], 12[6], 13[2], 14[5], 15[8], 16[5], 17[2], 18[4], 19, 20[5], 21[3], 22[2], 23, 24, 25[6], 26[5], 27[3], 28, 29[2], 30[5]
7:1[2], 2[5], 3[4], 4[6], 5[3], 6[2], 7[3], 8[4], 9[5], 10, 11[3], 12, 13[2], 14[5], 15[4], 16[4], 17[4], 18[4], 19[2], 20[4], 21[5], 22, 23, 24[3], 25[4], 28, 29[5], 30[6], 31[4], 32[3], 33[5], 34[6], 35[8], 36[3], 37[8], 38[5]
8:1, 2[3], 3[4], 4[5], 5[3], 7[6], 8[4], 9[5], 10[2], 11[3], 12, 13, 14[5], 15[7], 16[6], 17[3], 18[4], 19[2], 20[4], 21[6], 22[4], 23[4], 24[6], 25[8], 26[4], 27, 28[3], 29[4], 30[3], 31[6], 32[2], 33[4], 34, 35[5], 36[2]
9:1[2], 2, 3[3], 4[2], 5[4], 6[4], 7[5], 8[3], 9[8], 10[7], 11[3], 12[3], 13[4], 14[4], 15[5], 16[2], 17[4], 18[5], 19[8], 20[4], 21[3], 22[3], 23[6], 24[5]
10:1[2], 2[2], 3[2], 4[4], 5, 6[4], 7[6], 8, 9[2], 11[4], 12[4], 13[3], 14[3], 15[6], 16[3], 17[5], 18[3], 19[4]
11:1, 2[4], 3[3], 4[5], 5[3], 6[3], 7[3], 9[4], 10[4], 12, 13[4], 14[2], 16[4], 17[3], 18[3], 19[4], 21, 22[4], 24[2], 25[2], 26[3], 27, 28[2], 29[5], 30[5], 31, 32, 38, 39[2], 40[4], 41, 42[2], 44[2], 45[2], 46[5], 47[4]
12:1, 2[3], 3[2], 4[3], 5, 6[6], 7[3], 8[4]

LEVITICUS

13:1, 2[5], 3[9], 4[6], 5[6], 6[6], 7[4], 8[4], 9[2], 10[5], 11[2], 12[5], 13[3], 15[3], 16[2], 17[4], 18[2], 19[3], 20[5], 21[3], 22[2], 23[2], 24[2], 25[7], 26[4], 27[5], 28[5], 29[2], 30[5], 31[7], 32[6], 33[3], 34[7], 35[2], 36[4], 37[3], 38, 39[4], 40, 41, 42, 43[6], 44, 45[2], 46[3], 47[2], 48, 49[6], 50[3], 51[7], 52[2], 53[5], 54[3], 55[5], 56[7], 57[4], 58[3], 59[3]
14:1, 2[4], 3[5], 4, 5[2], 6[8], 7[3], 8, 9, 10[2], 11[6], 12[3], 13[8], 14[8], 15[3], 16[4], 17[9], 18[6], 19[3], 20[5], 22[2], 23[6], 24[6], 25[9], 26[3], 27[3], 28[9], 29[5], 30[3], 31[5], 32[2], 33, 34[3], 35[3], 36[7], 37[5], 38[5], 39[5], 40[4], 41[3], 42[2], 43[4], 44[4], 45[6], 46[3], 47[2], 48[7], 49, 50[2], 51[8], 52[8], 53[4], 54, 55, 57
15:1, 2, 4, 5, 6[2], 7[3], 8[2], 9, 10[2], 11[2], 12[2], 14[6], 15[5], 16, 17[2], 18[2], 19, 21, 22, 23, 24, 25[5], 26[3], 27, 29[5], 30[6], 31, 32, 33[2]
16:1[4], 2[7], 3, 4[3], 5[3], 6, 7[5], 8[4], 9[2], 10[5], 11[4], 12[3], 13[7], 14[5], 15[8], 16[6], 17[4], 18[8], 19[3], 20[5], 21[8], 22[3], 23[4], 24[4], 25[3], 26[3], 27[7], 28, 29[3], 30[2], 32[5], 33[7], 34[2]
17:1, 2[3], 3[3], 4[6], 5[9], 6[9], 8[2], 9[4], 10[2], 11[6], 12, 13[3], 14[7], 15
18:1, 2[2], 3[4], 4, 5, 6, 7[2], 8, 9[2], 10, 11, 12, 13, 14, 15, 16, 17, 18, 21[3], 24, 25[3], 27[3], 28[2], 29, 30
19:1, 2[3], 3, 4, 5, 6[4], 7, 8[2], 9[3], 10[2], 12[2], 13[2], 14[3], 15[4], 16[2], 18[2], 21[4], 22[5], 23[2], 24[3], 25[4], 26, 27[2], 28[2], 29[2], 30, 31, 32[4], 34[3], 36[2], 37
20:1, 2[5], 4[3], 6, 7, 8, 10[3], 11, 15, 16[2], 17, 18, 19, 22, 23[2], 24, 25, 26
21:1[4], 5, 6[4], 8[2], 9[2], 10[3], 12[5], 15, 16, 17, 21[5], 22[3], 23[3], 24
22:1, 2[3], 3[4], 4[3], 6[2], 7[2], 8, 9, 10[3], 11, 12[2], 13, 14[4], 15[3], 16[2], 17, 18[4], 19[3], 21, 22[3], 24, 25, 26, 27[3], 29, 30[3], 31, 32[2], 33[2]
23:1, 2[3], 3[4], 4[2], 5[3], 6[4], 7, 8[2], 9, 10[5], 11[5], 12[3], 13[4], 14, 15[5], 16[3], 17[2], 18[4], 19[2], 20[7], 21, 22[5], 23, 24[4], 25, 26, 27[2], 28, 30, 32[2], 33, 34[4], 35, 36[3], 37[3], 38[3], 39[7], 40[5], 41[3], 43[3], 44[3]
24:1, 2[3], 3[7], 4[3], 6[2], 7[2], 8[2], 9[3], 10[4], 11[5], 12[2], 13, 14[2], 15, 16[7], 22[2], 23[4]
25:1, 2[4], 3, 4[3], 5[2], 6[2], 7[2], 8[2], 9[6], 10[3], 11, 12[3], 13, 15[4], 16[7], 17, 18, 19, 20, 21, 22[3], 23[2], 24[2], 26, 27[4], 28[3], 30[4], 31[5], 32[5], 33[8], 34[2], 38[3], 40, 41, 42, 44, 45[2], 46, 47[3], 50[5], 51[2], 52[2], 53, 54, 55[3]
26:1, 2, 4[3], 5[4], 6[3], 7, 8, 10[2], 13[3], 16[2], 19, 20[2], 25[4], 26, 29[2], 30, 31, 32, 33, 34[2], 36[2], 38[2], 39, 40, 41[2], 42, 43[2], 44[2], 45[5], 46[4]
27:1, 2[3], 3[3], 5[2], 6[2], 7, 8[3], 9[2], 10, 11[3], 12[2], 14[3], 15[2], 16[2], 17, 18[6], 19[3], 20[2], 21[5], 22[2], 23[5], 24[5], 25[3], 26[4], 28[3], 30[8], 31, 32[6], 33, 34[3]

NUMBERS

1:1[8], 2[5], 4, 5[4], 6, 7, 8, 9, 10[3], 11, 12, 13, 14, 15, 16[3], 18[6], 19[2], 20[4], 21, 22[4], 23, 24[4], 25, 26[4], 27, 28[4], 29, 30[4], 31, 32[5], 33, 34[4], 35, 36[4], 37, 38[4], 39, 40[4], 41, 42[4], 43, 44[2], 45[2], 47[2], 48, 49[3], 50[6], 51[5], 52, 53[7], 54[2]
2:1, 2[4], 3[7], 5[3], 7[3], 9, 10[6], 12[4], 14[4], 16[2], 17[6], 18[6], 20[4], 22[4], 24[2], 25[6], 27[4], 29[4], 31, 32[3], 33[3], 34[3]
3:1[3], 2[3], 3[4], 4[5], 5, 6[2], 7[6], 8[7], 9[2], 10, 11, 12[6], 13[6], 14[2], 15[2], 16[2], 17, 18[2], 19, 20[4], 21[6], 22[2], 23[3], 24[5], 25[11], 26[9], 27[10], 28[4], 29[4], 30[6], 31[8], 32[7], 33[5], 34[2], 35[7], 36[8], 37[2], 38[9], 39[4], 40[5], 41[9], 42[3], 43[2], 44, 45[7], 46[4], 47[4], 48[2], 49[2], 50[5], 51[4]
4:1, 2[4], 3[4], 4[5], 5[3], 6[2], 7[5], 8[2], 9[3], 10, 11[2], 12[2], 13[2], 14[8], 15[9], 16[12], 17, 18[4], 19, 20, 21, 22[3], 23[4], 24[3], 25[10], 26[9], 27[4], 28[8], 29[2], 30[4], 31[7], 32[4], 33[8], 34[5], 35[4], 37[7], 38[2], 39[4], 40, 41[6], 42[3], 43[4], 45[5], 46[3], 47[6], 49[4]
5:1, 2[3], 3[2], 4[4], 5, 6[2], 7[2], 8[7], 9[3], 10, 11, 12, 13[2], 14[2], 15[3], 16[2], 17[6], 18[9], 19[3], 21[6], 22[2], 23[2], 24[5], 25[6], 26[6], 27[4], 28, 29, 30[4], 31
6:1, 2[2], 4[4], 5[7], 6[2], 7, 8[2], 9[3], 10[5], 11[4], 12[4], 13[6], 14[3], 16[2], 17[4], 18[10], 19[7], 20[5], 21[5], 22, 23, 24, 25, 26, 27
7:1[5], 2[4], 3[3], 4, 5[4], 6[3], 7, 8[4], 9[3], 10[5], 11[3], 12[3], 13[3], 15, 16, 17[3], 18[2], 19[3], 21, 22, 23[3], 24[3], 25[3], 27, 28, 29[3], 30[3], 31[3], 33, 34, 35[3], 36[3], 37[3], 39, 40, 41[3], 42[3], 43[3], 45, 46, 47[3], 48[3], 49[3], 51, 52, 53[3], 54[3], 55[3], 57, 58, 59[3], 60[3], 61[3], 63, 64, 65[3], 66[3], 67[3], 69, 70, 71[3], 72[3], 73[3], 75, 76, 77[3], 78[3], 79[3], 81, 82, 83[3], 84[4], 85[3], 86[5], 87[7], 88[9], 89[6]
8:1, 2[3], 3[3], 4[6], 5, 6[2], 9[5], 10[4], 11[5], 12[7], 13[2], 14[3], 15[4], 16[3], 17[4], 18[3], 19[10], 20[6], 21[2], 22[5], 23, 24[4], 25[2], 26[4]

NUMBERS

9:1[5], 2[2], 3[3], 4[2], 5[6], 6[2], 7[3], 8, 9, 10[3], 11[2], 12[3], 13[5], 14[7], 15[9], 16[2], 17[6], 18[7], 19[5], 20[6], 21[5], 22[3], 23[10]
10:1, 2[4], 3[4], 4[2], 5[2], 6[3], 7, 8[3], 9[3], 10[5], 11[6], 12[4], 13[3], 14[5], 15[4], 16[4], 17[4], 18[3], 19[4], 20[4], 21[4], 22[4], 23[4], 24[4], 25[6], 26[4], 27[4], 28[2], 29[5], 31, 32[2], 33[6], 34[3], 35, 36
11:1[7], 2[3], 3[4], 4[2], 5[6], 7[3], 8[3], 9[4], 10[4], 11[2], 12[2], 16[6], 17[3], 18[4], 20, 21, 22[4], 23[2], 24[7], 25[4], 26[9], 27, 28[2], 29[2], 30[2], 31[7], 32[4], 33[6], 34[2], 35
12:1, 2[2], 3[4], 4[3], 5[5], 6, 8[2], 9[2], 10[2], 11, 12, 13, 14[2], 15[2], 16[2]
13:1, 2[2], 3[4], 4[2], 5[2], 6[2], 7[2], 8[2], 9[2], 10[2], 11[3], 12[2], 13[2], 14[2], 15[2], 16[4], 17[2], 18[2], 19, 20[6], 21[2], 22[2], 23[3], 24[4], 25, 26[6], 27[2], 28[4], 29[10], 30, 31[2], 32[5], 33[3]
14:1[2], 2[3], 3[2], 5[3], 6[3], 7[3], 8, 9[4], 10[6], 11[2], 12, 13[2], 14, 15[2], 16[3], 17, 18[6], 19[2], 20, 21[3], 22, 23, 24, 25[6], 26, 27[2], 28, 30[3], 31, 33[2], 34[3], 35, 36[4], 37[4], 38[4], 39[2], 40[5], 41[2], 42, 43[5], 44[5], 45[2]
15:1, 2[2], 3[4], 4[2], 5[2], 6, 7[2], 8, 10, 12, 13[2], 14, 15[4], 16, 17, 18[2], 19[3], 20[3], 21[2], 22, 23[4], 24[6], 25[5], 26[4], 27, 28[3], 29[2], 30[4], 31[2], 32[3], 33, 35[4], 36[3], 37, 38[4], 39[2], 41[3]
16:1[5], 2[3], 3[4], 5, 7[3], 9[6], 10[2], 11, 12, 13, 14, 15, 16, 17, 18[3], 19[7], 20, 22[3], 23, 24[2], 25, 26[2], 27[2], 28, 29[3], 30[4], 31, 32[2], 33[3], 34[2], 35[2], 36, 37[5], 38[4], 39[3], 40[5], 41[5], 42[6], 43[2], 44, 46[4], 47[5], 48[3], 49[2], 50[4]
17:1, 2[3], 3[3], 4[3], 5[3], 6[2], 7[3], 8[4], 9[3], 10[3], 11, 12, 13[2]
18:1[4], 2[3], 3[5], 4[5], 5[5], 6[6], 7[3], 8[5], 9[2], 10, 11[3], 12[7], 13[2], 15[4], 16[3], 17[5], 18[3], 19[5], 20[2], 21[5], 22[3], 23[5], 24[5], 25, 26[5], 27[4], 28[4], 29[3], 30[6], 31[2], 32[3]
19:1, 2[4], 3[2], 4[3], 5, 6[4], 7[4], 8, 9[5], 10[5], 11, 12[4], 13[4], 14[3], 16, 17[2], 18[4], 19[5], 20[5], 21[2], 22[2]
20:1[5], 2, 3[2], 4[2], 6[7], 7, 8[5], 9[2], 10[2], 11[3], 12[4], 13[3], 14[2], 15, 16[2], 17[7], 18, 19[2], 22[2], 23[3], 24[3], 27[3], 28[3], 29[2]
21:1[4], 2, 3[5], 4[6], 5[2], 6[3], 7[5], 8, 9, 10, 11[2], 12, 13[6], 14[5], 15[4], 16[3], 18[7], 20[3], 21, 22[5], 23, 24[5], 25[3], 26[4], 27, 28[3], 29, 31[2], 32[2], 33[3], 34[2]
22:1[2], 2[2], 3[2], 4[6], 5[6], 6, 7[4], 8[2], 10, 11[2], 12, 13[3], 14, 16, 18[3], 19, 20[2], 21[2], 22[3], 23[9], 24[3], 25[5], 26[4], 27[4], 28[3], 29, 30, 31[5], 32[2], 33, 34[3], 35[5], 36[2], 38, 40, 41[4]
23:3, 5, 6, 7[3], 8, 9[5], 10[5], 12, 13, 14[2], 15, 16, 17[2], 19, 21[2], 22, 24[4], 26, 28
24:1[2], 2, 3[2], 4[3], 6[5], 7, 8[2], 11, 13[3], 14, 15[2], 16[5], 17[2], 19, 20[2], 21, 22, 24
25:1[2], 2[3], 3[2], 4[7], 5, 6[8], 7[4], 8[6], 9, 10, 11[5], 13[2], 14[5], 15[3], 16, 17, 18[5]
26:1[4], 2[3], 3[2], 4[5], 5[6], 6[4], 7[2], 8, 9[4], 10[2], 11, 12[7], 13[4], 14[2], 15[7], 16[4], 17[4], 18[2], 19[2], 20[7], 21[5], 22, 23[5], 24[4], 25, 26[7], 27[2], 28, 29[5], 30[5], 31[4], 32[4], 33[3], 34, 35[7], 36[3], 37[3], 38[7], 39[4], 40[5], 41, 42[4], 43[2], 44[7], 45[5], 46[2], 47[2], 48[5], 49[4], 50, 51[2], 52, 53[2], 54[2], 55[3], 56[2], 57[7], 58[12], 59[2], 61, 62[2], 63[3], 64[3], 65[4]
27:1[8], 2[6], 3[4], 4[2], 5, 6, 7[2], 8, 11[2], 12[3], 14[6], 15, 16[4], 17[2], 18[3], 19[2], 20[2], 21[5], 22[3], 23[2]
28:1, 2, 3[3], 4[3], 5, 6, 7[6], 8[5], 9[3], 10[2], 11[3], 13, 14[4], 15[3], 16[4], 17[2], 18, 19[2], 21, 23[2], 24[5], 25, 26[3], 27[3], 29, 30, 31
29:1[4], 2[2], 4, 5, 6[4], 7, 8[2], 10, 11[4], 12[3], 13[2], 14[2], 15, 16[2], 17[2], 18[4], 19[3], 20[2], 21[4], 22, 23[2], 24[4], 25[2], 26[2], 27[4], 28, 29[2], 30[4], 31, 32[2], 33[4], 34, 35, 36[2], 37[4], 38, 39, 40[2]
30:1[5], 2, 3, 5[2], 7, 8[2], 12[3], 13, 14, 16[3]
31:1, 2[2], 3[4], 4[2], 5, 6[8], 7[3], 8[4], 9[3], 11[2], 12[8], 13[4], 14[4], 15, 16[6], 17, 18, 19[3], 21[6], 22[6], 23[5], 24[2], 25, 26[5], 27[3], 28[6], 29[2], 30[9], 31[2], 32[4], 36[2], 37[2], 38[2], 39[2], 40[2], 41[4], 42[2], 43[2], 47[6], 48[3], 49[2], 50[2], 51[2], 52[5], 53, 54[7]
32:1[5], 2[5], 4[3], 6[2], 7[4], 8, 9[6], 10[2], 11[2], 12[4], 13[5], 14[2], 15, 17[4], 18, 20, 21, 22[4], 23, 25[2], 26, 27, 28[5], 29[5], 30, 31[3], 32[3], 33[12], 34, 37, 38, 39[3], 40, 41[2], 42
33:1[4], 2[2], 3[8], 4[3], 5, 6[2], 8[4], 10, 11[2], 12, 14, 15, 16, 36, 37[2], 38[8], 40[5], 44, 47, 48[2], 49, 50[2], 51[2], 52[2], 53[3], 54[7], 55[3]
34:1, 2[5], 3[4], 4[4], 5[4], 6[2], 7, 8[3], 9[2], 11[5], 12[4], 13[5], 14[7], 15[3], 16, 17[5], 18, 19[4], 20[3], 21[2], 22[4], 23[5], 24[4], 25[4], 26[4], 27[4], 28[4], 29[4]
35:1[2], 2[5], 3[2], 4[5], 5[9], 6[3], 7[2], 8[4], 9, 10[2], 11, 12[3], 14, 15[3], 16, 17, 18, 19[2], 21[2], 24[3], 25[9], 26[3], 27[5], 28[7], 30[2], 31, 32[4], 33[5], 34[3]

NUMBERS

36:1[10], 2[5], 3[7], 4[6], 5[5], 6[5], 7[5], 8[5], 9[3], 10[2], 11, 12[5], 13[6]

DEUTERONOMY

1:1[4], 2, 3[6], 4[3], 5, 6, 7[12], 8[3], 10[2], 11, 14, 15, 16[2], 17[5], 18, 19[4], 20[3], 21[3], 22, 23, 24[2], 25[3], 26[2], 27[4], 28[4], 30, 31[3], 32, 33, 34[2], 36[3], 37, 38, 40[3], 41[3], 42, 43[3], 44, 45[2], 46
2:1[4], 2, 4[3], 7[3], 8[5], 9[3], 10[2], 11[2], 12[4], 13[2], 14[6], 15[3], 16[2], 17, 18, 19[4], 20, 21[2], 22[2], 23[2], 24[2], 25[4], 26, 27[3], 29[4], 30, 31, 33, 34[3], 35[3], 36[5], 37[6]
3:1[2], 2[2], 3[2], 4[2], 6, 7[3], 8[5], 9[2], 10[3], 11[5], 12[4], 13[5], 14[3], 16[8], 17[5], 18[3], 20[3], 21[3], 22, 23, 25, 26[2], 27, 28, 29
4:1[4], 2[3], 3[3], 4, 5[2], 6[2], 7, 9[2], 10[6], 11[3], 12[5], 14[2], 15[4], 16[2], 17[4], 18[5], 19[6], 20[2], 21[2], 23[4], 24, 25[4], 26, 27[4], 28, 29, 30[2], 31[2], 32[5], 33[3], 34[2], 35, 36[2], 39[2], 40[2], 41, 42, 43[5], 44[2], 45[4], 46[4], 47[3], 48[2], 49[4]
5:1, 2, 3, 4[4], 5[5], 6[3], 8[3], 9[5], 11[3], 12[2], 14[3], 15[4], 16[3], 22[6], 23[5], 24[3], 25[2], 26[4], 27[2], 28[5], 31[4], 32[3], 33[3]
6:1[5], 2[2], 3[2], 4, 5, 7, 9, 10[2], 12[3], 13, 14[2], 15[5], 16, 17[2], 18[4], 19, 20[4], 21, 22, 23, 24[2], 25
7:1[9], 2, 4[2], 6[4], 7[2], 8[5], 9[2], 11[3], 12[3], 13[5], 15[2], 16[2], 18, 19[8], 20[2], 21, 22[3], 23, 25[3]
8:1[3], 2[3], 3[2], 5, 6[2], 7, 10[2], 11, 14[3], 15, 16, 17, 18, 19, 20[4]
9:2[3], 3[2], 4[4], 5[5], 6, 7[5], 8[2], 9[6], 10[9], 11[5], 12[2], 13, 15[4], 16[3], 17, 18[4], 19[3], 20[2], 21[4], 22, 23[4], 24[2], 25[3], 26, 27, 28[4]
10:1[3], 2[4], 3[3], 4[10], 5[4], 6[3], 8[6], 9[2], 10[4], 11[3], 12[3], 13[2], 14[4], 15, 16, 17, 18[3], 19[2], 20, 22[2]
11:1, 2[2], 3[2], 4[4], 5, 6[5], 7[2], 8[2], 9[2], 10[2], 11[2], 12[7], 13, 14[3], 17[5], 19, 20, 21[5], 22, 23, 24[5], 25[4], 27[2], 28[3], 29[4], 30[7], 31[2], 32
12:1[5], 2[4], 3[2], 4, 5[2], 6, 7[2], 8, 9[3], 10[2], 11[3], 12[2], 14[2], 15[6], 16[2], 17[2], 18[5], 19[2], 20, 21[3], 22[4], 23[5], 24, 25[2], 26[2], 27[8], 28[2], 29[2], 31[3]
13:2[2], 3[3], 4, 5[7], 6[2], 7[6], 9[2], 10[3], 12, 13[2], 14, 15[6], 16[6], 17[3], 18[4]
14:1[3], 2[4], 4[4], 5[7], 6[4], 7[7], 8[3], 9, 12[3], 13[3], 15[4], 16[3], 17[3], 18[4], 21[2], 22[2], 23[5], 24[4], 25[3], 26, 27, 28[3], 29[6]
15:1, 2[3], 4[3], 5[2], 6, 7, 9[3], 10, 11[2], 12, 14, 15[2], 17, 18, 19[4], 20[3], 21, 22[4], 23[2]
16:1[5], 2[6], 3[5], 4[3], 5[2], 6[6], 7[3], 8[2], 9[3], 10[4], 11[7], 13, 14[4], 15[5], 16[6], 17[2], 18[2], 19[4], 20[2], 21[2], 22
17:1[2], 2[3], 3[2], 4, 6[2], 7[5], 8[2], 9[4], 10[2], 11[6], 12[5], 13, 14[3], 15, 16[3], 18[3], 19[3], 20[5]
18:1[5], 2, 3[6], 4[3], 5[3], 6[3], 7[4], 8, 9[3], 10, 12[2], 13, 14, 15[2], 16[5], 17, 20[2], 21[2], 22[6]
19:1[3], 2[2], 3[2], 4[2], 5[5], 6[4], 8[2], 9, 10, 12[3], 13, 14[2], 15[3], 17[5], 18[2], 19
20:1[2], 2[3], 4, 5[3], 6, 7, 8[2], 9[4], 11, 13[3], 14[7], 15[2], 16[2], 17[7], 18, 19[4], 20[2]
21:1[3], 2, 3[4], 4[4], 5[5], 6[4], 8, 9[3], 10, 11, 13, 15[3], 16[5], 17[6], 18[2], 19[2], 20, 21, 23[2]
22:4, 5[2], 6[7], 7[2], 9[2], 12, 15[7], 16[2], 17[4], 18, 19[2], 20[2], 21[4], 22[3], 23, 24[4], 25[3], 26[2], 27[2], 29[2]
23:1[3], 2[4], 3[4], 4[2], 5[4], 8[3], 9, 10[2], 11[2], 12, 14[2], 15, 17[2], 18[5], 20[2], 21[2], 23, 25[2]
24:3[2], 4[3], 6[2], 7, 8[3], 9[2], 11[2], 12, 13[3], 15[2], 16[4], 17[3], 18, 19[6], 20[4], 21[4], 22
25:1[3], 2[2], 4[2], 5[3], 6[2], 7[4], 8, 9[2], 10, 11[4], 15[2], 16, 17, 18[2], 19[4]
26:1[2], 2[6], 3[4], 4[4], 5, 6, 7[2], 8, 10[4], 11[3], 12[7], 13[6], 14[3], 15, 16, 17, 18, 19
27:1[3], 2[3], 3[4], 5, 6[3], 7, 8[2], 9[4], 10[2], 11[2], 12, 14[2], 15[6], 16, 17, 18[3], 19[3], 20, 21, 22[3], 23, 24, 25, 26[2]
28:1[4], 2[2], 3[2], 4[5], 7, 8[4], 9[3], 10[3], 11[6], 12[4], 13[5], 14[3], 15[2], 16[2], 18[4], 20[2], 21[3], 22[2], 23, 24[2], 25[3], 26[3], 27[5], 28, 29, 30, 32, 33, 34, 35[5], 36, 37, 38[2], 39[3], 40, 42, 43, 44[2], 45[2], 47[2], 48, 49[4], 50[3], 51[3], 52, 53[5], 54[3], 55[3], 56[4], 57, 58[2], 59[2], 60, 61[2], 62[3], 63[3], 64[4], 65[2], 67[3], 68[2]
29:1[6], 2[2], 3[2], 4, 5, 6, 7[2], 8[3], 9, 10[2], 11[2], 12[2], 15, 16[2], 18[2], 19[2], 20[5], 21[5], 22[5], 23[3], 24[2], 25[3], 27[3], 28, 29[3]
30:1[4], 2, 3[3], 4[2], 5[2], 6[3], 7, 8[2], 9[5], 10[4], 13[2], 14, 16[3], 18, 20[4]
31:2, 3[2], 4[3], 5[2], 6, 7[3], 8, 9[6], 10[4], 11[2], 12[3], 13[2], 14[5], 15[6], 16[4], 18, 19[2], 20, 21[2], 22[2], 23[3], 24, 25[4], 26[5], 27, 28, 29[5], 30[3]
32:1, 2[6], 3[2], 4, 5, 6, 7[2], 8[7], 9[2], 10[2], 12, 13[6], 14[4], 15, 18, 19[2], 22[4], 24[3], 25[5], 26, 27[3], 30, 32[2], 33[2], 35[2], 36, 38[2], 42[5], 43, 44[4], 46[2], 47, 48, 49[3], 50, 51[5], 52[3]
33:1[3], 2, 3, 4[2], 5[3], 7[2], 8, 11[2], 12[4], 13[4], 14[4], 15[4], 16[8], 17[7], 19[5], 20[3], 21[6], 23[4], 26[3], 27[3], 28, 29[3]
34:1[5], 2[3], 3[4], 4[2], 5[5], 6, 8[3], 9[4], 10, 11[4], 12[2]

JOSHUA

1:1[5], 2[2], 3, 4[8], 5, 6, 7[3], 8, 9, 10[2], 11[4], 12[3], 13[4], 14[2], 15[6], 17
2:1[2], 2[3], 3[3], 4[2], 5[4], 6[4], 7[4], 8, 9[5], 10[6], 11, 12, 14[3], 15[3], 16[3], 17, 18[2], 19[3], 21[2], 22[4], 23[3], 24[4]
3:1[2], 2[2], 3[6], 4, 5[2], 6[7], 7[2], 8[5], 9[3], 10[8], 11[4], 12, 13[10], 14[5], 15[7], 16[6], 17[7]
4:1[2], 2, 3[4], 4[2], 5[6], 7[6], 8[7], 9[6], 10[6], 11[6], 12[4], 13[2], 14[3], 15, 16[3], 17, 18[9], 19[4], 21, 23[4], 24[5]
5:1[10], 2[3], 3[3], 4[5], 5[4], 6[8], 7, 8[2], 9[4], 10[5], 11[5], 12[7], 14[3], 15[3]
6:1, 2[3], 3[2], 4[5], 5[7], 6[6], 7[4], 8[8], 9[7], 10[2], 11[5], 12[4], 13[9], 14[3], 15[6], 16[6], 17[5], 18[3], 19[4], 20[11], 21[3], 22[4], 23[2], 24[7], 25[2], 26[4], 27[2]
7:1[10], 2[3], 3[2], 4[2], 5[5], 6[5], 7[3], 9[4], 10, 11, 12[2], 13[4], 14[8], 15[3], 16[2], 17[5], 18[4], 19, 20, 21[4], 22[2], 23[4], 24[5], 25, 26[4]
8:1[3], 2[3], 3, 4[3], 5[3], 6[2], 7[3], 8[4], 9[2], 10[4], 11[4], 12[2], 13[8], 14[5], 15[2], 16[2], 17, 18[4], 19[3], 20[6], 21[5], 22[3], 23, 24[8], 25, 26[2], 27[4], 29[6], 30, 31[6], 32[4], 33[10], 34[5], 35[4]
9:1[11], 3, 5, 6[2], 7[2], 9[3], 10[2], 11[2], 12, 13, 14[3], 15[2], 16, 17[2], 18[6], 19[3], 20, 21[3], 23, 24[4], 26[2], 27[4]
10:1, 2[2], 4, 5[7], 6[5], 7[2], 8, 10[2], 11[4], 12[7], 13[6], 14[3], 15, 17, 18[2], 19[2], 20[2], 21[3], 22[3], 23[6], 24[5], 25, 26[2], 27[6], 28[6], 30[8], 32[6], 35[3], 37[6], 39[6], 40[6], 41, 42, 43
11:1[2], 2[7], 3[10], 4[2], 5, 6, 7[2], 8[3], 9, 10[3], 11[3], 12[6], 13, 14[5], 15[2], 16[8], 17[2], 19[3], 20[2], 21[4], 22[3], 23[3]
12:1[9], 2[8], 3[9], 4[3], 5[4], 6[8], 7[7], 8[12], 9[2], 10[2], 11[2], 12[2], 13[2], 14[2], 15[2], 16[2], 17[2], 18[2], 19[2], 20[2], 21[2], 22[2], 23[4], 24[2]
13:1, 2[3], 3[9], 4[6], 5[4], 6[5], 7[2], 8[4], 9[6], 10[4], 11[2], 12[3], 13[6], 14[3], 15[2], 16[6], 17, 19[2], 21[6], 22[4], 23[7], 24[2], 25[3], 26, 27[6], 28[3], 29[4], 30[2], 31[5], 32[3], 33[2]
14:1[9], 2[4], 3[3], 4[3], 5[3], 6[6], 7[3], 8[3], 9[2], 10[4], 11, 12[5], 13, 14[4], 15[3]
15:1[7], 2[3], 3[2], 4[3], 5[7], 6[5], 7[8], 8[13], 9[7], 10[3], 11[6], 12[5], 13[6], 14[2], 15[2], 17[2], 19[2], 20[3], 21[4], 32, 33, 46, 47[3], 48, 61, 62, 63[5]
16:1[5], 2, 3[5], 4, 5[5], 6[5], 8[7], 9[5], 10[3]
17:1[4], 2[10], 3[5], 4[7], 5[2], 6[3], 7[4], 8[3], 9[9], 10[3], 11[4], 12[3], 13[2], 14[2], 15[4], 16[6], 17, 18[3]
18:1[5], 2, 3[3], 4[2], 5[3], 6[3], 7[7], 8[4], 9[3], 10[3], 11[6], 12[7], 13[6], 14[7], 15[5], 16[11], 17[4], 18, 19[8], 20[5], 21[4], 28[2]
19:1[5], 8[5], 9[8], 10[3], 11[2], 12[2], 13, 14[4], 16[2], 17[2], 22[2], 23[4], 24[3], 27[4], 29[6], 31[3], 32[3], 33, 34[4], 35, 39[4], 40[3], 41, 46, 47[6], 48[3], 49[3], 50[4], 51[12]
20:1, 2[2], 3[2], 4[6], 5[2], 6[5], 7, 8[6], 9[6]
21:1[9], 2[4], 3[4], 4[9], 5[6], 6[6], 7[4], 8[4], 9[4], 10[5], 11[4], 12[4], 13[3], 17, 19[3], 20[6], 21, 23, 25, 26[3], 27[5], 28, 30, 32[2], 33[2], 34[5], 36, 38[2], 40[4], 41[4], 43[2], 44[2], 45[2]
22:1[3], 2[2], 3[3], 4[5], 5[5], 7[3], 8, 9[10], 10[5], 11[8], 12[3], 13[7], 14[3], 15[4], 16[5], 17[3], 18[3], 19[8], 20[3], 21[5], 22[3], 23[2], 24, 25[3], 27[3], 28[3], 29[4], 30[8], 31[10], 32[8], 33[5], 34[4]
23:1, 3[2], 4[2], 5[2], 6[4], 7, 8, 9, 10, 11, 12, 13[2], 14[4], 15[3], 16[5]
24:1[2], 2[6], 3[3], 6[3], 7[4], 8[3], 9[2], 11[8], 12[3], 13, 14[5], 15[7], 16[2], 17[5], 18[5], 19[2], 20, 21[2], 22[2], 23[2], 24[2], 25, 26[4], 27[3], 28, 29[3], 30[3], 31[6], 32[6], 33

JUDGES

1:1[4], 2[2], 3, 4[3], 5[2], 8[4], 9[5], 10[2], 11[2], 13, 15[2], 16[7], 17[3], 18[3], 19[5], 20, 21[4], 22[2], 23[3], 24[4], 25[6], 26[5], 27[5], 28, 29[2], 30[3], 31[2], 32[4], 33[6], 34[4], 35[3], 36[4]
2:1[2], 2, 4[4], 5[2], 6[3], 7[7], 8[3], 9[4], 10[2], 11[3], 12[5], 13, 14[4], 15[4], 16[2], 17[3], 18[7], 19, 20[2], 21, 22[2], 23[2]
3:1[3], 2[3], 3[5], 4[3], 5[2], 7[5], 8[4], 9[5], 10[3], 11[2], 12[7], 13[2], 14[2], 15[6], 17, 18[3], 19, 21, 22[6], 23[3], 24[2], 25[3], 26, 27[3], 28[3], 30[2], 31[2]
4:1[3], 2[4], 3[3], 4, 5[2], 6[4], 7[2], 9[3], 11[5], 12, 13[3], 14[3], 15[3], 16[6], 17[6], 18, 20[2], 21[3], 22[2], 23[2], 24[3]
5:1, 2[3], 3[2], 4[4], 5[3], 6[5], 7[2], 8, 9[3], 10, 11[9], 13[4], 14[2], 15[3], 16[4], 17, 18[3], 19[3], 20, 21[2], 22[4], 23[8], 24[3], 26[3], 28[3], 30[3], 31[2]
6:1[5], 2[5], 3[4], 4[2], 5, 6[3], 7[3], 8[4], 9[3], 10[3], 11[4], 12[3], 13[5], 14[3], 15, 16[2], 19[3], 20[4], 21[11], 22[2], 23, 24[2], 25[5], 26[6], 27[3], 28[7], 29, 30[4], 33[5], 34[2], 37[4], 38[4], 39[3], 40[2]
7:1[7], 2[3], 3[3], 4[5], 5[4], 6[3], 7[4], 8[4], 9[3], 10, 11[4], 12[7], 13[2], 14[3], 15[6], 16[2], 17[2], 18[4], 19[8], 20[7], 21[2], 22[6], 23[2], 24[4], 25[5]
8:1[2], 2[3], 3, 4, 5[2], 6[2], 7[3], 8[2], 9, 10[3], 11[4], 12[2], 13[2], 14[3], 15[2], 16[4], 17[3], 18, 19[2], 20, 21[2], 22[2], 23, 24, 25, 26[4], 28[3], 29, 32[3], 33, 34[3], 35[2]

JUDGES

9:1[3], 2[3], 3[2], 4, 5[2], 6[4], 7, 8[2], 9[2], 10[2], 11[2], 12[2], 13[2], 14[2], 15[4], 16, 17, 18[2], 20[4], 23[2], 24[4], 25[3], 26[2], 27[3], 28[4], 30[4], 31[2], 32[2], 33[4], 34, 35[5], 36[5], 37[3], 38, 39, 40[2], 42[3], 43[4], 44[7], 45[4], 46[4], 47[2], 48[3], 49[5], 51[5], 52[3], 54, 55, 56, 57[4]
10:1[2], 4, 6[11], 7[6], 8[5], 9[2], 10[2], 11[6], 12[3], 14[2], 15[2], 16[3], 17[2], 18[3]
11:1[2], 2, 3, 4, 5[3], 6, 7, 8[3], 9[3], 10[2], 11[3], 12[2], 13[3], 14[2], 15[3], 16[2], 17[3], 18[8], 19[2], 21[5], 22[3], 23[2], 24, 25, 26[2], 27[4], 28[3], 29[3], 30[2], 31[3], 32[2], 33[4], 35, 36[3], 37, 38, 39, 40[3]
12:1[2], 2, 3[2], 4[4], 5[4], 6[2], 7[2], 12[2], 13, 15[5]
13:1[6], 2[2], 3[3], 5[4], 6[2], 7[3], 8[3], 9[4], 10[3], 11[3], 12, 13[3], 14, 15[2], 16[4], 17[2], 18[2], 19[2], 20[7], 21[3], 23, 24[3], 25[3]
14:1[2], 2[2], 3[2], 4[3], 5, 6[2], 7, 8[4], 9[3], 10[2], 12[2], 14[3], 15[2], 16, 17[4], 18[4], 19[3]
15:1[2], 3, 4, 5[6], 6[4], 8[2], 9, 10, 11[3], 12[2], 13, 14[4], 16[2], 17, 18[4], 19[2], 20[2]
16:2[5], 3[5], 4, 5[2], 8[2], 9[4], 12[2], 13[2], 14[5], 18[4], 19, 20[2], 21[2], 22, 23[2], 24[2], 25[2], 26[4], 27[4], 28[2], 29[4], 30[5], 31[2]
17:2[3], 3[3], 4[3], 5, 7, 8[3], 10[2], 11[3], 12[3], 13
18:1[3], 2[4], 3[4], 6[2], 7[6], 9[2], 10, 11[2], 13, 14[2], 15[4], 16[4], 17[10], 18[5], 19, 20[6], 21[3], 22[4], 23, 24, 25[2], 26, 27[5], 28, 29[6], 30[8], 31[2]
19:1, 2, 3[2], 4, 5[3], 6[2], 7, 8[3], 9[4], 10, 11[3], 12[2], 14, 15, 16[3], 17[3], 18[3], 19, 20[2], 21, 22[8], 23[3], 25[5], 26[5], 27[7], 28[2], 29, 30[3]
20:1[4], 2[5], 3[3], 4[3], 5[2], 6[2], 8, 9, 10[3], 11[2], 12[2], 13[5], 14[3], 15[3], 17, 18[5], 19[2], 20[2], 21[3], 22[4], 23[5], 24[3], 25[4], 26[5], 27[4], 28[4], 30[3], 31[8], 32[5], 33[3], 34, 35[4], 36[4], 37[5], 38[3], 39[4], 40[5], 41[2], 42[6], 43[2], 45[3], 46, 47[3], 48[7]
21:1, 2[2], 4[2], 5[5], 6, 7, 8[4], 9[2], 10[7], 11, 12[3], 13[3], 14, 15[3], 16[3], 18, 19[5], 20[2], 21[4], 22, 23[2], 24

RUTH

1:1[4], 2[5], 4[5], 5, 6[3], 7[3], 8[2], 9[2], 13[2], 17, 19, 20, 21[3], 22[3]
2:1, 2[2], 3[4], 4[3], 5, 6[4], 7[4], 9[4], 10, 11[2], 12[2], 14[3], 15, 16, 17, 18, 19, 20[4], 21, 23[2]
3:2, 3[2], 4, 6, 7[2], 8, 10[3], 11, 13[7], 14[2], 15[2], 16, 18[3]
4:1[2], 2[2], 3[2], 4[2], 5[7], 6, 7, 8, 9[3], 10[7], 11[6], 12[3], 13, 14[2], 16, 17[3], 18

1 SAMUEL

1:1[4], 2[4], 3[4], 4, 5, 6, 7[2], 9[3], 10, 11[3], 12, 15, 16, 17, 18, 19[3], 20[2], 21[3], 22[2], 23[2], 24[3], 25, 26[2], 27, 28[3]
2:1[2], 2, 3, 4[2], 5, 6[2], 7, 8[9], 9[2], 10[6], 11[3], 12[2], 13[4], 14[4], 15[4], 16, 17[5], 18, 19, 20[3], 21[3], 22[4], 24, 25[4], 26[2], 27[2], 28[4], 29[2], 30[3], 31[2], 32, 33[3], 36
3:1[4], 3[4], 4, 6, 7[3], 8[4], 10, 11[2], 13, 14[2], 15[5], 17[3], 18, 19[2], 20, 21[4]
4:1[3], 2[4], 3[9], 4[8], 5[5], 6[9], 7[2], 8[5], 9, 10, 11[2], 12[2], 13[5], 14[4], 16[3], 17[4], 18[4], 19[2], 20[2], 21[3], 22[2]
5:1[2], 2[3], 3[4], 4[8], 5[2], 6[3], 7[3], 8[8], 9[5], 10[5], 11[6], 12[4]
6:1[4], 2[5], 3[2], 4[4], 5[2], 6[2], 7[2], 8[5], 9, 10[2], 11[6], 12[9], 13[2], 14[6], 15[9], 16[3], 17[3], 18[10], 19[7], 20, 21[4]
7:1[7], 2[4], 3[6], 4[2], 5, 6[3], 7[6], 8[4], 9[3], 10[4], 11[2], 12[2], 13[6], 14[6], 15, 17
8:2[2], 4, 5, 6[2], 7[3], 8[2], 9[2], 10[3], 11[2], 14, 15, 17, 18, 19[2], 20, 21[4], 22[2]
9:1[4], 2[2], 3[3], 4[4], 5[2], 7[3], 8[3], 9, 10[2], 11[3], 12[3], 13[4], 14[3], 15, 16[3], 17[2], 18[2], 19[2], 20, 21[5], 22[2], 23[2], 24[3], 25[4], 26[4], 27[4]
10:1, 2[4], 3, 5[5], 6[2], 10[2], 11[4], 12[2], 13, 14, 16[3], 17[2], 18[5], 19, 20[2], 21[3], 22[4], 23[2], 24[5], 25[5], 27
11:1[2], 2, 3[2], 4[5], 5[5], 6, 7[5], 8[2], 9[5], 10, 11[8], 12[2], 13, 14[2], 15[4]
12:2, 3, 5, 6[3], 7[3], 8[2], 9[7], 10[3], 11[2], 12[3], 13[2], 14[5], 15[6], 16, 17[3], 18[4], 19[2], 20[3], 22[2], 23[3], 24
13:2[2], 3[6], 4[3], 5[3], 6[3], 7[3], 8[2], 9, 10, 11[3], 12[2], 13[3], 14[3], 15, 16[2], 17[5], 18[5], 19[3], 20[2], 21[5], 22[3], 23[3]
14:1[4], 2[2], 3[5], 4[8], 5[3], 6[4], 10, 11[5], 12[4], 15[6], 16[2], 17, 18[3], 19[5], 20[2], 21[5], 22[3], 23[2], 24[4], 25[2], 26[5], 27[4], 28[4], 29, 30[3], 31[2], 32[5], 33[3], 34[4], 35[4], 36[3], 37[2], 38[2], 39[2], 40[2], 41[2], 43[2], 45[4], 46[2], 47[4], 48[2], 49[6], 50[5], 51[3], 52[2]
15:1[4], 2[2], 4, 5, 6[5], 7, 8[5], 9[6], 10[2], 11, 12, 13[3], 14[3], 15[7], 16, 17[3], 18[3], 19[5], 20[6], 21[5], 22[4], 23[3], 24[3], 25, 26[3], 27, 28[2], 29, 30[2], 31, 32[3], 33, 35[2]
16:1[2], 2[2], 3, 4[3], 5[3], 6, 7[6], 8, 9, 10, 11[2], 12, 13[4], 14[3], 16, 18[3], 19, 23[2]
17:1, 2[4], 3[3], 4[2], 5[2], 7, 8, 10[2], 11, 12[3], 13[6], 14[2], 16, 17, 18, 19[3], 20[6], 21[2], 22[4], 23[5], 24[2], 25[3],

1 SAMUEL

26[5], 27[2], 28[4], 30[3], 31, 34, 36[4], 37[7], 40[2], 41[3], 42, 43[2], 44[5], 45[5], 46[9], 47[3], 48[3], 49[3], 50[3], 51[3], 52[7], 53[2], 54[2], 55[3], 56[2], 57[4], 58[2]
18:1[2], 4, 5[4], 6[3], 7, 8[2], 10[4], 11[2], 12, 13, 14, 17[3], 18, 19[2], 20, 21[4], 22[2], 23, 24, 25[5], 26[2], 27[3], 28, 29, 30[3]
19:2, 3, 4, 5[2], 6[2], 8, 9[2], 10[4], 11, 13, 15[2], 16[2], 20[4], 21, 23, 24
20:3, 5[4], 6, 8, 11[2], 12, 13[2], 14[2], 15[4], 16[3], 18, 19[3], 20, 21[4], 22[3], 23[2], 24[3], 25[2], 27[4], 29[2], 30[3], 31[2], 34[3], 35[3], 36[2], 37[5], 38[2], 39[2], 40, 41[3], 42[4]
21:1[2], 2[3], 4[2], 5[5], 6[4], 7[4], 8, 9[5], 10, 11[3], 12, 13[2], 14, 15
22:1, 3, 4[3], 5[4], 6, 7, 8, 9[4], 10[3], 11[5], 13, 14[2], 15[2], 16, 17[8], 18[4], 19[6], 20[2], 21, 22[3]
23:1[2], 2[3], 3[2], 4[3], 5[2], 6, 8, 9[2], 10, 11[2], 12[3], 14[2], 15, 16, 17, 18[2], 19[4], 20[2], 21, 23[4], 24[3], 25[2], 26[2], 27[2], 28
24:1[2], 2[2], 3[4], 4[4], 6[4], 7, 8[3], 10[3], 11[2], 12[2], 13[3], 14, 15, 18, 19, 20, 21, 22
25:1[2], 2, 3[5], 4, 5, 7, 8, 9, 10, 13, 14[2], 15[2], 16[2], 20[3], 21, 22[3], 23[2], 24, 25, 26[2], 27, 28[4], 29[5], 30[2], 31, 32, 34[3], 36[2], 37[2], 38, 39[5], 40, 41[3], 42, 44
26:1[2], 2[2], 3[4], 5[6], 6[3], 7[4], 8[3], 9, 10[2], 11[4], 12[3], 13[2], 14[3], 15[3], 16[4], 19[7], 20[5], 21, 22[2], 23[3], 24[2]
27:1[3], 2[2], 3[2], 5[2], 6, 7[3], 8[6], 9[6], 10[5], 11[3]
28:1, 3[2], 4, 5[2], 6[2], 8[2], 9[3], 10[2], 11, 12[2], 13[3], 14, 15, 16, 17[3], 18[3], 19[7], 20[4], 21, 22, 23[3], 24[2]
29:1[2], 2[3], 3[6], 4[6], 6[4], 7[2], 8[2], 9[3], 10[2], 11[4]
30:1[3], 2, 3, 4, 5[3], 6[4], 7[3], 8, 9[2], 10, 11, 14[4], 15, 16[5], 17[3], 18, 20[2], 21[4], 22[2], 23[2], 24[2], 26[5], 29[4], 31
31:1[3], 2[2], 3[3], 7[7], 8[3], 9[4], 10[2], 11[2], 12[4]

2 SAMUEL

1:1[3], 2[3], 3, 4[4], 5, 6[2], 10[2], 11, 12[4], 13[2], 14, 15, 16, 18[4], 19[2], 20[5], 21[3], 22[6], 25[3], 26, 27[2]
2:1[3], 2[2], 3, 4[3], 5[2], 6, 7, 8[2], 9, 10, 11[2], 12[3], 13[9], 14, 15[2], 16, 17[2], 19[2], 21, 22, 23[6], 24[4], 25[2], 26[3], 27[2], 28, 29, 30, 31, 32
3:1[3], 2, 3[5], 4[4], 5, 6[3], 7, 8[3], 9, 10[3], 12, 14, 15, 17, 18[5], 19[3], 20, 21, 22, 23[3], 24, 25, 26, 27[3], 28[3], 29[3], 30, 31[2], 32[3], 33, 34, 35[2], 36[3], 37[3], 38, 39[3]
4:1, 2[6], 3, 4, 5[5], 6[3], 7[2], 8[6], 9[3], 11, 12[3]
5:1, 2, 3[3], 6[6], 7[3], 8[7], 9[2], 10, 12, 14, 17[3], 18[2], 19[4], 20[3], 22[2], 23[2], 24[6], 25[2]
6:1, 2[5], 3[4], 4[3], 5[2], 6[2], 7[3], 8[3], 9[3], 10[5], 11[5], 12[6], 13[2], 14, 15[5], 16[4], 17[5], 18[3], 19[4], 20[5], 21[4], 22, 23[2]
7:1[2], 2[3], 3[2], 4[2], 5, 6[2], 7[3], 8[3], 9[3], 10, 11[2], 13, 14[3], 18, 19, 23[2], 25, 26[3], 29[2]
8:1[3], 2[2], 3[2], 4, 5[2], 6[2], 7[2], 9, 11[2], 12[3], 13[2], 14, 16[3], 17[4], 18[3]
9:1, 2[2], 3[4], 4[4], 5[2], 6[2], 7, 9, 10[4], 11[4], 12, 13
10:1[2], 2[4], 3[3], 4[2], 5[2], 6[4], 7[2], 8[6], 9[4], 10[4], 11[2], 12[3], 13[3], 14[4], 15, 16[4], 17, 18[4], 19[3]
11:1[3], 2[4], 3[4], 5, 6, 7[2], 8[2], 9[3], 11[3], 12, 13, 14[2], 15[3], 16, 17[5], 18[2], 19[4], 20[3], 21[4], 22, 23[5], 24[4], 25[3], 26, 27[3]
12:1[3], 2, 3, 4[4], 5[3], 6, 7[3], 8, 9[6], 10[3], 11[2], 12, 13[2], 14[3], 15[2], 16[2], 17[2], 18[6], 19[2], 20[3], 21[2], 22[2], 24, 25[3], 26[2], 27, 28[4], 29, 30[4], 31[5]
13:1[2], 3, 4, 5, 6[2], 8, 10[4], 13[2], 15[2], 16, 17, 18[2], 23, 24[2], 25, 26, 27, 29[2], 30[2], 31[2], 32[5], 33[3], 34[4], 35[2], 36[2], 37, 39
14:1[2], 2, 3[2], 4[3], 5, 6[3], 7[4], 8[2], 9[4], 10, 11[5], 12[2], 13[4], 14, 15[5], 16[4], 17[4], 18[5], 19[8], 20[2], 21[2], 22[4], 24[2], 25[2], 26[3], 28, 29[2], 30, 32[2], 33[5]
15:2[4], 3, 4, 6[3], 7[2], 8[2], 9, 10[3], 12[3], 13[2], 14[3], 15[3], 16[3], 17[2], 18[4], 19[3], 21[4], 22[2], 23[7], 24[6], 25[5], 27[4], 28[2], 29, 30[2], 31[2], 32[3], 34[2], 35[3], 37
16:1[3], 2[7], 3[4], 4, 5[3], 6[3], 8[6], 9[3], 10[2], 11, 12[2], 13[2], 14[2], 15[2], 16[3], 18[2], 19, 21[2], 22[3], 23[3]
17:2[2], 3[3], 4[2], 5, 7, 8[2], 9[2], 10, 11[2], 12[3], 13, 14[8], 15[2], 16[4], 17, 19[3], 20[4], 21[2], 22[2], 23, 24, 25[2], 26, 27[4], 29[3]
18:1, 2[8], 3[2], 4[4], 5[5], 6[4], 7[2], 8[5], 9[7], 11[2], 12[4], 13, 14[3], 16[3], 17, 18[2], 19[3], 20, 21, 22, 23[2], 24[5], 25[3], 26[4], 27[6], 28[6], 29[3], 30, 31[2], 32[4], 33[3]
19:1, 2[4], 3[2], 4[2], 5[6], 7[2], 8[7], 9[7], 10, 11[6], 12[2], 13[2], 14[4], 15[3], 16[2], 17[3], 18[3], 19[4], 20[3], 21[2], 23[2], 24[5], 25[2], 26, 27[2], 28[2], 29[2], 30[2], 31[2], 32, 33, 34[2], 35[2], 36[2], 37[2], 38, 39[3], 40[4], 41[5], 42[4], 43[7]
20:1[2], 2[2], 3[4], 4[2], 5[2], 6, 7[4], 8[2], 9[2], 10[4], 12[6], 13[3], 14[2], 15[4], 16, 17[2], 18, 19[2], 21[6], 22[6], 23[4], 24[2], 25, 26

21:1[4], 2[8], 3[4], 4, 5[3], 6[3], 7[5], 8[7], 9[7], 10[7], 11[2], 12[6], 13[3], 14[5], 15[2], 16[3], 17[4], 18[4], 19[5], 20, 21[2], 22[3]
22:1[6], 2, 3[2], 4, 5[2], 6[2], 7, 8[2], 10, 11[2], 12, 13, 14[2], 16[8], 19[2], 21[2], 22[2], 25, 26[2], 27[2], 28[2], 29, 31[2], 32, 36, 41, 42, 43[4], 44[2], 47[3], 48, 49, 50, 51
23:1[6], 2[2], 3[3], 4[5], 6, 7[3], 8[7], 9[5], 10[4], 11[5], 12[4], 13[6], 14[2], 15[3], 16[6], 17[2], 18[3], 19, 20[3], 21[3], 22[2], 23[2], 24[3], 25[2], 26[3], 27[2], 28[2], 29[3], 30[2], 31[2], 32[2], 33[3], 34[5], 35[2], 36[2], 37[3], 39
24:1[2], 2[7], 3[6], 4[8], 5[4], 6, 7[5], 8[2], 9[6], 10[3], 11[4], 12, 14[3], 15[4], 16[9], 17[3], 18[3], 19[2], 20[3], 21[5], 22[2], 23[3], 24[4], 25[4]

1 KINGS

1:2[3], 3[2], 4[3], 5, 7[2], 8[4], 9[4], 10[2], 11[2], 12, 14, 15[5], 16[2], 17, 18, 19[5], 20[3], 21, 22[2], 23[5], 25[4], 26[2], 27[3], 28[2], 29[2], 30, 31[2], 32[4], 33[2], 34[3], 36[4], 37[3], 38[5], 39[4], 40[4], 41[4], 42[2], 44[7], 45[4], 46[2], 47[4], 48[2], 49, 50[2], 51[3], 52, 53
2:1, 2[2], 3[3], 4[2], 5[7], 6, 7[2], 8[4], 9, 10, 11, 12, 13[2], 15[3], 17[2], 18, 19[2], 20, 21, 22[4], 23, 24[2], 25[2], 26[4], 27[4], 28[4], 29[4], 30[4], 31[3], 32[6], 33[3], 34[2], 35[6], 36, 37[2], 38[3], 39[2], 42[4], 43[3], 44[3], 45[2], 46[4]
3:1[4], 2[3], 3[2], 4[2], 5, 8, 10[2], 11, 13, 15[3], 16, 17[2], 18[3], 19, 21[2], 22[6], 23[6], 24[2], 25[4], 26[5], 27[3], 28[4]
4:2[3], 3[3], 4[3], 5[4], 6[3], 7, 8, 9, 10[2], 11[3], 12[2], 13[4], 14, 15, 16, 17, 18, 19[6], 20[2], 21[5], 23, 24[4], 25, 28[3], 29[2], 30[4], 31[2], 33[3], 34[2]
5:1, 3[5], 4, 5[3], 6, 7[2], 8, 9[2], 12, 13, 14, 15, 16[4], 17[3], 18[2]
6:1[8], 2[5], 3[8], 4, 5[6], 6[8], 7[2], 8[7], 9[2], 10[2], 11[2], 13, 14, 15[9], 16[6], 17[2], 18[2], 19[5], 20[4], 21[3], 22[4], 23, 24[8], 25[2], 26[3], 27[12], 28, 29[2], 30[2], 31[4], 32[3], 33[3], 34[5], 35, 36, 37[5], 38[6]
7:2[6], 3, 5[2], 6[5], 7[4], 8[2], 9[5], 10, 11, 12[6], 14, 16[6], 17[5], 18[5], 19[4], 20[6], 21[7], 22[4], 23[2], 24[3], 25[5], 26[2], 27[3], 28[4], 29[4], 30[3], 31[6], 32[5], 33[3], 34[3], 35[7], 36[4], 37, 38, 39[8], 40[6], 41[10], 42[4], 43[2], 44, 45[5], 46[3], 47[3], 48[6], 49[7], 50[12], 51[10]
8:1[10], 2[4], 3[3], 4[8], 5[2], 6[9], 7[6], 8[5], 9[5], 10[5], 11[6], 12[2], 14[3], 15, 16[2], 17[3], 18, 19[2], 20[6], 21[4], 22[4], 25, 27[2], 28[3], 29[2], 30, 31, 32[2], 33, 34[2], 36[2], 37[2], 38, 39[2], 40[2], 43[2], 44[3], 46[3], 47[2], 48[3], 51[2], 52[2], 53[3], 54[3], 55, 56[2], 57, 59[5], 60[3], 61, 62[2], 63[5], 64[13], 65[3], 66[5]
9:1[4], 2[2], 3, 5[2], 7, 8, 9[3], 10[5], 11[2], 12, 13, 14, 15[5], 16[2], 17, 18[2], 19[2], 20[3], 21[2], 22, 23[4], 24, 25[5], 26[3], 27[3]
10:1[4], 3, 4[2], 5[5], 6, 7[3], 9[3], 10[2], 11, 12[5], 13, 14, 15[6], 17[3], 18[2], 19[6], 20[4], 21[4], 22[3], 23[2], 24, 26[2], 27[3], 28[2], 29[3]
11:1[2], 2[3], 4[2], 5[4], 6[3], 7[4], 9[2], 10, 11[2], 12, 13, 14[3], 15[3], 19[4], 20[2], 21[4], [illegible], 27[4], 28[4], 29[4], 30, 31[4], 32[2], 33[6], 34[2], 35, 36, 39, 40, 41[4], 42, 43
12:2[2], 3, 4, 5, 6, 8[3], 9, 10, 12[4], 13[3], 14[2], 15[7], 16[4], 17[2], 18, 19, 20[3], 21[5], 22[2], 23[4], 24[6], 26[2], 27[3], 28[2], 29[2], 30[2], 31[3], 32[8], 33[6]
13:1[3], 2[7], 3[5], 4[4], 5[7], 6[7], 7[2], 8[2], 9[3], 10, 11[4], 12, 13[2], 14[2], 17[3], 18[2], 20[4], 21[6], 22[4], 23[2], 24[5], 25[6], 26[9], 27, 28[7], 29[6], 31[2], 32[7], 33[5], 34[3]
14:1, 2[2], 3, 4, 5[2], 6[2], 7[2], 8[2], 10[4], 11[6], 12[2], 13[3], 14[2], 15[4], 16, 17[3], 18[4], 19[5], 20, 21[4], 22[2], 24[5], 25, 26[6], 27[5], 28[5], 29[5], 31
15:1[2], 2, 3[3], 4, 5[5], 6, 7[5], 8, 9, 10, 11[2], 12[3], 13, 14[2], 15[4], 18[10], 20[4], 22[2], 23[7], 24, 25[2], 26[3], 27[3], 28, 29[4], 30[2], 31[5], 33[2], 34[3]
16:1[3], 2[2], 3[4], 4[5], 5[5], 7[10], 8[2], 9, 10, 11, 12[4], 13[3], 14[5], 15[3], 16[5], 18[4], 19[3], 20[5], 21[3], 22[3], 23, 24[6], 25[2], 26[3], 27[5], 29[3], 30[3], 31[4], 32, 33[2], 34[6]
17:1[3], 2[2], 3, 4[2], 5[3], 6[4], 7[2], 8[2], 10[3], 12, 14[6], 15, 16[4], 17[4], 20[2], 21[2], 22[4], 23[3], 24[3]
18:1[4], 3[2], 4[2], 5[3], 6, 7, 9, 10[2], 12[3], 13[3], 15, 18[2], 19[3], 20[2], 21[3], 22[2], 23, 24[5], 25[2], 26[3], 28, 29[3], 30[4], 31[5], 32[4], 33[5], 34[4], 35[3], 36[4], 37, 38[8], 39[5], 40[2], 42[2], 43, 44[3], 45[2], 46[3]
19:1[2], 2[2], 4, 6, 7[4], 8[2], 9[2], 10[3], 11[11], 12[4], 13[2], 14[3], 15[2], 16[2], 17[2], 18, 19[2], 20, 21[3]
20:1, 2, 3, 4, 5, 6, 7[3], 8[2], 9[4], 10[3], 11, 12[3], 13[2], 14[5], 15[5], 16[3], 17[3], 19[4], 20[3], 21[3], 22[5], 23[4], 24, 25[2], 26[3], 27[4], 28[7], 29[5], 30[4], 31[3], 32, 33[2], 34, 35[5], 36[2], 37, 38[3], 39[4], 40, 41[3], 42, 43
21:1[2], 2, 3[2], 4[3], 6, 7[3], 8[3], 9[2], 10, 11[5], 12, 13[5], 15[2], 16[2], 17[3], 18, 19[4], 20[2], 21, 22[5], 23[3], 24[5], 25[2], 26[3], 28[3], 29[2]
22:2[3], 3[3], 4, 5[3], 6[5], 7, 8[4], 9[2], 10[5], 11[3], 12[3], 13[5], 14[2], 15[5], 16[3], 17[2], 18, 19[4], 20, 21, 22[2], 23[3], 24[4], 26[4], 27[2], 28, 29[2], 30[4], 31[2], 32[3], 33[3], 34[5], 35[7], 36[3], 37[2], 38[5], 39[7], 41[2], 42, 43[6], 44, 45[5], 46[4], 48, 49[2], 50, 51[2], 52[6], 53

2 KINGS

1:1, 2, 3[6], 4, 5, 6[3], 8, 9[3], 10, 11, 12, 13[3], 14[2], 15[3], 16[2], 17[4], 18[5]
2:1, 2[2], 3[3], 4[2], 5[3], 6[2], 7[2], 8, 12[2], 13[2], 14[4], 15[4], 16[2], 19[5], 21[4], 22[2], 23[2], 24[3]
3:1[2], 2[3], 3[2], 4[2], 5[2], 6, 7[2], 8[2], 9[5], 10[3], 11[5], 12[4], 13[6], 14[3], 15[3], 16, 17, 18[3], 20[4], 21[3], 22[6], 23[2], 24[4], 25[5], 26[3], 27
4:1[5], 2[2], 4, 5[2], 6[2], 7[3], 10, 11, 13[3], 15, 16, 17[2], 18[2], 21[3], 22[3], 25[2], 26, 27[5], 29[2], 30[3], 31[4], 32[2], 33[2], 34[4], 35[3], 37, 38[6], 39[2], 40[3], 41[3], 42[4], 43[2], 44[2]
5:1[3], 2[2], 3, 4[2], 5[2], 6[2], 7[2], 8[3], 9[2], 11[4], 12, 13, 14[3], 15[2], 16, 17, 18[5], 20[3], 21, 22[2], 24[3], 26, 27
6:1[3], 5[2], 6[3], 8, 9[3], 10[3], 11[3], 12[3], 14, 15[3], 17[4], 18[2], 19[3], 20[3], 21, 23[2], 25, 26[2], 27[3], 28, 29, 30[5], 31[2], 32[8], 33[3]
7:1[4], 2[3], 3[2], 4[5], 5[5], 6[9], 7[2], 8[2], 9[2], 10[5], 11[2], 12[7], 13[5], 14[3], 15[4], 16[5], 17[8], 18[3], 19[2], 20[2]
8:1[3], 2[5], 3[5], 4[4], 5[4], 6[7], 7[2], 8[3], 10, 11, 12[3], 13, 15, 16[3], 18[6], 19, 20, 21[5], 22[2], 23[5], 24, 25[3], 26, 27[7], 28[3], 29[4]
9:1[3], 2[2], 3[3], 4[3], 5[2], 6[5], 7[7], 8[2], 9[5], 10[3], 11[2], 12, 13[2], 14[2], 15[3], 17[2], 18[3], 19, 20[4], 21[2], 22, 24, 25[4], 26[7], 27[5], 28, 29[2], 31, 32, 33[2], 35[3], 36[5], 37[4]
10:1[2], 3, 5[5], 6[6], 7[2], 8[5], 9[2], 10[6], 11, 12[2], 13[6], 14[2], 15[2], 16, 17[2], 18, 19[3], 21[3], 22[2], 23[6], 24[2], 25[9], 26[2], 27[2], 29[3], 30[4], 31[3], 32[2], 33[5], 34[5], 36
11:1[2], 2[4], 3[3], 4[9], 5[4], 6[5], 7[5], 8[3], 9[6], 10[4], 11[8], 12[4], 13[6], 14[7], 15[10], 16[4], 17[6], 18[8], 19[14], 20[5]
12:1, 2[3], 3[3], 4[11], 5[3], 6[4], 7[6], 8[4], 9[11], 10[6], 11[9], 12[4], 13[5], 14[3], 15[2], 16[4], 18[6], 19[5], 20, 21[3]
13:1[3], 2[4], 3[5], 4[4], 5[4], 6[3], 7[3], 8[5], 10[2], 11[4], 12[5], 13, 14[3], 16[3], 17[5], 18[3], 19, 20[5], 21[4], 22, 23, 25[6]
14:1[2], 3[2], 4[3], 5[2], 6[9], 7[2], 8[2], 9[4], 11, 12, 13[5], 14[6], 15[5], 16, 17[2], 18[5], 20, 21, 22, 23[3], 24[4], 25[9], 26[2], 27[4], 28[5], 29
15:1, 3[2], 4[3], 5[7], 6[5], 7, 8[2], 9[4], 10[2], 11[5], 12[4], 13[2], 14[2], 15[5], 16[2], 17[2], 18[4], 19[3], 20[5], 21[5], 23[2], 24[4], 25[4], 26[5], 27[2], 28[4], 29[2], 30[4], 31[5], 32[3], 33, 34[2], 35[6], 36[5], 37[3], 38
16:1[3], 2[2], 3[7], 4[2], 6[2], 7[4], 8[6], 9[3], 10[5], 11[2], 12[5], 13[2], 14[9], 15[13], 16, 17[5], 18[7], 19[5], 20
17:1[2], 2[3], 4[3], 5[2], 6[5], 7[4], 8[5], 9[5], 11[4], 12, 13[5], 14[2], 15[2], 16[3], 17[3], 18[2], 19[3], 20[3], 21[3], 22[2], 23[2], 24[4], 25[3], 26[9], 27[5], 28[2], 29[3], 30[3], 31[3], 32[5], 33[3], 34[5], 35, 36[2], 37[4], 38, 39[2], 41
18:1[2], 2, 3[2], 4[5], 5[2], 6[2], 7[2], 8[5], 9[2], 10[3], 11[4], 12[4], 13[2], 14[2], 15[5], 16[6], 17[5], 18[6], 19[2], 20, 21, 22, 23, 24[2], 25[2], 26[6], 27[2], 28[4], 29, 30[4], 31[2], 32, 33[4], 34[2], 35[3], 36[2], 37[6]
19:1[2], 2[6], 3[2], 4[7], 5, 6[4], 7, 8, 10[2], 11, 12[3], 13[4], 14[6], 15[5], 16[2], 17[2], 18[2], 19[3], 20[2], 21[5], 22, 23[9], 24[2], 26[5], 28, 29[4], 30[2], 31[2], 32[2], 33[3], 35[5], 37[3]
20:1[3], 2[2], 4[3], 5[6], 6[2], 7, 8[5], 9[4], 10[2], 11[4], 12, 13[6], 14, 15, 16[2], 17[2], 18[2], 19[2], 20[6]
21:2[6], 3[2], 4[3], 5[4], 6[3], 7[3], 8[3], 9[3], 10[2], 11, 12, 13[3], 14[2], 15, 16[2], 17[5], 18[2], 19, 20[2], 21[2], 22[3], 23[2], 24[4], 25[5], 26
22:1, 2[5], 3[7], 4[7], 5[12], 6, 7, 8[7], 9[10], 10[4], 11[4], 12[6], 13[6], 14[7], 15[2], 16[5], 17, 18[4], 19[3], 20[2]
23:1[2], 2[13], 3[6], 4[13], 5[9], 6[9], 7[6], 8[12], 9[5], 10[3], 11[11], 12[11], 13[11], 14[3], 15[6], 16[8], 17[5], 18[2], 19[6], 20[3], 21[5], 22[5], 23[2], 24[12], 25[2], 26[3], 27[2], 28[5], 29[2], 30[3], 31, 32[2], 33[2], 34[2], 35[9], 36, 37[2]
24:2[8], 3[3], 4[2], 5[5], 7[5], 8, 9[2], 10[2], 11, 12[4], 13[9], 14[6], 15[4], 16[2], 17, 18, 19[2], 20[3]
25:1[4], 2[2], 3[6], 4[10], 5[4], 6[2], 7[2], 8[6], 9[4], 10[5], 11[9], 12[4], 13[9], 14[5], 15[4], 16[5], 17[8], 18[6], 19[11], 20[2], 21[2], 22[4], 23[8], 24[4], 25[6], 26[4], 27[7], 28[2], 29, 30[2]

1 CHRONICLES

1:5, 6, 7, 8, 9[2], 10, 12, 14[3], 15[3], 16[3], 17, 19[3], 23, 27, 28, 29, 31, 32[2], 33[2], 34, 35, 36, 37, 38, 39, 40[2], 41[2], 42[2], 43[5], 44, 45[2], 46[3], 48, 49, 50[3], 51, 54
2:1, 3[6], 4, 5, 6, 7[3], 8, 9, 10, 13[2], 14[2], 15[2], 16, 17[2], 18, 21[2], 22, 23[4], 24, 25[3], 26, 27[2], 28[2], 29[2], 30, 31[3], 32[2], 33[2], 42[5], 43, 44, 45[2], 47, 49[4], 50[4], 51[2], 52[2], 53[7], 54[5], 55[7]
3:1[5], 2[5], 3[2], 5, 9[3], 15[5], 16, 17, 19[2], 21[5], 22[2], 23, 24
4:1, 2[3], 3[2], 4[5], 5, 6, 7, 8[2], 10, 11[2], 12[2], 13[2], 14[2], 15[3], 16, 17[2], 18[5], 19[5], 20[2], 21[7], 22[2], 23[2], 24, 26, 27, 31, 33, 34, 35[3], 37[5], 38, 39[3], 40, 41[2], 42[2], 43[2]
5:1[7], 2[2], 3[2], 4, 6, 7[2], 8[3], 9[4], 10[3], 11[2], 12[2], 13, 14[8], 15[3], 16, 17[2], 18[4], 19, 20[2], 22[2], 23[3], 24[3], 25[4], 26[7]
6:1, 2, 3[2], 10[2], 15[2], 16, 17[2], 18, 19[3], 22, 25, 26, 28[2], 29, 31[4], 32[5], 33[4], 34[4], 35[4], 36[4], 37[4], 38[4], 39[2], 40[3], 41[3], 42[3], 43[3], 44[5], 45[3], 46[3], 47[4], 48[3], 49[6], 50, 54[4], 55[2], 56[4], 57[3], 60, 61[4], 62[5], 63[4], 64[2], 65[6], 66[4], 67, 70[4], 71[3], 72, 74, 76, 77[3], 78[4], 80
7:1, 2[2], 3[2], 4, 5, 6, 7[2], 8[2], 9[2], 10[2], 11[2], 12[2], 13[2], 14[3], 15[3], 16[2], 17[4], 19, 20, 21, 24[2], 28[4], 29[4], 30, 31[2], 33[2], 34, 35, 36, 38, 39, 40[5]
8:1[2], 2[2], 3, 6[4], 8, 10, 12[2], 13[3], 16, 18, 21, 25, 27, 28, 29, 34, 35, 38, 39[3], 40[2]
9:1[2], 2[4], 3[3], 4[6], 5[2], 6, 7[4], 8[6], 9[2], 10, 11[7], 12[8], 13[4], 14[5], 15[3], 16[7], 17[2], 18[3], 19[12], 20[3], 21[4], 22[2], 23[6], 24[2], 26[3], 27[3], 28[2], 29[8], 30[4], 31[6], 32[3], 33[4], 34, 35, 40, 41, 44
10:1[3], 2[3], 3[3], 5, 7[3], 8[3], 9[3], 10[2], 11, 12[4], 13[3], 14[3]
11:2, 3[5], 4[3], 5[3], 6[2], 7[2], 8[3], 9, 10[4], 11[4], 12[3], 13[3], 14[3], 15[6], 16[2], 17[3], 18[6], 19[2], 20[3], 21[3], 22[2], 23[3], 24[3], 25[2], 26[4], 27[2], 28[3], 29[2], 30[3], 31[3], 32[2], 33[2], 34[4], 35[3], 36[2], 37[2], 38[2], 39[4], 40[2], 41[2], 42[3], 43[2], 44[3], 45[2], 46[3], 47
12:1[3], 2[2], 3[5], 4[4], 5, 6, 7, 8[7], 9[3], 10[2], 11[2], 12[2], 13[2], 14[4], 15[4], 16[2], 17, 18[3], 19[4], 20, 21[3], 22, 23[6], 24[2], 25[2], 26, 27[2], 29[5], 30[2], 31, 32[3], 35, 37[5], 38
13:1, 2[4], 3[2], 4[4], 5[2], 6[3], 7[3], 9[3], 10[3], 11, 12, 13[4], 14[4]
14:2, 4, 8[2], 9[2], 10[2], 11[2], 13[2], 14, 15[4], 16[2], 17[3]
15:1[2], 2[4], 3[2], 4[2], 5[2], 6[2], 7[2], 8[2], 9[2], 10[2], 11[2], 12[6], 13[3], 14[4], 15[6], 16[4], 17[5], 18[2], 19, 21, 22[2], 23, 24[4], 25[6], 26[4], 27[6], 28[4], 29[5]
16:1[3], 2[5], 4[4], 5, 6[3], 7[2], 8[2], 10[2], 11, 12, 14[2], 15, 16, 17, 18[2], 23[2], 24, 25, 26[4], 28[3], 29[4], 30[2], 31[4], 32[3], 33[5], 34, 35, 36[3], 37[4], 38, 39[5], 40[5], 41[2], 42, 43
17:1[4], 3[2], 4, 5, 6, 7[3], 8[3], 9[2], 10[2], 16[2], 17, 18, 21, 23, 24[3], 27
18:1[3], 2, 3, 4, 5[2], 6[2], 7[2], 8[3], 9, 11[5], 12[3], 13[2], 15[3], 16[3], 17[5]
19:1[2], 2[4], 3[3], 4, 5[3], 6[2], 7[2], 8[2], 9[6], 10[3], 11[4], 12[2], 13[2], 14[3], 15[3], 16[6], 17[3], 18[4], 19[4]
20:1[6], 2[2], 3[4], 4[4], 5[4], 6[2], 7, 8[3]
21:2[3], 3[2], 4, 5[3], 6, 8, 9, 10, 11, 12[8], 13[3], 14, 15[7], 16[5], 17, 18[5], 19[3], 20, 21[2], 22[5], 23[5], 24[2], 25, 26[3], 27[3], 28[3], 29[6], 30[3]
22:1[4], 2[3], 3[4], 4, 5[2], 6, 7[2], 8[3], 10, 11[5], 12[6], 13[4], 14[6], 16[7], 17, 18[5], 19[10]
23:2[3], 3[2], 4[3], 5[2], 6, 7, 8[2], 9[3], 10[2], 11[2], 12, 13[3], 14[2], 15, 16[2], 17[3], 18[2], 19[5], 20[3], 21[2], 22, 23, 24[9], 25, 26[3], 27[2], 28[10], 29[4], 30, 31[6], 32[10]
24:1[3], 2, 3[2], 4[6], 5[5], 6[10], 7[2], 8[2], 9[2], 10[2], 11[2], 12[2], 13[2], 14[2], 15[2], 16[2], 17[2], 18[2], 19[4], 20[4], 21[2], 22[2], 23[5], 24[2], 25[2], 26[2], 27, 29, 30[4], 31[7]
25:1[6], 2[5], 3[3], 4, 5[4], 6[6], 7[3], 8[4], 9[2], 10, 11, 12, 13, 14, 15, 16, 17, 18, 19, 20, 21, 22, 23, 24, 25, 26, 27, 28, 29, 30, 31
26:1[5], 2[5], 3[3], 4[6], 5[3], 6, 7, 8[2], 10[4], 11[4], 12[5], 13[3], 14, 15, 16[4], 18, 19[4], 20[5], 21[4], 22[4], 23[4], 24[3], 26[7], 27[3], 28[5], 29[2], 30[5], 31[6], 32[4]
27:1[6], 2[3], 3[5], 4[3], 5[4], 6[2], 7[3], 8[3], 9[4], 10[4], 11[4], 12[4], 13[4], 14[4], 15[3], 16[6], 17[3], 18[2], 19[2], 20[4], 21[3], 22[3], 23[4], 24[4], 25[8], 26[4], 27[6], 28[5], 29[5], 30[4], 31[4], 32[2], 33[3], 34[3]
28:1[15], 2[6], 4[6], 5[4], 8[6], 9[4], 10[2], 11[8], 12[10], 13[10], 15[7], 16[2], 17[4], 18[7], 19[2], 20[5], 21[7]
29:1[5], 2[5], 3[3], 4[3], 5[4], 6[6], 7[2], 8[5], 9[3], 10[2], 11[8], 15, 17[2], 18[3], 19[2], 20[6], 21[3], 22[5], 23[2], 24[4], 25[2], 26, 27, 29[8], 30[3]

2 CHRONICLES

1:1[2], 2[4], 3[7], 4[2], 5[6], 6[4], 9[2], 11, 12[2], 13[3], 14[2], 15[3], 16[2], 17[3]
2:1[2], 2, 3, 4[8], 5, 6, 7, 9, 10, 11[2], 12[3], 14[3], 15[4], 17[3], 18[2]
3:1[6], 2[3], 3[6], 4[7], 5, 6[2], 7[6], 8[5], 9[3], 10, 11[8], 12[6], 13, 14, 15[3], 16[4], 17[9]
4:1[3], 2, 3[2], 4[5], 5[4], 6[5], 7[3], 8[3], 9[5], 10[4], 11[5], 12[10], 13[4], 14, 16[5], 17[3], 18[2], 19[5], 20[3], 21[3], 22[11]
5:1[9], 2[10], 3[4], 4[3], 5[7], 6[2], 7[9], 8[6], 9[6], 10[4], 11[3], 12[4], 13[7], 14[5]
6:1[2], 3[3], 4, 5[3], 7[3], 8, 9[2], 10[7], 11[4], 12[4], 13[3], 14[2], 16, 18[2], 19[3], 20[2], 21, 22, 23[2], 24[2], 25[3], 26, 27[2], 28[2], 30[2], 31, 32, 33[3], 34[2], 35, 37[2], 38[3], 39, 40, 41, 42[2]
7:1[6], 2[6], 3[8], 4[3], 5[3], 6[6], 7[10], 8[4], 9[4], 10[5], 11[5], 12, 13[2], 15, 18, 20, 21, 22[2]
8:1[3], 2[2], 4[2], 5[2], 6[5], 7[6], 8[2], 9, 10[2], 11[7], 12[4], 13[8], 14[8], 15[4], 16[7], 17[2], 18[3]
9:1[2], 3[3], 4[5], 5, 6[3], 8[2], 9[2], 10[2], 11[6], 12[2], 13, 14[2], 16[3], 17, 18[4], 19[4], 20[5], 21[3], 22[2], 23[3], 25[2], 26[5], 27[3], 29[9], 31
10:2[3], 4, 5, 6, 8[3], 9, 10[2], 12[4], 13[3], 14[2], 15[7], 16[4], 17[2], 18[2], 19
11:1[2], 2[3], 3, 4[3], 11, 13[2], 14[3], 15[3], 16[3], 17[3], 18[4], 20, 21, 22[2], 23
12:1[3], 2[2], 3[4], 4, 5[4], 6[3], 7[4], 8[3], 9[6], 10[5], 11[5], 12[2], 13[3], 14, 15[4], 16
13:1, 2, 3[2], 5[2], 6[3], 7[2], 8[4], 9[7], 10[5], 11[7], 12, 13, 14[4], 15[2], 16, 18[3], 19[3], 20[2], 22[4]
14:1[2], 2[2], 3[5], 4[3], 5[4], 6[2], 7[2], 9, 10[2], 11, 12[3], 13[3], 14[4], 15
15:1[2], 2, 3, 4, 5[2], 8[9], 9[2], 10[3], 11[3], 12, 13, 14, 15[2], 16[3], 17[2], 18[2], 19[2]
16:1[3], 2[4], 4[3], 6[3], 7[5], 8[3], 9[4], 10[3], 11[3], 12[3], 13, 14[3]
17:2[3], 3[2], 4[2], 5[2], 6[3], 7[2], 9[5], 10[4], 11[2], 13[2], 14[4], 15, 16[2], 18, 19[3]
18:2, 3, 4[3], 5[2], 6, 7[5], 8[2], 9[4], 10[2], 11[4], 12[4], 13, 14[2], 15[4], 16[2], 17, 18[4], 19, 20[2], 21[2], 22[3], 23[4], 25[4], 26[2], 27, 28[2], 29[4], 30[4], 31[4], 32[3], 33[4], 34[6]
19:1, 2[5], 3[2], 4[2], 5[2], 6[3], 7[3], 8[6], 9[2], 10, 11[9]
20:1[3], 2, 3, 4[3], 5[4], 6[2], 7[2], 9, 10[2], 13, 14[9], 15[2], 16[4], 17[3], 18[4], 19[6], 20[3], 21[5], 22[2], 23[3], 24[4], 25[3], 26[6], 27[2], 28[2], 29[4], 30, 31, 32[3], 33[3], 34[6], 36, 37[3]
21:1, 2[2], 3[2], 4[3], 6[6], 7[3], 8[2], 9[3], 10[4], 11[2], 12[4], 13[5], 14, 15, 16[5], 17[3], 18, 19[2], 20[3]
22:1[6], 2, 3[2], 4[4], 5[2], 6[3], 7[4], 8[4], 9[4], 10[3], 11[8], 12[2]
23:1[7], 2[4], 3[6], 4[5], 5[7], 6[7], 7[4], 8[6], 9[3], 10[8], 11[4], 12[6], 13[8], 14[8], 15[3], 16[3], 17[4], 18[11], 19[4], 20[14], 21[4]
24:2[4], 4[2], 5[6], 6[9], 7[5], 8[4], 9[4], 10[3], 11[7], 12[9], 13[3], 14[8], 16[2], 17[4], 18[2], 19, 20[7], 21[5], 22[3], 23[8], 24[4], 25[6], 26[2], 27[7]
25:2[2], 3[2], 4[7], 5, 7[3], 8[2], 9[5], 10, 11[2], 12[5], 13[3], 14[4], 15[4], 16[3], 17[3], 18[3], 19, 20[2], 21[2], 22, 23[6], 24[7], 25[2], 26[4], 27[2], 28
26:1[2], 2, 4[2], 5[3], 6[5], 7[3], 8[2], 9[4], 10[4], 11[6], 12[4], 13[2], 14, 15[2], 16[4], 17[2], 18[6], 19[6], 20[3], 21[7], 22[4], 23[3]
27:1, 2[5], 3[4], 4[2], 5[7], 6, 7[4], 9
28:1[2], 2[2], 3[7], 4[2], 5[5], 6[2], 7[4], 8[2], 9[3], 10[2], 11[3], 12[7], 13[2], 14[5], 15[5], 16, 17, 18[7], 19[2], 21[6], 22[2], 23[4], 24[7], 25, 26[3], 27[3]
29:1, 2[2], 3[5], 4[3], 5[4], 6[4], 7[5], 8[2], 9, 10, 11, 12[11], 13[2], 14[2], 15[6], 16[12], 17[10], 18[7], 19[3], 20[5], 21[6], 22[10], 23[4], 24[5], 25[8], 26[4], 27[7], 28[4], 29, 30[6], 31[4], 32[4], 33, 34[7], 35[7], 36[3]
30:1[4], 2[4], 3[2], 4[3], 5[2], 6[9], 7, 8[3], 9[2], 10[2], 12[6], 13[2], 14[3], 15[8], 16[6], 17[6], 18[3], 19[3], 20[2], 21[6], 22[5], 23, 24[3], 25[6], 26[3], 27[3]
31:1[6], 2[7], 3[9], 4[6], 5[6], 6[5], 7[4], 8[3], 9[3], 10[7], 11[2], 12[5], 13[5], 14[8], 15[4], 16[2], 17[4], 18[2], 19[8], 20, 21[4]
32:1[2], 3[3], 4[5], 5[3], 6[4], 7[2], 8[3], 10, 11[3], 12, 13[3], 14, 15, 16, 17[4], 18[4], 19[6], 20[3], 21[7], 22[5], 23[2], 24[2], 25, 26[5], 28, 30[3], 31[5], 32[7], 33[4]
33:2[6], 3[2], 4[3], 5[4], 6[5], 7[3], 8[6], 9[4], 10, 11[5], 12[2], 13, 14[6], 15[9], 16[3], 17[3], 18[8], 19[3], 22[3], 23, 25[4]
34:2[5], 3[7], 4[6], 5[2], 6, 7[5], 8[10], 9[7], 10[9], 11[3], 12[8], 13[3], 14[6], 15[6], 16[3], 17[7], 18[4], 19[3], 20[5], 21[7], 22[7], 23[2], 24[5], 25, 26[4], 27[2], 28[4], 29[2], 30[13], 31[5], 32[3], 33[6]
35:1[4], 2[4], 3[6], 4[3], 5[8], 6[4], 7[5], 8[6], 9[2], 10[4], 11[4], 12[7], 13[4], 14[7], 15[6], 16[7], 17[3], 18[6], 19[2], 20, 21, 22[3], 23[2], 24[2], 25[3], 26[4], 27[2]
36:1[3], 3[2], 4, 5[2], 7[3], 8[4], 9[2], 10[4], 12[5], 13, 14[7], 15, 16[3], 17[4], 18[7], 19[4], 20[3], 21[4], 22[6], 23[4]

EZRA

1:1[6], 2[3], 3[3], 4[3], 5[6], 7[5], 8[3], 9, 11[2]
2:1[4], 2[3], 3, 4, 5, 6[2], 7, 8, 9, 10, 11, 12, 13, 14, 15, 16, 17, 18, 19, 20, 21, 22, 23, 24, 25, 26, 27, 28, 29, 30, 31[2], 32, 33, 34, 35, 36[3], 37, 38, 39, 40[3], 41[2], 42[8], 43[4], 44[3], 45[3], 46[3], 47[3], 48[3], 49[3], 50[3], 51[3], 52[3], 53[3], 54[2], 55[4], 56[3], 57[4], 58[2], 60[3], 61[7], 62, 63[2], 64, 68[5], 69[2], 70[6]
3:1[4], 2[7], 3[3], 4[4], 5[5], 6[6], 7[4], 8[13], 9[5], 10[9], 11[6], 12[4], 13[8]
4:1[5], 2[3], 3[5], 4[4], 5[2], 6[3], 7[6], 8[3], 9[12], 10[6], 11[5], 12[6], 13[4], 14[3], 15[5], 16[3], 17[6], 18, 20, 22[2], 23[3], 24[4]
5:1[6], 2[4], 3[2], 4[2], 5[4], 6[6], 7, 8[5], 10[3], 11[3], 12[5], 13[3], 14[6], 15[2], 16[3], 17[4]
6:1[4], 2[3], 3[10], 4[2], 5[5], 6[3], 7[5], 8[5], 9[4], 10[3], 12, 13[2], 14[8], 15[5], 16[7], 17[3], 18[4], 19[5], 20[6], 21[5], 22[7]
7:1[4], 2[3], 3[3], 4[3], 5[5], 6[5], 7[8], 8[3], 9[5], 10[2], 11[8], 12[3], 13, 14[2], 15[3], 16[6], 17[2], 18[4], 19[4], 20[2], 21[7], 23[5], 24, 25[4], 26[3], 27[4], 28[4]
8:1[4], 2[3], 3[3], 4[2], 5[2], 6[2], 7[2], 8[2], 9[2], 10[2], 11[2], 12[2], 13, 14, 15[4], 17[5], 18[4], 19, 20[4], 21, 22[5], 24[2], 25[6], 28[5], 29[7], 30[7], 31[7], 33[11], 34, 35[4], 36[6]
9:1[14], 2[4], 3, 4[4], 5[2], 6, 7[5], 8, 9[4], 11[5], 12[2], 14
10:1[2], 2[4], 3[4], 5[2], 6[4], 7[2], 8[4], 9[8], 10[2], 11[4], 12, 13, 14[4], 15[3], 16[8], 17[3], 18[4], 19, 20, 21, 22, 23[2], 24[2], 25, 26, 27, 28, 29, 30, 31, 33, 34, 43

NEHEMIAH

1:1[5], 2[2], 3[5], 4, 5, 6[4], 7[3], 8[2], 9[3], 11[4]
2:1[5], 2, 3[5], 4[2], 5[3], 6[3], 7[4], 8[10], 9[5], 10[5], 12[2], 13[6], 14[4], 15[5], 16[7], 17[3], 18[2], 19[5], 20
3:1[6], 2[2], 3[6], 4[5], 5[2], 6[7], 7[6], 8[5], 9[3], 10[2], 11[5], 12[3], 13[7], 14[6], 15[12], 16[8], 17[4], 18[3], 19[6], 20[7], 21[6], 22[3], 23[2], 24[5], 25[8], 26[5], 27[3], 28[2], 29[4], 30[3], 31[7], 32[5]
4:1[2], 2[4], 3, 4, 5, 6[4], 7[5], 10[3], 11[2], 12, 13[4], 14[5], 15, 16[9], 17[3], 18[2], 19[6], 20[2], 21[5], 22[4], 23[2]
5:1[2], 3, 4, 5, 7[2], 8[2], 9[3], 11[5], 12, 13[3], 14[7], 15[4], 16[2], 17[2], 18[3]
6:1[5], 2[2], 3, 4, 5, 6[3], 7, 9, 10[8], 11, 14[3], 15[3], 16, 17[2], 18[4]
7:1[5], 2[2], 3[4], 4[3], 5[5], 6[4], 7[3], 8, 9, 10, 11[2], 12, 13, 14, 15, 16, 17, 18, 19, 20, 21, 22, 23, 24, 25, 26, 27, 28, 29, 30, 31, 32, 33[2], 34[2], 35, 36, 37, 38, 39[3], 40, 41, 42, 43[3], 44[2], 45[7], 46[4], 47[3], 48[3], 49[3], 50[3], 51[3], 52[3], 53[3], 54[3], 55[3], 56[2], 57[4], 58[3], 59[4], 60[2], 62[3], 63[6], 64, 65[2], 66, 70[5], 71[4], 72[2], 73[8]
8:1[7], 2[5], 3[9], 4[2], 5[4], 6[5], 7[4], 8[4], 9[10], 10[4], 11[3], 12[2], 13[9], 14[5], 15, 16[8], 17[6], 18[7]
9:1[2], 2[2], 3[5], 4[3], 5[2], 6[4], 7[4], 8[7], 9[2], 10, 11[6], 12[3], 14, 15[2], 19[6], 21, 22[4], 23[2], 24[7], 27[3], 28[2], 29, 30[3], 32[6], 35, 36[3], 37
10:1[2], 8, 9[3], 14[2], 28[10], 29[3], 30[2], 31[7], 32[3], 33[10], 34[10], 35[4], 36[6], 37[10], 38[10], 39[13]
11:1[5], 2[2], 3[7], 4[9], 5[7], 6, 7[8], 9[3], 10[2], 11[7], 12[8], 13[5], 14[2], 15[5], 16[5], 17[9], 18[2], 19[2], 20[4], 21[2], 22[10], 23[2], 24[5], 25[5], 27, 28, 30[3], 31, 35, 36
12:1[3], 7[3], 8[2], 9, 12[3], 22[6], 23[7], 24[5], 25[3], 26[7], 27[4], 28[4], 29[3], 30[5], 31[5], 32, 35[7], 36[3], 37[7], 38[7], 39[7], 40[4], 41, 42, 43[3], 44[12], 45[6], 46[2], 47[8]
13:1[6], 2[2], 3[2], 4[4], 5[12], 6[3], 7[3], 8[2], 9[5], 10[5], 11[2], 12[5], 13[6], 14[2], 15[3], 16[2], 17[2], 18, 19[6], 20, 21[2], 22[4], 24[3], 28[4], 29[4], 30[3], 31[2]

ESTHER

1:1, 2[3], 3[4], 4[2], 5[6], 6, 7[3], 8[4], 9[3], 10[6], 11[5], 12[3], 13[4], 14[5], 15[4], 16[8], 17[3], 18[4], 19[5], 20[2], 21[5], 22[3]
2:1, 2[2], 3[9], 4[4], 5[4], 6[2], 7, 8[6], 9[5], 11[2], 12[5], 13[4], 14[8], 15[8], 16[7], 17[4], 18[4], 19[3], 20, 21[4], 22[3], 23[4]
3:1[3], 2[3], 3[3], 6[4], 7[6], 8[4], 9[5], 10[4], 11[3], 12[9], 13[6], 14[2], 15[6]
4:1[2], 2[2], 3[2], 4, 5, 6[3], 7[4], 8[4], 9, 11[8], 13[2], 14[2], 16[3]
5:1[8], 2[7], 3[3], 4[3], 5[3], 6[4], 8[6], 9, 11[6], 12[4], 13[2], 14[5]
6:1[4], 2[4], 3[2], 4[6], 5[3], 6[4], 7[3], 8[5], 9[8], 10[5], 11[6], 12, 13[2], 14[2]
7:1[2], 2[5], 3[2], 4[2], 5[2], 6[3], 7[5], 8[10], 9[6], 10[2]
8:1[5], 2[2], 3[4], 4[3], 5[8], 6[2], 7[6], 8[6], 9[10], 10[2], 11[5], 12[4], 13[3], 14[4], 15[3], 16, 17[6]
9:1[10], 2[4], 3[7], 4[2], 5[3], 6[2], 10[5], 11[3], 12[7], 13[3], 14[2], 15[4], 16[3], 17[4], 18[5], 19[5], 20[3], 21[4], 22[4], 23, 24[6], 25[3], 26[2], 27, 28[2], 29[3], 30[4], 31[4], 32[2]
10:1[4], 2[7], 3[4]

JOB

1:1, 3[3], 5[3], 6[2], 7[3], 8[2], 9, 10[2], 12[3], 14[2], 15[4], 16[3], 17[5], 19[4], 20, 21[4]
2:1[3], 2[3], 3[2], 4, 6, 7[3], 8, 10[2], 11[3], 13
3:3[2], 4, 5[3], 6[4], 8, 9[4], 10, 11[3], 12[2], 14, 17[2], 18[3], 19[2], 20, 22, 24, 25
4:1, 3, 4, 6, 7, 8, 9[2], 10[6], 11[2], 13[2], 15, 16, 19[2]
5:1, 2[2], 3, 4, 5[3], 6[2], 7, 10[2], 12[2], 13[3], 14[3], 15[4], 16, 17[3], 20[2], 21[2], 22[2], 23[4], 25[2]
6:2, 3[2], 4[4], 5[2], 6, 7, 8, 10[2], 12, 14[2], 15, 16[2], 18, 19[2], 23[3], 26, 27
7:1, 2[2], 4[3], 8, 9[2], 11[2], 21[2]
8:1, 2, 3, 5, 6, 8[2], 11[2], 13[2], 16, 17[2], 19[2], 20, 22[2]
9:5, 6[2], 7[2], 8[3], 9[2], 13, 22[2], 23[3], 24[5], 26[3], 31
10:1, 3[3], 5, 9, 18[2], 19[2], 21[2], 22[2]
11:1, 2, 6, 7, 9[3], 17[2], 20[4]

Misc.

JEREMIAH

29:1[8], 2[6], 3[3], 4[2], 5, 7[4], 8[3], 9, 10, 11[2], 14[5], 15, 16[4], 17[4], 18[6], 19[3], 20[3], 21[5], 22[4], 23, 24, 25[6], 26[6], 28, 29[3], 30[2], 31[3], 32[5]
30:1[2], 2[2], 3[5], 4[2], 5, 7, 8, 9, 10[2], 11, 12, 14[3], 15, 17, 18[5], 19, 21[2], 23[4], 24[4]
31:1[4], 2[4], 3, 4, 5[2], 6[3], 7[4], 8[6], 9, 10[3], 11[2], 12[6], 13[2], 14[3], 15, 16[4], 17, 18[2], 19, 20, 21[2], 22[2], 23[5], 24, 25, 27[6], 28, 29[2], 30, 31[4], 32[5], 33[3], 34[4], 35[8], 36[2], 37[5], 38[7], 39[2], 40[9]
32:1[4], 2[5], 3[3], 4[4], 5[2], 6[2], 7[2], 8[9], 9[2], 10[3], 11[3], 12[12], 14[3], 15[2], 16[4], 17[2], 18[6], 19[3], 20, 21, 24[8], 25[4], 26[2], 27[2], 28[4], 29[2], 30[5], 31, 32[5], 33[2], 34, 35[4], 36[7], 39, 42[2], 43[2], 44[10]
33:1[5], 2[4], 4[7], 5[2], 6, 7[3], 9[5], 10[3], 11[16], 12[2], 13[12], 14[4], 15[2], 16[2], 17[3], 18[2], 19[2], 20[3], 21[2], 22[5], 23[2], 24[2], 25[2], 26[2]
34:1[6], 2[5], 3[2], 4[4], 5[4], 6, 7[3], 8[4], 10[3], 11[2], 12[3], 13[5], 14, 15, 17[7], 18[5], 19[8], 20[6], 21[4], 22[2]
35:1[4], 2[5], 3[4], 4[11], 5[3], 6, 7, 8[2], 11[5], 12[2], 13[5], 14[2], 15[2], 16[3], 17[4], 18[5], 19[3]
36:1[3], 2[4], 3[2], 4[4], 5[2], 6[8], 7[4], 8[6], 9[7], 10[13], 11[5], 12[9], 13[4], 14[9], 16[2], 18, 19, 20[8], 21[8], 22[4], 23[6], 24, 25[2], 26[7], 27[6], 28[3], 29[2], 30[6], 31[3], 32[6]
37:1[3], 2[5], 3[6], 4, 5, 6[3], 7[3], 8, 9[2], 10[2], 11[2], 12[3], 13[6], 14[2], 15[4], 16[2], 17[5], 19, 20[3], 21[8]
38:1[6], 2[5], 3[3], 4[8], 5[2], 6[6], 7[6], 8[2], 9[5], 10[4], 11[5], 12[2], 13[3], 14[6], 16[3], 17[4], 18[3], 19[3], 20[2], 21[2], 22[4], 23[3], 25[3], 26, 27[3], 28[3]
39:1[2], 2[5], 3[6], 4[9], 5[3], 6[4], 8[5], 9[7], 10[6], 11[2], 13[3], 14[5], 15[4], 16[3], 17[3], 18[2]
40:1[4], 2[3], 3[2], 4[2], 5[7], 6[3], 7[8], 8[6], 9[5], 10, 11[6], 12[2], 13[4], 14[4], 15[4], 16[2]
41:1[7], 2[7], 3[3], 4, 5[2], 6[2], 7[6], 8, 9[5], 10[9], 11[5], 12[3], 13[4], 14[2], 15[2], 16[10], 17, 18[5]
42:1[7], 2[2], 3[3], 4[3], 5[3], 6[4], 7[2], 8[6], 9[2], 10, 11[2], 13[2], 14[3], 15[4], 16[3], 17[5], 18[3], 19, 20[3], 21[3], 22[4]
43:1[4], 2[4], 3[3], 4[7], 5[5], 6[7], 7[3], 8[2], 9[5], 10[3], 11[3], 12[3], 13[5]
44:1[4], 2[4], 4, 6[2], 7[3], 8[4], 9[7], 11[2], 12[9], 13[4], 14[4], 15[4], 16[3], 17[3], 18[3], 19, 20[4], 21[6], 22[3], 23[3], 24[5], 25[3], 26[7], 27[4], 28[5], 29, 30[4]
45:1[6], 2[2], 3, 4, 5
46:1[4], 2[4], 3, 4[3], 5, 6[4], 7, 8[4], 9[6], 10[6], 11, 12[4], 13[4], 14, 15, 16[2], 17, 18[4], 20, 21[3], 22, 23[2], 24[4], 25[3], 26[5], 27, 28[2]
47:1[4], 2[7], 3[6], 4[6], 5, 6, 7[2]
48:1[2], 2, 5[3], 6[2], 8[4], 9, 10[2], 12[2], 13, 14, 15[3], 16, 17[2], 18, 19, 21, 24[2], 25[2], 26, 28[5], 29[2], 30, 31, 32[4], 33[3], 34[2], 35[2], 36[2], 37[2], 38[3], 39, 40, 41[3], 42, 43[3], 44[6], 45[7], 46, 47[4]
49:1[2], 2[4], 3, 4, 5, 6[3], 7[2], 8[2], 12[2], 13[2], 14[3], 15, 16[7], 17, 18[3], 19[4], 20[5], 21[5], 22[4], 23, 25[2], 26[2], 27[2], 28[4], 30, 31[2], 32[3], 34[5], 35[3], 36[3], 37[2], 38[3], 39[3]
50:1[5], 2, 3, 4[4], 5[4], 6, 7[4], 8[6], 9, 10, 11, 12[2], 13[2], 14[2], 15[2], 16[4], 17[2], 18[4], 20[3], 21[3], 22, 23[3], 24, 25[6], 26, 27[2], 28[5], 29[4], 30[2], 31[2], 32, 33[3], 34[3], 35[3], 36, 37[2], 38, 39[5], 40[2], 41[3], 42[4], 43[2], 44[4], 45[6], 46[5]
51:1[2], 2, 3, 4[3], 5[2], 6[3], 7[4], 9, 10[3], 11[9], 12[7], 13, 14, 15[3], 16[5], 17, 18[2], 19[4], 20, 21[2], 22[2], 23[2], 24[2], 25[3], 26, 27[7], 28[6], 29[3], 30, 31, 32[3], 33[4], 34, 35[3], 36, 39, 40, 41[3], 42[3], 44[2], 45[3], 46[3], 47[3], 48[5], 49[3], 50[2], 51[2], 52[3], 53[2], 54[2], 55[2], 56[2], 57[2], 58[5], 59[6], 60, 63, 64[2]
52:1, 2[2], 3[3], 4[4], 5[2], 6[7], 7[11], 8[4], 9[3], 10[3], 11[3], 12[6], 13[6], 14[5], 15[10], 16[4], 17[9], 18[6], 19[9], 20[5], 21[3], 22[4], 23[2], 24[6], 25[13], 26[3], 27[2], 28[2], 29, 30[5], 31[7], 32[2], 33, 34[3]

LAMENTATIONS

1:1[3], 2, 3[2], 4[2], 5[4], 6[2], 7[5], 9, 10[2], 11, 12[2], 13, 14[2], 15[5], 16[2], 17, 18, 19[2], 20, 21
2:1[5], 2[7], 3[2], 4[3], 5[2], 6[6], 7[7], 8[5], 9[4], 10[5], 11[7], 12[3], 13, 15[5], 16[2], 17[3], 18[3], 19[7], 20[5], 21[6], 22[2]
3:1[2], 3, 12, 13, 14, 18, 19[2], 22, 24, 25[2], 26[2], 27, 29, 31, 32, 33, 34[2], 35[3], 36, 37, 38[2], 39, 40, 41, 45[3], 48[2], 50, 51, 53, 55, 57, 58, 62[2], 64, 66[2]
4:1[5], 2[4], 3[5], 4[4], 5, 6[5], 8, 9[3], 10[4], 11[2], 12[7], 13[5], 14, 15, 16[5], 19[4], 20[4], 21[2], 22
5:6[3], 9[3], 10, 11[3], 12, 13[3], 14[3], 15, 16, 18[2]

EZEKIEL

1:1[7], 2[3], 3[9], 4[5], 5[3], 7[3], 8, 10[7], 12, 13[6], 14[2], 15[3], 16[4], 19[5], 20[5], 21[5], 22[6], 23[3], 24[6], 25, 26[7], 27[5], 28[10]
2:2, 3, 4
3:1, 4, 5, 7[2], 11[3], 12[3], 13[5], 14[4], 15[2], 16[3], 17[2], 18[3], 19, 21[2], 22[3], 23[5], 24, 26, 27
4:1, 2, 3[2], 4[4], 5[5], 6[2], 7, 8, 9[2], 11, 13[3], 16
5:1, 2[5], 4[4], 5[3], 6[2], 7[4], 8[4], 9, 10[6], 11, 12[4], 13, 14[2], 15[2], 16[2], 17[2]
6:1[2], 2, 3[7], 5[2], 6[2], 7[3], 8[3], 9[2], 10, 11[6], 12[3], 13[4], 14[3]
7:1[2], 2[5], 3, 4[2], 5, 6, 7[6], 9[2], 10[3], 12[5], 13[4], 14[3], 15[6], 16[2], 19[5], 20[2], 21[4], 22, 23[2], 24[4], 26[4], 27[6]
8:1[7], 2[4], 3[10], 4[4], 5[7], 6[2], 7[3], 8[2], 9, 10[3], 11[4], 12[7], 14[4], 16[12], 17[4]
9:1, 2[4], 3[7], 4[8], 5[2], 6[3], 7[4], 8, 9[7], 11[3]
10:1[5], 2[5], 3[6], 4[10], 5[5], 6[4], 7[4], 8[2], 9[5], 10, 11[2], 12[2], 13, 14[8], 15[3], 16[5], 17[2], 18[5], 19[8], 20[4], 21[2], 22[3]
11:1[8], 2, 3[2], 5[4], 6[2], 7[5], 8[2], 9[2], 10[3], 11[3], 12[3], 13[2], 14[2], 15[4], 16[4], 17[4], 18[2], 19, 21[2], 22[4], 23[7], 24[4], 25[3]
12:1[2], 2, 5, 6[3], 7[3], 8[3], 9[2], 10[3], 12[4], 13[2], 14, 15[3], 16[5], 17[2], 19[6], 20[3], 21[2], 22[2], 23[3], 24, 25[4], 26[2], 27[3], 28[3]
13:1[2], 2[3], 3[2], 4[2], 5[6], 6[3], 7, 8[2], 9[6], 12[2], 13, 14[5], 15[2], 16[2], 17, 18[5], 19[2], 20[4], 21, 22[4], 23
14:1, 2[2], 3, 4[6], 5, 6[2], 7[4], 8[2], 9[3], 10[4], 11[2], 12[2], 13[3], 14, 15[2], 16[2], 17, 18, 20, 21[5], 22, 23
15:1[2], 2[3], 4[4], 5, 6[6], 7, 8[2]
16:1[2], 3[2], 4, 5[3], 7[2], 8[2], 14[2], 15, 16[2], 19, 21, 22, 23, 25, 26, 27[3], 28[3], 29, 30[2], 31, 34, 35[2], 36[3], 41[2], 43[2], 44, 45, 48, 49[3], 53[4], 56, 57[4], 58, 59[3], 60, 62, 63
17:1[2], 2, 3[3], 4, 5[2], 6, 7, 9[5], 10[2], 11[2], 12[4], 13[3], 14, 15, 16[4], 17, 18[2], 19, 21[2], 22[4], 23[4], 24[8]
18:1[2], 2[3], 3, 4[5], 6[3], 7[3], 9, 10, 11, 12[3], 15[3], 16[3], 17[2], 19[4], 20[11], 21, 23[2], 24[3], 25[2], 27, 29[3], 30, 32[2]
19:1, 3, 4[2], 6[2], 7[3], 8[2], 9[2], 10, 11[3], 12[3], 13
20:1[6], 2[2], 3[3], 4, 5[6], 6[3], 7[3], 8[4], 9[2], 10[2], 12, 13[3], 14, 15[3], 17, 18[2], 19, 20, 21[2], 22[2], 23[3], 26[4], 27[2], 28[4], 29[2], 30[3], 31[2], 32[3], 33, 34[2], 35[2], 36[3], 37[3], 38[4], 39, 40[6], 41[3], 42[4], 44[2], 45[2], 46[4], 47[8], 48
21:1[2], 2[2], 3[4], 4[4], 5, 6, 7[2], 8[2], 9, 10, 11[2], 12[2], 13[3], 14[6], 15[3], 16[2], 17, 18[2], 19[5], 20[3], 21[6], 22[5], 23, 24[2], 26[4], 28[6], 29[2], 30[2], 31[2], 32[4]
22:1[2], 2, 3[3], 4, 6, 7[4], 9[2], 12, 13, 14[2], 15[2], 16[3], 17[2], 18[4], 19[2], 20[3], 21[2], 22[4], 23[2], 24[2], 25[4], 26[3], 27[2], 28[2], 29[4], 30[3], 31[2]
23:1[2], 2, 3, 4[2], 5[2], 7, 8, 9[3], 10, 12, 14[3], 15[3], 17[2], 19[3], 20[2], 21[3], 22, 23[3], 25[2], 27, 28[3], 29, 30, 31, 32, 33[2], 34[2], 35, 36, 37, 38, 39[2], 42[3], 44[2], 45[3], 46, 47, 48, 49[2]
24:1[6], 2[3], 3[2], 4[4], 5[4], 6[3], 7[3], 8, 9[3], 10[3], 11[4], 12, 14[2], 15[2], 16, 17[3], 18[3], 19, 20[2], 21[5], 22, 24, 25[3], 27
25:1[2], 2, 3[6], 4[2], 5[2], 6[3], 7[4], 8[3], 9[4], 10[5], 11, 12[2], 13[2], 14[2], 15[3], 16[5], 17
26:1[5], 2[2], 3[2], 4[2], 5[5], 6[3], 7[2], 8[3], 10[5], 11[3], 12[2], 13[2], 14[3], 15[6], 16[3], 17[2], 18[4], 19[3], 20[7], 21
27:1[2], 3[4], 4[2], 6[4], 7, 8, 9[4], 10, 11[2], 12, 13, 14, 15[2], 16[2], 17, 18[4], 21, 22, 23, 25[3], 26[3], 27[5], 28[3], 29[5], 30, 32[3], 33[4], 34[5], 35[2], 36[2]
28:1[2], 2[6], 6[2], 7[3], 8[4], 9, 10[4], 11[2], 12[3], 13[11], 14[4], 15, 16[5], 17, 18[5], 19, 20[2], 22[3], 23[4], 24[2], 25[5], 26
29:1[6], 3[3], 4[3], 5[7], 6[3], 8, 9[3], 10[3], 12[7], 13[4], 14[3], 15[4], 16[3], 17[6], 18, 19[3], 20[2], 21[6]
30:1[2], 2[2], 3[5], 4[2], 5[4], 6[5], 7[4], 8, 9[2], 10[3], 11[5], 12[7], 13[4], 15[2], 17[2], 18[3], 19, 20[6], 21[2], 22[3], 23[3], 24[3], 25[7], 26[4]
31:1[6], 3[2], 4[4], 5[3], 6[3], 7, 8[5], 9[3], 10[2], 11[3], 12[8], 13[4], 14[9], 15[8], 16[7], 17[3], 18[8]
32:1[6], 2[3], 3, 4[6], 5[2], 6[3], 7[4], 8[2], 9[3], 10, 11[3], 12[6], 13[4], 14, 15[3], 16[4], 17[5], 18[6], 19, 20[3], 21[4], 22, 23[5], 24[6], 25[7], 26[3], 27[6], 28[3], 29[3], 30[6], 31[2], 32[6]
33:1[2], 2[4], 3[4], 4[3], 5[2], 6[6], 7[2], 8[2], 9, 10, 11[4], 12[9], 13, 14, 15[3], 17[3], 18, 19, 20[2], 21[5], 22[4], 23[2], 24[3], 25[3], 26, 27[8], 28[3], 29[2], 30[6], 31
34:1[2], 2[6], 3[3], 4, 5[2], 6[3], 7[2], 8[3], 9[2], 10[4], 11, 12[2], 13[6], 14[2], 15, 16[2], 17[3], 18[4], 20[3], 21, 24[2], 25[4], 26[2], 27[6], 28[3], 29[3], 30[3], 31[2]
35:1[2], 3, 4, 5[6], 6, 8, 9, 10, 11, 12[2], 14[2], 15[3]
36:1[3], 2[3], 3[5], 4[11], 5[5], 6[8], 7[2], 10[3], 11, 13, 14, 15[5], 16[2], 17[2], 18[2], 19[2], 20[3], 21[2], 22[3], 23[5], 24, 26, 28, 29, 30[5], 32, 33[4], 34[2], 35[2], 36[4], 37[2], 38[4]
37:1[6], 2, 4[2], 5, 6, 7, 8[3], 9[4], 10, 11, 12[2], 13, 14[2], 15[2], 16[3], 18, 19[5], 20, 21[3], 22[2], 25, 26, 28[3]
38:1[2], 2[2], 3[2], 6[2], 8[5], 9, 10[2], 11, 12[5], 13[2], 14, 15, 16[3], 17[2], 18[3], 19[2], 20[13], 21, 22, 23[2]
39:1[2], 2[3], 4[5], 5[2], 6[2], 7[4], 8[2], 9[8], 10[4], 11[7], 12[2], 13[4], 14[5], 15[4], 16[3], 17[3], 18[5], 20, 21[2], 22[2], 23[4], 25[3], 27[2], 28[2], 29[2]
40:1[10], 2[4], 3[2], 4[3], 5[7], 6[7], 7[5], 8[2], 9[5], 10[3], 11[5], 12[4], 13[4], 14[3], 15[6], 16[3], 17[3], 18[6], 19[5], 20[5], 21[7], 22[4], 23[5], 24[4], 25[3], 26[2], 27[3], 28[3], 29[4], 30, 31[4], 32[3], 33[4], 34[4], 35, 36[6], 37[4], 38[5], 39[5], 40[6], 41[2], 42[5], 43[3], 44[11], 45[5], 46[9], 47[3], 48[5], 49[5]
41:1[6], 2[8], 3[5], 4[4], 5[4], 6[6], 7[9], 8[4], 9[5], 10[3], 11[7], 12[7], 13[4], 14[5], 15[9], 16[7], 17[3], 19[7], 20[4], 21[8], 22[7], 23[2], 24[3], 25[5], 26[6]
42:1[7], 2[3], 3[4], 4[2], 5[5], 6[6], 7[6], 8[4], 9[3], 10[7], 11[4], 12[8], 13[11], 14[4], 15[3], 16[3], 17[2], 18[2], 19[2], 20[3]
43:1[3], 2[5], 3[7], 4[6], 5[5], 6[2], 7[7], 8, 9[2], 10[3], 11[11], 12[7], 13[10], 14[7], 15[2], 16[2], 17[5], 18[4], 19[4], 20[5], 21[5], 22[4], 23, 24[3], 25, 26, 27[4]
44:1[4], 2[3], 3[7], 4[7], 5[8], 6[3], 7[2], 8, 9[2], 10, 11[6], 12[2], 13[2], 14[3], 15[8], 17[4], 19[5], 21, 22[2], 23[4], 27[5], 29[3], 30[6], 31
45:1[7], 2[2], 3[4], 4[7], 5[5], 6[5], 7[17], 8[4], 9[2], 11[8], 12, 13[3], 14[4], 15[3], 16[3], 17[10], 18[5], 19[11], 20[3], 21[4], 22[3], 23[4], 25[10]
46:1[8], 2[10], 3[6], 4[4], 5[3], 6[2], 7, 8[4], 9[14], 10[2], 11[4], 12[6], 13[2], 14[4], 15[3], 16[3], 17[2], 18[2], 19[7], 20[7], 21[4], 22[2], 23, 24[5]
47:1[12], 2[6], 3[5], 4[5], 5, 6[2], 7[4], 8[5], 9[2], 10[3], 11[2], 12[6], 13[4], 14, 15[5], 16[3], 17[6], 18[5], 19[5], 20[4], 21, 22[4], 23[2]
48:1[7], 2[3], 3[3], 4[3], 5[3], 6[3], 7[3], 8[9], 9[2], 10[8], 11[4], 12[3], 13[5], 14[3], 15[6], 16[5], 17[6], 18[7], 19[2], 20[4], 21[18], 22[9], 23[4], 24[3], 25[3], 26[3], 27[3], 28[6], 29[3], 30[3], 31[4], 32, 33, 34, 35[3]

DANIEL

1:1[2], 2[7], 3[5], 4[4], 5[5], 6, 7[3], 8[5], 9[2], 10[5], 11[2], 13[4], 15[4], 16[2], 18[5], 19[2], 20[2], 21
2:1[2], 2[7], 3[2], 4[4], 5[5], 6[4], 7[3], 8[3], 9[4], 10[4], 11[3], 12[2], 13[2], 14[3], 15[4], 16[3], 17, 18[3], 19[2], 20, 21[3], 22[3], 23, 24[6], 25[4], 26[3], 27[9], 28[3], 30[3], 31, 34, 35[11], 36[3], 37, 38[5], 39, 40, 41[5], 42[3], 43, 44[3], 45[11], 46, 47, 48[4], 49[5]
3:1[4], 2[13], 3[12], 5[4], 6[2], 7[8], 8, 9, 10[3], 11, 12[3], 13, 14, 15[5], 16, 17, 18, 19[2], 20[2], 21[2], 22[4], 23[2], 24[4], 25[5], 26[5], 27[4], 28[2], 29, 30[2]
4:1[2], 2[2], 5[2], 6[3], 7[6], 8[5], 9[5], 10[4], 11[5], 12[7], 13, 14[3], 15[8], 17[10], 18[5], 19[5], 20[4], 21[5], 22[2], 23[10], 24[4], 25[5], 26[3], 27, 28, 29[3], 30[5], 31[3], 32[4], 33[3], 34[3], 35[5], 36[2], 37
5:1[2], 2[4], 3[4], 4, 5[8], 6[2], 7[9], 8[4], 10[5], 11[8], 12[3], 13[5], 14[2], 15[5], 16[4], 17[4], 18, 19, 21[6], 23[4], 24[2], 25, 26[2], 27, 28, 29[2], 30[2], 31[2]
6:1[2], 2[2], 3[3], 4[2], 5, 6, 7[7], 8[4], 9[2], 10, 12[7], 13[4], 14[3], 15[5], 16[3], 17[5], 18[2], 19[3], 20[4], 21, 22, 23[3], 24[6], 25, 26[3], 27[2], 28[3]
7:1[4], 2[3], 3, 4[4], 5[2], 6[2], 7[4], 8[4], 9[5], 10[2], 11[5], 12[2], 13[4], 15[2], 16[3], 17, 18[4], 19[4], 20[2], 21[2], 22[6], 23[3], 24[2], 25[4], 26[2], 27[7], 28[3]
8:1[3], 2[3], 3[4], 4, 5[5], 6[3], 7[5], 8[3], 9[3], 10[4], 11[4], 12[3], 13[5], 14, 15[3], 16[2], 17[3], 18, 19[4], 20[2], 21[4], 22, 23[3], 24[2], 25, 26[4], 27[2]
9:1[6], 2[7], 3, 4[3], 6[3], 7[3], 9, 10[3], 11[4], 12, 13[2], 14[3], 15, 16, 17[2], 18, 20[3], 21[5], 23[4], 24[3], 25[6], 26[7], 27[8]
10:1[5], 4[4], 6[4], 7[3], 9[3], 10, 11, 12, 13[4], 14[2], 15, 16[3], 17, 18, 20[2], 21
11:1[2], 2[3], 4, 5[2], 6[7], 7[3], 8[2], 9[2], 11[5], 12, 13[3], 14[4], 15[5], 16, 17[2], 18[2], 19, 20[2], 21[3], 22[3], 23, 24[4], 25[4], 26, 27[2], 28, 29[4], 30[3], 31[3], 32[2], 33[2], 35[2], 36[3], 37[2], 38, 39[2], 40[7], 41[3], 42[2], 43[4], 44[2], 45[3]
12:1[3], 2[2], 3[3], 4[4], 5[6], 6[4], 7[5], 8, 9[3], 10[3], 11[3], 12, 13[3]

HOSEA

1:1[6], 2[6], 3, 4[5], 5[2], 6, 7[2], 10[7], 11[4]
2:3, 4, 5, 9[2], 10, 12[2], 13[2], 14, 15[4], 16, 17, 18[9], 20, 21[3], 22[4], 23
3:1[4], 3, 4, 5[4]
4:1[6], 3[6], 4, 5[3], 6, 8, 10, 11, 12, 13[4], 14, 15[2], 16, 19
5:1, 2, 4[3], 5, 6, 7, 8[2], 9[2], 10[2], 11, 12, 13, 14
6:1, 2, 3[5], 4, 5[3], 6, 7, 9[2], 10[2], 11
7:1[4], 3[2], 4[2], 5[2], 6[2], 8, 10[2], 12[2], 16[4]
8:1[3], 3[2], 6[2], 7[4], 8, 10[3], 12, 13[2], 14
9:2[3], 3, 4[4], 5[4], 6, 7[6], 8[3], 9, 10[3], 11[3], 13, 15, 16, 17
10:1[3], 3, 4[2], 5[5], 7[2], 8[6], 9[3], 10, 11, 12, 13[2], 14[2], 15
11:4, 5[2], 6, 7, 9[4], 10[3], 11[2], 12[2]
12:1[2], 2, 3[2], 4, 5[2], 7, 9[4], 10[3], 11[2], 12, 13
13:2[4], 3[7], 4[2], 5[2], 7, 8[2], 12, 13[3], 14[2], 15[4], 16
14:1, 2[2], 3[2], 5[2], 6, 7[4], 9[4]

JOEL

1:1[3], 2[2], 4[6], 5, 6[2], 7, 8, 9[6], 10[5], 11[4], 12[8], 13[4], 14[6], 15[4], 16[2], 17[4], 18[3], 19[6], 20[6]
2:1[5], 2[4], 3[2], 4[2], 5[4], 6, 7, 8, 9[4], 10[5], 11[3], 12, 13[2], 14, 15, 16[7], 17[7], 18, 19[2], 20[3], 21, 22[6], 23[6], 24[2], 25[5], 26[2], 27[2], 29[2], 30[2], 31[5], 32[5]
3:1, 2[2], 4, 6[3], 7, 8[4], 9[3], 10, 12[3], 13[4], 14[4], 15[3], 16[7], 17, 18[6], 19[2], 21

AMOS

1:1[6], 2[4], 3[2], 4[2], 5[7], 6[3], 7[2], 8[5], 9[4], 10[2], 11[3], 12, 13[4], 14[5], 15
2:1[4], 2[3], 3[4], 4[5], 5, 6[4], 7[7], 8[3], 9[4], 10[4], 11, 12[2], 14[4], 15[2], 16[2]
3:1[3], 2[2], 4, 5[2], 6[3], 7[2], 8[2], 9[8], 10, 11[2], 12[6], 13[3], 14[6], 15[5]
4:1[3], 2[2], 3[3], 5[2], 6, 7[3], 8, 9[2], 10[5], 11[2], 13[7]
5:2, 3[3], 4[2], 6[2], 7, 8[9], 9[4], 10, 11, 12[3], 13, 14[2], 15[5], 16[5], 17, 18[4], 19[2], 20[2], 22, 23[2], 25, 26[2], 27[2]
6:1[3], 2[2], 3[2], 4[5], 5[2], 6[2], 7[2], 8[5], 10[6], 11[3], 12[2], 14[5]
7:1[6], 2[2], 3[2], 4[3], 6[2], 7, 8[3], 9[4], 10[4], 11, 12, 13[2], 15[3], 16[3], 17[3]
8:1, 2[2], 3[3], 4[3], 5[5], 6[4], 7[2], 8[2], 9[4], 10[2], 11[5], 12[4], 13, 14[2]
9:1[8], 3[4], 4, 5[3], 6[7], 7[5], 8[7], 9[3], 10[3], 11[3], 12[3], 13[7], 14[4], 15

OBADIAH

1[4], 2, 3[4], 4[3], 5, 6, 7[3], 8[3], 9[2], 11[4], 12[5], 13[4], 14[2], 15[3], 16, 17, 18[5], 19[6], 20[6], 21[3]

JONAH

1:1[3], 3[5], 4[4], 5[6], 6, 7, 9[4], 10[4], 11[2], 12[2], 13[3], 14, 15[2], 16[3], 17[3]
2:1[2], 2[2], 3[4], 5[4], 6[3], 7, 9[2], 10[3]
3:1[3], 2, 3[2], 4, 5[3], 6, 7[2], 8, 10
4:2[2], 4, 5[5], 6[2], 7[3], 8[3], 9, 10[3]

MICAH

1:1[4], 2[2], 3[3], 4[4], 5[5], 6[4], 7[6], 8[2], 9, 10[2], 11[2], 12[3], 13[6], 14[2], 15, 16
2:1[2], 3, 4, 5[2], 7[3], 8[2], 9, 11[2], 12[5], 13[4]
3:1, 2[2], 3[3], 4, 5[2], 6[3], 7[2], 8[2], 9[2], 11[5], 12[4]
4:1[7], 2[7], 4[2], 5[3], 6, 7, 8[6], 10[4], 12[4], 13[3]
5:1[2], 2, 3[3], 4[7], 5[2], 6[5], 7[6], 8[6], 10[2], 11, 13[2], 14, 15
6:1[3], 2[3], 4[2], 5[3], 6[2], 7[3], 8, 9[4], 10[4], 11[2], 12[2], 14[2], 15, 16[5]
7:1[4], 2[2], 3[3], 4[3], 5, 6[5], 7[2], 8, 9[3], 10[3], 11[2], 12[3], 13[2], 14[4], 15[2], 16, 17[3], 18[2], 19[2], 20[3]

NAHUM

1:1[4], 2[3], 3[7], 4[3], 5[4], 6[2], 7[2], 8, 9[2], 11, 12, 14[4], 15[3]
2:1[2], 2[4], 3[5], 4[4], 5[2], 6[3], 7, 9[4], 10[3], 11[7], 12, 13[5]
3:1[2], 2[6], 3[3], 4[4], 5[3], 8[4], 10[2], 11, 12[3], 13[3], 14[3], 15[5], 16[2], 17[5], 18[2], 19[2]

HABAKKUK

1:1[2], 4[3], 5, 6[4], 8[3], 9[3], 10[2], 13[2], 14[3], 15, 17
2:1, 2[2], 3[2], 4, 8[5], 9, 11[4], 13[4], 14[6], 16[2], 17[5], 18[4], 19[3], 20[2]
3:1, 2[4], 3[8], 4[8], 5, 6[4], 7[3], 8[4], 9[2], 10[4], 11[3], 12[2], 13[6], 14[2], 15[2], 16[3], 17[8], 18[2], 19[2]

ZEPHANIAH

1:1[8], 2[2], 3[8], 4[5], 5[3], 6[2], 7[5], 8[4], 9[2], 10[5], 11, 12[2], 13, 14[6], 16[3], 17[2], 18[5]
2:2[7], 3[4], 4, 5[8], 6, 7[6], 8[3], 9[6], 10[2], 11[5], 13, 14[9], 15
3:1, 2[2], 3[2], 4[2], 5[3], 6, 8[7], 9[3], 10[2], 11, 12[3], 13, 14, 15[4], 17[2], 18[2], 20[3]

HAGGAI

1:1[11], 2[4], 3[3], 5, 7, 8[3], 9, 10[2], 11[8], 12[12], 13[4], 14[11], 15[4]
2:1[6], 2[5], 4[5], 5, 6[5], 7[2], 8[3], 9[4], 10[6], 11[3], 12[2], 13, 14, 15[2], 16[2], 17[2], 18[5], 19[6], 20[4], 21[2], 22[7], 23[4]

ZECHARIAH

1:1[7], 2, 3[3], 4[3], 5, 6[2], 7[9], 8[2], 9, 10[4], 11[5], 12[3], 13[2], 14[2], 15[2], 16[2], 17[2], 19[2], 20, 21[4]
2:2[2], 3, 4, 5[3], 6[6], 7, 8[4], 9, 10[2], 11[3], 12[2], 13
3:1[3], 2[4], 3, 4, 5[2], 6[2], 7, 8[2], 9[4], 10[3]
4:1, 2[3], 3[4], 4, 5, 6[3], 7, 8[2], 9[3], 10[6], 11[3], 12[2], 14[3]
5:2[2], 3[3], 4[7], 5, 6, 7[2], 8[4], 9[5], 10[2], 11
6:1, 2[2], 3[2], 4, 5[5], 6[5], 7[4], 8[2], 9[2], 10[4], 11[3], 12[5], 13[4], 14[4], 15[5]
7:1[5], 2[2], 3[5], 4[2], 5[4], 7[6], 8[2], 9, 10[4], 11, 12[5], 13, 14[3]
8:1[2], 2, 3[5], 4[2], 5[3], 6[4], 7[3], 8, 9[8], 10, 11[3], 12[5], 13, 14[2], 15, 16[3], 17, 18[2], 19[11], 20[2], 21[3], 22[2], 23[3]
9:1[8], 3[3], 4[2], 5, 6[2], 8, 9, 10[7], 11[2], 12, 13[2], 14[5], 15[3], 16[3], 17[2]
10:1[5], 2[2], 3[5], 4[3], 5[5], 6[3], 7, 9, 10[2], 11[7], 12[2]
11:1, 2[4], 3[4], 4[3], 5, 6[6], 7[5], 9[2], 10, 11[4], 13[6], 14, 15[2], 16[4], 17[3]
12:1[8], 2[2], 3[2], 4[3], 5[3], 6[5], 7[6], 8[5], 9, 10[3], 11[2], 12[5], 13[3], 14
13:1[2], 2[7], 3[2], 4, 6, 7[5], 8[3], 9[3]
14:1[3], 2[7], 3[2], 4[9], 5[8], 6, 7, 8[2], 9[2], 10[6], 12[3], 13[3], 14[2], 15[6], 16[4], 17[4], 18[5], 19[3], 20[7], 21[4]

MALACHI

1:1[3], 2[2], 3[2], 4[5], 5[2], 6, 7[2], 8[3], 9, 10[2], 11[7], 12[3], 13[4], 14[4]
2:2, 3, 4, 5, 6, 7[4], 8[4], 9[2], 10, 11[3], 12[6], 13[3], 14[3], 15[3], 16[3], 17[4]
3:1[5], 2, 3[2], 4[3], 5[7], 6, 7[2], 10[4], 11[5], 12, 13, 14, 15, 16[3], 17, 18[2]
4:1[4], 2[2], 3[4], 4[2], 5[4], 6[6]

MATTHEW

1:1[4], 6[3], 11, 16, 17[3], 18[2], 20[3], 22[2], 24[2]
2:1[3], 2[2], 3, 4[2], 5, 6[3], 7[2], 8, 9[4], 10, 11[2], 13[4], 14, 15[3], 16[5], 17, 19, 20[3], 21[2], 22[2], 23
3:1[2], 2, 3[5], 4, 5, 7[2], 10[4], 11, 12[2], 16[3]
4:1[3], 3[2], 4, 5[3], 6, 7, 8[4], 10, 11, 13[2], 14, 15[5], 16[2], 17, 18[2], 21, 22, 23[3], 24
5:1, 3[2], 5[2], 7, 8, 9[2], 10, 12, 13[3], 14[2], 15, 17[2], 18, 19[4], 20[3], 21, 22[2], 23, 24, 25[5], 26, 32, 33, 35[3], 39, 40, 45[5], 46[2], 47
6:2[3], 5[4], 7, 13[3], 16, 22[3], 23, 24[4], 25[2], 26[2], 28[2], 30[3], 32, 33, 34[5]
7:3[2], 4, 5[2], 6, 12[2], 13[3], 14[2], 19, 21[2], 25[3], 26, 27[4], 28, 29
8:1, 4[2], 6, 8[2], 11[2], 12[2], 13[2], 15, 16[2], 17, 18, 20[4], 22, 24[3], 26[2], 27[3], 28[4], 29, 31[2], 32[4], 33[3], 34
9:2[3], 3, 6[3], 8, 9, 10, 11, 13, 14[2], 15[5], 16[2], 17[3], 20, 22, 23[3], 24, 25[3], 26, 28[2], 33[3], 34[3], 35[4], 36, 37[2], 38[2]
10:2[4], 3[2], 4, 5[3], 6[2], 7, 8[3], 10, 13, 14, 15[2], 16, 17, 18, 20, 21[5], 22, 23[2], 24[2], 25[4], 27[2], 28[2], 29, 30, 35[2], 41[2], 42
11:2[2], 5[7], 7[3], 11[2], 12[4], 13[2], 16, 19, 20, 21, 22, 23, 24[2], 25, 27[5]
12:1[3], 2[2], 4[3], 5[5], 6, 7, 8[2], 10, 11, 12, 13[2], 14, 17, 18, 19, 21, 22, 23[2], 24[3], 28[2], 29, 31[2], 32[3], 33[3], 34[3], 35[3], 36, 38[2], 39[2], 40[4], 41[2], 42[6], 43, 45[2], 46, 50[2]
13:1[3], 2[2], 4[2], 6, 7, 10, 11[2], 14, 18[2], 19[4], 20[3], 21, 22[5], 23[2], 24, 25, 26[2], 27[2], 28, 29[2], 30[5], 31, 32[5], 33[2], 34, 35[3], 36[5], 37[2], 38[8], 39[7], 40[3], 41, 43[3], 44[2], 45, 47[2], 48[2], 49[5], 50, 52, 55
14:1[2], 2[2], 5, 6, 9[2], 10, 11, 12, 13[2], 15[3], 19[7], 20, 22[2], 23[2], 24[4], 25[3], 26[2], 28, 29[2], 30, 32[2], 33[2], 34, 35, 36
15:2[2], 3, 4, 6, 9, 10, 11[2], 12, 14[4], 17[3], 18[3], 19, 20, 21, 22, 24[2], 26, 27[2], 29, 31[6], 32[2], 33, 35[2], 36[4], 37, 39[2]
16:1[2], 2, 3[6], 4[2], 5, 6[3], 9[2], 10[2], 11[3], 12[4], 13[2], 14[2], 16[3], 18, 19[2], 20, 21[2], 23, 26, 27[2], 28
17:2[2], 5, 6, 9[4], 10, 12, 13[2], 14, 15[2], 18[2], 19, 22[2], 23, 25[3], 26, 27[2]
18:1[4], 2, 3, 4[2], 6[2], 7[2], 10, 11, 12[2], 13, 14, 16, 17[2], 20, 23, 26, 27[2], 28[2], 30, 34
19:1, 3, 4, 8[2], 10[2], 12, 13, 14, 17, 20, 21, 22, 23, 24[2], 28[4], 30
20:1[2], 2, 3[2], 4, 5, 6[2], 7, 8[5], 9, 10, 11[2], 12[2], 16[2], 17[2], 18[3], 19[2], 20, 21[3], 22[2], 23, 24[2], 25[2], 28, 30, 31[2]
21:1, 2, 3, 4, 5[2], 6, 7[2], 8[3], 9[5], 10, 11[2], 12[5], 13, 14[3], 15[5], 16, 17, 18[2], 19[2], 20[2], 21[2], 23[4], 25, 26, 28, 30, 31[5], 32[3], 34[4], 35, 36, 38[3], 39, 40[2], 41, 42[7], 43[2], 45, 46
22:2, 3, 4, 6, 7, 8, 9[2], 10[2], 11[2], 13[2], 15, 16[3], 19, 21[2], 23[2], 25, 26[3], 27, 28[2], 29[2], 30[2], 31[2], 32[6], 33, 34[2], 36[2], 37, 38, 39, 40[2], 41, 42, 44
23:1, 2[2], 5, 6[3], 7, 9, 13, 14, 15, 16[3], 17[3], 18[2], 19[3], 20, 21, 22, 23[3], 25[3], 26[2], 29[4], 30[3], 31[2], 32, 33, 35[6], 37, 39[2]
24:1[3], 3[5], 6, 8, 12, 13[2], 14[3], 15[3], 16, 17, 18, 20[2], 21[2], 22, 24, 26[2], 27[5], 28[2], 29[6], 30[6], 31[2], 32, 33, 36, 37[3], 38[4], 39[3], 40[3], 41[3], 43[3], 44, 49, 50, 51
25:1[2], 4, 5, 6, 8[2], 9, 10[3], 11, 13[3], 14, 16[2], 18, 19, 21, 23, 24, 25, 27, 28, 30, 31[3], 32, 33[3], 34[4], 37, 40[2], 41[2], 45, 46
26:2[3], 3[6], 5[2], 6[2], 9, 10, 11, 13, 14[2], 17[4], 18[3], 19[2], 20[2], 23[2], 24[2], 26, 27, 28[2], 29, 30, 31[3], 34, 35, 36, 37, 40, 41[2], 42, 44[2], 45[3], 47[3], 51, 52[2], 54, 55[2], 56[3], 57[3], 58[3], 59[2], 60, 61, 62, 63[4], 64[3], 65, 67, 69, 71, 72, 74[2], 75[2]
27:1[3], 2, 3[2], 4, 5[2], 6[4], 7, 8, 9[4], 10[2], 11[4], 12, 14, 15[2], 19, 20[2], 21[2], 23[2], 24[2], 25, 27[4], 29[2], 30[2], 31, 35, 37[2], 38[2], 40[3], 41[2], 42[2], 43, 44[2], 45[3], 46, 49, 50, 51[6], 52[2], 53[2], 54[3], 56[2], 57, 58[2], 59, 60[3], 61[2], 62[4], 64[6], 66[2]
28:1[6], 2[4], 4, 5[2], 6[2], 7, 8, 9, 11[4], 12[2], 14, 15[2], 16, 19[4], 20[2]

MARK

1:1[3], 2, 3[4], 4[3], 5[2], 7, 8, 10[3], 12[2], 13[3], 14[2], 15[3], 16[2], 19[2], 20[2], 21[2], 22, 24, 26, 27, 28, 29[2], 31[2], 32, 33[2], 34, 35, 38, 42, 44, 45[2]
2:1, 2[2], 3, 4[5], 5[2], 6, 9[2], 10[3], 12, 13[2], 14[2], 16, 17[2], 18[4], 19[4], 20[2], 21[3], 22[4], 23[3], 24[2], 26[5], 27[2], 28[2]
3:1, 2, 3[2], 4, 5[3], 6[2], 7, 9, 11, 17[3], 18[2], 20, 22[3], 27, 28, 29, 32, 35[2]
4:1[5], 4[3], 6, 7, 10[2], 11[2], 14[2], 15[3], 16, 17, 18, 19[4], 20, 26[2], 27, 28[5], 29[3], 30, 31[3], 32[3], 33, 35[3], 36[2], 37[2], 38[2], 39[3], 41[2]
5:1[4], 2[2], 3, 4[2], 5[2], 7, 8, 10, 11, 12[2], 13[5], 14[3], 15[2], 16[2], 18[2], 19, 21[2], 22[2], 23, 27, 29, 30, 31, 33[2], 35[3], 36[3], 37, 38[4], 39, 40[4], 41[2], 42[2]
6:2[2], 3[3], 6, 7, 11[2], 14[2], 15, 16, 22[4], 23, 24[2], 25[3], 26, 27[2], 28[2], 30, 33, 35[2], 36[2], 39, 41[4], 43[2], 44, 45[3], 47[4], 48[4], 49, 51[2], 52[2], 53[2], 54, 56[3]
7:1[2], 3[4], 4[2], 5[3], 7, 8[3], 9, 10, 13, 14, 15[2], 17[3], 18, 19[2], 20[2], 21, 23, 24, 26[2], 27[3], 28[3], 29, 30[2], 31[4], 33, 35, 36[2], 37[2]
8:1, 2, 3, 4, 6[4], 8, 10, 11, 13[2], 14[2], 15[3], 19, 20, 23[3], 26[2], 27[2], 28[2], 29, 31[3], 33[2], 34, 35[2], 36, 38[3]
9:1, 7, 9[3], 10[2], 11, 12, 14, 15, 16, 17, 20[2], 22[2], 24[2], 25[2], 26, 27, 28, 31[3], 33[2], 34[2], 35[2], 36, 42, 43, 44, 45, 46, 47, 48, 50
10:1[3], 2, 5, 6[2], 10[2], 14[2], 15, 17, 19, 21[2], 23, 24[2], 25[2], 29, 30, 31, 32[2], 33[4], 34, 35, 37, 38[2], 39[2], 41, 42, 44, 45, 46[2], 48, 49, 51, 52
11:1, 2, 3, 4[2], 5, 7, 8[3], 9[2], 10[4], 11[3], 12, 13, 15[5], 16, 17, 18[2], 19, 20[3], 21, 23, 27[4], 30, 32
12:1, 2[5], 4, 7[2], 8, 9[4], 10[4], 11, 12[2], 13[2], 14[2], 17[2], 18, 20, 21[2], 22[2], 23[2], 24[2], 25[2], 26[6], 27[4], 28[2], 29[3], 30[2], 31, 32[2], 33[4], 34, 35[3], 36[2], 37, 38[2], 39[3], 41[3], 43
13:1, 3[2], 4, 7, 8, 9, 10, 11, 12[4], 13[2], 14[3], 15[2], 16, 18, 19[2], 20[3], 22, 24[2], 25[2], 26[2], 27[4], 28, 29, 32[3], 33, 34[2], 35[4]
14:1[4], 2[2], 3[3], 4, 5, 7, 8, 9, 10[2], 12[3], 13, 14[5], 16[2], 17[2], 20[2], 21[2], 23, 24, 25[3], 26, 27[2], 30, 31, 35[2], 38[2], 39, 41[4], 43[4], 47, 49[2], 51, 52, 53[4], 54[4], 55[2], 60[2], 61[4], 62[3], 63, 64, 65[2], 66[3], 68[2], 72[4]
15:1[4], 2[2], 3, 7, 8, 9[2], 10, 11[2], 12[2], 14, 15, 16[3], 18, 19, 20, 21[2], 22[2], 25, 26[3], 27[2], 28[2], 29, 30, 31[2], 32[2], 33[3], 34, 37, 38[4], 39[3], 40[2], 42[4], 43[2], 44, 45[2], 46[3], 47
16:1[2], 2[6], 3[3], 4, 5[2], 6, 8, 9[2], 12, 13, 14, 15[2], 18, 19[2], 20[2]

LUKE

1:2[2], 3, 4, 5[4], 6[2], 8[2], 9[4], 10[3], 11[3], 13, 15[3], 16[2], 17[8], 18, 19[2], 20, 21[2], 22, 23, 25[4], 26[4], 27[6], 28[6], 30, 32[4], 33, 34, 35[5], 36, 38[3], 39, 40, 41[3], 42, 43, 44[2], 45, 46, 48, 51[2], 52, 53[2], 58, 59[3], 65, 66[2], 67, 68, 69, 70[2], 71, 72, 73, 74, 75, 76[4], 77, 78[2], 79[2], 80[3]
2:1, 4[3], 6, 7, 8[2], 9[4], 10, 11[2], 12, 13[2], 14, 15[3], 16, 17, 18, 20[2], 21[4], 22[3], 23[4], 24[2], 25[3], 26[2], 27[6], 31, 32[2], 34, 35, 36[2], 37, 38, 39[2], 40[2], 41[2], 42[2], 43[2], 44, 46[3], 50
3:1[4], 2[4], 3[3], 4[7], 5[2], 6, 7[2], 9[4], 10, 14, 15[2], 16[2], 17[2], 18, 19[2], 21[2], 22, 23[2], 24[5], 25[5], 26[5], 27[5], 28[5], 29[5], 30[5], 31[5], 32[5], 33[5], 34[5], 35[5], 36[5], 37[5], 38[4]
4:1[3], 2, 3[2], 5[3], 6[2], 8, 9[2], 12, 13[2], 14[3], 16[2], 17[4], 18[7], 19[2], 20[4], 22, 25[3], 27[3], 28, 29[3], 30, 31, 33, 34, 35[2], 36, 37[2], 38, 39, 40, 41, 42, 43, 44
5:1[3], 2[2], 3[4], 4, 5[2], 7[2], 9[2], 10, 13, 14, 15, 16, 17[3], 19[4], 21[2], 24[3], 27, 32, 33[3], 34[3], 35[2], 36[4], 37[3], 39
6:1[4], 2[2], 4[3], 5[2], 6, 7[2], 8[3], 9, 10[2], 15, 16[2], 17[3], 19, 20, 22, 23[2], 26, 29[2], 33, 35[4], 38, 39[3], 40, 41[2], 42[4], 45[4], 46, 48[3], 49[3]
7:1[2], 3[2], 6[2], 9, 10[2], 11, 12[4], 13, 14, 17, 18, 20, 22[7], 24[4], 28[2], 29[3], 30[2], 31[2], 32, 33, 34, 36[2], 37[2], 38[2], 39, 41[2], 44[2], 45, 47, 50
8:1[3], 3, 5[3], 7, 10[2], 11[3], 12[3], 13[2], 15[2], 16, 19, 21, 22[2], 23, 24[3], 25, 26[2], 27[2], 29[5], 31, 32, 33[5], 34[2], 35[3], 36, 37[4], 38[2], 39, 40, 41, 42, 44, 45, 47[2], 49[3], 51[4], 54
9:2[2], 5, 6[2], 7[2], 8, 10[2], 11[2], 12[4], 16[4], 18, 19[2], 20, 22[3], 24, 25, 26[2], 27, 29, 32, 34, 35, 36,

LUKE

37^2, 38, 42^3, 43, 44^2, 47, 48, 51, 52, 56, 57, 58^2, 60^2, 62^2

10:1, 2^4, 4, 6, 7^2, 9^2, 10^2, 11^2, 13, 14, 17^2, 19^2, 20, 21, 22^5, 23^2, 26, 27, 31, 32^2, 35^2, 36

11:7, 13, 14^3, 15^2, 20^2, 24, 26^2, 27^3, 28, 29^3, 30^2, 31^7, 32^3, 33, 34^3, 35, 36^2, 38, 39^4, 42^2, 43^3, 44, 45, 46, 47^2, 48, 49, 50^4, 51^4, 52, 53^2

12:1^3, 3^3, 4, 7, 8^2, 9, 10^2, 11, 12^2, 13^2, 15^2, 16, 22, 23^2, 24^2, 26, 27, 28^3, 30^2, 31, 32, 33, 36, 37, 38^2, 39^3, 40, 42, 45, 46^2, 48, 49, 53^{10}, 54^2, 55, 56^3, 58^6, 59

13:1, 2, 4, 7^2, 10^2, 14^5, 15^3, 16, 17^2, 18, 19^3, 20, 21, 22, 24, 25^4, 28^2, 29^5, 31^2, 32, 33, 34, 35^3

14:1^3, 2, 3^2, 5, 7, 8, 9, 10^2, 13^4, 14^2, 15, 18, 21^8, 22, 23^3, 28, 29, 32, 34, 35^2

15:1, 2, 4^2, 8, 9, 10^2, 12^2, 13, 16^2, 21, 22^2, 23, 25^2, 26, 27, 30

16:1, 3^2, 4, 5, 8^4, 9, 10, 11^2, 13^4, 14, 15, 16^3, 17, 21^3, 22^3, 24, 29, 30, 31^2

17:1, 2, 5^2, 6^3, 7, 9, 11, 14, 17, 20^3, 21, 22^4, 24^4, 26^3, 27^3, 28, 29, 30^2, 31^3, 34^2, 35^2, 36^3, 37^2

18:6^2, 8^2, 10^3, 11, 12, 13, 14, 16, 17, 20, 22, 24, 25, 27, 29, 30, 31^3, 32, 33, 34, 35, 36, 39, 43

19:2^2, 3, 5, 8^3, 10, 11, 15^2, 16, 18, 23, 24, 29^2, 30^2, 31, 33^3, 34, 35, 36, 37^5, 38^4, 39^2, 40, 41, 42, 43, 44^2, 45, 46, 47^5, 48

20:1^6, 4, 6, 9, 10^5, 13^2, 14^3, 15^3, 16, 17^5, 19^4, 20^2, 21^2, 25^2, 26, 27, 29, 30, 31^2, 32, 33, 34, 35^2, 36^4, 37^6, 38^2, 39, 42^2, 45^2, 46^5, 47

21:1^2, 4^2, 5, 6^2, 8, 9, 12, 20, 21^3, 22, 23, 24^5, 25^6, 26^2, 27, 29^2, 31, 35^2, 36, 37^4, 38^3

22:1^2, 2^2, 3^2, 4, 6^2, 7^2, 8, 10^2, 11^5, 13, 14^2, 16, 17, 18^3, 20^2, 21^2, 22, 24, 25^2, 26, 30, 31, 34, 37^2, 39, 40, 44, 47, 48, 49, 50^2, 52^3, 53^2, 54, 55^2, 56, 59, 60, 61^4, 63, 64, 66^4, 67, 69^3, 70

23:1, 2, 3^2, 4^2, 5^2, 6, 10, 12, 13^3, 14, 17, 19, 22, 23^2, 26^2, 29^5, 30^2, 31, 33^5, 35^3, 36, 37^2, 38^2, 39, 40^2, 41, 44^3, 45^4, 46, 47, 48^2, 49, 51^4, 52, 54^2, 55^2, 56^2

24:1^5, 2^2, 3^2, 5^3, 7^3, 9^3, 10^2, 12^2, 18^2, 19, 20, 21, 22, 24^2, 25, 27^3, 28, 29, 32^2, 33^2, 34, 35, 36, 44^4, 45, 46^2, 49^2, 53

JOHN

1:1^4, 2^2, 4^2, 5^2, 7^2, 9^2, 10^3, 12, 13^3, 14^4, 17, 18^3, 19^2, 20, 23^5, 24, 29^4, 32, 33^4, 34, 35, 36, 37, 39, 40, 41^2, 42, 43, 44, 45^3, 48, 49^2, 50, 51^2

2:1^2, 2, 3, 5, 6^3, 7^2, 8^2, 9^8, 10^2, 13, 14^2, 15^5, 17, 18, 20, 21, 22^3, 23^3

3:1^2, 2, 3, 4, 5^2, 6^2, 8^3, 13, 14^3, 16, 17^3, 18^2, 19^2, 20^2, 21, 22, 25, 26, 28, 29^5, 31^2, 34^2, 35^2, 36^3

4:1^2, 5, 6^2, 8, 9^3, 10, 11^2, 12, 14^2, 15, 17, 19, 20, 21^2, 22, 23^4, 25, 27, 28^3, 29, 30, 31, 33, 34, 35, 39^3, 40, 42^4, 45^4, 46, 47, 49, 50^2, 52^3, 53^3, 54

5:1, 2^2, 3^2, 4^4, 7^3, 9^3, 10^2, 11, 14, 15^2, 16^2, 18^3, 19^3, 20^2, 21^3, 22^2, 23^4, 25^4, 26^2, 27, 28^3, 29^2, 30^2, 32, 33, 36^4, 37, 39, 42, 44, 45

6:1^2, 4^2, 10^3, 11^4, 12, 13^2, 14^2, 16, 17, 18, 19^2, 21^3, 22^5, 23^2, 24, 25^2, 26^2, 27^3, 28, 29, 31, 32, 33^2, 35, 37, 38, 39^2, 40^3, 41^2, 42, 44^2, 45^2, 46^2, 49, 50, 51^4, 52, 53^2, 54, 57^2, 59, 62, 63^3, 64, 67, 68, 69^2, 71^2

7:1, 2, 3, 4, 7^2, 10, 11^2, 12^2, 13, 14^3, 15, 17, 18, 19^2, 20, 22^2, 23^3, 24, 26^2, 28, 31, 32^4, 35^4, 37^2, 38, 39^2, 40^2, 41, 42^3, 43, 45^2, 46, 47, 48^2, 49

8:1^2, 2^3, 3^2, 4, 5, 6, 8, 9^4, 10, 12^3, 13, 15, 16, 17, 18, 20^2, 22, 25^2, 26, 27, 28, 29, 32^2, 34, 35^3, 36, 39, 40, 41, 44^5, 45, 46, 48, 52^2, 53, 57, 59^2

9:3, 4^2, 5^3, 6^5, 7, 8, 11, 13, 14^2, 15, 16^2, 17, 18^2, 22^3, 24^2, 30, 32^2, 35, 40

10:1^3, 2^3, 3^2, 4, 5, 7^2, 8, 9, 10, 11^3, 12^6, 13^2, 14, 15^3, 19, 21^3, 22^2, 23, 24^2, 25, 31, 33, 35^2, 36^3, 37, 38^2, 40

11:1, 2, 4^2, 6, 8, 9^3, 10, 15, 17, 19, 20, 24^2, 25^2, 27^3, 28, 30, 31^3, 33^2, 36, 37^2, 38, 39^2, 40, 41^3, 42, 45^2, 46, 47^2, 48, 49, 50^2, 52, 54^2, 55^3, 56^2, 57^2

12:1^2, 2, 3^4, 5, 6^2, 7, 8, 9^2, 10, 11, 12^2, 13^3, 16, 17^2, 18, 19^2, 20, 21, 23^2, 24, 29, 31^2, 32, 34^3, 35^2, 36^2, 38^4, 42^3, 43^2, 46, 47^2, 48^3, 49, 50

13:1^5, 2^2, 3, 5^2, 16, 18, 22, 26^2, 27, 28, 29^3, 30, 31, 33, 38

14:4, 5, 6^4, 8, 9^2, 10^5, 11^3, 12, 13^2, 16, 17^2, 19, 22, 24^2, 26^3, 27, 28, 30, 31^3

15:1^2, 3, 4^2, 5^3, 6, 9, 15, 16, 18, 19^5, 20^2, 24, 25, 26^4, 27

16:2^2, 3, 4^2, 7^2, 8, 11, 13, 15, 16, 17, 20, 21^3, 23, 25^2, 26, 27, 28^4, 32^2, 33^2

17:1, 3, 4^2, 5^2, 6^2, 8, 9, 11^2, 12^3, 13, 14^3, 15^2, 16^2, 18^2, 19, 21, 22, 23, 24^2, 25, 26

18:1^2, 2, 3, 6, 9, 10^2, 11^2, 12^3, 13, 14^2, 15^3, 16^3, 17^2, 18, 19, 20^4, 22^3, 23, 24, 26^3, 27, 28^3, 31, 32, 33^3, 35, 36, 37^3, 38, 39^3

19:2, 3, 5^3, 6, 7^2, 8, 9, 11, 12, 13^3, 14^4, 15, 17^2, 18, 19^4, 20^3, 21^5, 23^3, 24^2, 25^2, 26, 27, 28, 30^2, 31^5, 32^4, 34, 36, 38^3, 39, 40^4, 41^2, 42^2

20:1^5, 2^3, 3, 4^2, 5, 6^2, 7^2, 8, 9^2, 10, 11^2, 12^5, 15, 18^2, 19^7, 20^2, 22, 24, 25^6, 26^2, 30, 31^2

21:1^2, 2, 4^3, 6^4, 7^3, 8^2, 10, 11^2, 12^2, 14^2, 16, 17^2, 20, 23, 24, 25^3

THE ACTS

1:1, 2^3, 3^2, 4^2, 5, 6, 7^3, 8^3, 12, 13^2, 14^2, 15^3, 16^2, 18^2, 19^2, 20, 21^2, 22, 24, 26^2

2:1, 2, 4^2, 6, 9, 10, 11, 14, 15^2, 16, 17, 19, 20^3, 21^2, 22, 23, 24, 25, 28, 29, 30^2, 31, 33^4, 34^2, 36, 37^2, 38^4, 39^2, 41, 42, 43, 46, 47^3

3:1^3, 2^3, 3, 6, 7, 8, 9, 10^2, 11^3, 12, 13^3, 14^2, 15^2, 16^2, 18, 19^3, 21^4, 22^2, 23, 24, 25^5

4:1^5, 2^3, 3, 4^3, 5, 6^3, 7, 8^2, 9^2, 10^3, 11^3, 13, 14, 15, 17, 18, 19, 20, 21, 22, 23, 24, 25^3, 26^4, 27^2, 30, 31^3, 32^2, 33^3, 34^2, 35, 36^3, 37^2

5:2^2, 3^3, 5, 6, 7, 8, 9^4, 10^2, 11, 12^3, 13^2, 14^2, 15^4, 16, 17^3, 18^2, 19^3, 20^3, 21^7, 22^2, 23^3, 24^4, 25^3, 26^3, 27^2, 29, 30, 32, 33, 34^4, 37^2, 40^2, 41^2, 42

6:1^5, 2^4, 3, 4^2, 5^3, 6, 7^5, 8, 9^3, 10^2, 12^4, 13, 14, 15^2

7:1, 2, 3, 4^2, 7, 8^3, 9, 10, 11, 13, 16^3, 17^3, 19^2, 22^2, 23, 24, 26, 28, 29, 30^2, 31^3, 32^4, 33^2, 34, 35^4, 36^3, 37^2, 38^5, 40, 41^2, 42^5, 43^2, 44^3, 45^4, 46, 48^2, 49^2, 51, 52^4, 53^2, 54, 55^3, 56^3, 58^2

8:1^3, 3, 4, 5, 6^2, 9^2, 10^3, 12^3, 13, 14^2, 15, 16^2, 17, 18^2, 19, 20, 21, 22, 23^2, 24, 25^4, 26^4, 27^2, 28, 29, 30, 32^3, 33, 34^2, 35, 36, 37, 38^3, 39^4, 40

9:1^3, 2, 4, 5^2, 6^2, 7, 8^2, 10, 11^3, 14, 15^3, 17^4, 19, 20^2, 21, 22^2, 23, 24, 25^2, 26, 27^4, 29^3, 30, 31^5, 32, 33, 35, 38, 39^3, 40, 41, 42

10:1^2, 2, 3^2, 6, 7, 9^4, 11^2, 12^2, 15^2, 16, 17^2, 19^2, 21^2, 22^3, 23, 24, 30, 31, 32^2, 36^2, 37, 38^2, 39^2, 40, 41^2, 42^2, 43, 44^2, 45^4, 47, 48^2

11:1^3, 2, 4^2, 5, 6^3, 9, 11, 12^2, 15^2, 16^3, 17^2, 18, 19^3, 20^2, 21^3, 22^2, 23^2, 24^2, 26^2, 28^3, 29^2, 30^2

12:1^2, 2^2, 3^2, 4, 5, 6^4, 7^4, 8, 9, 10^5, 11^5, 12^3, 13^2, 14^2, 16, 17^4, 18, 19, 20^2, 22^2, 23^4, 24

13:1^2, 2^3, 4, 5^3, 6, 7^3, 8^3, 9, 10^3, 11^4, 12^3, 14^2, 15^6, 17^3, 18^2, 19, 20^2, 21^3, 22, 24^2, 26^2, 27^2, 29, 30, 31, 32^2, 33^2, 34^2, 36, 38, 39, 40, 42^4, 43^3, 44^3, 45^2, 46^2, 47^4, 48^3, 49^3, 50^4, 51, 52^2

14:1^4, 2^3, 3^2, 4^4, 5^2, 6, 7, 9, 11^4, 12, 13^3, 14^2, 15^2, 18, 19^2, 20^3, 21, 22^4, 23, 25, 26^2, 27^3, 28

15:1^2, 2, 3^4, 4^2, 5^3, 6, 7^3, 8^2, 10^2, 11^2, 12^2, 14^2, 15^2, 16^2, 17^4, 18^2, 19, 21, 22^3, 23^3, 24, 26, 27, 28, 30^2, 31, 32, 33^2, 35^2, 36^2, 38, 39^2, 40^2, 41

16:1, 2, 3, 4^3, 5^2, 6^3, 7, 9, 10^3, 11, 12, 13^3, 14^3, 15, 17^4, 18^3, 19^3, 20, 22^2, 23, 24^2, 25, 26^3, 27^4, 31, 32^2, 33^2, 35^2, 36^3, 38^2, 39, 40^3

17:1, 2, 3, 4^2, 5^5, 6^3, 7, 8^3, 9, 10^3, 11^2, 13^3, 14^2, 16, 17^4, 18^3, 21, 22, 23, 24, 26^4, 27, 29^2, 30, 31^3, 32^2, 34^2

18:3, 4^3, 5^2, 6, 7, 8^4, 9^2, 11, 12^3, 13, 14, 16, 17^4, 18, 19^2, 22, 23^2, 24, 25^6, 26^2, 27^2, 28^2

19:1, 2, 4^2, 5^2, 6, 7, 8^4, 9^3, 10^3, 11, 12^3, 13^3, 14, 15, 16^2, 17^3, 19, 20, 21, 23, 24, 25, 27^3, 28, 29^2, 30^2, 31^2, 32^2, 33^4, 34^2, 35^6, 38^2, 41

20:1^2, 3, 4, 6, 7^4, 8, 9, 12, 15^3, 16^2, 17^2, 18, 19^3, 21^2, 22^2, 23, 24^4, 25, 26, 27, 28^4, 29, 31, 32, 35^3, 38^2

21:1, 3^2, 4, 5^2, 7, 8^4, 9, 11^5, 13^2, 14^2, 16, 17, 18^2, 19, 20^2, 21^3, 22, 24, 25, 26^5, 27^4, 28^4, 29^2, 30^4, 31^2, 32^2, 33, 34^4, 35^4, 36^2, 37^2, 38, 39, 40^4

22:2^2, 3^4, 4, 5^4, 7, 9^2, 10, 11^2, 12^2, 13, 14^2, 16^2, 17, 20^2, 21, 22, 23, 24^2, 25, 26^2, 27, 28, 29, 30^4

23:1, 2^2, 3^2, 5^2, 6^6, 7^3, 8^2, 9^2, 10^3, 11^2, 12, 14, 15^2, 16, 17^2, 18^2, 19^2, 20^2, 22^2, 23^2, 24, 26, 27, 28, 30^2, 31, 32^3, 33^2, 34^2

24:1^3, 5^4, 6, 7, 9, 10^2, 12^4, 13, 14^4, 15^2, 18, 20, 21^2, 22^2, 24, 26, 27

25:1, 2^3, 3, 6^2, 7, 8^3, 9, 10, 12, 14, 15^3, 16^4, 17^3, 18, 21, 22, 23^4, 24^2, 27

26:1, 2^2, 3, 4^2, 5^2, 6^2, 7, 8, 9, 10^2, 12, 13^3, 14^3, 16, 17^2, 18, 19, 20^2, 21^2, 22, 23^4, 25, 26, 27, 30^2

27:2, 3, 4, 5, 6, 7, 8^2, 9, 10, 11^4, 12^3, 13, 15^2, 16, 17^2, 18^2, 19^3, 21, 22, 23, 27^2, 29^2, 30^5, 31^3, 32^3, 33^2, 34, 37, 38^3, 39^3, 40^5, 41^5, 42^2, 43^2, 44^2

28:1, 2^3, 3^2, 4^3, 5^2, 7^3, 8, 9, 11, 13^2, 15^2, 16^4, 17^5, 19, 20, 21, 23^3, 24, 25^2, 27, 28^2, 29, 31^2

ROMANS

1:1, 2, 3^2, 4^4, 5, 6, 7, 8, 9, 10, 11, 12, 14^4, 15, 16^4, 17^2, 18^2, 20^4, 23^2, 24, 25^3, 26, 27^3, 32^2

2:1, 2, 3^2, 4^2, 5^2, 8, 9^2, 10^2, 12^2, 13^4, 14^5, 15^3, 16^2, 17, 18^2, 19, 20^4, 23^2, 24^2, 25^2, 26^3, 27^3, 28, 29^3

3:1, 2, 3, 5, 6, 7, 12, 13, 17, 19^3, 20^4, 21^4, 22, 23, 24, 25^2, 26, 27, 28^2, 29^4, 30, 31^2

4:1, 3, 4, 5, 6^2, 8^2, 9^2, 11^4, 12^3, 13^5, 14^2, 15, 16^6, 17, 18, 19, 20, 24

5:2, 5^2, 6, 10, 11, 12, 13^2, 14^2, 15^5, 16^3, 17, 18^3, 19, 20^2

6:4^3, 5^2, 6, 9, 12, 13, 14, 15, 17^2, 18, 19^2, 20, 21, 22, 23^2

7:1^2, 2^4, 4^3, 5^3, 6^3, 7^3, 8^2, 9^2, 10, 11, 12^2, 13, 14, 16, 19^2, 22^2, 23^2, 24, 25^4

8:1^2, 2^4, 3^4, 4^4, 5^6, 7^2, 8, 9^4, 10^2, 11^3, 12^2, 13^4, 14^2, 15^2, 16^2, 18^2, 19^4, 20^2, 21^4, 22, 23^4, 26^2, 27^5, 28, 29^2, 33, 34, 35, 36^2, 39

9:1^2, 3, 4^7, 5^2, 6, 7, 8^6, 9, 11^2, 12^2, 17^2, 20, 21^3, 22, 23^2, 24^2, 26^3, 27^4, 28^3, 29, 30^2, 31^2, 32^2

10:3, 4^2, 5^3, 6, 7^2, 8^2, 9^2, 10^2, 11, 12^3, 13^2, 15^2, 16, 17, 18^3

11:1^2, 2, 4^3, 5, 7^2, 8, 11, 12^6, 13^2, 15^5, 16^4, 17^3, 18^3, 19, 21, 22, 24^2, 25^2, 26, 28^3, 29, 33^3, 34^2

12:1, 2, 3^2, 4, 6^2, 11, 13, 16, 17, 19

13:1^2, 2^2, 3^3, 4^3, 8, 10^2, 11, 12^4, 13, 14^3

14:1, 6^6, 8^3, 9, 10, 11, 14, 17^2, 19, 20

15:1^2, 3, 4, 5, 6, 7, 8^4, 9^2, 11, 12^2, 13^3, 15^2, 16^6, 18, 19^3, 20, 25, 26, 27, 29^3, 30^3, 31, 32, 33

16:1, 2, 4^2, 5^2, 7, 8, 11^2, 12^3, 13, 14, 15, 16, 17, 18^2, 20^2, 22, 23^3, 24, 25^4, 26^5

S^2

1 CORINTHIANS

1:1, 2^2, 3, 4, 6, 7, 8^2, 9, 10^4, 11, 13, 16, 17^2, 18^3, 19^4, 20^4, 21^3, 22^2, 23^2, 24^2, 25^2, 26, 27^6, 28, 31

2:1, 4, 5^2, 6^2, 7^3, 8^2, 9^2, 10^2, 11^4, 12^4, 13^2, 14^3, 16^3

3:5, 6, 7, 10^2, 13^2, 16^2, 17^2, 19^2, 20^3, 22

4:1^2, 4, 5^5, 9^2, 13^3, 15, 17, 19^3, 20, 21

5:1, 4^2, 5^5, 6, 7, 8^3, 10^3

6:1^2, 2^4, 4, 6, 9^2, 10, 11^3, 12, 13^6, 14, 15^3, 17, 18, 19^2

7:1, 3^4, 4^4, 5, 8, 10^3, 11, 12^2, 13, 14^4, 15, 17, 19^2, 20, 22^2, 23, 25^2, 26, 28, 29, 31, 32^3, 33^2, 34^5, 35, 36, 39^3, 40

8:3, 4^2, 6, 7, 8^2, 10^2, 11, 12, 13

9:1, 2^2, 5^2, 7^3, 8^2, 9^4, 12, 13^4, 14^3, 16^2, 17, 18^3, 19, 20^5, 21, 22^2, 23, 24, 25, 26

10:1^2, 2^2, 3, 4, 5, 6, 7, 10, 11^2, 13, 16^6, 18^3, 19, 20^2, 21^5, 22, 25, 26^3, 28^3, 29, 31, 32^3, 33

11:2, 3^5, 6, 7^4, 8^4, 9^4, 10^2, 11^5, 12^4, 16, 17^2, 18, 20, 22, 23^3, 25^3, 26, 27^3, 29, 32^2, 34

12:3^3, 4, 5, 6, 7^2, 8^4, 9^3, 10^2, 11, 12^2, 14, 15^4, 16^4, 17^4, 18^2, 19, 21^4, 22, 23, 24, 25^3, 26^2, 27, 28, 30, 31

13:1, 2, 3, 6, 13

14:2, 4, 5, 7, 8^2, 9^2, 10, 11^2, 12^2, 15^4, 16^3, 17, 19, 21^2, 23, 25, 27, 28, 29^2, 30, 32^3, 33^2, 34^2, 35, 36, 37^3

15:1, 3, 4^2, 5, 6, 7, 9^3, 10^2, 12^2, 13, 15, 16, 20^2, 21^2, 23, 24^3, 26, 28, 29^3, 32^2, 34, 35, 39, 40^4, 41^3, 42^2, 45^2, 47^4, 48^2, 49^4, 50, 52^4, 54, 56^3, 57, 58^3

16:1^3, 2^2, 7^2, 10^2, 11, 12, 13, 15^4, 17, 19^3, 20, 21, 22, 23

S^2

2 CORINTHIANS

1:1^3, 2, 3^3, 4, 5, 6^2, 7^2, 9^2, 11^2, 12^3, 13, 14^2, 17^2, 19, 20^2, 22^2

2:2, 3, 4, 9, 10, 12, 14, 16^4, 17^2

3:3^4, 6^5, 7^4, 8^2, 9^2, 10, 13^2, 14^3, 15, 16^2, 17^3, 18^5

4:2^4, 4^5, 5, 6^5, 7^2, 10^4, 11, 13, 14, 15^3, 16, 18^4

5:1, 5^3, 6^2, 8^2, 10^2, 11^2, 14, 16^2, 18, 19^2, 21

6:1, 2^3, 3, 4, 6, 7^5, 13, 16^3, 17^2, 18

7:1^2, 6, 7^2, 8, 10^2, 12^2, 13^2, 15

8:1^2, 2^2, 4^4, 5^2, 6, 8^2, 9, 11, 16^2, 17, 18^3, 19^3, 21^3, 22, 23^3, 24^2

9:1^2, 2, 3, 5^2, 9, 10^2, 12^3, 13^2, 14

10:1, 2, 3^2, 4^2, 5^2, 7, 8, 12, 13^2, 14, 16^2, 17, 18

11:3^2, 5, 7, 9, 10^2, 13, 15, 17, 18, 20, 22, 24, 25, 26^4, 28^2, 30, 31, 32^4, 33

12:1, 2^3, 3^2, 6, 7^4, 8, 9, 11, 12, 14^5, 15^2, 18^2, 21

13:1^2, 2, 4^2, 5, 8^2, 10^2, 11, 13, 14^5

S^2

GALATIANS

1:1^2, 2^2, 3, 4, 6, 7, 10, 11, 12, 13^2, 14^2, 16, 19^2, 20, 21, 22, 23

2:2, 5^2, 7^4, 8^4, 9^4, 10^2, 11, 12^2, 13, 14^6, 15, 16^8, 17, 18, 19^2, 20^4, 21^2

3:1, 2^4, 3^2, 5^4, 7^2, 8^3, 10^5, 11^3, 12^2, 13^2, 14^4, 15, 16, 17^3, 18^2, 19^4, 21^3, 22^2, 23^2, 24, 26, 29

4:1, 2^2, 3^2, 4^3, 5^2, 6, 9, 13^3, 15, 16, 21^2, 22^2, 23^3, 24^3, 26, 27, 28, 29^2, 30^6, 31^2

5:1^2, 3, 4, 5^2, 7, 9, 10, 11^2, 13, 14, 16^3, 17^7, 18^2, 19^2, 21^2, 22^2, 24^2, 25^2

6:1, 2, 6, 8^3, 10, 12^2, 13, 14^3, 16, 17^2, 18

S

EPHESIANS

1:1^3, 2, 3, 4^2, 5^2, 6^3, 7^2, 9, 10^2, 11^2, 12, 13^2, 14^4, 15^2, 17^4, 18^5, 19^2, 20^2, 22^2, 23

2:2^6, 3^5, 7^2, 8, 11^3, 12^3, 13, 14, 15^2, 16^2, 18, 19^2, 20^3, 21^2, 22

3:1, 2^2, 3, 4, 5^2, 6^3, 7^3, 8^3, 9^4, 10^4, 11, 12, 14, 15, 16^2, 18, 19^2, 20, 21

4:1^3, 3^3, 7^2, 9^2, 10, 12^6, 13^7, 14, 15^2, 16^5, 17^2, 18^4, 21, 22^3, 23, 24, 26, 27, 28, 29^2, 30^2

5:5, 6^2, 8, 9^2, 10, 11, 13, 14, 16^2, 17^2, 18, 19, 20^2, 21, 22, 23^7, 24^2, 25, 26^2, 29^2, 32, 33

6:1, 2, 3, 4^2, 5, 6^3, 7, 8^2, 9, 10^2, 11^3, 12^2, 13^2, 14, 15^2, 16^3, 17^4, 18, 19^2, 21, 22, 23^3

S

PHILIPPIANS

1:1^3, 2, 5^2, 6, 7^2, 8, 10, 11^2, 12^3, 13, 14^3, 16, 17^3, 19^2, 22^2, 24, 27^3, 29, 30

2:1, 2, 4, 6, 7^2, 8^2, 10^2, 11^2, 15^3, 16^2, 17, 18, 19, 21, 22^3, 24, 28^2, 29, 30

3:1^2, 2, 3^3, 4^2, 5^5, 6^3, 8^3, 9^3, 10^2, 11^2, 14^3, 16^2, 18^2, 20^2, 21

4:1, 2^2, 3^2, 4, 5, 7, 9, 10^2, 15^2, 18, 21, 22, 23

S

COLOSSIANS

1:1, 2^2, 3, 4^2, 5^4, 6^3, 8, 9^2, 10^2, 12^3, 13^2, 14, 15^3, 18^7, 19, 20, 22, 23^3, 24^2, 25^2, 26, 27^4

2:1, 2^4, 3, 5^3, 6, 7, 8^3, 9^2, 10, 11^5, 12^3, 13, 14^2, 16^2, 17, 19^3, 20^3, 22^2, 23^3

3:1, 2, 5, 6^2, 7, 9, 10^2, 12, 14, 15^2, 16^2, 17^3, 18, 20, 22, 23, 24^4, 25

4:2, 3, 5, 7, 8, 11^2, 12, 14, 15^2, 16^3, 17^2, 18^2

S

1 THESSALONIANS

1:1^5, 3, 5, 6^3, 8^2, 9, 10^2

2:2, 4, 6, 8, 9, 13^3, 14^2, 15, 16^3, 17, 19

3:2, 5, 8, 9, 12, 13^2

4:1, 2, 3, 5^2, 6^2, 10, 15^4, 16^5, 17^4

5:1^2, 2^3, 5^4, 7^2, 8^3, 12, 14^2, 18, 19, 23^2, 26, 27^2, 28

S^2

2 THESSALONIANS

1:1^3, 2, 3, 4, 5^2, 7, 8, 9^3, 11^2, 12^3

2:1, 2, 3, 4, 7^2, 8^3, 9, 10^2, 12, 13^4, 14^2, 15

3:1^2, 3, 4^2, 5^3, 6^2, 16^2, 17^2, 18

S^2

1 TIMOTHY

1:1, 2, 5^2, 7, 8, 9^3, 11^2, 12, 14, 15, 17^2, 18

2:3, 4^2, 5, 7^2, 11, 12, 14^2

3:1, 2, 5, 6^2, 7^2, 8, 9^2, 10, 12^2, 13^2, 15^5, 16^5

4:1^3, 3, 5, 6^2, 8, 10^2, 12, 14^4, 16

5:1, 2^2, 8, 9^2, 10^2, 11, 14^3, 16, 17^2, 18^4, 21^2, 25

6:1^2, 2, 3^2, 5, 10^3, 12, 13, 14, 15^2, 16, 17, 19, 21

S^2

2 TIMOTHY

1:1^2, 2, 5, 6^2, 7, 8^4, 9, 10^2, 11, 12, 13, 14, 16^2, 18^2

2:1, 2^2, 4, 6^2, 7, 8^2, 9, 10^2, 14^3, 15, 18^3, 19^3, 21, 22, 24^2, 25^2, 26^2

3:1, 5, 7^2, 8^2, 11, 14, 15, 17

4:1^3, 2, 3, 4, 5, 6, 7, 8^2, 11, 13^3, 14^2, 17^5, 18, 19, 21, 22

S^5

TITUS

1:1^3, 2, 3, 4^3, 5, 6, 7, 9^2, 10, 12, 13, 14, 15

2:1, 2, 3, 4, 5, 8, 10, 11, 13^2

3:4, 5^2, 7, 9, 10, 13, 15

S^3

PHILEMON

2, 3, 5, 6^2, 7^2, 9, 13^2, 16^2, 20^2, 25

HEBREWS

1:1^2, 2, 3^5, 4, 5, 6^3, 7, 8^2, 9, 10^5, 12, 13

2:1^2, 2, 3^2, 4, 5^2, 6, 7^2, 9^3, 10, 12^2, 13, 14^4, 16^2, 17^2

3:1^2, 3^2, 6^4, 7, 8^3, 12, 13, 14^2, 15, 17

4:2^2, 3^3, 4^2, 9, 11, 12^5, 13, 14^2, 15, 16

5:2^2, 3, 6, 7, 8, 9, 10, 12^3, 13

6:1^3, 2^2, 4^2, 5^3, 6, 7^2, 10, 11^3, 12, 15, 16, 17^2, 18, 19^2, 20^2

7:1^3, 3, 4^3, 5^6, 6, 7^2, 10, 11^5, 12^2, 13, 15, 16^2, 17, 18^2, 19^3, 21^2, 25, 26, 27, 28^5

8:1^6, 2^3, 4, 5^4, 6, 7, 8^4, 9^5, 10^3, 11^3, 13

9:1, 2^5, 3^3, 4^6, 5^2, 6^3, 7^4, 8^4, 9^3, 10, 12^2, 13^5, 14^3, 15^6, 16^2, 17, 18, 19^5, 20^2, 21^3, 22, 23^3, 24^4, 25^2, 26^5, 27, 28^2

10:1^4, 2, 4, 5, 7^2, 8, 9^2, 10^3, 11, 12, 15, 16^2, 19^2, 20, 21, 23, 25^4, 26^2, 27, 29^4, 30^2, 31^2, 32, 34, 36^2, 38, 39^2

11:1^2, 2, 3^2, 7^4, 9^3, 12^4, 13^2, 17, 19, 21^2, 22^2, 23, 24, 25^2, 26^4, 27^2, 28^3, 29^2, 30, 31^2, 32^2, 33, 34^5, 37, 38^2, 39

12:1^2, 2^6, 5^3, 6, 7, 9, 11^2, 12^2, 13, 14, 15, 17, 18, 19^3, 20, 21, 22^3, 23^4, 24^3, 26^2, 27

13:3, 4, 6, 7^3, 8, 9, 10, 11^4, 12^2, 13, 15^2, 17, 19^2, 20^5, 22, 24^2

S

JAMES

1:1^2, 3, 6^2, 7, 9, 10^3, 11^6, 12^3, 17, 18, 20^2, 21, 22, 23, 25^2, 27^3

2:1^2, 3^2, 5^2, 6^2, 7, 8^2, 9, 10, 11, 12, 16, 19, 21, 23^2, 25^2, 26^2

3:1, 2^2, 3, 4^2, 5, 6^4, 7, 8, 9^2, 10, 11, 12, 14, 17, 18

4:4^4, 5^2, 6^2, 7, 10^2, 11^4, 14, 15

5:3^2, 4^5, 5, 6, 7^6, 8^2, 9^2, 10^3, 11^4, 12, 14^4, 15^3, 16, 17^2, 18^2, 19, 20^2

1 PETER

1:1, 2^4, 3^3, 5^2, 7^2, 9^2, 10^2, 11^3, 12^4, 13^4, 14, 17^2, 19, 20^2, 21, 22^3, 23, 24^4, 25^4

2:2^2, 3, 6, 7^5, 8, 9, 10, 11, 12^2, 13^2, 14^2, 15^2, 16, 17^2, 18^2, 24, 25

3:1^4, 3, 4^4, 5^2, 7^3, 12^5, 15^2, 17, 18^4, 19, 20^3, 21^6, 22

4:1^3, 2^4, 3^3, 4, 5^2, 6^3, 7, 8, 10^3, 11^2, 12, 14^2, 17^4, 18^3, 19^2

5:1^3, 2^2, 3, 4, 5^3, 6, 8, 9^3, 10, 12, 13

2 PETER

1:1, 2, 3, 4^3, 8, 10, 11, 12, 16, 17^2, 18, 19^2, 20, 21^3

2:1^2, 2, 4, 5^5, 6, 7^2, 9^4, 10^2, 11, 12, 13^2, 15^4, 16^3, 17, 18^2, 19^2, 20^6, 21^2, 22^4

3:2^5, 3, 4^4, 5^5, 6, 7^4, 8, 9, 10^8, 12^4, 15^2, 16, 17^2, 18

1 JOHN

1:1^2, 2^2, 3, 5, 6, 7^3, 8

2:1^2, 2^3, 4, 5, 7^4, 8^2, 9, 10, 13^3, 14^3, 15^6, 16^8, 17^3, 18^2, 20, 21^2, 22^3, 23^5, 24^4, 25, 27^2

3:1^3, 2, 4^3, 8^6, 10^3, 11^2, 13, 14, 16^2, 17, 19, 23, 24

4:1^2, 2^2, 3^2, 4, 5^3, 6^2, 9^2, 10, 14^4, 15, 16, 17

5:1, 2, 3, 4^3, 5^2, 6^2, 7^3, 8^3, 9^3, 10^3, 11, 12^2, 13^4, 14, 15, 19, 20^2

2 JOHN

1^4, 2, 3^4, 4, 5, 6^2, 7^2, 9^4, 13

3 JOHN

1^3, 3^3, 5, 6, 7, 8, 9^2, 10^2, 12, 14

JUDE

1^2, 3^3, 4^2, 5^3, 6^3, 7^2, 8, 9^4, 11^3, 12, 13^2, 14^2, 17^2, 18, 19, 20, 21^2, 23^3, 24, 25

REVELATION

1:1, 2^2, 3^2, 4^2, 5^6, 7, 8^4, 9^4, 10^2, 11^3, 12, 13^5, 15, 16, 17^2, 18, 19^3, 20^8

2:1^5, 5, 6^2, 7^5, 8^4, 9^2, 10, 11^3, 12^3, 14^2, 15^2, 16, 17^4, 18^3, 19^2, 23^2, 24^2, 26^2, 27, 28, 29^2

3:1^4, 2, 5^2, 6^2, 7^3, 9, 10^4, 12^4, 13^2, 14^7, 18^2, 20^2, 22^2

4:1, 2^2, 3, 4^2, 5^3, 6^4, 7^4, 8, 9, 10^3

5:1^3, 2^2, 3^2, 4, 5^6, 6^7, 7^3, 8^4, 9^2, 10, 11^5, 12, 13^5, 14^2

6:1^4, 3^2, 4, 5^2, 6^4, 7^3, 8^4, 9^5, 10, 12^3, 13^2, 14, 15^9, 16^5, 17

7:1^7, 2^6, 3^4, 4^3, 5^3, 6^3, 7^3, 8^3, 9^2, 10^2, 11^5, 13, 14^2, 15^2, 16, 17^3

8:1^2, 2, 3^4, 4^5, 5^4, 6^2, 7^3, 8^4, 9^5, 10^4, 11^5, 12^{10}, 13^6

9:1^4, 2^7, 3^4, 4^3, 5, 7^3, 8^2, 9^2, 11^4, 13^3, 14^4, 15^2, 16^4, 17^5, 18^4, 20^3

10:1, 2^2, 4^2, 5^3, 6^5, 7^5, 8^6, 9^2, 10^2

11:1^3, 2^4, 4^4, 6^2, 7^2, 8^2, 9, 10^2, 11, 13^6, 14^2, 15^3, 16, 18^6, 19^2

12:1^2, 4^5, 6^2, 7^2, 9^4, 10^3, 11^4, 12^4, 13^4, 14^4, 15^3, 16^5, 17^5

13:1^4, 2^4, 3^2, 4^4, 7, 8^5, 10^5, 11, 12^4, 13^2, 14^7, 15^6, 17^4, 18^3

14:1, 2^3, 3^5, 4^3, 5, 6^3, 7^3, 8^2, 9^2, 10^8, 11^3, 12^4, 13^3, 14^2, 15^5, 16^3, 17, 18^5, 19^6, 20^5

15:1^2, 2^5, 3^4, 5^3, 6^3, 7^3, 8^5

16:1^5, 2^5, 3^4, 4^2, 5^2, 6, 7, 8^2, 9, 10^3, 11, 12^6, 13^6, 14^5, 16, 17^4, 18, 19^6, 20, 21^4

17:1^4, 2^5, 3^2, 4, 5^3, 6^5, 7^5, 8^7, 9^3, 10, 11^3, 12^2, 13, 14^2, 15^2, 16^3, 17^2, 18^3

18:1, 2^3, 3^7, 6, 8, 9^3, 10, 11^2, 12, 14, 15^2, 17, 18, 19, 21, 22^2, 23^6, 24^2

19:1, 2^3, 4^3, 5, 6^4, 7^2, 8^2, 9^3, 10^3, 13, 14, 15^3, 17^5, 18^5, 19^4, 20^4, 21^4

20:1^2, 2^2, 3^3, 4^4, 5^4, 6^2, 7, 8^6, 9^5, 10^4, 11^2, 12^5, 13^3, 14^2, 15^2

21:1^2, 2, 3, 4, 5, 6^4, 8^4, 9^5, 10^2, 11, 12^4, 13^4, 14^5, 15^3, 16^8, 17^3, 18^3, 19^7, 20^8, 21^3, 22^3, 23^6, 24^4, 25, 26^2, 27

22:1^2, 2^8, 3^2, 5^2, 6^3, 7^2, 8^2, 9^2, 10^3, 13^4, 14^3, 16^4, 17^3, 18^3, 19^5, 21

THEE

4571

GENESIS

3:11^2, 15, 16, 17, 18
4:7, 12
6:14, 18^2, 19, 20, 21^3
7:1, 2
8:16, 17^2
12:1^2, 2^2, 3^3, 12^2, 13^2
13:8^2, 9^2, 15, 17
15:7^2
16:2, 5^2, 6
17:2^2, 4, 5, 6^3, 7^4, 8^2, 9, 10, 16, 18, 19, 20, 21
18:3, 10, 14, 25^2
19:5, 9, 17, 21, 22
20:6^2, 7, 9, 15^2, 16^2
21:12, 17, 22, 23
22:2^2, 17
23:6, 11^3, 13^2, 15
24:2, 3, 7, 8, 12, 14, 17, 23, 40, 41, 43, 45, 50, 51
25:30
26:2, 3^3, 24^2, 28^3, 29^3
27:3, 4, 7, 8, 10, 19, 21^2, 25, 28, 29^5, 37, 42^2, 45^2
28:2, 3^3, 4^3, 13, 14, 15^5, 22
29:18, 19, 25, 27
30:2, 14, 15, 16, 26^2, 27, 29, 30, 31
31:3, 12, 13, 16, 27, 32, 35, 38, 39, 41, 42, 44, 48, 49, 50, 51, 52
32:6, 9, 11, 12, 17^3, 26, 29
33:5, 10, 11^2, 12, 14, 15
35:1, 11, 12^2
37:10, 13, 14, 16
38:16^2, 17, 18, 25, 29
39:9
40:13, 14^2, 19^3
41:15, 39, 41, 44
42:37^2
43:4, 9^2, 29
44:8, 18, 32, 33
45:11
46:3, 4^2
47:4, 5, 6, 29^2
48:2, 4^4, 5^2, 9, 20^2, 22
49:8, 25^2
50:5, 6, 17^3

EXODUS

2:7^2, 9, 14
3:10, 12^3, 18
4:1, 5, 8, 12, 13, 14^2, 16, 18, 23
5:3
6:29
7:1, 2, 15, 16
8:4, 9^2, 11, 21, 29
9:15, 16^2, 30
10:17, 28
11:8^2
12:24, 48
13:5^2, 7^2, 9^2, 11^3, 14
14:12
15:7, 11^2, 17, 26^2
17:5, 6
18:6, 14, 18^2, 19^2, 22^2, 23
19:9^3, 24^2
20:2, 4, 12, 24^2
21:13
22:25
23:5, 7, 15, 20^3, 23^2, 25, 27^2, 28^2, 29^2, 30, 31, 33^2
24:12
25:9, 16, 21, 22^3, 40
26:30
27:8, 20
28:1
29:35, 42
30:6, 23, 34, 36, 37
31:6, 11
32:4, 7, 8, 10, 21, 32, 34^2
33:2, 3^2, 5^4, 12, 13^2, 14^2, 17, 18, 19^2, 22^2
34:1, 3, 9, 10, 11^2, 12, 15, 17, 18, 24, 27

LEVITICUS

9:2
10:9, 14, 15
19:13, 19, 33
21:8
24:2
25:6^2, 8^2, 15, 16, 35^2, 36, 39^2, 40^2, 41, 47^2

NUMBERS

5:19, 20, 21
6:24^2, 25^2, 26^2
10:2, 3, 4, 29, 31, 32, 35^2
11:15, 16, 17^3, 23
12:11, 13
14:12, 15, 17, 19
16:10^2
18:1^2, 2^4, 4, 7, 8^2, 9, 10, 11^2, 12, 19^4
19:2
20:17, 18
21:7, 8, 29
22:6, 9, 16^2, 17^2, 20^2, 28, 29, 30, 32, 33, 34, 35, 37^3, 38
23:3, 11, 13, 26, 27^2
24:9^2, 10, 11^2, 14, 22
27:12, 18

DEUTERONOMY

1:21^2, 31, 38
2:7^2, 9, 19, 25^4, 31
3:25, 26, 27
4:21, 23, 30, 31^2, 32, 35, 36^3, 37, 38^3, 40^4
5:6, 8, 12, 15^2, 16^3, 27, 28, 31^2
6:2, 3^2, 6, 10^2, 12, 15^2, 17, 18, 19, 20
7:1^2, 2, 4, 6, 11, 12, 13^4, 15^3, 16^2, 19, 20, 22^2, 23, 24, 25
8:1, 2^3, 3^4, 4, 5, 7, 10, 11, 14, 15^2, 16^4, 18
9:3^2, 4^2, 5, 6, 12, 14
10:1^2, 10, 12, 13, 21, 22
11:29
12:1, 7, 14, 15, 20, 21^3, 25^2, 28^3, 29, 30
13:1, 2, 5^3, 6, 7^2, 10^2, 12, 17^3, 18
14:2, 24^3, 27, 29^2
15:4^2, 5, 6^3, 7, 9^2, 10, 11, 12^3, 13, 14, 15^2, 16^4, 18^5
16:1, 4, 5, 9, 10, 15, 17, 18^2, 20, 21^2, 22
17:2, 4, 8^2, 9, 10^2, 11^3, 14, 15^3
18:9, 12, 14^2, 15^2, 18
19:1, 2^2, 3^2, 7^2, 8, 9^2, 10^2, 13, 14
20:1^2, 11^4, 12^2, 14, 15, 16, 17, 20
21:1, 23
22:2^2, 6, 7^2, 12
23:4^2, 5^2, 9, 13, 14^4, 15, 16, 20, 21^2, 22
24:4, 11, 13^2, 15^2, 18^2, 19, 22
25:3, 15, 17, 18^3, 19^2
26:1, 2, 11, 16, 18^2, 19
27:2^2, 3^2, 10
28:1^2, 2^2, 7^3, 8^3, 9^2, 10, 11^2, 12, 13^2, 14, 15^3, 20, 21^2, 22^2, 23, 24, 25, 27, 28, 29, 31, 35, 36^2, 37, 43^2, 44, 45^4, 46, 48^2, 49, 51^2, 52^3, 53^2, 55, 57, 60^2, 61, 64, 65, 66, 68^2
29:12, 13^3
30:1^3, 2, 3^3, 4^2, 5^3, 7^2, 8, 9^2, 11^2, 14, 15, 16^2
31:3^3, 6^3, 8^4, 23, 26
32:6^3, 7^2, 18^2, 49, 52
33:10, 27, 29^2
34:4

JOSHUA

1:5^4, 7, 9^2, 17^2
2:3, 14, 18, 19
3:7^2
5:2
7:10, 13, 19, 25
8:1, 2
9:25
10:8
13:6
14:6
17:15^2

JUDGES

1:3, 24^2
3:19, 20
4:6, 7, 9, 14, 19, 20, 22
5:14
6:12, 14, 16, 18^3, 23, 39
7:2, 4^6, 9
9:31, 32, 33
10:10, 15^2
11:8, 17, 19, 24, 27, 36
12:1^2
13:4, 15^3, 17
14:15, 16
15:2, 12^2, 13^3
16:5, 6^2, 9, 10, 12, 14, 15, 20, 28^2
17:2, 3, 10
18:3, 5, 19, 23, 24, 25
19:6, 8, 11, 20

RUTH

1:10, 16^2, 17
2:4, 9, 12, 19, 22
3:1^2, 3^3, 4^2, 11, 13^3, 15
4:4^3, 8, 12, 14, 15^3

1 SAMUEL

1:8, 14, 17, 23, 26
2:2, 15, 20, 34, 36
3:9, 17^4
8:7^2, 8
9:3, 16, 17, 18, 19^2, 20, 23^3, 24^2, 26, 27
10:1, 2, 3, 4^2, 6, 7^3, 8^3, 15
11:1, 3
12:10
13:13, 14
14:7^2, 36, 40
15:1, 16, 17, 18, 23, 25, 26^2, 28, 30
16:1, 2, 3^2, 15, 16^2, 22
17:37, 45, 46^3
18:17, 22^2
19:2^2, 3^2, 4, 17
20:4, 8, 9^3, 10, 12^2, 13^4, 21^2, 22^2, 23, 29^2, 37, 42
21:1, 2^2
22:3, 5
23:11, 12, 17^2, 27
24:4^2, 10^3, 11^2, 12^3, 13, 15, 17, 19
25:6, 8^2, 24, 25, 26, 28^2, 29, 30^2, 31, 32, 34, 40^2
26:6, 8, 11, 15, 19^2, 21, 23
27:5
28:2, 8^2, 10, 11, 15, 16, 18, 19, 22^2

1 SAMUEL

29:6^2, 8, 10
30:7, 15

2 SAMUEL

1:4, 9, 16, 26
2:21^3, 22^2
3:8, 12^2, 13^2, 21, 24, 25
5:2, 24
7:3, 8, 9^2, 11^3, 12, 15, 16, 20, 22^2, 23, 24, 26, 27^2, 29^2
9:7^2
10:3^2, 11^2
11:12, 20, 25
12:7^2, 8^3, 11, 14
13:5^3, 6, 13^3, 20, 24, 25, 26^2
14:2, 5, 8, 10^2, 11, 12, 17, 18^2, 19, 32^2
15:3, 7, 20^2, 26, 31, 35
16:4, 8, 9, 21
17:3, 11
18:11, 12, 14, 22, 31^2, 32^2, 33
19:6, 7^3, 33, 37^2, 38^2, 41
20:16, 21
22:30, 50
24:10, 12^3, 13^2, 17, 21, 23, 24

1 KINGS

1:12^2, 13, 14, 20, 30
2:4, 8^2, 14, 16, 17^2, 18, 20^3, 26^2, 36, 42^2, 43
3:5, 6^2, 12^5, 13^2
5:6
6:12
8:13^2, 23^2, 25, 26, 27, 28, 33^3, 35, 40, 43^2, 46, 47, 48^2, 50^2, 52
9:4, 5
10:8, 9^3
11:11^3, 31^2, 35, 37, 38^4
12:4, 10, 28
13:2^3, 7, 8, 16^3, 18, 21, 22
14:2^2, 3^2, 5, 6, 7^2, 8, 9^2, 12
15:19^2
16:2^2
17:3^2, 4, 9^2, 10, 11, 13, 18, 21
18:10^2, 12^3, 41, 44^2
19:7, 20^3
20:5, 6, 22, 25, 31, 32, 34^2, 35, 36, 37
21:2^3, 3, 4, 6^3, 7, 15, 20, 21
22:5, 13, 16, 18, 23, 24

2 KINGS

1:10, 12, 13
2:2^2, 4^2, 6^2, 9^3, 10^2, 16, 19
3:13^2, 14^2
4:2, 3, 4, 10, 13, 22, 24, 26^2, 29, 30
5:6^2, 10, 13^2, 15, 17, 22, 26^2, 27
6:1, 2, 3, 7, 17, 18, 27^2, 28
7:13
8:4, 9, 14
9:3, 5^2, 6, 11, 12, 18, 19, 26
14:10^2
18:23^2, 26, 27
19:9, 10, 19, 21^3, 28, 29
20:3^2, 5, 6, 14, 18
22:19, 20

1 CHRONICLES

11:2
12:18^2
14:15
16:18
17:2, 7, 8^3, 10^2, 11, 13, 18, 20^2, 21, 24, 25, 27^2
19:3^2, 12^2
21:8, 10^3, 11, 12, 17, 23^2
22:9, 11^2, 12^2, 15, 16
28:9^2, 10, 20^3, 21^2
29:12, 13, 14^2, 15, 16, 17, 18

2 CHRONICLES

1:7, 11, 12^4
2:11, 16
6:2, 14^2, 16, 18, 19, 24^2, 26, 31, 33^2, 34, 36, 37, 38, 39, 40
7:17^2, 18
9:7, 8^3
10:4, 10
14:11^3
16:3^2
18:3, 4, 12, 15, 17, 22, 23
19:2, 3
20:2, 6, 8, 9, 12
25:7, 8, 9, 16, 19^2
26:18
34:27, 28
35:21^4

EZRA

4:12
5:10
7:13, 18, 19
9:6, 15^2
10:4^2

NEHEMIAH

1:5, 6^2, 7, 8, 11^2
4:5^2
6:7, 10^2
9:6, 8, 10, 18, 26^2, 27, 28^2, 32, 35

ESTHER

3:11^2
5:3, 6

ESTHER

7:2
9:12

JOB

1:11, 15, 16, 17, 19
2:5
4:2, 5^2, 7
5:1, 19^2, 20, 23
7:20^2
8:6, 8, 10^2, 18, 22
10:3, 9, 13
11:3, 5, 6^2, 18, 19^2
12:7^2, 8^2
13:20
14:3, 5, 15
15:6^2, 11^2, 12, 17
16:3
17:3
18:4
22:4^3, 10^2, 11, 21, 22, 27, 28
26:4
30:20
33:1, 7^2, 12, 32, 33
35:3, 4^2
36:2, 4, 16, 17, 18^2
38:3, 17, 34, 35
39:9, 10
40:4, 7, 14^2, 15
41:3^2, 4
42:2, 4^2, 5^2, 7

PSALMS

2:7, 8
5:2, 3, 4, 10, 11^2
6:5^2
7:1, 7
9:1, 2, 10^2
10:14
16:1, 2
17:6, 7
18:1, 29, 49
20:1^2, 2^2, 4
21:4, 8, 11
22:4, 5^2, 10, 19, 22, 25, 27
25:1, 2, 3, 5, 16, 20, 21
27:8
28:1, 2
30:1, 2, 8, 9, 12^2
31:1, 14, 17, 19^2, 22
32:5, 6, 8^3, 9
33:22
35:10, 18^2
36:9, 10
37:4, 34
38:9^2, 15
39:5, 7, 12
40:5, 16^2
41:4
42:1, 6
43:4
44:5, 17
45:2, 4, 5, 7, 8, 14, 17
49:18
50:7, 8, 12, 15, 17, 21
51:4^2, 13
52:5^4, 9
53:5
54:6
55:22, 23
56:3, 9, 12
57:1, 9^2
59:9, 17
60:4
61:2
62:12
63:1^3, 2, 3, 4, 5, 6^2, 8
65:1^2, 2, 4
66:3, 4^2, 13, 15
67:3^2, 5^2
68:29
69:5, 6^2, 9, 13, 19
70:4^2
71:1, 6^2, 14, 19, 22^2, 23
72:5
73:22, 23, 25^2, 27^2
74:22, 23
75:1^2
76:10
77:16^2
79:6, 11, 12, 13
80:14, 18
81:7^3, 8, 9, 10, 16
83:2, 5
84:4, 5, 12
85:6
86:2, 3, 4, 5, 7, 8, 9, 12, 14
87:3, 7
88:1, 2, 9^2, 10, 13^2
89:8^2
90:8, 13
91:3, 4, 7, 10, 11^2, 12
94:20
101:1
102:1, 28
103:4
104:27
105:11
108:3^2
114:5
116:4, 7, 17, 19
118:21, 25^2, 28^2
119:7, 10, 11, 62, 63, 74, 76, 79, 108, 120, 126, 146, 164, 168, 169, 170, 175
120:3^2
121:3, 6, 7
122:6, 8

PSALMS

123:1
128:2, 5
130:1, 4
134:3
135:9
137:5, 6, 8
138:1^2, 4
139:12^2, 14, 15, 18, 20, 21^2
141:1^2, 2, 8^2
142:5
143:6^2, 8^2, 9
144:9^2
145:1, 2, 10^2, 15
147:13, 14

PROVERBS

1:10
2:1, 11^2, 12, 16
3:2, 3, 28, 29, 30
4:6^2, 8^2, 9, 11^2, 24^2, 25
5:17, 19
6:22^3, 24, 25
7:1, 5, 15^2
9:8^2
20:22
22:18, 19^2, 20, 21^2, 27
23:1, 7^2, 11, 22, 25
25:7, 8, 10, 16, 17^2, 22
27:2
29:17
30:6, 7, 9, 10

ECCLESIASTES

2:1
7:21
8:2
9:9
10:4, 16
11:9^2

SONG OF SOLOMON

1:3, 4^3, 9, 11
4:7
6:1, 13
7:5, 12, 13
8:1^2, 2^3, 5^4

ISAIAH

1:25
2:10
3:12^2
7:5, 11, 17
8:1
9:3
10:24^2
12:1, 6
14:3, 8, 9^3, 10, 11^2, 16^3, 29
16:4, 9
19:12
22:1, 3, 15, 16, 17^2, 18, 19^2
24:17
25:1, 3^2
26:3^2, 8^2, 9^2, 13^2, 16, 20
29:3^3, 11, 12
30:19^2, 21, 22
33:1^3, 2
36:8^2, 11, 12
37:9, 10, 22^3, 29, 30
38:3^2, 6, 7, 18^2, 19
39:3, 7
40:9
41:9^4, 10^4, 11^2, 12^2, 13^2, 14, 15
42:6^3
43:1^4, 2^3, 3, 4^2, 5^2, 23^2
44:2^3, 8, 21, 22, 24
45:2, 3^2, 4^2, 5, 14^5
47:3, 5, 9^2, 10, 11^3, 13^2, 15^2
48:5^2, 6, 9^2, 10^2, 17^2
49:6, 7, 8^4, 15, 16, 17^2, 18^3, 19, 23, 25, 26
51:16, 19^3, 23
52:1, 14
54:6, 7^2, 8^2, 9^2, 10^2, 14, 15, 17^2
55:5^3
57:8, 12, 13
58:8, 9, 11, 12, 14^2
59:12, 21
60:1, 2^2, 4, 5^2, 6, 7^2, 9, 10^3, 11, 12, 13, 14^4, 15^2, 19^2
62:4, 5^2
64:4, 5, 7, 9, 11
65:15

JEREMIAH

1:5^4, 7^2, 8^2, 10, 17^2, 18, 19^4
2:2, 17, 19^3, 21, 22^2, 28^2, 31, 35
3:19^2, 22
4:14, 18, 30^2
5:7
6:8^2, 23, 26^2, 27
7:16, 27^2
10:6, 7^3, 25
11:15, 17^2, 20
12:1^2, 3, 5^2, 6^3
13:1, 6, 12, 20, 21^3, 27
14:7, 20, 22
15:2, 5^2, 6^2, 11, 14, 19^2, 20^6, 21^2
16:2, 10, 19
17:4^2, 13, 16^2
18:2, 20, 23
19:2, 10
20:4, 12, 15
21:2, 13
22:6, 7, 21, 23, 24, 25, 26^2
23:33, 37
25:15

JEREMIAH

26:2
27:2
28:8, 15, 16
29:22, 26
30:2^2, 10, 11^6, 14^3, 15, 16^3, 17^3
31:3^2, 4, 21^2, 23
32:7^2, 8, 17, 20, 25
33:3^2
34:3, 4, 5^3, 14^3
36:2^3, 19, 28
37:18, 20^3
38:4, 10, 14, 15^2, 16^2, 20^4, 22^2, 25^5
39:12, 16, 17, 18^2
40:4^6, 5, 14, 15^3
42:2^2, 5, 6
43:2, 3
44:16
45:2, 5
46:14^2, 27, 28^5
48:2, 18, 27, 32, 43, 46
49:5^2, 9, 15, 16^2
50:21, 24, 31^2, 42
51:14^2, 20^2, 21^2, 22^3, 23^3, 25^4, 26, 36

LAMENTATIONS

1:22
2:13^5, 14^2, 15, 16, 17
3:57
4:21, 22
5:21

EZEKIEL

2:1, 3, 4, 6, 8^2
3:3, 4, 6^2, 7, 10, 11, 17, 22, 25^2, 27
4:1^2, 3^2, 5, 6, 8^2, 9^2, 15
5:1^3, 8^2, 9, 10^3, 11, 12^3, 14^2, 15^2, 17^3
7:3^4, 4^3, 6, 7, 8^4, 9^2
8:6, 13, 15
12:3, 6, 9
16:4, 5^3, 6^4, 7, 8^5, 9^3, 10^4, 11, 14, 17, 19^2, 23, 24^2, 27^3, 33, 34^3, 37, 38^2, 39^3, 40^3, 41^2, 42^2, 44, 57, 59, 60^2, 61, 62, 63
20:47^2
21:3^2, 4, 7, 16, 19, 29^3, 30, 31^3
22:4, 5^2, 6, 7^3, 9^3, 10^2, 11, 12, 13, 14, 15^3
23:22^2, 24^3, 25^2, 26, 27, 28, 29^2, 30
24:2, 13^2, 14, 16, 17, 26^2
25:4^3, 7^5
26:3^2, 8^3, 10, 14, 15, 16, 17^2, 19^3, 20^2, 21
27:5, 7, 8, 9^2, 10, 15, 21, 25, 26^2, 27^2, 30, 31^2, 32^2, 34, 35, 36
28:3, 4, 7, 8, 9^2, 13, 14, 15, 16^3, 17^3, 18^4, 19^2, 22^2
29:3, 4, 5^3, 7^2, 8^2, 10, 21
32:3^2, 4^4, 6, 7, 8, 10^2, 11
33:7, 30, 31^2
35:3^3, 6^3, 9, 11, 14, 15
36:12, 15
37:16, 18
38:3, 4^2, 6, 7, 9, 13, 15, 16^2, 17
39:1, 2^4, 4^2
40:4^2
44:5

DANIEL

1:12, 13
2:23^3, 29^2, 31, 37, 38, 39^2
3:12, 16, 18
4:9^2, 18, 19^2, 25^4, 26, 27, 31^2, 32^3
5:10, 14^3, 16, 23
6:7, 12, 13, 16, 20, 22
8:19
9:7^2, 8, 15, 16, 18, 22, 23
10:11^2, 14, 19, 20, 21
11:2

HOSEA

1:2
2:19^2, 20
3:3
4:5, 6
5:8
6:4^2, 11
8:2, 5
11:8^4, 9
12:9
13:5, 10, 11
14:3

JOEL

1:19, 20

AMOS

3:11
4:12^2
5:17
6:10
7:2, 5, 10, 12

OBADIAH

2, 3, 4, 5^2, 7^5, 10, 15

JONAH

1:8, 11, 14^3
2:7, 9
3:2
4:2^2, 3

MICAH
1:13, 15, 16[3]
2:11, 12
4:8, 9[2], 10, 11
5:2, 10, 13, 14
6:3[2], 4[3], 8[2], 13[3], 14, 15, 16
7:12, 17, 18

NAHUM
1:11, 12[2], 13, 14, 15
2:13
3:5, 6[3], 7[3], 13, 14, 15[3], 19[2]

HABAKKUK
1:2
2:7[2], 8, 16, 17
3:10

ZEPHANIAH
2:5
3:11, 12, 15, 17[3], 18, 19

HAGGAI
2:23[3]

ZECHARIAH
1:9
2:10, 11[2]
3:2[2], 4[2], 7, 8
9:9, 11, 12, 13
11:15
14:1, 5

MALACHI
1:7, 8
2:14
3:8, 13

MATTHEW
1:20
2:6, 13
3:14
4:6[2], 9, 10
5:23, 25[2], 26, 29[3], 30[3], 39, 40, 41, 42[2]
6:2, 4, 6, 18, 23
8:13, 19, 29
9:2, 5, 22
11:10, 21[2], 23, 24, 25
12:38, 47
14:4, 28
15:28
16:17, 18, 19, 22[2], 23
17:4, 27
18:8[3], 9[3], 15[3], 16[2], 17, 22, 26, 29, 32, 33
19:27
20:13, 14
21:5, 19, 23
23:37
25:21, 23, 24, 37[3], 38[3], 39[2], 44[2]
26:17, 33, 34, 35[2], 62, 63, 68, 73
27:13

MARK
1:2, 24[2], 37
2:5, 9, 11
3:32
5:7[2], 19[2], 23, 31, 34, 41
6:18, 22, 23
8:33
9:5, 17, 25, 43[2], 45[2], 47[2]
10:28, 49, 51, 52
11:14, 28
14:30, 31[2], 36, 60
15:4

LUKE
1:3, 13, 19[2], 28, 35[3]
2:48
3:22
4:6, 8, 10[2], 11, 34[2]
5:20, 23, 24
6:29, 30
7:14, 20, 27, 40, 47, 50
8:20, 28[2], 39, 45[2], 48
9:33, 38, 57, 61
10:13[2], 21, 35
11:7, 27, 35, 36
12:20, 58[3], 59
13:31[2], 34
14:9[2], 10[3], 12[2], 14, 18, 19
15:18, 29
16:2, 27
17:3, 4[2], 19
18:11, 28, 41, 42
19:21, 22, 43[4], 44[3]
20:2
22:11, 32, 33, 34, 64
23:43

JOHN
1:48[2], 50[2]
2:4
3:3, 5, 7, 11, 26
4:10[2], 26
5:10, 12, 14
6:30
7:20
8:10, 11
9:26, 37
10:33
11:8, 22, 28, 40, 41
13:8, 37, 38
16:30
17:1, 3, 4, 5, 7, 8, 11, 13, 21, 25[2]
18:26, 30, 34, 35
19:10[2], 11[2]
21:3, 15, 16, 17, 18[3], 20, 22, 23

THE ACTS
3:6
5:9
7:3[2], 27, 34, 35
8:20, 22, 34
9:5, 6, 17, 34
10:6, 19, 20, 22[2], 32, 33[2]
11:14
12:8
13:11, 33, 47
16:18
17:32
18:10[3]
21:21, 23, 24, 37, 39
22:10[2], 14, 18, 19, 21
23:3, 18[2], 20, 21, 30[2], 35
24:2, 4[2], 8, 14, 19, 25
25:26
26:2, 3[2], 14, 16[3], 17[2], 24
27:24[2]
28:21[2], 22

ROMANS
2:4, 27
4:17
9:17[2]
10:8
11:18, 21, 22
13:4
15:3, 9

1 CORINTHIANS
4:7
8:10
12:21

2 CORINTHIANS
6:2[2]
12:9

GALATIANS
3:8

EPHESIANS
5:14
6:3

PHILIPPIANS
4:3

1 TIMOTHY
1:3, 18[2]
3:14[2]
4:14[2], 16
5:21
6:13, 21

2 TIMOTHY
1:3, 4, 5[2], 6[2], 14
2:7
3:15
4:1, 11, 13, 21

TITUS
1:5[2]
2:15
3:12, 15

PHILEMON
4, 7, 8, 9, 10, 11[2], 16, 18[2], 19, 20, 21, 23

HEBREWS
1:5, 9
2:12
5:5
6:14[2]
8:5
13:5[2]

JAMES
2:18

2 JOHN
5[2], 13

3 JOHN
3, 13, 14[3]

JUDE
9

REVELATION
2:4, 5, 10, 14, 16, 20
3:3[2], 8, 9, 10, 16, 18
4:1
11:17[2]
14:15
15:4[2]
17:1, 7
18:14[2], 22[3], 23[2]
21:9

THEIR

846

GENESIS
1:21, 25
5:2
6:20[2]
7:14
8:19
9:23[4]
10:5[3], 20[4], 30, 31[4], 32[2]
11:7
12:5
13:6
14:6, 11[2], 24
17:7, 8, 9, 23
18:20, 22, 26
19:10, 33, 35, 36
20:8
24:52, 59
25:13[2], 16[4]
26:18
31:38, 43, 53
32:15
33:2, 6
34:13, 18, 20[2], 21, 23[2], 27, 28[3], 29[3]
35:4[3]
36:7[2], 19, 30, 40[3], 43[2]
37:2, 4, 12, 16, 21, 22, 25[2], 32
39:1
42:6, 24, 25, 26, 28, 29, 35[2], 36
43:2, 11, 15, 24[2], 26, 27, 28
44:3, 13
45:25, 27
46:5[3], 6[2], 17, 32[3]
47:1[2], 4, 9, 12, 17[2], 22[2], 30
48:6[2]
49:5, 6[4], 7[2], 28
50:8[3], 15, 17

EXODUS
1:11, 14[2]
2:11, 16, 17, 18, 23, 24
3:7[3]
4:5, 31[2]
5:4, 5, 6, 10, 21
6:4, 6, 14, 16, 17, 19, 25, 26
7:11, 12, 19[4], 22
8:7, 18, 26
10:7, 23
12:3, 34[4], 42, 51
13:20
14:10, 19, 22[2], 25, 26[2], 29[2]
16:1[2]
17:1
18:7, 23
19:7, 10, 14
21:32
22:23
23:24[3], 26, 27, 32, 33
25:20[3], 34[2], 36[2], 40
26:21, 25, 29, 32, 37
27:10[2], 11[2], 12[2], 14[2], 15[2], 16[2], 17[2], 18, 21
28:10[2], 12, 20, 21, 38, 42
29:10, 15, 19, 20[2], 25, 28[2], 45, 46[2]
30:12, 19[2], 21[3]
31:16
32:3, 4, 15, 25[2], 32, 34
33:6
34:13[3], 15[2], 16[4]
35:17, 18, 25
36:26, 30, 34, 36, 38[4]
37:9[3], 22[2]
38:10[3], 11[3], 12[3], 14[2], 15[2], 17[2], 19[5], 28
39:13, 14
40:15[3], 31[2], 36, 38

LEVITICUS
4:15
6:17
7:34, 36, 38
8:14, 16, 18, 22, 24[3], 25, 28
9:24
10:5, 19[2]
11:8[2], 11[2], 21, 27, 35, 36, 37, 38
13:38, 39
15:31[2]
16:16[3], 21[2], 22, 27[3], 34
17:5, 7[2]
18:3, 6, 9, 10, 29
20:4, 5, 11, 12, 13, 16, 17, 18, 19, 20, 24, 27
21:5[3], 6[3], 17
22:16, 25
23:4, 18[2]
24:14
25:32, 33, 34[2], 45
26:4, 13, 20, 36[2], 39[2], 40[3], 41[3], 43[2], 44[2], 45[3]

NUMBERS
1:2[4], 3, 16, 17, 18[4], 20[4], 22[4], 24[3], 26[3], 28[3], 30[3], 32[3], 34[3], 36[3], 38[3], 40[3], 42[3], 45, 47, 52[2]
2:2, 3, 9, 10, 16, 17, 18, 24, 25, 31, 32[2], 34[3]
3:4, 10, 15[2], 17, 18, 19, 20[2], 31, 37[3], 39, 40, 45
4:2[2], 22[2], 26[2], 27[3], 28, 29[2], 31[2], 32[6], 33, 34[2], 36, 38[2], 40[2], 42[2], 44, 46[2]
5:3, 7
6:15[2]
7:2, 3, 7, 8, 9, 10, 11, 87
8:7[2], 10, 12, 21, 22, 26[2]
9:17, 18, 20, 22
10:6[2], 12, 13, 14, 18, 22, 25, 28
11:10, 12, 33
13:2, 4, 33
14:1, 5, 6, 9, 23
15:12, 25[3], 38[2]
16:15, 22, 26, 27[4], 32[2], 38, 45
17:2[3], 3, 6[3], 10
18:11, 17[2], 20, 21, 23
20:6, 8[2], 11
21:2, 3, 18
22:7
24:2, 8
25:2[3], 18[2]
26:2, 12, 15, 20, 23, 26, 28, 35, 37, 38, 41, 42[2], 44, 48, 50, 55, 57, 59
27:5, 7[2], 14, 19
28:2, 14, 20, 28, 31
29:3, 6[2], 9, 11, 14, 18[3], 19, 21[3], 24[3], 27[3], 30[3], 33[3], 37[3]
30:9
31:9[4], 10[2], 29
32:17, 38
33:1, 2[4], 4[2], 12, 52[3]
34:14[4], 15
35:2, 3[2], 7
36:3, 4[2], 6, 11, 12[2]

DEUTERONOMY
1:8, 25
2:5, 9, 12, 21, 22, 23
4:10, 37, 38
5:29
7:5[4], 10, 16, 24[2], 25
9:5, 14, 27[2]
10:6, 11, 15
11:4[2], 6[3], 9
12:2, 3[4], 29, 30[2], 31[4]
13:13
14:8[2]
18:2[2], 18
19:1[2]
20:18[2]
21:5, 6
23:3, 6[2], 8
29:8, 17[2], 25, 28
31:7, 11, 13, 19, 20, 21[2], 28
32:5, 8, 20, 21, 27, 29, 30, 31, 32[3], 33, 35[2], 36, 37[2], 38[2]
33:29

JOSHUA
1:6
3:14
4:6, 18, 21
5:1, 6, 7[2], 8
7:6, 8[2], 11, 12[3], 16
8:13, 19, 33[2]
9:4, 5[2], 14, 16, 17[2]
10:5, 13, 19, 24, 40, 42
11:4, 6[2], 9[2], 13, 17, 20, 21, 23[2]
12:1, 7
13:8, 14, 15, 16, 23, 24, 25, 28[2], 29, 30, 31, 33
14:2, 4[3]
15:1, 2, 5, 12, 20, 32, 36, 41, 44, 46, 51, 54, 57, 59, 60, 62
16:4, 5[2], 8, 9
17:2[2], 4
18:2, 5[2], 7[2], 10, 11[2], 12, 20, 21, 24, 28[2]
19:1[2], 2, 6, 7, 8, 9, 10[2], 11, 15, 16[2], 17, 18, 22[2], 23[2], 24, 25, 30, 31[2], 32, 33, 38, 39[2], 40, 41, 47, 48[2], 49
21:3[2], 7, 8, 19, 20, 26, 33[2], 40[2], 41, 42, 43, 44[4]
22:6, 7[2], 9, 14
23:1, 2[4], 5, 7
24:1[3], 8

JUDGES
1:4, 7[3]
2:2, 3, 4, 10, 12, 14[2], 17[2], 18[2], 19[3], 20, 22
3:4, 6[5], 7, 25
5:18, 20, 22
6:5[3], 9
7:2, 6[3], 8[2], 12, 19, 20[2]
8:3, 10, 21, 26, 28, 33, 34[2]
9:3, 24[2], 26, 27[2], 57
10:12
12:2
13:20
14:17, 19
15:13
16:18, 23, 24, 25
18:1, 2[2], 8[2], 14, 16, 23, 26, 29
19:14, 21, 22
20:13, 22, 33[2], 42
21:2, 6, 22[2], 23

RUTH
1:9, 14

1 SAMUEL
1:19
2:20, 25, 33
5:9
6:6, 7, 10, 11, 13[2]
8:9, 22
9:16
10:4, 12, 21
11:4
12:9
14:30, 46
15:24
17:1, 18[2], 51, 53
18:27
21:13
22:17[2]
23:5
25:12
28:1, 23
29:1
30:2, 3[3], 4
31:9, 13

2 SAMUEL
1:23[2]
2:26
3:18, 30
4:12[2]
5:21
7:10, 23, 24
10:3, 4[3], 18
12:30
13:31, 36
15:11, 36
17:8
18:28
20:2, 3
22:46
23:17, 19

1 KINGS
2:4[3], 15, 33
4:8
6:27
7:25, 31, 33[4]
8:7, 23, 25, 34, 35, 37[2], 44, 45[3], 48[5], 49[3], 50, 66
9:9[2], 21
10:5, 29
11:2, 8
12:16, 27
13:11, 12
14:15[2], 22[2], 27, 30
15:16, 32
16:2, 13, 26
18:28, 37, 39
19:21
20:6, 23, 24, 25, 32[2]
22:10

2 KINGS
1:14
3:24, 27
5:24
6:20, 22, 23
7:7[4], 15
8:12[4], 21
10:7
11:12
13:3, 5
14:12
16:15[2]
17:7, 9[2], 14[3], 15, 16, 17[2], 19, 23, 25, 29[2], 31, 33, 34[2], 40, 41[4]
18:12, 27[2], 35, 36, 37
19:17, 18, 26
21:8, 14[2], 15
22:7, 17
23:2, 3[2], 9, 14
25:21, 23[2], 24

1 CHRONICLES
1:29
3:9, 19
4:3, 27, 31, 32, 33[3], 38[3], 39, 41[3], 42
5:7[3], 9, 10[2], 13[2], 15, 16, 20[2], 21[2], 22, 24[2], 25
6:19, 32[2], 33, 44, 48, 54[3], 57, 60[2], 62, 63, 64, 65, 66
7:2[2], 4[2], 5[2], 7[2], 9[3], 11, 21, 22, 28, 30, 32, 40
8:28, 32
9:1, 2[2], 6, 9[3], 13[2], 17, 19, 22[3], 23, 25[2], 26, 32, 34, 38[2]
10:7, 9, 10, 12
11:19[2], 21
12:30, 32[2], 39
13:2, 8
14:12
15:15, 16, 17, 18
16:21, 38
17:9, 22
19:4[2], 7
20:2
21:16
23:3[2], 11, 22, 24[2], 28, 32
24:2, 3[2], 4[2], 19[3], 30, 31[2]
25:1, 3, 6, 7
26:6, 8[2], 13
27:1[2]
28:15, 18
29:18, 20[2], 21

2 CHRONICLES
1:17
3:13[2]
4:4, 7, 16, 20
5:8, 12[2], 13
6:14, 16, 25, 26, 28[2], 34, 35[3], 36, 37, 38[5], 39[3]
7:3, 6[2], 10, 14[3], 22
8:8, 14[3]
9:4[2], 6
10:16
11:13, 14[2], 16[2]
13:10, 16, 18
14:4
15:4, 12[3], 15[2]
17:14
18:9
19:4, 10
20:13[3], 27, 33[2]
21:3
22:5
24:18[2], 24[2]
25:4, 5, 10, 15, 20
26:11, 13
28:6, 8, 15
29:6[2], 15, 23, 24, 30, 34
30:7, 16[2], 22, 27[2]
31:1, 2, 6, 15[2], 16[4], 17[3], 18[5], 19
32:13, 17
33:17
34:5, 6, 25, 30, 32, 33[2]
35:2, 10[2], 11, 15[3], 25
36:15, 17[2]

EZRA
1:6
2:59[2], 61, 62, 65[2], 66[2], 67[2], 69, 70[2]
3:8[2], 9[2], 10, 12
4:5, 7, 9, 17, 23
5:3, 5, 8, 10
6:12, 13, 18[2], 20, 22
7:13, 16, 17[2]
8:1, 19, 24, 26
9:1, 2[2], 11[2], 12[4]
10:16[2], 19[3]

NEHEMIAH
2:18
3:5[3], 18, 23
4:3, 4[2], 5[2], 13[4], 15
5:1[2], 5, 6, 8, 11[4], 14, 15
6:9, 14, 16
7:61[2], 63, 64, 67[2], 68[2], 69, 73[2]
8:6[3], 7, 12, 15, 16
9:2[2], 3[3], 4, 6, 9, 11, 15[2], 16, 17[3], 20[2], 21[2], 23[2], 24[2], 26, 27[3], 28, 29, 35[2], 37
10:10, 28[3], 29[2], 30
11:3, 9, 12, 14[2], 19, 25, 30, 31
12:7, 9, 24, 27, 42, 45
13:11, 13[2], 24, 25[3]

ESTHER
1:17[2], 20, 22
2:3, 12
3:8, 12
8:9[3], 11, 13
9:2[2], 5, 10, 15, 16[4], 22, 27[3], 28, 31[3]

JOB
1:4[2], 5[2], 13, 18
2:12[3]
3:8, 15
4:21
5:5, 12[2], 13, 15
6:17, 18
8:4, 8, 10
11:3, 20
12:18
14:12
15:18, 35
16:10
17:2, 4
19:12, 15
20:10
21:8[4], 9, 10[2], 11[2], 13, 16[2], 17, 29
22:6, 18
24:5[2], 11[2], 18, 23
27:23
29:9[2], 10[3], 23, 25
30:2, 4, 9[2], 12
31:16, 39
33:16
34:24, 25
36:9[2], 10, 11[2], 14, 15, 20
37:8
38:15, 40
39:3[2], 4
40:12, 13, 22
42:15[2]

PSALMS
2:3[2], 12
4:7[2]
5:9[4], 10[2], 11
7:7
9:5, 6, 10, 15
10:17
11:2[2], 6
16:4[3]
17:7, 10[2], 11, 14[3]
18:45
19:3, 4[2]
21:10[2], 12
22:13
26:10
28:3[2], 4[4], 8
33:15[2], 19
34:5, 15, 17
35:6, 7, 16, 17, 21, 25
36:7
37:14, 15[3], 18, 39
40:15
44:1, 3[2], 12
49:6[2], 8, 10, 11[5], 13[4], 14[2]
55:9, 15, 23
56:5
57:4
58:4, 6[2]
59:7[2], 12[3]
62:4
64:3[3], 8
65:7
68:27[2]
69:22[2], 23[2], 25[2], 27

PSALMS
70:3
72:14^2
73:4^2, 7, 9^2, 17, 20
74:4, 8
76:5^2
78:4, 5, 6, 7, 8^2, 12, 18^2, 28^2, 29, 30^3, 33^2, 35^2, 36^2, 37, 38, 44^2, 46^2, 47^2, 48^2, 50^2, 51, 53, 55, 57, 58^2, 63^2, 64^2
79:3, 10, 12^2
81:12^2, 14^2, 15
83:11^2, 16
85:2
89:17, 32^2
90:10, 16
91:12
93:3^2
94:23^2
95:10
98:8
99:8
102:17, 28
104:11, 12, 17, 21^2, 22, 27, 29^2
105:14, 24, 25, 29^2, 30^2, 31, 32, 33^3, 35^2, 36^2, 37
106:11, 15^2, 18, 20, 21, 25, 27, 29, 32, 35, 36, 37^2, 38^2, 39^2, 42^3, 43^2, 44^2
107:5, 6^2, 12, 13^2, 14, 17^2, 18, 19^2, 20, 26, 27, 28^2, 30, 38
109:10^2, 13, 25, 29
115:2, 4, 7, 9^2, 10^2, 11^2
119:70, 118
123:2
124:3, 6
125:3, 4, 5
129:3
132:12
135:12, 17
136:10, 21
140:2, 3^2, 9
141:4, 5, 6, 10
144:8, 11, 12
145:15, 19
147:3, 4
149:2, 5, 6^2, 8^2

PROVERBS
1:6, 15, 16, 18^2, 22, 31^2
2:15
4:16, 22
8:21
9:15
10:15
11:6, 20
14:24
17:6
18:19
20:29
21:12
22:23
23:11^2
24:2^2, 22
25:27
29:13, 16
30:5, 11^2, 12^2, 13^2, 14, 25, 26

ECCLESIASTES
2:3
3:11
4:1, 9
5:11, 13
9:1, 3, 6^6

ISAIAH
2:4^2, 7^4, 8^3
3:4, 8^2, 9^3, 10, 12, 16, 17, 18^4
5:12, 13^2, 14^3, 17, 21^2, 24^2, 25, 27^2, 28^3, 29
6:10^5, 13
8:12, 19, 21^2
9:17^2
10:2, 5, 13, 25, 29
11:7, 14
13:8, 10, 11^2, 16^4, 18^2, 20, 21, 22^2
14:1, 2^2, 9, 21, 25
15:2, 3^3, 4
16:10^2
18:2, 7
20:4, 5^2
21:14

ISAIAH
24:14
25:11^2
26:11, 14, 21
28:25
29:13^4, 14^2, 15^2, 19
30:6^2, 7, 26
31:3, 4
33:2, 7, 9, 23, 24
34:2, 3^4, 4, 7^2
35:10
36:12^2, 20, 21, 22
37:18, 19, 27
40:24, 26, 31
41:1, 17, 29^2
42:11, 15
43:9, 14
44:9^2, 18^2, 25
45:12, 20
46:1
47:9
49:9, 22^2, 23^2, 26^2
50:2, 3
51:7, 11
52:15
53:11
54:17
55:12
56:7^2, 11
57:2, 8
58:1^2, 2
59:5, 6^4, 7^3, 8, 18
60:8, 9^2, 10, 11
61:6, 7^2, 8, 9^2
62:6
63:3, 6, 8, 9, 10
65:2, 4, 6, 7^2, 22, 23
66:3^3, 4^2, 18^2, 24^2

JEREMIAH
1:8, 16^2, 17
2:11^2, 26^4, 27^3
3:17, 21^2, 24^4
4:16
5:3, 4, 5, 6^3, 16, 24, 27, 31
6:3^2, 10, 12^2, 19, 23, 27
7:18, 19, 24^2, 26^3, 28^2, 30, 31^2
8:1, 7, 10^2, 12, 19
9:3^2, 5, 8, 14^2, 16
10:7, 9, 15, 21
11:8^2, 10^2, 12, 14, 18, 22^2, 23
12:2^2, 14
13:10
14:3^4, 4, 6, 10^3, 11, 12, 14, 16^4
15:7, 8, 9
16:3^2, 4, 7^2, 15^2, 17^2, 18^3
17:1, 2^3, 23^2, 25
18:8, 15, 16, 17, 21^6, 22, 23^3
19:4, 5, 7^3, 9^4, 15
20:4, 5, 11
21:7^2
22:9
23:3, 8, 10^2, 11, 12^2, 16, 22^2, 26, 27^2, 31, 32^2
24:5, 7^2, 9, 10
25:12, 14^2, 36, 38
26:3
27:4, 8, 11^2
29:23
30:3, 9^2, 10, 20^2, 21^2
31:12, 13^2, 17, 23, 32, 33^3, 34^2
32:18, 22, 30^2, 32^4, 34, 35^2, 38, 39, 40, 44
33:8^2, 12, 20, 26
34:14, 16, 20^3, 21^2
35:14, 16
36:3^2, 6, 7, 15, 24, 31
37:7
38:18, 19, 23
40:7, 8, 9
41:5^3, 8
42:17
43:12
44:3, 5^2, 9, 12, 15
46:5, 10, 21^2, 25^2, 26, 27
47:3, 5
48:12, 13, 33, 34, 44
49:1, 3, 7, 20, 21, 29^5, 32^3, 35, 37^2
50:4, 5, 6^2, 7^2, 9, 27^2, 34^2, 37^2, 38, 42, 45
51:5, 18, 24, 30^2, 39^2, 55, 56

LAMENTATIONS
1:11, 14, 19^2, 22
2:10^2, 12^3, 15^2, 16, 18, 20
3:14, 46, 60^2, 61^2, 62, 63^3, 64
4:3, 7, 8^3, 10^2, 14, 20
5:7, 8, 12, 14

EZEKIEL
1:5, 7^2, 8^4, 9, 10, 11^3, 13, 16^3, 17, 18^2, 20, 22, 23^2, 24^2, 25^2, 26
2:3, 6^3
3:8^2, 9
4:4, 5, 12, 13, 17
5:10, 16
6:5, 9^4, 13^4, 14
7:11, 18, 19^7, 20^2, 24^2, 27^2
8:16^2, 17
9:10^2
10:8, 10, 11, 12^4, 16, 19, 21, 22^2
11:19, 20, 21^4, 22
12:3^2, 4^2, 5, 6, 7, 16, 19^2
13:2, 3, 17
14:3^4, 5^2, 10, 11^2, 14^2, 20^2, 22^2, 23^2
16:39, 40, 45^2, 47^2, 53, 55^2
19:4, 7^2, 8^2
20:4, 8, 16^2, 18^3, 24^2, 26, 28^4, 30
21:6, 14, 15^3, 23, 28, 29
22:6, 10, 26, 31^2
23:3^3, 4, 7, 8, 15^3, 17, 20, 24, 30, 36, 37^3, 39^2, 42^2, 45, 47^4
24:25^6
25:4^2
26:10, 16^3, 17
27:9, 11, 29, 30^2, 32, 35^2
28:7, 25, 26
29:7^2, 14, 16
30:11, 13
31:6^2, 14^4
32:2, 10, 14^2, 24^2, 25^2, 26, 27^5, 29, 30^3
33:2^2, 17, 29, 31^3
34:10^2, 13, 14, 23, 24, 27^2, 30
35:5^2
36:5^2, 7, 12, 17^4, 18, 19^2, 23
37:10, 20, 21, 23^5, 25^3, 27
38:16
39:22, 23^2, 24^2, 26^3, 27, 28^2
40:16, 22^3, 41, 44
41:16
42:4, 11^3, 14
43:7^4, 8^4, 9^2, 10, 11
44:10^2, 12^2, 13^2, 18^2, 19^2, 20^3, 22, 28^2
45:4, 8
46:16, 18
47:10^2, 12
48:29, 34

DANIEL
1:15, 16
2:30
3:21^4, 27^2, 28^2, 29
4:21
6:24^3
7:12^2
8:23
9:7
11:8^3, 32

HOSEA
1:7
2:5, 17
3:5^2
4:7, 8^2, 9^2, 12^3, 18, 19
5:4^2, 5, 6^2, 7, 15^2
7:2^3, 3^2, 6^2, 7^2, 10, 12, 14^2, 15, 16^3
8:4^2, 13^2
9:4^3, 6^2, 9^2, 10, 11, 12, 15^3, 16^2
10:2^3, 8, 10
11:3, 4, 6, 11
12:11
13:2^2, 6^2, 8, 16^2
14:4

JOEL
1:3^2, 17
2:6, 7, 10, 17, 22
3:6, 13, 15, 19, 21

AMOS
1:13, 15
2:4^2, 8
3:10
4:1
5:12
6:2, 4
7:11
8:7
9:4, 15^2

OBADIAH
12, 13^5, 17

JONAH
1:2
2:8
3:8, 10^2
4:11^2

MICAH
2:1^2, 9^2, 12, 13
3:2^3, 3^2, 4, 5^2, 7
4:3^2, 13^2
6:12^2, 16
7:4, 13, 16^4, 17, 19

NAHUM
2:2, 5, 7
3:3^2, 17

HABAKKUK
1:7^2, 8^3, 9, 15^2, 16^4, 17
2:15
3:11, 14

ZEPHANIAH
1:9, 12^2, 13^2, 17^2, 18^2
2:7^2, 8, 10, 14
3:6^3, 7^2, 13

HAGGAI
1:12^2, 14
2:14, 22

ZECHARIAH
1:21
2:9
5:6, 9
7:2, 11, 12
8:8, 12
9:16
10:2, 5, 6, 7^3, 9
11:3, 5, 6, 8, 16
12:5^2, 12^2, 13^2, 14
14:12^6

MALACHI
4:6

MATTHEW
1:21
2:11, 12
3:6
4:6, 20, 21^2, 22, 23
6:2, 5, 7, 14, 15, 16^2
7:6, 16, 20
8:22, 33, 34
9:2, 4, 29, 30, 35
10:17, 21
11:1, 5, 16
12:9, 25
13:15^5, 43, 54, 58
14:14
15:2, 8^3, 37
17:6, 8, 25
18:10, 31, 35
19:12
20:4, 8, 31, 34^2
21:7, 8, 41
22:5, 7, 16, 18, 22
23:3, 4, 5^3
25:1, 3, 4^2, 7
26:43, 67
27:39

MARK
1:5, 18, 19, 20, 23, 39
2:5, 6
3:4, 5
4:12, 15
5:17
6:6, 8^2, 26, 52

MARK
7:3, 6^2
8:3
9:34, 44, 46, 48
10:42
11:4, 7, 8
12:12, 15, 44
13:12
14:40, 46, 56, 59, 65
15:19, 29
16:14

LUKE
1:16, 20, 51, 52, 66, 77
2:8, 39, 44
3:15
4:11, 15, 29
5:2, 6, 7, 11, 15, 20, 22, 30
6:1, 8, 17, 22, 23, 26
7:21
8:3, 12
9:47, 60
11:17, 48
12:36, 42
13:1
14:4
16:4, 8
17:13
19:32, 35, 36, 40
20:23, 26
21:1, 4, 12
22:66
23:25, 48
24:5, 11, 16, 31^2, 45

JOHN
3:19
4:38
8:9
10:39
11:19, 46
12:40^4
13:12
15:22, 25
17:19, 20
18:8
19:3, 31
20:10

THE ACTS
1:9, 19, 26
2:37, 45, 46
4:5, 23, 24, 29
5:18
6:1, 6
7:19, 34, 39, 41, 54, 57, 58, 60
8:17, 36
9:24
10:9
11:18
12:17, 20^2, 25
13:3, 5, 18, 19, 22, 27, 33, 50, 51
14:2, 3, 5, 11, 13, 14, 16
15:3, 9, 13, 22, 26
16:19, 22, 24, 33
17:21, 26
18:3
19:18, 19
21:21, 24
22:22, 23, 30
23:16, 28, 29
25:19
26:18
27:13, 43
28:6, 27^5

ROMANS
1:21^2, 24^2, 26, 27^2, 28
2:15^3
3:3, 13^3, 15, 16, 18
10:3, 18^2
11:9, 10^2, 11, 12, 24, 27, 30
13:7
15:27^3
16:4, 5, 18

1 CORINTHIANS
3:19
8:7, 12
14:35
16:19

2 CORINTHIANS
3:14, 15
5:19
6:16
8:2^3, 3^2, 5, 14^2
9:14
11:15

GALATIANS
2:13

EPHESIANS
4:17, 18
5:24, 28^2

PHILIPPIANS
2:21
3:19^2

COLOSSIANS
2:2

1 THESSALONIANS
2:15, 16
5:13

2 THESSALONIANS
3:12

1 TIMOTHY
3:11, 12^2
4:2
5:4, 12
6:1

2 TIMOTHY
2:17
3:2, 9
4:3, 4, 16

TITUS
1:12, 15
2:4^2, 5, 9
3:13

HEBREWS
2:10, 15
3:10
5:14
7:5
8:9, 10^2, 12^3
10:16^2, 17
11:16, 35
12:10
13:7

JAMES
1:27
3:3

1 PETER
3:5, 12, 14
4:14, 19

2 PETER
2:2, 3, 8, 12, 13
3:3, 16

3 JOHN
6

JUDE
6^2, 13, 15^2, 16^2, 18

REVELATION
2:22
3:4
4:4, 10
6:11^2, 14
7:3, 9, 11, 14, 17
9:4, 5, 7^2, 8, 9, 10^2, 17, 18, 19^4, 20, 21^4
10:3, 4
11:5^2, 6, 7, 8, 9^2, 11, 12, 16^2
12:8, 11^2
13:16^2
14:1, 2, 5, 11, 13^2
15:6
16:10, 11^3
17:13, 17^2
18:11, 19
19:19, 21
20:4^2, 12, 13
21:3, 4, 8, 24
22:4

THEM 846

GENESIS
1:14, 15, 17, 22, 26, 27, 28^2
2:1, 19^2
3:7, 21
5:2^2
6:1, 2, 4, 7, 13^2, 19, 20, 21
7:13
9:1, 19
10:1
11:3, 6, 8, 9, 29, 31
12:3
13:6
14:8, 14, 15^3, 24
15:5, 10, 11, 13^2
18:2^2, 8^2, 16^2
19:1^2, 3^2, 5^2, 6, 8^2, 9, 10, 12, 13, 17, 18
20:14
21:27^2, 31
22:6, 8
23:8
24:28, 53, 56, 60

GENESIS
25:6, 26
26:15^2, 18^2, 27, 30, 31
27:9, 13, 14, 15
28:11
29:4, 5, 6, 7, 9^2
30:14, 35, 37, 40, 42
31:5, 9, 32, 33, 34^3, 55
32:2, 4, 16, 23^2
33:3, 13
34:8, 14, 21^3, 23
35:4, 5
36:7
37:6, 13, 17^2, 18, 22
38:26
39:14
40:3, 4^2, 5, 6^3, 8^2, 11, 17, 22
41:3, 6, 8^2, 19, 21^2, 23, 27, 30, 35^2
42:7^4, 9^2, 12, 14, 17, 18, 22, 23^2, 24^4, 25^2, 27, 28, 29, 36
43:2, 11, 16, 23, 24, 27, 32, 34

GENESIS
44:4^2, 6^2, 15
45:1, 15, 21^2, 22, 24, 26, 27
47:2, 6^3, 11, 17^2, 20, 21, 22^2, 24
48:6, 9^2, 10^3, 12, 13^2, 16^2, 20
49:7^2, 28^3, 29^2
50:12, 19, 21^2

EXODUS
1:7, 10^2, 11^2, 12, 14, 16, 17, 18, 19, 21
2:17^2, 25
3:8^2, 9, 13^2, 16, 22
4:20
5:4, 5, 7, 8, 9, 13, 14, 21
6:1^2, 3, 4^2, 13
7:5, 6, 13, 22
8:2, 14, 15, 19
9:2^2, 12, 17, 19, 27
10:2, 8, 10, 14^2, 19, 27
12:3, 16, 21, 33, 36, 38, 42
13:17, 21^3

EXODUS
14:3, 4, 7, 9^2, 10, 13, 17, 19^2, 20, 22, 23, 25^2, 28^2, 29
15:5, 7^2, 9^2, 10, 12, 13, 15, 16, 17^2, 19, 21, 25^2
16:3, 4, 12, 15, 16, 20^2, 23
17:2
18:8^2, 11, 16, 20^2, 21, 22, 25
19:10^2, 21, 22, 24, 25
20:5^3, 6, 11
21:1, 34
22:11, 23
23:23, 24^2, 29, 30, 31, 32
24:12, 14
25:3, 8^2, 12, 13, 14, 18, 28^2, 29, 40
26:1, 24, 37^2
27:6
28:9, 11, 14, 25, 26, 27, 33, 40^2, 41^4, 42
29:1^2, 2, 3^2, 4, 8, 9^2, 13^2, 17, 22, 24, 25^2, 29, 30, 33, 35, 46^2

EXODUS
30:5, 12^3, 13, 14, 21, 29^2, 30
31:5
32:2^2, 3, 4, 8^2, 10^2, 12^3, 13, 18^3, 19, 21, 24^2, 25, 27, 31, 34
34:31^2, 32, 33
35:1^2, 23, 26, 29, 33, 35^2
36:8^2, 14, 29, 36^2
37:4, 7, 15, 28
38:6, 25, 28
39:7, 18, 19, 20, 43
40:12, 14, 15

LEVITICUS
1:2, 12
2:12
3:4, 10, 15, 16
4:2, 9, 10, 20^2, 35
5:8
6:10, 17, 18
7:4, 5, 7, 34, 35, 36^2

LEVITICUS
8:6, 10, 11, 13^3, 26, 27, 28^2
9:2, 7, 13, 14, 22
10:1^2, 2, 3, 4, 5, 11, 17
11:1, 4^2, 9, 22, 24, 25, 26, 28, 31, 32, 33, 42, 43
13:58
14:6, 12, 23, 24, 40, 42, 45, 51
15:2, 14, 15, 29, 31
16:4, 7, 16, 21, 23, 28
17:2, 5^2, 7, 8, 16
18:2, 5, 29
19:2, 10, 31^2, 37
20:6, 8, 11^2, 12^2, 13^2, 16, 18, 22, 23, 27^2
21:1, 23
22:3, 9, 16^2, 18, 22, 25^2, 31
23:2, 10, 20, 22, 43
24:6, 12
25:2, 18, 31, 44, 45, 46^2, 51
26:3, 36^2, 39, 41^2, 43^2, 44^4
27:2

NUMBERS

1:3, 19, 21, 22, 23, 25, 27, 29, 31, 33, 35, 37, 39, 41, 43, 47, 49
2:4, 13, 15, 19, 21, 23, 26, 28, 30
3:6, 15, 16, 22^2, 32, 34, 43, 47, 48, 49^2, 51
4:8, 12^3, 19^2, 23, 26, 27, 29, 30, 36, 40, 44, 48
5:3, 4, 12, 23
6:2, 16, 19, 20, 23, 27
7:1^2, 2, 3, 5^2, 6, 9, 13, 19, 25, 31, 37, 43, 49, 55, 61, 67, 73, 79
8:6, 7^5, 8, 13, 15^2, 16, 17, 20, 21^3, 22
9:8
10:2^2, 3, 33^2, 34, 35
11:1^2, 3, 4, 12^2, 16^2, 17, 21, 22^4, 24, 25, 26^2, 28, 29, 31, 32
12:9
13:2, 3, 17^2, 26^2
14:2, 6, 9^2, 10, 11, 12^2, 13, 14^2, 16^2, 23, 28, 31, 40, 45^2
15:2, 18, 25, 26, 29, 38^2, 39
16:3^3, 7, 9, 15^2, 17, 18, 19, 21, 28, 30^2, 31, 32, 33^2, 34^2, 38^3, 45, 46, 49
17:2, 4
18:8, 11, 12^2, 18, 20, 24, 26^2, 30
19:9, 10, 21
20:6, 8, 10, 12, 13, 25, 26, 28
21:1, 3, 16, 30^2, 33
22:6^2, 8, 11^3, 12, 20
23:11, 13^4, 21, 22, 25^2, 27
24:8, 10
25:4, 8, 11, 17
26:3, 7, 10, 18, 22, 25, 27, 34, 37, 41, 43, 47, 50, 62^2, 64, 65^2
27:3, 7^2, 17^4
28:2, 3, 31
30:12^3, 14^2, 15^2
31:3, 6^2, 8, 13, 15, 27^2, 30, 36, 47, 51
32:7, 8, 9, 13, 15, 17, 19, 20, 28, 29^2, 33, 41
33:4, 51, 55, 56
34:2
35:2, 3, 5, 6, 7, 8^2, 10, 15
36:6

DEUTERONOMY

1:3, 8^2, 13, 15, 29, 39, 42
2:5, 6^2, 9, 11, 12^4, 14, 15^2, 19^2, 20, 21^3, 22^2, 23
3:4, 6, 14, 20, 22, 28
4:1, 3, 6, 7, 9, 10, 13, 14, 19^2, 31, 37
5:1^3, 9^3, 10, 22^2, 29^2, 30, 31^3
6:1, 7^2, 8, 9
7:2^5, 3, 5, 9, 10^2, 11, 12, 15^2, 16, 17, 18, 20, 21, 22, 23^2, 24, 25
8:19^2
9:3^4, 4^2, 5, 10, 12^2, 14, 17^2, 28^5
10:2, 4, 11, 15^2
11:4^2, 6, 9, 16, 18, 19^2, 20, 21, 22
12:3, 18, 22^2, 29^2, 30
13:2
14:7^2
17:3, 5, 19
18:2, 3, 12, 18^2
19:1, 9
20:1, 3^2, 17, 19^4, 20
21:5, 8, 10^2, 18
22:1^2, 4^2, 19, 22, 24^2
23:8
24:8
25:1, 5
26:13^2, 16
27:2, 3, 4, 5, 26
28:13, 14, 25^2, 26, 31, 32, 39^2, 41, 55, 57, 61
29:1, 2, 7, 9, 17, 25^2, 26^2, 28^2
30:1, 7, 17, 20
31:2, 3, 4^2, 5^2, 6, 7^2, 10, 16^2, 17^4, 20^2, 21^3, 23, 28
32:11^2, 19, 20, 21^2, 23^2, 24, 26^2, 28, 30^2, 35, 38, 41, 46
33:2^2, 11^2, 17, 27

JOSHUA

1:2, 6, 14, 15
2:4, 5^2, 6^2, 7^2, 8, 15, 16, 21, 22^2, 23
4:3^3, 5, 7, 8^3, 12
5:1, 5, 6, 7^2
6:6, 8, 13, 23, 26
7:2, 5^3, 11, 21^2, 23^3, 24, 25^2
8:3, 4, 5, 6^2, 9, 11, 12, 15, 16, 20, 22^3, 24, 33^3, 35
9:5, 8, 11^2, 15^4, 16^2, 18^2, 19^2, 20^3, 21^4, 22^2, 26^3, 27
10:1, 8^3, 9, 10^4, 11, 18, 19^3, 20^2, 24, 25, 26^3, 27^2, 28, 39, 41
11:4, 6^2, 7^2, 8^5, 9, 11, 12^3, 13, 14, 17^2, 20^2, 21
12:6
13:6, 8^2, 12, 14, 22^2, 33
14:1, 3, 12
15:63
17:4, 13, 15
18:1, 4^2, 7, 8, 10
19:9^2, 47, 49
20:4^2, 9
21:2, 11, 21, 42, 44^2
22:2, 4, 6^2, 7^2, 8, 12, 15, 30, 32, 33
23:2, 5^2, 7^3, 12^2, 16
24:5, 7^2, 8^2, 11, 12, 13, 25

JUDGES

1:1, 4, 22, 25, 28, 29, 30, 32, 33, 34
2:3, 10, 12^3, 14^3, 15^2, 16^2, 17, 18^5, 19^2, 21, 22, 23^2
3:1, 2, 4, 8, 9, 15, 23, 25, 27, 28
4:2
5:14, 21, 30, 31
6:1, 2, 3, 4, 8, 9, 20, 35
7:1, 4^2, 6, 17, 24
8:2, 4, 8, 10, 11, 12, 16, 19, 20, 23, 24, 25, 34
9:1, 7, 8, 9, 11, 13, 24, 25, 33, 38, 43^3, 44, 49^2, 51^2, 57
10:7, 14, 16
11:9, 11, 21, 24, 25, 26, 32^2, 33, 35
12:2, 3
13:1
14:9^2, 12, 14, 18, 19^2
15:3^2, 5, 7, 8, 11^2, 12
16:3^3, 8, 12, 23, 25, 26
17:4
18:1^2, 2, 4, 6, 7, 8, 9, 18, 21, 27, 31
19:6, 8, 14, 15, 23^2, 24^3, 25
20:13, 20, 25, 28, 32, 34, 40, 41, 42^3, 43^2, 45^3, 48
21:6, 7^2, 10, 12, 13, 14^2, 15, 16, 17, 18, 22^3, 23^3

RUTH

1:4, 5, 6, 9, 13^2, 19, 20
2:9, 16^2

1 SAMUEL

2:8^3, 10, 16, 23, 25, 30, 34
3:13
5:6^3, 8
6:6, 7, 10, 12, 15
7:10, 11
8:7, 8, 9^3, 11, 12, 14^2, 16, 21, 22
9:4^2, 11, 12, 14, 20, 22^3, 26
10:5, 6, 10, 18
11:2, 7^2, 8, 11, 12
12:5, 8, 9^2
13:16, 19
14:8, 9, 10, 11, 12, 21, 22, 32^2, 34^3, 36^2, 37, 47, 48^2
15:3, 4, 6, 9, 15, 18
16:5, 20
17:3, 8, 23^2, 31, 36, 39^2, 40
18:16, 27
19:8, 20
20:11, 21, 40
21:13
22:2, 4, 11
23:5, 26
24:7, 22
25:7^2, 14, 15, 16, 18, 20, 29, 43
26:12^2, 13
27:5
30:2, 8^2, 17^2, 19^2, 21, 22^2, 27^3, 28^3, 29^3, 30^3, 31
31:7, 12, 13

2 SAMUEL

1:10, 11, 18
2:5, 7, 14
3:22, 36
4:7, 9, 12^2
5:3, 19, 20, 21, 23^2
6:22
7:10^2, 21
8:1, 2^2, 4, 7
10:4, 5, 9, 10, 16, 19
11:23
12:11, 17, 31^2
13:9, 10, 11, 30
14:6
15:36^2
16:1
17:9, 17, 18^2, 20^2, 22
18:1, 4, 14, 31
19:3, 28
20:3^3, 8, 19
21:2^3, 6^2, 7, 9^2, 10^2, 12^2, 13
22:15^2, 18, 23, 28, 31, 38^2, 39^2, 40, 41, 42, 43^3, 49
23:6, 7, 18
24:1, 12

1 KINGS

1:20, 33, 40
2:7, 32
5:3, 9^4, 14, 18
6:12, 15, 16, 32^2, 35
7:6^2, 15, 25, 37, 46
8:21, 34, 35, 36, 37, 44, 46^3, 47^2, 48, 50^4, 52, 53
9:6, 7, 9^3, 13, 21
10:17, 29
11:2, 18, 24
12:5, 7^3, 9, 10, 14, 16, 17, 28
13:11, 12
14:15, 23, 27, 28^2
15:18^2, 22
18:4^2, 6, 13, 23^2, 26, 27, 28, 40^5
19:2, 21
20:15, 18^2, 19, 20, 23, 25, 27^2
21:8, 11^2
22:6, 10, 11, 13, 17

2 KINGS

1:2, 3, 5, 7, 12
2:11, 12, 16, 18, 24^3
3:9, 10, 13, 21, 24
4:31, 33, 39^2, 44
5:12, 22, 23^2, 24^2
6:4, 11, 16, 18, 19^2, 21^3, 22^2, 23^2, 33
7:10, 12, 15
9:11, 17, 18, 19, 20
10:1, 6^2, 7^2, 8, 14^4, 18, 22, 25^3, 26, 29, 32

2 KINGS

11:4^4, 5, 9, 15
12:5^2, 7, 11
13:3, 4, 7^2, 17, 18, 23^5
14:27
15:29
16:17
17:6, 7, 9, 10, 11, 12, 15^4, 16, 18, 20^3, 21, 22, 24, 25^2, 26^2, 27^2, 28, 29, 32^2, 35^4
18:11, 12^2, 13, 18, 19, 23, 27
19:6, 11, 12, 18
20:13^3, 15
21:3, 8^2, 9, 14, 21, 24
22:5^2, 7, 9, 15
23:4^2, 5, 12^2, 16, 19, 20
24:2, 3, 16, 20
25:13, 19, 20, 21^2, 22, 24^2

1 CHRONICLES

2:6, 23, 53
4:21, 41, 42
5:11, 20^3, 25, 26^2
6:55, 67, 78
7:3, 4, 9, 40
8:6, 7, 8, 32
9:20, 25, 27^2, 28^2, 29
10:7, 12
11:3, 14, 20
12:15, 17^2, 18^2, 19, 29, 32, 34, 39, 40
13:2
14:8, 10^2, 11, 14^3
15:2, 12, 18
16:10, 21, 41, 42
17:9^2
18:1, 4, 7, 11
19:4^2, 5, 6, 10, 16, 17^2
20:3
21:2, 6, 10
23:6, 22, 31
24:3, 6, 19
25:7
26:30, 31
27:23, 26
29:8

2 CHRONICLES

2:2, 11, 17, 18
3:10, 15, 16^2
4:4, 6^2, 7, 8, 9, 17
5:12^2
6:25^2, 26, 27, 28, 34, 36^3, 38
7:6, 19, 20^2, 22^4
8:2, 8^2, 18
9:8^2, 16
10:5, 7^2, 9, 10, 13, 14, 16, 17
11:11, 12, 14, 16, 23
12:5, 7^2, 10, 11^2
13:7, 9, 13^2, 16, 17
14:7, 9, 11, 13, 14^2
15:4, 6, 9, 15^2
16:8, 9
17:8^2, 9, 14
18:5, 9^2, 16, 31
19:2, 4, 9, 10
20:1, 10^2, 12, 16^2, 17, 23, 25^2, 27^2
21:3
22:8, 12
23:3, 8, 14
24:5, 13, 17, 19^3, 20, 23
25:5^3, 10, 12^2, 13, 14^3, 20
26:9, 14
27:5
28:5^2, 8, 9^3, 12, 13, 15^7, 23^2
29:3, 4, 5, 8, 21, 23, 24, 34
30:7, 9^2, 10^2, 12, 14, 17, 18
31:1, 6, 7, 11
32:1, 6^2, 18^2, 22, 26
33:3, 8, 11, 15, 22, 25
34:4^4, 12, 21, 23
35:2, 11, 13, 15, 25
36:7, 15, 17^2, 20

EZRA

1:5, 6, 7, 8, 9, 11
2:63, 65
3:3, 7^2
4:2, 3, 4, 5, 20, 23
5:1, 2^2, 3^2, 4, 5, 9, 10, 12, 14, 15
6:5, 9, 20, 21, 22^2
7:17, 24, 25^2
8:1, 13, 14, 15, 17^2, 20, 22^2, 24, 25, 28, 29^2, 30, 33
10:3, 6, 10, 14^2, 15, 16, 44

NEHEMIAH

1:2, 5, 9^3
2:9, 10, 17, 18, 20^2
3:2, 4^3, 5, 7, 9, 10, 27, 29
4:4, 8, 9^2, 11^2, 12, 14, 16, 21, 23
5:2, 5, 7^2, 8, 10, 11^2, 12^3, 15
6:3, 4, 8, 17
7:3^3, 5, 65
8:8, 10^2, 12, 16, 17
9:1, 6, 10, 11, 12^2, 13^2, 14^2, 15^4, 17^2, 18, 19^4, 20^2, 21, 22^2, 23, 24^3, 26^2, 27^5, 28^4, 29^3, 30^3, 31^2, 34, 35^2
10:31
11:23
12:9, 24, 27, 29, 31, 32, 36, 37, 38^3, 40, 43, 44, 47
13:2^2, 10, 11^2, 13, 15, 17, 21^2, 25^4, 29, 30

ESTHER

1:7
2:3, 15
3:4^2, 8, 11, 13
4:7, 8, 15
5:8, 11
8:11^2, 17

ESTHER

9:1^3, 2^2, 3, 5, 21, 22^2, 23, 24^3, 26, 27^2, 28, 31

JOB

1:4, 5^2, 6, 14, 15^2, 16, 17
2:1
3:8
4:19, 21
5:4
6:19
8:4
9:5
12:15, 23^2, 24, 25
14:21
15:19
17:4
20:15^2
21:8, 9, 17, 26, 29
22:17, 19, 20
24:5, 12, 17^2
26:8
29:22, 24
30:5, 31
32:8
34:25, 26
36:7, 9, 13, 31
37:4, 12, 15, 21
39:4, 14, 15^2
40:13
41:16
42:9, 15

PSALMS

2:4, 5^2, 9^2
5:6, 10^3, 11^3
6:10
7:1
9:6, 10, 12, 13, 20
10:2, 5
12:7^2
15:4
17:7^2
18:14^2, 17, 37, 38, 40, 41^2, 42^2
19:4, 11^2, 13
21:9^3, 12^2
22:4, 18, 25
24:6, 9
25:3, 14^2
28:1, 4^3, 5^2, 9^2
29:6
31:6, 15, 17, 19^2, 20^2
33:6, 18^2, 19
34:7^2, 9, 16^2, 17, 18, 19, 20, 22
35:1^2, 3, 4^2, 5^2, 6, 19^2, 20, 24, 25^2, 26^2, 27^2
36:8, 10
37:40^4
39:6
40:5, 14^2, 15
41:10
42:4
43:3^2
44:2^2, 3^2, 5, 7, 13
48:6
49:7, 14^2
50:21
53:3, 5^2
54:3, 4, 5
55:15^3, 19, 23
57:4
58:7^2, 8, 9
59:1, 8, 11^3, 12, 13^3, 14^2, 15
60:4
62:10
63:11
64:5, 6, 7, 8
65:3, 5, 9
68:1, 2, 3^2, 17, 18, 25
69:6, 9, 11, 14, 22, 24^2, 27, 28
70:2^2, 3
71:13^2
73:6^2, 10, 18^2, 27
74:8
75:8^2
78:4, 5, 6^2, 11, 13, 14, 15, 24^2, 25, 27, 29, 31^2, 34, 38, 42, 45^3, 49^2, 52, 53, 54, 55^2, 66, 72^2
79:3, 4
80:5^2
81:12, 16
82:4
83:4, 8, 9, 13, 15^2, 17^2
84:5, 7, 11
85:8, 9
86:5, 14
87:4
88:4, 8
89:7, 9, 11, 12, 23
90:5
94:23^3
97:10
99:3, 6^2, 7^2, 8^2
101:3
102:26^2
103:11, 13, 17, 18
104:8, 12, 22, 24, 27, 28
105:3, 14, 17, 24, 27, 32, 37, 38^2, 40, 44
106:8, 9, 10^3, 11, 15, 23^2, 26^2, 27, 29, 34, 36, 41^3, 42, 43, 45, 46^2
107:3, 5, 6, 7, 13, 14, 19, 20^2, 22, 28, 30, 32, 34, 38, 40
109:10, 15^2, 20, 25, 28^2, 29
111:2, 5, 6
115:8^3, 13
118:4, 7^2, 10, 11, 12, 19
119:63^2, 84, 93, 118, 129, 152, 165, 167
125:4, 5
126:1, 2

PSALMS

127:5
129:5, 6
132:12
135:18^3
136:11
139:16, 17, 18, 21, 22^2
140:9, 10^2
143:7, 12
144:6^2
145:15, 18, 19^2, 20
146:8
147:4, 11, 18, 20
148:5, 6, 13
149:3^2, 5, 9

PROVERBS

1:12, 15, 32^2
2:7
3:3^2, 18, 21, 27
4:21^2, 22
5:6, 13, 17
6:21^2
7:3^2
8:8, 9, 17
10:26
11:3^2, 6
12:6, 20, 26
14:3, 22
19:7
20:10, 12, 26
21:6, 7
22:2, 5, 18, 21, 23, 26^2
24:1, 11, 21, 22, 25^2
25:13
27:3
28:4, 13
30:5, 7, 27
31:29

ECCLESIASTES

2:5, 10, 14
3:12, 18, 19
4:16
5:11^2
7:11, 12, 18
8:11, 12
9:1, 5, 11, 12
10:15
11:8
12:1

SONG OF SOLOMON

3:4
4:2
5:3
6:6

ISAIAH

1:14, 23, 31
2:9
3:4, 9, 12
4:2
5:8, 11^2, 18, 20, 21, 22, 25^2, 26, 27, 30
6:13
7:19, 20
8:7, 12, 15, 19, 20
9:2, 10, 13, 16^2
10:1, 6, 10, 15, 19, 20, 22
11:6, 14^2
13:2, 3, 8, 15, 17
14:1^2, 2^4, 18, 20, 22, 25
16:4
17:2, 13, 14^2
18:6^2
19:3, 4, 12^2, 20^2, 22^2
23:1, 13, 18
24:8, 9
25:11
26:5, 11, 14, 16
27:4^2, 6, 7, 11^5
28:1, 6, 9, 13
29:1, 15
30:5, 6, 8, 22, 28
31:1, 2, 4
32:3^2
33:4
34:2^2, 7, 16, 17^2
35:1, 4
36:1, 4, 8
37:6, 11, 12, 19
38:21
39:2^3, 4
40:11, 22, 24^2, 26, 29
41:1^2, 2, 3, 12^3, 15, 16^3, 17^2, 22^5, 27, 28^2
42:5^2, 7, 9, 11, 12, 16^4, 22
43:9^3
44:7^2, 9, 11^2
45:8, 16, 21^2
47:6^2, 14
48:3^2, 5^2, 6, 7^2, 13, 14, 21^2
49:9, 10^4, 18^2, 26
50:6, 9
51:8^2, 17, 23^2
52:4, 5^2, 15
54:2
56:5^2, 7^2
57:6, 8, 13^2
59:8, 12, 20, 21
60:9, 14
61:1, 3^2, 7, 8, 9^2
62:12
63:3^2, 6, 7, 9^4, 10, 11, 12^2, 13, 19
65:1^2, 8, 21^2, 23
66:4, 19^2, 21

JEREMIAH

1:16, 17^2
2:3, 13, 25, 28, 37
3:2

JEREMIAH

4:12
5:3^2, 5, 6^2, 7^2, 13^2, 14, 19
6:10, 13^2, 15^2, 18, 21, 30^2
7:16, 22^2, 23, 25, 27^2, 28, 31, 33
8:2, 3^2, 4, 9, 10^2, 12, 13^3, 19
9:2, 7^2, 9, 10, 13, 14, 15^2, 16^3, 18, 22, 25
10:2, 5^2, 11, 14, 16, 18
11:3, 4^2, 5, 6, 7, 8^3, 10, 11^2, 12, 14^2, 20, 22, 23
12:2, 3^2, 4, 6, 14^2, 15^3
13:10^2, 12, 13, 14^2, 19, 20, 21, 24
14:10, 12^2, 13, 14^3, 15, 16^3, 17^2, 18
15:1^2, 2, 3, 4, 7^2, 8, 9, 10, 16, 19^2
16:3^2, 5, 6^2, 7^3, 8, 11^3, 15^2, 16^2, 21^2
17:11^2, 18^4, 20
18:8, 10, 15, 17^2, 19, 20^2, 22, 23^2
19:7^2, 9^2, 11^2
20:4^2, 5^3, 12
21:3, 4, 7^2
22:7, 9, 25^2
23:2^2, 3^2, 4^2, 8, 12^2, 14, 15^2, 17, 21, 22, 32^4, 33
24:1, 5, 6^6, 7, 8, 9^2, 10^2
25:4, 6^2, 9^3, 10, 14^2, 16, 18, 26, 27, 28, 30^2, 31
26:2, 3, 4, 5, 19
27:2, 3, 4, 8, 15, 17, 18^2, 22^3
28:3, 13
29:5^2, 9, 17^2, 18^3, 19^2, 21^2, 22, 23, 28^2, 31
30:3, 9, 16, 19^4, 20, 21
31:4, 5, 8^3, 9^2, 13^2, 28^2, 32^3, 34^2
32:13, 14, 18, 22^2, 23^2, 33^2, 35, 37^4, 39^3, 40^3, 41^3, 42^2, 44
33:5, 6^2, 7, 8, 9, 11^2, 13, 24^2, 26
34:8, 9, 10^2, 11, 13, 16, 20^2, 21, 22
35:2^3, 4, 5, 15^2, 16, 17^3
36:3, 6, 13, 14, 18^2, 25, 26, 31^2, 32
37:5, 10
38:4, 11, 26, 27
39:4, 5, 10
40:7, 9, 10, 11, 14
41:5, 6^3, 7^2, 8^2, 9, 10, 18
42:4, 9, 17^2
43:1, 9, 10^2, 12^2
44:4, 13, 21, 27^2, 30
45:5
46:5, 15, 21, 25, 26
47:2
48:39
49:2, 11, 20^2, 29, 32, 36, 37^4
50:6^2, 7^2, 20, 21, 27^2, 28, 33^3, 43, 44, 45^2
51:1^2, 17, 19, 39, 40
52:3, 17, 25, 26^2, 27^2

LAMENTATIONS

1:13, 17, 22
2:2, 21
3:20, 25, 64, 65^2, 66
4:4, 15, 16^2

EZEKIEL

1:18, 19, 20, 21
2:4^2, 5, 6, 7
3:4, 6, 9, 11^3, 13, 15^2, 17, 25^2, 26, 27
4:6, 9, 13
5:2, 3, 4^3, 6, 12, 13^2, 16
6:2, 10, 12, 14
7:11^2, 16^2, 18, 19, 20, 22, 27^2
8:11^2, 18
9:1, 2, 7, 8
10:1, 2, 13, 16^2, 17, 19^2
11:4, 5, 16^3, 19^2, 20, 21, 22^2, 24, 25
12:10^2, 11, 12, 14, 15^2, 16, 19, 23^2, 28
13:2, 6, 11, 15, 17, 20^3
14:3, 4^2
15:7^3
16:17, 18^2, 19, 20, 21^3, 27, 28, 33, 36, 37^4, 50, 53, 54, 61
17:12^2
18:19, 24, 26
19:11, 12
20:3, 4^3, 5^3, 6^3, 7, 8^2, 9^2, 10^2, 11^3, 12^3, 13^3, 14, 15^3, 17^3, 19, 21^4, 22, 23^3, 25, 26^2, 27, 28^2, 29, 38^2, 40^2
21:23^2, 29
22:26, 28^2, 30, 31^2
23:4, 6, 7^2, 12, 15, 16^3, 17^2, 22, 23^3, 24, 27, 28^2, 36, 37^2, 43, 45, 46^2, 47^2
24:3, 5, 20, 25, 27
25:2, 10, 12, 17^2
26:20^2
27:31
28:8, 18, 24^2, 25, 26^2
29:12, 14, 15, 16, 21
30:5, 9, 23, 26
31:14, 16, 17, 18
32:10, 12, 13^2, 15, 18^2, 20, 21, 22, 23, 24^2, 25^3, 26, 28, 29^2, 30^3, 31, 32
33:2, 6, 7, 10, 11, 17, 25, 27, 31, 32^2, 33
34:2, 3, 4, 6, 10^2, 11, 12, 13^4, 14, 15, 16, 20, 21, 23^3, 24, 25, 26, 27^2, 28^2, 29, 30
35:11^2, 13
36:12, 18, 19^2, 20, 23, 27, 37^2

THEY

1992, *846*

JOSHUA

17:4, 10, 13, 16[2], 18[2]
18:4[2], 5
19:2, 49, 50, 51
20:3, 4, 5, 7, 8
21:2, 9, 11, 12, 13, 20, 21, 27, 43
22:6, 9, 10, 15[2], 28
23:12, 13
24:1, 2, 7, 8, 22, 30, 32, 33

JUDGES

1:4, 5[3], 6, 7, 10, 16, 17, 19, 20, 22, 24, 25[2], 28, 32, 34, 35
2:3, 5[2], 9, 12, 13, 14, 15[2], 17[4], 19[2], 22
3:4[2], 6, 12, 24[2], 25[3], 26, 28, 29
4:12, 24
5:7, 8, 11[2], 14, 19, 20, 23, 30[2]
6:3, 4, 5[4], 29[3], 35
7:11, 19[2], 20, 21, 25[3]
8:1, 5, 18[3], 19, 24[2], 25[2], 28, 35
9:3, 4, 7, 8, 9, 25, 27, 31, 34, 36, 41, 42, 46, 51, 55
10:4, 8, 16
11:2, 6, 13, 17, 18, 21, 22
12:4, 6[2]
14:9, 11[2], 13, 14, 15
15:6, 10, 11, 12, 13[2]
16:2, 7, 11, 23, 24[2], 25[3], 30
17:4
18:2[3], 3[3], 5, 7[2], 8, 9, 12[2], 13, 15, 19, 21, 22, 23[2], 26, 27[2], 28[2], 29, 31
19:4, 5, 6, 8[2], 11, 14[2], 15, 21, 22, 25[2]
20:5, 6, 10[3], 22, 31, 32, 34, 36[3], 38, 39[2], 41, 42[2], 43, 45[2], 48[2]
21:5, 8, 12[2], 14[3], 17, 19, 20, 23[2], 24

RUTH

1:2, 4[2], 7, 9, 10, 11, 13, 14, 19[4], 22
2:4, 9[2], 21, 22
4:2, 17

1 SAMUEL

1:9[2], 19, 25
2:4, 5[2], 12, 14, 15, 20, 22, 25, 27, 30, 34
4:2[2], 4, 6[2], 7[2], 9, 10
5:2, 3[2], 4, 7, 8[3], 9[2], 10[2], 11
6:3, 4[2], 6[2], 11, 12, 13[2], 14, 16, 18, 19, 21
7:6, 7, 10, 11, 13
8:2, 6, 7[3], 8[3], 19
9:4[4], 5, 10, 11[2], 12, 13, 14[2], 20, 25, 26[2], 27
10:2, 4, 5, 10, 14, 21, 22, 23, 27
11:5[2], 7, 9[2], 11[2], 15[2]
12:4, 5, 9[2], 10, 21
13:5, 6, 21
14:9, 10, 11, 13, 15, 16, 17, 20, 21, 22[2], 25, 30, 31, 33[2], 36
15:3, 6, 9, 15, 18
16:6
17:11, 19, 24, 31, 51, 53
18:6, 7, 8[2], 20, 27, 30
19:1, 8, 20[2], 21[2], 22, 24
20:11, 41
21:11
22:1, 4, 11, 17
23:1[2], 12, 13, 18, 24, 25, 28
25:7, 8, 9, 11, 13, 16, 26, 40, 43
26:12[2], 19[3]
27:11
28:4, 8, 25[2]
29:5
30:2, 4, 10, 11[2], 12, 16[2], 19, 20, 21[3], 22[2], 24
31:7[2], 8, 9, 10[2], 13

2 SAMUEL

1:12[2], 23[3]
2:3, 4[3], 13, 16[2], 24, 28, 29, 32[2]
3:21, 23, 32
4:6[3], 7[2], 8, 12[2]
5:3, 8, 11, 17, 21
6:3, 4, 6, 13, 17
7:10
8:14
9:2
10:5, 6, 13, 14, 15[2], 16, 19[2]
11:1, 10, 20
12:18, 19, 20
13:9, 30, 32
14:6, 7[2], 11
15:11[2], 24, 29, 30[2], 36
16:22
17:8[2], 10, 17[2], 18[2], 20[4], 21[2], 22, 29
18:3[2], 17
19:3, 8, 14, 17
20:3, 7, 8, 14, 15[2], 18[3], 22[2]
21:5, 9[2], 13, 14[2]
22:18, 19, 39[2], 42, 45[2], 46
23:6, 7, 9
24:3, 5, 6[2], 7, 8[2], 13, 17

1 KINGS

1:1, 3, 7, 23, 25, 32, 39, 41, 44, 45, 53
2:7, 39
3:22, 24, 28[2]
4:21, 27, 28
5:1, 6, 12, 14, 17, 18
6:8, 10, 27
7:28, 47
8:1, 4, 8[3], 9, 25, 30, 33, 35[2], 36, 40[2], 42, 43, 46[2], 47[2], 50[2], 51, 52, 66
9:8, 9[2], 12, 22, 28
10:25, 29

1 KINGS

11:2[2], 18[3], 24, 29, 33, 41
12:3, 7[2], 8, 13, 20, 24, 27
13:11, 13, 20, 25, 27, 30
14:15, 18, 19, 22[2], 23, 24, 29
15:7, 8, 22, 23, 31
16:5, 13[2], 14, 17, 20, 27
18:6, 10[2], 26[3], 28, 29, 34[2], 39[2], 40
19:10, 14, 21
20:6[2], 12, 15, 16, 17, 18[2], 20, 23[2], 25, 29, 32, 33
21:12, 13, 14
22:1, 6, 32[2], 33, 37, 38, 39, 45, 48

2 KINGS

1:6, 8, 18
2:2, 4, 6, 7, 8[2], 9, 11, 14, 15[2], 16, 17[3], 18, 20
3:9, 21, 22, 23[2], 24[3], 25[3], 26, 27
4:39, 40[4], 41, 42, 43[2], 44
5:23, 24
6:4[2], 14, 16[2], 18, 20[4], 22, 23[2], 25
7:3, 4[2], 5[2], 6, 7, 8, 9, 10[3], 11, 12[3], 13[2], 14, 15
8:23
9:12, 13, 21, 27, 33, 35[2], 36, 37
10:4, 7, 8, 13, 14, 16, 20, 21, 24, 25, 26, 27, 34, 35
11:2, 7, 9, 12[2], 16, 17, 18, 19, 20
12:10[2], 11[2], 14, 15[3], 19, 21
13:5, 6, 8, 9, 12, 20, 21[3]
14:12, 15, 18, 19[2], 20, 28
15:6, 7, 11, 15, 16, 21, 26, 31, 36
16:5, 18, 19
17:8, 9, 10, 11, 12, 14, 15[3], 16, 17, 19, 21, 22, 24, 25, 26[3], 28[2], 29, 32, 33[2], 34[3], 40[2], 41
18:10, 12, 17[3], 18, 20, 27, 34, 35
19:3, 18[2], 26[2], 31, 35[2], 37
20:7, 14[2], 15[2], 18[2], 20
21:8, 9, 14, 15, 17, 25
22:7, 14, 17[2], 19, 20
23:1, 9, 18, 28
24:5
25:1, 6[2], 7, 14[2], 23[2], 26

1 CHRONICLES

4:14, 23, 28, 39, 40[2], 43
5:10[2], 16, 19, 20[3], 21, 22, 23, 25
6:31, 32[2], 33, 55, 56, 57, 65, 67[2]
7:2, 4, 21
8:6
9:1, 18, 23, 27, 28, 33, 38
10:7[2], 8, 9[2], 10, 12
11:3, 7, 14, 19
12:1[2], 2, 15[2], 19, 21[2], 33, 39, 40
13:2, 4, 7, 9
14:11[2], 12[2], 16
15:26
16:1[2], 20
17:9
19:6, 7, 11, 14, 15, 16[2], 17, 19[2]
20:4, 8
21:3[2], 5, 17[2]
22:4
23:11, 24, 25, 26, 32
24:4, 5
25:8
26:6, 8, 13, 14, 27, 31
28:21
29:8, 9[2], 21, 22, 29

2 CHRONICLES

1:17[2]
2:17
3:13
4:20
5:5, 9[2], 10, 13
6:21, 24, 26[2], 27, 31[2], 32, 34, 36[2], 37[2], 38[2]
7:3, 9[2], 22
8:9, 15, 18
9:24, 28, 29
10:3, 7[2]
11:4, 17[2]
12:2, 6, 7[2], 8[2], 15
13:11[2], 13, 14, 18
14:1, 7, 10, 13[3], 14[2], 15
15:4, 9[2], 10, 11[2], 12, 14, 15
16:4, 6, 11, 14[2]
17:9, 10
18:5, 9, 10, 14, 29, 31[2], 32
19:8, 10
20:2, 4, 8, 10[2], 11, 16, 20[2], 21, 22[2], 23, 24[2], 25[4], 26[2], 27, 28, 29, 34, 36, 37
21:17, 20
22:4, 9[4]
23:2[2], 6[3], 11, 15[2], 16, 20, 21
24:7, 8, 9, 10, 11[2], 13, 14[3], 16, 18, 19[2], 21, 23, 24[2], 25[4], 26, 27
25:10, 12, 13, 20, 21, 22, 26, 27[2], 28
26:18, 20, 23[2]
27:7, 9
28:5, 6, 15, 18, 23[2], 26, 27[2]
29:7, 15, 16, 17[4], 18, 19, 21, 22[5], 23[2], 24, 29, 30[2], 34
30:1, 3, 5[3], 9, 10, 14[2], 15, 16[2], 18, 22, 23
31:1, 4, 5, 6, 7, 8, 11, 18
32:3, 18[2], 19, 21, 32, 33
33:8, 10, 18, 19, 20
34:4, 9[3], 10[2], 11, 13, 14, 16, 17, 22[2], 24, 25[2], 28, 33
35:1, 6, 11, 12[3], 13[2], 14, 15, 24, 25, 27
36:8, 16, 19, 20

EZRA

1:6
2:59[3], 62[2], 63, 68, 69
3:3[2], 4, 6, 7[2], 8, 10, 11[2]
4:2, 6, 11, 13, 15, 23
5:5[2], 7, 11, 14
6:3, 8, 9, 10, 13, 14[2], 18
7:13
8:17[2], 18, 36[2]
9:2
10:5[2], 7[2], 17, 19[3], 44

NEHEMIAH

1:3
2:7, 18[2], 19
3:1[3], 6, 8, 13
4:2[4], 3, 5, 7, 11, 12[2], 17[2], 22
5:8[2], 12[2]
6:2, 4, 9, 10[2], 13[2], 16[2], 19
7:3, 5, 61[3], 64, 65, 67
8:1, 4, 6, 8, 9, 12, 14, 15, 18
9:3[2], 10, 11, 12, 15, 16, 18, 19, 21, 22, 23, 24[2], 25[2], 26[2], 27, 28[4], 29, 30, 35[2], 37
10:28, 29
11:30
12:27, 37, 39, 43, 47
13:1, 2, 3[2], 5, 9, 13, 15[2], 19, 21, 22[2], 29

ESTHER

1:7, 8, 17
2:3, 23
3:4[2], 6, 7, 8, 9, 14
4:12
6:1, 9, 14
7:8, 10
8:7
9:5, 10[2], 12, 14, 15, 16, 17, 18, 21, 22, 23, 26[2], 27, 31
10:2

JOB

1:15, 19
2:11[2], 12[3], 13[2]
3:18, 22
4:8, 9[2], 20[2], 21
5:4, 14
6:15, 17[3], 18, 20[3]
8:10, 22
9:5, 25[2], 26
11:6, 20
12:6, 7[2], 15[2], 25
14:12, 21
15:24, 35
16:10[3]
17:12, 16
18:20[2]
19:15, 18, 19, 23, 24
20:7
21:11, 12, 13, 14, 18, 26, 30
22:12
24:1, 2, 3[2], 4, 5, 6[2], 7[2], 8, 9, 10[2], 13[2], 16[3], 17, 24[2]
27:13
28:1, 4[2]
29:22, 23[2], 24[2]
30:1, 3, 5[2], 7[2], 8[2], 10[2], 11, 12[2], 13[3], 14[2], 15, 24
31:13
32:3, 4, 15[3], 16
34:19, 20, 25, 27, 28
35:9[2], 12
36:7[2], 8, 9, 10, 11[2], 12[3], 13, 14, 27
37:12
38:14, 35, 40, 41
39:2[2], 3[3], 4[3], 16
41:6, 17[3], 23[2], 25
42:11[2]

PSALMS

2:12
3:1[2]
5:9, 10
9:3, 10, 15[2]
10:2
11:2[2]
12:2[2]
14:1[2], 3[2], 4, 5
17:10[2], 11[2], 14
18:17, 18, 37, 38[2], 41, 44[2]
19:10
20:8
21:11[3]
22:4, 5[2], 7[3], 13, 16, 17, 18, 26, 29[2], 31
23:4
24:1
25:6, 19[2]
27:2
28:5
31:4, 11, 13[2]
32:6, 9
34:5, 10, 21
35:7[2], 11, 12, 13, 15[2], 16, 20[2], 21[2]
36:8, 12
37:2, 9, 19[2], 20[2], 22, 28, 40
38:4, 12[2], 16[2], 19[2], 20
39:6
40:5[2], 12
41:7, 8
42:3, 10
44:3, 10
45:8, 15[2]
48:4, 5[3]
49:6, 11, 14, 19
51:19
53:1, 3, 4[2], 5
54:3
55:3[2], 10, 19[2], 21

PSALMS

56:2, 5, 6[4], 7, 8
57:6[3]
58:3[2], 4, 8
59:t, 3, 4, 6[2], 7[2], 12, 13, 15
62:4[4], 9
63:10[2]
64:4[2], 5[3], 6[2], 7, 8, 9
65:8, 12, 13[2]
66:4, 6
68:24
69:4[2], 12, 21[2], 23, 26[2], 35, 36
71:10, 24[2]
72:5, 9, 16
73:5[2], 7, 8[2], 9, 11, 12, 19[2], 27
74:4, 6, 7[2], 8[2]
76:5
77:16
78:5, 7, 10, 17, 18, 19[2], 22, 29, 30, 32, 34[2], 35, 36[2], 37, 39, 40, 41, 42, 44, 53, 56, 57, 58
79:1[2], 2, 3, 7, 12
80:12, 16
81:12
82:5[3]
83:2, 3, 4, 5[2], 8, 10, 16
84:4[2], 7
86:17
88:5, 17[2]
89:15, 16[2], 31, 51
90:5[2], 10
91:12
92:7, 14[2]
94:4, 5, 6, 7, 11, 21
95:10, 11
97:7
98:7
99:6, 7
101:6
102:8, 26[2]
104:7[2], 8[2], 9[2], 11, 22, 28[2], 29[2], 30, 32
105:12, 13, 18, 27, 28, 38, 41, 44, 45
106:3, 7, 12[2], 13[2], 16, 19, 20, 21, 24[2], 28, 29, 32, 33, 34, 36, 37, 38, 39, 41, 42, 43
107:4[2], 6, 7, 11, 12, 13, 18, 19, 23, 26[2], 27, 28, 30[2], 36, 38, 39, 43
109:2, 3, 4, 5, 25[2], 27, 28
111:8, 10
115:5[4], 6[4], 7[5], 8
118:11[2], 12[2]
119:2, 3[2], 74[2], 78, 86, 87, 91, 98, 111, 126, 136, 150[2], 155, 158, 165
120:7
122:1, 6
124:3
125:1
126:2, 5
127:1, 5[2]
129:1, 2[2], 3, 8
130:6[2]
135:16[4], 17[2], 18
137:3[2]
138:4, 5
139:18, 20
140:2, 3, 5[2], 8, 10
141:6[2], 9
142:3, 6
144:5
145:7, 11
147:20
148:5

PROVERBS

1:9, 11, 18[2], 28[3], 29, 30[2], 31
2:15, 19
3:2, 22
4:16[3], 17, 19[2], 22
7:5
8:9, 32, 36
11:20
12:22
14:22
15:22
16:13
17:15
18:8, 21
19:7
21:7
22:18
23:3, 5, 30[2], 35[2]
26:22
28:4, 5, 28
30:24, 25, 26, 27
31:5

ECCLESIASTES

1:7, 16
2:3
3:18[2], 19
4:1[2], 3, 9, 10, 11, 16
5:1[2], 8, 11
7:29
8:10[2]
9:3[2], 5[2], 6
11:3, 6, 8
12:3, 5

SONG OF SOLOMON

1:6
3:8
5:7[2]
6:5, 9

ISAIAH

1:2, 4[3], 6, 14, 18[3], 23, 28, 29, 31
2:4[2], 6[2], 8, 19, 20
3:9[3], 10, 12, 16

ISAIAH

5:6, 8, 11, 12, 13, 24, 26, 29[2], 30
6:10, 13
7:19, 22
8:19, 20, 21[3], 22[2]
9:2, 3[2], 12, 13, 16, 18, 20[2], 21
10:1, 2, 4[2], 18, 29[2]
11:9, 14[3]
13:2, 5, 8[3], 14, 17, 18
14:1, 2[3], 7, 10, 16, 21
15:3, 5[2], 7[3]
16:7, 8[3]
17:2, 3, 9, 13
18:6
19:2, 3, 6, 8[2], 9[2], 10, 12, 13[2], 14, 20, 21, 22
20:5
21:14, 15
22:3, 9, 24
23:5, 13[2]
24:5, 6, 9, 14[3], 22[2]
26:11[2], 14[4], 16[2], 19
27:11, 13
28:7[5], 12, 13
29:9[2], 15, 23, 24[2]
30:1, 5, 6, 16, 18
31:1[3], 3
32:12
33:1[2], 12, 17, 23[2]
34:12, 17[2]
35:2, 10
36:5, 12, 19, 20, 21
37:3, 19[2], 27[2], 32, 36[2], 38
38:18
39:3[2], 4[2], 7[2]
40:17, 24[3], 31[4]
41:6, 11[3], 12, 20, 22, 29
42:9, 16[2], 17[2], 22[3], 24[2]
43:2, 9, 17[4], 21
44:4, 9[4], 11[3], 18[3]
45:6, 14[5], 16[2], 20
46:1, 2[3], 6[3], 7[2]
47:9, 14[2], 15[2]
48:2, 3[2], 7, 13, 21
49:9, 10, 15, 17, 19, 21, 22, 23[2], 26
50:9
51:5, 6, 11, 20[2]
52:5, 6, 8[2], 15[3]
54:15
56:10[3], 11[3], 12
57:2, 6[2], 12
58:2[3], 3, 12
59:4[2], 5, 6, 7, 8[2], 19
60:4[2], 6[3], 7, 11, 14[2], 21
61:3, 4[3], 7[2], 9
62:9[2], 12
63:8, 10, 13, 15, 19
65:11, 16, 21[2], 22[2], 23[2], 24[2], 25
66:3, 4[2], 5, 17, 18, 19, 20, 24[2]

JEREMIAH

1:15[2], 19[2]
2:5, 6, 8, 13, 15, 24[2], 26, 27[2], 28, 30
3:1, 16[3], 17[2], 18, 21[2]
4:2, 17, 22[5], 23, 24, 29, 30
5:2[2], 3[4], 4[2], 5, 7, 8, 10, 12, 15, 16, 17[4], 22[3], 23, 24, 26[3], 27, 28[6]
6:3[2], 9, 10[3], 14, 15[6], 16, 17, 19, 23[3], 28[3]
7:17, 18, 19[2], 24, 26[2], 27[2], 30, 31, 32
8:1, 2[8], 4, 5[2], 6, 9[2], 11, 12[6], 16, 17, 19
9:2, 3[4], 5[2], 6, 10[2], 13, 16, 17[2]
10:4[2], 5[4], 8, 9, 11, 15[2], 18, 20, 21, 25
11:8[2], 10[2], 11[2], 12[2], 14, 17, 19
12:1, 2[3], 4, 5[2], 6[3], 10[2], 11, 13[3], 16[3], 17
13:11[2], 12
14:2, 3[3], 4, 6, 10[2], 12[3], 14, 15, 16[2], 18
15:2, 7, 20[2]
16:4[5], 6, 10, 12, 16[2], 17, 18[2], 20, 21
17:13[2], 15, 19, 23[2], 25, 26
18:12, 15[2], 18, 20, 22
19:4[2], 5, 9[2], 11, 13, 15[2]
20:4, 10, 11[3]
21:6
22:7, 8, 9[2], 12, 18[2], 27[2], 28[2]
23:3, 4[2], 7, 8, 12, 13, 14[3], 16[2], 17[2], 21[2], 22[2], 26, 27, 32
24:2, 3, 7[2], 8, 10
25:5, 16, 18, 30, 33[2]
26:3, 10, 23, 24
27:10, 11, 14, 15, 16, 18, 22[2]
28:14[2]
29:6, 9, 17, 19, 23
30:3, 9, 14, 16[2], 17, 19[2]
31:1, 9[2], 12[2], 15, 16, 23, 24, 29, 32, 33, 34[2], 37
32:14, 23[3], 24, 29, 31, 32[2], 33[2], 34, 35[2], 38, 39, 40
33:5, 8[3], 9, 24[2]
34:5[2], 10, 11[2], 18[2], 22
35:6, 14, 17[2]
36:3, 7, 9, 15, 16[2], 17, 20[2], 24, 31
37:4, 5, 9, 10, 15, 21[2]
38:6[2], 7, 9[2], 13, 18, 19[2], 20, 22, 23, 25, 27
39:1, 4, 5[2], 14, 16
40:7, 8[2], 12
41:1, 7, 12, 13, 17, 18
42:5, 17
43:3, 5, 7[3]
44:2, 3[4], 5, 6, 9, 10[2], 12[4], 14[2]
46:6, 12, 15, 16, 17, 21[2], 22, 23[2]

JEREMIAH

48:2, 32, 34, 39, 45
49:9[3], 12, 23[2], 29[3]
50:3[2], 4[2], 5, 6[3], 7, 9, 16[2], 20, 33, 36[2], 37[2], 38[2], 42[3]
51:2, 4, 14, 18[2], 24, 26, 30[3], 32, 38[2], 39, 57, 58, 64
52:7, 9, 18[2]

LAMENTATIONS

1:2, 6, 8, 10, 11[2], 14, 19[2], 21[3]
2:7, 8, 10[2], 12[2], 14, 15, 16[2]
3:6, 23, 53
4:2, 3, 5[2], 7[2], 8, 9[2], 10, 14[2], 15[4], 16[2], 18, 19[2]
5:11, 13

EZEKIEL

1:5, 7, 8[2], 9[3], 10[3], 12[4], 16, 17[4], 18[2], 20, 24[3], 25
2:3, 4, 5[4], 6, 7[3]
3:6, 7, 9, 11[2], 15, 25, 26, 27
4:16[2], 17
5:6[2], 12, 13, 17
6:9[4], 10, 11, 13, 14
7:13, 14, 16, 18, 19[2], 20, 21, 22, 24, 25, 26, 27
8:6, 9, 12, 13, 16, 17[4], 18
9:2, 6, 7, 8, 9
10:10, 11[7], 12, 17[2], 19, 20, 22
11:7, 15, 16, 18[2], 20[2]
12:2[2], 3[2], 4, 11, 12, 15, 16[3], 19, 23, 27
13:6[3], 9[3], 10, 15, 21
14:5, 10, 11, 14, 15, 16[2], 18[2], 20[2], 22, 23
15:7, 8
16:33[2], 37, 39[2], 40[2], 41, 47, 50, 51, 52[2]
17:15, 21, 23
18:22
19:4, 9[2]
20:8[3], 9, 12, 13[3], 16, 20, 21[2], 24, 25, 26[2], 27, 28[4], 38[2], 49
21:7, 23, 29[2]
22:7[3], 9[2], 10[2], 12, 18[2], 20, 25[3], 26[2], 29
23:3[3], 4[2], 8[2], 10[2], 13, 17, 24[2], 25[3], 26, 29, 37[3], 38[2], 39[3], 40, 43, 44[3], 45[2], 47, 49
24:14, 25, 27
25:3, 4[3], 11, 13, 14[2], 17
26:4, 6, 12[3], 16[2], 17
27:5[2], 6, 10[3], 11[2], 12, 13[2], 14, 15, 16, 17[2], 21[2], 22[2], 29, 30, 31[2], 32, 35
28:3, 7[2], 8, 16, 17, 19, 22, 23, 24, 25[2], 26[3]
29:6, 7[2], 9, 13, 14, 15, 16[2], 20, 21
30:4, 6[2], 7, 8, 11, 19, 25, 26
31:14, 17[2]
32:3, 10, 12, 15, 16[2], 20, 21[2], 24, 25[2], 26, 27[3], 29, 30[2]
33:24, 27[2], 29[2], 31[5], 32[2], 33
34:5[3], 10, 12, 14[2], 19[2], 22, 25, 27, 28[2], 29, 30[2]
35:8, 12[2], 15
36:3, 7, 8, 11, 12, 13, 17, 18[2], 19, 20[4], 21, 35, 38
37:2, 9, 10, 11, 17, 19, 21, 22[2], 23[3], 24[2], 25[3], 27
38:8, 23
39:6, 9[2], 10[3], 11[2], 12, 14[2], 16, 23[2], 26[3], 28
40:10, 22, 38, 41, 42[2], 49
41:6[3]
42:6, 11[2], 13[2], 14[4]
43:7, 8[2], 10, 11[3], 18, 22[2], 24, 25, 26[2]
44:7, 10, 11[3], 12[2], 13[3], 15[2], 16[3], 17[3], 18[2], 19[5], 20[2], 21, 22[2], 23, 24[4], 25[2], 26, 29
45:8
46:6, 10[2], 15, 20[2]
47:9, 10, 11, 12[2], 22[2]
48:14, 19

DANIEL

1:4, 5, 16, 19
2:2, 7, 13, 18, 43[2], 46
3:3, 9, 12, 13, 19, 24, 25, 28
4:6, 7, 25[3], 26, 32[2]
5:3, 4, 8, 15[2], 20, 21, 23, 29
6:4, 12, 13, 16, 22, 23, 24[3]
7:5, 12, 13, 25, 26
9:7, 11
10:7
11:2, 6[2], 14, 21, 22, 25, 26, 27, 31[2], 33[2], 34[2]
12:3[2]

HOSEA

1:11
2:4, 8, 17, 21, 22, 23
4:2, 4, 7[2], 8[2], 10[3], 12, 13, 14[3], 18, 19
5:4[2], 6[2], 7[2], 15[2]
6:7[2], 9
7:1, 2[3], 3, 4, 6[2], 7, 10, 11[2], 12, 13[3], 14[4], 15, 16[2]
8:1, 4[4], 5, 7[2], 8, 9, 10[2], 12, 13[2]
9:3[2], 4[2], 6, 9, 10[2], 12, 16[2], 17[2]
10:1, 2, 3, 4, 8, 9, 10
11:2[3], 3, 4, 5, 7, 10, 11
12:1, 8, 11[2]
13:2[2], 3, 6[3], 16
14:7[2]

JOEL

1:18
2:4, 5, 7[4], 8[3], 9[4], 17
3:2, 3[2], 8, 19

AMOS

1:3, 6, 9, 13^{2}
2:4, 6, 8^{2}
3:3, 10
4:8
5:10^{2}, 12^{3}, 16^{2}
6:2, 6, 7, 9, 14
7:2
8:3, 12^{2}, 14^{2}
9:2^{2}, 3^{2}, 4, 12, 14^{3}, 15

OBADIAH

5^{3}, 7, 16^{4}, 18, 19^{3}

JONAH

1:7^{2}, 8, 11, 13, 14, 15
2:8
3:10

MICAH

1:5, 7, 16
2:1, 2^{2}, 6^{3}, 12, 13
3:3, 4^{2}, 5, 7, 10, 11
4:3^{2}, 4, 12^{2}
5:1, 4, 6, 15
7:1, 2^{2}, 3^{2}, 16, 17^{3}

NAHUM

1:10^{3}, 12^{2}
2:4^{3}, 5^{2}, 8^{2}
3:3, 7, 10, 12^{2}, 17^{2}

HABAKKUK

1:7, 8, 9^{2}, 10^{3}, 15^{3}, 16, 17
2:7
3:10, 11, 14

ZEPHANIAH

1:11, 13^{2}, 17^{2}
2:4, 7^{2}, 8, 10^{2}
3:3, 4, 7, 9, 12, 13, 19

HAGGAI

1:14
2:14

ZECHARIAH

1:4, 5^{2}, 6^{2}, 10, 11, 15
2:9
3:5, 8
4:10^{2}
5:9^{2}
6:7^{2}, 15
7:2, 11^{2}, 12^{2}, 13^{2}, 14^{2}
8:8^{2}
9:15^{3}, 16
10:2^{3}, 5^{2}, 6, 7, 8^{2}, 9^{2}, 12
11:5, 6, 12
12:2, 6, 10^{3}
13:2, 4, 9^{2}
14:12, 13, 21

MALACHI

1:4^{2}
2:7
3:3, 15^{2}, 16, 17
4:3

MATTHEW

1:11, 12, 18, 23
2:5, 9^{3}, 10^{2}, 11^{4}, 12^{2}, 13, 18, 20
4:6, 18, 20, 22, 24
5:4^{2}, 5, 6^{2}, 7, 8, 9, 10, 12, 16
6:2^{2}, 5^{3}, 7^{2}, 16^{3}, 26^{3}, 28^{3}
7:6, 15
8:16, 29, 32^{2}, 33, 34^{2}
9:2, 8, 11, 12^{2}, 15, 17, 24, 28, 31^{2}, 32^{2}, 36
10:17^{2}, 19, 23, 25^{2}, 36
11:7, 8, 18, 19, 20, 21
12:2, 3, 10^{2}, 14, 16, 24, 27, 36, 41, 45
13:5^{3}, 6^{3}, 13^{3}, 15^{2}, 16^{2}, 41, 48, 51, 54, 56, 57
14:5, 13, 15, 16, 17, 20^{2}, 21, 26^{2}, 32, 33, 34^{2}, 35, 36
15:2^{2}, 9, 12, 14, 18, 31^{2}, 32^{2}, 34, 37^{2}, 38
16:5, 7, 12, 14, 20, 28
17:6, 8^{2}, 9, 12^{2}, 14, 16, 22, 23^{2}, 24^{2}
18:19, 31
19:5, 6, 7, 11, 25
20:4, 7, 9^{2}, 10^{3}, 11^{2}, 18, 22, 24, 25, 29, 30, 31^{2}, 33, 34
21:1, 7, 15, 20, 25, 27, 31, 34, 36, 37, 38, 39, 41, 45, 46^{3}
22:3, 5, 8, 10, 15, 16, 19, 21, 22^{2}, 28, 30, 33, 34, 42
23:3^{2}, 4^{2}, 5^{2}, 25
24:9, 24, 26, 30, 31, 38
25:3, 5, 10^{2}, 44
26:4, 5, 8, 15, 19, 21, 22, 26, 30^{2}, 50, 52, 57, 60, 66, 67, 73
27:2^{2}, 4, 7, 9^{2}, 13, 15, 16, 17, 18, 20, 21, 22, 23, 28, 29^{3}, 30, 31^{2}, 32^{3}, 33, 34, 35^{3}, 36, 39, 47, 54^{2}, 66
28:8, 9^{2}, 10^{2}, 11, 12^{2}, 15^{2}, 17^{2}

MARK

1:5, 16, 18, 20, 21, 22, 27^{3}, 29^{2}, 30, 32, 34, 36, 37^{2}, 45
2:3, 4^{4}, 8, 12, 15, 16, 17^{2}, 18, 19^{2}, 20, 23, 24, 25
3:2^{2}, 4, 6, 8^{2}, 9, 10, 11, 12, 13, 14, 19, 20, 21^{2}, 28, 30, 32
4:10, 12^{3}, 15^{2}, 16^{2}, 17, 18, 20, 33, 34, 36^{2}, 38, 41
5:1, 13, 14^{2}, 15^{2}, 16, 17, 40, 42
6:3, 8, 12, 13, 29, 30^{2}, 31, 32, 34, 36^{2}, 37, 38^{2}, 40, 42, 43, 44, 49^{2}, 50, 51, 52, 53^{2}, 54^{2}, 55, 56^{2}
7:2^{2}, 3, 4^{4}, 7, 15, 32^{2}, 36^{2}
8:2, 3, 5, 6, 7, 8^{2}, 9, 14, 16, 19, 20, 22, 28, 30
9:1, 4, 6, 8^{2}, 9^{3}, 10, 11, 13^{2}, 15, 18^{2}, 20, 30, 31, 32, 34^{2}
10:4, 8^{2}, 13, 23, 26, 32^{4}, 33, 34, 37, 39, 41, 42, 46, 49
11:1, 4^{2}, 6^{2}, 7, 9^{2}, 12, 15, 18^{2}, 20^{2}, 27, 31, 32, 33
12:3, 4, 5, 6, 8, 12^{3}, 13, 14^{2}, 16^{2}, 17, 18, 23, 25^{2}, 26, 43, 44
13:9, 11, 26
14:1, 2, 5, 11^{2}, 12, 16, 18, 19, 22, 23, 26^{2}, 31, 32, 40, 46, 50, 53, 64, 70
15:4, 6, 13, 14, 16, 17, 19, 20^{2}, 21, 22, 23, 24^{2}, 25, 27, 29, 32, 35
16:1, 2, 3, 4^{2}, 5^{2}, 6, 8^{4}, 10, 11^{2}, 12, 13^{2}, 14^{2}, 17^{2}, 18^{4}, 20

LUKE

1:2, 6, 7^{2}, 22, 58, 59^{2}, 61, 62, 63, 66
2:6, 9, 16, 17^{2}, 18, 20, 22, 39^{2}, 42, 43^{2}, 44^{2}, 45^{2}, 46, 48^{2}, 50
4:2, 11, 22, 28^{2}, 29, 32, 36^{2}, 38, 40, 41
5:6^{2}, 7^{4}, 9, 11^{2}, 18, 19^{3}, 26^{2}, 31^{2}, 33, 35
6:3, 7, 11^{2}, 18^{2}, 22, 39, 44
7:4^{2}, 10, 14, 16, 20, 25, 31, 32, 42, 49
8:10^{2}, 12^{2}, 13^{3}, 14^{2}, 15, 16, 22, 23^{2}, 24^{2}, 25^{2}, 26, 31, 32, 34^{2}, 35^{2}, 36, 37, 40, 45, 53, 56
9:6, 10^{2}, 11, 12, 13, 14, 15, 17, 19, 27, 32^{3}, 33, 34^{2}, 36^{2}, 37, 40, 43^{2}, 45^{3}, 52, 53, 54, 56, 57
10:7, 8, 10, 13, 38
11:19, 26, 28, 29, 32, 33, 48, 49, 54
12:1, 4, 11, 24, 27^{3}, 36, 48
13:2, 4, 29
14:1, 4, 6, 7, 12, 14, 18
15:24
16:4, 9, 14, 15, 26^{2}, 28, 29, 30, 31^{2}
17:1, 13, 14^{2}, 21, 23, 27^{4}, 28^{6}, 37
18:9, 15^{2}, 24, 26, 33, 34^{2}, 37, 39, 43
19:7^{2}, 11^{2}, 25, 32, 33, 34, 35^{3}, 36, 37, 42, 44, 48
20:5, 6, 7^{2}, 10, 11, 12, 13^{2}, 14, 15, 16^{2}, 19^{2}, 20^{3}, 21, 24, 26^{2}, 27, 31, 35, 36^{2}, 40, 41
21:3, 7, 12, 16, 24, 27, 30
22:2^{2}, 5, 9, 13^{2}, 23, 25, 28, 35, 38, 49^{2}, 54, 55, 64^{2}, 65, 70, 71
23:2, 5, 12, 18, 21, 23, 24, 25, 26^{3}, 29, 30, 31, 33^{2}, 34^{3}, 56
24:1^{2}, 2, 3, 4, 5^{2}, 8, 11, 14, 15, 16, 19, 23^{3}, 24, 28^{2}, 29, 31, 32, 33, 35, 36, 37^{2}, 41, 42, 45, 52

JOHN

1:21, 22, 24, 25, 37, 38, 39
2:3^{2}, 7, 8, 12, 22, 23
3:21, 23, 26
4:24, 30, 35, 40, 45, 52
5:12, 23, 25, 29^{2}, 39^{2}
6:2, 9, 11, 12, 13, 14, 15, 19^{3}, 21^{2}, 23, 24, 25^{2}, 28, 30, 34, 42, 45, 60, 63^{2}, 64
7:25, 26, 30, 39, 40, 45, 52
8:3, 4, 6^{2}, 7, 9, 19, 25, 27, 33, 39, 41, 59
9:8, 10, 12, 13, 17, 18, 19, 22, 24, 26, 28, 34^{2}, 35, 39^{2}
10:4, 5^{2}, 6^{2}, 10^{2}, 16, 25, 27, 28, 39
11:13, 31, 34, 41, 42, 53, 56^{2}, 57
12:2, 9^{2}, 10, 12, 16^{2}, 18, 37, 39, 40, 42^{2}, 43
15:6, 20^{4}, 21^{2}, 22^{2}, 24^{2}, 25
16:2, 3^{2}, 9, 18, 19
17:3, 6^{2}, 7, 8^{2}, 9, 11, 13, 14, 16, 19, 21^{2}, 22, 23, 24^{2}
18:5, 6, 7, 18, 21, 25, 28^{4}, 30, 40
19:2, 3, 6, 15, 16, 18, 23, 24^{3}, 29, 31, 33^{2}, 37^{2}, 40, 42
20:2^{2}, 4, 9, 13^{3}, 20, 23^{2}, 29
21:3^{3}, 5, 6^{2}, 8, 9^{2}, 15, 25

THE ACTS

1:4, 6^{2}, 9, 10, 12, 13^{2}, 23, 24, 26
2:1, 2, 4, 7, 12, 18, 37^{2}, 41, 42, 46
3:2, 10^{2}
4:1, 2, 3, 7^{2}, 13^{5}, 14, 15^{2}, 17, 18, 21^{3}, 23, 24^{2}, 29, 31^{4}, 32
5:12, 15, 16, 17, 21^{3}, 22, 24, 26^{2}, 27^{2}, 33^{2}, 40^{4}, 41^{2}, 42
6:5, 6^{3}, 10, 11, 12
7:6, 7^{2}, 19^{2}, 25, 26, 35, 41, 52, 54^{3}, 57, 59
8:1, 4, 10, 11, 12^{2}, 14, 15^{2}, 16, 17^{2}, 25^{2}, 36^{2}, 38, 39
9:2, 8, 24, 26, 29, 30, 37^{2}, 38, 39
10:9, 10, 22, 24, 39, 45, 46, 48
11:2, 18^{2}, 19, 20, 22, 23, 26, 30
12:10^{3}, 15^{2}, 16^{2}, 19, 20, 25
13:2, 3^{2}, 4^{2}, 5^{3}, 6^{2}, 13, 14^{2}, 17, 21, 27^{3}, 28^{2}, 29^{2}, 45, 48, 51
14:1, 3, 6, 7, 11, 12, 14, 18^{2}, 21^{2}, 23^{3}, 24^{2}, 25^{2}, 26^{2}, 27^{2}, 28
15:2, 3^{2}, 4^{3}, 11, 13, 20, 23, 30^{4}, 31^{2}, 33^{2}, 36, 39
16:3, 4^{2}, 6, 7^{2}, 8, 19, 23^{2}, 31, 32, 37^{2}, 38^{3}, 39, 40^{3}
17:1^{2}, 6^{2}, 8^{2}, 9^{2}, 11, 13, 15^{2}, 19, 27^{2}, 32
18:3, 6, 20, 26
19:2, 3, 4, 5^{2}, 6, 10, 16, 19, 26, 28^{2}, 29, 32, 33, 34
20:8, 12, 18, 37, 38^{2}
21:5, 6, 12, 20^{3}, 21^{2}, 22, 24^{2}, 25^{2}, 27, 29^{2}, 30, 31, 32^{2}
22:2^{2}, 9^{2}, 18, 19, 22, 23, 24, 25, 29
23:4, 12^{2}, 13, 14, 20, 21^{3}, 24, 28, 30, 32, 33
24:12, 13^{2}, 14, 15, 19, 20
25:7, 14, 17, 18
26:5, 10, 18, 20, 30, 31^{2}
27:1, 12, 13^{2}, 17^{3}, 18, 27, 28^{2}, 29, 30^{2}, 36^{2}, 38^{2}, 39^{3}, 40^{2}, 41, 43, 44
28:1^{2}, 2, 4, 6^{3}, 10, 15, 17, 18, 21, 23, 25^{2}, 27^{2}, 28

ROMANS

1:20, 21^{2}, 22, 28, 32
3:9^{2}, 12^{2}, 13, 17
4:7, 11, 14, 17
5:17
8:5^{2}, 8, 14, 23
9:6, 7^{2}, 8, 26, 32^{2}
10:1, 2, 3, 14^{5}, 15^{2}, 16, 18
11:3^{2}, 8^{2}, 10, 11^{2}, 20, 23^{2}, 28^{2}, 31
13:2, 6
15:21^{2}, 27
16:18

1 CORINTHIANS

2:8^{2}, 14^{2}
3:20
7:8, 9, 14, 29^{2}, 30^{6}, 31
9:13^{2}, 14, 24, 25
10:4, 5, 6, 11, 18, 20, 33
11:19
12:19, 20
13:8^{2}
14:7, 21, 23, 34, 35
15:10, 11, 18, 23, 29^{2}, 35, 48^{2}
16:4, 15, 17, 18

2 CORINTHIANS

5:15
6:16
8:3, 5, 23
9:4, 5, 13
10:10, 12
11:12^{2}, 22^{3}, 23
12:21

GALATIANS

1:23, 24
2:4, 6^{2}, 7, 9^{2}, 10, 12, 14
3:7, 9
4:17^{2}
5:12, 21, 24
6:12^{2}, 13^{2}

EPHESIANS

4:14
5:31

PHILIPPIANS

3:18
4:2, 22

COLOSSIANS

1:16, 20
3:21
4:9

1 THESSALONIANS

1:9
2:14, 15, 16
5:3^{2}, 7^{2}

2 THESSALONIANS

2:10^{2}, 11, 12
3:12

1 TIMOTHY

1:3, 7^{2}, 20
2:15
3:13
5:7, 11^{2}, 12, 13^{2}, 17, 24, 25
6:2^{3}, 9, 10, 17, 18^{2}, 19

2 TIMOTHY

1:15
2:10, 14, 16, 23, 26
3:6, 9
4:3^{2}, 4

TITUS

1:10, 11, 13, 16^{3}
2:3, 4, 10
3:8, 9, 14

HEBREWS

1:4, 11^{2}, 12, 14
2:11
3:10^{2}, 11, 16, 18, 19
4:3, 5, 6
6:6^{2}
7:5^{2}, 23^{2}
8:9, 10, 11
9:15
10:1, 2
11:13, 14^{2}, 15^{3}, 16, 23^{2}, 29, 30, 35, 37^{3}, 38, 40
12:10, 19, 20, 25
13:10, 17^{3}, 24

JAMES

2:7, 12
3:3, 4^{2}
4:1
5:15

1 PETER

1:12
2:8, 12^{3}
3:1, 2, 10, 16^{2}
4:4, 6

2 PETER

1:8, 21
2:3, 10^{2}, 12, 13^{3}, 14, 18^{2}, 19^{2}, 20^{2}, 21
3:4, 5, 16^{2}

1 JOHN

2:19^{7}
4:1, 5^{2}

2 JOHN

1

3 JOHN

7

JUDE

10^{3}, 11, 12^{2}, 15, 18, 19

REVELATION

1:3, 7, 15
2:2, 9, 22, 24, 27
3:4^{2}, 9
4:4, 8^{2}, 11
5:9
6:4, 9, 10, 11^{2}
7:13, 14, 15, 16
8:7, 11
9:4, 5^{2}, 8, 9, 10, 11, 19, 20, 21
11:2, 3, 6, 7, 9, 10, 11, 12^{2}, 18
12:6, 11^{2}
13:4^{2}, 14
14:3, 4^{3}, 5, 11, 12, 13
15:3
16:4, 6^{2}, 9, 10, 14, 15
17:8^{2}, 14
18:9, 18, 19
19:3, 9
20:4^{2}, 6, 9, 13
21:3, 26, 27
22:4, 5^{2}, 14^{2}

THOU

859, *4771*

GENESIS

2:16, 17^{3}
3:9, 11^{3}, 12, 13, 14^{4}, 15, 16, 17^{3}, 18, 19^{5}
4:6, 7^{4}, 10, 11, 12^{2}, 14
6:14, 15, 16^{4}, 18^{2}, 19, 21^{2}
7:1, 2
8:16
10:19^{2}, 30
12:2, 11, 13, 18^{2}, 19
13:9^{2}, 10, 14, 15
14:23
15:2, 3, 5, 15^{2}
16:8^{2}, 11, 13
17:1, 4, 8, 9^{2}, 15, 19
18:5, 15, 23, 24, 28
19:12^{2}, 15, 17^{2}, 19^{2}, 21, 22, 34
20:3^{2}, 4, 6, 7^{5}, 9^{3}, 10^{2}, 13
21:22, 23^{3}, 26, 29, 30
22:2, 12^{3}, 16, 18
23:6^{2}, 13
24:3, 4, 5, 6^{2}, 7, 8, 14^{2}, 23, 31^{2}, 37, 38, 40, 41^{3}, 42, 44, 47, 58, 60^{2}
25:18
26:9, 10^{2}, 16, 29^{2}
27:10, 18, 19, 20, 21, 24, 32, 33, 36, 38, 40^{3}, 43, 45
28:1, 3, 4^{2}, 6, 13, 14, 15, 22
29:14, 15^{2}, 25^{2}, 27
30:15^{2}, 16, 26, 29, 30, 31^{2}
31:13^{2}, 24, 26^{2}, 27, 28, 29^{2}, 30^{3}, 31, 32^{2}, 36, 37^{2}, 39, 41, 42, 43, 44^{2}, 50^{2}, 52
32:10, 12, 17^{2}, 18, 26, 28, 29
33:8, 9, 10
35:1, 17
37:8^{2}, 10, 15
38:16^{2}, 17^{2}, 23, 29
39:9, 17
40:13^{2}
41:15, 39, 40^{2}
43:4, 5, 8, 9
44:4, 18, 21, 23
45:10^{4}, 11^{2}, 19
46:30
47:6, 8, 25, 30^{2}
48:6
49:3, 4^{3}, 6^{2}, 8, 9
50:5

EXODUS

2:13, 14^{2}
3:5, 10, 12, 14, 15, 18^{2}
4:9^{2}, 10, 12, 13, 15, 16, 17^{2}, 21^{2}, 22, 23, 25, 26
5:15, 22^{2}, 23
6:1, 29
7:2, 9, 15^{2}, 16^{2}, 17
8:2, 10, 21, 22
9:2, 14, 15, 17^{2}, 19, 29
10:2, 3, 4, 7, 25, 28^{2}, 29
12:44, 46
13:5, 6, 8, 10, 12^{2}, 13^{4}, 14
14:11^{2}, 15, 16
15:7^{2}, 10, 12, 13^{3}, 16, 17^{2}, 26
17:3, 5, 6
18:14^{2}, 17, 18^{3}, 19^{2}, 20, 21, 23^{2}
19:3, 6, 12, 23, 24^{2}
20:3, 4, 5, 7, 9, 10^{2}, 13, 14, 15, 16, 17^{2}, 19, 22, 24, 25^{4}, 26
21:1, 2, 14, 23
22:18, 21, 23, 25^{3}, 26^{2}, 28, 29^{2}, 30^{2}
23:1, 2^{2}, 3, 4^{2}, 5^{2}, 6, 7, 8, 9, 10, 11^{2}, 12^{2}, 14, 15^{3}, 16^{2}, 18, 19^{2}, 22, 24^{2}, 27, 30, 31, 32, 33
24:1, 12
25:11^{2}, 12, 13, 14, 16, 17, 18^{2}, 21^{2}, 23, 24, 25^{2}, 26, 28, 29^{2}, 30, 31, 37, 40
26:1^{2}, 4^{2}, 5^{2}, 6, 7^{2}, 9, 10, 11, 14, 15, 17, 18, 19, 22, 23, 26, 29^{2}, 30, 31, 32, 33^{2}, 34, 35^{2}, 36, 37^{2}
27:1, 2^{2}, 3^{2}, 4^{2}, 5, 6, 8, 9, 20
28:1, 2, 3, 9, 11^{2}, 12, 13, 14, 15^{3}, 17, 22, 23, 24, 25, 26^{2}, 27, 30, 31, 33, 36, 37, 39^{3}, 40^{3}, 41, 42
29:1, 2, 3, 4, 5, 6, 7, 8, 9^{2}, 10, 11, 12, 13, 14, 15, 16^{2}, 17, 18, 19, 20, 21, 22, 24, 25, 26, 27, 31, 34, 35^{2}, 36^{4}, 37, 38, 39^{2}, 41
30:1^{2}, 3^{2}, 4^{2}, 5, 6, 12^{3}, 16, 18^{3}, 23, 25, 26, 29, 30, 31, 35, 36, 37
31:13
32:7, 11, 13, 21, 22, 32^{2}
33:1^{2}, 3, 12^{5}, 16, 17^{2}, 20, 21, 23
34:1, 10, 11, 12^{2}, 14, 15^{2}, 16, 17, 18^{3}, 20^{4}, 21^{3}, 22, 24, 25, 26^{2}, 27
40:2, 3, 4^{2}, 5, 6, 7, 8, 9, 10, 11, 12, 13, 14, 15^{2}

LEVITICUS

2:4, 6, 8, 13^{3}, 14^{2}, 15
6:21^{2}, 27
8:3
9:3
10:9, 14
13:55, 57, 58
17:8
18:7^{2}, 8, 9, 10, 11, 12, 13, 14^{2}, 15^{2}, 16, 17^{2}, 18, 19, 20, 21^{2}, 22, 23
19:9^{2}, 10^{3}, 12, 13, 14, 15^{2}, 16^{2}, 17^{2}, 18^{2}, 19^{2}, 27, 32, 34
20:2, 16, 19
21:8
22:23
23:22^{4}
24:5, 6, 7, 15
25:3^{2}, 4, 5, 8, 9, 14, 15, 16^{2}, 17, 35, 36, 37, 39, 43, 44
27:12

NUMBERS

1:3, 49, 50
3:9, 10, 15, 41, 47^{2}, 48
4:23, 29, 30
5:19^{2}, 20^{2}
7:5
8:2, 7, 8, 9^{2}, 10, 12, 13, 14, 15, 26
10:2^{2}, 29, 31^{2}, 32
11:11^{2}, 12^{2}, 15, 16, 17, 18, 21, 23, 29
13:2, 27
14:13, 14^{3}, 15, 17, 19
15:5, 6, 7, 8, 10
16:11, 13^{2}, 14^{2}, 15, 16^{2}, 17, 22, 37
17:2, 3, 4, 10
18:1^{2}, 2^{2}, 7, 10, 15^{2}, 16, 17^{2}, 20^{2}, 30
20:8^{4}, 14, 18, 20
21:2, 29, 34^{2}
22:6^{2}, 12^{2}, 17, 20, 28, 29, 30, 32, 34, 35, 37
23:5, 11^{2}, 13^{2}, 18, 27
24:10, 11, 12, 21
26:54^{2}
27:7^{2}, 8, 13^{2}, 20
28:3, 4^{2}, 7, 8^{2}, 21
31:2, 26, 30

DEUTERONOMY

1:14, 31, 37
2:4, 7, 18, 19, 28, 31, 37
3:2^{2}, 21, 24, 27, 28
4:9, 10, 19^{2}, 25, 29^{3}, 30^{2}, 33, 35, 36, 38, 40^{2}
5:7, 8, 9, 11, 13, 14^{3}, 15, 17, 18, 19, 20, 21^{2}, 27^{2}, 31^{2}
6:2^{2}, 5, 7^{5}, 8, 9, 10, 11^{4}, 12, 13, 18^{2}, 21
7:1^{2}, 2^{2}, 3^{3}, 6, 11, 14, 15, 16^{2}, 17, 18, 19, 21, 22, 24^{2}, 25^{2}, 26^{4}
8:2^{2}, 3, 5, 6, 9^{3}, 10^{2}, 11, 12, 13, 14, 17, 18, 19
9:1, 2^{2}, 3, 4, 5, 6, 7^{2}, 12, 26^{2}, 28, 29
10:2^{2}, 20^{3}
11:1, 10^{2}, 14, 15, 19^{4}, 20, 29^{2}
12:5, 13^{2}, 14^{2}, 15, 17^{2}, 18^{4}, 19^{2}, 20^{2}, 21^{2}, 22, 23^{2}, 24^{2}, 25^{2}, 26^{2}, 27^{2}, 28, 29^{2}, 30^{2}, 31, 32
13:2, 3, 5, 6^{2}, 8^{3}, 9, 10, 12, 14, 15, 16, 18
14:2, 3, 21^{4}, 22, 23^{2}, 24, 25, 26^{4}, 27, 28, 29
15:1, 3, 5, 6^{3}, 7, 8, 9, 10^{3}, 11, 12, 13^{2}, 14^{2}, 15^{2}, 17^{2}, 18^{2}, 19^{2}, 20^{2}, 21, 22, 23^{2}
16:2, 3^{5}, 4, 5, 6^{2}, 7^{2}, 8^{2}, 9^{2}, 10^{2}, 11^{2}, 12^{3}, 13^{2}, 14^{2}, 15^{2}, 18, 19^{2}, 20^{2}, 21^{2}, 22
17:1, 4, 5, 7, 8, 9, 10^{2}, 11^{2}, 12, 14, 15^{3}
18:4, 9^{2}, 13, 14, 16, 21, 22
19:1, 2, 3, 7, 9^{2}, 13, 14^{2}, 19
20:1^{2}, 10, 12, 13, 14^{2}, 15, 16, 17, 19^{4}, 20^{3}
21:8, 9^{2}, 10^{2}, 11, 12, 13, 14^{5}, 21, 22, 23
22:1^{2}, 2^{3}, 3^{5}, 4^{2}, 6, 7^{2}, 8^{3}, 9^{2}, 10, 11, 12^{2}, 21, 22, 24, 26
23:6, 7^{3}, 12^{2}, 13^{3}, 15, 16, 18, 19, 20^{4}, 21^{2}, 22, 23^{3}, 24^{3}, 25^{3}
24:4, 7, 8, 10^{2}, 11^{2}, 12, 13, 14, 15, 17, 18^{2}, 19^{2}, 20^{2}, 21^{2}, 22^{2}
25:4, 12, 13, 14, 15^{2}, 18, 19^{2}
26:1, 2^{2}, 3, 5, 10^{2}, 11^{2}, 12, 13^{2}, 14, 15^{2}, 16, 17, 18, 19
27:2, 3^{3}, 4, 5^{2}, 6^{2}, 7, 8, 9, 10
28:1, 2, 3^{2}, 6^{4}, 8, 9, 10, 12^{2}, 13^{3}, 14, 15, 16^{2}, 19^{4}, 20^{4}, 21, 22, 24, 25, 27, 29^{3}, 30^{4}, 31^{2}, 33^{2}, 34^{2}, 36^{3}, 37, 38, 39, 40^{2}, 41^{2}, 43, 44^{2}, 45^{2}, 47, 48, 49, 51, 52, 53, 58^{2}, 60, 61, 62, 63, 64^{2}, 65, 66, 67^{4}, 68
29:12
30:1, 2, 5, 6, 8, 10^{2}, 12, 13, 14, 16^{2}, 17, 18, 19, 20^{4}
31:2, 3, 7^{2}, 11, 14, 16, 23
32:14, 15^{3}, 18, 50, 52^{2}
33:7, 8^{2}, 23, 29^{2}
34:4

JOSHUA

1:2, 6, 7^{4}, 8^{4}, 9^{2}, 16^{2}, 18
2:17, 18^{3}, 20^{2}
3:8
5:13, 15
6:3
7:7, 9, 10, 13, 19, 25
8:1, 2^{2}
10:12^{2}
11:6
13:1, 6
14:6, 9, 12
15:18, 19
17:14, 15, 17^{2}, 18^{2}

JUDGES

1:14, 15
4:8^{2}, 9, 20, 22
5:4^{2}, 12, 16, 21
6:4, 12, 14, 16, 17, 18, 23, 26, 36^{2}, 37^{2}
7:5, 10^{2}, 11
8:1^{3}, 18, 21, 22^{3}
9:8, 10, 12, 14, 32, 33^{3}, 36, 38^{2}
10:15
11:2^{2}, 8, 12^{2}, 23, 24, 25, 27, 30, 33, 35^{2}, 36
12:1, 5
13:3^{2}, 5, 7, 8, 11, 16^{3}, 18
14:3, 16^{2}
15:2, 11^{2}, 18
16:6, 10^{2}, 13^{3}, 15^{2}
17:2^{2}, 9
18:3^{2}, 19, 23, 25
19:9, 17^{2}

RUTH

1:15, 16^{2}, 17
2:8, 9^{2}, 10, 11^{3}, 12, 13^{2}, 14, 19^{2}, 21, 22
3:2, 4^{3}, 5, 9^{2}, 10^{3}, 11^{2}, 15, 16, 18
4:4^{2}, 5^{2}, 6, 11

1 SAMUEL

1:8^{2}, 11, 14, 17, 23
2:16, 32

1 SAMUEL

3:5, 6, 8, 9, 17
4:20
8:5
9:16, 21, 27
10:2[3], 3[2], 4, 5[3], 6, 7, 8[3]
12:4[2]
13:11[2], 13[2], 14
14:37, 43, 44
15:1, 7, 13, 17[2], 19, 23, 26, 28
16:1, 3[2], 4, 16
17:28[4], 33[2], 43, 45[2], 52, 56, 58[2]
18:17, 21
19:3, 5[2], 11[2], 17
20:2, 8[3], 13, 14, 15, 18, 19[3], 21, 23, 30[2], 31
21:1, 9[2]
22:12, 13[2], 16[2], 18, 23[2]
23:17
24:4, 9, 11[2], 14, 17[2], 18[3], 19, 20, 21[2]
25:6, 7, 17, 25, 31, 33, 34
26:11, 14[2], 15[2], 16, 25[2]
27:8
28:1[3], 2, 9[2], 12[2], 13, 15[2], 16, 18, 19, 21, 22[3]
29:4, 6, 7, 8, 9
30:8, 13[2], 15[2]

2 SAMUEL

1:3, 5, 8, 13, 14, 25, 26
2:20, 26[2], 27
3:7, 8, 13[3], 21, 24[2], 25[2], 34
5:2[3], 6[2], 19, 23, 24[2], 25
6:22
7:5, 8, 9, 12, 18, 19, 20, 21, 22, 23, 24[2], 25[2], 27, 28[2], 29
9:2, 7, 8, 10[2]
10:3, 11
11:10[2], 11, 19, 21, 25[2]
12:7, 9[2], 10, 12, 13, 14, 21[3]
13:4[2], 12, 13, 16
14:11, 13
15:2, 19[2], 20[2], 27, 33[2], 34[2], 35[3]
16:2, 7[2], 8[3], 10, 17, 21
17:3, 6, 8, 11
18:3[3], 11[2], 13, 20[3], 21, 22[2]
19:5, 6[3], 7, 13[2], 14, 19, 23, 25, 28, 29[2], 33, 38
20:4, 6, 9, 17, 19[2]
21:4, 17[2]
22:3, 26[2], 27[2], 28[2], 29, 36, 37, 40[2], 41, 44[2], 49[2]
24:13

1 KINGS

1:6, 11, 12, 13, 14, 16, 17, 18, 20[2], 24, 27, 42
2:2, 3[3], 5, 8, 9[3], 13, 15, 22, 26[3], 31, 37[3], 42[3], 43, 44[2]
3:6[3], 7, 8, 11, 13, 14
5:3, 6[3], 8, 9[3]
6:12[2]
8:18, 19, 24[2], 25[2], 26, 28, 29[2], 30[3], 32, 34[2], 35, 36[3], 39[4], 40, 43, 44[2], 45, 46, 48[2], 49, 51, 53[3]
9:3[2], 4, 13
11:11, 22[2], 37, 38
12:4, 7, 10[3]
13:8, 9, 14, 17[2], 18, 21
14:2, 5, 6[2], 8, 9, 12
16:2
17:4, 13, 18[2], 20, 24
18:7, 9, 11, 14, 17, 18[2], 36, 37[2]
19:9, 13, 15, 16[2]
20:5, 9, 13[2], 14, 22, 25, 34, 36[2], 39, 42
21:5, 7, 10, 19[3], 20[2], 22, 29
22:4[2], 11[2], 16, 19, 22, 25[2], 28, 30

2 KINGS

1:4[2], 6[3], 9, 16[3]
2:3, 5, 10[2], 23[2]
3:7[2]
4:1, 2, 4[3], 7, 13[2], 16[2], 23, 29, 40
5:6, 8, 10, 13, 25
6:9, 12, 22[3]
7:2, 19
8:1[2], 10, 12[3], 13, 14
9:2, 7, 18, 19, 25
10:5[2], 30
13:17[2], 19[4]
14:10[4]
17:26
18:14, 19, 20[3], 21, 23, 24
19:6, 10, 11[2], 15[3], 19[3], 20, 22[2], 23, 25[2], 28
20:1, 5, 9, 18, 19
22:18, 19[2], 20
23:17

1 CHRONICLES

4:10[2]
11:2[3], 5
12:18
14:10, 15[2]
17:4, 7[2], 8, 11, 16, 17, 18, 19, 21, 22[2], 23[2], 25[2], 26, 27
19:3, 12
21:22
22:8[3], 11, 12, 13[2], 14
28:3[2], 9[4], 20
29:10, 11, 12, 17

2 CHRONICLES

1:8, 9, 11[2]
2:3, 16[2]
6:8, 9, 15[2], 16[2], 17, 20[2], 21[2], 23, 25[2], 26, 27[3], 30[3], 31, 33, 34[2], 35, 36, 38[2], 39, 41
7:17
9:6

2 CHRONICLES

10:4, 7, 10[3]
13:4
14:11
16:7, 8, 9[2]
18:3[2], 10, 12, 15, 21[2], 24[2], 27, 29, 33
19:2, 3
20:6[2], 7, 9, 10, 11, 12, 15, 37
21:12, 15
24:6
25:8, 15, 16[3], 19[5]
26:18
34:26, 27[2], 28
35:21

EZRA

4:13, 15, 16
7:14, 16, 17, 19, 20, 25
9:11, 13, 14[2], 15
10:12

NEHEMIAH

1:6, 7, 8, 10
2:2, 4, 5, 6
5:12
6:6[3], 7, 8[2], 14
9:6[4], 7, 8, 10[2], 11[2], 12, 13, 15, 17[2], 19, 20, 21, 22, 23[2], 24, 27[3], 28[3], 29, 30[2], 31[2], 33[2], 34, 35[2], 36, 37

ESTHER

3:3
4:13, 14[3]
5:3, 14[2]
6:10[2], 13[2]

JOB

1:7, 8, 10[2]
2:2, 3[2], 9, 10
4:2, 3[2], 4, 5[2]
5:1, 17, 21[2], 22[2], 23, 24[2], 25, 26, 27
7:12, 14, 17[2], 18, 19, 20[2], 21[2]
8:2, 5, 6
9:12, 28, 31
10:2, 3[2], 4[2], 6, 7, 8, 9[2], 10, 11, 12, 13, 14[2], 15, 16[2], 17, 18
11:3, 4, 7[2], 8[2], 13, 15[2], 16, 17[2], 18[3], 19
13:22[2], 24, 25[2], 26, 27[2]
14:3, 5, 13[3], 15[2], 16[2], 17, 19[2], 20[2]
15:4, 5, 7[2], 8[2], 9[2], 13
16:3, 7, 8, 18
17:4[2], 14[2]
20:4
22:3[2], 6, 7[2], 9, 11, 13, 15, 23[3], 24, 25, 26, 27[2], 28, 29
26:2[3], 3[2], 4
30:20[2], 21[2], 22[2], 23
31:24
33:5, 8, 12, 13, 32
34:16, 17, 18, 32, 33[3]
35:2[2], 3, 5, 6[3], 7[2], 8, 14[3]
36:17, 21, 23, 24
37:6, 15, 16, 18
38:3, 4[2], 5, 11, 12, 16[2], 17, 18[2], 20[2], 21[2], 22[2], 31, 32[2], 33[2], 34, 35, 39
39:1[2], 2[2], 10, 11[2], 12, 13, 19[2], 20
40:7, 8[3], 9[2]
41:1[2], 2, 4, 5[2], 7
42:2, 4

PSALMS

2:7, 9[2]
3:3, 7[2]
4:1, 6, 7, 8
5:3, 4, 5, 6, 10, 11, 12[2]
6:3
7:6, 7
8:2[2], 3, 4[2], 5, 6[2]
9:2, 4[2], 5[3], 6[2], 10, 13
10:1[2], 13, 14[3], 15[2], 17[3]
12:7[2]
13:1[2]
16:2[2], 5, 10[2], 11
17:3[3], 6, 7, 14
18:25[2], 26[2], 27, 28, 35, 36, 39[2], 40, 43[2], 48[2]
19:12
21:2, 3[2], 4, 5, 6[2], 9, 10, 12[2], 13
22:1[2], 2, 3[2], 4, 9[2], 10, 15, 19, 21
23:4, 5[2]
25:5, 7, 17
27:8, 9
28:1
30:1, 2, 3[2], 7[2], 10, 11[2]
31:2, 3, 4, 5, 7[2], 8, 14, 19[2], 20[2], 22
32:5, 6, 7[3], 8
35:17, 22
36:6, 8
37:1, 3[2], 10, 34
38:15
39:5, 9, 11[2]
40:5, 6[3], 9, 11, 17
41:2, 3, 10, 11, 12
42:5[3], 9, 11[3]
43:2[2], 5[2]
44:1, 2[2], 3, 4, 7, 9, 10, 11, 12, 13, 14, 19, 23, 24
45:2, 7, 11, 16
48:7
49:16, 18
50:15, 16[2], 17, 18[2], 19, 20[2], 21[2]
51:4[3], 6[2], 8, 14, 15, 16[2], 17, 18, 19
52:1, 3, 4[2], 9
53:5
55:13, 23

PSALMS

56:2, 8[2], 13[2]
57:5, 11
59:5, 8[2], 16
60:1[3], 2[2], 3[2], 4, 8, 10[2]
61:3, 5[2], 6
62:5, 12
63:1, 7
65:2, 3, 4, 5, 8, 9[4], 10[4], 11[5]
66:3, 10[2], 11[2], 12[2]
67:4
68:7[2], 9[2], 10, 18[3], 28, 30, 35
69:5, 19, 26[2]
70:5
71:3[3], 5[2], 6, 7, 17, 20, 21, 22, 23
73:18[2], 20[2], 23, 24, 27
74:1, 2[3], 11, 13[2], 14, 15[2], 16, 17[2]
76:4, 7[3], 8, 10
77:4, 14[2], 15, 20
79:5, 11
80:1[2], 4, 5, 6, 8[2], 9, 12, 15, 17
81:7, 8, 9
82:8
83:1, 18
85:1[2], 2[2], 3[2], 5[2], 6
86:2, 5, 7, 9, 10[2], 13, 15, 17
88:5, 6, 7, 8[2], 10, 14[2], 18
89:2, 9[2], 10[2], 11, 12, 13, 17, 19, 26, 38[2], 39[2], 40[2], 42[2], 43, 44, 45[2], 46, 47, 49
90:1, 2[2], 3, 5, 8, 15, 17[2]
91:4, 5, 8, 9, 12, 13[2]
92:4, 8, 10
93:2
94:2, 12, 13
97:9[2]
99:4[2], 8[3]
101:2
102:10, 12, 13, 25, 26[2], 27
104:1[2], 6, 8, 9, 20, 24, 26, 27, 28[2], 29[2], 30[2], 35
106:4
108:5, 11[2]
109:6, 21[2], 27, 28
110:1, 2, 3, 4
114:5[4], 7
115:9
116:8, 16
118:13, 21, 28[2]
119:4, 12, 18, 21, 25, 26, 28, 32, 37, 49, 57, 65, 68, 75, 82, 84, 86, 90, 93, 98, 102, 114, 117, 118, 119, 132[2], 137, 138, 151, 152, 171
120:3
123:1
128:2[2], 5, 6
130:3, 4
132:8
137:8
138:2, 3, 7[2]
139:1, 2[2], 3, 4, 5, 8[2], 13[2], 19
140:6, 7
142:3, 5, 7
143:10
144:3[2]
145:15, 16

PROVERBS

1:10, 15
2:1, 2, 3, 4, 5, 9, 20
3:4, 15, 23, 24[3], 28, 31
4:8, 12[3]
5:2, 6[2], 9, 11, 19, 20
6:1[2], 2[2], 3, 6, 9[2], 22[3], 35
7:4
9:12[4]
14:7
19:19[2], 20
20:13[2], 22
22:18, 21, 24, 25, 26, 27, 29
23:1, 2, 5, 6[2], 8[2], 13, 14, 17, 19, 31, 34, 35
24:1, 6, 10, 11, 12, 13, 14, 19, 21, 24
25:7, 8, 16[2], 22
26:4, 12
27:1, 22, 23, 27
29:20
30:4, 6[2], 10, 32[3]
31:29

ECCLESIASTES

5:1, 2, 4[2], 5[2], 6, 7, 8
7:10[2], 16, 17[2], 18, 21, 22
8:4
9:9[2], 10
10:17
11:1, 2, 5[2], 6, 9
12:1

SONG OF SOLOMON

1:7[3], 8[2], 15[3], 16
2:17
4:1[3], 7, 9[2], 16
5:9[2]
6:1, 4
7:6
8:1, 12, 13, 14

ISAIAH

1:26
2:6
3:6[2]
7:3, 16
9:3, 4
12:1[3], 6
14:3, 4, 8, 10[2], 12[2], 13, 15, 19, 20[2], 29, 31
16:4
17:10[2], 11[2]
22:1, 2, 8, 16[3], 18
23:2, 4, 12[3], 16[2]

ISAIAH

25:1[2], 2, 4, 5
26:3, 7, 12[2], 14, 15[4], 20
27:8
29:4, 6
30:19, 22[2], 23
33:1[4], 2, 19[3]
36:4, 5[3], 6, 7, 8, 9
37:6, 10, 11[2], 16[3], 20[2], 21, 23[2], 24, 26[2], 29
38:1, 12, 13, 16, 17[2]
39:7, 8
40:27, 28[2]
41:8, 9[2], 10, 12, 14, 15, 16[2]
42:20
43:1, 2[3], 4[2], 22[2], 23[2], 24[4], 26[2]
44:2, 17, 21[3], 26, 28
45:3, 4, 5, 9, 10[2], 15
47:1, 5[2], 6[2], 7[2], 8, 10[3], 11[3], 12[3], 13, 15
48:4, 5, 6[2], 7[2], 8[3], 17, 18
49:3, 6[2], 9, 18, 20[2], 21, 23
51:9, 10, 12[2], 16, 17, 21, 22, 23
53:10
54:1[2], 3, 4[4], 6, 11, 14[3], 17
55:5[2]
57:6[2], 7[2], 8[5], 9, 10[4], 11[3], 13
58:3[2], 5, 7[4], 9[3], 10, 11, 12[2], 13, 14
60:5, 15, 16[2], 18
62:2, 3, 4[2], 8, 12
63:2, 14, 16[2], 17, 19
64:1[2], 3[2], 5[2], 7, 8[2], 12[2]
65:5

JEREMIAH

1:5, 7[2], 11, 12, 13, 17
2:2, 17[2], 18[2], 19, 20[2], 21, 22, 23[3], 25, 27[2], 28, 33[2], 35[2], 36[3], 37[2]
3:1, 2[3], 3[2], 4[2], 5[2], 6, 7, 12, 13, 19, 22
4:1[3], 2, 10, 14, 19, 30[6]
5:3[2], 15, 17, 19
6:8, 27
7:16, 17, 27[2], 28
8:4
10:6, 24
11:3, 14, 15[2], 18, 21
12:1, 2[2], 3[2], 5[4]
13:4, 12, 13, 21[2], 22, 25, 27
14:7, 8, 9[2], 17, 19[2], 22[2]
15:2, 5, 6[2], 10, 14, 15, 17, 18, 19[5]
16:2[2], 8, 10, 11
17:4[2], 14, 16, 17
18:22, 23
19:10
20:6[5], 7[2]
21:8
22:2, 6, 15[2], 21[2], 22, 23, 25
23:33, 37
24:3
25:27, 28, 30
26:4, 8, 9
27:13
28:6, 7, 13[2], 15, 16[2]
29:24, 25, 26, 27
30:10, 13[2], 15
31:4[2], 5, 18[3], 21, 22[2]
32:3, 17, 18, 22, 23[2], 24[2], 25
33:3, 24
34:3[2], 4, 5, 14
36:6[3], 14, 17, 19, 29[3]
37:13, 17, 20
38:15[2], 17[2], 18[2], 21, 23[2], 24, 25, 26
39:17[2], 18[2]
40:14, 16[2]
43:2
44:16
45:3, 4, 5[2]
46:11[2], 19, 27, 28
47:5, 6[2]
48:2, 7[2], 18, 27[2]
49:4, 12[3], 16[2]
50:24[4], 31
51:13, 20, 26, 61, 62[2], 63[2], 64

LAMENTATIONS

1:10, 21[3], 22
2:20, 21[2], 22
3:17, 42, 43[3], 44, 45, 56, 57[2], 58[2], 59[2], 60, 61
4:21
5:19, 20, 21, 22[2]

EZEKIEL

2:4, 6[2], 7, 8[2]
3:1, 5, 6, 18[2], 19[2], 20, 21[2], 25[2], 26, 27
4:1, 3[2], 4[3], 5, 6[2], 7[2], 8[2], 9[3], 10[2], 11[2], 12[2], 15
5:1, 2[3], 3, 11
7:2, 7
8:6[2], 12, 13, 15[2], 17
9:8, 11
11:13
12:2, 3[2], 4[2], 5, 6[3], 9, 10
13:2, 17[2]
16:4[3], 5[2], 6[2], 7[3], 8, 13[4], 15, 16, 17, 18, 19, 20[3], 21, 22[2], 24, 25, 26, 28[3], 29[2], 30, 31[2], 33, 34[2], 36, 37[3], 41, 43[2], 45[2], 47[2], 48[2], 51[2], 52[5], 54[3], 55, 58, 59, 61[2], 62, 63[2]
17:9
19:1
20:4[2]
21:6, 7[2], 14, 19[2], 25, 28[2], 30, 32[2]
22:2[4], 3, 4[4], 8, 12[3], 13, 16[2], 24
23:21, 27, 28, 30[2], 31, 32[3], 33, 34[2], 35[2], 36, 40, 41

EZEKIEL

24:13[2], 16, 19[2], 25, 27[2]
25:3, 6, 7
26:14[2], 17, 20, 21[3]
27:2, 3[2], 7, 25, 33[2], 34, 36
28:2[3], 3, 4, 5, 6, 8, 9[2], 10, 12, 13[2], 14[3], 15[2], 16, 17, 18, 19[2]
29:5[2], 7[2]
31:2, 10, 18[3]
32:2[3], 6, 9, 19[2], 28
33:7[2], 8[2], 9[2], 10, 12, 14, 27, 30, 32
35:4[2], 5, 6, 10, 11, 12[2], 15[2]
36:1, 12[2], 13, 14, 15[2]
37:3, 16, 18[2], 20
38:7[3], 8[2], 9[3], 10, 11, 13[2], 14, 15[2], 16, 17
39:1, 4[2], 5, 17
40:4[2]
43:10, 19, 20[2], 21, 22[2], 23[2], 24, 25
44:6
45:3, 18, 20
46:13[2], 14
47:6

DANIEL

1:13
2:23[2], 26, 30, 31, 34, 37, 38, 41[2], 43, 45, 47
3:10, 12[2], 18
4:18[2], 20, 22, 25, 26, 32, 35
5:13, 16[3], 18, 22[2], 23[3], 27
6:12, 13, 16, 20
8:20, 26
9:7, 23
10:12, 19, 20
12:4, 13[2]

HOSEA

2:16, 20, 23[2]
3:3[3]
4:5, 6[3], 15
5:3
9:1[2], 14
10:9, 13
12:6
13:4, 9, 10
14:1

AMOS

5:23
7:8, 12, 16[2], 17
8:2

OBADIAH

2, 3, 4[2], 5, 10, 11[2], 12[3], 13[2], 14[2], 15

JONAH

1:6, 8[2], 10, 14
2:2, 3, 6
4:2, 4, 9, 10[2]

MICAH

1:11, 13, 14
2:5, 7
4:8, 9, 10[3], 13
5:2[2], 12, 13
6:1, 14[3], 15[4]
7:19, 20[2]

NAHUM

1:14
3:8, 11[3], 16

HABAKKUK

1:2[2], 3, 12[3], 13[2]
2:7, 8, 10, 15, 16[2]
3:8, 9, 12[2], 13[2], 14, 15

ZEPHANIAH

3:7[2], 11[3], 15, 16

ZECHARIAH

1:3, 12[2], 14
2:2, 11
3:7[3], 8
4:2, 5, 7[2], 9, 13
5:2
6:10
13:3[2]

MALACHI

1:2
2:14

MATTHEW

1:20, 21
2:6, 13
3:14
4:3, 6[2], 7, 9, 10[2]
5:21, 22, 23, 25[2], 26[2], 27, 33, 36[2], 42, 43
6:2, 3, 5[2], 6[3], 17[2], 18
7:3, 4, 5[2]
8:2[2], 3, 4, 8, 13, 19, 29[2], 31
9:27
11:3, 23, 25
12:37[2]
13:10, 27, 28
14:28, 31[2], 33
15:5, 12, 22, 28
16:14, 16, 17, 18, 19[2], 23[2]
17:4, 25, 27[3]
18:15, 28, 32[2], 33
19:17[2], 18[4], 19, 21[3]
20:12, 13, 21, 30, 31
21:16[2], 21[2], 23
22:12, 16[3], 17, 37, 39, 44
23:26, 37
25:20, 21[3], 22, 23[2], 24[3], 25, 26[2], 27

MATTHEW

26:17, 25, 34, 39, 50, 53, 62, 63[2], 64, 68, 69, 70, 73, 75
27:4, 11[2], 13, 19, 40[2], 46

MARK

1:11, 24[3], 40[2], 41, 44
3:11
4:38
5:7[2], 8, 31[2], 35
6:22, 23, 25
7:11
8:29, 33
9:22, 23, 24, 25
10:18, 19, 21[3], 35, 47, 48, 51
11:21, 23[2], 28
12:14[2], 30, 31, 32, 34, 36
13:2
14:12[2], 30, 36, 37[2], 60, 61, 67, 68, 70[2], 72
15:2[2], 4, 29, 34

LUKE

1:4[2], 13, 14, 20[2], 28[2], 30, 31, 42, 76[2]
2:29, 31, 48
3:22
4:3, 7, 8[2], 9, 11, 12, 34[3], 41
5:10, 12[2], 13
6:41, 42[4]
7:6, 19, 20, 43, 44[2], 45, 46
8:28, 45
9:54, 57, 60
10:15, 21, 26, 27, 28[2], 35, 36, 37, 40, 41
11:27, 45
12:19, 20[2], 41, 58[3], 59[2]
13:9, 12, 15, 26
14:8[2], 9, 10[2], 12, 13, 14[2], 22
15:29, 30, 31
16:2, 5, 7, 25[2], 27
17:4, 6[2], 8
18:19, 20, 22[3], 38, 39, 41
19:17[3], 19, 21[4], 22[2], 23, 42[2], 44
20:2, 21[2], 39, 42
22:9, 32, 34[2], 42, 48, 58, 60, 61, 67, 70
23:3[2], 37, 39, 40[2], 42, 43
24:18

JOHN

1:19, 21[2], 22[2], 25[2], 33, 38, 42[2], 48[2], 49[2], 50[2]
2:10, 18[2], 20
3:2[2], 8, 10, 26
4:9, 10[2], 11[2], 12, 17, 18[3], 19, 27[2]
5:6, 14
6:25, 30[2], 68, 69
7:3, 4, 20, 52
8:5, 13, 25, 33, 48, 52[2], 53[2], 57[2]
9:17, 28, 34[2], 35, 37
10:24[2], 33, 36
11:3, 8, 21, 22, 26, 27, 32, 40[2], 41, 42[2]
12:34
13:6, 7[2], 8[2], 27, 36[3], 38[2]
14:5, 9[2], 10, 22
16:5, 29, 30[2]
17:2[3], 3, 4, 5, 6[2], 7, 8[2], 9, 11, 12, 15[2], 18, 21[2], 22, 23[3], 24[3], 25, 26
18:9, 17, 21, 22, 23, 25, 33, 34, 35, 37[2]
19:9, 10[2], 11, 12[2]
20:13, 15[4], 29[2]
21:12, 15[2], 16[2], 17[4], 18[6], 22

THE ACTS

1:6, 24[2]
2:27[2], 28[2], 34
4:24, 27
5:4[2]
7:28[2], 33
8:20, 21, 23, 30[2], 37[2]
9:4, 5[2], 6[2], 17[2]
10:6, 15, 33[2]
11:3, 9, 14
12:15
13:10[3], 11, 33, 35, 47
16:31
17:19, 20
21:20, 21, 22, 24, 37, 38
22:7, 8[2], 14, 15[2], 16, 26, 27
23:3[2], 4, 5, 11[2], 19, 20, 21, 22[2]
24:4, 10, 11
25:9, 10, 12[2], 22
26:1, 14, 15[2], 16, 24, 27[2], 28, 29
27:24
28:22

ROMANS

2:1[5], 3[2], 4, 17, 19, 21[4], 22[4], 23[2], 25[2]
3:4[2]
7:7
9:19, 20[2]
10:9[2]
11:17, 18[2], 19, 20, 22[2], 24
12:20
13:3[2], 4, 9[6]
14:4, 10[2], 15, 22

1 CORINTHIANS

4:7[5]
7:16[4], 21[2], 27[2], 28[2]
9:9
14:16[2], 17
15:36[2], 37[2]

GALATIANS

2:14[2]
4:7, 27[2]
5:14
6:1

EPHESIANS
5:14
6:3

COLOSSIANS
4:17[2]

1 TIMOTHY
1:3, 18
3:15[2]

1 TIMOTHY
4:6[3], 12, 16
5:18, 21
6:11, 12, 14

2 TIMOTHY
1:6, 8[2], 13, 15, 18
2:1, 2[2], 3
3:10, 14[3], 15
4:5, 13, 15

TITUS
1:5
2:1
3:8

PHILEMON
5, 12, 15, 17, 19, 21

HEBREWS
1:5, 9, 10, 11, 12[2]
2:6[2], 7[2], 8
5:5, 6

HEBREWS
7:17, 21
8:5
10:5[2], 6, 8
12:5[2]

JAMES
2:3[2], 8, 11[3], 18, 19[2], 20, 22
4:11[2], 12

3 JOHN
2, 3, 5[2], 6[2]

REVELATION
1:11, 19, 20[2]
2:2[2], 4, 5[2], 6[2], 9, 10[2], 13[2], 14, 15, 20
3:1[2], 3[3], 4, 8, 10, 11, 15[2], 16, 17[2], 18[3]
4:11[2]
5:9[2]
6:6, 10

REVELATION
7:14
10:11
11:17, 18
15:3, 4
16:5[2], 6
17:7, 8, 12, 15, 16, 18
18:14, 20
19:10
22:9

THY

4674 or 4675

GENESIS
3:10, 14[2], 15[2], 16[4], 17[3], 19
4:6, 9, 10, 11[2], 14
6:18[3]
7:1
8:16[3]
12:1[3], 2, 7, 13, 18, 19[2]
13:8, 15, 16[2]
14:20
15:1[2], 5, 13, 15, 18
16:5, 6[2], 9, 10, 11
17:5[2], 7[2], 8, 9, 10, 12, 13[2], 15, 19
18:3[2], 9, 10
19:12[2], 15[2], 17, 19[3]
20:6, 13, 16
21:12[3], 13
22:2, 12, 16, 17[2], 18, 20
23:6[2], 11, 15
24:2, 5, 7, 14[3], 17, 19, 23, 40, 43, 44, 46, 51, 60
25:23[2], 31
26:3[2], 4[3], 9, 10, 24[2]
27:3[2], 6[2], 9, 10, 13, 19[2], 20, 29[2], 31, 32[2], 35[2], 37, 39, 40[3], 42, 44, 45
28:2[2], 4, 13[2], 14[2]
29:15, 18
30:14, 15, 27, 28, 29, 31, 32, 33, 34
31:3[2], 8[2], 13, 30, 31, 32, 37[2], 38[3], 41[3]
32:4, 5, 6, 9[2], 10, 12, 18, 20, 27, 28, 29
33:5, 10[2]
35:1, 10[3], 11, 12
37:10[2], 13, 14, 32
38:8[2], 11, 13, 18[3], 24
39:19
40:13, 19[2]
41:40
42:10, 11, 13
43:28
44:7, 8, 9, 16, 18[2], 21, 23, 24, 27, 30, 31[2], 32, 33
45:9, 10[4], 11, 17
46:3, 30, 34
47:3, 4[2], 5[2], 6, 15, 29[2]
48:1, 2, 4, 5, 6, 11[2], 18, 22
49:4, 8[3], 18, 25, 26
50:6, 16, 17[2], 18

EXODUS
2:9, 13
3:5[2], 6, 18
4:6, 7, 9, 10, 12, 14, 15, 16, 19, 23[2]
5:15, 16[2], 23[2]
7:1[2], 2, 9, 19
8:2, 3[5], 4[2], 5, 9[3], 10, 11[3], 16, 21[3], 23
9:3, 14[2], 15, 19, 30
10:2[2], 4, 6[4], 29
11:8
12:24
13:5, 7, 8, 9, 11, 13, 14
14:16
15:6[2], 7, 8, 10, 12, 13[3], 16, 17, 26
17:5
18:6[2]
20:2, 5, 7, 9, 10[8], 12[4], 16, 17[3], 24[3], 25, 26
22:26, 28, 29[3], 30
23:6, 10, 11[3], 12[2], 13, 16[2], 17, 19[2], 25[2], 26[2], 31, 33
28:1, 2, 4, 41
29:12, 26
32:4, 7, 8, 11[2], 12[2], 13, 32
33:1, 5, 13[4], 15, 16[3], 18
34:9, 10, 16[2], 19, 20, 24[3], 26[2]

LEVITICUS
2:5, 7, 13[3], 14[2]
5:15, 18
6:6
9:7[2]
10:9, 13[2], 14[4], 15
16:2
18:7[3], 8[2], 9[3], 10[2], 11[3], 12[2], 13[2], 14, 15[2], 16[2], 20, 21[2]
19:9[2], 10[2], 12, 13, 14, 15, 16[2], 17[2], 18[2], 19[2], 27, 29, 32
20:19[2]
21:8, 17
23:22[2]
25:3[2], 4[2], 5[2], 6[4], 7[2], 11, 14[2], 15, 17, 25, 35, 36[2], 37[2], 39, 43, 44[2], 47, 53
27:2, 3[2], 4, 5, 6[2], 7, 8, 13, 15, 16, 17, 18, 19, 23, 25, 27

NUMBERS
5:19, 20, 21[3], 22[3]
11:11[2], 12, 15

NUMBERS
14:13, 14, 19, 20
16:10, 11, 16
18:1[3], 2[3], 3, 7, 8, 9, 11[3], 19[3], 20
20:8, 14, 16, 17[2], 19
21:22[2], 34
22:32
23:3, 15
24:5[2], 11, 12, 14, 21[2]
27:13[2]
31:2, 49
32:4, 5[2], 25, 27, 31

DEUTERONOMY
1:21[2], 31
2:7[4], 27, 30[2]
3:2, 24[5]
4:3, 9[6], 10, 19, 21, 23, 24, 25, 29[3], 30, 31[2], 37, 40[3]
5:6, 9, 11, 12, 13, 14[10], 15[2], 16[5], 20, 21[3]
6:2[5], 3, 5[3], 7, 9[2], 10[2], 13, 15[2], 18, 20, 21
7:1, 2, 3[2], 4, 6[2], 9, 12[2], 13[7], 16, 18, 19[2], 20, 21, 22, 23, 25
8:2, 3, 4[2], 5, 6, 7, 10, 11, 13[4], 14, 16[2], 18[2], 19
9:3[2], 4, 5[3], 6[2], 7, 12, 26[2], 27, 29[3]
10:9, 11, 12[5], 13, 14, 15, 20, 21[2], 22[2]
11:1, 10[2], 12[2], 14[2], 15[2], 20, 29
12:1, 7, 13, 14[2], 15[3], 17[8], 18[8], 20[4], 21[5], 25, 26[2], 27[4], 28[2], 29, 31
13:5, 6[7], 10, 12[2], 16, 17, 18[2]
14:2, 21[2], 22, 23[6], 24[2], 25, 26[3], 27, 28, 29[2]
15:3, 4, 5, 6, 7[8], 9[2], 10[2], 11[4], 12, 14[4], 15, 17[2], 18, 19[5], 20[2], 21, 22
16:1[2], 2, 3, 4, 5[2], 6, 7[2], 8, 10[3], 11[7], 13[2], 14[6], 15[2], 16[2], 17, 18[3], 20, 21, 22
17:1[2], 2[3], 5, 8[2], 12, 14, 15[3]
18:4[3], 5[2], 6, 9, 12, 13, 14, 15[2], 16
19:1[2], 2[2], 3[2], 8[4], 9, 10[2], 14[2]
20:1, 13, 14, 16, 17
21:1, 2[2], 5, 8[2], 10, 11, 13, 23[2]
22:1[2], 2[2], 3, 4, 5, 7, 8, 9[3], 12, 17
23:5[3], 6, 7, 13, 14[3], 16, 18[2], 19, 20[2], 21[2], 23[3], 24[3], 25[2]
24:4, 9, 10, 13, 14[4], 18, 19[2], 21
25:3, 13, 15[2], 16, 19[2]
26:1, 2[3], 3, 4, 5, 10[2], 11, 12, 13[3], 15[2], 16[2], 17, 19
27:[illegible], 5, 6[illegible], 7, [illegible], 10
28:1[2], 2, 4[5], 5[2], 7, 8[2], 9, 11[4], 12, 13, 15, 17[2], 18[4], 20, 23[2], 24, 26, 29, 31[2], 32[2], 33[2], 35[2], 36[2], 40, 42[2], 45, 46, 47, 48, 51[4], 52[6], 53[3], 55, 57, 58, 59[2], 62, 64, 65, 66[2]
29:5[2], 11[4], 12[2], 13
30:1, 2[3], 3[3], 4, 5[3], 6[4], 7, 9[5], 10[3], 14[2], 16[2], 19, 20[4]
31:3, 6, 11, 12[2], 14, 16, 27[2]
32:6, 7[2], 50[2]
33:3[3], 8[3], 9[2], 10[2], 18[2], 25[3], 26, 27, 29[2]
34:4

JOSHUA
1:5, 8[2], 9, 17, 18[2]
2:18[4], 19
5:15[2]
7:9, 10
8:1, 18
9:8, 9[2], 24[2]
10:6[2]
14:9[2]
24:12[2]

JUDGES
1:3
5:12, 14
6:14, 17, 25[2], 26, 30
7:10
8:15, 22[2]
9:38, 54
11:10, 17, 19, 24, 36[2]
13:12, 16, 17[2]
14:3, 13, 15[2]
15:2, 18
16:6, 15
17:10
18:19[2], 25[3]
19:19[2], 20

RUTH
1:10, 15[2], 16[2]
2:11[4], 12, 13, 14
3:3, 9, 12, 17
4:12, 15[2]

1 SAMUEL
1:8, 14, 17, 18, 26
2:1, 16, 27, 28, 29, 30[2], 31, 34
3:9, 10
4:17
8:5[2]
9:20[2]
10:2
12:19[2]
13:13[2], 14
14:7, 28
15:15, 21, 24, 30, 33[2]
16:11, 16, 19
17:17[2], 18, 28, 32, 34, 36, 44, 55, 58
19:11
20:1, 3[2], 4, 6, 7, 8[3], 10, 15, 18, 22, 30, 31, 42
22:14[2], 15, 16, 22, 23
23:10, 11[2], 20
24:9, 11[2], 16
25:7, 8[3], 26, 28, 29[2], 33, 35[2]
26:15[2], 17, 24
27:5
28:1, 2, 17, 19, 21[2], 22
29:6[3], 8, 10
31:4

2 SAMUEL
1:16[3], 19, 26
2:21[2], 22
3:8, 12, 25[2], 34[2]
4:8
5:1[2]
6:21
7:9, 12[4], 16[2], 19[2], 20, 21[2], 23[3], 24, 25, 26[2], 27[2], 28[2], 29[3]
9:2, 6, 7[2], 8, 9, 10[4], 11
10:3
11:8[2], 10, 11, 21, 24[2], 25
12:8[3], 9, 10, 11[3], 13
13:5[2], 7, 20[3], 24[2], 35
14:6, 11[2], 15, 17, 19[2], 20, 22[2], 31
15:2, 3, 8, 15, 19, 20, 21, 27, 34[3]
16:3, 4, 8[2], 17[3], 19[2], 21[2]
17:8[2], 10
18:28, 29
19:5[6], 6, 7[2], 14, 19, 20, 26[2], 27, 28, 29, 35[2], 36, 37[2]
20:6
22:36[2]
24:3, 10, 13[2], 23

1 KINGS
1:2, 12, 13, 14, 17[2], 19, 26[2], 27, 30, 47[2]
2:3, 4, 6, 7[2], 21, 37, 38, 39, 44
3:6, 7, 8[2], 9[3], 12, 13, 14[2], 22[2], 23[2]
5:5[3], 6[2], 8
6:12
8:19[2], 23, 24[2], 25[2], 26[2], 28[2], 29, 30[3], 32, 33[2], 34, 35, 36[4], 38, 39, 41[2], 42[3], 43[4], 44[2], 48, 49, 50, 51, 52[2], 53
9:3[2], 4, 5[2]
10:6[2], 7, 8[3], 9
11:11, 12[3], 13, 37
12:4[2], 7, 9, 10, 28
13:6, 21, 22[2]
14:9, 12
15:19[2]
16:3
17:12, 13, 19, 23, 24
18:8, 9, 10, 11, 12, 14, 18, 31, 36[2], 44
19:2, 10[2], 14[2], 15, 16
20:3[4], 4, 5[4], 6, 9, 31, 32, 33, 34, 39[2], 40[2], 42[3]
21:2, 5, 6, 19, 21
22:4[2], 13, 23, 30, 49

2 KINGS
1:10, 12, 13[2], 14
2:2, 3[2], 4, 5[2], 6, 9, 16[2]
3:7[2], 13[2]
4:1[2], 3, 4, 7[2], 24, 26, 29[2], 30, 36
5:8, 10, 15, 17[2], 18[2], 25, 27
6:3, 12, 22[2], 28, 29
8:9, 13
9:1, 7, 22
10:5, 15, 30
14:9, 10
15:12
16:7[2]
18:23, 24, 26, 27
19:4[3], 10, 22, 23, 27[4], 28[4]
20:3, 5[3], 6, 17, 18
22:9, 19, 20[2]

1 CHRONICLES
10:4
11:1[2], 2

1 CHRONICLES
12:18[2]
16:35[2]
17:11[4], 17, 18[2], 19, 21[2], 22, 23, 24[2], 25[2], 26, 27
19:3
21:8, 12, 17
22:11, 12
28:6, 9, 21
29:13, 17, 18, 19[3]

2 CHRONICLES
1:9, 10
2:8[2], 10, 14[2]
6:2, 9[2], 14, 15[2], 16[2], 17[2], 19[2], 20[2], 21[3], 23, 24[2], 25, 26, 27[4], 29, 30, 31, 32[4], 33[4], 34[2], 38, 39[2], 41[4], 42
7:12, 17, 18[2]
9:5, 6, 7[3], 8[3]
10:4[2], 7, 9, 10
14:11
16:3[2], 7
18:3, 12, 22, 29
20:7[2], 8, 9[2], 11, 37
21:12[2], 13[2], 14[4], 15[2]
25:18
34:16, 27, 28[2]

EZRA
4:11, 15
7:14, 18, 19, 20, 25[2], 26
9:10, 11, 14

NEHEMIAH
1:6[2], 7, 8, 10[4], 11[4]
2:2, 5[2], 6
9:5, 8, 14[2], 16, 17, 18, 19, 20[2], 25, 26[2], 27, 28, 29[3], 30[2], 31, 32, 34[3], 35
13:22

ESTHER
3:8
4:14[2]
5:3, 6[2]
7:2[2], 3
9:12[2]

JOB
1:11, 12, 18[2]
2:5
4:4, 6[4]
5:24[2], 25, 26, 27
8:2, 4, 5, 6, 7[2], 21[2]
10:5[2], 12, 17
11:3, 14, 15, 16, 18
13:21, 24
14:13
15:5, 10, 12, 13[2]
21:14
22:3, 5, 6, 23, 25, 26[2], 27[2], 28
30:21
33:5, 6, 8, 31, 33
34:33
35:4, 6, 8[2]
36:16, 19
37:17
38:3, 11, 12, 21, 34
39:9, 11, 12[2], 26, 27
40:7, 11
41:5
42:7

PSALMS
2:8
3:8[2]
4:6
5:5, 7[4], 8[2], 11
6:1, 4
8:1[2], 3[2], 6, 9
9:1, 2, 3, 10, 14[2], 19
10:5, 14
13:1, 5[2]
15:1[2]
16:11[2]
17:2, 4, 5, 7[2], 8, 13, 14[2], 15[2]
18:15[2], 35[3], 49
19:11, 13, 14
20:3[2], 4, 5[2]
21:1[2], 5, 6, 8, 12, 13
22:22
23:4[2]
24:6
25:4[2], 5, 6[2], 7[2], 11
26:3[2], 7, 8
27:8, 9[3], 11
28:2, 9
30:7[2], 9
31:1, 3, 7, 15, 16[3], 19, 20
32:4
33:22
34:13[2]
35:3, 24, 28[2]
36:5[2], 6[2], 7[2], 8[2], 9, 10[2]

PSALMS
37:5, 6[2]
38:1[2], 2
39:10, 12
40:5[2], 8[2], 10[5], 11[3], 16
41:12
42:3, 7[3], 10
43:3[4]
44:2, 3[2], 5, 8, 12[2], 17, 18, 22, 24, 26
45:2, 3[4], 4[2], 6[2], 7[2], 8, 9[2], 10, 11[2], 12, 16[2], 17
48:9[2], 10[3], 11
50:7, 8[2], 9[2], 14, 16, 19[2], 20
51:1[2], 4, 9, 11[2], 12[2], 13, 14, 15, 18
52:2, 5, 9[2]
54:1[2], 5, 6
55:22
56:8[2], 12
57:1, 5, 10[2], 11
59:11, 16[2]
60:3, 5[2]
61:4[2], 5, 8
63:2[2], 3, 4, 7, 8
65:4[3], 8, 11[2]
66:3[2], 4, 13
67:2[2]
68:7, 10[2], 23[2], 24, 28[2], 29, 35
69:7, 13[2], 16[2], 17[2], 24, 27, 29
70:4
71:2, 8[2], 15[2], 16, 17, 18[2], 19, 22, 24
72:1[2], 2[2]
73:15, 24, 28
74:1, 2, 3, 4, 7[2], 10, 11[3], 13, 18, 19[2], 21
75:1[2]
76:6, 7
77:11, 12[2], 13, 14, 15, 18, 19[3], 20
79:1, 2[2], 5, 6[2], 8, 9[2], 10, 11, 13[3]
80:2, 3, 4, 7, 15, 16, 17[2], 18, 19
81:10[2]
83:1, 3[2], 15[2], 16
84:1, 4, 10
85:1, 2, 3, 6, 7[2]
86:2, 4, 8, 9, 11[3], 12, 13, 16[2]
88:5, 7[2], 11[2], 12[2], 14, 15, 16[2]
89:1, 2, 4[2], 5[2], 8, 10, 12, 13[2], 14[2], 15, 16[2], 17, 19, 39, 46, 49[2], 50
90:4, 7, 8, 9, 11[2], 13, 14, 16[3]
91:4, 7[2], 9, 10, 11, 12
92:1, 2[2], 4[2], 5[2]
93:2, 5
94:5, 12, 18, 19
97:8
99:3
102:2, 10, 12, 14, 15, 24, 25, 27, 28
103:3, 4, 5[2]
104:7[2], 13, 24[2], 29, 30
106:4[2], 5[2], 7[2], 47[2]
108:4[2], 5, 6[2]
109:1, 21[2], 26, 27, 28
110:1, 2, 3[3], 5
115:1[3]
116:7, 16[2]
119:4, 5, 6, 7, 8, 9, 10, 11, 12, 13, 14, 15[2], 16[2], 17[2], 18, 19, 20, 21, 22, 23[2], 24, 25, 26, 27[2], 28, 29, 30, 31, 32, 33, 34, 35, 36, 37, 38[3], 39, 40[2], 41[3], 42, 43, 44, 45, 46, 47, 48[2], 49, 50, 51, 52, 53, 54, 55[2], 56, 57, 58[2], 59, 60, 61, 62, 63, 64[2], 65[2], 66, 67, 68, 69, 70, 71, 72, 73[2], 74, 75, 76[3], 77[2], 78, 79, 80, 81[2], 82, 83, 84, 85, 86, 87, 88[2], 89, 90, 91, 92, 93, 94, 95, 96, 97, 98, 99, 100, 101, 102, 103, 104, 105, 106, 107, 108, 109, 110, 111, 112, 113, 114, 116, 117, 118, 119, 120, 122, 123[2], 124[3], 125[2], 126, 127, 128, 129, 130, 131, 132, 133, 134, 135[3], 136, 137, 138, 139, 140[2], 141, 142[2], 143, 144, 145, 146, 147, 148, 149[2], 150, 151, 152, 153, 154, 155, 156[2], 157, 158, 159[2], 160[2], 161, 162, 163, 164, 165, 166[2], 167, 168[2], 169, 170, 171, 172[2], 173, 174[2], 175, 176[2]
121:3, 5[3], 7, 8[2]
122:2, 7[2], 9
128:3[3], 5, 6
132:8[2], 9[2], 10, 11[2], 12[2]
135:13[2]
137:9
138:2[6], 4, 7, 8
139:7[2], 10[2], 14, 16, 17, 20
140:13[2]

PSALMS
142:7
143:1[2], 2[2], 5[2], 7, 8, 10[2], 11[2], 12[2]
144:5
145:1, 2, 4[2], 5[2], 6[2], 7[2], 10[2], 11[2], 13[2]
146:10
147:12, 13[2], 14

PROVERBS
1:8[2], 9[2], 14, 15
2:3, 10
3:3, 6[2], 8[2], 9, 10[2], 22[2], 23[2], 24, 26[2], 28, 29
4:7, 10, 12, 13, 23, 26[2], 27
5:2, 8, 9, 10[2], 11[2], 16, 18[2]
6:1[2], 2[2], 3[2], 9, 11[2], 20[2], 21
7:3, 4, 15
9:11[2]
16:3[2]
19:18[2], 20
22:18, 19, 25, 27, 28
23:2, 8, 9, 16, 22[2], 25[2]
24:6, 10, 12, 13, 14[2], 27, 28[2], 34[2]
25:8, 9[2], 17[2]
27:10[3], 23[2], 26, 27[3]
29:17[2]
30:32
31:3[2], 8, 9

ECCLESIASTES
5:1, 2[2], 6[3]
7:9, 17, 21
9:7[4], 8[2], 9[4], 10[2]
10:4, 16[2], 17[2], 20[2]
11:1, 6, 9[3], 10[2]
12:1[2]

SONG OF SOLOMON
1:2, 3[2], 4, 7[2], 8[2], 10[2]
2:14[4]
4:1[2], 2, 3[4], 4, 5, 9, 10[2], 11[3], 13
5:9[2]
6:1[2], 5, 6, 7[2]
7:1[2], 2[2], 3, 4[2], 7[2], 8[2], 9
8:5, 13

ISAIAH
1:22[2], 23, 25[2], 26[2]
2:6
3:6, 12, 25[2]
4:1
6:7[2]
7:3, 11, 17[2]
8:8
10:22, 27[2], 30
14:3[2], 9, 11[2], 19, 20[2], 30[2]
16:3, [illegible]
17:10[2], 11[2]
19:12
20:2[3]
22:2, 3, 7, 18[2], 19[2], 21[3]
23:10
25:1[2], 12
26:8[2], 9, 11, 13, 16, 17, 19[2], 20[2]
29:4[3], 5
30:19, 20[2], 22[2], 23[2]
33:6, 23
36:8, 9, 11, 12
37:4[3], 10, 23, 24, 28[4], 29[4]
38:3, 5[4], 17, 18, 19
39:6, 7
40:9
41:10, 13[2], 14
43:1, 3[3], 4, 5, 23[2], 24[2], 25[2], 27[2]
44:3, 22[2], 24, 27, 28
45:3, 4, 9
47:2, 3[2], 6, 7, 9, 10[3], 12[2], 13, 15[2]
48:4[2], 17[2], 18[2], 19[2]
49:16, 17[2], 19[3], 22[2], 23[3], 25, 26[2]
51:13, 15, 16, 20[2], 22[2], 23[2]
52:1[2], 2, 7, 8
54:2[3], 3, 4[2], 5[2], 6, 8, 11[2], 12[3], 13[2], 15
55:5
57:6[2], 7, 8[2], 9[2], 10, 11, 12[2], 13
58:1, 7[2], 8[3], 10[3], 11[2], 13[2], 14
59:21[4]
60:1, 3[2], 4[3], 9[2], 10, 11, 14, 16[2], 17, 18[4], 19[3], 20[3], 21
62:2[3], 3, 4[3], 5[2], 6, 8[2], 11
63:2, 14, 15[6], 16, 17[3], 18[2], 19
64:1, 2[2], 3, 5, 7[2], 8, 9, 10, 12
66:9

JEREMIAH
1:9, 17
2:2, 16, 17, 19[2], 20[2], 23, 25[2], 28[4], 33[2], 34, 36, 37
3:2[2], 13[2]
4:7[2], 14, 18[3], 30[3]
5:7, 14, 17[7]
10:6, 17, 25[2]
11:13[2], 16, 20, 21

JEREMIAH

12:1, 6[2]
13:1, 4, 20, 22[2], 25[2], 26[3], 27[2]
14:7, 9, 19, 21[3]
15:11, 13[4], 15[2], 16[3], 17
17:3[4]
18:20, 23
20:3, 4, 6, 12
22:2[2], 7, 15, 17, 20[2], 21[3], 22[3], 23, 25, 26
27:2, 13
28:6
29:25
30:8[2], 10, 12[2], 13, 14[2], 15[2], 17
31:4, 7, 16[2], 17, 21
32:17, 21, 23[2]
34:5
37:18
38:16, 17, 20, 22[2], 23[2]
39:18[2]
40:2
42:2, 3, 5
45:5
46:12[2], 15, 27
47:6
48:7[2], 18[2], 32[3], 46[2]
49:4, 11[2], 16[2]
50:31
51:13, 36

LAMENTATIONS

1:10
2:13, 14[2], 19[2]
3:23, 55, 65
4:22
5:19

EZEKIEL

2:1, 8
3:3[2], 8[2], 9, 11, 19, 21, 26[2], 27
4:3, 4, 6, 7, 8, 9, 10, 15
5:1, 3, 11
6:2, 11
7:3, 4, 8, 9
9:8[2]
11:15[3]
12:3, 4, 6[2], 18[2]
13:4, 17[2]
16:3[4], 4[2], 5, 6[2], 7, 8[2], 9, 11[2], 12, 13, 14[2], 15[2], 16[2], 17, 18, 20[3], 22[3], 23, 25[4], 26[2], 27, 29, 33[3],

EZEKIEL

34, 36[6], 37[3], 39[3], 43[2], 45[2], 46[3], 47, 48[2], 49, 51[2], 52[4], 53, 55[2], 56[3], 57[2], 58, 60, 61[4], 63[2]
19:2, 10[2]
20:46[2]
21:2[2], 6, 12, 16, 30, 32
22:4[3], 12, 13[2], 15
23:21[3], 22[2], 25[5], 26[2], 27[2], 28, 29[4], 31, 32, 33, 35[3], 40
24:13[2], 14[2], 16, 17[3], 27
25:2, 4[2], 6
26:8, 9[2], 10[2], 11[3], 12[7], 13[2], 15, 18[2]
27:4[3], 5, 6, 7, 8[3], 9[2], 10[2], 11[4], 12[2], 13[2], 14, 15, 16[3], 17[2], 18[2], 19[2], 20, 21, 22[2], 23, 24[2], 25, 26, 27[10], 28, 33[3], 34[2]
28:4[2], 5[4], 7[2], 13[3], 15, 16, 17[3], 18[2], 21
29:2, 4[6], 5, 7, 10
31:2
32:2[2], 5[2], 6, 8, 9, 10, 12
33:2, 9, 12, 17, 30, 31, 32
35:2, 4, 8[3], 9, 11, 12
36:13, 14, 15
37:18
38:2, 4, 7, 9, 10, 13, 15
39:3[3], 4

DANIEL

1:12, 13
2:4, 28[3], 29[3], 30
3:12, 18
4:22[2], 25, 26, 27[2], 32
5:10[2], 11[4], 16, 17[2], 18, 23[5], 26, 28
6:16, 20
9:5[2], 6[2], 11[2], 13, 15, 16[5], 17[3], 18[2], 19[3], 23, 24[2]
10:12[3], 14
11:14
12:1[2], 9, 13[2]

HOSEA

2:6
4:4, 5, 6[2]
6:5
8:1, 5
9:1
10:13[2], 14[2]
12:6[2], 9

HOSEA

13:4, 10[3], 14[2]
14:1, 8

JOEL

2:17
3:11

AMOS

3:11[2]
4:12
5:23[2]
6:10
7:16, 17[4]
8:14
9:15

OBADIAH

4, 7[2], 9, 10[2], 12, 15

JONAH

1:6, 8
2:3[2], 4[2]

MICAH

1:11, 16[2]
4:9, 13
5:10[2], 11[2], 13[2], 14[2]
6:1, 8, 9, 13, 14
7:4[2], 5[2], 10, 11, 14[2], 15

NAHUM

1:13, 14[3], 15[2]
2:13, 13[3]
3:5[4], 9, 12, 13[3], 14, 16, 17[2], 18[3], 19[3]

HABAKKUK

1:13
2:10[2], 15, 16[2]
3:2[2], 8[2], 9[2], 11, 13

ZEPHANIAH

1:7
3:11[2], 15, 17

ZECHARIAH

3:8
9:9, 11[2], 13[2]
11:1[2]
14:1

MALACHI

1:6, 8[2]
2:14[3]

MATTHEW

1:20
4:6, 7, 10
5:23[2], 24[4], 29[3], 30[3], 36, 39, 40[2], 43
6:3[2], 4, 6[4], 9, 10[2], 17, 18[2], 22, 23
7:3, 4, 5, 22[3]
8:4, 13
9:2, 5, 6, 14, 18, 22
11:10[2], 26
12:2, 37[2], 47[2]
13:27
15:2, 4, 28
17:16
18:8[2], 15[2], 33
19:19[3]
20:14, 21[2]
21:5
22:37[4], 39, 44
23:37
24:3
25:21, 23, 25
26:18, 42, 52, 73

MARK

1:2[2], 25, 44[2]
2:5, 9[2], 11[2], 18
3:32[2]
5:9, 19, 23, 34[2], 35
6:18
7:5, 10[2], 29[2]
9:18, 38, 43, 45
10:19, 21, 37[3], 52[2]
12:30[6], 31, 36
14:70

LUKE

1:13[2], 31, 36, 38, 42, 44, 61
2:29[2], 30, 32, 35, 48
4:8, 11, 12, 23, 35
5:5, 14, 20, 23, 24
6:10, 29[2], 30, 41, 42[2]
7:27[2], 48, 50
8:20[2], 30, 48, 49
9:40, 41, 49
10:17, 21, 27[6]
11:23, 34[2], 36
12:20
13:26, 34
14:12[4]
15:19[2], 21[2], 27[2], 29, 30[2], 32
16:2, 6, 7, 25[2]

LUKE

17:3, 19[2]
18:20[2], 42[2]
19:5, 16, 18, 20, 39, 42[2], 44[2]
20:43
22:32[2]
23:42, 46

JOHN

4:16, 18, 42, 50[2], 51, 53
5:8, 10, 11, 12
7:3
8:13, 19
11:23
12:15, 28
13:37, 38
17:1[2], 6[2], 12, 14, 17[2], 26
18:11
19:26, 27
20:27[2]
21:18

THE ACTS

2:28, 35[2]
3:25
4:25, 27, 28[2], 29[2], 30
5:9
7:3[2], 32, 33[2]
8:20, 21, 22
9:13, 14, 15, 17, 34
10:4, 31
11:14
12:8[2]
14:10
16:31
18:9
22:13, 16, 18, 20
23:5
24:2, 4, 25
26:16

ROMANS

2:5, 17, 23, 25
3:4
4:18
8:36
9:7
10:8[2], 9
11:3
13:9
14:10[2], 15[3], 21
15:9

1 CORINTHIANS

7:16[2]
8:11
14:16
15:55[2]

GALATIANS

3:16
5:14

EPHESIANS

6:2

1 TIMOTHY

4:12, 15
5:23
6:20

2 TIMOTHY

1:4, 5[2]
4:5, 9, 21, 22

PHILEMON

2, 5, 6, 7, 13, 14[2], 21

HEBREWS

1:8[2], 9[2], 12, 13
2:7, 12
10:7, 9
11:18

JAMES

2:8, 18[2]

2 JOHN

4, 13

3 JOHN

2, 6

REVELATION

2:2[3], 4, 5, 9, 13, 19[3]
3:1, 2, 8, 9, 11, 15, 18
4:11
5:9
10:9[2]
11:17, 18[3]
14:15, 18
15:3[2], 4[2]
16:7
18:10, 14, 23[2]
19:10[2]
22:9[2]

TO *1519*

GENESIS

1:14, 15, 16[2], 17, 18[2], 29, 30[3]
2:5[2], 9[2], 10, 15[2], 19, 20[3], 21
3:6[3], 12, 16, 18, 21, 22, 23, 24
4:3, 4, 5, 8, 11, 14, 23[2], 26[3]
6:1[2], 4, 16, 17, 19, 20, 21, 22
7:2, 3, 4, 10
8:1, 6, 7, 8, 11, 13
9:8, 10, 11, 14, 15, 20
10:8, 19, 21
11:2, 3[2], 4, 5, 6[2], 7, 8, 31
12:5, 10, 11[3], 12, 14, 19[2]
13:3, 6, 9[3], 15[2]
14:1, 7, 10, 17, 21, 22, 23
15:3, 5, 6, 7[2], 15, 17
16:2, 3[2], 6, 7, 9, 16
17:1, 7[2], 8
18:2, 5, 7, 10, 11, 14, 16, 19, 21, 25[2], 27, 31
19:1[2], 5, 8, 9[2], 10[2], 11, 13, 17[2], 19, 20, 27, 29, 30, 31, 34
20:3[2], 6, 9, 13[2], 16
21:2, 3, 6, 17, 22, 23[2], 26
22:1, 5, 9, 10, 14, 19, 20, 23
23:2[2], 7[2], 8, 16
24:4, 5, 8, 9, 10, 11[2], 13, 14[2], 15[2], 16[2], 17, 20, 21, 22, 23, 25, 27, 30, 32, 33, 36, 37, 38, 41, 43[4], 44, 48, 49[2], 52[2], 53[3], 56, 63, 65
25:8, 11, 13, 16, 20[2], 22, 24, 30, 32[2], 33
26:4, 7[2], 8, 11, 23, 26, 27, 31, 32, 34, 35
27:1, 3, 4, 5[4], 8, 9, 10, 11, 12, 14, 20, 25[2], 29[2], 30, 37, 40, 42[2], 43[2], 45, 46
28:2[2], 4[2], 5, 6[2], 7, 9, 11, 12, 13[2], 14[4], 15, 20[2], 21
29:10, 13[3], 14, 19[2], 20, 23[2], 25[2], 26, 28, 29[2]
30:4, 9, 14, 15, 16, 18, 22, 24, 25[2], 32, 33, 34, 38[2], 41
31:3, 4, 7, 9, 10, 18[2], 19, 20, 24[2], 26[2], 28, 29[2], 31, 32, 35, 36, 51, 52, 54
32:3, 5, 6[3], 8, 9, 13, 30
33:3[2], 4, 8, 11, 14, 17, 18
34:1, 4, 6, 7, 8, 12, 14[2], 16, 17, 19, 21, 22[2], 25, 30[3]
35:1, 2, 3, 6, 12[2], 16[2], 17, 18, 19, 22, 26
36:4, 12[2], 14, 40, 43
37:7, 8, 9, 10[5], 12, 13, 14[2], 17, 18, 19, 22[2], 23, 25[3], 27, 28, 32, 35[2]
38:1[2], 8, 9[2], 11, 12, 13[2], 14[2], 15, 16, 20, 22, 23, 24, 25, 26, 27, 28, 29
39:1, 3, 5, 7, 8, 10[4], 11[2], 13, 14[2], 15, 17[2], 18, 19[2], 22, 23[2]
40:1, 5, 7, 8, 9[2], 20, 22
41:1, 8, 11, 12[4], 13[2], 15, 24, 25, 28, 32, 36, 43, 45, 52, 54, 55[2], 57[2]

GENESIS

42:3, 5, 6[2], 7, 9, 10, 12, 21, 24, 25[3], 27, 28, 30, 35, 37[2], 38
43:2, 6, 7, 15, 16, 19, 20, 21[2], 22, 23, 26[2], 30, 33[2]
44:2, 7, 11, 13, 14, 24, 29, 30, 31[2], 32, 33, 34
45:1, 4, 5, 7[2], 8, 9, 11, 21, 22[2], 23, 27
46:1, 3, 5, 18, 22, 28, 29[2], 32, 33
47:4, 6, 12, 21[2], 24
48:1, 4, 7, 11, 12, 17, 22
49:13[2], 15, 28, 29
50:2, 7, 10, 11, 14, 20[3], 24[3]

EXODUS

1:10, 11, 13, 15, 16, 21
2:1, 4[2], 5[2], 7[2], 8, 11, 13, 14, 15, 16, 18[2], 21, 23
3:1[3], 4, 6, 8[2], 13, 16, 18[2], 21
4:8[2], 9, 14, 16[2], 18[2], 20, 21, 23, 24[2], 25, 27[2]
5:2, 7, 8, 10, 12, 14, 16, 17, 21[3], 23[3]
6:1, 3, 4, 7[2], 8[4], 13, 16, 17, 19, 20, 23, 25[2], 26[2], 27[2], 28
7:1, 14, 15, 17, 18, 20, 23, 24
8:2, 5, 9, 10[2], 13, 18, 20, 22, 23, 25, 26[2], 27, 28, 29[3], 31
9:2, 5, 8, 16, 18[2]
10:3, 4[2], 5, 10, 26, 28
12:2, 3[2], 4[2], 13[2], 14, 16, 21, 23[2], 24[2], 25[2], 26, 29, 35, 37, 41[2], 42[2], 48, 49, 51
13:5, 6, 10, 11, 14, 15[2], 17[2], 21[3]
14:11[2], 12, 13[3], 20[2], 21, 23, 24, 27
15:17, 21, 23, 26[2], 27
16:3[3], 5, 8[2], 10, 13, 15[2], 16[2], 18, 21, 22, 23[3], 25[3], 27[2], 28, 32, 33, 34, 35
17:1[2], 3, 4, 9, 10[2], 11, 16
18:7, 8, 9, 12, 13[2], 14[2], 15, 18, 19, 21, 23[2], 24
19:2, 3, 10[2], 12[2], 13, 16, 17, 20, 21, 22, 23, 24
20:5, 8, 20
21:6, 7, 8[2], 12, 14, 15, 16, 17, 19, 29[3], 31, 36
22:5, 7, 8, 9, 10, 16, 17[2], 18, 19, 25[2], 26, 27, 29, 31
23:1, 2[3], 4, 5, 20[2], 24, 27
24:4, 12, 14
25:7, 9, 20, 25, 27, 29, 35
26:3[2], 7, 13, 28, 33
27:3, 5, 7, 20[2], 21
28:3, 8, 10, 11, 14, 21[2], 35, 36, 42, 43
29:1[2], 10, 29[2], 30, 33[2], 35[2], 36, 37[2], 38, 42, 44[2]
30:1, 4[2], 15, 16, 18, 20[3], 21[3], 31
31:4[2], 5[2], 10, 11, 14, 15[2], 16
32:1, 5[2], 6[3], 12[2], 13, 14, 19, 20, 27, 28, 29[2], 30

EXODUS

33:1[2], 5, 7, 8, 9, 11, 19, 22
34:2, 7, 12, 24, 29, 30, 34, 35
35:2[3], 9, 19[2], 21, 27, 29[2], 32[2], 33[2], 35
36:1[3], 2[2], 3, 5, 6, 7, 12, 18, 29[2], 33[2], 34
37:2, 3, 5, 9[2], 14, 15, 16, 21, 27[2], 29
38:5, 7, 18, 21[2], 26, 30
39:1, 3, 4, 5, 7, 14[3], 26, 30[2], 31, 32, 37, 41[2], 42
40:4, 5, 16, 17, 30, 35

LEVITICUS

1:4, 9, 14
2:2[3], 13
4:2, 3, 5, 16, 23, 27, 28, 35
5:4[2], 7, 10, 11, 12[2], 17
6:2, 4, 5, 25, 30
7:8, 35, 36, 38
8:5, 11, 12, 15, 31, 34[2]
9:1, 4[2], 16
10:7, 15, 17[2], 19
11:1, 7, 8, 21, 31, 37, 45, 47
12:2, 8
13:12, 15, 19, 59[2]
14:4[2], 7, 8, 11, 14, 17, 18, 19, 21[2], 22, 25, 28, 29[2], 31[2], 32[2], 34, 35, 36[2], 38, 41, 49, 57
15:1, 13, 14, 28, 29
16:10[3], 17, 27, 30, 32, 34
17:4, 5, 9, 11[2]
18:4, 6[3], 14, 17, 18[3], 19, 20, 21, 23[2]
19:4, 11, 20[2], 24, 29[3], 31
20:2[2], 3[2], 5, 6, 9, 10, 11, 12, 13, 15, 16, 22, 24, 27
21:4, 10, 11, 14, 17, 21[2], 24
22:2, 8, 16, 18, 21[2], 33
23:2, 11, 20, 22, 28, 37[2], 43
24:2[2], 16[2], 17, 19, 20, 21, 23
25:9, 15, 16, 23, 25, 26[2], 27, 28[2], 30, 38[2], 39, 46, 47, 50[2]
26:1, 5, 8, 21, 37, 44[2]
27:8, 14, 16, 17, 18, 19, 20, 24[2], 25, 27[2], 29

NUMBERS

1:3[2], 18, 20[3], 22[3], 24[3], 26[3], 28[3], 30[3], 32[3], 34[3], 36[3], 38[3], 40[3], 42[3], 45[2], 50, 51[2], 54
2:10, 18, 34[2]
3:3, 7, 8, 9, 10, 16, 20, 22, 34, 38, 46, 48[2], 51[2]
4:3, 7, 11, 14, 15[2], 16, 19[2], 20, 23[2], 24, 30, 31, 33, 37, 41, 45, 47, 49[3]
5:6, 8[2], 15, 19, 20, 21[2], 22[3], 24, 26, 27[2], 29
6:2[2], 4, 10[2], 21
7:1, 5[3], 7, 89
8:7, 12, 15, 19[4], 20, 21, 22, 24, 26
9:3[2], 5, 12, 13, 14[2], 20[2]

NUMBERS

10:3, 7, 8, 9, 10, 11, 13, 14, 18, 22, 28, 30[2], 31[2], 33, 35
11:4, 13, 14, 16, 18[2], 22[2], 23, 25
12:8[2]
13:16, 17, 21, 26[4], 30, 31, 32
14:3[2], 4, 7, 14[2], 16, 20, 22, 25, 28, 29, 30, 36[2], 38, 44
15:3, 12[3], 24, 28, 34, 35, 39, 41
16:5[3], 7, 9[5], 10, 12, 13, 16, 28, 31, 33, 40[3], 42
17:2[2], 5[2], 6, 8, 10
18:6[2], 7, 8, 11[2], 16[2], 19, 24[2], 28
20:5[3], 8, 12, 17[2], 21
21:3, 4, 5, 7, 8, 9, 15, 16, 18, 19[2], 20, 23[2], 29, 32, 33, 34
22:2, 5[2], 11, 13[2], 14, 16[2], 18, 20, 23, 26[3], 30, 32, 36, 37[3], 38, 40[2], 41
23:3[2], 11, 12, 14, 17, 20, 23
24:1[2], 2, 10, 11[2], 12, 13, 14, 25
25:1, 2
26:1, 2[2], 18, 22, 25, 27, 37, 43, 47, 50, 53, 54[4], 55, 56, 59
27:7, 8, 11, 14
28:2, 7, 22, 30
29:5, 9[2], 14, 15, 18, 21, 24, 27, 30, 33, 37, 40
30:2[2], 13, 14
31:4, 6[3], 13, 16, 21, 27, 28, 36, 50, 52
32:2, 6[2], 8, 14, 19, 20, 27, 29, 33[2], 39
33:2[2], 14, 53, 54[3], 55, 56[2]
34:4[5], 8, 9, 10, 11, 12, 13[2], 14[2], 18, 29
35:2, 3, 5, 6, 7, 8, 11, 16, 17, 18, 21, 24, 25, 30[3], 31, 32[2]
36:2[3], 3[2], 5, 6[2], 7[2], 9[2]

DEUTERONOMY

1:3, 5, 7[2], 8[2], 9, 14, 19, 27[2], 28, 30, 33[3], 35, 36[2], 38, 41[2], 45
2:4, 15, 16, 18, 22, 24, 25, 27, 31[2], 32, 34
3:1[2], 3, 7, 12, 18, 24[3], 28
4:1, 5, 9, 10, 13, 14[2], 19, 20, 25[2], 26[2], 30, 34[2], 36, 38[3]
5:4, 5, 12, 15, 23, 30, 31, 32[3]
6:1[2], 2, 3, 10[4], 19, 20, 23, 24[2], 25
7:1, 6, 9, 10[4], 11, 12[2], 13, 24, 25
8:1, 2[3], 3, 6[2], 16, 18
9:1[4], 4, 5, 6, 7, 8[2], 9, 10, 11, 18[2], 19, 20, 22, 23, 27, 28[2]
10:4, 6, 7, 8[4], 10, 11, 12[4], 13, 15, 20
11:4[2], 8, 9[2], 10, 11, 13[3], 16, 21, 22[4], 25, 28, 29[2], 31[2], 32
12:1[2], 5, 9[2], 10, 11[2], 13[2], 15, 19, 20, 21, 29, 30, 31[2], 32
13:2, 3, 5[4], 9[2], 10, 12, 17, 18[3]
14:2, 23[2], 24[2]
15:4, 5[2], 11[2], 15, 18
16:2, 6, 8, 9[3], 11, 17

DEUTERONOMY

17:6[2], 7[2], 10[3], 11[4], 12, 16[4], 17[2], 19[3], 20[3]
18:5[2], 8, 9, 10, 14, 16, 19, 20[2], 22
19:2, 3, 5[2], 8, 9[3], 14, 16, 19
20:1, 4[2], 5, 9, 10, 18, 19[2]
21:1, 5[2], 10, 11, 12, 16, 22[2]
22:2, 4, 6, 7, 14, 16, 21[2], 22, 27
23:2, 3, 4, 14[2], 19, 20[2], 21, 22
24:1, 3, 4[2], 5, 6[2], 8[2], 10, 11, 16[3], 17, 18, 19, 22
25:2[4], 5[2], 7[3], 8[2], 11, 19
26:2, 3, 5, 13[3], 14[2], 16, 17[4], 18, 19
27:12, 13, 18, 25, 26
28:1[3], 7, 11, 12[2], 13[2], 14[4], 15[3], 20, 21, 25, 31[2], 44[2], 45, 50, 55, 56, 58, 63[7]
29:1, 4[3], 8[2], 13[4], 18, 19[3], 21, 22, 27, 29
30:1[2], 2, 6, 10, 12, 16[4], 18[2], 19, 20[4]
31:4[2], 7[2], 11, 12, 13[2], 16, 21, 24, 28, 29[2]
32:8[2], 13, 16[2], 17[3], 21[4], 26, 30, 35, 40, 41, 43[2], 45, 46[2], 47
33:7, 9, 17, 24
34:1, 4, 5, 10, 11[4]

JOSHUA

1:1, 2[2], 5, 6, 7[4], 8[2], 11[3], 12[3], 18
2:1, 2[2], 3[2], 5, 6, 7, 16, 20, 23
3:1, 2, 5, 7, 8, 13, 14[2]
4:1, 6, 8, 10[2], 11, 13, 18, 21, 23
5:1, 8, 13, 14
6:5, 8, 15, 16, 17, 20, 25
7:2, 3[2], 6, 7[3], 13, 14[2], 19
8:1, 2, 3, 5, 8, 9, 10, 12, 14[2], 16, 20[3], 23, 24, 34
9:1, 2, 3, 6[2], 10[3], 11[2], 12, 15, 16, 20, 24, 25, 26
10:1[3], 6[3], 10[2], 11[2], 12, 13, 15, 18, 19, 20, 21[2], 24, 25, 27, 28, 32[2], 33, 35[2], 37[2], 38, 39[5], 43
11:1[4], 2, 3[3], 5, 6, 11, 14, 17, 20, 23[2]
12:3[2], 7[2]
13:1, 3, 4, 15, 31
14:1, 4, 7, 11[2], 12
15:1, 3[6], 6[2], 7, 8, 9[2], 10[2], 11[2], 12[2], 13[2], 15, 16[2], 17, 18[2], 20
16:1, 2[2], 3[2], 5, 6[2], 7[3]
17:1, 4[2], 5, 7, 8, 13[2], 14, 15, 17[2]
18:3[2], 4[2], 6, 8[2], 9[2], 10, 11, 12, 13[2], 15, 16[4], 17[2], 19, 20, 21, 28
19:1[2], 8[2], 10, 11[2], 12[2], 13[4], 14, 16, 17[2], 22, 23, 24, 26[2], 27[4], 29[4], 31, 32[2], 33, 34[5], 39, 40, 47, 48, 49, 50
20:2
21:2[2], 12, 13[2], 21, 27, 32, 33, 38, 43, 44, 45

JOSHUA

22:5[6], 7, 9[3], 10[2], 12[2], 13[2], 15[2], 16, 18[2], 23[3], 24[2], 26, 27[2], 28[3], 29, 31[2], 32, 33[2]
23:1, 4, 6[4], 7, 9, 12, 14, 15, 16
24:1, 4, 5, 9, 15, 16, 22, 29, 33

JUDGES

1:1[2], 7, 9, 12[2], 13, 14[3], 23, 28[2], 34[2], 36
2:1[2], 4, 6, 12, 19[3], 22
3:1, 2, 4[2], 6[2], 9, 10, 18, 27, 28
4:5, 7, 9, 10, 12, 17, 18[2], 19, 22
5:3, 11, 16, 23[2], 26[2], 29, 30[2]
6:5, 7, 11, 22, 25, 29, 31, 35
7:2, 3, 5, 6[2], 9, 10[2], 11, 17, 20, 22[2], 25
8:1, 3, 4, 8, 27, 33, 35[2]
9:1, 3, 7, 8, 9, 10, 11, 13, 16, 21, 24, 26, 29[2], 31, 33, 36, 42, 48, 49, 50, 51[2], 52, 53
10:1, 9, 12, 18[2]
11:3, 4, 5, 8, 9, 10, 12[2], 16, 20, 24, 27, 31, 32, 33, 34[2], 35, 36[2], 39[2], 40
12:1[2], 3, 6
13:5, 7[2], 9, 11, 12, 17, 20[2], 21[2], 23, 25
14:1, 2, 3, 5[2], 8[2], 9, 10, 11[2], 15[2], 17[2], 19[2], 20
15:1[3], 2, 4, 6, 10[4], 11[2], 12, 17
16:1, 3, 4, 5, 6[2], 8, 16, 19[2], 21, 22, 23[2], 25
17:3[2], 4, 8[3], 9, 11, 13
18:1, 2[4], 7[2], 8, 9[3], 10, 14[2], 15, 17, 19[2], 22, 30
19:1[2], 2, 3[3], 5[2], 7, 8, 9[3], 12, 13[2], 14, 15[3], 18[3], 22, 25[2], 27
20:1, 3, 4[2], 5, 8, 9, 10[3], 13[2], 14[2], 18[2], 20[2], 21, 23, 25, 28[2], 31[3], 36, 39, 40[2], 47, 48[2]
21:1, 2, 3[2], 4, 5[3], 7, 8[4], 12, 13[3], 18, 19, 21[2], 22[2], 23, 24[3]

RUTH

1:1[2], 7, 8, 12[2], 16[2], 17, 18, 19[3], 22
2:2, 3, 8, 10, 12, 15, 18, 19[2], 20[2], 23
3:2, 3, 6, 7, 8, 11, 13[2], 16[2], 17
4:1, 4[2], 5, 6, 7[2], 10[2], 15, 17

1 SAMUEL

1:3[2], 4[2], 6, 7, 8[2], 12, 19[2], 20, 21, 25, 28[2]
2:6, 8[2], 10, 11[2], 15[2], 16, 19[3], 20, 24, 28[4], 29, 33[2], 35, 36[2]
3:2[2], 3, 6, 8, 11, 15, 17, 19, 20[2], 21
4:1[2], 3, 4, 9, 12, 16, 18, 19
5:3, 4[2], 10[5], 11, 12
6:2[2], 3, 4[2], 7, 9[2], 10, 12[3], 13, 16, 18[2], 20[2], 21[2]
7:1, 2, 5, 6, 7, 8[2], 10, 14, 16[2], 17

1 SAMUEL

8:1, 4, 5, 6, 8, 11, 12^3, 13^3, 14, 15^2, 16, 19, 22
9:3, 5^2, 6, 7^3, 8^2, 9^2, 10, 11^2, 12^3, 13^2, 14^2, 16^2, 17, 18, 19^2, 21, 26^2, 27^2
10:1, 2^2, 3^3, 5^3, 8^4, 9^2, 10, 11^2, 13, 14^3, 17, 20, 21, 24, 25, 26
11:3^2, 4, 9^2, 10, 11, 12, 13^2, 14^2, 15
12:3, 7^2, 17, 19, 22, 23
13:2, 4, 5, 7, 8^2, 9, 10^2, 12, 13, 14, 17, 18^3, 20^2, 21, 22, 23
14:1^2, 4, 6^3, 7, 9, 12, 19, 20, 21, 25, 26, 27, 30, 31, 43, 45, 46
15:1^2, 2, 5, 6, 7, 11, 12^3, 13, 15, 16, 21, 22^2, 27, 28, 32, 34^3, 35
16:1, 2^2, 3, 4, 5^3, 6, 9, 10, 12^2, 13, 16^2, 17, 21, 22, 23
17:1^2, 8^3, 9^2, 13^2, 15, 17^2, 20^2, 23, 25, 26^2, 27, 32, 33^3, 39, 40, 43, 44^3, 45^3, 46, 48^3, 49, 52^3, 54, 58
18:1, 2, 4^4, 6^2, 8, 10, 11, 17^2, 18, 19^3, 21^2, 23^2, 25^3, 26, 27^2, 30
19:1^2, 2^2, 4, 5, 7, 10^2, 11^4, 14, 15^2, 18^3, 20, 22^2, 23^2
20:5^2, 6, 8, 9, 10, 12, 13^2, 17, 18^2, 19, 21, 24, 27^3, 28^2, 29, 30, 33^2, 35, 37, 38, 40, 41, 42
21:1^2, 2, 6, 7, 10, 11, 14, 15
22:1^2, 3, 8, 9^2, 11^2, 13, 15^2, 17^2, 18
23:3, 4, 5, 6^3, 7, 8^4, 9, 10^3, 13, 15, 16, 18, 19^2, 20^3, 23^2, 24, 25, 26^2
24:1, 2, 3^2, 4, 5, 6, 7, 8, 9, 10, 11, 16, 17
25:1, 5^2, 6^3, 8^2, 9^2, 14, 17, 22, 23, 26^2, 29^2, 30^3, 32^2, 33, 34, 35^2, 36, 37, 38, 39^3, 40^5, 41^2, 44
26:1, 2^2, 5, 6^5, 7, 8^2, 9, 10, 13, 14^3, 15^3, 16, 20^2, 23^2, 25^2
27:1, 4, 8, 9, 10, 11^2, 12
28:1^3, 2^2, 7^2, 8, 9^2, 10^2, 12, 14, 15^2, 17^3, 19
29:1, 4^3, 5, 9^2, 11^3
30:1^2, 3, 4, 7^2, 9, 11, 12, 13^2, 14, 15^3, 19^2, 21^5, 22, 24, 26^2, 27^3, 28^3, 29^3, 30^3, 31^3
31:8^2, 9, 10, 11, 12

2 SAMUEL

1:1, 2^3, 14^2, 26
2:1, 8, 10, 12, 14, 15, 19^2, 21^3, 22^3, 23^3, 24, 26, 29, 32
3:5, 6, 7, 8^3, 9^3, 10^3, 12^2, 13, 14^2, 16, 17, 19^3, 20^2, 23, 24, 25^3, 27^2, 31^2, 35^3, 37, 39
4:2, 3, 4^2, 5, 8^2, 10
5:1, 2, 3^2, 4, 6, 8, 11, 13, 17^2, 19, 20, 24, 25
6:2, 6^2, 8, 9, 19^3, 20^3, 21
7:1, 3, 4, 5, 6, 7, 8, 11^2, 17^2, 19, 21^2, 22, 23^5, 24^2, 27^2, 29
8:1, 2^4, 3, 5, 6, 7, 10^2
9:9^3, 10, 11
10:1, 2, 3^3, 4, 5, 14, 16, 17, 19^2
11:1^2, 2^2, 6^2, 8^2, 9, 11^3, 12^3, 13^2, 14^2, 16, 27
12:4^3, 5, 7, 9^2, 10, 14^2, 17^2, 18^2, 20, 22, 23^2, 27, 29
13:1, 2^2, 4, 5, 6, 7^2, 8, 9, 10, 11, 12, 13, 23, 24, 25, 30^2, 33^2, 3[illegible], 37, [illegible], [illegible]
14:2^2, 3, 4^2, 6, 7, 8, 10, 11^2, 15, 16, 17, 19^2, 20^3, 22, 23^2, 24^2, 25^2, 29^3, 31, 32^3, 33^3
15:1^2, 2, 3, 5^2, 6^2, 7, 8, 9, 13, 14, 15, 16, 19^2, 22, 26, 28, 29, 32^3, 34, 35
16:2^2, 4, 5, 10, 11^2, 15, 16, 17^2, 20, 21
17:6, 9, 11^2, 13, 14^2, 15, 17, 18, 20^3, 21, 23^2, 24, 25^2, 27^2, 29
18:11, 17, 18, 21, 22, 24, 28, 32, 33
19:5, 8, 11^6, 12, 13^2, 15^5, 16, 18^2, 19, 20^2, 21, 22^2, 24, 25^3, 26, 28, 31, 34, 37, 38, 40, 41, 42
20:1^2, 2, 3^2, 4, 5, 6, 7, 9^2, 10^2, 13, 14, 15, 18, 19, 21, 22^3
21:2^2, 9, 10, 16, 17, 18, 20, 22
22:4, 7, 21^2, 25^2, 31, 35, 40, 42, 44, 51^2
23:3, 5, 9, 10, 13, 16, 21, 23, 37
24:1, 2^2, 4, 6^4, 7^4, 8, 13^2, 15^2, 16^2, 18, 19, 21^3

1 KINGS

1:3, 4, 5, 8, 21, 23, 31^2, 33^2, 35, 38^2, 43, 44, 47, 48, 51, 52, 53^2
2:3^2, 4^2, 5^2, 6^2, 7, 8^4, 9^2, 13, 14, 17, 19^3, 21^2, 23, 24, 26^2, 28, 30, 32, 39, 40^3, 41, 42, 44^3
3:4^2, 5, 6, 7, 9^2, 11, 12, 14, 15^2, 18, 21, 25^2, 28
4:10, 11, 12^2, 13^2, 15, 24, 25, 28, 34
5:2, 5, 6^2, 7, 8^2, 9, 10, 11^2, 14, 17, 18
6:1^2, 3, 11, 12, 19, 38
7:7, 8, 9, 14^2, 16, 18, 23, 32, 34, 36, 41, 42, 45, 50
8:6, 10, 11, 13^2, 16^2, 17, 18, 25^2, 28^4, 30, 31^2, 32^3, 33, 36, 39^2, 43^3, 44, 46, 52, 53, 54, 56, 58^2, 61^2, 64
9:1^2, 2, 3, 4^2, 5, 8, 10, 11, 12, 14, 15, 19, 21, 28^2
10:1, 2^2, 6, 9^2, 10, 13, 14, 16, 17, 24^2, 27^2

1 KINGS

11:2, 4, 11, 13, 15^2, 17, 18^2, 19, 21^2, 22^2, 24, 25, 29, 31^2, 33^2, 36, 37, 38, 40
12:1^3, 2, 5, 7, 9, 11, 12^2, 14^2, 16^2, 18^4, 20, 21^4, 23, 24^4, 26, 27^2, 28^2, 30
13:1, 4^2, 5, 10, 11, 17^2, 20, 22, 23^2, 26, 27, 29^3, 31^2, 32, 34^2
14:2^3, 3, 4^2, 5^2, 6^2, 8, 9^2, 12, 13, 15^2, 16, 17^2, 18, 21^2, 22, 24, 25
15:4^2, 17^2, 18, 21, 25, 26, 27^2, 29^2, 30, 33, 34
16:1, 2^3, 7, 8, 11^2, 12, 13^2, 15, 18, 19^2, 21, 23, 26^3, 29, 31^3, 33^2, 34
17:1, 4, 7, 9^3, 10^3, 11^2, 15, 16, 17, 18^4, 24
18:1^2, 2, 5, 6, 9, 10, 12, 15, 16^2, 17, 19, 27, 29^2, 31, 36, 40, 42^3, 43, 44, 45^2, 46
19:2^2, 3^2, 9, 10, 14, 15^2, 16^2, 17, 20
20:2, 4, 6, 9, 12, 22, 26^3, 30, 31, 32, 33^2, 35, 42, 43^2
21:1, 2, 3, 4, 5, 8, 10, 14, 15^3, 16^4, 17, 18^2, 20^2, 22^2, 25, 26, 27, 28
22:2^2, 4^3, 5, 6, 12, 13, 15^2, 17, 24, 25, 26, 29, 32^2, 33, 36^2, 37, 41, 42, 48^2, 51, 52, 53^2

2 KINGS

1:3^3, 6^2, 7, 9, 10, 16^2, 17
2:1, 2^2, 3^2, 4^2, 5^2, 6, 7, 9, 11, 15^3, 18, 20, 22, 25^2
3:1, 3, 5, 7^2, 10, 12, 13^4, 15, 20, 21^2, 23, 24, 26, 27
4:1^2, 5, 6, 8^3, 10, 12, 13^3, 14, 16, 17, 18^2, 19^2, 20, 22, 23^2, 24, 25^3, 26, 27^3, 29, 31, 35, 37, 38, 39, 40^2, 44
5:5, 6^2, 7^4, 8^2, 10, 11, 13, 14, 15, 16, 17, 18, 21, 22, 24, 26^3
6:4, 7, 10, 18^2, 19^2, 20, 22, 23, 24, 28^2, 30, 31, 32^3
7:1, 3, 5^2, 6^3, 8, 9, 10, 11, 12^2, 16, 17^2, 18^3
8:1, 3^2, 5^5, 7, 9^2, 14^3, 15, 16, 17, 19^2, 21, 25, 26, 28, 29^2
9:1, 2, 4, 5^2, 10, 11^2, 12, 15^3, 16^2, 17, 18^3, 19^2, 22, 23, 25, 26, 27^2, 28, 29, 30, 32^2, 35
10:1^3, 2, 5, 6^4, 7^3, 9^2, 12, 13, 15^3, 17^3, 19^3, 21, 24, 25^4, 29^2, 30, 31^2, 32
11:4, 9^3, 10, 11, 13, 19, 21
12:1, 4^2, 5, 8^2, 11, 12^4, 14, 15, 17^2, 18, 20
13:1, 2, 7, 10, 16, 21
14:2, 3, 5, 6^3, 8, 9^4, 10, 11, 12^2, 13, 14, 19^2, 22, 23, 24, 25, 28
15:1, 2, 3, 9, 12, 13, 14, 16, 17, 18, 19, 20^2, 23, 24, 27, 28, 29, 32, 33, 34, 37
16:1, 2, 3^2, 5^2, 6^2, 7, 8, 9, 10^4, 11, 12, 15, 16
17:1, 4^2, 5, 9, 11^2, 13^2, 14, 17^4, 23, 26, 31, 35^2, 36, 37
18:1^2, 2, 3, 4, 6, 8, 9, 14^2, 16, 17^2, 18^2, 19, 22, 23^2, 25^2, 26, 27^4, 29, 31^2, 32, 37
19:1, 2, 3^2, 4, 5, 6, 7^2, 9, 10, 11, 16, 20^2, 21, 23^2, 25^2, 34, 35, 37
20:1, 2, 4^2, 10
21:1, 6^2, 7^2, 8^3, 9, 11, 14, 15, 16^2, 19
22:1, 2^2, 3^2, 4, 5^2, 6^2, 8, 9, 11, 13, 15, 17, 18^3
23:3^4, 4, 5^5, 6, 8, 9, 10^2, 11, 15^2, 16, 19^4, 20, 23, 25^2, 29, 30, 31, 32, 33, 34^2, 35^5, 36, 37
24:2^2, 3^2, 7, 8, 9, 12, 15^2, 16, 17, 18, 19, 20
25:1, 6^2, 7, 11, 12, 13, 20^2, 23^2, 24^3, 25, 26, 27^2, 28

1 CHRONICLES

1:10
2:21, 23, 35^2
4:27, 39^2, 42
5:1, 18^3, 20, 26
6:19, 32, 49^2, 56, 57, 62, 64
7:2, 11, 15, 21, 22, 23, 40^2
8:6
9:1, 9, 22, 25^2, 27, 29, 32
10:4, 8^2, 9^2, 11, 12, 13
11:1, 3^3, 4, 5, 10^2, 13, 15^2, 18^2, 21, 23, 25, 31
12:1^2, 8, 15, 16, 17^4, 18, 19^4, 20^2, 22^2, 23^6, 24, 31, 32^2, 33, 36, 38^3
13:2, 3, 5, 6^4, 9, 10, 11, 12, 13^2
14:1^2, 8, 11, 15^2, 16
15:2^3, 3^2, 14, 15, 16^3, 19, 21, 25, 26, 29^2
16:3^2, 4^3, 5, 7, 15, 17^2, 20^2, 21, 23, 25^2, 33, 35, 37, 38, 40^3, 41^2, 43^2
17:1^2, 3^2, 4, 5^2, 6^2, 10, 11^2, 15^2, 17^2, 18, 19, 20, 21^3, 24, 25, 27
18:1, 3, 5, 7, 10^3
19:1, 2^4, 3^4, 5, 6^2, 7, 15, 16, 19
20:1^2, 2, 3, 4
21:1, 2^4, 3, 4, 6, 11, 12^2, 15^2, 17, 18^2, 21^3, 22, 23, 24, 25, 30
22:2^3, 4, 5, 6, 7^2, 8, 9, 13, 17, 19^4
23:4, 5, 11, 13^3, 28, 30^2, 31^2
24:3, 4, 7^2, 8^2, 9^2, 10^2, 11^2, 12^2, 13^2, 14^2, 15^2, 16^2, 17^2, 18^2, 19^2

1 CHRONICLES

25:1^2, 2, 3^2, 5^2, 6^2, 9^2, 10, 11, 12, 13, 14, 15, 16, 17, 18, 19, 20, 21, 22, 23, 24, 25, 26, 27, 28, 29, 30, 31
26:12, 13, 14, 15^2, 16, 27, 31, 32
27:1, 23, 24
28:1, 2, 4^3, 5, 6, 7, 10, 11, 15, 20
29:2^2, 3^2, 4, 5^2, 8, 9, 12^2, 14, 16, 17, 19^3, 20, 22^2

2 CHRONICLES

1:2^3, 3, 4, 6, 8, 11, 13^2
2:1, 2^3, 3^3, 4^5, 6^2, 7^2, 8, 9^2, 10, 11, 12, 14^4, 16^3, 18^3
3:1, 2, 4, 8^2, 11^2, 12^2
4:2, 6^2, 7, 11, 12^2, 13, 16
5:2, 7, 11, 13^3, 14
6:4, 5^2, 6, 7, 8^2, 16^3, 19^3, 20, 22, 23, 24, 25^2, 31, 33^2, 34, 38
7:3, 6, 7, 10^2, 11, 12^2, 13, 17, 18, 20, 21
8:1, 2^2, 3, 6, 8, 13, 14^4, 17^2, 18^2
9:1^2, 5, 8^4, 11^2, 12^2, 13, 14, 15, 16, 18^2, 21, 23, 26
10:1^3, 2, 3, 6^2, 7^2, 9^2, 11, 12^2, 15, 16^3, 18^4
11:1^3, 2, 3, 4, 13, 14, 16^3, 18, 22^2
12:1, 2, 4^2, 5^3, 7, 10, 13^2, 14
13:1, 5^4, 8, 9, 11, 12, 13, 15
14:4^2, 11, 15
15:2, 5^2, 9, 12, 13
16:1^2, 2, 5, 7, 9^2, 12^2
17:4, 5, 7^7, 14, 15
18:2^4, 3, 4, 5^2, 11, 12^3, 14^3, 15^2, 16, 17, 23, 24, 25^2, 28, 29^2, 31^3, 32, 33
19:1^2, 2^2, 3, 4, 6, 8, 10
20:1^2, 3, 4^2, 6, 7, 11^3, 12, 16, 17^2, 18, 19, 21, 22^2, 23^2, 24, 25, 27^3, 28, 31, 36^3, 37^2
21:3, 4, 5, 6, 7^3, 11, 12, 13^2, 19, 20
22:1, 2, 3, 4, 5, 6^2, 7^2, 8^2, 9^2
23:2, 7, 8^3, 9, 10, 12, 13, 15, 17, 18
24:1, 4^2, 5^3, 6^2, 9^2, 11^2, 12^3, 14^2, 17, 19^2, 22, 23^2
25:1, 3^2, 5^3, 7^2, 8^2, 9^3, 10^3, 11, 13, 14^2, 16^2, 17, 18^4, 19^2, 21, 22^2, 23^2, 24, 27^2
26:2, 3, 4, 5, 8^2, 11^2, 13, 14, 15^2, 16^2, 18^3, 19, 20, 23
27:1, 2, 8
28:1, 5, 7, 8, 9, 10, 13^3, 15^5, 16, 23, 25^2
29:1, 2, 8^3, 10, 11^2, 15^2, 16^2, 17^2, 18, 20, 21, 24, 25, 27, 30, 32, 34
30:1^4, 2, 3, 5^3, 6^2, 7, 10^2, 11, 12^2, 13, 16, 17, 19^2, 20, 22, 23, 24^2, 27
31:1^2, 2^4, 3, 4, 7, 10^2, 11, 14, 15^4, 16, 17, 18, 19^3, 21
32:1, 2, 3, 5, 6^2, 8^2, 9, 11^2, 13, 14, 15, 17^2, 18^2, 20, 21, 23^2, 24, 25, 30, 31^2
33:1, 6^3, 7^2, 8^2, 9^2, 10^2, 11, 13, 14, 16, 18, 21
34:1, 2^2, 3^2, 7, 8, 9^2, 10^2, 11^3, 12, 15^2, 16^2, 17, 19, 21, 22^3, 23, 25, 26, 28^2, 31^3, 32^3, 33^3
35:2, 4^2, 5, 6, 7^2, 8^2, 10, 12^2, 13, 15, 16^3, 18, 20, 21^3, 22, 23, 24, 25, 26
36:2, 4^2, 5, 6^2, 7, 9, 10, 11, 15, 18, 20^2, 21^2, 23

EZRA

1:2, 3, 5^2
2:68^2
3:1, 2, 4, 6, 7^5, 8, 9, 10
4:2^2, 3^2, 5, 8, 12, 14, 17^2, 21^2, 22^2, 23^2
5:2, 3^3, 5^2, 8, 9^2, 10, 13, 17^3
6:5, 8, 9, 12^4, 13, 14^2, 17, 21, 22
7:6, 8, 9^3, 10^3, 11, 13^2, 14^2, 15, 18^3, 20, 21, 22^3, 24, 26^3, 27, 28
8:15^2, 17, 21, 22^2, 30^2, 31, 32, 36
9:1^2, 6^2, 7^4, 8^3, 9^4, 11^2, 12
10:3^3, 5^2, 8, 10, 13, 16

NEHEMIAH

1:1, 4, 9, 11^3
2:1, 4, 6, 7, 8^3, 9, 10, 11, 12, 13, 14^3, 16^5, 19
3:2, 5, 16, 19^2, 21, 31
4:1, 5, 6, 7^2, 8^3, 10, 11, 12, 14^2, 15^3, 16, 19^2, 22
5:5^2, 8, 9, 11, 12, 13, 14, 19
6:1, 2, 3, 6^2, 7^3, 10^2, 11, 14, 16, 19^2
7:1, 3, 5, 6^2, 63, 70, 71
8:1^2, 6, 7, 8, 12^4, 13, 15
9:8^3, 12, 15^2, 16, 17^5, 19^2, 20, 23^2, 26^2, 27, 28, 36
10:29^3, 31, 32, 33, 34^2, 35, 36^2, 37, 38
11:1^3, 2, 3, 17
12:22, 24^3, 27^3, 44, 45
13:3, 5^2, 7, 10, 13^2, 19^2, 22^2, 24, 26, 27^2, 28

ESTHER

1:1, 6, 7, 8^3, 9, 11^3, 12, 13, 15, 16^3, 17, 20^2, 21, 22^3
2:3, 8^3, 9^2, 11, 12^4, 13, 14, 15, 18^2, 21, 22
3:4^2, 6^2, 7^3, 8, 9^2, 11^3, 12^5, 13^5, 14, 15

ESTHER

4:4^2, 5^3, 6, 7^3, 8^6, 11^4, 12, 13, 14^2, 16, 17
5:1, 2, 3, 5^2, 6, 8^4, 12, 14^2
6:1, 2, 3, 4^2, 6^4, 7, 8, 9^4, 10^2, 11, 12^2, 13, 14
7:1, 2, 4^3, 5, 7^2
8:3, 5^2, 6^2, 7, 9^6, 11^7, 13^2
9:1^3, 2, 13^3, 14, 19, 21, 22^3, 23, 24^3, 27^2, 29, 30, 31
10:3

JOB

1:4^2, 5, 6, 7, 11, 15, 16, 17, 19
2:1^2, 2, 3, 5, 8, 11^3
3:8, 20, 23
4:2, 12, 14, 20
5:1, 4, 11^2, 26
6:7, 9, 14, 18, 24, 26
7:1, 3^2, 4, 9, 10, 20
8:5, 8, 22
9:14, 15, 18, 19, 26
10:19, 21
11:6
12:3, 4, 5, 8, 22, 24, 25
13:3^2, 6, 12, 23, 25, 26
14:15, 18, 21
15:8, 20, 24, 28
16:8, 11, 12
17:5, 14^2, 16
18:11, 14
19:3, 17, 20^2
20:2, 3, 6, 10, 18, 23
21:4, 13, 30^2, 31, 32
22:3^2, 7^2, 14, 19, 23
23:2, 3
24:5, 7, 10, 12, 17, 21, 23
25:5
26:4, 10
28:3, 11, 24, 25, 28
29:7, 10, 11, 12, 13^2, 15^2, 16
30:1, 6, 10, 21, 22^2, 23^2, 24, 29^2, 31
31:3^2, 5, 7, 11, 12, 16, 23, 24, 28, 30^2, 32, 36, 39
32:1, 10, 11^2, 19, 22
33:1, 6, 22, 23, 24, 25, 30^2, 32^2
34:4, 11^2, 16, 18^3, 19, 28, 31, 33
35:2, 9
36:2, 3, 6, 10, 27, 32
37:6^3, 13, 15
38:12, 14, 20^2, 26^2, 27^3, 34, 36, 40
39:9, 11, 17, 21
40:19
41:10, 13, 16, 17, 31, 32^2
42:7, 8

PSALMS

4:t
5:t, 1
6:t, 6
7:2, 6, 8^2, 9, 17^2
8:t, 6
9:t, 2, 6, 8, 11, 20
10:9, 14, 17, 18
11:t, 1^2
12:t
13:t
14:t, 2
15:3, 4, 5
16:2, 3^2, 10
17:11, 14
18:t, 3, 20^2, 24^2, 30, 34, 38, 41, 50^4
19:t, 4, 5, 10
20:t, 4
21:t, 11
22:t, 7, 11, 15, 19, 29, 30
23:2
25:7
27:2, 4^2, 13
28:1^2, 3, 4^3
29:6, 9
30:1, 3, 7, 8, 9, 12^2
31:t, 2^2, 11, 13, 16, 18
32:10
33:10, 11, 19^2
34:9, 16
35:4^2, 11, 12, 23, 24, 26
36:t, 2, 3^2, 10, 12
37:5, 7, 8, 14^2, 32, 34
38:t^2, 17, 22
39:t^2, 1, 4, 11
40:t, 4, 5, 8, 12, 13^2, 14^2
41:t, 6^2, 13
42:t, 4
43:3
44:t, 7, 9, 10, 13^2, 20, 25
45:t, 17
46:t, 9
47:t, 6
48:1, 10, 13
49:t, 4, 7, 10, 11, 18, 19
50:4^2, 8, 16^2, 19, 22, 23
51:t^2, 1, 6, 8
52:t^2, 3
53:t, 2, 5
54:t^2, 2
55:t, 1, 22
56:t
57:t
58:t, 5, 7
59:t^2, 4, 5^2
60:t^2, 1, 2, 3, 4
61:t, 2
62:t^2, 4, 9, 12^2
63:2, 9
64:t, 3, 8
65:t, 4, 8
66:t, 4, 8, 9, 12, 19
67:t, 1
68:t, 4, 16, 33

PSALMS

69:t, 10, 11, 16, 20, 21, 23, 26
70:t^3, 1^2, 2
71:1, 2, 3, 11, 13, 18^2
72:3, 8, 15
73:1^2, 10, 16, 24, 28^2
74:7, 14^2
75:t, 4, 9
76:t, 7, 8, 9^2, 11, 12
77:t^2, 2, 6, 9
78:1^2, 4^2, 5, 6^2, 10, 13^2, 16, 24, 25, 26, 48^2, 50^2, 52, 54^2, 55, 58^2, 63, 66, 71, 72
79:2, 3, 4^2, 11^2, 13
80:t, 3, 5, 7, 9, 19
81:t, 11
82:3
83:9^2, 12, 17
84:t, 7, 10
85:t, 4, 5, 8^2
86:5, 6, 11
87:4
88:t, 10, 15
89:1, 4, 7^2, 8, 19, 29, 33, 39, 40, 41, 42, 43, 44^2
90:2, 3, 11, 12, 15
91:11
92:1^2, 2, 15
94:1^2, 2
95:1, 7
96:2, 4^2, 13
98:9
100:5
101:3
102:4, 5, 13, 18, 20^3, 21, 22
103:8, 10, 17, 18^3
104:9, 11, 14, 15^2, 23, 26, 29, 33
105:8, 10, 13^2, 14, 22, 25^2, 39
106:8, 23, 26, 27^2, 29, 45, 46, 47^2, 48
107:4, 7, 8, 12, 15, 21, 23, 26^2, 27, 31, 36, 38, 40
109:t, 12^2, 16, 26, 31
111:4
112:9
113:3, 6, 9^2
115:16
116:17
118:8^2, 9^2, 19
119:4, 5, 9, 25, 27, 31, 35, 36, 38, 41, 42, 49, 58, 60, 62, 76, 91, 95, 103, 112, 121, 126, 128, 132, 135, 149, 154, 156, 159, 169, 170
121:3
122:4
124:6
125:4
127:2^3
130:2
132:4^2, 17
133:1, 2
135:7
136:3, 4, 5, 6, 7, 8, 9, 10, 13, 14, 16, 17, 25
137:6, 7, 8
139:t, 12
140:t, 4, 11
141:4^2
143:1, 3^2, 8^2, 9, 10
144:1^2, 4, 14
145:3, 4, 8, 9, 12^2, 18
146:4, 7
147:1, 6, 8, 9^2, 18
149:7, 8, 9
150:2

PROVERBS

1:2^2, 3, 4^3, 6, 16^2
2:2, 7, 12, 13, 14, 16
3:2, 8^2, 15, 18, 22, 27^2, 28, 32
4:1, 8, 9^2, 16, 20, 22, 27^2
5:1, 5, 13
6:4^2, 6, 10, 18, 24, 26, 29, 30
7:8, 15^2, 21, 22^2, 23, 24, 25, 27^2
8:4, 7, 9^2, 11^2, 13, 21, 29
9:4, 7, 9, 15, 16
10:3, 16^2, 23^2, 26^3, 29^2
11:1, 17, 18, 19^2, 20, 24, 29
12:4, 6, 8, 20, 21, 22
13:5, 14, 18, 19^3, 21, 22, 25
14:8, 15, 22, 23, 27, 29, 34
15:8, 18, 21, 24, 26, 28
16:5, 7, 12^2, 16^3, 17, 19^2, 23, 24^2, 30^2, 32
17:4^2, 15, 16^2, 21, 23, 25^2, 26^2
18:5^2, 9, 18, 19
19:6, 7, 10, 11, 23, 24, 27^2
20:2, 3, 10, 13, 17, 25^2
21:3^2, 5^2, 6, 7, 9, 15^3, 19, 20, 25
22:1, 7, 9, 16^3, 19^2, 20, 21, 25, 27
23:1, 2^2, 4, 7, 12, 21, 30
24:1, 8, 9, 11^2, 12^2, 13, 20, 21, 23^2, 25, 29^4, 33
25:2^2, 8^3, 9, 10, 13, 20, 21^2, 24, 25, 27^2
26:4, 5, 8, 11^2, 15^2, 17, 21^3
27:1, 4, 7, 14, 19^2, 21, 23^2, 24
28:10, 17^2, 20, 21, 22
29:7, 12, 15^2, 27^2
30:14, 17, 23
31:3, 4, 6, 8, 15^2, 19, 20^2, 25, 27

ECCLESIASTES

1:5, 6, 11, 13^3, 16, 17^2
2:1, 3^2, 6, 11, 12, 14, 15^2, 16, 20^2, 21, 26^5
3:1^2, 2^4, 3^4, 4^4, 5^4, 6^4, 7^4, 8^2, 10^2, 11, 12^2, 14, 15, 20, 21, 22
4:10^2, 14
5:1^3, 2, 4, 6^2, 11, 12, 13, 15, 18^3, 19^4

ECCLESIASTES

6:2^2, 6, 8
7:2^5, 5^2, 9, 11, 12, 14, 25^4, 27
8:1, 2, 3, 6, 8^2, 9, 11, 14^3, 15^3, 16^2, 17^3
9:1, 2^8, 3, 4^2, 10, 11^6
10:1, 3, 10^2, 15^2, 16
11:2^2, 7
12:5, 7, 10

SONG OF SOLOMON

1:7, 9
2:3, 4
3:3
4:6^2
5:2, 5^2, 6
6:2^3, 11^2
7:7^2, 8, 9, 12
8:2, 11, 13^2, 14^2

ISAIAH

1:11, 12^2, 14, 16, 17
2:2, 3^2, 19, 20^3, 21^2, 22
3:4, 8, 10, 12, 13^2, 15, 24
4:1, 3
5:1, 4, 5^2, 8^2, 22^2, 26
7:1^2, 3, 7, 13, 15, 16, 18, 21, 22, 23
8:2, 3, 4, 8, 10, 11, 12^2, 14^2, 19, 20^3, 21, 22
9:3, 7^2, 16
10:2^2, 3, 6^3, 7, 11, 12, 20, 26, 27, 28^2, 30, 31
11:10, 11^2, 16
13:5, 9, 10, 11, 14, 16, 18, 20, 22
14:1, 2, 3^2, 9, 11, 12, 15^2, 16, 19, 24
15:1^2, 2^3, 7
16:1^2, 4, 10, 12^3
17:4, 7^2, 8, 11^2, 12^2
18:1, 2^2, 6, 7
19:3^4, 14, 18, 19^2, 21, 22, 23
20:4, 6
21:2, 11, 14, 16
22:1, 4, 5, 7, 8, 10, 12^4, 13, 20, 21^2, 23, 24
23:1, 6, 7, 9^2, 11, 12, 13, 15^2, 17^2, 18^2
24:2, 9, 16, 18, 20, 21
25:2, 4^2, 11, 12^2
26:5^2, 8^2, 10, 14, 21
27:6, 7, 9, 12, 13^2
28:1^2, 2, 6^3, 9, 11, 12^2, 17^2, 19, 21, 24, 26
29:1^3, 11, 12, 14, 15, 20, 24
30:1^2, 2^3, 4, 6, 7^2, 8, 10^2, 11, 13^2, 14^2, 21^2, 28^3, 29^2, 30
31:1^2, 4, 9
32:4, 5, 6^4, 7
33:1^3, 4
34:1, 2, 5, 10, 12, 14, 17
35:4, 10
36:1, 2, 4, 6, 7^3, 8^2, 10, 11, 12^4, 14, 16^2, 17, 22
37:1, 3^2, 4, 5, 7^2, 9^2, 10, 11, 17, 21, 22, 24^2, 26^2, 35, 38
38:4, 5, 10, 12, 13, 16, 17, 19, 20^2, 22
39:1, 5, 6, 8
40:2, 14, 16, 17, 18, 20, 22, 23, 25, 29^2
41:1, 2^3, 6, 22, 23, 27^2
42:1, 2, 5, 7^2, 8^2, 9, 10, 17, 23^2, 24, 25
[illegible]:[illegible], 11, 20[illegible], 22, 24, 28[illegible]
44:13, 15, 19^2, 26^2, 27, 28^2
45:1^4, 9, 10, 11, 16, 18, 24
46:1, 4^2, 5, 8, 11
47:7, 8, 9, 11, 12, 14^2, 15
48:3, 5^2, 17, 18, 20, 21
49:5^3, 6^3, 7^3, 8^3, 9^2, 18, 20, 21, 22^2, 23
50:1, 2^2, 4^3, 6^2, 8
51:1^2, 4, 6, 8, 10, 13, 18, 23^2
52:4, 5, 8
53:1, 6, 7, 10^2
54:3, 4, 16
55:1, 4^2, 7, 10^2, 13
56:1^2, 3, 6^4, 7, 8, 9, 10, 11, 12
57:1^2, 6, 7, 8, 9, 11, 15^2, 18, 19^2, 21
58:2^2, 4^3, 5^4, 6^3, 7^3, 10, 12, 14
59:7^2, 18^4, 20
60:3^2, 4, 8, 9^2, 13
61:1^5, 2^2, 3^2, 11^2
62:8, 11
63:1, 5^2, 6, 7^3, 10, 12, 14^2, 17
64:2^3, 7
65:3^2, 5, 10, 12^2, 24
66:2^2, 5, 6, 8, 9^3, 12, 15, 19^3, 20, 23^4

JEREMIAH

1:2, 7, 8, 10^6, 12, 19
2:1, 7, 18^4, 24, 27^2, 28, 33, 36
3:1, 3, 5, 9, 12, 13, 14, 15, 16^2, 17^2, 18
4:3, 4, 7, 9, 11^4, 16, 22^2
5:1, 3^2, 7, 19, 31
6:1, 2, 6, 10, 13, 17, 19, 20^2
7:1, 2, 3, 6, 7^2, 10, 12, 14^3, 16, 18^4, 19^2, 27, 30, 31, 34
8:5, 6, 10^2, 14^2, 19
9:3, 5^2, 6, 8, 12, 15, 21
10:5, 7, 10, 13, 20^2, 22, 23, 24
11:1, 2, 4, 5, 8, 10^3, 11, 13^4, 15, 17^2, 19
12:9, 11, 12, 13, 14, 15^3, 16^3
13:2, 4, 6^3, 7, 10^3, 11^2, 16, 18, 21, 23
14:1, 3^2, 8, 10, 16^2

JEREMIAH

15:2[5], 3[3], 4, 5, 8[2], 9, 10[2], 11, 13, 14, 18, 20[2]
16:5, 7[2], 8[3], 9, 10, 21[2]
17:3, 4, 10[3], 16, 21, 24[3], 27[2]
18:1, 2[2], 3, 4[2], 5, 7[3], 8, 9[2], 11[3], 15[3], 16, 18, 19[2], 20[2], 21[2], 22, 23
19:5, 7[2], 9, 11, 12, 14[2]
20:3, 4[2], 5, 6[2], 15, 17, 18
21:2, 3, 9, 14
22:1, 3, 8, 16, 17[2], 20, 27[2]
23:3, 13, 21, 22, 27[3], 28, 32, 35[2], 37
24:1, 6, 7, 9[2], 10
25:1, 2, 4, 5, 6[3], 7[2], 12, 14[2], 15[2], 17, 18[2], 28[2], 29, 31[2], 32, 35[2]
26:2[2], 3, 4[2], 5[2], 6, 8[2], 11[2], 12[2], 15[2], 16[3], 17, 18, 19, 20, 21[2], 24[2]
27:2, 3[6], 4, 6, 8, 9[5], 10, 12[2], 16[3], 18[2], 20, 22[2]
28:1, 3, 4, 6, 9, 15
29:1[4], 3, 4, 6, 7, 8[2], 10[2], 11, 14, 18[3], 19, 20, 24, 25[2], 27, 31[2], 32
30:1, 3[3], 8, 11, 13, 21[2]
31:2[3], 6, 9[2], 12, 15, 17, 18, 21, 28[6], 32[2], 38, 39
32:1, 4, 5, 7, 8[2], 11, 19[3], 22[2], 23[2], 24[2], 29[2], 30, 31, 32[2], 33, 34, 35[4], 37, 40, 41, 44
33:2, 5[2], 7, 9, 11, 12, 14, 15, 17, 18[3], 21, 23, 26[2]
34:2, 3[2], 8, 9, 11, 12, 15, 16[2], 17[6], 20, 22[3]
35:2, 8, 9[2], 10, 11[2], 13[2], 14, 15[3], 19
36:1, 3, 8, 9[3], 16, 20, 21, 23, 25, 26, 27, 29[2], 30[3], 32
37:3, 7[4], 11, 12[2], 13, 14[3], 20[2]
38:2, 4, 8, 9[2], 11, 15, 16, 18, 19, 21, 22, 23[2], 25, 26[3], 27
39:4, 5[2], 7[2], 9, 11, 12, 16
40:1, 4[3], 5[2], 6, 7, 8[2], 9[2], 10, 12[2], 13[2], 14, 15
41:1[2], 4, 5[2], 6[3], 10[3], 12, 13, 15, 17[2]
42:4[2], 5[3], 6, 7, 8, 9, 11[2], 12[2], 15[2], 16, 17[2], 21, 22[2]
43:1[2], 2[2], 3[2], 4, 5, 7, 11[3]
44:1, 3[4], 5[2], 7[3], 8, 11, 12[2], 14[4], 17[2], 18[3], 19[2], 20[3], 24, 25[3], 28
45:3
46:1, 3, 13, 16[3], 19
47:1, 3, 4[2]
48:4, 9, 11, 12, 15, 16, 32, 33, 35[2], 39
49:2, 3, 9, 10, 12, 14, 24, 28, 29, 34, 37, 39
50:5[2], 6[2], 9, 16[2], 19, 21, 27, 28, 29[2], 33, 34, 39, 42
51:9, 11, 16, 24, 27, 29, 30, 31[3], 33, 35[2], 40, 49, 53, 61[2], 62, 63
52:1, 2, 3, 4, 9, 11, 15, 17, 26[2], 27, 31

LAMENTATIONS

1:2, 4, 11, 12, 14[2], 15, 17, 19, 21
2:2, 4, 6, 8[2], 10, 12, 13[3], 14, 17, 20
3:13, 14, 21, 25, 30, 32, 34, 35, 36, 37, 40, 64
4:2, 3, 4, 8
5:2[2], 6[3], 13, 19

EZEKIEL

1:1, 9, 11, 12, 20[2]
2:3[2]
3:2, 3, 5[2], 6[2], 11, 15, 16, 18[2], 26[2]
4:3, 4, 5, 8, 9, 10, 11
5:1[2], 7, 13, 16
6:3[4], 13
7:3, 8, 9, 13, 14[2], 19, 21, 24, 27
8:1, 3[3], 4, 7, 14, 17[4]
9:1, 3[2], 5, 8
10:5, 6, 11, 16
11:13, 16, 24
12:2[2], 3, 12, 13[2], 14, 17, 23, 25, 26, 27
13:5, 6, 13, 14, 16, 18[3], 19[3], 20[2], 21
14:4[2], 7[2], 12, 15, 19, 21
15:3[2], 6
16:2, 4, 5[3], 7[2], 17, 20, 21[2], 23, 25[2], 26[2], 33[2], 34, 41, 42, 55[3]
17:9, 12[3], 17, 21, 24
18:3, 6[2], 7[2], 9, 10, 12, 15, 16, 24, 30
19:3, 6, 9, 12, 14[2]
20:1[2], 3, 4, 6, 8, 10, 12, 13, 21[2], 26[2], 28[2], 31, 32, 35, 37, 42[2], 44[2], 47[2]
21:3, 4, 7, 10, 11[2], 17, 19, 20[2], 21, 22[6], 23[2], 24[2], 28, 29, 30, 31, 32
22:3, 4[2], 6[2], 9, 12, 18, 20[2], 27[3]
23:15[2], 17, 19, 21, 24, 27, 32, 37[2], 39[2], 40, 46, 48[2]
24:6[2], 7, 8[2], 9, 13, 14[3], 17, 19, 24, 26[2], 27
25:4, 7[2], 14[2], 15
26:1, 3[2], 5, 11, 13, 14, 15, 17[2], 20
27:5, 7, 9, 19, 30
28:8, 17, 18, 25
29:4, 5[2], 6, 7, 14, 16, 17, 18, 21
30:9, 10, 11, 13, 20, 21[5], 22
31:1, 2, 14[3], 15[2], 16[2], 18
32:1, 4, 6, 12, 14, 17, 20, 21, 24, 25, 27, 29, 30
33:2, 8, 9, 12, 13[2], 21, 22, 27[2], 30[2], 33
34:2, 5, 8, 10, 13, 15, 18[2], 25, 26, 28
35:11[2], 12
36:4[7], 5, 6[3], 8[2], 12, 15[2], 19[2], 20, 27, 28, 33, 37
37:2, 5, 7, 9, 12, 17, 22
38:9, 10, 11[2], 12[3], 13[5], 16, 18, 20
39:2, 3, 4[2], 11, 13, 14[2], 17[2], 24[2], 28
40:4[2], 13, 16[3], 23, 24, 26[2], 27, 28[2], 29, 31, 32, 33, 34, 35[2], 36, 37, 39, 40, 46[2], 48, 49
41:1, 7[2], 16, 17
42:11[2], 12, 14, 19, 20
43:1, 3[3], 10, 14[2], 18[2], 19[2]
44:3, 6[2], 7[2], 11[2], 12, 13[3], 15[3], 16[2], 17, 19, 20, 23, 24, 25, 27, 30
45:4, 8[2], 15, 17[2], 23, 25[4]
46:5[2], 7, 9, 11[5], 14, 17[3], 18, 20, 21
47:3, 4[2], 5, 6[2], 9, 10[3], 11, 12, 13, 14, 15, 19[2], 21, 22[2], 23
48:1[3], 28

DANIEL

1:2, 4, 7[3], 10, 11, 12[2], 14
2:2[2], 3, 4, 5, 9, 12, 13, 14[2], 15[2], 17[2], 21, 24, 26[2], 28, 29[3], 30[2], 34, 35, 39, 43, 44, 45[2]
3:2[3], 4, 9, 13, 16[2], 17, 19, 20[2], 26
4:2, 3, 6, 8, 11, 17[2], 18, 19[2], 20, 22, 25[2], 26, 27, 31, 32[2], 34, 35, 37
5:1, 2, 7[2], 8, 16, 17[3], 28
6:1, 3, 4, 6, 7[2], 8, 12, 14[2], 18, 20[3]
7:4, 5, 6, 11, 13, 22, 25, 26[2], 27
8:2, 4, 6, 7[2], 10[2], 11, 12, 13[2], 15, 16, 23, 25
9:2, 3, 4[2], 6[2], 7[2], 8[4], 9, 10, 16[2], 17, 21, 22, 23, 24[6], 25[2], 27
10:6, 7, 12[3], 13, 14, 20
11:1[2], 3, 4[2], 6[2], 10, 14, 15, 16, 17, 18[2], 21, 25, 27, 28, 34, 35[4], 36, 39, 44[2], 45
12:1, 2[2], 3, 4[2], 6[2], 7, 12

HOSEA

1:2, 4, 5, 10
2:1, 7, 9, 11, 13, 18, 21, 23
3:1[2], 2
4:6, 10[2], 12, 15, 17
5:2, 4, 5, 6, 12, 13[2], 14, 15
6:3
7:10[2], 11[2], 16
8:1, 5, 9, 11[2], 12, 13
9:3, 4, 10, 12, 13
10:1[2], 3, 6, 8[2], 11[2], 12[2]
11:2, 3, 4, 5, 7[2], 9
12:2[3], 6, 7, 9, 14
13:2, 6
14:2, 3, 8

JOEL

1:1, 19
2:2, 9, 12, 13, 17, 23, 25, 28, 32
3:4, 8[2], 11, 12[2], 18, 20

AMOS

1:6[2], 9
2:4, 7, 8, 10, 12
3:10, 14
4:1, 4, 7[3], 8, 10, 12
5:2, 3, 5[2], 6, 7, 16[2], 18, 26, 27
6:1[2], 2[2], 3, 5[2], 9, 10, 13
7:2, 4, 10[2], 14
8:4[2], 9[2], 12[4]
9:2

OBADIAH

3, 5[2], 7, 9, 14, 21

JONAH

1:2, 3[4], 4, 5, 6, 7, 13[2], 17
2:5, 6
3:3, 4, 5, 7
4:2, 3[2], 4, 6[2], 8[4], 9[3]

MICAH

1:1, 7[2], 9, 13[2], 14[2]
2:1, 6[2], 7
3:1, 8[2]
4:1, 2[2], 8, 10[2]
5:2, 10
6:8[3], 14
7:1, 9, 11, 12[4], 15, 20[2]

NAHUM

1:3
2:5
3:1, 7

HABAKKUK

1:3, 6, 8, 13, 17
2:1, 6[2], 9[2], 10, 12, 15, 18, 19[2]
3:9, 14[2], 19[2]

ZEPHANIAH

1:8, 10, 12, 18
2:15
3:1[2], 2, 4, 5, 8[3], 9[2], 16[2], 18, 19

HAGGAI

1:1, 4, 6, 8, 9
2:2[3], 5, 16[3], 17, 21

ZECHARIAH

1:6[3], 10[2], 11, 16, 21[4]
2:2[2], 3, 4, 9, 11
3:1, 4, 7
4:2, 4, 10
5:3[2], 10, 11
6:7[4], 14[4], 15
7:1, 2, 3[2], 5[2], 9, 11, 13
8:1, 10, 12, 13, 14[2], 15[2], 16, 19, 20, 21[3], 22[2], 23
9:10[2], 12[2]
10:1, 6
11:9, 13, 17
12:9[2]
13:1[2], 2[2], 3, 4[2], 5, 8
14:2, 5, 6, 7[2], 10, 13, 16[4], 17, 18, 19

MALACHI

1:1
2:2[3], 5, 8, 15, 16
3:1, 5[2], 10, 14, 16
4:6[2]

MATTHEW

1:11, 12, 17, 18, 19[2], 20
2:1, 2, 8, 12, 13[2], 16, 19, 22
3:5, 7[3], 9[3], 11, 13[2], 14[2], 15[2]
4:1, 3, 16, 17[2]
5:13[2], 17[3], 22, 23, 24, 25[2], 28, 32, 39, 41, 42, 44, 45
6:1, 5, 6, 16, 18, 24, 30[2]
7:2, 4, 5, 8, 11[2], 12[2], 13, 15, 22, 28
8:4, 9[3], 10, 18, 20, 21, 25, 28, 29[2], 31, 33, 34
9:2, 5[2], 6[2], 7, 10, 13[2], 14, 16, 24, 28[2], 29, 32
10:1[2], 6, 13, 17, 21[3], 22, 28[2], 34[2], 35, 42
11:1[3], 5, 7[2], 8, 9, 14, 15, 20, 23, 27
12:1[2], 2, 4, 10, 12, 13, 18, 25, 32, 39, 42, 46[2], 47
13:3, 9, 11[2], 12, 13, 17[2], 30[2], 31, 43, 48, 53
14:4, 5, 7, 9, 11[2], 15, 16, 18, 19[4], 22[2], 23, 29[2], 30
15:1, 5, 20, 26[3], 31[4], 32, 33, 35, 36[2]
16:3, 5[2], 11, 21, 22, 27
17:4, 9, 14[3], 16, 17, 19, 20, 24[2], 27
18:7, 8[2], 9[2], 11, 17[2], 21, 24, 25[3], 34
19:1, 3, 5, 7[2], 8, 10, 11, 12, 14, 21, 24[2]
20:1, 15, 17, 18[2], 19[4], 20, 22[2], 23[3], 28[3]
21:1, 9, 14, 15, 19, 21, 28[2], 30, 33, 34, 43, 44, 46
22:3[2], 5[2], 8, 9, 11, 13, 17, 23, 24, 34, 46
23:1[2], 4, 5, 7, 13, 15, 23[2], 34
24:1[2], 6, 9, 17, 18, 19, 21, 31, 43, 45, 49[2]
25:1, 6, 9, 10[2], 11, 15[4], 27[2], 45[2]
26:1, 2, 8, 9, 16, 17[2], 18, 22, 26, 27, 37, 45, 49, 53, 55[2], 57, 58, 59[2], 61[2], 73, 74[2]
27:1[2], 2, 3, 4[2], 6, 7, 14, 15, 19, 24, 26, 31, 32, 33, 34, 46, 48, 49, 51, 58[2], 60
28:1[2], 8, 9, 14, 20

MARK

1:7, 9, 17, 24[2], 34, 40[2], 44[2], 45[3]
2:2, 9[3], 10[2], 15, 17[2], 18, 23[2], 26[2]
3:4[4], 7, 9, 10, 14, 15[3], 21
4:1, 3, 4, 9, 11, 21[2], 23, 24, 25, 33, 34, 41
5:7, 14, 15, 16, 17[2], 19, 20, 32, 37, 38, 40, 43
6:2, 7, 8, 18, 21, 27, 28[2], 31, 34, 36, 37[2], 39, 41[3], 45[3], 46, 53, 55
7:2, 4, 5, 11[2], 12, 16, 27[2], 30, 32, 34, 37[2]
8:1, 2, 3, 6[3], 7, 11, 13, 14, 22[2], 26[2], 31, 32
9:5[2], 6, 14, 15, 18, 22, 23, 32, 33, 35, 41[2], 43[2], 45[2], 47[2]
10:2[2], 4[2], 7, 12, 13, 14, 17, 21, 24, 25[2], 28, 30, 32[2], 33[3], 40[3], 41, 42[2], 45[3], 46, 47, 49, 50
11:1, 7, 13, 15[2], 21, 23, 27[2], 28
12:1[2], 2, 12, 13, 14[2], 17[2], 23, 33[2], 36, 38
13:5, 9[2], 12[3], 14, 15, 16, 17[2], 21, 22, 27, 29, 34[3]
14:1, 5, 8[2], 10, 11, 14, 19[2], 21, 22, 23, 32[2], 33[2], 40, 45, 48, 53, 55[2], 64, 65[4], 69[2], 70, 71[2], 72
15:1, 8[2], 15[2], 18, 20, 21, 23, 36[2], 38, 45
16:8, 9, 15

LUKE

1:1, 3[2], 8, 9[2], 16, 17[4], 19[2], 20, 23[2], 25, 27[2], 38, 41, 43[2], 49, 50, 55[3], 56, 59[2], 62, 72[3], 73, 76, 77, 79[3]
2:1, 3, 5, 10, 14, 15[3], 22[4], 23, 24[2], 27, 29, 32, 38, 39[2], 41, 42, 44, 45, 46, 51
3:7[4], 8[3], 11, 12, 14, 16, 21, 23
4:6, 9, 10, 16[3], 18[7], 19, 20, 21, 31, 34[2], 41, 43
5:1[2], 7, 11, 12, 14[2], 15[2], 17[2], 18[2], 21, 23[2], 24, 25, 26, 32[2]
6:1, 2, 4[2], 6, 8, 9[4], 11, 12[3], 17[2], 19, 26, 27, 29, 30, 31[2], 33[2], 34[4], 35, 38, 42[2], 47
7:2, 4, 6, 7, 8[2], 10, 11, 12, 15[2], 19, 22, 24[2], 25, 26, 31, 32[2], 36, 38, 40, 42, 43, 44, 45, 47, 49, 50
8:1, 4, 5, 8, 10[2], 14, 18[2], 19, 20, 22, 24, 25, 27, 28, 29, 31, 32, 35[2], 37, 38, 39, 40, 49, 51, 53, 55
9:1, 2[2], 9, 10, 12, 13, 14, 16[3], 17, 18, 21, 23, 28[2], 33[2], 37, 40, 42, 45, 51[3], 52, 53, 54, 56[3], 57, 58, 59, 62
10:5, 6, 7, 15[2], 19, 22[2], 24[2], 25, 29, 30, 34[2], 35, 38, 40[2]
11:1[2], 4, 6[2], 10, 13[2], 14, 17, 26, 27, 29, 30, 31, 37[2], 42[2], 46, 53[3], 54
12:1, 5, 12, 13, 17, 19, 25, 26, 28[2], 32, 37[2], 39, 41, 42, 45[3], 47, 48, 49, 50, 51, 54, 55, 58[3]
13:12, 14, 15, 24[2], 25[3], 26, 32[2], 33[2]
14:1[2], 3, 6, 7, 8, 9[2], 12, 17[2], 18, 19, 21, 23, 26, 28[2], 29[2], 30[2], 31[2], 35
15:1, 12[2], 14, 15[2], 17[2], 18, 19, 20, 21, 22, 24, 25, 29
16:3, 4, 7, 9, 11, 13, 17[2], 21, 22, 26[2], 27
17:3, 4, 7, 10, 11[2], 14, 18[2], 22, 23, 31, 33
18:1[3], 10, 13, 14, 16, 18, 25[2], 30, 31, 33, 35, 40
19:3, 4[2], 5[2], 7, 8, 9, 10[2], 11, 12[2], 14, 15[3], 19, 24, 28, 29[2], 35, 37, 45, 47, 48
20:1, 9[3], 10, 16, 18, 19, 22, 27, 30, 33, 35, 46
21:7, 9, 12, 13, 14, 15, 16[2], 21, 23, 28[3], 29, 31, 34, 36[3], 38[2]
22:5, 6, 15, 23, 31, 33[2], 39, 44, 45, 47, 52
23:2[3], 4[2], 5, 7, 8[2], 11, 15, 20[2], 25, 30[3], 32[2], 33, 36, 43, 48, 51, 56
24:4, 5, 9, 11, 12, 13, 15, 17, 18, 20[2], 21, 24, 25, 26[2], 29, 30[2], 32[3], 33, 34, 46[2], 50, 51, 52

JOHN

1:7, 8, 12[3], 19, 22, 27, 31, 33, 38, 42, 47
2:2, 4, 7, 12, 13
3:2, 13, 17, 20, 21, 23, 26[2], 33
4:5[3], 7[2], 8, 10[2], 11, 15, 20, 23, 28, 32, 33[2], 34[2], 35, 38, 52
5:1, 7, 10, 16, 18, 26[2], 27, 35, 36, 40, 45
6:6, 11[2], 15, 17, 24, 31, 35, 37[2], 38, 44, 52, 68
7:1, 4[2], 19, 20, 24, 25, 30, 32, 45, 50
8:6, 26[3], 27, 31, 33, 37, 40, 41, 56, 59
9:11, 13, 26[2]
10:3, 10[3], 18[2], 24, 29, 31, 39
11:7, 8, 15, 19[2], 31, 38, 45, 46, 53[2], 54, 55[2], 56
12:1, 5, 10, 12[2], 13, 20, 21, 29, 38, 47[2]
13:2, 3, 5[2], 6, 10[2], 12, 14, 15, 19, 24, 26[2], 29, 33, 35
14:2, 18, 21, 26, 29[2]
15:25
16:5, 10, 12, 13, 16, 17, 19, 28, 32
17:1, 2, 4, 11, 13
18:6, 13[2], 14, 20, 31[3], 36, 37
19:4, 7, 10[2], 12, 16, 20, 21, 23, 27, 29, 33, 39, 40
20:2[3], 3, 4, 8, 15, 16, 17[3], 21, 27
21:1, 6, 9, 11, 14, 15, 16, 21, 22, 23

THE ACTS

1:1, 3[2], 6, 7, 16, 19, 22, 25
2:4, 7, 12, 14, 17, 21, 27, 28, 30[3], 37, 39[2], 45, 46, 47
3:2, 3, 5, 12, 13, 14, 23, 26
4:5, 9, 10, 15, 16[2], 17, 18, 19, 23, 24, 28[2], 30
5:2, 3[3], 9, 13, 14, 20, 21[2], 28, 29, 31[3], 32, 33[2], 34, 35[2], 36[3], 38, 39, 40, 41, 42
6:4[2], 7, 10, 12, 13
7:5[3], 7, 13, 14, 17, 19, 23, 26, 30, 31, 33, 34, 35[2], 38[2], 39, 40, 42[3], 43, 44, 46, 54, 60
8:2, 3, 5, 10[2], 11, 24, 25, 27[2], 29, 30, 32, 36, 38, 40
9:2[2], 4, 5, 6, 10, 13, 14, 15, 23, 24, 26[3], 27[2], 29, 30[2], 32[2], 35, 37, 38[3], 40, 43
10:2[3], 3, 5, 6, 8, 9, 11, 13, 21, 22[2], 28, 32, 33[2], 41[2], 42[3], 43, 48[2]
11:2, 3, 5, 13, 15, 18, 19, 20, 25[2], 26, 28, 29[2], 30
12:1, 3, 4[4], 10, 11, 12, 13, 17[2], 19[2], 20
13:2, 4, 5, 7, 8, 10, 11, 13[2], 14, 19, 22[3], 23, 24, 25, 26, 31, 34[2], 35, 42, 43[2], 44, 46[2], 47, 48
14:1, 3, 5[2], 9, 11, 16, 20, 21[3], 22, 23, 24, 26[2]
15:2, 4, 5[3], 6, 10[2], 12, 14, 15, 19, 22[2], 24, 25, 28[3], 29, 30, 34, 37, 38[2]
16:1, 3, 4, 6, 7[2], 8, 9, 10[2], 11[2], 12, 13, 15[2], 16[2], 18[2], 20, 21[2], 22, 23, 30, 32, 36[2], 39
17:1, 5[2], 7, 14[2], 15[2], 16, 18, 20, 21, 22, 23, 25, 26, 29, 30
18:1, 2, 5, 7, 9, 10, 12, 13[2], 14, 15, 19, 20, 22, 24, 26, 27[2]
19:1[2], 13, 17, 21[2], 27, 36[2], 40
20:1, 3[2], 6, 7[2], 13[3], 14, 15, 16[2], 17, 18, 20, 21[2], 24, 26, 27, 28[2], 30, 31, 32[4], 34, 35[4]
21:1, 3, 4[2], 7, 12[2], 13[4], 15, 17, 21[3], 23, 25, 26, 31, 33, 34, 37, 39
22:2, 3, 5[3], 6, 9, 10, 12, 17[2], 24, 25, 30
23:2, 3[3], 9, 10[3], 14, 15[3], 17, 18[3], 19, 20[2], 22, 23[2], 29[3], 30[3], 31, 32[3], 33[2], 35
24:2, 6[2], 8, 10, 11[2], 16, 17[2], 19, 23[3], 25, 27
25:1, 3[2], 6, 9[2], 10[2], 11, 13, 15, 16[3], 17, 19, 20, 21[3], 22, 24, 25[2], 26[2], 27[3]
26:1, 3[2], 7, 9[2], 10, 11, 12, 14[2], 16, 18[3], 20[2], 21, 22, 23, 28, 29
27:2, 3[2], 5, 12[4], 16, 21, 22, 27, 30, 31[2], 33, 34, 35[2], 39, 40, 42, 43[2], 44[2]
28:4, 6, 8[2], 13[2], 14, 15, 16[3], 17, 19[2], 20[2], 22, 23[2]

ROMANS

1:1, 3, 4[2], 5, 7[3], 10, 11[2], 13, 14[4], 15[2], 16[3], 17, 22, 23[2], 24[2], 28[3], 30
2:2, 4, 6[2], 7, 10[3], 16
3:15, 19, 25[2], 26
4:1, 2, 4, 5, 8, 9, 12, 13[2], 16[4], 18, 20, 21, 22, 23, 24
5:7, 10, 14[2], 16, 18
6:2, 11, 16[3], 19[3], 22
7:1, 2, 3[2], 4[3], 5, 10[2], 18[2], 23
8:1, 6[2], 7, 12[2], 15, 18, 20, 23, 27, 28[3], 29[2], 31, 33, 38, 39
9:3, 4, 11, 15, 20, 21, 22[3], 26, 30, 31
10:1, 2, 3, 4, 6, 7, 19, 21
11:2, 4[2], 5, 11[2], 13, 14, 23, 24, 25, 35, 36[2]
12:2, 3[5], 6[3], 9, 10, 13[2], 16, 17
13:2, 3[2], 4[2], 7[5], 8, 10, 11, 14
14:1, 4[2], 6[3], 7[2], 9, 11[2], 12, 13, 14[3], 18, 21[2], 22
15:1[2], 2, 5[2], 7, 8, 9, 12, 14, 15, 16, 17, 18[2], 20, 21, 22, 23, 24[3], 25, 26, 27, 28, 30
16:17, 25[4], 26[2], 27
S

1 CORINTHIANS

1:1, 2[2], 17[2], 18, 19, 21, 27[2], 28[2]
2:1, 2, 6, 12
3:2, 5, 8, 10, 18, 22
4:5, 6[3], 7, 8, 9[3], 14, 18, 19
5:5, 9, 11[2], 12[2]
6:1, 2, 3, 4[2], 5[2], 6, 7[2], 16
7:1, 2, 5, 8, 9[2], 11, 12[2], 13, 15, 17, 25, 26, 27, 32, 39[2]
8:2, 6, 8, 9, 10[2], 13[2]
9:2, 3, 4[2], 5, 6, 15, 16, 20, 21[3], 22[2], 25, 27
10:6, 7[2], 13[4], 15, 19, 20[2], 22, 27[2], 31, 32[3]
11:2, 6, 7, 10, 15, 16, 20, 22[3], 29, 33
12:3, 7[2], 8[2], 9[2], 10[5], 11, 13, 21, 22, 23, 24
13:3[2], 12
14:3, 6, 8, 9, 12, 22[2], 28[2], 30, 32, 34[2], 35, 37, 39[2]
15:3, 4, 9, 24, 32, 34[2], 38, 54, 57
16:1, 3, 7, 12[2], 15, 16

2 CORINTHIANS

1:2, 4, 8, 12, 15, 16[3], 17, 21, 23
2:1, 3, 6, 7, 9, 10[2], 12[2], 14, 16[2]
3:1[2], 3, 4, 5, 7, 13, 16, 18
4:2, 3, 6[2], 15
5:2, 8[2], 10, 12[2], 13, 18[2], 19, 20, 21
7:3[2], 9, 10[2], 11, 14[2]
8:1, 3, 4, 5, 7, 8, 10[2], 11, 12[2], 16, 19[2], 24
9:1[3], 2, 5, 8[2], 9, 10, 11[2]
10:2[2], 4, 5, 6, 7, 13[3], 14, 15, 16[3]
11:1, 2[2], 7, 8, 9[2], 15, 32
12:1[2], 2, 4, 6[2], 7[2], 11, 13[2], 14[4]
13:1, 2[2], 3, 7, 10[3]
S

GALATIANS

1:3, 4, 5, 10, 16, 17[2], 18[2]
2:1, 2, 3, 4, 5, 6[4], 8, 9[2], 10, 11[3], 14[2], 17, 19
3:5, 6, 10, 16[3], 18, 19, 22, 24, 29
4:5, 9[2], 15, 18, 20[2], 21, 24, 25
5:3[2], 13, 17
6:3, 8[2], 12[2], 13, 16

EPHESIANS

1:1[2], 2, 5[2], 6, 7, 9, 11, 12, 16, 19[2], 21, 22[2]
2:2[2], 7, 15, 17[2]
3:2, 7, 9, 10, 11, 16[2], 18, 19, 20[2]
4:3, 7, 14[2], 16, 19, 22, 27, 28[2], 29, 32
5:2, 12, 19[2], 21, 24, 27, 28
6:4, 5[2], 7[2], 11, 13[2], 16, 19, 20, 21, 23

PHILIPPIANS

1:1, 7, 14, 16[2], 19, 20, 21[3], 23[2], 24, 26, 28[2], 29[2], 30
2:6, 11, 13[2], 19, 23, 25[3], 30
3:1[3], 7, 13, 21[2]
4:11, 12[6], 17, 18, 19
S

COLOSSIANS

1:2, 3, 4, 9[2], 11, 12, 20, 22, 23, 25[3], 26, 27, 29
2:2, 14[2], 17, 20, 22, 23
3:9, 15, 16, 17, 21, 22, 23
4:3, 4, 6, 10, 17[2]
S

1 THESSALONIANS

1:2, 7, 8[2], 9[2], 10[2]
2:2, 4, 8, 15, 16[4], 17
3:1, 2[2], 4, 5, 6[2], 9, 12, 13
4:1[2], 4, 9, 11[3], 13, 17
5:9[2], 12, 13, 15

2 THESSALONIANS

1:3, 6[2], 7, 10[2], 12
2:13[3], 14
3:7, 8, 9[2]
S

1 TIMOTHY

1:3, 4, 7, 10, 11[2], 15, 16[2], 18, 20
2:4[2], 6, 12[3]
3:2[3], 3, 5, 8, 13, 14, 15
4:1, 3[3], 4, 8, 13[3], 15[2]
5:4[2], 11, 13[2], 14[2], 24
6:3[3], 16, 17, 18[2], 19, 20
S

2 TIMOTHY

1:1, 2, 4, 5, 8, 9[2], 10, 12
2:2[2], 4, 8, 14[2], 15[2], 20[2], 24, 25
3:2, 7[2], 15
4:3, 6, 8, 9, 10, 11, 12, 14, 16, 18, 21

TITUS

1:1, 3, 4, 7[2], 9[2], 14
2:3, 4[3], 5[2], 6, 8, 9[2], 11
3:1[5], 2[2], 5, 7, 8, 12[3], 14
S

PHILEMON

2[2], 3, 8, 11[3], 16, 19
S

HEBREWS

1:5[2], 13, 14
2:1[2], 3, 4, 5, 10, 11, 15, 17[3], 18
3:2, 5, 7, 13, 15, 18[2]
4:1, 6, 7[2], 9, 11, 12, 13, 16
5:1, 3, 5[2], 7, 11[2], 12, 14[2]
6:5, 6[3], 8, 10[2], 11, 13, 16, 17, 18[2]
7:2, 5[2], 13, 23, 25[3], 27
8:3[2], 4, 5[3], 9[2], 10[2], 11, 12, 13
9:9, 11[2], 13, 14[2], 19[2], 24, 26, 27, 28
10:1, 2, 7, 9, 15, 19, 20, 24[2], 31, 32, 39
11:6[2], 7, 8, 11, 15, 16, 19, 20, 24[2], 25[2], 29, 32, 34, 35
12:11, 19, 22, 23[3], 24[2]
13:2, 8, 10, 14, 15[2], 16[2], 18, 19[2], 21[2]
S

JAMES

1:1, 5, 12, 19[3], 21, 26, 27[2]
2:3[2], 5, 8, 9, 16
3:2, 10, 17
4:2, 5, 7, 8[2], 9[2], 12[2], 13[3], 15, 17[3]
5:1, 16, 17

1 PETER

1:1, 2, 3, 4, 5, 12, 13[2], 14, 17
2:4, 5[2], 8, 13[2], 15, 18[3], 23, 24
3:1, 7, 15[2], 18[2]
4:2[2], 3, 4, 5[2], 6[3], 9, 10, 11, 12, 19[2]
5:3, 5[2], 11

2 PETER

1:1, 3, 5[2], 6[3], 7[2], 10, 12, 13, 15, 17
2:4[2], 8, 9[3], 10, 12, 13, 17, 21[2], 22[3]
3:9[2], 11, 13, 15, 16, 18

1 JOHN

1:9[2]
2:6
3:5, 16
4:10, 11, 14, 16
5:11, 14

2 JOHN

8, 12[3]

3 JOHN

4, 5[2], 8[2], 9, 13, 14[2]

JUDE

1, 3[2], 4, 7, 13, 15[2], 24[2], 25

REVELATION

1:1[2], 4[2], 6, 8, 12, 13
2:7[2], 12, 14[3], 17[2], 19, 20[4], 21, 23, 26, 27
3:2, 7, 9[2], 10, 18, 20, 21[2]
4:3, 8, 9, 11
5:2[3], 3[2], 4[3], 5[2], 9[3], 12
6:2, 4[2], 8, 16, 17
7:2[3], 10, 14
8:2, 6, 13[2]
9:1, 5, 6, 9, 10, 14, 15
10:4, 5, 7[2]
11:6[4], 9, 10, 12, 13, 17[2], 18
12:2, 4[3], 5[2], 12, 14, 15, 17
13:3, 4, 5, 6, 7[2], 12, 14[3], 15, 16
14:4, 6[2], 7, 15[2], 18
15:8
16:1, 6, 8, 9, 14[2], 19
17:17[2]
18:6[2], 17
19:7, 8, 10, 17, 19
20:8[3], 12, 13
21:10, 15, 17, 23
22:6, 8, 12, 14, 16

UNTO

GENESIS

1:9, 28
2:19, 22, 24
3:1, 2, 4, 6, 9^2, 13, 14, 16, 17^2, 19^2, 21
4:3, 4, 5, 6, 7, 9, 10, 12, 13, 15, 18, 19, 23^2
6:1, 4, 13, 20, 21
7:1, 5, 9, 15
8:9^2, 12, 15, 20
9:1, 8, 17, 24, 25
10:1, 19^3, 21, 25, 30
11:4, 31
12:1^2, 4, 6^2, 7^4, 8^2, 11, 18
13:3, 4, 8, 10, 14, 17, 18
14:6, 14, 15, 21, 22
15:1, 4, 5, 7, 9, 10, 13, 18^2
16:2^2, 4, 5, 6, 9, 10, 11, 13
17:1, 7, 8, 9, 15, 17, 18, 21, 23
18:1, 6, 7^2, 9, 10, 13, 14, 21, 27, 29, 30, 31, 33
19:3, 5^3, 6, 8^2, 12, 14^2, 16, 18, 19, 20, 21, 31^2, 34, 37, 38
20:5, 6, 9^3, 10, 13^2, 14, 16^2, 17
21:1, 3, 5, 7, 9, 10, 12^3, 14, 17, 22, 23^3, 27, 29, 30
22:1, 3, 5, 7, 11, 12, 15, 19, 20
23:3, 5, 13, 14, 15, 16, 18, 20
24:2, 3, 4^2, 5^3, 6, 7^4, 10, 12, 14, 20, 24^2, 25, 29^2, 30^2, 36, 38^2, 39, 40, 42, 45^2, 47, 48, 50, 54, 56, 58, 60, 65
25:5, 6^2, 12, 17, 18, 23, 33^2
26:1^2, 2, 3^3, 4, 9, 10, 16, 24, 27, 29, 32, 33, 35
27:1^2, 6^2, 13, 18, 19, 20, 21, 22, 26, 31^2, 32, 34, 37^2, 38, 39, 42
28:1, 4, 5, 9^2, 22
29:4, 5, 6, 15, 20, 21^2, 23, 24, 25, 30, 34
30:1, 3, 4, 14, 15, 16, 17, 25^2, 27, 29, 30, 40
31:3^2, 4, 5, 11, 12, 13^2, 14, 16, 24, 29, 39, 43^3, 46, 52, 55
32:3, 4, 9^2, 10, 16, 18, 19, 27, 32
33:1^3, 9, 13, 14^2, 16
34:1, 3^2, 4, 6, 9^2, 11^3, 12, 14^2, 15, 16, 17, 20, 22, 23, 24^2
35:1^3, 2, 3, 4, 7, 9, 10, 11, 17, 20, 27^3, 29
36:5
37:2, 4, 6, 10, 13^2, 18, 22, 23, 26, 29, 30, 35, 36
38:2, 8^2, 9, 12, 14, 16^3, 18
39:8, 10, 14^4, 17^3, 19
40:6, 8^2, 12, 13, 14^2, 16, 20, 21
41:8, 9, 13, 14, 15, 17, 24, 25, 28^2, 32, 38, 39, 40, 41, 44, 50^2, 55^2, 56
42:1, 7^3, 9, 10, 12, 14^2, 18, 20, 22, 23, 25, 28^2, 29^3, 31, 33, 34, 36, 37
43:2, 3^2, 5, 8, 9, 11, 13, 23, 29^2, 32, 34
44:4^2, 6, 7, 8, 10, 15, 16, 17, 18, 20, 21^2, 22, 23, 24, 27, 32^2
45:1, 3, 4, 9^2, 10, 12, 17^3, 18, 24, 25, 27
46:1, 2, 15, 18, 20^2, 25^2, 28^2, 29, 30, 31^4, 34
47:2, 3^2, 4, 5^2, 8, 9^2, 15, 17, 18^2, 19, 23, 24, 26, 29, 31^2
48:2, 3^2, 4, 5^2, 7, 9^2, 10, 11, 13, 15, 17, 18, 21^2
49:1, 2, 6, 10, 11^2, 13, 15, 26, 28, 29^2, 33
50:4, 12, 15, 16, 17^3, 19, 20, 21, 24^2

EXODUS

1:9, 10, 18, 19^2
2:9, 10, 11, 20, 23, 25
3:2, 4, 8^3, 9, 10, 11^2, 12, 13^5, 14^3, 15^4, 16^2, 17^2, 18^2
4:1^2, 2, 4, 5, 6, 9, 10^2, 11, 15, 16, 18^2, 19, 21, 22, 23, 30
5:1, 3, 4^2, 15, 16, 21, 22
6:1, 2^2, 3^3, 6, 8, 9^2, 10, 11, 12, 13^4, 28, 29^3, 30
7:1, 2, 4, 7, 8^2, 9^2, 10, 13, 14, 15^2, 16^2, 19^2, 22
8:1^3, 5^2, 8, 9, 10, 12, 15, 16^2, 19^2, 20^2
9:1^2, 8^2, 12^2, 13^2, 22, 27, 29^2, 33
10:1^2, 3^2, 5, 6, 7^2, 8^2, 9, 10, 12, 21, 24, 25, 28
11:1, 5, 8^2, 9^2
12:1, 2, 3, 4, 14, 21, 23, 26, 29, 36, 42, 43, 49
13:1, 2, 3, 5, 8, 9, 11, 12, 14
14:1, 2, 10, 11, 13, 15^3, 22, 24, 26, 29
15:1^2, 11, 13, 25
16:1, 3, 4, 6, 9^2, 10, 11, 12, 15, 20, 23^2, 25, 28, 33, 35
17:2, 4^2, 5, 9, 14
18:5, 6^2, 8, 13, 14, 15^2, 16, 17, 19^2, 22, 26
19:3^2, 4^2, 5, 6^2, 8, 9^3, 10^2, 12, 14, 15, 21^2, 23, 24^2, 25^2
20:4, 5, 6, 19, 20, 21, 22^2, 23, 24^2, 26
21:6^2, 8, 9, 11, 31, 32, 34
22:7, 8^2, 9, 10, 11, 12, 17, 20^2, 23, 26, 27, 29, 31
23:13, 14, 22^2, 23, 27, 31^2, 33
24:1^2, 5, 12, 14^3, 16
25:1, 2, 22, 25, 33, 34
26:24, 33
27:21
28:1^2, 3^2, 4, 12, 28, 29, 35, 41, 42, 43^3
29:1^2, 4, 17^2, 18^2, 25, 28, 34, 35, 41, 42
30:3, 10, 11, 12, 14, 15, 16, 17, 20, 22, 23, 30, 31^2, 32, 34^2, 36, 37, 38
31:1, 12, 13, 14, 18
32:1^2, 2^2, 3, 7, 9, 13^2, 14, 17, 19, 21^2, 23, 24, 25, 26^2, 27, 30^2, 31, 33, 34^2
33:1^4, 3, 5^3, 7, 8, 11^2, 12^2, 15, 17
34:1^2, 2, 4^2, 7, 15, 16, 25, 26, 27, 31^2, 34
35:1, 4, 5, 22, 29, 30
36:2, 3, 5, 10^2, 13
37:26
38:4
39:21, 31, 33
40:1, 12, 13, 15, 32

LEVITICUS

1:1^2, 2^3, 9, 13, 15, 17
2:1, 2, 8^3, 9, 11, 12, 14, 16
3:3, 5, 6, 9, 11, 14
4:1, 2, 3, 4, 12, 31, 35
5:6, 7, 8, 12, 14, 15, 16, 18
6:1, 2, 5, 6^2, 8, 9, 11, 15, 17, 19, 20, 21, 22, 24, 25
7:5, 11, 14, 18, 20, 21, 22, 23, 25, 28, 29^3, 32, 34^2, 35, 38
8:1, 3, 4, 5, 7, 21, 28, 31
9:2, 3, 4, 6, 7^3, 8, 9, 12, 13, 18, 23
10:3, 4, 6^3, 8, 11, 12^3, 19
11:1^2, 2, 4, 5, 6, 10, 11, 12, 20, 23, 26, 27, 28, 29, 35, 38
12:1, 2, 6^2
13:1, 2^3, 9, 16^2, 49
14:1, 2, 23^2, 33^2
15:1, 2^2, 14^2, 26, 29^2
16:1, 2^2, 18, 22, 29, 31, 34
17:1, 2^4, 4^3, 5^4, 6, 7^2, 8, 9^2, 12, 14
18:1, 2^2, 19
19:1, 2^2, 4, 5, 21^2, 23, 25, 34
20:1, 2, 3, 4, 16, 24^2, 26
21:1^3, 2, 3, 6, 7, 8, 16, 17, 23^2, 24^2
22:1, 2^2, 3^3, 12, 13, 14^2, 15, 17, 18^4, 21, 22^2, 24, 26, 27, 29
23:1, 2^2, 6, 8, 9, 10^4, 12, 13, 14, 15, 16^2, 17, 18^2, 21, 22, 23, 24, 25, 26, 27^2, 32^2, 33, 34^2, 36^3, 37, 38, 39, 41, 44
24:1, 2, 3, 7, 9, 11, 13, 15
25:1, 2^3, 4, 5, 8^2, 10^4, 11, 12, 13, 14, 15^2, 16, 27^2, 28, 39, 40, 42, 47, 49, 50^2, 51, 52^3, 55
26:1, 5^2, 9, 14, 16, 18, 21^2, 23, 24, 27^2, 28, 31, 40, 41
27:1, 2^2, 3, 5, 6, 9^2, 11, 13, 14, 15, 16, 18^2, 19, 21, 22, 23^3, 24, 28^2, 30, 32

NUMBERS

1:1, 48, 50
2:1^2, 5
3:5, 6, 9^2, 11, 13, 14, 40, 44, 48, 51
4:1^2, 9, 17^2, 19^2, 21, 27, 30, 35, 39, 43, 47
5:1, 4, 5, 6, 7^2, 8^2, 9, 11, 12^2, 15, 19, 21
6:1, 2^3, 5, 6, 8, 12, 13, 14, 17, 21, 22, 23^3, 25
7:4, 5, 6, 7, 8^2, 9^2, 11, 89^2
8:1, 2^3, 4^3, 5, 7, 12, 13, 16^2, 19, 20^2, 22, 23, 24, 26
9:1, 4, 7, 8, 9, 10^2, 12, 14, 21
10:1, 4, 29^2, 30, 32^2, 36
11:2^2, 11, 12^3, 13^2, 16^3, 18, 20, 23^2, 25^2, 26, 29, 35
12:4^4, 6^2, 11, 13, 14
13:1, 2, 17, 21, 22, 23, 26^3, 27, 32
14:2, 3, 7, 11, 13, 16, 18, 19, 23, 26^2, 28, 35, 39, 40, 44, 45
15:1, 2^3, 3^2, 4, 7, 8, 10, 13, 14, 17, 18^2, 19, 21, 22, 24, 25, 33^2, 35, 37, 38, 39, 40
16:3, 5^4, 8, 9^2, 15, 16, 19^2, 20^2, 23, 24, 25, 26, 30, 32, 36, 37, 38, 40, 44, 46^2, 50^2
17:1, 2, 6, 9, 10, 12, 13
18:1, 2^2, 4^2, 7, 8^2, 9, 10, 11, 12, 13, 15, 17, 19^2, 20, 24^2, 25, 26^2, 27, 28, 30^2
19:1^2, 2, 3, 10^2, 21
20:5, 6^2, 7, 8, 10, 12, 14, 16, 18, 19, 22, 23, 24^2, 25, 26
21:2, 7, 8, 16, 17, 21, 24^2, 26, 29, 30^3, 34^2
22:4, 5, 7^2, 8^2, 9, 10^2, 12, 13, 14, 16, 17^2, 18, 19, 20^3, 25, 28^2, 29, 30^3, 32, 34, 35^2, 36, 37^3, 38^2, 39
23:1, 3, 4, 5, 6, 11^2, 13^2, 15, 16, 17, 18, 25, 26, 27^2, 28, 29
24:10, 11, 12^2, 14
25:2, 3, 4, 5^2, 6, 10, 12, 16
26:1^2, 52, 53, 59, 60
27:4, 6, 7, 8^2, 9, 10, 11^2, 12^2, 13, 15, 18
28:1, 2^3, 3^2, 6, 7, 8, 11, 13^2, 14^3, 15, 19^2, 24, 26, 27, 28^2, 29, 31
29:1, 2, 6^2, 8^2, 12, 13, 14, 36, 39
30:1, 2, 3
31:1, 2, 3^2, 12^3, 15, 21, 25, 28, 29, 30, 41, 43, 47, 48, 49
32:2^2, 5, 6, 9, 11^3, 16, 17, 18, 20, 22, 25, 29, 31, 33^2, 38, 40
33:7, 9, 49, 50, 51^2, 56^2
34:1, 2^2, 5, 8, 11, 13, 16, 17, 29
35:1, 2^2, 4, 6, 8, 9, 10^2, 12, 25, 29
36:2, 4, 8, 11, 13

DEUTERONOMY

1:1, 2, 3^3, 6, 7^3, 8^2, 9, 17, 20^3, 21, 22, 24, 25, 29, 35, 39, 41, 42^2, 43, 44, 45, 46
2:1, 2, 4, 5, 9^2, 12^2, 14, 17, 19, 22, 23, 26, 27, 29, 31, 35, 36^2, 37^4
3:2^3, 6, 8, 10, 12, 13, 14^2, 15, 16^4, 17, 20^3, 21^2, 26^2
4:1^2, 2, 4, 7, 10, 11, 12, 13, 15^2, 19^2, 20, 21, 23, 30, 31, 32, 35, 42, 45, 48, 49
5:1, 9^2, 10, 22^2, 23, 27^2, 28^3, 31
6:7, 10, 18, 21, 23
7:2, 3^2, 6^2, 8, 12^2, 13, 16, 18^2, 19, 23, 25
8:1, 18, 20
9:3, 5, 7, 10, 12, 13, 19, 26, 27
10:1^3, 3, 4^2, 7, 8^2, 10, 11^3
11:3^2, 4^3, 5, 6, 9^2, 12, 13, 21, 22, 24, 25, 29
12:4, 5^2, 7, 11, 18, 26, 31^2
13:2, 3, 4, 7^2, 8^2, 17
14:2^2, 7, 8, 10, 19, 21^3, 25
15:2, 5, 6, 8, 9^2, 10^2, 11, 12, 14, 16, 17^2, 18, 19, 21
16:1, 2, 7, 9, 10^2, 15, 21
17:1^2, 5, 9^2, 12^2, 14, 16
18:2, 3, 6, 12, 14^2, 15^3, 17, 18^2, 19
19:5, 8^2, 19^2
20:2^2, 3^2, 5, 6, 7, 8^2, 9, 10^2, 11^2, 14, 15, 18
21:2, 3, 4, 5, 6, 8^2, 11, 13, 18, 19^2, 20
22:1, 2^2, 5^2, 13, 15, 16^2, 19, 23, 24, 26, 29
23:5^2, 15^2, 18, 20^2, 21, 23, 25
24:9, 11, 13, 15^2
25:1, 3, 5^3, 7^2, 8, 9^2, 16, 17
26:1, 2, 3^5, 7, 11^2, 12, 13^2, 15, 17, 19
27:2, 3, 5, 6, 9, 14, 15
28:1, 2, 8, 9^2, 11, 12^3, 13, 15, 20, 21, 26^2, 31, 32, 35, 36, 45, 60, 64, 68^2
29:2^3, 4, 7^2, 8, 11, 13^4, 21, 24, 26, 29^2
30:2, 4, 10^2, 12, 13, 14, 18, 20^2
31:1, 2^2, 4^2, 5^2, 7^4, 9^2, 14, 16, 18, 20^2, 23, 28
32:3, 17, 22, 43, 46^2, 48, 49^2, 50^2, 52
33:2, 7, 9, 19, 26, 29^2
34:1^2, 2, 3, 4^5, 6, 9, 10

JOSHUA

1:1, 2, 3^2, 4^2, 6^2, 15, 17^2, 18
2:3, 4, 7, 8, 9, 10, 12^2, 16, 17, 18, 21, 22, 24
3:4, 5, 6, 7, 9, 15
4:1, 5^2, 7, 8^2, 9, 10, 12, 13, 15, 18^2, 21
5:2, 6^2, 9^2, 13^2, 14^2, 15
6:2, 6, 7, 8, 16, 19, 22^2, 25
7:2, 3, 5, 9, 10, 19^2, 22, 23^2, 24, 26^2
8:1, 2^2, 5, 18, 24, 27^2, 28, 29, 30, 31
9:3, 6^2, 7, 8^2, 9, 11, 12, 15, 17, 18, 19^2, 20, 21^2, 22, 25^2, 26, 27
10:3^4, 4, 6, 8, 9, 10, 11, 14, 15, 20, 22, 23, 24^2, 25, 28, 29, 30^2, 31, 34, 36, 41^2, 43
11:6, 8^3, 9, 14, 17, 23^2
12:1, 2, 3, 5, 6, 7^2
13:1, 3, 4, 5, 6^2, 7, 9, 10, 11, 14^2, 15, 24^2, 25, 26^2, 27, 29, 31, 33^2
14:3, 4, 6^3, 10, 13, 14
15:3, 4, 5, 8, 9, 10^2, 11^2, 13, 18^2, 46, 47, 63
16:1, 2, 3, 5, 6, 8, 10
17:7, 9, 14, 17
18:3, 10, 18
19:10, 12, 28, 33
20:1, 2, 4^2, 6^3
21:1^3, 2, 3, 8, 27, 34, 43^2, 44, 45
22:2, 3, 4^3, 5, 6, 7^2, 8^2, 9, 10, 13, 15^2, 19, 21, 24, 31, 32
23:1, 2, 3, 4^2, 5, 7, 8^2, 9, 11, 12^2, 13, 14, 16
24:2, 4^2, 6^2, 7, 10, 11, 15, 19, 21, 22, 23, 24, 27^4, 28

JUDGES

1:3, 14, 15, 20, 21, 24, 26, 33
2:1^2, 3, 4, 5, 6, 10, 12, 15, 17^2, 19, 20
3:3, 4, 9, 13, 15^2, 17, 19, 20^2, 26, 28
4:3, 6, 7, 8, 11, 13, 14, 16, 18^2, 19, 20, 21, 22
5:3, 18
6:4, 6, 7, 8^2, 10, 11, 12^2, 13, 15, 16, 17, 18, 19, 20, 23^2, 24^2, 25, 26, 27, 30, 31, 35^3, 36, 39
7:2, 4^4, 5^2, 7^2, 8, 9^2, 11^2, 13^2, 17, 19, 22, 24^2
8:1, 2, 5^2, 6, 8, 9, 14, 15^2, 18, 20, 22, 23, 24, 27, 35
9:1, 5, 7^3, 8, 9, 11, 12, 13, 14, 15, 16, 31, 36, 38, 40, 48, 52^2, 54^2, 55, 56
10:4, 10, 11, 14, 15^3
11:2, 6, 7^2, 8, 9, 10, 12, 13^3, 14, 15, 16, 17, 19^2, 22^2, 28, 29, 30, 32, 33, 34, 35, 36^2, 37, 39
12:1, 2, 3, 5, 6
13:3^2, 5, 6, 7, 8^2, 9, 10^3, 11^2, 12, 13^2, 15, 16^2, 17, 18, 19, 22, 23
14:3^2, 10, 12^2, 13, 14, 15^2, 16^2, 18^2, 19
15:7, 11^4, 12^3, 13, 14, 19
16:1, 5^2, 7, 9, 10, 11, 12, 13^2, 14, 15, 16, 17^2, 18, 23, 26, 28
17:2, 3^2, 4, 9^2, 10^2, 11
18:1^2, 2, 3, 4, 5, 6, 8^2, 10, 12, 13^2, 14, 15, 18, 19^3, 23^2, 24, 25, 26, 27^2, 29
19:2, 3, 5, 6, 9, 11, 12, 13, 18, 21, 23^2, 24^2, 25, 28^2, 30
20:1, 14, 26, 32, 36, 42, 45^2, 47
21:1, 5, 12, 13, 22^4, 23

RUTH

1:7, 8, 10^2, 14, 15^2, 18, 20
2:2^2, 3, 4, 5, 8, 9, 10, 11^3, 13^2, 14, 19, 20^3, 21, 22, 23
3:1, 3, 5^2, 6, 13, 17
4:1, 3, 8, 9^2, 12, 13, 14, 15, 16

1 SAMUEL

1:3, 5, 10, 11^2, 14, 21, 22, 23, 24, 26
2:10, 11, 14, 16, 20, 22, 23, 25, 27^3, 28, 34
3:1, 5, 7, 9, 14, 17^2
4:3, 7, 8, 9, 16, 20
5:1, 5, 8^2
6:5, 12, 14, 15, 17, 18^2
7:3^3, 5, 8, 9^2, 14, 17
8:4, 5, 6, 7^3, 8^2, 9^2, 10, 22^3
9:6, 10, 11, 16, 17, 19, 23^2, 24
10:2, 7, 8, 11, 14, 15, 16, 17, 18, 19
11:1, 3^2, 7, 9^2, 10^2, 12
12:1^3, 2, 5, 6, 8, 10, 12, 17, 18, 19^3, 20
13:12, 15, 17^2
14:1, 4, 6, 7, 8^2, 9^2, 10^2, 11, 12, 17, 18, 19^2, 23, 33, 34, 35^2, 36^2, 40^3, 41, 45, 52
15:1^2, 6, 10, 11, 13, 15, 16^2, 20, 21, 24, 26, 28, 32
16:1, 3^2, 5, 7, 10, 11^2, 15, 17, 19, 20
17:8^2, 13, 17, 18, 28, 34, 37, 39, 41, 43, 44, 46, 52^2, 55
18:1, 8, 18, 19
19:4^2, 6, 11, 17^2
20:2, 4, 5^2, 11, 12^2, 21, 22, 27, 29, 30^2, 31, 32, 36, 40^2
21:1, 2^2, 5, 8, 11, 14
22:2, 3, 5, 7, 8, 13, 15, 17, 22
23:2, 3, 17^2, 27
24:4^3, 6^2, 16, 19, 21, 22^2
25:5, 6, 7, 8, 11, 13, 15, 16, 19, 21, 22, 27^2, 31^2, 34, 35, 40^2
26:1
27:2, 5, 6^2, 8
28:1, 7, 8^2, 9, 11, 13^2, 14, 15, 18, 21^4, 22, 23
29:3^3, 4^2, 6^3, 8^2
30:13, 15, 17, 24, 25, 26
31:4

2 SAMUEL

1:3^2, 4, 5, 7, 8, 9, 10, 13, 14, 16, 26
2:1^2, 5^4, 6
3:2, 7, 8, 12, 16, 21^2, 24, 38
4:8, 9
5:1, 6^2, 14, 19
6:10, 12, 21, 23
7:2, 4, 8, 9, 17, 20, 24, 27, 28
8:10, 11, 15
9:2^2, 3^2, 4^2, 6, 7, 9^2, 11, 12
10:2^2, 3^3, 5, 13
11:4^2, 7, 10^3, 11, 16, 19, 20^2, 23^3, 25^2
12:1^3, 3, 4^2, 8, 11, 13^2, 14, 15^2, 18^2, 19, 21, 24, 31^2
13:4^2, 5^2, 6, 10, 11^2, 13, 14, 15, 16^3, 17, 20, 22, 25, 26, 28, 29, 35, 39
14:2, 3, 5, 8, 9, 10, 12, 15^2, 18, 21, 27, 30, 31^2, 32
15:2, 3, 4, 7^2, 9, 14, 15, 25, 26, 27, 33^2, 34, 36
16:2, 3, 4, 9, 10, 16^2, 18, 21^2, 22
17:1, 3, 6, 7, 11, 15, 20, 21
18:2, 4, 11, 12, 18, 20, 21, 23, 24, 26, 28, 30, 32
19:2, 7^2, 8, 11, 14, 19^2, 22, 23^2, 25, 27, 28, 29, 30^2, 33, 34^2, 35, 37, 38, 39, 41
20:2, 3^2, 8, 14, 16, 17^2, 21, 22^2
21:2^2, 3, 4, 6^2, 8, 17
22:1, 42, 45^2, 50, 51
23:10, 13, 16, 19
24:3^2, 9, 10, 11, 12^2, 13^2, 14, 17, 18^2, 21, 22^2, 23^2, 24^2, 25

1 KINGS

1:2, 11, 13^3, 15^2, 16, 17^2, 27, 30, 33, 42, 51, 53
2:5^2, 7, 9, 14, 16, 17, 18, 19^3, 20, 22, 26^2, 27, 28, 29, 30, 31, 36, 38, 39, 42^3
3:2, 6, 11, 12, 13, 16, 26
4:12, 21^2, 27, 28, 33
5:1, 3, 5^3, 6^2, 7, 9^2
6:12, 24
7:8, 9, 48
8:1, 2, 5, 6, 8, 15, 18^2, 19, 26, 28^2, 29, 33, 34^2, 40, 44, 46, 47, 48^3, 52^4, 54, 56, 58, 59, 63, 65, 66
9:2, 3, 8, 13, 16, 21, 24, 25
10:5, 12, 13
11:2^3, 8, 9, 11, 14, 18, 22, 24, 35, 36, 38^2, 40
12:3, 5, 7^2, 9, 10^5, 15^2, 16^2, 19, 20, 22, 23^2, 27^2, 28, 30, 32^2, 33
13:1, 2, 6, 7, 8, 11, 12, 13, 14, 15, 18^3, 20, 21, 22, 26^3, 34
14:5^2, 27
15:19, 20, 29
17:1, 2, 5, 8, 13^2, 18^2, 19, 20, 21, 23
18:1, 2, 5^3, 15, 17, 19, 20^2, 21, 22, 25, 30^3, 31, 40, 41, 44
19:2, 5, 8, 9^2, 13, 15, 18, 20, 21^2
20:2, 5, 6, 7, 8^2, 9, 10^2, 12, 13, 22, 23, 25, 28, 31, 34, 35, 36, 39^2, 40, 42
21:2^2, 3, 5, 6^3, 7, 8, 11^2, 19^2, 25
22:3, 4, 5, 6, 8, 13^2, 14, 15, 16, 18, 22, 24, 26, 30, 34, 38, 49

2 KINGS

1:2, 3, 5^2, 6^4, 7, 9^2, 11^2, 12, 13, 15^2, 16
2:2^2, 3, 4, 5, 6, 9, 10, 16, 18^2, 19, 21, 22, 23^2
3:3, 4, 13^2, 26
4:1^2, 2, 6^2, 9, 13^2, 16, 17, 19, 22, 25, 26, 33, 36, 38, 42
5:1, 3, 5, 6, 7, 10, 13, 14, 17^2, 19, 25, 26, 27^2
6:1, 2, 9, 11, 15, 18, 19, 21, 26, 28^2, 29, 33
7:4, 5, 10, 12, 15, 20
8:1, 3, 6, 8, 10^2, 12, 22
9:1, 5, 6, 11^2, 20
10:1, 6, 10, 17, 18, 19, 22, 23, 27, 30^2
11:15
12:7
13:4, 14, 15^2, 18, 23^2
14:6, 7, 13, 25
15:5, 12^2
16:6, 9
17:12, 23, 32, 34, 41
18:4, 8, 11, 14, 19, 21, 22, 26, 27, 32
19:3, 6, 9, 29
20:1^2, 2, 5, 6, 8, 11, 12, 13, 14^3, 16, 17, 19
21:15
22:6, 8, 13^2, 14, 15, 17, 20
23:1, 4, 5, 6, 21, 25, 35
24:7
25:2, 8, 17, 24

1 CHRONICLES

1:19
2:3, 9, 19
3:1, 4, 5
4:31, 33, 39, 41, 43
5:1, 8, 9, 13, 23^2, 26^2
6:48, 61, 63, 67, 71, 77
7:28
10:9, 14
11:1, 2
12:8, 16, 17^3, 18, 40
13:2^4, 5, 9
14:10, 14
15:2, 3, 12^2
16:8, 9^2, 16, 18, 23, 28^2, 29^2, 34, 40
17:2, 5, 7, 15, 26
18:3, 11
19:2, 3^2, 11, 14
20:8
21:5, 8, 9, 10, 11, 13, 15, 17, 18, 22, 23, 26
22:7, 8, 9
23:13, 25, 26, 31^2
26:6
28:1, 3, 6
29:1, 5, 12, 17, 18, 19, 21^2, 22, 24

2 CHRONICLES

1:2, 5, 7^2, 8^2, 9, 12
2:15
3:1
5:2, 3, 6, 7, 9
6:14, 17, 19, 20, 21, 25, 27, 30^2, 31, 34, 36, 37, 38, 40
7:8, 10, 12, 15, 21^2
8:11, 12, 15, 16
9:12, 26, 28
10:5^2, 7, 9, 10^3, 15, 16, 19
11:3, 14, 16, 23
12:5
13:7, 10, 11, 14
14:7, 9, 11, 13
15:2, 4, 11, 14, 19
16:4, 7
17:3, 16
18:3, 4, 5, 7^2, 14, 17, 20, 23, 29
19:4
20:9, 15, 21, 24, 26, 28, 33
21:10
23:3, 14
24:5, 6, 11, 17, 19, 20, 23
25:12, 13, 14, 15^2, 16^2
26:18^3, 21
27:5
28:9^2, 10, 13, 16, 20, 21, 23, 25
29:5, 7, 11, 30, 31
30:1, 5, 6, 8, 9^2, 10, 17, 21, 22, 27
31:6, 16
32:9^2, 13, 18, 23, 24^2, 25, 31
33:2, 13, 17, 18, 22
34:4, 6, 25, 26
35:1, 3^2, 8^2, 9, 12, 22
36:13

EZRA

1:8, 11
2:1^3, 63, 69
3:3, 5, 6, 7^2, 8^2, 11
4:1, 2^2, 3^3, 6, 7, 11^2, 12^2, 13, 15, 17^2, 18, 20, 23, 24
5:1^2, 3, 4, 6, 7^2, 8, 9, 12, 14, 15
6:5^2, 8, 10, 21, 22
7:7, 11, 12, 15, 22, 26, 28
8:17^3, 22, 25, 26, 28^3, 30, 31, 35^2, 36
9:4, 5, 6, 7, 9, 11, 12^2
10:1, 2, 4, 7^2, 9, 10, 11

NEHEMIAH

1:3, 9^3
2:1, 2, 3, 4, 5^3, 6, 7, 8, 17, 18, 20
3:1^2, 2, 4^3, 5, 7^2, 8^3, 9, 10^2, 12, 13, 15, 16^2, 17, 20, 24^2, 26, 27, 31, 32
4:6, 9, 12^2, 14, 15^2, 19, 20, 22
5:5, 7, 8^3, 14, 15, 16, 17
6:2, 3, 4, 5, 8, 10, 17^2, 18
7:3, 6, 65, 70
8:1, 3, 9^2, 10^3, 12, 13, 15, 17, 18^2
9:4, 14, 27, 28, 29^2, 32, 34, 36, 37, 38
10:28, 30, 35, 36, 37^2, 38, 39
11:30
12:37, 38, 39, 46, 47^2
13:4, 6, 12, 13, 16, 17, 21, 25^2, 27

ESTHER

1:1, 3, 5^2, 14, 15, 17, 18, 19
2:2, 3^2, 8^2, 9, 13^2, 14, 15, 16, 18, 22
3:3, 4^2, 8, 10, 11, 12, 14
4:6, 7, 8^4, 10^2, 11^2, 16
5:3, 4^2, 6, 12^2, 14^3
6:3, 4, 5, 6^2, 11, 13, 14
7:2, 5
8:1^2, 2, 6, 7, 9^4, 13
9:5, 12, 13, 20, 22, 23, 26, 27, 30
10:3

JOB

1:2, 7, 8, 12, 14
2:2, 3, 6, 7, 9, 10, 13
3:6, 20, 25
5:7, 8^2
6:22, 28
7:4, 20
8:5
9:12, 16
10:2, 3, 15
11:7, 19
12:8
13:2, 12, 20, 27
15:19
16:20
19:11
20:6, 29
21:14, 15, 33
22:2^2, 17, 21, 26, 27, 28
23:5
28:28
29:21
30:20, 26
31:10, 37^2
32:12, 21
33:22, 23, 24, 26^3, 31, 33
34:2, 10, 11, 14, 15, 28, 31, 34, 36, 37
35:3, 5, 6
37:3, 14, 19
38:17, 35, 41
39:4, 13^2
40:6, 7, 14, 19
41:3^2
42:4, 7, 8, 11

PSALMS

2:5, 7
3:4, 8

PSALMS

4:3
5:2^2, 3
7:t, 4
10:14
13:6
16:2, 6
17:1^2, 6
18:t, 6, 39, 41, 44, 49^2
19:2^2, 6
22:5, 22, 24, 27, 31
24:4
25:1, 10, 16
26:11
27:6, 8, 12
28:1, 2
29:1^2, 2^2, 11
30:2, 4, 8, 12
31:22
32:2, 5^2, 6^2, 9
33:2, 3
34:5, 11, 15, 18
35:3, 10, 23
36:5, 10
37:5
39:12
40:1, 3, 5, 15
41:2, 4, 8, 10
42:3, 7, 8, 9, 10
43:3, 4^2
44:3, 25
45:14^2
46:9
47:1, 6, 9
48:10, 14
50:1, 5, 14^2, 16
51:t, 1, 12, 13, 18
52:t
54:5, 6
55:2, 14
56:1, 4, 9, 11, 12
57:1^2, 2^2, 9, 10^2
59:13, 17
61:1, 2, 8
62:11, 12
65:1, 2, 4
66:1, 3^2, 4, 15, 17
67:1
68:4, 20, 29, 31, 32^2, 34, 35
69:1, 8^2, 13, 16, 18, 27
70:5
71:2, 7, 18, 19, 22, 23, 24
72:1, 8
74:3, 19, 20
75:1^2, 4
76:11^2
77:1^3
78:36, 46^2, 62
79:2^2, 12
80:6, 11^2
81:1^2, 8^2, 12, 13, 15
83:9^2
85:1, 8
86:3^2, 4, 5, 6, 8^2, 16^2
88:2, 3, 8, 9, 13
89:3, 6^2, 8, 26, 35, 49
90:12, 16^2
92:1^2
94:15
95:1, 2, 11
96:1^2, 2, 7^2, 8^2
98:1, 4, 5
99:7
100:1, 4
101:1, 2
102:1, 2, 12
103:7^2, 17, 20
104:8, 23, 33
105:1, 2^2, 9, 10, 11
106:1, 4, 25, 28, 31^2, 36, 37, 38, 47
107:1, 6, 13, 18, 19, 28, 30
108:3, 4
109:4, 12, 17, 19, 25
110:1
111:5, 9
112:4
113:3, 5
115:1^3, 8
116:2, 7, 12, 14, 18
118:1, 6, 18, 27, 29
119:6, 15, 20, 25, 28, 31, 33, 36, 38, 41, 48, 49, 58, 59, 62, 65, 72, 76, 77, 79, 90, 103, 105^2, 107, 112, 116, 117, 124, 130, 132^2, 146, 149
120:1, 3^2
121:1
122:1, 4^2
123:1, 2^2
125:3, 4, 5
130:1
132:2^2, 11
135:3, 4, 12, 18
136:1, 2, 22, 26
138:1, 6
139:6, 17
140:6, 13
141:1^4, 8
142:1^2, 5, 6
143:6, 7, 8, 9
144:9^2, 10
145:18
146:2, 10
147:1, 7^2, 19^2
148:14
149:1, 3

PROVERBS

1:5, 9, 23^2, 33
2:2, 10, 18^2, 19
3:5, 15, 22, 28, 34
4:4, 18, 20, 22
5:1, 9^2
6:16
7:4, 13, 24
8:4, 32
11:27
12:14, 15
14:6, 12
15:9, 10, 12
16:3, 22, 25
18:13
19:17
20:23
22:17, 21
23:12, 22
24:11, 14, 24
25:7
26:4
28:27
29:17
30:1^2, 5, 6, 10
31:3, 6^2, 24

ECCLESIASTES

1:6, 7
2:3, 17, 18
3:20
5:4
7:21
8:4, 9, 14
9:3, 13
12:7

SONG OF SOLOMON

1:13, 14
2:10
8:11

ISAIAH

1:4, 6, 9^2, 10, 11, 13, 14, 23
2:2
3:9^2, 11
5:8, 11, 18, 20, 21, 22, 26, 30
6:3, 6
7:3, 4, 10
8:1, 2, 3, 5, 19^4, 22
9:6^2, 13
10:1, 11, 21, 30
12:5
13:2, 15
14:10^2
15:4^2, 5, 8^2
16:1, 8
18:4, 6, 7
19:11, 16, 17, 20^2, 21
20:1
21:2, 4, 6, 9, 10, 16
22:11^2, 15^2
24:16
25:6
26:15
27:2, 12
28:5, 13, 15
29:2, 11, 15
30:10^2, 18, 19, 22
31:1, 4, 6, 7
32:9
33:2, 21
34:17
35:2
36:2, 3, 4, 10, 11^2
37:2, 3, 6^2, 14, 15, 21, 30
38:1^3, 2, 5, 7, 15
39:3^4
40:2, 9, 18, 20
41:9, 13
42:3, 5, 10, 12, 16, 24
44:5, 7, 17^2, 22
45:9, 10^2, 14^3, 19, 20, 22, 23
46:3, 7, 12
47:15
48:11, 12, 13, 16, 22
49:1, 3, 6
51:1, 2^2, 4^2, 7, 11, 16, 19
52:7
53:12
54:9
55:2, 3, 5, 7, 11
56:4, 5, 8
57:9, 18
59:16, 20
60:5^2, 7^2, 9, 10, 11, 13, 14, 19^2
61:1, 3^2, 7
62:11
63:5
65:1, 2, 11, 15
66:1, 19, 20, 24

JEREMIAH

1:3^2, 4, 5, 7, 9, 11, 12, 13, 14, 16, 17
2:3, 10, 17, 21, 27, 31^2
3:1, 2, 4, 6, 7, 10, 11, 14, 17, 18, 22, 25
4:1, 10, 12, 13, 18^2
5:5^2, 13, 19, 24
6:3, 4, 10, 12, 13^2, 19, 20
7:9, 12, 13, 14^2, 18, 21, 22, 23, 25^2, 26, 27^2, 28
8:4, 10^3
10:1, 6, 7, 11
11:2, 3, 5, 6, 7^2, 9, 11^2, 12^2, 13, 14, 17, 20
12:6, 8, 9, 11
13:1, 3, 6, 8, 11^2, 12^2, 13, 18, 27
14:2, 10, 11, 13, 14^3, 17
15:1, 2, 16, 18, 19^2, 20
16:1, 10, 11, 12, 15, 19, 20
17:15, 17, 19, 20, 24, 26, 27
18:8
19:2, 4, 5, 11, 12, 13^2
20:3, 8, 12, 13, 15
21:1^2, 3, 8, 9
22:6^2, 8, 13, 21
23:1, 5, 12, 14, 16^2, 17^2, 33, 38
24:3, 4, 7, 10
25:2, 3^3, 4, 5, 7, 15, 17, 27, 28, 30, 33
26:2^2, 3, 4, 5, 8, 10, 11, 12, 14, 15, 16, 23
27:1, 3, 4^2, 5^2, 9, 10, 14^3, 15, 16^2, 17
28:1, 5, 12, 15
29:1, 3, 4^2, 7, 9, 12^2, 19, 21, 25, 28, 30, 31
30:2, 9, 15, 17, 21^2
31:3, 6, 26, 32, 34, 38, 40^3
32:6, 7, 8, 12, 16^2, 18, 20, 24, 25, 26, 29^2, 31, 33, 35, 37
33:1, 3, 6, 9^2, 14, 15, 19, 22
34:1, 6, 8^2, 14^2, 16, 17, 20
35:1, 2^2, 5, 12, 14^3, 15^2, 16, 17^2, 18^2
36:1, 2^2, 3, 4, 9, 13, 14^2, 15, 16, 18, 19, 32
37:2, 3, 6, 7, 18, 19
38:1, 4^2, 12, 14^2, 15^3, 16, 17^2, 19, 20^2, 24, 25^5, 26, 27
39:12^2, 14, 15, 18
40:1, 2, 4^3, 5, 6, 7, 9, 10, 12, 14, 15, 16
41:1, 6, 8, 14
42:1, 2^2, 4^3, 7, 9^2, 10, 12, 20^4, 21
43:1, 2, 8, 10
44:4, 5, 8^2, 10, 12, 15, 16^2, 17^2, 18, 19^2, 20, 23, 24, 25, 29
45:1, 2, 4, 5
48:1, 9, 12, 27, 34^3, 46
49:2, 4, 14, 29, 31
50:15, 27, 29, 44
51:2, 6, 9, 24, 44, 48, 53
52:5, 9, 22, 32

LAMENTATIONS

1:12^2, 21, 22^2
2:1, 18
3:10, 25, 41, 64, 65
4:4, 15, 21
5:4, 16, 21

EZEKIEL

1:3, 16
2:1^2, 2^2, 3^2, 4^2, 7, 8, 9
3:1^2, 3, 4^3, 6, 7^2, 10^2, 11^2, 16, 17, 18, 22, 24, 27
4:3, 9, 15, 16
5:15
6:1, 10
7:1, 2, 7, 27
8:5, 6, 8, 9, 12, 13, 15, 17
9:4, 7, 9
10:2, 7, 13
11:1, 2, 5, 14, 15^2, 25
12:1, 6, 8, 9, 10, 11, 19, 21, 23, 28
13:1, 2, 3, 11, 12, 15, 18
14:1, 2, 4^2, 6, 10, 22
15:1
16:1, 3, 5, 6^2, 8, 20^2, 23, 24, 27, 29, 33, 34, 36, 37, 54, 60, 61
17:1, 2, 3, 11
18:1, 22
19:4
20:2, 3^2, 5^4, 6, 7, 8, 9, 15, 18, 23, 27^2, 29^2, 30, 31, 39, 45
21:1, 7, 8, 18, 23, 29^2
22:1, 4^2, 17, 23, 24, 28
23:1, 16, 27, 30, 36^2, 37, 38, 40, 43, 44^4
24:1, 3^2, 15, 18, 19, 20, 21, 24, 26, 27
25:1, 3, 8, 10
26:1, 2
27:1, 3
28:1, 2, 11, 12, 20, 24
29:1, 4^2, 10, 17, 19
30:1, 20
31:1, 2, 4, 8, 14, 17, 18
32:1, 2, 17, 18
33:1, 2, 7, 8, 10, 11, 12, 14, 16, 21, 23, 25, 27, 31, 32
34:1, 2^2, 18, 20
35:1, 3, 6, 15
36:1, 3, 6, 9, 11, 13, 16, 20, 22, 32
37:3, 4^2, 5, 9^2, 11, 12, 15, 18, 19, 21, 25
38:1, 7^2, 13, 14
39:4, 11, 17, 24, 28
40:4^2, 6, 14, 15, 19, 22, 45, 46
41:4, 17, 20, 22
42:13^2
43:6, 7, 18, 19^2, 24
44:2, 5^2, 11, 12, 13^2, 15^2, 16, 26, 27, 28, 30
45:1, 4, 7
46:4, 7, 12, 13, 14, 16, 20, 24
47:1, 2, 6, 8, 10, 14^2, 18, 21, 22^2
48:2, 3, 4, 5, 6, 7, 8^2, 9, 12, 14, 18, 23, 24, 25, 26, 27, 28, 29

DANIEL

1:1, 3, 7^2, 10, 21
2:3, 5, 9, 19, 21, 23^2, 24^3, 25^2, 26, 27, 46, 47
3:3, 14, 18, 24^2
4:1^2, 6, 7, 11, 16, 18, 20, 22, 26, 27, 34^2, 35, 36^4
5:13, 15, 17
6:2, 6, 15^2, 16, 19, 20, 21, 25^2, 26
7:5, 10, 16, 26
8:1^3, 6, 7, 13, 14^2, 17
9:3, 4, 6, 7^3, 25, 26
10:1, 11^4, 12, 15, 16, 19^2, 20
11:18
12:7

HOSEA

1:1, 2, 4, 6, 10^2
2:1, 14, 19^2, 20, 23
3:1, 3
4:12, 15
5:4, 12, 14
6:1, 3^2, 4^2
7:7, 13^2, 14
8:2, 11
9:4^2, 10, 17
10:1, 6, 15
11:2, 4
12:4, 14
13:7
14:1, 2, 5

JOEL

1:14, 20
2:13, 14, 19
3:6

AMOS

1:5
2:7
3:7
4:6, 8^2, 9, 10^2, 11, 12^2, 13
5:4, 15, 18, 25
6:2, 10, 14
7:1, 4, 8, 12, 15^2
8:1, 2
9:7

OBADIAH

15, 20

JONAH

1:1, 3^2, 5, 6, 8, 9, 10, 11^3, 12^2, 14, 16
2:1, 2, 7, 9, 10
3:1, 2^2, 3, 6, 8, 10
4:2^2, 9

MICAH

1:9^2, 12, 15^2
2:11
3:4, 6^2, 8
4:1, 8, 13^2
5:2, 3, 4
6:3, 5, 9
7:7, 8, 10, 15, 18, 20

NAHUM

3:13

HABAKKUK

1:2, 10, 11, 16^2
2:1, 5^2, 7, 15, 16, 19
3:13, 16

ZEPHANIAH

1:1
2:5, 11

HAGGAI

1:1, 9, 13
2:20

ZECHARIAH

1:1, 3^3, 4^2, 6, 7, 9, 14, 19
2:2, 4, 5, 8, 11
3:2, 4^2, 6
4:2, 5, 6^2, 7, 8, 9, 11, 12
5:2, 3, 5, 11
6:4, 5, 8, 9, 12, 15
7:1, 2, 3, 4, 5^2, 8
8:3, 11, 15, 18
9:9, 10, 12
11:7, 12, 13^2, 15^2
12:2
13:3, 6
14:5, 10^3, 17, 20, 21

MALACHI

1:6, 8, 9, 11^2, 14
2:2, 4, 12
3:3, 4, 7^2
4:2, 4

MATTHEW

1:17, 20^2, 24
2:5, 11
3:7, 9^2, 10, 11, 13, 15, 16
4:6, 7, 9, 10, 11, 19, 24
5:1, 15, 18, 20, 22, 26, 28, 32, 33, 34, 39, 44
6:2, 5, 8, 16^2, 18^2, 25, 27, 29, 33, 34
7:6, 7, 11, 14, 21, 23, 24, 26
8:4^2, 5, 7, 10, 11, 13^2, 15, 16, 18, 19, 20, 21, 22, 26, 32
9:2, 6, 8, 9, 11, 12, 15, 16, 18, 24, 28^2, 29, 37
10:1, 15, 23, 42^2
11:3, 4, 7, 9, 11, 16^2, 17^2, 21^2, 22, 23, 24, 25, 27, 28, 29
12:2, 3, 6, 11, 20, 22, 25, 28, 31^3, 36, 39, 45, 47, 48
13:2, 3, 10^2, 11^2, 17, 24^2, 27, 28^2, 31, 33^2, 34^2, 36^2, 37, 44, 45, 47, 51^2, 52^3, 57
14:2, 4, 16, 17, 22, 25, 27, 28, 31, 35
15:3, 8, 10, 12, 15^2, 22, 24, 28^2, 29, 30, 32, 33, 34
16:2, 4, 6, 8, 15, 17^2, 18, 19, 21^2, 22, 23^2, 24, 28
17:3, 4, 11, 12^2, 13, 20^4, 22, 26^2, 27
18:1, 2, 3, 7, 10, 13, 17^2, 18, 19, 22^2, 23, 24, 31, 32, 34, 35
19:3^2, 4, 7, 8, 9, 10, 11, 13, 14, 16, 17, 18, 20, 21, 23^2, 24, 26, 27, 28^2
20:1, 4, 6, 7^2, 8^2, 12, 14^2, 17, 18^2, 21^2, 22, 23, 25, 28, 32, 33
21:1^2, 2^2, 3, 5, 13, 16^2, 19, 21^3, 23, 24, 25, 27, 31^3, 32, 36, 37, 40, 41^2, 42, 43
22:1, 2, 4, 12, 16, 17, 19, 20, 21^4, 24, 25, 26, 29, 31, 37, 39, 42, 43, 44
23:13, 14, 15, 16, 23, 25, 27^2, 28, 29, 31, 34, 35, 36, 37, 38, 39
24:2^2, 3, 4, 13, 14, 19, 23, 26, 27, 34, 47
25:1, 8, 12, 14, 15, 20, 21, 22, 23, 26, 28, 29, 34, 36, 39, 40^4, 41, 44, 45
26:1, 3, 7, 10, 13, 14, 15^2, 17, 18, 21, 22, 24, 25, 29, 31, 33, 34^2, 35, 36^2, 38^2, 40^2, 45, 50, 52, 58, 62, 63, 64^2, 68, 69, 71, 73, 75
27:8, 11, 13, 15, 17^2, 19, 21^2, 22^2, 26, 27, 33, 45, 53, 55, 62, 64, 65
28:5, 10, 11, 12, 18^2, 20

MARK

1:5, 13, 17, 31, 32, 37, 38, 40, 41, 44^2
2:2, 3, 4, 5, 8, 11, 13, 14, 16, 17, 18, 19, 24, 25, 27
3:3, 4, 5, 8, 13^2, 23^2, 28^2, 31, 32
4:1, 2, 9, 11^3, 13, 21, 24^2, 33, 34, 35^2, 38, 39, 40
5:1, 8, 11, 19, 21^3, 31, 34, 36, 39, 41^2
6:2, 4, 7, 10, 11, 18, 22, 23^2, 24, 25, 30, 31, 33, 35, 37^2, 38, 45, 48^2, 50, 51
7:1, 6, 9, 14^3, 18, 27^2, 28, 29, 31, 32, 34
8:1^2, 12^2, 17, 19, 21, 22, 27, 29^2, 34^2
9:1^2, 4, 13^2, 17, 19, 20, 21, 23, 25, 29, 31, 35, 36, 41
10:1, 3, 5, 11, 14^2, 15, 18, 20, 21, 23, 24, 28, 29, 32, 33^2, 35, 36, 37^2, 38, 39^2, 42, 45, 49, 51^3, 52
11:1, 2, 3, 5, 6, 11, 14, 17, 21, 22, 23^2, 24, 28, 29, 33^2
12:1, 4, 6, 9, 13, 14, 15, 16^2, 17, 18, 19^2, 24, 26, 32, 34, 38, 43^3
13:1, 2, 13, 19, 30, 37^2
14:9, 10^2, 12, 13, 16, 18, 19, 20, 24, 25, 27, 29, 30^2, 34^2, 36, 37, 41, 48, 61, 65, 72
15:2, 6, 8, 9, 11, 12^2, 14, 15, 22, 41^2, 43, 44, 46
16:2, 6, 7, 12, 13, 14, 15, 19

LUKE

1:2, 3, 11, 13, 18, 19^2, 22^2, 26, 28, 30, 32, 34, 35, 38, 61, 74, 77, 80
2:4, 10, 11, 12, 15^2, 20, 26, 34, 38, 48, 49, 50, 51
3:2, 8^2, 9, 11, 12, 13, 14, 16, 18
4:3, 5, 6^2, 8, 9, 12, 17, 21, 23^2, 24, 26^3, 29, 39, 40, 42, 43
5:4, 5, 7, 10, 14, 20, 22, 24^2, 27, 31, 33, 34, 36
6:2, 5, 9, 10, 13, 23, 24, 25^2, 26, 27, 29, 35, 38, 39
7:2, 3, 6, 7, 8, 9^2, 13, 14, 19, 20^2, 21, 22, 24, 26, 28, 32^2, 40^2, 43, 44, 47, 48
8:3, 10, 21, 22^2, 25, 39^2, 47, 48
9:3, 11, 12, 13, 20, 33, 43, 48, 50, 57, 58, 59, 60, 62
10:2, 9^2, 11, 12, 13^2, 17, 18, 19, 20, 21, 23, 26, 28, 29, 35, 36, 37, 41
11:1, 2, 5^3, 8, 9^2, 13, 17, 24, 27, 30, 39, 41, 42, 43, 44, 45, 46, 47, 51^2, 52, 53
12:1, 4, 5, 8, 10, 11^2, 13, 14, 15, 16, 20, 22^2, 27, 31, 36^2, 37, 41^2, 44, 48
13:2, 7, 8, 12, 14, 18, 23^2, 24, 25^2, 31, 32, 34, 35^2
14:3, 7, 10, 15, 16, 18, 23, 24, 25
15:1, 3, 6, 7, 10, 12, 16, 18, 21, 27, 31
16:1^2, 2, 5^3, 6, 7, 9, 15, 28, 29, 30, 31
17:1^2, 5, 6, 7, 8, 14^2, 19, 22, 24, 37^2
18:1, 3, 7, 9, 13, 15, 16^2, 17, 19, 22^2, 29^2, 31^2, 32, 35, 40, 41, 42, 43
19:5, 8, 9, 13, 15, 17, 22, 24, 25, 26^2, 31, 32, 33, 39, 40, 42, 46
20:2, 3, 8, 15, 20, 22, 23, 25^3, 28^2, 34, 36, 38, 41, 42, 45
21:3, 4, 10, 23, 32
22:4, 6, 9, 10, 11^2, 13, 15, 16, 18, 19, 22, 25, 29^2, 33, 35, 36, 37, 38, 40, 43, 46, 47, 48, 49, 52, 61, 67, 70
23:1, 7, 14^2, 15, 17, 18, 22, 25, 28, 42, 43^2, 52
24:1, 5, 6, 9, 10, 12, 17, 18, 19^2, 25, 27, 28, 36^2, 38, 41, 44^2, 46

JOHN

1:11, 22, 25, 29, 33, 38^2, 39, 41, 43, 45, 46^2, 48^2, 49, 50^2, 51^2
2:3, 4, 5^2, 7, 8^2, 10, 16, 18^2, 19, 22, 24
3:2, 3^2, 4, 5, 7, 9, 10, 11, 26^2, 34
4:7, 8, 9, 10, 11, 13, 15, 16, 17, 19, 21, 25, 26^2, 30, 32, 34, 35, 36, 40, 42, 45, 47, 48, 49, 50^2, 52, 53
5:6, 8, 10, 11, 12, 14^2, 19^2, 22, 24^2, 25, 29^2, 33^2
6:5^2, 8, 12, 13, 16, 19, 20, 23, 25, 26, 27^2, 28, 29, 30, 32^2, 33, 34, 35, 36, 43, 45, 47, 53^2, 61, 63, 65^3, 67
7:3, 6, 8^2, 9, 10, 21, 22, 26, 33^2, 35, 37, 45, 50, 52, 53
8:1, 2, 3, 4, 7, 9, 10, 11, 12, 13, 14, 19, 21, 23, 24, 25^3, 28, 34, 39^2, 42, 48, 51, 52, 55, 57, 58^2
9:7, 10, 11, 12, 15, 17, 24, 29, 30, 34, 35, 37, 40, 41
10:1, 6^2, 7^2, 24, 26, 28, 35, 41
11:3, 4, 8, 11, 14, 15, 16, 18, 21, 23, 24, 25, 27, 29, 31, 32, 34, 39, 40^2, 44, 49, 54
12:16, 24, 25, 27, 32, 35, 50
13:1^2, 6, 7, 8, 9, 12, 16, 20, 21, 25, 27, 28, 29, 33, 34, 36, 37, 38
14:3, 5, 6^2, 8, 9, 10, 12^2, 22^3, 23^2, 25, 26, 27^2, 28^3
15:3, 7, 11, 15, 20, 21, 22, 26
16:1, 3, 4, 6, 7^2, 12, 14, 15, 17, 19, 20, 23, 25^2, 26, 29, 33
17:6, 8, 26
18:4, 5, 6, 11, 15, 16^2, 17, 21, 24, 25, 28, 29, 30^2, 31^2, 33, 35, 37^2, 38^3, 39^2
19:4, 5, 6, 9, 10^2, 11, 14, 15, 16, 26, 27
20:1, 2, 10, 13^2, 15^2, 16^2, 17^3, 18, 19^2, 20, 21, 22, 23, 25^2, 26, 28, 29
21:3^2, 5, 6, 7^2, 10, 12, 15^2, 16^2, 17^4, 18, 19, 22, 23

THE ACTS

1:2, 7, 8^2, 12, 19, 22
2:3, 14^2, 29^2, 34, 37, 38, 39, 41
3:5, 10, 11, 12, 14, 20, 22^4, 25, 26
4:1, 3, 8, 10, 19^3, 23, 29, 35
5:4^2, 8, 9, 16, 35, 38
6:2
7:2, 3, 13, 26, 31, 37^3, 38, 40, 41, 44, 45
8:1, 5, 6, 14, 20, 26^3, 29, 35, 36
9:1, 2, 4, 6, 11, 15^2, 17, 21, 27, 34, 38
10:3, 4, 7, 8, 9, 11, 15, 19, 21, 28^2, 29, 32, 36, 41, 42
11:4, 7, 11^2, 13, 17, 18, 19, 20, 21, 22, 23, 24, 26, 27, 29
12:5, 8^2, 10^2, 15, 17^3, 21
13:4, 6, 15, 20, 21, 22, 23, 31, 32^2, 33, 36, 38^2, 41, 47, 51
14:3, 6^2, 13, 15^2, 18, 27
15:2, 3, 7, 8, 13, 18, 20, 23, 25^2, 33, 36, 39, 40
16:10, 13, 14, 17, 19, 25, 32, 37, 38
17:2, 3, 5, 6, 10, 15^2, 18, 19, 23, 29, 31, 34
18:2, 6^2, 14, 21, 26^2
19:2^2, 3^3, 4, 12, 22, 24, 30, 31, 33
20:1, 6, 7, 13, 18, 20, 22, 24, 27, 28, 34, 38
21:1^3, 2, 8, 11, 18, 20, 31, 32, 37^2, 39, 40^2
22:1, 4, 5^2, 6, 7^2, 8, 10, 13^2, 15, 18, 20, 21^2, 22, 25, 27
23:3, 15, 17^2, 18^3, 21, 23, 24, 26
24:2, 4, 8, 10^2, 14, 23
25:6, 11^2, 12^2, 13, 14, 21, 22, 26
26:1, 6, 7, 11, 14, 16^2, 17, 18, 19, 20, 22, 23, 28, 32^2
27:1, 3, 8, 10, 21, 40
28:17, 19, 21, 25, 26, 28^2, 30

ROMANS

1:1, 10, 11, 13, 16, 19, 26
2:5, 8, 14
3:2, 7, 22
4:3, 6, 11
5:5, 15, 16, 18, 21^2
6:10^2, 11^2, 13^3, 16^2, 19^2, 22
7:4, 5, 10, 13, 16
9:12, 17, 19, 21^2, 23, 26, 29
10:3, 10^2, 12, 18, 20, 21
11:4, 8, 9, 11, 27, 35
12:1, 3, 19
13:1
14:6, 8^2
15:8, 9, 15, 19, 23, 25^2, 27, 29, 32
16:1, 4, 5, 19^2

1 CORINTHIANS

1:2, 3, 8, 9, 11, 18, 23^2, 24, 30
2:1, 7, 10, 14
3:1^4, 10
4:9, 11, 13, 17, 21
5:5, 9, 11
6:12, 17
7:1, 3^2, 10, 27
8:1, 4, 7^2
9:2, 11, 15, 16, 17, 19, 20
10:2, 11, 28^2
11:13, 14, 17, 23, 34
12:2, 21, 31
14:2^2, 3, 6, 11^2, 21, 26, 34, 36, 37

1 CORINTHIANS

15:1^{2}, 2, 3, 6, 28^{2}
16:3, 5, 9, 11, 12, 16

2 CORINTHIANS

1:1, 13, 15, 16, 20, 23
2:3, 4^{2}, 12, 14, 15, 16^{2}
3:15
4:4, 11
5:5, 11, 12, 15^{2}, 19^{3}
6:11, 13, 18
7:12^{2}
8:2, 5, 17
9:5, 12, 13^{2}, 15
10:13, 14
11:9
12:9, 17, 19, 20

GALATIANS

1:2, 6, 8^{2}, 9, 17, 20, 22
2:2, 7^{2}, 9^{3}, 14, 19
3:8, 23, 24
4:8, 13
5:2, 4, 13
6:6, 10^{2}, 11, 14^{2}
S

EPHESIANS

1:5, 9, 14, 15, 17
2:10, 16, 18, 21
3:3, 5^{2}, 7, 8, 10, 14, 20, 21
4:7, 8, 13^{2}, 16, 19, 29, 30
5:10, 20, 22^{2}, 24, 31
6:5, 9, 13, 19, 22
S

PHILIPPIANS

1:2, 11, 12^{2}, 29
2:8, 19, 27, 30
3:10, 11, 13, 15, 21^{2}
4:5, 6, 16, 20

COLOSSIANS

1:2, 6, 8, 10, 11, 12, 20
2:2
3:18, 20, 23
4:1, 3, 7, 8, 9, 10, 11^{2}

1 THESSALONIANS

1:1^{2}, 5, 9
2:1, 2, 8^{2}, 9^{2}, 12, 18
3:6, 11
4:7^{2}, 8, 9, 15^{2}
5:1, 15, 23, 27
S

2 THESSALONIANS

1:1, 2
2:1
3:9

1 TIMOTHY

1:2, 6, 17, 18, 20
2:4
3:14^{2}, 16
4:7, 8, 16^{2}
6:16

2 TIMOTHY

1:12, 14, 16, 18^{2}
2:9, 15, 16, 21^{2}, 24
3:9, 11, 15, 17
4:4, 8, 9, 10^{2}, 18
S

TITUS

1:3, 15^{2}, 16
2:9, 14
3:2, 8, 12^{2}, 13

PHILEMON

1, 13, 16, 19, 21, 22

HEBREWS

1:1, 2, 5, 8
2:3, 5, 10, 12^{2}, 17
3:6, 14
4:2^{2}, 13, 16
5:4, 5, 7, 9
6:1, 6, 8, 11, 17
7:3, 4, 19, 21, 25
8:5
9:20, 27, 28^{2}
10:24, 29, 30, 39
11:4, 26
12:2, 4, 5^{2}, 9, 11, 18^{2}, 22^{2}
13:6, 7, 13, 22

JAMES

1:23
2:2, 3, 16, 23
4:6
5:7

1 PETER

1:2^{2}, 3, 5, 7, 10, 12^{5}, 13, 22, 25
2:4, 7^{2}, 14^{2}, 24, 25
3:5, 7^{2}, 12, 19, 22
4:7, 12, 19
5:5, 10, 12

2 PETER

1:2, 3^{2}, 4, 11, 16, 19
2:4, 6, 9, 21, 22
3:1, 7, 12, 15^{2}, 16

1 JOHN

1:2^{2}, 3, 4, 5
2:1, 7, 8, 12, 13^{3}, 14^{2}, 21, 26
3:14
5:13, 16^{3}, 17

2 JOHN

1, 5, 10, 12^{2}

3 JOHN

1, 9, 13

JUDE

2, 3^{3}, 6, 11, 21, 24

REVELATION

1:1^{3}, 4, 5, 6, 11^{8}, 13, 15, 17
2:1, 5, 7, 8, 10, 11, 14, 16, 17, 18^{2}, 20, 23, 24^{2}, 26, 29
3:1, 6, 13, 14, 22
4:3, 6
5:5, 10, 13^{2}
6:2, 4, 8, 11^{2}, 13
7:10, 12, 13, 14, 17
8:3
9:1, 3, 7^{2}, 10, 19
10:4, 8, 9^{3}, 11
11:1, 2, 3, 12, 18
12:5, 11, 12, 13
13:2, 4^{2}, 5^{2}, 7, 15
14:4, 6, 13, 14, 20
15:7
16:8, 14, 19
17:1^{2}, 7, 13, 15, 17
18:5, 6, 18
19:1, 9^{3}, 10, 17
20:4
21:5, 6^{2}, 9, 11, 18
22:6^{2}, 9, 10, 16, 18^{3}

UP 4605, *507*

GENESIS

2:6, 21
4:8
7:11, 17^{2}
8:7, 13
13:1, 10, 14
14:22
17:22
18:2, 16
19:1, 2, 14, 27, 28, 30
20:18
21:14, 16, 18, 32
22:3^{2}, 4, 13^{2}, 19
23:3, 7
24:16, 54, 63, 64
25:8, 17, 34
26:23, 31
27:38
28:12, 18^{2}
29:11
31:10, 12, 17, 21, 35, 45, 55
32:22
33:1, 5
35:1, 3, 13, 14, 29
37:25, 28, 35
38:8, 12, 13
39:15, 16, 18
40:13, 19, 20
41:2, 3, 4, 5, 6, 18, 19, 20, 21, 22, 23, 27, 34, 35, 44, 48^{3}
43:2, 15, 29
44:4, 17, 24, 30, 33, 34
45:9, 25
46:4, 5, 29, 31
47:14
48:17
49:4^{2}, 9^{2}, 33^{2}
50:5, 6, 7^{2}, 9, 14, 23, 25

EXODUS

1:8, 10
2:17, 23
3:8, 17
7:12, 20
8:3, 4, 5, 6, 7, 20
9:10, 13, 16, 32
10:12, 14
12:6, 30, 31, 34, 38
13:18, 19
14:10, 16
15:7
16:13, 14, 23, 24, 33, 34
17:3, 10, 11, 12
19:3, 12, 13, 20^{2}, 23, 24^{2}
20:25, 26
22:2
24:1, 2, 4, 9, 12, 13^{2}, 15, 18
26:15, 30, 33
29:27
32:1^{2}, 4, 6^{2}, 8, 23, 30
33:1^{2}, 3, 5, 8, 10, 12, 15
34:2, 3, 4^{2}, 24
35:21, 26
36:2, 20
40:2, 8^{2}, 17, 18^{3}, 21, 28, 33^{2}, 36, 37^{2}

LEVITICUS

6:10
9:22
11:45
13:4, 5, 11, 21, 26, 31, 33, 37, 42, 50, 54
14:38, 46
19:16, 32
22:30
26:1^{2}, 38

NUMBERS

1:51
6:26
7:1
9:15, 17, 21^{2}, 22
10:11, 21, 35
11:32
13:17^{2}, 21, 30, 31^{2}, 32^{2}
14:1, 13, 36, 37, 40^{3}, 42, 44
15:19, 20
16:2, 3, 12, 13, 14, 24, 25, 27, 30, 32, 34, 37, 45
17:4, 7
18:26
19:9^{2}
20:4, 5, 11, 25, 27
21:3, 5, 17, 33
22:4^{2}, 13, 14, 20, 21, 41
23:7, 18^{2}, 24^{2}
24:2, 3, 8, 9, 15, 20, 21, 23, 25
25:4, 7
26:10
27:12
31:52
32:9, 11, 14
33:38

DEUTERONOMY

1:21, 22, 24, 26, 28^{2}, 41^{2}, 42, 43
2:13, 24
3:1, 27^{2}
4:19
5:5
6:7
8:14
9:1, 9, 23
10:1, 3
11:6, 17, 18, 19
14:25, 28
16:22
17:8, 20
18:15, 18
19:11, 15, 16
20:1
22:4, 14, 19
23:14
24:5
25:7^{2}, 9
27:2, 4, 5
28:7, 33, 43
29:22
30:12
31:5, 16
32:11, 17, 30, 34^{2}, 36, 38, 40, 49, 50
33:2
34:1

JOSHUA

2:6, 8, 10
3:6^{2}, 16
4:5, 8, 9, 16, 17, 18^{2}, 19, 23^{2}
5:1, 7, 13
6:1, 5, 6, 12, 20, 26^{2}
7:2^{2}, 3^{2}, 4, 10, 13, 16
8:1, 3, 7, 10^{2}, 11, 14, 20, 31
9:4
10:4, 5, 6, 9, 10, 12, 33, 36
11:6, 17
12:7
14:8
15:3^{2}, 6^{2}, 7^{2}, 8^{2}, 15
16:1
17:15
18:1, 11, 12^{2}, 17
19:10, 11, 12, 47
20:5
22:12, 33
24:17, 26, 32

JUDGES

1:1, 2, 3, 4, 16, 22, 36
2:1^{2}, 4, 16, 18
3:9, 15
4:5, 10^{2}, 12, 14
6:3^{2}, 5, 8, 13, 21, 35, 38
7:1
8:8, 11, 13, 20, 28
9:7, 18, 32, 33, 34, 35, 43, 48, 51
11:2, 13, 16, 31, 37
12:3
13:20
14:2, 19
15:5, 6, 9, 10^{2}, 13
16:3, 5, 8, 18^{2}, 29, 31
18:9, 12, 17, 30, 31
19:5, 7, 9, 10, 17, 27, 28^{3}, 30
20:3, 9, 18^{3}, 19, 23^{3}, 26, 28, 30, 31, 33, 38, 40^{2}
21:2, 5^{2}, 8, 19

RUTH

1:9, 14
2:15, 18
3:14
4:1, 5, 10

1 SAMUEL

1:3, 5, 6, 7, 9, 19, 21, 22^{2}, 24
2:6, 7, 8^{2}, 14, 19, 35
5:12
6:9, 10, 13, 20, 21
7:1, 7, 10
8:8
9:11, 13^{2}, 14^{2}, 19, 24, 26
10:3, 18, 25
11:1, 4
12:6
13:5, 15
14:9, 10^{2}, 12^{2}, 13, 21, 46
15:2, 6, 11, 12, 34
16:13
17:20, 23, 25^{2}
19:15
20:38
21:12
22:8
23:11, 12, 19, 29
24:7, 16, 22
25:5, 13, 35
26:19
27:8
28:8, 11^{2}, 14, 15, 25
29:9, 10^{2}, 11^{2}
30:4

2 SAMUEL

2:1^{3}, 2, 3, 22, 27, 32
3:10, 32
4:4, 12
5:8, 17, 19^{2}, 22, 23
6:2, 12, 15
7:6, 12
12:3^{4}, 11, 17
13:29, 34, 36
14:14
15:2, 20, 24, 30^{4}
17:16, 21
18:9, 18, 24^{2}, 28^{2}, 31, 33
19:34
20:2, 3, 15, 19, 20, 21
21:6, 8, 13
22:9, 40, 49^{2}
23:1, 8, 18
24:9, 11, 18, 19, 22

1 KINGS

1:35, 40, 45, 49
2:19, 34
3:15
6:8
7:21^{3}
8:1, 3, 4^{2}, 20, 35, 54
9:16, 24
10:5, 29
11:14, 15, 23, 26, 27
12:8, 10, 18, 24, 27, 28^{2}
13:4, 29
14:10, 14, 15, 16, 25
15:4, 17
16:17, 32, 34
17:7, 19
18:38, 41, 42^{2}, 43^{2}, 44, 46
20:1, 22, 26, 33
21:16, 21, 25
22:6, 12, 20, 29, 35, 38

2 KINGS

1:3, 4, 6^{2}, 7, 9, 13, 14, 16
2:1, 11, 13, 16, 23^{4}
3:7, 8, 21, 22, 24
4:21, 29, 34, 35, 36, 37
6:7, 24
7:5
8:12
9:1, 2, 8, 25, 27, 32
10:1, 5, 6, 15
12:10^{2}, 17^{2}
13:21
14:10, 11, 26
15:14, 16
16:5, 7^{2}, 9
17:3, 4, 5^{2}, 7, 10, 36
18:9, 13, 17^{2}, 25^{2}
19:4, 14, 22, 23, 24, 26, 28
20:5, 8, 17
21:3^{2}
22:4
23:2, 9, 29
24:1, 10
25:4, 6, 27

1 CHRONICLES

5:26
11:6, 11, 20
13:6^{2}
14:2, 8, 10^{2}, 11, 14
15:3, 12, 14, 16, 25, 28
17:5, 11
21:1, 16, 18^{2}, 19, 27
25:5
26:16
28:2

2 CHRONICLES

1:4, 6, 17
2:16
3:17
5:2, 4, 5^{2}, 13
6:10, 26
7:13, 20
8:11
9:4
10:8, 10, 18
11:4
12:2, 9
13:4, 6
16:1
17:6
18:2, 5, 11, 14, 19, 28, 34
20:16, 19, 23
21:4, 9, 16, 17
24:7, 23
25:14, 19, 21
26:16, 19
28:9, 12, 15, 24
29:7, 20
30:7, 27
32:5^{2}, 25
33:3, 14, 19
34:30
35:20
36:6, 15, 22, 23

EZRA

1:1, 3, 5^{2}, 11^{2}
2:1, 59, 63, 68
3:2
4:2, 12^{2}, 13, 16, 23
5:2, 3, 9, 11
6:1, 11
7:6, 7, 9, 13, 28
8:1
9:5, 6^{2}, 9
10:6, 10

NEHEMIAH

2:1, 15, 17, 18
3:1^{2}, 3, 6, 13, 14, 15, 19, 31, 32
4:3, 7, 14
5:2
6:1, 10
7:1, 5, 6, 61, 65
8:5, 6
9:3, 4, 5, 18
10:38
12:1, 31, 37^{2}

ESTHER

2:7, 20
5:9
7:7

JOB

1:5, 7, 16
2:2, 12^{2}
3:8, 10, 11
4:15
5:5^{2}, 11, 18
6:3, 4
7:9
8:11
9:7
10:15, 18
11:10, 15, 20
12:14, 15
13:19
14:10, 11, 17^{2}
15:30
16:4, 8, 12
17:8
18:16
19:8, 12
20:6, 15, 27
21:19
22:22, 23, 24, 26, 29
24:22
26:8
27:7, 16
28:4, 5
29:8
30:4, 12, 20, 22, 28
31:14, 18, 21, 29
33:5
34:7
36:13
37:7, 20
38:3, 8, 10, 34
39:4, 18, 27, 30
40:7, 23^{2}
41:10, 15, 25
42:8

PSALMS

3:1, 3
4:6
5:3
7:6
9:13
10:12
14:4
15:3
16:4
17:5, 7
18:8, 35, 39, 48^{2}
20:5
21:9
22:15
24:4, 7^{2}, 9^{2}
25:1
27:2, 5, 6, 10, 12
28:2, 5, 9
30:1, 3
31:8, 19
33:7
35:2, 11, 23, 25
39:6
40:2, 5, 12
41:8, 9, 10
44:5
47:5
53:4
54:3
56:1, 2
57:3, 8
59:1, 15
63:4
69:9, 15, 29
71:6, 20
74:3, 4, 5, 8, 15, 23
75:3, 4, 5, 7
77:9
78:21, 38, 48
80:2
81:3, 12
83:2
86:4
87:6
88:8, 15
89:2, 4, 42
90:5, 6
91:12
92:11
93:3^{3}
94:2, 16^{2}, 18
97:3
102:10, 16
104:8
105:35
106:9, 17, 18, 26, 30
107:25, 26
109:23
110:7
113:7
119:48, 117
121:1
122:4
123:1
124:2, 3
127:2^{2}
129:6
132:3
134:2
139:8, 21
140:10
141:2
143:8
144:12
145:14
147:2, 3, 6

PROVERBS

1:12
2:3, 7
3:20
7:1
8:23, 30
10:12, 14
13:22
15:1, 18
16:27
21:20
22:6
23:8
24:16
25:7
26:9, 24
28:25
29:21, 22
30:4, 13, 31, 32
31:28

ECCLESIASTES

[illegible]
3:2, 3
4:10^{2}, 15
10:4, 12
12:4

SONG OF SOLOMON

2:7, 10
3:5
4:2, 12
5:5
6:6
7:8, 12, 13
8:4, 5^{2}

ISAIAH

1:2, 6
2:3, 4, 12, 13, 14
3:13, 14
5:5, 6, 11, 13, 24, 26
6:1
7:1, 6
8:7^{2}, 16
9:11, 18^{2}
10:15^{2}, 24, 26^{2}, 28, 29, 30
11:12, 16
13:2, 14, 17
14:4, 8, 9^{2}, 22
15:2, 5^{3}, 7
18:3
19:5, 6
21:2
22:1
23:4^{2}, 13^{2}, 18
24:10, 14, 18, 22
25:8
26:11
27:9
28:4, 7, 21
30:26
32:9, 13
33:3, 10, 12
34:3, 10, 13
35:9
36:1, 10^{2}
37:4, 14, 23, 24, 25, 27, 29
38:22
39:6
40:9^{3}, 15, 26, 31

ISAIAH
41:2, 25
42:2, 11, 13, 15[2]
43:6
44:4, 11, 26, 27
45:8, 13, 20
47:13
48:13
49:6, 18, 19, 21, 22[2], 23
50:2, 9
51:6, 8, 17, 18
52:8
53:2
55:13[2]
57:7, 8[2], 14[3], 20
58:1, 12
59:19
60:4, 7, 10
61:1, 4
62:10[3]
63:11
64:7, 11

JEREMIAH
1:17
2:6, 24
3:2, 6
4:3, 6, 7, 13, 29
5:10, 17[3]
6:1, 4
7:13, 16, 25, 29
9:10[2], 12, 18, 21
10:17, 20, 25
11:7, 13, 14
12:17
13:19, 20
14:2, 6
15:9
16:14, 15
18:7, 15, 21
20:9
21:2
22:20[2], 22
23:4, 7, 8, 10
24:6
25:32
26:5, 10, 17
27:22
29:15, 19, 22
30:9, 13
31:6, 21, 28, 40
32:2, 3, 33
33:1, 15
34:21
35:11, 15
36:5, 20
37:10, 11
38:10, 13[2]
39:2, 5, 15
42:10
45:4
46:4, 7, 8[2], 9, 11
47:2, 6
48:5[2], 15, 44
49:5, 14, 19, 22, 28, 31
50:2, 3, 9, 21, 26, 32, 38, 41, 44
51:1[2], 3, 9, 11, 12[2], 14, 27[2], 34, 36, 42, 44, 53
52:7, 9, 31

LAMENTATIONS
1:14[2], 19
2:2, 5[2], 7, 10, 16, 17, 19, 22
3:41, 62, 63
4:5
5:12

EZEKIEL
1:13, 19[2], 20, 21[2]
3:12, 14
4:14
7:11
8:3, 5[2], 11
9:3
10:4, 15, 16[2], 17[2], 19[2]
11:1, 22, 23, 24[2]
13:5[2], 10
14:3, 4, 7
16:40
17:9[2], 14, 17, 24
18:6, 12, 15
19:1, 3, 6, 12[2]
20:5[2], 6, 15, 23, 28, 42
21:15, 22
22:30
23:22, 27, 46, 47
24:8
26:3[2], 8, 17, 19
27:2, 30, 32
28:2, 5, 12[2], 14, 17
29:4
30:21
31:4, 10[3], 14[2]
32:2, 3
33:25
34:4, 16, 18, 23, 29
36:3[2], 7, 13
37:6, 8, 10, 12, 13
38:11, 16, 18
39:2, 15
40:6, 22, 26, 31, 34, 37, 40, 49
41:16
43:5, 24
44:12
47:14

DANIEL
2:21, 44
3:1, 2, 3[2], 5, 7, 12, 14, 18, 22, 24
4:17, 34
5:19, 20, 23
6:23[2]
7:3, 4, 5, 8[2], 20
8:3[2], 8, 22[2], 23, 25, 26, 27
9:24
10:5
11:2[2], 3, 4[2], 6, 7, 10[2], 12, 14, 15, 20, 21, 23, 25[2]
12:1, 4, 7, 9, 11

HOSEA
1:11
2:6, 15
4:8, 15, 19
6:1, 2
8:4, 7, 8, 9
9:6, 12, 16
10:4, 8, 12
11:8
13:12, 15[2], 16

JOEL
1:6, 10, 12, 20
2:9, 20[2]
3:9[2], 12

AMOS
1:6, 9, 13
2:10, 11
3:1, 5, 10
4:10
5:1, 2
6:8, 10, 14
7:1, 4
8:4, 8, 10, 14
9:2, 5, 7, 11[3], 15

OBADIAH
1, 6, 14, 21

JONAH
1:2, 3, 12, 15, 17
2:6
4:6, 10

MICAH
2:4, 8, 13[2]
3:10
4:2, 3
5:3, 9, 14
6:4, 14
7:3, 6

NAHUM
1:4, 9
2:1, 7
3:3, 15

HABAKKUK
1:3, 6, 9, 15
2:4, 6, 7
3:10, 16

ZEPHANIAH
2:4
3:8

HAGGAI
1:8, 14

ZECHARIAH
1:18, 21[2]
2:1, 13
5:1, 5, 7, 9[2]
6:1, 12
9:3, 13, 16
10:11, 12
11:16, 17
14:10, 13, 16, 17, 18[2], 19

MALACHI
3:15, 17
4:1, 2

MATTHEW
3:9, 12, 16
4:1, 5, 6, 8, 16
5:1
6:19, 20
9:6, 16
10:17, 19, 21[2]
11:5
12:42
13:4, 5, 6, 7, 26, 28, 29[2]
14:12, 19, 20, 23
15:13, 29, 37
16:9, 10, 24
17:1, 8, 27[2]
19:20
20:17, 18
22:7, 24
23:13, 32
24:9, 43
26:52
27:37, 50

MARK
1:10, 31, 35
2:4, 9, 11, 12, 21
3:13, 26
4:4, 5, 6, 7, 8, 27, 32
5:29
6:29, 41, 43, 51
7:34
8:8, 19, 20, 24, 25, 34
9:2, 27
10:16, 21, 32, 33
11:20
12:19
13:9, 11, 12, 16
14:42, 60
15:37, 39, 41
16:18, 19

LUKE
1:66, 69
2:4, 28, 42
3:8, 20
4:5, 11, 16[2], 25, 29
5:23, 24, 25[2], 28
6:8, 20
7:15, 16
8:6, 7, 8, 37
9:16, 17, 23, 28, 51
10:25, 34
11:27, 31, 32
12:19, 21
13:11, 25
14:10
16:23
17:6, 13
18:10, 13, 21, 31
19:4, 5, 20, 21, 22, 28
20:28
21:1, 12, 28[2]
22:45
23:5, 46
24:33, 50, 51

JOHN
2:7, 13, 17, 19, 20
3:13, 14[2]
4:14, 35
5:1, 8, 9, 11, 12, 21
6:3, 5, 12, 39, 40, 44, 54, 62
7:8[2], 10[2], 14
8:7, 10, 28, 59
10:1, 31
11:31, 41, 55
12:20, 32, 34
13:18
17:1
18:11, 30
19:30
21:11

THE ACTS
1:2, 9, 10, 11[2], 13, 15, 22
2:14[2], 24, 30, 32
3:1, 6, 7, 8, 13, 22, 26
4:24, 26
5:5, 6, 10, 17, 30, 34, 36, 37
6:12, 13
7:20, 21, 37, 42, 43, 55
8:31, 39
9:40, 41
10:4, 9, 16, 26[2], 40
11:2, 10, 28
12:7[2], 23
13:1, 16, 22, 31, 33, 34, 43, 50
14:2, 11, 20
15:2, 5, 7, 16
16:22
17:13
18:22
20:9, 11, 32
21:4, 12, 15[2], 27
22:3, 13, 22
24:11, 12
25:9, 18
26:10, 30
27:15, 17, 27, 40[2]

ROMANS
1:24, 26
2:5
4:24
6:4
8:11[2], 32
9:17
10:7
14:4
15:16

1 CORINTHIANS
4:6, 18, 19
5:2
6:14[2]
8:1
10:7
13:4
15:15[2], 24, 35, 54

2 CORINTHIANS
2:7
4:14[2]
5:4
9:5
12:2, 4, 14

GALATIANS
1:17, 18
2:1, 2
3:23

EPHESIANS
2:6
4:8, 10, 15
6:4

COLOSSIANS
1:5, 24
2:7, 18

1 THESSALONIANS
2:16
4:17

1 TIMOTHY
2:8
3:6, 16
4:6
5:10
6:19

2 TIMOTHY
1:6
4:8

HEBREWS
1:12
5:7
7:27[2]
11:17[2], 19
12:12, 15

JAMES
4:10
5:15

1 PETER
1:13, 21
2:5[2]

2 PETER
1:13
3:1, 10

1 JOHN
3:17

JUDE
12, 20

REVELATION
4:1
8:4, 7[2]
10:4, 5, 9, 10
11:12[2]
12:5, 16
13:1, 11
14:11
15:1
16:12
18:21
19:3
20:3, 9, 13[2]

UPON 5921, *1909*

GENESIS
1:2[2], 11, 15, 17, 25, 26, 28, 29, 30
2:5, 21
3:14
4:15, 26
6:12[2], 17
7:3, 4, 6, 8, 10, 12, 14, 17, 18[2], 19, 21[2], 23, 24
8:4, 17[2], 19
9:2[5], 16[2], 17, 23
11:4, 8, 9
12:8, 11
15:11, 12[2]
16:5
17:17
18:6, 19, 27, 31
19:3, 9, 16[3], 23, 24[2], 25
22:2, 6, 9, 12, 17
24:15, 16, 18, 30, 47[2], 61
26:7, 10, 25
27:12, 13, 15, 16[2]
28:11, 18
29:2, 3, 32
30:3
31:10, 12, 17, 34, 35, 46, 54
32:31[2], 32
34:25, 27
35:5, 20
37:22, 27, 34
38:28, 29, 30
39:5, 7
40:6, 17
41:3, 5, 17, 42
42:1, 21
43:18, 30
44:21
45:14[2], 15
46:4
47:31
48:2, 14[2], 17, 18
50:1[2], 23

EXODUS
1:16
2:25
3:6, 12, 22[2]
4:9[2], 20, 31
5:3, 8, 9, 21
7:4, 5, 17, 19[5]
8:3[2], 4[2], 5, 7, 14, 18[2], 21[3]
9:3[6], 9[2], 10[2], 11[2], 14[3], 19[2], 22[3], 23[2], 33
10:6, 12, 13
11:1[2], 5
12:13[2], 23, 33, 34
13:9, 16
14:4[2], 17[4], 18[3], 22, 26[3], 29, 30, 31
15:9, 15, 16, 19, 26[2]
16:14
17:6
18:8
19:11, 16, 18, 20, 22, 24
20:5, 12, 25
21:14, 19, 22, 30
23:2, 25
24:11, 16
25:11, 21, 22, 30
26:4, 7, 32[2], 34
27:2, 4, 7
28:8, 12[2], 22, 23, 26, 29, 30[2], 33, 34, 35, 36, 37[2], 38[2], 41, 43[2]
29:5, 6[2], 7, 8, 10, 12, 13[2], 15, 16, 18, 19, 20[5], 21[5], 22, 25, 38
30:1, 4, 7, 8, 10[2], 32, 33
31:18
32:16, 20, 21, 29[3], 34
33:16, 21
34:1, 7[2], 28, 35
36:17[2]
37:3[2], 13, 16, 27
39:5, 15, 19, 24, 25, 30, 31, 43
40:4, 13, 19, 20, 22, 23, 29, 38

LEVITICUS
1:4, 5, 7[2], 8[2], 11, 12, 13, 17[3]
2:1, 2, 9, 15
3:2[2], 3, 5[2], 8[2], 9, 10, 11, 13[2], 14, 15, 16
4:4, 7, 8, 9, 10, 15, 18, 19, 24, 25, 26, 29, 30, 31, 33, 34, 35
5:9, 11
6:9, 10, 12[2], 13, 15[2], 27
7:2, 5, 20, 31
8:7[2], 8, 9[3], 11, 12, 13[2], 14, 15[2], 16[2], 18, 19, 21, 22, 23[3], 24[4], 25, 26, 27[2], 28, 30[5]
9:9, 10, 12, 13, 14, 17, 18, 20[2], 24
10:6, 7
11:20, 21[2], 27, 29, 32, 37, 38, 41, 42[3], 44, 46
13:25, 27, 29, 30, 43, 45, 50
14:7, 14[3], 17[4], 18, 20, 25[3], 28[4], 29, 48
15:8, 9, 20[2], 22, 24, 26
16:2[2], 4, 8, 9, 13[2], 14, 15, 18, 19, 21[2], 22, 25
17:6, 11
18:25
19:17, 19, 28
20:9, 11, 12, 13, 16, 27
21:5, 10, 12
22:3, 22
23:37
24:4, 6, 7, 14
25:21, 37
26:21, 25, 30, 35, 36, 37

NUMBERS
1:53
4:7, 8, 10, 11, 14[2], 25
5:14[2], 15, 25, 26, 30[2]
6:5, 7, 19, 25, 26, 27
7:9, 89
8:7, 10, 12, 24, 25
9:15, 18, 19, 20, 22
10:34
11:9[2], 11, 17[2], 25[2], 26, 29, 31
12:3, 10, 11
13:23
14:18, 36, 37
15:31, 32, 38, 39
16:3, 4, 7, 22, 33, 45
17:2, 3
18:5, 17
19:2, 13[2], 15, 18[4], 19, 20
20:6, 26, 28
21:8[2], 9, 15
22:22, 30
23:4
24:2
27:18, 20, 23
30:14
31:27
33:4
35:22, 23

DEUTERONOMY
1:36
2:25
4:7, 10, 13, 26, 30, 32, 36, 39, 40
5:9
6:8, 9, 22[3]
7:6, 7, 15[2], 16, 22
8:4
11:12, 18, 20[2], 21, 25[2], 29[2]
12:1, 2[2], 16, 19, 24, 27[2]
13:9, 17
14:2
15:23
17:7, 18
19:5, 10
21:23
22:6[2], 8, 12, 14, 19
23:13, 19[2], 20[2]
24:15[2]
26:6
27:3, 5, 8, 12, 13
28:8, 15, 20, 24, 45, 46[2], 48, 56, 60, 61
29:5[2], 20, 22, 27
30:1, 3, 7, 18
31:17
32:2[2], 23[2], 24, 35, 42
33:10, 16[2], 26, 28, 29
34:9

JOSHUA
1:3
2:6, 8, 9, 15[2], 19[2]
3:13, 16
4:5
7:6[2], 10
8:7, 20, 32
9:4, 5[2], 20
10:11, 12, 13, 18, 24[2], 26
11:4, 7
12:2
13:9
19:34
20:8
23:15[2]
24:7

JUDGES
3:10, 16, 22, 23
4:16
6:14, 20, 26, 28, 34, 37, 39[2], 40
7:5, 6, 25
8:21
9:5, 18, 24[2], 33, 44, 49, 53, 57[2]
11:29, 37, 38
12:1
13:19
14:6, 17, 19
15:12, 14[2], 16
16:3, 9, 12, 14, 17, 19, 20, 26, 27, 29, 30[2]
18:19, 25
19:14, 20, 27, 28
20:5, 37, 41, 48

RUTH
3:3, 15
4:5, 10

1 SAMUEL
1:9, 11
2:8, 10, 28, 34
4:12, 13, 19
5:3, 4[2], 6, 7[2]
6:8, 11
7:10
9:16, 24, 25
10:1, 6, 10
11:2, 6
13:12, 13
14:1, 13[2], 25, 32
15:19, 27
16:13, 16, 23
17:5, 6, 38, 39, 49, 51
18:4, 10, 17[2]
19:9, 20, 23
20:9, 25[3], 31
21:13
22:17, 18[2]
24:2, 12, 13
25:24[2], 39, 42
26:12
28:18, 23
30:14[3], 16, 17
31:2[2], 4, 5

2 SAMUEL
1:2, 6[2], 9[2], 10[2], 15, 16, 19, 21, 24
4:11
5:20, 23
6:3, 8
9:8
11:2[2], 21, 23, 24
12:16
13:18, 29
14:7
15:14, 32
16:1, 8, 22
17:2, 12[2], 14
18:9, 17, 28
20:8[2], 12
21:10[2]
22:7, 11[2], 28, 34
24:15, 16, 20

1 KINGS
1:13, 17, 20, 24, 30, 33, 35, 38, 44, 47
2:5, 12, 25, 29, 31, 32[2], 33[6], 34, 37, 44, 46
3:4, 26
5:5
6:32[3], 35
7:2[2], 3, 16, 17, 18[2], 19, 20[2], 22, 25[2], 29, 31, 38, 41, 42
8:31, 32, 36

1 KINGS
9:5^2, 9^2, 21, 25^2
10:20
12:4, 9, 32, 33^2
13:2^3, 3, 29
14:10
17:14, 19, 20, 21
18:1, 26, 28, 42
19:11, 19
20:30, 31, 38
21:4, 21, 27, 29
22:17

2 KINGS
2:9, 16
3:15, 22, 27
4:4^2, 5^2, 21, 29, 31, 32, 33, 34^3, 35
5:23
6:26, 30^2
7:6, 9, 17, 20
8:1
9:25, 37
11:12
12:11
13:13, 16^3, 18
16:13, 15^2, 17
18:21^2, 23
19:7
21:12
22:16^2, 20
23:6, 16, 20^2
24:3
25:6, 17^2

1 CHRONICLES
1:10
5:16
6:49
9:27
10:4
12:8, 18, 19
13:11
14:11, 14, 17
15:13, 15, 27
16:8, 40
19:17
20:2
21:14, 16, 26^2
22:8
28:2, 5, 19
29:25

2 CHRONICLES
1:6
4:4^2, 13, 14
6:13^2, 16, 20^2, 22, 23, 27
7:3^2, 22
9:19
10:4, 9, 11
12:7
13:4, 10, 11, 18
14:14
15:1, 5
17:10
18:16, 18, 23
19:2, 7, 10^2
20:9, 12, 14
22:8
23:11, 20
24:7, 9, 18, 20, 22, 27
25:13, 28
26:15, 16, 20
28:11, 15
29:8, 22^2, 23, 24, 27
32:8, 12, 25^2, 26
33:11
34:4, 5, 21, 24^2, 25, 28^2
35:3, 16
36:17^2

EZRA
3:3^2
5:5
6:19
7:6, 9^2, 17, 24, 26, 28
8:18, 22, 31
9:5, 13

NEHEMIAH
2:8, 12, 18
4:4, 12, 19
5:4, 18, 19
6:1, 14
8:2, 4, 16
9:1, 4, 10, 13, 32, 33
10:34
12:31^2, 38
13:18^3

ESTHER
1:6
2:15, 17
3:13
4:5
5:1
6:8^2
7:8
8:7^2, 12^2, 14, 17
9:2, 3, 13, 25, 27^3
10:1^2

JOB
1:12, 15, 17, 19, 20
2:11, 12, 13
3:4, 5, 6, 25
4:5, 14
5:10^2
6:28
7:1, 8, 17
8:9, 15
9:8, 33

JOB
10:1, 3, 16, 17
12:4, 21
13:11, 27
14:3, 22
15:21, 26^2, 29
16:9^2, 10^2, 13, 14^2, 15
18:8, 15
19:21^2, 25
20:4, 22, 23^2, 25
21:5, 9, 17
22:28
24:23
25:3
26:7, 9
27:9, 10, 22
28:9
29:3, 4, 13, 19, 22
30:12, 14^2, 15, 16^2, 22, 30
31:1, 10, 36
33:7, 15^2, 19, 27
34:14, 21, 23
36:28, 30
37:12
38:5, 24
39:28
40:4
41:8, 30, 33
42:11

PSALMS
2:6
3:7, 8
4:1, 4, 6
5:t
6:t, 2
7:5, 16^2
8:t
9:t, 13
11:2, 6
12:t
14:2, 4
17:6
18:3, 6, 10^2, 33
21:5, 12
22:t, 9, 10, 13, 17, 18, 29
24:2^2
25:16, 18
27:2, 5, 7
29:3^2, 10
30:10
31:9, 16, 17
32:4
33:14, 18^2, 22
34:15
35:8, 16
36:4
37:9, 12
40:2, 12, 17
41:2, 3
43:4
44:17
45:t, 3, 9
46:t
47:8
48:6
49:4
50:10, 15
51:1, 19
53:t, 2, 4
54:7
55:3, 4, 5, 10, 15, 16, 22
56:t, 12
59:9, 10
60:t
61:t
62:1, 5, 10
63:6
64:8
65:5, 12
66:11
67:1, 2, 4
68:4, 33
69:t, 9, 15, 24
72:6, 16
73:25
74:5
78:24, 27, 31, 49
79:6^3
80:t, 17^2, 18
81:t
84:t, 9
86:5, 7, 16
88:t, 7, 9
89:19, 22
90:17^2
91:13, 14, 15
92:3^3
94:23
99:6^2
101:6
102:7, 13
103:17
104:3, 27
105:1, 16, 38
106:29
107:40
109:25
112:2, 8
116:2, 3, 4, 13, 17
118:5, 7
119:49, 53, 87, 132, 135
121:5
123:2^2, 3^2
125:3, 5
128:6
129:3, 6, 8
132:11, 12, 18
133:2^2, 3
135:9^2
137:2

PSALMS
139:5
140:10
141:7
144:9
145:15, 18^2
147:7, 8, 15
149:5, 7^2, 9
150:5^2

PROVERBS
1:27, 28
3:3, 18
6:21, 28
7:3^2
8:27
9:3
10:6, 24
11:26
19:12, 17
23:5, 31, 34
24:25, 32
25:12, 20, 22
26:14^2, 27
28:22
30:19, 24, 32

ECCLESIASTES
5:2
7:20
8:6, 14, 16
9:12
10:7^2
11:1, 2, 3

SONG OF SOLOMON
1:6^2
2:8^2, 17
3:8
4:16
5:5, 15
6:13
7:5
8:5, 6^2, 9, 14

ISAIAH
1:25
2:12^2, 13^2, 14^2, 15^2, 16^2
3:26
4:5^3
5:6
6:1, 7
7:17^3, 19^2
8:7, 17
9:2, 6, 7^2, 8
10:12, 20^2, 26
11:2, 14^2
12:4
13:2
14:13, 16, 25, 26^2
15:9^3
16:5
18:2, 4, 6^2
19:1, 8, 12
20:3^2
21:3, 8, 13
22:22, 24, 25
23:17
24:17, 20, 21
26:16
28:4, 10^4, 13^4, 22, 27
29:10
30:6^2, 16^2, 17, 18, 25^2, 32
32:11, 13^2, 15
33:4, 20
34:2^2, 5^2, 11
35:10
36:8, 12
37:7
38:21
40:7, 22, 24, 31
41:25^3
42:1, 5, 25
43:2, 22
44:3^4, 19
45:12
46:1^2, 7
47:6, 9, 11^3, 13
48:2
49:13, 16, 22
50:10
51:5, 6, 11
52:7
53:5
55:6, 7
56:7
57:7
58:14
59:17, 21
60:1, 2^2
61:1
62:6
63:3
64:7
65:3, 7^2
66:4, 12^2, 20^3, 24

JEREMIAH
1:14
2:3, 15, 20, 34, 37
3:6, 12, 21
4:20, 29
5:3, 10, 12, 15
6:11^2, 12, 19, 21, 23, 26
7:20^5
8:2
9:3, 22
10:25^2
11:8, 11, 16, 23
12:12
13:1, 4, 13, 16, 22, 26
14:16, 22

JEREMIAH
15:5, 8^3, 14
16:4, 17
17:1^2, 2, 18, 25
18:22
19:3, 13, 15^2
22:2, 4, 23, 24, 30
23:2, 12, 17, 19, 40
24:6
25:13, 26, 29, 30, 33
26:15^3
27:2, 5
28:14
29:12, 16, 17
30:16, 18, 23
31:5, 6, 19, 20, 26, 39
32:19, 23, 29, 42^2
33:17, 21
35:17^2
36:4, 6, 30, 31^3
39:5, 16
40:2, 3, 4
42:12, 17, 18^2
43:10
44:2^2
45:5
46:16, 21
47:5
48:8, 18, 21^4, 22^3, 23^3, 24^3, 32^2, 37^2, 38, 43, 44^2
49:5, 8, 36, 37
50:15, 19, 35^4, 36^2, 37^4, 38^2, 42
51:12, 13, 25, 35^2, 42, 47, 52, 56^2, 60, 64
52:9, 22^2, 23

LAMENTATIONS
1:10, 14
2:10^2, 11
3:28, 47, 53, 55, 57
4:19
5:1, 18

EZEKIEL
1:3, 15, 17, 22, 26^2, 28
2:1, 2
3:14, 22, 24, 25
4:1, 4^3, 5, 8, 9
5:1^2, 13, 16^2, 17^2
6:3, 12, 13, 14
7:2, 3^3, 4, 8^2, 12, 14, 18^2, 26^2
8:1, 10
9:4, 6, 8^2, 10
10:11
11:5, 8, 13, 21, 23
12:6, 7, 12, 13
13:9, 15^2, 18
14:9, 13^2, 17, 19, 21, 22^2
16:5, 8, 11, 12, 14, 41, 43
17:19, 20, 22
18:6, 8, 11, 13^2, 15, 20^2
19:9
20:8, 13, 21
21:12^4, 29, 31
22:9, 20, 21, 22, 24, 31^2
23:6, 8, 9, 10, 12^2, 14, 15^2, 16, 20, 23, 41, 42^2, 46, 49
24:6, 7^2, 8, 11, 13, 17^2, 23^2
25:7, 11, 12, 13, 14, 16, 17^2
26:7, 14, 16, 19
27:11^2, 29, 30
28:7, 12, 14, 18, 23, 26
29:5, 7, 8
30:4, 9, 15, 25
31:12, 13^2
32:4^3, 5, 8, 11, 27
33:2, 3, 4, 5, 10, 22, 26
34:6^2, 13, 14^2
36:10, 11, 12, 18^2, 25, 29
37:1, 4, 6^2, 8, 9, 10, 16^2, 22
38:12^2, 15, 20^2, 22^3
39:2, 4, 5, 14, 17, 21, 25, 29
40:1, 2, 4, 16, 17, 26, 31, 34, 37, 43
41:25^2, 26
43:3, 12, 14, 20, 24, 27^2
44:4, 17, 18^2
45:19^3, 22
47:10, 12

DANIEL
1:13
2:10, 28, 29, 34, 46
3:27
4:5, 13, 21, 24, 28, 33
5:5
6:10, 17, 23
7:1, 2, 4, 6, 23
8:7, 10, 17
9:11, 12^2, 13, 14^2, 17, 24^2, 27
10:7, 10^2, 16
11:18, 24, 42
12:6, 7

HOSEA
1:4, 6, 7
2:4, 13, 23
4:13^2
5:1, 10
7:9, 12, 14
8:14
9:1
10:7, 11, 12, 14
12:14
13:13
14:3

JOEL
1:6
2:2, 8, 9^2, 28, 29^2
3:4, 7

AMOS
1:12
2:2, 5, 8
3:5, 9, 14
4:2, 7^3, 13
5:2, 8, 11
6:4^2, 12
7:7
8:2, 10^2
9:1, 4, 6, 8, 9, 15

OBADIAH
11, 15^2, 16, 17

JONAH
1:6^2, 7^2, 8, 12, 14
2:10
4:8

MICAH
1:3
2:1
3:11^2
4:11
5:1, 7, 9, 15
7:16, 19

NAHUM
1:15
2:7
3:3, 5, 6, 7, 18, 19

HABAKKUK
1:13
2:1^2, 2
3:1, 8, 19

ZEPHANIAH
1:4^2, 5, 17
2:2^2
3:8^2, 9

HAGGAI
1:9, 11^9
2:15

ZECHARIAH
1:7, 8, 16
2:9
3:5^2, 9
4:2^2, 3^2, 11^2
5:8, 11
6:8, 11, 13^2
9:9^2, 16
10:6
11:11, 17^2
12:4, 10^3
13:7
14:4, 12, 17, 20

MALACHI
1:7
2:2, 3
3:16

MATTHEW
3:16
4:13
6:19
7:24, 25^2, 26, 27
9:18
10:13, 27
11:29
12:2, 18
13:5
16:18
19:28
20:25
21:5
23:9, 18, 35^2, 36
24:2, 3
25:31
26:10
27:29, 30, 35
28:2

MARK
1:10
3:10
6:5, 17, 39, 48, 49
7:30, 32
8:23, 25
10:16, 27, 34, 42
11:7, 11
13:2, 3
14:67
15:19, 24

LUKE
1:12, 35, 58
2:9, 25, 40
3:22
4:18
5:1, 19, 24, 36
6:10, 48^2, 49
8:6, 43
9:38
10:6
11:20, 22
12:1, 3
13:4
17:31
18:13
19:35, 43, 44
20:1, 18
21:6, 23, 25, 34
22:25, 56, 61
23:26
24:1, 49

JOHN
1:32, 33, 36, 51
4:27

JOHN
9:15
11:38
12:35
18:4
19:29, 31

THE ACTS
1:8, 26
2:3, 17, 43
3:4
4:1, 33
5:11^2, 28
6:12
7:57, 59
8:16, 24
10:9
11:6, 19
12:7, 21^2
13:11, 40
15:10, 17, 28
16:23
18:6
19:6, 13
20:7
21:35
22:13
24:7
26:16
27:26, 29

ROMANS
2:9
3:22
4:9^2
5:12, 18^2
9:28
10:12, 13
11:32
13:4, 6
15:20

1 CORINTHIANS
1:2
3:12
7:35^2
9:16
10:11
12:23
15:10
16:2

2 CORINTHIANS
1:11, 23
3:15
5:2, 4
8:4, 22
11:28
12:9

GALATIANS
4:11
6:16

EPHESIANS
2:20
4:26
5:6

PHILIPPIANS
1:3
2:7, 17, 27

COLOSSIANS
3:5

1 THESSALONIANS
2:16
5:3^2

1 TIMOTHY
4:15

HEBREWS
6:7, 18
8:6
11:21

JAMES
2:21
4:3
5:1

1 PETER
4:14
5:7

2 PETER
2:1, 5

1 JOHN
1:1
3:1

JUDE
15

REVELATION
1:17
2:24
3:3, 10^2, 12^2
4:3, 4
5:7, 13
7:10
8:3, 7, 10^2
9:3
10:1, 2, 5^2, 8^2
11:10, 11^2, 16
12:1, 3
13:1^3, 8
14:14
16:1, 2^3, 3, 4, 8, 10, 12, 18, 21
17:1, 3, 5, 16
18:24
19:11, 14, 21
20:3, 4^2
21:5

US *2248*

GENESIS
1:26
3:22
5:29
11:3, 4^{4}, 7
19:5, 13, 31, 32, 34
20:9
23:6^{3}
24:23, 55, 65
26:10^{2}, 16, 22, 28^{3}, 29
31:14, 15, 37, 44, 50, 53
32:18, 20
33:12^{2}
34:9^{2}, 10, 14, 16, 17, 21^{4}, 22^{3}, 23^{2}
35:3
37:8^{2}, 17, 20, 21, 27
39:14^{2}, 17
41:12^{2}, 13
42:2, 21^{2}, 28, 30^{2}, 33
43:2, 3, 4, 5, 7, 18^{3}
44:25, 26^{2}, 27, 30, 31
47:15, 19^{2}, 25
50:15^{2}

EXODUS
1:10^{2}
2:14, 19^{2}
3:18^{2}
5:3^{3}, 8, 16, 17, 21
8:26, 27
10:7, 25, 26
13:14, 15, 16
14:5, 11^{3}, 12^{2}, 25
16:3, 7, 8
17:2, 3^{2}, 7, 9
19:23
20:19^{2}
24:14
32:1^{3}, 23^{3}
33:15, 16
34:9^{2}

NUMBERS
10:29, 31^{2}, 32^{2}
11:4, 13, 18^{2}
12:2, 11
13:27, 30
14:3^{2}, 4^{2}, 8^{3}, 9^{2}
16:13^{3}, 14^{2}, 34
20:5^{2}, 14, 15, 16, 17
21:5, 7
22:4, 14
27:4
31:49
32:5, 19

DEUTERONOMY
1:6, 14, 19, 20, 22^{3}, 25^{3}, 27^{4}, 41
2:29, 30, 32, 33, 36^{2}, 37
3:1
5:2, 3^{3}, 24, 25, 27
6:21, 23^{3}, 24^{2}, 25
9:28
13:2^{2}, 6, 13
26:3, 6^{3}, 8, 9^{2}, 15
29:7, 15^{2}, 29
30:12^{2}, 13^{2}
31:17^{2}
33:4

JOSHUA
1:16^{2}
2:9, 14, 17, 18, 20, 24
4:23
5:6, 13
7:7^{2}, 9, 25
8:5, 6^{2}
9:6, 7, 11^{2}, 20, 22^{2}, 25
10:6^{4}
17:4, 16
21:2
22:17, 19^{2}, 22, 23, 25, 26^{2}, 27^{2}, 28^{2}, 31, 34
24:17^{2}, 18, 27^{2}

JUDGES
1:1, 24
6:13^{6}
8:1^{2}, 21, 22^{2}
9:8, 10, 12, 14
10:15^{2}
11:8, 10, 19, 24
12:1
13:8^{2}, 15, 23^{3}
14:15^{2}
15:10^{2}, 11^{2}
16:5, 24, 25
18:19^{2}, 25
19:11, 13, 28
20:3, 8^{2}, 13, 18, 32^{2}, 39
21:1, 22

RUTH
2:20

1 SAMUEL
4:3^{5}, 7, 8^{2}
5:7^{2}, 10^{2}, 11
6:2, 9^{3}, 20
7:8^{2}, 12
8:5^{2}, 6^{2}, 19, 20^{2}
9:5^{2}, 6^{2}, 8, 9, 10, 27
10:16, 19, 27
11:1, 3^{2}, 10, 12, 14
12:4^{2}, 10, 12, 19
14:1, 6^{2}, 9, 10^{2}, 12, 17, 36^{3}
17:9
20:11, 42
21:5
23:19
25:7, 15, 16, 40
26:11
27:11
29:4^{2}, 9
30:22, 23^{3}

2 SAMUEL
2:14
5:2
10:12
11:23^{2}
13:25, 26
15:14^{3}, 19, 20
17:5
18:3^{5}
19:9^{2}, 10, 42^{2}, 43
20:6^{2}
21:4, 5^{2}, 6, 17
24:14

1 KINGS
3:18
5:6
8:57^{3}
12:4, 9, 10
18:23, 26
20:23, 31

2 KINGS
1:6^{2}
4:9, 10^{3}, 13
6:1, 2^{3}, 11, 16
7:4^{3}, 6^{2}, 9, 12, 13
9:5, 12
10:5
14:8
18:26, 30, 32
19:19
22:13^{2}

1 CHRONICLES
13:2^{2}, 3^{2}
15:13
16:35^{3}
19:13

2 CHRONICLES
10:4, 9, 10
13:10, 12
14:7^{3}, 11
20:9, 11^{3}, 12
25:17
29:10
32:7, 8^{2}, 11
34:21

EZRA
4:2^{2}, 3^{2}, 12, 14, 18
5:11, 17
8:17, 18^{2}, 21, 22, 23, 31^{2}
9:8^{3}, 9^{4}, 13^{3}, 14^{2}
10:3, 14

NEHEMIAH
2:17, 18, 19^{2}, 20
4:12^{2}, 15^{2}, 20^{2}, 22, 23
5:8, 10, 17^{2}
6:2, 7, 9, 10^{2}, 16
9:32, 33, 37
10:32
13:18

JOB
9:33^{2}
15:9, 10
21:14
22:17
31:15
34:4^{3}, 37
35:11^{2}
37:19

PSALMS
2:3^{2}
4:6^{2}
12:4
17:11
20:9
33:22
34:3
44:1, 5, 7^{2}, 9, 10^{2}, 11^{2}, 13^{2}, 14, 17, 19^{2}, 23, 26
46:7, 11
47:3, 4
54:t
60:1^{3}, 3, 10, 11
62:8
65:5
66:10^{2}, 11, 12
67:1^{3}, 6, 7
68:19, 28
74:1, 8, 9
78:3
79:4, 8^{2}, 9^{2}
80:2, 3, 6, 7, 18, 19
83:4, 12
85:4^{2}, 5, 6, 7^{2}, 13
90:12, 14, 15^{2}, 17^{2}
95:1^{2}, 2, 6^{2}
100:3
103:10^{2}, 12
106:47^{2}
108:11, 12
115:1^{2}, 12^{2}
117:2
118:27
119:4
122:1
123:2, 3^{2}
124:2, 3^{2}, 4, 6
126:3
136:23, 24
137:3^{5}, 8

PROVERBS
1:11^{3}, 12, 14^{2}
7:18^{2}

ECCLESIASTES
1:10
12:13

SONG OF SOLOMON
2:15
5:9
7:11^{2}, 12^{2}

ISAIAH
1:9, 18
2:3^{2}, 5
4:1
6:8
7:6^{3}
8:10
9:6^{2}
14:8, 10
17:14^{2}
22:13
25:9
26:12^{2}, 13
28:15
29:15^{2}
30:10^{2}, 11
32:15
33:2, 14^{2}, 21, 22
36:11, 15, 18
37:20
41:1, 22^{2}
43:9, 26
50:8
53:6
59:9^{2}, 11, 12^{2}
63:7, 16^{2}, 17
64:6, 7^{2}, 12

JEREMIAH
2:6^{2}, 27
3:25
4:5, 8, 13
5:12, 19, 24^{2}
6:4^{2}, 5^{2}, 24, 26
8:8, 14^{4}
9:18, 19
11:19^{2}
14:7, 9^{2}, 19^{2}, 21^{2}
16:10
18:18^{3}
21:2^{4}, 13
26:16
29:15, 28
31:6
35:6, 8, 9, 10, 11
36:17
37:3, 9
38:16, 25^{2}
40:10
41:8
42:2^{2}, 3, 5^{2}, 6, 20^{2}
43:3^{4}
44:16
46:16
48:2
50:5
51:9, 10

LAMENTATIONS
3:40, 41, 43, 45, 46, 47
4:17^{2}, 19^{2}
5:1, 4, 8^{2}, 16, 20^{2}, 21, 22^{2}

EZEKIEL
8:12
11:3, 15
24:19^{2}
33:10, 24
35:12
37:18

DANIEL
1:12
2:23
3:17^{2}
9:7, 8, 10, 11, 12^{3}, 13, 14, 16

HOSEA
6:1^{3}, 2^{2}, 3
10:3, 8^{2}
12:4
14:2, 3

AMOS
4:1
6:13
9:10

OBADIAH
1

JONAH
1:6, 7^{2}, 8^{2}, 11, 14^{2}

MICAH
3:11^{2}
4:2^{2}
5:1, 6
7:19

ZECHARIAH
1:6^{2}
8:21

MALACHI
1:2, 9
2:10

MATTHEW
1:23
3:15
6:11, 12, 13^{2}
8:25, 29, 31^{2}
9:27
13:36, 56
15:15, 23
17:4^{2}
20:7, 12, 30, 31
21:25, 38^{2}
22:17, 25
24:3
25:8, 9, 11
26:46, 63, 68
27:4, 25, 49

MARK
1:24^{2}, 38
4:35
5:12
6:3
9:5^{2}, 22^{2}, 38^{2}, 40
10:35, 37
12:7, 19
13:4
14:15, 42
15:36
16:3

LUKE
1:1, 2, 69, 71, 74, 78
2:15^{2}, 48
4:34^{2}
7:5, 16, 20
8:22
9:33^{2}, 49, 50^{2}
10:11, 17
11:1, 3, 4^{4}, 45
12:41
13:25
15:23
16:26^{2}
17:13
19:14
20:2, 6, 14, 22, 28
22:8, 67
23:18, 30^{2}, 39
24:22, 24, 29, 32^{3}

JOHN
1:14, 22
2:18
4:12, 25
6:34, 52
8:5
9:34
10:24^{2}
11:7, 15, 16, 50
14:8^{2}, 9, 22, 31
16:17
17:21
18:31
19:24

THE ACTS
1:17, 21^{2}, 22^{2}
2:29
3:4, 12
4:17
5:28
6:14
7:27, 38, 40^{3}
10:41, 42
11:13, 15, 17
13:33, 47
14:11, 17
15:7, 8, 9, 24, 25, 28, 36
16:9, 10, 14, 15^{2}, 16, 17^{2}, 21, 37^{4}
17:27
20:5, 14
21:5, 11, 16, 17, 18
23:9
24:4, 7
25:24
27:2, 6, 7, 20
28:2^{2}, 7^{2}, 10^{2}, 15^{2}

ROMANS
3:8
4:16, 24
5:5, 8^{2}
6:3
8:4, 18, 26, 31^{2}, 32^{2}, 34, 35, 37, 39
9:24, 29
12:6^{2}, 7
13:12^{2}, 13
14:7, 12, 13, 19
15:2, 7
16:6

1 CORINTHIANS
1:18, 30
2:10, 12
4:1, 6, 8, 9
5:7, 8
6:14
7:15
8:6, 8
10:8, 9
15:32, 57
16:16

2 CORINTHIANS
1:4, 5, 8, 10^{2}, 11^{2}, 14, 19, 20, 21^{2}, 22
2:11, 14^{2}
3:3, 6
4:7, 12, 14^{2}, 17
5:5^{2}, 14, 18^{2}, 19, 20, 21
6:12
7:1, 2, 6, 7, 9
8:4^{2}, 5, 7, 19^{2}, 20^{2}
9:11
10:2, 8, 13

GALATIANS
1:4, 23
2:4
3:13^{2}, 24
4:26
5:1, 25, 26
6:9, 10

EPHESIANS
1:3, 4, 5, 6, 8, 9
2:4, 5, 6^{2}, 7, 14
3:20
4:7
5:2^{2}

PHILIPPIANS
3:15, 16^{2}, 17

COLOSSIANS
1:8, 12, 13^{2}
2:14^{2}
4:3^{2}

1 THESSALONIANS
1:6, 9, 10
2:8, 13, 15, 16, 18
3:6^{4}
4:1, 7, 8
5:6^{2}, 8, 9, 10, 25

2 THESSALONIANS
1:7
2:2, 16^{2}
3:1, 6, 7, 9

1 TIMOTHY
6:8, 17

2 TIMOTHY
1:7, 9^{3}, 14
2:12

TITUS
2:12, 14^{2}
3:5, 6, 15

HEBREWS
1:2
2:3
4:1^{2}, 2, 11, 14, 16
6:1, 18, 20
7:26
9:12, 24
10:15, 20, 22, 23, 24
11:40^{2}
12:1^{4}, 9, 10, 28
13:13, 15, 18

JAMES
1:18
3:3
4:5

1 PETER
1:3, 12
2:21^{2}
3:18, 21
4:1, 3, 17
5:10

2 PETER
1:1, 3^{2}, 4
3:2

1 JOHN
1:2, 3, 7, 8, 9^{2}, 10
2:19^{5}, 25
3:1^{2}, 16, 18, 20, 21, 23, 24^{2}
4:6^{2}, 7, 9, 10, 11, 12^{2}, 13^{2}, 16, 19
5:11, 14, 15, 20

2 JOHN
2^{2}

3 JOHN
9, 10

REVELATION
1:5^{2}, 6
5:9, 10
6:16^{2}
19:7

WAS 1961, *2258*

GENESIS
1:2^{2}, 3, 4, 7, 9, 10, 11, 12^{2}, 15, 18, 21, 24, 25, 30, 31
2:5^{2}, 10, 19, 20, 23
3:1, 6^{2}, 10^{2}, 20, 23
4:2^{2}, 5, 18, 19, 20, 21^{2}, 22, 26
5:24, 32
6:5^{2}, 9, 11^{2}, 12
7:6^{2}, 12, 17^{2}, 22^{2}, 23^{2}
8:1, 2, 11, 13, 14
9:19, 21^{2}
10:9, 10, 19, 25^{3}, 30
11:1, 10, 29, 30
12:4, 6, 10^{2}, 11, 14^{2}, 15, 18
13:2, 6^{2}, 7, 10, 14
14:10, 14, 18
15:12, 17
16:1, 4, 5, 14, 16
17:1, 24^{2}, 25^{2}, 26
18:10, 15
19:22, 23
20:16
21:3, 5^{2}, 8^{2}, 11, 15, 20
22:20, 24
23:1, 17^{3}
24:1, 15, 16, 29, 33, 36, 67
25:1, 8, 10, 17, 20, 21^{2}, 26^{2}, 27^{2}, 29, 30
26:1^{2}, 7, 8, 28, 34
27:1, 30
28:7, 11, 17, 19
29:2, 12^{2}, 16^{2}, 17^{2}, 25, 31^{2}, 33, 34
30:2, 29, 30, 37
31:1^{2}, 2, 22^{2}, 31, 36, 39, 40, 48
32:7^{2}, 24, 25
34:19, 24, 28^{2}, 29
35:3, 4, 5, 8^{2}, 16, 17, 18, 19, 29
36:12, 22, 24, 32, 35, 39^{2}
37:1, 2^{2}, 3, 15, 23^{2}, 24^{2}, 29
38:1, 2, 5, 6, 7, 12, 13, 14^{2}, 16, 21^{2}, 22, 24, 25, 29, 30
39:1, 2^{3}, 3, 5, 6, 11, 13, 19, 20, 21, 22, 23^{2}
40:2, 3, 9, 10, 11, 15, 16^{2}, 17, 20
41:7, 8^{2}, 10, 12, 13, 24, 32, 37, 46, 48, 49, 53, 54^{2}, 55, 56, 57
42:1, 5, 6^{2}, 27, 35
43:1, 12^{2}, 18, 21, 26, 34
44:3, 12, 14
45:8, 16
47:13^{2}, 14, 18, 28
48:7, 14^{2}
49:7^{2}, 15^{2}, 26, 32, 33
50:9, 11, 15, 26

EXODUS
1:5, 7, 14, 15
2:2, 11, 12, 21
3:2, 6
4:6, 7, 14
5:13, 19
6:3
7:7, 15, 21^{2}, 22
8:15, 19, 24
9:7^{2}, 11, 24^{2}, 25, 26, 31^{3}, 33, 35
10:13, 15, 22
11:3, 6
12:29, 30^{3}, 34, 39, 40
13:17
14:5^{2}, 20
15:23
16:14, 15, 20, 24, 31^{2}
17:1
18:3, 4^{2}, 11
19:16, 18
20:21
22:13

EXODUS
24:10, 17, 18
25:40
26:30
27:8
29:33
31:17
32:16
33:7, 8
34:28, 34
35:23, 24
36:7, 9, 12, 15^{2}, 21
37:1, 6, 10, 22, 25^{3}
38:1^{2}, 18^{3}, 21, 23, 24^{2}, 25, 29
39:4, 5^{2}, 9^{2}, 10^{2}, 19, 23, 32
40:17, 35, 36, 37, 38^{2}

LEVITICUS
4:10
6:2, 3, 4, 27
8:4, 10, 16, 21, 25, 26, 29, 30
9:8, 15, 18
10:16^{2}, 18, 20
13:18
14:6, 48
15:10
16:27
17:15
19:20
21:10
24:10, 11
25:33, 50, 51
27:24

NUMBERS
1:44
3:16, 21, 27, 33, 35
6:12
7:9, 10, 12, 13^{2}, 17, 19, 23, 25^{2}, 29, 31, 35, 37^{2}, 41, 43, 47, 49^{2}, 53, 55, 59, 61^{2}, 65, 67^{2}, 71, 73^{2}, 77, 79^{2}, 83, 84^{2}, 86, 88^{2}, 89^{2}
8:4^{2}
9:14, 15^{2}, 16, 17, 20^{2}, 21^{4}, 22
10:11, 14, 15, 16, 17, 18, 19, 20, 22, 23, 24, 25^{2}, 26, 27, 34
11:1, 2, 4, 7, 8, 10^{2}, 18, 25, 26, 33^{3}
12:3, 9, 10, 15^{2}
13:20, 22, 24
14:16
15:34
16:15, 31, 42, 47, 48, 50
17:6, 8
19:13
20:1, 2, 13, 29
21:4, 24, 26, 35
22:3^{2}, 4, 22^{2}, 26, 27, 30^{2}, 36
24:10, 20
25:3, 8, 11, 13, 14^{3}, 15^{3}, 18
26:46, 59, 60, 62, 64, 65
27:3, 13
28:6
31:14, 16, 26, 32, 36^{2}, 37, 38, 39, 40, 41, 43, 52
32:1, 10, 13^{2}, 39
33:14, 39
35:23, 25^{2}, 26
36:2

DEUTERONOMY
1:34, 37
2:14, 15, 20, 36
3:3, 4, 8, 11^{2}, 13, 26
4:21, 35
8:2, 15
9:8, 9, 10, 19^{2}, 20, 21, 28
10:6
11:6
19:6
21:15
22:27
26:5
29:27
32:12, 50
33:5, 16, 21
34:7^{2}, 9

JOSHUA
1:5, 17
2:2, 5, 15
3:7
4:10
5:1, 13
6:1, 21, 24, 27^{2}
7:1, 16, 17, 18, 22, 26
8:11, 13, 17, 25, 29, 33, 35
9:5, 10, 24
10:2^{2}, 14, 17
11:10, 11, 19, 20, 22
12:4
13:1, 16, 23^{2}, 25, 29, 30, 33
14:2, 7^{2}, 11^{2}, 15^{2}
15:1^{2}, 2, 5^{2}, 9^{2}, 11, 12, 15
16:5^{2}
17:1^{3}, 2, 7, 9, 10^{2}
18:1, 12, 14^{2}, 15, 17, 19, 20^{2}
19:1, 9^{2}, 10, 18, 25, 33, 41
21:10
22:14, 17
24:26, 33

JUDGES
1:10, 11, 17, 19, 22, 23, 28, 36
2:14, 15, 18, 19, 20
3:8, 17, 20, 24, 25, 27, 30, 31
4:1, 2, 11, 12, 16, 17, 21, 22
5:8^{2}, 14, 15
6:3, 6, 11, 21, 22, 27, 28^{5}, 30, 34, 35, 38, 40^{2}
7:8, 13^{2}, 15
8:3^{2}, 11, 13, 20, 26^{2}, 28^{2}, 31, 32, 33
9:5, 6, 25, 30, 44, 45, 47, 51, 55

JUDGES
10:2, 5, 7, 9, 16
11:1^{2}, 5, 18, 34, 39
12:5, 7, 10, 12, 15
13:2^{3}, 6^{2}, 9, 16, 21
14:4, 8, 19, 20
15:14, 18, 19
16:2, 4, 9, 16, 20, 22, 27, 29
17:1^{2}, 6^{2}, 7^{2}, 11^{2}, 12
18:1, 7, 20, 28^{3}, 29^{2}, 31
19:1^{2}, 2, 10, 11, 15, 16, 26^{2}, 27, 29, 30^{2}
20:1, 3, 4, 27, 34^{2}, 38, 41
21:25^{2}

RUTH
1:1, 2, 3, 4, 5, 7, 18, 19
2:1, 3^{2}, 5, 6, 14, 15, 17, 18
3:7, 8
4:3, 7^{2}, 9^{2}, 13

1 SAMUEL
1:1^{2}, 2, 4, 10, 13, 18, 20, 24
2:13^{2}, 17, 22, 26
3:1^{2}, 2, 3^{2}, 7, 19, 20
4:2, 6, 10^{2}, 11, 15, 18, 19^{2}, 21
5:3, 4^{2}, 6, 7, 9^{2}, 11^{2}
6:1, 4, 9, 14, 15
7:2^{2}, 10, 13, 14, 17^{2}
8:1, 2
9:1^{2}, 2^{3}, 5, 9, 10, 24
10:9, 20, 21^{2}, 23
11:6, 11
12:8, 12, 15
13:3, 4, 7, 19, 22^{2}
14:3, 4^{2}, 5, 14, 15^{2}, 18, 19, 20^{2}, 25, 27, 35, 39, 42, 43, 50^{2}, 51^{2}, 52
15:9^{2}, 12
16:12, 23^{3}
17:3, 4, 5^{2}, 7, 12^{2}, 14, 20, 28, 40, 42, 50, 51
18:1, 4, 5, 6, 8, 10, 12^{3}, 14, 15, 19, 28, 29, 30
19:7, 8, 9, 16, 19, 20, 21, 23
20:19, 24, 25, 27^{2}, 30, 33, 34, 37, 41
21:1, 6^{3}, 7^{2}, 12
22:2^{3}, 4, 6, 9, 22
23:7^{2}, 13^{2}, 15^{2}
24:1^{2}, 3
25:2^{3}, 3^{4}, 7, 20, 21, 36^{2}, 37, 39, 44
26:4, 12, 16, 21, 24
27:4^{2}, 7
28:3, 5, 14, 20^{2}, 21
30:3, 6^{2}, 19, 25
31:3, 4, 5

2 SAMUEL
1:1, 2, 10^{4}, 26
2:10, 11^{2}, 16, 17^{2}, 18, 32
3:1, 2, 6, 7, 8, 22^{2}, 23, 26, 27, 35, 37
4:1, 2^{2}, 4^{3}
5:2, 4, 10, 13
6:3, 4, 7, 8, 9, 12, 13, 14, 20, 21
7:9, 19
8:16^{2}, 17, 18
9:2^{2}, 6, 12, 13
10:9, 17
11:1, 2, 4, 7, 26, 27
12:3, 4^{2}, 5, 15, 18^{2}, 19, 21^{2}, 22, 30^{2}
13:1, 2^{2}, 3^{2}, 6, 8, 15, 19, 21, 38, 39^{2}
14:1, 6, 25^{2}, 26^{2}, 27^{2}
15:2, 5, 12, 17, 30, 32
16:1, 5, 16, 23^{2}
17:6, 19, 22, 23^{2}, 25^{2}, 27
18:6, 7, 8, 9^{2}, 14, 29, 33
19:1, 2^{2}, 16, 18, 25, 32^{2}, 39
20:1, 8, 10, 13, 17, 23^{2}, 24^{2}, 25, 26
21:1, 7, 11, 14, 16, 18^{2}, 19^{2}, 20^{3}
22:8, 10, 11, 19, 24, 42
23:1, 2, 8, 9, 10, 11^{2}, 14^{2}, 16, 18, 19^{2}, 23, 24
24:1, 2, 11, 16, 25^{2}

1 KINGS
1:1, 4, 6, 15, 23, 51
2:5, 10, 12, 15^{2}, 26, 29^{2}, 34, 41^{2}, 46
3:2, 4, 12, 15, 17, 18^{3}, 21^{2}, 26, 28
4:1, 4, 5^{2}, 6^{2}, 15, 16, 19^{3}, 22, 31^{2}
5:1, 12, 13, 14
6:2, 3^{2}, 6^{3}, 7^{5}, 8, 17, 18^{3}, 20^{2}, 22, 24, 25, 26^{2}, 37, 38^{2}
7:1, 2, 3, 4, 5, 6^{2}, 7, 8, 10, 12, 14^{3}, 16^{2}, 20, 22^{2}, 23^{2}, 24, 25, 26^{2}, 27, 28, 29, 31^{2}, 32, 33, 35, 38, 47, 48, 51
8:9, 17, 18^{2}, 54, 57, 64^{3}
9:1, 25
10:2^{2}, 3, 5, 6, 7, 14, 19, 20, 21
11:4^{3}, 9^{2}, 14, 15^{2}, 20, 21, 25, 26, 27, 28^{2}, 30, 40, 42, 43
12:2^{2}, 15, 18, 20^{2}, 21
13:5, 6^{2}, 9, 17, 24^{2}, 26
14:6, 8, 21^{2}, 28, 30, 31^{2}
15:2, 3, 5, 6, 7, 10, 11, 14, 16, 22, 23, 24, 32
16:6, 9, 18, 28
17:1, 10, 11, 17^{2}
18:2, 3, 4, 7, 13, 26^{3}, 29^{2}, 30, 38, 45^{2}, 46
19:6, 11^{2}, 12, 13, 19
20:12, 16, 29^{2}, 36, 40^{2}, 41
21:1, 11, 15^{2}, 16, 25
22:13, 33, 35, 37, 42^{2}, 43, 47^{2}, 50

2 KINGS
1:2^{2}, 7, 8
2:17, 23
3:4, 5, 9, 20^{2}, 26, 27
4:8^{2}, 18, 31, 32^{2}, 36, 38, 41
5:1^{3}, 8, 11, 14
6:5^{2}, 11, 13, 15, 17, 25^{2}, 26
7:5, 7, 10, 15, 16
8:5, 6, 7^{2}, 11, 17, 18, 24, 26^{2}, 27, 29
9:15, 16, 21, 30, 33, 34
10:5^{2}, 12, 15, 21^{2}, 22, 30, 36
11:1, 2, 3, 14, 16, 20, 21
12:1, 2, 6, 9, 10^{3}, 12, 13, 16^{2}, 18
13:2, 3, 11, 13, 14, 19, 21, 23
14:2^{2}, 3, 5, 9^{3}, 12, 16, 20, 21, 24, 25, 26^{2}
15:2^{2}, 3, 5^{2}, 9, 12, 18, 24, 28, 33^{2}, 34, 38
16:2^{2}, 8, 10, 12, 14, 20
17:2, 7, 18^{2}, 23, 25
18:2^{2}, 3, 5, 7, 9, 10, 15, 18, 36, 37
19:2, 8, 37
20:1, 4, 13^{2}
21:1^{2}, 2, 15, 16, 18, 19^{2}, 20, 26
22:1^{2}, 2, 7^{2}, 9, 19
23:2, 11, 15, 22, 23, 25, 26, 31^{2}, 32, 36^{2}, 37
24:8^{2}, 9, 10, 18^{2}, 19
25:2, 3, 4, 13, 16, 17^{2}, 19, 21, 30

1 CHRONICLES
1:19^{3}, 39, 43, 44, 45, 46^{2}, 47, 48, 49, 50^{3}
2:3, 17, 19, 21, 24, 26^{2}, 29, 34, 42, 45^{2}, 49
3:10
4:3, 9, 11, 40, 41
5:1^{2}, 2, 6, 7, 20, 22
6:54
7:2, 9, 15^{2}, 16, 24, 25, 40
8:29, 34, 37
9:17, 20^{2}, 21, 27, 31, 35, 40
10:3, 4, 5
11:2, 6, 9, 12^{2}, 13^{2}, 16^{2}, 18, 20, 21^{2}, 23, 25
12:3, 14, 18, 22, 27, 40
13:4, 10, 11, 12
14:2, 8
15:22^{2}, 27
16:39
17:13, 17
18:15, 16, 17
19:10, 17
20:1, 2, 4, 5^{2}, 6^{3}
21:5, 6, 7, 15, 20, 30
22:7
23:1, 3, 8, 11, 13, 16, 28
24:21, 25, 29
25:1, 7
26:1, 10, 20, 24, 28, 31
27:2, 3, 4^{2}, 5, 6^{2}, 7, 8, 9, 10, 11, 12, 13, 14, 15, 16, 24, 25^{2}, 26, 27^{2}, 28^{2}, 29^{2}, 30^{2}, 31^{2}, 32^{2}, 33^{2}, 34^{2}
29:27

2 CHRONICLES
1:1^{2}, 3^{2}, 6, 11, 13
2:14
3:3^{2}, 4^{3}, 6, 8, 9, 11^{2}, 12^{2}, 15^{2}
4:3^{2}, 4, 5, 6, 11, 19
5:1, 3, 10, 13
6:7, 8^{2}
7:7^{3}
8:16^{3}
9:1^{2}, 2, 4, 5, 6, 9, 13, 19, 20, 31
10:2, 15, 18
11:1
12:13^{2}, 16
13:2^{2}, 7, 13, 14
14:1, 2, 5, 14
15:4, 5, 6, 8, 9, 15, 17, 19
16:3, 6, 10^{2}, 12^{2}, 14
17:3, 6, 15, 16, 18
18:14, 32
20:25, 26, 29, 30, 31^{2}, 32
21:1, 3, 4, 5, 6, 17^{2}, 20
22:2^{2}, 3, 6, 7^{2}, 8, 9, 10, 11, 12
23:15, 18, 19, 21
24:1^{2}, 2, 4, 11^{2}, 13, 15^{2}
25:1^{2}, 2, 3, 10^{2}, 14, 15, 18^{3}, 22
26:1, 3^{2}, 4, 13, 15^{2}, 16^{2}, 19^{2}, 20, 21^{3}
27:1^{2}, 2, 8
28:1^{2}, 5, 7, 9^{3}
29:1^{2}, 2, 6, 8, 25, 28, 32, 34, 35, 36
30:5, 12, 17, 18, 26^{2}, 27
31:1, 12^{2}, 14, 20
32:2^{2}, 4, 5, 14, 15, 21, 23, 24, 25^{2}, 31^{2}
33:1, 2, 12, 13^{2}, 19^{2}, 21, 22
34:1, 2, 3, 9, 14, 16, 17, 27, 30
35:10, 16, 18, 19, 24, 26
36:2, 5^{2}, 8, 9^{2}, 10, 11, 12, 16

EZRA
1:6
2:61, 64
3:1, 3, 6, 11, 12, 13
4:7, 14, 15, 20, 23
5:5, 7, 11, 14^{2}, 17
6:1, 2^{2}, 15^{2}
7:6, 8, 28^{2}
8:22, 23, 31, 33^{3}, 34, 35
10:9

NEHEMIAH
1:1, 11
2:1, 2, 10, 11, 12, 14^{2}, 18

NEHEMIAH
3:16, 25
4:1, 3, 6, 15, 18
5:1, 6, 14, 18^{3}
6:1, 6, 10, 13, 15, 16, 18
7:1, 2, 4, 7, 63, 64, 66, 72
8:1, 3, 5, 17, 18
10:29
11:9^{2}, 11, 14, 17, 22, 23, 24
12:8, 37, 43
13:1, 4, 5, 6, 13^{2}, 26^{2}, 28

ESTHER
1:2, 8, 10, 11, 12, 13, 14
2:1^{2}, 5^{2}, 7, 8^{2}, 12, 13, 15, 16, 20, 22, 23^{3}
3:4, 5, 12^{2}, 14, 15^{2}
4:1, 3, 4, 5^{2}, 6, 8
5:2^{2}, 9
6:2, 4
7:6, 7, 8^{2}, 10
8:1, 9, 13, 14, 15
9:1, 4, 11, 14, 22, 32
10:3

JOB
1:1^{3}, 3^{2}, 5, 6, 13, 16, 17, 18
2:1, 11, 13
3:3^{2}, 25, 26^{2}
4:4, 12, 16^{2}
8:7
15:7, 19
16:12
17:6
20:4
22:16
23:17
29:4^{2}, 5, 13, 14, 15^{2}, 16, 19, 20^{2}
30:2, 25^{2}
31:18, 23, 25
32:1, 2^{2}, 3, 5^{2}, 6, 12
33:27
42:7

PSALMS
4:1
7:4
18:7, 9, 12, 18, 23, 41
22:9, 10
30:7
31:11, 13
32:4
33:9
35:13
37:36
38:13, 14
39:2^{2}, 3^{2}, 9
50:21
51:5
53:5
55:12^{2}, 13, 18, 21
63:t
66:14, 17
68:8, 9, 11, 14
69:10, 12, 20
73:3, 16, 21^{2}, 22^{2}
74:5
76:8
77:3^{2}, 18
78:8, 21^{2}, 30, 35, 37, 59, 62
79:3
81:4
87:4, 5, 6
95:10
97:8
105:17, 18, 37, 38
106:9, 11, 18, 30, 31, 33, 40
107:12
114:2, 3
116:6, 10
119:67, 158
122:1
124:1, 2, 3
126:2
139:15^{2}, 16
142:t, 3, 4

PROVERBS
4:3
5:14
8:23^{2}, 24, 25, 27, 30^{2}
23:35
24:31^{2}

ECCLESIASTES
1:10, 12
2:3, 9, 10, 11^{2}, 15, 24
3:16^{2}
4:1
5:6
7:23
9:14, 15
12:7, 9, 10^{2}

SONG OF SOLOMON
2:3, 4
3:4
5:6
6:12
8:10, 11

ISAIAH
1:21
6:4
7:2^{2}
9:1
10:14, 26
11:16
14:28
21:3^{2}, 14
22:14, 25
23:13

ISAIAH
26:16
28:13
36:3, 21, 22
37:2, 8, 38
38:1, 8, 9, 20
39:1, 2^{3}
41:28^{2}
43:10, 12, 13
47:6
48:8, 16
49:21
50:2^{2}, 5
52:14
53:3, 5^{3}, 7^{2}, 8^{3}, 9, 12
57:17^{2}
59:15, 16^{2}, 17
63:3, 5^{2}, 8, 9, 10
65:1, 2
66:7

JEREMIAH
2:2, 3
3:21
4:23, 25, 26
7:12
8:16
11:19
13:7^{2}, 20
14:4, 5, 6
15:9, 16
17:16
18:4
20:1, 2, 7, 8, 9^{2}, 14
22:15, 16^{2}
25:1
26:20, 21, 24
28:1
31:11, 15, 18, 19^{3}, 26, 32
32:1, 2^{2}, 8, 9, 11^{2}
33:1
35:4^{2}
36:22, 23^{3}
37:5, 11, 13^{3}, 16
38:6^{2}, 7, 27, 28^{3}
39:2, 15
40:5
41:7, 9
44:6^{2}
46:2, 5, 21
48:13, 27^{2}
49:12, 21
51:5, 59
52:1^{2}, 2, 5, 6^{2}, 7^{2}, 8, 12, 17, 19^{2}, 20, 21^{3}, 22^{2}, 27, 34

LAMENTATIONS
1:1^{2}
2:5, 12
3:10, 14
4:6, 7, 20
5:10

EZEKIEL
1:1, 2, 3, 4, 5, 7, 12, 13^{2}, 16^{2}, 20^{3}, 21, 22, 25^{2}, 26^{3}, 28^{2}
2:9^{2}, 10^{2}
3:3, 14, 22
8:3, 4, 14
9:2, 3^{2}, 8
10:1, 4^{2}, 5, 7^{2}, 9, 13, 14^{2}, 17, 19, 21, 22
11:22
12:7
13:10
15:5^{2}
16:3, 4, 8, 13, 14, 15, 19, 36, 45, 49^{2}, 56, 57
17:7, 8
19:4, 5, 7, 8, 10, 11, 12^{2}
21:22
22:10
23:5, 11, 13, 17^{2}, 18^{2}, 40, 42, 43
24:18
25:3^{2}
26:2
27:7^{2}, 12, 16, 18, 20
28:13^{2}, 15, 17
29:18^{2}
30:22
31:3^{2}, 5, 7^{2}, 8
32:15, 25
33:22^{4}, 24
34:4^{4}, 6, 8, 16^{4}
35:10, 15
36:17, 23, 35, 36
37:1^{2}, 7^{2}, 8
40:1^{2}, 2, 3^{2}, 6^{2}, 7^{2}, 9, 12^{2}, 13, 18, 21, 23, 25, 27, 29, 33, 36, 40, 43, 44^{2}, 47, 48, 49
41:1, 2, 6, 7^{2}, 9^{4}, 10, 11^{3}, 12^{3}, 15, 18^{2}, 19^{2}, 22
42:1^{2}, 2^{2}, 3^{2}, 4, 6, 7^{2}, 8, 9, 11, 12
43:2, 3
44:1
46:19^{2}, 21, 23^{2}
47:5
48:35

DANIEL
1:4, 19
2:1, 3, 12, 14, 19, 26, 31^{2}, 32, 34, 35^{2}, 45
3:1, 19^{3}, 22, 24, 27
4:4, 8, 10, 11, 12^{2}, 19^{2}, 20, 21, 31, 33^{3}, 36^{2}
5:2, 3, 6, 9^{2}, 11, 13, 20^{2}, 21^{4}, 24^{2}, 25, 30
6:2, 3^{2}, 4^{2}, 10, 14, 17, 22, 23^{3}
7:4^{3}, 6, 7, 9^{2}, 10, 11, 14, 15, 19, 20, 22
8:2^{2}, 3, 4, 5, 7^{3}, 8^{2}, 11^{2}, 12, 17, 18^{2}, 26, 27^{2}

DANIEL
9:1, 20, 21
10:1^{4}, 2, 4, 6, 8^{2}, 9, 19
12:1^{2}, 6, 7

HOSEA
1:10
2:3, 7
7:1
8:6
9:8
10:14
11:1, 4
12:13
13:6

AMOS
1:1
2:9^{2}
4:7
7:1, 14^{3}

JONAH
1:4^{2}, 5^{2}, 11, 13, 17
2:6
3:3
4:1, 2^{2}, 6

MICAH
4:7

NAHUM
3:8^{3}, 9, 10

HABAKKUK
3:2, 3, 4^{2}, 8^{3}, 9, 14

ZEPHANIAH
3:18, 19

HAGGAI
2:15, 18

ZECHARIAH
1:15
3:3
5:7, 9
7:7, 14
8:2^{3}, 9, 10^{2}
10:2, 3
11:11^{2}, 13
13:6

MALACHI
1:2, 13
2:5^{2}, 6^{2}
3:16

MATTHEW
1:16, 18^{3}, 19, 22^{2}
2:1, 3, 9, 15^{2}, 16^{2}, 17^{2}, 18, 19, 22, 23
3:3, 4, 16
4:1, 2, 12, 14
5:1, 21, 27
6:29
7:25, 27
8:1, 3, 5, 13, 14, 16, 17, 23, 24^{2}, 26, 28, 30, 33
9:20, 22, 28, 33^{2}, 36
10:3
11:14
12:3, 4, 9, 10, 13, 17, 22, 40
13:6, 19, 26, 33, 35, 47, 48, 54
14:6, 9, 11, 14, 15, 23^{2}, 24^{2}, 29, 30
15:28, 37
16:20
17:2^{2}, 18, 25
18:11, 24, 27, 31^{2}, 34^{2}
19:8
20:8
21:4^{2}, 10^{2}, 23^{2}, 25, 33
22:7, 10, 12, 31, 35, 46
24:21
25:6, 10, 25, 35^{3}, 36^{2}, 42^{2}, 43
26:3, 6, 20, 56, 71^{2}
27:1, 3, 8, 9^{3}, 12, 15, 19, 24, 35, 45, 51, 54, 56, 57^{2}, 61, 63
28:2, 3, 5

MARK
1:6, 9, 13^{2}, 14, 23, 33, 42, 45
2:1^{2}, 2, 3, 4, 25, 27
3:1, 5
4:1^{2}, 6^{2}, 10, 15, 22, 35, 36, 37, 38, 39
5:2, 5, 11, 14^{2}, 15, 16, 18, 21^{2}, 26, 29^{2}, 33, 36, 39, 40, 42
6:2, 14^{2}, 20, 21, 26, 34, 35, 47^{2}, 48, 52, 55
7:17, 26, 30, 32, 35
8:8, 25
9:2, 7, 26, 28, 33
10:1, 14, 17, 22, 47
11:11, 12, 13, 18, 19, 27, 30, 32
12:11
13:19
14:1, 4, 32, 45, 49, 66
15:7, 25, 26, 28^{2}, 33^{2}, 38, 39, 40, 41, 42^{2}, 46, 47
16:1, 4^{2}, 6, 9, 11, 14, 19

LUKE
1:5^{3}, 7, 9, 12, 26, 27^{2}, 29, 36, 41, 64, 66, 67, 80
2:2^{2}, 4, 6, 7, 13, 17, 20, 21^{3}, 25^{4}, 26, 36^{2}, 37, 40, 42, 51
3:21, 23^{2}, 24^{5}, 25^{5}, 26^{5}, 27^{5}, 28^{5}, 29^{5}, 30^{5}, 31^{5}, 32^{5}, 33^{5}, 34^{5}, 35^{5}, 36^{5}, 37^{5}, 38^{4}
4:1, 16, 17^{2}, 25^{2}, 26^{2}, 27, 29, 32, 33, 38, 40, 41, 42
5:3, 9, 10, 12, 17^{2}, 18, 29, 36
6:3, 6^{2}, 10, 13, 16, 48, 49
7:2^{2}, 4, 6, 12^{3}, 15, 37, 41

LUKE

8:5, 6, 20, 24, 29^{2}, 32, 34, 35, 36^{2}, 40, 41, 47^{2}, 53, 56
9:7^{4}, 8, 17, 18, 29^{2}, 36^{2}, 42, 45, 51, 53
10:32, 33, 36, 40
11:1, 14^{3}, 30, 50
12:27
13:10, 11^{2}, 13, 21
14:2, 30
15:6, 20, 24^{2}, 25, 28, 30, 32^{3}
16:1^{2}, 19^{2}, 20^{2}, 22^{2}
17:10, 15, 16, 20, 26, 28
18:2, 3, 23^{2}, 24, 34, 35, 40
19:2^{3}, 3^{2}, 4, 7, 10, 11, 15, 22, 29, 37, 41
20:4, 6, 7
21:5, 37
22:14, 22, 23, 24, 37, 39, 40, 41, 44, 45, 47, 53, 56, 59, 66
23:7, 8^{2}, 19, 25, 38, 44^{2}, 45^{2}, 47^{2}, 50^{2}, 51, 53^{2}, 54, 55
24:6, 10, 12, 13, 18, 19, 23, 35, 44, 51

JOHN

1:1^{3}, 2, 3^{2}, 4^{2}, 6^{2}, 8^{2}, 9, 10^{2}, 14, 15^{2}, 17, 28, 30, 39, 40, 44
2:1^{2}, 2, 9^{2}, 13, 17, 20, 22, 23, 25
3:1, 23^{2}, 24, 26
4:6^{2}, 45, 46^{2}, 47^{2}, 51, 53, 54
5:1, 4, 5, 9^{2}, 10, 13^{2}, 15, 18, 35
6:4, 10, 16, 17^{2}, 21, 22, 24, 62, 71
7:2, 12, 30, 39^{2}, 42, 43
8:4, 9, 20, 44, 56, 58
9:1, 2, 8, 13, 14, 16, 19, 20, 22, 24, 25, 32^{2}
10:19, 22^{2}
11:1, 2^{2}, 6^{2}, 15, 18, 20, 30^{2}, 32^{2}, 33, 38, 39, 41, 44^{2}, 55
12:1, 2, 3, 5, 6^{2}, 9, 12, 16, 17, 21
13:1, 3, 5, 12, 21, 23, 30, 31
16:4
17:5, 12
18:1, 10, 13^{2}, 14^{2}, 15, 16, 18, 28, 37, 40
19:8, 14, 19, 20^{3}, 23, 29, 31^{2}, 32, 33, 41^{3}, 42
20:1, 7, 14, 24
21:4^{2}, 7^{2}, 11, 12, 14, 17

THE ACTS

1:2, 9, 16, 17, 19, 22, 23, 26
2:1, 6, 16, 24, 26, 31
3:2, 10, 11, 13, 20
4:3, 4, 11, 14, 21, 22^{2}, 31, 32, 33, 34, 35, 36
5:4^{3}, 7^{2}, 36
6:1
7:2, 4, 9, 12, 13^{2}, 20^{2}, 21, 22^{2}, 23, 24, 29, 38, 58
8:1^{3}, 8, 9^{2}, 13, 16, 18, 28, 32^{2}, 33, 40
9:9, 10, 18, 19^{2}, 24, 26^{2}, 28, 33, 36^{2}, 37, 38^{2}, 39^{2}, 42
10:1, 4, 7, 16^{2}, 18, 22, 25, 29, 30, 37, 38, 42, 45
11:2, 5, 10, 11, 17, 21, 22, 23, 24^{2}
12:5^{2}, 6, 9^{2}, 11, 12, 15, 18^{3}, 20^{2}, 23, 25
13:1^{2}, 6, 7, 12, 29, 31, 32, 36, 43, 46, 49
14:4, 5, 12, 13
15:5, 37, 39
16:1^{3}, 2, 3, 13, 15, 19, 26, 33, 35
17:1, 2, 13, 16, 34
18:3, 5^{2}, 12, 14, 25, 27^{2}, 28
19:1, 16, 17^{2}, 29, 32, 34
20:1, 3, 9^{2}, 11, 20
21:3, 8, 11, 30, 31, 33, 35^{2}, 37, 40
22:3, 6, 17^{2}, 20^{2}, 28, 29^{2}, 30
23:5, 7, 12, 27^{2}, 30, 31, 34^{2}
24:2, 24
25:1, 7, 15, 19, 23^{3}
26:4, 19, 26
27:1, 8, 9^{3}, 12, 15, 20, 25, 27, 33, 39, 41, 42
28:1, 6, 7, 9, 11, 16, 17, 18, 19

ROMANS

1:3, 13, 21, 27
4:3, 9, 10^{2}, 13, 18, 19, 20, 21, 22, 23^{2}, 25^{2}
5:13, 14, 16^{2}
6:4, 17
7:8, 9, 10, 13
8:3, 20
9:12, 25, 26
10:20^{2}
15:8, 20, 21
16:25

1 CORINTHIANS

1:6, 13
2:3, 4
7:20
10:4, 5
11:9, 23
13:11
15:4, 5, 6, 7, 8, 10^{3}, 45^{2}, 46
16:12, 17
S

2 CORINTHIANS

1:15, 17, 18, 19^{3}
2:6, 12

THE ACTS

3:7^{2}, 10, 11
5:19
7:7, 13
8:9, 11, 19
9:2
11:5, 9^{3}, 25^{2}, 33
12:4, 7, 13
13:4
S

GALATIANS

1:11, 12, 22
2:3^{2}, 7^{2}, 8, 9, 10, 11^{2}, 13
3:6, 17^{2}, 19^{3}, 24
4:4, 14, 23^{3}, 28, 29^{2}

EPHESIANS

3:5, 7

PHILIPPIANS

2:5, 7, 26, 27, 30
S

COLOSSIANS

1:23
2:14^{2}

1 THESSALONIANS

2:1, 3
S

2 THESSALONIANS

1:10
2:5
S

1 TIMOTHY

1:11, 13, 14
2:13, 14^{2}
3:16
4:14
S

2 TIMOTHY

1:9, 14, 16, 17
2:8
3:9
4:17
S^{2}

TITUS

S

PHILEMON

11

HEBREWS

2:2, 3, 9
3:2^{2}, 3, 5, 10, 17^{2}
4:2, 6, 15
5:4, 7^{2}
6:18
7:4, 10, 11, 20, 22, 28
8:5^{2}, 6
9:2^{2}, 4, 8^{2}, 9, 18, 23, 28
10:29
11:4, 5^{2}, 8, 11^{2}, 17, 18, 19, 21, 23^{3}, 24, 38
12:2, 17, 20, 21

JAMES

1:24
2:21, 22, 23^{3}, 25
5:17

1 PETER

1:11, 12, 20^{2}
2:22, 23
3:20
4:6

2 PETER

1:9
2:16, 22
3:6

1 JOHN

1:1, 2^{3}
3:5, 8, 12
4:9

JUDE

3^{2}

REVELATION

1:4, 8, 9, 10, 16, 18
2:8, 13^{2}
4:1^{2}, 2^{2}, 3^{2}, 6, 7^{2}, 8
5:3, 4, 11, 12
6:2, 4^{3}, 8^{2}, 11, 12
7:2
8:1, 3^{2}, 7^{2}, 8, 12^{2}
9:1, 3, 4, 5^{2}, 9, 10, 18
10:1^{2}, 4, 10^{2}
11:1, 8, 13, 19^{2}
12:4^{2}, 5^{2}, 7, 8, 9^{2}, 13, 17
13:2, 3, 5^{2}, 7^{2}, 12
14:5, 16, 20
15:5, 8^{2}
16:8, 10, 12, 18^{2}, 19, 21
17:4, 5, 8^{2}, 11
18:1, 16, 24
19:8, 11, 13, 20
20:4, 10, 11, 12, 15^{2}
21:1, 11, 18^{2}, 19, 21^{2}
22:2

WE

587, *2249*

GENESIS

3:2
11:4
13:8
19:2, 5, 9, 13, 32^{2}, 34
20:13
24:25, 50, 57
26:16, 22, 28^{2}, 29^{2}, 32
29:4, 5, 8^{2}, 27
31:15, 49
32:6
34:14, 15^{2}, 16^{4}, 17^{2}
37:7, 20^{2}, 26, 32
38:23
40:8
41:11^{2}, 12, 38
42:2, 11^{2}, 21^{3}, 31^{3}, 32
43:4, 5, 7^{2}, 8^{3}, 10^{2}, 18, 20, 21^{3}, 22^{2}
44:8^{3}, 9, 16^{5}, 20^{2}, 22, 24^{2}, 26^{4}
46:34
47:3, 4^{2}, 15, 18, 19^{4}, 25
50:15, 17, 18

EXODUS

1:9
3:18^{2}
5:3
8:26^{2}, 27
10:9^{3}, 25, 26^{4}
12:33
14:5^{2}, 12^{3}
15:24
16:3^{3}, 7, 8
17:2
19:8
20:19^{2}
24:3, 7, 14
32:1, 23
33:16

LEVITICUS

25:20^{2}

NUMBERS

9:7^{3}
10:29^{2}, 31, 32
11:5^{2}, 13, 20
12:11^{2}
13:27, 28, 30, 31^{2}, 32^{2}, 33^{3}
14:2^{2}, 7, 40^{2}
16:12, 14
17:12^{3}, 13
20:3, 4, 10, 15, 16^{2}, 17^{5}, 19
21:7^{2}, 22^{4}, 30^{2}
22:6
31:50
32:5, 16, 17^{2}, 18, 19, 31, 32

DEUTERONOMY

1:19^{3}, 22^{3}, 28^{3}, 41^{2}
2:1^{2}, 8^{2}, 13, 14^{2}, 33, 34^{2}, 35^{2}
3:1, 3, 4^{2}, 6^{2}, 7, 8, 12, 29
4:7
5:24^{2}, 25^{3}, 26, 27
6:21, 25
12:8
18:21
26:7
29:7, 8, 16^{2}, 29
30:12, 13

JOSHUA

1:16^{2}, 17^{2}
2:10, 11, 14, 17, 18, 19, 20
4:23
5:1
6:17
7:7
8:5, 6^{2}
9:6, 7, 8, 9, 11, 12^{2}, 13, 19^{2}, 20^{3}, 22, 24, 25
10:4
22:17, 23, 24, 26, 27, 28^{2}, 29, 31
24:15, 16, 17^{2}, 18, 21, 22, 24^{2}

JUDGES

1:3, 24^{2}
8:6, 15, 25
9:28^{2}, 38
10:10^{2}, 15^{2}
11:6, 8, 10, 19, 24
12:1
13:8, 12^{2}, 15, 17, 22^{2}
14:13, 15^{2}
15:10, 12^{2}, 13^{2}
16:2, 5^{3}
18:5^{3}, 9^{2}
19:12^{2}, 18, 22
20:8^{2}, 9^{2}, 10, 13
21:7^{3}, 16, 18, 22^{2}

RUTH

1:10
4:11

1 SAMUEL

5:8
6:2^{2}, 4, 9
7:6
8:19, 20
9:6, 7^{3}
10:14^{2}
11:1, 3^{2}, 10, 12
12:10^{3}, 19^{2}
14:8^{2}, 9^{2}, 10, 12
15:15
16:11
17:9, 10
20:42
23:3^{2}
25:7, 8, 15^{4}, 16
30:14^{2}, 22^{2}

2 SAMUEL

5:1
7:22
11:23
12:18^{2}
13:25
14:7^{2}, 14
15:14
16:20
17:6, 12^{2}, 13
18:3
19:6, 10, 42, 43^{2}
20:1^{2}
21:4, 5, 6

1 KINGS

3:18^{2}
8:47^{2}
12:4, 9, 16^{2}
17:12
18:5^{2}
20:23^{2}, 25^{2}, 31
22:3, 7, 8, 15^{2}

2 KINGS

2:16
3:8, 11
6:1, 2^{2}, 15, 28^{2}, 29^{2}
7:3^{2}, 4^{7}, 9^{4}, 10, 12^{2}
10:4, 5^{2}, 13^{2}
18:22, 26

1 CHRONICLES

11:1
12:18
13:3
15:13
16:35
17:20
29:13, 14^{2}, 15, 16

2 CHRONICLES

2:16^{2}
6:37^{2}
10:4, 9, 16^{2}
13:10, 11
14:7^{2}, 11^{2}
18:3, 5, 6, 7, 14
20:9, 12^{2}
25:9
28:13
29:18, 19
31:10

EZRA

4:2^{2}, 3, 14^{2}, 16
5:4, 8, 9, 10^{2}, 11
7:24
8:15, 21, 22, 23, 31, 32
9:7^{2}, 9, 10^{2}, 14, 15^{3}
10:2, 4, 12, 13^{2}

NEHEMIAH

1:6, 7
2:17^{2}, 20
4:1, 4, 6, 9, 10, 11, 15, 19, 21
5:2^{3}, 3^{2}, 4, 5, 8, 12^{2}, 16
9:33, 36^{2}, 37, 38
10:30, 31^{2}, 32, 34, 37, 39
13:27

ESTHER

1:15
7:4^{2}

JOB

2:10^{2}
4:2
5:27
8:9
9:32
15:9
18:2, 3
19:28
21:14, 15^{3}
28:22
31:31^{2}
32:13
36:26
37:5, 19^{2}, 23
38:35

PSALMS

12:4
20:5^{2}, 7, 8, 9
21:13
33:21, 22
35:25^{2}
36:9
44:1, 5^{2}, 8, 17^{2}, 20, 22^{2}
46:2
48:8^{2}, 9
55:14
60:12
65:4
66:6, 12
74:9
75:1^{2}
78:3, 4
79:4, 8, 13^{2}
80:3, 7, 14, 18^{2}, 19
90:7^{2}, 9, 10, 12, 14, 15
95:7
100:3^{2}
103:14
106:6^{3}
108:13
115:18
118:24, 26
123:3
124:7
126:1, 3
129:8
132:6^{2}, 7^{2}
137:1^{3}, 2, 4

PROVERBS

1:13^{2}
24:12

SONG OF SOLOMON

1:4^{3}, 11
6:1, 13
8:8^{2}, 9^{2}

ISAIAH

1:9^{2}
2:3
4:1
5:19^{2}
9:10^{2}
14:10
16:6
20:6^{2}
22:13
24:16
25:9^{3}
26:1, 8, 13, 17, 18^{4}
28:15^{4}
30:16^{2}
33:2
36:7, 11
38:20
41:22, 23^{2}, 26^{2}
42:24
46:5
51:23
53:2^{2}, 3^{2}, 4, 5, 6^{2}
56:12
58:3^{2}
59:9^{2}, 10^{5}, 11^{2}, 12
63:19
64:3, 5^{2}, 6^{2}, 8^{2}, 9^{2}

JEREMIAH

2:31^{2}
3:22, 25^{3}
4:13
5:12
6:16, 17, 24
7:10
8:8, 14^{2}, 15, 20
9:19^{3}
13:12
14:7, 9, 19, 20^{2}, 22
15:2
16:10
18:12^{2}
20:10^{3}
26:19
30:5
35:6, 8^{2}, 9, 10, 11^{2}
36:16
38:4, 25
41:8
42:2^{2}, 3^{2}, 5, 6^{3}, 13, 14^{3}, 20
44:16, 17^{4}, 18^{2}, 19^{2}, 25^{2}
48:14, 29
50:7
51:9, 51^{2}

LAMENTATIONS

2:16^{4}
3:22, 42
4:17, 18, 20^{2}
5:3, 4, 5, 6, 7, 9, 16, 21

EZEKIEL

11:3
20:32
21:10
33:10^{2}, 24
35:10
37:11

DANIEL

2:4, 7, 23, 36
3:16, 17, 18, 24
6:5^{2}
9:5, 6, 8, 9, 10, 11, 13^{2}, 14, 15^{2}, 18

HOSEA

6:2, 3^{2}
8:2
10:3^{2}
14:2, 3^{2}

AMOS

6:10, 13
8:5^{2}, 6

OBADIAH

1

JONAH

1:6, 7, 8, 11, 14^{2}
3:9

MICAH

2:4
4:2, 5
5:5

HABAKKUK

1:12

ZECHARIAH

1:11
8:23^{2}

MALACHI

1:4^{2}, 6, 7
2:10^{2}, 17
3:7, 8, 13, 14^{2}, 15

MATTHEW

2:2
3:9
6:12, 31^{3}
7:22
8:25, 29
9:14
11:3, 17^{2}
12:38
13:28
14:17
15:33
16:7
17:19, 27
19:27^{2}
20:18, 22
21:25, 26^{2}, 27
22:16
23:30^{2}
25:37, 38, 39, 44
26:17, 65
27:42, 63
28:13, 14

MARK

1:24
2:12
4:30^{2}, 38
5:9, 12
6:37
8:16
9:28, 38^{2}
10:28, 33, 35^{2}, 37, 39
11:31, 32, 33
12:14, 15^{2}
14:12, 58, 63
15:32

LUKE

1:71, 74
3:8, 10, 12, 14
4:23, 34
5:5, 26
7:19, 20, 32^{2}
8:24
9:12, 13^{2}, 49^{2}, 54
10:11
11:4
13:26
15:32
17:10^{2}
18:28, 31
19:14
20:5, 6, 21
22:8, 9, 49, 71^{2}
23:2, 41^{2}
24:21

JOHN

1:14, 16, 22, 41, 45
3:2, 11^{3}
4:22^{2}, 42^{2}
6:5, 28^{2}, 30, 42, 68, 69
7:27, 35
8:33, 41^{2}, 48, 52
9:20, 21^{2}, 24, 28, 29^{2}, 31, 40, 41
10:33
11:16, 47, 48
12:21, 34
13:29
14:5^{2}, 23
16:18, 30^{2}
17:11, 22
18:30
19:7, 15
20:2, 25
21:3, 24

THE ACTS

2:8^{2}, 11, 32, 37
3:12, 15
4:9, 12, 16^{2}, 20^{2}
5:23^{3}, 28, 29, 32
6:2, 3, 4, 11, 14
7:40
10:33, 39, 47
11:12
13:32, 46
14:15, 22

THE ACTS
15:10, 11[2], 19, 20, 24[2], 27, 36
16:10, 11, 12, 13[2], 16, 28
17:19, 20, 28[2], 29[2], 32
19:2, 13, 25, 40[2]
20:6[2], 13, 14, 15[3]
21:1[2], 2, 3[2], 4, 5[4], 6[2], 7[2], 8[2], 10, 12[2], 14, 15, 16, 17, 23[2], 25
23:9, 14[3], 15
24:2, 3, 5, 6, 8
26:14
27:1, 2, 3, 4[2], 5[2], 7[2], 15, 16, 18, 19, 20, 26, 27, 29, 37
28:10, 11, 12, 13[2], 14[2], 16, 21, 22[2]

ROMANS
1:5
2:2
3:5, 8[2], 9[2], 19, 28, 31[2]
4:1, 9, 24
5:1, 2[2], 3, 6, 8, 9, 10[3], 11[2]
6:1[2], 2, 4[2], 5[2], 6, 8[3], 15[2]
7:4, 5, 6[3], 7, 14
8:12, 15, 16, 17[2], 22, 23, 24, 25[3], 26[3], 28, 31, 36[2], 37
9:14, 29, 30

ROMANS
10:8
12:4, 5
13:11
14:8[6], 10
15:1, 4

1 CORINTHIANS
1:23
2:6, 7, 12[2], 13, 16
3:9
4:8, 9, 10[3], 11, 12[2], 13[2]
6:3
8:1[2], 4, 6[2], 8[4]
9:4, 5, 6, 11[2], 12[3], 25
10:6, 16[2], 17[2], 22[2]
11:16, 31[2], 32[3]
12:13[3], 23[2]
13:9[2], 12
15:11, 15[2], 19[2], 30, 32, 49[2], 51[2], 52

2 CORINTHIANS
1:4[2], 6[3], 8[3], 9[2], 10, 12, 13, 14, 24
2:11, 15, 16, 17[2]
3:1[2], 4, 5, 12[2], 18
4:1[3], 5, 7, 8[2], 11, 13[2], 16, 18

2 CORINTHIANS
5:1[2], 2, 3, 4[2], 6[3], 7, 8, 9[2], 10, 11[2], 12, 13[2], 14, 16[3], 20[2], 21
6:1, 9
7:2[3], 5[2], 13[2], 14
8:1, 4, 5, 6, 18, 22[2]
9:4[2]
10:2, 3[2], 7, 11[4], 12, 13, 14[3], 15
11:4, 6, 12, 21
12:18[2], 19[3]
13:4[2], 6, 7[2], 8, 9[3]

GALATIANS
1:8[2], 9
2:4, 5, 9, 10, 15, 16[2], 17[2]
3:14, 23, 24, 25
4:3[2], 5, 28, 31
5:5, 25
6:9[2], 10

EPHESIANS
1:4, 7, 11, 12
2:3, 5, 10[2], 18
3:12, 20
4:13, 14, 25
5:30
6:12

PHILIPPIANS
3:3, 16, 20

COLOSSIANS
1:3, 4, 9[2], 14, 28[2]

1 THESSALONIANS
1:2, 5, 7, 8, 9
2:2[2], 4[2], 5, 6[2], 7, 8, 9[2], 10, 11, 13, 17, 18
3:1[2], 3, 4[3], 6, 7, 8, 9[2], 10, 12
4:1, 2, 6, 10, 11, 14, 15[2], 17[2]
5:5, 10[2], 12, 14

2 THESSALONIANS
1:3, 4, 11
2:1, 13
3:2, 4[2], 6, 7, 8[2], 9, 10[2], 11, 12

1 TIMOTHY
1:8
2:2
4:10[2]
6:7[2]

2 TIMOTHY
2:11[2], 12[3], 13

TITUS
2:12
3:3, 5, 7

PHILEMON
7

HEBREWS
2:1[3], 3[2], 5, 8, 9
3:6[2], 14[2], 19
4:3, 13, 14, 15[2], 16
5:11
6:3, 9[2], 11, 18, 19
7:19
8:1[2]
9:5
10:10, 26[2], 30, 39
11:3
12:1, 9[3], 10, 25[2], 28[2]
13:6, 10, 14[2], 18[2]

JAMES
1:18
3:1, 2, 3[2], 9[2]
4:13, 15
5:11, 17

1 PETER
2:24
4:3

2 PETER
1:16[2], 18[2], 19
3:13

1 JOHN
1:1[3], 2, 3[2], 4, 5, 6[3], 7[2], 8[3], 9, 10[3]
2:1, 3[3], 5[2], 18, 28
3:1, 2[5], 11, 14[3], 16[2], 19[2], 21, 22[3], 23, 24
4:6[2], 9, 10, 11, 12, 13[2], 14, 16, 17[2], 19, 21
5:2[3], 3, 9, 14[2], 15[5], 18, 19[2], 20[3]

2 JOHN
4, 5[2], 6, 8[3]

3 JOHN
8[2], 12, 14

REVELATION
5:10
7:3
11:17

WERE 1961, *2258*

GENESIS
1:5, 7[2], 8, 13, 19, 23, 31
2:1, 4, 25[2]
3:7[2]
4:8
5:2, 4, 5, 8, 11, 14, 17, 20, 23, 27, 31
6:1, 2, 4[2]
7:10, 11[2], 18, 19[2], 20, 23[2]
8:2, 3, 5, 7, 8, 9, 11, 13
9:18, 23, 29
10:1, 5, 18, 21, 25, 29, 32
11:32
13:13
14:3, 5, 13, 17
17:23[2], 27
18:11
19:11, 36
20:8
21:16
23:1, 17[3], 20
24:10, 32, 54, 63
25:3, 4, 24[2]
26:35
27:1, 15, 23, 42
29:2, 3
30:35[2], 42[2]
31:10, 19
34:5[2], 7[2], 14, 25
35:2, 4[2], 5, 6, 22, 26, 28
36:5, 7[2], 11, 12, 13, 14, 15, 16, 18, 22, 23, 25
37:7, 27
38:27
39:20, 22
40:5, 6, 7, 10
41:21, 48, 50, 53
42:28, 35
43:18[2], 34
44:3, 4
45:3
46:12, 15, 20, 21, 22[2], 25, 26, 27[3], 31
48:5, 10
49:24
50:3, 4, 23

EXODUS
1:5, 7, 12
5:12, 14, 19
6:4, 16, 18, 20
7:20[3], 25
8:18
9:26, 32[2], 34
10:6, 8, 11, 14[2]
12:33, 37, 39
14:10, 11, 21, 22, 29
15:8[2], 23, 25, 27
17:12[2]
19:1, 2[2], 16
21:3, 29
22:21
23:9
24:10[2]
28:32
32:3, 15[3], 16, 25
34:1, 30
35:22, 25
36:6, 9, 15, 29, 30[2], 36, 38
37:9, 13, 14, 16, 17, 20, 22, 25
38:2, 9, 10[2], 11[2], 12, 14, 15, 16, 17[2], 19, 20, 25, 27
39:13, 14
40:37

LEVITICUS
8:28
10:12, 16
14:35
18:27, 28, 30
19:34
26:37

NUMBERS
1:1, 16, 20, 21[2], 22[2], 23[2], 24, 25[2], 26, 27[2], 28, 29[2], 30, 31[2], 32, 33[2], 34, 35[2], 36, 37[2], 38, 39[2], 40, 41[2], 42, 43[2], 44, 45[3], 46[2], 47

NUMBERS
2:4[2], 6[2], 8[2], 9[2], 11[2], 13[2], 15[2], 16[2], 19[2], 21[2], 23[2], 24[2], 26[2], 28[2], 30[2], 31[2], 32[3], 33
3:3, 17, 22[3], 28, 34[2], 39[2], 43[2], 49[2], 51
4:36[2], 37[2], 38, 40[2], 41, 42, 44[2], 45, 46, 48[2], 49[2]
6:12
7:2[3], 13, 86, 87, 88
8:21
9:1, 6[2], 15, 22
10:28
11:1, 26[2], 29, 31[3]
12:3, 8
13:3, 4, 22, 33[2]
14:3, 6, 29, 38
15:26, 32
16:34, 39[2], 49
18:27
19:18
21:32
22:3, 22, 29, 40
23:22
24:8
25:5, 6, 9
26:7[2], 9, 18, 19, 20, 21, 22, 25, 27, 28, 33, 34, 37, 40, 41[2], 43[2], 47[2], 50[2], 51, 54, 57, 62[3], 63
31:5, 8, 38, 39, 40, 48
33:9, 38
36:11, 12

DEUTERONOMY
1:41
2:11, 14[2], 15, 16
3:5
4:32, 46, 47
5:5, 29
6:21
7:7[2]
8:15
9:15
10:2, 19
24:9
25:17, 18
28:62, 67[2]
29:17
31:24, 30
32:27, 29
33:5
34:8

JOSHUA
2:4, 7, 8, 10, 22
3:15[2], 16, 17
4:1, 7[2], 11, 18[2], 23[2]
5:1[3], 4, 5[2], 6[2], 7, 8
6:23
7:12
8:11, 14, 15, 16[3], 22, 24[2], 25, 35
9:1, 10, 13, 16, 17, 24
10:1, 2, 11[2], 20, 26, 28, 30, 32, 35, 37[2], 39
11:2, 5, 11
13:21, 22, 31
14:4, 12[2]
15:4, 7, 11, 21
16:8, 9
17:2, 5, 9, 13
18:12, 14, 19, 21
19:8, 22, 33
20:9
21:4, 10, 19, 26, 33, 40[2], 41, 42[2]
22:9, 30
24:15

JUDGES
2:10, 12, 15
3:4, 19, 24, 25
4:13
5:6, 15[2], 16, 18, 22
6:5, 33
7:1[2], 6, 11, 12, 19[2]
8:4, 10[2], 18[2], 19, 21, 24, 26
9:29, 34, 35, 36, 40, 43, 44, 47, 48[2]
10:8, 17
11:3, 33

JUDGES
12:2, 5
13:23
15:14
16:2, 7, 9, 11, 12, 25, 27[2], 30[2]
17:2, 4
18:3, 7[2], 16, 17, 22[3], 26, 27, 30
19:10, 11, 14, 16, 22, 27
20:3, 11, 15[2], 16, 17[2], 31, 36, 41, 44, 46[2]
21:9[2], 13

RUTH
1:13, 19
4:11

1 SAMUEL
1:3
2:5[2], 12, 27
4:3, 4, 7, 11, 15, 19
5:4, 12
6:13, 15
7:7[2], 10, 13, 14
8:2
9:3, 4, 5, 14, 20, 22[2], 25, 27
10:14, 16
11:8, 9, 11[2]
13:2[2], 4, 6[2], 8, 11, 15, 16, 22
14:2[2], 14, 17[2], 20, 21[2], 24, 26, 27, 28, 31, 41, 49[2]
16:6
17:1, 2, 11, 13, 19, 24, 31
18:26
19:16
20:9
21:5
22:2, 6[2], 11
23:13, 24
25:1, 2, 7[2], 15[4], 16[2], 40, 43
26:12
27:2, 8
29:4
30:1, 2, 3, 4, 5, 9[2], 10, 16, 21[2], 27[3], 28[3], 29[3], 30[3], 31[2]
31:7[3]

2 SAMUEL
1:11, 12, 23[4]
2:3, 4, 18, 24
3:2, 5, 20, 23, 31, 34
4:1[2], 2, 3
5:13, 14
6:2
8:7, 17, 18
9:12
10:5, 8, 13, 14, 15, 16, 19[2]
11:16, 23
12:1, 31
13:18[2], 30
14:27
15:4, 11, 14, 16, 22, 24
16:6, 14
17:21, 22, 29
18:1, 7
19:9, 17, 28, 43
20:3, 8, 14, 15, 18, 25
21:2, 9, 13, 22
22:9, 13, 16, 18, 23
23:9[2], 11
24:9[2]

1 KINGS
1:8, 41, 49[2]
2:5, 11
3:16, 18
4:2, 4, 20, 28, 32
5:3, 14, 16
6:1, 24, 25, 31, 32, 34[3]
7:4, 5, 6, 9, 11, 17, 18, 19[2], 20, 24[2], 25, 28, 29[3], 30, 31, 32[2], 33, 34[2], 35, 41[2], 42, 45, 47
8:4, 5[2], 8[2], 10, 47
9:20[2], 21[2], 22, 23[2]
10:12, 19, 21[3]
11:29
12:1, 8, 10, 21, 31
14:4, 9, 20, 24
15:14, 18
16:15, 16, 21, 25, 30, 33

1 KINGS
20:1, 15, 23, 27[2], 30
21:8, 11
22:43, 48

2 KINGS
2:3, 5, 8, 9, 15, 22
3:14, 21[2]
4:6, 38, 40
5:3
6:20[2]
7:3, 5, 10
9:5
10:4, 6, 29[2]
11:2, 9, 10
12:3, 13
13:21
14:4, 14
15:4, 16[2], 35
16:17
17:2, 9, 15
18:5, 17
19:12, 18, 26[3], 35
21:11
23:3, 4, 7, 8[2], 12, 13[2], 16, 19, 20, 24[2]
24:16
25:4, 5, 10, 11, 13, 15, 19[3], 25, 26, 28

1 CHRONICLES
1:19, 23, 51
2:3, 4, 9, 16, 25, 27, 28, 33, 42, 50
3:1[2], 4, 5, 9, 15, 19, 24
4:3, 6, 7, 14, 17, 20[2], 21, 23, 24, 31, 32, 33[2], 38, 41, 43
5:3, 7, 9, 13, 17, 18, 20[3], 24
6:18, 48, 49, 60, 61[2], 63, 71, 77, 78
7:1, 2, 4, 5, 7, 11, 16, 17, 19, 21, 28, 40[2]
8:3, 8, 10, 13, 28, 35, 38, 39, 40
9:1[3], 2, 9, 17, 18, 19[2], 22[3], 24, 25[2], 26[2], 29, 31, 32, 33[2], 34, 41, 44
10:7[2]
11:4, 13, 26
12:1, 2, 8[2], 14, 20, 21[2], 23, 24, 27, 31, 32[3], 33, 38, 39, 40
14:12
15:19, 23, 24
16:19, 41[2], 42
18:7, 16, 17
19:5[2], 9[2], 14, 15, 16[2], 19
20:2, 3, 4, 6, 8
21:5, 16, 29
22:2
23:3, 4[2], 5, 7, 9, 10[2], 11, 14, 15, 17[2], 24[2], 27
24:4[3], 5[2], 19, 20, 26, 30
25:5, 6, 7[2], 9, 10, 11, 12, 13, 14, 15, 16, 17, 18, 19, 20, 21, 22, 23, 24, 25, 26, 27, 28, 29, 30, 31
26:2, 4, 6[2], 7, 8, 11, 12, 17, 21, 22, 26, 29, 30, 31[2], 32
27:1, 2, 4, 5, 7, 8, 9, 10, 11, 12, 13, 14, 15, 22, 28, 29, 31
29:8, 15

2 CHRONICLES
2:17[2]
3:11, 13
4:3, 4, 12[2], 13, 19, 22
5:5, 6, 9[2], 11[3], 12, 13
8:7[2], 8, 9, 10
9:11, 18[2], 20[3]
10:1, 8, 10
11:1, 13
12:3, 5, 15
13:13, 18
14:8, 13[3]
15:5, 17
16:8
17:10, 13
18:30
20:22[2], 24, 25, 33, 37[2]
21:2, 13, 16

2 CHRONICLES
22:4, 6, 11
23:8[2], 9, 14
24:14, 25
25:12, 24
26:12, 17
28:6, 15[2], 23
29:29, 31, 32, 33, 34[2], 35
30:8, 14, 15, 17[2], 21
31:1, 6, 13, 15, 19[3]
32:3, 9, 13, 18, 19
34:4, 12, 13[3], 32, 33
35:3, 7[2], 14, 15, 17, 18
36:20

EZRA
1:6, 11[2]
2:58, 59[2], 62[3], 65[2], 66
3:1, 5, 8, 12
5:1, 2, 6, 10, 14
6:1, 20[2], 21
8:3, 20, 35
9:1, 4, 9
10:15, 16, 18

NEHEMIAH
1:2, 9
2:13[2]
4:7[2], 16
5:2, 3, 4, 8, 15, 16, 17, 18
6:16[2], 18
7:1, 4[2], 60, 61[2], 64[2], 67, 73
8:3, 12, 13, 17
9:1, 17, 25, 26
10:1, 8
11:6, 12, 18, 19, 20, 21, 22, 36
12:7, 9, 12, 22, 23, 25, 26, 44, 46
13:10, 13

ESTHER
1:5[2], 6[2]
2:7, 8, 9, 12, 14, 19, 21, 23
3:1, 2, 3, 6, 12[2], 13
6:1, 14
8:9, 11
9:11, 15, 16, 18, 20

JOB
1:2, 5, 13, 14, 18
4:7
6:2, 20[2]
9:15, 21
16:4
18:20
19:23[2], 24
21:4
22:16
28:5
29:2, 5
30:3, 5, 7, 8[2]
31:20, 28
32:4, 15
33:21
34:35
39:16
42:15

PSALMS
14:2, 5, 7
17:12
18:7, 8, 11, 15[2], 17, 22, 37, 38
22:5[2]
33:6
34:5[2]
35:13
39:12
45:9
46:6
48:4, 5
50:12
53:2, 5, 6
55:18, 21[3]
68:25, 33
73:2
77:16[2]
78:29, 30, 37, 39, 57, 63
80:10[2]
81:6
90:2
105:12

PSALMS
106:35, 36, 39, 42, 43
119:5
126:1
139:16[2]
148:5

PROVERBS
8:24[2], 25, 31

ECCLESIASTES
2:7, 9
4:1
7:10
8:10

SONG OF SOLOMON
1:6
5:4
6:13

ISAIAH
5:18, 25
7:23
10:15
14:2
26:18, 20
27:13
30:4, 5
33:3
37:12, 19, 27[3], 36
41:5, 11
42:24
46:1[2]
51:13
52:14
53:3
63:19

JEREMIAH
1:1
4:25, 26
5:8
6:15[2]
8:12[2]
9:1
11:13
14:3, 4
15:16
20:2
22:24, 26
24:1, 2
26:9
29:1, 2
30:14, 15
31:2, 15
34:5, 7, 8, 15
36:16, 24, 28, 32
37:15, 21
40:1[2], 4, 6, 7[2], 11[2], 12, 13
41:2, 3[2], 7, 8, 9, 10, 11, 13[3], 16, 18
42:8, 16
43:5
44:17
49:2
50:11, 33
52:7, 14, 17, 20, 22, 23[2], 25[3], 30, 32

LAMENTATIONS
2:4, 6
4:5, 7[3], 10
5:12

EZEKIEL
1:1, 7, 9, 11[3], 16, 18[3], 19[2], 20, 21[2], 23, 27
7:13
8:16
9:6, 8
10:1, 12, 15, 17, 19, 20
14:14, 16, 18, 20
16:47, 50
17:6
19:12
20:9, 24, 25
22:6
23:2, 3, 4[3], 6, 7, 42
27:8[3], 9[2], 10, 11[2], 13, 15[2], 17, 19, 21, 22, 23, 24

EZEKIEL
29:13
31:5, 8[2], 9, 15, 17
32:27, 29
34:5[2]
36:19, 31
37:2[2]
40:7, 10[2], 12, 15, 16[3], 17[2], 21[2], 22[2], 25, 26[2], 29, 30, 31[2], 33[2], 34[2], 37[2], 38, 39, 40[2], 41, 42, 43, 44, 49
41:2, 6, 8, 9, 11, 16, 20, 21, 22, 25[3], 26
42:3, 5[2], 6, 8[2], 10, 11[2], 12
43:3
46:22[2]
47:3, 4[2], 5, 7

DANIEL
1:6, 20
2:34, 42
3:3, 20, 21[2], 27
4:10, 12, 21, 33
5:3, 6, 9, 12
6:18
7:4, 7, 8[2], 9, 10, 12, 19, 20
8:3
10:3, 5, 7, 12

HOSEA
2:23
4:7
5:10
8:12
9:10
12:8
13:6[2]

AMOS
4:7, 8, 11

OBADIAH
7

JONAH
1:5[2], 10
2:5

MICAH
1:13

NAHUM
3:9[2], 10[2]

HABAKKUK
3:6

HAGGAI
2:16[3]

ZECHARIAH
1:8[2]
6:1, 2
7:3
8:9, 13
10:2

MATTHEW
1:11, 12
2:11, 13, 16
3:6, 16
4:18, 24[3]
5:12
7:28
8:16[2], 32
9:25, 30, 31, 36
11:20, 21
12:1, 3, 4, 23
13:2, 6, 54, 57
14:20, 21, 26, 32, 33, 34, 35, 36
15:1, 12, 30, 37, 38
16:5
17:6, 14, 23, 24
18:6[3], 31
19:12[2], 13, 25
20:9, 24
21:1, 15
22:3, 8[2], 25, 33, 34, 41
24:24, 37, 38[2]
25:2[2], 3, 10
26:22, 26, 43, 51, 57, 71
27:17, 33, 38, 44, 52, 54[2], 55
28:11[2], 12, 15

MARK
1:5, 16, 19, 22, 27, 29, 32[2], 34, 36
2:2, 6, 12, 15, 25, 26
4:10, 33, 34, 36
5:13[2], 15, 40, 42
6:2, 3, 13, 31, 34, 42, 44, 50, 51, 54, 55, 56[2]
7:35, 37
8:8, 9
9:4, 6, 9, 15, 32, 42[2]
10:24, 26, 32[3]
11:12
12:14, 20, 41
13:22
14:4, 11, 21, 35, 40, 53
15:32, 40, 44
16:5, 8[2]

LUKE
1:2, 6, 7, 10, 23, 45, 65
2:6[2], 8, 9, 15, 18, 21, 22, 33, 47, 48
3:15[2], 21
4:2, 20[2], 25, 27, 28, 32, 36
5:2[2], 7, 9, 10, 17[2], 26[2]
6:3, 4, 11, 18[2]
7:10, 20, 21, 24, 39
8:1, 4[2], 23[2], 30, 33, 35[2], 37, 38, 40, 45, 56
9:10, 14, 17, 18, 30, 32[3], 37, 43
11:29, 52
12:1
13:1, 2, 4, 17[2]
14:7, 17, 24
16:14, 16
17:2[2], 9, 12, 14, 17, 27
18:9, 34
19:32, 33, 48
20:29
22:5, 44, 49, 52, 55
23:5, 6, 12[2], 23, 32, 33, 39, 48
24:4, 5, 10, 16, 21, 22, 24, 31, 33, 35, 37, 44, 53

JOHN
1:3, 13, 24[2], 28
2:6
3:19, 23
4:8, 40
5:35
6:2, 11, 12, 19, 22[2], 26, 64, 65
7:10[2]
8:33, 39, 42
9:10, 33, 40, 41
10:6, 41
11:25, 31, 52, 57
12:12, 16, 20
13:1
14:2
15:19
16:19
17:6
18:30, 36
19:11, 28, 36
20:19[2], 20, 26
21:2, 6, 8[2], 9, 11

THE ACTS
1:6, 13, 15
2:1, 2, 4, 5, 6, 7, 8, 12[2], 37, 41[2], 43, 44
3:10
4:6[2], 13, 26, 27, 31[2], 32, 34[2]
5:12[2], 14, 16[2], 17[2], 21, 33, 36, 37, 41
6:1, 7, 10
7:16, 30, 54
8:1, 4, 7[3], 12, 13, 14, 15, 16, 39
9:2, 8, 19, 21, 23, 26, 31[2]
10:12, 17, 18, 21, 27, 38, 45
11:1, 2, 10, 11, 19, 20[2], 26
12:3, 10, 12, 16
13:1, 5, 42, 45[2], 48[2], 52
14:6, 27
15:4[2], 10, 30, 33
16:2, 3, 4[2], 5, 6, 7, 12, 14, 26[3], 32, 38
17:11[2], 12, 14, 21
18:3, 5, 8, 14
19:3, 5, 7, 9, 12, 14, 21, 28, 31, 32
20:8[2], 12, 16, 18, 34
21:1, 5, 8, 17, 18, 24, 27[2], 30, 38
22:5, 9[2], 11
23:6, 9, 13
24:9
25:17
26:10, 14, 29, 31
27:4, 7, 11, 17, 27, 30, 36, 37, 39[2]
28:1, 7, 9, 10, 14, 17, 24

ROMANS
1:21
3:2
4:2, 17
5:6, 8, 10[2], 19
6:3[2], 17, 20[2]
7:5[2], 6
9:3, 25, 32
11:7, 19, 20
15:4[2]
16:7

1 CORINTHIANS
1:9, 13
3:2
4:9
5:3
6:11
7:7, 14
9:15
10:1, 2, 5, 6, 7, 9, 10
11:5
12:2[2], 17[4], 19[2]
15:11

2 CORINTHIANS
1:8
3:14
5:1, 14
7:5[4], 8, 9[2], 13
8:3
11:17
12:12, 13
13:2

GALATIANS
1:17, 22
2:2, 6, 12[2]
3:16, 23
4:3[2], 5
5:12

EPHESIANS
1:13
2:1, 3, 5, 12, 13, 17[2]
5:8

PHILIPPIANS
3:7, 12
4:10, 18

COLOSSIANS
1:16[2], 21

1 THESSALONIANS
1:5, 7
2:2[2], 4, 7, 8[2]
3:4, 7

2 THESSALONIANS
3:10

TITUS
3:3

PHILEMON
14

HEBREWS
2:15
3:5
4:3
5:8
6:4[2]
7:11, 21, 23[2]
8:4
9:6, 9, 15
10:32, 33[2]
11:3[2], 13[2], 23, 29, 30, 34, 35, 37[4]

JAMES
5:3

1 PETER
1:18
2:8, 10, 21, 24, 25
3:20[2]

2 PETER
1:16, 18, 21
2:1, 18
3:2, 4, 5

1 JOHN
2:19[2]
3:12

JUDE
4, 17

REVELATION
1:14[2]
4:1, 4, 5, 6, 8, 11
6:1, 9, 11[2], 14
7:4[2], 5[3], 6[3], 7[3], 8[3]
8:2, 5, 7, 8, 9[2], 10, 11
9:2, 7[4], 8, 9, 10, 15[2], 16, 17, 19, 20
10:1
11:13[2], 15, 18, 19
12:9, 14
13:2, 3
14:3[2], 4[2]
15:2, 8
16:9, 18[2], 20
17:8
18:14, 15, 19, 23[2], 24
19:6, 12[2], 14, 20, 21[2]
20:4, 5, 12[3], 13[3], 14
21:1, 19, 21[2]
22:2

WITH
5973, *4862*

GENESIS
3:6, 12
4:8
5:22, 24
6:3, 9, 11, 13[2], 14, 16, 18[2], 19
7:7, 13, 23
8:1, 16, 17[2], 18
9:4, 8, 9[2], 10[3], 11, 12
11:31
12:4, 13, 17
13:1, 5
14:2[2], 5, 8, 9[3], 13, 17, 24
15:14, 18
16:6, 11
17:3, 4, 12, 13, 19[2], 21, 22, 23, 27[2]
18:11, 16, 23, 25, 33
19:1, 9[2], 11, 30, 32, 33, 34[2], 35, 36
20:16[2]
21:6, 10[2], 19, 20, 22, 23[3]
22:3, 5
23:4[2], 8, 16
24:15, 32, 40, 45, 49, 54, 55, 58
25:30
26:3, 8, 10, 15, 20[2], 24, 28[2]
27:15, 34, 35, 37, 44
28:4, 15, 20
29:6, 9[2], 14, 19, 25, 27, 30
30:8[2], 15, 16[2], 20[2], 29, 33
31:3, 5, 6, 21, 23, 25, 26, 27[4], 32[2], 36, 38, 42, 50
32:4, 6, 7, 9, 10, 11, 15, 20, 24, 25, 28[2]
33:1, 5, 7, 10, 11, 13[2], 15[2]
34:2, 5, 6, 7, 8, 9, 10, 16, 20, 21, 22, 23, 26, 31[2]
35:2, 3, 6, 13, 14, 15, 22
37:2[3], 14[2], 25
38:14, 24, 25
39:2, 3, 7, 8, 10, 12, 14[2], 15, 18, 21, 23
40:4, 7, 14
41:6, 10, 12, 23, 27
42:4, 6, 13, 24, 25, 26, 32, 33, 38[2]
43:3, 4, 5, 6, 8, 16[2], 19, 32[2], 34
44:1, 9, 10, 16, 23, 26[2], 29, 30, 31[2], 33, 34
45:1, 5, 15, 23[2]
46:1, 4, 6, 7[2], 15, 26
47:12, 17, 29, 30
48:1, 12, 21, 22[2]
49:12[2], 25, 29, 30
50:7, 9, 10, 13, 14

EXODUS
1:1, 7, 10, 11, 13, 14[2], 20
2:3[2], 21, 24[3]
3:2, 8, 12, 17, 18, 20
4:12, 15[2]
5:3[3], 15
6:1[2], 4, 6[2]
7:11, 17, 22
8:2, 5, 7, 17, 18
9:9, 10, 15, 24
10:9[6], 10, 24, 26[2]
12:8[2], 9[4], 10, 11, 22, 38, 48
13:5, 7[2], 9, 13, 19[2]
14:6, 8, 11
15:8, 10, 19[2], 20[2]
16:3, 12, 18, 20, 31
17:2[2], 3, 5, 8, 9[2], 10, 13, 16
18:5, 6, 12, 18, 19, 22
19:9, 17, 24
20:19[2], 22, 23
21:3, 6, 8, 9, 14, 18[2], 20, 22, 29
22:14, 15, 16, 19, 24, 30[3]
23:1, 5, 11[2], 18, 32[2]
24:2, 3, 8, 14
25:2, 11, 13, 14, 20, 22[2], 24, 28[2], 33[2], 34, 39
26:1[2], 6, 29[2], 31, 32, 36, 37
27:2, 6, 8, 16, 17
28:1, 3, 6, 11[2], 15, 21[2], 28, 41
29:2[2], 3, 4, 5, 9, 12, 14, 21[2], 34, 40[2], 43
30:3, 5, 6, 10, 20, 28, 34, 36
31:3, 6, 8, 9, 18[2]
32:4, 11[2]
33:3, 9, 12, 14, 15, 16, 22
34:3, 5, 10, 12, 15, 20, 25, 27[2], 28, 29[2], 31, 32, 33, 34, 35
35:12, 14, 16, 23, 24, 25, 31, 35
36:8, 13, 34[2], 35, 36, 38[2]
37:2, 4, 9[2], 11, 15, 26, 28
38:2, 6, 7, 17, 23
39:3, 6, 14, 21, 23, 37[2]
40:3, 12, 14

LEVITICUS
1:12, 13, 16, 17
2:2, 4[2], 5, 7, 11, 13[2], 16
3:4, 10, 15
4:9, 11[2], 12, 20[3], 25, 30, 34
5:4[2], 15, 16, 18
6:6, 10, 16, 17, 21
7:4, 10, 12[4], 13, 17, 19, 24, 30
8:2, 6, 7[3], 13, 15, 17, 30[2], 31, 32
9:4, 11, 13
10:9, 14, 15[2], 16
11:43[2], 44
13:57
14:10, 16, 21, 27, 31, 37, 52[6]
15:3, 17, 18[2], 24, 33
16:3, 4[2], 10, 14[2], 15[2], 19, 24
17:13, 15
18:20[2], 22[2], 23
19:13, 19[2], 20, 22, 26, 33, 34
20:2, 5, 10[2], 11, 12, 13[2], 14, 15, 18, 20, 24, 27
21:9
22:6, 8, 11, 14
23:13, 17, 18[2], 20[2]
24:23
25:6, 23, 35[2], 36, 40, 41, 43, 45, 46, 50[2], 52, 53[2], 54
26:9, 39, 40, 42[3], 44

NUMBERS
1:2, 4, 5
2:2, 17, 31
3:1
4:5, 8, 11, 12, 32[2]
5:7, 13[2], 19[2], 20, 21, 23
6:15[2], 17, 20
7:13, 19, 25, 31, 37, 43, 49, 55, 61, 67, 73, 79, 87, 89
8:8[2], 26
9:11
10:3, 4, 8, 9, 10, 29, 32
11:15, 16, 17[2], 18, 33
12:8
13:23, 27, 31
14:8, 9, 10, 12, 21, 24, 27, 43
15:4, 5, 6, 9[2], 14, 15, 16, 24, 35, 36
16:2, 10, 13, 14, 18, 22, 30
17:4, 13
18:1[2], 2[2], 7, 11[2], 19[2]
19:4, 5, 12, 16
20:3, 11, 13, 18, 20[2]
21:18, 24
22:7, 8, 9, 12, 13, 14, 20, 21, 22, 27, 35[2], 39, 40
23:13, 17, 21
24:8
25:1, 14, 18
26:3, 10
27:21
28:5, 9, 12[3], 13, 20, 28
29:3, 9, 14
30:2, 8, 10
31:6, 8, 10, 14[2], 17, 18, 23, 35
32:19, 29, 30, 33
33:1, 3
34:2, 12
35:7, 16, 17, 18, 21, 23, 25

DEUTERONOMY
1:16, 37
2:5, 7, 9, 19, 24, 26
3:5, 13, 26, 27
4:11[2], 21, 23, 29[2], 37, 40[2]
5:2, 3[2], 4, 16, 22, 23, 24, 29[2], 33
6:3[2], 5[3], 18, 21
7:2, 3, 5[2], 8, 9, 23, 25
8:3, 16
9:8, 9, 10[2], 15, 20, 21, 26
10:9, 12[2], 14, 22
11:2, 9, 10, 13[2]
12:3, 12, 23, 25[2], 28[2]
13:3[2], 10, 15[2], 16
14:27, 29
15:3, 16, 19
16:3, 4, 10, 18
17:5, 19
18:1, 6, 11, 13
19:5[2], 13
20:1, 4, 12, 13, 20
21:3, 21
22:2, 3[3], 6, 7, 9, 10, 21, 22[2], 23, 24, 25[2], 28, 29
23:4[2], 11, 16, 23, 25
24:5, 12
25:3, 11
26:5, 8[5], 9, 15, 16[2]
27:1, 2, 3, 4, 14, 20, 21, 22, 23
28:22[7], 27[4], 28, 30, 32, 35, 40, 47[2], 68
29:1[2], 10, 12[2], 14, 15[4], 25
30:2[2], 6[2], 10[2]
31:6, 7, 8, 16[2], 20, 23, 27
32:12, 14[2], 15, 16[2], 21[4], 22, 24[4], 25, 34, 39, 42[2], 43
33:2, 8[2], 17, 20, 21[2], 23[2], 24
34:4

JOSHUA
1:5[2], 9, 17[2]
2:6, 14, 19
3:7[2]
4:3, 8
5:6, 13
6:4, 5[2], 8, 9[2], 10, 13[2], 16, 17, 20[2], 21, 24, 27
7:12, 15[2], 24, 25[3]
8:1, 5, 11, 24, 35
9:2[3], 6, 7, 11[2], 15[2], 16
10:1, 4[2], 7, 10, 11[2], 15, 20, 24, 28, 29, 30, 31, 32, 34, 35, 36, 37, 38, 39, 43
11:4[2], 6, 7, 9, 10, 11[2], 12, 14, 18, 19, 21
13:8, 21, 22
14:4, 8, 12
15:32, 36, 41, 44, 45, 46, 47[2], 51, 54, 57, 59, 60, 62, 63
16:9
18:24, 28
19:15, 16, 22, 30, 31, 38, 46, 47, 48
21:2, 8, 11, 13[2], 14[2], 15[2], 16[3], 17[2], 18[2], 19, 21[2], 22[2], 23[2], 24[2], 25[2], 26, 27[2], 28[2], 29[2], 30[2], 31[2], 32[3], 33, 34[2], 35[2], 36[2], 37[2], 38[2], 39[2], 41, 42
22:5[2], 8[8], 14, 15, 18, 24, 27[3], 30
23:4, 12
24:6, 8, 12[2], 25

JUDGES
1:3[3], 8, 16, 17, 18[3], 19, 21, 22, 25
2:1, 2, 18
3:27, 31
4:6, 7, 8[2], 9[2], 10[2], 13, 15, 18
5:15, 26
6:5, 12, 13, 16, 17, 26, 39
7:1, 2, 4[3], 5, 10, 11, 16, 18[2], 19
8:1[2], 4, 7[2], 10, 15, 16
9:1[2], 16, 19[2], 23, 26, 32, 33, 34, 35, 38, 39, 44, 45, 48[2], 52
11:3, 6, 8, 11, 12, 33, 34[2], 38, 39
12:1[2], 2, 4
13:9, 19
14:7, 11, 15, 18
15:1, 5, 6, 8, 13, 14, 16[2]
16:3, 7, 8, 9, 11, 13, 14[3], 15, 16, 21, 29[2], 30[2]
17:2, 10, 11
18:4, 7, 11, 16, 17[2], 19, 23, 25, 27[2], 28
19:3, 4, 5, 10[2], 19, 20, 24, 29
20:1, 37, 38, 40, 43, 48
21:5, 10[2], 12

RUTH
1:6, 7, 8[3], 10, 11, 18, 20, 22
2:4, 6, 19[2], 22, 23
3:1, 2

1 SAMUEL
1:24[2]
2:4, 13[2], 18, 19, 22, 26[2], 29
3:14, 19
4:4, 5, 8, 12[2], 19
5:6, 7, 8, 9, 12
6:11, 15, 19
7:3, 10
9:3, 5, 19, 24, 25
10:5, 6, 7, 26
11:1, 2, 7, 10
12:2, 7, 20, 24
13:2[2], 4, 5, 15, 16, 22[3]
14:2, 7, 17, 18, 20, 21[4], 27, 28, 32, 33, 34[2], 43, 45
15:6, 8, 25, 26, 30
16:1, 2, 5, 16, 18, 19, 20, 23
17:5, 9, 19, 20, 23, 25, 28, 32, 33, 37, 38[2], 39, 43, 45[3], 47, 50[2], 57
18:1, 6[3], 10, 11, 12, 14, 22, 28
19:3, 8[2], 9[2], 10, 13, 16
20:5, 8[2], 13[2], 16, 35[2], 41
21:1, 8
22:2, 3, 4, 6, 8, 17, 19[2], 23[2]
23:5[2], 6, 19, 23[2]
24:7, 8, 18
25:7, 15, 16, 25, 26, 29, 31, 33, 39, 42
26:2, 6[2], 8
27:2[2], 3[3], 5
28:1[2], 8, 12, 14[2], 19[2], 23
29:2, 3, 4[3], 6, 8, 9, 10[2]
30:1, 3, 4, 9, 14, 21, 22[2], 23
31:5

2 SAMUEL
1:2, 11, 17, 21, 24
2:3[2], 23
3:8, 12[2], 13, 16, 17, 20[2], 21, 22[2], 23, 27, 31[2]
5:3, 10
6:2[2], 12, 14[2], 15[2]
7:3, 7[2], 9, 12, 14[2], 22, 29
8:2[3], 10[2], 11
10:13, 17, 19
11:1, 4, 5, 9, 11, 13, 17
12:3[2], 9[2], 11, 17, 24, 30
13:11, 14, 18, 20, 24, 26[2], 27, 28, 31
14:2, 17, 19
15:11, 12, 14[2], 19[2], 20[2], 22, 23, 24, 27, 30, 31, 32, 33, 35, 36
16:1, 10, 14, 15, 17, 18, 21, 23[2]
17:2, 8, 10, 12, 16, 22, 24, 29
18:1, 2, 5[2], 14, 27
19:4, 7, 16, 17[2], 22, 25, 31, 33[2], 34, 36[2], 37, 38, 40, 41
20:8, 9, 15, 16
21:15[2], 16, 17, 18, 19
22:26[2], 27[2], 40
23:5[2], 6, 7[2], 9, 21[2]
24:2

1 KINGS
1:1, 7[2], 8, 14, 21, 22, 23, 31, 33, 34, 37[2], 40[3], 41, 44, 49, 51
2:4[2], 8[3], 9, 10, 32, 43
3:1, 6, 17, 18
4:13
5:6
6:8, 9, 10, 12, 15[3], 16, 18, 20, 21[2], 22[2], 28, 29, 30, 32, 35, 36
7:2, 3, 5, 7, 9, 12, 14, 18, 26, 31, 49
8:5, 9, 15[2], 21, 23[2], 24[3], 25, 46, 48[2], 54, 55, 57[2], 61, 62, 65
9:11[2], 16, 27
10:1, 2[3], 18, 22, 26
11:1, 4, 9, 16, 17, 18, 21, 22, 29, 38, 43
12:6, 8[2], 10, 11[3], 14[2], 18, 21
13:7, 8, 15, 16[3], 18, 19
14:3, 6, 8, 20, 22, 31[2]
15:3, 8, 14, 19, 20, 22, 24[2]
16:2, 6, 7, 13, 17, 18, 26, 28
17:18, 20
18:4, 13, 28, 32, 33, 35, 45
19:1, 10, 14, 19[2], 21
20:1, 20, 21, 34[2], 38
21:8[2], 13
22:4, 11, 13, 27[2], 31[2], 40, 44, 49, 50[2]

2 KINGS
1:8, 9, 11, 13, 14, 15[2]
2:1, 16
3:4, 7, 12, 13, 17, 19, 20, 26
4:13, 26[3]
5:1, 3, 5, 9[2], 23, 26
6:1, 3, 4, 8, 15, 16[2], 18[2], 22[2], 32, 33
7:2, 19
8:2, 4, 9, 12[3], 21, 24[2], 28

2 KINGS

9:13, 15, 18, 19, 24, 28
10:2[2], 6, 13, 15, 16, 23, 25, 31, 35
11:3, 4[2], 8[2], 9, 11, 14, 15, 20
12:15, 21
13:9, 13[2], 19, 23
14:10, 15, 16[2], 20, 22, 29[2]
15:7[2], 16, 19, 22, 25[2], 38[2]
16:15, 20[2]
17:15, 18, 35, 36, 38
18:7, 17, 26, 27, 28, 31, 37
19:1, 2, 6, 23, 24, 32, 37
20:3, 21
21:6, 11, 18
22:7, 14, 17
23:2, 3, 11, 14, 18, 24, 25[3]
24:4, 6
25:7, 9, 10, 11, 17, 24, 25[2], 28

1 CHRONICLES

2:23[2]
4:9, 10, 23
5:10, 18, 19[2], 20
6:32, 33, 57[2], 58[2], 59[2], 60[3], 64, 67[2], 68[2], 69[2], 70[2], 71[2], 72[2], 73[2], 74[2], 75[2], 76[3], 77[2], 78[2], 79[2], 80[2], 81[2]
7:4, 23, 28
8:12, 32
9:20, 25, 38
11:3, 9, 10[2], 13, 19, 23[2], 42
12:2, 19, 27, 33, 34[2], 37, 38, 39
13:1[2], 2, 8[7], 14
14:1, 12
15:15, 16[2], 18, 19, 20, 21, 24, 25, 27[2], 28[5]
16:5[3], 6, 16, 38, 41, 42[3]
17:2, 6, 8, 11, 20
18:10[2], 11
19:14, 17, 19
20:3[4], 4, 5
21:7, 20, 21
22:11, 13, 15, 16, 18
23:2, 5
24:5
25:1[3], 3, 6, 7, 9
26:16
27:32
28:1[3], 9[2], 20, 21[2]
29:2, 6, 8, 9[2], 17, 21, 22, 30

2 CHRONICLES

1:1, 3, 14
2:3[2], 7[2], 8, 12, 13, 14[2]
3:4, 5[2], 6, 7, 8, 9, 10
4:5, 9, 20
5:10, 12[3], 13[2]
6:4[2], 11, 14, 15[3], 16, 18, 36, 38[2], 41
7:3, 6, 8, 18
8:5, 18
9:1[3], 17, 18, 21, 25, 31
10:6, 8[2], 10, 11[2], 14[2], 18
12:1, 3[2], 16
13:3[2], 8, 9, 11, 12[2], 14, 17, 19[3]
14:1, 9, 11[3], 13
15:2[2], 6, 9[2], 12[2], 14[4], 15[2]
16:3, 8, 10[2], 13, 14
17:3, 8[2], 9, 14, 15, 16, 17[2], 18
18:1, 2[2], 3[2], 10, 12, 26[2], 30[3]
19:6, 7, 9, 11
20:1, 13, 17[2], 18, 19, 21, 25, 27, 28, 35, 36, 37
21:1[2], 3, 4, 7, 9[2], 14, 18
22:1, 5, 6, 7, 9, 12
23:1, 2, 7[2], 8, 13[2], 14, 18[2], 21
24:21, 24
25:2, 7[3], 13, 16, 19, 24, 28
26:2, 13, 17, 19, 23[2]
27:5, 9
28:5, 9, 10[2], 15, 18[2], 27
29:8, 10, 18[2], 24, 25[3], 26[2], 27[2], 29, 30[2], 35
30:6, 21[2], 23, 25
31:9, 21
32:3, 7[3], 8[2], 9, 18, 21[2], 33
33:6[2], 11, 20
34:6, 25, 31[2]
35:12, 13, 21[3], 22
36:10, 17, 19, 23

EZRA

1:3, 4[4], 5, 6[5], 11
2:2, 63[2]
3:9[2], 10[2], 11, 12, 13
4:2, 3
5:2, 8
6:4, 12, 16, 22
7:13, 16, 17[2], 18, 28
8:1, 3, 4, 5, 6, 7, 8, 9, 10, 11, 12, 13, 14, 17, 18, 19, 24, 33[2]
9:2, 11[3], 14[2]
10:3, 4, 12, 14, 16, 17

NEHEMIAH

1:3
2:3, 9, 12[2], 13, 17
3:1
4:13, 17[3], 22
5:7
6:5
7:7, 65
8:2, 6[2]
9:1[2], 4, 6, 8, 13, 24[2]
10:32, 38
11:25
12:1, 24, 27[5], 35, 36, 40, 41, 42, 43
13:2[2], 9, 11, 17, 25

ESTHER

1:6, 10, 11
2:6[2], 9, 12[3], 13, 20
3:1, 11, 12
4:1[2], 2, 13
5:9, 12[2], 14
6:14
7:1
8:3, 8[2], 10, 15[2]
9:5, 29, 30

JOB

1:4, 15, 17
2:7, 10, 11, 13
3:14, 15[2]
4:2, 18
5:14, 23[2]
7:5, 14
8:21[2], 22
9:2, 3, 14, 17, 18, 30, 35
10:2, 11[2], 13
12:2, 5, 12, 13, 16, 18
13:3, 17, 19
14:3, 5
15:2, 3[2], 10, 11[2], 20, 27
16:5, 8, 9, 10, 14, 16, 21
17:2, 3[2]
18:6
19:2, 4, 6, 16, 20, 22, 24
20:11, 26
21:8, 24, 25
22:4, 16, 18, 21
23:4, 6, 7, 14
24:8, 14, 22
25:2, 4
26:10, 12
27:11, 13, 14
28:14, 16[2], 19, 22
29:5, 6
30:1, 21, 30
31:1, 5, 13, 18[2], 20
32:14
33:19[2], 23, 26, 29, 30
34:8[2], 9, 23
35:4
36:4, 7, 18, 32
37:4, 5, 18, 22
38:8, 30, 32
39:4, 10, 19, 24
40:2, 9, 10[2], 15, 22, 24
41:1[2], 2, 4, 5[2], 7[2], 13, 15, 28
42:8, 11

PSALMS

2:9, 11[2]
3:4
4:4
5:4, 9, 12[2]
6:6[2]
7:4, 11, 14
8:5
9:1, 6
10:14
12:2[3], 4
13:6
15:3
17:10, 14, 15
18:25[2], 26[2], 32, 39
20:6
21:3, 6
22:13
23:4, 5
25:14, 19
26:4[2], 5, 7, 9[2]
27:7
28:3[2], 7
29:11
30:11
31:9, 10[2]
32:7, 8, 9
33:2[2], 3
34:3
35:1[2], 13, 16[2], 19, 26
36:8, 9
37:12, 24
38:7
39:1[2], 2, 3, 11, 12
41:12
42:4[4], 8, 10
44:1, 2, 9, 19
45:3, 7, 12, 15
46:3, 7, 11
47:1, 5[2], 7
48:7
50:5, 18[2]
51:7, 12, 19[2]
54:t, 4
55:18, 20
58:9
59:7
60:t[2], 5, 10
62:4
63:5[2]
64:7
65:4, 6, 9, 10, 11, 13[2]
66:13, 15[2], 17[2]
68:6, 13[2], 19, 25, 27, 30[2]
69:10, 28, 30[2]
71:8[2], 13, 22[2]
72:2[2], 19
73:7, 19, 23, 24
74:6
75:5
77:1[2], 6, 15
78:8, 14[2], 36[2], 37, 47[2], 58[2], 62, 71
80:5, 10, 16
81:2, 16[2]
83:5, 7, 8, 15[2], 16
85:5
86:12
87:4
88:4, 7
89:1, 3, 10, 20, 21, 24, 28, 32[2], 38, 45
90:5, 14
91:4, 8, 15, 16
92:3, 10
93:1[2]
94:20
95:2[2], 10
96:13[2]
98:5[2], 6, 9[2]
100:2[2], 4[2]
101:2, 6
102:9
103:4, 5, 10
104:1, 2[2], 6[2], 13, 28
105:9, 18, 25, 37, 40, 43[2]
106:4[2], 5, 6, 29, 32, 33, 38, 39[2], 43
107:9, 12, 22
108:1, 6, 11
109:2, 3, 14, 18[2], 29[3], 30
110:6
111:1
112:5, 9, 10
113:8[2]
116:7
118:7, 27
119:2, 7, 10, 13, 17, 34, 58, 65, 69, 78, 93, 98, 124, 145
120:4, 6
123:3, 4[2]
125:5
126:2[2], 6[2]
127:5
128:2
130:4, 7[2]
132:9, 15, 16, 18
136:12[2]
138:1, 3
139:3, 18, 21, 22
141:4
142:1[2], 7
143:2
147:7, 8, 14, 20
149:3, 4, 8[2]
150:3[2], 4[2]

PROVERBS

1:11, 13, 15, 31
2:1, 16
3:5, 9[2], 10[2], 30, 32
4:7, 23
5:10, 17, 18, 19, 20, 22
6:1, 2[2], 12, 13[3], 22, 25, 32
7:1, 5, 10, 13, 14, 16[3], 17, 18, 20, 21[2]
8:12, 18, 24, 30, 31
10:4, 10, 18, 22
11:2, 9, 10
12:11, 14, 21
13:10, 16, 20
14:1, 10, 14, 18
15:16
16:7, 8, 19[2]
17:1, 14
18:1, 3, 20[2]
19:2, 7, 23
20:8, 13, 17, 18, 19[2]
21:9, 19, 27
22:24[2]
23:1, 7, 11, 13, 14, 21
24:1, 4, 21, 28, 31
25:9, 24
26:17, 23, 24
27:14, 22
28:4, 20, 23
29:3, 9, 24
30:8, 16, 19, 22, 28
31:10, 16, 17, 21, 26

ECCLESIASTES

1:8[2], 11, 16
2:1, 3, 9
4:6[2], 8, 15
5:2, 10[2], 11, 17
6:3, 4[2], 10
7:11
8:12, 13, 15, 16
9:7[2], 9, 10
11:5
12:14

SONG OF SOLOMON

1:2, 6, 10[2], 11
2:3, 5[2], 13
3:6[2], 10, 11
4:8[2], 9[2], 13[2], 14[2]
5:1[3], 2[2], 5[2], 12, 14[2]
6:1, 4, 10
7:1, 2
8:9

ISAIAH

1:4, 6, 7, 13, 20, 22, 27[2]
3:10, 11, 14, 16[2], 17
5:2, 13, 18[2], 26
6:2[3], 4, 6, 10[3]
7:2[2], 4, 20, 24[2], 25
8:1, 10, 11
9:5[2], 7[2], 10, 12
10:22, 24, 33, 34
11:4[4], 6[2], 15
12:1, 3
13:9
14:1, 6, 19, 20, 21, 23, 30
15:3, 5
16:4, 9[2], 14
17:5, 10
18:1, 5
19:23, 24[2]
20:4
21:3, 7[2], 9, 14
22:2, 6, 12, 17, 21[2]
23:17
24:2[12], 9, 12
25:5, 11
26:9[2], 17, 18, 19
27:1, 5[2], 6, 8
28:1, 2, 11, 15[2], 18[2], 27[3], 28[2]
29:3, 6[3], 9[2], 13[2]
30:1, 24[2], 27, 28, 29, 30[3], 31, 32[2]
31:8
32:7
33:1[2], 5, 14[2], 21
34:3, 6[4], 7[4], 14, 15
35:2, 4[2], 7, 10
36:2, 12, 13, 16, 22
37:1, 2, 9, 25, 33, 38
38:3, 11, 12, 14
40:9, 10[2], 11[2], 12, 14, 19, 31
41:3, 4, 7[2], 10[2], 11, 12
43:2, 5, 23[3], 24[4]
44:5, 12[3], 13[3], 16
45:9[2], 17
47:6, 12[2], 15
48:10, 20
49:4[2], 18[2], 23, 25[2], 26[3]
50:3, 8, 11
51:11, 21
52:8, 12
53:3, 5, 9[2], 12[3]
54:1, 7, 8, 9, 11[3]
55:3, 12[2]
56:12
57:5, 8, 9, 15
58:4, 14
59:3[2], 6, 12, 17, 21
60:7, 9
61:8, 10[4]
62:11
63:1, 3, 11, 12
64:11
65:23
66:10[3], 11[2], 15[4], 16

JEREMIAH

1:8, 19
2:9[2], 22, 29, 35
3:1, 2[3], 9[2], 10, 15, 18, 20
4:8, 30[3]
5:17, 18
6:3, 11[3], 12, 26, 28
8:8, 19[2]
9:4, 8, 15, 18[2], 25
10:3, 4[4], 13, 24
11:5, 10, 15, 16, 19
12:1[2], 5[2], 6
13:12[2], 13, 17
14:3, 17[3], 18[2], 21
15:6, 7, 11, 14, 17, 20
16:8, 18
17:1[2], 18
18:6, 17, 18, 19, 23
19:4, 5, 10
20:4, 9, 11, 17, 18
21:2, 5[2], 7, 10
22:7, 14[2], 15, 16, 19
23:15
24:1, 7
25:6, 7, 26, 31[2]
26:11, 14, 21, 22, 23, 24
27:8[3], 18
28:4
29:13, 16, 18[3], 23
30:6[2], 11, 14[2], 23[2]
31:3[2], 4, 7, 8[3], 9[2], 14[2], 24, 27[2], 31[2], 32, 33
32:4, 5, 21[5], 22, 29, 30, 40, 41[2]
33:5[2], 21[2], 25
34:2, 3, 5, 8, 13, 22
36:18[2], 23
37:8, 10, 15
38:6, 10, 11, 13, 17, 18, 23, 25, 27
39:3, 7, 8, 9
40:4[2], 5, 6, 9
41:1, 2[2], 3[2], 5, 7, 9, 11, 12, 13[2], 15, 16
42:6, 8, 11, 17
43:6, 12, 13
44:8, 25[2]
46:4, 10, 22[2], 25, 28
47:5
48:7, 32, 33, 39
49:2, 3, 20
50:5, 39, 45
51:5, 14[2], 16, 20[2], 21[2], 22[3], 23[3], 28, 32, 34, 40, 42, 58, 59
52:13, 14, 22, 32

LAMENTATIONS

1:2, 16
2:1, 4, 10, 11
3:5, 9, 15[2], 16[2], 30, 41, 43, 44, 48
4:9[2], 14
5:6, 9

EZEKIEL

1:15
2:6
3:3, 4, 10, 22, 24, 25, 27
4:12, 16[2], 17
5:2[2], 11[2], 12[2]
6:9[2], 11[2]
7:15, 18, 27
8:11, 16, 17, 18
9:1[2], 2[2], 3, 7, 11
10:2[2], 4, 6, 7
11:6, 13
12:7, 12, 18[3], 19[2]
13:10, 11, 13, 14, 15, 22
14:11
16:8, 9[2], 10[4], 11, 13, 16, 17, 26, 28[2], 36[2], 37[2], 40[2], 41, 59, 60, 62
17:3, 7, 12, 13, 16, 17, 20, 21
18:7, 16
19:4, 11
20:6, 7, 15, 18, 31, 33[3], 34[3], 35, 36[2], 39[2], 40, 41, 44
21:6[2], 21, 22, 24
22:7, 11, 14, 28, 31
23:6, 7[4], 8, 10, 14, 15, 16, 17[2], 23, 24[2], 25, 29, 30, 33[3], 37, 40, 42[2], 43[2], 47[3]
24:4, 7, 12, 16, 26
25:6[2], 10, 15, 17
26:7[3], 8, 9, 11, 16, 20[3]
27:7, 9, 11, 12, 14, 16, 21, 22[2], 24, 31[2], 33
28:4[2], 16, 26
30:5, 11[2], 24
31:3[2], 4, 11, 14, 16, 17[2], 18[2]
32:2[2], 3, 4, 5, 6, 7, 18, 19, 21, 24, 25[2], 27[2], 28[2], 29[3], 30[4], 32[2]
33:25, 31
34:3, 4[2], 16, 18[2], 19[2], 21[3], 25, 29, 30
35:8[2], 13
36:5[2], 37, 38
37:6, 19[2], 23[3], 26[2], 27
38:4[2], 5[2], 6, 9, 13, 15, 22[3]
39:4, 9, 10, 14, 20[3]
40:3, 4[2]
41:13, 15, 16, 18
42:16[2], 17, 18, 19
43:2, 22
44:5[3], 17, 18, 19
45:2
46:14, 23
47:22
48:20, 34

DANIEL

1:2, 8[2], 9, 13, 19
2:5, 11, 14, 18, 22, 41, 43[3]
4:15[3], 23[3], 25[2], 32, 33
5:7, 16, 21[3], 29
6:14, 17[2], 20
7:7, 13, 19, 21
8:7, 18
9:3, 15, 22, 26, 27
10:5, 7, 13, 17, 20, 21
11:3, 6, 7, 8[2], 11[3], 13[2], 17[2], 22, 23[2], 25[2], 28, 30, 34[2], 38[2], 39[2], 40[3], 44

HOSEA

2:2, 3, 6, 7, 13, 18[3]
4:1, 3[2], 4, 5, 14[2], 18
5:5, 6[2], 7
6:8
7:3[2], 5[2], 14
9:8
11:4[2], 12[4]
12:1, 2, 3, 4
13:3, 16
14:2, 8

JOEL

1:8
2:12[4], 20, 24, 26
3:2, 4, 18[2]

AMOS

1:3, 11, 13, 14[2]
2:2[3], 3
3:15
4:2[2], 5, 9, 10
5:8, 14
6:6, 7, 8, 10, 11[2], 12
7:7, 9
8:3
9:1

OBADIAH

7

JONAH

1:3
2:6, 9
3:6, 8

MICAH

1:7
2:4, 8, 10
3:5, 10[2]
5:1, 6
6:2[2], 6[2], 7[2], 8, 11[2], 15
7:2, 3, 14

NAHUM

1:8
2:3, 7, 12[2]
3:12

HABAKKUK

1:15
2:6, 12, 14, 16, 19
3:9, 13, 14, 15, 16

ZEPHANIAH

1:3, 4, 8, 9, 12
3:8, 9, 14, 17[2]

HAGGAI

1:6[2], 12, 13
2:4, 5, 7, 12, 17[3]

ZECHARIAH

1:2, 6, 9, 13[2], 14[2], 15, 16, 19
2:1, 3, 7
3:3, 4, 5
4:1, 2, 4, 5, 7, 10
5:4, 5, 10
6:4
7:14
8:2[2], 4, 23[2]
9:4, 8, 13, 14, 15
10:5, 9, 11
11:10
12:3, 4[3]
13:6
14:5

MALACHI

1:8
2:3, 4, 5, 6, 13[4], 16, 17
3:9
4:2, 4, 6

MATTHEW

1:18, 23[2]
2:3, 10, 11
3:11[3], 12
4:21, 24[2]
5:22, 25[2], 28, 41
7:2[2]
8:11, 16[2], 24, 28, 29
9:10, 11, 15, 20, 32, 36
11:7
12:3, 4, 22, 30[2], 41, 42, 45, 46, 47
13:15[3], 20, 29, 56
14:7, 9, 14, 24
15:8[2], 20, 22, 30, 32
16:1, 27
17:3, 17
18:9, 16, 26, 27, 29
19:10, 26[2]
20:2, 13, 15, 20, 22[2], 23[2], 24
21:2, 25
22:10, 16, 25, 37[3]
23:4, 30
24:19, 30, 31, 49, 51
25:3, 4, 10, 16, 19, 27, 31
26:11, 15, 18, 20, 23, 29, 35, 36, 37, 38, 40, 47[2], 51, 52, 55[2], 58, 67, 69, 71, 72
27:7, 19, 22, 34, 38, 41, 44, 46, 48, 50, 54
28:8, 12, 20

MARK

1:6[2], 8[2], 13, 20, 23, 24, 26, 27, 29, 32, 36, 41
2:15, 16[2], 19[2], 25, 26
3:5, 6, 7, 14
4:10, 16, 24, 30, 33, 36
5:2, 3, 4, 5, 7[2], 15, 16, 18[2], 24, 40, 42
6:3, 9, 13, 22, 25, 26, 34, 50
7:2[2], 5, 6
8:2, 4, 10, 11, 14, 34, 38
9:1, 2, 4[2], 8, 10[2], 14, 16, 18, 19, 24, 47, 49[2], 50
10:27[3], 30, 38[2], 39, 41, 46
11:11, 31
12:30[4], 33[4]
13:17, 26
14:7, 14, 17, 18, 20, 31, 33, 43[2], 48[2], 49, 53, 54, 58, 65, 67
15:1, 7[2], 17, 19, 23, 27, 28, 31, 32, 34, 37, 41
16:10, 14, 17, 20[2]

LUKE

1:15, 25, 28, 30, 36, 37, 39, 41, 42, 51, 53, 56, 58, 66, 67
2:5[2], 13, 16, 36, 37, 40, 48, 51, 52
3:14, 16[3], 17
4:28, 32, 33, 34, 36, 38, 40
5:9, 10, 18, 19, 26, 29, 30, 34, 36
6:3, 4, 11[2], 17, 18, 38
7:6, 11, 12, 24, 30, 36, 38[3], 44[2], 46[2], 49
8:1, 7, 13, 14, 15, 16, 22, 23, 28[2], 29, 37, 38, 45
9:18, 30, 32[3], 41, 49
10:17, 27[4]
11:7, 20, 23[2], 31, 32, 37, 46[2]
12:13, 25, 46, 47, 48, 50, 58
13:1, 14
14:9, 10, 15, 18, 25, 31[2]
15:2, 6, 9, 13, 16, 17, 29, 30, 31
16:21
17:15, 20
18:7, 11, 27[2]
19:7, 23, 37, 44
20:1, 5
21:5, 20, 23, 25, 27, 34
22:4, 11, 14, 15[2], 21, 28, 33, 48, 49, 52, 53, 56, 59
23:9, 11, 18, 23, 32, 35, 43, 46, 55
24:1, 10, 15, 24, 29[2], 30, 32, 33, 44, 49, 52

JOHN

1:1, 2, 26, 31, 33[2], 39
2:4, 7
3:2, 22, 26
4:6, 9, 11, 27[2], 40
5:18
6:3, 13, 22, 66
7:33
8:6, 29, 38[2]
9:6, 37, 40
11:2[2], 16, 31, 33, 43, 44[2], 54
12:2, 3[2], 8, 17, 35, 40[2]
13:5, 8, 18, 33
14:9, 16, 17, 23, 25, 27, 30
15:27
16:4, 32
17:5[3], 12, 24
18:1, 2, 3, 5, 15, 18, 22, 26
19:3, 15[2], 18, 29, 32, 34, 40
20:7, 24, 26
21:3, 8

THE ACTS

1:4, 5[2], 14[3], 17, 18, 21, 22, 26
2:1, 4[2], 14, 28, 29, 30, 40, 46[2], 47
3:4, 8, 10, 25
4:8, 13, 14, 24, 27, 29, 31[2], 33
5:1, 12, 16, 17[2], 21, 23, 26, 28, 31
6:9
7:9[2], 19, 38[2], 45, 48, 54, 57[2], 60
8:6, 7[3], 11, 13, 20[2], 31, 37
9:7, 17, 19, 28, 39[2], 43
10:2, 6, 20, 23, 27, 35, 38[3], 41, 45, 46
11:2, 3, 12, 16[2], 21, 23, 26
12:2, 6, 17, 20[2], 25
13:1, 7, 9, 16, 17, 31, 45, 52[2]
14:4[2], 5, 10, 13, 15, 17, 18, 20, 23, 27, 28
15:2, 4, 22[2], 24, 25[2], 32, 35, 37, 38[2]
16:3, 11, 16, 28, 34
17:2, 4, 5, 11, 15, 17[4], 23, 24, 25, 34
18:2, 3, 8, 10, 12, 14, 18, 19, 20
19:4, 6, 25, 26, 29[2], 33, 34, 38
20:9, 14, 18, 19[2], 24, 28, 31, 34, 36
21:1, 5, 7, 8, 16[3], 18, 24[2], 26, 29, 33, 36, 40
22:9, 11, 22, 25, 28
23:15, 19, 21, 27, 32
24:1[2], 3, 7, 12, 18[2], 24, 26
25:5, 12, 23[2], 24[2]
26:8, 9, 12, 13, 24, 30
27:2, 10, 18, 19, 24, 39, 41
28:10[2], 14, 16, 20[2], 27[3], 31

ROMANS

1:4, 9, 12, 27, 29
2:11
3:13
5:1
6:4, 6, 8[2]
7:18, 21, 25[2]
8:16, 17[2], 18, 25, 26, 32
9:14, 22
10:9, 10[2]
11:17
12:8[3], 10, 15[2], 18, 21
14:15[2], 20
15:6, 10, 13, 14, 24, 30, 32[2], 33
16:14, 15, 16, 20, 24

1 CORINTHIANS

1:2, 17
2:1, 3, 4, 13
3:2[2], 9, 19
4:3, 8, 12, 21
5:4, 8[3], 9, 10[3], 11
6:6, 7, 9, 20
7:5, 12, 13, 23, 24
8:7
9:13, 23
10:5, 13, 20
11:5, 32
12:26[2], 30
13:1
14:5[2], 6, 15[4], 16, 18, 19, 21, 23, 39
15:10, 32, 35
16:4, 6, 7, 10, 11, 12, 14, 16, 19, 20, 21, 23, 24

2 CORINTHIANS

1:1, 12, 17, 21
2:1, 4, 7
3:3[2], 18
4:14
5:1, 2, 8
6:1, 14[3], 15[2], 16
7:3, 4, 8, 15
8:4, 18, 19[2], 22
9:4
10:2, 12
11:1[2], 2, 4, 9, 25, 32
12:16, 18
13:4, 11, 12, 14

GALATIANS

1:2, 16, 18
2:1[2], 3, 5, 12, 13[2], 20
3:9
4:18, 20, 25, 30
5:1, 24
6:11, 18

EPHESIANS

1:3, 13
2:5, 19
3:12, 16, 18, 19
4:2[2], 14, 19, 25, 28, 31
5:6, 7, 11, 18[2], 26
6:2, 3, 5, 6, 7, 9, 14, 15, 18[2], 23, 24

PHILIPPIANS

1:1, 4, 11, 20, 23, 25, 27
2:6, 12, 17, 18, 22[2], 23, 29
4:3[3], 6, 9, 14, 15, 21, 23

COLOSSIANS

1:9, 11[2]
2:4, 5, 7, 11, 12[2], 13, 19, 20, 22
3:1, 3, 4, 9, 16, 22
4:2, 6[2], 9, 18

1 THESSALONIANS

1:6
2:2, 4, 17
3:4, 13
4:11, 14, 16[3], 17[2], 18
5:3, 10, 26, 28

2 THESSALONIANS

1:6, 7[2], 9, 11
2:5, 8[2], 9, 10
3:1, 8, 10, 12, 14, 16, 17, 18

1 TIMOTHY

1:10, 14
2:9[2], 10, 11, 15
3:4, 6
4:2, 3, 4, 14
5:2
6:6, 10, 21

2 TIMOTHY

1:3, 4, 9
2:4, 10, 11[2], 12, 22
3:6[2]
4:2, 11[2], 13[2], 16, 17, 22[2]

TITUS

2:15
3:15[2]

PHILEMON

13, 19, 25

HEBREWS

1:9
2:4[2], 7, 9
3:10, 17[2]
4:2, 13, 15
5:2, 7
7:21
8:8[3], 9, 10
9:4, 11, 19, 21, 22, 23[2], 24, 25
10:1, 16, 22[2]
11:7, 9[2], 25, 31[2], 37
12:1[2], 7[2], 14, 17, 18, 20, 28
13:3, 5, 9[3], 12, 16, 17[2], 23, 25

JAMES

1:6, 11, 13, 17, 18, 21
2:1, 2, 22
3:4, 13[2]
4:4
5:14

1 PETER

1:7, 8, 12, 18, 19, 22
2:15, 18, 20
3:2, 6, 7, 15
4:1, 4, 13
5:5, 13, 14[2]

2 PETER

1:1, 18
2:3, 6, 7, 8, 13[2], 14, 16, 17, 20
3:6, 8, 10[2], 12, 17

1 JOHN

1:1, 2, 3[3], 6, 7
2:1, 19

2 JOHN

2, 3, 12

3 JOHN

10, 13

JUDE

9, 12, 14, 23, 24

REVELATION

1:7, 12, 13[2]
2:12, 16, 22, 23, 27
3:4, 17, 18, 20[2], 21[2]
4:1
5:1, 2, 12
6:8[5], 10
7:2, 9, 10
8:3, 4, 5, 7, 8, 13
9:19
10:1, 3
11:6
12:1, 2, 5, 9, 17[2]
13:4, 7, 10[2]
14:1, 2, 4, 7, 9, 10, 15, 18
15:2, 6, 8
16:8, 9
17:1, 2[2], 4, 6[3], 12, 14[2], 16
18:1, 2, 3, 8, 9, 16, 21
19:2, 13, 15[2], 17, 20[3], 21[2]
20:4, 6
21:3[3], 8, 9, 15, 16, 19
22:12, 21

YE

859, *5210*

GENESIS

3:1, 3[3], 4, 5[2]
4:23
9:4, 7
17:10, 11
18:5[3]
19:2, 8
22:5
24:49
26:27[2]
29:4, 5, 7
31:6
32:4, 19[2], 20
34:9, 10[2], 11, 12, 15, 17, 30
40:7
42:1, 7, 9[2], 12, 14, 15[2], 16[2], 19[2], 20, 22, 33, 34[3], 36[2], 38[2]
43:3, 5, 6[2], 7, 27, 29
44:4, 5, 10, 15[2], 19, 23, 27, 29[2]
45:4, 5, 9, 13[3], 17, 18, 19, 24
46:34[2]
47:23, 24
49:2
50:17, 20, 21, 25

EXODUS

1:16[2], 18, 22[2]
2:18, 20
3:12, 18, 21[2], 22[2]
4:15
5:4, 5, 7, 8[2], 11[2], 14, 17[3], 18, 19, 21
6:7
8:25, 28[2]
9:28, 30
10:2, 11[2], 24
11:7
12:3, 5, 6, 10[2], 11[2], 13, 14[2], 15[2], 17[2], 18, 20[2], 22, 24, 25[2], 26, 27, 31[2], 32, 46
13:3, 4, 19
14:2, 13[3], 14
15:21
16:3, 6, 7[2], 8, 12[3], 16, 23[2], 25, 26, 28, 29
17:2[2]
19:4, 5[2], 6, 12
20:20, 22, 23[2]
22:21, 22, 31[3]
23:9[2], 25
24:1, 14
25:2, 3, 9, 19
30:9[2], 32, 37
31:13[2], 14
32:30
33:5
34:13
35:1, 3, 5

LEVITICUS

1:2
2:11[2], 12
3:17
7:23, 24, 26, 32
8:32, 33, 35[2]
9:3, 6
10:6, 7[2], 9[2], 10, 11, 13, 14, 17, 18
11:2, 3, 4, 8[2], 9[2], 11[2], 13, 21, 22, 24, 33, 39, 42, 43[3], 44[3], 45
14:34
15:31
16:29, 30, 31
17:14
18:3[4], 4, 5, 24, 26, 28, 30[3]
19:2, 3, 4, 5[2], 6, 9, 11, 12, 15, 19, 23[2], 25, 26[2], 27, 28, 30, 33, 34, 35, 36, 37
20:7, 8, 15, 22, 23, 24, 25[2], 26[2]
22:19, 20, 22, 24[2], 25, 28, 29, 30, 31, 32
23:2, 3, 4, 6, 7[2], 8[2], 10[2], 12[2], 14[2], 15[2], 16[2], 17, 18, 19, 21[2], 22, 24, 25[2], 27, 28, 31, 32[2], 35, 36[3], 37, 38, 39[2], 40[2], 41[2], 42
24:22
25:2, 9, 10[3], 11, 12, 13, 14, 17, 18[2], 19, 20, 22[2], 23, 24, 44, 45, 46[2]
26:1[2], 2, 3, 5, 6, 7, 10, 12, 13, 14, 15[3], 16, 17[2], 18, 21, 23, 25[2], 26, 27, 29[2], 34, 35, 37, 38

NUMBERS

1:2
4:18, 27, 32
5:3[2]
6:23
9:3[2], 14
10:5, 6, 7[2], 9[4], 10
11:18[3], 19, 20
12:4, 8
13:2, 20
14:9[2], 28, 30, 31[2], 34[3], 41, 42, 43[2]
15:2, 12[2], 14, 15, 18, 19[2], 20[3], 21, 22, 29, 39[3], 40
16:3[2], 7[2], 8, 10, 11, 17, 26, 28, 30, 41
18:3, 5, 7, 26[2], 28[3], 29, 30, 31[2], 32[4]
19:3
20:4, 5, 8, 10, 12[2], 24
21:5, 17
22:19
25:5
27:8, 9, 10, 11, 14
28:2, 3, 11, 18, 19, 20, 23, 24, 25[2], 26[3], 27, 31
29:1[2], 2, 7[3], 8, 12[3], 13, 17, 35[2], 36, 39
31:4, 15, 19, 23[2], 24[3]
32:6, 7, 14, 15[2], 20[2], 22, 23[2], 29
33:51, 52, 53, 54[4], 55[3]
34:2, 6, 7, 8, 10, 13, 18
35:2, 4, 5, 6[3], 7[2], 8[3], 10, 11, 13[2], 14[2], 31, 32, 33[2], 34

DEUTERONOMY

1:6, 10, 11, 14, 17[3], 18, 19, 20, 22, 26, 27, 31[2], 32, 33, 39, 41[3], 42, 43, 45, 46[2]
2:3, 4[2], 6[4], 24
3:18, 19, 20, 22
4:1, 2[3], 4, 5[2], 11, 12[2], 14[2], 15[2], 16, 20, 22, 23, 25, 26[3], 27, 28
5:1, 5, 23[2], 24, 28, 32[2], 33[4]
6:1[2], 3, 14, 16[2], 17
7:5[2], 7[2], 12, 25
8:1[2], 19, 20[2]
9:7[2], 8, 16[2], 18, 21, 22, 23[2], 24
10:19[2]
11:2, 5, 8[3], 9, 10, 11, 13, 16, 17, 18, 19, 22, 23, 25, 27, 28[2], 31[2], 32
12:1[2], 2[2], 3[2], 4, 5, 6, 7[4], 8, 9, 10[2], 11[2], 12[2], 16[2]
13:3, 4[2], 13
14:1[2], 4, 6, 7, 8, 9[2], 10, 11, 12, 20, 21
17:16
18:15
19:19
20:2, 3[2], 18
22:24[2]
23:4
24:8, 9
25:17
27:2, 4[2], 12
28:62[3], 63, 68
29:2, 6[3], 7, 9[2], 10, 16[2], 17
30:18[2]
31:5, 13[2], 19, 27, 29[2]
32:1, 3, 6, 43, 46, 47[2], 51[2]

JOSHUA

1:11, 14, 15
2:5, 10[3], 12, 13, 14, 16
3:3[2], 4[3], 8[2], 10
4:3[3], 6, 7, 17, 22, 23, 24
6:3[2], 4, 5, 10[2], 18[3], 22
7:12, 13, 14
8:2, 4[2], 7, 8[3]
9:6, 7, 8[2], 11, 22[2], 23
10:19, 25
18:3, 6
22:2, 3, 4, 16[3], 18[2], 19, 24, 25[2], 27, 31[2]
23:3, 5, 6[2], 7, 8, 11, 12, 13, 14, 16[2]
24:6, 7, 8, 11, 13[5], 14, 15[2], 19, 20, 22[2], 27

JUDGES

2:2[4]
5:2, 3[2], 9, 10[2], 23[2]
6:10[2], 31[2]
7:17, 18
8:15, 18, 19, 24
9:7, 15, 16[3], 18, 19[2], 48
10:12, 13, 14
11:7[3], 9, 26
12:2, 3[2], 4
14:12, 13[2], 15, 18[2]
15:7, 10, 12
18:6, 8, 9, 10[2], 14[2], 18, 24[3]
19:24
20:7
21:11[2], 21, 22[2]

RUTH

1:8, 9, 11, 13[2], 21
4:2, 9, 10

1 SAMUEL

2:23, 24, 29
4:9[2]
6:3[2], 5[2], 6, 8, 21
7:3
8:17, 18[2], 22
9:13[3], 19
10:14, 19[2], 24
11:9[2], 10
12:1, 5, 11, 12[2], 13[2], 14[2], 15, 17[2], 20, 21[2], 25[3]
14:33, 38, 40
15:6, 32
17:8[2], 9, 25
18:25
21:14[2], 15
22:7, 13
23:21[2], 23
25:6, 13
26:16[2]
27:10
29:10
30:23

2 SAMUEL

1:21, 24
2:5[2], 6, 7
3:17, 38
7:7
11:15[2], 20[3], 21
13:28
15:10[2], 36[2]
16:10
19:10, 11, 12[3], 13, 22[2], 42, 43[2]
21:3, 4
24:2

1 KINGS

1:34, 35, 45
9:6[2]
11:2
12:6, 9, 24
18:18, 21, 24, 25
20:28, 33
22:3

2 KINGS

1:3, 5
2:3, 5, 16
3:17[4], 19
6:2, 11, 19, 32
7:1
9:11
10:6[3], 8, 9, 13
11:5, 6, 8[2]
12:7
17:12, 13, 27, 35, 36[3], 37[2], 38[2], 39
18:19, 22[2], 31[2], 32
19:6, 10, 29[2]
22:13, 18

1 CHRONICLES

12:17[2]
15:12[3], 13
16:9, 10, 13[2], 15, 19, 28, 35
17:6
22:19
28:8

2 CHRONICLES

7:19
10:6, 9
11:4
12:5
13:5, 8[2], 9, 11, 12[2]
15:2[4], 7
18:14, 25, 27, 30
19:6[2], 9, 10[2]
20:15[2], 16[2], 17[2], 20[3]
23:4, 7
24:5, 20[3]
28:9, 10, 11, 13[2]
29:5, 8, 11, 31
30:6, 7[2], 8, 9[2]
32:10[2], 12, 13
34:23, 26

EZRA

4:2, 3, 18, 21, 22
6:6, 8
7:25
8:28, 29[2]
9:11, 12
10:10

NEHEMIAH

1:8, 9
2:17, 19[2], 20
4:12, 14, 20[2]
5:7, 8, 9[2], 11
8:10, 11
13:17, 18, 21[2], 25

ESTHER

4:16
8:8

JOB

6:21[2], 26, 27[2]
12:2
13:2, 4[2], 5, 7, 8[2], 9, 10
16:2, 4
17:10
18:2
19:2, 3[3], 5, 21, 22, 28, 29[2]
21:27, 28, 29[2], 34
27:12[2]
32:6, 11, 13
34:2[2], 10, 18
42:7, 8

PSALMS

2:10[2], 12
4:2[3]
6:8
11:1
14:6
22:23[3]
24:7[3], 9[2]
27:8
29:1
30:4
31:23, 24
32:9, 11[2]
33:1
34:9, 11
47:1, 7
48:13[2]
49:1[2]
50:22
58:1[3], 2[2]
62:3[3], 8
66:1, 8, 16
68:13[2], 16[2], 26, 32, 34
82:2, 6, 7
90:3
94:8[3]
95:7
96:7
97:7, 10, 12
99:5
100:1, 3
103:20, 21[3]
104:35
105:2, 3, 6[2], 45
106:1, 48
111:1
112:1
113:1[2], 9
114:6[3]
115:11, 15
116:19
117:1[2], 2
119:115
134:1[2]
135:1[3], 2, 20, 21
139:19
146:1, 10
147:1, 20
148:1[2], 2[2], 3[2], 4[2], 7, 14
149:1, 9
150:1, 6

PROVERBS

1:22[2], 24, 25
4:1, 2
5:7
7:24
8:5[3], 32

SONG OF SOLOMON

1:5
2:7[2]
3:3, 5[2], 11
5:8[2]
6:13
8:4

ISAIAH

1:5[2], 10[2], 12, 15[2], 19[2], 20[2], 29[3], 30
2:3, 5, 22
3:10, 14, 15[2]
6:9[2]
7:9[2], 13[2]
8:9[5], 12[2]
10:3[3]
12:3, 4
13:2, 6
16:1, 7
18:2, 3[3]
19:11
21:5, 12[2], 13[2]
22:9[2], 10[2], 11[2], 14
23:1, 2, 6[2], 14
24:15
26:2, 4, 19
27:2, 12[2]
28:12, 14, 15, 18, 22, 23
29:1, 9
30:12, 15[2], 16[2], 17[2], 21[3], 22, 29
31:6
32:9[2], 10[2], 11[2], 20
33:11[2], 13[2]
34:1[2], 16
35:3
36:4, 7, 13, 16[2]
37:6, 10, 30[2]
40:1[2], 2, 3, 18[2], 21[3], 25
41:14, 23, 24
42:10, 17, 18[3]
43:10[2], 12, 18, 19
44:8[2], 23[3], 26
45:8, 11, 17, 19, 20, 21, 22
46:5, 8, 12
48:1, 6, 14, 16[2], 20[4]
49:1
50:1, 11[4]
51:14, 7[3]
52:3[2], 9, 11[5], 12
55:1[2], 2[2], 6[2], 12
56:1, 9[2], 12
57:3, 4[3], 14[2]
58:3, 4[3], 6
61:6[3], 7
62:6, 10, 11
65:11, 12[3], 13[3], 14, 15, 18
66:1, 5, 10[3], 11[2], 12[2], 13, 14

JEREMIAH

2:4, 7[2], 12[2], 29[2], 31
3:13, 16, 20, 22
4:4, 5[2], 10, 16
5:1[2], 10, 14, 19[3], 22[2], 31
6:1, 4, 6, 16[2], 18
7:2, 4, 5[2], 6, 8, 9[2], 12, 13[3], 14, 23[2]
8:8
9:4[2], 17, 20
10:1, 11
11:2, 4, 6, 13
12:9
13:15, 16, 17, 23
14:13[2]
16:12[2], 13[3]
17:4, 20[2], 22[2], 24, 27
18:6, 11, 13
19:3
20:13
21:3, 4, 11
22:3, 4, 5, 10, 26[2], 30
23:2, 17, 20, 35, 36[2], 38[3]
25:3, 4, 5, 7[2], 8, 27, 28, 29[2], 34[3]
26:4, 5, 11, 12, 15[3]
27:4, 9[2], 10, 13, 14, 15[2]

JEREMIAH
29:5, 6[2], 7, 8, 12[2], 13[2], 15, 19, 20[2], 26, 28
30:6, 22, 24
31:6, 7[2], 10
32:5[2], 36, 43
33:10, 20
34:14, 15[2], 16, 17
35:5, 6[2], 7[4], 13, 14, 15[3], 18
36:19
37:7, 10, 18
40:3, 10[3]
42:9, 10, 11, 13, 15[2], 16[3], 18[3], 19[2], 20[2], 21, 22[2]
44:2, 3, 7, 8[4], 9, 21[2], 22, 23[2], 25[2], 26, 29
46:3, 4, 9[2], 14[2]
48:14, 17[2], 20, 26, 28
49:3, 5, 8, 14, 28, 30
50:2, 11[4], 14, 29, 45
51:3[2], 27, 45[2], 46, 50

LAMENTATIONS
1:12
4:15

EZEKIEL
5:7
6:3, 7, 8[2], 13
7:4, 9
9:5[2], 7
11:5, 6[2], 7, 8, 10[2], 11, 12[2], 17
12:20, 22
13:2, 5, 7[3], 8, 9, 11, 12, 14[3], 18[2], 19, 20[2], 21, 22, 23[2]
14:8, 22[2], 23[2]
15:7
17:12, 21
18:2[2], 3, 19, 25, 31[2], 32
20:3, 7, 18, 20, 29, 30[2], 31[3], 32, 34, 38, 39[4], 41, 42, 43[4], 44[2]
21:24[3]
22:19, 21, 22[2]
23:40, 49[2]
24:21, 22[2], 23[2], 24[2]
25:5
30:2
33:10, 11[3], 20[2], 25[2], 26[4]
34:3[4], 4[6], 7, 9, 18[2], 19[2], 21[2], 31
35:9, 13
36:1, 3[2], 4, 6, 8[2], 9, 11, 22[2], 23, 25, 27, 28[2], 30, 31
37:4, 5, 6[2], 13, 14[2]
39:17, 18, 19[3], 20
44:6, 7[2], 8[2], 28, 30
45:1[2], 6, 10, 13[2], 14, 20, 21
47:13, 14, 18, 21, 22, 23
48:8, 9, 20, 29

DANIEL
1:10
2:5[2], 6[2], 8[2], 9[3]
3:5[2], 14, 15[5], 26

HOSEA
1:9, 10[2]
2:1
4:1, 15[2], 18
5:14, 8
9:5

HOSEA
10:13[3]
14:3

JOEL
1:2[2], 3, 5[2], 11[3], 13[3], 14
2:1, 12, 19, 22, 23, 26, 27
3:4[3], 5, 6[2], 7, 9, 11, 13, 17

AMOS
2:11, 12
3:13
4:1, 3[2], 5, 6, 8, 9, 10, 11[2]
5:1, 4[2], 6, 7, 11[5], 14[2], 22, 25, 26[2]
6:2[2], 3, 12, 13
8:4
9:7

OBADIAH
1, 16

MICAH
1:2, 10[2], 11
2:3[2], 6, 8, 9[2], 10
3:1, 6[2], 9
6:1, 2[2], 5, 9, 16[2]
7:5[2]

NAHUM
1:9
2:9

HABAKKUK
1:5[2]

ZEPHANIAH
1:11
2:3[3], 12[2]
3:8

HAGGAI
1:4, 6[8], 9[3]
2:3, 4, 5[2], 17

ZECHARIAH
1:3, 4[2]
2:9
3:10
6:15[2]
7:5[2], 6[3], 7
8:9, 13[2], 15, 16[2]
9:12
10:1
11:2, 12
14:5[3]

MALACHI
1:2, 5, 6, 7[3], 8[2], 10, 12[2], 13[4]
2:1, 2[3], 4, 8[3], 9, 13, 14, 16, 17[3]
3:1[2], 6, 7[2], 8[2], 9[2], 10, 12, 13, 14, 18
4:2, 3, 4

MATTHEW
2:8
3:2, 3
5:11, 13, 14, 20, 21, 27, 33, 38, 39, 43, 45, 46[2], 47[2], 48
6:1[2], 7, 8[3], 9, 14, 15, 16, 24, 25[3], 26, 28, 30, 32, 33
7:1, 2[3], 6, 7, 11, 12[2], 13, 16, 20, 23

MATTHEW
8:26[2]
9:4, 6, 13, 28, 38
10:5, 7, 8, 11[2], 12, 14, 16, 18, 19[2], 20, 22, 23[2], 27[3], 31[2]
11:4, 7, 8, 9, 14, 17[2], 28, 29
12:3, 5, 7[2], 34
13:14[2], 17[2], 18, 29[2], 30, 51
14:16
15:3, 5, 6, 7, 16, 17, 34
16:2, 3[3], 8[3], 9[2], 10, 11[2], 15
17:5, 20[2]
18:3[2], 10, 12, 18[2], 35
19:4, 28[2]
20:4, 6, 7[2], 22[3], 23, 25, 32
21:2, 3, 5, 13, 16, 21[3], 22[2], 24, 25, 28, 32[4], 42
22:9[2], 18[2], 29, 31, 42
23:3, 8[2], 10, 13[3], 14[2], 15[2], 16, 17, 19, 23[2], 24, 25, 27, 28[2], 29, 31[2], 32, 33[3], 34[2], 35, 37, 39[2]
24:2, 6[2], 9, 15, 20, 32, 33[2], 42, 44[2]
25:6, 9, 13, 30, 34, 35[3], 36[3], 40[2], 41, 42[2], 43[3], 45[2]
26:2, 10, 11[2], 15, 27, 31, 36, 38, 40, 41, 55[2], 64, 65, 66
27:17, 21, 24, 65[2]
28:5[2], 7, 13, 19

MARK
1:3, 15, 17
2:8, 10, 25
4:13[2], 24[2], 40[2]
5:39
6:10[2], 11, 31, 37, 38
7:8[2], 9[2], 11, 12, 13[2], 18[2]
8:5, 17[4], 18[3], 19, 20, 21, 29
9:16, 33, 41, 50
10:36, 38[3], 39[2], 42
11:2[2], 3[2], 5, 17, 24[4], 25[2], 26, 31
12:10, 15, 24[2], 26, 27
13:7[2], 9[2], 11[4], 13, 14, 18, 23, 28, 29[2], 33[2], 35[2]
14:6, 7[4], 13, 14, 27, 32, 34, 38[2], 48, 49, 62, 64[2], 71
15:9, 12[2]
16:6, 7, 15

LUKE
2:12, 49[2]
3:4
4:23
5:22, 24, 30, 34
6:2, 3, 20, 21[4], 22, 23, 24, 25[2], 31[2], 32[2], 33[2], 34[3], 35[2], 36, 37[3], 38, 46
7:22, 24, 25, 26, 32[2], 33, 34
8:18
9:4, 5, 13, 20, 55[2]
10:2, 5, 8, 10, 11, 23, 24[2]
11:2, 9, 13, 18, 39, 40, 41, 42[2], 43, 44, 46[3], 47, 48[3], 52[3]
12:1, 3[2], 5, 7, 11[3], 12, 22[2], 24, 26[2], 28, 29[4], 30, 31, 33, 36, 40[2], 51, 54[2], 55[2], 56[3], 57
13:2, 3[2], 4, 5[2], 25[2], 26, 27[2], 28, 32, 34, 35[2]
16:9, 11, 12, 13, 15

LUKE
17:6[2], 10[2], 22[2]
19:30[2], 31[2], 33, 46
20:5, 23
21:6, 8[2], 9, 14, 16, 17, 19, 20, 30, 31[3], 36[2]
22:10, 11, 26, 28, 30, 35, 40, 46[2], 51, 52, 53, 67, 68, 70
23:14[2]
24:5, 17[2], 38, 39, 41, 48, 49[2]

JOHN
1:26, 38, 51
3:7, 11, 12[2], 28
4:20, 21, 22[2], 32, 35, 38[2], 48[2]
5:20, 33, 34, 35, 37, 38[2], 39[2], 40[2], 42, 43[2], 44, 45, 46[2], 47[2]
6:26[3], 29, 36, 53[2], 62, 67
7:8, 19, 21, 22, 23, 28[3], 34[2], 36[2], 45, 47
8:14, 15, 19[3], 21[2], 22, 23[2], 24[3], 28[2], 31[2], 32, 33, 36, 37[2], 38[2], 39[2], 40, 41, 42, 43[2], 44[2], 45, 46, 47[2], 49, 54, 55
9:19, 27[3], 30, 41[3]
10:20, 25, 26[2], 32, 34, 36, 38[2]
11:15, 34, 39, 49, 56
12:8[2], 19[2], 35, 36[2]
13:10, 11, 12, 13[2], 14, 15, 17[3], 19, 33[2], 34[2], 35[2]
14:1, 3, 4[2], 7[3], 13, 14, 15, 17, 19[2], 20[2], 24, 28[3], 29
15:3, 4[2], 5[2], 7[3], 8[2], 9, 10[2], 12, 14[2], 16[3], 17, 18, 19[2], 27[2]
16:1, 4, 10, 12, 16[2], 17[2], 19[3], 20[2], 22, 23[2], 24[2], 26, 27, 31, 32, 33[2]
18:4, 7, 8, 29, 31, 39[2]
19:4, 6, 35
20:22, 23[2], 31[2]
21:5, 6, 10

THE ACTS
1:4, 5, 8[2], 11[3]
2:14[2], 15, 22[2], 23, 33, 36, 38
3:12[3], 13, 14, 16, 17, 19, 22, 25
4:7, 8, 10, 19
5:8, 9, 25, 28[2], 30, 35[2], 39[2]
6:3
7:4, 26[2], 37, 42[2], 43[2], 49, 51[3], 52
8:24[2]
10:21[2], 28, 29, 37
11:16
13:15[2], 16, 25, 39, 41[2], 46
14:15[2]
15:1[2], 7, 10, 24, 29[4]
16:15
17:22[2], 23
18:14, 15
19:2[2], 3, 15, 25, 26, 35, 36, 37, 39
20:18, 25, 34, 35
21:13
22:1, 3
23:15[2]
25:24
27:21, 31, 33
28:26[2]

ROMANS
1:6, 11
6:3, 11, 12, 13, 14, 16[4], 17[2], 18, 19, 20[2], 21[2], 22
7:1, 4[2]
8:9, 13[4], 15[2]
9:26
11:2, 25[2], 30
12:1, 2[2]
13:5, 6, 14
14:1
15:6, 7, 10, 11[2], 13, 14, 30
16:2[2], 17

1 CORINTHIANS
1:5, 7, 8, 9, 10[2], 13, 26, 30
3:2[2], 3[2], 4, 5, 9[2], 16[2], 17, 23
4:6, 8[4], 10[3], 15[2], 16, 21
5:2, 4, 6, 7[2], 10, 12
6:2[2], 3, 4, 7[3], 8, 9, 11[3], 15, 16, 19[3], 20
7:1, 5[2], 23[2], 35
8:12[2]
9:1, 2, 13, 24[2]
10:1, 7, 10, 13[2], 15, 20, 21[2], 27, 31[2]
11:1, 2, 17, 18, 20, 22[2], 25[2], 26[2], 33, 34
12:2[3], 27
14:1, 5[2], 9[3], 12[3], 18, 20, 23, 26, 31
15:1[2], 2[3], 11, 17, 58[2]
16:1, 3, 6, 13, 15, 16, 18, 20

2 CORINTHIANS
1:7[2], 11, 13[2], 14[2], 15, 24
2:4[2], 7, 8, 9, 10
3:2, 3
5:12, 20
6:1, 11, 12[2], 13, 14, 16, 17, 18
7:3, 9[4], 11[2], 15
8:7[2], 9[2], 11, 13, 24
9:3, 4, 5, 8
10:7
11:1, 4[4], 7, 19[2], 20
12:11, 13, 19, 20
13:3, 5[3], 6, 7[2], 9

GALATIANS
1:6, 9, 13
3:1, 2, 3[2], 4, 7, 26, 28, 29[2]
4:6, 8[2], 9[3], 10, 12[2], 13, 14, 15[2], 17, 21[2]
5:2, 4, 7[2], 10, 13, 15[2], 16, 17[2], 18[2]
6:1, 2, 11

EPHESIANS
1:13[4], 18
2:2, 5, 8, 11, 12, 13, 19, 22
3:2, 4[2], 13, 17, 19
4:1[2], 4, 17, 20, 21, 22, 24, 26, 30, 32
5:1, 5, 7, 8[2], 15, 17
6:4, 9, 11, 13, 16, 21, 22

PHILIPPIANS
1:7, 10[2], 12, 27, 30
2:2[2], 12, 15[2], 18, 22, 26, 28[2]
3:15, 17
4:9, 10[2], 14[2], 15[2], 16

COLOSSIANS
1:4, 5, 6, 7, 9, 10, 23[2]
2:1, 6[2], 7, 10, 11, 12, 20[2]
3:1, 3, 4, 7[2], 8, 9, 13, 15[2], 17, 23, 24[2]
4:1, 6[2], 10, 12, 16

1 THESSALONIANS
1:5, 6, 9
2:2, 5, 8, 9, 10, 11, 12, 13[3], 14[2], 19, 20
3:4, 6, 8
4:1[3], 2, 3, 9[2], 10[2], 11, 12[2], 13
5:1, 4, 5, 11

2 THESSALONIANS
1:4, 5[2], 12
2:2, 5, 6, 15
3:4, 6, 7, 13

HEBREWS
3:7, 15
4:7
5:11, 12[2]
6:10[2], 12
10:25, 29, 32[2], 33[2], 34[2], 36[3]
12:3, 4, 5, 7, 8[2], 17, 18, 22, 25
13:5, 23

JAMES
1:2, 4, 22
2:3, 4, 6, 7, 8[2], 9[2], 12, 16[2], 24
3:14
4:2[5], 3[3], 4[2], 5, 8[2], 13, 14, 15, 16
5:1, 3, 5[2], 6, 8, 9, 11, 12, 16

1 PETER
1:6[2], 8[3], 15, 16, 17, 18[2], 22[2]
2:2, 3, 5, 9[2], 15, 20[4], 21[2], 24, 25
3:1, 6[2], 7, 8, 9[2], 13, 14[2], 17
4:4, 7, 13[2], 14[2]
5:4, 5, 10, 12, 14

2 PETER
1:4, 8, 10[2], 12, 15, 19[2]
3:2, 11, 14[2], 17[3]

1 JOHN
1:3
2:1, 7[2], 13[3], 14[3], 18, 20[2], 21[2], 24[3], 27[3], 29[2]
3:5, 11, 15
4:2, 3, 4
5:13[3]

2 JOHN
6[2]

3 JOHN
12

JUDE
3, 5, 17, 20

REVELATION
2:10[2], 25
12:12[2]
18:4[2], 20
19:5[2], 18

YOU 5209

GENESIS
1:29[2]
9:2[2], 3[2], 7, 9[2], 10[2], 11, 12[2], 15
17:10[2], 11, 12
18:4
19:2, 7, 8[2], 14
22:5
23:4[2], 9
26:27
27:45
31:29
34:8, 9, 10[2], 15[2], 16[2]
35:2
37:6
40:8
41:55
42:2, 14, 16[2], 22, 34, 38
43:3, 5, 14, 23[2]
44:17[2], 23
45:4, 5, 7[2], 8, 12, 17, 18, 19
46:33
47:16, 23[2]
48:21[2]
49:1[2]
50:4, 20, 21, 24[2], 25

EXODUS
3:13, 14, 15, 16[2], 17, 19, 20
4:15
5:4, 10, 11, 18, 21
6:6[3], 7[3], 8[2]
7:4, 9[2]
8:28
9:8, 28
10:5[2], 10[3], 16, 24
11:1[3], 9
12:2[2], 13[4], 14, 16[2], 21, 22, 23, 25, 26, 31, 49
13:3, 19[2]
14:13, 14
16:4, 6, 8, 15, 23, 29[2], 32[2]
18:10
19:4[2]
20:20, 22, 23
22:24

EXODUS
23:13
24:8, 14[2]
26:33
29:42
30:32, 36
31:13[2], 14
32:29
35:2, 5, 10

LEVITICUS
1:2
8:33, 34
9:4, 6
10:7, 17
11:4, 5, 6, 7, 8, 10, 11, 12, 20, 23, 26, 27, 28, 29, 31, 35, 38, 45
14:34
16:29[2], 30[2], 31, 34
17:8, 10, 11, 12[2], 13
18:3, 6, 24, 26, 27, 28[2], 30
19:23, 25, 28, 34[3], 36
20:8, 14, 22[2], 23, 24[3], 25, 26
21:8
22:20, 25, 32, 33
23:10, 11, 15, 21, 27, 28, 32, 36, 40
25:2, 6, 10, 11, 12, 21, 38[2], 44, 45[2], 46
26:1[2], 4, 6, 7, 8[3], 9[4], 11[2], 12, 13[2], 16[2], 17[4], 18, 21, 22[3], 24[2], 25[2], 26, 28[2], 30, 33[2], 36, 38, 39

NUMBERS
1:4, 5
9:8, 10, 14
10:8, 9, 10, 29
11:18, 20[2]
12:6
13:17
14:25[2], 28, 29, 30, 32, 42, 43[2]
15:2, 14[2], 15[2], 16[2], 18, 23, 39, 41
16:3, 6, 7, 8, 9[3], 17, 24, 26, 45

NUMBERS
17:4, 5
18:4, 6, 7, 26, 27
20:10
22:8, 13[2], 19
25:18[2]
28:19, 22, 30, 31
29:1, 5, 8
32:21, 23, 24, 29[2], 30[2]
33:52, 53, 55[2], 56
34:2, 7, 17
35:11[2], 12, 29

DEUTERONOMY
1:7, 8, 9[2], 10, 11[3], 13[2], 15, 17, 18, 20, 22, 23, 29, 30[3], 33[3], 40[2], 42, 43, 44[3], 45
2:3, 4, 5, 13
3:18[2], 19, 20[2], 22
4:1[2], 2[2], 3, 4, 5, 8, 12, 13[2], 14, 15, 16, 20[2], 23[2], 26, 27[2], 34
5:4, 5[2], 30, 32, 33[2]
6:1, 14, 15, 20
7:4, 7[2], 8[3], 14, 21
8:19
9:8[2], 9, 10, 16[2], 19[2], 23[2], 24, 25
10:4, 15
11:4, 5, 8, 13, 14, 17[2], 22, 23, 25[4], 26, 27, 28, 31, 32
12:9, 10[2], 11, 12, 32
13:1, 3, 5[3], 7, 11, 13, 14
14:7, 8, 10, 19
15:4, 7
16:11
17:2, 7, 16
18:10
19:19, 20
20:4[3], 18
21:9, 21
22:21, 24
23:4, 10, 16
24:7, 8
26:11
27:1, 4
28:54, 56, 63[6], 68
29:4, 5[2], 10, 14, 18[2], 22

DEUTERONOMY
30:18, 19[2]
31:5, 19, 27, 29[2]
32:38, 46, 47

JOSHUA
1:3, 11[2], 13[3], 14, 15[2]
2:9[2], 10, 11, 12[2], 16[2]
3:4, 5, 10[2], 11, 12
4:2, 3[2], 5[2], 6, 23
5:9
6:10, 16
7:12[2], 13
8:8
9:7, 11, 12, 22, 23, 24[3]
18:3, 4, 6, 7, 8
20:2[2]
22:2[2], 4[2], 5, 16, 19, 25, 27, 28
23:3[2], 4, 5[2], 7, 9[3], 10[3], 12[2], 13[3], 14[2], 15[5], 16[3]
24:5, 7, 8[3], 9, 10[2], 11, 12[2], 13, 15[2], 20[3], 22, 23, 27

JUDGES
2:1[3], 3[2]
6:8[2], 9[4], 10
7:7
8:2, 3, 5, 19, 23[3], 24
9:2[4], 7, 15, 17[2], 19
10:11, 12[2], 13, 14
12:2
14:12[3]
15:7
19:9[2], 23, 24
20:12
21:21

RUTH
1:8, 9[2]
2:4, 7

1 SAMUEL
4:9
6:3[2], 4, 5, 21
7:3[2], 5
8:11, 18[2]

1 SAMUEL
9:12, 13
10:2, 15, 18[2], 19
11:2, 10[2]
12:1, 2[3], 3, 5, 7[2], 11, 12, 13, 14, 15, 17, 22, 23[2], 24
14:9, 12, 29
15:6[2]
17:8[2], 47
18:23
22:3, 7[2], 8[2]
23:22, 23
25:5, 19
30:24, 26

2 SAMUEL
1:21, 24
2:6[2]
3:17, 31
4:11
7:23
13:28[2]
15:27, 28
16:10, 20
17:21
18:2, 4
19:22
20:16
21:3, 4

1 KINGS
1:33
9:6
11:2
12:11[3], 14[2], 28
18:25
20:7
22:28

2 KINGS
1:6, 7[2]
2:18
5:7
6:19
7:12
10:2[3], 23

2 KINGS
11:5, 7
17:13, 36, 37, 38, 39
18:27, 29[2], 30, 32[2]
22:15, 18
25:24

1 CHRONICLES
12:17
13:2
22:18[2]
28:8

2 CHRONICLES
7:19
10:11[3], 14[2]
12:5
13:8[2], 9, 12
15:2[3]
19:6, 7, 10[2], 11[2]
20:15, 17[2]
23:4
24:20
28:10[3], 11
29:11
30:6, 8, 9
32:11, 14, 15[3]
34:23, 26
36:23

EZRA
1:3
4:2
5:3, 9
7:21, 24

NEHEMIAH
1:8, 9
4:12
5:10, 11
6:3
13:21, 27

ESTHER
8:8

JOB
6:28, 29
12:2, 3^{2}
13:2, 9, 10, 11^{2}
16:4^{2}, 5
17:10^{2}
27:5, 11
32:6, 12^{2}, 21
42:8^{3}

PSALMS
34:11
50:22
62:3
82:6
115:14^{2}
118:26
127:2
129:8^{2}

PROVERBS
1:23^{3}, 27
4:2
8:4

SONG OF SOLOMON
2:7
3:5
5:8
8:4

ISAIAH
1:15, 16^{2}
5:3, 5
7:13, 14
8:19
21:10
22:14
28:19
29:10, 11
30:11, 13, 16, 18^{2}, 20
31:7
32:11^{2}
33:11
35:4
36:12, 14^{2}, 15, 17, 18
40:21
41:24
42:9, 23
43:12
46:4^{2}
50:1, 10
51:2, 12
52:12
55:3, 12
59:2^{2}
61:6
65:12
66:5^{2}, 13

JEREMIAH
2:7, 9
3:12, 14^{3}, 15^{2}
4:8
5:15, 18, 25
6:17
7:3, 7, 13^{2}, 14, 15, 23^{2}, 25
8:17^{2}
10:1
11:4
14:13, 14
15:14
16:13^{2}
18:6, 11^{2}
21:4, 5, 8, 9, 14
23:2, 16^{2}, 17, 33, 38, 39^{4}, 40

JEREMIAH
25:3, 4, 5, 6, 27
26:4, 5, 13, 14, 15
27:9, 10^{3}, 14^{2}, 15^{2}, 16^{2}
29:7, 8^{2}, 9, 10^{3}, 11^{2}, 12, 14^{5}, 16, 21, 27, 31^{2}
34:16, 17^{2}, 21
35:14, 15^{2}, 18
37:7^{2}, 10, 19^{2}
38:5
40:3, 9
42:4^{4}, 10^{5}, 11^{3}, 12^{3}, 16^{2}, 18, 19^{2}, 21^{2}
44:4, 7^{2}, 10, 11, 23, 29^{3}
49:3, 30^{3}, 31
50:12

LAMENTATIONS
1:12, 18

EZEKIEL
5:7^{2}, 16^{2}, 17
6:3, 7, 9
11:7, 8, 9^{3}, 10, 11, 12, 15, 17^{3}, 19
13:8, 12, 15, 18
14:22, 23
18:30, 31^{2}
20:3, 20, 31^{2}, 33, 34^{2}, 35^{2}, 36, 37^{2}, 38, 39, 41^{4}, 42, 44
22:19, 20^{3}, 21^{2}, 22
23:49
24:24
33:20, 30
34:3, 17, 18
36:2, 3^{2}, 7, 9^{2}, 10, 11^{3}, 12, 13, 23, 24^{3}, 25^{2}, 26^{3}, 27^{2}, 29^{2}, 32, 33^{2}, 36
37:5, 6^{4}, 12^{2}, 13, 14^{2}
39:17, 19
43:27
44:6
45:9
47:14, 21, 22^{5}

DANIEL
2:9
3:4, 15
4:1
6:25

HOSEA
5:1, 13^{2}
10:12, 15
14:2

JOEL
2:19^{2}, 20, 23^{2}, 25^{2}, 26
3:13

AMOS
2:10^{2}, 13
3:1, 2^{2}
4:2^{2}, 5, 6, 7, 9, 10, 11
5:1, 14, 18^{2}, 27
6:14^{2}

JONAH
1:12^{2}

MICAH
1:2, 11
2:4, 10
3:1^{2}, 6^{2}, 9

HABAKKUK
1:5

ZEPHANIAH
2:2^{2}, 5
3:20^{3}

HAGGAI
1:4, 6, 10, 13
2:3, 4, 5^{2}, 15, 17, 19

ZECHARIAH
1:3
2:6, 8^{2}
4:9
6:7, 15
7:10
8:13, 14, 17, 23^{2}
9:12
11:7, 9

MALACHI
1:2, 6, 9, 10^{2}
2:1, 2, 3, 4, 9
3:5, 7, 10^{2}, 12
4:2, 5

MATTHEW
3:7, 9, 11^{2}
4:19
5:11^{3}, 12, 18, 20, 22, 28, 32, 34, 39, 44^{5}, 46
6:2, 5, 14, 16, 25, 27, 29, 30, 33
7:2, 6, 7^{2}, 9, 12, 15, 23
8:10, 11
9:29
10:13, 14, 15, 16, 17^{2}, 19^{2}, 20, 23^{2}, 27, 40, 42
11:9, 11, 17^{2}, 21, 22^{2}, 24, 28, 29
12:6, 11, 28, 31, 36
13:11, 17
15:7
16:11, 28
17:12, 17^{2}, 20^{2}
18:3, 10, 13, 18, 19^{2}, 35
19:8, 9, 23, 24, 28
20:4, 26^{2}, 27, 32
21:2, 3, 21, 24^{2}, 27, 31^{2}, 32, 43^{2}
22:31
23:3, 11, 13, 14, 15, 16, 23, 25, 27, 29, 34, 35, 36, 38, 39
24:2, 4, 9^{2}, 23, 25, 26, 34, 47
25:9, 12^{2}, 34, 40, 45
26:11, 13, 15, 21^{2}, 29^{2}, 32, 55, 64
27:17, 21
28:7^{2}, 14, 20^{2}

MARK
1:8^{2}, 17
3:28
4:11, 24^{2}
6:11^{3}
7:6, 14
8:12
9:1, 13, 19^{2}, 41^{2}
10:3, 5, 15, 29, 36, 43^{2}, 44
11:2, 3, 23, 24, 25, 29^{2}, 33
12:43
13:5, 9, 11^{3}, 21, 23, 30, 36, 37
14:7, 9, 13, 15, 18^{2}, 25, 28, 49
15:9
16:7^{2}

LUKE
2:10, 11, 12
3:7, 8, 13, 16^{2}
4:24, 25
6:9, 22^{3}, 24, 25^{2}, 26^{2}, 27^{2}, 28^{2}, 31, 32, 33, 38^{2}, 47

LUKE
7:9, 26, 28, 32^{2}
8:10
9:5, 27, 41^{2}, 48
10:3, 6, 8^{2}, 9, 10, 11^{2}, 12, 13, 14, 16^{2}, 19^{2}, 20, 24
11:5, 8, 9^{3}, 11, 20, 41, 42, 43, 44, 46, 51, 52
12:4, 5^{2}, 8, 11, 12, 14, 22, 25, 27, 28, 31, 32, 37, 44, 51
13:3, 5, 15, 24, 25^{2}, 27^{2}, 28, 35^{2}
14:5, 24, 28, 33
15:4, 7, 10
16:9^{2}, 12, 26^{2}
17:6, 7, 10, 21, 23, 34
18:8, 14, 17, 29
19:26, 30, 31, 40
20:3, 8
21:3, 12^{3}, 13, 15, 16, 32, 34
22:10, 12, 15, 16, 18, 19, 20, 26, 27, 29, 31^{2}, 35, 37, 53, 67, 68
23:14, 15
24:6, 36, 44^{2}, 49

JOHN
1:26, 51
2:5
3:12^{2}
4:35, 38
5:19, 24, 25, 38, 42^{2}, 45^{2}
6:26, 27, 32^{3}, 36, 47, 53^{2}, 61, 63, 64, 65, 70^{2}
7:7, 19^{2}, 22, 33
8:7, 24, 25, 26, 32, 34, 36, 37, 40, 45, 46, 51, 55, 58
9:27
10:1, 7, 25, 26, 32
12:8, 24, 35^{2}
13:12, 15^{2}, 16, 18, 19, 20, 21^{2}, 33^{2}, 34^{2}
14:2^{2}, 3^{2}, 9, 10, 12, 16^{2}, 17^{2}, 18^{2}, 20, 25^{2}, 26^{2}, 27^{3}, 28^{2}, 29, 30
15:3, 4, 7^{2}, 9, 11^{2}, 12, 14, 15^{3}, 16^{3}, 17, 18^{2}, 19^{2}, 20^{2}, 21, 26
16:1, 2^{2}, 3, 4^{4}, 5, 6, 7^{4}, 12, 13^{2}, 14, 15, 20, 22^{2}, 23^{2}, 25^{3}, 26^{2}, 27, 33
18:8, 39^{2}
19:4
20:19, 21^{2}, 26

THE ACTS
1:7, 8, 11
2:14, 22^{2}, 29, 38, 39
3:14, 16, 20, 22^{2}, 26^{3}
4:10^{2}, 11, 19
5:28, 38
6:3
7:37, 43
10:29
13:26^{2}, 32, 34, 38^{2}, 40, 41, 46^{2}
14:15^{2}
15:24, 25, 27, 28
16:36
17:3, 23
18:14, 21
19:13
20:18, 20^{3}, 26, 27, 28, 29, 32^{3}, 35
22:1, 25
23:15
24:21
25:5, 26
26:8
27:22^{2}, 34^{2}
28:20^{3}, 28

ROMANS
1:7, 8, 9, 10, 11^{2}, 12^{2}, 13^{3}, 15
2:24
6:14, 17
8:9, 10, 11^{2}
10:19^{2}
11:13
12:1, 3, 14, 18
15:5, 13, 14, 15^{2}, 22, 23, 24^{3}, 28, 29, 30, 32^{2}, 33
16:1, 2, 16, 17, 19, 20, 21, 22, 23^{2}, 24, 25

1 CORINTHIANS
1:3, 4, 6, 8, 10^{2}, 11^{2}, 12, 13, 14
2:1^{2}, 2, 3
3:1, 2, 3, 16, 18
4:3, 6, 8, 14^{2}, 15, 16, 17^{2}, 18, 19, 21
5:1, 2, 9, 11
6:1, 2, 5, 7, 11, 19
7:5, 28, 32, 35
9:2, 11, 12, 23
10:13^{2}, 27^{2}, 28
11:2^{2}, 3, 14, 17^{2}, 18, 19^{2}, 22^{3}, 23, 24, 30
12:1, 3, 21, 31
14:6^{3}, 25, 26, 36^{2}, 37
15:1^{2}, 2, 3, 12, 51
16:2, 5, 6, 7^{2}, 10, 12, 13, 15, 19^{2}, 20, 23, 24

2 CORINTHIANS
1:2, 7, 8, 13, 15, 16^{3}, 18, 19, 21, 23
2:1, 2, 3^{3}, 4^{2}, 5, 8, 9
3:1^{2}
4:12, 14
5:12^{2}, 20^{2}
6:1, 11, 17, 18
7:3^{2}, 4^{2}, 7, 8^{2}, 11, 12^{3}, 13, 14^{2}, 15^{2}, 16
8:1, 6, 10, 16, 17, 22, 23
9:1, 2, 3, 4, 5, 8, 14^{3}
10:1^{3}, 2, 9, 13, 14^{2}, 15, 16
11:2^{3}, 6, 7, 8, 9^{2}, 11, 20^{4}
12:11, 12, 13, 14^{3}, 15^{2}, 16^{2}, 17^{2}, 18, 19, 20^{2}, 21
13:1, 2^{2}, 3, 4, 5, 11, 13, 14

GALATIANS
1:3, 6, 7, 8^{2}, 9, 11, 20
2:5
3:1^{2}, 2, 5^{2}, 27
4:11^{2}, 12, 13, 15, 16, 17^{2}, 18, 19, 20^{2}
5:2^{2}, 4^{2}, 7, 8, 10^{2}, 12, 21^{2}
6:11, 12, 13

EPHESIANS
1:2, 16^{2}, 17
2:1, 17
3:1, 13, 16
4:1, 6, 31, 32
5:3, 6, 33
6:13, 21, 22

PHILIPPIANS
1:2, 3, 4, 6, 7^{2}, 8, 24, 25, 26, 27, 28, 29
2:5, 13, 17, 19, 25, 26
3:1^{2}, 15, 18^{2}
4:9, 18, 21, 22, 23

COLOSSIANS
1:2, 3, 5, 6^{2}, 7, 9, 21, 22, 24, 25, 27

COLOSSIANS
2:1, 4, 5, 8, 13^{2}, 16, 18
3:13, 16
4:7, 8, 9^{2}, 10^{2}, 12^{3}, 13, 14, 16, 18

1 THESSALONIANS
1:1, 2^{2}, 5^{2}, 8, 9
2:1, 2, 6, 7, 8^{2}, 9^{2}, 10, 11, 12, 13, 17, 18
3:2^{2}, 4^{2}, 5, 6^{2}, 7, 9, 11, 12^{2}
4:1^{2}, 2, 4, 6, 9, 10, 11, 13, 15
5:1, 4, 12^{4}, 14, 18, 23, 24, 27, 28

2 THESSALONIANS
1:2, 3^{2}, 4, 6, 7, 10, 11^{2}, 12
2:1, 3, 5^{2}, 13^{2}, 14, 17
3:1, 3^{2}, 4^{2}, 6, 7, 8, 9, 10^{2}, 11, 16^{2}, 18

2 TIMOTHY
4:22

TITUS
2:8
3:15

PHILEMON
3, 6, 22

HEBREWS
3:12, 13
4:1
5:12
6:9, 11
9:20
12:5, 7, 15
13:7^{2}, 17^{2}, 19^{2}, 21^{2}, 22^{2}, 23, 24^{2}, 25

JAMES
1:5, 26
2:6^{2}, 16
3:13
4:1, 7, 8, 10
5:1, 3, 4, 6, 13, 14, 19

1 PETER
1:2, 4, 10, 12^{2}, 13, 15, 20, 25
2:7, 9, 11, 12
3:13, 15^{2}, 16
4:4, 12^{2}, 14, 15
5:1, 2, 5, 6, 7, 10^{2}, 12, 13^{2}, 14

2 PETER
1:2, 8^{2}, 11, 12, 13^{2}, 16
2:1, 3, 13
3:1, 15

1 JOHN
1:2, 3, 4, 5
2:1, 7, 8^{2}, 12^{2}, 13^{3}, 14^{3}, 21, 24^{2}, 26^{2}, 27^{4}
3:7, 13
4:4
5:13

2 JOHN
3, 10, 12^{2}

JUDE
2, 3^{3}, 5, 12, 18, 24^{2}

REVELATION
1:4
2:10, 13, 23, 24^{2}
12:12
18:6, 20
22:16, 21

DICTIONARY

OF

THE HEBREW BIBLE

A CONCISE

DICTIONARY

OF THE WORDS IN

THE HEBREW BIBLE;

WITH THEIR RENDERINGS

IN THE

AUTHORIZED ENGLISH VERSION.

BY

JAMES STRONG, S.T.D., LL.D.

PREFACE.

This work, although prepared as a companion to the Exhaustive Concordance, to which it is specially adapted, is here paged and printed so that it can be bound separately, in the belief that a brief and simple Dictionary of the Biblical Hebrew and Chaldee will be useful to students and others, who do not care at all times to consult a more copious and elaborate Lexicon; and it will be particularly serviceable to many who are unable to turn conveniently and rapidly, amid the perplexities and details of foreign characters with which the pages of Gesenius and Fürst bristle, to the fundamental and essential points of information that they are seeking. Even scholars will find here, not only all of a strictly verbal character which they most frequently want in ordinary consultation of a lexicon, but numerous original suggestions, relations, and distinctions, carefully made and clearly put, which are not unworthy of their attention, especially in the affinities of roots and the classification of meanings. The portable form and moderate cost of the book, it is hoped, will facilitate its use with all classes. The vocabulary is complete as to the ground-forms that actually occur in the biblical text (or *Kethib*), with the pointing that properly belongs to them. Their designation by numbers will especially aid those who are not very familiar with the original language, and the Anglicizing and pronunciation of the words will not come amiss to multitudes who have some acquaintance with it. The addition of the renderings in the common version will greatly contribute to fixing and extending the varied significations and applications of the Hebrew and Chaldee words, as well as to correcting their occasionally wrong translations. On this account, as well as for the sake of precision and to prevent repetition, the use of the same terms in the preceding definitions has been avoided wherever practicable. The design of the volume, being purely *lexical*, does not include grammatical, archæological, or exegetical details, which would have swelled its size and encumbered its plan.

By observing the subjoined directions, in the associated use of the Main and Comparative Concordances, the reader will have substantially a Concordance-Dictionary of both the Authorized and the Revised English Versions, as well as of the Hebrew Bible.

PLAN OF THE BOOK.

1. All the original words are treated in their alphabetical Hebrew order, and are numbered regularly from the first to the last, each being known throughout by its appropriate number. This renders reference easy without recourse to the Hebrew characters.

2. Immediately after each word is given its exact equivalent in English letters, according to the system of transliteration laid down in the scheme here following, which is substantially that adopted in the Common English Version, only more consistently and uniformly carried out; so that the word could readily be turned back again into Hebrew from the form thus given it.

3. Next follows the precise pronunciation, according to the usual English mode of sounding syllables, so plainly indicated that none can fail to apprehend and apply it. The most approved sounds are adopted, as laid down in the annexed scheme of articulation, and in such a way that any good Hebraist would immediately recognize the word if so pronounced, notwithstanding the minor variations current among scholars in this respect.

4. Then ensues a tracing of the etymology, radical meaning, and applied signification of the word, justly but tersely analyzed and expressed, with any other important peculiarities in this regard.

5. In the case of proper names, the same method is pursued, and at this point the regular mode of Anglicizing it, after the general style of the Common English Version, is given, and a few words of explanation are added to identify it.

6. Finally (after the punctuation-mark :—) are given all the different renderings of the word in the Authorized English Version, arranged in the alphabetical order of the leading terms, and conveniently condensed according to the explanations given below.

By searching out these various renderings in the MAIN CONCORDANCE, to which this Dictionary is designed as a companion, and noting the passages to which the same number corresponding to that of any given Hebrew word is attached in the marginal column, the reader, whether acquainted with the original language or not, will obtain a complete *Hebrew Concordance* also, expressed in the words of the Common English Version. This is an advantage which no other Concordance or Lexicon affords.

HEBREW ARTICULATION.

The following explanations are sufficient to show the method of transliterating Hebrew words into English adopted in this *Dictionary*.

1. The Hebrew is read *from right to left*. The Alphabet consists of 22 letters (and their variations), which are all regarded as *consonants*, being enunciated by the aid of certain "points" or marks, mostly beneath the letters, and which serve as *vowels*. There is no distinction of *capitals*, *italics*, etc.

2. The letters are as follows:

No.	Form.	Name.	Transliteration and Power.
1.	א	'Aleph (*aw'-lef*)	**'** unappreciable
2.	ב	Bêyth (*bayth*)	**b**
3.	ג	Gîymel (*ghee'-mel*)	**g** hard = γ
4.	ד	Dâleth (*daw'-leth*)	**d** [cent
5.	ה	Hê' (*hay*)	**h**, often quies-
6.	ו	Vâv (*vawv*)	**v**, or **w** quies-
7.	ז	Zayin (*zah'-yin*)	**z**, as in *zeal* [cent
8.	ח	Chêyth (*khayth*)	German **ch** = χ [(nearly *kh*)
9.	ט	Têyth (*tayth*)	**ṭ** = תּ [cent
10.	י	Yôwd (*yode*)	**y**, often quies-
11.	כ, final ך	Kaph (*caf*)	**k** = ק
12.	ל	Lâmed (*law'-med*)	**l**
13.	מ, final ם	Mêm (*mame*)	**m**
14.	נ, final ן	Nûwn (*noon*)	**n**
15.	ס	Çâmek (*saw'-mek*)	**ç** = *s* sharp = שׂ
16.	ע	'Ayin (*ah'-yin*)	**'** peculiar *
17. {	פ, final ף	Phê' (*fay*)	**ph** = *f* = φ
	פּ	Pê' (*pay*)	**p**
18.	צ, final ץ	Tsâdêy (*tsaw-day'*)	**ts**
19.	ק	Qôwph (*cofe*)	**q** = *k* = כ
20.	ר	Rêysh (*raysh*)	**r**
21. {	שׂ	Sîyn (*seen*)	**s** sharp = ס = σ
	שׁ	Shîyn (*sheen*)	**sh**
22. {	ת	Thâv (*thawv*)	**th**, as in THin
	תּ	Tâv (*tawv*)	**t** = ט = τ [= ϑ

* The letter *'Ayin*, owing to the difficulty experienced by Occidentals in pronouncing it accurately (it is a deep guttural sound, like that made in *gargling*), is generally neglected (i.e. passed over silently) in reading. We have represented it to the eye (but not exactly to the ear) by the Greek *rough breathing* (for distinctness and typographical convenience, a reversed *apostrophe*) in order to distinguish it from *'Âleph*, which is likewise treated as silent, being similarly represented by the Greek *smooth breathing* (the *apostrophe*).

3. The *vowel-points* are the following:

Form.*	Name.		Representation and Power.
(ָ)	Qâmêts	(*caw-mates'*)	**â**, as in ALL
(ַ)	Pattach	(*pat'-takh*)	**a**, as in mAn, (*fãr*)
(ֲ)	Shᵉvâ'-Pattach	(*she-vaw' pat'-takh*)	**ă**, as in hAt
(ֵ)	Tsêrêy	(*tsay-ray'*)	**ê**, as in thEy = η
(ֶ)	Çegôwl	(*seg-ole'*)	{ **e**, as in *thEir* **e**, as in *mEn* = ε
(ֱ)	Shᵉvâ'-Çegôwl	(*she-vaw' seg-ole'*)	**ĕ**, as in *mEt*
(ְ)	Shᵉvâ' †	(*she-vaw'*)	{ ᵉ obscure, as in [*avErage* silent, as *e* in *madE*
(ִ)	Chîyriq	(*khee'-rik*)	{ **î**, as in *machIne* ‡ **i**, as in *supplIant*, [(*mïsery*, *hĭt*)
(ֹ)	Chôwlem §	(*kho'-lem*)	**ô**, as in *no* = ω
(ָ)	Short Qâmêts ‖		**o**, as in *nor* = ο
(ֳ)	Shᵉvâ'-Qâmêts	(*she-vaw' caw-mates'*)	**ŏ**, as in *not*
(ּ)	Shûwrêq *	(*shoo-rake'*)	**û**, as in *cruel*
(ֻ)	Qibbûts *	(*kib'-boots*)	**u**, as in *full*, *rūde*

* The parenthesis-marks ( ) are given here in order to show the place of the vowel-points, whether below, above, or in the middle of the letter.

† *Silent Shᵉvâ'* is not represented by any mark in our method of transliteration, as it is understood whenever there is no other vowel-point.

‡ *Chîyriq* is thus long only when it is followed by a quiescent *yôwd* (either expressed or implied).

§ *Chôwlem* is written *fully* only over *Vâv*, which is then quiescent (*w*); but when used "defectively" (without the *Vâv*) it may be written either over the left-hand corner of the letter to which it belongs, or over the right-hand corner of the following one.

‖ Short *Qâmêts* is found only *in unaccented syllables ending with a consonant sound.*

4. A point in the bosom of a letter is called *Dâgêsh'*, and is of two kinds, which must be carefully distinguished.

a. Dâgêsh *lenè* occurs only in the letters בּ, גּ, דּ, כּ, פּ, תּ, (technically vocalized *Bᵉgad'-Kᵉphath'*,) when they *begin* a clause or sentence, or are preceded by a consonant *sound;* and simply has the effect of removing their aspiration.†

b. Dâgêsh *fortè* may occur in any letter except א, ה, ח, ע or ר; it is equivalent to *doubling* the letter, and at the same time it removes the aspiration of a Bᵉgad-Kᵉphath letter.‡

5. The *Maqqêph'* (־), like a *hyphen*, unites words only for purposes of pronunciation (by removing the primary accent from all except the last of them), but does not affect their meaning or their grammatical construction.

* *Shûwrêq* is written only in the bosom of *Vâv*. Sometimes it is said to be "defectively" written (without the *Vâv*), and then takes the form of *Qibbûts*, which in such cases is called *vicarious*.

† In our system of transliteration Dâgêsh *lenè* is represented only in the letters פּ and תּ, because elsewhere it does not affect the pronunciation (with most Hebraists).

‡ A point in the bosom of הּ is called *Mappîyq* (*mappeek'*). It occurs only in the final vowelless letter of a few words, and we have represented it by *hh*. A Dâgêsh *fortè* in the bosom of וּ may easily be distinguished from the vowel *Shûwrêq* by noticing that in the former case the letter has a proper vowel-point accompanying it.

It should be noted that both kinds of Dâgêsh are often omitted in writing (being then said to be *implied*), but (in the case at least of Dâgêsh *fortè*) the word is (by most Hebraists) pronounced the same as if it were present.

ABBREVIATIONS EMPLOYED.

abb. = abbreviated, abbreviation
absol. = absolute, absolutely
abstr. = abstract, abstractly
act. = active, actively
adj. = adjective, adjectively
adv. = adverb, adverbial, adverbially
aff. = affix, affixed
affin. = affinity
appar. = apparent, apparently
arch. = architecture, architectural, architecturally
art. = article.
artif. = artificial, artificially
Ass. = Assyrian
A. V. = Authorized Version
Bab. = Babylon, Babylonia, Babylonian
caus. = causative, causatively
Chald. = Chaldaism, Chaldee
collat. = collateral, collaterally
collect. = collective, collectively
comp. = compare, comparative, comparatively, comparison
concr. = concrete, concretely
conjec. = conjecture, conjectural, conjecturally
conjug. = conjugation, conjugational, conjugationally
conjunc. = conjunction, conjunctional, conjunctionally
constr. = construct, construction, constructive, constructively
contr. = contracted, contraction
correl. = correlated, correlation, correlative, correlatively
corresp. = corresponding, correspondingly
def. = definite, definitely
denom. = denominative, denominatively
der. = derivation, derivative, derivatively
desc. = descendant, descendants
E. = East, Eastern
e. g. = *exempli gratiâ*, for example
Eg. = Egypt, Egyptian, Egyptians
ellip. = ellipsis, elliptical, elliptically
equiv. = equivalent, equivalently
err. = erroneous, erroneously, error
esp. = especial, especially
etym. = etymology, etymological, etymologically
euphem. = euphemism, euphemistic, euphemistically
euphon. = euphonically, euphonious
extern. = external, externally
infer. = inference, inferential, inferentially
fem. = feminine
fig. = figurative, figuratively
for. = foreign, foreigner
freq. = frequentative, frequentatively
fut. = future
gen. = general, generally, generical, generically
Gr. = Græcism, Greek
gut. = guttural
Heb. = Hebraism, Hebrew
i.e. = *id est*, that is
ident. = identical, identically
immed. = immediate, immediately
imper. = imperative, imperatively
impl. = implication, implied, impliedly
incept. = inceptive, inceptively
incl. = including, inclusive, inclusively
indef. = indefinite, indefinitely
infin. = infinitive
inhab. = inhabitant, inhabitants
ins. = inserted
intens. = intensive, intensively
intern. = internal, internally
interj. = interjection, interjectional, interjectionally
intr. = intransitive, intransitively
Isr. = Israelite, Israelites, Israelitish
Jerus. = Jerusalem
Levit. = Levitical, Levitically
lit. = literal, literally
marg. = margin, marginal (reading)
masc. = masculine
mean. = meaning
ment. = mental, mentally
mid. = middle
modif. = modified, modification
mor. = moral, morally
mus. = musical
nat. = native, natural, naturally, nature
neg. = negative, negatively
obj. = object, objective, objectively
or. = origin, original, originally
orth. = orthography, orthographical, orthographically
Pal. = Palestine
part. = participle
pass. = passive, passively
patron. = patronymic, patronymically
perh. = perhaps
perm. = permutation (of allied letters)
pers. = person, personal, personally
Pers. = Persia, Persian, Persians
phys. = physical, physically
plur. = plural
poet. = poetry, poetical, poetically
pos. = positive, positively
pref. = prefix, prefixed
prep. = preposition, prepositional, prepositionally
prim. = primitive
prob. = probable, probably
prol. = prolonged, prolongation
pron. = pronominal, pronominally, pronoun
prox. = proximate, proximately
rad. = radical
recip. = reciprocal, reciprocally
redupl. = reduplicated, reduplication
refl. = reflexive, reflexively
rel. = relative, relatively
relig. = religion, religious, religiously
second. = secondarily, secondary
signif. = signification, signifying
short. = shortened, shorter
sing. = singular
spec. = specific, specifically
streng. = strengthening
subdiv. = subdivision, subdivisional, subdivisionally
subj. = subject, subjective, subjectively
substit. = substituted.
superl. = superlative, superlatively
symb. = symbolical, symbolically
tech. = technical, technically
tran. = transitive, transitively
transc. = transcription
transp. = transposed, transposition
unc. = uncertain, uncertainly
var. = variation.

SIGNS EMPLOYED.

+ (*addition*) denotes a rendering in the A. V. of one or more Heb. words in connection with the one under consideration.

× (*multiplication*) denotes a rendering in the A. V. that results from an idiom peculiar to the Heb.

° (*degree*), appended to a Heb. word, denotes a vowel-pointing corrected from that of the text. (This mark is set in Heb. Bibles over syllables in which the vowels of the marg. have been inserted instead of those properly belonging to the text.)

( ) (*parenthesis*), in the renderings from the A. V., denotes a word or syllable sometimes given in connection with the principal word to which it is annexed.

[ ] (*bracket*), in the rendering from the A. V., denotes the inclusion of an additional word in the Heb.

Italics, at the end of a rendering from the A. V., denote an explanation of the variations from the usual form.

HEBREW AND CHALDEE DICTIONARY

ACCOMPANYING

THE EXHAUSTIVE CONCORDANCE.

א

1. אָב **'âb**, *awb;* a prim. word; *father* in a lit. and immed., or fig. and remote application):—chief, (fore-) father ([-less]), × patrimony, principal. Comp. names in "Abi-".

2. אַב **'ab** (Chald.), *ab;* corresp. to 1:—father.

3. אֵב **'êb**, *abe;* from the same as 24; a *green* plant:—greenness, fruit.

4. אֵב **'êb** (Chald.), *abe;* corresp. to 3:—fruit.

אֹב **'ôb**. See 178.

5. אֲבַגְתָא **'Ăbagthâ'**, *ab-ag-thaw';* of for. or.; *Abagtha*, a eunuch of Xerxes:—Abagtha.

6. אָבַד **'âbad**, *aw-bad';* a prim. root; prop. to *wander* away, i.e. *lose* oneself; by impl. to *perish* (caus. *destroy*):—break, destroy (-uction), + not escape, fail, lose, (cause to, make) perish, spend, × and surely, take, be undone, × utterly, be void of, have no way to flee.

7. אֲבַד **'ăbad** (Chald.), *ab-ad';* corresp. to 6:—destroy, perish.

8. אֹבֵד **'ôbêd**, *o-bade';* act. part. of 6; (concr.) *wretched* or (abstr.) *destruction:*—perish.

9. אֲבֵדָה **'ăbêdâh**, *ab-ay-daw';* from 6; concr. something *lost;* abstr. *destruction*, i.e. Hades:—lost. Comp. 10.

10. אֲבַדֹּה **'ăbaddôh**, *ab-ad-do';* the same as 9, miswritten for 11; a *perishing:*—destruction.

11. אֲבַדּוֹן **'ăbaddôwn**, *ab-ad-done';* intens. from 6; abstr. a *perishing;* concr. Hades:—destruction.

12. אַבְדָן **'abdân**, *ab-dawn';* from 6; a *perishing:*—destruction.

13. אׇבְדָן **'obdân**, *ob-dawn';* from 6; a *perishing:*—destruction.

14. אָבָה **'âbâh**, *aw-baw';* a prim. root; to *breathe* after, i.e. (fig.) to *be acquiescent:*—consent, rest content, will, be willing.

15. אָבֶה **'âbeh**, *aw-beh';* from 14; *longing:*—desire.

16. אֵבֶה **'êbeh**, *ay-beh';* from 14 (in the sense of *bending* towards); the *papyrus:*—swift.

17. אֲבוֹי **'ăbôwy**, *ab-o'ee;* from 14 (in the sense of *desiring*); *want:*—sorrow.

18. אֵבוּס **'êbûwç**, *ay-booce';* from 75; a *manger* or *stall:*—crib.

19. אִבְחָה **'ibchâh**, *ib-khaw';* from an unused root (appar. mean. to *turn*); *brandishing* of a sword:—point.

20. אֲבַטִּיחַ **'ăbaṭṭîyach**, *ab-at-tee'-akh;* of uncert. der.; a *melon* (only plur.):—melon.

21. אֲבִי **'Ăbîy**, *ab-ee';* from 1; *fatherly; Abi*, Hezekiah's mother:—Abi.

22. אֲבִיאֵל **'Ăbîy'êl**, *ab-ee-ale';* from 1 and 410; *father* (i.e. *possessor*) *of God; Abiel*, the name of two Isr.:—Abiel.

23. אֲבִיאָסָף **'Ăbîy'âçâph**, *ab-ee-aw-sawf';* from 1 and 622; *father of gathering* (i.e. *gatherer*); *Abiasaph*, an Isr.:—Abiasaph.

24. אָבִיב **'âbîyb**, *aw-beeb';* from an unused root (mean. to *be tender*); *green*, i.e. a young *ear* of grain; hence the name of the month *Abib* or Nisan:—Abib, ear, green ears of corn.

25. אֲבִי גִבְעוֹן **'Ăbîy Gib'ôwn**, *ab-ee' ghib-one';* from 1 and 1391; *father* (i.e. *founder*) *of Gibon; Abi-Gibon*, perh. an Isr.:—father of Gibeon.

26. אֲבִיגַיִל **'Ăbîygayil**, *ab-ee-gah'-yil*, or shorter אֲבִיגַל **'Ăbîygal**, *ab-ee-gal';* from 1 and 1524; *father* (i.e. *source*) *of joy; Abigail* or *Abigal*, the name of two Israelitesses:—Abigal.

27. אֲבִידָן **'Ăbîydân**, *ab-ee-dawn';* from 1 and 1777; *father of judgment* (i.e. *judge*); *Abidan*, an Isr.:—Abidan.

28. אֲבִידָע **'Ăbîydâ'**, *ab-ee-daw';* from 1 and 3045; *father of knowledge* (i.e. *knowing*); *Abida*, a son of Abraham by Keturah:—Abida, Abidah.

29. אֲבִיָּה **'Ăbîyâh**, *ab-ee-yaw';* or prol. אֲבִיָּהוּ **'Ăbîyâhûw**, *ab-ee-yaw'-hoo;* from 1 and 3050; *father* (i.e. *worshipper*) *of Jah; Abijah*, the name of several Isr. men and two Israelitesses:—Abiah, Abijah.

30. אֲבִיהוּא **'Ăbîyhûw'**, *ab-ee-hoo';* from 1 and 1931; *father* (i.e. *worshipper*) of *Him* (i.e. *God*); *Abihu*, a son of Aaron:—Abihu.

31. אֲבִיהוּד **'Ăbîyhûwd**, *ab-ee-hood';* from 1 and 1935; *father* (i.e. *possessor*) *of renown; Abihud*, the name of two Isr.:—Abihud.

32. אֲבִיהַיִל **'Ăbîyhayil**, *ab-ee-hah'-yil;* or (more correctly) אֲבִיחַיִל **'Ăbîychayil**, *ab-ee-khah'-yil;* from 1 and 2428; *father* (i.e. *possessor*) *of might; Abihail* or *Abichail*, the name of three Isr. and two Israelitesses:—Abihail.

33. אֲבִי הָעֶזְרִי **'Ăbîy hâ-'Ezrîy**, *ab-ee'-haw-ez-ree';* from 44 with the art. inserted; *father of the Ezrite;* an *Abiezrite* or descendant of Abiezer:—Abiezrite.

34. אֶבְיוֹן **'ebyôwn**, *eb-yone';* from 14, in the sense of *want* (espec. in feeling); *destitute:*—beggar, needy, poor (man).

35. אֲבִיּוֹנָה **'abîyôwnâh**, *ab-ee-yo-naw';* from 14; provocative of *desire;* the *caper* berry (from its *stimulative* taste):—desire.

אֲבִיחַיִל **'Ăbîychayil**. See 32.

36. אֲבִיטוּב **'Ăbîyṭûwb**, *ab-ee-toob';* from 1 and 2898; *father of goodness* (i.e. *good*); *Abitub*, an Isr.:—Abitub.

37. אֲבִיטַל **'Ăbîyṭâl**, *ab-ee-tal';* from 1 and 2919; *father of dew* (i.e. *fresh*); *Abital*, a wife of King David:—Abital.

38. אֲבִיָּם **'Ăbîyâm**, *ab-ee-yawm';* from 1 and 3220; *father of* (the) *sea* (i.e. *seaman*); *Abijam* (or Abijah), a king of Judah:—Abijam.

39. אֲבִימָאֵל **'Ăbîymâ'êl**, *ab-ee-maw-ale';* from 1 and an elsewhere unused (prob. for.) word; *father of Mael* (appar. some Arab tribe); *Abimael*, a son of Joktan:—Abimael.

40. אֲבִימֶלֶךְ **'Ăbîymelek**, *ab-ee-mel'-ek;* from 1 and 4428; *father of* (the) *king; Abimelek*, the name of two Philistine kings and of two Isr.:—Abimelech.

41. אֲבִינָדָב **'Ăbîynâdâb**, *ab-ee-naw-dawb';* from 1 and 5068; *father of generosity* (i.e. *liberal*); *Abinadab*, the name of four Isr.:—Abinadab.

42. אֲבִינֹעַם **'Ăbîynô'am**, *ab-ee-no'-am;* from 1 and 5278; *father of pleasantness* (i.e. *gracious*); *Abinoam*, an Isr.:—Abinoam.

אֲבִינֵר **'Ăbîynêr**. See 74.

43. אֶבְיָסָף **'Ebyâçâph**, *eb-yaw-sawf';* contr. from 23; *Ebjasaph*, an Isr.:—Ebiasaph.

44. אֲבִיעֶזֶר **'Ăbîy'ezer**, *ab-ee-ay'-zer;* from 1 and 5829; *father of help* (i.e. *helpful*); *Abiezer*, the name of two Isr.:—Abiezer.

45. אֲבִי־עַלְבוֹן **'Ăbîy-'albôwn**, *ab-ee-al-bone';* from 1 and an unused root of unc. der.; prob. *father of strength* (i.e. *valiant*); *Abialbon*, an Isr.:—Abialbon.

46. אָבִיר **'âbîyr**, *aw-beer';* from 82; *mighty* (spoken of God):—mighty (one).

47. אַבִּיר **'abbîyr**, *ab-beer';* for 46:—angel, bull, chiefest, mighty (one), stout [-hearted], strong (one), valiant.

48. אֲבִירָם **'Ăbîyrâm**, *ab-ee-rawm';* from 1 and 7311; *father of height* (i.e. *lofty*); *Abiram*, the name of two Isr.:—Abiram.

49. אֲבִישַׁג **'Ăbîyshag**, *ab-ee-shag';* from 1 and 7686; *father of error* (i.e. *blundering*); *Abishag*, a concubine of David:—Abishag.

50. אֲבִישׁוּעַ **'Ăbîyshûwac**, *ab-ee-shoo'-ah;* from 1 and 7771; *father of plenty* (i.e. *prosperous*); *Abishua*, the name of two Isr.:—Abishua.

51. אֲבִישׁוּר **'Ăbîyshûwr**, *ab-ee-shoor';* from 1 and 7791; *father of* (the) *wall* (i.e. perh. *mason*); *Abishur*, an Isr.:—Abishur.

52. אֲבִישַׁי **'Ăbîyshay**, *ab-ee-shah'ee;* or (shorter) אַבְשַׁי **'Abshay**, *ab-shah'ee;* from 1 and 7862; *father of a gift* (i.e. prob. *generous*); *Abishai*, an Isr.:—Abishai.

53. אֲבִישָׁלוֹם **'Ăbîyshâlôwm**, *ab-ee-shaw-lome';* or (short.) אַבְשָׁלוֹם **'Abshâlôwm**, *ab-shaw-lome';* from 1 and 7965; *father of peace* (i.e. *friendly*); *Abshalom*, a son of David; also (the fuller form) a later Isr.:—Abishalom, Absalom.

54. אֶבְיָתָר **'Ebyâthâr**, *eb-yaw-thawr';* contr. from 1 and 3498; *father of abundance* (i.e. *liberal*); *Ebjathar*, an Isr.:—Abiathar.

55. אָבַךְ **'âbak**, *aw-bak';* a prim. root; prob. to *coil* upward:—mount up.

56. אָבַל **'âbal**, *aw-bal';* a prim. root; to *bewail:*—lament, mourn.

57. אָבֵל **'âbêl**, *aw-bale';* from 56; *lamenting:*—mourn (-er, -ing).

58. אָבֵל **'âbêl**, *aw-bale';* from an unused root (mean. to *be grassy*); a *meadow:*—plain. Comp. also the prop. names beginning with Abel-.

59. אָבֵל **'Âbêl**, *aw-bale';* from 58; a *meadow; Abel*, the name of two places in Pal.:—Abel.

60. אֵבֶל **'êbel**, *ay'-bel;* from 56; *lamentation:*—mourning.

61. אֲבָל **'ăbâl**, *ab-awl';* appar. from 56 through the idea of *negation; nay*, i.e. *truly* or *yet:*—but, indeed, nevertheless, verily.

62. אָבֵל בֵּית־מַעֲכָה **'Âbêl Bêyth-Ma'ăkâh**, *aw-bale' bayth ma-a-kaw';* from 58 and 1004 and 4601; *meadow of Beth-Maakah; Abel of Beth-maakah*, a place in Pal.:—Abel-beth-maachah, Abel of Beth-maachah.

63. אָבֵל הַשִּׁטִּים **'Âbêl hash-Shiṭṭîym,** *aw-bale' hash-shit-teem';* from 58 and the plur. of 7848, with the art. ins.; *meadow of the acacias; Abel hash-Shittim,* a place in Pal.:—Abel-shittim.

64. אָבֵל כְּרָמִים **'Âbêl Kᵉrâmîym,** *aw-bale' ker-aw-meem';* from 58 and the plur. of 3754; *meadow of vineyards; Abel-Keramim,* a place in Pal.:—plain of the vineyards.

65. אָבֵל מְחוֹלָה **'Âbêl Mᵉchôwlâh,** *aw-bale' mekh-o-law';* from 58 and 4246; *meadow of dancing; Abel-Mecholah,* a place in Pal.:—Abel-meholah.

66. אָבֵל מַיִם **'Âbêl Mayim,** *aw-bale' mah'-yim;* from 58 and 4325; *meadow of water; Abel-Majim,* a place in Pal.:—Abel-maim.

67. אָבֵל מִצְרַיִם **'Âbêl Mitsrayim,** *aw-bale' mits-rah'-yim;* from 58 and 4714; *meadow of Egypt; Abel-Mitsrajim,* a place in Pal.:—Abel-mizraim.

68. אֶבֶן **'eben,** *eh'-ben;* from the root of 1129 through the mean. to *build; a stone:*—+ carbuncle, + mason, + plummet, [chalk-, hail-, head-, sling-] stone (-ny), (divers) weight (-s).

69. אֶבֶן **'eben** (Chald.), *eh'-ben;* corresp. to 68:—stone.

70. אֹבֶן **'ôben,** *o'-ben;* from the same as 68; *a pair of stones* (only dual); a potter's *wheel* or a midwife's *stool* (consisting alike of two horizontal disks with a support between):—wheel, stool.

71. אֲבָנָה **'Abânâh,** *ab-aw-naw';* perh. fem. of 68; *stony; Abanah,* a river near Damascus:—Abana. Comp. 549.

72. אֶבֶן הָעֵזֶר **'Eben hâ-'êzer,** *eh'-ben haw-e'-zer;* from 68 and 5828 with the art. ins.; *stone of the help; Eben-ha-Ezer,* a place in Pal.:—Ebenezer.

73. אַבְנֵט **'abnêṭ,** *ab-nate';* of uncert. deriv.; a *belt:*—girdle.

74. אַבְנֵר **'Abnêr,** *ab-nare';* or (fully) אֲבִינֵר **'Âbîynêr,** *ab-ee-nare';* from 1 and 5216; *father of light* (i.e. *enlightening*); *Abner,* an Isr.:—Abner.

75. אָבַס **'âbaç,** *aw-bas';* a prim. root; to *fodder:*—fatted, stalled.

76. אֲבַעְבֻּעָה **'aba'bû'âh,** *ab-ah-boo-aw';* (by redupl.) from an unused root (mean. to *belch* forth); an inflammatory *pustule* (as *eruption*):—blains.

77. אֶבֶץ **'Ebets,** *eh'-bets;* from an unused root prob. mean. to *gleam; conspicuous; Ebets,* a place in Pal.:—Abez.

78. אִבְצָן **'Ibtsân,** *ib-tsawn';* from the same as 76; *splendid; Ibtsan,* an Isr.:—Ibzan.

79. אָבַק **'âbaq,** *aw-bak';* a prim. root; prob. to *float* away (as vapor), but used only as denom. from 80; to *bedust,* i.e. *grapple:*—wrestle.

80. אָבָק **'âbâq,** *aw-bawk';* from root of 79; light *particles* (as *volatile*):—(small) dust, powder.

81. אֲבָקָה **'abâqâh,** *ab-aw-kaw';* fem. of 80:—powder.

82. אָבַר **'âbar,** *aw-bar';* a prim. root; to *soar:*—fly.

83. אֵבֶר **'êber,** *ay-ber';* from 82; a *pinion:*—[long-] wing (-ed).

84. אֶבְרָה **'ebrâh,** *eb-raw';* fem. of 83:—feather, wing.

85. אַבְרָהָם **'Abrâhâm,** *ab-raw-hawm';* contr. from 1 and an unused root (prob. mean. *to be populous*); *father of a multitude; Abraham,* the later name of Abram:—Abraham.

86. אַבְרֵךְ **'abrêk,** *ab-rake';* prob. an Eg. word mean. *kneel:*—bow the knee.

87. אַבְרָם **'Abrâm,** *ab-rawm';* contr. from 48; *high father; Abram,* the original name of Abraham:—Abram.

אַבְשַׁי **'Abshay.** See 52.

אַבְשָׁלוֹם **'Abshâlôwm.** See 53.

88. אֹבֹת **'ôbôth,** *o-both';* plur. of 178; water-*skins; Oboth,* a place in the Desert:—Oboth.

89. אָגֵא **'Âgê',** *aw-gay';* of uncert. der. [comp. 90]; *Agê,* an Isr.:—Agee.

90. אֲגַג **'Agag,** *ag-ag';* or אֲגָג **'Âgâg,** *ag-awg';* of uncert. der. [comp. 89]; *flame; Agag,* a title of Amalekitish kings:—Agag.

91. אֲגָגִי **'Âgâgîy,** *ag-aw-ghee';* patrial or patron. from 90; an *Agagite* or descendant (subject) of Agag:—Agagite.

92. אֲגֻדָּה **'âguddâh,** *ag-ood-daw';* fem. pass. part. of an unused root (mean. to *bind*); a *band, bundle, knot,* or *arch:*—bunch, burden, troop.

93. אֱגוֹז **'ĕgôwz,** *eg-oze';* prob. of Pers. or.; a *nut:*—nut.

94. אָגוּר **'Âgûwr,** *aw-goor';* pass. part. of 103; *gathered* (i.e. *received* among the sages); *Agur,* a fanciful name for Solomon:—Agur.

95. אֲגוֹרָה **'âgôwrâh,** *ag-o-raw';* from the same as 94; prop. something *gathered,* i.e. perh. a *grain* or *berry;* used only of a small (silver) *coin:*—piece [of] silver.

96. אֶגֶל **'egel,** *eh'-ghel;* from an unused root (mean. to *flow* down or together as drops); a *reservoir:*—drop.

97. אֶגְלַיִם **'Eglayim,** *eg-lah'-yim;* dual of 96; a *double pond; Eglajim,* a place in Moab:—Eglaim.

98. אֲגַם **'ăgam,** *ag-am';* from an unused root (mean. to *collect* as water); a *marsh;* hence a *rush* (as growing in swamps); hence a *stockade* of reeds:—pond, pool, standing [water].

99. אָגֵם **'âgêm,** *aw-game';* prob. from the same as 98 (in the sense of *stagnant* water); fig. *sad:*—pond.

100. אַגְמוֹן **'agmôwn,** *ag-mone';* from the same as 98; a marshy *pool* [others from a different root, a *kettle*]; by impl. a *rush* (as growing there); collect. a *rope* of rushes:—bulrush, caldron, hook, rush.

101. אַגָּן **'aggân,** *ag-gawn';* prob. from 5059; a *bowl* (as *pounded* out hollow):—basin, cup, goblet.

102. אַגָּף **'aggâph,** *ag-gawf';* prob. from 5062 (through the idea of *impending*); a *cover* or *heap;* i.e. (only plur.) *wings* of an army, or *crowds* of troops:—bands.

103. אָגַר **'âgar,** *aw-gar';* a prim. root; to *harvest:*—gather.

104. אִגְּרָא **'iggᵉrâ'** (Chald.), *ig-er-aw';* of Pers. or.; an *epistle* (as carried by a state courier or postman):—letter.

105. אֲגַרְטָל **'ăgarṭâl,** *ag-ar-tawl';* of uncert. der.; a *basin:*—charger.

106. אֶגְרֹף **'egrôph,** *eg-rofe';* from 1640 (in the sense of *grasping*); the *clenched* hand:—fist.

107. אִגֶּרֶת **'iggereth,** *ig-eh'-reth;* fem. of 104; an *epistle:*—letter.

108. אֵד **'êd,** *ade;* from the same as 181 (in the sense of *enveloping*); a *fog:*—mist, vapor.

109. אָדַב **'âdab,** *aw-dab';* a prim. root; to *languish:*—grieve.

110. אַדְבְּאֵל **'Adbᵉ'êl,** *ad-beh-ale';* prob. from 109 (in the sense of *chastisement*) and 410; *disciplined of God; Adbeël,* a son of Ishmael:—Adbeel.

111. אֲדַד **'Âdad,** *ad-ad';* prob. an orth. var. for 2301; *Adad* (or Hadad), an Edomite:—Hadad.

112. אִדּוֹ **'Iddôw,** *id-do;* of uncert. der.; *Iddo,* an Isr.:—Iddo.

אֱדוֹם **'Êdôwm.** See 123.

אֱדוֹמִי **'Êdôwmîy.** See 30.

113. אָדוֹן **'âdôwn,** *aw-done',* or (short.) אָדֹן **'âdôn,** *aw-done';* from an unused root (mean. to *rule*); *sovereign,* i.e. *controller* (human or divine):—lord, master, owner. Comp. also names beginning with "Adoni-".

114. אַדּוֹן **'Addôwn,** *ad-done';* prob. intens. for 113; *powerful; Addon,* appar. an Isr.:—Addon.

115. אֲדוֹרַיִם **'Âdôwrayim,** *ad-o-rah'-yim;* dual from 142 (in the sense of *eminence*); *double mound; Adorajim,* a place in Pal.:—Adoraim.

116. אֱדַיִן **'ĕdayin** (Chald.), *ed-ah'-yin;* of uncert. der.; *then* (of time):—now, that time, then.

117. אַדִּיר **'addîyr,** *ad-deer';* from 142; *wide* or (gen.) *large;* fig. *powerful:*—excellent, famous, gallant, glorious, goodly, lordly, mighty (-ier, one), noble, principal, worthy.

118. אֲדַלְיָא **'Âdalyâ',** *ad-al-yaw';* of Pers. der.; *Adalja,* a son of Haman:—Adalia.

119. אָדַם **'âdam,** *aw-dam';* to *show blood* (in the face), i.e. *flush* or turn rosy:—be (dyed, made) red (ruddy).

120. אָדָם **'âdâm,** *aw-dawm';* from 119; *ruddy,* i.e. a *human being* (an individual or the species, *mankind,* etc.):— × another, + hypocrite, + common sort, × low, man (mean, of low degree), person.

121. אָדָם **'Âdâm,** *aw-dawm';* the same as 120; *Adam,* the name of the first man, also of a place in Pal.:—Adam.

122. אָדֹם **'âdôm,** *aw-dome';* from 119; *rosy:*—red, ruddy.

123. אֱדֹם **'Êdôm,** *ed-ome';* or (fully) אֱדוֹם **'Êdôwm,** *ed-ome';* from 122; *red* [see Gen. 25 : 25]; *Edom,* the elder twin-brother of Jacob; hence the region (Idumæa) occupied by him:—Edom, Edomites, Idumea.

124. אֹדֶם **'ôdem,** *o'-dem;* from 119; *redness,* i.e. the *ruby, garnet,* or some other red gem:—sardius.

125. אֲדַמְדָּם **'ădamdâm,** *ad-am-dawm';* redupl. from 119; *reddish:*—(somewhat) reddish.

126. אַדְמָה **'Admâh,** *ad-maw';* contr. for 127; *earthy; Admah,* a place near the Dead Sea:—Admah.

127. אֲדָמָה **'ădâmâh,** *ad-aw-maw';* from 119; *soil* (from its gen. *redness*):—country, earth, ground, husband [-man] (-ry), land.

128. אֲדָמָה **'Âdâmâh,** *ad-aw-maw';* the same as 127; *Adamah,* a place in Pal.:—Adamah.

אַדְמוֹנִי **'admôwnîy.** See 132.

129. אֲדָמִי **'Âdâmîy,** *ad-aw-mee';* from 127; *earthy; Adami,* a place in Pal.:—Adami.

130. אֱדֹמִי **'Êdômîy,** *ed-o-mee';* or (fully) אֱדוֹמִי **'Êdôwmîy,** *ed-o-mee';* patron. from 123; an *Edomite,* or desc. from (or inhab. of) Edom:—Edomite. See 726.

131. אֲדֻמִּים **'Âdummîym,** *ad-oom-meem';* plur. of 121; *red* spots; *Adummim,* a pass in Pal.:—Adummim.

132. אַדְמֹנִי **'admônîy,** *ad-mo-nee',* or (fully) אַדְמוֹנִי **'admôwnîy,** *ad-mo-nee';* from 119; *reddish* (of the hair or the complexion):—red, ruddy.

133. אַדְמָתָא **'Admâthâ',** *ad-maw-thaw';* prob. of Pers. der.; *Admatha,* a Pers. nobleman:—Admatha.

134. אֶדֶן **'eden,** *eh'-den;* from the same as 113 (in the sense of *strength*); a *basis* (of a building, a column, etc.):—foundation, socket.

אָדֹן **'âdôn.** See 113.

135. אַדָּן **'Addân,** *ad-dawn';* intens. from the same as 134; *firm; Addan,* an Isr.:—Addan.

136. אֲדֹנָי **'Âdônây,** *ad-o-noy';* an emphatic form of 113; the *Lord* (used as a prop. name of God only):—(my) Lord.

137. אֲדֹנִי־בֶזֶק **'Âdônîy-Bezeq,** *ad-o''-nee-beh'-zek;* from 113 and 966; *lord of Bezek; Adoni-Bezek,* a Canaanitish king:—Adonibezek.

138. אֲדֹנִיָּה **'Âdônîyâh,** *ad-o-nee-yaw';* or. (prol.) אֲדֹנִיָּהוּ **'Âdônîyâhûw,** *ad-o-nee-yaw'-hoo;* from 113 and 3050; *lord* (i.e. worshipper) of Jah; *Adonijah,* the name of three Isr.:—Adonijah.

139. אֲדֹנִי־צֶדֶק **'Âdônîy-Tsedeq,** *ad-o''-nee-tseh'-dek;* from 113 and 6664; *lord of justice; Adoni-Tsedek,* a Canaanitish king:—Adonizedec.

140. אֲדֹנִיקָם **'Âdônîyqâm,** *ad-o-nee-kawm';* from 113 and 6965; *lord of rising* (i.e. *high*)*; Adonikam,* the name of one or two Isr.:—Adonikam

141. אֲדֹנִירָם **ʼAdônîyrâm**, *ad-o-nee-rawm'*; from 113 and 7311; *lord of height; Adoniram*, an Isr.:—Adoniram.

142. אָדַר **ʼâdar**, *aw-dar'*; a prim. root; to *expand*, i.e. *be great* or (fig.) *magnificent*:—(become) glorious, honourable.

143. אֲדָר **ʼĂdâr**, *ad-awr'*; prob. of for. der.; perh. mean. *fire; Adar*, the 12th Heb. month:—Adar.

144. אֲדָר **ʼĂdâr** (Chald.), *ad-awr'*; corresp. to 143:—Adar.

145. אֶדֶר **ʼeder**, *eh'-der*; from 142; *amplitude*, i.e. (concr.) a *mantle*; also (fig.) *splendor*:—goodly, robe.

146. אַדָּר **ʼAddâr**, *ad-dawr'*; intens. from 142; *ample; Addar*, a place in Pal.; also an Isr.:—Addar.

147. אִדַּר **ʼiddar** (Chald.), *id-dar'*; intens. from a root corresp. to 142; *ample*, i.e. a threshing-*floor*:—threshingfloor.

148. אֲדַרְגָּזֵר **ʼădargâzêr** (Chald.), *ad-ar"-gaw-zare'*; from the same as 147, and 1505; a *chief diviner*, or *astrologer*:—judge.

149. אַדְרַזְדָּא **ʼadrazdâʼ** (Chald.), *ad-raz-daw'*; prob. of Pers. or.; *quickly* or *carefully*:—diligently.

150. אֲדַרְכֹּן **ʼădarkôn**, *ad-ar-kone'*; of Pers. or.; a *daric* or Pers. coin:—dram.

151. אֲדֹרָם **ʼĂdôrâm**, *ad-o-rawm'*; contr. for 141; *Adoram* (or Adoniram), an Isr.:—Adoram.

152. אַדְרַמֶּלֶךְ **ʼAdrammelek**, *ad-ram-meh'-lek*; from 142 and 4428; *splendor of* (the) *king; Adrammelek*, the name of an Assyr. idol, also of a son of Sennacherib:—Adrammelech.

153. אֶדְרָע **ʼedraʽ** (Chald.), *ed-raw'*; an orth. var. for 1872; an *arm*, i.e. (fig.) *power*:—force.

154. אֶדְרֶעִי **ʼedreʽîy**, *ed-reh'-ee*; from the equivalent of 153; *mighty; Edrei*, the name of two places in Pal.:—Edrei.

155. אַדֶּרֶת **ʼaddereth**, *ad-deh'-reth*; fem. of 117; something *ample* (as a *large* vine, a *wide* dress); also the same as 145:—garment, glory, goodly, mantle, robe.

156. אָדַשׁ **ʼâdash**, *aw-dash'*; a prim. root; to *tread* out (grain):—thresh.

157. אָהַב **ʼâhab**, *aw-hab'*; or אָהֵב **ʼâhêb**, *aw-habe'*; a prim. root; to *have affection* for (sexually or otherwise):—(be-) love (-d, -ly, -r), like, friend.

158. אַהַב **ʼahab**, *ah'-hab*; from 157; *affection* (in a good or a bad sense):—love (-r).

159. אֹהַב **ʼôhab**, *o'-hab*; from 156; mean. the same as 158:—love.

160. אַהֲבָה **ʼahăbâh**, *ă-hab-aw'*; fem. of 158 and mean. the same:—love.

161. אֹהַד **ʼÔhad**, *o'-had*; from an unused root mean. to *be united; unity; Ohad*, an Isr.:—Ohad.

162. אֲהָהּ **ʼăhâhh**, *ă-haw'*; appar. a prim. word expressing *pain* exclamatorily; *Oh!*:—ah, alas.

163. אַהֲוָא **ʼAhăvâʼ**, *ă-hav-aw'*; prob. of for. or.; *Ahava*, a river of Babylonia:—Ahava.

164. אֵהוּד **ʼÊhûwd**, *ay-hood'*; from the same as 161; *united; Ehud*, the name of two or three Isr.:—Ehud.

165. אֱהִי **ʼĕhîy**, *e-hee'*; appar. an orth. var. for 346; *where*:—I will be (Hos. 13 : 10, 14) [*which is often the rendering of the same Heb. form from* 1961].

166. אָהַל **ʼâhal**, *aw-hal'*; a prim. root; to *be clear*:—shine.

167. אָהַל **ʼâhal**, *aw-hal'*; a denom. from 168; to *tent*:—pitch (remove) a tent.

168. אֹהֶל **ʼôhel**, *o'-hel*; from 166; a *tent* (as *clearly* conspicuous from a distance):—covering, (dwelling) (place), home, tabernacle, tent.

169. אֹהֶל **ʼÔhel**, *o'-hel*; the same as 168; *Ohel*, an Isr.:—Ohel.

170. אָהֳלָה **ʼOhŏlâh**, *ŏ-hol-aw'*; in form a fem. of 168, but in fact for אָהֳלָהּ **ʼOhŏlâhh**, *ŏ-hol-aw'*; from 168; *her tent* (i.e. idolatrous *sanctuary*); *Oholah*, a symbol. name for Samaria:—Aholah.

171. אָהֳלִיאָב **ʼOhŏlîyʼâb**, *ŏ"-hol-e-awb'*; from 168 and 1; *tent of* (his) *father; Oholiab*, an Isr.:—Aholiab.

172. אָהֳלִיבָה **ʼOhŏlîybâh**, *ŏ"-hol-ee-baw'*; (similarly with 170) for אָהֳלִיבָהּ **ʼOhŏlîybâhh**, *ŏ"-hol-e-baw'*; from 168; *my tent* (is) *in her; Oholibah*, a symbol. name for Judah:—Aholibah.

173. אָהֳלִיבָמָה **ʼOhŏlîybâmâh**, *ŏ"-hol-e-baw-maw'*; from 168 and 1116; *tent of* (the) *height; Oholibamah*, a wife of Esau:—Aholibamah.

174. אֲהָלִים **ʼăhâlîym**, *ă-haw-leem'*; or (fem.) אֲהָלוֹת **ʼăhâlôwth**, *ă-haw-loth'* (only used thus in the plur.); of for. or.; *aloe* wood (i.e. sticks):—(tree of lign-) aloes.

175. אַהֲרוֹן **ʼAhărôwn**, *ă-har-one'*; of uncert. deriv.; *Aharon*, the brother of Moses:—Aaron.

176. אוֹ **ʼôw**, *o*; presumed to be the "constr." or genitival form of אַו **ʼav**, *av*, short. for 185; *desire* (and so prob. in Prov. 31 : 4); hence (by way of alternative) *or*, also *if*:—also, and, either, if, at the least, × nor, or, otherwise, then, whether.

177. אוּאֵל **ʼÛwʼêl**, *oo-ale'*; from 176 and 410; *wish of God; Uel*, an Isr.:—Uel.

178. אוֹב **ʼôwb**, *obe*; from the same as 1 (appar. through the idea of *prattling* a father's name); prop. a *mumble*, i.e. a water-*skin* (from its hollow sound); hence a *necromancer* (ventriloquist, as from a jar):—bottle, familiar spirit.

179. אוֹבִיל **ʼôwbîyl**, *o-beel'*; prob. from 56; *mournful; Obil*, an Ishmaelite:—Obil.

180. אוּבָל **ʼûwbâl**, *oo-bawl'*; or (short.) אֻבָל **ʼûbâl**, *oo-bawl'*; from 2986 (in the sense of 2988); a *stream*:—river.

181. אוּד **ʼûwd**, *ood*; from an unused root mean. to *rake* together; a *poker* (for *turning* or *gathering* embers):—(fire-) brand.

182. אוֹדוֹת **ʼôwdôwth**, *o-dōth'*; or (short.) אֹדוֹת **ʼôdôwth**, *o-dōth'* (only thus in the plur.); from the same as 181; *turnings* (i.e. *occasions*); (adv.) on *account of*:—(be-) cause, concerning, sake.

183. אָוָה **ʼâvâh**, *aw-vaw'*; a prim. root; to *wish for*:—covet, (greatly) desire, be desirous, long, lust (after).

184. אָוָה **ʼâvâh**, *aw-vaw'*; a prim. root; to *extend* or *mark* out:—point out.

185. אַוָּה **ʼavvâh**, *av-vaw'*; from 183; *longing*:—desire, lust after, pleasure.

186. אוּזַי **ʼÛwzay**, *oo-zah'ee*; perh. by perm. for 5813, *strong; Uzai*, an Isr.:—Uzai.

187. אוּזָל **ʼÛwzâl**, *oo-zâwl'*; of uncert. der.; *Uzal*, a son of Joktan:—Uzal.

188. אוֹי **ʼôwy**, *ō'ee*; prob. from 183 (in the sense of *crying* out after); *lamentation*; also interj. *Oh!*:—alas, woe.

189. אֱוִי **ʼĔvîy**, *ev-ee'*; prob. from 183; *desirous; Evi*, a Midianitish chief:—Evi.

אוֹיֵב **ʼôwyêb**. See 341.

190. אוֹיָה **ʼôwyâh**, *o-yaw'*; fem. of 188:—woe.

191. אֱוִיל **ʼĕvîyl**, *ev-eel'*; from an unused root (mean. to be *perverse*); (fig.) *silly*:—fool (-ish) (man).

192. אֱוִיל מְרֹדַךְ **ʼĔvîyl Merôdak**, *ev-eel' mer-o-dak'*; of Chald. deriv. and prob. mean. *soldier of Merodak; Evil-Merodak*, a Babylonian king:—Evil-merodach.

193. אוּל **ʼûwl**, *ool*; from an unused root mean. to *twist*, i.e. (by impl.) *be strong*; the *body* (as being *rolled* together); also *powerful*:—mighty, strength.

194. אוּלַי **ʼûwlay**, *oo-lah'ee*; or (short.) אֻלַי **ʼûlay**, *oo-lah'ee*; from 176; *if not*; hence *perhaps*:—if so be, may be, peradventure, unless.

195. אוּלַי **ʼÛwlay**, *oo-lah'ee*: of Pers. der.; the *Ulai* (or Eulæus), a river of Persia:—Ulai.

196. אֱוִלִי **ʼĕvîlîy**, *ev-ee-lee'*; from 191; *silly, foolish*; hence (mor.) *impious*:—foolish.

197. אוּלָם **ʼûwlâm**, *oo-lawm'*; or (short.) אֻלָם **ʼûlâm**, *oo-lawm'*; from 481 (in the sense of *tying*); a *vestibule* (as *bound* to the building):—porch.

198. אוּלָם **ʼÛwlâm**, *oo-lawm'*; appar. from 481 (in the sense of *dumbness*); *solitary; Ulam*, the name of two Isr.:—Ulam.

199. אוּלָם **ʼûwlâm**, *oo-lawm'*; appar. a variation of 194; *however* or *on the contrary*:—as for, but, howbeit, in very deed, surely, truly, wherefore.

200. אִוֶּלֶת **ʼivveleth**, *iv-veh'-leth*; from the same as 191; *silliness*:—folly, foolishly (-ness).

201. אוֹמָר **ʼÔwmâr**, *o-mawr'*; from 559; *talkative; Omar*, a grandson of Esau:—Omar.

202. אוֹן **ʼôwn**, *ōne*; prob. from the same as 205 (in the sense of *effort*, but successful); *ability, power*, (fig.) *wealth*:—force, goods, might, strength, substance.

203. אוֹן **ʼÔwn**, *ōne*; the same as 202; *On*, an Isr.:—On.

204. אוֹן **ʼÔwn**, *ōne*; or (short.) אֹן **ʼÔn**, *ōne*; of Eg. der.; *On*, a city of Egypt:—On.

205. אָוֶן **ʼâven**, *aw'-ven*; from an unused root perh. mean. prop. to *pant* (hence to *exert* oneself, usually in vain; to *come to naught*); strictly *nothingness*; also *trouble, vanity, wickedness*; spec. an *idol*:—affliction, evil, false, idol, iniquity, mischief, mourners (-ing), naught, sorrow, unjust, unrighteous, vain, vanity, wicked (-ness.) Comp. 369.

206. אָוֶן **ʼÂven**, *aw'-ven*; the same as 205; *idolatry; Aven*, the contemptuous synonym of three places, one in Cœle-Syria, one in Egypt (On), and one in Pal. (Bethel):—Aven. See also 204, 1007.

207. אוֹנוֹ **ʼÔwnôw**, *o-no'*; or (short.) אֹנוֹ **ʼÔnôw**, *o-no'*; prol. from 202; *strong; Ono*, a place in Pal.:—Ono.

208. אוֹנָם **ʼÔwnâm**, *o-nawm'*; a var. of 209; *strong; Onam*, the name of an Edomite and of an Isr.:—Onam.

209. אוֹנָן **ʼÔwnân**, *o-nawn'*: a var. of 207; *strong; Onan*, a son of Judah:—Onan.

210. אוּפָז **ʼÛwphâz**, *oo-fawz'*; perh. a corruption of 211; *Uphaz*, a famous gold region:—Uphaz.

211. אוֹפִיר **ʼÔwphîyr**, *o-feer'*; or (short.) אֹפִיר **ʼÔphîyr**, *o-feer'*; and אוֹפִר **ʼÔwphîr**, *o-feer'*; of uncert. deriv.; *Ophir*, the name of a son of Joktan, and of a gold region in the East:—Ophir.

212. אוֹפָן **ʼôwphân**, *o-fawn'*; or (short.) אֹפָן **ʼôphân**, *o-fawn'*; from an unused root mean. to *revolve*; a *wheel*:—wheel.

אוֹפִר **ʼÔwphîr**. See 211.

213. אוּץ **ʼûwts**, *oots*; a prim. root; to *press*; (by impl.) to *be close, hurry, withdraw*:—(make) haste (-n, -y), labor, be narrow.

214. אוֹצָר **ʼôwtsâr**, *o-tsaw'*; from 686; a *depository*:—armory, cellar, garner, store (-house), treasure (-house) (-y).

215. אוֹר **ʼôwr**, *ore*; a prim. root; *to be* (caus. *make*) *luminous* (lit. and metaph.):—× break of day, glorious, kindle, (be, en-, give, show) light (-en, -ened), set on fire, shine.

216. אוֹר **ʼôwr**, *ore*; from 215; *illumination* or (concr.) *luminary* (in every sense, including *lightning, happiness*, etc.):—bright, clear, + day, light (-ning), morning, sun.

217. אוּר **ʼûwr**, *oor*; from 215; *flame*, hence (in the plur.) the *East* (as being the region of light):—fire, light. See also 224.

218. אוּר **ʼÛwr**, *oor*; the same as 217; *Ur*, a place in Chaldæa; also an Isr.:—Ur.

219. אוֹרָה **ʼôwrâh**, *o-raw'*; fem. of 216; *luminousness*, i.e. (fig.) *prosperity*; also a plant (as being *bright*):—herb light.

220. אֲוֵרָה **'âvêrâh**, *av-ay-raw'*; by transp. for 723; a *stall*:—cote.

221. אוּרִי **'Ûwrîy**, *oo-ree'*; from 217; *fiery; Uri*, the name of three Isr.:—Uri.

222. אוּרִיאֵל **'Ûwrîy'êl**, *oo-ree-ale'*; from 217 and 410; *flame of God; Uriel*, the name of two Isr.:—Uriel.

223. אוּרִיָּה **'Ûwrîyâh**, *oo-ree-yaw'*; or (prol.) אוּרִיָּהוּ **'Ûwrîyâhûw**, *oo-ree-yaw'-hoo*; from 217 and 3050; *flame of Jah; Urijah*, the name of one Hittite and five Isr.:—Uriah, Urijah.

224. אוּרִים **'Ûwrîym**, *oo-reem'*; plur. of 217; *lights; Urim*, the oracular brilliancy of the figures in the high-priest's breastplate:—Urim.

אוֹרְנָה **'Owrenâh**. See 728.

225. אוּת **'ûwth**, *ooth*; a prim. root; prop. to *come*, i.e. (impl.) to *assent*:—consent.

226. אוֹת **'ôwth**, *ōth*; prob. from 225 (in the sense of *appearing*); a *signal* (lit. or fig.), as a *flag, beacon, monument, omen, prodigy, evidence*, etc.:—mark, miracle, (en-) sign, token.

227. אָז **'âz**, *awz*; a demonstrative adv.; *at that time* or *place*; also as a conj., *therefore*:—beginning, for, from, hitherto, now, of old, once, since, then, at which time, yet.

228. אֲזָא **'ăzâ'** (Chald.), *az-aw'*; or אֲזָה **'ăzâh** (Chald.), *az-aw'*; to *kindle*; (by impl.) to *heat*:—heat, hot.

229. אֶזְבַּי **'Ezbay**, *ez-bah'ee*; prob. from 231; *hyssop-like; Ezbai*, an Isr.:—Ezbai.

230. אֲזַד **'ăzad** (Chald.), *az-awd'*; of uncert. der.; *firm*:—be gone.

231. אֵזוֹב **'êzôwb**, *ay-zobe'*; prob. of for. der.; *hyssop*:—hyssop.

232. אֵזוֹר **'êzôwr**, *ay-zore'*; from 246; something *girt*; a *belt*, also a *band*:—girdle.

233. אֲזַי **'ăzay**, *az-ah'ee*; prob. from 227; *at that time*:—then.

234. אַזְכָּרָה **'azkârâh**, *az-kaw-raw'*; from 2142; a *reminder*; spec. *remembrance-offering*:—memorial.

235. אָזַל **'âzal**, *aw-zal'*; a prim. root; to *go away*, hence to *disappear*:—fail, gad about, go to and fro [*but in Ezek.* 27 : 19 *the word is rendered by many* "from Uzal," *by others* "yarn"], be gone (spent).

236. אֲזַל **'ăzal** (Chald.), *az-al'*; the same as 235; to *depart*:—go (up).

237. אֶזֶל **'ezel**, *eh'-zel*; from 235; *departure; Ezel*, a memorial stone in Pal.:—Ezel.

238. אָזַן **'âzan**, *aw-zan'*; a prim. root; prob. to *expand*; but used only as a denom. from 241; to *broaden out the ear* (with the hand), i.e. (by impl.) to *listen*:—give (perceive by the) ear, hear (-ken). See 239.

239. אָזַן **'âzan**, *aw-zan'*; a prim. root [rather ident. with 238 through the idea of *scales* as if two ears]; to *weigh*, i.e. (fig.) *ponder*:—give good heed.

240. אָזֵן **'âzên**, *aw-zane'*; from 238; a *spade* or *paddle* (as having a *broad* end):—weapon.

241. אֹזֶן **'ôzen**, *o'-zen*; from 238; *broadness*, i.e. (concr.) the *ear* (from its form in man):—+advertise, audience, +displease, ear, hearing, +show.

242. אֻזֵּן שֶׁאֱרָה **'Uzzên She'ĕrâh**, *ooz-zane' sheh-er-aw'*; from 238 and 7609; *plat of Sheerah* (i.e. settled by him); *Uzzen-Sheërah*, a place in Pal.:—Uzzen-sherah.

243. אַזְנוֹת תָּבוֹר **'Aznôwth Tâbôwr**, *az-nōth' taw-bore'*; from 238 and 8396; *flats* (i.e. *tops*) *of Tabor* (i.e. situated on it); *Aznoth-Tabor*, a place in Pal.:—Aznoth-tabor.

244. אָזְנִי **'Oznîy**, *oz-nee'*; from 241; *having* (quick) *ears; Ozni*, an Isr.; also an *Oznite* (collect.), his desc.:—Ozni, Oznites.

245. אֲזַנְיָה **'Ăzanyâh**, *az-an-yaw'*; from 238 and 3050; *heard by Jah; Azanjah*, an Isr.:—Azaniah.

246. אֲזִקִּים **'ăziqqîym**, *az-ik-keem'*; a var. for 2131; *manacles*:—chains.

247. אָזַר **'âzar**, *aw-zar'*; a prim. root; to *belt*:—bind (compass) about, gird (up, with).

248. אֶזְרוֹעַ **'ezrôwa'**, *ez-ro'-ă*; a var. for 2220; the *arm*:—arm.

249. אֶזְרָח **'ezrâch**, *ez-rawkh'*; from 2224 (in the sense of *springing up*); a spontaneous *growth*, i.e. *native* (tree or persons):—bay tree, (home-) born (in the land), of the (one's own) country (nation).

250. אֶזְרָחִי **'Ezrâchîy**, *ez-raw-khee'*; patron. from 2246; an *Ezrachite* or desc. of Zerach:—Ezrahite.

251. אָח **'âch**, *awkh*; a prim. word; a *brother* (used in the widest sense of literal relationship and metaph. affinity or resemblance [like 1]):—another, brother (-ly), kindred, like, other. Comp. also the prop. names beginning with "Ah-" or "Ahi-".

252. אַח **'ach** (Chald.), *akh*; corresp. to 251:—brother.

253. אָח **'âch**, *awkh*; a var. for 162; *Oh!* (expressive of grief or surprise):—ah, alas.

254. אָח **'âch**, *awkh*; of uncert. der.; a *fire-pot* or chafing-dish:—hearth.

255. אֹחַ **'ôach**, *o'-akh*; prob. from 253; a *howler* or lonesome wild animal:—doleful creature.

256. אַחְאָב **'Ach'âb**, *akh-awb'*; once (by contr.) אֶחָב **'Echâb** (Jer. 29 : 22), *ekh-awb'*; from 251 and 1; *brother* [i.e. *friend*] *of* (his) *father; Achab*, the name of a king of Israel and of a prophet at Babylon:—Ahab.

257. אַחְבָּן **'Achbân**, *akh-bawn'*; from 251 and 995; *brother* (i.e. *possessor*) *of understanding; Achban*, an Isr.:—Ahban.

258. אָחַד **'âchad**, *aw-khad'*; perh. a prim. root; to *unify*, i.e. (fig.) *collect* (one's thoughts):—go one way or other.

259. אֶחָד **'echâd**, *ekh-awd'*; a numeral from 258; prop. *united*, i.e. *one*; or (as an ordinal) *first*:—a, alike, alone, altogether, and, any (-thing), apiece, a certain, [dai-] ly, each (one), + eleven, every, few, first, + highway, a man, once, one, only, other, some, together.

260. אָחוּ **'âchûw**, *aw'-khoo*; of unc. (perh. Eg.) der.; a *bulrush* or any marshy grass (particularly that along the Nile):—flag, meadow.

261. אֵחוּד **'Êchûwd**, *ay-khood'*; from 258; *united; Echud*, the name of three Isr.:—Ehud.

262. אַחְוָה **'achvâh**, *akh-vaw'*; from 2331 (in the sense of 2324); an *utterance*:—declaration.

263. אַחֲוָה **'achăvâh** (Chald.), *akh-av-aw'*; corresp. to 262; *solution* (of riddles):—showing.

264. אַחֲוָה **'achăvâh**, *akh-av-aw'*; from 251; *fraternity*:—brotherhood.

265. אֲחוֹחַ **'Ăchôwach**, *akh-o'-akh*; by redupl. from 251; *brotherly; Achoach*, an Isr.:—Ahoah.

266. אֲחוֹחִי **'Ăchôwchîy**, *akh-o-khee'*; patron. from 264; an *Achochite* or desc. of Achoach:—Ahohite.

267. אֲחוּמַי **'Ăchûwmay**, *akh-oo-mah'ee*; perh. from 251 and 4325; *brother* (i.e. *neighbour*) *of water; Achumai*, an Isr.:—Ahumai.

268. אָחוֹר **'âchôwr**, *aw-khore'*; or (short.) אָחֹר **'âchôr**, *aw-khore'*; from 299; the *hinder* part; hence (adv.) *behind, backward*; also (as facing north) the *West*:—after (-ward), back (part, -side, -ward), hereafter, (be-) hind (-er part), time to come, without.

269. אָחוֹת **'âchôwth**, *aw-khōth'*; irreg. fem. of 251; a *sister* (used very widely [like 250], lit. and fig.):—(an-) other, sister, together.

270. אָחַז **'âchaz**, *aw-khaz'*; a prim. root; to *seize* (often with the accessory idea of holding in possession):— + be affrighted, bar, (catch, lay, take) hold (back), come upon, fasten, handle, portion, (get, have or take) possess (-ion).

271. אָחָז **'Âchâz**, *aw-khawz'*; from 270; *possessor; Achaz*, the name of a Jewish king and of an Isr.:—Ahaz.

272. אֲחֻזָּה **'ăchuzzâh**, *akh-ooz-zaw'*; fem. pass. part. from 270; something *seized*, i.e. a *possession* (esp. of land):—possession.

273. אַחְזַי **'Achzay**, *akh-zah'ee*; from 270; *seizer; Achzai*, an Isr.:—Ahasai.

274. אֲחַזְיָה **'Ăchazyâh**, *akh-az-yaw'*; or (prol.) אֲחַזְיָהוּ **'Ăchazyâhûw**, *akh-az-yaw'-hoo*; from 270 and 3050; *Jah has seized; Achazjah*, the name of a Jewish and an Isr. king:—Ahaziah.

275. אֲחֻזָּם **'Ăchuzzâm**, *akh-ooz-zawm'*; from 270; *seizure; Achuzzam*, an Isr.:—Ahuzam.

276. אֲחֻזַּת **'Ăchuzzath**, *akh-ooz-zath'*; a var. of 272; *possession; Achuzzath*, a Philistine:—Ahuzzath.

277. אֲחִי **'Ăchîy**, *akh-ee'*; from 251; *brotherly; Achi*, the name of two Isr.:—Ahi.

278. אֵחִי **'Êchîy**, *ay-khee'*; prob. the same as 277; *Echi*, an Isr.:—Ehi.

279. אֲחִיאָם **'Ăchîy'âm**, *akh-ee-awm'*; from 251 and 517; *brother of the mother* (i.e. *uncle*); *Achiam*, an Isr.:—Ahiam.

280. אֲחִידָה **'ăchîydâh** (Chald.), *akh-ee-daw'*; corresp. to 2420, an *enigma*:—hard sentence.

281. אֲחִיָּה **'Ăchîyâh**, *akh-ee-yaw'*; or (prol.) אֲחִיָּהוּ **'Ăchîyâhûw**, *akh-ee-yaw'-hoo*; from 251 and 3050; *brother* (i.e. *worshipper*) *of Jah; Achijah*, the name of nine Isr.:—Ahiah, Ahijah.

282. אֲחִיהוּד **'Ăchîyhûwd**, *akh-ee-hood'*; from 251 and 1935; *brother* (i.e. *possessor*) *of renown; Achihud*, an Isr.:—Ahihud.

283. אַחְיוֹ **'Achyôw**, *akh-yo'*; prol. from 251; *brotherly; Achio*, the name of three Isr.:—Ahio.

284. אֲחִיחֻד **'Ăchîychûd**, *akh-ee-khood'*; from 251 and 2330; *brother of a riddle* (i.e. *mysterious*); *Achichud*, an Isr.:—Ahihud.

285. אֲחִיטוּב **'Ăchîyṭûwb**, *akh-ee-toob'*; from 251 and 2898; *brother of goodness; Achitub*, the name of several priests:—Ahitub.

286. אֲחִילוּד **'Ăchîylûwd**, *akh-ee-lood'*; from 251 and 3205; *brother of one born; Achilud*, an Isr.:—Ahilud.

287. אֲחִימוֹת **'Ăchîymôwth**, *akh-ee-mōth'*; from 251 and 4191; *brother of death; Achimoth*, an Isr.:—Ahimoth.

288. אֲחִימֶלֶךְ **'Ăchîymelek**, *akh-ee-meh'-lek*; from 251 and 4428; *brother of* (the) *king; Achimelek*, the name of an Isr. and of a Hittite:—Ahimelech.

289. אֲחִימַן **'Ăchîyman**, *akh-ee-man'*; or אֲחִימָן **'Ăchîymân**, *akh-ee-mawn'*; from 251 and 4480; *brother of a portion* (i.e. *gift*); *Achiman*, the name of an Anakite and of an Isr.:—Ahiman.

290. אֲחִימַעַץ **'Ăchîyma'ats**, *akh-ee-mah'-ats*; from 251 and the equiv. of 4619; *brother of anger; Achimaats*, the name of three Isr.:—Ahimaaz.

291. אַחְיָן **'Achyân**, *akh-yawn'*; from 251; *brotherly; Achjan*, an Isr.:—Ahian.

292. אֲחִינָדָב **'Ăchîynâdâb**, *akh-ee-naw-dawb'*; from 251 and 5068; *brother of liberality; Achinadab*, an Isr.:—Ahinadab.

293. אֲחִינֹעַם **'Ăchîynô'am**, *akh-ee-no'-am*; from 251 and 5278; *brother of pleasantness; Achinoam*, the name of two Israelitesses:—Ahinoam.

294. אֲחִיסָמָךְ **'Ăchîyçâmâk**, *akh-ee-saw-mawk'*; from 251 and 5564; *brother of support; Achisamak*, an Isr.:—Ahisamach.

295. אֲחִיעֶזֶר **'Ăchîy'ezer**, *akh-ee-eh'-zer*; from 251 and 5828; *brother of help: Achiezer*, the name of two Isr.:—Ahiezer.

296. אֲחִיקָם **'Ăchîyqâm**, *akh-ee-kawm'*; from 251 and 6965; *brother of rising* (i.e. *high*); *Achikam*, an Isr.:—Ahikam.

297. אֲחִירָם **'Ăchîyrâm**, *akh-ee-rawm'*; from 251 and 7311; *brother of height* (i.e. *high*); *Achiram*, an Isr.:—Ahiram.

298. אֲחִירָמִי **'Ăchîyrâmîy**, *akh-ee-raw-mee'*; patron. from 297; an *Achiramite* or desc. (collect.) of Achiram:—Ahiramites.

299. אֲחִירַע **'Ăchîyraʻ**, *akh-ee-rah'*; from 251 and 7451; *brother of wrong; Achira*, an Isr.:—Ahira.

300. אֲחִישַׁחַר **'Ăchîyshachar**, *akh-ee-shakh'-ar*; from 251 and 7837; *brother of* (the) *dawn; Achishachar*, an Isr.:—Ahishar.

301. אֲחִישָׁר **'Ăchîyshâr**, *akh-ee-shawr'*; from 251 and 7891; *brother of* (the) *singer; Achishar*, an Isr.:—Ahishar.

302. אֲחִיתֹפֶל **'Ăchîythôphel**, *akh-ee-tho'-fel;* from 251 and 8602; *brother of folly; Achithophel*, an Isr.:—Ahithophel.

303. אַחְלָב **'Achlâb**, *akh-lawb'*; from the same root as 2459; *fatness* (i.e. *fertile*); *Achlab*, a place in Pal.:—Ahlab.

304. אַחְלַי **'Achlay**, *akh-lah'ee;* the same as 305; *wishful; Achlai*, the name of an Israelitess and of an Isr.:—Ahlai.

305. אַחֲלַי **'achălay**, *akh-al-ah'ee;* or אַחֲלֵי **'achălêy**, *akh-al-ay':* prob. from 253 and a var. of 3863; *would that!*:—O that, would God.

306. אַחְלָמָה **'achlâmâh**, *akh-law'-maw;* perh. from 2492 (and thus *dream-stone*); a gem, prob. the *amethyst*:—amethyst.

307. אַחְמְתָא **'Achmᵉthâ'**, *akh-me-thaw';* of Pers. der.; *Achmetha* (i.e. *Ecbatana*), the summer capital of Persia:—Achmetha.

308. אֲחַסְבַּי **'Ăchaçbay**, *akh-as-bah'ee;* of uncert. der.; *Achasbai*, an Isr.:—Ahasbai.

309. אָחַר **'âchar**, *aw-khar';* a prim. root; to *loiter* (i.e. *be behind*); by impl. to *procrastinate*:—continue, defer, delay, hinder, be late (slack), stay (there), tarry (longer).

310. אַחַר **'achar**, *akh-ar';* from 309; prop. the *hind* part; gen. used as an adv. or conj., *after* (in various senses):—after (that, -ward), again, at, away from, back (from, -side), behind, beside, by, follow (after, -ing), forasmuch, from, hereafter, hinder end, + out (over) live, + persecute, posterity, pursuing, remnant, seeing, since, thence [-forth], when, with.

311. אַחַר **'achar** (Chald.), *akh-ar';* corresp. to 310; *after*:—[here-] after.

312. אַחֵר **'achêr**, *akh-air';* from 309; prop. *hinder;* gen. *next, other*, etc.:—(an-) other (man), following, next, strange.

313. אַחֵר **'Achêr**, *akh-air';* the same as 312; *Acher*, an Isr.:—Aher.

314. אַחֲרוֹן **'achărôwn**, *akh-ar-one';* or (short.) אַחֲרֹן **'achărôn**, *akh-ar-one';* from 309; *hinder:* gen. *late* or *last;* spec. (as facing the east) *western*:—after (-ward), to come, following, hind (-er, -ermost, -most), last, latter, rereward, ut(ter)most.

315. אַחְרַח **'Achrach**, *akh-rakh;* from 310 and 251, *after* (his) *brother: Achrach*, an Isr.:—Aharah.

316. אֲחַרְחֵל **'Ăcharchêl**, *akh-ar-kale';* from 310 and 2426; *behind* (the) *intrenchment* (i.e. *safe*); *Acharchel*, an Isr.:—Aharhel.

317. אָחֳרִי **'ochŏrîy** (Chald.), *okh-or-ee';* from 311; *other*:—(an-) other.

318. אָחֳרֵין **'ochŏrêyn** (Chald.), *okh-or-ane';* or (short.) אָחֳרֵן **'ochŏrên** (Chald.), *okh-or-ane';* from 317; *last*:—at last.

319. אַחֲרִית **'achărîyth**, *akh-ar-eeth';* from 310; the *last* or *end*, hence the *future;* also *posterity*:—(last, latter) end (time), hinder (utter) -most, length, posterity, remnant, residue, reward.

320. אַחֲרִית **'achărîyth** (Chald.), *akh-ar-eeth';* from 311; the same as 319; *later*:—latter.

321. אָחֳרָן **'ochŏrân** (Chald.), *okh-or-awn';* from 311; the same as 317; *other*:—(an-) other.

אָחֳרֵן **'ochŏrên**. See 318.

322. אֲחֹרַנִּית **'ăchôranniyth**, *akh-o-ran-neeth';* prol. from 268; *backwards*:—back (-ward, again).

323. אֲחַשְׁדַּרְפַּן **'ăchashdarpan**, *akh-ash-dar-pan';* of Pers. der.; a *satrap* or governor of a main province (of Persia):—lieutenant.

324. אֲחַשְׁדַּרְפַּן **ăchashdarpan** (Chald.), *akh-ash-dar-pan';* corresp. to 323:—prince.

325. אֲחַשְׁוֵרוֹשׁ **'Ăchashvêrôwsh**, *akh-ash-vay-rōsh';* or (short.) אֲחַשְׁרֹשׁ **'Achashrôsh**, *akh-ash-rōsh'* (Esth. 10 : 1); of Pers. or.; *Achashverosh* (i.e. Ahasuerus or Artaxerxes, but in this case Xerxes), the title (rather than name) of a Pers. king:—Ahasuerus.

326. אֲחַשְׁתָּרִי **'ăchashtârîy**, *akh-ash-taw-ree';* prob. of Pers. der.; an *achastarite* (i.e. courier); the designation (rather than name) of an Isr.:—Haakashtari [*includ. the art.*].

327. אֲחַשְׁתְּרָן **'ăchastârân**, *akh-ash-taw-rawn';* of Pers. or.; a *mule*:—camel.

328. אַט **'aṭ**, *at;* from an unused root perh. mean. to *move softly;* (as a noun) a *necromancer* (from their soft incantations), (as an adv.) *gently*:—charmer, gently, secret, softly.

329. אָטָד **'âṭâd**, *aw-tawd';* from an unused root prob. mean. to *pierce* or *make fast;* a *thorn*-tree (espec. the *buckthorn*):—Atad, bramble, thorn.

330. אֵטוּן **'êṭûwn**, *ay-toon';* from an unused root (prob. mean. to *bind*); prop. *twisted* (yarn), i.e. *tapestry*:—fine linen.

331. אָטַם **'âṭam**, *aw-tam';* a prim. root; to *close* (the lips or ears); by anal. to *contract* (a window by bevelled jambs):—narrow, shut, stop.

332. אָטַר **'âṭar**, *aw-tar';* a prim. root; to *close* up:—shut.

333. אָטֵר **'Âṭêr**, *aw-tare';* from 332; *maimed; Ater*, the name of three Isr.:—Ater.

334. אִטֵּר **'iṭṭêr**, *it-tare';* from 332; *shut* up, i.e. *impeded* (as to the use of the right hand):— + left-handed.

335. אַי **'ay**, *ah'ee;* perh. from 370; *where?* hence *how?*:—how, what, whence, where, whether, which (way).

336. אִי **'îy**, *ee;* prob. ident. with 335 (through the idea of a *query*); *not*:—island (Job 22 : 30).

337. אִי **'îy**, *ee;* short. from 188; *alas!*:—woe.

338. אִי **'îy**, *ee;* prob. ident. with 337 (through the idea of a *doleful* sound); a *howler* (used only in the plural), i.e. any solitary wild creature:—wild beast of the islands.

339. אִי **'îy**, *ee;* from 183; prop. a *habitable* spot (as *desirable*); dry *land*, a *coast*, an *island*:—country, isle, island.

340. אָיַב **'âyab**, *aw-yab';* a prim. root; to *hate* (as one of an opposite tribe or party); hence to *be hostile*:—be an enemy.

341. אֹיֵב **'ôyêb**, *o-yabe';* or (fully) אוֹיֵב **'ôwyêb**, *o-yabe';* act. part. of 340; *hating;* an *adversary*:—enemy, foe.

342. אֵיבָה **'êybâh**, *ay-baw';* from 340; *hostility*:—enmity, hatred.

343. אֵיד **'êyd**, *ade;* from the same as 181 (in the sense of *bending* down); *oppression;* by impl. *misfortune, ruin*:—calamity, destruction.

344. אַיָּה **'ayâh**, *ah-yaw';* perh. from 337; the *screamer*, i.e. a *hawk*:—kite, vulture.

345. אַיָּה **'Ayâh**, *ah-yaw';* the same as 344; *Ajah*, the name of two Isr.:—Aiah, Ajah.

346. אַיֵּה **'ayêh**, *ah-yay';* prol. from 335; *where?*:—where.

347. אִיּוֹב **'Îyôwb**, *ee-yobe';* from 340; *hated* (i.e. *persecuted*); *Ijob*, the patriarch famous for his patience:—Job.

348. אִיזֶבֶל **'Îyzebel**, *ee-zeh'-bel;* from 336 and 2083; *chaste; Izebel*, the wife of king Ahab:—Jezebel.

349. אֵיךְ **'êyk**, *ake;* also אֵיכָה **'êykâh**, *ay-kaw';* and אֵיכָכָה **'êykâkâh**, *ay-kaw'-kah;* prol. from 335; *how?* or *how!*; also *where*:—how, what.

350. אִי־כָבוֹד **Îy-kâbôwd**, *ee-kaw-bode';* from 336 and 3519; (there is) *no glory*, i.e. *inglorious; Ikabod*, a son of Phineas:—I-chabod.

351. אֵיכֹה **'êykôh**, *ay-kō;* prob. a var. for 349, but not as an interrogative; *where*:—where.

אֵיכָה **'êykâh;** אֵיכָכָה **'êykâkâh**. See 349.

352. אַיִל **'ayîl**, *ah'-yil;* from the same as 193; prop. *strength;* hence anything *strong;* spec. a *chief* (politically); also a *ram* (from his strength); a *pilaster* (as a strong support); an *oak* or other strong tree:—mighty (man), lintel, oak, post, ram, tree.

353. אֱיָל **'êyâl**, *eh-yawl';* a var. of 352; *strength*.—strength.

354. אַיָּל **'ayâl**, *ah-yawl';* an intens. form of 352 (in the sense of *ram*); a *stag* or male deer:—hart.

355. אַיָּלָה **'ayâlâh**, *ah-yaw-law';* fem. of 354; a *doe* or female deer:—hind.

356. אֵילוֹן **'Êylôwn**, *ay-lone';* or (short.) אֵלוֹן **'Êlôwn**, *ay-lone';* or אֵילֹן **'Êylôn**, *ay-lone';* from 352; *oak-grove; Elon*, the name of a place in Pal., and also of one Hittite, two Isr.:—Elon.

357. אַיָּלוֹן **'Ayâlôwn**, *ah-yaw-lone';* from 354. *deer-field; Ajalon*, the name of five places in Pal.:—Aijalon, Ajalon.

358. אֵילוֹן בֵּית חָנָן **'Êylôwn Bêyth Chânân**, *ay-lone' bayth-chaw-nawn';* from 356, 1004, and 2603; *oak-grove of* (the) *house of favor; Elon of Beth-chanan*, a place in Pal.:—Elon-beth-hanan.

359. אֵילוֹת **'Êylôwth**, *ay-lōth';* or אֵילַת **'Êylath**, *ay-lath';* from 352; *trees* or a *grove* (i.e. palms); *Eloth* or *Elath*, a place on the Red Sea:—Elath, Eloth.

360. אֱיָלוּת **'êyâlûwth**, *eh-yaw-looth';* fem. of 353; *power;* by impl. *protection*:—strength.

361. אֵילָם **'êylâm**, *ay-lawm';* or (short.) אֵלָם **'êlâm**, *ay-lawm';* or (fem.) אֵלַמָּה **'êlammâh**, *ay-lam-maw';* prob. from 352; a *pillar-space* (or colonnade), i.e. a *pale* (or portico):—arch.

362. אֵילִם **'Êylîm**, *ay-leem';* plur. of 352; *palm-trees; Elim*, a place in the Desert:—Elim.

363. אִילָן **'îylân** (Chald.), *ee-lawn';* corresp. to 356; a *tree*:—tree.

364. אֵיל פָּארָן **'Êyl Pâ'rân**, *ale paw-rawn';* from 352 and 6290; *oak of Paran; El-Paran*, a portion of the district of Paran:—El-paran.

אֵילֹן **'Êylôn**. See 356.

365. אַיֶּלֶת **'ayeleth**, *ah-yeh'-leth;* the same as 355; a *doe*:—hind, Aijeleth.

אַיִם **'ayim**. See 368.

366. אָיֹם **'âyôm**, *aw-yome';* from an unused root (mean. to *frighten*); *frightful*:—terrible.

367. אֵימָה **'êymâh**, *ay-maw';* or (short.) אֵמָה **'êmah**, *ay-maw';* from the same as 366; *fright;* concr. an *idol* (as a bugbear):—dread, fear, horror, idol, terrible, terror.

368. אֵימִים **'Êymîym**, *ay-meem';* plur. of 367; *terrors; Emim*, an early Canaanitish (or Moabitish) tribe:—Emims.

369. אַיִן **'ayin**, *ah'-yin;* as if from a prim. root mean. to *be nothing* or *not exist;* a *non-entity;* gen. used as a neg. particle:—else, except, fail, [father-] less, be gone, in [-curable], neither, never, no (where), none, nor (any, thing), not, nothing, to nought, past, un [-searchable], well-nigh, without. Comp. 370.

370. אַיִן **'ayin**, *ah-yin';* prob. ident. with 369 in the sense of *query* (comp. 336);—*where?* (only in connection with prep. pref., *whence*):—whence, where.

371. אִין **'îyn**, *een;* appar. a short. form of 369; but (like 370) interrog.; is it *not?*:—not

372. אִיעֶזֶר **'Îyʻezer**, *ee-eh'-zer;* from 336 and 5828; *helpless; Iezer*, an Isr.:—Jeezer.

373. אִיעֶזְרִי 'Îy'ezrîy, *ee-ez-ree';* patron. from 372; an *Iezrite* or desc. of Iezer:—Jeezerite.

374. אֵיפָה 'êyphâh, *ay-faw';* or (short.) אֵפָה **'êphâh**, *ay-faw';* of Eg. der.; an *ephah* or measure for grain; hence a *measure* in gen.:—ephah, (divers) measure (-s).

375. אֵיפֹה 'êyphôh, *ay-fō';* from 335 and 6311; *what place?;* also (of time) *when?;* or (of means) *how?*:—what manner, where.

376. אִישׁ 'îysh, *eesh;* contr. for 582 [or perh. rather from an unused root mean. to *be extant*]; a *man* as an individual or a male person; often used as an adjunct to a more definite term (and in such cases frequently not expressed in translation):—also, another, any (man), a certain, + champion, consent, each, every (one), fellow, [foot-, husband-] man, (good-, great, mighty) man, he, high (degree), him (that is), husband, man [-kind], + none, one, people, person, + steward, what (man) soever, whoso (-ever), worthy. Comp. 802.

377. אִישׁ 'îysh, *eesh;* denom. from 376; to *be a man*, i.e. act in a manly way:—show (one) self a man.

378. אִישׁ־בֹּשֶׁת 'Îysh-Bôsheth, *eesh-bō'-sheth;* from 376 and 1322; *man of shame; Ish-Bosheth*, a son of King Saul:—Ish-bosheth.

379. אִישְׁהוֹד 'Îyshhôwd *eesh-hode';* from 376 and 1935; *man of renown; Ishod*, an Isr.:—Ishod.

380. אִישׁוֹן 'îyshôwn, *ee-shone';* dimin. from 376; the *little man* of the eye; the *pupil* or *ball;* hence the *middle* (of night):—apple [of the eye], black, obscure.

אִישׁ־חַי **'Îysh-Chay.** See 381.

381. אִישׁ־חַיִל 'Îysh-Chayil, *eesh-khah'-yil;* from 376 and 2428; *man of might;* by defect. transcription (2 Sam. 23 : 20) אִישׁ־חַי **'Îsh-Chay**, *eesh-khah'ee;* as if from 376 and 2416; *living man; Ish-chail* (or *Ish-chai*), an Isr.:—a valiant man.

382. אִישׁ־טוֹב 'Îysh-Tôwb, *eesh-tobe';* from 376 and 2897; *man of Tob; Ish-Tob*, a place in Pal.:—Ish-tob.

אִישַׁי **'Îshay.** See 3448.

אִיתוֹן **'îthôwn.** See 2978.

383. אִיתַי 'îythay (Chald.), *ee-thah'ee;* corresp. to 3426; prop. *entity;* used only as a particle of affirmation, there *is:*—art thou, can, do ye, have, it be, there is (are), × we will not.

384. אִיתִיאֵל 'Îythîy'êl, *eeth-ee-ale';* perh. from 837 and 410; *God has arrived; Ithiel*, the name of an Isr., also of a symb. person:—Ithiel.

385. אִיתָמָר 'Îythâmâr, *eeth-aw-mawr';* from 339 and 8558; *coast of* the *palm*-tree; *Ithamar*, a son of Aaron:—Ithamar.

386. אֵיתָן 'êythân, *ay-thawn';* or (short.) אֵתָן **'êthân**, *ay-thawn';* from an unused root (mean. to *continue*); *permanence;* hence (concr.) *permanent;* spec. a *chieftain:*—hard, mighty, rough, strength, strong.

387. אֵיתָן 'Êythân, *ay-thawn';* the same as 386; *permanent; Ethan*, the name of four Isr.:—Ethan.

388. אֵיתָנִים 'Êythânîym, *ay-thaw-neem';* plur. of 386; always with the art.; the *permanent* brooks; *Ethanim*, the name of a month:—Ethanim.

389. אַךְ 'ak, *ak;* akin to 403; a particle of affirmation, *surely;* hence (by limitation) *only:*—also, in any wise, at least, but, certainly, even, howbeit, nevertheless, notwithstanding, only, save, surely, of a surety, truly, verily, + wherefore, yet (but).

390. אַכַּד 'Akkad, *ak-kad';* from an unused root prob. mean. to *strengthen;* a *fortress; Accad*, a place in Bab.:—Accad.

391. אַכְזָב 'akzâb, *ak-zawb';* from 3576; *falsehood;* by impl. *treachery:*—liar, lie.

392. אַכְזִיב 'Akzîyb, *ak-zeeb';* from 391; *deceitful* (in the sense of a winter-torrent which *fails* in summer); *Akzib*, the name of two places in Pal.:—Achzib.

393. אַכְזָר 'akzâr, *ak-zawr';* from an unused root (appar. mean. to *act harshly*); *violent;* by impl. *deadly;* also (in a good sense) *brave:*—cruel, fierce.

394. אַכְזָרִי 'akzârîy, *ak-zaw-ree';* from 393; *terrible:*—cruel (one).

395. אַכְזְרִיּוּת 'akzᵉrîyûwth, *ak-ze-ree-ooth';* from 394; *fierceness:*—cruel.

396. אֲכִילָה 'ăkîylâh, *ak-ee-law';* fem. from 398; something *eatable*, i.e. *food:*—meat.

397. אָכִישׁ 'Âkîysh, *aw-keesh';* of uncert. der.; *Akish*, a Philistine king:—Achish.

398. אָכַל 'âkal, *aw-kal';* a prim. root; to *eat* (lit. or fig.):— × at all, burn up, consume, devour (-er, up), dine, eat (-er, up), feed (with), food, × freely, × in . . . wise (-deed, plenty), (lay) meat, × quite.

399. אֲכַל 'ăkal (Chald.), *ak-al';* corresp. to 398:— + accuse, devour, eat.

400. אֹכֶל 'ôkel, *o'-kel;* from 398; *food:*—eating, food, meal [-time], meat, prey, victuals.

401. אֻכָל 'Ûkâl, *oo-kawl';* or אֻכָּל **'Ukkâl**, *ook-kawl';* appar. from 398; *devoured; Ucal*, a fancy name:—Ucal.

402. אָכְלָה 'oklâh, *ok-law';* fem. of 401; *food:*—consume, devour, eat, food, meat.

403. אָכֵן 'âkên, *aw-kane';* from 3559 [comp. 3651]; *firmly;* fig. *surely;* also (advers.) *but:*—but, certainly, nevertheless, surely, truly, verily.

404. אָכַף 'âkaph, *aw-kaf';* a prim. root; appar. mean. to *curve* (as with a burden); to *urge:*—crave.

405. אֶכֶף 'ekeph, *eh'-kef;* from 404; a *load;* by impl. a *stroke* (others *dignity*):—hand.

406. אִכָּר 'ikkâr, *ik-kawr';* from an unused root mean. to *dig;* a *farmer:*—husbandman, ploughman.

407. אַכְשָׁף 'Akshâph, *ak-shawf';* from 3784; *fascination; Acshaph*, a place in Pal.:—Achshaph.

408. אַל 'al, *al;* a neg. particle [akin to 3808]; *not* (the qualified negation, used as a deprecative); once (Job 24 : 25) as a noun, *nothing:*—nay, neither, + never, no, nor, not, nothing [worth], rather than.

409. אַל 'al (Chald.), *al;* corresp. to 408:—not.

410. אֵל 'êl, *ale;* short. from 352; *strength;* as adj. *mighty;* espec. the *Almighty* (but used also of any *deity*):—God (god), × goodly, × great, idol, might (-y one), power, strong. Comp. names in "-el."

411. אֵל 'êl, *ale;* a demonstr. particle (but only in a plur. sense) *these* or *those:*—these, those. Comp. 428.

412. אֵל 'êl (Chald.), *ale;* corresp. to 411:—these.

413. אֵל 'êl, *ale;* (but used only in the shortened constr. form אֶל **'el**, *el*); a prim. particle, prop. denoting motion *towards*, but occasionally used of a quiescent position, i.e. *near, with* or *among;* often in general, *to:*—about, according to, after, against, among, as for, at, because (-fore, -side), both . . . and, by, concerning, for, from, × hath, in (-to), near, (out) of, over, through, to (-ward), under, unto, upon, whether, with (-in).

414. אֵלָא 'Êlâ', *ay-law';* a var. of 424; *oak; Ela*, an Isr.:—Elah.

415. אֵל אֱלֹהֵי יִשְׂרָאֵל 'Êl 'ĕlôhêy Yisrâ'êl, *ale el-o-hay' yis-raw-ale';* from 410 and 430 and 3478; the *mighty God of Jisrael; El-Elohi-Jisrael*, the title given to a consecrated spot by Jacob:—El-elohe-israel.

416. אֵל בֵּית־אֵל 'Êl Bêyth-'Êl, *ale bayth-ale';* from 410 and 1008; the *God of Bethel; El-Bethel*, the title given to a consecrated spot by Jacob:—El-beth-el.

417. אֶלְגָּבִישׁ 'elgâbîysh, *el-gaw-beesh';* from 410 and 1378; *hail* (as if a *great pearl*):—great hail [-stones].

418. אַלְגּוּמִּים 'algûwmmîym, *al-goom-meem';* by transp. for 484; sticks of *algum* wood:—algum [trees].

419. אֶלְדָּד 'Eldâd, *el-dâd';* from 410 and 1780; *God has loved; Eldad*, an Isr.:—Eldad.

420. אֶלְדָּעָה 'Eldâ'âh, *el-daw-aw';* from 410 and 3045; *God of knowledge; Eldaah*, a son of Midian:—Eldaah.

421. אָלָה 'âlâh, *aw-law';* a prim. root [rather ident. with 422 through the idea of *invocation*]; to *bewail:*—lament.

422. אָלָה 'âlâh, *aw-law';* a prim. root; prop. to *adjure*, i.e. (usually in a bad sense) *imprecate:*—adjure, curse, swear.

423. אָלָה 'âlâh, *aw-law';* from 422; an *imprecation:*—curse, cursing, execration, oath, swearing.

424. אֵלָה 'êlâh, *ay-law';* fem. of 352; an *oak* or other strong tree:—elm, oak, teil tree.

425. אֵלָה 'Êlâh, *ay-law';* the same as 424; *Elah*, the name of an Edomite, of four Isr., and also of a place in Pal.:—Elah.

426. אֱלָהּ 'ĕlâhh (Chald.), *el-aw';* corresp. to 433; *God:*—God, god.

427. אַלָּה 'allâh, *al-law';* a var. of 424:—oak.

428. אֵלֶּה 'êl-leh, *ale'-leh;* prol. from 411; *these* or *those:*—an- (the) other; one sort, so, some, such, them, these (same), they, this, those, thus, which, who (-m).

429. אֵלֶּה 'êlleh (Chald.), *ale'-leh;* corresp. to 428:—these.

אֱלֹהַּ **'ĕlôahh.** See 433.

430. אֱלֹהִים 'ĕlôhîym, *el-o-heem';* plur. of 433; *gods* in the ordinary sense; but spec. used (in the plur. thus, esp. with the art.) of the supreme *God;* occasionally applied by way of deference to *magistrates;* and sometimes as a superlative:—angels, × exceeding, God (gods) (-dess, -ly), × (very) great, judges, × mighty.

431. אֲלוּ 'ălûw (Chald.), *al-oo';* prob. prol. from 412; *lo!:*—behold.

432. אִלּוּ 'illûw, *il-loo';* prob. from 408; *nay*, i.e. (softened) *if:*—but if, yea though.

433. אֱלוֹהַּ 'ĕlôwahh, *el-o'-ah;* rarely (short.) אֱלֹהַּ **'ĕlôahh**, *el-o'-ah;* prob. prol. (emphat.) from 410; a *deity* or the *Deity:*—God, god. See 430.

434. אֱלוּל 'ĕlûwl, *el-ool';* for 457; good for *nothing:*—thing of nought.

435. אֱלוּל 'Ĕlûwl, *el-ool';* prob. of for. der.; *Elul*, the sixth Jewish month:—Elul.

436. אֵלוֹן 'êlôwn, *ay-lone';* prol. from 352; an *oak* or other strong tree:—plain. See also 356.

437. אַלּוֹן 'allôwn, *al-lone';* a var. of 436:—oak.

438. אַלּוֹן 'Allôwn, *al-lone';* the same as 437; *Allon*, an Isr., also a place in Pal.:—Allon.

439. אַלּוֹן בָּכוּת 'Allôwn Bâkûwth, *al-lone' baw-kooth';* from 437 and a var. of 1068; *oak of weeping; Allon-Bakuth*, a monumental tree:—Allon-bachuth.

440. אֵלוֹנִי 'Êlôwnîy, *ay-lo-nee';* or rather (short.) אֵלֹנִי **'Êlônîy**, *ay-lo-nee';* patron. from 438; an *Elonite* or desc. (collect.) of Elon:—Elonites.

441. אַלּוּף 'allûwph, *al-loof';* or (short.) אַלֻּף **'allûph**, *al-loof';* from 502; *familiar;* a *friend*, also *gentle;* hence a *bullock* (as being tame; applied, although masc., to a *cow*); and so a *chieftain* (as notable like neat cattle):—captain, duke, (chief) friend, governor, guide, ox.

442. אָלוּשׁ 'Âlûwsh, *aw-loosh';* of uncert. der.; *Alush*, a place in the Desert:—Alush.

443. אֶלְזָבָד 'Elzâbâd, *el-zaw-bawd';* from 410 and 2064; *God has bestowed; Elzabad*, the name of two Isr.:—Elzabad.

444. אָלַח 'âlach, *aw-lakh';* a prim. root; to *muddle*, i.e. (fig. and intrans.) to *turn* (morally) *corrupt:*—become filthy.

445. אֶלְחָנָן 'Elchânân, *el-khaw-nawn';* from 410 and 2603; *God* (is) *gracious; Elchanan*, an Isr.:—Elkanan.

אֵלִי **'Êlîy.** See 1017.

446. אֱלִיאָב **'Êlîy'âb**, *el-ee-awb'*; from 410 and 1; *God of* (his) *father; Eliab*, the name of six Isr.:—Eliab.

447. אֱלִיאֵל **'Êlîy'êl**, *el-ee-ale'*; from 410 repeated; *God of* (his) *God; Eliel*, the name of nine Isr.:—Eliel.

448. אֱלִיאָתָה **'Êlîy'âthâh**, *el-ee-aw-thaw'*; or (contr.) אֱלִיָּתָה **'Êlîyâthâh**, *el-ee-yaw-thaw'*; from 410 and 225; *God of* (his) *consent; Eliathah*, an Isr.:—Eliathah.

449. אֱלִידָד **'Êlîydâd**, *el-ee-dawd'*; from the same as 419; *God of* (his) *love; Elidad*, an Isr.:—Elidad.

450. אֶלְיָדָע **'Elyâdâ'**, *el-yaw-daw'*; from 410 and 3045; *God* (is) *knowing; Eljada*, the name of two Isr. and of an Aramaean leader:—Eliada.

451. אַלְיָה **'alyâh**, *al-yaw'*; from 422 (in the orig. sense of *strength*); the *stout* part, i.e. the fat *tail* of the Oriental sheep:—rump.

452. אֵלִיָּה **'Êlîyâh**, *ay-lee-yaw'*; or prol. אֵלִיָּהוּ **'Êlîyâhûw**, *ay-lee-yaw'-hoo*; from 410 and 3050; *God of Jehovah; Elijah*, the name of the famous prophet and of two other Isr.:—Elijah, Eliah.

453. אֱלִיהוּ **'Êlîyhûw**, *el-ee-hoo'*; or (fully) אֱלִיהוּא **'Êlîyhûw'**, *el-ee-hoo'*; from 410 and 1931; *God of him; Elihu*, the name of one of Job's friends, and of three Isr.:—Elihu.

454. אֶלְיְהוֹעֵינַי **'Elyᵉhôw'êynay**, *el-ye-ho-ay-nah'ee*; or (short.) אֶלְיוֹעֵינַי **'Elyôw'êynay**, *el-yo-ay-nah'ee*; from 413 and 3068 and 5869; *towards Jehovah* (are) *my eyes; Eljehoenai* or *Eljoenai*, the name of seven Isr.:—Elihoenai, Elionai.

455. אֶלְיַחְבָּא **'Elyachbâ'**, *el-yakh-baw'*; from 410 and 2244; *God will hide; Eljachba*, an Isr.:—Eliahbah.

456. אֱלִיחֹרֶף **'Êlîychôreph**, *el-ee-kho'-ref*; from 410 and 2779; *God of autumn; Elichoreph*, an Isr.:—Elihoreph.

457. אֱלִיל **'ĕlîyl**, *el-eel'*; appar. from 408; good for *nothing*, by anal. *vain* or *vanity*; spec. an *idol*:—idol, no value, thing of nought.

458. אֱלִימֶלֶךְ **'Êlîymelek**, *el-ee-meh'-lek*; from 410 and 4428; *God of* (the) *king; Elimelek*, an Isr.—Elimelech.

459. אִלֵּין **'illêyn** (Chald.), *il-lane'*; or shorter אִלֵּן **'illên**, *il-lane'*; prol. from 412; *these*:—the, these.

460. אֶלְיָסָף **'Elyâçâph**, *el-yaw-sawf'*; from 410 and 3254; *God* (is) *gatherer; Eljasaph*, the name of two Isr.:—Eliasaph.

461. אֱלִיעֶזֶר **'Êlîy'ezer**, *el-ee-eh'-zer*; from 410 and 5828; *God of help; Eliezer*, the name of a Damascene and of ten Isr.:—Eliezer.

462. אֱלִיעֵינַי **'Êlîy'êynay**, *el-ee-ay-nah'ee*; prob. contr. for 454; *Elienai*, an Isr.:—Elienai.

463. אֱלִיעָם **'Êlîy'âm**, *el-ee-awm'*; from 410 and 5971; *God of* (the) *people; Eliam*, an Isr.:—Eliam.

464. אֱלִיפַז **'Êlîyphaz**, *el-ee-faz'*; from 410 and 6337; *God of gold; Eliphaz*, the name of one of Job's friends, and of a son of Esau:—Eliphaz.

465. אֱלִיפָל **'Êlîyphâl**, *el-ee-fawl'*; from 410 and 6419; *God of judgment; Eliphal*, an Isr.:—Eliphal.

466. אֱלִיפְלֵהוּ **'Êlîyphᵉlêhûw**, *el-ee-fe-lay'-hoo*; from 410 and 6395; *God of his distinction; Eliphelehu*, an Isr.:—Elipheleh.

467. אֱלִיפֶלֶט **'Êlîypheleṭ**, *el-ee-feh'-let*; or (short.) אֶלְפֶּלֶט **'Elpeleṭ**, *el-peh'-let*; from 410 and 6405; *God of deliverance; Eliphelet* or *Elpelet*, the name of six Isr.:—Eliphalet, Eliphelet, Elpalet.

468. אֱלִיצוּר **'Êlêytsûwr**, *el-ee-tsoor'*; from 410 and 6697; *God of* (the) *rock; Elitsur*, an Isr.:—Elizur.

469. אֱלִיצָפָן **'Êlîytsâphân**, *el-ee-tsaw-fawn'*; or (short.) אֶלְצָפָן **'Eltsâphân**, *el-tsaw-fawn'*; from 410 and 6845; *God of treasure; Elitsaphan* or *Eltsaphan*, an Isr.:—Elizaphan, Elzaphan.

470. אֱלִיקָא **'Êlîyqâ'**, *el-ee-kaw'*; from 410 and 6958; *God of rejection; Elika*, an Isr.:—Elika.

471. אֶלְיָקִים **'Elyâqîym**, *el-yaw-keem'*; from 410 and 6965; *God of raising; Eljakim*, the name of four Isr.:—Eliakim.

472. אֱלִישֶׁבַע **'Êlîysheba'**, *el-ee-sheh'-bah*; from 410 and 7651 (in the sense of 7650); *God of* (the) *oath; Elisheba*, the wife of Aaron:—Elisheba.

473. אֱלִישָׁה **'Êlîyshâh**, *el-ee-shaw'*; prob. of for. der.; *Elishah*, a son of Javan:—Elishah.

474. אֱלִישׁוּעַ **'Êlîyshûwa'**, *el-ee-shoo'-ah*; from 410 and 7769; *God of supplication* (or *of riches*); *Elishua*, a son of King David:—Elishua.

475. אֶלְיָשִׁיב **'Elyâshîyb**, *el-yaw-sheeb'*; from 410 and 7725; *God will restore; Eljashib*, the name of six Isr.:—Eliashib.

476. אֱלִישָׁמָע **'Êlîyshâmâ'**, *el-ee-shaw-maw'*; from 410 and 8085; *God of hearing; Elishama*, the name of seven Isr.:—Elishama.

477. אֱלִישָׁע **'Êlîyshâ'**, *el-ee-shaw'*; contr. for 474; *Elisha*, the famous prophet:—Elisha.

478. אֱלִישָׁפָט **'Êlîyshâphâṭ**, *el-ee-shaw-fawt'*; from 410 and 8199; *God of judgment; Elishaphat*, an Isr.:—Elishaphat.

אֱלִיָּתָה **'Êlîyâthâh**. See 448.

479. אִלֵּךְ **'illêk** (Chald.), *il-lake'*; prol. from 412; *these*:—these, those.

480. אַלְלַי **'alᵉlay**, *al-le-lah'ee*; by redupl. from 421; *alas!*:—woe.

481. אָלַם **'âlam**, *aw-lam'*; a prim. root; to *tie* fast; hence (of the mouth) to be *tongue-tied*:—bind, be dumb, put to silence.

482. אֵלֶם **'êlem**, *ay'-lem*; from 481; *silence* (i.e. mute justice):—congregation. Comp. 3128.

אֵלָם **'êlâm**. See 361.

אֻלָם **'âlûm**. See 485.

483. אִלֵּם **'illêm**, *il-lame'*; from 481; *speechless*:—dumb (man).

484. אַלְמֻגִּים **'almuggîym**, *al-moog-gheem'*; prob. of for. der. (used thus only in the plur.); *almug* (i.e. prob. sandal-wood) sticks:—almug trees. Comp. 418.

485. אֲלֻמָּה **'ălummâh**, *al-oom-maw'*; or (masc.) אָלֻם **'âlûm**, *aw-loom'*; pass. part. of 481; something *bound*; a *sheaf*:—sheaf.

486. אַלְמוֹדָד **'Almôwdâd**, *al-mo-dawd'*; prob. of for. der.:—*Almodad*, a son of Joktan:—Almodad.

487. אַלַּמֶּלֶךְ **'Allammelek**, *al-lam-meh'-lek*; from 427 and 4428; *oak of* (the) *king; Allammelek*, a place in Pal.:—Alammelech.

488. אַלְמָן **'almân**, *al-mawn'*; prol. from 481 in the sense of *bereavement; discarded* (as a divorced person):—forsaken.

489. אַלְמֹן **'almôn**, *al-mone'*; from 481 as in 488; *bereavement*:—widowhood.

490. אַלְמָנָה **'almânâh**, *al-maw-naw'*; fem. of 488; a *widow*; also a *desolate* place:—desolate house (palace), widow.

491. אַלְמָנוּת **'almânûwth**, *al-maw-nooth'*; fem. of 488; concr. a *widow*; abstr. *widowhood*:—widow, widowhood.

492. אַלְמֹנִי **'almônîy**, *al-mo-nee'*; from 489 in the sense of *concealment*; *some* one (i.e. *so and so*, without giving the name of the person or place):—one, and such.

אִלֵּן **'illên**. See 459.

אֵלֹנִי **'Êlônîy**. See 440.

493. אֶלְנַעַם **'Elna'am**, *el-nah'-am*; from 410 and 5276; *God* (is his) *delight; Elnaam*, an Isr.:—Elnaam.

494. אֶלְנָתָן **'Elnâthân**, *el-naw-thawn'*; from 410 and 5414; *God* (is the) *giver; Elnathan*, the name of four Isr.:—Elnathan.

495. אֶלָּסָר **'Ellâçâr**, *el-law-sawr'*; prob. of for. der.; *Ellasar*, an early country of Asia:—Ellasar.

496. אֶלְעָד **'El'âd**, *el-awd'*; from 410 and 5749; *God has testified; Elad*, an Isr.:—Elead.

497. אֶלְעָדָה **'El'âdâh**, *el-aw-daw'*; from 410 and 5710; *God has decked; Eladah*, an Isr.:—Eladah.

498. אֶלְעוּזַי **'El'ûwzay**, *el-oo-zah'ee*; from 410 and 5756 (in the sense of 5797); *God* (is) *defensive; Eluzai*, an Isr.:—Eluzai.

499. אֶלְעָזָר **'El'âzâr**, *el-aw-zawr'*; from 410 and 5826; *God* (is) *helper; Elazar*, the name of seven Isr.:—Eleazar.

500. אֶלְעָלֵא **'El'âlê'**, *el-aw-lay'*; or (more properly) אֶלְעָלֵה **'El'âlêh**, *el-aw-lay'*; from 410 and 5927; *God* (is) *going up; Elale* or *Elaleh*, a place east of the Jordan:—Elealeh.

501. אֶלְעָשָׂה **'El'âsâh**, *el-aw-saw'*; from 410 and 6213; *God has made; Elasah*, the name of four Isr.:—Elasah, Eleasah.

502. אָלַף **'âlaph**, *aw-lof'*; a prim. root, to *associate* with; hence to *learn* (and caus. to *teach*):—learn, teach, utter.

503. אָלַף **'âlaph**, *aw-laf'*; denom. from 505; caus. to *make a thousandfold*:—bring forth thousands.

504. אֶלֶף **'eleph**, *eh'-lef*; from 502; a *family*; also (from the sense of *yoking* or *taming*) an *ox* or *cow*:—family, kine, oxen.

505. אֶלֶף **'eleph**, *eh'-lef*; prop. the same as 504; hence (an ox's head being the first letter of the alphabet, and this eventually used as a numeral) a *thousand*:—thousand.

506. אֲלַף **'ălaph** (Chald.), *al-af'*; or אֶלֶף **'eleph**, (Chald.), *eh'-lef*; corresp. to 505:—thousand.

507. אֶלֶף **'Eleph**, *eh'-lef*; the same as 505; *Eleph*, a place in Pal.:—Eleph.

אַלֻּף **'allûph**. See 441.

אֶלְפֶּלֶט **'Elpeleṭ**. See 467.

508. אֶלְפַּעַל **'Elpa'al**, *el-pah'-al*; from 410 and 6466; *God* (is) *act; Elpaal*, an Isr.:—Elpaal.

509. אָלַץ **'âlats**, *aw-lats'*; a prim. root; to *press*:—urge.

אֶלְצָפָן **'Eltsâphân**. See 469.

510. אַלְקוּם **'alqûwm**, *al-koom'*; prob. from 408 and 6965; a *non-rising* (i.e. *resistlessness*):—no rising up.

511. אֶלְקָנָה **'Elqânâh**, *el-kaw-naw'*; from 410 and 7069; *God has obtained; Elkanah*, the name of seven Isr.:—Elkanah.

512. אֶלְקֹשִׁי **'Elqôshîy**, *el-ko-shee'*; patrial from a name of uncert. der.; an *Elkoshite* or native of Elkosh:—Elkoshite.

513. אֶלְתּוֹלַד **'Eltôwlad**, *el-to-lad'*; prob. from 410 and a masc. form of 8435 [comp. 8434]; *God* (is) *generator; Eltolad*, a place in Pal.:—Eltolad.

514. אֶלְתְּקֵא **'Eltᵉqê**, *el-te-kay'*; or (more prop.) אֶלְתְּקֵה **'Eltᵉqêh**, *el-te-kay'*; of uncert. der.; *Elteke* or *Elteke*, a place in Pal.:—Eltekeh.

515. אֶלְתְּקֹן **'Eltᵉqôn**, *el-te-kone'*; from 410 and 8626; *God* (is) *straight; Eltekon*, a place in Pal.:—Eltekon.

516. אַל תַּשְׁחֵת **'Al tashchêth**, *al tash-kayth'*; from 408 and 7843; *Thou must not destroy*; prob. the opening words of a popular song:—Al-taschith.

517. אֵם **'êm**, *ame*; a prim. word; a *mother* (as the *bond* of the family); in a wide sense (both lit. and fig.) [like 1]:—dam, mother, × parting.

518. אִם **'im**, *eem;* a prim. particle; used very widely as demonstr., *lo!;* interrog., *whether?;* or conditional, *if, although;* also *Oh that!, when;* hence as a neg., *not:*—(and, can-, doubtless, if, that) (not), + but, either, + except, + more (-over if, than), neither, nevertheless, nor, oh that, or, + save (only, -ing), seeing, since, sith, + surely (no more, none, not), though, + of a truth, + unless, + verily, when, whereas, whether, while, + yet.

519. אָמָה **'âmâh**, *aw-maw';* appar. a prim. word; a *maid-servant* or female slave:—(hand-) bondmaid (-woman,) maid (-servant).

אֵמָה **'êmâh**. See 367.

520. אַמָּה **'ammâh**, *am-maw';* prol. from 517; prop. a *mother* (i.e. *unit*) of measure, or the *fore-arm* (below the elbow), i.e. a *cubit;* also a door-*base* (as a *bond* of the entrance):—cubit, + hundred [*by exchange for* 3967], measure, post.

521. אַמָּה **'ammâh** (Chald.), *am-maw';* corresp. to 520:—cubit.

522. אַמָּה **'Ammâh**, *am-maw';* the same as 520; *Ammah*, a hill in Pal.:—Ammah.

523. אֻמָּה **ummâh**, *oom-maw';* from the same as 517; a *collection*, i.e. community of persons:—nation, people.

524. אֻמָּה **'ummâh** (Chald.), *oom-maw';* corresp. to 523:—nation.

525. אָמוֹן **'âmôwn**, *aw-mone';* from 539, prob. in the sense of *training; skilled*, i.e. an architect [like 542]:—one brought up.

526. אָמוֹן **'Âmôwn**, *aw-mone';* the same as 525; *Amon*, the name of three Isr.:—Amon.

527. אָמוֹן **'âmôwn**, *aw-mone';* a var. for 1995; a *throng* of people:—multitude.

528. אָמוֹן **'Âmôwn**, *aw-mone';* of Eg. der.; *Amon* (i.e. Ammon or Amn), a deity of Egypt (used only as an adjunct of 4996):—multitude, populous.

529. אֵמוּן **'êmûwn**, *ay-moon';* from 539; *established*, i.e. (fig.) *trusty;* also (abstr.) *trustworthiness:*—faith (-ful), truth.

530. אֱמוּנָה **'ĕmûwnâh**, *em-oo-naw';* or (short.) אֱמֻנָה **'ĕmûnâh**, *em-oo-naw';* fem. of 529; lit. *firmness;* fig. *security;* mor. *fidelity:*—faith (-ful, -ly, -ness, [man]), set office, stability, steady, truly, truth, verily.

531. אָמוֹץ **'Âmôwts**, *aw-mohts';* from 553; *strong; Amots*, an Isr.:—Amoz.

532. אָמִי **'Âmîy**, *aw-mee';* an abbrev. for 526; *Ami*, an Isr.:—Ami.

אֲמִינוֹן **'Ămîynôwn**. See 550.

533. אַמִּיץ **'ammîyts**, *am-meets';* or (short.) אַמִּץ **'ammîts**, *am-meets';* from 553; *strong* or (abstr.) *strength:*—courageous, mighty, strong (one).

534. אָמִיר **'âmîyr**, *aw-meer';* appar. from 559 (in the sense of *self-exaltation*); a *summit* (of a tree or mountain):—bough, branch.

535. אָמַל **'âmal**, *aw-mal';* a prim. root; to *droop;* by impl. to *be sick*, to *mourn:*—languish, be weak, wax feeble.

536. אֻמְלַל **'umlal**, *oom-lal';* from 535; *sick:*—weak.

537. אֲמֵלָל **'ămêlâl**, *am-ay-lawl';* from 535; *languid:*—feeble.

538. אֲמָם **'Ămâm**, *am-awm';* from 517; *gathering*-spot; *Amam*, a place in Pal.:—Amam.

539. אָמַן **'âman**, *aw-man';* a prim. root; prop. *to build up* or *support;* to *foster* as a parent or nurse; fig. to *render* (or *be*) *firm* or faithful, to *trust* or believe, to be *permanent* or quiet; mor. to *be true* or certain; once (Isa. 30 : 21; by interch. for 541) to *go to the right hand:*—hence assurance, believe, bring up, establish, + fail, be faithful (of long continuance, stedfast, sure, surely, trusty, verified), nurse, (-ing father), (put), trust, turn to the right.

540. אֲמַן **'ăman** (Chald.), *am-an';* corresp. to 539:—believe, faithful, sure.

541. אָמַן **'âman**, *aw-man';* denom. from 3225; to take the *right hand* road:—turn to the right. See 539.

542. אָמָן **'âmân**, *aw-mawn';* from 539 (in the sense of *training*); an *expert:*—cunning workman.

543. אָמֵן **'âmên**, *aw-mane';* from 539; *sure;* abstr. *faithfulness;* adv. *truly:*—Amen, so be it, truth.

544. אֹמֶן **'ômen**, *oh-men';* from 539; *verity:*—truth.

545. אָמְנָה **'omnâh**, *om-naw';* fem. of 544 (in the spec. sense of *training*); *tutelage:*—brought up.

546. אָמְנָה **'omnâh**, *om-naw';* fem. of 544 (in its usual sense); adv. *surely:*—indeed.

547. אֹמְנָה **'ômᵉnâh**, *o-me-naw';* fem. act. part. of 544 (in the orig. sense of *supporting*); a *column:*—pillar.

548. אֲמָנָה **'ămânâh**, *am-aw-naw';* fem. of 543; something *fixed*, i.e. a *covenant*, an *allowance:*—certain portion, sure.

549. אֲמָנָה **'Ămânâh**, *am-aw-naw';* the same as 548; *Amanah*, a mountain near Damascus:—Amana.

אֱמֻנָה **'ĕmûnâh**. See 530.

550. אַמְנוֹן **'Amnôwn**, *am-nohn';* or אֲמִינוֹן **'Ămîynôwn**, *am-ee-nohn';* from 539; *faithful; Amnon* (or Aminon), a son of David:—Amnon.

551. אָמְנָם **'omnâm**, *om-nawm';* adv. from 544; *verily:*—indeed, no doubt, surely, (it is, of a) true (-ly, -th).

552. אֻמְנָם **'umnâm**, *oom-nawm';* an orth. var. of 551:—in (very) deed; of a surety.

553. אָמַץ **'âmats**, *aw-mats';* a prim. root; to *be alert*, phys. (on foot) or ment. (in courage):—confirm, be courageous (of good courage, stedfastly minded, strong, stronger), establish, fortify, harden, increase, prevail, strengthen (self), make strong (obstinate, speed).

554. אָמֹץ **'âmôts**, *aw-mohts';* prob. from 553; of a *strong* color, i.e. *red* (others *fleet*):—bay.

555. אֹמֶץ **'ômets**, *o'-mets;* from 553; *strength:*—stronger.

אַמִּץ **'ammîts**. See 533.

556. אַמְצָה **'amtsâh**, *am-tsaw';* from 553; *force:*—strength.

557. אַמְצִי **'Amtsîy**, *am-tsee';* from 553; *strong; Amtsi*, an Isr.:—Amzi.

558. אֲמַצְיָה **'Ămatsyâh**, *am-ats-yaw';* or אֲמַצְיָהוּ **'Ămatsyâhûw**, *am-ats-yaw'-hoo;* from 553 and 3050; *strength of Jah; Amatsjah*, the name of four Isr.:—Amaziah.

559. אָמַר **'âmar**, *aw-mar';* a prim. root; to *say* (used with great latitude):—answer, appoint, avouch, bid, boast self, call, certify, challenge, charge, + (at the, give) command (ment), commune, consider, declare, demand, × desire, determine, × expressly, × indeed, × intend, name, × plainly, promise, publish, report, require, say, speak (against, of), × still, × suppose, talk, tell, term, × that is, × think, use [speech], utter, × verily, × yet.

560. אֲמַר **'ămar** (Chald.), *am-ar';* corresp. to 559:—command, declare, say, speak, tell.

561. אֵמֶר **'êmer**, *ay'-mer;* from 559; something *said:*—answer, × appointed unto him, saying, speech, word.

562. אֹמֶר **'ômer**, *o'-mer;* the same as 561:—promise, speech, thing, word.

563. אִמַּר **'immar** (Chald.), *im-mar';* perh. from 560 (in the sense of *bringing forth*); a *lamb:*—lamb.

564. אִמֵּר **'Immêr**, *im-mare';* from 559; *talkative; Immer*, the name of five Isr.:—Immer.

565. אִמְרָה **'imrâh**, *im-raw';* or אֶמְרָה **'emrâh**, *em-raw';* fem. of 561, and mean. the same:—commandment, speech, word.

566. אִמְרִי **'Imrîy**, *im-ree';* from 564; *wordy; Imri*, the name of two Isr.:—Imri.

567. אֱמֹרִי **'Ĕmôrîy**, *em-o-ree';* prob. a patron. from an unused name derived from 559 in the sense of *publicity*, i.e. prominence; thus a *mountaineer;* an *Emorite*, one of the Canaanitish tribes:—Amorite.

568. אֲמַרְיָה **'Ămaryâh**, *am-ar-yaw';* or (prol.) אֲמַרְיָהוּ **'Ămaryâhûw**, *am-ar-yaw'-hoo;* from 559 and 3050; *Jah has said* (i.e. promised); *Amarjah*, the name of nine Isr.:—Amariah.

569. אַמְרָפֶל **'Amrâphel**, *am-raw-fel';* of uncert. (perh. for.) der.; *Amraphel*, a king of Shinar:—Amraphel.

570. אֶמֶשׁ **'emesh**, *eh'-mesh;* time *past*, i.e. *yesterday* or *last night:*—former time, yesterday (-night).

571. אֱמֶת **'emeth**, *eh'-meth;* contr. from 539; *stability;* fig. *certainty, truth, trustworthiness:*—assured (-ly), establishment, faithful, right, sure, true (-ly, -th), verity.

572. אַמְתַּחַת **'amtachath**, *am-takh'-ath;* from 4969; prop. something *expansive*, i.e. a *bag:*—sack.

573. אֲמִתַּי **'Ămittay**, *am-it-tah'ee;* from 571; *veracious; Amittai*, an Isr.:—Amittai.

574. אֵמְתָנִי **'emtânîy** (Chald.), *em-taw-nee';* from a root corresp. to that of 4975; *well-loined* (i.e. burly) or *mighty:*—terrible.

575. אָן **'ân**, *awn;* or אָנָה **'ânâh**, *aw'-naw;* contr. from 370; *where?;* hence *whither?, when?;* also *hither* and *thither:*—+ any (no) whither, now, where, whither (-soever).

אֹן **'Ôn**. See 204.

576. אֲנָא **'ănâ'** (Chald.), *an-aw';* or אֲנָה **'ănâh** (Chald.), *an-aw';* corresp. to 589; *I:*—I, as for me.

577. אָנָּא **'ânnâ'**, *awn'-naw;* or אָנָּה **'ânnâh**, *awn'-naw;* appar. contr. from 160 and 4994: *oh now!:*—I (me) beseech (pray) thee, O.

אֲנָה **'ănâh**. See 576.

אָנָה **'ânâh**. See 575.

578. אָנָה **'ânâh**, *aw-naw';* a prim. root; to *groan:*—lament, mourn.

579. אָנָה **'ânâh**, *aw-naw';* a prim. root [perh. rather ident. with 578 through the idea of *contraction* in anguish]; to *approach;* hence to *meet* in various senses:—befall, deliver, happen, seek a quarrel.

אָנָּה **'ânnâh**. See 577.

580. אֲנוּ **'ănûw**, *an-oo';* contr. for 587; *we:*—we.

אֹנוֹ **Ônôw**. See 207.

581. אִנּוּן **'innûwn** (Chald.), *in-noon';* or (fem.) אִנִּין **'inniyn** (Chald.), *in-neen';* corresp. to 1992; *they:*—× are, them, these.

582. אֱנוֹשׁ **'ĕnôwsh**, *en-oshe';* from 605; prop. a *mortal* (and thus differing from the more dignified 120); hence a *man* in gen. (singly or collect.):—another, × [blood-] thirsty, certain, chap [-man], divers, fellow, × in the flower of their age, husband, (certain, mortal) man, people, person, servant, some (× of them), + stranger, those, + their trade. It is often unexpressed in the Engl. Version, especially when used in apposition with another word. Comp. 376.

583. אֱנוֹשׁ **'Ĕnôwsh**, *en-ohsh';* the same as 582; *Enosh*, a son of Seth:—Enos.

584. אָנַח **'ânach**, *aw-nakh';* a prim. root; to *sigh:*—groan, mourn, sigh.

585. אֲנָחָה **'ănâchâh**, *an-aw-khaw';* from 585; *sighing:*—groaning, mourn, sigh.

586. אֲנַחְנָא **'ănachnâ'** (Chald.), *an-akh'-naw;* or אֲנַחְנָה **'ănachnâh** (Chald.), *an-akh-naw';* corresp. to 587; *we:*—we.

587. אֲנַחְנוּ **'ănachnûw**, *an-akh'-noo*, appar. from 595; *we:*—ourselves, us, we.

588. אֲנָחֲרָת **'Ănâchărâth**, *an-aw-kha-rawth';* prob. from the same root as 5170; a *gorge* or narrow pass; *Anacharath*, a place in Pal.:—Anaharath.

589. אֲנִי **'ănîy**, *an-ee'*; contr. from 595; *I:*—I, (as for) me, mine, myself, we, × which, × who.

590. אֳנִי **'ŏnîy**, *on-ee'*; prob. from 579 (in the sense of *conveyance*); a *ship* or (collect.) a *fleet:*—galley, navy (of ships).

591. אֳנִיָּה **'ŏnîyâh**, *on-ee-yaw'*; fem. of 590; a *ship:*—ship ([-men]).

592. אֲנִיָּה **'ănîyâh**, *an-ee-yaw'*; from 578; *groaning:*—lamentation, sorrow.

אִנִּין **'innîyn**. See 581.

593. אֲנִיעָם **'Ănîy'âm**, *an-ee-awm'*; from 578 and 5971; *groaning* of (the) *people; Aniam*, an Isr.:—Aniam.

594. אֲנָךְ **'ănâk**, *an-awk'*; prob. from an unused root mean. to *be narrow;* according to most a plumb-*line*, and to others a *hook:*—plumbline.

595. אָנֹכִי **'ânôkîy**, *aw-no-kee'* (sometimes *aw-no'-kee*); a prim. pron.; *I:*—I, me, × which.

596. אָנַן **'ânan**, *aw-nan'*; a prim. root; to *mourn*, i.e. *complain:*—complain.

597. אָנַס **'ânaç**, *aw-nas'*; to *insist:*—compel.

598. אֲנַס **'ănaç** (Chald.), *an-as'*; corresp. to 597; fig. to *distress:*—trouble.

599. אָנַף **'ânaph**, *aw-naf'*; a prim. root; to *breathe* hard, i.e. *be enraged:*—be angry (displeased).

600. אֲנַף **'ănaph** (Chald.), *an-af'*; corresp. to 639 (only in the plur. as a sing.); the *face:*—face, visage.

601. אֲנָפָה **'ănâphâh**, *an-aw-faw'*; from 599; an unclean bird, perh. the *parrot* (from its *irascibility*):—heron.

602. אָנַק **'ânaq**, *aw-nak'*; a prim. root; to *shriek:*—cry, groan.

603. אֲנָקָה **'ănâqâh**, *an-aw-kaw'*, from 602; *shrieking:*—crying out, groaning, sighing.

604. אֲנָקָה **'ănâqâh**, *an-aw-kaw'*; the same as 603; some kind of lizard, prob. the *gecko* (from its *wail*):—ferret.

605. אָנַשׁ **'ânash**, *aw-nash'*; a prim. root; to *be frail, feeble*, or (fig.) *melancholy:*—desperate (-ly wicked), incurable, sick, woeful.

606. אֱנָשׁ **'ĕnâsh** (Chald.), *en-awsh'*; or אֱנַשׁ **'ĕnash** (Chald.), *en-ash'*; corresp. to 582; a *man:*—man, + whosoever.

אַנְתְּ **'ant**. See 859.

607. אַנְתָּה **'antâh** (Chald.), *an-taw'*; corresp. to 859; *thou:*—as for thee, thou.

608. אַנְתּוּן **'antûwn** (Chald.), *an-toon'*; plur. of 607; *ye:*—ye.

609. אָסָא **'Âçâ'**, *aw-saw'*; of uncert. der.; *Asa*, the name of a king and of a Levite:—Asa.

610. אָסוּךְ **'âçûwk**, *aw-sook'*; from 5480; *anointed*, i.e. an oil-*flask:*—pot.

611. אָסוֹן **'âçôwn**, *aw-sone'*; of uncert. der.; *hurt:*—mischief.

612. אֵסוּר **'êçûwr**, *ay-soor'*; from 631; a *bond* (espec. *manacles* of a prisoner):—band, + prison.

613. אֱסוּר **'ĕçûwr** (Chald.), *es-oor'*; corresp. to 612:—band, imprisonment.

614. אָסִיף **'âçîyph**, *aw-seef'*; or אָסִף **'âçiph**, *aw-seef'*; from 622; *gathered*, i.e. (abstr.) a *gathering* in of crops:—ingathering.

615. אָסִיר **'âçîyr**, *aw-sere'*; from 631; *bound*, i.e. a *captive:*—(those which are) bound, prisoner.

616. אַסִּיר **'aççîyr**, *as-sere'*; for 615:—prisoner.

617. אַסִּיר **'Aççîyr**, *as-sere'*; the same as 616; *prisoner; Assir*, the name of two Isr.:—Assir.

618. אָסָם **'âçâm**, *aw-sawm'*; from an unused root mean. to *heap* together; a *storehouse* (only in the plur.):—barn, storehouse.

619. אַסְנָה **'Açnâh**, *as-naw'*; of uncert. der.; *Asnah*, one of the Nethinim:—Asnah.

620. אָסְנַפַּר **'Oçnappar**, *os-nap-par'*; of for. der.; *Osnappar*, an Assyrian king:—Asnapper.

621. אָסְנַת **'Âçᵉnath**, *aw-se-nath'*; of Eg. der.; *Asenath*, the wife of Joseph:—Asenath.

622. אָסַף **'âçaph**, *aw-saf'*; a prim. root; to *gather* for any purpose; hence to *receive, take away*, i.e. remove (destroy, leave behind, put up, restore, etc.):—assemble, bring, consume, destroy, fetch, gather (in, together, up again), × generally, get (him), lose, put all together, receive, recover [another from leprosy], (be) rereward, × surely, take (away, into, up), × utterly, withdraw.

623. אָסָף **'Âçâph**, *aw-sawf'*; from 622; *collector; Asaph*, the name of three Isr., and of the family of the first:—Asaph.

אָסִף **'âçiph**. See 614.

624. אָסֻף **'âçûph**, *aw-soof'*; pass. part. of 622; *collected* (only in the plur.), i.e. a *collection* (of offerings):—threshold, Asuppim.

625. אֹסֶף **'ôçeph**, *o'-sef*; from 622; a *collection* (of fruits):—gathering.

626. אֲסֵפָה **'ăçêphâh**, *as-ay-faw'*; from 622; a *collection* of people (only adv.):—× together.

627. אֲסֻפָּה **'ăçuppâh**, *as-up-paw'*; fem. of 624; a *collection* of (learned) men (only in the plur.):—assembly.

628. אֲסַפְסֻף **'açpᵉçûph**, *as-pes-oof'*; by redupl. from 624; *gathered up together*, i.e. a promiscuous *assemblage* (of people):—mixt multitude.

629. אָסְפַּרְנָא **'ocparnâ'** (Chald.), *os-par-naw'*; of Pers. der.; *diligently:*—fast, forthwith, speed (-ily).

630. אַסְפָּתָא **'Açpâthâ'**, *as-paw-thaw'*; of Pers. der.; *Aspatha*, a son of Haman:—Aspatha.

631. אָסַר **'âçar**, *aw-sar'*; a prim. root; to *yoke* or *hitch;* by anal. to *fasten* in any sense, to *join* battle:—bind, fast, gird, harness, hold, keep, make ready, order, prepare, prison (-er), put in bonds, set in array, tie.

632. אֱסָר **'ĕçâr**, *es-awr'*; or אִסָּר **'iççâr**, *is-sawr'*; from 631; an *obligation* or *vow* (of abstinence):—binding, bond.

633. אֱסָר **'ĕçâr** (Chald.), *es-awr'*; corresp. to 632 in a legal sense; an *interdict:*—decree.

634. אֵסַר־חַדּוֹן **'Êçar-Chaddôwn**, *ay-sar' chad-dohn'*; of for. der.; *Esar-chaddon*, an Assyr. king:—Esar-haddon.

635. אֶסְתֵּר **'Eçtêr**, *es-tare'*; of Pers. der.; *Ester*, the Jewish heroine:—Esther.

636. אָע **'â'** (Chald.), *aw*; corresp. to 6086; a *tree* or *wood:*—timber, wood.

637. אַף **'aph**, *af*; a prim. particle; mean. *accession* (used as an adv. or conj.); *also* or *yea;* adversatively *though:*—also, + although, and (furthermore, yet), but, even, + how much less (more, rather than), moreover, with, yea.

638. אַף **'aph** (Chald.), *af*; corresp. to 637:—also.

639. אַף **'aph**, *af*; from 599; prop. the *nose* or *nostril;* hence the *face*, and occasionally a *person;* also (from the rapid breathing in passion) *ire:*—anger (-gry), + before, countenance, face, + forbearing, forehead, + [long-] suffering, nose, nostril, snout, × worthy, wrath.

640. אָפַד **'âphad**, *aw-fad'*; a prim. root [rather a denom. from 646]; to *gird* on (the ephod):—bind, gird.

אֵפֹד **'êphôd**. See 646.

641. אֵפֹד **'Êphôd**, *ay-fode'*; the same as 646 short.; *Ephod*, an Isr.:—Ephod.

642. אֲפֻדָּה **'êphuddâh**, *ay-food-daw'*; fem. of 646; a *girding* on (of the ephod); hence gen. a *plating* (of metal):—ephod, ornament.

643. אַפֶּדֶן **'appeden**, *ap-peh'-den*; appar. of for. der.; a *pavilion* or palace-tent:—palace.

644. אָפָה **'âphâh**, *aw-faw'*; a prim. root; to *cook*, espec. to *bake:*—bake, (-r, [-meats]).

אֵפָה **'êphâh**. See 374.

645. אֵפוֹ **'ephôw**, *ay-fo'*; or אֵפוֹא **'êphôw'**, *ay-fo'*; from 6311; strictly a demonstrative particle, *here;* but used of time, *now* or *then:*—here, now, where?

646. אֵפוֹד **'êphôwd**, *ay-fode'*; rarely אֵפֹד **'êphôd**, *ay-fode'*; prob. of for. der.; a *girdle;* spec. the *ephod* or high-priest's shoulder-piece; also gen. an *image:*—ephod.

647. אֲפִיחַ **'Ăphîyach**, *af-ee'-akh*; perh. from 6315; *breeze; Aphiach*, an Isr.:—Aphiah.

648. אָפִיל **'âphîyl**, *aw-feel'*; from the same as 651 (in the sense of *weakness*); *unripe:*—not grown up.

649. אַפַּיִם **'Appayim**, *ap-pah'-yim*; dual of 639; *two nostrils; Appajim*, an Isr.:—Appaim.

650. אָפִיק **'âphîyq**, *aw-feek'*; from 622; prop. *containing*, i.e. a *tube;* also a *bed* or *valley* of a stream; also a *strong* thing or a *hero:*—brook, channel, mighty, river, + scale, stream, strong piece.

אֹפִיר **'Ôphîyr**. See 211.

651. אָפֵל **'âphêl**, *aw-fale'*; from an unused root mean. to *set* as the sun; *dusky:*—very dark.

652. אֹפֶל **'ôphel**, *o'-fel*; from the same as 651; *dusk:*—darkness, obscurity, privily.

653. אֲפֵלָה **'ăphêlâh**, *af-ay-law'*; fem. of 651; *duskiness*, fig. *misfortune;* concr. *concealment:*—dark, darkness, gloominess, × thick.

654. אֶפְלָל **'Ephlâl**, *ef-lawl'*; from 6419; *judge; Ephlal*, an Isr.:—Ephlal.

655. אֹפֶן **'ôphen**, *o'-fen*; from an unused root mean. to *revolve;* a *turn*, i.e. a *season:*—+ fitly.

אֹפָן **'ôphân**. See 212.

656. אָפֵס **'âphêç**, *aw-face'*; a prim. root; to *disappear*, i.e. *cease:*—be clean gone (at an end, brought to nought), fail.

657. אֶפֶס **'epheç**, *eh'-fes*; from 656; *cessation*, i.e. an *end* (espec. of the earth); often used adv. *no further;* also (like 6466) the *ankle* (in the dual), as being the extremity of the leg or foot:—ankle, but (only), end, howbeit, less than nothing, nevertheless (where), no, none (beside), not (any, -withstanding), thing of nought, save (-ing), there, uttermost part, want, without (cause).

658. אֶפֶס דַּמִּים **'Epheç Dammîym**, *eh'-fes dam-meem'*; from 657 and the plur. of 1818; *boundary of blood*-drops; *Ephes-Dammim*, a place in Pal.:—Ephes-dammim.

659. אֶפַע **'ẹpha'**, *eh'-fah*; from an unused root prob. mean. to *breathe;* prop. a *breath*, i.e. *nothing:*—of nought.

660. אֶפְעֶה **'eph'eh**, *ef-eh'*; from 659 (in the sense of *hissing*); an *asp* or other venomous serpent:—viper.

661. אָפַף **'âphaph**, *aw-faf'*; a prim. root; to *surround:*—compass.

662. אָפַק **'âphaq**, *aw-fak'*; a prim. root; to *contain*, i.e. (reflex.) *abstain:*—force (oneself), restrain.

663. אֲפֵק **'Ăphêq**, *af-ake'*; or אֲפִיק **'Ăphîyq**, *af-eek'*; from 662 (in the sense of *strength*); *fortress; Aphek* (or *Aphik*), the name of three places in Pal.:—Aphek, Aphik.

664. אֲפֵקָה **'Ăphêqâh**, *af-ay-kaw'*; fem. of 663; *fortress; Aphekah*, a place in Pal.:—Aphekah.

665. אֵפֶר **'êpher**, *ay'-fer*; from an unused root mean. to *bestrew; ashes:*—ashes.

666. אֲפֵר **'ăphêr**, *af-ayr'*; from the same as 665 (in the sense of *covering*); a *turban:*—ashes.

667. אֶפְרֹחַ **'ephrôach**, *ef-ro'-akh*; from 6524 (in the sense of *bursting* the shell); the *brood* of a bird:—young (one).

668. אַפִּרְיוֹן **'appiryôwn**, *ap-pir-yone'*; prob. of Eg. der.; a *palanquin:*—chariot.

669. אֶפְרַיִם **'Ephrayim**, *ef-rah'-yim*; dual of a masc. form of 672; *double fruit; Ephrajim*, a son of Joseph; also the tribe descended from him, and its territory:—Ephraim, Ephraimites

670. אֲפָרְסַי **'Âphâr^eçay** (Chald.), *af-aw-re-sah'-ee;* of for. or. (only in the plur.); an *Apharesite* or inhabitant of an unknown region of Assyria:—Apharsite.

671. אֲפַרְסְכַי **'Âpharç^ekay** (Chald.), *af-ar-sek-ah'ee;* or אֲפַרְסַתְכַי **'Âpharçathkay** (Chald.), *af-ar-sath-kah'ee;* of for. or. (only in the plur.); an *Apharsekite* or *Apharsathkite,* an unknown Assyrian tribe:—Apharsachites, Apharsathchites.

672. אֶפְרָת **'Ephrâth,** *ef-rawth';* or אֶפְרָתָה **'Ephrâthâh,** *ef-raw'-thaw;* from 6509; *fruitfulness; Ephrath,* another name for Bethlehem; once (Psa. 132 : 6) perh. for *Ephraim;* also of an Israelitish woman:—Ephrath, Ephratah.

673. אֶפְרָתִי **'Ephrâthîy,** *ef-rawth-ee';* patrial from 672; an *Ephrathite* or an *Ephraimite:*—Ephraimite, Ephrathite.

674. אַפְּתֹם **'app^ethôm** (Chald.), *ap-pe-thome';* of Pers. or.; *revenue;* others *at the last:*—revenue.

675. אֶצְבּוֹן **'Etsbôwn,** *ets-bone';* or אֶצְבֹּן **'Etsbôn,** *ets-bone';* of uncert. der.; *Etsbon,* the name of two Isr.:—Ezbon.

676. אֶצְבַּע **'etsba',** *ets-bah';* from the same as 6648 (in the sense of *grasping*); some thing to *seize* with, i.e. a *finger;* by anal. a *toe:*—finger, toe.

677. אֶצְבַּע **'etsba'** (Chald.), *ets-bah';* corresp. to 676:—finger, toe.

678. אָצִיל **'âtsîyl,** *aw-tseel';* from 680 (in its secondary sense of *separation*); an *extremity* (Isa. 41 : 9), also a *noble:*—chief man, noble.

679. אַצִּיל **'atstsîyl,** *ats-tseel';* from 680 (in its primary sense of *uniting*); a *joint* of the hand (i.e. *knuckle*); also (accord. to some) a *party-wall* (Ezek. 41 : 8):—[arm] hole, great.

680. אָצַל **'âtsal,** *aw-tsal';* a prim. root; prop. to *join;* used only as a denom. from 681; to *separate;* hence to *select, refuse, contract:*—keep, reserve, straiten, take.

681. אֵצֶל **'êtsel,** *ay'-tsel;* from 680 (in the sense of *joining*); a *side;* (as a prep.) *near:*—at, (hard) by, (from) (beside), near (unto), toward, with. See also 1018.

682. אָצֵל **'Âtsêl,** *aw-tsale';* from 680; *noble; Atsel,* the name of an Isr., and of a place in Pal.:—Azal, Azel.

683. אֲצַלְיָהוּ **'Atsalyâhûw,** *ats-al-yaw'-hoo;* from 680 and 3050 prol.; *Jah has reserved; Atsaljah,* an Isr.:—Azaliah.

684. אֹצֶם **'Ôtsem,** *o'-tsem;* from an unused root prob. mean. to *be strong; strength* (i.e. *strong*); *Otsem,* the name of two Isr.:—Ozem.

685. אֶצְעָדָה **'ets'âdâh,** *ets-aw-daw';* a var. from 6807; prop. a *step-chain;* by anal. a *bracelet:*—bracelet, chain.

686. אָצַר **'âtsar,** *aw-tsar';* a prim. root; to *store up:*—(lay up in) store, (make) treasure (-r).

687. אֵצֶר **'Êtser,** *ay'-tser;* from 686; *treasure; Etser,* an Idumæan:—Ezer.

688. אֶקְדָּח **'eqdâch,** *ek-dawkh';* from 6916; *burning,* i.e. a *carbuncle* or other fiery gem:—carbuncle.

689. אַקּוֹ **'aqqôw,** *ak-ko';* prob. from 602; *slender,* i.e. the *ibex:*—wild goat.

690. אֲרָא **'Ărâ',** *ar-aw';* prob. for 738; *lion; Ara,* an Isr.:—Ara.

691. אֶרְאֵל **'er'êl,** *er-ale';* prob. for 739; a h[illegible] (collect.):—valiant one.

692. אַרְאֵלִי **'Ar'êlîy,** *ar-ay-lee';* from 691; *heroic; Areli* (or an *Arelite,* collect.), an Isr. and his desc.:—Areli, Arelites.

693. אָרַב **'ârab,** *aw-rab';* a prim. root; to *lurk:*—(lie in) ambush (-ment), lay (lie in) wait.

694. אֲרָב **'Ărâb,** *ar-awb';* from 693; *ambush; Arab,* a place in Pal.:—Arab.

695. אֶרֶב **'ereb,** *eh'-reb;* from 693; *ambuscade:*—den, lie in wait.

696. אֹרֶב **'ôreb,** *o'-reb:* the same as 695:—wait.

אַרְבֵּאל **'Arbê'l.** See 1009.

697. אַרְבֶּה **'arbeh,** *ar-beh';* from 7235; a *locust* (from its rapid *increase*):—grasshopper, locust.

698. אָרֳבָה **'orŏbâh,** *or-ob-aw';* fem. of 696 (only in the plur.); *ambuscades:*—spoils.

699. אֲרֻבָּה **'ărubbâh,** *ar-oob-baw';* fem. part. pass. of 693 (as if for *lurking*); a *lattice;* (by impl.) a *window, dove-cot* (because of the pigeon-holes), *chimney* (with its apertures for smoke), *sluice* (with openings for water):—chimney, window.

700. אֲרֻבּוֹת **'Ărubbôwth,** *ar-oob-both;* plur. of 699; *Arubboth,* a place in Pal.:—Arubboth.

701. אַרְבִּי **'Arbîy,** *ar-bee';* patrial from 694; an *Arbite* or native of Arab:—Arbite.

702. אַרְבַּע **'arba',** *ar-bah';* masc. אַרְבָּעָה **'arbâ'âh,** *ar-baw-aw';* from 7251; *four:*—four.

703. אַרְבַּע **'arba'** (Chald.), *ar-bah';* corresp. to 702:—four.

704. אַרְבַּע **'Arba',** *ar-bah';* the same as 702; *Arba,* one of the Anakim:—Arba.

אַרְבָּעָה **'arbâ'âh.** See 702.

705. אַרְבָּעִים **'arbâ'îym,** *ar-baw-eem';* multiple of 702; *forty:*—forty.

706. אַרְבַּעְתַּיִם **'arba'tayim,** *ar-bah-tah'-yim;* dual of 702; *fourfold:*—fourfold.

707. אָרַג **'ârag,** *aw-rag';* a prim. root; to *plait* or *weave:*—weaver (-r).

708. אֶרֶג **'ereg,** *eh'-reg;* from 707; a *weaving;* a *braid;* also a *shuttle:*—beam, weaver's shuttle.

709. אַרְגֹּב **'Argôb,** *ar-gobe';* from the same as 7263; *stony; Argob,* a district of Pal.:—Argob.

710. אַרְגְּוָן **'arg^evân,** *arg-ev-awn';* a var. for 713; *purple:*—purple.

711. אַרְגְּוָן **'arg^evân** (Chald.), *arg-ev-awn';* corresp. to 710:—scarlet.

712. אַרְגַּז **'argâz,** *ar-gawz';* perh. from 7264 (in the sense of being *suspended*); a *box* (as a pannier):—coffer.

713. אַרְגָּמָן **'argâmân,** *ar-gaw-mawn';* of for. or.; *purple* (the color or the dyed stuff):—purple.

714. אַרְדְּ **'Ard,** *ard;* from an unused root prob. mean. to *wander; fugitive; Ard,* the name of two Isr.:—Ard.

715. אַרְדּוֹן **'Ardôwn,** *ar-dohn';* from the same as 714; *roaming; Ardon,* an Isr.:—Ardon.

716. אַרְדִּי **'Ardîy,** *ar-dee';* patron. from 714; an *Ardite* (collect.) or desc. of Ard:—Ardites.

717. אָרָה **'ârâh,** *aw-raw';* a prim. root; to *pluck:*—gather, pluck.

718. אֲרוּ **'ărûw** (Chald.), *ar-oo';* prob. akin to 431; *lo!:*—behold, lo.

719. אַרְוַד **'Arvad,** *ar-vad';* prob. from 7300; a refuge for the *roving; Arvad,* an island-city of Pal.:—Arvad.

720. אֲרוֹד **'Ărôwd,** *ar-ode';* an orth. var. of 719; *fugitive; Arod,* an Isr.:—Arod.

721. אַרְוָדִי **'Arvâdîy,** *ar-vaw-dee';* patrial from 719; an *Arvadite* or citizen of Arvad:—Arvadite.

722. אֲרוֹדִי **'Ărôwdîy,** *ar-o-dee';* patron. from 721; an *Arodite* or desc. of Arod:—Arodi, Arodites.

723. אֻרְוָה **'urvâh,** *oor-vaw';* or, אֲרָיָה **'ărâyâh,** *ar-aw-yah';* from 717 (in the sense of *feeding*); a *herding-place* for an animal:—stall.

724. אֲרוּכָה **'ărûwkâh,** *ar-oo-kaw';* or אֲרֻכָה **'ărûkâh,** *ar-oo-kaw';* fem. pass. part. of 748 (in the sense of *restoring* to soundness); *wholeness* (lit. or fig.):—health, made up, perfected.

725. אֲרוּמָה **'Ărûwmâh,** *ar-oo-maw';* a var. of 7316; *height; Arumah,* a place in Pal.:—Arumah.

726. אֲרוֹמִי° **'Ărôwmîy,** *ar-o-mee';* a clerical error for 130; an *Edomite* (as in the marg.):—Syrian.

727. אָרוֹן **'ârôwn,** *aw-rone';* or אָרֹן **'ârôn,** *aw-rone';* from 717 (in the sense of *gathering*); a *box:*—ark, chest, coffin.

728. אֲרַוְנָה **'Ăravnâh,** *ar-av-naw';* or (by transp.) אוֹרְנָה° **'Ôwrnâh,** *ore-naw';* or אֲנִיָּה° **'Arnîyah,** *ar-nee-yaw';* all by orth. var. for 771; *Aravnah* (or *Arnijah* or *Ornah*), a Jebusite:—Araunah.

729. אָרַז **'âraz,** *aw-raz';* a prim. root; to be *firm;* used only in the pass. participle as a denom. from 730; of *cedar:*—made of cedar.

730. אֶרֶז **'erez,** *eh'-rez;* from 729; a *cedar* tree (from the tenacity of its roots):—cedar (tree).

731. אַרְזָה **'arzâh,** *ar-zaw';* fem. of 730; *cedar* wainscoting:—cedar work.

732. אָרַח **'ârach,** *aw-rakh';* a prim. root; to *travel:*—go, wayfaring (man).

733. אָרַח **'Ârach,** *aw-rakh';* from 732; *way-faring; Arach,* the name of three Isr.:—Arah.

734. אֹרַח **'ôrach,** *o'-rakh;* from 732; a well trodden *road* (lit. or fig.); also a *caravan:*—manner, path, race, rank, traveller, troop, [by-, high-] way.

735. אֹרַח **'ôrach** (Chald.), *o'-rakh;* corresp. to 734; a *road:*—way.

736. אֹרְחָה **'ôr^echâh,** *o-rekh-aw';* fem. act. part. of 732; a *caravan:*—(travelling) company.

737. אֲרֻחָה **'ărûchâh,** *ar-oo-khaw';* fem. pass. part. of 732 (in the sense of *appointing*); a *ration* of food:—allowance, diet, dinner, victuals.

738. אֲרִי **'ărîy,** *ar-ee';* or (prol.) אַרְיֵה **'aryêh,** *ar-yay';* from 717 (in the sense of *violence*); a *lion:*—(young) lion, + pierce [*from the marg.*].

739. אֲרִיאֵל **'ărîy'êl,** *ar-ee-ale';* or אֲרִאֵל **'ărî'êl,** *ar-ee-ale';* from 738 and 410; *lion of God,* i.e. *heroic:*—lionlike men.

740. אֲרִיאֵל **'Ărî'êl,** *ar-ee-ale';* the same as 739; *Ariel,* a symb. name for Jerusalem, also the name of an Isr.:—Ariel.

741. אֲרִאֵיל **'ărî'êyl,** *ar-ee-ale';* either by transposition for 739 or, more prob., an orth. var. for 2025; the *altar* of the Temple:—altar.

742. אֲרִידַי **'Ărîyday,** *ar-ee-dah'-ee;* of Pers. or.; *Aridai,* a son of Haman:—Aridai.

743. אֲרִידָתָא **'Ărîydâthâ',** *ar-ee-daw-thaw';* of Pers. or.; *Aridatha,* a son of Haman:—Aridatha.

אַרְיֵה **'aryêh.** See 738.

744. אַרְיֵה **'aryêh** (Chald.), *ar-yay';* corresp. to 738:—lion.

745. אַרְיֵה **'Aryêh,** *ar-yay';* the same as 738; *lion; Arjeh,* an Isr.:—Arieh.

אֲרָיָה **'ărâyâh.** See 723.

746. אַרְיוֹךְ **'Ăryôwk,** *ar-yoke';* of for. or.; *Arjok,* the name of two Babylonians:—Arioch.

747. אֲרִיסַי **'Ărîyçay,** *ar-ee-sah'-ee;* of Pers. or.; *Arisai,* a son of Haman:—Arisai.

748. אָרַךְ **'ârak,** *aw-rak';* a prim. root; to *be* (caus. *make*) *long* (lit. or fig.):—defer, draw out, lengthen, (be, become, make, pro-) long, + (out-, over-) live, tarry (long).

749. אֲרַךְ **'ărak** (Chald.), *ar-ak';* prop. corresp. to 748, but used only in the sense of *reaching* to a given point; to *suit:*—be meet.

750. אָרֵךְ **'ârêk,** *aw-rake';* from 748; *long:*—long [-suffering, -winged], patient, slow [to anger].

751. אֶרֶךְ **'Erek,** *eh'-rek;* from 748; *length; Erek,* a place in Bab.:—Erech.

752. אָרֹךְ **'ârôk,** *aw-roke';* from 748; *long:*—long.

753. אֹרֶךְ **'ôrek,** *o'-rek;* from 748; *length:*—+ for ever, length, long.

754. אַרְכָא **'arkâ'** (Chald.), *ar-kaw';* or אַרְכָּה **'arkâh** (Chald.), *arkaw';* from 749; *length:*—lengthening, prolonged.

755. אַרְכֻבָה **'arkûbâh** (Chald.), *ar-koo-baw'* from an unused root corresp. to 7392 (in the sense of *bending* the knee); the *knee:*—knee.

אֲרֻכָה **'ărûkâh.** See 724.

756. אַרְכְּוַי **'Ark^evay** (Chald.), *ar-kev-ah'ee;* patrial from 751; an *Arkevite* (collect.) or native of Erek:—Archevite.

757 אַרְכִּי **'Arkîy,** *ar-kee';* patrial from another place (in Pal.) of similar name with 751; an *Arkite* or native of Erek:—Archi, Archite.

758. אֲרָם **'Ărâm,** *arawm';* from the same as 759; the *highland; Aram* or Syria, and its inhabitants; also the name of a son of Shem, a grandson of Nahor, and of an Isr.:—Aram, Mesopotamia, Syria, Syrians.

759. אַרְמוֹן **'armôwn,** *ar-mone';* from an unused root (mean. to *be elevated*); a *citadel* (from its *height*):—castle, palace. Comp. 2038.

760. אֲרַם צוֹבָה **'Ăram Tsôbâh,** *ar-am' tso-baw';* from 758 and 6678; *Aram of Tsoba* (or Cœle-Syria):—Aram-zobah.

761. אֲרַמִּי **'Ărammîy,** *ar-am-mee';* patrial from 758; an *Aramite* or Aramæan:—Syrian, Aramitess.

762. אֲרָמִית **'Ărâmîyth,** *ar-aw-meeth';* fem. of 761; (only adv.) *in Aramæan:*—in the Syrian language (tongue), in Syriack.

763. אֲרַם נַהֲרַיִם **'Ăram Nahărayim,** *ar-am' nah-har-ah'-yim;* from 758 and the dual of 5104; *Aram of* (the) *two rivers* (Euphrates and Tigris) or Mesopotamia:—Aham-naharaim, Mesopotamia.

764. אַרְמֹנִי **'Armônîy,** *ar-mo-nee';* from 759; *palatial; Armoni,* an Isr.:—Armoni.

765. אֲרָן **'Ărân,** *ar-awn';* from 7442; *stridulous; Aran,* an Edomite:—Aran.

766. אֹרֶן **'ôren,** *o'-ren;* from the same as 765 (in the sense of *strength*); the *ash* tree (from its toughness):—ash.

767. אֹרֶן **'Ôren,** *o'-ren;* the same as 766; *Oren,* an Isr.:—Oren.

אָרֹן **'ârôn.** See 727.

768. אַרְנֶבֶת **'arnebeth,** *ar-neh'-beth;* of uncert. der.; the *hare:*—hare.

769. אַרְנוֹן **'Arnôwn,** *ar-nohn';* or אַרְנֹן **'Arnôn,** *ar-nohn';* from 7442; a *brawling* stream; the *Arnon,* a river east of the Jordan; also its territory:—Arnon.

אֲרַנְיָה **'Arnîyah.** See 728.

770. אַרְנָן **'Arnân,** *ar-nawn';* prob. from the same as 769; *noisy; Arnan,* an Isr.:—Arnan.

771. אָרְנָן **'Ornân,** *or-nawn';* prob. from 766; *strong; Ornan,* a Jebusite:—Ornan. See 728.

772. אֲרַע **'ăra'** (Chald.), *ar-ah';* corresp. to 776; the *earth;* by impl. (fig.) *low:*—earth, inferior.

773. אַרְעִית **'ar'îyth** (Chald.), *arh-eeth';* fem. of 772; the *bottom:*—bottom.

774. אַרְפָּד **'Arpâd,** *ar-pawd';* from 7502; *spread* out; *Arpad,* a place in Syria:—Arpad, Arphad.

775. אַרְפַּכְשַׁד **'Arpakshad,** *ar-pak-shad';* prob. of for. or.; *Arpakshad,* a son of Noah; also the region settled by him:—Arphaxad.

776. אֶרֶץ **'erets,** *eh'-rets;* from an unused root prob. mean. to *be firm;* the *earth* (at large, or partitively a *land*):— × common, country, earth, field, ground, land, × nations, way, + wilderness, world.

777. אַרְצָא **'artsâ',** *ar-tsaw';* from 776; *earthiness; Artsa,* an Isr :—Arza.

778. אֲרַק **'ăraq** (Chald.), *ar-ak';* by transmutation for 772; the *earth:*—earth.

779. אָרַר **'ârar,** *aw-rar';* a prim. root; to *execrate:*— × bitterly curse.

780. אֲרָרַט **'Ărâraṭ,** *ar-aw-rat';* of for. or.; *Ararat* (or rather Armenia):—Ararat, Armenia.

781. אָרַשׂ **'âras,** *aw-ras';* a prim. root; to *engage* for matrimony:—betroth, espouse.

782. אֲרֶשֶׁת **'ăresheth,** *ar-eh'-sheth;* from 781 (in the sense of *desiring* to possess); a *longing* for:—request.

783. אַרְתַּחְשַׁשְׁתָּא **'Artachshashtâ',** *ar-takh-shash-taw';* or אַרְתַּחְשַׁשְׁתְּא **'Artachshasht',** *ar-takh-shasht';* or by perm. אַרְתַּחְשַׁסְתְּא **'Artachshaçt',** *ar-takh-shast';* of for. or.; *Artachshasta* (or Artaxerxes), a title (rather than name) of several Pers. kings:—Artaxerxes.

784. אֵשׁ **'êsh,** *aysh;* a prim. word; *fire* (lit. or fig.):—burning, fiery, fire, flaming, hot.

785. אֶשָּׁא **'êsh** (Chald.), *aysh;* corresp. to 784:—flame.

786. אִשׁ **'îsh,** *eesh;* ident. (in or. and formation) with 784; *entity;* used only adv., there *is* or *are:*—are there, none can. Comp. 3426.

787. אשׁ **'ôsh** (Chald.), *ohsh;* corresp. (by transp. and abb.) to 803; a *foundation:*—foundation.

788. אַשְׁבֵּל **'Ashbêl,** *ash-bale';* prob. from the same as 7640; *flowing; Ashbel,* an Isr.:—Ashbel.

789. אַשְׁבֵּלִי **'Ashbêlîy,** *ash-bay-lee';* patron. from 788; an *Ashbelite* (collect.) or desc. of Ashbel:—Ashbelites.

790. אֶשְׁבָּן **'Eshbân,** *esh-bawn';* prob. from the same as 7644; *vigorous; Eshban,* an Idumæan:—Eshban.

791. אַשְׁבֵּעַ **'Ashbêa',** *ash-bay'-ah;* from 7650; *adjurer; Asbeă,* an Isr.:—Ashbea.

792. אֶשְׁבַּעַל **'Eshba'al,** *esh-bah'-al;* from 376 and 1168; *man of Baal; Eshbaal* (or Ishbosheth), a son of King Saul:—Eshbaal.

793. אֶשֶׁד **'eshed,** *eh'-shed;* from an unused root mean. to *pour;* an *outpouring:*—stream.

794. אֲשֵׁדָה **'ăshêdâh,** *ash-ay-daw';* fem. of 793; a *ravine:*—springs.

795. אַשְׁדּוֹד **'Ashdôwd,** *ash-dode';* from 7703; *ravager; Ashdod,* a place in Pal.:—Ashdod.

796. אַשְׁדּוֹדִי **'Ashdôwdîy,** *ash-do-dee';* patrial from 795; an *Ashdodite* (often collect.) or inhabitant of Ashdod.:—Ashdodites, of Ashdod.

797. אַשְׁדּוֹדִית **'Ashdôwdîyth,** *ash-do-deeth';* fem. of 796; (only adv.) *in the language of Ashdod:*—in the speech of Ashdod.

798. אַשְׁדּוֹת הַפִּסְגָּה **'Ashdôwth hap-Piçgâh,** *ash-doth' hap-pis-gaw';* from the plur. of 794 and 6449 with the art. interposed; *ravines of the Pisgah; Ashdoth-Pisgah,* a place east of the Jordan:—Ashdoth-pisgah.

799. אֶשְׁדָּת **'eshdâth,** *esh-dawth';* from 784 and 1881; a *fire-law:*—fiery law.

800. אֶשָּׁה **'eshshâh,** *esh-shaw';* fem. of 784; *fire:*—fire.

801. אִשָּׁה **'ishshâh,** *ish-shaw';* the same as 800, but used in a liturgical sense; prop. a *burnt-offering;* but occasionally of any *sacrifice:*—(offering, sacrifice), (made) by fire.

802. אִשָּׁה **'ishshâh,** *ish-shaw';* fem. of 376 or 582; irregular plur. נָשִׁים **nâshîym,** *naw-sheem';* a *woman* (used in the same wide sense as 582):—[adulter]ess, each, every, female, × many, + none, one, + together, wife, woman. Often unexpressed in English.

803. אֲשׁוּיָה **'ăshûwyâh,** *ash-oo-yah';* fem. pass. part. from an unused root mean. to *found; foundation:*—foundation.

804. אַשּׁוּר **'Ashshûwr,** *ash-shoor';* or אַשֻּׁר **'Ashshûr,** *ash-shoor';* appar. from 833 (in the sense of *successful*); *Ashshur,* the second son of Shem; also his desc. and the country occupied by them (i.e. Assyria), its region and its empire:—Asshur, Assur, Assyria, Assyrians. See 838.

805. אֲשׁוּרִי **'Ăshûwrîy,** *ash-oo-ree';* or אַשּׁוּרִי **'Ashshûwrîy,** *ash-shoo-ree';* from a patrial word of the same form as 804; an *Ashurite* (collect.) or inhab. of Ashur, a district in Pal.:—Asshurim, Ashurites.

806. אַשְׁחוּר **'Ashchûwr,** *ash-khoor';* prob. from 7835; *black; Ashchur,* an Isr.:—Ashur.

807. אֲשִׁימָא **'Ăshîymâ',** *ash-ee-maw';* of for. or.; *Ashima,* a deity of Hamath:—Ashima.

אֲשֵׁירָה **'ăshêyrah.** See 842.

808. אָשִׁישׁ **'âshîysh,** *aw-sheesh';* from the same as 784 (in the sense of *pressing* down firmly; comp. 803); a (ruined) *foundation:*—foundation.

809. אֲשִׁישָׁה **'ăshîyshâh,** *ash-ee-shaw';* fem. of 808; something closely *pressed* together, i.e. a *cake* of raisins or other comfits:—flagon.

810. אֶשֶׁךְ **'eshek,** *eh'-shek;* from an unused root (prob. mean. to *bunch* together); a *testicle* (as a *lump*):—stone.

811. אֶשְׁכּוֹל **'eshkôwl,** *esh-kole';* or אֶשְׁכֹּל **'eshkôl,** *esh-kole';* prob. prol. from 810; a *bunch of grapes* or other fruit:—cluster (of grapes).

812. אֶשְׁכֹּל **'Eshkôl,** *esh-kole';* the same as 811; *Eshcol,* the name of an Amorite, also of a valley in Pal.:—Eshcol.

813. אַשְׁכְּנַז **'Ashk^enaz,** *ash-ken-az';* of for. or.; *Ashkenaz,* a Japhethite, also his desc.:—Ashkenaz.

814. אֶשְׁכָּר **'eshkâr,** *esh-cawr';* for 7939; a *gratuity:*—gift, present.

815. אֵשֶׁל **'êshel,** *ay'-shel;* from a root of uncert. signif.; a *tamarisk* tree; by extens. a *grove* of any kind:—grove, tree.

816. אָשַׁם **'âsham,** *aw-sham';* or אָשֵׁם **'âshêm,** *aw-shame';* a prim. root; to *be guilty;* by impl. to *be punished* or *perish:*— × certainly, be (-come, made) desolate, destroy, × greatly, be (-come, found, hold) guilty, offend (acknowledge offence), trespass.

817. אָשָׁם **'âshâm,** *aw-shawm';* from 816; *guilt;* by impl. a *fault;* also a *sin-offering:*—guiltiness, (offering for) sin, trespass (offering).

818. אָשֵׁם **'âshêm,** *aw-shame';* from 816; *guilty;* hence *presenting a sin-offering:*—one which is faulty, guilty.

819 אַשְׁמָה **'ashmâh,** *ash-maw';* fem. of 817; *guiltiness,* a *fault,* the *presentation of a sin-offering:*—offend, sin, (cause of) trespass (-ing, offering).

אַשְׁמוּרָה **'ashmûrâh.** See 821.

820. אַשְׁמָן **'ashmân,** *ash-mawn';* prob. from 8081; a *fat* field:—desolate place.

821. אַשְׁמֻרָה **'ashmûrâh,** *ash-moo-raw';* or אַשְׁמוּרָה **'ashmûwrâh,** *ash-moo-raw';* or אַשְׁמֹרֶת **'ashmôreth,** *ash-mo'-reth;* (fem.) from 8104; a night *watch:*—watch.

822. אֶשְׁנָב **'eshnâb,** *esh-nawb';* appar. from an unused root (prob. mean. to *leave interstices*); a latticed *window:*—casement, lattice.

823. אַשְׁנָה **'Ashnâh,** *ash-naw';* prob. a var. for 3466; *Ashnah,* the name of two places in Pal.:—Ashnah.

824. אֶשְׁעָן **'Esh'ân,** *esh-awn';* from 8172; *support; Eshan,* a place in Pal.:—Eshean.

825. אַשָּׁף **'ashshâph,** *ash-shawf';* from an unused root (prob. mean. to *lisp,* i.e. *practise enchantment*); a *conjurer:*—astrologer.

826. אַשָּׁף **'ashshâph** (Chald.), *ash-shawf';* corresp. to 825:—astrologer.

827. אַשְׁפָּה **'ashpâh,** *ash-paw';* perh. (fem.) from the same as 825 (in the sense of *covering*); a *quiver* or arrow-case:—quiver.

828. אַשְׁפְּנַז **'Ashp^enaz,** *ash-pen-az';* of for. or.; *Ashpenaz,* a Bab. eunuch:—Ashpenaz.

829. אֶשְׁפָּר **'eshpâr,** *esh-pawr';* of uncert. der.; a measured *portion:*—good piece (of flesh).

830. אַשְׁפֹּת **'ashpôth**, *ash-pohth'*; or אַשְׁפּוֹת **'ashpôwth**, *ash-pohth'*; or (contr.) שְׁפֹת **sh^ephôth**, *shef-ohth'*; plur. of a noun of the same form as 827, from 8192 (in the sense of *scraping*); a heap of *rubbish* or *filth*:—dung (hill).

831. אַשְׁקְלוֹן **'Ashq^elôwn**, *ash-kel-one'*; prob. from 8254 in the sense of *weighing-place* (i.e. *mart*); *Ashkelon*, a place in Pal.:—Ashkelon, Askalon.

832. אֶשְׁקְלוֹנִי **'Eshq^elôwnîy**, *esh-kel-o-nee'*; patrial from 831; an *Ashkelonite* (collect.) or inhab. of Ashkelon:—Eshkalonites.

833. אָשַׁר **'ashar**, *aw-shar'*; or אָשֵׁר **'âshêr**, *aw-share'*; a prim. root; to *be straight* (used in the widest sense, espec. to *be level*, *right*, *happy*); fig. to *go forward*, *be honest*, *prosper*:—(call, be) bless (-ed, happy), go, guide, lead, relieve.

834. אֲשֶׁר **'asher**, *ash-er'*; a prim. rel. pron. (of every gend. and numb.); *who*, *which*, *what*, *that*; also (as adv. and conjunc.) *when*, *where*, *how*, *because*, *in order that*, etc.:— × after, × alike, as (soon as), because, × every, for, + forasmuch, + from whence, + how (-soever), × if, (so) that ([thing] which, wherein), × though, + until, + whatsoever, when, where (+ -as, -in, -of, -on, -soever, -with), which, whilst, + whither (-soever), who (-m, -soever, -se). As it is indeclinable, it is often accompanied by the personal pron. expletively, used to show the connection.

835. אֶשֶׁר **'esher**, *eh'-sher*; from 833; *happiness*; only in masc. plur. constr. as interjec., how *happy!*:—blessed, happy.

836. אָשֵׁר **'Âshêr**, *aw-share'*; from 833; *happy*; *Asher*, a son of Jacob, and the tribe descended from him, with its territory; also a place in Pal.:—Asher.

837. אֹשֶׁר **'ôsher**, *o'-sher*; from 833; *happiness*:—happy.

838. אָשֻׁר **'âshûr**, *aw-shoor'*; or אַשֻּׁר **ashshûr**, *ash-shoor'*; from 833 in the sense of *going*; a *step*:—going, step.

839. אָשֻׁר **'âshûr**, *ash-oor'*; contr. for 8391; the *cedar* tree or some other light elastic wood:—Ashurite.

אַשֻּׁר **'Ashshûr**. See 804, 838.

840. אֲשַׂרְאֵל **'Ăsar'êl**, *as-ar-ale'*; by orth. var. from 833 and 410; *right of God*; *Asarel*, an Isr.:—Asareel.

841. אֲשַׂרְאֵלָה **'Asar'êlâh**, *as-ar-ale'-aw*; from the same as 840; *right towards God*; *Asarelah*, an Isr.:—Asarelah. Comp. 3480.

842. אֲשֵׁרָה **'ăshêrâh**, *ash-ay-raw'*; or אֲשֵׁירָה **'ăshêyrâh**, *ash-ay-raw'*; from 833; *happy*; *Asherah* (or Astarte) a Phœnician goddess; also an *image* of the same:—grove. Comp. 6253.

843. אָשֵׁרִי **'Âshêrîy**, *aw-shay-ree'*; patron. from 836; an *Asherite* (collect.) or desc. of Asher:—Asherites.

844. אַשְׂרִיאֵל **'Asrîy'êl**, *as-ree-ale'*; an orth. var. for 840; *Asriel*, the name of two Isr.:—Ashriel, Asriel.

845. אַשְׂרִאֵלִי **'Asrî'êlîy**, *as-ree-ale-ee'*; patron. from 844; an *Asrielite* (collect.) or desc. of Asriel:—Asrielites.

846. אֻשַּׁרְנָא **'ushsharnâ'** (Chald.), *oosh-ar-naw'*; from a root corresp. to 833; a *wall* (from its uprightness):—wall.

847. אֶשְׁתָּאֹל **'Eshtâ'ôl**, *esh-taw-ole'*; or אֶשְׁתָּאוֹל **'Eshtâ'ôwl**, *esh-taw-ole'*; prob. from 7592; *intreaty*; *Eshtaol*, a place in Pal.:—Eshtaol.

848. אֶשְׁתָּאֻלִי **'Eshtâ'ûlîy**, *esh-taw-oo-lee'*; patrial from 847; an *Eshtaolite* (collect.) or inhab. of Eshtaol:—Eshtaulites.

849. אֶשְׁתַּדּוּר **'eshtaddûwr** (Chald.), *esh-tad-dure'*; from 7712 (in a bad sense); *rebellion*:—sedition.

850. אֶשְׁתּוֹן **'Eshtôwn**, *esh-tone'*; prob. from the same as 7764; *restful*; *Eshton*, an Isr.:—Eshton.

851. אֶשְׁתְּמֹעַ **'Esht^emôa'**, *esh-tem-o'-ah*; or אֶשְׁתְּמוֹעַ **'Esht^emôwa'**, *esh-tem-o'-ah*; or אֶשְׁתְּמֹה **'Esht^emôh**, *esh-tem-o'*; from 8085 (in the sense of *obedience*); *Eshtemoa* or *Eshtemoh*, a place in Pal.:—Eshtemoa, Eshtemoh.

אַתְּ **'ath**. See 859.

852. אָת **'âth** (Chald.), *awth*; corresp. to 226; a *portent*:—sign.

853. אֵת **'êth**, *ayth*; appar. contr. from 226 in the demonstr. sense of *entity*; prop. *self* (but gen. used to point out more def. the object of a verb or prep., *even* or *namely*):—[*as such unrepresented in English.*]

854. אֵת **'êth**, *ayth*; prob. from 579; prop. *nearness* (used only as a prep. or adv.), *near*; hence gen. *with*, *by*, *at*, *among*, etc.:—against, among, before, by, for, from, in (-to), (out) of, with. Often with another prep. prefixed.

855. אֵת **'êth**, *ayth*; of uncert. der.; a *hoe* or other digging implement:—coulter, plowshare.

אַתָּ **'attâ**. See 859.

אָתָא **'âthâ'**. See 857.

856. אֶתְבַּעַל **'Ethba'al**, *eth-bah'-al*; from 854 and 1168; *with Baal*; *Ethbaal*, a Phœnician king:—Ethbaal.

857. אָתָה **'âthâh**, *aw-thaw'*; or אָתָא **'âthâ'**, *aw-thaw'*; a prim. root [collat. to 225 contr.]; to *arrive*:—(be-, things to) come (upon), bring.

858. אָתָה **'âthâh** (Chald.), *aw-thaw'*; or אָתָא **'âthâ'** (Chald.), *aw-thaw'*; corresp. to 857:—(be-) come, bring.

859. אַתָּה **'attâh**, *at-taw'*; or (short.) אַתָּ **'attâ**, *at-taw'*; or אַתְּ **'ath**, *ath*; fem. (irreg.) sometimes אַתִּי **'attîy**, *at-tee'*; plur. masc. אַתֶּם **'attem**, *at-tem'*; fem. אַתֶּן **'atten**, *at-ten'*; or אַתֵּנָה **'attênâh**, *at-tay'-naw*; or אַתֵּנָּה **'attênnâh**, *at-tane'-naw*; a prim. pron. of the sec. pers.; *thou* and *thee*, or (plur.) *ye* and *you*:—thee, thou, ye, you.

860. אָתוֹן **'athôwn**, *aw-thone'*; prob. from the same as 386 (in the sense of *patience*); a female *ass* (from its docility):—(she) ass.

861. אַתּוּן **'attûwn** (Chald.), *at-toon'*; prob. from the corresp. to 784; prob. a *fire-place*, i.e. *furnace*:—furnace.

862. אַתּוּק **'attûwq**, *at-tooke'*; or אַתִּיק **'attîyq**, *at-teek'*; from 5423 in the sense of *decreasing*; a *ledge* or offset in a building:—gallery.

אַתִּי **'attîy**. See 859.

863. אִתַּי **'Ittay**, *it-tah'ee*; or אִיתַי **'Iythay**, *ee-thah'ee*; from 854; *near*; *Ittai* or *Ithai*, the name of a Gittite and of an Isr.:—Ithai, Ittai.

864. אֵתָם **'Êthâm**, *ay-thawm'*; of Eg. der.; *Etham*, a place in the Desert:—Etham.

אַתֶּם **'attem**. See 859.

865. אֶתְמוֹל **'ethmôwl**, *eth-mole'*; or אִתְמוֹל **'ithmôwl**, *ith-mole'*; or אֶתְמוּל **'ethmûwl**, *eth-mool'*; prob. from 853 or 854 and 4136; *heretofore*; def. *yesterday*:— + before (that) time, + heretofore, of late (old), + times past, yester[day].

אַתֶּן **atten**. See 859.

866. אֶתְנָה **'ethnâh**, *eth-naw'*; from 8566; a *present* (as the price of harlotry):—reward.

אַתֵּנָה **'attênâh**, or אַתֵּנָּה **'attênnâh**. See 859.

867. אֶתְנִי **'Ethnîy**, *eth-nee'*; perh. from 866; *munificence*; *Ethni*, an Isr.:—Ethni.

868. אֶתְנַן **'ethnan**, *eth-nan'*; the same as 866; a *gift* (as the price of harlotry or idolatry):—hire, reward.

869. אֶתְנַן **'Ethnan**, *eth-nan'*; the same as 868 in the sense of 867; *Ethnan*, an Isr.:—Ethnan.

870. אֲתַר **'âthar** (Chald.), *ath-ar'*; from a root corresp. to that of 871; a *place*; (adv.) *after*:—after, place.

871. אֲתָרִים **'Âthârîym**, *ath-aw-reem'*; plur. from an unused root (prob. mean. to *step*); *places*; *Atharim*, a place near Pal.:—spies.

ב

872. בְּאָה **b^e'âh**, *bĕ-aw'*; from 935; an *entrance* to a building:—entry.

873. בִּאוּשׁ **bî'ûwsh** (Chald.) *be-oosh'*; from 888; *wicked*:—bad.

874. בָּאַר **bâ'ar**, *baw-ar'*; a prim. root; to *dig*; by anal. to *engrave*; fig. to *explain*:—declare, (make) plain (-ly).

875. בְּאֵר **b^e'êr**, *bĕ-ayr'*; from 874; a *pit*; espec. a *well*:—pit, well.

876. בְּאֵר **B^e'êr**, *bĕ-ayr'*; the same as 875; *Beër*, a place in the Desert, also one in Pal.:—Beer.

877. בֹּאר **bô'r**, *bore*; from 874; a *cistern*:—cistern.

878. בְּאֵרָא **B^e'êrâ'**, *bĕ-ay-raw'*; from 875; a *well*; *Beëra*, an Isr.:—Beera.

879. בְּאֵר אֵלִים **B^e'êr 'Êlîym**, *bĕ-ayr' ay-leem'*; from 875 and the plur. of 410; *well of heroes*; *Beër-Elim*, a place in the Desert:—Beer-elim.

880. בְּאֵרָה **B^e'êrâh**, *bĕ-ay-raw'*; the same as 878; *Beërah*, an Isr.:—Beerah.

881. בְּאֵרוֹת **B^e'êrôwth**, *bĕ-ay-rohth'*; fem. plur. of 875; *wells*; *Beëroth*, a place in Pal.:—Beeroth.

882. בְּאֵרִי **B^e'êrîy**, *bĕ-ay-ree'*; from 875; *fountained*; *Beëri*, the name of a Hittite and of an Isr.:—Beeri.

883. בְּאֵר לַחַי רֹאִי **B^e'êr la-Chay Rô'îy**, *bĕ-ayr' lakh-ah'ee ro-ee'*; from 875 and 2416 (with pref.) and 7203; *well of a living* (One) *my Seer*; *Beër-Lachai-Roï*, a place in the Desert:—Beer-lahai-roi.

884. בְּאֵר שֶׁבַע **B^e'êr Sheba'**, *bĕ-ayr' sheh'-bah*; from 875 and 7651 (in the sense of 7650); *well of an oath*; *Beër-Sheba*, a place in Pal.:—Beer-shebah.

885. בְּאֵרֹת בְּנֵי־יַעֲקָן **B^e'êrôth B^enêy-Ya'âqan**, *bĕ-ay-roth' bĕ-nay' yah-a-can'*; from the fem. plur. of 875, and the plur. contr. of 1121, and 3292; *wells of* (the) *sons of Jaakan*; *Beëroth-Bene-Jaakan*, a place in the Desert:—Beeroth of the children of Jaakan.

886. בְּאֵרֹתִי **B^e'êrôthîy**, *bĕ-ay-ro-thee'*; patrial from 881; a *Beërothite* or inhab. of Beëroth:—Beerothite.

887. בָּאַשׁ **bâ'ash**, *baw-ash'*; a prim. root; to *smell* bad; fig. to *be offensive* morally:—(make to) be abhorred (had in abomination, loathsome, odious), (cause a, make to) stink (-ing savour), × utterly.

888. בְּאֵשׁ **b^e'êsh** (Chald.), *bĕ-aysh'*; corresp. to 887:—displease.

889. בְּאֹשׁ **b^e'ôsh**, *bĕ-oshe'*; from 877; a *stench*:—stink.

890. בָּאְשָׁה **bo'shâh**, *bosh-aw'*; fem. of 889; *stink-weed* or any other noxious or useless plant:—cockle.

891. בְּאֻשִׁים **b^e'ûshîym**, *bĕ-oo-sheem'*; plur. of 889; *poison-berries*:—wild grapes.

892. בָּבָה **bâbâh**, *baw-baw'*; fem. act. part. of an unused root mean. to *hollow* out; something *hollowed* (as a *gate*), i.e. the *pupil* of the eye:—apple [of the eye].

893. בֵּבַי **Bêbay**, *bay-bah'ee*; prob. of for. or.; *Bebai*, an Isr.:—Bebai.

894. בָּבֶל **Bâbel**, *baw-bel'*; from 1101; *confusion*; *Babel* (i.e. Babylon), including Babylonia and the Bab. empire:—Babel, Babylon.

895. בָּבֶל **Bâbel** (Chald.), *baw-bel'*; corresp. to 894:—Babylon.

896. בַּבְלִי **Bablîy** (Chald.), *bab-lee'*; patrial from 895; a *Babylonian*:—Babylonia.

897. בַּג **bag**, *bag;* a Pers. word; *food:*—spoil [*from the marg. for* 957.]

898. בָּגַד **bâgad**, *baw-gad';* a prim. root; to *cover* (with a garment); fig. to *act covertly;* by impl. to *pillage:*—deal deceitfully (treacherously, unfaithfully), offend, transgress (-or), (depart), treacherous (dealer, -ly, man), unfaithful (-ly, man), × very.

899. בֶּגֶד **beged**, *behg'-ed;* from 898; a *covering,* i.e. clothing; also *treachery* or *pillage:*—apparel, cloth (-es, -ing), garment, lap, rag, raiment, robe, × very [treacherously], vesture, wardrobe.

900. בֹּגְדוֹת **bôg^edôwth**, *bohg-ed-ōhth';* fem. plur. act. part. of 898; *treacheries:*—treacherous.

901. בָּגוֹד **bâgôwd**, *baw-gode';* from 898; *treacherous:*—treacherous.

902. בִּגְוַי **Bigvay**, *big-vah'ee;* prob. of for. or.; *Bigvai,* an Isr.:—Bigvai.

903. בִּגְתָא **Bigthâ'**, *big-thaw';* of Pers. der.; *Bigtha,* a eunuch of Xerxes:—Bigtha.

904. בִּגְתָן **Bigthân**, *big-thawn';* or בִּגְתָנָא **Bigthânâ'**, *big-thaw'-naw;* of similar deriv. to 903; *Bigthan* or *Bigthana,* a eunuch of Xerxes:—Bigthan, Bigthana.

905. בַּד **bad**, *bad;* from 909; prop. *separation;* by impl. a *part* of the body, *branch* of a tree, *bar* for carrying; fig. *chief* of a city; espec. (with prep. pref.) as adv., *apart, only, besides:*—alone, apart, bar, besides, branch, by self, of each alike, except, only, part, staff, strength.

906. בַּד **bad**, *bad;* perh. from 909 (in the sense of *divided* fibres); flaxen *thread* or yarn; hence a *linen* garment:—linen.

907. בַּד **bad**, *bad;* from 908; a *brag* or *lie;* also a *liar:*—liar, lie.

908. בָּדָא **bâdâ'**, *baw-daw';* a prim. root; (fig.) to *invent:*—devise, feign.

909. בָּדַד **bâdad**, *baw-dad';* a prim. root; to *divide,* i.e. (reflex.) *be solitary:*—alone.

910. בָּדָד **bâdâd**, *baw-dawd';* from 909; *separate;* adv. *separately:*—alone, desolate, only, solitary.

911. בְּדַד **B^edad**, *bed-ad';* from 909; *separation; Bedad,* an Edomite:—Bedad.

912. בֵּדְיָה **Bêd^eyâh**, *bay-dĕ-yaw';* prob. shortened for 5662; *servant of Jehovah; Bedejah,* an Isr.:—Bedeiah.

913. בְּדִיל **b^edîyl**, *bed-eel';* from 914; *alloy* (because *removed* by smelting); by anal. *tin:*—+ plummet, tin.

914. בָּדַל **bâdal**, *baw-dal';* a prim. root; to *divide* (in var. senses lit. or fig., *separate, distinguish, differ, select,* etc.):—(make, put) difference, divide (asunder), (make) separate (self, -ation), sever (out), × utterly.

915. בָּדָל **bâdâl**, *baw-dawl';* from 914; a *part:*—piece.

916. בְּדֹלַח **b^edôlach**, *bed-o'-lakh;* prob. from 914; something in *pieces,* i.e. *bdellium,* a (fragrant) gum (perh. *amber*); others a *pearl:*—bdellium.

917. בְּדָן **B^edân**, *bed-awn';* prob. short. for 5658; *servile; Bedan,* the name of two Isr.:—Bedan.

918. בָּדַק **bâdaq**, *baw-dak';* a prim. root; to *gap* open; used only as a denom. from 919; to *mend* a breach:—repair.

919. בֶּדֶק **bedeq**, *beh'-dek;* from 918; a *gap* or *leak* (in a building or a ship):—breach, + calker.

920. בִּדְקַר **Bidqar**, *bid-car';* prob. from 1856 with prep. pref.; *by stabbing,* i.e. *assassin; Bidkar,* an Isr.:—Bidkar.

921. בְּדַר **b^edar** (Chald.), *bed-ar';* corresp. (by transp.) to 6504; to *scatter:*—scatter.

922. בֹּהוּ **bôhûw**, *bo'-hoo;* from an unused root (mean. to *be empty*); a *vacuity,* i.e. (superficially) an undistinguishable *ruin:*—emptiness, void.

923. בַּהַט **bahaṭ**, *bah'-hat;* from an unused root (prob. mean. to *glisten*); white *marble* or perh. *alabaster:*—red [marble].

924. בְּהִילוּ **b^ehîylûw** (Chald.), *bĕ-hee-loo';* from 927; a *hurry;* only adv. *hastily:*—in haste.

925. בָּהִיר **bâhîyr**, *baw-here';* from an unused root (mean. to *be bright*); *shining:*—bright.

926. בָּהַל **bâhal**, *baw-hal';* a prim. root; to *tremble* inwardly (or *palpitate*), i.e. (fig.) *be* (caus. *make*) (suddenly) *alarmed* or *agitated;* by impl. to *hasten* anxiously:—be (make) affrighted (afraid, amazed, dismayed, rash), (be, get, make) haste (-n, -y, -ily), (give) speedy (-ily), thrust out, trouble, vex.

927. בְּהַל **b^ehal** (Chald.), *bĕ-hal';* corresp. to 926; to *terrify, hasten:*—in haste, trouble.

928. בֶּהָלָה **behâlâh**, *beh-haw-law';* from 926; *panic, destruction:*—terror, trouble.

929. בְּהֵמָה **b^ehêmâh**, *bĕ-hay-maw';* from an unused root (prob. mean. to *be mute*); prop. a *dumb* beast; espec. any large quadruped or *animal* (often collect.):—beast, cattle.

930. בְּהֵמוֹת **b^ehêmôwth**, *bĕ-hay-mōhth';* in form a plur. of 929, but really a sing. of Eg. der.; a *water-ox,* i.e. the *hippopotamus* or Nile-horse:—Behemoth.

931. בֹּהֶן **bôhen**, *bo'-hen;* from an unused root appar. mean. to *be thick;* the *thumb* of the hand or *great toe* of the foot:—thumb, great toe.

932. בֹּהַן **Bôhan**, *bo'-han;* an orth. var. of 931; *thumb; Bohan,* an Isr.:—Bohan.

933. בֹּהַק **bôhaq**, *bo'-hak;* from an unused root mean. to *be pale;* white *scurf:*—freckled spot.

934. בַּהֶרֶת **bôhereth**, *bo-heh'-reth;* fem. act. part. of the same as 925; a *whitish* spot on the skin:—bright spot.

935. בּוֹא **bôw'**, *bo;* a prim. root; to *go* or *come* (in a wide variety of applications):—abide, apply, attain, × be, befall, + besiege, bring (forth, in, into, to pass), call, carry, × certainly, (cause, let, thing for) to come (against, in, out, upon, to pass), depart, × doubtless again, + eat, + employ, (cause to) enter (in, into, -tering, -trance, -try), be fallen, fetch, + follow, get, give, go (down, in, to war), grant, + have, × indeed, [in-]vade, lead, lift [up], mention, pull in, put, resort, run (down), send, set, × (well) stricken [in age], × surely, take (in), way.

בּוּב **bûwb**. See 892, 5014.

936. בּוּז **bûwz**, *booz;* a prim. root; to *disrespect:*—contemn, despise, × utterly.

937. בּוּז **bûwz**, *booz;* from 936; *disrespect:*—contempt (-uously), despised, shamed.

938. בּוּז **Bûwz**, *booz;* the same as 937; *Buz,* the name of a son of Nahor, and of an Isr.:—Buz.

939. בּוּזָה **bûwzâh**, *boo-zaw';* fem. pass. part. of 936; something *scorned;* an object of *contempt:*—despised.

940. בּוּזִי **Bûwzîy**, *boo-zee';* patron. from 938; a *Buzite* or desc. of Buz:—Buzite.

941. בּוּזִי **Bûwzîy**, *boo-zee';* the same as 940, *Buzi,* an Isr.:—Buzi.

942. בַּוַּי **Bavvay**, *bav-vah'ee;* prob. of Pers. or.; *Bavvai,* an Isr.:—Bavai.

943. בּוּךְ **bûwk**, *book;* a prim. root; to *involve* (lit. or fig.):—be entangled (perplexed).

944. בּוּל **bûwl**, *bool;* for 2981; *produce* (of the earth, etc.):—food, stock.

945. בּוּל **Bûwl**, *bool;* the same as 944 (in the sense of *rain*); *Bul,* the eighth Heb. month:—Bul.

בּוּם **bûwm**. See 1116.

946. בּוּנָה **Bûwnâh**, *boo-naw';* from 995; *discretion; Bunah,* an Isr.:—Bunah.

בּוּנִי **Bûwnîy**. See 1138.

947. בּוּס **bûwç**, *boos;* a prim. root; to *trample* (lit. or fig.):—loath, tread (down, under [foot]), be polluted.

948. בּוּץ **bûwts**, *boots;* from an unused root (of the same form) mean. to *bleach,* i.e. (intrans.) *be white;* prob. *cotton* (of some sort):—fine (white) linen.

949. בּוֹצֵץ **Bôwtsêts**, *bo-tsates';* from the same as 948; *shining; Botsets,* a rock near Michmash:—Bozez.

950. בּוּקָה **bûwqâh**, *boo-kaw';* fem. pass. part. of an unused root (mean. to *be hollow*); *emptiness* (as adj.):—empty.

951. בּוֹקֵר **bôwkêr**, *bo-kare';* prop. act. part. from 1239 as denom. from 1241; a *cattle-tender:*—herdman.

952. בּוּר **bûwr**, *boor;* a prim. root; to *bore,* i.e. (fig.) *examine:*—declare.

953. בּוֹר **bôwr**, *bore;* from 952 (in the sense of 877); a pit *hole* (espec. one used as a *cistern* or *prison*):—cistern, dungeon, fountain, pit, well.

954. בּוֹשׁ **bûwsh**, *boosh;* a prim. root; prop. to *pale,* i.e. by impl. to *be ashamed;* also (by impl.) to *be disappointed,* or *delayed:*—(be, make, bring to, cause, put to, with, a-) shame (-d), be (put to) confounded (-fusion), become dry, delay, be long.

955. בּוּשָׁה **bûwshâh**, *boo-shaw';* fem. part. pass. of 954; *shame:*—shame.

956. בּוּת **bûwth** (Chald.), *booth;* appar. denom. from 1005; to *lodge* over night:—pass the night.

957. בַּז **baz**, *baz;* from 962; *plunder:*—booty, prey, spoil (-ed).

958. בָּזָא **bâzâ'**, *baw-zaw';* a prim. root; prob. to *cleave:*—spoil.

959. בָּזָה **bâzâh**, *baw-zaw';* a prim. root; to *disesteem:*—despise, disdain, contemn (-ptible), + think to scorn, vile person.

960. בָּזֹה **bâzôh**, *baw-zo';* from 959; *scorned:*—despise.

961. בִּזָּה **bizzâh**, *biz-zaw';* fem. of 957; *booty:*—prey, spoil.

962. בָּזַז **bâzaz**, *baw-zaz';* a prim. root; to *plunder:*—catch, gather, (take) for a prey, rob (-ber), spoil, take (away, spoil), × utterly.

963. בִּזָּיוֹן **bizzâyôwn**, *biz-zaw-yone';* from 959:—*disesteem:*—contempt.

964. בִּזְיוֹתְיָה **bizyôwth^eyâh**, *biz-yo-thĕ-yaw';* from 959 and 3050; *contempts of Jah; Bizjothjah,* a place in Pal.:—Bizjothjah.

965. בָּזָק **bâzâq**, *baw-zawk';* from an unused root mean. to *lighten;* a *flash* of lightning:—flash of lightning.

966. בֶּזֶק **Bezeq**, *beh'-zek;* from 965; *lightning; Bezek,* a place in Pal.:—Bezek.

967. בָּזַר **bâzar**, *baw-zar';* a prim. root; to *disperse:*—scatter.

968. בִּזְתָא **Bizthâ'**, *biz-thaw';* of Pers. or.; *Biztha,* a eunuch of Xerxes:—Biztha.

969. בָּחוֹן **bâchôwn'**, *baw-khone';* from 974; an *assayer* of metals:—tower.

970. בָּחוּר **bâchûwr**, *baw-khoor';* or בָּחֻר **bâchûr**, *baw-khoor';* part. pass. of 977; prop. *selected,* i.e. a *youth* (often collect.):—(choice) young (man), chosen, × hole.

בְּחוּרוֹת **b^echûwrôwth**. See 979.

בַּחוּרִים **Bachûwrîym**. See 980.

971. בַּחִין **bachîyn**, *bakh-een';* another form of 975; a watch-*tower* of besiegers:—tower.

972. בָּחִיר **bâchîyr**, *baw-kheer';* from 977; *select:*—choose, chosen one, elect.

973. בָּחַל **bâchal**, *baw-khal';* a prim. root; to *loathe:*—abhor, get hastily [*from the marg. for* 926].

974. בָּחַן **bâchan**, *baw-khan';* a prim. root; to *test* (espec. metals); gen. and fig. to *investigate:*—examine, prove, tempt, try (trial).

975. בַּחַן **bachan**, *bakh'-an;* from 974 (in the sense of keeping a *look-out*); a watch-*tower:*—tower.

976. בֹּחַן **bôchan**, *bo'-khan;* from 974; *trial:*—tried.

977. בָּחַר **bâchar**, *baw-khar';* a prim. root; prop. to *try,* i.e. (by impl.) *select:*—acceptable, appoint, choose (choice), excellent, join, be rather, require.

בָּחֻר **bâchûr**. See 970.

978. בַּחֲרוּמִי **Bachărûwmîy**, *bakh-ar-oo-mee';* patrial from 980 (by transp.); a *Bacharumite* or inhab. of Bachurim:—Baharumite.

979. בְּחֻרוֹת **b^echûrôwth**, *bekh-oo-rothe';* or בְּחוּרוֹת **b^echûwrôwth**, *bekh-oo-roth';* fem. plur. of 970; also (masc. plur.) בְּחֻרִים **b^echûrîym**, *bekh-oo-reem';* youth (collect. and abstr.):—young men, youth.

980. בַּחֻרִים **Bachûrîym**, *bakh-oo-reem'*; or בַּחוּרִים **Bachûwrîym**, *bakh-oo-reem'*; masc. plur. of 970; *young men; Bachurim*, a place in Pal.:—Bahurim.

981. בָּטָא **bâṭâʼ**, *baw-taw'*; or בָּטָה **bâṭâh**, *baw-taw'*; a prim. root; to *babble*; hence to *vociferate* angrily:—pronounce, speak (unadvisedly).

982. בָּטַח **bâṭach**, *baw-takh'*; a prim. root; prop. to *hie* for refuge [but not so *precipitately* as 2620]; fig. to *trust*, be *confident* or *sure*:—be bold (confident, secure, sure), careless (one, woman), put confidence, (make to) hope, (put, make to) trust.

983. בֶּטַח **beṭach**, *beh'-takh*; from 982; prop. a place of *refuge*; abstr. *safety*, both the fact (*security*) and the feeling (*trust*); often (adv. with or without prep.) *safely*:—assurance, boldly, (without) care (-less), confidence, hope, safe (-ly, -ty), secure, surely.

984. בֶּטַח **Beṭach**, *beh'-takh*; the same as 983; *Betach*, a place in Syria:—Betah.

985. בִּטְחָה **biṭchâh**, *bit-khaw'*; fem. of 984; *trust*:—confidence.

986. בִּטָּחוֹן **biṭṭâchôwn**, *bit-taw-khone'*; from 982; *trust*:—confidence, hope.

987. בַּטֻּחוֹת **baṭṭûchôwth**, *bat-too-khōth'*; fem. plur. from 982; *security*:—secure.

988. בָּטֵל **bâṭêl**, *baw-tale'*; a prim. root; to *desist* from labor:—cease.

989. בְּטֵל **beṭêl** (Chald.), *bet-ale'*; corresp. to 988; to *stop*:—(cause, make to), cease, hinder.

990. בֶּטֶן **beṭen**, *beh'-ten*; from an unused root prob. mean. to *be hollow*; the *belly*, espec. the *womb*; also the *bosom* or *body* of anything:—belly, body, + as they be born, + within, womb.

991. בֶּטֶן **Beṭen**, *beh'-ten*; the same as 990; *Beten*, a place in Pal.:—Beten.

992. בֹּטֶן **bôṭen**, *bo'-ten*; from 990; (only in plur.) a *pistachio*-nut (from its form):—nut.

993. בְּטֹנִים **Beṭônîym**, *bet-o-neem'*; prob. plur. from 992; *hollows*: *Betonim*, a place in Pal.:—Betonim.

994. בִּי **bîy**, *bee*; perh. from 1158 (in the sense of *asking*); prop. a *request*; used only adv. (always with "my Lord"); *Oh that!*; *with leave*, or *if it please*:—alas, O, oh.

995. בִּין **bîyn**, *bene*; a prim. root; to *separate* mentally (or *distinguish*), i.e. (gen.) *understand*:—attend, consider, be cunning, diligently, direct, discern, eloquent, feel, inform, instruct, have intelligence, know, look well to, mark, perceive, be prudent, regard, (can) skill (-ful), teach, think, (cause, make to, get, give, have) understand (-ing), view, (deal) wise (-ly, man).

996. בֵּין **bêyn**, *bane* (sometimes in the plur. masc. or fem.); prop. the constr. contr. form of an otherwise unused noun from 995; a *distinction*; but used only as a prep., *between* (repeated before each noun, often with other particles); also as a conj., *either . . . or*:—among, asunder, at, between (-twixt . . . and), + from (the widest), × in, out of, whether (it be . . . or), within.

997. בֵּין **bêyn** (Chald.), *bane*; corresp. to 996:—among, between.

998. בִּינָה **bîynâh**, *bee-naw'*; from 995; *understanding*:—knowledge, meaning, × perfectly, understanding, wisdom.

999. בִּינָה **bîynâh** (Chald.), *bee-naw'*; corresp. to 998:—knowledge.

1000. בֵּיצָה **bêytsâh**, *bay-tsaw'*; from the same as 948; an *egg* (from its whiteness):—egg.

1001. בִּירָא **bîyrâʼ** (Chald.), *bee-raw'*; corresp. to 1002; a *palace*:—palace.

1002. בִּירָה **bîyrâh**, *bee-raw'*; of for. or.; a *castle* or *palace*:—palace.

1003. בִּירָנִית **bîyrânîyth**, *bee-raw-neeth'*; from 1002; a *fortress*:—castle.

1004. בַּיִת **bayith**, *bah'-yith*; prob. from 1129 abbrev.; a *house* (in the greatest var. of applications, espec. *family*, etc.):—court, daughter, door, + dungeon, family, + forth of, × great as would contain, hangings, home[born], [winter]house (-hold), inside (-ward), palace, place, + prison, + steward, + tablet, temple, web, + within (-out).

1005. בַּיִת **bayith** (Chald.), *bah-yith*; corresp. to 1004:—house.

1006. בַּיִת **Bayith**, *bah'-yith*; the same as 1004; *Bajith*, a place in Pal.:—Bajith.

1007. בֵּית אָוֶן **Bêyth ʼÂven**, *bayth aw'-ven*; from 1004 and 205; *house of vanity*; *Beth-Aven*, a place in Pal.:—Beth-aven.

1008. בֵּית־אֵל **Bêyth-ʼÊl**, *bayth-ale'*; from 1004 and 410; *house of God*; *Beth-El*, a place in Pal.:—Beth-el.

1009. בֵּית אַרְבֵּאל **Bêyth ʼArbêʼl**, *bayth arbale'*; from 1004 and 695 and 410; *house of God's ambush*; *Beth-Arbel*, a place in Pal.:—Beth-Arbel.

1010. בֵּית בַּעַל מְעוֹן **Bêyth Baʽal Meʽôwn**, *bayth bah'-al mĕ-own'*; from 1004 and 1168 and 4583; *house of Baal* of (the) *habitation of* [appar. by transp.]; or (shorter) בֵּית מְעוֹן **Bêyth Meʽôwn**, *bayth mĕ-own'*; *house of habitation of* (Baal); *Beth-Baal-Meön*, a place in Pal.:—Beth-baal-meon. Comp. 1186 and 1194.

1011. בֵּית בִּרְאִי **Bêyth Birʼîy**, *bayth bir-ee'*; from 1004 and 1254; *house of a creative* one; *Beth-Biri*, a place in Pal.:—Beth-birei.

1012. בֵּית בָּרָה **Bêyth Bârâh**, *bayth baw-raw'*; prob. from 1004 and 5679; *house of* (the) *ford*; *Beth-Barah*, a place in Pal.:—Beth-barah.

1013. בֵּית־גָּדֵר **Bêyth-Gâdêr**, *bayth-gaw-dare'*; from 1004 and 1447; *house of* (the) *wall*; *Beth-Gader*, a place in Pal.:—Beth-gader.

1014. בֵּית גָּמוּל **Bêyth Gâmûwl**, *bayth gaw-mool'*; from 1004 and the pass. part. of 1576; *house of* (the) *weaned*; *Beth-Gamul*, a place E. of the Jordan:—Beth-gamul.

1015. בֵּית דִּבְלָתַיִם **Bêyth Diblâthayim**, *bayth dib-law-thah'-yim*; from 1004 and the dual of 1690; *house of* (the) *two fig-cakes*; *Beth-Diblathajim*, a place E. of the Jordan:—Beth-diblathaim.

1016. בֵּית־דָּגוֹן **Bêyth-Dâgôwn**, *bayth-daw-gohn'*; from 1004 and 1712; *house of Dagon*; *Beth-Dagon*, the name of two places in Pal.:—Beth-dagon.

1017. בֵּית הָאֱלִי **Bêyth hâ-ʼÊlîy**, *bayth haw-el-ee'*; patrial from 1008 with the art. interposed; a *Beth-elite*, or inhab. of Bethel:—Bethelite.

1018. בֵּית הָאֵצֶל **Bêyth hâ-ʼêtsel**, *bayth haw-ay-tsel'*; from 1004 and 681 with the art. interposed; *house of the side*; *Beth-ha-Etsel*, a place in Pal.:—Beth-ezel.

1019. בֵּית הַגִּלְגָּל **Bêyth hag-Gilgâl**, *bayth hag-gil-gawl'*; from 1004 and 1537 with the article interposed; *house of the Gilgal* (or *rolling*); *Beth-hag-Gilgal*, a place in Pal.:—Beth-gilgal.

1020. בֵּית הַיְשִׁימוֹת **Bêyth ha-Yeshîymôwth**, *bayth hah-yesh-ee-mōth'*; from 1004 and the plur. of 3451 with the art. interposed; *house of the deserts*; *Beth-ha-Jeshimoth*, a town E. of the Jordan:—Beth-jeshimoth.

1021. בֵּית הַכֶּרֶם **Bêyth hak-Kerem**, *bayth hak-keh'-rem*; from 1004 and 3754 with the art. interposed; *house of the vineyard*; *Beth-hak-Kerem*, a place in Pal.:—Beth-haccerem.

1022. בֵּית הַלַּחְמִי **Bêyth hal-Lachmîy**, *bayth hal-lakh-mee'*; patrial from 1035 with the art. ins.; a *Beth-lechemite*, or native of Bethlechem:—Bethlehemite.

1023. בֵּית הַמֶּרְחָק **Bêyth ham-Merchâq**, *bayth ham-mer-khawk'*; from 1004 and 4801 with the art. interposed; *house of the breadth*; *Beth-ham-Merchak*, a place in Pal.:—place that was far off.

1024 בֵּית הַמַּרְכָּבוֹת **Bêyth ham-Markâbôwth**, *bayth ham-mar-kaw-both'*; or (short.) בֵּית מַרְכָּבוֹת **Bêyth Markâbôwth**, *bayth mar-kaw-both'*; from 1004 and the plur. of 4818 (with or without the art. interposed); *place of* (the) *chariots*; *Beth-ham-Markaboth* or *Beth-Markaboth*, a place in Pal.:—Beth-marcaboth.

1025. בֵּית הָעֵמֶק **Bêyth hâ-ʽÊmeq**, *bayth haw-Ay'-mek*; from 1004 and 6010 with the art. interposed; *house of the valley*; *Beth-ha-Emek*, a place in Pal.:—Beth-emek.

1026. בֵּית הָעֲרָבָה **Bêyth hâ-ʽĂrâbâh**, *bayth haw-ar-aw-baw'*; from 1004 and 6160 with the art. interposed; *house of the Desert*; *Beth-ha-Arabah*, a place in Pal.:—Beth-arabah.

1027. בֵּית הָרָם **Bêyth hâ-Râm**, *bayth haw-rawm'*; from 1004 and 7311 with the art. interposed; *house of the height*; *Beth-ha-Ram*, a place E. of the Jordan:—Beth-aram.

1028. בֵּית הָרָן **Bêyth hâ-Rân**, *bayth haw-rawn'*; prob. for 1027; *Beth-ha-Ran*, a place E. of the Jordan:—Beth-haran.

1029. בֵּית הַשִּׁטָּה **Bêyth hash-Shiṭṭâh**, *bayth hash-shit-taw'*; from 1004 and 7848 with the art. interposed; *house of the acacia*; *Beth-hash-Shittah*, a place in Pal.:—Beth-shittah.

1030. בֵּית הַשִּׁמְשִׁי **Bêyth hash-Shimshîy**, *bayth hash-shim-shee'*; patrial from 1053 with the art. inserted; a *Beth-shimshite*, or inhab. of Bethshemesh:—Bethshemite.

1031. בֵּית חָגְלָה **Bêyth Choglâh**, *bayth chog-law'*; from 1004 and the same as 2295; *house of a partridge*; *Beth-Choglah*, a place in Pal.:—Beth-hoglah.

1032. בֵּית חוֹרוֹן **Bêyth Chôwrôwn**, *bayth kho-rone'*; from 1004 and 2356; *house of hollowness*; *Beth-Choron*, the name of two adjoining places in Pal.:—Beth-horon.

בֵּית חָנָן **Bêyth Chânân**. See 358.

1033. בֵּית כַּר **Bêyth Kar**, *bayth kar*; from 1004 and 3733; *house of pasture*; *Beth-Car*, a place in Pal.:—Beth-car.

1034. בֵּית לְבָאוֹת **Bêyth Lebâʼôwth**, *bayth leb-aw-ōth'*; from 1004 and the plur. of 3833; *house of lionesses*; *Beth-Lebaoth*, a place in Pal.:—Beth-lebaoth. Comp. 3822.

1035. בֵּית לֶחֶם **Bêyth Lechem**, *bayth leh'-khem*; from 1004 and 3899; *house of bread*; *Beth-Lechem*, a place in Pal.:—Beth-lehem.

1036. בֵּית לְעַפְרָה **Bêyth le-ʽAphrâh**, *bayth lĕ-af-raw'*; from 1004 and the fem. of 6083 (with prep. interposed); *house to* (i.e. *of*) *dust*; *Beth-le-Aphrah*, a place in Pal.:—house of Aphrah.

1037. בֵּית מִלּוֹא **Bêyth Millôwʼ**, *bayth mil-lo'*; or בֵּית מִלֹּא **Bêyth Millôʼ**, *bayth mil-lo'*; from 1004 and 4407; *house of* (the) *rampart*; *Beth-Millo*, the name of two citadels:—house of Millo.

1038. בֵּית מַעֲכָה **Bêyth Maʽăkâh**, *bayth mah-ak-aw'*; from 1004 and 4601; *house of Maakah*; *Beth-Maakah*, a place in Pal.:—Beth-maachah.

1039. בֵּית נִמְרָה **Bêyth Nimrâh**, *bayth nim-raw'*; from 1004 and the fem. of 5246; *house of* (the) *leopard*; *Beth-Nimrah*, a place east of the Jordan:—Beth-nimrah. Comp. 5247.

1040. בֵּית עֵדֶן **Bêyth ʽÊden**, *bayth ay'-den*; from 1004 and 5730; *house of pleasure*; *Beth-Eden*, a place in Syria:—Beth-eden.

1041. בֵּית עַזְמָוֶת **Bêyth ʽAzmâveth**, *bayth az-maw'-veth*; from 1004 and 5820; *house of Azmaveth*, a place in Pal.:—Beth-azmaveth. Comp. 5820.

1042. בֵּית עֲנוֹת **Bêyth ʽĂnôwth**, *bayth an-ōth'*; from 1004 and a plur. from 6030; *house of replies*; *Beth-Anoth*, a place in Pal.:—Beth-anoth.

1043. בֵּית עֲנָת **Bêyth ʽĂnâth**, *bayth an-awth'*; an orth. var. for 1042; *Beth-Anath*, a place in Pal.:—Beth-anath.

1044. בֵּית עֵקֶד **Bêyth ʽÊqed**, *bayth ay'-ked*; from 1004 and a deriv. of 6123; *house of* (the) *binding* (for sheep-shearing); *Beth-Eked*, a place in Pal.:—shearing-house.

1045. בֵּית עַשְׁתָּרוֹת **Bêyth ʿAshtârôwth**, *bayth ash-taw-rōth'*; from 1004 and 6252; *house of Ashtoreths; Beth-Ashtaroth*, a place in Pal.:—house of Ashtaroth. Comp. 1203, 6252.

1046. בֵּית פֶּלֶט **Bêyth Pelet**, *bayth peh'-let*; from 1004 and 6412; *house of escape; Beth-Palet*, a place in Pal.:—Beth-palet.

1047. בֵּית פְּעוֹר **Bêyth Peʿôwr**, *bayth pĕ-ore'*; from 1004 and 6465; *house of Peor; Beth-Peor*, a place E. of the Jordan:—Beth-peor.

1048. בֵּית פַּצֵּץ **Bêyth Patstsêts**, *bayth pats-tsates'*; from 1004 and a der. from 6327; *house of dispersion; Beth-Patstsets*, a place in Pal.:—Beth-pazzez.

1049. בֵּית צוּר **Bêyth Tsûwr**, *bayth tsoor'*; from 1004 and 6697; *house of* (the) *rock; Beth-Tsur*, a place in Pal.:—Beth-zur.

1050. בֵּית רְחוֹב **Bêyth Rechôwb**, *bayth rĕ-khobe'*; from 1004 and 7339; *house of* (the) *street; Beth-Rechob*, a place in Pal.:—Beth-rehob.

1051. בֵּית רָפָא **Bêyth Râphâ'**, *bayth raw-faw'*; from 1004 and 7497; *house of* (the) *giant; Beth-Rapha*, an Isr.:—Beth-rapha.

1052. בֵּית שְׁאָן **Bêyth Sheʾân**, *bayth shĕ-awn'*; or בֵּית שָׁן **Bêyth Shân**, *bayth shawn'*; from 1004 and 7599; *house of ease; Beth-Shean* or *Beth-Shan*, a place in Pal.:—Beth-shean, Beth-Shan.

1053. בֵּית שֶׁמֶשׁ **Bêyth Shemesh**, *bayth sheh'-mesh*; from 1004 and 8121; *house of* (the) *sun; Beth-Shemesh*, a place in Pal.:—Beth-shemesh.

1054. בֵּית תַּפּוּחַ **Bêyth Tappûwach**, *bayth tap-poo'-akh*; from 1004 and 8598; *house of* (the) *apple; Beth-Tappuach*, a place in Pal.:—Beth-tappuah.

1055. בִּיתָן **bîythân**, *bee-thawn'*; prob. from 1004; a *palace* (i.e. *large house*):—palace.

1056. בָּכָא **Bâkâ'**, *baw-kaw'*; from 1058; *weeping; Baca*, a valley in Pal.:—Baca.

1057. בָּכָא **bâkâ'**, *baw-kaw'*; the same as 1056; the *weeping* tree (some gum-distilling tree, perh. the *balsam*):—mulberry tree.

1058. בָּכָה **bâkâh**, *baw-kaw'*; a prim. root; to *weep*; gen. to *bemoan*:— × at all, bewail, complain, make lamentation, × more, mourn, × sore, × with tears, weep.

1059. בֶּכֶה **bekeh**, *beh'-keh*; from 1058; a *weeping*:— × sore.

1060. בְּכוֹר **bekôwr**, *bek-ore'*; from 1069; *firstborn*; hence *chief*:—eldest (son), firstborn (-ling).

1061. בִּכּוּר **bikkûwr**, *bik-koor'*; from 1069; the *first-fruits* of the crop:—first fruit (-ripe [fig.]), hasty fruit.

1062. בְּכוֹרָה **bekôwrâh**, *bek-o-raw'*; or (short.) בְּכֹרָה **bekôrâh**, *bek-o-raw'*; fem. of 1060; the *firstling* of man or beast; abstr. *primogeniture*:—birthright, firstborn (-ling).

1063. בִּכּוּרָה **bikkûwrâh**, *bik-koo-raw'*; fem. of 1061; the *early fig*:—firstripe (fruit).

1064. בְּכוֹרַת **Bekôwrath**, *bek-o-rath'*; fem. of 1062; *primogeniture; Bekorath*, an Isr.:—Bechorath.

1065. בְּכִי **bekîy**, *bek-ee'*; from 1058; a *weeping*; by analogy, a *dripping*:—overflowing, × sore, (continual) weeping, wept.

1066. בֹּכִים **Bôkîym**, *bo-keem'*; plur. act. part. of 1058; (with the art.) the *weepers; Bokim*, a place in Pal.:—Bochim.

1067. בְּכִירָה **bekîyrâh**, *bek-ee-raw'*; fem. from 1069; the *eldest* daughter:—firstborn.

1068. בְּכִית **bekîyth**, *bek-eeth'*; from 1058; a *weeping*:—mourning.

1069. בָּכַר **bâkar**, *baw-kar'*; a prim. root; prop. to *burst* the womb, i.e. (caus.) *bear* or *make early fruit* (of woman or tree); also (as denom. from 1061) to *give the birthright*:—make firstborn, be firstling, bring forth first child (new fruit).

1070. בֶּכֶר **beker**, *beh'-ker*; from 1069 (in the sense of *youth*); a young *camel*:—dromedary.

1071. בֶּכֶר **Beker**, *beh'-ker*; the same as 1070; *Beker*, the name of two Isr.:—Becher.

1072. בִּכְרָה **bikrâh**, *bik-raw'*; fem. of 1070; a young *she-camel*:—dromedary.

בְּכֹרָה **bekôrâh**. See 1062.

1073. בַּכֻּרָה **bakkûrâh**, *bak-koo-raw'*; by orth. var. for 1063; a *first-ripe* fig:—first-ripe.

1074. בֹּכְרוּ **Bôkerûw**, *bo-ker-oo'*; from 1069; *first-born; Bokeru*, an Isr.:—Bocheru.

1075. בִּכְרִי **Bikrîy**, *bik-ree'*; from 1069; *youthful; Bikri*, an Isr.:—Bichri.

1076. בַּכְרִי **Bakrîy**, *bak-ree'*; patron. from 1071; a *Bakrite* (collect.) or desc. of Beker:—Bachrites.

1077. בַּל **bal**, *bal*; from 1086; prop. a *failure*; by impl. *nothing*; usually (adv.) *not* at all; also *lest*:—lest, neither, no, none (that . . .), not (any), nothing.

1078. בֵּל **Bêl**, *bale*; by contr. for 1168; *Bel*, the Baal of the Babylonians:—Bel.

1079. בָּל **bâl** (Chald.), *bawl*; from 1080; prop. *anxiety*, i.e. (by impl.) the *heart* (as its seat):—heart.

1080. בְּלָא **belâ'** (Chald.), *bel-aw'*; corresp. to 1086 (but used only in a mental sense); to *afflict*:—wear out.

1081. בַּלְאֲדָן **Bal'âdân**, *bal-ad-awn'*; from 1078 and 113 (contr.); *Bel* (is his) *lord; Baladan*, the name of a Bab. prince:—Baladan.

1082. בָּלַג **bâlag**, *baw-lag'*; a prim. root; to *break off* or *loose* (in a favorable or unfavorable sense), i.e. *desist* (from grief) or *invade* (with destruction):—comfort, (recover) strength (-en).

1083. בִּלְגָּה **Bilgâh**, *bil-gaw'*; from 1082; *desistance; Bilgah*, the name of two Isr.:—Bilgah.

1084. בִּלְגַּי **Bilgay**, *bil-gah'ee*; from 1082; *desistant; Bilgai*, an Isr.:—Bilgai.

1085. בִּלְדַּד **Bildad**, *bil-dad'*; of uncert. der.; *Bildad*, one of Job's friends:—Bildad.

1086. בָּלָה **bâlâh**, *baw-law'*; a prim. root; to *fail*; by impl. to *wear out, decay* (caus. *consume, spend*):—consume, enjoy long, become (make, wax) old, spend, waste.

1087. בָּלֶה **bâleh**, *baw-leh'*; from 1086; *worn out*:—old.

1088. בָּלָה **Bâlâh**, *baw-law'*; fem. of 1087; *failure; Balah*, a place in Pal.:—Balah.

1089. בָּלַהּ **bâlahh**, *baw-lah'*; a prim. root [rather by transp. for 926]; to *palpitate*; hence (caus.) to *terrify*:—trouble.

1090. בִּלְהָה **Bilhâh**, *bil-haw'*; from 1089; *timid; Bilhah*, the name of one of Jacob's concubines; also of a place in Pal.:—Bilhah.

1091. בַּלָּהָה **ballâhâh**, *bal-law-haw'*; from 1089; *alarm*; hence *destruction*:—terror, trouble.

1092. בִּלְהָן **Bilhân**, *bil-hawn'*; from 1089; *timid; Bilhan*, the name of an Edomite and of an Isr.:—Bilhan.

1093. בְּלוֹ **belôw** (Chald.), *bel-o'*; from a root corresp. to 1086; *excise* (on articles consumed):—tribute.

1094. בְּלוֹא **belôw'**, *bel-o'*; or (fully) בְּלוֹי **belôwy**, *bel-o'ee*; from 1086; (only in plur. constr.) *rags*:—old.

1095. בֵּלְטְשַׁאצַּר **Bêlṭeshaʼtstsar**, *bale-tesh-ats-tsar'*; of for. der.; *Belteshatstsar*, the Bab. name of Daniel:—Belteshazzar.

1096. בֵּלְטְשַׁאצַּר **Bêlṭeshaʼtstsar** (Chald.), *bale-tesh-ats-tsar'*; corresp. to 1095:—Belteshazzar.

1097. בְּלִי **belîy**, *bel-ee'*; from 1086; prop. *failure*, i.e. *nothing* or *destruction*; usually (with prep.) *without, not yet, because not, as long as*, etc.:—corruption, ig[norantly], for lack of, where no . . . is, so that no, none, not, un[awares], without.

1098. בְּלִיל **belîyl**, *bel-eel'*; from 1101; *mixed*, i.e. (spec.) *feed* (for cattle):—corn, fodder, provender.

1099. בְּלִימָה **belîymâh**, *bel-ee-mah'*; from 1097 and 4100; (as indef.) *nothing whatever*:—nothing.

1100. בְּלִיַּעַל **belîyaʿal**, *bel-e-yah'-al*; from 1097 and 3276; *without profit, worthlessness*; by extens. *destruction, wickedness* (often in connection with 376, 802, 1121, etc.):—Belial, evil, naughty, ungodly (men), wicked.

1101. בָּלַל **bâlal**, *baw-lal'*; a prim. root; to *overflow* (spec. with oil); by impl. to *mix*; also (denom. from 1098) to *fodder*:—anoint, confound, × fade, mingle, mix (self), give provender, temper.

1102. בָּלַם **bâlam**, *baw-lam'*; a prim. root; to *muzzle*:—be held in.

1103. בָּלַס **bâlaç**, *baw-las'*; a prim. root; to *pinch* sycamore figs (a process necessary to ripen them):—gatherer.

1104. בָּלַע **bâlaʿ**, *baw-lah'*; a prim. root; to *make away with* (spec. by *swallowing*); gen. to *destroy*:—cover, destroy, devour, eat up, be at end, spend up, swallow down (up).

1105. בֶּלַע **belaʿ**, *beh'-lah*; from 1104; a *gulp*; fig. *destruction*:—devouring, that which he hath swallowed up.

1106. בֶּלַע **Belaʿ**, *beh'-lah*; the same as 1105; *Bela*, the name of a place, also of an Edomite and of two Isr.:—Bela.

1107. בִּלְעֲדֵי **bilʿadêy**, *bil-ad-ay'*; or בַּלְעֲדֵי **balʿadêy**, *bal-ad-ay'*; constr. plur. from 1077 and 5703; *not till*, i.e. (as prep. or adv.) *except, without, besides*:—beside, not (in), save, without.

1108. בַּלְעִי **Balʿiy**, *bel-ee'*; patronym. from 1106: a *Belaite* (collect.) or desc. of Bela:—Belaites.

1109. בִּלְעָם **Bilʿâm**, *bil-awm'*; prob. from 1077 and 5971; *not* (of the) *people*, i.e. *foreigner; Bilam*, a Mesopotamian prophet; also a place in Pal.:—Balaam, Bileam.

1110. בָּלַק **bâlaq**, *baw-lak'*; a prim. root; to *annihilate*:—(make) waste.

1111. בָּלָק **Bâlâq**, *baw-lawk'*; from 1110; *waster; Balak*, a Moabitish king:—Balak.

1112. בֵּלְשַׁאצַּר **Bêlshaʼtstsar**, *bale-shats-tsar'*; or בֵּלְאשַׁצַּר **Bêl'shatstsar**, *bale-shats-tsar'*; of for. or. (comp. 1095); *Belshatstsar*, a Bab. king:—Belshazzar.

1113. בֵּלְשַׁאצַּר **Bêlshaʼtstsar** (Chald.), *bale-shats-tsar'*; corresp. to 1112:—Belshazzar.

1114. בִּלְשָׁן **Bilshân**, *bil-shawn'*; of uncert. der.; *Bilshan*, an Isr.:—Bilshan.

1115. בִּלְתִּי **biltîy**, *bil-tee'*; constr. fem. of 1086 (equiv. to 1097); prop. a *failure of*, i.e. (used only as a neg. particle, usually with prep. pref.) *not, except, without, unless, besides, because not, until*, etc.:—because un[satiable], beside, but, + continual, except, from, lest, neither, no more, none, not, nothing, save, that no, without.

1116. בָּמָה **bâmâh**, *baw-maw'*; from an unused root (mean. to *be high*); an *elevation*:—height, high place, wave.

1117. בָּמָה **Bâmâh**, *baw-maw'*; the same as 1116; *Bamah*, a place in Pal.:—Bamah. See also 1120.

1118. בִּמְהָל **Bimhâl**, *bim-hawl'*; prob. from 4107 with prep. pref.; *with pruning; Bimhal*, an Isr.:—Bimhal.

1119. בְּמוֹ **bemôw**, *bem-o'*; prol. for prep. pref.; *in, with, by*, etc.:—for, in, into, through.

1120. בָּמוֹת **Bâmôwth**, *baw-mōth'*; plur. of 1116; *heights*; or (fully) בָּמוֹת בַּעַל **Bâmôwth Baʿal**, *baw-mōth' bah'-al*; from the same and 1168; *heights of Baal; Bamoth* or *Bamoth-Baal*, a place E. of the Jordan:—Bamoth, Bamoth-baal.

1121. בֵּן **bên**, *bane*; from 1129; a *son* (as a *builder* of the family name), in the widest sense (of lit. and fig. relationship, including *grandson, subject, nation, quality* or *condition*, etc., [like 1, 251, etc.]):—+ afflicted, age, [Ahoh-] [Ammon-] [Hachmon-] [Lev-]ite, [anoint-]ed one, appointed to, (+) ar, row, [Assyr-] [Babylon-] [Egypt-] [Grec-]ian, one born, bough, branch, breed, + (young) bullock, + (young) calf, × came up in, child, colt, × common, × corn, daughter, × of first, + firstborn, foal, + very fruitful, + postage, × in, + kid, + lamb, (+) man, meet, + mighty, + nephew, old, (+) people, + rebel, + robber, × servant born, × soldier, son, + spark, + steward, + stranger, × surely, them of, + tumultuous one, + valiant[-est], whelp, worthy, young (one), youth.

1122. בֵּן **Bên**, *bane;* the same as 1121; *Ben,* an Isr.:—Ben.

1123. בֵּן **bên** (Chald.), *bane;* corresp. to 1121:—child, son, young.

1124. בְּנָא **bᵉnâʼ** (Chald.), *ben-aw';* or בְּנָה **bᵉnâh** (Chald.), *ben-aw';* corresp. to 1129; to *build:*—build, make.

1125. בֶּן־אֲבִינָדָב **Ben-ʼĂbîynâdâb**, *ben-ab-ee''-naw-dawb';* from 1121 and 40; (the) *son of Abinadab; Ben-Abinadab,* an Isr.:—the son of Abinadab.

1126. בֶּן־אוֹנִי **Ben-ʼÔwnîy**, *ben-o-nee';* from 1121 and 205; *son of my sorrow; Ben-Oni,* the original name of Benjamin:—Ben-oni.

1127. בֶּן־גֶּבֶר **Ben-Geber**, *ben-gheh'-ber;* from 1121 and 1397; *son of* (the) *hero; Ben-Geber,* an Isr.:—the son of Geber.

1128. בֶּן־דֶּקֶר **Ben-Deqer**, *ben-deh'-ker;* from 1121 and a der. of 1856; *son of piercing* (or *of a lance*); *Ben-Deker,* an Isr.:—the son of Dekar.

1129. בָּנָה **bânâh**, *baw-naw';* a prim. root; to *build* (lit. and fig.):—(begin to) build (-er), obtain children, make, repair, set (up), × surely.

1130. בֶּן־הֲדַד **Ben-Hădad**, *ben-had-ad';* from 1121 and 1908; *son of Hadad; Ben-Hadad,* the name of several Syrian kings:—Ben-hadad.

1131. בִּנּוּי **Binnûwy**, *bin-noo'ee;* from 1129; *built up; Binnui,* an Isr.:—Binnui.

1132. בֶּן־זוֹחֵת **Ben-Zôwchêth**, *ben-zo-khayth';* from 1121 and 2105; *son of Zocheth; Ben-Zocheth,* an Isr.:—Ben-zoketh.

1133. בֶּן־חוּר **Ben-Chûwr**, *ben-khoor';* from 1121 and 2354; *son of Chur; Ben-Chur,* an Isr.:—the son of Hur.

1134. בֶּן־חַיִל **Ben-Chayil**, *ben-khah'-yil;* from 1121 and 2428; *son of might; Ben-Chail,* an Isr.:—Ben-hail.

1135. בֶּן־חָנָן **Ben-Chânân**, *ben-khaw-nawn';* from 1121 and 2605; *son of Chanan; Ben-Chanan,* an Isr.:—Ben-hanan.

1136. בֶּן־חֶסֶד **Ben-Cheçed**, *ben-kheh'-sed;* from 1121 and 2617; *son of kindness; Ben-Chesed,* an Isr.:—the son of Hesed.

1137. בָּנִי **Bânîy**, *baw-nee';* from 1129; *built; Bani,* the name of five Isr.:—Bani.

1138. בֻּנִּי **Bunnîy**, *boon-nee';* or (fuller) בּוּנִי **Bûwnîy**, *boo-nee';* from 1129; *built; Bunni* or *Buni,* an Isr.:—Bunni.

1139. בְּנֵי־בְרַק **Bᵉnêy-Bᵉraq**, *ben-ay'-ber-ak';* from the plur. constr. of 1121 and 1300; *sons of lightning, Bene-berak,* a place in Pal.:—Bene-barak.

1140. בִּנְיָה **binyâh**, *bin-yaw';* fem. from 1129; a *structure:*—building.

1141. בְּנָיָה **Bᵉnâyâh**, *ben-aw-yaw';* or (prol.) בְּנָיָהוּ **Bᵉnâyâhûw**, *ben-aw-yaw'-hoo;* from 1129 and 3050; *Jah has built; Benajah,* the name of twelve Isr.:—Benaiah.

1142. בְּנֵי יַעֲקָן **Bᵉnêy Yaʻăqân**, *ben-ay' yah-ak-awn';* from the plur. of 1121 and 3292; *sons of Yaakan; Bene-Jaakan,* a place in the Desert:—Bene-jaakan.

1143. בֵּנַיִם **bênayim**, *bay-nah'-yim;* dual of 996; a *double interval,* i.e. the space between two armies:—+ champion.

1144. בִּנְיָמִין **Binyâmîyn**, *bin-yaw-mene';* from 1121 and 3225; *son of* (the) *right hand; Binjamin,* youngest son of Jacob; also the tribe descended from him, and its territory:—Benjamin.

1145. בֶּן־יְמִינִי **Ben-yᵉmîynîy**, *ben-yem-ee-nee';* sometimes (with the art. ins.) בֶּן־הַיְמִינִי **Ben-ha-yᵉmînîy**, *ben-hah-yem-ee-nee';* with 376 ins. (1 Sam. 9 : 1) בֶּן־אִישׁ יְמִינִי **Ben-ʼÎysh Yᵉmîynîy**, *ben-eesh' yem-ee-nee'; son of a man of Jemini;* or short. (1 Sam. 9 : 4; Esth. 2 : 5) אִישׁ יְמִינִי **ʼÎysh Yᵉmîynîy**, *eesh yem-ee-nee'; a man of Jemini;* or (1 Sam. 20 : 1) simply יְמִינִי **Yᵉmînîy**, *yem-ee-nee'; a Jeminite;* (plur. בְּנֵי יְמִינִי **Bᵉnîy Yᵉmîynîy**, *ben-ay' yem-ee-nee';*) patron. from 1144; a *Benjaminite,* or descendant of Benjamin:—Benjamite, of Benjamin.

1146. בִּנְיָן **binyân**, *bin-yawn';* from 1129; an *edifice:*—building.

1147. בִּנְיָן **binyân** (Chald.), *bin-yawn';* corresp. to 1146:—building.

1148. בְּנִינוּ **Bᵉnîynûw**, *ben-ee-noo';* prob. from 1121 with pron. suff.; *our son; Beninu,* an Isr.:—Beninu.

1149. בְּנַס **bᵉnaç** (Chald.), *ben-as';* of uncert. affin.; to *be enraged:*—be angry.

1150. בִּנְעָא **Binʻâʼ**, *bin-aw';* or בִּנְעָה **Binʻâh**, *bin-aw';* of uncert. der.; *Bina* or *Binah,* an Isr.:—Binea, Bineah.

1151. בֶּן־עַמִּי **Ben-ʻAmmîy**, *ben-am-mee';* from 1121 and 5971 with pron. suff.; *son of my people; Ben-Ammi,* a son of Lot:—Ben-ammi.

1152. בְּסוֹדְיָה **Bᵉçôwdᵉyâh**, *bes-o-deh-yaw';* from 5475 and 3050 with prep. pref.; *in* (the) *counsel of Jehovah; Besodejah,* an Isr.:—Besodeiah.

1153. בְּסַי **Bᵉçay**, *bes-ah'-ee;* from 947; *domineering; Besai,* one of the Nethinim:—Besai.

1154. בֶּסֶר **bêçer**, *beh'-ser;* from an unused root mean. to *be sour;* an *immature* grape:—unripe grape.

1155. בֹּסֶר **bôçer**, *bo'-ser;* from the same as 1154:—sour grape.

1156. בְּעָא **bᵉʻâʼ** (Chald.), *beh-aw';* or בְּעָה **bᵉʻâh** (Chald.), *beh-aw';* corresp. to 1158; to *seek* or *ask:*—ask, desire, make [petition], pray, request, seek.

1157. בְּעַד **bᵉʻad**, *beh-ad';* from 5704 with prep. pref.; *in up to* or *over against;* gen. *at, beside, among, behind, for,* etc.:—about, at, by (means of), for, over, through, up (-on), within.

1158. בָּעָה **bâʻâh**, *baw-aw';* a prim. root; to *gush* over, i.e. to *swell;* (fig.) to *desire* earnestly; by impl. to *ask:*—cause, inquire, seek up, swell out, boil.

1159. בָּעוּ **bâʻûw** (Chald.), *baw-oo';* from 1156; a *request:*—petition.

1160. בְּעוֹר **Bᵉʻôwr**, *beh-ore';* from 1197 (in the sense of *burning*); a *lamp; Beör,* the name of the father of an Edomitish king; also of that of Balaam:—Beor.

1161. בִּעוּתִים **biʻûwthîym**, *be-oo-theme';* masc. plur. from 1204; *alarms:*—terrors.

1162. בֹּעַז **Bôʻaz**, *bo'-az;* from an unused root of uncert. mean.; *Boaz,* the ancestor of David; also the name of a pillar in front of the temple:—Boaz.

1163. בָּעַט **bâʻaṭ**, *baw-at';* a prim. root; to *trample* down, i.e. (fig.) *despise:*—kick.

1164. בְּעִי **bᵉʻîy**, *beh-ee';* from 1158; a *prayer:*—grave.

1165. בְּעִיר **bᵉʻîyr**, *beh-ere';* from 1197 (in the sense of *eating*): cattle:—beast, cattle.

1166. בָּעַל **bâʻal**, *baw-al';* a prim. root; to *be master;* hence (as denom. from 1167) to *marry:*—Beulah have dominion (over), be husband, marry (-ried, × wife).

1167. בַּעַל **baʻal**, *bah'-al;* from 1166; a *master;* hence a *husband,* or (fig.) *owner* (often used with another noun in modifications of this latter sense):—+ archer, + babbler, + bird, captain, chief man, + confederate, + have to do, + dreamer, those to whom it is due, + furious, those that are given to it, great, + hairy, he that hath it, have, + horseman, husband, lord, man, + married, master, person, + sworn, they of.

1168. בַּעַל **Baʻal**, *bah'-al;* the same as 1167; *Baal,* a Phœnician deity:—Baal, [*plur.*] Baalim.

1169. בְּעֵל **bᵉʻêl** (Chald.), *beh-ale';* corresp. to 1167:—+ chancellor.

1170. בַּעַל בְּרִית **Baʻal Bᵉrîyth**, *bah'-al ber-eeth';* from 1168 and 1285; *Baal of* (the) *covenant; Baal-Berith,* a special deity of the Shechemites:—Baal-berith.

1171. בַּעַל גָּד **Baʻal Gâd**, *bah'-al gawd;* from 1168 and 1409; *Baal of Fortune; Baal-Gad,* a place in Syria:—Baal-gad.

1172. בַּעֲלָה **baʻălâh**, *bah-al-aw';* fem. of 1167; a *mistress:*—that hath, mistress.

1173. בַּעֲלָה **Baʻălâh**, *bah-al-aw';* the same as 1172; *Baalah,* the name of three places in Pal.:—Baalah.

1174. בַּעַל הָמוֹן **Baʻal Hâmôwn**, *bah'-al haw-mone';* from 1167 and 1995; *possessor of a multitude; Baal-Hamon,* a place in Pal.:—Baal-hamon.

1175. בְּעָלוֹת **Bᵉʻâlôwth**, *beh-aw-lōth';* plur. of 1172; *mistresses; Beälōth,* a place in Pal.:—Bealoth, in Aloth [*by mistake for a plur. from 5927 with prep. pref.*].

1176. בַּעַל זְבוּב **Baʻal Zᵉbûwb**, *bah'-al zeb-oob';* from 1168 and 2070; *Baal of* (the) *Fly; Baal-Zebub,* a special deity of the Ekronites:—Baal-zebub.

1177. בַּעַל חָנָן **Baʻal Chânân**, *bah'-al khaw-nawn';* from 1167 and 2603; *possessor of grace; Baal-Chanan,* the name of an Edomite, also of an Isr.:—Baal-hanan.

1178. בַּעַל חָצוֹר **Baʻal Châtsôwr**, *bah'-al khaw-tsore';* from 1167 and a modif. of 2691; *possessor of a village; Baal-Chatsor,* a place in Pal.:—Baal-hazor.

1179. בַּעַל חֶרְמוֹן **Baʻal Chermôwn**, *bah'-al kher-mone';* from 1167 and 2768; *possessor of Hermon; Baal-Chermon,* a place in Pal.:—Baal-hermon.

1180. בַּעֲלִי **Baʻălîy**, *bah-al-ee';* from 1167 with pron. suff.; *my master; Baali,* a symbolical name for Jehovah:—Baali.

1181. בַּעֲלֵי בָמוֹת **Baʻălêy Bâmôwth**, *bah-al-ay' baw-mōth';* from the plur. of 1168 and the plur. of 1116; *Baals of* (the) *heights; Baale-Bamoth,* a place E. of the Jordan:—lords of the high places.

1182. בְּעֶלְיָדָע **Bᵉʻelyâdâʻ**, *beh-el-yaw-daw';* from 1168 and 3045; *Baal has known; Beëljada,* an Isr.:—Beeliada.

1183. בְּעַלְיָה **Bᵉʻalyâh**, *beh-al-yaw';* from 1167 and 3050; *Jah* (is) *master; Bealjah,* an Isr.:—Bealiah.

1184. בַּעֲלֵי יְהוּדָה **Baʻălêy Yᵉhûwdâh**, *bah-al-ay' yeh-hoo-daw';* from the plur. of 1167 and 3063; *masters of Judah; Baale-Jehudah,* a place in Pal.:—Baale of Judah.

1185. בַּעֲלִיס **Baʻăliç**, *bah-al-ece';* prob. from a der. of 5965 with prep. pref.; *in exultation; Baalis,* an Ammonitish king:—Baalis.

1186. בַּעַל מְעוֹן **Baʻal Mᵉʻôwn**, *bah-al meh-one';* from 1168 and 4583; *Baal of* (the) *habitation* (of) [comp. 1010]; *Baal-Meön,* a place E. of the Jordan:—Baal-meon.

1187. בַּעַל פְּעוֹר **Baʻal Pᵉʻôwr**, *bah'-al peh-ore';* from 1168 and 6465; *Baal of Peor; Baal-Peör,* a Moabitish deity:—Baal-peor.

1188. בַּעַל פְּרָצִים **Baʻal Pᵉrâtsîym**, *bah'-al per-aw-tseem';* from 1167 and the plur. of 6556; *possessor of breaches; Baal-Peratsim,* a place in Pal.:—Baal-perazim.

1189. בַּעַל צְפוֹן **Baʻal Tsᵉphôwn**, *bah'-al tsef-one';* from 1168 and 6828 (in the sense of *cold*) [according to others an Eg. form of *Typhon,* the destroyer]; *Baal of winter; Baal-Tsephon,* a place in Egypt:—Baal-zephon.

1190. בַּעַל שָׁלִשָׁה **Ba'al Shâlîshâh**, *bah'-al shaw-lee-shaw'*; from 1168 and 8031; *Baal of Shalishah; Baal-Shalishah*, a place in Pal.:—Baal-shalisha.

1191. בַּעֲלָת **Ba'âlâth**, *bah-al-awth'*; a modif. of 1172; *mistressship; Baalath*, a place in Pal.:—Baalath.

1192. בַּעֲלַת בְּאֵר **Ba'âlath Be'êr**, *bah-al-ath' beh-ayr'*; from 1172 and 875; *mistress of a well; Baalath-Beër*, a place in Pal.:—Baalath-beer.

1193. בַּעַל תָּמָר **Ba'al Tâmâr**, *bah'-al taw-mawr'*, from 1167 and 8558; *possessor of* (the) *palm-tree; Baal-Tamar*, a place in Pal.:—Baal-tamar.

1194. בְּעֹן **Be'ôn**, *beh-ohn'*; prob. a contr. of 1010; *Beön*, a place E. of the Jordan:—Beon.

1195. בַּעֲנָא **Ba'ănâ'**, *bah-an-aw'*; the same as 1196; *Baana*, the name of four Isr.:—Baana, Baanah.

1196. בַּעֲנָה **Ba'ănâh**, *bah-an-aw'*; from a der. of 6031 with prep. pref.; *in affliction:—Baanah*, the name of four Isr.:—Baanah.

1197. בָּעַר **bâ'ar**, *baw-ar'*; a prim. root; to *kindle*, i.e. *consume* (by fire or by eating); also (as denom. from 1198) to *be (-come) brutish:*—be brutish, bring (put, take) away, burn, (cause to) eat (up), feed, heat, kindle, set ([on fire]), waste.

1198. בַּעַר **ba'ar**, *bah'-ar*; from 1197; prop. *food* (as *consumed*); i.e. (by exten.) of cattle *brutishness;* (concr.) *stupid:*—brutish (person), foolish.

1199. בָּעֲרָא **Bâ'ărâ'**, *bah-ar-aw'*; from 1198; *brutish; Baara*, an Israelitish woman:—Baara.

1200. בְּעֵרָה **be'êrâh**, *bě-ay-raw'*; from 1197; a *burning:*—fire.

1201. בַּעְשָׁא **Ba'shâ'**, *bah-shaw'*; from an unused root mean. to *stink; offensiveness; Basha*, a king of Israel:—Baasha.

1202. בַּעֲשֵׂיָה **Ba'ăsêyâh**, *bah-as-ay-yaw'*; from 6213 and 3050 with prep. pref.; *in* (the) *work of Jah; Baasejah*, an Isr.:—Baaseiah.

1203. בְּעֶשְׁתְּרָה **Be'eshterâh**, *beh-esh-ter-aw'*; from 6251 (as sing. of 6252) with prep. pref.; *with Ashtoreth; Beështerah*, a place E. of the Jordan:—Beeshterah.

1204. בָּעַת **bâ'ath**, *baw-ath'*; a prim. root; to *fear:*—affright, be (make) afraid, terrify, trouble.

1205. בְּעָתָה **be'âthâh**, *beh-aw-thaw'*; from 1204; *fear:*—trouble.

1206. בֹּץ **bôts**, *botse*; prob. the same as 948; *mud* (as *whitish* clay):—mire.

1207. בִּצָּה **bitstsâh**, *bits-tsaw'*; intens. from 1206; a *swamp:*—fen, mire (-ry place).

1208. בָּצוֹר° **bâtsôwr**, *baw-tsore'*; from 1219; *inaccessible*, i.e. *lofty:*—vintage [*by confusion with* 1210].

1209. בֵּצַי **Bêtsay**, *bay-tsah'ee*; perh. the same as 1153; *Betsai*, the name of two Isr.:—Bezai.

1210. בָּצִיר **bâtsîyr**, *baw-tseer'*; from 1219; *clipped*, i.e. the *grape crop:*—vintage.

1211. בֶּצֶל **betsel**, *beh'-tsel*; from an unused root appar. mean. to *peel;* an *onion:*—onion.

1212. בְּצַלְאֵל **Betsal'êl**, *bets-al-ale'*; prob. from 6738 and 410 with prep. pref.; *in* (the) *shadow* (i.e. protection) *of God; Betsalel;* the name of two Isr.:—Bezaleel.

1213. בַּצְלוּת **Batslûwth**, *bats-looth'*; or
בַּצְלִית **Batslîyth**, *bats-leeth'*; from the same as 1211; a *peeling; Batsluth* or *Batslith;* an Isr.:—Bazlith, Bazluth.

1214. בָּצַע **bâtsa'**, *baw-tsah'*; a prim. root to *break* off, i.e. (usually) *plunder;* fig. to *finish*, or (intrans.) *stop:*—(be) covet (-ous), cut (off), finish, fulfill, gain (greedily), get, be given to [covetousness], greedy, perform, be wounded.

1215. בֶּצַע **betsa'**, *beh'-tsah*; from 1214; *plunder;* by extens. *gain* (usually unjust):—covetousness, (dishonest) gain, lucre, profit.

1216. בָּצֵק **bâtsêq**, *baw-tsake'*; a prim. root; perh. to *swell* up, i.e. *blister:*—swell.

1217. בָּצֵק **bâtsêq**, *baw-tsake'*; from 1216; *dough* (as *swelling* by fermentation):—dough, flour.

1218. בָּצְקַת **Botsqath**, *bots-cath'*; from 1216; a *swell* of ground; *Botscath*, a place in Pal.:—Bozcath, Boskath.

1219. בָּצַר **bâtsar**, *baw-tsar'*; a prim. root; to *clip* off; spec. (as denom. from 1210) to *gather* grapes; also to *be isolated* (i.e. *inaccessible* by height or fortification):—cut off, (de-) fenced, fortify, (grape) gather (-er), mighty things, restrain, strong, wall (up), withhold.

1220. בֶּצֶר **betser**, *beh'-tser*; from 1219; strictly a *clipping*, i.e. *gold* (as *dug* out):—gold defence.

1221. בֶּצֶר **Betser**, *beh'-tser*; the same as 1220. an *inaccessible* spot; *Betser*, a place in Pal.; also an Isr.:—Bezer.

1222. בְּצַר **betsar**, *bets-ar'*; another form for 1220; *gold:*—gold.

1223. בָּצְרָה **botsrâh**, *bots-raw'*; fem. from 1219; an *enclosure*, i.e. *sheep-fold:*—Bozrah.

1224. בָּצְרָה **Botsrâh**, *bots-raw'*; the same as 1223; *Botsrah*, a place in Edom:—Bozrah.

1225. בִּצָּרוֹן **bitstsârôwn**, *bits-tsaw-rone'*; masc. intens. from 1219; a *fortress:*—stronghold.

1226. בַּצֹּרֶת **batstsôreth**, *bats-tso'-reth*; fem. intens. from 1219; *restraint* (of rain), i.e. *drought:*—dearth, drought.

1227. בַּקְבּוּק **Baqbûwq**, *bak-book'*; the same as 1228; *Bakbuk*, one of the *Nethinim:*—Bakbuk.

1228. בַּקְבֻּק **baqbûk**, *bak-book'*; from 1238; a *bottle* (from the gurgling in *emptying*):—bottle, cruse.

1229. בַּקְבֻּקְיָה **Baqbukyâh**, *bak-book-yaw'*; from 1228 and 3050; *emptying* (i.e. *wasting*) *of Jah; Bakbukjah*, an Isr.:—Bakbukiah.

1230. בַּקְבַּקַּר **Baqbaqqar**, *bak-bak-kar'*; redupl. from 1239; *searcher; Bakbakkar*, an Isr.:—Bakbakkar.

1231. בֻּקִּי **Buqqîy**, *book-kee'*; from 1238; *wasteful; Bukki*, the name of two Isr.:—Bukki.

1232. בֻּקִּיָּה **Buqqîyâh**, *book-kee-yaw'*; from 1238 and 3050; *wasting of Jah; Bukkijah*, an Isr.:—Bukkiah.

1233. בְּקִיעַ **beqîya'**, *bek-ee'-ah*; from 1234; a *fissure:*—breach, cleft.

1234. בָּקַע **bâqa'**, *baw-kah'*; a prim. root; to *cleave;* gen. to *rend, break, rip* or *open:*—make a breach, break forth (into, out, in pieces, through, up), be ready to burst, cleave (asunder), cut out, divide, hatch, rend (asunder), rip up, tear, win.

1235. בֶּקַע **beqa'**, *beh'-kah*; from 1234; a *section* (half) of a shekel, i.e. a *beka* (a weight and a coin):—bekah, half a shekel.

1236. בִּקְעָא **biq'â'** (Chald.), *bik-aw'*; corresp. to 1237:—plain.

1237. בִּקְעָה **biq'âh**, *bik-aw'*; from 1234; prop. a *split*, i.e. a wide level *valley* between mountains:—plain, valley.

1238. בָּקַק **bâqaq**, *baw-kah'*; a prim. root; to *pour* out, i.e. to *empty*, fig. to *depopulate;* by anal. to *spread* out (as a fruitful vine):—(make) empty (out), fail, × utterly, make void.

1239. בָּקַר **bâqar**, *baw-kar'*; a prim. root; prop. to *plough*, or (gen.) *break* forth, i.e. (fig.) to *inspect, admire, care for, consider:*—(make) inquire (-ry), (make) search, seek out.

1240. בְּקַר **beqar** (Chald.), *bek-ar'*; corresp. to 1239:—inquire, make search.

1241. בָּקָר **bâqâr**, *baw-kawr'*; from 1239; a *beeve* or animal of the ox kind of either gender (as used for *ploughing*); collect. a *herd:*—beeve, bull (+ -ock), + calf, + cow, great [cattle], + heifer, herd, kine, ox.

1242. בֹּקֶר **bôqer**, *bo'-ker*; from 1239; prop. *dawn* (as the *break* of day); gen. *morning:*—(+) day, early, morning, morrow.

1243. בַּקָּרָה **baqqârâh**, *bak-kaw-raw'*; intens. from 1239; a *looking after:*—seek out.

1244. בִּקֹּרֶת **biqqôreth**, *bik-ko-reth*; from 1239; prop. *examination*, i.e. (by impl.) *punishment:*—scourged.

1245. בָּקַשׁ **bâqash**, *baw-kash'*; a prim. root; to *search* out (by any method, spec. in worship or prayer); by impl. to *strive after:*—ask, beg, beseech, desire, enquire, get, make inquisition, procure, (make) request, require, seek (for).

1246. בַּקָּשָׁה **baqqâshâh**, *bak-kaw-shaw'*; from 1245; a *petition:*—request.

1247. בַּר **bar** (Chald.), *bar*; corresp. to 1121; a *son, grandson*, etc.:— × old, son.

1248. בַּר **bar**, *bar*; borrowed (as a title) from 1247; the *heir* (apparent to the throne):—son.

1249. בַּר **bar**, *bar*; from 1305 (in its various senses); *beloved;* also *pure, empty:*—choice, clean, clear, pure.

1250. בָּר **bâr**, *bawr*; or
בַּר **bar**, *bar*; from 1305 (in the sense of *winnowing*): *grain* of any kind (even while standing in the field); by extens. the open *country:*—corn, wheat.

1251. בַּר **bar** (Chald.), *bar*; corresp. to 1250; a *field:*—field.

1252. בֹּר **bôr**, *bore*; from 1305; *purity:*—cleanness, pureness.

1253. בֹּר **bôr**, *bore*; the same as 1252; vegetable *lye* (from its *cleansing*); used as a *soap* for washing, or a *flux* for metals:— × never so, purely.

1254. בָּרָא **bârâ'**, *baw-raw'*; a prim. root; (absol.) to *create;* (qualified) to *cut* down (a wood), *select, feed* (as formative processes):—choose, create (creator), cut down, dispatch, do, make (fat).

1255. בְּרֹאדַךְ בַּלְאֲדָן **Berô'dak Bal'ădân**, *ber-o-dak' bal-ad-awn'*; a var. of 4757; *Berodak-Baladan*, a Bab. king:—Berodach-baladan.

בִּרְאִי **Bir'îy**. See 1011.

1256. בְּרָאיָה **Berâ'yâh**, *ber-aw-yaw'*; from 1254 and 3050; *Jah has created; Berajah*, an Isr.:—Beraiah.

1257. בַּרְבֻּר **barbûr**, *bar-boor'*; by redupl. from 1250; a *fowl* (as fattened on *grain*):—fowl.

1258. בָּרַד **bârad**, *baw-rad'*; a prim. root, to *hail:*—hail.

1259. בָּרָד **bârâd**, *baw-rawd'*; from 1258; *hail:*—hail ([stones]).

1260. בֶּרֶד **Bered**, *beh'-red*; from 1258; *hail; Bered*, the name of a place south of Pal., also of an Isr.:—Bered.

1261. בָּרֹד **bârôd**, *baw-rode'*; from 1258; *spotted* (as if with *hail*):—grisled.

1262. בָּרָה **bârâh**, *baw-raw'*; a prim. root; to *select;* also (as denom. from 1250) to *feed;* also (as equiv. to 1305) to *render clear* (Eccl. 3 : 18):—choose, (cause to) eat, manifest, (give) meat.

1263. בָּרוּךְ **Bârûwk**, *baw-rook'*; pass. part. from 1288; *blessed; Baruk*, the name of three Isr.:—Baruch.

1264. בְּרוֹם **berôwm**, *ber-ome'*; prob. of for. or. *damask* (stuff of variegated thread):—rich apparel.

1265. בְּרוֹשׁ **berôwsh**, *ber-ōsh'*; of uncert. der.; a *cypress* (?) tree; hence a *lance* or a *musical* instrument (as made of that wood):—fir (tree).

1266. בְּרוֹת **berôwth**, *ber-ōth'*; a var. of 1265; the *cypress* (or some elastic tree):—fir.

1267. בָּרוּת **bârûwth**, *baw-rooth'*; from 1262; *food:*—meat.

1268. בֵּרוֹתָה **Bêrôwthâh**, *bay-ro-thaw'*; or
בֵּרֹתַי **Bêrôthay**, *bay-ro-thah'ee*; prob. from 1266; *cypress* or *cypresslike; Berothah* or *Berothai*, a place north of Pal.:—Berothah, Berothai.

1269. בִּרְזוֹת° **Birzôwth**, *beer-zoth'*; prob. fem. plur. from an unused root (appar. mean. to *pierce*); *holes; Birzoth*, an Isr.:– Birzavith [*from the marg.*].

1270. בַּרְזֶל **barzel**, *bar-zel'*; perh. from the root of 1269; *iron* (as *cutting*); by extens. an iron *implement*:—(ax) head, iron.

1271. בַּרְזִלַּי **Barzillay**, *bar-zil-lah'ee*; from 1270; *iron* hearted; *Barzillai*, the name of three Isr.:—Barzillai.

1272. בָּרַח **bârach**, *baw-rakh'*; a prim. root; to *bolt*, i.e. fig. to *flee* suddenly:—chase (away); drive away, fain, flee (away), put to flight, make haste, reach, run away, shoot.

בָּרִחַ **bârîach**. See 1281.

1273. בַּרְחֻמִי **Barchûmîy**, *bar-khoo-mee'*; by transp. for 978; a *Barchumite*, or native of *Bachurim*:—Barhumite.

1274. בְּרִי **beriy**, *ber-ee'*; from 1262; *fat*:—fat.

1275. בֵּרִי **Bêrîy**, *bay-ree'*; prob. by contr. from 882; *Beri*, an Isr.:—Beri.

1276. בֵּרִי **Bêrîy**, *bay-ree'*; of uncert. der.; (only in the plur. and with the art.) the *Berites*, a place in Pal.:—Berites.

1277. בָּרִיא **bârîyʼ**, *baw-ree'*; from 1254 (in the sense of 1262); *fatted* or *plump*:—fat ([fleshed], -ter), fed, firm, plenteous, rank.

1278. בְּרִיאָה **berîyʼâh**, *ber-ee-aw'*; fem. from 1254; a *creation*, i.e. a *novelty*:—new thing.

1279. בִּרְיָה **biryâh**, *beer-yaw'*; fem. from 1262; *food*:—meat.

1280. בְּרִיחַ **berîyach**, *ber-ee'-akh*; from 1272; a *bolt*:—bar, fugitive.

1281. בָּרִיחַ **bârîyach**, *baw-ree'-akh*; or (short.)

בָּרִחַ **bârîach**, *baw-ree'-akh*; from 1272; a *fugitive*, i.e. the *serpent* (as *fleeing*), and the constellation by that name:—crooked, noble, piercing.

1282. בָּרִיחַ **Bârîyach**, *baw-ree'-akh*; the same as 1281; *Bariach*, an Isr.:—Bariah.

1283. בְּרִיעָה **Berîyʻâh**, *ber-ee'-aw*; appar. from the fem. of 7451 with prep. pref.; *in trouble; Beriah*, the name of four Isr.:—Beriah.

1284. בְּרִיעִי **Berîyʻîy**, *ber-ee-ee'*; patron. from 1283; a *Beriite* (collect.) or desc. of Beriah:—Beerites.

1285. בְּרִית **berîyth**, *ber-eeth'*; from 1262 (in the sense of *cutting* [like 1254]); a *compact* (because made by passing between *pieces* of flesh):—confederacy, [con-]feder[-ate], covenant, league.

1286. בְּרִית **Berîyth**, *ber-eeth'*; the same as 1285; *Berith*, a Shechemitish deity:—Berith.

1287. בֹּרִית **bôrîyth**, *bo-reeth'*; fem. of 1253; vegetable *alkali*:—sope.

1288. בָּרַךְ **bârak**, *baw-rak'*; a prim. root; to *kneel*; by impl. to *bless* God (as an act of adoration), and (vice-versa) man (as a benefit); also (by euphemism) to *curse* (God or the king, as treason):—× abundantly, × altogether, × at all, blaspheme, bless, congratulate, curse, × greatly, × indeed, kneel (down), praise, salute, × still, thank.

1289. בְּרַךְ **berak** (Chald.), *ber-ak'*; corresp. to 1288:—bless, kneel.

1290. בֶּרֶךְ **berek**, *beh'-rek*; from 1288; a *knee*:—knee.

1291. בֶּרֶךְ **berek** (Chald.), *beh'-rek*; corresp. to 1290:—knee.

1292. בָּרַכְאֵל **Bârakʼêl**, *baw-rak-ale'*; from 1288 and 410, *God has blessed; Barakel*, the father of one of Job's friends:—Barachel.

1293. בְּרָכָה **Berâkâh**, *ber-aw-kaw'*; from 1288; *benediction*; by impl. *prosperity*:—blessing, liberal, pool, present.

1294. בְּרָכָה **Berâkâh**, *ber-aw-kaw'*; the same as 1293; *Berakah*, the name of an Isr., and also of a valley in Pal.:—Berachah.

1295. בְּרֵכָה **berêkâh**, *ber-ay-kaw'*; from 1288; a *reservoir* (at which camels *kneel* as a resting-place):—(fish-) pool.

1296. בֶּרֶכְיָה **Berekyâh**, *beh-rek-yaw'*; or

בֶּרֶכְיָהוּ **Berekyâhûw**, *beh-rek-yaw'-hoo*; from 1290 and 3050; *knee* (i.e. *blessing*) of *Jah; Berekjah*, the name of six Isr.:—Berachiah, Berechiah.

1297. בְּרַם **beram**, (Chald.) *ber-am'*; perh. from 7313 with prep. pref.; prop. *highly*, i.e. *surely*; but used adversatively, *however*:—but, nevertheless, yet.

1298. בֶּרַע **Beraʻ**, *beh'-rah*; of uncert. der.; *Bera*, a Sodomitish king:—Bera.

1299. בָּרַק **bâraq**, *baw-rak'*; a prim. root; to *lighten* (lightning):—cast forth.

1300. בָּרָק **bârâq**, *baw-rawk'*; from 1299; *lightning*; by anal. a *gleam*; concr. a *flashing* sword:—bright, glitter (-ing, sword), lightning.

1301. בָּרָק **Bârâq**, *baw-rawk'*; the same as 1300; *Barak*, an Isr.:—Barak.

1302. בַּרְקוֹס **Barqôwç**, *bar-kose'*; of uncert. der.; *Barkos*, one of the Nethimim:—Barkos.

1303. בַּרְקָן **barqân**, *bar-kawn'*; from 1300; a *thorn* (perh. as burning *brightly*):—brier.

1304. בָּרְקַת **bâreqeth**, *baw-reh'-keth*; or

בָּרְקַת **bârekath**, *baw-rek-ath'*; from 1300; a gem (as *flashing*), perh. the *emerald*:—carbuncle.

1305. בָּרַר **bârar**, *baw-rar'*; a prim. root; to *clarify* (i.e. *brighten*), *examine*, *select*:—make bright, choice, chosen, cleanse (be clean), clearly, polished, (shew self) pure (-ify), purge (out).

1306. בִּרְשַׁע **Birshaʻ**, *beer-shah'*; prob. from 7562 with prep. pref.; *with wickedness*; *Birsha*, a king of Gomorrah:—Birsha.

1307. בֵּרֹתִי **Bêrôthîy**, *bay-ro-thee'*; patrial from 1268; a *Berothite*, or inhabitant of Berothai:—Berothite.

1308. בְּשׂוֹר **Besôwr**, *bes-ore'*; from 1319; *cheerful*; *Besor*, a stream of Pal.:—Besor.

1309. בְּשׂוֹרָה **besôwrâh**, *bes-o-raw'*; or (short.)

בְּשֹׂרָה **besôrâh**, *bes-o-raw'*; fem. from 1319; glad *tidings*; by impl. *reward for good news*:—reward for tidings.

1310. בָּשַׁל **bâshal**, *baw-shal'*; a prim. root; prop. to *boil* up; hence to *be done* in cooking; fig. to *ripen*:—bake, boil, bring forth, is ripe, roast, seethe, sod (be sodden).

1311. בָּשֵׁל **bâshêl**, *baw-shale'*; from 1310, *boiled*:—× at all, sodden.

1312. בִּשְׁלָם **Bishlâm**, *bish-lawm'*; of for. der.; *Bishlam*, a Pers.:—Bishlam.

1313. בָּשָׂם **bâsâm**, *baw-sawm'*; from an unused root mean. to *be fragrant*; [comp. 5561] the *balsam* plant:—spice.

1314. בֶּשֶׂם **besem**, *beh'-sem*; or

בֹּשֶׂם **bôsem**, *bo'-sem*; from the same as 1313; *fragrance*; by impl. *spicery*; also the *balsam* plant:—smell, spice, sweet (odour).

1315. בָּשְׂמַת **Bosmath**, *bos-math'*; fem. of 1314 (the second form); *fragrance*; *Bosmath*, the name of a wife of Esau, and of a daughter of Solomon:—Bashemath, Basmath.

1316. בָּשָׁן **Bâshân**, *baw-shawn'*; of uncert. der.; *Bashan* (often with the art.), a region E. of the Jordan:—Bashan.

1317. בָּשְׁנָה **boshnâh**, *bosh-naw'*; fem. from 954; *shamefulness*:—shame.

1318. בָּשַׁס **bâshaç**, *baw-shas'*; a prim. root; to *trample* down:—tread.

1319. בָּשַׂר **bâsar**, *baw-sar'*; a prim. root; prop. to *be fresh*, i.e. *full* (*rosy*, fig. *cheerful*); to *announce* (glad news):—messenger, preach, publish, shew forth, (bear, bring, carry, preach, good, tell good) tidings.

1320. בָּשָׂר **bâsâr**, *baw-sawr'*; from 1319; *flesh* (from its *freshness*); by extens. *body*, *person*; also (by euphem.) the *pudenda* of a man:—body, [fat, lean] flesh [-ed], kin, [man-] kind, + nakedness, self, skin.

1321. בְּשַׂר **besar** (Chald.), *bes-ar'*; corresp. to 1320:—flesh.

בְּשֹׂרָה **besôrâh**. See 1309.

1322. בֹּשֶׁת **bôsheth**, *bo'-sheth*; from 954; *shame* (the feeling and the condition, as well as its cause); by impl. (spec.) an *idol*:—ashamed, confusion, + greatly, (put to) shame (-ful thing).

1323. בַּת **bath**, *bath*; from 1129 (as fem. of 1121); a *daughter* (used in the same wide sense as other terms of relationship, lit. and fig.):—apple [of the eye], branch, company, daughter, × first, × old, + owl, town, village.

1324. בַּת **bath**, *bath*; prob. from the same as 1327; a *bath* or Heb. measure (as a means of *division*) of liquids:—bath.

1325. בַּת **bath** (Chald.), *bath*; corresp. to 1324:—bath.

1326. בָּתָה **bâthâh**, *baw-thaw'*; prob. an orth. var. for 1327; *desolation*:—waste.

1327. בַּתָּה **battâh**, *bat-taw'*; fem. from an unused root (mean. to *break* in pieces); *desolation*:—desolate.

1328. בְּתוּאֵל **Bethûwʼêl**, *beth-oo-ale'*; appar. from the same as 1326 and 410; *destroyed of God; Bethuel*, the name of a nephew of Abraham, and of a place in Pal.:—Bethuel. Comp. 1329.

1329. בְּתוּל **Bethûwl**, *beth-ool'*; for 1328; *Bethul* (i.e. *Bethuel*), a place in Pal.:—Bethuel.

1330. בְּתוּלָה **bethûwlâh**, *beth-oo-law'*; fem. pass. part. of an unused root mean. to *separate*; a *virgin* (from her *privacy*); sometimes (by continuation) a *bride*; also (fig.) a *city* or *state*:—maid, virgin.

1331. בְּתוּלִים **bethûwlîym**, *beth-oo-leem'*; masc. plur. of the same as 1330; (collect. and abstr.) *virginity*; by impl. and concr. the *tokens* of it:—× maid, virginity.

1332. בִּתְיָה **Bithyâh**, *bith-yaw'*; from 1323 and 3050; *daughter* (i.e. worshipper) *of Jah; Bithjah*, an Eg. woman:—Bithiah.

1333. בָּתַק **bâthaq**, *baw-thak'*; a prim. root; to *cut* in pieces:—thrust through.

1334. בָּתַר **bâthar**, *baw-thar'*; a prim. root, to *chop* up:—divide.

1335. בֶּתֶר **bether**, *beh'-ther*; from 1334; a *section*:—part, piece.

1336. בֶּתֶר **Bether**, *beh'-ther*; the same as 1335; *Bether*, a (*craggy*) place in Pal.:—Bether.

1337. בַּת רַבִּים **Bath Rabbîym**, *bath rabbeem'*; from 1323 and a masc. plur. from 7227; the *daughter* (i.e. *city*) *of Rabbah*:—Bath-rabbim.

1338. בִּתְרוֹן **Bithrôwn**, *bith-rone'*; from 1334; (with the art.) the *craggy* spot; *Bithron*, a place E. of the Jordan:—Bithron.

1339. בַּת־שֶׁבַע **Bath-Shebaʻ**, *bath-sheh'-bah*; from 1323 and 7651 (in the sense of 7650); *daughter of an oath; Bath-Sheba*, the mother of Solomon:—Bath-sheba.

1340. בַּת־שׁוּעַ **Bath-Shûwaʻ**, *bath-shoo'-ah*; from 1323 and 7771; *daughter of wealth; Bath-shuă*, the same as 1339:—Bath-shua.

ג

1341. גֵּא **gêʼ**, *gay'*; for 1343; *haughty*:—proud.

1342. גָּאָה **gâʼâh**, *gaw-aw'*; a prim. root; to *mount* up; hence in gen. to *rise*, (fig.) be *majestic*:—gloriously, grow up, increase, be risen, triumph.

1343. גֵּאֶה **gêʼeh**, *gay-eh'*; from 1342; *lofty*; fig. *arrogant*:—proud.

1344. גֵּאָה **gêʼâh**, *gay-aw'*; fem. from 1342; *arrogance*:—pride.

1345. גְּאוּאֵל **Geʼûwʼêl**, *gheh-oo-ale'*; from 1342 and 410; *majesty of God; Geüel*, an Isr.:—Geuel.

1346. גַּאֲוָה **ga'ăvâh**, *gah-av-aw'*; from 1342; *arrogance* or *majesty;* by impl. (concr.) *ornament:*—excellency, haughtiness, highness, pride, proudly, swelling.

1347. גָּאוֹן **gâ'ôwn**, *gaw-ohn'*; from 1342; the same as 1346:—arrogancy, excellency (-lent), majesty, pomp, pride, proud, swelling.

1348. גֵּאוּת **gê'ûwth**, *gay-ooth'*; from 1342; the same as 1346:—excellent things, lifting up, majesty, pride, proudly, raging.

1349. גַּאֲיוֹן **ga'ăyôwn**, *gah-ăh-yone'*; from 1342: *haughty:*—proud.

1350. גָּאַל **gâ'al**, *gaw-al'*; a prim. root, *to redeem* (according to the Oriental law of kinship), i.e. to *be the next of kin* (and as such to *buy back* a relative's property, *marry* his widow, etc.):—× in any wise, × at all, avenger, deliver, (do, perform the part of near, next) kinsfolk (-man), purchase, ransom, redeem (-er), revenger.

1351. גָּאַל **gâ'al**, *gaw-al'*; a prim. root, [rather ident. with 1350, through the idea of *freeing*, i.e. *repudiating*]; *to soil* or (fig.) *desecrate:*—defile, pollute, stain.

1352. גֹּאֶל **gô'el**, *go'-el*; from 1351; *profanation:*—defile.

1353. גְּאֻלָּה **geullâh**, *gheh-ool-law'*; fem. pass. part. of 1350; *redemption* (including the right and the object); by impl. *relationship:*—kindred, redeem, redemption, right.

1354. גַּב **gab**, *gab*; from an unused root mean. *to hollow* or *curve;* the *back* (as *rounded* [comp. 1460 and 1479]; by anal. the *top* or *rim*, a *boss*, a *vault*, *arch* of eye, *bulwarks*, etc.:—back, body, boss, eminent (higher) place, [eye] brows, nave, ring.

1355. גַּב **gab** (Chald.), *gab*; corresp. to 1354:—back.

1356. גֵּב **gêb**, *gabe*; from 1461; a *log* (as *cut* out); also *well* or *cistern* (as *dug*):—beam, ditch, pit.

1357. גֵּב **gêb**, *gabe*; prob. from 1461 [comp. 1462]; a *locust* (from its *cutting*):—locust.

1358. גֹּב **gôb** (Chald.), *gobe*; from a root corresp. to 1461; a *pit* (for wild animals) (as *cut* out):—den.

1359. גֹּב **Gôb**, *gobe*; or (fully)

גּוֹב **Gôwb**, *gobe'*; from 1461; *pit; Gob*, a place in Pal.:—Gob.

1360. גֶּבֶא **gebe**, *geh'-beh*; from an unused root mean. prob. *to collect;* a *reservoir;* by anal. a *marsh:*—marish, pit.

1361. גָּבַהּ **gâbahh**, *gaw-bah'*; a prim. root; to *soar*, i.e. *be lofty;* fig. *to be haughty:*—exalt, be haughty, be (make) high (-er), lift up, mount up, be proud, raise up great height, upward.

1362. גָּבָהּ **gâbâhh**, *gaw-bawh'*; from 1361; *lofty* (lit. or fig.):—high, proud.

1363. גֹּבַהּ **gôbahh**, *go'-bah*; from 1361; *elation, grandeur, arrogance:*—excellency, haughty, height, high, loftiness, pride.

1364. גָּבֹהַּ **gâbôahh**, *gaw-bo'-ah*; or (fully)

גָּבוֹהַּ **gâbôwahh**, *gaw-bo'-ah*; from 1361; *elevated* (or *elated*), *powerful, arrogant:*—haughty, height, high (-er), lofty, proud, × exceeding proudly.

1365. גַּבְהוּת **gabhûwth**, *gab-hooth'*; from 1361; *pride:*—loftiness, lofty.

1366. גְּבוּל **gebûwl**, *gheb-ool'*; or (short.)

גְּבֻל **gebûl**, *gheb-ool'*; from 1379; prop. a *cord* (as *twisted*), i.e. (by impl.) a *boundary;* by extens. the *territory* inclosed:—border, bound, coast, × great, landmark, limit, quarter, space.

1367. גְּבוּלָה **gebûwlâh**, *gheb-oo-law'*; or (short.)

גְּבֻלָה **gebûlâh**, *gheb-oo-law'*; fem. of 1366; a *boundary, region:*—border, bound, coast, landmark, place.

1368. גִּבּוֹר **gibbôwr**, *ghib-bore'*; or (short.)

גִּבֹּר **gibbôr**, *ghib-bore'*; intens. from the same as 1397; *powerful;* by impl. *warrior, tyrant:*—champion, chief, × excel, giant, man, mighty (man, one), strong (man), valiant man.

1369. גְּבוּרָה **gebûwrâh**, *gheb-oo-raw'*; fem. pass. part. from the same as 1368; *force* (lit. or fig.); by impl. *valor, victory:*—force, mastery, might, mighty (act, power), power, strength.

1370. גְּבוּרָה **gebûwrâh** (Chald.), *gheb-oo-raw'*; corresp. to 1369; *power:*—might.

1371. גִּבֵּחַ **gibbêach**, *ghib-bay'-akh*; from an unused root mean. to *be high* (in the forehead); *bald* in the forehead:—forehead bald.

1372. גַּבַּחַת **gabbachath**, *gab-bakh'-ath*; from the same as 1371; *baldness* in the forehead; by anal. a *bare spot* on the right side of cloth:—bald forehead, × without.

1373. גַּבַּי **Gabbay**, *gab-bah'ee*; from the same as 1354; *collective:*—*Gabbai*, an Isr.:—Gabbai.

1374. גֵּבִים **Gêbîym**, *gay-beem'*; plur. of 1356; *cisterns; Gebim*, a place in Pal.:—Gebim.

1375. גְּבִיעַ **gebîya'**, *gheb-ee'-ah*; from an unused root (mean. *to be convex*); a *goblet;* by anal. the *calyx* of a flower:—house, cup, pot.

1376. גְּבִיר **gebîyr**, *gheb-eer'*; from 1396; a *master:*—lord.

1377. גְּבִירָה **gebîyrâh**, *gheb-ee-raw'*; fem. of 1376; a *mistress:*—queen.

1378. גָּבִישׁ **gâbîysh**, *gaw-beesh'*; from an unused root (prob. mean. *to freeze*); *crystal* (from its resemblance to *ice*):—pearl.

1379. גָּבַל **gâbal**, *gaw-bal'*; a prim. root; prop. to *twist* as a rope; only (as a denom. from 1366) to *bound* (as by a line):—be border, set (bounds about).

1380. גְּבַל **Gebal**, *gheb-al'*; from 1379 (in the sense of a *chain* of hills); a *mountain; Gebal*, a place in Phœnicia:—Gebal.

1381. גְּבָל **Gebâl**, *gheb-awl'*; the same as 1380; *Gebal*, a region in Idumæa:—Gebal.

גְּבֻלָה **gebûlâh**. See 1367.

1382. גִּבְלִי **Giblîy**, *ghib-lee'*; patrial from 1380; a *Gebalite*, or inhab. of Gebal:—Giblites, stone-squarer.

1383. גַּבְלֻת **gablûth**, *gab-looth'*; from 1379; a twisted *chain* or *lace:*—end.

1384. גִּבֵּן **gibbên**, *gib-bane'*; from an unused root mean. to be *arched* or *contracted; hunch-backed:*—crookbackt.

1385. גְּבִינָה **gebînah**, *gheb-ee-naw'*; fem. from the same as 1384; *curdled* milk:—cheese.

1386. גַּבְנֹן **gabnôn**, *gab-nohn'*; from the same as 1384; a *hump* or *peak* of hills:—high.

1387. גֶּבַע **Geba'**, *gheh'-bah*; from the same as 1375, a *hillock; Geba*, a place in Pal.:—Gaba, Geba, Gibeah.

1388. גִּבְעָא **Gib'â'**, *ghib-aw'*; by perm. for 1389; a *hill; Giba*, a place in Pal.:—Gibeah.

1389. גִּבְעָה **gib'âh**, *ghib-aw'*; fem. from the same as 1387; a *hillock:*—hill, little hill.

1390. גִּבְעָה **Gib'âh**, *ghib-aw'*; the same as 1389; *Gibah;* the name of three places in Pal.:—Gibeah, the hill.

1391. גִּבְעוֹן **Gib'ôwn**, *ghib-ohn'*; from the same as 1387; *hilly; Gibon*, a place in Pal.:—Gibeon.

1392. גִּבְעֹל **gib'ôl**, *ghib-ole'*; prol. from 1375; the *calyx* of a flower:—bolled.

1393. גִּבְעֹנִי **Gib'ônîy**, *ghib-o-nee'*; patrial from 1391; a *Gibonite*, or inhab. of Gibon:—Gibeonite.

1394. גִּבְעַת **Gib'ath**, *ghib-ath'*; from the same as 1375; *hilliness; Gibath:*—Gibeath.

1395. גִּבְעָתִי **Gib'âthîy**, *ghib-aw-thee'*; patrial from 1390; a *Gibathite*, or inhab. of Gibath:—Gibeathite.

1396. גָּבַר **gâbar**, *gaw-bar'*; a prim. root; to *be strong;* by impl. *to prevail, act insolently:*—exceed, confirm, be great, be mighty, prevail, put to more [strength], strengthen, be stronger, be valiant.

1397. גֶּבֶר **geber**, *gheh'-ber*; from 1396; prop. a *valiant* man or *warrior;* gen. a *person* simply:—every one, man, × mighty.

1398. גֶּבֶר **Geber**, *gheh'-ber*; the same as 1397; *Geber*, the name of two Isr.:—Geber.

1399. גְּבַר **gebar**, *gheb-ar'*; from 1396; the same as 1397; a person:—man.

1400. גְּבַר **gebar** (Chald.), *gheb-ar'*; corresp. to 1399:—certain, man.

1401. גִּבָּר **gibbâr** (Chald.), *ghib-bawr'*; intens. of 1400; *valiant*, or *warrior:*—mighty.

1402. גִּבָּר **Gibbâr**, *ghib-bawr'*; intens. of 1399; *Gibbar*, an Isr.:—Gibbar.

גְּבֻרָה **gebûrâh**. See 1369.

1403. גַּבְרִיאֵל **Gabrîy'êl**, *gab-ree-ale'*; from 1397 and 410; *man of God; Gabriel*, an archangel:—Gabriel.

1404. גְּבֶרֶת **gebereth**, *gheb-eh'-reth*; fem. of 1376; *mistress:*—lady, mistress.

1405. גִּבְּתוֹן **Gibbethôwn**, *ghib-beth-one'*; intens. from 1389; a *hilly* spot; *Gibbethon*, a place in Pal.:—Gibbethon.

1406. גָּג **gâg**, *gawg*; prob. by redupl. from 1342; a *roof;* by anal. the *top* of an altar:—roof (of the house), (house) top (of the house).

1407. גַּד **gad**, *gad*; from 1413 (in the sense of *cutting*); *coriander* seed (from its furrows):—coriander.

1408. גַּד **Gad**, *gad*; a var. of 1409; *Fortune*, a Bab. deity:—that troop.

1409. גָּד **gâd**, *gawd*; from 1464 (in the sense of *distributing*); *fortune:*—troop.

1410. גָּד **Gâd**, *gawd*; from 1464; *Gad*, a son of Jacob, includ. his tribe and its territory; also a prophet:—Gad.

1411. גְּדָבָר **gedâbâr** (Chald.), *ghed-aw-bawr'*; corresp. to 1489; a *treasurer:*—treasurer.

1412. גֻּדְגֹּדָה **Gudgôdâh**, *gud-go'-daw*; by redupl. from 1413 (in the sense of *cutting*) *cleft; Gudgodah*, a place in the Desert:—Gudgodah.

1413. גָּדַד **gâdad**, *gaw-dad'*; a prim. root [comp. 1464]; to *crowd;* also to *gash* (as if by *pressing* into):—assemble (selves by troops), gather (selves together, self in troops), cut selves.

1414. גְּדַד **gedad** (Chald.), *ghed-ad'*; corresp. to 1413; to *cut down:*—hew down.

גְּדֻדָה **gedûdâh**. See 1417.

1415. גָּדָה **gâdâh**, *gaw-daw'*; from an unused root (mean. to *cut* off); a *border* of a river (as *cut* into by the stream):—bank.

גַּדָּה **Gaddâh**. See 2693.

1416. גְּדוּד **gedûwd**, *ghed-ood'*; from 1413; a *crowd* (espec. of soldiers):—army, band (of men), company, troop (of robbers).

1417. גְּדוּד **gedûwd**, *ghed-ood'*; or (fem.)

גְּדֻדָה **gedûdâh**, *ghed-oo-daw'*; from 1413; a *furrow* (as *cut*):—furrow.

1418. גְּדוּדָה **gedûwdâh**, *ghed-oo-daw'*; fem. part. pass. of 1413; an *incision:*—cutting.

1419. גָּדוֹל **gâdôwl**, *gaw-dole'*; or (short.)

גָּדֹל **gâdôl**, *gaw-dole'*; from 1431; *great* (in any sense); hence *older;* also *insolent:*—+ aloud, elder (-est), + exceeding (-ly), + far, (man of) great (man, matter, thing, -er, -ness), high, long, loud, mighty, more, much, noble, proud thing, × sore, (×) very.

1420. גְּדוּלָה **gedûwlâh**, *ghed-oo-law'*; or (short.) גְּדֻלָּה **gedullâh**, *ghed-ool-law'*; or (less accurately)

גְּדוּלָּה **gedûwllâh**, *ghed-ool-law'*; fem. of 1419; *greatness;* (concr.) *mighty acts:*—dignity, great things (-ness), majesty.

1421. גִּדּוּף **giddûwph**, *ghid-doof'*; or (short.)

גִּדֻּף **giddûph**, *ghid-doof'*; and (fem.)

גִּדּוּפָה **giddûphâh**, *ghid-doo-faw'*; or

גִּדֻּפָה **giddûphâh**, *ghid-doo-faw'*; from 1422; *vilification:*—reproach, reviling.

1422. גְּדוּפָה **gᵉdûwphâh**, *ghed-oo-faw'*; fem. pass. part. of 1442; a *revilement*:—taunt.

גְּדוֹר **Gᵉdôwr**. See 1446.

1423. גְּדִי **gᵉdîy**, *ghed-ee'*; from the same as 1415; a young *goat* (from *browsing*):—kid.

1424. גָּדִי **Gâdîy**, *gaw-dee'*; from 1409; *fortunate*; *Gadi*, an Isr.:—Gadi.

1425. גָּדִי **Gâdîy**, *gaw-dee'*; patron. from 1410; a *Gadite* (collect.) or desc. of Gad:—Gadites, children of Gad.

1426. גַּדִּי **Gaddîy**, *gad-dee'*; intens. for 1424; *Gaddi*, an Isr.:—Gaddi.

1427. גַּדִּיאֵל **Gaddîy'êl**, *gad-dee-ale'*; from 1409 and 410; *fortune of God*; *Gaddiel*, an Isr.:—Gaddiel.

1428. גִּדְיָה **gidyâh**, *ghid-yaw'*; or

גַּדְיָה **gadyâh**, *gad-yaw'*; the same as 1415; a river *brink*:—bank.

1429. גְּדִיָּה **gᵉdîyâh**, *ghed-ee-yaw'*; fem. of 1423; a young female *goat*:—kid.

1430. גָּדִישׁ **gâdîysh**, *gaw-deesh'*; from an unused root (mean. to *heap* up); a *stack* of sheaves; by anal. a *tomb*:—shock (stack) (of corn), tomb.

1431. גָּדַל **gâdal**, *gaw-dal'*; a prim. root; prop. to *twist* [comp. 1434], i.e. to *be* (caus. *make*) *large* (in various senses, as in body, mind, estate or honor, also in pride):—advance, boast, bring up, exceed, excellent, be (-come, do, give, make, wax), great (-er, come to . . . estate, + things), grow (up), increase, lift up, magnify (-ifical), be much set by, nourish (up), pass, promote, proudly [spoken], tower.

1432. גָּדֵל **gâdêl**, *gaw-dale'*; from 1431; *large* (lit. or fig.):—great, grew.

1433. גֹּדֶל **gôdel**, *go'-del*; from 1431; *magnitude* (lit. or fig.):—greatness, stout (-ness).

1434. גְּדִל **gᵉdîl**, *ghed-eel'*; from 1431 (in the sense of *twisting*); *thread*, i.e. a *tassel* or *festoon*:—fringe, wreath.

1435. גִּדֵּל **Giddêl**, *ghid-dale'*; from 1431; *stout*; *Giddel*, the name of one of the Nethinim, also of one of "Solomon's servants":—Giddel.

גָּדֹל **gâdôl**. See 1419.

גְּדֻלָּה **gᵉdullâh**. See 1420.

1436. גְּדַלְיָה **Gᵉdalyâh**, *ghed-al-yaw'*; or (prol.)

גְּדַלְיָהוּ **Gᵉdalyâhûw**, *ghed-al-yaw'-hoo*; from 1431 and 3050; *Jah has become great*; *Gedaliah*, the name of five Isr.:—Gedaliah.

1437. גִּדַּלְתִּי **Giddaltîy**, *ghid-dal'-tee*; from 1431; *I have made great*; *Giddalti*, an Isr.:—Giddalti.

1438. גָּדַע **gâdaʻ**, *gaw-dah'*; a prim. root; to *fell* a tree; gen. to *destroy* anything:—cut (asunder, in sunder, down, off), hew down.

1439. גִּדְעוֹן **Gidʻôwn**, *ghid-ohn'*; from 1438; *feller* (i.e. *warrior*); *Gidon*, an Isr.:—Gideon.

1440. גִּדְעֹם **Gidʻôm**, *ghid-ohm'*; from 1438; a *cutting* (i.e. *desolation*); *Gidom*, a place in Pal.:—Gidom.

1441. גִּדְעֹנִי **Gidʻônîy**, *ghid-o-nee'*; from 1438; *warlike* [comp. 1439]; *Gidoni*, an Isr.:—Gideoni.

1442. גָּדַף **gâdaph**, *gaw-daf'*; a prim. root; to *hack* (with words), i.e. *revile*:—blaspheme, reproach.

גִּדּוּף **giddûph**, and

גִּדּוּפָה **giddûphâh**. See 1421.

1443. גָּדַר **gâdar**, *gaw-dar'*; a prim. root; to *wall* in or around:—close up, fence up, hedge, inclose, make up [a wall], mason, repairer.

1444. גֶּדֶר **geder**, *gheh'-der*; from 1443; a *circumvallation*:—wall.

1445. גֶּדֶר **Geder**, *gheh'-der*; the same as 1444; *Geder*, a place in Pal.:—Geder.

1446. גְּדֹר **Gᵉdôr**, *ghed-ore'*; or (fully)

גְּדוֹר **Gᵉdôwr**, *ghed-ore'*; from 1443; *inclosure*; *Gedor*, a place in Pal.; also the name of three Isr.:—Gedor.

1447. גָּדֵר **gâdêr**, *gaw-dare'*; from 1443; a *circumvallation*; by impl. an *inclosure*:—fence, hedge, wall.

1448. גְּדֵרָה **gᵉdêrâh**, *ghed-ay-raw'*; fem. of 1447; *inclosure* (espec. for flocks):—[sheep-] cote (fold) hedge, wall.

1449. גְּדֵרָה **Gᵉdêrâh**, *ghed-ay-raw'*; the same as 1448; (with the art.) *Gederah*, a place in Pal.:—Gederah, hedges.

1450. גְּדֵרוֹת **Gᵉdêrôwth**, *ghed-ay-rohth'*; plur. of 1448; *walls*; *Gederoth*, a place in Pal.:—Gederoth.

1451. גְּדֵרִי **Gᵉdêrîy**, *ghed-ay-ree'*; patrial from 1445; a *Gederite*, or inhab. of Geder:—Gederite.

1452. גְּדֵרָתִי **Gᵉdêrâthîy**, *ghed-ay-raw-thee'*; patrial from 1449; a *Gederathite*, or inhab. of Gederah:—Gederathite.

1453. גְּדֵרֹתַיִם **Gᵉdêrôthayim**, *ghed-ay-ro-thah'-yim*; dual of 1448; *double wall*; *Gederothajim*, a place in Pal.:—Gederothaim.

1454. גֵּה **gêh**, *gay*; prob. a clerical error for 2088; *this*:—this.

1455. גָּהָה **gâhâh**, *gaw-haw'*; a prim. root; to *remove* (a bandage from a wound, i.e. *heal* it):—cure.

1456. גֵּהָה **gêhâh**, *gay-haw'*; from 1455; a *cure*:—medicine.

1457. גָּהַר **gâhar**, *gaw-har'*; a prim. root; to *prostrate* oneself:—cast self down, stretch self.

1458. גַּו **gav**, *gav*; another form for 1460; the *back*:—back.

1459. גַּו **gav** (Chald.), *gav*; corresp. to 1460; the *middle*:—midst, same, there- (where-) in.

1460. גֵּו **gêv** *gave*; from 1342 [corresp. to 1354]; the *back*; by anal. the *middle*:— + among, back, body.

1461. גּוּב **gûwb**, *goob*; a prim. root; to *dig*:—husbandman.

1462. גּוֹב **gôwb**, *gobe*; from 1461; the *locust* (from its *grubbing* as a larve):—grasshopper, × great.

1463. גּוֹג **Gôwg**, *gohg*; of uncert. der.; *Gog*, the name of an Isr., also of some northern nation:—Gog.

1464. גּוּד **gûwd**, *goode*; a prim. root [akin to 1413]; to *crowd* upon, i.e. *attack*:—invade, overcome.

1465. גֵּוָה **gêvâh**, *gay-vaw'*; fem. of 1460; the *back*, i.e. (by extens.) the *person*:—body.

1466. גֵּוָה **gêvah**, *gay-vaw'*; the same as 1465; *exaltation*; (fig.) *arrogance*:—lifting up, pride.

1467. גֵּוָה **gêvâh** (Chald.), *gay-vaw'*; corresp. to 1466:—pride.

1468. גּוּז **gûwz**, *gooz*; a prim. root [comp. 1494]; prop. to *shear* off; but used only in the (fig.) sense of *passing* rapidly:—bring, cut off.

1469. גּוֹזָל **gôwzâl**, *go-zawl'*; or (short.)

גֹּזָל **gôzâl**, *go-zawl'*; from 1497; a *nestling* (as being comparatively *nude* of feathers):—young (pigeon).

1470. גּוֹזָן **Gôwzân**, *go-zawn'*; prob. from 1468; a *quarry* (as a place of *cutting* stones); *Gozan*, a province of Assyria:—Gozan.

1471. גּוֹי **gôwy**, *go'ee*; rarely (short.)

גֹּי **gôy**, *go'-ee*; appar. from the same root as 1465 (in the sense of *massing*); a foreign *nation*; hence a *Gentile*; also (fig.) a *troop* of animals, or a *flight* of locusts:—Gentile, heathen, nation, people.

1472. גְּוִיָּה **gᵉvîyâh**, *ghev-ee-yaw'*; prol. for 1465; a *body*, whether alive or dead:—(dead) body, carcase, corpse.

1473. גּוֹלָה **gôwlâh**, *go-law'*; or (short.)

גֹּלָה **gôlah**, *go-law'*; act. part. fem. of 1540; *exile*; concr. and coll. *exiles*:—(carried away), captive (-ity), removing.

1474. גּוֹלָן **Gôwlân**, *go-lawn'*; from 1473; *captive*; *Golan*, a place east of the Jordan:—Golan.

1475. גּוּמָּץ **gûwmmâts**, *goom-mawts'*; of uncert. der.; a *pit*:—pit.

1476. גּוּנִי **Gûwnîy**, *goo-nee'*; prob. from 1598; *protected*; *Guni*, the name of two Isr.:—Guni.

1477. גּוּנִי **Gûwnîy**, *goo-nee'*; patron. from 1476; a *Gunite* (collect. with art. pref.) or desc. of Guni:—Gunites.

1478. גָּוַע **gâvaʻ**, *gaw-vah'*; a prim. root; to *breathe* out, i.e. (by impl.) *expire*:—die, be dead, give up the ghost, perish.

1479. גּוּף **gûwph**, *goof*; a prim. root; prop. to *hollow* or *arch*, i.e. (fig.) *close*; to *shut*:—shut.

1480. גּוּפָה **gûwphâh**, *goo-faw'*; from 1479; a *corpse* (as *closed* to sense):—body.

1481. גּוּר **gûwr**, *goor*; a prim. root; prop. to *turn* aside from the road (for a lodging or any other purpose), i.e. *sojourn* (as a guest); also to *shrink*, *fear* (as in a *strange* place); also to *gather* for hostility (as *afraid*):—abide, assemble, be afraid, dwell, fear, gather (together), inhabitant, remain, sojourn, stand in awe, (be) stranger, × surely.

1482. גּוּר **gûwr**, *goor*; or (short.)

גֻּר **gûr**, *goor*; perh. from 1481; a *cub* (as still *abiding* in the lair), espec. of the lion:—whelp, young one.

1483. גּוּר **Gûwr**, *goor*; the same as 1482; *Gur*, a place in Pal.:—Gur.

1484. גּוֹר **gôwr**, *gore*; or (fem.)

גֹּרָה **gôrah**, *go-raw'*; a var. of 1482:—whelp.

1485. גּוּר־בַּעַל **Gûwr-Baʻal**, *goor-bah'-al*; from 1481 and 1168; *dwelling of Baal*; *Gur-Baal*, a place in Arabia:—Gur-baal.

1486. גּוֹרָל **gôwrâl**, *go-rawl'*; or (short.)

גֹּרָל **gôral**, *go-ral'*; from an unused root mean. to *be rough* (as stone); prop. a *pebble*, i.e. a *lot* (small stones being used for that purpose); fig. a *portion* or *destiny* (as if determined by lot):—lot.

1487. גּוּשׁ **gûwsh**, *goosh*; or rather (by perm.)

גִּישׁ **gîysh**, *gheesh*; of uncert. der.; a *mass* of earth:—clod.

1488. גֵּז **gêz**, *gaze*; from 1494; a *fleece* (as *shorn*); also mown *grass*:—fleece, mowing, mown grass.

1489. גִּזְבָּר **gizbâr**, *ghiz-bawr'*; of for. der.; *treasurer*:—treasurer.

1490. גִּזְבָּר **gizbâr** (Chald.), *ghiz-bawr'*; corresp. to 1489:—treasurer.

1491. גָּזָה **gâzâh**, *gaw-zaw'*; a prim. root [akin to 1468]; to *cut* off, i.e. *portion* out:—take.

1492. גַּזָּה **gazzâh**, *gaz-zaw'*; fem. from 1494; a *fleece*:—fleece.

1493. גִּזוֹנִי **Gizôwnîy**, *ghee-zo-nee'*; patrial from the unused name of a place appar. in Pal.; a *Gizonite* or inhab. of Gizoh:—Gizonite.

1494. גָּזַז **gâzaz**, *gaw-zaz'*; a prim. root [akin to 1468]; to *cut* off; spec. to *shear* a flock, or *shave* the hair; fig. to *destroy* an enemy:—cut off (down), poll, shave, ([sheep-]) shear (-er).

1495. גָּזֵז **Gâzêz** *gaw-zaze'*; from 1494; *shearer*; *Gazez*, the name of two Isr.:—Gazez.

1496. גָּזִית **gâzîyth**, *gaw-zeeth'*; from 1491; something *cut*, i.e. *dressed* stone:—hewed, hewn stone, wrought.

1497. גָּזַל **gâzal**, *gaw-zal'*; a prim. root; to *pluck* off; spec. to *flay*, *strip* or *rob*:—catch, consume, exercise [robbery], pluck (off), rob, spoil, take away (by force, violence), tear.

1498. גָּזֵל **gâzêl**, *gaw-zale'*; from 1497; *robbery*, or (concr.) *plunder*:—robbery, thing taken away by violence.

1499. גֵּזֶל **gêzel**, *ghe'-zel*; from 1497; *plunder*, i.e. *violence*:—violence, violent perverting.

גֹּזָל **gôzâl**. See 1469.

1500. גְּזֵלָה **g^{e}zêlâh**, *ghez-ay-law';* fem. of 1498 and mean. the same:—that (he had robbed) [which he took violently away], spoil, violence.

1501. גָּזָם **gâzâm**, *gaw-zawm';* from an unused root mean. to *devour;* a kind of *locust:*—palmer-worm.

1502. גַּזָּם **Gazzâm**, *gaz-zawm';* from the same as 1501; *devourer:*—Gazzam, one of the Nethinim:—Gazzam.

1503. גֶּזַע **gezaʿ**, *geh'-zah;* from an unused root mean. to *cut* down (trees); the *trunk* or *stump* of a tree (as felled or as planted):—stem, stock.

1504. גָּזַר **gâzar**, *gaw-zar';* a prim. root; to *cut* down or off; (fig.) to *destroy, divide, exclude* or *decide:*—cut down (off), decree, divide, snatch.

1505. גְּזַר **g^{e}zar** (Chald.), *ghez-ar';* corresp. to 1504; to *quarry; determine:*—cut out, soothsayer.

1506. גֶּזֶר **gezer**, *gheh'-zer;* from 1504; something *cut off;* a *portion:*—part, piece.

1507. גֶּזֶר **Gezer**, *gheh'-zer;* the same as 1506; *Gezer,* a place in Pal.:—Gazer, Gezer.

1508. גִּזְרָה **gizrâh**, *ghiz-raw';* fem. of 1506; the *figure* or person (as if *cut* out); also an *inclosure* (as *separated*):—polishing, separate place.

1509. גְּזֵרָה **g^{e}zêrâh**, *ghez-ay-raw';* from 1504; a *desert* (as *separated*):—not inhabited.

1510. גְּזֵרָה **g^{e}zêrâh** (Chald.), *ghez-ay-raw';* from 1505 (as 1504); a *decree:*—decree.

1511. גִּזְרִי **Gizrîy** (in the marg.), *ghiz-ree';* patrial from 1507; a *Gezerite* (collect.) or inhab. of Gezer; but better (as in the text) by transp.

גִּרְזִי **Girzîy**, *gher-zee';* patrial of 1630; a *Girzite* (collect.) or member of a native tribe in Pal.:—Gezrites.

גִּחוֹן **Gîchôwn**. See 1521.

1512. גָּחוֹן **gâchôwn**, *gaw-khone';* prob. from 1518; the external *abdomen, belly* (as the *source* of the fœtus [comp. 1521]):—belly.

גֵּחֲזִי **Gêchăzîy**. See 1522.

גָּחֹל **gâchol**. See 1513.

1513. גֶּחֶל **gechel**, *geh'-khel;* or (fem.)

גַּחֶלֶת **gacheleth**, *gah-kheh'-leth;* from an unused root mean. to *glow* or *kindle;* an *ember:*—(burning) coal.

1514. גַּחַם **Gacham**, *gah'-kham;* from an unused root mean. to *burn; flame; Gacham,* a son of Nahor:—Gaham.

1515. גַּחַר **Gachar**, *gah'-khar;* from an unused root mean. to *hide; lurker; Gachar,* one of the Nethinim:—Gahar.

גֹּי **gôy**. See 1471.

1516. גַּיְא **gay'**, *gah'ee;* or (short.)

גַּי **gay**, *gah'ee;* prob. (by transm.) from the same root as 1466 (abbrev.); a *gorge* (from its *lofty* sides; hence narrow, but not a gully or winter-torrent):—valley.

1517. גִּיד **gîyd**, *gheed;* prob. from 1464; a *thong* (as *compressing*); by anal. a *tendon:*—sinew.

1518. גִּיחַ **gîyach**, *ghee'-akh;* or (short.)

גֹּחַ **gôach**, *go'-akh;* a prim. root; to *gush* forth (as water), gen. to *issue:*—break forth, labor to bring forth, come forth, draw up, take out.

1519. גִּיחַ **gîyach** (Chald.), *ghee'-akh;* or (short.)

גּוּחַ **gûwach** (Chald.), *goo'-akh;* corresp. to 1518; to *rush* forth:—strive.

1520. גִּיחַ **Gîyach**, *ghee'-akh;* from 1518; a *fountain; Giach,* a place in Pal.:—Giah.

1521. גִּיחוֹן **Gîychôwn**, *ghee-khone';* or (short.)

גִּחֹן **Gîchôwn**, *ghee-khone';* from 1518; *stream; Gichon,* a river of Paradise; also a valley (or pool) near Jerusalem:—Gihon.

1522. גֵּיחֲזִי **Gêychăzîy**, *gay-khah-zee';* or

גֵּחֲזִי **Gêchăzîy**, *gay-khah-zee';* appar. from 1516 and 2372; *valley of a visionary; Gechazi,* the servant of Elisha:—Gehazi.

1523. גִּיל **gîyl**, *gheel;* or (by perm.)

גּוּל **gûwl**, *gool;* a prim. root; prop. to *spin* round (under the influence of any violent emotion), i.e. usually *rejoice,* or (as *cringing*) *fear:*—be glad, joy, be joyful, rejoice.

1524. גִּיל **gîyl**, *gheel;* from 1523; a *revolution* (of time, i.e. an *age*); also *joy:*—× exceedingly, gladness, × greatly, joy, rejoice (-ing), sort.

1525. גִּילָה **gîylâh**, *ghee-law';* or

גִּילַת **gîylath**, *ghee-lath';* fem. of 1524; *joy:*—joy, rejoicing.

גִּילֹה **Gîylôh**. See 1542.

1526. גִּילֹנִי **Gîylônîy**, *ghee-lo-nee';* patrial from 1542; a *Gilonite* or inhab. of Giloh:—Gilonite.

1527. גִּינַת **Gîynath**, *ghee-nath';* of uncert. der.; *Ginath,* an Isr.:—Ginath.

1528. גִּיר **gîyr** (Chald.), *gheer;* corresp. to 1615; *lime:*—plaster.

גֵּיר **gêyr**. See 1616.

1529. גֵּישָׁן **Gêyshân**, *gay-shawn';* from the same as 1487; *lumpish; Geshan,* an Isr.:—Geshan.

1530. גַּל **gal**, *gal;* from 1556; something *rolled,* i.e. a *heap* of stone or dung (plur. *ruins*); by anal. a *spring* of water (plur. *waves*):—billow, heap, spring, wave.

1531. גֹּל **gôl**, *gole;* from 1556; a *cup* for oil (as *round*):—bowl.

גְּלָא **g^{e}lâ'**. See 1541.

1532. גַּלָּב **gallâb**, *gal-lawb';* from an unused root mean. to *shave;* a *barber:*—barber.

1533. גִּלְבֹּעַ **Gilbôaʿ**, *ghil-bo'-ah;* from 1530 and 1158; *fountain of ebullition; Gilboa,* a mountain of Pal.:—Gilboa.

1534. גַּלְגַּל **galgal**, *gal-gal';* by redupl. from 1556; a *wheel;* by anal. a *whirlwind;* also *dust* (as *whirled*):—heaven, rolling thing, wheel.

1535. גַּלְגַּל **galgal** (Chald.), *gal-gal';* corresp. to 1534; a *wheel:*—wheel.

1536. גִּלְגָּל **gilgâl**, *ghil-gawl';* a var. of 1534:—wheel.

1537. גִּלְגָּל **Gilgâl**, *ghil-gawl';* the same as 1536 (with the art. as a prop. noun); *Gilgal.* the name of three places in Pal.:—Gilgal. See also 1019.

1538. גֻּלְגֹּלֶת **gulgôleth**, *gul-go'-leth;* by redupl. from 1556; a *skull* (as *round*); by impl. a *head* (in enumeration of persons):—head, every man, poll, skull.

1539. גֶּלֶד **geled**, *ghe'-led;* from an unused root prob. mean. to *polish;* the (human) *skin* (as *smooth*):—*skin.*

1540. גָּלָה **gâlâh**, *gaw-law';* a prim. root; to *denude* (espec. in a disgraceful sense); by impl. to *exile* (captives being usually *stripped*); fig. to *reveal:*— + advertise, appear, bewray, bring, (carry, lead, go) captive (into captivity), depart, disclose, discover, exile, be gone, open, × plainly, publish, remove, reveal, × shamelessly, shew, × surely, tell, uncover.

1541. גְּלָה **g^{e}lâh** (Chald.), *ghel-aw';* or

גְּלָא **g^{e}lâ'** (Chald.), *ghel-aw';* corresp. to 1540:—bring over, carry away, reveal.

גֹּלָה **gôlâh**. See 1473.

1542. גִּלֹה **Gîlôh**, *ghee-lo';* or (fully)

גִּילֹה **Gîylôh**, *ghee-lo';* from 1540; *open; Giloh,* a place in Pal.:—Giloh.

1543. גֻּלָּה **gullâh**, *gool-law';* fem. from 1556; a *fountain, bowl* or *globe* (all as *round*):—bowl, pommel, spring.

1544. גִּלּוּל **gillûwl**, *ghil-lool';* or (short.)

גִּלֻּל **gillûl**, *ghil-lool';* from 1556; prop. a *log* (as *round*); by impl. an *idol:*—idol.

1545. גְּלוֹם **g^{e}lôwm**, *ghel-ome';* from 1563; *clothing* (as *wrapped*):—clothes.

1546. גָּלוּת **gâlûwth**, *gaw-looth';* fem. from 1540; *captivity;* concr. *exiles* (collect.):—(they that are carried away) captives (-ity.)

1547. גָּלוּת **gâlûwth** (Chald.), *gaw-looth';* corresp. to 1546:—captivity.

1548. גָּלַח **gâlach**, *gaw-lakh';* a prim. root; prop. to *be bald,* i.e. (caus.) to *shave;* fig. to *lay waste:*—poll, shave (off).

1549. גִּלָּיוֹן **gillâyôwn**, *ghil-law-yone';* or

גִּלְיוֹן **gilyôwn**, *ghil-yone';* from 1540; a *tablet* for writing (as *bare*); by anal. a *mirror* (as a *plate*):—glass, roll.

1550. גָּלִיל **gâlîyl**, *gaw-leel';* from 1556; a *valve* of a folding door (as *turning*); also a *ring* (as *round*):—folding, ring.

1551. גָּלִיל **Gâlîyl**, *gaw-leel';* or (prol.)

גָּלִילָה **Gâlîylâh**, *gaw-lee-law';* the same as 1550; a *circle* (with the art.); *Galil* (as a special *circuit*) in the North of Pal.:—Galilee.

1552. גְּלִילָה **g^{e}lîylâh**, *ghel-ee-law';* fem. of 1550; a *circuit* or *region:*—border, coast, country.

1553. גְּלִילוֹת **G^{e}lîylôwth**, *ghel-ee-lowth';* plur. of 1552; *circles; Geliloth,* a place in Pal.:—Geliloth.

1554. גַּלִּים **Gallîym**, *gal-leem';* plur. of 1530; *springs; Gallim,* a place in Pal.:—Gallim.

1555. גָּלְיַת **Golyath**, *gol-yath';* perh. from 1540; *exile; Goljath,* a Philistine:—Goliath.

1556. גָּלַל **gâlal**, *gaw-lal';* a prim. root; to *roll* (lit. or fig.):—commit, remove, roll (away, down, together), run down, seek occasion, trust, wallow.

1557. גָּלָל **gâlâl**, *gaw-lawl';* from 1556; *dung* (as in *balls*):—dung.

1558. גָּלָל **gâlâl**, *gaw-lawl';* from 1556; a *circumstance* (as *rolled* around); only used adv., on *account* of:—because of, for (sake).

1559. גָּלָל **Gâlâl**, *gaw-lawl';* from 1556, in the sense of 1560; *great; Galal,* the name of two Isr.:—Galal.

1560. גְּלָל **g^{e}lâl** (Chald.), *ghel-awl';* from a root corresp. to 1556; *weight* or *size* (as if *rolled*):—great.

1561. גֵּלֶל **gêlel**, *gay'-lel;* a var. of 1557; *dung* (plur. *balls* of dung):—dung.

1562. גִּלֲלַי **Gîlălay**, *ghe-lal-ah'ee;* from 1561; *dungy; Gilalai,* an Isr.:—Gilalai.

1563. גָּלַם **gâlam**, *gaw-lam';* a prim. root; to *fold:*—wrap together.

1564. גֹּלֶם **gôlem**, *go'-lem;* from 1563; a *wrapped* (and unformed *mass,* i.e. as the *embryo*):—substance yet being unperfect.

1565. גַּלְמוּד **galmûwd**, *gal-mood';* prob. by prol. from 1563; *sterile* (as *wrapped* up too hard); fig. *desolate:*—desolate, solitary.

1566. גָּלַע **gâlaʿ**, *gaw-lah';* a prim. root; to *be obstinate:*—(inter-) meddle (with).

1567. גַּלְעֵד **Galʿêd**, *gal-ade';* from 1530 and 5707; *heap of testimony; Galed,* a memorial cairn E. of the Jordan:—Galeed.

1568. גִּלְעָד **Gilʿâd**, *ghil-awd';* prob. from 1567; *Gilad,* a region E. of the Jordan; also the name of three Isr.:—Gilead, Gileadite.

1569. גִּלְעָדִי **Gilʿâdîy**, *ghil-aw-dee';* patron. from 1568; a *Giladite* or desc. of Gilad:—Gileadite.

1570. גָּלַשׁ **gâlash**, *gaw-lash';* a prim. root; prob. to *caper* (as a goat):—appear.

1571. גַּם **gam**, *gam;* by contr. from an unused root mean. to *gather;* prop. *assemblage;* used only adv. *also, even, yea, though;* often repeated as correl. *both . . . and:*—again, alike, also, (so much) as (soon), both (so) . . . and, but, either . . . or, even, for all, (in) likewise (manner), moreover, nay . . . neither, one, then (-refore), though, what, with, yea.

1572. גָּמָא **gâmâ'**, *gaw-maw';* a prim. root (lit. or fig.) to *absorb:*—swallow, drink.

1573. גֹּמֶא **gôme'**, *go'-meh;* from 1572; prop. an *absorbent,* i.e. the *bulrush* (from its *porosity*); spec. the *papyrus:*—(bul-) rush.

1574. גֹּמֶד **gômed**, *go'-med;* from an unused root appar. mean. to *grasp;* prop. a *span:*—cubit.

1575. גַּמָּד **gammâd**, *gam-mawd'*; from the same as 1574; a *warrior* (as *grasping* weapons):—Gammadims.

1576. גְּמוּל **g^emûwl**, *ghem-ool'*; from 1580; *treatment*, i.e. an *act* (of good or ill); by impl. *service* or *requital*:— + as hast served, benefit, desert, deserving, that which he hath given, recompence, reward.

1577. גָּמוּל **gâmûwl**, *gaw-mool'*; pass. part. of 1580; *rewarded*; *Gamul*, an Isr.:—Gamul. See also 1014.

1578. גְּמוּלָה **g^emûwlâh**, *ghem-oo-law'*; fem. of 1576; mean. the same:—deed, recompence, such a reward.

1579. גִּמְזוֹ **Gimzôw**, *ghim-zo'*; of uncert. der.; *Gimzo*, a place in Pal.:—Gimzo.

1580. גָּמַל **gâmal**, *gaw-mal'*; a prim. root; to *treat* a person (well or ill), i.e. *benefit* or *requite*; by impl. (of *toil*) to *ripen*, i.e. (spec.) to *wean*:—bestow on, deal bountifully, do (good), recompense, requite, reward, ripen, + serve, wean, yield.

1581. גָּמָל **gâmâl**, *gaw-mawl'*; appar. from 1580 (in the sense of *labor* or *burden-bearing*): a *camel*:—camel.

1582. גְּמַלִּי **G^emallîy**, *ghem-al-lee'*; prob. from 1581; *camel-driver*; *Gemalli*, an Isr.:—Gemalli.

1583. גַּמְלִיאֵל **Gamlîy'êl**, *gam-lee-ale'*; from 1580 and 410; *reward of God*; *Gamliel*, an Isr.:—Gamaliel.

1584. גָּמַר **gâmar**, *gaw-mar'*; a prim. root; to *end* (in the sense of *completion* or *failure*):—cease, come to an end, fail, perfect, perform.

1585. גְּמַר **g^emar** (Chald.), *ghem-ar'*; corresp. to 1584:—perfect.

1586. גֹּמֶר **Gômer**, *go'-mer*; from 1584; *completion*; *Gomer*, the name of a son of Japheth and of his desc.; also of a Hebrewess:—Gomer.

1587. גְּמַרְיָה **G^emaryâh**, *ghem-ar-yaw'*; or

גְּמַרְיָהוּ **G^emaryâhûw**, *ghem-ar-yaw'-hoo*; from 1584 and 3050; *Jah has perfected*; *Gemarjah*, the name of two Isr.:—Gemariah.

1588. גַּן **gan**, *gan*; from 1598; a *garden* (as *fenced*):—garden.

1589. גָּנַב **gânab**, *gaw-nab'*; a prim. root; to *thieve* (lit. or fig.); by impl. to *deceive*:—carry away, × indeed, secretly bring, steal (away), get by stealth.

1590. גַּנָּב **gannâb**, *gaw-nab'*; from 1589; a *stealer*:—thief.

1591. גְּנֵבָה **g^enêbâh**, *ghen-ay-baw'*; from 1589; *stealing*, i.e. (concr.) something *stolen*:—theft.

1592. גְּנֻבַת **G^enûbath**, *ghen-oo-bath'*; from 1589; *theft*; *Genubath*, an Edomitish prince:—Genubath.

1593. גַּנָּה **gannâh**, *gan-naw'*; fem. of 1588; a *garden*:—garden.

1594. גִּנָּה **ginnâh**, *ghin-naw'*; another form for 1593:—garden.

1595. גֶּנֶז **genez**, *gheh'-nez*; from an unused root mean. to *store*; *treasure*; by impl. a *coffer*:—chest, treasury.

1596. גְּנַז **g^enaz** (Chald.), *ghen-az'*; corresp. to 1595; *treasure*:—treasure.

1597. גִּנְזַךְ **ginzak**, *ghin-zak'*; prol. from 1595; a *treasury*:—treasury.

1598. גָּנַן **gânan**, *gaw-nan'*; a prim. root; to *hedge* about, i.e. (gen.) *protect*:—defend.

1599. גִּנְּתוֹן **Ginn^ethôwn**, *ghin-neth-ōne*; or

גִּנְּתוֹ **Ginn^ethôw**, *ghin-neth-o'*; from 1598; *gardener*; *Ginnethon* or *Ginnetho*, an Isr.:—Ginnetho, Ginnethon.

1600. גָּעָה **gâ'âh**, *gaw-aw'*; a prim. root; to *bellow* (as cattle):—low.

1601. גֹּעָה **Gô'âh**, *go-aw'*; fem. act. part. of 1600; *lowing*; *Goah*, a place near Jerus.:—Goath.

1602. גָּעַל **gâ'al**, *gaw-al'*; a prim. root; to *detest*; by impl. to *reject*:—abhor, fail, lothe, vilely cast away.

1603. גַּעַל **Ga'al**, *gah'-al*; from 1602; *loathing*; *Gaal*, an Isr.:—Gaal.

1604. גֹּעַל **gô'al**, *go'-al*; from 1602; *abhorrence*:—loathing.

1605. גָּעַר **gâ'ar**, *gaw-ar'*; a prim. root; to *chide*:—corrupt, rebuke, reprove.

1606. גְּעָרָה **g^e'ârâh**, *gheh-aw-raw'*; from 1605; a *chiding*:—rebuke (-ing), reproof.

1607. גָּעַשׁ **gâ'ash**, *gaw-ash'*; a prim. root to *agitate* violently:—move, shake, toss, trouble.

1608. גַּעַשׁ **Ga'ash**, *ga'-ash*; from 1607; a *quaking*; *Gaash*, a hill in Pal.:—Gaash.

1609. גַּעְתָּם **Ga'tâm**, *gah-tawm'*; of uncert. der.; *Gatam*, an Edomite:—Gatam.

1610. גַּף **gaph**, *gaf*; from an unused root mean. to *arch*; the *back*; by extens. the *body* or self:— + highest places, himself.

1611. גַּף **gaph** (Chald.), *gaf*; corresp. to 1610:—a *wing*:—wing.

1612. גֶּפֶן **gephen**, *gheh'-fen*; from an unused root mean. to *bend*; a *vine* (as *twining*), esp. the grape:—vine, tree.

1613. גֹּפֶר **gôpher**, *go'-fer*; from an unused root, prob. mean. to *house in*; a kind of tree or wood (as used for *building*), appar. the *cypress*:—gopher.

1614. גָּפְרִית **gophrîyth**, *gof-reeth'*; prob. fem. of 1613; prop. cypress-*resin*; by anal. *sulphur* (as equally inflammable):—brimstone.

1615. גִּיר **gîr**, *gheer*; perh. from 3564; *lime* (from being *burned* in a kiln:—chalk [-stone].

1616. גֵּר **gêr**, *gare*; or (fully)

גֵּיר **gêyr**, *gare*; from 1481; prop. a *guest*; by impl. a *foreigner*:—alien, sojourner, stranger.

גּוּר **gûr**. See 1482.

1617. גֵּרָא **Gêrâ'**, *gay-raw'*; perh. from 1626; a *grain*; *Gera*, the name of six Isr.:—Gera.

1618. גָּרָב **gârâb**, *gaw-rawb'*; from an unused root mean. to *scratch*; *scurf* (from *itching*):—scab, scurvy.

1619. גָּרֵב **Gârêb**, *gaw-rabe'*; from the same as 1618; *scabby*; *Gareb*, the name of an Isr., also of a hill near Jerus.:—Gareb.

1620. גַּרְגַּר **gargar**, *gar-gar'*; by redupl. from 1641; a *berry* (as if a pellet of *rumination*):—berry.

1621. גַּרְגְּרוֹת **garg^erôwth**, *gar-gher-owth'*; fem. plur. from 1641; the *throat* (as used in *rumination*):—neck.

1622. גִּרְגָּשִׁי **Girgâshîy**, *ghir-gaw-shee'*; patrial from an unused name [of uncert. der.]; a *Girgashite*, one of the native tribes of Canaan:—Girgashite, Girgasite.

1623. גָּרַד **gârad**, *gaw-rad'*; a prim. root; to *abrade*:—scrape.

1624. גָּרָה **gârâh**, *gaw-raw'*; a prim. root; prop. to *grate*, i.e. (fig.) to *anger*:—contend, meddle, stir up, strive.

1625. גֵּרָה **gêrâh**, *gay-raw'*; from 1641; the *cud* (as *scraping* the throat):—cud.

1626. גֵּרָה **gêrâh**, *gay-raw'*; from 1641 (as in 1625); prop. (like 1620) a *kernel* (round as if *scraped*), i.e. a *gerah* or small weight (and coin):—gerah.

גֹּרָה **gôrâh**. See 1484.

1627. גָּרוֹן **gârôwn**, *gaw-rone'*; or (short.)

גָּרֹן **gârôn**, *gaw-rone'*; from 1641; the *throat* [comp. 1621] (as *roughened* by swallowing):— × aloud, mouth, neck, throat.

1628. גֵּרוּת **gêrûwth**, *gay-rooth'*; from 1481; a (temporary) *residence*:—habitation.

1629. גָּרַז **gâraz**, *gaw-raz'*; a prim. root; to *cut* off:—cut off.

1630. גְּרִזִים **G^erîziym**, *gher-ee-zeem'*; plur. of an unused noun from 1629 [comp. 1511], cut up (i.e. *rocky*); *Gerizim*, a mountain of Pal.:—Gerizim.

1631. גַּרְזֶן **garzen**, *gar-zen'*; from 1629; an *axe*:—ax.

1632. גָּרֹל **gârôl**, *gaw-role'*; from the same as 1486; *harsh*:—man of great [*as in the marg. which reads* 1419].

גֹּרָל **gôrâl**. See 1486.

1633. גָּרַם **gâram**, *gaw-ram'*; a prim. root; to *be spare* or *skeleton-like*; used only as a denom. from 1634; (caus.) to *bone*, i.e. *denude* (by extens. *craunch*) the bones:—gnaw the bones, break.

1634. גֶּרֶם **gerem**, *gheh'-rem*; from 1633; a *bone* (as the *skeleton* of the body); hence *self*, i.e. (fig.) *very*:—bone, strong, top.

1635. גְּרַם **gerem** (Chald.), *gheh'-rem*; corresp. to 1634; a *bone*:—bone.

1636. גַּרְמִי **Garmîy**, *gar-mee'*; from 1634; *bony*, i.e. *strong*:—Garmite.

1637. גֹּרֶן **gôren**, *go'-ren*; from an unused root mean. to *smooth*; a threshing-*floor* (as made *even*); by anal. any open *area*:—(barn, corn, threshing-) floor, (threshing-, void) place.

גֹּרֶן **gârôn**. See 1627.

1638. גָּרַס **gâraç**, *gaw-ras'*; a prim. root; to *crush*; also (intrans. and fig.) to *dissolve*:—break.

1639. גָּרַע **gâra'**, *gaw-rah'*; a prim. root; to *scrape* off; by impl. to *shave*, *remove*, *lessen* or *withhold*:—abate, clip, (di-) minish, do (take) away, keep back, restrain, make small, withdraw.

1640. גָּרַף **gâraph**, *gaw-raf'*; a prim. root; to *bear* off violently:—sweep away.

1641. גָּרַר **gârar**, *gaw-rar'*; a prim. root; to *drag* off roughly; by impl. to *bring up* the cud (i.e. *ruminate*); by anal. to *saw*:—catch, chew, × continuing, destroy, saw.

1642. גְּרָר **G^erâr**, *gher-awr'*; prob. from 1641; a *rolling* country; *Gerar*, a Philistine city:—Gerar.

1643. גֶּרֶשׂ **geres**, *gheh'-res*; from an unused root mean. to *husk*; a *kernel* (collect.), i.e. *grain*:—beaten corn.

1644. גָּרַשׁ **gârash**, *gaw-rash'*; a prim. root; to *drive* out from a possession; espec. to *expatriate* or *divorce*:—cast up (out), divorced (woman), drive away (forth, out), expel, × surely put away, trouble, thrust out.

1645. גֶּרֶשׁ **geresh**, *gheh'-resh*; from 1644; *produce* (as if *expelled*):—put forth.

1646. גְּרֻשָׁה **g^erushah**, *gher-oo-shaw'*; fem. pass. part. of 1644; (abstr.) *dispossession*:—exaction.

1647. גֵּרְשֹׁם **Gêr^eshôm**, *gay-resh-ome'*; for 1648; *Gereshom*, the name of four Isr.:—Gershom.

1648. גֵּרְשׁוֹן **Gêr^eshown**, *gay-resh-one'*; or

גֵּרְשׁוֹם **Gêr^eshôwm**, *gay-resh-ome'*; from 1644; a *refugee*; *Gereshon* or *Gereshom*, an Isr.:—Gershon, Gershom.

1649. גֵּרְשֻׁנִּי **Gêr^eshunnîy**, *gay-resh-oon-nee'*; patron. from 1648; a *Gereshonite* or desc. of Gereshon:—Gershonite, sons of Gershon.

1650. גְּשׁוּר **G^eshûwr**, *ghesh-oor'*; from an unused root (mean. to *join*); *bridge*; *Geshur*, a district of Syria:—Geshur, Geshurite.

1651. גְּשׁוּרִי **G^eshûwrîy**, *ghe-shoo-ree'*; patrial from 1650; a *Geshurite* (also collect.) or inhab. of Geshur:—Geshuri, Geshurites.

1652. גָּשַׁם **gâsham**, *gaw-sham'*; a prim. root; to *shower* violently:—(cause to) rain.

1653. גֶּשֶׁם **geshem**, *gheh'-shem*; from 1652; a *shower*:—rain, shower.

1654. גֶּשֶׁם **Geshem**, *gheh'-shem*; or (prol.)

גַּשְׁמוּ **Gashmûw**, *gash-moo'*; the same as 1653; *Geshem* or *Gashmu*, an Arabian:—Geshem, Gashmu.

1655. גֶּשֶׁם **geshem** (Chald.), *gheh'-shem*; appar. the same as 1653; used in a peculiar sense, the *body* (prob. for the [fig.] idea of a *hard rain*):—body.

1656. גֹּשֶׁם **gôshem**, *go'-shem;* from 1652; equiv. to 1653:—rained upon.

גַּשְׁמוּ **Gashmûw**. See 1654.

1657. גֹּשֶׁן **Gôshen**, *go'-shen;* prob. of Eg. or.; *Goshen*, the residence of the Isr. in Egypt; also a place in Pal.:—Goshen.

1658. גִּשְׁפָּא **Gishpâ'**, *ghish-paw';* of uncert. der.; *Gishpa*, an Isr.:—Gispa.

1659. גָּשַׁשׁ **gâshash**, *gaw-shash';* a prim. root; appar. to *feel* about:—grope.

1660. גַּת **gath**, *gath;* prob. from 5059 (in the sense of *treading* out grapes); a wine-*press* (or vat for holding the grapes in pressing them):—(wine-) press (fat).

1661. גַּת **Gath**, *gath;* the same as 1660; *Gath*, a Philistine city:—Gath.

1662. גַּת־הַחֵפֶר **Gath-ha-Chêpher**, *gath-hah-khay'-fer;* or (abridged)

גִּתָּה־חֵפֶר **Gittâh-Chêpher**, *ghit-taw-khay'-fer;* from 1660 and 2658 with the art. ins.; *wine-press of* (the) *well; Gath-Chepher*, a place in Pal.:—Gath-kephr, Gittah-kephr.

1663. גִּתִּי **Gittîy**, *ghit-tee';* patrial from 1661; a *Gittite* or inhab. of Gath:—Gittite.

1664. גִּתַּיִם **Gittayim**, *ghit-tah'-yim;* dual of 1660; *double wine-press; Gittajim*, a place in Pal.:—Gittaim.

1665. גִּתִּית **Gittîyth**, *ghit-teeth';* fem. of 1663; a *Gittite* harp:—Gittith.

1666. גֶּתֶר **Gether**, *gheh'-ther;* of uncert. der.; *Gether*, a son of Aram, and the region settled by him:—Gether.

1667. גַּת־רִמּוֹן **Gath-Rimmôwn**, *gath-rim-mone';* from 1660 and 7416; *wine-press of* (the) *pomegranate; Gath-Rimmon*, a place in Pal.:—Gath-rimmon.

ד

1668. דָּא **dâ'** (Chald.), *daw;* corresp. to 2088; *this:*—one . . . another, this.

1669. דָּאַב **dâ'ab**, *daw-ab';* a prim. root; to *pine:*—mourn, sorrow (-ful).

1670. דְּאָבָה **deʼâbâh**, *dĕh-aw-baw';* from 1669; prop. *pining;* by anal. *fear:*—sorrow.

1671. דְּאָבוֹן **deʼâbôwn**, *dĕh-aw-bone';* from 1669; *pining:*—sorrow.

1672. דָּאַג **dâ'ag**, *daw-ag';* a prim. root; *be anxious:*—be afraid (careful, sorry), sorrow, take thought.

1673. דֹּאֵג **Dô'êg**, *do-ayg';* or (fully)

דּוֹאֵג **Dôw'êg**, *do-ayg';* act. part. of 1672; *anxious; Doëg*, an Edomite:—Doeg.

1674. דְּאָגָה **deʼâgâh**, *dĕh-aw-gaw';* from 1672; *anxiety:*—care (-fulness), fear, heaviness, sorrow.

1675. דָּאָה **dâ'âh**, *daw-aw';* a prim. root; to *dart*, i.e. *fly* rapidly:—fly.

1676. דָּאָה **dâ'âh**, *daw-aw';* from 1675; the *kite* (from its rapid *flight*):—vulture. See 7201.

1677. דֹּב **dôb**, *dobe;* or (fully)

דּוֹב **dôwb**, *dobe;* from 1680; the *bear* (as slow):—bear.

1678. דֹּב **dôb** (Chald.), *dobe;* corresp. to 1677:—bear.

1679. דֹּבֶא **dôbe'**, *do'-beh;* from an unused root (comp. 1680) (prob. mean. to *be sluggish*, i.e. *restful*); *quiet:*—strength.

1680. דָּבַב **dâbab**, *daw-bab';* a prim. root (comp. 1679); to *move* slowly, i.e. *glide:*—cause to speak.

1681. דִּבָּה **dibbâh**, *dib-baw';* from 1680 (in the sense of *furtive* motion); *slander:*—defaming, evil report, infamy, slander.

1682. דְּבוֹרָה **debôwrâh**, *deb-o-raw';* or (short.)

דְּבֹרָה **debôrâh**, *deb-o-raw';* from 1696 (in the sense of *orderly* motion); the *bee* (from its *systematic* instincts):—bee.

1683. דְּבוֹרָה **Debôwrâh**, *deb-o-raw';* or (short.)

דְּבֹרָה **Debôrâh**, *deb-o-raw';* the same as 1682; *Deborah*, the name of two Hebrewesses:—Deborah.

1684. דְּבַח **debach** (Chald.), *deb-akh';* corresp. to 2076; to *sacrifice* (an animal):—offer [sacrifice].

1685. דְּבַח **debach** (Chald.), *deb-akh';* from 1684; a *sacrifice:*—sacrifice.

1686. דִּבְיוֹן **dibyôwn**, *dib-yone';* in the marg. for the textual reading

חֶרְיוֹן **cheryôwn**, *kher-yone';* both (in the plur. only and) of uncert. der.; prob. some cheap vegetable, perh. a bulbous root:—dove's dung.

1687. דְּבִיר **debîyr**, *deb-eer';* or (short.)

דְּבִר **debîr**, *deb-eer';* from 1696 (appar. in the sense of *oracle*); the *shrine* or innermost part of the sanctuary:—oracle.

1688. דְּבִיר **Debîyr**, *deb-eer';* or (short.)

דְּבִר **Debîr** (Josh. 13 : 26 [but see 3810]), *deb-eer';* the same as 1687; *Debir*, the name of an Amoritish king and of two places in Pal.:—Debir.

1689. דִּבְלָה **Diblâh**, *dib-law';* prob. an orth. err. for 7247; *Diblah*, a place in Syria:—Diblath.

1690. דְּבֵלָה **debêlâh**, *deb-ay-law';* from an unused root (akin to 2082) prob. mean. to *press* together; a *cake* of pressed figs:—cake (lump) of figs.

1691. דִּבְלַיִם **Diblayim**, *dib-lah'-yim;* dual from the masc. of 1690; *two cakes; Diblajim*, a symbol. name:—Diblaim.

דִּבְלָתַיִם **Diblâthayim**. See 1015.

1692. דָּבַק **dâbaq**, *daw-bak';* a prim. root; prop. to *impinge*, i.e. *cling* or *adhere;* fig. to *catch* by pursuit:—abide fast, cleave (fast together), follow close (hard after), be joined (together), keep (fast), overtake, pursue hard, stick, take.

1693. דְּבַק **debaq** (Chald.), *deb-ak';* corresp. to 1692; to *stick* to:—cleave.

1694. דֶּבֶק **debeq**, *deh'-bek;* from 1692; a *joint;* by impl. *solder:*—joint, solder.

1695. דָּבֵק **dâbêq**, *daw-bake';* from 1692; *adhering:*—cleave, joining, stick closer.

1696. דָּבַר **dâbar**, *daw-bar';* a prim. root; perh. prop. to *arrange;* but used fig. (of words) to *speak;* rarely (in a destructive sense) to *subdue:*—answer, appoint, bid, command, commune, declare, destroy, give, name, promise, pronounce, rehearse, say, speak, be spokesman, subdue, talk, teach, tell, think, use [entreaties], utter, × well, × work.

1697. דָּבָר **dâbâr**, *daw-bawr';* from 1696; a *word;* by impl. a *matter* (as *spoken* of) or *thing;* adv. a *cause:*—act, advice, affair, answer, × any such (thing), + because of, book, business, care, case, cause, certain rate, + chronicles, commandment, × commune (-ication), + concern [-ing], + confer, counsel, + dearth, decree, deed, × disease, due, duty, effect, + eloquent, errand, [evil favoured-] ness, + glory, + harm, hurt, + iniquity, + judgment, language, + lying, manner, matter, message, [no] thing, oracle, × ought, × parts, + pertaining, + please, portion, + power, promise, provision, purpose, question, rate, reason, report, request, × (as hast) said, sake, saying, sentence, + sign, + so, some [uncleanness], somewhat to say, + song, speech, × spoken, talk, task, + that, × there done, thing (concerning), thought, + thus, tidings, what [-soever], + wherewith, which, word, work.

1698. דֶּבֶר **deber**, *deh'-ber;* from 1696 (in the sense of *destroying*); a *pestilence:*—murrain, pestilence, plague.

1699. דֹּבֶר **dôber**, *do'-ber;* from 1696 (in its original sense); a *pasture* (from its *arrangement* of the flock):—fold, manner.

דְּבִר **debîr** or **Debîr**. See 1687, 1688.

1699'. דִּבֵּר **dibbêr**, *dib-bare';* for 1697:—word.

1700. דִּבְרָה **dibrâh**, *dib-raw';* fem. of 1697; a *reason, suit* or *style:*—cause, end, estate, order, regard.

1701. דִּבְרָה **dibrâh** (Chald.), *dib-raw';* corresp. to 1700:—intent, sake.

דְּבֹרָה **debôrâh** or **Debôrâh**. See 1682, 1683.

1702. דֹּבְרָה **dôberâh**, *do-ber-aw';* fem. act. part. of 1696 in the sense of *driving* [comp. 1699]; a *raft:*—float.

1703. דַּבָּרָה **dabbârâh**, *dab-baw-raw';* intens. from 1696; a *word:*—word.

1704. דִּבְרִי **Dibrîy**, *dib-ree';* from 1697; *wordy; Dibri*, an Isr.:—Dibri.

1705. דָּבְרַת **Dâberath**, *daw-ber-ath';* from 1697 (perh. in the sense of 1699); *Daberath*, a place in Pal.:—Dabareh, Daberath.

1706. דְּבַשׁ **debash**, *deb-ash';* from an unused root mean. to *be gummy; honey* (from its *stickiness*); by anal. *syrup:*—honey ([-comb]).

1707. דַּבֶּשֶׁת **dabbesheth**, *dab-beh'-sheth;* intens. from the same as 1706; a sticky *mass*, i.e. the *hump* of a camel:—hunch [of a camel].

1708. דַּבֶּשֶׁת **Dabbesheth**, *dab-beh'-sheth;* the same as 1707; *Dabbesheth*, a place in Pal.:—Dabbesheth.

1709. דָּג **dâg**, *dawg;* or (fully)

דָּאג **dâ'g** (Neh. 13 : 16), *dawg;* from 1711; a *fish* (as *prolific*); or perh. rather from 1672 (as *timid*); but still better from 1672 (in the sense of *squirming*, i.e. moving by the vibratory action of the tail); a *fish* (often used collect.):—fish.

1710. דָּגָה **dâgâh**, *daw-gaw';* fem. of 1709, and mean. the same:—fish.

1711. דָּגָה **dâgâh**, *daw-gaw';* a prim. root; to *move rapidly;* used only as a denom. from 1709; to *spawn*, i.e. *become numerous:*—grow.

1712. דָּגוֹן **Dâgôwn**, *daw-gohn';* from 1709; the *fish-god; Dagon*, a Philistine deity:—Dagon.

1713. דָּגַל **dâgal**, *daw-gal';* a prim. root; to *flaunt*, i.e. *raise a flag;* fig. to *be conspicuous:*—(set up, with) banners, chiefest.

1714. דֶּגֶל **degel**, *deh'-gel;* from 1713; a *flag:*—banner, standard.

1715. דָּגָן **dâgân**, *daw-gawn';* from 1711; prop. *increase*, i.e. *grain:*—corn ([floor]), wheat.

1716. דָּגַר **dâgar**, *daw-gar';* a prim. root; to *brood* over eggs or young:—gather, sit.

1717. דַּד **dad**, *dad;* appar. from the same as 1730; the *breast* (as the seat of *love*, or from its shape):—breast, teat.

1718. דָּדָה **dâdâh**, *daw-daw';* a doubtful root; to *walk gently:*—go (softly, with).

1719. דְּדָן **Dedân**, *ded-awn';* or (prol.)

דְּדָנֶה **Dedâneh** (Ezek. 25 : 13), *deh-daw'-neh;* of uncert. der.; *Dedan*, the name of two Cushites and of their territory:—Dedan.

1720. דְּדָנִים **Dedânîym**, *ded-aw-neem';* plur. of 1719 (as patrial); *Dedanites*, the desc. or inhab. of Dedan:—Dedanim.

1721. דֹּדָנִים **Dôdânîym**, *do-daw-neem';* or (by orth. err.)

רֹדָנִים **Rôdânîym** (1 Chron. 1 : 7), *ro-daw-neem';* a plur. of uncert. der.; *Dodanites*, or desc. of a son of Javan:—Dodanim.

1722. דְּהַב **dehab** (Chald.), *deh-hab';* corresp. to 2091; *gold:*—gold (-en).

1723. דַּהֲוָא **Dahăvâ'** (Chald.), *dah-hav-aw';* of uncert. der.; *Dahava*, a people colonized in Samaria:—Dehavites.

1724. דָּהַם **dâham**, *daw-ham';* a prim. root (comp. 1740); to *be dumb*, i.e. (fig.) *dumbfounded:*—be astonished.

1725. דָּהַר **dâhar**, *daw-har';* a prim. root; to *curvet* or move irregularly:—pranse.

1726. דַּהֲהַר **dahăhar**, *dah-hah-har';* by redupl. from 1725; a *gallop:*—pransing.

דּוֹאֵג **Dôw'êg**. See 1673.

1727. דּוּב **dûwb**, *doob;* a prim. root; to *mope*, i.e. (fig.) *pine:*—sorrow.

דּוֹב **dôwb**. See 1677.

1728. דַּוָּג **davvâg**, *dav-vawg';* an orth. var. of 1709 as a denom. [1771]; a *fisherman:*—fisher.

1729. דּוּגָה **dûwgâh**, *doo-gaw';* fem. from the same as 1728; prop. *fishery*, i.e. a *hook* for fishing:—fish [hook].

1730. דּוֹד **dôwd**, *dode;* or (short.) דֹּד **dôd**, *dode;* from an unused root mean. prop. to *boil*, i.e. (fig.) to *love;* by impl. a *love-token, lover, friend;* spec. an *uncle:*—(well-) beloved, father's brother, love, uncle.

1731. דּוּד **dûwd**, *dood;* from the same as 1730; a *pot* (for *boiling*); also (by resemblance of shape) a *basket:*—basket, caldron, kettle, (seething) pot.

1732. דָּוִד **Dâvîd**, *daw-veed';* rarely (fully) דָּוִיד **Dâvîyd**, *daw-veed';* from the same as 1730; *loving; David*, the youngest son of Jesse.—David.

1733. דּוֹדָה **dôwdâh**, *do-daw';* fem. of 1730; an *aunt:*—aunt, father's sister, uncle's wife.

1734. דּוֹדוֹ **Dôwdôw**, *do-do';* from 1730; *loving; Dodo*, the name of three Isr.:—Dodo.

1735. דּוֹדָוָהוּ **Dôwdâvâhûw**, *do-daw-vaw'-hoo;* from 1730 and 3050; *love of Jah; Dodavah*, an Isr.:—Dodavah.

1736. דּוּדַי **dûwday**, *doo-dah'-ee;* from 1731; a *boiler* or *basket;* also the *mandrake* (as *aphrodisiac*):—basket, mandrake.

1737. דּוֹדַי **Dôwday**, *do-dah'ee;* formed like 1736; *amatory; Dodai*, an Isr.:—Dodai.

1738. דָּוָה **dâvâh**, *daw-vaw';* a prim. root; to *be sick* (as if in menstruation):—infirmity.

1739. דָּוֶה **dâveh**, *daw-veh';* from 1738; *sick* (espec. in menstruation):—faint, menstruous cloth, she that is sick, having sickness.

1740. דּוּחַ **dûwach**, *doo'-akh;* a prim. root; to *thrust* away; fig. to *cleanse:*—cast out, purge, wash.

1741. דְּוַי **d^{e}vay**, *dev-ah'ee;* from 1739; *sickness;* fig. *loathing:*—languishing, sorrowful.

1742. דַּוָּי **davvây**, *dav-voy';* from 1739; *sick;* fig. *troubled:*—faint.

דָּוִיד **Dâvîyd**. See 1732.

1743. דּוּךְ **dûwk**, *dook;* a prim. root; to *bruise* in a mortar:—beat.

1744. דּוּכִיפַת **dûwkîyphath**, *doo-kee-fath';* of uncert. der.; the *hoopoe* or else the *grouse:*—lapwing.

1745. דּוּמָה **dûwmâh**, *doo-maw';* from an unused root mean. to *be dumb* (comp. 1820); *silence;* fig. *death:*—silence.

1746. דּוּמָה **Dûwmâh**, *doo-maw';* the same as 1745; *Dumah*, a tribe and region of Arabia:—Dumah.

1747. דּוּמִיָּה **dûwmîyâh**, *doo-me-yaw';* from 1820; *stillness;* adv. *silently;* abstr. *quiet, trust:*—silence, silent, waiteth.

1748. דּוּמָם **dûwmâm**, *doo-mawm';* from 1826; *still;* adv. *silently:*—dumb, silent, quietly wait.

דּוּמֶשֶׂק° **Dûwmesheq**. See 1833.

1749. דּוֹנַג **dôwnag**, *do-nag';* of uncert. der.; *wax:*—wax.

1750. דּוּץ **dûwts**, *doots;* a prim. root; to *leap:*—be turned.

1751. דּוּק **dûwq** (Chald.), *dook;* corresp. to 1854; to *crumble:*—be broken to pieces.

1752. דּוּר **dûwr**, *dure;* a prim. root; prop. to *gyrate* (or move in a circle), i.e. to *remain:*—dwell.

1753. דּוּר **dûwr** (Chald.), *dure;* corresp. to 1752; to *reside:*—dwell.

1754. דּוּר **dûwr**, *dure;* from 1752; a *circle, ball* or *pile:*—ball, turn, round about.

1755. דּוֹר **dôwr**, *dore;* or (short.) דֹּר **dôr**, *dore;* from 1752; prop. a *revolution* of time, i.e. an *age* or generation; also a *dwelling:*—age, × evermore, generation, [n-]ever, posterity.

1756. דּוֹר **Dôwr**, *dore;* or (by perm.) דֹּאר **Dô'r** (Josh. 17 : 11; 1 Kings 4 : 11), *dore;* from 1755; *dwelling; Dor*, a place in Pal.:—Dor.

1757. דּוּרָא **Dûwrâ'** (Chald.), *doo-raw';* prob. from 1753; *circle* or *dwelling; Dura*, a place in Bab.:—Dura.

1758. דּוּשׁ **dûwsh**, *doosh;* or דּוֹשׁ **dôwsh**, *dōsh;* or דִּישׁ **dîysh**, *deesh;* a prim. root; to *trample* or *thresh:*—break, tear, thresh, tread out (down), at grass [Jer. 50 : 11, *by mistake for* 1877].

1759. דּוּשׁ **dûwsh** (Chald.), *doosh;* corresp. to 1758; to *trample:*—tread down.

1760. דָּחָה **dâchâh**, *daw-khaw';* or דָּחַח **dâchach** (Jer. 23 : 12), *daw-khakh';* a prim. root; to *push* down:—chase, drive away (on), overthrow, outcast, × sore, thrust, totter.

1761. דַּחֲוָה **dachăvâh** (Chald.), *dakh-av-aw';* from the equiv. of 1760; prob. a musical *instrument* (as being *struck*):—instrument of music.

1762. דְּחִי **d^{e}chîy**, *deh-khee';* from 1760; a *push*, i.e. (by impl.) a *fall:*—falling.

1763. דְּחַל **d^{e}chal** (Chald.), *deh-khal';* corresp. to 2119; to *slink*, i.e. (by impl.) to *fear*, or (caus.) *be formidable:*—make afraid, dreadful, fear, terrible.

1764. דֹּחַן **dôchan**, *do'-khan;* of uncert. der.; *millet:*—millet.

1765. דָּחַף **dâchaph**, *daw-khaf';* a prim. root; to *urge*, i.e. *hasten:*—(be) haste (-ned), pressed on.

1766. דָּחַק **dâchaq**, *daw-khak';* a prim. root; to *press*, i.e. *oppress:*—thrust, vex.

1767. דַּי **day**, *dahee;* of uncert. der.; *enough* (as noun or adv.), used chiefly with prep. in phrases:—able, according to, after (ability), among, as (oft as), (more than) enough, from, in, since, (much as is) sufficient (-ly), too much, very, when.

1768. דִּי **dîy** (Chald.), *dee;* appar. for 1668; *that*, used as rel., conj., and espec. (with prep.) in adv. phrases; also as a prep. *of:*—× as, but, for (-asmuch +), + now, of, seeing, than, that, therefore, until, + what (-soever), when, which, whom, whose.

1769. דִּיבוֹן **Dîybôwn**, *dee-bone';* or (short.) דִּיבֹן **Dîybôn**, *dee-bone';* from 1727; *pining:*—*Dibon*, the name of three places in Pal.:—Dibon. [*Also, with* 1410 *added*, Dibon-gad.]

1770. דִּיג **dîyg**, *deeg;* denom. from 1709; to *fish:*—fish.

1771. דַּיָּג **dayâg**, *dah-yawg';* from 1770; a *fisherman:*—fisher.

1772. דַּיָּה **dayâh**, *dah-yaw';* intens. from 1675; a *falcon* (from its *rapid* flight):—vulture.

1773. דְּיוֹ **d^{e}yôw**, *deh-yo';* of uncert. der.; *ink:*—ink.

1774. דִּי זָהָב **Dîy zâhâb**, *dee zaw-hawb';* as if from 1768 and 2091; *of gold; Dizahab*, a place in the Desert:—Dizahab.

1775. דִּימוֹן **Dîymôwn**, *dee-mone';* perh. for 1769; *Dimon*, a place in Pal.:—Dimon.

1776. דִּימוֹנָה **Dîymôwnâh**, *dee-mo-naw';* fem. of 1775; *Dimonah*, a place in Pal.:—Dimonah.

1777. דִּין **dîyn**, *deen;* or (Gen. 6 : 3) דּוּן **dûwn**, *doon;* a prim. root [comp. 113]; to *rule;* by impl. to *judge* (as umpire); also to *strive* (as at law):—contend, execute (judgment), judge, minister judgment, plead (the cause), at strife, strive.

1778. דִּין **dîyn** (Chald.), *deen;* corresp. to 1777; to *judge:*—judge.

1779. דִּין **dîyn**, *deen;* or (Job 19 : 29) דּוּן **dûwn**, *doon;* from 1777; *judgment* (the suit, justice, sentence or tribunal); by impl. also *strife:*—cause, judgment, plea, strife.

1780. דִּין **dîyn** (Chald.), *deen;* corresp. to 1779:—judgment.

1781. דַּיָּן **dayân**, *dah-yawn';* from 1777; a *judge* or *advocate:*—judge.

1782. דַּיָּן **dayân** (Chald.), *dah-yawn';* corresp. to 1781:—judge.

1783. דִּינָה **Dîynâh**, *dee-naw';* fem. of 1779; *justice; Dinah*, the daughter of Jacob:—Dinah.

1784. דִּינַי **Dîynay** (Chald.), *dee-nah'ee;* patrial from an uncert. prim.; a *Dinaite* or inhab. of some unknown Ass. province:—Dinaite.

דִּיפַת **Dîyphath**. See 7384.

1785. דָּיֵק **dâyêq**, *daw-yake';* from a root corresp. to 1751; a *battering*-tower:—fort.

1786. דַּיִשׁ **dayîsh**, *dah'-yish;* from 1758; *threshing*-time:—threshing.

1787. דִּישׁוֹן **Dîyshôwn**, דִּישֹׁן **Dîyshôn**, דִּשׁוֹן **Dîshôwn**, or דִּשֹׁן **Dîshôn**, *dee-shone';* the same as 1788; *Dishon*, the name of two Edomites:—Dishon.

1788. דִּישֹׁן **dîyshôn**, *dee-shone';* from 1758; the *leaper*, i.e. an *antelope:*—pygarg.

1789. דִּישָׁן **Dîyshân**, *dee-shawn';* another form of 1787; *Dishan*, an Edomite:—Dishan, Dishon.

1790. דַּךְ **dak**, *dak;* from an unused root (comp. 1794); *crushed*, i.e. (fig.) *injured:*—afflicted, oppressed.

1791. דֵּךְ **dêk** (Chald.), *dake;* or דָּךְ **dâk** (Chald.), *dawk;* prol. from 1668; *this:*—the same, this.

1792. דָּכָא **dâkâ'**, *daw-kaw';* a prim. root (comp. 1794); to *crumble;* trans. to *bruise* (lit. or fig.):—beat to pieces, break (in pieces), bruise, contrite, crush, destroy, humble, oppress, smite.

1793. דַּכָּא **dakkâ'**, *dak-kaw';* from 1792; *crushed* (lit. *powder*, or fig. *contrite*):—contrite, destruction.

1794. דָּכָה **dâkâh**, *daw-kaw';* a prim. root (comp. 1790, 1792); to *collapse* (phys. or mentally):—break (sore), contrite, crouch.

1795. דַּכָּה **dakkâh**, *dak-kaw';* from 1794 like 1793; *mutilated:*—+ wounded.

1796. דֳּכִי **dŏkîy**, *dok-ee';* from 1794; a *dashing* of surf:—wave.

1797. דִּכֵּן **dikkên** (Chald.), *dik-kane';* prol. from 1791; *this:*—same, that, this.

1798. דְּכַר **d^{e}kar** (Chald.), *dek-ar';* corresp. to 2145; prop. a *male*, i.e. of sheep:—ram.

1799. דִּכְרוֹן **dikrôwn** (Chald.), *dik-rone';* or דָּכְרָן **dokrân**, *dok-rawn'* (Chald.); corresp. to 2146; a *register:*—record.

1800. דַּל **dal**, *dal;* from 1809; prop. *dangling*, i.e. (by impl.) *weak* or *thin:*—lean, needy, poor (man), weaker.

1801. דָּלַג **dâlag**, *daw-lag';* a prim. root; to *spring:*—leap.

1802. דָּלָה **dâlâh**, *daw-law';* a prim. root (comp. 1809); prop. to *dangle*, i.e. to *let down* a bucket (for *drawing* out water); fig. to *deliver:*—draw (out), × enough, lift up.

1803. דַּלָּה **dallâh**, *dal-law';* from 1802; prop. something *dangling*, i.e. a loose *thread* or *hair;* fig. *indigent:*—hair, pining sickness, poor (-est sort).

1804. דָּלַח **dâlach**, *daw-lakh';* a prim. root; to *roil* water:—trouble.

1805. דְּלִי **d^{e}lîy**, *del-ee';* or דֳּלִי **dŏlîy**, *dol-ee';* from 1802; a *pail* or *jar* (for *drawing* water):—bucket.

1806. דְּלָיָה **D^{e}lâyâh**, *del-aw-yaw';* or (prol.) דְּלָיָהוּ **D^{e}lâyâhhûw**, *del-aw-yaw'-hoo;* from 1802 and 3050; *Jah has delivered; Delajah*, the name of five Isr.:—Dalaiah, Delaiah.

1807. דְּלִילָה **D^{e}lîylâh**, *del-ee-law';* from 1809; *languishing:*—*Delilah*, a Philistine woman:—Delilah.

1808. דָּלִיָּה **dâlîyâh**, *daw-lee-yaw';* from 1802; something *dangling*, i.e. a *bough:*—branch.

1809. דָּלַל **dâlal**, *daw-lal';* a prim. root (comp. 1802); to *slacken* or *be feeble;* fig. to *be oppressed:*—bring low, dry up, be emptied, be not equal, fail, be impoverished, be made thin.

1810. דִּלְעָן **Dil'ân**, *dil-awn'*; of uncert. der.; *Dilan*, a place in Pal.:—Dilean.

1811. דָּלַף **dâlaph**, *daw-laf'*; a prim. root; to *drip*; by impl. to *weep*:—drop through, melt, pour out.

1812. דֶּלֶף **deleph**, *deh'-lef*; from 1811; a *dripping*:—dropping.

1813. דַּלְפוֹן **Dalphôwn**, *dal-fone'*; from 1811; *dripping*; *Dalphon*, a son of Haman:—Dalphon.

1814. דָּלַק **dâlaq**, *daw-lak'*; a prim. root; to *flame* (lit. or fig.):—burning, chase, inflame, kindle, persecute (-or), pursue hotly.

1815. דְּלַק **delaq** (Chald.), *del-ak'*; corresp. to 1814:—burn.

1816. דַּלֶּקֶת **dalleqeth**, *dal-lek'-keth*; from 1814; a *burning* fever:—inflammation.

1817. דֶּלֶת **deleth**, *deh'-leth*; from 1802; something *swinging*, i.e. the *valve* of a door:—door (two-leaved), gate, leaf, lid. [In Psa. 141:3, *dâl*, irreg.]

1818. דָּם **dâm**, *dawm*; from 1826 (comp. 119); *blood* (as that which when shed causes *death*) of man or an animal; by anal. the *juice* of the grape; fig. (espec. in the plur.) *bloodshed* (i.e. *drops* of blood):—blood (-y, -guiltiness, [-thirsty]), + innocent.

1819. דָּמָה **dâmâh**, *daw-maw'*; a prim. root; to *compare*; by impl. to *resemble*, *liken*, *consider*:—compare, devise, (be) like (-n), mean, think, use similitudes.

1820. דָּמָה **dâmâh**, *daw-maw'*; a prim. root; to *be dumb* or *silent*; hence to *fail* or *perish*; trans. to *destroy*:—cease, be cut down (off), destroy, be brought to silence, be undone, × utterly.

1821. דְּמָה **demâh** (Chald.), *dem-aw'*; corresp. to 1819; to *resemble*:—be like.

1822. דֻּמָּה **dummâh**, *doom-maw'*; from 1820; *desolation*; concr. *desolate*:—destroy.

1823. דְּמוּת **demûwth**, *dem-ooth'*; from 1819; *resemblance*; concr. *model*, *shape*; adv. *like*:—fashion, like (-ness, as), manner, similitude.

1824. דְּמִי **demîy**, *dem-ee'*; or
דֳּמִי **dŏmîy**, *dom-ee'*; from 1820; *quiet*:—cutting off, rest, silence.

1825. דִּמְיוֹן **dimyôwn**, *dim-yone'*; from 1819; *resemblance*:— × like.

1826. דָּמַם **dâmam**, *daw-mam'*; a prim. root [comp. 1724, 1820]; to *be dumb*; by impl. to *be astonished*, to *stop*; also to *perish*:—cease, be cut down (off), forbear, hold peace, quiet self, rest, be silent, keep (put to) silence, be (stand) still, tarry, wait.

1827. דְּמָמָה **demâmâh**, *dem-aw-maw'*; fem. from 1826; *quiet*:—calm, silence, still.

1828. דֹּמֶן **dômen**, *do'-men*; of uncert. der.; *manure*:—dung.

1829. דִּמְנָה **Dimnâh**, *dim-naw'*; fem. from the same as 1828; a *dung-heap*; *Dimnah*, a place in Pal.:—Dimnah.

1830. דָּמַע **dâma'**, *daw-mah'*; a prim. root; to *weep*:— × sore, weep.

1831. דֶּמַע **dema'**, *deh'-mah*; from 1830; a *tear*; fig. *juice*:—liquor.

1832. דִּמְעָה **dim'âh**, *dim-aw'*; fem. of 1831; *weeping*:—tears.

1833. דְּמֶשֶׁק **demesheq**, *dem-eh'-shek*; by orth. var. from 1834; *damask* (as a fabric of Damascus):—in Damascus.

1834. דַּמֶּשֶׂק **Dammeseq**, *dam-meh'-sek*; or
דּוּמֶשֶׂק **Dûwmeseq**, *doo-meh'-sek*; or
דַּרְמֶשֶׂק **Darmeseq**, *dar-meh'-sek*; of for. or.; *Damascus*, a city of Syria:—Damascus.

1835. דָּן **Dân**, *dawn*; from 1777; *judge*; *Dan*, one of the sons of Jacob; also the tribe descended from him, and its territory; likewise a place in Pal. colonized by them:—Dan.

1836. דֵּן **dên** (Chald.), *dane*; an orth. var. of 1791; *this*:—[afore-] time, + after this manner, here [-after], one . . . another, such, there [-fore], these, this (matter), + thus, where [-fore], which.

דָּנִאֵל **Dânî'êl.** See 1841.

1837. דַּנָּה **Dannâh**, *dan-naw'*; of uncert. der.; *Dannah*, a place in Pal.:—Dannah.

1838. דִּנְהָבָה **Dinhâbâh**, *din-haw-baw'*; of uncert. der.; *Dinhabah*, an Edomitish town:—Dinhaban.

1839. דָּנִי **Dânîy**, *daw-nee'*; patron. from 1835; a *Danite* (often collect.) or desc. (or inhab.) of Dan:—Danites, of Dan.

1840. דָּנִיֵּאל **Dânîyê'l**, *daw-nee-yale'*; in Ezek.
דָּנִאֵל **Dânî'êl**, *daw-nee-ale'*; from 1835 and 410; *judge of God*; *Daniel* or *Danijel*, the name of two Isr.:—Daniel.

1841. דָּנִיֵּאל **Dânîyê'l** (Chald.), *daw-nee-yale'*; corresp. to 1840; *Danijel*, the Heb. prophet:—Daniel.

1842. דָּן יַעַן **Dân Ya'an**, *dawn yah'-an*; from 1835 and (appar.) 3282; *judge of purpose*; *Dan-Jaan*, a place in Pal.:—Dan-jaan.

1843. דֵּעַ **dêa'**, *day'-ah*; from 3045; *knowledge*:—knowledge, opinion.

1844. דֵּעָה **dê'âh**, *day-aw'*; fem. of 1843; *knowledge*:—knowledge.

1845. דְּעוּאֵל **De'ûw'êl**, *deh-oo-ale'*; from 3045 and 410; *known of God*; *Deüel*, an Isr.:—Deuel.

1846. דָּעַךְ **dâ'ak**, *daw-ak'*; a prim. root; to *be extinguished*; fig. to *expire* or *be dried up*:—be extinct, consumed, put out, quenched.

1847. דַּעַת **da'ath**, *dah'-ath*; from 3045; *knowledge*:—cunning, [ig-] norantly, know (-ledge), [un-] awares (wittingly).

1848. דֳּפִי **dŏphîy**, *dof'-ee*; from an unused root (mean. to *push* over); a *stumbling-block*:—slanderest.

1849. דָּפַק **dâphaq**, *daw-fak'*; a prim. root; to *knock*; by anal. to *press* severely:—beat, knock, overdrive.

1850. דָּפְקָה **Dophqâh**, *dof-kaw'*; from 1849; a *knock*; *Dophkah*, a place in the Desert:—Dophkah.

1851. דַּק **daq**, *dak*; from 1854; *crushed*, i.e. (by impl.) *small* or *thin*:—dwarf, lean [-fleshed], very little thing, small, thin.

1852. דֹּק **dôq**, *doke*; from 1854; something *crumbling*, i.e. *fine* (as a *thin* cloth):—curtain.

1853. דִּקְלָה **Diqlâh**, *dik-law'*; of for. or.; *Diklah*, a region of Arabia:—Diklah.

1854. דָּקַק **dâqaq**, *daw-kak'*; a prim. root [comp. 1915]; to *crush* (or intrans.) *crumble*:—beat in pieces (small), bruise, make dust, (into) × powder, (be, very) small, stamp (small).

1855. דְּקַק **deqaq** (Chald.), *dek-ak'*; corresp. to 1854; to *crumble* or (trans.) *crush*:—break to pieces.

1856. דָּקַר **dâqar**, *daw-kar'*; a prim. root; to *stab*; by anal. to *starve*; fig. to *revile*:—pierce, strike (thrust) through, wound.

1857. דֶּקֶר **Deqer**, *deh'-ker*; from 1856; a *stab*; *Deker*, an Isr.:—Dekar.

1858. דַּר **dar**, *dar*; appar. from the same as 1865; prop. a *pearl* (from its sheen as rapidly *turned*); by anal. *pearl-stone*, i.e. mother-of-pearl or alabaster:— × white.

1859. דָּר **dâr** (Chald.), *dawr*; corresp. to 1755; an *age*:—generation.

דֹּר **dôr.** See 1755.

1860. דְּרָאוֹן **derâ'ôwn**, *der-aw-one'*; or
דֵּרָאוֹן **dêrâ'ôwn**, *day-raw-one'*; from an unused root (mean. to *repulse*); an object of *aversion*:—abhorring, contempt.

1861. דָּרְבוֹן **dorbôwn**, *dor-bone'* [also *dor-bawn'*]; of uncert. der.; a *goad*:—goad.

1862. דַּרְדַּע **Darda'**, *dar-dah'*; appar. from 1858 and 1843; *pearl of knowledge*; *Darda*, an Isr.:—Darda.

1863. דַּרְדַּר **dardar**, *dar-dar'*; of uncert. der.; a *thorn*:—thistle.

1864. דָּרוֹם **dârôwm**, *daw-rome'*; of uncert. der.; the *south*; poet. the *south wind*:—south.

1865. דְּרוֹר **derôwr**, *der-ore'*; from an unused root (mean. to *move rapidly*); *freedom*; hence *spontaneity* of outflow, and so *clear*:—liberty, pure.

1866. דְּרוֹר **derôwr**, *der-ore'*; the same as 1865, applied to a bird; the *swift*, a kind of swallow:—swallow.

1867. דָּרְיָוֶשׁ **Dâreyâvêsh**, *daw-reh-yaw-vaysh'*; of Pers. or.; *Darejavesh*, a title (rather than name) of several Persian kings:—Darius.

1868. דָּרְיָוֶשׁ **Dâreyâvêsh** (Chald.), *daw-reh-yaw-vaysh'*; corresp. to 1867:—Darius.

1869. דָּרַךְ **dârak**, *daw-rak'*; a prim. root; to *tread*; by impl. to *walk*; also to *string* a bow (by treading on it in bending):—archer, bend, come, draw, go (over), guide, lead (forth), thresh, tread (down), walk.

1870. דֶּרֶךְ **derek**, *deh'-rek*; from 1869; a *road* (as *trodden*); fig. a *course* of life or *mode* of action, often adv.:—along, away, because of, + by, conversation, custom, [east-] ward, journey, manner, passenger, through, toward, [high-] [path-] way [-side], whither [-soever].

1871. דַּרְכְּמוֹן **darkemôwn**, *dar-kem-one'*; of Pers. or.; a "*drachma*," or coin:—dram.

1872. דְּרָע **derâ'** (Chald.), *der-aw'*; corresp. to 2220; an *arm*:—arm.

1873. דָּרַע **Dâra'**, *daw-rah'*; prob. contr. from 1862; *Dara*, an Isr.:—Dara.

1874. דַּרְקוֹן **Darqôwn**, *dar-kone'*; of uncert. der.; *Darkon*, one of "Solomon's servants":—Darkon.

1875. דָּרַשׁ **dârash**, *daw-rash'*; a prim. root; prop. to *tread* or *frequent*; usually to *follow* (for pursuit or search); by impl. to *seek* or *ask*; spec. to *worship*:—ask, × at all, care for, × diligently, inquire, make inquisition, [necro-] mancer, question, require, search, seek [for, out], × surely.

1876. דָּשָׁא **dâshâ**, *daw-shaw'*; a prim. root; to *sprout*:—bring forth, spring.

1877. דֶּשֶׁא **deshe'**, *deh'-sheh*; from 1876; a *sprout*; by anal. *grass*:—(tender) grass, green, (tender) herb.

1878. דָּשֵׁן **dâshên**, *daw-shane'*; a prim. root; to *be fat*; trans. to *fatten* (or regard as fat); spec. to *anoint*; fig. to *satisfy*; denom. (from 1880) to *remove* (fat) *ashes* (of sacrifices):—accept, anoint, take away the (receive) ashes (from), make (wax) fat.

1879. דָּשֵׁן **dâshên**, *daw-shane'*; from 1878; *fat*; fig. *rich*, *fertile*:—fat.

1880. דֶּשֶׁן **deshen**, *deh'-shen*; from 1878; the *fat*; abstr. *fatness*, i.e. (fig.) *abundance*; spec. the (fatty) *ashes* of sacrifices:—ashes, fatness.

1881. דָּת **dâth**, *dawth*; of uncert. (perh. for.) der.; a royal *edict* or statute:—commandment, commission, decree, law, manner.

1882. דָּת **dâth** (Chald.), *dawth*; corresp. to 1881; decree, law.

1883. דֶּתֶא **dethe'** (Chald.), *deh'-thay*; corresp. to 1877:—tender grass.

1884. דְּתָבָר **dethâbâr** (Chald.), *deth-aw-bawr'*; of Pers. or.; mean. one *skilled in law*; a *judge*:—counsellor.

1885. דָּתָן **Dâthân**, *daw-thawn'*; of uncert. der.; *Dathan*, an Isr.:—Dathan.

1886. דֹּתָן **Dôthân**, *do'-thawn*; or (Chaldaizing dual)
דֹּתַיִן **Dôthayin** (Gen. 37 : 17), *do-thah'-yin*; of uncert. der.; *Dothan*, a place in Pal.:—Dothan.

ה

1887. הֵא **hê'**, *hay*; a prim. particle; *lo!*:—behold, lo.

1888. הֵא **hê'** (Chald.), *hay*; or
הָא **hâ'** (Chald.), *haw*; corresp. to 1887:—even, lo.

1889. הֶאָח **heâch**, *heh-awkh'*; from 1887 and 253; *aha!*:—ah, aha, ha.

הָאֲרָרִי **Hâ'rârîy.** See 2043.

1890. הַבְהָב **habhâb**, *hab-hawb'*; by redupl. from 3051; *gift* (in sacrifice), i.e. *holocaust*:—offering.

1891. הָבַל **hâbal**, *haw-bal'*; a prim. root; to *be vain* in act, word, or expectation; spec. to *lead astray:*—be (become, make) vain.

1892. הֶבֶל **hebel**, *heh'-bel*; or (rarely in the abs.) הֲבֵל **hăbêl**, *hab-ale'*; from 1891; *emptiness* or *vanity;* fig. something *transitory* and *unsatisfactory;* often used as an adv.:— × altogether, vain, vanity.

1893. הֶבֶל **Hebel**, *heh'-bel*; the same as 1892; *Hebel*, the son of Adam:—Abel.

1894. הֹבֶן **hôben**, *ho'-ben*; only in plur., from an unused root mean. to *be hard; ebony:*—ebony.

1895. הָבַר **hâbar**, *haw-bar'*; a prim. root of uncert. (perh. for.) der.; to *be a horoscopist:*— + (astro-) loger.

1896. הֵגֵא **Hêgê'**, *hay-gay'*; or (by perm.) הֵגַי **Hêgay**, *hay-gah'ee*; prob. of Pers. or.; *Hege* or *Hegai*, a eunuch of Xerxes:—Hegai, Hege.

1897. הָגָה **hâgâh**, *haw-gaw'*; a prim. root [comp. 1901]; to *murmur* (in pleasure or anger); by impl. to *ponder:*—imagine, meditate, mourn, mutter, roar, × sore, speak, study, talk, utter.

1898. הָגָה **hâgâh**, *haw-gaw'*; a prim. root; to *remove;*—stay, take away.

1899. הֶגֶה **hegeh**, *heh'-geh*; from 1897; a *muttering* (in sighing, thought, or as thunder):—mourning, sound, tale.

1900. הָגוּת **hâgûwth**, *haw-gooth'*; from 1897; *musing:*—meditation.

1901. הָגִיג **hâgîyg**, *haw-gheeg'*; from an unused root akin to 1897; prop. a *murmur*, i.e. *complaint:*—meditation, musing.

1902. הִגָּיוֹן **higgâyôwn**, *hig-gaw-yone'*; intens. from 1897; a *murmuring* sound, i.e. a musical notation (prob. similar to the modern *affetuoso* to indicate solemnity of movement); by impl. a *machination:*—device, Higgaion, meditation, solemn sound.

1903. הָגִין **hâgîyn**, *haw-gheen'*; of uncert. der.; perh. *suitable* or *turning:*—directly.

1904. הָגָר **Hâgâr**, *haw-gawr'*; of uncert. (perh. for.) der.; *Hagar*, the mother of Ishmael:—Hagar.

1905. הַגְרִי **Hagrîy**, *hag-ree'*; or (prol.) הַגְרִיא **Hagrî'**, *hag-ree'*; perh. patron. from 1904; a *Hagrite* or member of a certain Arabian clan:—Hagarene, Hagarite, Haggeri.

1906. הֵד **hêd**, *hade*; for 1959; a *shout:*—sounding again.

1907. הַדָּבָר **haddâbâr** (Chald.), *had-daw-bawr'*; prob. of for. or.; a *vizier:*—counsellor.

1908. הֲדַד **Hădad**, *had-ad'*; prob. of for. or. [comp. 111]; *Hadad*, the name of an idol, and of several kings of Edom:—Hadad.

1909. הֲדַדְעֶזֶר **Hădad'ezer**, *had-ad-eh'-zer*; from 1908 and 5828; *Hadad* (is his) *help; Hadadezer*, a Syrian king:—Hadadezer. Comp. 1928.

1910. הֲדַדְרִמּוֹן **Hădadrimmôwn**, *had-ad-rim-mone'*; from 1908 and 7417; *Hadad-Rimmon*, a place in Pal.:—Hadad-rimmon.

1911. הָדָה **hâdâh**, *haw-daw'*; a prim. root [comp. 3034]; to *stretch forth* the hand:—put.

1912. הֹדוּ **Hôdûw**, *ho'-doo*; of for. or.; *Hodu* (i.e. Hindû-stan):—India.

1913. הֲדוֹרָם **Hădôwrâm**, *had-o-rawm'*; or הֲדֹרָם **Hădôrâm**, *had-o-rawm'*; prob. of for. der.; *Hadoram*, a son of Joktan, and the tribe descended from him:—Hadoram.

1914. הִדַּי **Hidday**, *hid-dah'ee*; of uncert. der.; *Hiddai*, an Isr.:—Hiddai.

1915. הָדַךְ **hâdak**, *haw-dak'*; a prim. root [comp. 1854]; to *crush* with the foot:—tread down.

1916. הֲדֹם **hădôm**, *had-ome'*; from an unused root mean. to *stamp* upon; a *footstool:*—[foot-] stool.

1917. הַדָּם **haddâm** (Chald.), *had-dawm'*; from a root corresp. to that of 1916; something *stamped* to pieces, i.e. a *bit:*—piece.

1918. הֲדַס **hădaç**, *had-as'*; of uncert. der.; the *myrtle:*—myrtle (tree).

1919. הֲדַסָּה **Hădaççâh**, *had-as-saw'*; fem. of 1918; *Hadassah* (or Esther):—Hadassah.

1920. הָדַף **hâdaph**, *haw-daf'*; a prim. root; to *push* away or down:—cast away (out), drive, expel, thrust (away).

1921. הָדַר **hâdar**, *haw-dar'*; a prim. root; to *swell* up (lit. or fig., act. or pass.); by impl. to *favor* or *honour, be high* or *proud:*—countenance, crooked place, glorious, honour, put forth.

1922. הֲדַר **hădar** (Chald.), *had-ar'*; corresp. to 1921; to *magnify* (fig.):—glorify, honour.

1923. הֲדַר **hădar** (Chald.), *had-ar'*; from 1922; *magnificence:*—honour, majesty.

1924. הֲדַר **Hădar**, *had-ar'*; the same as 1926; *Hadar*, an Edomite:—Hadar.

1925. הֶדֶר **heder**, *heh'-der*; from 1921; *honour;* used (fig.) for the *capital* city (Jerusalem):—glory.

1926. הָדָר **hâdâr**, *haw-dawr'*; from 1921; *magnificence*, i.e. ornament or splendor:—beauty, comeliness, excellency, glorious, glory, goodly, honour, majesty.

1927. הֲדָרָה **hădârâh**, *had-aw-raw'*; fem. of 1926; *decoration:*—beauty, honour.

הֲדֹרָם **Hădôrâm**. See 1913.

1928. הֲדַרְעֶזֶר **Hădar'ezer**, *had-ar-eh'-zer*; from 1924 and 5828; *Hadar* (i.e. *Hadad*, 1908) is his *help; Hadarezer* (i.e. Hadadezer, 1909), a Syrian king:—Hadarezer.

1929. הָהּ **hâhh**, *haw*; a short. form of 162; *ah!* expressing grief:—woe worth.

1930. הוֹ **hôw**, *ho*; by perm. from 1929; *oh!:*—alas.

1931. הוּא **hûw'**, *hoo*; of which the fem. (beyond the Pentateuch) is הִיא **hîy'**, *he;* a prim. word, the third pers. pron. sing., *he* (*she* or *it*); only expressed when emphatic or without a verb; also (intens.) *self*, or (esp. with the art.) the *same;* sometimes (as demonstr.) *this* or *that;* occasionally (instead of copula) *as* or *are:*—he, as for her, him (-self), it, the same, she (herself), such, that (. . . it), these, they, this, those, which (is), who.

1932. הוּא **hûw** (Chald.), *hoo;* or (fem.) הִיא **hîy'** (Chald.), *he;* corresp. to 1931:— × are, it, this.

1933. הָוָא **hâvâ'**, *haw-vaw'*; or הָוָה **hâvâh**, *haw-vaw'*; a prim. root [comp. 183, 1961] supposed to mean prop. to *breathe;* to *be* (in the sense of existence):—be, × have.

1934. הֲוָא **hăvâ'** (Chald.), *hav-aw'*; or הֲוָה **hăvâh** (Chald.), *hav-aw'*; corresp. to 1933; to *exist;* used in a great variety of applications (especially in connection with other words):—be, become, + behold, + came (to pass), + cease, + cleave, + consider, + do, + give, + have + judge, + keep, + labour, + mingle (self), + put, + see, + seek, + set, + slay, + take heed, tremble, + walk, + would.

1935. הוֹד **hôwd**, *hode*; from an unused root; *grandeur* (i.e. an imposing form and appearance):—beauty, comeliness, excellency, glorious, glory, goodly, honour, majesty.

1936. הוֹד **Hôwd**, *hode*; the same as 1935; *Hod*, an Isr.:—Hod.

1937. הוֹדְוָה **Hôwdᵉvâh**, *ho-dev-aw'*; a form of 1938; *Hodevah* (or Hodevjah), an Isr.:—Hodevah.

1938. הוֹדַוְיָה **Hôwdavyâh**, *ho dav-yaw'*; from 1935 and 3050; *majesty of Jah; Hodavjah*, the name of three Isr.:—Hodaviah.

1939. הוֹדַיְוָהוּ **Howdayᵉvâhûw**, *ho-dah-yeh-vaw'-hoo*; a form of 1938; *Hodajvah*, an Isr.:—Hodaiah.

1940. הוֹדִיָּה **Hôwdîyâh**, *ho-dee-yaw'*; a form for the fem. of 3064; a *Jewess:*—Hodiah.

1941. הוֹדִיָּה **Hôwdîyâh**, *ho-dee-yaw'*; a form of 1938; *Hodijah*, the name of three Isr.:—Hodijah.

הָוָה **hâvâh**. See 1933.

הֲוָה **hăvâh**. See 1934.

1942. הַוָּה **havvâh**, *hav-vaw'*; from 1933 (in the sense of eagerly *coveting* and *rushing* upon; by impl. of *falling*); *desire;* also *ruin:*—calamity, iniquity, mischief, mischievous (thing), naughtiness, naughty, noisome, perverse thing, substance, very wickedness.

1943. הֹוָה **hôvâh**, *ho-vaw'*; another form for 1942; *ruin:*—mischief.

1944. הוֹהָם **Hôwhâm**, *ho-hawm'*; of uncert. der.; *Hoham*, a Canaanitish king:—Hoham.

1945. הוֹי **hôwy**, *hoh'ee*; a prol. form of 1930 [akin to 188]; *oh!:*—ah, alas, ho, O, woe.

1946. הוּךְ **hûwk** (Chald.), *hook;* corresp. to 1981; to *go;* caus. to *bring:*—bring again, come, go (up).

1947. הוֹלֵלָה **hôwlêlâh**, *ho-lay-law'*; fem. act. part. of 1984; *folly:*—madness.

1948. הוֹלֵלוּת **hôwlêlûwth**, *ho-lay-looth'*; from act. part. of 1984; *folly:*—madness.

1949. הוּם **hûwm**, *hoom;* a prim. root [comp. 2000]; to *make an uproar*, or *agitate* greatly:—destroy, move, make a noise, put, ring again.

1950. הוֹמָם **Hôwmâm**, *ho-mawm'*; from 2000; *raging; Homam*, an Edomitish chieftain:—Homam. Comp. 1967.

1951. הוּן **hûwn**, *hoon;* a prim. root; prop. to *be naught*, i.e. (fig.) to *be* (caus. *act*) *light:*—be ready.

1952. הוֹן **hôwn**, *hone;* from the same as 1951 in the sense of 202; *wealth;* by impl. *enough:*—enough, + for nought, riches, substance, wealth.

1953. הוֹשָׁמָע **Hôwshâmâ'**, *ho-shaw-maw'*; from 3068 and 8085; *Jehovah has heard; Hoshama*, an Isr.:—Hoshama.

1954. הוֹשֵׁעַ **Hôwshêă'**, *ho-shay'-ah*; from 3467; *deliverer; Hosheä*, the name of five Isr.:—Hosea, Hoshea, Oshea.

1955. הוֹשַׁעְיָה **Hôwsha'yâh**, *ho-shah-yaw'*; from 3467 and 3050; *Jah has saved; Hoshajah*, the name of two Isr.:—Hoshaiah.

1956. הוֹתִיר **Hôwthîyr**, *ho-theer'*; from 3498; *he has caused to remain; Hothir*, an Isr.:—Hothir.

1957. הָזָה **hâzâh**, *haw-zaw'*; a prim. root [comp. 2372]; to *dream:*—sleep.

1958. הִי **hîy**, *he;* for 5092; *lamentation:*—woe.

הִיא **hîy'**. See 1931, 1932.

1959. הֵידָד **hêydâd**, *hay-dawd'*; from an unused root (mean. to *shout*); *acclamation:*—shout (-ing).

1960. הֻיְּדָה **huyᵉdâh**, *hoo-yed-aw'*; from the same as 1959; prop. an *acclaim*, i.e. a *choir* of singers:—thanksgiving.

1961. הָיָה **hâyâh**, *haw-yaw'*; a prim. root [comp. 1933]; to *exist*, i.e. *be* or *become, come to pass* (always emphatic, and not a mere copula or auxiliary):—beacon, × altogether, be (-come, accomplished, committed, like), break, cause, come (to pass), continue, do, faint, fall, + follow, happen, × have, last, pertain, quit (one-)self, require, × use.

1962. הַיָּה **hayâh**, *hah-yaw'*; another form for 1943; *ruin:*—calamity.

1963. הֵיךְ **hêyk**, *hake;* another form for 349; *how?:*—how.

1964. הֵיכָל **hêykâl**, *hay-kawl'*; prob. from 3201 (in the sense of *capacity*); a large public building, such as a *palace* or *temple:*—palace, temple.

1965. הֵיכַל **hêykal** (Chald.), *hay-kal'*; corresp. to 1964:—palace, temple.

1966. הֵילֵל **hêylêl**, *hay-lale'*; from 1984 (in the sense of *brightness*); the *morning-star:*—lucifer.

1967. הֵימָם **Hêymâm**, *hay-mawm'*; another form for 1950; *Hemam*, an Idumæan:—Hemam.

1968. הֵימָן **Hêymân**, *hay-mawn'*; prob. from 539; *faithful; Heman*, the name of at least two Isr.:—Heman.

1969. הִין **hîyn**, *heen*; prob. of Eg. or.; a *hin* or liquid measure:—hin.

1970. הָכַר **hâkar**, *haw-kar'*; a prim. root; appar. to *injure*:—make self strange.

1971. הַכָּרָה **hakkârâh**, *hak-kaw-raw'*; from 5234; *respect*, i.e. partiality:—shew.

הַל **hal**. See 1973.

1972. הָלָא **hâlâ'**, *haw-law'*; prob. denom. from 1973; to *remove* or be *remote*:—cast far off.

1973. הָלְאָה **hâl^eâh**, *haw-leh-aw'*; from the prim. form of the art. [הַל **hal**]; *to the distance*, i.e. *far away*; also (of time) *thus far*:—back, beyond, (hence-) forward, hitherto, thenceforth, yonder.

1974. הִלּוּל **hillûwl**, *hil-lool'*; from 1984 (in the sense of *rejoicing*); a *celebration* of thanksgiving for harvest:—merry, praise.

1975. הַלָּז **hallâz**, *hal-lawz'*; from 1976; *this* or *that*:—side, that, this.

1976. הַלָּזֶה **hallâzeh**, *hal-law-zeh'*; from the art. [see 1973] and 2088; *this very*:—this.

1977. הַלֵּזוּ **hallêzûw**, *hal-lay-zoo'*; another form of 1976; *that*:—this.

1978. הָלִיךְ **hâlîyk**, *haw-leek'*; from 1980; a *walk*, i.e. (by impl.) a *step*:—step.

1979. הֲלִיכָה **hălîykâh**, *hal-ee-kaw'*; fem. of 1978; a *walking*; by impl. a *procession* or *march*, a *caravan*:—company, going, walk, way.

1980. הָלַךְ **hâlak**, *haw-lak'*; akin to 3212; a prim. root; to *walk* (in a great variety of applications, lit. and fig.):—(all) along, apace, behave (self), come, (on) continually, be conversant, depart, + be eased, enter, exercise (self), + follow, forth, forward, get, go (about, abroad, along, away, forward, on, out, up and down), + greater, grow, be wont to haunt, lead, march, × more and more, move (self), needs, on, pass (away), be at the point, quite, run (along), + send, speedily, spread, still, surely, + tale-bearer, + travel (-ler), walk (abroad, on, to and fro, up and down, to places), wander, wax, way-] faring man, × be weak, whirl.

1981. הֲלַךְ **hălak** (Chald.), *hal-ak'*; corresp. to 1980 [comp. 1946]; to *walk*:—walk.

1982. הֵלֶךְ **hêlek**, *hay'-lek*; from 1980; prop. a *journey*, i.e. (by impl.) a *wayfarer*; also a *flowing*:—× dropped, traveller.

1983. הֲלָךְ **hălâk** (Chald.), *hal-awk'*; from 1981; prop. a *journey*, i.e. (by impl.) *toll* on goods at a road:—custom.

1984. הָלַל **hâlal**, *haw-lal'*; a prim. root; to *be clear* (orig. of sound, but usually of color); to *shine*; hence to *make a show*, to *boast*; and thus to *be* (clamorously) *foolish*; to *rave*; causat. to *celebrate*; also to *stultify*:—(make) boast (self), celebrate, commend, (deal, make), fool (-ish, -ly), glory, give [light], be (make, feign self) mad (against), give in marriage, [sing, be worthy of] praise, rage, renowned, shine.

1985. הִלֵּל **Hillêl**, *hil-layl'*; from 1984; *praising* (namely God); *Hillel*, an Isr.:—Hillel.

1986. הָלַם **hâlam**, *haw-lam'*; a prim. root; to *strike* down; by impl. to *hammer*, *stamp*, *conquer*, *disband*:—beat (down), break (down), overcome, smite (with the hammer).

1987. הֵלֶם **Hêlem**, *hay'-lem*; from 1986; *smiter*; *Helem*, the name of two Isr.:—Helem.

1988. הֲלֹם **hălôm**, *hal-ome'*; from the art. [see 1973]; *hither*:—here, hither (-[to]), thither.

1989. הַלְמוּת **halmûwth**, *hal-mooth'*; from 1986; a *hammer* (or *mallet*):—hammer.

1990. הָם **Hâm**, *hawm*; of uncert. der.; *Ham*, a region of Pal.:—Ham.

1991. הֵם **hêm**, *haym*; from 1993; *abundance*, i.e. *wealth*:—any of theirs.

1992. הֵם **hêm**, *haym*; or (prol.)

הֵמָּה **hêmmâh**, *haym'-maw*; masc. plur. from 1931; *they* (only used when emphatic):—it, like, × (how, so) many (soever, more as) they (be), (the) same, × so, × such, their, them, these, they, those, which, who, whom, withal, ye.

1993. הָמָה **hâmâh**, *haw-maw'*; a prim. root [comp. 1949]; to *make a loud sound* (like Engl. "hum"); by impl. to *be in great commotion* or *tumult*, to *rage*, *war*, *moan*, *clamor*:—clamorous, concourse, cry aloud, be disquieted, loud, mourn, be moved, make a noise, rage, roar, sound, be troubled, make in tumult, tumultuous, be in an uproar.

1994. הִמּוֹ **himmôw** (Chald.), *him-mo'*; or (prol.)

הִמּוֹן **himmôwn** (Chald.), *him-mone'*; corresp. to 1992; *they*:—× are, them, those.

1995. הָמוֹן **hâmôwn**, *haw-mone'*; or

הָמֹן **hâmôn** (Ezek. 5 : 7), *haw-mone'*; from 1993; a *noise*, *tumult*, *crowd*; also *disquietude*, *wealth*:—abundance, company, many, multitude, multiply, noise, riches, rumbling, sounding, store, tumult.

הַמֹּלֶכֶת **ham-môleketh**. See 4447.

1996. הֲמוֹן גּוֹג **Hămôwn Gôwg**, *ham-one' gohg*; from 1995 and 1463; the *multitude of Gog*; the fanciful name of an emblematic place in Pal.:—Hamon-gog.

1997. הֲמוֹנָה **Hămôwnâh**, *ham-o-naw'*; fem. of 1995; *multitude*; *Hamonah*, the same as 1996:—Hamonah.

הֲמוּנֵךְ° **hămûwnêk**. See 2002.

1998. הֶמְיָה **hemyâh**, *hem-yaw'*; from 1993; *sound*:—noise.

1999. הֲמֻלָּה **hămullâh**, *ham-ool-law'*; or (too fully)

הֲמוּלָּה **hămûwllâh** (Jer. 11 : 16), *ham-ool-law'*; fem. pass. part. of an unused root mean. to *rush* (as rain with a windy roar); a *sound*:—speech, tumult.

הַמֶּלֶךְ **ham-melek**. See 4429.

2000. הָמַם **hâmam**, *haw-mam'*; a prim. root [comp. 1949, 1993]; prop. to *put in commotion*; by impl. to *disturb*, *drive*, *destroy*:—break, consume, crush, destroy, discomfit, trouble, vex.

הָמֹן **hâmôn**. See 1995.

2001. הָמָן **Hâmân**, *haw-mawn'*; of for. der.; *Haman*, a Pers. vizier:—Haman.

2002. הַמְנִיךְ **hamnîyk** (Chald.), *ham-neek'*; but the text is

הֲמוּנֵךְ° **hămûwnêk**, *ham-oo-nayk'*; of for. or.; a *necklace*:—chain.

2003. הָמָס **hâmâç**, *haw-mawce'*; from an unused root appar. mean. to *crackle*; a dry *twig* or *brushwood*:—melting.

2004. הֵן **hên**, *hane*; fem. plur. from 1931; *they* (only used when emphatic):—× in, such like, (with) them, thereby, therein, (more than) they, wherein, in which, whom, withal.

2005. הֵן **hên**, *hane*; a prim. particle; *lo!*; also (as expressing surprise) *if*:—behold, if, lo, though.

2006. הֵן **hên** (Chald.), *hane*; corresp. to 2005: *lo!* also *there* [-fore], [un-] *less*, *whether*, *but*, *if*:—(that) if, or, whether.

2007. הֵנָּה **hênnâh**, *hane'-naw*; prol. for 2004; *themselves* (often used emphat. for the copula, also in indirect relation):—× in, × such (and such things), their, (into) them, thence, therein, these, they (had), on this side, those, wherein.

2008. הֵנָּה **hênnâh**, *hane'-naw*; from 2004; *hither* or *thither* (but used both of place and time):—here, hither [-to], now, on this (that) side, + since, this (that) way, thitherward, + thus far, to . . . fro, + yet.

2009. הִנֵּה **hinnêh**, *hin-nay'*; prol. for 2005; *lo!*:—behold, lo, see.

2010. הֲנָחָה **hănâchâh**, *han-aw-khaw'*; from 5117; *permission* of rest, i.e. *quiet*:—release.

2011. הִנֹּם **Hinnôm**, *hin-nome'*; prob. of for. or.; *Hinnom*, appar. a Jebusite:—Hinnom.

2012. הֵנַע **Hêna'**, *hay-nah'*; prob. of for. der. *Hena*, a place appar. in Mesopotamia:—Hena.

2013. הָסָה **hâçâh**, *haw-saw'*; a prim. root; to *hush*:—hold peace (tongue), (keep) silence, be silent, still.

2014. הֲפֻגָה **hăphûgâh**, *haf-oo-gaw'*; from 6318; *relaxation*:—intermission.

2015. הָפַךְ **haphak**, *haw-fak'*; a prim. root; to *turn* about or over; by impl. to *change*, *overturn*, *return*, *pervert*:—× become, change, come, be converted, give, make [a bed], overthrow (-turn), perverse, retire, tumble, turn (again, aside, back, to the contrary, every way).

2016. הֶפֶךְ **hephek**, *heh'-fek*; or

הֵפֶךְ **hêphek**, *hay'-fek*; from 2015; a *turn*, i.e. the *reverse*:—contrary.

2017. הֹפֶךְ **hôphek**, *ho'-fek*; from 2015; an *upset*, i.e. (abstr.) *perversity*:—turning of things upside down.

2018. הֲפֵכָה **hăphêkâh**, *haf-ay-kaw'*; fem. of 2016; *destruction*:—overthrow.

2019. הֲפַכְפַּךְ **hăphakpak**, *haf-ak-pak'*; by redupl. from 2015; *very perverse*:—froward.

2020. הַצָּלָה **hatstsâlâh**, *hats-tsaw-law'*; from 5337; *rescue*:—deliverance.

2021. הֹצֶן **hôtsen**, *ho'-tsen*; from an unused root mean. appar. to *be sharp* or *strong*; a *weapon* of war:—chariot.

2022. הַר **har**, *har*; a short. form of 2042; a *mountain* or *range* of hills (sometimes used fig.):—hill (country), mount (-ain), × promotion.

2023. הֹר **Hôr**, *hore*; another form for 2022; *mountain*; *Hor*, the name of a peak in Idumæa and of one in Syria:—Hor.

2024. הָרָא **Hârâ'**, *haw-raw'*; perh. from 2022; *mountainousness*; *Hara*, a region of Media:—Hara.

2025. הַרְאֵל **har'êl**, *har-ale'*; from 2022 and 410; *mount of God*; fig. the *altar* of burnt-offering:—altar. Comp. 739.

2026. הָרַג **hârag**, *haw-rag'*; a prim. root; to *smite* with deadly intent:—destroy, out of hand, kill, murder (-er), put to [death], make [slaughter], slay (-er), × surely.

2027. הֶרֶג **hereg**, *heh'-reg*; from 2026; *slaughter*:—be slain, slaughter.

2028. הֲרֵגָה **hărêgâh**, *har-ay-gaw'*; fem. of 2027; *slaughter*:—slaughter.

2029. הָרָה **hârâh**, *haw-raw'*; a prim. root; to *be* (or *become*) *pregnant*, *conceive* (lit. or fig.):—been, be with child, conceive, progenitor.

2030. הָרֶה **hâreh**, *haw-reh'*; or

הָרִי **hârîy** (Hos. 14 : 1), *haw-ree'*; from 2029; *pregnant*:—(be, woman) with child, conceive, × great.

2031. הַרְהֹר **harhôr** (Chald.), *har-hor'*; from a root corresp. to 2029; a mental *conception*:—thought.

2032. הֵרוֹן **hêrôwn**, *hay-rone'*; or

הֵרָיוֹן **hêrâyôwn**, *hay-raw-yone'*; from 2029; *pregnancy*:—conception.

2033. הֲרוֹרִי **Hărôwrîy**, *har-o-ree'*; another form for 2043; a *Harorite* or mountaineer:—Harorite.

2034. הֲרִיסָה **hărîyçâh**, *har-ee-saw'*; from 2040; something *demolished*:—ruin.

2035. הֲרִיסוּת **hărîyçûwth**, *har-ee-sooth'*; from 2040; *demolition*:—destruction.

2036. הֹרָם **Hôrâm**, *ho-rawm'*; from an unused root (mean. to *tower up*); *high; Horam*, a Canaanitish king:—Horam.

2037. הָרֻם **Hârûm**, *haw-room'*; pass. part. of the same as 2036; *high; Harum*, an Isr.:—Harum.

2038. הַרְמוֹן **harmôwn**, *har-mone'*; from the same as 2036; a *castle* (from its height):—palace.

2039. הָרָן **Hârân**, *haw-rawn'*; perh. from 2022; *mountaineer; Haran*, the name of two men:—Haran.

2040. הָרַס **hâraç**, *haw-ras'*; a prim. root; to *pull* down or in pieces, *break, destroy*:—beat down, break (down, through), destroy, overthrow, pluck down, pull down, ruin, throw down, × utterly.

2041. הֶרֶס **hereç**, *heh'-res*; from 2040; *demolition*:—destruction.

2042. הָרָר **hârâr**, *haw-rawr'*; from an unused root mean. to *loom* up; a *mountain*:—hill, mount (-ain).

2043. הֲרָרִי **Hărârîy** *hah-raw-ree'*; or
הָרָרִי **Hârârîy** (2 Sam. 23 : 11), *haw-raw-ree'*; or
הָאֲרָרִי **Hâ'rârîy** (2 Sam. 23 : 34, last clause), *haw-raw-ree'*; appar. from 2042; a *mountaineer*:—Hararite.

2044. הָשֵׁם **Hâshêm**, *haw-shame'*; perh. from the same as 2828; *wealthy; Hashem*, an Isr.:—Hashem.

2045. הַשְׁמָעוּת **hâshmâ'ûwth**, *hashmaw-ooth'*; from 8085; *announcement*:—to cause to hear.

2046. הִתּוּךְ **hittûwk**, *hit-took'*; from 5413; a *melting*:—is melted.

2047. הֲתָךְ **Hăthâk**, *hath-awk'*; prob. of for. or.; *Hathak*, a Pers. eunuch:—Hatach.

2048. הָתַל **hâthal**, *haw-thal'*; a prim. root; to *deride*; by impl. to *cheat*:—deal deceitfully, deceive, mock.

2049. הָתֹל **hâthôl**, *haw-thole'*; from 2048 (only in plur. collect.); a *derision*:—mocker.

2050. הָתַת **hâthath'**, *haw-thath'*; a prim. root; prop. to *break* in upon, i.e. to *assail*:—imagine mischief.

ו

2051. וְדָן **Vedân**, *ved-awn'*; perh. for 5730; *Vedan* (or Aden), a place in Arabia:—Dan also.

2052. וָהֵב **Vâhêb**, *vaw-habe'*; of uncert. der.; *Vaheb*, a place in Moab:—what he did.

2053. וָו **vâv**, *vaw*; prob. a *hook* (the name of the sixth Heb. letter):—hook.

2054. וָזָר **vâzâr**, *vaw-zawr'*; presumed to be from an unused root mean. to *bear guilt*; *crime*:—× strange.

2055. וַיְזָתָא **Vayezâthâ'**, *vah-yez-aw'-thaw*; of for. or.; *Vajezatha*, a son of Haman:—Vajezatha.

2056. וָלָד **vâlâd**, *vaw-lawd'*; for 3206; a *boy*:—child.

2057. וַנְיָה **Vanyâh**, *van-yaw'*; perh. for 6043; *Vanjah*, an Isr.:—Vaniah.

2058. וָפְסִי **Vophçîy**, *vof-see'*; prob. from 3254; *additional; Vophsi*, an Isr.:—Vophsi.

2059. וַשְׁנִי **Vashnîy**, *vash-nee'*; prob. from 3461; *weak; Vashni*, an Isr.:—Vashni.

2060. וַשְׁתִּי **Vashtîy**, *vash-tee'*; of Pers. or.; *Vashti*, the queen of Xerxes:—Vashti.

ז

2061. זְאֵב **ze'êb**, *zeh-abe'*; from an unused root mean. to *be yellow*; a *wolf*:—wolf.

2062. זְאֵב **Ze'êb**, *zeh-abe'*; the same as 2061; *Zeëb*, a Midianitish prince:—Zeeb.

2063. זֹאת **zô'th**, *zothe'*; irreg. fem. of 2089; *this* (often used adv.):—hereby (-in, -with), it, likewise, the one (other, same), she, so (much), such (deed), that, therefore, these, this (thing), thus.

2064. זָבַד **zâbad**, *zaw-bad'*; a prim. root; to *confer*:—endure.

2065. זֶבֶד **zebed**, *zeh'-bed*; from 2064; a *gift*:—dowry.

2066. זָבָד **Zâbâd**, *zaw-bawd'*; from 2064; *giver; Zabad*, the name of seven Isr.:—Zabad.

2067. זַבְדִּי **Zabdîy**, *zab-dee'*; from 2065; *giving; Zabdi*, the name of four Isr.:—Zabdi.

2068. זַבְדִּיאֵל **Zabdîy'êl**, *zab-dee-ale'*; from 2065 and 410; *gift of God; Zabdiel*, the name of two Isr.:—Zabdiel.

2069. זְבַדְיָה **Zebadyâh**, *zeb-ad-yaw'*; or
זְבַדְיָהוּ **Zebadyâhûw**, *zeb-ad-yaw'-hoo*; from 2064 and 3050; *Jah has given; Zebadjah*, the name of nine Isr.:—Zebadiah.

2070. זְבוּב **zebûwb**, *zeb-oob'*; from an unused root (mean. to *flit*); a *fly* (espec. one of a stinging nature):—fly.

2071. זָבוּד **Zâbûwd**, *zaw-bood'*; from 2064; *given; Zabud*, an Isr.:—Zabud.

2072. זַבּוּד **Zabbûwd**, *zab-bood'*; a form of 2071; *given; Zabbud*, an Isr.:—Zabbud.

2073. זְבוּל **zebûwl**, *ze-bool'*; or
זְבֻל **zebûl**, *zeb-ool'*; from 2082; a *residence*:—dwell in, dwelling, habitation.

2074. זְבוּלוּן **Zebûwlûwn**, *zeb-oo-loon'*; or
זְבֻלוּן **Zebûlûwn**, *zeb-oo-loon'*; or
זְבוּלֻן **Zebûwlûn**, *zeb-oo-loon'*; from 2082; *habitation; Zebulon*, a son of Jacob; also his territory and tribe:—Zebulun.

2075. זְבוּלֹנִי **Zebûwlônîy**, *zeb-oo-lo-nee'*; patron. from 2074; a *Zebulonite* or desc. of Zebulun:—Zebulonite.

2076. זָבַח **zâbach**, *zaw-bakh'*; a prim. root; to *slaughter* an animal (usually in sacrifice):—kill, offer, (do) sacrifice, slay.

2077. זֶבַח **zebach**, *zeh'-bakh*; from 2076; prop. a *slaughter*, i.e. the *flesh* of an animal; by impl. a *sacrifice* (the victim or the act):—offer (-ing), sacrifice.

2078. זֶבַח **Zebach**, *zeh'-bakh*; the same as 2077; *sacrifice; Zebach*, a Midianitish prince:—Zebah.

2079. זַבַּי **Zabbay**, *zab-bah'ee*; prob. by orth. err. for 2140; *Zabbai* (or Zaccai), an Isr.:—Zabbai.

2080. זְבִידָה **Zebîydâh**, *zeb-ee-daw'*; fem. from 2064; *giving; Zebidah*, an Israelitess:—Zebudah.

2081. זְבִינָא **Zebîynâ'**, *zeb-ee-naw'*; from an unused root (mean. to *purchase*); *gainfulness; Zebina*, an Isr.:—Zebina.

2082. זָבַל **zâbal**, *zaw-bal'*; a prim. root; appar. prop. to *inclose*, i.e. to *reside*:—dwell with.

2083. זְבֻל **Zebûl**, *zeb-ool'*; the same as 2073; *dwelling; Zebul*, an Isr.:—Zebul. Comp. 2073.

זְבֻלוּן **Zebûlûwn**. See 2074.

2084. זְבַן **zeban** (Chald.), *zeb-an'*; corresp. to the root of 2081; to *acquire* by purchase:—gain.

2085. זָג **zâg**, *zawg*; from an unused root prob. mean. to *inclose*; the *skin* of a grape:—husk.

2086. זֵד **zêd**, *zade'*; from 2102; *arrogant*:—presumptuous, proud.

2087. זָדוֹן **zâdôwn**, *zaw-done'*; from 2102; *arrogance*:—presumptuously, pride, proud (man).

2088. זֶה **zeh**, *zeh*; a prim. word; the masc. demonst. pron., *this* or *that*:—he, × hence, × here, it (-self), × now, × of him, the one . . . the other, × than the other, (× out of) the (self) same, such (an one) that, these, this (hath, man), on this side . . . on that side, × thus, very, which. Comp. 2063, 2090, 2097, 2098.

2089. זֶה **zeh** (1 Sam. 17 : 34), *zeh*; by perm. for 7716; a *sheep*:—lamb.

2090. זֹה **zôh**, *zo*; for 2088; *this* or *that*:—as well as another, it, this, that, thus and thus.

2091. זָהָב **zâhâb**, *zaw-hawb'*; from an unused root mean. to *shimmer*; *gold*; fig. something *gold-colored* (i.e. *yellow*), as *oil*, a *clear sky*:—gold (-en), fair weather.

2092. זָהַם **zâham**, *zaw-ham'*; a prim. root; to be *rancid*, i.e. (trans.) to *loathe*:—abhor.

2093. זַהַם **Zaham**, *zah'-ham*; from 2092; *loathing; Zaham*, an Isr.:—Zaham.

2094. זָהַר **zâhar**, *zaw-har'*; a prim. root; to *gleam*; fig. to *enlighten* (by caution):—admonish, shine, teach, (give) warn (-ing).

2095. זְהַר **zehar** (Chald.), *zeh-har'*; corresp. to 2094; (pass.) *be admonished*:—take heed.

2096. זֹהַר **zôhar**, *zo'-har*; from 2094; *brilliancy*:—brightness.

2097. זוֹ **zôw**, *zo*; for 2088; *this* or *that*:—that, this.

2098. זוּ **zûw**, *zoo*; for 2088; *this* or *that*:—that this, × wherein, which, whom.

2099. זִו **Zîv**, *zeev'*; prob. from an unused root mean. to *be prominent*; prop. *brightness* [comp. 2122], i.e. (fig.) the month of *flowers; Ziv* (corresp. to Ijar or May):—Zif.

2100. זוּב **zûwb**, *zoob*; a prim. root; to *flow* freely (as water), i.e. (spec.) to *have a* (sexual) *flux*; fig. to *waste* away; also to *overflow*:—flow, gush out, have a (running) issue, pine away, run.

2101. זוֹב **zôwb**, *zobe*; from 2100; a seminal or menstrual *flux*:—issue.

2102. זוּד **zûwd**, *zood*; or (by perm.)
זִיד **zîyd**, *zeed*; a prim. root; to *seethe*; fig. to *be insolent*:—be proud, deal proudly, presume, (come) presumptuously, sod.

2103. זוּד **zûwd** (Chald.), *zood*; corresp. to 2102; to *be proud*:—in pride.

2104. זוּזִים **Zûwzîym**, *zoo-zeem'*; plur. prob. from the same as 2123; *prominent; Zuzites*, an aboriginal tribe of Pal.:—Zuzims.

2105. זוֹחֵת **Zôwchêth**, *zo-khayth'*; of uncert. or.; *Zocheth*, an Isr.:—Zoheth.

2106. זָוִית **zâvîyth**, *zaw-veeth'*; appar. from the same root as 2099 (in the sense of *prominence*); an *angle* (as *projecting*), i.e. (by impl.) a *corner-column* (or *anta*):—corner (stone).

2107. זוּל **zûwl**, *zool*; a prim. root [comp. 2151]; prob. to *shake* out, i.e. (by impl.) to *scatter* profusely; fig. to *treat lightly*:—lavish, despise.

2108. זוּלָה **zûwlâh**, *zoo-law'*; from 2107; prop. *scattering*, i.e. *removal*; used adv. *except*:—beside, but, only, save.

2109. זוּן **zûwn** *zoon*; a prim. root; perh. prop. to *be plump*, i.e. (trans.) to *nourish*:—feed.

2110. זוּן **zûwn** (Chald.), *zoon*; corresp. to 2109:—feed.

2111. זוּעַ **zûwa'**, *zoo'-ah*; a prim. root; prop. to *shake* off, i.e. (fig.) to *agitate* (as with fear):—move, tremble, vex.

2112. זוּעַ **zûwa'** (Chald.), *zoo'-ah*; corresp. to 2111; to *shake* (with fear):—tremble.

2113. זְוָעָה **zevâ'âh**, *zev-aw-aw'*; from 2111; *agitation, fear*:—be removed, trouble, vexation. Comp. 2189.

2114. זוּר **zûwr**, *zoor*; a prim. root; to *turn* aside (espec. for lodging); hence to *be a foreigner, strange, profane*; spec. (act. part.) to *commit adultery*:—(come from) another (man, place), fanner, go away, (e-) strange (-r, thing, woman).

2115. זוּר **zûwr**, *zoor*; a prim. root [comp. 6695]; to *press* together, *tighten*:—close, crush, thrust together.

2116. זוּרֶה **zûwreh**, *zoo-reh'*; from 2115; *trodden* on:—that which is crushed.

2117. זָזָא **zâzâ'**, *zaw-zaw'*; prob. from the root of 2123; *prominent; Zaza*, an Isr.:—Zaza.

2118. זָחַח **zâchach**, *zaw-khakh'*; a prim. root; to *shove* or *displace*:—loose.

2119. זָחַל **zâchal**, *zaw-khal'*; a prim. root; to *crawl*; by impl. to *fear*:—be afraid, serpent, worm.

2120. זֹחֶלֶת **Zôcheleth**, *zo-kheh'-leth*; fem. act. part. of 2119; *crawling* (i.e. *serpent*); *Zocheleth*, a boundary stone in Pal.:—Zoheleth.

2121. זֵידוֹן **zêydôwn**, *zay-dohn'*; from 2102; *boiling* of water, i.e. *wave*:—proud.

2122. זִיו **zîyv** (Chald.), *zeev*; corresp. to 2099; (fig.) *cheerfulness*:—brightness, countenance.

2123. זִיז **zîyz**, *zeez*; from an unused root appar. mean. to *be conspicuous*; *fulness* of the breast; also a moving *creature*:—abundance, wild beast.

2124. זִיזָא **Zîyzâ'**, *zee-zaw'*; appar. from the same as 2123; *prominence*, *Ziza*, the name of two Isr.:—Ziza.

2125. זִיזָה **Zîyzâh**, *zee-zaw'*; another form for 2124; *Zizah*, an Isr.:—Zizah.

2126. זִינָא **Zîynâ'**, *zee-naw'*; from 2109; well *fed*; or perh. an orth. err. for 2124; *Zina*, an Isr.:—Zina.

2127. זִיעַ **Zîyaʽ**, *zee'-ah*; from 2111; *agitation*; *Zia*, an Isr.:—Zia.

2128. זִיף **Zîyph**, *zeef*; from the same as 2203; *flowing*; *Ziph*, the name of a place in Pal.; also of an Isr.:—Ziph.

2129. זִיפָה **Zîyphâh**, *zee-faw'*; fem. of 2128; a *flowing*; *Ziphah*, an Isr.:—Ziphah.

2130. זִיפִי **Zîyphîy**, *zee-fee'*; patrial from 2128; a *Ziphite* or inhab. of Ziph:—Ziphim, Ziphite.

2131. זִיקָה **zîyqâh** (Isa. 50 : 11), *zee-kaw'* (fem.); and
זִק **zîq**, *zeek*; or
זֵק **zêq**, *zake*; from 2187; prop. what *leaps* forth, i.e. *flash* of fire, or a burning *arrow*; also (from the orig. sense of the root) a *bond*:—chain, fetter, firebrand, spark.

2132. זַיִת **zayith**, *zah'-yith*; prob. from an unused root [akin to 2099]; an *olive* (as yielding *illuminating* oil), the tree, the branch or the berry:—olive (tree, -yard), Olivet.

2133. זֵיתָן **Zêythân**, *zay-thawn'*; from 2132; *olive* grove; *Zethan*, an Isr.:—Zethan.

2134. זַךְ **zak**, *zak*; from 2141; *clear*:—clean, pure.

2135. זָכָה **zâkâh**, *zaw-kaw'*; a prim. root [comp. 2141]; to *be translucent*; fig. to *be innocent*:—be (make) clean, cleanse, be clear, count pure.

2136. זָכוּ **zâkûw** (Chald.), *zaw-koo'*; from a root corresp. to 2135; *purity*:—innocency.

2137. זְכוּכִית **zᵉkûwkîyth**, *zek-oo-keeth'*; from 2135; prop. *transparency*, i.e. *glass*:—crystal.

2138. זָכוּר **zâkûwr**, *zaw-koor'*; prop. pass. part. of 2142, but used for 2145; a *male* (of man or animals):—males, men-children.

2139. זַכּוּר **Zakkûwr**, *zak-koor'*; from 2142; *mindful*; *Zakkur*, the name of seven Isr.:—Zaccur, Zacchur.

2140. זַכַּי **Zakkay**, *zak-kah'ee*; from 2141; *pure*; *Zakkai*, an Isr.:—Zaccai.

2141. זָכַךְ **zâkak**, *zaw-kak'*; a prim. root [comp. 2135]; to *be transparent* or *clean* (phys. or mor.):—be (make) clean, be pure (-r).

2142. זָכַר **zâkar**, *zaw-kar'*; a prim. root; prop. to *mark* (so as to be recognized), i.e. to *remember*; by impl. to *mention*; also (as denom. from 2145) to *be male*:— × burn [incense], × earnestly, be male, (make) mention (of), be mindful, recount, record (-er), remember, make to be remembered, bring (call, come, keep, put) to (in) remembrance, × still, think on, × well.

2143. זֵכֶר **zêker**, *zay'-ker*; or
זֶכֶר **zeker**, *zeh'-ker*; from 2142; a *memento*, abstr. *recollection* (rarely if ever); by impl. *commemoration*:—memorial, memory, remembrance, scent.

2144. זֶכֶר **Zeker**, *zeh'-ker*; the same as 2143; *Zeker*, an Isr.:—Zeker.

2145. זָכָר **zâkâr**, *zaw-kawr'*; from 2142; prop. *remembered*, i.e. a *male* (of man or animals, as being the most noteworthy sex):— × him, male, man (child, -kind).

2146. זִכְרוֹן **zikrôwn**, *zik-rone'*; from 2142; a *memento* (or memorable thing, day or writing):—memorial, record.

2147. זִכְרִי **Zikrîy**, *zik-ree'*; from 2142; *memorable*; *Zicri*, the name of twelve Isr.:—Zichri.

2148. זְכַרְיָה **Zᵉkaryâh**, *zek-ar-yaw'*; or
זְכַרְיָהוּ **Zᵉkaryâhûw**, *zek-ar-yaw'-hoo*; from 2142 and 3050; *Jah has remembered*; *Zecarjah*, the name of twenty-nine Isr.:—Zachariah, Zechariah.

2149. זֻלּוּת **zullûwth**, *zool-looth'*; from 2151; prop. a *shaking*, i.e. perh. a *tempest*:—vilest.

2150. זַלְזַל **zalzal**, *zal-zal'*; by redupl. from 2151; *tremulous*, i.e. a *twig*:—sprig.

2151. זָלַל **zâlal**, *zaw-lal'*; a prim. root [comp. 2107]; to *shake* (as in the wind), i.e. to *quake*; fig. to *be loose* morally, *worthless* or *prodigal*:—blow down, glutton, riotous (eater), vile.

2152. זַלְעָפָה **zalʽâphâh**, *zal-aw-faw'*; or
זִלְעָפָה **zilʽâphâph**, *zil-aw-faw'*; from 2196; a *glow* (of wind or anger); also a *famine* (as *consuming*):—horrible, horror, terrible.

2153. זִלְפָּה **Zilpâh**, *zil-paw'*; from an unused root appar. mean. to *trickle*, as myrrh; fragrant *dropping*; *Zilpah*, Leah's maid:—Zilpah.

2154. זִמָּה **zimmâh**, *zim-maw'*; or
זַמָּה **zammâh**, *zam-maw'*; from 2161; a *plan*, espec. a bad one:—heinous crime, lewd (-ly, -ness), mischief, purpose, thought, wicked (device, mind, -ness).

2155. זִמָּה **Zimmâh**, *zim-maw'*; the same as 2154; *Zimmah*, the name of two Isr.:—Zimmah.

2156. זְמוֹרָה **zᵉmôwrâh**, *zem-o-raw'*; or
זְמֹרָה **zᵉmôrâh**, *zem-o-raw'* (fem.); and
זְמֹר **zᵉmôr**, *zem-ore'* (masc.): from 2168; a *twig* (as *pruned*):—vine, branch, slip.

2157. זַמְזֹם **Zamzôm**, *zam-zome'*; from 2161; *intriguing*; a *Zamzumite*, or native tribe of Pal.:—Zamzummim.

2158. זָמִיר **zâmîyr**, *zaw-meer'*; or
זָמִר **zâmîr**, *zaw-meer'*; and (fem.)
זְמִרָה **zᵉmîrâh**, *zem-ee-raw'*; from 2167; a *song* to be accompanied with instrumental music:—psalm (-ist), singing, song.

2159. זָמִיר **zâmîyr**, *zaw-meer'*; from 2168; a *twig* (as *pruned*):—branch.

2160. זְמִירָה **Zᵉmîyrâh**, *zem-ee-raw'*; fem. of 2158; *song*; *Zemirah*, an Isr.:—Zemira.

2161. זָמַם **zâmam**, *zaw-mam'*; a prim. root; to *plan*, usually in a bad sense:—consider, devise, imagine, plot, purpose, think (evil).

2162. זָמָם **zâmâm**, *zaw-mawm'*; from 2161; a *plot*:—wicked device.

2163. זָמַן **zâman**, *zaw-man'*; a prim. root; to *fix* (a time):—appoint.

2164. זְמַן **zᵉman** (Chald.), *zem-an'*; corresp. to 2163; to *agree* (on a time and place):—prepare.

2165. זְמָן **zᵉmân**, *zem-awn'*; from 2163; an *appointed* occasion:—season, time.

2166. זְמָן **zᵉmân** (Chald.), *zem-awn'*; from 2165; the same as 2165:—season, time.

2167. זָמַר **zâmar**, *zaw-mar'*; a prim. root [perh. ident. with 2168 through the idea of *striking* with the fingers]; prop. to *touch* the strings or parts of a musical instrument, i.e. *play* upon it; to make *music*, accompanied by the voice; hence to *celebrate* in song and music:—give praise, sing forth praises, psalms.

2168. זָמַר **zâmar**, *zaw-mar'*; a prim. root [comp. 2167, 5568, 6785]; to *trim* (a vine):—prune.

2169. זֶמֶר **zemer**, *zeh'-mer*; appar. from 2167 or 2168; a *gazelle* (from its lightly *touching* the ground):—chamois.

2170. זְמָר **zᵉmâr** (Chald.), *zem-awr'*; from a root corresp. to 2167; instrumental *music*:—musick.

זָמִר **zâmîr**. See 2158.

זְמֹר **zᵉmôr**. See 2156.

2171. זַמָּר **zammâr** (Chald.), *zam-mawr'*; from the same as 2170; an instrumental *musician*:—singer.

2172. זִמְרָה **zimrâh**, *zim-raw'*; from 2167; a *musical* piece or *song* to be accompanied by an instrument:—melody, psalm.

2173 זִמְרָה **zimrâh**, *zim-raw'*; from 2168; *pruned* (i.e. *choice*) fruit:—best fruit.

זְמִרָה **zᵉmîrâh**. See 2158.

זְמֹרָה **zᵉmôrâh**. See 2156.

2174. זִמְרִי **Zimrîy**, *zim-ree'*; from 2167; *musical*; *Zimri*, the name of five Isr., and of an Arabian tribe:—Zimri.

2175. זִמְרָן **Zimrân**, *zim-rawn'*; from 2167; *musical*; *Zimran*, a son of Abraham by Keturah:—Zimran.

2176. זִמְרָת **zimrâth**, *zim-rawth'*; from 2167; instrumental *music*; by impl. *praise*:—song.

2177. זַן **zan**, *zan*; from 2109; prop. *nourished* (or fully *developed*), i.e. a *form* or *sort*:—divers kinds, × all manner of store.

2178. זַן **zan** (Chald.), *zan*; corresp. to 2177; *sort*:—kind.

2179. זָנַב **zânab**, *zaw-nab'*; a prim. root mean. to *wag*; used only as a denom. from 2180; to *curtail*, i.e. *cut* off the rear:—smite the hindmost.

2180. זָנָב **zânâb**, *zaw-nawb'*; from 2179 (in the orig. sense of *flapping*); the *tail* (lit. or fig.):—tail.

2181. זָנָה **zânâh**, *zaw-naw'*; a prim. root [highly *fed* and therefore *wanton*]; to *commit adultery* (usually of the female, and less often of simple fornication, rarely of involuntary ravishment); fig. to *commit idolatry* (the Jewish people being regarded as the spouse of Jehovah):—(cause to) commit fornication, × continually, × great, (be an, play the) harlot, (cause to be, play the) whore, (commit, fall to) whoredom, (cause to) go a-whoring, whorish.

2182. זָנוֹחַ **Zânôwach**, *zaw-no'-akh*; from 2186; *rejected*; *Zanoach*, the name of two places in Pal.:—Zanoah.

2183. זָנוּן **zânûwn**, *zaw-noon'*; from 2181; *adultery*; fig. *idolatry*:—whoredom.

2184. זְנוּת **zᵉnûwth**, *zen-ooth'*; from 2181; *adultery*, i.e. (fig.) *infidelity*, *idolatry*:—whoredom.

2185. זֹנוֹת **zônôwth**, *zo-noth'*; regarded by some as if from 2109 or an unused root, and applied to military *equipments*; but evidently the fem. plur. act. part. of 2181; *harlots*:—armour.

2186. זָנַח **zânach**, *zaw-nakh'*; a prim. root mean. to *push* aside, i.e. *reject*, *forsake*, *fail*:—cast away (off), remove far away (off).

2187. זָנַק **zânaq**, *zaw-nak'*; a prim. root; prop. to *draw together* the feet (as an animal about to dart upon its prey), i.e. to *spring* forward:—leap.

2188. זֵעָה **zêʽâh**, *zay-aw'*; from 2111 (in the sense of 3154); *perspiration*:—sweat.

2189. זַעֲוָה **zaʽăvâh**, *zah-av-aw'*; by transp. for 2113; *agitation*, *maltreatment*:— × removed, trouble.

2190. זַעֲוָן **Zaʽăvân**, *zah-av-awn'*; from 2111; *disquiet*; *Zaavan*, an Idumæan:—Zaavan.

2191. זְעֵיר **zᵉʽêyr**, *zeh-ayr'*; from an unused root [akin (by perm.) to 6819], mean. to *dwindle*; *small*:—little.

2192. זְעֵיר **zᵉʽêyr** (Chald.), *zeh-ayr'*; corresp. to 2191:—*little*.

2193. זָעַךְ **zâʽak**, *zaw-ak'*; a prim. root; to *extinguish*:—be extinct.

2194. זָעַם **zâʽam**, *zaw-am'*; a prim. root; prop. to *foam* at the mouth, i.e. to *be enraged*:—abhor, abominable, (be) angry, defy, (have) indignation.

2195. זַעַם **zaʻam**, *zah'-am*; from 2194; strictly *froth* at the mouth, i.e. (fig.) *fury* (espec. of God's displeasure with sin):—angry, indignation, rage.

2196. זָעַף **zâʻaph**, *zaw-af'*; a prim. root; prop. to *boil* up, i.e. (fig.) to *be peevish* or *angry*:—fret, sad, worse liking, be wroth.

2197. זַעַף **zaʻaph**, *zah'-af*; from 2196; *anger*:—indignation, rage (-ing), wrath.

2198. זָעֵף **zâʻêph**, *zaw-afe'*; from 2196; *angry*:—displeased.

2199. זָעַק **zâʻaq**, *zaw-ak'*; a prim. root; to *shriek* (from anguish or danger); by anal. (as a herald) to *announce* or *convene* publicly:—assemble, call (together), (make a) cry (out), come with such a company, gather (together), cause to be proclaimed.

2200. זְעִק **zeʻiq** (Chald.), *zeh'-eek*; corresp. to 2199; to *make an outcry*:—cry.

2201. זַעַק **zaʻaq**, *zah'-ak*; and (fem.)

זְעָקָה **zeʻâqâh**, *zeh-aw-kaw'*; from 2199; a *shriek* or *outcry*:—cry (-ing).

2202. זִפְרֹן **Ziphrôn**, *zi-frone'*; from an unused root (mean. to *be fragrant*); *Ziphron*, a place in Pal.:—Ziphron.

2203. זֶפֶת **zepheth**, *zeh'-feth*; from an unused root (mean. to *liquify*); *asphalt* (from its tendency to *soften* in the sun):—pitch.

זִק **zîq**, or זֵק **zêq**. See 2131.

2204. זָקֵן **zâqên**, *zaw-kane'*; a prim. root; to *be old*:—aged man, be (wax) old (man).

2205. זָקֵן **zâqên**, *zaw-kane'*; from 2204; *old*:—aged, ancient (man), elder (-est), old (man, men and . . . women), senator.

2206. זָקָן **zâqân**, *zaw-kawn'*; from 2204; the *beard* (as indicating *age*):—beard.

2207. זֹקֶן **zôqen**, *zo'-ken*; from 2204; old *age*:—age.

2208. זָקֻן **zâqûn**, *zaw-koon'*; prop. pass. part. of 2204 (used only in the plur. as a noun); *old age*:—old age.

2209. זִקְנָה **ziqnâh**, *zik-naw'*; fem. of 2205; old *age*:—old (age).

2210 זָקַף **zâqaph**, *zaw-kaf'*; a prim. root; to *lift*, i.e. (fig.) *comfort*:—raise (up).

2211. זְקַף **zeqaph** (Chald.), *zek-af'*; corresp. to 2210; to *hang*, i.e. *impale*:—set up.

2212. זָקַק **zâqaq**, *zaw-kak'*; a prim. root; to *strain*, (fig.) *extract*, *clarify*:—fine, pour down, purge, purify, refine.

2213. זֵר **zêr**, *zare*; from 2237 (in the sense of *scattering*); a *chaplet* (as *spread* around the top), i.e. (spec.) a border *moulding*:—crown.

2214. זָרָא **zârâʼ**, *zaw-raw'*; from 2114 (in the sense of *estrangement*) [comp. 2219]; *disgust*:—loathsome.

2215. זָרַב **zârab**, *zaw-rab'*; a prim. root; to *flow* away:—wax warm.

2216. זְרֻבָּבֶל **Zerubbâbel**, *zer-oob-baw-bel'*; from 2215 and 894; *descended of* (i.e. from) *Babylon*, i.e. born there; *Zerubbabel*, an Isr.:—Zerubbabel.

2217. זְרֻבָּבֶל **Zerubbâbel** (Chald.), *zer-oob-baw-bel'*; corresp. to 2216:—Zerubbabel.

2218. זֶרֶד **Zered**, *zeh'-red*; from an unused root mean. to *be exuberant* in growth; lined with *shrubbery*; *Zered*, a brook E. of the Dead Sea:—Zared, Zered.

2219. זָרָה **zârâh**, *zaw-raw'*; a prim. root [comp. 2114; to *toss* about; by impl. to *diffuse*, *winnow*:—cast away, compass, disperse, fan, scatter (away), spread, strew, winnow.

2220. זְרוֹעַ **zerôwaʻ**, *zer-o'-ah*; or (short.)

זְרֹעַ **zerôaʻ**, *zer-o'-ah*; and (fem.)

זְרוֹעָה **zerôwʻâh**, *zer-o-aw'*; or

זְרֹעָה **zerôʻâh**, *zer-o-aw'*; from 2232; the *arm* (as *stretched* out), or (of animals) the *foreleg*; fig. *force*:—arm, + help, mighty, power, shoulder, strength.

2221. זֵרוּעַ **zêrûwaʻ**, *zay-roo'-ah*; from 2232; something *sown*, i.e. a *plant*:—sowing, thing that is sown.

2222. זַרְזִיף **zarzîyph**, *zar-zeef'*; by redupl. from an unused root mean. to *flow*; a *pouring rain*:—water.

זְרוֹעָה **zerôwʻâh**. See 2220.

2223. זַרְזִיר **zarzîyr**, *zar-zeer'*; by redupl. from 2115; prop. tightly *girt*, i.e. prob. a *racer*, or some fleet animal (as being *slender* in the waist):— + greyhound.

2224. זָרַח **zârach**, *zaw-rakh'*; a prim. root; prop. to *irradiate* (or shoot forth beams), i.e. to *rise* (as the sun); spec. to *appear* (as a symptom of leprosy):—arise, rise (up), as soon as it is up.

2225. זֶרַח **zerach**, *zeh'-rakh*; from 2224; a *rising* of light:—rising.

2226. זֶרַח **Zerach**, *zeh'-rakh*; the same as 2225: *Zerach*, the name of three Isr., also of an Idumæan and an Ethiopian prince:—Zarah, Zerah.

2227. זַרְחִי **Zarchîy**, *zar-khee'*; patron. from 2226; a *Zarchite* or desc. of Zerach:—Zarchite.

2228. זְרַחְיָה **Zerachyâh**, *zer-akh-yaw'*; from 2225 and 3050; *Jah has risen*; *Zerachjah*, the name of two Isr.:—Zerahiah.

2229. זָרַם **zâram**, *zaw-ram'*; a prim. root; to *gush* (as water):—carry away as with a flood, pour out.

2230. זֶרֶם **zerem**, *zeh'-rem*; from 2229; a *gush* of water:—flood, overflowing, shower, storm, tempest.

2231. זִרְמָה **zirmâh**, *zir-maw'*; fem. of 2230; a *gushing* of fluid (semen):—issue.

2232. זָרַע **zâraʻ**, *zaw-rah'*; a prim. root; to *sow*; fig. to *disseminate*, *plant*, *fructify*:—bear, conceive seed, set with, sow (-er), yield.

2233. זֶרַע **zeraʻ**, *zeh'-rah*; from 2232; *seed*; fig. *fruit*, *plant*, *sowing-time*, *posterity*:—× carnally, child, fruitful, seed (-time), sowing-time.

2234. זְרַע **zeraʻ** (Chald.), *zer-ah'*; corresp. to 2233; *posterity*:—seed.

זְרֹעַ **zerôaʻ**. See 2220.

2235. זֵרֹעַ **zêrôaʻ**, *zay-ro'-ah*; or

זֵרָעֹן **zêrâʻôn**, *zay-raw-ohn'*; from 2232; something *sown* (only in the plur.), i.e. a *vegetable* (as food):—pulse.

זְרֹעָה **zerʻôâh**. See 2220.

2236. זָרַק **zâraq**, *zaw-rak'*; a prim. root; to *sprinkle* (fluid or solid particles):—be here and there, scatter, sprinkle, strew.

2237. זָרַר **zârar**, *zaw-rar'*; a prim. root [comp. 2114]; perh. to *diffuse*, i.e. (spec.) to *sneeze*:—sneeze.

2238. זֶרֶשׁ **Zeresh**, *zeh'-resh*; of Pers. or.; *Zeresh*, Haman's wife:—Zeresh.

2239. זֶרֶת **zereth**, *zeh'-reth*; from 2219; the *spread* of the fingers, i.e. a *span*:—span.

2240. זַתּוּא **Zattûwʼ**, *zat-too'*; of uncert. der.; *Zattu*, an Isr.:—Zattu.

2241. זֵתָם **Zêthâm**, *zay-thawm'*; appar. a var. for 2133; *Zetham*, an Isr.:—Zetham.

2242. זֵתַר **Zêthar**, *zay-thar'*; of Pers. or.; *Zethar*, a eunuch of Xerxes:—Zethar.

ח

2243. חֹב **chôb**, *khobe*; by contr. from 2245; prop. a *cherisher*, i.e. the *bosom*:—bosom.

2244. חָבָא **châbâʼ**, *khaw-baw'*; a prim. root [comp. 2245]; to *secrete*:— × held, hide (self), do secretly.

2245. חָבַב **châbab**, *khaw-bab'*; a prim. root [comp. 2244, 2247]; prop. to *hide* (as in the bosom), i.e. to *cherish* (with affection):—love.

2246. חֹבָב **Chôbâb**, *kho-bawb'*; from 2245; *cherished*; *Chobab*, father-in-law of Moses:—Hobab.

2247. חָבָה **châbah**, *khaw-bah'*; a prim. root [comp. 2245]; to *secrete*:—hide (self).

2248. חֲבוּלָה **chăbûwlâh** (Chald.), *khab-oo-law'*; from 2255; prop. *overthrown*, i.e. (morally) *crime*:—hurt.

2249. חָבוֹר **Châbôwr**, *khaw-bore'*; from 2266; *united*; *Chabor*, a river of Assyria:—Habor.

2250. חַבּוּרָה **chabbûwrâh**, *khab-boo-raw'*; or

חַבֻּרָה **chabbûrâh**, *khab-boo-raw'*; or

חֲבֻרָה **chăbûrâh**, *khab-oo-raw'*; from 2266; prop. *bound* (with stripes), i.e. a *weal* (or black-and-blue mark itself):—blueness, bruise, hurt, stripe, wound.

2251. חָבַט **châbaṭ**, *khaw-bat'*; a prim. root; to *knock* out or off:—beat (off, out), thresh.

2252. חֲבַיָּה **Chăbayâh**, *khab-ah-yaw'*; or

חֲבָיָה **Chăbâyâh**, *khab-aw-yaw'*; from 2247 and 3050; *Jah has hidden*; *Chabajah*, an Isr.:—Habaiah.

2253. חֶבְיוֹן **chebyôwn**, *kheb-yone'*; from 2247; a *concealment*:—hiding.

2254. חָבַל **châbal**, *khaw-bal'*; a prim. root; to *wind* tightly (as a rope), i.e. to *bind*; spec. by a *pledge*; fig. to *pervert*, *destroy*; also to *writhe* in pain (espec. of parturition):— × at all, band, bring forth, (deal) corrupt (-ly), destroy, offend, lay to (take a) pledge, spoil, travail, × very, withhold.

2255. חֲבַל **chăbal** (Chald.), *khab-al'*; corresp. to 2254; to *ruin*:—destroy, hurt.

2256. חֶבֶל **chebel**, *kheh'-bel*; or

חֵבֶל **chêbel**, *khay'-bel*; from 2254; a *rope* (as *twisted*), espec. a measuring *line*; by impl. a *district* or *inheritance* (as *measured*); or a *noose* (as of *cords*); fig. a *company* (as if *tied* together); also a *throe* (espec. of parturition); also *ruin*:—band, coast, company, cord, country, destruction, line, lot, pain, pang, portion, region, rope, snare, sorrow, tackling.

2257. חֲבַל **chăbal** (Chald.), *khab-al'*; from 2255; *harm* (personal or pecuniary):—damage, hurt.

2258. חֲבֹל **chăbôl**, *khab-ole'*; or (fem.)

חֲבֹלָה **chăbôlâh**, *khab-o-law'*; from 2254; a *pawn* (as security for debt):—pledge.

2259. חֹבֵל **chôbêl**, *kho-bale'*; act. part. from 2254 (in the sense of handling *ropes*); a *sailor*:—pilot, shipmaster.

2260. חִבֵּל **chibbêl**, *khib-bale'*; from 2254 (in the sense of furnished with *ropes*); a *mast*:—mast.

2261. חֲבַצֶּלֶת **chăbatstseleth**, *khab-ats-tseh'-leth*; of uncert. der.; prob. *meadow-saffron*:—rose.

2262. חֲבַצַּנְיָה **Chăbatstsanyâh**, *khab-ats-tsan-yaw'*; of uncert. der.; *Chabatstsanjah*, a Rechabite:—Habazaniah.

2263. חָבַק **châbaq**, *khaw-bak'*; a prim. root; to *clasp* (the hands or in embrace):—embrace, fold.

2264. חִבֻּק **chibbûq**, *khib-book'*; from 2263; a *clasping* of the hands (in idleness):—fold.

2265. חֲבַקּוּק **Chăbaqqûwq**, *khab-ak-kook'*; by redupl. from 2263; *embrace*; *Chabakkuk*, the prophet:—Habakkuk.

2266. חָבַר **châbar**, *khaw-bar'*; a prim. root; to *join* (lit. or fig.); spec. (by means of spells) to *fascinate*:—charm (-er), be compact, couple (together), have fellowship with, heap up, join (self, together), league.

2267. חֶבֶר **cheber**, *kheh'-ber*; from 2266; a *society*; also a *spell*:— + charmer (-ing), company, enchantment, × wide.

2268. חֶבֶר **Cheber**, *hheh'-ber*; the same as 2267; *community*; *Cheber*, the name of a Kenite and of three Isr.:—Heber.

2269. חֲבַר **chăbar** (Chald.), *khab-ar'*; from a root corresp. to 2266; an *associate*:—companion, fellow.

2270. חָבֵר **châbêr**, *khaw-bare'*; from 2266; an *associate*:—companion, fellow, knit together.

2271. חַבָּר **chabbâr**, *khab-bawr'*; from 2266; a *partner*:—companion.

2272. חֲבַרְבֻּרָה **chăbarbûrâh**, *khab-ar-boo-raw'*; by redupl. from 2266; a *streak* (like a *line*), as on the tiger:—spot.

2273. חַבְרָה **chabrâh** (Chald.), *khab-raw'*; fem. of 2269; an *associate:*—other.

2274. חֶבְרָה **chebrâh**, *kheb-raw'*; fem. of 2267; *association:*—company.

2275. חֶבְרוֹן **Chebrôwn**, *kheb-rone'*; from 2267; seat of *association; Chebron*, a place in Pal., also the name of two Isr.:—Hebron.

2276. חֶבְרוֹנִי **Chebrôwnîy**, *kheb-ro-nee'*; or חֶבְרֹנִי **Chebrônîy**, *kheb-ro-nee'*; patron. from 2275; *Chebronite* (collect.), an inhab. of Chebron:—Hebronites.

2277. חֶבְרִי **Chebrîy**, *kheb-ree'*; patron. from 2268; a *Chebrite* (collect.) or desc. of Cheber:—Heberites.

2278. חֲבֶרֶת **chăbereth**, *khab-eh'-reth*; fem. of 2270; a *consort:*—companion.

2279. חֹבֶרֶת **chôbereth**, *kho-beh'-reth*; fem. act. part. of 2266; a *joint:*—which coupleth, coupling.

2280. חָבַשׁ **châbash**, *khaw-bash'*; a prim. root; to *wrap* firmly (espec. a turban, compress, or *saddle*); fig. to *stop*, to *rule:*—bind (up), gird about, govern, healer, put, saddle, wrap about.

2281. חָבֵת **châbêth**, *khaw-bayth'*; from an unused root prob. mean. to *cook* [comp. 4227]; something *fried*, prob. a griddle-*cake:*—pan.

2282. חַג **chag**, *khag*; or חָג **châg**, *khawg*; from 2287; a *festival*, or a *victim* therefor:—(solemn) feast (day), sacrifice, solemnity.

2283. חָגָא **châgâ'**, *khaw-gaw'*; from an unused root mean. to *revolve* [comp. 2287]; prop. *vertigo*, i.e. (fig.) *fear:*—terror.

2284. חָגָב **châgâb**, *khaw-gawb'*; of uncert. der.; a *locust:*—locust.

2285. חָגָב **Châgâb**, *khaw-gawb'*; the same as 2284; *locust; Chagab*, one of the Nethinim:—Hagab.

2286. חֲגָבָא **Chăgâbâ'**, *khag-aw-baw'*; or חֲגָבָה **Chăgâbâh**, *khag-aw-baw'*; fem. of 2285; *locust; Chagaba* or *Chagabah*, one of the Nethinim:—Hagaba, Hagabah.

2287. חָגַג **châgag**, *khaw-gag'*; a prim. root [comp. 2283, 2328]; prop. to move in a *circle*, i.e. (spec.) to *march* in a sacred procession, to *observe* a festival; by impl. to *be giddy:*—celebrate, dance, (keep, hold) a (solemn) feast (holiday), reel to and fro.

2288. חֲגָו **chăgâv**, *khag-awv'*; from an unused root mean. to take *refuge*; a *rift* in rocks:—cleft.

2289. חָגוֹר **châgôwr**, *khaw-gore'*; from 2296; *belted:*—girded with.

2290. חֲגוֹר **chăgôwr**, *khag-ore'*; or חֲגֹר **chăgôr**, *khag-ore'*; and (fem.) חֲגוֹרָה **chăgôwrâh**, *khag-o-raw'*; or חֲגֹרָה **chăgôrâh**, *khag-o-raw'*; from 2296; a *belt* (for the waist):—apron, armour, gird (-le).

2291. חַגִּי **Chaggîy**, *khag-ghee'*; from 2287; *festive; Chaggi*, an Isr.; also (patron.) a *Chaggite*, or desc. of the same:—Haggi, Haggites.

2292. חַגַּי **Chaggay**, *khag-gah'ee*; from 2282; *festive; Chaggai*, a Heb. prophet:—Haggai.

2293. חַגִּיָּה **Chaggîyâh**, *khag-ghee-yaw'*; from 2282 and 3050; *festival of Jah; Chaggijah*, an Isr.:—Haggiah.

2294. חַגִּית **Chaggîyth**, *khag-gheeth'*; fem. of 2291; *festive; Chaggith*, a wife of David:—Haggith.

2295. חָגְלָה **Choglâh**, *khog-law'*; of uncert. der.; prob. a *partridge; Choglah*, an Israelitess:—Hoglah. See also 1031.

2296. חָגַר **châgar**, *khaw-gar'*; a prim. root; to *gird* on (as a belt, armor, etc.):—be able to put on, be afraid, appointed, gird, restrain, × on every side.

2297. חַד **chad**, *khad*; abridged from 259; *one:*—one.

2298. חַד **chad** (Chald.), *khad*; corresp. to 2297; as card. *one*; as art. *single*; as ord. *first*; adv. *at once:*—a, first, one, together.

2299. חַד **chad**, *khad*; from 2300; *sharp:*—sharp.

2300. חָדַד **châdad**, *khaw-dad'*; a prim. root; to *be* (caus. *make*) *sharp* or (fig.) *severe:*—be fierce, sharpen.

2301. חֲדַד **Chădad**, *khad-ad'*; from 2300; *fierce; Chadad*, an Ishmaelite:—Hadad.

2302. חָדָה **châdâh**, *khaw-daw'*; a prim. root; to *rejoice:*—make glad, be joined, rejoice.

2303. חַדּוּד **chaddûwd**, *khad-dood'*; from 2300; a *point:*—sharp.

2304. חֶדְוָה **chedvâh**, *khed-vaw'*; from 2302; *rejoicing:*— gladness, joy.

2305. חֶדְוָה **chedvâh** (Chald.), *khed-vaw'*; corresp. to 2304:—*joy*.

2306. חֲדִי **chădîy** (Chald.), *khad-ee'*; corresp. to 2373; a *breast:*—breast.

2307. חָדִיד **Châdîyd**, *khaw-deed'*; from 2300; a *peak; Chadid*, a place in Pal.:—Hadid.

2308. חָדַל **châdal**, *khaw-dal'*; a prim. root; prop. to *be flabby*, i.e. (by impl.) *desist*; (fig.) *be lacking* or *idle:*—cease, end, fail, forbear, forsake, leave (off), let alone, rest, be unoccupied, want.

2309. חֶדֶל **chedel**, *kheh'-del*; from 2308; *rest*, i.e. the state of the *dead:*—world.

2310. חָדֵל **châdêl**, *khaw-dale'*; from 2308; *vacant*, i.e. *ceasing* or *destitute:*—he that forbeareth, frail, rejected.

2311. חַדְלַי **Chadlay**, *khad-lah'ee*; from 2309; *idle; Chadlai*, an Isr.:—Hadlai.

2312. חֵדֶק **chêdeq**, *khay'-dek*; from an unused root mean. to *sting*; a *prickly* plant:—brier, thorn.

2313. חִדֶּקֶל **Chiddeqel**, *khid-deh'-kel*; prob. of for. or.; the *Chiddekel* (or Tigris) river:—Hiddekel.

2314. חָדַר **châdar**, *khaw-dar'*; a prim. root; prop. to *inclose* (as a room), i.e. (by anal.) to *beset* (as in a siege):—enter a privy chamber.

2315. חֶדֶר **cheder**, *kheh'-der*; from 2314; an *apartment* (usually lit.):—([bed] inner) chamber, innermost (-ward) part, parlour, + south, × within.

2316. חֲדַר **Chădar**, *khad-ar'*; another form for 2315; *chamber; Chadar*, an Ishmaelite:—Hadar.

2317. חַדְרָךְ **Chadrâk**, *khad-rawk'*; of uncert. der.; *Chadrak*, a Syrian deity:—Hadrach.

2318. חָדַשׁ **châdash**, *khaw-dash'*; a prim. root; *to be new*; caus. to *rebuild:*—renew, repair.

2319. חָדָשׁ **châdâsh**, *khaw-dawsh'*; from 2318; *new:*—fresh, new thing.

2320. חֹדֶשׁ **chôdesh**, *kho'-desh*; from 2318; the *new* moon; by impl. a *month:*—month (-ly), new moon.

2321. חֹדֶשׁ **Chôdesh**, *kho'-desh*; the same as 2320; *Chodesh*, an Israelitess:—Hodesh.

2322. חֲדָשָׁה **Chădâshâh**, *khad-aw-shaw'*; fem. of 2319; *new; Chadashah*, a place in Pal.:—Hadashah.

2323. חֲדָת **chădath** (Chald.), *khad-ath'*; corresp. to 2319; *new:*—new.

2324. חֲוָא **chăvâ'** (Chald.), *khav-aw'*; corresp. to 2331; to *show:*—shew.

2325. חוּב **chûwb**, *khoob*; also חָיַב **châyab**, *khaw-yab'*; a prim. root; prop. perh. to *tie*, i.e. (fig. and reflex.) to *owe*, or (by impl.) to *forfeit:*—make endanger.

2326. חוֹב **chôwb**, *khobe*; from 2325; *debt:*—debtor.

2327. חוֹבָה **chôwbâh**, *kho-baw'*; fem. act. part. of 2247; *hiding* place; *Chobah*, a place in Syria:—Hobah.

2328. חוּג **chûwg**, *khoog*; a prim. root [comp. 2287]; to describe a *circle:*—compass.

2329. חוּג **chûwg**, *khoog*; from 2328; a *circle:*—circle, circuit, compass.

2330. חוּד **chûwd**, *khood*; a prim. root; prop. to *tie* a knot, i.e. (fig.) to *propound* a *riddle:*—put forth.

2331. חָוָה **châvâh**, *khaw-vah'*; a prim. root; [comp. 2324, 2421]; prop. to *live*; by impl. (intens.) to *declare* or *show:*—show.

2332. חַוָּה **Chavvâh**, *khav-vaw'*; causat. from 2331; *life-giver; Chavvah* (or Eve), the first woman:—Eve.

2333. חַוָּה **chavvâh**, *khav-vaw'*; prop. the same as 2332 (*life-giving*, i.e. *living-place*); by impl. an encampment or *village:*—(small) town.

2334. חַוּוֹת יָעִיר **Chavvôwth Yâ'îyr**, *khavvothe' yaw-eer'*; from the plur. of 2333 and a modification of 3265; *hamlets of Jair*, a region of Pal.:—[Bashan-] Havoth-jair.

2335. חוֹזַי **Chôwzay**, *kho-zah'ee*; from 2374; *visionary; Chozai*, an Isr.:—the seers.

2336. חוֹחַ **chôwach**, *kho'-akh*; from an unused root appar. mean. to *pierce*; a *thorn*; by anal. a *ring* for the nose:—bramble, thistle, thorn.

2337. חָוָח **châvâch**, *khaw-vawkh'*; perh. the same as 2336; a *dell* or *crevice* (as if *pierced* in the earth):—thicket.

2338. חוּט **chûwṭ** (Chald.), *khoot*; corresp. to the root of 2339, perh. as a denom.; to *string* together, i.e. (fig.) to *repair:*—join.

2339. חוּט **chûwṭ**, *khoot*; from an unused root prob. mean. to *sew*; a *string*; by impl. a measuring *tape:*—cord, fillet, line, thread.

2340. חִוִּי **Chivvîy**, *khiv-vee'*; perh. from 2333; a *villager*; a *Chivvite*, one of the aboriginal tribes of Pal.:—Hivite.

2341. חֲוִילָה **Chăvîylâh**, *khav-ee-law'*; prob. from 2342; *circular; Chavilah*, the name of two or three eastern regions; also perh. of two men:—Havilah.

2342. חוּל **chûwl**, *khool*; or חִיל **chîyl**, *kheel*; a prim. root; prop. to *twist* or *whirl* (in a circular or spiral manner), i.e. (spec.) to *dance*, to *writhe* in pain (espec. of parturition) or fear; fig. to *wait*, to *pervert:*—bear, (make to) bring forth, (make to) calve, dance, drive away, fall grievously (with pain), fear, form, great, grieve, (be) grievous, hope, look, make, be in pain, be much (sore) pained, rest, shake, shapen, (be) sorrow (-ful), stay, tarry, travail (with pain), tremble, trust, wait carefully (patiently), be wounded.

2343. חוּל **Chûwl**, *khool*; from 2342; a *circle; Chul*, a son of Aram; also the region settled by him:—Hul.

2344. חוֹל **chôwl**, *khole*; from 2342; *sand* (as *round* or whirling particles):—sand.

2345. חוּם **chûwm**, *khoom*; from an unused root mean. to *be warm*, i.e. (by impl.) *sunburnt* or *swarthy* (blackish):—brown.

2346. חוֹמָה **chôwmâh**, *kho-maw'*; fem. act. part. of an unused root appar. mean. to *join*; a *wall* of protection:—wall, walled.

2347. חוּס **chûwç**, *khoos*; a prim. root; prop. to *cover*, i.e. (fig.) to *compassionate:*—pity, regard, spare.

2348. חוֹף **chôwph**, *khofe*; from an unused root mean. to *cover*; a *cove* (as a *sheltered* bay):—coast [of the sea], haven, shore, [sea-] side.

2349. חוּפָם **Chûwphâm**, *khoo-fawm'*; from the same as 2348; *protection: Chupham*, an Isr.:—Hupham.

2350. חוּפָמִי **Chûwphâmîy**, *khoo-faw-mee'*; patron. from 2349; a *Chuphamite* or desc. of Chupham:—Huphamites.

2351. חוּץ **chûwts**, *khoots*; or (short.) חֻץ **chûts**, *khoots*; (both forms fem. in the plur.) from an unused root mean. to *sever*; prop. *separate* by a wall, i.e. *outside, outdoors:*—abroad, field, forth, highway, more, out (-side, -ward), street, without.

חוֹק **chôwq**. See 2436.

חוּקֹק **Chûwqôq**. See 2712.

2352. חוּר **chûwr**, *khoor;* or (short.)
חֻר **chûr**, *khoor;* from an unused root prob. mean. to *bore;* the *crevice* of a serpent; the *cell* of a prison:—hole.

2353. חוּר **chûwr**, *khoor;* from 2357; *white* linen:—white.

2354. חוּר **Chûwr**, *khoor;* the same as 2353 or 2352; *Chur*, the name of four Isr. and one Midianite:—Hur.

2355. חוֹר **chôwr**, *khore;* the same as 2353; *white* linen:—network. Comp. 2715.

2356. חוֹר **chôwr**, *khore;* or (short.)
חֹר **chôr**, *khore;* the same as 2352; a *cavity, socket, den:*—cave, hole.

2357. חָוַר **châvar**, *khaw-var';* a prim. root; to *blanch* (as with shame):—wax pale.

2358. חִוָּר **chivvâr** (Chald.), *khiv-vawr';* from a root corresp. to 2357; *white:*—white.
חוֹרוֹן **Chôwrôwn**. See 1032.
חוֹרִי **chôwrîy**. See 2753.

2359. חוּרִי **Chûwrîy**, *khoo-ree';* prob. from 2353; *linen*-worker; *Churi*, an Isr.:—Huri.

2360. חוּרַי **Chûwray**, *khoo-rah'ee;* prob. an orth. var. for 2359; *Churai*, an Isr.:—Hurai.

2361. חוּרָם **Chûwrâm**, *khoo-rawm';* prob. from 2353; *whiteness*, i.e. noble; *Churam*, the name of an Isr. and two Syrians:—Huram. Comp. 2438.

2362. חַוְרָן **Chavrân**, *khav-rawn';* appar. from 2357 (in the sense of 2352); *cavernous; Chavran*, a region E. of the Jordan:—Hauran.

2363. חוּשׁ **chûwsh**, *koosh;* a prim. root; to *hurry;* fig. to *be eager* with excitement or enjoyment:—(make) haste (-n), ready.

2364. חוּשָׁה **Chûwshâh**, *khoo-shaw';* from 2363; *haste; Chushah*, an Isr.:—Hushah.

2365. חוּשַׁי **Chûwshay**, *khoo-shah'ee;* from 2363; *hasty; Chushai*, an Isr.:—Hushai.

2366. חוּשִׁים **Chûwshîym**, *khoo-sheem';* or
חֻשִׁים **Chûshîym**, *khoo-shem';* or
חֻשִׁם **Chûshîm**, *khoo-sheem';* plur. from 2363; *hasters; Chushim*, the name of three Isr.:—Hushim.

2367. חוּשָׁם **Chûwshâm**, *khoo-shawm';* or
חֻשָׁם **Chûshâm**, *khoo-shawm';* from 2363; *hastily; Chusham*, an Idumæan:—Husham.

2368. חוֹתָם **chôwthâm**, *kho-thawm';* or
חֹתָם **chôthâm**, *kho-thawm';* from 2856; a *signature*-ring:—seal, signet.

2369. חוֹתָם **Chôwthâm**, *kho-thawm',* the same as 2368; *seal; Chotham*, the name of two Isr.:—Hotham, Hothan.

2370. חֲזָא **chăzâ'** (Chald.), *khaz-aw';* or
חֲזָה **chăzâh** (Chald.), *khaz-aw';* corresp. to 2372; to *gaze* upon; mentally to *dream, be usual* (i.e. *seem*):—behold, have [a dream], see, be wont.

2371. חֲזָאֵל **Chăzâ'êl**, *khaz-aw-ale';* or
חֲזָהאֵל **Chăzâh'êl**, *khaz-aw-ale';* from 2372 and 410; *God has seen; Chazaël*, a king of Syria:—Hazael.

2372. חָזָה **châzâh**, *khaw-zaw';* a prim. root; to *gaze* at; mentally to *perceive, contemplate* (with pleasure); spec. to *have a vision of:*—behold, look, prophesy, provide, see.

2373. חָזֶה **châzeh**, *khaw-zeh';* from 2372; the *breast* (as most *seen* in front):—breast.

2374. חֹזֶה **chôzeh**, *kho-zeh';* act. part. of 2372; a *beholder* in vision; also a *compact* (as *looked upon* with approval):—agreement, prophet, see that, seer, [star-] gazer.
חֲזָהאֵל **Chăzâh'êl**. See 2371.

2375. חֲזוֹ **Chăzow**, *khaz-o';* from 2372; *seer; Chazo*, a nephew of Abraham:—Hazo.

2376. חֵזֵו **chêzev** (Chald.), *khay'-zev;* from 2370; a *sight:*—look, vision.

2377. חָזוֹן **châzôwn**, *khaw-zone';* from 2372; a *sight* (mentally), i.e. a *dream, revelation*, or *oracle:*—vision.

2378. חָזוֹת **châzôwth**, *khaw-zooth';* from 2372; a *revelation:*—vision.

2379. חֲזוֹת **chăzôwth** (Chald.), *khaz-oth';* from 2370; a *view:*—sight.

2380. חָזוּת **châzûwth**, *khaw-zooth';* from 2372; a *look;* hence (fig.) striking *appearance, revelation*, or (by impl.) *compact:*—agreement, notable (one), vision.

2381. חֲזִיאֵל **Chăzîy'êl**, *khaz-ee-ale';* from 2372 and 410; *seen of God; Chaziel*, a Levite:—Haziel.

2382. חֲזָיָה **Chăzâyâh**, *khaz-aw-yaw';* from 2372 and 3050; *Jah has seen; Chazajah*, an Isr.:—Hazaiah.

2383. חֶזְיוֹן **Chezyôwn**, *khez-yone';* from 2372; *vision; Chezjon*, a Syrian:—Hezion.

2384. חִזָּיוֹן **chizzâyôwn**, *khiz-zaw-yone';* from 2372; a *revelation*, espec. by *dream:*—vision.

2385. חֲזִיז **châzîyz**, *khaw-zeez';* from an unused root mean. to *glare;* a *flash* of lightning:—bright cloud, lightning.

2386. חֲזִיר **chăzîyr**, *khaz-eer';* from an unused root prob. mean. to *inclose;* a *hog* (perh. as *penned*):—boar, swine.

2387. חֵזִיר **Chêzîyr**, *khay-zeer';* from the same as 2386; perh. *protected; Chezir*, the name of two Isr.:—Hezir.

2388. חָזַק **châzaq**, *khaw-zak';* a prim. root; to *fasten* upon; hence to *seize, be strong* (fig. *courageous*, causat. *strengthen, cure, help, repair, fortify*), *obstinate;* to *bind, restrain, conquer:*—aid, amend, × calker, catch, cleave, confirm, be constant, constrain, continue, be of good (take) courage (-ous, -ly), encourage (self), be established, fasten, force, fortify, make hard, harden, help, (lay) hold (fast), lean, maintain, play the man, mend, become (wax) mighty, prevail, be recovered, repair, retain, seize, be (wax) sore, strengthen (self), be stout, be (make, shew, wax) strong (-er), be sure, take (hold), be urgent, behave self valiantly, withstand.

2389. חָזָק **châzâq**, *khaw-zawk';* from 2388; *strong* (usu. in a bad sense, *hard, bold, violent*):—harder, hottest, + impudent, loud, mighty, sore, stiff [-hearted], strong (-er).

2390. חָזֵק **châzêq**, *khaw-zake';* from 2388; *powerful:*— × wax louder. stronger.

2391. חֵזֶק **chêzeq**, *khay'-zek;* from 2388; *help:*—strength.

2392. חֹזֶק **chôzeq**, *kho'-zek;* from 2388; *power:*—strength.

2393. חֶזְקָה **chezqâh**, *khez-kaw';* fem. of 2391; prevailing *power:*—strength (-en self), (was) strong.

2394. חָזְקָה **chozqâh**, *khoz-kaw';* fem. of 2392; *vehemence* (usu. in a bad sense):—force, mightily, repair. sharply.

2395. חִזְקִי **Chizqîy**, *khiz-kee';* from 2388; *strong; Chizki*, an Isr.:—Hezeki.

2396. חִזְקִיָּה **Chizqîyâh**, *khiz-kee-yaw';* or
חִזְקִיָּהוּ **Chizqîyâhûw**, *khiz-kee-yaw'-hoo;* also
יְחִזְקִיָּה **Y^echizqîyâh**, *yekh-iz-kee-yaw';* or
יְחִזְקִיָּהוּ **Y^echizqîyâhûw**, *yekh-iz-kee-yaw'-hoo;* from 2388 and 3050; *strengthened of Jah; Chizkijah*, a king of Judah, also the name of two other Isr.:—Hezekiah, Hizkiah, Hizkijah. Comp. 3169.

2397. חָח **châch**, *khawkh;* once (Ezek. 29 : 4)
חָחִי **châchîy**, *khakh-ee';* from the same as 2336; a *ring* for the nose (or lips):—bracelet, chain, hook.
חָחִי **châchîy**. See 2397.

2398. חָטָא **châṭâ'**, *khaw-taw';* a prim. root; prop. to *miss;* hence (fig. and gen.) to *sin;* by infer. to *forfeit, lack, expiate, repent*, (causat.) *lead astray, condemn:*—bear the blame, cleanse, commit [sin], by fault, harm he hath done, loss, miss, (make) offend (-er), offer for sin, purge, purify (self), make reconciliation, (cause, make) sin (-ful, -ness), trespass,

2399. חֵטְא **chêṭ'**, *khate;* from 2398; a *crime* or its *penalty:*—fault, × grievously, offence, (punishment of) sin.

2400. חַטָּא **chaṭṭâ'**, *khat-taw';* intens. from 2398; a *criminal*, or one accounted *guilty:*—offender, sinful, sinner.

2401. חֲטָאָה **chăṭâ'âh**, *khat-aw-aw';* fem. of 2399; an *offence*, or a *sacrifice* for it:—sin (offering), sinful.

2402. חַטָּאָה **chaṭṭâ'âh** (Chald.), *khat-taw-aw';* corresp. to 2401; an *offence*, and the *penalty* or *sacrifice* for it:—sin (offering).

2403. חַטָּאָה **chaṭṭâ'âh**, *khat-taw-aw';* or
חַטָּאת **chaṭṭâ'th**, *khat-tawth';* from 2398; an *offence* (sometimes habitual *sinfulness*), and its penalty, occasion, sacrifice, or expiation; also (concr.) an *offender:*—punishment (of sin), purifying (-fication for sin), sin (-ner, offering).

2404. חָטַב **châṭab**, *khaw-tab';* a prim. root; to *chop* or *carve* wood:—cut down, hew (-er), polish.

2405. חֲטֻבָה **chăṭûbâh**, *khat-oo-baw';* fem. pass. part. of 2404; prop. a *carving;* hence a *tapestry* (as figured):—carved.

2406. חִטָּה **chiṭṭâh**, *khit-taw';* of uncert. der.; *wheat*, whether the grain or the plant:—wheat (-en).

2407. חַטּוּשׁ **Chaṭṭûwsh**, *khat-toosh';* from an unused root of uncert. signif.; *Chattush*, the name of four or five Isr.:—Hattush.

2408. חֲטִי **chăṭîy** (Chald.), *khat-ee';* from a root corresp. to 2398; an *offence:*—sin.

2409. חַטָּיָא **chaṭṭâyâ'** (Chald.), *khat-taw-yaw';* from the same as 2408; an *expiation:*—sin offering.

2410. חֲטִיטָא **Chăṭîyṭa'**, *khat-ee-taw';* from an unused root appar. mean. to *dig out; explorer; Chatita*, a temple porter:—Hatita.

2411. חַטִּיל **Chaṭṭîyl**, *khat-teel';* from an unused root appar. mean. to *wave; fluctuating; Chattil*, one of "Solomon's servants":—Hattil.

2412. חֲטִיפָא **Chăṭîyphâ'**, *khat-ee-faw';* from 2414; *robber; Chatipha*, one of the Nethinim:—Hatipha.

2413. חָטַם **châṭam**, *khaw-tam';* a prim. root; to *stop:*—refrain.

2414. חָטַף **châṭaph**, *khaw-taf';* a prim. root; to *clutch;* hence to *seize* as a prisoner:—catch.

2415. חֹטֶר **chôṭer**, *kho'-ter;* from an unused root of uncert. signif.; a *twig:*—rod.

2416. חַי **chay**, *khah'ee;* from 2421; *alive;* hence *raw* (flesh); *fresh* (plant, water, year), *strong;* also (as noun, espec. in the fem. sing. and masc. plur.) *life* (or living thing), whether lit. or fig.:— + age, alive, appetite, (wild) beast, company, congregation, life (-time), live (-ly), living (creature, thing), maintenance, + merry, multitude, + (be) old, quick, raw, running, springing, troop.

2417. חַי **chay** (Chald.), *khah'ee;* from 2418; *alive;* also (as noun in plur.) *life:*—life, that liveth, living.

2418. חֲיָא **chăyâ'** (Chald.), *khah-yaw';* or
חֲיָה **chăyâh** (Chald.), *khah-yaw';* corresp. to 2421; to *live:*—live, keep alive.

2419. חִיאֵל **Chîy'êl**, *khee-ale';* from 2416 and 410; *living of God; Chiel*, an Isr.:—Hiel.
חָיָב **châyab**. See 2325.

2420. חִידָה **chîydâh**, *khee-daw';* from 2330; a *puzzle;* hence a *trick, conundrum, sententious maxim:*—dark saying (sentence, speech), hard question, proverb, riddle.

2421. חָיָה **châyâh**, *khaw-yaw'*; a prim. root [comp. 2331, 2424]; to *live*, whether lit. or fig.; causat. to *revive*:—keep (leave, make) alive, × certainly, give (promise) life, (let, suffer to) live, nourish up, preserve (alive), quicken, recover, repair, restore (to life), revive, (× God) save (alive, life, lives), × surely, be whole.

2422. חָיֶה **châyeh**, *khaw-yeh'*; from 2421; *vigorous*:—lively.

2423. חֵיוָא **chêyvâ'** (Chald.), *khay-vaw'*; from 2418; an *animal*:—beast.

2424. חַיּוּת **chayûwth**, *khah-yooth'*; from 2421; *life*:— × living.

2425. חָיַי **châyay**, *khaw-yah'ee*; a prim. root [comp. 2421]; to *live*; causat. to *revive*:—live, save life.

2426. חֵיל **chêyl**, *khale*; or (short.)

חֵל **chêl**, *khale*; a collat. form of 2428; an *army*; also (by anal.) an *intrenchment*:—army, bulwark, host, + poor, rampart, trench, wall.

חִיל **chîyl**. See 2342.

2427. חִיל **chîyl**, *kheel*; and (fem.)

חִילָה **chîylâh**, *khee-law'*; from 2342; a *throe* (espec. of childbirth):—pain, pang, sorrow.

2428. חַיִל **chayil**, *khah'-yil*; from 2342; prob. a *force*, whether of men, means or other resources; an *army*, *wealth*, *virtue*, *valor*, *strength*:—able, activity, (+) army, band of men (soldiers), company, (great) forces, goods, host, might, power, riches, strength, strong, substance, train, (+) valiant (-ly), valour, virtuous (-ly), war, worthy (-ily).

2429. חַיִל **chayil** (Chald.), *khah'-yil*; corresp. to 2428; an *army*, or *strength*:—aloud, army, × most [mighty], power.

2430. חֵילָה **chêylâh**, *khay-law'*; fem. of 2428; an *intrenchment*:—bulwark.

2431. חֵילָם **Chêylâm**, *khay-lawm'*; or

חֵלָאם **Chêl'âm**, *khay-lawm'*; from 2428; *fortress*; *Chelam*, a place E. of Pal.:—Helam.

2432. חִילֵן **Chîylên**, *khee-lane'*; from 2428; *fortress*; *Chilen*, a place in Pal.:—Hilen.

2433. חִין **chîyn**, *kheen*; another form for 2580; *beauty*:—comely.

2434. חַיִץ **chayits**, *khah'-yits*; another form for 2351; a *wall*:—wall.

2435. חִיצוֹן **chîytsôwn**, *khee-tsone'*; from 2434; prop. the (outer) *wall side*; hence *exterior*; fig. *secular* (as opposed to sacred):—outer, outward, utter, without.

2436. חֵיק **chêyq**, *khake*, or

חֵק **chêq**, *khake*; and

חוֹק **chôwq**, *khoke*; from an unused root, appar. mean. to *inclose*; the *bosom* (lit. or fig.):—bosom, bottom, lap, midst, within.

2437. חִירָה **Chîyrâh**, *khee-raw'*; from 2357 in the sense of *splendor*; *Chirah*, an Adullamite:—Hirah.

2438. חִירָם **Chîyrâm**, *khee-rawm'*, or

חִירוֹם **Chîyrôwm**, *khee-rome'*; another form of 2361; *Chiram* or *Chirom*, the name of two Tyrians:—Hiram, Huram.

2439. חִישׁ **chîysh**, *kheesh*; another form for 2363; to *hurry*:—make haste.

2440. חִישׁ **chîysh**, *kheesh*; from 2439; prop. a *hurry*; hence (adv.) *quickly*:—soon.

2441. חֵךְ **chêk**, *khake*; prob. from 2596 in the sense of *tasting*; prop. the *palate* or inside of the mouth; hence the *mouth* itself (as the organ of speech, taste and kissing):—(roof of the) mouth, taste.

2442. חָכָה **châkâh**, *khaw-kaw'*; a prim. root [appar. akin to 2707 through the idea of *piercing*]; prop. to *adhere* to; hence to await:—long, tarry, wait.

2443. חַכָּה **chakkâh**, *khak-kaw'*; prob. from 2442; a *hook* (as *adhering*):—angle, hook.

2444. חֲכִילָה **Chakîylâh**, *khak-ee-law'*; from the same as 2447; *dark*; *Chakilah*, a hill in Pal.:—Hachilah.

2445. חַכִּים **chakkîym** (Chald.), *khak-keem'*; from a root corresp. to 2449; *wise*, i.e. a *Magian*:—wise.

2446. חֲכַלְיָה **Chăkalyâh**, *khak-al-yaw'*; from the base of 2447 and 3050; *darkness of Jah*; *Chakaljah*, an Isr.:—Hachaliah.

2447. חַכְלִיל **chaklîyl**, *khak-leel'*; by redupl. from an unused root appar. mean. to *be dark*; darkly *flashing* (only of the eyes); in a good sense, *brilliant* (as stimulated by wine):—red.

2448. חַכְלִלוּת **chaklîlûwth**, *khak-lee-looth'*; from 2447; *flash* (of the eyes); in a bad sense, *blearedness*:—redness.

2449. חָכַם **châkam**, *khaw-kam'*; a prim. root, to *be wise* (in mind, word or act):—× exceeding, teach wisdom, be (make self, shew self) wise, deal (never so) wisely, make wiser.

2450. חָכָם **châkâm**, *khaw-kawm'*; from 2449; *wise*, (i.e. intelligent, skilful or artful):—cunning (man), subtil, ([un-]), wise ([hearted], man).

2451. חָכְמָה **chokmâh**, *khok-maw'*; from 2449; *wisdom* (in a good sense):—skilful, wisdom, wisely, wit.

2452. חָכְמָה **chokmâh** (Chald.), *khok-maw'*; corresp. to 2451; *wisdom*:—wisdom.

2453. חַכְמוֹנִי **Chakmôwnîy**, *khak-mo-nee'*; from 2449; *skilful*; *Chakmoni*, an Isr.:—Hachmoni, Hachmonite.

2454. חָכְמוֹת **chokmôwth**, *khok-mōth'*; or

חַכְמוֹת **chakmôwth**, *khak-mōth'*; collat. forms of 2451; *wisdom*:—wisdom, every wise [woman].

חֵל **chêl**. See 2426.

2455. חֹל **chôl**, *khole*; from 2490; prop. *exposed*; hence *profane*:—common, profane (place), unholy.

2456. חָלָא **châlâ'**, *khaw-law'*; a prim. root [comp. 2470]; to *be sick*:—be diseased.

2457. חֶלְאָה **chel'âh**, *khel-aw'*; from 2456; prop. *disease*; hence *rust*:—scum.

2458. חֶלְאָה **Chel'âh**, *khel-aw'*; the same as 2457; *Chelah*, an Israelitess:—Helah.

2459. חֶלֶב **cheleb**, *kheh'-leb*; or

חֵלֶב **chêleb**, *khay'-leb*; from an unused root mean. to *be fat*; *fat*, whether lit. or fig.; hence the *richest* or *choice* part:— × best, fat (-ness), × finest, grease, marrow.

2460. חֵלֶב **Chêleb**, *khay'-leb*; the same as 2459; *fatness*; *Cheleb*, an Isr.:—Heleb.

2461. חָלָב **châlâb**, *khaw-lawb'*; from the same as 2459; *milk* (as the *richness* of kine):—+ cheese, milk, sucking.

2462. חֶלְבָּה **Chelbâh**, *khel-baw'*; fem. of 2459; *fertility*; *Chelbah*, a place in Pal.:—Helbah.

2463. חֶלְבּוֹן **Chelbôwn**, *khel-bone'*; from 2459; *fruitful*; *Chelbon*, a place in Syria:—Helbon.

2464. חֶלְבְּנָה **chelbᵉnâh**, *khel-ben-aw'*; from 2459; *galbanam*, an odorous gum (as if *fatty*):—galbanum.

2465. חֶלֶד **cheled**, *kheh'-led*; from an unused root appar. mean. to *glide* swiftly; *life* (as a *fleeting* portion of time); hence the *world* (as *transient*):—age, short time, world.

2466. חֵלֶד **chêled**, *khay'-led*; the same as 2465; *Cheled*, an Isr.:—Heled.

2467. חֹלֶד **chôled**, *kho'-led*; from the same as 2465; a *weasel* (from its *gliding* motion):—weasel.

2468. חֻלְדָּה **Chuldâh**, *khool-daw'*; fem. of 2467; *Chuldah*, an Israelitess:—Huldah.

2469. חֶלְדַּי **Chelday**, *khel-dah'-ee*; from 2466; *worldliness*; *Cheldai*, the name of two Isr.:—Heldai.

2470. חָלָה **châlâh**, *khaw-law'*; a prim. root [comp. 2342, 2470, 2490]; prop. to *be rubbed* or *worn*; hence (fig.) to *be weak*, *sick*, *afflicted*; or (causat.) to *grieve*, *make sick*; also to *stroke* (in flattering), *entreat*:—beseech, (be) diseased, (put to) grief, be grieved, (be) grievous, infirmity, intreat, lay to, put to pain, × pray, make prayer, be (fall, make) sick, sore, be sorry, make suit (× supplication), woman in travail, be (become) weak, be wounded.

2471. חַלָּה **challâh**, *khal-law'*; from 2490; a *cake* (as usually *punctured*):—cake.

2472. חֲלוֹם **chălôwm**, *khal-ome'*; or (short.)

חֲלֹם **chălôm**, *khal-ome'*; from 2492; a *dream*:—dream (-er).

2473. חֹלוֹן **Chôlôwn**, *kho-lone'*; or (short.)

חֹלֹן **Chôlôn**, *kho-lone'*; prob. from 2344; *sandy*; *Cholon*, the name of two places in Pal.:—Holon.

2474. חַלּוֹן **challôwn**, *khal-lone'*; a *window* (as *perforated*):—window

2475. חֲלוֹף **chălôwph**, *khal-ofe'*; from 2498; prop *surviving*, by impl. (collect.) *orphans*:— × destruction.

2476. חֲלוּשָׁה **chălûwshâh**, *khal-oo-shaw'*; fem. pass. part. of 2522; *defeat*:—being overcome.

2477. חֲלַח **Chălach**, *khal-akh'*; prob. of for. or.; *Chalach*, a region of Assyria:—Halah.

2478. חַלְחוּל **Chalchûwl**, *khal-khool'*; by redupl. from 2342; *contorted*; *Chalchul*, a place in Pal.:—Halhul.

2479. חַלְחָלָה **chalchâlâh**, *khal-khaw-law'*; fem. from the same as 2478; *writhing* (in childbirth); by impl. *terror*:—(great, much) pain.

2480. חָלַט **châlaṭ**, *khaw-lat'*; a prim. root; to *snatch* at:—catch.

2481. חֲלִי **chălîy**, *khal-ee'*; from 2470; a *trinket* (as *polished*):—jewel, ornament.

2482. חֲלִי **Chălîy**, *khal-ee'*; the same as 2481; *Chali*, a place in Pal.:—Hali.

2483. חֳלִי **chŏlîy**, *khol-ee'*; from 2470; *malady*, *anxiety*, *calamity*:—disease, grief, (is) sick (-ness).

2484. חֶלְיָה **chelyâh**, *khel-yaw'*; fem. of 2481; a *trinket*:—jewel.

2485. חָלִיל **châlîyl**, *khaw-leel'*; from 2490; a *flute* (as *perforated*):—pipe.

2486. חָלִילָה **châlîylâh**, *khaw-lee'-law*; or

חָלִלָה **châlîlâh**, *khaw-lee'-law*; a directive from 2490; lit. *for a profaned* thing; used (interj.) *far be it!*:—be far, (× God) forbid.

2487. חֲלִיפָה **chălîyphâh**, *khal-ee-faw'*; from 2498; *alternation*:—change, course.

2488. חֲלִיצָה **chălîytsâh**, *khal-ee-tsaw'*; from 2502; *spoil*:—armour.

2489. חֵלְכָא **chêlᵉkâ'**, *khay-lek-aw'*; or

חֵלְכָה **chêlᵉkâh**, *khay-lek-aw'*; appar. from an unused root prob. mean. to *be dark* or (fig.) *unhappy*; a *wretch*, i.e. unfortunate:—poor.

2490. חָלַל **châlal**, *khaw-lal'*; a prim. root [comp. 2470]; prop. to *bore*, i.e. (by impl.) to *wound*, to *dissolve*; fig. to *profane* (a person, place or thing), to *break* (one's word), to *begin* (as if by an "opening wedge"); denom. (from 2485) to *play* (the flute):—begin (× men began), defile, × break, defile, × eat (as common things), × first, × gather the grape thereof, × take inheritance, pipe, player on instruments, pollute, (cast as) profane (self), prostitute, slay (slain), sorrow, stain, wound.

2491. חָלָל **châlâl**, *khaw-lawl'*; from 2490; *pierced* (espec. to death); fig. *polluted*:—kill, profane, slain (man), × slew, (deadly) wounded.

חָלִלָה **châlîlâh**. See 2486.

2492. חָלַם châlam, *khaw-lam'*; a prim. root; prop. to *bind* firmly, i.e. (by impl.) to *be* (causat. to *make*) *plump;* also (through the fig. sense of *dumbness*) to *dream:*—(cause to) dream (-er), be in good liking, recover.

2493. חֵלֶם chêlem (Chald.), *khay'-lem;* from a root corresp. to 2492; a *dream:*—dream.

2494. חֵלֶם Chêlem, *khay'-lem;* from 2492; a *dream; Chelem*, an Isr.:—Helem. Comp. 2469.

2495. חַלָּמוּת challâmûwth, *khal-law-mooth'*; from 2492 (in the sense of *insipidity*); prob. *purslain:*—egg.

2496. חַלָּמִישׁ challâmîysh, *khal-law-meesh'*; prob. from 2492 (in the sense of *hardness*); *flint:*—flint (-y), rock.

2497. חֵלֹן Chêlôn, *khay-lone'*, from 2428; *strong Chelon*, an Isr.:—Helon.

2498. חָלַף châlaph, *khaw-laf'*; a prim. root; prop. to *slide* by, i.e. (by impl.) to *hasten away, pass* on, *spring* up, *pierce* or *change:*—abolish, alter, change, cut off, go on forward, grow up, be over, pass (away, on, through), renew, sprout, strike through.

2499. חֲלַף chălaph (Chald.), *khal-af'*; corresp. to 2498; to *pass* on (of time):—pass.

2500. חֵלֶף chêleph, *khay'-lef;* from 2498; prop. *exchange;* hence (as prep.) *instead* of:—× for.

2501. חֶלֶף Cheleph, *kheh'-lef;* the same as 2500; *change; Cheleph*, a place in Pal.:—Heleph.

2502. חָלַץ châlats, *khaw-lats'*; a prim. root; to *pull* off; hence (intens.) to *strip*, (reflex.) to *depart;* by impl. to *deliver, equip* (for fight); *present, strengthen:*—arm (self), (go, ready) armed (× man, soldier), deliver, draw out, make fat, loose, (ready) prepared, put off, take away, withdraw self.

2503. חֶלֶץ Chelets, *kheh'-lets;* or

חֵלֶץ Chêlets, *khay'-lets;* from 2502; perh. *strength; Chelets*, the name of two Isr.:—Heles.

2504. חָלָץ châlâts, *khaw-lawts'*; from 2502 (in the sense of *strength*); only in the dual; the *loins* (as the seat of vigor):—loins, reins.

2505. חָלַק châlaq, *khaw-lak'*; a prim. root; to *be smooth* (fig.); by impl. (as smooth stones were used for *lots*) to *apportion* or *separate:*—deal, distribute, divide, flatter, give, (have, im-) part (-ner), take away a portion, receive, separate self, (be) smooth (-er).

2506. חֵלֶק chêleq, *khay'-lek;* from 2505; prop. *smoothness* (of the tongue); also an *allotment:*—flattery, inheritance, part, × partake, portion.

2507. חֵלֶק Chêleq, *khay'-lek;* the same as 2506; *portion; Chelek*, an Isr.:—Helek.

2508. חֲלָק chălâq (Chald.), *khal-awk'*; from a root corresp. to 2505; a *part:*—portion.

2509. חָלָק châlâq, *khaw-lawk'*; from 2505; *smooth* (espec. of tongue):—flattering, smooth.

2510. חָלָק Châlâq, *khaw-lawk'*; the same as 2509; *bare; Chalak*, a mountain of Idumæa:—Halak.

2511. חַלָּק challâq, *khal-lawk'*; from 2505; *smooth:*—smooth.

2512. חַלֻּק challûq, *khal-look'*; from 2505; *smooth:*—smooth.

2513. חֶלְקָה chelqâh, *khel-kaw'*; fem. of 2506; prop. *smoothness;* fig. *flattery;* also an *allotment:*—field, flattering (-ry), ground, parcel, part, piece of land ([ground]), plat, portion, slippery place, smooth (thing).

2514. חֲלַקָּה chălaqqâh, *khal-ak-kaw'*; fem. from 2505; *flattery:*—flattery.

2515. חֲלֻקָּה chăluqqâh, *khal-ook-kaw'*; fem. of 2512; a *distribution:*—division.

2516. חֶלְקִי Chelqîy, *khel-kee'*; patron. from 2507; a *Chelkite* or desc. of Chelek:—Helkites.

2517. חֶלְקַי Chelqay, *khel-kah'ee;* from 2505; *apportioned; Chelkai*, an Isr.:—Helkai.

2518. חִלְקִיָּה Chilqîyâh, *khil-kee-yaw'*; or

חִלְקִיָּהוּ Chilqîyâhûw, *khil-kee-yaw'-hoo;* from 2506 and 3050; *portion of Jah; Chilhijah*, the name of eight Isr.:—Hilkiah.

2519. חֲלַקְלַקָּה chălaqlaqqâh, *khal-ak-lak-kaw'*; by redupl. from 2505; prop. something *very smooth;* i.e. a *treacherous* spot; fig. *blandishment:*—flattery, slippery.

2520. חֶלְקַת Chelqath, *khel-kath'*; a form of 2513; *smoothness; Chelkath*, a place in Pal.:—Helkath.

2521. חֶלְקַת הַצֻּרִים Chelqath hats-Tsûrîym, *khel-kath' hats-tsoo-reem'*; from 2520 and the plur. of 6697, with the art. inserted; *smoothness of the rocks; Chelkath Hatsturim*, a place in Pal.:—Helkath-hazzurim.

2522. חָלַשׁ châlash, *khaw-lash'*; a prim. root; to *prostrate;* by impl. to *overthrow, decay:*—discomfit, waste away, weaken.

2523. חַלָּשׁ challâsh, *khal-lawsh'*; from 2522; *frail:*—weak.

2524. חָם châm, *khawm;* from the same as 2346; a *father-in-law* (as in *affinity*):—father in law.

2525. חָם châm, *khawm;* from 2552; *hot:*—hot, warm.

2526. חָם Châm, *khawm;* the same as 2525; *hot* (from the tropical habitat); *Cham*, a son of Noah; also (as a patron.) his desc. or their country:—Ham.

2527. חֹם chôm, *khome;* from 2552; *heat:*—heat, to be hot (warm).

2528. חֱמָא chĕmâ' (Chald.), *khem-aw'*; or

חֲמָה chămâh (Chald.), *kham-aw'*; corresp. to 2534; *anger:*—fury.

חֱמָא chêmâ'. See 2534.

2529. חֶמְאָה chem'âh, *khem-aw'*; or (short.)

חֵמָה chêmâh, *khay-maw'*; from the same root as 2346; curdled *milk* or *cheese:*—butter.

2530. חָמַד châmad, *khaw-mad'*; a prim. root; to *delight* in:—beauty, greatly beloved, covet, delectable thing, (× great) delight, desire, goodly, lust, (be) pleasant (thing), precious (thing).

2531. חֶמֶד chemed, *kheh'-med;* from 2530; *delight:*—desirable, pleasant.

2532. חֶמְדָּה chemdâh, *khem-daw'*; fem. of 2531; *delight:*—desire, goodly, pleasant, precious.

2533. חֶמְדָּן Chemdân, *khem-dawn'*; from 2531; *pleasant; Chemdan*, an Idumæan:—Hemdan.

2534. חֵמָה chêmâh, *khay-maw'*; or (Dan. 11 : 44)

חֵמָא chêmâ', *khay-maw'*; from 3179; *heat;* fig. *anger, poison* (from its *fever*):—anger, bottles, hot displeasure, furious (-ly, -ry), heat, indignation, poison, rage, wrath (-ful). See 2529.

2535. חַמָּה chammâh, *kham-maw'*; from 2525; *heat;* by impl. the *sun:*—heat, sun.

2536. חַמּוּאֵל Chammûw'êl, *kham-moo-ale'*; from 2535 and 410; *anger of God; Chammuel*, an Isr.:—Hamuel.

2537. חֲמוּטַל Chămûwṭal, *kham-oo-tal'*; or

חֲמִיטַל Chămîyṭal, *kham-ee-tal'*; from 2524 and 2919; *father-in-law of dew; Chamutal* or *Chamital*, an Israelitess:—Hamutal.

2538. חָמוּל Châmûwl, *khaw-mool'*; from 2550; *pitied; Chamul*, an Isr.:—Hamul.

2539. חָמוּלִי Châmûwlîy, *khaw-moo-lee'*; patron. from 2538: a *Chamulite* (collect.) or desc. of Chamul:—Hamulites.

2540. חַמּוֹן Chammôwn, *kham-mone'*; from 2552; *warm* spring; *Chammon*, the name of two places in Pal.:—Hammon.

2541. חָמוֹץ châmôwts, *khaw-motse'*; from 2556; prop. *violent;* by impl. a *robber:*—oppressed.

2542. חַמּוּק chammûwq, *kham-mook'*; from 2559; a *wrapping*, i.e. *drawers:*—joints.

2543. חֲמוֹר chămôwr, *kham-ore'*; or (short.)

חֲמֹר chămôr, *kham-ore;* from 2560; a male *ass* (from its dun *red*):—(he) ass.

2544. חֲמוֹר Chămôwr, *kham-ore'*; the same as 2543; *ass; Chamor*, a Canaanite:—Hamor.

2545. חֲמוֹת chămôwth, *kham-ōth'*; or (short.)

חֲמֹת chămôth, *kham-ōth'*; fem. of 2524; a *mother-in-law:*—mother in law.

2546. חֹמֶט chômeṭ, *kho'-met;* from an unused root prob. mean. to *lie low;* a *lizard* (as *creeping*):—snail.

2547. חֻמְטָה Chumṭâh, *khoom-taw'*; fem. of 2546; *low; Chumtah*, a place in Pal.:—Humtah.

2548. חָמִיץ châmîyts, *khaw-meets'*; from 2556; *seasoned*, i.e. *salt* provender:—clean.

2549. חֲמִישִׁי chămîyshîy, *kham-ee-shee'*; or

חֲמִשִּׁי chamishshîy, *kham-ish-shee'*; ord. from 2568; *fifth;* also a *fifth:*—fifth (part).

2550. חָמַל châmal, *khaw-mal'*; a prim. root; to *commiserate;* by impl. to *spare:*—have compassion, (have) pity, spare.

2551. חֶמְלָה chemlâh, *khem-law'*; from 2550; *commiseration:*—merciful, pity.

2552. חָמַם châmam, *khaw-mam'*; a prim. root; to *be hot* (lit. or fig.):—enflame self, get (have) heat, be (wax) hot, (be, wax) warm (self, at).

2553. חַמָּן chammân, *kham-mawn'*; from 2535; a *sun-pillar:*—idol, image.

2554. חָמַס châmaç, *khaw-mas'*; a prim. root; to *be violent;* by impl. to *maltreat:*—make bare, shake off, violate, do violence, take away violently, wrong, imagine wrongfully.

2555. חָמָס châmâç, *khaw-mawce'*; from 2554; *violence;* by impl. *wrong;* by meton. unjust *gain:*—cruel (-ty), damage, false, injustice, × oppressor, unrighteous, violence (against, done), violent (dealing), wrong.

2556. חָמֵץ châmêts, *khaw-mates'*; a prim. root; to *be pungent;* i.e. in taste (*sour*, i.e. lit. *fermented*, or fig. *harsh*), in color (*dazzling*):—cruel (man), dyed, be grieved, leavened.

2557. חָמֵץ châmêtz, *khaw-mates'*; from 2556; *ferment*, (fig.) *extortion:*—leaven, leavened (bread).

2558. חֹמֶץ chômets, *kho'-mets;* from 2556; *vinegar:*—vinegar.

2559. חָמַק châmaq, *khaw-mak'*; a prim. root; prop. to *enwrap;* hence to *depart* (i.e. turn about):—go about, withdraw self.

2560. חָמַר châmar, *khaw-mar'*; a prim. root; prop. to *boil* up; hence to *ferment* (with scum); to *glow* (with redness); as denom. (from 2564) to *smear* with pitch:—daub, foul, be red, trouble.

2561. חֶמֶר chemer, *kheh'-mer;* from 2560; *wine* (as *fermenting*):—× pure, red wine.

2562. חֲמַר chămar (Chald.), *kham-ar'*; corresp. to 2561; *wine:*—wine.

חֲמֹר chămôr. See 2543.

2563. חֹמֶר chômer, *kho'-mer;* from 2560; prop. a *bubbling* up, i.e. of water, a *wave;* of earth, *mire* or *clay* (cement); also a *heap;* hence a *chomer* or dry measure:—clay, heap, homer, mire, motion, mortar.

2564. חֵמָר chêmâr, *khay-mawr'*; from 2560; *bitumen* (as *rising* to the surface):—slime (-pit).

2565. חֲמֹרָה chămôrâh, *kham-o-raw'*; from 2560 [comp. 2563]; a *heap:*—heap.

2566. חַמְרָן Chamrân, *kham-rawn'*; from 2560; *red; Chamran*, an Idumæan:—Amran.

2567. חִמֵּשׁ châmash, *khaw-mash'*; a denom. from 2568; to *tax a fifth:*—take up the fifth part.

2568. חָמֵשׁ **châmêsh**, *khaw-maysh'*; masc.

חֲמִשָּׁה **chămishshâh**, *kham-ish-shaw'*; a prim. numeral; *five:*—fif [-teen], fifth, five (× apiece).

2569. חֹמֶשׁ **chômesh**, *kho'-mesh;* from 2567; a *fifth* tax:—fifth part.

2570. חֹמֶשׁ **chômesh**, *kho'-mesh;* from an unused root prob. mean. to *be stout;* the *abdomen* (as *obese*):—fifth [rib].

2571. חָמֻשׁ **châmûsh**, *khaw-moosh';* pass. part. of the same as 2570; *staunch*, i.e. able bodied *soldiers:*—armed (men), harnessed.

חֲמִשָּׁה **chămishshâh**. See 2568.

חֲמִשִּׁי **chămishshîy**. See 2549.

2572. חֲמִשִּׁים **chămishshîym**, *kham-ish-sheem';* multiple of 2568; *fifty:*—fifty.

2573. חֵמֶת **chêmeth**, *khay'-meth;* from the same as 2346; a skin *bottle* (as *tied* up):—bottle.

2574. חֲמָת **Chămâth**, *kham-awth';* from the same as 2346; *walled; Chamath*, a place in Syria:—Hamath, Hemath.

חֲמֹת **chămôth**. See 2545.

2575. חַמַּת **Chammath**, *kham-math';* a var. for the first part of 2576; *hot* springs; *Chammath*, a place in Pal.:—Hammath.

2576. חַמֹּת דֹּאר **Chammôth Dô'r**, *kham-moth' dore;* from the plur. of 2535 and 1756; *hot* springs *of Dor; Chammath-Dor*, a place in Pal.:—Hamath-Dor.

2577. חֲמָתִי **Chămâthîy**, *kham-aw-thee';* patrial from 2574; a *Chamathite* or native of *Chamath:*—Hamathite.

2578. חֲמַת צוֹבָה **Chămath Tsôwbâh**, *kham-ath' tso-baw';* from 2574 and 6678; *Chamath of Tsobah; Chamath-Tsobah;* prob. the same as 2574:—Hamath-Zobah.

2579. חֲמַת רַבָּה **Chămath Rabbâh**, *kham-ath' rab-baw';* from 2574 and 7237; *Chamath of Rabbah; Chamath-Rabbah*, prob. the same as 2574.

2580. חֵן **chên**, *khane;* from 2603; *graciousness*, i.e. subj. (*kindness, favor*) or objective (*beauty*):—favour, grace (-ious), pleasant, precious, [well-] favoured.

2581. חֵן **Chên**, *khane;* the same as 2580; *grace; Chen*, a fig. name for an Isr.:—Hen.

2582. חֵנָדָד **Chênâdâd**, *khay-naw-dawd';* prob. from 2580 and 1908; *favor of Hadad; Chenadad*, an Isr.:—Henadad.

2583. חָנָה **chânâh**, *khaw-naw';* a prim. root [comp. 2603]; prop. to *incline;* by impl. to *decline* (of the slanting rays of evening); spec. to *pitch* a tent; gen. to *encamp* (for abode or siege):—abide (in tents), camp, dwell, encamp, grow to an end, lie, pitch (tent), rest in tent.

2584. חַנָּה **Channâh**, *khan-naw';* from 2603; *favored; Channah*, an Israelitess:—Hannah.

2585. חֲנוֹךְ **Chănôwk**, *khan-oke';* from 2596; *initiated; Chanok*, an antediluvian patriach:—Enoch.

2586. חָנוּן **Chânûwn**, *khaw-noon';* from 2603; *favored; Chanun*, the name of an Ammonite and of two Isr.:—Hanun.

2587. חַנּוּן **channûwn**, *khan-noon';* from 2603; *gracious:*—gracious.

2588. חָנוּת **chânûwth**, *khaw-nooth';* from 2583; prop. a *vault* or *cell* (with an arch); by impl. a *prison:*—cabin.

2589. חַנּוֹת **channôwth**, *khan-nōth';* from 2603 (in the sense of *prayer*); *supplication:*—be gracious, intreated.

2590. חָנַט **chânaṭ**, *khaw-nat';* a prim. root; to *spice;* by impl. to *embalm;* also to *ripen:*—embalm, put forth.

2591. חִנְטָא **chinṭâ'** (Chald.), *khint-taw';* corresp. to 2406; *wheat:*—wheat.

2592. חַנִּיאֵל **Channîy'êl**, *khan-nee-ale';* from 2603 and 410; *favor of God; Channiel*, the name of two Isr.:—Hanniel.

2593. חָנִיךְ **chânîyk**, *kaw-neek';* from 2596; *initiated;* i.e. *practised:*—trained.

2594. חֲנִינָה **chănîynâh**, *khan-ee-naw';* from 2603; *graciousness:*—favour.

2595. חֲנִית **chănîyth**, *khan-eeth';* from 2583; a *lance* (for *thrusting*, like *pitching* a tent):—javelin, spear.

2596. חָנַךְ **chânak**, *khaw-nak';* a prim. root; prop. to *narrow* [comp. 2614]; fig. to *initiate* or *discipline:*—dedicate, train up.

2597. חֲנֻכָּא **chănukkâ'** (Chald.), *chan-ook-kaw';* corresp. to 2598; *consecration:*—dedication.

2598. חֲנֻכָּה **chănukkâh**, *khan-ook-kaw';* from 2596; *initiation*, i.e. *consecration:*—dedicating (-tion).

2599. חֲנֹכִי **Chănôkîy**, *khan-o-kee';* patron. from 2585; a *Chanokite* (collect.) or desc. of Chanok:—Hanochites.

2600. חִנָּם **chinnâm**, *khin-nawm';* from 2580; *gratis*, i.e. devoid of cost, reason or advantage:—without a cause (cost, wages), causeless, to cost nothing, free (-ly), innocent, for nothing (nought), in vain.

2601. חֲנַמְאֵל **Chănam'êl**, *khan-am-ale';* prob. by orth. var. for 2606; *Chanamel*, an Isr.:—Hanameel.

2602. חֲנָמָל **chănâmâl**, *khan-aw-mawl';* of uncert. der.; perh. the *aphis* or plant-louse:—frost.

2603. חָנַן **chânan**, *khaw-nan';* a prim. root [comp. 2583]; prop. to *bend* or stoop in kindness to an inferior; to *favor, bestow;* causat. to *implore* (i.e. move to favor by petition):—beseech, × fair, (be, find, shew) favour (-able), be (deal, give, grant (gracious (-ly), intreat, (be) merciful, have (shew) mercy (on, upon), have pity upon, pray, make supplication, × very.

2604. חֲנַן **chănan** (Chald.), *khan-an';* corresp. to 2603; to *favor* or (causat.) to *entreat:*—shew mercy, make supplication.

2605. חָנָן **Chânân**, *khaw-nawn';* from 2603; *favor; Chanan*, the name of seven Isr.:—Canan.

2606. חֲנַנְאֵל **Chănan'êl**, *khan-an-ale';* from 2603 and 410; *God has favored; Chananel*, prob. an Isr., from whom a tower of Jerusalem was named:—Hananeel.

2607. חֲנָנִי **Chănânîy**, *khan-aw-nee';* from 2603; *gracious; Chanani*, the name of six Isr.:—Hanani.

2608. חֲנַנְיָה **Chănanyâh**, *khan-an-yaw';* or

חֲנַנְיָהוּ **Chănanyâhûw**, *khan-an-yaw'-hoo;* from 2603 and 3050; *Jah has favored; Chananjah*, the name of thirteen Isr.:—Hananiah.

2609. חָנֵס **Chânêç**, *khaw-nace';* of Eg. der.; *Chanes*, a place in Egypt:—Hanes.

2610. חָנֵף **chânêph**, *khaw-nafe';* a prim. root; to *soil*, espec. in a moral sense:—corrupt, defile, × greatly, pollute, profane.

2611. חָנֵף **chânêph**, *khaw-nafe';* from 2610; *soiled* (i.e. with sin), *impious:*—hypocrite (-ical).

2612. חֹנֶף **chôneph**, *kho'-nef;* from 2610; moral *filth*, i.e. *wickedness:*—hypocrisy.

2613. חֲנֻפָה **chănûphâh**, *khan-oo-faw';* fem. from 2610; *impiety:*—profaneness.

2614. חָנַק **chânaq**, *khaw-nak';* a prim. root [comp. 2596]; to *be narrow;* by impl. to *throttle*, or (reflex.) to *choke* oneself to death (by a rope):—hang self, strangle.

2615. חַנָּתֹן **Channâthôn**, *khan-naw-thone';* prob. from 2603; *favored; Channathon*, a place in Pal.:—Hannathon.

2616. חָסַד **châçad**, *khaw-sad';* a prim. root; prop. perh. to *bow* (the neck only [comp. 2603] in courtesy to an equal), i.e. to *be kind;* also (by euphem. [comp. 1288], but rarely) to *reprove:*—shew self merciful, put to shame.

2617. חֶסֶד **cheçed**, *kheh'-sed;* from 2616; *kindness;* by impl. (towards God) *piety;* rarely (by opp.) *reproof*, or (subject.) *beauty:*—favour, good deed (-liness, -ness), kindly, (loving-) kindness, merciful (kindness), mercy, pity, reproach, wicked thing.

2618. חֶסֶד **Cheçed**, *kheh'-sed;* the same as 2617; *favor; Chesed*, an Isr.:—Hesed.

2619. חֲסַדְיָה **Chăçadyâh**, *khas-ad-yaw';* from 2617 and 3050; *Jah has favored; Chasadjah*, an Isr.:—Hasadiah.

2620. חָסָה **châçâh**, *khaw-saw';* a prim. root; to *flee* for protection [comp. 982]; fig. to *confide* in:—have hope, make refuge, (put) trust.

2621. חֹסָה **Chôçâh**, *kho-saw';* from 2620; *hopeful; Chosah*, an Isr.; also a place in Pal.:—Hosah.

2622. חָסוּת **châçûwth**, *khaw-sooth';* from 2620; *confidence:*—trust.

2623. חָסִיד **châçîyd**, *khaw-seed';* from 2616; prop. *kind*, i.e. (religiously) *pious* (a saint):—godly (man), good, holy (one), merciful, saint, [un-] godly.

2624. חֲסִידָה **chăçîydâh**, *khas-ee-daw';* fem. of 2623; the *kind* (maternal) bird, i.e. a *stork:*— × feather, stork.

2625. חָסִיל **châçîyl**, *khaw-seel';* from 2628; the *ravager*, i.e. a *locust:*—caterpillar.

2626. חָסִין **chăçîyn**, *khas-een';* from 2630; prop. *firm*, i.e. (by impl.) *mighty:*—strong.

2627. חַסִּיר **chaççîyr** (Chald.), *khas-seer';* from a root corresp. to 2637; *deficient:*—wanting.

2628. חָסַל **châçal**, *khaw-sal';* a prim. root; to *eat* off:—consume.

2629. חָסַם **châçam**, *khaw-sam';* a prim. root; to *muzzle;* by anal. to *stop* the nose:—muzzle, stop.

2630. חָסַן **châçan**, *khaw-san';* a prim. root; prop. to (be) *compact;* by impl. to *hoard:*—lay up.

2631. חֲסַן **chăçan** (Chald.), *khas-an';* corresp. to 2630; to *hold* in occupancy:—possess.

2632. חֱסֵן **chêçen** (Chald.), *khay'-sen;* from 2631; *strength:*—power.

2633. חֹסֶן **chôçen**, *kho'-sen;* from 2630; *wealth:*—riches, strength, treasure.

2634. חָסֹן **châçôn**, *khaw-sone';* from 2630; *powerful:*—strong.

2635. חֲסַף **chăçaph** (Chald.), *khas-af';* from a root corresp. to that of 2636; a *clod:*—clay.

2636. חַסְפַּס **chaçpaç**, *khas-pas';* redupl. from an unused root mean. appar. to *peel;* a *shred* or *scale:*—round thing.

2637. חָסֵר **châçêr**, *khaw-sare';* a prim. root; to *lack;* by impl. to *fail, want, lessen:*—be abated, bereave, decrease, (cause to) fail, (have) lack, make lower, want.

2638. חָסֵר **châçêr**, *khaw-sare';* from 2637; *lacking;* hence *without:*—destitute, fail, lack, have need, void, want.

2639. חֶסֶר **cheçer**, *kheh'-ser;* from 2637; *lack;* hence *destitution:*—poverty, want.

2640. חֹסֶר **chôçer**, *kho'-ser;* from 2637; *poverty:*—in want of.

2641. חַסְרָה **Chaçrâh**, *khas-raw';* from 2637; *want:*—Chasrah, an Isr.:—Hasrah.

2642. חֶסְרוֹן **cheçrôwn**, *khes-rone';* from 2637; *deficiency:*—wanting.

2643. חַף **chaph**, *khaf;* from 2653 (in the moral sense of *covered* from soil); *pure:*—innocent.

2644. חָפָא **châphâ'**, *khaw-faw';* an orth. var. of 2645; prop. to *cover*, i.e. (in a sinister sense) to *act covertly:*—do secretly.

2645. חָפָה **châphâh**, *khaw-faw';* a prim. root [comp. 2644, 2653]; to *cover;* by impl. to *veil*, to *incase, protect:*—ceil, cover, overlay.

2646. חֻפָּה **chuppâh**, *khoop-paw';* from 2645; a *canopy:*—chamber, closet, defence.

2647. חֻפָּה **Chuppâh**, *khoop-paw';* the same as 2646; *Chuppah*, an Isr.:—Huppah.

2648. חָפַז **châphaz**, *khaw-faz'*; a prim. root; prop. to *start* up suddenly, i.e. (by impl.) to *hasten* away, to *fear*:—(make) haste (away), tremble.

2649. חִפָּזוֹן **chippâzôwn**, *khip-paw-zone'*; from 2648; *hasty flight*:—haste.

2650. חֻפִּים **Chuppiym**, *khoop-peem'*; plur. of 2646 [comp. 2349]; *Chuppim*, an Isr.:—Huppim.

2651. חֹפֶן **chôphen**, *kho'-fen*; from an unused root of uncert. signif.; a *fist* (only in the dual):—fists, (both) hands, hand [-ful].

2652. חָפְנִי **Chophnîy**, *khof-nee'*; from 2651; perh. *pugilist*; *Chophni*, an Isr.:—Hophni.

2653. חֹפַף **chôphaph**, *khaw-faf'*; a prim. root [comp. 2645, 3182]; to *cover* (in protection):—cover.

2654. חָפֵץ **châphêts**, *khaw-fates'*; a prim. root; prop. to *incline* to; by impl. (lit. but rarely) to *bend*; fig. to *be pleased* with, *desire*:—× any at all, (have, take) delight, desire, favour, like, move, be (well) pleased, have pleasure, will, would.

2655. חָפֵץ **châphêts**, *khaw-fates'*; from 2654; *pleased* with:—delight in, desire, favour, please, have pleasure, whosoever would, willing, wish.

2656. חֵפֶץ **chêphets**, *khay'-fets*; from 2654; *pleasure*; hence (abstr.) *desire*; concr. a *valuable* thing; hence (by extens.) a *matter* (as something in mind):—acceptable, delight (-some), desire, things desired, matter, pleasant (-ure), purpose, willingly.

2657. חֶפְצִי בָהּ **Chephtsîy bâhh**, *khef-tsee' baw*; from 2656 with suffixes; *my delight* (is) *in her*; *Cheptsi-bah*, a fanciful name for Pal.:—Hephzi-bah.

2658. חָפַר **châphar**, *khaw-far'*; a prim. root; prop. to *pry* into; by impl. to *delve*, to *explore*:—dig, paw, search out, seek.

2659. חָפֵר **châphêr**, *khaw-fare'*; a prim. root [perh. rath. the same as 2658 through the idea of *detection*]; to *blush*; fig. to *be ashamed*, *disappointed*; causat. to *shame*, *reproach*:—be ashamed, be confounded, be brought to confusion (unto shame), come (be put to) shame, bring reproach.

2660. חֵפֶר **Chêpher**, *khay'-fer*; from 2658 or 2659; a *pit* or *shame*; *Chepher*, a place in Pal.; also the name of three Isr.:—Hepher.

2661. חֲפֹר **chăphôr**, *khaf-ore'*; from 2658; a *hole*; only in connection with 6512, which ought rather to be joined as one word, thus

חֲפַרְפֵּרָה **chăpharpêrâh**, *khaf-ar-pay-raw'*; by redupl. from 2658; a *burrower*, i.e. prob. a *rat*:— + mole.

2662. חֶפְרִי **Chephrîy**, *khef-ree'*; patron. from 2660; a *Chephrite* (collect.) or desc. of *Chepher*:—Hepherites.

2663 חֲפָרַיִם **Chăphârayîm**, *khaf-aw-rah'-yim*; dual of 2660; *double pit*; *Chapharajim*, a place in Pal.:—Haphraim.

חֲפַרְפֵּרָה **chăpharpêrâh**. See 2661.

2664. חָפַשׂ **châphas**, *khaw-fas'*; a prim. root; to *seek*; causat. to *conceal* oneself (i.e. let be sought), or *mask*:—change, (make) diligent (search), disguise self, hide, search (for, out).

2665. חֵפֶשׂ **chêphes**, *khay'-fes*; from 2664; something *covert*, i.e. a *trick*:—search.

2666. חָפַשׁ **châphash**, *khaw-fash'*; a prim. root; to *spread* loose, fig. to *manumit*:—be free.

2667. חֹפֶשׁ **Chôphesh**, *kho'-fesh*; from 2666; something *spread* loosely, i.e. a *carpet*:—precious.

2668. חֻפְשָׁה **chuphshâh**, *khoof-shaw'*; from 2666; *liberty* (from slavery):—freedom.

2669. חָפְשׁוּת **chôphshûwth**, *khof-shooth'*; and

חָפְשִׁית **chophshîyth**, *khof-sheeth'*; from 2666; *prostration* by sickness (with 1004, a *hospital*):—several.

2670. חָפְשִׁי **chophshîy**, *khof-shee'*; from 2666; *exempt* (from bondage, tax or care):—free, liberty.

2671. חֵץ **chêts**, *khayts*; from 2686; prop. a *piercer*, i.e. an *arrow*; by impl. a *wound*; fig. (of God) thunder-*bolt*; (by interchange for 6086) the *shaft* of a spear:— + archer, arrow, dart, shaft, staff, wound.

חֻץ **chûts**. See 2351.

2672. חָצַב **châtsab**, *khaw-tsab'*; or

חָצֵב **châtsêb**, *khaw-tsabe'*; a prim. root; to *cut* or carve (wood, stone or other material); by impl. to *hew*, *split*, *square*, *quarry*, *engrave*:—cut, dig, divide, grave, hew (out, -er), make, mason.

2673. חָצָה **châtsâh**, *khaw-tsaw'*; a prim. root [comp. 2686]; to *cut* or *split* in two; to *halve*:—divide, × live out half, reach to the midst, part.

2674. חָצוֹר **Châtsôwr**, *khaw-tsore'*; a collect. form of 2691; *village*; *Chatsor*, the name (thus simply) of two places in Pal. and of one in Arabia:—Hazor.

2675. חָצוֹר חֲדַתָּה **Châtsôwr Chădattâh**, *khaw-tsore' khad-at-taw'*; from 2674 and a Chaldaizing form of the fem. of 2319 [comp. 2323]; *new Chatsor*, a place in Pal.:—Hazor, Hadattah [*as if two places*].

2676. חָצוֹת **châtsôwth**, *khaw-tsoth'*; from 2673; the *middle* (of the night):—mid [-night].

2677. חֵצִי **chêtsîy**, *khay-tsee'*; from 2673; the *half* or *middle*:—half, middle, mid [-night], midst, part, two parts.

2678. חִצִּי **chitstsîy**, *khits-tsee'*; or

חֵצִי **chêtsîy**, *chay-tsee'*; prol. from 2671; an *arrow*:—arrow.

2679. חֲצִי הַמְּנֻחוֹת **Chătsîy ham-Menûchôwth**, *chat-tsee' ham-men-oo-khoth'*; from 2677 and the plur. of 4496, with the art. interposed; *midst of the resting-places*; *Chatsi-ham-Menuchoth*, an Isr.:—half of the Manahethites.

2680. חֲצִי הַמְּנַחְתִּי **Chătsîy ham-Menachtîy**, *khat-see' ham-men-akh-tee'*; patron. from 2679; a *Chatsi-ham-Menachtite* or desc. of Chatsi-ham-Menuchoth:—half of the Manahethites.

2681. חָצִיר **châtsîyr**, *khaw-tseer'*; a collat. form of 2691; a *court* or *abode*:—court.

2682. חָצִיר **châtsîyr**, *khaw-tseer'*; perh. orig. the same as 2681, from the *greenness* of a court-yard; *grass*; also a *leek* (collect.):—grass, hay, herb, leek.

2683. חֵצֶן **chêtsen**, *khay'-tsen*; from an unused root mean. to hold *firmly*; the *bosom* (as *comprised* between the arms):—bosom.

2684. חֹצֶן **chôtsen**, *kho'-tsen*; a collat. form of 2683, and mean. the same:—arm, lap.

2685. חֲצַף **chătsaph** (Chald.), *khats-af'*; a prim. root; prop. to *shear* or cut close; fig. to *be severe*:—hasty, be urgent.

2686. חָצַץ **châtsats**, *khaw-tsats'*; a prim. root [comp. 2673]; prop. to *chop* into, pierce or sever; hence to *curtail*, to *distribute* (into ranks); as denom. from 2671, to *shoot* an arrow:—archer, × bands, cut off in the midst.

2687. חָצָץ **châtsâts**, *khaw-tsawts'*; from 2687; prop. something *cutting*; hence *gravel* (as *grit*); also (like 2671) an *arrow*:—arrow, gravel (stone).

2688. חַצְצוֹן תָּמָר **Chatsetsôwn Tâmâr**, *khats-ets-one' taw-mawr'*; or

חַצֲצֹן תָּמָר **Chatsătsôn Tâmâr**, *khats-ats-one' taw-mawr'*; from 2686 and 8558; *division* [i.e. perh. *row*] *of* (the) *palm-tree*; *Chatsetson-tamar*, a place in Pal.:—Hazezon-tamar.

2689. חֲצֹצְרָה **chătsôtserâh**, *khats-o-tser-aw'*; by redupl. from 2690; a *trumpet* (from its *sundered* or quavering note):—trumpet (-er).

2690. חָצַר **châtsar**, *khaw-tsar'*; a prim. root; prop. to *surround* with a stockade, and thus *separate* from the open country; but used only in the redupl. form

חֲצֹצֵר **chătsôtsêr**, *khast-o-tsare'*; or (2 Chron. 5 : 12)

חֲצֹרֵר **chătsôrêr**, *hhats-o-rare'*; as dem. from 2689; to *trumpet*, i.e. blow on that instrument:—blow, sound, trumpeter.

2691. חָצֵר **châtsêr**, *khaw-tsare'* (masc. and fem.); from 2690 in its original sense; a *yard* (as *inclosed* by a fence); also a *hamlet* (as similarly *surrounded* with walls):—court, tower, village.

2692. חֲצַר אַדָּר **Chătsar Addâr**, *khats-ar' ad-dawr'*; from 2691 and 146; (the) *village of Addar*; *Chatsar-Addar*, a place in Pal.:—Hazar-addar.

2693. חֲצַר גַּדָּה **Chătsar Gaddâh**, *khats-ar' gad-daw'*; from 2691 and a fem. of 1408; (the) *village of* (female) *Fortune*; *Chatsar-Gaddah*, a place in Pal.:—Hazar-gaddah.

2694. חֲצַר הַתִּיכוֹן **Chătsar hat-Tîykôwn**, *khats-ar' hat-tee-kone'*; from 2691 and 8484 with the art. interposed; *village of the middle*; *Chatsar-hat-Tikon*, a place in Pal.:—Hazar-hatticon.

2695. חֶצְרוֹ **Chetsrôw**, *khets-ro'*; by an orth. var. for 2696; *inclosure*; *Chetsro*, an Isr.:—Hezro, Hezrai.

2696. חֶצְרוֹן **Chetsrôwn**, *khets-rone'*; from 2691; *court-yard*; *Chetsron*, the name of a place in Pal.; also of two Isr.:—Hezron.

2697. חֶצְרוֹנִי **Chetsrôwnîy**, *khets-ro-nee'*; patron. from 2696; a *Chetsronite* or (collect.) desc. of Chetsron:—Hezronites.

2698. חֲצֵרוֹת **Chătsêrowth**, *khats-ay-roth'*; fem. plur. of 2691; *yards*; *Chatseroth*, a place in Pal.:—Hazeroth.

2699. חֲצֵרִים **Chătsêrîym**, *khats-ay-reem'*; plur. masc. of 2691; *yards*; *Chatserim*, a place in Pal.:—Hazerim.

2700. חֲצַרְמָוֶת **Chătsarmâveth**, *khats-ar-maw'-veth*; from 2691 and 4194; *village of death*; *Chatsarmaveth*, a place in Arabia:—Hazarmaveth.

2701. חֲצַר סוּסָה **Chătsar Çûwçâh**, *khats-ar' soo-saw'*; from 2691 and 5484; *village of cavalry*; *Chatsar-Susah*, a place in Pal.:—Hazar-susah.

2702. חֲצַר סוּסִים **Chătsar Çûwçîym**, *khats-ar' soo-seem'*; from 2691 and the plur. of 5483; *village of horses*; *Chatsar-Susim*, a place in Pal.:—Hazar-susim.

2703. חֲצַר עֵינוֹן **Chătsar ʻÊynôwn**, *khats-ar' ay-none'*; from 2691 and a der. of 5869; *village of springs*; *Chatsar-Enon*, a place in Pal.:—Hazar-enon.

2704. חֲצַר עֵינָן **Chătsar ʻÊynân**, *khats-ar' ay-nawn'*; from 2691 and the same as 5881; *village of springs*; *Chatsar-Enan*, a place in Pal.:—Hazar-enan.

2705. חֲצַר שׁוּעָל **Chătsar Shûwʻâl**, *khats-ar' shoo-awl'*; from 2691 and 7776; *village of* (the) *fox*; *Chatsar-Shual*, a place in Pal.:—Hazar-shual.

חֵק **chêq**. See 2436.

2706. חֹק **chôq**, *khoke*; from 2710; an *enactment*; hence an *appointment* (of time, space quantity, labor or usage):—appointed, bound, commandment, convenient, custom, decree (-d), due, law, measure, × necessary, ordinance (-nary), portion, set time, statute, task.

2707. חָקָה **châqah**, *khaw-kaw'*; a prim. root; to *carve*; by impl. to *delineate*; also to *intrench*:—carved work, portrayed, set a print.

2708. חֻקָּה **chuqqâh**, *khook-kaw'*; fem. of 2706, and mean. substantially the same:—appointed, custom, manner, ordinance, site, statute.

2709. חֲקוּפָא **Chăqûwphâʼ**, *khah-oo-faw'*; from an unused root prob. mean. to *bend*; *crooked*; *Chakupha*, one of the Nethinim:—Hakupha.

2710. חָקַק **châqaq**, *khaw-kak'*; a prim. root; prop. to *hack*, i.e. *engrave* (Judg. 5 : 14, to *be a scribe* simply); by impl. to *enact* (laws being *cut* in stone or metal tablets in primitive times) or (gen.) *prescribe*:—appoint, decree, governor, grave, lawgiver, note, pourtray, print, set.

2711. חֵקֶק **chêqeq**, *khay'-kek*; from 2710; an *enactment*, a *resolution*:—decree, thought.

2712. חֻקֹּק **Chuqqôq**, *khook-koke'*; or (fully) חוּקֹק **Chûwqôq**, *khoo-koke'*; from 2710; *appointed*; *Chukkok* or *Chukok*, a place in Pal.:—Hukkok, Hukok.

2713. חָקַר **châqar**, *khaw-kar'*; a prim. root; prop. to *penetrate*; hence to *examine intimately*:—find out, (make) search (out), seek (out), sound, try.

2714. חֵקֶר **chêqer**, *khay'-ker*; from 2713; *examination*, *enumeration*, *deliberation*:—finding out, number, [un-] search (-able, -ed out, -ing).

2715. חֹר **chôr**, *khore*; or (fully) חוֹר **chôwr**, *khore*; from 2787; prop. *white* or *pure* (from the *cleansing* or *shining* power of fire [comp. 2751]); hence (fig.) *noble* (in rank):—noble.

חֻר **chûr**. See 2352.

2716. חֶרֶא **chereʼ**, *kheh'-reh*; from an unused (and vulg.) root prob. mean. to *evacuate* the bowels; *excrement*:—dung. Also חֲרִי° **chărîy**, *khar-ee'*.

2717. חָרַב **chârab**, *khaw-rab'*; or חָרֵב **chârêb**, *khaw-rabe'*; a prim. root; to *parch* (through drought), i.e. (by anal.) to *desolate*, *destroy*, *kill*:—decay, (be) desolate, destroy (-er), (be) dry (up), slay, × surely, (lay, lie, make) waste.

2718. חֲרַב **chărab** (Chald.), *khar-ab'*; a root corresp. to 2717; to *demolish*:—destroy.

2719. חֶרֶב **chereb**, *kheh'-reb*; from 2717; *drought*; also a *cutting* instrument (from its *destructive* effect), as a *knife*, *sword*, or other sharp implement:—axe, dagger, knife, mattock, sword, tool.

2720. חָרֵב **chârêb**, *khaw-rabe'*; from 2717; *parched* or *ruined*:—desolate, dry, waste.

2721. חֹרֶב **chôreb**, *kho'-reb*; a collat. form of 2719; *drought* or *desolation*:—desolation, drought, dry, heat, × utterly, waste.

2722. חֹרֵב **Chôrêb**, *kho-rabe'*; from 2717; *desolate*; *Choreb*, a (gen.) name for the Sinaitic mountains:—Horeb.

2723. חָרְבָּה **chorbâh**, *khor-baw'*; fem. of 2721; prop. *drought*, i.e. (by impl.) a *desolation*:—decayed place, desolate (place, -tion), destruction, (laid) waste (place).

2724. חָרָבָה **chârâbâh**, *khaw-raw-baw'*; fem. of 2720; a *desert*:—dry (ground, land).

2725. חֲרָבוֹן **chărâbôwn**, *khar-aw-bone'*; from 2717; parching *heat*:—drought.

2726. חַרְבוֹנָא **Charbôwnâʼ**, *khar-bo-naw'*; or חַרְבוֹנָה **Charbôwnâh**, *khar-bo-naw'*; of Pers. or.; *Charbona* or *Charbonah*, a eunuch of Xerxes:—Harbona, Harbonah.

2727. חָרַג **chârag**, *khaw-rag'*; a prim. root; prop. to *leap* suddenly, i.e. (by impl.) to *be dismayed*:—be afraid.

2728. חַרְגֹּל **chargôl**, *khar-gole'*; from 2727; the *leaping* insect, i.e. a *locust*:—beetle.

2729. חָרַד **chârad**, *khaw-rad'*; a prim. root; to *shudder* with terror; hence to *fear*; also to *hasten* (with anxiety):—be (make) afraid, be careful, discomfit, fray (away), quake, tremble.

2730. חָרֵד **chârêd**, *khaw-rade'*; from 2729; *fearful*; also *reverential*:—afraid, trembling.

2731. חֲרָדָה **chărâdâh**, *khar-aw-daw'*; fem. of 2730; *fear*, *anxiety*:—care, × exceedingly, fear, quaking, trembling.

2732. חֲרָדָה **Chărâdâh**, *khar-aw-daw'*; the same as 2731; *Charadah*, a place in the Desert:—Haradah.

2733. חֲרֹדִי **Chărôdîy**, *khar-o-dee'*; patrial from a deriv. of 2729 [comp. 5878]; a *Charodite*, or inhab. of *Charod*:—Harodite.

2734. חָרָה **chârâh**, *khaw-raw'*; a prim. root [comp. 2787]; to *glow* or grow warm; fig. (usually) to *blaze* up, of anger, zeal, jealousy:—be angry, burn, be displeased, × earnestly, fret self, grieve, be (wax) hot, be incensed, kindle, × very, be wroth. See 8474.

2735. חֹר הַגִּדְגָּד **Chôr hag-Gidgâd**, *khore hag-ghid-gawd'*; from 2356 and a collat. (masc.) form of 1412, with the art. interposed; *hole of the cleft*; *Chor-hag-Gidgad*, a place in the Desert:—Hor-hagidgad.

2736. חַרְהֲיָה **Charhăyâh**, *khar-hah-yaw'*; from 2734 and 3050; *fearing Jah*; *Charhajah*, an Isr.:—Harhaiah.

2737. חָרוּז **chârûwz**, *khaw-rooz'*; from an unused root mean. to *perforate*; prop. *pierced*, i.e. a *bead* of pearl, gems or jewels (as strung):—chain.

2738. חָרוּל **chârûwl**, *khaw-rool'*; or (short.) חָרֻל **chârûl**, *khaw-rool'*; appar. pass. part. of an unused root prob. mean. to *be prickly*; prop. *pointed*, i.e. a *bramble* or other thorny weed:—nettle.

חֹרוֹן **chôrôwn**. See 1032, 2772.

2739. חֲרוּמַף **chărûwmaph**, *khar-oo-maf'*; from pass. part. of 2763 and 639; *snub-nosed*; *Charumaph*, an Isr.:—Harumaph.

2740. חָרוֹן **chârôwn**, *khaw-rone'*; or (short.) חָרֹן **chârôn**, *khaw-rone'*; from 2734; a *burning* of anger:—sore displeasure, fierce (-ness), fury, (fierce) wrath (-ful).

2741. חֲרוּפִי **Chărûwphîy**, *khar-oo-fee'*; a patrial from (prob.) a collat. form of 2756; a *Charuphite* or inhab. of Charuph (or Chariph):—Haruphite.

2742. חָרוּץ **chârûwts**, *khaw-roots'*; or חָרֻץ **chârûts**, *khaw-roots'*; pass. part. of 2782; prop. *incised* or (act.) *incisive*; hence (as noun masc. or fem.) a *trench* (as dug), *gold* (as mined), a *threshing-sledge* (having sharp teeth); (fig.) *determination*; also *eager*:—decision, diligent, (fine) gold, pointed things, sharp, threshing instrument, wall.

2743. חָרוּץ **Chârûwts**, *khaw-roots'*; the same as 2742; *earnest*; *Charuts*, an Isr.:—Haruz.

2744. חַרְחוּר **Charchûwr**, *khar-khoor'*; a fuller form of 2746; *inflammation*; *Charchur*, one of the Nethinim:—Harhur.

2745. חַרְחַס **Charchaç**, *khar-khas'*; from the same as 2775; perh. *shining*; *Charchas*, an Isr.:—Harhas.

2746. חַרְחֻר **charchûr**, *khar-khoor'*; from 2787; *fever* (as *hot*):—extreme burning.

2747. חֶרֶט **chereṭ**, *kheh'-ret*; from a prim. root mean. to *engrave*; a *chisel* or *graver*; also a *style* for writing:—graving tool, pen.

חָרִט **chârîṭ**. See 2754.

2748. חַרְטֹם **charṭôm**, *khar-tome'*; from the same as 2747; a *horoscopist* (as *drawing* magical lines or circles):—magician.

2749. חַרְטֹם **charṭôm** (Chald.), *khar-tome'*; the same as 2748:—magician.

2750. חֳרִי **chŏrîy**, *khor-ee'*; from 2734; a *burning* (i.e. intense) anger:—fierce, × great, heat.

חֲרִי° **chărîy**. See 2716.

2751. חֹרִי **chôrîy**, *kho-ree'*; from the same as 2353; *white* bread:—white.

2752. חֹרִי **Chôrîy**, *kho-ree'*; from 2356; *cave-dweller* or troglodyte; a *Chorite* or aboriginal Idumæan:—Horims, Horites.

2753. חֹרִי **Chôrîy**, *kho-ree'*; or חוֹרִי **Chôwrîy**, *kho-ree'*; the same as 2752; *Chori*, the name of two men:—Hori.

2754. חָרִיט **chârîyṭ**, *khaw-reet'*; or חָרִט **chârîṭ**, *khaw-reet'*; from the same as 2747; prop. *cut* out (or *hollow*), i.e. (by impl.) a *pocket*:—bag, crisping pin.

2755. חֲרֵי־יוֹנִים **chărêy-yôwnîym**, *khar-ay'-yo-neem'*; from the plur. of 2716 and the plur. of 3123; *excrements of doves* [or perh. rather the plur. of a single word חֲרָאיוֹן **chărâʼyôwn**, *khar-aw-yone'*; of similar or uncert. deriv.], prob. a kind of vegetable:—doves' dung.

2756. חָרִיף **Chârîyph**, *khaw-reef'*; from 2778; *autumnal*; *Chariph*, the name of two Isr.:—Hariph.

2757. חָרִיץ **chârîyts**, *khaw-reets'*; or חָרִץ **chârîts**, *khaw-reets'*; from 2782; prop. *incisure* or (pass.) *incised* [comp. 2742]; hence a *threshing-sledge* (with *sharp* teeth): also a *slice* (as cut):— + cheese, harrow.

2758. חָרִישׁ **chârîysh**, *khaw-reesh'*; from 2790; *ploughing* or its season:—earing (time), ground.

2759. חֲרִישִׁי **chărîyshîy**, *khar-ee-shee'*; from 2790 in the sense of *silence*; *quiet*, i.e. *sultry* (as noun fem. the *sirocco* or hot east wind):—vehement.

2760. חָרַךְ **chârak**, *khaw-rak'*; a prim. root; to *braid* (i.e. to *entangle* or snare) or *catch* (game) in a net:—roast.

2761. חֲרַךְ **chărak** (Chald.), *khar-ak'*; a root prob. allied to the equiv. of 2787; to *scorch*:—singe.

2762. חֶרֶךְ **cherek**, *kheh'-rek*; from 2760; prop. a *net*, i.e. (by anal.) *lattice*:—lattice.

חָרֻל **chârûl**. See 2738.

2763. חָרַם **charam**, *khaw-ram'*; a prim. root; to *seclude*; spec. (by a ban) to *devote* to relig. uses (espec. destruction); phys. and reflex. to be *blunt* as to the nose:—make accursed, consecrate, (utterly) destroy, devote, forfeit, have a flat nose, utterly (slay, make away).

2734. חֵרֶם **chêrem**, *khay'-rem*; or (Zech. 14 : 11) חֶרֶם **cherem**, *kheh'-rem*; from 2763; phys. (as *shutting in*) a *net* (either lit. or fig.); usually a *doomed* object; abstr. *extermination*:—(ac-) curse (-d, -d thing), dedicated thing, things which should have been utterly destroyed, (appointed to) utter destruction, devoted (thing), net.

2765. חֳרֵם **Chŏrêm**, *khor-ame'*; from 2763; *devoted*; *Chorem*, a place in Pal.:—Horem.

2766. חָרִם **Chârim**, *khaw-reem'*; from 2763; *snub-nosed*; *Charim*, an Isr.:—Harim.

2767. חָרְמָה **Chormâh**, *khor-maw'*; from 2763; *devoted*; *Chormah*, a place in Pal.:—Hormah.

2768. חֶרְמוֹן **Chermôwn**, *kher-mone'*; from 2763; *abrupt*; *Chermon*, a mount of Pal.:—Hermon.

2769. חֶרְמוֹנִים **Chermôwnîym**, *kher-mo-neem'*; plur. of 2768; *Hermons*, i.e. its peaks:—the Hermonites.

2770. חֶרְמֵשׁ **chermêsh**, *kher-mashe'*; from 2763; a *sickle* (as *cutting*):—sickle.

2771. חָרָן **Chârân**, *kaw-rawn'*; from 2787; *parched*; *Charan*, the name of a man and also of a place:—Haran.

חָרֹן **chârôn**. See 2740.

2772. חֹרֹנִי **Chôrônîy**, *kho-ro-nee'*; patrial from 2773; a *Choronite* or inhab. of Choronaim:—Horonite.

2773. חֹרֹנַיִם **Chôrônayim**, *kho-ro-nah'-yim*; dual of a deriv. from 2356; *double cave-town*; *Choronajim*, a place in Moab:—Horonaim.

2774. חַרְנֶפֶר **Charnepher**, *khar-neh'-fer*; of uncert. der.; *Charnepher*, an Isr.:—Harnepher.

2775. חֶרֶס **chereç**, *kheh'-res*; or (with a directive enclitic) חַרְסָה **charçâh**, *khar'-saw*; from an unused root mean. to *scrape*; the *itch*; also [perh. from the mediating idea of 2777] the *sun*:—itch, sun.

2776. חֶרֶס **Chereç**, *kheh'-res*; the same as 2775; *shining*; *Cheres*, a mount. in Pal.:—Heres.

2777. חַרְסוּת **charçûwth**, *khar-sooth'*; from 2775 (appar. in the sense of a red *tile* used for scraping); a *potsherd*, i.e. (by impl.) a *pottery;* the name of a gate at Jerus.:—east.

2778. חָרַף **châraph**, *khaw-raf'*; a prim. root; to *pull* off, i.e. (by impl.) to *expose* (as by *stripping*); spec. to *betroth* (as if a surrender); fig. to carp at, i.e. *defame;* denom. (from 2779) to spend the *winter:*—betroth, blaspheme, defy, jeopard, rail, reproach, upbraid.

2779. חֹרֶף **chôreph**, *kho'-ref;* from 2778; prop. the *crop* gathered, i.e. (by impl.) the *autumn* (and winter) season; fig. *ripeness* of age:—cold, winter ([-house]), youth.

2780. חָרֵף **Chârêph**, *khaw-rafe'*; from 2778; *reproachful; Chareph*, an Isr.:—Hareph.

2781. חֶרְפָּה **cherpâh**, *kher-paw'*; from 2778; *contumely, disgrace*, the *pudenda:*—rebuke, reproach (-fully), shame.

2782. חָרַץ **chârats**, *khaw-rats'*; a prim root; prop. to *point* sharply, i.e. (lit.) to *wound;* fig. to *be alert*, to *decide:*—bestir self, decide, decree, determine, maim, move.

2783. חֲרַץ **chărats** (Chald.), *khar-ats'*; from a root corresp. to 2782 in the sense of *vigor;* the *loin* (as the seat of strength):—loin.

חָרֻץ **chârûts**. See 2742.

2784. חַרְצֻבָּה **chartsubbâh**, *khar-tsoob-baw'*; of uncert. der.; a *fetter;* fig. a *pain:*—band.

חָרִיץ **chârîts**. See 2757.

2785. חַרְצַן **chartsan**, *khar-tsan'*; from 2782; a *sour* grape (as *sharp* in taste):—kernel.

2786. חָרַק **châraq**, *khaw-rak'*; a prim. root; to *grate* the teeth:—gnash.

2787. חָרַר **chârar**, *khaw-rar'*; a prim. root; to *glow*, i.e. lit. (to *melt, burn, dry* up) or fig. (to *show* or *incite passion:*—be angry, burn, dry, kindle.

2788. חָרֵר **chârêr**, *khaw-rare'*; from 2787; *arid:*—parched place.

2789. חֶרֶס **cheres**, *kheh'-res;* a collat. form mediating between 2775 and 2791; a piece of *pottery:*—earth (-en), (pot-) sherd, + stone.

2790. חָרַשׁ **chârash**, *khaw-rash'*; a prim. root; to *scratch*, i.e. (by impl.) to *engrave, plough;* hence (from the use of tools) to *fabricate* (of any material); fig. to *devise* (in a bad sense); hence (from the idea of secrecy) to be *silent*, to *let alone;* hence (by impl.) to *be deaf* (as an accompaniment of dumbness):— × altogether, cease, conceal, be deaf, devise, ear, graven, imagine, leave off speaking, hold peace, plow (-er, -man), be quiet, rest, practise secretly, keep silence, be silent, speak not a word, be still, hold tongue, worker.

2791. חֶרֶשׁ **cheresh**, *kheh'-resh;* from 2790; magical *craft;* also *silence:*—cunning, secretly.

2792. חֶרֶשׁ **Cheresh**, *kheh'-resh;* the same as 2791:—*Cheresh*, a Levite:—Heresh.

2793. חֹרֶשׁ **chôresh**, *kho'-resh;* from 2790; a *forest* (perh. as furnishing the material for fabric):—bough, forest, shroud, wood.

2794. חֹרֵשׁ **chôrêsh**, *kho-rashe'*; act. part. of 2790; a *fabricator* or mechanic:—artificer.

2795. חֵרֵשׁ **chêrêsh**, *khay-rashe'*; from 2790; *deaf* (whether lit. or spir.):—deaf.

2796. חָרָשׁ **chârâsh**, *khaw-rawsh'*; from 2790; a *fabricator* of any material:—artificer, (+) carpenter, craftsman, engraver, maker, + mason, skilful, (+) smith, worker, workman, such as wrought.

2797. חַרְשָׁא **Charshâ'**, *khar-shaw'*; from 2792; *magician; Charsha*, one of the Nethinim:—Harsha.

2798. חֲרָשִׁים **Chărâshîym**, *khar-aw-sheem'*; plur. of 2796; *mechanics*, the name of a valley in Jerus.:—Charashim, craftsmen.

2799. חֲרֹשֶׁת **chărôsheth**, *khar-o'-sheth;* from 2790; mechanical *work:*—carving, cutting.

2800. חֲרֹשֶׁת **Chărôsheth**, *khar-o'-sheth;* the same as 2799; *Charosheth*, a place in Pal.:—Harosheth.

2801. חָרַת **chârath**, *khaw-rath'*; a prim. root; to *engrave:*—graven.

2802. חֶרֶת **Chereth**, *kheh'-reth;* from 2801 [but equiv. to 2793]; *forest; Chereth*, a thicket in Pal.:—Hereth.

2803. חָשַׁב **châshab**, *khaw-shab'*; a prim. root; prop. to *plait* or interpenetrate, i.e. (lit.) to *weave* or (gen.) to *fabricate;* fig. to *plot* or contrive (usually in a malicious sense); hence (from the mental effort) to *think, regard, value, compute:*—(make) account (of), conceive, consider, count, cunning (man, work, workman), devise, esteem, find out, forecast, hold, imagine, impute, invent, be like, mean, purpose, reckon (-ing be made), regard, think.

2804. חֲשַׁב **chăshab** (Chald.), *khash-ab'*; corresp. to 2803; to *regard:*—repute.

2805. חֵשֶׁב **chêsheb**, *khay'-sheb;* from 2803; a *belt* or strap (as being interlaced):—curious girdle.

2806. חֲשַׁבְדָּנָה **Chashbaddânâh**, *khash-bad-daw'-naw;* from 2803 and 1777; *considerate judge; Chasbaddanah*, an Isr.:—Hasbadana.

2807. חֲשׁוּבָה **Chăshûbâh**, *khash-oo-baw'*; from 2803; *estimation; Chashubah*, an Isr.:—Hashubah.

2808. חֶשְׁבּוֹן **cheshbôwn**, *khesh-bone'*; from 2803; prop. *contrivance;* by impl. *intelligence:*—account, device, reason.

2809. חֶשְׁבּוֹן **Cheshbôwn**, *khesh-bone'*; the same as 2808; *Cheshbon*, a place E. of the Jordan:—Heshbon.

2810. חִשָּׁבוֹן **chishshâbôwn**, *khish-shaw-bone'*; from 2803; a *contrivance*, i.e. actual (a warlike *machine*) or mental (a *machination*):—engine, invention.

2811. חֲשַׁבְיָה **Chăshabyâh**, *khash-ab-yaw';* or

חֲשַׁבְיָהוּ **Chăshabyâhûw**, *khash-ab-yaw'-hoo;* from 2803 and 3050; *Jah has regarded; Chashabjah*, the name of nine Isr.:—Hashabiah.

2812. חֲשַׁבְנָה **Chăshabnâh**, *khash-ab-naw'*; fem. of 2808; *inventiveness; Chashnah*, an Isr.:—Hashabnah.

2813. חֲשַׁבְנְיָה **Chăshabnᵉyâh**, *khash-ab-neh-yaw'*; from 2808 and 3050; *thought of Jah; Chashabneiah*, the name of two Isr.:—Hashabniah.

2814. חָשָׁה **châshâh**, *khaw-shaw'*; a prim. root; to *hush* or keep quiet:—hold peace, keep silence, be silent, (be) still.

2815. חַשּׁוּב **Chashshûwb**, *khash-shoob'*; from 2803; *intelligent; Chashshub*, the name of two or three Isr.:—Hashub, Hasshub.

2816. חֲשׁוֹךְ **chăshôwk** (Chald.), *khash-oke'*; from a root corresp. to 2821; the *dark:*—darkness.

2817. חֲשׂוּפָא **Chăsûwphâ'**, *khas-oo-faw';* or

חֲשֻׂפָא **Chăsûphâ'**, *khas-oo-faw'*; from 2834; *nakedness; Chasupha*, one of the Nethinim:—Hashupha, Hasupha.

חָשׁוּק **chăshûwq**. See 2838.

2818. חֲשַׁח **chăshach** (Chald.), *khash-akh'*; a collat. root to one corresp. to 2363 in the sense of *readiness;* to *be necessary* (from the idea of *convenience*) or (transit.) to *need:*—careful, have need of.

2819. חַשְׁחוּת **chashchûwth**, *khash-khooth'*; from a root corresp. to 2818; *necessity:*—be needful.

חֲשֵׁיכָה **chăshêykâh**. See 2825.

חֻשִׁים **Chûshîym**. See 2366.

2820. חָשַׂךְ **châsak**, *khaw-sak'*; a prim root; to *restrain* or (reflex.) *refrain;* by impl. to *refuse, spare, preserve;* also (by interch. with 2821) to *observe:*—assuage, × darken, forbear, hinder, hold back, keep (back), punish, refrain, reserve, spare, withhold.

2821. חָשַׁךְ **châshak**, *khaw-shak'*; a prim. root; to *be dark* (as *withholding* light); transit. to *darken:*—be black, be (make) dark, darken, cause darkness, be dim, hide.

2822. חֹשֶׁךְ **chôshek**, *kho-shek'*; from 2821; the *dark;* hence (lit.) *darkness;* fig. *misery, destruction, death, ignorance, sorrow, wickedness:*—dark (-ness), night, obscurity.

2823. חָשֹׁךְ **châshôk**, *khaw-shoke'*; from 2821; *dark* (fig. i.e. *obscure*):—mean.

2824. חֶשְׁכָה **cheshkâh**, *khesh-kaw'*; from 2821; *darkness:*—dark.

2825. חֲשֵׁכָה **chăshêkâh**, *khash-ay-kaw';* or

חֲשֵׁיכָה **chăshêykâh**, *khash-ay-kaw'*; from 2821; *darkness;* fig. *misery:*—darkness.

2826. חָשַׁל **châshal**, *khaw-shal'*; a prim. root; to *make* (intrans. *be*) *unsteady*, i.e. *weak:*—feeble.

2827. חֲשַׁל **chăshal** (Chald.), *khash-al'*; a root corresp. to 2826; to *weaken*, i.e. *crush:*—subdue.

2828. חָשֻׁם **Châshûm**, *khaw-shoom'*; from the same as 2831; *enriched; Chashum*, the name of two or three Isr.:—Hashum.

חֻשָׁם **Chûshâm**. See 2367.

חֻשִׁם **Chûshîm**. See 2366.

2829. חֶשְׁמוֹן **Cheshmôwn**, *khesh-mone'*; the same as 2831; *opulent; Cheshmon*, a place in Pal.:—Heshmon.

2830. חַשְׁמַל **chashmal**, *khash-mal'*; of uncert. der.; prob. *bronze* or polished spectrum metal:—amber.

2831. חַשְׁמַן **chashman**, *khash-man'*; from an unused root (prob. mean. *firm* or *capacious* in resources); appar. *wealthy:*—princes.

2832. חַשְׁמֹנָה **Chashmônâh**, *khash-mo-naw'*; fem. of 2831; *fertile; Chasmonah*, a place in the Desert:—Hashmonah.

2833. חֹשֶׁן **chôshen**, *kho'-shen;* from an unused root prob. mean. to *contain* or *sparkle;* perh. a *pocket* (as holding the Urim and Thummim), or *rich* (as containing gems), used only of the *gorget* of the highpriest:—breastplate.

2834. חָשַׂף **châsaph**, *khaw-saf'*; a prim. root; to *strip* off, i.e. gen. to *make naked* (for exertion or in disgrace), to *drain* away or *bail up* (a liquid):—make bare, clean, discover, draw out, take, uncover.

2835. חָשִׂף **châsiph**, *khaw-seef'*; from 2834; prop. *drawn off*, i.e. separated; hence a small *company* (as divided from the rest):—little flock.

2836. חָשַׁק **châshaq**, *khaw-shak'*; a prim. root; to *cling*, i.e. *join*, (fig.) to *love, delight* in; ellipt. (or by interch. for 2820) to *deliver:*—have a delight, (have a) desire, fillet, long, set (in) love.

2837. חֵשֶׁק **chêsheq**, *khay'-shek;* from 2836; *delight:*—desire, pleasure.

2838. חָשֻׁק **châshûq**, *khaw-shook';* or

חָשׁוּק **châshûwq**, *khaw-shook'*; pass. part. of 2836; *attached*, i.e. a fence-*rail* or rod connecting the posts or pillars:—fillet.

2839. חִשֻּׁק **chishshûq**, *khish-shook'*; from 2836; *conjoined*, i.e. a wheel-*spoke* or rod connecting the hub with the rim:—felloe.

2840. חִשֻּׁר **chishshûr**, *khish-shoor'*; from an unused root mean. to *bind* together; *combined*, i.e. the *nave* or hub of a wheel (as holding the spokes together):—spoke.

2841. חַשְׁרָה **chashrâh**, *khash-raw'*; from the same as 2840; prop. a *combination* or gathering, i.e. of watery *clouds:*—dark.

חֲשֻׂפָא **Chăsûphâ'**. See 2817.

2842. חָשַׁשׁ **châshash**, *khaw-shash'*; by var. for 7179; dry *grass:*—chaff.

2843. חֻשָׁתִי **Chûshâthîy**, *khoo-shaw-thee'*; patron. from 2364; a *Chushathite* or desc. of Chushah:—Hushathite.

2844. חַת chath, *khath;* from 2865; concr. *crushed;* also *afraid;* abstr. *terror:*—broken, dismayed, dread, fear.

2845. חֵת Chêth, *khayth;* from 2865; *terror; Cheth,* an aboriginal Canaanite:—Heth.

2846. חָתָה châthâh, *khaw-thaw';* a prim. root; to lay *hold* of; espec. to *pick* up fire:—heap, take (away).

2847. חִתָּה chittâh, *khit-taw';* from 2865; *fear:*—terror.

2848. חִתּוּל chittûwl, *khit-tool';* from 2853; *swathed,* i.e. a *bandage:*—roller.

2849. חַתְחַת chathchath, *khath-khath';* from 2844; *terror:*—fear.

2850. חִתִּי Chittîy, *khit-tee';* patron. from 2845; a *Chittite,* or desc. of Cheth:—Hittite, Hittites.

2851. חִתִּית chittîyth, *khit-teeth';* from 2865; *fear:*—terror.

2852. חָתַךְ châthak, *khaw-thak';* a prim. root; prop. to *cut* off, i.e. (fig.) to *decree:*—determine.

2853. חָתַל châthal, *khaw-thal';* a prim. root; to *swathe:*— × at all, swaddle.

2854. חֲתֻלָּה chăthullâh, *khath-ool-law';* from 2853; a *swathing* cloth (fig.):—swaddling band.

2855. חֶתְלֹן Chethlôn, *kheth-lone';* from 2853; *enswathed; Chethlon,* a place in Pal.:—Hethlon.

2856. חָתַם châtham, *khaw-tham';* a prim. root; to *close* up; espec. to *seal:*—make an end, mark, seal (up), stop.

2857. חֲתַם chătham (Chald.), *khath-am';* a root corresp. to 2856; to *seal:*—seal.

חֹתָם chôthâm. See 2368.

2858. חֹתֶמֶת chôthemeth, *kho-the-meth;* fem. act. part. of 2856; a *seal:*—signet.

2859. חָתַן châthan, *khaw-than';* a prim. root; to *give* (a daughter) *away* in marriage; hence (gen.) to *contract affinity* by marriage:—join in affinity, father in law, make marriages, mother in law, son in law.

2860. חָתָן châthân, *khaw-thawn';* from 2859; a *relative* by marriage (espec. through the bride); fig. a *circumcised* child (as a species of religious espousal):—bridegroom, husband, son in law.

2861. חֲתֻנָּה chăthunnâh, *khath-oon-naw';* from 2859; a *wedding:*—espousal.

2862. חָתַף châthaph, *khaw-thaf';* a prim. root; to *clutch:*—take away.

2863. חֶתֶף chetheph, *kheh'-thef;* from 2862; prop. *rapine;* fig. *robbery:*—prey.

2864. חָתַר châthar, *khaw-thar';* a prim. root; to *force* a passage, as by burglary; fig. with oars:—dig (through), row.

2865. חָתַת châthath, *khaw-thath';* a prim. root; prop. to *prostrate;* hence to *break* down, either (lit.) by violence, or (fig.) by confusion and fear:—abolish, affright, be (make) afraid, amaze, beat down, discourage, (cause to) dismay, go down, scare, terrify.

2866. חֲתַת chăthath, *khath-ath';* from 2865; *dismay:*—casting down.

2867. חֲתַת Chăthath, *khath-ath';* the same as 2866; *Chathath,* an Isr.:—Hathath.

ט

2868. טְאֵב ṭᵉ'êb (Chald.), *teh-abe';* a prim. root; to *rejoice:*—be glad.

2869. טָב ṭâb (Chald.), *tawb;* from 2868; the same as 2896; *good:*—fine, good.

2870. טָבְאֵל ṭâbᵉ'êl, *taw-beh-ale';* from 2895 and 410; *pleasing* (to) *God; Tabeël,* the name of a Syrian and of a Persian:—Tabeal, Tabeel.

2871. טָבוּל ṭâbûwl, *taw-bool';* pass. part. of 2881; prop. *dyed,* i.e. a *turban* (prob. as of colored stuff):—dyed attire.

2872. טַבּוּר ṭabbûwr, *tab-boor';* from an unused root mean. to *pile* up; prop. *accumulated;* i.e. (by impl.) a *summit:*—middle, midst.

2873. טָבַח ṭâbach, *taw-bakh';* a prim. root; to *slaughter* (animals or men):—kill, (make) slaughter, slay.

2874. טֶבַח ṭebach, *teh'-bakh;* from 2873; prop. something *slaughtered;* hence a *beast* (or *meat,* as butchered); abstr. *butchery* (or concr. a place of slaughter):— × beast, slaughter, × slay, × sore.

2875. טֶבַח Ṭebach, *teh'-bakh;* the same as 2874; *massacre; Tebach,* the name of a Mesopotamian and of an Isr.:—Tebah.

2876. טַבָּח ṭabbâch, *tab-bawkh';* from 2873; prop. a *butcher;* hence a *lifeguardsman* (because acting as executioner); also a *cook* (as usually slaughtering the animal for food):—cook, guard.

2877. טַבָּח ṭabbâch (Chald.), *tab-bawkh';* the same as 2876; a *lifeguardsman:*—guard.

2878. טִבְחָה ṭibchâh, *tib-khaw';* fem. of 2874 and mean. the same:—flesh, slaughter.

2879. טַבָּחָה ṭabbâchâh, *tab-baw-khaw';* fem. of 2876; a female *cook:*—cook.

2880. טִבְחַת Ṭibchath, *tib-khath';* from 2878; *slaughter; Tibchath,* a place in Syria:—Tibhath.

2881. טָבַל ṭâbal, *taw-bal';* a prim. root; to *dip:*—dip, plunge.

2882. טְבַלְיָהוּ Ṭᵉbalyâhûw, *teb-al-yaw'-hoo;* from 2881 and 3050; *Jah has dipped; Tebaljah,* an Isr.:—Tebaliah.

2883. טָבַע ṭâbaʻ, *taw-bah';* a prim. root; to *sink:*—drown, fasten, settle, sink.

2884. טַבָּעוֹת Ṭabbâʻôwth, *tab-baw-othe';* plur. of 2885; *rings; Tabbaoth,* one of the Nethinim:—Tabbaoth.

2885. טַבַּעַת ṭabbaʻath, *tab-bah'-ath;* from 2883; prop. a *seal* (as *sunk* into the wax), i.e. *signet* (for sealing); hence (gen.) a *ring* of any kind:—ring.

2886. טַבְרִמּוֹן Ṭabrimmôwn, *tab-rim-mone';* from 2895 and 7417; *pleasing* (to) *Rimmon; Tabrimmon,* a Syrian:—Tabrimmon.

2887. טֵבֵת Ṭêbeth, *tay'-beth;* prob. of for. der.; *Tebeth,* the tenth Heb. month:—Tebeth.

2888. טַבַּת Ṭabbath, *tab-bath';* of uncert. der.; *Tabbath,* a place E. of the Jordan:—Tabbath.

2889. טָהוֹר ṭâhôwr, *taw-hore';* or

טָהֹר ṭâhôr, *taw-hore';* from 2891; *pure* (in a phys., chem., cerem. or moral sense):—clean, fair, pure (-ness).

2890. טְהוֹר ṭᵉhôwr, *teh-hore';* from 2891; *purity:*—pureness.

2891. טָהֵר ṭâhêr, *taw-hare';* a prim. root; prop. to *be bright;* i.e. (by impl.) to *be pure* (phys. *sound, clear, unadulterated;* Levit. *uncontaminated;* mor. *innocent* or *holy*):—be (make, make self, pronounce) clean, cleanse (self), purge, purify (-ier, self).

2892. טֹהַר ṭôhar, *to'-har;* from 2891; lit. *brightness;* ceremon. *purification:*—clearness, glory, purifying.

2893. טָהֳרָה ṭohŏrâh, *toh-or-aw';* fem. of 2892; cerem. *purification;* moral *purity:*— × is cleansed, cleansing, purification (-fying).

2894. טוּא ṭûw', *too;* a prim. root; to *sweep away:*—sweep.

2895. טוֹב ṭowb, *tobe;* a prim. root, to *be* (trans. *do* or *make*) *good* (or *well*) in the widest sense:—be (do) better, cheer, be (do, seem) good, (make) goodly, × please, (be, do, go, play) well.

2896. טוֹב ṭôwb, *tobe;* from 2895; *good* (as an adj.) in the widest sense; used likewise as a noun, both in the masc. and the fem., the sing. and the plur. (*good,* a *good* or *good* thing, a *good* man or woman; the *good, goods* or *good* things, *good* men or women), also as an adv. (*well*):—beautiful, best, better, bountiful, cheerful, at ease, × fair (word), (be in) favour, fine, glad, good (deed, -lier, liest, -ly, -ness, -s), graciously, joyful, kindly, kindness, liketh (best), loving, merry, × most, pleasant, + pleaseth, pleasure, precious, prosperity, ready, sweet, wealth, welfare, (be) well ([-favoured]).

2897. טוֹב Ṭôwb, *tobe;* the same as 2896; *good; Tob,* a region appar. E. of the Jordan:—Tob.

2898. טוּב ṭûwb, *toob;* from 2895; *good* (as a noun), in the widest sense, espec. *goodness* (superl. concr. the *best*), *beauty, gladness, welfare:*—fair, gladness, good (-ness, thing, -s), joy, go well with.

2899. טוֹב אֲדֹנִיָּהוּ Ṭôwb Ădônîyâhûw, *tobe ado-nee-yah'-hoo;* from 2896 and 138; *pleasing* (to) *Adonijah; Tob-Adonijah,* an Isr.:—Tob-adonijah.

2900. טוֹבִיָּה Ṭôwbîyâh, *to-bee-yaw';* or

טוֹבִיָּהוּ Ṭôwbîyâhûw, *to-bee-yaw'-hoo;* from 2896 and 3050; *goodness of Jehovah; Tobijah,* the name of three Isr. and of one Samaritan:—Tobiah, Tobijah.

2901. טָוָה ṭâvâh, *taw-vaw';* a prim. root; to *spin:*—spin.

2902. טוּחַ ṭûwach, *too'-akh;* a prim. root; to *smear,* espec. with lime:—daub, overlay, plaister, smut.

2903. טוֹטָפָה ṭôwphâphâh, *to-faw-faw';* from an unused root mean. to *go around* or *bind;* a *fillet* for the forehead:—frontlet.

2904. טוּל ṭûwl, *tool;* a prim. root; to *pitch* over or *reel;* hence (transit.) to *cast* down or out:—carry away, (utterly) cast (down, forth, out), send out.

2905. טוּר ṭûwr, *toor;* from an unused root mean. to *range* in a reg. manner; a *row;* hence a *wall:*—row.

2906. טוּר ṭûwr (Chald.), *toor;* corresp. to 6697; a *rock* or hill:—mountain.

2907. טוּשׂ ṭûws, *toos;* a prim. root; to *pounce* as a bird of prey:—haste.

2908. טְוָת ṭᵉvâth (Chald.), *tev-awth';* from a root corresp. to 2901; *hunger* (as *twisting*):—fasting.

2909. טָחָה ṭâchâh, *taw-khaw';* a prim. root; to *stretch* a bow, as an *archer:*—[bow-]shot.

2910. טֻחָה ṭûwchâh, *too-khaw';* from 2909 (or 2902) in the sense of *overlaying;* (in the plur. only) the *kidneys* (as being *covered*); hence (fig.) the inmost *thought:*—inward parts.

2911. טְחוֹן ṭᵉchôwn, *tekh-one';* from 2912; a hand *mill;* hence a *millstone:*—to grind.

2912. טָחַן ṭâchan, *taw-khan';* a prim. root; to *grind* meal; hence to *be a concubine* (that being their employment):—grind (-er).

2913. טַחֲנָה ṭachănâh, *takh-an-aw';* from 2912; a hand *mill;* hence (fig.) *chewing:*—grinding.

2914. טְחֹר ṭᵉchôr, *tekh-ore';* from an unused root mean. to *burn;* a *boil* or ulcer (from the inflammation), espec. a tumor in the anus or pudenda (the piles):—emerod.

2915. טִיחַ ṭîyach, *tee'-akh;* from (the equiv. of) 2902; mortar or *plaster:*—daubing.

2916. טִיט ṭîyṭ, *teet;* from an unused root mean. appar. to *be sticky* [rath. perh. a denom. from 2894, through the idea of dirt to be *swept away*]; *mud* or *clay;* fig. *calamity:*—clay, dirt, mire.

2917. טִין ṭîyn (Chald.), *teen;* perh. by interch. for a word corresp. to 2916; *clay:*—miry.

2918. טִירָה ṭîyrâh, *tee-raw';* fem. of (an equiv. to) 2905; a *wall;* hence a *fortress* or a *hamlet:*—(goodly) castle, habitation, palace, row.

2919. טַל ṭal, *tal;* from 2926; *dew* (as *covering* vegetation):—dew.

2920. טַל ṭal (Chald.), *tal;* the same as 2919:—dew.

2921. טָלָא ṭâlâ', *taw-law';* a prim. root; prop. to *cover* with pieces; i.e. (by impl.) to *spot* or *variegate* (as tapestry):—clouted, with divers colours, spotted.

2922. טְלָא ṭᵉlâ', *tel-aw';* appar. from 2921 in the (orig.) sense of *covering* (for protection); a *lamb* [comp. 2924]:—lamb.

2923. טְלָאִים **Telâ'îym**, *tel-aw-eem'*; from the plur. of 2922; *lambs; Telaim*, a place in Pal.:—Telaim.

2924. טָלֶה **ṭâleh**, *taw-leh'*; by var. for 2922; a *lamb:*—lamb.

2925. טַלְטֵלָה **ṭalṭêlâh**, *tal-tay-law'*; from 2904; *overthrow* or *rejection:*—captivity.

2926. טָלַל **ṭâlal**, *taw-lal'*; a prim. root; prop. to *strew* over, i.e. (by impl.) to *cover* in or *plate* (with beams):—cover.

2927. טְלַל **ṭelal** (Chald.), *tel-al'*; corresp. to 2926; to *cover* with shade:—have a shadow.

2928. טֶלֶם **Telem**, *teh'-lem*; from an unused root mean. to *break* up or treat violently; *oppression; Telem*, the name of a place in Idumæa, also of a temple doorkeeper:—Telem.

2929. טַלְמוֹן **Ṭalmôwn**, *tal-mone'*; from the same as 2728; *oppressive; Talmon*, a temple doorkeeper:—Talmon.

2930. טָמֵא **ṭâmê'**, *taw-may'*; a prim. root; to *be foul*, espec. in a cerem. or mor. sense (*contaminated*):—defile (self), pollute (self), be (make, make self, pronounce) unclean, × utterly.

2931. טָמֵא **ṭâmê'**, *taw-may'*; from 2930; *foul* in a relig. sense:—defiled, + infamous, polluted (-tion), unclean.

2932. טֻמְאָה **ṭum'âh**, *toom-aw'*; from 2930; relig. *impurity:*—filthiness, unclean (-ness).

2933. טָמָה **ṭâmâh**, *taw-maw'*; a collat. form of 2930; to *be impure* in a relig. sense:—be defiled, be reputed vile.

2934. טָמַן **ṭâman**, *taw-man'*; a prim. root; to *hide* (by covering over):—hide, lay privily, in secret.

2935. טֶנֶא **ṭene'**, *teh'-neh*; from an unused root prob. mean. to *weave*; a *basket* (of interlaced osiers):—basket.

2936. טָנַף **ṭânaph**, *taw-naf'*; a prim. root; to *soil:*—defile.

2937. טָעָה **ṭâ'âh**, *taw-aw'*; a prim. root; to *wander*; causat. to *lead astray:*—seduce.

2938. טָעַם **ṭâ'am**, *taw-am'*; a prim. root; to *taste*; fig. to *perceive:*— × but, perceive, taste.

2939. טְעַם **ṭe'am** (Chald.), *teh-am'*; corresp. to 2938; to *taste*; causat. to *feed:*—make to eat, feed.

2940. טַעַם **ṭa'am**, *tah'-am*; from 2938; prop. a *taste*, i.e. (fig.) *perception*; by impl. *intelligence*; transit. a *mandate:*—advice, behaviour, decree, discretion, judgment, reason, taste, understanding.

2941. טַעַם **ṭa'am** (Chald.), *tah'-am*; from 2939; prop. a *taste*, i.e. (as in 2940) a judicial *sentence:*—account, × to be commanded, commandment, matter.

2942. טְעֵם **ṭe'êm** (Chald.), *teh-ame'*; from 2939, and equiv. to 2941; prop. *flavor*; fig. *judgment* (both subj. and obj.); hence *account* (both subj. and obj.):— + chancellor, + command, commandment, decree, + regard, taste, wisdom.

2943. טָעַן **ṭâ'an**, *taw-an'*; a prim. root; to *load* a beast:—lade.

2944. טָעַן **ṭâ'an**, *taw-an'*; a prim. root; to *stab:*—thrust through.

2945. טַף **ṭaph**, *taf*; from 2952 (perh. referring to the *tripping* gait of children); a *family* (mostly used collect. in the sing.):—(little) children (ones), families.

2946. טָפַח **ṭâphach**, *taw-fakh'*; a prim. root; to *flatten* out or *extend* (as a tent); fig. to *nurse* a child (as *promotive* of growth); or perh. a denom. from 2947, from *dandling* on the palms:—span, swaddle.

2947. טֶפַח **ṭêphach**, *tay'-fakh*; from 2946; a *spread* of the hand, i.e. a *palm-breadth* (not "span" of the fingers); archit. a *corbel* (as a supporting palm):—coping, hand-breadth.

2948. טֹפַח **ṭôphach**, *to'-fakh*; from 2946 (the same as 2947):—hand-breadth (broad).

2949. טִפֻּח **ṭippûch**, *tip-pookh'*; from 2946; *nursing:*—span long.

2950. טָפַל **ṭâphal**, *taw-fal'*; a prim. root; prop. to *stick* on as a patch; fig. to *impute* falsely:—forge (-r), sew up.

2951. טִפְסַר **ṭiphçar**, *tif-sar'*; of for. der.; a military *governor:*—captain.

2952. טָפַף **ṭâphaph**, *taw-faf'*; a prim. root; appar. to *trip* (with short steps) coquettishly:—mince.

2953. טְפַר **ṭephar** (Chald.), *tef-ar'*; from a root corresp. to 6852, and mean. the same as 6856; a finger-*nail*; also a *hoof* or *claw:*—nail.

2954. טָפַשׁ **ṭâphash**, *taw-fash'*; a prim. root; prop. appar. to *be thick*; fig. to *be stupid:*—be fat.

2955. טָפַת **Ṭâphath**, *taw-fath'*; prob. from 5197; a *dropping* (of ointment); *Taphath*, an Israelitess:—Taphath.

2956. טָרַד **ṭârad**, *taw-rad'*; a prim. root; to *drive* on; fig. to *follow* close:—continual.

2957. טְרַד **ṭerad** (Chald.), *ter-ad'*; corresp. to 2956; to *expel:*—drive.

2958. טְרוֹם **ṭerôwm**, *ter-ome'*; a var. of 2962; *not yet:*—before.

2959. טָרַח **ṭârach**, *taw-rakh'*; a prim. root; to *overburden:*—weary.

2960. טֹרַח **ṭôrach**, *to'-rakh*; from 2959; a *burden:*—cumbrance, trouble.

2961. טָרִי **ṭârîy**, *taw-ree'*; from an unused root appar. mean. to *be moist*; prop. *dripping*; hence *fresh* (i.e. recently made such):—new, putrefying.

2962. טֶרֶם **ṭerem**, *teh'-rem*; from an unused root appar. mean. to *interrupt* or *suspend*; prop. *non-occurrence*; used adv. *not yet* or *before:*—before, ere, not yet.

2963. טָרַף **ṭâraph**, *taw-raf'*; a prim. root; to *pluck* off or *pull* to pieces; causat. to *supply* with food (as in morsels):—catch, × without doubt, feed, ravin, rend in pieces, × surely, tear (in pieces).

2964. טֶרֶף **ṭereph**, *teh'-ref*; from 2963; something *torn*, i.e. a fragment, e.g. a *fresh* leaf, *prey, food:*—leaf, meat, prey, spoil.

2965. טָרָף **ṭârâph**, *taw-rawf'*; from 2963; recently *torn* off, i.e. *fresh:*—pluckt off.

2966. טְרֵפָה **ṭerêphâh**, *ter-ay-faw'*; fem. (collect.) of 2964; *prey*, i.e. flocks devoured by animals:—ravin, (that which was) torn (of beasts, in pieces).

2967. טַרְפְּלַי **Ṭarpelay** (Chald.), *tar-pel-ah'ee*; from a name of for. der.; a *Tarpelite* (collect.) or inhab. of Tarpel, a place in Assyria:—Tarpelites.

י

2968. יָאַב **yâ'ab**, *yaw-ab'*; a prim. root; to *desire:*—long.

2969. יָאָה **yâ'âh**, *yaw-aw'*; a prim. root; to *be suitable:*—appertain.

יְאֹר **ye'ôwr**. See 2975.

2970. יַאֲזַנְיָה **Ya'ăzanyâh**, *yah-az-an-yaw'*; or

יַאֲזַנְיָהוּ **Ya'ăzanyâhûw**, *yah-az-an-yaw'-hoo*; from 238 and 3050; *heard of Jah; Jaazanjah*, the name of four Isr.:—Jaazaniah. Comp. 3153.

2971. יָאִיר **Yâ'îyr**, *yaw-ere'*; from 215; *enlightener; Jaïr*, the name of four Isr.:—Jair.

2972. יָאִרִי **Yâ'irîy**, *yaw-ee-ree'*; patron. from 2971; a *Jaïrite* or desc. of Jair:—Jairite.

2973. יָאַל **yâ'al**, *yaw-al'*; a prim. root; prop. to *be slack*, i.e. (fig.) to *be foolish:*—dote, be (become, do) foolish (-ly).

2974. יָאַל **yâ'al**, *yaw-al'*; a prim. root [prob. rather the same as 2973 through the idea of mental *weakness*]; prop. to *yield*, espec. *assent*; hence (pos.) to *undertake* as an act of volition:—assay, begin, be content, please, take upon, × willingly, would.

2975. יְאֹר **ye'ôr**, *yeh-ore'*; of Eg. or.; a *channel*, e.g. a fosse, canal, shaft; spec. the *Nile*, as the one river of Egypt, including its collat. trenches; also the *Tigris*, as the main river of Assyria:—brook, flood, river, stream.

2976. יָאַשׁ **yâ'ash**, *yaw-ash'*; a prim. root; to *desist*, i.e. (fig.) to *despond:*—(cause to) despair, one that is desperate, be no hope.

2977. יֹאשִׁיָּה **Yô'shîyâh**, *yo-shee-yaw'*; or

יֹאשִׁיָּהוּ **Yô'shîyâhûw**, *yo-she-yaw'-hoo*; from the same root as 803 and 3050; *founded of Jah; Joshijah*, the name of two Isr.:—Josiah.

2978. יְאִתוֹן **ye'îthôwn**, *yeh-ee-thone'*; from 857; an *entry:*—entrance.

2979. יְאָתְרַי **ye'âtheray**, *yeh-aw-ther-ah'ee*; from the same as 871; *stepping; Jeätherai*, an Isr.:—Jeaterai.

2980. יָבַב **yâbab**, *yaw-bab*; a prim. root; to *bawl:*—cry out.

2981. יְבוּל **yebûwl**, *yeb-ool'*; from 2986; *produce*, i.e. a *crop* or (fig.) *wealth:*—fruit, increase.

2982. יְבוּס **Yebûwç**, *yeb-oos'*; from 947; *trodden*, i.e. threshing-place; *Jebus*, the aboriginal name of Jerus.:—Jebus.

2983. יְבוּסִי **Yebûwçîy**, *yeb-oo-see'*; patrial from 2982; a *Jebusite* or inhab. of Jebus:—Jebusite (-s).

2984. יִבְחַר **Yibchar**, *yib-khar'*; from 977; *choice; Jibchar*, an Isr.:—Ibhar.

2985. יָבִין **Yâbîyn**, *yaw-bene'*; from 995; *intelligent; Jabin*, the name of two Canaanitish kings:—Jabin.

יָבֵישׁ **Yâbêysh**. See 3003.

2986. יָבַל **yâbal**, *yaw-bal'*; a prim. root; prop. to *flow*; causat. to *bring* (espec. with pomp):—bring (forth), carry, lead (forth).

2987. יְבַל **yebal** (Chald.), *yeb-al'*; corresp. to 2986; to *bring:*—bring, carry.

יֹבֵל **yôbêl**. See 3104.

2988. יָבָל **yâbâl**, *yaw-bawl'*; from 2986; a *stream:*—[water-] course, stream.

2989. יָבָל **Yâbâl**, *yaw-bawl'*; the same as 2988; *Jabal*, an antediluvian:—Jabal.

יֹבֵל **yôbêl**. See 3104.

2990. יַבֵּל **yabbêl**, *yab-bale'*; from 2986; having *running* sores:—wen.

2991. יִבְלְעָם **Yible'âm**, *yib-leh-awm'*; from 1104 and 5971; *devouring people; Jibleäm*, a place in Pal.:—Ibleam.

2992. יָבַם **yâbam**, *yaw-bam'*; a prim. root of doubtful mean.; used only as a denom. from 2993; to *marry* a (deceased) brother's widow:—perform the duty of a husband's brother, marry.

2993. יָבָם **yâbâm**, *yaw-bawm'*; from (the orig. of) 2992; a *brother-in-law:*—husband's brother.

2994. יְבֵמֶת **yebêmeth**, *yeb-ay'-meth*; fem. part. of 2992; a *sister-in-law:*—brother's wife, sister in law.

2995. יַבְנְאֵל **Yabne'êl**, *yab-neh-ale'*; from 1129 and 410; *built of God; Jabneël*, the name of two places in Pal.:—Jabneel.

2996. יַבְנֶה **Yabneh**, *yab-neh'*; from 1129; a *building; Jabneh*, a place in Pal.:—Jabneh.

2997. יִבְנְיָה **Yibneyâh**, *yib-neh-yaw'*; from 1129 and 3050; *built of Jah; Jibnejah*, an Isr.:—Ibneiah.

2998. יִבְנִיָּה **Yibnîyâh**, *yib-nee-yaw'*; from 1129 and 3050; *building of Jah; Jibnijah*, an Isr.:—Ibnijah.

2999. יַבֹּק **Yabbôq**, *yab-boke'*; prob. from 1238; *pouring* forth; *Jabbok*, a river E. of the Jordan:—Jabbok.

3000. יְבֶרֶכְיָהוּ **Yeberekyâhûw**, *yeb-eh-rek-yaw'-hoo*; from 1288 and 3050: *blessed of Jah; Jeberekjah*, an Isr.:—Jeberechiah.

3001. יָבֵשׁ **yâbêsh**, *yaw-bashe'*; a prim. root; to *be ashamed, confused* or *disappointed*; also (as failing) to *dry* up (as water) or *wither* (as herbage):—be ashamed, clean, be confounded, (make) dry (up), (do) shame (-fully), × utterly, wither (away).

3002. יָבֵשׁ **yâbêsh**, *yaw-bashe'*; from 3001: *dry*:—dried (away), dry.

3003. יָבֵשׁ **Yâbêsh**, *yaw-bashe'*; the same as 3002 (also

יָבֵישׁ **Yâbêysh**, *yaw-bashe'*; often with the addition of 1568, i.e. *Jabesh of Gilad*); *Jabesh*, the name of an Isr. and of a place in Pal.:—Jabesh ([-Gilead]).

3004. יַבָּשָׁה **yabbâshâh**, *yab-baw-shaw'*; from 3001; *dry* ground:—dry (ground, land).

3005. יִבְשָׂם **Yibsâm**, *yib-sawm'*; from the same as 1314; *fragrant; Jibsam*, an Isr.:—Jibsam.

3006. יַבֶּשֶׁת **yabbesheth**, *yab-beh'-sheth*; a var. of 3004; *dry* ground:—dry land.

3007. יַבֶּשֶׁת **yabbesheth** (Chald.), *yab-beh'-sheth*; corresp. to 3006; *dry* land:—earth.

3008. יִגְאָל **Yig'âl**, *yig-awl'*; from 1350; *avenger; Jigal*, the name of three Isr.:—Igal, Igeal.

3009. יָגַב **yâgab**, *yaw-gab'*; a prim. root; to *dig* or plough:—husbandman.

3010. יָגֵב **yâgêb**, *yaw-gabe'*; from 3009; a ploughed *field*:—field.

3011. יָגְבְּהָה **Yogbᵉhâh**, *yog-beh-haw'*; fem. from 1361; *hillock; Jogbehah*, a place E. of the Jordan:—Jogbehah.

3012. יִגְדַּלְיָהוּ **Yigdalyâhûw**, *yig-dal-yaw'-hoo*; from 1431 and 3050; *magnified of Jah; Jigdaljah*, an Isr.:—Igdaliah.

3013. יָגָה **yâgâh**, *yaw-gaw'*; a prim. root; to *grieve*:—afflict, cause grief, grieve, sorrowful, vex.

3014. יָגָה **yâgâh**, *yaw-gaw'*; a prim. root [prob. rather the same as 3013 through the common idea of *dissatisfaction*]; to *push* away:—be removed.

3015. יָגוֹן **yâgôwn**, *yaw-gohn'*; from 3013; *affliction*:—grief, sorrow.

3016. יָגוֹר **yâgôwr**, *yaw-gore'*; from 3025; *fearful*:—afraid, fearest.

3017. יָגוּר **Yâgûwr**, *yaw-goor'*; prob. from 1481; a *lodging; Jagur*, a place in Pal.:—Jagur.

3018. יְגִיעַ **yᵉgîyaʻ**, *yeg-ee'-ah*; from 3021; *toil*; hence a *work, produce, property* (as the result of labor):—labour, work.

3019. יָגִיעַ **yâgîyaʻ**, *yaw-ghee'-ah*; from 3021; *tired*:—weary.

3020. יׇגְלִי **Yoglîy**, *yog-lee'*; from 1540; *exiled; Jogli*, an Isr.:—Jogli.

3021. יָגַע **yâgaʻ**, *yaw-gah'*; a prim. root; prop. to *gasp*; hence to *be exhausted*, to *tire*, to *toil*:—faint, (make to) labour, (be) weary.

3022. יָגָע **yâgâʻ**, *yaw-gaw'*; from 3021; *earnings* (as the product of toil):—that which he laboured for.

3023. יָגֵעַ **yâgêaʻ**, *yaw-gay'-ah*; from 3021; *tired*; hence (trans.) *tiresome*:—full of labour, weary.

3024. יְגִעָה **yᵉgîʻâh**, *yeg-ee-aw'*; fem. of 3019; *fatigue*:—weariness.

3025. יָגֹר **yâgôr**, *yaw-gore'*; a prim. root; to *fear*:—be afraid, fear.

3026. יְגַר שָׂהֲדוּתָא **Yᵉgar Sahădûwthâ'** (Chald.), *yegar' sah-had-oo-thaw'*; from a word derived from an unused root (mean. to *gather*) and a der. of a root corresp. to 7717; *heap of the testimony; Jegar-Sahadutha*, a cairn E. of the Jordan:—Jegar-Sahadutha.

3027. יָד **yâd**, *yawd*; a prim. word; a *hand* (the *open* one [indicating *power, means, direction*, etc.], in distinction from 3709, the *closed* one); used (as noun, adv., etc.) in a great variety of applications, both lit. and fig., both proximate and remote [as follow]:—(+ be) able, × about, + armholes, at, axletree, because of, beside, border, × bounty, + broad, [broken-] handed, × by, charge, coast, + consecrate, + creditor, custody, debt, dominion, × enough, + fellowship, force, × from, hand [-staves, -y work], × he, himself, × in, labour, + large, ledge, [left-] handed, means, × mine, ministry, near, × of, × order, ordinance, × our, parts, pain, power, × presumptuously, service, side, sore, state, stay, draw with strength, stroke, + swear, terror, × thee, × by them, × themselves, × thine own, × thou, through, × throwing, + thumb, times, × to, × under, × us, × wait on, [way-] side, where, + wide, × with (him, me, you), work, + yield, × yourselves.

3028. יַד **yad** (Chald.), *yad*; corresp. to 3027:—hand, power.

3029. יְדָא **yᵉdâ'** (Chald.), *yed-aw'*; corresp. to 3034; to *praise*:—(give) thank (-s).

3030. יִדְאֲלָה **Yidălâh**, *yid-al-aw'*; of uncert. der. *Jidalah*, a place in Pal.:—Idalah.

3031. יִדְבָּשׁ **Yidbâsh**, *yid-bawsh'*; from the same as 1706; perh. *honeyed; Jidbash*, an Isr.:—Idbash.

3032. יָדַד **yâdad**, *yaw-dad'*; a prim. root; prop. to *handle* [comp. 3034], i.e. to *throw*, e.g. lots:—cast.

3033. יְדִדוּת **yᵉdîdûwth**, *yed-ee-dooth'*; from 3039; prop. *affection*; concr. a *darling* object:—dearly beloved.

3034. יָדָה **yâdâh**, *yaw-daw'*; a prim. root; used only as denom. from 3027; lit. to *use* (i.e. hold out) *the hand*; phys. to *throw* (a stone, an arrow) at or away; espec. to *revere* or *worship* (with extended hands); intens. to *bemoan* (by wringing the hands):—cast (out), (make) confess (-ion), praise, shoot, (give) thank (-ful, -s, -sgiving).

3035. יִדּוֹ **Yiddôw**, *yid-do'*; from 3034; *praised; Jiddo*, an Isr.:—Iddo.

3036. יָדוֹן **Yâdôwn**, *yaw-done'*; from 3034; *thankful; Jadon*, an Isr.:—Jadon.

3037. יַדּוּעַ **Yaddûwaʻ**, *yad-doo'-ah*; from 3045; *knowing; Jaddua*, the name of two Isr.:—Jaddua.

3038. יְדוּתוּן **Yᵉdûwthûwn**, *yed-oo-thoon'*; or

יְדֻתוּן **Yᵉdûthûwn**, *yed-oo-thoon'*; or

יְדִיתוּן **Yᵉdiythûwn**, *yed-ee-thoon'*; prob. from 3034; *laudatory; Jeduthun*, an Isr.:—Jeduthun.

3039. יְדִיד **yᵉdîyd**, *yed-eed'*; from the same as 1730; *loved*:—amiable, (well-) beloved, loves.

3040. יְדִידָה **Yᵉdîydâh**, *yed-ee-daw'*; fem. of 3039; *beloved; Jedidah*, an Israelitess:—Jedidah.

3041. יְדִידְיָה **Yᵉdîydᵉyâh**, *yed-ee-deh-yaw'*; from 3039 and 3050; *beloved of Jah; Jedidejah*, a name of Solomon:—Jedidiah.

3042. יְדָיָה **Yᵉdâyâh**, *yed-aw-yaw'*; from 3034 and 3050; *praised of Jah; Jedajah*, the name of two Isr.:—Jedaiah.

3043. יְדִיעֲאֵל **Yᵉdîyʻăêl**, *yed-ee-ah-ale'*; from 3045 and 410; *knowing God; Jediaël*, the name of three Isr.:—Jediael.

3044. יִדְלָף **Yidlâph**, *yid-lawf'*; from 1811; *tearful; Jidlaph*, a Mesopotamian:—Jidlaph.

3045. יָדַע **yâdaʻ**, *yaw-dah'*; a prim. root; to *know* (prop. to ascertain by *seeing*); used in a great variety of senses, fig., lit., euphem. and infer. (including *observation, care, recognition*; and causat. *instruction, designation, punishment*, etc.) [as follow]:—acknowledge, acquaintance (-ted with), advise, answer, appoint, assuredly, be aware, [un-] awares, can [-not], certainly, for a certainty, comprehend, consider, × could they, cunning, declare, be diligent, (can, cause to) discern, discover, endued with, familiar friend, famous, feel, can have, be [ig-] norant, instruct, kinsfolk, kinsman, (cause to, let, make) know, (come to give, have, take) knowledge, have [knowledge], (be, make, make to be, make self) known, + be learned, + lie by man, mark, perceive, privy to, × prognosticator, regard, have respect, skilful, shew, can (man of) skill, be sure, of a surety, teach, (can) tell, understand, have [understanding], × will be, wist, wit, wot.

3046. יְדַע **yᵉdaʻ** (Chald.), *yed-ah'*; corresp. to 3045:—certify, know, make known, teach.

3047. יָדָע **Yâdâʻ**, *yaw-daw'*; from 3045; *knowing; Jada*, an Isr.:—Jada.

3048. יְדַעְיָה **Yᵉdaʻyâh**, *yed-ah-yaw'*; from 3045 and 3050; *Jah has known; Jedajah*, the name of two Isr.:—Jedaiah.

3049. יִדְּעֹנִי **yiddᵉʻônîy**, *yid-deh-o-nee'*; from 3045; prop. a *knowing* one; spec. a *conjurer*; (by impl.) a *ghost*:—wizard.

3050. יָהּ **Yâhh**, *yaw*; contr. for 3068, and mean. the same; *Jah*, the sacred name:—Jah, the Lord, most vehement. Cp. names in "-iah," "-jah."

3051. יָהַב **yâhab**, *yaw-hab'*; a prim. root; to *give* (whether lit. or fig.); gen. to *put*; imper. (reflex.) *come*:—ascribe, bring, come on, give, go, set, take.

3052. יְהַב **yᵉhab** (Chald.), *yeh-hab'*; corresp. to 3051:—deliver, give, lay, + prolong, pay, yield.

3053. יְהָב **yᵉhâb**, *yeh-hawb'*; from 3051; prop. what is *given* (by Providence), i.e. a *lot*:—burden.

3054. יָהַד **yâhad**, *yaw-had'*; denom. from a form corresp. to 3061; to *Judaize*, i.e. become Jewish:—become Jews.

3055. יְהֻד **Yᵉhûd**, *yeh-hood'*; a briefer form of one corresp. to 3061; *Jehud*, a place in Pal.:—Jehud.

3056. יֶהְדַּי **Yehday**, *yeh-dah'ee*; perh. from a form corresp. to 3061; *Judaistic; Jehdai*, an Isr.:—Jehdai.

3057. יְהֻדִיָּה **Yᵉhûdîyâh**, *yeh-hoo-dee-yaw'*; fem. of 3064; *Jehudijah*, a Jewess:—Jehudijah.

3058. יֵהוּא **Yêhûw'**, *yay-hoo'*; from 3068 and 1931; *Jehovah* (is) *He; Jehu*, the name of five Isr.:—Jehu.

3059. יְהוֹאָחָז **Yᵉhôw'âchâz**, *yeh-ho-aw-khawz'*; from 3068 and 270; *Jehovah-seized; Jehoăchaz*, the name of three Isr.:—Jehoahaz. Comp. 3099.

3060. יְהוֹאָשׁ **Yᵉhôw'âsh**, *yeh-ho-awsh'*; from 3068 and (perh.) 784; *Jehovah-fired; Jehoăsh*, the name of two Isr. kings:—Jehoash Comp. 3101.

3061. יְהוּד **Yᵉhûwd** (Chald.), *yeh-hood'*; contr. from a form corresp. to 3063; prop. *Judah*, hence *Judæa*:—Jewry, Judah, Judea.

3062. יְהוּדָאִי **Yᵉhûwdâ'îy** (Chald.), *yeh-hoo-daw-ee'*; patrial from 3061; a *Jehudaite* (or Judaite), i.e. Jew:—Jew.

3063. יְהוּדָה **Yᵉhûwdâh**, *yeh-hoo-daw'*; from 3034; *celebrated; Jehudah* (or Judah), the name of five Isr.; also of the tribe descended from the first, and of its territory:—Judah.

3064. יְהוּדִי **Yᵉhûwdîy**, *yeh-hoo-dee'*; patron. from 3063; a *Jehudite* (i.e. Judaite or Jew), or desc. of Jehudah (i.e. Judah):—Jew.

3065. יְהוּדִי **Yᵉhûwdîy**, *yeh-hoo-dee'*; the same as 3064; *Jehudi*, an Isr.:—Jehudi.

3066. יְהוּדִית **Yᵉhûwdîyth**, *yeh-hoo-deeth'*; fem. of 3064; the *Jewish* (used adv.) language:—in the Jews' language.

3067. יְהוּדִית **Yᵉhûwdîyth**, *yeh-hoo-deeth'*; the same as 3066; *Jewess; Jehudith*, a Canaanitess:—Judith.

3068. יְהֹוָה **Yᵉhôvâh**, *yeh-ho-vaw'*; from 1961; (the) self-*Existent* or Eternal; *Jehovah*, Jewish national name of God:—Jehovah, the Lord. Comp. 3050, 3069.

3069. יְהֹוִה **Yᵉhôvîh**, *yeh-ho-vee'*; a var. of 3068 [used after 136, and pronounced by Jews as 430, in order to prevent the repetition of the same sound, since they elsewhere pronounce 3068 as 136]:—God.

3070. יְהֹוָה יִרְאֶה **Yᵉhôvâh yireh**, *yeh-ho-vaw' yir-eh'*; from 3068 and 7200; *Jehovah will see* (to it); *Jehovah-Jireh*, a symbolical name for Mt. Moriah:—Jehovah-jireh.

3071. יְהֹוָה נִסִּי **Yᵉhôvâh niççîy**, *yeh-ho-vaw' nis-see'*; from 3068 and 5251 with pron. suffix.; *Jehovah* (is) *my banner; Jehovah-Nissi*, a symbolical name of an altar in the Desert.—Jehovah-nissi.

3072. יְהֹוָה צִדְקֵנוּ **Yᵉhôvâh tsidqênûw**, *yeh-ho-vaw' tsid-kay'-noo*; from 3068 and 6664 with pron. suffix.; *Jehovah* (is) *our right; Jehovah-Tsidkenu*, a symbolical epithet of the Messiah and of Jerus.:—the Lord our righteousness.

3073. יְהוָֹה שָׁלוֹם **Yᵉhôvâh shâlôwm**, *yeh-ho-vaw' shaw-lome'*; from 3068 and 7965; *Jehovah* (is) *peace; Jehovah-Shalom*, a symbolical name of an altar in Pal.:—Jehovah-shalom.

3074. יְהוָֹה שָׁמָּה **Yᵉhôvâh shâmmâh**, *yeh-ho-vaw' shawm'-maw*; from 3068 and 8033 with directive enclitic; *Jehovah* (is) *thither; Jehovah-Shammah*, a symbol. title of Jerus.:—Jehovah-shammah.

3075. יְהוֹזָבָד **Yᵉhôwzâbâd**, *yeh-ho-zaw-bawd'*; from 3068 and 2064; *Jehovah-endowed; Jehozabad*, the name of three Isr.:—Jehozabad. Comp. 3107.

3076. יְהוֹחָנָן **Yᵉhôwchânân**, *yeh-ho-khaw-nawn'*; from 3068 and 2603; *Jehovah-favored; Jehochanan*, the name of eight Isr.:—Johanan, Johanan. Comp. 3110.

3077. יְהוֹיָדָע **Yᵉhôwyâdâʻ**, *yeh-ho-yaw-daw'*; from 3068 and 3045; *Jehovah-known; Jehojada*, the name of three Isr.:—Jehoiada. Comp. 3111.

3078. יְהוֹיָכִין **Yᵉhôwyâkîyn**, *yeh-ho-yaw-keen'*; from 3068 and 3559; *Jehovah will establish; Jehojakin*, a Jewish king:—Jehoiachin. Comp. 3112.

3079. יְהוֹיָקִים **Yᵉhôwyâqîym**, *yeh-ho-yaw-keem'*; from 3068 abbrev. and 6965; *Jehovah will raise; Jehojakim*, a Jewish king:—Jehoiakim. Comp. 3113.

3080. יְהוֹיָרִיב **Yᵉhôwyârîyb**, *yeh-ho-yaw-reeb'*; from 3068 and 7378; *Jehovah will contend; Jehojarib*, the name of two Isr.:—Jehoiarib. Comp. 3114.

3081. יְהוּכַל **Yᵉhûwkal**, *yeh-hoo-kal'*; from 3201; *potent; Jehukal*, an Isr.:—Jehucal. Comp. 3116.

3082. יְהוֹנָדָב **Yᵉhôwnâdâb**, *yeh-ho-naw-dawb'*; from 3068 and 5068; *Jehovah-largessed; Jehonadab*, the name of an Isr. and of an Arab:—Jehonadab, Jonadab. Comp. 3122.

3083. יְהוֹנָתָן **Yᵉhôwnâthân**, *yeh-ho-naw-thawn'*; from 3068 and 5414; *Jehovah-given; Jehonathan*, the name of four Isr.:—Jonathan. Comp. 3129.

3084. יְהוֹסֵף **Yᵉhôwçêph**, *yeh-ho-safe'*; a fuller form of 3130; *Jehoseph* (i.e. Joseph), a son of Jacob:—Joseph.

3085. יְהוֹעַדָּה **Yᵉhôwʻaddâh**, *yeh-ho-ad-daw'*; from 3068 and 5710; *Jehovah-adorned; Jehoäddah*, an Isr.:—Jehoada.

3086. יְהוֹעַדִּין **Yᵉhôwʻaddîyn**, *yeh-ho-ad-deen'*; or

יְהוֹעַדָּן **Yᵉhôwaddân**, *yeh-ho-ad-dawn'*; from 3068 and 5727; *Jehovah-pleased; Jehoäddin* or *Jehoäddan*, an Israelitess:—Jehoaddan.

3087. יְהוֹצָדָק **Yᵉhôwtsâdâq**, *yeh-ho-tsaw-dawk'*; from 3068 and 6663; *Jehovah-righted; Jehotsadak*, an Isr.:—Jehozadek, Josedech. Comp. 3136.

3088. יְהוֹרָם **Yᵉhôwrâm**, *yeh-ho-rawm'*; from 3068 and 7311; *Jehovah-raised; Jehoram*, the name of a Syrian and of three Isr.:—Jehoram, Joram. Comp. 3141.

3089. יְהוֹשֶׁבַע **Yᵉhôwshebaʻ**, *yeh-ho-sheh'-bah*; from 3068 and 7650; *Jehovah-sworn; Jehosheba*, an Israelitess:—Jehosheba. Comp. 3090.

3090. יְהוֹשַׁבְעַת **Yᵉhôwshabʻath**, *yeh-ho-shab-ath'*; a form of 3089; *Jehoshabath*, an Israelitess:—Jehoshabeath.

3091. יְהוֹשׁוּעַ **Yᵉhôwshûwaʻ**, *yeh-ho-shoo'-ah*; or

יְהוֹשֻׁעַ **Yᵉhôwshûʻa**, *yeh-ho-shoo'-ah*; from 3068 and 3467; *Jehovah-saved; Jehoshuä* (i.e. Joshua), the Jewish leader:—Jehoshua, Jehoshuah, Joshua. Comp. 1954, 3442.

3092. יְהוֹשָׁפָט **Yᵉhôwshâphâṭ**, *yeh-ho-shaw-fawt'*; from 3068 and 8199; *Jehovah-judged; Jehoshaphat*, the name of six Isr.; also of a valley near Jerus.:—Jehoshaphat. Comp. 3146.

3093. יָהִיר **yâhîyr**, *yaw-here'*; prob. from the same as 2022; *elated*; hence *arrogant*:—haughty, proud.

3094. יְהַלֶּלְאֵל **Yᵉhallelʼêl**, *yeh-hal-lel-ale'*; from 1984 and 410; *praising God; Jehallelel*, the name of two Isr.:—Jehaleleel, Jehalelel.

3095. יַהֲלֹם **yahălôm**, *yah-hal-ome'*; from 1986 (in the sense of *hardness*); a precious stone, prob. *onyx*:—diamond.

3096. יַהַץ **Yahats**, *yah'-hats*; or

יַהְצָה **Yahtsâh**, *yah'-tsaw*; or (fem.)

יַהְצָה **Yahtsâh**, *yah-tsaw'*; from an unused root mean. to *stamp*; perh. *threshing*-floor; *Jahats* or *Jahtsah*, a place E. of the Jordan:—Jahaz, Jahaza, Jahzah.

3097. יוֹאָב **Yôwʼâb**, *yo-awb'*; from 3068 and 1; *Jehovah-fathered; Joäb*, the name of three Isr.:—Joab.

3098. יוֹאָח **Yôwʼâch**, *yo-awkh'*; from 3068 and 251; *Jehovah-brothered; Joach*, the name of four Isr.:—Joah.

3099. יוֹאָחָז **Yôwʼâchâz**, *yo-aw-khawz'*; a form of 3059; *Joächaz*, the name of two Isr.:—Jehoahaz, Joahaz.

3100. יוֹאֵל **Yôwʼêl**, *yo-ale'*; from 3068 and 410; *Jehovah* (is his) *God; Joël*, the name of twelve Isr.:—Joel.

3101. יוֹאָשׁ **Yôwʼâsh**, *yo-awsh'*; or

יֹאָשׁ **Yôʼâsh** (2 Chron. 24 : 1), *yo-awsh'*; a form of 3060; *Joäsh*, the name of six Isr.:—Joash.

3102. יוֹב **Yôwb**, *yobe*; perh. a form of 3103, but more prob. by err. transc. for 3437; *Job*, an Isr.:—Job.

3103. יוֹבָב **Yôwbâb**, *yo-bawb'*; from 2980; *howler; Jobab*, the name of two Isr. and of three foreigners:—Jobab.

3104. יוֹבֵל **yôwbêl**, *yo-bale'*; or

יֹבֵל **yôbêl**, *yo-bale'*; appar. from 2986; the *blast* of a horn (from its *continuous* sound); spec. the *signal* of the silver trumpets; hence the instrument itself and the festival thus introduced:—jubile, ram's horn, trumpet.

3105. יוּבַל **yûwbal**, *yoo-bal'*; from 2986; a *stream*:—river.

3106. יוּבָל **Yûwbâl**, *yoo-bawl'*; from 2986; *stream; Jubal*, an antediluvian:—Jubal.

3107. יוֹזָבָד **Yôwzâbâd**, *yo-zaw-bawd'*; a form of 3075; *Jozabad*, the name of ten Isr:—Josabad, Jozabad.

3108. יוֹזָכָר **Yôwzâkâr**, *yo-zaw-kawr'*; from 3068 and 2142; *Jehovah-remembered; Jozacar*, an Isr.:—Jozachar.

3109. יוֹחָא **Yôwchâʼ**, *yo-khaw'*; prob. from 3068 and a var. of 2421; *Jehovah-revived; Jocha*, the name of two Isr.:—Joha.

3110. יוֹחָנָן **Yôwchânân**, *yo-khaw-nawn'*; a form of 3076; *Jochanan*, the name of nine Isr.:—Johanan.

יוּטָה **Yûwṭâh**. See 3194.

3111. יוֹיָדָע **Yôwyâdâʻ**, *yo-yaw-daw'*; a form of 3077; *Jojada*, the name of two Isr.:—Jehoiada, Joiada.

3112. יוֹיָכִין **Yôwyâkîyn**, *yo-yaw-keen'*; a form of 3078; *Jojakin*, an Isr. king:—Jehoiachin.

3113. יוֹיָקִים **Yôwyâqîym**, *yo-yaw-keem'*; a form of 3079; *Jojakim*, an Isr.:—Joiakim. Comp. 3137.

3114. יוֹיָרִיב **Yôwyârîyb**, *yo-yaw-reeb'*; a form of 3080; *Jojarib*, the name of four Isr.:—Joiarib.

3115. יוֹכֶבֶד **Yôwkebed**, *yo-keh'-bed*; from 3068 contr. and 3513; *Jehovah-gloried; Jokebed*, the mother of Moses:—Jochebed.

3116. יוּכַל **Yûwkal**, *yoo-kal'*; a form of 3081; *Jukal*, an Isr.:—Jucal.

3117. יוֹם **yôwm**, *yome*; from an unused root mean. to *be hot*; a *day* (as the *warm* hours), whether lit. (from sunrise to sunset, or from one sunset to the next), or fig. (a space of time defined by an associated term), [often used adv.]:—age, + always, + chronicles, continually (-ance), daily, ([birth-], each, to) day, (now a, two) days (agone), + elder, × end, + evening, + (for) ever (-lasting, -more), × full, life, as (so) long as (. . . live), (even) now, + old, + outlived, + perpetually, presently, + remaineth, × required, season, × since, space, then, (process of) time, + as at other times, + in trouble, weather, (as) when, (a, the, within a) while (that), × whole (+ age), (full) year (-ly), + younger.

3118. יוֹם **yôwm** (Chald.), *yome*; corresp. to 3117; a *day*:—day (by day), time.

3119. יוֹמָם **yôwmâm**, *yo-mawm'*; from 3117; *daily*:—daily, (by, in the) day (-time).

3120. יָוָן **Yâvân**, *yaw-vawn'*; prob. from the same as 3196; *effervescing* (i.e. hot and active); *Javan*, the name of a son of Joktan, and of the race (*Ionians*, i.e. Greeks) descended from him, with their territory; also of a place in Arabia:—Javan.

3121. יָוֵן **yâvên**, *yaw-ven'*; from the same as 3196; prop. *dregs* (as *effervescing*); hence *mud*:—mire, miry.

3122. יוֹנָדָב **Yôwnâdâb**, *yo-naw-dawb'*; a form of 3082; *Jonadab*, the name of an Isr. and of a Rechabite:—Jonadab.

3123. יוֹנָה **yôwnâh**, *yo-naw'*; prob. from the same as 3196; a *dove* (appar. from the *warmth* of their mating):—dove, pigeon.

3124. יוֹנָה **Yônâh**, *yo-naw'*; the same as 3123; *Jonah*, an Isr.:—Jonah.

3125. יְוָנִי **Yᵉvânîy**, *yev-aw-nee'*; patron. from 3121; a *Jevanite*, or desc. of Javan:—Grecian.

3126. יוֹנֵק **yôwnêq**, *yo-nake'*; act. part. of 3243; a *sucker*; hence a *twig* (of a tree felled and sprouting):—tender plant.

3127. יוֹנֶקֶת **yôwneqeth**, *yo-neh'-keth*; fem. of 3126; a *sprout*:—(tender) branch, young twig.

3128. יוֹנַת אֵלֶם רְחֹקִים **yôwnath ʼêlem rᵉchôqîym**, *yo-nath' ay'-lem rekh-o-keem'*; from 3123 and 482 and the plur. of 7350; *dove of* (the) *silence* (i.e. *dumb* Israel) *of* (i.e. among) *distances* (i.e. strangers); the title of a ditty (used for a name of its melody):—Jonath-elem-rechokim.

3129. יוֹנָתָן **Yôwnâthân**, *yo-naw-thawn'*; a form of 3083; *Jonathan*, the name of ten Isr.:—Jonathan.

3130. יוֹסֵף **Yôwçêph**, *yo-safe'*; fut. of 3254; *let him add* (or perh. simply act. part. *adding*); *Joseph*, the name of seven Isr.:—Joseph. Comp. 3084.

3131. יוֹסִפְיָה **Yôwçiphyâh**, *yo-sif-yaw'*; from act. part. of 3254 and 3050; *Jah* (is) *adding; Josiphjah*, an Isr.:—Josiphiah.

3132. יוֹעֵאלָה **Yôwʻêʼlâh**, *yo-ay-law'*; perh. fem. act. part. of 3276; *furthermore; Joelah*, an Isr.:—Joelah.

3133. יוֹעֵד **Yôwʻêd**, *yo-ade'*; appar. act. part. of 3259; *appointer; Joed*, an Isr.:—Joed.

3134. יוֹעֶזֶר **Yôwʻezer**, *yo-eh'-zer*; from 3068 and 5828; *Jehovah* (is his) *help; Joezer*, an Isr.:—Joezer.

3135. יוֹעָשׁ **Yôwʻâsh**, *yo-awsh'*; from 3068 and 5789; *Jehovah-hastened; Joash*, the name of two Isr.:—Joash.

3136. יוֹצָדָק **Yôwtsâdâq**, *yo-tsaw-dawk'*; a form of 3087; *Jotsadak*, an Isr.:—Jozadak.

3137. יוֹקִים **Yôwqîym**, *yo-keem'*; a form of 3113; *Jokim*, an Isr.:—Jokim.

3138. יוֹרֶה **yôwreh**, *yo-reh'*; act. part. of 3384; *sprinkling*; hence a *sprinkling* (or autumnal showers):—first rain, former [rain].

3139. יוֹרָה **Yôwrâh**, *yo-raw'*; from 3384; *rainy; Jorah*, an Isr.:—Jorah.

3140. יוֹרַי **Yôwray**, *yo-rah'-ee*; from 3384; *rainy; Jorai*, an Isr.:—Jorai.

3141. יוֹרָם **Yôwrâm**, *yo-rawm'*; a form of 3088; *Joram*, the name of three Isr. and one Syrian:—Joram.

3142. יוּשַׁב חֶסֶד **Yûwshab Cheçed**, *yoo-shab' kheh'-sed*; from 7725 and 2617; *kindness will be returned; Jushab-Chesed*, an Isr.:—Jushab-hesed.

3143. יוֹשִׁבְיָה **Yôwshîbyâh**, *yo-shib-yaw'*; from 3427 and 3050; *Jehovah will cause to dwell; Joshibjah*, an Isr.:—Josibiah.

3144. יוֹשָׁה **Yôwshâh**, *yo-shaw'*; prob. a form of 3145; *Joshah*, an Isr.:—Joshah.

3145. יוֹשַׁוְיָה **Yôwshavyâh**, *yo-shav-yaw'*; from 3068 and 7737; *Jehovah-set; Joshavjah*, an Isr.:—Joshaviah. Comp. 3144.

3146. יוֹשָׁפָט **Yôwshâphâṭ**, *yo-shaw-fawt'*; a form of 3092; *Joshaphat*, an Isr.:—Joshaphat.

3147. יוֹתָם **Yôwthâm**, *yo-thawm'*; from 3068 and 8535; *Jehovah (is) perfect; Jotham*, the name of three Isr.:—Jotham.

3148. יוֹתֵר **yôwthêr**, *yo-thare'*; act. part. of 3498; prop. *redundant;* hence *over and above*, as adj., noun, adv. or conj. [as follows]:—better, more (-over), over, profit.

3149. יְזַוְאֵל **Yᵉzav'êl**, *yez-av-ale'*; from an unused root (mean. to *sprinkle*) and 410; *sprinkled of God; Jezavel*, an Isr.:—Jeziel [*from the marg.*].

3150. יִזִּיָּה **Yizzîyâh**, *yiz-zee-yaw'*; from the same as the first part of 3149 and 3050; *sprinkled of Jah; Jizzijah*, an Isr.:—Jeziah.

3151. יָזִיז **Yâzîyz**, *yaw-zeez'*; from the same as 2123; *he will make prominent; Jaziz*, an Isr.:—Jaziz.

3152. יִזְלִיאָה **Yizlîy'ah**, *yiz-lee-aw'*; perh. from an unused root (mean. to *draw up*); *he will draw out; Jizliah*, an Isr.:—Jezliah.

3153. יְזַנְיָה **Yᵉzanyâh**, *yez-an-yaw'*; or
יְזַנְיָהוּ **Yᵉzanyâhûw**, *yez-an-yaw'-hoo*; prob. for 2970; *Jezanjah*, an Isr.:—Jezaniah.

3154. יֶזַע **yezaʿ**, *yeh'-zah;* from an unused root mean to *ooze; sweat*, i.e. (by impl.) a *sweating* dress:—any thing that causeth sweat.

3155. יִזְרָח **Yizrâch**, *yiz-rawkh'*; a var. for 250; a *Jizrach* (i.e. Ezrachite or Zarchite) or desc. of Zerach:—Izrahite.

3156. יִזְרַחְיָה **Yizrachyâh**, *yiz-rakh-yaw'*; from 2224 and 3050; *Jah will shine; Jizrachjah*, the name of two Isr.:—Izrahiah, Jezrahiah.

3157. יִזְרְעֶאל **Yizrᵉʿeʾl**, *yiz-reh-ale'*; from 2232 and 410; *God will sow; Jizreël*, the name of two places in Pal. and of two Isr.:—Jezreel.

3158. יִזְרְעֵאלִי **Yizrᵉʿêʾlîy**, *yiz-reh-ay-lee'*; patron. from 3157; a *Jizreëlite* or native of Jizreel:—Jezreelite.

3159. יִזְרְעֵאלִית **Yizrᵉʿêʾlîyth**, *yiz-reh-ay-leeth'*; fem. of 3158; a *Jezreëlitess:*—Jezreelitess.

3160. יְחֻבָּה **Yᵉchubbâh**, *yekh-oob-baw'*; from 2247; *hidden; Jechubbah*, an Isr.:—Jehubbah.

3161. יָחַד **yâchad**, *yaw-khad'*; a prim. root; to be (or become) *one:*—join, unite.

3162. יַחַד **yachad**, *yakh'-ad*; from 3161; prop. a *unit*, i.e. (adv.) *unitedly:*—alike, at all (once), both, likewise, only, (al-) together, withal.

3163. יַחְדּוֹ **Yachdôw**, *yakh-doe'*; from 3162 with pron. suffix; *his unity*, i.e. (adv.) *together; Jachdo*, an Isr.:—Jahdo.

3164. יַחְדִּיאֵל **Yachdîy'êl**, *yakh-dee-ale'*; from 3162 and 410; *unity of God; Jachdiël*, an Isr.:—Jahdiel.

3165. יֶחְדִּיָּהוּ **Yechdîyâhûw**, *yekh-dee-yaw'-hoo;* from 3162 and 3050; *unity of Jah; Jechdijah*, the name of two Isr.:—Jehdeiah.

יְחַוְאֵל **Yᵉchav'êl**. See 3171.

3166. יַחֲזִיאֵל **Yachăzîy'êl**, *yakh-az-ee-ale'*; from 2372 and 410; *beheld of God; Jachaziël*, the name of five Isr.:—Jahaziel, Jahziel.

3167. יַחְזְיָה **Yachzᵉyâh**, *yakh-zeh-yaw'*; from 2372 and 3050; *Jah will behold; Jachzejah*, an Isr.:—Jahaziah.

3168. יְחֶזְקֵאל **Yᵉchezqê'l**, *yekh-ez-kale'*; from 2388 and 410; *God will strengthen; Jechezkel*, the name of two Isr.:—Ezekiel, Jehezekel.

3169. יְחִזְקִיָּה **Yᵉchizqîyâh**, *yekh-iz-kee-yaw'*; or
יְחִזְקִיָּהוּ **Yᵉchizqîyâhûw**, *yekh-iz-kee-yaw'-hoo*; from 3388 and 3050; *strengthened of Jah; Jechizkijah*, the name of five Isr.:—Hezekiah, Jehizkiah. Comp. 2396.

3170. יַחְזֵרָה **Yachzêrâh**, *yakh-zay-raw'*; from the same as 2386; perh. *protection; Jachzerah*, an Isr.:—Jahzerah.

3171. יְחִיאֵל **Yᵉchîy'êl**, *yekh-ee-ale'*; or (2 Chron. 29 : 14)
יְחַוְאֵל **Yᵉchav'êl**, *yekh-av-ale'*; from 2421 and 410; *God will live; Jechiël* (or *Jechavel*), the name of eight Isr.:—Jehiel.

3172. יְחִיאֵלִי **Yᵉchîy'êlîy**, *yekh-ee-ay-lee'*; patron. from 3171; a *Jechiëlite* or desc. of Jechiel:—Jehieli.

3173. יָחִיד **yâchîyd**, *yaw-kheed'*; from 3161; prop. *united*, i.e. *sole;* by impl. *beloved;* also *lonely;* (fem.) the *life* (as not to be replaced):—darling, desolate, only (child, son), solitary.

3174. יְחִיָּה **Yᵉchîyâh**, *yekh-ee-yaw'*; from 2421 and 3050; *Jah will live; Jechijah*, an Isr.:—Jehiah.

3175. יָחִיל **yâchîyl**, *yaw-kheel'*; from 3176; *expectant:*—should hope.

3176. יָחַל **yâchal**, *yaw-chal'*; a prim. root; to *wait;* by impl. to *be patient, hope:*—(cause to, have, make to) hope, be pained, stay, tarry, trust, wait.

3177. יַחְלְאֵל **Yachlᵉ'êl**, *yakh-leh-ale'*; from 3176 and 410; *expectant of God; Jachleël*, an Isr.:—Jahleel.

3178. יַחְלְאֵלִי **Yachlᵉ'êlîy**, *yakh-leh-ay-lee'*; patron. from 3177; a *Jachleëlite* or desc. of Jachleel.:—Jahleelites.

3179. יָחַם **yâcham**, *yaw-kham'*; a prim. root; prob. to *be hot;* fig. to *conceive:*—get heat, be hot, conceive, be warm.

3180. יַחְמוּר **yachmûwr**, *yakh-moor'*; from 2560; a kind of *deer* (from the color; comp. 2543):—fallow deer.

3181. יַחְמַי **Yachmay**, *yakh-mah'-ee;* prob. from 3179; *hot; Jachmai*, an Isr.:—Jahmai.

3182. יָחֵף **yâchêph**, *yaw-khafe'*; from an unused root mean. to *take off the shoes; unsandalled:*—barefoot, being unshod.

3183. יַחְצְאֵל **Yachtsᵉ'êl**, *yakh-tseh-ale'*; from 2673 and 410; *God will allot; Jachtseël*, an Isr.:—Jahzeel. Comp. 3185.

3184. יַחְצְאֵלִי **Yachtsᵉ'êlîy**, *yakh-tseh-ay-lee'*; patron. from 3183; a *Jachtseëlite* (collect.) or desc. of Jachtseel:—Jahzeelites.

3185. יַחְצִיאֵל **Yachtsîy'êl**, *yakh-tsee-ale'*; from 2673 and 410; *allotted of God; Jachtsiël*, an Isr.:—Jahziel. Comp. 3183.

3186. יָחַר **yâchar**, *yaw-khar'*; a prim. root; to *delay:*—tarry longer.

3187. יָחַשׂ **yâchas**, *yaw-khas'*; a prim. root; to *sprout;* used only as denom. from 3188; to *enroll* by pedigree:—(number after, number throughout the) genealogy (to be reckoned), be reckoned by genealogies.

3188. יַחַשׂ **yachas**, *yakh'-as;* from 3187; a *pedigree* or family list (as *growing* spontaneously):—genealogy.

3189. יַחַת **Yachath**, *yakh'-ath;* from 3161; *unity; Jachath*, the name of four Isr.:—Jahath.

3190. יָטַב **yâṭab**, *yaw-tab'*; a prim. root; to *be* (causat.) *make well*, lit. (*sound, beautiful*) or fig. (*happy, successful, right*):—be accepted, amend, use aright, benefit, be (make) better, seem best, make cheerful, be comely, + be content, diligent (-ly), dress, earnestly, find favour, give, be glad, do (be, make) good ([-ness]), be (make) merry, please (+ well), shew more [kindness], skilfully, × very small, surely, make sweet, thoroughly, tire, trim, very, be (can, deal, entreat, go, have) well [said, seen].

3191. יְטַב **yᵉṭab** (Chald.), *yet-ab'*; corresp. to 3190:—seem good.

3192. יָטְבָה **Yoṭbâh**, *yot-baw'*; from 3190; *pleasantness; Jotbah*, a place in Pal.:—Jotbah.

3193. יָטְבָתָה **Yoṭbâthâh**, *yot-baw'-thaw;* from 3192; *Jotbathah*, a place in the Desert:—Jotbath, Jotbathah.

3194. יֻטָּה **Yuṭṭâh**, *yoot-taw'*; or
יוּטָה **Yûwṭâh**, *yoo-taw';* from 5186; *extended; Juttah* (or *Jutah*), a place in Pal.:—Juttah.

3195. יְטוּר **Yᵉṭûwr**, *yet-oor'*; prob. from the same as 2905; *encircled* (i.e. inclosed); *Jetur*, a son of Ishmael:—Jetur.

3196. יַיִן **yayin**, *yah'-yin;* from an unused root mean. to *effervesce; wine* (as fermented); by impl. *intoxication:*—banqueting, wine, wine [-bibber].

3197. יַךְ **yak**, *yak;* by err. transc. for 3027; a *hand* or *side:*—[way-] side.

יָכוֹל **yâkôwl**. See 3201.

יְכוֹנְיָה **Yᵉkôwnᵉyâh**. See 3204.

3198. יָכַח **yâkach**, *yaw-kahh'*; a prim. root; to *be right* (i.e. correct); recip. to *argue;* causat. to *decide, justify* or *convict:*—appoint, argue, chasten, convince, correct (-ion), daysman, dispute, judge, maintain, plead, reason (together), rebuke, reprove (-r), surely, in any wise.

יְכִילְיָה **Yᵉkîylᵉyâh**. See 3203.

3199. יָכִין **Yâkîyn**, *yaw-keen'*; from 3559; *he* (or *it*) *will establish; Jakin*, the name of three Isr. and of a temple pillar:—Jachin.

3200. יָכִינִי **Yâkîyniy**, *yaw-kee-nee'*; patron. from 3199; a *Jakinite* (collect.) or desc. of Jakin:—Jachinites.

3201. יָכֹל **yâkôl**, *yaw-kole'*; or (fuller)
יָכוֹל **yâkôwl**, *yaw-kole'*; a prim. root; to *be able*, lit. (*can, could*) or mor. (*may, might*):—be able, any at all (ways), attain, can (away with, [-not]), could, endure, might, overcome, have power, prevail, still, suffer.

3202. יְכֵל **yᵉkêl** (Chald.), *yek-ale'*; or
יְכִיל **yᵉkîyl** (Chald.), *yek-eel'*; corresp. to 3201:—be able, can, couldest, prevail.

3203. יְכָלְיָה **Yᵉkolyâh**, *yek-ol-yaw'*; and
יְכָלְיָהוּ **Yᵉkolyâhûw**, *yek-ol-yaw'-hoo*; or (2 Ch. 26 : 3)
יְכִילְיָה **Yᵉkîylᵉyâh**, *yek-ee-leh-yaw'*; from 3201 and 3050; *Jah will enable; Jekoljah* or *Jekiljah*, an Israelitess:—Jecholiah, Jecoliah.

3204. יְכָנְיָה **Yᵉkonyâh**, *yek-on-yaw'*; and
יְכָנְיָהוּ **Yᵉkonyâhûw**, *yek-on-yaw'-hoo;* or (Jer. 27 : 20)
יְכוֹנְיָה **Yᵉkôwnᵉyâh**, *yek-o-neh-yaw'*; from 3559 and 3050; *Jah will establish; Jekonjah*, a Jewish king:—Jeconiah. Comp. 3659.

3205. יָלַד **yâlad**, *yaw-lad'*; a prim. root; to *bear* young; causat. to *beget;* med. to *act as midwife;* spec. to *show lineage:*—bear, beget, birth ([-day]), born, (make to) bring forth (children, young), bring up, calve, child, come, be delivered (of a child), time of delivery, gender, hatch, labour, (do the office of a) midwife, declare pedigrees, be the son of, (woman in, woman that) travail (-eth, -ing woman).

3206. יֶלֶד **yeled**, *yeh'-led;* from 3205; something *born*, i.e. a *lad* or *offspring:*—boy, child, fruit, son, young man (one).

3207. יַלְדָּה **yaldâh**, *yal-daw'*; fem. of 3206; a *lass:*—damsel, girl.

3208. יַלְדוּת **yaldûwth**, *yal-dooth'*; abstr. from 3206; *boyhood* (or *girlhood*):—childhood, youth.

3209. יִלּוֹד **yillôwd**, *yil-lode'*; pass. from 3205; *born:*—born.

3210. יָלוֹן **Yâlôwn**, *yaw-lone'*; from 3885; *lodging; Jalon*, an Isr.:—Jalon.

3211. יָלִיד **yâlîyd**, *yaw-leed'*; from 3205; *born:*—([home-]) born, child, son.

3212. יָלַךְ **yâlak**, *yaw-lak'*; a prim. root [comp. 1980]; to *walk* (lit. or fig.); causat. to *carry* (in various senses):—× again, away, bear, bring, carry (away), come (away), depart, flow, + follow (-ing), get (away, hence, him), (cause to, make) go (away, -ing, -ne, one's way, out), grow, lead (forth), let down, march, prosper, + pursue, cause to run, spread, take away ([-journey]), vanish, (cause to) walk (-ing), wax, × be weak.

3213. יָלַל yâlal, *yaw-lal';* a prim. root; to *howl* (with a wailing tone) or *yell* (with a boisterous one):—(make to) howl, be howling.

3214. יְלֵל y^{e}lêl, *yel-ale';* from 3213; a *howl:*—howling.

3215. יְלָלָה y^{e}lâlâh, *yel-aw-law';* fem. of 3214; a *howling:*—howling.

3216. יָלַע yâlaʻ, *yaw-lah';* a prim. root; to *blurt* or utter inconsiderately:—devour.

3217. יַלֶּפֶת yallepheth, *yal-leh'-feth;* from an unused root appar. mean. to *stick* or *scrape; scurf* or *tetter:*—scabbed.

3218. יֶלֶק yeleq, *yeh'-lek;* from an unused root mean. to *lick up;* a *devourer;* spec. the young *locust:*—cankerworm, caterpillar.

3219. יַלְקוּט yalqûwṭ, *yal-koot';* from 3950; a travelling *pouch* (as if for gleanings):—scrip.

3220. יָם yâm, *yawm;* from an unused root mean. to *roar;* a *sea* (as breaking in *noisy* surf) or large body of water; spec. (with the art.) the *Mediterranean;* sometimes a large *river,* or an artificial *basin;* locally, the *west,* or (rarely) the *south:*—sea (× -faring man, [-shore]), south, west (-ern, side, -ward).

3221. יָם yâm (Chald.), *yawm;* corresp. to 3220:—sea.

3222. יֵם yêm, *yame;* from the same as 3117; a *warm* spring:—mule.

3223. יְמוּאֵל Y^{e}mûwʼêl, *yem-oo-ale';* from 3117 and 410; *day of God; Jemuel,* an Isr.:—Jemuel.

3224. יְמִימָה Y^{e}mîymâh, *yem-ee-maw';* perh. from the same as 3117; prop. *warm,* i.e. *affectionate;* hence *dove* [comp. 3123]; *Jemimah,* one of Job's daughters:—Jemimah.

3225. יָמִין yâmîyn, *yaw-meen';* from 3231; the *right* hand or side (leg, eye) of a person or other object (as the *stronger* and more dexterous); locally, the *south:*— + left-handed, right (hand, side), south.

3226. יָמִין Yâmîyn, *yaw-meen';* the same as 3225; *Jamin,* the name of three Isr.:—Jamin. See also 1144.

3227. יְמִינִי y^{e}mîynîy, *yem-ee-nee';* for 3225; *right:*—(on the) right (hand).

3228. יְמִינִי Y^{e}mîynîy, *yem-ee-nee';* patron. from 3226; a *Jeminite* (collect.) or desc. of Jamin:—Jaminites. See also 1145.

3229. יִמְלָא Yimlâʼ, *yeem-law';* or

יִמְלָה Yimlâh, *yim-law';* from 4390; *full; Jimla* or *Jimlah,* an Isr.:—Imla, Imlah.

3230. יַמְלֵךְ Yamlêk, *yam-lake';* from 4427; *he will make king; Jamlek,* an Isr.:—Jamlech.

3231. יָמַן yâman, *yaw-man';* a prim. root; to *be* (phys.) *right* (i.e. firm); but used only as denom. from 3225 and transit., to *be right-handed* or *take the right-hand* side:—go (turn) to (on, use) the right hand.

3232. יִמְנָה Yimnâh, *yim-naw';* from 3231; *prosperity* (as betokened by the *right* hand); *Jimnah,* the name of two Isr.; also (with the art.) of the posterity of one of them:—Imna, Imnah, Jimnah, Jimnites.

3233. יְמָנִי y^{e}mânîy, *yem-aw-nee';* from 3231; *right* (i.e. at the right hand):—(on the) right (hand).

3234. יִמְנָע Yimnâʻ, *yim-naw';* from 4513; *he will restrain; Jimna,* an Isr.:—Imna.

3235. יָמַר yâmar, *yaw-mar';* a prim. root; to *exchange;* by impl. to *change places:*—boast selves, change.

3236. יִמְרָה Yimrâh, *yim-raw';* prob. from 3235; *interchange; Jimrah,* an Isr.:—Imrah.

3237. יָמַשׁ yâmash, *yaw-mash';* a prim. root; to *touch:*—feel.

3238. יָנָה yânâh, *yaw-naw';* a prim. root; to *rage* or *be violent:* by impl. to *suppress,* to *maltreat:*—destroy, (thrust out by) oppress (-ing, -ion, -or), proud, vex, do violence.

3239. יָנוֹחַ Yânôwach, *yaw-no'-akh;* or (with enclitic)

יָנוֹחָה Yânôwchâh, *yaw-no'-khaw;* from 3240; *quiet; Janoäch* or *Janochah,* a place in Pal.:—Janoah, Janohah.

יָנוּם Yânûm. See 3241.

3240. יָנַח yânach, *yaw-nakh';* a prim. root; to *deposit;* by impl. to *allow to stay:*—bestow, cast down, lay (down, up), leave (off), let alone (remain), pacify, place, put, set (down), suffer, withdraw, withhold. (The Hiphil forms with the *dagesh* are here referred to, in accordance with the older grammarians; but if any distinction of the kind is to be made, these should rather be referred to 5117, and the others here.)

3241. יָנִים Yânîym, *yaw-neem';* from 5123; *asleep; Janim,* a place in Pal.:—Janum [*from the marg.*].

3242. יְנִיקָה y^{e}nîyqâh, *yen-ee-kaw';* from 3243; a *sucker* or sapling:—young twig.

3243. יָנַק yânaq, *yaw-nak';* a prim. root; to *suck;* causat. to *give milk:*—milch, nurse (-ing mother), (give, make to) suck (-ing child, -ling).

3244. יַנְשׁוּף yanshûwph, *yan-shoof';* or

יַנְשׁוֹף yanshôwph, *yan-shofe';* appar. from 5398; an unclean (aquatic) bird; prob. the *heron* (perh. from its *blowing* cry, or because the *night*-heron is meant [comp. 5399]):—(great) owl.

3245. יָסַד yâçad, *yaw-sad';* a prim. root; to *set* (lit. or fig.); intens. to *found;* reflex. to *sit* down together, i.e. *settle, consult:*—appoint, take counsel, establish, (lay the, lay for a) found (-ation), instruct, lay, ordain, set, × sure.

3246. יְסֻד y^{e}çud, *yes-ood';* from 3245; a *foundation* (fig. i.e. *beginning*):— × began.

3247. יְסוֹד y^{e}çôwd, *yes-ode';* from 3245; a *foundation* (lit. or fig.):—bottom, foundation, repairing.

3248. יְסוּדָה y^{e}çûwdâh, *yes-oo-daw';* fem. of 3246; a *foundation:*—foundation.

3249. יָסוּר yâçûwr, *yaw-soor';* from 5493; *departing:*—they that depart.

3250. יִסּוֹר yiççôwr, *yis-sore';* from 3256; a *reprover:*—instruct.

3251. יָסַךְ yâçak, *yaw-sak';* a prim. root; to *pour* (intrans.):—be poured.

3252. יִסְכָּה Yiçkâh, *yis-kaw';* from an unused root mean. to *watch; observant; Jiskah,* sister of Lot:—Iscah.

3253. יִסְמַכְיָהוּ Yiçmakyâhûw, *yis-mak-yaw-hoo';* from 5564 and 3050; *Jah will sustain; Jismakjah,* an Isr.:—Ismachiah.

3254. יָסַף yâçaph, *yaw-saf';* a prim. root; to *add* or *augment* (often adv. to *continue* to do a thing):—add, × again, × any more, × cease, × come more, + conceive again, continue, exceed, × further, × gather together, get more, give moreover, × henceforth, increase (more and more), join, × longer (bring, do, make, much, put), × (the, much, yet) more (and more), proceed (further), prolong, put, be [strong-] er, × yet, yield.

3255. יְסַף y^{e}çaph (Chald.), *yes-af';* corresp. to 3254:—add.

3256. יָסַר yâçar, *yaw-sar';* a prim. root; to *chastise,* lit. (with blows) or fig. (with words); hence to *instruct:*—bind, chasten, chastise, correct, instruct, punish, reform, reprove, sore, teach.

3257. יָע yâʻ, *yaw;* from 3261; a *shovel:*—shovel.

3258. יַעְבֵּץ Yaʻbêts, *yah-bates';* from an unused root prob. mean. to *grieve; sorrowful; Jabets,* the name of an Isr., and also of a place in Pal.:—Jabez.

3259. יָעַד yâʻad, *yaw-ad';* a prim. root; to *fix* upon (by agreement or appointment); by impl. to *meet* (at a stated time), to *summon* (to trial), to *direct* (in a certain quarter or position), to *engage* (for marriage):—agree, (make an) appoint (-ment, a time), assemble (selves), betroth, gather (selves, together), meet (together), set (a time).

יֶעְדּוֹ Y^{e}ʻdôw. See 3260.

3260. יֶעְדִּי Y^{e}ʻdîy, *yed-ee';* from 3259; *appointed; Jedi,* an Isr.:—Iddo [*from the marg.*] See 3035.

3261. יָעָה yâʻâh, *yaw-aw';* a prim. root; appar to *brush* aside:—sweep away.

3262. יְעוּאֵל Y^{e}ʻûwʼêl, *yeh-oo-ale';* from 3261 and 410; *carried away of God; Jeüel,* the name of four Isr.:—Jehiel, Jeiel, Jeuel. Comp. 3273.

3263. יְעוּץ Y^{e}ʻûwts, *yeh-oots';* from 5779; *counsellor; Jeüts,* an Isr.:—Jeuz.

3264. יָעוֹר yâʻôwr, *yaw-ore';* a var. of 3293; a *forest:*—wood.

3265. יָעוּר Yâʻûwr, *yaw-oor';* appar. pass. part. of the same as 3293; *wooded; Jaür,* an Isr.:—Jair [*from the marg.*].

3266. יְעוּשׁ Y^{e}ʻûwsh, *yeh-oosh';* from 5789; *hasty; Jeüsh,* the name of an Edomite and of four Isr.:—Jehush, Jeush. Comp. 3274.

3267. יָעַז yâʻaz, *yaw-az';* a prim. root; to *be bold* or *obstinate:*—fierce.

3268. יַעֲזִיאֵל Yaʻăzîyʼêl, *yah-az-ee-ale';* from 3267 and 410; *emboldened of God; Jaaziël,* an Isr.:—Jaaziel.

3269. יַעֲזִיָּהוּ Yaʻăzîyâhûw, *yah-az-ee-yaw'-hoo;* from 3267 and 3050; *emboldened of Jah; Jaazijah,* an Isr.:—Jaaziah.

3270. יַעֲזִיר Yaʻăzêyr, *yah-az-ayr';* or

יַעְזֵר Yaʻzêr, *yah-zare';* from 5826; *helpful; Jaazer* or *Jazer,* a place E. of the Jordan:—Jaazer, Jazer.

3271. יָעַט yâʻaṭ, *yaw-at';* a prim. root; to *clothe:*—cover.

3272. יְעַט y^{e}ʻaṭ (Chald.), *yeh-at';* corresp. to 3289; to *counsel;* reflex. to *consult:*—counsellor, consult together.

3273. יְעִיאֵל Y^{e}ʻîyʼêl, *yeh-ee-ale';* from 3261 and 410; *carried away of God; Jeïel,* the name of six Isr.:—Jeiel, Jehiel. Comp. 3262.

יָעִיר Yâʻîyr. See 3265.

3274. יְעִישׁ Y^{e}ʻîysh, *yeh-eesh';* from 5789; *hasty; Jeïsh,* the name of an Edomite and of an Isr.:—Jeush [*from the marg.*]. Comp. 3266.

3275. יַעְכָּן Yaʻkân, *yah-kawn';* from the same as 5912; *troublesome; Jakan,* an Isr.:—Jachan.

3276. יָעַל yâʻal, *yaw-al';* a prim. root; prop. to *ascend;* fig. to *be valuable* (obj. *useful,* subj. *benefited*):— × at all, set forward, can do good, (be, have) profit (-able).

3277. יָעֵל yâʻêl, *yaw-ale';* from 3276; an *ibex* (as *climbing*):—wild goat.

3278. יָעֵל Yâʻêl, *yaw-ale';* the same as 3277; *Jaël,* a Canaanite:—Jael.

3279. יַעְלָא Yaʻălâʼ, *yah-al-aw';* or

יַעֲלָה Yaʻălâh, *yah-al-aw';* the same as 3280 or direct from 5976; *Jaala* or *Jaalah,* one of the Nethinim:—Jaala, Jaalah.

3280. יַעֲלָה yaʻălâh, *yah-al-aw';* fem. of 3277:—roe.

3281. יַעְלָם Yaʻlâm, *yah-lawm';* from 5956; *occult; Jalam,* an Edomite:—Jalam.

3282. יַעַן yaʻan, *yah'-an;* from an unused root mean. to *pay attention;* prop. *heed;* by impl. *purpose* (sake or account); used adv. to indicate the *reason* or cause:—because (that), forasmuch (+ as), seeing then, + that, + whereas, + why.

3283. יָעֵן yâʻên, *yaw-ane';* from the same as 3282; the *ostrich* (prob. from its *answering* cry:—ostrich.

3284. יַעֲנָה yaʻănâh, *yah-an-aw';* fem. of 3283, and mean. the same:— + owl.

3285. יַעְנַי Yaʻănay, *yah-an-ah'ee;* from the same as 3283; *responsive; Jaanai,* an Isr.:—Jaanai.

3286. יָעַף yâʻaph, *yaw-af';* a prim. root; to *tire* (as if from wearisome *flight*):—faint, cause to fly, (be) weary (self).

3287. יָעֵף yâʻêph, *yaw-afe';* from 3286; *fatigued;* fig. *exhausted:*—faint, weary.

3288. יְעָף y^{e}ʻâph, *yeh-awf';* from 3286; *fatigue* (adv. utterly *exhausted*):—swiftly.

3289. יָעַץ yâʻats, *yaw-ats';* a prim. root; to *advise;* reflex. to *deliberate* or *resolve:*—advertise, take advice, advise (well), consult, (give take) counsel (-lor), determine, devise, guide, purpose.

3290. יַעֲקֹב **Ya‛ăqôb**, *yah-ak-obe'*; from 6117; *heel*-catcher (i.e. supplanter); *Jaakob*, the Israelitish patriarch:—Jacob.

3291. יַעֲקֹבָה **Ya‛ăqôbâh**, *yah-ak-o'-baw*; from 3290; *Jaakobah*, an Isr.:—Jaakobah.

3292. יַעֲקָן **Ya‛ăqân**, *yah-ak-awn'*; from the same as 6130; *Jaakan*, an Idumæan:—Jaakan. Comp. 1142.

3293. יַעַר **ya‛ar**, *yah'-ar*; from an unused root prob. mean. to *thicken* with verdure; a *copse* of bushes; hence a *forest*; hence *honey* in the *comb* (as hived in trees):—[honey-] comb, forest, wood.

3294. יַעְרָה **Ya‛râh**, *yah-raw'*; a form of 3295; *Jarah*, an Isr.:—Jarah.

3295. יַעֲרָה **ya‛ărâh**, *yah-ar-aw'*; fem. of 3293, and mean. the same:—[honey-] comb, forest.

3296. יַעֲרֵי אֹרְגִים **Ya‛ărêy 'Orᵉgîym**, *yah-ar-ay' o-reg-eem'*; from the plur. of 3293 and the masc. plur. part. act. of 707; *woods of weavers*; *Jaare-Oregim*, an Isr.:—Jaare-oregim.

3297. יְעָרִים **Yᵉ‛ârîym**, *yeh-aw-reem'*; plur. of 3293; *forests*; *Jeärim*, a place in Pal.:—Jearim. Comp. 7157.

3298. יַעֲרֶשְׁיָה **Ya‛ăreshyâh**, *yah-ar-esh-yaw'*; from an unused root of uncert. signif. and 3050; *Jaareshjah*, an Isr.:—Jaresiah.

3299. יַעֲשׂוּ **Ya‛ăsûw**, *yah-as-oo'*; from 6213; *they will do*; *Jaasu*, an Isr.:—Jaasau.

3300. יַעֲשִׂיאֵל **Ya‛ăsîy'êl**, *yah-as-ee-ale'*; from 6213 and 410; *made of God*; *Jaasiel*, an Isr.:—Jaasiel, Jasiel.

3301. יִפְדְיָה **Yiphdᵉyâh**, *yif-deh-yaw'*; from 6299 and 3050; *Jah will liberate*; *Jiphdejah*, an Isr.:—Iphedeiah.

3302. יָפָה **yâphâh**, *yaw-faw'*; a prim. root; prop. to *be bright*, i.e. (by impl.) *beautiful*:—be beautiful, be (make self) fair (-r), deck.

3303. יָפֶה **yâpheh**, *yaw-feh'*; from 3302; *beautiful* (lit. or fig.):—+ beautiful, beauty, comely, fair (-est, one), + goodly, pleasant, well.

3304. יְפֵה־פִיָּה **yᵉphêh-phîyâh**, *yef-eh' fee-yaw'*; from 3302 by redupl.; *very beautiful*:—very fair.

3305. יָפוֹ **Yâphô**, *yaw-fo'*; or

יָפוֹא **Yâphôw'** (Ezra 3 : 7), *yaw-fo'*; from 3302; *beautiful*; *Japho*, a place in Pal.:—Japha, Joppa.

3306. יָפַח **yâphach**, *yaw-fakh'*; a prim. root; prop. to *breathe* hard, i.e. (by impl.) to *sigh*:—bewail self.

3307. יָפֵחַ **yâphêach**, *yaw-fay'-akh*; from 3306; prop. *puffing*, i.e. (fig.) *meditating*:—such as breathe out.

3308. יֳפִי **yŏphîy**, *yof-ee'*; from 3302; *beauty*:—beauty.

3309. יָפִיעַ **Yâphîya‛**, *yaw-fee'-ah*; from 3313; *bright*; *Japhia*, the name of a Canaanite, an Isr., and a place in Pal.:—Japhia.

3310. יַפְלֵט **Yaphlêṭ**, *yaf-late'*; from 6403; *he will deliver*; *Japhlet*, an Isr.:—Japhlet.

3311. יַפְלֵטִי **Yaphlêṭîy**, *yaf-lay-tee'*; patron. from 3310; a *Japhletite* or desc. of Japhlet:—Japhleti.

3312. יְפֻנֶּה **Yᵉphunneh**, *yef-oon-neh'*; from 6437; *he will be prepared*; *Jephunneh*, the name of two Isr.:—Jephunneh.

3313. יָפַע **yâpha‛**, *yaw-fah'*; a prim. root; to *shine*:—be light, shew self, (cause to) shine (forth).

3314. יִפְעָה **yiph‛âh**, *yif-aw'*; from 3313; *splendor* or (fig.) *beauty*:—brightness.

3315. יֶפֶת **Yepheth**, *yeh'-feth*; from 6601; *expansion*; *Jepheth*, a son of Noah; also his posterity:—Japheth.

3316. יִפְתָּח **Yiphtâch**, *yif-tawkh'*; from 6605; *he will open*; *Jiphtach*, an Isr.; also a place in Pal.:—Jephthah, Jiphtah.

3317. יִפְתַּח־אֵל **Yiphtach-'êl**, *yif-tach-ale'*; from 6605 and 410; *God will open*; *Jiphtach-el*, a place in Pal.:—Jiphthah-el.

3318. יָצָא **yâtsâ'**, *yaw-tsaw'*; a prim. root; to *go* (causat. *bring*) *out*, in a great variety of applications, lit. and fig., direct and proxim.:—× after, appear, × assuredly, bear out, × begotten, break out, bring forth (out, up), carry out, come (abroad, out, thereat, without), + be condemned, depart (-ing, -ure), draw forth, in the end, escape, exact, fail, fall (out), fetch forth (out), get away (forth, hence, out), (able to, cause to, let) go abroad (forth, on, out), going out, grow, have forth (out), issue out, lay (lie) out, lead out, pluck out, proceed, pull out, put away, be risen, × scarce, send with commandment, shoot forth, spread, spring out, stand out, × still, × surely, take forth (out), at any time, × to [and fro], utter.

3319. יְצָא **yᵉtsâ'** (Chald.), *yets-aw'*; corresp. to 3318:—finish.

3320. יָצַב **yâtsab**, *yaw-tsab'*; a prim. root; to *place* (any thing so as to stay); reflex. to *station*, *offer*, *continue*:—present selves, remaining, resort, set (selves), (be able to, can, with-) stand (fast, forth, -ing, still, up).

3321. יְצַב **yᵉtsêb** (Chald.), *yets-abe'*; corresp. to 3320; to *be firm*; hence to *speak surely*:—truth.

3322. יָצַג **yâtsag**, *yaw-tsag'*; a prim. root; to *place* permanently:—establish, leave, make, present, put, set, stay.

3323. יִצְהָר **yitshâr**, *yits-hawr'*; from 6671; *oil* (as producing *light*); fig. *anointing*:—+ anointed, oil.

3324. יִצְהָר **Yitshâr**, *yits-hawr'*; the same as 3323; *Jitshar*, an Isr.:—Izhar.

3325. יִצְהָרִי **Yitshârîy**, *yits-haw-ree'*; patron. from 3324; a *Jitsharite* or desc. of Jitshar:—Izeharites, Izharites.

3326. יָצוּעַ **yâtsûwa‛**, *yaw-tsoo'-ah*; pass. part. of 3331; *spread*, i.e. a *bed*; (arch.) an *extension*, i.e. *wing* or *lean-to* (a single story or collect.):—bed, chamber, couch.

3327. יִצְחָק **Yitschâq**, *yits-khawk'*; from 6711; *laughter* (i.e. *mockery*); *Jitschak* (or Isaac), son of Abraham:—Isaac. Comp. 3446.

3328. יִצְחַר **Yitschar**, *yits-khar'*; from the same as 6713; *he will shine*; *Jitschar*, an Isr.:—and Zehoar [*from the marg.*].

3329. יָצִיא **yâtsîy'**, *yaw-tsee'*; from 3318; *issue*, i.e. offspring:—those that came forth.

3330. יַצִּיב **yatstsîyb** (Chald.), *yats-tseeb'*; from 3321; *fixed*, *sure*; concr. *certainty*:—certain (-ty), true, truth.

יָצִיעַ **yâtsîya‛**. See 3326.

3331. יָצַע **yâtsa‛**, *yaw-tsah'*; a prim. root; to *strew* as a surface:—make [one's] bed, × lie, spread.

3332. יָצַק **yâtsaq**, *yaw-tsak'*; a prim. root; prop. to *pour* out (trans. or intrans.); by impl. to *melt* or *cast* as metal; by extens. to *place* firmly, to *stiffen* or grow hard:—cast, cleave fast, be (as) firm, grow, be hard, lay out, molten, overflow, pour (out), run out, set down, stedfast.

3333. יְצֻקָה **yᵉtsûqâh**, *yets-oo-kaw'*; pass. part. fem. of 3332; *poured* out, i.e. *run* into a mould:—when it was cast.

3334. יָצַר **yâtsar**, *yaw-tsar'*; a prim. root; to *press* (intrans.), i.e. *be narrow*; fig. *be in distress*:—be distressed, be narrow, be straitened (in straits), be vexed.

3335. יָצַר **yâtsar**, *yaw-tsar'*; prob. identical with 3334 (through the *squeezing* into shape); ([comp. 3331]); to *mould* into a form; espec. as a *potter*; fig. to *determine* (i.e. form a resolution):—× earthen, fashion, form, frame, make (-r), potter, purpose.

3336. יֵצֶר **yêtser**, *yay'-tser*; from 3335; a *form*; fig. *conception* (i.e. purpose):—frame, thing framed, imagination, mind, work.

3337. יֵצֶר **Yêtser**, *yay'-tser*; the same as 3336; *Jetser*, an Isr.:—Jezer.

3338. יָצֻר **yâtsûr**, *yaw-tsoor'*; pass. part. of 3335; *structure*, i.e. limb or part:—member.

3339. יִצְרִי **Yitsrîy**, *yits-ree'*; from 3335; *formative*; *Jitsri*, an Isr.:—Isri.

3340. יִצְרִי **Yitsrîy**, *yits-ree'*; patron. from 3337; a *Jitsrite* (collect.) or desc. of Jetser:—Jezerites.

3341. יָצַת **yâtsath**, *yaw-tsath'*; a prim. root; to *burn* or *set on fire*; fig. to *desolate*:—burn (up), be desolate, set (on) fire ([fire]), kindle.

3342. יֶקֶב **yeqeb**, *yeh'-keb*; from an unused root mean. to *excavate*; a *trough* (as dug out); spec. a wine-*vat* (whether the lower one, into which the juice drains; or the upper, in which the grapes are crushed):—fats, presses, press-fat, wine (-press).

3343. יְקַבְצְאֵל **Yᵉqabtsᵉ'êl**, *yek-ab-tseh-ale'*; from 6908 and 410; *God will gather*; *Jekabtseël*, a place in Pal.:—Jekabzeel. Comp. 6909.

3344. יָקַד **yâqad**, *yaw-kad'*; a prim. root; to *burn*:—(be) burn (-ing), × from the hearth, kindle.

3345. יְקַד **yᵉqad** (Chald.), *yek-ad'*; corresp. to 3344:—burning.

3346. יְקֵדָא **yᵉqêdâ'** (Chald.), *yek-ay-daw'*; from 3345; a *conflagration*:—burning.

3347. יָקְדְעָם **Yoqdᵉ‛âm**, *yok-deh-awm'*; from 3344 and 5971; *burning of* (the) *people*; *Jokdeäm*, a place in Pal.:—Jokdeam.

3348. יָקֶה **Yâqeh**, *yaw-keh'*; from an unused root prob. mean. to *obey*; *obedient*; *Jakeh*, a symbolical name (for Solomon):—Jakeh.

3349. יִקְּהָה **yiqqâhâh**, *yik-kaw-haw'*; from the same as 3348; *obedience*:—gathering, to obey.

3350. יְקוֹד **yᵉqôwd**, *yek-ode'*; from 3344; a *burning*:—burning.

3351. יְקוּם **yᵉqûwm**, *yek-oom'*; from 6965; prop. *standing* (extant), i.e. by impl. a *living thing*:—(living) substance.

3352. יָקוֹשׁ **yâqôwsh**, *yaw-koshe'*; from 3369; prop. *entangling*; hence a *snarer*:—fowler.

3353. יָקוּשׁ **yâqûwsh**, *yaw-koosh'*; pass. part. of 3369; prop. *entangled*, i.e. by impl. (intrans.) a *snare*, or (trans.) a *snarer*:—fowler, snare.

3354. יְקוּתִיאֵל **Yᵉqûwthîy'êl**, *yek-ooth-ee'-ale*; from the same as 3348 and 410; *obedience of God*; *Jekuthiël*, an Isr.:—Jekuthiel.

3355. יָקְטָן **Yoqṭân**, *yok-tawn'*; from 6994; *he will be made little*; *Joktan*, an Arabian patriarch:—Joktan.

3356. יָקִים **Yâqîym**, *yaw-keem'*; from 6965; *he will raise*; *Jakim*, the name of two Isr.:—Jakim. Comp. 3079.

3357. יַקִּיר **yaqqîyr**, *yak-keer'*; from 3365; *precious*:—dear.

3358. יַקִּיר **yaqqîyr** (Chald.) *yak-keer'*; corresp. to 3357:—noble, rare.

3359. יְקַמְיָה **Yᵉqamyâh**, *yek-am-yaw'*; from 6965 and 3050; *Jah will rise*; *Jekamjah*, the name of two Isr.:—Jekamiah. Comp. 3079.

3360. יְקַמְעָם **Yᵉqam‛âm**, *yek-am'-awm*; from 6965 and 5971; (the) *people will rise*; *Jekamam*, an Isr.:—Jekameam. Comp. 3079, 3361.

3361. יָקְמְעָם **Yoqmᵉ‛âm**, *yok-meh-awm'*; from 6965 and 5971; (the) *people will be raised*; *Jokmeäm*, a place in Pal.:—Jokmeam. Comp. 3360, 3362.

3362. יָקְנְעָם **Yoqnᵉ‛âm**, *yok-neh-awm'*; from 6969 and 5971; (the) *people will be lamented*; *Jokneäm*, a place in Pal.:—Jokneam.

3363. יָקַע **yâqa‛**, *yaw-kah'*; a prim. root; prop. to *sever* oneself, i.e. (by impl.) to *be dislocated*; fig. to *abandon*; causat. to *impale* (and thus allow to drop to pieces by *rotting*):—be alienated, depart, hang (up), be out of joint.

3364. יָקַץ **yâqats**, *yaw-kats'*; a prim. root; to *awake* (intrans.):—(be) awake (-d).

יָקַף **yâqaph**. See 5362.

3365. יָקַר **yâqar**, *yaw-kar'*; a prim. root; prop. appar. to *be heavy*, i.e. (fig.) *valuable*; causat. to *make rare* (fig. to *inhibit*):—be (make) precious, be prized, be set by, withdraw.

3366. יְקָר **yᵉqâr**, *yek-awr'*; from 3365; *value*, i.e. (concr.) *wealth*; abstr. *costliness*, *dignity*:—honour, precious (things), price.

3367. יְקָר **yᵉqâr** (Chald.), *yek-awr'*; corresp. to 3366:—glory, honour.

3368. יָקָר **yâqâr**, *yaw-kawr'*; from 3365; *valuable* (obj. or subj.):—brightness, clear, costly, excellent, fat, honourable women, precious, reputation.

3369. יָקֹשׁ **yâqôsh**, *yaw-koshe'*; a prim. root; to *ensnare* (lit. or fig.):—fowler (lay a) snare.

3370. יָקְשָׁן **Yoqshân**, *yok-shawn'*; from 3369; *insidious; Jokshan*, an Arabian patriarch:—Jokshan.

3371. יָקְתְאֵל **Yoqthᵉ'êl**, *yok-theh-ale'*; prob. from the same as 3348 and 410; *veneration of God* [comp. 3354]; *Joktheël*, the name of a place in Pal., and of one in Idumæa:—Joktheel.

יָרָא **yârâ'**. See 3384.

3372. יָרֵא **yârê'**, *yaw-ray'*; a prim. root; to *fear;* mor. to *revere;* caus. to *frighten:*—affright, be (make) afraid, dread (-ful), (put in) fear (-ful, -fully, -ing), (be had in) reverence (-end), × see, terrible (act, -ness, thing).

3373. יָרֵא **yârê'**, *yaw-ray'*; from 3372; *fearing;* mor. *reverent:*—afraid, fear (-ful).

3374. יִרְאָה **yir'âh**, *yir-aw'*; fem. of 3373; *fear* (also used as infin.); mor. *reverence:*—× dreadful, × exceedingly, fear (-fulness).

3375. יִרְאוֹן **Yirôwn**, *yir-ohn'*; from 3372; *fearfulness; Jiron*, a place in Pal.:—Iron.

3376. יִרְאִיָּיה **Yir'îyâyh**, *yir-ee-yaw'*; from 3373 and 3050; *fearful of Jah; Jirijah*, an Isr.:—Irijah.

3377. יָרֵב **Yârêb**, *yaw-rabe'*; from 7378; *he will contend; Jareb*, a symbolical name for Assyria:—Jareb. Comp. 3402.

3378. יְרֻבַּעַל **Yᵉrubba'al**, *yer-oob-bah'-al*; from 7378 and 1168; *Baal will contend; Jerubbaal*, a symbol. name of Gideon:—Jerubbaal.

3379. יָרָבְעָם **Yârob'âm**, *yaw-rob-awm'*; from 7378 and 5971; (the) *people will contend; Jarobam*, the name of two Isr. kings:—Jeroboam.

3380. יְרֻבֶּשֶׁת **Yᵉrubbesheth**, *yer-oob-beh'-sheth*; from 7378 and 1322; *shame* (i.e. the idol) *will contend; Jerubbesheth*, a symbol. name for Gideon:—Jerubbesheth.

3381. יָרַד **yârad**, *yaw-rad'*; a prim. root; to *descend* (lit. to *go downwards;* or conventionally to a lower region, as the shore, a boundary, the enemy, etc.; or fig. to *fall*); causat. to *bring down* (in all the above applications):—× abundantly, bring down, carry down, cast down, (cause to) come (-ing) down, fall (down), get down, go (-ing) down (-ward), hang down, × indeed, let down, light (down), put down (off), (cause to, let) run down, sink, subdue, take down.

3382. יֶרֶד **Yered**, *yeh'-red*; from 3381; a *descent; Jered*, the name of an antediluvian, and of an Isr.:—Jared.

3383. יַרְדֵּן **Yardên**, *yar-dane'*; from 3381; a *descender; Jarden*, the principal river of Pal.:—Jordan.

3384. יָרָה **yârâh**, *yaw-raw'*; or (2 Chr. 26 : 15)

יָרָא **yârâ'**, *yaw-raw'*; a prim. root; prop. to *flow* as water (i.e. to *rain*); trans. to *lay* or *throw* (espec. an arrow, i.e. to *shoot*); fig. to ***point*** out (as if by *aiming* the finger), to *teach:*—(+) archer, cast, direct, inform, instruct, lay, shew, shoot, teach (-er, -ing), through.

3385. יְרוּאֵל **Yᵉrûw'êl**, *yer-oo-ale'*; from 3384 and 410; *founded of God; Jeruel*, a place in Pal.:—Jeruel

3386. יָרוֹחַ **Yârôwach**, *yaw-ro'-akh*; perh. denom. from 3394; (born at the) new *moon; Jaroäch*, an Isr.:—Jaroah.

3387. יָרוֹק **yârôwq**, *yaw-roke'*; from 3417; *green*, i.e. an herb:—green thing.

3388. יְרוּשָׁא **Yᵉrûwshâ'**, *yer-oo-shaw'*; or

יְרוּשָׁה **Yᵉrûwshâh**, *yer-oo-shaw'*; fem. pass. part. of 3423; *possessed; Jerusha* or *Jerushah*, an Israelitess:—Jerusha, Jerushah.

3389. יְרוּשָׁלַם **Yᵉrûwshâlaim**, *yer-oo-shaw-lah'-im*; rarely

יְרוּשָׁלַיִם **Yᵉrûwshâlayim**, *yer-oo-shaw-lah'-yim*; a dual (in allusion to its two main hills [the true pointing, at least of the former reading, seems to be that of 3390]); prob. from (the pass. part. of) 3384 and 7999; *founded peaceful; Jerushalaïm* or *Jerushalem*, the capital city of Pal.:—Jerusalem.

3390. יְרוּשְׁלֶם **Yᵉrûwshâlêm** (Chald.), *yer-oo-shaw-lame'*; corresp. to 3389:—Jerusalem.

3391. יֶרַח **yerach**, *yeh'-rakh*; from an unused root of uncert. signif.; a *lunation*, i.e. *month:*—month, moon.

3392. יֶרַח **Yerach**, *yeh'-rakh*; the same as 3391; *Jerach*, an Arabian patriarch:—Jerah.

3393. יְרַח **yᵉrach** (Chald.), *yeh-rakh'*; corresp. to 3391; a *month:*—month.

3394. יָרֵחַ **yârêach**, *yaw-ray'-akh*; from the same as 3391; the *moon:*—moon.

יְרֵחוֹ **Yᵉrêchôw**. See 3405.

3395. יְרֹחָם **Yᵉrôcham**, *yer-o-khawm'*; from 7355; *compassionate; Jerocham*, the name of seven or eight Isr.:—Jeroham.

3396. יְרַחְמְאֵל **Yᵉrachmᵉ'êl**, *yer-akh-meh-ale'*; from 7355 and 410; *God will compassionate; Jerachmeël*, the name of three Isr.:—Jerahmeel.

3397. יְרַחְמְאֵלִי **Yᵉrachmᵉ'êlîy**, *yer-akh-meh-ay-lee'*; patron. from 3396; a *Jerachmeëlite* or desc. of Jerachmeel:—Jerahmeelites.

3398. יַרְחָע **Yarchâ'**, *yar-khaw'*; prob. of Eg. or.; *Jarcha*, an Eg.:—Jarha.

3399. יָרַט **yâraṭ**, *yaw-rat'*; a prim. root; to *precipitate* or *hurl* (*rush*) headlong; (intrans.) to *be rash:*—be perverse, turn over.

3400. יְרִיאֵל **Yᵉrîy'êl**, *yer-ee-ale'*; from 3384 and 410; *thrown of God; Jeriël*, an Isr.:—Jeriel. Comp. 3385.

3401. יָרִיב **yârîyb**, *yaw-rebe'*; from 7378; lit. *he will contend;* prop. adj. *contentious;* used as noun, an *adversary:*—that contend (-eth), that strive.

3402. יָרִיב **Yârîyb**, *yaw-rebe'*; the same as 3401; *Jarib*, the name of three Isr.:—Jarib.

3403. יְרִיבַי **Yᵉrîybay**, *yer-eeb-ah'ee*; from 3401; *contentious; Jeribai*, an Isr.:—Jeribai.

3404. יְרִיָּה **Yᵉrîyâh**, *yer-ee-yaw'*; or

יְרִיָּהוּ **Yᵉrîyâhûw**, *yer-ee-yaw'-hoo*; from 3384 and 3050; *Jah will throw; Jerijah*, an Isr.:—Jeriah, Jerijah.

3405. יְרִיחוֹ **Yᵉrîychôw**, *yer-ee-kho'*; or

יְרֵחוֹ **Yᵉrêchôw** *yer-ay-kho'*; or var. (1 Kings 16 : 34)

יְרִיחֹה **Yᵉrîychôh**, *yer-ee-kho'*; perh. from 3394; *its month;* or else from 7306; *fragrant; Jericho* or *Jerecho*, a place in Pal.:—Jericho.

3406. יְרִימוֹת **Yᵉrîymôwth**, *yer-ee-mohth'*; or

יְרֵימוֹת **Yᵉrêymôwth**, *yer-ay-mohth'*; or

יְרֵמוֹת **Yᵉrêmôwth**, *yer-ay-mohth'*; fem. plur. from 7311; *elevations; Jerimoth* or *Jeremoth*, the name of twelve Isr.:—Jeremoth, Jerimoth, and Ramoth [*from the marg.*].

3407. יְרִיעָה **yᵉrîy'âh**, *yer-ee-aw'*; from 3415; a *hanging* (as *tremulous*):—curtain.

3408. יְרִיעוֹת **Yᵉrîy'ôwth**, *yer-ee-ohth'*; plur. of 3407; *curtains; Jerioth*, an Israelitess:—Jerioth.

3409. יָרֵךְ **yârêk**, *yaw-rake'*; from an unused root mean. to *be soft;* the *thigh* (from its fleshy *softness*); by euphem. the *generative parts;* fig. a *shank, flank, side:*—× body, loins, shaft, side, thigh.

3410. יַרְכָא **yarkâ'** (Chald.), *yar-kaw'*; corresp. to 3411; a *thigh:*—thigh.

3411. יְרֵכָה **yᵉrêkâh**, *yer-ay-kaw'*; fem. of 3409; prop. the *flank;* but used only fig., the *rear* or *recess:*—border, coast, part, quarter, side.

3412. יַרְמוּת **Yarmûwth**, *yar-mooth'*; from 7311; *elevation; Jarmuth*, the name of two places in Pal.:—Jarmuth.

יְרֵמוֹת **Yᵉrêmôwth**. See 3406.

3413. יְרֵמַי **Yᵉrêmay**, *yer-ay-mah'ee*; from 7311; *elevated; Jeremai*, an Isr.:—Jeremai.

3414. יִרְמְיָה **Yirmᵉyâh**, *yir-meh-yaw'*; or

יִרְמְיָהוּ **Yirmᵉyâhûw**, *yir-meh-yaw'-hoo*; from 7311 and 3050; *Jah will rise; Jirmejah*, the name of eight or nine Isr.:—Jeremiah.

3415. יָרַע **yâra'**, *yaw-rah'*; a prim. root; prop. to *be broken* up (with any violent action), i.e. (fig.) to *fear:*—be grievous [*only Isa.* 15 : 4; *the rest belong* to 7489].

3416. יִרְפְּאֵל **Yirpᵉ'êl**, *yir-peh-ale'*; from 7495 and 410; *God will heal; Jirpeël*, a place in Pal.:—Irpeel.

3417. יָרַק **yâraq**, *yaw-rak'*; a prim. root; to *spit:*— × but, spit.

3418. יֶרֶק **yereq**, *yeh'-rek*; from 3417 (in the sense of *vacuity* of color); prop. *pallor*, i.e. hence the yellowish *green* of young and sickly vegetation; concr. *verdure*, i.e. grass or vegetation:—grass, green (thing).

3419. יָרָק **yârâq**, *yaw-rawk'*; from the same as 3418; prop. *green;* concr. a *vegetable:*—green, herbs.

יַרְקוֹן **Yarqôwn**. See 4313.

3420. יֵרָקוֹן **yêrâqôwn**, *yay-raw-kone'*; from 3418; *paleness*, whether of persons (from fright), or of plants (from drought):—mildew, paleness.

3421. יָרְקְעָם **Yorqᵉ'âm**, *yor-keh-awm'*; from 7324 and 5971; *people will be poured forth; Jorkeäm*, a place in Pal.:—Jorkeam.

3422. יְרַקְרַק **yᵉraqraq**, *yer-ak-rak'*; from the same as 3418; *yellowishness:*—greenish, yellow.

3423. יָרַשׁ **yârash**, *yaw-rash'*; or

יָרֵשׁ **yârêsh**, *yaw-raysh'*; a prim. root; to *occupy* (by *driving* out previous tenants, and *possessing* in their place); by impl. to *seize*, to *rob*, to *inherit;* also to *expel*, to *impoverish*, to *ruin:*—cast out, consume, destroy, disinherit, dispossess, drive (-ing) out, enjoy, expel, × without fail, (give to, leave for) inherit (-ance, -or), + magistrate, be (make) poor, come to poverty, (give to, make to) possess, get (have) in (take) possession, seize upon, succeed, × utterly.

3424. יְרֵשָׁה **yᵉrêshâh**, *yer-ay-shaw'*; from 3423; *occupancy:*—possession.

3425. יְרֻשָּׁה **yᵉrushshâh**, *yer-oosh-shaw'*; from 3423; something *occupied;* a *conquest;* also a *patrimony:*—heritage, inheritance, possession.

3426. יֵשׁ **yêsh**, *yaysh*; perh. from an unused root mean. to *stand* out, or *exist; entity;* used adv. or as a copula for the substantive verb (1961); there *is* or *are* (or any other form of the verb to *be*, as may suit the connection):—(there) are, (he, it, shall, there, there may, there shall, there should) be, thou do, had, hast, (which) hath, (I, shalt, that) have, (he, it, there) is, substance, it (there) was, (there) were, ye will, thou wilt, wouldest.

3427. יָשַׁב **yâshab**, *yaw-shab'*; a prim. root; prop. to *sit* down (spec. as judge. in ambush, in quiet); by impl. to *dwell*, to *remain;* causat. to *settle*, to *marry:*—(make to) abide (-ing), continue, (cause to, make to) dwell (-ing), ease self, endure, establish, × fail, habitation, haunt, (make to) inhabit (-ant), make to keep [house], lurking, × marry (-ing), (bring again to) place, remain, return, seat, set (-tle), (down-) sit (-down, still, -ting down, -ting [place] -uate), take, tarry.

3428. יֶשֶׁבְאָב **Yesheb'âb**, *yeh-sheb-awb'*; from 3427 and 1; *seat of* (his) *father; Jeshebab*, an Isr.:—Jeshebeab.

3429. יֹשֵׁב בַּשֶּׁבֶת **Yôshêb bash-Shebeth**, *yo-shabe' bash-sheh'-beth*; from the act. part. of 3427 and 7674, with a prep. and the art. interposed; *sitting in the seat; Josheb-bash-Shebeth*, an Isr.:—that sat in the seat.

3430. יִשְׁבּוֹ בְּנֹב **Yishbôw bᵉ-Nôb**, *yish-bo' beh-nobe;* from 3427 and 5011, with a pron. suffix and a prep. interposed; *his dwelling (is) in Nob; Jishbo-be-Nob,* a Philistine:—Ishbi-benob [*from the marg.*].

3431. יִשְׁבַּח **Yishbach**, *yish-bakh';* from 7623; *he will praise; Jishbach,* an Isr.:—Ishbah.

3432. יָשֻׁבִי **Yâshûbîy**, *yaw-shoo-bee';* patron. from 3437; a *Jashubite,* or desc. of Jashub:—Jashubites.

3433. יָשֻׁבִי לֶחֶם **Yâshûbîy Lechem**, *yaw-shoo'-bee leh'-khem;* from 7725 and 3899; *returner of bread; Jashubi-Lechem,* an Isr.:—Jashubi-lehem. [Prob. the text should be pointed

יֹשְׁבֵי לֶחֶם **Yôshᵉbêy Lechem**, *yo-sheh-bay' leh'-khem,* and rendered "(they were) inhabitants of Lechem," i.e. of Beth-lehem (by contraction). Comp. 3902.]

3434. יָשָׁבְעָם **Yâshobʻâm**, *yaw-shob-awm';* from 7725 and 5971; *people will return; Jashobam,* the name of two or three Isr.:—Jashobeam.

3435. יִשְׁבָּק **Yishbâq**, *yish-bawk';* from an unused root corresp. to 7662; *he will leave; Jishbak,* a son of Abraham:—Ishbak.

3436. יָשְׁבְּקָשָׁה **Yoshbᵉqâshâh**, *yosh-bek-aw-shaw';* from 3427 and 7186; *a hard seat; Joshbekashah,* an Isr.:—Joshbekashah.

3437. יָשׁוּב **Yâshûwb**, *yaw-shoob';* or

יָשִׁיב **Yâshîyb**, *yaw-sheeb';* from 7725; *he will return; Jashub,* the name of two Isr.:—Jashub.

3438. יִשְׁוָה **Yishvâh**, *yish-vaw';* from 7737; *he will level; Jishvah,* an Isr.:—Ishvah, Isvah.

3439. יְשׁוֹחָיָה **Yᵉshôwchâyâh**, *yesh-o-khaw-yaw';* from the same as 3445 and 3050; *Jah will empty; Jeshochajah,* an Isr.:—Jeshoaiah.

3440. יִשְׁוִי **Yishvîy**, *yish-vee';* from 7737; *level; Jishvi,* the name of two Isr.:—Ishuai, Ishvi, Isui, Jesui.

3441. יִשְׁוִי **Yishvîy**, *yish-vee';* patron. from 3440; a *Jishvite* (collect.) or desc. of Jishvi:—Jesuites.

3442. יֵשׁוּעַ **Yêshûwaʻ**, *yay-shoo'-ah;* for 3091; *he will save; Jeshua,* the name of ten Isr., also of a place in Pal.:—Jeshua.

3443. יֵשׁוּעַ **Yêshûwaʻ** (Chald.), *yay-shoo'-ah;* corresp. to 3442:—Jeshua.

3444. יְשׁוּעָה **yᵉshûwʻâh**, *yesh-oo'-aw;* fem. pass. part. of 3467; something *saved,* i.e. (abstr.) *deliverance;* hence *aid, victory, prosperity:*—deliverance, health, help (-ing), salvation, save, saving (health), welfare.

3445. יֶשַׁח **yeshach**, *yeh'-shakh;* from an unused root mean. to *gape* (as the empty stomach); *hunger:*—casting down.

3446. יִשְׂחָק **Yischâq**, *yis-khawk';* from 7831; *he will laugh; Jischak,* the heir of Abraham:—Isaac. Comp. 3327.

3447. יָשַׁט **yâshaṭ**, *yaw-shat';* a prim. root; to *extend:*—hold out.

3448. יִשַׁי **Yîshay**, *yee-shah'ee;* by Chald. אִישַׁי **ʼÎyshay**, *ee-shah'ee;* from the same as 3426; *extant; Jishai,* David's father:—Jesse.

יָשִׁיב **Yâshîyb**. See 3437.

3449. יִשִּׁיָּה **Yishshîyâh**, *yish-shee-yaw';* or

יִשִּׁיָּהוּ **Yishshîyâhûw**, *yish-shee-yaw'-hoo;* from 5383 and 3050; *Jah will lend; Jishshijah,* the name of five Isr.:—Ishiah, Isshiah, Ishijah, Jesiah.

3450. יְשִׂימָאֵל **Yᵉsîymâʼêl**, *yes-eem-aw-ale';* from 7760 and 410; *God will place; Jesimaël,* an Isr.:—Jesimael.

3451. יְשִׁימָה **yᵉshîymâh**, *yesh-ee-maw';* from 3456; *desolation:*—let death seize [*from the marg.*].

3452. יְשִׁימוֹן **yᵉshîymôwn**, *yesh-ee-mone';* from 3456; a *desolation:*—desert, Jeshimon, solitary, wilderness.

יְשִׁימוֹת **yᵉshîymôwth**. See 1020, 3451.

3453. יָשִׁישׁ **yâshîysh**, *yaw-sheesh';* from 3486; an *old* man:—(very) aged (man), ancient, very old.

3454. יְשִׁישַׁי **Yᵉshîyshay**, *yesh-ee-shah'ee;* from 3453; *aged; Jeshishai,* an Isr.:—Jeshishai.

3455. יָשַׂם **yâsam**, *yaw-sam';* a prim root; to *place;* intrans. to *be placed:*—be put (set).

3456. יָשַׁם **yâsham**, *yaw-sham';* a prim. root; to *lie waste:*—be desolate.

3457. יִשְׁמָא **Yishmâʼ**, *yish-maw';* from 3456; *desolate; Jishma,* an Isr.:—Ishma.

3458. יִשְׁמָעֵאל **Yishmâʻêʼl**, *yish-maw-ale';* from 8085 and 410; *God will hear; Jishmaël,* the name of Abraham's oldest son, and of five Isr.:—Ishmael.

3459. יִשְׁמְעֵאלִי **Yishmâʻêʼlîy**, *yish-maw-ay-lee';* patron. from 3458; a *Jishmaëlite* or desc. of Jishmael:—Ishmaelite.

3460. יִשְׁמַעְיָה **Yishmaʻyâh**, *yish-mah-yaw';* or

יִשְׁמַעְיָהוּ **Yishmaʻyâhûw**, *yish-mah-yaw'-hoo;* from 8085 and 3050; *Jah will hear; Jishmajah,* the name of two Isr.:—Ishmaiah.

3461. יִשְׁמְרַי **Yishmᵉray**, *yish-mer-ah'ee;* from 8104; *preservative; Jishmerai,* an Isr.:—Ishmerai.

3462. יָשֵׁן **yâshên**, *yaw-shane';* a prim. root; prop. to *be slack* or *languid,* i.e. (by impl.) *sleep* (fig. to *die*); also to *grow old, stale* or *inveterate:*—old (store), remain long, (make to) sleep.

3463. יָשֵׁן **yâshên**, *yaw-shane';* from 3462; *sleepy:*—asleep, (one out of) sleep (-eth, -ing), slept.

3464. יָשֵׁן **Yâshên**, *yaw-shane';* the same as 3463; *Jashen,* an Isr.:—Jashen.

3465. יָשָׁן **yâshân**, *yaw-shawn';* from 3462; *old:*—old.

3466. יְשָׁנָה **Yᵉshânâh**, *yesh-aw-naw';* fem. of 3465; *Jeshanah,* a place in Pal.:—Jeshanah.

3467. יָשַׁע **yâshaʻ**, *yaw-shah';* a prim. root; prop. to *be open, wide* or *free,* i.e. (by impl.) to *be safe;* causat. to *free* or *succor:*— × at all, avenging, defend, deliver (-er), help, preserve, rescue, be safe, bring (having) salvation, save (-iour), get victory.

3468. יֶשַׁע **yeshaʻ**, *yeh'-shah;* or

יֵשַׁע **yêshaʻ**, *yay'-shah;* from 3467; *liberty, deliverance, prosperity:*—safety, salvation, saving.

3469. יִשְׁעִי **Yishʻîy**, *yish-ee';* from 3467; *saving; Jishi,* the name of four Isr.:—Ishi.

3470. יְשַׁעְיָה **Yᵉshaʻyâh**, *yesh-ah-yaw';* or

יְשַׁעְיָהוּ **Yᵉshaʻyâhûw**, *yesh-ah-yaw'-hoo;* from 3467 and 3050; *Jah has saved; Jeshajah,* the name of seven Isr.:—Isaiah, Jesaiah, Jeshaiah.

3471. יָשְׁפֵה **yâshᵉphêh**, *yaw-shef-ay';* from an unused root mean. to *polish;* a gem supposed to be *jasper* (from the resemblance in name):—jasper.

3472. יִשְׁפָּה **Yishpâh**, *yish-paw';* perh. from 8192; *he will scratch; Jishpah,* an Isr.:—Ispah.

3473. יִשְׁפָּן **Yishpân**, *yish-pawn';* prob. from the same as 8227; *he will hide; Jishpan,* an Isr.:—Ishpan.

3474. יָשַׁר **yâshar**, *yaw-shar';* a prim. root; to *be straight* or *even;* fig. to *be* (causat. to *make*) *right, pleasant, prosperous:*—direct, fit, seem good (meet), + please (well), be (esteem, go) right (on), bring (look, make, take the) straight (way), be upright (-ly).

3475. יֵשֶׁר **Yêsher**, *yay'-sher;* from 3474; the *right; Jesher,* an Isr.:—Jesher.

3476. יֹשֶׁר **yôsher**, *yo'-sher;* from 3474; the *right:*—equity, meet, right, upright (-ness).

3477. יָשָׁר **yâshâr**, *yaw-shawr';* from 3474; *straight* (lit. or fig.):—convenient, equity, Jasher, just, meet (-est), + pleased well right (-eous), straight, (most) upright (-ly, -ness).

3478. יִשְׂרָאֵל **Yisrâʼêl**, *yis-raw-ale';* from 8280 and 410; *he will rule as God; Jisraël,* a symbolical name of Jacob; also (typically) of his posterity:—Israel.

3479. יִשְׂרָאֵל **Yisrâʼêl** (Chald.), *yis-raw-ale'* corresp. to 3478:—Israel.

3480. יְשַׂרְאֵלָה **Yᵉsarʼêlâh**, *yes-ar-ale'-aw;* by var. from 3477 and 410 with directive enclitic; *right towards God; Jesarelah,* an Isr.:—Jesharelah. Comp. 841.

3481. יִשְׂרְאֵלִי **Yisrᵉʼêlîy**, *yis-reh-ay-lee';* patron. from 3478; a *Jisreëlite* or desc. of Jisrael:—of Israel, Israelite.

3482. יִשְׂרְאֵלִית **Yisrᵉʼêlîyth**, *yis-reh-ay-leeth';* fem. of 3481; a *Jisreëlitess* or female desc. of Jisrael:—Israelitish.

3483. יִשְׁרָה **yishrâh**, *yish-raw';* fem. of 3477; *rectitude:*—uprightness.

3484. יְשֻׁרוּן **Yᵉshûrûwn**, *yesh-oo-roon';* from 3474; *upright; Jeshurun,* a symbol. name for Israel:—Jeshurun.

3485. יִשָּׂשכָר **Yissâᵉkâr**, *yis-saw-kawr'* (strictly *yis-saws-kawr'*); from 5375 and 7939; *he will bring a reward; Jissaskar,* a son of Jacob:—Issachar.

3486. יָשֵׁשׁ **yâshêsh**, *yaw-shaysh';* from an unused root mean. to *blanch; gray*-haired, i.e. an *aged* man:—stoop for age.

3487. יַת **yath** (Chald.), *yath;* corresp. to 853; a sign of the object of a verb: + whom.

3488. יְתִב **yᵉthîyb** (Chald.), *yeth-eeb';* corresp. to 3427; to *sit* or *dwell:*—dwell, (be) set, sit.

3489. יָתֵד **yâthêd**, *yaw-thade';* from an unused root mean. to *pin* through or *fast;* a *peg:*—nail, paddle, pin, stake.

3490. יָתוֹם **yâthôwm**, *yaw-thome';* from an unused root mean. to *be lonely;* a *bereaved* person:—fatherless (child), orphan.

3491. יָתוּר **yâthûwr**, *yaw-thoor';* pass. part. of 3498; prop. what is *left,* i.e. (by impl.) a *gleaning:*—range.

3492. יַתִּיר **Yattîyr**, *yat-teer';* from 3498; *redundant; Jattir,* a place in Pal.:—Jattir.

3493. יַתִּיר **yattîyr** (Chald.) *yat-teer';* corresp. to 3492; *preeminent;* adv. *very:*—exceeding (-ly), excellent.

3494. יִתְלָה **Yithlâh**, *yith-law';* prob. from 8518; *it will hang,* i.e. be high; *Jithlah,* a place in Pal.:—Jethlah.

3495. יִתְמָה **Yithmâh**, *yith-maw';* from the same as 3490; *orphanage; Jithmah,* an Isr.:—Ithmah.

3496. יַתְנִיאֵל **Yathnîyʼêl**, *yath-nee-ale';* from an unused root mean. to *endure,* and 410; *continued of God; Jathniël,* an Isr.:—Jathniel.

3497. יִתְנָן **Yithnân**, *yith-nawn';* from the same as 8577; *extensive; Jithnan,* a place in Pal.:—Ithnan.

3498. יָתַר **yâthar**, *yaw-thar';* a prim. root; to *jut* over or *exceed;* by impl. to *excel;* (intrans.) to *remain* or *be left;* causat. to *leave, cause to abound, preserve:*—excel, leave (a remnant), left behind, too much, make plenteous, preserve, (be, let) remain (-der, -ing, -nant), reserve, residue, rest.

3499. יֶתֶר **yether**, *yeh'-ther;* from 3498; prop. an *overhanging,* i.e. (by impl.) an *excess, superiority, remainder;* also a small *rope* (as hanging free):—+ abundant, cord, exceeding, excellency (-ent), what they leave, that hath left, plentifully, remnant, residue, rest, string, with.

3500. יֶתֶר **Yether**, *yeh'-ther;* the same as 3499 *Jether,* the name of five or six Isr. and of one Midianite:—Jether, Jethro. Comp. 3503.

3501. יִתְרָא **Yithrâʼ**, *yith-raw';* by var. for 3502; *Jithra,* an Isr. (or Ishmaelite):—Ithra.

3502. יִתְרָה **yithrâh**, *yith-raw';* fem. of 3499; prop. *excellence,* i.e. (by impl.) *wealth:*—abundance, riches.

3503. יִתְרוֹ **Yithrôw**, *yith-ro';* from 3499 with pron. suffix; *his excellence; Jethro,* Moses' father-in-law:—Jethro. Comp. 3500.

3504. יִתְרוֹן **yithrôwn**, *yith-rone';* from 3498; *preeminence, gain:*—better, excellency (-leth), profit (-able).

3505. יִתְרִי **Yithrîy**, *yith-ree';* patron. from 3500; a *Jithrite* or desc. of Jether:—Ithrite.

3506. יִתְרָן **Yithrân**, *yith-rawn';* from 3498; *excellent; Jithran,* the name of an Edomite and of an Isr.:—Ithran.

3507. יִתְרְעָם **Yithreʻâm**, *yith-reh-awm';* from 3499 and 5971; *excellence of people; Jithreām,* a son of David:—Ithream.

3508. יֹתֶרֶת **yôthereth**, *yo-theh'-reth;* fem. act. part. of 3498; the *lobe* or *flap* of the liver (as if redundant or outhanging):—caul.

3509. יְתֵת **Yethêth**, *yeh-thayth';* of uncert. der.; *Jetheth,* an Edomite:—Jetheth.

כ

3510. כָּאַב **kâʼab**, *kaw-ab';* a prim. root; prop. to feel *pain;* by impl. to *grieve;* fig. to *spoil:*—grieving, mar, have pain, make sad (sore), (be) sorrowful.

3511. כְּאֵב **keʼêb**, *keh-abe';* from 3510; *suffering* (phys. or mental), *adversity:*—grief, pain, sorrow.

3512. כָּאָה **kâʼâh**, *kaw-aw';* a prim. root; to *despond:* causat. to *deject:*—broken, be grieved, make sad.

3513. כָּבַד **kâbad**, *kaw-bad';* or

כָּבֵד **kâbêd**, *kaw-bade';* a prim. root; to *be heavy,* i.e. in a bad sense (*burdensome, severe, dull*) or in a good sense (*numerous, rich, honorable*); causat. to *make weighty* (in the same two senses):—abounding with, more grievously afflict, boast, be chargeable, × be dim, glorify, be (make) glorious (things), glory, (very) great, be grievous, harden, be (make) heavy, be heavier, lay heavily, (bring to, come to, do, get, be had in) honour (self), (be) honourable (man), lade, × more be laid, make self many, nobles, prevail, promote (to honour), be rich, be (go) sore, stop.

3514. כֹּבֶד **kôbed**, *ko'-bed;* from 3513; *weight, multitude, vehemence:*—grievousness, heavy, great number.

3515. כָּבֵד **kâbêd**, *kaw-bade';* from 3513; *heavy;* fig. in a good sense (*numerous*) or in a bad sense (*severe, difficult, stupid*):—(so) great, grievous, hard (-ened), (too) heavy (-ier), laden, much, slow, sore, thick.

3516. כָּבֵד **kâbêd**, *kaw-bade';* the same as 3515; the *liver* (as the *heaviest* of the viscera):—liver.

כָּבֹד **kâbôd**. See 3519.

3517. כְּבֵדֻת **kebêdûth**, *keb-ay-dooth';* fem. of 3515; *difficulty:*—× heavily.

3518. כָּבָה **kâbâh**, *kaw-baw';* a prim. root; to *expire* or (causat.) to *extinguish* (fire, light, anger):—go (put) out, quench.

3519. כָּבוֹד **kâbôwd**, *kaw-bode';* rarely

כָּבֹד **kâbôd**, *kaw-bode';* from 3513; prop. *weight;* but only fig. in a good sense, *splendor* or *copiousness:*—glorious (-ly), glory, honour (-able).

3520. כְּבוּדָּה **kebûwddâh**, *keb-ood-daw';* irreg. fem. pass. part. of 3513; *weightiness,* i.e. *magnificence, wealth:*—carriage, all glorious, stately.

3521. כָּבוּל **Kâbûwl**, *kaw-bool';* from the same as 3525 in the sense of *limitation; sterile; Cabul,* the name of two places in Pal.:—Cabul.

3522. כַּבּוֹן **Kabbôwn**, *kab-bone';* from an unused root mean. to *heap up; hilly; Cabbon,* a place in Pal.:—Cabbon.

3523. כְּבִיר **kebîyr**, *keb-eer;* from 3527 in the orig. sense of *plaiting;* a *matrass* (of intertwined materials):—pillow.

3524. כַּבִּיר **kabbîyr**, *kab-beer';* from 3527; *vast,* whether in extent (fig. of power, *mighty;* of time, *aged*), or in number, *many:*—+ feeble, mighty, most, much, strong, valiant.

3525. כֶּבֶל **kebel**, *keh'-bel;* from an unused root mean. to *twine* or braid together; a *fetter:*—fetter.

3526. כָּבַס **kâbaç**, *kaw-bas';* a prim. root; to *trample;* hence to *wash* (prop. by stamping with the feet), whether lit. (including the *fulling* process) or fig.:—fuller, wash (-ing).

3527. כָּבַר **kâbar**, *kaw-bar';* a prim. root; prop. to *plait* together, i.e. (fig.) to *augment* (espec. in number or quantity, to *accumulate*):—in abundance, multiply.

3528. כְּבָר **kebâr**, *keb-awr';* from 3527; prop. *extent* of time, i.e. a *great while;* hence *long ago, formerly, hitherto:*—already, (seeing that which), now.

3529. כְּבָר **Kebâr**, *keb-awr';* the same as 3528; *length; Kebar,* a river of Mesopotamia:—Chebar. Comp. 2249.

3530. כִּבְרָה **kibrâh**, *kib-raw';* fem. of 3528; prop. *length,* i.e. a *measure* (of uncert. dimension):—× little.

3531. כְּבָרָה **kebârâh**, *keb-aw-raw';* from 3527 in its orig. sense; a *sieve* (as netted):—sieve.

3532. כֶּבֶשׂ **kebes**, *keh-bes';* from an unused root mean. to *dominate;* a *ram* (just old enough to *butt*):—lamb, sheep.

3533. כָּבַשׁ **kâbash**, *kaw-bash';* a prim. root; to *tread* down; hence neg. to *disregard;* pos. to *conquer, subjugate, violate:*—bring into bondage, force, keep under, subdue, bring into subjection.

3534. כֶּבֶשׁ **kebesh**, *keh'-besh;* from 3533; a *footstool* (as trodden upon):—footstool.

3535. כִּבְשָׂה **kibsâh**, *kib-saw';* or

כַּבְשָׂה **kabsâh**, *kab-saw';* fem. of 3532; a *ewe:*—(ewe) lamb.

3536. כִּבְשָׁן **kibshân**, *kib-shawn';* from 3533; a smelting *furnace* (as *reducing* metals):—furnace.

3537. כַּד **kad**, *kad;* from an unused root mean. to *deepen;* prop. a *pail;* but gen. of earthenware; a *jar* for domestic purposes:—barrel, pitcher.

3538. כְּדַב **kedab** (Chald.), *ked-ab';* from a root corresp. to 3576; *false:*—lying.

3539. כַּדְכֹּד **kadkôd**, *kad-kode';* from the same as 3537 in the sense of *striking fire* from a metal forged; a *sparkling* gem, prob. the ruby:—agate.

3540. כְּדָרְלָעֹמֶר **Kedorlâʻômer**, *ked-or-law-o'-mer;* of for. or.; *Kedorlaomer,* an early Pers. king:—Chedorlaomer.

3541. כֹּה **kôh**, *ko;* from the prefix *k* and 1931; prop. *like this,* i.e. by impl. (of manner) *thus* (or *so*); also (of place) *here* (or *hither*); or (of time) *now:*—also, here, + hitherto, like, on the other side, so (and much), such, on that manner, (on) this (manner, side, way, way and that way), + mean while, yonder.

3542. כָּה **kâh** (Chald.), *kaw;* corresp. to 3541:—hitherto.

3543. כָּהָה **kâhâh**, *kaw-haw';* a prim. root; to *be weak,* i.e. (fig.) to *despond* (causat. *rebuke*), or (of light, the eye) to *grow dull:*—darken, be dim, fail, faint, restrain, × utterly.

3544. כֵּהֶה **kêheh**, *kay-heh';* from 3543; *feeble, obscure:*—somewhat dark, darkish, wax dim, heaviness, smoking.

3545. כֵּהָה **kêhâh**, *kay-haw';* fem. of 3544; prop. a *weakening;* fig. *alleviation,* i.e. cure:—healing.

3546. כְּהַל **kehal** (Chald.), *keh-hal';* a root corresp. to 3201 and 3557; to *be able:*—be able, could.

3547. כָּהַן **kâhan**, *kaw-han';* a prim. root, appar. mean. to *mediate* in religious services; but used only as denom. from 3548; to *officiate* as a priest; fig. to *put on regalia:*—deck, be (do the office of a, execute the, minister in the) priest ('s office).

3548. כֹּהֵן **kôhên**, *ko-hane';* act. part. of 3547; lit. one *officiating,* a *priest;* also (by courtesy) an *acting priest* (although a layman):—chief ruler, × own, priest, prince, principal officer.

3549. כָּהֵן **kâhên** (Chald.), *kaw-hane';* corresp. to 3548:—priest.

3550. כְּהֻנָּה **kehunnâh**, *keh-hoon-naw';* from 3547; *priesthood:*—priesthood, priest's office.

3551. כַּו **kav** (Chald.), *kav;* from a root corresp. to 3854 in the sense of *piercing;* a *window* (as a perforation):—window.

3552. כּוּב **Kûwb**, *koob;* of for. der.; *Kub,* a country near Egypt:—Chub.

3553. כּוֹבַע **kôwbaʻ**, *ko'-bah;* from an unused root mean. to be *high* or *rounded;* a *helmet* (as *arched*):—helmet. Comp. 6959.

3554. כָּוָה **kâvâh**, *kaw-vaw';* a prim. root; prop. to *prick* or *penetrate;* hence to *blister* (as smarting or eating into):—burn.

כּוֹחַ **kôwach**. See 3581.

3555. כְּוִיָּה **kevîyâh**, *kev-ee-yaw';* from 3554; a *branding:*—burning.

3556. כּוֹכָב **kôwkâb**, *ko-kawb';* prob. from the same as 3522 (in the sense of *rolling*) or 3554 (in the sense of *blazing*); a *star* (as *round* or as *shining*); fig. a *prince:*—star ([-gazer]).

3557. כּוּל **kûwl**, *kool;* a prim. root; prop. to *keep in;* hence to *measure;* fig. to *maintain* (in various senses):—(be able to, can) abide, bear, comprehend, contain, feed, forbearing, guide, hold (-ing in), nourish (-er), be present, make provision, receive, sustain, provide sustenance (victuals).

3558. כּוּמָז **kûwmâz**, *koo-mawz';* from an unused root mean. to *store* away; a *jewel* (prob. gold beads):—tablet.

3559. כּוּן **kûwn**, *koon;* a prim. root; prop. to *be erect* (i.e. stand perpendicular); hence (causat.) to *set up,* in a great variety of applications, whether lit. (*establish, fix, prepare, apply*), or fig. (*appoint, render sure, proper* or *prosperous*):—certain (-ty), confirm, direct, faithfulness, fashion, fasten, firm, be fitted, be fixed, frame, be meet, ordain, order, perfect, (make) preparation, prepare (self), provide, make provision, (be, make) ready, right, set (aright, fast, forth), be stable, (e-) stablish, stand, tarry, × very deed.

3560. כּוּן **Kûwn**, *koon;* prob. from 3559; *established; Kun,* a place in Syria:—Chun.

3561. כַּוָּן **kavvân**, *kav-vawn';* from 3559; something *prepared,* i.e. a sacrificial *wafer:*—cake.

3562. כּוֹנַנְיָהוּ **Kôwnanyâhûw**, *ko-nan-yaw'-hoo;* from 3559 and 3050; *Jah has sustained; Conanjah,* the name of two Isr.:—Conaniah, Cononiah. Comp. 3663.

3563. כּוֹס **kôwç**, *koce;* from an unused root mean. to *hold* together; a *cup* (as a container), often fig. a *lot* (as if a potion); also some unclean bird, prob. an *owl* (perh. from the cup-like cavity of its eye):—cup, (small) owl. Comp. 3599.

3564. כּוּר **kûwr**, *koor;* from an unused root mean. prop. to *dig* through; a *pot* or *furnace* (as if excavated):—furnace. Comp. 3600.

כּוֹר **kôwr**. See 3733.

3565. כּוֹר עָשָׁן **Kôwr ʻÂshân**, *kore aw-shawn';* from 3564 and 6227; *furnace of smoke; Cor-Ashan,* a place in Pal.:—Chor-ashan.

3566. כּוֹרֶשׁ **Kôwresh**, *ko'-resh;* or (Ezra 1 : 1 [last time], 2)

כֹּרֶשׁ **Kôresh**, *ko'-resh;* from the Pers.; *Koresh* (or Cyrus), the Pers. king:—Cyrus.

3567. כּוֹרֶשׁ **Kôwresh** (Chald.), *ko'-resh;* corresp. to 3566:—Cyrus.

3568. כּוּשׁ **Kûwsh**, *koosh;* prob. of for. or.; *Cush* (or Ethiopia), the name of a son of Ham, and of his territory; also of an Isr.:—Chush, Cush, Ethiopia.

3569. כּוּשִׁי **Kûwshîy**, *koo-shee';* patron. from 3568; a *Cushite*, or desc. of Cush:—Cushi, Cushite, Ethiopian (-s).

3570. כּוּשִׁי **Kûwshîy**, *koo-shee';* the same as 3569; *Cushi*, the name of two Isr.:—Cushi.

3571. כּוּשִׁית **Kûwshîyth**, *koo-sheeth';* fem. of 3569; a *Cushite woman:*—Ethiopian.

3572. כּוּשָׁן **Kûwshân**, *koo-shawn';* perh. from 3568; *Cushan*, a region of Arabia:—Cushan.

3573. כּוּשַׁן רִשְׁעָתַיִם **Kûwshan Rishʿâthâyim**, *koo-shan' rish-aw-thah'-yim;* appar. from 3572 and the dual of 7564; *Cushan of double wickedness; Cushan-Rishathajim*, a Mesopotamian king:—Chushan-rishathayim.

3574. כּוֹשָׁרָה **kôwshârâh**, *ko-shaw-raw';* from 3787; *prosperity;* in plur. *freedom:*—× chain.

3575. כּוּת **Kûwth**, *kooth;* or (fem.)

כּוּתָה **Kûwthâh**, *koo-thaw';* of for. or.; *Cuth* or *Cuthah*, a province of Assyria:—Cuth.

3576. כָּזַב **kâzab**, *kaw-zab';* a prim. root; to *lie* (i.e. *deceive*), lit. or fig.:—fail, (be found a, make a) liar, lie, lying, be in vain.

3577. כָּזָב **kâzâb**, *kaw-zawb';* from 3576; *falsehood;* lit. (*untruth*) or fig. (*idol*):—deceitful, false, leasing, + liar, lie, lying.

3578. כֹּזְבָא **Kôzᵉbâʾ**, *ko-zeb-aw';* from 3576; *fallacious; Cozeba*, a place in Pal.:—Choseba.

3579. כָּזְבִּי **Kozbîy**, *koz-bee';* from 3576; *false; Cozbi*, a Midianitess:—Cozbi.

3580. כְּזִיב **Kᵉzîyb**, *kez-eeb';* from 3576; *falsified; Kezib*, a place in Pal.:—Chezib.

3581. כֹּחַ **kôach**, *ko'-akh;* or (Dan. 11 : 6)

כּוֹחַ **kôwach**, *ko'-akh;* from an unused root mean. to *be firm; vigor*, lit. (*force*, in a good or a bad sense) or fig. (*capacity, means, produce*); also (from its hardiness) a large *lizard:*—ability, able, chameleon, force, fruits, might, power (-ful), strength, substance, wealth.

3582. כָּחַד **kâchad**, *kaw-khad';* a prim. root; to *secrete*, by act or word; hence (intens.) to *destroy:*—conceal, cut down (off), desolate, hide.

3583. כָּחַל **kâchal**, *kaw-khal';* a prim. root; to *paint* (with stibium):—paint.

3584. כָּחַשׁ **kâchash**, *kaw-khash';* a prim. root; to *be untrue*, in word (to *lie, feign, disown*) or deed (to *disappoint, fail, cringe*):—deceive, deny, dissemble, fail, deal falsely, be found liars, (be-) lie, lying, submit selves.

3585. כַּחַשׁ **kachash**, *kakh'-ash;* from 3584; lit. a *failure* of flesh, i.e. *emaciation;* fig. *hypocrisy:*—leanness, lies, lying.

3586. כֶּחָשׁ **kechâsh**, *kekh-awsh';* from 3584; *faithless:*—lying.

3587. כִּי **kîy**, *kee;* from 3554; a *brand* or *scar:*—burning.

3588. כִּי **kîy**, *kee;* a prim. particle [the full form of the prepositional prefix] indicating *causal* relations of all kinds, antecedent or consequent; (by impl.) very widely used as a rel. conj. or adv. [as below]; often largely modified by other particles annexed:—and, + (forasmuch, inasmuch, where-) as, assured [-ly], + but, certainly, doubtless, + else, even, + except, for, how, (because, in, so, than) that, + nevertheless, now, rightly, seeing, since, surely, then, therefore, + (al-) though, + till, truly, + until, when, whether, while, whom, yea, yet.

3589. כִּיד **kîyd**, *keed;* from a prim, root mean. to *strike:* a *crushing;* fig. *calamity:*—destruction.

3590. כִּידוֹד **kîydôwd**, *kee-dode';* from the same as 3589 [comp. 3539]; prop. something *struck* off, i.e. a *spark* (as struck):—spark.

3591. כִּידוֹן **kîydôwn**, *kee-dohn';* from the same as 3589; prop. something to *strike* with, i.e. a *dart* (perh. smaller than 2595):—lance, shield, spear, target.

3592. כִּידוֹן **Kîydôwn**, *kee-dohn';* the same as 3591; *Kidon*, a place in Pal.:—Chidon.

3593. כִּידוֹר **kîydôwr**, *kee-dore';* of uncert. der.; perh. *tumult:*—battle.

3594. כִּיּוּן **Kîyûwn**, *kee-yoon';* from 3559; prop. a *statue*, i.e. idol; but used (by euphemism) for some heathen deity (perh. corresp. to Priapus or Baal-peor):—Chiun.

3595. כִּיּוֹר **kîyôwr**, *kee-yore';* or

כִּיֹּר **kîyôr**, *kee-yore';* from the same as 3564; prop. something *round* (as *excavated* or *bored*), i.e. a chafing-*dish* for coals or a *caldron* for cooking; hence (from similarity of form) a *washbowl;* also (for the same reason) a *pulpit* or platform:—hearth, laver, pan, scaffold.

3596. כִּילַי **kîylay**, *kee-lah'ee;* or

כֵּלַי **kêlay**, *kay-lah'ee;* from 3557 in the sense of *withholding; niggardly:*—churl.

3597. כֵּילַף **kêylaph**, *kay-laf';* from an unused root mean. to *clap* or strike with noise; a *club* or sledge-hammer:—hammer.

3598. כִּימָה **Kîymâh**, *kee-maw';* from the same as 3558; a *cluster* of stars, i.e. the *Pleiades:*—Pleiades, seven stars.

3599. כִּיס **kîyç**, *keece;* a form for 3563; a *cup;* also a *bag* for money or weights.—bag, cup, purse.

3600. כִּיר **kîyr**, *keer;* a form for 3564 (only in the dual); a cooking *range* (consisting of two parallel stones, across which the boiler is set):—ranges for pots.

כִּיֹּר **kîyôr**. See 3595.

3601. כִּישׁוֹר **kîyshôwr**, *kee-shore';* from 3787; lit. a *director*, i.e. the *spindle* or shank of a distaff (6418), by which it is twirled:—spindle.

3602. כָּכָה **kâkâh**, *kaw'-kaw;* from 3541; *just so*, referring to the previous or following context:—after that (this) manner, this matter, (even) so, in such a case, thus.

3603. כִּכָּר **kikkâr**, *kik-kawr';* from 3769; a *circle*, i.e. (by impl.) a circumjacent *tract* or region, espec. the *Ghôr* or valley of the Jordan; also a (round) *loaf;* also a *talent* (or large [round] coin):—loaf, morsel, piece, plain, talent.

3604. כִּכֵּר **kikkêr** (Chald.), *kik-kare';* corresp. to 3603; a *talent:*—talent.

3605. כֹּל **kôl**, *kole;* or (Jer. 33 : 8)°

כּוֹל **kôwl**, *kole;* from 3634; prop. the *whole;* hence *all, any* or *every* (in the sing. only, but often in a plur. sense):—(in) all (manner, [ye]), altogether, any (manner), enough, every (one, place, thing), howsoever, as many as, [no-] thing, ought, whatsoever, (the) whole, whoso (-ever).

3606. כֹּל **kôl** (Chald.), *kole;* corresp. to 3605:—all, any, + (forasmuch) as, + be- (for this) cause, every, + no (manner, -ne), + there (where) -fore, + though, what (where, who) -soever, (the) whole.

3607. כָּלָא **kâlâʾ**, *kaw-law';* a prim. root; to *restrict*, by act (*hold* back or in) or word (*prohibit*):—finish, forbid, keep (back), refrain, restrain, retain, shut up, be stayed, withhold.

3608. כֶּלֶא **keleʾ**, *keh'-leh;* from 3607; a *prison:*—prison. Comp. 3610, 3628.

3609. כִּלְאָב **Kilʾâb**, *kil-awb';* appar. from 3607 and 1; *restraint of* (his) *father; Kilab*, an Isr.:—Chileab.

3610. כִּלְאַיִם **kilʾayim**, *kil-ah'-yim;* dual of 3608 in the original sense of *separation; two heterogeneities:*—divers seeds (-e kinds), mingled (seed).

3611. כֶּלֶב **keleb**, *keh'-leb;* from an unused root mean. to *yelp*, or else to *attack;* a *dog;* hence (by euphemism) a male *prostitute:*—dog.

3612. כָּלֵב **Kâlêb**, *kaw-labe';* perh. a form of 3611, or else from the same root in the sense of *forcible; Caleb*, the name of three Isr.:—Caleb.

3613. כָּלֵב אֶפְרָתָה **Kâlêb ʾEphrâthâh**, *kaw-labe' ef-raw'-thaw;* from 3612 and 672; *Caleb-Ephrathah*, a place in Eg. (if the text is correct):—Caleb-ephrathah.

3614. כָּלִבּוֹ° **Kâlibbôw**, *kaw-lib-bo';* prob. by err. transc. for

כָּלֵבִי **Kâlêbîy**, *kaw-lay-bee';* patron. from 3612; a *Calebite* or desc. of Caleb:—of the house of Caleb.

3615. כָּלָה **kâlâh**, *kaw-law';* a prim. root; to *end*, whether intrans. (to *cease*, be *finished*, *perish*) or trans. (to *complete*, *prepare*, *consume*):—accomplish, cease, consume (away), determine, destroy (utterly), be (when . . . were) done, (be an) end (of), expire, (cause to) fail, faint, finish, fulfil, × fully, × have, leave (off), long, bring to pass, wholly reap, make clean riddance, spend, quite take away, waste.

3616. כָּלֶה **kâleh**, *kaw-leh';* from 3615; *pining:*—fail.

3617. כָּלָה **kâlâh**, *kaw-law';* from 3615; a *completion;* adv. *completely;* also *destruction:*—altogether, (be, utterly) consume (-d), consummation (-ption), was determined, (full, utter) end, riddance.

3618. כַּלָּה **kallâh**, *kal-law';* from 3634; a *bride* (as if *perfect*); hence a *son's wife:*—bride, daughter-in-law, spouse.

כְּלוּא **kᵉlûwʾ**. See 3628.

3619. כְּלוּב **kᵉlûb**, *kel-oob';* from the same as 3611; a bird-*trap* (as furnished with a *clap*-stick or treadle to spring it); hence a *basket* (as resembling a wicker cage):—basket, cage.

3620. כְּלוּב **Kᵉlûwb**, *kel-oob';* the same as 3619; *Kelub*, the name of two Isr.:—Chelub.

3621. כְּלוּבַי **Kᵉlûwbay**, *kel-oo-bay'ee;* a form of 3612; *Kelubai*, an Isr.:—Chelubai.

3622. כְּלוּהַי **Kᵉlûwhay**, *kel-oo-hah'ee;* from 3615; *completed; Keluhai*, an Isr.:—Chelluh.

3623. כְּלוּלָה **kᵉlûwlâh**, *kel-oo-law';* denom pass. part. from 3618; *bridehood* (only in the plur.):—espousal.

3624. כֶּלַח **kelach**, *keh'-lakh;* from an unused root mean. to *be complete; maturity:*—full (old) age.

3625. כֶּלַח **Kelach**, *keh'-lakh;* the same as 3624; *Kelach*, a place in Assyria:—Calah.

3626. כָּל־חֹזֶה **Kol-Chôzeh**, *kol-kho-zeh';* from 3605 and 2374; *every seer; Col-Chozeh*, an Isr.:—Col-hozeh.

3627. כְּלִי **kᵉlîy**, *kel-ee';* from 3615; something *prepared*, i.e. any *apparatus* (as an implement, utensil, dress, vessel or weapon):—armour ([-bearer]), artillery, bag, carriage, + furnish, furniture, instrument, jewel, that is made of, × one from another, that which pertaineth, pot, + psaltery, sack, stuff, thing, tool, vessel, ware, weapon, + whatsoever.

3628. כְּלִיא **kᵉlîyʾ**, *kel-ee';* or

כְּלוּא **kᵉlûwʾ**, *kel-oo';* from 3607 [comp. 3608]; a *prison:*—prison.

3629. כִּלְיָה **kilyâh**, *kil-yaw';* fem. of 3627 (only in the plur.); a *kidney* (as an essential *organ*); fig. the *mind* (as the interior self):—kidneys, reins.

3630. כִּלְיוֹן **Kilyôwn**, *kil-yone';* a form of 3631; *Kiljon*, an Isr.:—Chilion.

3631. כִּלָּיוֹן **killâyôwn**, *kil-law-yone';* from 3615; *pining, destruction:*—consumption, failing.

3632. כָּלִיל **kâlîyl**, *kaw-leel';* from 3634; *complete;* as noun, the *whole* (spec. a sacrifice *entirely consumed*); as adv. *fully:*—all, every whit, flame, perfect (-ion), utterly, whole burnt offering (sacrifice), wholly.

3633. כַּלְכֹּל **Kalkôl**, *kal-kole';* from 3557; *sustenance; Calcol*, an Isr.:—Calcol, Chalcol.

3634. כָּלַל **kâlal**, *kaw-lal';* a prim. root; to *complete:*—(make) perfect.

3635. כְּלַל **kᵉlal** (Chald.), *kel-al'*; corresp. to 3634; to *complete*:—finish, make (set) up.

3636. כְּלָל **Kᵉlâl**, *kel-awl'*; from 3634; *complete*; *Kelal*, an Isr.:—Chelal.

3637. כָּלַם **kâlam**, *kaw-lawm'*; a prim. root; prop. to *wound*; but only fig., to *taunt* or *insult*:—be (make) ashamed, blush, be confounded, be put to confusion, hurt, reproach, (do, put to) shame.

3638. כִּלְמָד **Kilmâd**, *kil-mawd'*; of for. der.; *Kilmad*, a place appar. in the Assyrian empire:—Chilmad.

3639. כְּלִמָּה **kᵉlimmâh**, *kel-im-maw'*; from 3637; *disgrace*:—confusion, dishonour, reproach, shame.

3640. כְּלִמּוּת **kᵉlimmûwth**, *kel-im-mooth'*; from 3639; *disgrace*:—shame.

3641. כַּלְנֶה **Kalneh**, *kal-neh'*; or

כַּלְנֵה **Kalnêh**, *kal-nay'*; also

כַּלְנוֹ **Kalnôw**, *kal-no'*; of for. der.; *Calneh* or *Calno*, a place in the Assyrian empire:—Calneh, Calno. Comp. 3656.

3642. כָּמַהּ **kâmahh**, *kaw-mah'*; a prim. root; to *pine* after:—long.

3643. כִּמְהָם **Kimhâm**, *kim-hawm'*; from 3642; *pining*; *Kimham*, an Isr.:—Chimham.

3644. כְּמוֹ **kᵉmôw**, *kem-o'*; or

כָּמוֹ **kâmôw**, *kaw-mo'*; a form of the pref. *k*, but used separately [comp. 3651]; *as*, *thus*, *so*:—according to, (such) as (it were, well as), in comparison of, like (as, to, unto), thus, when, worth.

3645. כְּמוֹשׁ **Kᵉmôwsh**, *kem-oshe'*; or (Jer. 48 : 7)

כְּמִישׁ **Kᵉmîysh**, *kem-eesh'*; from an unused root mean. to *subdue*; the *powerful*; *Kemosh*, the god of the Moabites:—Chemosh.

3646. כַּמֹּן **kammôn**, *kam-mone'*; from an unused root mean. to *store* up or *preserve*; "*cummin*" (from its use as a *condiment*):—cummin.

3647. כָּמַס **kâmaç**, *kaw-mas'*; a prim. root; to *store* away, i.e. (fig.) in the memory:—lay up in store.

3648. כָּמַר **kâmar**, *kaw-mar'*; a prim. root; prop. to *intertwine* or *contract*, i.e. (by impl.) to *shrivel* (as with heat); fig. to *be* deeply *affected* with passion (love or pity):—be black, be kindled, yearn.

3649. כָּמָר **kâmâr**, *kaw-mawr'*; from 3648; prop. an *ascetic* (as if *shrunk* with self-maceration), i.e. an idolatrous *priest* (only in plur.):—Chemarims, (idolatrous) priests.

3650. כִּמְרִיר **kimrîyr**, *kim-reer'*; redupl. from 3648; *obscuration* (as if from *shrinkage* of light), i.e. an *eclipse* (only in plur.):—blackness.

3651. כֵּן **kên**, *kane*; from 3559; prop. *set* upright; hence (fig. as adj.) *just*; but usually (as adv. or conj.) *rightly* or *so* (in various applications to manner, time and relation; often with other particles):—+ after that (this, -ward, -wards), as . . . as, + [for-] asmuch as yet, + be (for which) cause, + following, howbeit, in (the) like (manner, -wise), × the more, right, (even) so, state, straightway, such (thing), surely, + there (where) -fore, this, thus, true, well, × you.

3652. כֵּן **kên** (Chald.), *kane*; corresp. to 3651; *so*:—thus.

3653. כֵּן **kên**, *kane*; the same as 3651, used as a noun; a *stand*, i.e. pedestal or station:—base, estate, foot, office, place, well.

3654. כֵּן **kên**, *kane*; from 3661 in the sense of *fastening*; a *gnat* (from infixing its sting; used only in plur. [and irreg. in Exod. 8 : 17, 18; Heb. 13 : 14]):—lice, × manner.

3655. כָּנָה **kânâh**, *kaw-naw'*; a prim. root; to *address* by an additional name; hence, to *eulogize*:—give flattering titles, surname (himself).

3656. כַּנֶּה **Kanneh**, *kan-neh'*; for 3641; *Canneh*, a place in Assyria:—Canneh.

3657. כַּנָּה **kannâh**, *kan-naw'*; from 3661; a *plant* (as *set*):—× vineyard.

3658. כִּנּוֹר **kinnôwr**, *kin-nore'*; from an unused root mean. to *twang*; a *harp*:—harp.

3659. כָּנְיָהוּ **Konyâhûw**, *kon-yaw'-hoo*; for 3204; *Conjah*, an Isr. king:—Coniah.

3660. כְּנֵמָא **kᵉnêmâ'** (Chald.), *ken-ay-maw'*; corresp. to 3644; *so* or *thus*:—so, (in) this manner (sort), thus.

3661. כָּנַן **kânan**, *kaw-nan'*; a prim. root; to *set* out, i.e. *plant*:—× vineyard.

3662. כְּנָנִי **Kᵉnânîy**, *ken-aw-nee'*; from 3661; *planted*; *Kenani*, an Isr.:—Chenani.

3663. כְּנַנְיָה **Kᵉnanyâh**, *ken-an-yaw'*; or

כְּנַנְיָהוּ **Kᵉnanyâhûw**, *ken-an-yaw'-hoo*; from 3661 and 3050; *Jah has planted*; *Kenanjah*, an Isr.:—Chenaniah.

3664. כָּנַס **kânaç**, *kaw-nas'*; a prim. root; to *collect*; hence, to *enfold*:—gather (together), heap up, wrap self.

3665. כָּנַע **kânaʻ**, *kaw-nah'*; a prim. root; prop. to *bend* the knee; hence to *humiliate*, *vanquish*:—bring down (low), into subjection, under, humble (self), subdue.

3666. כִּנְעָה **kinʻâh**, *kin-aw'*; from 3665 in the sense of *folding* [comp. 3664]; a *package*:—wares.

3667. כְּנַעַן **Kᵉnaʻan**, *ken-ah'-an*; from 3665; *humiliated*; *Kenaan*, a son of Ham; also the country inhabited by him:—Canaan, merchant, traffick.

3668. כְּנַעֲנָה **Kᵉnaʻănâh**, *ken-ah-an-aw'*; fem. of 3667; *Kenaanah*, the name of two Isr.:—Chenaanah.

3669. כְּנַעֲנִי **Kᵉnaʻănîy**, *ken-ah-an-ee'*; patrial from 3667; a *Kenaanite* or inhabitant of Kenaan; by impl. a *pedlar* (the Canaanites standing for their neighbors the Ishmaelites, who conducted mercantile caravans):—Canaanite, merchant, trafficker.

3670. כָּנַף **kânaph**, *kaw-naf'*; a prim. root; prop. to *project* laterally, i.e. prob. (reflex.) to *withdraw*:—be removed.

3671. כָּנָף **kânâph**, *kaw-nawf'*; from 3670; an *edge* or *extremity*; spec. (of a bird or army) a *wing*, (of a garment or bed-clothing) a *flap*, (of the earth) a *quarter*, (of a building) a *pinnacle*:—+ bird, border, corner, end, feather [-ed], × flying, + (one an-) other, overspreading, × quarters, skirt, × sort, uttermost part, wing ([-ed]).

3672. כִּנְּרוֹת **Kinnᵉrôwth**, *kin-ner-ōth'*; or

כִּנֶּרֶת **Kinnereth**, *kin-neh'-reth*; respectively plur. and sing. fem. from the same as 3658; perh. *harp-shaped*; *Kinneroth* or *Kinnereth*, a place in Pal.:—Chinnereth, Chinneroth, Cinneroth.

3673. כָּנַשׁ **kânash** (Chald.), *kaw-nash'*; corresp. to 3664; to *assemble*:—gather together.

3674. כְּנָת **kᵉnâth**, *ken-awth'*; from 3655; a *colleague* (as having the same title):—companion.

3675. כְּנָת **kᵉnâth** (Chald.), *ken-awth'*; corresp. to 3674:—companion.

3676. כֵּס **kêç**, *kace*; appar. a contr. for 3678, but prob. by err. transc. for 5251:—sworn.

3677. כֶּסֶא **keçeʼ**, *keh'-seh*; or

כֶּסֶה **keçeh**, *keh'-seh*; appar. from 3680; prop. *fulness* or the *full moon*, i.e. its festival:—(time) appointed.

3678. כִּסֵּא **kiççêʼ**, *kis-say'*; or

כִּסֵּה **kiççêh**, *kis-say'*; from 3680; prop. *covered*, i.e. a *throne* (as *canopied*):—seat, stool, throne.

3679. כַּסְדַּי **Kaçday**, *kas-dah'ee*; for 3778:—Chaldean.

3680. כָּסָה **kâçâh**, *kaw-saw'*; a prim. root; prop. to *plump*, i.e. *fill up* hollows; by impl. to *cover* (for clothing or secrecy):—clad self, close, clothe, conceal, cover (self), (flee to) hide, overwhelm. Comp. 3780.

כֶּסֶה **keçeh**. See 3677.

כִּסֵּה **kiççêh**. See 3678.

3681. כָּסוּי **kâçûwy**, *kaw-soo'ee*; pass. part. of 3680; prop. *covered*, i.e. (as noun) a *covering*:—covering.

3682. כְּסוּת **kᵉçûwth**, *kes-ooth'*; from 3680; a *cover* (garment); fig. a *veiling*:—covering, raiment, vesture.

3683. כָּסַח **kâçach**, *kaw-sakh'*; a prim. root; to *cut off*:—cut down (up).

3684. כְּסִיל **kᵉçîyl**, *kes-eel'*; from 3688; prop. *fat*, i.e. (fig.) stupid or *silly*:—fool (-ish).

3685. כְּסִיל **Kᵉçîyl**, *kes-eel'*; the same as 3684; any notable *constellation*; spec. *Orion* (as if a *burly* one):—constellation, Orion.

3686. כְּסִיל **Kᵉçîyl**, *kes-eel'*; the same as 3684; *Kesil*, a place in Pal.:—Chesil.

3687. כְּסִילוּת **kᵉçîylûwth**, *kes-eel-ooth'*; from 3684; *silliness*:—foolish.

3688. כָּסַל **kâçal**, *kaw-sal'*; a prim. root; prop. to *be fat*, i.e. (fig.) *silly*:—be foolish.

3689. כֶּסֶל **keçel**, *keh'-sel*; from 3688; prop. *fatness*, i.e. by impl. (lit.) the *loin* (as the seat of the leaf *fat*) or (gen.) the *viscera*; also (fig.) *silliness* or (in a good sense) *trust*:—confidence, flank, folly, hope, loin.

3690. כִּסְלָה **kiçlâh**, *kis-law'*; fem. of 3689; in a good sense, *trust*; in a bad one, *silliness*:—confidence, folly.

3691. כִּסְלֵו **Kiçlêv**, *kis-lave'*; prob. of for. or.; *Kisleu*, the 9th Heb. month:—Chisleu.

3692. כִּסְלוֹן **Kiçlôwn**, *kis-lone'*; from 3688; *hopeful*; *Kislon*, an Isr.:—Chislon.

3693. כְּסָלוֹן **Kᵉçâlôwn**, *kes-aw-lone'*; from 3688; *fertile*; *Kesalon*, a place in Pal.:—Chesalon.

3694. כְּסֻלּוֹת **Kᵉçullôwth**, *kes-ool-lōth'*; fem. plur. of pass. part. of 3688; *fattened*, *Kesulloth*, a place in Pal.:—Chesulloth.

3695. כַּסְלֻחִים **Kaçlûchîym**, *kas-loo'-kheem*; a plur. prob. of for. der.; *Casluchim*, a people cognate to the Eg.:—Casluhim.

3696. כִּסְלֹת תָּבֹר **Kiçlôth Tâbôr**, *kis-lōth' taw-bore'*; from the fem. plur. of 3689 and 8396; *flanks of Tabor*; *Kisloth-Tabor*, a place in Pal.:—Chisloth-tabor.

3697. כָּסַם **kâçam**, *kaw-sam'*; a prim. root; to *shear*:—× only, poll. Comp. 3765.

3698. כֻּסֶּמֶת **kuççemeth**, *koos-seh'-meth*; from 3697; *spelt* (from its bristliness as if just *shorn*):—fitches, rie.

3699. כָּסַס **kâçaç**, *kaw-sas'*; a prim. root; to *estimate*:—make count.

3700. כָּסַף **kâçaph**, *kaw-saf'*; a prim. root; prop. to *become pale*, i.e. (by impl.) to *pine* after; also to *fear*:—[have] desire, be greedy, long, sore.

3701. כֶּסֶף **keçeph**, *keh'-sef*; from 3700; *silver* (from its *pale* color); by impl. *money*:—money, price, silver (-ling).

3702. כְּסַף **kᵉçaph** (Chald.), *kes-af'*; corresp. to 3701:—money, silver.

3703. כָּסִפְיָא **Kâçiphyâʼ**, *kaw-sif-yaw'*; perh. from 3701; *silvery*; *Casiphja*, a place in Bab.:—Casiphia.

3704. כֶּסֶת **keçeth**, *keh'-seth*; from 3680; a *cushion* or pillow (as *covering* a seat or bed):—pillow.

3705. כְּעַן **kᵉʻan** (Chald.), *keh-an'*; prob. from 3652; *now*:—now.

3706. כְּעֶנֶת **kᵉʻeneth** (Chald.), *keh-eh'-neth*; or

כְּעֶת **kᵉʻeth** (Chald.), *keh-eth'*; fem. of 3705; *thus* (only in the formula "and *so forth*"):—at such a time.

3707. כָּעַס **kâʻaç**, *kaw-as'*; a prim. root; to *trouble*; by impl. to *grieve*, *rage*, *be indignant*:—be angry, be grieved, take indignation, provoke (to anger, unto wrath), have sorrow, vex, be wroth.

3708. כַּעַס **kaʻaç**, *kah'-as*; or (in Job)

כַּעַשׂ **kaʻas**, *kah'-as*; from 3707; *vexation*:—anger, angry, grief, indignation, provocation, provoking, × sore, sorrow, spite, wrath.

כְּעֶת **kᵉʻeth**. See 3706.

3709. כַּף **kaph**, *kaf;* from 3721; the hollow *hand* or palm (so of the *paw* of an animal, of the *sole*, and even of the *bowl* of a dish or sling, the *handle* of a bolt, the *leaves* of a palm-tree); fig. *power:*—branch, + foot, hand ([-ful], -dle, [-led]), hollow, middle, palm, paw, power, sole, spoon.

3710. כֵּף **kêph**, *kafe;* from 3721; a hollow *rock:*—rock.

3711. כָּפָה **kâphâh**, *kaw-faw';* a prim. root; prop. to *bend*, i.e. (fig.) to *tame* or subdue:—pacify.

3712. כִּפָּה **kippâh**, *kip-paw';* fem. of 3709; a *leaf* of a palm-tree:—branch.

3713. כְּפוֹר **kᵉphôwr**, *kef-ore';* from 3722; prop. a *cover*, i.e. (by impl.) a *tankard* (or *covered* goblet); also white *frost* (as *covering* the ground):—bason, hoar (-y) frost.

3714. כָּפִיס **kâphîyç**, *kaw-fece';* from an unused root mean. to *connect;* a *girder:*—beam.

3715. כְּפִיר **kᵉphîyr**, *kef-eer';* from 3722; a *village* (as *covered* in by walls); also a young *lion* (perh. as *covered* with a mane):—(young) lion, village. Comp. 3723.

3716. כְּפִירָה **Kᵉphîyrâh**, *kef-ee-raw';* fem. of 3715; the *village* (always with the art.); *Kephirah*, a place in Pal.:—Chephirah.

3717. כָּפַל **kâphal**, *kaw-fal';* a prim. root; to *fold* together; fig. to *repeat:*—double.

3718. כֶּפֶל **kephel**, *keh'-fel;* from 3717; a *duplicate:*—double.

3719. כָּפַן **kâphan**, *kaw-fan';* a prim. root; to *bend:*—bend.

3720. כָּפָן **kâphân**, *kaw-fawn';* from 3719; *hunger* (as making to *stoop* with emptiness and pain):—famine.

3721. כָּפַף **kâphaph**, *kaw-faf';* a prim. root; to *curve:*—bow down (self).

3722. כָּפַר **kâphar**, *kaw-far';* a prim. root; to *cover* (spec. with bitumen); fig. to *expiate* or *condone*, to *placate* or *cancel:*—appease, make (an) atonement, cleanse, disannul, forgive, be merciful, pacify, pardon, to *pitch*, purge (away), put off, (make) reconcile (-liation).

3723. כָּפָר **kâphâr**, *kaw-fawr';* from 3722; a *village* (as *protected* by walls):—village. Comp. 3715.

3724. כֹּפֶר **kôpher**, *ko'-fer;* from 3722; prop. a *cover*, i.e. (lit.) a *village* (as *covered* in); (spec.) *bitumen* (as used for *coating*), and the *henna* plant (as used for *dyeing*); fig. a *redemption*-price:—bribe, camphire, pitch, ransom, satisfaction, sum of money, village.

3725. כִּפֻּר **kippûr**, *kip-poor';* from 3722; *expiation* (only in plur.):—atonement.

3726. כְּפַר הָעַמּוֹנִי **Kᵉphar hâ-ʿAmmôwnîy**, *kef-ar' haw-am-mo-nee';* from 3723 and 5984, with the art. interposed; *village of the Ammonite; Kefar-ha-Ammoni*, a place in Pal.:—Chefar-haamonai.

3727. כַּפֹּרֶת **kappôreth**, *kap-po'-reth;* from 3722; a *lid* (used only of the *cover* of the sacred Ark):—mercy seat.

3728. כָּפַשׁ **kâphash**, *kaw-fash';* a prim. root; to *tread* down; fig. to *humiliate:*—cover.

3729. כְּפַת **kᵉphath** (Chald.), *kef-ath';* a root of uncert. correspondence; to *fetter:*—bind.

3730. כַּפְתֹּר **kaphtôr**, *kaf-tore';* or (Am. 9 : 1)

כַּפְתּוֹר **kaphtôwr**, *kaf-tore';* prob. from an unused root mean. to *encircle;* a *chaplet;* but used only in an architectonic sense, i.e. the *capital* of a column, or a wreath-like *button* or *disk* on the candelabrum:—knop, (upper) lintel.

3731. כַּפְתֹּר **Kaphtôr**, *kaf-tore';* or (Am. 9 : 7)

כַּפְתּוֹר **Kaphtôwr**, *kaf-tore';* appar. the same as 3730; *Caphtor* (i.e. a *wreath*-shaped island), the original seat of the Philistines:—Caphtor.

3732. כַּפְתֹּרִי **Kaphtôrîy**, *kaf-to-ree';* patrial from 3731; a *Caphtorite* (collect.) or native of Caphtor:—Caphthorim, Caphtorim (-s).

3733. כַּר **kar**, *kar;* from 3769 in the sense of *plumpness;* a *ram* (as *full-grown* and *fat*), including a *battering-ram* (as *butting*); hence a *meadow* (as *for sheep*); also a *pad* or camel's saddle (as *puffed out*):—captain, furniture, lamb, (large) pasture, ram. See also 1033, 3746.

3734. כֹּר **kôr**, *kore;* from the same as 3564; prop. a deep round *vessel*, i.e. (spec.) a *cor* or measure for things dry:—cor, measure. Chald. the same.

3735. כָּרָא **kârâʼ** (Chald.), *kaw-raw';* prob. corresp. to 3738 in the sense of *piercing* (fig.); to *grieve:*—be grieved.

3736. כַּרְבֵּל **karbêl**, *kar-bale';* from the same as 3525; to *gird* or *clothe:*—clothed.

3737. כַּרְבְּלָא **karbᵉlâʼ** (Chald.), *kar-bel-aw';* from a verb corresp. to that of 3736; a *mantle:*—hat.

3738. כָּרָה **kârâh**, *kaw-raw';* a prim. root; prop. to *dig;* fig. to *plot;* gen. to *bore* or open:—dig, × make (a banquet), open.

3739. כָּרָה **kârâh**, *kaw-raw';* usually assigned as a prim. root, but prob. only a special application of 3738 (through the common idea of *planning* implied in a bargain); to *purchase:*—buy, prepare.

3740. כֵּרָה **kêrâh**, *kay-raw';* from 3739; a *purchase:*—provision.

3741. כָּרָה **kârâh**, *kaw-raw';* fem. of 3733; a *meadow:*—cottage.

3742. כְּרוּב **kᵉrûwb**, *ker-oob';* of uncert. der.; a *cherub* or imaginary figure:—cherub, [plur.] cherubims.

3743. כְּרוּב **Kᵉrûwb**, *ker-oob';* the same as 3742; *Kerub*, a place in Bab.:—Cherub.

3744. כָּרוֹז **kârôwz** (Chald.), *kaw-roze';* from 3745; a *herald:*—herald.

3745. כְּרַז **kᵉraz** (Chald.), *ker-az';* prob. of Greek or. (κηρύσσω); to *proclaim:*—make a proclamation.

3746. כָּרִי **kârîy**, *kaw-ree';* perh. an abridged plur. of 3733 in the sense of *leader* (of the flock); a *life-guardsman:*—captains, Cherethites [*from the marg.*].

3747. כְּרִית **Kᵉrîyth**, *ker-eeth';* from 3772; a *cut; Kerith*, a brook of Pal.:—Cherith.

3748. כְּרִיתוּת **kᵉrîythûwth**, *ker-ee-thooth';* from 3772; a *cutting* (of the matrimonial bond), i.e. *divorce:*—divorce (-ment).

3749. כַּרְכֹּב **karkôb**, *kar-kobe';* expanded from the same as 3522; a *rim* or top margin:—compass.

3750. כַּרְכֹּם **karkôm**, *kar-kome';* prob. of for. or.; the *crocus:*—saffron.

3751. כַּרְכְּמִישׁ **Karkᵉmîysh**, *kar-kem-eesh';* of for. der.; *Karkemish*, a place in Syria:—Carchemish.

3752. כַּרְכַּס **Karkaç**, *kar-kas';* of Pers. or.; *Karkas*, a eunuch of Xerxes:—Carcas.

3753. כַּרְכָּרָה **karkârâh**, *kar-kaw-raw';* from 3769; a *dromedary* (from its *rapid* motion as if dancing):—swift beast.

3754. כֶּרֶם **kerem**, *keh'-rem;* from an unused root of uncert. mean.; a *garden* or *vineyard:*—vines, (increase of the) vineyard (-s), vintage. See also 1021.

3755. כֹּרֵם **kôrêm**, *ko-rame';* act. part. of an imaginary denom. from 3754; a *vinedresser:*—vine dresser [*as one or two words*].

3756. כַּרְמִי **Karmîy**, *kar-mee';* from 3754; *gardener; Karmi*, the name of three Isr.:—Carmi.

3757. כַּרְמִי **Karmîy**, *kar-mee';* patron. from 3756; a *Karmite* or desc. of *Karmi:*—Carmites.

3758. כַּרְמִיל **karmîyl**, *kar-mele';* prob. of for. or.; *carmine*, a deep red:—crimson.

3759. כַּרְמֶל **karmel**, *kar-mel';* from 3754; a planted *field* (garden, orchard, vineyard or park); by impl. garden *produce:*—full (green) ears (of corn), fruitful field (place), plentiful (field).

3760. כַּרְמֶל **Karmel**, *kar-mel';* the same as 3759; *Karmel*, the name of a hill and of a town in Pal.:—Carmel, fruitful (plentiful) field, (place).

3761. כַּרְמְלִי **Karmᵉlîy**, *kar-mel-ee';* patron from 3760; a *Karmelite* or inhab. of Karmel (the town):—Carmelite.

3762. כַּרְמְלִית **Karmᵉlîyth**, *kar-mel-eeth';* fem of 3761; a *Karmelitess* or female in hab. of Karmel:—Carmelitess.

3763. כְּרָן **Kᵉrân**, *ker-awn';* of uncert. der.: *Keran*, an aboriginal Idumæan:—Cheran.

3764. כָּרְסֵא **korçêʼ** (Chald.), *kor-say';* corresp. to 3678; a *throne:*—throne.

3765. כִּרְסֵם **kirçêm**, *kir-same';* from 3697; to *lay waste:*—waste.

3766. כָּרַע **kâraʻ**, *kaw-rah';* a prim. root; to *bend* the knee; by impl. to *sink*, to *prostrate:*—bow (down, self), bring down (low), cast down, couch, fall, feeble, kneeling, sink, smite (stoop) down, subdue, × very.

3767. כָּרָע **kârâʻ**, *kaw-raw';* from 3766; the *leg* (from the knee to the ankle) of men or locusts (only in the dual):—leg.

3768. כַּרְפַּס **karpaç**, *kar-pas';* of for. or.; *byssus* or fine vegetable wool:—green.

3769. כָּרַר **kârar**, *kaw-rar';* a prim. root; to *dance* (i.e. *whirl*):—dance (-ing).

3770. כְּרֵשׂ **kᵉrês**, *ker-ace';* by var. from 7164; the *paunch* or belly (as *swelling* out):—belly.

כֹּרֶשׁ **Kôresh.** See 3567.

3771. כַּרְשְׁנָא **Karshᵉnâʼ**, *kar-shen-aw';* of for. or.; *Karshena*, a courtier of Xerxes:—Carshena.

3772. כָּרַת **kârath**, *kaw-rath';* a prim. root; to *cut* (off, down or asunder); by impl. to *destroy* or *consume;* spec. to *covenant* (i.e. make an alliance or bargain, orig. by cutting flesh and passing between the pieces):—be chewed, be con- [feder-] ate, covenant, cut (down, off), destroy, fail, feller, be freed, hew (down), make a league ([covenant]), × lose, perish, × utterly, × want.

3773. כָּרֻתָה **kârûthâh**, *kaw-rooth-aw';* pass. part. fem. of 3772; something *cut*, i.e. a hewn *timber:*—beam.

3774. כְּרֵתִי **Kᵉrêthîy**, *ker-ay-thee';* prob. from 3772 in the sense of *executioner;* a *Kerethite* or *life-guardsman* [comp. 2876] (only collect. in the sing. as plur.):—Cherethims, Cherethites.

3775. כֶּשֶׂב **keseb**, *keh'-seb;* appar. by transp. for 3532; a young *sheep:*—lamb, sheep.

3776. כִּשְׂבָּה **kisbâh**, *kis-baw';* fem. of 3775; a young *ewe:*—lamb.

3777. כֶּשֶׂד **Kesed**, *keh'-sed;* from an unused root of uncert. mean.; *Kesed*, a relative of Abraham:—Chesed.

3778. כַּשְׂדִּי **Kasdîy**, *kas-dee'* (occasionally with enclitic

כַּשְׂדִּימָה **Kasdîymâh**, *kas-dee'-maw; towards* the *Kasdites:*—into Chaldea), patron. from 3777 (only in the plur.); a *Kasdite*, or desc. of Kesed; by impl. a *Chaldæan* (as if so descended); also an *astrologer* (as if proverbial of that people:—Chaldeans, Chaldees, inhabitants of Chaldea.

3779. כַּשְׂדַּי **Kasday** (Chald.), *kas-dah'ee;* corresp. to 3778; a *Chaldæan* or inhab. of Chaldæa; by impl. a *Magian* or professional astrologer:—Chaldean.

3780. כָּשָׂה **kâsâh**, *kaw-saw';* a prim. root; to *grow fat* (i.e. be *covered* with flesh):—be covered. Comp. 3680.

3781. כַּשִּׁיל **kashshîyl**, *kash-sheel';* from 3782; prop. a *feller*, i.e. an *axe:*—ax.

3782. כָּשַׁל **kâshal**, *kaw-shal';* a prim. root; to *totter* or *waver* (through weakness of the legs, espec. the ankle); by impl. to *falter, stumble*, faint or fall:—bereave [*from the marg.*], cast down, be decayed, (cause to) fail, (cause, make to) fall (down, -ing), feeble, be (the) ruin (-ed, of), (be) overthrown, (cause to) stumble, × utterly, be weak.

3783. כִּשָּׁלוֹן **kishshâlôwn**, *kish-shaw-lone';* from 3782; prop. a *tottering*, i.e. *ruin:*—fall.

3784. כָּשַׁף **kâshaph**, *kaw-shaf'*; a prim. root; prop. to *whisper* a spell, i.e. to *inchant* or practise magic:—sorcerer, (use) witch (-craft).

3785. כֶּשֶׁף **kesheph**, *keh'-shef*; from 3784; *magic:*—sorcery, witchcraft.

3786. כַּשָּׁף **kashshâph**, *kash-shawf'*; from 3784; a *magician:*—sorcerer.

3787. כָּשֵׁר **kâshêr**, *kaw-share'*; a prim. root prop. to be *straight* or *right;* by impl. to *be acceptable;* also to *succeed* or prosper:—direct, be right, prosper.

3788. כִּשְׁרוֹן **kishrôwn**, *kish-rone'*; from 3787; *success, advantage:*—equity, good, right.

3789. כָּתַב **kâthab**, *kaw-thab'*; a prim. root; to *grave;* by impl. to *write* (describe, inscribe, prescribe, subscribe):—describe, record, prescribe, subscribe, write (-ing, -ten).

3790. כְּתַב **kethab** (Chald.), *keth-ab'*; corresp. to 3789:—write (-ten).

3791. כָּתָב **kâthâb**, *kaw-thawb'*; from 3789; something *written*, i.e. a *writing, record* or *book:*—register, scripture, writing.

3792. כְּתָב **kethâb** (Chald.), *keth-awb'*; corresp. to 3791:—prescribing, writing (-ten).

3793. כְּתֹבֶת **kethôbeth**, *keth-o'-beth*; from 3789; a *letter* or other *mark* branded on the skin:—× any [mark].

3794. כִּתִּי **Kittîy**, *kit-tee'*; or

כִּתִּיִּי **Kittîyîy**, *kit-tee-ee'*; patrial from an unused name denoting Cyprus (only in the plur.); a *Kittite* or Cypriote; hence an *islander* in gen., i.e. the Greeks or Romans on the shores opposite Pal.:—Chittim, Kittim.

3795. כָּתִית **kâthîyth**, *kaw-theeth'*; from 3807; *beaten*, i.e. pure (oil):—beaten.

3796. כֹּתֶל **kôthel**, *ko'-thel*; from an unused root mean. to *compact;* a *wall* (as *gathering* inmates):—wall.

3797. כְּתַל **kethal** (Chald.), *keth-al'*; corresp. to 3796:—wall.

3798. כִּתְלִישׁ **Kithlîysh**, *kith-leesh'*; from 3796 and 376; *wall of a man; Kithlish*, a place in Pal.:—Kithlish.

3799. כָּתַם **kâtham**, *kaw-tham'*; a prim. root; prop. to *carve* or *engrave*, i.e. (by impl.) to *inscribe* indelibly:—mark.

3800. כֶּתֶם **kethem**, *keh'-them*; from 3799; prop. something *carved* out, i.e. *ore;* hence *gold* (pure as originally mined):—([most] fine, pure) gold (-en wedge).

3801. כְּתֹנֶת **kethôneth**, *keth-o'-neth*; or

כֻּתֹּנֶת **kuttôneth**, *koot-to'-neth*; from an unused root mean. to *cover* [comp. 3802]; a *shirt:*—coat, garment, robe.

3802. כָּתֵף **kâthêph**, *kaw-thafe'*; from an unused root mean. to *clothe;* the *shoulder* (proper, i.e. upper end of the arm; as being the spot where the garments hang); fig. *side-piece* or lateral projection of anything:—arm, corner, shoulder (-piece), side, undersetter.

3803. כָּתַר **kâthar**, *kaw-thar'*; a prim. root; to *enclose;* hence (in a friendly sense) to *crown*, (in a hostile one) to *besiege;* also to *wait* (as restraining oneself):—beset round, compass about, be crowned inclose round, suffer.

3804. כֶּתֶר **kether**, *keh'-ther*; from 3803; prop. a *circlet*, i.e. a *diadem:*—crown.

3805. כֹּתֶרֶת **kôthereth**, *ko-theh'-reth*; fem. act. part. of 3803; the *capital* of a column:—chapiter.

3806. כָּתַשׁ **kâthash**, *kaw-thash'*; a prim. root; to *butt* or *pound:*—bray.

3807. כָּתַת **kâthath**, *kaw-thath'*; a prim. root; to *bruise* or violently *strike:*—beat (down, to pieces), break in pieces, crushed, destroy, discomfit, smite, stamp.

ל

3808. לֹא **lô'**, *lo*; or

לוֹא **lôw'**, *lo*; or

לֹה **lôh** (Deut. 3 : 11), *lo;* a prim. particle; *not* (the simple or abs. negation); by impl. *no;* often used with other particles (as follows):—× before, + or else, ere, + except, ig [-norant], much, less, nay, neither, never, no ([-ne], -r, [-thing]), (× as though . . . , [can-], for) not (out of), of nought, otherwise, out of, + surely, + as truly as, + of a truth, + verily, for want, + whether, without.

3809. לָא **lâ'** (Chald.), *law;* or

לָה **lâh** (Chald.) (Dan. 4 : 32), *law;* corresp. to 3808:—or even, neither, no (-ne, -r), ([can-]) not, as nothing, without.

לֻא **lû'**. See 3863.

3810. לֹא דְבַר **Lô' Debar**, *lo deb-ar'*; or

לוֹ דְבַר **Lôw Debar** (2 Sam. 9 : 4, 5), *lo deb-ar'*; or

לִדְבִר **Lidbîr** (Josh. 13 : 26), *lid-beer'* [prob. rather

לֹדְבַר **Lôdebar**, *lo-deb-ar'*]; from 3808 and 1699; *pastureless; Lo-Debar*, a place in Pal.:—Debir, Lo-debar.

3811. לָאָה **lâ'âh**, *law-aw'*; a prim. root; to *tire;* (fig.) to *be* (or *make*) *disgusted:*—faint, grieve, lothe, (be, make) weary (selves).

3812. לֵאָה **Lê'âh**, *lay-aw'*; from 3811; *weary; Leah*, a wife of Jacob:—Leah.

לְאוֹם **le'owm**. See 3816.

3813. לָאַט **lâ'aṭ**, *law-at'*; a prim. root; to *muffle:*—cover.

3814. לָאט **lâ'ṭ**, *lawt*; from 3813 (or perh. for act. part. of 3874); prop. *muffled*, i.e. *silently:*—softly.

3815. לָאֵל **Lâ'êl**, *law-ale'*; from the prep. pref. and 410; (belonging) *to God; Laël* an Isr.:—Lael.

3816. לְאֹם **le'ôm**, *leh-ome'*; or

לְאוֹם **le'ôwm**, *leh-ome'*; from an unused root mean. to *gather;* a *community:*—nation, people.

3817. לְאֻמִּים **Le'ummîym**, *leh-oom-meem'*; plur. of 3816; *communities; Leüm mim*, an Arabian:—Leummim.

3818. לֹא עַמִּי **Lô' 'Ammîy**, *lo am-mee'*; from 3808 and 5971 with pron. suffix; *not my people; Lo-Ammi*, the symbol. name of a son of Hosea:—Lo-ammi.

3819. לֹא רֻחָמָה **Lô' Rûchâmâh**, *lo roo-khaw-maw'*; from 3808 and 7355; *not pitied; Lo-Ruchamah*, the symbol. name of a daughter of Hosea:—Lo-ruhamah.

3820. לֵב **lêb**, *labe*, a form of 3824; the *heart;* also used (fig.) very widely for the feelings, the will and even the intellect; likewise for the *centre* of anything:— + care for, comfortably, consent, × considered, courag [-eous], friend [-ly], ([broken-], [hard-], [merry-], [stiff-], [stout-], double) heart ([-ed]), × heed, × I, kindly, midst, mind (-ed), × regard ([-ed)], × themselves, × unawares, understanding, × well, willingly, wisdom.

3821. לֵב **lêb** (Chald.), *labe;* corresp. to 3820:—heart.

3822. לְבָאוֹת **Lebâ'ôwth**, *leb-aw-ōth'*; plur. of 3833; *lionesses; Lebaoth*, a place in Pal.:—Lebaoth. See also 1034.

3823. לָבַב **lâbab**, *law-bab'*; a prim. root; prop. to *be enclosed* (as if with *fat*); by impl. (as denom. from 3824) to *unheart*, i.e. (in a good sense) *transport* (with love), or (in a bad sense) *stultify;* also (as denom. from 3834) to *make cakes:*—make cakes, ravish, be wise.

3824. לֵבָב **lêbâb**, *lay-bawb'*; from 3823; the *heart* (as the most interior organ); used also like 3820:— + bethink themselves, breast, comfortably, courage, ([faint], [tender-] heart ([-ed]), midst, mind, × unawares, understanding.

3825. לְבַב **lebab** (Chald.), *leb-ab'*; corresp. to 3824:—heart.

לְבִבָה **lebîbâh**. See 3834.

3826. לִבָּה **libbâh**, *lib-baw'*; fem. of 3820; the *heart:*—heart.

3827. לַבָּה **labbâh**, *lab-baw'*; for 3852; *flame:*—flame.

3828. לְבוֹנָה **lebôwnâh**, *leb-o-naw'*; or

לְבֹנָה **lebônâh**, *leb-o-naw'*; from 3836; *frankincense* (from its *whiteness* or perh. that of its smoke):—(frank-) incense.

3829. לְבוֹנָה **Lebôwnâh**, *leb-o-naw'*; the same as 3828; *Lebonah*, a place in Pal.:—Lebonah.

3830. לְבוּשׁ **lebûwsh**, *leb-oosh'*; or

לְבֻשׁ **lebûsh**, *leb-oosh'*; from 3847; a *garment* (lit. or fig.); by impl. (euphem.) a *wife:*—apparel, clothed with, clothing, garment, raiment, vestment, vesture.

3831. לְבוּשׁ **lebûwsh** (Chald.), *leb-oosh'*; corresp. to 3830:—garment.

3832. לָבַט **lâbaṭ**, *law-bat'*; a prim. root; to *overthrow;* intrans. to *fall:*—fall.

לֻבִּי **Lubbîy**. See 3864.

3833. לָבִיא **lâbîy'**, *law-bee'*; or (Ezek. 19 : 2)

לְבִיָּא **lebîyâ'**, *leb-ee-yaw'*; irreg. masc. plur.

לְבָאִים **lebâ'îym**, *leb-aw-eem'*; irreg. fem. plur.

לְבָאוֹת **lebâ'ôwth**, *leb-aw-ōth'*; from an unused root mean. to *roar;* a *lion* (prop. a lioness as the fiercer [although not a *roarer;* comp. 738]):—(great, old, stout) lion, lioness, young [lion].

3834. לָבִיבָה **lâbîybâh**, *law-bee-baw'*; or rather

לְבִבָה **lebîbâh**, *leb-ee-baw'*; from 3823 in its orig. sense of *fatness* (or perh. of *folding*); a *cake* (either as *fried* or *turned*):—cake.

3835. לָבַן **lâban**, *law-ban'*; a prim. root; to *be* (or *become*) *white;* also (as denom. from 3843) to *make bricks:*—make brick, be (made, make) white (-r).

3836. לָבָן **lâbân**, *law-bawn'*; or (Gen. 49 : 12)

לָבֵן **lâbên**, *law-bane'*; from 3835; *white:*—white.

3837. לָבָן **Lâbân**, *law-bawn'*; the same as 3836; *Laban*, a Mesopotamian; also a place in the Desert:—Laban.

לַבֵּן **Labbên**. See 4192.

3838. לְבָנָא **Lebânâ'**, *leb-aw-naw'*; or

לְבָנָה **Lebânâh**, *leb-aw-naw'*; the same as 3842; *Lebana* or *Lebanah*, one of the Nethinim:—Lebana, Lebanah.

3839. לִבְנֶה **libneh**, *lib-neh'*; from 3835; some sort of *whitish* tree, perh. the *storax:*—poplar.

3840. לִבְנָה **libnâh**, *lib-naw'*; from 3835; prop. *whiteness*, i.e. (by impl.) *transparency:*—paved.

3841. לִבְנָה **Libnâh**, *lib-naw'*; the same as 3839; *Libnah*, a place in the Desert and one in Pal.:—Libnah.

3842. לְבָנָה **lebânâh**, *leb-aw-naw'*; from 3835; prop. (the) *white*, i.e. the *moon:*—moon. See also 3838.

3843. לְבֵנָה **lebênâh**, *leb-ay-naw'*; from 3835; a *brick* (from the *whiteness* of the clay):—(altar of) brick, tile.

לְבֹנָה **lebônâh**. See 3828.

3844. לְבָנוֹן **Lebânôwn**, *leb-aw-nohn'*; from 3825; (the) *white* mountain (from its snow); *Lebanon*, a mountain range in Pal.:—Lebanon.

3845. לִבְנִי **Libnîy**, *lib-nee'*; from 3835; *white; Libni*, an Isr.:—Libni.

3846. לִבְנִי **Libnîy**, *lib-nee'*; patron. from 3845; a *Libnite* or desc. of Libni (collect.):—Libnites.

3847. לָבַשׁ **lâbash**, *law-bash'*; or

לָבֵשׁ **lâbêsh**, *law-bashe'*; a prim. root; prop. *wrap* around, i.e. (by impl.) to *put on* a garment or *clothe* (oneself, or another), lit. or fig.:—(in) apparel, arm, array (self), clothe (self), come upon, put (on, upon), wear.

3848. לְבַשׁ **lᵉbash** (Chald.), *leb-ash'*; corresp. to 3847:—clothe.

לְבֻשׁ **lᵉbûsh**. See 3830.

3849. לֹג **lôg**, *lohg*; from an unused root appar. mean. to *deepen* or *hollow* [like 3537]; a *log* or measure for liquids:—log [of oil].

3850. לֹד **Lôd**, *lode*; from an unused root of uncert. signif.; *Lod*, a place in Pal.:—Lod.

לִדְבִר **Lidbîr**. See 3810.

3851. לַהַב **lahab**, *lah'-hab*; from an unused root mean. to *gleam*; a *flash*; fig. a sharply polished *blade* or *point* of a weapon:—blade, bright, flame, glittering.

3852. לֶהָבָה **lehâbâh**, *leh-aw-baw'*; or

לַהֶבֶת **lahebeth**, *lah-eh'-beth*; fem. of 3851, and mean. the same:—flame (-ming), head [of a spear].

3853. לְהָבִים **Lᵉhâbîym**, *leh-haw-beem'*; plur. of 3851; *flames*; *Lehabim*, a son of Mizrain, and his descend.:—Lehabim.

3854. לַהַג **lahag**, *lah'-hag*; from an unused root mean. to *be eager*; intense mental *application*:—study.

3855. לַהַד **Lahad**, *lah'-had*; from an unused root mean. to *glow* [comp. 3851] or else to *be earnest* [comp. 3854]; *Lahad*, an Isr.:—Lahad.

3856. לָהַהּ **lâhahh**, *law-hah'*; a prim. root mean. prop. to *burn*, i.e. (by impl.) to *be rabid* (fig. *insane*); also (from the *exhaustion* of frenzy) to *languish*:—faint, mad.

3857. לָהַט **lâhaṭ**, *law-hat'*; a prim. root; prop. to *lick*, i.e. (by impl.) to *blaze*:—burn (up), set on fire, flaming, kindle.

3858. לַהַט **lahaṭ**, *lah'-hat*; from 3857; a *blaze*; also (from the idea of *enwrapping*) *magic* (as *covert*):—flaming, enchantment.

3859. לָהַם **lâham**, *law-ham'*; a prim. root; prop. to *burn* in, i.e. (fig.) to *rankle*:—wound.

3860. לָהֵן **lâhên**, *law-hane'*; from the pref. prep. mean. *to* or *for* and 2005; pop. *for if*; hence *therefore*:—for them [*by mistake for prep. suffix*].

3861. לָהֵן **lâwhên** (Chald.), *law-hane'*; corresp. to 3860; *therefore*; also *except*:—but, except, save, therefore, wherefore.

3862. לַהֲקָה **lahăqâh**, *lah-hak-aw'*; prob. from an unused root mean. to *gather*; an *assembly*:—company.

לוֹא **lôwʼ**. See 3808.

3863. לוּא **lûwʼ**, *loo*; or

לֻא **lûʼ**, *loo*; or

לוּ **lûw**, *loo*; a conditional particle; *if*; by impl. (interj. as a wish) *would that!*:—if (haply), peradventure, I pray thee, though, I would, would God (that).

3864. לוּבִי **Lûwbîy**, *loo-bee'*; or

לֻבִּי **Lubbîy** (Dan. 11 : 43), *loob-bee'*; patrial from a name prob. derived from an unused root mean. to *thirst*, i.e. a *dry* region; appar. a *Libyan* or inhab. of interior Africa (only in plur.):—Lubim (-s), Libyans.

3865. לוּד **Lûwd**, *lood*; prob. of for. der.; *Lud*, the name of two nations:—Lud, Lydia.

3866. לוּדִי **Lûwdîy**, *loo-dee'*; or

לוּדִיִּי **Lûwdîyîy**, *loo-dee-ee'*; patrial from 3865; a *Ludite* or inhab. of Lud (only in plur.):—Ludim, Lydians.

3867. לָוָה **lâvâh**, *law-vaw'*; a prim. root; prop. to *twine*, i.e. (by impl.) to *unite*, to *remain*; also to *borrow* (as a form of *obligation*) or (caus.) to *lend*:—abide with, borrow (-er), cleave, join (self), lend (-er).

3868. לוּז **lûwz**, *looz*; a prim. root; to *turn aside* [comp. 3867, 3874 and 3885], i.e. (lit.) to *depart*, (fig.) *be perverse*:—depart, froward, perverse (-ness).

3869. לוּז **lûwz**, *looz*; prob. of for. or; some kind of *nut*-tree, perh. the *almond*:—hazel.

3870. לוּז **Lûwz**, *looz*; prob. from 3869 (as growing there); *Luz*, the name of two places in Pal.:—Luz.

3871. לוּחַ **lûwach**, *loo'-akh*; or

לֻחַ **lûach**, *loo'-akh*; from a prim. root; prob. mean. to *glisten*; a *tablet* (as *polished*), of stone, wood or metal:—board, plate, table.

3872. לוּחִית **Lûwchîyth**, *loo-kheeth'*; or

לֻחוֹת° **Lûchôwth** (Jer. 48 : 5), *loo-khoth'*; from the same as 3871; *floored*; *Luchith*, a place E. of the Jordan:—Luhith.

3873. לוֹחֵשׁ **Lôwchêsh**, *lo-khashe'*; act. part. of 3907; (the) *enchanter*; *Lochesh*, an Isr.:—Hallohesh, Haloshesh [*includ. the art.*].

3874. לוּט **lûwṭ**, *loot*; a prim. root; to *wrap* up:—cast, wrap.

3875. לוֹט **lôwṭ**, *lote*; from 3874; a *veil*:—covering.

3876. לוֹט **Lôwṭ**, *lote*; the same as 3875; *Lot*, Abraham's nephew:—Lot.

3877. לוֹטָן **Lôwṭân**, *lo-tawn'*; from 3875; *covering*; *Lotan*, an Idumæan:—Lotan.

3878. לֵוִי **Lêvîy**, *lay-vee'*; from 3867; *attached*; *Levi*, a son of Jacob:—Levi. See also 3879, 3881.

3879. לֵוִי **Lêvîy** (Chald.), *lay-vee'*; corresp. to 3880:—Levite.

3880. לִוְיָה **livyâh**, *liv-yaw'*; from 3867; something *attached*, i.e. a *wreath*:—ornament.

3881. לֵוִיִּי **Lêvîyîy**, *lay-vee-ee'*; or

לֵוִי **Lêvîy**, *lay-vee'*; patron. from 3878; a *Leviite* or desc. of Levi:—Levite.

3882. לִוְיָתָן **livyâthân**, *liv-yaw-thawn'*; from 3867; a *wreathed* animal, i.e. a *serpent* (espec. the *crocodile* or some other large sea-monster); fig. the constellation of the *dragon*; also as a symbol of *Bab.*:—leviathan, mourning.

3883. לוּל **lûwl**, *lool*; from an unused root mean. to *fold* back; a *spiral* step:—winding stair. Comp. 3924.

3884. לוּלֵא **lûwlêʼ**, *loo-lay'*; or

לוּלֵי **lûwlêy**, *loo lay'*; from 3863 and 3808; *if not*:—except, had not, if (... not), unless, were it not that.

3885. לוּן **lûwn**, *loon*; or

לִין **lîyn**, *leen*; a prim. root; to *stop* (usually over night); by impl. to *stay* permanently; hence (in a bad sense) to be *obstinate* (espec. in words, to *complain*):—abide (all night), continue, dwell, endure, grudge, be left, lie all night, (cause to) lodge (all night, in, -ing, this night), (make to) murmur, remain, tarry (all night, that night).

3886. לוּעַ **lûwaʻ**, *loo'-ah*; a prim. root; to *gulp*; fig. to *be rash*:—swallow down (up).

3887. לוּץ **lûwts**, *loots*; a prim. root; prop. to *make mouths* at, i.e. to *scoff*; hence (from the effort to pronounce a foreign language) to *interpret*, or (gen.) *intercede*:—ambassador, have in derision, interpreter, make a mock, mocker, scorn (-er, -ful), teacher.

3888. לוּשׁ **lûwsh**, *loosh*; a prim. root; to *knead*:—knead.

3889. לוּשׁ° **Lûwsh**, *loosh*; from 3888; *kneading*; *Lush*, a place in Pal.:—Laish [*from the marg.*]. Comp. 3919.

3890. לְוָת **lᵉvâth** (Chald.), *lev-awth'*; from a root corresp. to 3867; prop. *adhesion*, i.e. (as prep.) *with*:—× thee.

לֻחוֹת **Lûchôwth**. See 3872.

לָז **lâz**, and

לָזֶה **lâzeh**. See 1975 and 1976.

3891. לְזוּת **lᵉzûwth**, *lez-ooth'*; from 3868; *perverseness*:—perverse.

3892. לַח **lach**, *lakh*; from an unused root mean. to *be new*; *fresh*, i.e. unused or undried:—green, moist.

3893. לֵחַ **lêach**, *lay'-akh*; from the same as 3892; *freshness*, i.e. vigor:—natural force.

לֻחַ **lûach**. See 3871.

3894. לָחוּם **lâchûwm**, *law-khoom'*; or

לָחֻם **lâchûm**, *law-khoom'*; pass. part. of 3898; prop. *eaten*, i.e. *food*; also *flesh*, i.e. *body*:—while . . . is eating, flesh.

3895. לְחִי **lᵉchîy**, *lekh-ee'*; from an unused root mean. to *be soft*; the *cheek* (from its *fleshiness*); hence the *jaw*-bone:—cheek (bone), jaw (bone).

3896. לֶחִי **Lechîy**, *lekh'-ee*; a form of 3895; *Lechi*, a place in Pal.:—Lehi. Comp. also 7437.

3897. לָחַךְ **lâchak**, *law-khak'*; a prim. root; to *lick*:—lick (up).

3898. לָחַם **lâcham**, *law-kham'*; a prim. root; to *feed* on; fig. to *consume*; by impl. to *battle* (as *destruction*):—devour, eat, × ever, fight (-ing), overcome, prevail, (make) war (-ring).

3899. לֶחֶם **lechem**, *lekh'-em*; from 3898; *food* (for man or beast), espec. *bread*, or *grain* (for making it):—([shew-]) bread, × eat, food, fruit, loaf, meat, victuals. See also 1036.

3900. לְחֶם **lᵉchem** (Chald.), *lekh-em'*; corresp. to 3899:—feast.

3901. לָחֶם **lâchem**, *law-khem'*; from 3898; *battle*:—war.

לָחֻם **lâchûm**. See 3894.

3902. לַחְמִי **Lachmîy**, *lakh-mee'*; from 3899; *foodful*; *Lachmi*, a Philis.; or rather prob. a brief form (or perh. err. transc.) for 1022:—Lahmi. See also 3433.

3903. לַחְמָס **Lachmâç**, *lakh-maws'*; prob. by err. transc. for

לַחְמָם° **Lachmâm**, *lakh-mawm'*; from 3899; *food-like*; *Lachmam* or *Lachmas*, a place in Pal.:—Lahmam.

3904. לְחֵנָה **lᵉchênâh** (Chald.), *lekh-ay-naw'*; from an unused root of uncert. mean.; a *concubine*:—concubine.

3905. לָחַץ **lâchats**, *law-khats'*; a prim. root; prop. to *press*, i.e. (fig.) to *distress*:—afflict, crush, force, hold fast, oppress (-or), thrust self.

3906. לַחַץ **lachats**, *lakh'-ats*; from 3905; *distress*:—affliction, oppression.

3907. לָחַשׁ **lâchash**, *law-khash'*; a prim. root; to *whisper*; by impl. to *mumble* a spell (as a magician):—charmer, whisper (together).

3908. לַחַשׁ **lachash**, *lakh'-ash*; from 3907; prop. a *whisper*, i.e. by impl. (in a good sense) a private *prayer*, (in a bad one) an *incantation*; concr. an *amulet*:—charmed, earring, enchantment, orator, prayer.

3909. לָט **lâṭ**, *lawt*; a form of 3814 or else part. from 3874; prop. *covered*, i.e. *secret*; by impl. *incantation*; also *secrecy* or (adv.) *covertly*:—enchantment, privily, secretly, softly.

3910. לֹט **lôṭ**, *lote*; prob. from 3874; a gum (from its *sticky* nature), prob. *ladanum*:—myrrh.

3911. לְטָאָה **lᵉṭâʼâh**, *let-aw-aw'*; from an unused root mean. to *hide*; a kind of *lizard* (from its *covert* habits):—lizard.

3912. לְטוּשִׁם **Lᵉṭûwshîm**, *let-oo-sheem'*; masc. plur. of pass. part. of 3913; *hammered* (i.e. *oppressed*) ones; *Letushim*, an Arabian tribe:—Letushim.

3913. לָטַשׁ **lâṭash**, *law-tash'*; a prim. root; prop. to *hammer* out (an edge), i.e. to *sharpen*:—instructer, sharp (-en), whet.

3914. לֹיָה **lôyâh**, *lo-yaw'*; a form of 3880; a *wreath*:—addition.

3915. לַיִל **layil**, *lah'-yil*; or (Isa. 21 : 11)

לֵיל **lêyl**, *lale*; also

לַיְלָה **layᵉlâh**, *lah'-yel-aw*; from the same as 3883; prop. a *twist* (away of the light), i.e. *night*; fig. *adversity*:—([mid-]) night (season).

3916. לֵילְיָא **leylᵉyâʼ** (Chald.), *lay-leh-yaw'*; corresp. to 3915:—night.

3917. לִילִית **lîylîyth**, *lee-leeth'*; from 3915; a *night* spectre:—screech owl.

3918. לַיִשׁ **layish**, *lah'-yish;* from 3888 in the sense of *crushing;* a lion (from his destructive *blows*):—(old) lion.

3919. לַיִשׁ **Layish**, *lah'-yish;* the same as 3918; *Laïsh,* the name of two places in Pal.:—Laish. Comp. 3889.

3920. לָכַד **lâkad**, *law-kad';* a prim. root; to *catch* (in a net, trap or pit); gen. to *capture* or occupy; also to *choose* (by lot); fig. to *cohere:*—× at all, catch (self), be frozen, be holden, stick together, take.

3921. לֶכֶד **leked**, *leh'-ked;* from 3920; something to *capture* with, i.e. a *noose:*—being taken.

3922. לֵכָה **lêkâh**, *lay-kaw';* from 3212; a *journey; Lekah,* a place in Pal.:—Lecah.

3923. לָכִישׁ **Lâchîysh**, *law-keesh';* from an unused root of uncert. mean.; *Lakish,* a place in Pal.:—Lachish.

3924. לֻלָאָה **lûlâ'âh**, *loo-law-aw';* from the same as 3883; a *loop:*—loop.

3925. לָמַד **lâmad**, *law-mad';* a prim. root; prop. to *goad,* i.e. (by impl.) to *teach* (the rod being an Oriental *incentive*):—[un-] accustomed, × diligently, expert, instruct, learn, skilful, teach (-er, -ing).

לִמֻּד **limmûd**. See 3928.

3926. לְמוֹ **lᵉmôw**, *lem-o';* a prol. and separable form of the pref. prep.; *to* or *for:*—at, for, to, upon.

3927. לְמוּאֵל **Lᵉmûw'êl**, *lem-oo-ale';* or

לְמוֹאֵל **Lᵉmôw'êl**, *lem-o-ale';* from 3926 and 410; (belonging) *to God; Lemuël* or *Lemoël,* a symbol. name of Solomon:—Lemuel.

3928. לִמּוּד **limmûwd**, *lim-mood';* or

לִמֻּד **limmûd**, *lim-mood';* from 3925; *instructed:*—accustomed, disciple, learned, taught, used.

3929. לֶמֶךְ **Lemek**, *leh'-mek;* from an unused root of uncert. mean.; *Lemek,* the name of two antediluvian patriarchs:—Lamech.

3930. לֹעַ **lôaᵉ**, *lo'ah* from 3886; the *gullet:*—throat.

3931. לָעַב **lâᵉab**, *law-ab';* a prim. root; to *deride:*—mock.

3932. לָעַג **lâᵉag**, *law-ag';* a prim. root; to *deride;* by impl. (as if imitating a foreigner) to *speak unintelligibly:*—have in derision, laugh (to scorn), mock (on), stammering.

3933. לַעַג **laᵉag**, *lah'-ag;* from 3932; *derision, scoffing:*—derision, scorn (-ing).

3934. לָעֵג **lâᵉêg**, *law-ayg';* from 3932; a *buffoon;* also a *foreigner:*—mocker, stammering.

3935. לַעְדָּה **Laᵉdâh**, *lah-daw';* from an unused root of uncert. mean.; *Ladah,* an Isr.:—Laadah.

3936. לַעְדָּן **Laᵉdân**, *lah-dawn';* from the same as 3935; *Ladan,* the name of two Isr.:—Laadan.

3937. לָעַז **lâᵉaz**, *law-az';* a prim. root; to *speak in a foreign tongue:*—strange language.

3938. לָעַט **lâᵉaṭ**, *law-at';* a prim. root; to *swallow* greedily; causat. to *feed:*—feed.

3939. לַעֲנָה **laᵉănâh**, *lah-an-aw';* from an unused root supposed to mean to *curse;* *wormwood* (regarded as *poisonous,* and therefore *accursed*):—hemlock, wormwood.

3940. לַפִּיד **lappîyd**, *lap-peed';* or

לַפִּד **lappîd**, *lap-peed';* from an unused root prob. mean. to *shine;* a *flambeau, lamp* or *flame:*—(fire-) brand, (burning) lamp, lightning, torch.

3941. לַפִּידוֹת **Lappîydôwth**, *lap-pee-dōth';* fem. plur. of 3940; *Lappidoth,* the husband of Deborah:—Lappidoth.

3942. לִפְנַי **liphnay**, *lif-nah'ee;* from the pref. prep. (*to* or *for*) and 6440; *anterior:*—before.

3943. לָפַת **lâphath**, *law-fath';* a prim. root; prop. to *bend,* i.e. (by impl.) to *clasp;* also (reflex.) to *turn* around or aside:—take hold, turn aside (self).

3944. לָצוֹן **lâtsôwn**, *law-tsone';* from 3887; *derision:*—scornful (-ning).

3945. לָצַץ **lâtsats**, *law-tsats';* a prim. root; to *deride:*—scorn.

3946. לַקּוּם **Laqqûwm**, *lak-koom';* from an unused root thought to mean to *stop* up by a barricade; perh. *fortification; Lakkum,* a place in Pal.:—Lakum.

3947. לָקַח **lâqach**, *law-kakh';* a prim. root; to *take* (in the widest variety of applications):—accept, bring, buy, carry away, drawn, fetch, get, infold, × many, mingle, place, receive (-ing), reserve, seize, send for, take (away, -ing, up), use, win.

3948. לֶקַח **leqach**, *leh'-kakh;* from 3947; prop. something *received,* i.e. (mentally) *instruction* (whether on the part of the teacher or hearer); also (in an act. and sinister sense) *inveiglement:*—doctrine, learning, fair speech.

3949. לִקְחִי **Liqchîy**, *lik-khee';* from 3947; *learned; Likchi,* an Isr.:—Likhi.

3950. לָקַט **lâqaṭ**, *law-kat';* a prim. root; prop. to *pick* up, i.e. (gen.) to *gather;* spec. to *glean:*—gather (up), glean.

3951. לֶקֶט **leqeṭ**, *leh'-ket;* from 3950; the *gleaning:*—gleaning.

3952. לָקַק **lâqaq**, *law-kak';* a prim. root; to *lick* or *lap:*—lap, lick.

3953. לָקַשׁ **lâqash**, *law-kash';* a prim. root; to *gather* the *after* crop:—gather.

3954. לֶקֶשׁ **leqesh**, *leh'-kesh;* from 3953; the *after crop:*—latter growth.

3955. לְשַׁד **lᵉshad**, *lesh-ad';* from an unused root of uncert. mean.; appar. *juice,* i.e. (fig.) *vigor;* also a sweet or fat *cake:*—fresh, moisture.

3956. לָשׁוֹן **lâshôwn**, *law-shone';* or

לָשֹׁן **lâshôn**, *law-shone';* also (in plur.) fem.

לְשֹׁנָה **lᵉshônâh**, *lesh-o-naw';* from 3960; the *tongue* (of man or animals), used lit. (as the instrument of licking, eating, or speech), and fig. (speech, an ingot, a fork of flame, a cove of water):—+ babbler, bay, + evil speaker, language, talker, tongue, wedge.

3957. לִשְׁכָּה **lishkâh**, *lish-kaw';* from an unused root of uncert. mean.; a *room* in a building (whether for storage, eating, or lodging):—chamber, parlour. Comp. 5393.

3958. לֶשֶׁם **leshem**, *leh'-shem;* from an unused root of uncert. mean.; a *gem,* perh. the *jacinth:*—ligure.

3959. לֶשֶׁם **Leshem**, *leh'-shem;* the same as 3958; *Leshem,* a place in Pal.:—Leshem.

3960. לָשַׁן **lâshan**, *law-shan';* a prim. root; prop. to *lick;* but used only as a denom. from 3956; to *wag the tongue,* i.e. to *calumniate:*—accuse, slander.

3961. לִשָּׁן **lishshân** (Chald.) *lish-shawn';* corresp. to 3956; *speech,* i.e. a *nation:*—language.

3962. לֶשַׁע **Leshaᵉ**, *leh'-shah;* from an unused root thought to mean to *break* through; a boiling *spring; Lesha,* a place prob. E. of the Jordan:—Lasha.

3963. לֶתֶךְ **lethek**, *leh'-thek;* from an unused root of uncert. mean.; a *measure* for things dry:—half homer.

מ

מַה **ma-**, or

מָה **mâ-**. See 4100.

3964. מָא **mâ'** (Chald.) *maw;* corresp. to 4100; (as indef.) *that:*—+ what.

3965. מַאֲבוּס **maᵉăbûwç**, *mah-ab-ooce';* from 75; a *granary:*—storehouse.

3966. מְאֹד **mᵉ'ôd**, *meh-ode';* from the same as 181; prop. *vehemence,* i.e. (with or without prep.) *vehemently;* by impl. *wholly, speedily,* etc. (often with other words as an intensive or superlative; espec. when repeated):—diligently, especially, exceeding (-ly), far, fast, good, great (-ly), × louder and louder, might (-ily, -y), (so) much, quickly, (so) sore, utterly, very (+ much, sore), well.

3967. מֵאָה **mê'âh**, *may-aw';* or

מֵאיָה **mê'yâh**, *may-yaw';* prob. a prim. numeral; a *hundred;* also as a multiplicative and a fraction:—hundred ([-fold], -th), + sixscore.

3968. מֵאָה **Mê'âh**, *may-aw';* the same as 3967; *Meäh,* a tower in Jerus.:—Meah.

3969. מְאָה **mᵉ'âh** (Chald.), *meh-aw';* corresp. to 3967:—hundred.

3970. מַאֲוַי **ma'ăvay**, *mah-av-ah'ee;* from 183; a *desire:*—desire.

מוֹאל **môw'l**. See 4136.

3971. מאוּם **m'ûwm**, *moom;* usually

מוּם **mûwm**, *moom;* as if pass. part. from an unused root prob. mean. to *stain;* a *blemish* (phys. or mor.):—blemish, blot, spot.

3972. מְאוּמָה **mᵉ'ûwmâh**, *meh-oo'-maw;* appar. a form of 3971; prop. a *speck* or *point,* i.e. (by impl.) *something;* with neg. *nothing:*—fault, + no (-ught), ought, somewhat, any ([no-]) thing.

3973. מָאוֹס **mâ'ôwç**, *maw-oce';* from 3988; *refuse:*—refuse.

3974. מָאוֹר **mâ'ôwr**, *maw-ore';* or

מָאֹר **mâ'ôr**, *maw-ore';* also (in plur.) fem.

מְאוֹרָה **mᵉ'ôwrâh**, *meh-o-raw';* or

מְאֹרָה **mᵉ'ôrâh**, *meh-o-raw';* from 215; prop. a *luminous* body or *luminary,* i.e. (abstr.) *light* (as an element); fig. *brightness,* i.e. *cheerfulness;* spec. a *chandelier:*—bright, light.

3975. מְאוּרָה **mᵉ'ûwrâh**, *meh-oo-raw';* fem. pass. part. of 215; something *lighted,* i.e. an *aperture;* by impl. a *crevice* or *hole* of a serpent):—den.

3976. מֹאזֵן **mô'zên**, *mo-zane';* from 239; (only in the dual) a pair of *scales:*—balances.

3977. מֹאזֵן **mô'zên** (Chald.) *mo-zane';* corresp. to 3976:—balances.

מֵאיָה **mê'yâh**. See 3967.

3978. מַאֲכָל **ma'ăkâl**, *mah-ak-awl';* from 398; an *eatable* (includ. provender, flesh and fruit):—food, fruit, ([bake-]) meat (-s), victual.

3979. מַאֲכֶלֶת **ma'ăkeleth**, *mah-ak-eh'-leth;* from 398; something to *eat* with, i.e. a *knife:*—knife.

3980. מַאֲכֹלֶת **ma'ăkôleth**, *mah-ak-o'-leth;* from 398; something *eaten* (by fire), i.e. *fuel:*—fuel.

3981. מַאֲמָץ **ma'ămâts**, *mah-am-awts';* from 553; *strength,* i.e. (plur.) *resources:*—force.

3982. מַאֲמַר **ma'ămar**, *mah-am-ar';* from 559; something (authoritatively) *said,* i.e. an *edict:*—commandment, decree.

3983. מֵאמַר **mê'mar** (Chald.), *may-mar';* corresp. to 3982:—appointment, word.

3984. מָאן **mâ'n** (Chald.), *mawn;* prob. from a root corresp. to 579 in the sense of an *inclosure* by sides; a *utensil:*—vessel.

3985. מָאֵן **mâ'ên**, *maw-ane';* a prim. root; to *refuse:*—refuse, × utterly.

3986. מָאֵן **mâ'ên**, *maw-ane';* from 3985; *unwilling:*—refuse.

3987. מֵאֵן **mê'ên**, *may-ane';* from 3985; *refractory:*—refuse.

3988. מָאַס **mâ'aç**, *maw-as';* a prim. root; to *spurn;* also (intrans.) to *disappear:*—abhor, cast away (off), contemn, despise, disdain, (become) loathe (-some), melt away, refuse, reject, reprobate, × utterly, vile person.

3989. מַאֲפֶה **ma'ăpheh**, *mah-af-eh';* from 644; something *baked,* i.e. a *batch:*—baken.

3990. מַאֲפֵל **ma'ăphêl**, *mah-af-ale';* from the same as 651; something *opaque:*—darkness.

3991. מַאְפֵלְיָה **ma'phêlᵉyâh**, *mah-af-ay-leh-yaw';* prol. fem. of 3990; *opaqueness:*—darkness.

3992. מָאַר **mâ'ar**, *maw-ar'*, a prim. root; to *be bitter* or (causat.) to *embitter*, i.e. *be painful:*—fretting, picking.

מָאֹר **mâ'ôr**. See 3974.

3993. מַאֲרָב **ma'ărâb**, *mah-ar-awb'*; from 693; an *ambuscade:*—lie in ambush, ambushment, lurking place, lying in wait.

3994. מְאֵרָה **meêrâh**, *meh-ay-raw'*; from 779; an *execration:*—curse.

מְאֹרָה **me'ôrâh**. See 3974.

3995. מִבְדָּלָה **mibdâlâh**, *mib-daw-law'*; from 914; a *separation*, i.e. (concr.) a *separate* place:—separate.

3996. מָבוֹא **mâbôw'**, *maw-bo'*; from 935; an *entrance* (the place or the act); spec. (with or without 8121) *sunset* or the *west;* also (adv. with prep.) *towards:*—by which came, as cometh, in coming, as men enter into, entering, entrance into, entry, where goeth, going down, + westward. Comp. 4126.

3997. מְבוֹאָה **mebôwâh**, *meb-o-aw'*; fem. of 3996; a *haven:*—entry.

3998. מְבוּכָה **mebûwkâh**, *meb-oo-kaw'*; from 943; *perplexity:*—perplexity.

3999. מַבּוּל **mabbûwl**, *mab-bool'*; from 2986 in the sense of *flowing;* a *deluge:*—flood.

4000. מָבוֹן **mâbôwn**, *maw-bone'*; from 995; *instructing:*—taught.

4001. מְבוּסָה **mebûwçâh**, *meb-oo-saw'*; from 947; a *trampling:*—treading (trodden) down (under foot).

4002. מַבּוּעַ **mabbûwa'**, *mab-boo'-ah*; from 5042; a *fountain:*—fountain, spring.

4003. מְבוּקָה **mebûwqâh**, *meb-oo-kah'*; from the same as 950; *emptiness:*—void.

4004. מִבְחוֹר **mibchôwr**, *mib-khore'*; from 977; *select*, i.e. well fortified:—choice.

4005. מִבְחָר **mibchâr**, *mib-khawr'*; from 977; *select*, i.e. best:—choice (-st), chosen.

4006. מִבְחָר **Mibchâr**, *mib-khawr'*; the same as 4005; *Mibchar*, an Isr.:—Mibhar.

4007. מַבָּט **mabbâṭ**, *mab-bawt'*; or

מֶבָּט **mebbâṭ**, *meb-bawt'*; from 5027; something *expected*, i.e. (abstr.) *expectation:*—expectation.

4008. מִבְטָא **mibṭâ'**, *mib-taw'*; from 981; a rash *utterance* (hasty vow):—(that which . . .) uttered (out of).

4009. מִבְטָח **mibṭâch**, *mib-tawkh'*; from 982; prop. a *refuge*, i.e. (obj.) *security*, or (subj.) *assurance:*—confidence, hope, sure, trust.

4010. מַבְלִיגִית **mablîygîyth**, *mab-leeg-eeth'*; from 1082; *desistance* (or rather *desolation*):—comfort self.

4011. מִבְנֶה **mibneh**, *mib-neh'*; from 1129; a *building:*—frame.

4012. מְבֻנַּי **Mebunnay**, *meb-oon-nah'ee*; from 1129; *built* up; *Mebunnai*, an Isr.:—Mebunnai.

4013. מִבְצָר **mibtsâr**, *mib-tsawr'*; also (in plur.) fem. (Dan. 11 : 15)

מִבְצָרָה **mibtsârâh**, *mib-tsaw-raw'*; from 1219; a *fortification, castle*, or *fortified* city; fig. a *defender:*—(de-, most) fenced, fortress, (most) strong (hold).

4014. מִבְצָר **Mibtsâr**, *mib-tsawr'*; the same as 4013; *Mibtsar*, an Idumæan:—Mibzar.

מִבְצָרָה **mibtsârâh**. See 4013.

4015. מִבְרָח **mibrâch**, *mib-rawkh'*; from 1272; a *refugee:*—fugitive.

4016. מָבֻשׁ **mâbûsh**, *maw-boosh'*; from 954; (plur.) the (male) *pudenda:*—secrets.

4017. מִבְשָׂם **Mibsâm**, *mib-sawm'*, from the same as 1314; *fragrant; Mibsam*, the name of an Ishmaelite and of an Isr.:—Mibsam.

4018. מְבַשְּׁלָה **mebashshelâh**, *meb-ash-shel-aw'*; from 1310; a cooking *hearth:*—boiling-place.

מָג **Mâg**. See 7248. 7249.

4019. מַגְבִּישׁ **Magbîysh**, *mag-beesh'*; from the same as 1378; *stiffening; Magbish*, an Isr., or a place in Pal.:—Magbish.

4020. מִגְבָּלָה **migbâlâh**, *mig-baw-law'*; from 1379; a *border:*—end.

4021. מִגְבָּעָה **migbâ'âh**, *mig-baw-aw'*; from the same as 1389; a *cap* (as *hemispherical*):—bonnet.

4022. מֶגֶד **meged**, *meh'-ghed*; from an unused root prop. mean. to *be eminent;* prop. a *distinguished* thing; hence something *valuable*, as a product or fruit:—pleasant, precious fruit (thing).

4023. מְגִדּוֹן **Megiddôwn** (Zech. 12 : 11), *meg-id-dōne'*; or

מְגִדּוֹ **Megiddôw**, *meg-id-do'*; from 1413; *rendezvous; Megiddon* or *Megiddo*, a place in Pal.:—Megiddo, Megiddon.

4024. מִגְדּוֹל **Migdôwl**, *mig-dole'*; or

מִגְדֹּל **Migdôl**, *mig-dole'*; prob. of Eg. or.; *Migdol*, a place in Eg.:—Migdol, tower.

4025. מַגְדִּיאֵל **Magdîy'êl**, *mag-dee-ale'*; from 4022 and 410; *preciousness of God; Magdiël*, an Idumæan:—Magdiel.

4026. מִגְדָּל **migdâl**, *mig-dawl'*; also (in plur.) fem.

מִגְדָּלָה **migdâlâh**, *mig-daw-law'*; from 1431; a *tower* (from its size or height); by anal. a *rostrum;* fig. a (pyramidal) *bed* of flowers:—castle, flower, pulpit, tower. Comp. the names following.

מִגְדֹּל **Migdôl**. See 4024.

מִגְדָּלָה **migdâlâh**. See 4026.

4027. מִגְדַּל־אֵל **Migdal-'Êl**, *mig-dal-ale'*; from 4026 and 410· *tower of God; Migdal-El*, a place in Pal.:—Migdal-el.

4028. מִגְדַּל־גָּד **Migdal-Gâd**, *migdal-gawd'*; from 4026 and 1408; *tower of Fortune; Migdal-Gad*, a place in Pal.:—Migdal-gad.

4029. מִגְדַּל־עֵדֶר **Migdal-'Êder**, *mig-dal'-ay'-der;* from 4026 and 5739; *tower of a flock; Migdal-Eder*, a place in Pal.:—Migdal-eder, tower of the flock.

4030. מִגְדָּנָה **migdânâh**, *mig-daw-naw'*; from the same as 4022; *preciousness*, i.e. a *gem:*—precious thing, present.

4031. מָגוֹג **Mâgôwg**, *maw-gogue'*; from 1463; *Magog*, a son of Japheth; also a barbarous northern region:—Magog.

4032. מָגוֹר **mâgôwr**, *maw-gore'*; or (Lam. 2 : 22)

מָגוּר **mâgûwr**, *maw-goor'*; from 1481 in the sense of *fearing;* a *fright* (obj. or subj.):—fear, terror. Comp. 4036.

4033. מָגוּר **mâgûwr**, *maw-goor'*; or

מָגֻר **mâgûr**, *maw-goor'*; from 1481 in the sense of *lodging;* a temporary *abode;* by extens. a permanent *residence:*—dwelling, pilgrimage, where sojourn, be a stranger. Comp. 4032.

4034. מְגוֹרָה **megôwrâh**, *meg-o-raw'*; fem. of 4032; *affright:*—fear.

4035. מְגוּרָה **megûwrâh**, *meg-oo-raw'*; fem. of 4032 or of 4033; a *fright;* also a *granary:*—barn, fear.

4036. מָגוֹר מִסָּבִיב **Mâgôwr miç-Çâbîyb**, *maw-gore' mis-saw-beeb'*; from 4032 and 5439 with the prep. inserted; *affright from around; Magor-mis-Sabib*, a symbol. name of Pashur:—Magor-missabib.

4037. מַגְזֵרָה **magzêrâh**, *mag-zay-raw'*; from 1504; a *cutting* implement, i.e. a *blade:*—axe.

4038. מַגָּל **maggâl**, *mag-gawl'*; from an unused root mean. to *reap;* a *sickle:*—sickle.

4039. מְגִלָּה **megillâh**, *meg-il-law'*; from 1556; a *roll:*—roll, volume.

4040. מְגִלָּה **megillâh** (Chald.), *meg-il-law'*; corresp. to 4039:—roll.

4041. מְגַמָּה **megammâh**, *meg-am-maw'*; from the same as 1571; prop. *accumulation*, i.e. *impulse* or *direction:*—sup up.

4042. מָגַן **mâgan**, *maw-gan'*; a denom. from 4043; prop. to *shield;* encompass with; fig. to *rescue*, to *hand* safely *over* (i.e. *surrender*):—deliver.

4043. מָגֵן **mâgên**, *maw-gane'*; also (in plur.) fem.

מְגִנָּה **meginnâh**, *meg-in-naw'*; from 1598; a *shield* (i.e. the small one or *buckler*); fig. a *protector;* also the scaly *hide* of the crocodile:—× armed, buckler, defence, ruler, + scale, shield.

4044. מְגִנָּה **meginnâh**, *meg-in-naw'*; from 4042; a *covering* (in a bad sense), i.e. *blindness* or obduracy:—sorrow. See also 4043.

4045. מִגְעֶרֶת **mig'ereth**, *mig-eh'-reth;* from 1605; *reproof* (i.e. curse):—rebuke.

4046. מַגֵּפָה **maggêphâh**, *mag-gay-faw'*; from 5062; a *pestilence;* by anal. *defeat:*—(× be) plague (-d), slaughter, stroke.

4047. מַגְפִּיעָשׁ **Magpîy'âsh**, *mag-pee-awsh'*; appar. from 1479 or 5062 and 6211; *exterminator of* (the) *moth; Magpiash*, an Isr.:—Magpiash.

4048. מָגַר **mâgar**, *maw-gar'*; a prim. root; to *yield up;* intens. to *precipitate:*—cast down, terror.

4049. מְגַר **megar** (Chald.), *meg-ar'*; corresp. to 4048; to *overthrow:*—destroy.

4050. מְגֵרָה **megêrâh**, *meg-ay-raw'*; from 1641; a *saw:*—axe, saw.

4051. מִגְרוֹן **Migrôwn**, *mig-rone'*; from 4048; *precipice; Migron*, a place in Pal.:—Migron.

4052. מִגְרָעָה **migrâ'âh**, *mig-raw-aw'*; from 1639; a *ledge* or offset:—narrowed rest.

4053. מִגְרָפָה **migrâphâh**, *mig-raw-faw'*; from 1640; something *thrown off* (by the spade), i.e. a *clod:*—clod.

4054. מִגְרָשׁ **migrâsh**, *mig-rawsh'*; also (in plur.) fem. (Ezek. 27 : 28)

מִגְרָשָׁה **migrâshâh**, *mig-raw-shaw'*; from 1644; a *suburb* (i.e. open country whither flocks are *driven* for pasture); hence the *area* around a building, or the *margin* of the sea:—cast out, suburb.

4055. מַד **mad**, *mad;* or

מֵד **mêd**, *made;* from 4058; prop. *extent*, i.e. *height;* also a *measure;* by impl. a *vesture* (as measured); also a *carpet:*—armour, clothes, garment, judgment, measure, raiment, stature.

4056. מַדְבַּח **madbach** (Chald.), *mad-bakh'*; from 1684; a sacrificial *altar:*—altar.

4057. מִדְבָּר **midbâr**, *mid-bawr'*; from 1696 in the sense of *driving;* a *pasture* (i.e. open field, whither cattle are driven); by impl. a *desert;* also *speech* (including its organs):—desert, south, speech, wilderness.

4058. מָדַד **mâdad**, *maw-dad'*; a prim. root; prop. to *stretch;* by impl. to *measure* (as if by *stretching* a line); fig. to *be extended:*—measure, mete, stretch self.

4059. מִדַּד **middad**, *mid-dad'*; from 5074; *flight:*—be gone.

4060. מִדָּה **middâh**, *mid-daw'*; fem. of 4055; prop. *extension*, i.e. height or breadth; also a *measure* (including its standard); hence a *portion* (as measured) or a *vestment;* spec. *tribute* (as measured):—garment, measure (-ing, meteyard, piece, size, (great) stature, tribute, wide.

4061. מִדָּה **middâh** (Chald.), *mid-daw'*; or

מִנְדָּה **mindâh** (Chald.), *min-daw'*; corresp. to 4060; *tribute* in money:—toll, tribute.

4062. מַדְהֵבָה **madhêbâh**, *mad-hay-baw'*; perh. from the equiv. of 1722; *gold-making*, i.e. *exactress:*—golden city.

4063. מֶדֶו **medev**, *meh'-dev;* from an unused root mean. to *stretch;* prop. *extent*, i.e. *measure;* by impl. a *dress* (as measured):—garment.

4064. מַדְוֶה **madveh**, *mad-veh'*; from 1738; *sickness:*—disease.

4065. מַדּוּחַ **maddûwach**, *mad-doo'-akh;* from 5080; *seduction:*—cause of banishment.

4066. מָדוֹן **mâdôwn**, *maw-dohn'*; from 1777; a *contest* or quarrel:—brawling, contention (-ous), discord, strife. Comp. 4079, 4090.

4067. מָדוֹן **mâdôwn**, *maw-dohn'*; from the same as 4063; *extensiveness*, i.e. height:—stature.

4068. מָדוֹן **Mâdôwn**, *maw-dohn'*; the same as 4067; *Madon*, a place in Pal.:—Madon.

4069. מַדּוּעַ **maddûwaʿ**, *mad-doo'-ah*; or

מַדֻּעַ **maddûaʿ**, *mad-doo'-ah*; from 4100 and the pass. part. of 3045; *what* (is) *known?*; i.e. (by impl.) (adv.) *why?*:—how, wherefore, why.

4070. מְדוֹר **meᵉdôwr** Chald.), *med-ore'*; or

מְדֹר **meᵉdôr** (Chald.), *med-ore'*; or

מְדָר **meᵉdâr** (Chald.), *med-awr'*; from 1753; a *dwelling*:—dwelling.

4071. מְדוּרָה **meᵉdûwrâh**, *med-oo-raw'*; or

מְדֻרָה **meᵉdûrâh**, *med-oo-raw'*; from 1752 in the sense of *accumulation*; a *pile* of fuel:—pile (for fire).

4072. מִדְחֶה **midcheh**, *mid-kheh'*; from 1760; *overthrow*:—ruin.

4073. מְדַחְפָה **meᵉdachphâh**, *med-akh-faw'*; from 1765; a *push*, i.e. ruin:—overthrow.

4074. מָדַי **Mâday**, *maw-dah'ee*; of for. der.; *Madai*, a country of central Asia:—Madai, Medes, Media.

4075. מָדַי **Mâday**, *maw-dah'ee*; patrial from 4074; a *Madian* or native of Madai:—Mede.

4076. מָדַי **Mâday** (Chald.), *maw-dah'ee*; corresp. to 4074:—Mede (-s).

4077. מָדַי **Mâday** (Chald.), *maw-dah'ee*; corresp. to 4075:—Median.

4078. מַדַּי **madday**, *mad-dah'ee*; from 4100 and 1767; *what* (is) *enough*, i.e. *sufficiently*:—sufficiently.

4079. מִדְיָן **midyân**, *mid-yawn'*; a var. for 4066:—brawling, contention (-ous).

4080. מִדְיָן **Midyân** ,*mid-yawn'*; the same as 4079; *Midjan*, a son of Abraham; also his country and (collect.) his descend.:—Midian, Midianite.

4081. מִדִּין **Middiyn**, *mid-deen'*, a var. for 4080: Middin.

4082. מְדִינָה **meᵉdîynâh**, *med-ee-naw'*; from 1777; prop. a *judgeship*, i.e. *jurisdiction*; by impl. a *district* (as ruled by a judge); gen. a *region*:—(× every) province.

4083. מְדִינָה **meᵉdîynâh** (Chald.), *med-ee-naw'*; corresp. to 4082:—province.

4084. מִדְיָנִי **Midyânîy**, *mid-yaw-nee'*; patron. or patrial from 4080; a *Midjanite* or descend. (native) of Midjan:—Midianite. Comp. 4092.

4085. מְדֹכָה **meᵉdôkâh**, *med-o-kaw'*; from 1743; a *mortar*:—mortar.

4086. מַדְמֵן **Madmên**, *mad-mane'*; from the same as 1828; *dunghill*; *Madmen*, a place in Pal.:—Madmen.

4087. מַדְמֵנָה **madmênâh**, *mad-may-naw'*; fem. from the same as 1828; a *dunghill*:—dunghill.

4088. מַדְמֵנָה **Madmênâh**, *mad-may-naw'*; the same as 4087; *Madmenah*, a place in Pal.:—Madmenah.

4089. מַדְמַנָּה **Madmannâh**, *mad-man-naw'*; a var. for 4087; *Madmannah*, a place in Pal.:—Madmannah.

4090. מְדָן **meᵉdân**, *med-awn'*; a form of 4066:—discord, strife.

4091. מְדָן **Meᵉdân**, *med-awn'*; the same as 4090; *Medan*, a son of Abraham:—Medan.

4092. מְדָנִי **Meᵉdânîy**, *med-aw-nee'*; a var. of 4084:—Midianite.

4093. מַדָּע **maddâʿ**, *mad-daw'*; or

מַדַּע **maddaʿ**, *mad-dah'*; from 3045; *intelligence* or *consciousness*:—knowledge, science, thought.

מֹדָע **môdâʿ**. See 4129.

מַדֻּעַ **madûaʿ**. See 4069.

4094. מַדְקָרָה **madqârâh**, *mad-kaw-raw'*; from 1856; a *wound*:—piercing.

מְדֹר **meᵉdôr**. See 4070.

4095. מַדְרֵגָה **madrêgâh**, *mad-ray-gaw'*; from an unused root mean. to *step*; prop. a *step*; by impl. a *steep* or inaccessible place:—stair, steep place.

מְדֻרָה **meᵉdûrâh**. See 4071.

4096. מִדְרָךְ **midrâk**, *mid-rawk'*; from 1869; a *treading*, i.e. a place for stepping on:—[foot-] breadth.

4097. מִדְרָשׁ **midrâsh**, *mid-rawsh'*; from 1875; prop. an *investigation*, i.e. (by impl.) a *treatise* or elaborate compilation:—story.

4098. מְדֻשָּׁה **meᵉdushshâh**, *med-oosh-shaw'*; from 1758; a *threshing*, i.e. (concr. and fig.) *down-trodden* people:—threshing.

4099. מְדָתָא **Meᵉdâthâ**, *med-aw-thaw'*; of Pers. or.; *Medatha*, the father of Haman:—Hammedatha [*includ. the art.*].

4100. מָה **mâh**, *maw*; or מַה **mah**, *mah*; or מָ־ **mâ**, *maw*; or מַ־ **ma**, *mah*; also מֶה **meh**, *meh*; a prim. particle; prop. interrog. *what?* (includ. *how? why? when?*); but also exclam. *what!* (includ. *how!*), or indef. *what* (includ. *whatever*, and even rel. *that which*); often used with prefixes in various adv. or conj. senses:—how (long, oft, [-soever]), [no-] thing, what (end, good, purpose, thing), whereby (-fore, -in, -to, -with), (for) why.

4101. מָה **mâh** (Chald.), *maw*; corresp. to 4100:—how great (mighty), that which, what (-soever), why.

4102. מָהַהּ **mâhahh**, *maw-hah'*; appar. a denom. from 4100; prop. to *question* or hesitate, i.e. (by impl.) to *be reluctant*:—delay, linger, stay selves, tarry.

4103. מְהוּמָה **meᵉhûwmâh**, *meh-hoo-maw'*; from 1949; *confusion* or uproar:—destruction, discomfiture, trouble, tumult, vexation, vexed.

4104. מְהוּמָן **Meᵉhûwmân**, *meh-hoo-mawn'*; of Pers. or.; *Mehuman*, a eunuch of Xerxes:—Mehuman.

4105. מְהֵיטַבְאֵל **Meᵉhêyṭabʼêl**, *meh-hay-tab-ale'*; from 3190 (augmented) and 410; *bettered of God*; *Mehetabel*, the name of an Edomitish man and woman:—Mehetabeel, Mehetabel.

4106. מָהִיר **mâhîyr**, *maw-here'*; or

מָהִר **mâhîr**, *maw-here'*; from 4116; *quick*; hence *skilful*:—diligent, hasty, ready.

4107. מָהַל **mâhal**, *maw-hal'*; a prim. root; prop. to *cut down* or *reduce*, i.e. by impl. to *adulterate*:—mixed.

4108. מַהְלֵךְ **mahlêk**, *mah-lake'*; from 1980; a *walking* (plur. collect.), i.e. *access*:—place to walk.

4109. מַהֲלָךְ **mahălâk**, *mah-hal-awk'*; from 1980; a *walk*, i.e. a *passage* or a *distance*:—journey, walk.

4110. מַהֲלָל **mahălâl**, *mah-hal-awl'*; from 1984; *fame*:—praise.

4111. מַהֲלַלְאֵל **Mahălalʼêl**, *mah-hal-al-ale'*; from 4110 and 410; *praise of God*; *Mahalalel*, the name of an antediluvian patriarch and of an Isr.:—Mahalaleel.

4112. מַהֲלֻמָּה **mahălummâh**, *mah-hal-oom-maw'*; from 1986; a *blow*:—stripe, stroke.

4113. מַהֲמֹרָה **mahămôrâh**, *mah-ham-o-raw'*; from an unused root of uncert. mean.; perh. an *abyss*:—deep pit.

4114. מַהְפֵּכָה **mahpêkâh**, *mah-pay-kaw'*; from 2015; a *destruction*:—when ... overthrew, overthrow (-n).

4115. מַהְפֶּכֶת **mahpeketh**, *mah-peh'-keth*; from 2015; a *wrench*, i.e. the *stocks*:—prison, stocks.

4116. מָהַר **mâhar**, *maw-har'*; a prim. root; prop. to *be liquid* or *flow* easily, i.e. (by impl.); *to hurry* (in a good or a bad sense); often used (with another verb) adv. *promptly*:—be carried headlong, fearful, (cause to make, in, make) haste (-n, -ily, (be) hasty, (fetch, make ready) × quickly, rash, × shortly, (be so) × soon, make speed, × speedily, × straightway, × suddenly, swift.

4117. מָהַר **mâhar**, *maw-har'*; a prim. root (perh. rather the same as 4116 through the idea of *readiness* in assent): to *bargain* (for a wife), i.e. to *wed*:—endow, × surely.

4118. מַהֵר **mahêr**, *mah-hare'*; from 4116; prop. *hurrying*; hence (adv.) *in a hurry*:—hasteth, hastily, at once, quickly, soon, speedily, suddenly.

מָהִר **mâhîr**. See 4106.

4119. מֹהַר **môhar**, *mo'-har*; from 4117; a *price* (for a wife):—dowry.

4120. מְהֵרָה **meᵉhêrâh**, *meh-hay-raw'*; fem. of 4118; prop. a *hurry*; hence (adv.) *promptly*:—hastily, quickly, shortly, soon, make (with) speed (-ily), swiftly.

4121. מַהֲרַי **Mahăray**, *mah-har-ah'ee*; from 4116; *hasty*; *Maharai*, an Isr.:—Maharai.

4122. מַהֵר שָׁלָל חָשׁ בַּז **Mahêr Shâlâl Châsh Baz**, *mah-hare' shaw-lawl' khawsh baz*; from 4118 and 7998 and 2363 and 957; *hasting* (is he [the enemy] to the) *booty*, *swift* (to the) *prey*; *Maher-Shalal-Chash-Baz*; the symbol. name of the son of Isaiah:—Maher-shalal-hash-baz.

4123. מַהֲתַלָּה **mahăthallâh**, *mah-hath-al-law'*; from 2048; a *delusion*:—deceit.

4124. מוֹאָב **Môwʼâb**, *mo-awb*; from a prol. form of the prep. pref. *m-* and 1; *from* (her [the mother's]) *father*; *Moäb*, an incestuous son of Lot; also his territory and desc.:—Moab.

4125. מוֹאָבִי **Môwʼâbîy**, *mo-aw-bee'*; fem.

מוֹאָבִיָּה **Môwʼâbîyah**, *mo-aw-bee-yaw'*; or

מוֹאָבִית **Môwâbîyth**, *mo-aw-beeth'*; patron. from 4124; a *Moäbite* or *Moäbitess*, i.e. a desc. from Moab:—(woman) of Moab, Moabite (-ish, -ss).

מוֹאל **môwʼl**. See 4136.

4126. מוֹבָא **môwbâʼ**, *mo-baw'*; by transp. for 3996; an *entrance*:—coming.

4127. מוּג **mûwg**, *moog*; a prim. root; to *melt*, i.e. lit. (to *soften*, flow down, *disappear*), or fig. (to *fear*, *faint*):—consume, dissolve, (be) faint (-hearted), melt (away), make soft.

4128. מוּד **mûwd**, *mood*; a prim. root; to *shake*:—measure.

4129. מוֹדַע **môwdaʿ**, *mo-dah'*; or rather

מֹדָע **môdâʿ**, *mo-daw'*; from 3045; an *acquaintance*:—kinswoman.

4130. מוֹדַעַת **môwdaʻath**, *mo-dah'-ath*; from 3045; *acquaintance*:—kindred.

4131. מוֹט **môwṭ**, *mote*; a prim. root; to *waver*, by impl. to *slip*, *shake*, *fall*:—be carried, cast, be out of course, be fallen in decay, × exceedingly, fall (-ing down), be (re-) moved, be ready shake, slide, slip.

4132. מוֹט **môwṭ**, *mote*; from 4131; a *wavering*, i.e. *fall*; by impl. a *pole* (as shaking): hence a *yoke* (as essentially a bent pole):—bar, be moved, staff, yoke.

4133. מוֹטָה **môwṭâh**, *mo-taw'*; fem. of 4131; a *pole*; by impl. an *ox-bow*; hence a *yoke* (either lit. or fig.):—bands, heavy, staves, yoke.

4134. מוּךְ **mûwk**, *mook*; a prim. root; to *become thin*, i.e. (fig.) *be impoverished*:—be (waxen) poor (-er).

4135. מוּל **mûwl**, *mool*; a prim. root; to *cut* short, i.e. *curtail* (spec. the prepuce, i.e. to *circumcise*); by impl. to *blunt*; fig. to *destroy*:—circumcise (-ing, selves), cut down (in pieces), destroy, × must needs.

4136. מוּל **mûwl**, *mool*; or
מוֹל **môwl** (Deut. 1 : 1), *mole*; or
מוֹאל **môwʼl** (Neh. 12 : 38), *mole*; or
מֻל **mûl** (Num. 22 : 5), *mool*; from 4135; prop. *abrupt*, i.e. a *precipice*; by impl. the *front*; used only adv. (with prep. pref.) *opposite*:—(over) against, before, [fore-] front, from, [God-] ward, toward, with.

4137. מוֹלָדָה **Môwlâdâh**, *mo-law-daw'*; from 3205; *birth*; *Moladah*, a place in Pal.:—Moladah.

4138. מוֹלֶדֶת **môwledeth**, *mo-leh'-deth*; from 3205; *nativity* (plur. *birth-place*); by impl. *lineage*, *native country*; also *offspring*, *family*:—begotten, born, issue, kindred, native (-ity).

4139. מוּלָה **mûwlâh**, *moo-law'*; from 4135; *circumcision*:—circumcision.

4140. מוֹלִיד **Môwlîyd**, *mo-leed'*; from 3205; *genitor*; *Molid*, an Isr.:—Molid.
מוּם **muwm**. See 3971.
°מוּמְכָן **Môwmûkân**. See 4462.

4141. מוּסָב **mûwçâb**, *moo-sawb'*; from 5437; a *turn*, i.e. *circuit* (of a building):—winding about.

4142. מוּסַבָּה **mûwçabbâh**, *moo-sab-baw'*; or
מֻסַבָּה **mûçabbâh**, *moo-sab-baw'*; fem. of 4141; a *reversal*, i.e. the *backside* (of a gem), *fold* (of a double-leaved door), *transmutation* (of a name):—being changed, inclosed, be set, turning.

4143. מוּסָד **mûwçâd**, *moo-sawd'*; from 3245; a *foundation*:—foundation.

4144. מוֹסָד **môwçâd**, *mo-sawd'*; from 3245; a *foundation*:—foundation.

4145. מוּסָדָה **mûwçâdâh**, *moo-saw-daw'*; fem. of 4143; a *foundation*; fig. an *appointment*:—foundation, grounded. Comp. 4328.

4146. מוֹסָדָה **môwçâdâh**, *mo-saw-daw'*; or
מֹסָדָה **môçâdâh** *mo-saw-daw'*; fem. of 4144; a *foundation*:—foundation.

4147. מוֹסֵר **môwçêr**, *mo-sare'*; also (in plur.) fem.
מוֹסֵרָה **môwçêrâh**, *mo-say-raw'*; or
מֹסְרָה **môçᵉrâh**, *mo-ser-aw'*; from 3256; prop. *chastisement*, i.e. (by impl.) a *halter*; fig. *restraint*:—band, bond.

4148. מוּסָר **mûwçâr**, *moo-sawr'*; from 3256; prop. *chastisement*; fig. *reproof*, *warning* or *instruction*; also *restraint*:—bond, chastening ([-eth]), chastisement, check, correction, discipline, doctrine, instruction, rebuke.

4149. מוֹסֵרָה **Môwçêrâh**, *mo-say-raw'*; or (plur.)
מֹסְרוֹת **Môçᵉrôwth**, *mo-ser-othe'*; fem. of 4147; *correction* or *corrections*; *Moserah* or *Moseroth*, a place in the Desert:—Mosera, Moseroth.

4150. מוֹעֵד **môwʻêd**, *mo-ade'*; or
מֹעֵד **môʻêd** *mo-ade'*; or (fem.)
מוֹעָדָה **môwʻâdâh** (2 Chron. 8 : 13), *mo-aw-daw'*; from 3259; prop. an *appointment*, i.e. a fixed *time* or season; spec. a *festival*; conventionally a *year*; by implication, an *assembly* (as convened for a definite purpose); technically the *congregation*; by extension, the *place of meeting*; also a *signal* (as appointed beforehand):—appointed (sign, time), (place of, solemn) assembly, congregation, (set, solemn) feast, (appointed, due) season, solemn (-ity), synagogue, (set) time (appointed).

4151. מוֹעָד **môwʻâd**, *mo-awd'*; from 3259; prop. an *assembly* [as in 4150]; fig. a *troop*:—appointed time.

4152. מוּעָדָה **mûwʻâdâh**, *moo-aw-daw'*; from 3259; an *appointed* place, i.e. *asylum*:—appointed.

4153. מוֹעַדְיָה **Môwʻadyâh**, *mo-ad-yaw'*; from 4151 and 3050; *assembly of Jah*; *Moădjah*, an Isr.:—Moadiah. Comp. 4573.

4154. מוּעֶדֶת **mûwʻedeth**, *moo-ay'-deth*; fem. pass. part. of 4571; prop. *made to slip*, i.e. *dislocated*:—out of joint.

4155. מוּעָף **mûwʻâph**, *moo-awf'*; from 5774; prop. *covered*, i.e. *dark*; abstr. *obscurity*, i.e. *distress*:—dimness.

4156. מוֹעֵצָה **môwʻêtsâh**, *mo-ay-tsaw'*; from 3289; a *purpose*:—counsel, device.

4157. מוּעָקָה **mûwʻâqâh**, *moo-aw-kaw'*; from 5781; *pressure*, i.e. (fig.) *distress*:—affliction.

4158. °מוֹפַעַת **Môwphaʻath** (Jer. 48 : 21), *mo-fah'-ath*; or
מֵיפַעַת **mêyphaath**, *may-fah'-ath*; or
מֵפַעַת **mêphaath**, *may-fah'-ath*; from 3313; *illuminative*; *Mophaath* or *Mephaath*, a place in Pal.:—Mephaath.

4159. מוֹפֵת **môwphêth**, *mo-faith'*; or
מֹפֵת **môphêth**, *mo-faith'*; from 3302 in the sense of *conspicuousness*; a *miracle*; by impl. a *token* or *omen*:—miracle, sign, wonder (-ed at).

4160. מוּץ **mûwts**, *moots*; a prim. root; to *press*, i.e. (fig.) to *oppress*:—extortioner.

4161. מוֹצָא **môwtsâʼ**, *mo-tsaw'*; or
מֹצָא **môtsâʼ**, *mo-tsaw'*; from 3318; a *going forth*, i.e. (the act) an *egress*, or (the place) an *exit*; hence a *source* or *product*; spec. *dawn*, the *rising* of the sun (the *East*), *exportation*, *utterance*, a *gate*, a *fountain*, a *mine*, a *meadow* (as producing grass):—brought out, bud, that which came out, east, going forth, goings out, that which (thing that) is gone out, outgoing, proceeded out, spring, vein, [water-] course [springs].

4162. מוֹצָא **môwtsâʼ**, *mo-tsaw'*; the same as 4161; *Motsa*, the name of two Isr.:—Moza.

4163. מוֹצָאָה **môwtsâʼâh**, *mo-tsaw-aw'*; fem. of 4161; a family *descent*; also a *sewer* [marg.; comp. 6675]:—draught house; going forth.

4164. מוּצַק **mûwtsaq**, *moo-tsak'*; or
מוּצָק **mûwtsâq**, *moo-tsawk'*; from 3332; *narrowness*; fig. *distress*:—anguish, is straitened, straitness.

4165. מוּצָק **mûwtsâq**, *moo-tsawk'*; from 5694; prop. *fusion*, i.e. lit. a *casting* (of metal); fig. a *mass* (of clay):—casting, hardness.

4166. מוּצָקָה **mûwtsâqâh**, *moo-tsaw-kaw'*; or
מֻצָקָה **mûtsâqâh**, *moo-tsaw-kaw'*; from 3332; prop. something *poured* out, i.e. a *casting* (of metal); by impl. a *tube* (as cast):—when it was cast, pipe.

4167. מוּק **mûwq**, *mook*; a prim. root; to *jeer*, i.e. (intens.) *blaspheme*:—be corrupt.

4168. מוֹקֵד **môwqêd**, *mo-kade'*; from 3344; a *fire* or *fuel*; abstr. a *conflagration*:—burning, hearth.

4169. °מוֹקְדָה **môwqᵉdâh**, *mo-ked-aw'*; fem. of 4168; *fuel*:—burning.

4170. מוֹקֵשׁ **môwqêsh**, *mo-kashe'*; or
מֹקֵשׁ **môqêsh**, *mo-kashe'*; from 3369; a *noose* (for catching animals) (lit. or fig.); by impl. a *hook* (for the nose):—be ensnared, gin, (is) snare (-d), trap.

4171. מוּר **mûwr**, *moor*; a prim. root; to *alter*; by impl. to *barter*, to *dispose of*:—× at all, (ex-) change, remove.

4172. מוֹרָא **môwrâʼ**, *mo-raw'*; or
מֹרָא **môrâʼ**, *mo-raw'*; or
מֹרָה **môrâh** (Psa. 9 : 20), *mo-raw'*; from 3372; *fear*; by impl. a *fearful* thing or deed:—dread, (that ought to be) fear (-ed), terribleness, terror.

4173. מוֹרַג **môwrag**, *mo-rag'*; or
מֹרַג **môrag**, *mo-rag'*; from an unused root mean. to *triturate*; a threshing *sledge*:—threshing instrument.

4174. מוֹרָד **môwrâd**, *mo-rawd'*; from 3381; a *descent*; arch. an ornamental *appendage*, perh. a *festoon*:—going down, steep place, thin work.

4175. מוֹרֶה **môwreh**, *mo-reh'*; from 3384; an *archer*; also *teacher* or *teaching*; also the *early rain* [see 3138]:—(early) rain.

4176. מוֹרֶה **Môwreh**, *mo-reh'*; or
מֹרֶה **Môreh**, *mo-reh'*; the same as 4175; *Moreh*, a Canaanite; also a hill (perh. named from him):—Moreh.

4177. מוֹרָה **môwrâh**, *mo-raw'*; from 4171 in the sense of *shearing*; a *razor*:—razor.

4178. מוֹרָט **môwrâṭ**, *mo-rawt'*; from 3399; *obstinate*, i.e. independent:—peeled.

4179. מוֹרִיָּה **Môwrîyâh**, *mo-ree-yaw'*; or
מֹרִיָּה **Môrîyâh**, *mo-ree-yaw'*; from 7200 and 3050; *seen of Jah*; *Morijah*, a hill in Pal.:—Moriah.

4180. מוֹרָשׁ **môwrâsh**, *mo-rawsh'*; from 3423; a *possession*; fig. *delight*:—possession, thought.

4181. מוֹרָשָׁה **môwrâshâh**, *mo-raw-shaw'*; fem. of 4180; a *possession*:—heritage, inheritance, possession.

4182. מוֹרֶשֶׁת גַּת **Môwresheth Gath**, *mo-reh'-sheth gath*; from 3423 and 1661; *possession of Gath*; *Moresheth-Gath*, a place in Pal.:—Moresheth-gath.

4183. מוֹרַשְׁתִּי **Morashtîy**, *mo-rash-tee'*; patrial from 4182; a *Morashtite* or inhab. of Moresheth-Gath:—Morashthite.

4184. מוּשׁ **mûwsh**, *moosh*; a prim. root; to *touch*:—feel, handle.

4185. מוּשׁ **mûwsh**, *moosh*; a prim. root [perh. rather the same as 4184 through the idea of receding by *contact*]; to *withdraw* (both lit. and fig., whether intrans. or trans.):—cease, depart, go back, remove, take away.

4186. מוֹשָׁב **môwshâb**, *mo-shawb'*; or
מֹשָׁב **môshâb**, *mo-shawb'*; from 3427; a *seat*; fig. a *site*; abstr. a *session*; by extension an *abode* (the place or the time); by impl. *population*:—assembly, dwell in, dwelling (-place), wherein (that) dwelt (in), inhabited place, seat, sitting, situation, sojourning.

4187. מוּשִׁי **Mûwshîy**, *moo-shee'*; or
מֻשִּׁי **Mushshîy**, *mush-shee'*; from 4184; *sensitive*; *Mushi*, a Levite:—Mushi.

4188. מוּשִׁי **Mûwshîy**, *moo-shee'*; patron. from 4187; a *Mushite* (collect.) or desc. of Mushi:—Mushites.

4189. מוֹשְׁכָה **môwshᵉkâh**, *mo-shek-aw'*; act part. fem. of 4900; something *drawing*, i.e. (fig.) a *cord*:—band.

4190. מוֹשָׁעָה **môwshâʻâh**, *mo-shaw-aw'*; from 3467; *deliverance*:—salvation.

4191. מוּת **mûwth**, *mooth*; a prim. root; to *die* (lit. or fig.); causat. to *kill*:—× at all, × crying, (be) dead (body, man, one), (put to, worthy of) death, destroy (-er), (cause to, be like to, must) die, kill, necro [-mancer], × must needs, slay, × surely, × very suddenly, × in [no] wise.

4192. מוּת **Mûwth** (Psa. 48 : 14), *mooth;* or
מוּת לַבֵּן **Mûwth lab-bên**, *mooth lab-bane';* from 4191 and 1121 with the prep. and art. interposed; "*To die for the son*", prob. the title of a popular song:—death, Muth-labben.

4193. מוֹת **môwth** (Chald.), *mohth;* corresp. to 4194; *death:*—death.

4194. מָוֶת **mâveth**, *maw'-veth;* from 4191; *death* (nat. or violent); concr. the *dead*, their place or state (*hades*); fig. *pestilence, ruin:*—(be) dead ([-ly]), death, die (-d).

מוּת לַבֵּן **Mûwth lab-bên.** See 4192.

4195. מוֹתָר **môwthar**, *mo-thar';* from 3498; lit. *gain;* fig. *superiority:*—plenteousness, preeminence, profit.

4196. מִזְבֵּחַ **mizbêach**, *miz-bay'-akh;* from 2076; an *altar:*—altar.

4197. מֶזֶג **mezeg**, *meh'-zeg;* from an unused root mean. to *mingle* (water with wine); *tempered* wine:—liquor.

4198. מָזֶה **mâzeh**, *maw-zeh';* from an unused root mean. to *suck* out; *exhausted:*—burnt.

4199. מִזָּה **Mizzâh**, *miz-zaw';* prob. from an unused root mean. to *faint* with fear; *terror; Mizzah*, an Edomite:—Mizzah.

4200. מֶזֶו **mezev**, *meh'-zev;* prob. from an unused root mean. to *gather* in; a *granary:*—garner.

4201. מְזוּזָה **mezûwzâh**, *mez-oo-zaw';* or
מְזֻזָה **mezûzâh**, *mez-oo-zaw';* from the same as 2123; a *door-post* (as *prominent*):—(door, side) post.

4202. מָזוֹן **mâzôwn**, *maw-zone';* from 2109; *food:*—meat, victual.

4203. מָזוֹן **mâzôwn** (Chald.), *maw-zone';* corresp. to 4202:—meat.

4204. מָזוֹר **mâzôwr**, *maw-zore';* from 2114 in the sense of *turning aside* from truth; *treachery*, i.e. a *plot:*—wound.

4205. מָזוֹר **mâzôwr**, *maw-zore';* or
מָזֹר **mâzôr**, *maw-zore';* from 2115 in the sense of *binding* up; a *bandage*, i.e. *remedy;* hence a *sore* (as needing a compress):—bound up, wound.

מְזֻזָה **mezûzâh.** See 4201.

4206. מָזִיחַ **mâzîyach**, *maw-zee'-akh;* or
מֵזַח **mêzach**, *may-zakh';* from 2118; a *belt* (as movable):—girdle, strength.

4207. מַזְלֵג **mazlêg**, *maz-layg';* or (fem.)
מִזְלָגָה **mizlâgâh**, *miz-law-gaw';* from an unused root mean. to *draw* up; a *fork:*—fleshhook.

4208. מַזָּלָה **mazzâlâh**, *maz-zaw-law';* appar. from 5140 in the sense of *raining;* a *constellation*, i.e. Zodiacal sign (perh. as affecting the weather):—planet. Comp. 4216.

4209. מְזִמָּה **mezimmâh**, *mez-im-maw';* from 2161; a *plan*, usually evil (*machination*), sometimes good (*sagacity*):—(wicked) device, discretion, intent, witty invention, lewdness, mischievous (device), thought, wickedly.

4210. מִזְמוֹר **mizmôwr**, *miz-more';* from 2167; prop. instrumental *music;* by impl. a *poem* set to notes:—psalm.

4211. מַזְמֵרָה **mazmêrâh**, *maz-may-raw';* from 2168; a *pruning-knife:*—pruning-hook.

4212. מְזַמְּרָה **mezammerâh**, *mez-am-mer-aw';* from 2168; a *tweezer* (only in the plur.):—snuffers.

4213. מִזְעָר **mizʻâr**, *miz-awr';* from the same as 2191; *fewness;* by impl. as superl. *diminutiveness:*—few, × very.

מָזֹר **mâzôr.** See 4205.

4214. מִזְרֶה **mizreh**, *miz-reh';* from 2219; a winnowing *shovel* (as scattering the chaff):—fan.

4215. מְזָרֶה **mezâreh**, *mez-aw-reh';* appar. from 2219; prop. a *scatterer*, i.e. the north *wind* (as dispersing clouds; only in plur.):—north.

4216. מַזָּרָה **mazzârâh**, *maz-zaw-raw';* appar. from 5144 in the sense of *distinction;* some noted *constellation* (only in the plur.), perh. collect. the *zodiac:*—Mazzoroth. Comp. 4208.

4217. מִזְרָח **mizrâch**, *miz-rawkh';* from 2224; *sunrise*, i.e. the *east:*—east (side, -ward), (sun-) rising (of the sun).

4218. מִזְרָע **mizrâʻ**, *miz-raw';* from 2232; a planted *field:*—thing sown.

4219. מִזְרָק **mîzrâq**, *miz-rawk';* from 2236; a *bowl* (as if for sprinkling):—bason, bowl.

4220. מֵחַ **mêach**, *may'-akh;* from 4229 in the sense of *greasing; fat;* fig. *rich:*—fatling (one).

4221. מֹחַ **môach**, *mo'-akh;* from the same as 4220; *fat*, i.e. marrow:—marrow.

4222. מָחָא **mâchâ'**, *maw-khaw';* a prim. root; to *rub* or *strike* the hands together (in exultation):—clap.

4223. מְחָא **mechâ'** (Chald.), *mekh-aw';* corresp. to 4222; to *strike* in pieces; also to *arrest;* spec. to *impale:*—hang, smite, stay.

4224. מַחֲבֵא **machăbê'**, *makh-ab-ay';* or
מַחֲבֹא **machăbô'**, *makh-ab-o';* from 2244; a *refuge:*—hiding (lurking) place.

4225. מַחְבֶּרֶת **machbereth**, *makh-beh'-reth;* from 2266; a *junction*, i.e. seam or sewed piece:—coupling.

4226. מְחַבְּרָה **mechabberâh**, *mekh-ab-ber-aw';* from 2266; a *joiner*, i.e. brace or cramp:—coupling, joining.

4227. מַחֲבַת **machăbath**, *makh-ab-ath';* from the same as 2281; a *pan* for baking in:—pan.

4228. מַחֲגֹרֶת **machăgôreth**, *makh-ag-o'-reth;* from 2296; a *girdle:*—girding.

4229. מָחָה **mâchâh**, *maw-khaw';* a prim. root; prop. to *stroke* or *rub;* by impl. to *erase;* also to *smooth* (as if with oil), i.e. *grease* or make fat; also to *touch*, i.e. reach to:—abolish, blot out, destroy, full of marrow, put out, reach unto, × utterly, wipe (away, out).

4230. מְחוּגָה **mechûwgâh**, *mekh-oo-gaw';* from 2328; an instrument for marking a circle, i.e. *compasses:*—compass.

4231. מָחוֹז **mâchôwz**, *maw-khoze';* from an unused root mean. to *enclose;* a *harbor* (as *shut* in by the shore):—haven.

4232. מְחוּיָאֵל **Mechûwyâ'êl**, *mekh-oo-yaw-ale';* or
מְחִיָּיאֵל **Mechîyyâ'êl**, *mekh-ee-yaw-ale';* from 4229 and 410; *smitten of God; Mechujael* or *Mechijael*, an antediluvian patriarch:—Mehujael.

4233. מַחֲוִים **Machăvîym**, *makh-av-eem';* appar. a patrial, but from an unknown place (in the plur. only for a sing.); a *Machavite* or inhab. of some place named Machaveh:—Mahavite.

4234. מָחוֹל **mâchôwl**, *maw-khole';* from 2342; a (round) *dance:*—dance (-cing).

4235. מָחוֹל **Mâchôwl**, *maw-khole';* the same as 4234; *dancing; Machol*, an Isr.:—Mahol.

מְחוֹלָה **mechôwlâh.** See 65, 4246.

4236. מַחֲזֶה **machăzeh**, *makh-az-eh';* from 2372; a *vision:*—vision.

4237. מֶחֱזָה **mechĕzâh**, *mekh-ez-aw';* from 2372; a *window:*—light.

4238. מַחֲזִיאוֹת **Machăzîy'ôwth**, *makh-az-ee-oth';* fem. plur. from 2372; *visions; Machazioth*, an Isr.:—Mahazioth.

4239. מְחִי **mechîy**, *mekh-ee';* from 4229; a *stroke*, i.e. battering-*ram:*—engines.

4240. מְחִידָא **Mechîydâ'**, *mekh-ee-daw';* from 2330; *junction; Mechida*, one of the Nethinim:—Mehida.

4241. מִחְיָה **michyâh**, *mikh-yaw';* from 2421; *preservation of life;* hence *sustenance;* also the live flesh, i.e. the *quick:*—preserve life, quick, recover selves, reviving, sustenance, victuals.

מְחִיָּיאֵל **Mechîyyâ'êl.** See 4232.

4242. מְחִיר **mechîyr**, *mekh-eer';* from an unused root mean. to *buy; price, payment, wages:*—gain, hire, price, sold, worth.

4243. מְחִיר **Mechîyr**, *mekh-eer';* the same as 4242; *price; Mechir*, an Isr.:—Mehir.

4244. מַחְלָה **Machlâh**, *makh-law';* from 2470; *sickness; Machlah*, the name appar. of two Israelitesses:—Mahlah.

4245. מַחֲלֶה **machăleh**, *makh-al-eh';* or (fem.)
מַחֲלָה **machălâh**, *makk-al-aw';* from 2470; *sickness:*—disease, infirmity, sickness.

4246. מְחוֹלָה **mechôwlâh**, *mekh-o-law';* fem. of 4234; a *dance:*—company, dances (-cing).

4247. מְחִלָּה **mechillâh**, *mekh-il-law';* from 2490; a *cavern* (as if excavated):—cave.

4248. מַחְלוֹן **Machlôwn**, *makh-lone';* from 2470; *sick; Machlon*, an Isr.:—Mahlon.

4249. מַחְלִי **Machlîy**, *makh-lee';* from 2470; *sick; Machli*, the name of two Isr.:—Mahli.

4250. מַחְלִי **Machlîy**, *makh-lee';* patron. from 4249; a *Machlite* or (collect.) desc. of Machli:—Mahlites.

4251. מַחֲלוּי **machlûy**, *makh-loo'ee;* from 2470; a *disease:*—disease.

4252. מַחֲלָף **machălâph**, *makh-al-awf';* from 2498; a (sacrificial) *knife* (as *gliding* through the flesh):—knife.

4253. מַחְלָפָה **machlâphâh**, *makh-law-faw';* from 2498; a *ringlet* of hair (as *gliding* over each other):—lock.

4254. מַחֲלָצָה **machălâtsâh**, *makh-al-aw-tsaw';* from 2502; a *mantle* (as easily *drawn off*):—changeable suit of apparel, change of raiment.

4255. מַחְלְקָה **machleqâh** (Chald.), *makh-lek-aw';* corresp. to 4256; a *section* (of the Levites):—course.

4256. מַחֲלֹקֶת **machălôqeth**, *makh-al-o'-keth;* from 2505; a *section* (of Levites, people or soldiers):—company, course, division, portion. See also 5555.

4257. מַחֲלַת **machălath**, *makh-al-ath';* from 2470; *sickness; Machalath*, prob. the title (initial word) of a popular song:—Mahalath.

4258. מַחֲלַת **Machălath**, *makh-al-ath';* the same as 4257; *sickness; Machalath*, the name of an Ishmaelitess and of an Israelitess:—Mahalath.

4259. מְחֹלָתִי **Mechôlâthîy**, *mekh-o-law-thee';* patrial from 65; a *Mecholathite* or inhab. of Abel-Meholah:—Mecholathite.

4260. מַחֲמָאָה **machămâ'âh**, *makh-am-aw-aw';* a denom. from 2529; something *buttery* (i.e. unctuous and pleasant), as (fig.) *flattery:*—× than butter.

4261. מַחְמָד **machmâd**, *makh-mawd';* from 2530; *delightful;* hence a *delight*, i.e. object of affection or desire:—beloved, desire, goodly, lovely, pleasant (thing).

4262. מַחְמֻד **machmûd**, *makh-mood';* or
מַחְמוּד **machmûwd**, *makh-mood';* from 2530; *desired;* hence a *valuable:*—pleasant thing.

4263. מַחְמָל **machmâl**, *makh-mawl';* from 2550; prop. *sympathy;* (by paronomasia with 4261) *delight:*—pitieth.

4264. מַחֲנֶה **machăneh**, *makh-an-eh';* from 2583; an *encampment* (of travellers or troops); hence an *army*, whether lit. (of soldiers) or fig. (of dancers, angels, cattle, locusts, stars; or even the sacred courts):—army, band, battle, camp, company, drove, host, tents.

4265. מַחֲנֵה־דָן **Machănêh-Dân**, *makh-an-ay'-dawn;* from 4264 and 1835; *camp of Dan; Machaneh-Dan*, a place in Pal.:—Mahaneh-dan.

4266. מַחֲנַיִם **Machănayim**, *makh-an-ah'-yim;* dual of 4264; *double camp; Machanajim*, a place in Pal.:—Mahanaim.

4267. מַחֲנַק **machănaq**, *makh-an-ak';* from 2614; *choking:*—strangling.

4268. מַחֲסֶה **machăçeh**, *makh-as-eh';* or מַחְסֶה **machçeh**, *makh-seh';* from 2620; a *shelter* (lit. or fig.):—hope, (place of) refuge, shelter, trust.

4269. מַחְסוֹם **machçôwm**, *makh-sohm';* from 2629; a *muzzle:*—bridle.

4270. מַחְסוֹר **machçôwr**, *makh-sore';* or מַחְסֹר **machçôr**, *makh-sore';* from 2637; *deficiency;* hence *impoverishment:*—lack, need, penury, poor, poverty, want.

4271. מַחְסֵיָה **Machçêyâh**, *makh-say-yaw';* from 4268 and 3050; *refuge of* (i.e. *in*) *Jah; Machsejah*, an Isr.:—Maaseiah.

4272. מָחַץ **mâchats**, *maw-khats';* a prim. root; to *dash* asunder; by impl. to *crush, smash* or violently *plunge;* fig. to *subdue* or *destroy:*—dip, pierce (through), smite (through), strike through, wound.

4273. מַחַץ **machats**, *makh'-ats;* from 4272; a *contusion:*—stroke.

4274. מַחְצֵב **machtsêb**, *makh-tsabe';* from 2672; prop. a *hewing;* concr. a *quarry:*—hewed (-n).

4275. מֶחֱצָה **mechĕtsâh**, *mekh-ets-aw';* from 2673; a *halving:*—half.

4276. מַחֲצִית **machătsîyth**, *makh-ats-eeth';* from 2673; a *halving* or the *middle:*—half (so much), mid [-day].

4277. מָחַק **mâchaq**, *maw-khak';* a prim. root; to *crush:*—smite off.

4278. מֶחְקָר **mechqâr**, *mekh-kawr';* from 2713; prop. *scrutinized,* i.e. (by impl.) a *recess:*—deep place.

4279. מָחָר **mâchar**, *maw-khar';* prob. from 309; prop. *deferred,* i.e. the *morrow;* usually (adv.) *tomorrow;* indef. *hereafter:*—time to come, tomorrow.

4280. מַחֲרָאָה **machărâ'âh**, *makh-ar-aw-aw';* from the same as 2716; a *sink:*—draught house.

4281. מַחֲרֵשָׁה **machărêshâh**, *makh-ar-ay-shaw';* from 2790; prob. a *pick-axe:*—mattock.

4282. מַחֲרֶשֶׁת **machăresheth**, *makh-ar-eh'-sheth;* from 2790; prob. a *hoe:*—share.

4283. מָחֳרָת **mochŏrâth**, *mokh-or-awth';* or מָחֳרָתָם **mochŏrâthâm** (1 Sam. 30 : 17), *mokh-or-aw-thawm';* fem. from the same as 4279; the *morrow* or (adv.) *tomorrow:*—morrow, next day.

4284. מַחֲשָׁבָה **machăshâbâh**, *makh-ash-aw-baw';* or מַחֲשֶׁבֶת **machăshebeth**, *makh-ash-eh'-beth;* from 2803; a *contrivance*, i.e. (concr.) a *texture, machine,* or (abstr.) *intention, plan* (whether bad, a *plot;* or good, *advice*):—cunning (work), curious work, device (-sed), imagination, invented, means, purpose, thought.

4285. מַחְשָׁךְ **machshâk**, *makh-shawk';* from 2821; *darkness;* concr. a *dark place:*—dark (-ness, place).

4286. מַחְשֹׂף **machsôph**, *makh-sofe';* from 2834; a *peeling:*—made appear.

4287. מַחַת **Machath**, *makh'-ath;* prob. from 4229; *erasure; Machath,* the name of two Isr.:—Mahath.

4288. מְחִתָּה **mechittâh**, *mekh-it-taw';* from 2846; prop. a *dissolution;* concr. a *ruin,* or (abstr.) *consternation:*—destruction, dismaying, ruin, terror.

4289. מַחְתָּה **machtâh**, *makh-taw';* the same as 4288 in the sense of *removal;* a *pan* for live coals:—censer, firepan, snuffdish.

4290. מַחְתֶּרֶת **machtereth**, *makh-teh'-reth;* from 2864; a *burglary;* fig. *unexpected examination:*—breaking up, secret search.

4291. מְטָא **meṭâ'** (Chald.), *met-aw';* or מְטָה **meṭâh** (Chald.), *met-aw';* appar. corresp. to 4672 in the intrans. sense of being found *present;* to *arrive, extend* or *happen:*—come, reach.

4292. מַטְאֲטֵא **maṭ'ăṭê'**, *mat-at-ay';* appar. a denom. from 2916; a *broom* (as removing *dirt* [comp. Engl. "to dust", i.e. remove dust]):—besom.

4293. מַטְבֵּחַ **maṭbêach**, *mat-bay'-akh;* from 2873; *slaughter:*—slaughter.

4294. מַטֶּה **maṭṭeh**, *mat-teh';* or (fem.) מַטָּה **maṭṭâh**, *mat-taw';* from 5186; a *branch* (as *extending*); fig. a *tribe;* also a *rod,* whether for chastising (fig. *correction*), ruling (a *sceptre*), throwing (a *lance*), or walking (a *staff;* fig. a *support* of life, e.g. bread):—rod, staff, tribe.

4295. מַטָּה **maṭṭâh**, *mat'-taw;* from 5786 with directive enclitic appended; *downward, below* or *beneath;* often adv. with or without prefixes:—beneath, down (-ward), less, very low, under (-neath).

4296. מִטָּה **miṭṭâh**, *mit-taw';* from 5186; a *bed* (as *extended*) for sleeping or eating; by anal. a *sofa, litter* or *bier:*—bed ([-chamber]), bier.

4297. מֻטֶּה **muṭṭeh**, *moot-teh';* from 5186; a *stretching,* i.e. *distortion* (fig. *iniquity*):—perverseness.

4298. מֻטָּה **muṭṭâh**, *moot-taw';* from 5186; *expansion:*—stretching out.

4299. מַטְוֶה **maṭveh**, *mat-veh';* from 2901; something *spun:*—spun.

4300. מְטִיל **meṭîyl**, *met-eel';* from 2904 in the sense of *hammering* out; an iron *bar* (as *forged*):—bar.

4301. מַטְמוֹן **maṭmôwn**, *mat-mone';* or מַטְמֹן **maṭmôn**, *mat-mone';* or מַטְמֻן **maṭmûn**, *mat-moon';* from 2934; a *secret* storehouse; hence a *secreted* valuable (buried); gen. *money:*—hidden riches, (hid) treasure (-s).

4302. מַטָּע **maṭṭâ'**, *mat-taw';* from 5193; something *planted,* i.e. the place (a *garden* or vineyard), or the thing (a *plant,* fig. of men); by impl. the act, *planting:*—plant (-ation, -ing).

4303. מַטְעָם **maṭ'am**, *mat-am';* or (fem.) מַטְעַמָּה **maṭ'ammâh**, *mat-am-maw';* from 2938; a *delicacy:*—dainty (meat), savoury meat.

4304. מִטְפַּחַת **miṭpachath**, *mit-pakh'-ath;* from 2946; a wide *cloak* (for a woman):—vail, wimple.

4305. מָטַר **mâṭar**, *maw-tar';* a prim. root; to *rain:*—(cause to) rain (upon).

4306. מָטָר **mâṭâr**, *maw-tawr';* from 4305; *rain:*—rain.

4307. מַטָּרָא **maṭṭârâ'**, *mat-taw-raw';* or מַטָּרָה **maṭṭârâh**, *mat-taw-raw';* from 5201; a *jail* (as a *guard*-house); also an *aim* (as being closely *watched*):—mark, prison.

4308. מַטְרֵד **Maṭrêd**, *mat-rade';* from 2956; *propulsive; Matred,* an Edomitess:—Matred.

4309. מַטְרִי **Maṭrîy**, *mat-ree';* from 4305; *rainy; Matri,* an Isr.:—Matri.

4310. מִי **mîy**, *me;* an interrog. pron. of persons, as 4100 is of things, *who?* (occasionally, by a peculiar idiom, of things); also (indef.) *whoever;* often used in oblique construction with pref. or suff.:—any (man), × he, × him, + O that! what, which, who (-m, -se, -soever), + would to God.

4311. מֵידְבָא **Mêydebâ'**, *may-deb-aw';* from 4325 and 1679; *water of quiet; Medeba,* a place in Pal.:—Medeba.

4312. מֵידָד **Mêydâd**, *may-dawd';* from 3032 in the sense of *loving; affectionate; Medad,* an Isr.:—Medad.

4313. מֵי הַיַּרְקוֹן **Mêy hay-Yarqôwn**, *may hah'-ee-yar-kone';* from 4325 and 3420 with the art. interposed; *water of the yellowness; Me-haj-Jarkon,* a place in Pal.:—Me-jarkon.

4314. מֵי זָהָב **Mêy Zâhâb**, *may zaw-hawb';* from 4325 and 2091, *water of gold; Me-Zahab,* an Edomite:—Mezahab.

4315. מֵיטָב **mêyṭâb**, *may-tawb';* from 3190; the *best* part:—best.

4316. מִיכָא **Mîykâ'**, *mee-kaw';* a var. for 4318; *Mica,* the name of two Isr.:—Micha.

4317. מִיכָאֵל **Mîykâ'êl**, *me-kaw-ale';* from 4310 and (the pref. der. from) 3588 and 410; *who* (is) *like God?; Mikael,* the name of an archangel and of nine Isr.:—Michael.

4318. מִיכָה **Mîykâh**, *mee-kaw';* an abbrev. of 4320; *Micah,* the name of seven Isr.:—Micah, Micaiah, Michah.

4319. מִיכָהוּ **Mîykâhûw**, *me-kaw'-hoo;* a contr. for 4321; *Mikehu,* an Isr. prophet:—Micaiah (2 Chron. 18 : 8).

4320. מִיכָיָה **Mîykâyâh**, *me-kaw-yaw';* from 4310 and (the pref. der. from) 3588 and 3050; *who* (is) *like Jah?; Micajah,* the name of two Isr.:—Micah, Michaiah. Comp. 4318.

4321. מִיכָיְהוּ **Mîykâyehûw**, *me-kaw-yeh-hoo';* or מִכָיְהוּ **Mikâyehûw** (Jer. 36 : 11), *me-kaw-yeh-hoo';* abbrev. for 4322; *Mikajah,* the name of three Isr.:—Micah, Micaiah, Michaiah.

4322. מִיכָיָהוּ **Mîykâyâhûw**, *me-kaw-yaw'-hoo;* for 4320; *Mikajah,* the name of an Isr. and an Israelitess:—Michaiah.

4323. מִיכָל **mîykâl**, *me-kawl';* from 3201; prop. a *container,* i.e. a *streamlet:*—brook.

4324. מִיכָל **Mîykâl**, *me-kawl';* appar. the same as 4323; *rivulet; Mikal,* Saul's daughter:—Michal.

4325. מַיִם **mayim**, *mah'-yim;* dual of a prim. noun (but used in a sing. sense); *water;* fig. *juice;* by euphem. *urine, semen:*— + piss, wasting, water (-ing, [-course, -flood, -spring]).

4326. מִיָּמִן **Mîyâmîn**, *me-yaw-meem';* a form for 4509; *Mijamin,* the name of three Isr.:—Miamin, Mijamin.

4327. מִין **mîyn**, *meen;* from an unused root mean. to *portion* out; a *sort,* i.e. *species:*—kind. Comp. 4480.

4328. מְיֻסָּדָה **meyuççâdâh**, *meh-yoos-saw-daw';* prop. fem. pass. part. of 3245; something *founded,* i.e. a *foundation:*—foundation.

4329. מֵיסָךְ **mêyçâk**, *may-sawk';* from 5526; a *portico* (as *covered*):—covert.

מֵיפַעַת **Mêypha'ath**. See 4158.

4330. מִיץ **mîyts**, *meets;* from 4160; *pressure:*—churning, forcing, wringing.

4331. מֵישָׁא **Mêyshâ'**, *may-shaw';* from 4185; *departure; Mesha,* a place in Arabia; also an Isr.:—Mesha.

4332. מִישָׁאֵל **Mîyshâ'êl**, *mee-shaw-ale';* from 4310 and 410 with the abbrev. insep. rel. [see 834] interposed; *who* (is) *what God* (is)?; *Mishaël,* the name of three Isr.:—Mishael.

4333. מִישָׁאֵל **Mîyshâ'êl** (Chald.), *mee-shaw-ale';* corresp. to 4332; *Mishaël,* an Isr.:—Mishael.

4334. מִישׁוֹר **mîyshôwr**, *mee-shore';* or מִישֹׁר **mîyshôr**, *mee-shore';* from 3474; a *level,* i.e. a *plain* (often used [with the art. pref.] as a prop. name of certain districts); fig. *concord;* also *straightness,* i.e. (fig.) *justice* (sometimes adv. *justly*):—equity, even place, plain, right (-eously), (made) straight, uprightness.

4335. מֵישַׁךְ **Mêyshak**, *may-shak';* borrowed from 4336; *Meshak,* an Isr.:—Meshak.

4336. מֵישַׁךְ **Mêyshak** (Chald.), *may-shak';* of for. or. and doubtful signif.; *Meshak,* the Bab. name of 4333:—Meshak.

4337. מֵישָׁע **Mêyshâ'**, *may-shah';* from 3467; *safety; Mesha,* an Isr.:—Mesha.

4338. מֵישַׁע **Mêysha'**, *may-shaw';* a var. for 4337; *safety; Mesha,* a Moabite:—Mesha.

4339. מֵישָׁר **mêyshâr**, *may-shawr';* from 3474; *evenness,* i.e. (fig.) *prosperity* or *con-*

cord; also *straightness,* i.e. (fig.) *rectitude* (only in plur. with sing. sense; often adv.):—agreement, aright, that are equal, equity, (things that are) right (-eously, things), sweetly, upright (-ly, -ness).

4340. מֵיתָר **mêythâr**, *may-thawr';* from 3498; a *cord* (of a tent) [comp. 3499] or the *string* (of a bow):—cord, string.

4341. מַכְאֹב **mak'ôb**, *mak-obe';* sometimes מַכְאוֹב **mak'ôwb**, *mak-obe';* also (fem. Isa. 53 : 3) מַכְאֹבָה **mak'ôbâh**, *mak-o-baw';* from 3510; *anguish* or (fig.) *affliction:*—grief, pain, sorrow.

4342. מַכְבִּיר **makbîyr**, *mak-beer';* trans. part. of 3527; *plenty:*—abundance.

4343. מַכְבֵּנָא **Makbênâ'**, *mak-bay-naw';* from the same as 3522; *knoll; Macbena,* a place in Pal. settled by him:—Machbenah.

4344. מַכְבַּנַּי **Makbannay**, *mak-ban-nah'ee;* patrial from 4343; a *Macbannite* or native of Macbena:—Machbanai.

4345. מַכְבֵּר **makbêr**, *mak-bare';* from 3527 in the sense of *covering* [comp. 3531]; a *grate:*—grate.

4346. מַכְבָּר **makbâr**, *mak-bawr';* from 3527 in the sense of *covering;* a cloth (as *netted* [comp. 4345]):—thick cloth.

4347. מַכָּה **makkâh**, *mak-kaw';* or (masc.) מַכֶּה **makkeh**, *mak-keh';* (plur. only) from 5221; a *blow* (in 2 Chron. 2 : 10, of the *flail*); by impl. a *wound;* fig. *carnage,* also *pestilence:*—beaten, blow, plague, slaughter, smote, × sore, stripe, stroke, wound ([-ed]).

4348. מִכְוָה **mikvâh**, *mik-vaw';* from 3554; a *burn:*—that burneth, burning.

4349. מָכוֹן **mâkôwn**, *maw-kone';* from 3559; prop. a *fixture,* i.e. a *basis;* gen. a *place,* esp. as an *abode:*—foundation, habitation, (dwelling-, settled) place.

4350. מְכוֹנָה **m^ekôwnâh**, *mek-o-naw';* or מְכֹנָה **m^ekônâh**, *mek-o-naw';* fem. of 4349; a *pedestal,* also a *spot:*—base.

4351. מְכוּרָה **m^ekûwrâh**, *mek-oo-raw';* or מְכֹרָה **m^ekôrâh**, *mek-o-raw';* from the same as 3564 in the sense of *digging; origin* (as if a mine):—birth, habitation, nativity.

4352. מָכִי **Mâkîy**, *maw-kee';* prob. from 4134; *pining; Maki,* an Isr.:—Machi.

4353. מָכִיר **Mâkîyr**, *maw-keer';* from 4376; *salesman; Makir,* an Isr.:—Machir.

4354. מָכִירִי **Mâkîyrîy**, *maw-kee-ree';* patron. from 4353; a *Makirite* or descend. of Makir:—of Machir.

4355. מָכַךְ **mâkak**, *maw-kak';* a prim. root; to *tumble* (in ruins); fig. to *perish:*—be brought low, decay.

4356. מִכְלָאָה **miklâ'âh**, *mik-law-aw';* or מִכְלָה **miklâh**, *mik-law';* from 3607; a *pen* (for flocks):—([sheep-]) fold. Comp. 4357.

4357. מִכְלָה **miklâh**, *mik-law';* from 3615; *completion* (in plur. concr. adv. *wholly*):—perfect. Comp. 4356.

4358. מִכְלוֹל **miklôwl**, *mik-lole';* from 3634; *perfection* (i.e. concr. adv. *splendidly*):—most gorgeously, all sorts.

4359. מִכְלָל **miklâl**, *mik-lawl';* from 3634; *perfection* (of beauty):—perfection.

4360. מִכְלֻל **miklûl**, *mik-lool';* from 3634; something *perfect,* i.e. a splendid *garment:*—all sorts.

4361. מַכֹּלֶת **makkôleth**, *mak-ko'-leth;* from 398; *nourishment:*—food.

4362. מִכְמַן **mikman**, *mik-man';* from the same as 3646 in the sense of *hiding; treasure* (as *hidden*):—treasure.

4363. מִכְמָס **Mikmâç** (Ezra 2 : 27; Neh. 7 : 31), *mik-maws';* or מִכְמָשׁ **Mikmâsh**, *mik-mawsh';* or מִכְמַשׁ **Mikmash** (Neh. 11 : 31), *mik-mash';* from 3647; *hidden; Mikmas* or *Mikmash,* a place in Pal.:—Mikmas, Mikmash.

4364. מַכְמָר **makmâr**, *mak-mawr';* or מִכְמֹר **mikmôr**, *mik-more';* from 3648 in the sense of *blackening* by heat; a (hunter's) *net* (as *dark* from concealment):—net.

4365. מִכְמֶרֶת **mikmereth**, *mik-meh'-reth;* or מִכְמֹרֶת **mikmôreth**, *mik-mo'-reth;* fem. of 4364; a (fisher's) *net:*—drag, net.

מִכְמָשׁ **Mikmâsh**. See 4363.

4366. מִכְמְתָת **Mikm^ethâth**, *mik-meth-awth';* appar. from an unused root mean. to *hide; concealment; Mikmethath,* a place in Pal.:—Michmethath.

4367. מַכְנַדְבַי **Maknadbay**, *mak-nad-bah'ee;* from 4100 and 5068 with a particle interposed; *what* (is) *like* (a) *liberal* (man)?; *Maknadbai,* an Isr.:—Machnadebai.

מְכֹנָה **m^ekônâh**. See 4350.

4368. מְכֹנָה **M^ekônâh**, *mek-o-naw';* the same as 4350; a *base; Mekonah,* a place in Pal.:—Mekonah.

4369. מְכֻנָה **m^ekûnâh**, *mek-oo-naw';* the same as 4350; a *spot:*—base.

4370. מִכְנָס **miknâç**, *mik-nawce';* from 3647 in the sense of *hiding;* (only in dual) *drawers* (from *concealing* the private parts):—breeches.

4371. מֶכֶס **mekeç**, *meh'-kes;* prob. from an unused root mean. to *enumerate;* an *assessment* (as based upon a *census*):—tribute.

4372. מִכְסֶה **mikçeh**, *mik-seh';* from 3680; a *covering,* i.e. weather-*boarding:*—covering.

4373. מִכְסָה **mikçâh**, *mik-saw';* fem. of 4371; an *enumeration;* by impl. a *valuation:*—number, worth.

4374. מְכַסֶּה **m^ekaççeh**, *mek-as-seh';* from 3680; a *covering,* i.e. *garment;* spec. a *coverlet* (for a bed), an *awning* (from the sun); also the *omentum* (as covering the intestines):—clothing, to cover, that which covereth.

4375. מַכְפֵּלָה **Makpêlâh**, *mak-pay-law';* from 3717; a *fold; Makpelah,* a place in Pal.:—Machpelah.

4376. מָכַר **mâkar**, *maw-kar';* a prim. root; to *sell,* lit. (as merchandise, a daughter in marriage, into slavery), or fig. (to *surrender*):—× at all, sell (away, -er, self).

4377. מֶכֶר **meker**, *meh'-ker;* from 4376; *merchandise;* also *value:*—pay, price, ware.

4378. מַכָּר **makkâr**, *mak-kawr';* from 5234; an *acquaintance:*—acquaintance.

4379. מִכְרֶה **mikreh**, *mik-reh';* from 3738; a *pit* (for salt):—[salt-] pit.

4380. מְכֵרָה **m^ekêrâh**, *mek-ay-raw';* prob. from the same as 3564 in the sense of *stabbing;* a *sword:*—habitation.

מְכֹרָה **m^ekôrâh**. See 4351.

4381. מִכְרִי **Mikrîy**, *mik-ree';* from 4376; *salesman; Mikri,* an Isr.:—Michri.

4382. מְכֵרָתִי **M^ekêrâthîy**, *mek-ay-raw-thee';* patrial from an unused name (the same as 4380) of a place in Pal.; a *Mekerathite,* or inhab. of Mekerah:—Mecherathite.

4383. מִכְשׁוֹל **mikshôwl**, *mik-shole';* or מִכְשֹׁל **mikshôl**, *mik-shole';* masc. from 3782; a *stumbling-block,* lit. or fig. (*obstacle, enticement* [spec. an idol], *scruple*):—caused to fall, offence, × [no-] thing offered, ruin, stumbling-block.

4384. מַכְשֵׁלָה **makshêlâh**, *mak-shay-law';* fem. from 3782; a *stumbling-block,* but only fig. (*fall, enticement* [idol]):—ruin, stumbling-block.

4385. מִכְתָּב **miktâb**, *mik-tawb';* from 3789; a thing *written,* the *characters,* or a *document* (letter, copy, edict, poem):—writing.

4386. מְכִתָּה **m^ekittâh**, *mek-it-taw';* from 3807; a *fracture:*—bursting.

4387. מִכְתָּם **miktâm**, *mik-tawm';* from 3799; an *engraving,* i.e. (techn.) a *poem:*—Michtam.

4388. מַכְתֵּשׁ **maktêsh**, *mak-taysh';* from 3806; a *mortar;* by anal. a *socket* (of a tooth):—hollow place, mortar.

4389. מַכְתֵּשׁ **Maktêsh**, *mak-taysh';* the same as 4388; *dell;* the *Maktesh,* a place in Jerus.:—Maktesh.

מֻל **mûl**. See 4136.

4390. מָלֵא **mâlê'**, *maw-lay';* or מָלָא **mâlâ'** (Esth. 7 : 5), *maw-law';* a prim. root, to *fill* or (intrans.) *be full* of, in a wide application (lit. and fig.):—accomplish, confirm, + consecrate, be at an end, be expired, be fenced, fill, fulfil, (be, become, × draw, give in, go) full (-ly, -ly set, tale), [over-] flow, fulness, furnish, gather (selves, together), presume, replenish, satisfy, set, space, take a [hand-] full, + have wholly.

4391. מְלָא **m^elâ'** (Chald.), *mel-aw';* corresp. to 4390; to *fill:*—fill, be full.

4392. מָלֵא **mâlê'**, *maw-lay';* from 4390; *full* (lit. or fig.) or *filling* (lit.); also (concr.) *fulness;* adv. *fully:*— × she that was with child, fill (-ed, -ed with), full (-ly), multitude, as is worth.

4393. מְלֹא **m^elô'**, *mel-o';* rarely מְלוֹא **m^elôw'**, *mel-o';* or מְלוֹ **m^elôw** (Ezek. 41 : 8), *mel-o';* from 4390; *fulness* (lit. or fig.):— × all along, × all that is (there-) in, fill, (× that whereof . . . was) full, fulness, [hand-] full, multitude.

מִלֹּא **Millô'**. See 4407.

4394. מִלֻּא **millû'**, *mil-loo';* from 4390; a *fulfilling* (only in plur.), i.e. (lit.) a *setting* (of gems), or (techn.) *consecration* (also concr. a dedicatory *sacrifice*):—consecration, be set.

4395. מְלֵאָה **m^elê'âh**, *mel-ay-aw';* fem. of 4392; something *fulfilled,* i.e. *abundance* (of produce):—(first of ripe) fruit, fulness.

4396. מִלֻּאָה **millû'âh**, *mil-loo-aw';* fem. of 4394; a *filling,* i.e. *setting* (of gems):—inclosing, setting.

4397. מַלְאָךְ **mal'âk**, *mal-awk';* from an unused root mean. to *despatch* as a deputy; a *messenger;* spec. of God, i.e. an *angel* (also a prophet, priest or teacher):—ambassador, angel, king, messenger.

4398. מַלְאַךְ **mal'ak** (Chald.), *mal-ak';* corresp. to 4397; an *angel:*—angel.

4399. מְלָאכָה **m^elâ'kâh**, *mel-aw-kaw';* from the same as 4397; prop. *deputyship,* i.e. ministry; gen. *employment* (never servile) or work (abstr. or concr.); also *property* (as the result of *labor*):—business, + cattle, + industrious, occupation, (+ -pied), + officer, thing (made), use, (manner of) work ([-man], -manship).

4400. מַלְאֲכוּת **mal'âkûwth**, *mal-ak-ooth';* from the same as 4397; a *message:*—message.

4401. מַלְאָכִי **Mal'âkîy**, *mal-aw-kee';* from the same as 4397; *ministrative; Malaki,* a prophet:—Malachi.

4402. מִלֵּאת **millê'th**, *mil-layth';* from 4390; *fulness,* i.e. (concr.) a *plump* socket (of the eye):— × fitly.

4403. מַלְבּוּשׁ **malbûwsh**, *mal-boosh';* or מַלְבֻּשׁ **malbûsh**, *mal-boosh';* from 3847; a *garment,* or (collect.) *clothing:*—apparel, raiment, vestment.

4404. מַלְבֵּן **malbên**, *mal-bane';* from 3835 (denom.); a *brick-kiln:*—brickwork.

4405. מִלָּה **millâh**, *mil-law';* from 4448 (plur. masc. as if from מִלֶּה **milleh**, *mil-leh'*); a *word;* collect. a *discourse;* fig. a *topic:*— + answer, by-word, matter, any thing (what) to say, to speak (-ing), speak, talking, word.

4406. מִלָּה **millâh** (Chald.), *mil-law'*; corresp. to 4405; a *word, command, discourse*, or *subject*:—commandment, matter, thing, word.

מִלֹו **m^elôw**. See 4393.

מְלֹוא **m^elôw'**. See 4393.

4407. מִלֹּוא **millôw'**, *mil-lo'*; or

מִלֹּא **mil-lô'** (2 Kings 12 : 20), *mil-lo'*; from 4390; a *rampart* (as *filled* in), i.e. the *citadel*:—Millo. See also 1037.

4408. מַלּוּחַ **mallûwach**, *mal-loo'-akh*; from 4414; *sea-purslain* (from its *saltness*):—mallows.

4409. מַלּוּךְ **Mallûwk**, *mal-luke'*; or

מַלּוּכִי° **Mallûwkîy** (Neh. 12 : 14), *mal-loo-kee'*; from 4427; *regnant*; *Malluk*, the name of five Isr.:—Malluch, Melichu [*from the marg.*].

4410. מְלוּכָה **m^elûwkâh**, *mel-oo-kaw'*; fem. pass. part. of 4427; something *ruled*, i.e. a *realm*:—kingdom, king's, × royal.

4411. מָלֹון **mâlôwn**, *maw-lone'*; from 3885; a *lodgment*, i.e. *caravanserai* or *encampment*:—inn, place where . . . lodge, lodging (place).

4412. מְלוּנָה **m^elûwnâh**, *mel-oo-naw'*; fem. from 3885; a *hut*, a *hammock*:—cottage, lodge.

4413. מַלֹּותִי **Mallôwthîy**, *mal-lo'-thee*; appar. from 4448; *I have talked* (i.e. *loquacious*):—*Mallothi*, an Isr.:—Mallothi.

4414. מָלַח **mâlach**, *maw-lakh'*; a prim. root; prop. to *rub* to pieces or pulverize; intrans. to *disappear* as dust; also (as denom. from 4417) to *salt* whether intern. (to *season* with salt) or extern. (to *rub* with salt):— × at all, salt, season, temper together, vanish away.

4415. מְלַח **m^elach** (Chald.), *mel-akh'*; corresp. to 4414; to *eat* salt, i.e. (gen.) *subsist*:— + have maintenance.

4416. מְלַח **m^elach** (Chald.), *mel-akh'*; from 4415; *salt*:— + maintenance, salt.

4417. מֶלַח **melach**, *meh'-lakh*; from 4414; prop. *powder*, i.e. (spec.) *salt* (as easily pulverized and dissolved:—salt ([-pit]).

4418. מָלָח **mâlâch**, *maw-lawkh'*; from 4414 in its orig. sense; a *rag* or old garment:—rotten rag.

4419. מַלָּח **mallâch**, *mal-lawkh'*; from 4414 in its second. sense; a *sailor* (as following "the salt"):—mariner.

4420. מְלֵחָה **m^elêchâh**, *mel-ay-khaw'*; from 4414 (in its denom. sense); prop. *salted* (i.e. land [776 being understood]), i.e. a *desert*:—barren land (-ness), salt [land].

4421. מִלְחָמָה **milchâmâh**, *mil-khaw-maw'*; from 3898 (in the sense of *fighting*); a *battle* (i.e. the *engagement*); gen. *war* (i.e. *warfare*):—battle, fight, (-ing), war ([-rior]).

4422. מָלַט **mâlaṭ**, *maw-lat'*; a prim. root; prop. to *be smooth*, i.e. (by impl.) to *escape* (as if by *slipperiness*); causat. to *release* or *rescue*; spec. to *bring forth* young, *emit* sparks:—deliver (self), escape, lay, leap out, let alone, let go, preserve, save, × speedily, × surely.

4423. מֶלֶט **meleṭ**, *meh'-let*; from 4422, *cement* (from its plastic *smoothness*):—clay.

4424. מְלַטְיָה **M^elaṭyâh**, *mel-at-yaw'*; from 4423 and 3050; (whom) *Jah has delivered*; *Melatjah*, a Gibeonite:—Melatiah.

4425. מְלִילָה **m^elîylâh**, *mel-ee-law'*; from 4449 (in the sense of *cropping* [comp. 4135]); a *head* of grain (as *cut* off):—ear.

4426. מְלִיצָה **m^elîytsâh**, *mel-ee-tsaw'*; from 3887; an *aphorism*; also a *satire*:—interpretation, taunting.

4427. מָלַךְ **mâlak**, *maw-lak'*; a prim. root; to *reign*; incept. to *ascend the throne*; causat. to *induct* into royalty; hence (by impl.) to *take counsel*:—consult, × indeed, be (make, set a, set up) king, be (make) queen, (begin to, make to) reign (-ing), rule, × surely.

4428. מֶלֶךְ **melek**, *meh'-lek*; from 4427; a *king*:—king, royal.

4429. מֶלֶךְ **Melek**, *meh'-lek*; the same as 4428; *king*; *Melek*, the name of two Isr.:—Melech, Hammelech [*by includ. the art.*].

4430. מֶלֶךְ **melek** (Chald.), *meh'-lek*; corresp. to 4428; a *king*:—king, royal.

4431. מְלַךְ **m^elak** (Chald.), *mel-ak'*; from a root corresp. to 4427 in the sense of *consultation*; *advice*:—counsel.

4432. מֹלֶךְ **Môlek**, *mo'-lek*; from 4427; *Molek* (i.e. king), the chief deity of the Ammonites:—Molech. Comp. 4445.

4433. מַלְכָּא **malkâ'** (Chald.), *mal-kaw'*; corresp. to 4436; a *queen*:—queen.

4434. מַלְכֹּדֶת **malkôdeth**, *mal-ko'-deth*; from 3920; a *snare*:—trap.

4435. מִלְכָּה **Milkâh**, *mil-kaw'*; a form of 4436; *queen*; *Milcah*, the name of a Hebrewess and of an Isr.:—Milcah.

4436. מַלְכָּה **malkâh**, *mal-kaw'*; fem. of 4428; a *queen*:—queen.

4437. מַלְכוּ **malkûw** (Chald.), *mal-koo'*; corresp. to 4438; *dominion* (abstr. or concr.):—kingdom, kingly, realm, reign.

4438. מַלְכוּת **malkûwth**, *mal-kooth'*; or

מַלְכֻת **malkûth**, *mal-kooth'*; or (in plur.)

מַלְכֻיָּה **malkûyâh**, *mal-koo-yâh'*; from 4427; a *rule*; concr. a *dominion*:—empire, kingdom, realm, reign, royal.

4439. מַלְכִּיאֵל **Malkîy'êl**, *mal-kee-ale'*; from 4428 and 410; *king of* (i.e. appointed by) *God*; *Malkiël*, an Isr.:—Malchiel.

4440. מַלְכִּיאֵלִי **Malkîy'êlîy**, *mal-kee-ay-lee'*; patron. from 4439; a *Malkiëlite* or desc. of Malkiel:—Malchielite.

4441. מַלְכִּיָּה **Malkîyâh**, *mal-kee-yaw'*; or

מַלְכִּיָּהוּ **Malkîyâhûw** (Jer. 38 : 6), *mal-kee-yaw'-hoo*; from 4428 and 3050; *king of* (i.e. appointed by) *Jah*; *Malkijah*, the name of ten Isr.:—Malchiah, Malchijah.

4442. מַלְכִּי־צֶדֶק **Malkîy-Tsedeq**, *mal-kee-tseh'-dek*; from 4428 and 6664; *king of right*; *Malki-Tsedek*, an early king in Pal.:—Melchizedek.

4443. מַלְכִּירָם **Malkîyrâm**, *mal-kee-rawm'*; from 4428 and 7311; *king of a high* one (i.e. of exaltation); *Malkiram*, an Isr.:—Malchiram.

4444. מַלְכִּישׁוּעַ **Malkîyshûwa'**, *mal-kee-shoo'-ah*; from 4428 and 7769; *king of wealth*; *Malkishua*, an Isr.:—Malchishua.

4445. מַלְכָּם **Malkâm**, *mal-kawm'*; or

מִלְכּוֹם **Milkôwm**, *mil-kome'*; from 4428 for 4432; *Malcam* or *Milcom*, the national idol of the Ammonites:—Malcham, Milcom.

4446. מְלֶכֶת **m^eleketh**, *mel-eh'-keth*; from 4427; a *queen*:—queen.

4447. מֹלֶכֶת **Môleketh**, *mo-leh'-keth*; fem. act. part. of 4427; *queen*; *Moleketh*, an Israelitess:—Hammoleketh [*includ. the art.*].

4448. מָלַל **mâlal**, *maw-lal'*; a prim. root; to *speak* (mostly poet.) or *say*:—say, speak, utter.

4449. מְלַל **m^elal** (Chald.), *mel-al'*; corresp. to 4448; to *speak*:—say, speak (-ing).

4450. מִלֲלַי **Mîlălay**, *mee-lal-ah'ee*; from 4448; *talkative*; *Milalai*, an Isr.:—Milalai.

4451. מַלְמָד **malmâd**, *mal-mawd'*; from 3925; a *goad* for oxen:—goad.

4452. מָלַץ **mâlats**, *maw-lats'*; a prim. root; to *be smooth*, i.e. (fig.) *pleasant*:—be sweet.

4453. מֶלְצָר **meltsâr**, *mel-tsawr'*; of Pers. der.; the *butler* or other officer in the Bab. court:—Melzar.

4454. מָלַק **mâlaq**, *maw-lak'*; a prim. root; to *crack* a joint; by impl. to *wring* the neck of a fowl (without separating it):—wring off.

4455. מַלְקוֹחַ **malqôwach**, *mal-ko'-akh*; from 3947; trans. (in dual) the *jaws* (as taking food); intrans. *spoil* [and captives] (as taken):—booty, jaws, prey.

4456. מַלְקוֹשׁ **malqôwsh**, *mal-koshe'*; from 3953; the spring *rain* (comp. 3954); fig. *eloquence*:—latter rain.

4457. מֶלְקָח **melqâch**, *mel-kawkh'*; or

מַלְקָח **malqâch**, *mal-kawkh'*; from 3947; (only in dual) *tweezers*:—snuffers, tongs.

4458. מֶלְתָּחָה **meltâchâh**, *mel-taw-khaw'*; from an unused root mean. to *spread* out; a *wardrobe* (i.e. room where clothing is *spread*):—vestry.

4459. מַלְתָּעָה **maltâ'âh**, *mal-taw-aw'*; transp. for 4973; a *grinder*, i.e. back *tooth*:—great tooth.

4460. מַמְּגֻרָה **mamm^egûrâh**, *mam-meg-oo-raw'*; from 4048 (in the sense of *depositing*); a *granary*:—barn.

4461. מֵמַד **mêmad**, *may-mad'*; from 4058; a *measure*:—measure.

4462. מְמוּכָן **M^emûwkân**, *mem-oo-kawn'*; or (transp.)

מוֹמֻכָן° **Môwmûkân** (Esth. 1 : 16), *mo-moo-kawn'*; of Pers. der.; *Memucan* or *Momucan*, a Pers. satrap:—Memucan.

4463. מָמוֹת **mâmôwth**, *maw-mothe'*; from 4191; a mortal *disease*; concr. a *corpse*:—death.

4464. מַמְזֵר **mamzêr**, *mam-zare'*; from an unused root mean. to *alienate*; a *mongrel*, i.e. born of a Jewish father and a heathen mother:—bastard.

4465. מִמְכָּר **mimkâr**, *mim-kawr'*; from 4376; *merchandise*; abstr. a *selling*:— × ought, (that which cometh of) sale, that which . . . sold, ware.

4466. מִמְכֶּרֶת **mimkereth**, *mim-keh'-reth*; fem. of 4465; a *sale*:— + sold as.

4467. מַמְלָכָה **mamlâkâh**, *mam-law-kaw'*; from 4427; *dominion*, i.e. (abstr.) the estate (*rule*) or (concr.) the country (*realm*):—kingdom, king's, reign, royal.

4468. מַמְלָכוּת **mamlâkûwth**, *mam-law-kooth'*; a form of 4467 and equiv. to it:—kingdom, reign.

4469. מַמְסָךְ **mamçâk**, *mam-sawk'*; from 4537; *mixture*, i.e. (spec.) wine *mixed* (with water or spices):—drink-offering, mixed wine.

4470. מֶמֶר **memer**, *meh'-mer*; from an unused root mean. to *grieve*; *sorrow*:—bitterness.

4471. מַמְרֵא **Mamrê'**, *mam-ray'*; from 4754 (in the sense of *vigor*); *lusty*; *Mamre*, an Amorite:—Mamre.

4472. מַמְרֹר **mamrôr**, *mam-rore'*; from 4843; a *bitterness*, i.e. (fig.) calamity:—bitterness.

4473. מִמְשַׁח **mimshach**, *mim-shakh'*; from 4886, in the sense of *expansion*; *outspread* (i.e. with outstretched wings):—anointed.

4474. מִמְשָׁל **mimshâl**, *mim-shawl'*; from 4910; a *ruler* or (abstr.) *rule*:—dominion, that ruled.

4475. מֶמְשָׁלָה **memshâlâh**, *mem-shaw-law'*; fem. of 4474; *rule*; also (concr. in plur.) a *realm* or a *ruler*:—dominion, government, power, to rule.

4476. מִמְשָׁק **mimshâq**, *mim-shawk'*; from the same as 4943; a *possession*:—breeding.

4477. מַמְתַּק **mamtaq**, *mam-tak'*; from 4985; something *sweet* (lit. or fig.):—(most) sweet.

4478. מָן **mân**, *mawn*; from 4100; lit. a *whatness* (so to speak), i.e. *manna* (so called from the question about it):—manna.

4479. מָן **mân** (Chald.), *mawn*; from 4101; *who* or *what* (prop. interrog., hence also indef. and rel.):—what, who (-msoever, + -so).

4480. מִן **min**, *min*; or

מִנִּי **minnîy**, *min-nee'*; or

מִנֵּי **minnêy** (constr. plur.), *min-nay'* (Isa. 30 : 11); for 4482; prop. a *part* of; hence

(prep.), *from* or *out of* in many senses (as follows):—above, after, among, at, because of, by (reason of), from (among), in, × neither, × nor, (out) of, over, since, × then, through, × whether, with.

4481. מִן **min** (Chald.), *min;* corresp. to 4480:—according, after, + because, + before, by, for, from, × him, × more than, (out) of, part, since, × these, to, upon, + when.

4482. מֵן **mên**, *mane;* from an unused root mean. to *apportion;* a *part;* hence a musical *chord* (as parted into strings):—in [the same] (Psa. 68 : 23), stringed instrument (Psa. 150 : 4), whereby (Psa. 45 : 8 [*defective plur.*]).

4483. מְנָא **mᵉnâʼ** (Chald.), *men-aw';* or

מְנָה **mᵉnâh** (Chald.), *men-aw';* corresp. to 4487; to *count, appoint:*—number, ordain, set.

4484. מְנֵא **menêʼ** (Chald.), *men-ay';* pass. part. of 4483; *numbered:*—Mene.

4485. מַנְגִּינָה **mangîynâh**, *man-ghee-naw';* from 5059; a *satire:*—music.

מִנְדָּה **mindâh**. See 4061.

4486. מַנְדַּע **mandaʻ** (Chald.), *man-dah';* corresp. to 4093; *wisdom* or *intelligence:*—knowledge, reason, understanding.

מְנָה **mᵉnâh**. See 4483.

4487. מָנָה **mânâh**, *maw-naw';* a prim. root; prop. to *weigh* out; by impl. to *allot* or *constitute* officially; also to *enumerate* or enroll:—appoint, count, number, prepare, set, tell.

4488. מָנֶה **mâneh**, *maw-neh';* from 4487; prop. a fixed *weight* or measured amount, i.e. (techn.) a *maneh* or mina:—maneh, pound.

4489. מֹנֶה **môneh**, *mo-neh';* from 4487; prop. something *weighed* out, i.e. (fig.) a *portion* of time, i.e. an *instance:*—time.

4490. מָנָה **mânâh**, *maw-naw';* from 4487; prop. something *weighed* out, i.e. (gen.) a *division;* spec. (of food) a *ration;* also a *lot:*—such things as belonged, part, portion.

4491. מִנְהָג **minhâg**, *min-hawg';* from 5090; the *driving* (of a chariot):—driving.

4492. מִנְהָרָה **minhârâh**, *min-haw-raw';* from 5102; prop. a *channel* or fissure, i.e. (by impl.) a *cavern:*—den.

4493. מָנוֹד **mânôwd**, *maw-node';* from 5110; a *nodding* or *toss* (of the head in derision):—shaking.

4494. מָנוֹחַ **mânôwach**, *maw-no'-akh;* from 5117; *quiet,* i.e. (concr.) a *settled spot,* or (fig.) a *home:*—(place of) rest.

4495. מָנוֹחַ **Mânôwach**, *maw-no'-akh;* the same as 4494; *rest; Manoäch,* an Isr.:—Manoah.

4496. מְנוּחָה **menûwchâh**, *men-oo-khaw';* or

מְנֻחָה **mᵉnûchâh**, *men-oo-khaw';* fem. of 4495; *repose* or (adv.) *peacefully;* fig. *consolation* (spec. *matrimony*); hence (concr.) an *abode:*—comfortable, ease, quiet, rest (-ing place), still.

4497. מָנוֹן **mânôwn**, *maw-nohn';* from 5125; a *continuator,* i.e. *heir:*—son.

4498. מָנוֹס **mânôwç**, *maw-noce';* from 5127; a *retreat* (lit. or fig.); abstr. a *fleeing:*—× apace, escape, way to flee, flight, refuge.

4499. מְנוּסָה **mᵉnuwçâh**, *men-oo-saw';* or

מְנֻסָה **mᵉnûçâh**, *men-oo-saw';* fem. of 4498; *retreat:*—fleeing, flight.

4500. מָנוֹר **mânôwr**, *maw-nore';* from 5214; a *yoke* (prop. for *ploughing*), i.e. the *frame* of a loom:—beam.

4501. מְנוֹרָה **menôwrâh**, *men-o-raw';* or

מְנֹרָה **mᵉnôrâh**, *men-o-raw';* fem. of 4500 (in the orig. sense of 5216); a *chandelier:*—candlestick.

4502. מִנְּזָר **minnᵉzâr**, *min-ez-awr';* from 5144; a *prince:*—crowned.

4503. מִנְחָה **minchâh**, *min-khaw';* from an unused root mean. to *apportion,* i.e. *bestow;* a *donation;* euphem. *tribute;* spec. a sacrificial *offering* (usually bloodless and voluntary):—gift, oblation, (meat) offering, present, sacrifice.

4504. מִנְחָה **minchâh** (Chald.), *min-khaw';* corresp. to 4503; a sacrificial *offering:*—oblation, meat offering.

מְנֻחָה **mᵉnûchâh**. See 4496.

מְנֻחוֹת **Mᵉnûchôwth**. See 2679.

4505. מְנַחֵם **Mᵉnachêm**, *men-akh-ame';* from 5162; *comforter; Menachem,* an Isr.:—Menahem.

4506. מָנַחַת **Mânachath**, *maw-nakh'-ath;* from 5117; *rest; Manachath,* the name of an Edomite and of a place in Moab:—Manahath.

מְנַחְתִּי **Mᵉnachtîy**. See 2680.

4507. מְנִי **Mᵉnîy**, *men-ee';* from 4487; the *Apportioner,* i.e. Fate (as an idol):—number.

מִנִּי **minnîy**. See 4480, 4482.

4508. מִנִּי **Minnîy**, *min-nee';* of for. der.; *Minni,* an Armenian province:—Minni.

מְנָיוֹת **mᵉnâyôwth**. See 4521.

4509. מִנְיָמִין **Minyâmîyn**, *min-yaw-meen';* from 4480 and 3225; *from* (the) *right hand; Minjamin,* the name of two Isr.:—Miniamin. Comp. 4326.

4510. מִנְיָן **minyân** (Chald.), *min-yawn';* from 4483; *enumeration:*—number.

4511. מִנִּית **Minnîyth**, *min-neeth';* from the same as 4482; *enumeration; Minnith,* a place E. of the Jordan:—Minnith.

4512. מִנְלֶה **minleh**, *min-leh';* from 5239; *completion,* i.e. (in produce) *wealth:*—perfection.

מְנֻסָה **mᵉnûçâh**. See 4499.

4513. מָנַע **mânaʻ**, *maw-nah';* a prim. root; to *debar* (neg. or pos.) from benefit or injury:—deny, keep (back), refrain, restrain, withhold.

4514. מַנְעוּל **manʻûwl**, *man-ool';* or

מַנְעֻל **manʻûl**, *man-ool';* from 5274; a *bolt:*—lock.

4515. מִנְעָל **manʻâl**, *man-awl';* from 5274; a *bolt:*—shoe.

4516. מַנְעַם **manʻam**, *man-am';* from 5276; a *delicacy:*—dainty.

4517. מְנַעַנְעַ **mᵉnaʻnaʻ**, *men-ah-ah';* from 5128; a *sistrum* (so called from its *rattling* sound):—cornet.

4518. מְנַקִּית **mᵉnaqqîyth**, *men-ak-keeth';* from 5352; a *sacrificial basin* (for holding blood):—bowl.

מְנֹרָה **mᵉnôrâh**. See 4501.

4519. מְנַשֶּׁה **Mᵉnashsheh**, *men-ash-sheh';* from 5382; *causing to forget; Menashsheh,* a grandson of Jacob, also the tribe desc. from him, and its territory:—Manasseh.

4520. מְנַשִּׁי **Mᵉnashshîy**, *men-ash-shee';* from 4519; a *Menashshite* or desc. of Menashsheh:—of Manasseh, Manassites.

4521. מְנָת **mᵉnâth**, *men-awth';* from 4487; an *allotment* (by courtesy, law or providence):—portion.

4522. מַס **maç**, *mas;* or

מִס **miç**, *mees;* from 4549; prop. a *burden* (as causing to *faint*), i.e. a *tax* in the form of forced *labor:*—discomfited, levy, task [-master], tribute (-tary).

4523. מָס **mâç**, *mawce;* from 4549; *fainting,* i.e. (fig.) *disconsolate:*—is afflicted.

4524. מֵסַב **mêçab**, *may-sab';* plur. masc.

מְסִבִּים **mᵉçibbîym**, *mes-ib-beem';* or fem.

מְסִבּוֹת **mᵉçibbôwth**, *mes-ib-bohth';* from 5437; a *divan* (as *enclosing* the room); abstr. (adv.) *around:*—that compass about, (place) round about, at table.

מְסֻבָּה **mûçabbâh**. See 4142.

4525. מַסְגֵּר **maçgêr**, *mas-gare';* from 5462; a *fastener,* i.e. (of a person) a *smith,* (of a thing) a *prison:*—prison, smith.

4526. מִסְגֶּרֶת **miçgereth**, *mis-gheh'-reth;* from 5462; something *enclosing,* i.e. a *margin* (of a region, of a panel); concr. a *stronghold:*—border, close place, hole.

4527. מַסַּד **maççad**, *mas-sad';* from 3245; a *foundation:*—foundation.

מוֹסָדָה **môçâdâh**. See 4146.

4528. מִסְדְּרוֹן **miçdᵉrôwn**, *mis-der-ohn';* from the same as 5468; a *colonnade* or internal portico (from its *rows* of pillars):—porch.

4529. מָסָה **mâçâh**, *maw-saw';* a prim. root; to *dissolve:*—make to consume away, (make to) melt, water.

4530. מִסָּה **miççâh**, *mis-saw';* from 4549 (in the sense of *flowing*); *abundance,* i.e. (adv.) *liberally:*—tribute.

4531. מַסָּה **maççâh**, *mas-saw';* from 5254; a *testing,* of men (judicial) or of God (querulous):—temptation, trial.

4532. מַסָּה **Maççâh**, *mas-saw';* the same as 4531; *Massah,* a place in the Desert:—Massah.

4533. מַסְוֶה **maçveh**, *mas-veh';* appar. from an unused root mean. to *cover;* a *veil:*—vail.

4534. מְסוּכָה **mᵉçûwkâh**, *mes-oo-kaw';* for 4881; a *hedge:*—thorn hedge.

4535. מַסָּח **maççâch**, *mas-sawkh';* from 5255 in the sense of *staving* off; a *cordon,* (adv.) or (as a) military *barrier:*—broken down.

4536. מִסְחָר **miçchâr**, *mis-khawr';* from 5503; *trade:*—traffic.

4537. מָסַךְ **mâçak**, *maw-sak';* a prim. root; to *mix,* espec. wine (with spices):—mingle.

4538. מֶסֶךְ **meçek**, *meh'-sek;* from 4537; a *mixture,* i.e. of wine with spices:—mixture.

4539. מָסָךְ **mâçâk**, *maw-sawk';* from 5526; a *cover,* i.e. *veil:*—covering, curtain, hanging.

4540. מְסֻכָּה **mᵉçukkâh**, *mes-ook-kaw';* from 5526; a *covering,* i.e. garniture:—covering.

4541. מַסֵּכָה **maççêkâh**, *mas-say-kaw';* from 5258; prop. a *pouring* over, i.e. *fusion* of metal (espec. a *cast* image); by impl. a *libation,* i.e. league; concr. a *coverlet* (as if *poured* out):—covering, molten (image), vail.

4542. מִסְכֵּן **miçkên**, *mis-kane';* from 5531; *indigent:*—poor (man).

4543. מִסְכְּנָה **miçkᵉnâh**, *mis-ken-aw';* by transp. from 3664; a *magazine:*—store (-house), treasure.

4544. מִסְכֵּנֻת **miçkênûth**, *mis-kay-nooth';* from 4542; *indigence:*—scarceness.

4545. מַסֶּכֶת **maççeketh**, *mas-seh'-keth;* from 5259 in the sense of *spreading* out; something *expanded,* i.e. the *warp* in a loom (as *stretched* out to receive the woof):—web.

4546. מְסִלָּה **mᵉçillâh**, *mes-il-law';* from 5549; a *thoroughfare* (as *turnpiked*), lit. or fig.; spec. a *viaduct,* a *staircase:*—causeway, course, highway, path, terrace.

4547. מַסְלוּל **maçlûwl**, *mas-tool';* from 5549; a *thoroughfare* (as turnpiked):—highway.

4548. מַסְמֵר **maçmêr**, *mas-mare';* or

מִסְמֵר **miçmêr**, *mis-mare';* also (fem.)

מַסְמְרָה **maçmᵉrâh**, *mas-mer-aw';* or

מִסְמְרָה **miçmᵉrâh**, *mis-mer-aw';* or even

מַשְׂמְרָה **masmᵉrâh** (Eccles. 12 : 11), *mas-mer-aw';* from 5568; a *peg* (as *bristling* from the surface):—nail.

4549. מָסַס **mâçaç**, *maw-sas'*; a prim. root; to *liquefy*; fig. to *waste* (with disease), to *faint* (with fatigue, fear or grief):—discourage, faint, be loosed, melt (away), refuse, × utterly.

4550. מַסַּע **maççaʻ**, *mas-sah'*; from 5265; a *departure* (from *striking* the tents), i.e. march (not necessarily a single day's travel); by impl. a *station* (or point of *departure*):—journey (-ing).

4551. מַסָּע **maççâʻ**, *mas-saw'*; from 5265 in the sense of *projecting*; a *missile* (spear or arrow); also a *quarry* (whence stones are, as it were, *ejected*):—before it was brought, dart.

4552. מִסְעָד **miçʻâd**, *mis-awd'*; from 5582; a *balustrade* (for stairs):—pillar.

4553. מִסְפֵּד **miçpêd**, *mis-pade'*; from 5594; a *lamentation*:—lamentation, one mourneth, mourning, wailing.

4554. מִסְפּוֹא **miçpôwʼ**, *mis-po'*; from an unused root mean. to *collect*; *fodder*:—provender.

4555. מִסְפָּחָה **miçpâchâh**, *mis-paw-khaw'*; from 5596; a *veil* (as *spread* out):—kerchief.

4556. מִסְפַּחַת **miçpachath**, *mis-pakh'-ath*; from 5596; *scurf* (as *spreading* over the surface):—scab.

4557. מִסְפָּר **miçpâr**, *mis-pawr'*; from 5608; a *number*, def. (arithmetical) or indef. (large, *innumerable*; small, a *few*); also (abstr.) *narration*:— + abundance, account, × all, × few, [in-] finite, (certain) number (-ed), tale, telling, + time.

4558. מִסְפָּר **Miçpâr**, *mis-pawr'*; the same as 4457; *number*; *Mispar*, an Isr.:—Mizpar. Comp. 4559.

מֹסֵרוֹת **Môçêrowth**. See 4149.

4559. מִסְפֶּרֶת **Miçpereth**, *mis-peh'-reth*; fem. of 4457; *enumeration*; *Mispereth*, an Isr.:—Mispereth. Comp. 4458.

4560. מָסַר **mâçar**, *maw-sar'*; a prim. root; to *sunder*, i.e. (trans.) *set apart*, or (reflex.) *apostatize*:—commit, deliver.

4561. מֹסָר **môçâr**, *mo-sawr'*; from 3256; *admonition*:—instruction.

4562. מַסֹּרֶת **mâçôreth**, *maw-so'-reth*; from 631; a *band*:—bond.

4563. מִסְתּוֹר **miçtôwr**, *mis-tore'*; from 5641; a *refuge*:—covert.

4564. מַסְתֵּר **maçtêr**, *mas-tare'*; from 5641; prop. a *hider*, i.e. (abstr.) a hiding, i.e. *aversion*:—hid.

4565. מִסְתָּר **miçtâr**, *mis-tawr'*; from 5641; prop. a *concealer*, i.e. a *covert*:—secret (-ly, place).

מְעָא **meʻâʼ**. See 4577.

4566. מַעְבָּד **maʻbâd**, *mah-bawd'*; from 5647; an *act*:—work.

4567. מַעְבָּד **maʻbâd** (Chald.), *mah-bawd'*; corresp. to 4566; an *act*:—work.

4568. מַעֲבֶה **maʻăbeh**, *mah-ab-eh'*; from 5666; prop. *compact* (part of soil), i.e. *loam*:—clay.

4569. מַעֲבָר **maʻăbâr**, *mah-ab-awr'*; or fem.

מַעֲבָרָה **maʻăbârâh**, *mah-ab-aw-raw'*; from 5674; a *crossing*-place (of a river, a *ford*; of a mountain, a *pass*); abstr. a *transit*, i.e. (fig.) *overwhelming*:—ford, place where . . . pass, passage.

4570. מַעְגָּל **maʻgâl**, *mah-gawl'*; or fem.

מַעְגָּלָה **maʻgâlâh**, *mah-gaw-law'*; from the same as 5696; a *track* (lit. or fig.); also a *rampart* (as *circular*):—going, path, trench, way ([-side]).

4571. מָעַד **mâʻad**, *maw-ad'*; a prim. root; to *waver*:—make to shake, slide, slip.

מוֹעֵד **môʻêd**. See 4150.

4572. מַעֲדַי **Maʻăday**, *mah-ad-ah'ee*; from 5710; *ornamental*; *Maadai*, an Isr.:—Maadai.

4573. מַעַדְיָה **Maʻadyâh**, *mah-ad-yaw'*; from 5710 and 3050; *ornament of Jah*; *Maadjah*, an Isr.:—Maadiah. Comp. 4153.

4574. מַעֲדָן **maʻădân**, *mah-ad-awn'*; or (fem.)

מַעֲדַנָּה **maʻădannâh**, *mah-ad-an-naw'*; from 5727; a *delicacy* or (abstr.) *pleasure* (adv. *cheerfully*):—dainty, delicately, delight.

4575. מַעֲדַנָּה **maʻădannâh**, *mah-ad-an-naw'*; by transp. from 6029; a *bond*, i.e. *group*:—influence.

4576. מַעְדֵּר **maʻdêr**, *mah-dare'*; from 5737; a (weeding) *hoe*:—mattock.

4577. מְעָה **meʻâh** (Chald.), *meh-aw'*; or

מְעָא **meʻâʼ** (Chald.), *meh-aw'*; corresp. to 4578; only in plur. the *bowels*:—belly.

4578. מֵעֶה **mêʻâh**, *may-aw'*; from an unused root prob. mean. to *be soft*; used only in plur. the *intestines*, or (collect.) the *abdomen*, fig. *sympathy*; by impl. a *vest*; by extens. the *stomach*, the *uterus* (or of men, the seat of generation), the *heart* (fig.):—belly, bowels, × heart, womb.

4579. מֵעָה **mêʻâh**, *may-aw'*; fem. of 4578; the *belly*, i.e. (fig.) interior:—gravel.

4580. מָעוֹג **mâʻôwg**, *maw-ogue'*; from 5746; a *cake* of bread (with 3934 a *table-buffoon*, i.e. *parasite*):—cake, feast.

4581. מָעוֹז **mâʻôwz**, *maw-oze'* (also

מָעוּז **mâʻûwz**, *maw-ooz'*); or

מָעֹז **mâʻôz**, *maw-oze'* (also

מָעֻז **mâʻûz**, *maw-ooz'*); from 5810; a *fortified* place; fig. a *defence*:—force, fort (-ress), rock, strength (-en), (× most) strong (hold).

4582. מָעוֹךְ **Mâʻôwk**, *maw-oke'*; from 4600; *oppressed*; *Maok*, a Philistine:—Maoch.

4583. מָעוֹן **mâʻôwn**, *maw-ohn'*; or

מָעִין **mâʻîyn** (1 Chron. 4 : 41), *maw-een'*; from the same as 5772; an *abode*, of God (the Tabernacle or the Temple), men (their home) or animals (their lair); hence a *retreat* (asylum):—den, dwelling ([-] place), habitation.

4584. מָעוֹן **Mâʻôwn**, *maw-ohn'*; the same as 4583; a *residence*; *Maon*, the name of an Isr. and of a place in Pal.:—Maon, Maonites. Comp. 1010, 4586.

4585 מְעוֹנָה **meʻôwnâh**, *meh-o-naw'*; or

מְעֹנָה **meʻônâh**, *meh-o-naw'*; fem. of 4583, and mean. the same:—den, habitation, (dwelling) place, refuge.

4586. מְעוּנִי **Meʻûwnîy**, *meh-oo-nee'*; or

מְעִינִי **Meʻîynîy**, *meh-ee-nee'*; prob. patrial from 4584; a *Meünite*, or inhab. of Maon (only in plur.):—Mehunim (-s), Meunim.

4587. מְעוֹנֹתַי **Meʻôwnôthay**, *meh-o-no-thah'ee*; plur. of 4585; *habitative*; *Meonothai*, an Isr.:—Meonothai.

4588. מָעוּף **mâʻûwph**, *maw-oof'*; from 5774 in the sense of *covering* with shade [comp. 4155]; *darkness*:—dimness.

4589. מָעוֹר **mâʻôwr**, *maw-ore'*; from 5783; *nakedness*, i.e. (in plur.) the *pudenda*:—nakedness.

מָעֹז **mâʻôz**. See 4583.

מָעֻז **mâʻûz**. See 4583.

4590. מַעַזְיָה **Maʻazyâh**, *mah-az-yaw'*; or

מַעַזְיָהוּ **Maʻazyâhûw**, *mah-az-yaw'-hoo*; prob. from. 5756 (in the sense of *protection*) and 3050; *rescue of Jah*; *Maazjah*, the name of two Isr.:—Maaziah.

4591. מָעַט **mâʻaṭ**, *maw-at'*; a prim. root; prop. to *pare* off, i.e. *lessen*; intrans. to *be* (or caus. to *make*) *small* or *few* (or fig. *ineffective*):—suffer to decrease, diminish, (be, × borrow a, give, make) few (in number, -ness), gather least (little), be (seem) little, (× give the) less, be minished, bring to nothing.

4592. מְעַט **meʻaṭ**, *meh-at'*; or

מְעָט **meʻâṭ**, *meh-awt'*; from 4591; a *little* or *few* (often adv. or compar.):—almost, (some, very) few (-er, -est), lightly, little (while), (very) small (matter, thing), some, soon, × very.

4593. מָעֹט **mâʻôṭ**, *maw-ote'*; pass. adj. of 4591; *thinned* (as to the edge), i.e. *sharp*:—wrapped up.

4594. מַעֲטֶה **maʻăṭeh**, *mah-at-eh'*; from 5844; a *vestment*:—garment.

4595. מַעֲטָפָה **maʻăṭâphâh**, *mah-at-aw-faw'*; from 5848; a *cloak*:—mantle.

4596. מְעִי **meʻîy**, *meh-ee'*; from 5753; a *pile* of rubbish (as *contorted*), i.e. a *ruin* (comp. 5856):—heap.

4597. מָעַי **Mâʻai**, *maw-ah'ee*; prob. from 4578; *sympathetic*; *Maai*, an Isr.:—Maai.

4598. מְעִיל **meʻîyl**, *meh-eel'*; from 4603 in the sense of *covering*; a *robe* (i.e. upper and outer *garment*):—cloke, coat, mantle, robe.

מֵעִים **mêʻîym**. See 4578.

מְעִין **meʻîyn** (Chald.). See 4577.

4599. מַעְיָן **maʻyân**, *mah-yawn'*; or

מַעְיְנוֹ **maʻyenôw** (Psa. 114 : 8), *mah-yen-o'*; or (fem.)

מַעְיָנָה **maʻyânâh**, *mah-yaw-naw'*; from 5869 (as a denom. in the sense of a *spring*); a *fountain* (also collect.), fig. a *source* (of satisfaction):—fountain, spring, well.

מְעִינִי **Meʻîynîy**. See 4586.

4600. מָעַךְ **mâʻak**, *maw-ak'*; a prim. root; to *press*, i.e. to *pierce*, *emasculate*, *handle*:—bruised, stuck, be pressed.

4601. מַעֲכָה **Maʻăkâh**, *mah-ak-aw'*; or

מַעֲכָת **Maʻăkâth** (Josh. 13 : 13), *mah-ak-awth'*; from 4600; *depression*; *Maakah* (or *Maakath*), the name of a place in Syria, also of a Mesopotamian, of three Isr., and of four Israelitesses and one Syrian woman:—Maachah, Maachathites. See also 1038.

4602. מַעֲכָתִי **Maʻăkâthîy**, *mah-ak-aw-thee'*; patrial from 4601; a *Maakathite*, or inhab. of Maakah:—Maachathite.

4603. מָעַל **mâʻal**, *maw-al'*; a prim. root; prop. to *cover* up; used only fig. to *act covertly*, i.e. *treacherously*:—transgress, (commit, do a) trespass (-ing).

4604. מַעַל **maʻal**, *mah'-al*; from 4603; *treachery*, i.e. sin:—falsehood, grievously, sore, transgression, trespass, × very.

4605. מַעַל **maʻal**, *mah'-al*; from 5927; prop. the *upper* part, used only adv. with pref. *upward*, *above*, *overhead*, *from the top*, etc.:—above, exceeding (-ly), forward, on (× very) high, over, up (-on, -ward), very.

מֵעַל **mêʻal**. See 5921.

4606. מֵעָל **mêʻâl** (Chald.), *may-awl'*; from 5954; (only in plur. as sing.) the *setting* (of the sun):—going down.

4607. מֹעַל **môʻal**, *mo'-al*; from 5927; a *raising* (of the hands):—lifting up.

4608. מַעֲלֶה **maʻăleh**, *mah-al-eh'*; from 5927; an *elevation*, i.e. (concr.) *acclivity* or *platform*; abstr. (the relation or state) a *rise* or (fig.) *priority*:—ascent, before, chiefest, cliff, that goeth up, going up, hill, mounting up, stairs.

4609. מַעֲלָה **maʻălâh**, *mah-al-aw'*; fem. of 4608; *elevation*, i.e. the act (lit. a *journey* to a higher place, fig. a *thought* arising), or (concr.) the condition (lit. a *step* or *grade*-mark, fig. a *superiority* of station); spec. a climactic *progression* (in certain Psalms):—things that come up, (high) degree, deal, go up, stair, step, story.

4610. מַעֲלֵה עַקְרַבִּים **Ma'ălêh 'Aqrabbîym,** *mah-al-ay' ak-rab-beem';* from 4608 and (the plur. of) 6137; *Steep of Scorpions,* a place in the Desert:—Maaleh-accrabim, the ascent (going up) of Akrabbim.

4611. מַעֲלָל **ma'ălâl,** *mah-al-awl';* from 5953; an *act* (good or bad):—doing, endeavour, invention, work.

4612. מַעֲמָד **ma'ămâd,** *mah-am-awd';* from 5975; (fig.) a *position:*—attendance, office, place, state.

4613. מָעֳמָד **mo'ŏmâd,** *moh-om-awd';* from 5975; lit. a *foothold:*—standing.

4614. מַעֲמָסָה **ma'ămâçâh,** *mah-am-aw-saw';* from 6006; *burdensomeness:*—burdensome.

4615. מַעֲמָק **ma'ămâq,** *mah-am-awk';* from 6009; a *deep:*—deep, depth.

4616. מַעַן **ma'an,** *mah'-an;* from 6030; prop. *heed,* i.e. *purpose;* used only adv., *on account of* (as a motive or an aim), teleologically *in order that:*—because of, to the end (intent) that, for (to, . . . 's sake), + lest, that, to.

4617. מַעֲנֶה **ma'ăneh,** *mah-an-eh';* from 6030; a *reply* (favorable or contradictory):—answer, × himself.

4618. מַעֲנָה **ma'ănâh,** *mah-an-aw';* from 6031, in the sense of *depression* or *tilling;* a *furrow:*— + acre, furrow.

מְעֹנָה **me'ônâh.** See 4585.

4619. מַעַץ **Ma'ats,** *mah'-ats;* from 6095; *closure; Maats,* an Isr.:—Maaz.

4620. מַעֲצֵבָה **ma'ătsêbâh,** *mah-ats-ay-baw';* from 6087; *anguish:*—sorrow.

4621. מַעֲצָד **ma'ătsâd,** *mah-ats-awd';* from an unused root mean. to *hew;* an *axe:*—ax, tongs.

4622. מַעְצוֹר **ma'tsôwr,** *mah-tsore';* from 6113; obj. a *hindrance:*—restraint.

4623. מַעְצָר **ma'tsâr,** *mah-tsawr';* from 6113; subj. *control:*—rule.

4624. מַעֲקֶה **ma'ăqeh,** *mah-ak-eh';* from an unused root mean. to *repress;* a *parapet:*—battlement.

4625. מַעֲקָשׁ **ma'ăqâsh,** *mah-ak-awsh';* from 6140; a *crook* (in a road):—crooked thing.

4626. מַעַר **ma'ar,** *mah'-ar;* from 6168; a *nude* place, i.e. (lit.) the *pudenda,* or (fig.) a vacant *space:*—nakedness, proportion.

4627. מַעֲרָב **ma'ărâb,** *mah-ar-awb';* from 6148, in the sense of *trading; traffic;* by impl. mercantile *goods:*—market, merchandise.

4628. מַעֲרָב **ma'ărâb,** *mah-ar-awb';* or (fem.)

מַעֲרָבָה **ma'ărâbâh,** *mah-ar-aw-baw';* from 6150, in the sense of *shading;* the *west* (as the region of the *evening* sun):—west.

4629. מַעֲרֶה **ma'ăreh,** *mah-ar-eh';* from 6168; a *nude* place, i.e. a *common:*—meadows.

4630. מַעֲרָה° **ma'ărâh,** *mah-ar-aw';* fem. of 4629; an *open* spot:—army [*from the marg.*].

4631. מְעָרָה **me'ârâh,** *meh-aw-raw';* from 5783; a *cavern* (as dark):—cave, den, hole.

4632. מְעָרָה **Me'ârâh,** *meh-aw-raw';* the same as 4631; *cave; Meärah,* a place in Pal.:—Mearah.

4633. מַעֲרָךְ **ma'ărâk,** *mah-ar-awk';* from 6186; an *arrangement,* i.e. (fig.) mental *disposition:*—preparation.

4634. מַעֲרָכָה **ma'ărâkâh,** *mah-ar-aw-kaw';* fem. of 4633; an *arrangement;* concr. a *pile;* spec. a military *array:*—army, fight, be set in order, ordered place, rank, row.

4635. מַעֲרֶכֶת **ma'ăreketh,** *mah-ar-eh'-keth;* from 6186; an *arrangement,* i.e. (concr.) a *pile* (of loaves):—row, shewbread.

4636. מַעֲרֹם **ma'ărôm,** *mah-ar-ome';* from 6191, in the sense of *stripping; bare:*—naked.

4637. מַעֲרָצָה **ma'ărâtsâh,** *mah-ar-aw-tsaw';* from 6206; *violence:*—terror.

4638. מַעֲרָת **Ma'ărâth,** *mah-ar-awth';* a form of 4630; *waste; Maarath,* a place in Pal.:—Maarath.

4639. מַעֲשֶׂה **ma'ăseh,** *mah-as-eh';* from 6213; an *action* (good or bad); gen. a *transaction;* abstr. *activity;* by impl. a *product* (spec. a *poem*) or (gen.) *property:*—act, art, + bakemeat, business, deed, do (-ing), labour, thing made, ware of making, occupation, thing offered, operation, possession, × well, ([handy-, needle-, net-]) work, (-ing, -manship), wrought.

4640. מַעֲשַׂי **Ma'say,** *mah-as-ah'ee;* from 6213; *operative; Maasai,* an Isr.:—Maasiai.

4641. מַעֲשֵׂיָה **Ma'ăsêyâh,** *mah-as-ay-yaw';* or

מַעֲשֵׂיָהוּ **Ma'ăsêyâhûw,** *mah-as-ay-yaw'-hoo;* from 4639 and 3050; *work of Jah; Maasejah,* the name of sixteen Isr.:—Maaseiah.

4642. מַעֲשַׁקָּה **ma'ăshaqqâh,** *mah-ash-ak-kaw';* from 6231; *oppression:*—oppression, × oppressor.

4643. מַעֲשֵׂר **ma'ăsêr,** *mah-as-ayr';* or

מַעֲשַׂר **ma'ăsar,** *mah-as-ar';* and (in plur.) fem.

מַעַשְׂרָה **ma'asrâh,** *mah-as-raw';* from 6240; a *tenth;* espec. a *tithe:*—tenth (part), tithe (-ing).

4644. מֹף **Môph** *mofe;* of Eg. or.; *Moph,* the capital of Lower Egypt:—Memphis. Comp. 5297.

מְפִבֹשֶׁת **Mephîbôsheth.** See 4648.

4645. מִפְגָּע **miphgâ',** *mif-gaw';* from 6293; an *object of attack:*—mark.

4646. מַפָּח **mappâch,** *map-pawkh';* from 5301; a *breathing out* (of life), i.e. expiring:—giving up.

4647. מַפֻּחַ **mappûach,** *map-poo'-akh;* from 5301; the *bellows* (i.e. *blower*) of a forge:—bellows.

4648. מְפִיבֹשֶׁת **Mephîybôsheth,** *mef-ee-bo'-sheth;* or

מְפִבֹשֶׁת **Mephîbôsheth,** *mef-ee-bo'-sheth;* prob. from 6284 and 1322; *dispeller of shame* (i.e. of Baal); *Mephibosheth,* the name of two Isr.:—Mephibosheth.

4649. מֻפִּים **Muppîym,** *moop-peem';* a plur. appar. from 5130; *wavings; Muppim,* an Isr.:—Muppim. Comp. 8206.

4650. מֵפִיץ **mêphîyts,** *may-feets';* from 6327; a *breaker,* i.e. mallet:—maul.

4651. מַפָּל **mappâl,** *map-pawl';* from 5307; a *falling* off, i.e. chaff; also something *pendulous,* i.e. a flap:—flake, refuse.

4652. מִפְלָאָה **miphlâ'âh,** *mif-law-aw';* from 6381; a *miracle:*—wondrous work.

4653. מִפְלַגָּה **miphlaggâh,** *mif-lag-gaw';* from 6385; a *classification:*—division.

4654. מַפָּלָה **mappâlâh,** *map-paw-law';* or

מַפֵּלָה **mappêlâh,** *map-pay-law';* from 5307; something *fallen,* i.e. a *ruin:*—ruin (-ous).

4655. מִפְלָט **miphlâṭ,** *mif-lawt';* from 6403; an *escape:*—escape.

4656. מִפְלֶצֶת **miphletseth,** *mif-leh'-tseth;* from 6426; a *terror,* i.e. an idol:—idol.

4657. מִפְלָשׂ **miphlâs,** *mif-lawce';* from an unused root mean. to *balance;* a *poising:*—balancing.

4658. מַפֶּלֶת **mappeleth,** *map-peh'-leth;* from 5307; *fall,* i.e. *decadence;* concr. a *ruin;* spec. a *carcase:*—carcase, fall, ruin.

4659. מִפְעָל **miph'âl,** *mif-awl';* or (fem.)

מִפְעָלָה **miph'âlâh,** *mif-aw-law';* from 6466; a *performance:*—work.

4660. מַפָּץ **mappâts,** *map-pawts';* from 5310; a *smiting* to pieces:—slaughter.

4661. מַפֵּץ **mappêts,** *map-pates';* from 5310; a *smiter,* i.e. a war club:—battle ax.

4662. מִפְקָד **miphqâd,** *mif-kawd';* from 6485; an *appointment,* i.e. *mandate;* concr. a designated *spot;* spec. a *census:*—appointed place, commandment, number.

4663. מִפְקָד **Miphqâd,** *mif-kawd';* the same as 4662; *assignment; Miphkad,* the name of a gate in Jerus.:—Miphkad.

4664. מִפְרָץ **miphrâts,** *mif-rawts';* from 6555; a *break* (in the shore), i.e. a *haven:*—breach.

4665. מִפְרֶקֶת **miphreketh,** *mif-reh'-keth;* from 6561; prop. a *fracture,* i.e. *joint* (*vertebra*) of the neck:—neck.

4666. מִפְרָשׂ **miphrâs,** *mif-rawce';* from 6566; an *expansion:*—that which . . . spreadest forth, spreading.

4667. מִפְשָׂעָה **miphsâ'âh,** *mif-saw-aw';* from 6585; a *stride,* i.e. (by euphem.) the *crotch:*—buttocks.

מֹפֵת **môphêth.** See 4159.

4668. מַפְתֵּחַ **maphtêach,** *maf-tay'-akh;* from 6605; an *opener,* i.e. a *key:*—key.

4669. מִפְתָּח **miphtâch,** *mif-tawkh';* from 6605; an *aperture,* i.e. (fig.) *utterance:*—opening.

4670. מִפְתָּן **miphtân,** *mif-tawn';* from the same as 6620; a *stretcher,* i.e. a *sill:*—threshold.

4671. מֹץ **môts,** *motes;* or

מוֹץ **môwts** (Zeph. 2 : 2), *motes;* from 4160; *chaff* (as *pressed* out, i.e. *winnowed* or [rather] threshed loose):—chaff.

4672. מָצָא **mâtsâ',** *maw-tsaw';* a prim. root; prop. to *come forth to,* i.e. *appear* or *exist;* trans. to *attain,* i.e. *find* or *acquire;* fig. to *occur, meet* or *be present:*— + be able, befall, being, catch, × certainly, (cause to) come (on, to, to hand), deliver, be enough (cause to) find (-ing, occasion, out), get (hold upon), × have (here), be here, hit, be left, light (up-) on, meet (with), × occasion serve, (be) present, ready, speed, suffice, take hold on.

מֹצָא **môtsâ'.** See 4161.

4673. מַצָּב **matstsâb,** *mats-tsawb';* from 5324; a fixed *spot;* fig. an *office,* a military *post:*—garrison, station, place where . . . stood.

4674. מֻצָּב **mutstsâb,** *moots-tsawb';* from 5324; a *station,* i.e. military *post:*—mount.

4675. מַצָּבָה **matstsâbâh,** *mats-tsaw-baw';* or

מִצָּבָה **mitstsâbâh,** *mits-tsaw-baw';* fem. of 4673; a military *guard:*—army, garrison.

4676. מַצֵּבָה **matstsêbâh,** *mats-tsay-baw';* fem. (causat.) part. of 5324; something *stationed,* i.e. a *column* or (memorial *stone*); by anal. an *idol:*—garrison, (standing) image, pillar.

4677. מְצֹבָיָה **Metsôbâyâh,** *mets-o-baw-yaw';* appar. from 4672 and 3050; *found of Jah; Metsobajah,* a place in Pal.:—Mesobaite.

4678. מַצֶּבֶת **matstsebeth,** *mats-tseh'-beth;* from 5324; something *stationary,* i.e. a monumental *stone;* also the *stock* of a tree:—pillar, substance.

4679. מְצַד **metsad,** *mets-ad';* or

מְצָד **metsâd,** *mets-awd';* or (fem.)

מְצָדָה **metsâdâh,** *mets-aw-daw';* from 6679; a *fastness* (as a *covert* of ambush):—castle, fort, (strong) hold, munition.

מְצֻדָה **metsûdâh.** See 4686.

4680. מָצָה **mâtsâh,** *maw-tsaw';* a prim. root; to *suck* out; by impl. to *drain,* to *squeeze* out:—suck, wring (out).

4681. מֹצָה **Môtsâh,** *mo-tsaw';* act. part. fem. of 4680; *drained; Motsah,* a place in Pal.:—Mozah.

4682. מַצָּה **matstsâh,** *mats-tsaw';* from 4711 in the sense of *greedily* devouring for sweetness; prop. *sweetness;* concr. *sweet* (i.e. not soured or bittered with yeast); spec. an *unfermented cake* or loaf, or (ellipt.) the festival of *Passover* (because no leaven was then used):—unleavened (bread, cake), without leaven.

4683. מַצָּה **matstsâh,** *mats-tsaw';* from 5327; a *quarrel:*—contention, debate, strife.

4684. מִצְהָלָה **matshâlâh**, *mats-haw-law';* from 6670; a *whinnying* (through impatience for battle or lust):—neighing.

4685. מָצוֹד **mâtsôwd**, *maw-tsode';* or (fem.)
מְצוֹדָה **m^e tsôwdâh**, *mets-o-daw';* or
מְצֹדָה **m^e tsôdâh**, *mets-o-daw';* from 6679; a *net* (for *capturing* animals or fishes); also (by interch. for 4679) a *fastness* or (besieging) *tower:*—bulwark, hold, munition, net, snare.

4686. מָצוּד **mâtsûwd**, *maw-tsood';* or (fem.)
מְצוּדָה **m^e tsûwdâh**, *mets-oo-daw';* or
מְצֻדָה **m^e tsûdâh**, *mets-oo-daw';* for 4685; a *net*, or (abstr.) *capture;* also a *fastness:*—castle, defence, fort (-ress), (strong) hold, be hunted, net, snare, strong place.

4687. מִצְוָה **mitsvâh**, *mits-vaw';* from 6680; a *command*, whether human or divine (collect. the *Law*):—(which was) commanded (-ment), law, ordinance, precept.

4688. מְצוֹלָה **m^e tsôwlâh**, *mets-o-law';* or
מְצֹלָה **m^e tsôlâh**, *mets-o-law';* also
מְצוּלָה **m^e tsûwlâh**, *mets-oo-law';* or
מְצֻלָה **m^e tsûlâh**, *mets-oo-law';* from the same as 6683; a *deep* place (of water or mud):—bottom, deep, depth.

4689. מָצוֹק **mâtsôwq**, *maw-tsoke';* from 6693; a *narrow* place, i.e. (abstr. and fig.) *confinement* or *disability:*—anguish, distress, straitness.

4690. מָצוּק **mâtsûwq**, *maw-tsook';* or
מָצֻק **mâtsûq**, *maw-tsook';* from 6693; something *narrow*, i.e. a *column* or *hill-top:*—pillar, situate.

4691. מְצוּקָה **m^e tsûwqâh**, *mets-oo-kaw';* or
מְצֻקָה **m^e tsûqâh**, *mets-oo-kaw';* fem. of 4690; *narrowness*, i.e. (fig.) *trouble:*—anguish, distress.

4692. מָצוֹר **mâtsôwr**, *maw-tsore';* or
מָצוּר **mâtsûwr**, *maw-tsoor';* from 6696; something *hemming* in, i.e. (obj.) a *mound* (of besiegers), (abstr.) a *siege*, (fig.) *distress;* or (subj.) a *fastness:*—besieged, bulwark, defence, fenced, fortress, siege, strong (hold), tower.

4693. מָצוֹר **mâtsôwr**, *maw-tsore';* the same as 4692 in the sense of a *limit; Egypt* (as the *border* of Pal.):—besieged places, defence, fortified.

4694. מְצוּרָה **m^e tsûwrâh**, *mets-oo-raw';* or
מְצֻרָה **m^e tsûrâh**, *mets-oo-raw';* fem. of 4692; a *hemming* in, i.e. (obj.) a *mound* (of siege), or (subj.) a *rampart* (of protection), (abstr.) *fortification:*—fenced (city), fort, munition, strong hold.

4695. מַצּוּת **matstsûwth**, *mats-tsooth';* from 5327; a *quarrel:*—that contended.

4696. מֵצַח **mêtsach**, *may'-tsakh;* from an unused root mean. to be *clear*, i.e. *conspicuous;* the *forehead* (as *open* and *prominent*):—brow, forehead, + impudent.

4697. מִצְחָה **mitschâh**, *mits-khaw';* from the same as 4696; a *shin-piece* of armor (as *prominent*), only plur.:—greaves.

מְצִלָה **m^e tsôlah**. See 4688.

מְצֻלָה **m^e tsûlâh**. See 4688.

4698. מְצִלָּה **m^e tsillâh**, *mets-il-law';* from 6750; a *tinkler*, i.e. a *bell:*—bell.

4699. מְצֻלָּה **m^e tsullâh**, *mets-ool-law';* from 6751; *shade:*—bottom.

4700. מְצֵלֶת **m^e tsêleth**, *mets-ay'-leth;* from 6750; (only dual) double *tinklers*, i.e. cymbals:—cymbals.

4701. מִצְנֶפֶת **mitsnepheth**, *mits-neh'-feth;* from 6801; a *tiara*, i.e. official *turban* (of a king or high priest):—diadem, mitre.

4702. מַצָּע **matstsâ'**, *mats-tsaw';* from 3331; a *couch:*—bed.

4703. מִצְעָד **mits'âd**, *mits-awd';* from 6805; a *step;* fig. *companionship:*—going, step.

4704. מִצְּעִירָה **mitstsᵉ'îyrâh**, *mits-tseh-ee-raw';* fem. of 4705; prop. *littleness:* concr. *diminutive:*—little.

4705. מִצְעָר **mits'âr**, *mits-awr';* from 6819; *petty* (in size or number); adv. a *short* (time):—little one (while), small.

4706. מִצְעָר **Mits'âr**, *mits-awr';* the same as 4705; *Mitsar*, a peak of Lebanon:—Mizar.

4707. מִצְפֶּה **mitspeh**, *mits-peh';* from 6822; an *observatory*, espec. for military purposes:—watch tower.

4708. מִצְפֶּה **Mitspeh**, *mits-peh';* the same as 4707; *Mitspeh*, the name of five places in Pal.:—Mizpeh, watch tower. Comp. 4709.

4709. מִצְפָּה **Mitspah**, *mits-paw';* fem. of 4708; *Mitspah*, the name of two places in Pal.:—Mitspah. [This seems rather to be only an orth. var. of 4708 when "in pause".]

4710. מִצְפֻּן **mitspûn**, *mits-poon';* from 6845; a *secret* (place or thing, perh. *treasure*):—hidden thing.

4711. מָצַץ **mâtsats**, *maw-tsats';* a prim. root; to *suck:*—milk.

מוּצָקָה **mûtsâqâh**. See 4166.

4712. מֵצַר **mêtsar**, *may-tsar';* from 6896; something *tight*, i.e. (fig.) *trouble:*—distress, pain, strait.

מָצֻק **mâtsûq**. See 4690.

מְצֻקָה **m^e tsûqâh**. See 4691.

מְצֻרָה **m^e tsûrâh**. See 4694.

4713. מִצְרִי **Mitsrîy**, *mits-ree';* from 4714; a *Mitsrite*, or inhab. of Mitsrajim:—Egyptian, of Egypt.

4714. מִצְרַיִם **Mitsrayim**, *mits-rah'-yim;* dual of 4693; *Mitsrajim*, i.e. Upper and Lower Egypt:—Egypt, Egyptians, Mizraim.

4715. מִצְרֵף **mitsrêph**, *mits-rafe';* from 6884; a *crucible:*—fining pot.

4716. מַק **maq**, *mak;* from 4743; prop. a *melting*, i.e. *putridity:*—rottenness, stink.

4717. מַקָּבָה **maqqâbâh**, *mak-kaw-baw';* from 5344; prop. a *perforatrix*, i.e. a *hammer* (as *piercing*):—hammer.

4718. מַקֶּבֶת **maqqebeth**, *mak-keh'-beth;* from 5344; prop. a *perforator*, i.e. a *hammer* (as *piercing*); also (intrans.) a *perforation*, i.e. a *quarry:*—hammer, hole.

4719. מַקֵּדָה **Maqqêdâh**, *mak-kay-daw';* from the same as 5348 in the denom. sense of *herding* (comp. 5349); *fold; Makkedah*, a place in Pal.:—Makkedah.

4720. מִקְדָּשׁ **miqdâsh**, *mik-dawsh';* or
מִקְּדָשׁ **miqqedâsh** (Exod. 15 : 17), *mik-ked-awsh';* from 6942; a *consecrated* thing or place, espec. a *palace*, *sanctuary* (whether of Jehovah or of idols) or *asylum:*—chapel, hallowed part, holy place, sanctuary.

4721. מַקְהֵל **maqhêl**, *mak-hale';* or (fem.)
מַקְהֵלָה **maqhêlâh**, *mak-hay-law';* from 6950; an *assembly:*—congregation.

4722. מַקְהֵלֹת **Maqhêlôth**, *mak-hay-loth';* plur. of 4721 (fem.); *assemblies; Makheloth*, a place in the Desert:—Makheloth.

4723. מִקְוֶה **miqveh**, *mik-veh';* or
מִקְוֵה **miqvêh** (1 Kings 10 : 28), *mik-vay';* or
מִקְוֵא **miqvê'** (2 Chron. 1 : 16), *mik-vay';* from 6960; something *waited* for, i.e. *confidence* (obj. or subj.); also a *collection*, i.e. (of water) a *pond*, or (of men and horses) a *caravan* or *drove:*—abiding, gathering together, hope, linen yarn, plenty [of water], pool.

4724. מִקְוָה **miqvâh**, *mik-vaw';* fem. of 4723; a *collection*, i.e. (of water) a *reservoir:*—ditch.

4725. מָקוֹם **mâqôwm**, *maw-kome';* or
מָקֹם **mâqôm**, *maw-kome';* also (fem.)
מְקוֹמָה **m^e qôwmâh**, *mek-o-mah';* or
מְקֹמָה **m^e qômâh**, *mek-o-mah';* from 6965; prop. a *standing*, i.e. a *spot;* but used widely of a *locality* (gen. or spec.); also (fig.) of a *condition* (of body or mind):—country, × home, × open, place, room, space, × whither [-soever].

4726. מָקוֹר **mâqôwr**, *maw-kore';* or
מָקֹר **mâqôr**, *maw-kore';* from 6979; prop. something *dug*, i.e. a (gen.) *source* (of water, even when naturally flowing; also of tears, blood [by euphem. of the female *pudenda*]; fig. of happiness, wisdom, progeny):—fountain, issue, spring, well (-spring).

4727. מִקָּח **miqqâch**, *mik-kawkh';* from 3947; *reception:*—taking.

4728. מַקָּחָה **maqqâchâh**, *mak-kaw-khaw';* from 3947; something *received*, i.e. *merchandise* (purchased):—ware.

4729. מִקְטָר **miqṭâr**, *mik-tawr';* from 6999; something to *fume* (incense) on, i.e. a *hearth* place:—to burn . . . upon.

מְקַטְּרָה **m^e qaṭṭ^e râh**. See 6999.

4730. מִקְטֶרֶת **miqṭereth**, *mik-teh'-reth;* fem. of 4729; something to *fume* (incense) in, i.e. a *coal-pan:*—censer.

4731. מַקֵּל **maqqêl**, *mak-kale';* or (fem.)
מַקְּלָה **maqq^e lâh**, *mak-kel-aw';* from an unused root mean. appar. to *germinate;* a *shoot*, i.e. *stick* (with leaves on, or for walking, striking, guiding, divining):—rod, ([hand-]) staff.

4732. מִקְלוֹת **Miqlôwth**, *mik-lohth'* (or perh. *mik-kel-ohth'*); plur. of (fem.) 4731; *rods; Mikloth*, a place in the Desert:—Mikloth.

4733. מִקְלָט **miqlâṭ**, *mik-lawt';* from 7038 in the sense of *taking* in; an *asylum* (as a *receptacle*):—refuge.

4734. מִקְלַעַת **miqla'ath**, *mik-lah'-ath;* from 7049; a *sculpture* (prob. in bass-relief):—carved (figure), carving, graving.

מָקֹם **mâqôm**. See 4725.

מְקֹמָה **m^e qômâh**. See 4725.

4735. מִקְנֶה **miqneh**, *mik-neh';* from 7069; something *bought*, i.e. *property*, but only live *stock;* abstr. *acquisition:*—cattle, flock, herd, possession, purchase, substance.

4736. מִקְנָה **miqnâh**, *mik-naw';* fem. of 4735; prop. a *buying*, i.e. *acquisition;* concr. a piece of *property* (land or living); also the *sum* paid:—(he that is) bought, possession, piece, purchase.

4737. מִקְנֵיָהוּ **Miqnêyâhûw**, *mik-nay-yaw'-hoo;* from 4735 and 3050; *possession of Jah; Miknejah*, an Isr.:—Mikneiah.

4738. מִקְסָם **miqçâm**, *mik-sawm';* from 7080; an *augury:*—divination.

4739. מָקַץ **Mâqats**, *maw-kats';* from 7112; *end; Makats*, a place in Pal.:—Makaz.

4740. מַקְצוֹעַ **maqtsôwa'**, *mak-tso'-ah;* or
מַקְצֹעַ **maqtsôa'**, *mak-tso'-ah;* or (fem.)
מַקְצֹעָה **maqtsô'âh**, *mak-tso-aw';* from 7106 in the denom. sense of *bending;* an *angle* or recess:—corner, turning.

4741. מַקְצֻעָה **maqtsû'âh**, *mak-tsoo-aw';* from 7106; a *scraper*, i.e. a carving *chisel:*—plane.

4742. מְקֻצְעָה **m^e quts'âh**, *mek-oots-aw';* from 7106 in the denom. sense of *bending;* an *angle:*—corner.

4743. מָקַק **mâqaq**, *maw-kak';* a prim. root; to *melt;* fig. to *flow*, *dwindle*, *vanish:*—consume away, be corrupt, dissolve, pine away.

מָקֹר **mâqôr**. See 4726.

4744. מִקְרָא **miqrâ'**, *mik-raw';* from 7121; something *called* out, i.e. a public *meeting* (the act, the persons, or the place); also a *rehearsal:*—assembly, calling, convocation, reading.

4745. מִקְרֶה **miqreh**, *mik-reh';* from 7136; something *met* with, i.e. an *accident* or *fortune:*—something befallen, befalleth, chance, event, hap (-peneth).

4746. מְקָרֶה **mᵉqâreh**, *mek-aw-reh'*; from 7136; prop. something *meeting*, i.e. a *frame* (of timbers):—building.

4747. מְקֵרָה **mᵉqêrâh**, *mek-ay-raw'*; from the same as 7119; a *cooling* off:— × summer.

מֹקֵשׁ **môqêsh**. See 4170.

4748. מִקְשֶׁה **miqsheh**, *mik-sheh'*; from 7185 in the sense of *knotting* up round and hard; something *turned* (rounded), i.e. a *curl* (of tresses):— × well [set] hair.

4749. מִקְשָׁה **miqshâh**, *mik-shaw'*; fem. of 4748; *rounded* work, i.e. moulded by *hammering* (*repoussé*):—beaten (out of one piece, work), upright, whole piece.

4750. מִקְשָׁה **miqshâh**, *mik-shaw'*; denom. from 7180; lit. a *cucumbered* field, i.e. a *cucumber* patch:—garden of cucumbers.

4751. מַר **mar**, *mar*; or (fem.)

מָרָה **mârâh**, *maw-raw'*; from 4843; *bitter* (lit. or fig.); also (as noun) *bitterness*, or (adv.) *bitterly*:— + angry, bitter (-ly, -ness), chafed, discontented, × great, heavy.

4752. מַר **mar**, *mar*; from 4843 in its orig. sense of *distillation*; a *drop*:—drop.

4753. מֹר **môr**, *more*; or

מוֹר **môwr**, *more*; from 4843; *myrrh* (as *distilling* in drops, and also as *bitter*):—myrrh.

4754. מָרָא **mârâʼ**, *maw-raw'*; a prim. root; to *rebel*; hence (through the idea of *maltreating*) to *whip*, i.e. *lash* (self with wings, as the ostrich in running):—be filthy, lift up self.

4755. מָרָא **Mârâʼ**, *maw-raw'*; for 4751 fem.; *bitter*; *Mara*, a symbol. name of Naomi:—Mara.

4756. מָרֵא **mârêʼ** (Chald.), *maw-ray'*; from a root corresp. to 4754 in the sense of *domineering*; a *master*:—lord, Lord.

מֹרָא **môrâʼ**. See 4172.

4757. מְרֹאדַךְ בַּלְאֲדָן **Mᵉrôʼdak Balʼădân**, *mer-o-dak' bal-aw-dawn'*; of for. der.; *Merodak-Baladan*, a Bab. king:—Merodach-baladan. Comp. 4781.

4758. מַרְאֶה **marʼeh**, *mar-eh'*; from 7200; a *view* (the act of seeing); also an *appearance* (the thing seen), whether (real) a *shape* (espec. if handsome, *comeliness*; often plur. the *looks*), or (mental) a *vision*:— × apparently, appearance (-reth), × as soon as beautiful (-ly), countenance, fair, favoured, form, goodly, to look (up) on (to), look [-eth], pattern, to see, seem, sight, visage, vision.

4759. מַרְאָה **marʼâh**, *mar-aw'*; fem. of 4758; a *vision*; also (causat.) a *mirror*:—looking glass, vision.

4760. מֻרְאָה **murʼâh**, *moor-aw'*; appar. fem. pass. causat. part. of 7200; something *conspicuous*, i.e. the *craw* of a bird (from its *prominence*):—crop.

מְרֹאוֹן **Mᵉrʼôwn**. See 8112.

4761. מַרְאָשָׁה **marʼâshâh**, *mar-aw-shaw'*; denom. from 7218; prop. *headship*, i.e. (plur. for collect.) *dominion*:—principality.

4762 מַרְאֵשָׁה **Marʼêshâh**, *mar-ay-shaw'*; or

מָרֵשָׁה **Marêshâh**, *mar-ay-shaw'*; formed like 4761; *summit*; *Mareshah*, the name of two Isr. and of a place in Pal.:—Mareshah.

4763. מְרַאֲשָׁה **mᵉraʼăshâh** *mer-ah-ash-aw'*; formed like 4761; prop. a *head-piece*, i.e. (plur. for adv.) *at* (or *as*) the *head-rest* (or pillow):—bolster, head, pillow. Comp. 4772.

4764. מֵרַב **Mêrâb**, *may-rawb'*; from 7231; *increase*; *Merab*, a daughter of Saul:—Merab.

4765. מַרְבַד **marbad**, *mar-bad'*; from 7234; a *coverlet*:—covering of tapestry.

4766. מַרְבֶּה **marbeh**, *mar-beh'*; from 7235; prop. *increasing*; as noun, *greatness*, or (adv.) *greatly*:—great, increase.

4767. מִרְבָּה **mirbâh**, *meer-baw'*; from 7235; *abundance*, i.e. a great quantity:—much.

4768. מַרְבִּית **marbîyth**, *mar-beeth'*; from 7235; a *multitude*; also *offspring*; spec. *interest* (on capital):—greatest part, greatness, increase, multitude.

4769. מַרְבֵּץ **marbêts**, *mar-bates'*; from 7257; a *reclining* place, i.e. *fold* (for flocks):—couching place, place to lie down.

4770. מַרְבֵּק **marbêq**, *mar-bake'*; from an unused root mean. to *tie* up; a *stall* (for cattle):— × fat (-ted), stall.

מֹרַג **môrag**. See 4173.

4771. מַרְגּוֹעַ **margôwaʻ**, *mar-go'-ah*; from 7280; a *resting* place:—rest.

4772. מַרְגְּלָה **margᵉlâh**, *mar-ghel-aw'*; denom. from 7272; (plur. for collect.) a *foot-piece*, i.e. (adv.) *at the foot*, or (direct.) the *foot* itself:—feet. Comp. 4763.

4773. מַרְגֵּמָה **margêmâh**, *mar-gay-maw'*; from 7275; a *stone*-heap:—sling.

4774. מַרְגֵּעָה **margêʻâh**, *mar-gay-aw'*; from 7280; *rest*:—refreshing.

4775. מָרַד **mârad**, *maw-rad'*; a prim. root; to *rebel*:—rebel (-lious).

4776. מְרַד **mᵉrad** (Chald.), *mer-ad'*; from a root corresp. to 4775; *rebellion*:—rebellion.

4777. מֶרֶד **mered**, *meh'-red*; from 4775; *rebellion*:—rebellion.

4778. מֶרֶד **Mered**, *meh'-red*; the same as 4777; *Mered*, an Isr.:—Mered.

4779. מָרָד **mârâd** (Chald.), *maw-rawd'*; from the same as 4776; *rebellious*:—rebellious.

4780. מַרְדּוּת **mardûwth**, *mar-dooth'*; from 4775; *rebelliousness*:— × rebellious.

4781. מְרֹדָךְ **Mᵉrôdâk**, *mer-o-dawk'*; of for. der.; *Merodak*, a Bab. idol:—Merodach. Comp. 4757.

4782. מָרְדְּכַי **Mordᵉkay**, *mor-dek-ah'ee*; of for. der.; *Mordecai*, an Isr.:—Mordecai.

4783. מֻרְדָּף **murdâph**, *moor-dawf'*; from 7291; *persecuted*:—persecuted.

4784. מָרָה **mârâh**, *maw-raw'*; a prim. root; to *be* (caus. *make*) *bitter* (or unpleasant); (fig.) to *rebel* (or resist; causat. to *provoke*):—bitter, change, be disobedient, disobey, grievously, provocation, provoke (-ing), (be) rebel (against, -lious).

4785. מָרָה **Mârâh**, *maw-raw'*; the same as 4751 fem.; *bitter*; *Marah*, a place in the Desert:—Marah.

מֹרֶה **Môreh**. See 4175.

4786. מֹרָה **môrâh**, *mo-raw'*; from 4843; *bitterness*, i.e. (fig.) *trouble*:—grief.

4787. מָרָּה **morrâh**, *mor-raw'*; a form of 4786; *trouble*:—bitterness.

4788. מָרוּד **mârûwd**, *maw-rood'*; from 7300 in the sense of *maltreatment*; an *outcast*; (abstr.) *destitution*:—cast out, misery.

4789. מֵרוֹז **Mêrôwz**, *may-roze'*; of uncert. der.; *Meroz*, a place in Pal.:—Meroz.

4790. מְרוֹחַ **mᵉrôwach**, *mer-o-akh'*; from 4799; *bruised*, i.e. *emasculated*:—broken.

4791. מָרוֹם **mârôwm**, *maw-rome'*; from 7311; *altitude*, i.e. concr. (an *elevated place*), abstr. (*elevation*), fig. (*elation*), or adv. (*aloft*):—(far) above, dignity, haughty, height, (most, on) high (one, place), loftily, upward.

4792. מֵרוֹם **Mêrôwm**, *may-rome'*; formed like 4791; *height*; *Merom*, a lake in Pal.:—Merom.

4793. מֵרוֹץ **mêrôwts**, *may-rotes'*; from 7323; a *run* (the trial of speed):—race.

4794. מְרוּצָה **mᵉrûwtsâh**, *mer-oo-tsaw'*; or

מְרֻצָה **mᵉrûtsâh**, *mer-oo-tsaw'*; fem. of 4793; a *race* (the act), whether the manner or the progress:—course, running. Comp. 4835.

4795. מָרוּק **mârûwq**, *maw-rook'*; from 4838; prop. *rubbed*; but used abstr., a *rubbing* (with perfumery):—purification.

מְרוֹר **mᵉrôwr**. See 4844.

מְרוֹרָה **mᵉrôwrâh**. See 4846.

4796. מָרוֹת **Mârôwth**, *maw-rohth'*; plur. of 4751 fem.; *bitter* springs; *Maroth*, a place in Pal.:—Maroth.

4797. מִרְזַח **mirzach**, *meer-zakh'*; from an unused root mean. to *scream*; a *cry*, i.e. (of joy), a *revel*:—banquet.

4798. מַרְזֵחַ **marzêach**, *mar-zay'-akh*; formed like 4797; a *cry*, i.e. (of grief) a *lamentation*:—mourning.

4799. מָרַח **mârach**, *maw-rakh'*; a prim. root; prop. to *soften* by rubbing or pressure; hence (medicinally) to *apply* as an emollient:—lay for a plaister.

4800. מֶרְחָב **merchâb**, *mer-khawb'*; from 7337; *enlargement*, either lit. (an *open space*, usually in a good sense), or fig. (*liberty*):—breadth, large place (room).

4801. מֶרְחָק **merchâq**, *mer-khawk'*; from 7368; *remoteness*, i.e. (concr.) a *distant* place; often (adv.) *from afar*:— (a-, dwell in, very) far (country, off). See also 1023.

4802. מַרְחֶשֶׁת **marchesheth**, *mar-kheh'-sheth*; from 7370; a *stew-pan*:—fryingpan.

4803. מָרַט **mâraṭ**, *maw-rat'*; a prim. root; to *polish*; by impl. to *make bald* (the head), to *gall* (the shoulder); also, to *sharpen*:—bright, furbish, (have his) hair (be) fallen off, peeled, pluck off (hair).

4804. מְרַט **mᵉraṭ** (Chald.), *mer-at'*; corresp. to 4803; to *pull* off:—be plucked.

4805. מְרִי **mᵉrîy**, *mer-ee'*; from 4784; *bitterness*, i.e. (fig.) *rebellion*; concr. *bitter*, or *rebellious*:—bitter, (most) rebel (-lion, -lious).

4806. מְרִיא **mᵉrîyʼ**, *mer-ee'*; from 4754 in the sense of *grossness*, through the idea of *domineering* (comp. 4756); *stall-fed*; often (as noun) a *beeve*:—fat (fed) beast (cattle, -ling).

4807. מְרִיב בַּעַל **Mᵉrîyb Baʻal**, *mer-eeb' bah'-al*; from 7378 and 1168; *quarreller of Baal*; *Merib-Baal*, an epithet of Gideon:—Merib-baal. Comp. 4810.

4808. מְרִיבָה **mᵉrîybâh**, *mer-ee-baw'*; from 7378; *quarrel*:—provocation, strife.

4809. מְרִיבָה **Mᵉrîybâh**, *mer-ee-baw'*; the same as 4808; *Meribah*, the name of two places in the Desert:—Meribah.

4810. מְרִי בַעַל **Mᵉrîy Baʻal**, *mer-ee' bah'-al*; from 4805 and 1168; *rebellion of* (i.e. *against*) *Baal*; *Meri-Baal*, an epithet of Gideon:—Meri-baal. Comp. 4807.

4811. מְרָיָה **Mᵉrâyâh**, *mer-aw-yaw'*; from 4784; *rebellion*; *Merajah*, an Isr.:—Meraiah. Comp. 3236.

מֹרִיָּה **Môrîyâh**. See 4179.

4812. מְרָיוֹת **Mᵉrâyôwth**, *mer-aw-yohth'*; plur. of 4811; *rebellious*; *Merajoth*, the name of two Isr.:—Meraioth.

4813. מִרְיָם **Miryâm**, *meer-yawm'*; from 4805; *rebelliously*; *Mirjam*, the name of two Israelitesses:—Miriam.

4814. מְרִירוּת **mᵉrîyrûwth**, *mer-ee-rooth'*; from 4843; *bitterness*, i.e. (fig.) *grief*:—bitterness.

4815. מְרִירִי **mᵉrîyrîy**, *mer-ee-ree'*; from 4843; *bitter*, i.e. *poisonous*:—bitter.

4816. מֹרֶךְ **môrek**, *mo'-rek*; perh. from 7401; *softness*, i.e. (fig.) *fear*:—faintness.

4817. מֶרְכָּב **merkâb**, *mer-kawb'*; from 7392; a *chariot*; also a *seat* (in a vehicle):—chariot, covering, saddle.

4818. מֶרְכָּבָה **merkâbâh**, *mer-kaw-baw'*; fem. of 4817; a *chariot*:—chariot. See also 1024.

4819. מַרְכֹּלֶת **markôleth**, *mar-ko'-leth*; from 7402; a *mart*:—merchandise.

4820. מִרְמָה **mirmâh**, *meer-maw'*; from 7411 in the sense of *deceiving; fraud:*—craft, deceit (-ful, -fully), false, feigned, guile, subtilly, treachery.

4821. מִרְמָה **Mirmâh**, *meer-maw'*; the same as 4820; *Mirmah*, an Isr.:—Mirma.

4822. מְרֵמוֹת **Merêmôwth**, *mer-ay-mohth'*; plur. from 7311; *heights; Meremoth*, the name of two Isr.:—Meremoth.

4823. מִרְמָס **mirmâç**, *meer-mawce'*; from 7429; *abasement* (the act or the thing):—tread (down) -ing, (to be) trodden (down) under foot.

4824. מֵרֹנֹתִי **Mêrônôthîy**, *may-ro-no-thee'*; patrial from an unused noun; a *Meronothite*, or inhab. of some (otherwise unknown) Meronoth:—Meronothite.

4825. מֶרֶס **Mereç**, *meh'-res*; of for. der.; *Meres*, a Pers.:—Meres.

4826. מַרְסְנָא **Marçenâ'**, *mar-sen-aw'*; of for. der.; *Marsena*, a Pers.:—Marsena.

4827. מֵרַע **mêra'**, *may-rah'*; from 7489; used as (abstr.) noun, *wickedness:*—do mischief.

4828. מֵרֵעַ **mêrêa'**, *may-ray'-ah*; from 7462 in the sense of *companionship;* a *friend:*—companion, friend.

4829. מִרְעֶה **mir'eh**, *meer-eh'*; from 7462 in the sense of *feeding; pasture* (the place or the act); also the *haunt* of wild animals:—feeding place, pasture.

4830. מִרְעִית **mir'îyth**, *meer-eeth'*; from 7462 in the sense of *feeding; pasturage;* concr. a *flock:*—flock, pasture.

4831. מַרְעֲלָה **Mar'âlâh**, *mar-al-aw'*; from 7477; perh. *earthquake; Maralah*, a place in Pal.:—Maralah.

4832. מַרְפֵּא **marpê'**, *mar-pay'*; from 7495; prop. *curative*, i.e. lit. (concr.) a *medicine*, or (abstr.) a *cure;* fig. (concr.) *deliverance*, or (abstr.) *placidity:*—([in-]) cure (-able), healing (-lth), remedy, sound, wholesome, yielding.

4833. מִרְפָּשׂ **mirpâs**, *meer-paws'*; from 7515; *muddled* water:—that which . . . have fouled.

4834. מָרַץ **mârats**, *maw-rats'*; a prim. root; prop. to *press*, i.e. (fig.) to be *pungent* or vehement; to *irritate:*—embolden, be forcible, grievous, sore.

4835. מְרוּצָה **merûtsâh**, *mer-oo-tsaw'*; from 7533; *oppression:*—violence. See also 4794.

4836. מַרְצֵעַ **martsêa'**, *mar-tsay'-ah*; from 7527; an *awl:*—aul.

4837. מַרְצֶפֶת **martsepheth**, *mar-tseh'-feth*; from 7528; a *pavement:*—pavement.

4838. מָרַק **mâraq**, *maw-rak'*; a prim. root; to *polish;* by impl. to *sharpen;* also to *rinse:*—bright, furbish, scour.

4839. מָרָק **mârâq**, *maw-rawk'*; from 4838; *soup* (as if a *rinsing*):—broth. See also 6564.

4840. מֶרְקָח **merqâch**, *mer-kawkh'*; from 7543; a *spicy* herb:—× sweet.

4841. מֶרְקָחָה **merqâchâh**, *mer-kaw-khaw'*, fem. of 4840; abstr. a *seasoning* (with spicery); concr. an *unguent-kettle* (for preparing spiced oil):—pot of ointment, × well.

4842. מִרְקַחַת **mirqachath**, *meer-kakh'-ath*; from 7543; an aromatic *unguent;* also an *unguent-pot:*—prepared by the apothecaries' art, compound, ointment.

4843. מָרַר **mârar**, *maw-rar'*; a prim. root; prop. to *trickle* [see 4752]; but used only as a denom. from 4751; to *be* (causat. *make*) *bitter* (lit. or fig.):—(be, be in, deal, have, make) bitter (-ly, -ness), be moved with choler, (be, have sorely, it) grieved (-eth), provoke, vex.

4844. מְרֹר **merôr**, *mer-ore'*; or

מְרוֹר **merôwr**, *mer-ore'*; from 4843; a *bitter* herb:—bitter (-ness).

4845. מְרֵרָה **merêrâh**, *mer-ay-raw'*; from 4843; *bile* (from its bitterness):—gall.

4846. מְרֹרָה **merôrâh**, *mer-o-raw'*; or

מְרוֹרָה **merôwrâh**, *mer-o-raw'*; from 4843; prop. *bitterness;* concr. a *bitter thing;* spec. *bile;* also *venom* (of a serpent):—bitter (thing), gall.

4847. מְרָרִי **Merârîy**, *mer-aw-ree'*; from 4843; *bitter; Merari*, an Isr.:—Merari. See also 4848.

4848. מְרָרִי **Merârîy**, *mer-aw-ree'*; from 4847; a *Merarite* (collect.), or desc. of Merari:—Merarites.

מָרֵשָׁה **Mârêshâh**. See 4762.

4849. מִרְשַׁעַת **mirsha'ath**, *meer-shah'-ath*; from 7561; a female *wicked doer:*—wicked woman.

4850. מְרָתַיִם **Merâthayim**, *mer-aw-thah'-yim*; dual of 4751 fem.; *double bitterness; Merathajim*, an epithet of Babylon:—Merathaim.

4851. מַשׁ **Mash**, *mash*; of for. der.; *Mash*, a son of Aram, and the people desc. from him:—Mash.

4852. מֵשָׁא **Mêshâ'**, *may-shaw'*; of for. der.; *Mesha*, a place in Arabia:—Mesha.

4853. מַשָּׂא **massâ'**, *mas-saw'*; from 5375; a *burden;* spec. *tribute*, or (abstr.) *porterage;* fig. an *utterance*, chiefly a *doom*, espec. *singing;* mental, *desire:*—burden, carry away, prophecy, × they set, song, tribute.

4854. מַשָּׂא **Massâ'**, *mas-saw'*; the same as 4853; *burden; Massa*, a son of Ishmael:—Massa.

4855. מַשָּׁא **mashshâ'**, *mash-shaw'*; from 5383; a *loan;* by impl. *interest* on a debt:—exaction, usury.

4856. מַשֹּׂא **massô'**, *mas-so'*; from 5375; *partiality* (as a *lifting* up):—respect.

4857. מַשְׁאָב **mash'âb**, *mash-awb'*; from 7579; a *trough* for cattle to drink from:—place of drawing water.

מְשֹׁאָה **meshô'âh**. See 4875.

4858. מַשָּׂאָה **massâ'âh**, *mas-saw-aw'*; from 5375; a *conflagration* (from the *rising* of smoke):—burden.

4859. מַשָּׁאָה **mashshâ'âh**, *mash-shaw-aw'*; fem. of 4855; a *loan:*—× any [-thing], debt.

מַשָּׁאָה **mashshû'âh**. See 4876.

4860. מַשָּׁאוֹן **mashshâ'ôwn**, *mash-shaw-ohn'*; from 5377; *dissimulation:*—deceit.

4861. מִשְׁאָל **Mish'âl**, *mish-awl'*; from 7592; *request; Mishal*, a place in Pal.:—Mishal, Misheal. Comp. 4913.

4862. מִשְׁאָלָה **mish'âlâh**, *mish-aw-law'*; from 7592; a *request:*—desire, petition.

4863. מִשְׁאֶרֶת **mish'ereth**, *mish-eh'-reth*; from 7604 in the orig. sense of *swelling;* a *kneading-trough* (in which the dough *rises*):—kneading trough, store.

4864. מַשְׂאֵת **mas'êth**, *mas-ayth'*; from 5375; prop. (abstr.) a *raising* (as of the hands in prayer), or *rising* (of flame); fig. an *utterance;* concr. a *beacon* (as *raised*); a *present* (as taken), *mess*, or *tribute;* fig. a *reproach* (as a burden):—burden, collection, sign of fire, (great) flame, gift, lifting up, mess, oblation, reward.

מֹשָׁב **môshâb**. See 4186.

מְשֻׁבָה **meshûbâh**. See 4878.

4865. מִשְׁבְּצָה **mishbetsâh**, *mish-bets-aw'*; from 7660; a *brocade;* by anal. a (reticulated) *setting* of a gem:—ouch, wrought.

4866. מִשְׁבֵּר **mishbêr**, *mish-bare'*; from 7665; the *orifice* of the womb (from which the fœtus *breaks* forth):—birth, breaking forth.

4867. מִשְׁבָּר **mishbâr**, *mish-bawr'*; from 7665; a *breaker* (of the sea):—billow, wave.

4868. מִשְׁבָּת **mishbâth**, *mish-bawth'*; from 7673; *cessation*, i.e. destruction:—sabbath.

4869. מִשְׂגָּב **misgâb**, *mis-gawb'*; from 7682; prop. a *cliff* (or other *lofty* or *inaccessible* place); abstr. *altitude;* fig. a *refuge:*—defence, high fort (tower), refuge.

4869; *Misgab*, a place in Moab:—Misgab.

4870. מִשְׁגֶּה **mishgeh**, *mish-gay'*; from 7686; an *error:*—oversight.

4871. מָשָׁה **mâshâh**, *maw-shaw'*; a prim. root; to *pull* out (lit. or fig.):—draw (out).

4872. מֹשֶׁה **Môsheh**, *mo-sheh'*; from 4871; *drawing* out (of the water), i.e. *rescued; Mosheh*, the Isr. lawgiver:—Moses.

4873. מֹשֶׁה **Môsheh** (Chald.), *mo-sheh'*; corresp. to 4872:—Moses.

4874. מַשֶּׁה **mashsheh**, *mash-sheh'*; from 5383; a *debt:*— + creditor.

4875. מְשׁוֹאָה **meshôw'âh**, *mesh-o-aw'*; or

מְשֹׁאָה **meshô'âh**, *mesh-o-aw'*; from the same as 7722; (a) *ruin*, abstr. (the act) or concr. (the wreck):—desolation, waste.

4876. מַשּׁוּאָה **mashshûw'âh**, *mash-shoo-aw'*; or

מַשֻּׁאָה **mashshû'âh**, *mash-shoo-aw'*; for 4875; *ruin:*—desolation, destruction.

4877. מְשׁוֹבָב **Meshôwbâb**, *mesh-o-bawb'*; from 7725; *returned; Meshobab*, an Isr.:—Meshobab.

4878. מְשׁוּבָה **meshûwbâh**, *mesh-oo-baw'*; or

מְשֻׁבָה **meshûbâh**, *mesh-oo-baw'*; from 7725; *apostasy:*—backsliding, turning away.

4879. מְשׁוּגָה **meshûwgâh**, *mesh-oo-gaw'*; from an unused root mean. to *stray;* mis*take:*—error.

4880. מָשׁוֹט **mâshôwṭ**, *maw-shote'*; or

מִשּׁוֹט **mishshôwṭ**, *mish-shote'*; from 7751; an *oar:*—oar.

4881. מְשׂוּכָה **mesûwkâh**, *mes-oo-kaw'*; or

מְשֻׂכָה **mesûkâh**, *mes-oo-kaw'*; from 7753; a *hedge:*—hedge.

4882. מְשׁוּסָה **meshûwçâh**, *mesh-oo-saw'*; from an unused root mean. to *plunder; spoliation:*—spoil.

4883. מַשּׂוֹר **massôwr**, *mas-sore'*; from an unused root mean. to *rasp;* a *saw:*—saw.

4884. מְשׂוּרָה **mesûwrâh**, *mes-oo-raw'*; from an unused root mean. appar. to *divide;* a *measure* (for liquids):—measure.

4885. מָשׂוֹשׂ **mâsôws**, *maw-soce'*; from 7797; *delight*, concr. (the cause or object) or abstr. (the feeling):—joy, mirth, rejoice.

4886. מָשַׁח **mâshach**, *maw-shakh'*; a prim. root; to *rub* with oil, i.e. to *anoint;* by impl. to *consecrate;* also to *paint:*—anoint, paint.

4887. מְשַׁח **meshach** (Chald.), *mesh-akh'*; from a root corresp. to 4886; *oil:*—oil.

4888. מִשְׁחָה **mishchâh**, *meesh-khaw'*; or

מָשְׁחָה **moshchâh**, *mosh-khaw'*; from 4886; *unction* (the act); by impl. a consecratory *gift:*—(to be) anointed (-ing), ointment.

4889. מַשְׁחִית **mashchîyth**, *mash-kheeth'*; from 7843; *destructive*, i.e. (as noun) *destruction*, lit. (spec. a *snare*) or fig. (*corruption*):—corruption, (to) destroy (-ing), destruction, trap, × utterly.

4890. מִשְׂחָק **mischâq**, *mis-khawk'*; from 7831; a *laughing-stock:*—scorn.

4891. מִשְׁחָר **mishchâr**, *mish-khawr'*; from 7836 in the sense of day *breaking; dawn:*—morning.

4892. מַשְׁחֵת **mashchêth**, *mash-khayth'*; for 4889; *destruction:*—destroying.

4893. מִשְׁחָת **mishchâth**, *mish-khawth'*; or

מָשְׁחָת **moshchâth**, *mosh-khawth'*; from 7843; *disfigurement:*—corruption, marred.

4894. מִשְׁטוֹחַ **mishṭôwach**, *mish-to'-akh*; or

מִשְׁטַח **mishṭach**, *mish-takh'*; from 7849; a *spreading*-place:—(to) spread (forth, -ing, upon).

4895. מַשְׂטֵמָה **mastêmâh**, *mas-tay-maw'*; from the same as 7850; *enmity:*—hatred.

4896. מִשְׁטָר **mishṭâr**, *mish-tawr'*; from 7860; *jurisdiction:*—dominion.

4897. מֶשִׁי **meshîy**, *meh'-shee*; from 4871; *silk* (as *drawn* from the cocoon):—silk.

מֻשִׁי **Mûshîy**. See 4187.

4898. מְשֵׁיזַבְאֵל **Meshêyzab'êl**, *mesh-ay-zab-ale'*; from an equiv. to 7804 and 410; *delivered of God; Meshezabel*, an Isr.:—Meshezabeel.

4899. מָשִׁיחַ **mâshîyach**, *maw-shee'-akh*; from 4886; *anointed;* usually a *consecrated* person (as a king, priest, or saint); spec. the *Messiah:*—anointed, Messiah.

4900. מָשַׁךְ **mâshak**, *maw-shak'*; a prim. root; to *draw*, used in a great variety of applications (includ. to *sow*, to *sound*, to *prolong*, to *develop*, to *march*, to *remove*, to *delay*, to *be tall*, etc.):—draw (along, out), continue, defer, extend, forbear, × give, handle, make (pro-, sound) long, × sow, scatter, stretch out.

4901. מֶשֶׁךְ **meshek**, *meh'-shek*; from 4900; a *sowing;* also a *possession:*—precious, price.

4902. מֶשֶׁךְ **Meshek**, *meh'-shek*; the same in form as 4901, but prob. of for. der.; *Meshek*, a son of Japheth, and the people desc. from him:—Mesech, Meshech.

4903. מִשְׁכַּב **mishkab** (Chald.), *mish-kab'*; corresp. to 4904; a *bed:*—bed.

4904. מִשְׁכָּב **mishkâb**, *mish-kawb'*; from 7901; a *bed* (fig. a *bier*); abstr. *sleep;* by euphem. carnal *intercourse:*—bed ([-chamber]), couch, lieth (lying) with.

מְשֻׂכָה **mesûkâh**. See 4881.

4905. מַשְׂכִּיל **maskîyl**, *mas-keel'*; from 7919; *instructive*, i.e. a *didactic* poem:—Maschil.

מַשְׁכִּים **mashkîym**. See 7925.

4906. מַשְׂכִּית **maskîyth**, *mas-keeth'*; from the same as 7906; a *figure* (carved on stone, the wall, or any object); fig. *imagination:*—conceit, image (-ry), picture, × wish.

4907. מִשְׁכַּן **mishkan** (Chald.), *mish-kan'*; corresp. to 4908; *residence:*—habitation.

4908. מִשְׁכָּן **mishkân**, *mish-kawn'*; from 7931; a *residence* (includ. a shepherd's *hut*, the *lair* of animals, fig. the *grave;* also the *Temple*); spec. the *Tabernacle* (prop. its wooden walls):—dwelleth, dwelling (place), habitation, tabernacle, tent.

4909. מַשְׂכֹּרֶת **maskôreth**, *mas-koh'-reth*; from 7936; *wages* or a *reward:*—reward, wages.

4910. מָשַׁל **mâshal**, *maw-shal'*; a prim. root; to *rule:*—(have, make to have) dominion, governor, × indeed, reign, (bear, cause to, have) rule (-ing, -r), have power.

4911. מָשַׁל **mâshal**, *maw-shal'*; denom. from 4912; to *liken*, i.e. (trans.) to use figurative language (an allegory, adage, song or the like); intrans. to *resemble:*—be (-come) like, compare, use (as a) proverb, speak (in proverbs), utter.

4912. מָשָׁל **mâshâl**, *maw-shawl'*; appar. from 4910 in some orig. sense of *superiority* in mental action; prop. a pithy *maxim*, usually of a metaphorical nature; hence a *simile* (as an adage, poem, discourse):—byword, like, parable, proverb.

4913. מָשָׁל **Mâshâl**, *maw-shawl'*; for 4861; *Mashal*, a place in Pal.:—Mashal.

4914. מְשׁוֹל **meshôwl**, *mesh-ol'*; from 4911; a *satire:*—byword.

4915. מֹשֶׁל **môshel**, *mo'-shel*; (1) from 4910; *empire;* (2) from 4911; a *parallel:*—dominion, like.

מִשְׁלוֹשׁ **mishlôwsh**. See 7969.

4916. מִשְׁלוֹחַ **mishlôwach**, *mish-lo'-akh*; or

מִשְׁלֹחַ **mishlôach**, *mish-lo'-akh*; also

מִשְׁלָח **mishlâch**, *mish-lawkh'*; from 7971; a *sending* out, i.e. (abstr.) *presentation* (favorable), or *seizure* (unfavorable); also (concr.) a place of *dismissal*, or a *business* to be discharged:—to lay, to put, sending (forth), to set.

4917. מִשְׁלַחַת **mishlachath**, *mish-lakh'-ath*; fem. of 4916; a *mission*, i.e. (abstr. and favorable) *release*, or (concr. and unfavorable) an *army:*—discharge, sending.

4918. מְשֻׁלָּם **Meshullâm**, *mesh-ool-lawm'*; from 7999; *allied; Meshullam*, the name of seventeen Isr.:—Meshullam.

4919. מְשִׁלֵּמוֹת **Meshillêmôwth**, *mesh-il-lay-mohth'*; plur. from 7999; *reconciliations:*—*Meshillemoth*, an Isr.:—Meshillemoth. Comp. 4921.

4920. מְשֶׁלֶמְיָה **Meshelemyâh**, *mesh-eh-lem-yaw'*; or

מְשֶׁלֶמְיָהוּ **Meshelemyâhûw**, *mesh-eh-lem-yaw'-hoo*; from 7999 and 3050; *ally of Jah; Meshelemjah*, an Isr.:—Meshelemiah.

4921. מְשִׁלֵּמִית **Meshillêmîyth**, *mesh-il-lay-meeth'*; from 7999; *reconciliation; Meshillemith*, an Isr.:—Meshillemith. Comp. 4919.

4922. מְשֻׁלֶּמֶת **Meshullemeth**, *mesh-ool-leh'-meth*; fem. of 4918; *Meshullemeth*, an Israelitess:—Meshullemeth.

4923. מְשַׁמָּה **meshammâh**, *mesh-am-maw'*; from 8074; a *waste* or *amazement:*—astonishment, desolate.

4924. מַשְׁמָן **mashmân**, *mash-mawn'*; from 8080; *fat*, i.e. (lit. and abstr.) *fatness;* but usually (fig. and concr.) a *rich* dish, a *fertile* field, a *robust* man:—fat (one, -ness, -test, -test place).

4925. מִשְׁמַנָּה **Mishmannâh**, *mish-man-naw'*; from 8080; *fatness; Mashmannah*, an Isr.:—Mishmannah.

4926. מִשְׁמָע **mishmâʻ**, *mish-maw'*; from 8085; a *report:*—hearing.

4927. מִשְׁמָע **Mishmâʻ**, *mish-maw'*; the same as 4926; *Mishma*, the name of a son of Ishmael, and of an Isr.:—Mishma.

4928. מִשְׁמַעַת **mishmaʻath**, *mish-mah'-ath*; fem. of 4926; *audience*, i.e. the royal *court;* also *obedience*, i.e. (concr.) a *subject:*—bidding, guard, obey.

4929. מִשְׁמָר **mishmâr**, *mish-mawr'*; from 8104; a *guard* (the man, the post, or the *prison*); fig. a *deposit;* also (as observed) a *usage* (abstr.), or an *example* (concr.):—diligence, guard, office, prison, ward, watch.

4930. מַשְׂמְרָה **masmerâh**, *mas-mer-aw'*; for 4548 fem.; a *peg:*—nail.

4931. מִשְׁמֶרֶת **mishmereth**, *mish-meh'-reth*; fem. of 4929; *watch*, i.e. the act (*custody*) or (concr.) the *sentry*, the *post;* obj. *preservation*, or (concr.) *safe;* fig. *observance*, i.e. (abstr.) *duty*, or (obj.) a *usage* or *party:*—charge, keep, to be kept, office, ordinance, safeguard, ward, watch.

4932. מִשְׁנֶה **mishneh**, *mish-neh'*; from 8138; prop. a *repetition*, i.e. a *duplicate* (*copy* of a document), or a *double* (in amount); by impl. a *second* (in order, rank, age, quality or location):—college, copy, double, fatlings, next, second (order), twice as much.

4933. מְשִׁסָּה **mechiççâh**, *mesh-is-saw'*; from 8155; *plunder:*—booty, spoil.

4934. מִשְׁעוֹל **mishʻôwl**, *mish-ole'*; from the same as 8168; a *hollow*, i.e. a narrow passage:—path.

4935. מִשְׁעִי **mishʻîy**, *mish-ee'*; prob. from 8159; *inspection:*—to supple.

4936. מִשְׁעָם **Mishʻâm**, *mish-awm'*; appar. from 8159; *inspection; Misham*, an Isr.:—Misham.

4937. מִשְׁעֵן **mishʻên**, *mish-ane'*; or

מִשְׁעָן **mishʻân**, *mish-awn'*; from 8172; a *support* (concr.), i.e. (fig.) a *protector* or *sustenance:*—stay.

4938. מִשְׁעֵנָה **mishʻênâh**, *mish-ay-naw'*; or

מִשְׁעֶנֶת **mishʻeneth**, *mish-eh'-neth*; fem. of 4937; *support* (abstr.), i.e. (fig.) *sustenance* or (concr.) a *walking-stick:*—staff.

4939. מִשְׂפָּח **mispâch**, *mis-pawkh'*; from 5596; *slaughter:*—oppression.

4940. מִשְׁפָּחָה **mishpâchâh**, *mish-paw-khaw'*; from 8192 [comp. 8198]; a *family*, i.e. circle of relatives; fig. a *class* (of persons), a *species* (of animals) or *sort* (of things); by extens. a *tribe* or *people:*—family, kind (-red).

4941. מִשְׁפָּט **mishpâṭ**, *mish-pawt'*; from 8199; prop. a *verdict* (favorable or unfavorable) pronounced judicially, espec. a *sentence* or formal decree (human or [partic.] divine *law*, individual or collect.), includ. the act, the place, the suit, the crime, and the penalty; abstr. *justice*, includ. a partic. *right*, or *privilege* (statutory or customary), or even a *style:*— + adversary, ceremony, charge, × crime, custom, desert, determination, discretion, disposing, due, fashion, form, to be judged, judgment, just (-ice, -ly), (manner of) law (-ful), manner, measure, (due) order, ordinance, right, sentence, usest, × worthy, + wrong.

4942. מִשְׁפָּת **mishpâth**, *mish-pawth'*; from 8192; a *stall* for cattle (only dual):—burden, sheepfold.

4943. מֶשֶׁק **mesheq**, *meh'-shek*; from an unused root mean. to *hold; possession:*— + steward.

4944. מַשָּׁק **mashshâq**, *mash-shawk'*; from 8264; a *traversing*, i.e. rapid *motion:*—running to and fro.

4945. מַשְׁקֶה **mashqeh**, *mash-keh'*; from 8248; prop. *causing to drink*, i.e. a *butler;* by impl. (intrans.) *drink* (itself); fig. a *well-watered* region:—butler (-ship), cupbearer, drink (-ing), fat pasture, watered.

4946. מִשְׁקוֹל **mishqôwl**, *mish-kole'*; from 8254; *weight:*—weight.

4947. מַשְׁקוֹף **mashqôwph**, *mash-kofe'*; from 8259 in its orig. sense of *overhanging;* a *lintel:*—lintel, upper door post.

4948. מִשְׁקָל **mishqâl**, *mish-kawl'*; from 8254; *weight* (numerically estimated); hence, *weighing* (the act):—(full) weight.

4949. מִשְׁקֶלֶת **mishqeleth**, *mish-keh'-leth*; or

מִשְׁקֹלֶת **mishqôleth**, *mish-ko'-leth*; fem. of 4948 or 4947; a *weight*, i.e. a *plummet* (with line attached):—plummet.

4950. מִשְׁקָע **mishqâʻ**, *mish-kaw'*; from 8257; a *settling* place (of water), i.e. a pond:—deep.

4951. מִשְׂרָה **misrâh**, *mis-raw'*; from 8280; *empire:*—government.

4952. מִשְׁרָה **mishrâh**, *mish-raw'*; from 8281 in the sense of *loosening; maceration*, i.e. steeped *juice:*—liquor.

4953. מַשְׁרוֹקִי **mashrôwqîy** (Chald.), *mash-ro-kee'*; from a root corresp. to 8319; a (musical) *pipe* (from its *whistling* sound):—flute.

4954. מִשְׁרָעִי **Mishrâʻîy**, *mish-raw-ee'*; patrial from an unused noun from an unused root; prob. mean. to *stretch* out; *extension;* a *Mishraite*, or inhab. (collect.) of Mishra:—Mishraites.

4955. מִשְׂרָפָה **misrâphâh**, *mis-raw-faw'*; from 8313; *combustion*, i.e. *cremation* (of a corpse), or *calcination* (of lime):—burning.

4956. מִשְׂרְפוֹת מַיִם **Misrephôwth mayim**, *mis-ref-ohth' mah'-yim*; from the plur. of 4955 and 4325; *burnings of water; Misrephoth-Majim*, a place in Pal.:—Misrephoth-mayim.

4957. מַשְׂרֵקָה **Masrêqâh**, *mas-ray-kaw'*; a form for 7796 used denom.; *vineyard; Masrekah*, a place in Idumæa:—Masrekah.

4958. מַשְׂרֵת **masrêth**, *mas-rayth'*; appar. from an unused root mean. to *perforate*, i.e. hollow out; a *pan:*—pan.

4959. מָשַׁשׁ **mâshash**, *maw-shash'*; a prim. root; to *feel* of; by impl. to *grope:*—feel, grope, search.

4960. מִשְׁתֶּה **mishteh**, *mish-teh'*; from 8354; *drink;* by impl. *drinking* (the act); also (by impl.), a *banquet* or (gen.) *feast:*—banquet, drank, drink, feast ([-ed], -ing).

4961. מִשְׁתֵּה **mishteh** (Chald.), *mish-teh'*; corresp. to 4960; a *banquet:*—banquet.

4962. מַת **math**, *math*; from the same as 4970; prop. an *adult* (as of full length); by impl. a *man* (only in the plur.):— + few, × friends, men, persons, × small.

4963. מַתְבֵּן **mathbên**, *math-bane'*; denom. from 8401; *straw* in the heap:—straw.

4964. מֶתֶג **metheg**, *meh'-theg*; from an unused root mean. to *curb*; a *bit*:—bit, bridle.

4965. מֶתֶג הָאַמָּה **Metheg hâ-'Ammâh**, *meh'-theg haw-am-maw'*; from 4964 and 520 with the art. interposed; *bit of the metropolis*; *Metheg-ha-Ammah*, an epithet of Gath:—Metheg-ammah.

4966. מָתוֹק **mâthôwq**, *maw-thoke'*; or

מָתוּק **mâthûwq**, *maw-thook'*; from 4985; *sweet*:—sweet (-er, -ness).

4967. מְתוּשָׁאֵל **Methûwshâ'êl**, *meth-oo-shaw-ale'*; from 4962 and 410, with the rel. interposed; *man who* (is) *of God*; *Methushaël*, an antediluvian patriarch:—Methusael.

4968. מְתוּשֶׁלַח **Methûwshelach**, *meth-oo-sheh'-lakh*; from 4962 and 7973; *man of a dart*; *Methushelach*, an antediluvian patriarch:—Methuselah.

4969. מָתַח **mâthach**, *maw-thakh'*; a prim. root; to *stretch* out:—spread out.

4970. מָתַי **mâthay**, *maw-thah'ee*; from an unused root mean. to *extend*; prop. *extent* (of time); but used only adv. (espec. with other particles pref.), *when* (either rel. or interrog.):—long, when.

מְתִים **methîym**. See 4962.

4971. מַתְכֹנֶת **mathkôneth**, *math-ko'-neth*; or

מַתְכֻּנֶת **mathkûneth**, *math-koo'-neth*; from 8505 in the transferred sense of *measuring*; *proportion* (in size, number or ingredients):—composition, measure, state, tale.

4972. מַתְּלָאָה **mattelâ'âh**, *mat-tel-aw-aw'*; from 4100 and 8513; *what a trouble!*:—what a weariness.

4973. מְתַלְּעָה **methallecâh**, *meth-al-leh-aw'*; contr. from 3216; prop. a *biter*, i.e. a *tooth*:—cheek (jaw) tooth, jaw.

4974. מְתֹם **methôm**, *meth-ohm'*; from 8552; *wholesomeness*; also (adv.) *completely*:—men [*by reading* 4962], soundness.

מֶתֶן **Methen**. See 4981.

4975. מֹתֶן **môthen**, *mo'-then*; from an unused root mean. to *be slender*; prop. the *waist* or small of the back; only in plur. the *loins*:—+ greyhound, loins, side.

4976. מַתָּן **mattân**, *mat-tawn'*; from 5414; a *present*:—gift, to give, reward.

4977. מַתָּן **Mattân**, *mat-tawn'*; the same as 4976; *Mattan*, the name of a priest of Baal, and of an Isr.:—Mattan.

4978. מַתְּנָא **mattenâ'** (Chald.), *mat-ten-aw'*; corresp. to 4979:—gift.

4979. מַתָּנָה **mattânâh**, *mat-taw-naw'*; fem. of 4976; a *present*; spec. (in a good sense) a sacrificial *offering*, (in a bad sense) a *bribe*:—gift.

4980. מַתָּנָה **Mattânâh**, *mat-taw-naw'*; the same as 4979; *Mattanah*, a place in the Desert:—Mattanah.

4981. מִתְנִי **Mithnîy**, *mith-nee'*; prob. patrial from an unused noun mean. *slenderness*; a *Mithnite*, or inhab. of Methen:—Mithnite.

4982. מַתְּנַי **Mattenay**, *mat-ten-ah'ee*; from 4976; *liberal*; *Mattenai*, the name of three Isr.:—Mattenai.

4983. מַתַּנְיָה **Mattanyâh**, *mat-tan-yaw'*; or

מַתַּנְיָהוּ **Mattanyâhûw**, *mat-tan-yaw'-hoo*; from 4976 and 3050; *gift of Jah*; *Mattanjah*, the name of ten Isr.:—Mattaniah.

מָתְנַיִם **mothnayim**. See 4975.

4984. מִתְנַשֵּׂא **mithnassê'**, *mith-nas-say'*; from 5375; (used as abstr.) supreme *exaltation*:—exalted.

4985. מָתַק **mâthaq**, *maw-thak'*; a prim. root; to *suck*, by impl. to *relish*, or (intrans.) *be sweet*:—be (made, × take) sweet.

4986. מֶתֶק **metheq**, *meh'-thek*; from 4985; fig. *pleasantness* (of discourse):—sweetness.

4987. מֹתֶק **môtheq**, *mo'-thek*; from 4985; *sweetness*:—sweetness.

4988. מָתָק **mâthâq**, *maw-thawk'*; from 4985; a *dainty*, i.e. (gen.) *food*:—feed sweetly.

4989. מִתְקָה **Mithqâh**, *mith-kaw'*; fem. of 4987; *sweetness*; *Mithkah*, a place in the Desert:—Mithcah.

4990. מִתְרְדָת **Mithredâth**, *mith-red-awth'*; of Pers. origin; *Mithredath*, the name of two Persians:—Mithredath.

4991. מַתָּת **mattâth**, *mat-tawth'*; fem. of 4976 abbrev.; a *present*:—gift, reward.

4992. מַתַּתָּה **Mattattâh**, *mat-tat-taw'*; for 4993; *gift of Jah*; *Mattattah*, an Isr.:—Mattathah.

4993. מַתִּתְיָה **Mattithyâh**, *mat-tith-yaw'*; or

מַתִּתְיָהוּ **Mattithyâhûw**, *mat-tith-yaw'-hoo*; from 4991 and 3050; *gift of Jah*; *Mattithjah*, the name of four Isr.:—Mattithiah.

נ

4994. נָא **nâ'**, *naw*; a prim. particle of incitement and entreaty, which may usually be rendered *I pray*, *now* or *then*; added mostly to verbs (in the Imperat. or Fut.), or to interj., occasionally to an adv. or conj.:—I beseech (pray) thee (you), go to, now, oh.

4995. נָא **nâ'**, *naw*; appar. from 5106 in the sense of *harshness* from refusal; prop. *tough*, i.e. *uncooked* (flesh):—raw.

4996. נֹא **Nô'**, *no*; of Eg. origin; *No* (i.e. *Thebes*), the capital of Upper Egypt:—No. Comp. 528.

4997. נֹאד **nô'd**, *node*; or

נוֹאד **nô'wd**, *node*; also (fem.)

נֹאדָה **nô'dâh**, *no-daw'*; from an unused root of uncert. signif.; a (skin or leather) *bag* (for fluids):—bottle.

נְאַדְרַי **ne'dârîy**. See 142.

4998. נָאָה **nâ'âh**, *naw-aw'*; a prim. root; prop. to *be at home*, i.e. (by impl.) to be *pleasant* (or *suitable*), i.e. *beautiful*:—be beautiful, become, be comely.

4999. נָאָה **nâ'âh**, *naw-aw'*; from 4998; a *home*; fig. a *pasture*:—habitation, house, pasture, pleasant place.

5000. נָאוֶה **nâ'veh**, *naw-veh'*; from 4998 or 5116; *suitable*, or *beautiful*:—becometh, comely, seemly.

5001. נָאַם **nâ'am**, *naw-am'*; a prim. root; prop. to *whisper*, i.e. (by impl.) to *utter* as an oracle:—say.

5002. נְאֻם **ne'ûm**, *neh-oom'*; from 5001; an *oracle*:—(hath) said, saith.

5003. נָאַף **nâ'aph**, *naw-af'*; a prim. root; to *commit adultery*; fig. to *apostatize*:—adulterer (-ess), commit (-ing) adultery, woman that breaketh wedlock.

5004. נִאֻף **ni'ûph**, *nee-oof'*; from 5003; *adultery*:—adultery.

5005. נַאֲפוּף **na'aphûwph**, *nah-af-oof'*; from 5003; *adultery*:—adultery.

5006. נָאַץ **nâ'ats**, *naw-ats'*; a prim. root; to *scorn*; or (Eccles. 12 : 5) by interch. for 5132, to *bloom*:—abhor, (give occasion to) blaspheme, contemn, despise, flourish, × great, provoke.

5007. נְאָצָה **ne'âtsâh**, *neh-aw-tsaw'*; or

נֶאָצָה **ne'âtsâh**, *neh-aw-tsaw'*; from 5006; *scorn*:—blasphemy.

5008. נָאַק **nâ'aq**, *naw-ak'*; a prim. root; to *groan*:—groan.

5009. נְאָקָה **ne'âqâh**, *neh-aw-kaw'*; from 5008; a *groan*:—groaning.

5010. נָאַר **nâ'ar**, *naw-ar'*; a prim. root; to *reject*:—abhor, make void.

5011. נֹב **Nôb**, *nobe*; the same as 5108; *fruit*; *Nob*, a place in Pal.:—Nob.

5012. נָבָא **nâbâ'**, *naw-baw'*; a prim. root; to *prophesy*, i.e. speak (or sing) by inspiration (in prediction or simple discourse):—prophesy (-ing), make self a prophet.

5013. נְבָא **nebâ'** (Chald.), *neb-aw'*; corresp. to 5012:—prophesy.

5014. נָבַב **nâbab**, *naw-bab'*; a prim. root; to *pierce*; to *be hollow*, or (fig.) *foolish*:—hollow, vain.

5015. נְבוֹ **Nebôw**, *neb-o'*; prob. of for. der.; *Nebo*, the name of a Bab. deity, also of a mountain in Moab, and of a place in Pal.:—Nebo.

5016. נְבוּאָה **nebûw'âh**, *neb-oo-aw'*; from 5012; a *prediction* (spoken or written):—prophecy.

5017. נְבוּאָה **nebûw'âh** (Chald.), *neb-oo-aw*; corresp. to 5016; inspired *teaching*:—prophesying.

5018. נְבוּזַרְאֲדָן **Nebûwzarădân**, *neb-oo-zar-ad-awn'*; of for. or.; *Nebuzaradan*, a Bab. general:—Nebuzaradan.

5019. נְבוּכַדְנֶאצַּר **Nebûwkadne'tstsar**, *neb-oo-kad-nets-tsar'*; or

נְבֻכַדְנֶאצַּר **Nebûkadne'tstsar** (2 Kings 24 : 1, 10), *neb-oo-kad-nets-tsar'*; or

נְבוּכַדְנֶצַּר **Nebûwkadnetstsar** (Esth. 2 : 6; Dan. 1 : 18), *neb-oo-kad-nets-tsar'*; or

נְבוּכַדְרֶאצַּר **Nebûwkadre'tstsar**, *neb-oo-kad-rets-tsar'*; or

נְבוּכַדְרֶאצּוֹר **Nebûwkadre'tstsôwr** (Ezra 2 : 1; Jer. 49 : 28), *neb-oo-kad-rets-tsore'*; of for. der.; *Nebukadnetstsar* (or *-retstsar*, or *-retstsor*), king of Babylon:—Nebuchadnezzar, Nebuchadrezzar.

5020. נְבוּכַדְנֶצַּר **Nebûwkadnetstsar** (Chald.), *neb-oo-kad-nets-tsar'*; corresp. to 5019:—Nebuchadnezzar.

5021. נְבוּשַׁזְבָּן **Nebûwshazbân**, *neb-oo-shaz-bawn'*; of for. der.; *Nebushazban*, Nebuchadnezzar's chief eunuch:—Nebushazban.

5022. נָבוֹת **Nâbôwth**, *naw-both'*; fem. plur. from the same as 5011; *fruits*; *Naboth*, an Isr.:—Naboth.

5023. נְבִזְבָּה **nebizbâh** (Chald.), *neb-iz-baw'*; of uncert. der.; a *largess*:—reward.

5024. נָבַח **nâbach**, *naw-bakh'*; a prim. root; to *bark* (as a dog):—bark.

5025. נֹבַח **Nôbach**, *no'-bach*; from 5024; a *bark*; *Nobach*, the name of an Isr., and of a place E. of the Jordan:—Nobah.

5026. נִבְחַז **Nibchaz**, *nib-khaz'*; of for. or.; *Nibchaz*, a deity of the Avites:—Nibhaz.

5027. נָבַט **nâbaṭ**, *naw-bat'*; a prim. root; to *scan*, i.e. look intently at; by impl. to *regard* with pleasure, favor or care:—(cause to) behold, consider, look (down), regard, have respect, see.

5028. נְבָט **Nebâṭ**, *neb-awt'*; from 5027; *regard*; *Nebat*, the father of Jeroboam I:—Nebat.

5029. נְבִיא **nebîy'** (Chald.), *neb-ee'*; corresp. to 5030; a *prophet*:—prophet.

5030. נָבִיא **nâbîy'**, *naw-bee'*; from 5012; a *prophet* or (gen.) *inspired* man:—prophecy, that prophesy, prophet.

5031. נְבִיאָה **nebîy'âh**, *neb-ee-yaw'*; fem. of 5030; a *prophetess* or (gen.) *inspired* woman; by impl. a *poetess*; by association a *prophet's wife*:—prophetess.

5032. נְבָיוֹת **Nebâyôwth**, *neb-aw-yoth'*; or

נְבָיֹת **Nebâyôth**, *neb-aw-yoth'*; fem. plur. from 5107; *fruitfulnesses*; *Nebajoth*, a son of Ishmael, and the country settled by him:—Nebaioth, Nebajoth.

5033. נֵבֶךְ **nêbek**, *nay'-bek*; from an unused root mean. to *burst* forth; a *fountain*:—spring.

5034. נָבֵל **nâbêl**, *naw-bale'*; a prim. root; to *wilt*; gen. to *fall away*, *fail*, *faint*; fig. to *be foolish* or (mor.) *wicked*; causat. to *despise*, *disgrace*:—disgrace, dishonour, lightly esteem, fade (away, -ing), fall (down, -ing, off), do foolishly, come to nought, × surely, make vile, wither.

5035. נֶבֶל **nebel**, *neh'-bel*; or

נֵבֶל **nêbel**, *nay'-bel*; from 5034; a *skin-bag* for liquids (from *collapsing* when empty);

hence, a *vase* (as similar in shape when full); also a *lyre* (as having a body of like form):—bottle, pitcher, psaltery, vessel, viol.

5036. נָבָל **nâbâl**, *naw-bawl'*; from 5034; *stupid; wicked* (espec. *impious*):—fool (-ish, -ish man, -ish woman), vile person.

5037. נָבָל **Nâbâl**, *naw-bawl'*; the same as 5036; *dolt; Nabal*, an Isr.:—Nabal.

5038. נְבֵלָה **nᵉbêlâh**, *neb-ay-law'*; from 5034; a *flabby* thing, i.e. a *carcase* or *carrion* (human or bestial, often collect.); fig. an *idol*:—(dead) body, (dead) carcase, dead of itself, which died, (beast) that (which) dieth of itself.

5039. נְבָלָה **nᵉbâlâh**, *neb-aw-law'*; fem. of 5036; *foolishness*, i.e. (mor.) *wickedness*; concr. a *crime;* by extens. *punishment*:—folly, vile, villany.

5040. נַבְלוּת **nablûwth**, *nab-looth'*; from 5036; prop. *disgrace*, i.e. the (female) *pudenda*:—lewdness.

5041. נְבַלַּט **Nᵉballâṭ**, *neb-al-lawt'*; appar. from 5036 and 3909; *foolish secrecy; Neballat*, a place in Pal.:—Neballat.

5042. נָבַע **nâbaᶜ**, *naw-bah'*; a prim. root; to *gush* forth; fig. to *utter* (good or bad words); spec. to *emit* (a foul odor):—belch out, flowing, pour out, send forth, utter (abundantly).

5043. נֶבְרְשָׁא **nebrᵉshâ'** (Chald.), *neb-reh-shaw'*; from an unused root mean. to *shine;* a *light;* plur. (collect.) a *chandelier*:—candlestick.

5044. נִבְשָׁן **Nibshân**, *nib-shawn'*; of uncert. der.; *Nibshan*, a place in Pal.:—Nibshan.

5045. נֶגֶב **negeb**, *neh'-gheb;* from an unused root mean. to *be parched;* the *south* (from its drought); spec. the *Negeb* or southern district of Judah, occasionally, *Egypt* (as south to Pal.):—south (country, side, -ward).

5046. נָגַד **nâgad**, *naw-gad'*; a prim. root; prop. to *front*, i.e. stand boldly out opposite; by impl. (causat.), to *manifest;* fig. to *announce* (always by word of mouth to one present); spec. to *expose, predict, explain, praise*:—bewray, × certainly, certify, declare (-ing), denounce, expound, × fully, messenger, plainly, profess, rehearse, report, shew (forth), speak, × surely, tell, utter.

5047. נְגַד **nᵉgad** (Chald.), *neg-ad'*; corresp. to 5046; to *flow* (through the idea of *clearing* the way):—issue.

5048. נֶגֶד **neged**, *neh'-ghed;* from 5046; a *front*, i.e. part opposite; spec. a *counterpart*, or mate; usually (adv., espec. with prep.) *over against* or *before*:—about, (over) against, × aloof, × far (off), × from, over, presence, × other side, sight, × to view.

5049. נֶגֶד **neged** (Chald.), *neh'-ghed;* corresp. to 5048; *opposite*:—toward.

5050. נָגַהּ **nâgahh**, *naw-găh'*; a prim. root; to *glitter;* causat. to *illuminate*:—(en-) lighten, (cause to) shine.

5051. נֹגַהּ **nôgahh**, *no'-găh;* from 5050; *brilliancy* (lit. or fig.):—bright (-ness), light, (clear) shining.

5052. נֹגַהּ **Nôgahh**, *no'-găh;* the same as 5051; *Nogah*, a son of David:—Nogah.

5053. נֹגַהּ **nôgahh** (Chald.), *no'-găh;* corresp. to 5051; *dawn*:—morning.

5054. נְגֹהָה **nᵉgôhâh**, *neg-o-haw';* fem. of 5051; *splendor*:—brightness.

5055. נָגַח **nâgach**, *naw-gakh'*; a prim. root; to *but* with the horns; fig. to *war* against:—gore, push (down, -ing).

5056. נַגָּח **naggâch**, *nag-gawkh';* from 5055; *butting*, i.e. *vicious*:—used (wont) to push.

5057. נָגִיד **nâgîyd**, *naw-gheed';* or

נָגִד **nâgid**, *naw-gheed';* from 5046; a *commander* (as occupying the *front*), civil, military or religious; gen. (abstr. plur.), *honorable themes*:—captain, chief, excellent thing, (chief) governor, leader, noble, prince, (chief) ruler.

5058. נְגִינָה **nᵉgîynâh**, *neg-ee-naw';* or

נְגִינַת **nᵉgîynath** (Psa. 61 : title), *neg-ee-nath';* from 5059; prop. instrumental *music;* by impl. a stringed *instrument;* by extens. a *poem* set to music; spec. an *epigram*:—stringed instrument, musick, Neginoth [*plur.*], song.

5059. נָגַן **nâgan**, *naw-gan';* a prim. root; prop. to *thrum*, i.e. *beat* a tune with the fingers; espec. to *play* on a stringed instrument; hence (gen.) to *make music*:—player on instruments, sing to the stringed instruments, melody, ministrel, play (-er, -ing).

5060. נָגַע **nâgaᶜ**, *naw-gah';* a prim. root; prop. to *touch*, i.e. *lay the hand upon* (for any purpose; euphem., to *lie with* a woman); by impl. to *reach* (fig. to *arrive, acquire*); violently, to *strike* (punish, defeat, destroy, etc.):—beat, (× be able to) bring (down), cast, come (nigh), draw near (nigh), get up, happen, join, near, plague, reach (up), smite, strike, touch.

5061. נֶגַע **negaᶜ**, *neh'-gah;* from 5060; a *blow* (fig. *infliction*); also (by impl.) a *spot* (concr. a *leprous* person or dress):—plague, sore, stricken, stripe, stroke, wound.

5062. נָגַף **nâgaph**, *naw-gaf';* a prim. root; to *push, gore, defeat, stub* (the toe), *inflict* (a disease):—beat, dash, hurt, plague, slay, smite (down), strike, stumble, × surely, put to the worse.

5063. נֶגֶף **negeph**, *neh'-ghef;* from 5062; a *trip* (of the foot); fig. an *infliction* (of disease):—plague, stumbling.

5064. נָגַר **nâgar**, *naw-gar';* a prim. root; to *flow;* fig. to *stretch* out; causat. to *pour* out or down; fig. to *deliver* over:—fall, flow away, pour down (out), run, shed, spilt, trickle down.

5065. נָגַשׂ **nâgas**, *naw-gas';* a prim. root; to *drive* (an animal, a workman, a debtor, an army); by impl. to *tax, harass, tyrannize*:—distress, driver, exact (-or), oppress (-or), × raiser of taxes, taskmaster.

5066. נָגַשׁ **nâgash**, *naw-gash';* a prim. root; to *be* or *come* (causat. *bring*) *near* (for any purpose); euphem. to *lie with* a woman; as an enemy, to *attack;* relig. to *worship;* causat. to *present;* fig. to *adduce* an argument; by reversal, to *stand back*:—(make to) approach (nigh), bring (forth, hither, near), (cause to) come (hither, near, nigh), give place, go hard (up), (be, draw, go) near (nigh), offer, overtake, present, put, stand.

5067. נֵד **nêd**, *nade;* from 5110 in the sense of *piling* up; a *mound*, i.e. *wave*:—heap.

5068. נָדַב **nâdab**, *naw-dab';* a prim. root; to *impel;* hence to *volunteer* (as a soldier), to *present* spontaneously:—offer freely, be (give, make, offer self) willing (-ly).

5069. נְדַב **nᵉdab** (Chald.), *ned-ab';* corresp. to 5068; *be* (or *give*) *liberal* (*-ly*):—(be minded of . . . own) freewill (offering), offer freely (willingly).

5070. נָדָב **Nâdâb**, *naw-dawb';* from 5068; *liberal; Nadab*, the name of four Isr.:—Nadab.

5071. נְדָבָה **nᵉdâbâh**, *ned-aw-baw';* from 5068; prop. (abstr.) *spontaneity*, or (adj.) *spontaneous;* also (concr.) a *spontaneous* or (by infer., in plur.) *abundant* gift:—free (-will) offering, freely, plentiful, voluntary (-ily, offering), willing (-ly, offering).

5072. נְדַבְיָה **Nᵉdabyâh**, *ned-ab-yaw';* from 5068 and 3050; *largess of Jah; Nedabjah*, an Isr.:—Nedabiah.

5073. נִדְבָּךְ **nidbâk** (Chald.), *nid-bawk';* from a root mean. to *stick;* a *layer* (of building materials):—row.

5074. נָדַד **nâdad**, *naw-dad';* a prim. root; prop. to *wave* to and fro (rarely to *flap* up and down); fig. to *rove, flee*, or (caus.) to *drive* away:—chase (away), × could not, depart, flee (× apace, away), (re-) move, thrust away, wander (abroad, -er, -ing).

5075. נְדַד **nᵉdad** (Chald.), *ned-ad';* corresp. to 5074; to *depart*:—go from.

5076. נָדֻד **nâdûd**, *naw-dood';* pass. part. of 5074; prop. *tossed;* abstr. a *rolling* (on the bed):—tossing to and fro.

5077. נָדָה **nâdâh**, *naw-daw';* or

נָדָא° **nâdâ'** (2 Kings 17 : 21), *naw-daw';* a prim. root; prop. to *toss;* fig. to *exclude*, i.e. banish, postpone, prohibit:—cast out, drive, put far away.

5078. נֵדֶה **nêdeh**, *nay'-deh;* from 5077 in the sense of freely *flinging* money; a *bounty* (for prostitution):—gifts.

5079. נִדָּה **niddâh**, *nid-daw';* from 5074; prop. *rejection;* by impl. *impurity*, espec. personal (menstruation) or moral (idolatry, incest):—× far, filthiness, × flowers, menstruous (woman), put apart, × removed (woman), separation, set apart, unclean (-ness, thing, with filthiness).

5080. נָדַח **nâdach**, *naw-dakh';* a prim. root; to *push* off; used in a great variety of applications, lit. and fig. (to expel, mislead, strike, inflict, etc.):—banish, bring, cast down (out), chase, compel, draw away, drive (away, out, quite), fetch a stroke, force, go away, outcast, thrust away (out), withdraw.

5081. נָדִיב **nâdîyb**, *naw-deeb';* from 5068; prop. *voluntary*, i.e. generous; hence, *magnanimous;* as noun, a *grandee* (sometimes a *tyrant*):—free, liberal (things), noble, prince, willing ([hearted]).

5082. נְדִיבָה **nᵉdîybâh**, *ned-ee-baw';* fem. of 5081; prop. *nobility*, i.e. reputation:—soul.

5083. נָדָן **nâdân**, *naw-dawn';* prob. from an unused root mean. to *give;* a *present* (for prostitution):—gift.

5084. נָדָן **nâdân**, *naw-dawn';* of uncert. der.; a *sheath* (of a sword):—sheath.

5085. נִדְנֶה **nidneh** (Chald.), *nid-neh';* from the same as 5084; a *sheath;* fig. the *body* (as the receptacle of the soul):—body.

5086. נָדַף **nâdaph**, *naw-daf';* a prim. root; to *shove* asunder, i.e. *disperse*:—drive (away, to and fro), thrust down, shaken, tossed to and fro.

5087. נָדַר **nâdar**, *naw-dar';* a prim. root; to *promise* (pos., to do or give something to God):—(make a) vow.

5088. נֶדֶר **neder**, *neh'-der;* or

נֵדֶר **nêder**, *nay'-der;* from 5087; a *promise* (to God); also (concr.) a thing *promised*:—vow ([-ed]).

5089. נֹהַּ **nôahh**, *no'-ăh;* from an unused root mean. to *lament; lamentation*:—wailing.

5090. נָהַג **nâhag**, *naw-hag';* a prim. root; to *drive* forth (a person, an animal or chariot), i.e. *lead, carry away;* reflex. to *proceed* (i.e. impel or guide oneself); also (from the *panting* induced by effort), to *sigh*:—acquaint, bring (away), carry away, drive (away), lead (away, forth), (be) guide, lead (away, forth).

5091. נָהָה **nâhâh**, *naw-haw';* a prim. root; to *groan*, i.e. *bewail;* hence (through the idea of *crying* aloud) to *assemble* (as if on proclamation):—lament, wail.

5092. נְהִי **nᵉhîy**, *neh-hee';* from 5091; an *elegy*:—lamentation, wailing.

5093. נִהְיָה **nihyâh**, *nih-yaw';* fem. of 5092; *lamentation*:—doleful.

5094. נְהִיר° **nᵉhîyr** (Chald.), *neh-heere';* or

נְהִירוּ **nehîyrûw** (Chald.), *neh-hee-roo';* from the same as 5105; *illumination*, i.e. (fig.) wisdom:—light.

5095. נָהַל **nâhal**, *naw-hal';* a prim. root; prop. to run with a *sparkle*, i.e. *flow;* hence (trans.) to *conduct*, and (by infer.) to *protect, sustain*:—carry, feed, guide, lead (gently, on).

5096. נַהֲלָל **Nahălâl**, *năh-hal-awl';* or

נַהֲלֹל **Nahălôl**, *năh-hal-ole';* the same as 5097; *Nahalal* or *Nahalol*, a place in Pal.:—Nahalal, Nahallal, Nahalol.

5097. נַהֲלֹל **nahălôl**, *năh-hal-ole';* from 5095; *pasture*:—bush.

5098. נָהַם **nâham**, *naw-ham';* a prim. root; to *growl*:—mourn, roar (-ing).

5099. נַהַם **naham**, *năh'-ham;* from 5098; a *snarl*:—roaring.

5100. נְהָמָה **nᵉhâmâh**, *neh-haw-maw'*; fem. of 5099; *snarling*:—disquietness, roaring.

5101. נָהַק **nâhaq**, *naw-hak'*; a prim. root; to *bray* (as an ass), *scream* (from hunger):—bray.

5102. נָהַר **nâhar**, *naw-har'*; a prim. root; to *sparkle*, i.e. (fig.) *be cheerful*; hence (from the *sheen* of a running stream) to *flow*, i.e. (fig.) *assemble*:—flow (together), be lightened.

5103. נְהַר **nᵉhar** (Chald.), *neh-har'*; from a root corresp. to 5102; a *river*, espec. the Euphrates:—river, stream.

5104. נָהָר **nâhâr**, *naw-hawr'*; from 5102; a *stream* (includ. the *sea*; espec. the Nile, Euphrates, etc.); fig., *prosperity*:—flood, river.

5105. נְהָרָה **nᵉhârâh**, *neh-haw-raw'*; from 5102 in its orig. sense; *daylight*:—light.

5106. נוּא **nûw'**, *noo*; a prim. root; to *refuse*, *forbid*, *dissuade*, or *neutralize*:—break, disallow, discourage, make of none effect.

5107. נוּב **nûwb**, *noob*; a prim. root; to *germinate*, i.e. (fig.) to (causat. *make*) *flourish*; also (of words), to *utter*:—bring forth (fruit), make cheerful, increase.

5108. נוֹב° **nôwb**, *nobe*; or

נֵיב **nêyb**, *nabe*; from 5107; *produce*, lit. or fig.:—fruit.

5109. נוֹבַי° **Nôwbay**, *no-bah'ee*; from 5108; *fruitful*; *Nobai*, an Isr.:—Nebai [*from the marg.*].

5110. נוּד **nûwd**, *nood*; a prim. root; to *nod*, i.e. *waver*; fig. to *wander*, *flee*, *disappear*; also (from *shaking* the head in sympathy), to *console*, *deplore*, or (from *tossing* the head in scorn) *taunt*:—bemoan, flee, get, mourn, make to move, take pity, remove, shake, skip for joy, be sorry, vagabond, way, wandering.

5111. נוּד **nûwd** (Chald.), *nood*; corresp. to 5116; to *flee*:—get away.

5112. נוֹד **nôwd**, *node* [only defect.

נֹד **nôd**, *node*]; from 5110; *exile*:—wandering.

5113. נוֹד **Nôwd**, *node*; the same as 5112; *vagrancy*; *Nod*, the land of Cain:—Nod.

5114. נוֹדָב **Nôwdâb**, *no-dawb'*; from 5068; *noble*; *Nodab*, an Arab tribe:—Nodab.

5115. נָוָה **nâvâh**, *naw-vaw'*; a prim. root; to *rest* (as at home); causat. (through the implied idea of *beauty* [comp. 5116]), to *celebrate* (with praises):—keep at home, prepare an habitation.

5116. נָוֶה **nâveh**, *naw-veh'*; or (fem.)

נָוָה **nâvâh**, *naw-vaw'*; from 5115; (adj.) *at home*; hence (by impl. of satisfaction) *lovely*; also (noun) a *home*, of God (temple), men (residence), flocks (pasture), or wild animals (*den*):—comely, dwelling (place), fold, habitation, pleasant place, sheepcote, stable, tarried.

5117. נוּחַ **nûwach**, *noo'-akh*; a prim. root; to *rest*, i.e. *settle* down; used in a great variety of applications, lit. and fig., intrans., trans. and causat. (to *dwell*, *stay*, *let fall*, *place*, *let alone*, *withdraw*, *give comfort*, etc.):—cease, be confederate, lay, let down, (be) quiet, remain, (cause to, be at, give, have, make to) rest, set down. Comp. 3241.

5118. נוּחַ **nûwach**, *noo'-akh*; or

נוֹחַ **nôwach**, *no'-akh*; from 5117; *quiet*:—rest (-ed, -ing place).

5119. נוֹחָה **Nôwchâh**, *no-chaw'*; fem. of 5118; *quietude*; *Nochah*, an Isr.:—Nohah.

5120. נוּט **nûwṭ**, *noot*; to *quake*:—be moved.

5121. נָוִית **Nâvîyth**, *naw-veeth'*; from 5115; *residence*; *Navith*, a place in Pal.:—Naioth [*from the marg.*].

5122. נְוָלוּ **nᵉvâlûw** (Chald.), *nev-aw-loo'*; or

נְוָלִי **nᵉvâlîy** (Chald.), *nev-aw-lee'*; from an unused root prob. mean. to be *foul*; a *sink*:—dunghill.

5123. נוּם **nûwm**, *noom*; a prim. root; to *slumber* (from drowsiness):—sleep, slumber.

5124 נוּמָה **nûwmâh**, *noo-maw'*; from 5123; *sleepiness*:—drowsiness.

5125. נוּן **nûwn**, *noon*; a prim. root; to *resprout*, i.e. propagate by shoots; fig., to *be perpetual*:—be continued.

5126. נוּן **Nûwn**, *noon*; or

נוֹן **Nôwn** (1 Chron. 7 : 27), *nohn*; from 5125; *perpetuity*; *Nun* or *Non*, the father of Joshua:—Non, Nun.

5127. נוּס **nûwç**, *noos*; a prim. root; to *flit*, i.e. *vanish* away (subside, escape; causat. chase, impel, deliver):— × abate, away, be displayed, (make to) flee (away, -ing), put to flight, × hide, lift up a standard.

5128. נוּעַ **nûwaʻ**, *noo'-ah*; a prim. root; to *waver*, in a great variety of applications, lit. and fig. (as subjoined):—continually, fugitive, × make to [go] up and down, be gone away, (be) move (-able, -d), be promoted, reel, remove, scatter, set, shake, sift, stagger, to and fro, be vagabond, wag, (make) wander (up and down).

5129. נוֹעַדְיָה **Nôwʻadyâh**, *no-ad-yaw'*; from 3259 and 3050; *convened of Jah*; *Noädjah*, the name of an Isr., and a false prophetess:—Noadiah.

5130. נוּף **nûwph**, *noof*; a prim. root; to *quiver* (i.e. *vibrate* up and down, or *rock* to and fro); used in a great variety of applications (includ. sprinkling, beckoning, rubbing, bastinadoing, sawing, waving, etc.):—lift up, move, offer, perfume, send, shake, sift, strike, wave.

5131. נוֹף **nôwph**, *nofe*; from 5130; *elevation*:—situation. Comp. 5297.

5132. נוּץ **nûwts**, *noots*; a prim. root; prop. to *flash*; hence, to *blossom* (from the brilliancy of color); also, to *fly* away (from the quickness of motion):—flee away, bud (forth).

5133. נוֹצָה **nôwtsâh**, *no-tsaw'*; or

נֹצָה **nôtsâh**, *no-tsaw'*; fem. act. part. of 5327 in the sense of *flying*; a *pinion* (or wing feather); often (collect.) *plumage*:—feather (-s), ostrich.

5134. נוּק **nûwq**, *nook*; a prim. root; to *suckle*:—nurse.

5135. נוּר **nûwr** (Chald.), *noor*; from an unused root (corresp. to that of 5216) mean. to *shine*; *fire*:—fiery, fire.

5136. נוּשׁ **nûwsh**, *noosh*; a prim. root; to *be sick*, i.e. (fig.) *distressed*:—be full of heaviness.

5137. נָזָה **nâzâh**, *naw-zaw'*; a prim. root; to *spirt*, i.e. *besprinkle* (espec. in expiation):—sprinkle.

5138. נָזִיד **nâzîyd**, *naw-zeed'*; from 2102; something *boiled*, i.e. *soup*:—pottage.

5139. נָזִיר **nâzîyr**, *naw-zeer'*; or

נָזִר **nâzir**, *naw-zeer'*; from 5144; *separate*, i.e. consecrated (as *prince*, a *Nazirite*); hence (fig. from the latter) an *unpruned* vine (like an unshorn Nazirite):—Nazarite [*by a false alliteration with Nazareth*], separate (-d), vine undressed.

5140. נָזַל **nâzal**, *naw-zal'*; a prim. root; to *drip*, or *shed* by trickling:—distil, drop, flood, (cause to) flow (-ing), gush out, melt, pour (down), running water, stream.

5141. נֶזֶם **nezem**, *neh'-zem*; from an unused root of uncert. mean.; a nose-*ring*:—earring, jewel.

5142. נְזַק **nᵉzaq** (Chald.), *nez-ak'*; corresp. to the root of 5143; to *suffer* (causat. *inflict*) *loss*:—have (en-) damage, hurt (-ful).

5143. נֵזֶק **nêzeq**, *nay'-zek*; from an unused root mean. to *injure*; *loss*:—damage.

5144. נָזַר **nâzar**, *naw-zar'*; a prim. root; to *hold aloof*, i.e. (intrans.) *abstain* (from food and drink, from impurity, and even from divine worship [i.e. *apostatize*]); spec. to *set apart* (to sacred purposes), i.e. *devote*:—consecrate, separate (-ing, self).

5145. נֶזֶר **nezer**, *neh'-zer*; or

נֵזֶר **nêzer**, *nay'-zer*; from 5144; prop. something *set apart*, i.e. (abstr.) *dedication* (of a priest or Nazirite); hence (concr.) unshorn *locks*; also (by impl.) a *chaplet* (espec. of royalty):—consecration, crown, hair, separation.

5146. נֹחַ **Nôach**, *no'-akh*; the same as 5118; *rest*; *Noäch*, the patriarch of the flood:—Noah.

5147. נַחְבִּי **Nachbîy**, *nakh-bee'*; from 2247; *occult*; *Nachbi*, an Isr.:—Nakbi.

5148. נָחָה **nâchâh**, *naw-khaw'*; a prim. root; to *guide*; by impl. to *transport* (into exile, or as colonists):—bestow, bring, govern, guide, lead (forth), put, straiten.

5149. נְחוּם **Nᵉchûwm**, *neh-khoom'*; from 5162; *comforted*; *Nechum*, an Isr.:—Nehum.

5150. נִחוּם **nichûwm**, *nee-khoom'*; or

נִחֻם **nichûm**, *nee-khoom'*; from 5162; prop. *consoled*; abstr. *solace*:—comfort (-able), repenting.

5151. נַחוּם **Nachûwm**, *nakh-oom'*; from 5162; *comfortable*; *Nachum*, an Isr. prophet:—Nahum.

5152. נָחוֹר **Nâchôwr**, *naw-khore'*; from the same as 5170; *snorer*; *Nachor*, the name of the grandfather and a brother of Abraham:—Nahor.

5153. נָחוּשׁ **nâchûwsh**, *naw-khoosh'*; appar. pass. part. of 5172 (perh. in the sense of *ringing*, i.e. bell-metal; or from the *red* color of the throat of a serpent [5175, as denom.] when hissing); *coppery*, i.e. (fig.) hard:—of brass.

5154. נְחוּשָׁה **nᵉchûwshâh**, *nekh-oo-shaw'*; or

נְחֻשָׁה **nᵉchûshâh**, *nekh-oo-shaw'*; fem. of 5153; *copper*:—brass, steel. Comp. 5176.

5155. נְחִילָה **nᵉchîylah**, *nekh-ee-law'*; prob. denom. from 2485; a *flute*:—[*plur.*] Nehiloth.

5156. נְחִיר **nᵉchîyr**, *nekh-eer'*; from the same as 5170; a *nostril*:—[*dual*] nostrils.

5157. נָחַל **nâchal**, *naw-khal'*; a prim. root; to *inherit* (as a [fig.] mode of descent), or (gen.) to *occupy*; causat. to *bequeath*, or (gen.) *distribute*, *instate*:—divide, have ([inheritance]), take as an heritage, (cause to, give to, make to) inherit, (distribute for, divide [for, for an, by], give for, have, leave for, take [for]) inheritance, (have in, cause to, be made to) possess (-ion).

5158. נַחַל **nachal**, *nakh'-al*; or (fem.)

נַחְלָה **nachlâh** (Psa. 124 : 4), *nakh'-law*; or

נַחֲלָה **nachălâh** (Ezek. 47 : 19; 48 : 28), *nakh-al-aw'*; from 5157 in its orig. sense; a *stream*, espec. a winter *torrent*; (by impl.) a (narrow) *valley* (in which a brook runs); also a *shaft* (of a mine):—brook, flood, river, stream, valley.

5159. נַחֲלָה **nachălâh**, *nakh-al-aw'*; from 5157 (in its usual sense); prop. something *inherited*, i.e. (abstr.) *occupancy*, or (concr.) an *heirloom*; gen. an *estate*, *patrimony* or *portion*:—heritage, to inherit, inheritance, possession. Comp. 5158.

5160. נַחֲלִיאֵל **Nachălîy'êl**, *nakh-al-ee-ale'*; from 5158 and 410; *valley of God*; *Nachaliël*, a place in the Desert:—Nahaliel.

5161. נֶחֱלָמִי **Nechĕlâmîy**, *nekh-el-aw-mee'*; appar. a patron. from an unused name (appar. pass. part. of 2492); *dreamed*; a *Nechelamite*, or descend. of Nechlam:—Nehelamite.

5162. נָחַם **nâcham**, *naw-kham'*; a prim. root; prop. to *sigh*, i.e. *breathe* strongly; by impl. to *be sorry*, i.e. (in a favorable sense) to *pity*, *console* or (reflex.) *rue*; or (unfavorably) to *avenge* (oneself):—comfort (self), ease [one's self], repent (-er, -ing, self).

5163. נַחַם **Nacham**, *nakh'-am*; from 5162; *consolation*; *Nacham*, an Isr.:—Naham.

5164. נֹחַם **nôcham**, *no'-kham*; from 5162; *ruefulness*, i.e. desistance:—repentance.

5165. נֶחָמָה **nechâmâh**, *nekh-aw-maw'*; from 5162; *consolation*:—comfort.

5166. נְחֶמְיָה **Nᵉchemyâh**, *nekh-em-yaw'*; from 5162 and 3050; *consolation of Jah*; *Nechemjah*, the name of three Isr.:—Nehemiah.

5167. נַחֲמָנִי **Nachămânîy**, *nakh-am-aw-nee'*; from 5162; *consolatory*; *Nachamani*, an Isr.:—Nahamani.

5168. נַחְנוּ **nachnûw**, *nakh-noo'*; for 587; *we*:—we.

5169. נָחַץ **nâchats**, *naw-khats'*; a prim. root; to *be urgent:*—require haste.

5170. נַחַר **nachar**, *nakh'-ar*; and (fem.)

נַחֲרָה **nachărâh**, *nakh-ar-aw'*; from an unused root mean. to *snort* or *snore;* a *snorting:*—nostrils, snorting.

5171. נַחֲרַי **Nachăray**, *nakh-ar-ah'ee;* or

נַחְרַי **Nachray**, *nakh-rah'ee;* from the same as 5170; *snorer; Nacharai* or *Nachrai*, an Isr.:—Naharai, Nahari.

5172. נָחַשׁ **nâchash**, *naw-khash';* a prim. root; prop. to *hiss*, i.e. *whisper* a (magic) spell; gen. to *prognosticate:*— × certainly, divine, enchanter, (use) × enchantment, learn by experience, × indeed, diligently observe.

5173. נַחַשׁ **nachash**, *nakh'-ash;* from 5172; an *incantation* or *augury:*—enchantment.

5174. נְחָשׁ **nᵉchâsh** (Chald.), *nekh-awsh';* corresp. to 5154; *copper:*—brass.

5175. נָחָשׁ **nâchâsh**, *naw-khawsh';* from 5172; a *snake* (from its *hiss*):—serpent.

5176. נָחָשׁ **Nâchâsh**, *naw-khawsh';* the same as 5175; *Nachash*, the name of two persons appar. non-Isr.:—Nahash.

נְחֻשָׁה **nᵉchûshâh**. See 5154.

5177. נַחְשׁוֹן **Nachshôwn**, *nakh-shone';* from 5172; *enchanter; Nachshon*, an Isr.:—Naashon, Nahshon.

5178. נְחֹשֶׁת **nᵉchôsheth**, *nekh-o'-sheth;* for 5154; *copper;* hence, something made of that metal, i.e. *coin*, a *fetter;* fig. *base* (as compared with gold or silver):—brasen, brass, chain, copper, fetter (of brass), filthiness, steel.

5179. נְחֻשְׁתָּא **Nᵉchushtâ'**, *nekh-oosh-taw';* from 5178; *copper; Nechushta*, an Israelitess:—Nehushta.

5180. נְחֻשְׁתָּן **Nᵉchushtân**, *nekh-oosh-tawn';* from 5178; something made *of copper*, i.e. the copper *serpent* of the Desert:—Nehushtan.

5181. נָחַת **nâchath**, *naw-khath';* a prim. root; to *sink*, i.e. *descend;* causat., to *press* or *lead* down:—be broken, (cause to) come down, enter, go down, press sore, settle, stick fast.

5182. נְחַת **nᵉchath** (Chald.), *nekh-ath';* corresp. to 5181; to *descend;* causat., to *bring away, deposit, depose:*—carry, come down, depose, lay up, place.

5183. נַחַת **nachath**, *nakh'-ath;* from 5182; a *descent*, i.e. imposition, unfavorable (*punishment*) or favorable (*food*); also (intrans.; perh. from 5117), *restfulness:*—lighting down, quiet (-ness), to rest, be set on.

5184. נַחַת **Nachath**, *nakh'-ath;* the same as 5183; *quiet; Nachath*, the name of an Edomite and of two Isr.:—Nahath.

5185. נָחֵת **nâchêth**, *naw-khayth';* from 5181; *descending:*—come down.

5186. נָטָה **nâṭâh**, *naw-taw';* a prim. root; to *stretch* or spread out; by impl. to *bend* away (includ. mor. deflection); used in a great variety of application (as follows):— + afternoon, apply, bow (down, -ing), carry aside, decline, deliver, extend, go down, be gone, incline, intend, lay, let down, offer, outstretched, overthrown, pervert, pitch, prolong, put away, shew, spread (out), stretch (forth, out), take (aside), turn (aside, away), wrest, cause to yield.

5187. נְטִיל **nᵉṭîyl**, *net-eel';* from 5190; *laden:*—that bear.

5188. נְטִיפָה **nᵉṭîyphâh**, *net-ee-faw';* from 5197; a *pendant* for the ears (espec. of pearls):—chain, collar.

5189. נְטִישָׁה **nᵉṭîyshâh**, *net-ee-shaw';* from 5203; a *tendril* (as an offshoot):—battlement, branch, plant.

5190. נָטַל **nâṭal**, *naw-tal';* a prim root; to *lift;* by impl. to *impose:*—bear, offer, take up.

5191. נטל **nᵉṭal** (Chald.), *net-al';* corresp. to 5190; to *raise:*—take up.

5192. נֵטֶל **nêṭel**, *nay'-tel;* from 5190; a *burden:*—weighty.

5193. נָטַע **nâṭaʿ**, *naw-tah';* a prim. root; prop. to *strike* in, i.e. *fix;* spec. to *plant* (lit. or fig.):—fastened, plant (-er).

5194. נֶטַע **neṭaʿ**, *neh'-tah;* from 5193; a *plant;* collect., a *plantation;* abstr., a *planting:*—plant.

5195. נָטִיעַ **nâṭîaʿ**, *naw-tee'-ah;* from 5193; a *plant:*—plant.

5196. נְטָעִים **Nᵉṭâʿîym**, *net-aw-eem';* plur. of 5194; *Netaïm*, a place in Pal.:—plants.

5197. נָטַף **nâṭaph**, *naw-taf';* a prim. root; to *ooze*, i.e. *distil* gradually; by impl. to *fall in drops;* fig. to *speak* by inspiration:—drop (-ping), prophesy (-et).

5198. נָטָף **nâṭâph**, *naw-tawf';* from 5197; a *drop;* spec., an aromatic *gum* (prob. *stacte*):—drop, stacte.

5199. נְטֹפָה **Nᵉṭôphâh**, *net-o-faw';* from 5197; *distillation; Netophah*, a place in Pal.:—Netophah.

5200. נְטֹפָתִי **Nᵉṭôphâthîy**, *net-o-faw-thee';* patron. from 5199; a *Netophathite*, or inhab. of Netophah:—Netophathite.

5201. נָטַר **nâṭar**, *naw-tar';* a prim. root; to *guard;* fig., to *cherish* (anger):—bear grudge, keep (-er), reserve.

5202. נְטַר **nᵉṭar** (Chald.), *net-ar';* corresp. to 5201; to *retain:*—keep.

5203. נָטַשׁ **nâṭash**, *naw-tash';* a prim. root; prop. to *pound*, i.e. *smite;* by impl. (as if beating out, and thus expanding) to *disperse;* also, to *thrust* off, down, out or upon (includ. *reject, let alone, permit, remit*, etc.):—cast off, drawn, let fall, forsake, join [battle], leave (off), lie still, loose, spread (self) abroad, stretch out, suffer.

5204. נִי **nîy**, *nee;* a doubtful word; appar. from 5091; *lamentation:*—wailing.

5205. נִיד **nîyd**, *need;* from 5110; *motion* (of the lips n speech):—moving.

5206. נִידָה **nîydâh**, *nee-daw';* fem. of 5205; *removal*, i.e. exile:—removed.

5207. נִיחוֹחַ **nîychôwach**, *nee-kho'-akh;* or

נִיחֹחַ **nîychôach**, *nee-kho'-akh;* from 5117; prop. *restful*, i.e. *pleasant;* abstr. *delight:*—sweet (odour).

5208. נִיחוֹחַ **nîychôwach** (Chald.), *nee-kho'-akh;* or (shorter)

נִיחֹחַ **nîychôach** (Chald.), *nee-kho'-akh;* corresp. to 5207; *pleasure:*—sweet odour (savour).

5209. נִין **nîyn**, *neen;* from 5125; *progeny:*—son.

5210. נִינְוֵה **Nîynᵉvêh**, *nee-nev-ay';* of for. or.; *Nineveh*, the capital of Assyria:—Nineveh.

5211. נִיס **nîyç**, *neece;* from 5127; *fugitive:*—that fleeth.

5212. נִיסָן **Nîyçân**, *nee-sawn';* prob. of for. or.; *Nisan*, the first month of the Jewish sacred year:—Nisan.

5213. נִיצוֹץ **nîytsôwts**, *nee-tsotes';* from 5340; a *spark:*—spark.

5214. נִיר **nîyr**, *neer;* a root prob. ident. with that of 5216, through the idea of the *gleam* of a fresh furrow; to *till* the soil:—break up.

5215. נִיר **nîyr**, *neer;* or

נִר **nîr**, *neer;* from 5214; prop. *ploughing*, i.e. (concr.) freshly *ploughed* land:—fallow ground, ploughing, tillage.

5216. נִיר **nîyr**, *neer;* or

נִר **nîr**, *neer;* also

נֵיר **nêyr**, *nare;* or

נֵר **nêr**, *nare;* or (fem.)

נֵרָה **nêrâh**, *nay-raw';* from a prim. root [see 5214; 5135] prop. mean. to *glisten;* a *lamp* (i.e. the burner) or *light* (lit. or fig.):—candle, lamp, light.

5217. נָכָא **nâkâ'**, *naw-kaw';* a prim. root; to *smite*, i.e. *drive away:*—be viler.

5218. נָכֵא **nâkê'**, *naw-kay';* or

נָכָא **nâkâ'**, *naw-kaw';* from 5217; *smitten*, i.e. (fig.) *afflicted:*—broken, stricken, wounded.

5219. נְכֹאת **nᵉkô'th**, *nek-ohth';* from 5218; prop. a *smiting*, i.e. (concr.) an aromatic *gum* [perh. *styrax*] (as *powdered*):—spicery (-ces).

5220. נֶכֶד **neked**, *neh'-ked;* from an unused root mean. to *propagate; offspring:*—nephew, son's son.

5221. נָכָה **nâkâh**, *naw-kaw';* a prim. root; to *strike* (lightly or severely, lit. or fig.):—beat, cast forth, clap, give [wounds], × go forward, × indeed, kill, make [slaughter], murderer, punish, slaughter, slay (-er, -ing), smite (-r, -ing), strike, be stricken, (give) stripes, × surely, wound.

5222. נֵכֶה **nêkeh**, *nay-keh';* from 5221; a *smiter*, i.e. (fig.) *traducer:*—abject.

5223. נָכֶה **nâkeh**, *naw-keh';* *smitten*, i.e. (lit.) maimed, or (fig.) dejected:—contrite, lame.

5224. נְכוֹ **Nᵉkôw**, *nek-o';* prob. of Eg. or.; *Neko* an Eg. king:—Necho. Comp. 6549.

5225. נָכוֹן **Nâkôwn**, *naw-kone';* from 3559; *prepared; Nakon*, prob. an Isr.:—Nachon.

5226. נֵכַח **nêkach**, *nay'-kakh;* from an unused root mean. to *be straightforward;* prop. the *fore* part; used adv., *opposite:*—before, over against.

5227. נֹכַח **nôkach**, *no'-kakh;* from the same as 5226; prop., the *front* part; used adv. (espec. with prep.), *opposite, in front of, forward, in behalf of:*—(over) against, before, direct [-ly], for, right (on).

5228. נָכֹחַ **nâkôach**, *naw-ko'-akh;* from the same as 5226; *straightforward*, i.e. (fig.), *equitable, correct*, or (abstr.), *integrity:*—plain, right, uprightness.

5229. נְכֹחָה **nᵉkôchâh**, *nek-o-khaw';* fem. of 5228; prop. *straightforwardness*, i.e. (fig.) *integrity*, or (concr.) *a truth:*—equity, right (thing), uprightness.

5230. נָכַל **nâkal**, *naw-kal';* a prim root; to *defraud*, i.e. *act treacherously:*—beguile, conspire, deceiver, deal subtilly.

5231. נֵכֶל **nêkel**, *nay'-kel;* from 5230; *deceit:*—wile.

5232. נְכַס **nᵉkaç** (Chald.), *nek-as';* corresp. to 5233:—goods.

5233. נֶכֶס **nekeç**, *neh'-kes;* from an unused root mean. to *accumulate; treasure:*—riches, wealth.

5234. נָכַר **nâkar**, *naw-kar';* a prim. root; prop. to *scrutinize*, i.e. look intently at; hence (with *recognition* implied), to *acknowledge, be acquainted with, care for, respect, revere*, or (with *suspicion* implied), to *disregard, ignore, be strange* toward, *reject, resign, dissimulate* (as if ignorant or disowning):—acknowledge, × could, deliver, discern, dissemble, estrange, feign self to be another, know, take knowledge (notice), perceive, regard, (have) respect, behave (make) self strange (-ly).

5235. נֶכֶר **neker**, *neh'-ker;* or

נֹכֶר **nôker**, *no'-ker;* from 5234; something *strange*, i.e. unexpected *calamity:*—strange.

5236. נֵכָר **nêkâr**, *nay-kawr';* from 5234; *foreign*, or (concr.) a *foreigner*, or (abstr.) *heathendom:*—alien, strange (+ -er).

5237. נָכְרִי **nokrîy**, *nok-ree';* from 5235 (second form); *strange*, in a variety of degrees and applications (*foreign, non-relative, adulterous, different, wonderful*):—alien, foreigner, outlandish, strange (-r, woman).

5238. נְכֹת **nᵉkôth**, *nek-ôth';* prob. for 5219; *spicery*, i.e. (gen.) *valuables:*—precious things.

5239. נָלָה **nâlâh**, *naw-law';* appar. a prim. root; to *complete:*—make an end.

5240. נְמִבְזֶה **nᵉmibzeh**, *nem-ib-zeh';* from 959; *despised:*—vile.

5241. נְמוּאֵל **Nᵉmûwʼêl**, *nem-oo-ale'*; appar. for 3223; *Nemuel*, the name of two Isr.:—Nemuel.

5242. נְמוּאֵלִי **Nᵉmûwʼêlîy**, *nem-oo-ay-lee'*; from 5241; a *Nemuelite*, or desc. of Nemuel:—Nemuelite.

5243. נָמַל **nâmal**, *naw-mal'*; a prim. root; to *become clipped* or (spec.) *circumcised*:—(branch to) be cut down (off), circumcise.

5244. נְמָלָה **nᵉmâlâh**, *nem-aw-law'*; fem. from 5243; an *ant* (prob. from its almost *bisected* form):—ant.

5245. נְמַר **nᵉmar** (Chald.), *nem-ar'*; corresp. to 5246:—leopard.

5246 נָמֵר **nâmêr**, *naw-mare'*; from an unused root mean. prop. to *filtrate*, i.e. *be limpid* [comp. 5247 and 5249]; and thus to *spot* or *stain* as if by dripping; a *leopard* (from its stripes):—leopard.

נִמְרֹד **Nimrôd**. See 5248.

5247. נִמְרָה **Nimrâh**, *nim-raw'*; from the same as 5246; *clear* water; *Nimrah*, a place E. of the Jordan:—Nimrah. See also 1039, 5249.

5248. נִמְרוֹד **Nimrôwd**, *nim-rode'*; or

נִמְרֹד **Nimrôd**, *nim-rode'*; prob. of for. or.; *Nimrod*, a son of Cush:—Nimrod.

5249. נִמְרִים **Nimrîym**, *nim-reem'*; plur. of a masc. corresp. to 5247; *clear waters*; *Nimrim*, a place E. of the Jordan:—Nimrim. Comp. 1039.

5250. נִמְשִׁי **Nimshîy**, *nim-shee'*; prob. from 4871; *extricated*; *Nimshi*, the (grand-) father of Jehu:—Nimshi.

5251. נֵס **nêç**, *nace*; from 5264; a *flag*; also a *sail*; by impl. a *flagstaff*; gen. a *signal*; fig. a *token*:—banner, pole, sail, (en-) sign, standard.

5252. נְסִבָּה **nᵉçibbâh**, *nes-ib-baw'*; fem. part. pass. of 5437; prop. an *environment*, i.e. *circumstance* or *turn* of affairs:—cause.

5253. נָסַג **nâçag**, *naw-sag'*; a prim. root; to *retreat*:—departing away, remove, take (hold), turn away.

נְסָה **nᵉçâh**. See 5375.

5254. נָסָה **nâçâh**, *naw-saw'*; a prim. root; to *test*; by impl. to *attempt*:—adventure, assay, prove, tempt, try.

5255. נָסַח **nâçach**, *naw-sakh'*; a prim. root; to *tear* away:—destroy, pluck, root.

5256. נְסַח **nᵉçach** (Chald.), *nes-akh'*; corresp. to 5255:—pull down.

5257. נְסִיךְ **nᵉçîyk**, *nes-eek'*; from 5258; prop. something *poured* out, i.e. a *libation*; also a molten *image*; by impl. a *prince* (as *anointed*):—drink offering, duke, prince (-ipal).

5258. נָסַךְ **nâçak**, *naw-sak'*; a prim. root; to *pour* out, espec. a libation, or to *cast* (metal); by anal. to *anoint* a king:—cover, melt, offer, (cause to) pour (out), set (up).

5259. נָסַךְ **nâçak**, *naw-sak'*; a prim. root [prob. identical with 5258 through the idea of fusion]; to *interweave*, i.e. (fig.) to *overspread*:—that is spread.

5260. נְסַךְ **nᵉçak** (Chald.), *nes-ak'*; corresp. to 5258; to *pour* out a libation:—offer.

5261. נְסַךְ **nᵉçak** (Chald.), *nes-ak'*; corresp. to 5262; a *libation*:—drink offering.

5262. נֶסֶךְ **neçek**, *neh'-sek*; or

נֵסֶךְ **nêçek**, *nay'-sek*; from 5258; a *libation*; also a *cast idol*:—cover, drink offering, molten image.

נִסְמָן **niçmân**. See 5567.

5263. נָסַס **nâçaç**, *naw-sas'*; a prim. root; to *wane*, i.e. *be sick*.

5264. נָסַס **nâçaç**, *naw-sas'*; a prim. root; to *gleam* from afar, i.e. to *be conspicuous* as a signal; or rather perh. a denom. from 5251 [and ident. with 5263, through the idea of a flag as *fluttering* in the wind]; to *raise a beacon*:—lift up as an ensign, standard bearer.

5265. נָסַע **nâçaʻ**, *naw-sah'*; a prim. root; prop. to *pull* up, espec. the tent-pins, i.e. *start* on a journey:—cause to blow, bring, get, (make to) go (away, forth, forward, onward, out), (take) journey, march, remove, set aside (forward), × still, be on his (go their) way.

5266. נָסַק **nâçaq**, *naw-sak'*; a prim. root; to *go* up:—ascend.

5267. נְסַק **nᵉçaq** (Chald.), *nes-ak'*; corresp. to 5266:—take up.

5268. נִסְרֹךְ **Niçrôk**, *nis-roke'*; of for. or.; *Nisrok*, a Bab. idol:—Nisroch.

5269. נֵעָה **Nêʻâh**, *nay-aw'*; from 5128; *motion*; *Neäh*, a place in Pal.:—Neah.

5270. נֹעָה **Nôʻâh**, *no-aw'*; from 5128; *movement*; *Noäh*, an Israelitess:—Noah.

5271. נָעוּר **nâʻûwr**, *naw-oor'*; or

נָעֻר **nâʻûr**, *naw-oor'*; and (fem.)

נְעֻרָה **nᵉʻûrâh**, *neh-oo-raw'*; prop. pass. part. from 5288 as denom.; (only in plur. collect. or emphat.) *youth*, the state (*juvenility*) or the persons (*young* people):—childhood, youth.

5272. נְעִיאֵל **Nᵉʻîyʼêl**, *neh-ee-ale'*; from 5128 and 410; *moved of God*; *Neïel*, a place in Pal.:—Neiel.

5273. נָעִים **nâʻîym**, *naw-eem'*; from 5276; *delightful* (obj. or subj., lit. or fig.):—pleasant (-ure), sweet.

5274. נָעַל **nâʻal**, *naw-al'*; a prim. root; prop. to *fasten* up, i.e. with a bar or cord; hence (denom. from 5275), to *sandal*, i.e. furnish with slippers:—bolt, inclose, lock, shod, shut up.

5275. נַעַל **naʻal**, *nah'-al*; or (fem.)

נַעֲלָה **naʻălâh**, *nah-al-aw'*; from 5274; prop. a sandal *tongue*; by extens. a *sandal* or slipper (sometimes as a symbol of occupancy, a refusal to marry, or of something valueless):—dryshod, (pair of) shoe ([-latchet], -s).

5276. נָעֵם **nâʻêm**, *naw-ame'*; a prim. root; to *be agreeable* (lit. or fig.):—pass in beauty, be delight, be pleasant, be sweet.

5277. נַעַם **Naʻam**, *nah'-am*; from 5276; *pleasure*; *Naam*, an Isr.:—Naam.

5278. נֹעַם **nôʻam**, *no'-am*; from 5276; *agreeableness*, i.e. *delight*, *suitableness*, *splendor* or *grace*:—beauty, pleasant (-ness).

5279. נַעֲמָה **Naʻămâh**, *nah-am-aw'*; fem. of 5277; *pleasantness*; *Naamah*, the name of an antediluvian woman, of an Ammonitess, and of a place in Pal.:—Naamah.

5280. נַעֲמִי **Naʻămîy**, *nah-am-ee'*; patron. from 5283; a *Naamanite*, or desc. of Naaman (collect.):—Naamites.

5281. נׇעֳמִי **Noʻŏmîy**, *nō-om-ee'*; from 5278; *pleasant*; *Noömi*, an Israelitess:—Naomi.

5282. נַעֲמָן **naʻămân**, *nah-am-awn'*; from 5276; *pleasantness* (plur. as concr.):—pleasant.

5283. נַעֲמָן **Naʻămân**, *nah-am-awn'*; the same as 5282; *Naaman*, the name of an Isr. and of a Damascene:—Naaman.

5284. נַעֲמָתִי **Naʻămâthîy**, *nah-am-aw-thee'*; patrial from a place corresp. in name (but not ident.) with 5279; a *Naamathite*, or inhab. of Naamah:—Naamathite

5285. נַעֲצוּץ **naʻătsûwts**, *nah-ats-oots'*; from an unused root mean. to *prick*; prob. a *brier*; by impl. a *thicket* of thorny bushes:—thorn.

5286. נָעַר **nâʻar**, *naw-ar'*; a prim. root; to *growl*:—yell.

5287. נָעַר **nâʻar**, *naw-ar'*; a prim. root [prob. ident. with 5286, through the idea of the *rustling* of mane, which usually accompanies the lion's roar]; to *tumble* about:—shake (off, out, self), overthrow, toss up and down.

5288. נַעַר **naʻar**, *nah'-ar*; from 5287; (concr.) a *boy* (as active), from the age of infancy to adolescence; by impl. a *servant*; also (by interch. of sex), a *girl* (of similar latitude in age):—babe, boy, child, damsel [*from the marg.*], lad, servant, young (man).

5289. נַעַר **naʻar**, *nah'-ar*; from 5287 in its der. sense of *tossing* about; a *wanderer*:—young one.

5290. נֹעַר **nôʻar**, *no'-ar*; from 5287; (abstr.) *boyhood* [comp. 5288]:—child, youth.

נָעֻר **nâʻûr**. See 5271.

5291. נַעֲרָה **naʻărâh**, *nah-ar-aw'*; fem. of 5288; a *girl* (from infancy to adolescence):—damsel, maid (-en), young (woman).

5292. נַעֲרָה **Naʻărâh**, *nah-ar-aw'*; the same as 5291; *Naarah*, the name of an Israelitess, and of a place in Pal.:—Naarah, Naarath.

נְעֻרָה **nᵉʻûrâh**. See 5271.

5293. נַעֲרַי **Naʻăray**, *nah-ar-ah'ee*; from 5288; *youthful*; *Naarai*, an Isr.:—Naarai.

5294. נְעַרְיָה **Nᵉʻaryâh**, *neh-ar-yaw'*; from 5288 and 3050; *servant of Jah*; *Neärjah*, the name of two Isr.:—Neariah.

5295. נַעֲרָן **Naʻărân**, *nah-ar-awn'*; from 5288; *juvenile*; *Naaran*, a place in Pal.:—Naaran.

5296. נְעֹרֶת **nᵉʻôreth**, *neh-o'-reth*; from 5287; something *shaken* out, i.e. *tow* (as the refuse of flax):—tow.

נַעֲרָתָה **Naʻărâthâh**. See 5292.

5297. נֹף **Nôph**, *nofe*; a var. of 4644; *Noph*, the capital of Upper Egypt:—Noph.

5298. נֶפֶג **Nepheg**, *neh'-feg*; from an unused root prob. mean. to *spring* forth; a *sprout*; *Nepheg*, the name of two Isr.:—Nepheg.

5299. נָפָה **nâphâh**, *naw-faw'*; from 5130 in the sense of *lifting*; a *height*; also a *sieve*:—border, coast, region, sieve.

5300. נְפוּשְׁסִים° **Nᵉphûwshᵉçîym**, *nef-oo-shes-eem'*; for 5304; *Nephushesim*, a Temple-servant:—Nephisesim [*from the marg.*].

5301. נָפַח **nâphach**, *naw-fakh'*; a prim. root; to *puff*, in various applications (lit., to *inflate*, *blow* hard, *scatter*, *kindle*, *expire*; fig., to *disesteem*):—blow, breath, give up, cause to lose [life], seething, snuff.

5302. נֹפַח **Nôphach**, *no'-fakh*; from 5301; a *gust*; *Nophach*, a place in Moab:—Nophah.

5303. נְפִיל **nᵉphîyl**, *nef-eel'*; or

נְפִל **nᵉphil**, *nef-eel'*; from 5307; prop., a *feller*, i.e. a *bully* or *tyrant*:—giant.

5304. נְפִיסִים° **Nᵉphîyçîym**, *nef-ee-seem'*; plur. from an unused root mean. to *scatter*; *expansions*; *Nephisim*, a Temple-servant:—Nephusim [*from the marg.*].

5305. נָפִישׁ **Nâphîysh**, *naw-feesh'*; from 5314; *refreshed*; *Naphish*, a son of Ishmael, and his posterity:—Naphish.

5306. נֹפֶךְ **nôphek**, *no'-fek*; from an unused root mean. to *glisten*; *shining*; a gem, prob. the *garnet*:—emerald.

5307. נָפַל **nâphal**, *naw-fal'*; a prim. root; to *fall*, in a great variety of applications (intrans. or causat., lit. or fig.):—be accepted, cast (down, self, [lots], out), cease, die, divide (by lot), (let) fail, (cause to, let, make, ready to) fall (away, down, -en, -ing), fell (-ing), fugitive, have [inheritance], inferior, be judged [*by mistake for* 6419], lay (along), (cause to) lie down, light (down), be (× hast) lost, lying, overthrow, overwhelm, perish, present (-ed, -ing), (make to) rot, slay, smite out, × surely, throw down.

5308. נְפַל **nᵉphal** (Chald.), *nef-al'*; corresp. to 5307:—fall (down), have occasion.

5309. נֶפֶל **nephel**, *neh'-fel*; or

נֵפֶל **nêphel**, *nay'-fel*; from 5307; something *fallen*, i.e. an *abortion*:—untimely birth.

נְפִל **nᵉphîl**. See 5303.

5310. נָפַץ **nâphats**, *naw-fats'*; a prim. root; to *dash* to pieces, or *scatter*:—be beaten in sunder, break (in pieces), broken, dash (in pieces), cause to be discharged, dispersed, be overspread, scatter.

5311. נֶפֶץ **nephets**, *neh'-fets*; from 5310; a *storm* (as dispersing):—scattering.

5312. נְפַק **nᵉphaq** (Chald.), *nef-ak'*; a prim. root; to *issue*; causat., to *bring out*:—come (go, take) forth (out).

5313. נִפְקָא **niphqâ'** (Chald.), *nif-kaw'*; from 5312; an *outgo*, i.e. expense:—expense.

5314. נָפַשׁ **nâphash**, *naw-fash'*; a prim. root; to *breathe;* pass., to *be breathed* upon, i.e. (fig.) *refreshed* (as if by a current of air):—(be) refresh selves (-ed).

5315. נֶפֶשׁ **nephesh**, *neh'-fesh;* from 5314; prop. a *breathing* creature, i.e. *animal* or (abstr.) *vitality;* used very widely in a lit., accommodated or fig. sense (bodily or mental):—any, appetite, beast, body, breath, creature, × dead (-ly), desire, × [dis-] contented, × fish, ghost, + greedy, he, heart (-y), (hath, × jeopardy of) life (× in jeopardy), lust, man, me, mind, mortally, one, own, person, pleasure, (her-, him-, my-, thy-) self, them (your) -selves, + slay, soul, + tablet, they, thing, (× she) will, × would have it.

5316. נֶפֶת **nepheth**, *neh'-feth;* for 5299; a *height:*—country.

5317. נֹפֶת **nôpheth**, *no'-feth;* from 5130 in the sense of *shaking* to pieces; a *dripping* i.e. of *honey* (from the comb):—honeycomb.

5318. נֶפְתּוֹחַ **Nephtôwach**, *nef-to'-akh;* from 6605; *opened*, i.e. a *spring; Nephtoäch*, a place in Pal.:—Neptoah.

5319. נַפְתּוּל **naphtûwl**, *naf-tool';* from 6617; prop. *wrestled;* but used (in the plur.) trans., a *struggle:*—wrestling.

5320. נַפְתֻּחִים **Naphtûchîym**, *naf-too-kheem';* plur. of for. or.; *Naphtuchim*, an Eg. tribe:—Naptuhim.

5321. נַפְתָּלִי **Naphtâlîy**, *naf-taw-lee';* from 6617; *my wrestling; Naphtali*, a son of Jacob, with the tribe descended from him, and its territory:—Naphtali.

5322. נֵץ **nêts**, *nayts;* from 5340; a *flower* (from its *brilliancy*); also a *hawk* (from its *flashing* speed):—blossom, hawk.

5323. נָצָא **nâtsâ'**, *naw-tsaw';* a prim. root; to *go away:*—flee.

5324. נָצַב **nâtsab**, *naw-tsab';* a prim. root; to *station*, in various applications (lit. or fig.):—appointed, deputy, erect, establish, × Huzzah [*by mistake for a prop. name*], lay, officer, pillar, present, rear up, set (over, up), settle, sharpen, stablish, (make to) stand (-ing, still, up, upright), best state.

נְצִב **n^{e}tsîb**. See 5333.

5325. נִצָּב **nitstsâb**, *nits-tsawb';* pass. part. of 5324; *fixed*, i.e. a *handle:*—haft.

5326. נִצְבָּה **nitsbâh** (Chald.), *nits-baw';* from a root corresp. to 5324; *fixedness*, i.e. *firmness:*—strength.

5327. נָצָה **nâtsâh**, *naw-tsaw';* a prim. root; prop. to *go forth*, i.e. (by impl.) to *be expelled*, and (consequently) *desolate;* causat. to *lay waste;* also (spec.), to *quarrel:*—be laid waste, ruinous, strive (together).

נֹצָה **nôtsâh**. See 5133.

5328. נִצָּה **nitstsâh**, *nits-tsaw';* fem. of 5322; a *blossom:*—flower.

נְצוּרָה **n^{e}tsûwrâh**. See 5341.

5329. נָצַח **nâtsach**, *naw-tsakh';* a prim. root; prop. to *glitter* from afar, i.e. to be *eminent* (as a superintendent, espec. of the Temple services and its music); also (as denom. from 5331), to *be permanent:*—excel, chief musician (singer), oversee (-r), set forward.

5330. נְצַח **n^{e}tsach** (Chald.), *nets-akh';* corresp. to 5329; to *become chief:*—be preferred.

5331. נֶצַח **netsach**, *neh'-tsakh;* or

נֵצַח **nêtsach**, *nay'-tsakh;* from 5329; prop. a *goal*, i.e. the bright object at a distance travelled towards; hence (fig.), *splendor*, or (subj.) *truthfulness*, or (obj.) *confidence;* but usually (adv.), *continually* (i.e. to the most distant point of view):—alway (-s), constantly, end, (+ n-) ever (more), perpetual, strength, victory.

5332. נֵצַח **Nêtsach**, *nay'-tsakh;* prob. ident. with 5331, through the idea of *brilliancy* of color; *juice* of the grape (as blood red):—blood, strength.

5333. נְצִיב **n^{e}tsîyb**, *nets-eeb';* or

נְצִב **n^{e}tsib**, *nets-eeb';* from 5324; something *stationary*, i.e. a *prefect*, a military *post*, a *statue:*—garrison, officer, pillar.

5334. נְצִיב **N^{e}tsîyb**, *nets-eeb';* the same as 5333; *station; Netsib*, a place in Pal.:—Nezib.

5335. נְצִיחַ **n^{e}tsîyach**, *nets-ee'-akh;* from 5329; *conspicuous; Netsiach*, a Temple-servant:—Neziah.

5336. נָצִיר **nâtsîyr**, *naw-tsere';* from 5341; prop. *conservative;* but used pass., *delivered:*—preserved.

5337. נָצַל **nâtsal**, *naw-tsal';* a prim. root; to *snatch* away, whether in a good or a bad sense:— × at all, defend, deliver (self), escape, × without fail, part, pluck, preserve, recover, rescue, rid, save, spoil, strip, × surely, take (out).

5338. נְצַל **n^{e}tsal** (Chald.), *nets-al';* corresp. to 5337; to *extricate:*—deliver, rescue.

5339. נִצָּן **nitstsân**, *nits-tsawn';* from 5322; a *blossom:*—flower.

5340. נָצַץ **nâtsats**, *naw-tsats';* a prim. root; to *glare*, i.e. *be bright*-colored:—sparkle.

5341. נָצַר **nâtsar**, *naw-tsar';* a prim. root; to *guard*, in a good sense (to *protect, maintain, obey*, etc.) or a bad one (to *conceal*, etc.):—besieged, hidden thing, keep (-er, -ing), monument, observe, preserve (-r), subtil, watcher (-man).

5342. נֵצֶר **nêtser**, *nay'-tser;* from 5341 in the sense of *greenness* as a striking color; a *shoot;* fig., a *descendant:*—branch.

5343. נְקֵא **n^{e}qê'** (Chald.), *nek-ay';* from a root corresp. to 5352; *clean:*—pure.

5344. נָקַב **nâqab**, *naw-kab';* a prim. root; to *puncture*, lit. (to *perforate*, with more or less violence) or fig. (to *specify, designate, libel*):—appoint, blaspheme, bore, curse, express, with holes, name, pierce, strike through.

5345. נֶקֶב **neqeb**, *neh'-keb;* a *bezel* (for a gem):—pipe.

5346. נֶקֶב **Neqeb**, *neh'-keb;* the same as 5345; *dell; Nekeb*, a place in Pal.:—Nekeb.

5347. נְקֵבָה **n^{e}qêbâh**, *nek-ay-baw';* from 5344; *female* (from the sexual form):—female, woman.

5348. נָקֹד **nâqôd**, *naw-kode';* from an unused root mean. to *mark* (by *puncturing* or *branding*); *spotted:*—speckled.

5349. נֹקֵד **nôqêd**, *no-kade';* act. part. from the same as 5348; a *spotter* (of sheep or cattle), i.e. the owner or tender (who thus marks them):—herdman, sheepmaster.

5350. נִקֻּד **niqqud**, *nik-kood';* from the same as 5348; a *crumb* (as *broken* to spots); also a *biscuit* (as *pricked*):—cracknel, mouldy.

5351. נְקֻדָּה **n^{e}quddâh**, *nek-ood-daw';* fem. of 5348; a *boss:*—stud.

5352. נָקָה **nâqâh**, *naw-kaw';* a prim. root; to *be* (or *make*) *clean* (lit. or fig.); by impl. (in an adverse sense) to *be bare*, i.e. *extirpated:*—acquit × at all, × altogether, be blameless, cleanse, (be) clear (-ing), cut off, be desolate, be free, be (hold) guiltless, be (hold) innocent, × by no means, be quit, be (leave) unpunished, × utterly, × wholly.

5353. נְקוֹדָא **N^{e}qôwdâ'**, *nek-o-daw';* fem. of 5348 (in the fig. sense of *marked*); *distinction; Nekoda*, a Temple-servant:—Nekoda.

5354. נָקַט **nâqaṭ**, *naw-kat';* a prim. root; to *loathe:*—weary.

5355. נָקִי **nâqîy**, *naw-kee';* or

נָקִיא **nâqîy'** (Joel 4 : 19; Jonah 1 : 14), *naw-kee';* from 5352; *innocent:*—blameless, clean, clear, exempted, free, guiltless, innocent, quit.

5356. נִקָּיוֹן **niqqâyôwn**, *nik-kaw-yone';* or

נִקָּיֹן **niqqâyôn**, *nik-kaw-yone';* from 5352; *clearness* (lit. or fig.):—cleanness, innocency.

5357. נָקִיק **nâqîyq**, *naw-keek';* from an unused root mean. to *bore;* a *cleft:*—hole.

5358. נָקַם **nâqam**, *naw-kam';* a prim. root; to *grudge*, i.e. *avenge* or *punish:*—avenge (-r, self), punish, revenge (self), × surely, take vengeance.

5359. נָקָם **nâqâm**, *naw-kawm';* from 5358; *revenge:*— + avenged, quarrel, vengeance.

5360. נְקָמָה **n^{e}qâmâh**, *nek-aw-maw';* fem. of 5359; *avengement*, whether the act or the passion:— + avenge, revenge (-ing), vengeance.

5361. נָקַע **nâqa'**, *naw-kah';* a prim. root; to *feel aversion:*—be alienated.

5362. נָקַף **nâqaph**, *naw-kaf';* a prim. root; to *strike* with more or less violence (*beat, fell, corrode*); by impl. (of attack) to *knock together*, i.e. *surround* or *circulate:*—compass (about, -ing), cut down, destroy, go round (about), inclose, round.

5363. נֹקֶף **nôqeph**, *no'-kef;* from 5362; a *threshing* (of olives):—shaking.

5364. נִקְפָּה **niqpâh**, *nik-paw';* from 5362; prob. a *rope* (as *encircling*):—rent.

5365. נָקַר **nâqar**, *naw-kar';* a prim. root; to *bore* (*penetrate, quarry*):—dig, pick out, pierce, put (thrust) out.

5366. נְקָרָה **n^{e}qârâh**, *nek-aw-raw';* from 5365; a *fissure:*—cleft, clift.

5367. נָקַשׁ **nâqash**, *naw-kash';* a prim. root; to *entrap* (with a noose), lit. or fig.:—catch. (lay a) snare.

5368. נְקַשׁ **n^{e}qash** (Chald.), *nek-ash';* corresp. to 5367; but used in the sense of 5362; to *knock:*—smote.

נֵר **nêr**. נִר **nîr**. See 5215, 5216.

5369. נֵר **Nêr**, *nare;* the same as 5216; *lamp; Ner*, an Isr.:—Ner.

5370. נֵרְגַּל **Nêrgal**, *nare-gal';* of for. or.; *Nergal*, a Cuthite deity:—Nergal.

5371. נֵרְגַּל שַׁרְאֶצֶר **Nêrgal Shar'etser**, *nare-gal' shar-eh'-tser;* from 5370 and 8272; *Nergal-Sharetser*, the name of two Bab.:—Nergal-sharezer.

5372. נִרְגָּן **nirgân**, *neer-gawn';* from an unused root mean. to *roll* to pieces; a *slanderer:*—talebearer, whisperer.

5373. נֵרְדְּ **nêrd**, *nayrd;* of for. or.; *nard*, an aromatic:—spikenard.

נֵרָה **nêrâh**. See 5216.

5374. נֵרִיָּה **Nêrîyâh**, *nay-ree-yaw';* or

נֵרִיָּהוּ **Nêrîyâhûw**, *nay-ree-yaw'-hoo;* from 5216 and 3050; *light of Jah; Nerijah*, an Isr.:—Neriah.

5375. נָשָׂא **nâsâ'**, *naw-saw';* or

נָסָה **nâçâh** (Psa. 4 : 6 [7]), *naw-saw';* a prim. root; to *lift*, in a great variety of applications, lit. and fig., absol. and rel. (as follows):—accept, advance, arise, (able to, [armour], suffer to) bear (-er, up), bring (forth), burn, carry (away), cast, contain, desire, ease, exact, exalt (self), extol, fetch, forgive, furnish, further, give, go on, help, high, hold up, honourable (+ man), lade, lay, lift (self) up, lofty, marry, magnify, × needs, obtain, pardon, raise (up), receive, regard, respect, set (up), spare, stir up, + swear, take (away, up), × utterly, wear, yield.

5376. נְשָׂא **n^{e}sâ'** (Chald.), *nes-aw';* corresp. to 5375:—carry away, make insurrection, take.

5377. נָשָׁא **nâshâ'**, *naw-shaw';* a prim. root; to *lead astray*, i.e. (mentally) to *delude*, or (morally) to *seduce:*—beguile, deceive, × greatly, × utterly.

5378. נָשָׁא **nâshâ'**, *naw-shaw';* a prim. root [perh. ident. with 5377, through the idea of *imposition*]; to *lend* on interest; by impl. to *dun* for debt:—× debt, exact, giver of usury.

נָשִׂא **nâsî'**. See 5387.

נְשֻׂאָה **n^{e}sû'âh**. See 5385.

5379. נִשֵּׂאת **nissê'th**, *nis-sayth';* pass. part. fem. of 5375; something *taken*, i.e. a *present:*—gift.

5380. נָשַׁב **nâshab**, *naw-shab';* a prim. root; to *blow;* by impl. to *disperse:*—(cause to) blow, drive away.

5381. נָשַׂג **nâsag**, *naw-sag'*; a prim. root; to *reach* (lit. or fig.):—ability, be able, attain (unto), (be able to, can) get, lay at, put, reach, remove, wax rich, × surely, (over-) take (hold of, on, upon).

5382. נָשָׁה **nâshâh**, *naw-shaw'*; a prim. root; to *forget*; fig., to *neglect*; causat., to *remit, remove*:—forget, deprive, exact.

5383. נָשָׁה **nâshâh**, *naw-shaw'*; a prim. root [rather ident. with 5382, in the sense of 5378]; to *lend* or (by reciprocity) *borrow* on security or interest:—creditor, exact, extortioner, lend, usurer, lend on (taker of) usury.

5384. נָשֶׁה **nâsheh**, *naw-sheh'*; from 5382, in the sense of *failure*; *rheumatic* or *crippled* (from the incident to Jacob):—which shrank.

5385. נְשׂוּאָה **n^esûw'âh**, *nes-oo-aw'*; or rather

נְשֻׂאָה **n^esû'âh**, *nes-oo-aw'*; fem. pass. part. of 5375; something *borne*, i.e. a *load*:—carriage.

5386. נְשִׁי **n^eshîy**, *nesh-ee'*; from 5383; a *debt*:—debt.

5387. נָשִׂיא **nâsîy'**, *naw-see'*; or

נָשִׂא **nâsî'**, *naw-see'*; from 5375; prop. an *exalted* one, i.e. a *king* or *sheik*; also a rising *mist*:—captain, chief, cloud, governor, prince, ruler, vapour.

5388. נְשִׁיָּה **n^eshîyâh**, *nesh-ee-yaw'*; from 5382; *oblivion*:—forgetfulness.

נָשִׁים **nâshîym**. See 802.

5389. נָשִׁין **nâshîyn** (Chald.), *naw-sheen'*; irreg. plur. fem. of 606:—women.

5390. נְשִׁיקָה **n^eshîyqâh**, *nesh-ee-kaw'*; from 5401; a *kiss*:—kiss.

5391. נָשַׁךְ **nâshak**, *naw-shak'*; a prim. root; to *strike* with a sting (as a serpent); fig., to *oppress* with interest on a loan:—bite, lend upon usury.

5392. נֶשֶׁךְ **neshek**, *neh'-shek*; from 5391; *interest* on a debt:—usury.

5393. נִשְׁכָּה **nishkâh**, *nish-kaw'*; for 3957; a *cell*:—chamber.

5394. נָשַׁל **nâshal**, *naw-shal'*; a prim. root; to *pluck* off, i.e. *divest, eject*, or *drop*:—cast (out), drive, loose, put off (out), slip.

5395. נָשַׁם **nâsham**, *naw-sham'*; a prim. root; prop. to *blow* away, i.e. *destroy*:—destroy.

5396. נִשְׁמָא **nishmâ'** (Chald.), *nish-maw'*; corresp. to 5397; vital *breath*:—breath.

5397. נְשָׁמָה **n^eshâmâh**, *nesh-aw-maw'*; fr. 5395; a *puff*, i.e. *wind*, angry or vital *breath*, divine *inspiration, intellect*. or (concr.) an *animal*:—blast, (that) breath (-eth), inspiration, soul, spirit.

5398. נָשַׁף **nâshaph**, *naw-shaf'*; a prim. root; to *breeze*, i.e. *blow* up fresh (as the wind):—blow.

5399. נֶשֶׁף **nesheph**, *neh'-shef*; from 5398; prop. a *breeze*, i.e. (by impl.) *dusk* (when the evening breeze prevails):—dark, dawning of the day (morning), night, twilight.

5400. נָשַׂק **nâsaq**, *naw-sak'*; a prim. root; to *catch* fire:—burn, kindle.

5401. נָשַׁק **nâshaq**, *naw-shak'*; a prim. root [ident. with 5400, through the idea of *fastening* up; comp. 2388, 2836]; to *kiss*, lit. or fig. (*touch*); also (as a mode of *attachment*), to *equip* with weapons:—armed (men), rule, kiss, that touched.

5402. נֶשֶׁק **nesheq**, *neh'-shek*; or

נֵשֶׁק **nêsheq**, *nay'-shek*; from 5401; military *equipment*, i.e. (collect.) *arms* (offensive or defensive), or (concr.) an *arsenal*:—armed men, armour (-y), battle, harness, weapon.

5403. נְשַׁר **n^eshar** (Chald.), *nesh-ar'*; corresp. to 5404; an *eagle*:—eagle.

5404. נֶשֶׁר **nesher**, *neh'-sher*; from an unused root mean. to *lacerate*; the *eagle* (or other large bird of prey):—eagle.

5405. נָשַׁת **nâshath**, *naw-shath'*; a prim. root; prop. to *eliminate*, i.e. (intrans.) to *dry* up:—fail.

נְתִבָה **n^ethîbâh**. See 5410.

5406. נִשְׁתְּוָן **nisht^evân**, *nish-tev-awn'*; prob. of Pers. or.; an *epistle*:—letter.

5407. נִשְׁתְּוָן **nisht^evân** (Chald.), *nish-tev-awn'*; corresp. to 5406:—letter.

נְתוּן **Nathûwn**. See 5411.

5408. נָתַח **nâthach**, *naw-thakh'*; a prim. root; to *dismember*:—cut (in pieces), divide, hew in pieces.

5409. נֵתַח **nêthach**, *nay'-thakh*; from 5408; a *fragment*:—part, piece.

5410. נָתִיב **nâthîyb**, *naw-theeb'*; or (fem.)

נְתִיבָה **n^ethîybâh**, *neth-ee-baw'*; or

נְתִבָה **n^ethîbâh** (Jer. 6 : 16), *neth-ee-baw'*; from an unused root mean. to *tramp*; a (beaten) *track*:—path ([-way]), × travel [-ler], way.

5411. נָתִין **Nâthîyn**, *naw-theen'*; or

נָתוּן **Nâthûwn** (Ezra 8 : 17), *naw-thoon'* (the prop. form, as pass. part.), from 5414; one *given*, i.e. (in the plur. only) the *Nethinim*, or Temple-servants (as *given* up to that duty):—Nethinims.

5412. נְתִין **N^ethîyn** (Chald.), *netheen'*; corresp. to 5411:—Nethinims.

5413. נָתַךְ **nâthak**, *naw-thak'*; a prim. root; to *flow* forth (lit. or fig.); by impl. to *liquefy*:—drop, gather (together), melt, pour (forth, out).

5414. נָתַן **nâthan**, *naw-than'*; a prim. root; to *give*, used with great latitude of application (*put, make*, etc.):—add, apply, appoint, ascribe, assign, × avenge, × be ([healed]), bestow, bring (forth, hither), cast, cause, charge, come, commit consider, count, + cry, deliver (up), direct, distribute do, × doubtless, × without fail, fasten, frame, × get, give (forth, over, up), grant, hang (up), × have, × indeed, lay (unto charge, up), (give) leave, lend, let (out), + lie, lift up, make, + O that, occupy, offer, ordain, pay, perform, place, pour, print, × pull, put (forth), recompense, render, requite, restore, send (out), set (forth), shew, shoot forth (up). + sing, + slander, strike, [sub-] mit, suffer, × surely, × take, thrust, trade, turn, utter, + weep, × willingly, + withdraw, + would (to) God, yield.

5415. נְתַן **n^ethan** (Chald.), *neth-an'*; corresp. to 5414; *give*:—bestow, give, pay.

5416. נָתָן **Nâthân**, *naw-thawn'*; from 5414; *given*; *Nathan*, the name of five Isr.:—Nathan.

5417. נְתַנְאֵל **N^ethanê'l**, *neth-an-ale'*; from 5414 and 410; *given of God*; *Nethanel*, the name of ten Isr.:—Nethaneel.

5418. נְתַנְיָה **N^ethanyâh**, *neth-an-yaw'*; or

נְתַנְיָהוּ **N^ethanyâhûw**, *neth-an-yaw'-hoo*; from 5414 and 3050; *given of Jah*; *Nethanjah*, the name of four Isr.:—Nethaniah.

5419. נְתַן־מֶלֶךְ **N^ethan-Melek**, *neth-an' meh'-lek*; from 5414 and 4428; *given of* (the) *king*; *Nethan-Melek*, an Isr.:—Nathan-melech.

5420. נָתַס **nâthaç**, *naw-thas'*; a prim. root; to *tear* up:—mar.

5421. נָתַע **nâtha'**, *naw-thah'*; for 5422; to *tear* out:—break.

5422. נָתַץ **nâthats**, *naw-thats'*; a prim. root; to *tear* down:—beat down, break down (out), cast down, destroy, overthrow, pull down, throw down.

5423. נָתַק **nâthaq**, *naw-thak'*; a prim. root; to *tear* off:—break (off), burst, draw (away), lift up, pluck (away, off), pull (out), root out.

5424. נֶתֶק **netheq**, *neh'-thek*; from 5423; *scurf*:—(dry) scall.

5425. נָתַר **nâthar**, *naw-thar'*; a prim. root; to *jump*, i.e. be violently *agitated*; causat., to *terrify, shake off, untie*:—drive asunder, leap, (let) loose, × make, move, undo.

5426. נְתַר **n^ethar** (Chald.), *neth-ar'*; corresp. to 5425:—shake off.

5427. נֶתֶר **nether**, *neh'-ther*; from 5425; mineral *potash* (so called from *effervescing* with acid):—nitre.

5428. נָתַשׁ **nâthash**, *naw-thash'*; a prim. root; to *tear* away:—destroy, forsake, pluck (out, up, by the roots), pull up, root out (up), × utterly.

ס

5429. סְאָה **ç^e'âh**, *seh-aw'*; from an unused root mean. to *define*; a *seäh*, or certain measure (as *determinative*) for grain:—measure.

5430. סְאוֹן **ç^e'ôwn**, *seh-own'*; from 5431; perh. a military *boot* (as a protection from *mud*):—battle.

5431. סָאַן **çâ'an**, *saw-an'*; a prim. root; to *be miry*; used only as denom. from 5430; to *shoe*, i.e. (act. part.) a *soldier* shod:—warrior.

5432. סַאסְּאָה **ça'ç^e'âh**, *sah-seh-aw'*; for 5429; *measurement*, i.e. *moderation*:—measure.

5433. סָבָא **çâbâ'**, *saw-baw'*; a prim. root; to *quaff* to satiety, i.e. *become tipsy*:—drunkard, fill self, Sabean, [wine-] bibber.

5434. סְבָא **Ç^ebâ'**, *seb-aw'*; of for. or.; *Seba*, a son of Cush, and the country settled by him:—Seba.

5435. סֹבֶא **çôbe'**, *so'-beh*; from 5433; *potation*, concr. (*wine*), or abstr. (*carousal*):—drink, drunken, wine.

5436. סְבָאִי **Ç^ebâ'îy**, *seb-aw-ee'*; patrial from 5434; a *Sebaite*, or inhab. of Seba:—Sabean.

5437. סָבַב **çâbab**, *saw-bab'*; a prim. root; to *revolve, surround* or *border*; used in various applications, lit. and fig. (as follows):—bring, cast, fetch, lead, make, walk, × whirl, × round about, be about on every side, apply, avoid, beset (about), besiege, bring again, carry (about), change, cause to come about, × circuit, (fetch a) compass (about, round), drive, environ, × on every side, beset (close, come, compass, go, stand) round about, remove, return, set, sit down, turn (self) (about, aside, away, back).

5438. סִבָּה **çibbâh**, *sib-baw'*; from 5437; a (providential) *turn* (of affairs):—cause.

5439. סָבִיב **çâbîyb**, *saw-beeb'*; or (fem.)

סְבִיבָה **ç^ebîybâh**, *seb-ee-baw'*; from 5437; (as noun) a *circle, neighbor*, or *environs*; but chiefly (as adv., with or without prep.) *around*:—(place, round) about, circuit, compass, on every side.

5440. סָבַךְ **çâbak**, *saw-bak'*; a prim. root; to *entwine*:—fold together, wrap.

5441. סֹבֶךְ **çôbek**, *so'-bek*; from 5440; a *copse*:—thicket.

5442. סְבָךְ **ç^ebâk**, *seb-awk'*; from 5440; a *copse*:—thick (-et).

5443. סַבְּכָא **çabb^ekâ'** (Chald.), *sab-bek-aw'*; or

שַׂבְּכָא **sabb^ekâ'** (Chald.), *sab-bek-aw'*; from a root corresp. to 5440; a *lyre*:—sackbut.

5444. סִבְּכַי **Çibb^ekay**, *sib-bek-ah'ee*; from 5440; *copse-like*; *Sibbecai*, an Isr.:—Sibbecai, Sibbechai.

5445. סָבַל **çâbal**, *saw-bal'*; a prim. root; to *carry* (lit. or fig.), or (reflex.) *be burdensome*; spec. to *be gravid*:—bear, be a burden, carry, strong to labour.

5446. סְבַל **ç^ebal** (Chald.), *seb-al'*; corresp. to 5445; to *erect*:—strongly laid.

5447. סֵבֶל **çêbel**, *say'-bel*; from 5445; a *load* (lit. or fig.):—burden, charge.

5448. סֹבֶל **çôbel**, *so'-bel* [only in the form

סֻבָּל **çubbâl**, *soob-bawl'*]; from 5445; a *load* (fig.):—burden.

5449. סַבָּל **çabbâl**, *sab-bawl'*; from 5445; a *porter*:—(to bear, bearer of) burden (-s).

5450. סְבָלָה **ç^ebâlâh**, *seb-aw-law'*; from 5447; *porterage*:—burden.

5451. סִבֹּלֶת **çibbôleth**, *sib-bo'-leth*; for 7641; an *ear* of grain:—Sibboleth.

5452. סְבַר **ç^ebar** (Chald.), *seb-ar'*; a prim. root; to *bear in mind*, i.e. *hope*:—think.

5453. סִבְרַיִם **Çibrayim**, *sib-rah'-yim*; dual from a root corresp. to 5452; *double hope*; *Sibrajim*, a place in Syria:—Sibraim.

5454. סַבְתָּא **Çabtâ'**, *sab-taw'*; or

סַבְתָּה **Çabtâh**, *sab-taw'*; prob. of for. der.; *Sabta* or *Sabtah*, the name of a son of Cush, and the country occupied by his posterity:—Sabta, Sabtah.

5455. סַבְתְּכָא **Çabtᵉkâ'**, *sab-tek-aw'*; prob. of for. der.; *Sabteca*, the name of a son of Cush, and the region settled by him:—Sabtecha, Sabtechah.

5456. סָגַד **çâgad**, *saw-gad'*; a prim. root; to *prostrate* oneself (in homage):—fall down.

5457. סְגִד **çᵉgîd** (Chald.), *seg-eed'*; corresp. to 5456:—worship.

5458. סְגוֹר **çᵉgôwr**, *seg-ore'*; from 5462; prop. *shut up*, i.e. the *breast* (as inclosing the heart); also *gold* (as generally *shut* up safely):—caul, gold.

5459. סְגֻלָּה **çᵉgullâh**, *seg-ool-law'*; fem. pass. part. of an unused root mean. to *shut up*; *wealth* (as closely *shut* up):—jewel, peculiar (treasure), proper good, special.

5460. סְגַן **çᵉgan** (Chald.), *seg-an'*; corresp. to 5461:—governor.

5461. סָגָן **çâgân**, *saw-gawn'*; from an unused root mean. to *superintend*; a *præfect* of a province:—prince, ruler.

5462. סָגַר **çâgar**, *saw-gar'*; a prim. root; to *shut* up; fig. to *surrender*:—close up, deliver (up), give over (up), inclose, × pure, repair, shut (in, self, out, up, up together), stop, × straitly.

5463. סְגַר **çᵉgar** (Chald.), *seg-ar'*; corresp. to 5462:—shut up.

5464. סַגְרִיד **çagrîyd**, *sag-reed'*; prob. from 5462 in the sense of *sweeping* away; a pouring rain:—very rainy.

5465. סַד **çad**, *sad*; from an unused root mean. to *estop*; the *stocks*:—stocks.

5466. סָדִין **çâdîyn**, *saw-deen'*; from an unused root mean. to *envelop*; a *wrapper*, i.e. *shirt*:—fine linen, sheet.

5467. סְדֹם **Çᵉdôm**, *sed-ome'*; from an unused root mean. to *scorch*; *burnt* (i.e. *volcanic* or *bituminous*) district; *Sedom*, a place near the Dead Sea:—Sodom.

5468. סֶדֶר **çeder**, *seh'-der*; from an unused root mean. to *arrange*; *order*:—order.

5469. סַהַר **çahar**, *sah'-har*; from an unused root mean. to *be round*; *roundness*:—round.

5470. סֹהַר **çôhar**, *so'-har*; from the same as 5469; a *dungeon* (as *surrounded* by walls):—prison.

5471. סוֹא **Çôw'**, *so*; of for. der.; *So*, an Eg. king:—So.

5472. סוּג **çûwg**, *soog*; a prim. root; prop. to *flinch*, i.e. (by impl.) to *go back*, lit. (to *retreat*) or fig. (to *apostatize*):—backslider, drive, go back, turn (away, back).

5473. סוּג **çûwg**, *soog*; a prim. root [prob. rather ident. with 5472 through the idea of *shrinking* from a hedge; comp. 7735]; to *hem* in, i.e. *bind*:—set about.

סוּג° **çûwg**. See 5509.

5474. סוּגַר **çûwgar**, *soo-gar'*; from 5462; an *inclosure*, i.e. *cage* (for an animal):—ward.

5475. סוֹד **çôwd**, *sode*; from 3245; a *session*, i.e. *company* of persons (in close deliberation); by impl. *intimacy*, *consultation*, a *secret*:—assembly, counsel, inward, secret (counsel).

5476. סוֹדִי **Çôwdîy**, *so-dee'*; from 5475; a *confidant*; *Sodi*, an Isr.:—Sodi.

5477. סוּחַ **Çûwach**, *soo'-akh*; from an unused root mean. to *wipe* away; *sweeping*; *Suăch*, an Isr.:—Suah.

5478. סוּחָה **çûwchâh**, *soo-khaw'*; from the same as 5477; something *swept* away, i.e. *filth*:—torn.

סוּט **çûwṭ**. See 7750.

5479. סוֹטַי **Çôwṭay**, *so-tah'ee*; from 7750; *roving*; *Sotai*, one of the Nethinim:—Sotai.

5480. סוּךְ **çûwk**, *sook*; a prim. root; prop. to *smear* over (with oil), i.e. *anoint*:—anoint (self), × at all.

סוֹלְלָה **çôwlᵉlâh**. See 5550.

5481. סוּמְפּוֹנְיָה **çûwmpôwnᵉyâh** (Chald.), *soom-po-neh-yaw'*; or

סוּמְפֹּנְיָה **çûwmpônᵉyâh** (Chald.), *soom-po-neh-yaw'*; or

סִיפֹנְיָא° **çîyphônᵉyâ'** (Dan. 3 : 10) (Chald.), *see-fo-neh-yaw'*; of Greek origin (συμφωνία); a *bagpipe* (with a double pipe):—dulcimer.

5482. סְוֵנֵה **Çᵉvênêh**, *sev-ay-nay'* [rather to be written

סְוֵנָה **Çᵉvênâh**, *sev-ay'-naw*; for

סְוֵן **Çᵉvên**, *sev-ane'*; i.e. *to Seven*]; of Eg. der.; *Seven*, a place in Upper Eg.:—Syene.

5483. סוּס **çûwç**, *soos*; or

סֻס **çûç**, *soos*; from an unused root mean. to *skip* (prop. for joy); a *horse* (as leaping); also a *swallow* (from its rapid *flight*):—crane, horse ([-back, -hoof]). Comp. 6571.

5484. סוּסָה **çûwçâh**, *soo-saw'*; fem. of 5483; a *mare*:—company of horses.

5485. סוּסִי **Çûwçîy**, *soo-see'*; from 5483; *horse-like*; *Susi*, an Isr.:—Susi.

5486. סוּף **çûwph**, *soof*; a prim. root; to *snatch* away, i.e. *terminate*:—consume, have an end, perish, × be utterly.

5487. סוּף **çûwph** (Chald.), *soof*; corresp. to 5486; to *come to an end*:—consume, fulfil.

5488. סוּף **çûwph**, *soof*; prob. of Eg. or.; a *reed*, espec. the *papyrus*:—flag, Red [sea], weed. Comp. 5489.

5489. סוּף **Çûwph**, *soof*; for 5488 (by ellipsis of 3220); the *Reed* (*Sea*):—Red sea.

5490. סוֹף **çôwph**, *sofe*; from 5486; a *termination*:—conclusion, end, hinder part.

5491. סוֹף **çôwph** (Chald.), *sofe*; corresp. to 5490:—end.

5492. סוּפָה **çûwphâh**, *soo-faw'*; from 5486; a *hurricane*:—Red Sea, storm, tempest, whirlwind, Red sea.

5493. סוּר **çûwr**, *soor*; or

שׂוּר **sûwr** (Hos. 9 : 12), *soor*; a prim. root; to *turn* off (lit. or fig.):—be [-head], bring, call back, decline, depart, eschew, get [you], go (aside), × grievous, lay away (by), leave undone, be past, pluck away, put (away, down), rebel, remove (to and fro), revolt, × be sour, take (away, off), turn (aside, away, in), withdraw, be without.

5494. סוּר **çûwr**, *soor*; prob. pass. part. of 5493; *turned* off, i.e. *deteriorated*:—degenerate.

5495. סוּר **Çûwr**, *soor*; the same as 5494; *Sur*, a gate of the Temple:—Sur.

5496. סוּת **çûwth**, *sooth*; perh. denom. from 7898; prop. to *prick*, i.e. (fig.) stimulate; by impl. to *seduce*:—entice, move, persuade, provoke, remove, set on, stir up, take away.

5497. סוּת **çûwth**, *sooth*; prob. from the same root as 4533; *covering*, i.e. *clothing*:—clothes.

5498. סָחַב **çâchab**, *saw-khab'*; a prim. root; to *trail* along:—draw (out), tear.

5499. סְחָבָה **çᵉchâbâh**, *seh-khaw-baw'*; from 5498; a *rag*:—cast clout.

5500. סָחָה **çâchâh**, *saw-khaw'*; a prim. root; to *sweep* away:—scrape.

5501. סְחִי **çᵉchîy**, *seh-khee'*; from 5500; *refuse* (as *swept* off):—offscouring.

סָחִישׁ **çâchîysh**. See 7823.

5502. סָחַף **çâchaph**, *saw-khaf'*; a prim. root; to *scrape* off:—sweep (away).

5503. סָחַר **çâchar**, *saw-khar'*; a prim. root; to *travel* round (spec. as a *pedlar*); intens. to *palpitate*:—go about, merchant (-man), occupy with, pant, trade, traffick.

5504. סַחַר **çachar**, *sakh'-ar*; from 5503; *profit* (from trade):—merchandise.

5505. סָחַר **çâchar**, *saw-khar'*; from 5503; an *emporium*; abstr. *profit* (from trade):—mart, merchandise.

5506. סְחֹרָה **çᵉchôrâh**, *sekh-o-raw'*; from 5503; *traffic*:—merchandise.

5507. סֹחֵרָה **çôchêrâh**, *so-khay-raw'*; prop. act. part. fem. of 5503; something *surrounding* the person, i.e. a *shield*:—buckler.

5508. סֹחֶרֶת **çôchereth**, *so-kheh'-reth*; similar to 5507; prob. a (black) *tile* (or *tessara*) for laying borders with:—black marble.

סֵט **çêṭ**. See 7750.

5509. סִיג **çîyg**, *seeg*; or

סוּג° **çûwg** (Ezek. 22 : 18), *soog*; from 5472 in the sense of *refuse*; *scoria*:—dross.

5510. סִיוָן **Çîyvân**, *see-vawn'*; prob. of Pers. or.; *Sivan*, the third Heb. month:—Sivan.

5511. סִיחוֹן **Çîychôwn**, *see-khone'*; or

סִיחֹן **Çîychôn**, *see-khone'*; from the same as 5477; *tempestuous*; *Sichon*, an Amoritish king:—Sihon.

5512. סִין **Çîyn**, *seen*; of uncert. der.; *Sin*, the name of an Eg. town and (prob.) desert adjoining:—Sin.

5513. סִינִי **Çîynîy**, *see-nee'*; from an otherwise unknown name of a man; a *Sinite*, or descend. of one of the sons of Canaan:—Sinite.

5514. סִינַי **Çîynay**, *see-nah'ee*; of uncert. der.; *Sinai*, a mountain of Arabia:—Sinai.

5515. סִינִים **Çîynîym**, *see-neem'*; plur. of an otherwise unknown name; *Sinim*, a distant Oriental region:—Sinim.

5516. סִיסְרָא **Çîyçᵉrâ'**, *see-ser-aw'*; of uncert. der.; *Sisera*, the name of a Canaanitish king and of one of the Nethinim:—Sisera.

5517. סִיעָא **Çîyʻâ'**, *see-ah'*; or

סִיעֲהָא **Çîyʻăhâ'**, *see-ah-haw'*; from an unused root mean. to *converse*; *congregation*; *Sia*, or *Siaha*, one of the Nethinim:—Sia, Siaha.

סִיפֹנְיָא° **çîyphônᵉyâ'**. See 5481.

5518. סִיר **çîyr**, *seer*; or (fem.)

סִירָה **çîyrâh**, *see-raw'*; or

סִרָה **çîrâh** (Jer. 52 : 18), *see-raw'*; from a prim. root mean. to *boil* up; a *pot*; also a *thorn* (as springing up rapidly); by impl. a *hook*:—caldron, fishhook, pan, ([wash-]) pot, thorn.

5519. סָךְ **çâk**, *sawk*; from 5526; prop. a *thicket* of men, i.e. a *crowd*:—multitude.

5520. סֹךְ **çôk**, *soke*; from 5526; a *hut* (as of *entwined* boughs); also a *lair*:—covert, den, pavilion, tabernacle.

5521. סֻכָּה **çukkâh**, *sook-kaw'*; fem. of 5520; a *hut* or *lair*:—booth, cottage, covert, pavilion, tabernacle, tent.

5522. סִכּוּת **çikkûwth**, *sik-kooth'*; fem. of 5519; an (idolatrous) *booth*:—tabernacle.

5523. סֻכּוֹת **Çukkôwth**, *sook-kohth'*; or

סֻכֹּת **Çukkôth**, *sook-kohth'*; plur. of 5521; *booths*; *Succoth*, the name of a place in Egypt and of three in Pal.:—Succoth.

5524. סֻכּוֹת בְּנוֹת **Çukkôwth bᵉnôwth**, *sook-kohth' ben-ohth'*; from 5523 and the (irreg.) plur. of 1323; *booths of* (*the*) *daughters*; *brothels*, i.e. idolatrous *tents* for impure purposes:—Succoth-benoth.

5525. סֻכִּי **Çukkîy**, *sook-kee'*; patrial from an unknown name (perh. 5520); a *Sukkite*, or inhab. of some place near Eg. (i.e. *hut-dwellers*):—Sukkiims.

5526. סָכַךְ **çâkak**, *saw-kak'*; or

שָׂכַךְ **sâkak** (Exod. 33 : 22), *saw-kak'*; a prim. root; prop. to *entwine* as a screen; by impl. to *fence* in, *cover* over, (fig.) *protect*:—cover, defence, defend, hedge in, join together, set, shut up.

5527. סְכָכָה **Çᵉkâkâh**, *sek-aw-kaw'*; from 5526; *inclosure; Secacah*, a place in Pal.:—Secacah.

5528. סָכַל **çâkal**, *saw-kal'*; for 3688; to *be silly*:—do (make, play the, turn into) fool (-ish, -ishly, -ishness).

5529. סֶכֶל **çekel**, *seh'-kel*; from 5528; *silliness*; concr. and collect. *dolts*:—folly.

5530. סָכָל **çâkâl**, *saw-kawl'*; from 5528; *silly*:—fool (-ish), sottish.

5531. סִכְלוּת **çiklûwth**, *sik-looth'*; or

שִׂכְלוּת **siklûwth** (Eccl. 1 : 17), *sik-looth'*; from 5528; *silliness*:—folly, foolishness.

5532. סָכַן **çâkan**, *saw-kan'*; a prim. root; to *be familiar* with; by impl. to *minister* to, *be serviceable* to, to *cherish*, *be customary*:—acquaint (self), be advantage, × ever, (be, [un-]) profit (-able), treasurer, be wont.

5533. סָכַן **çâkan**, *saw-kan'*; prob. a denom. from 7915; prop. *to cut*, i.e. *damage*; also to *grow* (caus. *make*) *poor*:—endanger, impoverish.

5534. סָכַר **çâkar**, *saw-kar'*; a prim. root; to *shut* up; by impl. to *surrender*:—stop, give over. See also 5462; 7936.

5535. סָכַת **çâkath**, *saw-kath'*; a prim. root; to *be silent*; by impl. to *observe* quietly:—take heed.

סֻכֹּת **Çukkôth**. See 5523.

5536. סַל **çal**, *sal*; from 5549; prop. a willow *twig* (as *pendulous*), i.e. an *osier*; but only as woven into a *basket*:—basket.

5537. סָלָא **çâlâ'**, *saw-law'*; a prim. root; to *suspend* in a balance, i.e. *weigh*:—compare.

5538. סִלָּא **Çillâ'**, *sil-law'*; from 5549; an *embankment*; *Silla*, a place in Jerus.:—Silla.

5539. סָלַד **çâlad**, *saw-lad'*; a prim. root; prob. to *leap* (with joy), i.e. *exult*:—harden self.

5540. סֶלֶד **Çeled**, *seh'-led*; from 5539; *exultation*; *Seled*, an Isr.:—Seled.

5541. סָלָה **çâlâh**, *saw-law'*; a prim. root; to *hang* up, i.e. *weigh*, or (fig.) *contemn*:—tread down (under foot), value.

5542. סֶלָה **çelâh**, *seh'-law*; from 5541; *suspension* (of music), i.e. *pause*:—Selah.

5543. סַלּוּ **Çallûw**, *sal-loo'*; or

סַלּוּא **Çallûw'**, *sal-loo'*; or

סָלוּא **Çâlûw**, *saw-loo'*; or

סַלַּי **Çallay**, *sal-lah'ee*; from 5541; *weighed*; *Sallu* or *Sallai*, the name of two Isr.:—Sallai, Sallu, Salu.

5544. סִלּוֹן **çillôwn**, *sil-lone'*; or

סַלּוֹן **çallôwn**, *sal-lone'*; from 5541; a *prickle* (as if *pendulous*):—brier, thorn.

5545. סָלַח **çâlach**, *saw-lakh'*; a prim. root; to *forgive*:—forgive, pardon, spare.

5546. סַלָּח **çallâch**, *sal-lawkh'*; from 5545; *placable*:—ready to forgive.

סַלַּי **Çallay**. See 5543.

5547. סְלִיחָה **çᵉlîychâh**, *sel-ee-khaw'*; from 5545; *pardon*:—forgiveness, pardon.

5548. סַלְכָה **Çalkâh**, *sal-kaw'*; from an unused root mean. to *walk*; *walking*; *Salcah*, a place E. of the Jordan:—Salcah, Salchah.

5549. סָלַל **çâlal**, *saw-lal'*; a prim. root; to *mound* up (espec. a turnpike); fig. to *exalt*; reflex. to *oppose* (as by a dam):—cast up, exalt (self), extol, make plain, raise up.

5550. סֹלְלָה **çôlᵉlâh**, *so-lel-aw'*; or

סוֹלְלָה **çôwlᵉlâh**, *so-lel-aw'*; act. part. fem. of 5549, but used pass.; a military *mound*, i.e. *rampart* of besiegers:—bank, mount.

5551. סֻלָּם **çullâm**, *sool-lawm'*; from 5549; a *stair-case*:—ladder.

5552. סַלְסִלָּה **çalçillâh**, *sal-sil-law'*; from 5541; a *twig* (as *pendulous*):—basket.

5553. סֶלַע **çelaʻ**, *seh'-lah*; from an unused root mean. to be *lofty*; a craggy *rock*, lit. or fig. (a *fortress*):—(ragged) rock, stone (-ny), strong hold.

5554. סֶלַע **Çelaʻ**, *seh'-lah*; the same as 5553; *Sela*, the rock-city of Idumæa:—rock, Sela (-h).

5555. סֶלַע הַמַּחְלְקוֹת **Çelaʻ ham-machlᵉqôwth**, *seh'-lah ham-makh-lek-ôth'*; from 5553 and the plur. of 4256 with the art. interposed; *rock of the divisions*; *Sela-ham-Machlekoth*, a place in Pal.:—Sela-hammalekoth.

5556. סָלְעָם **çolʻâm**, *sol-awm'*; appar. from the same as 5553 in the sense of *crushing* as with a rock, i.e. consuming; a kind of *locust* (from its *destructiveness*):—bald locust.

5557. סָלַף **çâlaph**, *saw-laf'*; a prim. root; prop. to *wrench*, i.e. (fig.) to *subvert*:—overthrow, pervert.

5558. סֶלֶף **çeleph**, *seh'-lef*; from 5557; *distortion*, i.e. (fig.) *viciousness*:—perverseness.

5559. סְלִק **çᵉlîq** (Chald.), *sel-eek'*; a prim. root; to *ascend*:—come (up).

5560. סֹלֶת **çôleth**, *so'-leth*; from an unused root mean. to *strip*; *flour* (as *chipped* off):—(fine) flour, meal.

5561. סַם **çam**, *sam*; from an unused root mean. to *smell* sweet; an *aroma*:—sweet (spice).

5562. סַמְגַּר נְבוֹ **Çamgar Nᵉbôw**, *sam-gar' neb-o'*; of for. or.; *Samgar-Nebo*, a Bab. general:—Samgar-nebo.

5563. סְמָדַר **çᵉmâdar**, *sem-aw-dar'*; of uncert. der.; a vine *blossom*; used also adv. *abloom*:—tender grape.

5564. סָמַךְ **çâmak**, *saw-mak'*; a prim. root; to *prop* (lit. or fig.); reflex. to *lean* upon or *take hold* of (in a favorable or unfavorable sense):—bear up, establish, (up-) hold, lay, lean, lie hard, put, rest self, set self, stand fast, stay (self), sustain.

5565. סְמַכְיָהוּ **Çᵉmakyâhûw**, *sem-ak-yaw'-hoo*; from 5564 and 3050; *supported of Jah*; *Semakjah*, an Isr.:—Semachiah.

5566. סֶמֶל **çemel**, *seh'-mel*; or

סֵמֶל **çêmel**, *say'-mel*; from an unused root mean. to *resemble*; a *likeness*:—figure, idol, image.

5567. סָמַן **çâman**, *saw-man'*; a prim. root; to *designate*:—appointed.

5568. סָמַר **çâmar**, *saw-mar'*; a prim. root; to *be erect*, i.e. *bristle* as hair:—stand up, tremble.

5569. סָמָר **çâmâr**, *saw-mawr'*; from 5568; *bristling*, i.e. *shaggy*:—rough.

5570. סְנָאָה **Çᵉnâ'âh**, *sen-aw-aw'*; from an unused root mean. to *prick*; *thorny*; *Senaah*, a place in Pal.:—Senaah, Hassenaah [*with the art.*].

סְנֻאָה **çᵉnû'âh**. See 5574.

5571. סַנְבַלַּט **Çanballat**, *san-bal-lat'*; of for. or.; *Sanballat*, a Pers. satrap of Samaria:—Sanballat.

5572. סְנֶה **çᵉneh**, *sen-eh'*; from an unused root mean. to *prick*; a *bramble*:—bush.

5573. סֶנֶה **Çeneh**, *seh'-neh*; the same as 5572; *thorn*; *Seneh*, a crag in Pal.:—Seneh.

סַנָּה **Çannâh**. See 7158.

5574. סְנוּאָה **Çᵉnûw'âh**, *sen-oo-aw'*; or

סְנֻאָה **Çᵉnû'âh**, *sen-oo-aw'*; from the same as 5570; *pointed*; (used with the art. as a prop. name) *Senuah*, the name of two Isr.:—Hasenuah [*includ. the art.*], Senuah.

5575. סַנְוֵר **çanvêr**, *san-vare'*; of uncert. der.; (in plur.) *blindness*:—blindness.

5576. סַנְחֵרִיב **Çanchêrîyb**, *san-khay-reeb'*; of for. or.; *Sancherib*, an Ass. king:—Sennacherib.

5577. סַנְסִן **çançîn**, *san-seen'*; from an unused root mean. to be *pointed*; a *twig* (as *tapering*):—bough.

5578. סַנְסַנָּה **Çançannâh**, *san-san-naw'*; fem. of a form of 5577; a *bough*; *Sansannah*, a place in Pal.:—Sansannah.

5579. סְנַפִּיר **çᵉnappîyr**, *sen-ap-peer'*; of uncert. der.; a *fin* (collect.):—fins.

5580. סָס **çâç**, *sawce*; from the same as 5483; a *moth* (from the *agility* of the fly):—moth.

סוּס **çûç**. See 5483.

5581. סִסְמַי **Çiçmay**, *sis-mah'ee*; of uncert. der.; *Sismai*, an Isr.:—Sisamai.

5582. סָעַד **çâʻad**, *saw-ad'*; a prim. root; to *support* (mostly fig.):—comfort, establish, hold up, refresh self, strengthen, be upholden.

5583. סְעַד **çᵉʻad** (Chald.), *seh-ad'*; corresp. to 5582; to *aid*:—helping.

5584. סָעָה **çâʻâh**, *saw-aw'*; a prim. root; to *rush*:—storm.

5585. סָעִיף **çâʻîyph**, *saw-eef'*; from 5586; a *fissure* (of rocks); also a *bough* (as *subdivided*):—(outmost) branch, clift, top.

5586. סָעַף **çâʻaph**, *saw-af'*; a prim. root; prop. to *divide* up; but used only as denom. from 5585, to *disbranch* (a tree):—top.

5587. סָעִף **çâʻîph**, *saw-eef'*; or

שָׂעִף **sâʻîph**, *saw-eef'*; from 5586; *divided* (in mind), i.e. (abstr.) a *sentiment*:—opinion.

5588. סֵעֵף **çêʻêph**, *say-afe'*; from 5586; *divided* (in mind), i.e. (concr.) a *skeptic*:—thought.

5589. סְעַפָּה **çᵉʻappâh**, *seh-ap-paw'*; fem. of 5585; a *twig* or *branch*:—bough. Comp. 5634.

5590. סָעַר **çâʻar**, *saw-ar'*; a prim. root; to *rush* upon; by impl. to *toss* (trans. or intrans., lit. or fig.):—be (toss with) tempest (-uous), be sore troubled, come out as a (drive with the, scatter with a) whirlwind.

5591. סַעַר **çaʻar**, *sah'-ar*; or (fem.)

סְעָרָה **çᵉʻârâh**, *seh-aw-raw'*; from 5590; a *hurricane*:—storm (-y), tempest, whirlwind.

5592. סַף **çaph**, *saf*; from 5605, in its original sense of *containing*; a *vestibule* (as a *limit*); also a *dish* (for holding blood or wine):—bason, bowl, cup, door (post), gate, post, threshold.

5593. סַף **Çaph**, *saf*; the same as 5592; *Saph*, a Philistine:—Saph. Comp. 5598.

5594. סָפַד **çâphad**, *saw-fad'*; a prim. root; prop. to *tear* the hair and *beat* the breasts (as Orientals do in grief); gen. to *lament*; by impl. to *wail*:—lament, mourn (-er), wail.

5595. סָפָה **çâphâh**, *saw-faw'*; a prim. root; prop. to *scrape* (lit. to *shave*; but usually fig.) together (i.e. to *accumulate* or *increase*) or away (i.e. to *scatter*, *remove* or *ruin*; intrans. to *perish*):—add, augment, consume, destroy, heap, join, perish, put.

5596. סָפַח **çâphach**, *saw-fakh'*; or

שָׂפַח **sâphach** (Isa. 3 : 17), *saw-fakh'*; a prim. root; prop. to *scrape* out, but in certain peculiar senses (of *removal* or *association*):—abiding, gather together, cleave, put, smite with a scab.

5597. סַפַּחַת **çappachath**, *sap-pakh'-ath*; from 5596; the *mange* (as making the hair fall off):—scab.

5598. סִפַּי **Çippay**, *sip-pah'ee*; from 5592; *bason-like*; *Sippai*, a Philistine:—Sippai. Comp. 5593.

5599. סָפִיחַ **çâphîyach**, *saw-fee'-akh*; from 5596; something (spontaneously) *falling* off, i.e. a *self-sown* crop; fig. a *freshet*:—(such) things as (which) grow (of themselves), which groweth of its own accord (itself).

5600. סְפִינָה **çᵉphîynâh**, *sef-ee-naw'*; from 5603; a (sea-going) *vessel* (as *ceiled* with a deck):—ship.

5601. סַפִּיר **çappîyr**, *sap-peer'*; from 5608; a *gem* (perh. as used for *scratching* other substances), prob. the *sapphire*:—sapphire.

5602. סֵפֶל **çêphel**, *say'-fel*; from an unused root mean. to *depress*; a *basin* (as *deepened* out):—bowl, dish.

5603. סָפַן **çâphan**, *saw-fan'*; a prim. root; to *hide* by covering; spec. to *roof* (pass. part. as noun, a *roof*) or *wainscot*; fig. to *reserve*:—cieled, cover, seated.

5604. סִפֻּן **çippûn**, *sip-poon'*; from 5603; a *wainscot*:—cieling.

5605. סָפַף **çâphaph**, *saw-faf'*; a prim. root; prop. to *snatch* away, i.e. *terminate*; but used only as denom. from 5592 (in the sense of a *vestibule*), to *wait at* the *threshold*:—be a doorkeeper.

5606. סָפַק **çâphaq**, *saw-fak'*; or

שָׂפַק **sâphaq** (1 Kings 20 : 10; Job 27 : 23; Isa. 2 : 6), *saw-fak'*; a prim. root; to *clap* the hands (in token of compact, derision, grief, indignation or punishment); by impl. of satisfaction, to *be enough*; by impl. of excess, to *vomit*:—clap, smite, strike, suffice, wallow.

5607. סֵפֶק **çêpheq**, *say'-fek*; or

שֶׂפֶק **sepheq** (Job 20 : 22; 36 : 18), *seh'-fek*; from 5606; *chastisement*; also *satiety*:—stroke, sufficiency.

5608. סָפַר **çâphar**, *saw-far'*; a prim. root; prop. to *score* with a mark as a tally or record, i.e. (by impl.) to *inscribe*, and also to *enumerate*; intens. to *recount*, i.e. *celebrate*:—commune, (account, declare, number, + penknife, reckon, scribe, shew forth, speak, talk, tell (out), writer.

5609. סְפַר **çᵉphar** (Chald.), *sef-ar'*; from a root corresp. to 5608; a *book*:—book, roll.

5610. סְפָר **çᵉphâr**, *sef-awr'*; from 5608; a *census*:—numbering.

5611. סְפָר **Çᵉphâr**, *sef-awr'*; the same as 5610; *Sephar*, a place in Arabia:—Sephar.

5612. סֵפֶר **çêpher**, *say'-fer*; or (fem.)

סִפְרָה **çiphrâh** (Psa. 56 : 8 [9]), *sif-raw'*; from 5608; prop. *writing* (the art or a document); by impl. a *book*:—bill, book, evidence, × learn [-ed] (-ing), letter, register, scroll.

5613. סָפֵר **çâphêr** (Chald.), *saw-fare'*; from the same as 5609; a *scribe* (secular or sacred):—scribe.

5614. סְפָרָד **Çᵉphârâd**, *sef-aw-rawd'*; of for. der.; *Sepharad*, a region of Ass.:—Sepharad.

סִפְרָה **çiphrâh**. See 5612.

5615. סְפֹרָה **çᵉphôrâh**, *sef-o-raw'*; from 5608; a *numeration*:—number.

5616. סְפַרְוִי **Çᵉpharvîy**, *sef-ar-vee'*; patrial from 5617; a *Sepharvite* or inhab. of Sepharvain:—Sepharvite.

5617. סְפַרְוַיִם **Çᵉpharvayim** (dual), *sef-ar-vah'-yim*; or

סְפָרִים° **Çᵉphârîym** (plur.), *sef-aw-reem'*; of for. der.; *Sepharvajim* or *Spharim*, a place in Ass.:—Sepharvaim.

5618. סֹפֶרֶת **Çôphereth**, *so-feh'-reth*; fem. act. part. of 5608; a *scribe* (prop. female); *Sophereth*, a temple servant:—Sophereth.

5619. סָקַל **çâqal**, *saw-kal'*; a prim. root; prop. to *be weighty*; but used only in the sense of *lapidation* or its contrary (as if a *de*lapidation):—(cast, gather out, throw) stone (-s), × surely.

5620. סַר **çar**, *sar*; from 5637 contr.; *peevish*:—heavy, sad.

5621. סָרָב **çârâb**, *saw-rawb'*; from an unused root mean. to *sting*; a thistle:—brier.

5622. סַרְבַּל **çarbal** (Chald.), *sar-bal'*; of uncert. der.; a *cloak*:—coat.

5623. סַרְגוֹן **Çargôwn**, *sar-gōne'*; of for. der.; *Sargon*, an Ass. king:—Sargon.

5624. סֶרֶד **Çered**, *seh'-red*; from a prim. root mean. to *tremble*; *trembling*; *Sered*, an Isr.:—Sered.

5625. סַרְדִּי **Çardîy**, *sar-dee'*; patron. from 5624; a *Seredite* (collect.) or desc. of Sered:—Sardites.

5626. סִירָה **Çîrâh**, *see-raw'*; from 5493; *departure*; *Sirah*, a cistern so-called:—Sirah. See also 5518.

5627. סָרָה **çârâh**, *saw-raw'*; from 5493; *apostasy*, *crime*; fig. *remission*:— × continual, rebellion, revolt ([-ed]), turn away, wrong.

5628. סָרַח **çârach**, *saw-rakh'*; a prim. root; to *extend* (even to *excess*):—exceeding, hand, spread, stretch self, banish.

5629. סֶרַח **çerach**, *seh'-rakh*; from 5628; a *redundancy*:—remnant.

5630. סִרְיֹן **çiryôn**, *sir-yone'*; for 8302; a coat of *mail*:—brigandine.

5631. סָרִיס **çârîyç**, *saw-reece'*; or

סָרִס **çârîç**, *saw-reece'*; from an unused root mean. to *castrate*; a *eunuch*; by impl. *valet* (espec. of the female apartments), and thus a *minister* of state:—chamberlain, eunuch, officer. Comp. 7249.

5632. סָרֵךְ **çârêk** (Chald.), *saw-rake'*; of for. or.; an *emir*:—president.

5633. סֶרֶן **çeren**, *seh'-ren*; from an unused root of unc. mean.; an *axle*; fig. a *peer*:—lord, plate.

5634. סַרְעַפָּה **çarʻappâh**, *sar-ap-paw'*; for 5589; a *twig*:—bough.

5635. סָרַף **çâraph**, *saw-raf'*; a prim. root; to *cremate*, i.e. to *be* (near) *of kin* (such being privileged to kindle the pyre):—burn.

5636. סַרְפָּד **çarpâd**, *sar-pawd'*; from 5635; a *nettle* (as stinging like a *burn*):—brier.

5637. סָרַר **çârar**, *saw-rar'*; a prim. root; to *turn away*, i.e. (morally) *be refractory*:—× away, backsliding, rebellious, revolter (-ing), slide back, stubborn, withdrew.

5638. סְתָו° **çᵉthâv**, *seth-awv'*; from an unused root mean. to *hide*; *winter* (as the dark season):—winter.

5639. סְתוּר **Çᵉthûwr**, *seth-oor'*; from 5641; *hidden*; *Sethur*, an Isr.:—Sethur.

5640. סָתַם **çâtham**, *saw-tham'*; or

שָׂתַם **sâtham** (Num. 24 : 15), *saw-tham'*; a prim. root; to *stop* up; by impl. to *repair*; fig. to *keep secret*:—closed up, hidden, secret, shut out (up), stop.

5641. סָתַר **çâthar**, *saw-thar'*; a prim. root; to *hide* (by covering), lit. or fig.:—be absent, keep close, conceal, hide (self), (keep) secret, × surely.

5642. סְתַר **çᵉthar** (Chald.), *seth-ar'*; corresp. to 5641; to *conceal*; fig. to *demolish*:—destroy, secret thing.

5643. סֵתֶר **çêther**, *say'-ther*; or (fem.)

סִתְרָה **çithrâh** (Deut. 32 : 38), *sith-raw'*; from 5641; a *cover* (in a good or a bad, a lit. or a fig. sense):—backbiting, covering, covert, × disguise [-th], hiding place, privily, protection, secret (-ly, place).

5644. סִתְרִי **Çithrîy**, *sith-ree'*; from 5643; *protective*; *Sithri*, an Isr.:—Zithri.

ע

5645. עָב **ʻâb**, *awb* (masc. and fem.); from 5743; prop. an *envelope*, i.e. *darkness* (or *density*, 2 Chron. 4 : 17); spec. a (scud) *cloud*; also a *copse*:—clay, (thick) cloud, × thick, thicket. Comp. 5672.

5646. עָב **ʻâb**, *awb*; or

עֹב **ʻôb**, *obe*; from an unused root mean. to *cover*; prop. equiv. to 5645; but used only as an arch. term, an *architrave* (as *shading* the pillars):—thick (beam, plant).

5647. עָבַד **ʻâbad**, *aw-bad'*; a prim. root; to *work* (in any sense); by impl. to *serve*, *till*, (caus.) *enslave*, etc.:— × be, keep in bondage, be bondmen, bond-service, compel, do, dress, ear, execute, + husbandman, keep, labour (-ing man), bring to pass, (cause to, make to) serve (-ing, self), (be, become) servant (-s), do (use) service, till (-er), transgress [*from margin*], (set a) work, be wrought, worshipper.

5648. עֲבַד **ʻăbad** (Chald.), *ab-ad'*; corresp. to 5647; to *do*, *make*, *prepare*, *keep*, etc.:—× cut, do, execute, go on, make, move, work.

5649. עֲבַד **ʻăbad** (Chald.), *ab-ad'*; from 5648; a *servant*:—servant.

5650. עֶבֶד **ʻebed**, *eh'-bed*; from 5647; a *servant*:—× bondage, bondman, [bond-] servant, (man-) servant.

5651. עֶבֶד **ʻEbed**, *eh'-bed*; the same as 5650; *Ebed*, the name of two Isr.:—Ebed.

5652. עֲבָד **ʻăbâd**, *ab-awd'*; from 5647; a *deed*:—work.

5653. עַבְדָּא **ʻAbdâ'**, *ab-daw'*; from 5647; *work*; *Abda*, the name of two Isr.:—Abda.

5654. עֹבֵד אֱדוֹם **ʻÔbêd 'Ědôwm**, *o-bade' edome'*; from the act. part. of 5647 and 123; *worker of Edom*; *Obed-Edom*, the name of five Isr.:—Obed-edom.

5655. עַבְדְּאֵל **ʻAbdᵉ'êl**, *ab-deh-ale'*; from 5647 and 410; *serving God*; *Abdeël*, an Isr.:—Abdeel. Comp. 5661.

5656. עֲבֹדָה **ʻăbôdâh**, *ab-o-daw'*; or

עֲבוֹדָה **ʻăbôwdâh**, *ab-o-daw'*; from 5647; *work* of any kind:—act, bondage, + bondservant, effect, labour, ministering (-try), office, service (-ile, -itude), tillage, use, work, × wrought.

5657. עֲבֻדָּה **ʻăbuddâh**, *ab-ood-daw'*; pass. part. of 5647; something *wrought*, i.e. (concr.) *service*:—household, store of servants.

5658. עַבְדוֹן **ʻAbdôwn**, *ab-dohn'*; from 5647; *servitude*; *Abdon*, the name of a place in Pal. and of four Isr.:—Abdon. Comp. 5683.

5659. עַבְדוּת **ʻabdûwth**, *ab-dooth'*; from 5647; *servitude*:—bondage.

5660. עַבְדִּי **ʻAbdîy**, *ab-dee'*; from 5647; *serviceable*; *Abdi*, the name of two Isr.:—Abdi.

5661. עַבְדִיאֵל **ʻAbdîy'êl**, *ab-dee-ale'*; from 5650 and 410; *servant of God*; *Abdiël*, an Isr.:—Abdiel. Comp. 5655.

5662. עֹבַדְיָה **ʻÔbadyâh**, *o-bad-yaw'*; or

עֹבַדְיָהוּ **ʻÔbadyâhûw**, *o-bad-yaw'-hoo*; act. part. of 5647 and 3050; *serving Jah*; *Obadjah*, the name of thirteen Isr.:—Obadiah.

5663. עֶבֶד מֶלֶךְ **ʻEbed Melek**, *eh'-bed meh'-lek*; from 5650 and 4428; *servant of a king*; *Ebed-Melek*, a eunuch of king Zedekeah:—Ebed-melech.

5664. עֲבֵד נְגוֹ **ʻĂbêd Nᵉgôw**, *ab-ade' neg-o'*; the same as 5665; *Abed-Nego*, the Bab. name of one of Daniel's companions:—Abed-nego.

5665. עֲבֵד נְגוֹא **ʻĂbêd Nᵉgôw'** (Chald.), *ab-ade' neg-o'*; of for. or.; *Abed-Nego*, the name of Azariah:—Abed-nego.

5666. עָבָה **ʻâbâh**, *aw-baw'*; a prim. root; to *be dense*:—be (grow) thick (-er).

5667. עֲבוֹט **ʻăbôwṭ**, *ab-ote'*; or

עֲבֹט **ʻăbôṭ**, *ab-ote'*; from 5670; a *pawn*:—pledge.

5668. עָבוּר **ʻâbûwr**, *aw-boor'*; or

עָבֻר **ʻâbûr**, *aw-boor'*; pass. part. of 5674; prop. *crossed*, i.e. (abstr.) *transit*; used only adv. on *account* of, in *order* that:—because of, for (. . . 's sake), (intent) that, to.

5669. עָבוּר **‘âbûwr**, *aw-boor'*; the same as 5668; *passed*, i.e. *kept* over; used only of *stored* grain:—old corn.

5670. עָבַט **‘âbaṭ**, *aw-bat'*; a prim. root; to *pawn*; caus. to *lend* (on security); fig. to *entangle*:—borrow, break [*ranks*], fetch [*a pledge*], lend, × surely.

5671. עַבְטִיט **‘abṭîyṭ**, *ab-teet'*; from 5670; something *pledged*, i.e. (collect.) *pawned* goods:—thick clay [*by a false etym.*].

5672. עֲבִי **‘ăbîy**, *ab-ee'*; or

עֳבִי **‘ŏbîy**, *ob-ee'*; from 5666; *density*, i.e. *depth* or *width*:—thick (-ness). Comp. 5645.

5673. עֲבִידָה **‘ăbîydâh** (Chald.), *ab-ee-daw'*; from 5648; *labor* or *business*:—affairs, service, work.

5674. עָבַר **‘âbar**, *aw-bar'*; a prim. root; to *cross* over; used very widely of any *transition* (lit. or fig.; trans., intrans., intens. or causat.); spec. to *cover* (in copulation):—alienate, alter, × at all, beyond, bring (over, through), carry over, (over-) come (on, over), conduct (over), convey over, current, deliver, do away, enter, escape, fail, gender, get over, (make) go (away, beyond, by, forth, his way, in, on, over, through), have away (more), lay, meddle, overrun, make partition, (cause to, give, make to, over) pass (-age, along, away, beyond, by, -enger, on, out, over, through), (cause to, make) + proclaim (-amation), perish, provoke to anger, put away, rage, + raiser of taxes, remove, send over, set apart, + shave, cause to (make) sound, × speedily, × sweet smelling, take (away), (make to) transgress (-or), translate, turn away, [way-] faring man, be wrath.

5675. עֲבַר **‘ăbar** (Chald.), *ab-ar'*; corresp. to 5676:—beyond, this side.

5676. עֵבֶר **‘êber**, *ay'-ber*; from 5674; prop. a region *across*; but used only adv. (with or without a prep.) on the *opposite* side (espec. of the Jordan; usually mean. the *east*):— × against, beyond, by, × from, over, passage, quarter, (other, this) side, straight.

5677. עֵבֶר **‘Êber**, *ay'-ber*; the same as 5676; *Eber*, the name of two patriarchs and four Isr.:—Eber, Heber.

5678. עֶבְרָה **‘ebrâh**, *eb-raw'*; fem. of 5676; an *outburst* of passion:—anger, rage, wrath.

5679. עֲבָרָה **‘ăbârâh**, *ab-aw-raw'*; from 5674; a *crossing*-place:—ferry, plain [*from the marg.*].

5680. עִבְרִי **‘Ibrîy**, *ib-ree'*; patron. from 5677; an *Eberite* (i.e. Hebrew) or desc. of Eber:—Hebrew (-ess, woman).

5681. עִבְרִי **‘Ibrîy**, *ib-ree'*; the same as 5680; *Ibri*, an Isr.:—Ibri.

5682. עֲבָרִים **‘Ăbârîym**, *ab-aw-reem'*; plur. of 5676; regions *beyond*; *Abarim*, a place in Pal.:—Abarim, passages.

5683. עֶבְרֹן **‘Ebrôn**, *eb-rone'*; from 5676; *transitional*; *Ebron*, a place in Pal.:—Hebron. Perh. a clerical error for 5658.

5684. עֶבְרֹנָה **‘Ebrônâh**, *eb-raw-naw'*; fem. of 5683; *Ebronah*, a place in the Desert:—Ebronah.

5685. עָבַשׁ **‘âbash**, *aw-bash'*; a prim. root; to *dry* up:—be rotten.

5686. עָבַת **‘âbath**, *aw-bath'*; a prim. root; to *interlace*, i.e. (fig.) to *pervert*:—wrap up.

5687. עָבֹת **‘âbôth**, *aw-both'*; or

עָבוֹת **‘âbôwth**, *aw-both'*; from 5686; *intwined*, i.e. *dense*:—thick.

5688. עֲבֹת **‘ăbôth**, *ab-oth'*; or

עֲבוֹת **‘ăbôwth**, *ab-oth'*; or (fem.)

עֲבֹתָה **‘ăbôthâh**, *ab-oth-aw'*; the same as 5687; something *intwined*, i.e. a *string*, *wreath* or *foliage*:—band, cord, rope, thick bough (branch), wreathen (chain).

5689. עָגַב **‘âgab**, *aw-gab'*; a prim. root; to *breathe* after, i.e. to *love* (sensually):—dote, lover.

5690. עֶגֶב **‘egeb**, *eh'-gheb*; from 5689; *love* (concr.), i.e. *amative* words:—much love, very lovely.

5691. עֲגָבָה **‘ăgâbâh**, *ag-aw-baw'*; from 5689; *love* (abstr.), i.e. *amorousness*:—inordinate love.

5692. עֻגָּה **‘uggâh**, *oog-gaw'*; from 5746; an *ash-cake* (as *round*):—cake (upon the hearth).

עָגוֹל **‘âgôwl**. See 5696.

5693. עָגוּר **‘âgûwr**, *aw-goor'*; pass. part. [but with act. sense] of an unused root mean. to *twitter*; prob. the *swallow*:—swallow.

5694. עָגִיל **‘âgîyl**, *aw-gheel'*; from the same as 5696; something *round*, i.e. a *ring* (for the ears):—earring.

5695. עֵגֶל **‘êgel**, *ay'-ghel*; from the same as 5696; a (male) *calf* (as *frisking* round), espec. one nearly grown (i.e. a *steer*):—bullock, calf.

5696. עָגֹל **‘âgôl**, *aw-gole'*; or

עָגוֹל **‘âgôwl**, *aw-gole'*; from an unused root mean. to *revolve*, *circular*:—round.

5697. עֶגְלָה **‘eglâh**, *eg-law'*; fem. of 5695; a (female) *calf*, espec. one nearly grown (i.e. a *heifer*):—calf, cow, heifer.

5698. עֶגְלָה **‘Eglâh**, *eg-law'*; the same as 5697; *Eglah*, a wife of David:—Eglah.

5699. עֲגָלָה **‘ăgâlâh**, *ag-aw-law'*; from the same as 5696; something *revolving*, i.e. a wheeled *vehicle*:—cart, chariot, wagon.

5700. עֶגְלוֹן **‘Eglôwn**, *eg-lawn'*; from 5695; *vituline*; *Eglon*, the name of a place in Pal. and of a Moabitish king:—Eglon.

5701. עָגַם **‘âgam**, *aw-gam'*; a prim. root; to *be sad*:—grieve.

5702. עָגַן **‘âgan**, *aw-gan'*; a prim. root; to *debar*, i.e. from marriage:—stay.

5703. עַד **‘ad**, *ad*; from 5710; prop. a (peremptory) *terminus*, i.e. (by impl.) *duration*, in the sense of *advance* or *perpetuity* (substantially as a noun, either with or without a prep.):—eternity, ever (-lasting, -more), old, perpetually, + world without end.

5704. עַד **‘ad**, *ad*; prop. the same as 5703 (used as a prep., adv. or conj.; especially with a prep.); *as far* (or *long*, or *much*) *as*, whether of space (*even unto*) or time (*during*, *while*, *until*) or degree (*equally with*):—against, and, as, at, before, by (that), even (to), for (-asmuch as), [hither-] to, + how long, into, as long (much) as, (so) that, till, toward, until, when, while, (+ as) yet.

5705. עַד **‘ad** (Chald.), *ad*; corresp. to 5704; × and, at, for, [hither-] to, on, till, (un-) to, until, within.

5706. עַד **‘ad**, *ad*; the same as 5703 in the sense of the *aim* of an attack; *booty*:—prey.

5707. עֵד **‘êd**, *ayd*; from 5749 contr.; concr. a *witness*; abstr. *testimony*; spec. a *recorder*, i.e. *prince*:—witness.

5708. עֵד **‘êd**, *ayd*; from an unused root mean. to *set* a period [comp. 5710, 5749]; the *menstrual* flux (as periodical); by impl. (in plur.) *soiling*:—filthy.

עֹד **‘ôd**. See 5750.

5709. עֲדָא **‘ădâ’** (Chald.), *ad-aw'*; or

עֲדָה **‘ădâh** (Chald.), *ad-aw'*; corresp. to 5710:—alter, depart, pass (away), remove, take (away).

עֹדֵד **‘ôdêd**. See 5752.

5710. עָדָה **‘âdâh**, *aw-daw'*; a prim. root; to *advance*, i.e. *pass* on or *continue*; causat. to *remove*; spec. to *bedeck* (i.e. bring an ornament upon):—adorn, deck (self), pass by, take away.

5711. עָדָה **‘Âdâh**, *aw-daw'*; from 5710; *ornament*; *Adah*, the name of two women:—Adah.

5712. עֵדָה **‘êdâh**, *ay-daw'*; fem. of 5707 in the orig. sense of *fixture*; a stated *assemblage* (spec. a *concourse*, or gen. a *family* or *crowd*):—assembly, company, congregation, multitude, people, swarm. Comp. 5713.

5713. עֵדָה **‘êdâh**, *ay-daw'*; fem. of 5707 in its techn. sense; *testimony*:—testimony, witness. Comp. 5712.

5714. עִדּוֹ **‘Iddôw**, *id-do'*; or

עִדּוֹא **‘Iddôw’**, *id-do'*; or

עִדִּיא **‘Iddîy’**, *id-dee'*; from 5710; *timely*; *Iddo* (or *Iddi*), the name of five Isr.:—Iddo. Comp. 3035, 3260.

5715. עֵדוּת **‘êdûwth**, *ay-dooth'*; fem. of 5707; *testimony*:—testimony, witness.

5716. עֲדִי **‘ădîy**, *ad-ee'*; from 5710 in the sense of *trappings*; *finery*; gen. an *outfit*; spec. a *headstall*:— × excellent, mouth, ornament.

5717. עֲדִיאֵל **‘Ădîy’êl**, *ad-ee-ale'*; from 5716 and 410; *ornament of God*; *Adiël*, the name of three Isr.:—Adiel.

5718. עֲדָיָה **‘Ădâyâh**, *ad-aw-yaw'*; or

עֲדָיָהוּ **‘Ădâyâhûw**, *ad-aw-yaw'-hoo*; from 5710 and 3050; *Jah has adorned*; *Adajah*, the name of eight Isr.:—Adaiah.

5719. עָדִין **‘âdîyn**, *aw-deen'*; from 5727; *voluptuous*:—given to pleasures.

5720. עָדִין **‘Âdîyn**, *aw-deen'*; the same as 5719; *Adin*, the name of two Isr.:—Adin.

5721. עֲדִינָא **‘Ădîynâ’**, *ad-ee-naw'*; from 5719; *effeminacy*; *Adina*, an Isr.:—Adina.

5722. עֲדִינוֹ **‘ădîynôw**, *ad-ee-no'*; prob. from 5719 in the orig. sense of *slender* (i.e. a spear); *his spear*:—Adino.

5723. עֲדִיתַיִם **‘Ădîythayim**, *ad-ee-thah'-yim*; dual of a fem. of 5706; *double prey*; *Adithajim*, a place in Pal.:—Adithaim.

5724. עַדְלַי **‘Adlay**, *ad-lah'ee*; prob. from an unused root of uncert. mean.; *Adlai*, an Isr.:—Adlai.

5725. עֲדֻלָּם **‘Ădullâm**, *ad-ool-lawm'*; prob. from the pass. part. of the same as 5724; *Adullam*, a place in Pal.:—Adullam.

5726. עֲדֻלָּמִי **‘Ădullâmîy**, *ad-ool-law-mee'*; patrial from 5725; an *Adullamite* or native of Adullam:—Adullamite.

5727. עָדַן **‘âdan**, *aw-dan'*; a prim. root; to be *soft* or *pleasant*; fig. and reflex. to *live voluptuously*:—delight self.

5728. עֲדֶן **‘ăden**, *ad-en'*; or

עֲדֶנָּה **‘ădennâh**, *ad-en'-naw*; from 5704 and 2004; *till now*:—yet.

5729. עֶדֶן **‘Eden**, *eh'-den*; from 5727; *pleasure*; *Eden*, a place in Mesopotamia:—Eden.

5730. עֵדֶן **‘êden**, *ay'-den*; or (fem.)

עֶדְנָה **‘ednâh**, *ed-naw'*; from 5727; *pleasure*:—delicate, delight, pleasure. See also 1040.

5731. עֵדֶן **‘Êden**, *ay'-den*; the same as 5730 (masc.); *Eden*, the region of Adam's home:—Eden.

5732. עִדָּן **‘iddân** (Chald.), *id-dawn'*; from a root corresp. to that of 5708; a set *time*; techn. a *year*:—time.

5733. עַדְנָא **‘Adnâ’**, *ad-naw'*; from 5727; *pleasure*; *Adna*, the name of two Isr.:—Adna.

5734. עַדְנָה **‘Adnâh**, *ad-naw'*; from 5727; *pleasure*; *Adnah*, the name of two Isr.:—Adnah.

5735. עֲדְעָדָה **‘Ad‘âdâh**, *ad-aw-daw'*; from 5712; *festival*; *Adadah*, a place in Pal.:—Adadah.

5736. עָדַף **‘âdaph**, *aw-daf'*; a prim. root; to *be* (causat. *have*) *redundant*:—be more, odd number, be (have) over (and above), overplus, remain.

5737. עָדַר **‘âdar**, *aw-dar'*; a prim. root; to *arrange*, as a battle, a vineyard (to *hoe*); hence to *muster*, and so to *miss* (or find *wanting*):—dig, fail, keep (rank), lack.

5738. עֶדֶר **‘Eder**, *eh'-der*; from 5737; an *arrangement* (i.e. drove); *Eder*, an Isr.:—Ader.

5739. עֵדֶר **‘êder**, *ay'-der*; from 5737; an *arrangement*, i.e. *muster* (of animals):—drove, flock, herd.

5740. עֵדֶר **ʻÊder**, *ay'-der;* the same as 5739; *Eder*, the name of an Isr. and of two places in Pal.:—Edar, Eder.

5741. עַדְרִיאֵל **ʻAdrîyʼêl**, *ad-ree-ale';* from 5739 and 410; *flock of God; Adriel*, an Isr.:—Adriel.

5742. עָדָשׁ **ʻâdâsh**, *aw-dawsh';* from an unused root of uncert. mean.; a *lentil:*—lentile.

עַוָּא **ʻAvvâʼ**. See 5755.

5743. עוּב **ʻûwb**, *oob;* a prim. root; to be *dense* or *dark*, i.e. to *becloud:*—cover with a cloud.

5744. עוֹבֵד **ʻÔwbêd**, *o-bade';* act. part. of 5647; *serving; Obed*, the name of five Isr.:—Obed.

5745. עוֹבָל **ʻÔwbâl**, *o-bawl';* of for. der.; *Obal*, a son of Joktan:—Obal.

5746. עוּג **ʻûwg**, *oog;* a prim. root; prop. to *gyrate;* but used only as denom. from 5692, to *bake* (round cakes on the hearth):—bake.

5747. עוֹג **ʻÔwg**, *ogue;* prob. from 5746; *round; Og*, a king of Bashan:—Og.

5748. עוּגָב **ʻûwgâb**, *oo-gawb';* or

עֻגָּב **ʻuggâb**, *oog-gawb';* from 5689 in the orig. sense of *breathing;* a *reed*-instrument of music:—organ.

5749. עוּד **ʻûwd**, *ood;* a prim. root; to *duplicate* or *repeat;* by impl. to *protest, testify* (as by reiteration); intens. to *encompass, restore* (as a sort of reduplication):—admonish, charge, earnestly, lift up, protest, call (take) to record, relieve, rob, solemnly, stand upright, testify, give warning, (bear, call to, give, take to) witness.

5750. עוֹד **ʻôwd**, *ode;* or

עֹד **ʻôd**, *ode;* from 5749; prop. *iteration* or *continuance;* used only adv. (with or without prep.), *again, repeatedly, still, more:*—again, × all life long, at all, besides, but, else, further (-more), henceforth, (any) longer, (any) more (-over), × once, since, (be) still, when, (good, the) while (having being), (as, because, whether, while) yet (within).

5751. עוֹד **ʻôwd** (Chald.), *ode;* corresp. to 5750:—while.

5752. עוֹדֵד **ʻÔwdêd**, *o-dade';* or

עֹדֵד **ʻÔdêd**, *o-dade';* from 5749; *reiteration; Oded*, the name of two Isr.:—Oded.

5753. עָוָה **ʻâvâh**, *aw-vaw';* a prim. root; to *crook*, lit. or fig. (as follows):—do amiss, bow down, make crooked, commit iniquity, pervert, (do) perverse (-ly), trouble, × turn, do wickedly, do wrong.

5754. עַוָּה **ʻavvâh**, *av-vaw';* intens. from 5753 abbrev.; *overthrow:*— × overturn.

5755. עִוָּה **ʻIvvâh**, *iv-vaw';* or

עַוָּא **ʻAvvâʼ** (2 Kings 17 : 24), *av-vaw';* for 5754; *Ivvah* or *Avva*, a region of Ass.:—Ava, Ivah.

עָוֹון **ʻâvôwn**. See 5771.

5756. עוּז **ʻûwz**, *ooz;* a prim. root; to *be strong;* causat. to *strengthen*, i.e. (fig.) to *save* (by flight):—gather (self, self to flee), retire.

5757. עַוִּי **ʻAvvîy**, *av-vee';* patrial from 5755; an *Avvite* or native of Avvah (only plur.):—Avims, Avites.

5758. עִוְיָא **ʻivyâʼ** (Chald.), *iv-yaw';* from a root corresp. to 5753; *perverseness:*—iniquity.

5759. עֲוִיל **ʻăvîyl**, *av-eel';* from 5764; a *babe:*—young child, little one.

5760. עֲוִיל **ʻăvîyl**, *av-eel';* from 5765; *perverse* (morally):—ungodly.

5761. עַוִּים **ʻAvvîym**, *av-veem';* plur. of 5757; *Avvim* (as inhabited by Avvites), a place in Pal. (with the art. pref.):—Avim.

5762. עֲוִית **ʻĂvîyth**, *av-veeth';* or [perh.

עַיּוֹת° **ʻAyôwth**, *ah-yōth'*, as if plur. of 5857]

עֲיוּת° **ʻAyûwth**, *ah-yōth';* from 5753; *ruin; Avvith* (or *Avvoth*), a place in Pal.:—Avith.

5763. עוּל **ʻûwl**, *ool;* a prim. root; to *suckle*, i.e. *give milk:*—milch, (ewe great) with young.

5764. עוּל **ʻûwl**, *ool;* from 5763; a *babe:*—sucking child, infant.

5765. עָוַל **ʻâval**, *aw-val';* a prim. root; to *distort* (morally):—deal unjustly, unrighteous.

עוֹל **ʻôwl**. See 5923.

5766. עֶוֶל **ʻevel**, *eh'-vel;* or

עָוֶל **ʻâvel**, *aw'-vel;* and (fem.)

עַוְלָה **ʻavlâh**, *av-law';* or

עוֹלָה **ʻôwlâh**, *o-law';* or

עֹלָה **ʻôlâh**, *o-law';* from 5765; (moral) *evil:*—iniquity, perverseness, unjust (-ly), unrighteousness (-ly), wicked (-ness).

5767. עַוָּל **ʻavvâl**, *av-vawl';* intens. from 5765; *evil* (morally):—unjust, unrighteous, wicked.

עוֹלָה **ʻôwlâh**. See 5930.

5768. עוֹלֵל **ʻôwlêl**, *o-lale';* or

עֹלָל **ʻôlâl**, *o-lawl';* from 5763; a *suckling:*—babe, (young) child, infant, little one.

5769. עוֹלָם **ʻôwlâm**, *o-lawm';* or

עֹלָם **ʻôlâm**, *o-lawm';* from 5956; prop. *concealed*, i.e. the *vanishing* point; gen. time *out of mind* (past or fut.), i.e. (practically) *eternity;* freq. adv. (espec. with prep. pref.) *always:*—alway (-s), ancient (time), any more, continuance, eternal, (for, [n-]) ever (-lasting, -more, of old), lasting, long (time), (of) old (time), perpetual, at any time, (beginning of the) world (+ without end). Comp. 5331, 5703.

5770. עָוַן° **ʻâvan**, *aw-van';* denom. from 5869; to *watch* (with jealousy):—eye.

5771. עָוֹן **ʻâvôn**, *aw-vone';* or

עָווֹן **ʻâvôwn** (2 Kings 7 : 9; Psa. 51 : 5 [7]), *aw-vone';* from 5753; *perversity*, i.e. (moral) *evil:*—fault, iniquity, mischief, punishment (of iniquity), sin.

5772. עוֹנָה **ʻôwnâh**, *o-naw';* from an unused root appar. mean. to *dwell* together; (sexual) *cohabitation:*—duty of marriage.

5773. עַוְעֶה **ʻavʻeh**, *av-eh';* from 5753; *perversity:*— × perverse.

5774. עוּף **ʻûwph**, *oof;* a prim root; to *cover* (with wings or obscurity); hence (as denom. from 5775) to *fly;* also (by impl. of dimness) to *faint* (from the darkness of swooning):—brandish, be (wax) faint, flee away, fly (away), × set, shine forth, weary.

5775. עוֹף **ʻôwph**, *ofe;* from 5774; a *bird* (as *covered* with feathers, or rather as *covering* with wings), often collect.:—bird, that flieth, flying, fowl.

5776. עוֹף **ʻôwph** (Chald.), *ofe;* corresp. to 5775:—fowl.

5777. עוֹפֶרֶת **ʻôwphereth**, *o-feh'-reth;* or

עֹפֶרֶת **ʻôphereth**, *o-feh'-reth;* fem. part. act. of 6080; *lead* (from its *dusty* color):—lead.

5778. עוֹפַי° **ʻÔwphay**, *o-fah'-ee;* from 5775; *birdlike; Ephai*, an Isr.:—Ephai [*from marg.*].

5779. עוּץ **ʻûwts**, *oots;* a prim. root; to *consult:*—take advice ([counsel] together).

5780. עוּץ **ʻÛwts**, *oots;* appar. from 5779; *consultation; Uts*, a son of Aram, also a Seirite, and the regions settled by them:—Uz.

5781. עוּק **ʻûwq**, *ook;* a prim. root; to *pack:*—be pressed.

5782. עוּר **ʻûwr**, *oor;* a prim. root [rather ident. with 5783 through the idea of *opening* the eyes]; to *wake* (lit. or fig.):—(a-) wake (-n, up), lift up (self), × master, raise (up), stir up (self).

5783. עוּר **ʻûwr**, *oor;* a prim. root; to (*be*) *bare:*—be made naked.

5784. עוּר **ʻûwr** (Chald.), *oor; chaff* (as the *naked* husk):—chaff.

5785. עוֹר **ʻôwr**, *ore;* from 5783; *skin* (as *naked*); by impl. *hide, leather:*—hide, leather, skin.

5786. עָוַר **ʻâvar**, *aw-var';* a prim. root [rather denom. from 5785 through the idea of a *film* over the eyes]; to *blind:*—blind, put out. See also 5895.

5787. עִוֵּר **ʻivvêr**, *iv-vare';* intens. from 5786; *blind* (lit. or fig.):—blind (men, people).

עוֹרֵב **ʻôwrêb**. See 6159.

5788. עִוָּרוֹן **ʻivvârôwn**, *iv-vaw-rone';* and (fem.)

עַוֶּרֶת **ʻavvereth**, *av-veh'-reth;* from 5787; *blindness:*—blind (-ness).

5789. עוּשׁ **ʻûwsh**, *oosh;* a prim. root; to *hasten:*—assemble self.

5790. עוּת **ʻûwth**, *ooth;* for 5789; to *hasten*, i.e. *succor:*—speak in season.

5791. עָוַת **ʻâvath**, *aw-vath';* a prim. root; to *wrest:*—bow self, (make) crooked, falsifying, overthrow, deal perversely, pervert, subvert, turn upside down.

5792. עַוָּתָה **ʻavvâthâh**, *av-vaw-thaw';* from 5791; *oppression:*—wrong.

5793. עוּתַי **ʻÛwthay**, *oo-thah'-ee;* from 5790; *succoring; Uthai*, the name of two Isr.:—Uthai.

5794. עַז **ʻaz**, *az;* from 5810; *strong, vehement, harsh:*—fierce, + greedy, mighty, power, roughly, strong.

5795. עֵז **ʻêz**, *aze;* from 5810; a she-*goat* (as *strong*), but masc. in plur. (which also is used ellipt. for *goats' hair*):—(she) goat, kid.

5796. עֵז **ʻêz** (Chald.), *aze;* corresp. to 5795:—goat.

5797. עֹז **ʻôz**, *oze;* or (fully)

עוֹז **ʻôwz**, *oze;* from 5810; *strength* in various applications (*force, security, majesty, praise*):—boldness, loud, might, power, strength, strong.

5798. עֻזָּא **ʻUzzâʼ**, *ooz-zaw';* or

עֻזָּה **ʻUzzâh**, *ooz-zaw';* fem. of 5797; *strength; Uzza* or *Uzzah*, the name of five Isr.:—Uzza, Uzzah.

5799. עֲזָאזֵל **ʻăzâʼzêl**, *az-aw-zale';* from 5795 and 235; *goat of departure;* the *scape-goat:*—scapegoat.

5800. עָזַב **ʻâzab**, *aw-zab';* a prim. root; to *loosen*, i.e. *relinquish, permit*, etc.:—commit self, fail, forsake, fortify, help, leave (destitute, off), refuse, × surely.

5801. עִזָּבוֹן **ʻizzâbôwn**, *iz-zaw-bone';* from 5800 in the sense of *letting go* (for a price, i.e. *selling*); *trade*, i.e. the place (*mart*) or the payment (*revenue*):—fair, ware.

5802. עַזְבּוּק **ʻAzbûwq**, *az-book';* from 5794 and the root of 950; *stern depopulator; Azbuk*, an Isr.:—Azbuk.

5803. עַזְגָּד **ʻAzgâd**, *az-gawd';* from 5794 and 1409; *stern troop; Azgad*, an Isr.:—Azgad.

5804. עַזָּה **ʻAzzâh**, *az-zaw';* fem. of 5794; *strong; Azzah*, a place in Pal.:—Azzah, Gaza.

5805. עֲזוּבָה **ʻăzûwbâh**, *az-oo-baw';* fem. pass. part. of 5800; *desertion* (of inhabitants):—forsaking.

5806. עֲזוּבָה **ʻĂzûwbâh**, *az-oo-baw';* the same as 5805; *Azubah*, the name of two Israelitesses:—Azubah.

5807. עֱזוּז **ʻĕzûwz**, *ez-ooz';* from 5810; *forcibleness:*—might, strength.

5808. עִזּוּז **ʻizzûwz**, *iz-zooz';* from 5810; *forcible;* collect. and concr. an *army:*—power, strong.

5809. עַזּוּר **ʻAzzûwr**, *az-zoor';* or

עַזֻּר **ʻAzzûr**, *az-zoor';* from 5826; *helpful; Azzur*, the name of three Isr.:—Azur, Azzur.

5810. עָזַז **'âzaz**, *aw-zaz'*; a prim. root; to *be stout* (lit. or fig.):—harden, impudent, prevail, strengthen (self), be strong.

5811. עָזָז **'Âzâz**, *aw-zawz'*; from 5810; *strong; Azaz*, an Isr.:—Azaz.

5812. עֲזַזְיָהוּ **'Ăzazyâhûw**, *az-az-yaw'-hoo*; from 5810 and 3050; *Jah has strengthened; Azazjah*, the name of three Isr.:—Azaziah.

5813. עֻזִּי **'Uzzîy**, *ooz-zee'*; from 5810; *forceful; Uzzi*, the name of six Isr.:—Uzzi.

5814. עֻזִּיָּא **'Uzzîyâ'**, *ooz-zee-yaw'*; perh. for 5818; *Uzzija*, an Isr.:—Uzzia.

5815. עֲזִיאֵל **'Ăzîy'êl**, *az-ee-ale'*; from 5756 and 410; *strengthened of God; Aziël*, an Isr.:—Aziel. Comp. 3268.

5816. עֻזִּיאֵל **'Uzzîy'êl**, *ooz-zee-ale'*; from 5797 and 410; *strength of God; Uzziël*, the name of six Isr.:—Uzziel.

5817. עָזִּיאֵלִי **'Ozzîy'êlîy**, *oz-zee-ay-lee'*; patron. from 5816; an *Uzziëlite* (collect.) or desc. of Uzziel:—Uzzielites.

5818. עֻזִּיָּה **'Uzzîyâh**, *ooz-zee-yaw'*; or

עֻזִּיָּהוּ **'Uzzîyâhûw**, *ooz-zee-yaw'-hoo*; from 5797 and 3050; *strength of Jah; Uzzijah*, the name of five Isr.:—Uzziah.

5819. עֲזִיזָא **'Ăzîyzâ'**, *az-ee-zaw'*; from 5756; *strengthfulness; Aziza*, an Isr.:—Aziza.

5820. עַזְמָוֶת **'Azmâveth**, *az-maw'-veth*; from 5794 and 4194; *strong one of death; Azmaveth*, the name of three Isr. and of a place in Pal.:—Azmaveth. See also 1041.

5821. עַזָּן **'Azzân**, *az-zawn'*; from 5794; *strong one; Azzan*, an Isr.:—Azzan.

5822. עָזְנִיָּה **'ozniyâh**, *oz-nee-yaw'*; prob. fem. of 5797; prob. the *sea-eagle* (from its *strength*):—ospray.

5823. עָזַק **'âzaq**, *aw-zak'*; a prim. root; to *grub over*:—fence about.

5824. עִזְקָא **'izqâ'** (Chald.), *iz-kaw'*; from a root corresp. to 5823; a *signet*-ring (as engraved):—signet.

5825. עֲזֵקָה **'Ăzêqâh**, *az-ay-kaw'*; from 5823; *tilled; Azekah*, a place in Pal.:—Azekah.

5826. עָזַר **'âzar**, *aw-zar'*; a prim. root; to *surround*, i.e. *protect* or *aid*:—help, succour.

5827. עֶזֶר **'Ezer**, *eh'-zer*; from 5826; *help; Ezer*, the name of two Isr.:—Ezer. Comp. 5829.

5828. עֵזֶר **'êzer**, *ay'-zer*; from 5826; *aid*:—help.

5829. עֵזֶר **'Êzer**, *ay'-zer*; the same as 5828; *Ezer*, the name of four Isr.:—Ezer. Comp. 5827.

עַזּוּר **'Azzûr**. See 5809.

5830. עֶזְרָא **'Ezrâ'**, *ez-raw'*; a var. of 5833; *Ezra*, an Isr.:—Ezra.

5831. עֶזְרָא **'Ezrâ'** (Chald.), *ez-raw'*; corresp. to 5830; *Ezra*, an Isr.:—Ezra.

5832. עֲזַרְאֵל **'Ăzar'êl**, *az-ar-ale'*; from 5826 and 410; *God has helped; Azarel*, the name of five Isr.:—Azarael, Azareel.

5833. עֶזְרָה **'ezrâh**, *ez-raw'*; or

עֶזְרָת **'ezrâth** (Psa. 60 : 11 [13]; 108 : 12 [13]), *ez-rawth'*; fem. of 5828; *aid*:—help (-ed, -er).

5834. עֶזְרָה **'Ezrâh**, *ez-raw'*; the same as 5833; *Ezrah*, an Isr.:—Ezrah.

5835. עֲזָרָה **'ăzârâh**, *az-aw-raw'*; from 5826 in its orig. mean. of *surrounding*; an *inclosure*; also a *border*:—court, settle.

5836. עֶזְרִי **'Ezrîy**, *ez-ree'*; from 5828; *helpful; Ezri*, an Isr.:—Ezri.

5837. עַזְרִיאֵל **'Azrîy'êl**, *az-ree-ale'*; from 5828 and 410; *help of God; Azriël*, the name of three Isr.:—Azriel.

5838. עֲזַרְיָה **'Ăzaryâh**, *az-ar-yaw'*; or

עֲזַרְיָהוּ **'Ăzaryâhûw**, *az-ar-yaw'-hoo*; from 5826 and 3050; *Jah has helped; Azarjah*, the name of nineteen Isr.:—Azariah.

5839. עֲזַרְיָה **'Ăzaryâh** (Chald.), *az-ar-yaw'*; corresp. to 5838; *Azarjah*, one of Daniel's companions:—Azariah.

5840. עַזְרִיקָם **'Azrîyqâm**, *az-ree-kawm'*; from 5828 and act. part. of 6965; *help of an enemy; Azrikam*, the name of four Isr.:—Azrikam.

5841. עַזָּתִי **'Azzâthîy**, *az-zaw-thee'*; patrial from 5804; an *Azzathite* or inhab. of Azzah:—Gazathite, Gazite.

5842. עֵט **'êṭ**, *ate*; from 5860 (contr.) in the sense of *swooping*, i.e. *side-long stroke*; a *stylus* or marking stick:—pen.

5843. עֵטָא **'êṭâ'** (Chald.), *ay-taw'*; from 3272; *prudence*:—counsel.

5844. עָטָה **'âṭâh**, *aw-taw'*; a prim. root; to *wrap*, i.e. *cover, veil, clothe* or *roll*:—array self, be clad, (put a) cover (-ing, self), fill, put on, × surely, turn aside.

5845. עֲטִין **'ăṭîyn**, *at-een'*; from an unused root mean. appar. to *contain*; a *receptacle* (for milk, i.e. *pail*; fig. *breast*):—breast.

5846. עֲטִישָׁה **'ăṭîyshâh**, *at-ee-shaw'*; from an unused root mean. to *sneeze*; *sneezing*:—sneezing.

5847. עֲטַלֵּף **'ăṭallêph**, *at-al-lafe'*; of uncert. der.; a *bat*:—bat.

5848. עָטַף **'âṭaph**, *aw-taf'*; a prim. root; to *shroud*, i.e. *clothe* (whether trans. or reflex.); hence (from the idea of *darkness*) to *languish*:—cover (over), fail, faint, feebler, hide self, be overwhelmed, swoon.

5849. עָטַר **'âṭar**, *aw-tar'*; a prim. root; to *encircle* (for attack or protection); espec. to *crown* (lit. or fig.):—compass, crown.

5850. עֲטָרָה **'ăṭârâh**, *at-aw-raw'*; from 5849; a *crown*:—crown.

5851. עֲטָרָה **'Ăṭârâh**, *at-aw-raw'*; the same as 5850; *Atarah*, an Israelitess:—Atarah.

5852. עֲטָרוֹת **'Ăṭârôwth**, *at-aw-rōth'*; or

עֲטָרֹת **'Ăṭârôth**, *at-aw-rōth'*; plur. of 5850; *Ataroth*, the name (thus simply) of two places in Pal.:—Ataroth.

5853. עַטְרוֹת אַדָּר **'Aṭrôwth 'Addâr**, *at-rōth' ad-dawr'*; from the same as 5852 and 146; *crowns of Addar; Atroth-Addar*, a place in Pal.:—Ataroth-adar (-addar).

5854. עַטְרוֹת בֵּית יוֹאָב **'Aṭrôwth bêyth Yôw'âb**, *at-rōth' bayth yo-awb'*; from the same as 5852 and 1004 and 3097; *crowns of the house of Joäb; Atroth-beth-Joäb*, a place in Pal.:—Ataroth the house of Joab.

5855. עַטְרוֹת שׁוֹפָן **'Aṭrôwth Shôwphân**, *at-rōth' sho-fawn'*; from the same as 5852 and a name otherwise unused [being from the same as 8226] mean. *hidden; crowns of Shophan; Atroth-Shophan*, a place in Pal.:—Atroth, Shophan [*as if two places*].

5856. עִי **'iy**, *ee*; from 5753; a *ruin* (as if overturned):—heap.

5857. עַי **'Ay**, *ah'ee*; or (fem.)

עַיָּא **'Ayâ** (Neh. 11 : 31), *ah-yaw'*; or

עַיָּת **'Ayâth** (Isa. 10 : 28), *ah-yawth'*; for 5856; *Ai, Aja* or *Ajath*, a place in Pal.:—Ai, Aija, Aijath, Hai.

5858. עֵיבָל **'Êybâl**, *ay-bawl'*; perh. from an unused root prob. mean. to be *bald; bare; Ebal*, a mountain of Pal.:—Ebal.

עַיָּה **'Ayâh**. See 5857.

5859. עִיּוֹן **'Iyôwn**, *ee-yone'*; from 5856; *ruin; Ijon*, a place in Pal.:—Ijon.

5860. עִיט **'iyṭ**, *eet*; a prim. root; to *swoop* down upon (lit. or fig.):—fly, rail.

5861. עַיִט **'ayiṭ**, *ah'-yit*; from 5860; a *hawk* or other bird of prey:—bird, fowl, ravenous (bird).

5862. עֵיטָם **'Êyṭâm**, *ay-tawm'*; from 5861; *hawk-ground; Etam*, a place in Pal.:—Etam.

5863. עִיֵּי הָעֲבָרִים **'Iyêy hâ-'Ăbârîym**, *ee-yay' haw-ab-aw-reem'*; from the plur. of 5856 and the plur. of the act. part. of 5674 with the art. interposed; *ruins of the passers; Ije-ha-Abarim*, a place near Pal.:—Ije-abarim.

5864. עִיִּים **'Iyîym**, *ee-yeem'*; plur. of 5856; *ruins; Ijim*, a place in the Desert:—Iim.

5865. עֵילוֹם **'êylôwm**, *ay-lome'*; for 5769:—ever.

5866. עִילַי **'Îylay**, *ee-lah'ee*; from 5927; *elevated; Ilai*, an Isr.:—Ilai.

5867. עֵילָם **'Êylâm**, *ay-lawm'*; or

עוֹלָם **'Ôwlâm** (Ezra 10 : 2; Jer. 49 : 36), *o-lawm'*; prob. from 5956; *hidden*, i.e. *distant; Elam*, a son of Shem, and his descend., with their country; also of six Isr.:—Elam.

5868. עֲיָם **'ăyâm**, *ah-yawm'*; of doubtful or. and authenticity; prob. mean. *strength*:—mighty.

5869. עַיִן **'ayin**, *ah'-yin*; prob. a prim. word; an *eye* (lit. or fig.); by anal. a *fountain* (as the *eye* of the landscape):—affliction, outward appearance, + before, + think best, colour, conceit, + be content, countenance, + displease, eye ([-brow], [-d], -sight), face, + favour, fountain, furrow [*from the marg.*], × him, + humble, knowledge, look, (+ well), × me, open (-ly), + (not) please, presence, + regard, resemblance, sight, × thee, × them, + think, × us, well, × you (-rselves).

5870. עַיִן **'ayin** (Chald.), *ah'-yin*; corresp. to 5869; an *eye*:—eye.

5871. עַיִן **'Ayin**, *ah'-yin*; the same as 5869; *fountain; Ajin*, the name (thus simply) of two places in Pal.:—Ain.

5872. עֵין גֶּדִי **'Êyn Gedîy**, *ane geh'-dee*; from 5869 and 1423; *fountain of a kid; En-Gedi*, a place in Pal.:—En-gedi.

5873. עֵין גַּנִּים **'Êyn Ganniym**, *ane gan-neem'*; from 5869 and the plur. of 1588; *fountain of gardens; En-Gannim*, a place in Pal.:—En-gannim.

5874. עֵין־דֹּאר **'Êyn-Dô'r**, *ane-dore'*; or

עֵין דּוֹר **'Êyn Dôwr**, *ane dore*; or

עֵין־דֹּר **'Êyn-Dôr**, *ane-dore'*; from 5869 and 1755; *fountain of dwelling; En-Dor*, a place in Pal.:—En-dor.

5875. עֵין הַקּוֹרֵא **'Êyn haq-Qôwrê'**, *ane hak-ko-ray'*; from 5869 and the act. part. of 7121; *fountain of One calling; En-hak-Korè*, a place near Pal.:—En-hakhore.

עֵינוֹן **'Êynôwn**. See 2703.

5876. עֵין חַדָּה **'Êyn Chaddâh**, *ane khad-daw'*; from 5869 and the fem. of a der. from 2300; *fountain of sharpness; En-Chaddah*, a place in Pal.:—En-haddah.

5877. עֵין חָצוֹר **'Êyn Châtsôwr**, *ane khaw-tsore'*; from 5869 and the same as 2674; *fountain of a village; En-Chatsor*, a place in Pal.:—En-hazor.

5878. עֵין חֲרֹד **'Êyn Chărôd**, *ane khar-ode'*; from 5869 and a der. of 2729; *fountain of trembling; En-Charod*, a place in Pal.:—well of Harod.

5879. עֵינַיִם **'Êynayim**, *ay-nah'-yim*; or

עֵינָם **'Êynâm**, *ay-nawm'*; dual of 5869; *double fountain; Enajim* or *Enam*, a place in Pal.:—Enaim, openly (Gen. 38 : 21).

5880. עֵין מִשְׁפָּט **'Êyn Mishpâṭ**, *ane mish-pawt'*; from 5869 and 4941; *fountain of judgment; En-Mishpat*, a place near Pal.:—En-mishpat.

5881. עֵינָן **'Êynân**, *ay-nawn'*; from 5869; *having eyes; Enan*, an Isr.:—Enan. Comp. 2704.

5882. עֵין עֶגְלַיִם **'Êyn 'Eglayim**, *ane eg-lah'-yim*; from 5869 and the dual of 5695; *fountain of two calves; En-Eglajim*, a place in Pal.:—En-eglaim.

5883. עֵין רֹגֵל **'Êyn Rôgêl**, *ane ro-gale'*; from 5869 and the act. part. of 7270; *fountain of a traveller; En-Rogel*, a place near Jerus.:—En-rogel.

5884. עֵין רִמּוֹן **'Êyn Rimmôwn**, *ane rim-mone'*; from 5869 and 7416; *fountain of a pomegranate; En-Rimmon*, a place in Pal.:—En-rimmon.

5885. עֵין שֶׁמֶשׁ **'Êyn Shemesh**, *ane sheh'-mesh*; from 5869 and 8121; *fountain of* the *sun; En-Shemesh*, a place in Pal.:—En-shemesh.

5886. עֵין תַּנִּים **'Êyn Tanniym**, *ane tan-neem'*; from 5869 and the plur. of 8565; *fountain of jackals; En-Tannim*, a pool near Jerus.:—dragon well.

5887. עֵין תַּפּוּחַ **'Êyn Tappûwach**, *ane tap-poo'-akh*; from 5869 and 8598; *fountain of an apple*-tree; *En-Tappuäch*, a place in Pal.:—En-tappuah.

5888. עָיֵף **'âyêph**, *aw-yafe'*; a prim. root; to *languish*:—be wearied.

5889. עָיֵף **'âyêph**, *aw-yafe'*; from 5888; *languid*:—faint, thirsty, weary.

5890. עֵיפָה **'êyphâh**, *ay-faw'*; fem. from 5774; *obscurity* (as if from *covering*):—darkness.

5891. עֵיפָה **'Êyphâh**, *ay-faw'*; the same as 5890; *Ephah*, the name of a son of Midian, and of the region settled by him; also of an Isr. and of an Israelitess:—Ephah.

5892. עִיר **'iyr**, *eer*; or (in the plur.)

עָר **'âr**, *awr*; or

עָיַר **'âyar** (Judg. 10 : 4), *aw-yar'*; from 5782 a *city* (a place guarded by *waking* or a watch) in the widest sense (even of a mere *encampment* or *post*):—Ai [*from marg.*], city, court [*from marg.*], town.

5893. עִיר **'Îyr**, *eer*; the same as 5892; *Ir*, an Isr.:—Ir.

5894. עִיר **'îyr** (Chald.), *eer*; from a root corresp. to 5782; a *watcher*, i.e. an *angel* (as guardian):—watcher.

5895. עַיִר **'ayir**, *ah'-yeer*; from 5782 in the sense of *raising* (i.e. *bearing* a burden); prop. a young *ass* (as just broken to a load); hence an ass-*colt*:—(ass) colt, foal, young ass.

5896. עִירָא **'Îyrâ'**, *ee-raw'*; from 5782; *wakefulness; Ira*, the name of three Isr.:—Ira.

5897. עִירָד **'Îyrâd**, *ee-rawd'*; from the same as 6166; *fugitive; Irad*, an antediluvian:—Irad.

5898. עִיר הַמֶּלַח **'Îyr ham-Melach**, *eer ham-meh'-lakh*; from 5892 and 4417 with the art. of substance interp.; *city of (the) salt; Ir-ham-Melach*, a place near Pal.:—the city of salt.

5899. עִיר הַתְּמָרִים **'Îyr hat-Temârîym**, *eer hat-tem-aw-reem'*; from 5892 and the plur. of 8558 with the art. interp.; *city of the palmtrees; Ir-hat-Temarim*, a place in Pal.:—the city of palmtrees.

5900. עִירוּ **'Îyrûw**, *ee-roo'*; from 5892; a *citizen; Iru*, an Isr.:—Iru.

5901. עִירִי **'Îyrîy**, *ee-ree'*; from 5892; *urbane; Iri*, an Isr.:—Iri.

5902. עִירָם **'Îyrâm**, *ee-rawm'*; from 5892; *citywise; Iram*, an Idumæan:—Iram.

5903. עֵירֹם **'êyrôm**, *ay-rome'*; or

עֵרֹם **'êrôm**, *ay-rome'*; from 6191; *nudity*:—naked (-ness).

5904. עִיר נָחָשׁ **'Îyr Nâchâsh**, *eer naw-khawsh'*; from 5892 and 5175; *city of a serpent; Ir-Nachash*, a place in Pal.:—Ir-nahash.

5905. עִיר שֶׁמֶשׁ **'Îyr Shemesh**, *eer sheh'-mesh*; from 5892 and 8121; *city of* the *sun; Ir-Shemesh*, a place in Pal.:—Ir-shemesh.

5906. עַיִשׁ **'Ayish**, *ah'-yish*; or

עָשׁ **'Âsh**, *awsh*; from 5789; the constellation of the Great *Bear* (perh. from its *migration* through the heavens):—Arcturus.

עַיָּת **'Ayâth**. See 5857.

5907. עַכְבּוֹר **'Akbôwr**, *ak-bore'*; prob. for 5909; *Akbor*, the name of an Idumæan and two Isr.:—Achbor.

5908. עַכָּבִישׁ **'akkâbîysh**, *ak-kaw-beesh'*; prob. from an unused root in the lit. sense of *entangling*; a *spider* (as *weaving* a network):—spider.

5909. עַכְבָּר **'akbâr**, *ak-bawr'*; prob. from the same as 5908 in the secondary sense of *attacking*; a *mouse* (as *nibbling*):—mouse.

5910. עַכּוֹ **'Akkôw**, *ak-ko'*; appar. from an unused root mean. to *hem* in; *Akko* (from its situation on a *bay*):—Accho.

5911. עָכוֹר **'Âkôwr**, *aw-kore'*; from 5916; *troubled; Akor*, the name of a place in Pal.:—Achor.

5912. עָכָן **'Âkân**, *aw-kawn'*; from an unused root mean. to *trouble; troublesome; Akan*, an Isr.:—Achan. Comp. 5917.

5913. עָכַס **'âkaç**, *aw-kas'*; a prim. root; prop. to *tie*, spec. with fetters; but used only as denom. from 5914; to *put on anklets*:—make a tinkling ornament.

5914. עֶכֶס **'ekeç**, *eh'-kes*; from 5913; a *fetter*; hence an *anklet*:—stocks, tinkling ornament.

5915. עַכְסָה **'Akçâh**, *ak-saw'*; fem. of 5914; *anklet; Aksah*, an Israelitess:—Achsah.

5916. עָכַר **'âkar**, *aw-kar'*; a prim. root; prop. to *roil* water; fig. to *disturb* or *afflict*:—trouble, stir.

5917. עָכָר **'Âkâr**, *aw-kawr'*; from 5916; *troublesome; Akar*, an Isr.:—Achar. Comp. 5912.

5918. עָכְרָן **'Okrân**, *ok-rawn'*; from 5916; *muddler; Okran*, an Isr.:—Ocran.

5919. עַכְשׁוּב **'akshûwb**, *ak-shoob'*; prob. from an unused root mean. to *coil*; an *asp* (from lurking *coiled* up):—adder.

5920. עַל **'al**, *al*; from 5927; prop. the *top*; spec. the *Highest* (i.e. *God*); also (adv.) *aloft, to Jehovah*:—above, high, most High.

5921. עַל **'al**, *al*; prop. the same as 5920 used as a prep. (in the sing. or plur., often with pref., or as conj. with a particle following); *above, over, upon*, or *against* (yet always in this last relation with a downward aspect) in a great variety of applications (as follow):—above, according to (-ly), after, (as) against, among, and, × as, at, because of, beside (the rest of), between, beyond the time, × both and, by (reason of), × had the charge of, concerning for, in (that), (forth, out) of, (from) (off), (up) on, over, than, through (-out), to, touching, × with.

5922. עַל **'al** (Chald.), *al*; corresp. to 5921:—about, against, concerning, for, [there-] fore, from, in, × more, of, (there-, up-) on, (in-) to, + why with.

5923. עֹל **'ôl**, *ole*; or

עוֹל **'ôwl**, *ole*; from 5953; a *yoke* (as *imposed* on the neck), lit. or fig.:—yoke.

5924. עֵלָּא **'êllâ'** (Chald.), *ale-law'*; from 5922; *above*:—over.

5925. עֻלָּא **'Ullâ'**, *ool-law'*; fem. of 5923; *burden; Ulla*, an Isr.:—Ulla.

5926. עִלֵּג **'illêg**, *il-layg'*; from an unused root mean. to *stutter; stuttering*:—stammerer.

5927. עָלָה **'âlâh**, *aw-law'*; a prim. root; to *ascend*, intrans. (*be high*) or act. (*mount*); used in a great variety of senses, primary and secondary, lit. and fig. (as follow):—arise (up). (cause to) ascend up, at once, break [*the day*] (up), bring (up), (cause to) burn, carry up, cast up, + shew, climb (up), (cause to, make to) come (up), cut off, dawn, depart, exalt, excel, fall, fetch up, get up, (make to) go (away, up), grow (over), increase, lay, leap, levy, lift (self) up, light, [make] up, × mention, mount up, offer, make to pay, + perfect, prefer, put (on), raise, recover, restore, (make to) rise (up), scale, set (up), shoot forth (up), (begin to) spring (up), stir up, take away (up), work.

5928. עֲלָה **'âlâh** (Chald.), *al-aw'*; corresp. to 5930; a *holocaust*:—burnt offering.

5929. עָלֶה **'âleh**, *aw-leh'*; from 5927; a *leaf* (as *coming up* on a tree); collect. *foliage*:—branch, leaf.

5930. עֹלָה **'ôlâh**, *o-law'*; or

עוֹלָה **'ôwlâh**, *o-law'*; fem. act. part. of 5927; a *step* or (collect. *stairs*, as *ascending*); usually a *holocaust* (as *going up* in smoke):—ascent, burnt offering (sacrifice), go up to. See also 5766.

5931. עִלָּה **'illâh** (Chald.), *il-law'*; fem. from a root corresp. to 5927; a *pretext* (as *arising* artificially):—occasion.

5932. עַלְוָה **'alvâh**, *al-vaw'*; for 5766; moral *perverseness*:—iniquity.

5933. עַלְוָה **'Alvâh**, *al-vaw'*; or

עַלְיָה **'Alyâh**, *al-yaw'*; the same as 5932; *Alvah* or *Aljah*, an Idumæan:—Aliah, Alvah.

5934. עָלוּם **'âlûwm**, *aw-loom'*; pass. part. of 5956 in the denom. sense of 5958; (only in plur. as abstr.) *adolescence*; fig. *vigor*:—youth.

5935. עַלְוָן **'Alvân**, *al-vawn'*; or

עַלְיָן **'Alyân**, *al-yawn'*; from 5927; *lofty; Alvan* or *Aljan*, an Idumæan:—Alian, Alvan.

5936. עֲלוּקָה **'âlûwqâh**, *al-oo-kaw'*; fem. pass. part. of an unused root mean. to *suck*; the *leech*:—horse-leech.

5937. עָלַז **'âlaz**, *aw-laz'*; a prim. root; to *jump* for joy, i.e. *exult*:—be joyful, rejoice, triumph.

5938. עָלֵז **'âlêz**, *aw-laze'*; from 5937; *exultant*:—that rejoiceth.

5939. עֲלָטָה **'âlâṭâh**, *al-aw-taw'*; fem. from an unused root mean. to *cover*; *dusk*:—dark, twilight.

5940. עֱלִי **'ĕlîy**, *el-ee'*; from 5927; a *pestle* (as *lifted*):—pestle.

5941. עֵלִי **'Êlîy**, *ay-lee'*; from 5927; *lofty; Eli*, an Isr. high-priest:—Eli.

5942. עִלִּי **'illîy**, *il-lee'*; from 5927; *high*, i.e. compar.:—upper.

5943. עִלַּי **'illay** (Chald.), *il-lah'ee*; corresp. to 5942; *supreme* (i.e. *God*):—(most) high.

עַלְיָה **'Alyâh**. See 5933.

5944. עֲלִיָּה **'âlîyâh**, *al-ee-yaw'*; fem. from 5927; something *lofty*, i.e. a *stair-way*; also a *second-story* room (or even one on the roof); fig. the *sky*:—ascent, (upper) chamber, going up, loft, parlour.

5945. עֶלְיוֹן **'elyôwn**, *el-yone'*; from 5927; an *elevation*, i.e. (adj.) *lofty* (compar.); as title, the *Supreme*:—(Most, on) high (-er, -est), upper (-most).

5946. עֶלְיוֹן **'elyôwn** (Chald.), *el-yone'*; corresp. to 5945; the *Supreme*:—Most high.

5947. עַלִּיז **'alliyz**, *al-leez'*; from 5937; *exultant*:—joyous, (that) rejoice (-ing).

5948. עֲלִיל **'âlîyl**, *al-eel'*; from 5953 in the sense of *completing*; prob. a *crucible* (as *working* over the metal):—furnace.

5949. עֲלִילָה **'âlîylâh**, *al-ee-law'*; or

עֲלִלָה **'âlilâh**, *al-ee-law'*; from 5953 in the sense of *effecting*; an *exploit* (of God), or a *performance* (of man, often in a bad sense); by impl. an *opportunity*:—act (-ion), deed, doing, invention, occasion, work.

5950. עֲלִילִיָּה **'âlîylîyâh**, *al-ee-lee-yaw'*; for 5949; (miraculous) *execution*:—work.

עַלְיָן **'Alyân**. See 5935.

5951. עֲלִיצוּת **'âlîytsûwth**, *al-ee-tsooth'*; from 5970; *exultation*:—rejoicing.

5952. עַלִּית **'alliyth**, *al-leeth'*; from 5927; a *second-story* room:—chamber. Comp. 5944.

5953. עָלַל **'âlal**, *aw-lal'*; a prim. root; to *effect* thoroughly; spec. to *glean* (also fig.); by impl. (in a bad sense) to *overdo*, i.e. maltreat, be saucy to, pain, impose (also lit.):—abuse, affect, × child, defile, do, glean, mock, practise, throughly, work (wonderfully).

5954. עֲלַל **ʻălal** (Chald.), *al-al'*; corresp. to 5953 (in the sense of *thrusting* oneself in), to *enter*; caus. to *introduce*:—bring in, come in, go in.

עֹלָל **ʻôlâl**. See 5768.

עֲלִילָה **ʻălîlâh**. See 5949.

5955. עֹלֵלָה **ʻôlêlâh**, *o-lay-law'*; fem. act. part. of 5953; only in plur. *gleanings*; by extens. *gleaning-time*:—(gleaning) (of the) grapes, grapegleanings.

5956. עָלַם **ʻâlam**, *aw-lam'*; a prim. root; to *veil from sight*, i.e. *conceal* (lit. or fig.):—× any ways, blind, dissembler, hide (self), secret (thing).

5957. עָלַם **ʻâlam** (Chald.), *aw-lam'*; corresp. to 5769; *remote* time, i.e. the *future* or *past* indefinitely; often adv. *forever*:—for ([n-]) ever (lasting), old.

5958. עֶלֶם **ʻelem**, *eh'-lem*; from 5956; prop. something *kept out of sight* [comp. 5959], i.e. a *lad*:—young man, stripling.

עֹלָם **ʻôlâm**. See 5769.

5959. עַלְמָה **ʻalmâh**, *al-maw'*; fem. of 5958; a *lass* (as *veiled* or *private*):—damsel, maid, virgin.

5960. עַלְמוֹן **ʻAlmôwn**, *al-mone'*; from 5956; *hidden*; *Almon*, a place in Pal. See also 5963.

5961. עֲלָמוֹת **ʻĂlâmôwth**, *al-aw-mōth'*; plur. of 5959; prop. *girls*, i.e. the *soprano* or female voice, perh. *falsetto*:—Alamoth.

עַלְמוּת **ʻalmûwth**. See 4192.

5962. עַלְמִי **ʻAlmîy** (Chald.), *al-mee'*; patrial from a name corresp. to 5867 contr.; an *Elamite* or inhab. of Elam:—Elamite.

5963. עַלְמֹן דִּבְלָתָיְמָה **ʻAlmôn Diblâthâyᵉmâh**, *al-mone' dib-law-thaw'-yem-aw*; from the same as 5960 and the dual of 1690 [comp. 1015] with enclitic of direction; *Almon towards Diblathajim*; *Almon-Diblathajemah*, a place in Moab:—Almon-dilathaim.

5964. עָלֶמֶת **ʻÂlemeth**, *aw-leh'-meth*; from 5956; a *covering*; *Alemeth*, the name of a place in Pal. and of two Isr.:—Alameth, Alemeth.

5965. עָלַס **ʻâlaç**, *aw-las'*; a prim. root; to *leap* for joy, i.e. *exult*, *wave* joyously:—× peacock, rejoice, solace self.

5966. עָלַע **ʻâlaʻ**, *aw-lah'*; a prim. root; to *sip* up:—suck up.

5967. עֲלַע **ʻălaʻ** (Chald.), *al-ah'*; corresp. to 6763; a *rib*:—rib.

5968. עָלַף **ʻâlaph**, *aw-laf'*; a prim. root; to *veil* or *cover*; fig. to *be languid*:—faint, overlaid, wrap self.

5969. עֻלְפֶּה **ʻulpeh**, *ool-peh'*; from 5968; an *envelope*, i.e. (fig.) *mourning*:—fainted.

5970. עָלַץ **ʻâlats**, *aw-lats'*; a prim. root; to *jump* for joy, i.e. *exult*:—be joyful, rejoice, triumph.

5971. עַם **ʻam**, *am*; from 6004; a *people* (as a congregated *unit*); spec. a *tribe* (as those of Israel); hence (collect.) *troops* or *attendants*; fig. a *flock*:—folk, men, nation, people.

5972. עַם **ʻam** (Chald.), *am*; corresp. to 5971:—people.

5973. עִם **ʻim**, *eem*; from 6004; adv. or prep., *with* (i.e. in *conjunction* with), in varied applications; spec. *equally with*; often with prep. pref. (and then usually unrepresented in English):—accompanying, against, and, as (× long as), before, beside, by (reason of), for all, from (among, between), in, like, more than, of, (un-) to, with (-al).

5974. עִם **ʻim** (Chald.), *eem*; corresp. to 5973:—by, from, like, to (-ward), with.

5975. עָמַד **ʻâmad**, *aw-mad'*; a prim. root; to *stand*, in various relations (lit. and fig., intrans. and trans.):—abide (behind), appoint, arise, cease, confirm, continue, dwell, be employed, endure, establish, leave, make, ordain, be [over], place, (be) present (self), raise up, remain, repair, + serve, set (forth, over, -tle, up), (make to, make to be at a, with-) stand (by, fast, firm, still, up), (be at a) stay (up), tarry.

5976 עָמַד **ʻâmad**, *aw-mad'*; for 4571; to *shake*:—be at a stand.

5977. עֹמֶד **ʻômed**, *o'-med*; from 5975; a *spot* (as being *fixed*):—place, (+ where) stood, upright.

5978. עִמָּד **ʻimmâd**, *im-mawd'*; prol. for 5973; along *with*:—against, by, from, in, + me, + mine, of, + that I take, unto, upon, with (-in).

עַמֻּד **ʻammûd**. See 5982.

5979. עֶמְדָּה **ʻemdâh**, *em-daw'*; from 5975; a *station*, i.e. domicile:—standing.

5980. עֻמָּה **ʻummâh**, *oom-maw'*; from 6004; *conjunction*, i.e. *society*; mostly adv. or prep. (with prep. pref.), *near*, *beside*, *along with*:—(over) against, at, beside, hard by, in points.

5981. עֻמָּה **ʻUmmâh**, *oom-maw'*; the same as 5980; *association*; *Ummah*, a place in Pal.:—Ummah.

5982. עַמּוּד **ʻammûwd**, *am-mood'*; or

עַמֻּד **ʻammûd**, *am-mood'*; from 5975; a *column* (as *standing*); also a *stand*, i.e. platform:—× apiece, pillar.

5983. עַמּוֹן **ʻAmmôwn**, *am-mone'*; from 5971; *tribal*, i.e. *inbred*; *Ammon*, a son of Lot; also his posterity and their country:—Ammon, Ammonites.

5984. עַמּוֹנִי **ʻAmmôwnîy**, *am-mo-nee'*; patron. from 5983; an *Ammonite* or (adj.) *Ammonitish*:—Ammonite (-s).

5985. עַמּוֹנִית **ʻAmmôwnîyth**, *am-mo-neeth'*; fem. of 5984; an *Ammonitess*:—Ammonite (-ss).

5986. עָמוֹס **ʻÂmôwç**, *aw-moce'*; from 6006; *burdensome*; *Amos*, an Isr. prophet:—Amos.

5987. עָמוֹק **ʻÂmôwq**, *aw-moke'*; from 6009; *deep*; *Amok*, an Isr.:—Amok.

5988. עַמִּיאֵל **ʻAmmîyʼêl**, *am-mee-ale'*; from 5971 and 410; *people of God*; *Ammiël*, the name of three or four Isr.:—Ammiel.

5989. עַמִּיהוּד **ʻAmmîyhûwd**, *am-mee-hood'*; from 5971 and 1935; *people of splendor*; *Ammihud*, the name of three Isr.:—Ammihud.

5990. עַמִּיזָבָד **ʻAmmîyzâbâd**, *am-mee-zaw-bawd'*; from 5971 and 2064; *people of endowment*; *Ammizabad*, an Isr.:—Ammizabad.

5991. עַמִּיחוּר **ʻAmmîychûwr**, *am-mee-khoor'*; from 5971 and 2353; *people of nobility*; *Ammichur*, a Syrian prince:—Ammihud [*from the marg.*].

5992. עַמִּינָדָב **ʻAmmîynâdâb**, *am-mee-naw-dawb'*; from 5971 and 5068; *people of liberality*; *Amminadab*, the name of four Isr.:—Amminadab.

5993. עַמִּי נָדִיב **ʻAmmîy Nâdîyb**, *am-mee' naw-deeb'*; from 5971 and 5081; *my people* (is) *liberal*; *Ammi-Nadib*, prob. an Isr.:—Amminadib.

5994. עֲמִיק **ʻămîyq** (Chald.), *am-eek'*; corresp. to 6012; *profound*, i.e. unsearchable:—deep.

5995. עָמִיר **ʻâmîyr**, *aw-meer'*; from 6014; a *bunch* of grain:—handful, sheaf.

5996. עַמִּישַׁדַּי **ʻAmmîyshadday**, *am-mee-shad-dah'ee*; from 5971 and 7706; *people of* (the) *Almighty*; *Ammishaddai*, an Isr.:—Ammishaddai.

5997. עָמִית **ʻâmîyth**, *aw-meeth'*; from a prim. root mean. to *associate*; *companionship*; hence (concr.) a *comrade* or kindred man:—another, fellow, neighbour.

5998. עָמַל **ʻâmal**, *aw-mal'*; a prim. root; to *toil*, i.e. *work severely* and with irksomeness:—[take] labour (in).

5999. עָמָל **ʻâmâl**, *aw-mawl'*; from 5998; *toil*, i.e. *wearing effort*; hence *worry*, wheth. of body or mind:—grievance (-vousness), iniquity, labour, mischief, miserable (-sery), pain (-ful), perverseness, sorrow, toil, travail, trouble, wearisome, wickedness.

6000. עָמָל **ʻÂmâl**, *aw-mawl'*; the same as 5999; *Amal*, an Isr.:—Amal.

6001. עָמֵל **ʻâmêl**, *aw-male'*; from 5998; *toiling* concr. a *laborer*; fig. *sorrowful*:—that laboureth, that is a misery, had taken [labour], wicked, workman.

6002. עֲמָלֵק **ʻĂmâlêq**, *am-aw-lake'*; prob. of for. or.; *Amalek*, a descend. of Esau; also his posterity and their country:—Amalek.

6003. עֲמָלֵקִי **ʻĂmâlêqîy**, *am-aw-lay-kee'*; patron. from 6002; an *Amalekite* (or collect. the *Amalekites*) or desc. of Amalek:—Amalekite (-s).

6004. עָמַם **ʻâmam**, *aw-mam'*; a prim. root; to *associate*; by impl. to *overshadow* (by *huddling* together):—become dim, hide.

6005. עִמָּנוּאֵל **ʻImmânûwʼêl**, *im-maw-noo-ale'*; from 5973 and 410 with suff. pron. ins.; *with us* (is) *God*; *Immanuel*, a typ. name of Isaiah's son:—Immanuel.

6006. עָמַס **ʻâmaç**, *aw-mas'*; or

עָמַשׂ **ʻâmas**, *aw-mas'*; a prim. root; to *load*, i.e. *impose* a burden (or fig. infliction):—be borne, (heavy) burden (self), lade, load, put.

6007. עֲמַסְיָה **ʻĂmaçyâh**, *am-as-yaw'*; from 6006 and 3050; *Jah has loaded*; *Amasjah*, an Isr.:—Amasiah.

6008. עַמְעָד **ʻAmʻâd**, *am-awd'*; from 5971 and 5703; *people of time*; *Amad*, a place in Pal.:—Amad.

6009. עָמַק **ʻâmaq**, *aw-mak'*; a prim. root; to *be* (causat. *make*) *deep* (lit. or fig.):—(be, have, make, seek) deep (-ly), depth, be profound.

6010. עֵמֶק **ʻêmeq**, *ay'-mek*; from 6009; a *vale* (i.e. broad *depression*):—dale, vale, valley [*often used as a part of proper names*]. See also 1025.

6011. עֹמֶק **ʻômeq**, *o'-mek*; from 6009; *depth*:—depth.

6012. עָמֵק **ʻâmêq**, *aw-make'*; from 6009; *deep* (lit. or fig.):—deeper, depth, strange.

6013. עָמֹק **ʻâmôq**, *aw-moke'*; from 6009; *deep* (lit. or fig.):—(× exceeding) deep (thing)

6014. עָמַר **ʻâmar**, *aw-mar'*; a prim. root; prop. appar. to *heap*; fig. to *chastise* (as if *piling* blows); spec. (as denom. from 6016) to *gather* grain:—bind sheaves, make merchandise of.

6015. עֲמַר **ʻămar** (Chald.), *am-ar'*; corresp. to 6785; *wool*:—wool.

6016. עֹמֶר **ʻômer**, *o'-mer*; from 6014; prop. a *heap*, i.e. a *sheaf*; also an *omer*, as a dry measure:—omer, sheaf.

6017. עֲמֹרָה **ʻĂmôrâh**, *am-o-raw'*; from 6014; a (ruined) *heap*; *Amorah*, a place in Pal.:—Gomorrah.

6018. עָמְרִי **ʻOmrîy**, *om-ree'*; from 6014; *heaping*; *Omri*, an Isr.:—Omri.

6019. עַמְרָם **ʻAmrâm**, *am-rawm'*; prob. from 5971 and 7311; *high people*; *Amram*, the name of two Isr.:—Amram.

6020. עַמְרָמִי **ʻAmrâmîy**, *am-raw-mee'*; patron. from 6019; an *Amramite* or desc. of Amram:—Amramite.

עָמַשׂ **ʻâmas**. See 6006.

6021. עֲמָשָׂא **ʻĂmâsâʼ**, *am-aw-saw'*; from 6006; *burden*; *Amasa*, the name of two Isr.:—Amasa.

6022. עֲמָשַׂי **ʻĂmâsay**, *am-aw-sah'ee*; from 6006; *burdensome*; *Amasai*, the name of three Isr.:—Amasai.

6023. עֲמַשְׁסַי **ʻĂmashçay**, *am-ash-sah'ee*; prob. from 6006; *burdensome*; *Amashsay*, an Isr.:—Amashai.

6024. עֲנָב **ʻĂnâb**, *an-awb'*; from the same as 6025; *fruit*; *Anab*, a place in Pal.:—Anab.

6025. עֵנָב **ʻênâb**, *ay-nawb'*; from an unused root prob. mean. to *bear* fruit; a *grape*:—(ripe) grape, wine.

6026. עָנַג **ʻânag**, *aw-nag'*; a prim. root; to be *soft* or pliable, i.e. (fig.) *effeminate* or luxurious:—delicate (-ness), (have) delight (self), sport self.

6027. עֹנֶג **ʻôneg**, *o'-neg*; from 6026; *luxury*:—delight, pleasant.

6028. עָנֹג **ʻânôg**, *aw-nogue'*; from 6026; *luxurious*:—delicate.

6029. עָנַד **'ânad**, *aw-nad'*; a prim. root; to *lace* fast:—bind, tie.

6030. עָנָה **'ânâh**, *aw-naw'*; a prim. root; prop. to *eye* or (gen.) to *heed*, i.e. *pay attention;* by impl. to *respond;* by extens. to *begin* to speak; spec. to *sing, shout, testify, announce:*—give account, afflict [*by mistake for* 6031], (cause to, give) answer, bring low [*by mistake for* 6031], cry, hear, Leannoth, lift up, say, × scholar, (give a) shout, sing (together by course), speak, testify, utter, (bear) witness. See also 1042, 1043.

6031. עָנָה **'ânâh**, *aw-naw'*; a prim. root [possibly rather ident. with 6030 through the idea of *looking* down or *browbeating*]; to *depress* lit. or fig., trans. or intrans. (in various applications, as follow):—abase self, afflict (-ion, self), answer [*by mistake for* 6030], chasten self, deal hardly with, defile, exercise, force, gentleness, humble (self), hurt, ravish, sing [*by mistake for* 6030], speak [*by mistake for* 6030], submit self, weaken, × in any wise.

6032. עֲנָה **'ănâh** (Chald.), *an-aw'*; corresp. to 6030:—answer, speak.

6033. עֲנָה **'ănâh** (Chald.), *an-aw'*; corresp. to 6031:—poor.

6034. עֲנָה **'Ănâh**, *an-aw'*; prob. from 6030; an *answer; Anah*, the name of two Edomites and one Edomitess:—Anah.

6035. עָנָו **'ânâv**, *aw-nawv'*; or [by intermixture with 6041]

עָנָיו **'ânâyv**, *aw-nawv'*; from 6031; *depressed* (fig.), in mind (*gentle*) or circumstances (*needy*, espec. *saintly*):—humble, lowly, meek, poor°. Comp. 6041.

6036. עָנוּב **'Ânûwb**, *aw-noob'*; pass. part. from the same as 6025; *borne* (as fruit); *Anub*, an Isr.:—Anub.

6037. עַנְוָה **'anvâh**, *an-vaw'*; fem. of 6035; *mildness* (royal); also (concr.) *oppressed:*—gentleness, meekness.

6038. עֲנָוָה **'ănâvâh**, *an-aw-vaw'*; from 6035; *condescension*, human and subj. (*modesty*), or divine and obj. (*clemency*):—gentleness, humility, meekness.

6039. עֱנוּת **'ĕnûwth**, *en-ooth'*; from 6031; *affliction:*—affliction.

6040. עֳנִי **'ŏnîy**, *on-ee'*; from 6031; *depression*, i.e. misery:—afflicted (-ion), trouble.

6041. עָנִי **'ânîy**, *aw-nee'*; from 6031; *depressed*, in mind or circumstances [practically the same as 6035, although the marg. constantly disputes this, making 6035 subj. and 6041 obj.]:—afflicted, humble°, lowly°, needy, poor.

6042. עֻנִּי **'Unnîy**, *oon-nee'*; from 6031; *afflicted; Unni*, the name of two Isr.:—Unni.

6043. עֲנָיָה **'Ănâyâh**, *an-aw-yaw'*; from 6030; *Jah has answered; Anajah*, the name of two Isr.:—Anaiah.

עָנָיו **'ânâyv**. See 6035.

6044. עָנִים **'Ânîym**, *aw-neem'*; for plur. of 5869; *fountains; Anim*, a place in Pal.:—Anim.

6045. עִנְיָן **'inyân**, *in-yawn'*; from 6031; *ado*, i.e. (gen.) *employment* or (spec.) an *affair:*—business, travail.

6046. עָנֵם **'Ânêm**, *aw-name'*; from the dual of 5869; *two fountains; Anem*, a place in Pal.:—Anem.

6047. עֲנָמִים **'Ănâmîm**, *an-aw-meem'*; as if plur. of some Eg. word; *Anamim*, a son of Mizraim and his desc., with their country:—Anamim.

6048. עֲנַמֶּלֶךְ **'Ănammelek**, *an-am-meh'-lek*; of for. or.; *Anammelek*, an Assyrian deity:—Anammelech.

6049. עָנַן **'ânan**, *aw-nan'*; a prim. root; to *cover;* used only as denom. from 6051, to *cloud* over; fig. to *act covertly*, i.e. practise magic:—× bring, enchanter, Meonemin, observe (-r of) times, soothsayer, sorcerer.

6050. עֲנַן **'ănan** (Chald.), *an-an'*; corresp. to 6051:—cloud.

6051. עָנָן **'ânân**, *aw-nawn'*; from 6049; a *cloud* (as *covering* the sky), i.e. the *nimbus* or thunder-cloud:—cloud (-y).

6052. עָנָן **'Ânân**, *aw-nawn'*; the same as 6051; *cloud; Anan*, an Isr.:—Anan.

6053. עֲנָנָה **'ănânâh**, *an-aw-naw'*; fem. of 6051; *cloudiness:*—cloud.

6054. עֲנָנִי **'Ănânîy**, *an-aw-nee'*; from 6051; *cloudy; Anani*, an Isr.:—Anani.

6055. עֲנַנְיָה **'Ănanyâh**, *an-an-yaw'*; from 6049 and 3050; *Jah has covered; Ananjah*, the name of an Isr. and of a place in Pal.:—Ananiah.

6056. עֲנַף **'ănaph** (Chald.), *an-af'*; or

עֶנֶף **'eneph** (Chald.), *eh'-nef*; corresp. to 6057:—bough, branch.

6057. עָנָף **'ânâph**, *aw-nawf'*; from an unused root mean. to *cover;* a *twig* (as *covering* the limbs):—bough, branch.

6058. עָנֵף **'ânêph**, *aw-nafe'*; from the same as 6057; *branching:*—full of branches.

6059. עָנַק **'ânaq**, *aw-nak'*; a prim. root; prop. to *choke;* used only as denom. from 6060, to *collar*, i.e. adorn with a necklace; fig. to *fit out* with supplies:—compass about as a chain, furnish, liberally.

6060. עָנָק **'ânâq**, *aw-nawk'*; from 6059; a *necklace* (as if *strangling*):—chain.

6061. עָנָק **'Ânâq**, *aw-nawk'*; the same as 6060; *Anak*, a Canaanite:—Anak.

6062. עֲנָקִי **'Ănâqîy**, *an-aw-kee'*; patron. from 6061; an *Anakite* or desc. of Anak:—Anakim.

6063. עָנֵר **'Ânêr**, *aw-nare'*; prob. for 5288; *Aner*, an Amorite, also a place in Pal.:—Aner.

6064. עָנַשׁ **'ânash**, *aw-nash'*; a prim. root; prop. to *urge;* by impl. to *inflict* a penalty, spec. to *fine:*—amerce, condemn, punish, × surely.

6065. עֲנַשׁ **'ănash** (Chald.), *an-ash'*; corresp. to 6066; a *mulct:*—confiscation.

6066. עֹנֶשׁ **'ônesh**, *o'-nesh*; from 6064; a *fine:*—punishment, tribute.

עֶנֶת **'eneth**. See 3706.

6067. עֲנָת **'Ănâth**, *an-awth'*; from 6030; *answer; Anath*, an Isr.:—Anath.

6068. עֲנָתוֹת **'Ănâthôwth**, *an-aw-thōth'*; plur. of 6067; *Anathoth*, the name of two Isr., also of a place in Pal.:—Anathoth.

6069. עַנְתֹתִי **'Anthôthîy**, *an-tho-thee'*; or

עַנְּתוֹתִי **'Annethôwthîy**, *an-ne-tho-thee'*; patrial from 6068; an *Antothite* or inhab. of Anathoth:—of Anathoth, Anethothite, Anetothite, Antothite.

6070. עַנְתֹתִיָּה **'Anthôthîyâh**, *an-tho-thee-yaw'*; from the same as 6068 and 3050; *answers of Jah; Anthothijah*, an Isr.:—Antothijah.

6071. עָסִיס **'âçîyç**, *aw-sees'*; from 6072; *must* or fresh grape-juice (as just *trodden* out):—juice, new (sweet) wine.

6072. עָסַס **'âçaç**, *aw-sas'*; a prim. root; to *squeeze* out juice; fig. to *trample:*—tread down.

6073. עֳפֶא **'ŏphe'**, *of-eh'*; from an unused root mean. to *cover;* a *bough* (as covering the tree):—branch.

6074. עֳפִי **'ŏphîy** (Chald.), *of-ee'*; corresp. to 6073; a *twig;* bough, i.e. (collect.) *foliage:*—leaves.

6075. עָפַל **'âphal**, *aw-fal'*; a prim. root; to *swell;* fig. *be elated:*—be lifted up, presume.

6076. עֹפֶל **'ôphel**, *o'-fel*; from 6075; a *tumor;* also a *mound*, i.e. fortress:—emerod, fort, strong hold, tower.

6077. עֹפֶל **'Ôphel**, *o'-fel*; the same as 6076; *Ophel*, a ridge in Jerus.:—Ophel.

6078. עׇפְנִי **'Ophnîy**, *of-nee'*; from an unused noun [denoting a place in Pal.; from an unused root of uncert. mean.]; an *Ophnite* (collect.) or inhab. of Ophen:—Ophni.

6079. עַפְעַף **'aph'aph**, *af-af'*; from 5774; an *eyelash* (as *fluttering*); fig. morning *ray:*—dawning, eye-lid.

6080. עָפַר **'âphar**, *aw-far'*; a prim. root; mean. either to *be gray* or perh. rather to *pulverize;* used only as denom. from 6083, to *be dust:*—cast [dust].

6081. עֵפֶר **'Êpher**, *ay'-fer*; prob. a var. of 6082; *gazelle; Epher*, the name of an Arabian and of two Isr.:—Epher.

6082. עֹפֶר **'ôpher**, *o'-fer*; from 6080; a *fawn* (from the *dusty* color):—young roe [hart].

6083. עָפָר **'âphâr**, *aw-fawr'*; from 6080; *dust* (as *powdered* or *gray*); hence *clay, earth, mud:*—ashes, dust, earth, ground, morter, powder, rubbish.

עַפְרָה **'Aphrâh**. See 1036.

6084. עׇפְרָה **'Ophrâh**, *of-raw'*; fem. of 6082; *female fawn; Ophrah*, the name of an Isr. and of two places in Pal.:—Ophrah.

6085. עֶפְרוֹן **'Ephrôwn**, *ef-rone'*; from the same as 6081; *fawn-like; Ephron*, the name of a Canaanite and of two places in Pal.:—Ephron, Ephrain [*from the marg.*].

עֹפֶרֶת **'ôphereth**. See 5777.

6086. עֵץ **'êts**, *ates;* from 6095; a *tree* (from its *firmness*); hence *wood* (plur. *sticks*):—+ carpenter, gallows, helve, + pine, plank, staff, stalk, stick, stock, timber, tree, wood.

6087. עָצַב **'âtsab**, *aw-tsab'*; a prim. root; prop. to *carve*, i.e. *fabricate* or *fashion;* hence (in a bad sense) to *worry, pain* or *anger:*—displease, grieve, hurt, make, be sorry, vex, worship, wrest.

6088. עֲצַב **'ătsab** (Chald.), *ats-ab'*; corresp. to 6087; to *afflict:*—lamentable.

6089. עֶצֶב **'etseb**, *eh'-tseb*; from 6087; an earthen *vessel;* usually (painful) *toil;* also a *pang* (whether of body or mind):—grievous, idol, labor, sorrow.

6090. עֹצֶב **'ôtseb**, *o'-tseb*; a var. of 6089; an *idol* (as fashioned); also *pain* (bodily or mental):—idol, sorrow, × wicked.

6091. עָצָב **'âtsâb**, *aw-tsawb'*; from 6087; an (idolatrous) *image:*—idol, image.

6092. עָצֵב **'âtsêb**, *aw-tsabe'*; from 6087; a (hired) *workman:*—labour.

6093. עִצָּבוֹן **'itstsâbôwn**, *its-tsaw-bone'*; from 6087; *worrisomeness*, i.e. *labor* or *pain:*—sorrow, toil.

6094. עַצֶּבֶת **'atstsebeth**, *ats-tseh'-beth*; from 6087; an *idol;* also a *pain* or *wound:*—sorrow, wound.

6095. עָצָה **'âtsâh**, *aw-tsaw'*; a prim. root; prop. to *fasten* (or *make firm*), i.e. to *close* (the eyes):—shut.

6096. עָצֶה **'âtseh**, *aw-tseh'*; from 6095; the *spine* (as giving *firmness* to the body):—back bone.

6097. עֵצָה **'êtsâh**, *ay-tsaw'*; fem. of 6086; *timber:*—trees.

6098. עֵצָה **'êtsâh**, *ay-tsaw'*; from 3289; *advice;* by impl. *plan;* also *prudence:*—advice, advisement, counsel ([-lor]), purpose.

6099. עָצוּם **'âtsûwm**, *aw-tsoom'*; or

עָצֻם **'âtsûm**, *aw-tsoom'*; pass. part. of 6105; *powerful* (spec. a *paw*); by impl. *numerous:*—+ feeble, great, mighty, must, strong.

6100. עֶצְיוֹן גֶּבֶר **'Etsyôwn** (shorter

עֶצְיֹן **'Etsyôn**) **Geber**, *ets-yone' gheh'-ber*; from 6096 and 1397; *backbone-like of a man; Etsjon-Geber*, a place on the Red Sea:—Ezion-gaber, Ezion-geber.

6101. עָצַל **'âtsal**, *aw-tsal'*; a prim. root; to *lean* idly, i.e. to be *indolent* or *slack:*—be slothful.

6102. עָצֵל **'âtsêl**, *aw-tsale'*; from 6101; *indolent:*—slothful, sluggard.

6103. עַצְלָה **'atslâh**, *ats-law'*; fem. of 6102; (as abstr.) *indolence:*—slothfulness.

6104. עַצְלוּת **'atslûwth**, *ats-looth'*; from 6101; *indolence:*—idleness.

6105. עָצַם **'âtsam**, *aw-tsam'*; a prim. root; to *bind* fast, i.e. *close* (the eyes); intrans.

to *be* (causat. *make*) *powerful* or *numerous;* denom. (from 6106) to *craunch* the bones:—break the bones, close, be great, be increased, be (wax) mighty (-ier), be more, shut, be (-come, make) strong (-er).

6106. עֶצֶם **ʻetsem**, *eh'-tsem;* from 6105; a *bone* (as *strong*); by extens. the *body;* fig. the *substance*, i.e. (as pron.) *selfsame:*—body, bone, × life, (self-) same, strength, × very.

6107. עֶצֶם **ʻEtsem**, *eh'-tsem;* the same as 6106; *bone; Etsem*, a place in Pal.:—Azem, Ezem.

6108. עֹצֶם **ʻôtsem**, *o'-tsem;* from 6105; *power;* hence *body:*—might, strong, substance.

עָצֻם **ʻâtsûm**. See 6099.

6109. עָצְמָה **ʻotsmâh**, *ots-maw';* fem. of 6108; *powerfulness;* by extens. *numerousness:*—abundance, strength.

6110. עַצֻּמָה **ʻatstsûmâh**, *ats-tsoo-maw';* fem. of 6099; a *bulwark*, i.e. (fig.) *argument:*—strong.

6111. עַצְמוֹן **ʻAtsmôwn**, *ats-mone';* or

עַצְמֹן **ʻAtsmôn**, *ats-mone';* from 6107; *bone-like; Atsmon*, a place near Pal.:—Azmon.

6112. עֵצֶן **ʻêtsen**, *ay'-tsen;* from an unused root mean. to *be sharp* or *strong;* a *spear:*—Eznite [*from the marg.*].

6113. עָצַר **ʻâtsar**, *aw-tsar';* a prim. root; to *inclose;* by anal. to *hold back;* also to *maintain, rule, assemble:*— × be able, close up, detain, fast, keep (self close, still), prevail, recover, refrain, × reign, restrain, retain, shut (up), slack, stay, stop, withhold (self).

6114. עֶצֶר **ʻetser**, *eh'-tser;* from 6113; *restraint:*— + magistrate.

6115. עֹצֶר **ʻôtser**, *o'-tser;* from 6113; *closure;* also *constraint:*— × barren, oppression, × prison.

6116. עֲצָרָה **ʻatsârâh**, *ats-aw-raw';* or

עֲצֶרֶת **ʻatsereth**, *ats-eh'-reth;* from 6113; an *assembly*, espec. on a *festival* or *holiday:*—(solemn) assembly (meeting).

6117. עָקַב **ʻâqab**, *aw-kab';* a prim. root; prop. to *swell* out or up; used only as denom. from 6119, to *seize by the heel;* fig. to *circumvent* (as if *tripping* up the heels); also to *restrain* (as if holding by the heel):—take by the heel, stay, supplant, × utterly.

6118. עֵקֶב **ʻêqeb**, *ay'-keb;* from 6117 in the sense of 6119; a *heel*, i.e. (fig.) the *last* of anything (used adv. *for ever*); also *result*, i.e. *compensation;* and so (adv. with prep. or rel.) on *account of:*— × because, by, end, for, if, reward.

6119. עָקֵב **ʻâqêb**, *aw-kabe';* or (fem.)

עִקְּבָה **ʻiqqᵉbâh**, *ik-keb-aw';* from 6117; a *heel* (as *protuberant*); hence a *track;* fig. the *rear* (of an army):—heel, [horse-] hoof, last, lier in wait [*by mistake for* 6120], (foot-) step.

6120. עָקֵב **ʻâqêb**, *aw-kabe';* from 6117 in its denom. sense; a *lier in wait:*—heel [*by mistake for* 6119].

6121. עָקֹב **ʻâqôb**, *aw-kobe';* from 6117; in the orig. sense, a *knoll* (as *swelling* up); in the denom. sense (trans.) *fraudulent* or (intrans.) *tracked:*—crooked, deceitful, polluted.

6122. עָקְבָה **ʻoqbâh**, *ok-baw';* fem. of an unused form from 6117 mean. a *trick; trickery:*—subtilty.

6123. עָקַד **ʻâqad**, *aw-kad';* a prim. root; to *tie* with thongs:—bind.

עֵקֶד **ʻÊqed**. See 1044.

6124. עָקֹד **ʻâqôd**, *aw-kode';* from 6123; *striped* (with *bands*):—ring straked.

6125. עָקָה **ʻâqâh**, *aw-kaw';* from 5781; *constraint:*—oppression.

6126. עַקּוּב **ʻAqqûwb**, *ak-koob';* from 6117; *insidious; Akkub*, the name of five Isr.:—Akkub.

6127. עָקַל **ʻâqal**, *aw-kal';* a prim. root; to *wrest:*—wrong.

6128. עֲקַלְקַל **ʻăqalqal**, *ak-al-kal';* from 6127; *winding:*—by [-way], crooked way.

6129. עֲקַלָּתוֹן **ʻăqallâthôwn**, *ak-al-law-thone';* from 6127; *tortuous:*—crooked.

6130. עָקָן **ʻÂqân**, *aw-kawn';* from an unused root mean. to *twist; tortuous; Akan*, an Idumæan:—Akan. Comp. 3292.

6131. עָקַר **ʻâqar**, *aw-kar';* a prim. root; to *pluck* up (espec. by the roots); spec. to *hamstring;* fig. to *exterminate:*—dig down, hough, pluck up, root up.

6132. עֲקַר **ʻăqar** (Chald.), *ak-ar';* corresp. to 6131:—pluck up by the roots.

6133. עֵקֶר **ʻêqer**, *ay'-ker;* from 6131; fig. a *transplanted* person, i.e. naturalized citizen:—stock.

6134. עֵקֶר **ʻÊqer**, *ay'-ker;* the same as 6133; *Eker*, an Isr.:—Eker.

6135. עָקָר **ʻâqâr**, *aw-kawr';* from 6131; *sterile* (as if *extirpated* in the generative organs):—(× male or female) barren (woman).

6136. עִקַּר **ʻiqqar** (Chald.), *ik-kar';* from 6132; a *stock:*—stump.

6137. עַקְרָב **ʻaqrâb**, *ak-rawb';* of uncert. der.; a *scorpion;* fig. a *scourge* or knotted whip:—scorpion.

6138. עֶקְרוֹן **ʻEqrôwn**, *ek-rone';* from 6131; *eradication; Ekron*, a place in Pal.:—Ekron.

6139. עֶקְרוֹנִי **ʻEqrôwnîy**, *ek-ro-nee';* or

עֶקְרֹנִי **ʻEqrônîy**, *ek-ro-nee';* patrial from 6138; an *Ekronite* or inhab. of Ekron:—Ekronite.

6140. עָקַשׁ **ʻâqash**, *aw-kash';* a prim. root; to *knot* or *distort;* fig. to *pervert* (act or declare perverse):—make crooked, (prove, that is) perverse (-rt).

6141. עִקֵּשׁ **ʻiqqêsh**, *ik-kashe';* from 6140; *distorted;* hence *false:*—crooked, froward, perverse.

6142. עִקֵּשׁ **ʻÎqqêsh**, *ik-kashe';* the same as 6141; *perverse; Ikkesh*, an Isr.:—Ikkesh.

6143. עִקְּשׁוּת **ʻiqqᵉshûwth**, *ik-kesh-ooth';* from 6141; *perversity:*— × froward.

עָר **ʻâr**. See 5892.

6144. עָר **ʻÂr**, *awr;* the same as 5892; a *city; Ar*, a place in Moab:—Ar.

6145. עָר **ʻâr**, *awr;* from 5782; a *foe* (as *watchful* for mischief):—enemy.

6146. עָר **ʻâr** (Chald.), *awr;* corresp. to 6145:—enemy.

6147. עֵר **ʻÊr**, *ayr;* from 5782; *watchful; Er*, the name of two Isr.:—Er.

6148. עָרַב **ʻârab**, *aw-rab';* a prim. root; to *braid*, i.e. *intermix;* techn. to *traffic* (as if by barter); also to *give* or *be security* (as a kind of exchange):—engage, (inter-) meddle (with), mingle (self), mortgage, occupy, give pledges, be (-come, put in) surety, undertake.

6149. עָרֵב **ʻârêb**, *aw-rabe';* a prim. root [rather identical with 6148 through the idea of close *association*]; to be *agreeable:*—be pleasant (-ing), take pleasure in, be sweet.

6150. עָרַב **ʻârab**, *aw-rab';* a prim. root [rather identical with 6148 through the idea of *covering* with a texture]; to *grow dusky* at sundown:—be darkened, (toward) evening.

6151. עֲרַב **ʻărab** (Chald.), *ar-ab';* corresp. to 6148; to *commingle:*—mingle (self), mix.

6152. עֲרָב **ʻĂrâb**, *ar-awb';* or

עֲרַב **ʻĂrab**, *ar-ab';* from 6150 in the fig. sense of *sterility; Arab* (i.e. *Arabia*), a country E. of Pal.:—Arabia.

6153. עֶרֶב **ʻereb**, *eh'-reb;* from 6150; *dusk:*— + day, even (-ing, tide), night.

6154. עֵרֶב **ʻêreb**, *ay'-reb;* or

עֶרֶב **ʻereb** (1 Kings 10 : 15), (with the art. pref.), *eh'-reb;* from 6148; the *web* (or transverse threads of cloth); also a *mixture*, (or *mongrel* race):—Arabia, mingled people, mixed (multitude), woof.

6155. עָרָב **ʻârâb**, *aw-rawb';* from 6148; a *willow* (from the use of osiers as wattles):—willow.

6156. עָרֵב **ʻârêb**, *aw-rabe';* from 6149; *pleasant:*—sweet.

6157. עָרֹב **ʻârôb**, *aw-robe';* from 6148; a *mosquito* (from its *swarming*):—divers sorts of flies, swarm.

6158. עֹרֵב **ʻôrêb**, *o-rabe';* or

עוֹרֵב **ʻôwrêb**, *o-rabe';* from 6150; a *raven* (from its *dusky* hue):—raven.

6159. עֹרֵב **ʻÔrêb**, *o-rabe';* or

עוֹרֵב **ʻÔwrêb**, *o-rabe';* the same as 6158; *Oreb*, the name of a Midianite and of a cliff near the Jordan:—Oreb.

6160. עֲרָבָה **ʻărâbâh**, *ar-aw-baw';* from 6150 (in the sense of *sterility*); a *desert;* espec. (with the art. pref.) the (generally) sterile valley of the Jordan and its continuation to the Red Sea:—Arabah, champaign, desert, evening, heaven, plain, wilderness. See also 1026.

6161. עֲרֻבָּה **ʻărubbâh**, *ar-oob-baw';* fem. pass. part. of 6148 in the sense of a *bargain* or *exchange;* something given as *security*, i.e. (lit.) a *token* (of safety) or (metaph.) a *bondsman:*—pledge, surety.

6162. עֲרָבוֹן **ʻărâbôwn**, *ar-aw-bone';* from 6148 (in the sense of *exchange*); a *pawn* (given as security):—pledge.

6163. עֲרָבִי **ʻĂrâbîy**, *ar-aw-bee';* or

עַרְבִי **ʻArbîy**, *ar-bee';* patrial from 6152; an *Arabian* or inhab. of Arab (i.e. Arabia):—Arabian.

6164. עַרְבָתִי **ʻArbâthîy**, *ar-baw-thee';* patrial from 1026; an *Arbathite* or inhab. of (Beth-) Arabah:—Arbathite.

6165. עָרַג **ʻârag**, *aw-rag';* a prim. root; to *long* for:—cry, pant.

6166. עֲרָד **ʻĂrâd**, *ar-awd';* from an unused root mean. to *sequester* itself; *fugitive; Arad*, the name of a place near Pal., also of a Canaanite and an Isr.:—Arad.

6167. עֲרָד **ʻărâd** (Chald.), *ar-awd';* corresp. to 6171; an *onager:*—wild ass.

6168. עָרָה **ʻârâh**, *aw-raw';* a prim. root; to *be* (caus. *make*) *bare;* hence to *empty*, *pour* out, *demolish:*—leave destitute, discover, empty, make naked, pour (out), rase, spread self, uncover.

6169. עָרָה **ʻârâh**, *aw-raw';* fem. from 6168; a *naked* (i.e. level) plot:—paper reed.

6170. עֲרוּגָה **ʻărûwgâh**, *ar-oo-gaw';* or

עֲרֻגָה **ʻărûgâh**, *ar-oo-gaw';* fem. pass. part. of 6165; something *piled* up (as if [fig.] *raised* by mental aspiration), i.e. a *parterre:*—bed, furrow.

6171. עָרוֹד **ʻârôwd**, *aw-rode';* from the same as 6166; an *onager* (from his *lonesome* habits):—wild ass.

6172. עֶרְוָה **ʻervâh**, *er-vaw';* from 6168; *nudity*, lit. (espec. the *pudenda*) or fig. (*disgrace, blemish*):—nakedness, shame, unclean (-ness).

6173. עַרְוָה **ʻarvâh** (Chald.), *ar-vaw';* corresp. to 6172; *nakedness*, i.e. (fig.) *impoverishment:*—dishonour.

6174. עָרוֹם **ʻârôwm**, *aw-rome';* or

עָרֹם **ʻârôm**, *aw-rome';* from 6191 (in its orig. sense); *nude*, either partially or totally:—naked.

6175. עָרוּם **ʻârûwm**, *aw-room';* pass. part. of 6191; *cunning* (usually in a bad sense):—crafty, prudent, subtil.

6176. עֲרוֹעֵר **ʻărôwʻêr**, *ar-o-ayr';* or

עַרְעָר **ʻarʻâr**, *ar-awr';* from 6209 redupl.; a *juniper* (from its *nudity* of situation):—heath.

6177. עֲרוֹעֵר **ʻĂrôwʻêr**, *ar-o-ayr';* or

עֲרֹעֵר **ʻĂrôʻêr**, *ar-o-ayr';* or

עַרְעוֹר **ʻArʻôwr**, *ar-ore';* the same as 6176; *nudity* of situation; *Aroër*, the name of three places in or near Pal.:—Aroer.

6178. עָרוּץ **ʻârûwts**, *aw-roots'*; pass. part. of 6206; *feared*, i.e. (concr.) a *horrible* place or *chasm*:—cliffs.

6179. עֵרִי **ʻÊrîy**, *ay-ree'*; from 5782; *watchful*; *Eri*, an Isr.:—Eri.

6180. עֵרִי **ʻÊrîy**, *ay-ree'*; patron. of 6179; an *Erite* (collect.) or desc. of Eri:—Erites.

6181. עֶרְיָה **ʻeryâh**, *er-yaw'*; for 6172; *nudity*:—bare, naked, × quite.

6182. עֲרִיסָה **ʻărîyçâh**, *ar-ee-saw'*; from an unused root mean. to *comminute*; *meal*:—dough.

6183. עָרִיף **ʻârîyph**, *aw-reef'*; from 6201; the *sky* (as *drooping* at the horizon):—heaven.

6184. עָרִיץ **ʻârîyts**, *aw-reets'*; from 6206; *fearful*, i.e. *powerful* or *tyrannical*:—mighty, oppressor, in great power, strong, terrible, violent.

6185. עֲרִירִי **ʻărîyrîy**, *ar-e-ree'*; from 6209; *bare*, i.e. destitute (of children):—childless.

6186. עָרַךְ **ʻârak**, *aw-rak'*; a prim. root; to set in a *row*, i.e. *arrange*, put in *order* (in a very wide variety of applications):—put (set) (the battle, self) in array, compare, direct, equal, esteem, estimate, expert [in war], furnish, handle, join [battle], ordain, (lay, put, reckon up, set) (in) order, prepare, tax, value.

6187. עֵרֶךְ **ʻêrek**, *eh'-rek*; from 6186; a *pile*, *equipment*, *estimate*:—equal, estimation, (things that are set in) order, price, proportion, × set at, suit, taxation, × valuest.

6188. עָרֵל **ʻârêl**, *aw-rale'*; a prim. root; prop. to *strip*; but used only as denom. from 6189; to *expose* or *remove* the *prepuce*, whether lit. (to *go naked*) or fig. (to *refrain* from using):—count uncircumcised, foreskin to be uncovered.

6189. עָרֵל **ʻârêl**, *aw-rale'*; from 6188; prop. *exposed*, i.e. projecting loose (as to the prepuce); used only techn. *uncircumcised* (i.e. still having the prepuce uncurtailed):—uncircumcised (person).

6190. עָרְלָה **ʻorlâh**, *or-law'*; fem. of 6189; the *prepuce*:—foreskin, + uncircumcised.

6191. עָרַם **ʻâram**, *aw-ram'*; a prim. root; prop. to *be* (or *make*) *bare*; but used only in the der. sense (through the idea perh. of *smoothness*) to *be cunning* (usually in a bad sense):— × very, beware, take crafty [counsel], be prudent, deal subtilly.

6192. עָרַם **ʻâram**, *aw-ram'*; a prim. root; to *pile* up:—gather together.

6193. עֹרֶם **ʻôrem**, *o'-rem*; from 6191; a *stratagem*:—craftiness.

עֵרֹם **ʻÊrôm**. See 5903.

עָרֹם **ʻârôm**. See 6174.

6194. עָרֵם **ʻârêm** (Jer. 50 : 26), *aw-rame'*; or (fem.)

עֲרֵמָה **ʻărêmâh**, *ar-ay-maw'*; from 6192; a *heap*; spec. a *sheaf*:—heap (of corn), sheaf.

6195. עָרְמָה **ʻormâh**, *or-maw'*; fem. of 6193; *trickery*; or (in a good sense) *discretion*:—guile, prudence, subtilty, wilily, wisdom.

עֲרֵמָה **ʻarêmâh**. See 6194.

6196. עַרְמוֹן **ʻarmôwn**, *ar-mone'*; prob. from 6191; the *plane* tree (from its *smooth* and shed bark):—chestnut tree.

6197. עֵרָן **ʻÊrân**. *ay-rawn'*; prob. from 5782; *watchful*; *Eran*, an Isr.:—Eran.

6198. עֵרָנִי **ʻÊrânîy**, *ay-raw-nee'*; patron. from 6197; an *Eranite* or desc. (collect.) of Eran:—Eranites.

עַרְעוֹר **ʻArʻôwr**. See 6177.

6199. עַרְעָר **ʻarʻâr**, *ar-awr'*; from 6209; *naked*, i.e. (fig.) *poor*:—destitute. See also 6176.

עֲרֹעֵר **ʻĂrôʻêr**. See 6177.

6200. עֲרֹעֵרִי **ʻĂrôʻêrîy**, *ar-o-ay-ree'*; patron. from 6177; an *Aroërite* or inhab. of Aroër:—Aroerite.

6201. עָרַף **ʻâraph**, *aw-raf'*; a prim. root; to *droop*; hence to *drip*:—drop (down).

6202. עָרַף **ʻâraph**, *aw-raf'*; a prim. root [rather ident. with 6201 through the idea of *sloping*]; prop. to *bend* downward; but used only as a denom. from 6203, to *break the neck*; hence (fig.) to *destroy*:—that is beheaded, break down, break (cut off, strike off) neck.

6203. עֹרֶף **ʻôreph**, *o-ref'*; from 6202; the *nape* or back of the neck (as *declining*); hence the *back* generally (whether lit. or fig.):—back ([stiff-]) neck ([-ed]).

6204. עָרְפָּה **ʻOrpâh**, *or-paw'*; fem. of 6203; *mane*; *Orpah*, a Moabitess:—Orpah.

6205. עֲרָפֶל **ʻărâphel**, *ar-aw-fel'*; prob. from 6201; *gloom* (as of a *lowering* sky):—(gross, thick) dark (cloud, -ness).

6206. עָרַץ **ʻârats**, *aw-rats'*; a prim. root; to *awe* or (intrans.) to *dread*; hence to *harass*:—be affrighted (afraid, dread, feared, terrified), break, dread, fear, oppress, prevail, shake terribly.

6207. עָרַק **ʻâraq**, *aw-rak'*; a prim. root; to *gnaw*, i.e. (fig.) *eat* (by hyberbole); also (part.) a *pain*:—fleeing, sinew.

6208. עַרְקִי **ʻArqîy**, *ar-kee'*; patrial from an unused name mean. a *tush*; an *Arkite* or inhab. of Erek:—Arkite.

6209. עָרַר **ʻârar**, *aw-rar'*; a prim. root; to *bare*; fig. to *demolish*:—make bare, break, raise up [*perh. by clerical error for* RAZE], × utterly.

6210. עֶרֶשׂ **ʻeres**, *eh'-res*; from an unused root mean. perh. to *arch*; a *couch* (prop. with a *canopy*):—bed (-stead), couch.

6211. עָשׁ **ʻâsh**, *awsh*; from 6244; a *moth*:—moth. See also 5906.

6211'. עֲשַׂב **ʻăsab** (Chald.), *as-ab'*; 6212:—grass.

6212. עֶשֶׂב **ʻeseb**, *eh'-seb*; from an unused root mean. to *glisten* (or *be green*); *grass* (or any tender shoot):—grass, herb.

6213. עָשָׂה **ʻâsâh**, *aw-saw'*; a prim. root; to *do* or *make*, in the broadest sense and widest application (as follows):—accomplish, advance, appoint, apt, be at, become, bear, bestow, bring forth, bruise, be busy, × certainly, have the charge of, commit, deal (with), deck, + displease, do, (ready) dress (-ed), (put in) execute (-ion), exercise, fashion, + feast, [fight-] ing man, + finish, fit, fly, follow, fulfil, furnish, gather, get, go about, govern, grant, great, + hinder, hold ([a feast]), × indeed, + be industrious, + journey, keep, labour, maintain, make, be meet, observe, be occupied, offer, + officer, pare, bring (come) to pass, perform, practise, prepare, procure, provide, put, requite, × sacrifice, serve, set, shew, × sin, spend, × surely, take, × throughly, trim, × very, + vex, be [warr-] ior, work (-man), yield, use.

6214. עֲשָׂהאֵל **ʻĂsâhʼêl**, *as-aw-ale'*; from 6213 and 410; *God has made*; *Asahel*, the name of four Isr.:—Asahel.

6215. עֵשָׂו **ʻÊsâv**, *ay-sawv'*; appar. a form of the pass. part. of 6213 in the orig. sense of *handling*; *rough* (i.e. sensibly *felt*); *Esav*, a son of Isaac, including his posterity:—Esau.

6216. עָשׁוֹק **ʻâshôwq**, *aw-shoke'*; from 6231; *oppressive* (as noun, a *tyrant*):—oppressor.

6217. עָשׁוּק **ʻâshûwq**, *aw-shook'*; or

עָשֻׁק **ʻâshûq**, *aw-shook'*; pass. part. of 6231; used in plur. masc. as abstr. *tyranny*:—oppressed (-ion). [*Doubtful.*]

6218. עָשׂוֹר **ʻâsôwr**, *aw-sore'*; or

עָשֹׂר **ʻâsôr**, *aw-sore'*; from 6235; *ten*; by abbrev. ten *strings*, and so a *decachord*:—(instrument of) ten (strings, -th).

6219. עָשׁוֹת **ʻâshôwth**, *aw-shōth'*; from 6245; *shining*, i.e. polished:—bright.

6220. עַשְׁוָת **ʻAshvâth** *ash-vawth'*; for 6219; *bright*; *Ashvath*, an Isr.:—Ashvath.

6221. עֲשִׂיאֵל **ʻĂsîyʼêl**, *as-ee-ale'*; from 6213 and 410; *made of God*; *Asiël*, an Isr.:—Asiel.

6222. עֲשָׂיָה **ʻĂsâyâh**, *aw-saw-yaw'*; from 6213 and 3050; *Jah has made*; *Asajah*, the name of three or four Isr.:—Asaiah.

6223. עָשִׁיר **ʻâshîyr**, *aw-sheer'*; from 6238; *rich*, whether lit. or fig. (*noble*):—rich (man)

6224. עֲשִׂירִי **ʻăsîyrîy**. *as-ee-ree'*; from 6235; *tenth*; by abbrev. *tenth month* or (fem.) *part*:—tenth (part).

6225. עָשַׁן **ʻâshan**, *aw-shan'*; a prim. root; to *smoke*, whether lit. or fig.:—be angry (be on a) smoke.

6226. עָשֵׁן **ʻâshên**, *aw-shane'*; from 6225; *smoky*:—smoking.

6227. עָשָׁן **ʻâshân**, *aw-shawn'*; from 6225; *smoke*, lit. or fig. (*vapor*, *dust*, *anger*):—smoke (-ing).

6228. עָשָׁן **ʻÂshân**, *aw-shawn'*; the same as 6227; *Ashan*, a place in Pal.:—Ashan.

6229. עָשַׂק **ʻâsaq**, *aw-sak'*; a prim. root (ident. with 6231); to *press upon*, i.e. *quarrel*:—strive with.

6230. עֵשֶׂק **ʻêseq**, *ay'-sek*; from 6229; *strife*:—Esek.

6231. עָשַׁק **ʻâshaq**, *aw-shak'*; a prim. root (comp. 6229); to *press* upon, i.e. *oppress*, *defraud*, *violate*, *overflow*:—get deceitfully, deceive, defraud, drink up, (use) oppress ([-ion], -or), do violence (wrong).

6232. עֵשֶׁק **ʻÊsheq**, *ay-shek'*; from 6231; *oppression*; *Eshek*, an Isr.:—Eshek.

6233. עֹשֶׁק **ʻôsheq**, *o'-shek*; from 6231; *injury*, *fraud*, (subj.) *distress*, (concr.) *unjust gain*:—cruelly, extortion, oppression, thing [deceitfully gotten].

עָשֻׁק **ʻâshûq**. See 6217.

6234. עָשְׁקָה **ʻoshqâh**, *osh-kaw'*; fem. of 6233; *anguish*:—oppressed.

6235. עֶשֶׂר **ʻeser**, *eh'-ser*; masc.

עֲשָׂרָה **ʻăsârâh**, *as-aw-raw'*; from 6237; *ten* (as an *accumulation* to the extent of the digits):—ten, [fif-, seven-] teen.

6236. עֲשַׂר **ʻăsar** (Chald.), *as-ar'*; masc.

עַשְׂרָה **ʻasrâh** (Chald.), *as-raw'*; corresp. to 6235; *ten*:—ten, + twelve.

6237. עָשַׂר **ʻâsar**, *aw-sar'*; a prim. root (ident. with 6238); to *accumulate*; but used only as denom. from 6235; to *tithe*, i.e. take or give a tenth:— × surely, give (take) the tenth, (have, take) tithe (-ing, -s), × truly.

6238. עָשַׁר **ʻâshar**, *aw-shar'*; a prim. root; prop. to *accumulate*; chiefly (spec.) to *grow* (caus. *make*) *rich*:—be (-come, en-, make, make self, wax) rich, make [1 Kings 22 : 48 *marg.*]. See 6240.

6239. עֹשֶׁר **ʻôsher**, *o'-sher*; from 6238; *wealth*:—× far [richer], riches.

6240. עָשָׂר **ʻâsâr**, *aw-sawr'*; for 6235; *ten* (only in combination), i.e. *-teen*; also (ordinal) *-teenth*:—[eigh-, fif-, four-, nine-, seven-, six-, thir-] teen (-th), + eleven (-th), + sixscore thousand, + twelve (-th).

עָשֹׂר **ʻâsôr**. See 6218.

6241. עִשָּׂרוֹן **ʻissârôwn**, *is-saw-rone'*; or

עִשָּׂרֹן **ʻissârôn**, *is-saw-rone'*; from 6235; (fractional) a *tenth* part:—tenth deal.

6242. עֶשְׂרִים **ʻesrîym**, *es-reem'*; from 6235; *twenty*; also (ordinal) *twentieth*:—[six-] score, twenty (-ieth).

6243. עֶשְׂרִין **ʻesrîyn** (Chald.), *es-reen'*; corresp. to 6242:—twenty.

6244. עָשֵׁשׁ **ʻâshêsh**, *aw-shaysh'*; a prim. root; prob. to *shrink*, i.e. *fail*:—be consumed.

6245. עָשַׁת **ʻâshath**, *aw-shath'*; a prim. root; prob. to be *sleek*, i.e. *glossy*; hence (through the idea of *polishing*) to *excogitate* (as if *forming* in the mind):—shine, think.

6246. עֲשִׁית **ʻăshîth** (Chald.), *ash-eeth'*; corresp. to 6245; to *purpose*;—think.

6247. עֶשֶׁת **ʻesheth**, *eh'-sheth*; from 6245; a *fabric*:—bright.

6248. עַשְׁתּוּת **ʻashtûwth**, *ash-tooth'*; from 6245; *cogitation*:—thought.

6249. עַשְׁתֵּי **ʻashtêy**, *ash-tay'*; appar. masc. plur. constr. of 6247 in the sense of an *after-*

thought; (used only in connection with 6240 in lieu of 259) *eleven* or (ordinal) *eleventh:*—+ eleven (-th).

6250. עֶשְׁתֹּנָה **ʻeshtônâh**, *esh-to-naw';* from 6245; *thinking:*—thought.

6251. עַשְׁתְּרָה **ʻashtᵉrâh**, *ash-ter-aw';* prob. from 6238; *increase:*—flock.

6252. עַשְׁתָּרוֹת **ʻAshtârôwth**, *ash-taw-rōth',* or

עַשְׁתָּרֹת **ʻAshtârôth**, *ash-taw-rōth';* plur. of 6251; *Ashtaroth,* the name of a Sidonian deity, and of a place E. of the Jordan:—Ashtaroth, Astaroth. See also 1045, 6253, 6255.

6253. עַשְׁתֹּרֶת **ʻAshtôreth**, *ash-to'-reth;* prob. for 6251; *Ashtoreth,* the Phœnician goddess of love (and *increase*):—Ashtoreth.

6254. עַשְׁתְּרָתִי **ʻAshtᵉrâthîy**, *ash-ter-aw-thee';* patrial from 6252; an *Ashterathite* or inhab. of Ashtaroth:—Ashterathite.

6255. עַשְׁתְּרֹת קַרְנַיִם **ʻAshtᵉrôth Qarnayim**, *ash-ter-ōth' kar-nah'-yim;* from 6252 and the dual of 7161; *Ashtaroth of* (the) *double horns* (a symbol of the deity); *Ashteroth-Karnaïm,* a place E. of the Jordan:—Ashtoreth Karnaim.

6256. עֵת **ʻêth**, *ayth;* from 5703; *time,* espec. (adv. with prep.) *now, when,* etc.:—+ after, [al-] ways, × certain, + continually, + evening, long, (due) season, so [long] as, [even-, evening-, noon-] tide, ([meal-], what) time, when.

6257. עָתַד **ʻâthad**, *aw-thad';* a prim. root; to *prepare:*—make fit, be ready to become.

עַתֻּד **ʻattûd**. See 6260.

6258. עַתָּה **ʻattâh**, *at-taw';* from 6256; at *this time,* whether adv., conj. or expletive:—henceforth, now, straightway, this time, whereas.

6259. עָתוּד **ʻâthûwd**, *aw-thood';* pass. part. of 6257; *prepared:*—ready, treasures.

6260. עַתּוּד **ʻattûwd**, *at-tood';* or

עַתֻּד **ʻattûd**, *at-tood';* from 6257; *prepared,* i.e. *full grown;* spoken only (in plur.) of *he-goats,* or (fig.) *leaders* of the people:—chief one, (he) goat, ram.

6261. עִתִּי **ʻittîy**, *it-tee';* from 6256; *timely:*—fit.

6262. עַתַּי **ʻAttay**, *at-tah'ee;* for 6261; *Attai,* the name of three Isr.:—Attai.

6263. עֲתִיד **ʻăthîyd** (Chald.), *ath-eed';* corresp. to 6264; *prepared:*—ready.

6264. עָתִיד **ʻâthîyd**, *aw-theed';* from 6257; *prepared;* by impl. *skilful;* fem. plur. the *future;* also *treasure:*—things that shall come, ready, treasures.

6265. עֲתָיָה **ʻĂthâyâh**, *ath-aw-yaw';* from 5790 and 3050; *Jah has helped; Athajah,* an Isr.:—Athaiah.

6266. עָתִיק **ʻâthîyq**, *aw-theek';* from 6275; prop. *antique,* i.e. *venerable* or *splendid:*—durable.

6267. עַתִּיק **ʻattîyq**, *at-teek';* from 6275; *removed,* i.e. *weaned;* also *antique:*—ancient, drawn.

6268. עַתִּיק **ʻattîyq** (Chald.), *at-teek';* corresp. to 6267; *venerable:*—ancient.

6269. עֲתָךְ **ʻĂthâk**, *ath-awk';* from an unused root mean. to *sojourn; lodging; Athak,* a place in Pal.:—Athach.

6270. עַתְלַי **ʻAthlay**, *ath-lah'ee;* from an unused root mean. to *compress; constringent; Athlai,* an Isr.:—Athlai.

6271. עֲתַלְיָה **ʻĂthalyâh**, *ath-al-yaw';* or

עֲתַלְיָהוּ **ʻĂthalyâhûw**, *ath-al-yaw'-hoo;* from the same as 6270 and 3050; *Jah has constrained; Athaljah,* the name of an Israelitess and two Isr.:—Athaliah.

6272. עָתַם **ʻâtham**, *aw-tham';* a prim. root; prob. to *glow,* i.e. (fig.) *be desolated:*—be darkened.

6273. עָתְנִי **ʻOthnîy**, *oth-nee';* from an unused root mean. to *force; forcible; Othni,* an Isr.:—Othni.

6274. עָתְנִיאֵל **ʻOthnîyʼêl**, *oth-nee-ale';* from the same as 6273 and 410; *force of God; Othniël,* an Isr.:—Othniel.

6275. עָתַק **ʻâthaq**, *aw-thak';* a prim. root; to *remove* (intrans. or trans.); fig. to *grow old;* spec. to *transcribe:*—copy out, leave off, become (wax) old, remove.

6276. עָתֵק **ʻâthêq**, *aw-thake';* from 6275; *antique,* i.e. *valued:*—durable.

6277. עָתָק **ʻâthâq**, *aw-thawk';* from 6275 in the sense of *license; impudent:*—arrogancy, grievous (hard) things, stiff.

6278. עֵת קָצִין **ʻÊth Qâtsîyn**, *ayth kaw-tseen';* from 6256 and 7011; *time of a judge; Eth-Katsin,* a place in Pal.:—Ittah-kazin [*by includ. directive enclitic*].

6279. עָתַר **ʻâthar**, *aw-thar';* a prim. root [rather denom. from 6281]; to burn *incense* in worship, i.e. *intercede* (recipr. *listen* to prayer):—intreat, (make) pray (-er).

6280. עָתַר **ʻâthar**, *aw-thar';* a prim. root; to *be* (caus. *make*) *abundant:*—deceitful, multiply.

6281. עֶתֶר **ʻEther**, *eh'-ther;* from 6280; *abundance; Ether,* a place in Pal.:—Ether.

6282. עָתָר **ʻâthâr**, *aw-thawr';* from 6280; *incense* (as increasing to a *volume* of smoke); hence (from 6279) a *worshipper:*—suppliant, thick.

6283. עֲתֶרֶת **ʻăthereth**, *ath-eh'-reth;* from 6280; *copiousness:*—abundance.

פ

פֹּא **pôʼ**. See 6311.

6284. פָּאָה **pâʼâh**, *paw-aw';* a prim. root; to *puff,* i.e. *blow* away:—scatter into corners.

6285. פֵּאָה **pêʼâh**, *pay-aw';* fem. of 6311; prop. *mouth* in a fig. sense, i.e. *direction, region, extremity:*—corner, end, quarter, side.

6286. פָּאַר **pâʼar**, *paw-ar';* a prim. root; to *gleam,* i.e. (causat.) *embellish;* fig. to *boast;* also to *explain* (i.e. make clear) oneself; denom. from 6288, to *shake* a tree:—beautify, boast self, go over the boughs, glorify (self), glory, vaunt self.

6287. פְּאֵר **pᵉʼêr**, *peh-ayr';* from 6286; an *embellishment,* i.e. fancy *head-dress:*—beauty, bonnet, goodly, ornament, tire.

6288. פְּאֹרָה **pᵉʼôrâh**, *peh-o-raw';* or

פֹּרָאה **pôrâʼh**, *po-raw';* or

פֻּארָה **pûʼrâh**, *poo-raw';* from 6286; prop. *ornamentation,* i.e. (plur.) *foliage* (includ. the limbs) as *bright* green:—bough, branch, sprig.

6289. פָּארוּר **pâʼrûwr**, *paw-roor';* from 6286; prop. *illuminated,* i.e. a *glow;* as noun, a *flush* (of anxiety):—blackness.

6290. פָּארָן **Pâʼrân**, *paw-rawn';* from 6286; *ornamental; Paran,* a desert of Arabia:—Paran.

6291. פַּג **pag**, *pag;* from an unused root mean. to *be torpid,* i.e. *crude;* an *unripe* fig:—green fig.

6292. פִּגּוּל **piggûwl**, *pig-gool';* or

פִּגֻּל **piggûl**, *pig-gool';* from an unused root mean. to *stink;* prop. *fetid,* i.e. (fig.) *unclean* (ceremonially):—abominable (-tion, thing).

6293. פָּגַע **pâgaʻ**, *paw-gah';* a prim. root; to *impinge,* by accident or violence, or (fig.) by importunity:—come (betwixt), cause to entreat, fall (upon), make intercession, intercessor, intreat, lay, light [upon], meet (together), pray, reach, run.

6294. פֶּגַע **pegaʻ**, *peh'-gah;* from 6293; *impact* (casual):—chance, occurrent.

6295. פַּגְעִיאֵל **Pagʻîyʼêl**, *pag-ee-ale';* from 6294 and 410; *accident of God; Pagiël,* an Isr.:—Pagiel.

6296. פָּגַר **pâgar**, *paw-gar';* a prim. root; to *relax,* i.e. become *exhausted:*—be faint.

6297. פֶּגֶר **peger**, *peh'-gher;* from 6296; a *carcase* (as *limp*), whether of man or beast; fig. an idolatrous *image:*—carcase, corpse, dead body.

6298. פָּגַשׁ **pâgash**, *paw-gash';* a prim. root; to *come in contact with,* whether by accident or violence; fig. to *concur:*—meet (with, together).

6299. פָּדָה **pâdâh**, *paw-daw';* a prim. root; to *sever,* i.e. *ransom;* gener. to *release, preserve:*—× at all, deliver, × by any means, ransom, (that are to be, let be) redeem (-ed), rescue, × surely.

6300. פְּדַהְאֵל **Pᵉdahʼêl**, *ped-ah-ale';* from 6299 and 410; *God has ransomed; Pedahel,* an Isr.:—Pedahel.

6301. פְּדָהצוּר **Pᵉdâhtsûwr**, *ped-aw-tsoor';* from 6299 and 6697; a *rock* (i.e. God) *has ransomed; Pedahtsur,* an Isr.:—Pedahzur.

6302. פָּדוּי **pâdûwy**, *paw-doo'ee;* pass. part. of 6299; *ransomed* (and so occurring under 6299); as abstr. (in plur. masc.) a *ransom:*—(that are) to be (that were) redeemed.

6303. פָּדוֹן **Pâdôwn**, *paw-done';* from 6299; *ransom; Padon,* one of the Nethinim:—Padon.

6304. פְּדוּת **pᵉdûwth**, *ped-ooth';* or

פְּדֻת **pᵉdûth**, *ped-ooth';* from 6929; *distinction;* also *deliverance:*—division, redeem, redemption.

6305. פְּדָיָה **Pᵉdâyâh**, *ped-aw-yaw';* or

פְּדָיָהוּ **Pᵉdâyâhûw**, *ped-aw-yaw'-hoo;* from 6299 and 3050; *Jah has ransomed; Pedajah,* the name of six Isr.:—Pedaiah.

6306. פִּדְיוֹם **pidyôwm**, *pid-yome';* or

פִּדְיֹם **pidyôm**, *pid-yome';* also

פִּדְיוֹן **pidyôwn**, *pid-yone';* or

פִּדְיֹן **pidyôn**, *pid-yone';* from 6299; a *ransom:*—ransom, that were redeemed, redemption.

6307. פַּדָּן **Paddân**, *pad-dawn';* from an unused root mean. to *extend;* a *plateau;* or

פַּדַּן אֲרָם **Paddan ʼĂrâm**, *pad-dan' ar-awm';* from the same and 758; the *table-land of Aram; Paddan* or *Paddan-Aram,* a region of Syria:—Padan, Padan-aram.

6308. פָּדַע **pâdaʻ**, *paw-dah';* a prim. root; to *retrieve:*—deliver.

6309. פֶּדֶר **peder**, *peh'-der;* from an unused root mean. to *be greasy; suet:*—fat.

פְּדֻת **pᵉdûth**. See 6304.

6310. פֶּה **peh**, *peh;* from 6284; the *mouth* (as the means of *blowing*), whether lit. or fig. (particularly *speech*); spec. *edge, portion* or *side;* adv. (with prep.) *according to:*—accord (-ing as, -ing to), after, appointment, assent, collar, command (-ment), × eat, edge, end, entry, + file, hole, × in, mind, mouth, part, portion, × (should) say (-ing), sentence, skirt, sound, speech, × spoken, talk, tenor, × to, + two-edged, wish, word.

6311. פֹּה **pôh**, *po;* or

פֹּא **pôʼ** (Job 38 : 11), *po;* or

פּוֹ **pôw**, *po;* prob. from a prim. insep. particle פּ **p** (of demonstrative force) and 1931; *this place* (French *içi*), i.e. *here* or *hence:*—here, hither, the one (other, this, that) side.

פוֹא **pôwʼ**. See 375.

6312. פּוּאָה **Pûwʼâh**, *poo-aw';* or

פֻּוָּה **Puvvâh**, *poov-vaw';* from 6284; *blast; Puäh* or *Puvvah,* the name of two Isr.:—Phuvah, Pua, Puah.

6313. פּוּג **pûwg**, *poog;* a prim. root; to *be sluggish:*—cease, be feeble, faint, be slacked.

6314. פּוּגָה **pûwgâh**, *poo-gaw';* from 6313; *intermission:*—rest.

פֻּוָּה **Puvvâh**. See 6312.

6315. פּוּחַ **pûwach**, *poo'-akh;* a prim. root; to *puff,* i.e. blow with the breath or air; hence to *fan* (as a breeze), to *utter,* to *kindle* (a fire), to *scoff:*—blow (upon), break, puff, bring into a snare, speak, utter.

6316. פּוּט **Pûwṭ**, *poot;* of for. or.; *Put,* a son of Ham, also the name of his descendants or their region, and of a Persian tribe:—Phut, Put.

6317. פּוּטִיאֵל **Pûwṭîy'êl**, *poo-tee-ale'*; from an unused root (prob. mean. to *disparage*) and 410; *contempt of God; Putiël*, an Isr.:—Putiel.

6318. פּוֹטִיפַר **Pôwṭîyphar**, *po-tee-far'*; of Eg. der.; *Potiphar*, an Eg.:—Potiphar.

6319. פּוֹטִי פֶרַע **Pôwṭîy Pheraʻ**, *po'-tee feh'-rah*; of Eg. der.; *Poti-Phera*, an Eg.:—Poti-pherah.

6320. פּוּךְ **pûwk**, *pook*; from an unused root mean. to *paint; dye* (spec. *stibium* for the eyes):—fair colours, glistering, paint [-ed] (-ing).

6321. פּוֹל **pôwl**, *pole*; from an unused root mean. to *be thick*; a *bean* (as *plump*):—beans.

6322. פּוּל **Pûwl**, *pool*; of for. or.; *Pul*, the name of an Ass. king and of an Ethiopian tribe:—Pul.

6323. פּוּן **pûwn**, *poon*; a prim. root mean. to *turn*, i.e. *be perplexed*:—be distracted.

6324. פּוּנִי **Pûwnîy**, *poo-nee'*; patron. from an unused name mean. a *turn*; a *Punite* (collect.) or desc. of an unknown Pun:—Punites.

6325. פּוּנֹן **Pûwnôn**, *poo-none'*; from 6323; *perplexity; Punon*, a place in the Desert:—Punon.

6326. פּוּעָה **Pûw'âh**, *poo-aw'*; from an unused root mean. to *glitter; brilliancy; Puäh*, an Israelitess:—Puah.

6327. פּוּץ **pûwts**, *poots*; a prim. root; to *dash* in pieces, lit. or fig. (espec. to *disperse*):—break (dash, shake) in (to) pieces, cast (abroad), disperse (selves), drive, retire, scatter (abroad), spread abroad.

6328. פּוּק **pûwq**, *pook*; a prim. root; to *waver*:—stumble, move.

6329. פּוּק **pûwq**, *pook*; a prim. root [rather ident. with 6328 through the idea of *dropping* out; comp. 5312]; to *issue*, i.e. *furnish*; causat. to *secure*; fig. to *succeed*:—afford, draw out, further, get, obtain.

6330. פּוּקָה **pûwqâh**, *poo-kaw'*; from 6328; a *stumbling-block*:—grief.

6331. פּוּר **pûwr**, *poor*; a prim. root; to *crush*:—break, bring to nought, × utterly take.

6332. פּוּר **Pûwr**, *poor*; also (plur.)

פּוּרִים **Pûwrîym**, *poo-reem'*; or

פֻּרִים **Purîym**, *poo-reem'*; from 6331; a *lot* (as by means of a broken piece):—Pur, Purim.

6333. פּוּרָה **pûwrâh**, *poo-raw'*; from 6331; a *wine-press* (as *crushing* the grapes):—winepress.

פּוּרִים **Pûwrîym**. See 6332.

6334. פּוֹרָתָא **Pôwrâthâ'**, *po-raw-thaw'*; of Pers. or.; *Poratha*, a son of Haman:—Poratha.

6335. פּוּשׁ **pûwsh**, *poosh*; a prim. root; to *spread*; fig. *act proudly*:—grow up, be grown fat, spread selves, be scattered.

6336. פּוּתִי **Pûwthîy**, *poo-thee'*; patron. from an unused name mean. a *hinge*; a *Puthite* (collect.) or descend. of an unknown Puth:—Puhites [*as if from* 6312].

6337. פָּז **pâz**, *pawz*; from 6338; *pure* (gold); hence *gold* itself (as refined):—fine (pure) gold.

6338. פָּזַז **pâzaz**, *paw-zaz'*; a prim. root; to *refine* (gold):—best [gold].

6339. פָּזַז **pâzaz**, *paw-zaz'*; a prim. root [rather ident. with 6338]; to *solidify* (as if by *refining*); also to *spring* (as if *separating* the limbs):—leap, be made strong.

6340. פָּזַר **pâzar**, *paw-zar'*; a prim. root; to *scatter*, whether in enmity or bounty:—disperse, scatter (abroad).

6341. פַּח **pach**, *pakh*; from 6351; a (metallic) *sheet* (as *pounded* thin); also a spring *net* (as spread out like a *lamina*):—gin, (thin) plate, snare

6342. פָּחַד **pâchad**, *paw-kkad'*; a prim. root: to *be startled* (by a sudden alarm); hence to *fear* in general:—be afraid, stand in awe, (be in) fear, make to shake.

6343. פַּחַד **pachad**, *pakh'-ad*; from 6342; a (sudden) *alarm* (prop. the object feared, by impl. the feeling):- -dread (-ful), fear, (thing) great [fear, -ly feared], terror.

6344. פַּחַד **pachad**, *pakh'-ad*; the same as 6343; a *testicle* (as a cause of *shame* akin to fear):—stone.

6345. פַּחְדָּה **pachdâh**, *pakh-daw'*; fem. of 6343; *alarm* (i.e. *awe*):—fear.

6346. פֶּחָה **pechâh**, *peh-khaw'*; of for. or.; a *prefect* (of a city or small district):—captain, deputy, governor.

6347. פֶּחָה **pechâh** (Chald.), *peh-khaw'*; corresp. to 6346:—captain, governor.

6348. פָּחַז **pâchaz**, *paw-khaz'*; a prim. root; to *bubble* up or *froth* (as boiling water), i.e. (fig.) to *be unimportant*:—light.

6349. פַּחַז **pachaz**, *pakh'-az*; from 6348; *ebullition*, i.e. froth (fig. lust):—unstable.

6350. פַּחֲזוּת **pachăzûwth**, *pakh-az-ooth'*; from 6348; *frivolity*:—lightness.

6351. פָּחַח **pâchach**, *paw-khakh'*; a prim. root; to *batter* out; but used only as denom. from 6341, to *spread a net*:—be snared.

6352. פֶּחָם **pechâm**, *peh-khawm'*; perh. from an unused root prob. mean. to *be black*; a *coal*, whether charred or live:—coals.

6353. פֶּחָר **pechâr** (Chald.), *peh-khawr'*; from an unused root prob. mean. to *fashion*; a *potter*:—potter.

6354. פַּחַת **pachath**, *pakh'-ath*; prob. from an unused root appar. mean. to *dig*; a *pit*, espec. for catching animals:—hole, pit, snare,

6355. פַּחַת מוֹאָב **Pachath Môw'âb**, *pakh'-ath mo-awb'*; from 6354 and 4124; *pit of Moäb; Pachath-Moäb*, an Isr.:—Pahath-moab.

6356. פְּחֶתֶת **pᵉchetheth**, *pekh-eh'-theth*; from the same as 6354; a *hole* (by mildew in a garment):—fret inward.

6357. פִּטְדָה **piṭdâh**, *pit-daw'*; of for. der.; a *gem*, prob. the *topaz*:—topaz.

6358. פָּטוּר **pâṭûwr**, *paw-toor'*; pass. part. of 6362; *opened*, i.e. (as noun) a *bud*:—open.

6359. פָּטִיר **pâṭîyr**, *paw-teer'*; from 6362; *open*, i.e. *unoccupied*:—free.

6360. פַּטִּישׁ **paṭṭîysh**, *pat-teesh'*; intens. from an unused root mean. to *pound*; a *hammer*:—hammer.

6361. פַּטִּישׁ **paṭṭîysh** (Chald.), *pat-teesh'*; from a root corresp. to that of 6360; a *gown* (as if *hammered* out wide):—hose.

6362. פָּטַר **pâṭar**, *paw-tar'*; a prim. root; to *cleave* or burst through, i.e. (caus.) to *emit*, whether lit. or fig. (*gape*):—dismiss, free, let (shoot) out, slip away.

6363. פֶּטֶר **peṭer**, *peh'-ter*; or

פִּטְרָה **piṭrâh**, *pit-raw'*; from 6362; a *fissure*, i.e. (concr.) *firstling* (as *opening* the matrix):—firstling, openeth, such as open.

6364. פִּי־בֶסֶת **Pîy-Beceth**, *pee beh'-seth*; of Eg. or.; *Pi-Beseth*, a place in Eg.:—Pi-beseth.

6365. פִּיד **pîyd**, *peed*; from an unused root prob. mean. to *pierce*; (fig.) *misfortune*:—destruction, ruin.

6366. פֵּיָה **pêyâh**, *pay-aw'*; or

פִּיָה **pîyâh**, *pee-yaw'*; fem. of 6310; an *edge*:—(two-) edge (-d).

6367. פִּי הַחִירֹת **Pi ha-Chîyrôth**, *pee hah-khee-rōth'*; from 6310 and the fem. plur. of a noun (from the same root as 2356), with the art. interp.; *mouth of the gorges; Pi-ha-Chiroth*, a place in Eg.:—Pi-hahiroth. [In Num. 14 ; 19 without Pi-.]

6368. פִּיחַ **pîyach**, *pee'-akh*; from 6315; a *powder* (as easily *puffed away*), i.e. *ashes* or *dust*:—ashes.

6369. פִּיכֹל **Pîykôl**, *pee-kole'*; appar. from 6310 and 3605; *mouth of all; Picol*, a Philistine:—Phichol.

6370. פִּילֶגֶשׁ **pîylegesh**, *pee-leh'-ghesh*; or

פִּלֶגֶשׁ **pîlegesh**, *pee-leh'-ghesh*; of uncert. der.; a *concubine*; also (masc.) a *paramour*:—concubine, paramour.

6371. פִּימָה **pîymâh**, *pee-maw'*; prob. from an unused root mean. to *be plump; obesity*:—collops.

6372. פִּינְחָס **Pîynᵉchâç**, *pee-nekh-aws'*; appar. from 6310 and a var. of 5175; *mouth of a serpent; Pinechas*, the name of three Isr.:—Phinehas.

6373. פִּינֹן **pîynôn**, *pee-none'*; prob. the same as 6325; *Pinon*, an Idumæan:—Pinon.

6374. פִּיפִיָּה **pîyphîyâh**, *pee-fee-yaw'*; for 6366; an *edge* or *tooth*:—tooth, × two-edged

6375. פִּיק **pîyq**, *peek*; from 6329; a *tottering*:—smite together.

6376. פִּישׁוֹן **Pîyshôwn**, *pee-shone'*; from 6335; *dispersive; Pishon*, a river of Eden:—Pison.

6377. פִּיתוֹן **Pîythôwn**, *pee-thone'*; prob. from the same as 6596; *expansive; Pithon*, an Isr.:—Pithon.

6378. פַּךְ **pak**, *pak*; from 6379; a *flask* (from which a liquid may *flow*):—box, vial.

6379. פָּכָה **pâkâh**, *paw-kaw'*; a prim. root; to *pour*:—run out.

6380. פֹּכֶרֶת צְבָיִים **Pôkereth Tsᵉbâyîym**, *po-keh'-reth tseb-aw-yeem'*; from the act. part. (of the same form as the first word) fem. of an unused root (mean. to *entrap*) and plur. of 6643; *trap of gazelles; Pokereth-Tsebajim*, one of the "servants of Solomon":—Pochereth of Zebaim.

6381. פָּלָא **pâlâ'**, *paw-law'*; a prim. root; prop. perh. to *separate*, i.e. *distinguish* (lit. or fig.); by impl. to *be* (causat. *make*) *great, difficult, wonderful*:—accomplish, (arise . . . too, be too) hard, hidden, things too high, (be, do, do a, shew) marvellous (-ly, -els, things, work), miracles, perform, separate, make singular, (be, great, make) wonderful (-ers, -ly, things, works), wondrous (things, works, -ly).

6382. פֶּלֶא **pele'**, *peh'-leh*; from 6381; a *miracle*:—marvellous thing, wonder (-ful, -fully).

6383. פִּלְאִי **pil'îy**, *pil-ee'*; or

פָּלִיא **pâlîy'**, *paw-lee'*; from 6381; *remarkable*:—secret, wonderful.

6384. פַּלֻּאִי **Pallû'îy**, *pal-loo-ee'*; patron. from 6396; a *Palluïte* (collect.) or desc. of Pallu:—Palluites.

פְּלָאיָה **Pᵉlâ'yâh**. See 6411.

פִּלְאֶסֶר **Pil'eçer**. See 8407.

6385. פָּלַג **pâlag**, *paw-lag'*; a prim. root; to *split* (lit. or fig.):—divide.

6386. פְּלַג **pᵉlag** (Chald.), *pel-ag'*; corresp. to 6385:—divided.

6387. פְּלַג **pᵉlag** (Chald.), *pel-ag'*; from 6386; a *half*:—dividing.

6388. פֶּלֶג **peleg**, *peh'-leg*; from 6385; a *rill* (i.e. small *channel* of water, as in irrigation):—river, stream.

6389. פֶּלֶג **Peleg**, *peh'-leg*; the same as 6388; *earthquake; Peleg*, a son of Shem:—Peleg.

6390. פְּלַגָּה **pᵉlaggâh**, *pel-ag-gaw'*; from 6385; a *runlet*, i.e. *gully*:—division, river.

6391. פְּלֻגָּה **pᵉluggâh**, *pel-oog-gaw'*; from 6385; a *section*:—division.

6392. פְּלֻגָּה **pᵉluggâh** (Chald.), *pel-oog-gaw'*; corresp. to 6391:—division.

פִּלֶגֶשׁ **pîlegesh**. See 6370.

6393. פְּלָדָה **pᵉlâdâh**, *pel-aw-daw'*; from an unused root mean. to *divide*; a *cleaver*, i.e. iron *armature* (of a chariot):—torch.

6394. פִּלְדָּשׁ **Pildâsh**, *pil-dawsh'*; of uncert. der.; *Pildash*, a relative of Abraham:—Pildash.

6395. פָּלָה **pâlâh**, *paw-law'*; a prim. root; to *distinguish* (lit. or fig.):—put a difference, show marvellous, separate, set apart, sever, make wonderfully.

6396. פַּלּוּא **Pallûwʼ**, *pal-loo'*; from 6395; *distinguished; Pallu*, an Isr.:—Pallu, Phallu.

6397. פְּלוֹנִי **Pelôwnîy**, *pel-o-nee'*; patron. from an unused name (from 6395) mean. *separate;* a *Pelonite* or inhab. of an unknown Palon:—Pelonite.

6398. פָּלַח **pâlach**, *paw-lakh'*; a prim. root; to *slice*, i.e. *break* open or *pierce:*—bring forth, cleave, cut, shred, strike through.

6399. פְּלַח **pelach** (Chald.), *pel-akh'*; corresp. to 6398; to *serve* or worship:—minister, serve.

6400. פֶּלַח **pelach**, *peh'-lakh*; from 6398; a *slice:*—piece.

6401. פִּלְחָא **Pilchâʼ**, *pil-khaw'*; from 6400; *slicing; Pilcha*, an Isr.:—Pilcha.

6402. פָּלְחָן **polchân** (Chald.), *pol-khawn'*; from 6399; *worship:*—service,

6403. פָּלַט **pâlaṭ**, *paw-lat'*; a prim. root; to *slip* out, i.e. *escape;* causat. to *deliver:*—calve, carry away safe, deliver, (cause to) escape.

6404. פֶּלֶט **Peleṭ**, *peh'-let*; from 6403; *escape; Pelet*, the name of two Isr.:—Pelet. See also 1046.

פָּלֵט **pâlêṭ**. See 6412.

6405. פַּלֵּט **pallêṭ**, *pal-late'*; from 6403; *escape:*—deliverance, escape.

פְּלֵטָה **pelêṭâh**. See 6413.

6406. פַּלְטִי **Palṭîy**, *pal-tee'*; from 6403; *delivered; Palti*, the name of two Isr.:—Palti, Phalti.

6407. פַּלְטִי **Palṭîy**, *pal-tee'*; patron. from 6406; a *Paltite* or desc. of Palti:—Paltite.

6408. פִּלְטַי **Pilṭay**, *pil-tah'ee*; for 6407; *Piltai*, an Isr.:—Piltai.

6409. פַּלְטִיאֵל **Palṭîyʼêl**, *pal-tee-ale'*; from the same as 6404 and 410; *deliverance of God; Paltiël*, the name of two Isr.:—Paltiel, Phaltiel.

6410. פְּלַטְיָה **Pelaṭyâh**, *pel-at-yaw'*; or

פְּלַטְיָהוּ **Pelaṭyâhûw**, *pel-at-yaw'-hoo*; from 6403 and 3050; *Jah has delivered; Pelatjah*, the name of four Isr.:—Pelatiah.

פָּלִיא **pâlîyʼ**. See 6383.

6411. פְּלָיָה **Pelâyâh**, *pel-aw-yaw'*; or

פְּלָאיָה **Pelâʼyâh**, *pel-aw-yaw'*; from 6381 and 3050; *Jah has distinguished; Pelajah*, the name of three Isr.:—Pelaiah.

6412. פָּלִיט **pâlîyṭ**, *paw-leet'*; or

פָּלֵיט **pâlêyṭ**, *paw-late'*; or

פָּלֵט **pâlêṭ**, *paw-late'*; from 6403; a *refugee:*—(that have) escape (-d, -th), fugitive.

6413. פְּלֵיטָה **pelêyṭâh**, *pel-ay-taw'*; or

פְּלֵטָה **pelêṭâh**, *pel-ay-taw'*; fem. of 6412; *deliverance;* concr. an *escaped portion:*—deliverance, (that is) escape (-d), remnant.

6414. פָּלִיל **pâlîyl**, *paw-leel'*; from 6419; a *magistrate:*—judge.

6415. פְּלִילָה **pelîylâh**, *pel-ee-law'*; fem. of 6414; *justice:*—judgment.

6416. פְּלִילִי **pelîylîy**, *pel-ee-lee'*; from 6414; *judicial:*—judge.

6417. פְּלִילִיָּה **pelîylîyâh**, *pel-ee-lee-yaw'*; fem. of 6416; *judicature:*—judgment.

6418. פֶּלֶךְ **pelek**, *peh'-lek*; from an unused root mean. to *be round;* a *circuit* (i.e. *district*); also a *spindle* (as *whirled*); hence a *crutch:*—(di-) staff, part.

6419. פָּלַל **pâlal**, *paw-lal'*; a prim. root; to *judge* (officially or mentally); by extens. to *intercede, pray:*—intreat, judge (-ment), (make) pray (-er, -ing), make supplication.

6420. פָּלָל **Pâlâl**, *paw-lawl'*; from 6419; *judge; Palal*, an Isr.:—Palal.

6421. פְּלַלְיָה **Pelalyâh**, *pel-al-yaw'*; from 6419 and 3050; *Jah has judged; Pelaljah*, an Isr.:—Pelaliah.

6422. פַּלְמוֹנִי **palmôwnîy**, *pal-mo-nee'*; prob. for 6423; a *certain* one, i.e. so-and-so:—certain.

פִּלְנְאֶסֶר **Pilneʼeçer**. See 8407.

6423. פְּלֹנִי **pelônîy**, *pel-o-nee'*; from 6395; *such* a one, i.e. a specified *person:*—such.

פִּלְנֶסֶר **Pilneçer**. See 8407.

6424. פָּלַס **pâlaç**, *paw-las'*; a prim. root; prop. to *roll* flat, i.e. *prepare* (a road); also to *revolve*, i.e. *weigh* (mentally):—make, ponder, weigh.

6425. פֶּלֶס **peleç**, *peh'-les*; from 6424; a *balance:*—scales, weight.

פְּלֶסֶר **Peleçer**. See 8407.

6426. פָּלַץ **pâlats**, *paw-lats'*; a prim. root; prop. perh. to *rend*, i.e. (by impl.) to *quiver:*—tremble.

6427. פַּלָּצוּת **pallâtsûwth**, *pal-law-tsooth'*; from 6426; *affright:*—fearfulness, horror, trembling.

6428. פָּלַשׁ **pâlash**, *paw-lash'*; a prim. root; to *roll* (in dust):—roll (wallow) self.

6429. פְּלֶשֶׁת **Pelesheth**, *pel-eh'-sheth;* from 6428; *rolling*, i.e. *migratory; Pelesheth*, a region of Syria:—Palestina, Palestine, Philistia, Philistines.

6430. פְּלִשְׁתִּי **Pelishtîy**, *pel-ish-tee'*; patrial from 6429; a *Pelishtite* or inhab. of Pelesheth:—Philistine.

6431. פֶּלֶת **Peleth**, *peh'-leth;* from an unused root mean. to *flee; swiftness; Peleth*, the name of two Isr.:—Peleth.

6432. פְּלֵתִי **Pelêthîy**, *pel-ay-thee'*; from the same form as 6431; a *courier* (collect.) or official *messenger:*—Pelethites.

6433. פֻּם **pûm** (Chald.), *poom;* prob. for 6310; the *mouth* (lit. or fig.):—mouth.

6434. פֵּן **pên**, *pane;* from an unused root mean. to *turn;* an *angle* (of a street or wall):—corner.

6435. פֵּן **pên**, *pane;* from 6437; prop. *removal;* used only (in the constr.) adv. as conj. *lest:*—(lest) (peradventure), that . . . not.

6436. פַּנַּג **pannag**, *pan-nag'*; of uncert. der.; prob. *pastry:*—Pannag.

6437. פָּנָה **pânâh**, *paw-naw'*; a prim. root; to *turn;* by impl. to *face*, i.e. *appear, look*, etc.:—appear, at [even-] tide, behold, cast out, come on, × corner, dawning, empty, go away, lie, look, mark, pass away, prepare, regard, (have) respect (to), (re-) turn (aside, away, back, face, self), × right [early].

פָּנֶה **pâneh**. See 6440.

6438. פִּנָּה **pinnâh**, *pin-naw'*; fem. of 6434; an *angle;* by impl. a *pinnacle;* fig. a *chieftain:*—bulwark, chief, corner, stay, tower.

6439. פְּנוּאֵל **Penûwʼêl**, *pen-oo-ale'*; or (more prop.)

פְּנִיאֵל **Penîyʼêl**, *pen-ee-ale'*; from 6437 and 410; *face of God; Penuël* or *Peniël*, a place E. of Jordan; also (as Penuel) the name of two Isr.:—Peniel, Penuel.

פָּנִי° **pânîy**. See 6443.

6440. פָּנִים **pânîym**, *paw-neem'*; plur. (but always as sing.) of an unused noun

[פָּנֶה **pâneh**, *paw-neh'*; from 6437]; the *face* (as the part that *turns*); used in a great variety of applications (lit. and fig.); also (with prep. pref.) as a prep. (*before*, etc.):—+ accept, a- (be-) fore (-time), against, anger, × as (long as), at, + battle, + because (of), + beseech, countenance, edge, + employ, endure, + enquire, face, favour, fear of, for, forefront (-part), form (-er time, -ward), from, front, heaviness, × him (-self), + honourable, + impudent, + in, it, look [-eth] (-s), × me, + meet, × more than, mouth, of, off, (of) old (time), × on, open, + out of, over against, the partial, person, + please, presence, propect, was purposed, by reason, of, + regard, right forth, + serve, × shewbread, sight, state, straight, + street, × thee, × them (-selves), through (+ -out), till, time (-s) past, (un-) to (-ward), + upon, upside (+ down), with (-in, + -stand), × ye, × you.

6441. פְּנִימָה **penîymâh**, *pen-ee'-maw;* from 6440 with directive enclitic; *faceward*, i.e. *indoors:*—(with-) in (-ner part, -ward).

6442. פְּנִימִי **penîymîy**, *pen-ee-mee'*; from 6440; *interior:*—(with-) in (-ner, -ward).

6443. פָּנִין **pânîyn**, *paw-neen'*; or

פָּנִי° **pânîy**, *paw-nee'*; from the same as 6434; prob. a *pearl* (as *round*):—ruby.

6444. פְּנִנָּה **Peninnâh**, *pen-in-naw'*; prob. fem. from 6443 contr.; *Peninnah*, an Israelitess:—Peninnah.

6445. פָּנַק **pânaq**, *paw-nak'*; a prim. root; to *enervate:*—bring up.

6446. פַּס **paç**, *pas;* from 6461; prop. the *palm* (of the hand) or *sole* (of the foot) [comp. 6447]; by impl. (plur.) a *long and sleeved* tunic (perh. simply a *wide* one; from the orig. sense of the root, i.e. of *many breadths*):—(divers) colours.

6447. פַּס **paç** (Chald.), *pas;* from a root corresp. to 6461; the *palm* (of the hand, as being *spread* out):—part.

6448. פָּסַג **pâçag**, *paw-sag'*; a prim. root; to *cut up*, i.e. (fig.) *contemplate:*—consider.

6449. פִּסְגָּה **Piçgâh**, *pis-gaw';* from 6448; a *cleft; Pisgah*, a mt. E. of Jordan:—Pisgah.

6450. פַּס דַּמִּים **Paç Dammîym**, *pas dam-meem';* from 6446 and the plur. of 1818; *palm* (i.e. *dell*) *of bloodshed; Pas-Dammim*, a place in Pal.:—Pas-dammim. Comp. 658.

6451. פִּסָּה **piççâh**, *pis-saw'*; from 6461; *expansion*, i.e. *abundance:*—handful.

6452. פָּסַח **pâçach**, *paw-sakh'*; a prim. root; to *hop*, i.e. (fig.) *skip* over (or *spare*); by impl. to *hesitate;* also (lit.) to *limp*, to *dance:*—halt, become lame, leap, pass over.

6453. פֶּסַח **peçach**, *peh'-sakh;* from 6452; a *pretermission*, i.e. *exemption;* used only tech. of the Jewish *Passover* (the festival or the victim):—passover (offering).

6454. פָּסֵחַ **Pâçêach**, *paw-say'-akh;* from 6452; *limping; Paseäch*, the name of two Isr.:—Paseah, Phaseah.

6455. פִּסֵּחַ **piççêach**, *pis-say'-akh;* from 6452; *lame:*—lame.

6456. פְּסִיל **peçîyl**, *pes-eel';* from 6458; an *idol:*—carved (graven) image, quarry.

6457. פָּסַךְ **Pâçak**, *paw-sak';* from an unused root mean. to *divide; divider; Pasak*, an Isr.:—Pasach.

6458. פָּסַל **pâçal**, *paw-sal'*; a prim. root; to *carve*, whether wood or stone:—grave, hew.

6459. פֶּסֶל **peçel**, *peh'-sel;* from 6458; an *idol:*—carved (graven) image.

6460. פְּסַנְטֵרִין **peçanṭêrîyn** (Chald.), *pes-an-tay-reen'*; or

פְּסַנְתֵּרִין **peçantêrîyn**, *pes-an-tay-reen';* a transliteration of the Gr. ψαλτήριον *psaltēriŏn;* a *lyre:*—psaltery.

6461. פָּסַס **pâçaç**, *paw-sas'*; a prim. root; prob. to *disperse*, i.e. (intrans.) *disappear:*—cease.

6462. פִּסְפָּה **Piçpâh**, *pis-paw';* perh. from 6461; *dispersion; Pispah*, an Isr.:—Pispah.

6463. פָּעָה **pâʻâh**, *paw-aw';* a prim. root; to *scream:*—cry.

6464. פָּעוּ **Pâʻûw**, *paw-oo';* or

פָּעִי **Pâʻîy**, *paw-ee';* from 6463; *screaming; Paü* or *Paï*, a place in Edom:—Pai, Pau.

6465. פְּעוֹר **Pᵉʻôwr**, *peh-ore'*; from 6473; a *gap*; *Peör*, a mountain E. of Jordan; also (for 1187) a deity worshipped there:—Peor. See also 1047.

פָּעִי **Pâʻîy**. See 6464.

6466. פָּעַל **pâʻal**, *paw-al'*; a prim. root; to *do* or *make* (systematically and habitually), espec. to *practise*:—commit, [evil-] do (-er), make (-r), ordain, work (-er), wrought.

6467. פֹּעַל **pôʻal**, *po'-al*; from 6466; an *act* or *work* (concr.):—act, deed, do, getting, maker, work.

6468. פְּעֻלָּה **pᵉʻullâh**, *peh-ool-law'*; fem. pass. part. of 6466; (abstr.) *work*:—labour, reward, wages, work.

6469. פְּעֻלְּתַי **Pᵉʻullᵉthay**, *peh-ool-leh-thah'ee*; from 6468; *laborious*; *Peüllethai*, an Isr.:—Peulthai.

6470. פָּעַם **pâʻam**, *paw-am'*; a prim. root; to *tap*, i.e. beat regularly; hence (gen.) to *impel* or *agitate*:—move, trouble.

6471. פַּעַם **paʻam**, *pah'-am*; or (fem.)

פַּעֲמָה **paʻămâh**, *pah-am-aw'*; from 6470; a *stroke*, lit. or fig. (in various applications, as follow):—anvil, corner, foot (-step), going, [hundred-] fold, × now, (this) + once, order, rank, step, + thrice, ([often-], second, this, two) time (-s), twice, wheel.

6472. פַּעֲמֹן **paʻămôn**, *pah-am-one'*; from 6471; a *bell* (as *struck*):—bell.

6473. פָּעַר **pâʻar**, *paw-ar'*; a prim. root; to *yawn*, i.e. *open* wide (lit. or fig.):—gape, open (wide).

6474. פַּעֲרַי **Paʻăray**, *pah-ar-ah'ee*; from 6473; *yawning*; *Paarai*, an Isr.:—Paarai.

6475. פָּצָה **pâtsâh**, *paw-tsaw'*; a prim. root; to *rend*, i.e. *open* (espec. the mouth):—deliver, gape, open, rid, utter.

6476. פָּצַח **pâtsach**, *paw-tsakh'*; a prim. root; to *break* out (in joyful sound):—break (forth, forth into joy), make a loud noise.

6477. פְּצִירָה **pᵉtsîyrâh**, *pets-ee-raw'*; from 6484; *bluntness*:— + file.

6478. פָּצַל **pâtsal**, *paw-tsal'*; a prim. root; to *peel*:—pill.

6479. פְּצָלָה **pᵉtsâlâh**, *pets-aw-law'*; from 6478; a *peeling*:—strake.

6480. פָּצַם **pâtsam**, *paw-tsam'*; a prim. root; to *rend* (by earthquake):—break.

6481. פָּצַע **pâtsaʻ**, *paw-tsah'*; a prim. root; to *split*, i.e. *wound*:—wound.

6482. פֶּצַע **petsaʻ**, *peh'-tsah*; from 6481; a *wound*:—wound (-ing).

פַּצֵּץ **Patstsets**. See 1048.

6483. פִּצֵּץ **Pitstsêts**, *pits-tsates'*; from an unused root mean. to *dissever*; *dispersive*; *Pitstsets*, a priest:—Apses [*includ. the art.*].

6484. פָּצַר **pâtsar**, *paw-tsar'*; a prim. root; to *peck* at, i.e. (fig.) *stun* or *dull*:—press, urge, stubbornness.

6485. פָּקַד **pâqad**, *paw-kad'*; a prim. root; to *visit* (with friendly or hostile intent); by anal. to *oversee*, *muster*, *charge*, *care for*, *miss*, *deposit*, etc.:—appoint, × at all, avenge, bestow, (appoint to have the, give a) charge, commit, count, deliver to keep, be empty, enjoin, go see, hurt, do judgment, lack, lay up look, make × by any means, miss, number, officer, (make) overseer. have (the) oversight, punish, reckon, (call to) remember (-brance), set (over), sum, × surely, visit, want.

פִּקֻּד **piqqûd**. See 6490.

6486. פְּקֻדָּה **pᵉquddâh**, *pek-ood-daw'*; fem. pass. part. of 6485; *visitation* (in many senses, chiefly official):—account, (that have the) charge, custody, that which . . . laid up, numbers, office (-r), ordering, oversight, + prison, reckoning, visitation.

6487. פִּקָּדוֹן **piqqâdôwn**, *pik-kaw-done'*; from 6485; a *deposit*:—that which was delivered (to keep), store.

6488. פְּקִדֻת **pᵉqîdûth**, *pek-ee-dooth'*; from 6496; *supervision*:—ward.

6489. פְּקוֹד **Pᵉqôwd**, *pek-ode'*; from 6485; *punishment*; *Pekod*, a symbol. name for Bab.:—Pekod.

6490. פִּקּוּד **piqqûwd**, *pik-kood'*; or

פִּקֻּד **piqqûd**, *pik-kood'*; from 6485; prop. *appointed*, i.e. a *mandate* (of God; plur. only, collect. for the *Law*):—commandment, precept, statute.

6491. פָּקַח **pâqach**, *paw-kakh'*; a prim. root; to *open* (the senses, espec. the eyes); fig. to *be observant*:—open.

6492. פֶּקַח **Peqach**, *peh'-kakh*; from 6491; *watch*; *Pekach*, an Isr. king:—Pekah.

6493. פִּקֵּחַ **piqqêach**, *pik-kay'-akh*; from 6491; *clear-sighted*; fig. *intelligent*:—seeing, wise.

6494. פְּקַחְיָה **Pᵉqachyâh**, *pek-akh-yaw'*; from 6491 and 3050; *Jah has observed*; *Pekachjah*, an Isr. king:—Pekahiah.

6495. פְּקַח־קוֹחַ **pᵉqach-qôwach**, *pek-akh-ko'-akh*; from 6491 redoubled; *opening* (of a dungeon), i.e. *jail-delivery* (fig. *salvation* from sin):—opening of the prison.

6496. פָּקִיד **pâqîyd**, *paw-keed'*; from 6485; a *superintendent* (civil, military or religious):—which had the charge, governor, office, overseer, [that] was set.

6497. פֶּקַע **peqaʻ**, *peh'-kah*; from an unused root mean. to *burst*; only used as an architect. term of an ornament similar to 6498, a *semi-globe*:—knop.

6498. פַּקֻּעָה **paqqûʻâh**, *pak-koo-aw'*; from the same as 6497; the *wild cucumber* (from *splitting* open to shed its seeds):—gourd.

6499. פַּר **par**, *par*; or

פָּר **pâr**, *pawr*; from 6565; a *bullock* (appar. as *breaking* forth in wild strength, or perh. as *dividing* the hoof):—(+ young) bull (-ock), calf, ox.

6500. פָּרָא **pârâʼ**, *paw-raw'*; a prim. root; to *bear fruit*:—be fruitful.

6501. פֶּרֶא **pereʼ**, *peh'-reh*; or

פֶּרֶה **pereh** (Jer. 2 : 24), *peh'-reh*; from 6500 in the secondary sense of *running* wild; the *onager*:—wild (ass).

פֹּרָאה **pôrâʼh**. See 6288.

6502. פִּרְאָם **Pirʼâm**, *pir-awm'*; from 6501; *wildly*; *Piram*, a Canaanite:—Piram.

6503. פַּרְבָּר **Parbâr**, *par-bawr'*; or

פַּרְוָר **Parvâr**, *par-vawr'*; of for or.; *Parbar* or *Parvar*, a quarter of Jerus.:—Parbar, suburb.

6504. פָּרַד **pârad**, *paw-rad'*; a prim. root; to *break* through, i.e. *spread* or *separate* (oneself):—disperse, divide, be out of joint, part, scatter (abroad), separate (self), sever self, stretch, sunder.

6505. פֶּרֶד **pered**, *peh'-red*; from 6504; a *mule* (perh. from his *lonely* habits):—mule.

6506. פִּרְדָּה **pirdâh**, *pir-daw'*; fem. of 6505; a *she-mule*:—mule.

6507. פְּרֻדָה **pᵉrûdâh**, *per-oo-daw'*; fem. pass. part. of 6504; something *separated*, i.e. a *kernel*:—seed.

6508. פַּרְדֵּס **pardêç**, *par-dace'*; of for. or.; a *park*:—forest, orchard.

6509. פָּרָה **pârâh**, *paw-raw'*; a prim. root; to *bear fruit* (lit. or fig.):—bear, bring forth (fruit), (be, cause to be, make) fruitful, grow, increase.

6510. פָּרָה **pârâh**, *paw-raw'*; fem. of 6499; a *heifer*:—cow, heifer, kine.

6511. פָּרָה **Pârâh**, *paw-raw'*; the same as 6510; *Parah*, a place in Pal.:—Parah.

פֶּרֶה **pereh**. See 6501.

6512. פֵּרָה **pêrâh**, *pay-raw'*; from 6331; a *hole* (as *broken*, i.e. dug):— + mole. Comp. 2661.

6513. פֻּרָה **Pûrâh**, *poo-raw*; for 6288; *foliage*; *Purah*, an Isr.:—Phurah.

6514. פְּרוּדָא **Pᵉrûwdâʼ**, *per-oo-daw'*; or

פְּרִידָא **Pᵉrîydâʼ**, *per-ee-daw'*; from 6504; *dispersion*; *Peruda* or *Perida*, one of "Solomon's servants":—Perida, Peruda.

פְּרוֹזִי **pᵉrôwzîy**. See 6521.

6515. פָּרוּחַ **Pârûwach**, *paw-roo'-akh*; pass. part. of 6524; *blossomed*; *Paruäch*, an Isr.:—Paruah.

6516. פַּרְוַיִם **Parvayim**, *par-vah'-yim*; of for. or.; *Parvajim*, an Oriental region:—Parvaim.

6517. פָּרוּר **pârûwr**, *paw-roor'*; pass. part. of 6565 in the sense of *spreading* out [comp. 6524]; a *skillet* (as *flat* or *deep*):—pan, pot.

פַּרְוָר **Parvâr**. See 6503.

6518. פָּרָז **pâraz**, *paw-rawz'*; from an unused root mean. to *separate*, i.e. *decide*; a *chieftain*:—village.

6519. פְּרָזָה **pᵉrâzâh**, *per-aw-zaw'*; from the same as 6518; an *open* country:—(unwalled) town (without walls), unwalled village.

6520. פְּרָזוֹן **pᵉrâzôwn**, *per-aw-zone'*; from the same as 6518; *magistracy*, i.e. *leadership* (also concr. *chieftains*):—village.

6521. פְּרָזִי **pᵉrâzîy**, *per-aw-zee'*; or

פְּרוֹזִי **pᵉrôwzîy**, *per-o-zee'*; from 6519; a *rustic*:—village.

6522. פְּרִזִּי **Pᵉrizzîy**, *per-iz-zee'*; for 6521; inhab. *of the open country*; a *Perizzite*, one of the Canaanitish tribes:—Perizzite.

6523. פַּרְזֶל **parzel** (Chald.), *par-zel'*; corresp. to 1270; *iron*:—iron.

6524. פָּרַח **pârach**, *paw-rakh'*; a prim. root; to *break* forth as a bud, i.e. *bloom*; gen. to *spread*; spec. to *fly* (as extending the wings); fig. to *flourish*:— × abroad, × abundantly, blossom, break forth (out), bud, flourish, make fly, grow, spread, spring (up).

6525. פֶּרַח **perach**, *peh'-rakh*; from 6524; a *calyx* (nat. or artif.); gen. *bloom*:—blossom, bud, flower.

6526. פִּרְחַח **pirchach**, *pir-khakh'*; from 6524; *progeny*, i.e. a *brood*:—youth.

6527. פָּרַט **pârat**, *paw-rat'*; a prim. root; to *scatter* words, i.e. *prate* (or *hum*):—chant.

6528. פֶּרֶט **peret**, *peh'-ret*; from 6527; a *stray* or *single* berry:—grape.

6529. פְּרִי **pᵉrîy**, *per-ee'*; from 6509; *fruit* (lit. or fig.):—bough, ([first-]) fruit ([-ful]), reward.

פְּרִידָא **Pᵉrîydâʼ**. See 6514.

פֻּרִים **Pûrîym**. See 6332.

6530. פְּרִיץ **pᵉrîyts**, *per-eets'*; from 6555; *violent*, i.e. a *tyrant*:—destroyer, ravenous, robber.

6531. פֶּרֶךְ **perek**, *peh'-rek*; from an unused root mean. to *break* apart; *fracture*, i.e. *severity*:—cruelty, rigour.

6532. פֹּרֶכֶת **pôreketh**, *po-reh'-keth*; fem. act. part. of the same as 6531; a *separatrix*, i.e. (the sacred) *screen*:—vail.

6533. פָּרַם **pâram**, *paw-ram'*; a prim. root; to *tear*:—rend.

6534. פַּרְמַשְׁתָּא **Parmashtâʼ**, *par-mash-taw'*; of Pers. or.; *Parmashta*, a son of Haman:—Parmasta.

6535. פַּרְנַךְ **Parnak**, *par-nak'*; of uncert. der.; *Parnak*, an Isr.:—Parnach.

6536. פָּרַס **pâraç**, *paw-ras'*; a prim. root; to *break* in pieces, i.e. (usually without violence) to *split*, *distribute*:—deal, divide, have hoofs, part, tear.

6537. פְּרַס **pᵉraç** (Chald.), *per-as'*; corresp. to 6536; to *split* up:—divide, [U-] pharsin.

6538. פֶּרֶס **pereç**, *peh'-res*; from 6536; a *claw*; also a kind of *eagle*:—claw, ossifrage.

6539. פָּרַס **Pâraç**, *paw-ras'*; of for. or.; *Paras* (i.e. *Persia*), an Eastern country, including its inhab.:—Persia, Persians.

6540. פָּרַס **Pâraç** (Chald.), *paw-ras'*; corresp. to 6539:—Persia, Persians.

6541. פַּרְסָה **parçâh**, *par-saw'*; fem. of 6538; a *claw* or split *hoof*:—claw, [cloven-] footed, hoof.

6542. פַּרְסִי **Parçîy**, *par-see'*; patrial from 6539; a *Parsite* (i.e. *Persian*), or inhab. of Peres:—Persian.

6543. פַּרְסִי **Parçîy** (Chald.), *par-see'*; corresp. to 6542:—Persian.

6544. פָּרַע **pâra'**, *paw-rah'*; a prim. root; to *loosen*; by impl. to *expose*, *dismiss*; fig. *absolve*, *begin*:—avenge, avoid, bare, go back, let, (make) naked, set at nought, perish, refuse, uncover.

6545. פֶּרַע **pera'**, *peh'-rah*; from 6544; the *hair* (as *dishevelled*):—locks.

6546. פַּרְעָה **par'âh**, *par-aw'*; fem. of 6545 (in the sense of *beginning*); *leadership* (plur. concr. *leaders*):— + avenging, revenge.

6547. פַּרְעֹה **Par'ôh**, *par-o'*; of Eg. der.; *Paroh*, a gen. title of Eg. kings:—Pharaoh.

6548. פַּרְעֹה חָפְרַע **Par'ôh Chophra'**, *par-o' khof-rah'*; of Eg. der.; *Paroh-Chophra*, an Eg. king:—Pharaoh-hophra.

6549. פַּרְעֹה נְכֹה **Par'ôh N^ekôh**, *par-o' nek-o'*; or

פַּרְעֹה נְכוֹ **Par'ôh N^ekôw**, *par-o' nek-o'*; of Eg. der.; *Paroh-Nekoh* (or *-Neko*), an Eg. king:—Pharaoh-necho, Pharaoh-nechoh.

6550. פַּרְעֹשׁ **par'ôsh**, *par-oshe'*; prob. from 6544 and 6211; a *flea* (as the *isolated insect*):—flea.

6551. פַּרְעֹשׁ **Par'ôsh**, *par-oshe'*; the same as 6550; *Parosh*, the name of four Isr.:—Parosh, Pharosh.

6552. פִּרְעָתוֹן **Pir'âthôwn**, *pir-aw-thone'*; from 6546; *chieftaincy*; *Pirathon*, a place in Pal.:—Pirathon.

6553. פִּרְעָתוֹנִי **Pir'âthôwnîy**, *pir-aw-tho-nee'*; or

פִּרְעָתֹנִי **Pir'âthônîy**, *pir-aw-tho-nee'*; patrial from 6552; a *Pirathonite* or inhab. of Pirathon:—Pirathonite.

6554. פַּרְפַּר **Parpar**, *par-par'*; prob. from 6565 in the sense of *rushing*; *rapid*; *Parpar*, a river of Syria:—Pharpar.

6555. פָּרַץ **pârats**, *paw-rats'*; a prim. root; to *break* out (in many applications, direct and indirect, lit. and fig.):—× abroad, (make a) breach, break (away, down, -er, forth, in, up), burst out come (spread) abroad, compel, disperse, grow, increase, open, press, scatter, urge.

6556. פֶּרֶץ **perets**, *peh'-rets*; from 6555; a *break* (lit. or fig.):—breach, breaking forth (in), × forth, gap.

6557. פֶּרֶץ **Perets**, *peh'-rets*; the same as 6556; *Perets*, the name of two Isr.:—Perez, Pharez.

6558. פַּרְצִי **Partsîy**, *par-tsee'*; patron. from 6557; a *Partsite* (collect.) or desc. of Perets:—Pharzites.

6559. פְּרָצִים **p^erâtsîym**, *per-aw-tseem'*; plur. of 6556; *breaks*; *Peratsim*, a mountain in Pal.:—Perazim.

6560. פֶּרֶץ עֻזָּא **Perets 'Uzzâ'**, *peh'-rets ooz-zaw'*; from 6556 and 5798; *break of Uzza*; *Perets-Uzza*, a place in Pal.:—Perez-uzza.

6561. פָּרַק **pâraq**, *paw-rak'*; a prim. root; to *break* off or *craunch*; fig. to *deliver*:—break (off), deliver, redeem, rend (in pieces), tear in pieces.

6562. פְּרַק **p^eraq** (Chald.), *per-ak'*; corresp. to 6561; to *discontinue*:—break off.

6563. פֶּרֶק **pereq**, *peh'-rek*; from 6561; *rapine*; also a *fork* (in roads):—crossway, robbery.

6564. פָּרָק° **pârâq**, *paw-rawk'*; from 6561; *soup* (as full of *crumbed* meat):—broth. See also 4832.

6565. פָּרַר **pârar**, *paw-rar'*; a prim. root; to *break* up (usually fig., i.e. to *violate*, *frustrate*):— × any ways, break (asunder), cast off, cause to cease, × clean, defeat, disannul, disappoint, dissolve, divide, make of none effect, fail, frustrate, bring (come) to nought, × utterly, make void.

6566. פָּרַשׂ **pâras**, *paw-ras'*; a prim. root; to *break* apart, *disperse*, etc.:—break, chop in pieces, lay open, scatter, spread (abroad, forth, selves, out), stretch (forth, out).

6567. פָּרַשׁ **pârash**, *paw-rash'*; a prim. root; to *separate*, lit. (to *disperse*) or fig. (to *specify*); also (by impl.) to *wound*:—scatter, declare, distinctly, shew, sting.

6568. פְּרַשׁ **p^erash** (Chald.), *per-ash'*; corresp. to 6567; to *specify*:—distinctly.

6569. פֶּרֶשׁ **peresh**, *peh'-resh*; from 6567; *excrement* (as *eliminated*):—dung.

6570. פֶּרֶשׁ **Peresh**, *peh'-resh*; the same as 6569; *Peresh*, an Isr.:—Peresh.

6571. פָּרָשׁ **pârâsh**, *paw-rawsh'*; from 6567; a *steed* (as *stretched* out to a vehicle, not single nor for mounting [comp. 5483]); also (by impl.) a *driver* (in a chariot), i.e. (collect.) cavalry:—horseman.

6572. פַּרְשֶׁגֶן **parshegen**, *par-sheh'-ghen*; or

פַּתְשֶׁגֶן **pathshegen**, *path-sheh'-gen*; of for. or.; a *transcript*:—copy.

6573. פַּרְשֶׁגֶן **parshegen** (Chald.), *par-sheh'-ghen*; corresp. to 6572:—copy.

6574. פַּרְשְׁדֹן **parsh^edôn**, *par-shed-one'*; perh. by compounding 6567 and 6504 (in the sense of *straddling*) [comp. 6576]; the *crotch* (or *anus*):—dirt.

6575. פָּרָשָׁה **pârâshâh**, *paw-raw-shaw'*; from 6567; *exposition*:—declaration, sum.

6576. פַּרְשֵׁז **parshêz**, *par-shaze'*; a root appar. formed by compounding 6567 and that of 6518 [comp. 6574]; to *expand*:—spread.

6577. פַּרְשַׁנְדָּתָא **Parshandâthâ'**, *par-shan-daw-thaw'*; of Pers. or.; *Parshandatha*, a son of Haman:—Parshandatha.

6578. פְּרָת **P^erâth**, *per-awth'*; from an unused root mean. to *break* forth; *rushing*; *Perath* (i.e. *Euphrates*), a river of the East:—Euphrates.

פֹּרָת **pôrâth**. See 6509.

6579. פַּרְתַּם **partam**, *par-tam'*; of Pers. or.; a *grandee*:—(most) noble, prince.

6580. פַּשׁ **pash**, *pash*; prob. from an unused root mean. to *disintegrate*; *stupidity* (as a result of *grossness* or of *degeneracy*):—extremity.

6581. פָּשָׂה **pâsâh**, *paw-saw'*; a prim. root; to *spread*:—spread.

6582. פָּשַׁח **pâshach**, *paw-shakh'*; a prim. root; to *tear* in pieces:—pull in pieces.

6583. פַּשְׁחוּר **Pashchûwr**, *pash-khoor'*; prob. from 6582; *liberation*; *Pashchur*, the name of four Isr.:—Pashur.

6584. פָּשַׁט **pâshaṭ**, *paw-shat'*; a prim. root; to *spread* out (i.e. *deploy* in hostile array); by anal. to *strip* (i.e. *unclothe*, *plunder*, *flay*, etc.):—fall upon, flay, invade, make an invasion, pull off, put off, make a road, run upon, rush, set, spoil, spread selves (abroad), strip (off, self).

6585. פָּשַׂע **pâsa'**, *paw-sah'*; a prim. root; to *stride* (from *spreading* the legs), i.e. *rush* upon:—go.

6586. פָּשַׁע **pâsha'**, *paw-shah'*; a prim. root [rather ident. with 6585 through the idea of *expansion*]; to *break* away (from just authority), i.e. *trespass*, *apostatize*, *quarrel*:—offend, rebel, revolt, transgress (-ion, -or).

6587. פֶּשַׂע **pesa'**, *peh'-sah*; from 6585; a *stride*:—step.

6588. פֶּשַׁע **pesha'**, *peh'-shah*; from 6586; a *revolt* (national, moral or religious):—rebellion, sin, transgression, trespass.

6589. פָּשַׂק **pâsaq**, *paw-sak'*; a prim. root; to *dispart* (the feet or lips), i.e. *become licentious*:—open (wide).

6590. פְּשַׁר **p^eshar** (Chald.), *pesh-ar'*; corresp. to 6622; to *interpret*:—make [interpretations], interpreting.

6591. פְּשַׁר **p^eshar** (Chald.), *pesh-ar'*; from 6590; an *interpretation*:—interpretation.

6592. פֵּשֶׁר **pêsher**, *pay'-sher*; corresp. to 6591:—interpretation.

6593. פִּשְׁתֶּה **pishteh**, *pish-teh'*; from the same as 6580 as in the sense of *comminuting*; *linen* (i.e. the thread, as *carded*):—flax, linen.

6594. פִּשְׁתָּה **pishtâh**, *pish-taw'*; fem. of 6593; *flax*; by impl. a *wick*:—flax, tow.

6595. פַּת **path**, *path*; from 6626; a *bit*:—meat, morsel, piece.

6596. פֹּת **pôth**, *pohth*; or

פֹּתָה **pothâh** (Ezek. 13 : 19), *po-thaw'*; from an unused root mean. to *open*; a *hole*, i.e. *hinge* or the female *pudenda*:—hinge, secret part.

פְּתָאִי **p^ethâ'iy**. See 6612.

6597. פִּתְאוֹם **pith'ôwm**, *pith-ome'*; or

פִּתְאֹם **pith'ôm**, *pith-ome'*; from 6621; *instantly*:—straightway, sudden (-ly).

6598. פַּתְבַּג **pathbag**, *pathbag'*; of Pers. or.; a *dainty*:—portion (provision) of meat.

6599. פִּתְגָּם **pithgâm**, *pith-gawm'*; of Pers. or.; a (judicial) *sentence*:—decree, sentence.

6600. פִּתְגָּם **pithgâm** (Chald.), *pith-gawm'*; corresp. to 6599; a *word*, *answer*, *letter* or *decree*:—answer, letter, matter, word.

6601. פָּתָה **pâthâh**, *paw-thaw'*; a prim. root; to *open*, i.e. *be* (causat. *make*) *roomy*; usually fig. (in a mental or moral sense) to *be* (causat. *make*) *simple* or (in a sinister way) *delude*:—allure, deceive, enlarge, entice, flatter, persuade, silly (one).

6602. פְּתוּאֵל **P^ethûw'êl**, *peth-oo-ale'*; from 6601 and 410; *enlarged of God*; *Pethuël*, an Isr.:—Pethuel.

6603. פִּתּוּחַ **pittûwach**, *pit-too'-akh*; or

פִּתֻּחַ **pittûach**, *pit-too'-akh*; pass. part. of 6605; *sculpture* (in low or high relief or even intaglio):—carved (work) (are, en-) grave (-ing, -n).

6604. פְּתוֹר **P^ethôwr**, *peth-ore'*; of for. or.; *Pethor*, a place in Mesopotamia:—Pethor.

6605. פָּתַח **pâthach**, *paw-thakh'*; a prim. root; to *open* wide (lit. or fig.); spec. to *loosen*, *begin*, *plough*, *carve*:—appear, break forth, draw (out), let go free, (en-) grave (-n), loose (self), (be, be set) open (-ing), put off, ungird, unstop, have vent.

6606. פְּתַח **p^ethach** (Chald.), *peth-akh'*; corresp to 6605; to *open*:—open.

6607. פֶּתַח **pethach**, *peh'-thakh*; from 6605; an *opening* (lit.), i.e. *door* (*gate*) or *entrance way*:—door, entering (in), entrance (-ry), gate, opening, place.

6608. פֵּתַח **pêthach**, *pay'-thakh*; from 6605; *opening* (fig.) i.e. *disclosure*:—entrance.

פָּתֻחַ **pâthûach**. See 6603.

6609. פְּתִחָה **p^ethikhâh**, *peth-ee-khaw'*; from 6605; something *opened*, i.e. a *drawn* sword:—drawn sword.

6610. פִּתְחוֹן **pithchôwn**, *pith-khone'*; from 6605; *opening* (the act):—open (-ing).

6611. פְּתַחְיָה **P^ethachyâh**, *peth-akh-yaw'*; from 6605 and 3050; *Jah has opened*; *Pethachjah*, the name of four Isr.:—Pethakiah.

6612. פְּתִי **p^ethîy**, *peth-ee'*; or

פֶּתִי **pethîy**, *peh'-thee*; or

פְּתָאִי **p^ethâ'iy**, *peth-aw-ee'*; from 6601; *silly* (i.e. *seducible*):—foolish, simple (-icity, one).

6613. פְּתַי **p^ethay** (Chald.), *peth-ah'-ee*; from a root corresp. to 6601; *open*, i.e. (as noun) *width*:—breadth.

6614. פְּתִיגִיל **p^ethîygîyl**, *peth-eeg-eel'*; of uncert. der.; prob. a figured *mantle* for holidays:—stomacher.

6615. פְּתַיּוּת **p^ethayûwth**, *peth-ah-yooth'*; from 6612; *silliness* (i.e. *seducibility*):—simple.

6616. פָּתִיל **pâthîyl**, *paw-theel'*; from 6617; *twine*:—bound, bracelet, lace, line, ribband, thread, wire.

6617. פָּתַל **pâthal**, *paw-thal'*; a prim. root; to *twine*, i.e. (lit.) to *struggle* or (fig.) *be* (morally) *tortuous*:—(shew self) froward, shew self unsavoury, wrestle.

6618. פְּתַלְתֹּל **pᵉthaltôl**, *peth-al-tole'*; from 6617; *tortuous* (i.e. crafty):—crooked.

6619. פִּתֹם **Pîthôm**, *pee-thome'*; of Eg. der.; *Pithom*, a place in Eg.:—Pithom.

6620. פֶּתֶן **pethen**, *peh'-then*; from an unused root mean. to *twist*; an *asp* (from its *contortions*):—adder.

6621. פֶּתַע **pethaʻ**, *peh'-thah*; from an unused root mean. to *open* (the eyes); a *wink*, i.e. *moment* [comp. 6597] (used only [with or without prep.] adv. *quickly* or *unexpectedly*):—at an instant suddenly, × very.

6622. פָּתַר **pâthar**, *paw-thar'*; a prim. root; to *open* up, i.e. (fig.) *interpret* (a dream):—interpret (-ation, -er).

6623. פִּתְרוֹן **pithrôwn**, *pith-rone'*; or

פִּתְרֹן **pithrôn**, *pith-rone'*; from 6622; *interpretation* (of a dream):—interpretation.

6624. פַּתְרוֹס **Pathrôwç**, *path-roce'*; of Eg. der.; *Pathros*, a part of Eg.:—Pathros.

6625. פַּתְרֻסִי **Pathrûçîy**, *path-roo-see'*; patrial from 6624; a *Pathrusite*, or inhab. of Pathros:—Pathrusim.

פַּתְשֶׁגֶן **pathshegen**. See 6572.

6626. פָּתַת **pâthath**, *paw-thath'*; a prim. root; to *open*, i.e. *break*:—part.

צ

6627. צָאָה **tsâ'âh**, *tsaw-aw'*; from 3318; *issue*, i.e. (human) *excrement*:—that (which) cometh from (out).

צֹאָה **tsô'âh**. See 6675.

צְאוֹן° **tsᵉ'ôwn**. See 6629.

6628. צֶאֱל **tse'el**, *tseh'-el*; from an unused root mean. to *be slender*; the *lotus* tree:—shady tree.

6629. צֹאן **tsô'n**, *tsone*; or

צְאוֹן° **tsᵉ'ôwn** (Psa. 144 : 13), *tseh-one'*; from an unused root mean. to *migrate*; a collect. name for a *flock* (of sheep or goats); also fig. (of men):—(small) cattle, flock (+ -s), lamb (+ -s), sheep ([-cote, -fold, -shearer, -herds]).

6630. צַאֲנָן **Tsa'ănân**, *tsah-an-awn'*; from the same as 6629 used denom.; *sheep pasture*; *Zaanan*, a place in Pal.:—Zaanan.

6631. צֶאֱצָא **tse'ĕtsâ'**, *tseh-ets-aw'*; from 3318; *issue*, i.e. *produce*, *children*:—that which cometh forth (out), offspring.

6632. צָב **tsâb**, *tsawb*; from an unused root mean. to *establish*; a *palanquin* or *canopy* (as a *fixture*); also a species of *lizard* (prob. as clinging *fast*):—covered, litter, tortoise.

6633. צָבָא **tsâbâ'**, *tsaw-baw'*; a prim. root; to *mass* (an army or servants):—assemble, fight, perform, muster, wait upon, war.

6634. צְבָא **tsᵉbâ'** (Chald.), *tseb-aw'*; corresp. to 6633 in the fig. sense of *summoning* one's wishes; to *please*:—will, would.

6635. צָבָא **tsâbâ'**, *tsaw-baw'*; or (fem.)

צְבָאָה **tsᵉbâ'âh**, *tseb-aw-aw'*; from 6633; a *mass* of persons (or fig. things), espec. reg. organized for war (an *army*); by impl. a *campaign*, lit. or fig. (spec. *hardship*, *worship*):—appointed time, (+) army, (+) battle, company, host, service, soldiers, waiting upon, war (-fare).

6636. צְבֹאִים **Tsᵉbô'îym**, *tseb-o-eem'*; or (more correctly)

צְבִיִּים° **Tsᵉbiyîym**, *tseb-ee-yeem'*; or

צְבִיִּם° **Tsᵉbîyîm**, *tseb-ee-yeem'*; plur. of 6643; *gazelles*; *Tseboïm* or *Tsebijim*, a place in Pal.:—Zeboiim, Zeboim.

6637. צֹבֵבָה **Tsôbêbâh**, *tso-bay-baw'*; fem. act. part. of the same as 6632; the *canopier* (with the art.); *Tsobebah*, an Israelitess:—Zobebah.

6638. צָבָה **tsâbâh**, *tsaw-baw'*; a prim. root; to *amass*, i.e. *grow turgid*; spec. to *array* an army against:—fight, swell.

6639. צָבֶה **tsâbeh**, *tsaw-beh'*; from 6638; *turgid*:—swell.

צֹבָה **Tsôbâh**. See 6678.

6640. צְבוּ **tsᵉbûw** (Chald.), *tseb-oo'*; from 6634; prop. *will*; concr. an *affair* (as a matter of *determination*):—purpose.

6641. צָבוּעַ **tsâbûwaʻ**, *tsaw-boo'-ah*; pass. part. of the same as 6648; *dyed* (in stripes), i.e. the *hyena*:—speckled.

6642. צָבַט **tsâbaṭ**, *tsaw-bat'*; a prim. root; to *grasp*, i.e. *hand* out:—reach.

6643. צְבִי **tsᵉbîy**, *tseb-ee'*; from 6638 in the sense of *prominence*; *splendor* (as *conspicuous*); also a *gazelle* (as *beautiful*):—beautiful (-ty), glorious (-ry), goodly, pleasant, roe (-buck).

6644. צִבְיָא **Tsibyâ'**, *tsib-yaw'*; for 6645; *Tsibja*, an Isr.:—Zibia.

6645. צִבְיָה **Tsibyâh**, *tsib-yaw'*; for 6646; *Tsibjah*, an Israelitess:—Zibiah.

6646. צְבִיָּה **tsᵉbîyâh**, *tseb-ee-yaw'*; fem. of 6643; a *female* gazelle:—roe.

צְבִיִּים° (or צְבִיִּם) **Tsᵉbîyîym**. See 6636.

צְבָיִם° **Tsᵉbâyim**. See 6380.

6647. צְבַע **tsᵉbaʻ** (Chald.), *tseb-ah'*; a root corresp. to that of 6648; to *dip*:—wet.

6648. צֶבַע **tsebaʻ**, *tseh'-bah*; from an unused root mean. to *dip* (into coloring fluid); a *dye*:—divers, colours.

6649. צִבְעוֹן **Tsibʻôwn**, *tsib-one'*; from the same as 6648; *variegated*; *Tsibon*, an Idumæan:—Zibeon.

6650. צְבֹעִים **Tsᵉbôʻîym**, *tseb-o-eem'*; plur. of 6641; *hyenas*; *Tseboïm*, a place in Pal.:—Zeboim.

6651. צָבַר **tsâbar**, *tsaw-bar'*; a prim. root; to *aggregate*:—gather (together), heap (up), lay up.

6652. צִבֻּר **tsibbûr**, *tsib-boor'*; from 6551; a *pile*:—heap.

6653. צֶבֶת **tsebeth**, *tseh'-beth*; from an unused root appar. mean. to *grip*; a *lock* of stalks:—handful.

6654. צַד **tsad**, *tsad*; contr. from an unused root mean. to *sidle* off; a *side*; fig. an *adversary*:—(be-) side.

6655. צַד **tsad** (Chald.), *tsad*; corresp. to 6654; used adv. (with prep.) at or upon the *side* of:—against, concerning.

6656. צְדָא **tsᵉdâ'** (Chald.), *tsed-aw'*; from an unused root corresp. to 6658 in the sense of *intentness*; a (sinister) *design*:—true.

6657. צְדָד **Tsᵉdâd**, *tsed-awd'*; from the same as 6654; a *siding*; *Tsedad*, a place near Pal.:—Zedad.

6658. צָדָה **tsâdâh**, *tsaw-daw'*; a prim. root; to *chase*; by impl. to *desolate*:—destroy, hunt, lie in wait.

צֵדָה **tsêdâh**. See 6720.

6659. צָדוֹק **Tsâdôwq**, *tsaw-doke'*; from 6663; *just*; *Tsadok*, the name of eight or nine Isr.:—Zadok.

6660. צְדִיָּה **tsᵉdîyâh**, *tsed-ee-yaw'*; from 6658; *design* [comp. 6656]:—lying in wait.

6661. צִדִּים **Tsiddîym**, *tsid-deem'*; plur. of 6654; *sides*; *Tsiddim* (with the art.), a place in Pal.:—Ziddim.

6662. צַדִּיק **tsaddîyq**, *tsad-deek'*; from 6663; *just*:—just, lawful, righteous (man).

צִידֹנִי° **Tsîdônîy**. See 6722.

6663. צָדַק **tsâdaq**, *tsaw-dak'*; a prim. root; to *be* (causat. *make*) *right* (in a moral or forensic sense):—cleanse, clear self, (be, do) just (-ice, -ify, -ify self), (be, turn to) righteous (-ness).

6664. צֶדֶק **tsedeq**, *tseh'-dek*; from 6663; the *right* (nat., mor. or legal); also (abstr.) *equity* or (fig.) *prosperity*:—× even, (× that which is altogether) just (-ice), ([un-]) right (-eous) (cause, -ly, -ness).

6665. צִדְקָה **tsidqâh** (Chald.), *tsid-kaw'*; corresp. to 6666; *beneficence*:—righteousness.

6666. צְדָקָה **tsᵉdâqâh**, *tsed-aw-kaw'*; from 6663; *rightness* (abstr.), subj. (*rectitude*), obj. (*justice*), mor. (*virtue*) or fig. (*prosperity*):—justice, moderately, right (-eous) (act, -ly, -ness).

6667. צִדְקִיָּה **Tsidqîyâh**, *tsid-kee-yaw'*; or

צִדְקִיָּהוּ **Tsidqîyâhûw**, *tsid-kee-yaw'-hoo*; from 6664 and 3050; *right of Jah*; *Tsidkijah*, the name of six Isr.:—Zedekiah, Zidkijah.

6668. צָהַב **tsâhab**, *tsaw-hab'*; a prim. root; to *glitter*, i.e. *be golden* in color:—× fine.

6669. צָהֹב **tsâhôb**, *tsaw-obe'*; from 6668; *golden* in color:—yellow.

6670. צָהַל **tsâhal**, *tsaw-hal'*; a prim. root; to *gleam*, i.e. (fig.) *be cheerful*; by transf. to *sound* clear (of various animal or human expressions):—bellow, cry aloud (out), lift up, neigh, rejoice, make to shine, shout.

6671. צָהַר **tsâhar**, *tsaw-har'*; a prim. root; to *glisten*; used only as denom. from 3323, to *press* out *oil*:—make oil.

6672. צֹהַר **tsôhar**, *tso'-har*; from 6671; a *light* (i.e. *window*); dual *double light*, i.e. *noon*:—midday, noon (-day, -tide), window.

6673. צַו **tsav**, *tsav*; or

צָו **tsâv**, *tsawv*; from 6680; an *injunction*:—commandment, precept.

6674. צוֹא **tsôw'**, *tso*; or

צֹא **tsô'**, *tso*; from an unused root mean. to *issue*; *soiled* (as if *excrementitious*):—filthy.

6675. צוֹאָה **tsôw'âh**, *tso-aw'*; or

צֹאָה **tsô'âh**, *tso-aw'*; fem. of 6674; *excrement*; gen. *dirt*; fig. *pollution*:—dung, filth (-iness). Marg. for 2716.

6676. צַוַּאר **tsavva'r** (Chald.), *tsav-var'*; corresp. to 6677:—neck.

6677. צַוָּאר **tsavvâ'r**, *tsav-vawr'*; or

צַוָּר **tsavvâr** (Neh. 3 : 5), *tsav-vawr'*; or

צַוְּרֹן **tsavvârôn** (Cant. 4 : 9), *tsav-vaw-rone'*; or (fem.)

צַוָּארָה **tsavvâ'râh** (Mic. 2 : 3), *tsav-vaw-raw'*; intens. from 6696 in the sense of *binding*; the back of the *neck* (as that on which burdens are *bound*):—neck.

6678. צוֹבָא **Tsôwbâ'**, *tso-baw'*; or

צוֹבָה **Tsôwbâh**, *tso-baw'*; or

צֹבָה **Tsôbâh**, *tso-baw'*; from an unused root mean. to *station*; a *station*; *Zoba* or *Zobah*, a region of Syria:—Zoba, Zobah.

6679. צוּד **tsûwd**, *tsood*; a prim. root; to *lie* alongside (i.e. in wait); by impl. to *catch* an animal (fig. men); (denom. from 6718) to *victual* (for a journey):—chase, hunt, sore, take (provision).

6680. צָוָה **tsâvâh**, *tsaw-vaw'*; a prim. root; (intens.) to *constitute*, *enjoin*:—appoint, (for-) bid, (give a) charge, (give a, give in, send with) command (-er, -ment), send a messenger, put, (set) in order.

6681. צָוַח **tsâvach**, *tsaw-vakh'*; a prim. root; to *screech* (exultingly):—shout.

6682. צְוָחָה **tsᵉvâchâh**, *tsev-aw-khaw'*; from 6681; a *screech* (of anguish):—cry (-ing).

6683. צוּלָה **tsûwlâh**, *tsoo-law'*; from an unused root mean. to *sink*; an *abyss* (of the sea):—deep.

6684. צוּם **tsûwm**, *tsoom*; a prim. root; to *cover* over (the mouth), i.e. to *fast*:—× at all, fast.

6685. צוֹם **tsôwm**, *tsome*; or

צֹם **tsôm**, *tsome*; from 6684; a *fast*:—fast (-ing).

6686. צוּעָר **Tsûw'âr**, *tsoo-awr'*; from 6819; *small; Tsuär*, an Isr.:—Zuar.

6687. צוּף **tsûwph**, *tsoof*; a prim. root; to *overflow*:—(make to over-) flow, swim.

6688. צוּף **tsûwph**, *tsoof*; from 6687; *comb* of honey (from *dripping*):—honeycomb.

6689. צוּף **Tsûwph**, *tsoof*; or

צוֹפַי **Tsôwphay**, *tso-fah'ee*; or

צִיף° **Tsîyph**, *tseef*; from 6688; *honey-comb; Tsuph* or *Tsophai* or *Tsiph*, the name of an Isr. and of a place in Pal.:—Zophai, Zuph.

6690. צוֹפַח **Tsôwphach**, *tso-fakh'*; from an unused root mean. to *expand, breadth; Tsophach*, an Isr.:—Zophah.

צוֹפַי **Tsôwphay**. See 6689.

6691. צוֹפַר **Tsôwphar**, *tso-far'*; from 6852; *departing; Tsophar*, a friend of Job:—Zophar.

6692. צוּץ **tsûwts**, *tsoots*; a prim. root; to *twinkle*, i.e. *glance*; by anal. to *blossom* (fig. *flourish*):—bloom, blossom, flourish, shew self.

6693. צוּק **tsûwq**, *tsook*; a prim. root; to *compress*, i.e. (fig.) *oppress, distress*:—constrain, distress, lie sore, (op-) press (-or), straiten.

6694. צוּק **tsûwq**, *tsook*; a prim. root [rather ident. with 6693 through the idea of *narrowness* (of orifice)]; to *pour* out, i.e. (fig.) *smelt, utter*:—be molten, pour.

6695. צוֹק **tsôwq**, *tsoke*; or (fem.)

צוּקָה **tsûwqâh**, *tsoo-kaw'*; from 6693; a *strait*, i.e. (fig.) *distress*:—anguish, × troublous.

6696. צוּר **tsûwr**, *tsoor*; a prim. root; to *cramp*, i.e. *confine* (in many applications, lit. and fig., formative or hostile):—adversary, assault, beset, besiege, bind (up), cast, distress, fashion, fortify, inclose, lay siege, put up in bags.

6697. צוּר **tsûwr**, *tsoor*; or

צֻר **tsûr**, *tsoor*; from 6696; prop. a *cliff* (or sharp rock, as *compressed*); gen. a *rock* or *boulder*; fig. a *refuge*; also an *edge* (as *precipitous*):—edge, × (mighty) God (one), rock, × sharp, stone, × strength, × strong. See also 1049.

6698. צוּר **Tsûwr**, *tsoor*; the same as 6697; *rock; Tsur*, the name of a Midianite and of an Isr.:—Zur.

צוֹר **Tsôwr**. See 6865.

צַוָּר **tsavvâr**. See 6677.

6699. צוּרָה **tsûwrâh**, *tsoo-raw'*; fem. of 6697; a *rock* (Job 28 : 10); also a *form* (as if *pressed* out):—form, rock.

צַוָּרֹן **tsavvârôn**. See 6677.

6700. צוּרִיאֵל **Tsûwrîy'êl**, *tsoo-ree-ale'*; from 6697 and 410; *rock of God; Tsuriël*, an Isr.:—Zuriel.

6701. צוּרִישַׁדַּי **Tsûwrîyshadday**, *tsoo-ree-shad-dah'ee*; from 6697 and 7706; *rock of* (the) *Almighty; Tsurishaddai*, an Isr.:—Zurishaddai.

6702. צוּת **tsûwth**, *tsooth*; a prim. root; to *blaze*:—burn.

6703. צַח **tsach**, *tsakh*; from 6705; *dazzling*, i.e. *sunny, bright*, (fig.) *evident*:—clear, dry, plainly, white.

צִחָא **Tsîchâ'**. See 6727.

6704. צִחֶה **tsîcheh**, *tsee-kheh'*; from an unused root mean. to *glow; parched*:—dried up.

6705. צָחַח **tsâchach**, *tsaw-khakh'*; a prim. root; to *glare*, i.e. *be dazzling* white:—be whiter.

6706. צְחִיחַ **tsᵉchîyach**, *tsekh-ee'-akh*; from 6705; *glaring*, i.e. *exposed* to the bright sun:—higher place, top.

6707. צְחִיחָה **tsᵉchîychâh**, *tsekh-ee-khaw'*; fem. of 6706; a *parched* region, i.e. the *desert*:—dry land.

6708. צְחִיחִי° **tsᵉchîychîy**, *tsekh-ee-khee'*; from 6706; *bare spot*, i.e. in the *glaring sun*:—higher place.

6709. צַחֲנָה **tsachănâh**, *tsakh-an-aw'*; from an unused root mean. to *putrefy; stench*:—ill savour.

6710. צַחְצָחָה **tsachtsâchâh**, *tsakh-tsaw-khaw'*; from 6705; a *dry* place, i.e. *desert*:—drought.

6711. צָחַק **tsâchaq**, *tsaw-khak'*; a prim. root; to *laugh* outright (in merriment or scorn); by impl. to *sport*:—laugh, mock, play, make sport.

6712. צְחֹק **tsᵉchôq**, *tsekh-oke'*; from 6711; *laughter* (in pleasure or derision):—laugh (-ed to scorn).

6713. צַחַר **tsachar**, *tsakh'-ar*; from an unused root mean. to *dazzle; sheen*, i.e. *whiteness*:—white.

6714. צֹחַר **Tsôchar**, *tso'-khar*; from the same as 6713; *whiteness; Tsochar*, the name of a Hittite and of an Isr.:—Zohar. Comp. 3328.

6715. צָחֹר **tsâchôr**, *tsaw-khore'*; from the same as 6713; *white*:—white.

6716. צִי **tsîy**, *tsee*; from 6680; a *ship* (as a *fixture*):—ship.

6717. צִיבָא **Tsîybâ'**, *tsee-baw'*; from the same as 6678; *station; Tsiba*, an Isr.:—Ziba.

6718. צַיִד **tsayid**, *tsah'-yid*; from a form of 6679 and mean. the same; the *chase*; also *game* (thus taken); (gen.) *lunch* (espec. for a journey):— × catcheth, food, × hunter, (that which he took in) hunting, venison, victuals.

6719. צַיָּד **tsayâd**, *tsah'-yawd*; from the same as 6718; a *huntsman*:—hunter.

6720. צֵידָה **tsêydâh**, *tsay-daw'*; or

צֵדָה **tsêdâh**, *tsay-daw'*; fem. of 6718; *food*:—meat, provision, venison, victuals.

6721. צִידוֹן **Tsîydôwn**, *tsee-done'*; or

צִידֹן **Tsîydôn**, *tsee-done'*; from 6679 in the sense of *catching* fish; *fishery; Tsidon*, the name of a son of Canaan, and of a place in Pal.:—Sidon, Zidon.

6722. צִידֹנִי (or צִדֹנִי°) **Tsîydônîy**, *tsee-do-nee'*; patrial from 6721; a *Tsidonian* or inhab. of Tsidon:—Sidonian, of Sidon, Zidonian.

6723. צִיָּה **tsîyâh**, *tsee-yaw'*; from an unused root mean. to *parch; aridity*; concr. a *desert*:—barren, drought, dry (land, place), solitary place, wilderness.

6724. צִיוֹן **tsîyôwn**, *tsee-yone'*; from the same as 6723; a *desert*:—dry place.

6725. צִיּוּן **tsîyûwn**, *tsee-yoon'*; from the same as 6723 in the sense of *conspicuousness* [comp. 5329]; a monumental or guiding *pillar*:—sign, title, waymark.

6726. צִיּוֹן **Tsîyôwn**, *tsee-yone'*; the same (reg.) as 6725; *Tsijon* (as a permanent *capital*), a mountain of Jerus.:—Zion.

6727. צִיחָא **Tsîychâ'**, *tsee-khaw'*; or

צִחָא **Tsîchâ'**, *tsee-khaw'*; as if fem. of 6704; *drought; Tsicha*, the name of two Nethinim:—Ziha.

6728. צִיִּי **tsîyîy**, *tsee-ee'*; from the same as 6723; a *desert-dweller*, i.e. *nomad* or wild *beast*:—wild beast of the desert, that dwell in (inhabiting) the wilderness.

6729. צִינֹק **tsîynôq**, *tsee-noke'*; from an unused root mean. to *confine*; the *pillory*:—stocks.

6730. צִיעֹר **Tsîy'ôr**, *tsee-ore'*; from 6819; *small; Tsior*, a place in Pal.:—Zior.

צִיף° **Tsîyph**. See 6689.

6731. צִיץ **tsîyts**, *tseets*; or

צִץ **tsîts**, *tseets*; from 6692; prop. *glistening*, i.e. a burnished *plate*; also a *flower* (as *bright* colored); a *wing* (as *gleaming* in the air):—blossom, flower, plate, wing.

6732. צִיץ **Tsîyts**, *tseets*; the same as 6731; *bloom; Tsits*, a place in Pal.:—Ziz.

6733. צִיצָה **tsîytsâh**, *tsee-tsaw'*; fem. of 6731; a *flower*:—flower

6734. צִיצִת **tsîytsîth**, *tsee-tseeth'*; fem. of 6731; a *floral* or *wing*-like projection, i.e. a *fore-lock* of hair, a *tassel*:—fringe, lock.

צִיקְלַג **Tsîyqᵉlag**. See 6860.

6735. צִיר **tsîyr**, *tseer*; from 6696; a *hinge* (as *pressed* in turning); also a *throe* (as a phys. or mental *pressure*); also a *herald* or errand-doer (as *constrained* by the principal):—ambassador, hinge, messenger, pain, pang, sorrow. Comp. 6736.

6736. צִיר **tsîyr**, *tseer*; the same as 6735; a *form* (of beauty; as if *pressed* out, i.e. carved); hence an (idolatrous) *image*:—beauty, idol.

6737. צָיַר **tsâyar**, *tsaw-yar'*; a denom. from 6735 in the sense of *ambassador*; to *make an errand*, i.e. *betake* oneself:—make as if . . . had been ambassador.

6738. צֵל **tsêl**, *tsale*; from 6751; *shade*, whether lit. or fig.:—defence, shade (-ow).

6739. צְלָא **tsᵉlâ'** (Chald.), *tsel-aw'*; prob. corresp. to 6760 in the sense of *bowing; pray*:—pray.

6740. צָלָה **tsâlâh**, *tsaw-law'*; a prim. root; to *roast*:—roast.

6741. צִלָּה **Tsillâh**, *tsil-law'*; fem. of 6738; *Tsillah*, an antediluvian woman:—Zillah.

6742. צְלוּל° **tsᵉlûwl**, *tsel-ool'*; from 6749 in the sense of *rolling*; a (round or flattened) *cake*:—cake.

6743. צָלַח **tsâlach**, *tsaw-lakh'*; or

צָלֵחַ **tsâlêach**, *tsaw-lay'-akh*; a prim. root; to *push* forward, in various senses (lit. or fig., trans. or intrans.):—break out, come (mightily), go over, be good, be meet, be profitable, (cause to, effect, make to, send) prosper (-ity, -ous, -ously).

6744. צְלַח **tsᵉlach** (Chald.), *tsel-akh'*; corresp. to 6743; to *advance* (trans. or intrans.):—promote, prosper.

6745. צֵלָחָה **tsêlâchâh**, *tsay-law-khaw'*; from 6743; something *protracted* or flattened out, i.e. a *platter*:—pan.

6746. צְלֹחִית **tsᵉlôchîyth**, *tsel-o-kheeth'*; from 6743; something *prolonged* or tall, i.e. a *vial* or salt-*cellar*:—cruse.

6747. צַלַּחַת **tsallachath**, *tsal-lakh'-ath*; from 6743; something *advanced* or deep, i.e. a *bowl*; fig. the *bosom*:—bosom, dish.

6748. צָלִי **tsâlîy**, *tsaw-lee'*; pass. part. of 6740; *roasted*:—roast.

6749. צָלַל **tsâlal**, *tsaw-lal'*; a prim. root; prop. to *tumble* down, i.e. *settle* by a waving motion:—sink. Comp. 6750, 6751.

6750. צָלַל **tsâlal**, *tsaw-lal'*; a prim. root [rather ident. with 6749 through the idea of *vibration*]; to *tinkle*, i.e. *rattle* together (as the ears in *reddening* with shame, or the teeth in *chattering* with fear):—quiver, tingle.

6751. צָלַל **tsâlal**, *tsaw-lal'*; a prim. root [rather ident. with 6749 through the idea of *hovering* over (comp. 6754)]; to *shade*, as twilight or an opaque object:—begin to be dark, shadowing.

6752. צֵלֶל **tsêlel**, *tsay'-lel*; from 6751; *shade*:—shadow.

6753. צְלֶלְפּוֹנִי **Tsᵉlelpôwnîy**, *tsel-el-po-nee'*; from 6752 and the act. part. of 6437; *shade-facing; Tselelponi*, an Israelitess:—Hazelelponi [*includ. the art.*].

6754. צֶלֶם **tselem**, *tseh'-lem*; from an unused root mean. to *shade*; a *phantom*, i.e. (fig.) *illusion, resemblance*; hence a representative *figure*, espec. an *idol*:—image, vain shew.

6755. צֶלֶם **tselem** (Chald.), *tseh'-lem*; or

צְלֵם **tsᵉlem** (Chald.), *tsel-em'*; corresp. to 6754; an idolatrous *figure*:—form, image.

6756. צַלְמוֹן **Tsalmôwn**, *tsal-mone'*; from 6754; *shady; Tsalmon*, the name of a place in Pal. and of an Isr.:—Zalmon.

6757. צַלְמָוֶת **tsalmâveth**, *tsal-maw'-veth*; from 6738 and 4194; *shade of death*, i.e. the *grave* (fig. *calamity*):—shadow of death.

6758. צַלְמֹנָה **Tsalmônâh**, *tsal-mo-naw'*; fem. of 6757; *shadiness; Tsalmonah*, a place in the Desert:—Zalmonah.

6759. צַלְמֻנָּע **Tsalmunnâʻ**, *tsal-moon-naw';* from 6738 and 4513; *shade has been denied; Tsalmunna,* a Midianite:—Zalmunna.

6760. צָלַע **tsâlaʻ**, *tsaw-lah';* a prim. root; prob. to *curve;* used only as denom. from 6763, to *limp* (as if *one-sided*):—halt.

6761. צֶלַע **tselaʻ**, *tseh'-lah;* from 6760; a *limping* or *fall* (fig.):—adversity, halt (-ing).

6762. צֶלַע **Tselaʻ**, *tseh'-lah;* the same as 6761; *Tsela,* a place in Pal.:—Zelah.

6763. צֵלָע **tsêlâʻ**, *tsay-law';* or (fem.)

צַלְעָה **tsalʻâh**, *tsal-aw';* from 6760; a *rib* (as *curved*), lit. (of the body) or fig. (of a door, i.e. *leaf*); hence a *side,* lit. (of a person) or fig. (of an object or the sky, i.e. *quarter*); arch. a (espec. floor or ceiling) *timber* or *plank* (single or collect., i.e. a *flooring*):—beam, board, chamber, corner, leaf, plank, rib, side (chamber).

6764. צָלָף **Tsâlâph**, *tsaw-lawf';* from an unused root of unknown mean.; *Tsalaph,* an Isr.:—Zalaph.

6765. צְלָפְחָד **Tselophchâd**, *tsel-of-chawd';* from the same as 6764 and 259; *Tselophchad,* an Isr.:—Zelophehad.

6766. צֶלְצַח **Tseltsach**, *tsel-tsakh';* from 6738 and 6703; *clear shade; Tseltsach,* a place in Pal.:—Zelzah.

6767. צְלָצַל **tselâtsal**, *tsel-aw-tsal';* from 6750 redupl.; a *clatter,* i.e. (abstr.) *whirring* (of wings); (concr.) a *cricket;* also a *harpoon* (as *rattling*), a *cymbal* (as *clanging*):—cymbal, locust, shadowing, spear.

6768. צֶלֶק **Tseleq**, *tseh'-lek;* from an unused root mean. to *split; fissure; Tselek,* an Isr.:—Zelek.

6769. צִלְּתַי **Tsillethay**, *tsil-leth-ah'ee;* from the fem. of 6738; *shady; Tsillethai,* the name of two Isr.:—Zilthai.

צֹם **tsôm**. See 6685.

6770. צָמֵא **tsâmêʼ**, *tsaw-may';* a prim. root; to *thirst* (lit. or fig.):—(be a-, suffer) thirst (-y).

6771. צָמֵא **tsâmêʼ**, *tsaw-may';* from 6770; *thirsty* (lit. or fig.):—(that) thirst (-eth, -y).

6772. צָמָא **tsâmâʼ**, *tsaw-maw';* from 6770; *thirst* (lit. or fig.):—thirst (-y).

6773. צִמְאָה **tsimʼâh**, *tsim-aw';* fem. of 6772; *thirst* (fig. of libidinousnes):—thirst.

6774. צִמָּאוֹן **tsimmâʼôwn**, *tsim-maw-one';* from 6771; a *thirsty* place, i.e. *desert:*—drought, dry ground, thirsty land.

6775. צָמַד **tsâmad**, *tsaw-mad';* a prim. root; to *link,* i.e. *gird;* fig. to *serve,* (mentally) *contrive:*—fasten, frame, join (self).

6776. צֶמֶד **tsemed**, *tseh'-med;* a *yoke* or *team* (i.e. pair); hence an *acre* (i.e. day's task for a yoke of cattle to plough):—acre, couple, × together, two [asses], yoke (of oxen).

6777. צַמָּה **tsammâh**, *tsam-maw';* from an unused root mean. to *fasten* on; a *veil:*—locks.

6778. צַמּוּק **tsammûwq**, *tsam-mook';* from 6784; a cake of *dried* grapes:—bunch (cluster) of raisins.

6779. צָמַח **tsâmach**, *tsaw-makh';* a prim. root; to *sprout* (trans. or intrans., lit. or fig.):—bear, bring forth, (cause to, make to) bud (forth), (cause to, make to) grow (again, up), (cause to) spring (forth, up).

6780. צֶמַח **tsemach**, *tseh'-makh;* from 6779; a *sprout* (usually concr.), lit. or fig.:—branch, bud, that which (where) grew (upon), spring (-ing).

6781. צָמִיד **tsâmîyd**, *tsaw-meed';* or

צָמִד **tsâmîd**, *tsaw-meed';* from 6775; a *bracelet* or *arm-clasp;* gen. a *lid:*—bracelet, covering.

6782. צַמִּים **tsammîym**, *tsam-meem';* from the same as 6777; a *noose* (as *fastening*); fig. *destruction:*—robber.

6783. צְמִיתֻת **tsemîythûth**, *tsem-ee-thooth';* or

צְמִתֻת **tsemîthûth**, *tsem-ee-thooth';* from 6789; *excision,* i.e. *destruction;* used only (adv.) with prep. pref. *to extinction,* i.e. *perpetually:*—ever.

6784. צָמַק **tsâmaq**, *tsaw-mak';* a prim. root; to *dry* up:—dry.

6785. צֶמֶר **tsemer**, *tseh'-mer;* from an unused root prob. mean. to *be shaggy; wool:*—wool (-len).

6786. צְמָרִי **Tsemârîy**, *tsem-aw-ree';* patrial from an unused name of a place in Pal.; a *Tsemarite* or branch of the Canaanites:—Zemarite.

6787. צְמָרַיִם **Tsemârayim**, *tsem-aw-rah'-yim;* dual of 6785; *double fleece; Tsemarajim,* a place in Pal.:—Zemaraim.

6788. צַמֶּרֶת **tsammereth**, *tsam-meh'-reth;* from the same as 6785; *fleeciness,* i.e. *foliage:*—highest branch, top.

6789. צָמַת **tsâmath**, *tsaw-math';* a prim. root; to *extirpate* (lit. or fig.):—consume, cut off, destroy, vanish.

צְמִתֻת **tsemîthûth**. See 6783.

6790. צִן **Tsîn**, *tseen;* from an unused root mean. to *prick; a crag; Tsin,* a part of the Desert:—Zin.

6791. צֵן **tsên**, *tsane;* from an unused root mean. to *be prickly;* a *thorn;* hence a *thorn-hedge:*—thorn.

6792. צֹנֵא **tsônêʼ**, *tso-nay';* or

צֹנֶה **tsôneh**, *tso-neh';* for 6629; a *flock:*—sheep.

6793. צִנָּה **tsinnâh**, *tsin-naw';* fem. of 6791; a *hook* (as *pointed*); also a (large) *shield* (as if guarding by *prickliness*); also *cold* (as *piercing*):—buckler, cold, hook, shield, target.

6794. צִנּוּר **tsinnûwr**, *tsin-noor';* from an unused root perh. mean. to *be hollow;* a *culvert:*—gutter, water-spout.

6795. צָנַח **tsânach**, *tsaw-nakh';* a prim. root; to *alight;* (trans.) to *cause to descend,* i.e. *drive* down:—fasten, light [from off].

6796. צָנִין **tsânîyn**, *tsaw-neen';* or

צָנִן **tsânîn**, *tsaw-neen';* from the same as 6791; a *thorn:*—thorn.

6797. צָנִיף **tsânîyph**, *tsaw-neef';* or

צָנוֹף° **tsânôwph**, *tsaw-nofe';* or (fem.)

צָנִיפָה **tsânîyphâh**, *tsaw-nee-faw';* from 6801; a *head-dress* (i.e. piece of cloth *wrapped* around):—diadem, hood, mitre.

6798. צָנַם **tsânam**, *tsaw-nam';* a prim. root; to *blast* or *shrink:*—withered.

6799. צְנָן **Tsenân**, *tsen-awn';* prob. for 6630; *Tsenan,* a place near Pal.:—Zenan.

צָנִן **tsânîn**. See 6796.

6800. צָנַע **tsânaʻ**, *tsaw-nah';* a prim. root; to *humiliate:*—humbly, lowly.

6801. צָנַף **tsânaph**, *tsaw-naf';* a prim. root; to *wrap,* i.e. *roll* or *dress:*—be attired, × surely, violently turn.

6802. צְנֵפָה **tsenêphâh**, *tsen-ay-faw';* from 6801; a *ball:*— × toss.

6803. צִנְצֶנֶת **tsintseneth**, *tsin-tseh'-neth;* from the same as 6791; a *vase* (prob. a vial *tapering* at the top):—pot.

6804. צַנְתָּרָה **tsantârâh**, *tsan-taw-raw';* prob. from the same as 6794; a *tube:*—pipe.

6805. צָעַד **tsâʻad**, *tsaw-ad';* a prim. root; to *pace,* i.e. *step* regularly; (upward) to *mount;* (along) to *march;* (down and caus.) to *hurl:*—bring, go, march (through), run over.

6806. צַעַד **tsaʻad**, *tsah'-ad;* from 6804; a *pace* or regular *step:*—pace, step.

6807. צְעָדָה **tseʻâdâh**, *tseh-aw-daw';* fem. of 6806; a *march;* (concr.) an (ornamental) *ankle-chain:*—going, ornament of the legs.

6808. צָעָה **tsâʻâh**, *tsaw-aw';* a prim. root; to *tip* over (for the purpose of *spilling* or *pouring* out), i.e. (fig.) *depopulate;* by impl. to *imprison* or *conquer;* (reflex.) to *lie down* (for coition):—captive exile, travelling, (cause to) wander (-er).

צָעוֹר° **tsâʻôwr**. See 6810.

6809. צָעִיף **tsâʻîyph**, *tsaw-eef';* from an unused root mean. to *wrap* over; a *veil:*—vail.

6810. צָעִיר **tsâʻîyr**, *tsaw-eer';* or

צָעוֹר° **tsâʻôwr**, *tsaw-ore';* from 6819; *little;* (in number) *few;* (in age) *young,* (in value) *ignoble:*—least, little (one), small (one), + young (-er, -est).

6811. צָעִיר **Tsâʻîyr**, *tsaw-eer';* the same as 6810; *Tsaïr,* a place in Idumæa:—Zair.

6812. צְעִירָה **tseʻîyrâh**, *tseh-ee-raw';* fem. of 6810; *smallness* (of age), i.e. *juvenility:*—youth.

6813. צָעַן **tsâʻan**, *tsaw-an';* a prim. root; to *load* up (beasts), i.e. to *migrate:*—be taken down.

6814. צֹעַן **Tsôʻan**, *tso'-an;* of Eg. der.; *Tsoän,* a place in Eg.:—Zoan.

6815. צַעֲנַנִּים **Tsaʻănannîym**, *tsah-an-an-neem';* or (dual)

צַעֲנַיִם° **Tsaʻănayim**, *tsah-an-ah'-yim;* plur. from 6813; *removals; Tsaanannim* or *Tsaanajim,* a place in Pal.:—Zaannannim, Zaanaim.

6816. צַעְצֻעַ **tsaʻtsuaʻ**, *tsah-tsoo'-ah;* from an unused root mean. to *bestrew* with carvings; *sculpture:*—image [work].

6817. צָעַק **tsâʻaq**, *tsaw-ak';* a prim. root; to *shriek;* (by impl.) to *proclaim* (an assembly):— × at all, call together, cry (out), gather (selves) (together).

6818. צַעֲקָה **tsaʻăqâh**, *tsah-ak-aw';* from 6817; a *shriek:*—cry (-ing).

6819. צָעַר **tsâʻar**, *tsaw-ar';* a prim. root; to *be small,* i.e. (fig.) *ignoble:*—be brought low, little one, be small.

6820. צֹעַר **Tsôʻar**, *tso'-ar;* from 6819; *little; Tsoär,* a place E. of the Jordan:—Zoar.

6821. צָפַד **tsâphad**, *tsaw-fad';* a prim. root; to *adhere:*—cleave.

6822. צָפָה **tsâphâh**, *tsaw-faw';* a prim. root; prop. to *lean* forward, i.e. to *peer* into the distance; by impl. to *observe, await:*—behold, espy, look up (well), wait for, (keep the) watch (-man).

6823. צָפָה **tsâphâh**, *tsaw-faw';* a prim. root [prob. rather ident. with 6822 through the idea of *expansion* in outlook transf. to act]; to *sheet* over (espec. with metal):—cover, overlay.

6824. צָפָה **tsâphâh**, *tsaw-faw';* from 6823; an *inundation* (as *covering*):— × swimmest.

6825. צְפוֹ **Tsephôw**, *tsef-o';* or

צְפִי **Tsephîy**, *tsef-ee';* from 6822; *observant; Tsepho* or *Tsephi,* an Idumæan:—Zephi, Zepho.

6826. צִפּוּי **tsippûwy**, *tsip-poo'ee;* from 6823; *encasement* (with metal):—covering, overlaying.

6827. צְפוֹן **Tsephôwn**, *tsef-one';* prob. for 6837; *Tsephon,* an Isr.:—Zephon.

6828. צָפוֹן **tsâphôwn**, *tsaw-fone';* or

צָפֹן **tsâphôn**, *tsaw-fone';* from 6845; prop. *hidden,* i.e. *dark;* used only of the *north* as a quarter (*gloomy* and *unknown*):—north (-ern, side, -ward, wind).

6829. צָפוֹן **Tsâphôwn**, *tsaw-fone';* the same as 6828; *boreal; Tsaphon,* a place in Pal.:—Zaphon.

6830. צְפוֹנִי **tsephôwnîy**, *tsef-o-nee';* from 6828; *northern:*—northern.

6831. צְפוֹנִי **Tsephôwnîy**, *tsef-o-nee';* patron. from 6827; a *Tsephonite,* or (collect.) descend. of Tsephon:—Zephonites.

6832. צְפוּעַ° **tsephûwaʻ**, *tsef-oo'-ah;* from the same as 6848; *excrement* (as *protruded*):—dung.

6833. צִפּוֹר **tsippôwr**, *tsip-pore';* or

צִפֹּר **tsippôr**, *tsip-pore';* from 6852; a little *bird* (as *hopping*):—bird, fowl, sparrow.

6834. צִפּוֹר **Tsippôwr**, *tsip-pore'*; the same as 6833; *Tsippor*, a Moabite:—Zippor.

6835. צַפַּחַת **tsappachath**, *tsap-pakh'-ath*; from an unused root mean. to *expand*; a *saucer* (as *flat*):—cruse.

6836. צְפִיָּה **tsᵉphîyâh**, *tsef-ee-yaw'*; from 6822; *watchfulness:*—watching.

6837. צִפְיוֹן **Tsiphyôwn**, *tsif-yone'*; from 6822; *watch*-tower; *Tsiphjon*, an Isr.:—Ziphion. Comp. 6827.

6838. צַפִּיחִת **tsappîychîth**, *tsap-pee-kheeth'*; from the same as 6835; a flat thin *cake:*—wafer.

6839. צֹפִים **Tsôphîym**, *tso-feem'*; plur. of act. part. of 6822; *watchers; Tsophim*, a place E. of the Jordan:—Zophim.

6840. צָפִין° **tsâphîyn**, *tsaw-feen'*; from 6845; a *treasure* (as *hidden*):—hid.

6841. צְפִיר **tsᵉphîyr** (Chald.), *tsef-eer'*; corresp. to 6842; a he-*goat:*—he [goat].

6842. צָפִיר **tsâphîyr**, *tsaw-feer'*; from 6852; a male *goat* (as *prancing*):—(he) goat.

6843. צְפִירָה **tsᵉphîyrâh**, *tsef-ee-raw'*; fem. formed like 6842; a *crown* (as *encircling* the head); also a *turn* of affairs (i.e. *mishap*):—diadem, morning.

6844. צָפִית **tsâphîyth**, *tsaw-feeth'*; from 6822; a *sentry:*—watchtower.

6845. צָפַן **tsâphan**, *tsaw-fan'*; a prim. root; to *hide* (by *covering* over); by impl. to *hoard* or *reserve*; fig. to *deny*; spec. (favorably) to *protect*, (unfavorably) to *lurk:*—esteem, hide (-den one, self), lay up, lurk (be set) privily, (keep) secret (-ly, place).

צָפֹן **tsâphôn**. See 6828.

6846. צְפַנְיָה **Tsᵉphanyâh**, *tsef-an-yaw'*; or

צְפַנְיָהוּ **Tsᵉphanyâhûw**, *tsef-an-yaw'-hoo*; from 6845 and 3050; *Jah has secreted; Tsephanjah*, the name of four Isr.:—Zephaniah.

6847. צָפְנַת פַּעְנֵחַ **Tsophnath Paʿnêach**, *tsof-nath' pah-nay'-akh*; of Eg. der.; *Tsophnath-Paneäch*, Joseph's Eg. name:—Zaphnath-paaneah.

6848. צֶפַע **tsephaʿ**, *tseh'-fah*; or

צִפְעֹנִי **tsiphʿônîy**, *tsif-o-nee'*; from an unused root mean. to *extrude*; a *viper* (as *thrusting* out the tongue, i.e. *hissing*):—adder, cockatrice.

6849. צְפִעָה **tsᵉphiʿâh**, *tsef-ee-aw'*; fem. from the same as 6848; an *outcast* thing:—issue.

צִפְעֹנִי **tsiphʿônîy**. See 6848.

6850. צָפַף **tsâphaph**, *tsaw-faf'*; a prim. root; to *coo* or *chirp* (as a bird):—chatter, peep, whisper.

6851. צַפְצָפָה **tsaphtsâphâh**, *tsaf-tsaw-faw'*; from 6687; a *willow* (as growing in *overflowed* places):—willow tree.

6852. צָפַר **tsâphar**, *tsaw-far'*; a prim. root; to *skip* about, i.e. *return:*—depart early.

6853. צְפַר **tsᵉphar** (Chald.), *tsef-ar'*; corresp. to 6833; a *bird.*—bird.

צִפֹּר **tsippôr**. See 6833.

6854. צְפַרְדֵּעַ **tsᵉphardêaʿ**, *tsef-ar-day'-ah*; from 6852 and a word elsewhere unused mean. a *swamp*; a *marsh-leaper*, i.e. *frog:*—frog.

6855. צִפֹּרָה **Tsippôrâh**, *tsip-po-raw'*; fem. of 6833; *bird; Tsipporah*, Moses' wife:—Zipporah.

6856. צִפֹּרֶן **tsippôren**, *tsip-po'-ren*; from 6852 (in the denom. sense [from 6833] of *scratching*); prop. a *claw*, i.e. (human) *nail;* also the *point* of a style (or pen, tipped with adamant):—nail, point.

6857. צְפַת **Tsᵉphath**, *tsef-ath'*; from 6822; *watch*-tower; *Tsephath*, a place in Pal.:—Zephath.

6858. צֶפֶת **tsepheth**, *tseh'-feth*; from an unused root mean. to *encircle;* a *capital* of a column:—chapiter.

6859. צְפָתָה **Tsᵉphâthâh**, *tsef-aw'-thaw*; the same as 6857; *Tsephathah*, a place in Pal.:—Zephathah.

צִץ **tsîts**. See 6732.

6860. צִקְלַג **Tsiqlâg**, *tsik-lag'*; or

צִיקְלַג **Tsîyqᵉlag** (1 Chron. 12 : 1, 20), *tsee-kel-ag'*; of uncert. der.; *Tsiklag* or *Tsikelag*, a place in Pal.:—Ziklag.

6861. צִקְלֹן **tsiqlôn**, *tsik-lone'*; from an unused root mean. to *wind;* a *sack* (as *tied* at the mouth):—husk.

6862. צַר **tsar**, *tsar*; or

צָר **tsâr**, *tsawr*; from 6887; *narrow;* (as a noun) a *tight* place (usually fig., i.e. *trouble*); also a *pebble* (as in 6864); (trans.) an *opponent* (as *crowding*):—adversary, afflicted (-tion), anguish, close, distress, enemy, flint, foe, narrow, small, sorrow, strait, tribulation, trouble.

6863. צֵר **Tsêr**, *tsare*; from 6887; *rock; Tser*, a place in Pal.:—Zer.

6864. צֹר **tsôr**, *tsore*; from 6696; a *stone* (as if *pressed* hard or to a point); (by impl. of use) a *knife:*—flint, sharp stone.

6865. צֹר **Tsôr**, *tsore*; or

צוֹר **Tsôwr**, *tsore*; the same as 6864; a *rock; Tsor*, a place in Pal.:—Tyre, Tyrus.

צֻר **tsûr**. See 6697.

6866. צָרַב **tsârab**, *tsaw-rab'*; a prim. root; to *burn:*—burn.

6867. צָרֶבֶת **tsârebeth**, *tsaw-reh'-beth*; from 6866; *conflagration* (of fire or disease):—burning, inflammation.

6868. צְרֵדָה **Tsᵉrêdâh**, *tser-ay-daw'*; or

צְרֵדָתָה **Tsᵉrêdâthâh**, *tser-ay-daw'-thaw*; appar. from an unused root mean. to *pierce; puncture; Tseredah*, a place in Pal.:—Zereda, Zeredathah.

6869. צָרָה **tsârâh**, *tsaw-raw'*; fem. of 6862; *tightness* (i.e. fig. *trouble*); trans. a female *rival:*—adversary, adversity, affliction, anguish, distress, tribulation, trouble.

6870. צְרוּיָה **Tsᵉrûwyâh**, *tser-oo-yaw'*; fem. part. pass. from the same as 6875; *wounded; Tserujah*, an Israelitess:—Zeruiah.

6871. צְרוּעָה **Tsᵉrûwʿâh**, *tser-oo-aw'*; fem. pass. part. of 6879; *leprous; Tseruäh*, an Israelitess:—Zeruah.

6872. צְרוֹר **tsᵉrôwr**, *tser-ore'*; or (shorter)

צְרֹר **tsᵉrôr**, *tser-ore'*; from 6887; a *parcel* (as *packed* up); also a *kernel* or *particle* (as if a *package*):—bag, × bendeth, bundle, least grain, small stone.

6873. צָרַח **tsârach**, *tsaw-rakh'*; a prim. root; to *be clear* (in tone, i.e. *shrill*), i.e. to *whoop:*—cry, roar.

6874. צְרִי **Tsᵉrîy**, *tser-ee'*; the same as 6875; *Tseri*, an Isr.:—Zeri. Comp. 3340.

6875. צְרִי **tsᵉrîy**, *tser-ee'*; or

צֳרִי **tsŏrîy**, *tsor-ee'*; from an unused root mean. to *crack* [as by *pressure*], hence to *leak; distillation*, i.e. *balsam:*—balm.

6876. צֹרִי **Tsôrîy**, *tso-ree'*; patrial from 6865; a *Tsorite* or inhab. of Tsor (i.e. *Syrian*):—(man) of Tyre.

6877. צְרִיחַ **tsᵉrîyach**, *tser-ee'-akh*; from 6873 in the sense of *clearness* of vision; a *citadel:*—high place, hold.

6878. צֹרֶךְ **tsôrek**, *tso'-rek*; from an unused root mean. to *need; need:*—need.

6879. צָרַע **tsâraʿ**, *tsaw-rah'*; a prim. root; to *scourge*, i.e. (intrans. and fig.) to *be stricken with leprosy:*—leper, leprous.

6880. צִרְעָה **tsirʿâh**, *tsir-aw'*; from 6879; a *wasp* (as *stinging*):—hornet.

6881. צָרְעָה **Tsorʿâh**, *tsor-aw'*; appar. another form for 6880; *Tsorah*, a place in Pal.:—Zareah, Zorah, Zoreah.

6882. צָרְעִי **Tsorʿîy**, *tsor-ee'*; or

צָרְעָתִי **Tsorʿâthîy**, *tsor-aw-thee'*; patrial from 6881; a *Tsorite* or *Tsorathite*, i.e. inhab. of Tsorah:—Zorites, Zareathites, Zorathites.

6883. צָרַעַת **tsâraʿath**, *tsaw-rah'-ath*; from 6879; *leprosy:*—leprosy.

6884. צָרַף **tsâraph**, *tsaw-raf'*; a prim. root; to *fuse* (metal), i.e. *refine* (lit. or fig.):—cast, (re-) fine (-er), founder, goldsmith, melt, pure, purge away, try.

6885. צֹרְפִי **Tsôrᵉphîy**, *tso-ref-ee'*; from 6884; *refiner; Tsorephi* (with the art.), an Isr.:—goldsmith's.

6886. צָרְפַת **Tsârᵉphath**, *tsaw-ref-ath'*; from 6884; *refinement; Tsarephath*, a place in Pal.:—Zarephath.

6887. צָרַר **tsârar**, *tsaw-rar'*; a prim. root; to *cramp*, lit. or fig., trans. or intrans. (as follows):—adversary, (be in) afflict (-ion), besiege, bind (up), (be in, bring) distress, enemy, narrower, oppress, pangs, shut up, be in a strait (trouble), vex.

6888. צְרֵרָה **Tsᵉrêrâh**, *tser-ay-raw'*; appar. by erroneous transcription for 6868; *Tsererah* for *Tseredah:*—Zererath.

6889. צֶרֶת **Tsereth**, *tseh'-reth*; perh. from 6671; *splendor; Tsereth*, an Isr.:—Zereth.

6890. צֶרֶת הַשַּׁחַר **Tsereth hash-Shachar**, *tseh'-reth hash-shakh'-ar*; from the same as 6889 and 7837 with the art. interposed; *splendor of the dawn; Tsereth-hash-Shachar*, a place in Pal.:—Zareth-shahar.

6891. צָרְתָן **Tsârᵉthân**, *tsaw-reth-awn'*; perh. for 6868; *Tsarethan*, a place in Pal.:—Zarthan.

ק

6892. קֵא **qêʾ**, *kay*; or

קִיא **qîyʾ**, *kee*; from 6958; *vomit;*—vomit.

6893. קָאַת **qâʾath**, *kaw-ath'*; from 6958; prob. the *pelican* (from *vomiting*):—cormorant.

6894. קַב **qab**, *kab*; from 6895; a *hollow*, i.e. vessel used as a (dry) *measure:*—cab.

6895. קָבַב **qâbab**, *kaw-bab'*; a prim. root; to *scoop* out, i.e. (fig.) to *malign* or *execrate* (i.e. *stab* with words):—× at all, curse.

6896. קֵבָה **qêbâh**, *kay-baw'*; from 6895; the *paunch* (as a *cavity*) or first stomach of ruminants:—maw.

6897. קֹבָה **qôbâh**, *ko'-baw*; from 6895; the *abdomen* (as a *cavity*):—belly.

6898. קֻבָּה **qubbâh**, *koob-baw'*; from 6895; a *pavilion* (as a domed *cavity*):—tent.

6899. קִבּוּץ **qibbûwts**, *kib-boots'*; from 6908; a *throng:*—company.

6900. קְבוּרָה **qᵉbûwrâh**, *keb-oo-raw'*; or

קְבֻרָה **qᵉbûrâh**, *keb-oo-raw'*; fem. pass. part. of 6912; *sepulture;* (concr.) a *sepulchre:*—burial, burying place, grave, sepulchre.

6901. קָבַל **qâbal**, *kaw-bal'*; a prim. root; to *admit*, i.e. *take* (lit. or fig.):—choose, (take) hold, receive, (under-) take.

6902. קְבַל **qᵉbal** (Chald.), *keb-al'*; corresp. to 6901; to *acquire:*—receive, take.

6903. קְבֵל **qᵉbêl** (Chald.), *keb-ale'*; or

קֳבֵל **qŏbêl** (Chald.), *kob-ale'*; corresp. to 6905; (adv.) *in front of;* usually (with other particles) *on account of*, *so as, since, hence:*—+ according to, + as, + because, before, + for this cause, + forasmuch as, + by this means, over against, by reason of, + that, + therefore, + though, + wherefore.

6904. קֹבֶל **qôbel**, *ko'-bel*; from 6901 in the sense of *confronting* (as standing *opposite* in order to receive); a *battering-ram:*—war.

6905. קָבָל **qâbâl**, *kaw-bawl'*; from 6901 in the sense of *opposite* [see 6904]; the *presence*, i.e. (adv.) *in front of:*—before.

6906. קָבַע **qâbaʿ**, *kaw-bah'*; a prim. root; to *cover*, i.e. (fig.) *defraud:*—rob, spoil.

6907. קֻבַּעַת **qubbaʻath**, *koob-bah'-ath;* from 6906; a *goblet* (as deep like a *cover*):—dregs.

6908. קָבַץ **qâbats**, *kaw-bats';* a prim. root; to *grasp*, i.e. *collect:*—assemble (selves), gather (bring) (together, selves together, up), heap, resort, × surely, take up.

6909. קַבְצְאֵל **Qabtsᵉʼêl**, *kab-tseh-ale';* from 6908 and 410; *God has gathered; Kabtseël*, a place in Pal.:—Kabzeel. Comp. 3343.

6910. קְבֻצָה **qᵉbûtsâh**, *keb-oo-tsaw';* fem. pass. part. of 6908; a *hoard:*— × gather.

6911. קִבְצַיִם **Qibtsayim**, *kib-tsah'-yim;* dual from 6908; a *double heap; Kibtsajim*, a place in Pal.:—Kibzaim.

6912. קָבַר **qâbar**, *kaw-bar';* a prim. root; to *inter:*— × in any wise, bury (-ier).

6913. קֶבֶר **qeber**, *keh'-ber;* or (fem.)

קִבְרָה **qibrâh**, *kib-raw';* from 6912; a *sepulchre:*—burying place, grave, sepulchre.

קְבֻרָה **qᵉbûrâh**. See 6900.

6914. קִבְרוֹת הַתַּאֲוָה **Qibrôwth hat-Taʼăvâh**, *kib-rōth' hat-tah-av-aw';* from the fem. plur. of 6913 and 8378 with the art. interposed; *graves of the longing; Kibroth-hat-Taavh*, a place in the Desert:—Kibroth-hattaavah.

6915. קָדַד **qâdad**, *kaw-dad';* a prim. root; to *shrivel* up, i.e. *contract* or *bend* the body (or neck) in deference:—bow (down) (the) head, stoop.

6916. קִדָּה **qiddâh**, *kid-daw';* from 6915; *cassia* bark (as in *shrivelled* rolls):—cassia.

6917. קָדוּם **qâdûwm**, *kaw-doom';* pass. part. of 6923; a *pristine* hero:—ancient.

6918. קָדוֹשׁ **qâdôwsh**, *kaw-doshe';* or

קָדֹשׁ **qâdôsh**, *kaw-doshe';* from 6942; *sacred* (ceremonially or morally); (as noun) *God* (by eminence), an *angel*, a *saint*, a *sanctuary:*—holy (One), saint.

6919. קָדַח **qâdach**, *kaw-dakh';* a prim. root to *inflame:*—burn, kindle.

6920. קַדַּחַת **qaddachath**, *kad-dakh'-ath;* from 6919; *inflammation*, i.e. febrile disease:—burning ague, fever.

6921. קָדִים **qâdîym**, *kaw-deem';* or

קָדִם **qâdîm**, *kaw-deem';* from 6923; the *fore* or front part; hence (by orientation) the *East* (often adv. *eastward*, for brevity the *east wind*):—east (-ward, wind).

6922. קַדִּישׁ **qaddîysh** (Chald.), *kad-deesh';* corresp. to 6918.—holy (One), saint.

6923. קָדַם **qâdam**, *kaw-dam';* a prim. root; to *project* (one self), i.e. *precede;* hence to *anticipate, hasten, meet* (usually for help):—come (go, [flee]) before, + disappoint, meet, prevent.

6924. קֶדֶם **qedem**, *keh'-dem;* or

קֵדְמָה **qêdmâh**, *kayd'-maw;* from 6923; the *front*, of place (absol. the *fore part*, rel. the *East*) or time (*antiquity*); often used adv. (*before, anciently, eastward*):—aforetime, ancient (time), before, east (end, part, side, -ward), eternal, × ever (-lasting), forward, old, past. Comp. 6926.

6925. קֳדָם **qŏdâm** (Chald.), *kod-awm';* or

קְדָם **qᵉdâm** (Chald.) (Dan. 7 : 13), *ked-awm';* corresp. to 6924; *before:*—before, × from, × I (thought), × me, + of, × it pleased, presence.

קָדִם **qâdîm**. See 6921.

6926. קִדְמָה **qidmâh**, *kid-maw';* fem. of 6924; the *forward* part (or rel.) *East* (often adv. *on the east* or *in front*):—east (-ward).

6927. קַדְמָה **qadmâh**, *kad-maw';* from 6923; *priority* (in time); also used adv. (*before*):—afore, antiquity, former (old) estate.

6928. קַדְמָה **qadmâh** (Chald.), *kad-maw';* corresp. to 6927; *former* time:—afore [-time], ago.

קֵדְמָה **qêdmâh**. See 6924.

6929. קֵדְמָה **Qêdᵉmâh**, *kayd'-maw;* from 6923; *precedence; Kedemah*, a son of Ishmael:—Kedemah.

6930. קַדְמוֹן **qadmôwn**, *kad-mone';* from 6923; *eastern:*—east.

6931. קַדְמוֹנִי **qadmôwnîy**, *kad-mo-nee';* or

קַדְמֹנִי **qadmônîy**, *kad-mo-nee';* from 6930; (of time) *anterior* or (of place) *oriental:*—ancient, they that went before, east, (thing of) old.

6932. קְדֵמוֹת **Qᵉdêmôwth**, *ked-ay-mothe';* from 6923; *beginnings; Kedemoth*, a place in eastern Pal.:—Kedemoth.

6933. קַדְמַי **qadmay** (Chald.), *kad-mah'ee;* from a root corresp. to 6923; *first:*—first.

6934. קַדְמִיאֵל **Qadmîyʼêl**, *kad-mee-ale';* from 6924 and 410; *presence of God; Kadmiël*, the name of three Isr.:—Kadmiel.

קַדְמֹנִי **qadmônîy**. See 6931.

6935. קַדְמֹנִי **Qadmônîy**, *kad-mo-nee';* the same as 6931; *ancient*, i.e. aboriginal; *Kadmonite* (collect.), the name of a tribe in Pal.:—Kadmonites.

6936. קָדְקֹד **qodqôd**, *kod-kode';* from 6915; the *crown* of the head (as the part most *bowed*):—crown (of the head), pate, scalp, top of the head.

6937. קָדַר **qâdar**, *kaw-dar';* a prim. root; to *be ashy*, i.e. *dark*-colored; by impl. to *mourn* (in sackcloth or sordid garments):—be black (-ish), be (make) dark (-en), × heavily, (cause to) mourn.

6938. קֵדָר **Qêdâr**, *kay-dawr';* from 6937; *dusky* (of the skin or the tent); *Kedar*, a son of Ishmael; also (collect.) *bedawin* (as his descendants or representatives):—Kedar.

6939. קִדְרוֹן **Qidrôwn**, *kid-rone';* from 6937; *dusky* place; *Kidron*, a brook near Jerus.:—Kidron.

6940. קַדְרוּת **qadrûwth**, *kad-rooth';* from 6937; *duskiness:*—blackness.

6941. קְדֹרַנִּית **qᵉdôranniyth**, *ked-o-ran-neeth';* adv. from 6937; *blackish ones* (i.e. *in sackcloth*); used adv. in *mourning* weeds:—mournfully.

6942. קָדַשׁ **qâdâsh**, *kaw-dash';* a prim. root; to *be* (causat. *make, pronounce* or *observe* as) *clean* (ceremonially or morally):—appoint, bid, consecrate, dedicate, defile, hallow, (be, keep) holy (-er, place), keep, prepare, proclaim, purify, sanctify (-ied one, self), × wholly.

6943. קֶדֶשׁ **Qedesh**, *keh'-desh;* from 6942; a *sanctum; Kedesh*, the name of four places in Pal.:—Kedesh.

6944. קֹדֶשׁ **qôdesh**, *ko'-desh;* from 6942; a *sacred* place or thing; rarely abstr. *sanctity:*—consecrated (thing), dedicated (thing), hallowed (thing), holiness, (× most) holy (× day, portion, thing), saint, sanctuary.

6945. קָדֵשׁ **qâdêsh**, *kaw-dashe';* from 6942; a (quasi) *sacred* person, i.e. (techn.) a (male) *devotee* (by prostitution) to licentious idolatry:—sodomite, unclean.

6946. קָדֵשׁ **Qâdêsh**, *kaw-dashe';* the same as 6945; *sanctuary; Kadesh*, a place in the Desert:—Kadesh. Comp. 6947.

קָדֹשׁ **qâdôsh**. See 6918.

6947. קָדֵשׁ בַּרְנֵעַ **Qâdêsh Barnêaʻ**, *kaw-dashe' bar-nay'-ah;* from the same as 6946 and an otherwise unused word (appar. compounded of a correspondent to 1251 and a deriv. of 5128) mean. *desert of a fugitive; Kadesh of* (the) *Wilderness of Wandering; Kadesh-Barneä*, a place in the Desert:—Kadesh-barnea.

6948. קְדֵשָׁה **qᵉdêshâh**, *ked-ay-shaw';* fem. of 6945; a female *devotee* (i.e. *prostitute*):—harlot, whore.

6949. קָהָה **qâhâh**, *kaw-haw';* a prim. root; to be *dull:*—be set on edge, be blunt.

6950. קָהַל **qâhal**, *kaw-hal';* a prim. root; to *convoke:*—assemble (selves) (together), gather (selves) (together).

6951. קָהָל **qâhâl**, *kaw-hawl';* from 6950; *assemblage* (usually concr.):—assembly, company, congregation, multitude.

6952. קְהִלָּה **qᵉhillâh**, *keh-hil-law';* from 6950; an *assemblage:*—assembly, congregation.

6953. קֹהֶלֶת **qôheleth**, *ko-heh'-leth;* fem. of act. part. from 6950; a (female) *assembler* (i.e. lecturer); abstr. *preaching* (used as a "nom de plume", *Koheleth*):—preacher.

6954. קְהֵלָתָה **Qᵉhêlâthâh**, *keh-hay-law'-thaw;* from 6950; *convocation; Kehelathah*, a place in the Desert:—Kehelathah.

6955. קְהָת **Qᵉhâth**, *keh-hawth';* from an unused root mean. to *ally* oneself; *allied; Kehath*, an Isr.:—Kohath.

6956. קֳהָתִי **Qŏhâthîy**, *ko-haw-thee';* patron. from 6955; a *Kohathite* (collect.) or desc. of Kehath:—Kohathites.

6957. קַו **qav**, *kav;* or

קָו **qâv**, *kawv;* from 6960 [comp. 6961]; a *cord* (as *connecting*), espec. for measuring; fig. a *rule;* also a *rim*, a musical *string* or *accord:*—line. Comp. 6978.

6958. קוֹא **qôwʼ**, *ko;* or

קָיָה **qâyâh** (Jer. 25 : 27), *kaw-yaw';* a prim. root; to *vomit:*—spue (out), vomit (out, up, up again).

6959. קוֹבַע **qôwbaʻ**, *ko'-bah* or *ko-bah';* a form collat. to 3553; a *helmet:*—helmet.

6960. קָוָה **qâvâh**, *kaw-vaw';* a prim. root; to *bind* together (perh. by *twisting*), i.e. *collect;* (fig.) to *expect:*—gather (together), look, patiently, tarry, wait (for, on, upon).

6961. קָוֶה **qâveh**, *kaw-veh';* from 6960; a (measuring) *cord* (as if for *binding*):—line.

קוֹחַ **qôwach**. See 6495.

6962. קוּט **qûwṭ**, *koot;* a prim. root; prop. to *cut off*, i.e. (fig.) *detest:*—be grieved, lothe self.

6963. קוֹל **qôwl**, *kole;* or

קֹל **qôl**, *kole;* from an unused root mean. to *call* aloud; a *voice* or *sound:*— + aloud, bleating, crackling, cry (+ out), fame, lightness, lowing, noise, + hold peace, [pro-] claim, proclamation, + sing, sound, + spark, thunder (-ing), voice, + yell.

6964. קוֹלָיָה **Qôwlâyâh**, *ko-law-yaw';* from 6963 and 3050; *voice of Jah; Kolajah*, the name of two Isr.:—Kolaiah.

6965. קוּם **qûwm**, *koom;* a prim. root; to *rise* (in various applications, lit., fig., intens. and caus.):—abide, accomplish, × be clearer, confirm, continue, decree, × be dim, endure, × enemy, enjoin, get up, make good, help, hold, (help to) lift up (again), make, × but newly, ordain, perform, pitch, raise (up), rear (up), remain, (a-) rise (up) (again, against), rouse up, set (up), (e-) stablish, (make to) stand (up), stir up, strengthen, succeed, (as-, make) sure (-ly), (be) up (-hold, -rising).

6966. קוּם **qûwm** (Chald.), *koom;* corresp. to 6965:—appoint, establish, make, raise up self, (a-) rise (up), (make to) stand, set (up).

6967. קוֹמָה **qôwmâh**, *ko-maw';* from 6965; *height:*— × along, height, high, stature, tall.

6968. קוֹמְמִיּוּת **qôwmᵉmîyûwth**, *ko-mem-ee-yooth';* from 6965; *elevation*, i.e. (adv.) *erectly* (fig.):—upright.

6969. קוּן **qûwn**, *koon;* a prim. root; to *strike* a musical note, i.e. *chant* or *wail* (at a funeral):—lament, mourning woman.

6970. קוֹעַ **Qôwaʻ**, *ko'-ah;* prob. from 6972 in the orig. sense of *cutting* off; *curtailment; Koä*, a region of Bab.:—Koa.

6971. קוֹף **qôwph**, *kofe;* or

קֹף **qôph**, *kofe;* prob. of for. or.; a *monkey:*—ape.

6972. קוּץ **qûwts**, *koots;* a prim. root; to *clip* off; used only as denom. from 7019; to *spend the harvest* season:—summer.

6973. קוּץ **qûwts**, *koots;* a prim. root [rather ident. with 6972 through the idea of *severing* oneself from (comp. 6962)]; to be (caus. *make*) *dis-*

gusted or *anxious*:—abhor, be distressed, be grieved, loathe, vex, be weary.

6974. קוּץ **qûwts**, *koots;* a prim. root [rather ident. with 6972 through the idea of *abruptness* in starting up from sleep (comp. 3364)]; to *awake* (lit. or fig.):—arise, (be) (a-) wake, watch.

6975. קוֹץ **qôwts**, *kotse;* or

קֹץ **qôts**, *kotse;* from 6972 (in the sense of *pricking*); a *thorn:*—thorn.

6976. קוֹץ **Qôwts**, *kotse;* the same as 6975; *Kots*, the name of two Isr.:—Koz, Hakkoz [*includ. the art.*].

6977. קְוֻצָּה **qᵉvutstsâh**, *kev-oots-tsaw';* fem. pass. part. of 6972 in its orig. sense; a *forelock* (as *shorn*):—lock.

6978. קַו־קַו **qav-qav**, *kav-kav';* from 6957 (in the sense of a *fastening*); *stalwart:*—× meted out.

6979. קוּר **qûwr**, *koor;* a prim. root; to *trench;* by impl. to *throw forth;* also (denom. from 7023) to *wall up*, whether lit. (to *build* a wall) or fig. (to *estop*):—break down, cast out, destroy, dig.

6980. קוּר **qûwr**, *koor;* from 6979; (only plur.) *trenches*, i.e. a *web* (as if so formed):—web.

6981. קוֹרֵא **Qôwrêʼ**, *ko-ray';* or

קֹרֵא **Qôrêʼ** (1 Chron. 26 : 1), *ko-ray';* act. part. of 7121; *crier; Korè*, the name of two Isr.:—Kore.

6982. קוֹרָה **qôwrâh**, *ko-raw';* or

קֹרָה **qôrâh**, *ko-raw';* from 6979; a *rafter* (forming *trenches* as it were); by impl. a *roof:*—beam, roof.

6983. קוֹשׁ **qôwsh**, *koshe;* a prim. root; to *bend;* used only as denom. for 3369, to *set a trap:*—lay a snare.

6984. קוּשָׁיָהוּ **qûwshâyâhûw**, *koo-shaw-yaw'-hoo;* from the pass. part. of 6983 and 3050; *entrapped of Jah; Kushajah*, an Isr.:—Kushaiah.

6985. קַט **qaṭ**, *kat;* from 6990 in the sense of *abbreviation;* a *little*, i.e. (adv.) *merely:*—very.

6986. קֶטֶב **qeṭeb**, *keh'-teb;* from an unused root mean. to *cut* off; *ruin:*—destroying, destruction.

6987. קֹטֶב **qôṭeb**, *ko'-teb;* from the same as 6986; *extermination:*—destruction.

6988. קְטוֹרָה **qᵉṭôwrâh**, *ket-o-raw';* from 6999; *perfume:*—incense.

6989. קְטוּרָה **Qᵉṭûwrâh**, *ket-oo-raw';* fem. pass. part. of 6999; *perfumed; Keturah*, a wife of Abraham:—Keturah.

6990. קָטַט **qâṭaṭ**, *kaw-tat';* a prim. root; to *clip* off, i.e. (fig.) *destroy:*—be cut off.

6991. קָטַל **qâṭal**, *kaw-tal';* a prim. root; prop. to *cut* off, i.e. (fig.) *put to death:*—kill, slay.

6992. קְטַל **qᵉṭal** (Chald.), *ket-al';* corresp. to 6991; to *kill:*—slay.

6993. קֶטֶל **qeṭel**, *keh'-tel;* from 6991; a violent *death:*—slaughter.

6994. קָטֹן **qâṭôn**, *kaw-tone';* a prim. root [rather denom. from 6996]; to *diminish*, i.e. *be* (caus. *make*) *diminutive* or (fig.) *of no account:*—be a (make) small (thing), be not worthy.

6995. קֹטֶן **qôṭen**, *ko'-ten;* from 6994; a *pettiness*, i.e. the *little finger:*—little finger.

6996. קָטָן **qâṭân**, *kaw-tawn';* or

קָטֹן **qâṭôn**, *kaw-tone';* from 6962; *abbreviated*, i.e. *diminutive*, lit. (in quantity, size or number) or fig. (in age or importance):—least, less (-ser), little (one), small (-est, one, quantity, thing), young (-er, -est).

6997. קָטָן **Qâṭân**, *kaw-tawn';* the same as 6996; *small; Katan*, an Isr.:—Hakkatan [*includ. the art.*].

6998. קָטַף **qâṭaph**, *kaw-taf';* a prim. root; to *strip* off:—crop off, cut down (up), pluck.

6999. קָטַר **qâṭar**, *kaw-tar';* a prim. root [rather ident. with 7000 through the idea of fumigation in a *close* place and perh. thus *driving* out the occupants]; to *smoke*, i.e. turn into fragrance by fire (espec. as an act of worship):—burn (incense, sacrifice) (upon), (altar for) incense, kindle, offer (incense, a sacrifice).

7000. קָטַר **qâṭar**, *kaw-tar';* a prim. root; to *inclose:*—join.

7001. קְטַר **qᵉṭar** (Chald.), *ket-ar';* from a root corresp. to 7000; a *knot* (as *tied* up), i.e. (fig.) a *riddle;* also a *vertebra* (as if a knot):—doubt, joint.

7002. קִטֵּר **qiṭṭêr**, *kit-tare';* from 6999; *perfume:*—incense.

7003. קִטְרוֹן **Qiṭrôwn**, *kit-rone';* from 6999; *fumigative; Kitron*, a place in Pal.:—Kitron.

7004. קְטֹרֶת **qᵉṭôreth**, *ket-o'-reth;* from 6999; a *fumigation:*—(sweet) incense, perfume.

7005. קַטָּת **Qaṭṭâth**, *kat-tawth';* from 6996; *littleness, Kattath*, a place in Pal.:—Kattath.

7006. קָיָה **qâyâh**, *kaw-yaw';* a prim. root; to *vomit:*—spue.

7007. קַיִט **qâyiṭ** (Chald.), *kah'-yit;* corresp. to 7019; *harvest:*—summer.

7008. קִיטוֹר **qîyṭôwr**, *kee-tore';* or

קִיטֹר **qîyṭôr**, *kee-tore';* from 6999; a *fume*, i.e. *cloud:*—smoke, vapour.

7009. קִים **qîym**, *keem;* from 6965; an *opponent* (as *rising* against one), i.e. (collect.) enemies:—substance.

7010. קְיָם **qᵉyâm** (Chald.), *keh-yawm';* from 6966; an *edict* (as *arising* in law):—decree, statute.

7011. קַיָּם **qayâm** (Chald.), *kah-yawm';* from 6966; *permanent* (as *rising* firmly):—stedfast, sure.

7012. קִימָה **qîymâh**, *kee-maw';* from 6965; an *arising:*—rising up.

קִימוֹשׁ **Qîymôwsh.** See 7057.

7013. קַיִן **qayin**, *kah'-yin;* from 6969 in the orig. sense of *fixity;* a *lance* (as *striking fast*):—spear.

7014. קַיִן **Qayin**, *kah'-yin;* the same as 7013 (with a play upon the affinity to 7069); *Kajin*, the name of the first child, also of a place in Pal., and of an Oriental tribe:—Cain, Kenite (-s).

7015. קִינָה **qîynâh**, *kee-naw';* from 6969; a *dirge* (as accompanied by *beating* the breasts or on instruments):—lamentation.

7016. קִינָה **Qîynâh**, *kee-naw';* the same as 7015; *Kinah*, a place in Pal.:—Kinah.

7017. קֵינִי **Qêynîy**, *kay-nee';* or

קִינִי **Qîynîy** (1 Chron. 2 : 55), *kee-nee';* patron. from 7014; a *Kenite* or member of the tribe of Kajin:—Kenite.

7018. קֵינָן **Qêynân**, *kay-nawn';* from the same as 7064; *fixed; Kenan*, an antediluvian:—Cainan, Kenan.

7019. קַיִץ **qayits**, *kah'-yits;* from 6972; *harvest* (as the *crop*), whether the product (grain or fruit) or the (dry) season:—summer (fruit, house).

7020. קִיצוֹן **qîytsôwn**, *kee-tsone';* from 6972; *terminal:*—out- (utter-) most.

7021. קִיקָיוֹן **qîyqâyôwn**, *kee-kaw-yone';* perh. from 7006; the *gourd* (as *nauseous*):—gourd.

7022. קִיקָלוֹן **qîyqâlôwn**, *kee-kaw-lone';* from 7036; intense *disgrace:*—shameful spewing.

7023. קִיר **qîyr**, *keer;* or

קִר **qîr** (Isa. 22 : 5), *keer;* or (fem.)

קִירָה **qîyrâh**, *kee-raw';* from 6979; a *wall* (as built in a *trench*):— + mason, side, town, × very, wall.

7024. קִיר **Qîyr**, *keer;* the same as 7023; *fortress; Kir*, a place in Ass.; also one in Moab:—Kir. Comp. 7025.

7025. קִיר חֶרֶשׂ **Qîyr Cheres**, *keer kheh'-res;* or (fem. of the latter word)

קִיר חֲרֶשֶׂת **Qîyr Chăreseth**, *keer khar-eh'-seth;* from 7023 and 2789; *fortress of earthenware; Kir-Cheres* or *Kir-Chareseth*, a place in Moab:—Kir-haraseth, Kir-hareseth, Kir-haresh, Kir-heres.

7026. קֵירֹס **Qêyrôç**, *kay-roce';* or

קֵרֹס **Qêrôç**, *kay-roce';* from the same as 7166; *ankled; Keros*, one of the Nethinim:—Keros.

7027. קִישׁ **Qîysh**, *keesh;* from 6983; a *bow; Kish*, the name of five Isr.:—Kish.

7028. קִישׁוֹן **Qîyshôwn**, *kee-shone';* from 6983; *winding; Kishon*, a river of Pal.:—Kishon, Kison.

7029. קִישִׁי **Qîyshîy**, *kee-shee';* from 6983; *bowed; Kishi*, an Isr.:—Kishi.

7030. קִיתָרֹס° **qîythârôç** (Chald.), *kee-thaw-roce';* of Gr. origin (κίθαρις); a *lyre:*—harp.

7031. קַל **qal**, *kal;* contr. from 7043; *light;* (by impl.) *rapid* (also adv.):—light, swift (-ly).

7032. קָל **qâl** (Chald.), *kawl;* corresp. to 6963:—sound, voice.

קֹל **qôl.** See 6963.

7033. קָלָה **qâlâh**, *kaw-law';* a prim. root [rather ident. with 7034 through the idea of *shrinkage* by heat]; to *toast*, i.e. *scorch* partially or slowly:—dried, loathsome, parch, roast.

7034. קָלָה **qâlâh**, *kaw-law';* a prim. root; to *be light* (as implied in *rapid* motion), but fig. only (*be* [caus. *hold*] *in contempt*):—base, contemn, despise, lightly esteem, set light, seem vile.

7035. קָלַהּ **qâlahh**, *kaw-lah';* for 6950; to *assemble:*—gather together.

7036. קָלוֹן **qâlôwn**, *kaw-lone';* from 7034; *disgrace;* (by impl.) the *pudenda:*—confusion, dishonour, ignominy, reproach, shame.

7037. קַלַּחַת **qallachath**, *kal-lakh'-ath;* appar. but a form for 6747; a *kettle:*—caldron.

7038. קָלַט **qâlaṭ**, *kaw-lat';* a prim. root; to *maim:*—lacking in his parts.

7039. קָלִי **qâlîy**, *kaw-lee';* or

קָלִיא **qâlîyʼ**, *kaw-lee';* from 7033; *roasted* ears of grain:—parched corn.

7040. קַלַּי **Qallay**, *kal-lah'ee;* from 7043; *frivolous; Kallai*, an Isr.:—Kallai.

7041. קֵלָיָה **Qêlâyâh**, *kay-law-yaw';* from 7034; *insignificance; Kelajah*, an Isr.:—Kelaiah.

7042. קְלִיטָא **Qᵉlîyṭâʼ**, *kel-ee-taw';* from 7038; *maiming; Kelita*, the name of three Isr.:—Kelita.

7043. קָלַל **qâlal**, *kaw-lal';* a prim. root; to *be* (caus. *make*) *light*, lit. (*swift, small, sharp*, etc.) or fig. (*easy, trifling, vile*, etc.):—abate, make bright, bring into contempt, (ac-) curse, despise, (be) ease (-y, -ier), (be a, make, make somewhat, move, seem a, set) light (-en, -er, -ly, -ly afflict, -ly esteem, thing), × slight [-ly], be swift (-er), (be, be more, make, re-) vile, whet.

7044. קָלָל **qâlâl**, *kaw-lawl';* from 7043; *brightened* (as if *sharpened*):—burnished, polished.

7045. קְלָלָה **qᵉlâlâh**, *kel-aw-law';* from 7043; *vilification:*—(ac-) curse (-d, -ing).

7046. קָלַס **qâlaç**, *kaw-las';* a prim. root; to *disparage*, i.e. ridicule:—mock, scoff, scorn.

7047. קֶלֶס **qeleç**, *keh'-les;* from 7046; a *laughing-stock:*—derision.

7048. קַלָּסָה **qallâçâh**, *kal-law-saw';* intens. from 7046; *ridicule:*—mocking.

7049. קָלַע **qâlaʻ**, *kaw-lah';* a prim. root; to *sling;* also to *carve* (as if a *circular* motion, or into *light* forms):—carve, sling (out).

7050. קֶלַע **qelaʻ**, *keh'-lah;* from 7049; a *sling;* also a (door) *screen* (as if *slung* across), or the *valve* (of the door) itself:—hanging, leaf, sling.

7051. קַלָּע **qallâʻ**, *kal-law';* intens. from 7049; a *slinger:*—slinger.

7052. קְלֹקֵל **q^{e}lôqêl**, *kel-o-kale'*; from 7043; *insubstantial*:—light.

7053. קִלְּשׁוֹן **qill^{e}shôwn**, *kil-lesh-one'*; from an unused root mean. to *prick*; a *prong*, i.e. hay-*fork*:—fork.

7054. קָמָה **qâmâh**, *kaw-maw'*; fem. of act. part. of 6965; something that *rises*, i.e. a *stalk* of grain:—(standing) corn, grown up, stalk.

7055. קְמוּאֵל **Q^{e}mûw'êl**, *kem-oo-ale'*; from 6965 and 410; *raised of God*; *Kemuël*, the name of a relative of Abraham, and of two Isr.:—Kemuel.

7056. קָמוֹן **Qâmôwn**, *kaw-mone'*; from 6965; an *elevation*; *Kamon*, a place E. of the Jordan:—Camon.

7057. קִמּוֹשׁ **qimmôwsh**, *kim-moshe'*; or

קִימוֹשׁ **qîymôwsh**, *kee-moshe'*; from an unused root mean. to *sting*; a *prickly* plant:—nettle. Comp. 7063.

7058. קֶמַח **qemach**, *keh'-makh*; from an unused root prob. mean. to *grind*; *flour*:—flour, meal.

7059. קָמַט **qâmaṭ**, *kaw-mat'*; a prim. root; to *pluck*, i.e. destroy:—cut down, fill with wrinkles.

7060. קָמַל **qâmal**, *kaw-mal'*; a prim. root; to *wither*:—hew down, wither.

7061. קָמַץ **qâmats**, *kaw-mats'*; a prim. root; to *grasp* with the hand:—take an handful.

7062. קֹמֶץ **qômets**, *ko'-mets*; from 7061; a *grasp*, i.e. *handful*:—handful.

7063. קִמָּשׁוֹן **qimmâshôwn**, *kim-maw-shone'*; from the same as 7057; a *prickly* plant:—thorn.

7064. קֵן **qên**, *kane*; contr. from 7077; a *nest* (as *fixed*), sometimes includ. the *nestlings*; fig. a *chamber* or *dwelling*:—nest, room.

7065. קָנָא **qânâ'**, *kaw-naw'*; a prim. root; to *be* (caus. *make*) *zealous*, i.e. (in a bad sense) *jealous* or *envious*:—(be) envy (-ious), be (move to, provoke to) jealous (-y), × very, (be) zeal (-ous).

7066. קְנָא **q^{e}nâ'** (Chald.), *ken-aw'*; corresp. to 7069; to *purchase*:—buy.

7067. קַנָּא **qannâ'**, *kan-naw'*; from 7065; *jealous*:—jealous. Comp. 7072.

7068. קִנְאָה **qin'âh**, *kin-aw'*; from 7065; *jealousy* or *envy*:—envy (-ied), jealousy, × sake, zeal.

7069. קָנָה **qânâh**, *kaw-naw'*; a prim. root; to *erect*, i.e. *create*; by extens. to *procure*, espec. by purchase (caus. *sell*); by impl. to *own*:—attain, buy (-er), teach to keep cattle, get, provoke to jealousy, possess (-or), purchase, recover, redeem, × surely, × verily.

7070. קָנֶה **qâneh**, *kaw-neh'*; from 7069; a *reed* (as *erect*); by resemblance a *rod* (espec. for measuring), *shaft*, *tube*, *stem*, the *radius* (of the arm), *beam* (of a steelyard):—balance, bone, branch, calamus, cane, reed, × spearman, stalk.

7071. קָנָה **Qânâh**, *kaw-naw'*; fem. of 7070; *reediness*; *Kanah*, the name of a stream and of a place in Pal.:—Kanah.

7072. קַנּוֹא **qannôw'**, *kan-no'*; for 7067; *jealous* or *angry*:—jealous.

7073. קְנַז **Q^{e}naz**, *ken-az'*; prob. from an unused root mean. to *hunt*; *hunter*; *Kenaz*, the name of an Edomite and of two Isr.:—Kenaz.

7074. קְנִזִּי **Q^{e}nizzîy**, *ken-iz-zee'*; patron. from 7073; a *Kenizzite* or desc. of Kenaz:—Kenezite, Kenizzites.

7075. קִנְיָן **qinyân**, *kin-yawn'*; from 7069; *creation*, i.e. (concr.) *creatures*; also *acquisition*, *purchase*, *wealth*:—getting, goods, × with money, riches, substance.

7076. קִנָּמוֹן **qinnâmôwn**, *kin-naw-mone'*; from an unused root (mean. to *erect*); *cinnamon* bark (as in *upright* rolls):—cinnamon.

7077. קָנַן **qânan**, *kaw-nan'*; a prim. root; to *erect*; but used only as denom. from 7064; to *nestle*, i.e. *build* or *occupy* as a nest:—make . . . nest.

7078. קֶנֶץ **qenets**, *keh'-nets*; from an unused root prob. mean. to *wrench*; *perversion*:—end.

7079. קְנָת **Q^{e}nâth**, *ken-awth'*; from 7069; *possession*; *Kenath*, a place E. of the Jordan:—Kenath.

7080. קָסַם **qâçam**, *kaw-sam'*; a prim. root; prop. to *distribute*, i.e. *determine* by lot or magical scroll; by impl. to *divine*:—divine (-r, -ation), prudent, soothsayer, use [divination].

7081. קֶסֶם **qeçem**, *keh'-sem*; from 7080; a *lot*; also *divination* (includ. its *fee*), *oracle*:—(reward of) divination, divine sentence, witchcraft.

7082. קָסַס **qâçaç**, *kaw-sas'*; a prim. root; to *lop* off:—cut off.

7083. קֶסֶת **qeçeth**, *keh'-seth*; from the same as 3563 (or as 7185); prop. a *cup*, i.e. an *ink-stand*:—inkhorn.

7084. קְעִילָה **Q^{e}'îylâh**, *keh-ee-law'*; perh. from 7049 in the sense of *inclosing*; *citadel*; *Keïlah*, a place in Pal.:—Keilah.

7085. קַעֲקַע **qa'ăqa'**, *kah-ak-ah'*; from the same as 6970; an *incision* or gash:— + mark.

7086. קְעָרָה **q^{e}'ârâh**, *keh-aw-raw'*; prob. from 7167; a *bowl* (as *cut* out hollow):—charger, dish.

קֹף **qôph**. See 6971.

7087. קָפָא **qâphâ'**, *kaw-faw'*; a prim. root; to *shrink*, i.e. *thicken* (as unracked wine, curdled milk, clouded sky, frozen water):—congeal, curdle, dark°, settle.

7088. קָפַד **qâphad**, *kaw-fad'*; a prim. root; to *contract*, i.e. roll together:—cut off.

7089. קְפָדָה **q^{e}phâdâh**, *kef-aw-daw'*; from 7088; *shrinking*, i.e. terror:—destruction.

7090. קִפּוֹד **qippôwd**, *kip-pode'*; or

קִפֹּד **qippôd**, *kip-pode'*; from 7088; a species of bird, perh. the *bittern* (from its *contracted* form):—bittern.

7091. קִפּוֹז **qippôwz**, *kip-poze'*; from an unused root mean. to *contract*, i.e. *spring* forward; an *arrow-snake* (as *darting* on its prey):—great owl.

7092. קָפַץ **qâphats**, *kaw-fats'*; a prim. root; to *draw together*, i.e. close; by impl. to *leap* (by *contracting* the limbs); spec. to *die* (from *gathering* up the feet):—shut (up), skip, stop, take out of the way.

7093. קֵץ **qêts**, *kates*; contr. from 7112; an *extremity*; adv. (with prep. pref.) *after*:— + after, (utmost) border, end, [in-] finite, × process.

קוֹץ **qôts**. See 6975.

7094. קָצַב **qâtsab**, *kaw-tsab'*; a prim. root; to *clip*, or (gen.) *chop*:—cut down, shorn.

7095. קֶצֶב **qetseb**, *keh'-tseb*; from 7094; *shape* (as if *cut* out); *base* (as if there *cut* off):—bottom, size.

7096. קָצָה **qâtsâh**, *kaw-tsaw'*; a prim. root; to *cut* off; (fig.) to *destroy*; (partially) to *scrape* off:—cut off, cut short, scrape (off).

7097. קָצֶה **qâtseh**, *kaw-tseh'*; or (neg. only)

קֵצֶה **qêtseh**, *kay'-tseh*; from 7096; an *extremity* (used in a great variety of applications and idioms; comp. 7093):— × after, border, brim, brink, edge, end, [in-] finite, frontier, outmost coast, quarter, shore, (out-) side, × some, ut (-ter-) most (part).

7098. קָצָה **qâtsâh**, *kaw-tsaw'*; fem. of 7097; a *termination* (used like 7097):—coast, corner, (selv-) edge, lowest, (uttermost) part.

7099. קֶצֶו **qetsev**, *keh'-tsev*; and (fem.)

קִצְוָה **qitsvâh**, *kits-vaw'*; from 7096; a *limit* (used like 7097, but with less variety):—end, edge, uttermost part.

7100. קֶצַח **qetsach**, *keh'-tsakh*; from an unused root appar. mean. to *incise*; *fennel-flower* (from its *pungency*):—fitches.

7101. קָצִין **qâtsîyn**, *kaw-tseen'*; from 7096 in the sense of *determining*; a *magistrate* (as *deciding*) or other *leader*:—captain, guide, prince, ruler. Comp. 6278.

7102. קְצִיעָה **q^{e}tsîy'âh**, *kets-ee-aw'*; from 7106; *cassia* (as *peeled*; plur. the *bark*):—cassia.

7103. קְצִיעָה **Q^{e}tsîy'âh**, *kets-ee-aw'*; the same as 7102; *Ketsiah*, a daughter of Job:—Kezia.

7104. קְצִיץ **Q^{e}tsîyts**, *kets-eets'*; from 7112; *abrupt*; *Keziz*, a valley in Pal.:—Keziz.

7105. קָצִיר **qâtsîyr**, *kaw-tseer'*; from 7114; *severed*, i.e. *harvest* (as *reaped*), the crop, the time, the reaper, or fig.; also a *limb* (of a tree, or simply *foliage*):—bough, branch, harvest (man).

7106. קָצַע **qâtsa'**, *kaw-tsah'*; a prim. root; to *strip* off, i.e. (partially) *scrape*; by impl. to *segregate* (as an angle):—cause to scrape, corner.

7107. קָצַף **qâtsaph**, *kaw-tsaf'*; a prim. root; to *crack* off, i.e. (fig.) *burst* out in rage:—(be) anger (-ry), displease, fret self, (provoke to) wrath (come), be wroth.

7108. קְצַף **q^{e}tsaph** (Chald.), *kets-af'*; corresp. to 7107; to *become enraged*:—be furious.

7109. קְצַף **q^{e}tsaph** (Chald.), *kets-af'*; from 7108; *rage*:—wrath.

7110. קֶצֶף **qetseph**, *keh'-tsef*; from 7107; a *splinter* (as *chipped* off); fig. *rage* or *strife*:—foam, indignation, × sore, wrath.

7111. קְצָפָה **q^{e}tsâphâh**, *kets-aw-faw'*; from 7107; a *fragment*:—bark [-ed].

7112. קָצַץ **qâtsats**, *kaw-tsats'*; a prim. root; to *chop* off (lit. or fig.):—cut (asunder, in pieces, in sunder, off), × utmost.

7113. קְצַץ **q^{e}tsats** (Chald.), *kets-ats'*; corresp. to 7112:—cut off.

7114. קָצַר **qâtsar**, *kaw-tsar'*; a prim. root; to *dock* off, i.e. *curtail* (trans. or intrans., lit. or fig.); espec. to *harvest* (grass or grain):— × at all, cut down, much discouraged, grieve, harvestman, lothe, mourn, reap (-er), (be, wax) short (-en, -er), straiten, trouble, vex.

7115. קֹצֶר **qôtser**, *ko'-tser*; from 7114; *shortness* (of spirit), i.e. impatience:—anguish.

7116. קָצֵר **qâtsêr**, *kaw-tsare'*; from 7114; *short* (whether in size, number, life, strength or temper):—few, hasty, small, soon.

7117. קְצָת **q^{e}tsâth**, *kets-awth'*; from 7096; a *termination* (lit. or fig.); also (by impl.) a *portion*; adv. (with prep. pref.) *after*:—end, part, × some.

7118. קְצָת **q^{e}tsâth** (Chald.), *kets-awth'*; corresp. to 7117:—end, partly.

7119. קַר **qar**, *kar*; contr. from an unused root mean. to *chill*; *cool*; fig. *quiet*:—cold, excellent [*from the marg.*].

קִר **qîr**. See 7023.

7120. קֹר **qôr**, *kore*; from the same as 7119; *cold*:—cold.

7121. קָרָא **qârâ'**, *kaw-raw'*; a prim. root [rather ident. with 7122 through the idea of *accosting* a person met]; to *call* out to (i.e. prop. *address* by name, but used in a wide variety of applications):—bewray [self], that are bidden, call (for, forth, self, upon), cry (unto), (be) famous, guest, invite, mention, (give) name, preach, (make) proclaim (-ation), pronounce, publish, read, renowned, say.

7122. קָרָא **qârâ'**, *kaw-raw'*; a prim. root; to *encounter*, whether accidentally or in a hostile manner:—befall, (by) chance, (cause to) come (upon), fall out, happen, meet.

7123. קְרָא **q^{e}râ'** (Chald.), *ker-aw'*; corresp. to 7121:—call, cry, read.

7124. קֹרֵא **qôrê'**, *ko-ray'*; prop. act. part. of 7121; a *caller*, i.e. *partridge* (from its *cry*):—partridge. See also 6981.

7125. קִרְאָה **qir'âh**, *keer-aw'*; from 7122; an *encountering*, accidental, friendly or hostile (also adv. *opposite*):— × against (he come), help, meet, seek, × to, × in the way.

7126. קָרַב **qârab**, *kaw-rab'*; a prim. root; to *approach* (caus. *bring near*) for whatever purpose:—(cause to) approach, (cause to) bring (forth, near), (cause to) come (near, nigh), (cause to) draw near (nigh), go (near), be at hand, join, be near, offer, present, produce, make ready, stand, take.

7127. קְרֵב **qᵉrêb** (Chald.), *ker-abe'*; corresp. to 7126:—approach, come (near, nigh), draw near.

7128. קְרָב **qᵉrâb**, *ker-awb'*; from 7126; hostile *encounter:*—battle, war.

7129. קְרָב **qᵉrâb** (Chald.), *ker-awb'*; corresp. to 7128:—war.

7130. קֶרֶב **qereb**, *keh'-reb*; from 7126; prop. the *nearest* part, i.e. the *centre*, whether lit., fig. or adv. (espec. with prep.):— × among, × before, bowels, × unto charge, + eat (up), × heart, × him, × in, inward (× -ly, part, -s, thought), midst, + out of, purtenance, × therein, × through, × within self.

7131. קָרֵב **qârêb**, *kaw-rabe'*; from 7126; *near:*—approach, come (near, nigh), draw near.

קָרֹב **qârôb**. See 7138.

7132. קְרָבָה **qᵉrâbâh**, *ker-aw-baw'*; from 7126; *approach:*—approaching, draw near.

7133. קָרְבָּן **qorbân**, *kor-bawn'*; or

קֻרְבָּן **qurbân**, *koor-bawn'*; from 7126; something *brought near* the altar, i.e. a sacrificial *present:*—oblation, that is offered, offering.

7134. קַרְדֹּם **qardôm**, *kar-dome'*; perh. from 6923 in the sense of *striking* upon; an *axe:*—ax.

7135. קָרָה **qârâh**, *kaw-raw'*; fem. of 7119; *coolness:*—cold.

7136. קָרָה **qârâh**, *kaw-raw'*; a prim. root; to *light upon* (chiefly by accident); caus. to *bring about;* spec. to *impose* timbers (for roof or floor):—appoint, lay (make) beams, befall, bring, come (to pass unto), floor, [hap] was, happen (unto), meet, send good speed.

7137. קָרֶה **qâreh**, *kaw-reh'*; from 7136; an (unfortunate) *occurrence*, i.e. some accidental (ceremonial) *disqualification:*—uncleanness that chanceth.

קֹרָה **qôrâh**. See 6982.

7138. קָרוֹב **qârôwb**, *kaw-robe'*; or

קָרֹב **qârôb**, *kaw-robe'*; from 7126; *near* (in place, kindred or time):—allied, approach, at hand, + any of kin, kinsfolk (-sman), (that is) near (of kin), neighbour, (that is) next, (them that come) nigh (at hand), more ready, short (-ly).

7139. קָרַח **qârach**, *kaw-rakh'*; a prim. root; to *depilate:*—make (self) bald.

7140. קֶרַח **qerach**, *keh'-rakh*; or

קֹרַח **qôrach**, *ko'-rakh*; from 7139; *ice* (as if bald, i.e. *smooth*); hence, *hail;* by resemblance, rock *crystal:*—crystal, frost, ice.

7141. קֹרַח **Qôrach**, *ko'-rakh*; from 7139; *ice; Korach*, the name of two Edomites and three Isr.:—Korah.

7142. קֵרֵחַ **qêrêach**, *kay-ray'-akh*; from 7139; *bald* (on the back of the head):—bald (head).

7143. קָרֵחַ **Qârêach**, *kaw-ray'-akh*; from 7139; *bald; Kareăch*, an Isr.:—Careah, Kareah.

7144. קָרְחָה **qorchâh**, *kor-khaw'*; or

קָרְחָא **qorchâ'** (Ezek. 27 : 31), *kor-khaw'*; from 7139; *baldness:*—bald (-ness), × utterly.

7145. קָרְחִי **Qorchîy**, *kor-khee'*; patron. from 7141; a *Korchite* (collect.) or desc. of Korach:—Korahite, Korathite, sons of Kore, Korhite.

7146. קָרַחַת **qârachath**, *kaw-rakh'-ath*; from 7139; a *bald* spot (on the back of the head); fig. a *threadbare* spot (on the back side of the cloth):—bald head, bare within.

7147. קְרִי **qᵉrîy**, *ker-ee'*; from 7136; hostile *encounter:*—contrary.

7148. קָרִיא **qârîy'**, *kaw-ree'*; from 7121; *called*, i.e. *select:*—famous, renowned.

7149. קִרְיָא **qiryâ'** (Chald.), *keer-yaw'*; or

קִרְיָה **qiryâh** (Chald.), *keer-yaw'*; corresp. to 7151:—city.

7150. קְרִיאָה **qᵉrîy'âh**, *ker-ee-aw'*; from 7121; a *proclamation:*—preaching.

7151. קִרְיָה **qiryâh**, *kir-yaw'*; from 7136 in the sense of *flooring*, i.e. building; a *city:*—city.

7152. קְרִיּוֹת **Qᵉrîyôwth**, *ker-ee-yōth'*; plur. of 7151; *buildings; Kerioth*, the name of two places in Pal.:—Kerioth, Kirioth.

7153. קִרְיַת אַרְבַּע **Qiryath 'Arba'**, *keer-yath' ar-bah'*; or (with the art. interposed)

קִרְיַת הָאַרְבַּע **Qiryath hâ-'Arba'** (Neh. 11 : 25), *keer-yath' haw-ar-bah'*; from 7151 and 704 or 702; *city of Arba*, or *city of the four* (giants); *Kirjath-Arba* or *Kirjath-ha-Arba*, a place in Pal.:—Kirjath-arba.

7154. קִרְיַת בַּעַל **Qiryath Ba'al**, *keer-yath' bah'-al;* from 7151 and 1168; *city of Baal; Kirjath-Baal*, a place in Pal.:—Kirjath-baal.

7155. קִרְיַת חֻצוֹת **Qiryath Chûtsôwth**, *keer-yath' khoo-tsōth'*; from 7151 and the fem. plur. of 2351; *city of streets; Kirjath-Chutsoth*, a place in Moab:—Kirjath-huzoth.

7156. קִרְיָתַיִם **Qiryâthayim**, *keer-yaw-thah'-yim;* dual of 7151; *double city; Kirjathaïm*, the name of two places in Pal.:—Kiriathaim, Kirjathaim.

7157. קִרְיַת יְעָרִים **Qiryath Yᵉ'ârîym**, *keer-yath' yeh-aw-reem'*; or (Jer. 26 : 20) with the art. interposed; or (Josh. 18 : 28) simply the former part of the word; or

קִרְיַת עָרִים **Qiryath 'Ârîym**, *keer-yath' aw-reem'*; from 7151 and the plur. of 3293 or 5892; *city of forests*, or *city of towns; Kirjath-Jeärim* or *Kirjath-Arim*, a place in Pal.:—Kirjath, Kirjath-jearim, Kirjath-arim.

7158. קִרְיַת סַנָּה **Qiryath Çannâh**, *keer-yath' san-naw'*; or

קִרְיַת סֵפֶר **Qiryath Çêpher**, *keer-yath' say'-fer;* from 7151 and a simpler fem. from the same as 5577, or (for the latter name) 5612; *city of branches*, or *of a book; Kirjath-Sannah* or *Kirjath-Sepher*, a place in Pal.:—Kirjath-sannah, Kirjath-sepher.

7159. קָרַם **qâram**, *kaw-ram'*; a prim. root; to *cover:*—cover.

7160. קָרַן **qâran**, *kaw-ran'*; a prim. root; to *push* or gore; used only as denom. from 7161, to *shoot out horns;* fig. *rays:*—have horns, shine.

7161. קֶרֶן **qeren**, *keh'-ren;* from 7160; a *horn* (as *projecting*); by impl. a *flask, cornet;* by resembl. an elephant's *tooth* (i.e. *ivory*), a *corner* (of the altar), a *peak* (of a mountain), a *ray* (of light); fig. *power:*— × hill, horn.

7162. קֶרֶן **qeren** (Chald.), *keh'-ren;* corresp. to 7161; a *horn* (lit. or for sound):—horn, cornet.

7163. קֶרֶן הַפּוּךְ **qeren hap-pûwk**, *keh'-ren hap-pook'*; from 7161 and 6320; *horn of cosmetic; Keren-hap-Puk*, one of Job's daughters:—Keren-happuch.

7164. קָרַס **qâraç**, *kaw-ras'*; a prim. root; prop. to *protrude;* used only as denom. from 7165 (for alliteration with 7167), to *hunch*, i.e. be humpbacked:—stoop.

7165. קֶרֶס **qereç**, *keh'-res;* from 7164; a *knob* or belaying-pin (from its swelling form):—tache.

קֵרֹס **Qêrôç**. See 7026.

7166. קַרְסֹל **qarçôl**, *kar-sole'*; from 7164; an *ankle* (as a *protuberance* or joint):—foot.

7167. קָרַע **qâra'**, *kaw-rah'*; a prim. root; to *rend*, lit. or fig. (*revile, paint* the eyes, as if enlarging them):—cut out, rend, × surely, tear.

7168. קֶרַע **qera'**, *keh'-rah;* from 7167; a *rag:*—piece, rag.

7169. קָרַץ **qârats**, *kaw-rats'*; a prim. root; to *pinch*, i.e. (partially) to *bite* the lips, *blink* the eyes (as a gesture of malice), or (fully) to *squeeze* off (a piece of clay in order to mould a vessel from it):—form, move, wink.

7170. קְרַץ **qᵉrats** (Chald.), *ker-ats'*; corresp. to 7171 in the sense of a *bit* (to "eat the *morsels* of" any one, i.e. *chew* him up [fig.] by *slander*):— + accuse

7171. קֶרֶץ **qerets**, *keh'-rets;* from 7169; *extirpation* (as if by *constriction*):—destruction.

7172. קַרְקַע **qarqa'**, *kar-kah';* from 7167; *floor* (as if a pavement of pieces or *tesseræ*), of a building or the sea:—bottom, (× one side of the) floor.

7173. קַרְקַע **Qarqa'**, *kar-kah';* the same as 7172; *ground-floor; Karka* (with the art. pref.), a place in Pal.:—Karkaa.

7174. קַרְקֹר **Qarqôr**, *kar-kore';* from 6979; *foundation; Karkor*, a place E. of the Jordan:—Karkor.

7175. קֶרֶשׁ **qeresh**, *keh'-resh;* from an unused root mean. to *split* off; a *slab* or plank; by impl. a *deck* of a ship:—bench, board.

7176. קֶרֶת **qereth**, *keh'-reth;* from 7136 in the sense of building; a *city:*—city.

7177. קַרְתָּה **Qartâh**, *kar-taw';* from 7176; *city; Kartah*, a place in Pal.:—Kartah.

7178. קַרְתָּן **Qartân**, *kar-tawn';* from 7176; *city-plot; Kartan*, a place in Pal.:—Kartan.

7179. קַשׁ **qash**, *kash;* from 7197; *straw* (as *dry*):—stubble.

7180. קִשֻּׁא **qishshû'**, *kish-shoo';* from an unused root (mean. to be *hard*); a *cucumber* (from the difficulty of *digestion*):—cucumber.

7181. קָשַׁב **qâshab**, *kaw-shab';* a prim. root; to *prick up* the ears, i.e. *hearken:*—attend, (cause to) hear (-ken), give heed, incline, mark (well), regard.

7182. קֶשֶׁב **qesheb**, *keh'-sheb;* from 7181; a *hearkening:*— × diligently, hearing, much heed, that regarded.

7183. קַשָּׁב **qashshâb**, *kash-shawb';* or

קַשֻּׁב **qashshûb**, *kash-shoob';* from 7181; *hearkening:*—attent (-ive).

7184. קָשָׂה **qâsâh**, *kaw-saw';* or

קַשְׂוָה **qasvâh**, *kas-vaw';* from an unused root mean. to be *round;* a *jug* (from its shape):—cover, cup.

7185. קָשָׁה **qâshâh**, *kaw-shaw';* a prim. root; prop. to *be dense*, i.e. tough or *severe* (in various applications):—be cruel, be fiercer, make grievous, be ([ask a], be in, have, seem, would) hard (-en, [labour], -ly, thing), be sore, (be, make) stiff (-en, [-necked]).

7186. קָשֶׁה **qâsheh**, *kaw-sheh';* from 7185; *severe* (in various applications):—churlish, cruel, grievous, hard ([-hearted], thing), heavy, + impudent, obstinate, prevailed, rough (-ly), sore, sorrowful, stiff ([-necked]), stubborn, + in trouble.

7187. קְשׁוֹט **qᵉshôwṭ** (Chald.), *kesh-ote';* or

קְשֹׁט **qᵉshôṭ** (Chald.), *kesh-ote';* corresp. to 7189; *fidelity:*—truth.

7188. קָשַׁח **qâshach**, *kaw-shakh';* a prim. root; to *be* (caus. *make*) *unfeeling:*—harden.

7189. קֹשֶׁט **qôsheṭ**, *ko'-shet;* or

קֹשְׁטְ **qôshṭ**, *kōsht;* from an unused root mean. to *balance; equity* (as evenly *weighed*), i.e. *reality:*—certainty, truth.

קֹשֹׁט **qôshôṭ**. See 7187.

7190. קְשִׁי **qᵉshîy**, *kesh-ee';* from 7185; *obstinacy:*—stubbornness.

7191. קִשְׁיוֹן **Qishyôwn**, *kish-yone';* from 7190; *hard ground; Kishjon*, a place in Pal.:—Kishion, Keshon.

7192. קְשִׂיטָה **qᵉsîyṭah**, *kes-ee-taw';* from an unused root (prob. mean. to *weigh* out); an *ingot* (as definitely *estimated* and stamped for a coin):—piece of money (silver).

7193. קַשְׂקֶשֶׂת **qasqeseth**, *kas-keh'-seth;* by redupl. from an unused root mean. to *shale* off as bark; a *scale* (of a fish); hence a coat of *mail* (as composed of or covered with jointed *plates* of metal):—mail, scale.

7194. קָשַׁר **qâshar**, *kaw-shar';* a prim. root; to *tie*, phys. (*gird, confine, compact*) or ment. (in *love, league*):—bind (up), (make a) conspire (-acy, -ator), join together, knit, stronger, work [treason].

7195. קֶשֶׁר **qesher**, *keh'-sher;* from 7194; an (unlawful) *alliance:*—confederacy, conspiracy, treason.

7196. קִשֻּׁר **qishshûr**, *kish-shoor';* from 7194; an (ornamental) *girdle* (for women):—attire, headband.

7197. קָשַׁשׁ **qâshash**, *kaw-shash';* a prim. root; to *become sapless* through drought; used only as denom. from 7179; to *forage* for straw, stubble or wood; fig. to *assemble:*—gather (selves) (together).

7198. קֶשֶׁת **qesheth**, *keh'-sheth;* from 7185 in the orig. sense (of 6983) of *bending;* a *bow,* for *shooting* (hence fig. *strength*) or the *iris:*—× arch (-er), + arrow, bow ([-man, -shot]).

7199. קַשָּׁת **qashshâth**, *kash-shawth';* intens. (as denom.) from 7198; a *bowman:*—× archer.

ר

7200. רָאָה **râ'âh**, *raw-aw';* a prim. root; to *see,* lit. or fig. (in numerous applications, direct and implied, trans., intrans. and causat.):—advise self, appear, approve, behold, × certainly, consider, discern, (make to) enjoy, have experience, gaze, take heed, × indeed, × joyfully, lo, look (on, one another, one on another, one upon another, out, up, upon), mark, meet, × be near, perceive, present, provide, regard, (have) respect, (fore-, cause to, let) see (-r, -m, one another), shew (self), × sight of others, (e-) spy, stare, × surely, × think, view, visions.

7201. רָאָה **râ'âh**, *raw-aw';* from 7200; a *bird* of prey (prob. the *vulture,* from its sharp *sight*):—glede. Comp. 1676.

7202. רָאֶה **râ'eh**, *raw-eh';* from 7200; *seeing,* i.e. experiencing:—see.

7203. רֹאֶה **rô'eh**, *ro-eh';* act. part. of 7200; a *seer* (as often rendered); but also (abstr.) a *vision:*—vision.

7204. רֹאֵה **Rô'êh**, *ro-ay';* for 7203; *prophet; Roëh,* an Isr.:—Haroeh [*includ. the art.*].

7205. רְאוּבֵן **Re'ûwbên**, *reh-oo-bane';* from the imper. of 7200 and 1121; *see ye a son; Reüben,* a son of Jacob:—Reuben.

7206. רְאוּבֵנִי **Re'ûwbênîy**, *reh-oo-bay-nee';* patron. from 7205; a *Reübenite* or desc. of Reüben:—children of Reuben, Reubenites.

7207. רַאֲוָה **ra'ăvâh**, *rah-av-aw';* from 7200; *sight,* i.e. satisfaction:—behold.

7208. רְאוּמָה **Re'ûwmâh**, *reh-oo-maw';* fem. pass. part. of 7213; *raised; Reümah,* a Syrian woman:—Reumah.

7209. רְאִי **re'îy**, *reh-ee';* from 7200; a *mirror* (as *seen*):—looking glass.

7210. רֳאִי **rô'îy**, *ro-ee';* from 7200; *sight,* whether abstr. (*vision*) or concr. (a *spectacle*):—gazingstock, look to, (that) see (-th).

7211. רְאָיָה **Re'âyâh**, *reh-aw-yaw';* from 7200 and 3050; *Jah has seen; Reäjah,* the name of three Isr.:—Reaia, Reaiah.

7212. רְאִית **re'îyth**, *reh-eeth';* from 7200; *sight:*—beholding.

7213. רָאַם **râ'am**, *raw-am';* a prim. root; to *rise:*—be lifted up.

7214. רְאֵם **re'êm**, *reh-ame';* or

רְאֵים **re'êym**, *reh-ame';* or

רֵים **rêym**, *rame;* or

רֵם **rêm**, *rame;* from 7213; a wild *bull* (from its *conspicuousness*):—unicorn.

7215. רָאמָה **râ'mâh**, *raw-maw';* from 7213; something *high* in value, i.e. perh. *coral:*—coral.

7216. רָאמוֹת **Râ'môwth**, *raw-mōth';* or

רָאמֹת **Râmôth**, *raw-mōth';* plur. of 7215; *heights; Ramoth,* the name of two places in Pal.:—Ramoth.

7217. רֵאשׁ **rê'sh** (Chald.), *raysh;* corresp. to 7218; the *head;* fig. the *sum:*—chief, head, sum.

7218. רֹאשׁ **rô'sh**, *roshe;* from an unused root appar. mean. to *shake;* the *head* (as most easily *shaken*), whether lit. or fig. (in many applications, of place, time, rank, etc.):—band, beginning, captain, chapiter, chief (-est place, man, things), company, end, × every [man], excellent, first, forefront, ([be-]) head, height, (on) high (-est part, [priest]), × lead, × poor, principal, ruler, sum, top.

7219. רֹאשׁ **rô'sh**, *roshe;* or

רוֹשׁ **rôwsh** (Deut. 32 : 32), *roshe;* appar. the same as 7218; a poisonous *plant,* prob. the *poppy* (from its conspicuous *head*); gen. *poison* (even of serpents):—gall, hemlock, poison, venom.

7220. רֹאשׁ **Rô'sh**, *roshe;* prob. the same as 7218; *Rosh,* the name of an Isr. and of a for. nation:—Rosh.

רֵאשׁ **rê'sh**. See 7389.

7221. רִאשָׁה **rî'shâh**, *ree-shaw';* from the same as 7218; a *beginning:*—beginning.

7222. רֹאשָׁה **rô'shâh**, *ro-shaw';* fem. of 7218; the *head:*—head [-stone].

7223. רִאשׁוֹן **rî'shôwn**, *ree-shone';* or

רִאשֹׁן **rî'shôn**, *ree-shone';* from 7221; *first,* in place, time or rank (as adj. or noun):—ancestor, (that were) before (-time), beginning, eldest, first, fore [-father] (-most), former (thing), of old time, past.

7224. רִאשֹׁנִי **rî'shônîy**, *ree-sho-nee';* from 7223; *first:*—first.

7225. רֵאשִׁית **rê'shîyth**, *ray-sheeth';* from the same as 7218; the *first,* in place, time, order or rank (spec. a *firstfruit*):—beginning, chief (-est), first (-fruits, part, time), principal thing.

7226. רַאֲשֹׁת **ra'ăshôth**, *rah-ash-ōth';* from 7218; a *pillow* (being for the *head*):—bolster.

7227. רַב **rab**, *rab;* by contr. from 7231; *abundant* (in quantity, size, age, number, rank, quality):—(in) abound (-undance, -ant, -antly), captain, elder, enough, exceedingly, full, great (-ly, man, one), increase, long (enough, [time]), (do, have) many (-ifold, things, a time), ([ship-]) master, mighty, more, (too, very) much, multiply (-tude), officer, often [-times], plenteous, populous, prince, process [of time], suffice (-ient).

7228. רַב **rab**, *rab;* by contr. from 7232; an *archer* [or perh. the same as 7227]:—archer.

7229. רַב **rab** (Chald.), *rab;* corresp. to 7227:—captain, chief, great, lord, master, stout.

רִב **rîb**. See 7378.

7230. רֹב **rôb**, *robe;* from 7231; *abundance* (in any respect):—abundance (-antly), all, × common [sort], excellent, great (-ly, -ness, number), huge, be increased, long, many, more in number, most, much, multitude, plenty (-ifully), × very [age].

7231. רָבַב **râbab**, *raw-bab';* a prim. root; prop. to *cast* together [comp. 7241], i.e. *increase,* espec. in number; also (as denom. from 7233) to *multiply by the myriad:*—increase, be many (-ifold), be more, multiply, ten thousands.

7232. רָבַב **râbab**, *raw-bab';* a prim. root [rather ident. with 7231 through the idea of *projection*]; to *shoot* an arrow:—shoot.

7233. רְבָבָה **rebâbâh**, *reb-aw-baw';* from 7231; *abundance* (in number), i.e. (spec.) a *myriad* (whether def. or indef.):—many, million, × multiply, ten thousand.

7234. רָבַד **râbad**, *raw-bad';* a prim. root; to *spread:*—deck.

7235. רָבָה **râbâh**, *raw-baw';* a prim. root; to *increase* (in whatever respect):—[bring in] abundance (× -antly), + archer [*by mistake for* 7232], be in authority, bring up, × continue, enlarge, excel, exceeding (-ly), be full of, (be, make) great (-er, -ly, × -ness), grow up, heap, increase, be long, (be, give, have, make, use) many (a time), (any, be, give, give the, have) more (in number), (ask, be, be so, gather, over, take, yield) much (greater, more), (make to) multiply, nourish, plenty (-eous), × process [of time], sore, store, thoroughly, very.

7236. רְבָה **rebâh** (Chald.), *reb-aw';* corresp. to 7235:—make a great man, grow.

7237. רַבָּה **Rabbâh**, *rab-baw';* fem. of 7227; *great; Rabbah,* the name of two places in Pal., E. and W.:—Rabbah, Rabbath.

7238. רְבוּ **rebûw** (Chald.), *reb-oo';* from a root corresp. to 7235; *increase* (of dignity):—greatness, majesty.

7239. רִבּוֹ **ribbôw**, *rib-bo';* from 7231; or

רִבּוֹא **ribbôw'**, *rib-bo';* from 7231; a *myriad,* i.e. indef. *large number:*—great things, ten ([eight] -een, [for] -ty, + sixscore, + threescore, × twenty, [twen] -ty) thousand.

7240. רִבּוֹ **ribbôw** (Chald.), *rib-bo';* corresp. to 7239:—× ten thousand times ten thousand.

7241. רָבִיב **râbîyb**, *raw-beeb';* from 7231; a *rain* (as an *accumulation* of drops):—shower.

7242. רָבִיד **râbîyd**, *raw-beed';* from 7234; a *collar* (as *spread* around the neck):—chain.

7243. רְבִיעִי **rebîy'îy**, *reb-ee-ee';* or

רְבִעִי **rebî'îy**, *reb-ee-ee';* from 7251; *fourth;* also (fractionally) a *fourth:*—foursquare, fourth (part).

7244. רְבִיעַי **rebîy'ay** (Chald.), *reb-ee-ah'ee;* corresp. to 7243:—fourth.

7245. רַבִּית **Rabbîyth**, *rab-beeth';* from 7231; *multitude; Rabbith,* a place in Pal.:—Rabbith.

7246. רָבַךְ **râbak**, *raw-bak';* a prim. root; to *soak* (bread in oil):—baken, (that which is) fried.

7247. רִבְלָה **Riblâh**, *rib-law';* from an unused root mean. to *be fruitful; fertile; Riblah,* a place in Syria:—Riblah.

7248. רַב־מָג **Rab-Mâg**, *rab-mawg';* from 7227 and a for. word for a Magian; *chief Magian; Rab-Mag,* a Bab. official:—Rab-mag.

7249. רַב־סָרִיס **Rab-Çârîyç**, *rab-saw-reece';* from 7227 and a for. word for a eunuch; *chief chamberlain; Rab-Saris,* a Bab. official:—Rab-saris.

7250. רָבַע **râba'**, *raw-bah';* a prim. root; to *squat* or *lie out flat,* i.e. (spec.) in copulation:—let gender, lie down.

7251. רָבַע **râba'**, *raw-bah';* a prim. root [rather ident. with 7250 through the idea of *sprawling* "at all fours" (or possibly the reverse is the order of deriv.); comp. 702]; prop. to *be four* (sided); used only as denom. of 7253; to *be quadrate:*—(four-) square (-d).

7252. רֶבַע **reba'**, *reh'-bah;* from 7250; *prostration* (for sleep):—lying down.

7253. רֶבַע **reba'**, *reh'-bah;* from 7251; a *fourth* (part or side):—fourth part, side, square.

7254. רֶבַע **Reba'**, *reh'-bah;* the same as 7253; *Reba,* a Midianite:—Reba.

7255. רֹבַע **rôba'**, *ro'-bah;* from 7251; a *quarter:*—fourth part.

7256. רִבֵּעַ **ribbêa'**, *rib-bay'-ah;* from 7251; a descendant of the *fourth* generation, i.e. *great great grandchild:*—fourth.

רְבִעִי **rebîy'îy**. See 7243.

7257. רָבַץ **râbats**, *raw-bats';* a prim. root; to *crouch* (on all four legs folded, like a recumbent animal); by impl. to *recline, repose, brood, lurk, imbed:*—crouch (down), fall down, make a fold, lay, (cause to, make to) lie (down), make to rest, sit.

7258. רֶבֶץ **rebets**, *reh'-bets;* from 7257; a *couch* or place of repose:—where each lay, lie down in, resting place.

7259. רִבְקָה **Ribqâh**, *rib-kaw'*; from an unused root prob. mean. to *clog* by tying up the fetlock; *fettering* (by beauty); *Ribkah*, the wife of Isaac:—Rebekah.

7260. רַבְרַב **rabrab** (Chald.), *rab-rab'*; from 7229; *huge* (in size); *domineering* (in character):—(very) great (things).

7261. רַבְרְבָן **rabrᵉbân** (Chald.), *rab-reb-awn'*; from 7260; a *magnate*:—lord, prince.

7262. רַבְשָׁקֵה **Rabshâqêh**, *rab-shaw-kay'*; from 7227 and 8248; *chief butler*; *Rabshakeh*, a Bab. official:—Rabshakeh.

7263. רֶגֶב **regeb**, *reh'-gheb*; from an unused root mean. to *pile* together; a *lump* of clay:—clod.

7264. רָגַז **râgaz**, *raw-gaz'*; a prim. root; to *quiver* (with any violent emotion, espec. anger or fear):—be afraid, stand in awe, disquiet, fall out, fret, move, provoke, quake, rage, shake, tremble, trouble, be wroth.

7265. רְגַז **rᵉgaz** (Chald.), *reg-az'*; corresp. to 7264:—provoke unto wrath.

7266. רְגַז **rᵉgaz** (Chald.), *reg-az'*; from 7265; violent *anger*:—rage.

7267. רֹגֶז **rôgez**, *ro'-ghez*; from 7264; *commotion*, *restlessness* (of a horse), *crash* (of thunder), *disquiet*, *anger*:—fear, noise, rage, trouble (-ing), wrath.

7268. רַגָּז **raggâz**, *rag-gawz'*; intens. from 7264; *timid*:—trembling.

7269. רָגְזָה **rogzâh**, *rog-zaw'*; fem. of 7267; *trepidation*:—trembling.

7270. רָגַל **râgal**, *raw-gal'*; a prim. root; to *walk* along; but only in spec. applications, to *reconnoitre*, to *be a tale-bearer* (i.e. slander); also (as denom. from 7272) to *lead about*:—backbite, search, slander, (e-) spy (out), teach to go, view.

7271. רְגַל **rᵉgal** (Chald.), *reg-al'*; corresp. to 7272:—foot.

7272. רֶגֶל **regel**, *reh'-gel*; from 7270; a *foot* (as used in *walking*); by impl. a *step*; by euphem. the *pudenda*:— × be able to endure, × according as, × after, × coming, × follow, ([broken-]) foot ([-ed, -stool]), × great toe, × haunt, × journey, leg, + piss, + possession, time.

7273. רַגְלִי **raglîy**, *rag-lee'*; from 7272; a *footman* (soldier):—(on) foot (-man).

7274. רֹגְלִים **Rôgᵉlîym**, *ro-gel-eem'*; plur. of act. part. of 7270; *fullers* (as *tramping* the cloth in washing); *Rogelim*, a place E. of the Jordan:—Rogelim.

7275. רָגַם **râgam**, *raw-gam'*; a prim. root [comp. 7263, 7321, 7551]; to *cast* together (stones), i.e. to *lapidate*:— × certainly, stone.

7276. רֶגֶם **Regem**, *reh'-gem*; from 7275; *stone-heap*; *Regem*, an Isr.:—Regem.

7277. רִגְמָה **rigmâh**, *rig-maw'*; fem. of the same as 7276; a *pile* (of stones), i.e. (fig.) a *throng*:—council.

7278. רֶגֶם מֶלֶךְ **Regem Melek**, *reh'-gem meh'-lek*; from 7276 and 4428; *king's heap*; *Regem-Melek*, an Isr.:—Regem-melech.

7279. רָגַן **râgan**, *raw-gan'*; a prim. root; to *grumble*, i.e. *rebel*:—murmur.

7280. רָגַע **râgaʿ**, *raw-gah'*; a prim. root; prop. to *toss* violently and suddenly (the sea with waves, the skin with boils); fig. (in a favorable manner) to *settle*, i.e. quiet; spec. to *wink* (from the motion of the eye-lids):—break, divide, find ease, be a moment, (cause, give, make to) rest, make suddenly.

7281. רֶגַע **regaʿ**, *reh'-gah*; from 7280; a *wink* (of the eyes), i.e. a very *short space* of time:—instant, moment, space, suddenly.

7282. רָגֵעַ **râgêaʿ**, *raw-gay'-ah*; from 7280; *restful*, i.e. peaceable:—that are quiet.

7283. רָגַשׁ **râgash**, *raw-gash'*; a prim. root; to *be tumultuous*:—rage.

7284. רְגַשׁ **rᵉgash** (Chald.), *reg-ash'*; corresp. to 7283; to *gather* tumultuously:—assemble (together).

7285. רֶגֶשׁ **regesh**, *reh'-ghesh*; or (fem.)

רִגְשָׁה **rigshâh**, *rig-shaw'*; from 7283; a tumultuous *crowd*:—company, insurrection.

7286. רָדַד **râdad**, *raw-dad'*; a prim. root; to *tread* in pieces, i.e. (fig.) to *conquer*, or (spec.) to *overlay*:—spend, spread, subdue.

7287. רָדָה **râdâh**, *raw-daw'*; a prim. root; to *tread* down, i.e. *subjugate*; spec. to *crumble* off:—(come to, make to) have dominion, prevail against, reign, (bear, make to) rule, (-r, over), take.

7288. רַדַּי **Radday**, *rad-dah'ee*; intens. from 7287; *domineering*; *Raddai*, an Isr.:—Raddai.

7289. רָדִיד **râdîyd**, *raw-deed'*; from 7286 in the sense of *spreading*; a *veil* (as expanded):—vail, veil.

7290. רָדַם **râdam**, *raw-dam'*; a prim. root; to *stun*, i.e. *stupefy* (with sleep or death):—(be fast a-, be in a deep, cast into a dead, that) sleep (-er, -eth).

7291. רָדַף **râdaph**, *raw-daf'*; a prim. root; to *run after* (usually with hostile intent; fig. [of time] *gone by*):—chase, put to flight, follow (after, on), hunt, (be under) persecute (-ion, -or), pursue (-r).

7292. רָהַב **râhab**, *raw-hab'*; a prim. root; to *urge* severely, i.e. (fig.) *importune*, *embolden*, *capture*, *act insolently*:—overcome, behave self proudly, make sure, strengthen.

7293. רַהַב **rahab**, *rah'-hab*; from 7292; *bluster* (-*er*):—proud, strength.

7294. רַהַב **Rahab**, *rah'-hab*; the same as 7293; *Rahab* (i.e. *boaster*), an epithet of Egypt:—Rahab.

7295. רָהָב **râhâb**, *raw-hawb'*; from 7292; *insolent*:—proud.

7296. רֹהַב **rôhab**, *ro'-hab*; from 7292; *pride*:—strength.

7297. רָהָה **râhâh**, *raw-haw'*; a prim. root; to *fear*:—be afraid.

7298. רַהַט **rahaṭ**, *rah'-hat*; from an unused root appar. mean. to *hollow out*; a *channel* or watering-box; by resemblance a *ringlet* of hair (as forming parallel lines):—gallery, gutter, trough.

7299. רֵו **rêv** (Chald.), *rave*; from a root corresp. to 7200; *aspect*:—form.

רוּב° **rûwb**. See 7378.

7300. רוּד **rûwd**, *rood*; a prim. root; to *tramp* about, i.e. *ramble* (free or disconsolate):—have the dominion, be lord, mourn, rule.

7301. רָוָה **râvâh**, *raw-vaw'*; a prim. root; to *slake* the thirst (occasionally of other appetites):—bathe, make drunk, (take the) fill, satiate, (abundantly) satisfy, soak, water (abundantly).

7302. רָוֶה **râveh**, *raw-veh'*; from 7301; *sated* (with drink):—drunkenness, watered.

7303. רוֹהֲגָה° **Rôwhăgâh**, *ro-hag-aw'*; from an unused root prob. mean. to *cry* out; *outcry*; *Rohagah*, an Isr.:—Rohgah.

7304. רָוַח **râvach**, *raw-vakh'*; a prim. root [rather ident. with 7306]; prop. to *breathe* freely, i.e. *revive*; by impl. to *have ample room*:—be refreshed, large.

7305. רֶוַח **revach**, *reh'-vakh*; from 7304; *room*, lit. (an *interval*) or fig. (*deliverance*):—enlargement, space.

7306. רוּחַ **rûwach**, *roo'-akh*; a prim. root; prop. to *blow*, i.e. *breathe*; only (lit.) to *smell* or (by impl. *perceive* (fig. to *anticipate*, *enjoy*):—accept, smell, × touch, make of quick understanding.

7307. רוּחַ **rûwach**, *roo'-akh*; from 7306; *wind*; by resemblance *breath*, i.e. a sensible (or even violent) exhalation; fig. *life*, *anger*, *unsubstantiality*; by extens. a *region* of the sky; by resemblance *spirit*, but only of a rational being (includ. its expression and functions):—air, anger, blast, breath, × cool, courage, mind, × quarter, × side, spirit ([-ual]), tempest, × vain, ([whirl-]) wind (-y).

7308. רוּחַ **rûwach** (Chald.), *roo'-akh*; corresp. to 7307:—mind, spirit, wind.

7309. רְוָחָה **rᵉvâchâh**, *rev-aw-khaw'*; fem. of 7305; *relief*:—breathing, respite.

7310. רְוָיָה **rᵉvâyâh**, *rev-aw-yaw'*; from 7301; *satisfaction*:—runneth over, wealthy.

7311. רוּם **rûwm**, *room*; a prim. root; to *be high* act. to *rise* or *raise* (in various applications, lit. or fig.):—bring up, exalt (self), extol, give, go up, haughty, heave (up), (be, lift up on, make on, set up on, too) high (-er, one), hold up, levy, lift (-er) up, (be) lofty, (× a-) loud, mount up, offer (up), + presumptuously, (be) promote (-ion), proud, set up, tall (-er), take (away, off, up), breed worms.

7312. רוּם **rûwm**, *room*; or

רֻם **rûm**, *room*; from 7311; (lit.) *elevation* or (fig.) *elation*:—haughtiness, height, × high.

7313. רוּם **rûwm** (Chald.), *room*; corresp. to 7311; (fig. only):—extol, lift up (self), set up.

7314. רוּם **rûwm** (Chald.), *room*; from 7313; (lit.) *altitude*:—height.

7315. רוֹם **rôwm**, *rome*; from 7311; *elevation*, i.e. (adv.) *aloft*:—on high.

7316. רוּמָה **Rûwmâh**, *roo-maw'*; from 7311; *height*; *Rumah*, a place in Pal.:—Rumah.

7317. רוֹמָה **rôwmâh**, *ro-maw'*; fem. of 7315; *elation*, i.e. (adv.) *proudly*:—haughtily.

7318. רוֹמָם **rôwmâm**, *ro-mawm'*; from 7426; *exaltation*, i.e. (fig. and spec.) *praise*:—be extolled.

7319. רוֹמְמָה **rôwmᵉmâh**, *ro-mem-aw'*; fem. act. part. of 7426; *exaltation*, i.e. *praise*:—high.

7320. רוֹמַמְתִּי עֶזֶר **Rôwmamtîy ʿEzer** (or רֹמַמְתִּי **Rômamtîy**), *ro-mam'-tee eh'-zer*; from 7311 and 5828; *I have raised up a help*; *Romamti-Ezer*, an Isr.:—Romamti-ezer.

7321. רוּעַ **rûwaʿ**, *roo-ah'*; a prim. root; to *mar* (espec. by breaking); fig. to *split* the ears (with sound), i.e. *shout* (for alarm or joy):—blow an alarm, cry (alarm, aloud, out), destroy, make a joyful noise, smart, shout (for joy), sound an alarm, triumph.

7322. רוּף **rûwph**, *roof*; a prim. root; prop. to *triturate* (in a mortar), i.e. (fig.) to *agitate* (by concussion):—tremble.

7323. רוּץ **rûwts**, *roots*; a prim. root; to *run* (for whatever reason, espec. to *rush*):—break down, divide speedily, footman, guard, bring hastily, (make) run (away, through), post, stretch out.

7324. רוּק **rûwq**, *rook*; a prim. root; to *pour* out (lit. or fig.), i.e. *empty*:— × arm, cast out, draw (out), (make) empty, pour forth (out).

7325. רוּר **rûwr**, *roor*; a prim. root; to *slaver* (with spittle), i.e. (by analogy) to *emit* a fluid (ulcerous or natural):—run.

7326. רוּשׁ **rûwsh**, *roosh*; a prim. root; to *be destitute*:—lack, needy, (make self) poor (man).

רוֹשׁ **rôwsh**. See 7219.

7327. רוּת **Rûwth**, *rooth*; prob. for 7468; *friend*; *Ruth*, a Moabitess:—Ruth.

7328. רָז **râz** (Chald.), *rawz*; from an unused root prob. mean. to *attenuate*, i.e. (fig.) *hide*; a *mystery*:—secret.

7329. רָזָה **râzâh**, *raw-zaw'*; a prim. root; to *emaciate*, i.e. *make* (*become*) *thin* (lit. or fig.):—famish, wax lean.

7330. רָזֶה **râzeh**, *raw-zeh'*; from 7329; *thin*:—lean.

7331. רְזוֹן **Rᵉzôwn**, *rez-one'*; from 7336; *prince*; *Rezon*, a Syrian:—Rezon.

7332. רָזוֹן **râzôwn**, *raw-zone'*; from 7329; *thinness*:—leanness, × scant.

7333. רָזוֹן **râzôwn**, *raw-zone'*; from 7336; a *dignitary*:—prince.

7334. רָזִי **râzîy**, *raw-zee'*; from 7329; *thinness*:—leanness.

7335. רָזַם **râzam**, *raw-zam'*; a prim. root; to *twinkle* the eye (in mockery):—wink.

7336. רָזַן **râzan**, *raw-zan'*; a prim. root; prob. to be *heavy*, i.e. (fig.) *honorable*:—prince, ruler.

7337. רָחַב **râchab**, *raw-khab'*; a prim. root; to *broaden* (intrans. or trans., lit. or fig.):—be an en- (make) large (-ing), make room, make (open) wide.

7338. רַחַב **rachab**, *rakh'-ab*; from 7337; a *width*:—breadth, broad place.

7339. רְחֹב **rᵉchôb**, *rekh-obe'*; or

רְחוֹב **rᵉchôwb**, *rekh-obe'*; from 7337; a *width*, i.e. (concr.) *avenue* or *area*:—broad place (way), street. See also 1050.

7340. רְחֹב **Rᵉchôb**, *rekh-obe'*; or

רְחוֹב **Rᵉchôwb**, *rekh-obe'*; the same as 7339; *Rechob*, the name of a place in Syria, also of a Syrian and an Isr.:—Rehob.

7341. רֹחַב **rôchab**, *ro'-khab*; from 7337; *width* (lit. or fig.):—breadth, broad, largeness, thickness, wideness.

7342. רָחָב **râchâb**, *raw-khawb'*; from 7337; *roomy*, in any (or every) direction, lit. or fig.:—broad, large, at liberty, proud, wide.

7343. רָחָב **Râchâb**, *raw-khawb'*; the same as 7342; *proud*; *Rachab*, a Canaanitess:—Rahab.

7344. רְחֹבוֹת **Rᵉchôbôwth**, *rekh-o-bōth'*; or

רְחֹבֹת **Rᵉchôbôth**, *rekh-o-bōth'*; plur. of 7339; *streets*; *Rechoboth*, a place in Assyria and one in Pal.:—Rehoboth.

7345. רְחַבְיָה **Rᵉchabyâh**, *rekh-ab-yaw'*; or

רְחַבְיָהוּ **Rᵉchabyâhûw**, *rekh-ab-yaw'-hoo*; from 7337 and 3050; *Jah has enlarged*; *Rechabjah*, an Isr.:—Rehabiah.

7346. רְחַבְעָם **Rᵉchabʻâm**, *rekh-ab-awm'*; from 7337 and 5971; *a people has enlarged*; *Rechabam*, an Isr. king:—Rehoboam.

רְחֹבֹת **Rᵉchôbôth**. See 7344.

7347. רֵחֶה **rêcheh**, *ray-kheh'*; from an unused root mean. to *pulverize*; a *mill*-stone:—mill (stone).

רְחוֹב **Rᵉchôwb**. See 7339, 7340.

7348. רְחוּם **Rᵉchûwm**, *rekh-oom'*; a form of 7349; *Rechum*, the name of a Pers. and of three Isr.:—Rehum.

7349. רַחוּם **rachûwm**, *rakh-oom'*; from 7355; *compassionate*:—full of compassion, merciful.

7350. רָחוֹק **râchôwq**, *raw-khoke'*; or

רָחֹק **râchôq**, *raw-khoke'*; from 7368; *remote*, lit. or fig., of place or time; spec. *precious*; often used adv. (with prep.):—(a-) far (abroad, off), long ago, of old, space, great while to come.

7351. רְחִיט° **rᵉchîyṭ**, *rekh-eet'*; from the same as 7298; a *panel* (as resembling a *trough*):—rafter.

7352. רַחִיק **rachîyq** (Chald.), *rakh-eek'*; corresp. to 7350:—far.

7353. רָחֵל **râchêl**, *raw-kale'*; from an unused root mean. to *journey*; a *ewe* [the *females* being the predominant element of a flock] (as a good *traveller*):—ewe, sheep.

7354. רָחֵל **Râchêl**, *raw-khale'*; the same as 7353; *Rachel*, a wife of Jacob:—Rachel.

7355. רָחַם **râcham**, *raw-kham'*; a prim. root; to *fondle*; by impl. to *love*, espec. to *compassionate*:—have compassion (on, upon), love, (find, have, obtain, shew) mercy (-iful, on, upon), (have) pity, Ruhamah, × surely.

7356. רַחַם **racham**, *rakh'-am*; from 7355; *compassion* (in the plur.); by extens. the *womb* (as *cherishing* the fœtus); by impl. a *maiden*:—bowels, compassion, damsel, tender love, (great, tender) mercy, pity, womb.

7357. רַחַם **Racham**, *rakh'-am*; the same as 7356; *pity*; *Racham*, an Isr.:—Raham.

7358. רֶחֶם **rechem**, *rekh'-em*; from 7355; the *womb* [comp. 7356]:—matrix, womb.

7359. רְחֵם **rᵉchêm** (Chald.), *rekh-ame'*; corresp. to 7356; (plur.) *pity*:—mercy.

7360. רָחָם **râchâm**, *raw-khawm'*; or (fem.)

רָחָמָה **râchâmâh**, *raw-khaw-maw'*; from 7355; a kind of *vulture* (supposed to be *tender* towards its young):—gier-eagle.

7361. רַחֲמָה **rachămâh**, *rakh-am-aw'*; fem. of 7356; a *maiden*:—damsel.

7362. רַחְמָנִי **rachmânîy**, *rakh-maw-nee'*; from 7355; *compassionate*:—pitiful.

7363. רָחַף **râchaph**, *raw-khaf'*; a prim. root; to *brood*; by impl. to *be relaxed*:—flutter, move, shake.

7364. רָחַץ **râchats**, *raw-khats'*; a prim. root; to *lave* (the whole or a part of a thing):—bathe (self), wash (self).

7365. רְחַץ **rᵉchats** (Chald.), *rekh-ats'*; corresp. to 7364 [prob. through the accessory idea of *ministering* as a servant at the bath]; to *attend* upon:—trust.

7366. רַחַץ **rachats**, *rakh'-ats*; from 7364; a *bath*:—wash[-pot].

7367. רַחְצָה **rachtsâh**, *rakh-tsaw'*; fem. of 7366; a *bathing* place:—washing.

7368. רָחַק **râchaq**, *raw-khak'*; a prim. root; to *widen* (in any direction), i.e. (intrans.) *recede* or (trans.) *remove* (lit. or fig., of place or relation):—(a-, be, cast, drive, get, go, keep [self], put, remove, be too, [wander], withdraw) far (away, off), loose, × refrain, very, (be) a good way (off).

7369. רָחֵק **râchêq**, *raw-khake'*; from 7368; *remote*:—that are far.

רָחֹק **râchôq**. See 7350.

7370. רָחַשׁ **râchash**, *raw-khash'*; a prim. root; to *gush*:—indite.

7371. רַחַת **rachath**, *rakh'-ath*; from 7306; a *winnowing-fork* (as *blowing* the chaff away):—shovel.

7372. רָטַב **râṭab**, *raw-tab'*; a prim. root; to *be moist*:—be wet.

7373. רָטֹב **râṭôb**, *raw-tobe'*; from 7372; *moist* (with sap):—green.

7374. רֶטֶט **reṭeṭ**, *reh'-tet*; from an unused root mean. to *tremble*; *terror*:—fear.

7375. רוּטֲפַשׁ **rûwṭăphash**, *roo-taf-ash'*; a root compounded from 7373 and 2954; to *be rejuvenated*:—be fresh.

7376. רָטַשׁ **râṭash**, *raw-tash'*; a prim. root; to *dash* down:—dash (in pieces).

7377. רִי **rîy**, *ree*; from 7301; *irrigation*, i.e. a shower:—watering.

7378. רִיב **rîyb**, *reeb*; or

רוּב° **rûwb**, *roob*; a prim. root; prop. to *toss*, i.e. *grapple*; mostly fig. to *wrangle*, i.e. *hold a controversy*; (by impl.) to *defend*:—adversary, chide, complain, contend, debate, × ever, × lay wait, plead, rebuke, strive, × thoroughly.

7379. רִיב **rîyb**, *reeb*; or

רִב **rîb**, *reeb*; from 7378; a *contest* (personal or legal):— + adversary, cause, chiding, contend (-tion), controversy, multitude [*from the marg.*], pleading, strife, strive (-ing), suit.

7380. רִיבַי **Rîybay**, *ree-bah'ee*; from 7378; *contentious*; *Ribai*, an Isr.:—Ribai.

7381. רֵיחַ **rêyach**, *ray'-akh*; from 7306; *odor* (as if *blown*):—savour, scent, smell.

7382. רֵיחַ **rêyach** (Chald.), *ray'-akh*; corresp. to 7381:—smell.

רֵים **rêym**. See 7214.

רֵיעַ **rêyaʻ**. See 7453.

7383. רִיפָה **rîyphâh**, *ree-faw'*; or

רִפָה **rîphâh**, *ree-faw'*; from 7322; (only plur.), *grits* (as *pounded*):—ground corn, wheat.

7384. רִיפַת **Rîyphath**, *ree-fath'*; or (prob. by orth. error)

דִּיפַת **Dîyphath**, *dee-fath'*; of for. or.; *Riphath*, a grandson of Japheth and his desc.:—Riphath.

7385. רִיק **rîyq**, *reek*; from 7324; *emptiness*; fig. a *worthless* thing; adv. *in vain*:—empty, to no purpose, (in) vain (thing), vanity.

7386. רֵיק **rêyq**, *rake*; or (shorter)

רֵק **rêq**, *rake*; from 7324; *empty*; fig. *worthless*:—emptied (-ty), vain (fellow, man).

7387. רֵיקָם **rêyqâm**, *ray-kawm'*; from 7386; *emptily*; fig. (obj.) *ineffectually*, (subj.) *undeservedly*:—without cause, empty, in vain, void.

7388. רִיר **rîyr**, *reer*; from 7325; *saliva*; by resemblance *broth*:—spittle, white [of an egg].

7389. רֵישׁ **rêysh**, *raysh*; or

רֵאשׁ **rêʼsh**, *raysh*; or

רִישׁ **rîysh**, *reesh*; from 7326; *poverty*:—poverty.

7390. רַךְ **rak**, *rak*; from 7401; *tender* (lit. or fig.); by impl. *weak*:—faint [-hearted], soft, tender ([-hearted], one), weak.

7391. רֹךְ **rôk**, *roke*; from 7401; *softness* (fig.):—tenderness.

7392. רָכַב **râkab**, *raw-kab'*; a prim. root; to *ride* (on an animal or in a vehicle); caus. to *place upon* (for riding or gen.), to *despatch*:—bring (on [horse-] back), carry, get [oneself] up, on [horse-] back, put, (cause to, make to) ride (in a chariot, on, -r), set.

7393. רֶכֶב **rekeb**, *reh'-keb*; from 7392; a *vehicle*; by impl. a *team*; by extens. *cavalry*; by analogy a *rider*, i.e. the upper millstone:—chariot, (upper) millstone, multitude [*from the marg.*], wagon.

7394. רֵכָב **Rêkâb**, *ray-kawb'*; from 7392; *rider*; *Rekab*, the name of two Arabs and of two Isr.:—Rechab.

7395. רַכָּב **rakkâb**, *rak-kawb'*; from 7392; a *charioteer*:—chariot man, driver of a chariot, horseman.

7396. רִכְבָּה **rikbâh**, *rik-baw'*; fem. of 7393; a *chariot* (collect.):—chariots.

7397. רֵכָה **Rêkâh**, *ray-kaw'*; prob. fem. from 7401; *softness*; *Rekah*, a place in Pal.:—Rechah.

7398. רְכוּב **rᵉkûwb**, *rek-oob'*; from pass. part. of 7392; a *vehicle* (as *ridden* on):—chariot.

7399. רְכוּשׁ **rᵉkûwsh**, *rek-oosh'*; or

רְכֻשׁ **rᵉkûsh**, *rek-oosh'*; from pass. part. of 7408; *property* (as *gathered*):—good, riches, substance.

7400. רָכִיל **râkîyl**, *raw-keel'*; from 7402; a *scandal-monger* (as *travelling* about):—slander, carry tales, talebearer.

7401. רָכַךְ **râkak**, *raw-kak'*; a prim. root; to *soften* (intrans. or trans.), used fig.:—(be) faint ([-hearted]), mollify, (be, make) soft (-er), be tender.

7402. רָכַל **râkal**, *raw-kal'*; a prim. root; to *travel* for trading:—(spice) merchant.

7403. רָכָל **Râkâl**, *raw-kawl'*; from 7402; *merchant*; *Rakal*, a place in Pal.:—Rachal.

7404. רְכֻלָּה **rᵉkullâh**, *rek-ool-law'*; fem. pass. part. of 7402; *trade* (as *peddled*):—merchandise, traffic.

7405. רָכַס **râkaç**, *raw-kas'*; a prim. root; to *tie*:—bind.

7406. רֶכֶס **rekeç**, *reh'-kes*; from 7405; a mountain *ridge* (as of *tied* summits):—rough place.

7407. רֹכֶס **rôkeç**, *ro'-kes*; from 7405; a *snare* (as of *tied* meshes):—pride.

7408. רָכַשׁ **râkash**, *raw-kash'*; a prim. root; to *lay up*, i.e. collect:—gather, get.

7409. רֶכֶשׁ **rekesh**, *reh'-kesh*; from 7408; a *relay* of animals on a post-route (as *stored* up for that purpose); by impl. a *courser*:—dromedary, mule, swift beast.

רְכֻשׁ **rᵉkûsh**. See 7399.

רֵם **rêm**. See 7214.

7410. רָם **Râm**, *rawm;* act. part. of 7311; *high; Ram,* the name of an Arabian and of an Isr.:—Ram. See also 1027.

רֻם **rûm**. See 7311.

7411. רָמָה **râmâh**, *raw-maw';* a prim. root; to *hurl;* spec. to *shoot;* fig. to *delude* or *betray* (as if causing to fall):—beguile, betray, [bow-] man, carry, deceive, throw.

7412. רְמָה **rᵉmâh** (Chald.), *rem-aw';* corresp. to 7411; to *throw, set,* (fig.) *assess:*—cast (down), impose.

7413. רָמָה **râmâh**, *raw-maw';* fem. act. part. of 7311; a *height* (as a seat of idolatry):—high place.

7414. רָמָה **Râmâh**, *raw-maw';* the same as 7413; *Ramah,* the name of four places in Pal.:—Ramah.

7415. רִמָּה **rimmâh**, *rim-maw';* from 7426 in the sense of *breeding* [comp. 7311]; a *maggot* (as rapidly *bred*), lit. or fig.:—worm.

7416. רִמּוֹן **rimmôwn**, *rim-mone';* or

רִמֹּן **rimmôn**, *rim-mone';* from 7426; a *pomegranate,* the tree (from its *upright* growth) or the fruit (also an artificial ornament):—pomegranate.

7417. רִמּוֹן **Rimmôwn**, *rim-mone';* or (shorter)

רִמֹּן **Rimmôn**, *rim-mone';* or

רִמּוֹנוֹ **Rimmôwnôw** (1 Chron. 6 : 62 [77]), *rim-mo-no';* the same as 7416; *Rimmon,* the name of a Syrian deity, also of five places in Pal :—Remmon, Rimmon. The addition "-methoar" (Josh. 19 : 13) is

הַמְּתֹאָר **ham-mᵉthô'âr**, *ham-meth-o-awr';* pass. part. of 8388 with the art.; *the* (one) *marked off,* i.e. *which pertains;* mistaken for part of the name.

רָמוֹת **Râmôwth**. See 7418, 7433.

7418. רָמוֹת־נֶגֶב **Râmôwth-Negeb**, *raw-mōth-neh'-gheb;* or

רָמַת נֶגֶב **Râmath Negeb**, *raw'-math neh'-gheb;* from the plur. or construct. of 7413 and 5045; *heights* (or *height*) *of the South; Ramoth-Negeb* or *Ramath-Negeb,* a place in Pal.:—south Ramoth, Ramath of the south.

7419. רָמוּת **râmûwth**, *raw-mooth';* from 7311; a *heap* (of carcases):—height.

7420. רֹמַח **rômach**, *ro'-makh;* from an unused root mean. to *hurl;* a *lance* (as *thrown*); espec. the iron *point:*—buckler, javelin, lancet, spear.

7421. רַמִּי **rammîy**, *ram-mee';* for 761; a *Ramite,* i.e. Aramæan:—Syrian.

7422. רַמְיָה **Ramyâh**, *ram-yaw';* from 7311 and 3050; *Jah has raised; Ramjah,* an Isr.:—Ramiah.

7423. רְמִיָּה **rᵉmîyâh**, *rem-ee-yaw';* from 7411; *remissness, treachery:*—deceit (-ful, -fully), false, guile, idle, slack, slothful.

7424. רַמָּךְ **rammâk**, *ram-mawk';* of for. or.; a brood *mare:*—dromedary.

7425. רְמַלְיָהוּ **Rᵉmalyâhûw**, *rem-al-yaw'-hoo;* from an unused root and 3050 (perh. mean. to *deck*); *Jah has bedecked; Remaljah,* an Isr.:—Remaliah.

7426. רָמַם **râmam**, *raw-mam';* a prim. root; to *rise* (lit. or fig.):—exalt, get [oneself] up, lift up (self), mount up.

7427. רֹמֵמֻת **rômêmûth**, *ro-may-mooth';* from the act. part. of 7426; *exaltation:*—lifting up of self.

רִמֹּן **rimmôn**. See 7416.

7428. רִמֹּן פֶּרֶץ **Rimmôn Perets**, *rim-mone' peh'-rets;* from 7416 and 6556; *pomegranate of the breach; Rimmon-Perets,* a place in the Desert:—Rimmon-parez.

7429. רָמַס **râmac**, *raw-mas';* a prim. root; to *tread* upon (as a potter, in walking or abusively):—oppressor, stamp upon, trample (under feet), tread (down, upon).

7430. רָמַשׂ **râmas**, *raw-mas';* a prim. root; prop. to *glide* swiftly, i.e. to *crawl* or *move* with short steps; by analogy to *swarm:*—creep, move.

7431. רֶמֶשׂ **remes**, *reh'-mes;* from 7430; a *reptile* or any other rapidly moving animal:—that creepeth, creeping (moving) thing.

7432. רֶמֶת **Remeth**, *reh'-meth;* from 7411; *height; Remeth,* a place in Pal.:—Remeth.

7433. רָמֹת (or רָמוֹת **Râmôwth**) גִּלְעָד **Râmôth Gil'âd** (2 Chron. 22 : 5), *raw-mōth' gil-awd';* from the plur. of 7413 and 1568; *heights of Gilad; Ramoth-Gilad,* a place E. of the Jordan:—Ramoth-gilead, Ramoth in Gilead. See also 7216.

7434. רָמַת הַמִּצְפֶּה **Râmath ham-Mitspeh**, *raw-math' ham-mits-peh';* from 7413 and 4707 with the art. interp.; *height of the watch-tower; Ramath-ham-Mitspeh,* a place in Pal.:—Ramath-mizpeh.

7435. רָמָתִי **Râmâthîy**, *raw-maw-thee';* patron. of 7414; a *Ramathite* or inhab. of Ramah:—Ramathite.

7436. רָמָתַיִם צוֹפִים **Râmâthayim Tsôwphîym**, *raw-maw-thah'-yim tso-feem';* from the dual of 7413 and the plur. of the act. part. of 6822; *double height of watchers; Ramathajim-Tsophim,* a place in Pal.:—Ramathaim-zophim.

7437. רָמַת לֶחִי **Râmath Lechîy**, *raw'-math lekh'-ee;* from 7413 and 3895; *height of a jaw-bone; Ramath-Lechi,* a place in Pal.:—Ramath-lehi.

רָן **Rân**. See 1028.

7438. רֹן **rôn**, *rone;* from 7442; a *shout* (of deliverance):—song.

7439. רָנָה **rânâh**, *raw-naw';* a prim. root; to *whiz:*—rattle.

7440. רִנָּה **rinnâh**, *rin-naw';* from 7442; prop. a *creaking* (or shrill sound), i.e. *shout* (of joy or grief):—cry, gladness, joy, proclamation, rejoicing, shouting, sing (-ing), triumph.

7441. רִנָּה **Rinnâh**, *rin-naw';* the same as 7440; *Rinnah,* an Isr.:—Rinnah.

7442. רָנַן **rânan**, *raw-nan';* a prim. root; prop. to *creak* (or emit a stridulous sound), i.e. to *shout* (usually for joy):—aloud for joy, cry out, be joyful, (greatly, make to) rejoice, (cause to) shout (for joy), (cause to) sing (aloud, for joy, out), triumph.

7443. רֶנֶן **renen**, *reh'-nen;* from 7442; an *ostrich* (from its *wail*):—× goodly.

7444. רַנֵּן **rannên**, *ran-nane';* intens. from 7442; *shouting* (for joy):—singing.

7445. רְנָנָה **rᵉnânâh**, *ren-aw-naw';* from 7442; a *shout* (for joy):—joyful (voice), singing, triumphing.

7446. רִסָּה **Riççâh**, *ris-saw';* from 7450; a *ruin* (as *dripping* to pieces); *Rissah,* a place in the Desert:—Rissah.

7447. רָסִיס **râçîyç**, *raw-sees';* from 7450; prop. *dripping* to pieces, i.e. a *ruin;* also a dew-*drop:*—breach, drop.

7448. רֶסֶן **reçen**, *reh'-sen;* from an unused root mean. to *curb;* a *halter* (as *restraining*); by impl. the *jaw:*—bridle.

7449. רֶסֶן **Reçen**, *reh'-sen;* the same as 7448; *Resen,* a place in Ass.:—Resen.

7450. רָסַס **râçaç**, *raw-sas';* a prim. root; to *comminute;* used only as denom. from 7447, to *moisten* (with drops):—temper.

7451. רַע **ra'**, *rah;* from 7489; *bad* or (as noun) *evil* (nat. or mor.):—adversity, affliction, bad, calamity, + displease (-ure), distress, evil ([-favouredness], man, thing), + exceedingly, × great, grief (-vous), harm, heavy, hurt (-ful), ill (favoured), + mark, mischief (-vous), misery, naught (-ty), noisome, + not please, sad (-ly), sore, sorrow, trouble, vex, wicked (-ly, -ness, one), worse (-st), wretchedness, wrong. [Incl. fem. רָעָה **râ'âh**; as adj. or noun.]

7452. רֵעַ **rêa'**, *ray'-ah;* from 7321; a *crash* (of thunder), *noise* (of war), *shout* (of joy):—× aloud, noise, shouted.

7453. רֵעַ **rêa'**, *ray'-ah;* or

רֵיעַ **rêya'**, *ray'-ah;* from 7462; an *associate* (more or less close):—brother, companion, fellow, friend, husband, lover, neighbour, × (an-) other.

7454. רֵעַ **rêa'**, *ray'-ah;* from 7462; a *thought* (as *association* of ideas):—thought.

7455. רֹעַ **rôa'**, *ro'-ah;* from 7489; *badness* (as *marring*), phys. or mor.:— × be so bad, badness, (× be so) evil, naughtiness, sadness, sorrow, wickedness.

7456. רָעֵב **râ'êb**, *raw-abe';* a prim. root; to *hunger:*—(suffer to) famish, (be, have, suffer, suffer to) hunger (-ry).

7457. רָעֵב **râ'êb**, *raw-abe';* from 7456; *hungry* (more or less intensely):—hunger bitten, hungry.

7458. רָעָב **râ'âb**, *raw-awb';* from 7456; *hunger* (more or less extensive):—dearth, famine, + famished, hunger.

7459. רְעָבוֹן **rᵉ'âbôwn**, *reh-aw-bone';* from 7456; *famine:*—famine.

7460. רָעַד **râ'ad**, *raw-ad';* a prim. root; to *shudder* (more or less violently):—tremble.

7461. רַעַד **ra'ad**, *rah'-ad;* or (fem.)

רְעָדָה **rᵉ'âdâh**, *reh-aw-daw';* from 7460; a *shudder:*—fear, trembling.

7462. רָעָה **râ'âh**, *raw-aw';* a prim. root; to *tend* a flock, i.e. *pasture* it; intrans. to *graze* (lit. or fig.); gen. to *rule;* by extens. to *associate* with (as a friend):— × break, companion, keep company with, devour, eat up, evil entreat, feed, use as a friend, make friendship with, herdman, keep [sheep] (-er), pastor, + shearing house, shepherd, wander, waste.

7463. רֵעֶה **rê'eh**, *ray-eh';* from 7462; a (male) *companion:*—friend.

7464. רֵעָה **rê'âh**, *ray'-aw;* fem. of 7453; a female *associate:*—companion, fellow.

7465. רֹעָה **rô'âh**, *ro-aw';* for 7455; *breakage:*—broken, utterly.

7466. רְעוּ **Rᵉ'ûw**, *reh-oo';* for 7471 in the sense of 7453; *friend; Reü,* a postdiluvian patriarch:—Reu.

7467. רְעוּאֵל **Rᵉ'ûw'êl**, *reh-oo-ale';* from the same as 7466 and 410; *friend of God; Reüel,* the name of Moses' father-in-law, also of an Edomite and an Isr.:—Raguel, Reuel.

7468. רְעוּת **rᵉ'ûwth**, *reh-ooth';* from 7462 in the sense of 7453; a female *associate;* gen. an *additional* one:— + another, mate, neighbour.

7469. רְעוּת **rᵉ'ûwth**, *reh-ooth';* prob. from 7462; a *feeding* upon, i.e. grasping after:—vexation.

7470. רְעוּת **rᵉ'ûwth** (Chald.), *reh-ooth';* corresp. to 7469; *desire:*—pleasure, will.

7471. רְעִי **rᵉ'îy**, *reh-ee';* from 7462; *pasture:*—pasture.

7472. רֵעִי **Rê'îy**, *ray-ee';* from 7453; *social; Reï,* an Isr.:—Rei.

7473. רֹעִי **rô'îy**, *ro-ee';* from act. part. of 7462; *pastoral;* as noun, a *shepherd:*—shepherd.

7474. רַעְיָה **ra'yâh**, *rah-yaw';* fem. of 7453; a female *associate:*—love.

7475. רַעְיוֹן **ra'yôwn**, *rah-yone';* from 7462 in the sense of 7469; *desire:*—vexation.

7476. רַעְיוֹן **ra'yôwn** (Chald.), *rah-yone';* corresp. to 7475; a *grasp,* i.e. (fig.) mental *conception:*—cogitation, thought.

7477. רָעַל **râ'al**, *raw-al';* a prim. root; to *reel,* i.e. (fig.) to *brandish:*—terribly shake.

7478. רַעַל **ra'al**, *rah'-al;* from 7477; a *reeling* (from intoxication):—trembling.

7479. רַעֲלָה **ra'ălâh**, *rah-al-aw';* fem. of 7478; a long *veil* (as *fluttering*):—muffler.

7480. רְעֵלָיָה **Rᵉ'êlâyâh**, *reh-ay-law-yaw';* from 7477 and 3050; *made to tremble* (i.e. *fearful*) *of Jah; Reëlajah,* an Isr.:—Reeliah.

7481. רָעַם **râ'am**, *raw-am';* a prim. root; to *tumble,* i.e. *be* violently *agitated;* spec.

to *crash* (of thunder); fig. to *irritate* (with anger):—make to fret, roar, thunder, trouble.

7482. רַעַם **ra'am**, *rah'-am;* from 7481; a *peal* of thunder:—thunder.

7483. רַעְמָה **ra'mâh**, *rah-maw';* fem. of 7482; the *mane* of a horse (as *quivering* in the wind):—thunder.

7484. רַעְמָה **Ra'mâh**, *rah-maw';* the same as 7483; *Ramah*, the name of a grandson of Ham, and of a place (perh. founded by him):—Raamah.

7485. רַעַמְיָה **Ra'amyâh**, *rah-am-yaw';* from 7481 and 3050; *Jah has shaken; Raamjah*, an Isr.:—Raamiah.

7486. רַעְמְסֵס **Ra'm^eçêç**, *rah-mes-ace';* or

רַעַמְסֵס **Ra'amçêç**, *rah-am-sace';* of Eg. or.; *Rameses* or *Raamses*, a place in Egypt:—Raamses, Rameses.

7487. רַעֲנַן **ra'ânan** (Chald.), *rah-aw-nan';* corresp. to 7488; *green*, i.e. (fig.) *prosperous:*—flourishing.

7488. רַעֲנָן **ra'ânân**, *rah-an-awn';* from an unused root mean. to *be green; verdant;* by anal. *new;* fig. *prosperous:*—green, flourishing.

7489. רָעַע **râ'a'**, *raw-ah';* a prim. root; prop. to *spoil* (lit. by *breaking* to pieces); fig. to *make* (or *be*) *good for nothing*, i.e. *bad* (phys., soc. or mor.):—afflict, associate selves [*by mistake for* 7462], break (down, in pieces), + displease, (be, bring, do) evil (doer, entreat, man), show self friendly [*by mistake for* 7462], do harm, (do) hurt, (behave self, deal) ill, × indeed, do mischief, punish, still, vex, (do) wicked (doer, -ly), be (deal, do) worse.

7490. רְעַע **r^e'a'** (Chald.), *reh-ah';* corresp. to 7489:—break, bruise.

7491. רָעַף **râ'aph**, *raw-af';* a prim. root; to *drip:*—distil, drop (down).

7492. רָעַץ **râ'ats**, *raw-ats';* a prim. root; to *break* in pieces; fig. *harass:*—dash in pieces, vex.

7493. רָעַשׁ **râ'ash**, *raw-ash;* a prim. root; to *undulate* (as the earth, the sky, etc.; also a field of grain), partic. through fear; spec. to *spring* (as a locust):—make afraid, (re-) move, quake, (make to) shake, (make to) tremble.

7494. רַעַשׁ **ra'ash**, *rah'-ash;* from 7493; *vibration, bounding, uproar:*—commotion, confused noise, earthquake, fierceness, quaking, rattling, rushing, shaking.

7495. רָפָא **râphâ'**, *raw-faw';* or

רָפָה **râphâh**, *raw-faw';* a prim. root; prop. to *mend* (by stitching), i.e. (fig.) to *cure:*—cure, (cause to) heal, physician, repair, × thoroughly, make whole. See 7503.

7496. רָפָא **râphâ'**, *raw-faw';* from 7495 in the sense of 7503; prop. *lax*, i.e. (fig.) a *ghost* (as *dead;* in plur. only):—dead, deceased.

7497. רָפָא **râphâ'**, *raw-faw';* or

רָפָה **râphâh**, *raw-faw';* from 7495 in the sense of *invigorating;* a *giant:*—giant, Rapha, Rephaim (-s). See also 1051.

7498. רָפָא **Râphâ'**, *raw-faw';* or

רָפָה **Râphâh**, *raw-faw';* prob. the same as 7497; *giant; Rapha* or *Raphah*, the name of two Isr.:—Rapha.

7499. רְפֻאָה **r^ephû'âh**, *ref-oo-aw';* fem. pass. part. of 7495; a *medicament:*—heal [-ed], medicine.

7500. רִפְאוּת **riph'ûwth**, *rif-ooth';* from 7495; a *cure:*—health.

7501. רְפָאֵל **R^ephâ'êl**, *ref-aw-ale';* from 7495 and 410; *God has cured; Rephaël*, an Isr.:—Rephael.

7502. רָפַד **râphad**, *raw-fad';* a prim. root; to *spread* (a bed); by impl. to *refresh:*—comfort, make [a bed], spread.

7503. רָפָה **râphâh**, *raw-faw';* a prim. root; to *slacken* (in many applications, lit. or fig.):—abate, cease, consume, draw [toward evening], fail, (be) faint, be (wax) feeble, forsake, idle, leave, let alone (go, down), (be) slack, stay, be still, be slothful, (be) weak (-en). See 7495.

7504. רָפֶה **râpheh**, *raw-feh';* from 7503; *slack* (in body or mind):—weak.

רָפָה **râphâh, Râphâh**. See 7497, 7498.

רִפָה **riphâh**. See 7383.

7505. רָפוּא **Râphûw'**, *raw-foo';* pass. part. of 7495; *cured; Raphu*, an Isr.:—Raphu.

7506. רֶפַח **Rephach**, *reh'-fakh;* from an unused root appar. mean. to *sustain; support; Rephach*, an Isr.:—Rephah.

7507. רְפִידָה **r^ephîydâh**, *ref-ee-daw';* from 7502; a *railing* (as *spread* along):—bottom.

7508. רְפִידִים **R^ephîydîym**, *ref-ee-deem';* plur. of the masc. of the same as 7507; *ballusters; Rephidim*, a place in the Desert:—Rephidim.

7509. רְפָיָה **R^ephâyâh**, *ref-aw-yaw';* from 7495 and 3050; *Jah has cured; Rephajah*, the name of five Isr.:—Rephaiah.

7510. רִפְיוֹן **riphyôwn**, *rif-yone';* from 7503; *slackness:*—feebleness.

7511. רָפַס **râphaç**, *raw-fas';* a prim. root; to *trample*, i.e. *prostrate:*—humble self, submit self.

7512. רְפַס **r^ephaç** (Chald.), *ref-as';* corresp. to 7511:—stamp.

7513. רַפְסֹדָה **raphçôdâh**, *raf-so-daw';* from 7511; a *raft* (as *flat* on the water):—flote.

7514. רָפַק **râphaq**, *raw-fak';* a prim. root; to *recline:*—lean.

7515. רָפַשׂ **râphas**, *raw-fas';* a prim. root; to *trample*, i.e. *roil* water:—foul, trouble.

7516. רֶפֶשׁ **rephesh**, *reh'-fesh;* from 7515; *mud* (as *roiled*):—mire.

7517. רֶפֶת **repheth**, *reh'-feth;* prob. from 7503; a *stall* for cattle (from their *resting* there):—stall.

7518. רַץ **rats**, *rats;* contr. from 7533; a *fragment:*—piece.

7519. רָצָא **râtsâ'**, *raw-tsaw';* a prim. root; to *run;* also to *delight* in:—accept, run.

7520. רָצַד **râtsad**, *raw-tsad';* a prim. root; prob. to *look askant*, i.e. (fig.) *be jealous:*—leap.

7521. רָצָה **râtsâh**, *raw-tsaw';* a prim. root; to *be pleased with;* spec. to *satisfy* a debt:—(be) accept (-able), accomplish, set affection, approve, consent with, delight (self), enjoy, (be, have a) favour (-able), like, observe, pardon, (be, have, take) please (-ure), reconcile self.

7522. רָצוֹן **râtsôwn**, *raw-tsone';* or

רָצֹן **râtsôn**, *raw-tsone';* from 7521; *delight* (espec. as shown):—(be) acceptable (-ance, -ed), delight, desire, favour, (good) pleasure, (own, self, voluntary) will, as . . . (what) would.

7523. רָצַח **râtsach**, *raw-tsakh';* a prim. root; prop. to *dash* in pieces, i.e. *kill* (a human being), espec. to *murder:*—put to death, kill, (man-) slay (-er), murder (-er).

7524. רֶצַח **retsach**, *reh'-tsakh;* from 7523; a *crushing;* spec. a *murder-cry:*—slaughter, sword.

7525. רִצְיָא **Ritsyâ'**, *rits-yaw';* from 7521; *delight; Ritsjah*, an Isr.:—Rezia.

7526. רְצִין **R^etsîyn**, *rets-een';* prob. for 7522; *Retsin*, the name of a Syrian and of an Isr.:—Rezin.

7527. רָצַע **râtsa'**, *raw-tsah';* a prim. root; to *pierce:*—bore.

7528. רָצַף **râtsaph**, *raw-tsaf';* a denom. from 7529; to *tessellate*, i.e. embroider (as if with bright stones):—pave.

7529. רֶצֶף **retseph**, *reh'-tsef;* for 7565; a red-hot *stone* (for baking):—coal.

7530. רֶצֶף **Retseph**, *reh'-tsef;* the same as 7529; *Retseph*, a place in Ass.:—Rezeph.

7531. רִצְפָּה **ritspâh**, *rits-paw';* fem. of 7529; a hot *stone;* also a tessellated *pavement:*—live coal, pavement.

7532. רִצְפָּה **Ritspâh**, *rits-paw';* the same as 7531; *Ritspah*, an Israelitess:—Rizpah.

7533. רָצַץ **râtsats**, *raw-tsats';* a prim. root; to *crack* in pieces, lit. or fig.:—break, bruise, crush, discourage, oppress, struggle together.

7534. רַק **raq**, *rak;* from 7556 in its orig. sense; *emaciated* (as if *flattened* out):—lean ([-fleshed]), thin.

7535. רַק **raq**, *rak;* the same as 7534 as a noun; prop. *leanness*, i.e. (fig.) limitation; only adv. *merely*, or conj. *although:*—but, even, except, howbeit howsoever, at the least, nevertheless, nothing but, notwithstanding, only, save, so [that], surely, yet (so), in any wise.

7536. רֹק **rôq**, *roke;* from 7556; *spittle:*—spit (-ting, -tle).

7537. רָקַב **râqab**, *raw-kab';* a prim. root; to *decay* (as by worm-eating):—rot.

7538. רָקָב **râqâb**, *raw-kawb';* from 7537; *decay* (by *caries*):—rottenness (thing).

7539. רִקָּבוֹן **riqqâbôwn**, *rik-kaw-bone';* from 7538; *decay* (by *caries*):—rotten.

7540. רָקַד **râqad**, *raw-kad';* a prim. root; prop. to *stamp*, i.e. to *spring* about (wildly or for joy):—dance, jump, leap, skip.

7541. רַקָּה **raqqâh**, *rak-kaw';* fem. of 7534; prop. *thinness*, i.e. the *side* of the head:—temple.

7542. רַקּוֹן **Raqqôwn**, *rak-kone';* from 7534 *thinness; Rakkon*, a place in Pal.:—Rakkon.

7543. רָקַח **râqach**, *raw-kakh';* a prim. root; to *perfume:*—apothecary, compound, make [ointment], prepare, spice.

7544. רֶקַח **reqach**, *reh'-kakh;* from 7543; prop. *perfumery*, i.e. (by impl.) *spicery* (for flavor):—spiced.

7545. רֹקַח **rôqach**, *ro'-kakh;* from 7542; an *aromatic:*—confection, ointment.

7546. רַקָּח **raqqâch**, *rak-kawkh';* from 7543; a male *perfumer:*—apothecary.

7547. רַקֻּחַ **raqqûach**, *rak-koo'-akh;* from 7543; a *scented* substance:—perfume.

7548. רַקָּחָה **raqqâchâh**, *rak-kaw-khaw';* fem. of 7547; a female *perfumer:*—confectioner.

7549. רָקִיעַ **râqîya'**, *raw-kee'-ah;* from 7554; prop. an *expanse*, i.e. the *firmament* or (apparently) visible arch of the sky:—firmament.

7550. רָקִיק **râqîyq**, *raw-keek';* from 7556 in its orig. sense; a thin *cake:*—cake, wafer.

7551. רָקַם **râqam**, *raw-kam';* a prim. root; to *variegate* color, i.e. *embroider;* by impl. to *fabricate:*—embroiderer, needlework, curiously work.

7552. רֶקֶם **Reqem**, *reh'-kem;* from 7551; *versicolor; Rekem*, the name of a place in Pal., also of a Midianite and an Isr.:—Rekem.

7553. רִקְמָה **riqmâh**, *rik-maw';* from 7551; *variegation* of color; spec. *embroidery:*—broidered (work), divers colours, (raiment of) needlework (on both sides).

7554. רָקַע **râqa'**, *raw-kah';* a prim. root; to *pound* the earth (as a sign of passion); by analogy to *expand* (by hammering); by impl. to *overlay* (with thin sheets of metal):—beat, make broad, spread abroad (forth, over, out, into plates), stamp, stretch.

7555. רִקֻּעַ **riqqûa'**, *rik-koo'-ah;* from 7554; *beaten* out, i.e. a (metallic) *plate:*—broad.

7556. רָקַק **râqaq**, *raw-kak';* a prim. root; to *spit:*—spit.

7557. רַקַּת **Raqqath**, *rak-kath';* from 7556 in its orig. sense of *diffusing;* a *beach* (as *expanded* shingle); *Rakkath*, a place in Pal.:—Rakkath.

7558. רִשְׁיוֹן **rishyôwn**, *rish-yone';* from an unused root mean. to *have leave;* a *permit:*—grant.

7559. רָשַׁם **râsham**, *raw-sham';* a prim. root; to *record:*—note.

7560. רְשַׁם **r^esham** (Chald.), *resh-am';* corresp. to 7559:—sign, write.

7561. רָשַׁע **râsha'**, *raw-shah';* a prim. root; to *be* (caus. *do* or *declare*) *wrong;* by impl to *disturb*, *violate*:—condemn, make trouble, vex, be (commit, deal, depart, do) wicked (-ly, -ness).

7562. רֶשַׁע **resha'**, *reh'-shah*; from 7561; a *wrong* (espec. moral):—iniquity, wicked (-ness).

7563. רָשָׁע **râshâ'**, *raw-shaw'*; from 7561; morally *wrong*; concr. an (actively) *bad* person:— + condemned, guilty, ungodly, wicked (man), that did wrong.

7564. רִשְׁעָה **rish'âh**, *rish-aw'*; fem. of 7562; *wrong* (espec. moral):—fault, wickedly (-ness).

7565. רֶשֶׁף **resheph**, *reh'-shef*; from 8313; a live *coal*; by analogy *lightning*; fig. an *arrow* (as *flashing* through the air); spec. *fever*:—arrow, (burning) coal, burning heat, + spark, hot thunderbolt.

7566. רֶשֶׁף **Resheph**, *reh'-shef*; the same as 7565; *Resheph*, an Isr.:—Resheph.

7567. רָשַׁשׁ **râshash**, *raw-shash'*; a prim. root; to *demolish*:—impoverish.

7568. רֶשֶׁת **resheth**, *reh'-sheth*; from 3423; a *net* (as *catching* animals):—net [-work].

7569. רַתּוֹק **rattôwq**, *rat-toke'*; from 7576; a *chain*:—chain.

7570. רָתַח **râthach**, *raw-thakh'*; a prim. root; to *boil*:—boil.

7571. רֶתַח **rethach**, *reh'-thakh*; from 7570; a *boiling*:— × [boil] well.

7572. רַתִּיקָה **rattîyqâh**, *rat-tee-kaw'*; from 7576; a *chain*:—chain.

7573. רָתַם **râtham**, *raw-tham'*; a prim. root: to *yoke* up (to the pole of a vehicle):—bind.

7574. רֶתֶם **rethem**, *reh'-them*; or
רֹתֶם **rôthem**, *ro'-them*; from 7573; the Spanish *broom* (from its pole-like stems):—juniper (tree).

7575. רִתְמָה **Rithmâh**, *rith-maw'*; fem. of 7574; *Rithmah*, a place in the Desert:—Rithmah.

7576. רָתַק **râthaq**, *raw-thak'*; a prim. root; to *fasten*:—bind.

7577. רְתֻקָה **rethûqâh**, *reth-oo-kaw'*; fem. pass. part. of 7576; something *fastened*, i.e. a *chain*:—chain.

7578. רְתֵת **rethêth**, *reth-ayth'*; for 7374; *terror*:—trembling.

ש

7579. שָׁאַב **shâ'ab**, *shaw-ab'*; a prim. root; to *bale* up water:—(woman to) draw (-er, water).

7580. שָׁאַג **shâ'ag**, *shaw-ag'*; a prim. root; to *rumble* or *moan*:— × mightily, roar.

7581. שְׁאָגָה **she'âgâh**, *sheh-aw-gaw'*; from 7580; a *rumbling* or *moan*:—roaring.

7582. שָׁאָה **shâ'âh**, *shaw-aw'*; a prim. root; to *rush*; by impl. to *desolate*:—be desolate, (make a) rush (-ing), (lay) waste.

7583. שָׁאָה **shâ'âh**, *shaw-aw'*; a prim. root [rather ident. with 7582 through the idea of *whirling* to giddiness]; to *stun*, i.e. (intrans.) *be astonished*:—wonder.

7584. שַׁאֲוָה **sha'ăvâh**, *shah-av-aw'*; from 7582; a *tempest* (as *rushing*):—desolation.

7585. שְׁאוֹל **she'ôwl**, *sheh-ole'*; or
שְׁאֹל **she'ôl**, *sheh-ole'*; from 7592; *hades* or the world of the dead (as if a subterranean *retreat*), includ. its accessories and inmates:—grave, hell, pit.

7586. שָׁאוּל **Shâ'ûwl**, *shaw-ool'*; pass. part. of 7592; *asked*; *Shaül*, the name of an Edomite and two Isr.:—Saul, Shaul.

7587. שָׁאוּלִי **Shâ'ûwlîy**, *shaw-oo-lee'*; patron. from 7856; a *Shaülite* or desc. of Shaul:—Shaulites.

7588. שָׁאוֹן **shâ'ôwn**, *shaw-one'*; from 7582; *uproar* (as of *rushing*); by impl. *destruction*:— × horrible, noise, pomp, rushing, tumult (× -uous).

7589. שְׁאָט **she'âṭ**, *sheh-awt'*; from an unused root mean. to *push* aside; *contempt*:—despite (-ful).

7590. שָׁאט **shâ't**, *shawt*; for act. part. of 7750 [comp. 7589]; one *contemning*:—that (which) despise (-d).

7591. שְׁאִיָּה **she'îyâh**, *sheh-ee-yaw'*; from 7582; *desolation*:—destruction.

7592. שָׁאַל **shâ'al**, *shaw-al'*; or
שָׁאֵל **shâ'êl**, *shaw-ale'*; a prim. root; to *inquire*; by impl. to *request*; by extens. to *demand*:—ask (counsel, on), beg, borrow, lay to charge, consult, demand, desire, × earnestly, enquire, + greet, obtain leave, lend, pray, request, require, + salute, × straitly, × surely, wish.

7593. שְׁאֵל **she'êl** (Chald.), *sheh-ale'*; corresp. to 7592:—ask, demand, require.

7594. שְׁאָל **She'âl**, *sheh-awl'*; from 7592; *request*; *Sheäl*, an Isr.:—Sheal.
שְׁאֹל **she'ôl**. See 7585.

7595. שְׁאֵלָא **she'êlâ'** (Chald.), *sheh-ay-law'*; from 7593; prop. a *question* (at law), i.e. judicial *decision* or mandate:—demand.

7596. שְׁאֵלָה **she'êlâh**, *sheh-ay-law'*; or
שֵׁלָה **shêlâh** (1 Sam. 1 : 17), *shay-law'*; from 7592; a *petition*; by impl. a *loan*:—loan, petition, request.

7597. שְׁאַלְתִּיאֵל **She'altîy'êl**, *sheh-al-tee-ale'*; or
שַׁלְתִּיאֵל **Shaltîy'êl**, *shal-tee-ale'*; from 7592 and 410; *I have asked God*; *Sheältiël*, an Isr.:—Shalthiel, Shealtiel.

7598. שְׁאַלְתִּיאֵל **She'altîy'êl** (Chald.), *sheh-al-tee-ale'*; corresp. to 7597:—Shealtiel.

7599. שָׁאַן **shâ'an**, *shaw-an'*; a prim. root; to *loll*, i.e. *be peaceful*:—be at ease, be quiet rest. See also 1052.

7600. שַׁאֲנָן **sha'ănân**, *shah-an-awn'*; from 7599; *secure*; in a bad sense, *haughty*:—that is at ease, quiet, tumult. Comp. 7946.

7601 שָׁאַס **shâ'aç**, *shaw-as'*; a prim. root; to *plunder*:—spoil.

7602. שָׁאַף **shâ'aph**, *shaw-af'*; a prim. root; to *inhale* eagerly; fig. to *covet*; by impl. to *be angry*; also to *hasten*:—desire (earnestly), devour, haste, pant, snuff up, swallow up.

7603. שְׂאֹר **se'ôr**, *seh-ore'*; from 7604; *barm* or yeast-cake (as *swelling* by fermentation):—leaven.

7604. שָׁאַר **shâ'ar**, *shaw-ar'*; a prim. root; prop. to *swell* up, i.e. *be* (caus. *make*) *redundant*:—leave, (be) left, let, remain, remnant, reserve, the rest.

7605. שְׁאָר **she'âr**, *sheh-awr'*; from 7604; a *remainder*:— × other, remnant, residue, rest.

7606. שְׁאָר **she'âr** (Chald.), *sheh-awr'*; corresp. to 7605:— × whatsoever more, residue, rest.

7607. שְׁאֵר **she'êr**, *sheh-ayr'*; from 7604; *flesh* (as *swelling* out), as living or for food; gen. *food* of any kind; fig. *kindred* by blood:—body, flesh, food, (near) kin (-sman, -swoman), near (nigh) [of kin].

7608. שַׁאֲרָה **sha'ărâh**, *shah-ar-aw'*; fem. of 7607; female *kindred* by blood:—near kinswomen.

7609. שֶׁאֱרָה **She'ĕrâh**, *sheh-er-aw'*; the same as 7608; *Sheërah*, an Israelitess:—Sherah.

7610. שְׁאָר יָשׁוּב **She'âr Yâshûwb**, *sheh-awr' yaw-shoob'*; from 7605 and 7725; *a remnant will return*; *Sheär-Jashub*, the symbol. name of one of Isaiah's sons:—Shear-jashub.

7611. שְׁאֵרִית **she'êrîyth**, *sheh-ay-reeth'*; from 7604; a *remainder* or residual (surviving, final) portion:—that had escaped, be left, posterity, remain (-der), remnant, residue, rest.

7612. שֵׁאת **shê'th**, *shayth*; from 7582; *devastation*:—desolation.

7613. שְׂאֵת **se'êth**, *seh-ayth'*; from 5375; an *elevation* or leprous scab; fig. *elation* or cheerfulness; *exaltation* in rank or character:—be accepted, dignity, excellency, highness, raise up self, rising.

7614. שְׁבָא **Shebâ'**, *sheb-aw'*; of for. or.; *Sheba*, the name of three early progenitors of tribes and of an Ethiopian district:—Sheba, Sabeans.

7615. שְׁבָאִי **Shebâ'îy**, *sheb-aw-ee'*; patron. from 7614; a *Shebaïte* or desc. of Sheba:—Sabean.

7616. שָׁבָב **shâbâb**, *shaw-bawb'*; from an unused root mean. to *break* up; a *fragment*, i.e. *ruin*:—broken in pieces.

7617. שָׁבָה **shâbâh**, *shaw-baw'*; a prim. root; to *transport* into captivity:—(bring away, carry, carry away, lead, lead away, take) captive (-s), drive (take) away.

7618. שְׁבוּ **shebûw**, *sheb-oo'*; from an unused root (prob. ident. with that of 7617 through the idea of *subdivision* into flashes or streamers [comp. 7632]) mean. to *flame*; a *gem* (from its sparkle), prob. the *agate*:—agate.

7619. שְׁבוּאֵל **Shebûw'êl**, *sheb-oo-ale'*; or
שׁוּבָאֵל **Shûwbâ'êl**, *shoo-baw-ale'*; from 7617 (abbrev.) or 7725 and 410; *captive* (or *returned*) *of God*; *Shebuël* or *Shubaël*, the name of two Isr.:—Shebuel, Shubael.

7620. שָׁבוּעַ **shâbûwa'**, *shaw-boo'-ah*; or
שָׁבֻעַ **shâbûa'**, *shaw-boo'-ah*; also (fem.)
שְׁבֻעָה **shebû'âh**, *sheb-oo-aw'*; prop. pass. part. of 7650 as a denom. of 7651; lit. *sevened*, i.e. a *week* (spec. of years):—seven, week.

7621. שְׁבוּעָה **shebûw'âh**, *sheb-oo-aw'*; fem. pass. part. of 7650; prop. something *sworn*, i.e. an *oath*:—curse, oath, × sworn.

7622. שְׁבוּת **shebûwth**, *sheb-ooth'*; or
שְׁבִית **shebîyth**, *sheb-eeth'*; from 7617; *exile*: concr. *prisoners*; fig. a *former state* of prosperity:—captive (-ity).

7623. שָׁבַח **shâbach**, *shaw-bakh'*; a prim. root; prop. to *address* in a loud tone, i.e. (spec.) *loud*; fig. to *pacify* (as if by words):—commend, glory, keep in, praise, still, triumph.

7624. שְׁבַח **shebach** (Chald.), *sheb-akh'*; corresp. to 7623; to *adulate*, i.e. *adore*:—praise.

7625. שְׁבַט **shebaṭ** (Chald.), *sheb-at'*; corresp. to 7626; a *clan*:—tribe.

7626. שֵׁבֶט **shêbeṭ**, *shay'-bet*; from an unused root prob. mean. to *branch* off; a *scion*, i.e. (lit.) a *stick* (for punishing, writing, fighting, ruling, walking, etc.) or (fig.) a *clan*:— × correction, dart, rod, sceptre, staff, tribe.

7627. שְׁבָט **Shebâṭ**, *sheb-awt'*; of for. or.; *Shebat*, a Jewish month:—Sebat.

7628. שְׁבִי **shebîy**, *sheb-ee'*; from 7618; *exiled*; *captured*; as noun, *exile* (abstr. or concr. and collect.); by extens. *booty*:—captive (-ity), prisoners, × take away, that was taken.

7629. שֹׁבִי **Shôbîy**, *sho-bee'*; from 7617; *captor*; *Shobi*, an Ammonite:—Shobi.

7630. שֹׁבַי **Shôbay**, *sho-bah'ee*; for 7629; *Shobai*, an Isr.:—Shobai.

7631. שְׂבִיב **sebîyb** (Chald.), *seb-eeb'*; corresp. to 7632:—flame.

7632. שָׁבִיב **shâbîyb**, *shaw-beeb'*; from the same as 7616; *flame* (as *split* into tongues):—spark.

7633. שִׁבְיָה **shibyâh**, *shib-yaw'*; fem. of 7628; *exile* (abstr. or concr. and collect.):—captives (-ity).

7634. שָׁבְיָה **Shobyâh**, *shob-yaw'*; fem. of the same as 7629; *captivation*; *Shobjah*, an Isr.:—Shachia [*from the marg.*].

7635. שָׁבִיל **shâbîyl**, *shaw-beel'*; from the same as 7640; a *track* or passage-way (as if *flowing* along):—path.

7636. שָׁבִיס **shâbîyç**, *shaw-beece'*; from an unused root mean. to *interweave*; a *netting* for the hair:—caul.

7637. שְׁבִיעִי **shᵉbîyʻîy**, *sheb-ee-ee';* or

שְׁבִעִי **shᵉbîʻîy**, *sheb-ee-ee';* ordinal from 7657; *seventh:*—seventh (time).

שְׁבִית **shᵉbîyth**. See 7622.

7638. שָׂבָךְ **sâbâk**, *saw-bawk';* from an unused root mean. to *intwine;* a *netting* (ornament to the capital of a column):—net.

שַׂבְּכָא **sabbᵉkâʼ**. See 5443.

7639. שְׂבָכָה **sᵉbâkâh**, *seb-aw-kaw';* fem. of 7638; a *net-work*, i.e. (in hunting) a *snare*, (in arch.) a *ballustrade;* also a *reticulated* ornament to a pillar:—checker, lattice, network, snare, wreath (-enwork).

7640. שֹׁבֶל **shôbel**, *show'-bel;* from an unused root mean. to *flow;* a lady's *train* (as *trailing* after her):—leg.

7641. שִׁבֹּל **shibbôl**, *shib-bole;* or (fem.)

שִׁבֹּלֶת **shibbôleth**, *shib-bo'-leth;* from the same as 7640; a *stream* (as *flowing*); also an *ear* of grain (as *growing* out); by anal. a *branch:*—branch, channel, ear (of corn), ([water-]) flood, Shibboleth. Comp. 5451.

7642. שַׁבְלוּל **shablûwl**, *shab-lool';* from the same as 7640; a *snail* (as if *floating* in its own slime):—snail.

שִׁבֹּלֶת **shibbôleth**. See 7641.

7643. שְׂבָם **Sᵉbâm**, *seb-awm';* or (fem.)

שִׂבְמָה **Sibmâh**, *sib-maw';* prob. from 1313; *spice; Sebam* or *Sibmah*, a place in Moab:—Shebam, Shibmah, Sibmah.

7644. שֶׁבְנָא **Shebnâʼ**, *sheb-naw';* or

שֶׁבְנָה **Shebnâh**, *sheb-naw';* from an unused root mean. to *grow; growth; Shebna* or *Shebnah*, an Isr.:—Shebna, Shebnah.

7645. שְׁבַנְיָה **Shᵉbanyâh**, *sheb-an-yaw';* or

שְׁבַנְיָהוּ **Shᵉbanyâhûw**, *sheb-an-yaw'-hoo;* from the same as 7644 and 3050; *Jah has grown* (i.e. *prospered*); *Shebanjah*, the name of three or four Isr.:—Shebaniah.

7646. שָׂבַע **sâbaʻ**, *saw-bah';* or

שָׂבֵעַ **sâbêaʻ**, *saw-bay'-ah;* a prim. root; to *sate*, i.e. *fill* to satisfaction (lit. or fig.):—have enough, fill (full, self, with), be (to the) full (of), have plenty of, be satiate, satisfy (with), suffice, be weary of.

7647. שָׂבָע **sâbâʻ**, *saw-baw';* from 7646; *copiousness:*—abundance, plenteous (-ness, -ly).

7648. שֹׂבַע **sôbaʻ**, *so'-bah;* from 7646; *satisfaction* (of food or [fig.] joy):—fill, full (-ness), satisfying, be satisfied.

7649. שָׂבֵעַ **sâbêaʻ**, *saw-bay'-ah;* from 7646; *satiated* (in a pleasant or disagreeable sense):—full (of), satisfied (with).

7650. שָׁבַע **shâbaʻ**, *shaw-bah';* a prim. root; prop. to *be complete*, but used only as a denom. from 7651; to *seven* oneself, i.e. *swear* (as if by repeating a declaration seven times):—adjure, charge (by an oath, with an oath), feed to the full [*by mistake for* 7646], take an oath, × straitly, (cause to, make to) swear.

7651. שֶׁבַע **shebaʻ**, *sheh'-bah;* or (masc.)

שִׁבְעָה **shibʻâh**, *shib-aw';* from 7650; a prim. cardinal number; *seven* (as the sacred *full* one); also (adv.) *seven times;* by impl. a *week;* by extens. an *indefinite* number:—(+ by) seven ([-fold], -s, [-teen, -teenth], -th, times). Comp. 7658.

7652. שֶׁבַע **shebaʻ**, *sheh'-bah;* the same as 7651; *seven; Sheba*, the name of a place in Pal., and of two Isr.:—Sheba.

שָׁבֻעַ **shâbûaʻ**. See 7620.

7653. שִׂבְעָה **sibʻâh**, *sib-aw';* fem. of 7647; *satiety:*—fulness.

7654. שָׂבְעָה **sobʻâh**, *sob-aw';* fem. of 7648; *satiety:*—(to have) enough, × till . . . be full, [un-] satiable, satisfy, × sufficiently.

שִׁבְעָה **shibʻâh**. See 7651.

7655. שִׁבְעָה **shibʻâh** (Chald.), *shib-aw';* corresp. to 7651:—seven (times).

7656. שִׁבְעָה **Shibʻâh**, *shib-aw';* masc. of 7651; *seven (-th); Shebah*, a well in Pal.:—Shebah.

שְׁבֻעָה **shᵉbûʻâh**. See 7620.

שְׁבִעִי **shᵉbîyʻîy**. See 7637.

7657. שִׁבְעִים **shibʻîym**, *shib-eem';* multiple of 7651; *seventy:*—seventy, threescore and ten (+ -teen).

7658. שִׁבְעָנָה **shibʻânâh**, *shib-aw-naw';* prol. for the masc. of 7651; *seven:*—seven.

7659. שִׁבְעָתַיִם **shibʻâthayim**, *shib-aw-thah'-yim;* dual (adv.) of 7651; *seven-times:*—seven (-fold, times).

7660. שָׁבַץ **shâbats**, *shaw-bats';* a prim. root; to *interweave* (colored) threads in squares; by impl. (*of reticulation*) to *inchase* gems in gold:—embroider, set.

7661. שָׁבָץ **shâbâts**, *shaw-bawts';* from 7660; *intanglement*, i.e. (fig.) *perplexity:*—anguish.

7662. שְׁבַק **shᵉbaq** (Chald.), *sheb-ak';* corresp. to the root of 7733; to *quit*, i.e. allow to remain:—leave, let alone.

7663. שָׂבַר **sâbar**, *saw-bar';* erroneously

שָׁבַר **shâbar** (Neh. 2 : 13, 15), *shaw-bar';* a prim. root; to *scrutinize;* by impl. (of *watching*) to *expect* (with hope and patience):—hope, tarry, view, wait.

7664. שֵׂבֶר **sêber**, *say'-ber;* from 7663; *expectation:*—hope.

7665. שָׁבַר **shâbar**, *shaw-bar';* a prim. root; to *burst* (lit. or fig.):—break (down, off, in pieces, up), broken ([-hearted]), bring to the birth, crush, destroy, hurt, quench, × quite, tear, view [*by mistake for* 7663].

7666. שָׁבַר **shâbar**, *shaw-bar';* denom. from 7668; to *deal* in grain:—buy, sell.

7667. שֶׁבֶר **sheber**, *sheh'-ber;* or

שֵׁבֶר **shêber**, *shay'-ber;* from 7665; a *fracture*, fig. *ruin;* spec. a *solution* (of a dream):—affliction, breach, breaking, broken [-footed, -handed], bruise, crashing, destruction, hurt, interpretation, vexation.

7668. שֶׁבֶר **sheber**, *sheh'-ber;* the same as 7667; *grain* (as if *broken* into kernels):—corn, victuals.

7669. שֶׁבֶר **Sheber**, *sheh'-ber;* the same as 7667; *Sheber*, an Isr.:—Sheber.

7670. שִׁבְרוֹן **shibrôwn**, *shib-rone';* from 7665; *rupture*, i.e. a *pang;* fig. *ruin:*—breaking, destruction.

7671. שְׁבָרִים **Shᵉbârîym**, *sheb-aw-reem';* plur. of 7667; *ruins; Shebarim*, a place in Pal.:—Shebarim.

7672. שְׁבַשׁ **shᵉbash** (Chald.), *sheb-ash';* corresp. to 7660; to *intangle*, i.e. *perplex:*—be astonished.

7673. שָׁבַת **shâbath**, *shaw-bath';* a prim. root; to *repose*, i.e. *desist* from exertion; used in many impl. relations (caus., fig. or spec.):—(cause to, let, make to) cease, celebrate, cause (make) to fail, keep (sabbath), suffer to be lacking, leave, put away (down), (make to) rest, rid, still, take away.

7674. שֶׁבֶת **shebeth**, *sheh'-beth;* from 7673; *rest, interruption, cessation:*—cease, sit still, loss of time.

7675. שֶׁבֶת **shebeth**, *sheh'-beth;* infin. of 3427; prop. *session;* but used also concr. an *abode* or *locality:*—place, seat. Comp. 3429.

7676. שַׁבָּת **shabbâth**, *shab-bawth';* intens. from 7673; *intermission*, i.e. (spec.) the *Sabbath:*—(+ every) sabbath.

7677. שַׁבָּתוֹן **shabbâthôwn**, *shab-baw-thone';* from 7676; a *sabbatism* or special holiday:—rest, sabbath.

7678. שַׁבְּתַי **Shabbᵉthay**, *shab-beth-ah'ee;* from 7676; *restful; Shabbethai*, the name of three Isr.:—Shabbethai.

7679. שָׂגָא **sâgâʼ**, *saw-gaw';* a prim. root; to *grow*, i.e. (caus.) to *enlarge*, (fig.) *laud:*—increase, magnify.

7680. שְׂגָא **sᵉgâʼ** (Chald.), *seg-aw';* corresp. to 7679; to *increase:*—grow, be multiplied.

7681. שָׁגֵא **Shâgêʼ**, *shaw-gay';* prob. from 7686; *erring; Shagè*, an Isr.:—Shage.

7682. שָׂגַב **sâgab**, *saw-gab';* a prim. root; to *be* (caus. *make*) *lofty*, espec. *inaccessible;* by impl. *safe, strong;* used lit. and fig.:—defend, exalt, be excellent, (be, set on) high, lofty, be safe, set up (on high), be too strong.

7683. שָׁגַג **shâgag**, *shaw-gag';* a prim. root; to *stray*, i.e. (fig.) *sin* (with more or less apology):— × also for that, deceived, err, go astray, sin ignorantly.

7684. שְׁגָגָה **shᵉgâgâh**, *sheg-aw-gaw';* from 7683; a *mistake* or inadvertent *transgression:*—error, ignorance, at unawares, unwittingly.

7685. שָׂגָה **sâgâh**, *saw-gaw';* a prim. root; to *enlarge* (espec. upward, also fig.):—grow (up), increase.

7686. שָׁגָה **shâgâh**, *shaw-gaw';* a prim. root; to *stray* (caus. *mislead*), usually (fig.) to *mistake*, espec. (mor.) to *transgress;* by extens. (through the idea of intoxication) to *reel*, (fig.) *be enraptured:*—(cause to) go astray, deceive, err, be ravished, sin through ignorance, (let, make to) wander.

7687. שְׂגוּב **Sᵉgûwb**, *seg-oob';* from 7682; *aloft; Segub*, the name of two Isr.:—Segub.

7688. שָׁגַח **shâgach**, *shaw-gakh';* a prim. root; to *peep*, i.e. *glance* sharply at:—look (narrowly).

7689. שַׂגִּיא **saggîyʼ**, *sag-ghee';* from 7679; (superlatively) *mighty:*—excellent, great.

7690. שַׂגִּיא **saggîyʼ** (Chald.), *sag-ghee';* corresp. to 7689; *large* (in size, quantity or number, also adv.):—exceeding, great (-ly), many, much, sore, very.

7691. שְׁגִיאָה **shᵉgîyʼâh**, *sheg-ee-aw';* from 7686; a moral *mistake:*—error.

7692. שִׁגָּיוֹן **shiggâyôwn**, *shig-gaw-yone';* or

שִׁגָּיֹנָה **shiggâyônâh**, *shig-gaw-yo-naw';* from 7686; prop. *aberration*, i.e. (tech.) a *dithyramb* or rambling poem:—Shiggaion, Shigionoth.

7693. שָׁגַל **shâgal**, *shaw-gal';* a prim. root; to *copulate* with:—lie with, ravish.

7694. שֵׁגָל **shêgâl**, *shay-gawl';* from 7693; a *queen* (from cohabitation):—queen.

7695. שֵׁגָל **shêgâl** (Chald.), *shay-gawl';* corresp. to 7694; a (legitimate) *queen:*—wife.

7696. שָׁגַע **shâgaʻ**, *shaw-gah';* a prim. root; to *rave* through insanity:—(be, play the) mad (man).

7697. שִׁגָּעוֹן **shiggâʻôwn**, *shig-gaw-yone';* from 7696; *craziness:*—furiously, madness.

7698. שֶׁגֶר **sheger**, *sheh'-ger;* from an unused root prob. mean. to *eject;* the *fœtus* (as finally *expelled*):—that cometh of, increase.

7699. שַׁד **shad**, *shad;* or

שֹׁד **shôd**, *shode;* prob. from 7736 (in its orig. sense) contr.; the *breast* of a woman or animal (as *bulging*):—breast, pap, teat.

7700. שֵׁד **shêd**, *shade;* from 7736; a *dæmon* (as *malignant*):—devil.

7701. שֹׁד **shôd**, *shode;* or

שׁוֹד **shôwd** (Job 5 : 21), *shode;* from 7736; *violence, ravage:*—desolation, destruction, oppression, robbery, spoil (-ed, -er, -ing), wasting.

7702. שָׂדַד **sâdad**, *saw-dad'*; a prim. root; to *abrade*, i.e. *harrow* a field:—break clods, harrow.

7703. שָׁדַד **shâdad**, *shaw-dad'*; a prim. root; prop. to *be burly*, i.e. (fig.) *powerful* (pass. *impregnable*); by impl. to *ravage:*—dead, destroy (-er), oppress, robber, spoil (-er), × utterly, (lay) waste.

7704. שָׂדֶה **sâdeh**, *saw-deh'*; or

שָׂדַי **sâday**, *saw-dah'ee*; from an unused root mean. to *spread* out; a *field* (as *flat*):—country, field, ground, land, soil, × wild.

7705. שִׁדָּה **shiddâh**, *shid-dah'*; from 7703; a *wife* (as *mistress* of the house):—× all sorts, musical instrument.

7706. שַׁדַּי **Shadday**, *shad-dah'ee*; from 7703; the *Almighty:*—Almighty.

7707. שְׁדֵיאוּר **Shedêy'ûwr**, *shed-ay-oor'*; from the same as 7704 and 217; *spreader of light; Shedejur*, an Isr.:—Shedeur.

7708. שִׂדִּים **Siddîym**, *sid-deem'*; plur. from the same as 7704; *flats; Siddim*, a valley in Pal.:—Siddim.

7709. שְׁדֵמָה **shedêmâh**, *shed-ay-maw'*; appar. from 7704; a cultivated *field:*—blasted, field.

7710. שָׁדַף **shâdaph**, *shaw-daf'*; a prim. root; to *scorch:*—blast.

7711. שְׁדֵפָה **shedêphâh**, *shed-ay-faw'*; or

שִׁדָּפוֹן **shiddâphôwn**, *shid-daw-fone'*; from 7710; *blight:*—blasted (-ing).

7712. שְׁדַר **shedar** (Chald.), *shed-ar'*; a prim. root; to *endeavor:*—labour.

7713. שְׂדֵרָה **sedêrâh**, *sed-ay-raw'*; from an unused root mean. to *regulate*; a *row*, i.e. *rank* (of soldiers), *story* (of rooms):—board, range.

7714. שַׁדְרַךְ **Shadrak**, *shad-rak'*; prob. of for. or.; *Shadrak*, the Bab. name of one of Daniel's companions:—Shadrach.

7715. שַׁדְרַךְ **Shadrak** (Chald.), *shad-rak'*; the same as 7714:—Shadrach.

7716. שֶׂה **seh**, *seh*; or

שֵׂי **sêy**, *say*; prob. from 7582 through the idea of *pushing* out to graze; a member of a flock, i.e. a *sheep* or *goat:*—(lesser, small) cattle, ewe, lamb, sheep.

7717. שָׂהֵד **sâhêd**, *saw-hade'*; from an unused root mean. to *testify*; a *witness:*—record.

7718. שֹׁהַם **shôham**, *sho'-ham*; from an unused root prob. mean. to *blanch*; a gem, prob. the *beryl* (from its *pale* green color):—onyx.

7719. שֹׁהַם **Shôham**, *sho'-ham*; the same as 7718; *Shoham*, an Isr.:—Shoham.

7720. שַׂהֲרֹן **sahărôn**, *sah-har-one'*; from the same as 5469; a round *pendant* for the neck:—ornament, round tire like the moon.

°שַׁו **shav**. See 7723.

7721. שׂוֹא **sôw'**, *so*; from an unused root (akin to 5375 and 7722) mean. to *rise*; a *rising:*—arise.

7722. שׁוֹא **shôw'**, *sho*; or (fem.)

שׁוֹאָה **shôw'âh**, *sho-aw'*; or

שֹׁאָה **shô'âh**, *sho-aw'*; from an unused root mean. to *rush* over; a *tempest*; by impl. *devastation:*—desolate (-ion), destroy, destruction, storm, wasteness.

7723. שָׁוְא **shâv'**, *shawv*; or

°שַׁו **shav**, *shav*; from the same as 7722 in the sense of *desolating*; *evil* (as *destructive*), lit. (*ruin*) or mor. (espec. *guile*); fig. *idolatry* (as false, subj.), *uselessness* (as deceptive, obj.; also adv. in *vain*):—false (-ly), lie, lying, vain, vanity.

7724. שְׁוָא **Shevâ'**, *shev-aw'*; from the same as 7723; *false*; *Sheva*, an Isr.:—Sheva.

7725. שׁוּב **shûwb**, *shoob*; a prim. root; to *turn* back (hence, away) trans. or intrans., lit. or fig. (not necessarily with the idea of *return* to the starting point); gen. to *retreat*; often adv. *again:*—([break, build, circumcise, dig, do anything, do evil, feed, lay down, lie down, lodge, make, rejoice, send, take, weep]) × again, (cause to) answer (+ again), × in any case (wise), × at all, averse, bring (again, back, home again), call [to mind], carry again (back), cease, × certainly, come again (back) × consider, + continually, convert, deliver (again), + deny, draw back, fetch home again, × fro, get [oneself] (back) again, × give (again), go again (back, home), [go] out, hinder, let, [see] more, × needs, be past, × pay, pervert, pull in again, put (again, up again), recall, recompense, recover, refresh, relieve, render (again), × repent, requite, rescue, restore, retrieve, (cause to, make to) return, reverse, reward, + say nay, send back, set again, slide back, still, × surely, take back (off), (cause to, make to) turn (again, self again, away, back, back again, backward, from, off), withdraw.

שׁוּבָאֵל **Shûwbâ'êl**. See 7619.

7726. שׁוֹבָב **shôwbâb**, *sho-bawb'*; from 7725; *apostate*, i.e. idolatrous:—backsliding, frowardly, turn away [*from marg.*].

7727. שׁוֹבָב **Shôwbâb**, *sho-bawb'*; the same as 7726; *rebellious*; *Shobab*, the name of two Isr.:—Shobab.

7728. שׁוֹבֵב **shôwbêb**, *sho-babe'*; from 7725; *apostate*, i.e. heathenish or (actually) heathen:—backsliding.

7729. שׁוּבָה **shûwbâh**, *shoo-baw'*; from 7725; a *return:*—returning.

7730. שׂוֹבֶךְ **sôwbek**, *so'-bek*; for 5441; a *thicket*, i.e. interlaced branches:—thick boughs.

7731. שׁוֹבָךְ **Shôwbâk**, *sho-bawk'*; perh. for 7730; *Shobak*, a Syrian:—Shobach.

7732. שׁוֹבָל **Shôwbâl**, *sho-bawl'*; from the same as 7640; *overflowing*; *Shobal*, the name of an Edomite and two Isr.:—Shobal.

7733. שׁוֹבֵק **Shôwbêq**, *sho-bake'*; act. part. from a prim. root mean. to *leave* (comp. 7662); *forsaking*; *Shobek*, an Isr.:—Shobek.

7734. שׂוּג **sûwg**, *soog*; a prim. root; to *retreat:*—turn back.

7735. שׂוּג **sûwg**, *soog*; a prim. root; to *hedge* in:—make to grow.

7736. שׁוּד **shûwd**, *shood*; a prim. root; prop. to *swell* up, i.e. fig. (by impl. of *insolence*) to *devastate:*—waste.

שׁוֹד **shôwd**. See 7699, 7701.

7737. שָׁוָה **shâvâh**, *shaw-vaw'*; a prim. root; prop. to *level*, i.e. *equalize*; fig. to *resemble*; by impl. to *adjust* (i.e. counterbalance, be suitable, compose, place, yield, etc.):—avail, behave, bring forth, compare, countervail, (be, make) equal, lay, be (make, a-) like, make plain, profit, reckon.

7738. °שָׁוָה **shâvâh**, *shaw-vaw'*; a prim. root; to *destroy:*— × substance [*from the marg.*].

7739. שְׁוָה **shevâh** (Chald.), *shev-aw'*; corresp. to 7737; to *resemble:*—make like.

7740. שָׁוֵה **Shâvêh**, *shaw-vay'*; from 7737; *plain*; *Shaveh*, a place in Pal.:—Shaveh.

7741. שָׁוֵה קִרְיָתַיִם **Shâvêh Qiryâthayim**, *shaw-vay' kir-yaw-thah'-yim*; from the same as 7740 and the dual of 7151; *plain of a double city; Shaveh-Kirjathajim*, a place E. of the Jordan:—Shaveh Kiriathaim.

7742. שׂוּחַ **sûwach**, *soo'-akh*; a prim. root; to *muse* pensively:—meditate.

7743. שׁוּחַ **shûwach**, *shoo'-akh*; a prim. root; to *sink*, lit. or fig.:—bow down, incline, humble.

7744. שׁוּחַ **Shûwach**, *shoo'-akh*; from 7743; *dell*; *Shûăch*, a son of Abraham:—Shuah.

7745 שׁוּחָה **shûwchâh**, *shoo-khaw'*; from 7743; a *chasm:*—ditch, pit.

7746. שׁוּחָה **Shûwchâh**, *shoo-khaw'*; the same as 7745; *Shuchah*, an Isr.:—Shuah.

7747. שׁוּחִי **Shuchîy**, *shoo-khee'*; patron. from 7744; a *Shuchite* or desc. of Shuach:—Shuhite.

7748. שׁוּחָם **Shûwchâm**, *shoo-khawm'*; from 7743; *humbly*; *Shucham*, an Isr.:—Shuham.

7749. שׁוּחָמִי **Shûwchâmîy**, *shoo-khaw-mee'*; patron. from 7748; a *Shuchamite* (collect.):—Shuhamites.

7750. שׂוּט **sûwṭ**, *soot*; or (by perm.)

סוּט **çûwṭ**, *soot*; a primitive root; to *detrude*, i.e. (intrans. and fig.) *become derelict* (wrongly practise; namely, idolatry):—turn aside to.

7751. שׁוּט **shûwṭ**, *shoot*; a prim. root; prop. to *push* forth; (but used only fig.) to *lash*, i.e. (the sea with oars) to *row*; by impl. to *travel:*—go (about, through, to and fro), mariner, rower, run to and fro.

7752. שׁוֹט **shôwṭ**, *shote*; from 7751; a *lash* (lit. or fig.):—scourge, whip.

7753. שׂוּךְ **sûwk**, *sook*; a prim. root; to *entwine*, i.e. *shut* in (for formation, protection or restraint):—fence, (make an) hedge (up).

7754. שׂוֹךְ **sôwk**, *soke*; or (fem.)

שׂוֹכָה **sôwkâh**, *so-kaw'*; from 7753; a *branch* (as *interleaved*):—bough.

7755. שׂוֹכֹה **Sôwkôh**, *so-ko'*; or

שֹׂכֹה **Sôkôh**, *so-ko'*; or

שׂוֹכוֹ **Sôwkôw**, *so-ko'*; from 7753; *Sokoh* or *Soko*, the name of two places in Pal.:—Shocho, Shochoh, Sochoh, Soco, Socoh.

7756. שׂוּכָתִי **Sûwkâthîy**, *soo-kaw-thee'*; prob. patron. from a name corresp. to 7754 (fem.); a *Sukathite* or desc. of an unknown Isr. named Sukah:—Suchathite.

7757. שׁוּל **shûwl**, *shool*; from an unused root mean. to *hang* down; a *skirt*; by impl. a bottom *edge:*—hem, skirt, train.

7758. שׁוֹלָל **shôwlâl**, *sho-lawl'*; or

°שֵׁילָל **shêylâl** (Mic. 1 : 8), *shay-lawl'*; from 7997; *nude* (espec. bare-foot); by impl. *captive:*—spoiled, stripped.

7759. שׁוּלַמִּית **Shûwlammîyth**, *shoo-lam-meeth'*; from 7999; *peaceful* (with the art. always pref., making it a pet name); the *Shulammith*, an epithet of Solomon's queen:—Shulamite.

7760. שׂוּם **sûwm**, *soom*; or

שִׂים **sîym**, *seem*; a prim. root; to *put* (used in a great variety of applications, lit., fig., infer. and ellip.):— × any wise, appoint, bring, call [a name], care, cast in, change, charge, commit, consider, convey, determine, + disguise, dispose, do, get, give, heap up, hold, impute, lay (down, up), leave, look, make (out), mark, + name, × on, ordain, order, + paint, place, preserve, purpose, put (on), + regard, rehearse, reward, (cause to) set (on, up), shew, + stedfastly, take, × tell, + tread down, ([over-]) turn, × wholly, work.

7761. שׂוּם **sûwm** (Chald.), *soom*; corresp. to 7760:— + command, give, lay, make, + name, + regard, set.

7762. שׁוּם **shûwm**, *shoom*; from an unused root mean. to *exhale*; *garlic* (from its rank *odor*):—garlic.

7763. שׁוֹמֵר **Shôwmêr**, *sho-mare'*; or

שֹׁמֵר **Shômêr**, *sho-mare'*; act. part. of 8104; *keeper*; *Shomer*, the name of two Isr.:—Shomer.

7764. שׁוּנִי **Shûwnîy**, *shoo-nee'*; from an unused root mean. to *rest*; *quiet*; *Shuni*, an Isr.:—Shuni.

7765. שׁוּנִי **Shûwnîy**, *shoo-nee'*; patron. from 7764; a Shunite (collect.) or desc. of Shuni:—Shunites.

7766. שׁוּנֵם **Shûwnêm**, *shoo-name'*; prob. from the same as 7764; *quietly*; *Shunem*, a place in Pal.:—Shunem.

7767. שׁוּנַמִּית **Shûwnammîyth**, *shoo-nam-meeth'*; patrial from 7766; a *Shunammitess*, or female inhab. of Shunem:—Shunamite.

7768. שָׁוַע **shâvaʻ**, *shaw-vah'*; a prim. root; prop. to *be free*; but used only causat. and reflex. to *halloo* (for help, i.e. *freedom* from some trouble):—cry (aloud, out), shout.

7769. שׁוּעַ **shûwaʻ**, *shoo'-ah*; from 7768; a *halloo*:—cry, riches.

7770. שׁוּעַ **Shûwaʻ**, *shoo'-ah*; the same as 7769; *Shuä*, a Canaanite:—Shua, Shuah.

7771. שׁוֹעַ **shôwaʻ**, *sho'-ah*; from 7768 in the orig. sense of *freedom*; a *noble*, i.e. *liberal*, *opulent*; also (as noun in the derived sense) a *halloo*:—bountiful, crying, rich.

7772. שׁוֹעַ **Shôwaʻ**, *sho'-ah*; the same as 7771; *rich*; *Shoä*, an Oriental people:—Shoa.

7773. שֶׁוַע **shevaʻ**, *sheh'-vah*; from 7768; a *halloo*:—cry.

7774. שׁוּעָא **Shûwʻâʼ**, *shoo-aw'*; from 7768; *wealth*; *Shuä*, an Israelitess:—Shua.

7775. שַׁוְעָה **shavʻâh**, *shav-aw'*; fem. of 7773; a *hallooing*:—crying.

7776. שׁוּעָל **shûwʻâl**, *shoo-awl'*; or

שֻׁעָל **shûʻâl**, *shoo-awl'*; from the same as 8168; a *jackal* (as a *burrower*):—fox.

7777. שׁוּעָל **Shûwʻâl**, *shoo-awl'*; the same as 7776; *Shuäl*, the name of an Isr. and of a place in Pal.:—Shual.

7778. שׁוֹעֵר **shôwʻêr**, *sho-are'*; or

שֹׁעֵר **shôʻêr**, *sho-are'*; act. part. of 8176 (as denom. from 8179); a *janitor*:—door-keeper, porter.

7779. שׁוּף **shûwph**, *shoof*; a prim. root; prop. to *gape*, i.e. *snap* at; fig. to *overwhelm*:—break, bruise, cover.

7780. שׁוֹפָךְ **Shôwphâk**, *sho-fawk'*; from 8210; *poured*; *Shophak*, a Syrian:—Shophach.

7781. שׁוּפָמִי **Shûwphâmîy**, *shoo-faw-mee'*; patron. from 8197; a *Shuphamite* (collect.) or desc. of Shephupham:—Shuphamite.

שׁוֹפָן **Shôwphân**. See 5855.

7782. שׁוֹפָר **shôwphâr**, *sho-far'*; or

שֹׁפָר **shôphâr**, *sho-far'*; from 8231 in the orig. sense of *incising*; a *cornet* (as giving a *clear* sound) or curved horn:—cornet, trumpet.

7783. שׁוּק **shûwq**, *shook*; a prim. root; to *run* after or over, i.e. *overflow*:—overflow, water.

7784. שׁוּק **shûwq**, *shook*; from 7783; a *street* (as *run* over):—street.

7785. שׁוֹק **shôwq**, *shoke*; from 7783; the (lower) *leg* (as a *runner*):—hip, leg, shoulder, thigh.

7786. שׂוּר **sûwr**, *soor*; a prim. root; prop. to *vanquish*; by impl. to *rule* (caus. *crown*):—make princes, have power, reign. See 5493.

7787. שׂוּר **sûwr**, *soor*; a prim. root [rather ident. with 7786 through the idea of *reducing* to pieces; comp. 4883]; to *saw*:—cut.

7788. שׁוּר **shûwr**, *shoor*; a prim. root; prop. to *turn*, i.e. *travel* about (as a harlot or a merchant):—go, sing. See also 7891.

7789. שׁוּר **shûwr**, *shoor*; a prim. root [rather ident. with 7788 through the idea of *going round* for inspection]; to *spy* out, i.e. (gen.) *survey*, (for evil) *lurk for*, (for good) *care for*:—behold, lay wait, look, observe, perceive, regard, see.

7790. שׁוּר **shûwr**, *shoor*; from 7789; a *foe* (as *lying in wait*):—enemy.

7791. שׁוּר **shûwr**, *shoor*; from 7788; a *wall* (as *going about*):—wall.

7792. שׁוּר **shûwr** (Chald.), *shoor*; corresp. to 7791:—wall.

7793. שׁוּר **Shûwr**, *shoor*; the same as 7791; *Shur*, a region of the Desert:—Shur.

7794. שׁוֹר **shôwr**, *shore*; from 7788; a *bullock* (as a *traveller*):—bull (-ock), cow, ox, wall [*by mistake for* 7791].

7795. שׂוֹרָה **sôwrâh**, *so-raw'*; from 7786 in the prim. sense of 5493; prop. a *ring*, i.e. (by analogy) a *row* (adv.):—principal.

שׂוֹרֵק **sôwrêq**. See 8321.

7796. שׂוֹרֵק **Sôwrêq**, *so-rake'*; the same as 8321; a *vine*; *Sorek*, a valley in Pal.:—Sorek.

7797. שׂוּשׂ **sûws**, *soos*; or

שִׂישׂ **sîys**, *sece*; a prim. root; to *be bright*, i.e. *cheerful*:—be glad, × greatly, joy, make mirth, rejoice.

7798. שַׁוְשָׁא **Shavshâʼ**, *shav-shaw'*; from 7797; *joyful*; *Shavsha*, an Isr.:—Shavsha.

7799. שׁוּשַׁן **shûwshan**, *shoo-shan'*; or

שׁוֹשָׁן **shôwshân**, *sho-shawn'*; or

שֹׁשָׁן **shôshân**, *sho-shawn'*; and (fem.)

שׁוֹשַׁנָּה **shôwshannâh**, *sho-shan-naw'*; from 7797; a *lily* (from its *whiteness*), as a flower or arch. ornament; also a (straight) *trumpet* (from the *tubular* shape):—lily, Shoshannim.

7800. שׁוּשַׁן **Shûwshan**, *shoo-shan'*; the same as 7799; *Shushan*, a place in Persia:—Shushan.

7801. שׁוּשַׁנְכִי **Shûwshankîy** (Chald.), *shoo-shan-kee'*; of for. or.; a *Shushankite* (collect.) or inhab. of some unknown place in Ass.:—Susanchites.

7802. שׁוּשַׁן עֵדוּת **Shûwshan ʻÊdûwth**, *shoo-shan' ay-dooth'*; or (plur. of former)

שׁוֹשַׁנִּים עֵדוּת **Shôwshannîym ʻÊdûwth**, *sho-shan-neem' ay-dooth'*; from 7799 and 5715; *lily* (or *trumpet*) *of assemblage*; *Shushan-Eduth* or *Shoshannim-Eduth*, the title of a popular song:—Shoshannim-Eduth, Shushan-eduth.

שׁוּשַׁק **Shûwshaq**. See 7895.

7803. שׁוּתֶלַח **Shûwthelach**, *shoo-theh'-lakh*; prob. from 7582 and the same as 8520; *crash of breakage*; *Shuthelach*, the name of two Isr.:—Shuthelah.

7804. שְׁזַב **shᵉzab** (Chald.), *shez-ab'*; corresp. to 5800; to *leave*, i.e. (caus.) *free*:—deliver.

7805. שָׁזַף **shâzaph**, *shaw-zaf'*; a prim. root; to *tan* (by sun-burning); fig. (as if by a piercing ray) to *scan*:—look up, see.

7806. שָׁזַר **shâzar**, *shaw-zar'*; a prim. root; to *twist* (a thread of straw):—twine.

7807. שַׁח **shach**, *shakh*; from 7817; *sunk*, i.e. *downcast*:— + humble.

7808. שֵׂחַ **sêach**, *say'-akh*; for 7879; *communion*, i.e. (reflex.) *meditation*:—thought.

7809. שָׁחַד **shâchad**, *shaw-khad'*; a prim. root; to *donate*, i.e. *bribe*:—hire, give a reward.

7810. שַׁחַד **shachad**, *shakh'-ad*; from 7809; a *donation* (venal or redemptive):—bribe (-ry), gift, present, reward.

7811. שָׂחָה **sâchâh**, *saw-khaw'*; a prim. root; to *swim*; caus. to *inundate*:—(make to) swim.

7812. שָׁחָה **shâchâh**, *shaw-khaw'*; a prim. root; to *depress*, i.e. *prostrate* (espec. reflex. in homage to royalty or God):—bow (self) down, crouch, fall down (flat), humbly beseech, do (make) obeisance, do reverence, make to stoop, worship.

7813. שָׂחוּ **sâchûw**, *saw'-khoo*; from 7811; a *pond* (for *swimming*):—to swim in.

7814. שְׂחוֹק **sᵉchôwq**, *sekh-oke'*; or

שְׂחֹק **sᵉchôq**, *sekh-oke'*; from 7832; *laughter* (in merriment or defiance):—derision, laughter (-ed to scorn, -ing), mocked, sport.

7815. שְׁחוֹר **shᵉchôwr**, *shekh-ore'*; from 7835; *dinginess*, i.e. perh. *soot*:—coal.

שִׁחוֹר **shîchôwr**. See 7883.

שָׁחוֹר **shâchôwr**. See 7838.

7816. שְׁחוּת **shᵉchûwth**, *shekh-ooth'*; from 7812; *pit*:—pit.

7817. שָׁחַח **shâchach**, *shaw-khakh'*; a prim. root; to *sink* or *depress* (reflex. or caus.):—bend, bow (down), bring (cast) down, couch, humble self, be (bring) low, stoop.

7818. שָׂחַט **sâchaṭ**, *saw-khat'*; a prim. root; to *tread* out, i.e. *squeeze* (grapes):—press.

7819. שָׁחַט **shâchaṭ**, *shaw-khat'*; a prim. root; to *slaughter* (in sacrifice or massacre):—kill, offer, shoot out, slay, slaughter.

7820. שָׁחַט **shâchaṭ**, *shaw-khat'*; a prim. root [rather ident. with 7819 through the idea of *striking*]; to *hammer* out:—beat.

7821. שְׁחִיטָה **shᵉchîyṭâh**, *shekh-ee-taw'*; from 7819; *slaughter*:—killing.

7822. שְׁחִין **shᵉchîyn**, *shekh-een'*; from an unused root prob. mean. to *burn*; *inflammation*, i.e. an *ulcer*:—boil, botch.

7823. שָׁחִיס **shâchîyç**, *shaw-khece'*; or

סָחִישׁ **çâchîysh**, *saw-kheesh'*; from an unused root appar. mean. to *sprout*, *after-growth*:—(that) which springeth of the same.

7824. שָׁחִיף **shâchîyph**, *shaw-kheef'*; from the same as 7828; a *board* (as *chipped* thin):—cieled with.

7825. שְׁחִית **shᵉchîyth**, *shekh-eeth'*; from 7812; a *pit*-fall (lit. or fig.):—destruction, pit.

7826. שַׁחַל **shachal**, *shakh'-al*; from an unused root prob. mean. to *roar*; a *lion* (from his characteristic *roar*):—(fierce) lion.

7827. שְׁחֵלֶת **shᵉchêleth**, *shekh-ay'-leth*; appar. from the same as 7826 through some obscure idea, perh. that of *peeling* off by concussion of sound; a *scale* or shell, i.e. the aromatic *mussel*:—onycha.

7828. שַׁחַף **shachaph**, *shakh'-af*; from an unused root mean. to *peel*, i.e. *emaciate*; the *gull* (as *thin*):—cuckoo.

7829. שַׁחֶפֶת **shachepheth**, *shakh-eh'-feth*; from the same as 7828; *emaciation*:—consumption.

7830. שַׁחַץ **shachats**, *shakh'-ats*; from an unused root appar. mean. to *strut*; *haughtiness* (as evinced by the attitude):— × lion, pride.

7831. שַׁחֲצוֹם **Shachatsôwm**, *shakh-ats-ome'*; from the same as 7830; *proudly*; *Shachatsom*, a place in Pal.:—Shahazimah [*from the marg.*].

7832. שָׂחַק **sâchaq**, *saw-khak'*; a prim. root; to *laugh* (in pleasure or detraction); by impl. to *play*:—deride, have in derision, laugh, make merry, mock (-er), play, rejoice, (laugh to) scorn, be in (make) sport.

7833. שָׁחַק **shâchaq**, *shaw-khak'*; a prim. root; to *comminute* (by trituration or attrition):—beat, wear.

7834. שַׁחַק **shachaq**, *shakh'-ak*; from 7833; a *powder* (as *beaten* small); by anal. a thin *vapor*; by extens. the *firmament*:—cloud, small dust, heaven, sky.

שְׂחֹק **sᵉchôq**. See 7814.

7835. שָׁחַר **shâchar**, *shaw-khar'*; a prim. root [rather ident. with 7836 through the idea of the *duskiness* of early dawn]; to *be dim* or dark (in color):—be black.

7836. שָׁחַר **shâchar**, *shaw-khar'*; a prim. root; prop. to *dawn*, i.e. (fig.) *be* (up) *early* at any task (with the impl. of earnestness); by extens. to *search* for (with painstaking):—[do something] betimes, enquire early, rise (seek) betimes, seek diligently) early, in the morning).

7837. שַׁחַר **shachar**, *shakh'-ar*; from 7836; *dawn* (lit., fig. or adv.):—day (-spring), early, light, morning, whence riseth.

שִׁחֹר **Shîchôr**. See 7883.

7838. שָׁחֹר **shâchôr**, *shaw-khore'*; or

שָׁחוֹר **shâchôwr**, *shaw-khore'*; from 7835; prop. *dusky*, but also (absol.) *jetty*:—black.

7839. שַׁחֲרוּת **shachărûwth**, *shakh-ar-ooth';* from 7836; a *dawning*, i.e. (fig.) *juvenescence:*—youth.

7840. שְׁחַרְחֹרֶת **shᵉcharchôreth**, *shekh-ar-kho'-reth;* from 7835; *swarthy:*—black.

7841. שְׁחַרְיָה **Shᵉcharyâh**, *shekh-ar-yaw';* from 7836 and 3050; *Jah has sought; Shecharjah*, an Isr.:—Shehariah.

7842. שַׁחֲרַיִם **Shachărayim**, *shakh-ar-ah'-yim;* dual of 7837; *double dawn; Shacharajim*, an Isr.:—Shaharaim.

7843. שָׁחַת **shâchath**, *shaw-khath';* a prim. root; to *decay*, i.e. (caus.) *ruin* (lit. or fig.):—batter, cast off, corrupt (-er, thing), destroy (-er, -uction), lose, mar, perish, spill, spoiler, × utterly, waste (-r).

7844. שְׁחַת **shᵉchath** (Chald.), *shekh-ath';* corresp. to 7843:—corrupt, fault.

7845. שַׁחַת **shachath**, *shakh'-ath;* from 7743; a *pit* (espec. as a trap); fig. *destruction:*—corruption, destruction, ditch, grave, pit.

7846. שֵׂט **sêṭ**, *sayte;* or

סֵט **çêṭ**, *sayt;* from 7750; a *departure* from right, i.e. *sin:*—revolter, that turn aside.

7847. שָׂטָה **sâṭâh**, *saw-taw';* a prim. root; to *deviate* from duty:—decline, go aside, turn.

7848. שִׁטָּה **shiṭṭâh**, *shit-taw';* fem. of a deriv. [only in the plur.

שִׁטִּים **shiṭṭîym**, *shit-teem'*, mean. the *sticks* of wood] from the same as 7850; the *acacia* (from its *scourging* thorns):—shittah, shittim. See also 1029.

7849. שָׁטַח **shâṭach**, *shaw-takh';* a prim. root; to *expand:*—all abroad, enlarge, spread, stretch out.

7850. שֹׁטֵט **shôṭêṭ**, *sho-tate';* act. part. of an otherwise unused root mean. (prop. to *pierce;* but only as a denom. from 7752) to *flog;* a *goad:*—scourge.

7851. שִׁטִּים **Shiṭṭîym**, *shit-teem';* the same as the plur. of 7848; *acacia* trees; *Shittim*, a place E. of the Jordan:—Shittim.

7852. שָׂטַם **sâṭam**, *saw-tam';* a prim. root; prop. to *lurk* for, i.e. *persecute:*—hate, oppose self against.

7853. שָׂטַן **sâṭan**, *saw-tan';* a prim. root; to *attack*, (fig.) *accuse:*—(be an) adversary, resist.

7854. שָׂטָן **sâṭân**, *saw-tawn';* from 7853; an *opponent;* espec. (with the art. pref.) *Satan*, the arch-enemy of good:—adversary, Satan, withstand.

7855. שִׂטְנָה **siṭnâh**, *sit-naw';* from 7853; *opposition* (by letter):—accusation.

7856. שִׂטְנָה **Siṭnâh**, *sit-naw';* the same as 7855; *Sitnah*, the name of a well in Pal.:—Sitnah.

7857. שָׁטַף **shâṭaph**, *shaw-taf';* a prim. root; to *gush;* by impl. to *inundate, cleanse;* by anal. to *gallop, conquer:*—drown, (over-) flow (-whelm), rinse, run, rush, (throughly) wash (away).

7858. שֶׁטֶף **sheṭeph**, *sheh'-tef;* or

שֵׁטֶף **shêṭeph**, *shay'-tef;* from 7857; a *deluge* (lit. or fig.):—flood, outrageous, overflowing.

7859. שְׁטַר **shᵉṭar** (Chald.), *shet-ar';* of uncert. der.: a *side:*—side.

7860. שֹׁטֵר **shôṭêr**, *sho-tare';* act. part. of an otherwise unused root prob. mean. to *write;* prop. a *scribe*, i.e. (by anal. or impl.) an official *superintendent* or *magistrate:*—officer, overseer, ruler.

7861. °שִׁטְרַי **Shiṭray**, *shit-rah'ee;* from the same as 7860; *magisterial; Shitrai*, an Isr.:—Shitrai.

7862. שַׁי **shay**, *shah'ee;* prob. from 7737; a *gift* (as *available*):—present.

7863. שִׂיא **sîy'**, *see;* from the same as 7721 by perm.; *elevation:*—excellency.

7864. שְׁיָא **Shᵉyâ'**, *sheh-yaw';* for 7724; *Sheja*, an Isr.:—Sheva [*from the marg.*].

7865. שִׂיאֹן **Sîy'ôn**, *see-ohn';* from 7863; *peak; Sion*, the summit of Mt. Hermon:—Sion.

7866. שִׁיאוֹן **Shî'yôwn**, *shee-ohn';* from the same as 7722; *ruin; Shijon*, a place in Pal.:—Shihon.

7867. שִׂיב **sîyb**, *seeb;* a prim. root; prop. to *become aged*, i.e. (by impl.) to *grow gray:*—(be) grayheaded.

7868. שִׂיב **sîyb** (Chald.), *seeb;* corresp. to 7867:—elder.

7869. שֵׂיב **sêyb**, *sabe;* from 7867; old *age:*—age.

7870. שִׁיבָה **shîybâh**, *shee-baw';* by perm. from 7725; a *return* (of property):—captivity.

7871. שִׁיבָה **shîybâh**, *shee-baw';* from 3427; *residence:*—while . . . lay.

7872. שֵׂיבָה **sêybâh**, *say-baw';* fem. of 7869; old *age:*—(be) gray (grey, hoar, -y) hairs (head, -ed), old age.

7873. שִׂיג **sîyg**, *seeg;* from 7734; a *withdrawal* (into a private place):—pursuing.

7874. שִׂיד **sîyd**, *seed;* a prim. root prob. mean. to *boil* up (comp. 7736); used only as denom. from 7875; to *plaster:*—plaister.

7875. שִׂיד **sîyd**, *seed;* from 7874; *lime* (as *boiling* when slacked):—lime, plaister.

7876. שָׁיָה **shâyâh**, *shaw-yaw';* a prim. root; to *keep* in memory:—be unmindful. [Render Deut. 32 : 18, "A Rock bore thee, *thou must recollect;* and (yet) thou hast forgotten," etc.]

7877. שִׁיזָא **Shîyzâ'**, *shee-zaw';* of unknown der.; *Shiza*, an Isr.:—Shiza.

7878. שִׂיחַ **sîyach**, *see'-akh;* a prim. root; to *ponder*, i.e. (by impl.) *converse* (with oneself, and hence aloud) or (trans.) *utter:*—commune, complain, declare, meditate, muse, pray, speak, talk (with).

7879. שִׂיחַ **sîyach**, *see'-akh;* from 7878; a *contemplation;* by impl. an *utterance:*—babbling, communication, complaint, meditation, prayer, talk.

7880. שִׂיחַ **sîyach**, *see'-akh;* from 7878; a *shoot* (as if *uttered* or put forth), i.e. (gen.) *shrubbery:*—bush, plant, shrub.

7881. שִׂיחָה **sîychâh**, *see-khaw';* fem. of 7879; *reflection;* by extens. *devotion:*—meditation, prayer.

7882. שִׁיחָה **shîychâh**, *shee-khaw';* for 7745; a *pit*-fall:—pit.

7883. שִׁיחוֹר **Shîychôwr**, *shee-khore';* or

שִׁחוֹר **Shîchôwr**, *shee-khore';* or

שִׁחֹר **Shîchôr**, *shee-khore';* prob. from 7835; *dark*, i.e. *turbid; Shichor*, a stream of Egypt:—Shihor, Sihor.

7884. שִׁיחוֹר לִבְנָת **Shîychôwr Libnâth**, *shee-khore' lib-nawth';* from the same as 7883 and 3835; *darkish whiteness; Shichor-Libnath*, a stream of Pal.:—Shihor-libnath.

7885. שַׁיִט **shayiṭ**, *shah' yit;* from 7751; an *oar;* also (comp. 7752) a *scourge*° (fig.):—oar, scourge.

7886. שִׁילֹה **Shîylôh**, *shee-lo';* from 7951; *tranquil; Shiloh*, an epithet of the Messiah:—Shiloh.

7887. שִׁילֹה **Shîylôh**, *shee-lo';* or

שִׁלֹה **Shîlôh**, *shee-lo';* or

שִׁילוֹ **Shîylôw**, *shee-lo';* or

שִׁלוֹ **Shîlôw**, *shee-lo';* from the same as 7886; *Shiloh*, a place in Pal.:—Shiloh.

7888. שִׁילוֹנִי **Shiylôwnîy**, *shee-lo-nee';* or

שִׁילֹנִי **Shîylônîy**, *shee-lo-nee';* or

שִׁלֹנִי **Shîlônîy**, *shee-lo-nee';* from 7887; a *Shilonite* or inhab. of Shiloh:—Shilonite.

שֵׁילָל **shêylâl**. See 7758.

7889. °שִׁימוֹן **Shîymôwn**, *shee-mone';* appar. for 3452; *desert; Shimon*, an Isr.:—Shimon.

7890. °שַׁיִן **shayin**, *shah'-yin;* from an unused root mean. to *urinate; urine:*—piss.

7891. שִׁיר **shiyr**, *sheer;* or (the orig. form)

°שׁוּר **shûwr** (1 Sam. 18 : 6), *shoor;* a prim. root [rather ident. with 7788 through the idea of *strolling* minstrelsy]: to *sing:*—behold [*by mistake for* 7789], sing (-er, -ing man, -ing woman).

7892. שִׁיר **shîyr**, *sheer;* or fem.

שִׁירָה **shîyrâh**, *shee-raw';* from 7891; a *song;* abstr. *singing:*—musical (-ick), × sing (-er, -ing), song.

שִׂישׂ **sîys**. See 7797.

7893. שַׁיִשׁ **shayish**, *shah'-yish;* from an unused root mean. to *bleach*, i.e. *whiten; white*, i.e. *marble:*—marble. See 8336.

7894. שִׁישָׁא **Shîyshâ'**, *shee-shaw';* from the same as 7893; *whiteness; Shisha*, an Isr.:—Shisha.

7895. שִׁישַׁק **Shîyshaq**, *shee-shak';* or

°שׁוּשַׁק **Shûwshaq**, *shoo-shak';* of Eg. der.; *Shishak*, an Eg. king:—Shishak.

7896. שִׁית **shîyth**, *sheeth;* a prim. root; to *place* (in a very wide application):—apply, appoint, array, bring, consider, lay (up), let alone, × look, make, mark, put (on), + regard, set, shew, be stayed, × take.

7897. שִׁית **shîyth**, *sheeth;* from 7896; a *dress* (as *put* on):—attire.

7898. שַׁיִת **shayith**, *shah'-yith;* from 7896; *scrub* or *trash*, i.e. wild *growth* of weeds or briers (as if *put* on the field):—thorns.

7899. שֵׂךְ **sêk**, *sake;* from 5526 in the sense of 7753; a *brier* (as of a hedge):—prick.

7900. שֹׂךְ **sôk**, *soke;* from 5526 in the sense of 7753; a *booth* (as *interlaced*):—tabernacle.

7901. שָׁכַב **shâkab**, *shaw-kab';* a prim. root; to *lie* down (for rest, sexual connection, decease or any other purpose):— × at all, cast down, ([over-]) lay (self) (down), (make to) lie (down, down to sleep, still, with), lodge, ravish, take rest, sleep, stay.

7902. שְׁכָבָה **shᵉkâbâh**, *shek-aw-baw';* from 7901; a *lying* down (of dew, or for the sexual act):— × carnally, copulation, × lay, seed.

7903. שְׁכֹבֶת **shᵉkôbeth**, *shek-o'-beth;* from 7901; a (sexual) *lying* with:— × lie.

7904. שָׁכָה **shâkâh**, *shaw-kaw';* a prim. root; to *roam* (through lust):—in the morning [*by mistake for* 7925].

7905. שֻׂכָּה **sukkâh**, *sook-kaw';* fem. of 7900 in the sense of 7899; a *dart* (as pointed like a *thorn*):—barbed iron.

7906. שֵׂכוּ **Sêkûw**, *say'-koo;* from an unused root appar. mean. to *surmount;* an *observatory* (with the art.); *Seku*, a place in Pal.:—Sechu.

7907. שֶׂכְוִי **sekvîy**, *sek-vee';* from the same as 7906; *observant*, i.e. (concr.) the *mind:*—heart.

7908. שְׁכוֹל **shᵉkôwl**, *shek-ole';* infin. of 7921: *bereavement:*—loss of children, spoiling.

7909. שַׁכּוּל **shakkuwl**, *shak-kool';* or

שַׁכֻּל **shakkul**, *shak-kool';* from 7921; *bereaved:*—barren, bereaved (robbed) of children (whelps).

7910. שִׁכּוֹר **shikkôwr**, *shik-kore';* or

שִׁכֹּר **shikkôr**, *shik-kore';* from 7937; *intoxicated*, as a state or a habit:—drunk (-ard, -en, -en man).

7911. שָׁכַח **shâkach**, *shaw-kakh';* or

שָׁכֵחַ **shâkêach**, *shaw-kay'-akh*, a prim. root; to *mislay*, i.e. to *be oblivious* of, from want of memory or attention:— × at all, (cause to) forget.

7912. שְׁכַח **shᵉkach** (Chald.), *shek-akh';* corresp. to 7911 through the idea of disclosure of a *covered* or *forgotten* thing; to *discover* (lit. or fig.):—find.

7913. שָׁכֵחַ **shâkêach**, *shaw-kay'-akh;* from 7911; *oblivious:*—forget.

7914. שְׂכִיָּה **sᵉkîyâh**, *sek-ee-yaw';* fem. from the same as 7906; a *conspicuous* object:—picture.

7915. שַׂכִּין **sakkîyn**, *sak-keen';* intens. perh. from the same as 7906 in the sense of 7753; a *knife* (as *pointed* or edged):—knife.

7916. שָׂכִיר **sâkîyr**, *saw-keer';* from 7936; a man *at wages* by the day or year:—hired (man, servant), hireling.

7917. שְׂכִירָה **sᵉkîyrâh**, *sek-ee-raw';* fem. of 7916; a *hiring:*—that is hired.

7918. שָׁכַךְ **shâkak**, *shaw-kak';* a prim. root; to *weave* (i.e. *lay*) a trap; fig. (through the idea of *secreting*) to *allay* (passions; phys. *abate* a flood):—appease, assuage, make to cease, pacify, set.

7919. שָׂכַל **sâkal**, *saw-kal';* a prim. root; to *be* (caus. *make* or *act*) *circumspect* and hence *intelligent:*—consider, expert, instruct, prosper, (deal) prudent (-ly), (give) skill (-ful), have good success, teach, (have, make to) understand (-ing), wisdom, (be, behave self, consider, make) wise (-ly), guide wittingly.

7920. שְׂכַל **sᵉkal** (Chald.), *sek-al';* corresp. to 7919:—consider.

7921. שָׁכֹל **shâkôl**, *shaw-kole';* a prim. root; prop. to *miscarry*, i.e. *suffer abortion;* by anal. to *bereave* (lit. or fig.):—bereave (of children), barren, cast calf (fruit, young), be (make) childless, deprive, destroy, × expect, lose children, miscarry, rob of children, spoil.

7922. שֶׂכֶל **sekel**, *seh'-kel;* or

שֵׂכֶל **sêkel**, *say'-kel;* from 7919; *intelligence;* by impl. *success:*—discretion, knowledge, policy, prudence, sense, understanding, wisdom, wise.

שַׁכֻּל **shakkûl**. See 7909.

שִׂכְלוּת **siklûwth**. See 5531.

7923. שִׁכֻּלִים **shikkulîym**, *shik-koo-leem';* plur. from 7921; *childlessness* (by continued bereavements):—to have after loss of others.

7924. שׇׂכְלְתָנוּ **soklᵉthânûw** (Chald.), *sok-leth-aw-noo';* from 7920; *intelligence:*—understanding.

7925. שָׁכַם **shâkam**, *shaw-kam';* a prim. root: prop. to *incline* (the shoulder to a burden); but used only as denom. from 7926; lit. to *load up* (on the back of man or beast), i.e. to *start early* in the morning:—(arise, be up, get [oneself] up, rise up) early (betimes), morning.

7926. שְׁכֶם **shᵉkem**, *shek-em';* from 7925; the *neck* (between the shoulders) as the place of burdens; fig. the *spur* of a hill:—back, × consent, portion, shoulder.

7927. שְׁכֶם **Shᵉkem**, *shek-em';* the same as 7926; *ridge; Shekem*, a place in Pal.:—Shechem.

7928. שֶׁכֶם **Shekem**, *sheh'-kem;* for 7926; *Shekem*, the name of a Hivite and two Isr.:—Shechem.

7929. שִׁכְמָה **shikmâh**, *shik-maw';* fem. of 7926; the *shoulder*-bone:—shoulder blade.

7930. שִׁכְמִי **Shikmîy**, *shik-mee';* patron. from 7928; a *Shikmite* (collect.), or desc. of Shekem:—Shichemites.

7931. שָׁכַן **shâkan**, *shaw-kan';* a prim. root [appar. akin (by transm.) to 7901 through the idea of *lodging;* comp. 5531, 7925]; to *reside* or permanently stay (lit. or fig.):—abide, continue, (cause to, make to) dwell (-er), have habitation, inhabit, lay, place, (cause to) remain, rest, set (up).

7932. שְׁכַן **shᵉkan** (Chald.), *shek-an';* corresp. to 7931:—cause to dwell, have habitation.

7933. שֶׁכֶן **sheken**, *sheh'-ken;* from 7931; a *residence:*—habitation.

7934. שָׁכֵן **shâkên**, *shaw-kane';* from 7931; a *resident;* by extens. a fellow-*citizen:*—inhabitant, neighbour, nigh.

7935. שְׁכַנְיָה **Shᵉkanyâh**, *shek-an-yaw';* or (prol.)

שְׁכַנְיָהוּ **Shᵉkanyâhûw**, *shek-an-yaw'-hoo;* from 7931 and 3050; *Jah has dwelt; Shekanjah*, the name of nine Isr.:—Shecaniah, Shechaniah.

7936. שָׂכַר **sâkar**, *saw-kar';* or (by perm.)

סָכַר **çâkar** (Ezra 4 : 5), *saw-kar';* a prim. root [appar. akin (by prosthesis) to 3739 through the idea of temporary *purchase;* comp. 7937]; to *hire:*—earn wages, hire (out self), reward, × surely.

7937. שָׁכַר **shâkar**, *shaw-kar';* a prim root; to *become tipsy;* in a qualified sense, to *satiate* with a stimulating drink or (fig.) influence:—(be filled with) drink (abundantly), (be, make) drunk (-en), be merry. [Superlative of 8248.]

7938. שֶׂכֶר **seker**, *seh'-ker;* from 7936; *wages:*—reward, sluices.

7939. שָׂכָר **sâkâr**, *saw-kawr';* from 7936; *payment* of contract; concr. *salary, fare, maintenance;* by impl. *compensation, benefit:*—hire, price, reward [-ed], wages, worth.

7940. שָׂכָר **Sâkar**, *saw-kar';* the same as 7939; *recompense; Sakar*, the name of two Isr.:—Sacar.

7941. שֵׁכָר **shêkâr**, *shay-kawr';* from 7937; an *intoxicant*, i.e. intensely alcoholic *liquor:*—strong drink, + drunkard, strong wine.

שִׁכּוֹר **shikkôr**. See 7910.

7942. שִׁכְּרוֹן **Shikkᵉrôwn**, *shik-ker-one';* for 7943; *drunkenness; Shikkeron*, a place in Pal.:—Shicron.

7943. שִׁכָּרוֹן **shikkârôwn**, *shik-kaw-rone';* from 7937; *intoxication:*—(be) drunken (-ness).

7944. שַׁל **shal**, *shal;* from 7952 abbrev.; a *fault:*—error.

7945. שֶׁל **shel**, *shel;* for the rel. 834; used with prep. pref., and often followed by some pron. aff.; on *account* of, *what*soever, *which*soever:—cause, sake.

7946. שַׁלְאֲנָן **shalʼănân**, *shal-an-awn';* for 7600; *tranquil:*—being at ease.

7947. שָׁלַב **shâlab**, *shaw-lab';* a prim. root; to *space* off; intens. (*evenly*) to *make equidistant:*—equally distant, set in order.

7948. שָׁלָב **shâlâb**, *shaw-lawb';* from 7947; a *spacer* or raised *interval*, i.e. the *stile* in a frame or panel:—ledge.

7949. שָׁלַג **shâlag**, *shaw-lag';* a prim. root; prop. mean. to be *white;* used only as denom. from 7950; to be *snow-white* (with the linen clothing of the slain):—be as snow.

7950. שֶׁלֶג **sheleg**, *sheh'-leg;* from 7949; *snow* (prob. from its *whiteness*):—snow (-y).

7951. שָׁלָה **shâlâh**, *shaw-law';* or

שָׁלַו **shâlav** (Job 3 : 26), *shaw-lav';* a prim. root; to be *tranquil*, i.e. *secure* or *successful:*—be happy, prosper, be in safety.

7952. שָׁלָה **shâlâh**, *shaw-law';* a prim. root [prob. rather ident. with 7953 through the idea of *educing*]; to *mislead:*—deceive, be negligent.

7953. שָׁלָה **shâlâh**, *shaw-law';* a prim. root [rather cognate (by contr.) to the base of 5394, 7997 and their congeners through the idea of *extracting*]; to *draw* out or off, i.e. *remove* (the soul by death):—take away.

7954. שְׁלָה **shᵉlâh** (Chald.), *shel-aw';* corresp. to 7951; to *be secure:*—at rest.

שִׁלֹה **Shîlôh**. See 7887.

7955. שָׁלָה **shâlâh** (Chald.), *shaw-law';* from a root corresp. to 7952; a *wrong:*—thing amiss.

שֵׁלָה **shêlâh**. See 7596.

7956. שֵׁלָה **Shêlâh**, *shay-law';* the same as 7596 (shortened); *request; Shelah*, the name of a postdiluvian patriarch and of an Isr.:—Shelah.

7957. שַׁלְהֶבֶת **shalhebeth**, *shal-heh'-beth;* from the same as 3851 with sibilant pref.; a *flare* of fire:—(flaming) flame.

שָׁלֵו **shâlav**. See 7951.

7958. שְׂלָו **sᵉlâv**, *sel-awv';* or

שְׂלָיו **sᵉlâyv**, *sel-awv';* by orth. var. from 7951 through the idea of *sluggishness;* the *quail* collect. (as *slow* in flight from its weight):—quails.

7959. שֶׁלֶו **shelev**, *sheh'-lev;* from 7951; *security:*—prosperity.

שִׁלוֹ **Shîlôw**. See 7887.

7960. שָׁלוּ **shâlûw** (Chald.), *shaw-loo';* or

שָׁלוּת **shâlûwth** (Chald.), *shaw-looth';* from the same as 7955; a *fault:*—error, × fail, thing amiss.

7961. שָׁלֵו **shâlêv**, *shaw-lave';* or

שָׁלֵיו **shâlêyv**, *shaw-lave';* fem.

שְׁלֵוָה **shᵉlêvâh**, *shel-ay-vaw';* from 7951; *tranquil;* (in a bad sense) *careless;* abstr. *security;*—(being) at ease, peaceable, (in) prosper (-ity), quiet (-ness), wealthy.

7962. שַׁלְוָה **shalvâh**, *shal-vaw';* from 7951; *security* (genuine or false):—abundance, peace (-ably), prosperity, quietness.

7963. שְׁלֵוָה **shᵉlêvâh** (Chald.), *shel-ay-vaw';* corresp. to 7962; *safety:*—tranquillity. See also 7961.

7964. שִׁלּוּחַ **shillûwach**, *shil-loo'-akh;* or

שִׁלֻּחַ **shillûach**, *shil-loo'-akh;* from 7971; (only in plur.) a *dismissal*, i.e. (of a wife) *divorce* (espec. the document); also (of a daughter) *dower:*—presents, have sent back.

7965. שָׁלוֹם **shâlôwm**, *shaw-lome';* or

שָׁלֹם **shâlôm**, *shaw-lome';* from 7999; *safe*, i.e. (fig.) *well, happy, friendly;* also (abstr.) *welfare*, i.e. health, prosperity, peace:—× do, familiar, × fare, favour, + friend, × greet, (good) health, (× perfect, such as be at) peace (-able, -ably), prosper (-ity, -ous), rest, safe (-ly), salute, welfare, (× all is, be) well, × wholly.

7966. שִׁלּוּם **shillûwm**, *shil-loom';* or

שִׁלֻּם **shillûm**, *shil-loom';* from 7999; a *requital*, i.e. (secure) *retribution*, (venal) a *fee:*—recompense, reward.

7967. שַׁלּוּם **Shallûwm**, *shal-loom';* or (shorter)

שַׁלֻּם **Shallûm**, *shal-loom';* the same as 7966; *Shallum*, the name of fourteen Isr.:—Shallum.

שְׁלוֹמִית **Shᵉlôwmîyth**. See 8019.

7968. שַׁלּוּן **Shallûwn**, *shal-loon';* prob. for 7967; *Shallun*, an Isr.:—Shallum.

7969. שָׁלוֹשׁ **shâlôwsh**, *shaw-loshe';* or

שָׁלֹשׁ **shâlôsh**, *shaw-loshe';* masc.

שְׁלוֹשָׁה **shᵉlôwshâh**, *shel-o-shaw';* or

שְׁלֹשָׁה **shᵉlôshâh**, *shel-o-shaw';* a prim. number; *three;* occasionally (ordinal) *third*, or (multipl.) *thrice:*— + fork, + often [-times], third, thir [-teen, -teenth], three, + thrice. Comp. 7991.

7970. שְׁלוֹשִׁים **shᵉlôwshîym**, *shel-o-sheem';* or

שְׁלֹשִׁים **shᵉlôshîym**, *shel-o-sheem';* multiple of 7969; *thirty;* or (ordinal) *thirtieth:*—thirty, thirtieth. Comp. 7991.

שָׁלוּת **shâlûwth**. See 7960.

7971. שָׁלַח **shâlach**, *shaw-lakh';* a prim. root; to *send* away, for, or out (in a great variety of applications):— × any wise, appoint, bring (on the way), cast (away, out), conduct, × earnestly, forsake, give (up), grow long, lay, leave, let depart (down, go, loose), push away, put (away, forth, in, out), reach forth, send (away, forth, out), set, shoot (forth, out), sow, spread, stretch forth (out).

7972. שְׁלַח **shᵉlach** (Chald.), *shel-akh';* corresp. to 7971:—put, send.

7973. שֶׁלַח **shelach**, *sheh'-lakh;* from 7971; a *missile* of attack, i.e. *spear;* also (fig.) a *shoot* of growth, i.e. *branch:*—dart, plant, × put off, sword, weapon.

7974. שֶׁלַח **Shelach**, *sheh'-lakh;* the same as 7973; *Shelach,* a postdiluvian patriarch:—Salah, Shelah. Comp. 7975.

7975. שִׁלֹּחַ **Shilôach**, *shee-lo'-akh;* or (in imitation of 7974)

שֶׁלַח **Shelach** (Neh. 3 : 15), *sheh'-lakh;* from 7971; *rill; Shiloäch,* a fountain of Jerus.:—Shiloah, Siloah.

שִׁלֻּחַ **shillûach**. See 7964.

7976. שִׁלֻּחָה **shilluchâh**, *shil-loo-khaw';* fem. of 7964; a *shoot:*—branch.

7977. שִׁלְחִי **Shilchîy**, *shil-khee';* from 7973; *missive,* i.e. *armed; Shilchi,* an Isr.:—Shilhi.

7978. שִׁלְחִים **Shilchîym**, *shil-kheem';* plur. of 7973; *javelins* or *sprouts; Shilchim,* a place in Pal.:—Shilhim.

7979. שֻׁלְחָן **shulchân**, *shool-khawn';* from 7971; a *table* (as *spread* out); by impl. a *meal:*—table.

7980. שָׁלַט **shâlaṭ**, *shaw-lat';* a prim. root; to *dominate,* i.e. *govern;* by impl. to *permit:*—(bear, have) rule, have dominion, give (have) power.

7981. שְׁלֵט **sheleṭ** (Chald.), *shel-ate';* corresp. to 7980:—have the mastery, have power, bear rule, be (make) ruler.

7982. שֶׁלֶט **sheleṭ**, *sheh'-let;* from 7980; prob. a *shield* (as *controlling,* i.e. protecting the person):—shield.

7983. שִׁלְטוֹן **shilṭôwn**, *shil-tone';* from 7980; a *potentate:*—power.

7984. שִׁלְטוֹן **shilṭôwn** (Chald.), *shil-tone';* or

שִׁלְטֹן **shilṭôn**, *shil-tone';* corresp. to 7983:—ruler.

7985. שָׁלְטָן **sholṭân** (Chald.), *shol-tawn';* from 7981; *empire* (abstr. or concr.):—dominion.

7986. שַׁלֶּטֶת **shalleṭeth**, *shal-leh'-teth;* fem. from 7980; a *vixen:*—imperious.

7987. שְׁלִי **shelîy**, *shel-ee';* from 7951; *privacy:*—+ quietly.

7988. שִׁלְיָה **shilyâh**, *shil-yaw';* fem. from 7953; a *fœtus* or *babe* (as *extruded* in birth):—young one.

שְׁלָיו **selâyv**. See 7958.

שַׁלֵיו **shalêyv**. See 7961.

7989. שַׁלִּיט **shallîyṭ**, *shal-leet';* from 7980; *potent;* concr. a *prince* or *warrior:*—governor, mighty, that hath power, ruler.

7990. שַׁלִּיט **shallîyṭ** (Chald.), *shal-leet';* corresp. to 7989; *mighty;* abstr. *permission;* concr. a *premier:*—captain, be lawful, rule (-r).

7991. שָׁלִישׁ **shâlîysh**, *shaw-leesh';* or

שָׁלוֹשׁ° **shâlôwsh** (1 Chron. 11 : 11; 12 : 18), *shaw-loshe';* or

שָׁלֹשׁ° **shâlôsh** (2 Sam. 23 : 13), *shaw-loshe';* from 7969; a *triple,* i.e. (as a musical instrument) a *triangle* (or perh. rather *three*-stringed lute); also (as an indef. great quantity) a *three-fold* measure (perh. a *treble* ephah); also (as an officer) a general of the *third* rank (upward, i.e. the highest):—captain, instrument of musick, (great) lord, (great) measure, prince, three [*from the marg.*].

7992. שְׁלִישִׁי **shelîyshîy**, *shel-ee-shee';* ordinal from 7969; *third;* fem. a *third* (part); by extens. a *third* (day, year or time); spec. a *third*-story cell):—third (part, rank, time), three (years old).

7993. שָׁלַךְ **shâlak**, *shaw-lak';* a prim. root; to *throw* out, down or away (lit. or fig.):—adventure, cast (away, down, forth, off, out), hurl, pluck, throw.

7994. שָׁלָךְ **shâlâk**, *shaw-lawk';* from 7993; *bird of prey,* usually thought to be the *pelican* (from *casting* itself into the sea):—cormorant.

7995. שַׁלֶּכֶת **shalleketh**, *shal-leh'-keth;* from 7993; a *felling* (of trees):—when cast.

7996. שַׁלֶּכֶת **Shalleketh**, *shal-leh'-keth;* the same as 7995; *Shalleketh,* a gate in Jerus.:—Shalleketh.

7997. שָׁלַל **shâlal**, *shaw-lal';* a prim. root; to *drop* or *strip;* by impl. to *plunder:*—let fall, make self a prey, × of purpose, (make a, [take]) spoil.

7998. שָׁלָל **shâlâl**, *shaw-lawl';* from 7997; *booty:*—prey, spoil.

7999. שָׁלַם **shâlam**, *shaw-lam';* a prim. root; to *be safe* (in mind, body or estate); fig. to *be* (caus. *make*) *completed;* by impl. to *be friendly;* by extens. to *reciprocate* (in various applications):—make amends, (make an) end, finish, full, give again, make good, (re-) pay (again), (make) (to) (be at) peace (-able), that is perfect, perform, (make) prosper (-ous), recompense, render, requite, make restitution, restore, reward, × surely.

8000. שְׁלַם **shelam** (Chald.), *shel-am';* corresp. to 7999; to *complete,* to *restore:*—deliver, finish.

8001. שְׁלָם **shelâm** (Chald.), *shel-awm';* corresp. to 7965; *prosperity:*—peace.

8002. שֶׁלֶם **shelem**, *sheh'-lem;* from 7999; prop. *requital,* i.e. a (voluntary) sacrifice in *thanks:*—peace offering.

8003. שָׁלֵם **shâlêm**, *shaw-lame';* from 7999; *complete* (lit. or fig.); espec. *friendly:*—full, just, made ready, peaceable, perfect (-ed), quiet, Shalem [*by mistake for a name*], whole.

8004. שָׁלֵם **Shâlêm**, *shaw-lame';* the same as 8003; *peaceful; Shalem,* an early name of Jerus.:—Salem.

שָׁלֹם **shâlôm**. See 7965.

8005. שִׁלֵּם **shillêm**, *shil-lame';* from 7999; *requital:*—recompense.

8006. שִׁלֵּם **Shillêm**, *shil-lame';* the same as 8005; *Shillem,* an Isr.:—Shillem.

שִׁלֻּם **shillûm**. See 7966.

שַׁלֻּם **Shallûm**. See 7967.

8007. שַׂלְמָא **Salmâ'**, *sal-maw';* prob. for 8008; *clothing; Salma,* the name of two Isr.:—Salma.

8008. שַׂלְמָה **salmâh**, *sal-maw';* transp. for 8071; a *dress:*—clothes, garment, raiment.

8009. שַׂלְמָה **Salmâh**, *sal-maw';* the same as 8008; *clothing; Salmah,* an Isr.:—Salmon. Comp. 8012.

8010. שְׁלֹמֹה **Shelômôh**, *shel-o-mo';* from 7965; *peaceful; Shelomoh,* David's successor:—Solomon.

8011. שִׁלֻּמָה **shillumâh**, *shil-loo-maw';* fem. of 7966; *retribution:*—reward.

8012. שַׂלְמוֹן **Salmôwn**, *sal-mone';* from 8008; *investiture; Salmon,* an Isr.:—Salmon. Comp. 8009.

8013. שְׁלֹמוֹת **Shelômôwth**, *shel-o-môth';* fem. plur. of 7965; *pacifications; Shelomoth,* the name of two Isr.:—Shelomith [*from the marg.*], Shelomoth. Comp. 8019.

8014. שַׁלְמַי **Salmay**, *sal-mah'ee;* from 8008; *clothed; Salmai,* an Isr.:—Shalmai.

8015. שְׁלֹמִי **Shelômîy**, *shel-o-mee';* from 7965; *peaceable; Shelomi,* an Isr.:—Shelomi.

8016. שִׁלֵּמִי **Shillêmîy**, *shil-lay-mee';* patron. from 8006; a *Shilemite* (collect.) or desc. of Shillem:—Shillemites.

8017. שְׁלֻמִיאֵל **Shelûmîy'êl**, *shel-oo-mee-ale';* from 7965 and 410; *peace of God; Shelumiël,* an Isr.:—Shelumiel.

8018. שֶׁלֶמְיָה **Shelemyâh**, *shel-em-yaw';* or

שֶׁלֶמְיָהוּ **Shelemyâhuw**, *shel-em-yaw'-hoo;* from 8002 and 3050; *thank-offering of Jah; Shelemjah,* the name of nine Isr.:—Shelemiah.

8019. שְׁלֹמִית **Shelômîyth**, *shel-o-meeth';* or

שְׁלוֹמִית **Shelôwmîyth** (Ezra 8 : 10), *shel-o-meeth';* from 7965; *peaceableness; Shelomith,* the name of five Isr. and three Israelitesses:—Shelomith.

8020. שַׁלְמַן **Shalman**, *shal-man';* of for. der.; *Shalman,* a king appar. of Assyria:—Shalman. Comp. 8022.

8021. שַׁלְמֹן **shalmôn**, *shal-mone';* from 7999; a *bribe:*—reward.

8022. שַׁלְמַנְאֶסֶר **Shalman'eçer**, *shal-man-eh'-ser;* of for. der.; *Shalmaneser,* an Ass. king:—Shalmaneser. Comp. 8020.

8023. שִׁלֹנִי **Shîlônîy**, *shee-lo-nee';* the same as 7888; *Shiloni,* an Isr.:—Shiloni.

8024. שֵׁלָנִי **Shêlânîy**, *shay-law-nee';* from 7956; a *Shelanite* (collect.), or desc. of Shelah:—Shelanites.

8025. שָׁלַף **shâlaph**, *shaw-laf';* a prim. root; to *pull* out, up or off:—draw (off), grow up, pluck off.

8026. שֶׁלֶף **sheleph**, *sheh'-lef;* from 8025; *extract; Sheleph,* a son of Jokthan:—Sheleph.

8027. שָׁלַשׁ **shâlash**, *shaw-lash';* a prim. root perh. orig. to *intensify,* i.e. *treble;* but appar. used only as denom. from 7969, to *be* (caus. *make*) *triplicate* (by restoration, in portions, strands, days or years):—do the third time, (divide into, stay) three (days, -fold, parts, years old).

8028. שֶׁלֶשׁ **Shelesh**, *sheh'-lesh;* from 8027; *triplet; Shelesh,* an Isr.:—Shelesh.

שָׁלֹשׁ **shâlôsh**. See 7969.

8029. שִׁלֵּשׁ **shillêsh**, *shil-laysh';* from 8027; a desc. of the *third* degree, i.e. *great grandchild:*—third [generation].

8030. שִׁלְשָׁה **Shilshâh**, *shil-shaw';* fem. from the same as 8028; *triplication; Shilshah,* an Isr.:—Shilshah.

8031. שָׁלִשָׁה **Shâlîshâh**, *shaw-lee-shaw';* fem. from 8027; *trebled* land; *Shalishah,* a place in Pal.:—Shalisha.

שְׁלֹשָׁה **shâlôshâh**. See 7969.

8032. שִׁלְשׁוֹם **shilshôwm**, *shil-shome';* or

שִׁלְשֹׁם **shilshôm**, *shil-shome';* from the same as 8028; *trebly,* i.e. (in time) *day before yesterday:*—+ before (that time, -time), excellent things [*from the marg.*], + heretofore, three days, + time past.

שְׁלֹשִׁים **shelôshîym**. See 7970.

שַׁלְתִּיאֵל **Shaltîy'êl**. See 7597.

8033. שָׁם **shâm**, *shawm;* a prim. particle [rather from the rel. 834]; *there* (transf. to time) *then;* often *thither,* or *thence:*—in it, + thence, there (-in, + of, + out), + thither, + whither.

8034. שֵׁם **shêm**, *shame;* a prim. word [perh. rather from 7760 through the idea of definite and conspicuous *position;* comp. 8064]; an *appellation,* as a mark or memorial of individuality; by impl. *honor, authority, character:*— + base, [in-] fame [-ous], name (-d), renown, report.

8035. שֵׁם **Shêm**, *shame;* the same as 8034; *name; Shem,* a son of Noah (often includ. his posterity):—Sem, Shem.

8036. שֻׁם **shum** (Chald.), *shoom;* corresp. to 8034:—name.

8037. שַׁמָּא **Shammâ'**, *sham-maw';* from 8074; *desolation; Shamma,* an Isr.:—Shamma.

8038. שֶׁמְאֵבֶר **Shem'êber**, *shem-ay'-ber;* appar. from 8034 and 83; *name of pinion,* i.e. *illustrious; Shemeber,* a king of Zeboim:—Shemeber.

8039. שִׁמְאָה **Shim'âh**, *shim-aw';* perh. for 8093; *Shimah,* an Isr.:—Shimah. Comp. 8043.

8040. שְׂמֹאול **semôwl**, *sem-ole';* or

שְׂמֹאל **semô'l**, *sem-ole';* a prim. word [rather perh. from the same as 8071 (by insertion of א) through the idea of *wrapping* up]; prop. *dark* (as *enveloped*), i.e. the *north;* hence (by orientation) the *left* hand:—left (hand, side).

8041. שָׂמַאל **sâma'l**, *saw-mal';* a prim. root [rather denom. from 8040]; to use the *left* hand or pass in that direction):—(go, turn) (on the, to the) left.

8042. שְׂמָאלִי **s^{e}mâ'lîy**, *sem-aw-lee'*; from 8040; situated on the *left* side:—left.

8043. שִׁמְאָם **Shim'âm**, *shim-awm'*; for 8039 [comp. 38]; *Shimam*, an Isr.:—Shimeam.

8044. שַׁמְגַּר **Shamgar**, *sham-gar'*; of uncert. der.; *Shamgar*, an Isr. judge:—Shamgar.

8045. שָׁמַד **shâmad**, *shaw-mad'*; a prim. root; to *desolate*:—destroy (-uction), bring to nought, overthrow, perish, pluck down, × utterly.

8046. שְׁמַד **sh^{e}mad** (Chald.), *shem-ad'*; corresp. to 8045:—consume.

שָׁמֶה **shâmeh**. See 8064.

8047. שַׁמָּה **shammâh**, *sham-maw'*; from 8074; *ruin*; by impl. *consternation*:—astonishment, desolate (-ion), waste, wonderful thing.

8048. שַׁמָּה **Shammâh**, *sham-maw'*; the same as 8047; *Shammah*, the name of an Edomite and four Isr.:—Shammah.

8049. שַׁמְהוּת **Shamhûwth**, *sham-hooth'*; for 8048; *desolation*; *Shamhuth*, an Isr.:—Shamhuth.

8050. שְׁמוּאֵל **Sh^{e}mûw'êl**, *shem-oo-ale'*; from the pass. part. of 8085 and 410; *heard of God*; *Shemuël*, the name of three Isr.:—Samuel, Shemuel.

שְׁמוֹנֶה **sh^{e}môwneh**. See 8083.

שְׁמוֹנָה **sh^{e}môwnâh**. See 8083.

שְׁמוֹנִים **sh^{e}môwnîym**. See 8084.

8051. שַׁמּוּעַ **Shammûwaʿ**, *sham-moo'-ah*; from 8074; *renowned*; *Shammua*, the name of four Isr.:—Shammua, Shammuah.

8052. שְׁמוּעָה **sh^{e}mûwʿâh**, *shem-oo-aw'*; fem. pass. part. of 8074; something *heard*, i.e. an *announcement*:—bruit, doctrine, fame, mentioned, news, report, rumor, tidings.

8053. שָׁמוּר° **Shâmûwr**, *shaw-moor'*; pass. part. of 8103; *observed*; *Shamur*, an Isr.:—Shamir [*from the marg.*].

8054. שַׁמּוֹת **Shammôwth**, *sham-mōth'*; plur. of 8047; *ruins*; *Shammoth*, an Isr.:—Shamoth.

8055. שָׂמַח **sâmach**, *saw-makh'*; a prim. root; prob. to *brighten up*, i.e. (fig.) *be* (caus. *make*) *blithe* or *gleesome*:—cheer up, be (make) glad, (have, make) joy (-ful), be (make) merry, (cause to, make to) rejoice, × very.

8056. שָׂמֵחַ **sâmêach**, *saw-may'-akh*; from 8055; *blithe* or *gleeful*:—(be) glad, joyful, (making) merry ([-hearted], -ily), rejoice (-ing).

8057. שִׂמְחָה **simchâh**, *sim-khaw'*; from 8056; *blithesomeness* or *glee*, (religious or festival):—× exceeding (-ly), gladness, joy (-fulness), mirth, pleasure, rejoice (-ing).

8058. שָׁמַט **shâmaṭ**, *shaw-mat'*; a prim. root; to *fling* down; incipiently to *jostle*; fig. to *let alone*, *desist*, *remit*:—discontinue, overthrow, release, let rest, shake, stumble, throw down.

8059. שְׁמִטָּה **sh^{e}miṭṭâh**, *shem-it-taw'*; from 8058; *remission* (of debt) or *suspension* of labor):—release.

8060. שַׁמַּי **Shammay**, *sham-mah'ee*; from 8073; *destructive*; *Shammai*, the name of three Isr.:—Shammai.

8061. שְׁמִידָע **Sh^{e}mîydâʿ**, *shem-ee-daw'*; appar. from 8034 and 3045; *name of knowing*; *Shemida*, an Isr.:—Shemida, Shemidah.

8062. שְׁמִידָעִי **Sh^{e}mîydâʿîy**, *shem-ee-daw-ee'*; patron. from 8061; a *Shemidaïte* (collect.) or desc. of Shemida:—Shemidaites.

8063. שְׂמִיכָה **s^{e}mîykâh**, *sem-ee-kaw'*; from 5564; a *rug* (as *sustaining* the Oriental sitter):—mantle.

8064. שָׁמַיִם **shâmayim**, *shaw-mah'-yim*; dual of an unused sing.

שָׁמֶה **shâmeh**, *shaw-meh'*; from an unused root mean. to *be lofty*; the *sky* (as *aloft*; the dual perh. alluding to the visible arch in which the clouds move, as well as to the higher ether where the celestial bodies revolve):—air, × astrologer, heaven (-s).

8065. שָׁמַיִן **shâmayin** (Chald.), *shaw-mah'-yin*; corresp. to 8064:—heaven.

8066. שְׁמִינִי **sh^{e}mîynîy**, *shem-ee-nee'*; from 8083; *eight*:—eight.

8067. שְׁמִינִית **sh^{e}mîynîyth**, *shem-ee-neeth'*; fem. of 8066; prob. an *eight*-stringed lyre:—Sheminith.

8068. שָׁמִיר **shâmîyr**, *shaw-meer'*; from 8104 in the orig. sense of *pricking*; a *thorn*; also (from its *keenness* for scratching) a gem, prob. the *diamond*:—adamant (stone), brier, diamond.

8069. שָׁמִיר **Shâmîyr**, *shaw-meer'*; the same as 8068; *Shamir*, the name of two places in Pal.:—Shamir. Comp. 8053.

8070. שְׁמִירָמוֹת **Sh^{e}mîyrâmôwth**, *shem-ee-raw-mōth'*; or

°שְׁמָרִימוֹת **Sh^{e}mârîymôwth**, *shem-aw-ree-mōth'*; prob. from 8034 and plur. of 7413; *name of heights*; *Shemiramoth*, the name of two Isr.:—Shemiramoth.

8071. שִׂמְלָה **simlâh**, *sim-law'*; perh. by perm. for the fem. of 5566 (through the idea of a *cover* assuming the shape of the object beneath); a *dress*, espec. a *mantle*:—apparel, cloth (-es, -ing), garment, raiment. Comp. 8008.

8072. שַׂמְלָה **Samlâh**, *sam-law'*; prob. for the same as 8071; *Samlah*, an Edomite:—Samlah.

8073. שַׁמְלַי° **Shamlay**, *sham-lah'ee*; for 8014; *Shamlai*, one of the Nethinim:—Shalmai [*from the marg.*].

8074. שָׁמֵם **shâmêm**, *shaw-mame'*; a prim. root; to *stun* (or intrans. *grow numb*), i.e. *devastate* or (fig.) *stupefy* (both usually in a passive sense):—make amazed, be astonied, (be an) astonish (-ment), (be, bring into, unto, lay, lie, make) desolate (-ion, places), be destitute, destroy (self), (lay, lie, make) waste, wonder.

8075. שְׁמַם **sh^{e}mam** (Chald.), *shem-am'*; corresp. to 8074:—be astonied.

8076. שָׁמֵם **shâmêm**, *shaw-mame'*; from 8074; *ruined*:—desolate.

8077. שְׁמָמָה **sh^{e}mâmâh**, *shem-aw-maw'*; or

שִׁמָמָה **shimămâh**, *shee-mam-aw'*; fem. of 8076; *devastation*; fig. *astonishment*:—(laid, × most) desolate (-ion), waste.

8078. שִׁמָּמוֹן **shimmâmôwn**, *shim-maw-mone'*; from 8074; *stupefaction*:—astonishment.

8079. שְׂמָמִית **s^{e}mâmîyth**, *sem-aw-meeth'*; prob. from 8074 (in the sense of *poisoning*); a *lizard* (from the superstition of its noxiousness):—spider.

8080. שָׁמַן **shâman**, *shaw-man'*; a prim. root; to *shine*, i.e. (by anal.) *be* (caus. *make*) *oily* or *gross*:—become (make, wax) fat.

8081. שֶׁמֶן **shemen**, *sheh'-men*; from 8080; *grease*, espec. liquid (as from the olive, often perfumed); fig. *richness*:—anointing, × fat (things), × fruitful, oil ([-ed]), ointment, olive, + pine.

8082. שָׁמֵן **shâmên**, *shaw-mane'*; from 8080; *greasy*, i.e. *gross*; fig. *rich*:—fat, lusty, plenteous.

8083. שְׁמֹנֶה **sh^{e}môneh**, *shem-o-neh'*; or

שְׁמוֹנֶה **sh^{e}môwneh**, *shem-o-neh'*; fem.

שְׁמֹנָה **sh^{e}mônâh**, *shem-o-naw'*; or

שְׁמוֹנָה **sh^{e}môwnâh**, *shem-o-naw'*; appar. from 8082 through the idea of *plumpness*; a cardinal number, *eight* (as if a *surplus* above the "perfect" seven); also (as ordinal) *eighth*:—eight ([-een, -eenth]), eighth.

8084. שְׁמֹנִים **sh^{e}mônîym**, *shem-o-neem'*; or

שְׁמוֹנִים **sh^{e}môwnîym**, *shem-o-neem'*; mult. from 8083; *eighty*; also *eightieth*:—eighty (-ieth), fourscore.

8085. שָׁמַע **shâmaʿ**, *shaw-mah'*; a prim. root; to *hear* intelligently (often with impl. of attention, obedience, etc.; caus. to *tell*, etc.):—× attentively, call (gather) together, × carefully, × certainly, consent, consider, be content, declare, × diligently, discern, give ear, (cause to, let, make to) hear (-ken, tell), × indeed, listen, make (a) noise, (be) obedient, obey, perceive, (make a) proclaim (-ation), publish, regard, report, shew (forth), (make a) sound, × surely, tell, understand, whosoever [heareth], witness.

8086. שְׁמַע **sh^{e}maʿ** (Chald.), *shem-ah'*; corresp. to 8085:—hear, obey.

8087. שֶׁמַע **Shemaʿ**, *sheh'-mah*; for the same as 8088; *Shema*, the name of a place in Pal. and of four Isr.:—Shema.

8088. שֵׁמַע **shêmaʿ**, *shay'-mah*; from 8085; something *heard*, i.e. a *sound*, *rumor*, *announcement*; abstr. *audience*:—bruit, fame, hear (-ing), loud, report, speech, tidings.

8089. שֹׁמַע **shômaʿ**, *sho'-mah*; from 8085; a *report*:—fame.

8090. שְׁמָע **Sh^{e}mâʿ**, *shem-aw'*; for 8087; *Shema*, a place in Pal.:—Shema.

8091. שָׁמָע **Shâmâʿ**, *shaw-maw'*; from 8085; *obedient*; *Shama*, an Isr.:—Shama.

8092. שִׁמְעָא **Shimʿâ'**, *shim-aw'*; for 8093; *Shima*, the name of four Isr.:—Shimea, Shimei, Shamma.

8093. שִׁמְעָה **Shimʿâh**, *shim-aw'*; fem. of 8088; *annunciation*; *Shimah*, an Isr.:—Shimeah.

8094. שְׁמָעָה **Sh^{e}mâʿâh**, *shem-aw-aw'*; for 8093; *Shemaah*, an Isr.:—Shemaah.

8095. שִׁמְעוֹן **Shimʿôwn**, *shim-ōne'*; from 8085; *hearing*; *Shimon*, one of Jacob's sons, also the tribe desc. from him:—Simeon.

8096. שִׁמְעִי **Shimʿîy**, *shim-ee'*; from 8088; *famous*; *Shimi*, the name of twenty Isr.:—Shimeah [*from the marg.*], Shimei, Shimhi, Shimi.

8097. שִׁמְעִי **Shimʿîy**, *shim-ee'*; patron. from 8096; a *Shimite* (collect.) or desc. of Shimi:—of Shimi, Shimites.

8098. שְׁמַעְיָה **Sh^{e}maʿyâh**, *shem-aw-yaw'*; or

שְׁמַעְיָהוּ **Sh^{e}maʿyâhûw**, *shem-aw-yaw'-hoo*; from 8085 and 3050; *Jah has heard*; *Shemajah*, the name of twenty-five Isr.:—Shemaiah.

8099. שִׁמְעֹנִי **Shimʿônîy**, *shim-o-nee'*; patron. from 8095; a *Shimonite* (collect.) or desc. of Shimon:—tribe of Simeon, Simeonites.

8100. שִׁמְעָת **Shimʿâth**, *shim-awth'*; fem. of 8088; *annunciation*; *Shimath*, an Ammonitess:—Shimath.

8101. שִׁמְעָתִי **Shimʿâthîy**, *shim-aw-thee'*; patron. from 8093; a *Shimathite* (collect.) or desc. of Shimah:—Shimeathites.

8102. שֶׁמֶץ **shemets**, *sheh'-mets*; from an unused root mean. to *emit a sound*; an *inkling*:—a little.

8103. שִׁמְצָה **shimtsâh**, *shim-tsaw'*; fem. of 8102; scornful *whispering* (of hostile spectators):—shame.

8104. שָׁמַר **shâmar**, *shaw-mar'*; a prim. root; prop. to *hedge* about (as with thorns), i.e. *guard*; gen. to *protect*, *attend to*, etc.:—beware, be circumspect, take heed (to self), keep (-er, self), mark, look narrowly, observe, preserve, regard, reserve, save (self), sure, (that lay) wait (for), watch (-man).

8105. שֶׁמֶר **shemer**, *sheh'-mer*; from 8104; something *preserved*, i.e. the *settlings* (plur. only) of wine:—dregs, (wines on the) lees.

8106. שֶׁמֶר **Shemer**, *sheh'-mer*; the same as 8105; *Shemer*, the name of three Isr.:—Shamer, Shemer.

8107. שִׁמֻּר **shimmûr**, *shim-moor'*; from 8104; an *observance*:—× be (much) observed.

שֹׁמֵר **Shômêr**. See 7763.

8108. שָׁמְרָה **shomrâh**, *shom-raw'*; fem. of an unused noun from 8104 mean. a *guard*; *watchfulness*:—watch.

8109. שְׁמֻרָה **sh^{e}mûrâh**, *shem-oo-raw'*; fem. of pass. part. of 8104; something *guarded*, i.e. an *eye-lid*:—waking.

8110. שִׁמְרוֹן **Shimrôwn**, *shim-rone'*; from 8105 in its orig. sense; *guardianship*; *Shimron*, the name of an Isr. and of a place in Pal.:—Shimron.

8111. שֹׁמְרוֹן **Shômᵉrown**, *sho-mer-ōne'*; from the act. part. of 8104; *watch-station; Shomeron*, a place in Pal.:—Samaria.

8112. שִׁמְרוֹן מְראוֹן **Shimrôwn Mᵉrôʼwn**, *shim-rone' mer-one'*; from 8110 and a der. of 4754; *guard of lashing; Shimron-Meron*, a place in Pal.:—Shimon-meron.

8113. שִׁמְרִי **Shimrîy**, *shim-ree'*; from 8105 in its orig. sense; *watchful; Shimri*, the name of four Isr.:—Shimri.

8114. שְׁמַרְיָה **Shᵉmaryâh**, *shem-ar-yaw'*; or

שְׁמַרְיָהוּ **Shᵉmaryâhûw**, *shem-ar-yaw'-hoo*; from 8104 and 3050; *Jah has guarded; Shemarjah*, the name of four Isr.:—Shamariah, Shemariah.

שְׁמָרִימוֹת° **Shᵉmârîymôwth**. See 8070.

8115. שָׁמְרַיִן **Shomrayin** (Chald.), *shom-rah'-yin*; corresp. to 8111; *Shomraïn*, a place in Pal.:—Samaria.

8116. שִׁמְרִית **Shimrîyth**, *shim-reeth'*; fem. of 8113; *female guard; Shimrith*, a Moabitess:—Shimrith.

8117. שִׁמְרֹנִי **Shimrônîy**, *shim-ro-nee'*; patron. from 8110; a *Shimronite* (collect.) or desc. of Shimron:—Shimronites.

8118. שֹׁמְרֹנִי **Shômᵉrônîy**, *sho-mer-o-nee'*; patrial from 8111; a *Shomeronite* (collect.) or inhab. of Shomeron:—Samaritans.

8119. שִׁמְרָת **Shimrâth**, *shim-rawth'*; from 8104; *guardship; Shimrath*, an Isr.:—Shimrath.

8120. שְׁמַשׁ **shᵉmash** (Chald.), *shem-ash'*; corresp. to the root of 8121 through the idea of *activity* implied in day-light; to *serve*:—minister.

8121. שֶׁמֶשׁ **shemesh**, *sheh'-mesh*; from an unused root mean. to be *brilliant*; the *sun*; by impl. the *east*; fig. a *ray*, i.e. (arch.) a notched *battlement*:— + east side (-ward), sun ([rising]), + west (-ward), window. See also 1053.

8122. שֶׁמֶשׁ **shemesh** (Chald.), *sheh'-mesh*; corresp. to 8121; the *sun*:—sun.

8123. שִׁמְשׁוֹן **Shimshôwn**, *shim-shone'*; from 8121; *sunlight; Shimshon*, an Isr.:—Samson.

שִׁמְשִׁי **Shimshîy**. See 1030.

8124. שִׁמְשַׁי **Shimshay** (Chald.), *shim-shah'ee*; from 8122; *sunny; Shimshai*, a Samaritan: Shimshai.

8125. שַׁמְשְׁרַי **Shamshᵉray**, *sham-sher-ah'ee*; appar. from 8121; *sunlike; Shamsherai*, an Isr.:—Shamsherai.

8126. שֻׁמָתִי **Shûmâthîy**, *shoo-maw-thee'*; patron. from an unused name from 7762 prob. mean. *garlic*-smell; a *Shumathite* (collect.) or desc. of Shumah:—Shumathites.

8127. שֵׁן **shên**, *shane*; from 8150; a *tooth* (as *sharp*); spec. (for 8143) *ivory*; fig. a *cliff*:—crag, × forefront, ivory, × sharp, tooth.

8128. שֵׁן **shên** (Chald.), *shane*; corresp. to 8127; a *tooth*:—tooth.

8129. שֵׁן **Shên**, *shane*; the same as 8127; *crag; Shen*, a place in Pal.:—Shen.

8130. שָׂנֵא **sânêʼ**, *saw-nay'*; a prim. root; to *hate* (personally):—enemy, foe, (be) hate (-ful, -r), odious, × utterly.

8131. שְׂנֵא **sᵉnêʼ** (Chald.), *sen-ay'*; corresp. to 8130:—hate.

8132. שָׁנָא **shânâʼ**, *shaw-naw'*; a prim. root; to *alter*:—change.

8133. שְׁנָא **shᵉnâʼ** (Chald.), *shen-aw'*; corresp. to 8132:—alter, change, (be) diverse.

שְׁנָא **shênâʼ**. See 8142.

8134. שִׁנְאָב **Shinʼâb**, *shin-awb'*; prob. from 8132 and 1; a *father has turned; Shinab*, a Canaanite:—Shinab.

8135. שִׂנְאָה **sinʼâh**, *sin-aw'*; from 8130; *hate*:— + exceedingly, hate (-ful, -red).

8136. שִׁנְאָן **shinʼân**, *shin-awn'*; from 8132; *change*, i.e. *repetition*:— × angels.

8137. שֶׁנְאַצַּר **Shenatstsar**, *shen-ats-tsar'*; appar. of Bab. or.; *Shenatstsar*, an Isr.:—Senazar.

8138. שָׁנָה **shânâh**, *shaw-naw'*; a prim. root; to *fold*, i.e. *duplicate* (lit. or fig.); by impl. to *transmute* (trans. or intrans.):—do (speak, strike) again, alter, double, (be given to) change, disguise, (be) diverse, pervert, prefer, repeat, return, do the second time.

8139. שְׁנָה **shᵉnâh** (Chald.), *shen-aw'*; corresp. to 8142:—sleep.

8140. שְׁנָה **shᵉnâh** (Chald.), *shen-aw'*; corresp. to 8141:—year.

8141. שָׁנֶה **shâneh** (in plur. only), *shaw-neh'*; or (fem.)

שָׁנָה **shânâh**, *shaw-naw'*; from 8138; a *year* (as a *revolution* of time):— + whole age, × long, + old, year (× -ly).

8142. שֵׁנָה **shênâh**, *shay-naw'*; or

שֵׁנָא **shênâʼ** (Psa. 127 : 2), *shay-naw'*; from 3462; *sleep*:—sleep.

8143. שֶׁנְהַבִּים **shenhabbîym**, *shen-hab-beem'*; from 8127 and the plur. appar. of a for. word; prob. *tooth of elephants*, i.e. *ivory tusk*:—ivory.

8144. שָׁנִי **shânîy**, *shaw-nee'*; of uncert. der.; *crimson*, prop. the insect or its color, also stuff dyed with it:—crimson, scarlet (thread).

8145. שֵׁנִי **shênîy**, *shay-nee'*; from 8138; prop. *double*, i.e. *second*; also adv. *again*:—again, either [of them], (an-) other, second (time).

8146. שָׂנִיא **sânîyʼ**, *saw-nee'*; from 8130; *hated*:—hated.

8147. שְׁנַיִם **shᵉnayim**, *shen-ah'-yim*; dual of 8145; fem.

שְׁתַּיִם **shᵉttayim**, *shet-tah'-yim*; *two*; also (as ordinal) *twofold*:—both, couple, double, second, twain, + twelfth, + twelve, + twenty (sixscore) thousand, twice, two.

8148. שְׁנִינָה **shᵉnîynâh**, *shen-ee-naw'*; from 8150; something *pointed*, i.e. a *gibe*:—byword, taunt.

8149. שְׁנִיר **Shᵉnîyr**, *shen-eer'*; or

סְנִיר **Sᵉnîyr**, *sen-eer'*; from an unused root mean. to *be pointed*; *peak*; *Shenir* or *Senir*, a summit of Lebanon:—Senir, Shenir.

8150. שָׁנַן **shânan**, *shaw-nan'*; a prim. root; to *point* (trans. or intrans.); intens. to *pierce*; fig. to *inculcate*:—prick, sharp (-en), teach diligently, whet.

8151. שָׁנַס **shânaç**, *shaw-nas'*; a prim. root; to *compress* (with a belt):—gird up.

8152. שִׁנְעָר **Shinʻâr**, *shin-awr'*; prob. of for. der.; *Shinar*, a plain in Bab.:—Shinar.

8153. שְׁנָת **shᵉnâth**, *shen-awth'*; from 3462; *sleep*:—sleep.

8154. שָׁסָה **shâçâh**, *shaw-saw'*; or

שָׁשָׂה **shâsâh** (Isa. 10 : 13), *shaw-saw'*; a prim. root; to *plunder*:—destroyer, rob, spoil (-er).

8155. שָׁסַס **shâçaç**, *shaw-sas'*; a prim. root; to *plunder*:—rifle, spoil.

8156. שָׁסַע **shâçaʻ**, *shaw-sah'*; a prim. root; to *split* or *tear*; fig. to *upbraid*:—cleave, (be) cloven ([footed]), rend, stay.

8157. שֶׁסַע **sheçaʻ**, *sheh'-sah*; from 8156; a *fissure*:—cleft, clovenfooted.

8158. שָׁסַף **shâçaph**, *shaw-saf'*; a prim. root; to *cut* in pieces, i.e. slaughter:—hew in pieces.

8159. שָׁעָה **shâʻâh**, *shaw-aw'*; a prim. root; to *gaze* at or about (prop. for help); by impl. to *inspect*, *consider*, *compassionate*, *be nonplussed* (as looking around in amazement) or *bewildered*:—depart, be dim, be dismayed, look (away), regard, have respect, spare, turn.

8160. שָׁעָה **shâʻâh** (Chald.), *shaw-aw'*; from a root corresp. to 8159; prop. a *look*, i.e. a *moment*:—hour.

שְׂעוֹר **sᵉʻôwr**. See 8184.

שְׂעוֹרָה **sᵉʻôwrâh**. See 8184.

8161. שַׁעֲטָה **shaʻățâh**, *shah'-at-aw*; fem. from an unused root mean. to *stamp*; a *clatter* (of hoofs):—stamping.

8162. שַׁעַטְנֵז **shaʻațnêz**, *shah-at-naze'*; prob. of for. der.; *linsey-woolsey*, i.e. cloth of linen and wool carded and spun together:—garment of divers sorts, linen and woollen.

8163. שָׂעִיר **sâʻîyr**, *saw-eer'*; or

שָׂעִר **sâʻîr**, *saw-eer'*; from 8175; *shaggy*; as noun, a *he-goat*; by anal. a *faun*:—devil, goat, hairy, kid, rough, satyr.

8164. שָׂעִיר **sâʻîyr**, *saw-eer'*; formed the same as 8163; a *shower* (as *tempestuous*):—small rain.

8165. שֵׂעִיר **Sêʻîyr**, *say-eer'*; formed like 8163; *rough*; *Seïr*, a mountain of Idumæa and its aboriginal occupants, also one in Pal.:—Seir.

8166. שְׂעִירָה **sᵉʻîyrâh**, *seh-ee-raw'*; fem. of 8163; a *she-goat*:—kid.

8167. שְׂעִירָה **Sᵉʻîyrâh**, *seh-ee-raw'*; formed as 8166; *roughness*; *Seïrah*, a place in Pal.:—Seirath.

8168. שֹׁעַל **shôʻal**, *sho'-al*; from an unused root mean. to *hollow* out; the *palm*; by extens. a *handful*:—handful, hollow of the hand.

שׁוּעָל **shûʻâl**. See 7776.

8169. שַׁעַלְבִים **Shaʻalbîym**, *shah-al-beem'*; or

שַׁעֲלַבִּין **Shaʻălabbîyn**, *shah-al-ab-been'*; plur. from 7776; *fox-holes*; *Shaalbim* or *Shaalabbin*, a place in Pal.:—Shaalabbin, Shaalbim.

8170. שַׁעַלְבֹנִי **Shaʻalbônîy**, *shah-al-bo-nee'*; patrial from 8169; a *Shaalbonite* or inhab. of Shaalbin:—Shaalbonite.

8171. שַׁעֲלִים **Shaʻălîym**, *shah-al-eem'*; plur. of 7776; *foxes*; *Shaalim*, a place in Pal.:—Shalim.

8172. שָׁעַן **shâʻan**, *shaw-an'*; a prim. root; to *support* one's self:—lean, lie, rely, rest (on, self), stay.

8173. שָׁעַע **shâʻaʻ**, *shaw-ah'*; a prim. root; (in a good acceptation) to *look* upon (with complacency), i.e. *fondle*, *please* or *amuse* (self); (in a bad one) to *look* about (in dismay), i.e. *stare*:—cry (out) [*by confusion with* 7768], dandle, delight (self), play, shut.

שָׂעִף **sâʻîph**. See 5587.

8174. שַׁעַף **Shaʻaph**, *shah'-af*; from 5586; *fluctuation*; *Shaaph*, the name of two Isr.:—Shaaph.

8175. שָׂעַר **sâʻar**, *saw-ar'*; a prim. root; to *storm*; by impl. to *shiver*, i.e. *fear*:—be (horribly) afraid, fear, hurl as a storm, be tempestuous, come like (take away as with) a whirlwind.

8176. שָׁעַר **shâʻar**, *shaw-ar'*; a prim. root; to *split* or *open*, i.e. (lit., but only as denom. from 8179) to *act as gate-keeper* (see 7778); (fig.) to *estimate*:—think.

8177. שְׂעַר **sᵉʻar** (Chald.), *seh-ar'*; corresp. to 8181; *hair*:—hair.

8178. שַׂעַר **saʻar**, *sah'-ar*; from 8175; a *tempest*; also a *terror*:—affrighted, × horribly, × sore, storm. See 8181.

8179. שַׁעַר **shaʻar**, *shah'-ar*; from 8176 in its orig. sense; an *opening*, i.e. *door* or *gate*:—city, door, gate, port (× -er).

8180. שַׁעַר **shaʻar**, *shah'-ar*; from 8176; a *measure* (as a *section*):—[hundred-] fold.

שָׂעִר **sâʻîr**. See 8163.

8181. שֵׂעָר **sêʻâr**, *say-awr'*; or

שַׂעַר **saʻar** (Isa. 7 : 20), *sah'-ar*; from 8175 in the sense of *dishevelling*; *hair* (as if *tossed* or *bristling*):—hair (-y), × rough.

שֹׁעֵר **shôʻêr**. See 7778.

8182. שֹׁעָר **shôʻâr**, *sho-awr'*; from 8176; *harsh* or *horrid*, i.e. *offensive*:—vile.

8183. שְׂעָרָה **sᵉʻârâh**, *seh-aw-raw'*; fem. of 8178; a *hurricane*:—storm, tempest.

8184. שְׂעֹרָה **s^e'ôrâh**, *seh-o-raw'*; or שְׂעוֹרָה **s^e'ôwrâh**, *seh-o-raw'* (fem. mean. the *plant*); and (masc. mean. the *grain*); also שְׂעֹר **s^e'ôr**, *seh-ore'*; or שְׂעוֹר **s^e'ôwr**, *seh-ore'*; from 8175 in the sense of *roughness*; *barley* (as *villose*):—barley.

8185. שַׂעֲרָה **sa'ărâh**, *sah-ar-aw'*; fem. of 8181; *hairiness*:—hair.

8186. שַׁעֲרוּרָה **sha'ărûwrâh**, *shah-ar-oo-raw'*; or שַׁעֲרִירִיָּה **sha'ărîyrîyâh**, *shah-ar-ee-ree-yaw'*; or שַׁעֲרֻרִת **sha'ărûrîth**, *shah-ar-oo-reeth'*; fem. from 8176 in the sense of 8175; something *fearful*:—horrible thing.

8187. שְׁעַרְיָה **She'aryâh**, *sheh-ar-yaw'*; from 8176 and 3050; *Jah has stormed*; *Sheărjah*, an Isr.:—Sheariah.

8188. שְׂעֹרִים **S^e'ôrîym**, *seh-o-reem'*; masc. plur. of 8184; *barley* grains; *Seŏrim*, an Isr.:—Seorim.

8189. שַׁעֲרַיִם **Sha'ărayim**, *shah-ar-ah'-yim*; dual of 8179; *double gates*; *Shaarajim*, a place in Pal.:—Shaaraim.

שַׁעֲרִירִיָּה° **sha'ărîyrîyâh**. See 8186.

שַׁעֲרֻרִת **sha'ărûrîth**. See 8186.

8190. שַׁעַשְׁגַז **Sha'ashgaz**, *shah-ash-gaz'*; of Pers. der.; *Shaashgaz*, a eunuch of Xerxes:—Shaashgaz.

8191. שַׁעְשֻׁעַ **sha'shûa'**, *shah-shoo'-ah*; from 8173; *enjoyment*:—delight, pleasure.

8192. שָׁפָה **shâphâh**, *shaw-faw'*; a prim. root; to *abrade*, i.e. *bare*:—high, stick out.

8193. שָׂפָה **sâphâh**, *saw-faw'*; or (in dual and plur.) שֶׂפֶת **sepheth**, *sef-eth'*; prob. from 5595 or 8192 through the idea of *termination* (comp. 5490); the *lip* (as a natural boundary); by impl. *language*; by anal. a *margin* (of a vessel, water, cloth, etc.):—band, bank, binding, border, brim, brink, edge, language, lip, prating, ([sea-]) shore, side, speech, talk, [vain] words.

8194. שָׁפָה **shâphâh**, *shaw-faw'*; from 8192 in the sense of *clarifying*; a *cheese* (as *strained* from the whey):—cheese.

8195. שְׁפוֹ **Sh^ephôw**, *shef-o'*; or שְׁפִי **Sh^ephîy**, *shef-ee'*; from 8192; *baldness* [comp. 8205]; *Shepho* or *Shephi*, an Idumæan:—Shephi, Shepho.

8196. שְׁפוֹט **sh^ephôwṭ**, *shef-ote'*; or שְׁפוּט **sh^ephûwṭ**, *shef-oot'*; from 8199; a judicial *sentence*, i.e. *punishment*:—judgment.

8197. שְׁפוּפָם **Sh^ephûwphâm**, *shef-oo-fawm'*; or שְׁפוּפָן **Sh^ephûwphân**, *shef-oo-fawn'*; from the same as 8207; *serpent-like*; *Shephupham* or *Shephuphan*, an Isr.:—Shephuphan, Shupham.

8198. שִׁפְחָה **shiphchâh**, *shif-khaw'*; fem. from an unused root mean. to *spread* out (as a *family*; see 4940); a *female slave* (as a member of the *household*):—(bond-, hand-) maid (-en, -servant), wench, bondwoman, womanservant.

8199. שָׁפַט **shâphaṭ**, *shaw-fat'*; a prim. root; to *judge*, i.e. pronounce *sentence* (for or against); by impl. to *vindicate* or *punish*; by extens. to *govern*; pass. to *litigate* (lit. or fig.):— + avenge, × that condemn, contend, defend, execute (judgment), (be a) judge (-ment), × needs, plead, reason, rule.

8200. שְׁפַט **sh^ephaṭ** (Chald.), *shef-at'*; corresp. to 8199; to *judge*:—magistrate.

8201. שֶׁפֶט **shepheṭ**, *sheh'-fet*; from 8199; a *sentence*, i.e. *infliction*:—judgment.

8202. שָׁפָט **Shâphâṭ**, *shaw-fawt'*; from 8199; *judge*; *Shaphat*, the name of four Isr.:—Shaphat.

8203. שְׁפַטְיָה **Sh^ephaṭyâh**, *shef-at-yaw'*; or שְׁפַטְיָהוּ **Sh^ephaṭyâhûw**, *shef-at-yaw'-hoo*; from 8199 and 3050; *Jah has judged*; *Shephatjah*, the name of ten Isr.:—Shephatiah.

8204. שִׁפְטָן **Shiphṭân**, *shif-tawn'*; from 8199; *judge-like*; *Shiphtan*, an Isr.:—Shiphtan.

8205. שְׁפִי **sh^ephîy**, *shef-ee'*; from 8192; *bareness*; concr. a *bare* hill or plain:—high place, stick out.

8206. שֻׁפִּים **Shuppîym**, *shoop-peem'*; plur. of an unused noun from the same as 8207 and mean. the same; *serpents*; *Shuppim*, an Isr.:—Shuppim.

8207. שְׁפִיפֹן **sh^ephîyphôn**, *shef-ee-fone'*; from an unused root mean. the same as 7779; a kind of *serpent* (as *snapping*), prob. the *cerastes* or horned adder:—adder.

8208. שָׁפִיר **Shaphîyr**, *shaf-eer'*; from 8231; *beautiful*; *Shaphir*, a place in Pal.:—Saphir.

8209. שַׁפִּיר **shappîyr** (Chald.), *shap-peer'*; intens. of a form corresp. to 8208; *beautiful*:—fair.

8210. שָׁפַךְ **shâphak**, *shaw-fak'*; a prim. root; to *spill* forth (blood, a libation, liquid metal; or even a solid, i.e. to *mound* up); also (fig.) to *expend* (life, soul, complaint, money, etc.); intens. to *sprawl* out:—cast (up), gush out, pour (out), shed (-der, out), slip.

8211. שֶׁפֶךְ **shephek**, *sheh'-fek*; from 8210; an *emptying* place, e.g. an *ash-heap*:—are poured out.

8212. שָׁפְכָה **shophkâh**, *shof-kaw'*; fem. of a der. from 8210; a *pipe* (for *pouring* forth, e.g. wine), i.e. the *penis*:—privy member.

8213. שָׁפֵל **shâphêl**, *shaw-fale'*; a prim. root; to *depress* or *sink* (espec. fig. to *humiliate*, intrans. or trans.):—abase, bring (cast, put) down, debase, humble (self), be (bring, lay, make, put) low (-er).

8214. שְׁפַל **sh^ephal** (Chald.), *shef-al'*; corresp. to 8213:—abase, humble, put down, subdue.

8215. שְׁפַל **sh^ephal** (Chald.), *shef-al'*; from 8214; *low*:—basest.

8216. שֵׁפֶל **shêphel**, *shay'-fel*; from 8213; an *humble* rank:—low estate (place).

8217. שָׁפָל **shâphâl**, *shaw-fawl'*; from 8213; *depressed*, lit. or fig.:—base (-st), humble, low (-er, -ly).

8218. שִׁפְלָה **shiphlâh**, *shif-law'*; fem. of 8216; *depression*:—low place.

8219. שְׁפֵלָה **sh^ephêlâh**, *shef-ay-law'*; from 8213; *Lowland*, i.e. (with the art.) the maritime slope of Pal.:—low country, (low) plain, vale (-ley).

8220. שִׁפְלוּת **shiphlûwth**, *shif-looth'*; from 8213; *remissness*:—idleness.

8221. שְׁפָם **Sh^ephâm**, *shef-awm'*; prob. from 8192; *bare spot*; *Shepham*, a place in or near Pal.:—Shepham.

8222. שָׂפָם **sâphâm**, *saw-fawm'*; from 8193; the *beard* (as a *lip-piece*):—beard, (upper) lip.

8223. שָׁפָם **Shâphâm**, *shaw-fawm'*; formed like 8221; *baldly*; *Shapham*, an Isr.:—Shapham.

8224. שִׂפְמוֹת **Siphmôwth**, *sif-mōth'*; fem. plur. of 8221; *Siphmoth*, a place in Pal.:—Siphmoth.

8225. שִׁפְמִי **Shiphmîy**, *shif-mee'*; patrial from 8221; a *Shiphmite* inhab. of Shepham:—Shiphmite.

8226. שָׂפַן **sâphan**, *saw-fan'*; a prim. root; to *conceal* (as a valuable):—treasure.

8227. שָׁפָן **shâphân**, *shaw-fawn'*; from 8226; a species of *rock-rabbit* (from its *hiding*), i.e. prob. the *hyrax*:—coney.

8228. שֶׁפַע **shepha'**, *sheh'-fah*; from an unused root mean. to *abound*; *resources*:—abundance.

8229. שִׁפְעָה **shiph'âh**, *shif-aw'*; fem. of 8228; *copiousness*:—abundance, company, multitude.

8230. שִׁפְעִי **Shiph'îy**, *shif-ee'*; from 8228; *copious*; *Shiphi*, an Isr.:—Shiphi.

שָׂפַק **sâphaq**. See 5606.

8231. שָׁפַר **shâphar**, *shaw-far'*; a prim. root; to *glisten*, i.e. (fig.) *be* (caus. *make*) *fair*:—× goodly.

8232. שְׁפַר **sh^ephar** (Chald.), *shef-ar'*; corresp. to 8231; to *be beautiful*:—be acceptable, please, + think good.

8233. שֶׁפֶר **shepher**, *sheh'-fer*; from 8231; *beauty*:—× goodly.

8234. שֶׁפֶר **Shepher**, *sheh'-fer*; the same as 8233; *Shepher*, a place in the Desert:—Shapper.

שׁוֹפָר **shôphâr**. See 7782.

8235. שִׁפְרָה **shiphrâh**, *shif-raw'*; from 8231; *brightness*:—garnish.

8236. שִׁפְרָה **Shiphrâh**, *shif-raw'*; the same as 8235; *Shiphrah*, an Israelitess:—Shiphrah.

8237. שַׁפְרוּר° **shaphrûwr**, *shaf-roor'*; from 8231; *splendid*, i.e. a *tapestry* or *canopy*.—royal pavilion.

8238. שְׁפַרְפַר **sh^epharphar** (Chald.), *shef-ar-far'*; from 8231; the *dawn* (as *brilliant* with aurora):— × very early in the morning.

8239. שָׁפַת **shâphath**, *shaw-fath'*; a prim. root; to *locate*, i.e. (gen.) *hang* on or (fig.) *establish*, *reduce*:—bring, ordain, set on.

8240. שָׁפָת **shâphâth**, *shaw-fawth'*; from 8239; a (double) *stall* (for cattle); also a (two-pronged) *hook* (for flaying animals on):—hook, pot.

8241. שֶׁצֶף **shetseph**, *sheh'-tsef*; from 7857 (for alliteration with 7110); an *outburst* (of anger):—little.

8242. שַׂק **saq**, *sak*; from 8264; prop. a *mesh* (as allowing a liquid to *run* through), i.e. coarse loose cloth or *sacking* (used in mourning and for bagging); hence a *bag* (for grain, etc.):—sack (-cloth, -clothes).

8243. שָׁק **shâq** (Chald.), *shawk*; corresp. to 7785; the *leg*:—leg.

8244. שָׂקַד **sâqad**, *saw-kad'*; a prim. root; to *fasten*:—bind.

8245. שָׁקַד **shâqad**, *shaw-kad'*; a prim. root; to *be alert*, i.e. *sleepless*; hence to *be on the lookout* (whether for good or ill):—hasten, remain, wake, watch (for).

8246. שָׁקַד **shâqad**, *shaw-kad'*; a denom. from 8247; to *be* (intens. *make*) *almond-shaped*:—make like (unto, after the fashion of) almonds.

8247. שָׁקֵד **shâqêd**, *shaw-kade'*; from 8245; the *almond* (tree or nut; as being the *earliest* in bloom):—almond (tree).

8248. שָׁקָה **shâqâh**, *shaw-kaw'*; a prim. root; to *quaff*, i.e. (caus.) to *irrigate* or *furnish a potion to*:—cause to (give, give to, let, make to) drink, drown, moisten, water. See 7937, 8354.

8249. שִׁקֻּו **shiqqûv**, *shik-koov'*; from 8248; (plur. collect.) a *draught*:—drink.

8250. שִׁקּוּי **shiqqûwy**, *shik-koo'ee*; from 8248; a *beverage*; *moisture*, i.e. (fig.) *refreshment*:—drink, marrow.

8251. שִׁקּוּץ **shiqqûwts**, *shik-koots'*; or שִׁקֻּץ **shiqqûts**, *shik-koots'*; from 8262; *disgusting*, i.e. *filthy*; espec. *idolatrous* or (concr.) an *idol*:—abominable filth (idol, -ation), detestable (thing).

8252. שָׁקַט **shâqaṭ**, *shaw-kat'*; a prim. root; to *repose* (usually fig.):—appease, idleness, (at, be at, be in, give) quiet (-ness), (be at, be in, give, have, take) rest, settle, be still.

8253. שֶׁקֶט **sheqeṭ**, *sheh'-ket*; from 8252; *tranquility*:—quietness.

8254. שָׁקַל **shâqal**, *shaw-kal'*; a prim. root; to *suspend* or *poise* (espec. in trade):—pay, receive (-r), spend, × throughly, weigh.

8255. שֶׁקֶל **sheqel**, *sheh'-kel;* from 8254; prob. a *weight;* used as a commercial standard:—shekel.

8256. שָׁקָם **shâqâm**, *shaw-kawm';* or (fem.)

שִׁקְמָה **shiqmâh**, *shik-maw';* of uncert. der.; a *sycamore* (usually the tree):—sycamore (fruit, tree).

8257. שָׁקַע **shâqa'**, *shaw-kah'* (abbrev. ° Am. 8 : 8); a prim. root; to *subside;* by impl. to *be overflowed, cease;* caus. to *abate, subdue:*—make deep, let down, drown, quench, sink.

8258. שְׁקַעְרוּרָה **shᵉqa'rûwrâh**, *shek-ah-roo-raw';* from 8257; a *depression:*—hollow strake.

8259. שָׁקַף **shâqaph**, *shaw-kaf';* a prim. root; prop. to *lean out* (of a window), i.e. (by impl.) *peep* or *gaze* (pass. *be a spectacle*):—appear, look (down, forth, out).

8260. שֶׁקֶף **sheqeph**, *sheh'-kef;* from 8259; a *loophole* (for *looking out*), to admit light and air:—window.

8261. שָׁקֻף **shâqûph**, *shaw-koof';* pass. part. of 8259; an *embrasure* or opening [comp. 8260] with bevelled jam:—light, window.

8262. שָׁקַץ **shâqats**, *shaw-kats';* a prim. root; to *be filthy*, i.e. (intens.) to *loathe, pollute:*—abhor, make abominable, have in abomination, detest, × utterly.

8263. שֶׁקֶץ **sheqets**, *sheh'-kets;* from 8262; *filth*, i.e. (fig. and spec.) an *idolatrous* object:—abominable (-tion).

שִׁקֻּץ **shiqqûts**. See 8251.

8264. שָׁקַק **shâqaq**, *shaw-kak';* a prim. root; to *course* (like a beast of prey); by impl. to *seek greedily:*—have appetite, justle one against another, long, range, run (to and fro).

8265. שָׂקַר **sâqar**, *saw-kar';* a prim. root; to *ogle*, i.e. *blink* coquettishly:—wanton.

8266. שָׁקַר **shâqar**, *shaw-kar';* a prim. root; to *cheat*, i.e. *be untrue* (usually in words):—fail, deal falsely, lie.

8267. שֶׁקֶר **sheqer**, *sheh'-ker;* from 8266; an *untruth;* by impl. a *sham* (often adv.):—without a cause, deceit (-ful), false (-hood, -ly), feignedly, liar, + lie, lying, vain (thing), wrongfully.

8268. שֹׁקֶת **shôqeth**, *sho'-keth;* from 8248; a *trough* (for *watering*):—trough.

8269. שַׂר **sar**, *sar;* from 8323; a *head* person (of any rank or class):—captain (that had rule), chief (captain), general, governor, keeper, lord, ([-task-]) master, prince (-ipal), ruler, steward.

8270. שֹׁר **shôr**, *shore;* from 8324; a *string* (as *twisted* [comp. 8306]), i.e. (spec.) the umbilical cord (also fig. as the centre of strength):—navel.

8271. שְׁרֵא **shᵉrê'** (Chald.), *sher-ay';* a root corresp. to that of 8293; to *free, separate;* fig. to *unravel, commence;* by impl. (of unloading beasts) to *reside:*—begin dissolve, dwell, loose.

8272. שַׁרְאֶצֶר **Shar'etser**, *shar-eh'-tser;* of for. der.; *Sharetser*, the name of an Ass. and an Isr.:—Sharezer.

8273. שָׁרָב **shârâb**, *shaw-rawb';* from an unused root mean. to *glare;* quivering *glow* (of the air), espec. the *mirage:*—heat, parched ground.

8274. שֵׁרֵבְיָה **Shêrêbyâh**, *shay-rayb-yaw';* from 8273 and 3050; *Jah has brought heat; Sherebjah*, the name of two Isr.:—Sherebiah.

8275. שַׁרְבִיט **sharbîyṭ**, *shar-beet';* for 7626; a *rod* of empire:—sceptre.

8276. שָׂרַג **sârag**, *saw-rag';* a prim. root; to *intwine:*—wrap together, wreath.

8277. שָׂרַד **sârad**, *saw-rad';* a prim. root; prop. to *puncture* [comp. 8279], i.e. (fig. through the idea of *slipping* out) to *escape* or survive:—remain.

8278. שְׂרָד **sᵉrâd**, *ser-awd';* from 8277; *stitching* (as *pierced* with a needle):—service.

8279. שֶׂרֶד **sered**, *seh'-red;* from 8277; a (carpenter's) *scribing-awl* (for *pricking* or scratching measurements):—line.

8280. שָׂרָה **sârâh**, *saw-raw';* a prim. root; to *prevail:*—have power (as a prince).

8281. שָׁרָה **shârâh**, *shaw-raw';* a prim. root; to *free:*—direct.

8282. שָׂרָה **sârâh**, *saw-raw';* fem. of 8269; a *mistress*, i.e. female noble:—lady, princess, queen.

8283. שָׂרָה **Sârâh**, *saw-raw';* the same as 8282; *Sarah*, Abraham's wife:—Sarah.

8284. שָׁרָה **shârâh**, *shaw-raw';* prob. fem. of 7791; a *fortification* (lit. or fig.):—sing [*by mistake for* 7891], wall.

8285. שֵׁרָה **shêrâh**, *shay-raw';* from 8324 in its orig. sense of *pressing;* a wrist-*band* (as *compact* or *clasping*):—bracelet.

8286. שְׂרוּג **Sᵉrûwg**, *ser-oog';* from 8276; *tendril; Serug*, a postdiluvian patriarch:—Serug.

8287. שָׁרוּחֶן **Shârûwchen**, *shaw-roo-khen';* prob. from 8281 (in the sense of *dwelling* [comp. 8271]) and 2580; *abode of pleasure; Sharuchen*, a plac in Pal.:—Sharuhen.

8288. שְׂרוֹךְ **sᵉrôwk**, *ser-oke';* from 8308; a *thong* (as *laced* or *tied*):—([shoe-]) latchet.

8289. שָׁרוֹן **Shârôwn**, *shaw-rone';* prob. abridged from 3474; *plain; Sharon*, the name of a place in Pal.:—Lasharon, Sharon.

8290. שָׁרוֹנִי **Shârôwnîy**, *shaw-ro-nee';* patrial from 8289; a *Sharonite* or inhab. of Sharon:—Sharonite.

8291. שַׂרוּק **sarûwq**, *sar-ook';* pass. part. from the same as 8321; a *grapevine:*—principal plant. See 8320, 8321.

8292. שְׁרוּקָה° **shᵉrûwqâh**, *sher-oo-kaw';* or (by perm.)

שְׁרִיקָה **shᵉrîyqâh**, *sher-ee-kaw';* fem. pass. part. of 8319; a *whistling* (in scorn); by anal. a *piping:*—bleating, hissing.

8293. שֵׁרוּת° **shêrûwth**, *shay-rooth';* from 8281 abbrev.; *freedom:*—remnant.

8294. שֶׂרַח **Serach**, *seh'-rakh;* by perm. for 5629; *superfluity; Serach*, an Israelitess:—Sarah, Serah.

8295. שָׂרַט **sâraṭ**, *saw-rat';* a prim. root; to *gash:*—cut in pieces, make [cuttings] pieces.

8296. שֶׂרֶט **sereṭ**, *seh'-ret;* and

שָׂרֶטֶת **sâreṭeth**, *saw-reh'-teth;* from 8295; an *incision:*—cutting.

8297. שָׂרַי **Sâray**, *saw-rah'ee;* from 8269; *dominative; Sarai*, the wife of Abraham:—Sarai.

8298. שָׁרַי **Shâray**, *shaw-rah'ee;* prob. from 8324; *hostile; Sharay*, an Isr.:—Sharai.

8299. שָׂרִיג **sârîyg**, *saw-reeg';* from 8276; a *tendril* (as *intwining*):—branch.

8300. שָׂרִיד **sârîyd**, *saw-reed';* from 8277; a *survivor:*— × alive, left, remain (-ing), remnant, rest.

8301. שָׂרִיד **Sârîyd**, *saw-reed';* the same as 8300; *Sarid*, a place in Pal.:—Sarid.

8302. שִׁרְיוֹן **shiryôwn**, *shir-yone';* or

שִׁרְיֹן **shiryôn**, *shir-yone';* and

שִׁרְיָן **shiryân**, *shir-yawn';* also (fem.)

שִׁרְיָה **shiryâh**, *shir-yaw';* and

שִׁרְיֹנָה **shiryônâh**, *shir-yo-naw';* from 8281 in the orig. sense of *turning;* a *corslet* (as if *twisted*):—breastplate, coat of mail, habergeon, harness. See 5030.

8303. שִׁרְיוֹן **Shiryôwn**, *shir-yone';* and

שִׂרְיֹן **Siryôn**, *sir-yone';* the same as 8302 (i.e. *sheeted* with snow); *Shirjon* or *Sirjon*, a peak of the Lebanon:—Sirion.

8304. שְׂרָיָה **Sᵉrâyâh**, *ser-aw-yaw';* or

שְׂרָיָהוּ **Sᵉrâyâhûw**, *ser-aw-yaw'-hoo;* from 8280 and 3050; *Jah has prevailed; Serajah*, the name of nine Isr.:—Seraiah.

8305. שְׂרִיקָה **sᵉrîyqâh**, *ser-ee-kaw';* from the same as 8321 in the orig. sense of *piercing; hetchelling* (or combing flax), i.e. (concr.) *tow* (by extens. *linen* cloth):—fine.

8306. שָׁרִיר **shârîyr**, *shaw-reer';* from 8324 in the orig. sense as in 8270 (comp. 8326); a *cord*, i.e. (by anal.) *sinew:*—navel.

8307. שְׁרִירוּת **shᵉrîyrûwth**, *sher-ee-rooth';* from 8324 in the sense of *twisted*, i.e. *firm; obstinacy:*—imagination, lust.

8308. שָׂרַךְ **sârak**, *saw-rak';* a prim. root; to *interlace:*—traverse.

8309. שְׁרֵמָה° **shᵉrêmâh**, *sher-ay-maw';* prob. by orth. error for 7709; a *common:*—field.

8310. שַׂרְסְכִים **Sarçᵉkîym**, *sar-seh-keem';* of for. der.; *Sarsekim*, a Bab. general:—Sarsechim.

8311. שָׂרַע **sâra'**, *saw-rah';* a prim. root; to *prolong*, i.e. (reflex.) *be deformed* by excess of members:—stretch out self, (have any) superfluous thing.

8312. שַׂרְעַף **sar'aph**, *sar-af';* for 5587; *cogitation:*—thought.

8313. שָׂרַף **sâraph**, *saw-raf';* a prim. root; to *be* (caus. *set*) *on fire:*—(cause to, make a) burn ([-ing], up), kindle, × utterly.

8314. שָׂרָף **sârâph**, *saw-rawf';* from 8313; *burning*, i.e. (fig.) *poisonous* (serpent); spec. a *saraph* or symbol. creature (from their copper color):—fiery (serpent), seraph.

8315. שָׂרָף **Sâraph**, *saw-raf';* the same as 8314; *Saraph*, an Isr.:—Saraph.

8316. שְׂרֵפָה **sᵉrêphâh**, *ser-ay-faw';* from 8313; *cremation:*—burning.

8317. שָׁרַץ **shârats**, *shaw-rats';* a prim. root; to *wriggle*, i.e. (by impl.) *swarm* or *abound:*—breed (bring forth, increase) abundantly (in abundance), creep, move.

8318. שֶׁרֶץ **sherets**, *sheh'-rets;* from 8317; a *swarm*, i.e. active mass of minute animals:—creep (-ing thing), move (-ing creature).

8319. שָׁרַק **shâraq**, *shaw-rak';* a prim. root; prop. to *be shrill*, i.e. to whistle or *hiss* (as a call or in scorn):—hiss.

8320. שָׂרֻק **sâruq**, *saw-rook';* from 8319; *bright red* (as *piercing* to the sight), i.e. *bay:*—speckled. See 8291.

8321. שֹׂרֵק **sôrêq**, *so-rake';* or

שׂוֹרֵק **sôwrêq**, *so-rake';* and (fem.)

שֹׂרֵקָה **sôrêqâh**, *so-ray-kaw';* from 8319 in the sense of *redness* (comp. 8320); a *vine stock* (prop. one yielding *purple* grapes, the richest variety):—choice (-st, noble) wine. Comp. 8291.

8322. שְׁרֵקָה **shᵉrêqâh**, *sher-ay-kaw';* from 8319; a *derision:*—hissing.

8323. שָׂרַר **sârar**, *saw-rar';* a prim. root; to *have* (trans. *exercise;* reflex. *get*) *dominion:*—× altogether, make self a prince, (bear) rule.

8324. שָׁרַר **shârar**, *shaw-rar';* a prim. root; to *be hostile* (only act. part. an *opponent*):—enemy.

8325. שָׁרָר **Shârâr**, *shaw-rawr';* from 8324; *hostile; Sharar*, an Isr.:—Sharar.

8326. שֹׁרֶר **shôrer**, *sho'-rer;* from 8324 in the sense of *twisting* (comp. 8270); the umbilical *cord*, i.e. (by extens.) a *bodice:*—navel.

8327. שָׁרַשׁ **shârash**, *shaw-rash';* a prim. root; to *root*, i.e. strike into the soil, or (by impl.) to pluck from it:—(take, cause to take) root (out).

8328. שֶׁרֶשׁ **sheresh**, *sheh'-resh;* from 8327; a *root* (lit. or fig.):—bottom, deep, heel, root.

8329. שֶׁרֶשׁ **Sheresh**, *sheh'-resh;* the same as 8328; *Sheresh*, an Isr.:—Sharesh.

8330. שֹׁרֶשׁ **shôresh** (Chald.), *sho'-resh;* corresp. to 8328:—root.

8331. שַׁרְשָׁה **sharshâh**, *shar-shaw';* from 8327; a *chain* (as *rooted*, i.e. *linked*):—chain. Comp. 8333.

8332. שְׁרֹשׁוּ **shᵉrôshûw** (Chald.), *sher-o-shoo';* from a root corresp. to 8327; *eradication*, i.e. (fig.) *exile:*—banishment.

8333. שַׁרְשְׁרָה **sharsherâh**, *shar-sher-aw'*; from 8327 [comp. 8331]; a *chain*; (arch.) prob. a *garland*:—chain.

8334. שָׁרַת **shârath**, *shaw-rath'*; a prim. root; to *attend* as a menial or worshipper; fig. to *contribute* to:—minister (unto), (do) serve (-ant, -ice, -itor), wait on.

8335. שָׁרֵת **shârêth**, *shaw-rayth'*; infin. of 8334; *service* (in the Temple):—minister (-ry).

8336. שֵׁשׁ **shêsh**, *shaysh*; or (for alliteration with 4897)

שְׁשִׁי **sheshîy**, *shesh-ee'*; for 7893; *bleached* stuff, i.e. *white* linen or (by anal.) marble:— × blue, fine ([twined]) linen, marble, silk.

8337. שֵׁשׁ **shêsh**, *shaysh*; masc.

שִׁשָּׁה **shishshâh**, *shish-shaw'*; a prim. number; *six* (as an overplus [see 7797] beyond five or the fingers of the hand); as ord. *sixth*:—six ([-teen, -teenth]), sixth.

8338. שָׁוְשָׁא **shâwshâw**, *shaw-shaw'*; a prim. root; appar. to *annihilate*:—leave but the sixth part [*by confusion with* 8341].

8339. שֵׁשְׁבַּצַּר **Shêshbatstsar**, *shaysh-bats-tsar'*; of for. der.; *Sheshbatstsar*, Zerubbabel's Pers. name:—Sheshbazzar.

8340. שֵׁשְׁבַּצַּר **Shêshbatstsar** (Chald.), *shaysh-bats-tsar'*; corresp. to 8339:—Sheshbazzar.

שָׁשָׂה **shâsâh**. See 8154.

8341. שָׁשָׁה **shâshâh**, *shaw-shaw'*; a denom. from 8337; to *sixth* or divide into sixths:—give the sixth part.

8342. שָׂשׂוֹן **sâsôwn**, *saw-sone'*; or

שָׂשֹׂן **sâsôn**, *saw-sone'*; from 7797; *cheerfulness*; spec. *welcome*:—gladness, joy, mirth, rejoicing.

8343. שָׁשַׁי **Shâshay**, *shaw-shah'ee*; perh. from 8336; *whitish*; *Shashai*, an Isr.:—Shashai.

8344. שֵׁשַׁי **Shêshay**, *shay-shah'ee*; prob. for 8343; *Sheshai*, a Canaanite:—Sheshai.

8345. שִׁשִּׁי **shishshîy**, *shish-shee'*; from 8337; *sixth*, ord. or (fem.) fractional:—sixth (part).

8346. שִׁשִּׁים **shishshîym**, *shish-sheem'*; multiple of 8337; *sixty*:—sixty, three score.

8347. שֵׁשַׁךְ **Shêshak**, *shay-shak'*; of for. der.; *Sheshak*, a symbol. name of Bab.:—Sheshach.

8348. שֵׁשָׁן **Shêshân**, *shay-shawn'*; perh. for 7799; *lily*; *Sheshan*, an Isr.:—Sheshan.

שֹׁשָׁן **Shôshân**. See 7799.

8349. שָׁשַׁק **Shâshaq**, *shaw-shak'*; prob. from the base of 7785; *pedestrian*; *Shashak*, an Isr.:—Shashak.

8350. שָׁשַׁר **shâshar**, *shaw-shar'*; perh. from the base of 8324 in the sense of that of 8320; *red* ochre (from its *piercing* color):—vermillion.

8351. שֵׁת **shêth** (Num. 24 : 17), *shayth*; from 7582; *tumult*:—Sheth.

8352. שֵׁת **Shêth**, *shayth*; from 7896; *put*, i.e. *substituted*; *Sheth*, third son of Adam:—Seth, Sheth.

8353. שֵׁת **shêth** (Chald.), *shayth*; or

שִׁת **shîth** (Chald.), *sheeth*; corresp. to 8337:—six (-th).

8354. שָׁתָה **shâthâh**, *shaw-thaw'*; a prim. root; to *imbibe* (lit. or fig.):— × assuredly, banquet, × certainly, drink (-er, -ing), drunk (× -ard), surely. [Prop. intensive of 8248.]

8355. שְׁתָה **shethâh** (Chald.), *sheth-aw'*; corresp. to 8354:—drink.

8356. שָׁתָה **shâthâh**, *shaw-thaw'*; from 7896; a *basis*, i.e. (fig.) political or moral *support*:—foundation, purpose.

8357. שֵׁתָה **shêthâh**, *shay-thaw'*; from 7896; the *seat* (of the person):—buttock.

8358. שְׁתִי **shethîy**, *sheth-ee'*; from 8354; *intoxication*:—drunkenness.

8359. שְׁתִי **shethîy**, *sheth-ee'*; from 7896; a *fixture*, i.e. the *warp* in weaving:—warp.

8360. שְׁתִיָּה **shethîyâh**, *sheth-ee-yaw'*; fem. of 8358; *potation*:—drinking.

שְׁתַּיִם **shettayim**. See 8147.

8361. שִׁתִּין **shittîyn** (Chald.), *shit-teen'*; corresp. to 8346 [comp. 8353]; *sixty*:—threescore.

8362. שָׁתַל **shâthal**, *shaw-thal'*; a prim. root; to *transplant*:—plant.

8363. שְׁתִל **shethîyl**, *sheth-eel'*; from 8362; a *sprig* (as if *transplanted*), i.e. *sucker*:—plant.

8364. שֻׁתַלְחִי **Shûthalchîy**, *shoo-thal-kee'*; patron. from 7803; a *Shuthalchite* (collect.) or desc. of Shuthelach:—Shuthalhites.

שָׂתַם **sâtham**. See 5640.

8365. שָׁתַם **shâtham**, *shaw-tham'*; a prim. root; to *unveil* (fig.):—be open.

8366. שָׁתַן **shâthan**, *shaw-than'*; a prim. root; (caus.) to *make water*, i.e. *urinate*:—piss.

8367. שָׁתַק **shâthaq**, *shaw-thak'*; a prim. root; to *subside*:—be calm, cease, be quiet.

8368. שָׂתַר **sâthar**, *saw-thar'*; a prim. root; to *break* out (as an eruption):—have in [one's] secret parts.

8369. שֵׁתָר **Shêthâr**, *shay-thawr'*; of for. der.; *Shethar*, a Pers. satrap:—Shethar.

8370. שְׁתַר בּוֹזְנַי **Shethar Bôwzenay**, *sheth-ar' bo-zen-ah'ee*; of for. der.; *Shethar-Bozenai*, a Pers. officer:—Shethar-boznai.

8371. שָׁתַת **shâthath**, *shaw-thath'*; a prim. root; to *place*, i.e. *array*; reflex. to *lie*:—be laid, set.

ת

8372. תָּא **tâ'**, *taw*; and (fem.)

תָּאָה **tâ'âh** (Ezek. 40 : 12), *taw-aw'*; from (the base of) 8376; a *room* (as *circumscribed*):—(little) chamber.

8373. תָּאַב **tâ'ab**, *taw-ab'*; a prim. root; to *desire*:—long.

8374. תָּאַב **tâ'ab**, *taw-ab'*; a prim. root [prob. rather ident. with 8373 through the idea of *puffing* disdainfully at; comp. 340]; to *loathe* (mor.):—abhor.

8375. תַּאֲבָה **ta'âbâh**, *tah-ab-aw'*; from 8374 [comp. 15]; *desire*:—longing.

8376. תָּאָה **tâ'âh**, *taw-aw'*; a prim. root; to *mark off*, i.e. (intens.) *designate*:—point out.

8377. תְּאוֹ **te'ôw**, *teh-o'*; and

תּוֹא **tôw'** (the orig. form), *toh*; from 8376; a species of *antelope* (prob. from the white stripe on the cheek):—wild bull (ox).

8378. תַּאֲוָה **ta'âvâh**, *tah-av-aw'*; from 183 (abbrev.); a *longing*; by impl. a *delight* (subj. *satisfaction*, obj. a *charm*):—dainty, desire, × exceedingly, × greedily, lust (ing), pleasant. See also 6914.

8379. תַּאֲוָה **ta'âvâh**, *tah-av-aw'*; from 8376; a *limit*, i.e. full extent:—utmost bound.

8380. תָּאוֹם **tâ'ôwm**, *taw-ome'*; or

תָּאֹם **tâ'ôm**, *taw-ome'*; from 8382; a *twin* (in plur. only), lit. or fig.:—twins.

8381. תַּאֲלָה **ta'âlâh**, *tah-al-aw'*; from 422; an *imprecation*:—curse.

8382. תָּאַם **tâ'am**, *taw-am'*; a prim. root; to *be complete*; but used only as denom. from 8380, to *be* (caus. *make*) *twinned*, i.e. (fig.) *duplicate* or (arch.) *jointed*:—coupled (together), bear twins.

תְּאֹם **tâ'ôm**. See 8380.

8383. תְּאֻן **te'ûn**, *teh-oon'*; from 205; *naughtiness*, i.e. *toil*:—lie.

8384. תְּאֵן **te'ên**, *teh-ane'*; or (in the sing., fem.)

תְּאֵנָה **te'ênâh**, *teh-ay-naw'*; perh. of for. der.; the *fig* (tree or fruit):—fig (tree).

8385. תַּאֲנָה **ta'ânâh**, *tah-an-aw'*; or

תֹּאֲנָה **tô'ânâh**, *to-an-aw'*; from 579; an *opportunity* or (subj.) *purpose*:—occasion.

8386. תַּאֲנִיָּה **ta'ânîyâh**, *tah-an-ee-yaw'*; from 578; *lamentation*:—heaviness, mourning.

8387. תַּאֲנַת שִׁלֹה **Ta'ânath Shilôh**, *tah-an-ath' shee-lo'*; from 8385 and 7887; *approach of Shiloh*; *Taanath-Shiloh*, a place in Pal.:—Taanath-shiloh.

8388. תָּאַר **tâ'ar**, *taw-ar'*; a prim. root; to *delineate*; reflex. to *extend*:—be drawn, mark out, [Rimmon-] methoar [*by union with* 7417].

8389. תֹּאַר **tô'ar**, *to'-ar*; from 8388; *outline*, i.e. *figure* or *appearance*:— + beautiful, × comely, countenance, + fair, × favoured, form, × goodly, × resemble, visage.

8390. תַּאֲרֵעַ **Ta'ârêa'**, *tah-ar-ay'-ah*; perh. from 772; *Taareä*, an Isr.:—Tarea. See 8475.

8391. תְּאַשּׁוּר **te'ashshûwr**, *teh-ash-shoor'*; from 833; a species of *cedar* (from its *erectness*):—box (tree).

8392. תֵּבָה **têbâh**, *tay-baw'*; perh. of for. der.; a *box*:—ark.

8393. תְּבוּאָה **tebûw'âh**, *teb-oo-aw'*; from 935; *income*, i.e. *produce* (lit. or fig.):—fruit, gain, increase, revenue.

8394. תָּבוּן **tâbûwn**, *taw-boon'*; and (fem.)

תְּבוּנָה **tebûwnâh**, *teb-oo-naw'*; or

תּוֹבֻנָה° **tôwbûnâh**, *to-boo-naw'*; from 995; *intelligence*; by impl. an *argument*; by extens. *caprice*:—discretion, reason, skilfulness, understanding, wisdom.

8395. תְּבוּסָה **tebûwçâh**, *teb-oo-saw'*; from 947: a *treading down*, i.e. *ruin*:—destruction.

8396. תָּבוֹר **Tâbôwr**, *taw-bore'*; from a root corresp. to 8406; *broken region*; *Tabor*, a mountain in Pal., also a city adjacent:—Tabor.

8397. תֶּבֶל **tebel**, *teh'-bel*; appar. from 1101; *mixture*, i.e. *unnatural* bestiality:—confusion.

8398. תֵּבֵל **têbêl**, *tay-bale'*; from 2986; the *earth* (as *moist* and therefore inhabited); by extens. the *globe*; by impl. its *inhabitants*; spec. a partic. *land*, as Babylonia, Pal.:—habitable part, world.

תּוּבַל **Tûbal**. See 8422.

8399. תַּבְלִית **tablîyth**, *tab-leeth'*; from 1086; *consumption*:—destruction.

8400. תְּבַלֻּל **teballûl**, *teb-al-lool'*; from 1101 in the orig. sense of *flowing*; a *cataract* (in the eye):—blemish.

8401. תֶּבֶן **teben**, *teh'-ben*; prob. from 1129; prop. *material*, i.e. (spec.) refuse *haum* or stalks of grain (as *chopped* in threshing and used for fodder):—chaff, straw, stubble.

8402. תִּבְנִי **Tibni**, *tib-nee'*; from 8401; *strawy*; *Tibni*, an Isr.:—Tibni.

8403. תַּבְנִית **tabnîyth**, *tab-neeth'*; from 1129; *structure*; by impl. a *model*, *resemblance*:—figure, form, likeness, pattern, similitude.

8404. תַּבְעֵרָה **Tab'êrâh**, *tab-ay-raw'*; from 1197; *burning*; *Taberah*, a place in the Desert:—Taberah.

8405. תֵּבֵץ **Têbêts**, *tay-bates'*; from the same as 948; *whiteness*; *Tebets*, a place in Pal.:—Thebez.

8406. תְּבַר **tebar** (Chald.), *teb-ar'*; corresp. to 7665; to *be fragile* (fig.):—broken.

8407. תִּגְלַת פִּלְאֶסֶר **Tiglath Pil'eçer**, *tig-lath' pil-eh'-ser*; or

תִּגְלַת פְּלֶסֶר **Tiglath Peleçer**, *tig-lath pel-eh-ser*; or

תִּלְּגַת פִּלְנְאֶסֶר **Tilgath Pilne'eçer**, *til-gath' pil-neh-eh'-ser*; or

תִּלְּגַת פִּלְנֶסֶר **Tilgath Pilneçer**, *til-gath' pil-neh'-ser*; of for. der.; *Tiglath-Pileser* or *Tilgath-pilneser*, an Assyr. king:—Tiglath-pileser, Tilgath-pilneser.

8408. תַּגְמוּל **tagmûwl**, *tag-mool'*; from 1580; a *bestowment*:—benefit.

8409. תִּגְרָה **tigrâh**, *tig-raw'*; from 1624; *strife*, i.e. *infliction*:—blow.

תֹּגַרְמָה **Tôgarmâh**. See 8425.

8410. תִּדְהָר **tidhâr**, *tid-hawr'*; appar. from 1725; *enduring*; a species of hard-wood or *lasting* tree (perh. *oak*):—pine (tree).

8411. תְּדִירָא **tᵉdîyrâ'** (Chald.), *ted-ee-raw'*; from 1753 in the orig. sense of *enduring*; *permanence*, i.e. (adv.) *constantly*:—continually.

8412. תַּדְמֹר **Tadmôr**, *tad-more'*; or

תַּמֹּר° **Tammôr** (1 Kings 9 : 18), *tam-more'*; appar. from 8558; *palm*-city; *Tadmor*, a place near Pal.:—Tadmor.

8413. תִּדְעָל **Tidᶜâl**, *tid-awl'*; perh. from 1763; *fearfulness*; *Tidal*, a Canaanite:—Tidal.

8414. תֹּהוּ **tôhûw**, *to'-hoo*; from an unused root mean. to lie *waste*; a *desolation* (of surface), i.e. *desert*; fig. a *worthless* thing; adv. in *vain*:—confusion, empty place, without form, nothing, (thing of) nought, vain, vanity, waste, wilderness.

8415. תְּהוֹם **tᵉhôwm**, *teh-home'*; or

תְּהֹם **tᵉhôm**, *teh-home'*; (usually fem.) from 1949; an *abyss* (as a *surging* mass of water), espec. the *deep* (the *main* sea or the subterranean *water-supply*):—deep (place), depth.

8416. תְּהִלָּה **tᵉhillâh**, *teh-hil-law'*; from 1984; *laudation*; spec. (concr.) a *hymn*:—praise.

8417. תָּהֳלָה **tohŏlâh**, *to-hol-aw'*; fem. of an unused noun (appar. from 1984) mean. *bluster*; *braggadocio*, i.e. (by impl.) *fatuity*:—folly.

8418. תַּהֲלֻכָה **tahălûkâh**, *tah-hal-oo-kaw'*; from 1980; a *procession*:— × went.

תְּהֹם **tᵉhôm**. See 8415.

8419. תַּהְפֻּכָה **tahpûkâh**, *tah-poo-kaw'*; from 2015; a *perversity* or *fraud*:—(very) froward (-ness, thing), perverse thing.

8420. תָּו **tâv**, *taw*; from 8427; a *mark*; by impl. a *signature*:—desire, mark.

8421. תּוּב **tûwb** (Chald.), *toob*; corresp. to 7725; to *come back*; spec. (trans. and ellip.) to *reply*:—answer, restore, return (an answer).

8422. תּוּבַל **Tûwbal**, *too-bal'*; or

תֻּבַל **Tûbal**, *too-bal'*; prob. of for. der.; *Tubal*, a postdiluvian patriarch and his posterity:—Tubal.

8423. תּוּבַל קַיִן **Tûwbal Qayin**, *too-bal' kah'-yin*; appar. from 2986 (comp. 2981) and 7014; *offspring of Cain*; *Tubal-Kajin*, an antediluvian patriarch:—Tubal-cain.

תּוֹבֻנָה° **tôwbûnâh**. See 8394.

8424. תּוּגָה **tûwgâh**, *too-gaw'*; from 3013; *depression* (of spirits); concr. a *grief*:—heaviness, sorrow.

8425. תּוֹגַרְמָה **Tôwgarmâh**, *to-gar-maw'*; or

תֹּגַרְמָה **Tôgarmâh**, *to-gar-maw'*; prob. of for. der.; *Togarmah*, a son of Gomer and his posterity:—Togarmah.

8426. תּוֹדָה **tôwdâh**, *to-daw'*; from 3034; prop. an *extension* of the hand, i.e. (by impl.) *avowal*, or (usually) *adoration*; spec. a *choir* of worshippers:—confession, (sacrifice of) praise, thanks (-giving, offering).

8427. תָּוָה **tâvâh**, *taw-vaw'*; a prim. root; to *mark* out, i.e. (prim.) *scratch* or (def.) *imprint*:—scrabble, set [a mark].

8428. תָּוָה **tâvâh**, *taw-vaw'*; a prim. root [or perh. ident. with 8427 through a similar idea from *scraping* to pieces]; to *grieve*:—limit [*by confusion with* 8427].

8429. תְּוַהּ **tᵉvahh** (Chald.), *tev-ah'*; corresp. to 8539 or perh. to 7582 through the idea of *sweeping* to ruin [comp. 8428]; to *amaze*, i.e. (reflex. by impl.) *take alarm*:—be astonied.

8430. תּוֹחַ **Tôwach**, *to'-akh*; from an unused root mean. to *depress*; *humble*; *Toăch*, an Isr.:—Toah.

8431. תּוֹחֶלֶת **tôwcheleth**, *to-kheh'-leth*; from 3176; *expectation*:—hope.

תּוֹךְ **tôwk**. See 8496.

8432. תָּוֶךְ **tâvek**, *taw'-vek*; from an unused root mean. to *sever*; a *bisection*, i.e. (by impl.) the *centre*:—among (-st), × between, half, × (there-, where-) in (-to), middle, mid [-night], midst (among), × out (of), × through, × with (-in).

8433. תּוֹכֵחָה **tôwkêchâh**, *to-kay-khaw'*; and

תּוֹכַחַת **tôwkachath**, *to-kakh'-ath*; from 3198; *chastisement*; fig. (by words) *correction*, *refutation*, *proof* (even in defence):—argument, × chastened, correction, reasoning, rebuke, reproof, × be (often) reproved.

תּוּכִּי **tûwkkîy**. See 8500.

8434. תּוֹלָד **Tôwlâd**, *to-lawd'*; from 3205; *posterity*; *Tolad*, a place in Pal.:—Tolad. Comp. 513.

8435. תּוֹלְדָה **tôwlᵉdâh**, *to-led-aw'*; or

תֹּלְדָה **tôlᵉdâh**, *to-led-aw'*; from 3205; (plur. only) *descent*, i.e. *family*; (fig.) *history*:—birth, generations.

8436. תּוּלוֹן° **Tûwlôn**, *too-lone'*; from 8524; *suspension*; *Tulon*, an Isr.:—Tilon [*from the marg.*].

8437. תּוֹלָל **tôwlâl**, *to-lawl'*; from 3213; *causing to howl*, i.e. an *oppressor*:—that wasted.

8438. תּוֹלָע **tôwlâᶜ**, *to-law'*; and (fem.)

תּוֹלֵעָה **tôwlêᶜâh**, *to-lay-aw'*; or

תּוֹלַעַת **tôwlaᶜath**, *to-lah'-ath*; or

תֹּלַעַת **tôlaᶜath**, *to-lah'-ath*; from 3216; a *maggot* (as *voracious*); spec. (often with ellips. of 8144) the crimson-*grub*, but used only (in this connection) of the color from it, and cloths dyed therewith:—crimson, scarlet, worm.

8439. תּוֹלָע **Tôwlâᶜ**, *to-law'*; the same as 8438; *worm*; *Tola*, the name of two Isr.:—Tola.

8440. תּוֹלָעִי **Tôwlâᶜîy**, *to-law-ee'*; patron. from 8439; a *Tolaïte* (collect.) or desc. of Tola:—Tolaites.

8441. תּוֹעֵבָה **tôwᶜêbâh**, *to-ay-baw'*; or

תֹּעֵבָה **tôᶜêbâh**, *to-ay-baw'*; fem. act. part. of 8581; prop. something *disgusting* (mor.), i.e. (as noun) an *abhorrence*; espec. *idolatry* or (concr.) an *idol*:—abominable (custom, thing), abomination.

8442. תּוֹעָה **tôwᶜâh**, *to-aw'*; fem. act. part. of 8582; *mistake*, i.e. (mor.) *impiety*, or (political) *injury*:—error, hinder.

8443. תּוֹעָפָה **tôwᶜâphâh**, *to-aw-faw'*; from 3286; (only in plur. collect.) *weariness*, i.e. (by impl.) *toil* (*treasure* so obtained) or *speed*:—plenty, strength.

8444. תּוֹצָאָה **tôwtsâ'âh**, *to-tsaw-aw'*; or

תֹּצָאָה **tôtsâ'âh**, *to-tsaw-aw'*; from 3318; (only in plur. collect.) *exit*, i.e. (geographical) *boundary*, or (fig.) *deliverance*, (act.) *source*:—border (-s), going (-s) forth (out), issues, outgoings.

8445. תּוֹקַהַת° **Tôwqahath**, *to-kah'-ath*; from the same as 3349; *obedience*; *Tokahath*, an Isr.:—Tikvath [*by correction for* 8616].

8446. תּוּר **tûwr**, *toor*; a prim. root; to *meander* (caus. *guide*) about, espec. for trade or reconnoitring:—chap [-man], sent to descry, be excellent, merchant [-man], search (out), seek, (e-) spy (out).

8447. תּוֹר **tôwr**, *tore*; or

תֹּר **tôr**, *tore*; from 8446; a *succession*, i.e. a *string* or (abstr.) *order*:—border, row, turn.

8448. תּוֹר **tôwr**, *tore*; prob. the same as 8447; a *manner* (as a sort of *turn*):—estate.

8449. תּוֹר **tôwr**, *tore*; or

תֹּר **tôr**, *tore*; prob. the same as 8447; a *ring-dove*, often (fig.) as a term of endearment:—(turtle) dove.

8450. תּוֹר **tôwr** (Chald.), *tore*; corresp. (by perm.) to 7794; a *bull*:—bu[illegible], ox.

8451. תּוֹרָה **tôwrâh**, *to-raw'*; or

תֹּרָה **tôrâh**, *to-raw'*; from 3384; a *precept* or *statute*, espec. the *Decalogue* or *Pentateuch*:—law.

8452. תּוֹרָה **tôwrâh**, *to-raw'*; prob. fem. of 8448; a *custom*:—manner.

8453. תּוֹשָׁב **tôwshâb**, *to-shawb'*; or

תֹּשָׁב **tôshâb** (1 Kings 17 : 1), *to-shawb'*; from 3427; a *dweller* (but not outlandish [5237]); espec. (as distinguished from a native citizen [act. part. of 3427] and a temporary inmate [1616] or mere lodger [3885]) resident *alien*:—foreigner, inhabitant, sojourner, stranger.

8454. תּוּשִׁיָּה **tûwshîyâh**, *too-shee-yaw'*; or

תֻּשִׁיָּה **tûshîyâh**, *too-shee-yaw'*; from an unused root prob. mean. to *substantiate*; *support* or (by impl.) *ability*, i.e. (direct) *help*, (in purpose) an *undertaking*, (intellectual) *understanding*:—enterprise, that which (thing as it) is, substance, (sound) wisdom, working.

8455. תּוֹתָח **tôwthâch**, *to-thawkh'*; from an unused root mean. to *smite*; a *club*:—darts.

8456. תָּזַז **tâzaz**, *taw-zaz'*; a prim. root; to *lop* off:—cut down.

8457. תַּזְנוּת **taznûwth**, *taz-nooth'*; or

תַּזְנֻת **taznûth**, *taz-nooth'*; from 2181; *harlotry*, i.e. (fig.) *idolatry*:—fornication, whoredom.

8458. תַּחְבֻּלָה **tachbûlâh**, *takh-boo-law'*; or

תַּחְבּוּלָה **tachbûwlâh**, *takh-boo-law'*; from 2254 as denom. from 2256; (only in plur.) prop. *steerage* (as a management of *ropes*), i.e. (fig.) *guidance* or (by impl.) a *plan*:—good advice, (wise) counsels.

8459. תֹּחוּ **Tôchûw**, *to'-khoo*; from an unused root mean. to *depress*; *abasement*, *Tochu*, an Isr.:—Tohu.

8460. תְּחוֹת **tᵉchôwth** (Chald.), *tekh-ōth'*; or

תְּחֹת **tᵉchôth** (Chald.), *tekh-ōth'*; corresp. to 8478; *beneath*:—under.

8461. תַּחְכְּמֹנִי **Tachkᵉmônîy**, *takh-kem-o-nee'*; prob. for 2453; *sagacious*; *Tachkemoni*, an Isr.:—Tachmonite.

8462. תְּחִלָּה **tᵉchillâh**, *tekh-il-law'*; from 2490 in the sense of *opening*; a *commencement*; rel. *original* (adv. *-ly*):—begin (-ning), first (time).

8463. תַּחֲלוּא **tachălûw'**, *takh-al-oo'*; or

תַּחֲלֻא **tachălû'**, *takh-al-oo'*; from 2456; a *malady*:—disease, × grievous, (that are) sick (-ness).

8464. תַּחְמָס **tachmâç**, *takh-mawce'*; from 2554; a species of unclean bird (from its *violence*), perh. an *owl*:—night hawk.

8465. תַּחַן **Tachan**, *takh'-an*; prob. from 2583; *station*; *Tachan*, the name of two Isr.:—Tahan.

8466. תַּחֲנָה **tachănâh**, *takh-an-aw'*; from 2583; (only plur. coll.) an *encampment*:—camp.

8467. תְּחִנָּה **tᵉchinnâh**, *tekh-in-naw'*; from 2603; *graciousness*; caus. *entreaty*:—favour, grace, supplication.

8468. תְּחִנָּה **Tᵉchinnâh**, *tekh-in-naw'*; the same as 8467; *Techinnah*, an Isr.:—Tehinnah.

8469. תַּחֲנוּן **tachănûwn**, *takh-an-oon'*; or (fem.)

תַּחֲנוּנָה **tachănûwnâh**, *takh-an-oo-naw'*; from 2603; earnest *prayer*:—intreaty, supplication.

8470. תַּחֲנִי **Tachănîy**, *takh-an-ee'*; patron. from 8465; a *Tachanite* (collect.) or desc. of Tachan:—Tahanites.

8471. תַּחְפַּנְחֵס **Tachpanchêç**, *takh-pan-khace'*; or
תְּחַפְנְחֵס **Teꞌchaphneꞌchêç** (Ezek. 30 : 18), *tekh-af-nekh-ace'*; or
תַּחְפְּנֵס **Tachpeꞌnêç** (Jer. 2 : 16), *takh-pen-ace'*; of Eg. der.; *Tachpanches*, *Techaphneches* or *Tachpenes*, a place in Egypt:—Tahapanes, Tahpanhes, Tehaphnehes.

8472. תַּחְפְּנֵיס **Tachpeꞌnêyç**, *takh-pen-ace'*; of Eg. der.; *Tachpenes*, an Eg. woman:—Tahpenes.

8473. תַּחְרָא **tachărâ'**, *takh-ar-aw'*; from 2734 in the orig. sense of 2352 or 2353; a linen *corslet* (as *white* or *hollow*):—habergeon.

8474. תַּחֲרָה **tachârâh**, *takh-aw-raw'*; a factitious root from 2734 through the idea of the *heat* of jealousy; to *vie* with a rival:—close, contend.

8475. תַּחְרֵעַ **Tachrêaꞌ**, *takh-ray'-ah*; for 8390; *Tachreä*, an Isr.:—Tahrea.

8476. תַּחַשׁ **tachash**, *takh'-ash*; prob. of for. der.; a (clean) animal with fur, prob. a species of *antelope*:—badger.

8477. תַּחַשׁ **Tachash**, *takh'-ash*; the same as 8476; *Tachash*, a relative of Abraham:—Thahash.

8478. תַּחַת **tachath**, *takh'-ath*; from the same as 8430; the *bottom* (as *depressed*); only adv. *below* (often with prep. pref. *underneath*), in *lieu of*, etc.:—as, beneath, × flat, in (-stead), (same) place (where . . . is), room, for . . . sake, stead of, under, × unto, × when . . . was mine, whereas, [where-] fore, with.

8479. תַּחַת **tachath** (Chald.), *takh'-ath*; corresp. to 8478:—under.

8480. תַּחַת **Tachath**, *takh'-ath*; the same as 8478; *Tachath*, the name of a place in the Desert, also of three Isr.:—Tahath.

תְּחֹת **teꞌchôth**. See 8460.

8481. תַּחְתּוֹן **tachtôwn**, *takh-tone'*; or
תַּחְתֹּן **tachtôn**, *takh-tone'*; from 8478; *bottommost*:—lower (-est), nether (-most).

8482. תַּחְתִּי **tachtîy**, *takh-tee'*; from 8478; *lowermost*; as noun (fem. plur.) the *depths* (fig. a *pit*, the *womb*):—low (parts, -er, -er parts, -est), nether (part).

8483. תַּחְתִּים חָדְשִׁי **Tachtîym Chodshîy**, *takh-teem' khod-shee'*; appar. from the plur. masc. of 8482 or 8478 and 2320; *lower* (ones) *monthly*; *Tachtim-Chodshi*, a place in Pal.:—Tahtim-hodshi.

8484. תִּיכוֹן **tîykôwn**, *tee-kone'*; or
תִּיכֹן **tîykôn**, *tee-kone'*; from 8432; *central*:—middle (-most), midst.

8485. תֵּימָא **Têymâ'**, *tay-maw'*; or
תֵּמָא **Têmâ'**, *tay-maw'*; prob. of for. der.; *Tema*, a son of Ishmael, and the region settled by him:—Tema.

8486. תֵּימָן **têymân**, *tay-mawn'*; or
תֵּמָן **têmân**, *tay-mawn'*; denom. from 3225; the *south* (as being on the *right* hand of a person facing the east):—south (side, -ward, wind).

8487. תֵּימָן **Têymân**, *tay-mawn'*; or
תֵּמָן **Têmân**, *tay-mawn'*; the same as 8486; *Teman*, the name of two Edomites, and of the region and desc. of one of them:—south, Teman.

8488. תֵּימְנִי **Têymeꞌnîy**, *tay-men-ee'*; prob. for 8489; *Temeni*, an Isr.:—Temeni.

8489. תֵּימָנִי **Têymânîy**, *tay-maw-nee'*; patron. from 8487; a *Temanite* or desc. of Teman:—Temani, Temanite.

8490. תִּימָרָה **tîymârâh**, *tee-maw-raw'*; or
תִּמָרָה **tîmârâh**, *tee-maw-raw'*; from the same as 8558; a *column*, i.e. cloud:—pillar.

8491. תִּיצִי **Tîytsîy**, *tee-tsee'*; patrial or patron. from an unused noun of uncert. mean.; a *Titsite* or desc. or inhab. of an unknown Tits:—Tizite.

8492. תִּירוֹשׁ **tîyrôwsh**, *tee-roshe'*; or
תִּירֹשׁ **tîyrôsh**, *tee-roshe'*; from 3423 in the sense of *expulsion*; *must* or fresh grape-juice (as just *squeezed* out); by impl. (rarely) fermented *wine*:—(new, sweet) wine.

8493. תִּירְיָא **Tîyreꞌyâ'**, *tee-reh-yaw'*; prob. from 3372; *fearful*; *Tirja*, an Isr.:—Tiria.

8494. תִּירָס **Tîyrâç**, *tee-rawce'*; prob. of for. der.; *Tiras*, a son of Japheth:—Tiras.

תִּירֹשׁ **tîyrôsh**. See 8492.

8495. תַּיִשׁ **tayish**, *tah'-yeesh*; from an unused root mean. to *butt*; a *buck* or he-goat (as given to *butting*):—he goat.

8496. תֹּךְ **tôk**, *toke*; or
תּוֹךְ **tôwk** (Psa. 72 : 14), *toke*; from the same base as 8432 (in the sense of *cutting* to pieces); *oppression*:—deceit, fraud.

8497. תָּכָה **tâkâh**, *taw-kaw'*; a prim. root; to *strew*, i.e. *encamp*:—sit down.

8498. תְּכוּנָה **teꞌkûwnâh**, *tek-oo-naw'*; fem. pass. part. of 8505; *adjustment*, i.e. *structure*; by impl. *equipage*:—fashion, store.

8499. תְּכוּנָה **teꞌkûwnâh**, *tek-oo-naw'*; from 8559; or prob. ident. with 8498; something *arranged* or *fixed*, i.e. a *place*:—seat.

8500. תֻּכִּי **tukkîy**, *took-kee'*; or
תּוּכִּי **tûwkkîy**, *took-kee'*; prob. of for. der.; some imported creature, prob. a *peacock*:—peacock.

8501. תָּכָךְ **tâkâk**, *taw-kawk'*; from an unused root mean. to *dissever*, i.e. *crush*:—deceitful.

8502. תִּכְלָה **tiklâh**, *tik-law'*; from 3615; *completeness*:—perfection.

8503. תַּכְלִית **taklîyth**, *tak-leeth'*; from 3615; *completion*; by impl. an *extremity*:—end, perfect (-ion).

8504. תְּכֵלֶת **teꞌkêleth**, *tek-ay'-leth*; prob. for 7827; the cerulean *mussel*, i.e. the color (*violet*) obtained therefrom or stuff dyed therewith:—blue.

8505. תָּכַן **tâkan**, *taw-kan'*; a prim. root; to *balance*, i.e. *measure* out (by weight or dimension); fig. to *arrange*, *equalize*, through the idea of *levelling* (ment. *estimate*, *test*):—bear up, direct, be ([un-]) equal, mete, ponder, tell, weigh.

8506. תֹּכֶן **tôken**, *to'-ken*; from 8505; a fixed *quantity*:—measure, tale.

8507. תֹּכֶן **Tôken**, *to'-ken*; the same as 8506; *Token*, a place in Pal.:—Tochen.

8508. תָּכְנִית **tokniyth**, *tok-neeth'*; from 8506; *admeasurement*, i.e. *consummation*:—pattern, sum.

8509. תַּכְרִיךְ **takrîyk**, *tak-reek'*; appar. from an unused root mean. to *encompass*; a *wrapper* or robe:—garment.

8510. תֵּל **têl**, *tale*; by contr. from 8524; a *mound*:—heap, × strength.

8511. תָּלָא **tâlâ'**, *taw-law'*; a prim. root; to *suspend*; fig. (through *hesitation*) to *be uncertain*; by impl. (of ment. *dependence*) to *habituate*:—be bent, hang (in doubt).

8512. תֵּל אָבִיב **Têl 'Âbîyb**, *tale aw-beeb'*; from 8510 and 24; *mound* of *green growth*; *Tel-Abib*, a place in Chaldæa:—Tel-abib.

8513. תְּלָאָה **teꞌlâ'âh**, *tel-aw-aw'*; from 3811; *distress*:—travail, travel, trouble.

8514. תַּלְאוּבָה **tal'ûwbâh**, *tal-oo-baw'*; from 3851; *desiccation*:—great drought.

8515. תְּלַאשָּׂר **Teꞌla'ssar**, *tel-as-sar'*; or
תְּלַשָּׂר **Teꞌlassar**, *tel-as-sar'*; of for. der.; *Telassar*, a region of Assyria:—Telassar.

8516. תַּלְבֹּשֶׁת **talbôsheth**, *tal-bo'-sheth*; from 3847; a *garment*:—clothing.

8517. תְּלַג **teꞌlag** (Chald.), *tel-ag'*; corresp. to 7950; *snow*:—snow.

תִּלְגַת **Tilgath**. See 8407.

תֹּלְדָה **tôlꞌdâh**. See 8435.

8518. תָּלָה **tâlâh**, *taw-law'*; a prim. root; to *suspend* (espec. to *gibbet*):—hang (up).

8519. תְּלוּנָה **teꞌlûwnâh**, *tel-oo-naw'*; or
תְּלֻנָּה **teꞌlunnâh**, *tel-oon-naw'*; from 3885 in the sense of *obstinacy*; a *grumbling*:—murmuring.

8520. תֶּלַח **Telach**, *teh'-lakh*; prob. from an unused root mean. to *dissever*; *breach*; *Telach*, an Isr.:—Telah.

8521. תֵּל חַרְשָׁא **Têl Charshâ'**, *tale khar-shaw'*; from 8510 and the fem. of 2798; *mound of workmanship*; *Tel-Charsha*, a place in Bab.:—Tel-haresha, Tel-harsa.

8522. תְּלִי **teꞌlîy**, *tel-ee'*; prob. from 8518; a *quiver* (as *slung*):—quiver.

8523. תְּלִיתַי **teꞌlîythay** (Chald.), *tel-ee-thah'ee*; or
תַּלְתִּי **taltîy** (Chald.), *tal-tee'*; ordinal from 8532; *third*:—third.

8524. תָּלַל **tâlal**, *taw-lal'*; a prim. root; to *pile* up, i.e. *elevate*:—eminent. Comp. 2048.

8525. תֶּלֶם **telem**, *teh'-lem*; from an unused root mean. to *accumulate*; a *bank* or *terrace*:—furrow, ridge.

8526. תַּלְמַי **Talmay**, *tal-mah'ee*; from 8525; *ridged*; *Talmai*, the name of a Canaanite and a Syrian:—Talmai.

8527. תַּלְמִיד **talmîyd**, *tal-meed'*; from 3925; a *pupil*:—scholar.

8528. תֵּל מֶלַח **Têl Melach**, *tale meh'-lakh*; from 8510 and 4417; *mound of salt*; *Tel-Melach*, a place in Bab.:—Tel-melah.

תְּלֻנָּה **teꞌlunnâh**. See 8519.

8529. תָּלַע **tâlaꞌ**, *taw-law'*; a denom. from 8438; to *crimson*, i.e. dye that color:—× scarlet.

תֹּלַעַת **tôla'ath**. See 8438.

8530. תַּלְפִּיָּה **talpîyâh**, *tal-pee-yaw'*; fem. from an unused root mean. to *tower*; something *tall*, i.e. (plur. collect.) *slenderness*:—armoury.

תְּלַשָּׂר **Teꞌlassar**. See 8515.

8531. תְּלַת **teꞌlath** (Chald.), *tel-ath'*; from 8532; a *tertiary* rank:—third.

8532. תְּלָת **teꞌlâth** (Chald.), *tel-awth'*; masc.
תְּלָתָה **teꞌlâthâh** (Chald.), *tel-aw-thaw'*; or
תְּלָתָא **teꞌlâthâ'** (Chald.), *tel-aw-thaw'*; corresp. to 7969; *three* or *third*:—third, three.

תַּלְתִּי **taliy**. See 8523.

8533. תְּלָתִין **teꞌlâthîyn** (Chald.), *tel-aw-theen'*; mult. of 8532; *ten times three*:—thirty.

8534. תַּלְתַּל **taltal**, *tal-tal'*; by redupl. from 8524 through the idea of *vibration*; a trailing *bough* (as *pendulous*):—bushy.

8535. תָּם **tâm**, *tawm*; from 8552; *complete*; usually (mor.) *pious*; spec. *gentle*, *dear*:—coupled together, perfect, plain, undefiled, upright.

8536. תָּם **tâm** (Chald.), *tawm*; corresp. to 8033; *there*:—× thence, there, × where.

8537. תֹּם **tôm**, *tome*; from 8552; *completeness*; fig. *prosperity*; usually (mor.) *innocence*:—full, integrity, perfect (-ion), simplicity, upright (-ly, -ness), at a venture. See 8550.

תֵּמָא **Têmâ'**. See 8485.

8538. תֻּמָּה **tummâh**, *toom-maw'*; fem. of 8537; *innocence*:—integrity.

8539. תָּמַהּ **tâmahh**, *taw-mah'*; a prim. root; to *be in consternation*:—be amazed, be astonished, marvel (-lously), wonder.

8540. תְּמַהּ **teꞌmahh** (Chald.), *tem-ah'*; from a root corresp. to 8539; a *miracle*:—wonder.

8541. תִּמָּהוֹן **timmâhôwn**, *tim-maw-hone'*; from 8539; *consternation*:—astonishment.

8542. תַּמּוּז **Tammûwz**, *tam-mooz'*; of uncert. der.; *Tammuz*, a Phœnician deity:—Tammuz.

8543. תְּמוֹל **temôwl**, *tem-ole'*; or
תְּמֹל **temôl**, *tem-ole'*; prob. for 865; prop. *ago*, i.e. a (short or long) *time since*; espec. *yesterday*, or (with 8032) *day before yesterday*:— + before (-time), + these [three] days, + heretofore, + time past, yesterday.

8544. תְּמוּנָה **temûwnâh**, *tem-oo-naw'*; or
תְּמֻנָה **temûnâh**, *tem-oo-naw'*; from 4327; *something portioned* (i.e. *fashioned*) out, as a *shape*, i.e. (indef.) *phantom*, or (spec.) *embodiment*, or (fig.) *manifestation* (of favor):—image, likeness, similitude.

8545. תְּמוּרָה **temûwrâh**, *tem-oo-raw'*; from 4171; *barter*, *compensation*:—(ex-) change (-ing), recompense, restitution.

8546. תְּמוּתָה **temûwthâh**, *tem-oo-thaw'*; from 4191; *execution* (as a doom):—death, die.

8547. תֶּמַח **Temach**, *teh'-makh*; of uncert. der.; *Temach*, one of the Nethinim:—Tamah, Thamah.

8548. תָּמִיד **tâmîyd**, *taw-meed'*; from an unused root mean. to *stretch*; prop. *continuance* (as indef. *extension*); but used only (attributively as adj.) *constant* (or adv. *constantly*); ellipt. the *regular* (daily) sacrifice:—alway (-s), continual (employment, -ly), daily, ([n-]) ever (-more), perpetual.

8549. תָּמִים **tâmîym**, *taw-meem'*; from 8552; *entire* (lit., fig. or mor.); also (as noun) *integrity*, *truth*:—without blemish, complete, full, perfect, sincerely (-ity), sound, without spot, undefiled, upright (-ly), whole.

8550. תֻּמִּים **Tummîym**, *toom-meem'*; plur. of 8537; *perfections*, i.e. (techn.) one of the epithets of the objects in the high-priest's breastplate as an emblem of *complete* Truth:—Thummim.

8551. תָּמַךְ **tâmak**, *taw-mak'*; a prim. root; to *sustain*; by impl. to *obtain*, *keep fast*; fig. to *help*, *follow close*:—(take, up-) hold (up), maintain, retain, stay (up).

תְּמֹל **temôl**. See 8543.

8552. תָּמַם **tâmam**, *taw-mam'*; a prim. root; to *complete*, in a good or a bad sense, lit. or fig., trans. or intrans. (as follows):—accomplish, cease, be clean [pass-] ed, consume, have done, (come to an, have an, make an) end, fail, come to the full, be all gone, × be all here, be (make) perfect, be spent, sum, be (shew self) upright, be wasted, whole.

תֵּמָן **têman**, **Têmân**. See 8486, 8487.

8553. תִּמְנָה **Timnâh**, *tim-naw'*; from 4487; a *portion* assigned; *Timnah*, the name of two places in Pal.:—Timnah, Timnath, Thimnathah.

תְּמֻנָה **temûnâh**. See 8544.

8554. תִּמְנִי **Timnîy**, *tim-nee'*; patrial from 8553; a *Timnite* or inhab. of Timnah:—Timnite.

8555. תִּמְנָע **Timnâʻ**, *tim-naw'*; from 4513; *restraint*; *Timna*, the name of two Edomites:—Timna, Timnah.

8556. תִּמְנַת חֶרֶס **Timnath Chereç**, *tim-nath kheh'-res*; or
תִּמְנַת סֶרַח **Timnath Çerach**, *tim-nath seh'-rakh*; from 8553 and 2775; *portion of* (the) *sun*; *Timnath-Cheres*, a place in Pal.:—Timnath-heres, Timnath-serah.

8557. תֶּמֶס **temeç**, *teh'-mes*; from 4529; *liquefaction*, i.e. *disappearance*:—melt.

8558. תָּמָר **tâmâr**, *taw-mawr'*; from an unused root mean. to *be erect*; a *palm* tree:—palm (tree).

8559. תָּמָר **Tâmâr**, *taw-mawr'*; the same as 8558; *Tamar*, the name of three women and a place:—Tamar.

8560. תֹּמֶר **tômer**, *to'-mer*; from the same root as 8558; a *palm* trunk:—palm tree.

8561. תִּמֹּר **timmôr** (plur. only), *tim-more'*; or (fem.)
תִּמֹּרָה **timmôrâh** (sing. and plur.), *tim-mo-raw'*; from the same root as 8558; (arch.) a *palm*-like pilaster (i.e. umbellate):—palm tree.

תַּמֹּר **Tammôr**. See 8412.

תִּמָרָה **tîmârâh**. See 8490.

8562. תַּמְרוּק **tamrûwq**, *tam-rook'*; or
תַּמְרֻק **tamrûq**, *tam-rook'*; or
תַּמְרִיק **tamrîyq**, *tam-reek'*; from 4838; prop. a *scouring*, i.e. *soap* or *perfumery* for the bath; fig. a *detergent*:— × cleanse, (thing for) purification (-fying).

8563. תַּמְרוּר **tamrûwr**, *tam-roor'*; from 4843; *bitterness* (plur. as collect.):— × most bitter (-ly).

תַּמְרֻק **tamrûq**, and
תַּמְרִיק **tamrîyq**. See 8562.

8564. תַּמְרוּר **tamrûwr**, *tam-roor'*; from the same root as 8558; an *erection*, i.e. *pillar* (prob. for a guide-board):—high heap.

8565. תַּן **tan**, *tan*; from an unused root prob. mean. to *elongate*; a *monster* (as preternaturally formed), i.e. a *sea-serpent* (or other huge marine animal); also a *jackal* (or other hideous land animal):—dragon, whale. Comp. 8577.

8566. תָּנָה **tânâh**, *taw-naw'*; a prim. root; to *present* (a mercenary inducement), i.e. *bargain* with (a harlot):—hire.

8567. תָּנָה **tânâh**, *taw-naw'*; a prim. root [rather ident. with 8566 through the idea of *attributing* honor]; to *ascribe* (praise), i.e. *celebrate*, *commemorate*:—lament, rehearse.

8568. תַּנָּה **tannâh**, *tan-naw'*; prob. fem. of 8565; a female *jackal*:—dragon.

8569. תְּנוּאָה **tenûwʼâh**, *ten-oo-aw'*; from 5106; *alienation*; by impl. *enmity*:—breach of promise, occasion.

8570. תְּנוּבָה **tenûwbâh**, *ten-oo-baw'*; from 5107; *produce*:—fruit, increase.

8571. תְּנוּךְ **tenûwk**, *ten-ook'*; perh. from the same as 594 through the idea of *protraction*; a *pinnacle*, i.e. *extremity*:—tip.

8572. תְּנוּמָה **tenûwmâh**, *ten-oo-maw'*; from 5123; *drowsiness*, i.e. *sleep*:—slumber (-ing).

8573. תְּנוּפָה **tenûwphâh**, *ten-oo-faw'*; from 5130; a *brandishing* (in threat); by impl. *tumult*; spec. the official *undulation* of sacrificial offerings:—offering, shaking, wave (offering).

8574. תַּנּוּר **tannûwr**, *tan-noor'*; from 5216; a *fire-pot*:—furnace, oven.

8575. תַּנְחוּם **tanchûwm**, *tan-khoom'*; or
תַּנְחֻם **tanchûm**, *tan-khoom'*; and (fem.)
תַּנְחוּמָה **tanchûwmâh**, *tan-khoo-maw'*; from 5162; *compassion*, *solace*:—comfort, consolation.

8576. תַּנְחֻמֶת **Tanchûmeth**, *tan-khoo'-meth*; for 8575 (fem.); *Tanchumeth*, an Isr.:—Tanhumeth.

8577. תַּנִּין **tannîyn**, *tan-neen'*; or
תַּנִּים **tannîym** (Ezek. 29 : 3), *tan-neem'*; intens. from the same as 8565; a marine or land *monster*, i.e. *sea-serpent* or *jackal*:—dragon, sea-monster, serpent, whale.

8578. תִּנְיָן **tinyân** (Chald.), *tin-yawn'*; corresp. to 8147; *second*:—second.

8579. תִּנְיָנוּת **tinyânûwth** (Chald.), *tin-yaw-nooth'*; from 8578; a *second time*:—again.

8580. תַּנְשֶׁמֶת **tanshemeth**, *tan-sheh'-meth*; from 5395; prop. a hard *breather*, i.e. the name of two unclean creatures, a lizard and a bird (both perh. from changing color through their *irascibility*), prob. the *tree-toad* and the *water-hen*:—mole, swan.

8581. תָּעַב **tâʻab**, *taw-ab'*; a prim. root; to *loathe*, i.e. (mor.) *detest*:—(make to be) abhor (-red), (be, commit more, do) abominable (-y), × utterly.

תֹּעֵבָה **tôʻêbâh**. See 8441.

8582. תָּעָה **tâʻâh**, *taw-aw'*; a prim. root; to *vacillate*, i.e. *reel* or *stray* (lit. or fig.); also caus. of both:—(cause to) go astray, deceive, dissemble, (cause to, make to) err, pant, seduce, (make to) stagger, (cause to) wander, be out of the way.

8583. תֹּעוּ **Tôʻûw**, *to'-oo*; or
תֹּעִי **Tôʻîy**, *to'-ee*; from 8582; *error*; *Toü* or *Toï*, a Syrian king:—Toi, Tou.

8584. תְּעוּדָה **teʻûwdâh**, *teh-oo-daw'*; from 5749; *attestation*, i.e. a *precept*, *usage*:—testimony.

8585. תְּעָלָה **teʻâlâh**, *teh-aw-law'*; from 5927; a *channel* (into which water is *raised* for irrigation); also a *bandage* or *plaster* (as placed *upon* a wound):—conduit, cured, healing, little river, trench, watercourse.

8586. תַּעֲלוּל **taʻălûwl**, *tah-al-ool'*; from 5953; *caprice* (as a fit *coming on*), i.e. *vexation*; concr. a *tyrant*:—babe, delusion.

8587. תַּעֲלֻמָּה **taʻălummâh**, *tah-al-oom-maw'*; from 5956; a *secret*:—thing that is hid, secret.

8588. תַּעֲנוּג **taʻănûwg**, *tah-an-oog'*; or
תַּעֲנֻג **taʻănûg**, *tah-an-oog'*; and (fem.)
תַּעֲנֻגָה **taʻănûgâh**, *tah-an-oog-aw'*; from 6026; *luxury*:—delicate, delight, pleasant.

8589. תַּעֲנִית **taʻănîyth**, *tah-an-eeth'*; from 6031; *affliction* (of self), i.e. *fasting*:—heaviness.

8590. תַּעֲנָךְ **Taʻănâk**, *tah-an-awk'*; or
תַּעְנָךְ **Taʻnâk**, *tah-nawk'*; of uncert. der.; *Taanak* or *Tanak*, a place in Pal.:—Taanach, Tanach.

8591. תָּעַע **tâʻaʻ**, *taw-ah'*; a prim. root; to *cheat*; by anal. to *maltreat*:—deceive, misuse.

8592. תַּעֲצֻמָה **taʻătsûmâh**, *tah-ats-oo-maw'*; from 6105; *might* (plur. collect.):—power.

8593. תַּעַר **taʻar**, *tah'-ar*; from 6168; a *knife* or *razor* (as *making* bare); also a *scabbard* (as *being bare*, i.e. empty):—[pen-] knife, rasor, scabbard, shave, sheath.

8594. תַּעֲרֻבָה **taʻărûbâh**, *tah-ar-oo-baw'*; from 6148; *suretyship*, i.e. (concr.) a *pledge*:— + hostage.

8595. תַּעְתֻּעַ **taʻtûaʻ**, *tah-too'-ah*; from 8591; a *fraud*:—error.

8596. תֹּף **tôph**, *tofe*; from 8608 contr.; a *tambourine*:—tabret, timbrel.

8597. תִּפְאָרָה **tiphʼârâh**, *tif-aw-raw'*; or
תִּפְאֶרֶת **tiphʼereth**, *tif-eh'-reth*; from 6286; *ornament* (abstr. or concr., lit. or fig.):—beauty (-iful), bravery, comely, fair, glory (-ious), honour, majesty.

8598. תַּפּוּחַ **tappûwach**, *tap-poo'-akh*; from 5301; an *apple* (from its *fragrance*), i.e. the fruit or the tree (prob. includ. others of the *pome* order, as the quince, the orange, etc.):—apple (tree). See also 1054.

8599. תַּפּוּחַ **Tappûwach**, *tap-poo'-akh*; the same as 8598; *Tappûach*, the name of two places in Pal., also of an Isr.:—Tappuah.

8600. תְּפוֹצָה **tephôwtsâh**, *tef-o-tsaw'*; from 6327; a *dispersal*:—dispersion.

8601. תֻּפִין **tûphîyn**, *too-feen'*; from 644; *cookery*, i.e. (concr.) a *cake*:—baked piece.

8602. תָּפֵל **tâphêl**, *taw-fale'*; from an unused root mean. to *smear*; *plaster* (as *gummy*) or *slime*; (fig.) *frivolity*:—foolish things, unsavoury, untempered.

8603. תֹּפֶל **Tôphel**, *to'-fel*; from the same as 8602; *quagmire*; *Tophel*, a place near the Desert:—Tophel.

8604. תִּפְלָה **tiphlâh**, *tif-law'*; from the same as 8602; *frivolity*:—folly, foolishly.

8605. תְּפִלָּה **tᵉphillâh**, *tef-il-law'*; from 6419; *intercession, supplication*; by impl. a *hymn*:—prayer.

8606. תִּפְלֶצֶת **tiphletseth**, *tif-leh'-tseth*; from 6426; *fearfulness*:—terrible.

8607. תִּפְסַח **Tiphçach**, *tif-sakh'*; from 6452; *ford*; *Tiphsach*, a place in Mesopotamia:—Tipsah.

8608. תָּפַף **tâphaph**, *taw-faf'*; a prim. root; to *drum*, i.e. play (as) on the tambourine:—taber, play with timbrels.

8609. תָּפַר **tâphar**, *taw-far'*; a prim. root; to *sew*:—(women that) sew (together).

8610. תָּפַשׂ **tâphas**, *taw-fas'*; a prim. root; to *manipulate*, i.e. *seize*; chiefly to *capture, wield*; spec. to *overlay*; fig. to *use* unwarrantably:—catch, handle, (lay, take) hold (on, over), stop, × surely, surprise, take.

8611. תֹּפֶת **tôpheth**, *to'-feth*; from the base of 8608; a *smiting*, i.e. (fig.) *contempt*:—tabret.

8612. תֹּפֶת **Tôpheth**, *to'-feth*; the same as 8611; *Topheth*, a place near Jerus.:—Tophet, Topheth.

8613. תָּפְתֶּה **Tophteh**, *tof-teh'*; prob. a form of 8612; *Tophteh*, a place of cremation:—Tophet.

8614. תִּפְתָּי **tiphtay** (Chald.), *tif-tah'ee*; perh. from 8199; *judicial*, i.e. a *lawyer*:—sheriff.

תּוֹצָאָה **tôtsâ'âh**. See 8444.

8615. תִּקְוָה **tiqvâh**, *tik-vaw'*; from 6960; lit. a *cord* (as an *attachment* [comp. 6961]); fig. *expectancy*:—expectation ([-ted]), hope, live, thing that I long for.

8616. תִּקְוָה **Tiqvâh**, *tik-vaw'*; the same as 8615; *Tikvah*, the name of two Isr.:—Tikvah.

8617. תְּקוּמָה **tᵉqûwmâh**, *tek-oo-maw'*; from 6965; *resistfulness*:—power to stand.

8618. תְּקוֹמֵם **tᵉqôwmêm**, *tek-o-mame'*; from 6965; an *opponent*:—rise up against.

8619. תָּקוֹעַ **tâqôwaʻ**, *taw-ko'-ah*; from 8628 (in the musical sense); a *trumpet*:—trumpet.

8620. תְּקוֹעַ **Tᵉqôwaʻ**, *tek-o'-ah*; a form of 8619; *Tekoä*, a place in Pal.:—Tekoa, Tekoah.

8621. תְּקוֹעִי **Tᵉqôwʻîy**, *tek-o-ee'*; or

תְּקֹעִי **Tᵉqôʻîy**, *tek-o-ee'*; patron. from 8620; a *Tekoïte* or inhab. of Tekoah:—Tekoite.

8622. תְּקוּפָה **tᵉqûwphâh**, *tek-oo-faw'*; or

תְּקֻפָה **tᵉqûphâh**, *tek-oo-faw'*; from 5362; a *revolution*, i.e. (of the sun) *course*, (of time) *lapse*:—circuit, come about, end.

8623. תַּקִּיף **taqqîyph**, *tak-keef'*; from 8630; *powerful*:—mightier.

8624. תַּקִּיף **taqqîyph** (Chald.), *tak-keef'*; corresp. to 8623:—mighty, strong.

8625. תְּקַל **tᵉqal** (Chald.), *tek-al'*; corresp. to 8254; to *balance*:—Tekel, be weighed.

8626. תָּקַן **tâqan**, *taw-kan'*; a prim. root; to *equalize*, i.e. *straighten* (intrans. or trans.); fig. to *compose*:—set in order, make straight.

8627. תְּקַן **tᵉqan** (Chald.), *tek-an'*; corresp. to 8626; to *straighten* up, i.e. *confirm*:—establish.

8628. תָּקַע **tâqaʻ**, *taw-kah'*; a prim. root; to *clatter*, i.e. *slap* (the hands together), *clang* (an instrument); by anal. to *drive* (a nail or tent-pin, a dart, etc.); by impl. to *become bondsman* (by hand-clasping):—blow ([a trumpet]), cast, clap, fasten, pitch [tent], smite, sound, strike, × suretiship, thrust.

8629. תֵּקַע **têqaʻ**, *tay-kah'*; from 8628; a *blast* of a trumpet:—sound.

תְּקֹעִי **Tᵉqôʻîy**. See 8621.

8630. תָּקַף **tâqaph**, *taw-kaf'*; a prim. root; to *overpower*:—prevail (against).

8631. תְּקֵף **tᵉqêph** (Chald.), *tek-afe'*; corresp. to 8630; to *become* (caus. *make*) *mighty* or (fig.) *obstinate*:—make firm, harden, be (-come) strong.

8632. תְּקֹף **tᵉqôph** (Chald.), *tek-ofe'*; corresp. to 8633; *power*:—might, strength.

8633 תֹּקֶף **tôqeph**, *to'-kef*; from 8630; *might* or (fig.) *positiveness*:—authority, power, strength.

תְּקֻפָה **tᵉqûphâh**. See 8622.

תֹּר **tôr**. See 8447, 8449.

8634. תַּרְאֲלָה **Tar'âlâh**, *tar-al-aw'*; prob. for 8653; a *reeling*; *Taralah*, a place in Pal.:—Taralah.

8635. תַּרְבּוּת **tarbûwth**, *tar-booth'*; from 7235; *multiplication*, i.e. *progeny*:—increase.

8636. תַּרְבִּית **tarbîyth**, *tar-beeth'*; from 7235; *multiplication*, i.e. *percentage* or *bonus* in addition to principal:—increase, unjust gain.

8637. תִּרְגַּל **tirgal**, *teer-gal'*; a denom. from 7270; to *cause to walk*:—teach to go.

8638. תִּרְגַּם **tirgam**, *teer-gam'*; a denom. from 7275 in the sense of *throwing* over; to *transfer*, i.e. *translate*:—interpret.

תֹּרָה **tôrâh**. See 8451.

8639. תַּרְדֵּמָה **tardêmâh**, *tar-day-maw'*; from 7290; a *lethargy* or (by impl.) *trance*:—deep sleep.

8640. תִּרְהָקָה **Tirhâqâh**, *teer-haw'-kaw*; of for. der.; *Tirhakah*, a king of Kush:—Tirhakah.

8641. תְּרוּמָה **tᵉrûwmâh**, *ter-oo-maw'*; or

תְּרֻמָה **tᵉrûmâh** (Deut. 12 : 11), *ter-oo-maw'*; from 7311; a *present* (as offered up), espec. in *sacrifice* or as *tribute*:—gift, heave offering ([shoulder]), oblation, offered (-ing).

8642. תְּרוּמִיָּה **tᵉrûwmîyâh**, *ter-oo-mee-yaw'*; formed as 8641; a sacrificial *offering*:—oblation.

8643. תְּרוּעָה **tᵉrûwʻâh**, *ter-oo-aw'*; from 7321; *clamor*, i.e. *acclamation* of joy or a *battle-cry*; espec. *clangor* of trumpets, as an *alarum*:—alarm, blow (-ing) (of, the) (trumpets), joy, jubile, loud noise, rejoicing, shout (-ing), (high, joyful) sound (-ing).

8644. תְּרוּפָה **tᵉrûwphâh**, *ter-oo-faw'*, from 7322 in the sense of its congener 7495; a *remedy*:—medicine.

8645. תִּרְזָה **tirzâh**, *teer-zaw'*; prob. from 7329; a species of tree (appar. from its *slenderness*), perh. the *cypress*:—cypress.

8646. תֶּרַח **Terach**, *teh'-rakh*; of uncert. der.; *Terach*, the father of Abraham; also a place in the Desert:—Tarah, Terah.

8647. תִּרְחֲנָה **Tirchânâh**, *teer-khan-aw'*; of uncert. der.; *Tirchanah*, an Isr.:—Tirhanah.

8648. תְּרֵין **tᵉrêyn** (Chald.), *ter-ane'*; fem.

תַּרְתֵּין **tartêyn**, *tar-tane'*; corresp. to 8147; *two*:—second, + twelve, two.

8649. תָּרְמָה **tormâh**, *tor-maw'*; and

תַּרְמוּת **tarmûwth**, *tar-mooth'*; or

תַּרְמִית **tarmîyth**, *tar-meeth'*; from 7411; *fraud*:—deceit (-ful), privily.

תְּרֻמָה **tᵉrûmâh**. See 8641.

8650. תֹּרֶן **tôren**, *to'-ren*; prob. for 766; a *pole* (as a mast or flag-staff):—beacon, mast.

8651. תְּרַע **tᵉraʻ** (Chald.), *ter-ah'*; corresp. to 8179; a *door*; by impl. a *palace*:—gate mouth.

8652. תָּרָע **târâʻ** (Chald.), *taw-raw'*; from 8651; a *doorkeeper*:—porter.

8653. תַּרְעֵלָה **tarʻêlâh**, *tar-ay-law'*; from 7477; *reeling*:—astonishment, trembling.

8654. תִּרְעָתִי **Tirʻâthîy**, *teer-aw-thee'*; patrial from an unused name mean. *gate*; a *Tirathite* or inhab. of an unknown Tirah:—Tirathite.

8655. תְּרָפִים **tᵉrâphîym**, *ter-aw-feme'*; plur. per. from 7495; a *healer*; *Teraphim* (sing. or plur.) a family idol:—idols (-atry), images, teraphim.

8656. תִּרְצָה **Tirtsâh**, *teer-tsaw'*; from 7521; *delightsomeness*; *Tirtsah*, a place in Pal.; also an Israelitess:—Tirzah.

8657. תֶּרֶשׁ **Teresh**, *teh'-resh*; of for. der.; *Teresh*, a eunuch of Xerxes:—Teresh.

8658. תַּרְשִׁישׁ **tarshîysh**, *tar-sheesh'*; prob. of for. der. [comp. 8659]; a gem, perh. the *topaz*:—beryl.

8659. תַּרְשִׁישׁ **Tarshîysh**, *tar-sheesh'*; prob. the same as 8658 (as the region of the stone, or the reverse); *Tarshish*, a place on the Mediterranean, hence the epithet of a *merchant* vessel (as if for or from that port); also the name of a Persian and of an Isr.:—Tarshish, Tharshish.

8660. תִּרְשָׁתָא **Tirshâthâ'**, *teer-shaw-thaw'*; of for. der.; the title of a Pers. deputy or *governor*:—Tirshatha.

תַּרְתֵּין **tartêyn**. See 8648.

8661. תַּרְתָּן **Tartân**, *tar-tawn'*; of for. der.; *Tartan*, an Assyrian:—Tartan.

8662. תַּרְתָּק **Tartâq**, *tar-tawk'*; of for. der.; *Tartak*, a deity of the Avvites:—Tartak.

8663. תְּשֻׁאָה **tᵉshûʼâh**, *tesh-oo-aw'*; from 7722; a *crashing* or loud *clamor*:—crying, noise, shouting, stir.

תֹּשָׁב **tôshâb**. See 8453.

8664. תִּשְׁבִּי **Tishbîy**, *tish-bee'*; patrial from an unused name mean. *recourse*; a *Tishbite* or inhab. of Tishbeh (in Gilead):—Tishbite.

8665. תַּשְׁבֵּץ **tashbêts**, *tash-bates'*; from 7660; *checkered* stuff (as *reticulated*):—broidered.

8666. תְּשׁוּבָה **tᵉshûwbâh**, *tesh-oo-baw'*; or

תְּשֻׁבָה **tᵉshûbâh**, *tesh-oo-baw'*; from 7725; a *recurrence* (of time or place); a *reply* (as *returned*):—answer, be expired, return.

8667. תְּשׂוּמֶת **tᵉsûwmeth**, *tes-oo-meth'*; from 7760; a *deposit*, i.e. *pledging*:—+ fellowship.

8668. תְּשׁוּעָה **tᵉshûwʻâh**, *tesh-oo-aw'*; or

תְּשֻׁעָה **tᵉshûʻâh**, *tesh-oo-aw'*; from 7768 in the sense of 3467; *rescue* (lit. or fig., pers., national or spir.):—deliverance, help, safety, salvation, victory.

8669. תְּשׁוּקָה **tᵉshûwqâh**, *tesh-oo-kaw'*; from 7783 in the orig. sense of *stretching* out after; a *longing*:—desire.

8670. תְּשׁוּרָה **tᵉshûwrâh**, *tesh-oo-raw'*; from 7788 in the sense of *arrival*; a *gift*:—present.

תַּשְׁחֵת **tashchêth**. See 516.

תּוּשִׁיָּה **tûshîyâh**. See 8454.

8671. תְּשִׁיעִי **tᵉshîyʻîy**, *tesh-ee-ee'*; ord. from 8672; *ninth*:—ninth.

תְּשֻׁעָה **tᵉshûʻâh**. See 8668.

8672. תֵּשַׁע **têshaʻ**, *tay'-shah*; or (masc.)

תִּשְׁעָה **tishʻâh**, *tish-aw'*; perh. from 8159 through the idea of a *turn* to the next or full number ten; *nine* or (ord.) *ninth*:—nine (+ -teen, + -teenth, -th).

8673. תִּשְׁעִים **tishʻîym**, *tish-eem'*; multiple from 8672; *ninety*:—ninety.

8674. תַּתְּנַי **Tattᵉnay**, *tat-ten-ah'ee*; of for. der.; *Tattenai*, a Persian:—Tatnai.

PLACES WHERE THE HEBREW AND THE ENGLISH BIBLES DIFFER IN THE DIVISION OF CHAPTERS AND VERSES.

Book	English.	Hebrew.
Genesis	31:55	32: 1
	32: 1-32	2-33
Exodus	8: 1-4	7:26-29
	5-32	8: 1-28
	22: 1	21:37
	2-31	22: 1-30
Leviticus	6: 1-7	5:20-26
	8-30	6: 1-23
Numbers	16:36-50	17: 1-15
	17: 1-13	16-28
	26: 1 (first clause)	25:19
	29:40	30: 1
	30: 1-16	2-17
Deuteronomy	5:18-33	5:17-30
	12:32	13: 1
	13: 1-18	2-19
	22:30	23: 1
	23: 1-25	2-26
	29: 1	28:69
	2-29	29: 1-28
Joshua	21:36, 37	(not in most copies)
	38-45	21:36-43
1 Samuel	19: 2 (first clause)	19: 1
	20:42	21: 1
	21: 1-15	2-16
	23:29	24: 1
	24: 1-22	2-23
2 Samuel	17:28 (first word)	29 (middle)
	18:33	19: 1
	19: 1-43	2-44
1 Kings	4:21-34	5: 1-14
	5: 1-18	15-32
	18:33 (l. half)	(first half)18:34
	20: 2 (l. half)	(first half)20: 3
	22:22 (f. clause)	(l. cl.)22:21
	43 (last half)	44
	44-53	45-54
2 Kings	11:21	12: 1
	12: 1-21	2-22
1 Chronicles	6: 1-15	5:27-41
	16-81	6: 1-66
2 Chronicles	2: 1	1:18
	2-18	2: 1-17
	14: 1	13:23
	2-15	14: 1-14
Nehemiah	4: 1-6	3:33-38
	7-23	4: 1-17
	9:38	10: 1
	10: 1-39	2-40
Job	41: 1-8	40:25-32
	9-34	41: 1-26
Psalms	3:*title*	3: 1
	1-8	2-9
	4:*title*	4: 1
	1-8	2-9
	5:*title*	5: 1
	1-12	2-13
	6:*title*	6: 1
	1-10	2-11
	7:*title*	7: 1
	1-17	2-18
	8:*title*	8: 1
	1-9	2-10
	9:*title*	9: 1
	1-20	2-21
	11:*title* (first clause)	11: 1
	12:*title*	12: 1
	1-8	2-9
	13:*title*	13: 1
	1-5	2-6
	6 (last half)	6
	14:*title* (first clause)	14: 1
	15:*title* (first clause)	15: 1
	16:*title* (first clause)	16: 1
	17:*title* (first clause)	17: 1
	18:*title*	18:1&(f.c.)2
	1-50	2-51
	19:*title*	19: 1
	1-14	2-15
Psalms	20:*title*	20: 1
	1-9	2-10
	21:*title*	21: 1
	1-13	2-14
	22:*title*	22: 1
	1-31	2-32
	23:*title* (first clause)	23: 1
	24-28:*title*.(first clause)	24-28: 1
	29:*title* (first clause)	29: 1
	30:*title*	30: 1
	1-12	2-13
	31:*title*	31: 1
	1-24	2-25
	32:*title* (first clause)	32: 1
	34:*title*	34: 1
	1-22	2-23
	35&37:*title*.(first word)	35&37: 1
	36:*title*	36: 1
	1-12	2-13
	38:*title*	38: 1
	1-22	2-23
	39:*title*	39: 1
	1-13	2-14
	40:*title*	40: 1
	1-17	2-18
	41:*title*	41: 1
	1:13	2-14
	42:*title*	42: 1
	1-11	2-12
	44:*title*	44: 1
	1-26	2-27
	45:*title*	45: 1
	1-17	2-18
	46:*title*	46: 1
	1-11	2-12
	47:*title*	47: 1
	1-9	2-10
	48:*title*	48: 1
	1-14	2-15
	49:*title*	49: 1
	1-20	2-21
	50:*title* (first clause)	50: 1
	51:*title*	51: 1&2
	1-19	2-21
	52:*title* (first clause)	52: 1 & 2
	1-9	2-11
	53:*title*	53: 1
	1-6	2-7
	54:*title*	54: 1 & 2
	1-7	2-9
	55:*title*	55: 1
	1-23	2-24
	56:*title*	56: 1
	1-23	2-24
	57:*title*	57: 1
	1-11	2-12
	58:*title*	58: 1
	1-11	2-12
	59:*title*	59: 1
	1-17	2-18
	60:*title*	60: 1 & 2
	1-12	3-14
	61:*title*	61: 1
	1-8	2-9
	62:*title*	62: 1
	1-12	2-13
	63:*title*	63: 1
	1-11	2-12
	64:*title*	64: 1
	1-10	2-11
	65:*title*	65: 1
	1-13	2-14
	66:*title* (first clause)	66: 1
	67:*title*	67: 1
	1-7	2-8
	68:*title*	68: 1
	1-35	2-36
	69:*title*	69: 1
	1-36	2-37
Psalms	70:*title*	70: 1
	1-5	2-6
	72:*title* (first word)	72: 1
	73:*title* (first clause)	73: 1
	74:*title* (first clause)	74: 1
	1-10	2-11
	76:*title*	76: 1
	1-12	2-13
	77:*title*	77: 1
	1-20	2-21
	78 & 79:*title*.(f. clause)	78&79: 1
	80:*title*	80: 1
	1-19	2-20
	81:*title*	81: 1
	1-16	2-17
	82:*title* (first clause)	82: 1
	83:*title*	83: 1
	1-18	2-19
	84:*title*	84: 1
	1-12	2-13
	85:*title*	85: 1
	1-13	2-14
	86 & 87:*title*.(first cl.)	86&87: 1
	88:*title*	88: 1
	1-18	2-19
	89:*title*	89: 1
	1-52	2-53
	90:*title* (first clause)	90: 1
	92:*title*	92: 1
	11-5	2-16
	98:*title* (first word)	98: 1
	100&101:*title*.(1st cl.)	100&101: 1
	102:*title*	102: 1
	1-28	2-29
	103:*title* (first word)	103: 1
	108:*title*	108: 1
	1-13	2-14
	109, 110, 120-134, 138 and 139:*title*.(first cl.) same	1
	140:*title*	140: 1
	1-13	2-14
	141:*title* (first clause)	141: 1
	142:*title*	142: 1
	1-6	2-7
	143:*title* (first clause)	143: 1
	144:*title* (first word)	144: 1
	145:*title* (first clause)	145: 1
Ecclesiastes	5: 1	4:17
	2-20	5: 1-19
Canticles	6:13	7: 1
	7: 1-13	2-14
Isaiah	9: 1	8:23
	2-21	9: 1-20
	64: 1	63:19
	2-12	64: 1-11
Jeremiah	9: 1	8:23
	2-26	9: 1-25
Ezekiel	20:45-49	21: 1-5
	21: 1-32	6-37
Daniel	4: 1-3	3:31-33
	4-37	4: 1-34
	5:31	6: 1
	6: 1-28	2-29
Hosea	1:10, 11	2: 1, 2
	2: 1-23	3-25
	11:12	12: 1
	12: 1-14	2-15
	13:16	14: 1
	14: 1-9	2-10
Joel	2:28-32	3: 1-5
	3: 1-21	4: 1-21
Jonah	1:17	2: 1
	2: 1-10	2-11
Micah	5: 1	4:14
	2-15	5: 1-14
Nahum	1:15	2: 1
	2: 1-13	2-14
Zechariah	1:18	2: 1-4
	2: 1-13	2-17
Malachi	4: 1-6	3:19-24

DICTIONARY

OF THE

GREEK TESTAMENT

Note regarding the Greek Dictionary: The numbering of Greek words skips 2717 and from 3202 to 3303. This error in numbering is part of the original edition of the Dictionary. Because the original numbering system (with these errors) has been used by so many Bible students and other Bible reference works, it has been left unchanged to avoid the confusion that would result from having an old and a new Strong's numbering system. The only error is the skipping of *numbers, not* the omission of Greek words. No Greek words that Strong listed in the original dictionary are missing from this exact reproduction of the original.

A CONCISE DICTIONARY

OF THE WORDS IN

THE GREEK TESTAMENT;

WITH THEIR RENDERINGS

IN THE

AUTHORIZED ENGLISH VERSION.

BY

JAMES STRONG, S.T.D., LL.D.

PREFACE.

THIS work is entirely similar in origin, method, and design, to the author's HEBREW DICTIONARY, and may be employed separately, for a corresponding purpose and with a like result, namely, to be serviceable to many who have not the wish or the ability to use a more copious Lexicon of New-Testament Greek. In this case also even scholars will find many suggestions and explanations not unworthy their attention.

PLAN OF THE BOOK.

1. All the original words are treated in their alphabetical Greek order, and are numbered regularly from the first to the last, each being known throughout by its appropriate number. This renders reference easy without recourse to the Greek characters.

2. Immediately after each word is given its exact equivalent in English letters, according to the system of transliteration laid down in the scheme here following, which is substantially that adopted in the Common English Version, only more consistently and uniformly carried out; so that the word could readily be turned back again into Greek from the form thus given it.

3. Next follows the precise pronunciation, according to the usual English mode of sounding syllables, so plainly indicated that none can fail to apprehend and apply it. The most approved sounds are adopted, as laid down in the annexed scheme of articulation, and in such a way that any good Græcist would immediately recognise the word if so pronounced, notwithstanding the minor variations current among scholars in this respect.

4. Then ensues a tracing of the etymology, radical meaning, and applied significations of the word, justly but tersely analyzed and expressed, with any other important peculiarities in this regard.

5. In the case of proper names, the same method is pursued, and at this point the regular mode of Anglicizing it, after the general style of the Common English Version, is given, and a few words of explanation are added to identify it.

6. Finally (after the punctuation-mark :—) are given all the different renderings of the word in the Authorized English Version, arranged in the alphabetical order of the leading terms, and conveniently condensed according to the explanations given below.

By searching out these various renderings in the MAIN CONCORDANCE, to which this Dictionary is designed as a companion, and noting the passages to which the same number corresponding to that of any given Greek word is attached in the marginal column, the reader, whether acquainted with the original language or not, will obtain a complete *Greek Concordance* also, expressed in the words of the Common English Version. This is an advantage which no other Concordance or Lexicon affords.

GREEK ARTICULATION.

THE following explanations are sufficient to show the mode of writing and pronouncing Greek words in English adopted in this *Dictionary*.

1. The *Alphabet* is as follows:

No.	Form.		Name.	Transliteration and Power.
1.	Α	α	Alpha (*al'-fah*)	a, as in ARM or [MAN*
2.	Β	β	Bēta (*bay'-tah*)	b
3.	Γ	γ	Gamma (*gam'-mah*)	g hard †
4.	Δ	δ	Dĕlta (*del'-tah*)	d
5.	Ε	ε	Ĕpsilŏn (*ep'-see-lon*)	ĕ, as in MET
6.	Ζ	ζ	Zēta (*dzay'-tah*)	z, as in ADZE‡
7.	Η	η	Ēta (*ay'-tah*)	ē, as in *they*
8.	Θ	θ or ϑ	Thēta (*thay'-tah*)	th, as in THIN§
9.	Ι	ι	Iōta (*ee-o'-tah*)	i, as in *ma-* [*chine* ‖
10.	Κ	κ or ϰ	Kappa (*cap'-pah*)	k
11.	Λ	λ	Lambda (*lamb'-dah*)	l
12.	Μ	μ	Mu (*moo*)	m
13.	Ν	ν	Nu (*noo*)	n
14.	Ξ	ξ	Xi (*ksee*)	x = *ks*
15.	Ο	ο	Omikrŏn (*om'-e-cron*)	ŏ, as in *not*
16.	Π	π	Pi (*pee*)	p
17.	Ρ	ρ	Rhō (*hro*)	r
18.	Σ	σ, final ς	Sigma (*sig'-mah*)	s sharp
19.	Τ	τ	Tau (*tŏw*)	t¶
20.	Υ	υ	Upsilŏn (*u'-pse-lon*)	u, as in *full*
21.	Φ	φ	Phi (*fee*)	ph = *f*
22.	Χ	χ	Chi (*khee*)	German ch *
23.	Ψ	ψ	Psi (*psee*)	ps
24.	Ω	ω	Omĕga (*o'-meg-ah*)	ō, as in *no.*

* α, when *final*, or before ρ final or followed by any *other* consonant, is sounded like *a* in ARM; elsewhere like *a* in MAN.

† γ, when followed by γ, κ, χ, or ξ, is sounded like *ng* in KING.

‡ ζ is always sounded like *dz*.

§ θ never has the guttural sound, like *th* in THIS.

‖ ι has the sound of *ee* when it *ends* an *accented* syllable; in other situations a more obscure sound, like *i* in AMIABLE or IMBECILE.

¶ τ never has a sibilant sound, like *t* in NATION, NATURE.

2. The mark ῾, placed over the *initial* vowel of a word, is called the *Rough Breathing*, and is equivalent to the English *h*, by which we have accordingly represented it. Its *absence* over an initial vowel is indicated by the mark ᾿, called the *Smooth Breathing*, which is unappreciable or silent, and is therefore not represented in our method of transliteration.†

3. The following are the Greek *diphthongs*, properly so called:‡

Form.	Transliteration and Power.	Form.	Transliteration and Power.
αι	ai (*ah'ee*) [ă + ē]	αυ	ow, as in *now*
ει	ei, as in HEIGHT	ευ	eu, as in FEUD
οι	oi, as in OIL	ου	ou, as in *through*.
υι	we, as in SWEET		

* From the difficulty of producing the true sound of χ, it is generally sounded like *k*.

† These signs are placed over the *second* vowel of a *diphthong*. The same is true of the accents.

The *Rough* Breathing always belongs to υ initial.

The Rough Breathing is always used with ρ, when it begins a word. If this letter be doubled in the middle of a word, the first takes the Smooth, and the second the Rough, Breathing.

As these signs cannot conveniently be written over the first letter of a word, when a *capital*, they are in such cases placed *before* it. This observation applies also to the *accents*. The aspiration *always* begins the syllable.

Occasionally, in consequence of a contraction (*crasis*), the Smooth Breathing is made to stand in the middle of a word, and is then called *Coro'nis*.

‡ The above are combinations of two *short* vowels, and are pronounced like their respective elements, but in more rapid succession than otherwise. Thus αι is midway between *i* in HIGH, and *ay* in SAY.

Besides these, there are what are called *improper* diphthongs, in which the former is a *long* vowel. In these,

ᾳ sounds like α		ηυ sounds like η + υ	
ῃ " " η		ωυ " " ω + υ.	
ῳ " " ω			

the second vowel, when ι, is written *under* the first (unless that be a capital), and is *silent*; when υ, it is sounded separately. When the initial is a capital, the ι is placed after it, but does not take the breathing nor accent.

The sign ¨, called *diær'esis*, placed over the *latter* of two vowels, indicates that they do *not* form a diphthong.

4. The *accent* (stress of voice) falls on the syllable where it is written.* It is of three forms: the *acute* (´), which is the only true accent; the *grave* (`) which is its substitute; and the *circumflex* (ˆ or ˜), which is the union of the two. The acute may stand on any one of the last *three* syllables, and in case it occurs on the final syllable, before another word in the same sentence, it is written as a grave. The grave is understood (but never written as such) on every other syllable. The circumflex is written on any syllable (necessarily the last or next to the last one of a word), formed by the contraction of two syllables, of which the *first* would properly have the acute.

5. The following *punctuation*-marks are used: the comma (,), the semicolon (·), the colon or period (.), the interrogation-point (;), and by some editors, also the exclamation-point, parentheses and quotation-marks.

* Every word (except a few monosyllables, called *Aton'ics*) must have one accent; several small words (called *Enclit'ics*) throw their accent (always as an acute) on the last syllable of the preceding word (in addition to its own accent, which still has the principal stress), where this is possible.

ABBREVIATIONS EMPLOYED.

abst. = abstract (-ly)
acc. = accusative (case)
adv. = adverb (-ial) (-ly)
aff. = affinity
alt. = alternate (-ly)
anal. = analogy
app. = apparent (-ly)
caus. = causative (-ly)
cer. = { ceremony / ceremonial (-ly) }
Chald. = Chaldee
Chr. = Christian
coll. = collective (-ly)
comp. = { comparative / comparatively / compare / compound (-s) }
concr. = concrete (-ly)
corr. = corresponding

dat. = dative (case)
der. = { derivation / derivative / derived }
dim. = diminutive
dir. = direct (-ly)
E. = East
eccl. = ecclesiastical (-ly)
Eg. = Egypt (-ian)
ell. = { ellipsis / elliptical (-ly) }
eq. = equivalent
esp. = especially
euph. = { euphemism / euphemistic / euphemistically }
ext. = extension
fem. = feminine
fig. = figurative (-ly)

for. = foreign
gen. = genitive (case)
Gr. = Greek
Heb. = { Hebraism / Hebrew }
i.e. = { *id est* / that is }
imper. = imperative
imperf. = imperfect
impers. = impersonal (-ly)
impl. = { implication / implied }
incl. = including
ind. = indicative (-ly)
indiv. = individual (-ly)
inf. = infinitive
inh. = inhabitant (-s)
intens. = intensive (-ly)
intr. = intransitive (-ly)

invol. = { involuntary / involuntarily }
irr. = irregular (-ly)
Isr. = { Israelite (-s) / Israelitish }
Jer. = Jerusalem
Lat. = Latin
lit. = literal (-ly)
mean. = meaning
ment. = mental (-ly)
mid. = middle (voice)
mor. = moral (-ly)
mult. = multiplicative
nat. = natural (-ly)
neg. = negative (-ly)
neut. = neuter
obj. = objective (-ly)
obs. = obsolete

or. = origin (-al) (-ly)
Pal. = Palestine
part. = participle
pass. = passive (-ly)
perh. = perhaps
pers. = person (-al) (-ly)
phys. = physical (-ly)
pl. = plural
pref. = prefix (-ed)
pos. = positive (-ly)
prim. = primary
prob. = probably
prol. = { prolongation / prolonged }
pron. = { pronominal (-ly) / pronoun }
prop. = properly
redupl. = { reduplicated / reduplication }

refl. = reflexive (-ly)
rel. = relative (-ly)
Rom. = Roman
sing. = singular
spec. = special (-ly)
subj. = subjective (-ly)
sup. = superlative (-ly)
tech. = technical (-ly)
term. = termination
trans. = transitive (-ly)
transp. = { transposed / transposition }
typ. = typical (-ly)
unc. = uncertain
var. = { variation / various }
voc. = vocative
vol. = { voluntarily / voluntary }

SIGNS EMPLOYED.

+ (*addition*) denotes a rendering in the A. V. of one or more Gr. words in connection with the one under consideration.

× (*multiplication*) denotes a rendering in the A. V. that results from an idiom peculiar to the Gr.

( ) (*parenthesis*), in the renderings from the A. V., denotes a word or syllable sometimes given in connection with the principal word to which it is annexed.

[ ] (*bracket*), in the rendering from the A. V., denotes the inclusion of an additional word in the Gr.

***Italics*, at the end of a rendering from the A. V., denote an explanation of the variations from the usual form.**

Greek

GREEK DICTIONARY OF THE NEW TESTAMENT.

A.

N. B.—The numbers *not in italics* refer to the words in the *Hebrew Dictionary*. Significations within quotation-marks are derivative representatives of the Greek.

1. Α α, **A a**, *al-fah*; of Heb. or.; the first letter of the alphabet; fig. only (from its use as a numeral) the *first:*—Alpha. Often used (usually ἀν **an**, before a vowel) also in composition (as a contraction from *427*) in the sense of *privation;* so in many words beginning with this letter; occasionally in the sense of *union* (as a contraction of *260*).

2. Ἀαρών **Aarōn**, *ah-ar-ohn';* of Heb. or. [175]; *Aaron*, the brother of Moses:—Aaron.

3. Ἀβαδδών **Abaddōn** *ab-ad-dohn';* of Heb. or. [11]; a destroying *angel:*—Abaddon.

4. ἀβαρής **abarēs**, *ab-ar-ace';* from *1* (as a neg. particle) and *922; weightless*, i.e. (fig.) *not burdensome:*—from being burdensome.

5. Ἀββᾶ **Abba**, *ab-bah';* of Chald. or. [2]; *father* (as a voc.):—Abba.

6. Ἄβελ **Abĕl**, *ab'-el;* of Heb. or. [1893]; *Abel*, the son of Adam:—Abel.

7. Ἀβιά **Abia**, *ab-ee-ah';* of Heb. or. [29]; *Abijah*, the name of two Isr.:—Abia.

8. Ἀβιάθαρ **Abiathar**, *ab-ee-ath'-ar;* of Heb. or. [54]; *Abiathar*, an Isr.:—Abiathar.

9. Ἀβιληνή **Abilēnē**, *ab-ee-lay-nay';* of for. or. [comp. 58]; *Abilene*, a region of Syria:—Abilene.

10. Ἀβιούδ **Abiŏud**, *ab-ee-ood';* of Heb. or. [31]; *Abihud*, an Isr.:—Abiud.

11. Ἀβραάμ **Abraam**, *ab-rah-am';* of Heb. or. [85]; *Abraham*, the Heb. patriarch:—Abraham. [In Acts 7 : 16 the text should prob. read *Jacob.*]

12. ἄβυσσος **abussŏs**, *ab'-us-sos;* from *1* (as a neg. particle) and a var. of *1037; depthless*, i.e. (spec.) (infernal) "*abyss*":—deep, (bottomless) pit.

13. Ἄγαβος **Agabŏs**, *ag'-ab-os;* of Heb. or. [comp. 2285]; *Agabus*, an Isr.:—Agabus.

14. ἀγαθοεργέω **agathŏĕrgĕō**, *ag-ath-er-gheh'-o;* from *18* and *2041;* to *work good:*—do good.

15. ἀγαθοποιέω **agathŏpŏiĕō**, *ag-ath-op-oy-eh'-o;* from *17;* to *be a well-doer* (as a favor or a duty):—(when) do good (well).

16. ἀγαθοποιΐα **agathŏpŏiia**, *ag-ath-op-oy-ee'-ah;* from *17; well-doing*, i.e. *virtue:*—well-doing.

17. ἀγαθοποιός **agathŏpŏiŏs**, *ag-ath-op-oy-os';* from *18* and *4160;* a *well-doer*, i.e. *virtuous:*—them that do well.

18. ἀγαθός **agathŏs**, *ag-ath-os';* a prim. word; "*good*" (in any sense, often as noun):—benefit, good (-s, things), well. Comp. *2570*.

19. ἀγαθωσύνη **agathōsunē**, *ag-ath-o-soo'-nay;* from *18; goodness*, i.e. *virtue* or *beneficence:*—goodness.

20. ἀγαλλίασις **agalliasis**, *ag-al-lee'-as-is;* from *21; exultation;* spec. *welcome:*—gladness, (exceeding) joy.

21. ἀγαλλιάω **agalliaō**, *ag-al-lee-ah'-o;* from ἄγαν **agan** (*much*) and *242;* prop. to *jump for joy*, i.e. *exult:*—be (exceeding) glad, with exceeding joy, rejoice (greatly).

22. ἄγαμος **agamŏs**, *ag'-am-os;* from *1* (as a neg. particle) and *1062; unmarried:*—unmarried.

23. ἀγανακτέω **aganaktĕō**, *ag-an-ak-teh'-o;* from ἄγαν **agan** (*much*) and ἄχθος **achthŏs** (*grief;* akin to the base of *43*); to *be greatly afflicted*, i.e. (fig.) *indignant:*—be much (sore) displeased, have (be moved with, with) indignation.

24. ἀγανάκτησις **aganaktēsis**, *ag-an-ak'-tay-sis;* from *23; indignation:*—indignation.

25. ἀγαπάω **agapaō**, *ag-ap-ah'-o;* perh. from ἄγαν **agan** (*much*) [or comp. 5689]; to *love* (in a social or moral sense):—(be-) love (-ed). Comp. *5368*.

26. ἀγάπη **agapē**, *ag-ah'-pay;* from *25; love*, i.e. *affection* or *benevolence;* spec. (plur.) a *love-feast:*—(feast of) charity ([-ably]), dear, love.

27. ἀγαπητός **agapētŏs**, *ag-ap-ay-tos';* from *25; beloved:*—(dearly, well) beloved, dear.

28. Ἄγαρ **Agar**, *ag'-ar;* of Heb. or. [1904]; *Hagar*, the concubine of Abraham:—Hagar.

29. ἀγγαρεύω **aggarĕuō**, *ang-ar-yew'-o;* of for. or. [comp. 104]; prop. to *be a courier*, i.e., (by impl.) to *press* into public service:—compel (to go).

30. ἀγγεῖον **aggĕiŏn**, *ang-eye'-on;* from ἄγγος **aggŏs** (a *pail*, perh. as *bent;* comp. the base of *43*); a *receptacle:*—vessel.

31. ἀγγελία **aggĕlia**, *ang-el-ee'-ah;* from *32;* an *announcement*, i.e. (by impl.) *precept:*—message.

32. ἄγγελος **aggĕlŏs**, *ang'-el-os;* from ἀγγέλλω **aggĕllō** [prob. der. from *71;* comp. *34*] (to *bring tidings*); a *messenger;* esp. an "*angel*"; by impl. a *pastor:*—angel, messenger.

33. ἄγε **agĕ**, *ag'-eh;* imper. of *71;* prop. *lead*, i.e. *come on:*—go to.

34. ἀγέλη **agĕlē**, *ag-el'-ay;* from *71* [comp. *32*]; a *drove:*—herd.

35. ἀγενεαλόγητος **agĕnĕalŏgētŏs**, *ag-en-eh-al-og'-ay-tos;* from *1* (as neg. particle) and *1075; unregistered* as to birth:—without descent.

36. ἀγενής **agĕnēs**, *ag-en-ace';* from *1* (as neg. particle) and *1085;* prop. *without kin*, i.e. (of unknown descent, and by impl.) *ignoble:*—base things.

37. ἁγιάζω **hagiazō**, *hag-ee-ad'-zo;* from *40;* to *make holy*, i.e. (cer.) *purify* or *consecrate;* (mentally) to *venerate:*—hallow, be holy, sanctify.

38. ἁγιασμός **hagiasmŏs**, *hag-ee-as-mos';* from *37;* prop. *purification*, i.e. (the state) *purity;* concr. (by Hebr.) a *purifier:*—holiness, sanctification.

39. ἅγιον **hagiŏn**, *hag'-ee-on;* neut. of *40;* a *sacred* thing (i.e. spot):—holiest (of all), holy place, sanctuary.

40. ἅγιος **hagiŏs**, *hag'-ee-os;* from ἅγος **hagŏs** (an *awful* thing) [comp. *53*, 2282]; *sacred* (phys. *pure*, mor. *blameless* or *religious*, cer. *consecrated*):—(most) holy (one, thing), saint.

41. ἁγιότης **hagiŏtēs**, *hag-ee-ot'-ace;* from *40; sanctity* (i.e. prop. the state):—holiness.

42. ἁγιωσύνη **hagiōsunē**, *hag-ee-o-soo'-nay;* from *40; sacredness* (i.e. prop. the quality):—holiness.

43. ἀγκάλη **agkalē**, *ang-kal'-ay;* from ἄγκος **agkŏs** (a *bend*, "ache"); an *arm* (as *curved*):—arm.

44. ἄγκιστρον **agkistrŏn**, *ang'-kis-tron;* from the same as *43;* a *hook* (as *bent*):—hook.

45. ἄγκυρα **agkura**, *ang'-koo-rah;* from the same as *43;* an "*anchor*" (as *crooked*):—anchor.

46. ἄγναφος **agnaphŏs**, *ag'-naf-os;* from *1* (as a neg. particle) and the same as *1102;* prop. *unfulled*, i.e. (by impl.) *new* (cloth):—new.

47. ἁγνεία **hagnĕia**, *hag-ni'-ah;* from *53; cleanliness* (the quality), i.e. (spec.) *chastity:*—purity.

48. ἁγνίζω **hagnizō**, *hag-nid'-zo;* from *53;* to *make clean*, i.e. (fig.) *sanctify* (cer. or mor.):—purify (self).

49. ἁγνισμός **hagnismŏs**, *hag-nis-mos';* from *48;* a *cleansing* (the act), i.e. (cer.) *lustration:*—purification.

50. ἀγνοέω **agnŏĕō**, *ag-no-eh'-o;* from *1* (as a neg. particle) and *3539; not to know* (through lack of information or intelligence); by impl. to *ignore* (through disinclination):—(be) ignorant (-ly), not know, not understand, unknown.

51. ἀγνόημα **agnŏēma**, *ag-no'-ay-mah;* from *50;* a thing *ignored*, i.e. *shortcoming:*—error.

52. ἄγνοια **agnŏia**, *ag'-noy-ah;* from *50; ignorance* (prop. the quality):—ignorance.

53. ἁγνός **hagnŏs**, *hag-nos';* from the same as *40;* prop. *clean*, i.e. (fig.) *innocent, modest, perfect:*—chaste, clean, pure.

54. ἁγνότης **hagnŏtēs**, *hag-not'-ace;* from *53; cleanness* (the state), i.e. (fig.) *blamelessness:*—pureness.

55. ἁγνῶς **hagnōs**, *hag-noce';* adv. from *53; purely*, i.e. *honestly:*—sincerely.

56. ἀγνωσία **agnōsia**, *ag-no-see'-ah;* from *1* (as neg. particle) and *1108; ignorance* (prop. the state):—ignorance, not the knowledge.

57. ἄγνωστος **agnōstŏs**, *ag'-noce-tos;* from *1* (as neg. particle) and *1110; unknown:*—unknown.

58. ἀγορά **agŏra**, *ag-or-ah';* from ἀγείρω **agĕirō** (to *gather;* prob. akin to *1453*); prop. the *town-square* (as a place of public resort); by impl. a *market* or *thoroughfare:*—market (-place), street.

59. ἀγοράζω **agŏrazō**, *ag-or-ad'-zo;* from *58;* prop. to *go to market*, i.e. (by impl.) to *purchase;* spec. to *redeem:*—buy, redeem.

60. ἀγοραῖος **agŏraiŏs**, *ag-or-ah'-yos;* from *58; relating to the market-place*, i.e. *forensic* (times); by impl. *vulgar:*—baser sort, low.

61. ἄγρα **agra**, *ag'-rah;* from *71;* (abstr.) a *catching* (of fish); also (concr.) a *haul* (of fish):—draught.

62. ἀγράμματος **agrammatŏs**, *ag-ram-mat-os;* from *1* (as neg. particle) and *1121; unlettered*, i.e. *illiterate:*—unlearned.

63. ἀγραυλέω **agraulĕō**, *ag-row-leh'-o;* from *68* and *832* (in the sense of *833*); to *camp out:*—abide in the field.

64. ἀγρεύω **agrĕuō**, *ag-rew'-o;* from *61;* to *hunt*, i.e. (fig.) to *entrap:*—catch.

65. ἀγριέλαιος **agriĕlaiŏs**, *ag-ree-el'-ah-yos;* from *66* and *1636;* an *oleaster:*—olive tree (which is) wild.

66. ἄγριος **agriŏs**, *ag'-ree-os;* from *68; wild* (as pertaining to the *country*), lit. (*natural*) or fig. (*fierce*):—wild, raging.

67. Ἀγρίππας **Agrippas**, *ag-rip'-pas;* appar. from *66* and *2462; wild-horse tamer; Agrippas*, one of the Herods:—Agrippa.

68. ἀγρός **agrŏs**, *ag-ros';* from *71;* a *field* (as a *drive* for cattle); gen. the *country;* spec. a *farm*, i.e. *hamlet:*—country, farm, piece of ground, land.

69. ἀγρυπνέω **agrupnĕō**, *ag-roop-neh'-o;* ultimately from *1* (as neg. particle) and *5258;* to *be sleepless*, i.e. *keep awake:*—watch.

70. ἀγρυπνία **agrupnia**, *ag-roop-nee'-ah;* from *69; sleeplessness*, i.e. a *keeping awake:*—watch.

71. ἄγω **agō**, *ag'-o;* a prim. verb; prop. to *lead;* by impl. to *bring, drive*, (reflex.) *go*, (spec.) *pass* (time), or (fig.) *induce:*—be, bring (forth), carry, (let) go, keep, lead away, be open.

72. ἀγωγή **agōgē**, *ag-o-gay';* redupl. from *71;* a *bringing up*, i.e. *mode of living:*—manner of life.

73. ἀγών agōn, *ag-one'*; from *71*; prop. a place of *assembly* (as if *led*), i.e. (by impl.) a *contest* (held there); fig. an *effort* or *anxiety*:—conflict, contention, fight, race.

74. ἀγωνία agōnia, *ag-o-nee'-ah*; from *73*; a *struggle* (prop. the state), i.e. (fig.) *anguish*:—agony.

75. ἀγωνίζομαι agōnizŏmai, *ag-o-nid'-zom-ahee*; from *73*; to *struggle*, lit. (to *compete* for a prize), fig. (to *contend* with an adversary), or gen. (to *endeavor* to accomplish something):—fight, labor fervently, strive.

76. Ἀδάμ Adam, *ad-am'*; of Heb. or. [121]; *Adam*, the first man; typ. (of Jesus) *man* (as his representative):—Adam.

77. ἀδάπανος adapanŏs, *ad-ap'-an-os*; from *1* (as neg. particle) and *1160*; *costless*, i.e. *gratuitous*:—without expense.

78. Ἀδδί Addi, *ad-dee'*; prob. of Heb. or. [comp. 5716]; *Addi*, an Isr.:—Addi.

79. ἀδελφή adĕlphē, *ad-el-fay'*; fem. of *80*; a *sister* (nat. or eccles.):—sister.

80. ἀδελφός adĕlphŏs, *ad-el-fos'*; from *1* (as a connective particle) and **δελφύς dĕlphus** (the *womb*); a *brother* (lit. or fig.) near or remote [much like 1]:—brother.

81. ἀδελφότης adĕlphŏtēs, *ad-el-fot'-ace*; from *80*; *brotherhood* (prop. the feeling of *brotherliness*), i.e. the (Christian) *fraternity*:—brethren, brotherhood.

82. ἄδηλος adēlŏs, *ad'-ay-los*; from *1* (as a neg. particle) and *1212*; *hidden*, fig. *indistinct*:—appear not, uncertain.

83. ἀδηλότης adēlŏtēs, *ad-ay-lot'-ace*; from *82*; *uncertainty*:— × uncertain.

84. ἀδήλως adēlōs, *ad-ay'-loce*; adv. from *82*; *uncertainly*:—uncertainly.

85. ἀδημονέω adēmŏnĕō, *ad-ay-mon-eh'-o*; from a der. of **ἀδέω adĕō**, (to be *sated* to loathing); to *be in distress* (of mind):—be full of heaviness, be very heavy.

86. ᾅδης haidēs, *hah'-dace*; from *1* (as a neg. particle) and *1492*; prop. *unseen*, i.e. "*Hades*" or the place (state) of departed souls:—grave, hell.

87. ἀδιάκριτος adiakritŏs, *ad-ee-ak'-ree-tos*; from *1* (as a neg. particle) and a der. of *1252*; prop. *undistinguished*, i.e. (act.) *impartial*:—without partiality.

88. ἀδιάλειπτος adialĕiptŏs, *ad-ee-al'-ipe-tos*; from *1* (as a neg. particle) and a der. of a compound of *1223* and *3007*; *unintermitted*, i.e. *permanent*:—without ceasing, continual.

89. ἀδιαλείπτως adialĕiptōs, *ad-ee-al-ipe'-toce*; adv. from *88*; *uninterruptedly*, i.e. *without omission* (on an appropriate occasion):—without ceasing.

90. ἀδιαφθορία adiaphthŏria, *ad-ee-af-thor-ee'-ah*; from a der. of a compound of *1* (as a neg. particle) and a der. of *1311*; *incorruptibleness*, i.e. (fig.) *purity* (of doctrine):—uncorruptness.

91. ἀδικέω adikĕō, *ad-ee-keh'-o*; from *94*; to *be unjust*, i.e. (act.) *do wrong* (mor., socially or phys.):—hurt, injure, be an offender, be unjust, (do, suffer, take) wrong.

92. ἀδίκημα adikēma, *ad-eek'-ay-mah*; from *91*; a *wrong* done:—evil doing, iniquity, matter of wrong.

93. ἀδικία adikia, *ad-ee-kee'-ah*; from *94*; (legal) *injustice* (prop. the quality, by impl. the act); mor. *wrongfulness* (of character, life or act):—iniquity, unjust, unrighteousness, wrong.

94. ἄδικος adikŏs, *ad'-ee-kos*; from *1* (as a neg. particle) and *1349*; *unjust*; by extens. *wicked*; by impl. *treacherous*; spec. *heathen*:—unjust, unrighteous.

95. ἀδίκως adikōs, *ad-ee'-koce*; adv. from *94*; *unjustly*:—wrongfully.

96. ἀδόκιμος adŏkimŏs, *ad-ok'-ee-mos*; from *1* (as a neg. particle) and *1384*; *unapproved*, i.e. *rejected*; by impl. *worthless* (lit. or mor.):—castaway, rejected, reprobate.

97. ἄδολος adŏlŏs, *ad'-ol-os*; from *1* (as a neg. particle) and *1388*; *undeceitful*, i.e. (fig.) *unadulterated*:—sincere.

98. Ἀδραμυττηνός Adramuttēnŏs, *ad-ram-oot-tay-nos'*; from **Ἀδραμύττειον Adramuttĕiŏn** (a place in Asia Minor); *Adramyttene* or belonging to Adramyttium:—of Adramyttium.

99. Ἀδρίας Adrias, *ad-ree'-as*; from **Ἀδρία Adria** (a place near its shore); the *Adriatic* sea (including the Ionian):—Adria.

100. ἁδρότης hadrŏtēs, *had-rot'-ace*; from **ἁδρός hadrŏs** (*stout*); *plumpness*, i.e. (fig.) *liberality*:—abundance.

101. ἀδυνατέω adunatĕō, *ad-oo-nat-eh'-o*; from *102*; to *be unable*, i.e. (pass.) *impossible*:—be impossible.

102. ἀδύνατος adunatŏs, *ad-oo'-nat-os*; from *1* (as a neg. particle) and *1415*; *unable*, i.e. *weak* (lit. or fig.); pass. *impossible*:—could not do, impossible, impotent, not possible, weak.

103. ᾄδω aidō, *ad'-o*; a prim. verb; to *sing*:—sing.

104. ἀεί aĕi, *ah-eye'*; from an obs. prim. noun (appar. mean. continued *duration*); "*ever*;" by qualification *regularly*; by impl. *earnestly*:—always, ever.

105. ἀετός aĕtŏs, *ah-et-os'*; from the same as *109*; an *eagle* (from its *wind*-like flight):—eagle.

106. ἄζυμος azumŏs, *ad'-zoo-mos*; from *1* (as a neg. particle) and *2219*; *unleavened*, i.e. (fig.) *uncorrupted*; (in the neut. plur.) spec. (by impl.) the *Passover* week:—unleavened (bread).

107. Ἀζώρ Azōr, *ad-zore'*; of Heb. or. [comp. 5809]; *Azor*, an Isr.:—Azor.

108. Ἄζωτος Azōtŏs, *ad'-zo-tos*; of Heb. or. [795]; *Azotus* (i.e. Ashdod), a place in Pal.:—Azotus.

109. ἀήρ aēr, *ah-ayr'*; from **ἄημι aēmi** (to *breathe* unconsciously, i.e. *respire*; by anal. to *blow*); "*air*" (as naturally *circumambient*):—air. Comp. *5594*.

ἀθά atha. See *3134*.

110. ἀθανασία athanasia, *ath-an-as-ee'-ah*; from a compound of *1* (as a neg. particle) and *2288*; *deathlessness*:—immortality.

111. ἀθέμιτος athĕmitŏs, *ath-em'-ee-tos*; from *1* (as a neg. particle) and a der. of **θέμις thĕmis** (*statute*; from the base of *5087*); *illegal*; by impl. *flagitious*:—abominable, unlawful thing.

112. ἄθεος athĕŏs, *ath'-eh-os*; from *1* (as a neg. particle) and *2316*; *godless*:—without God.

113. ἄθεσμος athĕsmŏs, *ath'-es-mos*; from *1* (as a neg. particle) and a der. of *5087* (in the sense of *enacting*); *lawless*, i.e. (by impl.) *criminal*:—wicked.

114. ἀθετέω athĕtĕō, *ath-et-eh'-o*; from a compound of *1* (as a neg. particle) and a der. of *5087*; to *set aside*, i.e. (by impl.) to *disesteem*, *neutralize* or *violate*:—cast off, despise, disannul, frustrate, bring to nought, reject.

115. ἀθέτησις athĕtēsis, *ath-et'-ay-sis*; from *114*; *cancellation* (lit. or fig.):—disannulling, put away.

116. Ἀθῆναι Athēnai, *ath-ay'-nahee*; plur. of **Ἀθήνη Athēnē** (the goddess of wisdom, who was reputed to have founded the city); *Athenæ*, the capital of Greece:—Athens.

117. Ἀθηναῖος Athēnaiŏs, *ath-ay-nah'-yos*; from *116*; an *Athenæan* or inhab. of Athenæ:—Athenian.

118. ἀθλέω athlĕō, *ath-leh'-o*; from **ἆθλος athlŏs** (a *contest* in the public lists); to *contend* in the competitive games:—strive.

119. ἄθλησις athlēsis, *ath'-lay-sis*; from *118*; a *struggle* (fig.):—fight.

120. ἀθυμέω athumĕō, *ath-oo-meh'-o*; from a comp. of *1* (as a neg. particle) and *2372*; to *be spiritless*, i.e. *disheartened*:—be dismayed.

121. ἄθωος athōŏs, *ath'-o-os*; from *1* (as a neg. particle) and a prob. der. of *5087* (mean. a *penalty*); *not guilty*:—innocent.

122. αἴγειος aigĕŏs, *ah'ee-ghi-os*; from **αἴξ aix**, (a *goat*); belonging to a *goat*:—goat.

123. αἰγιαλός aigialŏs, *ahee-ghee-al-os'*; from **ἀΐσσω aïssō** (to *rush*) and *251* (in the sense of the *sea*); a *beach* (on which the *waves dash*):—shore.

124. Αἰγύπτιος Aiguptiŏs, *ahee-goop'-tee-os*; from *125*; an *Ægyptian* or inhab. of Ægyptus:—Egyptian.

125. Αἴγυπτος Aiguptŏs, *ah'ee-goop-tos*; of uncert. der.; *Ægyptus*, the land of the Nile:—Egypt.

126. ἀΐδιος aïdiŏs, *ah-id'-ee-os*; from *104*; *everduring* (forward and backward, or forward only):—eternal, everlasting.

127. αἰδώς aidōs, *ahee-doce'*; perh. from *1* (as a neg. particle) and *1492* (through the idea of *downcast* eyes); *bashfulness*, i.e. (towards men), *modesty* or (towards God) *awe*:—reverence, shamefacedness.

128. Αἰθίοψ Aithiŏps, *ahee-thee'-ops*; from **αἴθω aithō** (to *scorch*) and **ὤψ ōps** (the *face*, from *3700*); an *Æthiopian* (as a *blackamoor*):—Ethiopian.

129. αἷμα haima, *hah'ee-mah*; of uncert. der.; *blood*, lit. (of men or animals), fig. (the *juice* of grapes) or spec. (the atoning *blood* of Christ); by impl. *bloodshed*, also *kindred*:—blood.

130. αἱματεκχυσία haimatĕkchusia, *hahee-mat-ek-khoo-see'-ah*; from *129* and a der. of *1632*; an *effusion of blood*:—shedding of blood.

131. αἱμοῤῥέω haimŏrrhĕō, *hahee-mor-hreh'-o*; from *129* and *4482*; to *flow blood*, i.e. *have a hæmorrhage*:—diseased with an issue of blood.

132. Αἰνέας Ainĕas, *ahee-neh'-as*; of uncert. der.; *Æněas*, an Isr.:—Æneas.

133. αἴνεσις ainĕsis, *ah'ee-nes-is*; from *134*; a *praising* (the act), i.e. (spec.) a *thank* (-offering):—praise.

134. αἰνέω ainĕō, *ahee-neh'-o*; from *136*; to *praise* (God):—praise.

135. αἴνιγμα ainigma, *ah'ee-nig-ma*; from a der. of *136* (in its prim. sense); an *obscure* saying ("enigma"), i.e. (abstr.) *obscureness*:— × darkly.

136. αἶνος ainŏs, *ah'ee-nos*; appar. a prim. word; prop. a *story*, but used in the sense of *1868*; *praise* (of God):—praise.

137. Αἰνών Ainōn, *ahee-nohn'*; of Hebr. or. [a der. of 5869, *place of springs*]; *Ænon*, a place in Pal.:—Ænon.

138. αἱρέομαι hairĕŏmai, *hahee-reh'-om-ahee*; prob. akin to *142*; to *take for oneself*, i.e. to *prefer*:—choose. Some of the forms are borrowed from a cognate **ἕλλομαι hellŏmai**, *hel'-lom-ahee*; which is otherwise obsolete.

139. αἵρεσις hairĕsis, *hah'ee-res-is*; from *138*; prop. a *choice*, i.e. (spec.) a *party* or (abstr.) *disunion*:—heresy [*which is the Gr. word itself*], sect.

140. αἱρετίζω hairĕtizō, *hahee-ret-id'-zo*; from a der. of *138*; to *make a choice*:—choose.

141. αἱρετικός hairĕtikŏs, *hahee-ret-ee-kos'*; from the same as *140*; a *schismatic*:—heretic [*the Gr. word itself*].

142. αἴρω airō, *ah'ee-ro*; a prim. verb; to *lift*; by impl. to *take up* or *away*; fig. to *raise* (the voice), *keep in suspense* (the mind); spec. to *sail* away (i.e. *weigh anchor*); by Heb. [comp. 5375] to *expiate* sin:—away with, bear (up), carry, lift up, loose, make to doubt, put away, remove, take (away, up).

143. αἰσθάνομαι aisthanŏmai, *ahee-sthan'-om-ahee*; of uncert. der.; to *apprehend* (prop. by the senses):—perceive.

144. αἴσθησις aisthēsis, *ah'ee-sthay-sis*; from *143*; *perception*, i.e. (fig.) *discernment*:—judgment.

145. αἰσθητήριον aisthētēriŏn, *ahee-sthay-tay'-ree-on*; from a der. of *143*; prop. an *organ of perception*, i.e. (fig.) *judgment*:—senses.

146. αἰσχροκερδής aischrŏkĕrdēs, *ahee-skhrok-er-dace'*; from *150* and **κέρδος kerdos** (*gain*); *sordid*:—given to (greedy of) filthy lucre.

147. αἰσχροκερδῶς aischrŏkĕrdōs, *ahee-skhrok-er-doce'*; adv. from *146*; *sordidly*:—for filthy lucre's sake.

148. αἰσχρολογία aischrŏlŏgia, *ahee-skhrol-og-ee'-ah*; from *150* and *3056*; *vile conversation*:—filthy communication.

149. αἰσχρόν aischrŏn, *ahee-skhron'*; neut. of *150*; a *shameful* thing, i.e. *indecorum*:—shame.

150. αἰσχρός aischrŏs, *ahee-skhros'*; from the same as *153*; *shameful*, i.e. *base* (spec. *venal*):—filthy.

151. αἰσχρότης aischrŏtēs, *ahee-skhrot'-ace*; from *150*; *shamefulness*, i.e. *obscenity*:—filthiness.

152. αἰσχύνη aischunē, *ahee-skhoo'-nay*; from *153*; *shame* or *disgrace* (abstr. or concr.):—dishonesty, shame.

153. αἰσχύνομαι aischunŏmai, *ahee-skhoo'-nom-ahee*; from **αἶσχος aischŏs** (*disfigurement*, i.e. *disgrace*); to *feel shame* (for oneself):—be ashamed.

154. αἰτέω aitĕō, *ahee-teh'-o*; of uncert. der.; to *ask* (in gen.):—ask, beg, call for, crave, desire, require. Comp. *4441*.

155. αἴτημα aitēma, *ah'ee-tay-mah*; from *154*; a *thing asked* or (abstr.) an *asking*:—petition, request, required.

156. αἰτία aitia, *ahee-tee'-a*; from the same as *154*; a *cause* (as if *asked* for), i.e. (logical) *reason* (motive, matter), (legal) *crime* (alleged or proved):—accusation, case, cause, crime, fault, [wh-]ere [-fore].

157. αἰτίαμα aitiama, *ahee-tee'-am-ah*; from a der. of *156*; a *thing charged*:—complaint.

158. αἴτιον aitiŏn, *ah'ee-tee-on*; neut. of *159*; a *reason* or *crime* [like *156*]:—cause, fault.

159. αἴτιος aitiŏs, *ah'ee-tee-os*; from the same as *154*; *causative*, i.e. (concr.) a *causer*:—author.

160. αἰφνίδιος aiphnidiŏs, *aheef-nid'-ee-os*; from a comp. of *1* (as a neg. particle) and *5316* [comp. *1810*] (mean. *non-apparent*); *unexpected*, i.e. (adv.) *suddenly*:—sudden, unawares.

161. αἰχμαλωσία aichmalōsia, *aheekh-mal-o-see'-ah*; from *164*; *captivity*:—captivity.

162. αἰχμαλωτεύω aichmalōtĕuō, *aheekh-mal-o-tew'-o*; from *164*; to *capture* [like *163*]:—lead captive.

163. αἰχμαλωτίζω aichmalōtizō, *aheekh-mal-o-tid'-zo*; from *164*: to *make captive*:—lead away captive, bring into captivity.

164. αἰχμαλωτός aichmalōtŏs, *aheekh-mal-o-tos'*; from **αἰχμή aichmē** (a *spear*) and a der. of the same as *259*; prop. a *prisoner of war*, i.e. (gen.) a *captive*:—captive.

165. αἰών aiōn, *ahee-ohn'*; from the same as *104*; prop. an *age*; by extens. *perpetuity* (also past); by impl. the *world*; spec. (Jewish) a Messianic period (present or future):—age, course, eternal, (for) ever (-more), [n-]ever, (beginning of the, while the) world (began, without end). Comp. *5550*.

166. αἰώνιος aiōniŏs, *ahee-o'-nee-os*; from *165*; *perpetual* (also used of past time, or past and future as well):—eternal, for ever, everlasting, world (began).

167. ἀκαθαρσία akatharsia, *ak-ath-ar-see'-ah*; from *169*; *impurity* (the quality), phys. or mor.:—uncleanness.

168. ἀκαθάρτης akathartēs, *ak-ath-ar'-tace*; from *169*; *impurity* (the state), mor.:—filthiness.

169. ἀκάθαρτος akathartŏs, *ak-ath'-ar-tos*; from *1* (as a neg. particle) and a presumed der. of *2508* (mean. *cleansed*); *impure* (cer., mor. [*lewd*] or spec. [*dæmonic*]):—foul, unclean.

170. ἀκαιρέομαι akairĕŏmai, *ak-ahee-reh'-om-ahee*; from a comp. of *1* (as a neg. particle) and *2540* (mean. *unseasonable*); to *be inopportune* (for oneself), i.e. to *fail of a proper occasion*:—lack opportunity.

171. ἀκαίρως akairōs, *ak-ah'ee-roce*; adv. from the same as *170*; *inopportunely*:—out of season.

172. ἄκακος akakŏs, *ak'-ak-os*; from *1* (as a neg. particle) and *2556*; *not bad*, i.e. (obj.) *innocent* or (subj.) *unsuspecting*:—harmless, simple.

173. ἄκανθα akantha, *ak'-an-thah*; prob. from the same as *188*; a *thorn*:—thorn.

174. ἀκάνθινος akanthinŏs, *ak-an'-thee-nos*; from *173*; *thorny*:—of thorns.

175. ἄκαρπος akarpŏs, *ak'-ar-pos*; from *1* (as a neg. particle) and *2590*; *barren* (lit. or fig.):—without fruit, unfruitful.

176. ἀκατάγνωστος akatagnōstŏs, *ak-at-ag'-noce-tos*; from *1* (as a neg. particle) and a der. of *2607*; *unblamable*:—that cannot be condemned.

177. ἀκατακάλυπτος akatakaluptŏs, *ak-at-ak-al'-oop-tos*; from *1* (as a neg. particle) and a der. of a comp. of *2596* and *2572*; *unveiled*:—uncovered.

178. ἀκατάκριτος akatakritŏs, *ak-at-ak'-ree-tos*; from *1* (as a neg. particle) and a der. of *2632*; *without* (legal) *trial*:—uncondemned.

179. ἀκατάλυτος akatalutŏs, *ak-at-al'-oo-tos*; from *1* (as a neg. particle) and a der. of *2647*; *indissoluble*, i.e. (fig.) *permanent*:—endless.

180. ἀκατάπαυστος akatapaustŏs, *ak-at-ap'-ow-stos*; from *1* (as a neg. particle) and a der. of *2664*; *unrefraining*:—that cannot cease.

181. ἀκαταστασία akatastasia, *ak-at-as-tah-see'-ah*; from *182*; *instability*, i.e. *disorder*:—commotion, confusion, tumult.

182. ἀκατάστατος akatastatŏs, *ak-at-as'-tat-os*; from *1* (as a neg. particle) and a der. of *2525*; *inconstant*:—unstable.

183. ἀκατάσχετος akataschĕtŏs, *ak-at-as'-khet-os*; from *1* (as a neg. particle) and a der. of *2722*; *unrestrainable*:—unruly.

184. Ἀκελδαμά Akeldama, *ak-el-dam-ah'*; of Chald. or. [mean. *field of blood*; corresp. to 2506 and 1818]; *Akeldama*, a place near Jerus.:—Aceldama.

185. ἀκέραιος akĕraiŏs, *ak-er'-ah-yos*; from *1* (as a neg. particle) and a presumed der. of *2767*: *unmixed*, i.e. (fig.) *innocent*:—harmless, simple.

186. ἀκλινής aklinēs, *ak-lee-nace'*; from *1* (as a neg. particle) and *2827*; *not leaning*, i.e. (fig.) *firm*:—without wavering.

187. ἀκμάζω akmazō, *ak-mad'-zo*; from the same as *188*; to *make a point*, i.e. (fig.) *mature*:—be fully ripe.

188. ἀκμήν akmēn, *ak-mane'*; accus. of a noun ("*acme*") akin to **ἀκή akē** (a *point*) and mean. the same; adv. *just* now, i.e. *still*:—yet.

189. ἀκοή akŏē, *ak-ŏ-ay'*; from *191*; *hearing* (the act, the sense or the thing heard):—audience, ear, fame, which ye heard, hearing, preached, report, rumor.

190. ἀκολουθέω akŏlŏuthĕō, *ak-ol-oo-theh'-o*; from *1* (as a particle of union) and **κέλευθος kĕlĕuthŏs** (a *road*); prop. to *be in the same way with*, i.e. to *accompany* (spec. as a disciple):—follow, reach.

191. ἀκούω akŏuō, *ak-oo'-o*; a prim. verb; to *hear* (in various senses):—give (in the) audience (of), come (to the ears), ([shall]) hear (-er, -ken), be noised, be reported, understand.

192. ἀκρασία akrasia, *ak-ras-ee'-a*; from *193*; *want of self-restraint*:—excess, incontinency.

193. ἀκράτης akratēs, *ak-rat'-ace*; from *1* (as a neg. particle) and *2904*; *powerless*, i.e. *without self-control*:—incontinent.

194. ἄκρατος akratŏs, *ak'-rat-os*; from *1* (as a neg. particle) and a presumed der. of *2767*; *undiluted*:—without mixture.

195. ἀκρίβεια akribĕia, *ak-ree'-bi-ah*; from the same as *196*; *exactness*:—perfect manner.

196. ἀκριβέστατος akribĕstatŏs, *ak-ree-bes'-ta-tos*; superlative of **ἀκρίβης akribēs** (a der. of the same as *206*); *most exact*:—most straitest.

197. ἀκριβέστερον akribĕstĕrŏn, *ak-ree-bes'-ter-on*; neut. of the comparative of the same as *196*; (adv.) *more exactly*:—more perfect (-ly).

198. ἀκριβόω akribŏō, *ak-ree-bŏ'-o*; from the same as *196*; to *be exact*, i.e. *ascertain*:—enquire diligently.

199. ἀκριβῶς akribōs, *ak-ree-boce'*; adv. from the same as *196*; *exactly*:—circumspectly, diligently, perfect (-ly).

200. ἀκρίς akris, *ak-rece'*; appar. from the same as *206*; a *locust* (as *pointed*, or as *lighting* on the *top* of vegetation):—locust.

201. ἀκροατήριον akrŏateriŏn, *ak-rŏ-at-ay'-ree-on*; from *202*; an *audience-room*:—place of hearing.

202. ἀκροατής akrŏatēs, *ak-rŏ-at-ace'*; from **ἀκροάομαι akrŏaŏmai** (to *listen*; appar. an intens. of *191*); a *hearer* (merely):—hearer.

203. ἀκροβυστία akrŏbustia, *ak-rob-oos-tee'-ah*; from *206* and prob. a modified form of **πόσθη pŏsthē** (the *penis* or male sexual organ); the *prepuce*; by impl. an *uncircumcised* (i.e. *gentile*, fig. *unregenerate*) state or person:—not circumcised, uncircumcised [*with 2192*], uncircumcision.

204. ἀκρογωνιαῖος akrŏgōniaiŏs, *ak-rog-o-nee-ah'-yos*; from *206* and *1137*; belonging to the extreme *corner*:—chief corner.

205. ἀκροθίνιον akrŏthiniŏn, *ak-roth-in'-ee-on*; from *206* and **θίς this** (a *heap*); prop. (in the plur.) the *top of the heap*, i.e. (by impl.) *best of the booty*:—spoils.

206. ἄκρον akrŏn, *ak'-ron*; neut. of an adj. prob. akin to the base of *188*; the *extremity*:—one end . . . other, tip, top, uttermost part.

207. Ἀκύλας Akulas, *ak-oo'-las*; prob. for Lat. *aquila* (an *eagle*); *Akulas*, an Isr.:—Aquila.

208. ἀκυρόω akurŏō, *ak-oo-rŏ'-o*; from *1* (as a neg. particle) and *2964*; to *invalidate*:—disannul, make of none effect.

209. ἀκωλύτως akōlutōs, *ak-o-loo'-toce*; adv. from a compound of *1* (as a neg. particle) and a der. of *2967*; in *an unhindered manner*, i.e. *freely*:—no man forbidding him.

210. ἄκων akōn, *ak'-ohn*; from *1* (as a neg. particle) and *1635*; *unwilling*:—against the will.

211. ἀλάβαστρον alabastrŏn, *al-ab'-as-tron*; neut. of **ἀλάβαστρος alabastrŏs** (of uncert. der.), the name of a stone; prop. an "*alabaster*" box, i.e. (by extens.) a perfume *vase* (of any material):—(alabaster) box.

212. ἀλαζονεία alazŏnĕia, *al-ad-zon-i'-a*; from *213*; *braggadocio*, i.e. (by impl.) *self-confidence*:—boasting, pride.

213. ἀλαζών alazōn, *al-ad-zone'*; from **ἄλη alē** (*vagrancy*); *braggart*:—boaster.

214. ἀλαλάζω alalazō, *al-al-ad'-zo*; from **ἀλαλή alalē** (a *shout*, "*halloo*"); to *vociferate*, i.e. (by impl.) to *wail*; fig. to *clang*:—tinkle, wail.

215. ἀλάλητος alalētŏs, *al-al'-ay-tos*; from *1* (as a neg. particle) and a der. of *2980*; *unspeakable*:—unutterable, which cannot be uttered.

216. ἄλαλος alalŏs, *al'-al-os*; from *1* (as a neg. particle) and *2980*; *mute*:—dumb.

217. ἅλας halas, *hal'-as*; from *251*; *salt*; fig. *prudence*:—salt.

218. ἀλείφω alĕiphō, *al-i'-fo*; from *1* (as particle of union) and the base of *3045*; to *oil* (with perfume):—anoint.

219. ἀλεκτοροφωνία alektŏrŏphōnia, *al-ek-tor-of-o-nee'-ah*; from *220* and *5456*; *cock-crow*, i.e. the third night-watch:—cockcrowing.

220. ἀλέκτωρ alĕktōr, *al-ek'-tore*; from **ἀλέκω** (to *ward off*); a *cock* or male fowl:—cock.

221. Ἀλεξανδρεύς Alĕxandrĕus, *al-ex-and-reuce'*; from **Ἀλεξάνδρεια** (the city so called); an *Alexandreian* or inhab. of Alexandria:—of Alexandria, Alexandrian.

222. Ἀλεξανδρῖνος Alĕxandrinŏs, *al-ex-an-dree'-nos*; from the same as 221; *Alexandrine*, or belonging to Alexandria:—of Alexandria.

223. Ἀλέξανδρος Alĕxandrŏs, *al-ex'-an-dros*; from the same as (the first part of) *220* and *435*; *man-defender*; *Alexander*, the name of three Isr. and one other man:—Alexander.

224. ἄλευρον alĕurŏn, *al'-yoo-ron*; from **ἀλέω alĕō** (to *grind*); *flour*:—meal.

225. ἀλήθεια alēthĕia, *al-ay'-thi-a*; from *227*; *truth*:—true, × truly, truth, verity.

226. ἀληθεύω alēthĕuō, *al-ayth-yoo'-o*; from *227*; to *be true* (in doctrine and profession):—speak (tell) the truth.

227. ἀληθής alēthēs, *al-ay-thace'*; from *1* (as a neg. particle) and *2990*; *true* (*as not concealing*):—true, truly, truth.

228. **ἀληθινός alēthinŏs**, *al-ay-thee-nos'*; from *227*; *truthful*:—true.

229. **ἀλήθω alēthō**, *al-ay'-tho*; from the same as *224*; to *grind*:—grind.

230. **ἀληθῶς alēthōs**, *al-ay-thoce'*; adv. from *227*; *truly*:—indeed, surely, of a surety, truly, of a (in) truth, verily, very.

231. **ἁλιεύς halĭeus**, *hal-ee-yoos'*; from *251*; a *sailor* (as engaged on the *salt* water), i.e. (by impl.) a *fisher*:—fisher (-man).

232. **ἁλιεύω halĭeuō**, *hal-ee-yoo'-o*; from *231*; to *be a fisher*, i.e. (by impl.) to *fish*:—go a-fishing.

233. **ἁλίζω halizō**, *hal-id'-zo*; from *251*; to *salt*:—salt.

234. **ἀλίσγεμα alisgĕma**, *al-is'-ghem-ah*; from **ἀλισγέω alisgĕō** (to *soil*); (cer.) *defilement*:—pollution.

235. **ἀλλά alla**, *al-lah'*; neut. plur. of *243*; prop. *other* things, i.e. (adv.) *contrariwise* (in many relations):—and, but (even), howbeit, indeed, nay, nevertheless, no, notwithstanding, save, therefore, yea, yet.

236. **ἀλλάσσω allassō**, *al-las'-so*; from *243*; to *make different*:—change.

237. **ἀλλαχόθεν allachŏthĕn**, *al-lakh-oth'-en*; from *243*; *from elsewhere*:—some other way.

238. **ἀλληγορέω allēgŏrĕō**, *al-lay-gor-eh'-o*; from *243* and **ἀγορέω agŏrĕō** (to *harangue* [comp. *58*]); to *allegorize*:—be an allegory [*the Gr. word itself*].

239. **ἀλληλουϊα allēlŏuïa**, *al-lay-loo'-ee-ah*; of Heb. or. [imper. of 1984 and 3050]; *praise ye Jah!*, an adoring exclamation:—alleluiah.

240. **ἀλλήλων allēlōn**, *al-lay'-lone*; Gen. plur. from *243* redupl.; *one another*:—each other, mutual, one another, (the other), (them-, your-) selves, (selves) together [*sometimes with 3326 or 4314*].

241. **ἀλλογενής allŏgĕnēs**, *al-log-en-ace'*; from *243* and *1085*; *foreign*, i.e. not a Jew:—stranger.

242. **ἅλλομαι hallŏmai**, *hal'-lom-ahee*; mid. of appar. a prim. verb; to *jump*; fig. to *gush*:—leap, spring up.

243. **ἄλλος allŏs**, *al'-los*; a prim. word; "*else*," i.e. *different* (in many applications):—more, one (another), (an-, some an-) other (-s, -wise).

244. **ἀλλοτριεπίσκοπος allotriĕpiskŏpŏs**, *al-lot-ree-ep-is'-kop-os*; from *245* and *1985*; *overseeing others'* affairs, i.e. a *meddler* (spec. in Gentile customs):—busybody in other men's matters.

245. **ἀλλότριος allŏtriŏs**, *al-lot'-ree-os*; from *243*; *another's*, i.e. not one's own; by extens. *foreign*, *not akin*, *hostile*:—alien, (an-) other (man's, men's), strange (-r).

246. **ἀλλόφυλος allŏphulŏs**, *al-lof'-oo-los*; from *243* and *5443*; *foreign*, i.e. (spec.) *Gentile*:—one of another nation.

247. **ἄλλως allōs**, *al'-loce*; adv. from *243*; *differently*:—otherwise.

248. **ἀλοάω alŏaō**, *al-o-ah'-o*; from the same as *257*; to *tread* out grain:—thresh, tread out the corn.

249. **ἄλογος alŏgŏs**, *al'-og-os*; from *1* (as a neg. particle) and *3056*; *irrational*:—brute, unreasonable.

250. **ἀλοή alŏē**, *al-ŏ-ay'*; of for. or. [comp. 174]; *aloes* (the gum):—aloes.

251. **ἅλς hals**, *halce*; a prim. word; "*salt*":—salt.

252. **ἁλυκός halukŏs**, *hal-oo-kos'*; from *251*; *briny*:—salt.

253. **ἀλυπότερος alupŏtĕrŏs**, *al-oo-pot'-er-os*; compar. of a comp. of *1* (as a neg. particle) and *3077*; *more without grief*:—less sorrowful.

254. **ἅλυσις halusis**, *hal'-oo-sis*; of uncert. der.; a *fetter* or *manacle*:—bonds, chain.

255. **ἀλυσιτελής alusitĕlēs**, *al-oo-sit-el-ace'*; from *1* (as a neg. particle) and the base of *3081*; *gainless*, i.e. (by impl.) *pernicious*:—unprofitable.

256. **'Αλφαῖος Alphaiŏs**, *al-fah'-yos*; of Heb. or. [comp. 2501]; *Alphæus*, an Isr.:—Alpheus.

257. **ἅλων halōn**, *hal'-ohn*; prob. from the base of *1507*; a threshing-*floor* (as *rolled* hard), i.e. (fig.) the *grain* (and chaff, as just threshed):—floor.

258. **ἀλώπηξ alōpēx**, *al-o'-pakes*; of uncert. der.; a *fox*, i.e. (fig.) a *cunning* person:—fox.

259. **ἅλωσις halōsis**, *hal'-o-sis*; from a collateral form of *138*; *capture*:—be taken.

260. **ἅμα hama**, *ham'-ah*; a prim. particle; prop. *at the "same" time*, but freely used as a prep. or adv. denoting close association:—also, and, together, with (-al).

261. **ἀμαθής amathēs**, *am-ath-ace'*; from *1* (as a neg. particle) and *3129*; *ignorant*:—unlearned.

262. **ἀμαράντινος amarantinŏs**, *am-ar-an'-tee-nos*; from *263*; "*amaranthine*", i.e. (by impl.) *fadeless*:—that fadeth not away.

263. **ἀμάραντος amarantŏs**, *am-ar'-an-tos*; from *1* (as a neg. particle) and a presumed der. of *3133*; *unfading*, i.e. (by impl.) *perpetual*:—that fadeth not away.

264. **ἁμαρτάνω hamartanō**, *ham-ar-tan'-o*; perh. from *1* (as a neg. particle) and the base of *3313*; prop. to *miss* the mark (and so *not share* in the prize), i.e. (fig.) to *err*, esp. (mor.) to *sin*.—for your faults, offend, sin, trespass.

265. **ἁμάρτημα hamartēma**, *ham-ar'-tay-mah*; from *264*; a *sin* (prop. concr.):—sin.

266. **ἁμαρτία hamartia**, *ham-ar-tee'-ah*; from *264*; *sin* (prop. abstr.):—offence, sin (-ful).

267. **ἀμάρτυρος amarturŏs**, *am-ar'-too-ros*; from *1* (as a neg. particle) and a form of *3144*; *unattested*:—without witness.

268. **ἁμαρτωλός hamartōlŏs**, *ham-ar-to-los'*; from *264*; *sinful*, i.e. a *sinner*:—sinful, sinner.

269. **ἄμαχος amachŏs**, *am'-akh-os*; from *1* (as a neg. particle) and *3163*; *peaceable*:—not a brawler.

270. **ἀμάω amaō**, *am-ah'-o*; from *260*; prop. to *collect*, i.e. (by impl.) *reap*:—reap down.

271. **ἀμέθυστος amĕthustŏs**, *am-eth'-oos-tos*; from *1* (as a neg. particle) and a der. of *3184*; the "*amethyst*" (supposed to *prevent intoxication*):—amethyst.

272. **ἀμελέω amĕlĕō**, *am-el-eh'-o*; from *1* (as a neg. particle) and *3199*; to *be careless* of:—make light of, neglect, be negligent, not regard.

273. **ἄμεμπτος amĕmptŏs**, *am'-emp-tos*; from *1* (as a neg. particle) and a der. of *3201*; *irreproachable*:—blameless, faultless, unblamable.

274. **ἀμέμπτως amĕmptōs**, *am-emp'-toce*; adv. from *273*; *faultlessly*:—blameless, unblamably.

275. **ἀμέριμνος amĕrimnŏs**, *am-er'-im-nos*; from *1* (as a neg. particle) and *3308*; *not anxious*:—without care (-fulness), secure.

276. **ἀμετάθετος amĕtathĕtŏs**, *am-et-ath'-et-os*; from *1* (as a neg. particle) and a der. of *3346*; *unchangeable*, or (neut. as abstr.) *unchangeability*:—immutable (-ility).

277. **ἀμετακίνητος amĕtakinētŏs**, *am-et-ak-in'-ay-tos*; from *1* (as a neg. particle) and a der. of *3334*; *immovable*:—unmovable.

278. **ἀμεταμέλητος amĕtamĕlētŏs**, *am-et-am-el'-ay-tos*; from *1* (as a neg. particle) and a presumed der. of *3338*; *irrevocable*:—without repentance, not to be repented of.

279. **ἀμετανόητος amĕtanŏētŏs**, *am-et-an-ŏ'-ay-tos*; from *1* (as a neg. particle) and a presumed der. of *3340*; *unrepentant*:—impenitent.

280. **ἄμετρος amĕtrŏs**, *am'-et-ros*; from *1* (as a neg. particle) and *3358*; *immoderate*:—(thing) without measure.

281. **ἀμήν amēn**, *am-ane'*; of Heb. or. [543]; prop. *firm*, i.e. (fig.) *trustworthy*; adv. *surely* (often as interj. *so be it*):—amen, verily.

282. **ἀμήτωρ amētōr**, *am-ay'-tore*; from *1* (as a neg. particle) and *3384*; *motherless*, i.e. *of unknown maternity*:—without mother.

283. **ἀμίαντος amiantŏs**, *am-ee'-an-tos*; from *1* (as a neg. particle) and a der. of *3392*; *unsoiled*, i.e. (fig.) *pure*:—undefiled.

284. **'Αμιναδάβ Aminadab**, *am-ee-nad-ab'*; of Heb. or. [5992]; *Aminadab*, an Isr.:—Aminadab.

285. **ἄμμος ammŏs**, *am'-mos*; perh. from *260*; *sand* (as *heaped* on the beach):—sand.

286. **ἀμνός amnŏs**, *am-nos'*; appar. a prim. word; a *lamb*:—lamb.

287. **ἀμοιβή amŏibē**, *am-oy-bay'*; from **ἀμείβω amĕibō** (to *exchange*); *requital*:—requite.

288. **ἄμπελος ampĕlŏs**, *am'-pel-os*; prob. from the base of *297* and that of *257*; a *vine* (as *coiling about* a support):—vine.

289. **ἀμπελουργός ampĕlŏurgŏs**, *am-pel-oor-gos'*; from *288* and *2041*; a *vine-worker*, i.e. *pruner*:—vine-dresser.

290. **ἀμπελών ampĕlōn**, *am-pel-ohn'*; from *288*; a *vineyard*:—vineyard.

291. **'Αμπλίας Amplias**, *am-plee'-as*; contr. for Lat. *ampliatus* [*enlarged*]; *Amplias*, a Rom. Chr.:—Amplias.

292. **ἀμύνομαι amunŏmai**, *am-oo'-nom-ahee*; mid. of a prim. verb; to *ward off* (for oneself), i.e. *protect*:—defend.

293. **ἀμφίβληστρον amphiblēstrŏn**, *am-fib'-lace-tron*; from a comp. of the base of *297* and *906*; a (fishing) *net* (as *thrown about* the fish):—net.

294. **ἀμφιέννυμι amphiĕnnumi**, *am-fee-en'-noo-mee*; from the base of *297* and **ἕννυμι hĕnnumi** (to *invest*); to *enrobe*:—clothe.

295. **'Αμφίπολις Amphipŏlis**, *am-fip'-ol-is*; from the base of *297* and *4172*; a *city surrounded* by a river; *Amphipolis*, a place in Macedonia:—Amphipolis.

296. **ἄμφοδον amphŏdŏn**, *am'-fod-on*; from the base of *297* and *3598*; a *fork* in the road:—where two ways meet.

297. **ἀμφότερος amphŏtĕrŏs**, *am-fot'-er-os*; compar. of **ἀμφί amphi** (*around*); (in plur.) *both*:—both.

298. **ἀμώμητος amōmētŏs**, *am-o'-may-tos*; from *1* (as a neg. particle) and a der. of *3469*; *unblameable*:—blameless.

299. **ἄμωμος amōmŏs**, *am'-o-mos*; from *1* (as a neg. particle) and *3470*; *unblemished* (lit. or fig.):—without blame (blemish, fault, spot), faultless, unblameable.

300. **'Αμών Amōn**, *am-one'*; of Heb. or. [526]; *Amon*, an Isr.:—Amon.

301. **'Αμώς Amōs**, *am-oce'*; of Heb. or. [531]; *Amos*, an Isr.:—Amos.

302. **ἄν an**, *an*; a prim. particle, denoting a *supposition*, *wish*, *possibility* or *uncertainty*:—[what-, where-, whither-, who-]soever. Usually unexpressed except by the subjunctive or potential mood. Also contr. for *1437*.

303. **ἀνά ana**, *an-ah'*; a prim. prep. and adv.; prop. *up*; but (by extens.) used (distributively) *severally*, or (locally) *at* (etc.):—and, apiece, by, each, every (man), in, through. In compounds (as a prefix) it often means (by impl.) *repetition*, *intensity*, *reversal*, etc.

304. **ἀναβαθμός anabathmŏs**, *an-ab-ath-mos'*; from *305* [comp. *898*]; a *stairway*:—stairs.

305. **ἀναβαίνω anabainō**, *an-ab-ah'ee-no*; from *303* and the base of *939*; to *go up* (lit. or fig.):—arise, ascend (up), climb (go, grow, rise, spring) up, come (up).

306. **ἀναβάλλομαι anaballŏmai**, *an-ab-al'-lom-ahee*; mid. from *303* and *906*; to *put off* (for oneself):—defer.

307. **ἀναβιβάζω anabibazō**, *an-ab-ee-bad'-zo*; from *303* and a der. of the base of *939*; to *cause to go up*, i.e. *haul* (a net):—draw.

308. **ἀναβλέπω anablĕpō**, *an-ab-lep'-o*; from *303* and *991*; to *look up*; by impl. to *recover sight*:—look (up), see, receive sight.

309. **ἀνάβλεψις anablĕpsis**, *an-ab'-lep-sis*; from *308*; *restoration of sight*:—recovering of sight.

310. **ἀναβοάω anabŏaō**, *an-ab-o-ah'-o*; from *303* and *994*; to *halloo*:—cry (aloud, out).

311. **ἀναβολή anabŏlē**, *an-ab-ol-ay'*; from *306*; a *putting off*:—delay.

312. ἀναγγέλλω **anaggĕllō**, *an-ang-el'-lo;* from *303* and the base of *32;* to *announce* (in detail):—declare, rehearse, report, show, speak, tell.

313. ἀναγεννάω **anagĕnnaō**, *an-ag-en-nah'-o;* from *303* and *1080;* to *beget* or (by extens.) *bear* (again):—beget, (bear) × again.

314. ἀναγινώσκω **anaginōskō**, *an-ag-in-oce'-ko;* from *303* and *1097;* to *know again,* i.e. (by extens.) to *read:*—read.

315. ἀναγκάζω **anagkazō**, *an-ang-kad'-zo;* from *318;* to *necessitate:*—compel, constrain.

316. ἀναγκαῖος **anagkaiŏs**, *an-ang-kah'-yos;* from *318; necessary;* by impl. *close* (of kin):—near, necessary, necessity, needful.

317. ἀναγκαστῶς **anagkastŏs**, *an-ang-kas-toce';* adv. from a der. of *315; compulsorily:*—by constraint.

318. ἀνάγκη **anagkē**, *an-ang-kay';* from *303* and the base of *43; constraint* (lit. or fig.); by impl. *distress:*—distress, must needs, (of) necessity (-sary), needeth, needful.

319. ἀναγνωρίζομαι **anagnōrizŏmai**, *an-ag-no-rid'-zom-ahee;* mid. from *303* and *1107;* to *make* (oneself) *known:*—be made known.

320. ἀνάγνωσις **anagnōsis**, *an-ag'-no-sis;* from *314;* (the act of) *reading:*—reading.

321. ἀνάγω **anagō**, *an-ag'-o;* from *303* and *71;* to *lead up;* by extens. to *bring out;* spec. to *sail away:*—bring (again, forth, up again), depart, launch (forth), lead (up), loose, offer, sail, set forth, take up.

322. ἀναδείκνυμι **anadĕiknumi**, *an-ad-ike'-noo-mee;* from *303* and *1166;* to *exhibit,* i.e. (by impl.) to *indicate, appoint:*—appoint, shew.

323. ἀνάδειξις **anadĕixis**, *an-ad'-ike-sis;* from *322;* (the act of) *exhibition:*—shewing.

324. ἀναδέχομαι **anadĕchŏmai**, *an-ad-ekh'-om-ahee;* from *303* and *1209;* to *entertain* (as a guest):—receive.

325. ἀναδίδωμι **anadidōmi**, *an-ad-eed'-om-ee;* from *303* and *1325;* to *hand over:*—deliver.

326. ἀναζάω **anazaō**, *an-ad-zah'-o;* from *303* and *2198;* to *recover life* (lit. or fig.):—(be a-) live again, revive.

327. ἀναζητέω **anazētĕō**, *an-ad-zay-teh'-o;* from *303* and *2212;* to *search* out:—seek.

328. ἀναζώννυμι **anazōnnumi**, *an-ad-zone'-noo-mee;* from *303* and *2224;* to *gird afresh:*—gird up.

329. ἀναζωπυρέω **anazōpurĕō**, *an-ad-zo-poor-eh'-o;* from *303* and a comp. of the base of *2226* and *4442;* to *re-enkindle:*—stir up.

330. ἀναθάλλω **anathallō**, *an-ath-al'-lo;* from *303* and θάλλω **thallō** (to *flourish*); to *revive:*—flourish again.

331. ἀνάθεμα **anathĕma**, *an-ath'-em-ah;* from *394;* a (religious) *ban* or (concr.) *excommunicated* (thing or person):—accursed, anathema, curse, × great.

332. ἀναθεματίζω **anathĕmatizō**, *an-ath-em-at-id'-zo;* from *331;* to *declare* or *vow* under penalty of execration:—(bind under a) curse, bind with an oath.

333. ἀναθεωρέω **anathĕōrĕō**, *an-ath-eh-o-reh'-o;* from *303* and *2334;* to *look again* (i.e. *attentively*) at (lit. or fig.):—behold, consider.

334. ἀνάθημα **anathēma**, *an-ath'-ay-mah;* from *394* [like *331*, but in a good sense]; a *votive* offering:—gift.

335. ἀναίδεια **anaidĕia**, *an-ah'-ee-die-ah';* from a comp. of *1* (as a neg. particle [comp. *427*]) and *127; impudence,* i.e. (by impl.) *importunity:*—importunity.

336. ἀναίρεσις **anairĕsis**, *an-ah'-ee-res-is;* from *337;* (the act of) *killing:*—death.

337. ἀναιρέω **anairĕō**, *an-ahee-reh'-o;* from *303* and (the act. of) *138;* to *take up,* i.e. *adopt;* by impl. to *take away* (violently), i.e. *abolish, murder:*—put to death, kill, slay, take away, take up.

338. ἀναίτιος **anaitiŏs**, *an-ah'-ee-tee-os;* from *1* (as a neg. particle) and *159* (in the sense of *156*); *innocent:*—blameless, guiltless.

339. ἀνακαθίζω **anakathizō**, *an-ak-ath-id'-zo;* from *303* and *2523;* prop. to *set up,* i.e. (reflex.) to *sit up:*—sit up.

340. ἀνακαινίζω **anakainizō**, *an-ak-ahee-nid'-zo;* from *303* and a der. of *2537;* to *restore:*—renew.

341. ἀνακαινόω **anakainŏō**, *an-ak-ahee-nŏ'-o;* from *303* and a der. of *2537;* to *renovate:*—renew.

342. ἀνακαίνωσις **anakainōsis**, *an-ak-ah'ee-no-sis;* from *341; renovation:*—renewing.

343. ἀνακαλύπτω **anakaluptō**, *an-ak-al-oop'-to;* from *303* (in the sense of *reversal*) and *2572;* to *unveil:*—open, ([un-]) taken away.

344. ἀνακάμπτω **anakamptō**, *an-ak-amp'-to;* from *303* and *2578;* to *turn back:*—(re-) turn.

345. ἀνάκειμαι **anakĕimai**, *an-ak-i'-mahee;* from *303* and *2749;* to *recline* (as a corpse or at a meal):—guest, lean, lie, sit (down, at meat), at the table.

346. ἀνακεφαλαίομαι **anakĕphalaiŏmai**, *an-ak-ef-al-ah'ee-om-ahee;* from *303* and *2775* (in its or. sense); to *sum up:*—briefly comprehend, gather together in one.

347. ἀνακλίνω **anaklinō**, *an-ak-lee'-no;* from *303* and *2827;* to *lean back:*—lay, (make) sit down.

348. ἀνακόπτω **anakŏptō**, *an-ak-op'-to;* from *303* and *2875;* to *beat back,* i.e. *check:*—hinder.

349. ἀνακράζω **anakrazō**, *an-ak-rad'-zo;* from *303* and *2896;* to *scream up* (aloud):—cry out.

350. ἀνακρίνω **anakrinō**, *an-ak-ree'-no;* from *303* and *2919;* prop. to *scrutinize,* i.e. (by impl.) *investigate, interrogate, determine:*—ask, question, discern, examine, judge, search.

351. ἀνάκρισις **anakrisis**, *an-ak'-ree-sis;* from *350;* a (judicial) *investigation:*—examination.

352. ἀνακύπτω **anakuptō**, *an-ak-oop'-to;* from *303* (in the sense of *reversal*) and *2955;* to *unbend,* i.e. *rise;* fig. *be elated:*—lift up, look up.

353. ἀναλαμβάνω **analambanō**, *an-al-am-ban'-o;* from *303* and *2983;* to *take up:*—receive up, take (in, unto, up).

354. ἀνάληψις **analēpsis**, *an-al'-ape-sis;* from *353; ascension:*—taking up.

355. ἀναλίσκω **analiskō**, *an-al-is'-ko;* from *303* and a form of the alternate of *138;* prop. to *use up,* i.e. *destroy:*—consume.

356. ἀναλογία **analŏgia**, *an-al-og-ee'-ah;* from a comp. of *303* and *3056; proportion:*—proportion.

357. ἀναλογίζομαι **analŏgizŏmai**, *an-al-og-id'-zom-ahee;* mid. from *356;* to *estimate,* i.e. (fig.) *contemplate:*—consider.

358. ἄναλος **analŏs**, *an'-al-os;* from *1* (as a neg. particle) and *251; saltless,* i.e. *insipid:*— × lose saltness.

359. ἀνάλυσις **analusis**, *an-al'-oo-sis;* from *360; departure:*—departure.

360. ἀναλύω **analuō**, *an-al-oo'-o;* from *303* and *3089;* to *break up,* i.e. *depart* (lit. or fig.):—depart, return.

361. ἀναμάρτητος **anamartētŏs**, *an-am-ar'-tay-tos;* from *1* (as a neg. particle) and a presumed der. of *264; sinless:*—that is without sin.

362. ἀναμένω **anemĕnō**, *an-am-en'-o;* from *303* and *3306;* to *await:*—wait for.

363. ἀναμιμνήσκω **anamimnēskō**, *an-am-im-nace'-ko;* from *303* and *3403;* to *remind;* reflex. to *recollect:*—call to mind, (bring to, call to, put in), remember (-brance).

364. ἀνάμνησις **anamnēsis**, *an-am'-nay-sis;* from *363; recollection:*—remembrance (again).

365. ἀνανεόω **ananĕŏō**, *an-an-neh-ŏ'-o;* from *303* and a der. of *3501;* to *renovate,* i.e. *reform:*—renew.

366. ἀνανήφω **ananēphō**, *an-an-ay'-fo;* from *303* and *3525;* to become *sober again,* i.e. (fig.) *regain* (one's) *senses:*—recover self.

367. Ἀνανίας **Ananias**, *an-an-ee'-as;* of Heb. or. [2608]; *Ananias,* the name of three Isr.:—Ananias.

368. ἀναντίρρητος **anantirrhētŏs**, *an-an-tir'-hray-tos;* from *1* (as a neg. particle) and a presumed der. of a comp. of *473* and *4483; indisputable:*—cannot be spoken against.

369. ἀναντιρρήτως **anantirrhētōs**, *an-an-tir-hray'-toce;* adv. from *368; promptly:*—without gainsaying.

370. ἀνάξιος **anaxiŏs**, *an-ax'-ee-os;* from *1* (as a neg. particle) and *514; unfit:*—unworthy.

371. ἀναξίως **anaxiōs**, *an-ax-ee'-oce;* adv. from *370; irreverently:*—unworthily.

372. ἀνάπαυσις **anapausis**, *an-ap'-ŏw-sis;* from *373; intermission;* by impl. *recreation:*—rest.

373. ἀναπαύω **anapauō**, *an-up-ŏw'-o;* from *303* and *3973;* (reflex.) to *repose* (lit. or fig. [*be exempt*], *remain*); by impl. to *refresh:*—take ease, refresh, (give, take) rest.

374. ἀναπείθω **anapĕithō**, *an-ap-i'-tho;* from *303* and *3982;* to *incite:*—persuade.

375. ἀναπέμπω **anapĕmpō**, *an-ap-em'-po;* from *303* and *3992;* to *send up* or *back:*—send (again).

376. ἀνάπηρος **anapĕrŏs**, *an-ap'-ay-ros;* from *303* (in the sense of *intensity*) and πῆρος **pērŏs** (*maimed*); *crippled:*—maimed.

377. ἀναπίπτω **anapipto**, *an-ap-ip'-to;* from *303* and *4098;* to *fall back,* i.e. *lie down, lean back:*—lean, sit down (to meat).

378. ἀναπληρόω **anaplērŏō**, *an-ap-lay-rŏ'-o;* from *303* and *4137;* to *complete;* by impl. to *occupy, supply;* fig. to *accomplish* (by coincidence or obedience):—fill up, fulfil, occupy, supply.

379. ἀναπολόγητος **anapŏlŏgētŏs**, *an-ap-ol-og'-ay-tos;* from *1* (as a neg. particle) and a presumed der. of *626; indefensible:*—without excuse, inexcuseable.

380. ἀναπτύσσω **anaptussō**, *an-ap-toos'-so;* from *303* (in the sense of *reversal*) and *4428;* to *unroll* (a scroll or volume):—open.

381. ἀνάπτω **anaptō**, *an-ap'-to;* from *303* and *681;* to *enkindle:*—kindle, light.

382. ἀναρίθμητος **anarithmētŏs**, *an-ar-ith'-may-tos;* from *1* (as a neg. particle) and a der. of *705; unnumbered,* i.e. *without number:*—innumerable.

383. ἀνασείω **anasĕiō**, *an-as-i'-o;* from *303* and *4579;* fig. to *excite:*—move, stir up.

384. ἀνασκευάζω **anaskĕuazō**, *an-ask-yoo-ad'-zo;* from *303* (in the sense of *reversal*) and a der. of *4632;* prop. to *pack up* (baggage), i.e. (by impl. and fig.) to *upset:*—subvert.

385. ἀνασπάω **anaspaō**, *an-as-pah'-o;* from *303* and *4685;* to *take up* or *extricate:*—draw up, pull out.

386. ἀνάστασις **anastasis**, *an-as'-tas-is;* from *450;* a *standing up* again, i.e. (lit.) a *resurrection* from death (individual, gen. or by impl. [its author]), or (fig.) a (moral) *recovery* (of spiritual truth):—raised to life again, resurrection, rise from the dead, that should rise, rising again.

387. ἀναστατόω **anastatŏō**, *an-as-tat-ŏ'-o;* from a der. of *450* (in the sense of *removal*); prop. to *drive out* of home, i.e. (by impl.) to *disturb* (lit. or fig.):—trouble, turn upside down, make an uproar.

388. ἀνασταυρόω **anastaurŏō**, *an-as-tŏw-rŏ'-o;* from *303* and *4717;* to *recrucify* (fig.):—crucify afresh.

389. ἀναστενάζω **anastĕnazō**, *an-as-ten-ad'-zo;* from *303* and *4727;* to *sigh deeply:*—sigh deeply.

390. ἀναστρέφω **anastrĕphō**, *an-as-tref'-o;* from *303* and *4762;* to *overturn;* also to *return;* by impl. to *busy* oneself, i.e. *remain, live:*—abide, behave self, have conversation, live, overthrow, pass, return, be used.

391. ἀναστροφή **anastrŏphē**, *an-as-trof-ay';* from *390; behavior:*—conversation.

392. ἀνατάσσομαι **anatassŏmai**, *an-at-as'-som-ahee;* from *303* and the mid. of *5021;* to *arrange:*—set in order.

393. ἀνατέλλω **anatĕllō**, *an-at-el'-lo;* from *303* and the base of *5056;* to (*cause to*) *arise:*—(a-, make to) rise, at the rising of, spring (up), be up.

394. ἀνατίθεμαι **anatithĕmai**, *an-at-ith'-em-ahee;* from *303* and the mid. of *5087;* to *set forth* (for oneself), i.e. *propound:*—communicate, declare.

395. ἀνατολή **anatŏlē**, *an-at-ol-ay'*; from *303*; a *rising* of light, i.e. *dawn* (fig.); by impl. the *east* (also in plur.):—dayspring, east, rising.

396. ἀνατρέπω **anatrĕpō**, *an-at-rep'-o*; from *303* and the base of *5157*; to *overturn* (fig.):—overthrow, subvert.

397. ἀνατρέφω **anatrĕphō**, *an-at-ref'-o*; from *303* and *5142*; to *rear* (phys. or ment.):—bring up, nourish (up).

398. ἀναφαίνω **anaphainō**, *an-af-ah'ee-no*; from *303* and *5316*; to *show*, i.e. (reflex.) *appear*, or (pass.) *have pointed* out:—(should) appear, discover.

399. ἀναφέρω **anaphĕrō**, *an-af-er'-o*; from *303* and *5342*; to *take up* (lit. or fig.):—bear, bring (carry, lead) up, offer (up).

400. ἀναφωνέω **anaphōnĕō**, *an-af-o-neh'-o*; from *303* and *5455*; to *exclaim*:—speak out.

401. ἀνάχυσις **anachusis**, *an-akh'-oo-sis*; from a comp. of *303* and χέω **chĕō** (to *pour*); prop. *effusion*, i.e. (fig.) *license*:—excess.

402. ἀναχωρέω **anachōrĕō**, *an-akh-o-reh'-o*; from *303* and *5562*; to *retire*:—depart, give place, go (turn) aside, withdraw self.

403. ἀνάψυξις **anapsuxis**, *an-aps'-ook-sis*; from *404*; prop. a *recovery of breath*, i.e. (fig.) *revival*:—revival.

404. ἀναψύχω **anapsuchō**, *an-aps-oo'-kho*; from *303* and *5594*; prop. to *cool off*, i.e. (fig.) *relieve*:—refresh.

405. ἀνδραποδιστής **andrapŏdistēs**, *an-drap-od-is-tace'*; from a der. of a comp. of *435* and *4228*; an *enslaver* (as bringing *men* to his *feet*):—menstealer.

406. Ἀνδρέας **Andrĕas**, *an-dreh'-as*; from *435*; *manly*; *Andreas*, an Isr.:—Andrew.

407. ἀνδρίζομαι **andrizŏmai**, *an-drid'-zom-ahee*; mid. from *435*; to *act manly*:—quit like men.

408. Ἀνδρόνικος **Andrŏnikŏs**, *an-dron'-ee-kos*; from *435* and *3534*; *man of victory*; *Andronicos*, an Isr.:—Andronicus.

409. ἀνδροφόνος **andrŏphŏnŏs**, *an-drof-on'-os*; from *435* and *5408*; a *murderer*:—manslayer.

410. ἀνέγκλητος **anĕgklētŏs**, *an-eng'-klay-tos*; from *1* (as a neg. particle) and a der. of *1458*; *unaccused*, i.e. (by impl.) *irreproachable*:—blameless.

411. ἀνεκδιήγητος **anĕkdiēgētŏs**, *an-ek-dee-ay'-gay-tos*; from *1* (as a neg. particle) and a presumed der. of *1555*; *not expounded* in full, i.e. *indescribable*:—unspeakable.

412. ἀνεκλάλητος **anĕklalētŏs**, *an-ek-lal'-ay-tos*; from *1* (as a neg. particle) and a presumed der. of *1583*; *not spoken out*, i.e. (by impl.) *unutterable*:—unspeakable.

413. ἀνέκλειπτος **anĕklĕiptŏs**, *an-ek'-lipe-tos*; from *1* (as a neg. particle) and a presumed der. of *1587*; *not left out*, i.e. (by impl.) *inexhaustible*:—that faileth not.

414. ἀνεκτότερος **anĕktŏtĕrŏs**, *an-ek-tot'-er-os*; compar. of a der. of *430*; *more endurable*:—more tolerable.

415. ἀνελεήμων **anĕlĕēmōn**, *an-eleh-ay'-mone*; from *1* (as a neg. particle) and *1655*; *merciless*:—unmerciful.

416. ἀνεμίζω **anemizō**, *an-em-id'-zo*; from *417*; to *toss with the wind*:—drive with the wind.

417. ἄνεμος **anĕmŏs**, *an'-em-os*; from the base of *109*; *wind*; (plur.) by impl. (the four) *quarters* (of the earth):—wind.

418. ἀνένδεκτος **anĕndĕktŏs**, *an-en'-dek-tos*; from *1* (as a neg. particle) and a der. of the same as *1735*; *unadmitted*, i.e. (by impl.) *not supposable*:—impossible.

419. ἀνεξερεύνητος **anĕxĕrĕunētŏs**, *an-ex-er-yoo'-nay-tos*; from *1* (as a neg. particle) and a presumed der. of *1830*; *not searched out*, i.e. (by impl.) *inscrutable*:—unsearchable.

420. ἀνεξίκακος **anĕxikakŏs**, *an-ex-ik'-ak-os*; from *430* and *2556*; *enduring of ill*, i.e. *forbearing*:—patient.

421. ἀνεξιχνίαστος **anĕxichniastŏs**, *an-ex-ikh-nee'-as-tos*; from *1* (as a neg. particle) and a presumed der. of a comp. of *1537* and a der. of *2487*; *not tracked out*, i.e. (by impl.) *untraceable*:—past finding out, unsearchable.

422. ἀνεπαίσχυντος **anĕpaischuntŏs**, *an-ep-ah'ee-skhoon-tos*; from *1* (as a neg. particle) and a presumed der. of a comp. of *1909* and *153*; *not ashamed*, i.e. (by impl.) *irreprehensible*:—that needeth not to be ashamed.

423. ἀνεπίληπτος **anĕpilēptŏs**, *an-ep-eel'-ape-tos*; from *1* (as a neg. particle) and a der. of *1949*; *not arrested*, i.e. (by impl.) *inculpable*:—blameless, unrebukeable.

424. ἀνέρχομαι **anĕrchŏmai**, *an-erkh'-om-ahee*; from *303* and *2064*; to *ascend*:—go up.

425. ἄνεσις **anĕsis**, *an'-es-is*; from *447*; *relaxation* or (fig.) *relief*:—eased, liberty, rest.

426. ἀνετάζω **anĕtazō**, *an-et-ad'-zo*; from *303* and ἐτάζω **ĕtazō** (to *test*); to *investigate* (judicially):—(should have) examine (-d).

427. ἄνευ **anĕu**, *an'-yoo*; a prim. particle; *without*:—without. Comp. *1*.

428. ἀνεύθετος **anĕuthĕtŏs**, *an-yoo'-the-tos*; from *1* (as a neg. particle) and *2111*; *not well set*, i.e. *inconvenient*:—not commodious.

429. ἀνευρίσκω **anĕuriskō**, *an-yoo-ris'-ko*; from *303* and *2147*; to *find out*:—find.

430. ἀνέχομαι **anĕchŏmai**, *an-ekh'-om-ahee*; mid. from *303* and *2192*; to *hold oneself up* against, i.e. (fig.) *put up* with:—bear with, endure, forbear, suffer.

431. ἀνέψιος **anĕpsiŏs**, *an-eps'-ee-os*; from *1* (as a particle of union) and an obsolete νέπος **nĕpŏs** (a *brood*); prop. *akin*, i.e. (spec.) a *cousin*:—sister's son.

432. ἄνηθον **anēthŏn**, *an'-ay-thon*; prob. of for. or.; *dill*:—anise.

433. ἀνήκω **anēkō**, *an-ay'-ko*; from *303* and *2240*; to *attain to*, i.e. (fig.) *be proper*:—convenient, be fit.

434. ἀνήμερος **anēmĕrŏs**, *an-ay'-mer-os*; from *1* (as a neg. particle) and ἥμερος **hēmĕrŏs** (*lame*); *savage*:—fierce.

435. ἀνήρ **anēr**, *an'-ayr*; a prim. word [comp. *444*]; a *man* (prop. as an individual male):—fellow, husband, man, sir.

436. ἀνθίστημι **anthistēmi**, *anth-is'-tay-mee*; from *473* and *2476*; to *stand against*, i.e. *oppose*:—resist, withstand.

437. ἀνθομολογέομαι **anthŏmŏlŏgĕŏmai**, *anth-om-ol-og-eh'-om-ahee*; from *473* and the mid. of *3670*; to *confess in turn*, i.e. *respond* in praise:—give thanks.

438. ἄνθος **anthŏs**, *anth'-os*; a prim. word; a *blossom*:—flower.

439. ἀνθρακιά **anthrakia**, *anth-rak-ee-ah'*; from *440*; a bed of burning *coals*:—fire of coals.

440. ἄνθραξ **anthrax**, *anth'-rax*; of uncert. der.; a live *coal*:—coal of fire.

441. ἀνθρωπάρεσκος **anthrōparĕskŏs**, *anth-ro-par'-es-kos*; from *444* and *700*; *man-courting*, i.e. *fawning*:—men-pleaser.

442. ἀνθρώπινος **anthrōpinŏs**, *anth-ro'-pee-nos*; from *444*; *human*:—human, common to man, man[-kind], [man-]kind, men's, after the manner of men.

443. ἀνθρωποκτόνος **anthrōpŏktŏnŏs**, *anth-ro-pok-ton'-os*; from *444* and κτείνω **ktĕinō** (to *kill*); a *manslayer*:—murderer. Comp. *5406*.

444. ἄνθρωπος **anthrōpŏs**, *anth'-ro-pos*; from *435* and ὤψ **ōps** (the *countenance*; from *3700*); *man-faced*, i.e. a *human* being:—certain, man.

445. ἀνθυπατεύω **anthupatĕuō**, *anth-oo-pat-yoo'-o*; from *446*; to *act as proconsul*:—be the deputy.

446. ἀνθύπατος **anthupatŏs**, *anth-oo'-pat-os*; from *473* and a superlative of *5228*; *instead* of the *highest* officer, i.e. (spec.) a Roman *proconsul*:—deputy.

447. ἀνίημι **aniēmi**, *an-ee'-ay-mee*; from *303* and ἵημι **hiēmi** (to *send*); to *let up*, i.e. (lit.) *slacken*, or (fig.) *desert*, *desist* from:—forbear, leave, loose.

448. ἀνίλεως **anilĕōs**, *an-ee'-leh-oce*; from *1* (as a neg. particle) and *2436*; *inexorable*:—without mercy.

449. ἄνιπτος **aniptŏs**, *an'-ip-tos*; from *1* (as a neg. particle) and a presumed der. of *3538*; *without ablution*:—unwashen.

450. ἀνίστημι **anistēmi**, *an-is'-tay-mee*; from *303* and *2476*; to *stand up* (lit. or fig., trans. or intrans.):—arise, lift up, raise up (again), rise (again), stand up (-right).

451. Ἄννα **Anna**, *an'-nah*; of Heb. or. [2584]; *Anna*, an Israelitess:—Anna.

452. Ἄννας **Annas**, *an'-nas*; of Heb. or. [2608]; *Annas* (i.e. *367*), an Isr.:—Annas.

453. ἀνόητος **anŏētŏs**, *an-o'-ay-tos*; from *1* (as a neg. particle) and a der. of *3539*; *unintelligent*; by impl. *sensual*:—fool (-ish), unwise.

454. ανοια **anŏia**, *an'-oy-ah*; from a comp. of *1* (as a neg. particle) and *3563*; *stupidity*; by impl. *rage*:—folly, madness.

455. ἀνοίγω **anŏigō**, *an-oy'-go*; from *303* and οἴγω **ŏigō** (to *open*); to *open up* (lit. or fig., in various applications):—open.

456. ἀνοικοδομέω **anŏikŏdŏmĕō**, *an-oy-kod-om-eh'-o*; from *303* and *3618*; to *rebuild*:—build again.

457. ἄνοιξις **anŏixis**, *an'-oix-is*; from *455*; *opening* (throat):—× open.

458. ἀνομία **anŏmia**, *an-om-ee'-ah*; from *459*; *illegality*, i.e. *violation of law* or (gen.) *wickedness*:—iniquity, × transgress (-ion of) the law, unrighteousness.

459. ἄνομος **anŏmŏs**, *an'-om-os*; from *1* (as a neg. particle) and *3551*; *lawless*, i.e. (neg.) *not subject to* (the Jewish) *law*; (by impl. a *Gentile*), or (pos.) *wicked*:—without law, lawless, transgressor, unlawful, wicked.

460. ἀνόμως **anŏmōs**, *an-om'-oce*; adv. from *459*; *lawlessly*, i.e. (spec.) *not amenable to* (the Jewish) *law*:—without law.

461. ἀνορθόω **anŏrthŏō**, *an-orth-o'-o*; from *303* and a der. of the base of *3717*; to *straighten up*:—lift (set) up, make straight.

462. ἀνόσιος **anŏsiŏs**, *an-os'-ee-os*; from *1* (as a neg. particle) and *3741*; *wicked*:—unholy.

463. ἀνοχή **anŏchē**, *an-okh-ay'*; from *430*; *self-restraint*, i.e. *tolerance*:—forbearance.

464. ἀνταγωνίζομαι **antagōnizŏmai**, *an-tag-o-nid'-zom-ahee*; from *473* and *75*; to *struggle against* (fig.) ["antagonize"]:—strive against.

465. ἀντάλλαγμα **antallagma**, *an-tal'-ag-mah*; from a comp. of *473* and *236*; an *equivalent* or *ransom*:—in exchange.

466. ἀνταναπληρόω **antanaplērŏō**, *an-tan-ap-lay-ro'-o*; from *473* and *378*; to *supplement*:—fill up.

467. ἀνταποδίδωμι **antapŏdidōmi**, *an-tap-od-ee'-do-mee*; from *473* and *591*; to *requite* (good or evil):—recompense, render, repay.

468. ἀνταπόδομα **antapŏdŏma**, *an-tap-od'-om-ah*; from *467*; a *requital* (prop. the thing):—recompense.

469. ἀνταπόδοσις **antapŏdŏsis**, *an-tap-od'-os-is*; from *467*; *requital* (prop. the act):—reward.

470. ἀνταποκρίνομαι **antapŏkrinŏmai**, *an-tap-ok-ree'-nom-ahee*; from *473* and *611*; to *contradict* or *dispute*:—answer again, reply against.

471. ἀντέπω **antĕpō**, *an-tep'-o*; from *473* and *2036*; to *refute* or *deny*:—gainsay, say against.

472. ἀντέχομαι **antĕchŏmai**, *an-tekh'-om-ahee*; from *473* and the mid. of *2192*; to *hold* oneself *opposite* to, i.e. (by impl.) *adhere to*; by extens. to *care for*:—hold fast, hold to, support.

473. ἀντί **anti**, *an-tee'*; a prim. particle; *opposite*, i.e. *instead* or *because* of (rarely *in addition* to):—for, in the room of. Often used in composition to denote *contrast*, *requital*, *substitution*, *correspondence*, etc.

474. ἀντιβάλλω **antiballō**, *an-tee-bal'-lo;* from *473* and *906;* to *bandy:*—have.

475. ἀντιδιατίθεμαι **antidiatithĕmai**, *an-tee-dee-at-eeth'-em-ahee;* from *473* and *1303;* to *set oneself opposite,* i.e. *be disputatious:*—that oppose themselves.

476. ἀντίδικος **antidikŏs**, *an-tid'-ee-kos;* from *473* and *1349;* an *opponent* (in a lawsuit); spec. *Satan* (as the arch-enemy):—adversary.

477. ἀντίθεσις **antithĕsis**, *an-tith'-es-is;* from a comp. of *473* and *5087;* *opposition,* i.e. a *conflict* (of theories):—opposition.

478. ἀντικαθίστημι **antikathistēmi**, *an-tee-kath-is'-tay-mee;* from *473* and *2525;* to *set down* (troops) *against,* i.e. *withstand:*—resist.

479. ἀντικαλέω **antikalĕō**, *an-tee-kal-eh'-o;* from *473* and *2564;* to *invite in return:*—bid again.

480. ἀντίκειμαι **antikĕimai**, *an-tik'-i-mahee;* from *473* and *2749;* to *lie opposite,* i.e. *be adverse* (fig. *repugnant*) to:—adversary, be contrary, oppose.

481. ἀντικρύ **antikru**, *an-tee-kroo';* prol. from *473;* *opposite:*—over against.

482. ἀντιλαμβάνομαι **antilambanŏmai**, *an-tee-lam-ban'-om-ahee;* from *473* and the mid. of *2983;* to *take* hold of *in turn,* i.e. *succor;* also to *participate:*—help, partaker, support.

483. ἀντίλεγω **antilĕgō**, *an-til'-eg-o;* from *473* and *3004;* to *dispute, refuse:*—answer again, contradict, deny, gainsay (-er), speak against.

484. ἀντίληψις **antilēpsis**, *an-til'-ape-sis;* from *482;* *relief:*—help.

485. ἀντιλογία **antilŏgia**, *an-tee-log-ee'-ah;* from a der. of *483;* *dispute, disobedience:*—contradiction, gainsaying, strife.

486. ἀντιλοιδορέω **antilŏidŏrĕō**, *an-tee-loy-dor-eh'-o;* from *473* and *3058;* to *rail in reply:*—revile again.

487. ἀντίλυτρον **antilutrŏn**, *an-til'-oo-tron;* from *473* and *3083;* a *redemption-price:*—ransom.

488. ἀντιμετρέω **antimĕtrĕō**, *an-tee-met-reh'-o;* from *473* and *3354;* to *mete in return:*—measure again.

489. ἀντιμισθία **antimisthia**, *an-tee-mis-thee'-ah;* from a comp. of *473* and *3408;* *requital, correspondence:*—recompense.

490. Ἀντιόχεια **Antiŏchĕia**, *an-tee-okh'-i-ah;* from Ἀντίοχος **Antiŏchus** (a Syrian king); *Antiochia,* a place in Syria:—Antioch.

491. Ἀντιοχεύς **Antiŏchĕus**, *an-tee-okh-yoos';* from *490;* an *Antiochian* or inhab. of Antiochia:—of Antioch.

492. ἀντιπαρέρχομαι **antiparĕrchŏmai**, *an-tee-par-er'-khom-ahee;* from *473* and *3928;* to *go along opposite:*—pass by on the other side.

493. Ἀντίπας **Antipas**, *an-tee'-pas;* contr. for a comp. of *473* and a der. of *3962;* *Antipas,* a Chr.:—Antipas.

494. Ἀντιπατρίς **Antipatris**, *an-tip-at-rece';* from the same as *493;* *Antipatris,* a place in Pal.:—Antipatris.

495. ἀντιπέραν **antipĕran**, *an-tee-per'-an;* from *473* and *4008;* *on the opposite side:*—over against.

496. ἀντιπίπτω **antipiptō**, *an-tee-pip'-to;* from *473* and *4098* (includ. its alt.); to *oppose:*—resist.

497. ἀντιστρατεύομαι **antistratĕuŏmai**, *an-tee-strat-yoo'-om-ahee;* from *473* and *4754;* (fig.) to *attack,* i.e. (by impl.) *destroy:*—war against.

498. ἀντιτάσσομαι **antitassŏmai**, *an-tee-tas'-som-ahee;* from *473* and the mid. of *5021;* to *range oneself against,* i.e. *oppose:*—oppose themselves, resist.

499. ἀντίτυπον **antitupŏn**, *an-teet'-oo-pon;* neut. of a comp. of *473* and *5179;* *corresponding* ["antitype"], i.e. a *representative, counterpart:*—(like) figure (whereunto).

500. ἀντίχριστος **antichristŏs**, *an-tee'-khris-tos:* from *473* and *5547;* an *opponent of the Messiah:*—antichrist.

501. ἀντλέω **antlĕō**, *ant-leh-o;* from ἄντλος **antlŏs** (the *hold* of a ship); to *bale* up (prop. bilge water), i.e. *dip* water (with a bucket, pitcher, etc.):—draw (out).

502. ἄντλημα **antlēma**, *ant'-lay-mah;* from *501;* a *baling-vessel:*—thing to draw with.

503. ἀντοφθαλμέω **antŏphthalmĕō**, *ant-of-thal-meh'-o;* from a comp. of *473* and *3788;* to *face:*—bear up into.

504. ἄνυδρος **anudrŏs**, *an'-oo-dros;* from *1* (as a neg. particle) and *5204;* *waterless,* i.e. *dry:*—dry, without water.

505. ἀνυπόκριτος **anupŏkritŏs**, *an-oo-pok'-ree-tos;* from *1* (as a neg. particle) and a presumed der. of *5271;* *undissembled,* i.e. *sincere:*—without dissimulation (hypocrisy), unfeigned.

506. ἀνυπότακτος **anupŏtaktŏs**, *an-oo-pot'-ak-tos;* from *1* (as a neg. particle) and a presumed der. of *5293;* *unsubdued,* i.e. *insubordinate* (in fact or temper):—disobedient, that is not put under, unruly.

507. ἄνω **anō**, *an'-o;* adv. from *473;* *upward* or *on the top:*—above, brim, high, up.

508. ἀνώγεον **anōgĕōn**, *an-ogue'-eh-on;* from *507* and *1093;* *above* the *ground,* i.e. (prop.) the *second floor* of a building; used for a *dome* or a *balcony* on the upper story:—upper room.

509. ἄνωθεν **anōthĕn**, *an'-o-then;* from *507;* *from above;* by anal. *from the first;* by impl. *anew:*—from above, again, from the beginning (very first), the top.

510. ἀνωτερικός **anōtĕrikŏs**, *an-o-ter-ee-kos';* from *511;* *superior,* i.e. (locally) *more remote:*—upper.

511. ἀνώτερος **anōtĕrŏs**, *an-o'-ter-os;* comp. degree of *507;* *upper,* i.e. (neut. as adv.) to a *more conspicuous* place, in a *former* part of the book:—above, higher.

512. ἀνωφέλες **anōphĕlĕs**, *an-o-fel'-ace;* from *1* (as a neg. particle) and the base of *5624;* *useless* or (neut.) *inutility:*—unprofitable (-ness).

513. ἀξίνη **axinē**, *ax-ee'-nay;* prob. from ἄγνυμι **agnumi** (to *break;* comp. *4486*); an *axe:*—axe.

514. ἄξιος **axiŏs**, *ax'-ee-os;* prob. from *71;* *deserving, comparable* or *suitable* (as if *drawing* praise):—due reward, meet, [un-] worthy.

515. ἀξιόω **axiŏō**, *ax-ee-ŏ'-o;* from *514;* to *deem entitled* or *fit:*—desire, think good, count (think) worthy.

516. ἀξίως **axiōs**, *ax-ee'-oce;* adv. from *514;* *appropriately:*—as becometh, after a godly sort, worthily (-thy).

517. ἀόρατος **aŏratŏs**, *ah-or'-at-os;* from *1* (as a neg. particle) and *3707;* *invisible:*—invisible (thing).

518. ἀπαγγέλλω **apaggĕllō**, *ap-ang-el'-lo;* from *575* and the base of *32;* to *announce:*—bring word (again), declare, report, shew (again), tell.

519. ἀπάγχομαι **apagchŏmai**, *ap-ang'-khom-ahee;* from *575* and ἄγχω **agchō** (to *choke;* akin to the base of *43*); to *strangle oneself off* (i.e. to death):—hang himself.

520. ἀπάγω **apagō**, *ap-ag'-o;* from *575* and *71;* to *take off* (in various senses):—bring, carry away, lead (away), put to death, take away.

521. ἀπαίδευτος **apaidĕutŏs**, *ap-ah'ee-dyoo-tos;* from *1* (as a neg. particle) and a der. of *3811;* *uninstructed,* i.e. (fig.) *stupid:*—unlearned.

522. ἀπαίρω **apairō**, *ap-ah'ee-ro;* from *575* and *142;* to *lift off,* i.e. *remove:*—take (away).

523. ἀπαιτέω **apaitĕō**, *ap-ah'ee-teh-o;* from *575* and *154;* to *demand back:*—ask again, require.

524. ἀπαλγέω **apalgĕō**, *ap-alg-eh'-o;* from *575* and ἀλγέω **algĕō** (to *smart*); to *grieve out,* i.e. *become apathetic:*—be past feeling.

525. ἀπαλλάσσω **apallassō**, *ap-al-las'-so;* from *575* and *236;* to *change away,* i.e. *release,* (reflex.) *remove:*—deliver, depart.

526. ἀπαλλοτριόω **apallŏtriŏō**, *ap-al-lot-ree-ŏ'-o;* from *575* and a der. of *245;* to *estrange away,* i.e. (pass. and fig.) to *be non-participant:*—alienate, be alien.

527. ἁπαλός **apalŏs**, *ap-al-os';* of uncert. der.; *soft:*—tender.

528. ἀπαντάω **apantaō**, *ap-an-tah'-o;* from *575* and a der. of *473;* to *meet away,* i.e. *encounter:*—meet.

529. ἀπάντησις **apantēsis**, *ap-an'-tay-sis;* from *528;* a (friendly) *encounter:*—meet.

530. ἅπαξ **hapax**, *hap'-ax;* prob. from *537;* *one* (or a *single*) *time* (numerically or conclusively):—once.

531. ἀπαράβατος **aparabatŏs**, *ap-ar-ab'-at-os;* from *1* (as a neg. particle) and a der. of *3845;* *not passing away,* i.e. *untransferable* (perpetual):—unchangeable.

532. ἀπαρασκεύαστος **aparaskĕuastŏs**, *ap-ar-ask-yoo'-as-tos;* from *1* (as a neg. particle) and a der. of *3903;* *unready:*—unprepared.

533. ἀπαρνέομαι **aparnĕŏmai**, *ap-ar-neh'-om-ahee;* from *575* and *720;* to *deny utterly,* i.e. *disown, abstain:*—deny.

534. ἀπάρτι **aparti**, *ap-ar'-tee;* from *575* and *737;* *from now,* i.e. *henceforth* (*already*):—from henceforth.

535. ἀπαρτισμός **apartismŏs**, *ap-ar-tis-mos';* from a der. of *534;* *completion:*—finishing.

536. ἀπαρχή **aparchē**, *ap-ar-khay';* from a comp. of *575* and *756;* a *beginning* of sacrifice, i.e. the (Jewish) *first-fruit* (fig.):—first-fruits.

537. ἅπας **hapas**, *hap'-as;* from *1* (as a particle of union) and *3956;* absolutely *all* or (sing.) *every* one:—all (things), every (one), whole.

538. ἀπατάω **apataō**, *ap-at-ah'-o;* of uncert. der.; to *cheat,* i.e. *delude:*—deceive.

539. ἀπάτη **apatē**, *ap-at'-ay;* from *538;* *delusion:*—deceit (-ful, -fulness), deceivableness (-ving).

540. ἀπάτωρ **apatōr**, *ap-at'-ore;* from *1* (as a neg. particle) and *3962;* *fatherless,* i.e. *of unrecorded paternity:*—without father.

541. ἀπαύγασμα **apaugasma**, *ap-ŏw'-gas-mah;* from a comp. of *575* and *826;* an *off-flash,* i.e. *effulgence:*—brightness.

542. ἀπείδω **apĕidō**, *ap-i'-do;* from *575* and the same as *1492;* to *see* fully:—see.

543. ἀπείθεια **apĕithĕia**, *ap-i'-thi-ah;* from *545;* *disbelief* (obstinate and rebellious):—disobedience, unbelief.

544. ἀπειθέω **apĕithĕō**, *ap-i-theh'-o;* from *545;* to *disbelieve* (wilfully and perversely):—not believe, disobedient, obey not, unbelieving.

545. ἀπειθής **apĕithēs**, *ap-i-thace';* from *1* (as a neg. particle) and *3982;* *unpersuadable,* i.e. *contumacious:*—disobedient.

546. ἀπειλέω **apĕilĕō**, *ap-i-leh'-o;* of uncert. der.; to *menace;* by impl. to *forbid:*—threaten.

547. ἀπειλή **apĕilē**, *ap-i-lay';* from *546;* a *menace:*— × straitly, threatening.

548. ἄπειμι **apĕimi**, *ap'-i-mee;* from *575* and *1510;* to *be away:*—be absent. Comp. *549.*

549. ἄπειμι **apĕimi**, *ap'-i-mee;* from *575* and εἶμι **ĕimi** (to *go*); to *go away:*—go. Comp. *548.*

550. ἀπειπόμην **apĕipŏmēn**, *ap-i-pom'-ane;* reflex. past of a comp. of *575* and *2036;* to *say off* for oneself, i.e. *disown:*—renounce.

551. ἀπείραστος **apĕirastŏs**, *ap-i'-ras-tos;* from *1* (as a neg. particle) and a presumed der. of *3987;* *untried,* i.e. *not temptable:*—not to be tempted.

552. ἄπειρος **apĕirŏs**, *ap'-i-ros;* from *1* (as a neg. particle) and *3984;* *inexperienced,* i.e. *ignorant:*—unskilful.

553. ἀπεκδέχομαι **apĕkdĕchŏmai**, *ap-ek-dekh'-om-ahee;* from *575* and *1551;* to *expect fully:*—look (wait) for.

554. ἀπεκδύομαι **apĕkduŏmai**, *ap-ek-doo'-om-ahee;* mid. from *575* and *1562;* to *divest wholly* oneself, or (for oneself) *despoil:*—put off, spoil.

555. ἀπέκδυσις **apĕkdusis**, *ap-ek'-doo-sis;* from *554;* *divestment:*—putting off.

556. ἀπελαύνω **apĕlaunō**, *ap-el-ŏw'-no;* from *575* and *1643;* to *dismiss:*—drive.

557. **ἀπελεγμός apĕlĕgmŏs**, *ap-el-eg-mos'*; from a comp. of *575* and *1651*; *refutation*, i.e. (by impl.) *contempt*:—nought.

558. **ἀπελεύθερος apĕlĕuthĕrŏs**, *ap-el-yoo'-ther-os*; from *575* and *1658*; one *freed away*, i.e. a *freedman*:—freeman.

559. **Ἀπελλῆς Apĕllēs**, *ap-el-lace'*; of Lat. or.; *Apelles*, a Chr.:—Apelles.

560. **ἀπελπίζω apĕlpizō**, *ap-el-pid'-zo*; from *575* and *1679*; to *hope out*, i.e. *fully expect*:—hope for again.

561. **ἀπέναντι apĕnanti**, *ap-en'-an-tee*; from *575* and *1725*; *from in front*, i.e. *opposite*, *before* or *against*:—before, contrary, over against, in the presence of.

ἀπέπω apĕpō. See *550*.

562. **ἀπέραντος apĕrantŏs**, *ap-er'-an-tos*; from *1* (as a neg. particle) and a secondary der. of *4008*; *unfinished*, i.e. (by impl.) *interminable*:—endless.

563. **ἀπερισπάστως apĕrispastōs**, *ap-er-is-pas-toce'*; adv. from a comp. of *1* (as a neg. particle) and a presumed der. of *4049*; *undistractedly*, i.e. *free from* (domestic) *solicitude*:—without distraction.

564. **ἀπερίτμητος apĕritmētŏs**, *ap-er-eet'-may-tos*; from *1* (as a neg. particle) and a presumed der. of *4059*; *uncircumcised* (fig.):—uncircumcised.

565. **ἀπέρχομαι apĕrchŏmai**, *ap-erkh'-om-ahee*; from *575* and *2064*; to *go off* (i.e. *depart*), *aside* (i.e. *apart*) or *behind* (i.e. *follow*), lit. or fig.:—come, depart, go (aside, away, back, out, . . . ways), pass away, be past.

566. **ἀπέχει apĕchĕi**, *ap-ekh'-i*; 3d pers. sing. pres. indic. act. of *568* used impers.; *it is sufficient*:—it is enough.

567. **ἀπέχομαι apĕchŏmai**, *ap-ekh'-om-ahee*; mid. (reflex.) of *568*; to *hold oneself off*, i.e. *refrain*:—abstain.

568. **ἀπέχω apĕchō**, *ap-ekh'-o*; from *575* and *2192*; (act.) to *have out*, i.e. *receive in full*; (intrans.) to *keep* (oneself) *away*, i.e. *be distant* (lit. or fig.):—be, have, receive.

569. **ἀπιστέω apistĕō**, *ap-is-teh'-o*; from *571*; to *be unbelieving*, i.e. (trans.) *disbelieve*, or (by impl.) *disobey*:—believe not.

570. **ἀπιστία apistia**, *ap-is-tee'-ah*; from *571*; *faithlessness*, i.e. (neg.) *disbelief* (*want of* Chr. *faith*), or (pos.) *unfaithfulness* (*disobedience*):—unbelief.

571. **ἄπιστος apistŏs**, *ap'-is-tos*; from *1* (as a neg. particle) and *4103*; (act.) *disbelieving*, i.e. *without* Chr. *faith* (spec. a *heathen*); (pass.) *untrustworthy* (person), or *incredible* (thing):—that believeth not, faithless, incredible thing, infidel, unbeliever (-ing).

572. **ἁπλότης haplŏtēs**, *hap-lot'-ace*; from *573*; *singleness*, i.e. (subj.) *sincerity* (*without dissimulation or self-seeking*), or (obj.) *generosity* (*copious bestowal*):—bountifulness, liberal (-ity), simplicity, singleness.

573. **ἁπλοῦς haplŏus**, *hap-looce'*; prob. from *1* (as a particle of union) and the base of *4120*; prop. *folded together*, i.e. *single* (fig. *clear*):—single.

574. **ἁπλῶς haplōs**, *hap-loce'*; adv. from *573* (in the obj. sense of *572*); *bountifully*:—liberally.

575. **ἀπό apŏ**, *apŏ'*; a prim. particle; "*off*," i.e. *away* (from something near), in various senses (of place, time, or relation; lit. or fig.):—(× here-) after, ago, at, because of, before, by (the space of), for (-th), from, in, (out) of, off, (up-) on (-ce), since, with. In composition (as a prefix) it usually denotes *separation*, *departure*, *cessation*, *completion*, *reversal*, etc.

576. **ἀποβαίνω apŏbainō**, *ap-ob-ah'ee-no*; from *575* and the base of *939*; lit. to *disembark*; fig. to *eventuate*:—become, go out, turn.

577. **ἀποβάλλω apŏballō**, *ap-ob-al'-lo*; from *575* and *906*; to *throw off*; fig. to *lose*:—cast away.

578. **ἀποβλέπω apŏblĕpō**, *ap-ob-lep'-o*; from *575* and *991*; to *look away* from everything else, i.e. (fig.) intently *regard*:—have respect.

579. **ἀπόβλητος apŏblētŏs**, *ap-ob'-lay-tos*; from *577*; *cast off*, i.e. (fig.) such as to *be rejected*:—be refused.

580. **ἀποβολή apŏbŏlē**, *ap-ob-ol-ay'*; from *577*; *rejection*; fig. *loss*:—casting away, loss.

581. **ἀπογενόμενος apŏgĕnŏmĕnŏs**, *ap-og-en-om'-en-os*; past part. of a comp. of *575* and *1096*; *absent*, i.e. *deceased* (fig. *renounced*):—being dead.

582. **ἀπογραφή apŏgraphē**, *ap-og-raf-ay'*; from *583*; an *enrollment*; by impl. an *assessment*:—taxing.

583. **ἀπογράφω apŏgraphō**, *ap-og-raf'-o*; from *575* and *1125*; to *write off* (a copy or list), i.e. *enrol*:—tax, write.

584. **ἀποδείκνυμι apŏdĕiknumi**, *ap-od-ike'-noo-mee*; from *575* and *1166*; to *show off*, i.e. *exhibit*; fig. to *demonstrate*, i.e. *accredit*:—(ap-) prove, set forth, shew.

585. **ἀπόδειξις apŏdĕixis**, *ap-od'-ike-sis*; from *584*; *manifestation*:—demonstration.

586. **ἀποδεκατόω apŏdĕkatŏō**, *ap-od-ek-at-ŏ'-o*; from *575* and *1183*; to *tithe* (as debtor or creditor):—(give, pay, take) tithe.

587. **ἀπόδεκτος apŏdĕktŏs**, *ap-od'-ek-tos*; from *588*; *accepted*, i.e. *agreeable*:—acceptable.

588. **ἀποδέχομαι apŏdĕchŏmai**, *ap-od-ekh'-om-ahee*; from *575* and *1209*; to *take fully*, i.e. *welcome* (persons), *approve* (things):—accept, receive (gladly).

589. **ἀποδημέω apŏdēmĕō**, *ap-od-ay-meh'-o*; from *590*; to *go abroad*, i.e. *visit a foreign land*:—go (travel) into a far country, journey.

590. **ἀπόδημος apŏdēmŏs**, *ap-od'-ay-mos*; from *575* and *1218*; *absent from* one's own *people*, i.e. a *foreign traveller*:—taking a far journey.

591. **ἀποδίδωμι apŏdidōmi**, *ap-od-eed'-o-mee*; from *575* and *1325*; to *give away*, i.e. *up*, *over*, *back*, etc. (in various applications):—deliver (again), give (again), (re-) pay (-ment be made), perform, recompense, render, requite, restore, reward, sell, yield.

592. **ἀποδιορίζω apŏdiŏrizō**, *ap-od-ee-or-id'-zo*; from *575* and a comp. of *1223* and *3724*; to *disjoin* (by a boundary, fig. a party):—separate.

593. **ἀποδοκιμάζω apŏdŏkimazō**, *ap-od-ok-ee-mad'-zo*; from *575* and *1381*; to *disapprove*, i.e. (by impl.) to *repudiate*:—disallow, reject.

594. **ἀποδοχή apŏdŏchē**, *ap-od-okh-ay'*; from *588*; *acceptance*:—acceptation.

595. **ἀπόθεσις apŏthĕsis**, *ap-oth'-es-is*; from *659*; a *laying aside* (lit. or fig.):—putting away (off).

596. **ἀποθήκη apŏthēkē**, *ap-oth-ay'-kay*; from *659*; a *repository*. i.e. *granary*:—barn, garner.

597. **ἀποθησαυρίζω apŏthēsaurizō**, *ap-oth-ay-sow-rid'-zo*; from *575* and *2343*; to *treasure away*:—lay up in store.

598. **ἀποθλίβω apŏthlibō**, *ap-oth-lee'-bo*; from *575* and *2346*; to *crowd* from (every side):—press.

599. **ἀποθνήσκω apŏthnēskō**, *ap-oth-nace'-ko*; from *575* and *2348*; to *die off* (lit. or fig.):—be dead, death, die, lie a-dying, be slain (× with).

600. **ἀποκαθίστημι apŏkathistēmi**, *ap-ok-ath-is'-tay-mee*; from *575* and *2525*; to *reconstitute* (in health, home or organization):—restore (again).

601. **ἀποκαλύπτω apŏkaluptō**, *ap-ok-al-oop'-to*; from *575* and *2572*; to take *off the cover*, i.e. *disclose*:—reveal.

602. **ἀποκάλυψις apŏkalupsis**, *ap-ok-al'-oop-sis*; from *601*; *disclosure*:—appearing, coming, lighten, manifestation, be revealed, revelation.

603. **ἀποκαραδοκία apŏkaradŏkia**, *ap-ok-ar-ad-ok-ee'-ah*; from a comp. of *575* and a comp. of **κάρα kara** (the *head*) and *1380* (in the sense of *watching*); *intense anticipation*:—earnest expectation.

604. **ἀποκαταλλάσσω apŏkatallassō**, *ap-ok-at-al-las'-so*; from *575* and *2644*; to *reconcile fully*:—reconcile.

605. **ἀποκατάστασις apŏkatastasis**, *ap-ok-at-as'-tas-is*; from *600*; *reconstitution*:—restitution.

606. **ἀπόκειμαι apŏkĕimai**, *ap-ok'-i-mahee*; from *575* and *2749*; to *be reserved*; fig. to *await*:—be appointed, (be) laid up.

607. **ἀποκεφαλίζω apŏkĕphalizō**, *ap-ok-ef-al-id'-zo*; from *575* and *2776*; to *decapitate*:—behead.

608. **ἀποκλείω apŏklĕiō**, *ap-ok-li'-o*; from *575* and *2808*; to *close fully*:—shut up.

609. **ἀποκόπτω apŏkŏptō**, *ap-ok-op'-to*; from *575* and *2875*; to *amputate*; reflex. (by irony) to *mutilate* (the privy parts):—cut off. Comp. *2699*.

610. **ἀπόκριμα apŏkrima**, *ap-ok'-ree-mah*; from *611* (in its orig. sense of *judging*); a judicial *decision*:—sentence.

611. **ἀποκρίνομαι apŏkrinŏmai**, *ap-ok-ree'-nom-ahee*; from *575* and **κρινω krino**; to *conclude for oneself*, i.e. (by impl.) to *respond*; by Hebr. [comp. 6030] to *begin to speak* (where an address is expected):—answer.

612. **ἀπόκρισις apŏkrisis**, *ap-ok'-ree-sis*; from *611*; a *response*:—answer.

613. **ἀποκρύπτω apŏkruptō**, *ap-ok-roop'-to*; from *575* and *2928*; to *conceal away* (i.e. *fully*); fig. to *keep secret*:—hide.

614. **ἀπόκρυφος apŏkruphŏs**, *ap-ok'-roo-fos*; from *613*; *secret*; by impl. *treasured*:—hid, kept secret.

615. **ἀποκτείνω apŏktĕinō**, *ap-ok-ti'-no*; from *575* and **κτείνω ktĕinō** (to *slay*); to *kill* outright; fig. to *destroy*:—put to death, kill, slay.

616. **ἀποκυέω apŏkuĕō**, *ap-ok-oo-eh'o*; from *575* and the base of *2949*; to *breed forth*, i.e. (by transf.) to *generate* (fig.):—beget, bring forth.

617. **ἀποκυλίω apŏkuliō**, *ap-ok-oo-lee'-o*; from *575* and *2947*; to *roll away*:—roll away (back).

618. **ἀπολαμβάνω apŏlambanō**, *ap-ol-am-ban'-o*; from *575* and *2983*; to *receive* (spec. in *full*, or as a host); also to *take aside*:—receive, take.

619. **ἀπόλαυσις apŏlausis**, *ap-ol'-ŏw-sis*; from a comp. of *575* and **λαύω lauō** (to *enjoy*); full *enjoyment*:—enjoy (-ment).

620. **ἀπολείπω apŏlĕipō**, *ap-ol-ipe'-o*; from *575* and *3007*; to *leave* behind (pass. *remain*); by impl. to *forsake*:—leave, remain.

621. **ἀπολείχω apŏlĕichō**, *ap-ol-i'-kho*; from *575* and **λείχω lĕichō** (to "*lick*"); to *lick* clean:—lick.

622. **ἀπόλλυμι apŏllumi**, *ap-ol'-loo-mee*; from *575* and the base of *3639*; to *destroy* fully (reflex. to *perish*, or *lose*), lit. or fig.:—destroy, die, lose, mar, perish.

623. **Ἀπολλύων Apŏlluōn**, *ap-ol-loo'-ohn*; act. part. of *622*; a *destroyer* (i.e. *Satan*);—Apollyon.

624. **Ἀπολλωνία Apŏllōnia**, *ap-ol-lo-nee'-ah*; from the pagan deity **Ἀπόλλων Apŏllōn** (i.e. the *sun*; from *622*); *Apollonia*, a place in Macedonia:—Apollonia.

625. **Ἀπολλώς Apŏllōs**, *ap-ol-loce'*; prob. from the same as *624*; *Apollos*, an Isr.:—Apollos.

626. **ἀπολογέομαι apŏlŏgĕŏmai**, *ap-ol-og-eh'-om-ahee*: mid. from a comp. of *575* and *3056*; to give an *account* (legal *plea*) of oneself, i.e. *exculpate* (self):—answer (for self), make defence, excuse (self), speak for self.

627. **ἀπολογία apŏlŏgia**, *ap-ol-og-ee'-ah*; from the same as *626*; a *plea* ("apology"):—answer (for self), clearing of self, defence.

628. **ἀπολούω apŏlŏuō**, *ap-ol-oo'-o*; from *575* and *3068*; to *wash* fully, i.e. (fig.) *have remitted* (reflex.):—wash (away).

629. **ἀπολύτρωσις apŏlutrōsis**, *ap-ol-oo'-tro-sis*; from a comp. of *575* and *3083*; (the act) *ransom* in full, i.e. (fig.) *riddance*, or (spec.) Chr. *salvation*:—deliverance, redemption.

630. **ἀπολύω apŏluō**, *ap-ol-oo'-o*; from *575* and *3089*; to *free* fully, i.e. (lit.) *relieve*, *release*, *dismiss* (reflex. *depart*), or (fig.) *let die*, *pardon*, or (spec.) *divorce*:—(let) depart, dismiss, divorce, forgive, let go, loose, put (send) away, release, set at liberty.

631. **ἀπομάσσομαι apŏmassŏmai**, *ap-om-as'-som-ahee*; mid. from *575* and **μάσσω massō** (to *squeeze*, *knead*, *smear*); to *scrape away*:—wipe off.

632. **ἀπονέμω apŏnĕmō**, *ap-on-em'-o*; from *575* and the base of *3551*; to *apportion*, i.e. *bestow*:—give.

633. **ἀπονίπτω apŏniptō**, *ap-on-ip'-to;* from *575* and *3538;* to *wash off* (reflex. one's own hands symbolically):—wash.

634. **ἀποπίπτω apŏpiptō**, *ap-op-ip'-to;* from *575* and *4098;* to *fall off:*—fall.

635. **ἀποπλανάω apŏplanaō**, *ap-op-lan-ah'-o;* from *575* and *4105;* to *lead astray* (fig.); pass. to *stray* (from truth):—err, seduce.

636. **ἀποπλέω apŏplĕō**, *ap-op-leh'-o;* from *575* and *4126;* to *set sail:*—sail away.

637. **ἀποπλύνω apŏplunō**, *ap-op-loo'-no;* from *575* and *4150;* to *rinse off:*—wash.

638. **ἀποπνίγω apŏpnigō**, *ap-op-nee'-go;* from *575* and *4155;* to *stifle* (by drowning or overgrowth):—choke.

639. **ἀπορέω apŏrĕō**, *ap-or-eh'-o;* from a comp. of *1* (as a neg. particle) and the base of *4198;* to *have no way* out, i.e. *be at a loss* (mentally):—(stand in) doubt, be perplexed.

640. **ἀπορία apŏria**, *ap-or-ee'-a;* from the same as *639;* a (state of) *quandary:*—perplexity.

641. **ἀποῤῥίπτω apŏrrhiptō**, *ap-or-hrip'-to;* from *575* and *4496;* to *hurl off,* i.e. *precipitate* (oneself):—cast.

642. **ἀπορφανίζω apŏrphanizō**, *ap-or-fan-id'-zo;* from *575* and a der. of *3737;* to *bereave wholly,* i.e. (fig.) *separate* (from intercourse):—take.

643. **ἀποσκευάζω apŏskĕuazō**, *ap-osk-yoo-ad'-zo;* from *575* and a der. of *4632;* to *pack up* (one's) *baggage:*—take up . . . carriages.

644. **ἀποσκίασμα apŏskiasma**, *ap-os-kee'-as-mah;* from a comp. of *575* and a der. of *4639;* a *shading off,* i.e. *obscuration:*—shadow.

645. **ἀποσπάω apŏspaō**, *ap-os-pah'-o;* from *575* and *4685;* to *drag forth,* i.e. (lit.) *unsheathe* (a sword), or rel. (with a degree of force implied) *retire* (pers. or factiously):—(with-) draw (away), after we were gotten from.

646. **ἀποστασία apŏstasia**, *ap-os-tas-ee'-ah;* fem. of the same as *647; defection* from truth (prop. the state) ["apostasy"]:—falling away, forsake.

647 **ἀποστάσιον apŏstasiŏn**, *ap-os-tas'-ee-on;* neut. of a (presumed) adj. from a der. of *868;* prop. something *separative,* i.e. (spec.) *divorce:*—(writing of) divorcement.

648. **ἀποστεγάζω apŏstĕgazō**, *ap-os-teg-ad'-zo;* from *575* and a der. of *4721;* to *unroof:*—uncover.

649. **ἀποστέλλω apŏstĕllō**, *ap-os-tel'-lo;* from *575* and *4724; set apart,* i.e. (by impl.) to *send out* (prop. on a mission) lit. or fig.:—put in, send (away, forth, out), set [at liberty].

650. **ἀποστερέω apŏstĕrĕō**, *ap-os-ter-eh'-o;* from *575* and **στερέω stĕrĕō** (to *deprive*); to *despoil:*—defraud, destitute, kept back by fraud.

651. **ἀποστολή apŏstŏlē**, *ap-os-tol-ay';* from *649, commission,* i.e. (spec.) *apostolate:*—apostleship.

652. **ἀπόστολος apŏstŏlŏs**, *ap-os'-tol-os;* from *649;* a *delegate;* spec. an *ambassador* of the Gospel; officially a *commissioner* of Christ ["*apostle*"] (with miraculous powers):—apostle, messenger, he that is sent.

653. **ἀποστοματίζω apŏstŏmatizō**, *ap-os-tom-at-id'-zo;* from *575* and a (presumed) der. of *4750;* to *speak off-hand* (prop. *dictate*), i.e. to *catechize* (in an invidious manner):—provoke to speak.

654. **ἀποστρέφω apŏstrĕphō**, *ap-os-tref'-o;* from *575* and *4762;* to *turn away* or *back* (lit. or fig.):—bring again, pervert, turn away (from).

655. **ἀποστυγέω apŏstugĕō**, *ap-os-toog-eh'-o;* from *575* and the base of *4767;* to *detest* utterly:—abhor.

656. **ἀποσυνάγωγος apŏsunagōgŏs**, *ap-os-oon-ag'-o-gos;* from *575* and *4864; excommunicated:*—(put) out of the synagogue (-s).

657. **ἀποτάσσομαι apŏtassŏmai**, *ap-ot-as'-som-ahee;* mid. from *575* and *5021;* lit. to *say adieu* (by departing or dismissing); fig. to *renounce:*—bid farewell, forsake, take leave, send away.

658. **ἀποτελέω apŏtĕlĕō**, *ap-ot-el-eh'-o;* from *575* and *5055;* to *complete entirely,* i.e. *consummate:*—finish.

659. **ἀποτίθημι apŏtithēmi**, *ap-ot-eeth'-ay-mee;* from *575* and *5087;* to *put away* (lit. or fig.):—cast off, lay apart (aside, down), put away (off).

660. **ἀποτινάσσω apŏtinassō**, *ap-ot-in-as'-so;* from *575* and **τινάσσω tinassō** (to *jostle*); to *brush off:*—shake off.

661. **ἀποτίνω apŏtinō**, *ap-ot-ee'-no;* from *575* and *5099;* to *pay* in full:—repay.

662. **ἀποτολμάω apŏtŏlmaō**, *ap-ot-ol-mah'-o;* from *575* and *5111;* to *venture* plainly:—be very bold.

663. **ἀποτομία apŏtŏmia**, *ap-ot-om-ee'-ah;* from the base of *664;* (fig.) *decisiveness,* i.e. *rigor:*—severity.

664. **ἀποτόμως apŏtŏmōs**, *ap-ot-om'-oce;* adv. from a der. of a comp. of *575* and **τέμνω tĕmnō** (to *cut*); *abruptly,* i.e. *peremptorily:*—sharply (-ness).

665. **ἀποτρέπω apŏtrĕpō**, *ap-ot-rep'-o;* from *575* and the base of *5157;* to *deflect,* i.e. (reflex.) *avoid:*—turn away.

666. **ἀπουσία apŏusia**, *ap-oo-see'-ah;* from the part. of *548;* a *being away:*—absence.

667. **ἀποφέρω appŏhĕrō**, *ap-of-er'-o;* from *575* and *5342;* to *bear off* (lit. or rel.):—bring, carry (away).

668. **ἀποφεύγω apŏphĕugō**, *ap-of-yoo'-go;* from *575* and *5343;* (fig.) to *escape:*—escape.

669. **ἀποφθέγγομαι apŏphthĕggŏmai**, *ap-of-theng'-om-ahee;* from *575* and *5350;* to *enunciate* plainly, i.e. *declare:*—say, speak forth, utterance.

670. **ἀποφορτίζομαι apŏphŏrtizŏmai**, *ap-of-or-tid'-zom-ahee;* from *575* and the mid. of *5412;* to *unload:*—unlade.

671. **ἀπόχρησις apŏchrēsis**, *ap-okh'-ray-sis;* from a comp. of *575* and *5530;* the act of *using up,* i.e. *consumption:*—using.

672. **ἀποχωρέω apŏchōrĕō**, *ap-okh-o-reh'-o;* from *575* and *5562;* to *go away:*—depart.

673. **ἀποχωρίζω apŏchōrizō**, *ap-okh-o-rid'-zo;* from *575* and *5563;* to *rend apart;* reflex. to *separate:*—depart (asunder).

674. **ἀποψύχω apŏpsuchō**, *ap-ops-oo'-kho;* from *575* and *5594;* to *breathe out,* i.e. *faint:*—hearts failing.

675. **Ἄππιος 'Appiŏs**, *ap'-pee-os;* of Lat. or.; (in the genitive, i.e. possessive case) *of Appius,* the name of a Roman:—Appii.

676. **ἀπρόσιτος aprŏsitŏs**, *ap-ros'-ee-tos;* from *1* (as a neg. particle) and a der. of a comp. of *4314* and **εἶμι ĕimi** (to *go*); *inaccessible:*—which no man can approach.

677. **ἀπρόσκοπος aprŏskŏpŏs**, *ap-ros'-kop-os;* from *1* (as a neg. particle) and a presumed der. of *4350;* act. *inoffensive,* i.e. *not leading into sin;* pass. *faultless,* i.e. *not led into sin:*—none (void of, without) offence.

678. **ἀπροσωπολήπτως aprŏsōpŏlēptōs**, *ap-ros-o-pol-ape'-toce;* adv. from a comp. of *1* (as a neg. particle) and a presumed der. of a presumed comp. of *4383* and *2983* [comp. *4381*]; in a way *not accepting* the *person,* i.e. *impartially:*—without respect of persons.

679. **ἄπταιστος aptaistŏs**, *ap-tah'ee-stos;* from *1* (as a neg. particle) and a der. of *4417; not stumbling,* i.e. (fig.) *without sin:*—from falling.

680. **ἅπτομαι haptŏmai**, *hap'-tom-ahee;* reflex. of *681;* prop. to *attach* oneself to, i.e. to *touch* (in many implied relations):—touch.

681. **ἅπτω haptō**, *hap'-to;* a prim. verb; prop. to *fasten* to, i.e. (spec.) to *set* on fire:—kindle, light.

682. **Ἀπφία Apphia**, *ap-fee'-a;* prob. of for. or.; *Apphia,* a woman of Colossæ:—Apphia.

683. **ἀπωθέομαι apōthĕŏmai**, *ap-o-theh'-om-ahee;* or **ἀπώθομαι apōthŏmai**, *ap-o'-thom-ahee;* from *575* and the mid. of **ὠθέω ōthĕō** or **ὤθω ōthō** (to *shove*); to *push off,* fig. to *reject:*—cast away, put away (from), thrust away (from).

684. **ἀπώλεια apōlĕia**, *ap-o'-li-a;* from a presumed der. of *622; ruin* or *loss* (phys., spiritual or eternal):—damnable (-nation), destruction, die, perdition, × perish, pernicious ways, waste.

685. **ἀρά ara**, *ar-ah';* prob. from *142;* prop. *prayer* (as *lifted* to Heaven), i.e. (by impl.) *imprecation:*—curse.

686. **ἄρα ara**, *ar'-ah;* prob. from *142* (through the idea of *drawing* a conclusion); a particle denoting an *inference* more or less decisive (as follows):—haply, (what) manner (of man), no doubt, perhaps, so be, then, therefore, truly, wherefore. Often used in connection with other particles, especially *1065* or *3767* (after) or *1487* (before). Comp. also *687.*

687. **ἆρα ara**, *ar'-ah;* a form of *686,* denoting an *interrogation* to which a negative answer is presumed:—therefore.

688. **Ἀραβία Arabia**, *ar-ab-ee'-ah;* of Heb. or. [6152]; *Arabia,* a region of Asia:—Arabia.

ἄραγε aragĕ. See *686* and *1065.*

689. **Ἀράμ Aram**, *ar-am';* of Heb. or. [7410]; *Aram* (i.e. *Ram*), an Isr.:—Aram.

690. **Ἄραψ 'Araps**, *ar'-aps;* from *688;* an *Arab* or native of Arabia:—Arabian.

691. **ἀργέω argĕō**, *arg-eh'-o;* from *692;* to *be idle,* i.e. (fig.) to *delay:*—linger.

692. **ἀργός argŏs**, *ar-gos';* from *1* (as a neg. particle) and *2041; inactive,* i.e. *unemployed;* (by impl.) *lazy, useless:*—barren, idle, slow.

693. **ἀργύρεος argurĕŏs**, *ar-goo'-reh-os;* from *696;* made *of silver:*—(of) silver.

694. **ἀργύριον arguriŏn**, *ar-goo'-ree-on;* neut. of a presumed der. of *696; silvery,* i.e. (by impl.) *cash;* spec. a *silverling* (i.e. *drachma* or *shekel*):—money, (piece of) silver (piece).

695. **ἀργυροκόπος argurŏkŏpŏs**, *ar-goo-rok-op'-os;* from *696* and *2875;* a *beater* (i.e. *worker*) *of silver:*—silversmith.

696. **ἄργυρος argurŏs**, *ar'-goo-ros;* from **ἀργός argŏs** (*shining*); *silver* (the metal, in the articles or coin):—silver.

697. **Ἄρειος Πάγος Arĕiŏs Pagŏs**, *ar'-i-os pag'-os;* from **Ἄρης Arēs** (the name of the Greek deity of war) and a der. of *4078; rock of Ares,* a place in Athens:—Areopagus, Mars' Hill.

698. **Ἀρεοπαγίτης Arĕŏpagitēs**, *ar-eh-op-ag-ee'-tace;* from *697;* an *Areopagite* or member of the court held on Mars' Hill:—Areopagite.

699. **ἀρέσκεια arĕskĕia**, *ar-es'-ki-ah;* from a der. of *700; complaisance:*—pleasing.

700. **ἀρέσκω arĕskō**, *ar-es'-ko;* prob. from *142* (through the idea of *exciting* emotion); to *be agreeable* (or by impl. to seek to be so):—please.

701. **ἀρεστός arĕstŏs**, *ar-es-tos';* from *700; agreeable;* by impl. *fit:*—(things that) please (-ing), reason.

702. **Ἀρέτας Arĕtas**, *ar-et'-as;* of for. or.; *Aretas,* an Arabian:—Aretas.

703. **ἀρέτη arĕtē**, *ar-et'-ay;* from the same as *730;* prop. *manliness* (*valor*), i.e. *excellence* (intrinsic or attributed):—praise, virtue.

704. **ἀρήν arēn**, *ar-ane';* perh. the same as *730;* a *lamb* (as a *male*):—lamb.

705. **ἀριθμέω arithmĕō**, *ar-ith-meh'-o;* from *706;* to *enumerate* or *count:*—number.

706. **ἀριθμός arithmŏs**, *ar-ith-mos';* from *142;* a *number* (as reckoned *up*):—number.

707. **Ἀριμαθαία Arimathaia**, *ar-ee-math-ah'ee-ah;* of Heb. or. [7414]; *Arimathæa* (or *Ramah*), a place in Pal.:—Arimathæa.

708. **Ἀρίσταρχος Aristarchŏs**, *ar-is'-tar-khos;* from the same as *712* and *757; best ruling; Aristarchus,* a Macedonian:—Aristarchus.

709. **ἀριστάω aristaō**, *ar-is-tah'-o;* from *712;* to *take the principal meal:*—dine.

710. **ἀριστερός aristĕrŏs**, *ar-is-ter-os';* appar. a comp. of the same as *712;* the *left* hand (as *second-best*):—left [hand].

711. **᾿Αριστόβουλος Aristŏbŏulŏs**, *ar-is-tob'-oo-los;* from the same as *712* and *1012; best counselling; Aristobulus,* a Chr.:—Aristobulus.

712. **ἄριστον aristŏn**, *ar'-is-ton;* appar. neut. of a superlative from the same as *730;* the *best* meal [or *breakfast;* perh. from **ἦρι ēri** (*"early"*)], i.e. *luncheon:*—dinner.

713. **ἀρκετός arkĕtŏs**, *ar-ket-os';* from *714; satisfactory:*—enough, suffice (-ient).

714. **ἀρκέω arkĕō**, *ar-keh'-o;* appar. a prim. verb [but prob. akin to *142* through the idea of *raising* a barrier]; prop. to *ward off,* i.e. (by impl.) to *avail* (fig. *be satisfactory*):—be content, be enough, suffice, be sufficient.

715. **ἄρκτος arktŏs**, *ark'-tos;* prob. from *714;* a *bear* (as *obstructing* by ferocity):—bear.

716. **ἅρμα harma**, *har'-mah;* prob. from *142* [perh. with *1* (as a particle of union) prefixed]; a *chariot* (as *raised* or fitted *together* [comp. *719*]):—chariot.

717. **᾿Αρμαγεδδών Armagĕddōn**, *ar-mag-ed-dohn';* of Heb. or. [2022 and 4023]; *Armageddon* (or *Har-Megiddon*), a symbol. name:—Armageddon.

718. **ἁρμόζω harmŏzō**, *har-mod'-zo;* from *719;* to *joint,* i.e. (fig.) to *woo* (reflex. to *betroth*):—espouse.

719. **ἁρμός harmŏs**, *har-mos';* from the same as *716;* an *articulation* (of the body):—joint.

720. **ἀρνέομαι arnĕŏmai**, *ar-neh'-om-ahee;* perh. from *1* (as a neg. particle) and the mid. of *4483;* to *contradict,* i.e. *disavow, reject, abnegate:*—deny, refuse.

721. **ἀρνίον arniŏn**, *ar-nee'-on;* diminutive from *704;* a *lambkin:*—lamb.

722. **ἀροτριόω arŏtriŏō**, *ar-ot-ree-ŏ'-o;* from *723;* to *plough:*—plow.

723. **ἄροτρον arŏtrŏn**, *ar'-ot-ron;* from **ἀρόω arŏō** (to *till*); a *plough:*—plow.

724. **ἁρπαγή harpagē**, *har-pag-ay';* from *726; pillage* (prop. abstr.):—extortion, ravening, spoiling.

725. **ἁρπαγμός harpagmŏs**, *har-pag-mos';* from *726; plunder* (prop. concr.):—robbery.

726. **ἁρπάζω harpazō**, *har-pad'-zo;* from a der. of *138;* to *seize* (in various applications):—catch (away, up), pluck, pull, take (by force).

727. **ἅρπαξ harpax**, *har'-pax;* from *726; rapacious:*—extortion, ravening.

728. **ἀῤῥαβών arrhabōn**, *ar-hrab-ohn';* of Heb. or. [6162]; a *pledge,* i.e. part of the purchase-money or property given in advance as *security* for the rest:—earnest.

729. **ἄῤῥαφος arrhaphŏs**, *ar'-hraf-os;* from *1* (as a neg. particle) and a presumed der. of the same as *4476; unsewed,* i.e. of a single piece:—without seam.

730. **ἄῤῥην arrhēn**, *ar'-hrane;* or

ἄρσην arsēn, *ar'-sane;* prob. from *142; male* (as stronger for *lifting*):—male, man.

731. **ἄῤῥητος arrhētŏs**, *ar'-hray-tos;* from *1* (as a neg. particle) and the same as *4490; unsaid,* i.e. (by impl.) *inexpressible:*—unspeakable.

732. **ἄῤῥωστος arrhōstŏs**, *ar'-hroce-tos;* from *1* (as a neg. particle) and a presumed der. of *4517; infirm:*—sick (folk, -ly).

733. **ἀρσενοκοίτης arsĕnŏkŏitēs**, *ar-sen-ok-oy'-tace;* from *730* and *2845;* a *sodomite:*—abuser of (that defile) self with mankind.

734. **᾿Αρτεμᾶς Artĕmas**, *ar-tem-as';* contr. from a comp. of *735* and *1435; gift of Artemis; Artemas* (or *Artemidorus*), a Chr.:—Artemas.

735. **῎Αρτεμις Artĕmis**, *ar'-tem-is;* prob. from the same as *736; prompt; Artemis,* the name of a Grecian goddess borrowed by the Asiatics for one of their deities:—Diana.

736. **ἀρτέμων artĕmōn**, *ar-tem'-ohn;* from a der. of *737;* prop. something *ready* [or else more remotely from *142* (comp. *740*); something *hung* up], i.e. (spec.) the *topsail* (rather *foresail* or *jib*) of a vessel:—mainsail.

737. **ἄρτι arti**, *ar'-tee;* adv. from a der. of *142* (comp. *740*) through the idea of *suspension;* just *now:*—this day (hour), hence [-forth], here [-after], hither [-to], (even) now, (this) present.

738. **ἀρτιγέννητος artigĕnnētŏs**, *ar-teeg-en'-nay-tos;* from *737* and *1084; just born,* i.e. (fig.) a *young convert:*—new born.

739. **ἄρτιος artiŏs**, *ar'-tee-os;* from *737; fresh,* i.e. (by impl.) *complete:*—perfect.

740. **ἄρτος artos**, *ar'-tos;* from *142; bread* (as *raised*) or a *loaf:*—(shew-) bread, loaf.

741. **ἀρτύω artuō**, *ar-too'-o;* from a presumed der. of *142;* to *prepare,* i.e. *spice* (with *stimulating* condiments):—season.

742. **᾿Αρφαξάδ Arphaxad**, *ar-fax-ad';* of Heb. or. [775]; *Arphaxad,* a post-diluvian patriarch:—Arphaxad.

743. **ἀρχάγγελος archaggĕlŏs**, *ar-khang'-el-os;* from *757* and *32;* a *chief angel:*—archangel.

744. **ἀρχαῖος archaiŏs**, *ar-khah'-yos;* from *746; original* or *primeval:*—(them of) old (time).

745. **᾿Αρχέλαος Archĕlaŏs**, *ar-khel'-ah-os;* from *757* and *2994; people-ruling; Archelaus,* a Jewish king:—Archelaus.

746. **ἀρχή archē**, *ar-khay';* from *756;* (prop. abstr.) a *commencement,* or (concr.) *chief* (in various applications of order, time, place or rank):—beginning, corner, (at the, the) first (estate), magistrate, power, principality, principle, rule.

747. **ἀρχηγός archēgŏs**, *ar-khay-gos';* from *746* and *71;* a *chief leader:*—author, captain, prince.

748. **ἀρχιερατικός archiĕratikŏs**, *ar-khee-er-at-ee-kos';* from *746* and a der. of *2413; high-priestly:*—of the high-priest.

749. **ἀρχιερεύς archiĕrĕus**, *ar-khee-er-yuce';* from *746* and *2409;* the *high-priest* (lit. of the Jews, typ. Christ); by extens. a *chief priest:*—chief (high) priest, chief of the priests.

750. **ἀρχιποίμην archipŏimēn**, *ar-khee-poy'-mane;* from *746* and *4166;* a *head shepherd:*—chief shepherd.

751. **῎Αρχιππος Archippŏs**, *ar'-khip-pos;* from *746* and *2462; horse-ruler; Archippus,* a Chr.:—Archippus.

752. **ἀρχισυνάγωγος archisunagōgŏs**, *ar-khee-soon-ag'-o-gos;* from *746* and *4864; director of the synagogue* services:—(chief) ruler of the synagogue.

753. **ἀρχιτέκτων architĕktōn**, *ar-khee-tek'-tone;* from *746* and *5045;* a *chief constructor,* i.e. "*architect*":—masterbuilder.

754. **ἀρχιτελώνης architĕlōnēs**, *ar-khee-tel-o'-nace;* from *746* and *5057;* a *principal tax-gatherer:*—chief among the publicans.

755. **ἀρχιτρίκλινος architriklinŏs**, *ar-khee-tree'-klee-nos;* from *746* and a comp. of *5140* and *2827* (a *dinner-bed,* because composed of three couches); *director of* the *entertainment:*—governor (ruler) of the feast.

756. **ἄρχομαι archŏmai**, *ar'-khom-ahee;* mid. of *757* (through the impl. of *precedence*); to *commence* (in order of time):—(rehearse from the) begin (-ning).

757. **ἄρχω archō**, *ar'-kho;* a prim. verb; to be *first* (in political rank or power):—reign (rule) over.

758. **ἄρχων archōn**, *ar'-khone;* pres. part. of *757;* a *first* (in rank or power):—chief (ruler), magistrate, prince, ruler.

759. **ἄρωμα "arōma,"** *ar'-o-mah;* from *142* (in the sense of *sending* off scent); an *aromatic:*—(sweet) spice.

760. **᾿Ασά Asa**, *as-ah';* of Heb. or. [609]; *Asa,* an Isr.:—Asa.

761. **ἀσάλευτος asalĕutŏs**, *as-al'-yoo-tos;* from *1* (as a neg. particle) and a der. of *4531; unshaken,* i.e. (by impl.) *immovable* (fig.):—which cannot be moved, unmovable.

762. **ἄσβεστος asbĕstŏs**, *as'-bes-tos;* from *1* (as a neg. particle) and a der. of *4570; not extinguished,* i.e. (by impl.) *perpetual:*—not to be quenched, unquenchable.

763. **ἀσέβεια asĕbĕia**, *as-eb'-i-ah;* from *765; impiety,* i.e. (by impl.) *wickedness:*—ungodly (-liness).

764. **ἀσεβέω asĕbĕō**, *as-eb-eh'-o;* from *765;* to be (by impl. *act*) *impious* or *wicked:*—commit (live, that after should live) ungodly.

765. **ἀσεβής asĕbēs**, *as-eb-ace';* from *1* (as a neg. particle) and a presumed der. of *4576; irreverent,* i.e. (by extens.) *impious* or *wicked:*—ungodly (man).

766. **ἀσέλγεια asĕlgĕia**, *as-elg'-i-a;* from a comp. of *1* (as a neg. particle) and a presumed **σελγής sĕlgēs** (of uncert. der., but appar. mean. *continent*); *licentiousness* (sometimes including other vices):—filthy, lasciviousness, wantonness.

767. **ἄσημος asēmŏs**, *as'-ay-mos;* from *1* (as a neg. particle) and the base of *4591; unmarked,* i.e. (fig.) *ignoble:*—mean.

768. **᾿Ασήρ Asēr**, *as-ayr';* of Heb. or. [836]; *Aser* (i.e. *Asher*), an Isr. tribe:—Aser.

769. **ἀσθένεια asthĕnĕia**, *as-then'-i-ah;* from *772; feebleness* (of body or mind); by impl. *malady;* mor. *frailty:*—disease, infirmity, sickness, weakness.

770. **ἀσθενέω asthĕnĕō**, *as-then-eh'-o;* from *772;* to *be feeble* (in any sense):—be diseased, impotent folk (man), (be) sick, (be, be made) weak.

771. **ἀσθένημα asthĕnēma**, *as-then'-ay-mah;* from *770;* a *scruple* of conscience:—infirmity.

772. **ἀσθενής asthĕnēs**, *as-then-ace';* from *1* (as a neg. particle) and the base of *4599; strengthless* (in various applications, lit., fig. and mor.):—more feeble, impotent, sick, without strength, weak (-er, -ness, thing).

773. **᾿Ασία Asia**, *as-ee'-ah;* of uncert. der.; *Asia,* i.e. *Asia Minor,* or (usually) only its western shore:—Asia.

774. **᾿Ασιανός Asianŏs**, *as-ee-an-os';* from *773;* an *Asian* (i.e. *Asiatic*) or inhab. of Asia:—of Asia.

775. **᾿Ασιάρχης Asiarchēs**, *as-ee ar'-khace;* from *773* and *746;* an *Asiarch* or president of the public festivities in a city of Asia Minor:—chief of Asia.

776. **ἀσιτία asitia**, *as-ee-tee'-ah;* from *777; fasting* (the state):—abstinence.

777. **ἄσιτος asitŏs**, *as'-ee-tos;* from *1* (as a neg. particle) and *4621; without* (taking) *food:*—fasting.

778. **ἀσκέω askĕō**, *as-keh'-o;* prob. from the same as *4632;* to *elaborate,* i.e. (fig.) *train* (by impl. *strive*):—exercise.

779. **ἀσκός askŏs**, *as-kos';* from the same as *778;* a leathern (or skin) *bag* used as a bottle:—bottle.

780. **ἀσμένως asmĕnōs**, *as-men'-oce;* adv. from a der. of the base of *2237; with pleasure:*—gladly.

781. **ἄσοφος asŏphŏs**, *as'-of-os;* from *1* (as a neg. particle) and *4680; unwise:*—fool.

782. **ἀσπάζομαι aspazŏmai**, *as-pad'-zom-ahee;* from *1* (as a particle of union) and a presumed form of *4685;* to *enfold* in the arms, i.e. (by impl.) to *salute,* (fig.) to *welcome:*—embrace, greet, salute, take leave.

783. **ἀσπασμός aspasmŏs**, *as-pas-mos';* from *782;* a *greeting* (in person or by letter):—greeting, salutation.

784. **ἄσπιλος aspilŏs**, *as'-pee-los;* from *1* (as a neg. particle) and *4695; unblemished* (phys. or mor.):—without spot, unspotted.

785. **ἀσπίς aspis**, *as-pece';* of uncert. der.; a *buckler* (or *round* shield); used of a serpent (as *coiling* itself), prob. the "*asp*":—asp.

786. **ἄσπονδος aspŏndŏs**, *as'-pon-dos;* from *1* (as a neg. particle) and a der. of *4689;* lit. *without libation* (which usually accompanied a treaty), i.e. (by impl.) *truceless:*—implacable, truce-breaker.

787. **ἀσσάριον assariŏn**, *as-sar'-ee-on;* of Lat. or.; an *assarius* or *as,* a Roman coin:—farthing.

788. **ἆσσον assŏn**, *as'-son;* neut. comparative of the base of *1451; more nearly,* i.e. *very near:*—close.

789. **῎Ασσος Assŏs**, *as'-sos;* prob. of for. or.; *Assus,* a city of Asia Minor:—Assos.

790. **ἀστατέω astatĕō**, *as-tat-eh'-o;* from *1* (as a neg. particle) and a der. of *2476;* to *be non-stationary,* i.e. (fig.) *homeless:*—have no certain dwelling-place.

791. **ἀστεῖος astĕiŏs**, *as-ti'-os;* from **ἄστυ astu** (a *city*); *urbane,* i.e. (by impl.) *handsome:*—fair.

792. **ἀστήρ astēr**, *as-tare';* prob. from the base of *4766;* a *star* (as *strown* over the sky), lit. or fig.:—star.

793. ἀστήρικτος astēriktŏs, *as-tay'-rik-tos;* from *1* (as a neg. particle) and a presumed der. of *4741; unfixed*, i.e. (fig.) *vacillating:*—unstable.

794. ἄστοργος astŏrgŏs, *as'-tor-gos;* from *1* (as a neg. particle) and a presumed der. of **στέργω stĕrgō** (to *cherish* affectionately); *hard-hearted* towards kindred:—without natural affection.

795. ἀστοχέω astŏchĕō, *as-tokh-eh'-o;* from a comp. of *1* (as a neg. particle) and **στόιχος stŏichŏs** (an *aim*); to *miss* the mark, i.e. (fig.) *deviate* from truth:—err, swerve.

796. ἀστραπή astrapē, *as-trap-ay';* from *797; lightning;* by anal. *glare:*—lightning, bright shining.

797. ἀστράπτω astraptō, *as-trap'-to;* prob. from *792;* to *flash* as lightning:—lighten, shine.

798. ἄστρον astrŏn, *as'-tron;* neut. from *792;* prop. a *constellation;* put for a single *star* (nat. or artificial):—star.

799. Ἀσύγκριτος Asugkritŏs, *as-oong'-kree-tos;* from *1* (as a neg. particle) and a der. of *4793; incomparable; Asyncritus*, a Chr.:—Asyncritus.

800. ἀσύμφωνος asumphōnŏs, *as-oom'-fo-nos;* from *1* (as a neg. particle) and *4850; inharmonious* (fig.):—agree not.

801. ἀσύνετος asunĕtŏs, *as-oon'-ay-tos;* from *1* (as a neg. particle) and *4908; unintelligent;* by impl. *wicked:*—foolish, without understanding.

802. ἀσύνθετος asunthĕtŏs, *as-oon'-thet-os;* from *1* (as a neg. particle) and a der. of *4934;* prop. *not agreed*, i.e. *treacherous* to compacts:—covenant-breaker.

803. ἀσφάλεια asphalĕia, *as-fal'-i-ah;* from *804; security* (lit. or fig.):—certainty, safety.

804. ἀσφαλής asphalēs, *as-fal-ace';* from *1* (as a neg. particle) and **σφάλλω sphallō** (to "*fail*"); *secure* (lit. or fig.):—certain (-ty), safe, sure.

805. ἀσφαλίζω asphalizō, *as-fal-id'-zo;* from *804;* to *render secure:*—make fast (sure).

806. ἀσφαλῶς asphalōs, *as-fal-oce';* adv. from *804; securely* (lit. or fig.):—assuredly, safely.

807. ἀσχημονέω aschēmŏnĕō, *as-kay-mon-eh'-o;* from *809;* to *be* (i.e. *act*) *unbecoming:*—behave self uncomely (unseemly).

808. ἀσχημοσύνη aschēmŏsunē, *as-kay-mos-oo'-nay;* from *809;* an *indecency;* by impl. the *pudenda:*—shame, that which is unseemly.

809. ἀσχήμων askēmōn, *as-kay'-mone;* from *1* (as a neg. particle) and a presumed der. of *2192* (in the sense of its congener *4976*); prop. *shapeless*, i.e. (fig.) *inelegant:*—uncomely.

810. ἀσωτία asōtia, *as-o-tee'-ah;* from a comp. of *1* (as a neg. particle) and a presumed der. of *4982;* prop. *unsavedness*, i.e. (by impl.) *profligacy:*—excess, riot.

811. ἀσώτως asōtōs, *as-o'-toce;* adv. from the same as *810; dissolutely:*—riotous.

812. ἀτακτέω ataktĕō, *at-ak-teh'-o;* from *813;* to *be* (i.e. *act*) *irregular:*—behave self disorderly.

813. ἄτακτος ataktŏs, *at'-ak-tos;* from *1* (as a neg. particle) and a der. of *5021; unarranged*, i.e. (by impl.) *insubordinate* (religiously):—unruly.

814. ἀτάκτως ataktōs, *at-ak'-toce;* adv. from *813; irregularly* (mor.):—disorderly.

815. ἄτεκνος atĕknŏs, *at'-ek-nos;* from *1* (as a neg. particle) and *5043; childless:*—childless, without children.

816. ἀτενίζω atĕnizō, *at-en-id'-zo;* from a comp. of *1* (as a particle of union) and **τείνω tĕinō** (to *stretch*); to *gaze* intently:—behold earnestly (stedfastly), fasten (eyes), look (earnestly, stedfastly, up stedfastly), set eyes.

817. ἄτερ atĕr, *at'-er;* a particle prob. akin to *427; aloof*, i.e. *apart* from (lit. or fig.):—in the absence of, without.

818. ἀτιμάζω atimazō, *at-im-ad'-zo;* from *820;* to *render infamous*, i.e. (by impl.) *contemn* or *maltreat:*—despise, dishonour, suffer shame, entreat shamefully.

819. ἀτιμία atimia, *at-ee-mee'-ah;* from *820; infamy*, i.e. (subj.) comparative *indignity*, (obj.) *disgrace:*—dishonour, reproach, shame, vile.

820. ἄτιμος atimŏs, *at'-ee-mos;* from *1* (as a neg. particle) and *5092;* (neg.) *unhonoured* or (pos.) *dishonoured:*—despised, without honour, less honourable [*comparative degree*].

821. ἀτιμόω atimŏō, *at-ee-mŏ'-o;* from *820;* used like *818*, to *maltreat:*—handle shamefully.

822. ἀτμίς atmis, *at-mece';* from the same as *109; mist:*—vapour.

823. ἄτομος atŏmŏs, *at'-om-os;* from *1* (as a neg. particle) and the base of *5114; uncut*, i.e. (by impl.) *indivisible* [an "*atom*" of time]:—moment.

824. ἄτοπος atŏpŏs, *at'-op-os;* from *1* (as a neg. particle) and *5117; out of place*, i.e. (fig.) *improper, injurious, wicked:*—amiss, harm, unreasonable.

825. Ἀττάλεια Attalĕia, *at-tal'-i-ah;* from **Ἄτταλος Attalŏs** (a king of Pergamus); *Attaleia*, a place in Pamphylia:—Attalia.

826. αὐγάζω augazō, *ŏw-gad'-zo;* from *827;* to *beam* forth (fig.):—shine.

827. αὐγή augē, *ŏwg'-ay;* of uncert. der.; a *ray* of light, i.e. (by impl.) *radiance, dawn:*—break of day.

828. Αὔγουστος Augŏustŏs, *ŏw'-goos-tos;* from Lat. ["august"]; *Augustus*, a title of the Rom. emperor:—Augustus.

829. αὐθάδης authadēs, *ŏw-thad'-ace;* from *846* and the base of *2237; self-pleasing*, i.e. *arrogant:*—self-willed.

830. αὐθαίρετος authairĕtŏs, *ŏw-thah'ee-ret-os;* from *846* and the same as *140; self-chosen*, i.e. (by impl.) *voluntary:*—of own accord, willing of self.

831. αὐθεντέω authĕntĕō, *ŏw-then-teh'-o;* from a comp. of *846* and an obsol. **ἕντης hĕntēs** (a *worker*); to *act of oneself*, i.e. (fig.) *dominate:*—usurp authority over.

832. αὐλέω aulĕō, *ŏw-leh'-o;* from *836;* to play the *flute:*—pipe.

833. αὐλή aulē, *ŏw-lay';* from the same as *109;* a *yard* (as open to the *wind*); by impl. a *mansion:*—court, ([sheep-]) fold, hall, palace.

834. αὐλητής aulētēs, *ŏw-lay-tace';* from *832;* a *flute-player:*—minstrel, piper.

835. αὐλίζομαι aulizŏmai, *ŏw-lid'-zom-ahee;* mid. from *833;* to *pass the night* (prop. in the open air):—abide, lodge.

836. αὐλός aulŏs, *ŏw-los';* from the same as *109*, a *flute* (as *blown*):—pipe.

837. αὐξάνω auxanō, *ŏwx-an'-o;* a prolonged form of a prim. verb; to *grow* ("*wax*"), i.e. *enlarge* (lit. or fig., act. or pass.):—grow (up), (give the) increase.

838. αὔξησις auxēsis, *ŏwx'-ay-sis;* from *837; growth:*—increase.

839. αὔριον auriŏn, *ŏw'-ree-on;* from a der. of the same as *109* (mean. a *breeze*, i.e. the morning *air*); prop. *fresh*, i.e. (adv. with ellipsis of *2250*) *to-morrow:*—(to-) morrow, next day.

840. αὐστηρός austērŏs, *ŏw-stay-ros';* from a (presumed) der. of the same as *109* (mean. *blown*); *rough* (prop. as a *gale*), i.e. (fig.) *severe:*—austere.

841. αὐτάρκεια autarkeia, *ŏw-tar'-ki-ah;* from *842; self-satisfaction*, i.e. (abstr.) *contentedness*, or (concr.) a *competence:*—contentment, sufficiency.

842. αὐτάρκης autarkēs, *ŏw-tar'-kace;* from *846* and *714; self-complacent*, i.e. *contented:*—content.

843. αὐτοκατάκριτος autŏkatakritŏs, *ŏw-tok-at-ak'-ree-tos;* from *846* and a der. of *2632; self-condemned:*—condemned of self.

844. αὐτόματος autŏmatŏs, *ŏw-tom'-at-os;* from *846* and the same as *3155; self-moved* ["automatic"], i.e. *spontaneous:*—of own accord, of self.

845. αὐτόπτης autŏptēs, *ŏw-top'-tace;* from *846* and *3700; self-seeing*, i.e. an *eye-witness:*—eye-witness.

846. αὐτός autŏs, *ŏw-tos';* from the particle **αὖ au** [perh. akin to the base of *109* through the idea of a *baffling* wind] (*backward*); the reflex. pron. *self*, used (alone or in the comp. *1438*) of the third pers., and (with the prop. pers. pron.) of the other persons:—her, it (-self), one, the other, (mine) own, said, ([self-], the) same, ([him-, my-, thy-]) self, [your-] selves, she, that, their (-s), them ([-selves]), there [-at, -by, -in, -into, -of, -on, -with], they, (these) things, this (man), those, together, very, which. Comp. *848*.

847. αὐτοῦ autŏu, *ŏw-too';* genitive (i.e. possessive) of *846*, used as an adv. of location; prop. belonging to the *same* spot, i.e. *in this* (or *that*) *place:*—(t-) here.

848. αὑτοῦ hautŏu, *how-too';* contr. for *1438; self* (in some oblique case or reflex. relation):—her (own), (of) him (-self), his (own), of it, thee, their (own), them (-selves), they.

849. αὐτόχειρ autŏchĕir, *ŏw-tokh'-ire;* from *846* and *5495; self-handed*, i.e. doing *personally:*—with . . . own hands.

850. αὐχμηρός auchmērŏs, *ŏwkh-may-ros';* from **αὐχμός auchmŏs** [prob. from a base akin to that of *109*] (*dust*, as *dried* by wind); prop. *dirty*, i.e. (by impl.) *obscure:*—dark.

851. ἀφαιρέω aphairĕō, *af-ahee-reh'-o;* from *575* and *138;* to *remove* (lit. or fig.):—cut (smite) off, take away.

852. ἀφανής aphanēs, *af-an-ace';* from *1* (as a neg. particle) and *5316; non-apparent:*—that is not manifest.

853. ἀφανίζω aphanizō, *af-an-id'-zo;* from *852;* to *render unapparent*, i.e. (act.) *consume* (*becloud*), or (pass.) *disappear* (*be destroyed*):—corrupt, disfigure, perish, vanish away.

854. ἀφανισμός aphanismŏs, *af-an-is-mos';* from *853; disappearance*, i.e. (fig.) *abrogation:*—vanish away.

855. ἄφαντος aphantŏs, *af'-an-tŏs;* from *1* (as a neg. particle) and a der. of *5316; non-manifested*, i.e. *invisible:*—vanished out of sight.

856. ἀφεδρών aphĕdrōn, *af-ed-rone';* from a comp. of *575* and the base of *1476;* a place of *sitting apart*, i.e. a *privy:*—draught.

857. ἀφειδία aphĕidia, *af-i-dee'-ah;* from a comp. of *1* (as a neg. particle) and *5339; unsparingness*, i.e. *austerity* (*ascetism*):—neglecting.

858. ἀφελότης aphĕlŏtēs, *af-el-ot'-ace;* from a comp. of *1* (as a neg. particle) and **φέλλος phĕllŏs** (in the sense of a *stone* as *stubbing* the foot); *smoothness*, i.e. (fig.) *simplicity:*—singleness.

859. ἄφεσις aphĕsis, *af'-es-is;* from *863; freedom;* (fig.) *pardon:*—deliverance, forgiveness, liberty, remission.

860. ἁφή haphē, *haf-ay';* from *680;* prob. a *ligament* (as *fastening*):—joint.

861. ἀφθαρσία aphtharsia, *af-thar-see'-ah;* from *862; incorruptibility;* gen. *unending existence;* (fig.) *genuineness:*—immortality, incorruption, sincerity.

862. ἄφθαρτος aphthartŏs, *af'-thar-tos;* from *1* (as a neg. particle) and a der. of *5351; undecaying* (in essence or continuance):—not (in-, un-) corruptible, immortal.

863. ἀφίημι aphiēmi, *af-ee'-ay-mee;* from *575* and **ἵημι hiemi** (to *send;* an intens. form of **εἶμι ĕimi**, to *go*); to *send forth*, in various applications (as follow):—cry, forgive, forsake, lay aside, leave, let (alone, be, go, have), omit, put (send) away, remit, suffer, yield up.

864. ἀφικνέομαι aphiknĕŏmai, *af-ik-neh'-om-ahee;* from *575* and the base of *2425;* to *go* (i.e. *spread*) *forth* (by rumor):—come abroad.

865. ἀφιλάγαθος aphilagathŏs, *af-il-ag'-ath-os;* from *1* (as a neg. particle) and *5358; hostile to virtue:*—despiser of those that are good.

866. ἀφιλάργυρος aphilargurŏs, *af-il-ar'-goo-ros;* from *1* (as a neg. particle) and *5366; unavaricious:*—without covetousness, not greedy of filthy lucre.

867. ἄφιξις aphixis, *af'-ix-is;* from *864;* prop. *arrival*, i.e. (by impl.) *departure:*—departing.

868. ἀφίστημι aphistēmi, *af-is'-tay-mee;* from *575* and *2476;* to *remove*, i.e. (act.) *instigate* to revolt;

usually (reflex.) to *desist*, *desert*, etc.:—depart, draw (fall) away, refrain, withdraw self.

869. **ἄφνω aphnō**, *af'-no;* adv. from *852* (contr.); *unawares*, i.e. *unexpectedly:*—suddenly.

870. **ἀφόβως aphŏbōs**, *af-ob'-oce;* adv. from a comp. of *1* (as a neg. particle) and *5401; fearlessly:*—without fear.

871. **ἀφομοιόω aphŏmŏiŏō**, *af-om-oy-ŏ'-o;* from *575* and *3666;* to *assimilate* closely:—make like.

872. **ἀφοράω aphŏraō**, *af-or-ah'-o;* from *575* and *3708;* to *consider* attentively:—look.

873. **ἀφορίζω aphŏrizō**, *af-or-id'-zo;* from *575* and *3724;* to *set off* by boundary, i.e. (fig.) *limit*, *exclude*, *appoint*, etc.:—divide, separate, sever.

874. **ἀφορμή aphŏrmē**, *af-or-may';* from a comp. of *575* and *3729;* a *starting*-point, i.e. (fig.) an *opportunity:*—occasion.

875. **ἀφρίζω aphrizō**, *af-rid'-zo;* from *876;* to *froth* at the mouth (in epilepsy):—foam.

876. **ἀφρός aphrŏs**, *af-ros';* appar. a prim. word; *froth*, i.e. *slaver:*—foaming.

877. **ἀφροσύνη aphrŏsunē**, *af-ros-oo'-nay;* from *878; senselessness*, i.e. (euphem.) *egotism;* (mor.) *recklessness:*—folly, foolishly (-ness).

878. **ἄφρων aphrōn**, *af'-rone;* from *1* (as a neg. particle) and *5424;* prop. *mindless*, i.e. *stupid*, (by impl.) *ignorant*, (spec.) *egotistic*, (practically) *rash*, or (mor.) *unbelieving:*—fool (-ish), unwise.

879. **ἀφυπνόω aphupnŏō**, *af-oop-nŏ'-o;* from a comp. of *575* and *5258;* prop. to *become awake*, i.e. (by impl.) to *drop* (off) in slumber:—fall asleep.

880. **ἄφωνος aphōnŏs**, *af'-o-nos;* from *1* (as a neg. particle) and *5456; voiceless*, i.e. *mute* (by nature or choice); fig. *unmeaning:*—dumb, without signification.

881. **Ἀχάζ Achaz**, *akh-adz';* of Heb. or. [271]; *Achaz*, an Isr.:—Achaz.

882. **Ἀχαΐα Achaia**, *ach-ah-ee'-ah;* of uncert. der.; *Achaïa* (i.e. *Greece*), a country of Europe:—Achaia.

883. **Ἀχαϊκός Achaïkŏs**, *ach-ah-ee-kos';* from *882;* an *Achaïan; Achaïcus*, a Chr.:—Achaicus.

884. **ἀχάριστος acharistŏs**, *ach-ar'-is-tos;* from *1* (as a neg. particle) and a presumed der. of *5483; thankless*, i.e. *ungrateful:*—unthankful.

885. **Ἀχείμ Achĕim**, *akh-ime';* prob. of Heb. or. [comp. 3137]; *Achim*, an Isr.:—Achim.

886. **ἀχειροποίητος achĕirŏpŏiētŏs**, *akh-i-rop-oy'-ay-tos;* from *1* (as a neg. particle) and *5499; unmanufactured*, i.e. *inartificial:*—made without (not made with) hands.

887. **ἀχλύς achlus**, *akh-looce';* of uncert. der.; *dimness* of sight, i.e. (prob.) a *cataract:*—mist.

888. **ἀχρεῖος achrĕiŏs**, *akh-ri'-os;* from *1* (as a neg. particle) and a der. of *5534* [comp. *5532*]; *useless*, i.e. (euphem.) *unmeritorious:*—unprofitable.

889. **ἀχρειόω achrĕiŏō**, *akh-ri-ŏ'-o;* from *888;* to *render useless*, i.e. *spoil:*—become unprofitable.

890. **ἄχρηστος achrēstŏs**, *akh'-race-tos;* from *1* (as a neg. particle) and *5543; inefficient*, i.e. (by impl.) *detrimental:*—unprofitable.

891. **ἄχρι achri**, *akh'-ree;* or **ἄχρις achris**, *akh'-rece;* akin to *206* (through the idea of a *terminus*); (of time) *until* or (of place) *up to:*—as far as, for, in (-to), till, (even, un-) to, until, while. Comp. *3360*.

892. **ἄχυρον achurŏn**, *akh'-oo-ron;* perh. remotely from **χέω chĕō** (to *shed* forth); *chaff* (as *diffusive*):—chaff.

893. **ἀψευδής apsĕudēs**, *aps-yoo-dace';* from *1* (as a neg. particle) and *5579; veracious:*—that cannot lie.

894. **ἄψινθος apsinthŏs**, *ap'-sin-thos;* of uncert. der.; *wormwood* (as a type of *bitterness*, i.e. [fig.] *calamity*):—wormwood.

895. **ἄψυχος apsuchŏs**, *ap'-soo-khos;* from *1* (as a neg. particle) and *5590; lifeless*, i.e. *inanimate* (mechanical):—without life.

B

896. **Βάαλ Baal**, *bah'-al;* of Heb. or. [1168]; *Baal*, a Phœnician deity (used as a symbol of idolatry):—Baal.

897. **Βαβυλών Babulōn**, *bab-oo-lone';* of Heb. or. [894]; *Babylon*, the capital of Chaldæa (lit. or fig. [as a type of tyranny]):—Babylon.

898. **βαθμός bathmŏs**, *bath-mos';* from the same as *899;* a *step*, i.e. (fig.) *grade* (of dignity):—degree.

899. **βάθος bathŏs**, *bath'-os;* from the same as *901; profundity*, i.e. (by impl.) *extent;* (fig.) *mystery:*—deep (-ness, things), depth.

900. **βαθύνω bathunō**, *bath-oo'-no;* from *901;* to *deepen:*—deep.

901. **βαθύς bathus**, *bath-oos';* from the base of *939; profound* (as *going* down), lit. or fig.:—deep, very early.

902. **βαΐον baïŏn**, *bah-ee'-on;* a diminutive of a der. prob. of the base of *939;* a palm *twig* (as *going* out far):—branch.

903. **Βαλαάμ Balaam**, *bal-ah-am';* of Heb. or. [1109]; *Balaam*, a Mesopotamian (symb. of a false teacher):—Balaam.

904. **Βαλάκ Balak**, *bal-ak';* of Heb. or. [1111]; *Balak*, a Moabite:—Balac.

905. **βαλάντιον balantiŏn**, *bal-an'-tee-on;* prob. remotely from *906* (as a *depository*); a *pouch* (for money):—bag, purse.

906. **βάλλω ballō**, *bal'-lo;* a prim. verb; to *throw* (in various applications, more or less violent or intense):—arise, cast (out), × dung, lay, lie, pour, put (up), send, strike, throw (down), thrust. Comp. *4496*.

907. **βαπτίζω baptizō**, *bap-tid'-zo;* from a der. of *911;* to *make whelmed* (i.e. *fully wet*); used only (in the N. T.) of ceremonial *ablution*, espec. (techn.) of the ordinance of Chr. *baptism:*—baptist, baptize, wash.

908. **βάπτισμα baptisma**, *bap'-tis-mah;* from *907; baptism* (techn. or fig.):—baptism.

909. **βαπτισμός baptismŏs**, *bap-tis-mos';* from *907; ablution* (cerem. or Chr.):—baptism, washing.

910. **Βαπτιστής Baptistēs**, *bap-tis-tace';* from *907;* a *baptizer*, as an epithet of Christ's forerunner:—Baptist.

911. **βάπτω baptō**, *bap'-to;* a prim. verb; to *whelm*, i.e. cover wholly with a fluid; in the N. T. only in a qualified or spec. sense, i.e. (lit.) to *moisten* (a part of one's person), or (by impl.) to *stain* (as with dye):—dip.

912. **Βαραββᾶς Barabbas**, *bar-ab-bas';* of Chald. or. [1347 and *5*]; *son of Abba; Bar-abbas*, an Isr.:—Barabbas.

913. **Βαράκ Barak**, *bar-ak';* of Heb. or. [1301]; *Barak*, an Isr.:—Barak.

914. **Βαραχίας Barachias**, *bar-akh-ee'-as;* of Heb. or. [1296]; *Barachias* (i.e. *Berechijah*), an Isr.:—Barachias.

915. **βάρβαρος barbarŏs**, *bar'-bar-os;* of uncert. der.; a *foreigner* (i.e. *non-Greek*):—barbarian (-rous).

916. **βαρέω barĕō**, *bar-eh'-o;* from *926;* to *weigh* down (fig.):—burden, charge, heavy, press.

917. **βαρέως barĕōs**, *bar-eh'-oce;* adv. from *926; heavily* (fig.):—dull.

918. **Βαρθολομαῖος Barthŏlŏmaiŏs**, *bar-thol-om-ah'-yos;* of Chald. or. [1247 and 8526]; *son of Tolmai; Bar-tholomæus*, a Chr. apostle:—Bartholomeus.

919. **Βαριησοῦς Bariēsŏus**, *bar-ee-ay-sooce';* of Chald. or. [1247 and 3091]; *son of Jesus* (or *Joshua*); *Bar-jesus*, an Isr.:—Barjesus.

920. **Βαριωνᾶς Bariōnas**, *bar-ee-oo-nas';* of Chald. or. [1247 and 3124]; *son of Jonas* (or *Jonah*); *Bar-jonas*, an Isr.:—Bar-jona.

921. **Βαρνάβας Barnabas**, *bar-nab'-as;* of Chald. or. [1247 and 5029]; *son of Nabas* (i.e. *prophecy*); *Barnabas*, an Isr.:—Barnabas.

922. **βάρος barŏs**, *bar'-os;* prob. from the same as *939* (through the notion of *going* down; comp. *899*); *weight;* in the N. T. only fig. a *load*, *abundance*, *authority:*—burden (-some), weight.

923. **Βαρσαβᾶς Barsabas**, *bar-sab-as';* of Chald. or. [1247 and prob. 6634]; *son of Sabas* (or *Tsaba*); *Bar-sabas*, the name of two Isr.:—Barsabas.

924. **Βαρτιμαῖος Bartimaiŏs**, *bar-tim-ah'-yos;* of Chald. or. [1247 and 2931]; *son of Timæus* (or the *unclean*); *Bar-timæus*, an Isr.:—Bartimæus.

925. **βαρύνω barunō**, *bar-oo'-no;* from *926;* to *burden* (fig.):—overcharge.

926. **βαρύς barus**, *bar-ooce';* from the same as *922; weighty*, i.e. (fig.) *burdensome*, *grave:*—grievous, heavy, weightier.

927. **βαρύτιμος barutimŏs**, *bar-oo'-tim-os;* from *926* and *5092;* highly *valuable:*—very precious.

928. **βασανίζω basanizō**, *bas-an-id'-zo;* from *931;* to *torture:*—pain, toil, torment, toss, vex.

929. **βασανισμός basanismŏs**, *bas-an-is-mos';* from *928; torture:*—torment.

930. **βασανιστής basanistēs**, *bas-an-is-tace';* from *928;* a *torturer:*—tormentor.

931. **βάσανος basanŏs**, *bas'-an-os;* perh. remotely from the same as *939* (through the notion of *going* to the bottom); a *touch-stone*, i.e. (by anal.) *torture:*—torment.

932. **βασιλεία basilĕia**, *bas-il-i'-ah;* from *935;* prop. *royalty*, i.e. (abstr.) *rule*, or (concr.) a *realm* (lit. or fig.):—kingdom, + reign.

933. **βασίλειον basilĕiŏn**, *bas-il'-i-on;* neut. of *934;* a *palace:*—king's court.

934. **βασίλειος basilĕiŏs**, *bas-il'-i-os;* from *935; kingly* (in nature):—royal.

935. **βασιλεύς basilĕus**, *bas-il-yooce';* prob. from *939* (through the notion of a *foundation* of power); a *sovereign* (abs., rel. or fig.):—king.

936. **βασιλεύω basilĕuō**, *bas-il-yoo'-o;* from *935;* to *rule* (lit. or fig.):—king, reign.

937. **βασιλικός basilikŏs**, *bas-il-ee-kos';* from *935; regal* (in relation), i.e. (lit.) belonging to (or befitting) the sovereign (as land, dress, or a *courtier*), or (fig.) *preeminent:*—king's, nobleman, royal.

938. **βασίλισσα basilissa**, *bas-il'-is-sah;* fem. from *936;* a *queen:*—queen.

939. **βάσις basis**, *bas'-ece;* from **βαίνω bainō** (to *walk*); a *pace* ("base"), i.e. (by impl.) the *foot:*—foot.

940. **βασκαίνω baskainō**, *bas-kah'-ee-no;* akin to *5335;* to *malign*, i.e. (by extens.) to *fascinate* (by false representations):—bewitch.

941. **βαστάζω bastazō**, *bas-tad'-zo;* perh. remotely der. from the base of *939* (through the idea of *removal*); to *lift*, lit. or fig. (*endure*, *declare*, *sustain*, *receive*, etc.):—bear, carry, take up.

942. **βάτος batŏs**, *bat'-os;* of uncert. der.; a *brier* shrub:—bramble, bush.

943. **βάτος batŏs**, *bat'-os;* of Heb. or. [1324]; a *bath*, or measure for liquids:—measure.

944. **βάτραχος batrachŏs**, *bat'-rakh-os;* of uncert. der.; a *frog:*—frog.

945. **βαττολογέω battŏlŏgĕō**, *bat-tol-og-eh'-o;* from **Βάττος Battŏs** (a proverbial stammerer) and *3056;* to *stutter*, i.e. (by impl.) to *prate* tediously:—use vain repetitions.

946. **βδέλυγμα bdĕlugma**, *bdel'-oog-mah;* from *948;* a *detestation*, i.e. (spec.) *idolatry:*—abomination.

947. **βδελυκτός bdĕluktŏs**, *bdel-ook-tos';* from *948; detestable*, i.e. (spec.) *idolatrous:*—abominable.

948. **βδελύσσω bdĕlussō**, *bdel-oos'-so;* from a (presumed) der. of **βδέω bdĕō** (to *stink*); to *be disgusted*, i.e. (by impl.) *detest* (espec. of idolatry):—abhor, abominable.

949. **βέβαιος bĕbaiŏs**, *beb'-ah-yos;* from the base of *939* (through the idea of *basality*); *stable* (lit. or fig.):—firm, of force, stedfast, sure.

950. **βεβαιόω bĕbaiŏō**, *beb-ah-yŏ'-o;* from *949;* to *stabilitate* (fig.):—confirm, (e-) stablish.

951. **βεβαίωσις bĕbaiōsis**, *beb-ah'-yo-sis;* from *950; stabiliment:*—confirmation.

952. **βέβηλος bĕbēlŏs**, *beb'-ay-los;* from the base of *939* and **βηλός bēlŏs** (a *threshold*); *accessible* (as by *crossing the door-way*), i.e. (by impl. of Jewish notions) *heathenish, wicked*:—profane (person).

953. **βεβηλόω bĕbēlŏō**, *beb-ay-lŏ'-o*; from *952*; to *desecrate*:—profane.

954. **Βεελζεβούλ Bĕĕlzĕbŏul**, *beh-el-zeb-ool'*; of Chald. or. [by parody upon 1176]; *dung-god; Beelzebul*, a name of Satan:—Beelzebub.

955. **Βελίαλ Bĕlial**, *bel-ee'-al*; of Heb. or. [1100]; *worthlessness; Belial*, as an epithet of Satan:—Belial.

956. **βέλος bĕlŏs**, *bel'-os*; from *906*; a *missile*, i.e. *spear* or *arrow*:—dart.

957. **βελτίον bĕltiŏn**, *bel-tee'-on*; neut. of a comp. of a der. of *906* (used for the comp. of *18*); *better*:—very well.

958. **Βενιαμίν Bĕniamin**, *ben-ee-am-een'*; of Heb. or. [1144]; *Benjamin*, an Isr.:—Benjamin.

959. **Βερνίκη Bĕrnikē**, *ber-nee'-kay*; from a provincial form of *5342* and *3529*; *victorious; Bernicè*, a member of the Herodian family:—Bernice.

960. **Βέροια Bĕrŏia**, *ber'-oy-ah*; perh. a provincial from a der. of *4008* [*Peræa*, i.e. the region *beyond* the coast-line]; *Beræa*, a place in Macedonia:—Berea.

961. **Βεροιαῖος Bĕrŏiaiŏs**, *ber-oy-ah'-yos*; from *960*; a *Beræœan* or native of Berœa:—of Berea.

962. **Βηθαβαρά Bēthabara**, *bay-thab-ar-ah'*; of Heb. or. [1004 and 5679]; *ferry-house; Bethabara* (i.e. *Bethabarah*), a place on the Jordan:—Bethabara.

963. **Βηθανία Bēthania**, *bay-than-ee'-ah*; of Chald. or.; *date-house; Beth-any*, a place in Pal.:—Bethany.

964. **Βηθεσδά Bēthĕsda**, *bay-thes-dah'*; of Chald. or. [comp. 1004 and 2617]; *house of kindness; Beth-esda*, a pool in Jerus.:—Bethesda.

965. **Βηθλεέμ Bēthlĕĕm**, *bayth-leh-em'*; of Heb. or. [1036]; *Bethleem* (i.e. *Beth-lechem*), a place in Pal.:—Bethlehem.

966. **Βηθσαϊδά Bēthsaida**, *bayth-sahee-dah'*; of Chald. or. [comp. 1004 and 6719]; *fishing-house; Beth-saïda*, a place in Pal.:—Bethsaida.

967. **Βηθφαγή Bēthphagē**, *bayth-fag-ay'*; of Chald. or. [comp. 1004 and 6291]; *fig-house; Beth-phagè*, a place in Pal.:—Bethphage.

968. **βῆμα bēma**, *bay'-ma*; from the base of *939*; a *step*, i.e. *foot-breath*; by impl. a *rostrum*, i.e. *tribunal*:—judgment-seat, set [foot] on, throne.

969. **βήρυλλος bērullŏs**, *bay'-rool-los*; of uncert. der.; a "*beryl*":—beryl.

970. **βία bia**, *bee'-ah*; prob. akin to *979* (through the idea of *vital* activity); *force*:—violence.

971. **βιάζω biazō**, *bee-ad'-zo*; from *970*; to *force*, i.e. (reflex.) to *crowd oneself* (into), or (pass.) to *be seized*:—press, suffer violence.

972. **βίαιος biaiŏs**, *bee'-ah-yos*; from *970*; *violent*:—mighty.

973. **βιαστής biastēs**, *bee-as-tace'*; from *971*; a *forcer*, i.e. (fig.) *energetic*:—violent.

974. **βιβλιαρίδιον bibliaridiŏn**, *bib-lee-ar-id'-ee-on*; a dimin. of *975*; a *booklet*:—little book.

975. **βιβλίον bibliŏn**, *bib-lee'-on*; a dimin. of *976*; a *roll*:—bill, book, scroll, writing.

976. **βίβλος biblŏs**, *bib'-los*; prop. the inner *bark* of the papyrus plant, i.e. (by impl.) a *sheet* or *scroll* of writing:—book.

977. **βιβρώσκω bibrōskō**, *bib-ro'-sko*; a reduplicated and prolonged form of an obsol. prim. verb [perh. causative of *1006*]; to *eat*:—eat.

978. **Βιθυνία Bithunia**, *bee-thoo-nee'-ah*; of uncert. der.; *Bithynia*, a region of Asia:—Bithynia.

979. **βίος biŏs**, *bee'-os*; a prim. word; *life*, i.e. (lit.) the present state of existence; by impl. the means of *livelihood*:—good, life, living.

980. **βιόω biŏō**, *bee-ŏ'-o*; from *979*; to *spend existence*:—live.

981. **βίωσις biōsis**, *bee'-o-sis*; from *980*; *living* (prop. the act, by impl. the mode):—manner of life.

982. **βιωτικός biōtikŏs**, *bee-o-tee-kos'*; from a der. of *980*; *relating to* the present *existence*:—of (pertaining to, things that pertain to) this life.

983. **βλαβερός blabĕrŏs**, *blab-er-os'*; from *984*; *injurious*:—hurtful.

984. **βλάπτω blaptō**, *blap'-to*; a prim. verb; prop. to *hinder*, i.e. (by impl.) to *injure*:—hurt.

985. **βλαστάνω blastanō**, *blas-tan'-o*; from **βλαστός blastŏs** (a *sprout*); to *germinate*; by impl. to *yield* fruit:—bring forth, bud, spring (up).

986. **Βλάστος Blastŏs**, *blas'-tos*; perh. the same as the base of *985*; *Blastus*, an officer of Herod Agrippa:—Blastus.

987. **βλασφημέω blasphēmĕō**, *blas-fay-meh'-o*; from *989*; to *vilify*; spec. to *speak impiously*:—(speak) blaspheme (-er, -mously, -my), defame, rail on, revile, speak evil.

988. **βλασφημία blasphēmia**, *blas-fay-me'-ah*; from *989*; *vilification* (espec. against God):—blasphemy, evil speaking, railing.

989. **βλάσφημος blasphēmŏs**, *blas'-fay-mos*; from a der. of *984* and *5345*; *scurrilous*, i.e. *calumnious* (against man), or (spec.) *impious* (against God):—blasphemer (-mous), railing.

990. **βλέμμα blĕmma**, *blem'-mah*; from *991*; *vision* (prop. concr.; by impl. abstr.):—seeing.

991. **βλέπω blĕpō**, *blep'-o*; a prim. verb; to *look* at (lit. or fig.):—behold, beware, lie, look (on, to), perceive, regard, see, sight, take heed. Comp. *3700*.

992. **βλητέος blētĕŏs**, *blay-teh'-os*; from *906*; fit *to be cast* (i.e. *applied*):—must be put.

993. **Βοανεργές Bŏanĕrgĕs**, *bŏ-an-erg-es'*; of Chald. or. [1123 and 7266]; *sons of commotion; Boänerges*, an epithet of two of the Apostles:—Boanerges.

994. **βοάω bŏaō**, *bŏ-ah'-o*; appar. a prol. form of a prim. verb; to *halloo*, i.e. *shout* (for help or in a tumultuous way):—cry.

995. **βοή bŏē**, *bŏ-ay'*; from *994*; a *halloo*, i.e. *call* (for aid, etc.):—cry.

996. **βοήθεια bŏēthĕia**, *bŏ-ay'-thi-ah*; from *998*; *aid*; spec. a rope or chain for *frapping* a vessel:—help.

997. **βοηθέω bŏēthĕō**, *bŏ-ay-theh'-o*; from *998*; to *aid* or *relieve*:—help, succour.

998. **βοηθός bŏēthŏs**, *bŏ-ay-thos'*; from *995* and **θέω thĕō** (to *run*); a *succorer*:—helper.

999. **βόθυνος bŏthunŏs**, *both'-oo-nos*; akin to *900*; a *hole* (in the ground); spec. a *cistern*:—ditch, pit.

1000. **βολή bŏlē**, *bol-ay'*; from *906*; a *throw* (as a measure of distance):—cast.

1001. **βολίζω bŏlizō**, *bol-id'-zo*; from *1002*; to *heave* the lead:—sound.

1002. **βολίς bŏlis**, *bol-ece'*; from *906*; a *missile*, i.e. *javelin*:—dart.

1003. **Βοόζ Bŏŏz**, *bŏ-oz'*; of Heb. or. [1162]; *Boöz*, (i.e. *Boäz*), an Isr.:—Booz.

1004. **βόρβορος bŏrbŏrŏs**, *bor'-bor-os*; of uncert. der.; *mud*:—mire.

1005. **βοῤῥᾶς borrhas**, *bor-hras'*; of uncert. der.; the *north* (prop. wind):—north.

1006. **βόσκω bŏskō**, *bos'-ko*; a prol. form of a prim. verb [comp. *977*, *1016*]; to *pasture*; by extens. to *fodder*; reflex. to *graze*:—feed, keep.

1007. **Βοσόρ Bŏsŏr**, *bos-or'*; of Heb. or. [1160]; *Bosor* (i.e. *Beŏr*), a Moabite:—Bosor.

1008. **βοτάνη bŏtanē**, *bot-an'-ay*; from *1006*; *herbage* (as if for *grazing*):—herb.

1009. **βότρυς bŏtrus**, *bot'-rooce*; of uncert. der.; a *bunch* (of grapes):—(vine) cluster (of the vine).

1010. **βουλευτής bŏulĕutēs**, *bool-yoo-tace'*; from *1011*; an *adviser*, i.e. (spec.) a *councillor* or member of the Jewish Sanhedrim:—counsellor.

1011. **βουλεύω bŏulĕuō**, *bool-yoo'-o*; from *1012*; to *advise*, i.e. (reflex.) *deliberate*, or (by impl.) *resolve*:—consult, take counsel, determine, be minded, purpose.

1012. **βουλή bŏulē**, *boo-lay'*; from *1014*; *volition*, i.e. (obj.) *advice*, or (by impl.) *purpose*:—+ advise, counsel, will.

1013. **βούλημα bŏulēma**, *boo'-lay-mah*; from *1014*; a *resolve*:—purpose, will.

1014. **βούλομαι boo'-lom-ahee**; mid. of a prim. verb; to "*will*," i.e. (reflex.) *be willing*:—be disposed, minded, intend, list, (be, of own) will (-ing). Comp. *2309*.

1015. **βουνός bŏunŏs**, *boo-nos'*; prob. of for. or.; a *hillock*:—hill.

1016. **βοῦς bŏus**, *booce*; prob. from the base of *1006*; an *ox* (as *grazing*), i.e. an animal of that species ("beef"):—ox.

1017. **βραβεῖον brabĕiŏn**, *brab-i'-on*; from **βραβεύς brabĕus** (an *umpire*; of uncert. der.); an *award* (of arbitration), i.e. (spec.) a *prize* in the public games:—prize.

1018. **βραβεύω brabĕuō**, *brab-yoo'-o*; from the same as *1017*; to *arbitrate*, i.e. (gen.) to *govern* (fig. *prevail*):—rule.

1019. **βραδύνω bradunō**, *brad-oo'-no*; from *1021*; to *delay*:—be slack, tarry.

1020. **βραδυπλοέω braduplŏĕō**, *brad-oo-plŏ-eh'-o*; from *1021* and a prol. form of *4126*; to *sail slowly*:—sail slowly.

1021. **βραδύς bradus**, *brad-ooce'*; of uncert. affin.; *slow*; fig. *dull*:—slow.

1022. **βραδύτης bradutēs**, *brad-oo'-tace*; from *1021*; *tardiness*:—slackness.

1023. **βραχίων brachiōn**, *brakh-ee'-own*; prop. comp. of *1024*, but appar. in the sense of **βράσσω brassō** (to *wield*); the *arm*, i.e. (fig.) *strength*:—arm.

1024. **βραχύς brachus**, *brakh-ooce'*; of uncert. affin.; *short* (of time, place, quantity, or number):—few words, little (space, while).

1025. **βρέφος brĕphŏs**, *bref'-os*; of uncert. affin.; an *infant* (prop. unborn) lit. or fig.:—babe, (young) child, infant.

1026. **βρέχω brĕchō**, *brekh'-o*; a prim. verb; to *moisten* (espec. by a shower):—(send) rain, wash.

1027. **βροντή brŏntē**, *bron-tay'*; akin to **βρέμω brĕmō** (to *roar*); *thunder*:—thunder (-ing).

1028. **βροχή brŏchē**, *brokh-ay'*; from 1026; *rain*:—rain.

1029. **βρόχος brŏchŏs**, *brokh'-os*; of uncert. der.; a *noose*:—snare.

1030. **βρυγμός brugmŏs**, *broog-mos'*; from *1031*; a *grating* (of the teeth):—gnashing.

1031. **βρύχω bruchō**, *broo'-kho*; a prim. verb; to *grate* the teeth (in pain or rage):—gnash.

1032. **βρύω bruō**, *broo'-o*; a prim. verb; to *swell* out, i.e. (by impl.) to *gush*:—send forth.

1033. **βρῶμα brōma**, *bro'-mah*; from the base of *977*; *food* (lit. or fig.), espec. (cer.) articles allowed or forbidden by the Jewish law:—meat, victuals.

1034. **βρώσιμος brōsimŏs**, *bro'-sim-os*; from *1035*; *eatable*:—meat.

1035. **βρῶσις brōsis**, *bro'-sis*; from the base of *977*; (abstr.) *eating* (lit. or fig.); by extens. (concr.) *food* (lit. or fig.):—eating, food, meat.

1036. **βυθίζω buthizō**, *boo-thid'-zo*; from *1037*; to *sink*; by impl. to *drown*:—begin to sink, drown.

1037. **βυθός buthŏs**, *boo-thos'*; a var. of *899*; *depth*, i.e. (by impl.) the *sea*:—deep.

1038. **βυρσεύς bursĕus**, *boorce-yooce'*; from **βύρσα bursa** (a *hide*); a *tanner*:—tanner.

1039. **βύσσινος bussinŏs**, *boos'-see-nos*; from *1040*; made of *linen* (neut. a linen *cloth*):—fine linen.

1040. **βύσσος bussŏs**, *boos'-sos*; of Heb. or. [948]; white *linen*:—fine linen.

1041. **βῶμος bōmŏs**, *bo'-mos*; from the base of *939*; prop. a *stand*, i.e. (spec.) an *altar*:—altar.

Γ

1042. **γαββαθά gabbatha**, *gab-bath-ah'*; of Chald. or. [comp. 1355]; *the knoll*; *gabbatha*, a vernacular term for the Roman tribunal in Jerus.:—Gabbatha.

1043. **Γαβριήλ Gabriēl**, *gab-ree-ale';* of Heb. or. 1403]; *Gabriel*, an archangel:—Gabriel.

1044. **γάγγραινα gaggraina**, *gang'-grahee-nah;* from **γραίνω grainō** (to *gnaw*); an *ulcer* ("gangrene"):—canker.

1045. **Γάδ Gad**, *gad;* of Heb. or. [1410]; *Gad*, a tribe of Isr.:—Gad.

1046. **Γαδαρηνός Gadarēnŏs**, *gad-ar-ay-nos';* from **Γαδαρά** (a town E. of the Jordan); a *Gadarene* or inhab. of Gadara:—Gadarene.

1047. **γάζα gaza**, *gad'-zah;* of for. or.; a *treasure:*—treasure.

1048. **Γάζα Gaza**, *gad'-zah;* of Heb. or. [5804]; *Gazah* (i.e. *'Azzah*), a place in Pal.:—Gaza.

1049. **γαζοφυλάκιον gazŏphulakiŏn**, *gad-zof-oo-lak'-ee-on;* from *1047* and *5438;* a *treasure-house*, i.e. a court in the temple for the collection-boxes:—treasury.

1050. **Γάϊος Gaïŏs**, *gah'-ee-os;* of Lat. or.; *Gaïus* (i.e. *Caius*), a Chr.:—Gaius.

1051. **γάλα gala**, *gal'-ah;* of uncert. affin.; *milk* (fig.):—milk.

1052. **Γαλάτης Galatēs**, *gal-at'-ace;* from *1053;* a *Galatian* or inhab. of Galatia:—Galatian.

1053. **Γαλατία Galatia**, *gal-at-ee'-ah;* of for. or.; *Galatia*, a region of Asia:—Galatia.

1054. **Γαλατικός Galatikŏs**, *gal-at-ee-kos';* from *1053;* *Galatic* or relating to Galatia:—of Galatia.

1055. **γαλήνη galēnē**, *gal-ay'-nay;* of uncert. der.; *tranquillity:*—calm.

1056. **Γαλιλαία Galilaia**, *gal-il-ah'-yah;* of Heb. or. [1551]; *Galilæa* (i.e. the heathen *circle*), a region of Pal.:—Galilee.

1057. **Γαλιλαῖος Galilaiŏs**, *gal-ee-lah'-yos;* from *1056;* *Galilæan* or belonging to Galilæa:—Galilæan, of Galilee.

1058. **Γαλλίων Galliōn**, *gal-lee'-own;* of Lat. or.; *Gallion* (i.e. *Gallio*), a Roman officer:—Gallio.

1059. **Γαμαλιήλ Gamaliēl**, *gam-al-ee-ale';* of Heb. or. [1583]; *Gamaliel* (i.e. *Gamliel*), an Isr.:—Gamaliel.

1060. **γαμέω gamĕō**, *gam-eh'-o;* from *1062;* to *wed* (of either sex):—marry (a wife).

1061. **γαμίσκω gamiskō**, *gam-is'-ko;* from *1062;* to *espouse* (a daughter to a husband):—give in marriage.

1062. **γάμος gamŏs**, *gam'-os;* of uncert. affin.; *nuptials:*—marriage, wedding.

1063. **γάρ gar**, *gar;* a prim. particle; prop. assigning a *reason* (used in argument, explanation or intensification; often with other particles):—and, as, because (that), but, even, for, indeed, no doubt, seeing, then, therefore, verily, what, why, yet.

1064. **γαστήρ gastēr**, *gas-tare';* of uncert. der.; the *stomach;* by anal. the *matrix;* fig. a *gourmand:*—belly, + with child, womb.

1065. **γέ gĕ**, *gheh;* a prim. particle of *emphasis* or *qualification* (often used with other particles prefixed):—and besides, doubtless, at least, yet.

1066. **Γεδεών Gĕdĕōn**, *ghed-eh-own';* of Heb. or. [1439]; *Gedeon* (i.e. *Gid[e]on*), an Isr.:—Gedeon.

1067. **γέεννα gĕĕnna**, *gheh'-en-nah;* of Heb. or [1516 and 2011]; *valley of* (the son of) *Hinnom; gehenna* (or *Ge-Hinnom*), a valley of Jerus., used (fig.) as a name for the place (or state) of everlasting punishment:—hell.

1068. **Γεθσημανῆ Gĕthsēmanē**, *gheth-say-man-ay';* of Chald. or. [comp. 1660 and 8081]; *oil-press; Gethsemane*, a garden near Jerus.:—Gethsemane.

1069. **γείτων gĕitōn**, *ghi'-tone;* from *1093;* a *neighbor* (as adjoining one's *ground*); by impl. a *friend:*—neighbour.

1070. **γελάω gĕlaō**, *ghel-ah'-o;* of uncert. affin.; to *laugh* (as a sign of joy or satisfaction):—laugh.

1071. **γέλως gĕlōs**, *ghel'-oce;* from *1070;* *laughter* (as a mark of gratification):—laughter.

1072. **γεμίζω gĕmizō**, *ghem-id'-zo;* trans. from *1073;* to *fill* entirely:—fill (be) full.

1073. **γέμω gĕmō**, *ghem'-o;* a prim. verb; to *swell* out, i.e. *be full:*—be full.

1074. **γενεά gĕnĕa**, *ghen-eh-ah';* from (a presumed der. of) *1085;* a *generation;* by impl. an *age* (the period or the persons):—age, generation, nation, time.

1075. **γενεαλογέω gĕnĕalŏgĕō**, *ghen-eh-al-og-eh'-o;* from *1074* and *3056;* to *reckon by generations*, i.e. *trace in genealogy:*—count by descent.

1076. **γενεαλογία gĕnĕalŏgia**, *ghen-eh-al-og-ee'-ah;* from the same as *1075;* *tracing by generations*, i.e. "*genealogy*":—genealogy.

1077. **γενέσια gĕnĕsia**, *ghen-es'-ee-ah;* neut. plur. of a der. of *1078;* *birthday* ceremonies:—birthday.

1078. **γένεσις genesis**, *ghen'-es-is;* from the same as *1074;* *nativity;* fig. *nature:*—generation, nature (-ral).

1079. **γενετή gĕnĕtē**, *ghen-et-ay';* fem. of a presumed der. of the base of *1074;* *birth:*—birth.

1080. **γεννάω gĕnnaō**, *ghen-nah'-o;* from a var. of *1085;* to *procreate* (prop. of the father, but by extens. of the mother); fig. to *regenerate:*—bear, beget, be born, bring forth, conceive, be delivered of, gender, make, spring.

1081. **γέννημα gĕnnēma**, *ghen'-nay-mah;* from *1080;* *offspring;* by anal. *produce* (lit. or fig.):—fruit, generation.

1082. **Γεννησαρέτ Gĕnnēsarĕt**, *ghen-nay-sar-et';* of Heb. or. [comp. 3672]; *Gennesaret* (i.e. *Kinnereth*), a lake and plain in Pal.:—Gennesaret.

1083. **γέννησις gĕnnēsis**, *ghen'-nay-sis;* from *1080;* *nativity:*—birth.

1084. **γεννητός gĕnnētŏs**, *ghen-nay-tos';* from *1080;* *born:*—they that are born.

1085. **γένος gĕnŏs**, *ghen'-os;* from *1096;* "*kin*" (abstr. or concr., lit. or fig., indiv. or coll.):—born, country (-man), diversity, generation, kind (-red), nation, offspring, stock.

1086. **Γεργεσηνός Gĕrgĕsēnŏs**, *gher-ghes-ay-nos';* of Heb. or. [1622]; a *Gergesene* (i.e. *Girgashite*) or one of the aborigines of Pal.:—Gergesene.

1087. **γερουσία gĕrŏusia**, *gher-oo-see'-ah;* from *1088;* the *eldership*, i.e. (collect.) the Jewish *Sanhedrim:*—senate.

1088. **γέρων gĕrōn**, *gher'-own;* of uncert. affin. [comp. *1094*]; *aged:*—old.

1089. **γεύομαι gĕuŏmai**, *ghyoo'-om-ahee;* a prim. verb; to *taste;* by impl. to *eat;* fig. to *experience* (good or ill):—eat, taste.

1090. **γεωργέω gĕōrgĕō**, *gheh-ore-gheh'-o;* from *1092;* to *till* (the soil):—dress.

1091. **γεώργιον gĕōrgiŏn**, *gheh-ore'-ghee-on;* neut. of a (presumed) der. of *1092;* *cultivable*, i.e. a *farm:*—husbandry.

1092. **γεωργός gĕōrgŏs**, *gheh-ore-gos';* from *1093* and the base of *2041;* a *land-worker*, i.e. *farmer:*—husbandman.

1093. **γῆ gē**, *ghay;* contr. from a prim. word; *soil;* by extens. a *region*, or the solid part or the whole of the *terrene* globe (includ. the occupants in each application):—country, earth (-ly), ground, land, world.

1094. **γῆρας gēras**, *ghay'-ras;* akin to *1088;* *senility:*—old age.

1095. **γηράσκω gēraskō**, *ghay-ras'-ko;* from *1094;* to *be senescent:*—be (wax) old.

1096. **γίνομαι ginŏmai**, *ghin'-om-ahee;* a prol. and mid. form of a prim. verb; to *cause to be* ("*gen*"-*erate*), i.e. (reflex.) to *become* (*come into being*), used with great latitude (lit., fig., intens., etc.):—arise, be assembled, be (come, -fall, -have self), be brought (to pass), (be) come (to pass), continue, be divided, be done, draw, be ended, fall, be finished, follow, be found, be fulfilled, + God forbid, grow, happen, have, be kept, be made, be married, be ordained to be, partake, pass, be performed, be published, require, seem, be showed, × soon as it was, sound, be taken, be turned, use, wax, will, would, be wrought.

1097. **γινώσκω ginōskō**, *ghin-oce'-ko;* a prol. form of a prim. verb; to "*know*" (absol.), in a great variety of applications and with many impl. (as follow, with others not thus clearly expressed):—allow, be aware (of), feel, (have) know (-ledge), perceive, be resolved, can speak, be sure, understand.

1098. **γλεῦκος glĕukŏs**, *glyoo'-kos;* akin to *1099;* *sweet* wine, i.e. (prop.) *must* (fresh juice), but used of the more saccharine (and therefore highly inebriating) fermented *wine:*—new wine.

1099. **γλυκύς glukus**, *gloo-koos';* of uncert. affin.; *sweet* (i.e. not bitter nor salt):—sweet, fresh.

1100. **γλῶσσα glōssa**, *gloce-sah';* of uncert. affin.; the *tongue;* by impl. a *language* (spec. one naturally unacquired):—tongue.

1101. **γλωσσόκομον glōssŏkŏmŏn**, *gloce-sok'-om-on;* from *1100* and the base of *2889;* prop. a *case* (to keep mouthpieces of wind-instruments in), i.e. (by extens.) a *casket* or (spec.) *purse:*—bag.

1102. **γναφεύς gnaphĕus**, *gnaf-yuce';* by var. for a der. from **κνάπτω knaptō** (to *tease* cloth); a cloth-*dresser:*—fuller.

1103. **γνήσιος gnēsiŏs**, *gnay'-see-os;* from the same as *1077;* *legitimate* (of birth), i.e. *genuine:*—own, sincerity, true.

1104. **γνησίως gnēsiōs**, *gnay-see'-oce;* adv. from *1103;* *genuinely*, i.e. *really:*—naturally.

1105. **γνόφος gnŏphŏs**, *gnof'-os;* akin to *3509;* *gloom* (as of a storm):—blackness.

1106. **γνώμη gnōmē**, *gno'-may;* from *1097;* *cognition*, i.e. (subj.) *opinion*, or (obj.) *resolve* (*counsel, consent*, etc.):—advice, + agree, judgment, mind, purpose, will.

1107. **γνωρίζω gnōrizō**, *gno-rid'-zo;* from a der. of *1097;* to *make known;* subj. to *know:*—certify, declare, make known, give to understand, do to wit, wot.

1108. **γνῶσις gnōsis**, *gno'-sis;* from *1097;* *knowing* (the act), i.e. (by impl.) *knowledge:*—knowledge, science.

1109. **γνώστης gnōstēs**, *gnoce'-tace;* from *1097;* a *knower:*—expert.

1110. **γνωστός gnōstŏs**, *gnoce-tos';* from *1097;* well *known:*—acquaintance, (which may be) known, notable.

1111. **γογγύζω gŏgguzō**, *gong-good'-zo;* of uncert. der.; to *grumble:*—murmur.

1112. **γογγυσμός gŏggusmŏs**, *gong-goos-mos';* from *1111;* a *grumbling:*—grudging, murmuring.

1113. **γογγυστής gŏggustēs**, *gong-goos-tace';* from *1111;* a *grumbler:*—murmurer.

1114. **γόης gŏēs**, *gŏ'-ace;* from **γοάω gŏaō** (to *wail*); prop. a *wizard* (as *muttering* spells), i.e. (by impl.) an *impostor:*—seducer.

1115. **Γολγοθᾶ Golgŏtha**, *gol-goth-ah';* of Chald. or. [comp. 1538]; *the skull; Golgotha*, a knoll near Jerus.:—Golgotha.

1116. **Γόμοῤῥα Gŏmŏrrha**, *gom'-or-hrhah;* of Heb. or. [6017]; *Gomorrha* (i.e. *'Amorah*), a place near the Dead Sea:—Gomorrha.

1117. **γόμος gŏmŏs**, *gom'-os;* from *1073;* a *load* (as *filling*), i.e. (spec.) a *cargo*, or (by extens.) *wares:*—burden, merchandise.

1118. **γονεύς gŏnĕus**, *gon-yooce';* from the base of *1096;* a *parent:*—parent.

1119. **γονύ gŏnu**, *gon-oo';* of uncert. affin.; the "*knee*":—knee (× -l).

1120. **γονυπετέω gŏnupĕtĕō**, *gon-oo-pet-eh'-o;* from a comp. of *1119* and the alt. of *4098;* to *fall* on the *knee:*—bow the knee, kneel down.

1121. **γράμμα gramma**, *gram'-mah;* from *1125;* a *writing*, i.e. a *letter, note, epistle, book*, etc.; plur. *learning:*—bill, learning, letter, scripture, writing, written.

1122. **γραμματεύς grammatĕus**, *gram-mat-yooce';* from *1121;* a *writer*, i.e. (professionally) *scribe* or *secretary:*—scribe, town-clerk.

1123. **γραπτός graptŏs**, *grap-tos';* from *1125;* *inscribed* (fig.):—written.

1124. **γραφή graphē**, *graf-ay';* from *1125;* a *document*, i.e. holy *Writ* (or its contents or a statement in it):—scripture.

1125. **γράφω graphō**, *graf'-o;* a prim. verb; to "*grave*", espec. to *write;* fig. to *describe:*—describe, write (-ing, -ten).

1126. **γραώδης graōdēs**, *grah-o'-dace;* from **γραῦς graus** (an *old woman*) and *1491; crone-like,* i.e. *silly:*—old wives'.

1127. **γρηγορεύω grēgŏrĕuō**, *gray-gor-yoo'-o;* from *1453;* to *keep awake,* i.e. *watch* (lit. or fig.):—be vigilant, wake, (be) watch (-ful).

1128. **γυμνάζω gumnazō**, *goom-nad'-zo;* from *1131;* to *practise naked* (in the games), i.e. *train* (fig.):—exercise.

1129. **γυμνασία gumnasia**, *goom-nas-ee'-ah;* from *1128; training,* i.e. (fig.) *asceticism:*—exercise.

1130. **γυμνητεύω gumnētĕuō**, *goom-nayt-yoo'-o;* from a der. of *1131;* to *strip,* i.e. (reflex.) *go poorly clad:*—be naked.

1131. **γυμνός gumnŏs**, *goom-nos';* of uncert. affin.; *nude* (absol. or rel., lit. or fig.):—naked.

1132. **γυμνότης gumnŏtēs**, *goom-not'-ace;* from *1131; nudity* (absol. or comp.):—nakedness.

1133. **γυναικάριον gunaikariŏn**, *goo-nahee-kar'-ee-on;* a dimin. from *1135;* a *little* (i.e. *foolish*) *woman:*—silly woman.

1134. **γυναικεῖος gunaikĕiŏs**, *goo-nahee-ki'-os;* from *1135; feminine:*—wife.

1135. **γυνή gunē**, *goo-nay';* prob. from the base of *1096;* a *woman;* spec. a *wife:*—wife, woman.

1136. **Γώγ Gōg**, *gogue;* of Heb. or. [1463]; *Gog,* a symb. name for some future Antichrist:—Gog.

1137. **γωνία gōnia**, *go-nee'-ah;* prob. akin to *1119;* an *angle:*—corner, quarter.

Δ

1138. **Δαβίδ Dabid**, *dab-eed';* of Heb. or. [1732]; *Dabid* (i.e. *David*), the Isr. king:—David.

1139. **δαιμονίζομαι daimŏnizŏmai**, *dahee-mon-id'-zom-ahee;* mid. from *1142;* to *be exercised by a dæmon:*—have a (be vexed with, be possessed with) devil (-s).

1140. **δαιμόνιον daimŏniŏn**, *dahee-mon'-ee-on;* neut. of a der. of *1142;* a *dæmonic being;* by extens. a *deity:*—devil, god.

1141. **δαιμονιώδης daimŏniōdēs**, *dahee-mon-ee-o'-dace;* from *1140* and *1142; dæmon-like:*—devilish.

1142. **δαίμων daimōn**, *dah'ee-mown;* from **δαίω daiō** (to *distribute* fortunes); a *dæmon* or supernatural spirit (of a bad nature):—devil.

1143. **δάκνω daknō**, *dak'-no;* a prol. form of a prim. root: to *bite,* i.e. (fig.) *thwart:*—bite.

1144. **δάκρυ dakru**, *dak'-roo;* or

δάκρυον dakruŏn, *dak'-roo-on;* of uncert. affin.; a *tear:*—tear.

1145. **δακρύω dakruō**, *dak-roo'-o;* from 1144; to *shed tears:*—weep. Comp. *2799.*

1146. **δακτύλιος daktuliŏs**, *dak-too'-lee-os;* from *1147;* a *finger-ring:*—ring.

1147. **δάκτυλος daktulŏs**, *dak'-too-los;* prob. from *1176;* a *finger:*—finger.

1148. **Δαλμανουθά Dalmanŏutha**, *dal-man-oo-thah';* prob. of Chald. or.; *Dalmanūtha,* a place in Pal.:—Dalmanutha.

1149. **Δαλματία Dalmatia**, *dal-mat-ee'-ah;* prob. of for. der.; *Dalmatia,* a region of Europe:—Dalmatia.

1150. **δαμάζω damazō**, *dam-ad'-zo;* a var. of an obs. prim. of the same mean.; to *tame:*—tame.

1151. **δάμαλις damalis**, *dam'-al-is;* prob. from the base of *1150;* a *heifer* (as *tame*):—heifer.

1152. **Δάμαρις Damaris**, *dam'-ar-is;* prob. from the base of *1150;* perh. *gentle; Damaris,* an Athenian woman:—Damaris.

1153. **Δαμασκηνός Damaskēnŏs**, *dam-as-kay-nos';* from *1154;* a *Damascene* or inhab. of Damascus:—Damascene.

1154. **Δαμασκός Damaskŏs**, *dam-as-kos';* of Heb. or. [1834]; *Damascus,* a city of Syria:—Damascus.

1155. **δανείζω danĕizō**, *dan-ide'-zo;* from *1156;* to *loan* on interest; reflex. to *borrow:*—borrow, lend.

1156. **δάνειον danĕiŏn**, *dan'-i-on;* from **δάνος danŏs** (a *gift*); prob. akin to the base of *1325;* a *loan:*—debt.

1157. **δανειστής danĕistēs**, *dan-ice-tace';* from *1155;* a *lender:*—creditor.

1158. **Δανιήλ Daniēl**, *dan-ee-ale';* of Heb. or. [1840]; *Daniel,* an Isr.:—Daniel.

1159. **δαπανάω dapanaō**, *dap-an-ah'-o;* from *1160;* to *expend,* i.e. (in a good sense) to *incur cost,* or (in a bad one) to *waste:*—be at charges, consume, spend.

1160. **δαπάνη dapanē**, *dap-an'-ay;* from **δάπτω daptō** (to *devour*); *expense* (as *consuming*):—cost.

1161. **δέ dĕ**, *deh;* a prim. particle (adversative or continuative); *but, and,* etc.:—also, and, but, moreover, now [*often unexpressed in English*].

1162. **δέησις dĕēsis**, *deh'-ay-sis;* from *1189;* a *petition:*—prayer, request, supplication.

1163. **δεῖ dĕi**, *die;* 3d pers. sing. act. pres. of *1210;* also **δεόν dĕŏn**, *deh-on';* neut. act. part. of the same; both used impers.; *it is* (*was,* etc.) *necessary* (as *binding*):—behoved, be meet, must (needs), (be) need (-ful), ought, should.

1164. **δεῖγμα dĕigma**, *dīgh'-mah;* from the base of *1166;* a *specimen* (as *shown*):—example.

1165. **δειγματίζω dĕigmatizō**, *dīgh-mat-id'-zo;* from *1164;* to *exhibit:*—make a shew.

1166. **δεικνύω dĕiknuō**, *dike-noo'-o;* a prol. form of an obs. prim. of the same mean.; to *show* (lit. or fig.):—shew.

1167. **δειλία dĕilia**, *di-lee'-ah;* from *1169; timidity:*—fear.

1168. **δειλιάω dĕiliaō**, *di-lee-ah'-o;* from *1167;* to *be timid:*—be afraid.

1169. **δειλός dĕilŏs**, *di-los';* from **δέος dĕŏs** (*dread*); *timid,* i.e. (by impl.) *faithless:*—fearful.

1170. **δεῖνα dĕina**, *di'-nah;* prob. from the same as *1171* (through the idea of forgetting the name as *fearful,* i.e. *strange*); *so and so* (when the person is not specified):—such a man.

1171. **δεινῶς dĕinōs**, *di-noce';* adv. from a der. of the same as *1169; terribly,* i.e. *excessively:*—grievously, vehemently.

1172. **δειπνέω dĕipnĕō**, *dipe-neh'-o;* from *1173;* to *dine,* i.e. take the principal (or evening) meal:—sup (× -per).

1173. **δεῖπνον dĕipnŏn**, *dipe'-non;* from the same as *1160; dinner,* i.e. the chief meal (usually in the evening):—feast, supper.

1174. **δεισιδαιμονέστερος dĕisidaimŏnĕstĕrŏs**, *dice-ee-dahee-mon-es'-ter-os;* the comp. of a der. of the base of *1169* and *1142; more religious* than others:—too superstitious.

1175. **δεισιδαιμονία dĕisidaimŏnia**, *dice-ee-dahee-mon-ee'-ah;* from the same as *1174; religion:*—superstition.

1176. **δέκα dĕka**, *dek'-ah;* a prim. number; *ten:*—[eight-] een, ten.

1177. **δεκαδύο dĕkaduŏ**, *dek-ad-oo'-ŏ;* from *1176* and *1417; two* and *ten,* i.e. *twelve:*—twelve.

1178. **δεκαπέντε dĕkapĕntĕ**, *dek-ap-en'-teh;* from *1176* and *4002; ten* and *five,* i.e. *fifteen:*—fifteen.

1179. **Δεκάπολις Dĕkapŏlis**, *dek-ap'-ol-is;* from *1176* and *4172;* the *ten-city* region; the *Decapolis,* a district in Syria:—Decapolis.

1180. **δεκατέσσαρες dĕkatĕssarĕs**, *dek-at-es'-sar-es;* from *1176* and *5064; ten* and *four,* i.e. *fourteen:*—fourteen.

1181. **δεκάτη dĕkatē**, *dek-at'-ay;* fem. of *1182;* a *tenth,* i.e. as a percentage or (tech.) *tithe:*—tenth (part), tithe.

1182. **δέκατος dĕkatŏs**, *dek'-at-os;* ordinal from *1176; tenth:*—tenth.

1183. **δεκατόω dĕkatŏō**, *dek-at-ŏ'-o;* from *1181;* to *tithe,* i.e. to *give* or *take a tenth:*—pay (receive) tithes.

1184. **δεκτός dĕktŏs**, *dek-tos';* from *1209; approved;* (fig.) *propitious:*—accepted (-table).

1185. **δελεάζω dĕlĕazō**, *del-eh-ad'-zo;* from the base of *1388;* to *entrap,* i.e. (fig.) *delude:*—allure, beguile, entice.

1186. **δένδρον dĕndrŏn**, *den'-dron;* prob. from **δρῦς drus** (an *oak*); a *tree:*—tree.

1187. **δεξιολάβος dĕxiŏlabŏs**, *dex-ee-ol-ab'-os;* from *1188* and *2983;* a *guardsman* (as if *taking the right*) or light-armed soldier:—spearman.

1188. **δεξιός dĕxiŏs**, *dex-ee-os';* from *1209;* the *right* side or (fem.) hand (as that which usually *takes*):—right (hand, side).

1189. **δέομαι dĕŏmai**, *deh'-om-ahee;* mid. of *1210;* to *beg* (as *binding oneself*), i.e. *petition:*—beseech, pray (to), make request. Comp. 4441.

δεόν dĕŏn. See *1163.*

1190. **Δερβαῖος Dĕrbaiŏs**, *der-bah'ee-os;* from *1191;* a *Derbæan* or inhab. of Derbe:—of Derbe.

1191. **Δέρβη Dĕrbē**, *der'-bay;* of for. or.; *Derbè,* a place in Asia Minor:—Derbe.

1192. **δέρμα dĕrma**, *der'-mah;* from 1194; a *hide:*—skin.

1193. **δερμάτινος dĕrmatinŏs**, *der-mat'-ee-nos;* from *1192;* made of *hide:*—leathern, of a skin.

1194. **δέρω dĕrō**, *der'-o;* a prim. verb; prop. to *flay,* i.e. (by impl.) to *scourge,* or (by anal.) to *thrash:*—beat, smite.

1195. **δεσμεύω dĕsmĕuō**, *des-myoo'-o;* from a (presumed) der. of *1196;* to *be a binder* (*captor*), i.e. to *enchain* (a prisoner), to *tie on* (a load):—bind.

1196. **δεσμέω dĕsmĕō**, *des-meh'-o;* from *1199;* to tie, i.e. *shackle:*—bind.

1197. **δεσμή dĕsmē**, *des-may';* from *1196;* a *bundle:*—bundle.

1198. **δέσμιος dĕsmiŏs**, *des'-mee-os;* from *1199;* a *captive* (as *bound*):—in bonds, prisoner.

1199. **δεσμόν dĕsmŏn**, *des-mon';* or

δεσμός dĕsmŏs, *des-mos';* neut. and masc. respectively from *1210;* a *band,* i.e. *ligament* (of the body) or *shackle* (of a prisoner); fig. an *impediment* or *disability:*—band, bond, chain, string.

1200. **δεσμοφύλαξ dĕsmŏphulax**, *des-mof-oo'-lax;* from *1199* and *5441;* a *jailer* (as *guarding* the *prisoners*):—jailor, keeper of the prison.

1201. **δεσμωτήριον dĕsmōtēriŏn**, *des-mo-tay'-ree-on;* from a der. of *1199* (equiv. to *1196*); a *place of bondage,* i.e. a *dungeon:*—prison.

1202. **δεσμώτης dĕsmōtēs**, *des-mo'-tace;* from the same as *1201;* (pass.) a *captive:*—prisoner.

1203. **δεσπότης dĕspŏtēs**, *des-pot'-ace;* perh. from *1210* and **πόσις pŏsis** (a *husband*); an absolute *ruler* ("despot"):—Lord, master.

1204. **δεῦρο dĕurŏ**, *dyoo'-rŏ;* of uncert. affin.; *here;* used also imper. *hither!;* and of time, *hitherto:*—come (hither), hither [-to].

1205. **δεῦτε dĕutĕ**, *dyoo'-teh;* from *1204* and an imper. form of **εἶμι ĕimi** (to *go*); *come hither!:*—come, × follow.

1206. **δευτεραῖος dĕutĕraiŏs**, *dyoo-ter-ah'-yos;* from *1208; secondary,* i.e. (spec.) on the *second* day:—next day.

1207. **δευτερόπρωτος dĕutĕrŏprōtŏs**, *dyoo-ter-op'-ro-tos;* from *1208* and *4413; second-first,* i.e. (spec.) a designation of the Sabbath immediately after the Paschal week (being the *second* after Passover day, and the *first* of the seven Sabbaths intervening before Pentecost):—second . . . after the first.

1208. **δεύτερος dĕutĕrŏs**, *dyoo'-ter-os;* as the comp. of *1417;* (ordinal) *second* (in time, place or rank; also adv.):—afterward, again, second (-arily, time).

1209. **δέχομαι dĕchŏmai**, *dekh'-om-ahee;* mid. of a prim. verb; to *receive* (in various applications, lit. or fig.):—accept, receive, take. Comp. *2983.*

1210. **δέω dĕō**, *deh'-o;* a prim. verb; to *bind* (in various applications, lit. or fig.):—bind, be in bonds, knit, tie, wind. See also *1163, 1189.*

1211. δή **dē**, *day;* prob. akin to *1161;* a particle of emphasis or explicitness; *now, then,* etc.:—also, and, doubtless, now, therefore.

1212. δῆλος **dēlŏs**, *day'-los;* of uncert. der.; *clear:*— + bewray, certain, evident, manifest.

1213. δηλόω **dēlŏō**, *day-lŏ'-o;* from *1212;* to *make plain* (by words):—declare, shew, signify.

1214. Δημᾶς **Dēmas**, *day-mas';* prob. for *1216;* *Demas,* a Chr.:—Demas.

1215. δημηγορέω **dēmēgŏrĕō**, *day-may-gor-eh'-o;* from a comp. of *1218* and *58;* to *be a people-gatherer,* i.e. to *address* a public assembly:—make an oration.

1216. Δημήτριος **Dēmētriŏs**, *day-may'-tree-os;* from Δημήτηρ **Dēmētēr** (*Ceres*); *Demetrius,* the name of an Ephesian and of a Chr.:—Demetrius.

1217. δημιουργός **dēmiŏurgŏs**, *day-me-oor-gos';* from *1218* and *2041;* a *worker* for the *people,* i.e. *mechanic* (spoken of the *Creator*):—maker.

1218. δῆμος **dēmŏs**, *day'-mos;* from *1210;* the *public* (as *bound* together socially):—people.

1219. δημόσιος **dēmŏsiŏs**, *day-mos'-ee-os;* from *1218;* *public;* (fem. sing. dat. as adv.) *in public:*—common, openly, publickly.

1220. δηνάριον **dēnariŏn**, *day-nar'-ee-on;* of Lat. or.; a *denarius* (or *ten asses*):—pence, penny [-worth].

1221. δήποτε **dēpŏtĕ**, *day'-pot-eh;* from *1211* and *4218;* a particle of generalization; *indeed, at any time:*—(what-) soever.

1222. δήπου **dēpŏu**, *day'-poo;* from *1211* and *4225;* a particle of asseveration; *indeed doubtless:*—verily.

1223. διά **dia**, *dee-ah';* a prim. prep. denoting the *channel* of an act; *through* (in very wide applications, local, causal or occasional):—after, always, among, at, to avoid, because of (that), briefly, by, for (cause) . . . fore, from, in, by occasion of, of, by reason of, for sake, that, thereby, therefore, × though, through (-out), to, wherefore, with (-in). In composition it retains the same general import.

Δία **Dia**. See *2203.*

1224. διαβαίνω **diabainō**, *dee-ab-ah'ee-no;* from *1223* and the base of *939;* to *cross:*—come over, pass (through).

1225. διαβάλλω **diaballō**, *dee-ab-al'-lo;* from *1223* and *906;* (fig.) to *traduce:*—accuse.

1226. διαβεβαιόομαι **diabĕbaiŏŏmai**, *dee-ab-eb-ahee-ŏ'-om-ahee;* mid. of a comp. of *1223* and *950;* to *confirm thoroughly* (by words), i.e. *asseverate:*—affirm constantly.

1227. διαβλέπω **diablĕpō**, *dee-ab-lep'-o;* from *1223* and *991;* to *look through,* i.e. *recover full vision:*—see clearly.

1228. διάβολος **diabŏlŏs**, *dee-ab'-ol-os;* from *1225;* a *traducer;* spec. *Satan* [comp. 7854]:—false accuser, devil, slanderer.

1229. διαγγέλλω **diaggĕllō**, *de-ang-gel'-lo;* from *1223* and the base of *32;* to *herald thoroughly:*—declare, preach, signify.

1230. διαγίνομαι **diaginŏmai**, *dee-ag-in'-om-ahee;* from *1223* and *1096;* to *elapse meanwhile:*— × after, be past, be spent.

1231. διαγινώσκω **diaginōskō**, *dee-ag-in-o'-sko;* from *1223* and *1097;* to *know thoroughly,* i.e. *ascertain exactly:*—(would) enquire, know the uttermost.

1232. διαγνωρίζω **diagnōrizō**, *dee-ag-no-rid'-zo;* from *1123* and *1107;* to *tell abroad:*—make known.

1233. διάγνωσις **diagnōsis**, *dee-ag'-no-sis;* from *1231;* (magisterial) *examination* ("diagnosis"):—hearing.

1234. διαγογγύζω **diagŏgguzō**, *dee-ag-ong-good'-zo;* from *1223* and *1111;* to *complain throughout* a crowd:—murmur.

1235. διαγρηγορέω **diagrēgŏrĕō**, *dee-ag-ray-gor-eh'-o;* from *1223* and *1127;* to *waken thoroughly:*—be awake.

1236. διάγω **diagō**, *dee-ag'-o;* from *1223* and *71;* to *pass* time or life:—lead life, living.

1237. διαδέχομαι **diadĕchŏmai**, *dee-ad-ekh'-om-ahee;* from *1223* and *1209;* to *receive in turn,* i.e. (fig.) *succeed to:*—come after.

1238. διάδημα **diadēma**, *dee-ad'-ay-mah;* from a comp. of *1223* and *1210;* a "*diadem*" (as *bound about* the head):—crown. Comp. *4735.*

1239. διαδίδωμι **diadidōmi**, *dee-ad-id'-o-mee;* from *1223* and *1325;* to *give throughout* a crowd, i.e. *deal out;* also to *deliver* over (as to a successor):—(make) distribute (-ion), divide, give.

1240. διάδοχος **diadŏchŏs**, *dee-ad'-okh-os;* from *1237;* a *successor* in office:—room.

1241. διαζώννυμι **diazōnnumi**, *dee-az-own'-noo-mee;* from *1223* and *2224;* to *gird tightly:*—gird.

1242. διαθήκη **diathēkē**, *dee-ath-ay'-kay;* from *1303;* prop. a *disposition,* i.e. (spec.) a *contract* (espec. a devisory *will*):—covenant, testament.

1243. διαίρεσις **dairĕsis**, *dee-ah'ee-res-is;* from *1244;* a *distinction* or (concr.) *variety:*—difference, diversity.

1244. διαιρέω **dairĕō**, *dee-ahee-reh'-o;* from *1223* and *138;* to *separate,* i.e. *distribute:*—divide.

1245. διακαθαρίζω **diakatharizō**, *dee-ak-ath-ar-id'-zo;* from *1223* and *2511;* to *cleanse perfectly,* i.e. (spec.) *winnow:*—throughly purge.

1246. διακατελέγχομαι **diakatĕlĕgchŏmai**, *dee-ak-at-el-eng'-khom-ahee;* mid. from *1223* and a comp. of *2596* and *1651;* to *prove downright,* i.e. *confute:*—convince.

1247. διακονέω **diakŏnĕō**, *dee-ak-on-eh'-o;* from *1249;* to *be an attendant,* i.e. *wait upon* (menially or as a host, friend or [fig.] teacher); techn. to *act as a* Chr. *deacon:*—(ad-) minister (unto), serve, use the office of a deacon.

1248. διακονία **diakŏnia**, *dee-ak-on-ee'-ah;* from *1249;* *attendance* (as a servant, etc.); fig. (eleemosynary) *aid,* (official) *service* (espec. of the Chr. teacher, or techn. of the *diaconate*):—(ad-) minister (-ing, -tration, -try), office, relief, service (-ing).

1249. διάκονος **diakŏnŏs**, *dee-ak'-on-os;* prob. from an obs. διάκω **diakō** (to *run* on errands; comp. *1377*); an *attendant,* i.e. (gen.) a *waiter* (at table or in other menial duties); spec. a Chr. *teacher* and *pastor* (techn. a *deacon* or *deaconess*):—deacon, minister, servant.

1250. διακόσιοι **diakŏsiŏi**, *dee-ak-os'-ee-oy;* from *1364* and *1540;* *two hundred:*—two hundred.

1251. διακούομαι **diakŏuŏmai**, *dee-ak-oo'-om-ahee;* mid. from *1223* and *191;* to *hear throughout,* i.e. *patiently listen* (to a prisoner's plea):—hear.

1252. διακρίνω **diakrinō**, *dee-ak-ree'-no;* from *1223* and *2919;* to *separate thoroughly,* i.e. (lit. and reflex.) to *withdraw* from, or (by impl.) *oppose;* fig. to *discriminate* (by impl. *decide*), or (reflex.) *hesitate:*—contend, make (to) differ (-ence), discern, doubt, judge, be partial, stagger, waver.

1253. διάκρισις **diakrisis**, *dee-ak'-ree-sis;* from *1252;* judicial *estimation:*—discern (-ing), disputation.

1254. διακωλύω **diakōluō**, *dee-ak-o-loo'-o;* from *1223* and *2967;* to *hinder altogether,* i.e. *utterly prohibit:*—forbid.

1255. διαλαλέω **dialalĕō**, *dee-al-al-eh'-o;* from *1223* and *2980;* to *talk throughout* a company, i.e. *converse* or (gen.) *publish:*—commune, noise abroad.

1256. διαλέγομαι **dialĕgŏmai**, *dee-al-eg'-om-ahee;* mid. from *1223* and *3004;* to *say thoroughly,* i.e. *discuss* (in argument or exhortation):—dispute, preach (unto), reason (with), speak.

1257. διαλείπω **dialĕipō**, *dee-al-i'-po;* from *1223* and *3007;* to *leave off in the middle,* i.e. *intermit:*—cease.

1258. διάλεκτος **dialĕktŏs**, *dee-al'-ek-tos;* from *1256;* a (mode of) *discourse,* i.e. "*dialect*":—language, tongue.

1259. διαλλάσσω **diallassō**, *dee-al-las'-so;* from *1223* and *236;* to *change thoroughly,* i.e. (ment.) to *conciliate:*—reconcile.

1260. διαλογίζομαι **dialŏgizŏmai**, *dee-al-og-id'-zom-ahee;* from *1223* and *3049;* to *reckon thoroughly,* i.e. (gen.) to *deliberate* (by reflection or discussion):—cast in mind, consider, dispute, muse, reason, think.

1261. διαλογισμός **dialŏgismŏs**, *dee-al-og-is-mos';* from *1260;* *discussion,* i.e. (internal) *consideration* (by impl. *purpose*), or (external) *debate:*—dispute, doubtful (-ing), imagination, reasoning, thought.

1262. διαλύω **dialuō**, *dee-al-oo'-o;* from *1223* and *3089;* to *dissolve utterly:*—scatter.

1263. διαμαρτύρομαι **diamarturŏmai**, *dee-am-ar-too'-rom-ahee;* from *1223* and *3140;* to *attest* or *protest earnestly,* or (by impl.) *hortatively:*—charge, testify (unto), witness.

1264. διαμάχομαι **diamachŏmai**, *dee-am-akh'-om-ahee;* from *1223* and *3164;* to *fight fiercely* (in altercation):—strive.

1265. διαμένω **diamĕnō**, *dee-am-en'-o;* from *1223* and *3306;* to *stay constantly* (in being or relation):—continue, remain.

1266. διαμερίζω **diamĕrizō**, *dee-am-er-id'-zo;* from *1223* and *3307;* to *partition thoroughly* (lit. in distribution, fig. in dissension):—cloven, divide, part.

1267. διαμερισμός **diamĕrismŏs**, *dee-am-er-is-mos';* from *1266;* *disunion* (of opinion and conduct):—division.

1268. διανέμω **dianĕmō**, *dee-an-em'-o;* from *1223* and the base of *3551;* to *distribute,* i.e. (of information) to *disseminate:*—spread.

1269. διανεύω **dianĕuō**, *dee-an-yoo'-o;* from *1223* and *3506;* to *nod* (or *express* by signs) *across* an intervening space:—beckon.

1270. διανόημα **dianŏēma**, *dee-an-ŏ'-ay-mah;* from a comp. of *1223* and *3539;* something *thought through,* i.e. a *sentiment:*—thought.

1271. διάνοια **dianŏia**, *dee-an'-oy-ah;* from *1223* and *3563;* *deep thought,* prop. the faculty (*mind* or its *disposition*), by impl. its exercise:—imagination, mind, understanding.

1272. διανοίγω **dianŏigō**, *dee-an-oy'-go;* from *1223* and *455;* to *open thoroughly,* lit. (as a first-born) or fig. (to *expound*):—open.

1273. διανυκτερεύω **dianuktĕrĕuō**, *dee-an-ook-ter-yoo'-o;* from *1223* and a der. of *3571;* to *sit up the whole night:*—continue all night.

1274. διανύω **dianuō**, *dee-an-oo'-o;* from *1223* and ἀνύω **anuō** (to *effect*); to *accomplish thoroughly:*—finish.

1275. διαπαντός **diapantŏs**, *dee-ap-an-tos';* from *1223* and the genit. of *3956;* *through all* time, i.e. (adv.) *constantly:*—alway (-s), continually.

1276. διαπεράω **diapĕraō**, *dee-ap-er-ah'-o;* from *1223* and a der. of the base of *4008;* to *cross entirely:*—go over, pass (over), sail over.

1277. διαπλέω **diaplĕō**, *dee-ap-leh'-o;* from *1223* and *4126;* to *sail through:*—sail over.

1278. διαπονέω **diapŏnĕō**, *dee-ap-on-eh'-o;* from *1223* and a der. of *4192;* to *toil through,* i.e. (pass.) *be worried:*—be grieved.

1279. διαπορεύομαι **diapŏrĕuŏmai**, *dee-ap-or-yoo'-om-ahee;* from *1223* and *4198;* to *travel through:*—go through, journey in, pass by.

1280. διαπορέω **diapŏrĕō**, *dee-ap-or-eh'-o;* from *1223* and *639;* to *be thoroughly nonplussed:*—(be in) doubt, be (much) perplexed.

1281. διαπραγματεύομαι **diapragmatĕuŏmai**, *dee-ap-rag-mat-yoo'-om-ahee;* from *1223* and *4231;* to *thoroughly occupy oneself,* i.e. (trans. and by impl.) to *earn* in business:—gain by trading.

1282. διαπρίω **diapriō**, *dee-ap-ree'-o;* from *1223* and the base of *4249;* to *saw asunder,* i.e. (fig.) to *exasperate:*—cut (to the heart).

1283. διαρπάζω **diarpazō**, *dee-ar-pad'-zo;* from *1223* and *726;* to *seize asunder,* i.e. *plunder:*—spoil.

1284. διαῤῥήσσω **diarrhēssō**, *dee-ar-hrayce'-so;* from *1223* and *4486;* to *tear asunder:*—break, rend.

1285. διασαφέω **diasaphĕō**, *dee-as-af-eh'-o;* from *1223* and σαφής **saphēs** (*clear*); to *clear thoroughly,* i.e. (fig.) *declare:*—tell unto.

1286. διασείω **diasĕiō**, *dee-as-i'-o;* from *1223* and *4579;* to *shake thoroughly,* i.e. (fig.) to *intimidate:*—do violence to.

1287. διασκορπίζω **diaskŏrpizō**, *dee-as-kor-pid'-zo;* from *1223* and *4650;* to *dissipate,* i.e. (gen.) to *rout* or *separate;* spec. to *winnow;* fig. to *squander:*—disperse, scatter (abroad), strew, waste.

1288. **διασπάω diaspaō**, *dee-as-pah'-o;* from *1223* and *4685;* to *draw apart*, i.e. *sever* or *dismember:*—pluck asunder, pull in pieces.

1289. **διασπείρω diaspĕirō**, *dee-as-pi'-ro;* from *1223* and *4687;* to *sow throughout*, i.e. (fig.) *distribute* in foreign lands:—scatter abroad.

1290. **διασπορά diaspŏra**, *dee-as-por-ah';* from *1289; dispersion*, i.e. (spec. and concr.) the (converted) Isr. *resident* in Gentile countries:—(which are) scattered (abroad).

1291. **διαστέλλομαι diastĕllŏmai**, *dee-as-tel'-lom-ahee;* mid. from *1223* and *4724;* to *set* (oneself) *apart* (fig. *distinguish*), i.e. (by impl.) to *enjoin:*—charge, that which was (give) commanded (-ment).

1292. **διάστημα diastēma**, *dee-as'-tay-mah;* from *1339;* an *interval:*—space.

1293. **διαστολή diastŏlē**, *dee-as-tol-ay';* from *1291;* a *variation:*—difference, distinction.

1294. **διαστρέφω diastrĕphō**, *dee-as-tref'-o;* from *1223* and *4762;* to *distort*, i.e. (fig.) *misinterpret*, or (mor.) *corrupt:*—perverse (-rt), turn away.

1295. **διασώζω diasōzō**, *dee-as-odze'-o;* from *1223* and *4982;* to *save thoroughly*, i.e. (by impl. or anal.) to *cure, preserve, rescue*, etc.:—bring safe, escape (safe), heal, make perfectly whole, save.

1296. **διαταγή diatagē**, *dee-at-ag-ay';* from *1299; arrangement*, i.e. *institution:*—instrumentality.

1297. **διάταγμα diatagma**, *dee-at'-ag-mah;* from *1299;* an *arrangement*, i.e. (authoritative) *edict:*—commandment.

1298. **διαταράσσω diatarassō**, *dee-at-ar-as'-so;* from *1223* and *5015;* to *disturb wholly*, i.e. *agitate* (with alarm):—trouble.

1299. **διατάσσω diatassō**, *dee-at-as'-so;* from *1223* and *5021;* to *arrange thoroughly*, i.e. (spec.) *institute, prescribe*, etc.:—appoint, command, give, (set in) order, ordain.

1300. **διατελέω diatĕlĕō**, *dee-at-el-eh'-o;* from *1223* and *5055;* to *accomplish thoroughly*, i.e. (subj.) to *persist:*—continue.

1301. **διατηρέω diatērĕō**, *dee-at-ay-reh'-o;* from *1223* and *5083;* to *watch thoroughly*, i.e. (pos. and trans.) to *observe* strictly, or (neg. and reflex.) to *avoid* wholly:—keep.

1302. **διατί diati**, *dee-at-ee';* from *1223* and *5101; through what* cause ?, i.e. *why?:*—wherefore, why.

1303. **διατίθεμαι diatithĕmai**, *dee-at-ith'-em-ahee;* mid. from *1223* and *5087;* to *put apart*, i.e. (fig.) *dispose* (by assignment, compact or bequest):—appoint, make, testator.

1304. **διατρίβω diatribō**, *dee-at-ree'-bo;* from *1223* and the base of *5147;* to *wear through* (time), i.e. *remain:*—abide, be, continue, tarry.

1305. **διατροφή diatrŏphē**, *dee-at-rof-ay';* from a comp. of *1223* and *5142; nourishment:*—food.

1306. **διαυγάζω diaugazō**, *dee-ŏw-gad'-zo;* from *1223* and *826;* to *glimmer through*, i.e. *break* (as day):—dawn.

1307. **διαφανής diaphanēs**, *dee-af-an-ace';* from *1223* and *5316; appearing through*, i.e. "*diaphanous*":—transparent.

1308. **διαφέρω diaphĕrō**, *dee-af-er'-o;* from *1223* and *5342;* to *bear through*, i.e. (lit.) *transport;* usually to *bear apart*, i.e. (obj.) to *toss about* (fig. *report*); subj. to "*differ*," or (by impl.) *surpass:*—be better, carry, differ from, drive up and down, be (more) excellent, make matter, publish, be of more value.

1309. **διαφεύγω diaphĕugō**, *dee-af-yoo'-go;* from *1223* and *5343;* to *flee through*, i.e. *escape:*—escape.

1310. **διαφημίζω diaphēmizō**, *dee-af-ay-mid'-zo;* from *1223* and a der. of *5345;* to *report thoroughly*, i.e. *divulgate:*—blaze abroad, commonly report, spread abroad, fame.

1311. **διαφθείρω diaphthĕirō**, *dee-af-thi'-ro;* from *1225* and *5351;* to *rot thoroughly*, i.e. (by impl.) to *ruin* (pass. *decay* utterly, fig. *pervert*):—corrupt, destroy, perish.

1312. **διαφθορά diaphthŏra**, *dee-af-thor-ah';* from *1311; decay:*—corruption.

1313. **διάφορος diaphŏrŏs**, *dee-af'-or-os;* from *1308; varying;* also *surpassing:*—differing, divers, more excellent.

1314. **διαφυλάσσω diaphulassō**, *dee-af-oo-las'-so;* from *1223* and *5442;* to *guard thoroughly*, i.e. *protect:*—keep.

1315. **διαχειρίζομαι diachĕirizŏmai**, *dee-akh-i-rid'-zom-ahee;* from *1223* and a der. of *5495;* to *handle thoroughly*, i.e. *lay* violent *hands* upon:—kill, slay.

1316. **διαχωρίζομαι diachōrizŏmai**, *dee-akh-o-rid'-zom-ahee;* from *1223* and the mid. of *5563;* to *remove* (oneself) *wholly*, i.e. *retire:*—depart.

1317. **διδακτικός didaktikŏs**, *did-ak-tik-os';* from *1318; instructive* ("didactic"):—apt to teach.

1318. **διδακτός didaktŏs**, *did-ak-tos';* from *1321;* (subj.) *instructed* or (obj.) *communicated* by teaching:—taught, which . . . teacheth.

1319. **διδασκαλία didaskalia**, *did-as-kal-ee'-ah;* from *1320; instruction* (the function or the information):—doctrine, learning, teaching.

1320. **διδάσκαλος didaskalŏs**, *did-as'-kal-os;* from *1321;* an *instructor* (gen. or spec.):—doctor, master, teacher.

1321. **διδάσκω didaskō**, *did-as'-ko;* a prol. (caus.) form of a prim. verb **δάω daō** (to *learn*); to *teach* (in the same broad application):—teach.

1322. **διδαχή didachē**, *did-akh-ay';* from *1321; instruction* (the act or the matter):—doctrine, hath been taught.

1323. **δίδραχμον didrachmŏn**, *did'-rakh-mon;* from *1364* and *1406;* a *double drachma* (*didrachm*):—tribute.

1324. **Δίδυμος Didumŏs**, *did'-oo-mos;* prol. from *1364; double*, i.e. *twin; Didymus*, a Chr.:—Didymus.

1325. **δίδωμι didōmi**, *did'-o-mee;* a prol. form of a prim. verb (which is used as an altern. in most of the tenses); to *give* (used in a very wide application, prop. or by impl., lit. or fig.; greatly modified by the connection):—adventure, bestow, bring forth, commit, deliver (up), give, grant, hinder, make, minister, number, offer, have power, put, receive, set, shew, smite (+ with the hand), strike (+ with the palm of the hand), suffer, take, utter, yield.

1326. **διεγείρω diĕgĕirō**, *dee-eg-i'-ro;* from *1223* and *1453;* to *wake fully*, i.e. *arouse* (lit. or fig.):—arise, awake, raise, stir up.

1327. **διέξοδος diĕxŏdŏs**, *dee-ex'-od-os;* from *1223* and *1841;* an *outlet through*, i.e. prob. an open *square* (from which roads diverge):—highway

1328. **διερμηνευτής diĕrmēnĕutēs**, *dee-er-main-yoo-tace';* from *1329;* an *explainer:*—interpreter.

1329. **διερμηνεύω diĕrmēnĕuō**, *dee-er-main-yoo'-o;* from *1223* and *2059;* to *explain thoroughly;* by impl. to *translate:*—expound, interpret (-ation).

1330. **διέρχομαι diĕrchŏmai**, *dee-er'-khom-ahee;* from *1223* and *2064;* to *traverse* (lit.):—come, depart, go (about, abroad, every where, over, through, throughout), pass (by, over, through, throughout), pierce through, travel, walk through.

1331. **διερωτάω diĕrōtaō**, *dee-er-o-tah'-o;* from *1223* and *2065;* to *question throughout*, i.e. *ascertain* by interrogation:—make enquiry for.

1332. **διετής diĕtēs**, *dee-et-ace';* from *1364* and *2094; of two years* (in age):—two years old.

1333. **διετία diĕtia**, *dee-et-ee'-a;* from *1332;* a space of *two years* (*biennium*):—two years.

1334. **διηγέομαι diēgĕŏmai**, *dee-ayg-eh'-om-ahee;* from *1223* and *2233;* to *relate fully:*—declare, shew, tell.

1335. **διήγεσις diēgĕsis**, *dee-ayg'-es-is;* from *1334;* a *recital:*—declaration.

1336. **διηνεκές diēnĕkĕs**, *dee-ay-nek-es';* neut. of a comp. of *1223* and a der. of an alt. of *5342; carried through*, i.e. (adv. with *1519* and *3588* pref.) *perpetually:*—+ continually, for ever.

1337. **διθάλασσος dithalassŏs**, *dee-thal'-as-sos;* from *1364* and *2281; having two seas*, i.e. a *sound* with a double outlet:—where two seas met.

1338. **διϊκνέομαι diïknĕŏmai**, *dee-ik-neh'-om-ahee;* from *1223* and the base of *2425;* to *reach through*, i.e. *penetrate:*—pierce.

1339. **διΐστημι diïstēmi**, *dee-is'-tay-mee;* from *1223* and *2476;* to *stand apart*, i.e. (reflex.) to *remove, intervene:*—go further, be parted, after the space of.

1340. **διϊσχυρίζομαι diïschurizŏmai**, *dee-is-khoo-rid'-zom-ahee;* from *1223* and a der. of *2478;* to *stout it through*, i.e. *asseverate:*—confidently (constantly) affirm.

1341. **δικαιοκρισία dikaiŏkrisia**, *dik-ah-yok-ris-ee'-ah;* from *1342* and *2920;* a *just sentence:*—righteous judgment.

1342. **δίκαιος dikaiŏs**, *dik'-ah-yos;* from *1349; equitable* (in character or act); by impl. *innocent, holy* (absol. or rel.):—just, meet, right (-eous).

1343. **δικαιοσύνη dikaiŏsunē**, *dik-ah-yos-oo'-nay;* from *1342; equity* (of character or act); spec. (Chr.) *justification:*—righteousness.

1344. **δικαιόω dikaiŏō**, *dik-ah-yŏ'-o;* from *1342;* to *render* (i.e. *show* or *regard* as) *just* or *innocent:*—free, justify (-ier), be righteous.

1345. **δικαίωμα dikaiōma**, *dik-ah'-yo-mah;* from *1344;* an *equitable deed;* by impl. a *statute* or *decision:*—judgment, justification, ordinance, righteousness.

1346. **δικαίως dikaiōs**, *dik-ah'-yoce;* adv. from *1342; equitably:*—justly, (to) righteously (-ness).

1347. **δικαίωσις dikaiōsis**, *dik-ah'-yo-sis;* from *1344; acquittal* (for Christ's sake):—justification.

1348. **δικαστής dikastēs**, *dik-as-tace';* from a der. of *1349;* a *judger:*—judge.

1349. **δίκη dikē**, *dee'-kay;* prob. from *1166; right* (as self-evident), i.e. *justice* (the principle, a decision, or its execution):—judgment, punish, vengeance.

1350. **δίκτυον diktuŏn**, *dik'-too-on;* prob. from a prim. verb **δίκω dikō** (to *cast*); a *seine* (for fishing):—net.

1351. **δίλογος dilŏgŏs**, *dil'-og-os;* from *1364* and *3056; equivocal*, i.e. telling a different story:—double tongued.

1352. **διό diŏ**, *dee-ŏ';* from *1223* and *3739; through which* thing, i.e. *consequently:*—for which cause, therefore, wherefore.

1353. **διοδεύω diŏdĕuō**, *dee-od-yoo'-o;* from *1223* and *3593;* to *travel through:*—go throughout, pass through.

1354. **Διονύσιος Diŏnusiŏs**, *dee-on-oo'-see-os;* from **Διόνυσος Diŏnusŏs** (*Bacchus*); *reveller; Dionysius*, an Athenian:—Dionysius.

1355. **διόπερ diŏpĕr**, *dee-op'-er;* from *1352* and *4007; on which very account:*—wherefore.

1356. **διοπετής diŏpĕtēs**, *dee-op-et'-ace;* from the alt. of *2203* and the alt. of *4098; sky-fallen* (i.e. an *aerolite*):—which fell down from Jupiter.

1357. **διόρθωσις diŏrthōsis**, *dee-or'-tho-sis;* from a comp. of *1223* and a der. of *3717*, mean. to *straighten thoroughly; rectification*, i.e. (spec.) the Messianic *restauration:*—reformation.

1358. **διορύσσω diŏrussō**, *dee-or-oos'-so;* from *1223* and *3736;* to *penetrate* burglariously:—break through (up).

Διός Diŏs. See *2203*.

1359. **Διόσκουροι Diŏskŏurŏi**, *dee-os'-koo-roy;* from the alt. of *2203* and a form of the base of *2877; sons of Jupiter*, i.e. the twins *Dioscuri:*—Castor and Pollux.

1360. **διότι diŏti**, *dee-ot'-ee;* from *1223* and *3754; on the very account that*, or *inasmuch as:*—because (that), for, therefore.

1361. **Διοτρεφής Diŏtrĕphēs**, *dee-ot-ref-ace';* from the alt. of *2203* and *5142; Jove-nourished; Diotrephes*, an opponent of Christianity:—Diotrephes.

1362. **διπλοῦς diplŏus**, *dip-looce';* from *1364* and (prob.) the base of *4119; two-fold:*—double, two-fold more.

1363. **διπλόω diplŏō**, *dip-lŏ'-o;* from *1362;* to *render two-fold:*—double.

1364. **δίς dis**, *dece;* adv. from *1417; twice:*—again, twice.

Δίς Dis. See *2203.*

1365. **διστάζω distazō**, *dis-tad'-zo;* from *1364;* prop. to *duplicate*, i.e. (ment.) to *waver* (in opinion):—doubt.

1366. **δίστομος distŏmŏs**, *dis'-tom-os;* from *1364* and *4750; double-edged:*—with two edges, two-edged.

1367. **δισχίλιοι dischilioi**, *dis-khil'-ee-oy;* from *1364* and *5507: two thousand:*—two thousand.

1368. **διϋλίζω diulizō**, *dee-oo-lid'-zo;* from *1223* and **ὑλίζω hulizō**, *hoo-lid'-zo* (to *filter*); to *strain out:*—strain at [*prob. by misprint*].

1369. **διχάζω dichazō**, *dee-khad'-zo;* from a der. of *1364;* to *make apart*, i.e. *sunder* (fig. *alienate*):—set at variance.

1370. **διχοστασία dichŏstasia**, *dee-khos-tas-ee'-ah;* from a der. of *1364* and *4714; disunion*, i.e. (fig.) *dissension:*—division, sedition.

1371. **διχοτομέω dichŏtŏmĕō**, *dee-khot-om-eh'-o;* from a comp. of a der. of *1364* and a der. of **τέμνω tĕmnō** (to *cut*); to *bisect*, i.e. (by extens.) to *flog* severely:—cut asunder (in sunder).

1372. **διψάω dipsaō**, *dip-sah'-o;* from a var. of *1373;* to *thirst* for (lit. or fig.):—(be, be a-) thirst (-y).

1373. **δίψος dipsŏs**, *dip'-sos;* of uncert. affin.; *thirst:*—thirst.

1374. **δίψυχος dipsuchŏs**, *dip'-soo-khos;* from *1364* and *5590; two-spirited*, i.e. *vacillating* (in opinion or purpose):—double minded.

1375. **διωγμός diōgmŏs**, *dee-ogue-mos';* from *1377; persecution:*—persecution.

1376. **διώκτης diōktēs**, *dee-oke'-tace;* from *1377; a persecutor:*—persecutor.

1377. **διώκω diōkō**, *dee-o'-ko;* a prol. (and caus.) form of a prim. verb **δίω diō** (to *flee;* comp. the base of *1169* and *1249*); to *pursue* (lit. or fig.); by impl. to *persecute:*—ensue, follow (after), given to, (suffer) persecute (-ion), press toward.

1378. **δόγμα dŏgma**, *dog'-mah;* from the base of *1380;* a *law* (civil, cer. or eccl.):—decree, ordinance.

1379. **δογματίζω dŏgmatizō**, *dog-mat-id'-zo;* from *1378;* to *prescribe* by statute, i.e. (reflex.) to *submit to* cer. *rule:*—be subject to ordinances.

1380. **δοκέω dŏkĕō**, *dok-eh'-o;* a prol. form of a prim. verb **δόκω dŏkō**, *dok'-o* (used only as an alt. in certain tenses; comp. the base of *1166*) of the same mean.; to *think;* by impl. to *seem* (truthfully or uncertainly):—be accounted, (of own) please (-ure), be of reputation, seem (good), suppose, think, trow.

1381. **δοκιμάζω dŏkimazō**, *dok-im-ad'-zo;* from *1384;* to *test* (lit. or fig.); by impl. to *approve:*—allow, discern, examine, × like, (ap-) prove, try.

1382. **δοκιμή dŏkimē**, *dok-ee-may';* from the same as *1384; test* (abstr. or concr.); by impl. *trustiness:*—experience (-riment), proof, trial.

1383. **δοκίμιον dŏkimiŏn**, *dok-im'-ee-on;* neut. of a presumed der. of *1382;* a *testing;* by impl. *trustworthiness:*—trial, trying.

1384. **δόκιμος dŏkimŏs**, *dok'-ee-mos;* from *1380;* prop. *acceptable* (*current* after assayal), i.e. *approved:*—approved, tried.

1385. **δοκός dŏkŏs**, *dok-os';* from *1209* (through the idea of *holding* up); a *stick* of timber:—beam.

δόκω dŏkō. See *1380.*

1386. **δόλιος dŏliŏs**, *dol'-ee-os;* from *1388; guileful:*—deceitful.

1387. **δολιόω dŏliŏō**, *dol-ee-ŏ'-o;* from *1386;* to *be guileful:*—use deceit.

1388. **δόλος dŏlŏs**, *dol'-os;* from an obs. prim. **δέλλω dĕllō** (prob. mean. to *decoy;* comp. *1185*); a *trick* (*bait*), i.e. (fig.) *wile:*—craft, deceit, guile, subtilty.

1389. **δολόω dŏlŏō**, *dol-ŏ'-o;* from *1388;* to *ensnare*, i.e. (fig.) *adulterate:*—handle deceitfully.

1390. **δόμα dŏma**, *dom'-ah;* from the base of *1325;* a *present:*—gift.

1391. **δόξα dŏxa**, *dox'-ah;* from the base of *1380; glory* (as very *apparent*), in a wide application (lit. or fig., obj. or subj.):—dignity, glory (-ious), honour, praise, worship.

1392. **δοξάζω dŏxazō**, *dox-ad'-zo;* from *1391;* to *render* (or *esteem*) *glorious* (in a wide application):—(make) glorify (-ious), full of (have) glory, honour, magnify.

1393. **Δορκάς Dŏrkas**, *dor-kas'; gazelle; Dorcas*, a Chr. woman:—Dorcas.

1394. **δόσις dŏsis**, *dos'-is;* from the base of *1325;* a *giving;* by impl. (concr.) a *gift:*—gift, giving.

1395. **δότης dŏtēs**, *dot'-ace;* from the base of *1325;* a *giver:*—giver.

1396. **δουλαγωγέω dŏulagōgĕō**, *doo-lag-ogue-eh'-o;* from a presumed comp. of *1401* and *71;* to *be a slave-driver*, i.e. to *enslave* (fig. *subdue*):—bring into subjection.

1397. **δουλεία dŏulĕia**, *doo-li'-ah;* from *1398; slavery* (cer. or fig.):—bondage.

1398. **δουλεύω dŏulĕuō**, *dool-yoo'-o;* from *1401;* to *be a slave* to (lit. or fig., invol. or vol.):—be in bondage, (do) serve (-ice).

1399. **δούλη dŏulē**, *doo'-lay;* fem. of *1401;* a *female slave* (invol. or vol.):—handmaid (-en).

1400. **δοῦλον dŏulŏn**, *doo'-lon;* neut. of *1401; subservient:*—servant.

1401. **δοῦλος dŏulŏs**, *doo'-los;* from *1210;* a *slave* (lit. or fig., invol. or vol.; frequently therefore in a qualified sense of *subjection* or *subserviency*):—bond (-man), servant.

1402. **δουλόω dŏulŏō**, *doo-lŏ'-o;* from *1401;* to *enslave* (lit. or fig.):—bring into (be under) bondage, × given, become (make) servant.

1403. **δοχή dŏchē**, *dokh-ay';* from *1209;* a *reception*, i.e. convivial *entertainment:*—feast.

1404. **δράκων drakōn**, *drak'-own;* prob. from an alt. form of **δέρκομαι dĕrkŏmai** (to *look*); a fabulous kind of *serpent* (perh. as supposed to *fascinate*):—dragon.

1405. **δράσσομαι drassŏmai**, *dras'-som-ahee;* perh. akin to the base of *1404* (through the idea of *capturing*); to *grasp*, i.e. (fig.) *entrap:*—take.

1406. **δραχμή drachmē**, *drakh-may';* from *1405;* a *drachma* or (silver) coin (as *handled*):—piece (of silver).

δρέμω drĕmō. See *5143.*

1407. **δρέπανον drĕpanŏn**, *drep'-an-on;* from **δρέπω drĕpō** (to *pluck*); a gathering *hook* (espec. for harvesting):—sickle.

1408. **δρόμος drŏmŏs**, *drom'-os;* from the alt. of *5143;* a *race*, i.e. (fig.) *career:*—course.

1409. **Δρούσιλλα Drŏusilla**, *droo'-sil-lah;* a fem. dimin. of *Drusus* (a Rom. name); *Drusilla*, a member of the Herodian family:—Drusilla.

δῦμι dumi. See *1416.*

1410. **δύναμαι dunamai**, *doo'-nam-ahee;* of uncert. affin.; to *be able* or *possible:*—be able, can (do, + -not), could, may, might, be possible, be of power.

1411. **δύναμις dunamis**, *doo'-nam-is;* from *1410; force* (lit. or fig.); spec miraculous *power* (usually by impl. a *miracle* itself):—ability, abundance, meaning, might (-ily, -y, -y deed), (worker of) miracle (-s), power, strength, violence, mighty (wonderful) work.

1412. **δυναμόω dunamŏō**, *doo-nam-ŏ'-o;* from *1411;* to *enable:*—strengthen.

1413. **δυνάστης dunastēs**, *doo-nas'-tace;* from *1410;* a *ruler* or *officer:*—of great authority, mighty, potentate.

1414. **δυνατέω dunatĕō**, *doo-nat-eh'-o;* from *1415;* to *be efficient* (fig.):—be mighty.

1415. **δυνατός dunatŏs**, *doo-nat-os';* from *1410; powerful* or *capable* (lit. or fig.); neut. *possible:*—able, could, (that is) mighty (man), possible, power, strong.

1416. **δύνω dunō**, *doo'-no;* or

δῦμι dumi, *doo'-mee;* prol. forms of an obs. prim. **δύω duō**, *doo'-o* (to *sink*); to *go 'down'":*—set.

1417. **δύο duŏ**, *doo'-ŏ;* a prim. numeral; "*two*":—both, twain, two.

1418. **δυσ- dus-**, *doos;* a prim. inseparable particle of uncert. der.; used only in composition as a pref.; *hard*, i.e. *with difficulty:*—+ hard, + grievous, *etc.*

1419. **δυσβάστακτος dusbastaktŏs**, *doos-bas'-tak-tos;* from *1418* and a der. of *941; oppressive:*—grievous to be borne.

1420. **δυσεντερία dusĕntĕria**, *doos-en-ter-ee'-ah;* from *1418* and a comp. of *1787* (mean. a *bowel*); a "*dysentery*":—bloody flux.

1421. **δυσερμήνευτος dusĕrmēnĕutŏs**, *doos-er-mane'-yoo-tos;* from *1418* and a presumed der. of *2059; difficult of explanation:*—hard to be uttered.

1422. **δύσκολος duskŏlŏs**, *doos'-kol-os;* from *1418* and **κόλον kŏlŏn** (*food*); prop. *fastidious about eating* (*peevish*), i.e. (gen.) *impracticable:*—hard.

1423. **δυσκόλως duskŏlōs**, *doos-kol'-oce;* adv. from *1422; impracticably:*—hardly.

1424. **δυσμή dusmē**, *doos-may';* from *1416;* the sun-set, i.e. (by impl.) the *western* region:—west.

1425. **δυσνόητος dusnŏētŏs**, *doos-nŏ'-ay-tos;* from *1418* and a der. of *3539; difficult of perception:*—hard to be understood.

1426. **δυσφημία dusphēmia**, *doos-fay-mee'-ah;* from a comp. of *1418* and *5345; defamation:*—evil report.

δύω duō. See *1416.*

1427. **δώδεκα dōdĕka**, *do'-dek-ah;* from *1417* and *1176; two* and *ten*, i.e. a *dozen:*—twelve.

1428. **δωδέκατος dōdĕkatŏs**, *do-dek'-at-os;* from *1427; twelfth:*—twelfth.

1429. **δωδεκάφυλον dōdĕkaphulŏn**, *do-dek-af'-oo-lon;* from *1427* and *5443;* the *commonwealth* of Israel:—twelve tribes.

1430. **δῶμα dōma**, *do'-mah;* from **δέμω dĕmō** (to *build*); prop. an *edifice*, i.e. (spec.) a *roof:*—housetop.

1431. **δωρεά dōrĕa**, *do-reh-ah';* from *1435;* a *gratuity:*—gift.

1432. **δωρεάν dōrĕan**, *do-reh-an';* acc. of *1431* as adv.; *gratuitously* (lit. or fig.):—without a cause, freely, for naught, in vain.

1433. **δωρέομαι dōrĕŏmai**, *do-reh'-om-ahee;* mid. from *1435;* to *bestow* gratuitously:—give.

1434. **δώρημα dōrēma**, *do'-ray-mah;* from *1433;* a *bestowment:*—gift.

1435. **δῶρον dōrŏn**, *do'-ron;* a *present;* spec. a *sacrifice:*—gift, offering.

E

1436. **ἔα ĕa**, *eh'-ah;* appar. imper. of *1439;* prop. *let it be*, i.e. (as interj.) *aha !:*—let alone.

1437. **ἐάν ĕan**, *eh-an';* from *1487* and *302;* a *conditional* particle; *in case* that, *provided*, etc.; often used in connection with other particles to denote *indefiniteness* or *uncertainty:*—before, but, except, (and) if, (if) so, (what-, whither-) soever, though, when (-soever), whether (or), to whom, [who-] so (-ever). See *3361.*

ἐάν μή ĕan mē. See *3361.*

1438. **ἑαυτοῦ hĕautŏu**, *heh-ŏw-too'* (incl. all the other cases); from a reflex. pron. otherwise obsol. and the gen. (dat. or acc.) of *846; him-* (*her-*, *it-*, *them-*, also [in conjunction with the pers. pron. of the other persons] *my-*, *thy-*, *our-*, *your-*) *self* (*selves*), etc.:—alone, her (own, -self), (he) himself, his (own), itself, one (to) another, our (thine) own (-selves), + that she had, their (own, own selves), (of) them (-selves), they, thyself, you, your (own, own conceits, own selves, -selves).

1439. **ἐάω ĕaō**, *eh-ah'-o;* of uncert. affin.; to *let be*, i.e. *permit* or *leave* alone:—commit, leave, let (alone), suffer. See also *1436.*

1440. **ἑβδομήκοντα hĕbdŏmēkŏnta**, *heb-dom-ay'-kon-tah;* from *1442* and a modified form of *1176; seventy:*—seventy, three score and ten.

1441. **ἑβδομηκοντακίς hĕbdŏmēkŏntakis**, *heb-dom-ay-kon-tak-is';* multiple adv. from *1440; seventy times:*—seventy times.

1442. **ἕβδομος hĕbdŏmŏs**, *heb'-dom-os;* ordinal from 2033; *seventh:*—seventh.

1443. **Ἐβέρ Ĕbĕr**, *eb-er';* of Heb. or. [5677]; *Eber*, a patriarch:—Eber.

1444. **Ἑβραϊκός Hĕbraïkŏs**, *heb-rah-ee-kos';* from 1443; *Hebraïc* or the *Jewish* language:—Hebrew.

1445. **Ἑβραῖος Hĕbraiŏs**, *heb-rah'-yos;* from 1443; a *Hebræan* (i.e. Hebrew) or *Jew:*—Hebrew.

1446. **Ἑβραΐς Hĕbraïs**, *heb-rah-is';* from 1443; the *Hebraistic* (i.e. *Hebrew*) or *Jewish* (*Chaldee*) language:—Hebrew.

1447. **Ἑβραϊστί Hĕbraïsti**, *heb-rah-is-tee';* adv. from 1446; *Hebraistically* or in the Jewish (Chaldee) language:—in (the) Hebrew (tongue).

1448. **ἐγγίζω ĕggizō**, *eng-id'-zo;* from 1451; to make *near*, i.e. (reflex.) *approach:*—approach, be at hand, come (draw) near, be (come, draw) nigh.

1449. **ἐγγράφω ĕggraphō**, *eng-graf'-o;* from 1722 and 1125; to "*engrave*", i.e. *inscribe:*—write (in).

1450. **ἔγγυος ĕgguŏs**, *eng'-goo-os;* from 1722 and **γυῖον guiŏn** (a *limb*); *pledged* (as if *articulated* by a member), i.e. a *bondsman:*—surety.

1451. **ἐγγύς ĕggus**, *eng-goos';* from a prim. verb **ἄγχω agchō** (to *squeeze* or *throttle;* akin to the base of 43); *near* (lit. or fig., of place or time):—from, at hand, near, nigh (at hand, unto), ready.

1452. **ἐγγύτερον ĕggutĕrŏn**, *eng-goo'-ter-on;* neut. of the comp. of 1451; *nearer:*—nearer.

1453. **ἐγείρω ĕgĕirō**, *eg-i'-ro;* prob. akin to the base of 58 (through the idea of *collecting* one's faculties); to *waken* (trans. or intrans.), i.e. *rouse* (lit. from sleep, from sitting or lying, from disease, from death; or fig. from obscurity, inactivity, ruins, nonexistence):—awake, lift (up), raise (again, up), rear up, (a-) rise (again, up), stand, take up.

1454. **ἔγερσις ĕgĕrsis**, *eg'-er-sis;* from 1453; a *resurgence* (from death):—resurrection.

1455. **ἐγκάθετος ĕgkathĕtŏs**, *eng-kath'-et-os;* from 1722 and a der. of 2524; *subinduced*, i.e. surreptitiously *suborned* as a lier-in-wait:—spy.

1456. **ἐγκαίνια ĕgkainia**, *eng-kah'ee-nee-ah;* neut. plur. of a presumed comp. from 1722 and 2537; *innovatives*, i.e. (spec.) *renewal* (of religious services after the Antiochian interruption):—dedication.

1457. **ἐγκαινίζω ĕgkainizō**, *eng-kahee-nid'-zo;* from 1456; to *renew*, i.e. *inaugurate:*—consecrate, dedicate.

1458. **ἐγκαλέω ĕgkalĕō**, *eng-kal-eh'-o;* from 1722 and 2564; to *call in* (as a debt or demand), i.e. *bring to account* (*charge*, *criminate*, etc.):—accuse, call in question, implead, lay to the charge.

1459. **ἐγκαταλείπω ĕgkatalĕipō**, *eng-kat-al-i'-po;* from 1722 and 2641; to *leave behind in* some place, i.e. (in a good sense) *let remain over*, or (in a bad one) to *desert:*—forsake, leave.

1460. **ἐγκατοικέω ĕgkatŏikĕō**, *eng-kat-oy-keh'-o;* from 1722 and 2730; to *settle down in* a place, i.e. *reside:*—dwell among.

1461. **ἐγκεντρίζω ĕgkĕntrizō**, *eng-ken-trid'-zo;* from 1722 and a der. of 2759; to *prick in*, i.e. *ingraft:*—graff in (-to).

1462. **ἔγκλημα ĕgklēma**, *eng'-klay-mah;* from 1458; an *accusation*, i.e. *offence* alleged:—crime laid against, laid to charge.

1463. **ἐγκομβόομαι ĕgkŏmbŏŏmai**, *eng-kom-bŏ'-om-ahee;* mid. from 1722 and **κομβόω kŏmbŏō** (to *gird*); to *engirdle* oneself (for labor), i.e. fig. (the apron being a badge of servitude) to *wear* (in token of mutual deference):—be clothed with.

1464. **ἐγκοπή ĕgkŏpē**, *eng-kop-ay';* from 1465; a *hindrance:*—× hinder.

1465. **ἐγκόπτω ĕgkŏptō**, *eng-kop'-to;* from 1722 and 2875; to *cut into*, i.e. (fig.) *impede*, *detain:*—hinder, be tedious unto.

1466. **ἐγκράτεια ĕgkratĕia**, *eng-krat'-i-ah;* from 1468; *self-control* (espec. *continence*):—temperance.

1467. **ἐγκρατεύομαι ĕgkratĕuŏmai**, *eng-krat-yoo'-om-ahee;* mid. from 1468; to *exercise self-restraint* (in diet and chastity):—can ([-not]) contain, be temperate.

1468. **ἐγκρατής ĕgkratēs**, *eng-krat-ace';* from 1722 and 2904; *strong in* a thing (*masterful*), i.e. (fig. and reflex.) *self-controlled* (in appetite, etc.):—temperate.

1469. **ἐγκρίνω ĕgkrinō**, *eng-kree'-no;* from 1722 and 2919; to *judge in*, i.e. *count* among:—make of the number.

1470. **ἐγκρύπτω ĕkgruptō**, *eng-kroop'-to;* from 1722 and 2928; to *conceal in*, i.e. *incorporate with:*—hid in.

1471. **ἔγκυος ĕgkuŏs**, *eng'-koo-os;* from 1722 and the base of 2949; *swelling inside*, i.e. *pregnant:*—great with child.

1472. **ἐγχρίω ĕgchriō**, *eng-khree'-o;* from 1722 and 5548; to *rub in* (oil), i.e. *besmear:*—anoint.

1473. **ἐγώ ĕgō**, *eg-o';* a prim. pron. of the first pers. *I* (only expressed when emphatic):—I, me. For the other cases and the plur. see 1691, 1698, 1700, 2248, 2249, 2254, 2257, etc.

1474. **ἐδαφίζω ĕdaphizō**, *ed-af-id'-zo;* from 1475; to *raze:*—lay even with the ground.

1475. **ἔδαφος ĕdaphŏs**, *ed'-af-os;* from the base of 1476; a *basis* (*bottom*), i.e. the *soil:*—ground.

1476. **ἑδραῖος hĕdraiŏs**, *hed-rah'-yos;* from a der. of **ἕζομαι hĕzŏmai** (to *sit*); *sedentary*, i.e. (by impl.) *immovable:*—settled, stedfast.

1477. **ἑδραίωμα hĕdraiōma**, *hed-rah'-yo-mah;* from a der. of 1476; a *support*, i.e. (fig.) *basis:*—ground.

1478. **Ἐζεκίας Ĕzĕkias**, *ed-zek-ee'-as;* of Heb. or. [2396]; *Ezekias* (i.e. *Hezekiah*), an Isr.:—Ezekias.

1479. **ἐθελοθρησκεία ĕthĕlŏthrēskĕia**, *eth-el-oth-race-ki'-ah;* from 2309 and 2356; *voluntary* (*arbitrary* and *unwarranted*) *piety*, i.e. *sanctimony:*—will worship.

ἐθέλω ĕthĕlō. See 2309.

1480. **ἐθίζω ĕthizō**, *eth-id'-zo;* from 1485; to *accustom*, i.e. (neut. pass. part.) *customary:*—custom.

1481. **ἐθνάρχης ĕthnarchēs**, *eth-nar'-khace;* from 1484 and 746; the *governor* [not king] *of a district:*—ethnarch.

1482. **ἐθνικός ĕthnikŏs**, *eth-nee-kos';* from 1484; *national* ("*ethnic*"), i.e. (spec.) a *Gentile:*—heathen (man).

1483. **ἐθνικῶς ĕthnikōs**, *eth-nee-koce';* adv. from 1482; *as a Gentile:*—after the manner of Gentiles.

1484. **ἔθνος ĕthnŏs**, *eth'-nos;* prob. from 1486; a *race* (as of the same *habit*), i.e. a *tribe;* spec. a *foreign* (*non-Jewish*) one (usually by impl. *pagan*):—Gentile, heathen, nation, people.

1485. **ἔθος ĕthŏs**, *eth'-os;* from 1486; a *usage* (prescribed by habit or law):—custom, manner, be wont.

1486. **ἔθω ĕthō**, *eth'-o;* a prim. verb; to *be used* (by habit or conventionality); neut. perf. part. *usage:*—be custom (manner, wont).

1487. **εἰ ĕi**, *i;* a prim. particle of conditionality; *if*, *whether*, *that*, etc.:—forasmuch as, if, that, ([al-]) though, whether. Often used in connection or composition with other particles, espec. as in 1489, 1490, 1499, 1508, 1509, 1512, 1513, 1536, 1537. See also 1437.

1488. **εἶ ĕi**, *i;* second pers. sing. pres. of 1510; thou *art:*—art, be.

1489. **εἴγε ĕigĕ**, *i'-gheh;* from 1487 and 1065; *if indeed*, *seeing that*, *unless*, (with neg.) *otherwise:*—if (so be that, yet).

1490. **εἰ δὲ μή(γε) ĕi dĕ mē(gĕ)**, *i deh may'-(gheh);* from 1487, 1161 and 3361 (sometimes with 1065 added); *but if not:*—(or) else, if (not, otherwise), otherwise.

1491. **εἶδος ĕidŏs**, *i'-dos*, from 1492; a *view*, i.e. *form* (lit. or fig.):—appearance, fashion, shape, sight.

1492. **εἴδω ĕidō**, *i'-do;* a prim. verb; used only in certain past tenses, the others being borrowed from the equiv. 3700 and 3708; prop. to *see* (lit. or fig.); by impl. (in the perf. only) to *know:*—be aware, behold, × can (+ not tell), consider, (have) know (-ledge), look (on), perceive, see, be sure, tell, understand, wist, wot. Comp. 3700.

1493. **εἰδωλεῖον ĕidōlĕiŏn**, *i-do-li'-on;* neut. of a presumed der. of 1497; an *image-fane:*—idol's temple.

1494. **εἰδωλόθυτον ĕidōlŏthutŏn**, *i-do-loth'-oo-ton;* neut. of a comp. of 1497 and a presumed der. of 2380; an *image-sacrifice*, i.e. part of an *idolatrous offering:*—(meat, thing that is) offered (in sacrifice, sacrificed) to (unto) idols.

1495. **εἰδωλολατρεία ĕidōlŏlatrĕia**, *i-do-lol-at-ri'-ah;* from 1497 and 2999; *image-worship* (lit. or fig.):—idolatry.

1496. **εἰδωλολάτρης ĕidōlŏlatrēs**, *i-do-lol-at'-race;* from 1497 and the base of 3000; an *image-* (*servant* or) *worshipper* (lit. or fig.):—idolater.

1497. **εἴδωλον ĕidōlŏn**, *i'-do-lon;* from 1491; an *image* (i.e. for worship); by impl. a heathen *god*, or (plur.) the *worship* of such:—idol.

1498. **εἴην ĕiēn**, *i'-ane;* optative (i.e. Eng. subjunctive) pres. of 1510 (includ. the other pers.); *might* (*could*, *would* or *should*) *be:*—mean, + perish, should be, was, were.

1499. **εἰ καί ĕi kai**, *i kahee;* from 1487 and 2532; *if also* (or *even*):—if (that), though.

1500. **εἰκῆ ĕikē**, *i-kay';* prob. from 1502 (through the idea of *failure*); *idly*, i.e. *without reason* (or *effect*):—without a cause, (in) vain (-ly).

1501. **εἴκοσι ĕikŏsi**, *i'-kos-ee;* of uncert. affin.; a *score:*—twenty.

1502. **εἴκω ĕikō**, *i'-ko;* appar. a prim. verb; prop. *to be weak*, i.e. *yield:*—give place.

1503. **εἴκω ĕikō**, *i'-ko;* appar. a prim. verb [perh. akin to 1502 through the idea of *faintness* as a copy]; to *resemble:*—be like.

1504. **εἰκών ĕikōn**, *i-kone';* from 1503; a *likeness*, i.e. (lit.) *statue*, *profile*, or (fig.) *representation*, *resemblance:*—image.

1505. **εἰλικρίνεια ĕilikrinĕia**, *i-lik-ree'-ni-ah;* from 1506; *clearness*, i.e. (by impl.) *purity* (fig.):—sincerity.

1506. **εἰλικρινής ĕilikrinēs**, *i-lik-ree-nace';* from **εἵλη hĕilē** (the sun's *ray*) and 2919; *judged by sunlight*, i.e. tested as *genuine* (fig.):—pure, sincere.

1507. **εἱλίσσω hĕilissō**, *hi-lis'-so;* a prol. form of a prim. but defective verb **εἵλω hĕilō** (of the same mean.); to *coil* or *wrap:*—roll together. See also 1667.

1508. **εἰ μή ĕi mē**, *i may;* from 1487 and 3361; *if not:*—but, except (that), if not, more than, save (only) that, saving, till.

1509. **εἰ μή τι ĕi mē ti**, *i may tee;* from 1508 and the neut. of 5100; *if not somewhat:*—except.

1510. **εἰμί ĕimi**, *i-mee';* first pers. sing. pres. indic.; a prol. form of a prim. and defective verb; I *exist* (used only when emphatic):—am, have been, × it is I, was. See also 1488, 1498, 1511, 1527, 2258, 2071, 2070, 2075, 2076, 2771, 2468, 5600.

1511. **εἶναι ĕinai**, *i'-nahee;* pres. infin. from 1510; *to exist:*—am, are, come, is, × lust after, × please well, there is, to be, was.

εἵνεκεν hĕinĕkĕn. See 1752.

1512. **εἴ περ ĕi pĕr**, *i per;* from 1487 and 4007; *if perhaps:*—if so be (that), seeing, though.

1513. **εἴ πως ĕi pōs**, *i poce;* from 1487 and 4458; *if somehow:*—if by any means.

1514. **εἰρηνεύω ĕirēnĕuō**, *i-rane-yoo'-o;* from 1515; *to be* (*act*) *peaceful:*—be at (have, live in) peace, live peaceably.

1515. **εἰρήνη ĕirēnē**, *i-ray'-nay;* prob. from a prim. verb **εἴρω ĕirō** (to *join*); *peace* (lit. or fig.); by impl. *prosperity:*—one, peace, quietness, rest, + set at one again.

1516. **εἰρηνικός ĕirēnikŏs**, *i-ray-nee-kos';* from 1515; *pacific;* by impl. *salutary:*—peaceable.

1517. **εἰρηνοποιέω ĕirēnŏpŏiĕō**, *i-ray-nop-oy-eh'-o;* from 1518; *to be a peace-maker*, i.e. (fig.) to *harmonize:*—make peace.

1518. **εἰρηνοποιός ĕirēnŏpŏiŏs**, *i-ray-nop-oy-os';* from 1515 and 4160; *pacificatory*, i.e. (subj.) *peaceable:*—peacemaker.

εἴρω ĕirō. See 1515, 4483, 5346.

1519. **εἰς ĕis**, *ice;* a prim. prep.; *to* or *into* (indicating the point reached or entered), of place, time, or (fig.) purpose (result, etc.); also in adv. phrases:—[abundant-] ly, against, among, as, at, [back-] ward, before, by, concerning, + continual, + far more exceeding, for [intent, purpose], fore, + forth, in (among, at, unto, -so much that, -to), to the intent that, + of one mind, + never, of, (up-) on, + perish, + set at one again, (so) that, therefore (-unto), throughout, till, to (be, the end, -ward), (here-) until (-to), . . . ward, [where-] fore, with. Often used in composition with the same general import, but only with verbs (etc.) expressing motion (lit. or fig.).

1520. **εἷς hĕis**, *hice;* (includ. the neut. [etc.] **ἕν hĕn**); a prim. numeral; *one:*—a (-n, -ny, certain), + abundantly, man, one (another), only, other, some. See also *1527, 3367, 3391, 3762.*

1521. **εἰσάγω ĕisagō**, *ice-ag'-o;* from *1519* and *71;* to *introduce* (lit. or fig.):—bring in (-to), (+ was to) lead into.

1522. **εἰσακούω ĕisakŏuō**, *ice-ak-oo'-o;* from *1519* and *191;* to *listen* to:—hear.

1523. **εἰσδέχομαι ĕisdĕchŏmai**, *ice-dekh'-om-ahee;* from *1519* and *1209;* to *take into* one's favor:—receive.

1524. **εἴσειμι ĕisĕimi**, *ice'-i-mee;* from *1519* and **εἶμι ĕimi** (to *go*); to *enter:*—enter (go) into.

1525. **εἰσέρχομαι ĕisĕrchŏmai**, *ice-er'-khom-ahee;* from *1519* and *2064;* to *enter* (lit. or fig.):—× arise, come (in, into), enter in (-to), go in (through).

1526. **εἰσί ĕisi**, *i-see';* 3d pers. plur. pres. indic. of *1510;* they *are:*—agree, are, be, dure, × is, were.

1527. **εἷς καθ' εἷς hĕis kath' hĕis**, *hice kath hice;* from *1520* repeated with *2596* inserted; *severally:*—one by one.

1528. **εἰσκαλέω ĕiskalĕō**, *ice-kal-eh'-o;* from *1519* and *2564;* to *invite* in:—call in.

1529. **εἴσοδος ĕisŏdŏs**, *ice'-od-os;* from *1519* and *3598;* an *entrance* (lit. or fig.):—coming, enter (-ing) in (to).

1530. **εἰσπηδάω ĕispēdaō**, *ice-pay-dah'-o;* from *1519* and **πηδάω pēdaō** (to *leap*); to *rush in:*—run (spring) in.

1531. **εἰσπορεύομαι ĕispŏrĕuŏmai**, *ice-por-yoo'-om-ahee;* from *1519* and *4198;* to *enter* (lit. or fig.):—come (enter) in, go into.

1532. **εἰστρέχω ĕistrĕchō**, *ice-trekh'-o;* from *1519* and *5143;* to *hasten inward:*—run in.

1533. **εἰσφέρω ĕisphĕrō**, *ice-fer'-o;* from *1519* and *5342;* to *carry inward* (lit. or fig.):—bring (in), lead into.

1534. **εἶτα ĕita**, *i'-tah;* of uncert. affin.; a particle of *succession* (in time or logical enumeration), *then, moreover:*—after that (-ward), furthermore, then. See also *1899.*

1535. **εἴτε ĕitĕ**, *i'-teh;* from *1487* and *5037;* if *too:*—if, or, whether.

1536. **εἴ τις ĕi tis**, *i tis;* from *1487* and *5100;* if *any:*—he that, if a (-ny) man ('s, thing, from any, ought), whether any, whosoever.

1537. **ἐκ ĕk**, *ek;* or

ἐξ ĕx, *ex;* a prim. prep. denoting *origin* (the point *whence* motion or action proceeds), *from, out* (of place, time or cause; lit. or fig.; direct or remote):—after, among, × are, at, betwixt (-yond), by (the means of), exceedingly, (+ abundantly above), for (-th), from (among, forth, up), + grudgingly, + heartily, × heavenly, × hereby, + very highly, in, . . . ly, (because, by reason) of, off (from), on, out among (from, of), over, since, × thenceforth, through, × unto, × vehemently, with (-out). Often used in composition, with the same general import; often of *completion.*

1538. **ἕκαστος hĕkastŏs**, *hek'-as-tos;* as if a superlative of **ἕκας hĕkas** (*afar*); *each* or *every:*—any, both, each (one), every (man, one, woman), particularly.

1539. **ἑκάστοτε hĕkastŏtĕ**, *hek-as'-tot-eh;* as if from *1538* and *5119;* at *every time:*—always.

1540. **ἑκατόν hĕkatŏn**, *hek-at-on';* of uncert. affin.; a *hundred:*—hundred.

1541. **ἑκατονταέτης hĕkatŏntaĕtēs**, *hek-at-on-tah-et'-ace;* from *1540* and *2094;* *centenarian:*—hundred years old.

1542. **ἑκατονταπλασίων hĕkatŏntaplasiŏn**, *hek-at-on-ta-plah-see'-own;* from *1540* and a presumed der. of *4111;* a *hundred times:*—hundredfold.

1543. **ἑκατοντάρχης hĕkatŏntarchēs**, *hek-at-on-tar'-khace;* or

ἑκατόνταρχος hĕkatŏntarchŏs, *hek-at-on'-tar-khos;* from *1540* and *757;* the *captain of one hundred men:*—centurion.

1544. **ἐκβάλλω ĕkballō**, *ek-bal'-lo;* from *1537* and *906;* to *eject* (lit. or fig.):—bring forth, cast (forth, out), drive (out), expel, leave, pluck (pull, take, thrust) out, put forth (out), send away (forth, out).

1545. **ἔκβασις ĕkbasis**, *ek'-bas-is;* from a comp. of *1537* and the base of *939* (mean. to *go out*); an *exit* (lit. or fig.):—end, way to escape.

1546. **ἐκβολή ĕkbŏlē**, *ek-bol-ay';* from *1544;* *ejection,* i.e. (spec.) a *throwing overboard* of the cargo:—+ lighten the ship.

1547. **ἐκγαμίζω ĕkgamizō**, *ek-gam-id'-zo;* from *1537* and a form of *1061* [comp. *1548*]; to *marry off* a daughter:—give in marriage.

1548. **ἐκγαμίσκω ĕkgamiskō**, *ek-gam-is'-ko;* from *1537* and *1061;* the same as *1547:*—give in marriage.

1549. **ἔκγονον ĕkgŏnŏn**, *ek'-gon-on;* neut. of a der. of a comp. of *1537* and *1096;* a *descendant,* i.e. (spec.) *grandchild:*—nephew.

1550. **ἐκδαπανάω ĕkdapanaō**, *ek-dap-an-ah'-o;* from *1537* and *1159;* to *expend* (wholly), i.e. (fig.) *exhaust:*—spend.

1551. **ἐκδέχομαι ĕkdĕchŏmai**, *ek-dekh'-om-ahee;* from *1537* and *1209;* to *accept from* some source, i.e. (by impl.) to *await:*—expect, look (tarry) for, wait (for).

1552. **ἔκδηλος ĕkdēlŏs**, *ek'-day-los;* from *1537* and *1212;* *wholly evident:*—manifest.

1553. **ἐκδημέω ĕkdēmĕō**, *ek-day-meh'-o;* from a comp. of *1537* and *1218;* to *emigrate,* i.e. (fig.) *vacate* or *quit:*—be absent.

1554. **ἐκδίδωμι ĕkdidōmi**, *ek-did-o'-mee;* from *1537* and *1325;* to *give forth,* i.e. (spec.) to *lease:*—let forth (out).

1555. **ἐκδιηγέομαι ĕkdiēgĕŏmai**, *ek-dee-ayg-eh'-om-ahee;* from *1537* and a comp. of *1223* and *2233;* to *narrate* through wholly:—declare.

1556. **ἐκδικέω ĕkdikĕō**, *ek-dik-eh'-o;* from *1558;* to *vindicate, retaliate, punish:*—a (re-) venge.

1557. **ἐκδίκησις ĕkdikēsis**, *ek-dik'-ay-sis;* from *1556;* *vindication, retribution:*—(a-, re-) venge (-ance), punishment.

1558. **ἔκδικος ĕkdikŏs**, *ek'-dik-os;* from *1537* and *1349;* carrying *justice out,* i.e. a *punisher:*—a (re-) venger.

1559. **ἐκδιώκω ĕkdiōkō**, *ek-dee-o'-ko;* from *1537* and *1377;* to *pursue out,* i.e. *expel* or *persecute* implacably:—persecute.

1560. **ἔκδοτος ĕkdŏtŏs**, *ek'-dot-os;* from *1537* and a der. of *1325;* *given out* or *over,* i.e. *surrendered:*—delivered.

1561. **ἐκδοχή ĕkdŏchē**, *ek-dokh-ay';* from *1551;* *expectation:*—looking for.

1562. **ἐκδύω ĕkduō**, *ek-doo'-o;* from *1537* and the base of *1416;* to cause to *sink out* of, i.e. (spec. as of clothing) to *divest:*—strip, take off from, unclothe.

1563. **ἐκεῖ ĕkĕi**, *ek-i';* of uncert. affin.; *there;* by extens. *thither:*—there, thither (-ward), (to) yonder (place).

1564. **ἐκεῖθεν ĕkĕithĕn**, *ek-i'-then;* from *1563;* *thence:*—from that place, (from) thence, there.

1565. **ἐκεῖνος ĕkĕinŏs**, *ek-i'-nos;* from *1563;* *that* one (or [neut.] thing); often intensified by the art. prefixed:—he, it, the other (same), selfsame, that (same, very), × their, × them, they, this, those. See also *3778.*

1566. **ἐκεῖσε ĕkĕisĕ**, *ek-i'-seh;* from *1563;* *thither:*—there.

1567. **ἐκζητέω ĕkzētĕō**, *ek-zay-teh'-o;* from *1537* and *2212;* to *search out,* i.e. (fig.) *investigate, crave, demand,* (by Hebr.) *worship:*—en- (re-) quire, seek after (carefully, diligently).

1568. **ἐκθαμβέω ĕkthambĕō**, *ek-tham-beh'-o;* from *1569;* to *astonish* utterly:—affright, greatly (sore) amaze.

1569. **ἔκθαμβος ĕkthambŏs**, *ek'-tham-bos;* from *1537* and *2285;* *utterly astounded:*—greatly wondering.

1570. **ἔκθετος ĕkthĕtŏs**, *ek'-thet-os;* from *1537* and a der. of *5087;* *put out,* i.e. *exposed* to perish:—cast out.

1571. **ἐκκαθαίρω ĕkkathairō**, *ek-kath-ah'ee-ro;* from *1537* and *2508;* to *cleanse thoroughly:*—purge (out).

1572. **ἐκκαίω ĕkkaiō**, *ek-kah'-yo;* from *1537* and *2545;* to *inflame* deeply:—burn.

1573. **ἐκκακέω ĕkkakĕō**, *ek-kak-eh'-o;* from *1537* and *2556;* to *be* (*bad* or) *weak,* i.e. (by impl.) to *fail* (in heart):—faint, be weary.

1574. **ἐκκεντέω ĕkkĕntĕō**, *ek-ken-teh'-o;* from *1537* and the base of *2759;* to *transfix:*—pierce.

1575. **ἐκκλάω ĕkklaō**, *ek-klah'-o;* from *1537* and *2806;* to *exscind:*—break off.

1576. **ἐκκλείω ĕkklĕiō**, *ek-kli'-o;* from *1537* and *2808;* to *shut out* (lit. or fig.):—exclude.

1577. **ἐκκλησία ĕkklēsia**, *ek-klay-see'-ah;* from a comp. of *1537* and a der. of *2564;* a *calling out,* i.e. (concr.) a popular *meeting,* espec. a religious *congregation* (Jewish *synagogue,* or Chr. community of members on earth or saints in heaven or both):—assembly, church.

1578. **ἐκκλίνω ĕkklinō**, *ek-klee'-no;* from *1537* and *2827;* to *deviate,* i.e. (absol.) to *shun* (lit. or fig.), or (rel.) to *decline* (from piety):—avoid, eschew, go out of the way.

1579. **ἐκκολυμβάω ĕkkŏlumbaō**, *ek-kol-oom-bah'-o;* from *1537* and *2860;* to *escape* by *swimming:*—swim out.

1580. **ἐκκομίζω ĕkkŏmizō**, *ek-kom-id'-zo;* from *1537* and *2865;* to *bear forth* (to burial):—carry out.

1581. **ἐκκόπτω ĕkkŏptō**, *ek-kop'-to;* from *1537* and *2875;* to *exscind;* fig. to *frustrate:*—cut down (off, out), hew down, hinder.

1582. **ἐκκρέμαμαι ĕkkrĕmamai**, *ek-krem'-am-ahee;* mid. from *1537* and *2910;* to *hang upon* the lips of a speaker, i.e. *listen closely:*—be very attentive.

1583. **ἐκλαλέω ĕklalĕō**, *ek-lal-eh'-o;* from *1537* and *2980;* to *divulge:*—tell.

1584. **ἐκλάμπω ĕklampō**, *ek-lam'-po;* from *1537* and *2989;* to be *resplendent:*—shine forth.

1585. **ἐκλανθάνομαι ĕklanthanŏmai**, *ek-lan-than'-om-ahee;* mid. from *1537* and *2990;* to be utterly *oblivious* of:—forget.

1586. **ἐκλέγομαι ĕklĕgŏmai**, *ek-leg'-om-ahee;* mid. from *1537* and *3004* (in its prim. sense); to *select;*—make choice, choose (out), chosen.

1587. **ἐκλείπω ĕklĕipō**, *ek-li'-po;* from *1537* and *3007;* to *omit,* i.e. (by impl.) *cease* (*die*):—fail.

1588. **ἐκλεκτός ĕklĕktŏs**, *ek-lek-tos';* from *1586;* *select;* by impl. *favorite:*—chosen, elect.

1589. **ἐκλογή ĕklŏgē**, *ek-log-ay';* from *1586;* (divine) *selection* (abstr. or concr.):—chosen, election.

1590. **ἐκλύω ĕkluō**, *ek-loo'-o;* from *1537* and *3089;* to *relax* (lit. or fig.):—faint.

1591. **ἐκμάσσω ĕkmassō**, *ek-mas'-so;* from *1537* and the base of *3145;* to *knead out,* i.e. (by anal.) to *wipe dry:*—wipe.

1592. **ἐκμυκτερίζω ĕkmuktĕrizō**, *ek-mook-ter-id'-zo;* from *1537* and *3456;* to *sneer* outright at:—deride.

1593. **ἐκνεύω ĕknĕuō**, *ek-nyoo'-o;* from *1537* and *3506;* (by anal.) to *slip off,* i.e. quietly *withdraw:*—convey self away.

1594. **ἐκνήφω ĕknēphō**, *ek-nay'-fo;* from *1537* and *3525;* (fig.) to *rouse* (oneself) *out* of stupor:—awake.

1595. **ἑκούσιον hĕkŏusiŏn**, *hek-oo'-see-on;* neut. of a der. from *1635;* *voluntariness:*—willingly.

1596. **ἑκουσίως hĕkŏusiŏs**, *hek-oo-see'-oce;* adv. from the same as *1595; voluntarily:*—wilfully, willingly.

1597. **ἔκπαλαι ĕkpalai**, *ek'-pal-ahee;* from *1537* and *3819; long ago, for a long while:*—of a long time, of old.

1598. **ἐκπειράζω ĕkpĕirazō**, *ek-pi-rad'-zo;* from *1537* and *3985;* to *test thoroughly:*—tempt.

1599. **ἐκπέμπω ĕkpĕmpō**, *ek-pem'-po;* from *1537* and *3992;* to *despatch:*—send away (forth).

ἐκπερισσοῦ ĕkpĕrissŏu. See *1537* and *4053*.

1600. **ἐκπετάννυμι ĕkpĕtannumi**, *ek-pet-an'-noo-mee;* from *1537* and a form of *4072;* to *fly out,* i.e. (by anal.) *extend:*—stretch forth.

1601. **ἐκπίπτω ĕkpiptō**, *ek-pip'-to;* from *1537* and *4098;* to *drop away;* spec. *be driven out* of one's course; fig. to *lose, become inefficient:*—be cast, fail, fall (away, off), take none effect.

1602. **ἐκπλέω ĕkplĕō**, *ek-pleh'-o;* from *1537* and *4126;* to *depart* by ship:—sail (away, thence).

1603. **ἐκπληρόω ĕkplērŏō**, *ek-play-rŏ'-o;* from *1537* and *4137;* to *accomplish* entirely:—fulfill.

1604. **ἐκπλήρωσις ĕkplērōsis**, *ek-play'-ro-sis;* from *1603; completion:*—accomplishment.

1605. **ἐκπλήσσω ĕkplēssō**, *ek-place'-so;* from *1537* and *4141;* to *strike* with astonishment:—amaze, astonish.

1606. **ἐκπνέω ĕkpnĕō**, *ek-pneh'-o;* from *1537* and *4154;* to *expire:*—give up the ghost.

1607. **ἐκπορεύομαι ĕkpŏrĕuŏmai**, *ek-por-yoo'-om-ahee;* from *1537* and *4198;* to *depart, be discharged, proceed, project:*—come (forth, out of), depart, go (forth, out), issue, proceed (out of).

1608. **ἐκπορνεύω ĕkpŏrnĕuō**, *ek-porn-yoo'-o;* from *1537* and *4203;* to *be utterly unchaste:*—give self over to fornication.

1609. **ἐκπτύω ĕkptuō**, *ek-ptoo'-o;* from *1537* and *4429;* to *spit out,* i.e. (fig.) *spurn:*—reject.

1610. **ἐκριζόω ĕkrizŏō**, *ek-rid-zŏ'-o;* from *1537* and *4492;* to *uproot:*—pluck up by the root, root up.

1611. **ἔκστασις ĕkstasis**, *ek'-stas-is;* from *1839;* a *displacement* of the mind, i.e. *bewilderment,* "*ecstasy*":— + be amazed, amazement, astonishment, trance.

1612. **ἐκστρέφω ĕkstrĕphō**, *ek-stref'-o;* from *1537* and *4762;* to *pervert* (fig.):—subvert.

1613. **ἐκταράσσω ĕktarassō**, *ek-tar-as'-so;* from *1537* and *5015;* to *disturb wholly:*—exceedingly trouble.

1614. **ἐκτείνω ĕktĕinō**, *ek-ti'-no;* from *1537* and **τείνω tĕinō** (to *stretch*); to *extend:*—cast, put forth, stretch forth (out).

1615. **ἐκτελέω ĕktĕlĕō**, *ek-tel-eh'-o;* from *1537* and *5055;* to *complete* fully:—finish.

1616. **ἐκτένεια ĕktĕnĕia**, *ek-ten'-i-ah;* from *1618; intentness:*— × instantly.

1617. **ἐκτενέστερον ĕktĕnĕstĕrŏn**, *ek-ten-es'-ter-on;* neut. of the comp. of *1618; more intently:*—more earnestly.

1618. **ἐκτενής ĕktĕnēs**, *ek-ten-ace';* from *1614; intent:*—without ceasing, fervent.

1619. **ἐκτενῶς ĕktĕnōs**, *ek-ten-oce';* adv. from *1618; intently:*—fervently.

1620. **ἐκτίθημι ĕktithēmi**, *ek-tith'-ay-mee;* from *1537* and *5087;* to *expose;* fig. to *declare:*—cast out, expound.

1621. **ἐκτινάσσω ĕktinassō**, *ek-tin-as'-so;* from *1537* and **τινάσσω tinassō** (to *swing*); to *shake violently:*—shake (off).

1622. **ἐκτός ĕktŏs**, *ek-tos';* from *1537;* the *exterior;* fig. (as a prep.) *aside from, besides:*—but, except (-ed), other than, out of, outside, unless, without.

1623. **ἕκτος hĕktŏs**, *hek'-tos;* ordinal from *1803; sixth:*—sixth.

1624. **ἐκτρέπω ĕktrĕpō**, *ek-trep'-o;* from *1537* and the base of *5157;* to *deflect,* i.e. *turn away* (lit. or fig.):—avoid, turn (aside, out of the way).

1625. **ἐκτρέφω ĕktrĕphō**, *ek-tref'-o;* from *1537* and *5142;* to *rear up* to maturity, i.e. (gen.) to *cherish* or *train:*—bring up, nourish.

1626. **ἔκτρωμα ĕktrōma**, *ek'-tro-mah;* from a comp. of *1537* and **τιτρώσκω titrōskō** (to *wound*); a *miscarriage* (*abortion*), i.e. (by anal.) *untimely birth:*—born out of due time.

1627. **ἐκφέρω ĕkphĕrō**, *ek-fer'-o;* from *1537* and *5342;* to *bear out* (lit. or fig.):—bear, bring forth, carry forth (out).

1628. **ἐκφεύγω ĕkphĕugō**, *ek-fyoo'-go;* from *1537* and *5343;* to *flee out:*—escape, flee.

1629. **ἐκφοβέω ĕkphŏbĕō**, *ek-fob-eh'-o;* from *1537* and *5399;* to *frighten utterly:*—terrify.

1630. **ἔκφοβος ĕkphŏbŏs**, *ek'-fob-os;* from *1537* and *5401; frightened out* of one's wits:—sore afraid, exceedingly fear.

1631. **ἐκφύω ĕkphuō**, *ek-foo'-o;* from *1537* and *5453;* to *sprout up:*—put forth.

1632. **ἐκχέω ĕkchĕō**, *ek-kheh'-o;* or (by var.)

ἐκχύνω ĕkchunō, *ek-khoo'-no;* from *1537* and **χέω chĕō** (to *pour*); to *pour forth;* fig. to *bestow:*—gush (pour) out, run greedily (out), shed (abroad, forth), spill.

1633. **ἐκχωρέω ĕkchōrĕō**, *ek-kho-reh'-o;* from *1537* and *5562;* to *depart:*—depart out.

1634. **ἐκψύχω ĕkpsuchō**, *ek-psoo'-kho;* from *1537* and *5594;* to *expire:*—give (yield) up the ghost.

1635. **ἑκών hĕkōn**, *hek-own';* of uncert. affin.; *voluntary:*—willingly.

1636. **ἐλαία ĕlaia**, *el-ah'-yah;* fem. of a presumed der. from an obsol. prim.; an *olive* (the tree or the fruit):—olive (berry, tree).

1637. **ἔλαιον ĕlaiŏn**, *el'-ah-yon;* neut. of the same as *1636;* olive *oil:*—oil.

1638. **ἐλαιών ĕlaiōn**, *el-ah-yone';* from *1636;* an *olive-orchard,* i.e. (spec.) the *Mt. of Olives:*—Olivet.

1639. **Ἐλαμίτης Ĕlamitēs**, *el-am-ee'-tace;* of Heb. or. [5867]; an *Elamite* or Persian:—Elamite.

1640. **ἐλάσσων ĕlassōn**, *el-as'-sone;* or

ἐλάττων ĕlattōn, *el-at-tone';* comp. of the same as *1646; smaller* (in size, quantity, age or quality):—less, under, worse, younger.

1641. **ἐλαττονέω ĕlattŏnĕō**, *el-at-ton-eh-o;* from *1640;* to *diminish,* i.e. *fall short:*—have lack.

1642. **ἐλαττόω ĕlattŏō**, *el-at-tŏ'-o;* from *1640;* to *lessen* (in rank or influence):—decrease, make lower.

1643. **ἐλαύνω ĕlaunō**, *el-ŏw'-no;* a prol. form of a prim. verb (obsol. except in certain tenses as an altern. of this) of uncert. affin.; to *push* (as wind, oars or dæmoniacal power):—carry, drive, row.

1644. **ἐλαφρία ĕlaphria**, *el-af-ree'-ah;* from *1645; levity* (fig.), i.e. *fickleness:*—lightness.

1645. **ἐλαφρός ĕlaphrŏs**, *el-af-ros';* prob. akin to *1643* and the base of *1640; light,* i.e. *easy:*—light.

1646. **ἐλάχιστος ĕlachistŏs**, *el-akh'-is-tos;* superl. of **ἔλαχυς ĕlachus** (*short*); used as equiv. to *3398; least* (in size, amount, dignity, etc.):—least, very little (small), smallest.

1647. **ἐλαχιστότερος ĕlachistŏtĕrŏs**, *el-akh-is-tot'-er-os;* comp. of *1646; far less:*—less than the least.

1648. **Ἐλεάζαρ Ĕlĕazar**, *el-eh-ad'-zar;* of Heb. or. [499]; *Eleazar,* an Isr.:—Eleazar.

1649. **ἔλεγξις ĕlĕgxis**, *el'-eng-xis;* from *1651; refutation,* i.e. *reproof:*—rebuke.

1650. **ἔλεγχος ĕlĕgchŏs**, *el'-eng-khos;* from *1651; proof, conviction:*—evidence, reproof.

1651. **ἐλέγχω ĕlĕgchō**, *el-eng'-kho;* of uncert. affin.; to *confute, admonish:*—convict, convince, tell a fault, rebuke, reprove.

1652. **ἐλεεινός ĕlĕĕinŏs**, *el-eh-i-nos';* from *1656; pitiable:*—miserable.

1653. **ἐλεέω ĕlĕĕō**, *el-eh-eh'-o;* from *1656;* to *compassionate* (by word or deed, spec. by divine grace):—have compassion (pity on), have (obtain, receive, shew) mercy (on).

1654. **ἐλεημοσύνη ĕlĕēmŏsunē**, *el-eh-ay-mos-oo'-nay;* from *1656; compassionateness,* i.e. (as exercised towards the poor) *beneficence,* or (concr.) a *benefaction:*—alms (-deeds).

1655. **ἐλεήμων ĕlĕēmōn**, *el-eh-ay'-mone;* from *1653; compassionate* (actively):—merciful.

1656. **ἔλεος ĕlĕŏs**, *el'-eh-os;* of uncert. affin.; *compassion* (human or divine, espec. active):—(+ tender) mercy.

1657. **ἐλευθερία ĕlĕuthĕria**, *el-yoo-ther-ee'-ah;* from *1658; freedom* (legitimate or licentious, chiefly mor. or cer.):—liberty.

1658. **ἐλεύθερος ĕlĕuthĕrŏs**, *el-yoo'-ther-os;* prob. from the alt. of *2064; unrestrained* (to *go* at pleasure), i.e. (as a citizen) *not a slave* (whether *freeborn* or *manumitted*), or (gen.) *exempt* (from obligation or liability):—free (man, woman), at liberty.

1659. **ἐλευθερόω ĕlĕuthĕrŏō**, *el-yoo-ther-ŏ'-o;* from *1658;* to *liberate,* i.e. (fig.) to *exempt* (from mor., cer. or mortal liability):—deliver, make free.

ἐλεύθω ĕlĕuthō. See *2064*.

1660. **ἔλευσις ĕlĕusis**, *el'-yoo-sis;* from the alt. of *2064;* an *advent:*—coming.

1661. **ἐλεφάντινος ĕlĕphantinŏs**, *el-ef-an'-tee-nos;* from **ἔλεφας ĕlĕphas** (an "*elephant*"); *elephantine,* i.e. (by impl.) composed of *ivory:*—of ivory.

1662. **Ἐλιακείμ Ĕliakĕim**, *el-ee-ak-ime';* of Heb. or. [471]; *Eliakim,* an Isr.:—Eliakim.

1663. **Ἐλιέζερ Ĕliĕzĕr**, *el-ee-ed'-zer;* of Heb. or. [461]; *Eliezer,* an Isr.:—Eliezer.

1664. **Ἐλιούδ Ĕliŏud**, *el-ee-ood';* of Heb. or. [410 and 1935]; *God of majesty; Eliud,* an Isr.:—Eliud.

1665. **Ἐλισάβετ Ĕlisabĕt**, *el-ee-sab'-et;* of Heb. or. [472]; *Elisabet,* an Israelitess:—Elisabeth.

1666. **Ἐλισσαῖος Ĕlissaiŏs**, *el-is-sah'-yos;* of Heb. or. [477]; *Elissæus,* an Isr.:—Elissæus.

1667. **ἑλίσσω hĕlissō**, *hel-is'-so;* a form of *1507;* to *coil* or *wrap:*—fold up.

1668. **ἕλκος hĕlkŏs**, *hel'-kos;* prob. from *1670;* an *ulcer* (as if drawn together):—sore.

1669. **ἑλκόω hĕlkŏō**, *hel-kŏ'-o;* from *1668;* to *cause to ulcerate,* i.e. (pass.) *be ulcerous:*—full of sores.

1670. **ἑλκύω hĕlkuō**, *hel-koo'-o;* or

ἕλκω hĕlkō, *hel'-ko;* prob. akin to *138;* to *drag* (lit. or fig.):—draw. Comp. *1667*.

1671. **Ἑλλάς Hĕllas**, *hel-las';* of uncert. affin.; *Hellas* (or *Greece*), a country of Europe:—Greece.

1672. **Ἕλλην Hĕllēn**, *hel'-lane;* from *1671;* a *Hellen* (*Grecian*) or inhab. of Hellas; by extens. a *Greek-speaking* person, espec. a *non-Jew:*—Gentile, Greek.

1673. **Ἑλληνικός Hĕllēnikŏs**, *hel-lay-nee-kos';* from *1672; Hellenic,* i.e. *Grecian* (in language):—Greek.

1674. **Ἑλληνίς Hĕllēnis**, *hel-lay-nis';* fem. of *1672;* a *Grecian* (i.e. *non-Jewish*) woman:—Greek.

1675. **Ἑλληνιστής Hĕllēnistēs**, *hel-lay-nis-tace';* from a der. of *1672;* a *Hellenist* or Greek-speaking Jew:—Grecian.

1676. **Ἑλληνιστί Hĕllēnisti**, *hel-lay-nis-tee';* adv. from the same as *1675; Hellenistically,* i.e. in the Grecian language:—Greek.

1677. **ἐλλογέω ĕllŏgĕō**, *el-log-eh'-o;* from *1722* and *3056* (in the sense of *account*); to *reckon in,* i.e. *attribute:*—impute, put on account.

ἕλλομαι hĕllŏmai. See *138*.

1678. **Ἐλμωδάμ Ĕlmōdam**, *el-mo-dam';* of Heb. or. [perh. for 486]; *Elmodam,* an Isr.:—Elmodam.

1679. **ἐλπίζω ĕlpizō**, *el-pid'-zo;* from *1680;* to *expect* or *confide:*—(have, thing) hope (-d) (for), trust.

1680. **ἐλπίς ĕlpis**, *el-pece';* from a prim. **ἔλπω ĕlpō** (to *anticipate,* usually with pleasure); *expectation* (abstr. or concr.) or *confidence:*—faith, hope.

1681. **Ἐλύμας Ĕlumas**, *el-oo'-mas;* of for. or.; *Elymas,* a wizard:—Elymas.

1682. **ἐλοΐ ĕlōï**, *el-o-ee';* of Chald. or. [426 with pron. suff.]; *my God:*—Eloi.

1683. **ἐμαυτοῦ ĕmautŏu**, *em-ŏw-too'*; gen. comp. of *1700* and *846*; *of myself* (so likewise the dat.

ἐμαυτῷ ĕmautōį, *em-ow-tō'*; and acc.

ἐμαυτόν ĕmautŏn, *em-ow-ton'*):—me, mine own (self), myself.

1684. **ἐμβαίνω ĕmbainō**, *em-ba'hee-no*; from *1722* and the base of *939*; to *walk on*, i.e. *embark* (aboard a vessel), *reach* (a pool):—come (get) into, enter (into), go (up) into, step in, take ship.

1685. **ἐμβάλλω ĕmballō**, *em-bal'-lo*; from *1722* and *906*; to *throw on*, i.e. (fig.) *subject to* (eternal punishment):—cast into.

1686. **ἐμβάπτω ĕmbaptō**, *em-bap'-to*; from *1722* and *911*; to *whelm on*, i.e. *wet* (a part of the person, etc.) by contact with a fluid:—dip.

1687. **ἐμβατεύω ĕmbatĕuō**, *em-bat-yoo'-o*; from *1722* and a presumed der. of the base of *939*; equiv. to *1684*; to *intrude on* (fig.):—intrude into.

1688. **ἐμβιβάζω ĕmbibazō**, *em-bib-ad'-zo*; from *1722* and **βιβάζω bibazō** (to *mount*; causat. of *1684*); to *place on*, i.e. *transfer* (aboard a vessel):—put in.

1689. **ἐμβλέπω ĕmblĕpō**, *em-blep'-o*; from *1722* and *991*; to *look on*, i.e. (rel.) to *observe* fixedly, or (absol.) to *discern* clearly:—behold, gaze up, look upon, (could) see.

1690. **ἐμβριμάομαι ĕmbrimaŏmai**, *em-brim-ah'-om-ahee*; from *1722* and **βριμάομαι brimaŏmai** (to *snort* with anger); to have *indignation on*, i.e. (trans.) to *blame*, (intrans.) to *sigh* with chagrin, (spec.) to sternly *enjoin*:—straitly charge, groan, murmur against.

1691. **ἐμέ ĕmĕ**, *em-eh'*; a prol. form of *3165*; *me*:—I, me, my (-self).

1692. **ἐμέω ĕmĕō**, *em-eh'-o*; of uncert. affin.; to *vomit*:—(will) spue.

1693. **ἐμμαίνομαι ĕmmainŏmai**, *em-mah'ee-nom-ahee*; from *1722* and *3105*; to *rave on*, i.e. *rage at*:—be mad against.

1694. **Ἐμμανουήλ Ĕmmanŏuēl**, *em-man-oo-ale'*; of Heb. or. [6005]; *God with us*; *Emmanuel*, a name of Christ:—Emmanuel.

1695. **Ἐμμαούς Ĕmmaŏus**, *em-mah-ooce'*; prob. of Heb. or. [comp. 3222]; *Emmaüs*, a place in Pal.:—Emmaus.

1696. **ἐμμένω ĕmmĕnō**, *em-men'-o*; from *1722* and *3306*; to *stay in* the same place, i.e. (fig.) to *persevere*:—continue.

1697. **Ἐμμόρ Ĕmmŏr**, *em-mor'*; of Heb. or. [2544]; *Emmor* (i.e. *Chamor*), a Canaanite:—Emmor.

1698. **ἐμοί ĕmŏi**, *em-oy'*; a prol. form of *3427*; to *me*:—I, me, mine, my.

1699. **ἐμός ĕmŏs**, *em-os'*; from the oblique cases of *1473* (*1698*, *1700*, *1691*); *my*:—of me, mine (own), my.

1700. **ἐμοῦ ĕmŏu**, *em-oo'*; a prol. form of *3450*; *of me*:—me, mine, my.

1701. **ἐμπαιγμός ĕmpaigmŏs**, *emp-aheeg-mos'*; from *1702*; *derision*:—mocking.

1702. **ἐμπαίζω ĕmpaizō**, *emp-aheed'-zo*; from *1722* and *3815*; to *jeer at*, i.e. *deride*:—mock.

1703. **ἐμπαίκτης ĕmpaiktēs**, *emp-aheek-tace'*; from *1702*; a *derider*, i.e. (by impl.) a *false teacher*:—mocker, scoffer.

1704. **ἐμπεριπατέω ĕmpĕripatĕō**, *em-per-ee-pat-eh'-o*; from *1722* and *4043*; to *perambulate on* a place, i.e. (fig.) to *be occupied among* persons:—walk in.

1705. **ἐμπίπλημι ĕmpiplēmi**, *em-pip'-lay-mee*; or

ἐμπλήθω ĕmplēthō, *em-play'-tho*; from *1722* and the base of *4118*; to *fill in* (up), i.e. (by impl.) to *satisfy* (lit. or fig.):—fill.

1706. **ἐμπίπτω ĕmpiptō**, *em-pip'-to*; from *1722* and *4098*; to *fall on*, i.e. (lit.) *be entrapped by*, or (fig.) *be overwhelmed with*:—fall among (into).

1707. **ἐμπλέκω ĕmplĕkō**, *em-plek'-o*; from *1722* and *4120*; to *entwine*, i.e. (fig.) *involve* with:—entangle (in, self with).

ἐμπλήθω ĕmplēthō. See *1705*.

1708. **ἐμπλοκή ĕmplŏkē**, *em-plok-ay'*; from *1707*; elaborate *braiding* of the hair:—plaiting.

1709. **ἐμπνέω ĕmpnĕō**, *emp-neh'-o*; from *1722* and *4154*; to *inhale*, i.e. (fig.) to *be animated by* (bent *upon*):—breathe.

1710. **ἐμπορεύομαι ĕmpŏrĕuŏmai**, *em-por-yoo'-om-ahee*; from *1722* and *4198*; to *travel in* (a country as a pedlar), i.e. (by impl.) to *trade*:—buy and sell, make merchandise.

1711. **ἐμπορία ĕmpŏria**, *em-por-ee'-ah*; fem. from *1713*; *traffic*:—merchandise.

1712. **ἐμπόριον ĕmpŏriŏn**, *em-por'-ee-on*; neut. from *1713*; a *mart* ("*emporium*"):—merchandise.

1713. **ἔμπορος ĕmpŏrŏs**, *em'-por-os*; from *1722* and the base of *4198*; a (wholesale) *tradesman*:—merchant.

1714. **ἐμπρήθω ĕmprēthō**, *em-pray'-tho*; from *1722* and **πρήθω prēthō** (to *blow* a flame); to *enkindle*, i.e. *set on fire*:—burn up.

1715. **ἔμπροσθεν ĕmprŏsthĕn**, *em'-pros-then*; from *1722* and *4314*; *in front of* (in place [lit. or fig.] or time):—against, at, before, (in presence, sight) of.

1716. **ἐμπτύω ĕmptuō**, *emp-too'-o*; from *1722* and *4429*; to *spit at* or *on*:—spit (upon).

1717. **ἐμφανής ĕmphanēs**, *em-fan-ace'*; from a comp. of *1722* and *5316*; *apparent in* self:—manifest, openly.

1718. **ἐμφανίζω ĕmphanizō**, *em-fan-id'-zo*; from *1717*; to *exhibit* (in person) or *disclose* (by words):—appear, declare (plainly), inform, (will) manifest, shew, signify.

1719. **ἔμφοβος ĕmphŏbŏs**, *em'-fob-os*; from *1722* and *5401*; *in fear*, i.e. *alarmed*:—affrighted, afraid, tremble.

1720. **ἐμφυσάω ĕmphusaō**, *em-foo-sah'-o*; from *1722* and **φυσάω phusaō** (to *puff*) [comp. *5453*]; to *blow at* or *on*:—breathe on.

1721. **ἔμφυτος ĕmphutŏs**, *em'-foo-tos*; from *1722* and a der. of *5453*; *implanted* (fig.):—engrafted.

1722. **ἐν ĕn**, *en*; a prim. prep. denoting (fixed) *position* (in place, time or state), and (by impl.) *instrumentality* (medially or constructively), i.e. a relation of *rest* (intermediate between *1519* and *1537*); "*in*," *at*, (up-) *on*, *by*, etc.:—about, after, against, + almost, × altogether, among, × as, at, before, between, (here-) by (+ all means), for (. . . sake of), + give self wholly to, (here-) in (-to, -wardly), × mightily, (because) of, (up-) on, [open-] ly, × outwardly, one, × quickly, × shortly, [speedi-] ly, × that, × there (-in, -on), through (-out), (un-) to (-ward), under, when, where (-with), while, with (-in). Often used in compounds, with substantially the same import; rarely with verbs of motion, and then not to indicate direction, except (elliptically) by a separate (and different) prep.

1723. **ἐναγκαλίζομαι ĕnagkalizŏmai**, *en-ang-kal-id'-zom-ahee*; from *1722* and a der. of *43*; to *take in* one's *arms*, i.e. *embrace*:—take up in arms.

1724. **ἐνάλιος ĕnaliŏs**, *en-al'-ee-os*; from *1722* and *251*; *in the sea*, i.e. *marine*:—thing in the sea.

1725. **ἔναντι ĕnanti**, *en'-an-tee*; from *1722* and *473*; *in front* (i.e. fig. *presence*) *of*:—before.

1726. **ἐναντίον ĕnantiŏn**, *en-an-tee'-on*; neut. of *1727*; (adv.) *in the presence* (*view*) *of*:—before, in the presence of.

1727. **ἐναντίος ĕnantiŏs**, *en-an-tee'-os*; from *1725*; *opposite*; fig. *antagonistic*:—(over) against, contrary.

1728. **ἐνάρχομαι ĕnarchŏmai**, *en-ar'-khom-ahee*; from *1722* and *756*; to *commence on*:—rule [*by mistake* for *757*].

1729. **ἐνδεής ĕndĕēs**, *en-deh-ace'*; from a comp. of *1722* and *1210* (in the sense of *lacking*); *deficient in*:—lacking.

1730. **ἔνδειγμα ĕndĕigma**, *en'-dighe-mah*; from *1731*; an *indication* (concr.):—manifest token.

1731. **ἐνδείκνυμι ĕndĕiknumi**, *en-dike'-noo-mee*; from *1722* and *1166*; to *indicate* (by word or act):—do, show (forth).

1732. **ἔνδειξις ĕndĕixis**, *en'-dike-sis*; from *1731*; *indication* (abstr.):—declare, evident token, proof.

1733. **ἕνδεκα hĕndĕka**, *hen'-dek-ah*; from (the neut. of) *1520* and *1176*; *one* and *ten*, i.e. *eleven*:—eleven.

1734. **ἑνδέκατος hĕndĕkatŏs**, *hen-dek'-at-os*; ord. from *1733*; *eleventh*:—eleventh.

1735. **ἐνδέχεται ĕndĕchĕtai**, *en-dekh'-et-ahee*; third pers. sing. pres. of a comp. of *1722* and *1209*; (impers.) *it is accepted in*, i.e. *admitted* (*possible*):—can (+ not) be.

1736. **ἐνδημέω ĕndēmĕō**, *en-day-meh'-o*; from a comp. of *1722* and *1218*; to *be in* one's own *country*, i.e. *home* (fig.):—be at home (present).

1737. **ἐνδιδύσκω ĕndiduskō**, *en-did-oos'-ko*; a prol. form of *1746*; to *invest* (with a garment):—clothe in, wear.

1738. **ἔνδικος ĕndikŏs**, *en'-dee-kos*; from *1722* and *1349*; *in the right*, i.e. *equitable*:—just.

1739. **ἐνδόμησις ĕndŏmēsis**, *en-dom'-ay-sis*; from a comp. of *1722* and a der. of the base of *1218*; a *housing in* (*residence*), i.e. *structure*:—building.

1740. **ἐνδοξάζω ĕndŏxazō**, *en-dox-ad'-zo*; from *1741*; to *glorify*:—glorify.

1741. **ἔνδοξος ĕndŏxŏs**, *en'-dox-os*; from *1722* and *1391*; *in glory*, i.e. *splendid*, (fig.) *noble*:—glorious, gorgeous [-ly], honourable.

1742. **ἔνδυμα ĕnduma**, *en'-doo-mah*; from *1746*, *apparel* (espec. the outer *robe*):—clothing, garment, raiment.

1743. **ἐνδυναμόω ĕndunamŏō**, *en-doo-nam-ŏ'-o*; from *1722* and *1412*; to *empower*:—enable, (increase in) strength (-en), be (make) strong.

1744. **ἐνδύνω ĕndunō**, *en-doo'-no*; from *1772* and *1416*; to *sink* (by impl. *wrap* [comp. *1746*]) *on*, i.e. (fig.) *sneak*:—creep.

1745. **ἔνδυσις ĕndusis**, *en'-doo-sis*; from *1746*; *investment* with clothing:—putting on.

1746. **ἐνδύω ĕnduō**, *en-doo'-o*, from *1722* and *1416* (in the sense of *sinking* into a garment); to *invest* with clothing (lit. or fig.):—array, clothe (with), endue, have (put) on.

ἐνέγκω ĕnĕgkō. See *5342*.

1747. **ἐνέδρα ĕnĕdra**, *en-ed'-rah*; fem. from *1722* and the base of *1476*; an *ambuscade*, i.e. (fig.) murderous *purpose*:—lay wait. See also *1749*.

1748. **ἐνεδρεύω ĕnĕdrĕuō**, *en-ed-ryoo'-o*; from *1747*; to *lurk*, i.e. (fig.) *plot* assassination:—lay wait for.

1749. **ἔνεδρον ĕnĕdrŏn**, *en'-ed-ron*; neut. of the same as *1747*; an *ambush*, i.e. (fig.) murderous *design*:—lying in wait.

1750. **ἐνειλέω ĕnĕilĕō**, *en-i-leh'-o*; from *1772* and the base of *1507*; to *enwrap*:—wrap in.

1751. **ἔνειμι ĕnĕimi**, *en'-i-mee*; from *1772* and *1510*; to *be within* (neut. part. plur.):—such things as . . . have. See also *1762*.

1752. **ἕνεκα hĕnĕka**, *hen'-ek-ah*; or

ἕνεκεν hĕnĕkĕn, *hen'-ek-en*; or

εἵνεκεν hĕinĕkĕn, *hi'-nek-en*; of uncert. affin.; *on account of*:—because, for (cause, sake), (where-) fore, by reason of, that.

1753. **ἐνέργεια ĕnĕrgĕia**, *en-erg'-i-ah*; from *1756*; *efficiency* ("*energy*"):—operation, strong, (effectual) working.

1754. **ἐνεργέω ĕnĕrgĕō**, *en-erg-eh'-o*; from *1756*; to *be active*, *efficient*:—do, (be) effectual (fervent), be mighty in, shew forth self, work (effectually in)

1755. **ἐνέργημα ĕnĕrgēma**, *en-erg'-ay-mah;* from *1754*: an *effect:*—operation, working.

1756. **ἐνεργής ĕnĕrgēs**, *en-er-gace';* from *1722* and *2041*: *active, operative:*—effectual, powerful.

1757. **ἐνευλογέω ĕnĕulŏgĕō**, *en-yoo-log-eh'-o;* from *1722* and *2127*; to *confer a benefit on:*—bless.

1758. **ἐνέχω ĕnĕchō**, *en-ekh'-o;* from *1722* and *2192*; to *hold in* or *upon*, i.e. *ensnare;* by impl. to *keep a grudge:*—entangle with, have a quarrel against, urge.

1759. **ἐνθάδε ĕnthadĕ**, *en-thad'-eh;* from a prol. form of *1722*; prop. *within*, i.e. (of place) *here, hither:*—(t-) here, hither.

1760. **ἐνθυμέομαι ĕnthumĕŏmai**, *en-thoo-meh'-om-ahee;* from a comp. of *1722* and *2372*; to *be inspirited*, i.e. *ponder:*—think.

1761. **ἐνθύμησις ĕnthumēsis**, *en-thoo'-may-sis;* from *1760*; *deliberation:*—device, thought.

1762. **ἔνι ĕni**, *en'-ee;* contr. for third pers. sing. pres. indic. of *1751*; impers. *there is* in or among:—be, (there) is.

1763. **ἐνιαυτός ĕniautŏs**, *en-ee-ŏw-tos';* prol. from a prim. **ἔνος ĕnŏs** (a *year*); a *year:*—year.

1764. **ἐνίστημι ĕnistēmi**, *en-is'-tay-mee;* from *1722* and *2476*; to *place on* hand, i.e. (reflex.) *impend*, (part.) be *instant:*—come, be at hand, present.

1765. **ἐνισχύω ĕnischuō**, *en-is-khoo'-o;* from *1722* and *2480*; to *invigorate* (trans. or reflex.):—strengthen.

1766. **ἔννατος ĕnnatŏs**, *en'-nat-os;* ord. from *1767*: *ninth:*—ninth.

1767. **ἐννέα ĕnnĕa**, *en-neh'-ah;* a prim. number; *nine:*—nine.

1768. **ἐννενηκονταεννέα ĕnnĕnēkŏntaĕnnĕa**, *en-nen-ay-kon-tah-en-neh'-ah;* from a (tenth) multiple of *1767* and *1767* itself; *ninety-nine:*—ninety and nine.

1769. **ἐννεός ĕnnĕŏs**, *en-neh-os';* from *1770*; *dumb* (as *making signs*), i.e. *silent* from astonishment:—speechless.

1770. **ἐννεύω ĕnnĕuō**, *en-nyoo'-o;* from *1722* and *3506*; to *nod at*, i.e. *beckon* or *communicate by gesture:*—make signs.

1771. **ἔννοια ĕnnŏia**, *en'-noy-ah;* from a comp. of *1722* and *3563*; *thoughtfulness*, i.e. moral *understanding:*—intent, mind.

1772. **ἔννομος ĕnnŏmŏs**, *en'-nom-os;* from *1722* and *3551*; (subj.) *legal*, or (obj.) *subject* to:—lawful, under law.

1773. **ἔννυχον ĕnnuchŏn**, *en'-noo-khon;* neut. of a comp. of *1722* and *3571*; (adv.) *by night:*—before day.

1774. **ἐνοικέω ĕnŏikĕō**, *en-oy-keh'-o;* from *1722* and *3611*; to *inhabit* (fig.):—dwell in.

1775. **ἑνότης hĕnŏtēs**, *hen-ot'-ace;* from *1520*; *oneness*, i.e. (fig.) *unanimity:*—unity.

1776. **ἐνοχλέω ĕnŏchlĕō**, *en-okh-leh'-o;* from *1722* and *3791*; to *crowd in*, i.e. (fig.) to *annoy:*—trouble.

1777. **ἔνοχος ĕnŏchŏs**, *en'-okh-os;* from *1758*; *liable* to (a condition, penalty or imputation):—in danger of, guilty of, subject to.

1778. **ἔνταλμα ĕntalma**, *en'-tal-mah;* from *1781*; an *injunction*, i.e. religious *precept:*—commandment.

1779. **ἐνταφιάζω ĕntaphiazō**, *en-taf-ee-ad'-zo;* from a comp. of *1722* and *5028*; to *inswathe* with cerements for interment:—bury.

1780. **ἐνταφιασμός ĕntaphiasmŏs**, *en-taf-ee-as-mos';* from *1779*; *preparation* for interment:—burying.

1781. **ἐντέλλομαι ĕntĕllŏmai**, *en-tel'-lom-ahee;* from *1722* and the base of *5056*; to *enjoin:*—(give) charge, (give) command (-ments), injoin.

1782. **ἐντεῦθεν ĕntĕuthĕn**, *ent-yoo'-then;* from the same as *1759*; *hence* (lit. or fig.); (repeated) *on both sides:*—(from) hence, on either side.

1783. **ἔντευξις ĕntĕuxis**, *ent'-yook-sis;* from *1793*; an *interview*, i.e. (spec.) *supplication:*—intercession, prayer.

1784. **ἔντιμος ĕntimŏs**, *en'-tee-mos;* from *1722* and *5092*; *valued* (fig.):—dear, more honourable, precious, in reputation.

1785. **ἐντολή ĕntŏlē**, *en-tol-ay';* from *1781*; *injunction*, i.e. an authoritative *prescription:*—commandment, precept.

1786. **ἐντόπιος ĕntŏpiŏs**, *en-top'-ee-os;* from *1722* and *5117*; a *resident:*—of that place.

1787. **ἐντός ĕntŏs**, *en-tos';* from *1722*; *inside* (adv. or noun):—within.

1788. **ἐντρέπω ĕntrĕpō**, *en-trep'-o;* from *1722* and the base of *5157*; to *invert*, i.e. (fig. and reflex.) in a good sense, to *respect;* or in a bad one, to *confound:*—regard, (give) reverence, shame.

1789. **ἐντρέφω ĕntrĕphō**, *en-tref'-o;* from *1722* and *5142*; (fig.) to *educate:*—nourish up in.

1790. **ἔντρομος ĕntrŏmŏs**, *en'-trom-os;* from *1722* and *5156*; *terrified:*— × quake, × trembled.

1791. **ἐντροπή ĕntrŏpē**, *en-trop-ay';* from *1788*; *confusion:*—shame.

1792. **ἐντρυφάω ĕntruphaō**, *en-troo-fah'-o;* from *1722* and *5171*; to *revel in:*—sporting selves.

1793. **ἐντυγχάνω ĕntugchanō**, *en-toong-khan'-o;* from *1722* and *5177*; to *chance upon*, i.e. (by impl.) *confer with;* by extens. to *entreat* (in favor or against):—deal with, make intercession.

1794. **ἐντυλίσσω ĕntulissō**, *en-too-lis'-so;* from *1722* and **τυλίσσω tulissō** (to *twist;* prob. akin to *1507*); to *entwine*, i.e. *wind* up in:—wrap in (together).

1795. **ἐντυπόω ĕntupŏō**, *en-too-pŏ'-o;* from *1722* and a der. of *5179*; to *enstamp*, i.e. *engrave:*—engrave.

1796. **ἐνυβρίζω ĕnubrizō**, *en-oo-brid'-zo;* from *1722* and *5195*; to *insult:*—do despite unto.

1797. **ἐνυπνιάζομαι ĕnupniazŏmai**, *en-oop-nee-ad'-zom-ahee;* mid. from *1798*; to *dream:*—dream (-er).

1798. **ἐνύπνιον ĕnupniŏn**, *en-oop'-nee-on;* from *1722* and *5258*; something seen *in sleep*, i.e. a *dream* (*vision* in a dream):—dream.

1799. **ἐνώπιον ĕnōpiŏn**, *en-o'-pee-on;* neut. of a comp. of *1722* and a der. of *3700*; *in the face* of (lit. or fig.):—before, in the presence (sight) of, to.

1800. **Ἐνώς Ĕnōs**, *en-oce';* of Heb. or. [583]; *Enos* (i.e. *Enosh*), a patriarch:—Enos.

1801. **ἐνωτίζομαι ĕnōtizŏmai**, *en-o-tid'-zom-ahee;* mid. from a comp. of *1722* and *3775*; to take *in one's ear*, i.e. to *listen:*—hearken.

1802. **Ἐνώχ Ĕnōk**, *en-oke';* of Heb. or. [2585]; *Enoch* (i.e. *Chanok*), an antediluvian:—Enoch.

ἐξ ĕx. See *1537*.

1803. **ἕξ hĕx**, *hex;* a prim. numeral; *six:*—six.

1804. **ἐξαγγέλλω ĕxaggĕllō**, *ex-ang-el'-lo;* from *1537* and the base of *32*; to *publish*, i.e. *celebrate:*—shew forth.

1805. **ἐξαγοράζω ĕxagŏrazō**, *ex-ag-or-ad'-zo;* from *1537* and *59*; to *buy up*, i.e. *ransom;* fig. to *rescue* from loss (*improve* opportunity):—redeem.

1806. **ἐξάγω ĕxagō**, *ex-ag'-o;* from *1537* and *71*; to *lead forth:*—bring forth (out), fetch (lead) out.

1807. **ἐξαιρέω ĕxairĕō**, *ex-ahee-reh'-o;* from *1537* and *138*; act. to *tear out;* mid. to *select;* fig. to *release:*—deliver, pluck out, rescue.

1808. **ἐξαίρω ĕxairō**, *ex-ah'ee-ro;* from *1537* and *142*; to *remove:*—put (take) away.

1809. **ἐξαιτέομαι ĕxaitĕŏmai**, *ex-ahee-teh'-om-ahee;* mid. from *1537* and *154*; to *demand* (for trial):—desire.

1810. **ἐξαίφνης ĕxaiphnēs**, *ex-ah'eef-nace;* from *1537* and the base of *160*; *of a sudden* (*unexpectedly*):—suddenly. Comp. *1819*.

1811. **ἐξακολουθέω ĕxakŏlŏuthĕō**, *ex-ak-ol-oo-theh'-o;* from *1537* and *190*; to *follow out*, i.e. (fig.) to *imitate, obey*, yield to:—follow.

1812. **ἑξακόσιοι hĕxakŏsiŏi**, *hex-ak-os'-ee-oy;* plur. ordinal from *1803* and *1540*; *six hundred:*—six hundred.

1813. **ἐξαλείφω ĕxalĕiphō**, *ex-al-i'-fo;* from *1537* and *218*; to *smear out*, i.e. *obliterate* (*erase* tears, fig. *pardon* sin):—blot out, wipe away.

1814. **ἐξάλλομαι ĕxallŏmai**, *ex-al'-lom-ahee;* from *1537* and *242*; to *spring forth:*—leap up.

1815. **ἐξανάστασις ĕxanastasis**, *ex-an-as'-tas-is;* from *1817*; a *rising from* death:—resurrection.

1816. **ἐξανατέλλω ĕxanatĕllō**, *ex-an-at-el'-lo;* from *1537* and *393*; to *start up out of* the ground, i.e. *germinate:*—spring up.

1817. **ἐξανίστημι ĕxanistēmi**, *ex-an-is'-tay-mee;* from *1537* and *450*; obj. to *produce*, i.e. (fig.) *beget;* subj. to *arise*, i.e. (fig.) *object:*—raise (rise) up.

1818. **ἐξαπατάω ĕxapataō**, *ex-ap-at-ah'-o;* from *1537* and *538*; to *seduce wholly:*—beguile, deceive.

1819. **ἐξάπινα ĕxapina**, *ex-ap'-ee-nah;* from *1537* and a der. of the same as *160*; *of a sudden*, i.e. *unexpectedly:*—suddenly. Comp. *1810*.

1820. **ἐξαπορέομαι ĕxapŏrĕŏmai**, *ex-ap-or-eh'-om-ahee;* mid. from *1537* and *639*; to *be utterly at a loss*, i.e. *despond:*—(in) despair.

1821. **ἐξαποστέλλω ĕxapŏstĕllō**, *ex-ap-os-tel'-lo;* from *1537* and *649*; to *send away forth*, i.e. (on a mission) to *despatch*, or (peremptorily) to *dismiss:*—send (away, forth, out).

1822. **ἐξαρτίζω ĕxartizō**, *ex-ar-tid'-zo;* from *1537* and a der. of *739*; to *finish out* (time); fig. to *equip fully* (a teacher):—accomplish, thoroughly furnish.

1823. **ἐξαστράπτω ĕxastraptō**, *ex-as-trap'-to;* from *1537* and *797*; to *lighten forth*, i.e. (fig.) to *be radiant* (of very white garments):—glistening.

1824. **ἐξαύτης ĕxautēs**, *ex-ŏw'-tace;* from *1537* and the gen. sing. fem. of *846* (*5610* being understood); *from that* hour, i.e. *instantly:*—by and by, immediately, presently, straightway.

1825. **ἐξεγείρω ĕxĕgĕirō**, *ex-eg-i'-ro;* from *1537* and *1453*; to *rouse fully*, i.e. (fig.) to *resuscitate* (from death), *release* (from infliction):—raise up.

1826. **ἔξειμι ĕxĕimi**, *ex'-i-mee;* from *1537* and **εἶμι ĕimi** (to *go*); to *issue*, i.e. *leave* (a place), *escape* (to the shore):—depart, get [*to land*], go out.

1827. **ἐξελέγχω ĕxĕlĕgchō**, *ex-el-eng'-kho;* from *1537* and *1651*; to *convict fully*, i.e. (by impl.) to *punish:*—convince.

1828. **ἐξέλκω ĕxĕlkō**, *ex-el'-ko;* from *1537* and *1670*; to *drag forth*, i.e. (fig.) to *entice* (to sin):—draw away.

1829. **ἐξέραμα ĕxĕrama**, *ex-er'-am-ah;* from a comp. of *1537* and a presumed **ἐράω ĕraō** (to *spue*); *vomit*, i.e. *food disgorged:*—vomit.

1830. **ἐξερευνάω ĕxĕrĕunaō**, *ex-er-yoo-nah'-o;* from *1537* and *2045*; to *explore* (fig.):—search diligently.

1831. **ἐξέρχομαι ĕxĕrchŏmai**, *ex-er'-khom-ahee;* from *1537* and *2064*; to *issue* (lit. or fig.):—come (forth, out), depart (out of), escape, get out, go (abroad, away, forth, out, thence), proceed (forth), spread abroad.

1832. **ἔξεστι ĕxĕsti**, *ex'-es-tee;* third pers. sing. pres. indic. of a comp. of *1537* and *1510*; so also **ἐξόν ĕxŏn**, *ex-on';* neut. pres. part. of the same (with or without some form of *1510* expressed); impers. *it is right* (through the fig. idea of *being out* in public):—be lawful, let, × may (-est).

1833. **ἐξετάζω ĕxĕtazō**, *ex-et-ad'-zo;* from *1537* and **ἐτάζω ĕtazō** (to *examine*); to *test thoroughly* (by questions), i.e. *ascertain* or *interrogate:*—ask, enquire, search.

1834. **ἐξηγέομαι ĕxēgĕŏmai**, *ex-ayg-eh'-om-ahee;* from *1537* and *2233*; to *consider out* (aloud), i.e. *rehearse, unfold:*—declare, tell.

1835. **ἑξήκοντα hĕxēkŏnta**, *hex-ay'-kon-tah;* the tenth multiple of *1803*; *sixty:*—sixty [-fold], threescore.

1836. **ἑξῆς hĕxēs**, *hex-ace';* from *2192* (in the sense of *taking hold* of, i.e. *adjoining*); *successive:*—after, following, × morrow, next.

1837. **ἐξηχέομαι ĕxēchĕŏmai**, *ex-ay-kheh'-om-ahee;* mid. from *1537* and *2278*; to "*echo*" *forth*, i.e. *resound* (*be* generally *reported*):—sound forth.

1838. **ἕξις hĕxis**, *hex'-is;* from *2192*; *habit*, i.e. (by impl.) *practice:*—use.

1839. **ἐξίστημι ĕxistēmi**, *ex-is'-tay-mee;* from *1537* and *2476*; to *put* (*stand*) *out* of wits, i.e. *astound*, or (reflex.) *become astounded*, *insane:*—amaze, be (make) astonished, be beside self (selves), bewitch, wonder.

1840. **ἐξισχύω ĕxischuō**, *ex-is-khoo'-o;* from *1537* and *2480*; to *have full strength*, i.e. *be entirely competent:*—be able.

1841. **ἔξοδος ĕxŏdŏs**, *ex'-od-os;* from *1537* and *3598*; an *exit*, i.e. (fig.) *death:*—decease, departing.

1842. **ἐξολοθρεύω ĕxŏlŏthrĕuō**, *ex-ol-oth-ryoo'-o;* from *1537* and *3645*; to *extirpate:*—destroy.

1843. **ἐξομολογέω ĕxŏmŏlŏgĕō**, *ex-om-ol-og-eh'-o;* from *1537* and *3670*; to *acknowledge* or (by impl. of *assent*) *agree fully:*—confess, profess, promise.

ἐξόν ĕxŏn. See *1832*.

1844. **ἐξορκίζω ĕxŏrkizō**, *ex-or-kid'-zo;* from *1537* and *3726*; to *exact an oath*, i.e. *conjure:*—adjure.

1845. **ἐξορκιστής ĕxŏrkistēs**, *ex-or-kis-tace';* from *1844*; *one that binds by an oath* (or *spell*), i.e. (by impl.) an "*exorcist*" (*conjurer*):—exorcist.

1846. **ἐξορύσσω ĕxŏrussō**, *ex-or-oos'-so;* from *1537* and *3736*; to *dig out*, i.e. (by extens.) to *extract* (an eye), *remove* (a roofing):—break up, pluck out.

1847. **ἐξουδενόω ĕxŏudĕnŏō**, *ex-oo-den-ŏ'-o;* from *1537* and a der. of the neut. of *3762*; to *make utterly nothing of*, i.e. *despise:*—set at nought. See also *1848*.

1848. **ἐξουθενέω ĕxŏuthĕnĕō**, *ex-oo-then-eh'-o;* a var. of *1847* and mean. the same:—contemptible, despise, least esteemed, set at nought.

1849. **ἐξουσία ĕxŏusia**, *ex-oo-see'-ah;* from *1832* (in the sense of *ability*); *privilege*, i.e. (subj.) *force*, *capacity*, *competency*, *freedom*, or (obj.) *mastery* (concr. *magistrate*, *superhuman*, *potentate*, *token of control*), delegated *influence:*—authority, jurisdiction, liberty, power, right, strength.

1850. **ἐξουσιάζω ĕxŏusiazō**, *ex-oo-see-ad'-zo;* from *1849*; to *control:*—exercise authority upon, bring under the (have) power of.

1851. **ἐξοχή ĕxŏchē**, *ex-okh-ay';* from a comp. of *1537* and *2192* (mean. to *stand out*); *prominence* (fig.):—principal.

1852. **ἐξυπνίζω ĕxupnizō**, *ex-oop-nid'-zo;* from *1853*; to *waken:*—awake out of sleep.

1853. **ἔξυπνος ĕxupnŏs**, *ex'-oop-nos;* from *1537* and *5258*; *awake:*— × out of sleep.

1854. **ἔξω ĕxō**, *ex'-o;* adv. from *1537*; *out* (*-side*, *of doors*), lit. or fig.:—away, forth, (with-) out (of, -ward), strange.

1855. **ἔξωθεν ĕxōthĕn**, *ex'-o-then;* from *1854*; *external* (*-ly*):—out (-side -ward, -wardly), (from) without.

1856. **ἐξωθέω ĕxōthĕō**, *ex-o-theh'-o;* or

ἐξώθω ĕxōthō, *ex-o'-tho;* from *1537* and **ὠθέω ōthĕō** (to *push*); to *expel*; by impl. to *propel:*—drive out, thrust in.

1857. **ἐξώτερος ĕxōtĕrŏs**, *ex-o'-ter-os;* comp. of *1854*; *exterior:*—outer.

1858. **ἑορτάζω hĕŏrtazō**, *heh-or-tad'-zo;* from *1859*; to *observe a festival:*—keep the feast.

1859. **ἑορτή hĕŏrtē**, *heh-or-tay';* of uncert. affin.; a *festival:*—feast, holyday.

1860. **ἐπαγγελία ĕpaggĕlia**, *ep-ang-el-ee'-ah;* from *1861*; an *announcement* (for information, assent or pledge; espec. a divine *assurance* of good):—message, promise.

1861. **ἐπαγγέλλω ĕpaggĕllō**, *ep-ang-el'-lo;* from *1909* and the base of *32*; to *announce upon* (reflex.), i.e. (by impl.) to *engage* to do something, to *assert* something respecting oneself:—profess, (make) promise.

1862. **ἐπάγγελμα ĕpaggĕlma**, *ep-ang'-el-mah;* from *1861*; a *self-committal* (by *assurance* of conferring some good):—promise.

1863. **ἐπάγω ĕpagō**, *ep-ag'-o;* from *1909* and *71*; to *superinduce*, i.e. *inflict* (an evil), *charge* (a crime):—bring upon.

1864. **ἐπαγωνίζομαι ĕpagōnizŏmai**, *ep-ag-o-nid'-zom-ahee;* from *1909* and *75*; to *struggle for:*—earnestly contend for.

1865. **ἐπαθροίζω ĕpathrŏizō**, *ep-ath-roid'-zo;* from *1909* and **ἀθροίζω athrŏizō** (to *assemble*); to *accumulate:*—gather thick together.

1866. **Ἐπαίνετος Ĕpainĕtŏs**, *ep-a'hee-net-os;* from *1867*; *praised*; *Epænetus*, a Chr.:—Epenetus.

1867. **ἐπαινέω ĕpainĕō**, *ep-ahee-neh'-o;* from *1909* and *134*; to *applaud:*—commend, laud, praise.

1868. **ἔπαινος ĕpainŏs**, *ep'-ahee-nos;* from *1909* and the base of *134*; *laudation;* concr. a *commendable* thing:—praise.

1869. **ἐπαίρω ĕpairō**, *ep-ahee'-ro;* from *1909* and *142*; to *raise up* (lit. or fig.):—exalt self, poise (lift, take) up.

1870. **ἐπαισχύνομαι ĕpaischunŏmai**, *ep-ahee-skhoo'-nom-ahee;* from *1909* and *153*; to *feel shame for* something:—be ashamed.

1871. **ἐπαιτέω ĕpaitĕō**, *ep-ahee-teh'-o;* from *1909* and *154*; to *ask for:*—beg.

1872. **ἐπακολουθέω ĕpakŏlŏuthĕō**, *ep-ak-ol-oo-theh'-o;* from *1909* and *190*; to *accompany:*—follow (after).

1873. **ἐπακούω ĕpakŏuō**, *ep-ak-oo'-o;* from *1909* and *191*; to *hearken* (favorably) *to:*—hear.

1874. **ἐπακροάομαι ĕpakrŏaŏmai**, *ep-ak-rŏ-ah'-om-ahee;* from *1909* and the base of *202*; to *listen* (intently) *to:*—hear.

1875. **ἐπάν ĕpan**, *ep-an';* from *1909* and *302*; a particle of indef. contemporaneousness; *whenever*, *as soon as:*—when.

1876. **ἐπάναγκες ĕpanagkĕs**, *ep-an'-ang-kes;* neut. of a presumed comp. of *1909* and *318*; (adv.) *on necessity*, i.e. *necessarily:*—necessary.

1877. **ἐπανάγω ĕpanagō**, *ep-an-ag'-o;* from *1909* and *321*; to *lead up on*, i.e. (techn.) to *put out* (to sea); (intrans.) to *return:*—launch (thrust) out, return.

1878. **ἐπαναμιμνήσκω ĕpanamimnēskō**, *ep-an-ah-mim-nace'-ko;* from *1909* and *363*; to *remind of:*—put in mind.

1879. **ἐπαναπαύομαι ĕpanapauŏmai**, *ep-an-ah-pŏw'-om-ahee;* mid. from *1909* and *373*; to *settle on*; lit. (*remain*) or fig. (*rely*):—rest in (upon).

1880. **ἐπανέρχομαι ĕpanĕrchŏmai**, *ep-an-er'-khom-ahee;* from *1909* and *424*; to *come up on*, i.e. *return:*—come again, return.

1881. **ἐπανίσταμαι ĕpanistamai**, *ep-an-is'-tam-ahee;* mid. from *1909* and *450*; to *stand up on*, i.e. (fig.) to *attack:*—rise up against.

1882. **ἐπανόρθωσις ĕpanŏrthōsis**, *ep-an-or'-tho-sis;* from a comp. of *1909* and *461*; a *straightening up again*, i.e. (fig.) *rectification* (*reformation*):—correction.

1883. **ἐπάνω ĕpanō**, *ep-an'-o;* from *1909* and *507*; *up above*, i.e. *over* or *on* (of place, amount, rank, etc.):—above, more than, (up-) on, over.

1884. **ἐπαρκέω ĕparkĕō**, *ep-ar-keh'-o;* from *1909* and *714*; to *avail for*, i.e. *help:*—relieve.

1885. **ἐπαρχία ĕparchia**, *ep-ar-khee'-ah;* from a comp. of *1909* and *757* (mean. a *governor* of a district, "eparch"); a special *region* of government, i.e. a Roman *præfecture:*—province.

1886. **ἔπαυλις ĕpaulis**, *ep'-ŏw-lis;* from *1909* and an equiv. of *833*; a *hut over* the head, i.e. a *dwelling*.

1887. **ἐπαύριον ĕpauriŏn**, *ep-ow'-ree-on;* from *1909* and *839*; occurring *on the succeeding* day, i.e. (*2250* being implied) *to-morrow:*—day following, morrow, next day (after).

1888. **ἐπαυτοφώρῳ ĕpautŏphōrōi**, *ep-ow-tof-o'-ro;* from *1909* and *846* and (the dat. sing. of) a der. of **φώρ phōr** (a *thief*); *in theft itself*, i.e. (by anal.) *in actual crime:*—in the very act.

1889. **Ἐπαφρᾶς Ĕpaphras**, *ep-af-ras';* contr. from *1891*; *Epaphras*, a Chr.:—Epaphras.

1890. **ἐπαφρίζω ĕpaphrizō**, *ep-af-rid'-zo;* from *1909* and *875*; to *foam upon*, i.e. (fig.) to *exhibit* (a vile passion):—foam out.

1891. **Ἐπαφρόδιτος Ĕpaphrŏditŏs**, *ep-af-rod'-ee-tos;* from *1909* (in the sense of *devoted* to) and **Ἀφροδίτη Aphrŏditē** (*Venus*); *Epaphroditus*, a Chr.:—Epaphroditus. Comp. *1889*.

1892. **ἐπεγείρω ĕpĕgĕirō**, *ep-eg-i'-ro;* from *1909* and *1453*; to *rouse upon*, i.e. (fig.) to *excite* against:—raise, stir up.

1893. **ἐπεί ĕpĕi**, *ep-i';* from *1909* and *1487*; *thereupon*, i.e. *since* (of time or cause):—because, else, for that (then, -asmuch as), otherwise, seeing that, since, when.

1894. **ἐπειδή ĕpĕidē**, *ep-i-day';* from *1893* and *1211*; *since now*, i.e. (of time) *when*, or (of cause) *whereas:*—after that, because, for (that, -asmuch as), seeing, since.

1895. **ἐπειδήπερ ĕpĕidēpĕr**, *ep-i-day'-per;* from *1894* and *4007*; *since indeed* (of cause):—forasmuch.

1896. **ἐπεῖδον ĕpĕidŏn**, *ep-i'-don;* and other moods and persons of the same tense; from *1909* and *1492*; to *regard* (favorably or otherwise):—behold, look upon.

1897. **ἐπείπερ ĕpĕipĕr**, *ep-i'-per;* from *1893* and *4007*; *since* indeed (of cause):—seeing.

1898. **ἐπεισαγωγή ĕpĕisagōgē**, *ep-ice-ag-o-gay';* from a comp. of *1909* and *1521*; a *superintroduction:*—bringing in.

1899. **ἔπειτα ĕpĕita**, *ep'-i-tah;* from *1909* and *1534*; *thereafter:*—after that (-ward), then.

1900. **ἐπέκεινα ĕpĕkĕina**, *ep-ek'-i-nah;* from *1909* and (the acc. plur. neut. of) *1565*; *upon those* parts of, i.e. *on the further side of:*—beyond.

1901. **ἐπεκτείνομαι ĕpĕktĕinŏmai**, *ep-ek-ti'-nom-ahee;* mid. from *1909* and *1614*; to *stretch* (oneself) forward *upon:*—reach forth.

1902. **ἐπενδύομαι ĕpĕnduŏmai**, *ep-en-doo'-om-ahee;* mid. from *1909* and *1746*; to *invest upon* oneself:—be clothed upon.

1903. **ἐπενδύτης ĕpĕndutēs**, *ep-en-doo'-tace;* from *1902*; a *wrapper*, i.e. outer garment:—fisher's coat.

1904. **ἐπέρχομαι ĕpĕrchŏmai**, *ep-er'-khom-ahee;* from *1909* and *2064*; to *supervene*, i.e. *arrive*, *occur*, *impend*, *attack*, (fig.) *influence:*—come (in, upon).

1905. **ἐπερωτάω ĕpĕrōtaō**, *ep-er-o-tah'-o;* from *1909* and *2065*; to *ask for*, i.e. *inquire*, *seek:*—ask (after, questions), demand, desire, question.

1906. **ἐπερώτημα ĕpĕrōtēma**, *ep-er-o'-tay-mah;* from *1905*; an *inquiry:*—answer.

1907. **ἐπέχω ĕpĕchō**, *ep-ekh'-o;* from *1909* and *2192*; to *hold upon*, i.e. (by impl.) to *retain*; (by extens.) to *detain*; (with impl. of *3563*) to *pay attention to:*—give (take) heed unto, hold forth, mark, stay.

1908. **ἐπηρεάζω ĕpērĕazō**, *ep-ay-reh-ad'-zo;* from a comp. of *1909* and (prob.) **ἀρειά arĕia** (*threats*); to *insult*, *slander:*—use despitefully, falsely accuse.

1909. **ἐπί ĕpi**, *ep-ee';* a prim. prep. prop. mean. *superimposition* (of time, place, order, etc.), as a relation of *distribution* [with the gen.], i.e. *over*, *upon*, etc.; of *rest* (with the dat.) *at*, *on*, etc.; of *direction* (with the acc.) *towards*, *upon*, etc.:—about (the times), above, after, against, among, as long as (touching), at, beside, × have charge of, (be-, [where-]) fore, in (a place, as much as, the time of, -to), (because) of, (up-) on (behalf of), over, (by, for) the space of, through (-out), (un-) to (-ward), with. In compounds it retains essentially the same import, *at*, *upon*, etc. (lit. or fig.).

1910. **ἐπιβαίνω ĕpibainō**, *ep-ee-bah'ee-no;* from *1909* and the base of *939*; to *walk upon*, i.e. *mount*, *ascend*, *embark*, *arrive:*—come (into), enter into, go abroad, sit upon, take ship.

1911. **ἐπιβάλλω ĕpiballō**, *ep-ee-bal'-lo;* from *1909* and *906*; to *throw upon* (lit. or fig., trans. or reflex.; usually with more or less force); spec. (with *1438* implied) to *reflect;* impers. to *belong to:*—beat into, cast (up-) on, fall, lay (on), put (unto), stretch forth, think on.

1912. **ἐπιβαρέω ĕpibarĕō,** *ep-ee-bar-eh'-o;* from *1909* and *916;* to *be heavy upon,* i.e. (pecuniarily) to *be expensive to;* fig. to *be severe towards:*—be chargeable to, overcharge.

1913. **ἐπιβιβάζω ĕpibibazō,** *ep-ee-bee-bad'-zo;* from *1909* and a redupl. deriv. of the base of *939* [comp. *307*]; to *cause to mount* (an animal):—set on.

1914. **ἐπιβλέπω ĕpiblĕpō,** *ep-ee-blep'-o;* from *1909* and *991;* to *gaze at* (with favor, pity or partiality):—look upon, regard, have respect to.

1915. **ἐπίβλημα ĕpiblēma,** *ep-ib'-lay-mah;* from *1911;* a *patch:*—piece.

1916. **ἐπιβοάω ĕpibŏaō,** *ep-ee-bo-ah'-o;* from *1909* and *994;* to *exclaim against:*—cry.

1917. **ἐπιβουλή ĕpibŏulē,** *ep-ee-boo-lay';* from a presumed comp. of *1909* and *1014;* a *plan against* someone, i.e. a *plot:*—laying (lying) in wait.

1918. **ἐπιγαμβρεύω ĕpigambrĕuō,** *ep-ee-gam-bryoo'-o;* from *1909* and a der. of *1062;* to *form affinity with,* i.e. (spec.) in a levirate way:—marry.

1919. **ἐπίγειος ĕpigĕiŏs,** *ep-ig'-i-os;* from *1909* and *1093; worldly* (phys. or mor.):—earthly, in earth, terrestrial.

1920. **ἐπιγίνομαι ĕpiginŏmai,** *ep-ig-in'-om-ahee;* from *1909* and *1096;* to *arrive upon,* i.e. *spring up* (as a wind):—blow.

1921. **ἐπιγινώσκω ĕpiginōskō,** *ep-ig-in-oce'-ko;* from *1909* and *1097;* to *know upon* some mark, i.e. *recognise;* by impl. to *become fully acquainted with,* to *acknowledge:*—(ac-, have, take) know (-ledge, well), perceive.

1922. **ἐπίγνωσις ĕpignōsis,** *ep-ig'-no-sis;* from *1921; recognition,* i.e. (by impl.) full *discernment, acknowledgment:*—(ac-) knowledge (-ing, -ment).

1923. **ἐπιγραφή ĕpigraphē,** *ep-ig-raf-ay';* from *1924;* an *inscription:*—superscription.

1924. **ἐπιγράφω ĕpigraphō,** *ep-ee-graf'-o;* from *1909* and *1125;* to *inscribe* (phys. or ment.):—inscription, write in (over, thereon).

1925. **ἐπιδείκνυμι ĕpidĕiknumi,** *ep-ee-dike'-noo-mee;* from *1909* and *1166;* to *exhibit* (phys. or ment.):—shew.

1926. **ἐπιδέχομαι ĕpidĕchŏmai,** *ep-ee-dekh'-om-ahee;* from *1909* and *1209;* to *admit* (as a guest or [fig.] teacher):—receive.

1927. **ἐπιδημέω ĕpidēmĕō,** *ep-ee-day-meh'-o;* from a comp. of *1909* and *1218;* to *make oneself at home,* i.e. (by extens.) to *reside* (in a foreign country):—[be] dwelling (which were) there, stranger.

1928. **ἐπιδιατάσσομαι ĕpidiatassŏmai,** *ep-ee-dee-ah-tas'-som-ahee;* mid. from *1909* and *1299;* to *appoint besides,* i.e. *supplement* (as a codicil):—add to.

1929. **ἐπιδίδωμι ĕpididōmi,** *ep-ee-did'-o-mee;* from *1909* and *1325;* to *give over* (by hand or surrender):—deliver unto, give, let (+ [her drive]), offer.

1930. **ἐπιδιορθόω ĕpidiŏrthŏō,** *ep-ee-dee-or-thŏ'-o;* from *1909* and a der. of *3717;* to *straighten further,* i.e. (fig.) *arrange additionally:*—set in order.

1931. **ἐπιδύω ĕpiduō,** *ep-ee-doo'-o;* from *1909* and *1416;* to *set* fully (as the sun):—go down.

1932. **ἐπιείκεια ĕpiĕikĕia,** *ep-ee-i'-ki-ah;* from *1933; suitableness,* i.e. (by impl.) *equity, mildness:*—clemency, gentleness.

1933. **ἐπιεικής ĕpiĕikēs,** *ep-ee-i-kace';* from *1909* and *1503; appropriate,* i.e. (by impl.) *mild:*—gentle, moderation, patient.

1934. **ἐπιζητέω ĕpizētĕō,** *ep-eed-zay-teh'-o;* from *1909* and *2212;* to *search* (*inquire*) *for;* intens to *demand,* to *crave:*—desire, enquire, seek (after, for).

1935. **ἐπιθανάτιος ĕpithanatiŏs,** *ep-ee-than-at'-ee-os;* from *1909* and *2288;* doomed to *death:*—appointed to death.

1936. **ἐπίθεσις ĕpithĕsis,** *ep-ith'-es-is;* from *2007;* an *imposition* (of hands officially):—laying (putting) on.

1937. **ἐπιθυμέω ĕpithumĕō,** *ep-ee-thoo-meh'-o;* from *1909* and *2372;* to set the *heart upon,* i.e. *long* for (rightfully or otherwise):—covet, desire, would fain, lust (after).

1938. **ἐπιθυμητής ĕpithumētēs,** *ep-ee-thoo-may-tace';* from *1937;* a *craver:*— + lust after.

1939. **ἐπιθυμία ĕpithumia,** *ep-ee-thoo-mee'-ah;* from *1937;* a *longing* (espec. for what is forbidden):—concupiscence, desire, lust (after).

1940. **ἐπικαθίζω ĕpikathizō,** *ep-ee-kath-id'-zo;* from *1909* and *2523;* to *seat upon:*—set on.

1941. **ἐπικαλέομαι ĕpikalĕŏmai,** *ep-ee-kal-eh'-om-ahee;* mid. from *1909* and *2564;* to *entitle;* by impl. to *invoke* (for aid, worship, testimony, decision, etc.):—appeal (unto), call (on, upon), surname.

1942. **ἐπικάλυμα ĕpikaluma,** *ep-ee-kal'-oo-mah;* from *1943;* a *covering,* i.e. (fig.) *pretext:*—cloke.

1943. **ἐπικαλύπτω ĕpikaluptō,** *ep-ee-kal-oop'-to;* from *1909* and *2572;* to *conceal,* i.e. (fig.) *forgive:*—cover.

1944. **ἐπικατάρατος ĕpikataratŏs,** *ep-ee-kat-ar'-at-os;* from *1909* and a der. of *2672; imprecated,* i.e. *execrable:*—accursed.

1945. **ἐπίκειμαι ĕpikĕimai,** *ep-ik'-i-mahee;* from *1909* and *2749;* to *rest upon* (lit. or fig.):—impose, be instant, (be) laid (there-, up-) on, (when) lay (on), lie (on), press upon.

1946. **Ἐπικούρειος Ĕpikŏurĕiŏs,** *ep-ee-koo'-ri-os;* from **Ἐπίκουρος Ĕpikŏurŏs** [comp. *1947*] (a noted philosopher); an *Epicurean* or follower of Epicurus:—Epicurean.

1947. **ἐπικουρία ĕpikŏuria,** *ep-ee-koo-ree'-ah;* from a comp. of *1909* and a (prol.) form of the base of *2877* (in the sense of *servant*); *assistance:*—help.

1948. **ἐπικρίνω ĕpikrinō,** *ep-ee-kree'-no;* from *1909* and *2919;* to *adjudge:*—give sentence.

1949. **ἐπιλαμβάνομαι ĕpilambanŏmai,** *ep-ee-lam-ban'-om-ahee;* mid. from *1909* and *2983;* to *seize* (for help, injury, attainment or any other purpose; lit. or fig.):—catch, lay hold (up-) on, take (by, hold of, on).

1950. **ἐπιλανθάνομαι ĕpilanthanŏmai,** *ep-ee-lan-than'-om-ahee;* mid. from *1909* and *2990;* to *lose out* of mind; by impl. to *neglect:*—(be) forget (-ful of).

1951. **ἐπιλέγομαι ĕpilĕgŏmai,** *ep-ee-leg'-om-ahee;* mid. from *1909* and *3004;* to *surname, select:*—call, choose.

1952. **ἐπιλείπω ĕpilĕipō,** *ep-ee-li'-po;* from *1909* and *3007;* to *leave upon,* i.e. (fig.) to *be insufficient for:*—fail.

1953. **ἐπιλησμονή ĕpilēsmŏnē,** *ep-ee-lace-mon-ay';* from a der. of *1950; negligence:*— × forgetful.

1954. **ἐπίλοιπος ĕpilŏipŏs,** *ep-il'-oy-pos;* from *1909* and *3062; left over,* i.e. *remaining:*—rest.

1955. **ἐπίλυσις ĕpilusis,** *ep-il'-oo-sis;* from *1956; explanation,* i.e. *application:*—interpretation.

1956. **ἐπιλύω ĕpiluō,** *ep-ee-loo'-o;* from *1909* and *3089;* to *solve further,* i.e. (fig.) to *explain, decide:*—determine, expound.

1957. **ἐπιμαρτυρέω ĕpimarturĕō,** *ep-ee-mar-too-reh'-o;* from *1909* and *3140;* to *attest further,* i.e. *corroborate:*—testify.

1958. **ἐπιμέλεια ĕpimĕlĕia,** *ep-ee-mel'-i-ah;* from *1959; carefulness,* i.e. kind *attention* (*hospitality*):— + refresh self.

1959. **ἐπιμελέομαι ĕpimĕlĕŏmai,** *ep-ee-mel-eh'-om-ahee;* mid. from *1909* and the same as *3199;* to *care for* (phys. or otherwise):—take care of.

1960. **ἐπιμελῶς ĕpimĕlōs,** *ep-ee-mel-oce';* adv. from a der. of *1959; carefully:*—diligently.

1961. **ἐπιμένω ĕpimĕnō,** *ep-ee-men'-o;* from *1909* and *3306;* to *stay over,* i.e. *remain* (fig. *persevere*):—abide (in), continue (in), tarry.

1962. **ἐπινεύω ĕpinĕuō,** *ep-een-yoo'-o;* from *1909* and *3506;* to *nod at,* i.e. (by impl.) to *assent:*—consent.

1963. **ἐπίνοια ĕpinŏia,** *ep-in'-oy-ah;* from *1909* and *3563; attention* of the mind, i.e. (by impl.) *purpose:*—thought.

1964. **ἐπιορκέω ĕpiŏrkĕō,** *ep-ee-or-keh'-o;* from *1965;* to *commit perjury:*—forswear self.

1965. **ἐπίορκος ĕpiŏrkŏs,** *ep-ee'-or-kos;* from *1909* and *3727;* on *oath,* i.e. (falsely) a *forswearer:*—perjured person.

1966. **ἐπιοῦσα ĕpiŏusa,** *ep-ee-oo'-sah;* fem. sing. part. of a comp. of *1909* and **εἶμι hĕimi** (to *go*); *supervening,* i.e. (*2250* or *3571* being expressed or implied) the *ensuing* day or night:—following, next.

1967. **ἐπιούσιος ĕpiŏusiŏs,** *ep-ee-oo'-see-os;* perh. from the same as *1966; to-morrow's;* but more prob. from *1909* and a der. of the pres. part. fem. of *1510; for subsistence,* i.e. *needful:*—daily.

1968. **ἐπιπίπτω ĕpipiptō,** *ep-ee-pip'-to;* from *1909* and *4098;* to *embrace* (with affection) or *seize* (with more or less violence; lit. or fig.):—fall into (on, upon), lie on, press upon.

1969. **ἐπιπλήσσω ĕpiplēssō,** *ep-ee-place'-so;* from *1909* and *4141;* to *chastise,* i.e. (with words) to *upbraid:*—rebuke.

1970. **ἐπιπνίγω ĕpipnigō,** *ep-ee-pnee'-go;* from *1909* and *4155;* to *throttle upon,* i.e. (fig.) *overgrow:*—choke.

1971. **ἐπιποθέω ĕpipŏthĕō,** *ep-ee-poth-eh'-o;* from *1909* and **ποθέω pŏthĕō** (to *yearn*); to *dote upon,* i.e. *intensely crave* possession (lawfully or wrongfully):—(earnestly) desire (greatly), (greatly) long (after), lust.

1972. **ἐπιπόθησις ĕpipŏthēsis,** *ep-ee-poth'-ay-sis;* from *1971;* a *longing for:*—earnest (vehement) desire.

1973. **ἐπιπόθητος ĕpipŏthētŏs,** *ep-ee-poth'-ay-tos;* from *1909* and a der. of the latter part of *1971; yearned upon,* i.e. *greatly loved:*—longed for.

1974. **ἐπιποθία ĕpipŏthia,** *ep-ee-poth-ee'-ah;* from *1971; intense longing:*—great desire.

1975. **ἐπιπορεύομαι ĕpipŏrĕuŏmai,** *ep-ee-por-yoo'-om-ahee;* from *1909* and *4198;* to *journey further,* i.e. *travel on* (*reach*):—come.

1976. **ἐπιῤῥάπτω ĕpirrhaptō,** *ep-ir-hrap'-to;* from *1909* and the base of *4476;* to *stitch upon,* i.e. *fasten* with the needle:—sew on.

1977. **ἐπιῤῥίπτω ĕpirrhiptō,** *ep-ir-hrip'-to;* from *1909* and *4496;* to *throw upon* (lit. or fig.):—cast upon.

1978. **ἐπίσημος ĕpisēmŏs,** *ep-is'-ay-mos;* from *1909* and some form of the base of *4591; remarkable,* i.e. (fig.) *eminent:*—notable, of note.

1979. **ἐπισιτισμός ĕpisitismŏs,** *ep-ee-sit-is-mos';* from a comp. of *1909* and a der. of *4621;* a *provisioning,* i.e. (concr.) *food:*—victuals.

1980. **ἐπισκέπτομαι ĕpiskĕptŏmai,** *ep-ee-skep'-tom-ahee;* mid. from *1909* and the base of *4649;* to *inspect,* i.e. (by impl.) to *select;* by extens. to *go to see, relieve:*—look out, visit.

1981. **ἐπισκηνόω ĕpiskēnŏō,** *ep-ee-skay-nŏ'-o;* from *1909* and *4637;* to *tent upon,* i.e. (fig.) *abide with:*—rest upon.

1982. **ἐπισκιάζω ĕpiskiazō,** *ep-ee-skee-ad'-zo;* from *1909* and a der. of *4639;* to *cast a shade upon,* i.e. (by anal.) to *envelop* in a haze of brilliancy; fig. to *invest* with preternatural influence:—overshadow.

1983. **ἐπισκοπέω ĕpiskŏpĕō,** *ep-ee-skop-eh'-o;* from *1909* and *4648;* to *oversee;* by impl. to *beware:*—look diligently, take the oversight.

1984. **ἐπισκοπή ĕpiskŏpē,** *ep-is-kop-ay';* from *1980; inspection* (for relief); by impl. *superintendence;* spec. the Chr. "*episcopate*":—the office of a "bishop", bishoprick, visitation.

1985. **ἐπίσκοπος ĕpiskŏpŏs,** *ep-is'-kop-os;* from *1909* and *4649* (in the sense of *1983*); a *superintendent,* i.e. Chr. officer in gen. charge of a (or the) church (lit. or fig.):—bishop, overseer.

1986. **ἐπισπάομαι ĕpispaŏmai,** *ep-ee-spah'-om-ahee;* from *1909* and *4685;* to *draw over,* i.e. (with *203* implied) *efface* the mark of *circumcision* (by recovering with the foreskin):—become uncircumcised.

1987. **ἐπίσταμαι ĕpistamai,** *ep-is'-tam-ahee;* appar. a mid. of *2186* (with *3563* implied); to *put* the mind *upon,* i.e. *comprehend,* or *be acquainted with:*—know, understand.

1988. **ἐπιστάτης ĕpistatēs**, *ep-is-tat'-ace;* from *1909* and a presumed der. of *2476;* an *appointee over*, i.e. *commander* (*teacher*):—master.

1989. **ἐπιστέλλω ĕpistĕllō**, *ep-ee-stel'-lo;* from *1909* and *4724;* to *enjoin* (by writing), i.e. (gen.) to *communicate by letter* (for any purpose):—write (a letter, unto).

1990. **ἐπιστήμων ĕpistēmōn**, *ep-ee-stay'-mone;* from *1987; intelligent:*—endued with knowledge.

1991. **ἐπιστηρίζω ĕpistērizō**, *ep-ee-stay-rid'-zo;* from *1909* and *4741;* to *support further*, i.e. *reëstablish:*—confirm, strengthen.

1992. **ἐπιστολή ĕpistŏlē**, *ep-is-tol-ay';* from *1989;* a *written message:*—"epistle", letter.

1993. **ἐπιστομίζω ĕpistŏmizō**, *ep-ee-stom-id'-zo;* from *1909* and *4750;* to put something *over* the *mouth*, i.e. (fig.) to *silence:*—stop mouths.

1994. **ἐπιστρέφω ĕpistrĕphō**, *ep-ee-stref'-o;* from *1909* and *4762;* to *revert* (lit., fig. or mor.):—come (go) again, convert, (re-) turn (about, again).

1995. **ἐπιστροφή ĕpistrŏphē**, *ep-is-trof-ay';* from *1994; reversion*, i.e. mor. *revolution:*—conversion.

1996. **ἐπισυνάγω ĕpisunagō**, *ep-ee-soon-ag'-o;* from *1909* and *4863;* to *collect upon* the same place:—gather (together).

1997. **ἐπισυναγωγή ĕpisunagōgē**, *ep-ee-soon-ag-o-gay';* from *1996;* a complete *collection;* spec. a Chr. *meeting* (for worship):—assembling (gathering) together.

1998. **ἐπισυντρέχω ĕpisuntrĕchō**, *ep-ee-soon-trekh'-o;* from *1909* and *4936;* to *hasten together upon* one place (or a partic. occasion):—come running together.

1999. **ἐπισύστασις ĕpisustasis**, *ep-ee-soo'-stas-is;* from the mid. of a comp. of *1909* and *4921;* a *conspiracy*, i.e. *concourse* (riotous or friendly):—that which cometh upon, + raising up.

2000. **ἐπισφαλής ĕpisphalēs**, *ep-ee-sfal-ace';* from a comp. of *1909* and **σφάλλω sphallō** (to *trip*); fig. *insecure:*—dangerous.

2001. **ἐπισχύω ĕpischuō**, *ep-is-khoo'-o;* from *1909* and *2480;* to *avail further*, i.e. (fig.) *insist stoutly:*—be the more fierce.

2002. **ἐπισωρεύω ĕpisōrĕuō**, *ep-ee-so-ryoo'-o;* from *1909* and *4987;* to *accumulate further*, i.e. (fig.) *seek* additionally:—heap.

2003. **ἐπιταγή ĕpitagē**, *ep-ee-tag-ay';* from *2004;* an *injunction* or *decree;* by impl. *authoritativeness:*—authority, commandment.

2004. **ἐπιτάσσω ĕpitassō**, *ep-ee-tas'-so;* from *1909* and *5021;* to *arrange upon*, i.e. *order:*—charge, command, injoin.

2005. **ἐπιτελέω ĕpitĕlĕō**, *ep-ee-tel-eh'-o;* from *1909* and *5055;* to *fulfill further* (or *completely*), i.e. *execute;* by impl. to *terminate, undergo:*—accomplish, do, finish, (make) (perfect), perform (× -ance).

2006. **ἐπιτήδειος ĕpitēdĕiŏs**, *ep-ee-tay'-di-os;* from **ἐπιτηδές ĕpitēdĕs** (*enough*); *serviceable*, i.e. (by impl.) *requisite:*—things which are needful.

2007. **ἐπιτίθημι ĕpitithēmi**, *ep-ee-tith'-ay-mee;* from *1909* and *5087;* to *impose* (in a friendly or hostile sense):—add unto, lade, lay upon, put (up) on, set on (up), + surname, × wound.

2008. **ἐπιτιμάω ĕpitimaō**, *ep-ee-tee-mah'-o;* from *1909* and *5091;* to *tax upon*, i.e. *censure* or *admonish;* by impl. *forbid:*—(straitly) charge, rebuke.

2009. **ἐπιτιμία ĕpitimia**, *ep-ee-tee-mee'-ah;* from a comp. of *1909* and *5092;* prop. *esteem*, i.e. *citizenship;* used (in the sense of *2008*) of a *penalty:*—punishment.

2010. **ἐπιτρέπω ĕpitrĕpō**, *ep-ee-trep'-o;* from *1909* and the base of *5157;* to *turn over* (*transfer*), i.e. *allow:*—give leave (liberty, license), let, permit, suffer.

2011. **ἐπιτροπή ĕpitrŏpē**, *ep-ee-trop-ay';* from *2010; permission*, i.e. (by impl.) full *power:*—commission.

2012. **ἐπίτροπος ĕpitrŏpŏs**, *ep-it'-rop-os;* from *1909* and *5158* (in the sense of *2011*); a *commissioner*, i.e. domestic *manager, guardian:*—steward, tutor.

2013. **ἐπιτυγχάνω ĕpitugchanō**, *ep-ee-toong-khan'-o;* from *1909* and *5177;* to *chance upon*, i.e. (by impl.) *attain:*—obtain.

2014. **ἐπιφαίνω ĕpiphainō**, *ep-ee-fah'ee-no;* from *1909* and *5316;* to *shine upon*, i.e. *become* (lit.) *visible* or (fig.) *known:*—appear, give light.

2015. **ἐπιφάνεια ĕpiphanĕia**, *ep-if-an'-i-ah;* from *2016;* a *manifestation*, i.e. (spec.) the *advent* of Christ (past or fut.):—appearing, brightness.

2016. **ἐπιφανής ĕpiphanēs**, *ep-if-an-ace';* from *2014; conspicuous*, i.e. (fig.) *memorable:*—notable.

2017. **ἐπιφαύω ĕpiphauō**, *ep-ee-fōw'-o;* a form of *2014;* to *illuminate* (fig.):—give light.

2018. **ἐπιφέρω ĕpiphĕrō**, *ep-ee-fer'-o;* from *1909* and *5342;* to *bear upon* (or *further*), i.e. *adduce* (pers. or judicially [*accuse, inflict*]), *superinduce:*—add, bring (against), take.

2019. **ἐπιφωνέω ĕpiphōnĕō**, *ep-ee-fo-neh'-o;* from *1909* and *5455;* to *call at* something, i.e. *exclaim:*—cry (against), give a shout.

2020. **ἐπιφώσκω ĕpiphōskō**, *ep-ee-foce'-ko;* a form of *2017;* to begin to *grow light:*—begin to dawn, × draw on.

2021. **ἐπιχειρέω ĕpichĕirĕō**, *ep-ee-khi-reh'-o;* from *1909* and *5495;* to put the *hand upon*, i.e. *undertake:*—go about, take in hand (upon).

2022. **ἐπιχέω ĕpichĕō**, *ep-ee-kheh'-o;* from *1909* and **χέω chĕō** (to *pour*); to *pour upon:*—pour in.

2023. **ἐπιχορηγέω ĕpichŏrēgĕō**, *ep-ee-khor-ayg-eh'-o;* from *1909* and *5524;* to *furnish besides*, i.e. fully *supply*, (fig.) *aid* or *contribute:*—add, minister (nourishment, unto).

2024. **ἐπιχορηγία ĕpichŏrēgia**, *ep-ee-khor-ayg-ee'-ah;* from *2023; contribution:*—supply.

2025. **ἐπιχρίω ĕpichriō**, *ep-ee-khree'-o;* from *1909* and *5548;* to *smear over:*—anoint.

2026. **ἐποικοδομέω ĕpŏikŏdŏmĕō**, *ep-oy-kod-om-eh'-o;* from *1909* and *3618;* to *build upon*, i.e. (fig.) to *rear up:*—build thereon (thereupon, on, upon).

2027. **ἐποκέλλω ĕpŏkĕllō**, *ep-ok-el'-lo;* from *1909* and **ὀκέλλω ŏkĕllō** (to *urge*); to *drive upon* the shore, i.e. to *beach* a vessel:—run aground.

2028. **ἐπονομάζω ĕpŏnŏmazō**, *ep-on-om-ad'-zo;* from *1909* and *3687;* to *name further*, i.e. *denominate:*—call.

2029. **ἐποπτεύω ĕpŏptĕuō**, *ep-opt-yoo'-o;* from *1909* and a der. of *3700;* to *inspect*, i.e. *watch:*—behold.

2030. **ἐπόπτης ĕpŏptēs**, *ep-op'-tace;* from *1909* and a presumed der. of *3700;* a *looker-on:*—eye-witness.

2031. **ἔπος ĕpŏs**, *ep'-os;* from *2036;* a *word:*—× say.

2032. **ἐπουράνιος ĕpŏuraniŏs**, *ep-oo-ran'-ee-os;* from *1909* and *3772; above* the *sky:*—celestial, (in) heaven (-ly), high.

2033. **ἑπτά hĕpta**, *hep-tah';* a prim. number; *seven:*—seven.

2034. **ἑπτάκις hĕptakis**, *hep-tak-is';* adv. from *2033; seven times:*—seven times.

2035. **ἑπτακισχίλιοι hĕptakischiliŏi**, *hep-tak-is-khil'-ee-oy;* from *2034* and *5507; seven times a thousand:*—seven thousand.

2036. **ἔπω ĕpō**, *ep'-o;* a prim. verb (used only in the def. past tense, the others being borrowed from *2046*, *4483* and *5346*); to *speak* or *say* (by word or writing):—answer, bid, bring word, call, command, grant, say (on), speak, tell. Comp. *3004*.

2037. **Ἔραστος Ĕrastŏs**, *er'-as-tos;* from **ἐράω ĕraō** (*to love*); *beloved; Erastus*, a Chr.:—Erastus.

2038. **ἐργάζομαι ĕrgazŏmai**, *er-gad'-zom-ahee;* mid. from *2041;* to *toil* (as a task, occupation, etc.), (by impl.) *effect, be engaged in* or *with*, etc.:—commit, do, labor for, minister about, trade (by), work.

2039. **ἐργασία ĕrgasia**, *er-gas-ee'-ah;* from *2040; occupation;* by impl. *profit, pains:*—craft, diligence, gain, work.

2040. **ἐργάτης ĕrgatēs**, *er-gat'-ace;* from *2041;* a *toiler;* fig. a *teacher:*—labourer, worker (-men).

2041. **ἔργον ĕrgŏn**, *er'-gon;* from a prim. (but obsol.) **ἔργω ĕrgō** (to *work*); *toil* (as an effort or occupation); by impl. an *act:*—deed, doing, labour, work.

2042. **ἐρεθίζω ĕrĕthizō**, *er-eth-id'-zo;* from a presumed prol. form of *2054;* to *stimulate* (espec. to anger):—provoke.

2043. **ἐρείδω ĕrĕidō**, *er-i'-do;* of obscure affin.; to *prop*, i.e. (reflex.) *get fast:*—stick fast.

2044. **ἐρεύγομαι ĕrĕugŏmai**, *er-yoog'-om-ahee;* of uncert. affin.; to *belch*, i.e. (fig.) to *speak out:*—utter.

2045. **ἐρευνάω ĕrĕunaō**, *er-yoo-nah'-o;* appar. from *2046* (through the idea of *inquiry*); to *seek*, i.e. (fig.) to *investigate:*—search.

2046. **ἐρέω ĕrĕō**, *er-eh'-o;* prob. a fuller form of *4483;* an alt. for *2036* in cert. tenses; to *utter*, i.e. *speak* or *say:*—call, say, speak (of), tell.

2047. **ἐρημία ĕrēmia**, *er-ay-mee'-ah;* from *2048; solitude* (concr.):—desert, wilderness.

2048. **ἔρημος ĕrēmŏs**, *er'-ay-mos;* of uncert. affin.; *lonesome*, i.e. (by impl.) *waste* (usually as a noun, *5561* being implied):—desert, desolate, solitary, wilderness.

2049. **ἐρημόω ĕrēmŏō**, *er-ay-mŏ'-o;* from *2048;* to *lay waste* (lit. or fig.):—(bring to, make) desolate (-ion), come to nought.

2050. **ἐρήμωσις ĕrēmōsis**, *er-ay'-mo-sis;* from *2049; despoliation:*—desolation.

2051. **ἐρίζω ĕrizō**, *er-id'-zo;* from *2054;* to *wrangle:*—strive.

2052. **ἐριθεία ĕrithĕia**, *er-ith-i'-ah;* perh. from the same as *2042;* prop. *intrigue*, i.e. (by impl.) *faction:*—contention (-ious), strife.

2053. **ἔριον ĕriŏn**, *er'-ee-on;* of obscure affin.; *wool:*—wool.

2054. **ἔρις ĕris**, *er'-is;* of uncert. affin.; a *quarrel*, i.e. (by impl.) *wrangling:*—contention, debate, strife, variance.

2055. **ἐρίφιον ĕriphiŏn**, *er-if'-ee-on;* from *2056;* a *kidling*, i.e. (gen.) *goat* (symbol. *wicked* person):—goat.

2056. **ἔριφος ĕriphŏs**, *er'-if-os;* perh. from the same as *2053* (through the idea of *hairiness*); a *kid* or (gen.) *goat:*—goat, kid.

2057. **Ἑρμᾶς Hĕrmas**, *her-mas';* prob. from *2060; Hermas*, a Chr.:—Hermas.

2058. **ἑρμηνεία hĕrmēnĕia**, *her-may-ni'-ah;* from the same as *2059; translation:*—interpretation.

2059. **ἑρμηνεύω hĕrmēnĕuō**, *her-mayn-yoo'-o;* from a presumed der. of *2060* (as the god of language); to *translate:*—interpret.

2060. **Ἑρμῆς Hĕrmēs**, *her-mace';* perh. from *2046; Hermes*, the name of the messenger of the Gr. deities; also of a Chr.:—Hermes, Mercury.

2061. **Ἑρμογένης Hĕrmŏgĕnēs**, *her-mog-en'-ace;* from *2060* and *1096; born of Hermes; Hermogenes*, an apostate Chr.:—Hermogenes.

2062. **ἑρπετόν hĕrpĕtŏn**, *her-pet-on';* neut. of a der. of **ἕρπω hĕrpō** (to *creep*); a *reptile*, i.e. (by Hebr. [comp. 7431]) a small *animal:*—creeping thing, serpent.

2063. **ἐρυθρός ĕruthrŏs**, *er-oo-thros';* of uncert. affin.; *red*, i.e. (with *2281*) the *Red* Sea:—red.

2064. **ἔρχομαι ĕrchŏmai**, *er'-khom-ahee;* mid. of a prim. verb (used only in the pres. and imperf. tenses, the others being supplied by a kindred [mid.] **ἐλεύθομαι ĕlĕuthŏmai**, *el-yoo'-thom-ahee;* or [act.] **ἔλθω ĕlthō**, *el'-tho;* which do not otherwise occur); to *come* or *go* (in a great variety of applications, lit. and fig.):—accompany, appear, bring, come enter, fall out, go, grow, × light, × next, pass, resort, be set.

2065. **ἐρωτάω ĕrōtaō**, *er-o-tah'-o;* appar. from *2046* [comp. *2045*]; to *interrogate;* by impl. to *request:*—ask, beseech, desire, intreat, pray. Comp. *4441*.

2066. ἐσθής **ĕsthēs**, *es-thace'*; from ἕννυμι **hĕnnumi** (to *clothe*); *dress:*—apparel, clothing, raiment, robe.

2067. ἔσθησις **ĕsthēsis**, *es'-thay-sis;* from a der. of *2066; clothing* (concr.):—garment.

2068. ἐσθίω **ĕsthiō**, *es-thee'-o;* strengthened for a prim. ἔδω **ĕdō** (to *eat*); used only in certain tenses, the rest being supplied by *5315;* to *eat* (usually lit.):—devour, eat, live.

2069. Ἐσλί **Ĕsli**, *es-lee';* of Heb. or. [prob. for 454]; *Esli*, an Isr.:—Esli.

2070. ἐσμέν **ĕsmĕn**, *es-men';* first pers. plur. indic. of *1510;* we *are:*—are, be, have our being, × have hope, + [the gospel] was [preached unto] us.

2071. ἔσομαι **ĕsŏmai**, *es'-om-ahee;* fut. of *1510; will be:*—shall (should) be (have), (shall) come (to pass), × may have, × fall, what would follow, × live long, × sojourn.

2072. ἔσοπτρον **ĕsŏptrŏn**, *es'-op-tron;* from *1519* and a presumed der. of *3700;* a *mirror* (for *looking into*):—glass. Comp. *2734*.

2073. ἑσπέρα **hĕspĕra**, *hes-per'-ah;* fem. of an adj. ἑσπερός **hĕspĕrŏs** (*evening*); the *eve* (*5610* being impl.):—evening (-tide).

2074. Ἐσρώμ **Ĕsrōm**, *es-rome;* of Heb. or. [2696]; *Esrom* (i.e. *Chetsron*), an Isr.:—Esrom.

2075. ἐστέ **ĕstĕ**, *es-teh';* second pers. plur. pres. indic. of *1510;* ye *are:*—be, have been, belong.

2076. ἐστί **ĕsti**, *es-tee';* third pers. sing. pres. indic. of *1510;* he (she or it) *is;* also (with neut. plur.) they *are:*—are, be (-long), call, × can [-not], come, consisteth, × dure for awhile, + follow, × have, (that) is (to say), make, meaneth, × must needs, + profit, + remaineth, + wrestle.

2077. ἔστω **ĕstō**, *es'-to;* second pers. sing. pres. imper. of *1510; be* thou; also

ἔστωσαν **ĕstōsan**, *es'-to-san;* third pers. of the same; *let* them *be:*—be.

2078. ἔσχατος **ĕschatŏs**, *es'-khat-os;* a superl. prob. from *2192* (in the sense of *contiguity*); *farthest, final* (of place or time):—ends of, last, latter end, lowest, uttermost.

2079. ἐσχάτως **ĕschatōs**, *es-khat'-oce;* adv. from *2078; finally*, i.e. (with *2192*) *at the extremity* of life:—point of death.

2080. ἔσω **ĕsō**, *es'-o;* from *1519; inside* (as prep. or adj.):—(with-) in (-ner, -to, -ward).

2081. ἔσωθεν **ĕsōthĕn**, *es'-o-then;* from *2080; from inside;* also used as equiv to *2080* (*inside*):—inward (-ly), (from) within, without.

2082. ἐσώτερος **ĕsōtĕrŏs**, *es-o'-ter-os;* compar. of *2080; interior:*—inner, within.

2083. ἑταῖρος **hĕtairŏs**, *het-ah'-ee-ros;* from ἔτης **ĕtēs** (a *clansman*); a *comrade:*—fellow, friend.

2084. ἑτερόγλωσσος **hĕtĕrŏglōssŏs**, *het-er-og'-loce-sos;* from *2087* and *1100; other-tongued*, i.e. a *foreigner:*—man of other tongue.

2085. ἑτεροδιδασκαλέω **hĕtĕrŏdidaskalĕō**, *het-er-od-id-as-kal-eh'-o;* from *2087* and *1320;* to *instruct differently:*—teach other doctrine (-wise).

2086. ἑτεροζυγέω **hĕtĕrŏzugĕō**, *het-er-od-zoog-eh'-o;* from a comp. of *2087* and *2218;* to *yoke* up *differently*, i.e. (fig.) to *associate discordantly:*—unequally yoke together with.

2087. ἕτερος **hĕtĕrŏs**, *het'-er-os;* of uncert. affin.; (an-, the) *other* or *different:*—altered, else, next (day), one, (an-) other, some, strange.

2088. ἑτέρως **hĕtĕrōs**, *het-er'-oce;* adv. from *2087; differently:*—otherwise.

2089. ἔτι **ĕti**, *et'-ee;* perh. akin to *2094;* "*yet,*" *still* (of time or degree):—after that, also, ever, (any) further, (t-) henceforth (more), hereafter, (any) longer, (any) more (-one), now, still, yet.

2090. ἑτοιμάζω **hĕtŏimazō**, *het-oy-mad'-zo;* from *2092;* to *prepare:*—prepare, provide, make ready. Comp. *2680*.

2091. ἑτοιμασία **hĕtŏimasia**, *het-oy-mas-ee'-ah;* from *2090; preparation:*—preparation.

2092. ἕτοιμος **hĕtŏimŏs**, *het-oy'-mos;* from an old noun ἔτεος **hĕtĕŏs** (*fitness*); *adjusted*, i.e. *ready:*—prepared, (made) ready (-iness, to our hand).

2093. ἑτοίμως **hĕtŏimōs**, *het'-oy-moce;* adv. from *2092; in readiness:*—ready.

2094. ἔτος **ĕtŏs**, *et'-os;* appar. a prim. word; a *year:*—year.

2095. εὖ **ĕu**, *yoo;* neut. of a prim. εὖς **ĕus** (*good*); (adv.) *well:*—good, well (done).

2096. Εὔα **Ĕua**, *yoo'-ah;* of Heb. or. [2332]; *Eua* (or *Eva*, i.e. *Chavvah*), the first woman:—Eve.

2097. εὐαγγελίζω **ĕuaggĕlizō**, *yoo-ang-ghel-id'-zo;* from *2095* and *32;* to *announce good* news ("evangelize") espec. the gospel:—declare, bring (declare, show) glad (good) tidings, preach (the gospel).

2098. εὐαγγέλιον **ĕuaggĕliŏn**, *yoo-ang-ghel'-ee-on;* from the same as *2097;* a *good message*, i.e. the *gospel:*—gospel.

2099. εὐαγγελιστής **ĕuaggĕlistēs**, *yoo-ang-ghel-is-tace';* from *2097;* a *preacher* of the gospel:—evangelist.

2100. εὐαρεστέω **ĕuarĕstĕō**, *yoo-ar-es-teh'-o;* from *2101;* to *gratify entirely:*—please (well).

2101. εὐάρεστος **ĕuarĕstŏs**, *yoo-ar'-es-tos;* from *2095* and *701; fully agreeable:*—acceptable (-ted), wellpleasing.

2102. εὐαρέστως **ĕuarĕstōs**, *yoo-ar-es'-toce;* adv. from *2101; quite agreeably:*—acceptably, + please well.

2103. Εὔβουλος **Ĕubŏulŏs**, *yoo'-boo-los;* from *2095* and *1014; good-willer; Eubulus*, a Chr.:—Eubulus.

2104. εὐγένης **ĕugĕnēs**, *yoog-en'-ace;* from *2095* and *1096; well born*, i.e. (lit.) *high* in rank, or (fig.) *generous:*—more noble, nobleman.

2105. εὐδία **ĕudia**, *yoo-dee'-ah;* fem. from *2095* and the alt. of *2203* (as the god of the weather); a *clear sky*, i e. *fine weather:*—fair weather.

2106. εὐδοκέω **ĕudŏkĕō**, *yoo-dok-eh'-o;* from *2095* and *1380;* to *think well* of, i.e. *approve* (an act); spec. to *approbate* (a person or thing):—think good, (be well) please (-d), be the good (have, take) pleasure, be willing.

2107. εὐδοκία **ĕudŏkia**, *yoo-dok-ee'-ah;* from a presumed comp. of *2095* and the base of *1380; satisfaction*, i.e. (subj.) *delight*, or (obj.) *kindness, wish, purpose:*—desire, good pleasure (will), × seem good.

2108. εὐεργεσία **ĕuĕrgĕsia**, *yoo-erg-es-ee'-ah;* from *2110; beneficence* (gen. or spec.):—benefit, good deed done.

2109. εὐεργετέω **ĕuĕrgĕtĕō**, *yoo-erg-et-eh'-o;* from *2110;* to *be philanthropic:*—do good.

2110. εὐεργέτης **ĕuĕrgĕtēs**, *yoo-erg-et'-ace;* from *2095* and the base of *2041;* a *worker of good*, i.e. (spec.) a *philanthropist:*—benefactor.

2111. εὔθετος **ĕuthĕtŏs**, *yoo'-thet-os;* from *2095* and a der. of *5087; well placed*, i.e. (fig.) *appropriate:*—fit, meet.

2112. εὐθέως **ĕuthĕōs**, *yoo-theh'-oce;* adv. from *2117; directly*, i.e. *at once* or *soon:*—anon, as soon as, forthwith, immediately, shortly, straightway.

2113. εὐθυδρομέω **ĕuthudrŏmĕō**, *yoo-thoo-drom-eh'-o;* from *2117* and *1408;* to *lay a straight course*, i.e. *sail direct:*—(come) with a straight course.

2114. εὐθυμέω **ĕuthumĕō**, *yoo-thoo-meh'-o;* from *2115;* to *cheer up*, i.e. (intrans.) *be cheerful;* neut. comp. (adv.) *more cheerfully:*—be of good cheer (merry).

2115. εὔθυμος **ĕuthumŏs**, *yoo'-thoo-mos;* from *2095* and *2372;* in *fine spirits*, i.e. *cheerful:*—of good cheer, the more cheerfully.

2116. εὐθύνω **ĕuthunō**, *yoo-thoo'-no;* from *2117;* to *straighten* (*level*); tech. to *steer:*—governor, make straight.

2117. εὐθύς **ĕuthus**, *yoo-thoos';* perh. from *2095* and *5087; straight*, i.e. (lit.) *level*, or (fig.) *true;* adv. (of time) *at once:*—anon, by and by, forthwith, immediately, straightway.

2118. εὐθύτης **ĕuthutēs**, *yoo-thoo'-tace;* from *2117; rectitude:*—righteousness.

2119. εὐκαιρέω **ĕukairĕō**, *yoo-kahee-reh'-o;* from *2121;* to *have good time*, i.e. *opportunity* or *leisure:*—have leisure (convenient time), spend time.

2120. εὐκαιρία **ĕukairia**, *yoo-kahee-ree'-ah;* from *2121;* a favorable *occasion:*—opportunity.

2121. εὔκαιρος **ĕukairŏs**, *yoo'-kahee-ros;* from *2095* and *2540; well-timed*, i.e. *opportune:*—convenient, in time of need.

2122. εὐκαίρως **ĕukairōs**, *yoo-kah'ee-roce;* adv. from *2121; opportunely:*—conveniently, in season.

2123. εὐκοπώτερος **ĕukŏpōtĕrŏs**, *yoo-kop-o'-ter-os;* comp. of a comp. of *2095* and *2873; better for toil*, i.e. *more facile:*—easier.

2124. εὐλάβεια **ĕulabĕia**, *yoo-lab'-i-ah;* from *2126;* prop. *caution*, i.e. (religiously) *reverence* (*piety*); by impl. *dread* (concr.):—fear (-ed).

2125. εὐλαβέομαι **ĕulabĕŏmai**, *yoo-lab-eh'-om-ahee;* mid. from *2126;* to *be circumspect*, i.e. (by impl.) to *be apprehensive;* religiously, to *reverence:*—(moved with) fear.

2126. εὐλαβής **ĕulabēs**, *yoo-lab-ace';* from *2095* and *2983; taking well* (*carefully*), i.e. *circumspect* (religiously, *pious*):—devout.

2127. εὐλογέω **ĕulŏgĕō**, *yoo-log-eh'-o;* from a comp. of *2095* and *3056;* to *speak well of*, i.e. (religiously) to *bless* (*thank* or *invoke a benediction upon, prosper*):—bless, praise.

2128. εὐλογητός **ĕulŏgētŏs**, *yoo-log-ay-tos';* from *2127; adorable:*—blessed.

2129. εὐλογία **ĕulŏgia**, *yoo-log-ee'-ah;* from the same as *2127; fine speaking*, i.e. *elegance of language; commendation* ("*eulogy*"), i.e. (reverentially) *adoration;* religiously, *benediction;* by impl. *consecration;* by extens. *benefit* or *largess:*—blessing (a matter of) bounty (× -tifully), fair speech.

2130. εὐμετάδοτος **ĕumĕtadŏtŏs**, *yoo-met-ad'-ot-os;* from *2095* and a presumed der. of *3330; good at imparting*, i.e. *liberal:*—ready to distribute.

2131. Εὐνίκη **Ĕunikē**, *yoo-nee'-kay;* from *2095* and *3529; victorious; Eunice*, a Jewess:—Eunice.

2132. εὐνόεω **ĕunŏĕō**, *yoo-nŏ-eh'-o;* from a comp. of *2095* and *3563;* to *be well-minded*, i.e. *reconcile:*—agree.

2133. εὔνοια **ĕunŏia**, *yoo'-noy-ah;* from the same as *2132; kindness;* euphem. *conjugal duty:*—benevolence, good will.

2134. εὐνουχίζω **ĕunŏuchizō**, *yoo-noo-khid'-zo*, from *2135;* to *castrate* (fig. *live unmarried*):—make . . . eunuch.

2135. εὐνοῦχος **ĕunŏuchŏs**, *yoo-noo'-khos;* from εὐνή **ĕunē** (a *bed*) and *2192;* a *castrated* person (such being employed in Oriental bed-chambers); by extens. an *impotent* or *unmarried* man; by impl. a *chamberlain* (*state-officer*):—eunuch.

2136. Εὐοδία **Ĕuŏdia**, *yoo-od-ee'-ah;* from the same as *2137; fine travelling; Euodia*, a Chr. woman:—Euodias.

2137. εὐοδόω **ĕuŏdŏō**, *yoo-od-ŏ'-o;* from a comp. of *2095* and *3598;* to *help* on the *road*, i.e. (pass.) *succeed in reaching;* fig. to *succeed* in business affairs:—(have a) prosper (-ous journey).

2138. εὐπειθής **ĕupĕithēs**, *yoo-pi-thace';* from *2095* and *3982; good* for *persuasion*, i.e. (intrans.) *compliant:*—easy to be intreated.

2139. εὐπερίστατος **ĕupĕristatŏs**, *yoo-per-is'-tat-os;* from *2095* and a der. of a presumed comp. of *4012* and *2476; well standing around*, i.e. (a *competitor*) *thwarting* (a racer) in every direction (fig. of sin in gen.):—which doth so easily beset.

2140. εὐποιΐα **ĕupŏiïa**, *yoo-poy-ee'-ah;* from a comp. of *2095* and *4160; well doing*, i.e. *beneficence:*—to do good.

2141. εὐπορέω **ĕupŏrĕō**, *yoo-por-eh'-o;* from a comp. of *2090* and the base of *4197;* (intrans.) to *be good* for *passing* through, i.e. (fig.) *have* pecuniary *means:*—ability.

2142. εὐπορία **ĕupŏria**, *yoo-por-ee'-ah;* from the same as *2141;* pecuniary *resources:*—wealth.

2143. **εὐπρέπεια ĕuprĕpĕia**, *yoo-prep'-i-ah;* from a comp. of *2095* and *4241;* *good suitableness*, i.e. *gracefulness:*—grace.

2144. **εὐπρόσδεκτος ĕuprŏsdĕktŏs**, *yoo-pros'-dek-tos;* from *2095* and a der. of *4327;* *well-received*, i.e. *approved, favorable:*—acceptable (-ted).

2145. **εὐπρόσεδρος ĕuprŏsĕdrŏs**, *yoo-pros'-ed-ros;* from *2095* and the same as *4332;* *sitting well towards*, i.e. (fig.) *assiduous* (neut. *diligent service*):—× attend upon.

2146. **εὐπροσωπέω ĕuprŏsōpĕō**, *yoo-pros-o-peh'-o;* from a comp. of *2095* and *4383;* *to be of good countenance*, i.e. (fig.) to *make a display:*—make a fair show.

2147. **εὑρίσκω hĕuriskō**, *hyoo-ris'-ko;* a prol. form of a prim.

εὕρω hĕurō, *hyoo'-ro;* which (together with another cognate form

εὑρέω hĕurĕō, *hyoo-reh'-o*) is used for it in all the tenses except the pres. and imperf.; to *find* (lit. or fig.):—find, get, obtain, perceive, see.

2148. **Εὐροκλύδων Ĕurŏkludōn**, *yoo-rok-loo'-dohn;* from **Εὖρος Ĕurŏs** (the *east* wind) and *2830;* a *storm from the East* (or S.E.), i.e. (in modern phrase) a *Levanter:*—Euroklydon.

2149. **εὐρύχωρος ĕuruchōrŏs**, *yoo-roo'-kho-ros;* from **εὐρύς ĕurus** (*wide*) and *5561;* *spacious:*—broad.

2150. **εὐσέβεια ĕusĕbĕia**, *yoo-seb'-i-ah;* from *2152;* *piety;* spec. the gospel scheme:—godliness, holiness.

2151. **εὐσεβέω ĕusĕbĕō**, *yoo-seb-eh'-o;* from *2152;* to *be pious*, i.e. (towards God) to *worship*, or (towards parents) to *respect* (*support*):—show piety, worship.

2152. **εὐσεβής ĕusĕbēs**, *yoo-seb-ace';* from *2095* and *4576;* *well-reverent*, i.e. *pious:*—devout, godly.

2153. **εὐσεβῶς ĕusĕbōs**, *yoo-seb-oce';* adv. from *2152;* *piously:*—godly.

2154. **εὔσημος ĕusēmŏs**, *yoo'-say-mos;* from *2095* and the base of *4591;* *well indicated*, i.e. (fig.) *significant:*—easy to be understood.

2155. **εὔσπλαγχνος ĕusplagchnŏs**, *yoo'-splangkh-nos;* from *2095* and *4698;* *well compassioned*, i.e. *sympathetic:*—pitiful, tender-hearted.

2156. **εὐσχημόνως ĕuschēmŏnōs**, *yoo-skhay-mon'-oce;* adv. from *2158;* *decorously:*—decently, honestly.

2157. **εὐσχημοσύνη ĕuschēmŏsunē**, *yoo-skhay-mos-oo'-nay;* from *2158;* *decorousness:*—comeliness.

2158. **εὐσχήμων ĕuschēmōn**, *yoo-skhay'-mone;* from *2095* and *4976;* *well-formed*, i.e. (fig.) *decorous*, *noble* (in rank):—comely, honourable.

2159. **εὐτόνως ĕutŏnōs**, *yoo-ton'-oce;* adv. from a comp. of *2095* and a der. of **τείνω tĕinō** (to *stretch*); *in a well-strung manner*, i.e. (fig.) *intensely* (in a good sense, *cogently;* in a bad one, *fiercely*):—mightily, vehemently.

2160. **εὐτραπελία ĕutrapĕlia**, *yoo-trap-el-ee'-ah;* from a comp. of *2095* and a der. of the base of *5157* (mean. *well-turned*, i.e. *ready at repartee, jocose*); *witticism*, i.e. (in a vulgar sense) *ribaldry:*—jesting.

2161. **Εὔτυχος Ĕutuchŏs**, *yoo'-too-khos;* from *2095* and a der. of *5177;* *well-fated*, i.e. *fortunate; Eutychus*, a young man:—Eutychus.

2162. **εὐφημία ĕuphēmia**, *yoo-fay-mee'-ah;* from *2163;* *good language* ("*euphemy*"), i.e. *praise* (*repute*):—good report.

2163. **εὔφημος ĕuphēmŏs**, *yoo'-fay-mos;* from *2095* and *5345;* *well spoken of*, i.e. *reputable:*—of good report.

2164. **εὐφορέω ĕuphŏrĕō**, *yoo-for-eh'-o;* from *2095* and *5409;* to *bear well*, i.e. *be fertile:*—bring forth abundantly.

2165. **εὐφραίνω ĕuphrainō**, *yoo-frah'ee-no;* from *2095* and *5424;* to *put* (mid. or pass. *be*) *in a good frame of mind*, i.e. *rejoice:*—fare, make glad, be (make) merry, rejoice.

2166. **Εὐφράτης Ĕuphratēs**, *yoo-frat'-ace;* of for. or. [comp. 6578]; *Euphrates*, a river of Asia:—Euphrates.

2167. **εὐφροσύνη ĕuphrŏsunē**, *yoo-fros-oo'-nay;* from the same as *2165;* *joyfulness:*—gladness, joy.

2168. **εὐχαριστέω ĕucharistĕō**, *yoo-khar-is-teh'-o;* from *2170;* *to be grateful*, i.e. (act.) to *express gratitude* (towards); spec. to *say grace* at a meal:—(give) thank (-ful, -s).

2169. **εὐχαριστία ĕucharistia**, *yoo-khar-is-tee'-ah;* from *2170;* *gratitude;* act. *grateful language* (to God, as an act of worship):—thankfulness, (giving of) thanks (-giving).

2170. **εὐχάριστος ĕucharistŏs**, *yoo-khar'-is-tos;* from *2095* and a der. of *5483;* *well favored*, i.e. (by impl.) *grateful:*—thankful.

2171. **εὐχή ĕuchē**, *yoo-khay';* from *2172;* prop. a *wish*, expressed as a *petition* to God, or in *votive* obligation:—prayer, vow.

2172. **εὔχομαι ĕuchŏmai**, *yoo'-khom-ahee;* mid. of a prim. verb; to *wish;* by impl. to *pray* to God:—pray, will, wish.

2173. **εὔχρηστος ĕuchrēstŏs**, *yoo'-khrays-tos;* from *2095* and *5543;* *easily used*, i.e. *useful:*—profitable, meet for use.

2174. **εὐψυχέω ĕupsuchĕō**, *yoo-psoo-kheh'-o;* from a comp. of *2095* and *5590;* *to be in good spirits*, i.e. *feel encouraged:*—be of good comfort.

2175. **εὐωδία ĕuōdia**, *yoo-o-dee'-ah;* from a comp. of *2095* and a der. of *3605;* *good-scentedness*, i.e. *fragrance:*—sweet savour (smell, -smelling).

2176. **εὐώνυμος ĕuōnumŏs**, *yoo-o'-noo-mos;* from *2095* and *3686;* prop. *well-named* (*good-omened*), i.e. the *left* (which was the *lucky* side among the pagan Greeks); neut. as adv. *at the left* hand:—(on the) left.

2177. **ἐφάλλομαι ĕphallŏmai**, *ef-al'-lom-ahee;* from *1909* and *242;* *to spring upon:*—leap on.

2178. **ἐφάπαξ ĕphapax**, *ef-ap'-ax;* from *1909* and *530;* *upon one occasion* (only):—(at) once (for all).

2179. **Ἐφεσῖνος Ĕphĕsinŏs**, *ef-es-ee'-nos;* from *2181;* *Ephesine*, or situated at Ephesus:—of Ephesus.

2180. **Ἐφέσιος Ĕphĕsiŏs**, *ef-es'-ee-os;* from *2181;* an *Ephesian* or inhab. of Ephesus:—Ephesian, of Ephesus.

2181. **Ἔφεσος Ĕphĕsŏs**, *ef'-es-os;* prob. of for. or.; *Ephesus*, a city of Asia Minor:—Ephesus.

2182. **ἐφευρέτης ĕphĕurĕtēs**, *ef-yoo-ret'-ace;* from a comp. of *1909* and *2147;* *a discoverer*, i.e. *contriver:*—inventor.

2183. **ἐφημερία ĕphēmĕria**, *ef-ay-mer-ee'-ah;* from *2184;* *diurnality*, i.e. (spec.) the quotidian *rotation* or *class* of the Jewish priests' service at the Temple, as distributed by families:—course.

2184. **ἐφήμερος ĕphēmĕrŏs**, *ef-ay'-mer-os;* from *1909* and *2250;* *for a day* ("ephemeral"), i.e. *diurnal:*—daily.

2185. **ἐφικνέομαι ĕphiknĕŏmai**, *ef-ik-neh'-om-ahee;* from *1909* and a cognate of *2240;* to *arrive upon*, i.e. *extend to:*—reach.

2186. **ἐφίστημι ĕphistēmi**, *ef-is'-tay-mee;* from *1909* and *2476;* to *stand upon*, i.e. *be present* (in various applications, friendly or otherwise, usually lit.):—assault, come (in, to, unto, upon), be at hand (instant), present, stand (before, by, over).

2187. **Ἐφραΐμ Ĕphraim**, *ef-rah-im';* of Heb. or. [669 or better 6085]; *Ephraïm*, a place in Pal.:—Ephraim.

2188. **ἐφφαθά ĕphphatha**, *ef-fath-ah';* of Chald. or. [6606]; *be opened!:*—Ephphatha.

2189. **ἔχθρα ĕchthra**, *ekh'-thrah;* fem. of *2190;* *hostility;* by impl. a reason for *opposition:*—enmity, hatred.

2190. **ἐχθρός ĕchthrŏs**, *ekh-thros';* from a prim. **ἔχθω ĕchthō** (to *hate*); *hateful* (pass. *odious*, or act. *hostile*); usually as a noun, an *adversary* (espec. *Satan*):—enemy, foe.

2191. **ἔχιδνα ĕchidna**, *ekh'-id-nah;* of uncert. or.; an *adder* or other poisonous snake (lit. or fig.):—viper.

2192. **ἔχω ĕchō**, *ekh'-o* (includ. an alt. form **σχέω schĕō**, *skheh'-o;* used in certain tenses only); a prim. verb; to *hold* (used in very various applications, lit. or fig., direct or remote; such as *possession, ability, contiguity, relation* or *condition*):—be (able, × hold, possessed with), accompany, + begin to amend, can (+ -not), × conceive, count, diseased, do, + eat, + enjoy, + fear, following, have, hold, keep, + lack, + go to law, lie, + must needs, + of necessity, + need, next, + recover, + reign, + rest, return, × sick, take for, + tremble, + uncircumcised, use.

2193. **ἕως hĕōs**, *heh'-oce;* of uncert. affin.; a conj., prep. and adv. of continuance, *until* (of time and place):—even (until, unto), (as) far (as), how long, (un-) til (-l), (hither-, un-, up) to, while (-s).

Z

2194. **Ζαβουλών Zabŏulōn**, *dzab-oo-lone';* of Heb. or. [2074]; *Zabulon* (i.e. *Zebulon*), a region of Pal.:—Zabulon.

2195. **Ζακχαῖος Zakchaiŏs**, *dzak-chah'ee-yos;* of Heb. or. [comp. 2140]; *Zacchæus*, an Isr.:—Zacchæus.

2196. **Ζαρά Zara**, *dzar-ah';* of Heb. or. [2226]; *Zara* (i.e. *Zerach*), an Isr.:—Zara.

2197. **Ζαχαρίας Zacharias**, *dzakh-ar-ee'-as;* of Heb. or. [2148]; *Zacharias* (i.e. *Zechariah*), the name of two Isr.:—Zacharias.

2198. **ζάω zaō**, *dzah'-o;* a prim. verb; to *live* (lit. or fig.):—life (-time), (a-) live (-ly), quick.

2199. **Ζεβεδαῖος Zĕbĕdaiŏs**, *dzeb-ed-ah'-yos;* of Heb. or. [comp. 2067]; *Zebedæus*, an Isr.:—Zebedee.

2200. **ζεστός zĕstŏs**, *dzes-tos';* from *2204;* *boiled*, i.e. (by impl.) *calid* (fig. *fervent*):—hot.

2201. **ζεῦγος zĕugŏs**, *dzyoo'-gos;* from the same as *2218;* a *couple*, i.e. a *team* (of oxen yoked together) or *brace* (of birds tied together):—yoke, pair.

2202. **ζευκτηρία zĕuktēria**, *dzyook-tay-ree'-ah;* fem. of a der. (at the second stage) from the same as *2218;* a *fastening* (*tiller-rope*):—band.

2203. **Ζεύς Zĕus**, *dzyooce;* of uncert. affin.; in the oblique cases there is used instead of it a (prob. cognate) name

Δίς Dis, *deece*, which is otherwise obsolete; *Zeus* or *Dis* (among the Latins *Jupiter* or *Jove*), the supreme deity of the Greeks:—Jupiter.

2204. **ζέω zĕō**, *dzeh'-o;* a prim. verb; to *be hot* (*boil*, of liquids; or *glow*, of solids), i.e. (fig.) *be fervid* (*earnest*):—be fervent.

2205. **ζῆλος zēlŏs**, *dzay'-los;* from *2204;* prop. *heat*, i.e. (fig.) "*zeal*" (in a favorable sense, *ardor;* in an unfavorable one, *jealousy*, as of a husband [fig. of God], or an enemy, *malice*):—emulation, envy (-ing), fervent mind, indignation, jealousy, zeal.

2206. **ζηλόω zēlŏō**, *dzay-lŏ'-o;* from *2205;* to *have warmth* of feeling for or against:—affect, covet (earnestly), (have) desire, (move with) envy, be jealous over, (be) zealous (-ly affect).

2207. **ζηλωτής zēlōtēs**, *dzay-lo-tace';* from *2206;* a "*zealot*":—zealous.

2208. **Ζηλωτής Zēlōtēs**, *dzay-lo-tace';* the same as *2208;* a *Zealot*, i.e. (spec.) *partisan* for Jewish political independence:—Zelotes.

2209. **ζημία zēmia**, *dzay-mee'-ah;* prob. akin to the base of *1150* (through the idea of *violence*); *detriment:*—damage, loss.

2210. **ζημιόω zēmiŏō**, *dzay-mee-ŏ'-o;* from *2209;* to *injure*, i.e. (reflex. or pass.) to *experience detriment:*—be cast away, receive damage, lose, suffer loss.

2211. **Ζηνᾶς Zēnas**, *dzay-nas';* prob. contr. from a poetic form of *2203* and *1435;* *Jove-given; Zenas*, a Chr.:—Zenas.

2212. **ζητέω zētĕō**, *dzay-teh'-o;* of uncert. affin.; to *seek* (lit. or fig.); spec. (by Heb.) to *worship* (God), or (in a bad sense) to *plot* (against life):—be (go) about, desire, endeavour, enquire (for), require, (× will) seek (after, for, means). Comp. *4441*.

2213. ζήτημα **zētēma**, *dzay'-tay-mah;* from 2212; a *search* (prop. concr.), i.e. (in words) a *debate:*- question.

2214. ζήτησις **zētēsis**, *dzay'-tay-sis;* from 2212; a *searching* (prop. the act), i.e. a *dispute* or its *theme:*—question.

2215. ζιζάνιον **zizaniŏn**, *dziz-an'-ee-on;* of uncert. or.; *darnel* or false grain:—tares.

2216. Ζοροβάβελ **Zŏrŏbabĕl**, *dzor-ob-ab'-el;* of Heb, or. [2216]; *Zorobabel* (i.e. *Zerubbabel*), an Isr.:—Zorobabel.

2217. ζόφος **zŏphŏs**, *dzof'-os;* akin to the base of 3509; *gloom* (as shrouding like a *cloud*):—blackness, darkness, mist.

2218. ζυγός **zugŏs**, *dzoo-gos';* from the root of ζεύγνυμι **zĕugnumi** (to *join*, espec. by a "yoke"); a *coupling*, i.e. (fig.) *servitude* (a *law* or *obligation*); also (lit.) the *beam* of the balance (as *connecting* the scales):—pair of balances, yoke.

2219. ζύμη **zumē**, *dzoo'-may;* prob. from 2204; *ferment* (as if *boiling* up):—leaven.

2220. ζυμόω **zumŏō**, *dzoo-mŏ'-o;* from 2219; to *cause to ferment:*—leaven.

2221. ζωγρέω **zōgrĕō**, *dzogue-reh'-o;* from the same as 2226 and 64; to *take alive* (*make a prisoner of war*), i.e. (fig.) to *capture* or *ensnare:*—take captive, catch.

2222. ζωή **zōē**, *dzo-ay';* from 2198; *life* (lit. or fig.):—life (-time). Comp. 5590.

2223. ζώνη **zōnē**, *dzo'-nay;* prob. akin to the base of 2218; a *belt;* by impl. a *pocket:*—girdle, purse.

2224. ζώννυμι **zōnnumi**, *dzone'-noo-mi;* from 2223; to *bind about* (espec. with a belt):—gird.

2225. ζωογονέω **zōŏgŏnĕō**, *dzo-og-on-eh'-o;* from the same as 2226 and a der. of 1096; to *engender alive* i.e. (by anal.) to *rescue* (pass. *be saved*) from death:—live, preserve.

2226. ζῶον **zōŏn**, *dzo'-on;* neut. of a der. of 2198; a *live* thing, i.e. an *animal:*—beast.

2227. ζωοποιέω **zōŏpŏiĕō**, *dzo-op-oy-eh'-o;* from the same as 2226 and 4160; to (*re-*) *vitalize* (lit. or fig.):—make alive, give life, quicken.

H

2228. ἤ **ē**, *ay;* a prim. particle of distinction between two connected terms; disjunctive, *or;* comparative, *than:*—and, but (either), (n-) either, except it be, (n-) or (else), rather, save, than, that, what, yea. Often used in connection with other particles. Comp. especially 2235, 2260, 2273.

2229. ἦ **ē**, *ay;* an adv. of *confirmation;* perh. intens. of 2228; used only (in the N. T.) before 3303; *assuredly:*—surely.

ἡ **hē**. See 3588.

ἥ **hē**. See 3739.

ᾗ **ē̦**. See 5600.

2230. ἡγεμονεύω **hēgĕmŏnĕuō**, *hayg-em-on-yoo'-o;* from 2232; to *act as ruler:*—be governor.

2231. ἡγεμονία **hēgĕmŏnia**, *hayg-em-on-ee'-ah;* from 2232; *government*, i.e. (in time) official *term:*—reign.

2232. ἡγεμών **hēgĕmōn**, *hayg-em-ohn';* from 2233; a *leader*, i.e. *chief* person (or fig. place) of a province:—governor, prince, ruler.

2233. ἡγέομαι **hēgĕŏmai**, *hayg-eh'-om-ahee;* mid. of a (presumed) strengthened form of 71; to *lead*, i.e. *command* (with official authority); fig. to *deem*, i.e. *consider:*—account, (be) chief, count, esteem, governor, judge, have the rule over, suppose, think.

2234. ἡδέως **hēdĕōs**, *hay-deh'-oce;* adv. from a der. of the base of 2237; *sweetly*, i.e. (fig.) *with pleasure:*—gladly.

2235. ἤδη **ēdē**, *ay'-day;* appar. from 2228 (or possibly 2229) and 1211; *even now:*—already, (even) now (already), by this time.

2236. ἥδιστα **hēdista**, *hay'-dis-tah;* neut. plur. of the superl. of the same as 2234; *with great pleasure:*—most (very) gladly.

2237. ἡδονή **hēdŏnē**, *hay-don-ay';* from ἁνδάνω **handanō** (to *please*); sensual *delight;* by impl. *desire:*—lust, pleasure.

2238. ἡδύοσμον **hēduŏsmŏn**, *hay-doo'-os-mon;* neut. of a comp. of the same as 2234 and 3744; a *sweet-scented* plant, i.e. *mint:*—mint.

2239. ἦθος **ēthŏs**, *ay'-thos;* a strengthened form of 1485; *usage*, i.e. (plur.) moral *habits:*—manners.

2240. ἥκω **hēkō**, *hay'-ko;* a prim. verb; to *arrive*, i.e. *be present* (lit. or fig.):—come.

2241. ἠλί **ēli**, *ay-lee';* of Heb. or. [410 with pron. suffix]; *my God:*—Eli.

2242. Ἡλί **Hēli**, *hay-lee';* of Heb. or. [5941]; *Heli* (i.e. *Eli*), an Isr.:—Heli.

2243. Ἡλίας **Hēlias**, *hay-lee'-as;* of Heb. or. [452]; *Helias* (i.e. *Elijah*), an Isr.:—Elias.

2244. ἡλικία **hēlikia**, *hay-lik-ee'-ah;* from the same as 2245; *maturity* (in years or size):—age, stature.

2245. ἡλίκος **hēlikŏs**, *hay-lee'-kos;* from ἧλιξ **hēlix** (a *comrade*, i.e. one of the same age); *as big as*, i.e. (interjectively) *how much:*—how (what) great.

2246. ἥλιος **hēliŏs**, *hay'-lee-os;* from ἕλη **hĕlē** (a *ray;* perh. akin to the alt. of 138); the *sun;* by impl. *light:*— + east, sun.

2247. ἧλος **hēlŏs**, *hay'-los;* of uncert. affin.; a *stud*, i.e. *spike:*—nail.

2248. ἡμᾶς **hēmas**, *hay-mas';* acc. plur. of 1473; *us:*—our, us, we.

2249. ἡμεῖς **hēmĕis**, *hay-mice';* nom. plur. of 1473; *we* (only used when emphatic):—us, we (ourselves).

2250. ἡμέρα **hēmĕra**, *hay-mer'-ah;* fem. (with 5610 implied) of a der. of ἧμαι **hēmai** (to *sit;* akin to the base of 1476) mean. *tame*, i.e. *gentle; day*, i.e. (lit.) the time space between dawn and dark, or the whole 24 hours (but several days were usually reckoned by the Jews as inclusive of the parts of both extremes); fig. a *period* (always defined more or less clearly by the context):—age, + alway, (mid-) day (by day, [-ly]), + for ever, judgment, (day) time, while, years.

2251. ἡμέτερος **hēmĕtĕrŏs**, *hay-met'-er-os;* from 2349; *our:*—our, your [*by a different reading*].

2252. ἤμην **ēmēn**, *ay'-mane;* a prol. form of 2358; I *was:*—be, was. [*Sometimes unexpressed.*]

2253. ἡμιθανής **hēmithanēs**, *hay-mee-than-ace';* from a presumed comp. of the base of 2255 and 2348; *half dead*, i.e. *entirely exhausted:*—half dead.

2254. ἡμῖν **hēmin**, *hay-meen';* dat. plur. of 1473; *to* (or *for, with, by*) *us:*—our, (for) us, we.

2255. ἥμισυ **hēmisu**, *hay'-mee-soo;* neut. of a der. from an inseparable pref. akin to 260 (through the idea of *partition* involved in *connection*) and mean. *semi-;* (as noun) *half:*—half.

2256. ἡμιώριον **hēmiōriŏn**, *hay-mee-o'-ree-on;* from the base of 2255 and 5610; a *half-hour:*—half an hour.

2257. ἡμῶν **hēmōn**, *hay-mone';* gen. plur. of 1473; *of* (or *from*) *us:*—our (company), us, we.

2258. ἦν **ēn**, *ane;* imperf. of 1510; *I* (*thou*, etc.) *was* (*wast* or *were*):— + agree, be, × have (+ charge of), hold, use, was (-t), were.

2259. ἡνίκα **hēnika**, *hay-nee'-kah;* of uncert. affin.; *at which time:*—when.

2260. ἤπερ **ēpĕr**, *ay'-per;* from 2228 and 4007; *than at all* (or *than perhaps, than indeed*):—than.

2261. ἤπιος **ēpiŏs**, *ay'-pee-os;* prob. from 2031; prop. *affable*, i.e. *mild* or *kind:*—gentle.

2262. Ἤρ **Ēr**, *ayr;* of Heb. or. [6147]; *Er*, an Isr.:—Er.

2263. ἤρεμος **ērĕmŏs**, *ay'-rem-os;* perh. by transposition from 2048 (through the idea of *stillness*); *tranquil:*—quiet.

2264. Ἡρώδης **Hērōdēs**, *hay-ro'-dace;* comp. of ἥρως **hērōs** (a "*hero*") and 1491; *heroic; Herodes*, the name of four Jewish kings:—Herod.

2265. Ἡρωδιανοί **Hērōdianŏi**, *hay-ro-dee-an-oy';* plur. of a der. of 2264; *Herodians*, i.e. partisans of Herodes:—Herodians.

2266. Ἡρωδιάς **Hērōdias**, *hay-ro-dee-as';* from 2264; *Herodias*, a woman of the Herodian family:—Herodias.

2267. Ἡρωδίων **Hērōdiōn**, *hay-ro-dee'-ohn;* from 2264; *Herodion*, a Chr.:—Herodion.

2268. Ἡσαΐας **Hēsaïas**, *hay-sah-ee'-as;* of Heb. or. [3470]; *Hesaias* (i.e. *Jeshajah*), an Isr.:—Esaias.

2269. Ἡσαῦ **Ēsau**, *ay-sŏw';* of Heb. or. [6215]; *Esau*, an Edomite:—Esau.

2270. ἡσυχάζω **hēsuchazō**, *hay-soo-khad'-zo;* from the same as 2272; to *keep still* (intrans.), i.e. *refrain* from labor, meddlesomeness or speech:—cease, hold peace, be quiet, rest.

2271. ἡσυχία **hēsuchia**, *hay-soo-khee'-ah;* fem. of 2272; (as noun) *stillness*, i.e. desistance from bustle or language:—quietness, silence.

2272. ἡσύχιος **hēsuchiŏs**, *hay-soo'-khee-os;* a prol. form of a comp. prob. of a der. of the base of 1476 and perh. 2192; prop. *keeping* one's *seat* (*sedentary*), i.e. (by impl.) *still* (*undisturbed, undisturbing*):—peaceable, quiet.

2273. ἤτοι **ētŏi**, *ay'-toy;* from 2228 and 5104; *either indeed:*—whether.

2274. ἡττάω **hēttaō**, *hayt-tah'-o;* from the same as 2276; to *make worse*, i.e. *vanquish* (lit. or fig.); by impl. to *rate lower:*—be inferior, overcome.

2275. ἥττημα **hēttēma**, *hayt'-tay-mah;* from 2274; a *deterioration*, i.e. (obj.) *failure* or (subj.) *loss:*—diminishing, fault.

2276. ἧττον **hēttŏn**, *hate'-ton;* neut. of comp. of ἧκα **hēka** (*slightly*) used for that of 2556; *worse* (as noun); by impl. *less* (as adv.):—less, worse.

2277. ἤτω **ētō**, *ay'-to;* third pers. sing. imperative of 1510; *let him* (or *it*) *be:*—let . . . be.

2278. ἠχέω **ēchĕō**, *ay-kheh'-o;* from 2279; to *make* a loud *noise*, i.e. *reverberate:*—roar, sound.

2279. ἦχος **ēchŏs**, *ay'-khos;* of uncert. affin.; a loud or confused *noise* ("*echo*"), i.e. *roar;* fig. a *rumor:*—fame, sound.

Θ

2280. Θαδδαῖος **Thaddaiŏs**, *thad-dah'-yos;* of uncert. or.; *Thaddæus*, one of the Apostles:—Thaddæus.

2281. θάλασσα **thalassa**, *thal'-as-sah;* prob. prol. from 251; the *sea* (gen. or spec.):—sea.

2282. θάλπω **thalpō**, *thal'-po;* prob. akin to θάλλω **thallō** (to *warm*); to *brood*, i.e. (fig.) to *foster:*—cherish.

2283. Θάμαρ **Thamar**, *tham'-ar;* of Heb. or. [8559]; *Thamar* (i.e. *Tamar*), an Israelitess:—Thamar.

2284. θαμβέω **thambĕō**, *tham-beh'-o;* from 2285; to *stupefy* (with surprise), i.e. *astound:*—amaze, astonish.

2285. θάμβος **thambŏs**, *tham'-bos;* akin to an obsol. τάφω **taphō** (to *dumbfound*); *stupefaction* (by surprise), i.e. *astonishment:*— × amazed, + astonished, wonder.

2286. θανάσιμος **thanasimŏs**, *than-as'-ee-mos;* from 2288; *fatal*, i.e. *poisonous:*—deadly.

2287. θανατήφορος **thanatēphŏrŏs**, *than-at-ay'-for-os;* from (the fem. form of) 2288 and 5342; *death-bearing*, i.e. *fatal:*—deadly.

2288. θάνατος **thanatŏs**, *than'-at-os;* from 2348; (prop. an adj. used as a noun) *death* (lit. or fig.):— × deadly, (be . . .) death.

2289. θανατόω **thanatŏō**, *than-at-ŏ'-o;* from 2288; to *kill* (lit. or fig.):—become dead, (cause to be) put to death, kill, mortify.

θάνω **thanō**. See 2348.

2290. θάπτω **thaptō**, *thap'-to;* a prim. verb; to *celebrate funeral rites*, i.e. *inter:*—bury.

2291. Θάρα **Thara**, *thar'-ah;* of Heb. or. [8646]; *Thara* (i.e. *Terach*), the father of Abraham:—Thara.

2292. **θαῤῥέω tharrhĕō**, *thar-hreh'-o;* another form for *2293;* to *exercise courage:*—be bold, × boldly, have confidence, be confident. Comp. *5111.*

2293. **θαρσέω tharsĕō**, *thar-seh'-o;* from *2294;* to *have courage:*—be of good cheer (comfort). Comp. *2292.*

2294. **θάρσος tharsŏs**, *thar'-sos;* akin (by transp.) to **θράσος thrasŏs** (*daring*); *boldness* (subj.):—courage.

2295. **θαῦμα thauma**, *thŏu'-mah;* appar. from a form of *2300;* *wonder* (prop. concr.; but by impl. abstr.):—admiration.

2296. **θαυμάζω thaumazō**, *thŏu-mad'-zo;* from *2295;* to *wonder;* by impl. to *admire:*—admire, have in admiration, marvel, wonder.

2297. **θαυμάσιος thaumasiŏs**, *thŏw-mas'-ee-os;* from *2295;* *wondrous,* i.e. (neut. as noun) a *miracle:*—wonderful thing.

2298. **θαυμαστός thaumastŏs**, *thŏw-mas-tos';* from *2296;* *wondered* at, i.e. (by impl.) *wonderful:*—marvel (-lous).

2299. **θεά thĕa**, *theh-ah';* fem. of *2316;* a female *deity:*—goddess.

2300. **θεάομαι thĕaŏmai**, *theh-ah'-om-ahee;* a prol. form of a prim. verb; to *look* closely at, i.e. (by impl.) to *perceive* (lit. or fig.); by extens. to *visit:*—behold, look (upon), see. Comp. *3700.*

2301. **θεατρίζω thĕatrizō**, *theh-at-rid'-zo;* from *2302;* to *expose as a spectacle:*—make a gazing stock.

2302. **θέατρον thĕatrŏn**, *theh'-at-ron;* from *2300;* *a place for public show* ("*theatre*"), i.e. general *audience-room;* by impl. a *show* itself (fig.):—spectacle, theatre.

2303. **θεῖον thĕiŏn**, *thi'-on;* prob. neut. of *2304* (in its or. sense of *flashing*); *sulphur:*—brimstone.

2304. **θεῖος thĕiŏs**, *thi'-os;* from *2316;* *godlike* (neut. as noun, *divinity*):—divine, godhead.

2305. **θειότης thĕiŏtēs**, *thi-ot'-ace;* from *2304;* *divinity* (abstr.):—godhead.

2306. **θειώδης thĕiōdēs**, *thi-o'-dace;* from *2303* and *1491;* *sulphur-like,* i.e. *sulphurous:*—brimstone.

θελέω thĕlĕō. See *2309.*

2307. **θέλημα thĕlēma**, *thel'-ay-mah;* from the prol. form of *2309;* a *determination* (prop. the thing), i.e. (act.) *choice* (spec. *purpose, decree;* abstr. *volition*) or (pass.) *inclination:*—desire, pleasure, will.

2308. **θέλησις thĕlēsis**, *thel'-ay-sis;* from *2309;* *determination* (prop. the act), i.e. *option:*—will.

2309. **θέλω thĕlō**, *thel'-o;* or **ἐθέλω ĕthelo**, *eth-el'-o;* in certain tenses **θελέω thĕlĕō**, *thel-eh'-o;* and **ἐθελέω ĕthĕlĕō**, *eth-el-eh'-o,* which are otherwise obsol.; appar. strengthened from the alt. form of *138;* to *determine* (as an act. *option* from subj. impulse; whereas *1014* prop. denotes rather a pass. *acquiescence* in obj. considerations), i.e., *choose* or *prefer* (lit. or fig.); by impl. to *wish,* i.e. *be inclined* to (sometimes adv. *gladly*); impers. for the fut. tense, to *be about to;* by Heb. to *delight in:*—desire, be disposed (forward), intend, list, love, mean, please, have rather, (be) will (have, -ling, -ling [ly]).

2310. **θεμέλιος thĕmĕliŏs**, *them-el'-ee-os;* from a der. of *5087;* something *put* down, i.e. a *substruction* (of a building, etc.), (lit. or fig.):—foundation.

2311. **θεμελιόω thĕmĕliŏō**, *them-el-ee-ŏ'-o;* from *2310;* to *lay a basis* for, i.e. (lit.) *erect,* or (fig.) *consolidate:*—(lay the) found (-ation), ground, settle.

2312. **θεοδίδακτος thĕŏdidaktŏs**, *theh-od-id'-ak-tos;* from *2316* and *1321;* *divinely instructed:*—taught of God.

2312'. **θεολόγος thĕŏlŏgŏs**, *theh-ol-og'-os;* from *2316* and *3004;* a "*theologian*":—divine.

2313. **θεομαχέω thĕŏmachĕō**, *theh-o-makh-eh'-o;* from *2314;* to *resist deity:*—fight against God.

2314. **θεόμαχος thĕŏmachŏs**, *theh-om'-akh-os;* from *2316* and *3164;* an *opponent of deity:*—to fight against God.

2315. **θεόπνευστος thĕŏpnĕustŏs**, *theh-op'-nvoo-stos;* from *2316* and a presumed der. of *4154;* *divinely breathed* in:—given by inspiration of God.

2316. **θεός thĕŏs**, *theh'-os;* of uncert. affin.; a *deity,* espec. (with *3588*) *the* supreme *Divinity;* fig. a *magistrate;* by Heb. *very:*— × exceeding, God, god [-ly, -ward].

2317. **θεοσέβεια thĕŏsĕbĕia**, *theh-os-eb'-i-ah;* from *2318;* *devoutness,* i.e. *piety:*—godliness.

2318. **θεοσεβής thĕŏsĕbēs**, *theh-os-eb-ace';* from *2316* and *4576;* *reverent of God,* i.e. *pious:*—worshipper of God.

2319. **θεοστυγής thĕŏstugēs**, *theh-os-too-gace';* from *2316* and the base of *4767;* *hateful to God,* i.e. *impious:*—hater of God.

2320. **θεότης thĕŏtēs**, *theh-ot'-ace;* from *2316;* *divinity* (abstr.):—godhead.

2321. **Θεόφιλος Thĕŏphilŏs**, *theh-of'-il-os;* from *2316* and *5384;* *friend of God; Theophilus,* a Chr.:—Theophilus.

2322. **θεραπεία thĕrapĕia**, *ther-ap-i'-ah;* from *2323;* *attendance* (spec. medical, i.e. *cure*); fig. and collec. *domestics:*—healing, household.

2323. **θεραπεύω thĕrapĕuō**, *ther-ap-yoo'-o;* from the same as *2324;* to *wait upon* menially, i.e. (fig.) to *adore* (God), or (spec.) to *relieve* (of disease):—cure, heal, worship.

2324. **θεράπων thĕrapōn**, *ther-ap'-ohn;* appar. a part. from an otherwise obsol. der. of the base of *2330;* a menial *attendant* (as if *cherishing*):—servant.

2325. **θερίζω thĕrizō**, *ther-id'-zo;* from *2330* (in the sense of the *crop*); to *harvest:*—reap.

2326. **θερισμός thĕrismŏs**, *ther-is-mos';* from *2325;* *reaping,* i.e. the *crop:*—harvest.

2327. **θεριστής thĕristēs**, *ther-is-tace';* from *2325;* a *harvester:*—reaper.

2328. **θερμαίνω thĕrmainō**, *ther-mah'ee-no;* from *2329;* to *heat* (oneself):—(be) warm (-ed, self).

2329. **θέρμη thĕrmē**, *ther'-may;* from the base of *2330;* *warmth:*—heat.

2330. **θέρος thĕrŏs**, *ther'-os;* from a prim. **θέρω thĕrō** (to *heat*); prop. *heat,* i.e. *summer:*—summer.

2331. **Θεσσαλονικεύς Thĕssalŏnikĕus**, *thes-sal-on-ik-yoos';* from *2332;* a *Thessalonican,* i.e. inhab. of Thessalonice:—Thessalonian.

2332. **Θεσσαλονίκη Thĕssalŏnikē**, *thes-sal-on-ee'-kay;* from **Θεσσαλός Thĕssalŏs** (a *Thessalian*) and *3529;* *Thessalonice,* a place in Asia Minor:—Thessalonica.

2333. **Θευδᾶς Thĕudas**, *thyoo-das';* of uncert. or.; *Theudas,* an Isr.:—Theudas.

θέω thĕō. See *5087.*

2334. **θεωρέω thĕōrĕō**, *theh-o-reh'-o;* from a der. of *2300* (perh. by add. of *3708*); to *be a spectator* of, i.e. *discern,* (lit., fig. [*experience*] or intens. [*acknowledge*]):—behold, consider, look on, perceive, see. Comp. *3700.*

2335. **θεωρία thĕōria**, *theh-o-ree'-ah;* from the same as *2334;* *spectatorship,* i.e. (concr.) a *spectacle:*—sight.

2336. **θήκη thēkē**, *thay'-kay;* from *5087;* a *receptacle,* i.e. *scabbard:*—sheath.

2337. **θηλάζω thēlazō**, *thay-lad'-zo;* from **θηλή thēlē** (the *nipple*); to *suckle;* by impl. to *suck:*—(give) suck (-ling).

2338. **θῆλυς thēlus**, *thay'-loos;* from the same as *2337;* *female:*—female, woman.

2339. **θήρα thēra**, *thay'-rah;* from **θήρ thēr** (a wild *animal,* as *game*); *hunting,* i.e. (fig.) *destruction:*—trap.

2340. **θηρεύω thērĕuō**, *thay-ryoo'-o;* from *2339;* to *hunt* (an animal), i.e. (fig.) to *carp at:*—catch.

2341. **θηριομαχέω thēriŏmachĕō**, *thay-ree-om-akh-eh'-o;* from a comp. of *2342* and *3164;* to *be a beast-fighter* (in the gladiatorial show), i.e. (fig.) to *encounter* (furious men):—fight with wild beasts.

2342. **θηρίον thēriŏn**, *thay-ree'-on;* dimin. from the same as *2339;* a *dangerous animal:*—(venomous, wild) beast.

2343. **θησαυρίζω thēsaurizō**, *thay-sŏw-rid'-zo;* from *2344;* to *amass* or *reserve* (lit. or fig.):—lay up (treasure), (keep) in store, (heap) treasure (together, up).

2344. **θησαυρός thēsaurŏs**, *thay-sow-ros';* from *5087;* a *deposit,* i.e. *wealth* (lit. or fig.):—treasure.

2345. **θιγγάνω thigganō**, *thing-gan'-o;* a prol. form of an obsol. prim. **θίγω thigō** (to *finger*); to *manipulate,* i.e. *have to do with;* by impl. to *injure:*—handle, touch.

2346. **θλίβω thlibō**, *thlee'-bo;* akin to the base of *5147;* to *crowd* (lit. or fig.):—afflict, narrow, throng, suffer tribulation, trouble.

2347. **θλῖψις thlipsis**, *thlip'-sis;* from *2346;* *pressure* (lit. or fig.):—afflicted (-tion), anguish, burdened, persecution, tribulation, trouble.

2348. **θνήσκω thnēskō**, *thnay'-sko;* a strengthened form of a simpler prim. **θάνω thanō**, *than'-o* (which is used for it only in certain tenses); to *die* (lit. or fig.):—be dead, die.

2349. **θνητός thnētŏs**, *thnay-tos';* from *2348;* *liable to die:*—mortal (-ity).

2350. **θορυβέω thŏrubĕō**, *thor-oo-beh'-o;* from *2351;* to *be in tumult,* i.e. *disturb, clamor:*—make ado (a noise), trouble self, set on an uproar.

2351. **θόρυβος thŏrubŏs**, *thor'-oo-bos;* from the base of *2360;* a *disturbance:*—tumult, uproar.

2352. **θραύω thrauō**, *thrŏw'-o;* a prim. verb; to *crush:*—bruise. Comp. *4486.*

2353. **θρέμμα thrĕmma**, *threm'-mah;* from *5142;* *stock* (as *raised* on a farm):—cattle.

2354. **θρηνέω thrēnĕō**, *thray-neh'-o;* from *2355;* to *bewail:*—lament, mourn.

2355. **θρῆνος thrēnŏs**, *thray'-nos;* from the base of *2360;* *wailing:*—lamentation.

2356. **θρησκεία thrēskĕia**, *thrace-ki'-ah;* from a der. of *2357;* ceremonial *observance:*—religion, worshipping.

2357. **θρῆσκος thrēskŏs**, *thrace'-kos;* prob. from the base of *2360;* *ceremonious* in worship (as *demonstrative*), i.e. *pious:*—religious.

2358. **θριαμβεύω thriambĕuō**, *three-am-byoo'-o;* from a prol. comp. of the base of *2360* and a der. of *680* (mean. a *noisy iambus,* sung in honor of Bacchus); to *make an acclamatory procession,* i.e. (fig.) to *conquer* or (by Hebr.) to *give victory:*—(cause) to triumph (over).

2359. **θρίξ thrix**, *threeks;* gen. **τριχός trichŏs**, etc.; of uncert. der.; *hair:*—hair. Comp. *2864.*

2360. **θροέω thrŏĕō**, *thrŏ-eh'-o,* from **θρέομαι thrĕŏmai** (to *wail*); to *clamor,* i.e. (by impl.) to *frighten:*—trouble.

2361. **θρόμβος thrŏmbŏs**, *throm'-bos;* perh. from *5142* (in the sense of *thickening*); a *clot:*—great drop.

2362. **θρόνος thrŏnŏs**, *thron'-os;* from **θράω thraō** (to *sit*); a stately *seat* ("*throne*"); by impl. *power* or (concr.) a *potentate:*—seat, throne.

2363. **Θυάτειρα Thuatĕira**, *thoo-at'-i-rah;* of uncert. der.; *Thyatira,* a place in Asia Minor:—Thyatira.

2364. **θυγάτηρ thugatēr**, *thoo-gat'-air;* appar. a prim. word [comp. "*daughter*"]; a *female child,* or (by Hebr.) *descendant* (or *inhabitant*):—daughter.

2365. **θυγάτριον thugatriŏn**, *thoo-gat'-ree-on;* from *2364;* a *daughterling:*—little (young) daughter.

2366. **θύελλα thuĕlla**, *thoo'-el-lah;* from *2380* (in the sense of *blowing*) a storm:—tempest.

2367. **θύϊνος thuïnŏs**, *thoo'-ee-nos;* from a der. of *2380* (in the sense of *blowing;* denoting a certain *fragrant* tree); made of *citron*-wood:—thyine.

2368. **θυμίαμα thumiama**, *thoo-mee'-am-ah;* from *2370;* an *aroma,* i.e. fragrant *powder* burnt in religious service; by impl. the *burning* itself:—incense, odour.

2369. **θυμιαστήριον thumiastēriŏn**, *thoo-mee-as-tay'-ree-on;* from a der. of *2370;* a *place of fumigation,* i.e. the *altar of incense* (in the Temple):—censer.

2370. θυμιάω **thumiaō**, *thoo-mee-ah'-o;* from a der. of *2380* (in the sense of *smoking*); to *fumigate*, i.e. *offer* aromatic *fumes*:—burn incense.

2371. θυμομαχέω **thumŏmachĕō**, *thoo-mom-akh-eh'-o;* from a presumed comp. of *2372* and *3164;* to *be in a furious fight*, i.e. (fig.) to *be exasperated*:—be highly displeased.

2372. θυμός **thumŏs**, *thoo-mos';* from *2380; passion* (as if *breathing* hard):—fierceness, indignation, wrath. Comp. *5590*.

2373. θυμόω **thumŏō**, *thoo-mŏ'-o;* from *2372;* to *put in a passion*, i.e. *enrage*:—be wroth.

2374. θύρα **thura**, *thoo'-rah;* appar. a prim. word [comp. "door"]; a *portal* or entrance (the opening or the closure, lit. or fig.):—door, gate.

2375. θυρεός **thurĕŏs**, *thoo-reh-os';* from *2374;* a large *shield* (as *door*-shaped):—shield.

2376. θυρίς **thuris**, *thoo-rece';* from *2374;* an *aperture*, i.e. *window*:—window.

2377. θυρωρός **thurōrŏs**, *thoo-ro-ros';* from *2374* and οὖρος **ŏurŏs** (a *watcher*); a *gate-warden*:—that kept the door, porter.

2378. θυσία **thusia**, *thoo-see'-ah;* from *2380; sacrifice* (the act or the victim, lit. or fig.):—sacrifice.

2379. θυσιαστήριον **thusiastēriŏn**, *thoo-see-as-tay'-ree-on;* from a der. of *2378;* a *place of sacrifice*, i.e. an *altar* (spec. or gen., lit. or fig.):—altar.

2380. θύω **thuō**, *thoo'-o;* a prim. verb; prop. to *rush* (*breathe* hard, *blow*, *smoke*), i.e. (by impl.) to *sacrifice* (prop. by fire, but gen.); by extens. to *immolate* (*slaughter* for any purpose):—kill, (do) sacrifice, slay.

2381. Θωμᾶς **Thōmas**, *tho-mas';* of Chald. or. [comp. 8380]; *the twin; Thomas*, a Chr.:—Thomas.

2382. θώραξ **thōrax**, *tho'-rax;* of uncert. affin.; the *chest* ("*thorax*"), i.e. (by impl.) a *corslet*:—breastplate.

I

2383. Ἰάειρος **Iaĕirŏs**, *ee-ah'-i-ros;* of Heb. or. [2971]; *Jäirus* (i.e. *Jair*), an Isr.:—Jairus.

2384. Ἰακώβ **Iakōb**, *ee-ak-obe';* of Heb. or. [3290]; *Jacob* (i.e. *Ja'akob*), the progenitor of the Isr.; also an Isr.:—Jacob.

2385. Ἰάκωβος **Iakōbŏs**, *ee-ak'-o-bos;* the same as *2384* Græcized; *Jacobus*, the name of three Isr.:—James.

2386. ἴαμα **iama**, *ee'-am-ah;* from *2390;* a *cure* (the effect):—healing.

2387. Ἰαμβρῆς **Iambrēs**, *ee-am-brace';* of Eg. or.; *Jambres*, an Eg.:—Jambres.

2388. Ἰαννά **Ianna**, *ee-an-nah';* prob. of Heb. or. [comp. 3238]; *Janna*, an Isr.:—Janna.

2389. Ἰαννῆς **Iannēs**, *ee-an-nace';* of Eg. or.; *Jannes*, an Eg.:—Jannes.

2390. ἰάομαι **iaŏmai**, *ee-ah'-om-ahee;* mid. of appar. a prim. verb; to *cure* (lit. or fig.):—heal, make whole.

2391. Ἰάρεδ **Iarĕd**, *ee-ar'-ed;* of Heb. or. [3382]; *Jared* (i.e. *Jered*), an antediluvian:—Jared.

2392. ἴασις **iasis**, *ee'-as-is;* from *2390; curing* (the act):—cure, heal (-ing).

2393. ἴασπις **iaspis**, *ee'-as-pis;* prob. of for. or. [see 3471]; "*jasper*", a gem:—jasper.

2394. Ἰάσων **Iasōn**, *ee-as'-oan;* fut. act. part. masc. of *2390; about to cure; Jason*, a Chr.:—Jason.

2395. ἰατρός **iatrŏs**, *ee-at-ros';* from *2390;* a *physician*:—physician.

2396. ἴδε **idĕ**, *id'-eh;* second pers. sing. imper. act. of *1492;* used as interj. to denote *surprise; lo!*:—behold, lo, see.

2397. ἰδέα **idĕa**, *id-eh'-ah;* from *1492;* a *sight* [comp. fig. "idea"], i.e. *aspect*:—countenance.

2398. ἴδιος **idiŏs**, *id'-ee-os;* of uncert. affin.: *pertaining to self*, i.e. one's *own;* by impl. *private* or *separate*:—× his acquaintance, when they were alone, apart, aside, due, his (own, proper, several), home, (her, our, thine, your) own (business), private (-ly), proper, severally, their (own).

2399. ἰδιώτης **idiōtēs**, *id-ee-o'-tace;* from *2398;* a *private* person, i.e. (by impl.) an *ignoramus* (comp. "idiot"):—ignorant, rude, unlearned.

2400. ἰδού **idŏu**, *id-oo';* second pers. sing. imper. mid. of *1492;* used as imper. *lo!*:—behold, lo, see.

2401. Ἰδουμαία **Idŏumaia**, *id-oo-mah'-yah;* of Heb. or. [123]; *Idumæa* (i.e. *Edom*), a region E. (and S.) of Pal.:—Idumæa.

2402. ἱδρώς **hidrōs**, *hid-roce';* a strengthened form of a prim. ἴδος **idŏs** (*sweat*); *perspiration*:—sweat.

2403. Ἰεζαβήλ **Iĕzabēl**, *ee-ed-zab-ale';* of Heb. or. [348]; *Jezabel* (i.e. *Jezebel*), a Tyrian woman (used as a synonym of a termagant or false teacher):—Jezabel.

2404. Ἱεράπολις **Hiĕrapŏlis**, *hee-er-ap'-ol-is;* from *2413* and *4172; holy city; Hierapolis*, a place in Asia Minor:—Hierapolis.

2405. ἱερατεία **hiĕratĕia**, *hee-er-at-i'-ah;* from *2407; priestliness*, i.e. the *sacerdotal function*:—office of the priesthood, priest's office.

2406. ἱεράτευμα **hiĕratĕuma**, *hee-er-at'-yoo-mah;* from *2407;* the *priestly fraternity*, i.e. a *sacerdotal order* (fig.):—priesthood.

2407. ἱερατεύω **hiĕratĕuō**, *hee-er-at-yoo'-o;* prol. from *2409;* to *be a priest*, i.e. *perform his functions*:—execute the priest's office.

2408. Ἱερεμίας **Hiĕrĕmias**, *hee-er-em-ee'-as;* of Heb. or. [3414]; *Hieremias* (i.e. *Jermijah*), an Isr.:—Jeremiah.

2409. ἱερεύς **hiĕrĕus**, *hee-er-yooce';* from *2413;* a *priest* (lit. or fig.):—(high) priest.

2410. Ἱεριχώ **Hiĕrichō**, *hee-er-ee-kho';* of Heb. or. [3405]; *Jericho*, a place in Pal.:—Jericho.

2411. ἱερόν **hiĕrŏn**, *hee-er-on';* neut. of *2413;* a *sacred* place, i.e. the entire precincts (whereas *3485* denotes the central *sanctuary* itself) of the *Temple* (at Jerus. or elsewhere):—temple.

2412. ἱεροπρεπής **hiĕrŏprĕpēs**, *hee-er-op-rep-ace';* from *2413* and the same as *4241; reverent*:—as becometh holiness.

2413. ἱερός **hiĕrŏs**, *hee-er-os';* of uncert. affin.; *sacred*:—holy.

2414. Ἱεροσόλυμα **Hiĕrŏsŏluma**, *hee-er-os-ol'-oo-mah;* of Heb. or. [3389]; *Hierosolyma* (i.e. *Jerushalaïm*), the capital of Pal.:—Jerusalem. Comp. *2419*.

2415. Ἱεροσολυμίτης **Hiĕrŏsŏlumitēs**, *hee-er-os-ol-oo-mee'-tace;* from *2414;* a *Hierosolymite*, i.e. inhab. of Hierosolyma:—of Jerusalem.

2416. ἱεροσυλέω **hiĕrŏsulĕō**, *hee-er-os-ool-eh'-o;* from *2417;* to *be a temple-robber* (fig.):—commit sacrilege.

2417. ἱερόσυλος **hiĕrŏsulŏs**, *hee-er-os'-oo-los;* from *2411* and *4813;* a *temple-despoiler*:—robber of churches.

2418. ἱερουργέω **hiĕrŏurgĕō**, *hee-er-oorg-eh'-o;* from a comp. of *2411* and the base of *2041;* to *be a temple-worker*, i.e. *officiate as a priest* (fig.):—minister.

2419. Ἱερουσαλήμ **Hiĕrŏusalēm**, *hee-er-oo-sal-ame';* of Heb. or. [3389]; *Hierusalem* (i.e. *Jerushalem*), the capital of Pal.:—Jerusalem. Comp. *2414*.

2420. ἱερωσύνη **hiĕrōsunē**, *hee-er-o-soo'-nay;* from *2413; sacredness*, i.e. (by impl.) the *priestly office*:—priesthood.

2421. Ἰεσσαί **Iĕssai**, *es-es-sah'ee;* of Heb. or. [3448]; *Jessæ* (i.e. *Jishai*), an Isr.:—Jesse.

2422. Ἰεφθάε **Iĕphthaĕ**, *ee-ef-thah'-eh;* of Heb. or. [3316]; *Jephthaë* (i.e. *Jiphtach*), an Isr.:—Jephthah.

2423. Ἰεχονίας **Iĕchŏnias**, *ee-ekh-on-ee'-as;* of Heb. or. [3204]; *Jechonias* (i.e. *Jekonjah*), an Isr.:—Jechonias.

2424. Ἰησοῦς **Iēsŏus**, *ee-ay-sooce';* of Heb. or. [3091]; *Jesus* (i.e. *Jehoshua*), the name of our Lord and two (three) other Isr.:—Jesus.

2425. ἱκανός **hikanŏs**, *hik-an-os';* from ἵκω **hikō** [ἱκάνω or ἱκνέομαι, akin to *2240*] (to *arrive*): *competent* (as if *coming* in season), i.e. *ample* (in amount) or *fit* (in character):—able, + content, enough, good, great, large, long (while), many, meet, much, security, sore, sufficient, worthy.

2426. ἱκανότης **hikanŏtēs**, *hik-an-ot'-ace;* from *2425; ability*:—sufficiency.

2427. ἱκανόω **hikanŏō**, *hik-an-ŏ'-o;* from *2425;* to *enable*, i.e. *qualify*:—make able (meet).

2428. ἱκετηρία **hikĕtēria**, *hik-et-ay-ree'-ah;* from a der. of the base of *2425* (through the idea of *approaching* for a favor); *intreaty*:—supplication.

2429. ἰκμάς **hikmas**, *hik-mas';* of uncert. affin.; *dampness*:—moisture.

2430. Ἰκόνιον **Ikŏniŏn**, *ee-kon'-ee-on;* perh. from *1504; image-like; Iconium*, a place in Asia Minor:—Iconium.

2431. ἱλαρός **hilarŏs**, *hil-ar-os';* from the same as *2436; propitious* or *merry* ("*hilarious*"), i.e. *prompt* or *willing*:—cheerful.

2432. ἱλαρότης **hilarŏtēs**, *hil-ar-ot'-ace;* from *2431; alacrity*:—cheerfulness.

2433. ἱλάσκομαι **hilaskŏmai**, *hil-as'-kom-ahee;* mid. from the same as *2436;* to *conciliate*, i.e. (trans.) to *atone* for (sin), or (intrans.) *be propitious*:—be merciful, make reconciliation for.

2434. ἱλασμός **hilasmŏs**, *hil-as-mos'; atonement*, i.e. (concr.) an *expiator*:—propitiation.

2435. ἱλαστήριον **hilastēriŏn**, *hil-as-tay'-ree-on;* neut. of a der. of *2433;* an *expiatory* (place or thing), i.e. (concr.) an atoning *victim*, or (spec.) the *lid* of the Ark (in the Temple):—mercyseat, propitiation.

2436. ἵλεως **hilĕōs**, *hil'-eh-oce;* perh. from the alt. form of *138; cheerful* (as *attractive*), i.e. *propitious;* adv. (by Hebr.) God be *gracious!*, i.e. (in averting some calamity) *far* be it:—be it far, merciful.

2437. Ἰλλυρικόν **Illurikŏn**, *il-loo-ree-kon';* neut. of an adj. from a name of uncert. der.; (the) *Illyrican* (shore), i.e. (as a name itself) *Illyricum*, a region of Europe:—Illyricum.

2438. ἱμάς **himas**, *hee-mas';* perh. from the same as *260;* a *strap*, i.e. (spec.) the *tie* (of a sandal) or the *lash* (of a scourge):—latchet, thong.

2439. ἱματίζω **himatizō**, *him-at-id'-zo;* from *2440;* to *dress*:—clothe.

2440. ἱμάτιον **himatiŏn**, *him-at'-ee-on;* neut. of a presumed der. of ἕννυμι **ĕnnumi** (to *put on*); a *dress* (inner or outer):—apparel, cloke, clothes, garment, raiment, robe, vesture.

2441. ἱματισμός **himatismŏs**, *him-at-is-mos';* from *2439; clothing*:—apparel (× -led), array, raiment, vesture.

2442. ἱμείρομαι **himĕirŏmai**, *him-i'-rom-ahee;* mid. from ἵμερος **himĕrŏs** (a *yearning;* of uncert. affin); to *long for*:—be affectionately desirous.

2443. ἵνα **hina**, *hin'-ah;* prob. from the same as the former part of *1438* (through the *demonstrative* idea; comp. *3588*); in order *that* (denoting the *purpose* or the *result*):—albeit, because, to the intent (that), lest, so as, (so) that, (for) to. Comp. *3363*.

ἵνα μή **hina mē**. See *3363*.

2444. ἱνατί **hinati**, *hin-at-ee';* from *2443* and *5101; for what* reason ?, i.e. *why?*:—wherefore, why.

2445. Ἰόππη **Iŏppē**, *ee-op'-pay;* of Heb. or. [3305]; *Joppe* (i.e. *Japho*), a place in Pal.:—Joppa.

2446. Ἰορδάνης **Iŏrdanēs**, *ee-or-dan'-ace;* of Heb. or. [3383]; the *Jordanes* (i.e. *Jarden*), a river of Pal.:—Jordan.

2447. ἰός **iŏs**, *ee-os';* perh. from εἶμι **ĕimi** (to *go*) or ἵημι **hiēmi** (to *send*); *rust* (as if *emitted* by metals); also *venom* (as *emitted* by serpents):—poison, rust.

2448. Ἰουδά **Iŏuda**, *ee-oo-dah'*; of Heb. or. [3063 or perh. 3194]; *Judah* (i.e. *Jehudah* or *Juttah*), a part of (or place in) Pal.:—Judah.

2449. Ἰουδαία **Iŏudaia**, *ee-oo-dah'-yah*; fem. of *2453* (with *1093* impl.); the *Judæan* land (i.e. *Judæa*), a region of Pal.:—Judæa.

2450. Ἰουδαΐζω **Iŏudaizō**, *ee-oo-dah-id'-zo*; from *2453*; *to become a Judæan*, i.e. "*Judaize*":—live as the Jews.

2451. Ἰουδαϊκός **Iŏudaikŏs**, *ee-oo-dah-ee-kos'*; from *2453*; *Judaïc*, i.e. *resembling a Judæan*:—Jewish.

2452. Ἰουδαϊκῶς **Iŏudaikōs**, *ee-oo-dah-ee-koce'*; adv. from *2451*; *Judaïcally* or *in a manner resembling a Judæan*:—as do the Jews.

2453. Ἰουδαῖος **Iŏudaiŏs**, *ee-oo-dah'-yos*; from *2448* (in the sense of *2455* as a country); *Judæan*, i.e. belonging to *Jehudah*:—Jew (-ess), of Judæa.

2454. Ἰουδαϊσμός **Iŏudaismŏs**, *ee-oo-dah-is-mos'*; from *2450*; "*Judaïsm*", i.e. the *Jewish faith* and usages:—Jews' religion.

2455. Ἰουδάς **Iŏudas**, *ee-oo-das'*; of Heb. or. [3063]; *Judas* (i.e. *Jehudah*), the name of ten Isr.; also of the posterity of one of them and its region:—Juda (-h, -s); Jude.

2456. Ἰουλία **Iŏulia**, *ee-oo-lee'-ah*; fem. of the same as *2457*; *Julia*, a Chr. woman:—Julia.

2457. Ἰούλιος **Iŏuliŏs**, *ee-oo'-lee-os*; of Lat. or.; *Julius*, a centurion:—Julius.

2458. Ἰουνίας **Iŏunias**, *ee-oo-nee'-as*; of Lat. or.; *Junias*, a Chr.:—Junias.

2459. Ἰοῦστος **Iŏustŏs**, *ee-ooce'-tos*; of Lat. or. ("*just*"); *Justus*, the name of three Chr.:—Justus.

2460. ἱππεύς **hippĕus**, *hip-yooce'*; from *2462*; an *equestrian*, i.e. member of a *cavalry* corps:—horseman.

2461. ἱππικόν **hippikŏn**, *hip-pee-kon'*; neut. of a der. of *2462*; the *cavalry* force:—horse [-men].

2462. ἵππος **hippŏs**, *hip'-pos*; of uncert. affin.; a *horse*:—horse.

2463. ἶρις **iris**, *ee'-ris*; perh. from *2046* (as a symb. of the female *messenger* of the pagan deities); a *rainbow* ("*iris*"):—rainbow.

2464. Ἰσαάκ **Isaak**, *ee-sah-ak'*; of Heb. or. [3327]; *Isaac* (i.e. *Jitschak*), the son of Abraham:—Isaac.

2465. ἰσάγγελος **isaggĕlŏs**, *ee-sang'-el-los*; from *2470* and *32*; *like an angel*, i.e. *angelic*:—equal unto the angels.

2466. Ἰσαχάρ **Isachar**, *ee-sakh-ar'*, of Heb. or. [3485]; *Isachar* (i.e. *Jissaskar*), a son of Jacob (fig. his desc.):—Issachar.

2467. ἴσημι **isēmi**, *is'-ay-mee*; assumed by some as the base of cert. irreg. forms of *1492*; *to know*:—know.

2468. ἴσθι **isthi**, *is'-thee*; sec. pers. imper. pres. of *1510*; *be* thou:—+ agree, be, × give thyself wholly to.

2469. Ἰσκαριώτης **Iskariōtēs**, *is-kar-ee-o'-tace*; of Heb. or. [prob. 377 and 7149]; *inhab. of Kerioth*; *Iscariotes* (i.e. *Keriothite*), an epithet of Judas the traitor:—Iscariot.

2470. ἴσος **isŏs**, *ee'-sos*; prob. from *1492* (through the idea of *seeming*); *similar* (in amount or kind):—+ agree, as much, equal, like.

2471. ἰσότης **isŏtēs**, *ee-sot'-ace*; *likeness* (in condition or proportion); by impl. *equity*:—equal (-ity).

2472. ἰσότιμος **isŏtimŏs**, *ee-sot'-ee-mos*; from *2470* and *5092*; *of equal value* or *honor*:—like precious.

2473. ἰσόψυχος **isŏpsuchŏs**, *ee-sop'-soo-khos*; from *2470* and *5590*; *of similar spirit*:—likeminded.

2474. Ἰσραήλ **Israēl**, *is-rah-ale'*; of Heb. or. [3478]; *Israel* (i.e. *Jisrael*), the adopted name of Jacob, includ. his desc. (lit. or fig.):—Israel.

2475. Ἰσραηλίτης **Israēlitēs**, *is-rah-ale-ee'-tace*; from *2474*; an "*Israelite*", i.e. desc. of Israel (lit. or fig.):—Israelite.

2476. ἵστημι **histēmi**, *his'-tay-mee*; a prol. form of a prim. στάω **staō**, *stah'-o* (of the same mean., and used for it in certain tenses); to *stand* (trans. or intrans.), used in various applications (lit. or fig.):—abide, appoint, bring, continue, covenant, establish, hold up, lay, present, set (up), stanch, stand (by, forth, still, up). Comp. *5087*.

2477. ἱστορέω **histŏrĕō**, *his-tor-eh'-o*; from a der. of *1492*; *to be knowing* (*learned*), i.e. (by impl.) to *visit* for information (*interview*):—see.

2478. ἰσχυρός **ischurŏs**, *is-khoo-ros'*; from *2479*; *forcible* (lit. or fig.):—boisterous, mighty (-ier), powerful, strong (-er, man), valiant.

2479. ἰσχύς **ischus**, *is-khoos'*; from a der. of ἰς **is** (*force*; comp. ἔσχον **ĕschŏn**, a form of *2192*); *forcefulness* (lit. or fig.):—ability, might ([-ily]), power, strength.

2480. ἰσχύω **ischuō**, *is-khoo'-o*; from *2479*; to *have* (or *exercise*) *force* (lit. or fig.):—be able, avail, can do ([-not]), could, be good, might, prevail, be of strength, be whole, + much work.

2481. ἴσως **isōs**, *ee'-soce*; adv. from *2470*; *likely*, i.e. *perhaps*:—it may be.

2482. Ἰταλία **Italia**, *ee-tal-ee'-ah*; prob. of for. or.; *Italia*, a region of Europe:—Italy.

2483. Ἰταλικός **Italikŏs**, *ee-tal-ee-kos'*; from *2482*; *Italic*, i.e. belonging to Italia:—Italian.

2484. Ἰτουραΐα **Itŏuraia**, *ee-too-rah'-yah*; of Heb. or. [3195]; *Ituræa* (i.e. *Jetur*), a region of Pal.:—Ituræa.

2485. ἰχθύδιον **ichthudiŏn**, *ikh-thoo'-dee-on*; dimin. from *2486*; a *petty fish*:—little (small) fish.

2486. ἰχθύς **ichthus**, *ikh-thoos'*; of uncert. affin.; a *fish*:—fish.

2487. ἴχνος **ichnŏs**, *ikh'-nos*; from ἰκνέομαι **iknĕŏmai** (to *arrive*; comp. *2240*); a *track* (fig.):—step.

2488. Ἰωάθαμ **Iōatham**, *ee-o-ath'-am*; of Heb. or. [3147]; *Joatham* (i.e. *Jotham*), an Isr.:—Joatham.

2489. Ἰωάννα **Iōanna**, *ee-o-an'-nah*; fem. of the same as *2491*; *Joanna*, a Chr.:—Joanna.

2490. Ἰωαννᾶς **Iōannas**, *ee-o-an-nas'*; a form of *2491*; *Joannas*, an Isr.:—Joannas.

2491. Ἰωάννης **Iōannēs**, *ee-o-an'-nace*; of Heb. or. [3110]; *Joannes* (i.e. *Jochanan*), the name of four Isr.:—John.

2492. Ἰώβ **Iōb**, *ee-obe'*; of Heb. or. [347]; *Job* (i.e. *Ijob*), a patriarch:—Job.

2493. Ἰωήλ **Iōēl**, *ee-o-ale'*; of Heb. or. [3100]; *Joel*, an Isr.:—Joel.

2494. Ἰωνάν **Iōnan**, *ee-o-nan'*; prob. for *2491* or *2495*; *Jonan*, an Isr.:—Jonan.

2495. Ἰωνᾶς **Iōnas**, *ee-o-nas'*; of Heb. or. [3124]; *Jonas* (i.e. *Jonah*), the name of two Isr.:—Jonas.

2496. Ἰωράμ **Iōram**, *ee-o-ram'*; of Heb. or. [3141]; *Joram*, an Isr.:—Joram.

2497. Ἰωρείμ **Iōrĕim**, *ee-o-rime'*; perh. for *2496*; *Jorim*, an Isr.:—Jorim.

2498. Ἰωσαφάτ **Iōsaphat**, *ee-o-saf-at'*; of Heb. or. [3092]; *Josaphat* (i.e. *Jehoshaphat*), an Isr.:—Josaphat.

2499. Ἰωσή **Iōsē**, *ee-o-say'*; gen. of *2500*; *Jose*, an Isr.:—Jose.

2500. Ἰωσῆς **Iōsēs**, *ee-o-sace'*; perh. for *2501*; *Joses*, the name of two Isr.:—Joses. Comp. *2499*.

2501. Ἰωσήφ **Iōsēph**, *ee-o-safe'*; of Heb. or. [3130]; *Joseph*, the name of seven Isr.:—Joseph.

2502. Ἰωσίας **Iōsias**, *ee-o-see'-as*; of Heb. or. [2977]; *Josias* (i.e. *Joshiah*), an Isr.:—Josias.

2503. ἰῶτα **iōta**, *ee-o'-tah*; of Heb. or. [the tenth letter of the Heb. alphabet]; "*iota*", the name of the ninth letter of the Gr. alphabet, put (fig.) for a very small part of anything:—jot.

K

2504. κἀγώ **kagō**, *kag-o'*; from *2532* and *1473* (so also the dat.

κἀμοί **kamŏi**, *kam-oy'*; and acc.

κἀμέ **kamĕ**, *kam-eh'*); *and* (or *also*, *even*, etc.) *I*, (*to*) *me*:—(and, even, even so, so) I (also, in like wise), both me, me also.

2505. καθά **katha**, *kath-ah'*; from *2596* and the neut. plur. of *3739*; *according to which* things, i.e. *just as*:—as.

2506. καθαίρεσις **kathairĕsis**, *kath-ah'ee-res-is*; from *2507*; *demolition*; fig. *extinction*:—destruction, pulling down.

2507. καθαιρέω **kathairĕō**, *kath-ahee-reh'-o*; from *2596* and *138* (includ. its alt.); to *lower* (or with violence) *demolish* (lit. or fig.):—cast (pull, put, take) down, destroy.

2508. καθαίρω **kathairō**, *kath-ah'ee-ro*; from *2513*; to *cleanse*, i.e. (spec.) to *prune*; fig. to *expiate*:—purge.

2509. καθάπερ **kathapĕr**, *kath-ap'-er*; from *2505* and *4007*; *exactly as*:—(even, as well) as.

2510. καθάπτω **kathaptō**, *kath-ap'-to*; from *2596* and *680*; to *seize upon*:—fasten on.

2511. καθαρίζω **katharizō**, *kath-ar-id'-zo*; from *2513*; to *cleanse* (lit. or fig.):—(make) clean (-se), purge, purify.

2512. καθαρισμός **katharismŏs**, *kath-ar-is-mos'*; from *2511*; a *washing* off, i.e. (cer.) *ablution*, (mor.) *expiation*:—cleansing, + purge, purification, (-fying).

2513. καθαρός **katharŏs**, *kath-ar-os'*; of uncert. affin.; *clean* (lit. or fig.):—clean, clear, pure.

2514. καθαρότης **katharŏtēs**, *kath-ar-ot'-ace*; from *2513*; *cleanness* (cer.):—purification.

2515. καθέδρα **kathĕdra**, *kath-ed'-rah*; from *2596* and the same as *1476*; a *bench* (lit. or fig.):—seat.

2516. καθέζομαι **kathĕzŏmai**, *kath-ed'-zom-ahee*; from *2596* and the base of *1476*; to *sit down*:—sit.

2517. καθεξῆς **kathĕxēs**, *kath-ex-ace'*; from *2596* and *1836*; *thereafter*, i.e. *consecutively*; as a noun (by ell. of noun) a *subsequent* person or time:—after (-ward), by (in) order.

2518. καθεύδω **kathĕudō**, *kath-yoo'-do*; from *2596* and εὕδω **hĕudō** (to *sleep*); to lie *down to rest*, i.e. (by impl.) to *fall asleep* (lit. or fig.):—(be a-) sleep.

2519. καθηγητής **kathēgētēs**, *kath-ayg-ay-tace'*; from a comp. of *2596* and *2233*; a *guide*, i.e. (fig.) a *teacher*:—master.

2520. καθήκω **kathēkō**, *kath-ay'-ko*; from *2596* and *2240*; to *reach to*, i.e. (neut. of pres. act. part., fig. as adj.) *becoming*:—convenient, fit.

2521. κάθημαι **kathēmai**, *kath'-ay-mahee*; from *2596* and ἧμαι **hēmai** (to *sit*; akin to the base of *1476*); to *sit down*; fig. to *remain*, *reside*:—dwell, sit (by, down).

2522. καθημερινός **kathēmĕrinŏs**, *kath-ay-mer-ee-nos'*; from *2596* and *2250*; *quotidian*:—daily.

2523. καθίζω **kathizō**, *kath-id'-zo*; another (act.) form for *2516*; to *seat down*, i.e. *set* (fig. *appoint*); intrans. to *sit* (down); fig. to *settle* (*hover*, *dwell*):—continue, set, sit (down), tarry.

2524. καθίημι **kathiēmi**, *kath-ee'-ay-mee*; from *2596* and ἵημι **hiēmi** (to *send*); to *lower*:—let down.

2525. καθίστημι **kathistēmi**, *kath-is'-tay-mee*; from *2596* and *2476*; to *place down* (permanently), i.e. (fig.) to *designate*, *constitute*, *convoy*:—appoint, be, conduct, make, ordain, set.

2526. καθό **kathŏ**, *kath-ŏ'*; from *2596* and *3739*; *according to which* thing, i.e. *precisely as*, *in proportion as*:—according to that, (inasmuch) as.

2526'. καθολικός, **kathŏlikŏs**, *kath-ol-ee-kos'*; from *2527*; *universal*:—general.

2527. καθόλου, **kathŏlŏu**, *kath-ol'-oo*; from *2596* and *3650*; *on the whole*, i.e. *entirely*:—at all.

2528. καθοπλίζω **kathŏplizō**, *kath-op-lid'-zo*; from *2596* and *3695*; to *equip fully* with armor:—arm.

2529. καθοράω **kathŏraō**, *kath-or-ah'-o*; from *2596* and *3708*; to *behold fully*, i.e. (fig.) *distinctly apprehend*:—clearly see.

2530. καθότι **kathŏti**, *kath-ot'-ee*; from *2596* and *3739* and *5100*; *according to which certain thing*, i.e. *as far* (or *inasmuch*) *as*:—(according, forasmuch) as, because (that).

2531. καθώς kathōs, *kath-oce'*; from *2596* and *5613*; *just* (or *inasmuch*) *as, that*:—according to, (according, even) as, how, when.

2532. καί kai, *kahee*; appar. a prim. particle, having a *copulative* and sometimes also a *cumulative* force; *and, also, even, so, then, too*, etc.; often used in connection (or composition) with other particles or small words:—and, also, both, but, even, for, if, indeed, likewise, moreover, or, so, that, then, therefore, when, yea, yet.

2533. Καϊάφας Kaïaphas, *kah-ee-af'-as*; of Chald. or.; *the dell*; *Caïaphas* (i.e. *Cajepha*), an Isr.:—Caiaphas.

2534. καίγε kaigĕ, *ka'hee-gheh*; from *2532* and *1065*; *and at least* (or *even, indeed*):—and, at least.

2535. Κάϊν Kaïn, *kah'-in*; of Heb. or. [7014]; *Caïn* (i.e. *Cajin*), the son of Adam:—Cain.

2536. Καϊνάν Kaïnan, *kah-ee-nan'*; of Heb. or. [7018]; *Caïnan* (i.e. *Kenan*), the name of two patriarchs:—Cainan.

2537. καινός kainŏs, *kahee-nos'*; of uncert. affin.; *new* (espec. in *freshness*; while *3501* is prop. so with respect to *age*):—new.

2538. καινότης kainŏtēs, *kahee-not'-ace*; from *2537*; *renewal* (fig.):—newness.

2539. καίπερ kaipĕr, *kah'ee-per*; from *2532* and *4007*; *and indeed*, i.e. *nevertheless* or *notwithstanding*:—and yet, although.

2540. καιρός kairŏs, *kahee-ros'*; of uncert. affin.; an *occasion*, i.e. *set* or *proper* time:— × always, opportunity, (convenient, due) season, (due, short, while) time, a while. Comp. *5550*.

2541. Καῖσαρ Kaisar, *kah'ee-sar*; of Lat. or.; *Cæsar*, a title of the Rom. emperor:—Cæsar.

2542. Καισάρεια Kaisarĕia, *kahee-sar'-i-a*; from *2541*; *Cæsaria*, the name of two places in Pal.:—Cæsarea.

2543. καίτοι kaitŏi, *kah'ee-toy*; from *2532* and *5104*; *and yet*, i.e. *nevertheless*:—although.

2544. καίτοιγε kaitŏigĕ, *kah'ee-toyg-eh*; from *2543* and *1065*; *and yet indeed*, i.e. *although really*:—nevertheless, though.

2545. καίω kaiō, *kah'-yo*; appar. a prim. verb; to *set on fire*, i.e. *kindle* or (by impl.) *consume*:—burn, light.

2546. κἀκεῖ kakĕi, *kak-i'*; from *2532* and *1563*; *likewise in that place*:—and there, there (thither) also.

2547. κἀκεῖθεν kakĕithĕn, *kak-i'-then*; from *2532* and *1564*; *likewise from that place* (or *time*):—and afterward (from) (thence), thence also.

2548. κἀκεῖνος kakĕinŏs, *kak-i'-nos*; from *2532* and *1565*; *likewise that* (or *those*):—and him (other, them), even he, him also, them (also), (and) they.

2549. κακία kakia, *kak-ee'-ah*; from *2556*; *badness*, i.e. (subj.) *depravity*, or (act.) *malignity*, or (pass.) *trouble*:—evil, malice (-iousness), naughtiness, wickedness.

2550. κακοήθεια kakŏēthĕia, *kak-ŏ-ay'-thi-ah*; from a comp. of *2556* and *2239*; *bad character*, i.e. (spec.) *mischievousness*:—malignity.

2551. κακολογέω kakŏlŏgĕō, *kak-ol-og-eh'-o*; from a comp. of *2556* and *3056*; to *revile*:—curse, speak evil of.

2552. κακοπάθεια kakŏpathĕia, *kak-op-ath'-i-ah*; from a comp. of *2556* and *3806*; *hardship*:—suffering affliction.

2553. κακοπαθέω kakŏpathĕō, *kak-op-ath-eh'-o*; from the same as *2552*; to *undergo hardship*:—be afflicted, endure afflictions (hardness), suffer trouble.

2554. κακοποιέω kakŏpŏiĕō, *kak-op-oy-eh'-o*; from *2555*; to *be a bad-doer*, i.e. (obj.) to *injure*, or (gen.) to *sin*:—do (-ing) evil.

2555. κακοποιός kakŏpŏiŏs, *kak-op-oy-os'*; from *2556* and *4160*; a *bad-doer*; (spec.) a *criminal*:—evil-doer, malefactor.

2556. κακός kakŏs, *kak-os'*; appar. a prim. word; *worthless* (*intrinsically* such; whereas *4190* prop. refers to *effects*), i.e. (subj.) *depraved*, or (obj.) *injurious*:—bad, evil, harm, ill, noisome, wicked.

2557. κακοῦργος kakŏurgŏs, *kak-oor'-gos*; from *2556* and the base of *2041*; a *wrong-doer*, i.e. *criminal*:—evil-doer, malefactor.

2558. κακουχέω kakŏuchĕō, *kak-oo-kheh'-o*; from a presumed comp. of *2556* and *2192*; to *maltreat*:—which suffer adversity, torment.

2559. κακόω kakŏō, *kak-ŏ'-o*; from *2556*; to *injure*; fig. to *exasperate*:—make evil affected, entreat evil, harm, hurt, vex.

2560. κακῶς kakōs, *kak-oce'*; adv. from *2556*; *badly* (phys. or mor.):—amiss, diseased, evil, grievously, miserably, sick, sore.

2561. κάκωσις kakōsis, *kak'-o-sis*; from *2559*; *maltreatment*:—affliction.

2562. καλάμη kalamē, *kal-am'-ay*; fem. of *2563*; a *stalk* of grain, i.e. (collect.) *stubble*:—stubble.

2563. κάλαμος kalamŏs, *kal'-am-os*; of uncert. affin.; a *reed* (the plant or its stem, or that of a similar plant); by impl. a *pen*:—pen, reed.

2564. καλέω kalĕō, *kal-eh'-o*; akin to the base of *2753*; to "*call*" (prop. aloud, but used in a variety of applications, dir. or otherwise):—bid, call (forth), (whose, whose sur-) name (was [called]).

2565. καλλιέλαιος kalliĕlaiŏs, *kal-le-el'-ah-yos*; from the base of *2566* and *1636*; a *cultivated olive* tree, i.e. a *domesticated* or *improved* one:—good olive tree.

2566. καλλίον kalliŏn, *kal-lee'-on*; neut. of the (irreg.) comp. of *2570*; (adv.) *better* than many:—very well.

2567. καλοδιδάσκαλος kalŏdidaskalŏs, *kal-od-id-as'-kal-os*; from *2570* and *1320*; a *teacher of* the *right*:—teacher of good things.

2568. Καλοὶ Λιμένες Kalŏi Limĕnĕs, *kal-oy' lee-men'-es*; plur. of *2570* and *3040*; *Good Harbors*, i.e. *Fairhaven*, a bay of Crete:—fair havens.

2569. καλοποιέω kalŏpŏiĕō, *kal-op-oy-eh'-o*; from *2570* and *4160*; to *do well*, i.e. live virtuously:—well doing.

2570. καλός kalŏs, *kal-os'*; of uncert. affin.; prop. *beautiful*, but chiefly (fig.) *good* (lit. or mor.), i.e. *valuable* or *virtuous* (for *appearance* or *use*, and thus distinguished from *18*, which is prop. *intrinsic*):— × better, fair, good (-ly), honest, meet, well, worthy.

2571. κάλυμα kaluma, *kal'-oo-mah*; from *2572*; a *cover*, i.e. *veil*:—vail.

2572. καλύπτω kaluptō, *kal-oop'-to*; akin to *2813* and *2928*; to *cover up* (lit. or fig.):—cover, hide.

2573. καλῶς kalōs, *kal-oce'*; adv. from *2570*; *well* (usually mor.):—(in a) good (place), honestly, + recover, (full) well.

2574. κάμηλος kamēlŏs, *kam'-ay-los*; of Heb. or. [1581]; a "*camel*":—camel.

2575. κάμινος kaminŏs, *kam'-ee-nos*; prob. from *2545*; a *furnace*:—furnace.

2576. καμμύω kammuō, *kam-moo'-o*; for a comp. of *2596* and the base of *3466*; to *shut down*, i.e. *close* the eyes:—close.

2577. κάμνω kamnō, *kam'-no*; appar. a prim. verb; prop. to *toil*, i.e. (by impl.) to *tire* (fig. *faint*, *sicken*):—faint, sicken, be wearied.

2578. κάμπτω kamptō, *kamp'-to*; appar. a prim. verb; to *bend*:—bow.

2579. κἄν kan, *kan*; from *2532* and *1437*; *and* (or *even*) *if*:—and (also) if (so much as), if but, at the least, though, yet.

2580. Κανᾶ Kana, *kan-ah'*; of Heb. or. [comp. 7071]; *Cana*, a place in Pal.:—Cana.

2581. Κανανίτης Kananitēs, *kan-an-ee'-tace*; of Chald. or. [comp. 7067]; *zealous*; *Cananitès*, an epithet:—Canaanite [*by mistake for a der. from 5477*].

2582. Κανδάκη Kandakē, *kan-dak'-ay*; of for. or.; *Candacè*, an Eg. queen:—Candace.

2583. κανών kanōn, *kan-ohn'*; from **κάνη kanē** (a straight *reed*, i.e. *rod*); a *rule* ("*canon*"), i.e. (fig.) a *standard* (of faith and practice); by impl. a *boundary*, i.e. (fig.) a *sphere* (of activity):—line, rule.

2584. Καπερναούμ Kapĕrnaŏum, *cap-er-nah-oom'*; of Heb. or. [prob. 3723 and 5151]; *Capernaüm* (i.e. *Caphanachum*), a place in Pal.:—Capernaum.

2585. καπηλεύω kapēlĕuō, *kap-ale-yoo'-o*; from **κάπηλος kapēlŏs** (a *huckster*); to *retail*, i.e. (by impl.) to *adulterate* (fig.):—corrupt.

2586. καπνός kapnŏs, *kap-nos'*; of uncert. affin.; *smoke*:—smoke.

2587. Καππαδοκία Kappadŏkia, *kap-pad-ok-ee'-ah*; of for. or.; *Cappadocia*, a region of Asia Minor:—Cappadocia.

2588. καρδία kardia, *kar-dee'-ah*; prol. from a prim. **κάρ kar** (Lat. *cor*, "*heart*"); the *heart*, i.e. (fig.) the *thoughts* or *feelings* (*mind*); also (by anal.) the *middle*:—(+ broken-) heart (-ed).

2589. καρδιογνώστης kardiŏgnōstēs, *kar-dee-og-noce'-tace*; from *2588* and *1097*; a *heart-knower*:—which knowest the hearts.

2590. καρπός karpŏs, *kar-pos'*; prob. from the base of *726*; *fruit* (as *plucked*), lit. or fig.:—fruit.

2591. Κάρπος Karpŏs, *kar'-pos*; perh. for *2590*; *Carpus*, prob. a Chr.:—Carpus.

2592. καρποφορέω karpŏphŏrĕō, *kar-pof-or-eh'-o*; from *2593*; to *be fertile* (lit. or fig.):—be (bear, bring forth) fruit (-ful).

2593. καρποφόρος karpŏphŏrŏs, *kar-pof-or'-os*; from *2590* and *5342*; *fruitbearing* (fig.):—fruitful.

2594. καρτερέω kartĕrĕō, *kar-ter-eh'-o*; from a der. of *2904* (transp.); to *be strong*, i.e. (fig.) *steadfast* (*patient*):—endure.

2595. κάρφος karphŏs, *kar'-fos*; from **κάρφω karphō** (to *wither*); a dry *twig* or *straw*:—mote.

2596. κατά kata, *kat-ah'*; a prim. particle; (prep.) *down* (in place or time), in varied relations (according to the case [gen., dat. or acc.] with which it is joined):—about, according as (to), after, against, (when they were) × alone, among, and, × apart, (even, like) as (concerning, pertaining to, touching), × aside, at, before, beyond, by, to the charge of, [charita-] bly, concerning, + covered, [dai-] ly, down, every, (+ far more) exceeding, × more excellent, for, from . . . to, godly, in (-asmuch, divers, every, -to, respect of), . . . by, after the manner of, + by any means, beyond (out of) measure, × mightily, more, × natural, of (up-) on (× part), out (of every), over against, (+ your) × own, + particularly, so, through (-oughout, -oughout every), thus, (un-) to (-gether, -ward), × uttermost, where (-by), with. In composition it retains many of these applications, and frequently denotes *opposition*, *distribution* or *intensity*.

2597. καταβαίνω katabainō, *kat-ab-ah'ee-no*; from *2596* and the base of *939*; to *descend* (lit. or fig.):—come (get, go, step) down, descend, fall (down).

2598. καταβάλλω kataballō, *kat-ab-al'-lo*; from *2596* and *906*; to *throw down*:—cast down, descend, fall (down).

2599. καταβαρέω katabarĕō, *kat-ab-ar-eh'-o*; from *2596* and *916*; to *impose upon*:—burden.

2600. κατάβασις katabasis, *kat-ab'-as-is*; from *2597*; a *declivity*:—descent.

2601. καταβιβάζω katabibazō, *kat-ab-ib-ad'-zo*; from *2596* and a der. of the base of *939*; to *cause to go down*, i.e. *precipitate*:—bring (thrust) down.

2602. καταβολή katabŏlē, *kat-ab-ol-ay'*; from *2598*; a *deposition*, i.e. *founding*; fig. *conception*:—conceive, foundation.

2603. καταβραβεύω katabrabĕuō, *kat-ab-rab-yoo'-o*; from *2596* and *1018* (in its orig. sense); to *award* the price *against*, i.e. (fig.) to *defraud* (of salvation):—beguile of reward.

2604. καταγγελεύς kataggĕlĕus, *kat-ang-gel-yooce'*; from *2605*; a *proclaimer*:—setter forth.

2605. καταγγέλλω kataggĕllō, *kat-ang-gel'-lo*; from *2596* and the base of *32*; to *proclaim*, *promulgate*:—declare, preach, shew, speak of, teach.

2606. καταγελάω katagĕlaō, *kat-ag-el-ah'-o*; to *laugh down*, i.e. *deride*:—laugh to scorn.

2607. καταγινώσκω kataginōskō, *kat-ag-in-o'-sko*; from *2596* and *1097*; to *note against*, i.e. *find fault with*:—blame, condemn.

2608. κατάγνυμι katagnumi, *kat-ag'-noo-mee*; from *2596* and the base of *4486*; *to rend in pieces*, i.e. *crack apart*:—break.

2609. κατάγω katagō, *kat-ag'-o*; from *2596* and *71*; to *lead down*; spec. to *moor* a vessel:—bring (down, forth), (bring to) land, touch.

2610. καταγωνίζομαι katagōnizŏmai, *kat-ag-o-nid'-zom-ahee*; from *2596* and *75*; to *struggle against*, i.e. (by impl.) to *overcome*:—subdue.

2611. καταδέω katadĕō, *kat-ad-eh'-o*; from *2596* and *1210*; to *tie down*, i.e. *bandage* (a wound):—bind up.

2612. κατάδηλος katadēlŏs, *kat-ad'-ay-los*; from *2596* intens. and *1212*; *manifest*:—far more evident.

2613. καταδικάζω katadikazō, *kat-ad-ik-ad'-zo*; from *2596* and a der. of *1349*; to *adjudge against*, i.e. *pronounce guilty*:—condemn.

2614. καταδιώκω katadiōkō, *kat-ad-ee-o'-ko*; from *2596* and *1377*; to *hunt down*, i.e. *search for*:—follow after.

2615. καταδουλόω katadŏulŏō, *kat-ad-oo-lŏ'-o*; from *2596* and *1402*; to *enslave utterly*:—bring into bondage.

2616. καταδυναστεύω katadunastĕuō, *kat-ad-oo-nas-tyoo'-o*; from *2596* and a der. of *1413*; to *exercise dominion against*, i.e. *oppress*:—oppress.

2617. καταισχύνω kataischunō, *kat-ahee-skhoo'-no*; from *2596* and *153*; to *shame down*, i.e. *disgrace* or (by impl.) *put to the blush*:—confound, dishonour, (be a-, make a-) shame (-d).

2618. κατακαίω katakaiō, *kat-ak-ah'ee-o*; from *2596* and *2545*; to *burn down* (to the ground), i.e. *consume wholly*:—burn (up, utterly).

2619. κατακαλύπτω katakaluptō, *kat-ak-al-oop'-to*; from *2596* and *2572*; to *cover wholly*, i.e. *veil*:—cover, hide.

2620. κατακαυχάομαι katakauchaŏmai, *kat-ak-ŏw-khah'-om-ahee*; from *2596* and *2744*; to *exult against* (i.e. *over*):—boast (against), glory, rejoice against.

2621. κατάκειμαι katakĕimai, *kat-ak'-i-mahee*; from *2596* and *2749*; to *lie down*, i.e. (by impl.) *be sick*; spec. to *recline* at a meal:—keep, lie, sit at meat (down).

2622. κατακλάω kataklaō, *kat-ak-lah'-o*; from *2596* and *2806*; to *break down*, i.e. *divide*:—break.

2623. κατακλείω kataklĕiō, *kat-ak-li'-o*; from *2596* and *2808*; to *shut down* (in a dungeon), i.e. *incarcerate*:—shut up.

2624. κατακληροδοτέω kataklērŏdŏtĕō, *kat-ak-lay-rod-ot-eh'-o*; from *2596* and a der. of a comp. of *2819* and *1325*; to *be a giver of lots to each*, i.e. (by impl.) to *apportion an estate*:—divide by lot.

2625. κατακλίνω kataklinō, *kat-ak-lee'-no*; from *2596* and *2827*; to *recline down*, i.e. (spec.) to *take a place* at table:—(make) sit down (at meat).

2626. κατακλύζω katakluzō, *kat-ak-lood'-zo*; from *2596* and the base of *2830*; to *dash* (*wash*) *down*, i.e. (by impl.) to *deluge*:—overflow.

2627. κατακλυσμός kataklusmŏs, *kat-ak-looce-mos'*; from *2626*; an *inundation*:—flood.

2628. κατακολουθέω katakŏlŏuthĕō, *kat-ak-ol-oo-theh'-o*; from *2596* and *190*; to *accompany closely*:—follow (after).

2629. κατακόπτω katakŏptō, *kat-ak-op'-to*; from *2596* and *2875*; to *chop down*, i.e. *mangle*:—cut.

2630. κατακρημνίζω katakrēmnizō, *kat-ak-rame-nid'-zo*; from *2596* and a der. of *2911*; to *precipitate down*:—cast down headlong.

2631. κατάκριμα katakrima, *kat-ak'-ree-mah*; from *2632*; an *adverse sentence* (the verdict):—condemnation.

2632. κατακρίνω katakrinō, *kat-ak-ree'-no*; from *2596* and *2919*; to *judge against*, i.e. *sentence*:—condemn, damn.

2633. κατάκρισις katakrisis, *kat-ak'-ree-sis*; from *2632*; *sentencing adversely* (the act):—condemn (-ation).

2634. κατακυριεύω katakuriĕuō, *kat-ak-oo-ree-yoo'-o*; from *2596* and *2961*; to *lord against*, i.e. *control, subjugate*:—exercise dominion over (lordship), be lord over, overcome.

2635. καταλαλέω katalalĕō, *kat-al-al-eh'-o*; from *2637*; to *be a traducer*, i.e. to *slander*:—speak against (evil of).

2636. καταλαλία katalalia, *kat-al-al-ee'-ah*; from *2637*; *defamation*:—backbiting, evil speaking.

2637 κατάλαλος katalalŏs, *kat-al'-al-os*; from *2596* and the base of *2980*; *talkative against*, i.e. a *slanderer*:—backbiter.

2638. καταλαμβάνω katalambanō, *kat-al-am-ban'-o*; from *2596* and *2983*; to *take eagerly*, i.e. *seize, possess*, etc. (lit. or fig.).—apprehend, attain, come upon, comprehend, find, obtain, perceive, (over-) take.

2639. καταλέγω katalĕgō, *kat-al-eg'-o*; from *2596* and *3004* (in its orig. mean.); to *lay down*, i.e. (fig.) to *enrol*:—take into the number.

2640. κατάλειμμα katalĕimma, *kat-al'-ime-mah*; from *2641*; a *remainder*, i.e. (by impl.) a *few*:—remnant.

2641. καταλείπω katalĕipō, *kat-al-i'-po*; from *2596* and *3007*; to *leave down*, i.e. *behind*; by impl. to *abandon, have remaining*:—forsake, leave, reserve.

2642. καταλιθάζω katalithazō, *kat-al-ith-ad'-zo*; from *2596* and *3034*; to *stone down*, i.e. *to death*:—stone.

2643. καταλλαγή katallagē, *kat-al-lag-ay'*; from *2644*; *exchange* (fig. *adjustment*), i.e. *restoration* to (the divine) favor:—atonement, reconciliation (-ing).

2644. καταλλάσσω katallassō, *kat-al-las'-so*; from *2596* and *236*; to *change mutually*, i.e. (fig.) to *compound* a difference:—reconcile.

2645. κατάλοιπος katalŏipŏs, *kat-al'-oy-pos*; from *2596* and *3062*; *left down* (*behind*), i.e. *remaining* (plur. the *rest*):—residue.

2646. κατάλυμα kataluma, *kat-al'-oo-mah*; from *2647*; prop. a *dissolution* (breaking up of a journey), i.e. (by impl.) a *lodging-place*:—guestchamber, inn.

2647. καταλύω kataluō, *kat-al-oo'-o*; from *2596* and *3089*; to *loosen down* (*disintegrate*), i.e. (by impl.) to *demolish* (lit. or fig.); spec. [comp. *2646*] to *halt* for the night:—destroy, dissolve, be guest, lodge, come to nought, overthrow, throw down.

2648. καταμανθάνω katamanthanō, *kat-am-an-than'-o*; from *2596* and *3129*; to *learn thoroughly*, i.e. (by impl.) to *note carefully*:—consider.

2649. καταμαρτυρέω katamarturĕō, *kat-am-ar-too-reh'-o*; from *2596* and *3140*; to *testify against*:—witness against.

2650. καταμένω katamĕnō, *kat-am-en'-o*; from *2596* and *3306*; to *stay fully*, i.e. *reside*:—abide.

2651. καταμόνας katamŏnas, *kat-am-on'-as*; from *2596* and acc. plur. fem. of *3441* (with *5561* impl.); *according to sole* places, i.e. (adv.) *separately*:—alone.

2652. κατανάθεμα katanathĕma, *kat-an-ath'-em-ah*; from *2596* (intens.) and *331*; an *imprecation*:—curse.

2653. καταναθεματίζω katanathĕmatizō, *kat-an-ath-em-at-id'-zo*; from *2596* (intens.) and *332*; to *imprecate*:—curse.

2654. καταναλίσκω katanaliskō, *kat-an-al-is'-ko*; from *2596* and *355*; to *consume utterly*:—consume.

2655. καταναρκάω katanarkaō, *kat-an-ar-kah'-o*; from *2596* and **ναρκάω narkaō** (to be *numb*); to *grow utterly torpid*, i.e. (by impl.) *slothful* (fig. *expensive*):—be burdensome (chargeable).

2656. κατανεύω katanĕuō, *kat-an-yoo'-o*; from *2596* and *3506*; to *nod down* (*towards*), i.e. (by anal.) to *make signs* to:—beckon.

2657. κατανοέω katanŏĕō, *kat-an-o-eh'-o*; from *2596* and *3539*; to *observe fully*:—behold, consider, discover, perceive.

2658. καταντάω katantaō, *kat-an-tah'-o*; from *2596* and a der. of *473*; to *meet against*, i.e. *arrive* at (lit. or fig.):—attain, come.

2659. κατάνυξις katanuxis, *kat-an'-oox-is*; from *2660*; a *prickling* (sensation, as of the limbs asleep), i.e. (by impl. [perh. by some confusion with *3506* or even with *3571*]) *stupor* (*lethargy*):—slumber.

2660. κατανύσσω katanussō, *kat-an-oos'-so*; from *2596* and *3572*; to *pierce thoroughly*, i.e. (fig.) to *agitate* violently ("sting to the quick"):—prick.

2661. καταξιόω kataxiŏō, *kat-ax-ee-ŏ'-o*; from *2596* and *515*; to *deem entirely deserving*:—(ac-) count worthy.

2662. καταπατέω katapatĕō, *kat-ap-at-eh'-o*; from *2596* and *3961*; to *trample down*; fig. to *reject* with disdain:—trample, tread (down, underfoot).

2663. κατάπαυσις katapausis, *kat-ap'-ŏw-sis*; from *2664*; *reposing down*, i.e. (by Hebr.) *abode*:—rest.

2664. καταπαύω katapauō, *kat-ap-ŏw'-o*; from *2596* and *3973*; to *settle down*, i.e. (lit.) to *colonize*, or (fig.) to (*cause to*) *desist*:—cease, (give) rest (-rain).

2665. καταπέτασμα katapĕtasma, *kat-ap-et'-as-mah*; from a comp. of *2596* and a congener of *4072*; something *spread thoroughly*, i.e. (spec.) the door *screen* (to the Most Holy Place) in the Jewish Temple:—vail.

2666. καταπίνω katapinō, *kat-ap-ee'-no*; from *2596* and *4095*; to *drink down*, i.e. *gulp entire* (lit. or fig.):—devour, drown, swallow (up).

2667. καταπίπτω katapiptō, *kat-ap-ip'-to*; from *2596* and *4098*; to *fall down*:—fall (down).

2668. καταπλέω kataplĕō, *kat-ap-leh'-o*; from *2596* and *4126*; to *sail down* upon a place, i.e. to *land* at:—arrive.

2669. καταπονέω katapŏnĕō, *kat-ap-on-eh'-o*; from *2596* and a der. of *4192*; to *labor down*, i.e. *wear with toil* (fig. *harass*):—oppress, vex.

2670. καταποντίζω katapŏntizō, *kat-ap-on-tid'-zo*; from *2596* and a der. of the same as *4195*; to *plunge down*, i.e. *submerge*:—drown, sink.

2671. κατάρα katara, *kat-ar'-ah*; from *2596* (intens.) and *685*; *imprecation, execration*:—curse (-d, -ing).

2672. καταράομαι kataraŏmai, *kat-ar-ah'-om-ahee*; mid. from *2671*; to *execrate*; by anal. to *doom*:—curse.

2673. καταργέω katargĕō, *kat-arg-eh'-o*; from *2596* and *691*; to *be* (*render*) *entirely idle* (*useless*), lit. or fig.:—abolish, cease, cumber, deliver, destroy, do away, become (make) of no (none, without) effect, fail, loose, bring (come) to nought, put away (down), vanish away, make void.

2674. καταριθμέω katarithmĕō, *kat-ar-ith-meh'-o*; from *2596* and *705*; to *reckon among*:—number with.

2675. καταρτίζω katartizō, *kat-ar-tid'-zo*; from *2596* and a der. of *739*; to *complete thoroughly*, i.e. *repair* (lit. or fig.) or *adjust*:—fit, frame, mend, (make) perfect (-ly join together), prepare, restore.

2676. κατάρτισις katartisis, *kat-ar'-tis-is*; from *2675*; *thorough equipment* (subj.):—perfection.

2677. καταρτισμός katartismŏs, *kat-ar-tis-mos'*; from *2675*; *complete furnishing* (obj.):—perfecting.

2678. κατασείω katasĕiō, *kat-as-i'-o*; from *2596* and *4579*; to *sway downward*, i.e. *make a signal*:—beckon.

2679. κατασκάπτω kataskaptō, *kat-as-kap'-to*; from *2596* and *4626*; to *undermine*, i.e. (by impl.) *destroy*:—dig down, ruin.

2680. κατασκευάζω kataskĕuazō, *kat-ask-yoo-ad'-zo*; from *2596* and a der. of *4632*; to *prepare thoroughly* (prop. by external *equipment*; whereas *2090* refers rather to internal *fitness*); by impl. to *construct, create*:—build, make, ordain, prepare.

2681. κατασκηνόω kataskēnŏō, *kat-as-kay-nŏ'-o*; from *2596* and *4637*; to *camp down*, i.e. *haunt*; fig. to *remain*:—lodge, rest.

2682. κατασκήνωσις kataskēnōsis, *kat-as-kay'-no-sis*; from *2681*; an *encamping*, i.e. (fig.) a *perch*:—nest.

2683. κατασκιάζω kataskiazō, *kat-as-kee-ad'-zo*; from *2596* and a der. of *4639*; to *overshade*, i.e. *cover*:—shadow.

2684. **κατασκοπέω kataskŏpĕō**, *kat-as-kop-eh'-o*; from *2685*; to *be a sentinel*, i.e. to *inspect insidiously*:—spy out.

2685. **κατάσκοπος kataskŏpŏs**, *kat-as'-kop-os*; from *2596* (intens.) and *4649* (in the sense of a *watcher*); a *reconnoiterer*:—spy.

2686. **κατασοφίζομαι katasŏphizŏmai**, *kat-as-of-id'-zom-ahee*; mid. from *2596* and *4679*; to *be crafty against*, i.e. *circumvent*:—deal subtilly with.

2687. **καταστέλλω katastĕllō**, *kat-as-tel'-lo*; from *2596* and *4724*; to *put down*, i.e. *quell*:—appease, quiet.

2688. **κατάστημα katastēma**, *kat-as'-tay-mah*; from *2525*; prop. a *position* or *condition*, i.e. (subj.) *demeanor*:—behaviour.

2689. **καταστολή katastŏlē**, *kat-as-tol-ay'*; from *2687*; a *deposit*, i.e. (spec.) *costume*:—apparel.

2690. **καταστρέφω katastrĕphō**, *kat-as-tref'-o*; from *2596* and *4762*; to *turn upside down*, i.e. *upset*:—overthrow.

2691. **καταστρηνιάω katastrēniaō**, *kat-as-tray-nee-ah'-o*; from *2596* and *4763*; to *become voluptuous against*:—begin to wax wanton against.

2692. **καταστροφή katastrŏphē**, *kat-as-trof-ay'*; from *2690*; an *overturn* ("*catastrophe*"), i.e. *demolition*; fig. *apostasy*:—overthrow, subverting.

2693. **καταστρώννυμι katastrōnnumi**, *kat-as-trone'-noo-mee*; from *2596* and *4766*; to *strew down*, i.e. (by impl.) to *prostrate* (*slay*):—overthrow.

2694. **κατασύρω katasurō**, *kat-as-oo'-ro*; from *2596* and *4951*; to *drag down*, i.e. *arrest* judicially:—hale.

2695. **κατασφάττω katasphattō**, *kat-as-fat'-to*; from *2596* and *4969*; to *kill down*, i.e. *slaughter*:—slay.

2696. **κατασφραγίζω katasphragizō**, *kat-as-frag-id'-zo*; from *2596* and *4972*; to *seal closely*:—seal.

2697. **κατάσχεσις kataschĕsis**, *kat-as'-khes-is*; from *2722*; a *holding down*, i.e. *occupancy*:—possession.

2698. **κατατίθημι katatithēmi**, *kat-at-ith'-ay-mee*; from *2596* and *5087*; to *place down*, i.e. *deposit* (lit. or fig.):—do, lay, shew.

2699. **κατατομή katatŏmē**, *kat-at-om-ay'*; from a comp. of *2596* and **τέμνω tĕmnō** (to *cut*); a *cutting down* (*off*), i.e. *mutilation* (ironically):—concision. Comp. *609*.

2700. **κατατοξεύω katatŏxĕuō**, *kat-at-ox-yoo'-o*; from *2596* and a der. of *5115*; to *shoot down* with an arrow or other missile:—thrust through.

2701. **κατατρέχω katatrĕchō**, *kat-at-rekh'-o*; from *2596* and *5143*; to *run down*, i.e. *hasten* from a tower:—run down.

καταφάγω kataphagō. See *2719*.

2702. **καταφέρω kataphĕrō**, *kat-af-er'-o*; from *2596* and *5342* (includ. its alt.); to *bear down*, i.e. (fig.) *overcome* (with drowsiness); spec. to *cast* a vote:—fall, give, sink down.

2703. **καταφεύγω kataphĕugō**, *kat-af-yoo'-go*; from *2596* and *5343*; to *flee down* (*away*):—flee.

2704. **καταφθείρω kataphthĕirō**, *kat-af-thi'-ro*; from *2596* and *5351*; to *spoil entirely*, i.e. (lit.) to *destroy*; or (fig.) to *deprave*:—corrupt, utterly perish.

2705. **καταφιλέω kataphilĕō**, *kat-af-ee-leh'-o*; from *2596* and *5368*; to *kiss earnestly*:—kiss.

2706. **καταφρονέω kataphrŏnĕō**, *kat-af-ron-eh'-o*; from *2596* and *5426*; to *think against*, i.e. *disesteem*:—despise.

2707. **καταφροντής kataphrŏntēs**, *kat-af-ron-tace'*; from *2706*; a *contemner*:—despiser.

2708. **καταχέω katachĕō**, *kat-akh-eh'-o*; from *2596* and **χέω chĕō** (to *pour*); to *pour down* (*out*):—pour.

2709. **καταχθόνιος katachthŏniŏs**, *kat-akh-thon'-ee-os*; from *2596* and **χθών chthōn** (the *ground*); *subterranean*, i.e. *infernal* (belonging to the world of departed spirits):—under the earth.

2710. **καταχράομαι katachraŏmai**, *kat-akh-rah'-om-ahee*; from *2596* and *5530*; to *overuse*, i.e. *misuse*:—abuse.

2711. **καταψύχω katapsuchō**, *kat-ap-soo'-kho*; from *2596* and *5594*; to *cool down* (*off*), i.e. *refresh*:—cool.

2712. **κατείδωλος katĕidōlŏs**, *kat-i'-do-los*; from *2596* (intens.) and *1497*; *utterly idolatrous*:—wholly given to idolatry.

κατελεύθω katĕlĕuthō. See *2718*.

2713. **κατέναντι katĕnanti**, *kat-en'-an-tee*; from *2596* and *1725*; *directly opposite*:—before, over against.

κατενέγκω katĕnĕgkō. See *2702*.

2714. **κατενώπιον katĕnōpiŏn**, *kat-en-o'-pee-on*; from *2596* and *1799*; *directly in front of*:—before (the presence of), in the sight of.

2715. **κατεξουσιάζω katĕxŏusiazō**, *kat-ex-oo-see-ad'-zo*; from *2596* and *1850*; to *have* (*wield*) *full privilege over*:—exercise authority.

2716. **κατεργάζομαι katĕrgazŏmai**, *kat-er-gad'-zom-ahee*; from *2596* and *2038*; to *work fully*, i.e. *accomplish*; by impl. to *finish*, *fashion*:—cause, do (deed), perform, work (out).

2718. **κατέρχομαι katĕrchŏmai**, *kat-er'-khom-ahee*; from *2596* and *2064* (includ. its alt.); to *come* (or *go*) *down* (lit. or fig.):—come (down), depart, descend, go down, land.

2719. **κατεσθίω katĕsthiō**, *kat-es-thee'-o*; from *2596* and *2068* (includ. its alt.); to *eat down*, i.e. *devour* (lit. or fig.):—devour.

2720. **κατευθύνω katĕuthunō**, *kat-yoo-thoo'-no*; from *2596* and *2116*; to *straighten fully*, i.e. (fig.) *direct*:—guide, direct.

2721. **κατεφίστημι katĕphistēmi**, *kat-ef-is'-tay-mee*; from *2596* and *2186*; to *stand over against*, i.e. *rush upon* (*assault*):—make insurrection against.

2722. **κατέχω katĕchō**, *kat-ekh'-o*; from *2596* and *2192*; to *hold down* (*fast*), in various applications (lit. or fig.):—have, hold (fast), keep (in memory), let, × make toward, possess, retain, seize on, stay, take, withhold.

2723. **κατηγορέω katēgŏrĕō**, *kat-ay-gor-eh'-o*; from *2725*; to *be a plaintiff*, i.e. to *charge* with some offence:—accuse, object.

2724. **κατηγορία katēgŏria**, *kat-ay-gor-ee'-ah*; from *2725*; a *complaint* ("category"), i.e. criminal *charge*:—accusation (× -ed).

2725. **κατήγορος katēgŏrŏs**, *kat-ay'-gor-os*; from *2596* and *58*; *against* one in the *assembly*, i.e. a *complainant* at law; spec. *Satan*:—accuser.

2726. **κατήφεια katēphĕia**, *kat-ay'-fi-ah*; from a comp. of *2596* and perh. a der. of the base of *5316* (mean. *downcast* in look); *demureness*, i.e. (by impl.) *sadness*:—heaviness.

2727. **κατηχέω katēchĕō**, *kat-ay-kheh'-o*; from *2596* and *2279*; to *sound down* into the ears, i.e. (by impl.) to *indoctrinate* ("*catechize*") or (gen.) to *apprise of*:—inform, instruct, teach.

2728. **κατιόω katiŏō**, *kat-ee-ŏ'-o*; from *2596* and a der. of *2447*; to *rust down*, i.e. *corrode*:—canker.

2729. **κατισχύω katischuō**, *kat-is-khoo'-o*; from *2596* and *2480*; to *overpower*:—prevail (against).

2730. **κατοικέω katŏikĕō**, *kat-oy-keh'-o*; from *2596* and *3611*; to *house permanently*, i.e. *reside* (lit. or fig.):—dwell (-er), inhabitant (-ter).

2731. **κατοίκησις katŏikēsis**, *kat-oy'-kay-sis*; from *2730*; *residence* (prop. the act; but by impl. concr. the mansion):—dwelling.

2732. **κατοικητήριον katŏikētēriŏn**, *kat-oy-kay-tay'-ree-on*; from a der. of *2730*; a *dwelling-place*:—habitation.

2733. **κατοικία katŏikia**, *kat-oy-kee'-ah*; *residence* (prop. the condition; but by impl. the abode itself):—habitation.

2734. **κατοπτρίζομαι katŏptrizŏmai**, *kat-op-trid'-zom-ahee*; mid. from a comp. of *2596* and a der. of *3700* [comp. *2072*]; to *mirror oneself*, i.e. to *see reflected* (fig.):—behold as in a glass.

2735. **κατόρθωμα katŏrthōma**, *kat-or'-tho-mah*; from a comp. of *2596* and a der. of *3717* [comp. *1357*]; something *made fully upright*, i.e. (fig.) *rectification* (spec. *good* public *administration*):—very worthy deed.

2736. **κάτω katō**, *kat'-o*; also (comp.)

κατωτέρω katōtĕrō, *kat-o-ter'-o* [comp. *2737*]; adv. from *2596*; *downwards*:—beneath, bottom, down, under.

2737. **κατώτερος katōtĕrŏs**, *kat-o'-ter-os*; comp. from *2736*; *inferior* (locally, of Hades):—lower.

2738. **καῦμα kauma**, *kŏw'-mah*; from *2545*; prop. a *burn* (concr.), but used (abstr.) of a *glow*:—heat.

2739. **καυματίζω kaumatizō**, *kŏw-mat-id'-zo*; from *2738*; to *burn*:—scorch.

2740. **καῦσις kausis**, *kŏw'-sis*; from *2545*; *burning* (the act):—be burned.

2741. **καυσόω kausŏō**, *kŏw-sŏ'-o*; from *2740*; to *set on fire*:—with fervent heat.

2742. **καύσων kausōn**, *kŏw'-sone*; from *2741*; a *glare*:—(burning) heat.

2743. **καυτηριάζω kautēriazō**, *kŏw-tay-ree-ad'-zo*; from a der. of *2545*; to *brand* ("*cauterize*"), i.e. (by impl.) to *render unsensitive* (fig.):—sear with a hot iron.

2744. **καυχάομαι kauchaŏmai**, *kŏw-khah'-om-ahee*; from some (obsol.) base akin to that of **αὐχέω auchĕō** (to *boast*) and *2172*; to *vaunt* (in a good or a bad sense):—(make) boast, glory, joy, rejoice.

2745. **καύχημα kauchēma**, *kŏw'-khay-mah*; from *2744*; a *boast* (prop. the object; by impl. the act) in a good or a bad sense:—boasting, (whereof) to glory (of), glorying, rejoice (-ing).

2746. **καύχησις kauchēsis**, *kŏw'-khay-sis*; from *2744*; *boasting* (prop. the act; by impl. the object), in a good or a bad sense:—boasting, whereof I may glory, glorying, rejoicing.

2747. **Κεγχρεαί Kĕgchrĕai**, *keng-khreh-a'hee*; prob. from **κέγχρος kĕgchrŏs** (*millet*); *Cenchreæ*, a port of Corinth:—Cenchrea.

2748. **Κεδρών Kĕdrōn**, *ked-rone'*; of Heb. or. [6939]; *Cedron* (i.e. *Kidron*), a brook near Jerus.:—Cedron.

2749. **κεῖμαι kĕimai**, *ki'-mahee*; mid. of a prim. verb; to *lie* outstretched (lit. or fig.):—be (appointed, laid up, made, set), lay, lie. Comp. *5087*.

2750. **κειρία kĕiria**, *ki-ree'-ah*; of uncert. affin.; a *swathe*, i.e. *winding-sheet*:—graveclothes.

2751. **κείρω kĕirō**, *ki'-ro*; a prim. verb; to *shear*:—shear (-er).

2752. **κέλευμα kĕlĕuma**, *kel'-yoo-mah*; from *2753*; a *cry* of incitement:—shout.

2753. **κελεύω kĕlĕuō**, *kel-yoo'-o*; from a prim. **κέλλω kĕllō** (to *urge* on); "hail"; to *incite* by word, i.e. *order*:—bid, (at, give) command (-ment).

2754. **κενοδοξία kĕnŏdŏxia**, *ken-od-ox-ee'-ah*; from *2755*; *empty glorying*, i.e. *self-conceit*:—vain-glory.

2755. **κενόδοξος kĕnŏdŏxŏs**, *ken-od'-ox-os*; from *2756* and *1391*; *vainly glorifying*, i.e. *self-conceited*:—desirous of vain-glory.

2756. **κενός kĕnŏs**, *ken-os'*; appar. a prim. word; *empty* (lit. or fig.):—empty, (in) vain.

2757. **κενοφωνία kĕnŏphōnia**, *ken-of-o-nee'-ah*; from a presumed comp. of *2756* and *5456*; *empty sounding*, i.e. *fruitless discussion*:—vain.

2758. **κενόω kĕnŏō**, *ken-ŏ'-o*; from *2756*; to *make empty*, i.e. (fig.) to *abase*, *neutralize*, *falsify*:—make (of none effect, of no reputation, void), be in vain.

2759. **κέντρον kĕntrŏn**, *ken'-tron*; from **κεντέω kĕntĕō** (to *prick*); a *point* ("*centre*"), i.e. a *sting* (fig. *poison*) or *goad* (fig. divine *impulse*):—prick, sting.

2760. **κεντυρίων kĕnturiōn**, *ken-too-ree'-ohn*; of Lat. or.; a *centurion*, i.e. *captain* of one hundred soldiers:—centurion.

2761. **κενῶς kĕnōs**, *ken-oce'*; adv. from *2756*; *vainly*, i.e. *to no purpose*:—in vain.

2762. **κεραία kĕraia**, *ker-ah'-yah*; fem. of a presumed der. of the base of *2768*; something *horn-like*, i.e. (spec.) the *apex* of a Heb. letter (fig. the least *particle*):—tittle.

2763. **κεραμεύς kĕramĕus**, *ker-am-yooce'*; from *2766*; a *potter*:—potter.

2764. κεραμικός **kĕramikŏs**, *ker-am-ik-os'*; from 2766; *made of clay*, i.e. *earthen*:—of a potter.

2765. κεράμιον **kĕramiŏn**, *ker-am'-ee-on*; neut. of a presumed der. of 2766; an *earthenware* vessel, i.e. *jar*:—pitcher.

2766. κέραμος **kĕramŏs**, *ker'-am-os*; prob. from the base of 2767 (through the idea of *mixing* clay and water); *earthenware*, i.e. a *tile* (by anal. a thin *roof* or *awning*):—tiling.

2767. κεράννυμι **kĕrannumi**, *ker-an'-noo-mee*; a prol. form of a more prim. κεράω **kĕraō**, *ker-ah'-o* (which is used in certain tenses); to *mingle*, i.e. (by impl.) to *pour* out (for drinking):—fill, pour out. Comp. 3396.

2768. κέρας **kĕras**, *ker'-as*; from a prim. κάρ **kar** (the *hair* of the head); a *horn* (lit. or fig.):—horn.

2769. κεράτιον **kĕratiŏn**, *ker-at'-ee-on*; neut. of a presumed der. of 2768; something *horned*, i.e. (spec.) the *pod* of the carob-tree:—husk.

κεράω **kĕraō**. See 2767.

2770. κερδαίνω **kĕrdainō**, *ker-dah'ee-no*; from 2771; to *gain* (lit. or fig.):—(get) gain, win.

2771. κέρδος **kĕrdŏs**, *ker'-dos*; of uncert. affin.; *gain* (pecuniary or gen.):—gain, lucre.

2772. κέρμα **kĕrma**, *ker'-mah*; from 2751; a *clipping* (*bit*), i.e. (spec.) a *coin*:—money.

2773. κερματιστής **kĕrmatistēs**, *ker-mat-is-tace'*; from a der. of 2772; a *handler of coins*, i.e. *money-broker*:—changer of money.

2774. κεφάλαιον **kĕphalaiŏn**, *kef-al'-ah-yon*; neut. of a der. of 2776; a *principal* thing, i.e. *main point*; spec. an *amount* (of money):—sum.

2775. κεφαλαιόω **kĕphalaiŏō**, *kef-al-ahee-ŏ'-o*; from the same as 2774; (spec.) to *strike on the head*:—wound in the head.

2776. κεφαλή **kĕphalē**, *kef-al-ay'*; prob. from the prim. κάπτω **kaptō** (in the sense of *seizing*); the *head* (as the part most readily *taken* hold of), lit. or fig.:—head.

2777. κεφαλίς **kĕphalis**, *kef-al-is'*; from 2776; prop. a *knob*, i.e. (by impl.) a *roll* (by extens. from the *end* of a stick on which the MS. was rolled):—volume.

2778. κῆνσος **kēnsŏs**, *kane'-sos*; of Lat. or.; prop. an *enrolment* ("*census*"), i.e. (by impl.) a *tax*:—tribute.

2779. κῆπος **kēpŏs**, *kay'-pos*; of uncert. affin.; a *garden*:—garden.

2780. κηπουρός **kēpŏurŏs**, *kay-poo-ros'*; from 2779 and οὖρος **ŏurŏs** (a *warden*); a *garden-keeper*, i.e. *gardener*:—gardener.

2781. κηρίον **kēriŏn**, *kay-ree'-on*; dimin. from κηός **kēŏs** (*wax*); a *cell* for honey, i.e. (collect.) the *comb*:—[honey-] comb.

2782. κήρυγμα **kērugma**, *kay'-roog-mah*; from 2784; a *proclamation* (espec. of the gospel; by impl. the *gospel* itself):—preaching.

2783. κῆρυξ **kērux**, *kay'-roox*; from 2784; a *herald*, i.e. of divine truth (espec. of the gospel):—preacher.

2784. κηρύσσω **kērussō**, *kay-roos'-so*; of uncert. affin.; to *herald* (as a public *crier*), espec. divine truth (the gospel):—preach (-er), proclaim, publish.

2785. κῆτος **kētŏs**, *kay'-tos*; prob. from the base of 5490; a huge *fish* (as *gaping* for prey):—whale.

2786. Κηφᾶς **Kēphas**, *kay-fas'*; of Chald. or. [comp. 3710]; *the Rock*; *Cephas* (i.e. *Kepha*), a surname of Peter:—Cephas.

2787. κιβωτός **kibōtŏs**, *kib-o-tos'*; of uncert. der.; a *box*, i.e. the sacred *ark* and that of Noah:—ark.

2788. κιθάρα **kithara**, *kith-ar'-ah*; of uncert. affin.; a *lyre*:—harp.

2789. κιθαρίζω **kitharizō**, *kith-ar-id'-zo*; from 2788; to *play on a lyre*:—harp.

2790. κιθαρῳδός **kitharōidŏs**, *kith-ar-o'-dos*; from 2788 and a der. of the same as 5603; a *lyre-singer* (*-player*), i.e. *harpist*:—harper.

2791. Κιλικία **Kilikia**, *kil-ik-ee'-ah*; prob. of for. or.; *Cilicia*, a region of Asia Minor:—Cilicia.

2792. κινάμωμον **kinamōmŏn**, *kin-am'-o-mon*; of for. or. [comp. 7076]; *cinnamon*:—cinnamon.

2793. κινδυνεύω **kindunĕuō**, *kin-doon-yoo'-o*; from 2794; to *undergo peril*:—be in danger, be (stand) in jeopardy.

2794. κίνδυνος **kindunŏs**, *kin'-doo-nos*; of uncert. der.; *danger*:—peril.

2795. κινέω **kinĕō**, *kin-eh'-o*; from κίω **kiō** (poetic for εἶμι **ĕimi**, to *go*); to *stir* (trans.), lit. or fig.:—(re-) move (-r), way.

2796. κίνησις **kinēsis**, *kin'-ay-sis*; from 2795; a *stirring*:—moving.

2797. Κίς **Kis**, *kis*; of Heb. or. [7027]; *Cis* (i.e. *Kish*), an Isr.:—Cis.

κίχρημι **kichrēmi**. See 5531.

2798. κλάδος **kladŏs**, *klad'-os*; from 2806; a *twig* or *bough* (as if broken off):—branch.

2799. κλαίω **klaiō**, *klah'-yo*; of uncert. affin.; to *sob*, i.e. *wail* aloud (whereas 1145 is rather to *cry* silently):—bewail, weep.

2800. κλάσις **klasis**, *klas'-is*; from 2806; *fracture* (the act):—breaking.

2801. κλάσμα **klasma**, *klas'-mah*; from 2806; a *piece* (*bit*):—broken, fragment.

2802. Κλαύδη **Klaudē**, *klŏw'-day*; of uncert. der.; *Claude*, an island near Crete:—Clauda.

2803. Κλαυδία **Klaudia**, *klŏw-dee'-ah*; fem. of 2804; *Claudia*, a Chr. woman:—Claudia.

2804. Κλαύδιος **Klaudiŏs**, *klŏw'-dee-os*; of Lat. or.; *Claudius*, the name of two Romans:—Claudius.

2805. κλαυθμός **klauthmŏs**, *klŏwth-mos'*; from 2799; *lamentation*:—wailing, weeping, × wept.

2806. κλάω **klaō**, *klah'-o*; a prim. verb; to *break* (spec. of bread):—break.

2807. κλείς **klĕis**, *klice*; from 2808; a *key* (as *shutting* a lock), lit. or fig.:—key.

2808. κλείω **klĕiō**, *kli'-o*; a prim. verb; to *close* (lit. or fig.):—shut (up).

2809. κλέμμα **klĕmma**, *klem'-mah*; from 2813; *stealing* (prop. the thing stolen, but used of the act):—theft.

2810. Κλεόπας **Klĕŏpas**, *kleh-op'-as*; prob. contr. from Κλεόπατρος **Klĕŏpatrŏs** (comp. of 2811 and 3962); *Cleopas*, a Chr.:—Cleopas.

2811. κλέος **klĕŏs**, *kleh'-os*; from a shorter form of 2564; *renown* (as if *being called*):—glory.

2812. κλέπτης **klĕptēs**, *klep'-tace*; from 2813; a *stealer* (lit. or fig.):—thief. Comp. 3027.

2813. κλέπτω **klĕptō**, *klep'-to*; a prim. verb; to *filch*:—steal.

2814. κλῆμα **klēma**, *klay'-mah*; from 2806; a *limb* or *shoot* (as if *broken* off):—branch.

2815. Κλήμης **Klēmēs**, *klay'-mace*; of Lat. or.; *merciful*; *Clemes* (i.e. *Clemens*), a Chr.:—Clement.

2816. κληρονομέω **klērŏnŏmĕō**, *klay-ron-om-eh'-o*; from 2818; to *be an heir* to (lit. or fig.):—be heir, (obtain by) inherit (-ance).

2817. κληρονομία **klērŏnŏmia**, *klay-ron-om-ee'-ah*; from 2818; *heirship*, i.e. (concr.) a *patrimony* or (gen.) a *possession*:—inheritance.

2818. κληρονόμος **klērŏnŏmŏs**, *klay-ron-om'-os*; from 2819 and the base of 3551 (in its orig. sense of *partitioning*, i.e. [reflex.] *getting* by apportionment); a *sharer by lot*, i.e. an *inheritor* (lit. or fig.); by impl. a *possessor*:—heir.

2819. κλῆρος **klērŏs**, *klay'-ros*; prob. from 2806 (through the idea of using *bits* of wood, etc., for the purpose); a *die* (for drawing chances); by impl. a *portion* (as if so secured); by extens. an *acquisition* (espec. a *patrimony*, fig.):—heritage, inheritance, lot, part.

2820. κληρόω **klērŏō**, *klay-rŏ'-o*; from 2819; to *allot*, i.e. (fig.) to *assign* (a privilege):—obtain an inheritance.

2821. κλῆσις **klēsis**, *klay'-sis*; from a shorter form of 2564; an *invitation* (fig.):—calling.

2822. κλητός **klētŏs**, *klay-tos'*; from the same as 2821; *invited*, i.e. *appointed*, or (spec.) a *saint*:—called.

2823. κλίβανος **klibanŏs**, *klib'-an-os*; of uncert. der.; an earthen *pot* used for baking in:—oven.

2824. κλίμα **klima**, *klee'-mah*; from 2827; a *slope*, i.e. (spec.) a "*clime*" or *tract* of country:—part, region.

2825. κλίνη **klinē**, *klee'-nay*; from 2827; a *couch* (for sleep, sickness, sitting or eating):—bed, table.

2826. κλινίδιον **klinidiŏn**, *klin-id'-ee-on*; neut. of a presumed der. of 2825; a *pallet* or *little couch*:—bed.

2827. κλίνω **klinō**, *klee'-no*; a prim. verb; to *slant* or *slope*, i.e. *incline* or *recline* (lit. or fig.):—bow (down), be far spent, lay, turn to flight, wear away.

2828. κλισία **klisia**, *klee-see'-ah*; from a der. of 2827; prop. *reclination*, i.e. (concr. and spec.) a *party* at a meal:—company.

2829. κλοπή **klŏpē**, *klop-ay'*; from 2813; *stealing*:—theft.

2830. κλύδων **kludōn**, *kloo'-dohn*; from κλύζω **kluzō** (to *billow* or *dash* over); a *surge* of the sea (lit. or fig.):—raging, wave.

2831. κλυδωνίζομαι **kludōnizŏmai**, *kloo-do-nid'-zom-ahee*; mid. from 2830; to *surge*, i.e. (fig.) to *fluctuate*:—toss to and fro.

2832. Κλωπᾶς **Klōpas**, *klo-pas'*; of Chald. or. (corresp. to 256); *Clopas*, an Isr.:—Clopas.

2833. κνήθω **knēthō**, *knay'-tho*; from a prim. κνάω **knaō** (to *scrape*); to *scratch*, i.e. (by impl.) to *tickle*:— × itching.

2834. Κνίδος **Knidŏs**, *knee'-dos*; prob. of for. or.; *Cnidus*, a place in Asia Minor:—Cnidus.

2835. κοδράντης **kŏdrantēs**, *kod-ran'-tace*; of Lat. or.; a *quadrans*, i.e. the fourth part of an as:—farthing.

2836. κοιλία **kŏilia**, *koy-lee'-ah*; from κοῖλος **kŏilŏs** ("*hollow*"); a *cavity*, i.e. (spec.) the *abdomen*; by impl. the *matrix*; fig. the *heart*:—belly, womb.

2837. κοιμάω **kŏimaō**, *koy-mah'-o*; from 2749; to *put to sleep*, i.e. (pass. or reflex.) to *slumber*; fig. to *decease*:—(be a-, fall a-, fall on) sleep, be dead.

2838. κοίμησις **kŏimēsis**, *koy'-may-sis*; from 2837; *sleeping*, i.e. (by impl.) *repose*:—taking of rest.

2839. κοινός **kŏinŏs**, *koy-nos'*; prob. from 4862; *common*, i.e. (lit.) shared by all or several, or (cer.) *profane*:—common, defiled, unclean, unholy.

2840. κοινόω **kŏinŏō**, *koy-nŏ'-o*; from 2839; to *make* (or *consider*) *profane* (cer.):—call common, defile, pollute, unclean.

2841. κοινωνέω **kŏinōnĕō**, *koy-no-neh'-o*; from 2844; to *share* with others (obj. or subj.):—communicate, distribute, be partaker.

2842. κοινωνία **kŏinōnia**, *koy-nohn-ee'-ah*; from 2844; *partnership*, i.e. (lit.) *participation*, or (social) *intercourse*, or (pecuniary) *benefaction*:—(to) communicate (-ation), communion, (contri-) distribution, fellowship.

2843. κοινωνικός **kŏinōnikŏs**, *koy-no-nee-kos'*; from 2844; *communicative*, i.e. (pecuniarily) *liberal*:—willing to communicate.

2844. κοινωνός **kŏinōnŏs**, *koy-no-nos'*; from 2839; a *sharer*, i.e. *associate*:—companion, × fellowship, partaker, partner.

2845. κοίτη **kŏitē**, *koy'-tay*; from 2749; a *couch*; by extens. *cohabitation*; by impl. the male *sperm*:—bed, chambering, × conceive.

2846. κοιτών **kŏitōn**, *koy-tone'*; from 2845; a *bedroom*:— + chamberlain.

2847. κόκκινος **kŏkkinŏs**, *kok'-kee-nos*; from 2848 (from the *kernel*-shape of the insect); *crimson-colored*:—scarlet (colour, coloured).

2848. κόκκος **kŏkkŏs**, *kok'-kos*; appar. a prim. word; a *kernel* of seed:—corn, grain.

2849. κολάζω **kŏlazō**, *kol-ad'-zo*; from κόλος **kŏlŏs** (*dwarf*); prop. to *curtail*, i.e. (fig.) to *chastise* (or *reserve* for infliction).—punish.

2850. **κολακεία kŏlakĕia**, *kol-ak-i'-ah;* from a der. of **κόλαξ kŏlax** (a *fawner*); *flattery:*— × flattering.

2851. **κόλασις kŏlasis**, *kol'-as-is;* from 2849; penal *infliction:*—punishment, torment.

2852. **κολαφίζω kŏlaphizō**, *kol-af-id'-zo;* from a der. of the base of 2849; to *rap* with the fist:—buffet.

2853. **κολλάω kŏllaō**, *kol-lah'-o;* from **κόλλα kŏlla** ("*glue*"); to *glue*, i.e. (pass. or reflex.) to *stick* (fig.):—cleave, join (self), keep company.

2854. **κολλούριον kŏllŏuriŏn**, *kol-loo'-ree-on;* neut. of a presumed der. of **κολλύρα kŏllura** (a *cake;* prob. akin to the base of 2853); prop. a *poultice* (as made of or in the form of *crackers*), i.e. (by anal.) a *plaster:*—eyesalve.

2855. **κολλυβιστής kŏllubistēs**, *kol-loo-bis-tace';* from a presumed der. of **κόλλυβος kŏllubŏs** (a small *coin;* prob. akin to 2854); a *coin-dealer:*—(money-) changer.

2856. **κολοβόω kŏlŏbŏō**, *kol-ob-ŏ'-o;* from a der. of the base of 2849; to *dock*, i.e. (fig.) *abridge:*—shorten.

2857. **Κολοσσαί Kŏlŏssai**, *kol-os-sah'ee;* appar. fem. plur. of **κολοσσός kŏlŏssŏs** ("*colossal*"); *Colossæ*, a place in Asia Minor:—Colosse.

2858. **Κολοσσαεύς Kŏlŏssaĕus**, *kol-os-sayoos';* fr. 2857; a *Colossæan*, i.e. inh. of Colossæ:—Colossian.

2859. **κόλπος kŏlpŏs**, *kol'-pos;* appar. a prim. word; the *bosom;* by anal. a *bay:*—bosom, creek.

2860. **κολυμβάω kŏlumbaō**, *kol-oom-bah'-o;* from **κόλυμβος kŏlumbŏs** (a *diver*); to *plunge* into water:—swim.

2861. **κολυμβήθρα kŏlumbēthra**, *kol-oom-bay'-thrah;* from 2860; a *diving-place*, i.e. *pond* for bathing (or swimming):—pool.

2862. **κολωνία kŏlōnia**, *kol-o-nee'-ah;* of Lat. or.; a Roman "*colony*" for veterans:—colony.

2863. **κομάω kŏmaō**, *kom-ah'-o;* from 2864; to *wear tresses* of hair:—have long hair.

2864. **κόμη kŏmē**, *kom'-ay;* appar. from the same as 2865; the *hair* of the head (*locks*, as *ornamental*, and thus differing from 2359, which prop. denotes merely the *scalp*):—hair.

2865. **κομίζω kŏmizō**, *kom-id'-zo;* from a prim. **κομέω kŏmĕō** (to *tend*, i.e. take care of); prop. to *provide* for, i.e. (by impl.) to *carry* off (as if from harm; gen. *obtain*):—bring, receive.

2866. **κομψότερον kŏmpsŏtĕrŏn**, *komp-sot'-er-on;* neut. compar. of a der. of the base of 2865 (mean. prop. *well dressed*, i.e. *nice*); fig. *convalescent:*— + began to amend.

2867. **κονιάω kŏniaō**, *kon-ee-ah'-o;* from **κονία kŏnia** (*dust;* by anal. *lime*); to *whitewash:*—whiten.

2868. **κονιορτός kŏniŏrtŏs**, *kon-ee-or-tos';* from the base of 2867 and **ὄρνυμι ŏrnumi** (to "*rouse*"); *pulverulence* (as *blown* about):—dust.

2869. **κοπάζω kŏpazō**, *kop-ad'-zo;* from 2873; to *tire*, i.e. (fig.) to *relax:*—cease.

2870. **κοπετός kŏpĕtŏs**, *kop-et-os';* from 2875; *mourning* (prop. by *beating* the breast):—lamentation.

2871. **κοπή kŏpē**, *kop-ay';* from 2875; *cutting*, i.e. *carnage:*—slaughter.

2872. **κοπιάω kŏpiaō**, *kop-ee-ah'-o;* from a der. of 2873; to *feel fatigue;* by impl. to *work hard:*—(bestow) labour, toil, be wearied.

2873. **κόπος kŏpŏs**, *kop'-os;* from 2875; a *cut*, i.e. (by anal.) *toil* (as *reducing* the strength), lit. or fig.; by impl. *pains:*—labour, + trouble, weariness.

2874. **κοπρία kŏpria**, *kop-ree'-ah;* from **κόπρος kŏprŏs** (*ordure;* perh. akin to 2875); *manure:*—dung (-hill).

2875. **κόπτω kŏptō**, *kop'-to;* a prim. verb; to "*chop*"; spec. to *beat* the breast in grief:—cut down, lament, mourn, (be-) wail. Comp. the base of 5114.

2876. **κόραξ kŏrax**, *kor'-ax;* perh. from 2880; a *crow* (from its *voracity*):—raven.

2877. **κοράσιον kŏrasiŏn**, *kor-as'-ee-on*, neut. of a presumed der. of **κόρη kŏrē** (a *maiden*); a (little) *girl:*—damsel, maid.

2878. **κορβᾶν kŏrban**, *kor-ban';* and **κορβανᾶς kŏrbanas**, *kor-ban-as';* of Heb. and Chald. or. respectively [7133]; a votive *offering* and *the offering;* a *consecrated present* (to the Temple fund); by extens. (the latter term) the *Treasury* itself, i.e. the room where the contribution boxes stood:—Corban, treasury.

2879. **Κορέ Kŏrĕ**, *kor-eh';* of Heb. or. [7141]; *Corè* (i.e. *Korach*), an Isr.:—Core.

2880. **κορέννυμι kŏrĕnnumi**, *kor-en'-noo-mee;* a prim. verb; to *cram*, i.e. *glut* or *sate:*—eat enough, full.

2881. **Κορίνθιος Kŏrinthiŏs**, *kor-in'-thee-os;* from 2882; a *Corinthian*, i.e. inhab. of Corinth:—Corinthian.

2882. **Κόρινθος Kŏrinthŏs**, *kor'-in-thos;* of uncert. der.; *Corinthus*, a city of Greece:—Corinth.

2883. **Κορνήλιος Kŏrnēliŏs**, *kor-nay'-lee-os;* of Lat. or.; *Cornelius*, a Roman:—Cornelius.

2884. **κόρος kŏrŏs**, *kor'-os;* of Heb. or. [3734]; a *cor*, i.e. a specific measure:—measure.

2885. **κοσμέω kŏsmĕō**, *kos-meh'-o;* from 2889; to *put in* proper *order*, i.e. *decorate* (lit. or fig.); spec. to *snuff* (a wick):—adorn, garnish, trim.

2886. **κοσμικός kŏsmikŏs**, *kos-mee-kos';* from 2889 (in its secondary sense); *terrene* ("*cosmic*"), lit. (*mundane*) or fig. (*corrupt*):—worldly.

2887. **κόσμιος kŏsmiŏs**, *kos'-mee-os;* from 2889 (in its prim. sense); *orderly*, i.e. *decorous:*—of good behaviour, modest.

2888. **κοσμοκράτωρ kŏsmŏkratōr**, *kos-mok-rat'-ore;* from 2889 and 2902; a *world-ruler*, an epithet of Satan:—ruler.

2889. **κόσμος kŏsmŏs**, *kos'-mos;* prob. from the base of 2865; orderly *arrangement*, i.e. *decoration;* by impl. the *world* (in a wide or narrow sense, includ. its inhab., lit. or fig. [mor.]):—adorning, world.

2890. **Κούαρτος Kŏuartŏs**, *koo'-ar-tos;* of Lat. or. (*fourth*); *Quartus*, a Chr.:—Quartus.

2891. **κοῦμι kŏumi**, *koo'-mee;* of Chald. or. [6966]; *cumi* (i.e. *rise!*):—cumi.

2892. **κουστωδία kŏustōdia**, *koos-to-dee'-ah;* of Lat. or.; "*custody*", i.e. a Roman *sentry:*—watch.

2893. **κουφίζω kŏuphizō**, *koo-fid'-zo;* from **κοῦφος kŏuphŏs** (*light* in weight); to *unload:*—lighten.

2894. **κόφινος kŏphinŏs**, *kof'-ee-nos;* of uncert. der.; a (small) *basket:*—basket.

2895. **κράββατος krabbatŏs**, *krab'-bat-os;* prob. of for. or.; a *mattress:*—bed.

2896. **κράζω krazō**, *krad'-zo;* a prim. verb; prop. to "*croak*" (as a raven) or *scream*, i.e. (gen.) to *call* aloud (*shriek*, *exclaim*, *intreat*):—cry (out).

2897. **κραιπάλη kraipalē**, *krahee-pal'-ay;* prob. from the same as 726; prop. a *headache* (as a *seizure* of pain) from drunkenness, i.e. (by impl.) a *debauch* (by anal. a *glut*):—surfeiting.

2898. **κρανίον kraniŏn**, *kran-ee'-on;* dimin. of a der. of the base of 2768; a *skull* ("*cranium*"):—Calvary, skull.

2899. **κράσπεδον kraspĕdŏn**, *kras'-ped-on;* of uncert. der.; a *margin*, i.e. (spec.) a *fringe* or *tassel:*—border, hem.

2900. **κραταιός krataiŏs**, *krat-ah-yos';* from 2904; *powerful:*—mighty.

2901. **κραταιόω krataiŏō**, *krat-ah-yŏ'-o;* from 2900; to *empower*, i.e. (pass.) *increase in vigor:*—be strenghtened, be (wax) strong.

2902. **κρατέω kratĕō**, *krat-eh'-o;* from 2904; to *use strength*, i.e. *seize* or *retain* (lit. or fig.):—hold (by, fast), keep, lay hand (hold) on, obtain, retain, take (by).

2903. **κράτιστος kratistŏs**, *krat'-is-tos;* superl. of a der. of 2904; *strongest*, i.e. (in dignity) *very honorable:*—most excellent (noble).

2904. **κράτος kratŏs**, *krat'-os;* perh. a prim. word; *vigor* ["great"] (lit. or fig.):—dominion, might [-ily], power, strength.

2905. **κραυγάζω kraugazō**, *krŏw-gad'-zo;* from 2906; to *clamor:*—cry out.

2906. **κραυγή kraugē**, *krŏw-gay';* from 2896; an *outcry* (in notification, tumult or grief):—clamour, cry (-ing).

2907. **κρέας krĕas**, *kreh'-as;* perh. a prim. word; (butcher's) *meat:*—flesh.

2908. **κρεῖσσον krĕissŏn**, *krice'-son;* neut. of an alt. form of 2909; (as noun) *better*, i.e. *greater advantage:*—better.

2909. **κρείττων krĕittōn**, *krite'-tohn;* compar. of a der. of 2904; *stronger*, i.e. (fig.) *better*, i.e. *nobler:*—best, better.

2910. **κρεμάννυμι krĕmannumi**, *krem-an'-noo-mee;* a prol. form of a prim. verb; to *hang:*—hang.

2911. **κρημνός krēmnŏs**, *krame-nos';* from 2910; *overhanging*, i.e. a *precipice:*—steep place.

2912. **Κρής Krēs**, *krace;* from 2914; a *Cretan*, i.e. inhab. of Crete:—Crete, Cretian.

2913. **Κρήσκης Krēskēs**, *krace'-kace;* of Lat. or.; *growing; Cresces* (i.e. *Crescens*), a Chr.:—Crescens.

2914. **Κρήτη Krētē**, *kray'-tay;* of uncert. der.; *Cretè*, an island in the Mediterranean:—Crete.

2915. **κριθή krithē**, *kree-thay';* of uncert. der.; *barley:*—barley.

2916. **κρίθινος krithinŏs**, *kree'-thee-nos;* from 2915; consisting *of barley:*—barley.

2917. **κρίμα krima**, *kree'-mah;* from 2919; a *decision* (the function or the effect, for or against ["crime"]):—avenge, condemned, condemnation, damnation, + go to law, judgment.

2918. **κρίνον krinŏn**, *kree'-non;* perh. a prim. word; a *lily:*—lily.

2919. **κρίνω krinō**, *kree'-no;* prop. to *distinguish*, i.e. *decide* (mentally or judicially); by impl. to *try*, *condemn*, *punish:*—avenge, conclude, condemn, damn, decree, determine, esteem, judge, go to (sue at the) law, ordain, call in question, sentence to, think.

2920. **κρίσις krisis**, *kree'-sis;* *decision* (subj. or obj., for or against); by extens. a *tribunal;* by impl. *justice* (spec. divine *law*):—accusation, condemnation, damnation, judgment.

2921. **Κρίσπος Krispŏs**, *kris'-pos;* of Lat. or.; "*crisp*"; *Crispus*, a Corinthian:—Crispus.

2922. **κριτήριον kritēriŏn**, *kree-tay'-ree-on;* neut. of a presumed der. of 2923; a *rule* of judging ("*criterion*"), i.e. (by impl.) a *tribunal:*—to judge, judgment (seat).

2923. **κριτής kritēs**, *kree-tace';* from 2919; a *judge* (gen. or spec.):—judge.

2924. **κριτικός kritikŏs**, *krit-ee-kos';* from 2923; *decisive* ("*critical*"), i.e. *discriminative:*—discerner.

2925. **κρούω krŏuō**, *kroo'-o;* appar. a prim. verb; to *rap:*—knock.

2926. **κρυπτή kruptē**, *kroop-tay';* fem. of 2927; a *hidden* place, i.e. *cellar* ("*crypt*"):—secret.

2927. **κρυπτός kruptŏs**, *kroop-tos';* from 2928; *concealed*, i.e. *private:*—hid (-den), inward [-ly], secret.

2928. **κρύπτω kruptō**, *kroop'-to;* a prim. verb; to *conceal* (prop. by *covering*):—hide (self), keep secret, secret [-ly].

2929. **κρυσταλλίζω krustallizō**, *kroos-tal-lid'-zo;* from 2930; to *make* (i.e. intrans. *resemble*) *ice* ("crystallize"):—be clear as crystal.

2930. **κρύσταλλος krustallŏs**, *kroos'-tal-los;* from a der. of **κρύος kruŏs** (*frost*); *ice*, i.e. (by anal.) rock "*crystal*":—crystal.

2931. **κρυφῆ kruphē**, *kroo-fay';* adv. from 2928; *privately:*—in secret.

2932. **κτάομαι ktaŏmai**, *ktah'-om-ahee;* a prim. verb; to *get*, i.e. *acquire* (by any means; *own*):—obtain, possess, provide, purchase.

2933. κτῆμα **ktēma**, *ktay'-mah;* from *2932;* an *acquirement*, i.e. *estate:*—possession.

2934. κτῆνος **ktēnŏs**, *ktay'-nos;* from *2932; property*, i.e. (spec.) a domestic *animal:*—beast.

2935. κτήτωρ **ktētōr**, *ktay'-tore;* from *2932;* an *owner:*—possessor.

2936. κτίζω **ktizō**, *ktid'-zo;* prob. akin to *2932* (through the idea of the *proprietorship* of the *manufacturer*); to *fabricate*, i.e. *found* (*form* originally):—create, Creator, make.

2937. κτίσις **ktisis**, *ktis'-is;* from *2936;* original *formation* (prop. the act; by impl. the thing, lit. or fig.):—building, creation, creature, ordinance.

2938. κτίσμα **ktisma**, *ktis'-mah;* from *2936;* an original *formation* (concr.), i.e. *product* (created thing):—creature.

2939. κτιστής **ktistēs**, *ktis-tace';* from *2936;* a *founder*, i.e. *God* (as author of all things):—Creator.

2940. κυβεία **kubĕia**, *koo-bi'-ah;* from κύβος **kubŏs** (a "*cube*", i.e. *die* for playing); *gambling*, i.e. (fig.) *artifice* or *fraud:*—sleight.

2941. κυβέρνησις **kubĕrnēsis**, *koo-ber'-nay-sis;* from κυβερνάω **kubĕrnaō** (of Lat. or., to *steer*); *pilotage*, i.e. (fig.) *directorship* (in the church):—government.

2942. κυβερνήτης **kubĕrnētēs**, *koo-ber-nay'-tace;* from the same as *2941; helmsman*, i.e. (by impl.) *captain:*—(ship) master.

2943. κυκλόθεν **kuklŏthĕn**, *koo-kloth'-en;* adv. from the same as *2945; from* the *circle*, i.e. *all around:*—(round) about.

κυκλός **kuklŏs**. See *2945*.

2944. κυκλόω **kuklŏō**, *koo-klŏ'-o;* from the same as *2945;* to *encircle*, i.e. *surround:*—compass (about), come (stand) round about.

2945. κύκλῳ **kuklōi**, *koo'-klo;* as if dat. of κύκλος **kuklŏs** (a *ring*, "*cycle*"; akin to *2947*); i.e. *in a circle* (by impl. of *1722*), i.e. (adv.) *all around:*—round about.

2946. κύλισμα **kulisma**, *koo'-lis-mah;* from *2947;* a *wallow* (the effect of *rolling*), i.e. *filth:*—wallowing.

2947. κυλιόω **kuliŏō**, *koo-lee-ŏ'-o;* from the base of *2949* (through the idea of *circularity;* comp. *2945*, *1507*); to *roll* about:—wallow.

2948. κυλλός **kullŏs**, *kool-los';* from the same as *2947; rocking* about, i.e. *crippled* (*maimed*, in feet or hands):—maimed.

2949. κῦμα **kuma**, *koo'-mah;* from κύω **kuō** (to *swell* [with young], i.e. *bend, curve*); a *billow* (as *bursting* or *toppling*):—wave.

2950. κύμβαλον **kumbalŏn**, *koom'-bal-on;* from a der. of the base of *2949;* a "*cymbal*" (as *hollow*):—cymbal.

2951. κύμινον **kuminŏn**, *koo'-min-on;* of for. or. [comp. 3646]; *dill* or *fennel* ("cummin"):—cummin.

2952. κυνάριον **kunariŏn**, *koo-nar'-ee-on;* neut. of a presumed der. of *2965;* a *puppy:*—dog.

2953. Κύπριος **Kupriŏs**, *koo'-pree-os;* from *2954;* a *Cyprian* (*Cypriot*), i.e. inhab. of Cyprus:—of Cyprus.

2954. Κύπρος **Kuprŏs**, *koo'-pros;* of uncert. or.; *Cyprus*, an island in the Mediterranean:—Cyprus.

2955. κύπτω **kuptō**, *koop'-to;* prob. from the base of *2949;* to *bend* forward:—stoop (down).

2956. Κυρηναῖος **Kurēnaiŏs**, *koo-ray-nah'-yos;* from *2957;* a *Cyrenæan*, i.e. inhab. of Cyrene:—of Cyrene, Cyrenian.

2957. Κυρήνη **Kurēnē**, *koo-ray'-nay;* of uncert. der.; *Cyrenè*, a region of Africa:—Cyrene.

2958. Κυρήνιος **Kurēniŏs**, *koo-ray'-nee-os;* of Lat. or.; *Cyrenius* (i.e. *Quirinus*), a Roman:—Cyrenius.

2959. Κυρία **Kuria**, *koo-ree'-ah;* fem. of *2962; Cyria*, a Chr. woman:—lady.

2960. κυριακός **kuriakŏs**, *koo-ree-ak-os';* from *2962; belonging to* the *Lord* (Jehovah or Jesus):—Lord's.

2961. κυριεύω **kuriĕuō**, *koo-ree-yoo'-o;* from *2962;* to *rule:*—have dominion over, lord, be lord of, exercise lordship over.

2962. κύριος **kuriŏs**, *koo'-ree-os;* from κῦρος **kurŏs** (*supremacy*); *supreme* in authority, i.e. (as noun) *controller;* by impl. *Mr.* (as a respectful title):—God, Lord, master, Sir.

2963. κυριότης **kuriŏtēs**, *koo-ree-ot'-ace;* from *2962; mastery*, i.e. (concr. and coll.) *rulers:*—dominion, government.

2964. κυρόω **kurŏō**, *koo-rŏ'-o;* from the same as *2962;* to *make authoritative*, i.e. *ratify:*—confirm.

2965. κύων **kuōn**, *koo'-ohn;* a prim. word; a *dog* ["*hound*"] (lit. or fig.):—dog.

2966. κῶλον **kōlŏn**, *ko'-lon;* from the base of *2849;* a *limb* of the body (as if *lopped*):—carcase.

2967. κωλύω **kōluō**, *ko-loo'-o;* from the base of *2849;* to *estop*, i.e. *prevent* (by word or act):—forbid, hinder, keep from, let, not suffer, withstand.

2968. κώμη **kōmē**, *ko'-may;* from *2749;* a *hamlet* (as if *laid* down):—town, village.

2969. κωμόπολις **kōmŏpŏlis**, *ko-mop'-ol-is;* from *2968* and *4172;* an unwalled *city:*—town.

2970. κῶμος **kōmŏs**, *ko'-mos;* from *2749;* a *carousal* (as if a *letting loose*):—revelling, rioting.

2971. κώνωψ **kōnōps**, *ko'-nopes;* appar. from a der. of the base of *2759* and a der. of *3700;* a *mosquito* (from its *stinging proboscis*):—gnat.

2972. Κῶς **Kōs**, *koce;* of uncert. or.; *Cos*, an island in the Mediterranean:—Cos.

2973. Κωσάμ **Kōsam**, *ko-sam';* of Heb. or. [comp. 7081]; *Cosam* (i.e. *Kosam*), an Isr.:—Cosam.

2974. κωφός **kōphŏs**, *ko-fos';* from *2875; blunted*, i.e. (fig.) of hearing (*deaf*) or speech (*dumb*):—deaf, dumb, speechless.

Λ

2975. λαγχάνω **lagchanō**, *lang-khan'-o;* a prol. form of a prim. verb, which is only used as an alt. in certain tenses; to *lot*, i.e. *determine* (by impl. *receive*) espec. by lot:—his lot be, cast lots, obtain.

2976. Λάζαρος **Lazarŏs**, *lad'-zar-os;* prob. of Heb. or. [499]; *Lazarus* (i.e. *Elazar*), the name of two Isr. (one imaginary):—Lazarus.

2977. λάθρα **lathra**, *lath'-rah;* adv. from *2990; privately:*—privily, secretly.

2978. λαῖλαψ **lailaps**, *lah'ee-laps;* of uncert. der.; a *whirlwind* (*squall*):—storm, tempest.

2979. λακτίζω **laktizō**, *lak-tid'-zo;* from adv. λάξ **lax** (*heelwise*); to *recalcitrate:*—kick.

2980. λαλέω **lalĕō**, *lal-eh'-o;* a prol. form of an otherwise obsol. verb; to *talk*, i.e. *utter* words:—preach, say, speak (after), talk, tell, utter. Comp. *3004*.

2981. λαλιά **lalia**, *lal-ee-ah';* from *2980; talk:*—saying, speech.

2982. λαμά **lama**, *lam-ah';* or

λαμμᾶ **lamma**, *lam-mah';* of Heb. or. [4100 with prep. pref.]; *lama* (i.e. *why*):—lama.

2983. λαμβάνω **lambanō**, *lam-ban'-o;* a prol. form of a prim. verb, which is used only as an alt. in certain tenses; to *take* (in very many applications, lit. and fig. [prop. obj. or act., to *get hold* of; whereas *1209* is rather subj. or pass., to *have offered* to one; while *138* is more violent, to *seize* or *remove*]):—accept, + be amazed, assay, attain, bring, × when I call, catch, come on (× unto), + forget, have, hold, obtain, receive (× after), take (away, up).

2984. Λάμεχ **Lamĕch**, *lam'-ekh;* of Heb. or. [3929]; *Lamech* (i.e. *Lemek*), a patriarch:—Lamech.

λαμμᾶ **lamma**. See *2982*.

2985. λαμπάς **lampas**, *lam-pas';* from *2989;* a "*lamp*" or *flambeau:*—lamp, light, torch.

2986. λαμπρός **lamprŏs**, *lam-pros';* from the same as *2985;* radiant; by anal. *limpid;* fig. *magnificent* or *sumptuous* (in appearance):—bright, clear, gay, goodly, gorgeous, white.

2987. λαμπρότης **lamprŏtēs**, *lam-prot'-ace;* from *2896; brilliancy:*—brightness.

2988. λαμπρῶς **lamprōs**, *lam-proce';* adv. from *2986; brilliantly*, i.e. (fig.) *luxuriously:*—sumptuously.

2989. λάμπω **lampō**, *lam'-po;* a prim. verb; to *beam*, i.e. *radiate* brilliancy (lit. or fig.):—give light, shine.

2990. λανθάνω **lanthanō**, *lan-than'-o;* a prol. form of a prim. verb, which is used only as an alt. in certain tenses; to *lie hid* (lit. or fig.); often used adv. *unwittingly:*—be hid, be ignorant of, unawares.

2991. λαξευτός **laxĕutŏs**, *lax-yoo-tos';* from a comp. of λᾶς **las** (a *stone*) and the base of *3584* (in its orig. sense of *scraping*); *rock-quarried:*—hewn in stone.

2992. λαός **laŏs**, *lah-os';* appar. a prim. word; a *people* (in gen.; thus differing from *1218*, which denotes one's *own* populace):—people.

2993. Λαοδίκεια **Laŏdikĕia**, *lah-od-ik'-i-ah;* from a comp. of *2992* and *1349; Laodicia*, a place in Asia Minor:—Laodicea.

2994. Λαοδικεύς **Laŏdikĕus**, *lah-od-ik-yooce';* from *2993;* a *Laodicean*, i.e. inhab. of Laodicia:—Laodicean.

2995. λάρυγξ **larugx**, *lar'-oongks;* of uncert. der.; the *throat* ("*larynx*"):—throat.

2996. Λασαία **Lasaia**, *las-ah'-yah;* of uncert. or.; *Lasæa*, a place in Crete:—Lasea.

2997. λάσχω **laschō**, *las'-kho;* a strengthened form of a prim. verb, which only occurs in this and another prol. form as alt. in certain tenses; to *crack* open (from a fall):—burst asunder.

2998. λατομέω **latŏmĕō**, *lat-om-eh'-o;* from the same as the first part of *2991* and the base of *5114;* to *quarry:*—hew.

2999. λατρεία **latrĕia**, *lat-ri'-ah;* from *3000; ministration* of God, i.e. *worship:*—(divine) service.

3000. λατρεύω **latrĕuō**, *lat-ryoo'-o;* from λάτρις **latris** (a hired *menial*); to *minister* (to God), i.e. *render* religious *homage:*—serve, do the service, worship (-per).

3001. λάχανον **lachanŏn**, *lakh'-an-on;* from λαχαίνω **lachainō** (to *dig*); a *vegetable:*—herb.

3002. Λεββαῖος **Lĕbbaiŏs**, *leb-bah'-yos;* of uncert. or.; *Lebbæus*, a Chr.:—Lebbæus.

3003. λεγεών **lĕgĕōn**, *leg-eh-ohn';* of Lat. or.; a "*legion*", i.e. Rom. *regiment* (fig.):—legion.

3004. λέγω **lĕgō**, *leg'-o;* a prim. verb; prop. to "*lay*" forth, i.e. (fig.) *relate* (in words [usually of systematic or set *discourse;* whereas *2036* and *5346* generally refer to an *individual* expression or speech respectively; while *4483* is prop. to *break silence* merely, and *2980* means an *extended* or random harangue]); by impl. to *mean:*—ask, bid, boast, call, describe, give out, name, put forth, say (-ing, on), shew, speak, tell, utter.

3005. λεῖμμα **lĕimma**, *lime'-mah;* from *3007;* a *remainder:*—remnant.

3006. λεῖος **lĕiŏs**, *li'-os;* appar. a prim. word; *smooth*, i.e. "*level*":—smooth.

3007. λείπω **lĕipō**, *li'-po;* a prim. verb; to *leave*, i.e. (intrans. or pass.) to *fail* or be *absent:*—be destitute (wanting), lack.

3008. λειτουργέω **lĕitŏurgĕō**, *li-toorg-eh'-o;* from *3011;* to be a *public servant*, i.e. (by anal.) to *perform* religious or charitable *functions* (*worship, obey, relieve*):—minister.

3009. λειτουργία **lĕitŏurgia**, *li-toorg-ee'-ah;* from *3008; public function* (as priest ["liturgy"] or almsgiver):—ministration (-try), service.

3010. λειτουργικός **lĕitŏurgikŏs**, *li-toorg-ik-os';* from the same as *3008; functional publicly* ("liturgic"), i.e. *beneficent:*—ministering.

3011. λειτουργός **lĕitŏurgŏs**, *li-toorg-os';* from a der. of *2992* and *2041;* a *public servant*, i.e. a *functionary* in the Temple or Gospel, or (gen.) a *worshipper* (of God) or *benefactor* (of man):—minister (-ed).

3012. λέντιον **lĕntiŏn**, *len'-tee-on;* of Lat. or.; a "*linen*" cloth, i.e. *apron:*—towel.

3013. λεπίς **lĕpis**, *lep-is';* from λέπω **lĕpō** (to *peel*); a *flake:*—scale.

3014. λέπρα **lĕpra**, *lep'-rah;* from the same as 3013; *scaliness*, i.e. "*leprosy*":—leprosy.

3015. λεπρός **lĕprŏs**, *lep-ros';* from the same as 3014; *scaly*, i.e. *leprous* (a *leper*):—leper.

3016. λεπτόν **lĕptŏn**, *lep-ton';* neut. of a der. of the same as 3013; something *scaled* (*light*), i.e. a small *coin:*—mite.

3017. Λευΐ **Lĕui**, *lyoo-ee';* of Heb. or. [3878]; *Levi*, the name of three Isr.:—Levi. Comp. 3018.

3018. Λευΐς **Lĕuis**, *lyoo-is';* a form of 3017; *Lewis* (i.e. *Levi*), a Chr.:—Levi.

3019. Λευΐτης **Lĕuitēs**, *lyoo-ee'-tace;* from 3017; a *Levite*, i.e. desc. of Levi:—Levite.

3020. Λευϊτικός **Lĕuitikŏs**, *lyoo-it'-ee-kos;* from 3019; *Levitic*, i.e. relating to the Levites:—Levitical.

3021. λευκαίνω **lĕukainō**, *lyoo-kah'ee-no;* from 3022; to *whiten:*—make white, whiten.

3022. λευκός **lĕukŏs**, *lyoo-kos';* from λύκη **lukē** ("*light*"); *white:*—white.

3023. λεών **lĕōn**, *leh-ohn';* a prim. word; a "*lion*":—lion.

3024. λήθη **lēthē**, *lay'-thay;* from 2990; *forgetfulness:*—+ forget.

3025. ληνός **lēnŏs**, *lay-nos';* appar. a prim. word; a *trough*, i.e. wine-*vat:*—winepress.

3026. λῆρος **lērŏs**, *lay'-ros;* appar. a prim. word; *twaddle*, i.e. an *incredible* story:—idle tale.

3027. λῃστής **lēstēs**, *lace-tace';* from ληΐζομαι **lēizŏmai** (to *plunder*); a *brigand:*—robber, thief.

3028. λῆψις **lēpsis**, *lape'-sis;* from 2983; *receipt* (the act):—receiving.

3029. λίαν **lian**, *lee'-an;* of uncert. affin.; *much* (adv.):—exceeding, great (-ly), sore, very (+ chiefest).

3030. λίβανος **libanŏs**, *lib'-an-os;* of for. or. [3828]; the *incense*-tree, i.e. (by impl.) *incense* itself:—frankincense.

3031. λιβανωτός **libanōtŏs**, *lib-an-o-tos';* from 3030; *frankincense*, i.e. (by extens.) a *censer* for burning it:—censer.

3032. Λιβερτῖνος **Libĕrtinŏs**, *lib-er-tee'-nos;* of Lat. or.; a Rom. *freedman:*—Libertine.

3033. Λιβύη **Libuē**, *lib-oo'-ay;* prob. from 3047; *Libye*, a region of Africa:—Libya.

3034. λιθάζω **lithazō**, *lith-ad'-zo;* from 3037; to *lapidate:*—stone.

3035. λίθινος **lithinŏs**, *lith'-ee-nos;* from 3037; *stony*, i.e. made of *stone:*—of stone.

3036. λιθοβολέω **lithŏbŏlĕō**, *lith-ob-ol-eh'-o;* from a comp. of 3037 and 906; to *throw stones*, i.e. *lapidate:*—stone, cast stones.

3037. λίθος **lithŏs**, *lee'-thos;* appar. a prim. word; a *stone* (lit. or fig.):—(mill-, stumbling-) stone.

3038. λιθόστρωτος **lithŏstrōtŏs**, *lith-os'-tro-tos;* from 3037 and a der. of 4766; *stone-strewed*, i.e. a tessellated *mosaic* on which the Rom. tribunal was placed:—Pavement.

3039. λικμάω **likmaō**, *lik-mah'-o;* from λικμός **likmŏs**, the equiv. of λίκνον **liknŏn** (a winnowing *fan* or basket); to *winnow*, i.e. (by anal.) to *triturate:*—grind to powder.

3040. λιμήν **limēn**, *lee-mane';* appar. a prim. word; a *harbor:*—haven. Comp. 2568.

3041. λίμνη **limnē**, *lim'-nay;* prob. from 3040 (through the idea of the nearness of shore); a *pond* (large or small):—lake.

3042. λιμός **limŏs**, *lee-mos';* prob. from 3007 (through the idea of *destitution*); a *scarcity* of food:—dearth, famine, hunger.

3043. λίνον **linŏn**, *lee'-non;* prob. a prim. word; *flax*, i.e. (by impl.) "*linen*":—linen.

3044. Λῖνος **Linŏs**, *lee'-nos;* perh. from 3043; *Linus*, a Chr.:—Linus.

3045. λιπαρός **liparŏs**, *lip-ar-os';* from λίπος **lipŏs** (*grease*); *fat*, i.e. (fig.) *sumptuous:*—dainty.

3046. λίτρα **litra**, *lee'-trah;* of Lat. or. [*libra*]; a *pound* in weight:—pound.

3047. λίψ **lips**, *leeps;* prob. from λείβω **lĕibō** (to *pour* a "libation"); the *south* (-west) wind (as bringing rain, i.e. (by extens.) the *south* quarter:—southwest.

3048. λογία **lŏgia**, *log-ee'-ah;* from 3056 (in the commercial sense); a *contribution:*—collection, gathering.

3049. λογίζομαι **lŏgizŏmai**, *log-id'-zom-ahee;* mid. from 3056; to *take an inventory*, i.e. *estimate* (lit. or fig.):—conclude, (ac-) count (of), + despise, esteem, impute, lay, number, reason, reckon, suppose, think (on).

3050. λογικός **lŏgikŏs**, *log-ik-os';* from 3056; *rational* ("*logical*"):—reasonable, of the word.

3051. λόγιον **lŏgiŏn**, *log'-ee-on;* neut. of 3052; an *utterance* (of God):—oracle.

3052. λόγιος **lŏgiŏs**, *log'-ee-os;* from 3056; *fluent*, i.e. an *orator:*—eloquent.

3053. λογισμός **lŏgismŏs**, *log-is-mos';* from 3049; *computation*, i.e. (fig.) *reasoning* (*conscience*, *conceit*):—imagination, thought.

3054. λογομαχέω **lŏgŏmachĕō**, *log-om-akh-eh'-o;* from a comp. of 3056 and 3164; to *be disputatious* (on trifles):—strive about words.

3055. λογομαχία **lŏgŏmachia**, *log-om-akh-ee'-ah;* from the same as 3054; *disputation* about trifles ("*logomachy*"):—strife of words.

3056. λόγος **lŏgŏs**, *log'-os;* from 3004; something *said* (including the *thought*); by impl. a *topic* (subject of discourse), also *reasoning* (the mental faculty) or *motive;* by extens. a *computation;* spec. (with the art. in John) the Divine *Expression* (i.e. *Christ*):—account, cause, communication, × concerning, doctrine, fame, × have to do, intent, matter, mouth, preaching, question, reason, + reckon, remove, say (-ing), shew, × speaker, speech, talk, thing, + none of these things move me, tidings, treatise, utterance, word, work.

3057. λόγχη **lŏgchē**, *long'-khay;* perh. a prim. word; a "*lance*":—spear.

3058. λοιδορέω **lŏidŏrĕō**, *loy-dor-eh'-o;* from 3060; to *reproach*, i.e. *vilify:*—revile.

3059. λοιδορία **lŏidŏria**, *loy-dor-ee'-ah;* from 3060; *slander* or *vituperation:*—railing, reproach [-fully].

3060. λοίδορος **lŏidŏrŏs**, *loy'-dor-os;* from λοιδός **lŏidŏs** (*mischief*); *abusive*, i.e. a *blackguard;*—railer, reviler.

3061. λοιμός **lŏimŏs**, *loy-mos';* of uncert. affin.; a *plague* (lit. the *disease*, or fig. a *pest*):—pestilence (-t).

3062. λοιποί **lŏipŏy**, *loy-poy';* masc. plur. of a der. of 3007; *remaining* ones:—other, which remain, remnant, residue, rest.

3063. λοιπόν **lŏipŏn**, *loy-pon';* neut. sing. of the same as 3062; something *remaining* (adv.):—besides, finally, furthermore, (from) henceforth, moreover, now, + it remaineth, then.

3064. λοιποῦ **lŏipŏu**, *loy-poo';* gen. sing. of the same as 3062; *remaining* time:—from henceforth.

3065. Λουκᾶς **Lŏukas**, *loo-kas';* contr. from Lat. *Lucanus; Lucas*, a Chr.:—Lucas, Luke.

3066. Λούκιος **Lŏukiŏs**, *loo'-kee-os;* of Lat. or.; *illuminative; Lucius*, a Chr.:—Lucius.

3067. λουτρόν **lŏutrŏn**, *loo-tron';* from 3068; a *bath*, i.e. (fig.) *baptism:*—washing.

3068. λούω **lŏuō**, *loo'-o;* a prim. verb; to *bathe* (the *whole* person; whereas 3538 means to wet a *part* only, and 4150 to wash, cleanse *garments* exclusively):—wash.

3069. Λύδδα **Ludda**, *lud'-dah;* of Heb. or. [3850]; *Lydda* (i.e. *Lod*), a place in Pal.:—Lydda.

3070. Λυδία **Ludia**, *loo-dee'-ah;* prop. fem. of Λύδιος **Ludiŏs** [of for. or.] (a *Lydian*, in Asia Minor); *Lydia*, a Chr. woman:—Lydia.

3071. Λυκαονία **Lukaŏnia**, *loo-kah-on-ee'-ah;* perh. remotely from 3074; *Lycaonia*, a region of Asia Minor:—Lycaonia.

3072. Λυκαονιστί **Lukaŏnisti**, *loo-kah-on-is-tee';* adv. from a der. of 3071; *Lycaonistically*, i.e. in the language of the Lycaonians:—in the speech of Lycaonia.

3073. Λυκία **Lukia**, *loo-kee'-ah;* prob. remotely from 3074; *Lycia*, a province of Asia Minor:—Lycia.

3074. λύκος **lukŏs**, *loo'-kos;* perh. akin to the base of 3022 (from the *whitish* hair); a *wolf:*—wolf.

3075. λυμαίνομαι **lumainŏmai**, *loo-mah'ee-nom-ahee;* mid. from a prob. der. of 3089 (mean. *filth*); prop. to *soil*, i.e. (fig.) *insult* (*maltreat*):—make havock of.

3076. λυπέω **lupĕō**, *loo-peh'-o;* from 3077; to *distress;* reflex. or pass. to *be sad:*—cause grief, grieve, be in heaviness, (be) sorrow (-ful), be (make) sorry.

3077. λύπη **lupē**, *loo'-pay;* appar. a prim. word; *sadness:*—grief, grievous, + grudgingly, heaviness, sorrow.

3078. Λυσανίας **Lusanias**, *loo-san-ee'-as;* from 3080 and ἀνία **ania** (*trouble*); *grief-dispelling; Lysanias*, a governor of Abilene:—Lysanias.

3079. Λυσίας **Lusias**, *loo-see'-as;* of uncert. affin.; *Lysias*, a Rom.:—Lysias.

3080. λύσις **lusis**, *loo'-sis;* from 3089; a *loosening*, i.e. (spec.) *divorce:*—to be loosed.

3081. λυσιτελεῖ **lusitĕlĕi**, *loo-sit-el-i';* third pers. sing. pres. indic. act. of a der. of a comp. of 3080 and 5056; impers. it *answers* the *purpose*, i.e. *is advantageous:*—it is better.

3082. Λύστρα **Lustra**, *loos'-trah;* of uncert. or.; *Lystra*, a place in Asia Minor:—Lystra.

3083. λύτρον **lutrŏn**, *loo'-tron;* from 3089; something to *loosen* with, i.e. a redemption *price* (fig. *atonement*):—ransom.

3084. λυτρόω **lutrŏō**, *loo-trŏ'-o;* from 3083; to *ransom* (lit. or fig.):—redeem.

3085. λύτρωσις **lutrōsis**, *loo'-tro-sis;* from 3084; a *ransoming* (fig.):—+ redeemed, redemption.

3086. λυτρωτής **lutrōtēs**, *loo-tro-tace';* from 3084; a *redeemer* (fig.):—deliverer.

3087. λυχνία **luchnia**, *lookh-nee'-ah;* from 3088; a *lamp-stand* (lit. or fig.):—candlestick.

3088. λύχνος **luchnŏs**, *lookh'-nos;* from the base of 3022; a portable *lamp* or other *illuminator* (lit. or fig.):—candle, light.

3089. λύω **luō**, *loo'-o;* a prim. verb; to "*loosen*" (lit. or fig.):—break (up), destroy, dissolve, (un-) loose, melt, put off. Comp. 4486.

3090. Λωΐς **Lōis**, *lo-ece';* of uncert. or.; *Loïs*, a Chr. woman:—Lois.

3091. Λώτ **Lōt**, *lote;* of Heb. or. [3876]; *Lot*, a patriarch:—Lot.

M

3092. Μαάθ **Maath**, *mah-ath';* prob. of Heb. or.; *Maath*, an Isr.:—Maath.

3093. Μαγδαλά **Magdala**, *mag-dal-ah';* of Chald. or. [comp. 4026]; *the tower; Magdala* (i.e. *Migdala*), a place in Pal.:—Magdala.

3094. Μαγδαληνή **Magdalēnē**, *mag-dal-ay-nay';* fem. of a der. of 3093; a female *Magdalene*, i.e. inhab. of Magdala:—Magdalene.

3095. μαγεία **magĕia**, *mag-i'-ah;* from 3096; "*magic*":—sorcery.

3096. μαγεύω **magĕuō**, *mag-yoo'-o;* from 3097; to *practice magic:*—use sorcery.

3097. μάγος **magŏs**, *mag'-os;* of for. or. [7248]; a *Magian*, i.e. Oriental *scientist;* by impl. a *magician:*—sorcerer, wise man.

3098. Μαγώγ **Magōg**, *mag-ogue';* of Heb. or. [4031]; *Magog*, a for. nation, i.e. (fig.) an Antichristian party:—Magog.

3099. Μαδιάν **Madian**, *mad-ee-an';* of Heb. or. [4080]; *Madian* (i.e. *Midian*), a region of Arabia:—Madian.

3100. μαθητεύω **mathētĕuō**, *math-ayt-yoo'-o;* from 3101; intrans. to *become a pupil;* trans. to *disciple*, i.e. enrol as scholar:—be disciple, instruct, teach.

3101. μαθητής **mathētēs**, *math-ay-tes';* from 3129; a *learner*, i.e. *pupil:*—disciple.

3102. μαθήτρια **mathētria**, *math-ay'-tree-ah;* fem. from 3101; a female *pupil:*—disciple.

3103. **Μαθουσάλα Mathŏusala**, *math-oo-sal'-ah;* of Heb. or. [4968]; *Mathusala* (i.e. *Methushelach*), an antediluvian:—Mathusala.

3104. **Μαϊνάν Maïnan**, *mahee-nan';* prob. of Heb. or.; *Maïnan*, an Isr.:—Mainan.

3105. **μαίνομαι mainŏmai**, *mah'ee-nom-ahee;* mid. from a prim. **μάω maō** (to *long* for; through the idea of insensate *craving*); to *rave* as a "maniac":—be beside self (mad).

3106. **μακαρίζω makarizō**, *mak-ar-id'-zo;* from *3107;* to *beatify*, i.e. *pronounce* (or *esteem*) *fortunate:*—call blessed, count happy.

3107. **μακάριος makariŏs**, *mak-ar'-ee-os;* a prol. form of the poetical **μάκαρ makar** (mean. the same); supremely *blest;* by extens. *fortunate, well off:*—blessed, happy (× -ier).

3108. **μακαρισμός makarismŏs**, *mak-ar-is-mos';* from *3106;* *beatification*, i.e. *attribution of good fortune:*—blessedness.

3109. **Μακεδονία Makĕdŏnia**, *mak-ed-on-ee'-ah;* from *3110;* *Macedonia*, a region of Greece:—Macedonia.

3110. **Μακεδών Makĕdōn**, *mak-ed'-ohn;* of uncert. der.; a *Macedon* (*Macedonian*), i.e. inhab. of Macedonia:—of Macedonia, Macedonian.

3111. **μάκελλον makĕllŏn**, *mak'-el-lon;* of Lat. or. [*macellum*]; a *butcher's stall, meat market* or *provision-shop:*—shambles.

3112. **μακράν makran**, *mak-ran';* fem. acc. sing. of *3117* (*3598* being implied); *at a distance* (lit. or fig.):—(a-) far (off), good (great) way off.

3113. **μακρόθεν makrŏthĕn**, *mak-roth'-en;* adv. from *3117;* *from a distance* or *afar:*—afar off, from far.

3114. **μακροθυμέω makrŏthumĕō**, *mak-roth-oo-meh'-o;* from the same as *3116;* to *be long-spirited*, i.e. (obj.) *forbearing* or (subj.) *patient:*—bear (suffer) long, be longsuffering, have (long) patience, be patient, patiently endure.

3115. **μακροθυμία makrŏthumia**, *mak-roth-oo-mee'-ah;* from the same as *3116;* *longanimity*, i.e. (obj.) *forbearance* or (subj.) *fortitude:*—longsuffering, patience.

3116. **μακροθυμώς makrŏthumōs**, *mak-roth-oo-moce';* adv. of a comp. of *3117* and *2372;* *with long* (*enduring*) *temper*, i.e. *leniently:*—patiently.

3117. **μακρός makrŏs**, *mak-ros';* from *3372;* *long* (in place [*distant*] or time [neut. plur.]):—far, long.

3118. **μακροχρόνιος makrŏchrŏniŏs**, *mak-rokh-ron'-ee-os;* from *3117* and *5550;* *long-timed*, i.e. *long-lived:*—live long.

3119. **μαλακία malakia**, *mal-ak-ee'-ah;* from *3120;* *softness*, i.e. *enervation* (*debility*):—disease.

3120. **μαλακός malakŏs**, *mal-ak-os';* of uncert. affin.; *soft*, i.e. *fine* (clothing); fig. a *catamite:*—effeminate, soft.

3121. **Μαλελεήλ Malĕlĕēl**, *mal-el-eh-ale';* of Heb. or [4111]; *Maleleël* (i.e. *Mahalalel*), an antediluvian:—Maleleel.

3122. **μάλιστα malista**, *mal'-is-tah;* neut. plur. of the superl. of an appar. prim. adv. **μάλα mala** (*very*); (adv.) *most* (*in the greatest degree*) or *particularly:*—chiefly, most of all, (e-) specially.

3123. **μᾶλλον mallŏn**, *mal'-lon;* neut. of the compar. of the same as *3122;* (adv.) *more* (*in a greater degree*) or *rather:*— + better, × far, (the) more (and more), (so) much (the more), rather.

3124. **Μάλχος Malchŏs**, *mal'-khos;* of Heb. or. [4429]; *Malchus*, an Isr.:—Malchus.

3125. **μάμμη mammē**, *mam'-may;* of nat. or. ["mammy"]; a *grandmother:*—grandmother.

3126. **μαμμωνᾶς mammōnas**, *mam-mo-nas';* of Chald. or. (*confidence*, i.e. fig. *wealth*, personified); *mammonas*, i.e. *avarice* (deified):—mammon.

3127. **Μαναήν Manaēn**, *man-ah-ane';* of uncert. or.; *Manaën*, a Chr.:—Manaen.

3128. **Μανασσῆς Manassēs**, *man-as-sace';* of Heb. or. [4519]; *Manasses* (i.e. *Menashsheh*), an Isr.:—Manasses.

3129. **μανθάνω manthanō**, *man-than'-o;* prol. from a prim. verb, another form of which, **μαθέω mathĕō**, is used as an alt. in cert. tenses; to *learn* (in any way):—learn, understand.

3130. **μανία mania**, *man-ee'-ah;* from *3105;* *craziness:*—[+ make] × mad.

3131. **μάννα manna**, *man'-nah;* of Heb. or. [4478]; *manna* (i.e. *man*), an edible gum:—manna.

3132. **μαντεύομαι mantĕuŏmai**, *mant-yoo'-om-ahee;* from a der. of *3105* (mean. a *prophet*, as supposed to *rave* through *inspiration*); to *divine*, i.e. *utter spells* (under pretence of foretelling):—by soothsaying.

3133. **μαραίνω marainō**, *mar-ah'ee-no;* of uncert. affin.; to *extinguish* (as fire), i.e. (fig. and pass.) to *pass away:*—fade away.

3134. **μαρὰν ἀθά maran atha**, *mar'-an ath'-ah;* of Chald. or. (mean. *our Lord has come*); *maranatha*, i.e. an exclamation of the approaching *divine judgment:*—Maran-atha.

3135. **μαργαρίτης margaritēs**, *mar-gar-ee'-tace;* from **μάργαρος margarŏs** (a pearl-*oyster*); a *pearl:*—pearl.

3136. **Μάρθα Martha**, *mar'-thah;* prob. of Chald. or. (mean. *mistress*); *Martha*, a Chr. woman:—Martha.

3137. **Μαρία Maria**, *mar-ee'-ah;* or
Μαριάμ Mariam, *mar-ee-am';* of Heb. or. [4813]; *Maria* or *Mariam* (i.e. *Mirjam*), the name of six Chr. females:—Mary.

3138. **Μάρκος Markŏs**, *mar'-kos;* of Lat. or.; *Marcus*, a Chr.:—Marcus, Mark.

3139. **μάρμαρος marmarŏs**, *mar'-mar-os;* from **μαρμαίρω marmairō** (to *glisten*); *marble* (as sparkling *white*):—marble.

μάρτυρ martur. See *3144.*

3140. **μαρτυρέω marturĕō**, *mar-too-reh'-o;* from *3144;* to *be a witness*, i.e. *testify* (lit. or fig.):—charge, give [*evidence*], bear record, have (obtain, of) good (honest) report, be well reported of, testify, give (have) testimony, (be, bear, give, obtain) witness.

3141. **μαρτυρία marturia**, *mar-too-ree'-ah;* from *3144;* *evidence* given (judicially or gen.):—record, report, testimony, witness.

3142. **μαρτύριον marturiŏn**, *mar-too'-ree-on;* neut. of a presumed der. of *3144;* something *evidential*, i.e. (gen.) *evidence* given or (spec.) the *Decalogue* (in the sacred Tabernacle):—to be testified, testimony, witness.

3143. **μαρτύρομαι marturŏmai**, *mar-too'-rom-ahee;* mid. from *3144;* to *be adduced as a witness*, i.e. (fig.) to *obtest* (in affirmation or exhortation):—take to record, testify.

3144. **μάρτυς martus**, *mar'-toos;* of uncert. affin.; a *witness* (lit. [judicially] or fig. [gen.]); by anal. a "*martyr*":—martyr, record, witness.

3145. **μασσάομαι massaŏmai**, *mas-sah'-om-ahee;* from a prim. **μάσσω massō** (to *handle* or *squeeze*); to *chew:*—gnaw.

3146. **μαστιγόω mastigŏō**, *mas-tig-ŏ'-o;* from *3148;* to *flog* (lit. or fig.):—scourge.

3147. **μαστίζω mastizō**, *mas-tid'-zo;* from *3149;* to *whip* (lit.):—scourge.

3148. **μάστιξ mastix**, *mas'-tix;* prob. from the base of *3145* (through the idea of *contact*); a *whip* (lit. the Roman *flagellum* for criminals; fig. a *disease*):—plague, scourging.

3149. **μαστός mastŏs**, *mas-tos';* from the base of *3145;* a (prop. female) *breast* (as if *kneaded* up):—pap.

3150. **ματαιολογία mataiŏlŏgia**, *mat-ah-yol-og-ee'-ah;* from *3151;* *random talk*, i.e. *babble:*—vain jangling.

3151. **ματαιολόγος mataiŏlŏgŏs**, *mat-ah-yol-og'-os;* from *3152* and *3004;* an *idle* (i.e. *senseless* or *mischievous*) *talker*, i.e. a *wrangler:*—vain talker.

3152. **μάταιος mataiŏs**, *mat'-ah-yos;* from the base of *3155;* *empty*, i.e. (lit.) *profitless*, or (spec.) an *idol:*—vain, vanity.

3153. **ματαιότης mataiŏtēs**, *mat-ah-yot'-ace;* from *3152;* *inutility;* fig. *transientness;* mor. *depravity:*—vanity.

3154. **ματαιόω mataiŏō**, *mat-ah-yŏ'-o;* from *3152;* to *render* (pass. *become*) *foolish*, i.e. (mor.) *wicked* or (spec.) *idolatrous:*—become vain.

3155. **μάτην matēn**, *mat'-ane;* accus. of a der. of the base of *3145* (through the idea of tentative *manipulation*, i.e. unsuccessful *search*, or else of *punishment*); *folly*, i.e. (adv.) *to no purpose:*—in vain.

3156. **Ματθαῖος Matthaiŏs**, *mat-thah'-yos;* a shorter form of *3161;* *Matthæus* (i.e. *Matthitjah*), an Isr. and Chr.:—Matthew.

3157. **Ματθάν Matthan**, *mat-than';* of Heb. or. [4977]; *Matthan* (i.e. *Mattan*), an Isr.:—Matthan.

3158. **Ματθάτ Matthat**, *mat-that';* prob. a shortened form of *3161;* *Matthat* (i.e. *Mattithjah*), the name of two Isr.:—Mathat.

3159. **Ματθίας Matthias**, *mat-thee'-as;* appar. a shortened form of *3161;* *Matthias* (i.e. *Mattithjah*), an Isr.:—Matthias.

3160. **Ματταθά Mattatha**, *mat-tath-ah';* prob. a shortened form of *3161* [comp. 4992]; *Mattatha* (i.e. *Mattithjah*), an Isr.:—Mattatha.

3161. **Ματταθίας Mattathias**, *mat-tath-ee'-as;* of Heb. or. [4993]; *Mattathias* (i.e. *Mattithjah*), an Isr. and Chr.:—Mattathias.

3162. **μάχαιρα machaira**, *makh'-ahee-rah;* prob. fem. of a presumed der. of *3163;* a *knife*, i.e. *dirk;* fig. *war*, judicial *punishment:*—sword.

3163. **μάχη machē**, *makh'-ay;* from *3164;* a *battle*, i.e. (fig.) *controversy:*—fighting, strive, striving.

3164. **μάχομαι machŏmai**, *makh'-om-ahee;* mid. of an appar. prim. verb; to *war*, i.e. (fig.) to *quarrel, dispute:*—fight, strive.

3165. **μέ mĕ**, *meh;* a shorter (and prob. orig.) form of *1691;* *me:*—I, me, my.

3166. **μεγαλαυχέω mĕgalauchĕō**, *meg-al-ŏw-kheh'-o;* from a comp. of *3173* and **αὐχέω auchĕō** (to *boast;* akin to *837* and *2744*); to *talk big*, i.e. *be grandiloquent* (*arrogant, egotistic*):—boast great things.

3167. **μεγαλεῖος mĕgalĕiŏs**, *meg-al-i'-os;* from *3173;* *magnificent*, i.e. (neut. plur. as noun) a conspicuous *favor*, or (subj.) *perfection:*—great things, wonderful works.

3168. **μεγαλειότης mĕgalĕiŏtēs**, *meg-al-i-ot'-ace;* from *3167;* *superbness*, i.e. *glory* or *splendor:*—magnificence, majesty, mighty power.

3169. **μεγαλοπρεπής mĕgalŏprĕpēs**, *meg-al-op-rep-ace';* from *3173* and *4241;* *befitting greatness* or *magnificence* (*majestic*):—excellent.

3170. **μεγαλύνω mĕgalunō**, *meg-al-oo'-no;* from *3173;* to *make* (or *declare*) *great*, i.e. *increase* or (fig.) *extol:*—enlarge, magnify, shew great.

3171. **μεγάλως mĕgalōs**, *meg-al'-oce;* adv. from *3173;* *much:*—greatly.

3172. **μεγαλωσύνη mĕgalōsunē**, *meg-al-o-soo'-nay;* from *3173;* *greatness*, i.e. (fig.) *divinity* (often *God* himself):—majesty.

3173. **μέγας mĕgas**, *meg'-as* [includ. the prol. forms, fem. **μεγάλη mĕgalē**, plur. **μεγάλοι mĕgalŏi**, etc.; comp. also *3176*, *3187*]; *big* (lit. or fig., in a very wide application):—(+ fear) exceedingly, great (-est), high, large, loud, mighty, + (be) sore (afraid), strong, × to years.

3174. **μέγεθος mĕgĕthŏs**, *meg'-eth-os;* from *3173;* *magnitude* (fig.):—greatness.

3175. **μεγιστᾶνες mĕgistanĕs**, *meg-is-tan'-es;* plur. from *3176;* *grandees:*—great men, lords.

3176. **μέγιστος mĕgistŏs**, *meg'-is-tos;* superl. of *3173;* *greatest* or *very great:*—exceeding great.

3177. **μεθερμηνεύω mĕthĕrmĕnĕuō**, *meth-er-mane-yoo'-o;* from *3326* and *2059;* to *explain over*, i.e. *translate:*—(by) interpret (-ation).

3178. **μέθη mĕthē**, *meth'-ay;* appar. a prim. word; an *intoxicant*, i.e. (by impl.) *intoxication:*—drunkenness.

3179. μεθίστημι **mĕthistēmi**, *meth-is'-tay-mee;* or (1 Cor. 13 : 2)

μεθιστάνω **mĕthistanō**, *meth-is-tan'-o;* from *3326* and *2476;* to *transfer*, i.e. *carry away*, *depose* or (fig.) *exchange*, *seduce:*—put out, remove, translate, turn away.

3180. μεθοδεία **mĕthŏdĕia**, *meth-od-i'-ah;* from a comp. of *3326* and *3593* [comp. "method"]; *travelling over*, i.e. *travesty* (*trickery*):—wile, lie in wait.

3181. μεθόριος **mĕthŏriŏs**, *meth-or'-ee-os;* from *3326* and *3725;* *bounded alongside*, i.e. *contiguous* (neut. plur. as noun, *frontier*):—border.

3182. μεθύσκω **mĕthuskō**, *meth-oos'-ko;* a prol. (trans.) form of *3184;* to *intoxicate:*—be drunk (-en).

3183. μέθυσος **mĕthusŏs**, *meth'-oo-sos;* from *3184;* *tipsy*, i.e. (as noun) a *sot:*—drunkard.

3184. μεθύω **mĕthuō**, *meth-oo'-o;* from another form of *3178;* to *drink* to *intoxication*, i.e. *get drunk:*—drink well, make (be) drunk (-en).

3185. μεῖζον **mĕizŏn**, *mide'-zon;* neut. of *3187;* (adv.) in a *greater* degree:—the more.

3186. μειζότερος **mĕizŏtĕrŏs**, *mide-zot'-er-os;* continued compar. of *3187;* *still larger* (fig.):—greater.

3187. μείζων **mĕizōn**, *mide'-zone;* irreg. compar. of *3173;* *larger* (lit. or fig., spec. in age):—elder, greater (-est), more.

3188. μέλαν **mĕlan**, *mel'-an;* neut. of *3189* as noun; *ink:*—ink.

3189. μέλας **mĕlas**, *mel'-as;* appar. a prim. word; *black:*—black.

3190. Μελεᾶς **Mĕlĕas**, *mel-eh-as';* of uncert. or.; *Meleas*, an Isr.:—Meleas.

μέλει **mĕlĕi**. See *3199*.

3191. μελετάω **mĕlĕtaō**, *mel-et-ah'-o;* from a presumed der. of *3199;* to *take care of*, i.e. (by impl.) *revolve* in the mind:—imagine, (pre-) meditate.

3192. μέλι **mĕli**, *mel'-ee;* appar. a prim. word; *honey:*—honey.

3193. μελίσσιος **mĕlissiŏs**, *mel-is'-see-os;* from *3192:* *relating to honey*, i.e. *bee* (comb):—honeycomb.

3194. Μελίτη **Mĕlitē**, *mel-ee'-tay;* of uncert. or.; *Melita*, an island in the Mediterranean:—Melita.

3195. μέλλω **mĕllō**, *mel'-lo;* a strengthened form of *3199* (through the idea of *expectation*); to *intend*, i.e. *be about* to be, do, or suffer something (of persons or things, espec. events; in the sense of *purpose*, *duty*, *necessity*, *probability*, *possibility*, or *hesitation*):—about, after that, be (almost), (that which is, things, + which was for) to come, intend, was to (be), mean, mind, be at the point, (be) ready, + return, shall (begin), (which, that) should (after, afterwards, hereafter) tarry, which was for, will, would, be yet.

3196. μέλος **mĕlŏs**, *mel'-os;* of uncert. affin.; a *limb* or *part* of the body:—member.

3197. Μελχί **Mĕlchi**, *mel-khee';* of Heb. or. [4428 with pron. suf., *my king*]; *Melchi* (i.e. *Malki*), the name of two Isr.:—Melchi.

3198. Μελχισεδέκ **Mĕlchisĕdĕk**, *mel-khis-ed-ek';* of Heb. or. [4442]; *Melchisedek* (i.e. *Malkitsedek*), a patriarch:—Melchisedec.

3199. μέλω **mĕlō**, *mel'-o;* a prim. verb; to *be of interest* to, i.e. to *concern* (only third pers. sing. pres. indic. used impers. *it matters*):—(take) care.

3200. μεμβράνα **mĕmbrana**, *mem-bran'-ah;* of Lat. or. ("*membrane*"); a (written) sheep-*skin:*—parchment.

3201. μέμφομαι **mĕmphŏmai**, *mem'-fom-ahee;* mid. of an appar. prim. verb; to *blame:*—find fault.

3202. μεμψίμοιρος **mĕmpsimŏirŏs**, *mem-psim'-oy-ros;* from a presumed der. of *3201* and μοῖρα **mŏira** (*fate;* akin to the base of *3313*); *blaming fate*, i.e. *querulous* (*discontented*):—complainer.

3303. μέν **mĕn**, *men;* a prim. particle; prop. indic. of *affirmation* or *concession* (*in fact*); usually followed by a *contrasted* clause with *1161* (*this* one, the *former*, etc.):—even, indeed, so, some, truly, verily. Often compounded with other particles in an *intensive* or *asseverative* sense.

3304. μενοῦνγε **mĕnŏungĕ**, *men-oon'-geh;* from *3303* and *3767* and *1065;* *so then at least:*—nay but, yea doubtless (rather, verily).

3305. μέντοι **mĕntŏi**, *men'-toy;* from *3303* and *5104;* *indeed though*, i.e. *however:*—also, but, howbeit, nevertheless, yet.

3306. μένω **mĕnō**, *men'-o;* a prim. verb; to *stay* (in a given place, state, relation or expectancy):—abide, continue, dwell, endure, be present, remain, stand, tarry (for), × thine own.

3307. μερίζω **mĕrizō**, *mer-id'-zo;* from *3313;* to *part*, i.e. (lit.) to *apportion*, *bestow*, *share*, or (fig.) to *disunite*, *differ:*—deal, be difference between, distribute, divide, give part.

3308. μέριμνα **mĕrimna**, *mer'-im-nah;* from *3307* (through the idea of *distraction*); *solicitude:*—care.

3309. μεριμνάω **mĕrimnaō**, *mer-im-nah'-o;* from *3308;* to *be anxious* about:—(be, have) care (-ful), take thought.

3310. μερίς **mĕris**, *mer-ece';* fem. of *3313;* a *portion*, i.e. *province*, *share* or (abstr.) *participation:*—part (× -akers).

3311. μερισμός **mĕrismŏs**, *mer-is-mos';* from *3307;* a *separation* or *distribution:*—dividing asunder, gift.

3312. μεριστής **mĕristēs**, *mer-is-tace';* from *3307;* an *apportioner* (*administrator*):—divider.

3313. μέρος **mĕrŏs**, *mer'-os;* from an obsol. but more prim. form of μείρομαι **mĕirŏmai** (to *get* as a *section* or *allotment*); a *division* or *share* (lit. or fig., in a wide application):—behalf, coast, course, craft, particular (+ -ly), part (+ -ly), piece, portion, respect, side, some sort (-what).

3314. μεσημβρία **mĕsēmbria**, *mes-ame-bree'-ah;* from *3319* and *2250;* *midday;* by impl. the *south:*—noon, south.

3315. μεσιτεύω **mĕsitĕuō**, *mes-it-yoo'-o;* from *3316;* to *interpose* (as arbiter), i.e. (by impl.) to *ratify* (as surety):—confirm.

3316. μεσίτης **mĕsitēs**, *mes-ee'-tace;* from *3319;* a *go-between*, i.e. (simply) an *internunciator*, or (by impl.) a *reconciler* (*intercessor*):—mediator.

3317. μεσονύκτιον **mĕsŏnuktiŏn**, *mes-on-ook'-tee-on;* neut. of a comp. of *3319* and *3571;* *midnight* (espec. as a watch):—midnight.

3318. Μεσοποταμία **Mĕsŏpŏtamia**, *mes-op-ot-am-ee'-ah;* from *3319* and *4215;* *Mesopotamia* (as lying between the Euphrates and the Tigris; comp. 763), a region of Asia:—Mesopotamia.

3319. μέσος **mĕsŏs**, *mes'-os;* from *3326;* *middle* (as adj. or [neut.] noun):—among, × before them, between, + forth, mid [-day, -night], midst, way.

3320. μεσότοιχον **mĕsŏtŏichŏn**, *mes-ot'-oy-khon;* from *3319* and *5109;* a *partition* (fig.):—middle wall.

3321. μεσουράνημα **mĕsŏuranēma**, *mes-oo-ran'-ay-mah;* from a presumed comp. of *3319* and *3772;* *mid-sky:*—midst of heaven.

3322. μεσόω **mĕsŏō**, *mes-ŏ'-o;* from *3319;* to *form* the *middle*, i.e. (in point of time), to *be half-way* over:—be about the midst.

3323. Μεσσίας **Mĕssias**, *mes-see'-as;* of Heb. or. [4899]; the *Messias* (i.e. *Mashiach*), or Christ:—Messias.

3324. μεστός **mĕstŏs**, *mes-tos';* of uncert. der.; *replete* (lit. or fig.):—full.

3325. μεστόω **mĕstŏō**, *mes-tŏ'-o;* from *3324;* to *replenish*, i.e. (by impl.) to *intoxicate:*—fill.

3326. μετά **mĕta**, *met-ah';* a prim. prep. (often used adv.); prop. denoting *accompaniment;* "*amid*" (local or causal); modified variously according to the case (gen. *association*, or acc. *succession*) with which it is joined; occupying an intermediate position between *575* or *1537* and *1519* or *4314;* less intimate than *1722*, and less close than *4862*):—after (-ward), × that he again, against, among, × and, + follow, hence, hereafter, in, of, (up-) on, + our, × and setting, since, (un-) to, + together, when, with (+ -out). Often used in composition, in substantially the same relations of *participation* or *proximity*, and *transfer* or *sequence*.

3327. μεταβαίνω **mĕtabainō**, *met-ab-ah'ee-no;* from *3326* and the base of *939;* to *change place:*—depart, go, pass, remove.

3328. μεταβάλλω **mĕtaballō**, *met-ab-al'-lo;* from *3326* and *906;* to *throw over*, i.e. (mid. fig.) to *turn about* in opinion:—change mind.

3329. μετάγω **mĕtagō**, *met-ag'-o;* from *3326* and *71;* to *lead over*, i.e. *transfer* (*direct*):—turn about.

3330. μεταδίδωμι **mĕtadidōmi**, *met-ad-id'-o-mee;* from *3326* and *1325;* to *give over*, i.e. *share:*—give, impart.

3331. μετάθεσις **mĕtathĕsis**, *met-ath'-es-is;* from *3346;* *transposition*, i.e. *transferral* (to heaven), *disestablishment* (of a law):—change, removing, translation.

3332. μεταίρω **mĕtairō**, *met-ah'ee-ro;* from *3326* and *142;* to *betake* oneself, i.e. *remove* (locally):—depart.

3333. μετακαλέω **mĕtakalĕō**, *met-ak-al-eh'-o;* from *3326* and *2564;* to *call elsewhere*, i.e. *summon:*—call (for, hither).

3334. μετακινέω **mĕtakinĕō**, *met-ak-ee-neh'-o;* from *3326* and *2795;* to *stir* to a place *elsewhere*, i.e. *remove* (fig.):—move away.

3335. μεταλαμβάνω **mĕtalambanō**, *met-al-am-ban'-o;* from *3326* and *2983;* to *participate;* gen. to *accept* (and use):—eat, have, be partaker, receive, take.

3336. μετάληψις **mĕtalēpsis**, *met-al'-ape-sis;* from *3335;* *participation:*—taking.

3337. μεταλλάσσω **mĕtallassō**, *met-al-las'-so;* from *3326* and *236;* to *exchange:*—change.

3338. μεταμέλλομαι **mĕtamĕllŏmai**, *met-am-el'-lom-ahee;* from *3326* and the mid. of *3199;* to *care afterwards*, i.e. *regret:*—repent (self).

3339. μεταμορφόω **mĕtamŏrphŏō**, *met-am-or-fŏ'-o;* from *3326* and *3445;* to *transform* (lit. or fig. "metamorphose"):—change, transfigure, transform.

3340. μετανοέω **mĕtanŏĕō**, *met-an-ŏ-eh'-o;* from *3326* and *3539;* to *think differently* or *afterwards*, i.e. *reconsider* (mor. *feel compunction*):—repent.

3341. μετάνοια **mĕtanŏia**, *met-an'-oy-ah;* from *3340;* (subj.) *compunction* (for guilt, includ. *reformation*); by impl. *reversal* (of [another's] decision):—repentance.

3342. μεταξύ **mĕtaxu**, *met-ax-oo';* from *3326* and a form of *4862;* *betwixt* (of place or person); (of time) as adj. *intervening*, or (by impl.) *adjoining:*—between, mean while, next.

3343. μεταπέμπω **mĕtapĕmpō**, *met-ap-emp'-o;* from *3326* and *3992;* to *send from elsewhere*, i.e. (mid.) to *summon* or *invite:*—call (send) for.

3344. μεταστρέφω **mĕtastrĕphō**, *met-as-tref'-o;* from *3326* and *4762;* to *turn across*, i.e. *transmute* or (fig.) *corrupt:*—pervert, turn.

3345. μετασχηματίζω **mĕtaschēmatizō**, *met-askh-ay-mat-id'-zo;* from *3326* and a der. of *4976;* to *transfigure* or *disguise;* fig. to *apply* (by accommodation) :—transfer, transform (self) ; to *change*.

3346. μετατίθημι **mĕtatithēmi**, *met-at-ith'-ay-mee;* from *3326* and *5087;* to *transfer*, i.e. (lit.) *transport*, (by impl.) *exchange*, (reflex.) *change sides*, or (fig.) *pervert:*—carry over, change, remove, translate, turn.

3347. μετέπειτα **mĕtĕpĕita**, *met-ep'-i-tah;* from *3326* and *1899;* *thereafter:*—afterward.

3348. μετέχω **mĕtĕchō**, *met-ekh'-o;* from *3326* and *2192;* to *share* or *participate;* by impl. *belong* to, *eat* (or *drink*):—be partaker, pertain, take part, use.

3349. μετεωρίζω **mĕtĕōrizō**, *met-eh-o-rid'-zo;* from a comp. of *3326* and a collat. form of *142* or perh. rather of *109* (comp. "meteor"); to *raise in mid-air*, i.e. (fig.) *suspend* (pass. *fluctuate* or *be anxious*):—be of doubtful mind.

3350. μετοικεσία **mĕtŏikĕsia**, *met-oy-kes-ee'-ah;* from a der. of a comp. of *3326* and *3624;* a *change of abode*, i.e. (spec.) *expatriation:*— × brought, carried (-ying) away (in-) to.

3351. **μετοικίζω mĕtŏikizō,** *met-oy-kid'-zo;* from the same as *3350;* to *transfer* as a *settler* or *captive,* i.e. *colonize* or *exile:*—carry away, remove into.

3352. **μετοχή mĕtŏchē,** *met-okh-ay';* from *3348;* *participation,* i.e. *intercourse:*—fellowship.

3353. **μέτοχος mĕtŏchŏs,** *met'-okh-os;* from *3348;* *participant,* i.e. (as noun) a *sharer;* by impl. an *associate:*—fellow, partaker, partner.

3354. **μετρέω mĕtrĕō,** *met-reh'-o;* from *3358;* to *measure* (i.e. ascertain in size by a fixed standard); by impl. to *admeasure* (i.e. allot by rule); fig. to *estimate:*—measure, mete.

3355. **μετρητής mĕtrētēs,** *met-ray-tace';* from *3354;* a *measurer,* i.e. (spec.) a certain standard *measure* of capacity for liquids:—firkin.

3356. **μετριοπαθέω mĕtriŏpathĕō,** *met-ree-op-ath-eh'-o;* from a comp. of the base of *3357* and *3806;* to *be moderate in passion,* i.e. *gentle* (to *treat indulgently*):—have compassion.

3357. **μετρίως mĕtriōs,** *met-ree'-oce;* adv. from a der. of *3358;* *moderately,* i.e. *slightly:*—a little.

3358. **μέτρον mĕtrŏn,** *met'-ron;* an appar. prim. word; a *measure* ("metre"), lit. or fig.; by impl. a limited *portion* (*degree*):—measure.

3359. **μέτωπον mĕtōpŏn,** *met'-o-pon;* from *3326* and **ὤψ ōps** (the *face*); the *forehead* (as *opposite the countenance*):—forehead.

3360. **μέχρι mĕchri,** *mekh'-ree;* or

μεχρίς mĕchris, *mekh-ris';* from *3372;* *as far as,* i.e. *up to* a certain point (as prep. of extent [denoting the *terminus,* whereas *891* refers espec. to the *space* of time or place intervening] or conj.):—till, (un-) to, until.

3361. **μή mē,** *may;* a prim. particle of qualified *negation* (whereas *3756* expresses an absolute denial); (adv.) *not,* (conj.) *lest;* also (as interrog. implying a *neg.* answer [whereas *3756* expects an *affirm.* one]) *whether:*—any, but (that), × forbear, + God forbid, + lack, lest, neither, never, no (× wise in), none, nor, [can-] not, nothing, that not, un [-taken], without. Often used in compounds in substantially the same relations. See also *3362, 3363, 3364, 3372, 3373, 3375, 3378.*

3362. **ἐὰν μή ĕan mē,** *eh-an' may;* i.e. *1437* and *3361;* *if not,* i.e. *unless:*— × before, but, except, if no, (if, + whosoever) not.

3363. **ἵνα μή hina mē,** *hin'-ah may;* i.e. *2443* and *3361;* *in order* (or *so*) *that not:*—albeit not, lest, that no (-t, [-thing]).

3364. **οὐ μή ŏu mē,** *oo may;* i.e. *3756* and *3361;* a double neg. strengthening the denial; *not at all:*—any more, at all, by any (no) means, neither, never, no (at all), in no case (wise), nor ever, not (at all, in any wise). Comp. *3378.*

3365. **μηδαμῶς mēdamōs,** *may-dam-oce';* adv. from a comp. of *3361* and **ἀμός amŏs** (*somebody*); *by no means:*—not so.

3366. **μηδέ mēdĕ,** *may-deh';* from *3361* and *1161;* *but not, not even;* in a continued negation, *nor:*—neither, nor (yet), (no) not (once, so much as).

3367. **μηδείς mēdĕis,** *may-dice';* includ. the irreg. fem. **μηδεμία mēdĕmia,** *may-dem-ee'-ah,* and the neut. **μηδέν mēdĕn,** *may-den';* from *3361* and *1520;* *not even one* (man, woman, thing):—any (man, thing), no (man), none, not (at all, any man, a whit), nothing, + without delay.

3368. **μηδέποτε mēdĕpŏtĕ,** *may-dep'-ot-eh;* from *3366* and *4218;* *not even ever:*—never.

3369. **μηδέπω mēdĕpō,** *may-dep'-o;* from *3366* and *4452;* *not even yet:*—not yet.

3370. **Μῆδος Mēdŏs,** *may'-dos;* of for. or. [comp. 4074]; a *Median,* or inhab. of Media:—Mede.

3371. **μηκέτι mēkĕti,** *may-ket'-ee;* from *3361* and *2089;* *no further:*—any longer, (not) henceforth, hereafter, no henceforward (longer, more, soon), not any more.

3372. **μῆκος mēkŏs,** *may'-kos;* prob. akin to *3173;* *length* (lit. or fig.):—length.

3373. **μηκύνω mēkunō,** *may-koo'-no;* from *3372;* to *lengthen,* i.e. (mid.) to *enlarge:*—grow up.

3374. **μηλωτή mēlōtē,** *may-lo-tay';* from **μῆλον mēlŏn** (a *sheep*); a *sheep-skin:*—sheepskin.

3375. **μήν mēn,** *mane;* a stronger form of *3303;* a particle of affirmation (only with *2229*); *assuredly:*—+ surely.

3376. **μήν mēn,** *mane;* a prim. word; a *month:*—month.

3377. **μηνύω mēnuō,** *may-noo'-o;* prob. from the same base as *3145* and *3415* (i.e. **μάω maō,** to *strive*); to *disclose* (through the idea of mental *effort* and thus calling to *mind*), i.e. *report, declare, intimate:*—shew, tell.

3378. **μὴ οὐκ mē ŏuk,** *may ook;* i.e. *3361* and *3756;* as interrog. and neg. *is it not that?:*—neither (followed by *no*), + never, not. Comp. *3364.*

3379. **μήποτε mēpŏtĕ,** *may'-pot-eh;* or

μή ποτε mē pŏtĕ, *may pot'-eh;* from *3361* and *4218;* *not ever;* also *if* (or *lest*) *ever* (or *perhaps*):—if peradventure, lest (at any time, haply), not at all, whether or not.

3380. **μήπω mēpō,** *may'-po;* from *3361* and *4452;* *not yet:*—not yet.

3381. **μήπως mēpōs,** *may'-poce;* or

μή πως mē pōs, *may poce;* from *3361* and *4458;* *lest somehow:*—lest (by any means, by some means, haply, perhaps).

3382. **μηρός mērŏs,** *may-ros';* perh. a prim. word; a *thigh:*—thigh.

3383. **μήτε mētĕ,** *may'-teh;* from *3361* and *5037;* *not too,* i.e. (in continued negation) *neither* or *nor;* also, *not even:*—neither, (n-) or, so much as.

3384. **μήτηρ mētēr,** *may'-tare;* appar. a prim. word; a "*mother*" (lit. or fig., immed. or remote):—mother.

3385. **μήτι mēti,** *may'-tee;* from *3361* and the neut. of *5100;* *whether at all:*—not [*the particle usually not expressed, except by the form of the question*].

3386. **μήτιγε mētigĕ,** *may'-tig-eh;* from *3385* and *1065;* *not at all then,* i.e. *not to say* (*the rather still*):—how much more.

3387. **μήτις mētis,** *may'-tis;* or

μή τις mē tis, *may tis;* from *3361* and *5100;* *whether any:*—any [*sometimes unexpressed except by the simple interrogative form of the sentence*].

3388. **μήτρα mētra,** *may'-trah;* from *3384;* the *matrix:*—womb.

3389. **μητραλῴας mētralō̜as,** *may-tral-o'-as;* from *3384* and the base of *257;* a *mother-thresher,* i.e. *matricide:*—murderer of mothers.

3390. **μητρόπολις mētrŏpŏlis,** *may-trop'-ol-is;* from *3384* and *4172;* a *mother city,* i.e. "*metropolis*":—chiefest city.

3391. **μία mia,** *mee'-ah;* irreg. fem. of *1520;* *one* or *first:*—a (certain), + agree, first, one, × other.

3392. **μιαίνω miainō,** *me-ah'ee-no;* perh. a prim. verb; to *sully* or *taint,* i.e. *contaminate* (cer. or mor.):—defile.

3393. **μίασμα miasma,** *mee'-as-mah;* from *3392* ("*miasma*"); (mor.) *foulness* (prop. the effect):—pollution.

3394. **μιασμός miasmŏs,** *mee-as-mos';* from *3392;* (mor.) *contamination* (prop. the act):—uncleanness.

3395. **μίγμα migma,** *mig'-mah;* from *3396;* a *compound:*—mixture.

3396. **μίγνυμι mignumi,** *mig'-noo-mee;* a prim. verb; to *mix:*—mingle.

3397. **μικρόν mikrŏn,** *mik-ron';* masc. or neut. sing. of *3398* (as noun); a *small* space of *time* or *degree:*—a (little) (while).

3398. **μικρός mikrŏs,** *mik-ros';* includ. the comp. **μικρότερος mikrŏtĕrŏs,** *mik-rot'-er-os;* appar. a prim. word; *small* (in size, quantity, number or (fig.) dignity):—least, less, little, small.

3399. **Μίλητος Milētŏs,** *mil'-ay-tos;* of uncert. or.; *Miletus,* a city of Asia Minor:—Miletus.

3400. **μίλιον miliŏn,** *mil'-ee-on;* of Lat. or.: a *thousand* paces, i.e. a "*mile*":—mile.

3401. **μιμέομαι mimĕŏmai,** *mim-eh'-om-ahee;* mid. from **μῖμος mimŏs** (a "*mimic*"); to *imitate:*—follow.

3402. **μιμητής mimētēs,** *mim-ay-tace';* from *3401;* an *imitator:*—follower.

3403. **μιμνήσκω mimnēskō,** *mim-nace'-ko;* a prol. form of *3415* (from which some of the tenses are borrowed); to *remind,* i.e. (mid.) to *recall to mind:*—be mindful, remember.

3404. **μισέω misĕō,** *mis-eh'-o;* from a prim. **μῖσος misŏs** (*hatred*); to *detest* (espec. to *persecute*); by extens. to *love less:*—hate (-ful).

3405. **μισθαποδοσία misthapŏdŏsia,** *mis-thap-od-os-ee'-ah;* from *3406;* *requital* (good or bad):—recompence of reward.

3406. **μισθαποδότης misthapŏdŏtēs,** *mis-thap-od-ot'-ace;* from *3409* and *591;* a *remunerator:*—rewarder.

3407. **μίσθιος misthiŏs,** *mis'-thee-os;* from *3408;* a *wage-earner:*—hired servant.

3408. **μισθός misthŏs,** *mis-thos';* appar. a prim. word; *pay* for service (lit. or fig.), good or bad:—hire, reward, wages.

3409. **μισθόω misthŏō,** *mis-tho'-o;* from *3408;* to *let* out for wages, i.e. (mid.) to *hire:*—hire.

3410. **μίσθωμα misthōma,** *mis'-tho-mah;* from *3409;* a *rented* building:—hired house.

3411. **μισθωτός misthōtŏs,** *mis-tho-tos';* from *3409;* a *wage-worker* (good or bad):—hired servant, hireling.

3412. **Μιτυλήνη Mitulēnē,** *mit-oo-lay'-nay;* for **μυτιλήνη mutilēnē** (*abounding in shell-fish*); *Mitylene* (or *Mytilene*), a town in the island Lesbos:—Mitylene.

3413. **Μιχαήλ Michaēl,** *mikh-ah-ale';* of Heb. or. [4317]; *Michaël,* an archangel:—Michael.

3414. **μνᾶ mna,** *mnah;* of Lat. or.; a *mna* (i.e. *mina*), a certain *weight:*—pound.

3415. **μνάομαι mnaŏmai,** *mnah'-om-ahee;* mid. of a der. of *3306* or perh. of the base of *3145* (through the idea of *fixture* in the mind or of mental *grasp*); to *bear in mind,* i.e. *recollect;* by impl. to *reward* or *punish:*—be mindful, remember, come (have) in remembrance. Comp. *3403.*

3416. **Μνάσων Mnasōn,** *mnah'-sohn;* of uncert. or.; *Mnason,* a Chr.:—Mnason.

3417. **μνεία mnĕia,** *mni'-ah;* from *3415* or *3403;* *recollection;* by impl. *recital:*—mention, remembrance.

3418. **μνῆμα mnēma,** *mnay'-mah;* from *3415;* a *memorial,* i.e. sepulchral *monument* (*burial-place*):—grave, sepulchre, tomb.

3419. **μνημεῖον mnēmĕiŏn,** *mnay-mi'-on;* from *3420;* a *remembrance,* i.e. *cenotaph* (*place of interment*):—grave, sepulchre, tomb.

3420. **μνήμη mnēmē,** *mnay'-may;* from *3403;* *memory:*—remembrance.

3421. **μνημονεύω mnēmŏnĕuō,** *mnay-mon-yoo'-o;* from a der. of *3420;* to *exercise memory,* i.e. *recollect;* by impl. to *punish;* also to *rehearse:*—make mention, be mindful, remember.

3422. **μνημόσυνον mnēmŏsunŏn,** *mnay-mos'-oo-non;* from *3421;* a *reminder* (*memorandum*), i.e. *record:*—memorial.

3423. **μνηστεύω mnēstĕuō,** *mnace-tyoo'-o;* from a der. of *3415;* to *give a souvenir* (engagement present), i.e. *betroth:*—espouse.

3424. **μογιλάλος mŏgilalŏs,** *mog-il-al'-os;* from *3425* and *2980;* *hardly talking,* i.e. *dumb* (*tongue-tied*):—having an impediment in his speech.

3425. **μόγις mŏgis,** *mog'-is;* adv. from a prim. **μόγος mŏgŏs** (*toil*); *with difficulty:*—hardly.

3426. **μόδιος mŏdiŏs,** *mod'-ee-os;* of Lat. or.; a *modius,* i.e. certain measure for things dry (the quantity or the utensil):—bushel.

3427. **μοί mŏi,** *moy;* the simpler form of *1698;* to *me:*—I, me, mine, my.

3428. **μοιχαλίς mŏichalis**, *moy-khal-is'*; a prol. form of the fem. of *3432*; an *adulteress* (lit. or fig.):—adulteress (-ous, -y).

3429. **μοιχάω mŏichaō**, *moy-khah'-o*; from *3432*; (mid.) to *commit adultery*:—commit adultery.

3430. **μοιχεία mŏichĕia**, *moy-khi'-ah*; from *3431*; *adultery*:—adultery.

3431. **μοιχεύω mŏichĕuō**, *moy-khyoo'-o*; from *3432*; to *commit adultery*:—commit adultery.

3432. **μοιχός mŏichŏs**, *moy-khos'*; perh. a prim. word; a (male) *paramour*; fig. *apostate*:—adulterer.

3433. **μόλις mŏlis**, *mol'-is*; prob. by var. for *3425*; *with difficulty*:—hardly, scarce (-ly), + with much work.

3434. **Μολόχ Mŏlŏch**, *mol-okh'*; of Heb. or. [4432]; *Moloch* (i.e. *Molek*), an idol:—Moloch.

3435. **μολύνω mŏlunō**, *mol-oo'-no*; prob. from *3189*; to *soil* (fig.):—defile.

3436. **μολυσμός mŏlusmŏs**, *mol-oos-mos'*; from *3435*; a *stain*, i.e. (fig.) *immorality*:—filthiness.

3437. **μομφή mŏmphē**, *mom-fay'*; from *3201*; *blame*, i.e. (by impl.) a *fault*:—quarrel.

3438. **μονή mŏnē**, *mon-ay'*; from *3306*; a *staying*, i.e. *residence* (the act or the place):—abode, mansion.

3439. **μονογενής mŏnŏgĕnēs**, *mon-og-en-ace'*; from *3441* and *1096*; *only-born*, i.e. *sole*:—only (begotten, child).

3440. **μόνον mŏnŏn**, *mon'-on*; neut. of *3441* as adv.; *merely*:—alone, but, only.

3441. **μόνος mŏnŏs**, *mon'-os*; prob. from *3306*; *remaining*, i.e. *sole* or *single*; by impl. *mere*:—alone, only, by themselves.

3442. **μονόφθαλμος mŏnŏphthalmŏs**, *mon-of'-thal-mos*; from *3441* and *3788*; *one-eyed*:—with one eye.

3443. **μονόω mŏnŏō**, *mon-ŏ'-o*; from *3441*; to *isolate*, i.e. *bereave*:—be desolate.

3444. **μορφή mŏrphē**, *mor-fay'*; perh. from the base of *3313* (through the idea of *adjustment* of parts); *shape*; fig. *nature*:—form.

3445. **μορφόω mŏrphŏō**, *mor-fŏ'-o*; from the same as *3444*; to *fashion* (fig.):—form.

3446. **μόρφωσις mŏrphōsis**, *mor'-fo-sis*; from *3445*; *formation*, i.e. (by impl.) *appearance* (*semblance* or [concr.] *formula*):—form.

3447. **μοσχοποιέω mŏschŏpŏiĕō**, *mos-khop-oy-eh'-o*; from *3448* and *4160*; to *fabricate* the image of a *bullock*:—make a calf.

3448. **μόσχος mŏschŏs**, *mos'-khos*; prob. strengthened for **ὄσχος ŏschŏs** (a *shoot*); a young *bullock*:—calf.

3449. **μόχθος mŏchthŏs**, *mokh'-thos*; from the base of *3425*; *toil*, i.e. (by impl.) *sadness*:—painfulness, travail.

3450. **μοῦ mŏu**, *moo*; the simpler form of *1700*; *of me*:—I, me, mine (own), my.

3451. **μουσικός mŏusikŏs**, *moo-sik-os'*; from **Μοῦσα Mŏusa** (a *Muse*); "*musical*", i.e. (as noun) a *minstrel*:—musician.

3452. **μυελός muĕlŏs**, *moo-el-os'*; perh. a prim. word; the *marrow*:—marrow.

3453. **μυέω muĕō**, *moo-eh'-o*; from the base of *3466*; to *initiate*, i.e. (by impl.) to *teach*:—instruct.

3454. **μῦθος muthŏs**, *moo'-thos*; perh. from the same as *3453* (through the idea of *tuition*); a *tale*, i.e. *fiction* ("*myth*"):—fable.

3455. **μυκάομαι mukaŏmai**, *moo-kah'-om-ahee*; from a presumed der. of **μύζω muzō** (to "*moo*"); to *bellow* (*roar*):—roar.

3456. **μυκτηρίζω muktērizō**, *mook-tay-rid'-zo*; from a der. of the base of *3455* (mean. *snout*, as that whence *lowing* proceeds); to *make mouths* at, i.e. *ridicule*:—mock.

3457. **μυλικός mulikŏs**, *moo-lee-kos'*; from *3458*; *belonging to a mill*:—mill [-stone].

3458. **μύλος mulŏs**, *moo'-los*; prob. ultimately from the base of *3433* (through the idea of *hardship*); a "*mill*", i.e. (by impl.) a *grinder* (*millstone*):—millstone.

3459. **μύλων mulōn**, *moo'-lone*; from *3458*; a *mill-house*:—mill.

3460. **Μύρα Mura**, *moo'-rah*; of uncert. der.; *Myra*, a place in Asia Minor:—Myra.

3461. **μυριάς murias**, *moo-ree'-as*; from *3463*; a *ten-thousand*; by extens. a "*myriad*" or indefinite number:—ten thousand.

3462. **μυρίζω murizō**, *moo-rid'-zo*; from *3464*; to *apply* (perfumed) *unguent* to:—anoint.

3463. **μύριοι muriŏi**, *moo'-ree-oi*; plur. of an appar. prim. word (prop. mean. *very many*); *ten thousand*; by extens. *innumerably* many:—ten thousand.

3464. **μύρον murŏn**, *moo'-ron*; prob. of for. or. [comp. 4753, *4666*]; "*myrrh*", i.e. (by impl.) *perfumed oil*:—ointment.

3465. **Μυσία Musia**, *moo-see'-ah*; of uncert. or.; *Mysia*, a region of Asia Minor:—Mysia.

3466. **μυστήριον mustēriŏn**, *moos-tay'-ree-on*; from a der. of **μύω muō** (to *shut* the mouth); a *secret* or "*mystery*" (through the idea of *silence* imposed by *initiation* into religious rites):—mystery.

3467. **μυωπάζω muōpazō**, *moo-ope-ad'-zo*; from a comp. of the base of *3466* and **ὤψ ōps** (the *face*; from *3700*); to *shut* the *eyes*, i.e. *blink* (*see indistinctly*):—cannot see afar off.

3468. **μώλωψ mōlōps**, *mo'-lopes*; from **μῶλος mōlŏs** ("*moil*"; prob. akin to the base of *3433*) and prob. **ὤψ ōps** (the *face*; from *3700*); a *mole* ("black eye") or *blow-mark*:—stripe.

3469. **μωμάομαι mōmaŏmai**, *mo-mah'-om-ahee*; from *3470*; to *carp* at, i.e. *censure* (*discredit*):—blame.

3470. **μῶμος mōmŏs**, *mo'-mos*; perh. from *3201*; a *flaw* or *blot*, i.e. (fig.) *disgraceful* person:—blemish.

3471. **μωραίνω mōrainō**, *mo-rah'ee-no*; from *3474*; to *become insipid*; fig. to *make* (pass. *act*) as a *simpleton*:—become fool, make foolish, lose savour.

3472. **μωρία mōria**, *mo-ree'-ah*; from *3474*; *silliness*, i.e. *absurdity*:—foolishness.

3473. **μωρολογία mōrŏlŏgia**, *mo-rol-og-ee'-ah*; from a comp. of *3474* and *3004*; *silly talk*, i.e. *buffoonery*:—foolish talking.

3474. **μωρός mōrŏs**, *mo-ros'*; prob. from the base of *3466*; *dull* or *stupid* (as if *shut* up), i.e. *heedless*, (mor.) *blockhead*, (appar.) *absurd*:—fool (-ish, × -ishness).

3475. **Μωσεύς Mōsĕus**, *moce-yoos'*; or
Μωσῆς Mōsēs, *mo-sace'*; or
Μωϋσῆς Mōüsēs, *mo-oo-sace'*; of Heb. or.; [4872]; *Moseus*, *Moses* or *Moüses* (i.e. *Mosheh*), the Heb. lawgiver:—Moses.

N

3476. **Ναασσών Naassōn**, *nah-as-sone'*; of Heb. or. [5177]; *Naasson* (i.e. *Nachshon*), an Isr.:—Naasson.

3477. **Ναγγαί Naggai**, *nang-gah'ee*; prob. of Heb. or. [comp. 5052]; *Nangæ* (i.e. perh. *Nogach*), an Isr.:—Nagge.

3478. **Ναζαρέθ Nazarĕth**, *nad-zar-eth'*; or
Ναζαρέτ Nazarĕt, *nad-zar-et'*; of uncert. der.; *Nazareth* or *Nazaret*, a place in Pal.:—Nazareth.

3479. **Ναζαρηνός Nazarēnŏs**, *nad-zar-ay-nos'*; from *3478*; a *Nazarene*, i.e. inhab. of Nazareth:—of Nazareth.

3480. **Ναζωραῖος Nazōraiŏs**, *nad-zo-rah'-yos*; from *3478*; a *Nazoræan*, i.e. inhab. of Nazareth; by extens. a *Christian*:—Nazarene, of Nazareth.

3481. **Ναθάν Nathan**, *nath-an'*; of Heb. or. [5416]; *Nathan*, an Isr.:—Nathan.

3482. **Ναθαναήλ Nathanaēl**, *nath-an-ah-ale'*; of Heb. or. [5417]; *Nathanaël* (i.e. *Nathanel*), an Isr. and Chr.:—Nathanael.

3483. **ναί nai**, *nahee*; a prim. particle of strong affirmation; *yes*:—even so, surely, truth, verily, yea, yes.

3484. **Ναΐν Naïn**, *nah-in'*; prob. of Heb. or. [comp. 4999]; *Naïn*, a place in Pal.:—Nain.

3485. **ναός naŏs**, *nah-os'*; from a prim. **ναίω naiō** (to *dwell*); a *fane*, *shrine*, *temple*:—shrine, temple. Comp. *2411*.

3486. **Ναούμ Naŏum**, *nah-oom'*; of Heb. or. [5151]; *Naüm* (i.e. *Nachum*), an Isr.:—Naum.

3487. **νάρδος nardŏs**, *nar'-dos*; of for. or. [comp. 5373]; "*nard*":—[spike-] nard.

3488. **Νάρκισσος Narkissŏs**, *nar'-kis-sos*; a flower of the same name, from **ναρκη narkē** (*stupefaction*, as a "narcotic"); *Narcissus*, a Roman:—Narcissus.

3489. **ναυαγέω nauagĕō**, *nŏw-ag-eh'-o*; from a comp. of *3491* and *71*; to *be shipwrecked* (*stranded*, "navigate"), lit. or fig.:—make (suffer) shipwreck.

3490. **ναύκληρος nauklērŏs**, *nŏw'-klay-ros*; from *3491* and *2819* ("clerk"); a *captain*:—owner of a ship.

3491. **ναῦς naus**, *nŏwce*; from **νάω naō** or **νέω nĕō** (to *float*); a *boat* (of any size):—ship.

3492. **ναύτης nautēs**, *now'-tace*; from *3491*; a *boatman*, i.e. *seaman*:—sailor, shipman.

3493. **Ναχώρ Nachōr**, *nakh-ore'*; of Heb. or. [5152]; *Nachor*, the grandfather of Abraham:—Nachor.

3494. **νεανίας nĕanias**, *neh-an-ee'-as*; from a der. of *3501*; a *youth* (up to about forty years):—young man.

3495. **νεανίσκος nĕaniskŏs**, *neh-an-is'-kos*; from the same as *3494*; a *youth* (under forty):—young man.

3496. **Νεάπολις Nĕapŏlis**, *neh-ap'-ol-is*; from *3501* and *4172*; *new town*; *Neäpolis*, a place in Macedonia:—Neapolis.

3497. **Νεεμάν Nĕĕman**, *neh-eh-man'*; of Heb. or. [5283]; *Neëman* (i.e. *Naaman*), a Syrian:—Naaman.

3498. **νεκρός nĕkrŏs**, *nek-ros'*; from an appar. prim. **νέκυς nĕkus** (a *corpse*); *dead* (lit. or fig.; also as noun):—dead.

3499. **νεκρόω nĕkrŏō**, *nek-rŏ'-o*; from *3498*; to *deaden*, i.e. (fig.) to *subdue*:—be dead, mortify.

3500. **νέκρωσις nĕkrōsis**, *nek'-ro-sis*; from *3499*; *decease*; fig. *impotency*:—deadness, dying.

3501. **νέος nĕŏs**, *neh'-os*; includ. the comp.
νεώτερος nĕōtĕrŏs, *neh-o'-ter-os*; a prim. word; "*new*", i.e. (of persons) *youthful*, or (of things) *fresh*; fig. *regenerate*:—new, young.

3502. **νεοσσός nĕŏssŏs**, *neh-os-sos'*; from *3501*; a *youngling* (*nestling*):—young.

3503. **νεότης nĕŏtēs**, *neh-ot'-ace*; from *3501*; *newness*, i.e. *youthfulness*:—youth.

3504. **νεόφυτος nĕŏphutŏs**, *neh-of'-oo-tos*; from *3501* and a der. of *5453*; *newly planted*, i.e. (fig.) a *young convert* ("*neophyte*"):—novice.

3505. **Νέρων Nĕrōn**, *ner'-ohn*; of Lat. or.; *Neron* (i.e. *Nero*), a Rom. emperor:—Nero.

3506. **νεύω nĕuō**, *nyoo'-o*; appar. a prim. verb; to "*nod*", i.e. (by anal.) to *signal*:—beckon.

3507. **νεφέλη nĕphĕlē**, *nef-el'-ay*; from *3509*; prop. *cloudiness*, i.e. (concr.) a *cloud*:—cloud.

3508. **Νεφθαλείμ Nĕphthalĕim**, *nef-thal-ime'*; of Heb. or. [5321]; *Nephthaleim* (i.e. *Naphthali*), a tribe in Pal.:—Nephthalim.

3509. **νέφος nĕphŏs**, *nef'-os*; appar. a prim. word; a *cloud*:—cloud.

3510. **νεφρός nĕphrŏs**, *nef-ros'*; of uncert. affin.; a *kidney* (plur.), i.e. (fig.) the inmost *mind*:—reins.

3511. **νεωκόρος nĕōkŏrŏs**, *neh-o-kor'-os*; from a form of *3485* and **κορέω kŏrĕō** (to *sweep*); a *temple-servant*, i.e. (by impl.) a *votary*:—worshipper.

3512. **νεωτερικός nĕōtĕrikŏs**, *neh-o-ter'-ik-os*; from the comp. of *3501*; *appertaining to younger* persons, i.e. *juvenile*:—youthful.

νεώτερος nĕōtĕrŏs. See *3501*.

3513. **νή nē**, *nay*; prob. an intens. form of *3483*; a particle of attestation (accompanied by the object invoked or appealed to in confirmation); *as sure as*:—I protest by.

3514. **νήθω nēthō**, *nay'-tho*; from **νέω nĕō** (of like mean.); to *spin*:—spin.

3515. νηπιάζω **nēpiazō**, *nay-pee-ad'-zo;* from 3516; to *act* as a *babe*, i.e. (fig.) *innocently:*—be a child.

3516. νήπιος **nēpiŏs**, *nay'-pee-os;* from an obsol. particle νη- **nē-** (implying *negation*) and 2031; *not speaking*, i.e. an *infant* (*minor*); fig. a *simple-minded* person, an *immature* Christian:—babe, child (+ -ish).

3517. Νηρεύς **Nērĕus**, *nare-yoos';* appar. from a der. of the base of 3491 (mean. *wet*); *Nereus*, a Chr.:—Nereus.

3518. Νηρί **Nēri**, *nay-ree';* of Heb. or. [5374]; *Neri* (i.e. *Nerijah*), an Isr.:—Neri.

3519. νησίον **nēsiŏn**, *nay-see'-on;* dimin. of 3520; an *islet:*—island.

3520. νῆσος **nēsŏs**, *nay'-sos;* prob. from the base of 3491; an *island:*—island, isle.

3521. νηστεία **nēstĕia**, *nace-ti'-ah;* from 3522; *abstinence* (from lack of food, or voluntary and religious); spec. the *fast* of the Day of Atonement:—fast (-ing.)

3522. νηστεύω **nēstĕuō**, *nace-tyoo'-o;* from 3523; to *abstain* from food (religiously):—fast.

3523. νῆστις **nēstis**, *nace'-tis;* from the insep. neg. particle νη- **nē-** (*not*) and 2068; *not eating*, i.e. *abstinent* from food (religiously):—fasting.

3524. νηφάλεος **nēphalĕŏs**, *nay-fal'-eh-os;* or
νηφάλιος **nēphaliŏs**, *nay-fal'-ee-os;* from 3525; *sober*, i.e. (fig.) *circumspect* —sober, vigilant.

3525. νήφω **nēphō**, *nay'-fo;* of uncert. affin.; to *abstain* from wine (*keep sober*), i.e. (fig.) *be discreet:*—be sober, watch.

3526. Νίγερ **Nigĕr**, *neeg'-er;* of Lat. or.; *black; Niger*, a Chr.:—Niger.

3527. Νικάνωρ **Nikanōr**, *nik-an'-ore;* prob. from 3528; *victorious; Nicanor*, a Chr.:—Nicanor.

3528. νικάω **nikaō**, *nik-ah'-o;* from 3529; to *subdue* (lit. or fig.):—conquer, overcome, prevail, get the victory.

3529. νίκη **nikē**, *nee'-kay;* appar. a prim. word; *conquest* (abstr.), i.e. (fig.) the *means of success:*—victory.

3530. Νικόδημος **Nikŏdēmŏs**, *nik-od'-ay-mos;* from 3534 and 1218; *victorious* among his *people; Nicodemus*, an Isr.:—Nicodemus.

3531. Νικολαΐτης **Nikŏlaïtēs**, *nik-ol-ah-ee'-tace;* from 3532; a *Nicolaïte*, i.e. adherent of *Nicolaüs:*—*Nicolaitane.*

3532. Νικόλαος **Nikŏlaŏs**, *nik-ol'-ah-os;* from 3534 and 2992; *victorious* over the *people; Nicolaüs*, a heretic:—Nicolaus.

3533. Νικόπολις **Nikŏpŏlis**, *nik-op'-ol-is;* from 3534 and 4172; *victorious city; Nicopolis*, a place in Macedonia:—Nicopolis.

3534. νῖκος **nikŏs**, *nee'-kos;* from 3529; a *conquest* (concr.), i.e. (by impl.) *triumph:*—victory.

3535. Νινευΐ **Ninĕui**, *nin-yoo-ee';* of Heb. or. [5210]; *Nineví* (i.e. *Nineveh*), the capital of Assyria:—Nineve.

3536. Νινευΐτης **Ninĕuitēs**, *nin-yoo-ee'-tace;* from 3535; a *Ninevite*, i.e. inhab. of Nineveh:—of Nineve, Ninevite.

3537. νιπτήρ **niptēr**, *nip-tare';* from 3538; a *ewer:*—bason.

3538. νίπτω **niptō**, *nip'-to;* to *cleanse* (espec. the hands or the feet or the face); cer. to *perform ablution:*—wash. Comp. 3068.

3539. νοιέω **nŏiĕō**, *noy-eh'-o;* from 3563; to *exercise* the *mind* (*observe*), i.e. (fig.) to *comprehend, heed:*—consider, perceive, think, understand.

3540. νόημα **nŏēma**, *nŏ'-ay-mah;* from 3539; a *perception*, i.e. *purpose*, or (by impl.) the *intellect, disposition*, itself:—device, mind, thought.

3541. νόθος **nŏthŏs**, *noth'-os;* of uncert. affin.; a *spurious* or *illegitimate* son:—bastard.

3542. νομή **nŏmē**, *nom-ay';* fem. from the same as 3551; *pasture*, i.e. (the act) *feeding* (fig. *spreading* of a gangrene), or (the food) *pasturage:*— × eat, pasture.

3543. νομίζω **nŏmizō**, *nom-id'-zo;* from 3551; prop. to *do* by *law* (*usage*), i.e. to *accustom* (pass. *be usual*); by extens. to *deem* or *regard:*—suppose, think, be wont.

3544. νομικός **nŏmikŏs**, *nom-ik-os';* from 3551; *according* (or *pertaining*) *to law*, i.e. *legal* (cer.); as noun, an *expert in* the (Mosaic) *law:*—about the law, lawyer.

3545. νομίμως **nŏmimōs**, *nom-im'-oce;* adv. from a der. of 3551; *legitimately* (spec. agreeably to the rules of the lists):—lawfully.

3546. νόμισμα **nŏmisma**, *nom'-is-mah;* from 3543; *what is reckoned* as of value (after the Lat. *numisma*), i.e. current *coin:*—money.

3547. νομοδιδάσκαλος **nŏmŏdidaskalŏs**, *nom-od-id-as'-kal-os;* from 3551 and 1320; an *expounder of* the (Jewish) *law*, i.e. a *Rabbi:*—doctor (teacher) of the law.

3548. νομοθεσία **nŏmŏthĕsia**, *nom-oth-es-ee'-ah;* from 3550; *legislation* (spec. the *institution of* the Mosaic *code*):—giving of the law.

3549. νομοθετέω **nŏmŏthĕtĕō**, *nom-oth-et-eh'-o;* from 3550; to *legislate*, i.e. (pass.) to *have* (the Mosaic) *enactments* injoined, *be sanctioned* (by them):—establish, receive the law.

3550. νομοθέτης **nŏmŏthĕtēs**, *nom-oth-et'-ace;* from 3551 and a der. of 5087; a *legislator:*—lawgiver.

3551. νόμος **nŏmŏs**, *nom'-os;* from a prim. νέμω **nĕmō** (to *parcel* out, espec. *food* or *grazing* to animals); *law* (through the idea of prescriptive *usage*), gen. (*regulation*), spec. (of Moses [includ. the volume]; also of the Gospel), or fig. (a *principle*):—law.

3552. νοσέω **nŏsĕō**, *nos-eh'-o;* from 3554; to *be sick*, i.e. (by impl. of a diseased appetite) to *hanker* after (fig. to *harp* upon):—dote.

3553. νόσημα **nŏsēma**, *nos'-ay-ma;* from 3552; an *ailment:*—disease.

3554. νόσος **nŏsŏs**, *nos'-os;* of uncert. affin.; a *malady* (rarely fig. of mor. *disability*):—disease, infirmity, sickness.

3555. νοσσιά **nŏssia**, *nos-see-ah';* from 3502; a *brood* (of chickens):—brood.

3556. νοσσίον **nŏssiŏn**, *nos-see'-on;* dimin. of 3502; a *birdling:*—chicken.

3557. νοσφίζομαι **nŏsphizŏmai**, *nos-fid'-zom-ahee;* mid. from νοσφί **nŏsphi** (*apart* or *clandestinely*); to *sequestrate* for oneself, i.e. *embezzle:*—keep back, purloin.

3558. νότος **nŏtŏs**, *not'-os;* of uncert. affin.; the *south (-west) wind;* by extens. the *southern quarter* itself:—south (wind).

3559. νουθεσία **nŏuthĕsia**, *noo-thes-ee'-ah;* from 3563 and a der. of 5087; calling *attention* to, i.e. (by impl.) mild *rebuke* or *warning:*—admonition.

3560. νουθετέω **nŏuthĕtĕō**, *noo-thet-eh'-o;* from the same as 3559; to *put in mind*, i.e. (by impl.) to *caution* or *reprove* gently:—admonish, warn.

3561. νουμηνία **nŏumēnia**, *noo-may-nee'-ah;* fem. of a comp. of 3501 and 3376 (as noun by impl. of 2250); the festival of *new moon:*—new moon.

3562. νουνεχῶς **nŏunĕchōs**, *noon-ekh-oce';* adv. from a comp. of the acc. of 3563 and 2192; in a *mind-having* way, i.e. *prudently:*—discreetly.

3563. νοῦς **nŏus**, *nooce;* prob. from the base of 1097; the *intellect*, i.e. *mind* (divine or human; in thought, feeling, or will); by impl. *meaning:*—mind, understanding. Comp. 5590.

3564. Νυμφᾶς **Numphas**, *noom-fas';* prob. contr. for a comp. of 3565 and 1435; *nymph-given* (i.e. *-born*); *Nymphas*, a Chr.:—Nymphas.

3565. νύμφη **numphē**, *noom-fay';* from. a prim. but obsol. verb νύπτω **nuptō** (to *veil* as a bride; comp. Lat. "*nupto*," to *marry*); a young *married* woman (as *veiled*), includ. a *betrothed* girl; by impl. a *son's wife:*—bride, daughter in law.

3566. νυμφίος **numphiŏs**, *noom-fee'-os;* from 3565; a *bride-groom* (lit. or fig.):—bridegroom.

3567. νυμφών **numphōn**, *noom-fohn';* from 3565; the *bridal* room:—bridechamber.

3568. νῦν **nun**, *noon;* a prim. particle of present time; "*now*" (as adv. of date, a transition or emphasis); also as noun or adj. *present* or *immediate:*—henceforth, + hereafter, of late, soon, present, this (time). See also 3569, 3570.

3569. τανῦν **tanun**, *tan-oon';* or
τὰ νῦν **ta nun**, *tah noon;* from neut. plur. of 3588 and 3568; *the* things *now*, i.e. (adv.) *at present:*—(but) now.

3570. νυνί **nuni**, *noo-nee';* a prol. form of 3568 for emphasis; *just now:*—now.

3571. νύξ **nux**, *noox;* a prim. word; "*night*" (lit. or fig.):—(mid-) night.

3572. νύσσω **nussō**, *noos'-so;* appar. a prim. word; to *prick* ("nudge"):—pierce.

3573. νυστάζω **nustazō**, *noos-tad'-zo;* from a presumed der. of 3506; to *nod*, i.e. (by impl.) to *fall asleep;* fig. to *delay:*—slumber.

3574. νυχθήμερον **nuchthēmĕrŏn**, *nookh-thay'-mer-on;* from 3571 and 2250; a *day-and-night*, i.e. full *day* of twenty-four hours:—night and day.

3575. Νῶε **Nōĕ**, *no'-eh;* of Heb. or. [5146]; *Noĕ*, (i.e. *Noäch*), a patriarch:—Noe.

3576. νωθρός **nōthrŏs**, *no-thros';* from a der. of 3541; *sluggish*, i.e. (lit.) *lazy*, or (fig.) *stupid:*—dull, slothful.

3577. νῶτος **nōtŏs**, *no'-tos;* of uncert. affin.; the *back:*—back.

Ξ

3578. ξενία **xĕnia**, *xen-ee'-ah;* from 3581; *hospitality*, i.e. (by impl.) a *place of entertainment:*—lodging.

3579. ξενίζω **xĕnizō**, *xen-id'-zo;* from 3581; to *be a host* (pass. a *guest*); by impl. *be* (*make, appear*) *strange:*—entertain, lodge, (think it) strange.

3580. ξενοδοχέω **xĕnŏdŏchĕō**, *xen-od-okh-eh'-o;* from a comp. of 3581 and 1209; to *be hospitable:*—lodge strangers.

3581. ξένος **xĕnŏs**, *xen'-os;* appar. a prim. word; *foreign* (lit. *alien*, or fig. *novel*); by impl. a *guest* or (vice-versa) *entertainer:*—host, strange (-r).

3582. ξέστης **xĕstēs**, *xes'-tace;* as if from ξέω **xĕō** (prop. to *smooth;* by impl. [of *friction*] to *boil* or *heat*); a *vessel* (as *fashioned* or for *cooking*) [or perh. by corruption from the Lat. *sextarius*, the *sixth* of a modius, i.e. about a *pint*], i.e. (spec.) a *measure* for liquids or solids, (by anal. a *pitcher*):—pot.

3583. ξηραίνω **xērainō**, *xay-rah'ee-no;* from 3584; to *desiccate;* by impl. to *shrivel*, to *mature:*—dry up, pine away, be ripe, wither (away).

3584. ξηρός **xērŏs**, *xay-ros';* from the base of 3582 (through the idea of *scorching*); *arid;* by impl. *shrunken, earth* (as opposed to water):—dry, land, withered.

3585. ξύλινος **xulinŏs**, *xoo'-lin-os;* from 3586; *wooden:*—of wood.

3586. ξύλον **xulŏn**, *xoo'-lon;* from another form of the base of 3582; *timber* (as fuel or material); by impl. a *stick, club* or *tree* or other wooden article or substance:—staff, stocks, tree, wood.

3587. ξυράω **xuraō**, *xoo-rah'-o;* from a der. of the same as 3586 (mean. a *razor*); to *shave* or "*shear*" the hair:—shave.

O

3588. ὁ **hŏ**, *hŏ;* includ. the fem.
ἡ **hē**, *hay;* and the neut.
τό **tŏ**, *tŏ*, in all their inflections; the def. article; *the* (sometimes to be supplied, at others omitted in English idiom):—the, this, that, one, he, she, it, etc.
ὅ **hŏ**. See 3739.

3589. ὀγδοήκοντα **ŏgdŏēkŏnta**, *og-dŏ-ay'-kon-tah;* from 3590; *ten times eight:*—fourscore.

3590. ὄγδοος **ŏgdŏŏs**, *og'-dŏ-os;* from 3638; the *eighth:*—eighth.

3591. ὄγκος **ŏgkŏs**, *ong'-kos;* prob. from the same as 43; a *mass* (as *bending* or *bulging* by its load), i.e. *burden* (*hindrance*):—weight.

3592. ὅδε **hŏdĕ**, *hod'-eh;* includ. the fem.

ἥδε **hēdĕ**, *hay'-deh;* and the neut.

τόδε **tŏdĕ**, *tod'-e;* from 3588 and 1161; the *same,* i.e. *this* or *that* one (plur. *these* or *those*); often used as pers. pron.:—he, she, such, these, thus.

3593. ὁδεύω **hŏdĕuō**, *hod-yoo'-o;* from 3598; to *travel:*—journey.

3594. ὁδηγέω **hŏdēgĕō**, *hod-ayg-eh'-o;* from 3595; to *show* the *way* (lit. or fig. [*teach*]):—guide, lead.

3595. ὁδηγός **hŏdēgŏs**, *hod-ayg-os';* from 3598 and 2233; a *conductor* (lit. or fig. [*teacher*]):—guide, leader.

3596. ὁδοιπορέω **hŏdŏipŏrĕō**, *hod-oy-por-eh'-o;* from a comp. of 3598 and 4198; to *be a wayfarer,* i.e. *travel:*—go on a journey.

3597. ὁδοιπορία **hŏdŏipŏria**, *hod-oy-por-ee'-ah;* from the same as 3596; *travel:*—journey (-ing).

3598. ὁδός **hŏdŏs**, *hod-os';* appar. a prim. word; a *road;* by impl. a *progress* (the route, act or distance); fig. a *mode* or *means:*—journey, (high-) way.

3599. ὀδούς **ŏdŏus**, *od-ooce';* perh. from the base of 2068; a "*tooth*":—tooth.

3600. ὀδυνάω **ŏdunaō**, *od-oo-nah'-o;* from 3601; to *grieve:*—sorrow, torment.

3601. ὀδύνη **ŏdunē**, *od-oo'-nay;* from 1416; *grief* (as *dejecting*):—sorrow.

3602. ὀδυρμός **ŏdurmŏs**, *od-oor-mos';* from a der. of the base of 1416; *moaning,* i.e. *lamentation:*—mourning.

3603. ὅ ἐστι **hŏ esti**, *hŏ es-tee';* from the neut. of 3739 and the third pers. sing. pres. ind. of 1510; *which is:*—called, which is (make), that is (to say).

3604. Ὀζίας **Ŏzias**, *od-zee'-as;* of Heb. or. [5818]; *Ozias* (i.e. *Uzzijah*), an Isr.:—Ozias.

3605. ὄζω **ŏzō**, *od'-zo;* a prim. verb (in a strengthened form); to *scent* (usually an ill "odor"):—stink.

3606. ὅθεν **hŏthĕn**, *hoth'-en;* from 3739 with the directive enclitic of source; *from which* place or source or cause (adv. or conj.):—from thence, (from) whence, where (-by, -fore, -upon).

3607. ὀθόνη **ŏthŏnē**, *oth-on'-ay;* of uncert. affin.; a *linen* cloth, i.e. (espec.) a *sail:*—sheet.

3608. ὀθόνιον **ŏthŏniŏn**, *oth-on'-ee-on;* neut. of a presumed der. of 3607; a linen *bandage:*—linen clothes.

3609. οἰκεῖος **ŏikĕiŏs**, *oy-ki'-os;* from 3624; *domestic,* i.e. (as noun), a *relative, adherent:*—(those) of the (his own) house (-hold).

3610. οἰκέτης **ŏikĕtēs**, *oy-ket'-ace;* from 3611; a fellow *resident,* i.e. menial *domestic:*—(household) servant.

3611. οἰκέω **ŏikĕō**, *oy-keh'-o;* from 3624; to *occupy a house,* i.e. *reside* (fig. *inhabit, remain, inhere*); by impl. to *cohabit:*—dwell. See also 3625.

3612. οἴκημα **ŏikēma**, *oy'-kay-mah;* from 3611; a *tenement,* i.e. (spec.) a *jail:*—prison.

3613. οἰκητήριον **ŏikētēriŏn**, *oy-kay-tay'-ree-on;* neut. of a presumed der. of 3611 (equiv. to 3612); a *residence* (lit. or fig.):—habitation, house.

3614. οἰκία **ŏikia**, *oy-kee'-ah;* from 3624; prop. *residence* (abstr.), but usually (concr.) an *abode* (lit. or fig.); by impl. a *family* (espec. *domestics*):—home, house (-hold).

3615. οἰκιακός **ŏikiakŏs**, *oy-kee-ak-os';* from 3614; *familiar,* i.e. (as noun) *relatives:*—they (them) of (his own) household.

3616. οἰκοδεσποτέω **ŏikŏdĕspŏtĕō**, *oy-kod-es-pot-eh'-o;* from 3617; to *be the head of* (i.e. *rule*) a *family:*—guide the house.

3617. οἰκοδεσπότης **ŏikŏdĕspŏtēs**, *oy-kod-es-pot'-ace;* from 3624 and 1203; *the head of a family:*—goodman (of the house), householder, master of the house.

3618. οἰκοδομέω **ŏikŏdŏmĕō**, *oy-kod-om-eh'-o;* from the same as 3619; to *be a house-builder,* i.e. *construct* or (fig.) *confirm:*—(be in) build (-er, -ing, up), edify, embolden.

3619. οἰκοδομή **ŏikŏdŏmē**, *oy-kod-om-ay';* fem. (abstr.) of a comp. of 3624 and the base of 1430; *architecture,* i.e. (concr.) a *structure;* fig. *confirmation:*—building, edify (-ication, -ing).

3620. οἰκοδομία **ŏikŏdŏmia**, *oy-kod-om-ee'-ah;* from the same as 3619; *confirmation:*—edifying.

3621. οἰκονομέω **ŏikŏnŏmĕō**, *oy-kon-om-eh'-o;* from 3623; to *manage* (a house, i.e. an estate):—be steward.

3622. οἰκονομία **ŏikŏnŏmia**, *oy-kon-om-ee'-ah;* from 3623; *administration* (of a household or estate); spec. a (religious) "*economy*":—dispensation, stewardship.

3623. οἰκονόμος **ŏikŏnŏmŏs**, *oy-kon-om'-os;* from 3624 and the base of 3551; a *house-distributor* (i.e. *manager*), or *overseer,* i.e. an employee in that capacity; by extens. a fiscal *agent* (*treasurer*); fig. a *preacher* (of the Gospel):—chamberlain, governor, steward.

3624. οἶκος **ŏikŏs**, *oy'-kos;* of uncert. affin.; a *dwelling* (more or less extensive, lit. or fig.); by impl. a *family* (more or less related, lit. or fig.):—home, house (-hold), temple.

3625. οἰκουμένη **ŏikŏumĕnē**, *oy-kou-men'-ay;* fem. part. pres. pass. of 3611 (as noun, by impl. of 1093); *land,* i.e. the (terrene part of the) *globe;* spec. the Roman *empire:*—earth, world.

3626. οἰκουρός **ŏikŏurŏs**, *oy-koo-ros';* from 3624 and οὖρος **ŏurŏs** (a *guard;* be "*ware*"); a *stayer at home,* i.e. *domestically inclined* (a "good housekeeper"):—keeper at home.

3627. οἰκτείρω **ŏiktĕirō**, *oyk-ti'-ro;* also (in certain tenses) prol.

οἰκτερέω **ŏiktĕrĕō**, *oyk-ter-eh'-o;* from οἶκτος **ŏiktŏs** (*pity*); to *exercise pity:*—have compassion on.

3628. οἰκτιρμός **ŏiktirmŏs**, *oyk-tir-mos';* from 3627; *pity:*—mercy.

3629. οἰκτίρμων **ŏiktirmōn**, *oyk-tir'-mone;* from 3627; *compassionate:*—merciful, of tender mercy.

οἶμαι **ŏimai**. See 3633.

3630. οἰνοπότης **ŏinŏpŏtēs**, *oy-nop-ot'-ace;* from 3631 and a der. of the alt. of 4095; a *tippler:*—winebibber.

3631. οἶνος **ŏinŏs**, *oy'-nos;* a prim. word (or perh. of Heb. or. [3196]); "*wine*" (lit. or fig.):—wine.

3632. οἰνοφλυγία **ŏinŏphlugia**, *oy-nof-loog-ee'-ah;* from 3631 and a form of the base of 5397; an *overflow* (or surplus) of *wine,* i.e. *vinolency* (*drunkenness*):—excess of wine.

3633. οἴομαι **ŏiŏmai**, *oy'-om-ahee;* or (shorter)

οἶμαι **ŏimai**, *oy'-mahee;* mid. appar. from 3634; to *make like* (oneself), i.e. *imagine* (*be of the opinion*):—suppose, think.

3634. οἷος **hŏiŏs**, *hoy'-os;* prob. akin to 3588, 3739, and 3745; *such* or *what sort* of (as a correl. or exclamation); espec. the neut. (adv.) with neg. not *so:*—so (as), such as, what (manner of), which.

οἴω **ŏiō**. See 5342.

3635. ὀκνέω **ŏknĕō**, *ok-neh'-o;* from ὄκνος **ŏknŏs** (*hesitation*); to *be slow* (fig. *loath*):—delay.

3636. ὀκνηρός **ŏknērŏs**, *ok-nay-ros';* from 3635; *tardy,* i.e. *indolent;* (fig.) *irksome:*—grievous, slothful.

3637. ὀκταήμερος **ŏktaēmĕrŏs**, *ok-tah-ay'-mer-os;* from 3638 and 2250; an *eight-day* old person or act:—the eighth day.

3638. ὀκτώ **ŏktō**, *ok-to';* a prim. numeral; "*eight*":—eight.

3639. ὄλεθρος **ŏlĕthrŏs**, *ol'-eth-ros;* from a prim. ὄλλυμι **ŏllumi** (to *destroy;* a prol. form); *ruin,* i.e. *death, punishment:*—destruction.

3640. ὀλιγόπιστος **ŏligŏpistŏs**, *ol-ig-op'-is-tos;* from 3641 and 4102; *incredulous,* i.e. *lacking confidence* (in Christ):—of little faith.

3641. ὀλίγος **ŏligŏs**, *ol-ee'-gos;* of uncert. affin.; *puny* (in extent, degree, number, duration or value); espec. neut. (adv.) *somewhat:*—+ almost, brief [-ly], few, (a) little, + long, a season, short, small, a while.

3642. ὀλιγόψυχος **ŏligŏpsuchŏs**, *ol-ig-op'-soo-khos;* from 3641 and 5590; *little-spirited,* i.e. *faint-hearted:*—feebleminded.

3643. ὀλιγωρέω **ŏligōrĕō**, *ol-ig-o-reh'-o;* from a comp. of 3641 and ὥρα **ōra** ("*care*"); to *have little regard* for, i.e. to *disesteem:*—despise.

3644. ὀλοθρευτής **ŏlŏthrĕutēs**, *ol-oth-ryoo-tace';* from 3645; a *ruiner,* i.e. (spec.) a venomous *serpent:*—destroyer.

3645. ὀλοθρεύω **ŏlŏthrĕuō**, *ol-oth-ryoo'-o;* from 3639; to *spoil,* i.e. *slay:*—destroy.

3646. ὁλοκαύτωμα **hŏlŏkautōma**, *hol-ok-ow'-to-mah;* from a der. of a comp. of 3650 and a der. of 2545; a *wholly-consumed* sacrifice ("holocaust"):—(whole) burnt offering.

3647. ὁλοκληρία **hŏlŏklēria**, *hol-ok-lay-ree'-ah;* from 3648; *integrity,* i.e. physical *wholeness:*—perfect soundness.

3648. ὁλόκληρος **hŏlŏklērŏs**, *hol-ok'-lay-ros;* from 3650 and 2819; *complete* in every *part,* i.e. perfectly *sound* (in body):—entire, whole.

3649. ὀλολύζω **ŏlŏluzō**, *ol-ol-ood'-zo;* a redupl. prim. verb; to "*howl*" or "*halloo*", i.e. *shriek:*—howl.

3650. ὅλος **hŏlŏs**, *hol'-os;* a prim. word; "*whole*" or "*all*", i.e. *complete* (in extent, amount, time or degree), espec. (neut.) as noun or adv.:—all, altogether, every whit, + throughout, whole.

3651. ὁλοτελής **hŏlŏtĕlēs**, *hol-ot-el-ace';* from 3650 and 5056; *complete* to the *end,* i.e. *absolutely perfect:*—wholly.

3652. Ὀλυμπᾶς **Olumpas**, *ol-oom-pas';* prob. a contr. from Ὀλυμπιόδωρος **Olumpiŏdōrŏs** (*Olympian-bestowed,* i.e. *heaven-descended*); *Olympas,* a Chr.:—Olympas.

3653. ὄλυνθος **ŏlunthŏs**, *ol'-oon-thos;* of uncert. der.; an *unripe* (because out of season) *fig:*—untimely fig.

3654. ὅλως **hŏlōs**, *hol'-oce;* adv. from 3650; *completely,* i.e. *altogether;* (by anal.) *everywhere;* (neg.) not *by any means:*—at all, commonly, utterly.

3655. ὄμβρος **ŏmbrŏs**, *om'-bros;* of uncert. affin.; a thunder *storm:*—shower.

3656. ὁμιλέω **hŏmilĕō**, *hom-il-eh'-o;* from 3658; to *be in company* with, i.e. (by impl.) to *converse:*—commune, talk.

3657. ὁμιλία **hŏmilia**, *hom-il-ee'-ah;* from 3658; *companionship* ("homily"), i.e. (by impl.) *intercourse:*—communication.

3658. ὅμιλος **hŏmilŏs**, *hom'-il-os;* from the base of 3674 and a der. of the alt. of 138 (mean. a *crowd*); *association together,* i.e. a *multitude:*—company.

3659. ὄμμα **ŏmma**, *om'-mah;* from 3700; a *sight,* i.e. (by impl.) the *eye:*—eye.

3660. ὀμνύω **ŏmnuō**, *om-noo'-o;* a prol. form of a prim. but obsol. ὄμω **ŏmō**, for which another prol. form (ὀμόω **ŏmŏō**, *om-ŏ'-o*) is used in certain tenses; to *swear,* i.e. *take* (or *declare on*) *oath:*—swear.

3661. ὁμοθυμαδόν **hŏmŏthumadŏn**, *hom-oth-oo-mad-on';* adv. from a comp. of the base of 3674 and 2372; *unanimously:*—with one accord (mind).

3662. ὁμοιάζω **hŏmŏiazō**, *hom-oy-ad'-zo;* from 3664; to *resemble:*—agree.

3663. ὁμοιοπαθής **hŏmŏiŏpathēs**, *hom-oy-op-ath-ace';* from 3664 and the alt. of 3958; *similarly affected:*—of (subject to) like passions.

3664. ὅμοιος **hŏmŏiŏs**, *hom'-oy-os;* from the base of 3674; *similar* (in appearance or character):—like, + manner.

3665. ὁμοιότης **hŏmŏiŏtēs**, *hom-oy-ot'-ace;* from 3664; *resemblance:*—like as, similitude.

3666. ὁμοιόω **hŏmŏiŏō**, *hom-oy-ŏ'-o;* from 3664; to *assimilate,* i.e. *compare;* pass. to *become similar:*—be (make) like, (in the) liken (-ess), resemble.

3667. ὁμοίωμα **hŏmŏiōma**, *hom-oy'-o-mah;* from 3666; a *form;* abstr. *resemblance:*—made like to, likeness, shape, similitude.

3668. **ὁμοίως hŏmŏiōs**, *hom-oy'-oce;* adv. from *3664; similarly:*—likewise, so.

3669. **ὁμοίωσις hŏmŏiōsis**, *hom-oy'-o-sis;* from *3666; assimilation*, i.e. *resemblance:*—similitude.

3670. **ὁμολογέω hŏmŏlŏgĕō**, *hom-ol-og-eh'-o;* from a comp. of the base of *3674* and *3056; to assent*, i.e. *covenant, acknowledge:*—con- (pro-) fess, confession is made, give thanks, promise.

3671. **ὁμολογία hŏmŏlŏgia**, *hom-ol-og-ee'-ah;* from the same as *3670; acknowledgment:*—con- (pro-) fession, professed.

3672. **ὁμολογουμένως hŏmŏlŏgŏumĕnōs**, *hom-ol-og-ŏw-men'-oce;* adv. of pres. pass. part. of *3670; confessedly:*—without controversy.

3673. **ὁμότεχνος hŏmŏtĕchnŏs**, *hom-ot'-ekh-nos;* from the base of *3674* and *5078;* a *fellow-artificer:*—of the same craft.

3674. **ὁμοῦ hŏmŏu**, *hom-oo';* gen. of **ὁμός hŏmŏs** (the *same;* akin to *260*) as adv.; *at the same* place or time:—together.

3675. **ὁμόφρων hŏmŏphrōn**, *hom-of'-rone;* from the base of *3674* and *5424; like-minded*, i.e. *harmonious:*—of one mind.

ὀμόω ŏmŏō. See *3660*.

3676. **ὅμως hŏmōs**, *hom'-oce;* adv. from the base of *3674; at the same* time, i.e. (conj.) *notwithstanding, yet still:*—and even, nevertheless, though but.

3677. **ὄναρ ŏnar**, *on'-ar;* of uncert. der.; a *dream:*—dream.

3678. **ὀνάριον ŏnariŏn**, *on-ar'-ee-on;* neut. of a presumed der. of *3688;* a *little ass:*—young ass.

ὀνάω ŏnaō. See *3685*.

3679. **ὀνειδίζω ŏnĕidizō**, *on-i-did'-zo;* from *3681;* to *defame*, i.e. *rail at, chide, taunt:*—cast in teeth, (suffer) reproach, revile, upbraid.

3680. **ὀνειδισμός ŏnĕidismŏs**, *on-i-dis-mos';* from *3679; contumely:*—reproach.

3681. **ὄνειδος ŏnĕidŏs**, *on'-i-dos;* prob. akin to the base of *3686; notoriety*, i.e. a *taunt* (*disgrace*):—reproach.

3682. **Ὀνήσιμος Ŏnēsimŏs**, *on-ay'-sim-os;* from *3685; profitable; Onesimus*, a Chr.:—Onesimus.

3683. **Ὀνησίφορος Ŏnēsiphŏrŏs**, *on-ay-sif'-or-os;* from a der. of *3685* and *5411; profit-bearer; Onesiphorus*, a Chr.:—Onesiphorus.

3684. **ὀνικός ŏnikŏs**, *on-ik-os';* from *3688; belonging to* an *ass*, i.e. *large* (so as to be turned by an ass):—millstone.

3685. **ὀνίνημι ŏninēmi**, *on-in'-ay-mee;* a prol. form of an appar. prim. verb

(ὄνομαι ŏnŏmai, to *slur*); for which another prol. form (**ὀνάω ŏnaō**) is used as an alt. in some tenses [unless indeed it be identical with the base of *3686* through the idea of *notoriety*]; to *gratify*, i.e. (mid.) to *derive pleasure* or *advantage* from:—have joy.

3686. **ὄνομα ŏnŏma**, *on'-om-ah;* from a presumed der. of the base of *1097* (comp. *3685*); a "*name*" (lit. or fig.) [*authority, character*]:—called, (+ sur-) name (-d).

3687. **ὀνομάζω ŏnŏmazō**, *on-om-ad'-zo;* from *3686;* to *name*, i.e. *assign an appellation;* by extens. to *utter, mention, profess:*—call, name.

3688. **ὄνος ŏnŏs**, *on'-os;* appar. a prim. word; a *donkey:*—ass.

3689. **ὄντως ŏntōs**, *on'-toce;* adv. of the oblique cases of *5607; really:*—certainly, clean, indeed, of a truth, verily.

3690. **ὄξος ŏxŏs**, *ox'-os;* from *3691; vinegar*, i.e. *sour* wine:—vinegar.

3691. **ὀξύς ŏxus**, *ox-oos';* prob. akin to the base of *188* ["*acid*"]; *keen;* by anal. *rapid:*—sharp, swift.

3692. **ὀπή ŏpē**, *op-ay';* prob. from *3700;* a *hole* (as if for light), i.e. *cavern;* by anal. a *spring* (of water):—cave, place.

3693. **ὄπισθεν ŏpisthĕn**, *op'-is-then;* from **ὄπις ŏpis** (*regard;* from *3700*) with enclitic of source; *from the rear* (as a secure *aspect*), i.e. *at the back* (adv. and prep. of place or time):—after, backside, behind.

3694. **ὀπίσω ŏpisō**, *op-is'-o;* from the same as *3693* with enclitic of direction; *to* the *back*, i.e. *aback* (as adv. or prep. of time or place; or as noun):—after, back (-ward), (+ get) behind, + follow.

3695. **ὁπλίζω hŏplizō**, *hop-lid'-zo;* from *3696;* to *equip* (with weapons [mid. and fig.]):—arm self.

3696. **ὅπλον hŏplŏn**, *hop'-lon;* prob. from a prim. **ἕπω hĕpō** (to be *busy* about); an *implement* or *utensil* or *tool* (lit. or fig., espec. offensive for war):—armour, instrument, weapon.

3697. **ὁποῖος hŏpŏiŏs**, *hop-oy'-os;* from *3739* and *4169;* of *what* kind *that*, i.e. *how* (*as*) *great* (*excellent*) (spec. as indef. correl. to anteced. def. *5108* of quality):—what manner (sort) of, such as, whatsoever.

3698. **ὁπότε hŏpŏtĕ**, *hop-ot'-eh;* from *3739* and *4218; what* (-ever) *then*, i.e. (of time) *as soon as:*—when.

3699. **ὅπου hŏpŏu**, *hop'-oo;* from *3739* and *4225; what* (-ever) *where*, i.e. *at whichever* spot:—in what place, where (-as, -soever), whither (+ soever).

3700. **ὀπτάνομαι ŏptanŏmai**, *op-tan'-om-ahee;* a (mid.) prol. form of the prim. (mid.)

ὄπτομαι ŏptŏmai, *op'-tom-ahee*, which is used for it in certain tenses; and both as alt. of *3708;* to *gaze* (i.e. with wide-open eyes, as at something remarkable; and thus differing from *991*, which denotes simply *voluntary* observation; and from *1492*, which expresses merely mechanical, passive or casual vision; while *2300*, and still more emphatically its intens. *2334*, signifies an earnest but more continued *inspection;* and *4648* a watching *from a distance*):—appear, look, see, shew self.

3701. **ὀπτασία ŏptasia**, *op-tas-ee'-ah;* from a presumed der. of *3700; visuality*, i.e. (concr.) an *apparition:*—vision.

ὄπτομαι ŏptŏmai. See *3700*.

3702. **ὀπτός ŏptŏs**, *op-tos';* from an obsol. verb akin to **ἕψω hĕpsō** (to "*steep*"); *cooked*, i.e. *roasted:*—broiled.

3703. **ὀπώρα ŏpōra**, *op-o'-rah;* appar. from the base of *3796* and *5610;* prop. *even-tide* of the (summer) season (*dog-days*), i.e. (by impl.) *ripe* fruit:—fruit.

3704. **ὅπως hŏpōs**, *hop'-oce;* from *3739* and *4459; what* (-ever) *how*, i.e. *in* the *manner that* (as adv. or conj. of coincidence, intentional or actual):—because, how, (so) that, to, when.

3705. **ὅραμα hŏrama**, *hor'-am-ah;* from *3708; something gazed at*, i.e. a *spectacle* (espec. supernat.):—sight, vision.

3706. **ὅρασις hŏrasis**, *hor'-as-is;* from *3708;* the act of *gazing*, i.e. (external) an *aspect* or (intern.) an inspired *appearance:*—sight, vision.

3707. **ὁρατός hŏratŏs**, *hor-at-os';* from *3708; gazed at*, i.e. (by impl.) *capable of being seen:*—visible.

3708. **ὁράω hŏraō**, *hor-ah'-o;* prop. to *stare* at [comp. *3700*], i.e. (by impl.) to *discern* clearly (phys. or ment.); by extens. to *attend* to; by Hebr. to *experience;* pass. to *appear:*—behold, perceive, see, take heed.

3709. **ὀργή ŏrgē**, *or-gay';* from *3713;* prop. *desire* (as a *reaching* forth or *excitement* of the mind), i.e. (by anal.) violent *passion* (*ire*, or [justifiable] *abhorrence*); by impl. *punishment:*—anger, indignation, vengeance, wrath.

3710. **ὀργίζω ŏrgizō**, *or-gid'-zo;* from *3709;* to *provoke* or *enrage*, i.e. (pass.) *become exasperated:*—be angry (wroth).

3711. **ὀργίλος ŏrgilŏs**, *org-ee'-los;* from *3709; irascible:*—soon angry.

3712. **ὀργυιά ŏrguia**, *org-wee-ah';* from *3713;* a *stretch* of the arms, i.e. a *fathom:*—fathom.

3713. **ὀρέγομαι ŏrĕgŏmai**, *or-eg'-om-ahee;* mid. of appar. a prol. form of an obsol. prim. [comp. *3735*]; to *stretch* oneself, i.e. *reach* out after (*long* for):—covet after, desire.

3714. **ὀρεινός ŏrĕinŏs**, *or-i-nos';* from *3735; mountainous*, i.e. (fem. by impl. of *5561*) the *Highlands* (of Judæa):—hill country.

3715. **ὄρεξις ŏrĕxis**, *or'-ex-is;* from *3713; excitement* of the mind, i.e. *longing* after:—lust.

3716. **ὀρθοποδέω ŏrthŏpŏdĕō**, *or-thop-od-eh'-o;* from a comp. of *3717* and *4228;* to *be straight-footed*, i.e. (fig.) to *go directly* forward:—walk uprightly.

3717. **ὀρθός ŏrthŏs**, *or-thos';* prob. from the base of *3735; right* (as *rising*), i.e. (perpendicularly) *erect* (fig. *honest*), or (horizontally) *level* or *direct:*—straight, upright.

3718. **ὀρθοτομέω ŏrthŏtŏmĕō**, *or-thot-om-eh'-o;* from a comp. of *3717* and the base of *5114;* to *make a straight cut*, i.e. (fig.) to *dissect* (*expound*) *correctly* (the divine message):—rightly divide.

3719. **ὀρθρίζω ŏrthrizō**, *or-thrid'-zo;* from *3722*, to *use* the *dawn*, i.e. (by impl.) to *repair betimes:*—come early in the morning.

3720. **ὀρθρινός ŏrthrinŏs**, *or-thrin-os';* from *3722; relating to* the *dawn*, i.e. *matutinal* (as an epithet of Venus, espec. brilliant in the early day):—morning.

3721. **ὄρθριος ŏrthriŏs**, *or'-three-os;* from *3722; in* the *dawn*, i.e. up *at day-break:*—early.

3722. **ὄρθρος ŏrthrŏs**, *or'-thros;* from the same as *3735; dawn* (as *sun-rise, rising* of light); by extens. *morn:*—early in the morning.

3723. **ὀρθῶς ŏrthōs**, *or-thoce';* adv. from *3717; in a straight* manner, i.e. (fig.) *correctly* (also mor.):—plain, right (-ly).

3724. **ὁρίζω hŏrizō**, *hor-id'-zo;* from *3725;* to *mark* out or *bound* ("*horizon*"), i.e. (fig.) to *appoint, decree, specify:*—declare, determine, limit, ordain.

3725. **ὅριον hŏriŏn**, *hor'-ee-on;* neut. of a der. of an appar. prim. **ὅρος hŏrŏs** (a *bound* or *limit*); a *boundary*-line, i.e. (by impl.) a *frontier* (*region*):—border, coast.

3726. **ὁρκίζω hŏrkizō**, *hor-kid'-zo;* from *3727;* to *put on oath*, i.e. *make swear;* by anal. to solemnly *enjoin:*—adjure, charge.

3727. **ὅρκος hŏrkŏs**, *hor'-kos;* from **ἕρκος hĕrkŏs** (a *fence;* perh. akin to *3725*); a *limit*, i.e. (sacred) *restraint* (spec. *oath*):—oath.

3728. **ὁρκωμοσία hŏrkōmŏsia**, *hor-ko-mos-ee'-ah;* from a comp. of *3727* and a der. of *3660; asseveration on oath:*—oath.

3729. **ὁρμάω hŏrmaō**, *hor-mah'-o;* from *3730;* to *start, spur* or *urge* on, i.e. (reflex.) to *dash* or *plunge:*—run (violently), rush.

3730. **ὁρμή hŏrmē**, *hor-may';* of uncert. affin.; a violent *impulse*, i.e. *onset:*—assault.

3731. **ὅρμημα hŏrmēma**, *hor'-may-mah;* from *3730;* an *attack*, i.e. (abstr.) *precipitancy:*—violence.

3732. **ὄρνεον ŏrnĕŏn**, *or'-neh-on;* neut. of a presumed der. of *3733;* a *birdling:*—bird, fowl.

3733. **ὄρνις ŏrnis**, *or'-nis;* prob. from a prol. form of the base of *3735;* a *bird* (as *rising* in the air), i.e. (spec.) a *hen* (or female domestic fowl):—hen.

3734. **ὁροθεσία hŏrŏthĕsia**, *hor-oth-es-ee'-ah;* from a comp. of the base of *3725* and a der. of *5087;* a *limit-placing*, i.e. (concr.) *boundary-line:*—bound.

3735. **ὄρος ŏrŏs**, *or'-os;* prob. from an obsol. **ὄρω ŏrō** (to *rise* or "*rear*"; perh. akin to *142;* comp. *3733*); a *mountain* (as *lifting* itself above the plain):—hill, mount (-ain).

3736. **ὀρύσσω ŏrussō**, *or-oos'-so;* appar. a prim. verb; to "*burrow*" in the ground, i.e. *dig:*—dig.

3737. **ὀρφανός ŏrphanŏs**, *or-fan-os';* of uncert. affin.; *bereaved* ("*orphan*"), i.e. *parentless:*—comfortless, fatherless.

3738. **ὀρχέομαι ŏrchĕŏmai**, *or-kheh'-om-ahee;* mid. from **ὄρχος ŏrchŏs** (a *row* or *ring*); to *dance* (from the *ranklike* or *regular* motion):—dance.

3739. **ὅς hŏs**, *hos;* includ. fem.

ἥ hē, *hay;* and neut.

ὅ hŏ, *hŏ;* prob. a prim. word (or perh. a form of the art. *3588*); the rel. (sometimes demonstrative) pron., *who, which, what, that:*—one, (an-, the) other, some, that, what, which, who (-m, -se), etc. See also *3757*.

3740. ὁσάκις **hŏsakis**, *hos-ak'-is;* multiple adv. from *3739;* *how* (i.e. with *302*, *so*) *many times* as:—as oft (-en) as.

3741. ὅσιος **hŏsiŏs**, *hos'-ee-os;* of uncert. affin.; prop. *right* (by intrinsic or divine character; thus distinguished from *1342*, which refers rather to *human* statutes and relations; from *2413*, which denotes formal *consecration;* and from *40*, which relates to *purity* from defilement), i.e. *hallowed* (*pious, sacred, sure*):—holy, mercy, shalt be.

3742. ὁσιότης **hŏsiŏtēs**, *hos-ee-ot'-ace;* from *3741;* *piety:*—holiness.

3743. ὁσίως **hŏsiōs**, *hos-ee-oce';* adv. from *3741;* *piously:*—holily.

3744. ὀσμή **ŏsmē**, *os-may';* from *3605;* *fragrance* (lit. or fig.):—odour, savour.

3745. ὅσος **hŏsŏs**, *hos'-os;* by redupl. from *3739;* *as* (*much, great, long*, etc.) *as:*—all (that), as (long, many, much) (as), how great (many, much), [in-] asmuch as, so many as, that (ever), the more, those things, what (great, -soever), wheresoever, wherewithsoever, which, × while, who (-soever).

3746. ὅσπερ **hŏspĕr**, *hos'-per;* from *3739* and *4007;* *who especially:*—whomsoever.

3747. ὀστέον **ŏstĕŏn**, *os-teh'-on;* or contr.

ὀστοῦν **ŏstŏun**, *os-toon';* of uncert. affin.; a *bone:*—bone.

3748. ὅστις **hŏstis**, *hos'-tis;* includ. the fem.

ἥτις **hētis**, *hay'-tis;* and the neut.

ὅ,τι **hŏ,ti**, *hot'-ee;* from *3739* and *5100;* *which some*, i.e. *any that;* also (def.) *which same:*—× and (they), (such) as, (they) that, in that they, what (-soever), whereas ye, (they) which, who (-soever). Comp. *3754*.

3749. ὀστράκινος **ŏstrakinŏs**, *os-tra'-kin-os;* from ὄστρακον **ŏstrakŏn** ["oyster"] (a *tile*, i.e. *terra cotta*); *earthen*-ware, i.e. *clayey;* by impl. *frail:*—of earth, earthen.

3750. ὄσφρησις **ŏsphrēsis**, *os'-fray-sis;* from a der. of *3605;* *smell* (the sense):—smelling.

3751. ὀσφύς **ŏsphus**, *os-foos';* of uncert. affin.; the *loin* (extern.), i.e. the *hip;* intern. (by extens.) *procreative power:*—loin.

3752. ὅταν **hŏtan**, *hot'-an;* from *3753* and *302;* *whenever* (implying *hypothesis* or more or less *uncertainty*); also caus. (conj.) *inasmuch as:*—as long (soon) as, that, + till, when (-soever), while.

3753. ὅτε **hŏtĕ**, *hot'-eh;* from *3739* and *5037;* at *which* (thing) *too*, i.e. *when:*—after (that), as soon as, that, when, while.

ὅ,τε **hŏ,tĕ**, *hŏ,t'-eh;* also fem.

ἥ,τε **hē,tĕ**, *hay'-teh;* and neut.

τό,τε **tŏ,tĕ**, *tot'-eh;* simply the art. *3588* followed by *5037;* so written (in some editions) to distinguish them from *3752* and *5119*.

3754. ὅτι **hŏti**, *hot'-ee;* neut. of *3748* as conj.; demonst. *that* (sometimes redundant); caus. *because:*—as concerning that, as though, because (that), for (that), how (that), (in) that, though, why.

3755. ὅτου **hŏtŏu**, *hot'-oo;* for the gen. of *3748* (as adv.); during *which same* time, i.e. *whilst:*—whiles.

3756. οὐ **ŏu**, *oo;* also (before a vowel)

οὐκ **ŏuk**, *ook;* and (before an aspirate)

οὐχ **ŏuch**, *ookh;* a prim. word; the absol. neg. [comp. *3361*] adv.; *no* or *not:*—+ long, nay, neither, never, no (× man), none, [can-] not, + nothing, + special, un ([-worthy]), when, + without, + yet but. See also *3364, 3372*.

3757. οὗ **hŏu**, *hoo;* gen. of *3739* as adv.; at *which* place, i.e. *where:*—where (-in), whither ([-soever]).

3758. οὐά **ŏua**, *oo-ah';* a prim. exclamation of surprise; "*ah*":—ah.

3759. οὐαί **ŏuai**, *oo-ah'ee;* a prim. exclamation of grief: "*woe*":—alas, woe.

3760. οὐδαμῶς **ŏudamōs**, *oo-dam-oce';* adv. from (the fem.) of *3762;* *by no means:*—not.

3761. οὐδέ **ŏudĕ**, *oo-deh';* from *3756* and *1161;* *not however*, i.e. *neither, nor, not even:*—neither (indeed), never, no (more, nor, not), nor (yet), (also, even, then) not (even, so much as), + nothing, so much as.

3762. οὐδείς **ŏudĕis**, *oo-dice';* includ. fem.

οὐδεμία **ŏudĕmia**, *oo-dem-ee'-ah;* and neut.

οὐδέν **ŏudĕn**, *oo-den';* from *3761* and *1520;* *not even one* (man, woman or thing), i.e. *none, nobody, nothing:*—any (man), aught, man, neither any (thing), never (man), no (man), none (+ of these things), not (any, at all, -thing), nought.

3763. οὐδέποτε **ŏudĕpŏtĕ**, *oo-dep'-ot-eh;* from *3761* and *4218;* *not even at any time*, i.e. *never at all:*—neither at any time, never, nothing at any time.

3764. οὐδέπω **ŏudĕpō**, *oo-dep'-o;* from *3761* and *4452;* *not even yet:*—as yet not, never before (yet), (not) yet.

3765. οὐκέτι **ŏukĕti**, *ook-et'-ee;* also (separately)

οὐκ ἔτι **ŏuk ĕti**, *ook et'-ee;* from *3756* and *2089;* *not yet, no longer:*—after that (not), (not) any more, henceforth (hereafter) not, no longer (more), not as yet (now), now no more (not), yet (not).

3766. οὐκοῦν **ŏukŏun**, *ook-oon';* from *3756* and *3767;* is it *not therefore* that, i.e. (affirm.) *hence* or *so:*—then.

3767. οὖν **ŏun**, *oon;* appar. a prim. word; (adv.) *certainly*, or (conj.) *accordingly:*—and (so, truly), but, now (then), so (likewise then), then, therefore, verily, wherefore.

3768. οὔπω **ŏupō**, *oo'-po;* from *3756* and *4452;* *not yet:*—hitherto not, (no . . .) as yet, not yet.

3769. οὐρά **ŏura**, *oo-rah';* appar. a prim. word; a *tail:*—tail.

3770. οὐράνιος **ŏuraniŏs**, *oo-ran'-ee-os;* from *3772;* *celestial*, i.e. *belonging to* or *coming from* the *sky:*—heavenly.

3771. οὐρανόθεν **ŏuranŏthĕn**, *oo-ran-oth'-en;* from *3772* and the enclitic of source; *from the sky:*—from heaven.

3772. οὐρανός **ŏuranŏs**, *oo-ran-os';* perh. from the same as *3735* (through the idea of *elevation*); the *sky;* by extens. *heaven* (as the abode of God); by impl. *happiness, power, eternity;* spec. the *Gospel* (*Christianity*):—air, heaven ([-ly]), sky.

3773. Οὐρβανός **Ŏurbanŏs**, *oor-ban-os';* of Lat. or.; *Urbanus* (*of the city*, "*urbane*"), a Chr.:—Urbanus.

3774. Οὐρίας **Ŏurias**, *oo-ree'-as;* of Heb. or. [223]; *Urias* (i.e. *Urijah*), a Hittite:—Urias.

3775. οὖς **ŏus**, *ooce;* appar. a prim. word; the *ear* (phys. or ment.):—ear.

3776. οὐσία **ŏusia**, *oo-see'-ah;* from the fem. of *5607;* *substance*, i.e. *property* (*possessions*):—goods, substance.

3777. οὔτε **ŏutĕ**, *oo'-teh;* from *3756* and *5037;* *not too*, i.e. *neither* or *nor;* by anal. *not even:*—neither, none, nor (yet), (no, yet) not, nothing.

3778. οὗτος **hŏutŏs**, *hoo'-tos;* includ. nom. masc. plur.

οὗτοι **hŏutŏi**, *hoo'-toy;* nom. fem. sing.

αὕτη **hautē**, *hŏw'-tay;* and nom. fem. plur.

αὗται **hautai**, *hŏw'-tahee;* from the art. *3588* and *846;* *the he* (*she* or *it*), i.e. *this* or *that* (often with art. repeated):—he (it was that), hereof, it, she, such as, the same, these, they, this (man, same, woman), which, who.

3779. οὕτω **hŏutō**, *hoo'-to;* or (before a vowel)

οὕτως **hŏutōs**, *hoo'-toce;* adv. from *3778;* *in this way* (referring to what precedes or follows):—after that, after (in) this manner, as, even (so), for all that, like (-wise), no more, on this fashion (-wise), so (in like manner), thus, what.

3780. οὐχί **ŏuchi**, *oo-khee';* intens. of *3756;* *not indeed:*—nay, not.

3781. ὀφειλέτης **ŏphĕilĕtēs**, *of-i-let'-ace;* from *3784;* an *ower*, i.e. person *indebted;* fig. a *delinquent;* mor. a *transgressor* (against God):—debtor, which owed, sinner.

3782. ὀφειλή **ŏphĕilē**, *of-i-lay';* from *3784;* *indebtedness*, i.e. (concr.) a *sum* owed; fig. *obligation*, i.e. (conjugal) *duty:*—debt, due.

3783. ὀφείλημα **ŏphĕilēma**, *of-i'-lay-mah;* from (the alt. of) *3784;* *something owed*, i.e. (fig.) a *due;* mor. a *fault:*—debt.

3784. ὀφείλω **ŏphĕilō**, *of-i'-lo;* or (in cert. tenses) its prol. form

ὀφειλέω **ŏphĕilĕō**, *of-i-leh'-o;* prob. from the base of *3786* (through the idea of *accruing*); to *owe* (pecuniarily); fig. to *be under obligation* (*ought, must, should*); mor. to *fail* in duty:—behove, be bound, (be) debt (-or), (be) due (-ty), be guilty (indebted), (must) need (-s), ought, owe, should. See also *3785*.

3785. ὄφελον **ŏphĕlŏn**, *of'-el-on;* first pers. sing. of a past tense of *3784;* *I ought* (*wish*), i.e. (interj.) *oh that!:*—would (to God.)

3786. ὄφελος **ŏphĕlŏs**, *of'-el-os;* from ὀφέλλω **ŏphĕllō** (to *heap* up, i.e. *accumulate* or *benefit*); *gain:*—advantageth, profit.

3787. ὀφθαλμοδουλεία **ŏphthalmŏdŏulĕia**, *of-thal-mod-oo-li'-ah;* from *3788* and *1397;* *sight-labor*, i.e. that needs watching (*remissness*):—eye-service.

3788. ὀφθαλμός **ŏphthalmŏs**, *of-thal-mos';* from *3700;* the *eye* (lit. or fig.); by impl. *vision;* fig. *envy* (from the jealous side-glance):—eye, sight.

3789. ὄφις **ŏphis**, *of'-is;* prob. from *3700* (through the idea of *sharpness* of vision); a *snake*, fig. (as a type of sly cunning) an artful *malicious* person, espec. *Satan:*—serpent.

3790. ὀφρύς **ŏphrus**, *of-roos';* perh. from *3700* (through the idea of the shading or proximity to the organ of *vision*); the eye-"*brow*" or *forehead*, i.e. (fig.) the *brink* of a precipice:—brow.

3791. ὀχλέω **ŏchlĕō**, *okh-leh'-o;* from *3793;* to *mob*, i.e. (by impl.) to *harass:*—vex.

3792. ὀχλοποιέω **ŏchlŏpŏiĕō**, *okh-lop-oy-eh'-o;* from *3793* and *4160;* to *make a crowd*, i.e. *raise a* public *disturbance:*—gather a company.

3793. ὄχλος **ŏchlŏs**, *okh'-los;* from a der. of *2192* (mean. a *vehicle*); a *throng* (as *borne* along); by impl. the *rabble;* by extens. a *class* of people; fig. a *riot:*—company, multitude, number (of people), people, press.

3794. ὀχύρωμα **ŏchurōma**, *okh-oo'-ro-mah;* from a remote der. of *2192* (mean. to *fortify*, through the idea of *holding* safely); a *castle* (fig. *argument*):—stronghold.

3795. ὀψάριον **ŏpsariŏn**, *op-sar'-ee-on;* neut. of a presumed der. of the base of *3702;* a *relish* to other food (as if cooked *sauce*), i.e. (spec.) *fish* (presumably salted and dried as a condiment):—fish.

3796. ὀψέ **ŏpsĕ**, *op-seh';* from the same as *3694* (through the idea of *backwardness*); (adv.) *late* in the day; by extens. *after the close of the day:*—(at) even, in the end.

3797. ὄψιμος **ŏpsimŏs**, *op'-sim-os;* from *3796;* *later*, i.e. *vernal* (showering):—latter.

3798. ὄψιος **ŏpsiŏs**, *op'-see-os;* from *3796;* *late;* fem. (as noun) *afternoon* (early eve) or *nightfall* (later eve):—even (-ing, [-tide]).

3799. ὄψις **ŏpsis**, *op'-sis;* from *3700;* prop. *sight* (the act), i.e. (by impl.) the *visage*, an external *show:*—appearance, countenance, face.

3800. ὀψώνιον **ŏpsōniŏn**, *op-so'-nee-on;* neut. of a presumed der. of the same as *3795;* *rations* for a soldier, i.e. (by extens.) his *stipend* or *pay:*—wages.

3801. ὁ ὢν καὶ ὁ ἦν καὶ ὁ ἐρχόμενος **hŏ ōn kai hŏ ēn kai hŏ ĕrchŏmĕnŏs**, *hŏ own kahee hŏ ane kahee hŏ er-khom'-en-os;* a phrase combining *3588* with the pres. part. and imperf. of *1510* and the pres. part. of *2064* by means of *2532;* *the one being and the* one that *was and the* one *coming*, i.e. *the Eternal*, as a divine epithet of Christ:—which art (is, was), and (which) wast (is, was), and art (is) to come (shalt be).

Π

3802. παγιδεύω **pagidĕuō**, *pag-id-yoo'-o;* from *3803;* to *ensnare* (fig.):—entangle.

3803. παγίς **pagis**, *pag-ece';* from *4078;* a *trap*

(as *fastened* by a noose or notch); fig. a *trick* or *stratagem* (*temptation*):—snare.

Πάγος Pagŏs. See *697.*

3804. **πάθημα pathēma**, *path'-ay-mah;* from a presumed der. of *3806;* something *undergone*, i.e. *hardship* or *pain;* subj. an *emotion* or *influence:*—affection, affliction, motion, suffering.

3805. **παθητός pathētŏs**, *path-ay-tos';* from the same as *3804;* *liable* (i.e. *doomed*) to experience *pain:*—suffer.

3806. **πάθος pathŏs**, *path'-os;* from the alt. of *3958;* prop. *suffering* ("*pathos*"), i.e. (subj.) a *passion* (espec. *concupiscence*):—(inordinate) affection, lust.

πάθω pathō. See *3958.*

3807. **παιδαγωγός paidagōgŏs**, *pahee-dag-o-gos';* from *3816* and a redupl. form of *71;* a *boy-leader*, i.e. a servant whose office it was to take the children to school; (by impl. [fig.] a *tutor* ["*pædagogue*"]):—instructor, schoolmaster.

3808. **παιδάριον paidariŏn**, *pahee-dar'-ee-on;* neut. of a presumed der. of *3816;* a *little boy:*—child, lad.

3809. **παιδεία paidĕia**, *pahee-di'-ah;* from *3811;* *tutorage*, i.e. *education* or *training;* by impl. disciplinary *correction:*—chastening, chastisement, instruction, nurture.

3810. **παιδευτής paidĕutēs**, *pahee-dyoo-tace';* from *3811;* a *trainer*, i.e. *teacher* or (by impl.) *discipliner:*—which corrected, instructor.

3811. **παιδεύω paidĕuō**, *pahee-dyoo'-o;* from *3816;* to *train* up a child, i.e. *educate*, or (by impl.) *discipline* (by punishment):—chasten (-ise), instruct, learn, teach.

3812. **παιδιόθεν paidiŏthĕn**, *pahee-dee-oth'-en;* adv. (of *source*) from *3813;* *from infancy:*—of a child.

3813. **παιδίον paidiŏn**, *pahee-dee'-on;* neut. dimin. of *3816;* a *childling* (of either sex), i.e. (prop.) an infant, or (by extens.) a half-grown *boy* or girl; fig. an *immature* Christian:—(little, young) child, damsel.

3814. **παιδίσκη paidiskē**, *pahee-dis'-kay;* fem. dimin. of *3816;* a *girl*, i.e. (spec.) a *female slave* or *servant:*—bondmaid (-woman), damsel, maid (-en).

3815. **παίζω paizō**, *paheed'-zo;* from *3816;* to *sport* (as a boy):—play.

3816. **παῖς pais**, *paheece;* perh. from *3817;* a *boy* (as often *beaten* with impunity), or (by anal.) a *girl*, and (gen.) a *child;* spec. a *slave* or *servant* (espec. a *minister* to a king; and by eminence to God):—child, maid (-en), (man) servant, son, young man.

3817. **παίω paiō**, *pah'-yo;* a prim. verb; to *hit* (as if by a single blow and less violently than *5180*); spec. to *sting* (as a scorpion):—smite, strike.

3818. **Πακατιανή Pakatianē**, *pak-at-ee-an-ay';* fem. of an adj. of uncert. der.; *Pacatianian*, a section of Phrygia:—Pacatiana.

3819. **πάλαι palai**, *pal'-ahee;* prob. another form for *3825* (through the idea of *retrocession*); (adv.) *formerly*, or (by rel.) *sometime since;* (ellipt. as adj.) *ancient:*—any while, a great while ago, (of) old, in time past.

3820. **παλαιός palaiŏs**, *pal-ah-yos';* from *3819;* *antique*, i.e. *not recent*, *worn out:*—old.

3821. **παλαιότης palaiŏtēs**, *pal-ah-yot'-ace;* from *3820;* *antiquatedness:*—oldness.

3822. **παλαιόω palaiŏō**, *pal-ah-yŏ'-o;* from *3820;* to *make* (pass. *become*) *worn out*, or *declare obsolete:*—decay, make (wax) old.

3823. **πάλη palē**, *pal'-ay;* from **πάλλω pallō** (to *vibrate;* another form for *906*); *wrestling:*—+ wrestle.

3824. **παλιγγενεσία paliggĕnĕsia**, *pal-ing-ghen-es-ee'-ah;* from *3825* and *1078;* (spiritual) *rebirth* (the state or the act), i.e. (fig.) spiritual *renovation;* spec. Messianic *restoration:*—regeneration.

3825. **πάλιν palin**, *pal'-in;* prob. from the same as *3823* (through the idea of *oscillatory* repetition); (adv.) *anew*, i.e. (of place) *back*, (of time) *once more*, or (conj.) *furthermore* or *on the other hand:*—again.

3826. **παμπληθεί pamplēthĕi**, *pam-play-thi';* dat. (adv.) of a comp. of *3956* and *4128;* *in full multitude*, i.e. *concertedly* or *simultaneously:*—all at once.

3827. **πάμπολυς pampŏlus**, *pam'-pol-ooce;* from *3956* and *4183;* *full many*, i.e. *immense:*—very great.

3828. **Παμφυλία Pamphulia**, *pam-fool-ee'-ah;* from a comp. of *3956* and *5443;* *every-tribal*, i.e. *heterogeneous* (*5561* being impl.); *Pamphylia*, a region of Asia Minor:—Pamphylia.

3829. **πανδοχεῖον pandŏchĕiŏn**, *pan-dokh-i'-on;* neut. of a presumed comp. of *3956* and a der. of *1209;* *all-receptive*, i.e. a public *lodging*-place (*caravanserai* or *khan*):—inn.

3830. **πανδοχεύς pandŏchĕus**, *pan-dokh-yoos';* from the same as *3829;* an *innkeeper* (*warden of a caravanserai*):—host.

3831. **πανήγυρις panēguris**, *pan-ay'-goo-ris;* from *3956* and a der. of *58;* a *mass-meeting*, i.e. (fig.) *universal companionship:*—general assembly.

3832. **πανοικί panŏiki**, *pan-oy-kee';* adv. from *3956* and *3624;* *with* the *whole family:*—with all his house.

3833. **πανοπλία panŏplia**, *pan-op-lee'-ah;* from a comp. of *3956* and *3696;* *full armor* ("*panoply*"):—all (whole) armour.

3834. **πανουργία panŏurgia**, *pan-oorg-ee'-ah;* from *3835;* *adroitness*, i.e. (in a bad sense) *trickery* or *sophistry:*—(cunning) craftiness, subtilty.

3835. **πανοῦργος panŏurgŏs**, *pan-oor'-gos;* from *3956* and *2041;* *all-working*, i.e. *adroit* (*shrewd*):—crafty.

3836. **πανταχόθεν pantachŏthĕn**, *pan-takh-oth'-en;* adv. (of *source*) from *3837;* *from all* directions:—from every quarter.

3837. **πανταχοῦ pantachŏu**, *pan-takh-oo';* gen. (as adv. of *place*) of a presumed der. of *3956;* *universally:*—in all places, everywhere.

3838. **παντελής pantĕlēs**, *pan-tel-ace';* from *3956* and *5056;* *full-ended*, i.e. *entire* (neut. as noun, *completion*):—+ in [no] wise, uttermost.

3839. **πάντη pantē**, *pan'-tay;* adv. (of *manner*) from *3956;* *wholly:*—always.

3840. **παντόθεν pantŏthĕn**, *pan-toth'-en;* adv. (of *source*) from *3956;* *from* (i.e. *on*) *all* sides:—on every side, round about.

3841. **παντοκράτωρ pantŏkratōr**, *pan-tok-rat'-ore;* from *3956* and *2904;* the *all-ruling*, i.e. *God* (as absolute and universal *sovereign*):—Almighty, Omnipotent.

3842. **πάντοτε pantŏtĕ**, *pan'-tot-eh;* from *3956* and *3753;* *every when*, i.e. *at all* times:—alway (-s), ever (-more).

3843. **πάντως pantōs**, *pan'-toce;* adv. from *3956;* *entirely;* spec. *at all events*, (with neg. following) *in* no *event:*—by all means, altogether, at all, needs, no doubt, in [no] wise, surely.

3844. **παρά para**, *par-ah';* a prim. prep.; prop. *near*, i.e. (with gen.) *from beside* (lit. or fig.), (with dat.) *at* (or *in*) the *vicinity* of (obj. or subj.), (with acc.) to the *proximity* with (local [espec. *beyond* or *opposed* to] or causal [*on account* of]):—above, against, among, at, before, by, contrary to, × friend, from, + give [such things as they], + that [she] had, × his, in, more than, nigh unto, (out) of, past, save, side . . . by, in the sight of, than, [there-] fore, with. In compounds it retains the same variety of application.

3845. **παραβαίνω parabainō**, *par-ab-ah'ee-no;* from *3844* and the base of *939;* to *go contrary to*, i.e. *violate* a command:—(by) transgress (-ion).

3846. **παραβάλλω paraballō**, *par-ab-al'-lo;* from *3844* and *906;* to *throw alongside*, i.e. (reflex.) to *reach* a place, or (fig.) to *liken:*—arrive, compare.

3847. **παράβασις parabasis**, *par-ab'-as-is;* from *3845;* *violation:*—breaking, transgression.

3848. **παραβάτης parabatēs**, *par-ab-at'-ace;* from *3845;* a *violator:*—breaker, transgress (-or).

3849. **παραβιάζομαι parabiazŏmai**, *par-ab-ee-ad'-zom-ahee;* from *3844* and the mid. of *971;* to *force contrary* to (nature), i.e. *compel* (by entreaty):—constrain.

3850. **παραβολή parabŏlē**, *par-ab-ol-ay';* from *3846;* a *similitude* ("*parable*"), i.e. (symbol.) *fictitious narrative* (of common life conveying a moral), *apothegm* or *adage:*—comparison, figure, parable, proverb.

3851. **παραβουλεύομαι parabŏulĕuŏmai**, *par-ab-ool-yoo'-om-ahee;* from *3844* and the mid. of *1011;* to *misconsult*, i.e. *disregard:*—not (to) regard (-ing).

3852. **παραγγελία paraggĕlia**, *par-ang-gel-ee'-ah;* from *3853;* a *mandate:*—charge, command.

3853. **παραγγέλλω paraggĕllō**, *par-ang-gel'-lo;* from *3844* and the base of *32;* to *transmit a message*, i.e. (by impl.) to *enjoin:*—(give in) charge, (give) command (-ment), declare.

3854. **παραγίνομαι paraginŏmai**, *par-ag-in'-om-ahee;* from *3844* and *1096;* to *become near*, i.e. *approach* (*have arrived*); by impl. to *appear* publicly:—come, go, be present.

3855. **παράγω paragō**, *par-ag'-o;* from *3844* and *71;* to *lead near*, i.e. (reflex. or intrans.) to *go along* or *away:*—depart, pass (away, by, forth).

3856. **παραδειγματίζω paradĕigmatizō**, *par-ad-igue-mat-id'-zo;* from *3844* and *1165;* to *show alongside* (the public), i.e. *expose to infamy;*—make a public example, put to an open shame.

3857. **παράδεισος paradĕisŏs**, *par-ad'-i-sos;* of Oriental or. [comp. 6508]; a *park*, i.e. (spec.) an *Eden* (place of future happiness, "*paradise*"):—paradise.

3858. **παραδέχομαι paradĕchŏmai**, *par-ad-ekh'-om-ahee;* from *3844* and *1209;* to *accept near*, i.e. *admit* or (by impl.) *delight* in:—receive.

3859. **παραδιατριβή paradiatribē**, *par-ad-ee-at-ree-bay';* from a comp. of *3844* and *1304;* *misemployment*, i.e. *meddlesomeness:*—perverse disputing.

3860. **παραδίδωμι paradidōmi**, *par-ad-id'-o-mee;* from *3844* and *1325;* to *surrender*, i.e. *yield up*, *intrust*, *transmit:*—betray, bring forth, cast, commit, deliver (up), give (over, up), hazard, put in prison, recommend.

3861. **παράδοξος paradŏxŏs**, *par-ad'-ox-os;* from *3844* and *1391* (in the sense of *seeming*); *contrary to expectation*, i.e. *extraordinary* ("*paradox*"):—strange.

3862. **παράδοσις paradŏsis**, *par-ad'-os-is;* from *3860;* *transmission*, i.e. (concr.) a *precept;* spec. the Jewish *traditionary law:*—ordinance, tradition.

3863. **παραζηλόω parazēlŏō**, *par-ad-zay-lŏ'-o;* from *3844* and *2206;* to *stimulate alongside*, i.e. *excite to rivalry:*—provoke to emulation (jealousy).

3864. **παραθαλάσσιος parathalassiŏs**, *par-ath-al-as'-see-os;* from *3844* and *2281;* *along* the *sea*, i.e. *maritime* (*lacustrine*):—upon the sea coast.

3865. **παραθεωρέω parathĕōrĕō**, *par-ath-eh-o reh'-o;* from *3844* and *2334;* to *overlook* or *disregard:*—neglect.

3866. **παραθήκη parathēkē**, *par-ath-ay'-kay;* from *3908;* a *deposit*, i.e. (fig.) *trust:*—committed unto.

3867. **παραινέω parainĕō**, *par-ahee-neh'-o;* from *3844* and *134;* to *mispraise*, i.e. *recommend* or *advise* (a different course):—admonish, exhort.

3868. **παραιτέομαι paraitĕŏmai**, *par-ahee-teh'-om-ahee;* from *3844* and the mid. of *154;* to *beg off*, i.e. *deprecate*, *decline*, *shun:*—avoid, (make) excuse, intreat, refuse, reject.

3869. **παρακαθίζω parakathizō**, *par-ak-ath-id'-zo;* from *3844* and *2523;* to *sit down near:*—sit.

3870. **παρακαλέω parakalĕō**, *par-ak-al-eh'-o;* from *3844* and *2564;* to *call near*, i.e. *invite*, *invoke* (by *imploration*, *hortation* or *consolation*):—beseech, call for, (be of good) comfort, desire, (give) exhort (-ation), intreat, pray.

3871. **παρακαλύπτω parakaluptō**, *par-ak-al-oop'-to;* from *3844* and *2572;* to *cover alongside*, i.e. *veil* (fig.):—hide.

3872. **παρακαταθήκη parakatathēkē**, *par-ak-at-ath-ay'-kay;* from a comp. of *3844* and *2698;* something *put down alongside*, i.e. a *deposit* (sacred *trust*):—that (thing) which is committed (un-) to (trust).

3873. **παράκειμαι parakĕimai**, *par-ak'-i-mahee;* from *3844* and *2749;* to *lie near*, i.e. *be at hand* (fig. *be prompt* or *easy*):—be present.

3874. **παράκλησις paraklēsis**, *par-ak'-lay-sis;* from *3870; imploration, hortation, solace:*—comfort, consolation, exhortation, intreaty.

3875. **παράκλητος paraklētŏs**, *par-ak'-lay-tos;* an *intercessor, consoler:*—advocate, comforter.

3876. **παρακοή parakŏē**, *par-ak-ŏ-ay';* from *3878; inattention*, i.e. (by impl.) *disobedience:*—disobedience.

3877. **παρακολουθέω parakŏlŏuthĕō**, *par-ak-ol-oo-theh'-o;* from *3844* and *190;* to *follow near*, i.e. (fig.) *attend* (as a result), *trace out, conform* to:—attain, follow, fully know, have understanding.

3878. **παρακούω parakŏuō**, *par-ak-oo'-o;* from *3844* and *191;* to *mishear*, i.e. (by impl.) to *disobey:*—neglect to hear.

3879. **παρακύπτω parakuptō**, *par-ak-oop'-to;* from *3844* and *2955;* to *bend beside*, i.e. *lean over* (so as to *peer within*):—look (into), stoop down.

3880. **παραλαμβάνω paralambanō**, *par-al-am-ban'-o;* from *3844* and *2983;* to *receive near*, i.e. *associate with* oneself (in any familiar or intimate act or relation); by anal. to *assume* an office; fig. to *learn:*—receive, take (unto, with).

3881. **παραλέγομαι paralĕgŏmai**, *par-al-eg'-om-ahee;* from *3844* and the mid. of *3004* (in its orig. sense); (spec.) to *lay* one's course *near*, i.e. *sail past:*—pass, sail by.

3882. **παράλιος paraliŏs**, *par-al'-ee-os;* from *3844* and *251; beside the salt* (sea), i.e. *maritime:*—sea coast.

3883. **παραλλαγή parallagē**, *par-al-lag-ay';* from a comp. of *3844* and *236; transmutation* (of phase or orbit), i.e. (fig.) *fickleness:*—variableness.

3884. **παραλογίζομαι paralŏgizŏmai**, *par-al-og-id'-zom-ahee;* from *3844* and *3049;* to *misreckon*, i.e. *delude:*—beguile, deceive.

3885. **παραλυτικός paralutikŏs**, *par-al-oo-tee-kos';* from a der. of *3886;* as if *dissolved*, i.e. "*paralytic*":—that had (sick of) the palsy.

3886. **παραλύω paraluō**, *par-al-oo'-o;* from *3844* and *3089;* to *loosen beside*, i.e. *relax* (perf. pas. part. *paralyzed* or *enfeebled*):—feeble, sick of the (taken with) palsy.

3887. **παραμένω paramĕnō**, *par-am-en'-o;* from *3844* and *3306;* to *stay near*, i.e. *remain* (lit. *tarry;* or fig. *be permanent, persevere*):—abide, continue.

3888. **παραμυθέομαι paramuthĕŏmai**, *par-am-oo-theh'-om-ahee;* from *3844* and the mid. of a der. of *3454;* to *relate near*, i.e. (by impl.) *encourage, console:*—comfort.

3889. **παραμυθία paramuthia**, *par-am-oo-thee'-ah;* from *3888; consolation* (prop. abstr.):—comfort.

3890. **παραμύθιον paramuthiŏn**, *par-am-oo'-thee-on;* neut. of *3889; consolation* (prop. concr.):—comfort.

3891. **παρανομέω paranŏmĕō**, *par-an-om-eh'-o;* from a comp. of *3844* and *3551;* to *be opposed to law*, i.e. to *transgress:*—contrary to law.

3892. **παρανομία paranŏmia**, *par-an-om-ee'-ah;* from the same as *3891; transgression:*—iniquity.

3893. **παραπικραίνω parapikrainō**, *par-ap-ik-rah'ee-no;* from *3844* and *4087;* to *embitter alongside*, i.e. (fig.) to *exasperate:*—provoke.

3894. **παραπικρασμός parapikrasmŏs**, *par-ap-ik-ras-mos';* from *3893; irritation:*—provocation.

3895. **παραπίπτω parapiptō**, *par-ap-ip'-to;* from *3844* and *4098;* to *fall aside*, i.e. (fig.) to *apostatize:*—fall away.

3896. **παραπλέω paraplĕō**, *par-ap-leh'-o;* from *3844* and *4126;* to *sail near:*—sail by.

3897. **παραπλήσιον paraplēsiŏn**, *par-ap-lay'-see-on;* neut. of a comp. of *3844* and the base of *4139* (as adv.); *close by*, i.e. (fig.) *almost:*—nigh unto.

3898. **παραπλησίως paraplēsiōs**, *par-ap-lay-see'-oce;* adv. from the same as *3897; in a manner near by*, i.e. (fig.) *similarly:*—likewise.

3899. **παραπορεύομαι parapŏrĕuŏmai**, *par-ap-or-yoo'-om-ahee;* from *3844* and *4198;* to *travel near:*—go, pass (by).

3900. **παράπτωμα paraptōma**, *par-ap'-to-mah;* from *3895;* a *side-slip* (*lapse* or *deviation*), i.e. (unintentional) *error* or (wilful) *transgression:*—fall, fault, offence, sin, trespass.

3901. **παραῤῥυέω pararrhuĕō**, *par-ar-hroo-eh'-o;* from *3844* and the alt. of *4482;* to *flow by*, i.e. (fig.) carelessly *pass* (*miss*):—let slip.

3902. **παράσημος parasēmŏs**, *par-as'-ay-mos;* from *3844* and the base of *4591; side-marked*, i.e. *labelled* (with a *badge* [*figure-head*] of a ship):—sign.

3903. **παρασκευάζω paraskĕuazō**, *par-ask-yoo-ad'-zo;* from *3844* and a der. of *4632;* to *furnish aside*, i.e. *get ready:*—prepare self, be (make) ready.

3904. **παρασκευή paraskĕuē**, *par-ask-yoo-ay';* as if from *3903; readiness:*—preparation.

3905. **παρατείνω paratĕinō**, *par-at-i'-no;* from *3844* and **τείνω tĕinō** (to *stretch*); to *extend along*, i.e. *prolong* (in point of time):—continue.

3906. **παρατηρέω paratērĕō**, *par-at-ay-reh'-o;* from *3844* and *5083;* to *inspect alongside*, i e. *note insidiously* or *scrupulously:*—observe, watch.

3907. **παρατήρησις paratērēsis**, *par-at-ay'-ray-sis;* from *3906; inspection*, i.e. *ocular evidence:*—observation.

3908. **παρατίθημι paratithēmi**, *par-at-ith'-ay-mee;* from *3844* and *5087;* to *place alongside*, i.e. *present* (food, truth); by impl. to *deposit* (as a trust or for protection):—allege, commend, commit (the keeping of), put forth, set before.

3909. **παρατυγχάνω paratugchanō**, *par-at-oong-khan'-o;* from *3844* and *5177;* to *chance near*, i.e. *fall in with:*—meet with.

3910. **παραυτίκα parautika**, *par-ŏw-tee'-kah;* from *3844* and a der. of *846; at the very* instant, i.e. *momentary:*—but for a moment.

3911. **παραφέρω paraphĕrō**, *par-af-er'-o;* from *3844* and *5342* (includ. its alt. forms); to *bear along* or *aside*, i.e. *carry off* (lit. or fig.); by impl. to *avert:*—remove, take away.

3912. **παραφρονέω paraphrŏnĕō**, *par-af-ron-eh'-o;* from *3844* and *5426;* to *misthink*, i.e. *be insane* (*silly*):—as a fool.

3913. **παραφρονία paraphrŏnia**, *par-af-ron-ee'-ah;* from *3912; insanity*, i.e. *foolhardiness:*—madness.

3914. **παραχειμάζω parachĕimazō**, *par-akh-i-mad'-zo;* from *3844* and *5492;* to *winter near*, i.e. *stay* with over the *rainy* season:—winter.

3915. **παραχειμασία parachĕimasia**, *par-akh-i-mas-ee'-ah;* from *3914;* a *wintering* over:—winter in.

3916. **παραχρῆμα parachrēma**, *par-akh-ray'-mah;* from *3844* and *5536* (in its orig. sense); *at the thing* itself, i.e. *instantly:*—forthwith, immediately, presently, straightway, soon.

3917. **πάρδαλις pardalis**, *par'-dal-is;* fem. of **πάρδος pardŏs** (a *panther*); a *leopard:*—leopard.

3918. **πάρειμι parĕimi**, *par'-i-mee;* from *3844* and *1510* (includ. its various forms); to *be near*, i.e. *at hand;* neut. pres. part. (sing.) *time being*, or (plur.) *property:*—come, × have, be here, + lack, (be here) present.

3919. **παρεισάγω parĕisagō**, *par-ice-ag'-o;* from *3844* and *1521;* to *lead in aside*, i.e. *introduce surreptitiously:*—privily bring in.

3920. **παρείσακτος parĕisaktŏs**, *par-ice'-ak-tos;* from *3919; smuggled in:*—unawares brought in.

3921. **παρεισδύνω parĕisdunō**, *par-ice-doo'-no;* from *3844* and a comp. of *1519* and *1416;* to *settle in alongside*, i.e. *lodge stealthily:*—creep in unawares.

3922. **παρεισέρχομαι parĕisĕrchŏmai**, *par-ice-er'-khom-ahee;* from *3844* and *1525;* to *come in alongside*, i.e. *supervene additionally* or *stealthily:*—come in privily, enter.

3923. **παρεισφέρω parĕisphĕrō**, *par-ice-fer'-o;* from *3844* and *1533;* to *bear in alongside*, i.e. *introduce simultaneously:*—give.

3924. **παρεκτός parĕktŏs**, *par-ek-tos';* from *3844* and *1622; near outside*, i.e. *besides:*—except, saving, without.

3925. **παρεμβολή parĕmbŏlē**, *par-em-bol-ay';* from a comp. of *3844* and *1685;* a *throwing in beside* (*juxtaposition*), i.e. (spec.) *battle-array, encampment* or *barracks* (tower Antonia):—army, camp, castle.

3926. **παρενοχλέω parĕnŏchlĕō**, *par-en-okh-leh'-o;* from *3844* and *1776;* to *harass further*, i.e. *annoy:*—trouble.

3927. **παρεπίδημος parĕpidēmŏs**, *par-ep-id'-ay-mos;* from *3844* and the base of *1927;* an *alien alongside*, i.e. a *resident foreigner:*—pilgrim, stranger.

3928. **παρέρχομαι parĕrchŏmai**, *par-er'-khom-ahee;* from *3844* and *2064;* to *come near* or *aside*, i.e. to *approach* (*arrive*), *go by* (or *away*), (fig.) *perish* or *neglect*, (caus.) *avert:*—come (forth), go, pass (away, by, over), past, transgress.

3929. **πάρεσις parĕsis**, *par'-es-is;* from *3935; prætermission*, i.e. *toleration:*—remission.

3930. **παρέχω parĕchō**, *par-ekh'-o;* from *3844* and *2192;* to *hold near*, i.e. *present, afford, exhibit, furnish occasion:*—bring, do, give, keep, minister, offer, shew, + trouble.

3931. **παρηγορία parēgŏria**, *par-ay-gor-ee'-ah;* from a comp of *3844* and a der. of *58* (mean. to *harangue* an assembly); an *address alongside*, i.e. (spec.) *consolation:*—comfort.

3932. **παρθενία parthĕnia**, *par-then-ee'-ah;* from *3933; maidenhood:*—virginity.

3933. **παρθένος parthĕnŏs**, *par-then'-os;* of unknown or.; a *maiden;* by impl. an unmarried *daughter:*—virgin.

3934. **Πάρθος Parthŏs**, *par'-thos;* prob. of for. or.; a *Parthian*, i.e. inhab. of Parthia:—Parthian.

3935. **παρίημι pariēmi**, *par-ee'-ay-mi;* from *3844* and **ἵημι hiēmi** (to *send*); to *let by*, i.e. *relax:*—hang down.

3936. **παρίστημι paristēmi**, *par-is'-tay-mee;* or prol. **παριστάνω paristanō**, *par-is-tan'-o;* from *3844* and *2476;* to *stand beside*, i.e. (trans.) to *exhibit, proffer*, (spec.) *recommend*, (fig.) *substantiate;* or (intrans.) to *be at hand* (or *ready*), *aid:*—assist, bring before, command, commend, give presently, present, prove, provide, shew, stand (before, by, here, up, with), yield.

3937. **Παρμενᾶς Parmĕnas**, *par-men-as';* prob. by contr. for **Παρμενίδης Parmĕnidēs** (a der. of a comp. of *3844* and *3306*); *constant; Parmenas*, a Chr.:—Parmenas.

3938. **πάροδος parŏdŏs**, *par'-od-os;* from *3844* and *3598;* a *by-road*, i.e. (act.) a *route:*—way.

3939. **παροικέω parŏikĕō**, *par-oy-keh'-o;* from *3844* and *3611;* to *dwell near*, i.e. *reside* as a *foreigner:*—sojourn in, be a stranger.

3940. **παροικία parŏikia**, *par-oy-kee'-ah;* from *3941; foreign residence:*—sojourning, × as strangers.

3941. **πάροικος parŏikŏs**, *par'-oy-kos;* from *3844* and *3624;* having a *home near*, i.e. (as noun) a *by-dweller* (*alien resident*):—foreigner, sojourn, stranger.

3942. **παροιμία parŏimia**, *par-oy-mee'-ah;* from a comp. of *3844* and perh. a der. of *3633;* appar. a state *alongside of supposition*, i.e. (concr.) an *adage;*

spec. an enigmatical or fictitious *illustration*:—parable, proverb.

3943. **πάροινος parŏinŏs**, *par'-oy-nos;* from 3844 and 3631; staying *near wine*, i.e. *tippling* (a *toper*):—given to wine.

3944. **παροίχομαι parŏichŏmai**, *par-oy'-khom-ahee;* from 3844 and **οἴχομαι ŏichŏmai** (to *depart*); to *escape along*, i.e. *be gone*:—past.

3945. **παρομοιάζω parŏmŏiazō**, *par-om-oy-ad'-zo;* from 3946; to *resemble*:—be like unto.

3946. **παρόμοιος parŏmŏiŏs**, *par-om'-oy-os;* from 3844 and 3664; *alike nearly*, i.e. *similar*:—like.

3947. **παροξύνω parŏxunō**, *par-ox-oo'-no;* from 3844 and a der. of 3691; to *sharpen alongside*, i.e. (fig.) to *exasperate*:—easily provoke, stir.

3948. **παροξυσμός parŏxusmŏs**, *par-ox-oos-mos';* from 3947 ("*paroxysm*"); *incitement* (to good), or *dispute* (in anger):—contention, provoke unto.

3949. **παροργίζω parŏrgizō**, *par-org-id'-zo;* from 3844 and 3710; to *anger alongside*, i.e. *enrage*:—anger, provoke to wrath.

3950. **παροργισμός parŏrgismŏs**, *par-org-is-mos';* from 3949; *rage*:—wrath.

3951. **παροτρύνω parŏtrunō**, *par-ot-roo'-no;* from 3844 and **ὀτρύνω ŏtrunō** (to *spur*); to *urge along*, i.e. *stimulate* (to hostility):—stir up.

3952. **παρουσία parŏusia**, *par-oo-see'-ah;* from the pres. part. of 3918; a *being near*, i.e. *advent* (often, *return*; spec. of Christ to punish Jerusalem, or finally the wicked); (by impl.) phys. *aspect*:—coming, presence.

3953. **παροψίς parŏpsis**, *par-op-sis';* from 3844 and the base of 3795; a *side-dish* (the receptacle):—platter.

3954. **παῤῥησία parrhēsia**, *par-rhay-see'-ah;* from 3956 and a der. of 4483; *all out-spokenness*, i.e. *frankness, bluntness, publicity;* by impl. *assurance*:—bold (× -ly, -ness, -ness of speech), confidence, × freely, × openly, × plainly (-ness).

3955. **παῤῥησιάζομαι parrhēsiazŏmai**, *par-hray-see-ad'-zom-ahee;* mid. from 3954; to *be frank* in utterance, or *confident* in spirit and demeanor:—be (wax) bold, (preach, speak) boldly.

3956. **πᾶς pas**, *pas;* includ. all the forms of declension; appar. a prim. word; *all, any, every*, the *whole*:—all (manner of, means), alway (-s), any (one), × daily, + ever, every (one, way), as many as, + no (-thing), × throughly, whatsoever, whole, whosoever.

3957. **πάσχα pascha**, *pas'-khah;* of Chald. or. [comp. 6453]; the *Passover* (the meal, the day, the festival or the special sacrifices connected with it):—Easter, Passover.

3958. **πάσχω paschō**, *pas'-kho;* includ. the forms **πάθω** (**pathō**, *path'-o*) and **πένθω** (**pĕnthō**, *pen'-tho*), used only in certain tenses for it; appar. a prim. verb; to *experience* a sensation or impression (usually painful):—feel, passion, suffer, vex.

3959. **Πάταρα Patara**, *pat'-ar-ah;* prob. of for. or.; *Patara*, a place in Asia Minor:—Patara.

3960. **πατάσσω patassō**, *pat-as'-so;* prob. prol. from 3817; to *knock* (gently or with a weapon or fatally):—smite, strike. Comp. 5180.

3961. **πατέω patĕō**, *pat-eh'-o;* from a der. prob. of 3817 (mean. a "*path*"); to *trample* (lit. or fig.):—tread (down, under foot).

3962. **πατήρ patēr**, *pat-ayr';* appar. a prim. word; a "*father*" (lit. or fig., near or more remote):—father, parent.

3963. **Πάτμος Patmŏs**, *pat'-mos;* of uncert. der.; *Patmus*, an islet in the Mediterranean:—Patmos.

3964. **πατραλῴας patralōˌas**, *pat-ral-o'-as;* from 3962 and the same as the latter part of 3389; a *parricide*:—murderer of fathers.

3965. **πατριά patria**, *pat-ree-ah';* as if fem. of a der. of 3962; paternal *descent*, i.e. (concr.) a *group* of families or a whole *race* (*nation*):—family, kindred, lineage.

3966. **πατριάρχης patriarchēs**, *pat-ree-arkh'-ace;* from 3965 and 757; a *progenitor* ("patriarch"):—patriarch.

3967. **πατρικός patrikŏs**, *pat-ree-kos';* from 3962; *paternal*, i.e. *ancestral*:—of fathers.

3968. **πατρίς patris**, *pat-rece';* from 3962; a *father-land*, i.e. *native town;* (fig.) heavenly *home*:—(own) country.

3969. **Πατρόβας Patrŏbas**, *pat-rob'-as;* perh. contr. for **Πατρόβιος Patrŏbiŏs** (a comp. of 3962 and 979); *father's life; Patrobas*, a Chr.:—Patrobas.

3970. **πατροπαράδοτος patrŏparadŏtŏs**, *pat-rop-ar-ad'-ot-os;* from 3962 and a der. of 3860 (in the sense of *handing over* or *down*); *traditionary*:—received by tradition from fathers.

3971. **πατρῷος patrōˌŏs**, *pat-ro'-os;* from 3962; *paternal*, i.e. *hereditary*:—of fathers.

3972. **Παῦλος Paulŏs**, *pŏw'-los;* of Lat. or.; (*little;* but remotely from a der. of 3973, mean. the same); *Paulus*, the name of a Rom. and of an apostle:—Paul, Paulus.

3973. **παύω pauō**, *pŏw'-o;* a prim. verb ("*pause*"); to *stop* (trans. or intrans.), i.e. *restrain, quit, desist, come to an end*:—cease, leave, refrain.

3974. **Πάφος Paphŏs**, *paf'-os;* of uncert. der.; *Paphus*, a place in Cyprus:—Paphos.

3975. **παχύνω pachunō**, *pakh-oo'-no;* from a der. of 4078 (mean. *thick*); to *thicken*, i.e. (by impl.) to *fatten* (fig. *stupefy* or *render callous*):—wax gross.

3976. **πέδη pĕdē**, *ped'-ay;* ultimately from 4228; a *shackle* for the feet:—fetter.

3977. **πεδινός pĕdinŏs**, *ped-ee-nos';* from a der. of 4228 (mean. the *ground*); *level* (as easy for the *feet*):—plain.

3978. **πεζεύω pĕzĕuō**, *ped-zyoo'-o;* from the same as 3979; to *foot* a journey, i.e. *travel* by land:—go afoot.

3979. **πεζῇ pĕzēˌ**, *ped-zay';* dat. fem. of a der. of 4228 (as adv.); *foot-wise*, i.e. by *walking*:—a- (on) foot.

3980. **πειθαρχέω pĕitharchĕō**, *pi-tharkh-eh'-o;* from a comp. of 3982 and 757; to *be persuaded* by a *ruler*, i.e. (gen.) to *submit* to authority; by anal. to *conform* to advice:—hearken, obey (magistrates).

3981. **πειθός pĕithŏs**, *pi-thos';* from 3982; *persuasive*:—enticing.

3982. **πείθω pĕithō**, *pi'-tho;* a prim. verb; to *convince* (by argument, true or false); by anal. to *pacify* or *conciliate* (by other fair means); reflex. or pass. to *assent* (to evidence or authority), to *rely* (by inward certainty):—agree, assure, believe, have confidence, be (wax) conflent, make friend, obey, persuade, trust, yield.

3983. **πεινάω pĕinaō**, *pi-nah'-o;* from the same as 3993 (through the idea of pinching *toil;* "*pine*"); to *famish* (absol. or comparatively); fig. to *crave*:—be an hungered.

3984. **πεῖρα pĕira**, *pi'-rah;* from the base of 4008 (through the idea of *piercing*); a *test*, i.e. *attempt, experience*:—assaying, trial.

3985. **πειράζω pĕirazō**, *pi-rad'-zo;* from 3984; to *test* (obj.), i.e. *endeavor, scrutinize, entice, discipline*:—assay, examine, go about, prove, tempt (-er), try.

3986. **πειρασμός pĕirasmŏs**, *pi-ras-mos';* from 3985; a putting to *proof* (by experiment [of good], *experience* [of evil], solicitation, discipline or provocation); by impl. *adversity*:—temptation, × try.

3987. **πειράω pĕiraō**, *pi-rah'-o;* from 3984; to *test* (subj.), i.e. (reflex.) to *attempt*:—assay.

3988. **πεισμονή pĕismŏnē**, *pice-mon-ay';* from a presumed der. of 3982; *persuadableness*, i.e. *credulity*:—persuasion.

3989. **πέλαγος pĕlagŏs**, *pel'-ag-os;* of uncert. affin.; deep or open *sea*, i.e. the *main*:—depth, sea.

3990. **πελεκίζω pĕlĕkizō**, *pel-ek-id'-zo;* from a der. of 4141 (mean. an *axe*); to *chop* off (the head), i.e. *truncate*:—behead.

3991. **πέμπτος pĕmptŏs**, *pemp'-tos;* from 4002; *fifth*:—fifth.

3992. **πέμπω pĕmpō**, *pem'-po;* appar. a prim. verb; to *dispatch* (from the subj. view or point of *departure*, whereas **ἵημι hiēmi** [as a stronger form of **εἶμι ĕimi**] refers rather to the obj. point or *terminus ad quem*, and 4724 denotes prop. the *orderly* motion involved), espec. on a temporary errand; also to *transmit, bestow*, or *wield*:—send, thrust in.

3993. **πένης pĕnēs**, *pen'-ace;* from a prim. **πένω pĕnō** (to *toil* for daily subsistence); *starving*, i.e. *indigent*:—poor. Comp. 4434.

3994. **πενθερά pĕnthĕra**, *pen-ther-ah';* fem. of 3995; a *wife's mother*:—mother in law, wife's mother.

3995. **πενθερός pĕnthĕrŏs**, *pen-ther-os';* of uncert. affin.; a *wife's father*:—father in law.

3996. **πενθέω pĕnthĕō**, *pen-theh'-o;* from 3997; to *grieve* (the feeling or the act):—mourn, (be-) wail.

3997. **πένθος pĕnthŏs**, *pen'-thos;* strengthened from the alt. of 3958; *grief*:—mourning, sorrow.

3998. **πεντιχρός pĕntichrŏs**, *pen-tikh-ros';* prol. from the base of 3993; *necessitous*:—poor.

3999. **πεντακίς pĕntakis**, *pen-tak-ece';* mult. adv. from 4002; *five times*:—five times.

4000. **πεντακισχίλιοι pĕntakischiliŏi**, *pen-tak-is-khil'-ee-oy;* from 3999 and 5507; *five times a thousand*:—five thousand.

4001. **πεντακόσιοι pĕntakŏsiŏi**, *pen-tak-os'-ee-oy;* from 4002 and 1540; *five hundred*:—five hundred.

4002. **πέντε pĕntĕ**, *pen'-teh;* a prim. number; "*five*":—five.

4003. **πεντεκαιδέκατος pĕntĕkaidĕkatŏs**, *pen-tek-ahee-dek'-at-os;* from 4002 and 2532 and 1182; *five and tenth*:—fifteenth.

4004. **πεντήκοντα pĕntēkŏnta**, *pen-tay'-kon-tah;* mult. of 4002; *fifty*:—fifty.

4005. **πεντηκοστή pĕntēkŏstē**, *pen-tay-kos-tay';* fem. of the ord. of 4004; *fiftieth* (2250 being implied) from Passover, i.e. the festival of "*Pentecost*":—Pentecost.

4006. **πεποίθησις pĕpŏithēsis**, *pep-oy'-thay-sis;* from the perf. of the alt. of 3958; *reliance*:—confidence, trust.

4007. **περ pĕr**, *per;* from the base of 4008; an enclitic particle significant of *abundance* (*thoroughness*), i.e. *emphasis; much, very* or *ever*:—[whom-] soever.

4008. **πέραν pĕran**, *per'-an;* appar. acc. of an obsol. der. of **πείρω pĕirō** (to "*pierce*"); *through* (as adv. or prep.), i.e. *across*:—beyond, farther (other) side, over.

4009. **πέρας pĕras**, *per'-as;* from the same as 4008; an *extremity*:—end, ut- (ter-) most part.

4010. **Πέργαμος Pĕrgamŏs**, *per'-gam-os;* from 4444; *fortified; Pergamus*, a place in Asia Minor:—Pergamos.

4011. **Πέργη Pĕrgē**, *perg'-ay;* prob. from the same as 4010; a *tower; Perga*, a place in Asia Minor:—Perga.

4012. **περί pĕri**, *per-ee';* from the base of 4008; prop. *through* (all over), i.e. *around;* fig. *with respect* to; used in various applications, of place, cause or time (with the gen. denoting the *subject* or *occasion* or *superlative* point; with the acc. the *locality, circuit, matter, circumstance* or general *period*):—(there-) about, above, against, at, on behalf of, × and his company, which concern, (as) concerning, for, × how it will go with, ([there-, where-]) of, on, over, pertaining (to), for sake, × (e-) state, (as) touching, [where-] by (in), with. In comp. it retains substantially the same mean. of circuit (*around*), excess (*beyond*), or completeness (*through*).

4013. **περιάγω pĕriagō**, *per-ee-ag'-o;* from *4012* and *71;* to *take around* (as a companion); reflex. to *walk around:*—compass, go (round) about, lead about.

4014. **περιαιρέω pĕriairĕō**, *per-ee-ahee-reh'-o;* from *4012* and *138* (incl. its alt.); to *remove* all *around*, i.e. *unveil, cast off* (anchor); fig. to *expiate:*—take away (up).

4015. **περιαστράπτω pĕriastraptō**, *per-ee-as-trap'-to;* from *4012* and *797;* to *flash* all *around*, i.e. *envelop in light:*—shine round (about).

4016. **περιβάλλω pĕriballō**, *per-ee-bal'-lo;* from *4012* and *906;* to *throw* all *around*, i.e. *invest* (with a palisade or with clothing):—array, cast about, clothe (-d me), put on.

4017. **περιβλέπω pĕriblĕpō**, *per-ee-blep'-o;* from *4012* and *991;* to *look* all *around:*—look (round) about (on).

4018. **περιβόλαιον pĕribŏlaiŏn**, *per-ib-ol'-ah-yon;* neut. of a presumed der. of *4016;* something *thrown around* one, i.e. a *mantle, veil:*—covering, vesture.

4019. **περιδέω pĕridĕō**, *per-ee-deh'-o;* from *4012* and *1210;* to *bind around* one, i.e. *enwrap:*—bind about.

περιδρέμω pĕridrĕmō. See *4063.*

περιέλλω pĕriĕllō. See *4014.*

περιέλθω pĕriĕlthō. See *4022.*

4020. **περιεργάζομαι pĕriĕrgazŏmai**, *per-ee-er-gad'-zom-ahee;* from *4012* and *2038;* to *work* all *around*, i.e. *bustle about* (*meddle*):—be a busybody.

4021. **περίεργος pĕriĕrgŏs**, *per-ee'-er-gos;* from *4012* and *2041;* *working all around*, i.e. *officious* (*meddlesome*, neut. plur. *magic*):—busybody, curious arts.

4022. **περιέρχομαι pĕriĕrchŏmai**, *per-ee-er'-khom-ahee;* from *4012* and *2064* (includ. its alt.); to *come* all *around*, i.e. *stroll, vacillate, veer:*—fetch a compass, vagabond, wandering about.

4023. **περιέχω pĕriĕchō**, *per-ee-ekh'-o;* from *4012* and *2192;* to *hold* all *around*, i.e. *include, clasp* (fig.):—+ astonished, contain, after [this manner].

4024. **περιζώννυμι pĕrizōnnumi**, *per-id-zone'-noo-mee;* from *4012* and *2224;* to *gird* all *around*, i.e. (mid. or pass.) to *fasten on one's belt* (lit. or fig.):—gird (about, self).

4025. **περίθεσις pĕrithĕsis**, *per-ith'-es-is;* from *4060;* a *putting* all *around*, i.e. *decorating* oneself with:—wearing.

4026. **περιΐστημι pĕriïstēmi**, *per-ee-is'-tay-mee;* from *4012* and *2476;* to *stand* all *around*, i.e. (near) to *be a bystander*, or (aloof) to *keep away* from:—avoid, shun, stand by (round about).

4027. **περικάθαρμα pĕrikatharma**, *per-ee-kath'-ar-mah;* from a comp. of *4012* and *2508;* something *cleaned* off all *around*, i.e. *refuse* (fig.):—filth.

4028. **περικαλύπτω pĕrikaluptō**, *per-ee-kal-oop'-to;* from *4012* and *2572;* to *cover* all *around*, i.e. *entirely* (the face, a surface):—blindfold, cover, overlay.

4029. **περίκειμαι pĕrikĕimai**, *per-ik'-i-mahee;* from *4012* and *2749;* to *lie* all *around*, i.e. *inclose, encircle, hamper* (lit. or fig.):—be bound (compassed) with, hang about.

4030. **περικεφαλαία pĕrikĕphalaia**, *per-ee-kef-al-ah'-yah;* fem. of a comp. of *4012* and *2776;* *encirclement of the head*, i.e. a *helmet:*—helmet.

4031. **περικρατής pĕrikratēs**, *per-ee-krat-ace';* from *4012* and *2904;* *strong* all *around*, i.e. a *master* (*manager*):—+ come by.

4032. **περικρύπτω pĕrikruptō**, *per-ee-kroop'-to;* from *4012* and *2928;* to *conceal* all *around*, i.e. *entirely:*—hide.

4033. **περικυκλόω pĕrikuklŏō**, *per-ee-koo-klŏ'-o;* from *4012* and *2944;* to *encircle* all *around*, i.e. *blockade completely:*—compass round.

4034. **περιλάμπω pĕrilampō**, *per-ee-lam'-po;* from *4012* and *2989;* to *illuminate* all *around*, i.e. *invest with a halo:*—shine round about.

4035. **περιλείπω pĕrilĕipō**, *per-ee-li'-po;* from *4012* and *3007;* to *leave* all *around*, i.e. (pass.) *survive:*—remain.

4036. **περίλυπος pĕrilupŏs**, *per-il'-oo-pos;* from *4012* and *3077;* *grieved* all *around*, i.e. *intensely sad:*—exceeding (very) sorry (-owful).

4037. **περιμένω pĕrimĕnō**, *per-ee-men'-o;* from *4012* and *3306;* to *stay around*, i.e. *await:*—wait for.

4038. **πέριξ pĕrix**, *per'-ix;* adv. from *4012;* all *around*, i.e. (as adj.) *circumjacent:*—round about.

4039. **περιοικέω pĕriŏikĕō**, *per-ee-oy-keh'-o;* from *4012* and *3611;* to *reside around*, i.e. *be a neighbor:*—dwell round about.

4040. **περίοικος pĕriŏikŏs**, *per-ee'-oy-kos;* from *4012* and *3624;* *housed around*, i.e. *neighboring* (ellipt. as noun):—neighbour.

4041. **περιούσιος pĕriŏusiŏs**, *per-ee-oo'-see-os;* from the pres. part. fem. of a comp. of *4012* and *1510;* *being beyond* usual, i.e. *special* (one's *own*):—peculiar.

4042. **περιοχή pĕriŏchē**, *per-ee-okh-ay';* from *4023;* a *being held around*, i.e. (concr.) a *passage* (of Scripture, as *circumscribed*):—place.

4043. **περιπατέω pĕripatĕō**, *per-ee-pat-eh'-o;* from *4012* and *3961;* to *tread* all *around*, i.e. *walk* at large (espec. as proof of ability); fig. to *live, deport oneself, follow* (as a companion or votary):—go, be occupied with, walk (about).

4044. **περιπείρω pĕripĕirō**, *per-ee-pi'-ro;* from *4012* and the base of *4008;* to *penetrate entirely*, i.e. *transfix* (fig.):—pierce through.

4045. **περιπίπτω pĕripiptō**, *per-ee-pip'-to;* from *4012* and *4098;* to *fall* into something that is all *around*, i.e. *light among* or *upon, be surrounded with:*—fall among (into).

4046. **περιποιέομαι pĕripŏiĕŏmai**, *per-ee-poy-eh'-om-ahee;* mid. from *4012* and *4160;* to *make around oneself*, i.e. *acquire* (*buy*):—purchase.

4047. **περιποίησις pĕripŏiēsis**, *per-ee-poy'-ay-sis;* from *4046;* *acquisition* (the act or the thing); by extens. *preservation:*—obtain (-ing), peculiar, purchased, possession, saving.

4048. **περιῤῥήγνυμι pĕrirrhēgnumi**, *per-ir-hrayg'-noo-mee;* from *4012* and *4486;* to *tear* all *around*, i.e. *completely away:*—rend off.

4049. **περισπάω pĕrispaō**, *per-ee-spah'-o;* from *4012* and *4685;* to *drag* all *around*, i.e. (fig.) to *distract* (with care):—cumber.

4050. **περισσεία pĕrissĕia**, *per-is-si'-ah;* from *4052;* *surplusage*, i.e. *superabundance:*—abundance (-ant, [-ly]), superfluity.

4051. **περίσσευμα pĕrissĕuma**, *per-is'-syoo-mah;* from *4052;* a *surplus*, or *superabundance:*—abundance, that was left, over and above.

4052. **περισσεύω pĕrissĕuō**, *per-is-syoo'-o;* from *4053;* to *superabound* (in quantity or quality), *be in excess, be superfluous;* also (trans.) to *cause to superabound* or *excel:*—(make, more) abound, (have, have more) abundance, (be more) abundant, be the better, enough and to spare, exceed, excel, increase, be left, redound, remain (over and above).

4053. **περισσός pĕrissŏs**, *per-is-sos';* from *4012* (in the sense of *beyond*); *superabundant* (in quantity) or *superior* (in quality); by impl. *excessive;* adv. (with *1537*) *violently;* neut. (as noun) *preeminence:*—exceeding abundantly above, more abundantly, advantage, exceedingly, very highly, beyond measure, more, superfluous, vehement [-ly].

4054. **περισσότερον pĕrissŏtĕrŏn**, *per-is-sot'-er-on;* neut. of *4055* (as adv.); in a *more superabundant* way:—more abundantly, a great deal, far more.

4055. **περισσότερος pĕrissŏtĕrŏs**, *per-is-sot'-er-os;* comp. of *4053;* *more superabundant* (in number, degree or character):—more abundant, greater (much) more, overmuch.

4056. **περισσοτέρως pĕrissŏtĕrōs**, *per-is-sot-er'-oce;* adv. from *4055;* *more superabundantly:*—more abundant (-ly), × the more earnest, (more) exceedingly, more frequent, much more, the rather.

4057. **περισσῶς pĕrissōs**, *per-is-soce';* adv. from *4053;* *superabundantly:*—exceedingly, out of measure, the more.

4058. **περιστερά pĕristĕra**, *per-is-ter-ah';* of uncert. der.; a *pigeon:*—dove, pigeon.

4059. **περιτέμνω pĕritĕmnō**, *per-ee-tem'-no;* from *4012* and the base of *5114;* to *cut around*, i.e. (spec.) to *circumcise:*—circumcise.

4060. **περιτίθημι pĕritithēmi**, *per-ee-tith'-ay-mee;* from *4012* and *5087;* to *place around;* by impl. to *present:*—bestow upon, hedge round about, put about (on, upon), set about.

4061. **περιτομή pĕritŏmē**, *per-it-om-ay';* from *4059;* *circumcision* (the rite, the condition or the people, lit. or fig.):—× circumcised, circumcision.

4062. **περιτρέπω pĕritrĕpō**, *per-ee-trep'-o;* from *4012* and the base of *5157;* to *turn around*, i.e. (ment.) to *craze:*—+ make mad.

4063. **περιτρέχω pĕritrĕchō**, *per-ee-trekh'-o;* from *4012* and *5143* (includ. its alt.); to *run around*, i.e. *traverse:*—run through.

4064. **περιφέρω pĕriphĕrō**, *per-ee-fer'-o;* from *4012* and *5342;* to *convey around*, i.e. *transport hither and thither:*—bear (carry) about.

4065. **περιφρονέω pĕriphrŏnĕō**, *per-ee-fron-eh'-o;* from *4012* and *5426;* to *think beyond*, i.e. *depreciate* (*contemn*):—despise.

4066. **περίχωρος pĕrichōrŏs**, *per-ikh'-o-ros;* from *4012* and *5561;* *around* the *region*, i.e. *circumjacent* (as noun, with *1093* impl. *vicinity*):—country (round) about, region (that lieth) round about.

4067. **περίψωμα pĕripsōma**, *per-ip'-so-mah;* from a comp. of *4012* and **ψάω psaō** (to *rub*); something *brushed* all *around*, i.e. *off-scrapings* (fig. *scum*):—offscouring.

4068. **περπερεύομαι pĕrpĕrĕuŏmai**, *per-per-yoo'-om-ahee;* mid. from **πέρπερος pĕrpĕrŏs** (*braggart;* perh. by redupl. of the base of *4008*); to *boast:*—vaunt itself.

4069. **Περσίς Pĕrsis**, *per-sece';* a *Persian* woman; *Persis*, a Chr. female:—Persis.

4070. **πέρυσι pĕrusi**, *per'-oo-si;* adv. from *4009;* the *by-gone*, i.e. (as noun) *last year:*—+ a year ago.

πετάομαι pĕtaŏmai. See *4072.*

4071. **πετεινόν pĕtĕinŏn**, *pet-i-non';* neut. of a der. of *4072;* a *flying* animal, i.e. *bird:*—bird, fowl.

4072. **πέτομαι pĕtŏmai**, *pet'-om-ahee;* or prol.

πετάομαι pĕtaŏmai, *pet-ah'-om-ahee;* or contr. **πτάομαι ptaŏmai**, *ptah'-om-ahee;* mid. of a prim. verb; to *fly:*—fly (-ing).

4073. **πέτρα pĕtra**, *pet'-ra;* fem. of the same as *4074;* a (mass of) *rock* (lit. or fig.):—rock.

4074. **Πέτρος Pĕtrŏs**, *pet'-ros;* appar. a prim. word; a (piece of) *rock* (larger than *3037*); as a name, *Petrus*, an apostle:—Peter, rock. Comp. *2786.*

4075. **πετρώδης pĕtrōdēs**, *pet-ro'-dace;* from *4073* and *1491;* *rock-like*, i.e. *rocky:*—stony.

4076. **πήγανον pēganŏn**, *pay'-gan-on;* from *4078;* *rue* (from its *thick* or *fleshy* leaves):—rue.

4077. **πηγή pēgē**, *pay-gay';* prob. from *4078* (through the idea of *gushing* plumply); a *fount* (lit. or fig.), i.e. *source* or *supply* (of water, blood, enjoyment) (not necessarily the original spring):—fountain, well.

4078. **πήγνυμι pēgnumi**, *payg'-noo-mee;* a prol. form of a prim. verb (which in its simpler form occurs only as an alt. in certain tenses); to *fix* ("*peg*"), i.e. (spec.) to *set up* (a tent):—pitch.

4079. **πηδάλιον pēdaliŏn**, *pay-dal'-ee-on;* neut. of a (presumed) der. of **πηδόν pēdŏn** (the *blade* of an oar; from the same as *3976*); a "*pedal*", i.e. *helm:*—rudder.

4080. **πηλίκος pēlikŏs**, *pay-lee'-kos;* a quantitative form (the fem.) of the base of *4225;* *how much* (as indef.), i.e. in size or (fig.) dignity:—how great (large).

4081. **πηλός pēlŏs**, *pay-los';* perh. a prim. word; *clay:*—clay.

4082. πήρα **pēra**, *pay'-rah;* of uncert. affin.; a *wallet* or leather *pouch* for food:—scrip.

4083. πῆχυς **pēchus**, *pay'-khoos;* of uncert. affin.; the *fore-arm*, i.e. (as a measure) a *cubit:*—cubit.

4084. πιάζω **piazō**, *pee-ad'-zo;* prob. another form of *971;* to *squeeze*, i.e. *seize* (gently by the hand [*press*], or officially [*arrest*], or in hunting [*capture*]):—apprehend, catch, lay hand on, take. Comp. *4085*.

4085. πιέζω **piĕzō**, *pee-ed'-zo;* another form for *4084;* to *pack:*—press down.

4086. πιθανολογία **pithanŏlŏgia**, *pith-an-ol-og-ee'-ah;* from a comp. of a der. of *3982* and *3056; persuasive language:*—enticing words.

4087. πικραίνω **pikrainō**, *pik-rah'ee-no;* from *4089;* to *embitter* (lit. or fig.):—be (make) bitter.

4088. πικρία **pikria**, *pik-ree'-ah;* from *4089; acridity* (espec. *poison*), lit. or fig.:—bitterness.

4089. πικρός **pikrŏs**, *pik-ros';* perh. from *4078* (through the idea of *piercing*); *sharp* (*pungent*), i.e. *acrid* (lit. or fig.):—bitter.

4090. πικρῶς **pikrōs**, *pik-roce';* adv. from *4089; bitterly*, i.e. (fig.) *violently:*—bitterly.

4091. Πιλάτος **Pilatŏs**, *pil-at'-os;* of Lat. or.; *close-pressed*, i.e. *firm; Pilatus*, a Rom.:—Pilate.

πίμπλημι **pimplēmi**. See *4130*.

4092. πίμπρημι **pimprēmi**, *pim'-pray-mee;* a redupl. and prol. form of a prim.

πρέω **prĕō**, *preh'-o* (which occurs only as an alt. in certain tenses); to *fire*, i.e. *burn* (fig. and pass. *become inflamed* with fever):—be (× should have) swollen.

4093. πινακίδιον **pinakidiŏn**, *pin-ak-id'-ee-on;* dimin. of *4094;* a *tablet* (for writing on):—writing table.

4094. πίναξ **pinax**, *pin'-ax;* appar. a form of *4109;* a *plate:*—charger, platter.

4095. πίνω **pinō**, *pee'-no;* a prol. form of

πίω **piō**, *pee'-o*, which (together with another form πόω **pŏō**, *pŏ'-o*) occurs only as an alt. in cert. tenses; to *imbibe* (lit. or fig.):—drink.

4096. πιότης **piŏtēs**, *pee-ot'-ace;* from πίων **piōn** (*fat;* perh. akin to the alt. of *4095* through the idea of *repletion*); *plumpness*, i.e. (by impl.) *richness* (*oiliness*):—fatness.

4097. πιπράσκω **pipraskō**, *pip-ras'-ko;* a redupl. and prol. form of

πράω **praō**, *prah'-o* (which occurs only as an alt. in cert. tenses); contr. from περάω **pĕraō** (to *traverse;* from the base of *4008*); to *traffic* (by *travelling*), i.e. *dispose* of as merchandise or into slavery (lit. or fig.):—sell.

4098. πίπτω **piptō**, *pip'-to;* a redupl. and contr. form of πέτω **pĕtō**, *pet'-o* (which occurs only as an alt. in cert. tenses); prob. akin to *4072* through the idea of *alighting;* to *fall* (lit or fig.):—fail, fall (down), light on.

4099. Πισιδία **Pisidia**, *pis-id-ee'-ah;* prob. of for. or.; *Pisidia*, a region of Asia Minor:—Pisidia.

4100. πιστεύω **pistĕuō**, *pist-yoo'-o;* from *4102;* to *have faith* (in, upon, or with respect to, a person or thing), i.e. *credit;* by impl. to *entrust* (espec. one's spiritual well-being to Christ):—believe (-r), commit (to trust), put in trust with.

4101. πιστικός **pistikŏs**, *pis-tik-os';* from *4102; trustworthy*, i.e. *genuine* (*unadulterated*):—spike-[nard].

4102. πίστις **pistis**, *pis'-tis;* from *3982; persuasion*, i.e. *credence;* mor. *conviction* (of *religious* truth, or the truthfulness of God or a religious teacher), espec. *reliance* upon Christ for salvation; abstr. *constancy* in such profession; by extens. the system of religious (Gospel) *truth* itself:—assurance, belief, believe, faith, fidelity.

4103. πιστός **pistŏs**, *pis-tos';* from *3982;* obj. *trustworthy;* subj. *trustful:*—believe (-ing, -r), faithful (-ly), sure, true.

4104. πιστόω **pistŏō**, *pis-tŏ'-o;* from *4103;* to *assure:*—assure of.

4105. πλανάω **planaō**, *plan-ah'-o;* from *4106;* to (prop. *cause* to) *roam* (from safety, truth, or virtue):—go astray, deceive, err, seduce, wander, be out of the way.

4106. πλάνη **planē**, *plan'-ay;* fem. of *4108* (as abstr.); obj. *fraudulence;* subj. a *straying* from orthodoxy or piety:—deceit, to deceive, delusion, error.

4107. πλανήτης **planētēs**, *plan-ay'-tace;* from *4108;* a *rover* ("planet"), i.e. (fig.) an *erratic* teacher:—wandering.

4108. πλάνος **planŏs**, *plan'-os;* of uncert. affin.; *roving* (as a *tramp*), i.e. (by impl.) an *impostor* or *misleader:*—deceiver, seducing.

4109. πλάξ **plax**, *plax;* from *4111;* a *moulding-board*, i.e. *flat* surface ("*plate*", or *tablet*, lit. or fig.):—table.

4110. πλάσμα **plasma**, *plas'-mah;* from *4111;* something *moulded:*—thing formed.

4111. πλάσσω **plassō**, *plas'-so;* a prim. verb; to *mould*, i.e. *shape* or *fabricate:*—form.

4112. πλαστός **plastŏs**, *plas-tos';* from *4111; moulded*, i.e. (by impl.) *artificial* or (fig.) *fictitious* (*false*):—feigned.

4113. πλατεῖα **platĕia**, *plat-i'-ah;* fem. of *4116;* a *wide* "*plat*" or "*place*", i.e. open *square:*—street.

4114. πλάτος **platŏs**, *plat'-os;* from *4116; width:*—breadth.

4115. πλατύνω **platunō**, *plat-oo'-no;* from *4116;* to *widen* (lit. or fig.):—make broad, enlarge.

4116. πλατύς **platus**, *plat-oos';* from *4111;* spread out "*flat*" ("plot"), i.e. *broad:*—wide.

4117. πλέγμα **plĕgma**, *pleg'-mah;* from *4120;* a *plait* (of hair):—broidered hair.

πλεῖον **plĕiŏn**. See *4119*.

4118. πλεῖστος **plĕistŏs**, *plice'-tos;* irreg. superl. of *4183;* the *largest number* or *very large:*—very great, most.

4119. πλείων **plĕiōn**, *pli -own;* neut.

πλεῖον **plĕiŏn**, *pli'-on;* or

πλέον **plĕŏn**, *pleh'-on;* compar. of *4183; more* in quantity, number, or quality; also (in plur.) the *major portion:*— × above, + exceed, more excellent, further, (very) great (-er), long (-er), (very) many, greater (more) part, + yet but.

4120. πλέκω **plĕkō**, *plek'-o;* a prim. word; to *twine* or *braid:*—plait.

πλέον **plĕŏn**. See 4119.

4121. πλεονάζω **plĕŏnazō**, *pleh-on-ad'-zo;* from *4119;* to *do*, *make* or *be more*, i.e. *increase* (trans. or intrans.); by extens. to *superabound:*—abound, abundant, make to increase, have over.

4122. πλεονεκτέω **plĕŏnĕktĕō**, *pleh-on-ek-teh'-o;* from *4123;* to *be covetous*, i.e. (by impl.) to *overreach:*—get an advantage, defraud, make a gain.

4123. πλεονέκτης **plĕŏnĕktēs**, *pleh-on-ek'-tace;* from *4119* and *2192; holding* (*desiring*) *more*, i.e. *eager for gain* (*avaricious*, hence a *defrauder*):—covetous.

4124. πλεονεξία **plĕŏnĕxia**, *pleh-on-ex-ee'-ah;* from *4123; avarice*, i.e. (by impl.) *fraudulency*, *extortion:*—covetous (-ness) practices, greediness.

4125. πλευρά **plĕura**, *plyoo-rah';* of uncert. affin.; a *rib*, i.e. (by extens.) *side:*—side.

4126. πλέω **plĕō**, *pleh'-o;* another form for

πλεύω **plĕuō**, *plyoo'-o*, which is used as an alt. in certain tenses; prob. a form of *4150* (through the idea of *plunging* through the water); to *pass* in a vessel:—sail. See also *4130*.

4127. πληγή **plēgē**, *play-gay';* from *4141;* a *stroke;* by impl. a *wound;* fig. a *calamity:*—plague, stripe, wound (-ed).

4128. πλῆθος **plēthŏs**, *play'-thos;* from *4130;* a *fulness*, i.e. a *large number*, *throng*, *populace:*—bundle, company, multitude.

4129. πληθύνω **plēthunō**, *play-thoo'-no;* from another form of *4128;* to *increase* (trans. or intrans.):—abound, multiply.

4130. πλήθω **plēthō**, *play'-tho;* a prol. form of a prim. πλέω **plĕō**, *pleh'-o* (which appears only as an alt. in certain tenses and in the redupl. form πίμπλημι **pimplēmi**); to "*fill*" (lit. or fig. [*imbue*, *influence*, *supply*]); spec. to *fulfil* (time):—accomplish, full (. . . come), furnish.

4131. πλήκτης **plēktēs**, *plake'-tace;* from *4141;* a *smiter*, i.e. *pugnacious* (*quarrelsome*):—striker.

4132. πλημμύρα **plēmmura**, *plame-moo'-rah;* prol. from *4130; flood-tide*, i.e. (by anal.) a *freshet:*—flood.

4133. πλήν **plēn**, *plane;* from *4119; moreover* (*besides*), i.e. *albeit*, *save that*, *rather*, *yet:*—but (rather), except, nevertheless, notwithstanding, save, than.

4134. πλήρης **plērēs**, *play'-race;* from *4130; replete*, or *covered* over; by anal. *complete:*—full.

4135. πληροφορέω **plērŏphŏrĕō**, *play-rof-or-eh'-o;* from *4134* and *5409;* to *carry* out *fully* (in evidence), i.e. *completely assure* (or *convince*), *entirely accomplish:*—most surely believe, fully know (persuade), make full proof of.

4136. πληροφορία **plērŏphŏria**, *play-rof-or-ee'-ah;* from *4135; entire confidence:*—(full) assurance.

4137. πληρόω **plērŏō**, *play-rŏ'-o;* from *4134;* to *make replete*, i.e. (lit.) to *cram* (a net), *level* up (a hollow), or (fig.) to *furnish* (or *imbue*, *diffuse*, *influence*), *satisfy*, *execute* (an office), *finish* (a period or task), *verify* (or *coincide* with a prediction), etc.:—accomplish, × after, (be) complete, end, expire, fill (up), fulfil, (be, make) full (come), fully preach, perfect, supply.

4138. πλήρωμα **plērōma**, *play'-ro-mah;* from *4137; repletion* or *completion*, i.e. (subj.) what *fills* (as contents, supplement, copiousness, multitude), or (obj.) what is *filled* (as container, performance, period):—which is put in to fill up, piece that filled up, fulfilling, full, fulness.

4139. πλησίον **plēsiŏn**, *play-see'-on;* neut. of a der. of πέλας **pĕlas** (*near*); (adv.) *close* by; as noun, a *neighbor*, i.e. *fellow* (as man, countryman, Chr. or friend):—near, neighbour.

4140. πλησμονή **plēsmŏnē**, *place-mon-ay';* from a presumed der. of *4130;* a *filling* up, i.e. (fig.) *gratification:*—satisfying.

4141. πλήσσω **plēssō**, *place'-so;* appar. another form of *4111* (through the idea of *flattening* out); to *pound*, i.e. (fig.) to *inflict* with (calamity):—smite. Comp. *5180*.

4142. πλοιάριον **plŏiariŏn**, *ploy-ar'-ee-on;* neut. of a presumed der. of *4143;* a *boat:*—boat, little (small) ship.

4143. πλοῖον **plŏiŏn**, *ploy'-on;* from *4126;* a *sailer*, i.e. *vessel:*—ship (-ping).

4144. πλόος **plŏŏs**, *plŏ'-os;* from *4126;* a *sail*, i.e. *navigation:*—course, sailing, voyage.

4145. πλούσιος **plŏusiŏs**, *ploo'-see-os;* from *4149; wealthy;* fig. *abounding* with:—rich.

4146. πλουσίως **plŏusiōs**, *ploo-see'-oce;* adv. from *4145; copiously:*—abundantly, richly.

4147. πλουτέω **plŏutĕō**, *ploo-teh'-o;* from *4148;* to *be* (or *become*) *wealthy* (lit. or fig.):—be increased with goods, (be made, wax) rich.

4148. πλουτίζω **plŏutizō**, *ploo-tid'-zo;* from *4149;* to *make wealthy* (fig.):—en- (make) rich.

4149. πλοῦτος **plŏutŏs**, *ploo'-tos;* from the base of *4130; wealth* (as *fulness*), i.e. (lit.) *money*, *possessions*, or (fig.) *abundance*, *richness*, (spec.) valuable *bestowment:*—riches.

4150. πλύνω **plunō**, *ploo'-no;* a prol. form of an obsol. πλύω **pluō** (to "*flow*"); to "*plunge*", i.e. *launder* clothing:—wash. Comp. *3068*, *3538*.

4151. πνεῦμα **pnĕuma**, *pnyoo'-mah;* from *4154;* a *current* of air, i.e. *breath* (*blast*) or a *breeze;* by anal. or fig. a *spirit*, i.e. (human) the rational *soul*, (by impl.) *vital principle*, mental *disposition*, etc., or (superhuman) an *angel*, *dæmon*, or (divine) *God*, Christ's *spirit*, the Holy *Spirit:*—ghost, life, spirit (-ual, -ually), mind. Comp. *5590*.

4152. **πνευματικός pnĕumatikŏs**, *pnyoo-mat-ik-os'*; from 4151; *non-carnal*, i.e. (humanly) *ethereal* (as opposed to gross), or (dæmoniacally) a *spirit* (concr.), or (divinely) *supernatural, regenerate, religious*:—spiritual. Comp. 5591.

4153. **πνευματικῶς pnĕumatikōs**, *pnyoo-mat-ik-oce'*; adv. from 4152; *non-physically*, i.e. *divinely, figuratively*:—spiritually.

4154. **πνέω pnĕō**, *pneh'-o*; a prim. word; to *breathe* hard, i.e. *breeze*:—blow. Comp. 5594.

4155. **πνίγω pnigō**, *pnee'-go*; strengthened from 4154; to *wheeze*, i.e. (caus. by impl.) to *throttle* or *strangle* (*drown*):—choke, take by the throat.

4156. **πνικτός pniktŏs**, *pnik-tos'*; from 4155; *throttled*, i.e. (neut. concr.) an animal *choked* to death (*not bled*):—strangled.

4157. **πνοή pnŏē**, *pno-ay'*; from 4154; *respiration*, a *breeze*:—breath, wind.

4158. **ποδήρης pŏdērēs**, *pod-ay'-race*; from 4228 and another element of uncert. affin.; a *dress* (2066 implied) *reaching* the *ankles*:—garment down to the foot.

4159. **πόθεν pŏthĕn**, *poth'-en*; from the base of 4213 with enclitic adv. of origin; *from which* (as interrog.) or *what* (as rel.) place, state, source or cause:—whence.

4160. **ποιέω pŏiĕō**, *poy-eh'-o*; appar. a prol. form of an obsol. prim.; to *make* or *do* (in a very wide application, more or less direct):—abide, + agree, appoint, × avenge, + band together, be, bear, + bewray, bring (forth), cast out, cause, commit, + content, continue, deal, + without any delay, (would) do (-ing), execute, exercise, fulfil, gain, give, have, hold, × journeying, keep, + lay wait, + lighten the ship, make, × mean, + none of these things move me, observe, ordain, perform, provide, + have purged, purpose, put, + raising up, × secure, shew, × shoot out, spend, take, tarry, + transgress the law, work, yield. Comp. 4238.

4161. **ποίημα pŏiēma**, *poy'-ay-mah*; from 4160; a *product*, i.e. *fabric* (lit. or fig.):—thing that is made, workmanship.

4162. **ποίησις pŏiēsis**, *poy'-ay-sis*; from 4160; *action*, i.e. *performance* (of the law):—deed.

4163. **ποιητής pŏiētēs**, *poy-ay-tace'*; from 4160; a *performer*; spec. a "*poet*":—doer, poet.

4164. **ποικίλος pŏikilŏs**, *poy-kee'-los*; of uncert. der.; *motley*, i.e. *various* in character:—divers, manifold.

4165. **ποιμαίνω pŏimainō**, *poy-mah'ee-no*; from 4166; to *tend* as a shepherd (or fig. *superviser*):—feed (cattle), rule.

4166. **ποιμήν pŏimēn**, *poy-mane'*; of uncert. affin.; a *shepherd* (lit. or fig.):—shepherd, pastor.

4167. **ποίμνη pŏimnē**, *poym'-nay*; contr. from 4165; a *flock* (lit. or fig.):—flock, fold.

4168. **ποίμνιον pŏimniŏn**, *poym'-nee-on*; neut. of a presumed der. of 4167; a *flock*, i.e. (fig.) *group* (of believers):—flock.

4169. **ποῖος pŏiŏs**, *poy'-os*; from the base of 4226 and 3634; individualizing interrog. (of character) *what* sort of, or (of number) *which* one:—what (manner of), which.

4170. **πολεμέω pŏlĕmĕō**, *pol-em-eh'-o*; from 4171; to *be* (engaged) in *warfare*, i.e. to *battle* (lit. or fig.):—fight, (make) war.

4171. **πόλεμος pŏlĕmŏs**, *pol'-em-os*; from **πέλομαι pĕlŏmai** (to *bustle*); *warfare* (lit. or fig.; a single encounter or a series):—battle, fight, war.

4172. **πόλις pŏlis**, *pol'-is*; prob. from the same as 4171, or perh. from 4183; a *town* (prop. with walls, of greater or less size):—city.

4173. **πολιτάρχης pŏlitarchēs**, *pol-it-ar'-khace*; from 4172 and 757; a *town-officer*, i.e. *magistrate*:—ruler of the city.

4174. **πολιτεία pŏlitĕia**, *pol-ee-ti'-ah*; from 4177 ("*polity*"); *citizenship*; concr. a *community*:—commonwealth, freedom.

4175. **πολίτευμα pŏlitĕuma**, *pol-it'-yoo-mah*; from 4176; a *community*, i.e. (abstr.) *citizenship* (fig.):—conversation.

4176. **πολιτεύομαι pŏlitĕuŏmai**, *pol-it-yoo'-om-ahee*; mid. of a der. of 4177; to *behave* as a citizen (fig.):—let conversation be, live.

4177. **πολίτης pŏlitēs**, *pol-ee'-tace*; from 4172; a *townsman*:—citizen.

4178. **πολλάκις pŏllakis**, *pol-lak'-is*; mult. adv. from 4183; *many times*, i.e. *frequently*:—oft (-en, -entimes, -times).

4179. **πολλαπλασίων pŏllaplasiōn**, *pol-lap-las-ee'-ohn*; from 4183 and prob. a der. of 4120; *manifold*, i.e. (neut. as noun) *very much more*:—manifold more.

4180. **πολυλογία pŏlulŏgia**, *pol-oo-log-ee'-ah*; from a comp. of 4183 and 3056; *loquacity*, i.e. *prolixity*:—much speaking.

4181. **πολυμέρως pŏlumĕrōs**, *pol-oo-mer'-oce*; adv. from a comp. of 4183 and 3313; *in many portions*, i.e. *variously* as to time and agency (*piecemeal*):—at sundry times.

4182. **πολυποίκιλος pŏlupŏikilŏs**, *pol-oo-poy'-kil-os*; from 4183 and 4164; *much variegated*, i.e. *multifarious*:—manifold.

4183. **πολύς pŏlus**, *pol-oos'*; includ. the forms from the alt. **πολλός pŏllŏs**; (sing.) *much* (in any respect) or (plur.) *many*; neut. (sing.) as adv. *largely*; neut. (plur.) as adv. or noun *often, mostly, largely*:—abundant, + altogether, common, + far (passed, spent), (+ be of a) great (age, deal, -ly, while), long, many, much, oft (-en [-times]), plenteous, sore, straitly. Comp. 4118, 4119.

4184. **πολύσπλαγχνος pŏlusplagchnŏs**, *pol-oo'-splankh-nos*; from 4183 and 4698 (fig.); *extremely compassionate*:—very pitiful.

4185. **πολυτελής pŏlutĕlēs**, *pol-oo-tel-ace'*; from 4183 and 5056; *extremely expensive*:—costly, very precious, of great price.

4186. **πολύτιμος pŏlutimŏs**, *pol-oot'-ee-mos*; from 4183 and 5092; *extremely valuable*:—very costly, of great price.

4187. **πολυτρόπως pŏlutrŏpōs**, *pol-oot-rop'-oce*; adv. from a comp. of 4183 and 5158; *in many ways*, i.e. *variously* as to method or form:—in divers manners.

4188. **πόμα pŏma**, *pom'-ah*; from the alt. of 4095; a *beverage*:—drink.

4189. **πονηρία pŏnēria**, *pon-ay-ree'-ah*; from 4190; *depravity*, i.e. (spec.) *malice*; plur. (concr.) *plots, sins*:—iniquity, wickedness.

4190. **πονηρός pŏnērŏs**, *pon-ay-ros'*; from a der. of 4192; *hurtful*, i.e. *evil* (prop. in effect or influence, and thus differing from 2556, which refers rather to *essential* character, as well as from 4550, which indicates *degeneracy* from original virtue); fig. *calamitous*; also (pass.) *ill*, i.e. *diseased*; but espec. (mor.) *culpable*, i.e. *derelict, vicious, facinorous*; neut. (sing.) *mischief, malice*, or (plur.) *guilt*; masc. (sing.) the *devil*, or (plur.) *sinners*:—bad, evil, grievous, harm, lewd, malicious, wicked (-ness). See also 4191.

4191. **πονηρότερος pŏnērŏtĕrŏs**, *pon-ay-rot'-er-os*; compar. of 4190; *more evil*:—more wicked.

4192. **πόνος pŏnŏs**, *pon'-os*; from the base of 3993; *toil*, i.e. (by impl.) *anguish*:—pain.

4193. **Ποντικός Pŏntikŏs**, *pon-tik-os'*; from 4195; a *Pontican*, i.e. native of Pontus:—born in Pontus.

4194. **Πόντιος Pŏntiŏs**, *pon'-tee-os*; of Lat. or.; appar. *bridged*; *Pontius*, a Rom.:—Pontius.

4195. **Πόντος Pŏntŏs**, *pon'-tos*; a *sea*; *Pontus*, a region of Asia Minor:—Pontus.

4196. **Πόπλιος Pŏpliŏs**, *pop'-lee-os*; of Lat. or.; appar. "*popular*"; *Poplius* (i.e. *Publius*), a Rom.:—Publius.

4197. **πορεία pŏrĕia**, *por-i'-ah*; from 4198; *travel* (by land); fig. (plur.) *proceedings*, i.e. *career*:—journey [-ing], ways.

4198. **πορεύομαι pŏrĕuŏmai**, *por-yoo'-om-ahee*; mid. from a der. of the same as 3984; to *traverse*, i.e. *travel* (lit. or fig.; espec. to *remove* [fig. *die*], *live*, etc.);—depart, go (away, forth, one's way, up), (make a, take a) journey, walk.

4199. **πορθέω pŏrthĕō**, *por-theh'-o*; prol. from **πέρθω pĕrthō** (to *sack*); to *ravage* (fig.):—destroy, waste.

4200. **πορισμός pŏrismŏs**, *por-is-mos'*; from a der. of **πόρος pŏrŏs** (a *way*, i.e. *means*); *furnishing* (*procuring*), i.e. (by impl.) *money-getting* (*acquisition*):—gain.

4201. **Πόρκιος Pŏrkiŏs**, *por'-kee-os*; of Lat. or.; appar. *swinish*; *Porcius*, a Rom.:—Porcius.

4202. **πορνεία pŏrnĕia**, *por-ni'-ah*; from 4203; *harlotry* (includ. *adultery* and *incest*); fig. *idolatry*:—fornication.

4203. **πορνεύω pŏrnĕuō**, *porn-yoo'-o*; from 4204; to *act the harlot*, i.e. (lit.) *indulge* unlawful *lust* (of either sex), or (fig.) *practise idolatry*:—commit (fornication).

4204. **πόρνη pŏrnē**, *por'-nay*; fem. of 4205; a *strumpet*; fig. an *idolater*:—harlot, whore.

4205. **πόρνος pŏrnŏs**, *por'-nos*; from **πέρνημι pĕrnēmi** (to *sell*; akin to the base of 4097); a (male) *prostitute* (as *venal*), i.e. (by anal.) a *debauchee* (*libertine*):—fornicator, whoremonger.

4206. **πόῤῥω pŏrrhō**, *por'-rho*; adv. from 4253; *forwards*, i.e. *at a distance*:—far, a great way off. See also 4207.

4207. **πόῤῥωθεν pŏrrhōthĕn**, *por'-rho-then*; from 4206 with adv. enclitic of source; *from far*, or (by impl.) *at a distance*, i.e. *distantly*:—afar off.

4208. **ποῤῥωτέρω pŏrrhōtĕrō**, *por-rho-ter'-o*; adv. compar. of 4206; *farther*, i.e. *a greater distance*:—further.

4209. **πορφύρα pŏrphura**, *por-foo'-rah*; of Lat. or.; the "*purple*" mussel, i.e. (by impl.) the *red-blue* color itself, and finally a garment dyed with it:—purple.

4210. **πορφυροῦς pŏrphurŏus**, *por-foo-rooce'*; from 4209; *purpureal*, i.e. *bluish red*:—purple.

4211. **πορφυρόπωλις pŏrphurŏpōlis**, *por-foo-rop'-o-lis*; fem. of a comp. of 4209 and 4453; *a female trader in purple* cloth:—seller of purple.

4212. **ποσάκις pŏsakis**, *pos-ak'-is*; mult. from 4214; *how many times*:—how oft (-en).

4213. **πόσις pŏsis**, *pos'-is*; from the alt. of 4095; a *drinking* (the act), i.e. (concr.) a *draught*:—drink.

4214. **πόσος pŏsŏs**, *pos'-os*; from an obsol. **πός pŏs** (*who, what*) and 3739; interrog. pron. (of amount) *how much* (*large, long* or [plur.] *many*):—how great (long, many), what.

4215. **ποταμός pŏtamŏs**, *pot-am-os'*; prob. from a der. of the alt. of 4095 (comp. 4224); a *current, brook* or *freshet* (as *drinkable*), i.e. *running water*:—flood, river, stream, water.

4216. **ποταμοφόρητος pŏtamŏphŏrētŏs**, *pot-am-of-or'-ay-tos*; from 4215 and a der. of 5409; *river-borne*, i.e. *overwhelmed by a stream*:—carried away of the flood.

4217. **ποταπός pŏtapŏs**, *pot-ap-os'*; appar. from 4219 and the base of 4226; interrog. *whatever*, i.e. of *what possible* sort:—what (manner of).

4218. **ποτέ pŏtĕ**, *pot-eh'*; from the base of 4225 and 5037; indef. adv., at *some time, ever*:—afore- (any, some-) time (-s), at length (the last), (+ n-) ever, in the old time, in time past, once, when.

4219. **πότε pŏtĕ**, *pot'-eh*; from the base of 4226 and 5037; interrog. adv., at *what time*:— + how long, when.

4220. **πότερον pŏtĕrŏn**, *pot'-er-on*; neut. of a compar. of the base of 4226; interrog. as adv., *which* (of two), i.e. *is it* this or that:—whether.

4221. **ποτήριον pŏtēriŏn**, *pot-ay'-ree-on*; neut. of a der. of the alt. of 4095; a *drinking-vessel*; by extens. the contents thereof, i.e. a *cupful* (*draught*); fig. a *lot* or *fate*:—cup.

4222. **ποτίζω pŏtizō**, *pot-id'-zo*; from a der. of the alt. of 4095; to *furnish drink, irrigate*:—give (make) to drink, feed, water.

4223. Ποτίολοι **Pŏtiŏlŏi**, *pot-ee'-ol-oy;* of Lat. or.; *little wells,* i.e. *mineral springs; Potioli* (i.e. *Puteoli*), a place in Italy:—Puteoli.

4224. πότος **pŏtŏs**, *pot'-os;* from the alt. of *4095;* a *drinking-bout* or *carousal:*—banqueting.

4225. πού **pŏu**, *poo;* gen. of an indef. pron. πός **pŏs** (*some*) otherwise obsol. (comp. *4214*); as adv. of place, *somewhere,* i.e. *nearly:*—about, a certain place.

4226. ποῦ **pŏu**, *poo;* gen. of an interrog. pron. πός **pŏs** (*what*) otherwise obsol. (perh. the same as *4225* used with the rising slide of inquiry); as adv. of place; *at* (by impl. *to*) *what* locality:—where, whither.

4227. Πούδης **Pŏudēs**, *poo'-dace;* of Lat. or.; *modest; Pudes* (i.e. *Pudens*), a Chr.:—Pudens.

4228. πούς **pŏus**, *pooce;* a prim word; a "*foot*" (fig. or lit.):—foot (-stool).

4229. πρᾶγμα **pragma**, *prag'-mah;* from *4238;* a *deed;* by impl. an *affair;* by extens. an *object* (material):—business, matter, thing, work.

4230. πραγματεία **pragmatĕia**, *prag-mat-i'-ah;* from *4231;* a *transaction,* i.e. *negotiation:*—affair.

4231. πραγματεύομαι **pragmatĕuŏmai**, *prag-mat-yoo'-om-ahee;* from *4229;* to *busy oneself* with, i.e. to *trade:*—occupy.

4232. πραιτώριον **praitōriŏn**, *prahee-to'-ree-on;* of Lat. or.; the *prætorium* or governor's *court-room* (sometimes includ. the whole *edifice* and *camp*):—(common, judgment) hall (of judgment), palace, prætorium.

4233. πράκτωρ **praktōr**, *prak'-tore;* from a der. of *4238;* a *practiser,* i.e. (spec.) an official *collector:*—officer.

4234. πρᾶξις **praxis**, *prax'-is;* from *4238; practice,* i.e. (concr.) an *act;* by extens. a *function:*—deed, office, work.

4235. πρᾷος **pra͵ŏs**, *prah'-os;* a form of *4239,* used in cert. parts; *gentle,* i.e. *humble:*—meek.

4236. πρᾳότης **pra͵ŏtēs**, *prah-ot'-ace;* from *4235; gentleness;* by impl. *humility:*—meekness.

4237. πρασιά **prasia**, *pras-ee-ah';* perh. from πράσον **prasŏn** (a *leek,* and so an *onion-patch*); a garden-*plot,* i.e. (by impl. of regular *beds*) a *row* (repeated in plur. by Hebr. to indicate an arrangement):—in ranks.

4238. πράσσω **prassō**, *pras'-so;* a prim. verb; to "*practise*", i.e. *perform repeatedly* or *habitually* (thus differing from *4160,* which prop. refers to a *single* act); by impl. to *execute, accomplish,* etc.; spec. to *collect* (dues), *fare* (personally):—commit, deeds, do, exact, keep, require, use arts.

4239. πραΰς **praüs**, *prah-ooce';* appar. a prim. word; *mild,* i.e. (by impl.) *humble:*—meek. See also *4235.*

4240. πραΰτης **praütēs**, *prah-oo'-tace;* from *4239; mildness,* i.e. (by impl.) *humility:*—meekness.

4241. πρέπω **prĕpō**, *prep'-o;* appar. a prim. verb; to *tower* up (*be conspicuous*), i.e. (by impl.) to *be suitable* or *proper* (third pers. sing. pres. indic., often used impers., it is *fit* or *right*):—become, comely.

4242. πρεσβεία **prĕsbĕia**, *pres-bi'-ah;* from *4243; seniority* (*eldership*), i.e. (by impl.) an *embassy* (concr. *ambassadors*):—ambassage, message.

4243. πρεσβεύω **prĕsbĕuō**, *pres-byoo'-o;* from the base of *4245;* to be a *senior,* i.e. (by impl.) *act as a representative* (fig. *preacher*):—be an ambassador.

4244. πρεσβυτέριον **prĕsbutĕriŏn**, *pres-boo-ter'-ee-on;* neut. of a presumed der. of *4245;* the *order of elders,* i.e. (spec.) Isr. *Sanhedrim* or Chr. "*presbytery*":—(estate of) elder (-s), presbytery.

4245. πρεσβύτερος **prĕsbutĕrŏs**, *pres-boo'-ter-os;* compar. of πρέσβυς **prĕsbus** (*elderly*); *older;* as noun, a *senior;* spec. an Isr. *Sanhedrist* (also fig. member of the celestial council) or Chr. "*presbyter*":—elder (-est), old.

4246. πρεσβύτης **prĕsbutēs**, *pres-boo'-tace;* from the same as *4245;* an *old man:*—aged (man), old man.

4247. πρεσβῦτις **prĕsbutis**, *pres-boo'-tis;* fem. of *4246;* an *old woman:*—aged woman.

πρήθω **prēthō**. See *4092.*

4248. πρηνής **prēnēs**, *pray-nace';* from *4253; leaning* (*falling*) *forward* ("*prone*"), i.e. *head foremost:*—headlong.

4249. πρίζω **prizō**, *prid'-zo;* a strengthened form of a prim. πρίω **priō** (to *saw*); to *saw* in two:—saw asunder.

4250. πρίν **prin**, *prin;* adv. from *4253; prior, sooner:*—before (that), ere.

4251. Πρίσκα **Priska**, *pris'-kah;* of Lat. or.; fem. of *Priscus, ancient; Priska,* a Chr. woman:—Prisca. See also *4252.*

4252. Πρίσκιλλα **Priscilla**, *pris'-cil-lah;* dimin. of *4251; Priscilla* (i.e. *little Prisca*), a Chr. woman:—Priscilla.

4253. πρό **prŏ**, *prŏ;* a prim. prep.; "*fore*", i.e. *in front of, prior* (fig. *superior*) *to:*—above, ago, before, or ever. In comp. it retains the same significations.

4254. προάγω **prŏagō**, *prŏ-ag'-o;* from *4253* and *71;* to *lead forward* (magisterially); intrans. to *precede* (in place or time [part. *previous*]):—bring (forth, out), go before.

4255. προαιρέομαι **prŏairĕŏmai**, *prŏ-ahee-reh'-om-ahee;* from *4253* and *138;* to *choose* for oneself *before* another thing (*prefer*), i.e. (by impl.) to *propose* (*intend*):—purpose.

4256. προαιτιάομαι **prŏaitiaŏmai**, *prŏ-ahee-tee-ah'-om-ahee;* from *4253* and a der. of *156;* to *accuse already,* i.e. *previously charge:*—prove before.

4257. προακούω **prŏakŏuō**, *prŏ-ak-oo'-o;* from *4253* and *191;* to *hear already,* i.e. *anticipate:*—hear before.

4258. προαμαρτάνω **prŏamartanō**, *prŏ-am-ar-tan'-o;* from *4253* and *264;* to *sin previously* (to conversion):—sin already, heretofore sin.

4259. προαύλιον **prŏauliŏn**, *prŏ-ŏw'-lee-on;* neut. of a presumed comp. of *4253* and *833;* a *fore-court,* i.e. *vestibule* (*alley-way*):—porch.

4260. προβαίνω **prŏbainō**, *prob-ah'ee-no;* from *4253* and the base of *939;* to *walk forward,* i.e. *advance* (lit. or in years):— + be of a great age, go farther (on), be well stricken.

4261. προβάλλω **prŏballō**, *prob-al'-lo;* from *4253* and *906;* to *throw forward,* i.e. *push to the front, germinate:*—put forward, shoot forth.

4262. προβατικός **prŏbatikŏs**, *prob-at-ik-os';* from *4263; relating to sheep,* i.e. (a *gate*) through which they were led into Jerusalem:—sheep (market).

4263. πρόβατον **prŏbatŏn**, *prob'-at-on;* prop. neut. of a presumed der. of *4260; something that walks forward* (a *quadruped*), i.e. (spec.) a *sheep* (lit. or fig.):—sheep ([-fold]).

4264. προβιβάζω **prŏbibazō**, *prob-ib-ad'-zo;* from *4253* and a redupl. form of *971;* to *force forward,* i.e. *bring to the front, instigate:*—draw, before instruct.

4265. προβλέπω **prŏblĕpō**, *prob-lep'-o;* from *4253* and *991;* to *look out beforehand,* i.e. *furnish in advance:*—provide.

4266. προγίνομαι **prŏginŏmai**, *prog-in'-om-ahee;* from *4253* and *1096;* to *be already,* i.e. *have previously transpired:*—be past.

4267. προγινώσκω **prŏginōskō**, *prog-in-oce'-ko;* from *4253* and *1097;* to *know beforehand,* i.e. *foresee:*—foreknow (ordain), know (before).

4268. πρόγνωσις **prŏgnōsis**, *prog'-no-sis;* from *4267; forethought:*—foreknowledge.

4269. πρόγονος **prŏgŏnŏs**, *prog'-on-os;* from *4266;* an *ancestor,* (*grand-*) *parent:*—forefather, parent.

4270. προγράφω **prŏgraphō**, *prog-raf'-o;* from *4253* and *1125;* to *write previously;* fig. to *announce, prescribe:*—before ordain, evidently set forth, write (afore, aforetime).

4271. πρόδηλος **prŏdēlŏs**, *prod'-ay-los;* from *4253* and *1212; plain before* all men, i.e. *obvious:*—evident, manifest (open) beforehand.

4272. προδίδωμι **prŏdidōmi**, *prod-id'-o-mee;* from *4253* and *1325;* to *give before* the other party has given:—first give.

4273. προδότης **prŏdŏtēs**, *prod-ot'-ace;* from *4272* (in the sense of *giving forward* into another's [the enemy's] hands); a *surrender:*—betrayer, traitor.

προδρέμω **prŏdrĕmō**. See *4390.*

4274. πρόδρομος **prŏdrŏmŏs**, *prod'-rom-os;* from the alt. of *4390;* a *runner ahead,* i.e. *scout* (fig. *precursor*):—forerunner.

4275. προείδω **prŏĕidō**, *pro-i'-do;* from *4253* and *1492; foresee:*—foresee, saw before.

προειρέω **prŏĕirĕō**. See *4280.*

4276. προελπίζω **prŏĕlpizō**, *prŏ-el-pid'-zo;* from *4253* and *1679;* to *hope in advance* of other confirmation:—first trust.

4277. προέπω **prŏĕpō**, *prŏ-ep'-o;* from *4253* and *2036;* to *say already,* to *predict:*—forewarn, say (speak, tell) before. Comp. *4280.*

4278. προενάρχομαι **prŏĕnarchŏmai**, *prŏ-en-ar'-khom-ahee;* from *4253* and *1728;* to *commence already:*—begin (before).

4279. προεπαγγέλλομαι **prŏĕpaggĕllŏmai**, *prŏ-ep-ang-ghel'-lom-ahee;* mid. from *4253* and *1861;* to *promise of old:*—promise before.

4280. προερέω **prŏĕrĕō**, *prŏ-er-eh'-o;* from *4253* and *2046;* used as alt. of *4277;* to *say already, predict:*—foretell, say (speak, tell) before.

4281. προέρχομαι **prŏĕrchŏmai**, *prŏ-er'-khom-ahee;* from *4253* and *2064* (includ. its alt.); to *go onward, precede* (in place or time):—go before (farther, forward), outgo, pass on.

4282. προετοιμάζω **prŏĕtŏimazō**, *prŏ-et-oy-mad'-zo;* from *4253* and *2090;* to *fit up in advance* (lit. or fig.):—ordain before, prepare afore.

4283. προευαγγελίζομαι **prŏĕuaggĕlizŏmai**, *prŏ-yoo-ang-ghel-id'-zom-ahee;* mid. from *4253* and *2097;* to *announce* glad news *in advance:*—preach before the gospel.

4284. προέχομαι **prŏĕchŏmai**, *prŏ-ekh-om-ahee;* mid. from *4253* and *2192;* to *hold* oneself *before* others, i.e. (fig.) to *excel:*—be better.

4285. προηγέομαι **prŏēgĕŏmai**, *prŏ-ay-geh'-om-ahee;* from *4253* and *2233;* to *lead the way* for others, i.e *show deference:*—prefer.

4286. πρόθεσις **prŏthĕsis**, *proth'-es-is;* from *4388;* a *setting forth,* i.e. (fig.) *proposal* (*intention*); spec. the *show*-bread (in the Temple) as *exposed* before God:—purpose, shew [-bread].

4287. προθέσμιος **prŏthĕsmiŏs**, *proth-es'-mee-os;* from *4253* and a der. of *5087; fixed beforehand,* i.e. (fem. with *2250* impl.) a *designated* day:—time appointed.

4288. προθυμία **prŏthumia**, *proth-oo-mee'-ah;* from *4289; predisposition,* i.e. *alacrity:*—forwardness of mind, readiness (of mind), ready (willing) mind.

4289. πρόθυμος **prŏthumŏs**, *proth'-oo-mos;* from *4253* and *2372; forward in spirit,* i.e. *predisposed;* neut. (as noun) *alacrity:*—ready, willing.

4290. προθύμως **prŏthumōs**, *proth-oo'-moce;* adv. from *4289; with alacrity:*—willingly.

4291. προΐστημι **prŏistēmi**, *prŏ-is'-tay-mee;* from *4253* and *2476;* to *stand before,* i.e. (in rank) to *preside,* or (by impl.) to *practise:*—maintain, be over, rule.

4292. προκαλέομαι **prŏkalĕŏmai**, *prok-al-eh'-om-ahee;* mid. from *4253* and *2564;* to *call forth to oneself* (*challenge*), i.e. (by impl.) to *irritate:*—provoke.

4293. προκαταγγέλλω **prŏkataggĕllō**, *prok-at-ang-ghel'-lo;* from *4253* and *2605;* to *announce beforehand,* i.e. *predict, promise:*—foretell, have notice (shew) before.

4294. προκαταρτίζω **prŏkatartizō**, *prok-at-ar-tid'-zo;* from *4253* and *2675;* to *prepare in advance:*—make up beforehand.

4295. πρόκειμαι **prŏkĕimai**, *prok'-i-mahee;* from *4253* and *2740;* to *lie before* the view, i.e. (fig.) to *be present* (to the mind), to *stand forth* (as an example or reward):—be first, set before (forth).

4296. προκηρύσσω prŏkērussō, *prok-ay-rooce'-so;* from *4253* and *2784;* to *herald* (i.e. *proclaim*) *in advance:*—before (first) preach.

4297. προκοπή prŏkŏpē, *prok-op-ay';* from *4298; progress,* i.e. *advancement* (subj. or obj.):—furtherance, profit.

4298. προκόπτω prŏkŏptō, *prok-op'-to;* from *4253* and *2875;* to *drive forward* (as if by beating), i.e. (fig. and intrans.) to *advance* (in amount, to *grow;* in time, to *be well along*):—increase, proceed, profit, be far spent, wax.

4299. πρόκριμα prŏkrima, *prok'-ree-mah;* from a comp. of *4253* and *2919;* a *prejudgment* (*prejudice*), i.e. *prepossession:*—prefer one before another.

4300. προκυρόω prŏkurŏō, *prok-oo-rŏ'-o;* from *4253* and *2964;* to *ratify previously:*—confirm before.

4301. προλαμβάνω prŏlambanō, *prol-am-ban'-o;* from *4253* and *2983;* to *take in advance,* i.e. (lit.) *eat before* others have an opportunity; (fig.) to *anticipate, surprise:*—come aforehand, overtake, take before.

4302. προλέγω prŏlĕgō, *prol-eg'-o;* from *4253* and *3004;* to *say beforehand,* i.e. *predict, forewarn:*—foretell, tell before.

4303. προμαρτύρομαι prŏmarturŏmai, *prom-ar-too'-rom-ahee;* from *4253* and *3143;* to *be a witness in advance,* i.e. *predict:*—testify beforehand.

4304. προμελετάω prŏmĕlĕtaō, *prom-el-et-ah'-o;* from *4253* and *3191;* to *premeditate:*—meditate before.

4305. προμεριμνάω prŏmĕrimnaō, *prom-er-im-nah'-o;* from *4253* and *3309;* to *care* (anxiously) *in advance:*—take thought beforehand.

4306. προνοέω prŏnŏĕō, *pron-ŏ-eh'-o;* from *4253* and *3539;* to *consider in advance,* i.e. *look* out for *beforehand* (act. by way of *maintenance* for others; mid. by way of *circumspection* for oneself):—provide (for).

4307. πρόνοια prŏnŏia, *pron'-oy-ah;* from *4306; forethought,* i.e. provident *care* or *supply:*—providence, provision.

4308. προοράω prŏŏraō, *prŏ-or-ah'-o;* from *4253* and *3708;* to *behold in advance,* i.e. (act.) to *notice* (another) *previously,* or (mid.) to *keep in* (one's own) *view:*—foresee, see before.

4309. προορίζω prŏŏrizō, *prŏ-or-id'-zo;* from *4253* and *3724;* to *limit in advance,* i.e. (fig.) *predetermine:*—determine before, ordain, predestinate.

4310. προπάσχω prŏpaschō, *prop-as'-kho;* from *4253* and *3958;* to *undergo* hardship *previously:*—suffer before.

4311. προπέμπω prŏpĕmpō, *prop-em'-po;* from *4253* and *3992;* to *send forward,* i.e. *escort* or *aid* in travel:—accompany, bring (forward) on journey (way), conduct forth.

4312. προπετής prŏpĕtēs, *prop-et-ace';* from a comp. of *4253* and *4098; falling forward,* i.e. *headlong* (fig. *precipitate*):—heady, rash [-ly].

4313. προπορεύομαι prŏpŏrĕuŏmai, *prop-or-yoo'-om-ahee;* from *4253* and *4198;* to *precede* (as guide or herald):—go before.

4314. πρός prŏs, *pros;* a strengthened form of *4253;* a prep. of direction; *forward to,* i.e. *toward* (with the genit. *the side* of, i.e. *pertaining to;* with the dat. *by the side of,* i.e. *near to;* usually with the accus. the place, time, occasion, or respect, which is the *destination* of the relation, i.e. *whither* or *for* which it is predicated):—about, according to, against, among, at, because of, before, between, ([where-]) by, for, × at thy house, in, for intent, nigh unto, of, which pertain to, that, to (the end that), + together, to ([you]) -ward, unto, with (-in). In comp. it denotes essentially the same applications, namely, motion *towards,* accession *to,* or nearness *at.*

4315. προσάββατον prŏsabbatŏn, *pros-ab'-bat-on;* from *4253* and *4521;* a *fore-sabbath,* i.e. the *Sabbath-eve:*—day before the sabbath. Comp. *3904.*

4316. προσαγορεύω prŏsagŏrĕuō, *pros-ag-or-yoo'-o;* from *4314* and a der. of *58* (mean. to *harangue*); to *address,* i.e. salute by *name:*—call.

4317. προσάγω prŏsagō, *pros-ag'-o;* from *4314* and *71;* to *lead towards,* i.e. (trans.) to *conduct near* (*summon, present*), or (intrans.) to *approach:*—bring, draw near.

4318. προσαγωγή prŏsagōgē, *pros-ag-ogue-ay';* from *4317* (comp. *72*); *admission:*—access.

4319. προσαιτέω prŏsaitĕō *pros-ahee-teh'-o;* from *4314* and *154;* to *ask repeatedly* (*importune*), i.e. *solicit:*—beg.

4320. προσαναβαίνω prŏsanabainō, *pros-an-ab-ah'ee-no;* from *4314* and *305;* to *ascend farther,* i.e. *be promoted* (*take an upper* [more honorable] *seat*):—go up.

4321. προσαναλίσκω prŏsanaliskō, *pros-an-al-is'-ko;* from *4314* and *355;* to *expend further:*—spend.

4322. προσαναπληρόω prŏsanaplērŏō, *pros-an-ap-lay-rŏ'-o;* from *4314* and *378;* to *fill up further,* i.e. *furnish fully:*—supply.

4323. προσανατίθημι prŏsanatithēmi, *pros-an-at-ith'-ay-mee;* from *4314* and *394;* to *lay up in addition,* i.e. (mid. and fig.) to *impart* or (by impl.) to *consult:*—in conference add, confer.

4324. προσαπειλέω prŏsapĕilĕō, *pros-ap-i-leh'-o;* from *4314* and *546;* to *menace additionally:*—threaten further.

4325. προσδαπανάω prŏsdapanaō, *pros-dap-an-ah'-o;* from *4314* and *1159;* to *expend additionally:*—spend more.

4326. προσδέομαι prŏsdĕŏmai, *pros-deh'-om-ahee;* from *4314* and *1189;* to *require additionally,* i.e. *want further:*—need.

4327. προσδέχομαι prŏsdĕchŏmai, *pros-dekh'-om-ahee;* from *4314* and *1209;* to *admit* (to intercourse, hospitality, credence or [fig.] endurance); by impl. to *await* (with confidence or patience):—accept, allow, look (wait) for, take.

4328. προσδοκάω prŏsdŏkaō, *pros-dok-ah'-o;* from *4314* and **δοκεύω dŏkĕuō** (to *watch*); to *anticipate* (in thought, hope or fear); by impl. to *await:*—(be in) expect (-ation), look (for), when looked, tarry, wait for.

4329. προσδοκία prŏsdŏkia, *pros-dok-ee'-ah;* from *4328; apprehension* (of evil); by impl. *infliction* anticipated:—expectation, looking after.

προσδρέμω prŏsdrĕmō. See *4370.*

4330. προσεάω prŏsĕaō, *pros-eh-ah'-o;* from *4314* and *1439;* to *permit further* progress:—suffer.

4331. προσεγγίζω prŏsĕggizō, *pros-eng-ghid'-zo;* from *4314* and *1448;* to *approach near:*—come nigh.

4332. προσεδρεύω prŏsĕdrĕuō, *pros-ed-ryoo'-o;* from a comp. of *4314* and the base of *1476;* to *sit near,* i.e. *attend* as a servant:—wait at.

4333. προσεργάζομαι prŏsĕrgazŏmai, *pros-er-gad'-zom-ahee;* from *4314* and *2038;* to *work additionally,* i.e. (by impl.) *acquire besides:*—gain.

4334. προσέρχομαι prŏsĕrchŏmai, *pros-er'-khom-ahee;* from *4314* and *2064* (includ. its alt.); to *approach,* i.e. (lit.) *come near, visit,* or (fig.) *worship, assent to:*—(as soon as he) come (unto), come thereunto, consent, draw near, go (near, to, unto).

4335. προσευχή prŏsĕuchē, *pros-yoo-khay';* from *4336; prayer* (*worship*); by impl. an *oratory* (*chapel*):— × pray earnestly, prayer.

4336. προσεύχομαι prŏsĕuchŏmai, *pros-yoo'-khom-ahee;* from *4314* and *2172;* to *pray to* God, i.e. *supplicate, worship:*—pray (× earnestly, for), make prayer.

4337. προσέχω prŏsĕchō, *pros-ekh'-o;* from *4314* and *2192;* (fig.) to *hold* the mind (*3563* impl.) *towards,* i.e. *pay attention to, be cautious about, apply oneself to, adhere to:*—(give) attend (-ance, -ance at, -ance to, unto), beware, be given to, give (take) heed (to, unto) have regard.

4338. προσηλόω prŏsēlŏō, *pros-ay-lŏ'-o;* from *4314* and a der. of *2247;* to *peg to,* i.e. *spike* fast:—nail to.

4339. προσήλυτος prŏsēlutŏs, *pros-ay'-loo-tos;* from the alt. of *4334;* an *arriver* from a foreign region, i.e. (spec.) an *acceder* (*convert*) to Judaism ("*proselyte*"):—proselyte.

4340. πρόσκαιρος prŏskairŏs, *pros'-kahee-ros;* from *4314* and *2540; for* the *occasion* only, i.e. *temporary:*—dur- [eth] for awhile, endure for a time, for a season, temporal.

4341. προσκαλέομαι prŏskalĕŏmai, *pros-kal-eh'-om-ahee;* mid. from *4314* and *2564;* to *call toward* oneself, i.e. *summon, invite:*—call (for, to, unto).

4342. προσκαρτερέω prŏskartĕrĕō, *pros-kar-ter-eh'-o;* from *4314* and *2594;* to *be earnest towards,* i.e. (to a thing) to *persevere, be constantly* diligent, or (in a place) to *attend* assiduously all the exercises, or (to a person) to *adhere* closely *to* (as a servitor):—attend (give self) continually (upon), continue (in, instant in, with), wait on (continually).

4343. προσκαρτέρησις prŏskartĕrēsis, *pros-kar-ter'-ay-sis;* from *4342; persistency:*—perseverance.

4344. προσκεφάλαιον prŏskĕphalaiŏn, *pros-kef-al'-ahee-on;* neut. of a presumed comp. of *4314* and *2776;* something *for* the *head,* i.e. a *cushion:*—pillow.

4345. προσκληρόω prŏsklērŏō, *pros-klay-rŏ'-o;* from *4314* and *2820;* to *give* a common *lot to,* i.e. (fig.) to *associate with:*—consort with.

4346. πρόσκλισις prŏsklisis, *pros'-klis-is;* from a comp. of *4314* and *2827;* a *leaning towards,* i.e. (fig.) *proclivity* (*favoritism*):—partiality.

4347. προσκολλάω prŏskŏllaō, *pros-kol-lah'-o;* from *4314* and *2853;* to *glue to,* i.e. (fig.) to *adhere:*—cleave, join (self).

4348. πρόσκομμα prŏskŏmma, *pros'-kom-mah;* from *4350;* a *stub,* i.e. (fig.) *occasion of apostasy:*—offence, stumbling (-block, [-stone]).

4349. προσκοπή prŏskŏpē, *pros-kop-ay';* from *4350;* a *stumbling,* i.e. (fig. and concr.) *occasion of sin:*—offence.

4350. προσκόπτω prŏskŏptō, *pros-kop'-to;* from *4314* and *2875;* to *strike at,* i.e. *surge against* (as water); spec. to *stub on,* i.e. *trip up* (lit. or fig.):—beat upon, dash, stumble (at).

4351. προσκυλίω prŏskuliō, *pros-koo-lee'-o;* from *4314* and *2947;* to *roll towards,* i.e. *block against:*—roll (to).

4352. προσκυνέω prŏskunĕō, *pros-koo-neh'-o;* from *4314* and a prob. der. of *2965* (mean. to *kiss,* like a dog *licking* his master's hand); to *fawn* or *crouch* to, i.e. (lit. or fig.) *prostrate* oneself in homage (do *reverence* to, *adore*):—worship.

4353. προσκυνητής prŏskunētēs, *pros-koo-nay-tace';* from *4352;* an *adorer:*—worshipper.

4354. προσλαλέω prŏslalĕō, *pros-lal-eh'-o;* from *4314* and *2980;* to *talk to,* i.e. *converse with:*—speak to (with).

4355. προσλαμβάνω prŏslambanō, *pros-lam-ban'-o;* from *4314* and *2983;* to *take* to oneself, i.e. *use* (food), *lead* (aside), *admit* (to friendship or hospitality):—receive, take (unto).

4356. πρόσληψις prŏslēpsis, *pros'-lape-sis;* from *4355; admission:*—receiving.

4357. προσμένω prŏsmĕnō, *pros-men'-o;* from *4314* and *3306;* to *stay further,* i.e. *remain* in a place, with a person; fig. to *adhere* to, *persevere* in:—abide still, be with, cleave unto, continue in (with).

4358. προσορμίζω prŏsŏrmizō, *pros-or-mid'-zo;* from *4314* and a der. of the same as *3730* (mean. to *tie* [*anchor*] or *lull*); to *moor to,* i.e. (by impl.) *land at:*—draw to the shore.

4359. προσοφείλω prŏsŏphĕilō, *pros-of-i'-lo;* from *4314* and *3784;* to *be indebted additionally:*—over besides.

4360. προσοχθίζω prŏsŏchthizō, *pros-okh-thid'-zo;* from *4314* and a form of **ὀχθέω ŏchthĕō** (to *be vexed* with something irksome); to *feel indignant at:*—be grieved with.

4361. πρόσπεινος prŏspĕinŏs, *pros'-pi-nos;* from *4314* and the same as *3983; hungering further,* i.e. *intensely hungry:*—very hungry.

4362. **προσπήγνυμι prŏspēgnumi**, *pros-payg'-noo-mee;* from *4314* and *4078;* to *fasten to*, i.e. (spec.) to *impale* (on a cross):—crucify.

4363. **προσπίπτω prŏspiptō**, *pros-pip'-to;* from *4314* and *4098;* to *fall towards*, i.e. (gently) *prostrate* oneself (in supplication or homage), or (violently) to *rush* upon (in storm):—beat upon, fall (down) at (before).

4364. **προσποιέομαι prŏspŏiĕŏmai**, *pros-poy-eh'-om-ahee;* mid. from *4314* and *4160;* to *do forward for oneself*, i.e. *pretend* (as if about to do a thing):—make as though.

4365. **προσπορεύομαι prŏspŏrĕuŏmai**, *pros-por-yoo'-om-ahee;* from *4314* and *4198;* to *journey towards*, i.e. *approach* [not the same as *4313*]:—go before.

4366. **προσρήγνυμι prŏsrēgnumi**, *pros-rayg'-noo-mee;* from *4314* and *4486;* to *tear towards*, i.e. *burst upon* (as a tempest or flood):—beat vehemently against (upon).

4367. **προστάσσω prŏstassō**, *pros-tas'-so;* from *4314* and *5021;* to *arrange towards*, i.e. (fig.) *enjoin:*—bid, command.

4368. **προστάτις prŏstatis**, *pros-tat'-is;* fem. of a der. of *4291;* a *patroness*, i.e. *assistant:*—succourer.

4369. **προστίθημι prŏstithēmi**, *pros-tith'-ay-mee;* from *4314* and *5087;* to *place additionally*, i.e. *lay beside, annex, repeat:*—add, again, give more, increase, lay unto, proceed further, speak to any more.

4370. **προστρέχω prŏstrĕchō**, *pros-trekh'-o;* from *4314* and *5143* (includ. its alt.); to *run towards*, i.e. *hasten* to meet or join:—run (thither to, to).

4371. **προσφάγιον prŏsphagiŏn**, *pros-fag'-ee-on;* neut. of a presumed der. of a comp. of *4314* and *5315;* something *eaten in addition* to bread, i.e. a *relish* (spec. *fish;* comp. *3795*):—meat.

4372. **πρόσφατος prŏsphatŏs**, *pros'-fat-os;* from *4253* and a der. of *4969;* *previously* (*recently*) *slain* (*fresh*), i.e. (fig.) *lately made:*—new.

4373. **προσφάτως prŏsphatōs**, *pros-fat'-oce;* adv. from *4372;* *recently:*—lately.

4374. **προσφέρω prŏsphĕrō**, *pros-fer'-o;* from *4314* and *5342* (includ. its alt.); to *bear towards*, i.e. *lead to, tender* (espec. to God), *treat:*—bring (to, unto), deal with, do, offer (unto, up), present unto, put to.

4375. **προσφιλής prŏsphilēs**, *pros-fee-lace';* from a presumed comp. of *4314* and *5368;* *friendly towards*, i.e. *acceptable:*—lovely.

4376. **προσφορά prŏsphŏra**, *pros-for-ah';* from *4374;* *presentation;* concr. an *oblation* (bloodless) or *sacrifice:*—offering (up).

4377. **προσφωνέω prŏsphōnĕō**, *pros-fo-neh'-o;* from *4314* and *5455;* to *sound towards*, i.e. *address, exclaim, summon:*—call unto, speak (un-) to.

4378. **πρόσχυσις prŏschusis**, *pros'-khoo-sis;* from a comp. of *4314* and **χέω chĕō** (to *pour*); a *shedding forth*, i.e. *affusion:*—sprinkling.

4379. **προσψαύω prŏspsauō**, *pros-psow'-o;* from *4314* and **ψαύω psauō** (to *touch*); to *impinge*, i.e. *lay a finger on* (in order to relieve):—touch.

4380. **προσωποληπτέω prŏsōpŏlēptĕō**, *pros-o-pol-ape-teh'-o;* from *4381;* to *favor an individual*, i.e. *show partiality:*—have respect to persons.

4381. **προσωπολήπτης prŏsōpŏlēptēs**, *pros-o-pol-ape'-tace;* from *4383* and *2983;* an *accepter* of a *face* (*individual*), i.e. (spec.) one *exhibiting partiality:*—respecter of persons.

4382. **προσωποληψία prŏsōpŏlēpsia**, *pros-o-pol-ape-see'-ah;* from *4381;* *partiality*, i.e. *favoritism:*—respect of persons.

4383. **πρόσωπον prŏsōpŏn**, *pros'-o-pon;* from *4314* and **ὤψ ōps** (the *visage;* from *3700*); the *front* (as being *towards view*), i.e. the *countenance, aspect, appearance, surface;* by impl. *presence, person:*—(outward) appearance, × before, countenance, face, fashion, (men's) person, presence.

4384. **προτάσσω prŏtassō**, *prot-as'-so;* from *4253* and *5021;* to *pre-arrange*, i.e. *prescribe:*—before appoint.

4385. **προτείνω prŏtĕinō**, *prot-i'-no;* from *4253* and **τείνω tĕinō** (to *stretch*); to *protend*, i.e. *tie prostrate* (for scourging):—bind.

4386. **πρότερον prŏtĕrŏn**, *prot'-er-on;* neut. of *4387* as adv. (with or without the art.); *previously:*—before, (at the) first, former.

4387. **πρότερος prŏtĕrŏs**, *prot'-er-os;* compar. of *4253;* *prior* or *previous:*—former.

4388. **προτίθεμαι prŏtithĕmai**, *prot-ith'-em-ahee;* mid. from *4253* and *5087;* to *place before*, i.e. (for oneself) to *exhibit;* (to oneself) to *propose* (*determine*):—purpose, set forth.

4389. **προτρέπομαι prŏtrĕpŏmai**, *prot-rep'-om-ahee;* mid. from *4253* and the base of *5157;* to *turn forward* for oneself, i.e. *encourage:*—exhort.

4390. **προτρέχω prŏtrĕchō**, *prot-rekh'-o;* from *4253* and *5143* (includ. its alt.); to *run forward*, i.e. *outstrip, precede:*—outrun, run before.

4391. **προϋπάρχω prŏüparchō**, *prŏ-oop-ar'-kho;* from *4253* and *5225;* to *exist before*, i.e. (adv.) to *be* or *do* something *previously:*—+ be before (-time).

4392. **πρόφασις prŏphasis**, *prof'-as-is;* from a comp. of *4253* and *5316;* an *outward showing*, i.e. *pretext:*—cloke, colour, pretence, show.

4393. **προφέρω prŏphĕrō**, *prof-er'-o;* from *4253* and *5342;* to *bear forward*, i.e. *produce:*—bring forth.

4394. **προφητεία prŏphētĕia**, *prof-ay-ti'-ah;* from *4396* ("*prophecy*"); *prediction* (scriptural or other):—prophecy, prophesying.

4395. **προφητεύω prŏphētĕuō**, *prof-ate-yoo'-o;* from *4396;* to *foretell* events, *divine, speak* under *inspiration, exercise* the prophetic *office:*—prophesy.

4396. **προφήτης prŏphētēs**, *prof-ay'-tace;* from a comp. of *4253* and *5346;* a *foreteller* ("*prophet*"); by anal. an *inspired speaker;* by extens. a *poet:*—prophet.

4397. **προφητικός prŏphētikŏs**, *prof-ay-tik-os';* from *4396;* *pertaining to a foreteller* ("*prophetic*"):—of prophecy, of the prophets.

4398. **προφῆτις prŏphētis**, *prof-ay'-tis;* fem. of *4396;* a *female foreteller* or an *inspired woman:*—prophetess.

4399. **προφθάνω prŏphthanō**, *prof-than'-o;* from *4253* and *5348;* to *get an earlier start of*, i.e. *anticipate:*—prevent.

4400. **προχειρίζομαι prŏchĕirizŏmai**, *prokh-i-rid'-zom-ahee;* mid. from *4253* and a der. of *5495;* to *handle* for oneself *in advance*, i.e. (fig.) to *purpose:*—choose, make.

4401. **προχειροτονέω prŏchĕirŏtŏnĕō**, *prokh-i-rot-on-eh'-o;* from *4253* and *5500;* to *elect in advance:*—choose before.

4402. **Πρόχορος Prŏchŏrŏs**, *prokh'-or-os;* from *4253* and *5525;* *before the dance; Prochorus*, a Chr.:—Prochorus.

4403. **πρύμνα prumna**, *proom'-nah;* fem. of **πρυμνύς prumnus** (*hindmost*); the *stern* of a ship:—hinder part, stern.

4404. **πρωΐ prōi**, *pro-ee';* adv. from *4253;* at *dawn;* by impl. the *day-break* watch:—early (in the morning), (in the) morning.

4405. **πρωΐα prōïa**, *pro-ee'-ah;* fem. of a der. of *4404* as noun; *day-dawn:*—early, morning.

4406. **πρώϊμος prōïmŏs**, *pro'-ee-mos;* from *4404;* *dawning*, i.e. (by anal.) *autumnal* (showering, the first of the rainy season):—early.

4407. **πρωϊνός prōïnŏs**, *pro-ee-nos';* from *4404;* pertaining to the *dawn*, i.e. *matutinal:*—morning.

4408. **πρῷρα prōra**, *pro'-ra;* fem. of a presumed der. of *4253* as noun; the *prow*, i.e. forward part of a vessel:—forepart (-ship).

4409. **πρωτεύω prōtĕuō**, *prote-yoo'-o;* from *4413;* to *be first* (in rank or influence):—have the preeminence.

4410. **πρωτοκαθεδρία prōtŏkathĕdria**, *pro-tok-ath-ed-ree'-ah;* from *4413* and *2515;* a *sitting first* (in the front row), i.e. *preeminence* in council:—chief (highest, uppermost) seat.

4411. **πρωτοκλισία prōtŏklisia**, *pro-tok-lis-ee'-ah;* from *4413* and *2828;* a *reclining first* (in the place of honor) at the dinner-bed, i.e. *preeminence* at meals:—chief (highest, uppermost) room.

4412. **πρῶτον prōtŏn**, *pro'-ton;* neut. of *4413* as adv. (with or without *3588*); *firstly* (in time, place, order, or importance):—before, at the beginning, chiefly, (at, at the) first (of all).

4413. **πρῶτος prōtŏs**, *pro'-tos;* contr. superl. of *4253;* *foremost* (in time, place, order or importance):—before, beginning, best, chief (-est), first (of all), former.

4414. **πρωτοστάτης prōtŏstatēs**, *pro-tos-tat'-ace;* from *4413* and *2476;* one *standing first* in the ranks, i.e. a *captain* (*champion*):—ringleader.

4415. **πρωτοτόκια prōtŏtŏkia**, *pro-tot-ok'-ee-ah;* from *4416;* *primogeniture* (as a privilege):—birthright.

4416. **πρωτοτόκος prōtŏtŏkŏs**, *pro-tot-ok'-os;* from *4413* and the alt. of *5088;* *first-born* (usually as noun, lit. or fig.):—firstbegotten (-born).

4417. **πταίω ptaiō**, *ptah'-yo;* a form of *4098;* to *trip*, i.e. (fig.) to *err, sin, fail* (of salvation):—fall, offend, stumble.

4418. **πτέρνα ptĕrna**, *pter'-nah;* of uncert. der.; the *heel* (fig.):—heel.

4419. **πτερύγιον ptĕrugiŏn**, *pter-oog'-ee-on;* neut. of a presumed der. of *4420;* a *winglet*, i.e. (fig.) *extremity* (top corner):—pinnacle.

4420. **πτέρυξ ptĕrux**, *pter'-oox;* from a der. of *4072* (mean. a *feather*); a *wing:*—wing.

4421. **πτηνόν ptēnŏn**, *ptay-non';* contr. for *4071;* a *bird:*—bird.

4422. **πτοέω ptŏĕō**, *ptŏ-eh'-o;* prob. akin to the alt. of *4098* (through the idea of causing to *fall*) or to *4072* (through that of causing to *fly* away); to *scare:*—frighten.

4423. **πτόησις ptŏēsis**, *ptŏ'-ay-sis;* from *4422;* *alarm:*—amazement.

4424. **Πτολεμαΐς Ptŏlĕmaïs**, *ptol-em-ah-is';* from **Πτολεμαῖος Ptŏlĕmaiŏs** (*Ptolemy*, after whom it was named); *Ptolemaïs*, a place in Pal.:—Ptolemais.

4425. **πτύον ptuŏn**, *ptoo'-on;* from *4429;* a *winnowing-fork* (as *scattering* like spittle):—fan.

4426. **πτύρω pturō**, *ptoo'-ro;* from a presumed der. of *4429* (and thus akin to *4422*); to *frighten:*—terrify.

4427. **πτύσμα ptusma**, *ptoos'-mah;* from *4429;* *saliva:*—spittle.

4428. **πτύσσω ptussō**, *ptoos'-so;* prob. akin to **πετάννυμι pĕtannumi** (to *spread;* and thus appar. allied to *4072* through the idea of *expansion*, and to *4429* through that of *flattening;* comp. *3961*); to *fold*, i.e. *furl* a scroll:—close.

4429. **πτύω ptuō**, *ptoo'-o;* a prim. verb (comp. *4428*); to *spit:*—spit.

4430. **πτῶμα ptōma**, *pto'-mah;* from the alt. of *4098;* a *ruin*, i.e. (spec.) lifeless *body* (*corpse, carrion*):—dead body, carcase, corpse.

4431. **πτῶσις ptōsis**, *pto'-sis;* from the alt. of *4098;* a *crash*, i.e. *downfall* (lit. or fig.):—fall.

4432. **πτωχεία ptōchĕia**, *pto-khi'-ah;* from *4433;* *beggary*, i.e. *indigence* (lit. or fig.):—poverty.

4433. **πτωχεύω ptōchĕuō**, *pto-khyoo'-o;* from *4434;* *to be a beggar*, i.e. (by impl.) to *become indigent* (fig.):—become poor.

4434. **πτωχός ptōchŏs**, *pto-khos';* from **πτώσσω ptōssō** (to *crouch;* akin to *4422* and the alt. of *4098*); a *beggar* (as *cringing*), i.e. *pauper* (strictly denoting absolute or public *mendicancy*, although also used in a qualified or relative sense; whereas *3993* prop. means only *straitened* circumstances in private), lit. (often as noun) or fig. (*distressed*):—beggar (-ly), poor.

4435. **πυγμή pugmē**, *poog-may';* from a prim. **πύξ pux** (the *fist* as a weapon); the clenched *hand*, le. (only in dat. as adv.) *with the fist* (hard *scrubbing*):—oft.

4436. Πύθων **Puthōn**, *poo'-thone;* from Πυθώ **Puthō** (the name of the region where Delphi, the seat of the famous *oracle*, was located); a *Python*, i.e. (by anal. with the supposed *diviner* there) *inspiration* (*soothsaying*):—divination.

4437. πυκνός **puknŏs**, *pook-nos';* from the same as 4635; *clasped* (*thick*), i.e. (fig.) *frequent;* neut. plur. (as adv.) *frequently:*—often (-er).

4438. πυκτέω **puktĕō**, *pook-teh'-o;* from a der. of the same as 4435; to *box* (with the fist), i.e. *contend* (as a boxer) at the games (fig.):—fight.

4439. πύλη **pulē**, *poo'-lay;* appar. a prim. word; a *gate*, i.e. the leaf or wing of a folding *entrance* (lit. or fig.):—gate.

4440. πυλών **pulōn**, *poo-lone';* from 4439; a *gateway*, *door-way* of a building or city; by impl. a *portal* or *vestibule:*—gate, porch.

4441. πυνθάνομαι **punthanŏmai**, *poon-than'-om-ahee;* mid. prol. from a prim. πύθω **puthō** (which occurs only as an alt. in certain tenses); to *question*, i.e. *ascertain* by inquiry (as a matter of *information* merely; and thus differing from 2065, which prop. means a *request* as a favor; and from 154, which is strictly a *demand* of something due; as well as from 2212, which implies a *search* for something hidden; and from 1189, which involves the idea of urgent *need*); by impl. to *learn* (by casual intelligence):—ask, demand, enquire, understand.

4442. πῦρ **pur**, *poor;* a prim. word; "*fire*" (lit. or fig., spec. *lightning*):—fiery, fire.

4443. πυρά **pura**, *poo-rah';* from 4442; a *fire* (concr.):—fire.

4444. πύργος **purgŏs**, *poor'-gos;* appar. a prim. word ("*burgh*"); a *tower* or *castle:*—tower.

4445. πυρέσσω **purĕssō**, *poo-res'-so;* from 4443; to *be on fire*, i.e. (spec.) to *have a fever:*—be sick of a fever.

4446. πυρετός **purĕtŏs**, *poo-ret-os';* from 4445; *inflamed*, i.e. (by impl.) *feverish* (as noun, *fever*):—fever.

4447. πύρινος **purinŏs**, *poo'-ree-nos;* from 4443; *fiery*, i.e. (by impl.) *flaming:*—of fire.

4448. πυρόω **purŏō**, *poo-rŏ'-o;* from 4442; to *kindle*, i.e. (pass.) to *be ignited*, *glow* (lit.), *be refined* (by impl.), or (fig.) to *be inflamed* (with anger, grief, lust):—burn, fiery, be on fire, try.

4449. πυῤῥάζω **purrhazō**, *poor-hrad'-zo;* from 4450; to *redden* (intrans.):—be red.

4450. πυῤῥός **purrhŏs**, *poor-hros';* from 4442; *fire-like*, i.e. (spec.) *flame-colored:*—red.

4451. πύρωσις **purōsis**, *poo'-ro-sis;* from 4448; *ignition*, i.e. (spec.) *smelting* (fig. *conflagration*, *calamity* as a *test*):—burning, trial.

4452. -πω **-pō**, *po;* another form of the base of 4458; an enclitic particle of indefiniteness; *yet, even;* used only in comp. See 3369, 3380, 3764, 3768, 4455.

4453. πωλέω **pōlĕō**, *po-leh'-o;* prob. ultimately from πέλομαι **pĕlŏmai** (to *be busy*, to *trade*); to *barter* (as a *pedlar*), i.e. to *sell:*—sell, whatever is sold.

4454. πῶλος **pōlŏs**, *po'-los;* appar. a prim. word; a "*foal*" or "*filly*", i.e. (spec.) a *young ass:*—colt.

4455. πώποτε **pōpŏtĕ**, *po'-pot-e;* from 4452 and 4218; *at any time*, i.e. (with neg. particle) *at no time:*—at any time, + never (. . . to any man), + yet never man.

4456. πωρόω **pōrŏō**, *po-rŏ'-o;* appar. from πῶρος **pōrŏs** (a kind of *stone*); to *petrify*, i.e (fig.) to *indurate* (*render stupid* or *callous*):—blind, harden.

4457. πώρωσις **pōrōsis**, *po'-ro-sis;* from 4456; *stupidity* or *callousness:*—blindness, hardness.

4458. -πώς **-pōs**, *poce;* adv. from the base of 4225; an enclitic particle of indefiniteness of manner; *somehow* or *anyhow;* used only in comp.:—haply, by any (some) means, perhaps. See 1513, 3381. Comp. 4459.

4459. πῶς **pōs**, *poce;* adv. from the base of 4226; an interrog. particle of manner; *in what way?* (sometimes the question is indirect, *how?*); also as exclamation, *how* much!:—how, after (by) what manner (means), that. [*Occasionally unexpressed in English.*]

P

4460. Ῥαάβ **Rhaab**, *hrah-ab';* of Heb. or. [7343]; *Raab* (i.e. *Rachab*), a Canaanitess:—Rahab. See also 4477.

4461. ῥαββί **rhabbi**, *hrab-bee';* of Heb. or. [7227 with pron. suffix]; *my master*, i.e. *Rabbi*, as an official title of honor:—Master, Rabbi.

4462. ῥαββονί **rhabbŏni**, *hrab-bon-ee';* or ῥαββουνί **rhabbŏuni**, *hrab-boo-nee';* of Chald. or.; corresp. to 4461:—Lord, Rabboni.

4463. ῥαβδίζω **rhabdizō**, *hrab-did'-zo;* from 4464; to *strike with a stick*, i.e. *bastinado:*—beat (with rods).

4464. ῥάβδος **rhabdŏs**, *hrab'-dos;* from the base of 4474; a *stick* or *wand* (as a *cudgel*, a *cane* or a *baton* of royalty):—rod, sceptre, staff.

4465. ῥαβδοῦχος **rhabdŏuchŏs**, *hrab-doo'-khos;* from 4464 and 2192; a *rod-* (the Lat. *fasces*) *holder*, i.e. a Rom. *lictor* (*constable* or *executioner*):—serjeant.

4466. Ῥαγαῦ **Rhagau**, *hrag-ŏw';* of Heb. or. [7466]; *Ragau* (i.e. *Reü*), a patriarch:—Ragau.

4467. ῥᾳδιούργημα **rhaidiŏurgēma**, *hrad-ee-oorg'-ay-mah;* from a comp. of ῥᾴδιος **rhaidiŏs** (*easy*, i.e. *reckless*) and 2041; *easy-going behavior*, i.e. (by extens.) a *crime:*—lewdness.

4468. ῥᾳδιουργία **rhaidiŏurgia**, *hrad-ee-oorg-ee'-a;* from the same as 4467; *recklessness*, i.e. (by extens.) *malignity:*—mischief.

4469. ῥακά **rhaka**, *rhak-ah';* of Chald. or. [comp. 7386]; O *empty* one, i.e. thou *worthless* (as a term of utter vilification):—Raca.

4470. ῥάκος **rhăkŏs**, *hrak'-os;* from 4486; a "*rag*," i.e. *piece* of cloth:—cloth.

4471. Ῥαμᾶ **Rhama**, *hram-ah';* of Heb. or. [7414]; *Rama* (i.e. *Ramah*), a place in Pal.:—Rama.

4472. ῥαντίζω **rhantizō**, *hran-tid'-zo;* from a der. of ῥαίνω **rhainō** (to *sprinkle*); to *render besprinkled*, i.e. *asperse* (cer. or fig.):—sprinkle.

4473. ῥαντισμός **rhantismŏs**, *hran-tis-mos';* from 4472; *aspersion* (cer. or fig.):—sprinkling.

4474. ῥαπίζω **rhapizō**, *hrap-id'-zo;* from a der. of a prim. ῥέπω **rhĕpō** (to *let fall*, "*rap*"); to *slap:*—smite (with the palm of the hand). Comp. 5180.

4475. ῥάπισμα **rhapisma**, *hrap'-is-mah;* from 4474; a *slap:*—(+ strike with the) palm of the hand, smite with the hand.

4476. ῥαφίς **rhaphis**, *hraf-ece';* from a prim. ῥάπτω **rhaptō** (to *sew;* perh. rather akin to the base of 4474 through the idea of *puncturing*); a *needle:*—needle.

4477. Ῥαχάβ **Rhachab**, *hrakh-ab';* from the same as 4460; *Rachab*, a Canaanitess:—Rachab.

4478. Ῥαχήλ **Rhachēl**, *hrakh-ale';* of Heb. or. [7354]; *Rachel*, the wife of Jacob:—Rachel.

4479. Ῥεβέκκα **Rhĕbĕkka**, *hreb-bek'-kah;* of Heb. or. [7259]; *Rebecca* (i.e. *Ribkah*), the wife of Isaac:—Rebecca.

4480. ῥέδα **rhĕda**, *hred'-ah;* of Lat. or.; a *rheda*, i.e. four-wheeled *carriage* (*wagon* for riding):—chariot.

4481. Ῥεμφάν **Rhĕmphan**, *hrem-fan';* by incorrect transliteration for a word of Heb. or. [3594]; *Remphan* (i.e. *Kijun*), an Eg. idol:—Remphan.

4482. ῥέω **rhĕō**, *hreh'-o;* a prim. verb; for some tenses of which a prol. form

ῥεύω **rhĕuō**, *hryoo'-o*, is used; to *flow* ("*run*", as water):—flow.

4483. ῥέω **rhĕō**, *hreh'-o;* for certain tenses of which a prol. form

ἐρέω **ĕrĕō**, *er-eh'-o*, is used; and both as alt. for 2036; perh. akin (or ident.) with 4482 (through the idea of *pouring* forth); to *utter*, i.e. *speak* or *say:*—command, make, say, speak (of). Comp. 3004.

4484. Ῥήγιον **Rhēgiŏn**, *hrayg'-ee-on;* of Lat. or.; *Rhegium*, a place in Italy:—Rhegium.

4485. ῥῆγμα **rhēgma**, *hrayg'-mah;* from 4486; something *torn*, i.e. a *fragment* (by impl. and abstr. a *fall*):—ruin.

4486. ῥήγνυμι **rhēgnumi**, *hrayg'-noo-mee;* or ῥήσσω **rhēssō**, *hrace'-so;* both prol. forms of ῥήκω **rhēkō** (which appears only in certain forms, and is itself prob. a strengthened form of ἄγνυμι **agnumi** [see in 2608]); to "*break*", "*wreck*" or "*crack*", i.e. (espec.) to *sunder* (by *separation* of the parts; 2608 being its intensive [with the prep. in comp.], and 2352 a *shattering* to minute fragments; but not a *reduction* to the constituent particles, like 3089) or *disrupt*, *lacerate;* by impl. to *convulse* (with *spasms*); fig. to *give vent* to joyful emotions:—break (forth), burst, rend, tear.

4487. ῥῆμα **rhēma**, *hray'-mah;* from 4483; an *utterance* (individ., collect. or spec.); by impl. a *matter* or *topic* (espec. of narration, command or dispute); with a neg. *naught* whatever:—+ evil, + nothing, saying, word.

4488. Ῥησά **Rhēsa**, *hray-sah';* prob. of Heb. or. [appar. for 7509]; *Resa* (i.e. *Rephajah*), an Isr.:—Rhesa.

4489. ῥήτωρ **rhētōr**, *hray'-tore;* from 4483; a *speaker*, i.e. (by impl.) a forensic *advocate:*—orator.

4490. ῥητῶς **rhētōs**, *hray-toce';* adv. from a der. of 4483; *out-spokenly*, i.e. *distinctly:*—expressly.

4491. ῥίζα **rhiza**, *hrid'-zah;* appar. a prim. word; a "*root*" (lit. or fig.):—root.

4492. ῥιζόω **rhizŏō**, *rhid-zŏ'-o;* from 4491; to *root* (fig. *become stable*):—root.

4493. ῥιπή **rhipē**, *hree-pay';* from 4496; a *jerk* (of the eye, i.e. [by anal.] an *instant*):—twinkling.

4494. ῥιπίζω **rhipizō**, *hrip-id'-zo;* from a der. of 4496 (mean. a *fan* or *bellows*); to *breeze up*, i.e. (by anal.) to *agitate* (into waves):—toss.

4495. ῥιπτέω **rhiptĕō**, *hrip-teh'-o;* from a der. of 4496; to *toss* up:—cast off.

4496. ῥίπτω **rhiptō**, *hrip'-to;* a prim. verb (perh. rather akin to the base of 4474, through the idea of sudden *motion*); to *fling* (prop. with a quick *toss*, thus differing from 906, which denotes a *deliberate* hurl; and from τείνω **tĕinō** [see in 1614], which indicates an *extended* projection); by qualification, to *deposit* (as if a load); by extens. to *disperse:*—cast (down, out), scatter abroad, throw.

4497. Ῥοβοάμ **Rhŏbŏam**, *hrob-ŏ-am';* of Heb. or. [7346]; *Roboäm* (i.e. *Rechabam*), an Isr.:—Roboam.

4498. Ῥόδη **Rhŏdē**, *hrod'-ay;* prob. for ῥοδή **rhŏdē** (a *rose*); *Rodè*, a servant girl:—Rhoda.

4499. Ῥόδος **Rhŏdŏs**, *hrod'-os;* prob. from ῥόδον **rhŏdŏn** (a *rose*); *Rhodus*, an island of the Mediterranean:—Rhodes.

4500. ῥοιζηδόν **rhŏizēdŏn**, *hroyd-zay-don';* adv. from a der. of ῥοῖζος **rhŏizŏs** (a *whir*); *whizzingly*, i.e. *with a crash:*—with a great noise.

4501. ῥομφαία **rhŏmphaia**, *hrom-fah'-yah;* prob. of for. or.; a *sabre*, i.e. a long and broad *cutlass* (any *weapon* of the kind, lit. or fig.):—sword.

4502. Ῥουβήν **Rhŏubēn**, *hroo-bane';* of Heb. or. [7205]; *Ruben* (i.e. *Reuben*), an Isr.:—Reuben.

4503. Ῥούθ **Rhŏuth**, *hrooth;* of Heb. or. [7327]; *Ruth*, a Moabitess:—Ruth.

4504. Ῥοῦφος **Rhŏuphŏs**, *hroo'-fos;* of Lat. or.; *red; Rufus*, a Chr.:—Rufus.

4505. ῥύμη **rhumē**, *hroo'-may;* prol. from 4506 in its orig. sense; an *alley* or *avenue* (as crowded):—lane, street.

4506. ῥύομαι **rhuŏmai**, *rhoo'-om-ahee;* mid. of an obsol. verb, akin to 4482 (through the idea of a *current;* comp. 4511); to *rush* or *draw* (for oneself), i.e. *rescue:*—deliver (-er).

4507. ῥυπαρία **rhuparia**, *hroo-par-ee'-ah;* from 4508; *dirtiness* (mor.):—filthiness.

4508. **ῥυπαρός rhuparŏs**, *rhoo-par-os'*; from *4509*; *dirty*, i.e. (rel.) *cheap* or *shabby*; mor. *wicked*:—vile.

4509. **ῥύπος rhupŏs**, *hroo'-pos*; of uncert. affin.; *dirt*, i.e. (mor.) *depravity*:—filth.

4510. **ῥυπόω rhupŏō**, *rhoo-pŏ'-o*; from *4509*; to *soil*, i.e. (intrans.) to *become dirty* (mor.):—be filthy.

4511. **ῥύσις rhusis**, *hroo'-sis*; from *4506* in the sense of its congener *4482*; a *flux* (of blood):—issue.

4512. **ῥυτίς rhutis**, *hroo-tece'*; from *4506*; a *fold* (as *drawing* together), i.e. a *wrinkle* (espec. on the face):—wrinkle.

4513. **Ῥωμαϊκός Rhōmaïkŏs**, *rho-mah-ee-kos'*; from *4514*; *Romaïc*, i.e. *Latin*:—Latin.

4514. **Ῥωμαῖος Rhōmaiŏs**, *hro-mah'-yos*; from *4516*; *Romœan*, i.e. *Roman* (as noun):—Roman, of Rome.

4515. **Ῥωμαϊστί Rhōmaïsti**, *hro-mah-is-tee'*; adv. from a presumed der. of *4516*; *Romaïstically*, i.e. *in* the *Latin* language:—Latin.

4516. **Ῥώμη Rhōmē**, *hro'-may*; from the base of *4517*; *strength*; *Roma*, the capital of Italy:—Rome.

4517. **ῥώννυμι rhōnnumi**, *hrone'-noo-mee*; prol. from **ῥώομαι rhōŏmai** (to *dart*; prob. akin to *4506*); to *strengthen*, i.e. (imper. pass.) *have health* (as a parting exclamation, *good-bye*):—farewell.

Σ

4518. **σαβαχθανί sabachthani**, *sab-akh-than-ee'*; of Chald. or. [7662 with pron. suff.]; *thou hast left me*; *sabachthani* (i.e. *shebakthani*), a cry of distress:—sabachthani.

4519. **σαβαώθ sabaōth**, *sab-ah-ōwth'*; of Heb. or. [6635 in fem. plur.]; *armies*; *sabaoth* (i.e. *tsebaoth*), a military epithet of God:—sabaoth.

4520. **σαββατισμός sabbatismŏs**, *sab-bat-is-mos'*; from a der. of *4521*; a "*sabbatism*", i.e. (fig.) the *repose* of Christianity (as a type of heaven):—rest.

4521. **σάββατον sabbatŏn**, *sab'-bat-on*; of Heb. or. [7676]; the *Sabbath* (i.e. *Shabbath*), or day of weekly *repose* from secular avocations (also the observance or institution itself); by extens. a *se'nnight*, i.e. the interval between two Sabbaths; likewise the plur. in all the above applications:—sabbath (day), week.

4522. **σαγήνη sagēnē**, *sag-ay'-nay*; from a der. of **σάττω sattō** (to *equip*) mean. *furniture*, espec. a *pack-saddle* (which in the East is merely a bag of *netted* rope); a "*seine*" for fishing:—net.

4523. **Σαδδουκαῖος Saddŏukaiŏs**, *sad-doo-kah'-yos*; prob. from *4524*; a *Sadducœan* (i.e. *Tsadokian*), or follower of a certain heretical Isr.:—Sadducee.

4524. **Σαδώκ Sadōk**, *sad-oke'*; of Heb. or. [6659]; *Sadoc* (i.e. *Tsadok*), an Isr.:—Sadoc.

4525. **σαίνω sainō**, *sah'ee-no*; akin to *4579*; to *wag* (as a dog its tail fawningly), i.e. (gen.) to *shake* (fig. *disturb*):—move.

4526. **σάκκος sakkŏs**, *sak'-kos*; of Heb. or. [8242]; "*sack*"-cloth, i.e. *mohair* (the material or garments made of it, worn as a sign of grief):—sackcloth.

4527. **Σαλά Sala**, *sal-ah'*; of Heb. or. [7974]; *Sala* (i.e. *Shelach*), a patriarch:—Sala.

4528. **Σαλαθιήλ Salathiēl**, *sal-ath-ee-ale'*; of Heb. or. [7597]; *Salathiël* (i.e. *Sheältiël*), an Isr.:—Salathiel.

4529. **Σαλαμίς Salamis**, *sal-am-ece'*; prob. from *4535* (from the *surge* on the shore); *Salamis*, a place in Cyprus:—Salamis.

4530. **Σαλείμ Salĕim**, *sal-ime'*; prob. from the same as *4531*; *Salim*, a place in Pal.:—Salim.

4531. **σαλεύω salĕuō**, *sal-yoo'-o*; from *4535*; to *waver*, i.e. *agitate*, *rock*, *topple* or (by impl.) *destroy*; fig. to *disturb*, *incite*:—move, shake (together), which can [-not] be shaken, stir up.

4532. **Σαλήμ Salēm**, *sal-ame'*; of Heb. or. [8004]; *Salem* (i.e. *Shalem*), a place in Pal.:—Salem.

4533. **Σαλμών Salmōn**, *sal-mone'*; of Heb. or. [8012]; *Salmon*, an Isr.:—Salmon.

4534. **Σαλμώνη Salmōnē**, *sal-mo'-nay*; perh. of similar or. to *4529*; *Salmone*, a place in Crete:—Salmone.

4535. **σάλος salŏs**, *sal'-os*; prob. from the base of *4525*; a *vibration*, i.e. (spec.) *billow*:—wave.

4536. **σάλπιγξ salpigx**, *sal'-pinx*; perh. from *4535* (through the idea of *quavering* or *reverberation*): a *trumpet*:—trump (-et).

4537. **σαλπίζω salpizō**, *sal-pid'-zo*; from *4536*; to *trumpet*, i.e. *sound a blast* (lit. or fig.):—(which are yet to) sound (a trumpet).

4538. **σαλπιστής salpistēs**, *sal-pis-tace'*; from *4537*; a *trumpeter*:—trumpeter.

4539. **Σαλώμη Salōmē**, *sal-o'-may*; prob. of Heb. or. [fem. from 7965]; *Salomè* (i.e. *Shelomah*), an Israelitess:—Salome.

4540. **Σαμάρεια Samarĕia**, *sam-ar'-i-ah*; of Heb. or. [8111]; *Samaria* (i.e. *Shomeron*), a city and region of Pal.:—Samaria.

4541. **Σαμαρείτης Samarĕitēs**, *sam-ar-i'-tace*; from *4540*; a *Samarite*, i.e. inhab. of Samaria:—Samaritan.

4542. **Σαμαρεῖτις Samarĕitis**, *sam-ar-i'-tis*; fem. of *4541*; a *Samaritess*, i.e. woman of Samaria:—of Samaria.

4543. **Σαμοθρᾴκη Samŏthraikē**, *sam-oth-rak'-ay*; from *4544* and **Θρᾴκη Thraikē** (*Thrace*); *Samo-thracè* (*Samos of Thrace*), an island in the Mediterranean:—Samothrac'

4544. **Σάμος Samŏs**, *sam'-os*; of uncert. affin.; *Samus*, an island of the Mediterranean:—Samos.

4545. **Σαμουήλ Samŏuēl**, *sam-oo-ale'*; of Heb. or. [8050]; *Samuel* (i.e. *Shemuel*), an Isr.:—Samuel.

4546. **Σαμψών Sampsōn**, *samp-sone'*; of Heb. or. [8123]; *Sampson* (i.e. *Shimshon*), an Isr.:—Samson.

4547. **σανδάλιον sandaliŏn**, *san-dal'-ee-on*; neut. of a der. of **σάνδαλον sandalŏn** (a "*sandal*"; of uncert. or.); a *slipper* or *sole-pad*:—sandal.

4548. **σανίς sanis**, *san-ece'*; of uncert. affin.; a *plank*:—board.

4549. **Σαούλ Saŏul**, *sah-ool'*; of Heb. or. [7586]; *Saül* (i.e. *Shaül*), the Jewish name of *Paul*:—Saul. Comp. *4569*.

4550. **σαπρός saprŏs**, *sap-ros'*; from *4595*; *rotten*, i.e. *worthless* (lit. or mor.):—bad, corrupt. Comp. *4190*.

4551. **Σαπφείρη Sapphĕirē**, *sap-fi'-ray*; fem. of *4552*; *Sapphirè*, an Israelitess:—Sapphira.

4552. **σάπφειρος sapphĕirŏs**, *sap'-fi-ros*; of Heb. or. [5601]; a "*sapphire*" or *lapis-lazuli* gem:—sapphire.

4553. **σαργάνη sarganē**, *sar-gan'-ay*; appar. of Heb. or. [8276]; a *basket* (as *interwoven* or *wicker-work*):—basket.

4554. **Σάρδεις Sardĕis**, *sar'-dice*; plur. of uncert. der.; *Sardis*, a place in Asia Minor:—Sardis.

4555. **σάρδινος sardinŏs**, *sar'-dee-nos*; from the same as *4556*; *sardine* (*3037* being impl.), i.e. a gem, so called:—sardine.

4556. **σάρδιος sardiŏs**, *sar'-dee-os*; prop. adj. from an uncert. base; *sardian* (*3037* being impl.), i.e. (as noun) the gem so called:—sardius.

4557. **σαρδόνυξ sardŏnux**, *sar-don'-oox*; from the base of *4556* and **ὄνυξ ŏnux** (the *nail* of a finger; hence the "*onyx*" stone); a "*sardonyx*", i.e. the gem so called:—sardonyx.

4558. **Σάρεπτα Sarĕpta**, *sar'-ep-tah*; of Heb. or. [6886]; *Sarepta* (i.e. *Tsarephath*), a place in Pal.:—Sarepta.

4559. **σαρκικός sarkikŏs**, *sar-kee-kos'*; from *4561*; *pertaining to flesh*, i.e. (by extens.) *bodily*, *temporal*, or (by impl.) *animal*, *unregenerate*:—carnal, fleshly.

4560. **σάρκινος sarkinŏs**, *sar'-kee-nos*; from *4561*; *similar to flesh*, i.e. (by anal.) *soft*:—fleshly.

4561. **σάρξ sarx**, *sarx*; prob. from the base of *4563*; *flesh* (as *stripped* of the skin), i.e. (strictly) the *meat* of an animal (as food), or (by extens.) the *body* (as opposed to the soul [or spirit], or as the symbol of what is external, or as the means of kindred), or (by impl.) *human nature* (with its frailties [phys. or mor.] and passions), or (spec.) a *human being* (as such):—carnal (-ly, + -ly minded), flesh ([-ly]).

4562. **Σαρούχ Sarŏuch**, *sar-ooch'*; of Heb. or. [8286]; *Saruch* (i.e. *Serug*), a patriarch:—Saruch.

4563. **σαρόω sarŏō**, *sar-ŏ'-o*; from a der. of **σαίρω sairō** (to *brush* off; akin to *4951*) mean. a *broom*; to *sweep*:—sweep.

4564. **Σάῤῥα Sarrha**, *sar'-hrah*; of Heb. or. [8283]; *Sarra* (i.e. *Sarah*), the wife of Abraham:—Sara, Sarah.

4565. **Σάρων Sarōn**, *sar'-one*; of Heb. or. [8289]; *Saron* (i.e. *Sharon*), a district of Pal.:—Saron.

4566. **Σατᾶν Satan**, *sat-an'*; of Heb. or. [7854]; *Satan*, i.e. the *devil*:—Satan. Comp. *4567*.

4567. **Σατανᾶς Satanas**, *sat-an-as'*; of Chald. or. corresp. to *4566* (with the def. affix); *the accuser*, i.e. the *devil*:—Satan.

4568. **σάτον satŏn**, *sat'-on*; of Heb. or. [5429]; a certain *measure* for things dry:—measure.

4569. **Σαῦλος Saulŏs**, *sŏw'-los*; of Heb. or., the same as *4549*; *Saulus* (i.e. *Shaül*), the Jewish name of *Paul*:—Saul.

σαυτοῦ sautŏu, etc. See *4572*.

4570. **σβέννυμι sbĕnnumi**, *sben'-noo-mee*; a prol. form of an appar. prim. verb; to *extinguish* (lit. or fig.):—go out, quench.

4571. **σέ sĕ**, *seh*; accus. sing. of *4771*; *thee*:—thee, thou, × thy house.

4572. **σεαυτοῦ sĕautŏu**, *seh-ŏw-too'*; gen. from *4571* and *846*; also dat. of the same, **σεαυτῷ sĕautōi**, *seh-ŏw-to'*; and acc. **σεαυτόν sĕautŏn**, *seh-ŏw-ton'*; likewise contr. **σαυτοῦ sautŏu**, *sŏw-too'*; **σαυτῷ sautōi**, *sŏw-to'*; and **σαυτόν sautŏn**, *sŏw-ton'*; respectively; *of* (*with*, *to*) *thyself*:—thee, thine own self, (thou) thy (-self).

4573. **σεβάζομαι sĕbazŏmai**, *seb-ad'-zom-ahee*; mid. from a der. of *4576*; to *venerate*, i.e. *adore*:—worship.

4574. **σέβασμα sĕbasma**, *seb'-as-mah*; from *4573*; something *adored*, i.e. an *object of worship* (god, altar, etc.):—devotion, that is worshipped.

4575. **σεβαστός sĕbastŏs**, *seb-as-tos'*; from *4573*; *venerable* (*august*), i.e. (as noun) a title of the Rom. *Emperor*, or (as adj.) *imperial*:—Augustus (-').

4576. **σέβομαι sĕbŏmai**, *seb'-om-ahee*; mid. of an appar. prim. verb; to *revere*, i.e. *adore*:—devout, religious, worship.

4577. **σειρά sĕira**, *si-rah'*; prob. from *4951* through its congener **εἴρω ĕirō** (to *fasten*; akin to *138*); a *chain* (as *binding* or *drawing*):—chain.

4578. **σεισμός sĕismŏs**, *sice-mos'*; from *4579*; a *commotion*, i.e. (of the air) a *gale*, (of the ground) an *earthquake*:—earthquake, tempest.

4579. **σείω sĕiō**, *si'-o*; appar. a prim. verb; to *rock* (*vibrate*, prop. sideways or to and fro), i.e. (gen.) to *agitate* (in any direction; cause to *tremble*); fig. to throw into a *tremor* (of fear or concern):—move, quake, shake.

4580. **Σεκοῦνδος Sĕkŏundŏs**, *sek-oon'-dos*; of Lat. or.; "*second*"; *Secundus*, a Chr.:—Secundus.

4581. **Σελεύκεια Sĕlĕukĕia**, *sel-yook'-i-ah*; from **Σέλευκος Sĕlĕukŏs** (*Seleucus*, a Syrian king); *Seleuceia*, a place in Syria:—Seleucia.

4582. **σελήνη sĕlēnē**, *sel-ay'-nay*; from **σέλας sĕlas** (*brilliancy*; prob. akin to the alt. of *138*, through the idea of *attractiveness*); the *moon*:—moon.

4583. **σεληνιάζομαι sĕlēniazŏmai**, *sel-ay-nee-ad'-zom-ahee*; mid. or pass. from a presumed der. of *4582*; to *be moon-struck*, i.e. *crazy*:—be lunatic.

4584. **Σεμεΐ Sĕmĕï**, *sem-eh-ee'*; of Heb. or. [8096]; *Semeï* (i.e. *Shimi*), an Isr.:—Semei.

4585. **σεμίδαλις sĕmidalis**, *sem-id'-al-is*; prob. of for. or.; fine wheaten *flour*:—fine flour.

4586. **σεμνός sĕmnŏs**, *sem-nos'*; from 4576; *venerable*, i.e. *honorable*:—grave, honest.

4587. **σεμνότης sĕmnŏtēs**, *sem-not'-ace*; from 4586; *venerableness*, i.e. *probity*:—gravity, honesty.

4588. **Σέργιος Sĕrgiŏs**, *serg'-ee-os*; of Lat. or.; *Sergius*, a Rom.:—Sergius.

4589. **Σήθ Sēth**, *sayth*; of Heb. or. [8352]; *Seth* (i.e. *Sheth*), a patriarch:—Seth.

4590. **Σήμ Sēm**, *same*; of Heb. or. [8035]; *Sem* (i.e. *Shem*), a patriarch:—Sem.

4591. **σημαίνω sēmainō**, *say-mah'ee-no*; from **σῆμα sēma** (a *mark*; of uncert. der.); to *indicate*:—signify.

4592. **σημεῖον sēmĕiŏn**, *say-mi'-on*; neut. of a presumed der. of the base of 4591; an *indication*, espec. cer. or supernat.:—miracle, sign, token, wonder.

4593. **σημειόω sēmĕiŏō**, *say-mi-ŏ'-o*; from 4592; to *distinguish*, i.e. *mark* (for avoidance):—note.

4594. **σήμερον sēmĕrŏn**, *say'-mer-on*; neut. (as adv.) of a presumed comp. of the art. 3588 (τ changed to σ) and 2250; on *the* (i.e. *this*) *day* (or *night* current or just passed); gen. *now* (i.e. at *present, hitherto*):—this (to-) day.

4595. **σήπω sēpō**, *say'-po*; appar. a prim. verb; to *putrefy*, i.e. (fig.) *perish*:—be corrupted.

4596. **σηρικός sērikŏs**, *say-ree-kos'*; from **Σήρ Sēr** (an Indian tribe from whom *silk* was procured; hence the name of the *silk-worm*); *Seric*, i.e. *silken* (neut. as noun, a *silky* fabric):—silk.

4597. **σής sēs**, *sace*; appar. of Heb. or. [5580]; a *moth*:—moth.

4598. **σητόβρωτος sētŏbrōtŏs**, *say-tob'-ro-tos*; from 4597 and a der. of 977; *moth-eaten*:—motheaten.

4599. **σθενόω sthĕnŏō**, *sthen-ŏ'-o*; from **σθένος sthĕnŏs** (bodily *vigor*; prob. akin to the base of 2476); to *strengthen*, i.e. (fig.) *confirm* (in spiritual knowledge and power):—strengthen.

4600. **σιαγών siagōn**, *see-ag-one'*; of uncert. der.; the *jaw*-bone, i.e. (by impl.) the *cheek* or side of the face:—cheek.

4601. **σιγάω sigaō**, *see-gah'-o*; from 4602; to *keep silent* (trans. or intrans.):—keep close (secret, silence), hold peace.

4602. **σιγή sigē**, *see-gay'*; appar. from **σίζω sizō** (to *hiss*, i.e. *hist* or *hush*); *silence*:—silence. Comp. 4623.

4603. **σιδήρεος sidērĕŏs**, *sid-ay'-reh-os*; from 4604; made *of iron*:—(of) iron.

4604. **σίδηρος sidērŏs**, *sid'-ay-ros*; of uncert. der.; *iron*:—iron.

4605. **Σιδών Sidōn**, *sid-one'*; of Heb. or. [6721]; *Sidon* (i.e. *Tsidon*), a place in Pal.:—Sidon.

4606. **Σιδώνιος Sidōniŏs**, *sid-o'-nee-os*; from 4605; a *Sidonian*, i.e. inhab. of Sidon:—of Sidon.

4607. **σικάριος sikariŏs**, *sik-ar'-ee-os*; of Lat. or.; a *dagger-man* or *assassin*; a *freebooter* (Jewish *fanatic* outlawed by the Romans):—murderer. Comp. 5406.

4608. **σίκερα sikĕra**, *sik'-er-ah*; of Heb. or. [7941]; an *intoxicant*, i.e. intensely fermented *liquor*:—strong drink.

4609. **Σίλας Silas**, *see'-las*; contr. for 4610; *Silas*, a Chr.:—Silas.

4610. **Σιλουανός Silŏuanŏs**, *sil-oo-an-os'*; of Lat. or.; "*silvan*"; *Silvanus*, a Chr.:—Silvanus. Comp. 4609.

4611. **Σιλωάμ Silōam**, *sil-o-am'*; of Heb. or. [7975]; *Siloäm* (i.e. *Shiloäch*), a pool of Jerus.:—Siloam.

4612. **σιμικίνθιον simikinthiŏn**, *sim-ee-kin'-thee-on*; of Lat. or.; a *semicinctium* or *half-girding*, i.e. narrow covering (*apron*):—apron.

4613. **Σίμων Simōn**, *see'-mone*; of Heb. or. [8095]; *Simon* (i.e. *Shimon*), the name of nine Isr.:—Simon. Comp. 4826.

4614. **Σινᾶ Sina**, *see-nah'*; of Heb. or. [5514]; *Sina* (i.e. *Sinai*), a mountain in Arabia:—Sina.

4615. **σίναπι sinapi**, *sin'-ap-ee*; perh. from **σίνομαι sinŏmai** (to *hurt*, i.e. *sting*); *mustard* (the plant):—mustard.

4616. **σινδών sindōn**, *sin-done'*; of uncert. (perh. for.) or.; *byssos*, i.e. bleached *linen* (the cloth or a garment of it):—(fine) linen (cloth).

4617. **σινιάζω siniazō**, *sin-ee-ad'-zo*; from **σινίον siniŏn** (a *sieve*); to *riddle* (fig.):—sift.

σῖτα sita. See 4621.

4618. **σιτευτός sitĕutŏs**, *sit-yoo-tos'*; from a der. of 4621; *grain-fed*, i.e. *fattened*:—fatted.

4619. **σιτιστός sitistŏs**, *sit-is-tos'*; from a der. of 4621; *grained*, i.e. *fatted*:—fatling.

4620. **σιτόμετρον sitŏmĕtrŏn**, *sit-om'-et-ron*; from 4621 and 3358; a *grain-measure*, i.e. (by impl.) *ration* (*allowance* of food):—portion of meat.

4621. **σῖτος sitŏs**, *see'-tos*; plur. irreg. neut.

σῖτα sita, *see'-tah*; of uncert. der.; *grain*, espec. *wheat*:—corn, wheat.

4622. **Σιών Siōn**, *see-own'*; of Heb. or. [6726]; *Sion* (i.e. *Tsijon*), a hill of Jerus.; fig. the *Church* (militant or triumphant):—Sion.

4623. **σιωπάω siōpaō**, *see-o-pah'-o*; from **σιωπή siōpē** (*silence*, i.e. a *hush*; prop. *muteness*, i.e. *involuntary* stillness, or *inability* to speak; and thus differing from 4602, which is rather a voluntary *refusal* or *indisposition* to speak, although the terms are often used synonymously); to *be dumb* (but not *deaf* also, like 2974 prop.); fig. to *be calm* (as *quiet* water):—dumb, (hold) peace.

4624. **σκανδαλίζω skandalizō**, *skan-dal-id'-zo* ("scandalize"); from 4625; to *entrap*, i.e. *trip* up (fig. *stumble* [trans.] or *entice* to sin, apostasy or displeasure):—(make to) offend.

4625. **σκάνδαλον skandalŏn**, *skan'-dal-on* ("scandal"); prob. from a der. of 2578; a *trap-stick* (*bent* sapling), i.e. *snare* (fig. *cause* of displeasure or sin):—occasion to fall (of stumbling), offence, thing that offends, stumblingblock.

4626. **σκάπτω skaptō**, *skap'-to*; appar. a prim. verb; to *dig*:—dig.

4627. **σκάφη skaphē**, *skaf'-ay*; a "*skiff*" (as if *dug* out), or *yawl* (carried aboard a large vessel for landing):—boat.

4628. **σκέλος skĕlŏs**, *skel'-os*; appar. from **σκέλλω skĕllō** (to *parch*; through the idea of *leanness*); the *leg* (as *lank*):—leg.

4629. **σκέπασμα skĕpasma**, *skep'-as-mah*; from a der. of **σκέπας skĕpas** (a *covering*; perh. akin to the base of 4649 through the idea of *noticeableness*); *clothing*:—raiment.

4630. **Σκευᾶς Skĕuas**, *skyoo-as'*; appar. of Lat. or.; *left-handed*; *Scevas* (i.e. *Scœvus*), an Isr.:—Sceva.

4631. **σκευή skĕuē**, *skyoo-ay'*; from 4632; *furniture*, i.e. spare *tackle*:—tackling.

4632. **σκεῦος skĕuŏs**, *skyoo'-os*; of uncert. affin.; a *vessel*, *implement*, *equipment* or *apparatus* (lit. or fig. [spec. a *wife* as contributing to the usefulness of the husband]):—goods, sail, stuff, vessel.

4633. **σκηνή skēnē**, *skay-nay'*; appar. akin to 4632 and 4639; a *tent* or cloth hut (lit. or fig.):—habitation, tabernacle.

4634. **σκηνοπηγία skēnŏpēgia**, *skay-nop-ayg-ee'-ah*; from 4636 and 4078; the *Festival of Tabernacles* (so called from the custom of erecting booths for temporary homes):—tabernacles.

4635. **σκηνοποιός skēnŏpŏiŏs**, *skay-nop-oy-os'*; from 4633 and 4160; a *manufacturer of tents*:—tentmaker.

4636. **σκῆνος skēnŏs**, *skay'-nos*; from 4633; a *hut* or temporary residence, i.e. (fig.) the human *body* (as the abode of the spirit):—tabernacle.

4637. **σκηνόω skēnŏō**, *skay-nŏ'-o*; from 4636; to *tent* or *encamp*, i.e. (fig.) to *occupy* (as a mansion) or (spec.) to *reside* (as God did in the Tabernacle of old, a symbol of protection and communion):—dwell.

4638. **σκήνωμα skēnōma**, *skay'-no-mah*; from 4637; an *encampment*, i.e. (fig.) the *Temple* (as God's residence), the *body* (as a tenement for the soul):—tabernacle.

4639. **σκία skia**, *skee'-ah*; appar. a prim. word; "*shade*" or a shadow (lit. or fig. [darkness of *error* or an *adumbration*]):—shadow.

4640. **σκιρτάω skirtaō**, *skeer-tah'-o*; akin to **σκαίρω skairō** (to *skip*); to *jump*, i.e. sympathetically *move* (as the *quickening* of a fœtus):—leap (for joy).

4641. **σκληροκαρδία sklērŏkardia**, *sklay-rok-ar-dee'-ah*; fem. of a comp. of 4642 and 2588; *hard-heartedness*, i.e. (spec.) *destitution of* (spiritual) *perception*:—hardness of heart.

4642. **σκληρός sklērŏs**, *sklay-ros'*; from the base of 4628; *dry*, i.e. *hard* or *tough* (fig. *harsh, severe*):—fierce, hard.

4643. **σκληρότης sklērŏtēs**, *sklay-rot'-ace*; from 4642; *callousness*, i.e. (fig.) *stubbornness*:—hardness.

4644. **σκληροτράχηλος sklērŏtrachēlŏs**, *sklay-rot-rakh'-ay-los*; from 4642 and 5137; *hard-naped*, i.e. (fig.) *obstinate*:—stiffnecked.

4645. **σκληρύνω sklērunō**, *sklay-roo'-no*; from 4642; to *indurate*, i.e. (fig.) *render stubborn*:—harden.

4646. **σκολιός skŏliŏs**, *skol-ee-os'*; from the base of 4628; *warped*, i.e. *winding*; fig. *perverse*:—crooked, froward, untoward.

4647. **σκόλοψ skŏlŏps**, *skol'-ops*; perh. from the base of 4628 and 3700; *withered* at the *front*, i.e. a *point* or *prickle* (fig. a bodily *annoyance* or *disability*):—thorn.

4648. **σκοπέω skŏpĕō**, *skop-eh'-o*; from 4649; to take *aim* at (*spy*), i.e. (fig.) *regard*:—consider, take heed, look at (on), mark. Comp. 3700.

4649. **σκοπός skŏpŏs**, *skop-os'* ("scope"); from **σκέπτομαι skĕptŏmai** (to *peer* about ["skeptic"]; perh. akin to 4626 through the idea of *concealment*; comp. 4629); a *watch* (*sentry* or *scout*), i.e. (by impl.) a *goal*:—mark.

4650. **σκορπίζω skŏrpizō**, *skor-pid'-zo*; appar. from the same as 4651 (through the idea of *penetrating*); to *dissipate*, i.e. (fig.) *put to flight, waste, be liberal*:—disperse abroad, scatter (abroad).

4651. **σκορπίος skŏrpiŏs**, *skor-pee'-os*; prob. from an obsol. **σκέρπω skĕrpō** (perh. strengthened from the base of 4649 and mean. to *pierce*); a "*scorpion*" (from its *sting*):—scorpion.

4652. **σκοτεινός skŏtĕinŏs**, *skot-i-nos'*; from 4655; *opaque*, i.e. (fig.) *benighted*:—dark, full of darkness.

4653. **σκοτία skŏtia**, *skot-ee'-ah*; from 4655; *dimness, obscurity* (lit. or fig.):—dark (-ness).

4654. **σκοτίζω skŏtizō**, *skot-id -zo*; from 4655; to *obscure* (lit. or fig.):—darken.

4655. **σκότος skŏtŏs**, *skot'-os*; from the base of 4639; *shadiness*, i.e. *obscurity* (lit. or fig.):—darkness.

4656. **σκοτόω skŏtŏō**, *skot-ŏ'-o*; from 4655; to *obscure* or *blind* (lit. or fig.):—be full of darkness.

4657. **σκύβαλον skubalŏn**, *skoo'-bal-on*; neut. of a presumed der. of 1519 and 2965 and 906; what is *thrown to the dogs*, i.e. *refuse* (*ordure*):—dung.

4658. **Σκύθης Skuthēs**, *skoo'-thace*; prob. of for. or.; a *Scythene* or *Scythian*, i.e. (by impl.) a *savage*:—Scythian.

4659. **σκυθρωπός skuthrōpŏs**, *skoo-thro-pos'*; from **σκυθρός skuthrŏs** (*sullen*) and a der. of 3700; *angry-visaged*, i.e. *gloomy* or affecting a *mournful* appearance:—of a sad countenance.

4660. **σκύλλω skullō**, *skool'-lo*; appar. a prim. verb; to *flay*, i.e. (fig.) to *harass*:—trouble (self).

4661. **σκῦλον skulŏn**, *skoo'-lon*; neut. from 4660; something *stripped* (as a *hide*), i.e. *booty*:—spoil.

4662. **σκωληκόβρωτος skōlēkŏbrōtŏs**, *sko-lay-kob'-ro-tos*; from 4663 and a der. of 977; *worm-eaten*, i.e. *diseased with maggots*:—eaten of worms.

4663. σκώληξ **skōlēx**, *sko'-lakes;* of uncert. der.; a *grub, maggot* or *earth-worm:*—worm.

4664. σμαράγδινος **smaragdinŏs**, *smar-ag'-dee-nos;* from 4665; consisting *of emerald:*—emerald.

4665. σμάραγδος **smaragdŏs**, *smar'-ag-dos;* of uncert. der.; the *emerald* or green gem so called:—emerald.

4666. σμύρνα **smurna**, *smoor'-nah;* appar. strengthened for 3464; *myrrh:*—myrrh.

4667. Σμύρνα **Smurna**, *smoor'-nah;* the same as 4666; *Smyrna*, a place in Asia Minor:—Smyrna.

4668. Σμυρναῖος **Smurnaiŏs**, *smoor-nah'-yos;* from 4667; a *Smyrnæan:*—in Smyrna.

4669. σμυρνίζω **smurnizō**, *smoor-nid'-zo;* from 4667; to *tincture with myrrh*, i.e. *embitter* (as a narcotic):—mingle with myrrh.

4670. Σόδομα **Sŏdŏma**, *sod'-om-ah;* plur. of Heb. or. [5467]; *Sodoma* (i.e. *Sedom*), a place in Pal.:—Sodom.

4671. σοί **sŏi**, *soy;* dat. of 4771; *to thee:*—thee, thine own, thou, thy.

4672. Σολομών or Σολομῶν **Sŏlŏmōn**, *sol-om-one';* of Heb. or. [8010]; *Solomon* (i.e. *Shelomoh*), the son of David:—Solomon.

4673. σορός **sŏrŏs**, *sor-os';* prob. akin to the base of 4987; a *funereal receptacle* (*urn, coffin*), i.e. (by anal.) a *bier:*—bier.

4674. σός **sŏs**, *sos;* from 4771; *thine:*—thine (own), thy (friend).

4675. σοῦ **sŏu**, *soo;* gen. of 4771; *of thee, thy:*—× home, thee, thine (own), thou, thy.

4676. σουδάριον **sŏudariŏn**, *soo-dar'-ee-on;* of Lat. or.; a *sudarium* (*sweat-cloth*), i.e. *towel* (for wiping the perspiration from the face, or binding the face of a corpse):—handkerchief, napkin.

4677. Σουσάννα **Sŏusanna**, *soo-san'-nah;* of Heb. or. [7799 fem.]; *lily; Susannah* (i.e. *Shoshannah*), an Israelitess:—Susanna.

4678. σοφία **sŏphia**, *sof-ee'-ah;* from 4680; *wisdom* (higher or lower, worldly or spiritual):—wisdom.

4679. σοφίζω **sŏphizō**, *sof-id'-zo;* from 4680; to *render wise;* in a sinister acceptation, to *form "sophisms"*, i.e. *continue plausible error:*—cunningly devised, make wise.

4680. σοφός **sŏphŏs**, *sof-os';* akin to σαφής **saphēs** (*clear*); *wise* (in a most gen. application):—wise. Comp. 5429.

4681. Σπανία **Spania**, *span-ee'-ah;* prob. of for. or.; *Spania*, a region of Europe:—Spain.

4682. σπαράσσω **sparassō**, *spar-as'-so;* prol. from σπαίρω **spairō** (to *gasp;* appar. strengthened from 4685 through the idea of *spasmodic* contraction); to *mangle*, i.e. *convulse* with epilepsy:—rend, tear.

4683. σπαργανόω **sparganŏō**, *spar-gan-ŏ'-o;* from σπάργανον **sparganŏn** (a *strip;* from a der. of the base of 4682 mean. to *strap* or *wrap* with strips); to *swathe* (an infant after the Oriental custom):—wrap in swaddling clothes.

4684. σπαταλάω **spatalaō**, *spat-al-ah'-o;* from σπατάλη **spatalē** (*luxury*); to *be voluptuous:*—live in pleasure, be wanton.

4685. σπάω **spaō**, *spah'-o;* a prim. verb; to *draw:*—draw (out).

4686. σπεῖρα **spĕira**, *spi'-rah;* of immed. Lat. or., but ultimately a der. of 138 in the sense of its cogn. 1507; a *coil* (*spira*, "spire"), i.e. (fig.) a *mass* of men (a Rom. military *cohort;* also [by anal.] a *squad* of Levitical janitors):—band.

4687. σπείρω **spĕirō**, *spi'-ro;* prob. strengthened from 4685 (through the idea of *extending*); to *scatter*, i.e. *sow* (lit. or fig.):—sow (-er), receive seed.

4688. σπεκουλάτωρ **spĕkŏulatōr**, *spek-oo-lat'-ore;* of Lat. or.; a *speculator*, i.e. military *scout* (*spy* or [by extens.] *life-guardsman*):—executioner.

4689. σπένδω **spĕndō**, *spen'-do;* appar. a prim. verb; to *pour* out as a libation, i.e. (fig.) to *devote* (one's life or blood, as a sacrifice) ("*spend*"):—(be ready to) be offered.

4690. σπέρμα **spĕrma**, *sper'-mah;* from 4687; something *sown*, i.e. *seed* (includ. the male "*sperm*"); by impl. *offspring;* spec. a *remnant* (fig. as if kept over for planting):—issue, seed.

4691. σπερμολόγος **spĕrmŏlŏgŏs**, *sper-mol-og'-os;* from 4690 and 3004; a *seed-picker* (as the crow), i.e. (fig.) a *sponger, loafer* (spec. a *gossip* or *trifler* in talk):—babbler.

4692. σπεύδω **spĕudō**, *spyoo'-do;* prob. strengthened from 4228; to "*speed*" ("study"), i.e. *urge* on (diligently or earnestly); by impl. to *await* eagerly:—(make, with) haste unto.

4693. σπήλαιον **spēlaiŏn**, *spay'-lah-yon;* neut. of a presumed der. of σπέος **spĕŏs** (a *grotto*); a *cavern;* by impl. a *hiding-place* or *resort:*—cave, den.

4694. σπιλάς **spilas**, *spee-las';* of uncert. der.; a *ledge* or *reef* of rock in the sea:—spot [*by confusion with* 4696].

4695. σπιλόω **spilŏō**, *spee-lŏ'-o;* from 4696; to *stain* or *soil* (lit. or fig.):—defile, spot.

4696. σπίλος **spilŏs**, *spee'-los;* of uncert. der.; a *stain* or *blemish*, i.e. (fig.) *defect, disgrace:*—spot.

4697. σπλαγχνίζομαι **splagchnizŏmai**, *splangkh-nid'-zom-ahee;* mid. from 4698; to have the *bowels* yearn, i.e. (fig.) *feel sympathy, to pity:*—have (be moved with) compassion.

4698. σπλάγχνον **splagchnŏn**, *splangkh'-non;* prob. strengthened from σπλήν **splēn** (the "*spleen*"); an *intestine* (plur.); fig. *pity* or *sympathy:*—bowels, inward affection, + tender mercy.

4699. σπόγγος **spŏggŏs**, *spong'-gos;* perh. of for. or.; a "*sponge*":—spunge.

4700. σποδός **spŏdŏs**, *spod-os';* of uncert. der.; *ashes:*—ashes.

4701. σπορά **spŏra**, *spor-ah';* from 4687; a *sowing*, i.e. (by impl.) *parentage:*—seed.

4702. σπόριμος **spŏrimŏs**, *spor'-ee-mos;* from 4703; *sown*, i.e. (neut. plur.) a planted *field:*—corn (-field).

4703. σπόρος **spŏrŏs**, *spor'-os;* from 4687; a *scattering* (of seed), i.e. (concr.) *seed* (as sown):—seed (× sown).

4704. σπουδάζω **spŏudazō**, *spoo-dad'-zo;* from 4710; to *use speed*, i.e. to *make effort, be prompt* or *earnest:*—do (give) diligence, be diligent (forward), endeavour, labour, study.

4705. σπουδαῖος **spŏudaiŏs**, *spoo-dah'-yos;* from 4710; *prompt, energetic, earnest:*—diligent.

4706. σπουδαιότερον **spŏudaiŏtĕrŏn**, *spoo-dah-yot'-er-on;* neut. of 4707 as adv.; *more earnestly* than others), i.e. very *promptly:*—very diligently.

4707. σπουδαιότερος **spŏudaiŏtĕrŏs**, *spoo-dah-yot'-er-os;* compar. of 4705; *more prompt, more earnest:*—more diligent (forward).

4708. σπουδαιοτέρως **spŏudaiŏtĕrōs**, *spoo-dah-yot-er'-oce;* adv. from 4707; *more speedily*, i.e. *sooner* than otherwise:—more carefully.

4709. σπουδαίως **spŏudaiōs**, *spoo-dah'-yoce;* adv. from 4705; *earnestly, promptly:*—diligently, instantly.

4710. σπουδή **spŏudē**, *spoo-day';* from 4692; "*speed*", i.e. (by impl.) *despatch, eagerness, earnestness:*—business, (earnest) care (-fulness), diligence, forwardness, haste.

4711. σπυρίς **spuris**, *spoo-rece';* from 4687 (as *woven*); a *hamper* or *lunch-receptacle:*—basket.

4712. στάδιον **stadiŏn**, *stad'-ee-on;* or masc. (in plur.) στάδιος **stadiŏs**, *stad'-ee-os;* from the base of 2476 (as *fixed*); a *stade* or certain measure of distance; by impl. a *stadium* or *race-course:*—furlong, race.

4713. στάμνος **stamnŏs**, *stam'-nos;* from the base of 2476 (as *stationary*); a *jar* or earthen *tank:*—pot.

4714. στάσις **stasis**, *stas'-is;* from the base of 2476; a *standing* (prop. the act), i.e. (by anal.) *position* (*existence*); by impl. a popular *uprising;* fig. *controversy:*—dissension, insurrection, × standing, uproar.

4715. στατήρ **statēr**, *stat-air';* from the base of 2476; a *stander* (*standard* of value), i.e. (spec.) a *stater* or certain coin:—piece of money.

4716. σταυρός **staurŏs**, *stŏw-ros';* from the base of 2476; a *stake* or *post* (as *set* upright), i.e. (spec.) a *pole* or *cross* (as an instrument of capital punishment); fig. *exposure to death*, i.e. *self-denial;* by impl. the *atonement* of Christ:—cross.

4717. σταυρόω **staurŏō**, *stŏw-rŏ'-o;* from 4716; to *impale* on the cross; fig. to *extinguish* (*subdue*) passion or selfishness:—crucify.

4718. σταφυλή **staphulē**, *staf-oo-lay';* prob. from the base of 4735; a *cluster* of grapes (as if *intertwined*):—grapes.

4719. στάχυς **stachus**, *stakh'-oos;* from the base of 2476; a *head* of grain (as *standing* out from the stalk):—ear (of corn).

4720. Στάχυς **Stachus**, *stakh'-oos;* the same as 4719; *Stachys*, a Chr.:—Stachys.

4721. στέγη **stĕgē**, *steg'-ay;* strengthened from a prim. τέγος **tĕgŏs** (a "*thatch*" or "*deck*" of a building); a *roof:*—roof.

4722. στέγω **stĕgō**, *steg'-o;* from 4721; to *roof* over, i.e. (fig.) to *cover* with silence (*endure* patiently):—(for-) bear, suffer.

4723. στεῖρος **stĕirŏs**, *sti'-ros;* a contr. from 4731 (as *stiff* and *unnatural*); "*sterile*":—barren.

4724. στέλλω **stĕllō**, *stel'-lo;* prob. strengthened from the base of 2476; prop. to *set* fast ("*stall*"), i.e. (fig.) to *repress* (reflex. *abstain* from associating with):—avoid, withdraw self.

4725. στέμμα **stĕmma**, *stem'-mah;* from the base of 4735; a *wreath* for show:—garland.

4726. στεναγμός **stĕnagmŏs**, *sten-ag-mos';* from 4727; a *sigh:*—groaning.

4727. στενάζω **stĕnazō**, *sten-ad'-zo;* from 4728; to *make* (intrans. *be*) *in straits*, i.e. (by impl.) to *sigh, murmur, pray* inaudibly:—with grief, groan, grudge, sigh.

4728. στενός **stĕnŏs**, *sten-os';* prob. from the base of 2476; *narrow* (from obstacles *standing* close about):—strait.

4729. στενοχωρέω **stĕnŏchōrĕō**, *sten-okh-o-reh'-o;* from the same as 4730; to *hem* in closely, i.e. (fig.) *cramp:*—distress, straiten.

4730. στενοχωρία **stĕnŏchōria**, *sten-okh-o-ree'-ah;* from a comp. of 4728 and 5561; *narrowness of room*, i.e. (fig.) *calamity:*—anguish, distress.

4731. στερεός **stĕrĕŏs**, *ster-eh-os';* from 2476; *stiff*, i.e. *solid, stable* (lit. or fig.):—stedfast, strong, sure.

4732. στερεόω **stĕrĕŏō**, *ster-eh-ŏ'-o;* from 4731; to *solidify*, i.e. *confirm* (lit. or fig.):—establish, receive strength, make strong.

4733. στερέωμα **stĕrĕōma**, *ster-eh'-o-mah;* from 4732; something *established*, i.e. (abstr.) *confirmation* (*stability*):—stedfastness.

4734. Στεφανᾶς **Stĕphanas**, *stef-an-as';* prob. contr. for στεφανωτός **stĕphanōtŏs** (*crowned;* from 4737); *Stephanas*, a Chr.:—Stephanas.

4735. στέφανος **stĕphanŏs**, *stef'-an-os;* from an appar. prim. στέφω **stĕphō** (to *twine* or *wreathe*); a *chaplet* (as a badge of royalty, a prize in the public games or a symbol of honor gen.; but more conspicuous and elaborate than the simple *fillet*, 1238), lit. or fig.:—crown.

4736. Στέφανος **Stĕphanŏs**, *stef'-an-os;* the same as 4735; *Stephanus*, a Chr.:—Stephen.

4737. στεφανόω **stephanŏō**, *stef-an-ŏ'-o;* from 4735; to *adorn with* an honorary *wreath* (lit. or fig.):—crown.

4738. στῆθος **stēthŏs**, *stay'-thos;* from 2476 (as *standing* prominently); the (entire extern.) *bosom*, i.e. *chest:*—breast.

4739. στήκω **stēkō**, *stay'-ko;* from the perf. tense of 2476; to *be stationary*, i.e. (fig.) to *persevere:*—stand (fast).

4740. στηριγμός **stērigmŏs**, *stay-rig-mos';* from 4741; *stability* (fig.):—stedfastness.

4741. **στηρίζω stērizō**, *stay-rid'-zo;* from a presumed der. of *2476* (like *4731*); to *set fast*, i.e. (lit.) to *turn resolutely* in a certain direction, or (fig.) to *confirm:*—fix, (e-) stablish, stedfastly set, strengthen.

4742. **στίγμα stigma**, *stig'-mah;* from a prim. **στίζω stizō** (to "*stick*", i.e. *prick*); a *mark* incised or punched (for recognition of ownership), i.e. (fig.) *scar* of service:—mark.

4743. **στιγμή stigmē**, *stig-may';* fem. of *4742;* a *point* of time, i.e. an *instant:*—moment.

4744. **στίλβω stilbō**, *stil'-bo;* appar. a prim. verb; to *gleam*, i.e. *flash* intensely:—shining.

4745. **στοά stŏa**, *stŏ-ah';* prob. from *2476;* a *colonnade* or interior *piazza:*—porch.

4746. **στοιβάς stŏibas**, *stoy-bas';* from a prim. **στείβω stĕibō** (to "*step*" or "*stamp*"); a *spread* (as if *tramped* flat) of loose materials for a couch, i.e. (by impl.) a *bough* of a tree so employed:—branch.

4747. **στοιχεῖον stŏichĕiŏn**, *stoy-khi'-on;* neut. of a presumed der. of the base of *4748;* something *orderly* in arrangement, i.e. (by impl.) a *serial* (*basal, fundamental, initial*) constituent (lit.), proposition (fig.):—element, principle, rudiment.

4748. **στοιχέω stŏichĕō**, *stoy-kheh'-o;* from a der. of **στείχω stĕichō** (to *range* in regular line); to *march* in (military) rank (*keep step*), i.e. (fig.) to *conform* to virtue and piety:—walk (orderly).

4749. **στολή stŏlē**, *stol-ay';* from *4724;* *equipment*, i.e. (spec.) a "*stole*" or long-fitting *gown* (as a mark of dignity):—long clothing (garment), (long) robe.

4750. **στόμα stŏma**, *stom'-a;* prob. strengthened from a presumed der. of the base of *5114;* the *mouth* (as if a *gash* in the face); by impl. *language* (and its relations); fig. an *opening* (in the earth); spec. the *front* or *edge* (of a weapon):—edge, face, mouth.

4751. **στόμαχος stŏmachŏs**, *stom'-akh-os;* from *4750;* an *orifice* (the *gullet*), i.e. (spec.) the "*stomach*":—stomach.

4752. **στρατεία stratĕia**, *strat-i'-ah;* from *4754;* military *service*, i.e. (fig.) the apostolic *career* (as one of hardship and danger):—warfare.

4753. **στράτευμα stratĕuma**, *strat'-yoo-mah;* from *4754;* an *armament*, i.e. (by impl.) a body of *troops* (more or less extensive or systematic):—army, soldier, man of war.

4754. **στρατεύομαι stratĕuŏmai**, *strat-yoo'-om-ahee;* mid. from the base of *4756;* to *serve* in a military campaign; fig. to *execute the apostolate* (with its arduous duties and functions), to *contend* with carnal inclinations:—soldier, (go to) war (-fare).

4755. **στρατηγός stratēgŏs**, *strat-ay-gos';* from the base of *4756* and *71* or *2233;* a *general*, i.e. (by impl. or anal.) a (military) *governor* (*prœtor*), the *chief* (*prœfect*) of the (Levitical) temple-wardens:—captain, magistrate.

4756. **στρατία stratia**, *strat-ee'-ah;* fem. of a der. of **στρατός stratŏs** (an *army;* from the base of *4766*, as *encamped*); *camp-likeness*, i.e. an *army*, i.e. (fig.) the *angels*, the celestial *luminaries:*—host.

4757. **στρατιώτης stratiōtēs**, *strat-ee-o'-tace;* from a presumed der. of the same as *4756;* a *camper-out*, i.e. a (common) *warrior* (lit. or fig.):—soldier.

4758. **στρατολογέω stratŏlŏgĕō**, *strat-ol-og-eh'-o;* from a comp. of the base of *4756* and *3004* (in its orig. sense); to *gather* (or *select*) as a *warrior*, i.e. *enlist* in the army:—choose to be a soldier.

4759. **στρατοπεδάρχης stratŏpĕdarchēs**, *strat-op-ed-ar'-khace;* from *4760* and *757;* a *ruler of an army*, i.e. (spec.) a Prætorian *prœfect:*—captain of the guard.

4760. **στρατόπεδον stratŏpĕdŏn**, *strat-op'-ed-on;* from the base of *4756* and the same as *3977;* a *camping-ground*, i.e. (by impl.) a body of *troops:*—army.

4761. **στρεβλόω strĕblŏō**, *streb-lŏ'-o;* from a der. of *4762;* to *wrench*, i.e. (spec.) to *torture* (by the rack), but only fig. to *pervert:*—wrest.

4762. **στρέφω strĕphō**, *stref'-o;* strengthened from the base of *5157;* to *twist*, i.e. *turn* quite around or *reverse* (lit. or fig.):—convert, turn (again, back again, self, self about).

4763. **στρηνιάω strēniaō**, *stray-nee-ah'-o;* from a presumed der. of *4764;* to *be luxurious:*—live deliciously.

4764. **στρῆνος strēnŏs**, *stray'-nos;* akin to *4731;* a "*straining*", "*strenuousness*" or "strength", i.e. (fig.) *luxury* (*voluptuousness*):—delicacy.

4765. **στρουθίον strŏuthiŏn**, *stroo-thee'-on;* dimin. of **στρουθός strŏuthŏs** (a *sparrow*); a *little sparrow:*—sparrow.

4766. **στρώννυμι strōnnumi**, *strone'-noo-mee;* or simpler **στρωννύω strōnnuō**, *strone-noo'-o;* prol. from a still simpler **στρόω strŏō**, *strŏ'-o* (used only as an alt. in certain tenses); prob. akin to *4731* through the idea of *positing*); to "*strew*", i.e. *spread* (as a carpet or couch):—make bed, furnish, spread, strew.

4767. **στυγνητός stugnētŏs**, *stoog-nay-tos';* from a der. of an obsol. appar. prim. **στύγω stugō** (to *hate*); *hated*, i.e. *odious:*—hateful.

4768. **στυγνάζω stugnazō**, *stoog-nad'-zo;* from the same as *4767;* to *render gloomy*, i.e. (by impl.) *glower* (*be overcast* with clouds, or *sombreness* of speech):—lower, be sad.

4769. **στῦλος stulŏs**, *stoo'-los;* from **στύω stuō** (to *stiffen;* prop. akin to the base of *2476*); a *post* ("*style*"), i.e. (fig.) *support:*—pillar.

4770. **Στωϊκός Stōïkŏs**, *sto-ik-os';* from *4745;* a "*Stoïc*" (as occupying a particular porch in Athens), i.e. adherent of a certain philosophy:—Stoick.

4771. **σύ su**, *soo;* the pers. pron. of the sec. pers. sing.; *thou:*—thou. See also *4571, 4671, 4675;* and for the plur. *5209, 5210, 5213, 5216.*

4772. **συγγένεια suggĕnĕia**, *soong-ghen'-i-ah;* from *4773;* *relationship*, i.e. (concr.) *relatives:*—kindred.

4773. **συγγενής suggĕnēs**, *soong-ghen-ace';* from *4862* and *1085;* a *relative* (by blood); by extens. a fellow *countryman:*—cousin, kin (-sfolk, -sman).

4774. **συγγνώμη suggnōmē**, *soong-gno'-may;* from a comp. of *4862* and *1097;* *fellow knowledge*, i.e. *concession:*—permission.

4775. **συγκάθημαι sugkathēmai**, *soong-kath'-ay-mahee;* from *4862* and *2521;* to *seat oneself* in company *with:*—sit with.

4776. **συγκαθίζω sugkathizō**, *soong-kath-id'-zo;* from *4862* and *2523;* to *give* (or *take*) *a seat* in company *with:*—(make) sit (down) together.

4777. **συγκακοπαθέω sugkakŏpathĕō**, *soong-kak-op-ath-eh'-o;* from *4862* and *2553;* to *suffer hardship* in company *with:*—be partaker of afflictions.

4778. **συγκακουχέω sugkakŏuchĕō**, *soong-kak-oo-kheh'-o;* from *4862* and *2558;* to *maltreat* in company *with*, i.e. (pass.) *endure persecution together:*—suffer affliction with.

4779. **συγκαλέω sugkalĕō**, *soong-kal-eh'-o;* from *4862* and *2564;* to *convoke:*—call together.

4780. **συγκαλύπτω sugkaluptō**, *soong-kal-oop'-to;* from *4862* and *2572;* to *conceal altogether:*—cover.

4781. **συγκάμπτω sugkamptō**, *soong-kamp'-to;* from *4862* and *2578;* to *bend together*, i.e. (fig.) to *afflict:*—bow down.

4782. **συγκαταβαίνω sugkatabainō**, *soong-kat-ab-ah'ee-no;* from *4862* and *2597;* to *descend* in company *with:*—go down with.

4783. **συγκατάθεσις sugkatathĕsis**, *soong-kat-ath'-es-is;* from *4784;* a *deposition* (of sentiment) in company *with*, i.e. (fig.) *accord* with:—agreement.

4784. **συγκατατίθεμαι sugkatatithĕmai**, *soong-kat-at-ith'-em-ahee;* mid. from *4862* and *2698;* to *deposit* (one's vote or opinion) in company *with*, i.e. (fig.) to *accord* with:—consent.

4785. **συγκαταψηφίζω sugkatapsēphizō**, *soong-kat-aps-ay-fid'-zo;* from *4862* and a comp. of *2596* and *5585;* to *count down* in company *with*, i.e. *enroll among:*—number with.

4786. **συγκεράννυμι sugkĕrannumi**, *soong-ker-an'-noo-mee;* from *4862* and *2767;* to *commingle*, i.e. (fig.) to *combine* or *assimilate:*—mix with, temper together.

4787. **συγκινέω sugkinĕō**, *soong-kin-eh'-o;* from *4862* and *2795;* to *move together*, i.e. (spec.) to *excite* as a mass (to sedition):—stir up.

4788. **συγκλείω sugklĕiō**, *soong-kli'-o;* from *4862* and *2808;* to *shut together*, i.e. *include* or (fig.) *embrace* in a common subjection to:—conclude, inclose, shut up.

4789. **συγκληρονόμος sugklērŏnŏmŏs**, *soong-klay-ron-om'-os;* from *4862* and *2818;* a *co-heir*, i.e. (by anal.) *participant in common:*—fellow (joint) -heir, heir together, heir with.

4790. **συγκοινωνέω sugkŏinōnĕō**, *soong-koy-no-neh'-o;* from *4862* and *2841;* to *share* in company *with*, i.e. *co-participate* in:—communicate (have fellowship) with, be partaker of.

4791. **συγκοινωνός sugkŏinōnŏs**, *soong-koy-no-nos';* from *4862* and *2844;* a *co-participant:*—companion, partake (-r, -r with).

4792. **συγκομίζω sugkŏmizō**, *soong-kom-id'-zo;* from *4862* and *2865;* to *convey together*, i.e. *collect* or *bear* away in company *with* others:—carry.

4793. **συγκρίνω sugkrinō**, *soong-kree'-no;* from *4862* and *2919;* to *judge* of one thing in connection *with* another, i.e. *combine* (spiritual ideas with appropriate expressions) or *collate* (one person with another by way of contrast or resemblance):—compare among (with).

4794. **συγκύπτω sugkuptō**, *soong-koop'-to;* from *4862* and *2955;* to *stoop altogether*, i.e. *be completely overcome* by:—bow together.

4795. **συγκυρία sugkuria**, *soong-koo-ree'-ah;* from a comp. of *4862* and **κυρέω kurĕō** (to *light* or *happen;* from the base of *2962*); *concurrence*, i.e. *accident:*—chance.

4796. **συγχαίρω sugchairō**, *soong-khah'ee-ro;* from *4862* and *5463;* to *sympathize in gladness*, *congratulate:*—rejoice in (with).

4797. **συγχέω sugchĕō**, *soong-kheh'-o;* or **συγχύνω sugchunō**, *soong-khoo'-no;* from *4862* and **χέω chĕō** (to *pour*) or its alt.; to *commingle* promiscuously, i.e. (fig.) to *throw* (an assembly) *into disorder*, to *perplex* (the mind):—confound, confuse, stir up, be in an uproar.

4798. **συγχράομαι sugchraŏmai**, *soong-khrah'-om-ahee;* from *4862* and *5530;* to *use jointly*, i.e. (by impl.) to *hold intercourse in common:*—have dealings with.

4799. **σύγχυσις sugchusis**, *soong'-khoo-sis;* from *4797;* *commixture*, i.e. (fig.) riotous *disturbance:*—confusion.

4800. **συζάω suzaō**, *sood-zah'-o;* from *4862* and *2198;* to continue to *live* in common *with*, i.e. *co-survive* (lit. or fig.):—live with.

4801. **συζεύγνυμι suzĕugnumi**, *sood-zyoog'-noo-mee;* from *4862* and the base of *2201;* to *yoke together*, i.e. (fig.) *conjoin* (in marriage):—join together.

4802. **συζητέω suzētĕō**, *sood-zay-teh'-o;* from *4862* and *2212;* to investigate *jointly*, i.e. *discuss, controvert, cavil:*—dispute (with), enquire, question (with), reason (together).

4803. **συζήτησις suzētēsis**, *sood-zay'-tay-sis;* from *4802;* *mutual questioning*, i.e. *discussion:*—disputation (-ting), reasoning.

4804. **συζητητής suzētētēs**, *sood-zay-tay-tace';* from *4802;* a *disputant*, i.e. *sophist:*—disputer.

4805. **σύζυγος suzugŏs**, *sood'-zoo-gos;* from *4801;* *co-yoked*, i.e. (fig.) as noun, a *colleague;* prob. rather as prop. name; *Syzygus*, a Chr.:—yokefellow.

4806. **συζωοποιέω suzōŏpŏiĕō**, *sood-zo-op-oy-eh'-o;* from *4862* and *2227;* to *reanimate conjointly* with (fig.):—quicken together with.

4807. **συκάμινος sukaminŏs**, *soo-kam'-ee-nos;* of Heb. or. [8256] in imitation of *4809;* a *sycamore-fig* tree:—sycamine tree.

4808. **συκῆ sukē**, *soo-kay';* from *4810;* a *fig-tree:*—fig tree.

4809. **συκομωραία sukŏmōraia**, *soo-kom-o-rah'-yah;* from *4810* and **μόρον mōrŏn** (the *mul-*

berry); the "*sycamore*"-fig tree:—sycamore tree. Comp. *4807*.

4810. **σῦκον sukŏn**, *soo'-kon;* appar. a prim. word; a *fig:*—fig.

4811. **συκοφαντέω sukŏphantĕō**, *soo-kof-an-teh'-o;* from a comp. of *4810* and a der. of *5316;* to *be a fig-informer* (reporter of the law forbidding the exportation of figs from Greece), "*sycophant*", i.e. (gen. and by extens.) to *defraud* (*exact* unlawfully, *extort*):—accuse falsely, take by false accusation.

4812. **συλαγωγέω sulagōgĕō**, *soo-lag-ogue-eh'-o;* from the base of *4813* and (the redupl. form of) *71;* to *lead* away as *booty*, i.e. (fig.) *seduce:*—spoil.

4813. **συλάω sulaō**, *soo-lah'-o;* from a der. of **σύλλω sullō** (to *strip;* prob. akin to *138;* comp. *4661*); to *despoil:*—rob.

4814. **συλλαλέω sullalĕō**, *sool-lal-eh'-o;* from *4862* and *2980;* to *talk together*, i.e. *converse:*—commune (confer, talk) with, speak among.

4815. **συλλαμβάνω sullambanō**, *sool-lam-ban'-o;* from *4862* and *2983;* to *clasp*, i.e. *seize* (*arrest, capture*); spec. to *conceive* (lit. or fig.); by impl. to *aid:*—catch, conceive, help, take.

4816. **συλλέγω sullĕgō**, *sool-leg'-o;* from *4862* and *3004* in its orig. sense; to *collect:*—gather (together, up).

4817. **συλλογίζομαι sullŏgizŏmai**, *sool-log-id'-zom-ahee;* from *4862* and *3049;* to *reckon together* (with oneself), i.e. *deliberate:*—reason with.

4818. **συλλυπέω sullupĕō**, *sool-loop-eh'-o;* from *4862* and *3076;* to *afflict jointly*, i.e. (pass.) *sorrow at* (on account of) some one:—be grieved.

4819. **συμβαίνω sumbainō**, *soom-bah'ee-no;* from *4862* and the base of *939;* to *walk* (fig. *transpire*) *together*, i.e. *concur* (*take place*):—be (-fall), happen (unto).

4820. **συμβάλλω sumballō**, *soom-bal'-lo;* from *4862* and *906;* to *combine*, i.e. (in speaking) to *converse, consult, dispute*, (mentally) to *consider*, (by impl.) to *aid*, (personally) to *join, attack:*—confer, encounter, help, make, meet with, ponder.

4821. **συμβασιλεύω sumbasilĕuō**, *soom-bas-il-yoo'-o;* from *4862* and *936;* to *be co-regent* (fig.):—reign with.

4822. **συμβιβάζω sumbibazō**, *soom-bib-ad'-zo;* from *4862* and **βιβάζω bibazō** (to *force;* caus. [by redupl.] of the base of *939*); to *drive together*, i.e. *unite* (in association or affection), (mentally) to *infer, show, teach:*—compact, assuredly gather, instruct, knit together, prove.

4823. **συμβουλεύω sumbŏulĕuō**, *soom-bool-yoo'-o;* from *4862* and *1011;* to *give* (or *take*) *advice jointly*, i.e. *recommend, deliberate* or *determine:*—consult, (give, take) counsel (together).

4824. **συμβούλιον sumbŏuliŏn**, *soom-boo'-lee-on;* neut. of a presumed der. of *4825;* *advisement;* spec. a *deliberative* body, i.e. the provincial *assessors* or lay-court:—consultation, counsel, council.

4825. **σύμβουλος sumbŏulŏs**, *soom'-boo-los;* from *4862* and *1012;* a *consultor*, i.e. *adviser:*—counsellor.

4826. **Συμεών Sumĕōn**, *soom-eh-one';* from the same as *4613;* *Symeon* (i.e. *Shimon*), the name of five Isr.:—Simeon, Simon.

4827. **συμμαθητής summathētēs**, *soom-math-ay-tace';* from a comp. of *4862* and *3129;* a *co-learner* (of Christianity):—fellowdisciple.

4828. **συμμαρτυρέω summarturĕō**, *soom-mar-too-reh'-o;* from *4862* and *3140;* to *testify jointly*, i.e. *corroborate* by (concurrent) evidence:—testify unto, (also) bear witness (with).

4829. **συμμερίζομαι summĕrizŏmai**, *soom-mer-id'-zom-ahee;* mid. from *4862* and *3307;* to *share jointly*, i.e. *participate* in:—be partaker with.

4830. **συμμέτοχος summĕtŏchŏs**, *soom-met'-okh-os;* from *4862* and *3353;* a *co-participant:*—partaker.

4831. **συμμιμητής summimētēs**, *soom-mim-ay-tace';* from a presumed comp. of *4862* and *3401;* a *co-imitator*, i.e. *fellow votary:*—follower together.

4832. **σύμμορφός summŏrphŏs**, *soom-mor-fos';* from *4862* and *3444;* *jointly formed*, i.e. (fig.) *similar:*—conformed to, fashioned like unto.

4833. **συμμορφόω summŏrphŏō**, *soom-mor-fŏ'-o;* from *4832;* to *render like*, i.e. (fig.) to *assimilate:*—make conformable unto.

4834. **συμπαθέω sumpathĕō**, *soom-path-eh'-o;* from *4835;* to *feel* "*sympathy*" with, i.e. (by impl.) to *commiserate:*—have compassion, be touched with a feeling of.

4835. **συμπαθής sumpathēs**, *soom-path-ace';* from *4841;* *having a fellow-feeling* ("*sympathetic*"), i.e. (by impl.) *mutually commiserative:*—having compassion one of another.

4836. **συμπαραγίνομαι sumparaginŏmai**, *soom-par-ag-in'-om-ahee;* from *4862* and *3854;* to *be present together*, i.e. to *convene;* by impl. to *appear in aid:*—come together, stand with.

4837. **συμπαρακαλέω sumparakalĕō**, *soom-par-ak-al-eh'-o;* from *4862* and *3870;* to *console jointly:*—comfort together.

4838. **συμπαραλαμβάνω sumparalambanō**, *soom-par-al-am-ban'-o;* from *4862* and *3880;* to *take along in company:*—take with.

4839. **συμπαραμένω sumparamĕnō**, *soom-par-am-en'-o;* from *4862* and *3887;* to *remain in company*, i.e. *still live:*—continue with.

4840. **συμπάρειμι sumparĕimi**, *soom-par'-i-mee;* from *4862* and *3918;* to *be at hand together*, i.e. *now present:*—be here present with.

4841. **συμπάσχω sumpaschō**, *soom-pas'-kho;* from *4862* and *3958* (includ. its alt.); to *experience pain jointly* or of the *same kind* (spec. *persecution;* to "*sympathize*"):—suffer with.

4842. **συμπέμπω sumpĕmpō**, *soom-pem'-po;* from *4862* and *3992;* to *despatch in company:*—send with.

4843. **συμπεριλαμβάνω sumpĕrilambanō**, *soom-per-ee-lam-ban'-o;* from *4862* and a comp. of *4012* and *2983;* to *take by inclosing altogether*, i.e. *earnestly throw the arms about one:*—embrace.

4844. **συμπίνω sumpinō**, *soom-pee'-no;* from *4862* and *4095;* to *partake a beverage in company:*—drink with.

4845. **συμπληρόω sumplērŏō**, *soom-play-rŏ'-o;* from *4862* and *4137;* to *implenish completely*, i.e. (of space) to *swamp* (a boat), or (of time) to *accomplish* (pass. *be complete*):—(fully) come, fill up.

4846. **συμπνίγω sumpnigō**, *soom-pnee'-go;* from *4862* and *4155;* to *strangle completely*, i.e. (lit.) to *drown*, or (fig.) to *crowd:*—choke, throng.

4847. **συμπολίτης sumpŏlitēs**, *soom-pol-ee'-tace;* from *4862* and *4177;* *a native of the same town*, i.e. (fig.) *co-religionist* (*fellow-Christian*):—fellow-citizen.

4848. **συμπορεύομαι sumpŏrĕuŏmai**, *soom-por-yoo'-om-ahee;* from *4862* and *4198;* to *journey together;* by impl. to *assemble:*—go with, resort.

4849. **συμπόσιον sumpŏsiŏn**, *soom-pos'-ee-on;* neut. of a der. of the alt. of *4844;* a *drinking*-party ("*symposium*"), i.e. (by extens.) a *room* of guests:—company.

4850. **συμπρεσβύτερος sumprĕsbutĕrŏs**, *soom-pres-boo'-ter-os;* from *4862* and *4245;* a *co-presbyter:*—presbyter, also an elder.

συμφάγω sumphagō. See *4906*.

4851. **συμφέρω sumphĕrō**, *soom-fer'-o;* from *4862* and *5342* (includ. its alt.); to *bear together* (*contribute*), i.e. (lit.) to *collect*, or (fig.) to *conduce;* espec. (neut. part. as noun) *advantage:*—be better for, bring together, be expedient (for), be good, (be) profit (-able for).

4852. **σύμφημι sumphēmi**, *soom'-fay-mee;* from *4862* and *5346;* to *say jointly*, i.e. *assent to:*—consent unto.

4853. **συμφυλέτης sumphulĕtēs**, *soom-foo-let'-ace;* from *4862* and a der. of *5443;* a *co-tribesman*, i.e. *native of the same country:*—countryman.

4854. **σύμφυτος sumphutŏs**, *soom'-foo-tos;* from *4862* and a der. of *5453;* *grown* along *with* (*connate*), i.e. (fig.) closely *united* to:—planted together.

4855. **συμφύω sumphuō**, *soom-foo'-o;* from *4862* and *5453;* pass. to *grow jointly:*—spring up with.

4856. **συμφωνέω sumphōnĕō**, *soom-fo-neh'-o;* from *4859;* to be *harmonious*, i.e. (fig.) to *accord* (*be suitable, concur*) or *stipulate* (by compact):—agree (together, with).

4857. **συμφώνησις sumphōnēsis**, *soom-fo'-nay-sis;* from *4856;* *accordance:*—concord.

4858. **συμφωνία sumphōnia**, *soom-fo-nee'-ah;* from *4859;* *unison* of sound ("*symphony*"), i.e. a *concert* of instruments (harmonious *note*):—music.

4859. **σύμφωνος sumphōnŏs**, *soom'-fo-nos;* from *4862* and *5456;* *sounding together* (*alike*), i.e. (fig.) *accordant* (neut. as noun, *agreement*):—consent.

4860. **συμψηφίζω sumpsēphizō**, *soom-psay-fid'-zo;* from *4862* and *5585;* to *compute jointly:*—reckon.

4861. **σύμψυχος sumpsuchŏs**, *soom'-psoo-khos;* from *4862* and *5590;* *co-spirited*, i.e. *similar in sentiment:*—like-minded.

4862. **σύν sun**, *soon;* a prim. prep. denoting *union;* *with* or *together* (but much closer than *3326* or *3844*), i.e. by association, companionship, process, resemblance, possession, instrumentality, addition etc.:—beside, with. In comp. it has similar applications, includ. *completeness*.

4863. **συνάγω sunagō**, *soon-ag'-o;* from *4862* and *71;* to *lead together*, i.e. *collect* or *convene;* spec. to *entertain* (hospitably):— + accompany, assemble (selves, together), bestow, come together, gather (selves together, up, together), lead into, resort, take in.

4864. **συναγωγή sunagōgē**, *soon-ag-o-gay';* from (the redupl. form of) *4863;* an *assemblage* of persons; spec. a Jewish "*synagogue*" (the meeting or the place); by anal. a Christian *church:*—assembly, congregation, synagogue.

4865. **συναγωνίζομαι sunagōnizŏmai**, *soon-ag-o-nid'-zom-ahee;* from *4862* and *75;* to *struggle* in company *with*, i.e. (fig.) to *be a partner* (*assistant*):—strive together with.

4866. **συναθλέω sunathlĕō**, *soon-ath-leh'-o;* from *4862* and *118;* to *wrestle* in company *with*, i.e. (fig.) to *seek jointly:*—labour with, strive together for.

4867. **συναθροίζω sunathrŏizō**, *soon-ath-royd'-zo;* from *4862* and **ἀθροίζω athrŏizō** (to *hoard*); to *convene:*—call (gather) together.

4868. **συναίρω sunairō**, *soon-ah'ee-ro;* from *4862* and *142;* to *make up together*, i.e. (fig.) to *compute* (an account):—reckon, take.

4869. **συναιχμάλωτος sunaichmalōtŏs**, *soon-aheekh-mal'-o-tos;* from *4862* and *164;* a *co-captive:*—fellowprisoner.

4870. **συνακολουθέω sunakŏlŏuthĕō**, *soon-ak-ol-oo-theh'-o;* from *4862* and *190;* to *accompany:*—follow.

4871. **συναλίζω sunalizō**, *soon-al-id'-zo;* from *4862* and **ἁλίζω halizō** (to *throng*); to *accumulate*, i.e. *convene:*—assemble together.

4872. **συναναβαίνω sunanabainō**, *soon-an-ab-ah'ee-no;* from *4862* and *305;* to *ascend* in company *with:*—come up with.

4873. **συνανάκειμαι sunanakĕimai**, *soon-an-ak'-i-mahee;* from *4862* and *345;* to *recline* in company *with* (at a meal):—sit (down, at the table, together) with (at meat).

4874. **συναναμίγνυμι sunanamignumi**, *soon-an-am-ig'-noo-mee;* from *4862* and a comp. of *303* and *3396;* to *mix up together*, i.e. (fig.) *associate with:*—(have, keep) company (with).

4875. **συναναπαύομαι sunanapauŏmai**, *soon-an-ap-ŏw'-om-ahee;* mid. from *4862* and *373;* to *recruit oneself* in company *with:*—refresh with.

4876. **συναντάω sunantaō**, *soon-an-tah'-o;* from *4862* and a der. of *473;* to *meet with;* fig. to *occur:*—befall, meet.

4877. **συνάντησις sunantēsis**, *soon-an'-tay-sis;* from *4876*; a *meeting with:*—meet.

4878. **συναντιλαμβάνομαι sunantilambanŏmai**, *soon-an-tee-lam-ban'-om-ahee;* from *4862* and *482*; to *take* hold of *opposite together*, i.e. *co-operate* (*assist*):—help.

4879. **συναπάγω sunapagō**, *soon-ap-ag'-o;* from *4862* and *520*; to *take off together*, i.e. *transport with* (*seduce*, pass. *yield*):—carry (lead) away with, condescend.

4880. **συναποθνήσκω sunapŏthnēskō**, *soon-ap-oth-nace'-ko;* from *4862* and *599*; to *decease* (lit.) in company *with*, or (fig.) similarly *to:*—be dead (die) with.

4881. **συναπόλλυμι sunapŏllumi**, *soon-ap-ol'-loo-mee;* from *4862* and *622*; to *destroy* (mid. or pass. *be slain*) in company *with:*—perish with.

4882. **συναποστέλλω sunapŏstĕllō**, *soon-ap-os-tel'-lo;* from *4862* and *649*; to *despatch* (on an errand) in company *with:*—send with.

4883. **συναρμολογέω sunarmŏlŏgĕō**, *soon-ar-mol-og-eh'-o;* from *4862* and a der. of a comp. of *719* and *3004* (in its orig. sense of *laying*); to *render close-jointed together*, i.e. *organize compactly:*—be fitly framed (joined) together.

4884. **συναρπάζω sunarpazō**, *soon-ar-pad'-zo;* from *4862* and *726*; to *snatch together*, i.e. *seize:*—catch.

4885. **συναυξάνω sunauxanō**, *soon-ŏwx-an'-o;* from *4862* and *837*; to *increase* (*grow up*) *together:*—grow together.

4886. **σύνδεσμος sundĕsmŏs**, *soon'-des-mos;* from *4862* and *1199*; a *joint tie*, i.e. *ligament*, (fig.) *uniting principle, control:*—band, bond.

4887. **συνδέω sundĕō**, *soon-deh'-o;* from *4862* and *1210*; to *bind with*, i.e. (pass.) *be a fellow-prisoner* (fig.):—be bound with.

4888. **συνδοξάζω sundŏxazō**, *soon-dox-ad'-zo;* from *4862* and *1392*; to *exalt* to dignity in company (i.e. *similarly*) *with:*—glorify together.

4889. **σύνδουλος sundŏulŏs**, *soon'-doo-los;* from *4862* and *1401*; a *co-slave*, i.e. *servitor* or *ministrant of the same master* (human or divine):—fellowservant.

συνδρέμω sundrĕmō. See *4936*.

4890. **συνδρομή sundrŏmē**, *soon-drom-ay';* from (the alt. of) *4936*; a *running together*, i.e. (riotous) *concourse:*—run together.

4891. **συνεγείρω sunĕgĕirō**, *soon-eg-i'-ro;* from *4862* and *1453*; to *rouse* (from death) in company *with*, i.e. (fig.) to *revivify* (spiritually) in resemblance to:—raise up together, rise with.

4892. **συνέδριον sunĕdriŏn**, *soon-ed'-ree-on;* neut of a presumed der. of a comp. of *4862* and the base of *1476*; a *joint session*, i.e. (spec.) the Jewish *Sanhedrim*; by anal. a subordinate *tribunal:*—council.

4893. **συνείδησις sunĕidēsis**, *soon-i'-day-sis;* from a prol. form of *4894*; *co-perception*, i.e. moral *consciousness:*—conscience.

4894. **συνείδω sunĕidō**, *soon-i'-do;* from *4862* and *1492*; to *see completely;* used (like its prim.) only in two past tenses, respectively mean. to *understand* or *become aware*, and to *be conscious* or (clandestinely) *informed of:*—consider, know, be privy, be ware of.

4895. **σύνειμι sunĕimi**, *soon'-i-mee;* from *4862* and *1510* (includ. its various inflections); to *be* in company *with*, i.e. *present* at the time:—be with.

4896. **σύνειμι sunĕimi**, *soon'-i-mee;* from *4862* and **εἶμι ĕimi** (to *go*); to *assemble:*—gather together.

4897. **συνεισέρχομαι sunĕisĕrchŏmai**, *soon-ice-er'-khom-ahee;* from *4862* and *1525*; to *enter* in company *with:*—go in with, go with into.

4898. **συνέκδημος sunĕkdēmŏs**, *soon-ek'-day-mos;* from *4862* and the base of *1553*; a *co-absentee* from home, i.e. *fellow-traveller:*—companion in travel, travel with.

4899. **συνεκλεκτός sunĕklĕktŏs**, *soon-ek-lek-tos';* from a comp. of *4862* and *1586*; *chosen* in company *with*, i.e. *co-elect* (*fellow Christian*):—elected together with.

4900. **συνελαύνω sunĕlaunō**, *soon-el-ow'-no;* from *4862* and *1643*; to *drive together*, i.e. (fig.) *exhort* (to reconciliation):— + set at one again.

4901. **συνεπιμαρτυρέω sunĕpimarturĕō**, *soon-ep-ee-mar-too-reh'-o;* from *4862* and *1957*; to *testify further jointly*, i.e. *unite in adding evidence:*—also bear witness.

4902. **συνέπομαι sunĕpŏmai**, *soon-ep'-om-ahee;* mid. from *4862* and a prim. **ἕπω hĕpō** (to *follow*); to *attend* (*travel*) in company *with:*—accompany.

4903. **συνεργέω sunĕrgĕō**, *soon-erg-eh'-o;* from *4904*; to *be a fellow-worker*, i.e. *co-operate:*—help (work) with, work (-er) together.

4904. **συνεργός sunĕrgŏs**, *soon-er-gos';* from a presumed comp. of *4862* and the base of *2041*; a *co-laborer*, i.e. *coadjutor:*—companion in labour, (fellow-) helper (-labourer, -worker), labourer together with, workfellow.

4905. **συνέρχομαι sunĕrchŏmai**, *soon-er'-khom-ahee;* from *4862* and *2064*; to *convene*, *depart* in company *with*, *associate* with, or (spec.) *cohabit* (conjugally):—accompany, assemble (with), come (together), come (company, go) with, resort.

4906. **συνεσθίω sunĕsthiō**, *soon-es-thee'-o;* from *4862* and *2068* (includ. its alt.); to *take food* in company *with:*—eat with.

4907. **σύνεσις sunĕsis**, *soon'-es-is;* from *4920*; a mental *putting together*, i.e. *intelligence* or (concr.) the *intellect:*—knowledge, understanding.

4908. **συνετός sunĕtŏs**, *soon-et'-os;* from *4920*; mentally *put* (or *putting*) *together*, i.e. *sagacious:*—prudent. Comp. *5429*.

4909. **συνευδοκέω sunĕudŏkĕō**, *soon-yoo-dok-eh'-o;* from *4862* and *2106*; to *think well of in common*, i.e. *assent* to, *feel gratified with:*—allow, assent, be pleased, have pleasure.

4910. **συνευωχέω sunĕuōchĕō**, *soon-yoo-o-kheh'-o;* from *4862* and a der. of a presumed comp. of *2095* and a der. of *2192* (mean. to *be in good condition*, i.e. [by impl.] to *fare well*, or *feast*); to *entertain* sumptuously in company *with*, i.e. (mid. or pass.) to *revel together:*—feast with.

4911. **συνεφίστημι sunĕphistēmi**, *soon-ef-is'-tay-mee;* from *4862* and *2186*; to *stand up together*, i.e. to *resist* (or *assault*) *jointly:*—rise up together.

4912. **συνέχω sunĕchō**, *soon-ekh'-o;* from *4862* and *2192*; to *hold together*, i.e. to *compress* (the ears, with a crowd or siege) or *arrest* (a prisoner); fig. to *compel, perplex, afflict, preoccupy:*—constrain, hold, keep in, press, lie sick of, stop, be in a strait, straiten, be taken with, throng.

4913. **συνήδομαι sunēdŏmai**, *soon-ay'-dom-ahee;* mid. from *4862* and the base of *2237*; to *rejoice* in *with* oneself, i.e. *feel satisfaction* concerning:—delight.

4914. **συνήθεια sunēthĕia**, *soon-ay'-thi-ah;* from a comp. of *4862* and *2239*; *mutual habituation*, i.e. *usage:*—custom.

4915. **συνηλικιώτης sunēlikiōtēs**, *soon-ay-lik-ee-o'-tace;* from *4862* and a der. of *2244*; a *co-aged* person, i.e. *alike* in years:—equal,

4916. **συνθάπτω sunthaptō**, *soon-thap'-to;* from *4862* and *2290*; to *inter* in company *with*, i.e. (fig.) to *assimilate* spiritually (to Christ by a sepulture as to sin):—bury with.

4917. **συνθλάω sunthlaō**, *soon-thlah'-o;* from *4862* and **θλάω thlaō** (to *crush*); to *dash together*, i.e. *shatter:*—break.

4918. **συνθλίβω sunthlibō**, *soon-thlee'-bo;* from *4862* and *2346*; to *compress*, i.e. *crowd* on all sides:—throng.

4919. **συνθρύπτω sunthruptō**, *soon-throop'-to;* from *4862* and **θρύπτω thruptō** (to *crumble*); to *crush together*, i.e. (fig.) to *dispirit:*—break.

4920. **συνίημι suniēmi**, *soon-ee'-ay-mee;* from *4862* and **ἵημι hiēmi** (to *send*); to *put together*, i.e. (mentally) to *comprehend;* by impl. to *act piously:*—consider, understand, be wise.

4921. **συνιστάω sunistaō**, *soon-is-tah'-o;* or (strengthened)

συνιστάνω sunistanō, *soon-is-tan'-o;* or

συνίστημι sunistēmi, *soon-is'-tay-mee;* from *4862* and *2476* (includ. its collat. forms); to *set together*, i.e. (by impl.) to *introduce* (favorably), or (fig.) to *exhibit;* intrans. to *stand near*, or (fig.) to *constitute:*—approve, commend, consist, make, stand (with).

4922. **συνοδεύω sunŏdĕuō**, *soon-od-yoo'-o;* from *4862* and *3593*; to *travel* in company *with:*—journey with.

4923. **συνοδία sunŏdia**, *soon-od-ee'-ah;* from a comp. of *4862* and *3598* ("*synod*"); *companionship* on a journey, i.e. (by impl.) a *caravan:*—company.

4924. **συνοικέω sunŏikĕō**, *soon-oy-keh'-o;* from *4862* and *3611*; to *reside together* (as a family):—dwell together.

4925. **συνοικοδομέω sunŏikŏdŏmĕō**, *soon-oy-kod-om-eh'-o;* from *4862* and *3618*; to *construct*, i.e. (pass.) to *compose* (in company with other Christians, fig.):—build together.

4926. **συνομιλέω sunŏmilĕō**, *soon-om-il-eh'-o;* from *4862* and *3656*; to *converse* mutually:—talk with.

4927. **συνομορέω sunŏmŏrĕō**, *soon-om-or-eh'-o;* from *4862* and a der. of a comp. of the base of *3674* and the base of *3725*; to *border together*, i.e. *adjoin:*—join hard.

4928. **συνοχή sunŏchē**, *soon-okh-ay';* from *4912*; *restraint*, i.e. (fig.) *anxiety:*—anguish, distress.

4929. **συντάσσω suntassō**, *soon-tas-so;* from *4862* and *5021*; to *arrange jointly*, i.e. (fig.) to *direct:*—appoint.

4930. **συντέλεια suntĕlĕia**, *soon-tel'-i-ah;* from *4931*; *entire completion*, i.e. *consummation* (of a dispensation):—end.

4931. **συντελέω suntĕlĕō**, *soon-tel-eh'-o;* from *4862* and *5055*; to *complete entirely;* gen. to *execute* (lit. or fig.):—end, finish, fulfil, make.

4932. **συντέμνω suntĕmnō**, *soon-tem'-no;* from *4862* and the base of *5114*; to *contract* by cutting, i.e. (fig.) *do concisely* (*speedily*):—(cut) short.

4933. **συντηρέω suntērĕō**, *soon-tay-reh'-o;* from *4862* and *5083*; to *keep* closely *together*, i.e. (by impl.) to *conserve* (from ruin); ment. to *remember* (and *obey*):—keep, observe, preserve.

4934. **συντίθεμαι suntithĕmai**, *soon-tith'-em-ahee;* mid. from *4862* and *5087*; to *place jointly*, i.e. (fig.) to *consent* (*bargain, stipulate*), *concur:*—agree assent, covenant.

4935. **συντόμως suntŏmōs**, *soon-tom'-oce;* adv. from a der. of *4932*; *concisely* (*briefly*):—a few words.

4936. **συντρέχω suntrĕchō**, *soon-trekh'-o;* from *4862* and *5143* (includ. its alt.); to *rush together* (hastily *assemble*) or *headlong* (fig.):—run (together, with).

4937. **συντρίβω suntribō**, *soon-tree'-bo;* from *4862* and the base of *5147*; to *crush completely*, i.e. to *shatter* (lit. or fig.):—break (in pieces), broken to shivers (+ -hearted), bruise.

4938. **σύντριμμα suntrimma**, *soon-trim'-mah;* from *4937*; *concussion* or utter *fracture* (prop. concr.), i.e. complete *ruin:*—destruction.

4939. **σύντροφος suntrŏphŏs**, *soon'-trof-os;* from *4862* and *5162* (in a pass. sense); a *fellow-nursling*, i.e. *comrade:*—brought up with.

4940. **συντυγχάνω suntugchanō**, *soon-toong-khan'-o;* from *4862* and *5177*; to *chance together*, i.e. *meet* with (*reach*):—come at.

4941. **Συντύχη Suntuchē**, *soon-too'-khay;* from *4940*; an *accident; Syntyche*, a Chr. female:—Syntyche.

4942. **συνυποκρίνομαι sunupŏkrinŏmai**, *soon-oo-pok-rin'-om-ahee;* from *4862* and *5271*; to *act hypocritically* in concert *with:*—dissemble with.

4943. **συνυπουργέω sunupŏurgĕō**, *soon-oop-oorg-eh'-o;* from *4862* and a der. of a comp. of *5259* and the base of *2041*; to *be a co-auxiliary*, i.e. *assist:*—help together.

4944. συνωδίνω **sunōdinō**, *soon-o-dee'-no;* from 4862 and 5605; to *have* (parturition) *pangs* in company (concert, simultaneously) *with*, i.e. (fig.) to *sympathize* (in expectation of relief from suffering):—travail in pain together.

4945. συνωμοσία **sunōmŏsia**, *soon-o-mos-ee'-ah*, from a comp. of 4862 and 3660; a *swearing together*, i.e. (by impl.) a *plot*:—conspiracy.

4946. Συράκουσαι **Surakŏusai**, *soo-rak'-oo-sahee;* plur. of uncert. der.; *Syracusæ*, the capital of Sicily:—Syracuse.

4947. Συρία **Suria**, *soo-ree'-ah;* prob. of Heb. or. [6865]; *Syria* (i.e. *Tsyria* or *Tyre*), a region of Asia:—Syria.

4948. Σύρος **Surŏs**, *soo'-ros;* from the same as 4947; a *Syran* (i.e. prob. *Tyrian*), a native of Syria:—Syrian.

4949. Συροφοίνισσα **Surŏphŏinissa**, *soo-rof-oy'-nis-sah;* fem. of a comp. of 4948 and the same as 5403; a *Syro-phœnician* woman, i.e. a female native of Phœnicia in Syria:—Syrophenician.

4950. σύρτις **surtis**, *soor'-tis;* from 4951; a *shoal* (from the sand *drawn* thither by the waves), i.e. the *Syrtis* Major or great bay on the N. coast of Africa:—quicksands.

4951. σύρω **surō**, *soo'-ro;* prob. akin to 138; to *trail*:—drag, draw, hale.

4952. συσπαράσσω **susparassō**, *soos-par-as'-so;* from 4862 and 4682; to *rend completely*, i.e. (by anal.) to *convulse* violently:—throw down.

4953. σύσσημον **sussēmŏn**, *soos'-say-mon;* neut. of a comp. of 4862 and the base of 4591; a *sign in common*, i.e. preconcerted *signal*:—token.

4954. σύσσωμος **sussōmŏs**, *soos'-so-mos;* from 4862 and 4983; *of a joint body*, i.e. (fig.) a *fellow-member* of the Christian community:—of the same body.

4955. συστασιαστής **sustasiastēs**, *soos-tas-ee-as-tace';* from a comp. of 4862 and a der. of 4714; a *fellow-insurgent*:—make insurrection with.

4956. συστατικός **sustatikŏs**, *soos-tat-ee-kos';* from a der. of 4921; *introductory*, i.e. *recommendatory*:—of commendation.

4957. συσταυρόω **sustaurŏō**, *soos-tow-rŏ'-o;* from 4862 and 4717; to *impale* in company *with* (lit. or fig.):—crucify with.

4958. συστέλλω **sustĕllō**, *soos-tel'-lo;* from 4862 and 4724; to *send* (*draw*) *together*, i.e. *enwrap* (*enshroud* a corpse for burial), *contract* (an interval):—short, wind up.

4959. συστενάζω **sustĕnazō**, *soos-ten-ad'-zo;* from 4862 and 4727; to *moan jointly*, i.e. (fig.) *experience a common calamity*:—groan together.

4960. συστοιχέω **sustŏichĕō**, *soos-toy-kheh'-o;* from 4862 and 4748; to *file together* (as soldiers in ranks), i.e. (fig.) to *correspond* to:—answer to.

4961. συστρατιώτης **sustratiōtēs**, *soos-trat-ee-o'-tace;* from 4862 and 4757; a *co-campaigner*, i.e. (fig.) an *associate* in Christian toil:—fellowsoldier.

4962. συστρέφω **sustrĕphō**, *soos-tref'-o;* from 4862 and 4762; to *twist together*, i.e. *collect* (a bundle, a crowd):—gather.

4963. συστροφή **sustrŏphē**, *soos-trof-ay';* from 4962; a *twisting together*, i.e. (fig.) a secret *coalition*, riotous *crowd*:— + band together, concourse.

4964. συσχηματίζω **suschēmatizō**, *soos-khay-mat-id'-zo;* from 4862 and a der. of 4976; to *fashion alike*, i.e. *conform* to the same pattern (fig.):—conform to, fashion self according to.

4965. Συχάρ **Suchar**, *soo-khar';* of Heb. or. [7941]; *Sychar* (i.e. *Shekar*), a place in Pal.:—Sychar.

4966. Συχέμ **Suchĕm**, *soo-khem';* of Heb. or. [7927]; *Sychem* (i.e. *Shekem*), the name of a Canaanite and of a place in Pal.:—Sychem.

4967. σφαγή **sphagē**, *sfag-ay';* from 4969; *butchery* (of animals for food or sacrifice, or [fig.] of men [*destruction*]):—slaughter.

4968. σφάγιον **sphagiŏn**, *sfag'-ee-on;* neut. of a der. of 4967; a *victim* (in sacrifice):—slain beast.

4969. σφάζω **sphazō**, *sfad'-zo;* a prim. verb; to *butcher* (espec. an animal for food or in sacrifice) or (gen.) to *slaughter*, or (spec.) to *maim* (violently):—kill, slay, wound.

4970. σφόδρα **sphŏdra**, *sfod'-rah;* neut. plur. of σφοδρός **sphŏdrŏs** (*violent*; of uncert. der.) as adv.; *vehemently*, i.e. in *a high degree*, *much*:—exceeding (-ly), greatly, sore, very.

4971. σφοδρῶς **sphŏdrōs**, *sfod-roce';* adv. from the same as 4970; *very much*:—exceedingly.

4972. σφραγίζω **sphragizō**, *sfrag-id'-zo;* from 4973; to *stamp* (with a signet or private mark) for security or preservation (lit. or fig.); by impl. to *keep secret*, to *attest*:—(set a, set to) seal up.

4973. σφραγίς **sphragis**, *sfrag-ece';* prob. strengthened from 5420; a *signet* (as *fencing* in or protecting from misappropriation); by impl. the *stamp* impressed (as a mark of privacy, or genuineness), lit. or fig.:—seal.

4974. σφυρόν **sphurŏn**, *sfoo-ron';* neut. of a presumed der. prob. of the same as σφαῖρα **sphaira** (a *ball*, "*sphere*"; comp. the fem. σφῦρα **sphura**, a *hammer*); the *ankle* (as *globular*):—ancle bone.

4975. σχεδόν **schĕdŏn**, *skhed-on';* neut. of a presumed der. of the alt. of 2192 as adv.; *nigh*, i.e. *nearly*:—almost.

σχέω **schĕō**. See 2192.

4976. σχῆμα **schēma**, *skhay'-mah;* from the alt. of 2192; a *figure* (as a *mode* or *circumstance*), i.e. (by impl.) external *condition*:—fashion.

4977. σχίζω **schizō**, *skhid'-zo;* appar. a prim. verb; to *split* or *sever* (lit. or fig.):—break, divide, open, rend, make a rent.

4978. σχίσμα **schisma**, *skhis'-mah;* from 4977; a *split* or *gap* ("*schism*"), lit. or fig.:—division, rent, schism.

4979. σχοινίον **schŏiniŏn**, *skhoy-nee'-on;* dimin. of σχοῖνος **schŏinŏs** (a *rush* or *flag*-plant; of uncert. der.); a *rushlet*, i.e. *grass-withe* or *tie* (gen.):—small cord, rope.

4980. σχολάζω **schŏlazō**, *skhol-ad'-zo;* from 4981; to *take a holiday*, i.e. *be at leisure* for (by impl. *devote oneself* wholly to); fig. to *be vacant* (of a house):—empty, give self.

4981. σχολή **schŏlē**, *skhol-ay';* prob. fem. of a presumed der. of the alt. of 2192; prop. *loitering* (as a *withholding* of oneself from work) or *leisure*, i.e. (by impl.) a "*school*" (as *vacation* from phys. employment):—school.

4982. σώζω **sōzō**, *sode'-zo;* from a prim. σῶς **sōs** (contr. for obsol. σάος **saŏs**, "*safe*"); to *save*, i.e. *deliver* or *protect* (lit. or fig.):—heal, preserve, save (self), do well, be (make) whole.

4983. σῶμα **sōma**, *so'-mah;* from 4982; the *body* (as a *sound* whole), used in a very wide application, lit. or fig.:—bodily, body, slave.

4984. σωματικός **sōmatikŏs**, *so-mat-ee-kos';* from 4983; *corporeal* or *physical*:—bodily.

4985. σωματικῶς **sōmatikōs**, *so-mat-ee-koce';* adv. from 4984; *corporeally* or *physically*:—bodily.

4986. Σώπατρος **Sōpatrŏs**, *so'-pat-ros;* from the base of 4982 and 3962; *of a safe father*; *Sopatrus*, a Chr.:—Sopater. Comp. 4989.

4987. σωρεύω **sōrĕuō**, *sore-yoo'-o;* from another form of 4673; to *pile up* (lit. or fig.):—heap, load.

4988. Σωσθένης **Sōsthĕnēs**, *soce-then'-ace;* from the base of 4982 and that of 4599; *of safe strength*; *Sosthenes*, a Chr.:—Sosthenes.

4989. Σωσίπατρος **Sōsipatrŏs**, *so-sip'-at-ros;* prol. for 4986; *Sosipatrus*, a Chr.:—Sosipater.

4990. σωτήρ **sōtēr**, *so-tare';* from 4982; a *deliverer*, i.e. God or Christ:—saviour.

4991. σωτηρία **sōtēria**, *so-tay-ree'-ah;* fem. of a der. of 4990 as (prop. abstr.) noun; *rescue* or *safety* (phys. or mor.):—deliver, health, salvation, save, saving.

4992. σωτήριον **sōtēriŏn**, *so-tay'-ree-on;* neut. of the same as 4991 as (prop. concr.) noun; *defender* or (by impl.) *defence*:—salvation.

4993. σωφρονέω **sōphrŏnĕō**, *so-fron-eh'-o;* from 4998; to *be of sound mind*, i.e. *sane*, (fig.) *moderate*:—be in right mind, be sober (minded), soberly.

4994. σωφρονίζω **sōphrŏnizō**, *so-fron-id'-zo;* from 4998; to *make of sound mind*, i.e. (fig.) to *discipline* or *correct*:—teach to be sober.

4995. σωφρονισμός **sōphrŏnismŏs**, *so-fron-is-mos';* from 4994; *discipline*, i.e. *self-control*:—sound mind.

4996. σωφρόνως **sōphrŏnōs**, *so-fron'-oce;* adv. from 4998; *with sound mind*, i.e. *moderately*:—soberly.

4997. σωφροσύνη **sōphrŏsunē**, *so-fros-oo'-nay;* from 4998; *soundness of mind*, i.e. (lit.) *sanity* or (fig.) *self-control*:—soberness, sobriety.

4998. σώφρων **sōphrōn**, *so'-frone;* from the base of 4982 and that of 5424; *safe* (*sound*) in *mind*, i.e. *self-controlled* (*moderate* as to opinion or passion):—discreet, sober, temperate.

T

τά **ta**. See 3588.

4999. Ταβέρναι **Tabĕrnai**, *tab-er'-nahee;* plur. of Lat. or.; *huts* or *wooden-walled* buildings; *Tabernæ*:—taverns.

5000. Ταβιθά **Tabitha**, *tab-ee-thah';* of Chald. or. [comp. 6646]; *the gazelle*; *Tabitha* (i.e. *Tabjetha*), a Chr. female:—Tabitha.

5001. τάγμα **tagma**, *tag'-mah;* from 5021; something orderly in *arrangement* (a *troop*), i.e. (fig.) a *series* or *succession*:—order.

5002. τακτός **taktŏs**, *tak-tos';* from 5021; *arranged*, i.e. *appointed* or *stated*:—set.

5003. ταλαιπωρέω **talaipōrĕō**, *tal-ahee-po-reh'-o*, from 5005; to *be wretched*, i.e. *realize* one's own *misery*:—be afflicted.

5004. ταλαιπωρία **talaipōria**, *tal-ahee-po-ree'-ah;* from 5005; *wretchedness*, i.e. *calamity*:—misery.

5005. ταλαίπωρος **talaipōrŏs**, *tal-ah'ee-po-ros;* from the base of 5007 and a der. of the base of 3984; *enduring trial*, i.e. *miserable*:—wretched.

5006. ταλαντιαῖος **talantiaiŏs**, *tal-an-tee-ah'-yos;* from 5007; *talent-like* in weight:—weight of a talent.

5007. τάλαντον **talantŏn**, *tal'-an-ton;* neut. of a presumed der. of the orig. form of τλάω **tlaō** (to *bear*; equiv. to 5342); a *balance* (as *supporting* weights), i.e. (by impl.) a certain *weight* (and thence a *coin* or rather *sum* of money) or "*talent*":—talent.

5008. ταλιθά **talitha**, *tal-ee-thah';* of Chald. or. [comp. 2924]; *the fresh*, i.e. *young girl*; *talitha* (*O maiden*):—talitha.

5009. ταμεῖον **tamĕiŏn**, *tam-i'-on;* neut. contr. of a presumed der. of ταμίας **tamias** (a *dispenser* or *distributor*; akin to τέμνω **tĕmnō**, to *cut*); a *dispensary* or *magazine*, i.e. a chamber on the ground-floor or interior of an Oriental house (gen. used for *storage* or *privacy*, a spot for retirement):—secret chamber, closet, storehouse.

τανῦν **tanun**. See 3568.

5010. τάξις **taxis**, *tax'-is;* from 5021; regular *arrangement*, i.e. (in time) fixed *succession* (of rank or character), official *dignity*:—order.

5011. ταπεινός **tapĕinŏs**, *tap-i-nos';* of uncert. der.; *depressed*, i.e. (fig.) *humiliated* (in circumstances or disposition):—base, cast down, humble, of low degree (estate), lowly.

5012. ταπεινοφροσύνη **tapĕinŏphrŏsunē**, *tap-i-nof-ros-oo'-nay;* from a comp. of 5011 and the base of 5424; *humiliation of mind*, i.e. *modesty*:—humbleness of mind, humility (of mind), lowliness (of mind).

5013. ταπεινόω **tapĕinŏō**, *tap-i-nŏ'-o;* from 5011; to *depress*; fig. to *humiliate* (in condition or heart):—abase, bring low, humble (self).

5014. ταπείνωσις **tapĕinōsis**, *tap-i'-no-sis;* from 5013; *depression* (in rank or feeling):—humiliation, be made low, low estate, vile.

5015. ταράσσω **tarassō**, *tar-as'-so;* of uncert. affin.; to *stir* or *agitate* (*roil* water):—trouble.

5016. **ταραχή tarachē**, *tar-akh-ay'*; fem. from *5015*; *disturbance*, i.e. (of water) *roiling*, or (of a mob) *sedition*:—trouble (-ing).

5017. **τάραχος tarachŏs**, *tar'-akh-os*; masc. from *5015*; *a disturbance*, i.e. (popular) *tumult*:—stir.

5018. **Ταρσεύς Tarsĕus**, *tar-syoos'*; from *5019*; a *Tarsean*, i.e. native of Tarsus:—of Tarsus.

5019. **Ταρσός Tarsŏs**, *tar-sos'*; perh. the same as **ταρσός tarsŏs** (a *flat* basket); *Tarsus*, a place in Asia Minor:—Tarsus.

5020. **ταρταρόω tartarŏō**, *tar-tar-ŏ'-o*; from **Τάρταρος Tartarŏs** (the deepest *abyss* of Hades); to *incarcerate* in eternal torment:—cast down to hell.

5021. **τάσσω tassō**, *tas'-so*; a prol. form of a prim. verb (which latter appears only in certain tenses); to *arrange* in an orderly manner, i.e. *assign* or *dispose* (to a certain position or lot):—addict, appoint, determine, ordain, set.

5022. **ταῦρος taurŏs**, *tŏw'-ros*; appar. a prim. word [comp. 8450, "*steer*"]; a *bullock*:—bull, ox.

5023. **ταῦτα tauta**, *tŏw'-tah*; nom. or acc. neut. plur. of *3778*; *these* things:— + afterward, follow, + hereafter, × him, the same, so, such, that, then, these, they, this, those, thus.

5024. **ταὐτά tauta**, *tow-tah'*; neut. plur. of *3588* and *846* as adv.; in *the same* way:—even thus, (manner) like, so.

5025. **ταύταις tautais**, *tŏw'-toheece*; and
ταύτας tautas, *tŏw'-tas*; dat. and acc. fem. plur. respectively of *3778*; (*to* or *with* or *by*, etc.) *these*:—hence, that, then, these, those.

5026. **ταύτῃ tautē**, *tŏw'-tay*; and
ταύτην tautēn, *tŏw'-tane*; and
ταύτης tautēs, *tŏw'-tace*; dat., acc. and gen. respectively of the fem. sing. of *3778*; (*towards* or *of*) *this*:—her, + hereof, it, that, + thereby, the (same), this (same).

5027. **ταφή taphē**, *taf-ay'*; fem. from *2290*; *burial* (the act):— × bury.

5028. **τάφος taphŏs**, *taf'-os*; masc. from *2290*; a *grave* (the place of interment):—sepulchre, tomb.

5029. **τάχα tacha**, *takh'-ah*; as if neut. plur. of *5036* (adv.); *shortly*, i.e. (fig.) *possibly*:—peradventure (-haps).

5030. **ταχέως tachĕōs**, *takh-eh'-oce*; adv. from *5036*; *briefly*, i.e. (in time) *speedily*, or (in manner) *rapidly*:—hastily, quickly, shortly, soon, suddenly.

5031. **ταχινός tachinŏs**, *takh-ee-nos'*; from *5034*; *curt*, i.e. *impending*:—shortly, swift.

5032. **τάχιον tachiŏn**, *takh'-ee-on*; neut. sing. of the compar. of *5036* (as adv.); *more swiftly*, i.e. (in manner) *more rapidly*, or (in time) *more speedily*:—out [run], quickly, shortly, sooner.

5033. **τάχιστα tachista**, *takh'-is-tah*; neut. plur. of the superl. of *5036* (as adv.); *most quickly*, i.e. (with *5613* pref.) *as soon* as possible:— + with all speed.

5034. **τάχος tachŏs**, *takh'-os*; from the same as *5036*; a *brief* space (of time), i.e. (with *1722* pref.) in *haste*:— + quickly, + shortly, + speedily.

5035. **ταχύ tachu**, *takh-oo'*; neut. sing. of *5036* (as adv.); *shortly*, i.e. *without delay*, *soon*, or (by surprise) *suddenly*, or (by impl. of ease) *readily*:—lightly, quickly.

5036. **ταχύς tachus**, *takh-oos'*; of uncert. affin.; *fleet*, i.e. (fig.) *prompt* or *ready*:—swift.

5037. **τέ tĕ**, *teh*; a prim. particle (enclitic) of connection or addition; *both* or *also* (prop. as correl. of *2532*):—also, and, both, even, then, whether. Often used in comp., usually as the latter part.

5038. **τεῖχος tĕichŏs**, *ti'-khos*; akin to the base of *5088*; a *wall* (as *formative* of a house):—wall.

5039. **τεκμήριον tĕkmēriŏn**, *tek-may'-ree-on*; neut. of a presumed der. of **τεκμάρ tĕkmar** (a *goal* or fixed *limit*); a *token* (as *defining* a fact), i.e. *criterion* of certainty:—infallible proof.

5040. **τεκνίον tĕkniŏn**, *tek-nee'-on*; dimin. of *5043*; an *infant*, i.e. (plur. fig.) *darlings* (Christian *converts*):—little children.

5041. **τεκνογονέω tĕknŏgŏnĕō**, *tek-nog-on-eh'-o*; from a comp. of *5043* and the base of *1096*; to *be a child-bearer*, i.e. *parent* (*mother*):—bear children.

5042. **τεκνογονία tĕknŏgŏnia**, *tek-nog-on-ee'-ah*; from the same as *5041*; *childbirth* (*parentage*), i.e. (by impl.) *maternity* (the performance of *maternal duties*):—childbearing.

5043. **τέκνον tĕknŏn**, *tek'-non*; from the base of *5088*; a *child* (as *produced*):—child, daughter, son.

5044. **τεκνοτροφέω tĕknŏtrŏphĕō**, *tek-not-rof-eh'-o*; from a comp. of *5043* and *5142*; *to be a child-rearer*, i.e. *fulfil* the duties of *a female parent*:—bring up children.

5045. **τέκτων tĕktōn**, *tek'-tone*; from the base of *5088*; an *artificer* (as *producer* of fabrics), i.e. (spec.) a *craftsman* in wood:—carpenter.

5046. **τέλειος tĕlĕiŏs**, *tel'-i-os*; from *5056*; *complete* (in various applications of labor, growth, mental and moral character, etc.); neut. (as noun, with *3588*) *completeness*:—of full age, man, perfect.

5047. **τελειότης tĕlĕiŏtēs**, *tel-i-ot'-ace*; from *5046*; (the state) *completeness* (ment. or mor.):—perfection (-ness).

5048. **τελειόω tĕlĕiŏō**, *tel-i-ŏ'-o*; from *5046*; to *complete*, i.e. (lit.) *accomplish*, or (fig.) *consummate* (in character):—consecrate, finish, fulfil, (make) perfect.

5049. **τελείως tĕlĕiōs**, *tel-i'-oce*; adv. from *5046*; *completely*, i.e. (of hope) *without wavering*:—to the end.

5050. **τελείωσις tĕlĕiōsis**, *tel-i'-o-sis*; from *5448*; (the act) *completion*, i.e. (of prophecy) *verification*, or (of expiation) *absolution*:—perfection, performance.

5051. **τελειωτής tĕlĕiōtēs**, *tel-i-o-tace'*; from *5048*; a *completer*, i.e. *consummater*:—finisher.

5052. **τελεσφορέω tĕlĕsphŏrĕō**, *tel-es-for-eh'-o*; from a comp. of *5056* and *5342*; *to be a bearer to completion* (maturity), i.e. to *ripen* fruit (fig.):—bring fruit to perfection.

5053. **τελευτάω tĕlĕutaō**, *tel-yoo-tah'-o*; from a presumed der. of *5055*; to *finish* life (by impl. of *979*), i.e. *expire* (*demise*):—be dead, decease, die.

5054. **τελευτή tĕlĕutē**, *tel-yoo-tay'*; from *5053*; *decease*:—death.

5055. **τελέω tĕlĕō**, *tel-eh'-o*; from *5056*; to *end*, i.e. *complete*, *execute*, *conclude*, *discharge* (a debt):—accomplish, make an end, expire, fill up, finish, go over, pay, perform.

5056. **τέλος tĕlŏs**, *tel'-os*; from a prim. **τέλλω tĕllō** (to *set out* for a definite point or *goal*); prop. the point aimed at as a *limit*, i.e. (by impl.) the *conclusion* of an act or state (*termination* [lit., fig. or indef.], *result* [immed., ultimate or prophetic], *purpose*); spec. an *impost* or *levy* (as *paid*):— + continual, custom, end (-ing), finally, uttermost. Comp. *5411*.

5057. **τελώνης tĕlōnēs**, *tel-o'-nace*; from *5056* and *5608*; a *tax-farmer*, i.e. *collector of* public *revenue*:—publican.

5058. **τελώνιον tĕlōniŏn**, *tel-o'-nee-on*; neut. of a presumed der. of *5057*; a *tax-gatherer's* place of business:—receipt of custom.

5059. **τέρας tĕras**, *ter'-as*; of uncert. affin.; a *prodigy* or *omen*:—wonder.

5060. **Τέρτιος Tĕrtiŏs**, *ter'-tee-os*; of Lat. or.; *third*; *Tertius*, a Chr.:—Tertius.

5061. **Τέρτυλλος Tĕrtullŏs**, *ter'-tool-los*; of uncert. der.; *Tertullus*, a Rom.:—Tertullus.

τέσσαρα tĕssara. See *5064*.

5062. **τεσσαράκοντα tĕssarakŏnta**, *tes-sar-ak'-on-tah*; the decade of *5064*; *forty*:—forty.

5063. **τεσσαρακονταετής tĕssarakŏntaĕtēs**, *tes-sar-ak-on-tah-et-ace'*; from *5062* and *2094*; *of forty years* of age:—(+ full, of) forty years (old).

5064. **τέσσαρες tĕssarĕs**, *tes'-sar-es*; neut.
τέσσαρα tĕssara, *tes'-sar-ah*; a plur. number; *four*:—four.

5065. **τεσσαρεσκαιδέκατος tĕssarĕskaidĕkatŏs**, *tes-sar-es-kahee-dek'-at-os*; from *5064* and *2532* and *1182*; *fourteenth*:—fourteenth.

5066. **τεταρταῖος tĕtartaiŏs**, *tet-ar-tah'-yos*; from *5064*; pertaining to the *fourth* day:—four days.

5067. **τέταρτος tĕtartŏs**, *tet'-ar-tos*; ord. from *5064*; *fourth*:—four (-th).

5068. **τετράγωνος tĕtragōnŏs**, *tet-rag'-o-nos*; from *5064* and *1137*; *four-cornered*, i.e. *square*:—foursquare.

5069. **τετράδιον tĕtradiŏn**, *tet-rad'-ee-on*; neut. of a presumed der. of **τέτρας tĕtras** (a *tetrad*; from *5064*); a *quaternion* or squad (picket) of four Rom. soldiers:—quaternion.

5070. **τετρακισχίλιοι tĕtrakischiliŏi**, *tet-rak-is-khil'-ee-oy*; from the mult. adv. of *5064* and *5507*; *four times a thousand*:—four thousand.

5071. **τετρακόσιοι tĕtrakŏsiŏi**, *tet-rak-os'-ee-oy*; neut. **τετρακόσια tĕtrakŏsia**, *tet-rak-os'-ee-ah*; plur. from *5064* and *1540*; *four hundred*:—four hundred.

5072. **τετράμηνον tĕtramēnŏn**, *tet-ram'-ay-non*; neut. of a comp. of *5064* and *3376*; a *four months'* space:—four months.

5073. **τετραπλόος tĕtraplŏŏs**, *tet-rap-lŏ'-os*; from *5064* and a der. of the base of *4118*; *quadruple*:—fourfold.

5074. **τετράπους tĕtrapŏus**, *tet-rap'-ooce*; from *5064* and *4228*; a *quadruped*:—fourfooted beast.

5075. **τετραρχέω tĕtrarchĕō**, *tet-rar-khch'-o*; from *5076*; *to be a tetrarch*:—(be) tetrarch.

5076. **τετράρχης tĕtrarchēs**, *tet-rar'-khace*; from *5064* and *757*; the *ruler of a fourth* part of a country ("*tetrarch*"):—tetrarch.

τεύχω tĕuchō. See *5177*.

5077. **τεφρόω tĕphrŏō**, *tef-rŏ'-o*; from **τέφρα tephra** (*ashes*); to *incinerate*, i.e. *consume*:—turn to ashes.

5078. **τέχνη tĕchnē**, *tekh'-nay*; from the base of *5088*; *art* (as *productive*), i.e. (spec.) a *trade*, or (gen.) *skill*:—art, craft, occupation.

5079. **τεχνίτης tĕchnitēs**, *tekh-nee'-tace*; from *5078*; an *artisan*; fig. a *founder* (*Creator*):—builder, craftsman.

5080. **τήκω tēkō**, *tay'-ko*; appar. a prim. verb; to *liquefy*:—melt.

5081. **τηλαυγῶς tēlaugōs**, *tay-lŏw-goce'*; adv. from a comp. of a der. of *5056* and *827*; in a *far-shining* manner, i.e. *plainly*:—clearly.

5082. **τηλικοῦτος tēlikŏutŏs**, *tay-lik-oo'-tos*; fem. **τηλικαύτη tēlikautē**, *tay-lik-ŏw'-tay*; from a comp. of *3588* with *2245* and *3778*; *such as this*, i.e. (in [fig.] magnitude) *so vast*:—so great, so mighty.

5083. **τηρέω tērĕō**, *tay-reh'-o*; from **τηρός tērŏs** (a *watch*; perh. akin to *2334*); to *guard* (from *loss* or *injury*, prop. by keeping *the eye* upon; and thus differing from *5442*, which is prop. to *prevent* escaping; and from *2892*, which implies a *fortress* or full military lines of apparatus), i.e. to *note* (a prophecy; fig. to *fulfil* a command); by impl. to *detain* (in custody; fig. to *maintain*); by extens. to *withhold* (for personal ends; fig. to *keep unmarried*):—hold fast, keep (-er), (ob-, pre-, re) serve, watch.

5084. **τήρησις tērēsis**, *tay'-ray-sis*; from *5083*; a *watching*, i.e. (fig.) *observance*, or (concr.) a *prison*:—hold.

τῇ tē, **τήν tēn**, **τῆς tēs**. See *3588*.

5085. **Τιβεριάς Tibĕrias**, *tib-er-ee-as'*; from *5086*; *Tiberias*, the name of a town and a lake in Pal.:—Tiberias.

5086. **Τιβέριος Tibĕriŏs**, *tib-er'-ee-os*; of Lat. or.; prob. *pertaining to the river Tiberis* or *Tiber*; *Tiberius*, a Rom. emperor:—Tiberius.

5087. **τίθημι tithēmi**, *tith'-ay-mee*; a prol. form of a prim.
θέω thĕō, *theh'-o* (which is used only as alt. in cert. tenses); to *place* (in the widest application, lit. and fig.; prop. in a passive or horizontal posture, and thus different from *2476*, which prop. denotes an upright and active position, while *2749* is prop. reflexive and utterly prostrate):— + advise, appoint, bow, commit, conceive, give, × kneel down, lay (aside,

down, up), make, ordain, purpose, put, set (forth), settle, sink down.

5088. τίκτω tiktō, *tik'-to;* a strengthened form of a prim. **τέκω tĕkō**, *tek'-o* (which is used only as alt. in certain tenses); to *produce* (from seed, as a mother, a plant, the earth, etc.), lit. or fig.:—bear, be born, bring forth, be delivered, be in travail.

5089. τίλλω tillō, *til'-lo;* perh. akin to the alt. of *138*, and thus to *4951;* to *pull* off:—pluck.

5090. Τίμαιος Timaiŏs, *tim'-ah-yos;* prob. of Chald. or. [comp. 2931]; *Timæus* (i.e. *Timay*), an Isr.:—Timæus.

5091. τιμάω timaō, *tim-ah'-o;* from *5093;* to *prize*, i.e. *fix a valuation* upon; by impl. to *revere:*—honour, value.

5092. τιμή timē, *tee-may';* from *5099;* a *value*, i.e. *money* paid, or (concr. and collect.) *valuables;* by anal. *esteem* (espec. of the highest degree), or the *dignity* itself:—honour, precious, price, some.

5093. τίμιος timiŏs, *tim'-ee-os;* includ. the comp.

τιμιώτερος timiōtĕrŏs, *tim-ee-o'-ter-os;* and the superl.

τιμιώτατος timiōtatŏs, *tim-ee-o'-tat-os;* from *5092;* *valuable*, i.e. (obj.) *costly*, or (subj.) *honored, esteemed*, or (fig.) *beloved:*—dear, honourable, (more, most) precious, had in reputation.

5094. τιμιότης timiŏtēs, *tim-ee-ot'-ace;* from *5093;* *expensiveness*, i.e. (by impl.) *magnificence:*—costliness.

5095. Τιμόθεος Timŏthĕŏs, *tee-moth'-eh-os;* from *5092* and *2316;* *dear to God; Timotheus*, a Chr.:—Timotheus, Timothy.

5096. Τίμων Timōn, *tee'-mone;* from *5092;* *valuable; Timon*, a Chr.:—Timon.

5097. τιμωρέω timōrĕō, *tim-o-reh'-o;* from a comp. of *5092* and **οὖρος ŏurŏs** (a *guard*); prop. to *protect* one's *honor*, i.e. to *avenge* (*inflict a penalty*):—punish.

5098. τιμωρία timōria, *tee-mo-ree'-ah;* from *5097;* *vindication*, i.e. (by impl.) a *penalty:*—punishment.

5099. τίνω tinō, *tee'-no;* strengthened for a prim.

τίω tiō, *tee'-o* (which is only used as an alt. in certain tenses); to *pay* a price, i.e. as a *penalty:*—be punished with.

5100. τὶς tis, *tis;* an enclit. indef. pron.; *some* or *any* person or object:—a (kind of), any (man, thing, thing at all), certain (thing), divers, he (every) man, one (× thing), ought, + partly, some (man, -body, -thing, -what), (+ that no-) thing, what (-soever), × wherewith, whom [-soever], whose ([-soever]).

5101. τίς tis, *tis;* prob. emphat. of *5100;* an interrog. pron., *who, which* or *what* (in direct or indirect questions):—every man, how (much), + no (-ne, thing), what (manner, thing), where ([-by, -fore, -of, -unto, -with, -withal]), whether, which, who (-m, -se), why.

5102. τίτλος titlŏs, *tit'-los;* of Lat. or.; a *titulus* or "*title*" (*placard*):—title.

5103. Τίτος Titŏs, *tee'-tos*, of Lat. or. but uncert. signif.; *Titus*, a Chr.:—Titus.

τίω tiō. See *5099.*

τό tŏ. See *3588.*

5104. τοί tŏi, *toy;* prob. for the dat. of *3588;* an enclit. particle of *asseveration* by way of contrast; *in sooth:*—[*used only with other particles in comp., as 2544, 3305, 5105, 5106*, etc.]

5105. τοιγαροῦν tŏigarŏun, *toy-gar-oon';* from *5104* and *1063* and *3767;* *truly for then*, i.e. *consequently:*—there- (where-) fore.

τοίγε tŏigĕ. See *2544.*

5106. τοίνυν tŏinun, *toy'-noon;* from *5104* and *3568;* *truly now*, i.e. *accordingly:*—then, therefore.

5107. τοιόσδε tŏiŏsdĕ, *toy-os'-deh* (includ. the other inflections); from a der. of *5104* and *1161;* *such-like then*, i.e. *so great:*—such.

5108. τοιοῦτος tŏiŏutŏs, *toy-oo'-tos* (includ. the other inflections); from *5104* and *3778;* *truly this*, i.e. *of this sort* (to denote character or individuality):—like, such (an one).

5109. τοῖχος tŏichŏs, *toy'-khos;* another form of *5038;* a *wall:*—wall.

5110. τόκος tŏkŏs, *tok'-os;* from the base of *5088;* *interest* on money loaned (as a *produce*):—usury.

5111. τολμάω tŏlmaō, *tol-mah'-o;* from **τόλμα tŏlma** (*boldness;* prob. itself from the base of *5056* through the idea of *extreme* conduct); to *venture* (obj. or in *act;* while *2292* is rather subj. or in *feeling*); by impl. to be *courageous:*—be bold, boldly, dare, durst.

5112. τολμηρότερον tŏlmērŏtĕrŏn, *tol-may-rot'-er-on;* neut. of the comp. of a der. of the base of *5111* (as adv.); *more daringly*, i.e. *with greater confidence* than otherwise:—the more boldly.

5113. τολμητής tŏlmētēs, *tol-may-tace';* from *5111;* a *daring* (*audacious*) man:—presumptuous.

5114. τομώτερος tŏmōtĕrŏs, *tom-o'-ter-os;* comp. of a der. of the prim. **τέμνω tĕmnō** (to *cut;* more comprehensive or decisive than *2875*, as if by a *single* stroke; whereas that implies repeated blows, like *hacking*); *more keen:*—sharper.

5115. τόξον tŏxŏn, *tox'-on;* from the base of *5088;* a *bow* (appar. as the simplest fabric):—bow.

5116. τοπάζιον tŏpaziŏn, *top-ad'-zee-on;* neut. of a presumed der. (alt.) of **τόπαζος tŏpazŏs** (a "*topaz*"; of uncert. or.); a gem, prob. the *chrysolite:*—topaz.

5117. τόπος tŏpŏs, *top'-os;* appar. a prim. word; a *spot* (gen. in *space*, but limited by occupancy; whereas *5561* is a larger but partic. *locality*), i.e. *location* (as a position, home, tract, etc.); fig. *condition, opportunity;* spec. a *scabbard:*—coast, licence, place, × plain, quarter, + rock, room, where.

5118. τοσοῦτος tŏsŏutŏs, *tos-oo'-tos;* from **τόσος tŏsŏs** (*so much;* appar. from *3588* and *3739*) and *3778* (includ. its variations); so *vast as this*, i.e. *such* (in quantity, amount, number or space):—as large, so great (long, many, much), these many.

5119. τότε tŏtĕ, *tot'-eh;* from (the neut. of) *3588* and *3753;* *the when*, i.e. *at the time* that (of the past or future, also in consecution):—that time, then.

5120. τοῦ tŏu, *too*, prop. the gen. of *3588;* sometimes used for *5127;* *of this person:*—his.

5121. τοὐναντίον tŏunantiŏn, *too-nan-tee'-on;* contr. for the neut. of *3588* and *1726;* *on the contrary:*—contrariwise.

5122. τοὔνομα tŏunŏma, *too'-no-mah;* contr. for the neut. of *3588* and *3686;* *the name* (is):—named.

5123. τουτέστι tŏutĕsti, *toot-es'-tee;* contr. for *5124* and *2076;* *that is:*—that is (to say).

5124. τοῦτο tŏutŏ, *too'-tŏ;* neut. sing. nom. or acc. of *3778;* *that* thing:—here [-unto], it, partly, self [-same], so, that (intent), the same, there [-fore, -unto], this, thus, where [-fore].

5125. τούτοις tŏutŏis, *too'-toice;* dat. plur. masc. or neut. of *3778;* to (*for, in, with* or *by*) *these* (persons or things):—such, them, there [-in, -with], these, this, those.

5126. τοῦτον tŏutŏn, *too'-ton;* acc. sing. masc. of *3778;* *this* (person, as obj. of verb or prep.):—him, the same, that, this.

5127. τούτου tŏutŏu, *too'-too;* gen. sing. masc. or neut. of *3778;* *of* (*from* or *concerning*) *this* (person or thing):—here [-by], him, it, + such manner of, that, thence [-forth], thereabout, this, thus.

5128. τούτους tŏutŏus, *too'-tooce;* acc. plur. masc. of *3778;* *these* (persons, as obj. of verb or prep.):—such, them, these, this.

5129. τούτῳ tŏutōi, *too'-to;* dat. sing. masc. or neut. of *3778;* *to* (*in, with* or *by*) *this* (person or thing):—here [-by, -in], him, one, the same, there [-in], this.

5130. τούτων tŏutōn, *too'-tone;* gen. plur. masc. or neut. of *3778;* *of* (*from* or *concerning*) *these* (persons or things):—such, their, these (things), they, this sort, those.

5131. τράγος tragŏs, *trag'-os;* from the base of *5176;* a *he-goat* (as a *gnawer*):—goat.

5132. τράπεζα trapĕza, *trap'-ed-zah;* prob. contr. from *5064* and *3979;* a *table* or *stool* (as being *four legged*), usually for food (fig. a *meal*); also a *counter* for money (fig. a broker's *office* for loans at interest):—bank, meat, table.

5133. τραπεζίτης trapĕzitēs, *trap-ed-zee'-tace;* from *5132;* a money-*broker* or *banker:*—exchanger.

5134. τραῦμα trauma, *trŏw'-mah;* from the base of **τιτρώσκω titrōskō** (to *wound;* akin to the base of *2352, 5147, 5149*, etc.); a *wound:*—wound.

5135. τραυματίζω traumatizō, *trŏw-mat-id'-zo;* from *5134;* to *inflict a wound:*—wound.

5136. τραχηλίζω trachēlizō, *trakh-ay-lid'-zo;* from *5137;* to *seize* by *the throat* or *neck*, i.e. to *expose* the *gullet* of a victim for killing (gen. to *lay bare*):—opened.

5137. τράχηλος trachēlŏs, *trakh'-ay-los;* prob. from *5143* (through the idea of *mobility*); the *throat* (*neck*), i.e. (fig.) *life:*—neck.

5138. τραχύς trachus, *trakh-oos';* perh. strengthened from the base of *4486* (as if *jagged* by rents); *uneven, rocky* (*reefy*):—rock, rough.

5139. Τραχωνῖτις Trachōnitis, *trakh-o-nee'-tis;* from a der. of *5138;* *rough* district; *Trachonitis*, a region of Syria:—Trachonitis.

5140. τρεῖς trĕis, *trice;* neut.

τρία tria, *tree'-ah;* a prim. (plur.) number; "*three*":—three.

5141. τρέμω trĕmō, *trem'-o;* strengthened from a prim. **τρέω trĕō** (to "*dread*", "*terrify*"); to "*tremble*" or *fear:*—be afraid, trembling.

5142. τρέφω trĕphō, *tref'-o;* a prim. verb (prop. **θρέφω thrĕphō**; but perh. strength. from the base of *5157* through the idea of *convolution*); prop. to *stiffen*, i.e. *fatten* (by impl. to *cherish* [with food, etc.], *pamper, rear*):—bring up, feed, nourish.

5143. τρέχω trĕchō, *trekh'-o;* appar. a prim. verb (prop. **θρέχω thrĕchō**; comp. *2359*); which uses **δρέμω drĕmō**, *drem'-o* (the base of *1408*) as alt. in certain tenses; to *run* or *walk hastily* (lit. or fig.):—have course, run.

5144. τριάκοντα triakŏnta, *tree-ak'-on-tah;* the decade of *5140;* *thirty:*—thirty.

5145. τριακόσιοι triakŏsiŏi, *tree-ak-os'-ee-oy;* plur. from *5140* and *1540;* *three hundred:*—three hundred.

5146. τρίβολος tribŏlŏs, *trib'-ol-os;* from *5140* and *956;* prop. a *crow-foot* (*three-pronged obstruction in war*), i.e. (by anal.) a *thorny plant* (*caltrop*):—brier, thistle.

5147. τρίβος tribŏs, *tree'-bos;* from **τρίβω tribō** (to "*rub*"; akin to **τείρω tĕirō**, **τρύω truō**, and the base of *5131, 5134*); a *rut* or worn *track:*—path.

5148. τριετία triĕtia, *tree-et-ee'-ah;* from a comp. of *5140* and *2094;* a *three years' period* (*triennium*):—space of three years.

5149. τρίζω trizō, *trid'-zo;* appar. a prim. verb; to *creak* (*squeak*), i.e. (by anal.) to *grate* the teeth (in frenzy):—gnash.

5150. τρίμηνον trimēnŏn, *trim'-ay-non;* neut. of a comp. of *5140* and *3376* as noun; a *three months'* space:—three months.

5151. τρίς tris, *trece;* adv. from *5140;* *three times:*—three times, thrice.

5152. τρίστεγον tristĕgŏn, *tris'-teg-on;* neut. of a comp. of *5140* and *4721* as noun; a *third roof* (*story*):—third loft.

5153. τρισχίλιοι trischiliŏi, *tris-khil'-ee-oy;* from *5151* and *5507;* *three times a thousand:*—three thousand.

5154. τρίτος tritŏs, *tree'-tos;* ord. from *5140;* *third;* neut. (as noun) a *third part*, or (as adv.) a (or the) *third* time, *thirdly:*—third (-ly).

τρίχες trichĕs, etc. See *2359.*

5155. τρίχινος trichinŏs, *trikh'-ee-nos;* from *2359;* *hairy*, i.e. made *of hair* (*mohair*):—of hair.

5156. τρόμος **trŏmŏs**, *trom'-os;* from *5141;* a "*trembling*", i.e. quaking with *fear:*— + tremble (-ing).

5157. τροπή **tropē**, *trop-ay';* from an appar. prim. τρέπω **trĕpō** (to *turn*); a *turn* ("trope"), i.e. *revolution* (fig. *variation*):—turning.

5158. τρόπος **trŏpŏs**, *trop'-os;* from the same as *5157;* a *turn*, i.e. (by impl.) *mode* or *style* (espec. with prep. or rel. pref. as adv. *like*); fig. *deportment* or *character:*—(even) as, conversation, [+ like] manner (+ by any) means, way.

5159. τροποφορέω **trŏpŏphŏrĕō**, *trop-of-or-eh'-o;* from *5158* and *5409;* to *endure* one's *habits:*—suffer the manners.

5160. τροφή **trŏphē**, *trof-ay';* from *5142;* *nourishment* (lit. or fig.); by impl. *rations* (*wages*):—food, meat.

5161. Τρόφιμος **Trŏphimŏs**, *trof'-ee-mos;* from *5160; nutritive; Trophimus*, a Chr.:—Trophimus.

5162. τροφός **trŏphŏs**, *trof-os';* from *5142;* a *nourisher*, i.e. *nurse:*—nurse.

5163. τροχιά **trŏchia**, *trokh-ee-ah';* from *5164;* a *track* (as a wheel-*rut*), i.e. (fig.) a *course* of conduct:—path.

5164. τροχός **trŏchŏs**, *trokh-os';* from *5143;* a *wheel* (as a *runner*), i.e. (fig.) a *circuit* of phys. effects:—course.

5165. τρύβλιον **trubliŏn**, *troob'-lee-on;* neut. of a presumed der. of uncert. affin.; a *bowl:*—dish.

5166. τρυγάω **trugaō**, *troo-gah'-o;* from a der. of τρύγω **trugō** (to *dry*) mean. ripe *fruit* (as if *dry*); to *collect* the vintage:—gather.

5167. τρυγών **trugōn**, *troo-gone';* from τρύζω **truzō** (to *murmur;* akin to *5149*, but denoting a *duller* sound); a *turtle-dove* (as *cooing*):—turtle-dove.

5168. τρυμαλιά **trumalia**, *troo-mal-ee-ah';* from a der. of τρύω **truō** (to *wear* away; akin to the base of *5134*, *5147* and *5176*); an *orifice*, i.e. a needle's *eye:*—eye. Comp. *5169*.

5169. τρύπημα **trupēma**, *troo'-pay-mah;* from a der. of the base of *5168;* an *aperture*, i.e. a needle's *eye:*—eye.

5170. Τρύφαινα **Truphaina**, *troo'-fahee-nah;* from *5172; luxurious; Tryphœna*, a Chr. woman:—Tryphena.

5171. τρυφάω **truphaō**, *troo-fah'-o;* from *5172;* to *indulge in luxury:*—live in pleasure.

5172. τρυφή **truphē**, *troo-fay';* from θρύπτω **thruptō** (to *break* up or [fig.] *enfeeble*, espec. the mind and body by indulgence); *effeminacy*, i.e. *luxury* or *debauchery:*—delicately, riot.

5173. Τρυφῶσα **Truphōsa**, *troo-fo'-sah;* from *5172; luxuriating; Tryphosa*, a Chr. female:—Tryphosa.

5174. Τρῳάς **Trōas**, *tro-as';* from Τρός **Trōs** (a *Trojan*); the *Troad* (or plain of Troy), i.e. *Troas*, a place in Asia Minor:—Troas.

5175. Τρωγύλλιον **Trōgulliŏn**, *tro-gool'-lee-on;* of uncert. der.; *Trogyllium*, a place in Asia Minor:—Trogyllium.

5176. τρώγω **trōgō**, *tro'-go;* prob. strength. from a collat. form of the base of *5134* and *5147* through the idea of *corrosion* or *wear;* or perh. rather of a base of *5167* and *5149* through the idea of a *craunching* sound; to *gnaw* or *chew*, i.e. (gen.) to *eat:*—eat.

5177. τυγχάνω **tugchanō**, *toong-khan'-o;* prob. for an obsol. τύχω **tuchō** (for which the mid. of another alt. τεύχω **tĕuchō** [to *make ready* or *bring to pass*] is used in cert. tenses; akin to the base of *5088* through the idea of *effecting;* prop. to *affect;* or (spec.) to *hit* or *light upon* (as a mark to be reached), i.e. (trans.) to *attain* or *secure* an object or end, or (intrans.) to *happen* (as if *meeting* with); but in the latter application only impers. (with *1487*), i.e. *perchance;* or (pres. part.) as adj. *usual* (as if commonly *met with*, with *3756*, *extraordinary*), neut. (as adv.) *perhaps;* or (with another verb) as adv. by *accident* (*as it were*):—be, chance, enjoy, little, obtain, × refresh . . . self, + special. Comp. *5180*.

5178. τυμπανίζω **tumpanizō**, *toom-pan-id'-zo;* from a der. of *5180* (mean. a *drum*, "*tympanum*"); to stretch on an instrument of *torture* resembling a drum, and thus *beat* to death:—torture.

5179. τύπος **tupŏs**, *too'-pos;* from *5180;* a *die* (as *struck*), i.e. (by impl.) a *stamp* or *scar;* by anal. a *shape*, i.e. a *statue*, (fig.) *style* or *resemblance;* spec. a *sampler* ("*type*"), i.e. a *model* (for imitation) or *instance* (for warning):—en- (ex-) ample, fashion, figure, form, manner, pattern, print.

5180. τύπτω **tuptō**, *toop'-to;* a prim. verb (in a strength. form); to "*thump*", i.e. *cudgel* or *pummel* (prop. with a stick or *bastinado*), but in any case by *repeated* blows; thus differing from *3817* and *3960*, which denote a [usually single] blow with the hand or any instrument, or *4141* with the *fist* [or a *hammer*], or *4474* with the *palm;* as well as from *5177*, an *accidental* collision); by impl. to *punish;* fig. to *offend* (the conscience):—beat, smite, strike, wound.

5181. Τύραννος **Turannŏs**, *too'-ran-nos;* a provincial form of the der. of the base of *2962;* a "*tyrant*"; *Tyrannus*, an Ephesian:—Tyrannus.

5182. τυρβάζω **turbazō**, *toor-bad'-zo;* from τύρβη **turbē** (Lat. *turba*, a *crowd;* akin to *2351*); to *make* "*turbid*", i.e. *disturb:*—trouble.

5183. Τύριος **Turiŏs**, *too'-ree-os;* from *5184;* a *Tyrian*, i.e. inhab. of Tyrus:—of Tyre.

5184. Τύρος **Turŏs**, *too'-ros;* of Heb. or. [6865]: *Tyrus* (i.e. *Tsor*), a place in Pal.:—Tyre.

5185. τυφλός **tuphlŏs**, *toof-los';* from *5187;* *opaque* (as if *smoky*), i.e. (by anal.) *blind* (phys. or ment.):—blind.

5186. τυφλόω **tuphlŏō**, *toof-lŏ'-o;* from *5185;* to *make blind*, i.e. (fig.) to *obscure:*—blind.

5187. τυφόω **tuphŏō**, *toof-ŏ'-o;* from a der. of *5188;* to envelop with *smoke*, i.e. (fig.) to *inflate* with self-conceit:—high-minded, be lifted up with pride, be proud.

5188. τυφώ **tuphō**, *too'-fo;* appar. a prim. verb; to make a *smoke*, i.e. slowly *consume* without flame:—smoke.

5189. τυφωνικός **tuphōnikŏs**, *too-fo-nee-kos';* from a der. of *5188; stormy* (as if *smoky*):—tempestuous.

5190. Τυχικός **Tuchikŏs**, *too-khee-kos';* from a der. of *5177; fortuitous*, i.e. *fortunate; Tychicus*, a Chr.:—Tychicus.

Υ

5191. ὑακίνθινος **huakinthinŏs**, *hoo-ak-in'-thee-nos;* from *5192;* "*hyacinthine*" or "*jacinthine*", i.e. deep *blue:*—jacinth.

5192. ὑάκινθος **huakinthŏs**, *hoo-ak'-in-thos;* of uncert. der.; the "*hyacinth*" or "*jacinth*", i.e. some gem of a deep *blue* color, prob. the *zirkon:*—jacinth.

5193. ὑάλινος **hualinŏs**, *hoo-al'-ee-nos;* from *5194; glassy*, i.e. *transparent:*—of glass.

5194. ὕαλος **hualŏs**, *hoo'-al-os;* perh. from the same as *5205* (as being transparent like *rain*); *glass:*—glass.

5195. ὑβρίζω **hubrizō**, *hoo-brid'-zo;* from *5196;* to *exercise violence*, i.e. *abuse:*—use despitefully, reproach, entreat shamefully (spitefully).

5196. ὕβρις **hubris**, *hoo'-bris;* from *5228; insolence* (as over-bearing), i.e. *insult*, *injury:*—harm, hurt, reproach.

5197. ὑβριστής **hubristēs**, *hoo-bris-tace';* from *5195;* an *insulter*, i.e. *maltreater:*—despiteful, injurious.

5198. ὑγιαίνω **hugiainō**, *hoog-ee-ah'ee-no;* from *5199;* to *have* sound *health*, i.e. *be well* (in body); fig. to be *uncorrupt* (*true* in doctrine):—be in health, (be safe and) sound, (be) whole (-some).

5199. ὑγιής **hugiēs**, *hoog-ee-ace';* from the base of *837; healthy*, i.e. *well* (in body); fig. *true* (in doctrine):—sound, whole.

5200. ὑγρός **hugrŏs**, *hoo-gros';* from the base of *5205; wet* (as if with *rain*), i.e. (by impl.) *sappy* (*fresh*):—green.

5201. ὑδριά **hudria**, *hoo-dree-ah';* from *5204;* a *water-jar*, i.e. *receptacle* for family supply:—waterpot.

5202. ὑδροποτέω **hudrŏpŏtĕō**, *hoo-drop-ot-eh'-o;* from a comp. of *5204* and a der. of *4095;* to *be a water-drinker*, i.e. to *abstain from vinous beverages:*—drink water.

5203. ὑδρωπικός **hudrōpikŏs**, *hoo-dro-pik-os';* from a comp. of *5204* and a der. of *3700* (as if *looking watery*); to be "*dropsical*":—have the dropsy.

5204. ὕδωρ **hudōr**, *hoo'-dore;* gen.

ὕδατος **hudatŏs**, *hoo'-dat-os*, etc.; from the base of *5205; water* (as if *rainy*) lit. or fig.:—water.

5205. ὑετός **huĕtŏs**, *hoo-et-os';* from a prim. ὕω **huō** (to *rain*); *rain*, espec. a *shower:*—rain.

5206. υἱοθεσία **huiŏthĕsia**, *hwee-oth-es-ee'-ah;* from a presumed comp. of *5207* and a der. of *5087;* the *placing* as a *son*, i.e. *adoption* (fig. Chr. *sonship* in respect to God):—adoption (of children, of sons).

5207. υἱός **huiŏs**, *hwee-os';* appar. a prim. word; a "*son*" (sometimes of animals), used very widely of immed., remote or fig. kinship:—child, foal, son.

5208. ὕλη **hulē**, *hoo-lay';* perh. akin to *3586;* a *forest*, i.e. (by impl.) *fuel:*—matter.

5209. ὑμᾶς **humas**, *hoo-mas';* acc. of *5210; you* (as the obj. of a verb or prep.):—ye, you (+ -ward), your (+ own).

5210. ὑμεῖς **humĕis**, *hoo-mice';* irreg. plur. of *4771; you* (as subj. of verb):—ye (yourselves), you.

5211. Ὑμεναῖος **Humĕnaiŏs**, *hoo-men-ah'-yos;* from Ὑμήν **Humēn** (the god of *weddings*); "*hymenæal*"; *Hymenæus*, an opponent of Christianity:—Hymenæus.

5212. ὑμέτερος **humĕtĕrŏs**, *hoo-met'-er-os;* from *5210; yours*, i.e. *pertaining to you:*—your (own).

5213. ὑμῖν **humin**, *hoo-min';* irreg. dat. of *5210;* to (*with* or *by*) *you:*—ye, you, your (-selves).

5214. ὑμνέω **humnĕō**, *hoom-neh'-o;* from *5215;* to *hymn*, i.e. sing a religious ode; by impl. to *celebrate* (God) in song:—sing an hymn (praise unto).

5215. ὕμνος **humnŏs**, *hoom'-nos;* appar. from a simpler (obsol.) form of ὕδέω **hudĕō** (to *celebrate;* prob. akin to *103;* comp. *5567*); a "*hymn*" or religious ode (one of the Psalms):—hymn.

5216. ὑμῶν **humōn**, *hoo-mone';* gen. of *5210; of* (*from* or *concerning*) *you:*—ye, you, your (own, -selves).

5217. ὑπάγω **hupagō**, *hoop-ag'-o;* from *5259* and *71;* to *lead* (oneself) *under*, i.e. *withdraw* or *retire* (as if *sinking* out of sight), lit. or fig.:—depart, get hence, go (a-) way.

5218. ὑπακοή **hupakŏē**, *hoop-ak-ŏ-ay';* from *5219; attentive hearkening*, i.e. (by impl.) *compliance* or *submission:*—obedience, (make) obedient, obey (-ing).

5219. ὑπακούω **hupakŏuō**, *hoop-ak-oo'-o;* from *5259* and *191;* to *hear under* (as a *subordinate*), i.e. to *listen attentively;* by impl. to *heed* or *conform* to a command or authority:—hearken, be obedient to, obey.

5220. ὕπανδρος **hupandrŏs**, *hoop'-an-dros;* from *5259* and *435;* in subjection *under a man*, i.e. a *married* woman:—which hath an husband.

5221. ὑπαντάω **hupantaō**, *hoop-an-tah'-o;* from *5259* and a der. of *473;* to *go opposite* (meet) *under* (*quietly*), i.e. to *encounter*, *fall in with:*—(go to) meet.

5222. ὑπάντησις **hupantēsis**, *hoop-an'-tay-sis;* from *5221;* an *encounter* or *concurrence* (with *1519* for infin., in order to *fall in with*):—meeting.

5223. ὕπαρξις **huparxis**, *hoop'-arx-is;* from *5225; existency* or *proprietorship*, i.e. (concr.) *property*, *wealth:*—goods, substance.

5224. ὑπάρχοντα **huparchŏnta**, *hoop-ar'-khon-tah;* neut. plur. of pres. part. act. of *5225* as noun; things *extant* or *in hand*, i.e. *property* or *possessions:*—goods, that which one has, things which (one) possesseth, substance, that hast.

5225. ὑπάρχω huparchō, *hoop-ar'-kho;* from 5259 and 756; to *begin under* (*quietly*), i.e. *come into existence* (*be present* or *at hand*); expletively, to *exist* (as copula or subordinate to an adj., part., adv. or prep., or as auxil. to principal verb):—after, behave, live.

5226. ὑπείκω hupĕikō, *hoop-i'-ko;* from 5259 and **εἴκω ĕikō** (to *yield*, be "*weak*"); to *surrender:*—submit self.

5227. ὑπεναντίος hupĕnantiŏs, *hoop-en-an-tee'-os;* from 5259 and 1727; *under* (*covertly*) *contrary* to, i.e. *opposed* or (as noun) an *opponent:*—adversary, against.

5228. ὑπέρ hupĕr, *hoop-er';* a prim. prep.; "*over*", i.e. (with the gen.) of place, *above, beyond, across*, or causal, *for* the sake of, *instead, regarding;* with the acc. *superior to*, more *than:*—(+ exceeding abundantly) above, in (on) behalf of, beyond, by, + very chiefest, concerning, exceeding (above, -ly), for, + very highly, more (than), of, over, on the part of, for sake of, in stead, than, to (-ward), very. In comp. it retains many of the above applications.

5229. ὑπεραίρομαι hupĕrairŏmai, *hoop-er-ah'ee-rom-ahee;* mid. from 5228 and 142; to *raise* oneself *over*, i.e. (fig.) to *become haughty:*—exalt self, be exalted above measure.

5230. ὑπέρακμος hupĕrakmŏs, *hoop-er'-ak-mos;* from 5228 and the base of 188; *beyond* the "*acme*", i.e. fig. (of a daughter) *past* the *bloom* (*prime*) of youth:— + pass the flower of (her) age.

5231. ὑπεράνω hupĕranō, *hoop-er-an'-o;* from 5228 and 507; *above upward*, i.e. *greatly higher* (in place or rank):—far above, over.

5232. ὑπεραυξάνω hupĕrauxanō, *hoop-er-owx-an'-o;* from 5228 and 837; to *increase above* ordinary degree:—grow exceedingly.

5233. ὑπερβαίνω hupĕrbainō, *hoop-er-bah'ee-no;* from 5228 and the base of 939; to *transcend*, i.e. (fig.) to *overreach:*—go beyond.

5234. ὑπερβαλλόντως hupĕrballŏntōs, *hoop-er-bal-lon'-toce;* adv. from pres. part. act. of 5235; *excessively:*—beyond measure.

5235. ὑπερβάλλω hupĕrballō, *hoop-er-bal'-lo;* from 5228 and 906; to *throw beyond* the usual mark, i.e. (fig.) to *surpass* (only act. part. *supereminent*):—exceeding, excel, pass.

5236. ὑπερβολή hupĕrbŏlē, *hoop-er-bol-ay';* from 5235; a *throwing beyond* others, i.e. (fig.) *supereminence;* adv. (with 1519 or 2596) *pre-eminently:*—abundance, (far more) exceeding, excellency, more excellent, beyond (out of) measure.

5237. ὑπερείδω hupĕrĕidō, *hoop-er-i'-do;* from 5228 and 1492; to *overlook*, i.e. *not punish:*—wink at.

5238. ὑπερέκεινα hupĕrĕkĕina, *hoop-er-ek'-i-nah;* from 5228 and the neut. plur. of 1565; *above those* parts, i.e. *still farther:*—beyond.

5239. ὑπερεκτείνω hupĕrĕktĕinō, *hoop-er-ek-ti'-no;* from 5228 and 1614; to *extend inordinately:*—stretch beyond.

5240. ὑπερεκχύνω hupĕrĕkchunō, *hoop-er-ek-khoo'-no;* from 5228 and the alt. form of 1632; to *pour out over*, i.e. (pass.) to *overflow:*—run over.

ὑπερεκπερισσοῦ hupĕrĕkpĕrissŏu. See 5228 and 1537 and 4053.

5241. ὑπερεντυγχάνω hupĕrĕntugchanō, *hoop-er-en-toong-khan'-o;* from 5228 and 1793; to *intercede in behalf of:*—make intercession for.

5242. ὑπερέχω hupĕrĕchō, *hoop-er-ekh'-o;* from 5228 and 2192; to *hold* oneself *above*, i.e. (fig.) to *excel;* part. (as adj., or neut. as noun) *superior, superiority:*—better, excellency, higher, pass, supreme.

5243. ὑπερηφανία hupĕrēphania, *hoop-er-ay-fan-ee'-ah;* from 5244; *haughtiness:*—pride.

5244. ὑπερήφανος hupĕrēphanŏs, *hoop-er-ay'-fan-os;* from 5228 and 5316; *appearing above* others (*conspicuous*), i.e. (fig.) *haughty:*—proud.

ὑπερλίαν hupĕrlian. See 5228 and 3029.

5245. ὑπερνικάω hupĕrnikaō, *hoop-er-nik-ah'-o;* from 5228 and 3528; to *vanquish beyond*, i.e. *gain* a decisive *victory:*—more than conquer.

5246. ὑπέρογκος hupĕrŏgkŏs, *hoop-er'-ong-kos;* from 5228 and 3591; *bulging over*, i.e. (fig.) *insolent:*—great swelling.

5247. ὑπεροχή hupĕrŏchē, *hoop-er-okh-ay';* from 5242; *prominence*, i.e. (fig.) *superiority* (in rank or character):—authority, excellency.

5248. ὑπερπερισσεύω hupĕrpĕrissĕuō, *hoop-er-per-is-syoo'-o;* from 5228 and 4052; to *superabound:*—abound much more, exceeding.

5249. ὑπερπερισσῶς hupĕrpĕrissōs, *hoop-er-per-is-soce';* from 5228 and 4057; *superabundantly*, i.e. *exceedingly:*—beyond measure.

5250. ὑπερπλεονάζω hupĕrplĕŏnazō, *hoop-er-pleh-on-ad'-zo;* from 5228 and 4121; to *superabound:*—be exceeding abundant.

5251. ὑπερυψόω hupĕrupsŏō, *hoop-er-oop-sŏ'-o;* from 5228 and 5312; to *elevate above* others, i.e. *raise* to the *highest* position:—highly exalt.

5252. ὑπερφρονέω hupĕrphrŏnĕō, *hoop-er-fron-eh'-o;* from 5228 and 5426; to *esteem* oneself *overmuch*, i.e. *be vain* or *arrogant:*—think more highly.

5253. ὑπερῷον hupĕrōiŏn, *hoop-er-o'-on;* neut. of a der. of 5228; a *higher* part of the house, i.e. apartment in the *third story:*—upper chamber (room).

5254. ὑπέχω hupĕchō, *hoop-ekh'-o;* from 5259 and 2192; to *hold* oneself *under*, i.e. *endure* with patience:—suffer.

5255. ὑπήκοος hupēkŏŏs, *hoop-ay'-kŏ-os;* from 5219; *attentively listening*, i.e. (by impl.) *submissive:*—obedient.

5256. ὑπηρετέω hupērĕtĕō, *hoop-ay-ret-eh'-o;* from 5257; to *be a subordinate*, i.e. (by impl.) *subserve:*—minister (unto), serve.

5257. ὑπηρέτης hupērĕtēs, *hoop-ay-ret'-ace;* from 5259 and a der. of **ἐρέσσω ĕrĕssō** (to *row*); an *under-oarsman*, i.e. (gen.) *subordinate* (*assistant, sexton, constable*):—minister, officer, servant.

5258. ὕπνος hupnŏs, *hoop'-nos;* from an obsol. prim. (perh. akin to 5259 through the idea of *subsilience*); *sleep*, i.e. (fig.) spiritual *torpor:*—sleep.

5259. ὑπό hupŏ, *hoop-ŏ';* a prim. prep.; *under*, i.e. (with the gen.) of place (*beneath*), or with verbs (the agency or means, *through*); (with the acc.) of place (whither [*underneath*] or where [*below*]) or time (when [*at*]):—among, by, from, in, of, under, with. In comp. it retains the same gen. applications, espec. of *inferior* position or condition, and spec. *covertly* or *moderately*.

5260. ὑποβάλλω hupŏballō, *hoop-ob-al'-lo;* from 5259 and 906; to *throw* in *stealthily*, i.e. *introduce* by collusion:—suborn.

5261. ὑπογραμμός hupŏgrammŏs, *hoop-og-ram-mos';* from a comp. of 5259 and 1125; an *underwriting*, i.e. *copy* for imitation (fig.):—example.

5262. ὑπόδειγμα hupŏdĕigma, *hoop-od'-igue-mah;* from 5263; an *exhibit* for imitation or warning (fig. *specimen, adumbration*):—en- (ex-) ample, pattern.

5263. ὑποδείκνυμι hupŏdĕiknumi, *hoop-od-ike'-noo-mee;* from 5259 and 1166; to *exhibit under* the eyes, i.e. (fig.) to *exemplify* (*instruct, admonish*):—show, (fore-) warn.

5264. ὑποδέχομαι hupŏdĕchŏmai, *hoop-od-ekh'-om-ahee;* from 5259 and 1209; to *admit under* one's roof, i.e. *entertain* hospitably:—receive.

5265. ὑποδέω hupŏdĕō, *hoop-od-eh'-o;* from 5259 and 1210; to *bind under* one's feet, i.e. *put on* shoes or sandals:—bind on, (be) shod.

5266. ὑπόδημα hupŏdēma, *hoop-od'-ay-mah;* from 5265; something *bound under* the feet, i.e. a *shoe* or *sandal:*—shoe.

5267. ὑπόδικος hupŏdikŏs, *hoop-od'-ee-kos;* from 5259 and 1349; *under sentence*, i.e. (by impl.) *condemned:*—guilty.

5268. ὑποζύγιον hupŏzugiŏn, *hoop-od-zoog'-ee-on;* neut. of a comp. of 5259 and 2218; an animal *under* the *yoke* (*draught-beast*), i.e. (spec.) a *donkey:*—ass.

5269. ὑποζώννυμι hupŏzōnnumi, *hoop-od-zone'-noo-mee;* from 5259 and 2224; to *gird under*, i.e. *frap* (a vessel with cables across the keel, sides and deck):—undergirt.

5270. ὑποκάτω hupŏkatō, *hoop-ok-at'-o;* from 5259 and 2736; *down under*, i.e. *beneath:*—under.

5271. ὑποκρίνομαι hupŏkrinŏmai, *hoop-ok-rin'-om-ahee;* mid. from 5259 and 2919; to *decide* (*speak* or *act*) *under* a false part, i.e. (fig.) *dissemble* (*pretend*):—feign.

5272. ὑπόκρισις hupŏkrisis, *hoop-ok'-ree-sis;* from 5271; *acting under* a feigned part, i.e. (fig.) *deceit* ("*hypocrisy*"):—condemnation, dissimulation, hypocrisy.

5273. ὑποκριτής hupŏkritēs, *hoop-ok-ree-tace';* from 5271; an *actor under* an assumed character (*stage-player*), i.e. (fig.) a *dissembler* ("*hypocrite*"):—hypocrite.

5274. ὑπολαμβάνω hupŏlambanō, *hoop-ol-am-ban'-o;* from 5259 and 2983; to *take* from *below*, i.e. *carry upward;* fig. to *take up*, i.e. *continue* a discourse or topic; ment. to *assume* (*presume*):—answer, receive, suppose.

5275. ὑπολείπω hupŏlĕipō, *hoop-ol-i'-po;* from 5295 and 3007; to *leave under* (*behind*), i.e. (pass.) to *remain* (*survive*):—be left.

5276. ὑπολήνιον hupŏlēniŏn, *hoop-ol-ay'-nee-on;* neut. of a presumed comp. of 5259 and 3025; vessel or receptacle *under* the *press*, i.e. lower *wine-vat:*—winefat.

5277. ὑπολιμπάνω hupŏlimpanō, *hoop-ol-im-pan'-o;* a prol. form for 5275; to *leave behind*, i.e. *bequeath:*—leave.

5278. ὑπομένω hupŏmĕnō, *hoop-om-en'-o;* from 5259 and 3306; to *stay under* (*behind*), i.e. *remain;* fig. to *undergo*, i.e. *bear* (trials), *have fortitude, persevere:*—abide, endure, (take) patient (-ly), suffer, tarry behind.

5279. ὑπομιμνήσκω hupŏmimnēskō, *hoop-om-im-nace'-ko;* from 5259 and 3403; to *remind quietly*, i.e. *suggest* to the (mid. one's own) memory:—put in mind, remember, bring to (put in) remembrance.

5280. ὑπόμνησις hupŏmnēsis, *hoop-om'-nay-sis;* from 5279; a *reminding* or (reflex.) *recollection:*—remembrance.

5281. ὑπομονή hupŏmŏnē, *hoop-om-on-ay';* from 5278; cheerful (or hopeful) *endurance, constancy:*—enduring, patience, patient continuance (waiting).

5282. ὑπονοέω hupŏnŏĕō, *hoop-on-ŏ-eh'-o;* from 5259 and 3539; to *think under* (*privately*), i.e. to *surmise* or *conjecture:*—think, suppose, deem.

5283. ὑπόνοια hupŏnŏia, *hoop-on'-oy-ah;* from 5282; *suspicion:*—surmising.

5284. ὑποπλέω hupŏplĕō, *hoop-op-leh'-o;* from 5259 and 4126; to *sail under* the lee of:—sail under.

5285. ὑποπνέω hupŏpnĕō, *hoop-op-neh'-o;* from 5259 and 4154; to *breathe gently*, i.e. *breeze:*—blow softly.

5286. ὑποπόδιον hupŏpŏdiŏn, *hoop-op-od'-ee-on;* neut. of a comp. of 5259 and 4228; something *under* the *feet*, i.e. a *foot-rest* (fig.):—footstool.

5287. ὑπόστασις hupŏstasis, *hoop-os'-tas-is;* from a comp. of 5259 and 2476; a *setting under* (*support*), i.e. (fig.) concr. *essence*, or abstr. *assurance* (obj. or subj.):—confidence, confident, person, substance.

5288. ὑποστέλλω hupŏstĕllō, *hoop-os-tel'-lo;* from 5259 and 4724; to *withhold under* (*out of sight*), i.e. (reflex.) to *cower* or *shrink*, (fig.) to *conceal* (*reserve*):—draw (keep) back, shun, withdraw.

5289. ὑποστολή hupŏstŏlē, *hoop-os-tol-ay';* from 5288; *shrinkage* (*timidity*), i.e. (by impl.) *apostasy:*—draw back.

5290. ὑποστρέφω hupŏstrĕphō, *hoop-os-tref'-o;* from 5259 and 4762; to *turn under* (*behind*), i.e. to *return* (lit. or fig.):—come again, return (again, back again), turn back (again).

5291. ὑποστρώννυμι hupŏstrōnnumi, *hoop-os-trone'-noo-mee;* from 5259 and 4766; to *strew underneath* (the feet as a carpet):—spread.

5292. ὑποταγή hupŏtagē, *hoop-ot-ag-ay'*; from *5293*; *subordination*:—subjection.

5293. ὑποτάσσω hupŏtassō, *hoop-ot-as'-so*; from *5259* and *5021*; to *subordinate*; reflex. to *obey*:—be under obedience (obedient), put under, subdue unto, (be, make) subject (to, unto), be (put) in subjection (to, under), submit self unto.

5294. ὑποτίθημι hupŏtithēmi, *hoop-ot-ith'-ay-mee*; from *5259* and *5087*; to *place underneath*, i.e. (fig.) to *hazard*, (reflex.) to *suggest*:—lay down, put in remembrance.

5295. ὑποτρέχω hupŏtrĕchō, *hoop-ot-rekh'-o*; from *5259* and *5143* (includ. its alt.); to *run under*, i.e. (spec.) to *sail past*:—run under.

5296. ὑποτύπωσις hupŏtupōsis, *hoop-ot-oop'-o-sis*; from a comp. of *5259* and a der. of *5179*; *typification under* (*after*), i.e. (concr.) a *sketch* (fig.) for imitation:—form, pattern.

5297. ὑποφέρω hupŏphĕrō, *hoop-of-er'-o*; from *5259* and *5342*; to *bear* from *underneath*, i.e. (fig.) to *undergo* hardship:—bear, endure.

5298. ὑποχωρέω hupŏchōrĕō, *hoop-okh-o-reh'-o*; from *5259* and *5562*; to *vacate down*, i.e. *retire* quietly:—go aside, withdraw self.

5299. ὑπωπιάζω hupōpiazō, *hoop-o-pee-ad'-zo*; from a comp. of *5259* and a der. of *3700*; to hit *under* the *eye* (*buffet* or *disable* an antagonist as a pugilist), i.e. (fig.) to *tease* or *annoy* (into compliance), *subdue* (one's passions):—keep under, weary.

5300. ὗς hus, *hoos*; appar. a prim. word; a *hog* ("*swine*"):—sow.

5301. ὕσσωπος hussōpŏs, *hoos'-so-pos*; of for. or. [231]; "*hyssop*":—hyssop.

5302. ὑστερέω hustĕrĕō, *hoos-ter-eh'-o*; from *5306*; to *be later*, i.e. (by impl.) to *be inferior*; gen. to *fall short* (*be deficient*):—come behind (short), be destitute, fail, lack, suffer need, (be in) want, be the worse.

5303. ὑστέρημα hustĕrēma, *hoos-ter'-ay-mah*; from *5302*; a *deficit*; spec. *poverty*:—that which is behind, (that which was) lack (-ing), penury, want.

5304. ὑστέρησις hustĕrēsis, *hoos-ter'-ay-sis*; from *5302*; a *falling short*, i.e. (spec.) *penury*:—want.

5305. ὕστερον hustĕrŏn, *hoos'-ter-on*; neut. of *5306* as adv.; *more lately*, i.e. *eventually*:—afterward, (at the) last (of all).

5306. ὕστερος hustĕrŏs, *hoos'-ter-os*; compar. from *5259* (in the sense of *behind*); *later*:—latter.

5307. ὑφαντός huphantŏs, *hoo-fan-tos'*; from **ὑφαίνω huphainō** (to *weave*); *woven*, i.e. (perh.) *knitted*:—woven.

5308. ὑψηλός hupsēlŏs, *hoop-say-los'*; from *5311*; *lofty* (in place or character):—high (-er, -ly) (esteemed).

5309. ὑψηλοφρονέω hupsēlŏphrŏnĕō, *hoop-say-lo-fron-eh'-o*; from a comp. of *5308* and *5424*; to *be lofty in mind*, i.e. *arrogant*:—be highminded.

5310. ὕψιστος hupsistŏs, *hoop'-sis-tos*; superl. from the base of *5311*; *highest*, i.e. (masc. sing.) the *Supreme* (God), or (neut. plur.) the *heavens*:—most high, highest.

5311. ὕψος hupsŏs, *hoop'-sos*; from a der. of *5228*; *elevation*, i.e. (abstr.) *altitude*, (spec.) the *sky*, or (fig.) *dignity*:—be exalted, height, (on) high.

5312. ὑψόω hupsŏō, *hoop-sŏ'-o*; from *5311*; to *elevate* (lit. or fig.):—exalt, lift up.

5313. ὕψωμα hupsōma, *hoop'-so-mah*; from *5312*; an *elevated* place or thing, i.e. (abstr.) *altitude*, or (by impl.) a *barrier* (fig.):—height, high thing.

Φ

5314. φάγος phagŏs, *fag'-os*; from *5315*; a *glutton*:—gluttonous.

5315. φάγω phagō, *fag'-o*; a prim. verb (used as an alt. of *2068* in cert. tenses); to *eat* (lit. or fig.):—eat, meat.

5316. φαίνω phainō, *fah'ee-no*; prol. for the base of *5457*; to *lighten* (*shine*), i.e. *show* (trans. or intrans., lit. or fig.):—appear, seem, be seen, shine, × think.

5317. Φάλεκ Phalĕk, *fal'-ek*; of Heb. or. [6389]; *Phalek* (i.e. *Peleg*), a patriarch:—Phalec.

5318. φανερός phanĕrŏs, *fan-er-os'*; from *5316*; *shining*, i.e. *apparent* (lit. or fig.); neut. (as adv.) *publicly*, *externally*:—abroad, + appear, known, manifest, open [+ -ly], outward ([+ -ly]).

5319. φανερόω phanĕrŏō, *fan-er-ŏ'-o*; from *5318*; to *render apparent* (lit. or fig.):—appear, manifestly declare, (make) manifest (forth), shew (self).

5320. φανερῶς phanĕrōs, *fan-er-oce'*; adv. from *5318*; *plainly*, i.e. *clearly* or *publicly*:—evidently, openly.

5321. φανέρωσις phanĕrōsis, *fan-er'-o-sis*; from *5319*; *exhibition*, i.e. (fig.) *expression*, (by extens.) a *bestowment*:—manifestation.

5322. φανός phanŏs, *fan-os'*; from *5316*; a *lightener*, i.e. *light*; *lantern*:—lantern.

5323. Φανουήλ Phanŏuēl, *fan-oo-ale'*; of Heb. or. [6439]; *Phanuēl* (i.e. *Penuēl*), an Isr.:—Phanuel.

5324. φαντάζω phantazō, *fan-tad'-zo*; from a der. of *5316*; to *make apparent*, i.e. (pass.) to *appear* (neut. part. as noun, a *spectacle*):—sight.

5325. φαντασία phantasia, *fan-tas-ee'-ah*; from a der. of *5324*; (prop. abstr.) a (vain) *show* ("fantasy"):—pomp.

5326. φάντασμα phantasma, *fan'-tas-mah*; from *5324*; (prop. concr.) a (mere) *show* ("phantasm"), i.e. *spectre*:—spirit.

5327. φάραγξ pharagx, *far'-anx*; prop. strength. from the base of *4008* or rather of *4486*; a *gap* or *chasm*, i.e. *ravine* (*winter-torrent*):—valley.

5328. Φαραώ Pharaō, *far-ah-o'*; of for. or. [6547]; *Pharaō* (i.e. *Pharoh*), an Eg. king:—Pharaoh.

5329. Φαρές Pharĕs, *far-es'*; of Heb. or. [6557]; *Phares* (i.e. *Perets*), an Isr.:—Phares.

5330. Φαρισαῖος Pharisaiŏs, *far-is-ah'-yos*; of Heb. or. [comp. 6567]; a *separatist*, i.e. exclusively *religious*; a *Pharisæan*, i.e. Jewish sectary:—Pharisee.

5331. φαρμακεία pharmakĕia, *far-mak-i'-ah*; from *5332*; *medication* ("pharmacy"), i.e. (by extens.) *magic* (lit. or fig.):—sorcery, witchcraft.

5332. φαρμακεύς pharmakĕus, *far-mak-yoos'*; from **φάρμακον pharmakŏn** (a *drug*, i.e. spellgiving *potion*); a *druggist* ("pharmacist") or *poisoner*, i.e. (by extens.) a *magician*:—sorcerer.

5333. φαρμακός pharmakŏs, *far-mak-os'*; the same as *5332*:—sorcerer.

5334. φάσις phasis, *fas'-is*; from *5346* (not the same as "phase", which is from *5316*); a *saying*, i.e. *report*:—tidings.

5335. φάσκω phaskō, *fas'-ko*; prol. from the same as *5346*; to *assert*:—affirm, profess, say.

5336. φάτνη phatnē, *fat'-nay*; from **πατέομαι patĕŏmai** (to *eat*); a *crib* (for fodder):—manger, stall.

5337. φαῦλος phaulŏs, *fŏw'-los*; appar. a prim. word; "*foul*" or "*flawy*", i.e. (fig.) *wicked*:—evil.

5338. φέγγος phĕggŏs, *feng'-gos*; prob. akin to the base of *5457* [comp. *5350*]; *brilliancy*:—light.

5339. φείδομαι phĕidŏmai, *fi'-dom-ahee*; of uncert. affin.; to *be chary* of, i.e. (subj.) to *abstain* or (obj.) to *treat leniently*:—forbear, spare.

5340. φειδομένως phĕidŏmĕnōs, *fi-dom-en'-oce*; adv. from part. of *5339*; *abstemiously*, i.e. *stingily*:—sparingly.

5341. φελόνης phĕlŏnēs, *fel-on'-ace*; by transp. for a der. prob. of *5316* (as *showing* outside the other garments); a *mantle* (*surtout*):—cloke.

5342. φέρω phĕrō, *fer'-o*; a prim. verb (for which other and appar. not cognate ones are used in certain tenses only; namely,

οἴω ŏiō, *oy'-o*; and

ἐνέγκω ĕnĕgkō, *en-eng'-ko*); to "*bear*" or *carry* (in a very wide application, lit. and fig., as follows):—be, bear, bring (forth), carry, come, + let her drive, be driven, endure, go on, lay, lead, move, reach, rushing, uphold.

5343. φεύγω phĕugō, *fyoo'-go*; appar. a prim. verb; to *run away* (lit. or fig.); by impl. to *shun*; by anal. to *vanish*:—escape, flee (away).

5344. Φῆλιξ Phēlix, *fay'-lix*; of Lat. or.; *happy*; *Phelix* (i.e. *Felix*), a Rom.:—Felix.

5345. φήμη phēmē, *fay'-may*; from *5346*; a *saying*, i.e. *rumor* ("fame"):—fame.

5346. φημί phēmi, *fay-mee'*; prop. the same as the base of *5457* and *5316*; to *show* or *make known* one's thoughts, i.e. *speak* or *say*:—affirm, say. Comp. *3004*.

5347. Φῆστος Phēstŏs, *face'-tos*; of Lat. der.; *festal*; *Phestus* (i.e. *Festus*), a Rom.:—Festus.

5348. φθάνω phthanō, *fthan'-o*; appar. a prim. verb; to *be beforehand*, i.e. *anticipate* or *precede*, by extens. to *have arrived* at:—(already) attain, come, prevent.

5349. φθαρτός phthartŏs, *fthar-tos'*; from *5351*; *decayed*, i.e. (by impl.) *perishable*:—corruptible.

5350. φθέγγομαι phthĕggŏmai, *ftheng'-gom-ahee*; prob. akin to *5338* and thus to *5346*; to *utter* a clear sound, i.e. (gen.) to *proclaim*:—speak.

5351. φθείρω phthĕirō, *fthi'-ro*; prob. strength. from **φθίω phthiō** (to *pine* or *waste*); prop. to *shrivel* or *wither*, i.e. to *spoil* (by any process) or (gen.) to *ruin* (espec. fig. by mor. influences, to *deprave*):—corrupt (self), defile, destroy.

5352. φθινοπωρινός phthinŏpōrinŏs, *fthin-op-o-ree-nos'*; from a der. of **φθίνω phthinō** (to *wane*; akin to the base of *5351*) and *3703* (mean. *late autumn*); *autumnal* (as *stripped* of leaves):—whose fruit withereth.

5353. φθόγγος phthŏggŏs, *fthong'-gos*; from *5350*; *utterance*, i.e. a *musical* note (vocal or instrumental):—sound.

5354. φθονέω phthŏnĕō, *fthon-eh'-o*; from *5355*; to *be jealous* of:—envy.

5355. φθόνος phthŏnŏs, *fthon'-os*; prob. akin to the base of *5351*; *ill-will* (as *detraction*), i.e. *jealousy* (*spite*):—envy.

5356. φθορά phthŏra, *fthor-ah'*; from *5351*; *decay*, i.e. *ruin* (spontaneous or inflicted, lit. or fig.):—corruption, destroy, perish.

5357. φιάλη phialē, *fee-al'-ay*; of uncert. affin.; a broad shallow *cup* ("phial"):—vial.

5358. φιλάγαθος philagathŏs, *fil-ag'-ath-os*; from *5384* and *18*; *fond to good*, i.e. a *promoter of virtue*:—love of good men.

5359. Φιλαδέλφεια Philadĕlphĕia, *fil-ad-el'-fee-ah*; from **Φιλάδελφος Philadĕlphŏs** (the same as *5361*), a king of Pergamos; *Philadelphia*, a place in Asia Minor:—Philadelphia.

5360. φιλαδελφία philadĕlphia, *fil-ad-el-fee'-ah*; from *5361*; *fraternal affection*:—brotherly love (kindness), love of the brethren.

5361. φιλάδελφος philadĕlphŏs, *fil-ad'-el-fos*; from *5384* and *80*; *fond of brethren*, i.e. *fraternal*:—love as brethren.

5362. φίλανδρος philandrŏs, *fil'-an-dros*; from *5384* and *435*; *fond of man*, i.e. *affectionate* as a wife:—love their husbands.

5363. φιλανθρωπία philanthrōpia, *fil-an-thro-pee'-ah*; from the same as *5364*; *fondness of mankind*, i.e. *benevolence* ("*philanthropy*"):—kindness, love towards man.

5364. φιλανθρώπως philanthrōpōs, *fil-an-thro'-poce*; adv. from a comp. of *5384* and *444*; *fondly to man* ("philanthropically"), i.e. *humanely*:—courteously.

5365. φιλαργυρία philarguria, *fil-ar-goo-ree'-ah*; from *5366*; *avarice*:—love of money.

5366. φιλάργυρος philargurŏs, *fil-ar'-goo-ros*; from *5384* and *696*; *fond of silver* (*money*), i.e. *avaricious*:—covetous.

5367. φίλαυτος philautŏs, *fil'-ŏw-tos*; from *5384* and *846*; *fond of self*, i.e. *selfish*:—lover of own self.

5368. φιλέω philĕō, *fil-eh'-o*; from *5384*; to *be a friend to* (*fond of* [an individual or an object]), i.e. *have affection* for (denoting *personal* attachment, as a matter of sentiment or feeling; while 25 is wider, embracing espec. the judgment and the *deliberate* assent of the will as a matter of principle, duty and propriety: the two thus stand related very much as 2309 and 1014, or as 2372 and 3563 respectively; the former being chiefly of the *heart* and the latter of the *head*); spec. to *kiss* (as a mark of tenderness):—kiss, love.

5369. φιλήδονος **philēdŏnŏs**, *fil-ay'-don-os;* from 5384 and 2237; *fond of pleasure*, i.e. *voluptuous:*—lover of pleasure.

5370. φίλημα **philēma**, *fil'-ay-mah;* from 5368; a *kiss:*—kiss.

5371. Φιλήμων **Philēmōn**, *fil-ay'-mone;* from 5368; *friendly; Philemon*, a Chr.:—Philemon.

5372. Φιλητός **Philētŏs**, *fil-ay-tos';* from 5368; *amiable; Philetus*, an opposer of Christianity:—Philetus.

5373. φιλία **philia**, *fil-ee'-ah;* from 5384; *fondness:*—friendship.

5374. Φιλιππήσιος **Philippēsiŏs**, *fil-ip-pay'-see-os;* from 5375; a *Philippesian* (*Philippian*), i.e. native of Philippi:—Philippian.

5375. Φίλιπποι **Philippŏi**, *fil'-ip-poy;* plur. of 5376; *Philippi*, a place in Macedonia:—Philippi.

5376. Φίλιππος **Philippŏs**, *fil'-ip-pos;* from 5384 and 2462; *fond of horses; Philippus*, the name of four Isr.:—Philip.

5377. φιλόθεος **philŏthĕŏs**, *fil-oth'-eh-os;* from 5384 and 2316; *fond of God*, i.e. *pious:*—lover of God.

5378. Φιλόλογος **Philŏlŏgŏs**, *fil-ol'-og-os;* from 5384 and 3056; *fond of words*, i.e. *talkative* (*argumentative, learned, "philological"*); *Philologus*, a Chr.:—Philologus.

5379. φιλονεικία **philŏnĕikia**, *fil-on-i-kee'-ah;* from 5380; *quarrelsomeness*, i.e. a *dispute:*—strife.

5380. φιλόνεικος **philŏnĕikŏs**, *fil-on'-i-kos;* from 5384 and νεῖκος **nĕikŏs** (a *quarrel;* prob. akin to 3534); *fond of strife*, i.e. *disputatious:*—contentious.

5381. φιλονεξία **philŏnĕxia**, *fil-on-ex-ee'-ah;* from 5382; *hospitableness:*—entertain strangers, hospitality.

5382. φιλόξενος **philŏxĕnŏs**, *fil-ox'-en-os;* from 5384 and 3581; *fond of guests*, i.e. *hospitable:*—given to (lover of, use) hospitality.

5383. φιλοπρωτεύω **philŏprōtĕuō**, *fil-op-rote-yoo'-o;* from a comp. of 5384 and 4413; *to be fond of being first*, i.e. *ambitious* of distinction:—love to have the preëminence.

5384. φίλος **philŏs**, *fee'-los;* prop. *dear*, i.e. a *friend;* act. *fond*, i.e. *friendly* (still as a noun, an *associate, neighbor*, etc.):—friend.

5385. φιλοσοφία **philŏsŏphia**, *fil-os-of-ee'-ah;* from 5386; "*philosophy*", i.e. (spec.) Jewish *sophistry:*—philosophy.

5386. φιλόσοφος **philŏsŏphŏs**, *fil-os'-of-os;* from 5384 and 4680; *fond of wise* things, i.e. a "*philosopher*":—philosopher.

5387. φιλόστοργος **philŏstŏrgŏs**, *fil-os'-tor-gos;* from 5384 and στοργή **stŏrgē** (*cherishing* one's kindred, espec. parents or children); *fond of* natural *relatives*, i.e. *fraternal* towards fellow Chr.:—kindly affectioned.

5388. φιλότεκνος **philŏtĕknŏs**, *fil-ot'-ek-nos;* from 5384 and 5043; *fond of* one's *children*, i.e. *maternal:*—love their children.

5389. φιλοτιμέομαι **philŏtimĕŏmai**, *fil-ot-im-eh'-om-ahee;* mid. from a comp. of 5384 and 5092; to be *fond of honor*, i.e. *emulous* (*eager* or *earnest* to do something):—labour, strive, study.

5390. φιλοφρόνως **philŏphrŏnōs**, *fil-of-ron'-oce;* adv. from 5391; *with friendliness of mind*, i.e. *kindly:*—courteously.

5391. φιλόφρων **philŏphrōn**, *fil-of'-rone;* from 5384 and 5424; *friendly of mind*, i.e. *kind:*—courteous.

5392. φιμόω **phimŏō**, *fee-mŏ'-o;* from φιμός **phimŏs** (a *muzzle*); to *muzzle:*—muzzle.

5393. Φλέγων **Phlĕgōn**, *fleg'-one;* act. part. of the base of 5395; *blazing; Phlegon*, a Chr.:—Phlegon.

5394. φλογίζω **phlŏgizō**, *flog-id'-zo;* from 5395; *to cause a blaze*, i.e. *ignite* (fig. to *inflame* with passion):—set on fire.

5395. φλόξ **phlŏx**, *flox;* from a prim. φλέγω **phlĕgō** (to "*flash*" or "*flame*"); a *blaze:*—flame (-ing).

5396. φλυαρέω **phluarĕō**, *floo-ar-eh'-o;* from 5397; *to be a babbler* or *trifler*, i.e. (by impl.) to *berate* idly or mischievously:—prate against.

5397. φλύαρος **phluarŏs**, *floo'-ar-os;* from φλύω **phluō** (to *bubble*); a *garrulous* person, i.e. *prater:*—tattler.

5398. φοβερός **phŏbĕrŏs**, *fob-er-os';* from 5401; *frightful*, i.e. (obj.) *formidable:*—fearful, terrible.

5399. φοβέω **phŏbĕō**, *fob-eh'-o;* from 5401; to *frighten*, i.e. (pass.) to *be alarmed;* by anal. to *be in awe* of, i.e. *revere:*—be (+ sore) afraid, fear (exceedingly), reverence.

5400. φόβητρον **phŏbētrŏn**, *fob'-ay-tron;* neut. of a der. of 5399; a *frightening* thing, i.e. *terrific* portent:—fearful sight.

5401. φόβος **phŏbŏs**, *fob'-os;* from a prim. φέβομαι **phĕbŏmai** (to *be* put in *fear*); *alarm* or *fright:*—be afraid, + exceedingly, fear, terror.

5402. Φοίβη **Phŏibē**, *foy'-bay;* fem. of φοῖβος **phŏibŏs** (*bright;* prob. akin to the base of 5457); *Phœbe*, a Chr. woman:—Phebe.

5403. Φοινίκη **Phŏinikē**, *foy-nee'-kay;* from 5404; *palm*-country; *Phœnice* (or *Phœnicia*), a region of Pal.:—Phenice, Phenicia.

5404. φοῖνιξ **phŏinix**, *foy'-nix;* of uncert. der.; a *palm*-tree:—palm (tree).

5405. Φοῖνιξ **Phŏinix**, *foy'-nix;* prob. the same as 5404; *Phœnix*, a place in Crete:—Phenice.

5406. φονεύς **phŏnĕus**, *fon-yooce';* from 5408; a *murderer* (always of *criminal* [or at least *intentional*] homicide; which 443 does not necessarily imply; while 4607 is a spec. term for a *public* bandit):—murderer.

5407. φονεύω **phŏnĕuō**, *fon-yoo'-o;* from 5406; *to be a murderer* (of):—kill, do murder, slay.

5408. φόνος **phŏnŏs**, *fon'-os;* from an obsol. prim. φένω **phĕnō** (to *slay*); *murder:*—murder, + be slain with, slaughter.

5409. φορέω **phŏrĕō**, *for-eh'-o;* from 5411; to *have a burden*, i.e. (by anal.) to *wear* as clothing or a constant accompaniment:—bear, wear.

5410. Φόρον **Phŏrŏn**, *for'-on;* of Lat. or.; a *forum* or market-place; only in comp. with 675, a *station* on the Appian road:—forum.

5411. φόρος **phŏrŏs**, *for'-os;* from 5342; a *load* (as *borne*), i.e. (fig.) a *tax* (prop. an individ. *assessment* on persons or property; whereas 5056 is usually a gen. *toll* on goods or travel):—tribute.

5412. φορτίζω **phŏrtizō**, *for-tid'-zo;* from 5414; to *load* up (prop. as a vessel or animal), i.e. (fig.) to *overburden* with ceremony (or spiritual anxiety):—lade, be heavy laden.

5413. φορτίον **phŏrtiŏn**, *for-tee'-on;* dimin. of 5414; an *invoice* (as part of *freight*), i.e. (fig.) a *task* or *service:*—burden.

5414. φόρτος **phŏrtŏs**, *for'-tos;* from 5342; something *carried*, i.e. the *cargo* of a ship:—lading.

5415. Φορτουνάτος **Phŏrtŏunatŏs**, *for-too-nat'-os;* of Lat. or.; "*fortunate*"; *Fortunatus*, a Chr.:—Fortunatus.

5416. φραγέλλιον **phragĕlliŏn**, *frag-el'-le-on;* neut. of a der. from the base of 5417; a *whip*, i.e. Rom. *lash* as a public punishment:—scourge.

5417. φραγελλόω **phragĕllŏō**, *frag-el-lŏ'-o;* from a presumed equiv. of the Lat. *flagellum;* to *whip*, i.e. *lash* as a public punishment:—scourge.

5418. φραγμός **phragmŏs**, *frag-mos';* from 5420; a *fence*, or inclosing *barrier* (lit. or fig.):—hedge (+ round about), partition.

5419. φράζω **phrazō**, *frad'-zo;* prob. akin to 5420 through the idea of *defining;* to *indicate* (by word or act), i.e. (spec.) to *expound:*—declare.

5420. φράσσω **phrassō**, *fras'-so;* appar. a strength. form of the base of 5424; to *fence* or inclose, i.e. (spec.) to *block* up (fig. to *silence*):—stop.

5421. φρέαρ **phrĕar**, *freh'-ar;* of uncert. der.; a *hole* in the ground (dug for obtaining or holding water or other purposes), i.e. a *cistern* or *well;* fig. an *abyss* (as a *prison*):—well, pit.

5422. φρεναπατάω **phrĕnapataō**, *fren-ap-at-ah'-o;* from 5423; to *be a mind-misleader*, i.e. *delude:*—deceive.

5423. φρεναπάτης **phrĕnapatēs**, *fren-ap-at-ace;* from 5424 and 539; a *mind-misleader*, i.e. *seducer:*—deceiver.

5424. φρήν **phrēn**, *frane;* prob. from an obsol. φράω **phraō** (to *rein* in or *curb;* comp. 5420); the *midrif* (as a *partition* of the body), i.e. (fig. and by impl. of sympathy) the *feelings* (or sensitive nature; by extens. [also in the plur.] the *mind* or cognitive faculties):—understanding.

5425. φρίσσω **phrissō**, *fris'-so;* appar. a prim. verb; to "*bristle*" or *chill*, i.e. *shudder* (*fear*):—tremble.

5426. φρονέω **phrŏnĕō**, *fron-eh'-o;* from 5424; to *exercise* the *mind*, i.e. *entertain* or *have* a *sentiment* or *opinion;* by impl. to *be* (mentally) *disposed* (more or less earnestly in a certain direction); intens. to *interest oneself* in (with concern or obedience):—set the affection on, (be) care (-ful), (be like-, + be of one, + be of the same, + let this) mind (-ed), regard, savour, think.

5427. φρόνημα **phrŏnēma**, *fron'-ay-mah;* from 5426; (mental) *inclination* or *purpose:*—(be, + be carnally, + be spiritually) mind (-ed).

5428. φρόνησις **phrŏnēsis**, *fron'-ay-sis;* from 5426; mental *action* or *activity*, i.e. intellectual or mor. *insight:*—prudence, wisdom.

5429. φρόνιμος **phrŏnimŏs**, *fron'-ee-mos;* from 5424; *thoughtful*, i.e. *sagacious* or *discreet* (implying a *cautious* character; while 4680 denotes *practical* skill or acumen; and 4908 indicates rather *intelligence* or mental acquirement); in a bad sense *conceited* (also in the compar.):—wise (-r).

5430. φρονίμως **phrŏnimōs**, *fron-im'-oce;* adv. from 5429; *prudently:*—wisely.

5431. φροντίζω **phrŏntizō**, *fron-tid'-zo;* from a der. of 5424; to *exercise thought*, i.e. *be anxious:*—be careful.

5432. φρουρέω **phrŏurĕō**, *froo-reh'-o;* from a comp. of 4253 and 3708; to *be a watcher in advance*, i.e. to *mount guard* as a sentinel (*post spies* at gates); fig. to *hem in, protect:*—keep (with a garrison). Comp. 5083.

5433. φρυάσσω **phruassō**, *froo-as'-so*, akin to 1032, 1031; to *snort* (as a spirited horse), i.e. (fig.) to *make a tumult:*—rage.

5434. φρύγανον **phruganŏn**, *froo'-gan-on;* neut. of a presumed der. of φρύγω **phrugō** (to *roast* or *parch;* akin to the base of 5395); something *desiccated*, i.e. a dry *twig:*—stick.

5435. Φρυγία **Phrugia**, *froog-ee'-ah;* prob. of for. or.; *Phrygia*, a region of Asia Minor:—Phrygia.

5436. Φύγελλος **Phugĕllŏs**, *foog'-el-los;* prob. from 5343; *fugitive; Phygellus*, an apostate Chr.:—Phygellus.

5437. φυγή **phugē**, *foog-ay';* from 5343; a *fleeing*, i.e. *escape:*—flight.

5438. φυλακή **phulakē**, *foo-lak-ay';* from 5442; a *guarding* or (concr. *guard*), the act, the person; fig. the place, the condition, or (spec.) the time (as a division of day or night), lit. or fig.:—cage, hold, (im-) prison (-ment), ward, watch.

5439. φυλακίζω **phulakizō**, *foo-lak-id'-zo;* from 5441; to *incarcerate:*—imprison.

5440. φυλακτήριον **phulaktēriŏn**, *foo-lak-tay'-ree-on;* neut. of a der. of 5442; a *guard-case*, i.e. "*phylactery*" for wearing slips of Scripture texts:—phylactery.

5441. φύλαξ **phulax**, *foo'-lax;* from 5442; a *watcher* or *sentry:*—keeper.

5442. φυλάσσω **phulassō**, *foo-las'-so;* prob. from 5443 through the idea of *isolation;* to *watch*, i.e.

be on guard (lit. or fig.); by impl. to *preserve, obey, avoid*:—beware, keep (self), observe, save. Comp. 5083.

5443. φυλή phulē, *foo-lay'*; from 5453 (comp. 5444); an *offshoot*, i.e. *race* or *clan*:—kindred, tribe.

5444. φύλλον phullŏn, *fool'-lon*; from the same as 5443; a *sprout*, i.e. *leaf*:—leaf.

5445. φύραμα phurama, *foo'-ram-ah*; from a prol. form of **φύρω phurō** (to *mix* a liquid with a solid; perh. akin to 5453 through the idea of *swelling* in bulk), mean to *knead*; a *mass* of dough:—lump.

5446. φυσικός phusikŏs, *foo-see-kos'*; from 5449; "*physical*", i.e. (by impl.) *instinctive*:—natural. Comp. 5591.

5447. φυσικῶς phusikōs, *foo-see-koce'*; adv. from 5446; "*physically*", i.e. (by impl.) *instinctively*:—naturally.

5448. φυσιόω phusiŏō, *foo-see-ŏ'-o*; from 5449 in the prim. sense of *blowing*; to *inflate*, i.e. (fig.) *make proud* (*haughty*):—puff up.

5449. φύσις phusis, *foo'-sis*; from 5453; *growth* (by *germination* or *expansion*), i.e. (by impl.) natural *production* (lineal *descent*); by extens. a *genus* or *sort*; fig. native *disposition, constitution* or *usage*:—([man-]) kind, nature ([-al]).

5450. φυσίωσις phusiōsis, *foo-see'-o-sis*; from 5448; *inflation*, i.e. (fig.) *haughtiness*:—swelling.

5451. φυτεία phutĕia, *foo-ti'-ah*; from 5452; trans-*planting*, i.e. (concr.) a *shrub* or *vegetable*:—plant.

5452. φυτεύω phutĕuō, *foot-yoo'-o*; from a der. of 5453; to *set out* in the earth, i.e. *implant*; fig. to *instil* doctrine:—plant.

5453. φύω phuō, *foo'-o*; a prim. verb; prob. orig. to "*puff*" or *blow*, i.e. to *swell* up; but only used in the impl. sense, to *germinate* or *grow* (*sprout, produce*), lit. or fig.:—spring (up).

5454. φωλεός phōlĕŏs, *fo-leh-os'*; of uncert. der.; a *burrow* or *lurking-place*:—hole.

5455. φωνέω phōnĕō, *fo-neh'-o*; from 5456; to emit a *sound* (animal, human or instrumental); by impl. to *address* in words or by name, also in imitation:—call (for), crow, cry.

5456. φωνή phōnē, *fo-nay'*; prob. akin to 5316 through the idea of *disclosure*; a *tone* (articulate, bestial or artificial); by impl. an *address* (for any purpose), *saying* or *language*:—noise, sound, voice.

5457. φῶς phōs, *foce*; from an obsol. **φάω phaō** (to *shine* or make *manifest*, espec. by *rays*; comp. 5316, 5346); *luminousness* (in the widest application, nat. or artificial, abstr. or concr., lit. or fig.):—fire, light.

5458. φωστήρ phōstēr, *foce-tare'*; from 5457; an *illuminator*, i.e. (concr.) a *luminary*, or (abstr.) *brilliancy*:—light.

5459. φωσφόρος phōsphŏrŏs, *foce-for'-os*; from 5457 and 5342; *light-bearing* ("phosphorus"), i.e. (spec.) the *morning-star* (fig.):—day star.

5460. φωτεινός phōtĕinŏs, *fo-ti-nos'*; from 5457; *lustrous*, i.e. *transparent* or *well-illuminated* (fig.):—bright, full of light.

5461. φωτίζω phōtizō, *fo-tid'-zo*; from 5457; to *shed rays*, i.e. to *shine* or (trans.) to *brighten* up (lit. or fig.):—enlighten, illuminate, (bring to, give) light, make to see.

5462. φωτισμός phōtismŏs, *fo-tis-mos'*; from 5461; *illumination* (fig.):—light.

X

5463. χαίρω chairō, *khah'ee-ro*; a prim. verb; to be "*cheer*"*ful*, i.e. calmly *happy* or well-off; impers. espec. as salutation (on meeting or parting), *be well*:—farewell, be glad, God speed, greeting, hail, joy (-fully), rejoice.

5464. χάλαζα chalaza, *khal'-ad-zah*; prob. from 5465; *hail*:—hail.

5465. χαλάω chalaō, *khal-ah'-o*; from the base of 5490; to *lower* (as into a *void*):—let down, strike.

5466. Χαλδαῖος Chaldaiŏs, *khal-dah'-yos*; prob. of Heb. or. [3778]; a *Chaldæan* (i.e. *Kasdi*), or native of the region of the lower Euphrates:—Chaldæan.

5467. χαλεπός chalĕpŏs, *khal-ep-os'*; perh. from 5465 through the idea of *reducing* the strength; *difficult*, i.e. *dangerous*, or (by impl.) *furious*:—fierce, perilous.

5468. χαλιναγωγέω chalinagōgĕō, *khal-in-agogue-eh'-o*; from a comp. of 5469 and the redupl. form of 71; to be a *bit-leader*, i.e. to *curb* (fig.):—bridle.

5469. χαλινός chalinŏs, *khal-ee-nos'*; from 5465; a *curb* or *head-stall* (as *curbing* the spirit):—bit, bridle.

5470. χάλκεος chalkĕŏs, *khal'-keh-os*; from 5475; *coppery*:—brass.

5471. χαλκεύς chalkĕus, *khalk-yooce'*; from 5475; a *copper-worker* or *brazier*:—coppersmith.

5472. χαλκηδών chalkēdōn, *khal-kay-dōhn'*; from 5475 and perh. 1491; *copper-like*, i.e. "*chalcedony*":—chalcedony.

5473. χαλκίον chalkiŏn, *khal-kee'-on*; dimin. from 5475; a *copper dish*:—brazen vessel.

5474. χαλκολίβανον chalkŏlibanŏn, *khal-kol-ib'-an-on*; neut. of a comp. of 5475 and 3030 (in the impl. mean. of *whiteness* or *brilliancy*); *burnished copper*, an alloy of copper (or gold) and silver having a brilliant lustre:—fine brass.

5475. χαλκός chalkŏs, *khal-kos'*; perh. from 5465 through the idea of *hollowing* out as a vessel (this metal being chiefly used for that purpose); *copper* (the substance, or some implement or coin made of it):—brass, money.

5476. χαμαί chamai, *kham-ah'ee*; adv. perh. from the base of 5490 through the idea of a *fissure* in the soil; *earthward*, i.e. *prostrate*:—on (to) the ground.

5477. Χαναάν Chanaan, *khan-ah-an'*; of Heb. or. [3667]; *Chanaan* (i.e. *Kenaan*), the early name of Pal.:—Chanaan.

5478. Χαναναῖος Chanaanaiŏs, *khan-ah-an-ah'-yos*; from 5477; a *Chanaanæan* (i.e. *Kenaanite*), or native of gentile Pal.:—of Canaan.

5479. χαρά chara, *khar-ah'*; from 5463; *cheerfulness*, i.e. calm *delight*:—gladness, × greatly, (× be exceeding) joy (-ful, -fully, -fulness, -ous).

5480. χάραγμα charagma, *khar'-ag-mah*; from the same as 5482; a *scratch* or *etching*, i.e. *stamp* (as a *badge* of servitude), or *sculptured* figure (*statue*):—graven, mark.

5481. χαρακτήρ charaktēr, *khar-ak-tare'*; from the same as 5482; a *graver* (the tool or the person), i.e. (by impl.) *engraving* (["*character*"], the *figure* stamped, i.e. an exact *copy* or [fig.] *representation*):—express image.

5482. χάραξ charax, *khar'-ax*; from **χαράσσω charassō** (to *sharpen* to a point; akin to 1125 through the idea of *scratching*); a *stake*, i.e. (by impl.) a *palisade* or *rampart* (military *mound* for circumvallation in a siege):—trench.

5483. χαρίζομαι charizŏmai, *khar-id'-zom-ahee*; mid. from 5485; to grant as a *favor*, i.e. gratuitously, in kindness, pardon or rescue:—deliver, (frankly) forgive, (freely) give, grant.

5484. χάριν charin, *khar'-in*; acc. of 5485 as prep.; through *favor* of, i.e. *on account* of:—be-(for) cause of, for sake of, + . . . fore, × reproachfully.

5485. χάρις charis, *khar'-ece*; from 5463; *graciousness* (as *gratifying*), of manner or act (abstr. or concr.; lit., fig. or spiritual; espec. the divine influence upon the heart, and its reflection in the life; including *gratitude*):—acceptable, benefit, favour, gift, grace (-ious), joy liberality, pleasure, thank (-s, -worthy).

5486. χάρισμα charisma, *khar'-is-mah*; from 5483; a (divine) *gratuity*, i.e. *deliverance* (from danger or passion); (spec.) a (spiritual) *endowment*, i.e. (subj.) religious *qualification*, or (obj.) miraculous *faculty*:—(free) gift.

5487. χαριτόω charitŏō, *khar-ee-tŏ'-o*; from 5485; to *grace*, i.e. indue with special *honor*:—make accepted, be highly favoured.

5488. Χαρράν Charrhan, *khar-hran'*; of Heb. or. [2771]; *Charrhan* (i.e. *Charan*), a place in Mesopotamia:—Charran.

5489. χάρτης chartēs, *khar'-tace*; from the same as 5482; a *sheet* ("chart") of writing-material (as to be *scribbled* over):—paper.

5490. χάσμα chasma, *khas'-mah*; from a form of an obsol. prim. **χάω chaō** (to "*gape*" or "*yawn*"); a "*chasm*" or *vacancy* (impassable *interval*):—gulf.

5491. χεῖλος chĕilŏs, *khi'-los*; from a form of the same as 5490; a *lip* (as a *pouring* place); fig. a *margin* (of water):—lip, shore.

5492. χειμάζω chĕimazō, *khi-mad'-zo*; from the same as 5494; to *storm*, i.e. (pass.) to *labor under a gale*:—be tossed with tempest.

5493. χείμαρρος chĕimarrhŏs, *khi'-mar-hros*; from the base of 5494 and 4482; a *storm-runlet*, i.e. *winter-torrent*:—brook.

5494. χειμών chĕimōn, *khi-mone'*; from a der. of **χέω chĕō** (to *pour*; akin to the base of 5490 through the idea of a *channel*), mean. a *storm* (as *pouring* rain); by impl. the *rainy* season, i.e. *winter*:—tempest, foul weather, winter.

5495. χείρ chĕir, *khire*; perh. from the base of 5494 in the sense of its congener the base of 5490 (through the idea of *hollowness* for grasping); the *hand* (lit. or fig. [*power*]; espec. [by Heb.] a *means* or *instrument*):—hand.

5496. χειραγωγέω chĕiragōgĕō, *khi-rag-ogue-eh'-o*; from 5497; to be a *hand-leader*, i.e. to *guide* (a blind person):—lead by the hand.

5497. χειραγωγός chĕiragōgŏs, *khi-rag-o-gos'*; from 5495 and a redupl. form of 71; a *hand-leader*, i.e. personal *conductor* (of a blind person):—some to lead by the hand.

5498. χειρόγραφον chĕirŏgraphŏn, *khi-rog'-raf-on*; neut. of a comp. of 5495 and 1125; something *hand-written* ("*chirograph*"), i.e. a *manuscript* (spec. a legal *document* or *bond* [fig.]):—handwriting.

5499. χειροποίητος chĕirŏpŏiētŏs, *khi-rop-oy'-ay-tos*; from 5495 and a der. of 4160; *manufactured*, i.e. *of human construction*:—made by (make with) hands.

5500. χειροτονέω chĕirŏtŏnĕō, *khi-rot-on-eh'-o*; from a comp. of 5495 and **τείνω tĕinō** (to *stretch*); to be a *hand-reacher* or *voter* (by raising the hand), i.e. (gen.) to *select* or *appoint*:—choose, ordain.

5501. χείρων chĕirōn, *khi'-rone*; irreg. comp. of 2556; from an obsol. equiv. **χέρης chĕrēs** (of uncert. der.); *more evil* or *aggravated* (phys., ment. or mor.):—sorer, worse.

5502. χερουβίμ chĕrŏubim, *kher-oo-beem'*; plur. of Heb. or. [3742]; "*cherubim*" (i.e. *cherubs* or *kerubim*):—cherubims.

5503. χήρα chēra, *khay'-rah*; fem. of a presumed der. appar. from the base of 5490 through the idea of *deficiency*; a *widow* (as *lacking* a husband), lit. or fig.:—widow.

5504. χθές chthĕs, *khthes*; of uncert. der.; "*yesterday*"; by extens. *in time past* or *hitherto*:—yesterday.

5505. χιλιάς chilias, *khil-ee-as'*; from 5507; *one thousand* ("*chiliad*"):—thousand.

5506. χιλίαρχος chiliarchŏs, *khil-ee-ar-khos*; from 5507 and 757; the *commander of a thousand* soldiers ("*chiliarch*"), i.e. *colonel*:—(chief, high) captain.

5507. χίλιοι chiliŏi, *khil'-ee-oy*; plur. of uncert. affin.; a *thousand*:—thousand.

5508. Χίος Chiŏs, *khee'-os*; of uncert. der.; *Chios*, an island in the Mediterranean:—Chios.

5509. χιτών chitōn, *khee-tone'*; of for. or. [3801]; a *tunic* or *shirt*:—clothes, coat, garment.

5510. χιών chiōn, *khee-one'*; perh. akin to the base of 5490 (5465) or 5494 (as *descending* or *empty*); *snow*:—snow.

5511. χλαμύς chlamus, *khlam-ooce'*; of uncert. der.; a military *cloak*:—robe.

5512. χλευάζω **chlĕuazō**, *khlyoo-ad'-zo;* from a der. prob. of *5491;* to *throw out* the *lip*, i.e. *jeer* at:—mock.

5513. χλιαρός **chliarŏs**, *khlee-ar-os';* from χλίω **chliō** (to *warm*); *tepid:*—lukewarm.

5514. Χλόη **Chlŏē**, *khlŏ'-ay;* fem. of appar. a prim. word; "*green*"; *Chloë*, a Chr. female:—Chloe.

5515. χλωρός **chlōrŏs**, *khlo-ros';* from the same as *5514;* *greenish*, i.e. *verdant*, *dun-colored:*—green, pale.

5516. χξϛ **chi xi stigma**, *khee zee stig'-ma;* the 22d, 14th and an obsol. letter (*4742* as a *cross*) of the Greek alphabet (intermediate between the 5th and 6th), used as numbers; denoting respectively 600, 60 and 6; 666 as a numeral:—six hundred threescore and six.

5517. χοϊκός **chŏïkŏs**, *khŏ-ik-os';* from *5522;* *dusty* or *dirty* (*soil*-like), i.e. (by impl.) *terrene:*—earthy.

5518. χοῖνιξ **chŏinix**, *khoy'-nix;* of uncert. der.; a *chœnix* or cert. dry measure:—measure.

5519. χοῖρος **chŏirŏs**, *khoy'-ros;* of uncert. der.; a *hog:*—swine.

5520. χολάω **chŏlaō**, *khol-ah'-o;* from *5521;* to *be bilious*, i.e. (by impl.) *irritable* (*enraged*, "choleric"):—be angry.

5521. χολή **chŏlē**, *khol-ay';* fem. of an equiv. perh. akin to the same as *5514* (from the *greenish* hue); "*gall*" or *bile*, i.e. (by anal.) *poison* or an *anodyne* (wormwood, poppy, etc.):—gall.

5522. χόος **chŏŏs**, *khŏ'-os;* from the base of *5494;* a *heap* (as *poured* out), i.e. *rubbish;* loose *dirt:*—dust.

5523. Χοραζίν **Chŏrazin**, *khor-ad-zin';* of uncert. der.; *Chorazin*, a place in Pal.:—Chorazin.

5524. χορηγέω **chŏrēgĕō**, *khor-ayg-eh'-o;* from a comp. of *5525* and *71;* to *be a dance-leader*, i.e. (gen.) to *furnish:*—give, minister.

5525. χορός **chŏrŏs**, *khor-os';* of uncert. der.; a *ring*, i.e. round *dance* ("choir"):—dancing.

5526. χορτάζω **chŏrtazō**, *khor-tad'-zo;* from *5528;* to *fodder*, i.e. (gen.) to *gorge* (*supply food* in abundance):—feed, fill, satisfy.

5527. χόρτασμα **chŏrtasma**, *khor'-tas-mah;* from *5526;* *forage*, i.e. *food:*—sustenance.

5528. χόρτος **chŏrtŏs**, *khor'-tos;* appar. a prim. word; a "*court*" or "*garden*", i.e. (by impl. of *pasture*) *herbage* or *vegetation:*—blade, grass, hay.

5529. Χουζᾶς **Chŏuzas**, *khood-zas';* of uncert. or.; *Chuzas*, an officer of Herod:—Chuza.

5530. χράομαι **chraŏmai**, *khrah'-om-ahee;* mid. of a prim. verb (perh. rather from *5495*, to *handle*); to *furnish* what is needed; (give an *oracle*, "*graze*" [touch slightly], *light* upon, etc.), i.e. (by impl.) to *employ* or (by extens.) to *act towards* one in a given manner:—entreat, use. Comp. *5531*, *5534*.

5531. χράω **chraō**, *khrah'-o;* prob. the same as the base of *5530;* to *loan:*—lend.

5532. χρεία **chrĕia**, *khri'-ah;* from the base of *5530* or *5534;* *employment*, i.e. an *affair;* also (by impl.) *occasion*, *demand*, *requirement* or *destitution:*—business, lack, necessary (-ity), need (-ful), use, want.

5533. χρεωφειλέτης **chrĕōphĕilĕtēs**, *khreh-o-fi-let'-ace;* from a der. of *5531* and *3781;* a *loan-ower*, i.e. *indebted* person:—debtor.

5534. χρή **chrē**, *khray;* third pers. sing. of the same as *5530* or *5531* used impers.; it *needs* (*must* or *should*) be:—ought.

5535. χρῄζω **chrēizō**, *khrade'-zo;* from *5532;* to *make* (i.e. *have*) *necessity*, i.e. *be in want* of:—(have) need.

5536. χρῆμα **chrēma**, *khray'-mah;* something *useful* or *needed*, i.e. *wealth*, *price:*—money, riches.

5537. χρηματίζω **chrēmatizō**, *khray-mat-id'-zo;* from *5536;* to *utter an oracle* (comp. the orig. sense of *5530*), i.e. divinely *intimate;* by impl. (comp. the secular sense of *5532*) to constitute a *firm* for business, i.e. (gen.) *bear* as a *title:*—be called, be admonished (warned) of God, reveal, speak.

5538. χρηματισμός **chrēmatismŏs**, *khray-mat-is-mos';* from *5537;* a divine *response* or *revelation:*—answer of God.

5539. χρήσιμος **chrēsimŏs**, *khray'-see-mos;* from *5540;* *serviceable:*—profit.

5540. χρῆσις **chrēsis**, *khray'-sis;* from *5530;* *employment*, i.e. (spec.) sexual *intercourse* (as an *occupation* of the body):—use.

5541. χρηστεύομαι **chrēstĕuŏmai**, *khraste-yoo'-om-ahee;* mid. from *5543;* to *show oneself useful*, i.e. *act benevolently:*—be kind.

5542. χρηστολογία **chrēstŏlŏgia**, *khrase-tol-og-ee'-ah;* from a comp. of *5543* and *3004;* *fair speech*, i.e. *plausibility:*—good words.

5543. χρηστός **chrēstŏs**, *khrase-tos';* from *5530;* *employed*, i.e. (by impl.) *useful* (in manner or morals):—better, easy, good (-ness), gracious, kind.

5544. χρηστότης **chrēstŏtēs**, *khray-stot'-ace;* from *5543;* *usefulness*, i.e. mor. *excellence* (in character or demeanor):—gentleness, good (-ness), kindness.

5545. χρίσμα **chrisma**, *khris'-mah;* from *5548;* an *unguent* or *smearing*, i.e. (fig.) the spec. *endowment* ("chrism") of the Holy Spirit:—anointing, unction.

5546. Χριστιανός **Christianŏs**, *khris-tee-an-os';* from *5547;* a *Christian*, i.e. follower of Christ:—Christian.

5547. Χριστός **Christŏs**, *khris-tos';* from *5548;* *anointed*, i.e. the *Messiah*, an epithet of Jesus:—Christ.

5548. χρίω **chriō**, *khree'-o;* prob. akin to *5530* through the idea of *contact;* to *smear* or *rub* with oil, i.e. (by impl.) to *consecrate* to an office or religious service:—anoint.

5549. χρονίζω **chrŏnizō**, *khron-id'-zo;* from *5550;* to *take time*, i.e. *linger:*—delay, tarry.

5550. χρόνος **chrŏnŏs**, *khron'-os;* of uncert. der.; a space of *time* (in gen., and thus prop. distinguished from *2540*, which designates a *fixed* or special occasion; and from *165*, which denotes a particular *period*) or *interval;* by extens. an individ. *opportunity;* by impl. *delay:*— + years old, season, space, (× often-) time (-s), (a) while.

5551. χρονοτριβέω **chrŏnŏtribĕō**, *khron-ot-rib-eh'-o;* from a presumed comp. of *5550* and the base of *5147;* to *be a time-wearer*, i.e. to *procrastinate* (*linger*):—spend time.

5552. χρύσεος **chrusĕŏs**, *khroo'-seh-os;* from *5557;* made *of gold:*—of gold, golden.

5553. χρυσίον **chrusiŏn**, *khroo-see'-on;* dimin. of *5557;* a *golden* article, i.e. gold plating, ornament, or coin:—gold.

5554. χρυσοδακτύλιος **chrusŏdaktuliŏs**, *khroo-sod-ak-too'-lee-os;* from *5557* and *1146;* *gold-ringed*, i.e. *wearing* a golden finger-ring or similar *jewelry:*—with a gold ring.

5555. χρυσόλιθος **chrusŏlithŏs**, *khroo-sol'-ee-thos;* from *5557* and *3037;* *gold-stone*, i.e. a *yellow gem* ("*chrysolite*"):—chrysolite.

5556. χρυσόπρασος **chrusŏprasŏs**, *khroo-sop'-ras-os;* from *5557* and πράσον **prasŏn** (a *leek*); a *greenish-yellow* gem ("*chrysoprase*"):—chrysoprase.

5557. χρυσός **chrusŏs**, *khroo-sos';* perh. from the base of *5530* (through the idea of the *utility* of the metal); *gold;* by extens. a *golden* article, as an ornament or coin:—gold.

5558. χρυσόω **chrusŏō**, *khroo-sŏ'-o;* from *5557;* to *gild*, i.e. *bespangle* with golden ornaments:—deck.

5559. χρώς **chrōs**, *khroce;* prob. akin to the base of *5530* through the idea of *handling;* the *body* (prop. its *surface* or *skin*):—body.

5560. χωλός **chōlŏs**, *kho-los';* appar. a prim. word; "*halt*", i.e. *limping:*—cripple, halt, lame.

5561. χώρα **chōra**, *kho'-rah;* fem. of a der. of the base of *5490* through the idea of *empty* expanse; *room*, i.e. a space of *territory* (more or less extensive; often includ. its inhab.):—coast, county, fields, ground, land, region. Comp. *5117*.

5562. χωρέω **chōrĕō**, *kho-reh'-o;* from *5561;* to *be* in (*give*) *space*, i.e. (intrans.) to *pass*, *enter*, or (trans.) to *hold*, *admit* (lit. or fig.):—come, contain, go, have place, (can, be room to) receive.

5563. χωρίζω **chōrizō**, *kho-rid'-zo;* from *5561;* to *place room* between, i.e. *part;* reflex. to *go away:*—depart, put asunder, separate.

5564. χωρίον **chōriŏn**, *kho-ree'-on;* dimin. of *5561;* a *spot* or *plot* of ground:—field, land, parcel of ground, place, possession.

5565. χωρίς **chōris**, *kho-rece';* adv. from *5561;* *at a space*, i.e. *separately* or *apart* from (often as prep.):—beside, by itself, without.

5566. χῶρος **chōrŏs**, *kho'-ros;* of Lat. or.; the *north-west* wind:—north west.

Ψ

5567. ψάλλω **psallō**, *psal'-lo;* prob. strengthened from ψάω **psaō** (to *rub* or *touch* the surface; comp. *5597*); to *twitch* or *twang*, i.e. to *play* on a stringed instrument (*celebrate* the divine worship *with music* and accompanying odes):—make melody, sing (psalms).

5568. ψαλμός **psalmŏs**, *psal-mos';* from *5567;* a set piece of *music*, i.e. a sacred *ode* (accompanied with the voice, harp or other instrument; a "*psalm*"); collect. the book of the *Psalms:*—psalm. Comp. *5603*.

5569. ψευδάδελφος **psĕudadĕlphŏs**, *psyoo-dad'-el-fos;* from *5571* and *80;* a *spurious brother*, i.e. *pretended associate:*—false brethren.

5570. ψευδαπόστολος **psĕudapŏstŏlŏs**, *psyoo-dap-os'-tol-os;* from *5571* and *652;* a *spurious apostle*, i.e. *pretended preacher:*—false teacher.

5571. ψευδής **psĕudēs**, *psyoo-dace';* from *5574;* *untrue*, i.e. *erroneous*, *deceitful*, *wicked:*—false, liar.

5572. ψευδοδιδάσκαλος **psĕudŏdidaskalŏs**, *psyoo-dod-id-as'-kal-os;* from *5571* and *1320;* a *spurious teacher*, i.e. *propagator* of *erroneous* Chr. *doctrine:*—false teacher.

5573. ψευδολόγος **psĕudŏlŏgŏs**, *psyoo-dol-og'-os;* from *5571* and *3004;* *mendacious*, i.e. *promulgating erroneous* Chr. *doctrine:*—speaking lies.

5574. ψεύδομαι **psĕudŏmai**, *psyoo'-dom-ahee;* mid. of an appar. prim. verb; to *utter an untruth* or attempt to *deceive* by falsehood:—falsely, lie.

5575. ψευδομάρτυρ **psĕudŏmartur**, *psyoo-dom-ar'-toor;* from *5571* and a kindred form of *3144;* a *spurious witness*, i.e. *bearer of untrue testimony:*—false witness.

5576. ψευδομαρτυρέω **psĕudŏmarturĕō**, *psyoo-dom-ar-too-reh'-o;* from *5575;* to *be an untrue testifier*, i.e. offer *falsehood in evidence:*—be a false witness.

5577. ψευδομαρτυρία **psĕudŏmarturia**, *psyoo-dom-ar-too-ree'-ah;* from *5575;* *untrue testimony:*—false witness.

5578. ψευδοπροφήτης **psĕudŏprŏphētēs**, *psyoo-dop-rof-ay'-tace;* from *5571* and *4396;* a *spurious prophet*, i.e. *pretended foreteller* or religious *impostor:*—false prophet.

5579. ψεῦδος **psĕudŏs**, *psyoo'-dos;* from *5574;* a *falsehood:*—lie, lying.

5580. ψευδόχριστος **psĕudŏchristŏs**, *psyoo-dokh'-ris-tos;* from *5571* and *5547;* a *spurious Messiah:*—false Christ.

5581. ψευδώνυμος **psĕudōnumŏs**, *psyoo-do'-noo-mos;* from *5571* and *3686;* *untruly named:*—falsely so called.

5582. ψεῦσμα **psĕusma**, *psyoos'-mah;* from *5574;* a *fabrication*, i.e. *falsehood:*—lie.

5583. ψεύστης **psĕustēs**, *psyoos-tace';* from *5574;* a *falsifier:*—liar.

5584. ψηλαφάω **psēlaphaō**, *psay-laf-ah'-o;* from the base of *5567* (comp. *5586*); to *manipulate*, i.e. *verify* by contact; fig. to *search* for:—feel after, handle, touch.

5585. ψηφίζω **psēphizō**, *psay-fid'-zo;* from *5586;* to *use pebbles* in enumeration, i.e. (gen.) to *compute:*—count.

5586. ψῆφος **psēphŏs**, *psay'-fos;* from the same as *5584;* a *pebble* (as worn smooth by *handling*), i.e.

(by impl. of use as a *counter* or *ballot*) a *verdict* (of acquittal) or *ticket* (of admission); a *vote:*—stone, voice.

5587. ψιθυρισμός **psithurismŏs**, *psith-oo-ris-mos';* from a der. of ψίθος **psithŏs** (a *whisper;* by impl. a *slander;* prob. akin to *5574*); *whispering*, i.e. secret *detraction:*—whispering.

5588. ψιθυριστής **psithuristēs**, *psith-oo-ris-tace';* from the same as *5587;* a secret *calumniator:*—whisperer.

5589. ψιχίον **psichiŏn**, *psikh-ee'-on;* dimin. from a der. of the base of *5567* (mean. a *crumb*); a *little bit* or *morsel:*—crumb.

5590. ψυχή **psuchē**, *psoo-khay';* from *5594; breath*, i.e. (by impl.) *spirit*, abstr. or concr. (the *animal* sentient principle only; thus distinguished on the one hand from *4151*, which is the rational and immortal *soul;* and on the other from *2222*, which is mere *vitality*, even of plants: these terms thus exactly correspond respectively to the Heb. 5315, 7307 and 2416):—heart (+ -ily), life, mind, soul, + us, + you.

5591. ψυχικός **psuchikŏs**, *psoo-khee-kos';* from *5590; sensitive*, i.e. *animate* (in distinction on the one hand from *4152*, which is the higher or *renovated* nature; and on the other from *5446*, which is the lower or *bestial* nature):—natural, sensual.

5592. ψύχος **psuchŏs**, *psoo'-khos;* from *5594; coolness:*—cold.

5593. ψυχρός **psuchrŏs**, *psoo-chros';* from *5592; chilly* (lit. or fig.):—cold.

5594. ψύχω **psuchō**, *psoo'-kho;* a prim. verb; to *breathe* (*voluntarily* but *gently;* thus differing on the one hand from *4154*, which denotes prop. a *forcible* respiration; and on the other from the base of *109*, which refers prop. to an inanimate *breeze*), i.e. (by impl. of reduction of temperature by evaporation) to *chill* (fig.):—wax cold.

5595. ψωμίζω **psōmizō**, *pso-mid'-zo;* from the base of *5596;* to *supply* with *bits*, i.e. (gen.) to *nourish:*—(bestow to) feed.

5596. ψωμίον **psōmiŏn**, *pso-mee'-on;* dim. from a der. of the base of *5597;* a *crumb* or *morsel* (as if *rubbed* off), i.e. a *mouthful:*—sop.

5597. ψώχω **psōchō**, *pso'-kho;* prol. from the same base as *5567;* to *triturate*, i.e. (by anal.) to *rub* out (kernels from husks with the fingers or hand):—rub.

Ω

5598. Ω ō, i.e. ὦμεγα **ōmĕga**, *o'-meg-ah;* the last letter of the Gr. alphabet, i.e. (fig.) the *finality:*—Omega.

5599. ὦ ō, *o;* a prim. interj.; as a sign of the voc. *O;* as a note of exclamation, *oh:*—O.

5600. ὦ ō, *o;* includ. the oblique forms, as well as ἦς **ēs**, *ace;* ᾖ ē, *ay*, etc.; the subjunctive of *1510;* (*may, might, can, could, would, should, must*, etc.; also with *1487* and its comp., as well as with other particles) *be:*—+ appear, are, (may, might, should) be, × have, is, + pass the flower of her age, should stand, were.

5601. Ὠβήδ **Ōbēd**, *o-bade';* of Heb. or. [5744]; *Obed*, an Isr.:—Obed.

5602. ὧδε **hōdĕ**, *ho'-deh;* from an adv. form of *3592; in this* same spot, i.e. *here* or *hither:*—here, hither, (in) this place, there.

5603. ᾠδή **ōidē**, *o-day';* from *103;* a *chant* or "*ode*" (the gen. term for any words sung; while *5215* denotes espec. a *religious* metrical composition, and *5568* still more spec. a *Heb.* cantillation):—song.

5604. ὠδίν **ōdin**, *o-deen';* akin to *3601;* a *pang* or *throe*, esp. of childbirth:—pain, sorrow, travail.

5605. ὠδίνω **ōdinō**, *o-dee'-no;* from *5604;* to *experience* the *pains* of parturition (lit. or fig.):—travail in (birth).

5606. ὦμος **ōmŏs**, *o'-mos;* perh. from the alt. of *5342;* the *shoulder* (as that on which burdens are *borne*):—shoulder.

5607. ὤν **ōn**, *oan;* includ. the fem.

οὖσα **ŏusa**, *oo'-sah;* and the neut.

ὄν **ŏn**, *on;* pres. part. of *1510; being:*—be, come, have.

5608. ὠνέομαι **ōnĕŏmai**, *o-neh'-om-ahee;* mid. from an appar. prim. ὦνος **ōnŏs** (a *sum* or *price*); to *purchase* (synon. with the earlier *4092*):—buy.

5609. ᾠόν **ōŏn**, *o-on';* appar. a prim. word; an "*egg*":—egg.

5610. ὥρα **hōra**, *ho'-rah;* appar. a prim. word; an "*hour*" (lit. or fig.):—day, hour, instant, season, × short, [even-] tide, (high) time.

5611. ὡραῖος **hōraiŏs**, *ho-rah'-yos;* from *5610; belonging* to the right *hour* or *season* (*timely*), i.e. (by impl.) *flourishing* (*beauteous* [fig.]):—beautiful.

5612. ὠρύομαι **ōruŏmai**, *o-roo'-om-ahee;* mid. of an appar. prim. verb; to "*roar*":—roar.

5613. ὡς **hōs**, *hoce;* prob. adv. of comp. from *3739; which how*, i.e. *in that manner* (very variously used, as follows):—about, after (that), (according) as (it had been, it were), as soon (as), even as (like), for, how (greatly), like (as, unto), since, so (that), that, to wit, unto, when ([-soever]), while, × with all speed.

5614. ὡσαννά **hōsanna**, *ho-san-nah';* of Heb. or. [3467 and 4994]; *oh save!; hosanna* (i.e. *hoshia-na*), an exclamation of adoration:—hosanna.

5615. ὡσαύτως **hōsautōs**, *ho-sōw'-toce;* from *5613* and an adv. from *846; as thus*, i.e. *in the same way:*—even so, likewise, after the same (in like) manner.

5616. ὡσεί **hōsĕi**, *ho-si';* from *5613* and *1487; as if:*—about, as (it had been, it were), like (as).

5617. Ὠσηέ **Hōsēĕ**, *ho-say-eh';* of Heb. or. [1954]; *Hoseë* (i.e. *Hosheä*), an Isr.:—Osee.

5618. ὥσπερ **hōspĕr**, *hoce'-per;* from *5613* and *4007; just as*, i.e. *exactly like:*—(even, like) as.

5619. ὡσπερεί **hōspĕrĕi**, *hoce-per-i';* from *5618* and *1487; just as if*, i.e. *as it were:*—as.

5620. ὥστε **hōstĕ**, *hoce'-teh;* from *5613* and *5037; so too*, i.e. *thus therefore* (in various relations of *consecution*, as follow):—(insomuch) as, so that (then), (insomuch) that, therefore, to, wherefore.

5621. ὠτίον **ōtiŏn**, *o-tee'-on;* dimin. of *3775;* an *earlet*, i.e. *one* of the ears, or perh. the *lobe* of the ear:—ear.

5622. ὠφέλεια **ōphĕlĕia**, *o-fel'-i-ah;* from a der. of the base of *5624; usefulness*, i.e. *benefit:*—advantage, profit.

5623. ὠφελέω **ōphĕlĕō**, *o-fel-eh'-o;* from the same as *5622;* to *be useful*, i.e. to *benefit:*—advantage, better, prevail, profit.

5624. ὠφέλιμος **ōphĕlimŏs**, *o-fel'-ee-mos;* from a form of *3786; helpful* or *serviceable*, i.e. *advantageous:*—profit (-able).

NOTE.

Owing to changes in the enumeration while in progress, there were no words left for Nos. *2717* and *3203–3302*, which were therefore silently dropped out of the vocabulary and references as redundant. This will occasion no practical mistake or inconvenience.

VARIATIONS

IN THE NUMBERING OF VERSES IN THE GREEK AND ENGLISH NEW TESTAMENT.

English.	Greek.
Mark 13: 8 (last clause)	(first clauses) 9
Luke 22: 66 (last word)	(first word) 67
John 1: 38 (all after first clause)	39
39	40
40	41
41	42
42	43
John 1: 43	44
44	45
45	46
46	47
47	48
48	49
49	50
John 1: 50	51
51	52
Acts 4: 6 (last clause)	(in) 5
13: 33 (former half)	(latter half) 32
1 Pet 2: 8 (first two clauses)	(last two clauses) 7

SUPPLEMENTS

THE LAWS OF THE BIBLE

I. FORMS OF GOVERNMENT

A. ***Patriarchal.*** The family being the unit of life, the father as head of the family was the authoritative ruler .... Judg. 11:29–40; Job 1:5

B. ***Theocracy.*** God was the direct ruler of His people .... Ex. 19:3–8

C. ***Government by judges.*** The people forgot God. God chastised them by selling them into slavery to their enemies. Upon repentance God raised up military chieftains as deliverers .... Judg. 2:13–18

D. ***Monarchy.*** This was begun by the coronation of Saul, reached its height in David and Solomon, and ended with the Babylonian captivity .... 1 Sam. 10:24

II. CITIZENSHIP UNDER THE THEOCRACY

A. ***Israelites.*** Those of Israel who ratified the covenant of Sinai, and later their children, were entitled to the rights of citizenship .... Ex. 19:5–8; Deut. 6:1–9

B. ***Moabites and Ammonites excluded*** .... Deut. 23:3

C. ***Edomites and Egyptians in the third generation were eligible*** .... Deut. 23:7, 8

III. LAWS OF THE THEOCRACY

A. ***Pertaining to citizenship***

1. Law applied equally to strangers as to natives .... Lev. 24:22; Num. 15:22–30
2. Jew not to marry a stranger .... Gen. 34:14
3. Strangers could own slaves .... Lev. 25:47–55

B. ***Pertaining to slavery***

1. Slaves obtained
   - a. Captured in war .... Num. 31:7–11
   - b. Inherited .... Lev. 25:46
   - c. Bought .... Ex. 21:2
   - d. Sold for debt or theft .. Ex. 22:3; Deut. 15:12
2. How to treat slaves
   - a. Israelites could be redeemed from slavery .... Lev. 25:47–55
   - b. Jewish slaves to be set free in Year of Jubilee ...... Lev. 25:39–41
   - c. Regarded as part of owner's household and possession .... Gen. 12:16; Ex. 20:17
   - d. Could be struck by master .... Ex. 21:20, 21
   - e. Fugitive not to be returned .... Deut. 23:15, 16; 1 Sam. 30:15
   - f. Freed if ill-treated ... Ex. 21:26, 27
   - g. To enjoy the Sabbath .... Ex. 20:10

C. ***Pertaining to taxation***

1. Census taken .... Luke 2:1–3
2. Purpose of taxes
   - a. Valuation of persons .. Lev. 27:1–13
   - b. Temple service ...... Ex. 30:11–16; 2 Chr. 24:6, 9
   - c. Taxes .... Matt. 22:15–21; Rom. 13:6, 7
3. Amount of taxes ...... 1 Sam. 8:10–18
4. Priests and attendants exempt .... Ezra 7:24

D. ***Military laws***

1. Age of soldiers .... Num. 1:2, 3; 26:2
2. Selective draft .... Num. 31:3–7
3. Exemption from service
   - a. Levites .... Num. 1:49
   - b. Certain individuals ... Deut. 20:5–7
   - c. Fainthearted .... Deut. 20:8
4. Cleanliness in camp .. Num. 31:19, 20; Deut. 23:9–14
5. Regulations in battle
   - a. Notice to be given Deut. 20:10, 11
   - b. Fruit trees spared Deut. 20:19, 20
   - c. Treatment of captives .... Num. 21:2, 3, 35; 31:17, 18; Deut. 20:14–18; Josh. 11:14
   - d. Plunder .... Deut. 20:14
   - e. Indemnity .... 2 Kin. 3:4

IV. CRIMINAL LAWS

A. *Crimes against the public*

1. Bribery .... Ex. 23:8; Deut. 16:19; Prov. 17:23
2. Contempt for the law ..... Num. 15:30; Deut. 6:16, 17
   Penalty .... Deut. 17:12, 13
3. Perjury .... Ex. 20:16; Lev. 19:12
   Penalty .... Deut. 19:16–20
4. Perverting or obstructing justice .... Ex. 23:1, 2, 6; Lev. 19:15; Ps. 82:2
   Penalty .... Deut. 16:19, 20
5. Conspiracy .... 2 Sam. 15:10–12

B. *Crimes of immoral acts*

1. Adultery .... Ex. 20:14; Deut. 5:18
   Penalty .... Lev. 20:10; Deut. 22:22–25
2. Rape .... Deut. 22:25, 26
   Penalty .... Deut. 22:25–29
3. Prostitution .... Deut. 23:17
   Penalty .... Lev. 19:29; 21:9
4. Seduction .... Ex. 22:16, 17
   Penalty .... Deut. 22:28, 29
5. Incest .... Lev. 18:6–18; Deut. 22:30
   Penalty .... Lev. 20:11–21
6. Sodomy .... Lev. 18:22, 23; Deut. 23:17
   Penalty .... Ex. 22:19; Lev. 20:13, 15, 16

C. *Crimes against persons*

1. Murder .... Ex. 20:13
   Penalty .... Gen. 9:6; Ex. 21:12
2. Manslaughter .... Ex. 21:12–14; Josh. 20:3–6
   Penalty .... Num. 35:11, 22–28
3. Assault .... Ex. 21:18–26
   Penalty .... Ex. 21:19–27; Lev. 24:19, 20
4. Kidnapping .... Ex. 21:16; Deut. 24:7
5. Slander .... Lev. 19:16

D. *Crimes against property*

1. Stealing .... Ex. 20:15; 22:1–12; Deut. 23:24, 25
2. Arson .... Ex. 22:6
3. Moving a landmark .... Deut. 19:14

V. LAWS PERTAINING TO DOMESTIC RELATIONS

A. *Marriage*

1. Ordained by God ...... Gen. 1:27, 28; 2:18, 24
2. Within the tribe .... Num. 36:6
3. Polygamy forbidden .... 1 Cor. 7:2; 1 Tim. 3:2
4. Marriage forbidden with:
   a. Stepmother .... Lev. 18:8; 20:11
   b. Aliens .... Ex. 34:13–17; Deut. 7:1–3
   c. Sister .... Lev. 20:17
   d. Aunt .... Lev. 20:19
   e. Grandchild .... Lev. 18:10
   f. Daughter-in-law .... Lev. 18:15
5. Divorce .... Lev. 21:7; 22:13; Is. 50:1; 1 Cor. 7:10, 11
   a. Not to remarry woman divorced by another man .... Deut. 24:1–4
   b. For committing adultery .... Jer. 3:8; Matt. 19:3–9; Mark 10:2–12; Luke 16:8

B. *Parent and child*

1. Father has authority over child .... Num. 30:3–5
2. Father to arrange marriage .... Gen. 24:2–4
3. Parents to educate .... Deut. 21:18–21; Prov. 22:6; Eph. 6:4
4. Parents to discipline .. Deut. 21:18–21; Prov. 22:15
5. Children to honor parents .. Ex. 20:12; 21:15
6. Children to be regarded as gift of God .... Gen. 33:5; 48:9; Josh. 24:3
7. Penalty for children who dishonor parents .... Lev. 20:9; Deut. 21:18–21

VI. ESTATES—DESCENT AND DISTRIBUTION LAWS

A. ***Inheritance***

1. Sons inherit father's estate .... Gen. 21:10–13; 1 Chr. 5:1
2. Double portion to firstborn .... Deut. 21:15–17
3. Wife not heir, but descends with property to next of kin ... Ruth 4:1–12
4. Daughters heirs when no sons .... Num. 27:8, 9
5. When no sons or daughters, inheritance to nearest relative Num. 27:9–11

B. ***Real property—titles***

1. Real estate
   a. Land divided among tribes .... Num. 26:52–56; Josh. 14:5
   b. Not transferable ..... Num. 36:6–9
   c. Not permanently sold .... Lev. 25:23–28
   d. Value of land according to years after Jubilee .... Lev. 25:15, 16
   e. Release of land .... Lev. 25:8–34
   f. Mode of transfer
      (1) Deed made .... Jer. 32:9–14
      (2) Taking off sandal ... Ruth 4:3–11
      (3) Deed delivered in presence of witnesses ...... Jer. 32:10, 12
      (4) Deed recorded ...... Jer. 32:14
2. Personal property (All property which is moveable, as against real property such as houses and lands)
   a. Sale recognized .... Lev. 25:14
   b. Pledges of:
      (1) Children given as .. 2 Kin. 4:1–7
      (2) Upper and lower millstone prohibited .... Deut. 24:6
      (3) Not retained overnight .... Ex. 22:26, 27; Deut. 24:13
      (4) Voluntary ...... Deut. 24:10, 11

VII. SOCIAL SECURITY AND WELFARE LAWS

A. ***Widows and orphans*** .... Ex. 22:22, 23; Deut. 14:28, 29; Acts 6:1–4; 1 Tim. 5:3–16

1. Widow to marry nearest relative .... Deut. 25:5–10
2. Widow and orphans not to be oppressed .... Zech. 7:9–12; Mal. 3:5

B. ***Neighbors*** .... Lev. 19:13

C. ***The poor*** .... Ex. 22:25–27; Lev. 19:9, 10; Deut. 15:7–11; Luke 3:11; 14:13, 14

D. ***Strangers or aliens*** ...... Lev. 19:33, 34; Deut. 24:19–22; Zech. 7:9–12

E. ***Poor and needy*** .... Deut. 24:14, 15

F. ***Servants*** .... Deut. 24:14, 15

G. ***Handicapped***

1. Blind .... Lev. 19:14; Deut. 27:18; Luke 14:13, 14
2. Deaf .... Lev. 19:14
3. Lame .... Luke 14:12–14

VIII. LAWS PERTAINING TO CONTRACTS

A. ***Debts*** .... Ex. 22:25; Deut. 15:1–3; Neh. 5:10, 11

B. ***With neighbors*** .... Deut. 15:1–3

C. ***With foreigners*** .... Deut. 15:1–3

D. ***Interest*** .... Ex. 22:25; Lev. 25:35–37; Deut. 23:19, 20; Ezek. 18:10–13

E. ***Loans*** .... Ex. 22:25; Deut. 23:19, 20; 2 Kin. 4:1–7; Neh. 5:2–5

F. ***Mortgages*** .... Neh. 5:2–5

G. ***Pledges*** (See VI. B. 2)

H. ***Sales*** .... Lev. 25:14

I. ***Sales of land*** .... Lev. 25:23–28; Ruth 4:3–11; Jer. 32:9–14

J. ***Of servitude*** .... Ex. 21:2–4; Deut. 15:12

K. ***Sureties*** .... Prov. 6:1, 2; 17:18

IX. RELIGIOUS LAWS

A. ***Clean and unclean meat*** . . . Lev. 11:2–31; Deut. 14:3–21

B. ***Forbidden foods***

1. Fat and blood . . . . Lev. 17:10–14
2. Flesh torn by beasts . . . . Ex. 22:31
3. Fruit of young trees . . . . Lev. 19:23–25

C. ***Sacred obligations***

1. Firstborn . . . . Ex. 34:19, 20
2. Firstfruits . . . . Ex. 34:26; Deut. 18:4
3. Tithes . . . . Gen. 14:19, 20; Lev. 27:30–33; 2 Chr. 31:4–12; Mal. 3:8–11; Matt. 23:23
4. Atonement money . . . . . . Ex. 30:12–16
5. Freewill offering . . . . Lev. 22:17–20; Num. 15:1–4

D. ***Sacred calendar***

1. Sabbath . . . . Gen. 2:1–3; Ex. 16:23; Lev. 23:3; Num. 28:9, 10; Deut. 5:12–15; Neh. 10:31; Ezek. 46:3
   a. Punishment for not keeping . . . . Num. 15:32–36
   b. Made for man . . . . Mark 2:23–28
   c. Healing on the Sabbath . . . . Luke 13:14–17; 14:3–5; John 5:8–16
2. Passover . . . . Ex. 12:1–14; Deut. 16:1–8; Ezek. 45:21, 24; Luke 22:7–18
3. Feast of Unleavened Bread . . Ex. 34:18
4. Feast of Weeks . . . . Deut. 16:9–11
5. Feast of Tabernacles . . Lev. 23:33–44; Num. 29:12–40; Deut. 16:13–17
6. Sabbatical (seventh) Year . . . . Ex. 21:2–6; 23:10, 11; Lev. 25:1–7; Deut. 15:1–14; 2 Chr. 36:21; Neh. 10:31
7. Day of Atonement . . . . . Lev. 23:26–32

E. ***Crimes against God***

1. Worship of false gods . . . . . . Ex. 20:1–5
   Penalty . . . . Ex. 22:20
2. Spiritualism . . . . Lev. 20:27
   Penalty . . . . Ex. 22:18
3. Blasphemy . . . . Lev. 24:16; Deut. 5:11
   Penalty . . . . Lev. 24:16

X. LAWS PERTAINING TO LEGAL PROCEDURE

A. ***Judges appointed*** . . . . Ex. 18:13–26; 2 Chr. 19:4–11

1. Moses, first judge . . . . . . Ex. 18:13–27
2. Priests judge in small matters . . . . Ex. 18:22
3. King as judge . . . . 1 Kin. 7:1–7

B. ***Submission of cases***

1. Ordinary cases submitted to judges . . . . Deut. 25:1, 2
2. Exceptional cases taken to Levitical priest for verdict . . . . . . Deut. 17:8–11
3. Extreme cases submitted to the LORD for decision . . . . . Num. 5:11–31; Deut. 21:1–9
4. Judges must not pervert justice . . . . Ex. 23:6–8
5. Bribery forbidden . . . . Deut. 16:18–20

C. ***Where courts were held***

1. At gate of city . . . . Deut. 21:19
2. In Hall of Judgment . . . . 1 Kin. 7:7

D. ***Judgments***

1. Regarded as from God . . . . . Deut. 1:17
2. Righteous to be justified and wicked condemned . . . . Deut. 25:1
3. Sentence to be executed Deut. 25:2, 3

E. ***Appeals***

1. To Moses . . . . Ex. 18:26
2. To priests . . . . Deut. 17:8–11
3. To the king . . . . 1 Kin. 3:16–27

F. ***Damages***

1. For disfiguring a person Lev. 24:19, 20
2. For stealing . . . . Ex. 22:4, 5
3. Kindling a fire which destroys property . . . . Ex. 22:6
4. Breach of trust . . . . Lev. 6:1–5
5. Killing an animal . . . . . . Ex. 21:35, 36; Lev. 24:18, 21

6. Loss of animal falling into pit .... Ex. 21:33, 34
7. Loss of borrowed property .. Ex. 22:14

G. *Methods of punishment*

1. Infliction in kind .... Gen. 9:6; Lev. 24:19, 20
2. Burning .... Lev. 20:14
3. Mutilation .... Deut. 25:11, 12
4. Hanging .... Deut. 21:22, 23
5. Stoning .... Lev. 24:16
6. Beating .... Deut. 25:2, 3
7. Excommunication .... Ezra 10:8
8. Imprisonment .... Ezra 7:26
9. Compensation for damages .... Ex. 21:19, 32, 36
10. Restitution for stolen or borrowed property .... Ex. 22:12, 14, 15

H. *Method of protection*

1. Cities of refuge appointed .... Num. 35:6–15
2. Protection till trial could be held .... Num. 35:12
3. Murderer unprotected Num. 35:30, 31
4. Unintentional manslayer remained in city of refuge till death of high priest .... Josh. 20:1–6

XI. TORT LAWS

A. *Assault* .... Ex. 21:18, 19

B. *Compensation* .... Ex. 21:18, 19, 32

C. *Damage by animals* .... Ex. 21:32

D. *Damage by fire* .... Ex. 22:6

E. *Injury to animals* .... Ex. 21:33–36; Lev. 24:18, 21

F. *Loss of borrowed property* Ex. 22:14, 15

G. *Personal injury* .... Lev. 24:19, 20

H. *Rights of strangers* .... Lev. 24:22

XII. LAWS OF SANITATION AND CLEANLINESS

A. *Cleansing of the woman after childbirth* .... Lev. 12:1–8

B. *Test for leprosy* .... Lev. 13:1–59

C. *Cleansing of the leper's house* .... Lev. 14:33–57

D. *Cleansing of males with discharge* .... Lev. 15:1–15

E. *Laws concerning the woman during menstruation* .... Lev. 15:24–33

XIII. LAWS PERTAINING TO ANIMALS

A. *Beasts of burden* .... Ex. 23:12; Deut. 25:4

B. *Beasts of the field* .... Ex. 23:11

C. *Mother and young* .... Lev. 22:28; Deut. 22:6, 7

D. *Enemy's animals* .... Ex. 23:4, 5; Deut. 22:4

XIV. LAWS CONCERNING INTEREST AND LOANS

Interest on money was called usury in biblical times. (Now usury means excess interest.)

A. *Taking of interest forbidden among Jews* .... Ex. 22:25; Deut. 23:19, 20

The money was borrowed for relief of distress.

B. *Allowed to be taken from foreigners* .... Deut. 23:20

Money was borrowed by foreigner to develop trade.

C. *Property returned without interest* .... Neh. 5:11–13

D. *Differing weights and measures forbidden* .... Deut. 25:13–16

TEACHINGS AND ILLUSTRATIONS OF CHRIST

Subject	*Reference*
Abiding in Christ	John 15:4–10
Ability	Matt. 25:14, 15
Ablution	Matt. 6:17, 18
Abode	John 14:23
Abraham	John 8:37, 56
Abstinence	Luke 21:34
Abundant life	John 10:10
Access to God	John 10:7, 9
Accountability	Luke 12:47, 48
Accusation, false	Matt. 5:11
Adultery	Matt. 5:27, 28
Adversity	Luke 24:46
Affliction	Matt. 24:7–12
Agreement	Matt. 18:19
Altar	Matt. 23:18, 19
Ambition	Luke 22:25–30
Angels	Matt. 13:39, 41
Anger	Matt. 5:22
Anxiety	Luke 12:22–31
Apostasy	Matt. 13:18–22 Luke 8:13
Apostles	Luke 11:49
Appearance	Matt. 6:16
Appearance, outward	Matt. 23:27, 28
Authority	Matt. 21:24 Luke 10:19
Avarice	Luke 12:16–21
Backsliding	Luke 9:62
Baptism	Acts 1:5 Matt. 28:19
Beatitudes	Matt. 5:3–11
Beelzebub	Matt. 10:25
Begging	Luke 16:3
Beneficence	Matt. 5:42
Betrayal	Matt. 26:21
Bigotry	Luke 18:9–14
Birds	Matt. 8:20
Blasphemy	Matt. 12:31, 32
Blessings	Matt. 5:3–11
Blind guides	Matt. 15:14
Borrowing	Matt. 5:42
Bread of life	John 6:32–35
Brothers	Matt. 23:8
Builders	Luke 6:47–49 Matt. 7:24
Burdens	Luke 11:46
Burial	Matt. 8:22
Caesar	Matt. 22:21
Call of God	Matt. 20:16
Called ones	Matt. 22:14
Capital and labor	Matt. 20:1–15
Capital punishment	Matt. 26:52
Care of God	Matt. 6:30, 33
Caution	Mark 4:24
Celibacy	Matt. 19:11, 12
Character	John 1:47
Charity	Luke 12:33
Cheating	Mark 10:19
Chosen	Matt. 22:14
Church	Matt. 18:17
Circumcision	John 7:22, 23
Cleansing	John 15:3
Coin	Matt. 22:19–21
Coldness	Matt. 24:12
Communication	Luke 24:17
Compassion	Matt. 15:32 Luke 10:33
Compromise	Matt. 5:25, 26
Conceit	Luke 18:10–12
Conduct, Christian	Matt. 5:16
Confessing Christ	Matt. 10:32, 33
Confession of sin	Luke 18:13, 14
Confidence	Mark 10:24
Conflict	Matt. 10:34–36
Conscience	John 8:7–9
Contention	Matt. 18:15–17
Contentment	John 6:43
Conversion	Matt. 13:15
Convict	John 16:8
Corruption, moral	Luke 11:39
Courage	Matt. 9:22
Covenant	Mark 14:24
Coveting	Mark 7:21, 22
Cross-bearing	Matt. 10:38
Crucifixion	Luke 9:22
Cup of water	Matt. 10:42
Dancing	Luke 15:25–27
Daniel	Matt. 24:15
Darkness	Luke 11:35
David	Matt. 12:3
Day	John 11:9
Deaf	Matt. 13:13–15
Death	Luke 9:22 John 8:51
Debts	Matt. 18:24
Deceivers	Matt. 24:4, 5
Decision	Matt. 6:24
Defilement	Matt. 15:11, 18, 19
Devil	Matt. 13:38, 39
Diligence	John 9:4
Disbelief	John 5:38
Discernment	Matt. 16:2, 3
Discipleship	Luke 14:33
Disputes	Mark 9:33, 34
Distress	Luke 21:23, 25
Divorce	Matt. 5:31, 32
Doctrine	Mark 7:7
Doubt	Matt. 21:21
Drunkard	Luke 7:34
Drunkenness	Luke 21:34
Dullness	Matt. 13:13
Duty	Luke 17:10
Dwelling places	John 14:2, 3
Earth	Matt. 5:18
Earthquakes	Mark 13:8
Economy	Matt. 15:37 John 6:12
Elect	Matt. 24:24, 31
Election	Matt. 25:34
Elijah	Matt. 17:11, 12
Employer	Matt. 20:1–16
Encouragement	Matt. 9:2
Endowments	Matt. 25:14, 15
Endurance	Matt. 10:22 Luke 21:19
Enemies	Matt. 5:43, 44
Eternal life	Matt. 19:29
Eternal sin	Mark 3:29
Etiquette	Luke 10:8
Evil	Matt. 15:19
Exaltation	Matt. 23:12
Example	John 13:15

Subject	*Reference*
Excuses	Luke 14:18–20
Extravagance	Luke 15:11–14
Fainting	Mark 8:2, 3
Faith	Matt. 6:25
	Mark 11:22
	Luke 7:50
Faithfulness	Matt. 25:21
Faithlessness	Matt. 25:24–30
False prophets	Matt. 24:11
False witness	Matt. 19:18
Farm	Matt. 22:2–6
Fasting	Matt. 6:16–18
Faultfinding	Matt. 7:3–5
Faults	Matt. 18:15
Fear of God	Matt. 10:28
Feast	Luke 14:8
Feet washing	John 13:12–15
Fellowship	Matt. 8:11
Flattery	Luke 6:26
Flesh	John 6:53
Flock	Matt. 26:31
Following Christ	Matt. 10:37, 38
Food	Matt. 6:11
	Matt. 6:25
	John 6:27
Fool	Matt. 5:22
Formalism	Matt. 23:23–28
Forsaking all	Luke 14:33
Foxes	Luke 9:58
Friends	Luke 11:5–8
Frugality	John 6:12
Fruitfulness	Matt. 13:23
Fruitlessness	Luke 13:6–9
Generosity	Matt. 25:34–40
Gentiles	Matt. 10:5–7
Gentleness	Matt. 5:5
Giving	Luke 6:38
Gladness	Luke 15:32
Glorifying God	Matt. 5:16
Gluttony	Luke 21:34
God	Matt. 19:17, 26
Godlessness	John 5:42, 44
Golden Rule	Matt. 7:12
Gospel	Luke 4:18
Grace	2 Cor. 12:9
Greatness	Matt. 5:19
Grumble	John 6:43
Guidance	John 16:13
Hairs numbered	Matt. 10:30
Hand of God	John 10:27–29
Happiness	Matt. 5:12
	John 13:16, 17
Harlots	Matt. 21:31
Harvest	Matt. 9:37, 38
Hatred	John 15:18, 19
Healing	Matt. 10:7, 8
	Mark 2:17
Heart	Matt. 13:19
Heaven	Luke 16:17
	John 3:13
Hell	Matt. 5:22
	Matt. 10:28
Helper	John 14:16
	John 15:26
Helpless	John 6:44
Hireling	John 10:11–13
Holy Spirit	John 14:26
Home	Mark 5:19
Honesty	Luke 8:15
	Mark 10:19
Honor of men	Matt. 6:2
Honor of parents	Matt. 15:3–6
Hospitality	Luke 14:12–14
Humility	John 13:14
	Matt. 11:29
Hunger, spiritual	Luke 6:21
	Matt. 5:6
Hypocrisy	Matt. 6:5
	Luke 6:42
Ignorance	Matt. 22:29
Immortality	Matt. 25:46
	John 11:25, 26
Impartiality of God	Matt. 5:45
Inconsistency	Matt. 7:3–5
	Luke 6:41, 42
Indecision	Luke 9:62
Indifference	Matt. 24:12
Industry	John 4:36
Infidelity	John 3:18
Influence	Matt. 5:13
Ingratitude	Luke 17:17, 18
Innocence	Matt. 10:16
Insincerity	Luke 16:15
Inspiration	Luke 12:12
Instability	Matt. 7:26, 27
Instruction	John 6:45
Insufficiency	Mark 10:21
Integrity	Luke 16:10
Intercession	John 17:9
Investment	Matt. 6:19, 20
Jealousy	Luke 15:25–30
John the Baptist	Luke 7:24–28
Jonah	Matt. 12:39–41
Joy	Matt. 25:21
	Luke 15:7, 10
Judge not	Matt. 7:1, 2
Judgment	Matt. 11:24
Judgment day	Matt. 25:31–46
Justice	John 5:30
Justification, self	Luke 16:15
Killing	Matt. 5:21, 22
Kindness	Luke 10:30–35
Kingdom	Luke 7:28
	John 18:36
Kiss	Luke 7:45
Knowledge	John 8:31, 32
Labor	Matt. 20:1–14
Laughter	Luke 6:21
Law	Luke 16:16
Lawsuit	Matt. 5:25, 40
Lawyers	Luke 11:46
Leaven	Matt. 16:6
	Luke 13:20, 21
Lending	Luke 6:34, 35
Lepers	Matt. 10:7, 8
Levite	Luke 10:30–32
Liars	John 8:44, 45
Liberality	Luke 6:30, 38
Liberty	Luke 4:18
Life	Matt. 6:25
	John 5:40
Light	Luke 11:33
	John 8:12
Living water	John 4:10
Log	Luke 6:41, 42
Loneliness	John 16:32
Lord's Supper	Matt. 26:26–29
Loss of soul	Matt. 16:25, 26
Lost opportunity	Matt. 25:7–12
Love	Matt. 22:37–40
Lukewarmness	Matt. 26:40, 41
Lunatic	Matt. 17:14, 15
Lust	Mark 4:18, 19
Magistrates	Luke 12:11, 58
Mammon	Matt. 6:24
Marriage	Matt. 19:4–6
	Mark 12:25
Martyrdom	John 16:1–3
Mary's choice	Luke 10:41, 42
Memorial	Matt. 26:13
Mercy	Matt. 5:7
	Luke 16:24
Minister	Luke 10:2

TEACHINGS OF CHRIST

Subject	*Reference*
Miracles	Matt. 12:28
Money lender, creditor	Luke 7:41, 42
Moses	Matt. 19:8
Moses' Law	John 7:19
Mother	Matt. 10:37
Mourn	Matt. 5:4
Murder	Matt. 15:19
Mysteries of Heaven	Matt. 13:11
Narrow way	Matt. 7:13, 14
Neglect	Luke 12:47
Neighbor	Matt. 19:19
Neutrality	Matt. 12:30
New birth	John 3:3, 5–8
Noah	Luke 17:26, 27
Oath	Matt. 5:33–37
Obedience	Matt. 12:50
Offering	Matt. 5:25
Offerings	Luke 21:3, 4
Opportunity	Matt. 5:25
Parables	Mark 4:11, 12
Paradise	Luke 23:43
Pardoning	Luke 6:37
Parents	Matt. 10:21
Patriotism	Matt. 22:21
Peace	Mark 9:50
Peacemakers	Matt. 5:9
Penitence	Luke 18:13
Perception	John 8:43
Perfection	Matt. 5:48
Persecution	Matt. 24:9
Perseverance	Matt. 10:22
Pharisaism	Matt. 23:2–33
Pharisee and tax collector	Luke 18:10–14
Pharisees	Matt. 5:20
Philanthropy	Luke 11:41
Physician	Matt. 9:12
Piety	John 1:47
Pleasing God	John 8:29
Pleasures	Luke 8:14
Poison	Mark 16:17, 18
Poll tax	Matt. 22:19–21
Polygamy	Matt. 19:8, 9
Poor	Mark 14:7
Power	Matt. 6:13
Prayer	Matt. 7:7–11
	Matt. 6:9–13
Preaching	Mark 16:15, 16
Procrastination	Matt. 25:3
Profit and loss	Matt. 16:26

Subject	*Reference*
Prophets	Matt. 10:41
	Matt. 7:15
Proselyte	Luke 23:15
Protection	Luke 18:3
Providence	Matt. 6:25–33
Prudence	Matt. 10:16–20
Punishment	Matt. 21:41
Purity	Matt. 5:8
Ransom	Matt. 20:28
Reaping	John 4:35–38
Receiving Christ	Mark 9:37
Reconciliation	Matt. 5:23, 24
Regeneration	Matt. 19:28
Rejecting Christ	John 3:18
Rejoicing	Luke 10:20
Release	Luke 4:18
Religion	Mark 7:6–8
	Matt. 25:34–36
Repentance	Matt. 11:21
	Luke 13:28
Reproof	Matt. 11:21–23
Resignation	Matt. 26:39
Responsibility	Luke 12:47, 48
Rest	Matt. 26:45
	Matt. 11:28–30
Resurrection	John 6:40
Retaliation	Matt. 5:39–44
Retribution	Matt. 23:34, 35
Reward	Matt. 10:42
Riches	Mark 4:19
Righteousness	Matt. 5:6, 20
	John 16:10
Robbers	Luke 10:30
	John 10:1
Robbery	Matt. 23:25
Sabbath	Matt. 12:5–8
Sackcloth	Matt. 11:21
Sacrifice	Matt. 12:7
Sacrilege	Matt. 21:13
Sadducees	Matt. 16:6
Salt	Matt. 5:13
	Mark 9:50
Salvation	Luke 19:19
	John 4:22
Samaritan	Luke 10:30–35
Sanctification	John 17:17
Satan	Matt. 4:10
	Mark 4:15
Scripture	Matt. 21:42
	Luke 4:21
Secrecy	Luke 12:2, 3

Subject	*Reference*
Security	Luke 6:47, 48
Seduction	Mark 13:22
Seeking the kingdom	Matt. 6:19, 20
Self-condemnation	Matt. 23:29–32
	Luke 19:20–24
Self-control	Matt. 5:21
Self-deception	Luke 12:16–21
Self-denial	Matt. 16:24–26
Self-exaltation	Matt. 23:12
Self-examination	Matt. 7:3–5
Selfishness	Luke 6:32–35
Self-righteousness	Matt. 23:23–27
Self-sacrifice	Matt. 16:25
Serpents	Matt. 23:33
	John 3:14
Service	Luke 22:27
Sheep	Luke 15:4–7
Shepherd	John 10:1–18
Sickness	Matt. 10:8
Signs	John 4:48
	Luke 11:16
Silence	Matt. 17:9
Sin	John 8:34
	Matt. 26:28
Sincerity	Matt. 5:13–16
Skepticism	John 20:27, 29
Slaves	Matt. 18:23
	John 15:15
Sleep	Mark 4:26, 27
	Mark 13:35, 36
Slothfulness	Matt. 25:26–30
Son of Man	Luke 9:22
Sorrow	Matt. 19:22
	John 16:6
Soul	Matt. 10:28
	Luke 12:19, 20
Soul winners	Matt. 4:19
Sowing	Mark 4:14
Speech	John 8:43
Spirit	Matt. 26:41
	Mark 5:8
Statement	Matt. 5:37
Steadfastness	Matt. 10:22
Stealing	Matt. 19:18
Steward	Luke 12:42, 43
	Luke 16:1–8
Stewardship	Luke 19:13–27
Stomach	Matt. 15:17
Strife	Luke 22:24

Subject	*Reference*
Stubbornness	John 5:40
Stumbling block	Matt. 23:13
Submission	Matt. 26:39, 42
Suffering	Matt. 26:38
Supper, The Lord's	Luke 22:14–20
Swearing	Matt. 23:16–22
Talents	Matt. 18:24
Taxes	Matt. 22:19–21
Tax collectors	Matt. 5:46, 47
Teaching	Matt. 28:19, 20 John 13:13–15
Temperance	Luke 21:34
Temptations	Matt. 4:1–11 Luke 8:13
Thieves	Matt. 6:19 John 10:1, 8
Timidness	Mark 4:40
Tithes	Luke 18:11, 12
Traditions	Mark 7:9, 13
Transgressions	Matt. 15:2
Treasures	Matt. 6:19–21
Tribulation	Matt. 24:9 John 16:33
Truth	John 14:6
Unbelievers	Luke 12:46
Uncharitableness	John 7:24
Unchastity	Matt. 5:31, 32
Uncleanness	Matt. 23:27
Unity	John 17:20, 21
Unpardonable sin	Matt. 12:31, 32
Vengeance	Matt. 5:39, 40
Vine	John 15:1, 4, 5
Visions	Matt. 17:9
Walks of Life	John 12:35 John 8:12
War	Matt. 24:26
Watchfulness	Matt. 24:42, 44 Luke 12:37–40
Wedding	Luke 14:8–10
Widow	Mark 12:43, 44
Wine	Luke 5:37–39
Wisdom	Luke 21:15
Witness	John 8:14
Witness, false	Matt. 19:18
Witnessing	Acts 1:8
Wives	Luke 14:20, 26
Worker	Matt. 10:10
Worldliness	Luke 21:34
Worm	Mark 9:43–48
Worries of the world	Matt. 13:22
Worship	Matt. 4:10
Yoke	Matt. 11:28, 29
Zacchaeus	Luke 19:5
Zeal	John 2:17

The Jewish Calendar

The Jews used two kinds of calendars:
Civil Calendar—official calendar of kings, childbirth, and contracts.
Sacred Calendar—from which festivals were computed.

NAMES OF MONTHS	CORRESPONDS WITH	NO. OF DAYS	MONTH OF CIVIL YEAR	MONTH OF SACRED YEAR
TISHRI	Sept.–Oct.	30 days	1st	7th
HESHVAN	Oct.–Nov.	29 or 30	2nd	8th
CHISLEV	Nov.–Dec.	29 or 30	3rd	9th
TEBETH	Dec.–Jan.	29	4th	10th
SHEBAT	Jan.–Feb.	30	5th	11th
ADAR	Feb.–Mar.	29 or 30	6th	12th
NISAN	Mar.–Apr.	30	7th	1st
IYAR	Apr.–May	29	8th	2nd
SIVAN	May–June	30	9th	3rd
TAMMUZ	June–July	29	10th	4th
AB	July–Aug.	30	11th	5th
*__ELUL__	Aug.–Sept.	29	12th	6th

The Jewish day was from sunset to sunset, in 8 equal parts:

FIRST WATCH .... SUNSET TO 9 P.M.
SECOND WATCH ... 9 P.M. TO MIDNIGHT
THIRD WATCH .... MIDNIGHT TO 3 A.M.
FOURTH WATCH ... 3 A.M. TO SUNRISE

FIRST WATCH .... SUNRISE TO 9 A.M.
SECOND WATCH ... 9 A.M. TO NOON
THIRD WATCH .... NOON TO 3 P.M.
FOURTH WATCH ... 3 P.M. TO SUNSET

*Hebrew months were alternately 30 and 29 days long. Their year, shorter than ours, had 354 days. Therefore, about every 3 years (7 times in 19 years) an extra 29-day-month, VEADAR, was added between ADAR and NISAN.

Jewish Feasts

Feast of	*Month on Jewish Calendar*	*Day*	*Corresponding Month*	*References*
*Passover (Unleavened Bread)	Nisan	14 21	Mar.–Apr.	Ex. 12:43—13:10; Matt. 26:17–20
*Pentecost (Firstfruits or Weeks)	Sivan	6 (50 days after Passover)	May–June	Deut. 16:9–12; Acts 2:1
Trumpets, *Rosh Hashanah*	Tishri	1, 2	Sept.–Oct.	Num. 29:1–6
Day of Atonement, *Yom Kippur*	Tishri	10	Sept.–Oct.	Lev. 23:26–32; Heb. 9:7
*Tabernacles (Booths or Ingathering)	Tishri	15–22	Sept.–Oct.	Neh. 8:13–18; John 7:2
Dedication (Lights), *Hanukkah*	Chislev	25 (8 days)	Nov.–Dec.	John 10:22
Purim (Lots)	Adar	14, 15	Feb.–Mar.	Esth. 9:18–32

*The three major feasts for which all males of Israel were required to travel to the Temple in Jerusalem (Ex. 23:14–19).

Monies and Weights

All values are approximate and are based upon a standard of $1,000 per troy ounce of gold and $20 per troy ounce of silver.

	Talent	*Mina*	*Shekel*	*Gerah*
Talent	91 lb. (troy) silver $21,840 gold $1,092,000			
Mina	60 minas	18.2 oz. (troy) silver $364 gold $18,200		
Shekel	3,000 shekels	50 shekels	.364 oz. (troy) silver $7.28 gold $364	
Gerah	60,000 gerahs	1,000 gerahs	20 gerahs	.0182 oz. (troy) silver $.36 gold $18.20

Drachma—.27 oz. (troy) gold $270; Bekah—.182 oz. (troy) silver $3.64

Conversion to current value—divide 1000 and 20 respectively into the current values of gold and silver. Multiply these factors with the corresponding values found in this chart and in the text.

New Testament Monies

	Denarius	*Copper Coin*	*Quadrans (penny)*	*Mite*
Denarius	1 day's wages			
Copper Coin	16 copper coins	1/16 day's wages		
Quadrans (penny)	64 pennies	4 pennies	1/64 day's wages	
Mite	128 mites	8 mites	2 mites	1/128 day's wages

Temple tax—2 days' wages

Measures of Length

	Rod (reed)	Pace	Cubit	Span	Handbreadth	Finger
Rod (reed)	9 ft. (Ezek. 10.5 ft.)					
Pace	3 paces	3 ft.				
Cubit	6 cubits	2 cubits	1.5 ft. (Ezek. 18 in.)			
Span	12 spans	4 spans	2 spans	9 in.		
Hand-breadth	36 hand-breadths	12 hand-breadths	6 hand-breadths	3 hand-breadths	3 in.	
Finger	144 fingers	48 fingers	24 fingers	12 fingers	4 fingers	.75 in.

A day's journey—20 mi.; a sabbath day's journey—3,637 ft.; some distance (a little way)—5 mi.; mile (Roman)—4,854 ft.; stadion (furlong)—606 ft.; fathom—6 ft.

Dry Measures

	Homer	Seah	Ephah	Omer
Homer (kor, measure)	6.524 bu.			
Seah (measure)	3 seahs	2.175 bu.		
Ephah	10 ephahs	3.33 ephahs	.652 bu.	
Omer (sheaf)	100 omers	33.33 omers	10 omers	2.087 qt.

Basket—1 peck

Liquid Measures

	Kor	Bath	Hin	Kab	Log
Kor	60 gal.				
Bath (measure)	10 baths	6 gal.			
Hin	60 hins	6 hins	1 gal.		
Kab	120 kabs	12 kabs	2 kabs	2 qt.	
Log	480 logs	48 logs	8 logs	4 logs	1 pt.

UNIVERSAL SUBJECT GUIDE TO THE BIBLE

A

SUBJECT	REFERENCE
Aaron—*bright*	
A. *Ancestry and family of:*	
Descendant of Levi	Ex. 6:16-20
Son of Amram and Jochebed	Ex. 6:20
Moses' older brother	Ex. 7:1, 7
Brother of Miriam	Ex. 15:20
Husband of Elisheba	Ex. 6:23
Father of Nadab, Abihu, Eleazar, and Ithamar	Ex. 6:23
B. *Position of:*	
Moses' helper	Ex. 4:13-31
Becomes "prophet" to Moses	Ex. 7:1, 2
God inspired	Ex. 12:1
Commissioned, with Moses to deliver Israelites from Egypt	Ex. 6:13, 26 Josh. 24:5
Inferior to that of Melchizedek	Heb. 7:11-19
C. *Special privileges of:*	
Appears before Pharaoh	Ex. 5:1-4
Performs miracles	Ex. 7:9, 10, 19, 20
Supports Moses' hands	Ex. 17:10-12
Ascends Mt. Sinai	Ex. 19:24 Ex. 24:1, 9
Sees God's glory	Ex. 24:9, 10
Judges Israel in Moses' absence	Ex. 24:14
Allowed inside the veil	Lev. 16:15
Blesses the people	Lev. 9:22
Intercedes for Miriam	Num. 12:10-12
D. *Sins of:*	
Tolerates idolatry	Ex. 32:1-4
Permits evil	Ex. 32:21-25
Conspires against Moses	Num. 12:1-16
With Moses, fails at Meribah	Num. 20:1-13, 24
E. *Character of:*	
A good speaker	Ex. 4:14
Weak in crises	Ex. 32:1-24
Subject to jealousy	Num. 12:1, 2
Conscious of guilt	Num. 12:11
Submissive	Lev. 10:1-7
A saint	Ps. 106:16
F. *Priesthood of:*	
Chosen by God	Ex. 28:1
Sons, in office	Lev. 8:1-36
Anointed with oil	Ex. 30:25, 30
Duties given	Ex. 30:7-10
Garments prescribed	Ex. 39:27-29
Ordained to teach	Lev. 10:8, 11
Set apart to offer sacrifices	Lev. 9:1-24 Heb. 5:1-4
Alone enters within the holy place	Ex. 30:10 Heb. 9:7, 25
Intercedes for others	Num. 16:46-48
Confirmed by God	Num. 17:8-10 Heb. 9:4
Hereditary	Num. 20:23-28
For lifetime	Heb. 7:23
Inferior to Melchizedek's	Heb. 7:11-19
G. *Death and descendants of:*	
Lives 123 years	Num. 33:39
Death	Num. 20:23, 24
Eleazar, son of, successor	Num. 20:25-28 Deut. 10:6
Aaronites—*descendants of Aaron*	
Fights with David	1 Chr. 12:27
Under Zadok	1 Chr. 27:17
Ab—*fifth month of the Jewish year*	
Aaron died in	Num. 33:38
See Jewish calendar	
Ab—*father*	
A part of many Hebrew names (e.g., Abinadab, Abner, Abijah)	1 Sam. 7:1
Abaddon—*a Hebrew word translated "destruction"*	
Designates ruin in	Job 31:12
Parallel with hell (Sheol) in	Job 26:6
Refers to death	Job 28:22
Personified	Rev. 9:11

SUBJECT	REFERENCE
Abagtha	
A eunuch under King Ahasuerus	Esth. 1:10
Abana—*a river flowing through Damascus*	
Spoken of highly by Naaman	2 Kin. 5:12
Abandon—*desert*	
A. *Required for:*	
Safety	Gen. 19:12-26 Acts 27:41-44
Salvation	Phil. 3:7-10
Service	Matt. 10:37-39
Sanctification	2 Cor. 6:14-18
Spiritual success	Heb. 11:24-27
B. *Aspects of:*	
Land, commanded	Gen. 12:1-5
Idolaters, justified	Ex. 32:1-10
One's ministry, rebuked	1 Kin. 19:3-18
Family, regretted	1 Sam. 30:1-6
The tabernacle, remembered	Jer. 7:12
Jerusalem, lamented	Matt. 23:37, 38
C. *Of men to judgment because of:*	
Sin	Gen. 6:5-7
Rebellion	1 Sam. 15:16-26
Unbelief	Matt. 23:37-39
Rejecting God	Rom. 1:21-32
Fornication	1 Cor. 5:1-5
Apostasy	Heb. 10:26-29
Abarim—*regions beyond*	
Moses sees the promised land from	Num. 27:12
Abasement—*degradation; humiliation*	
A. *As a judgment for:*	
Stubbornness	2 Kin. 14:8-14
Defaming God	2 Chr. 32:1-22
Pride	Is. 14:12-17
Hating Jews	Esth. 7:5-10
Arrogance	Dan. 4:33, 37 Acts 12:20-23
B. *As a virtue, seen in:*	
Nineveh's repentance	Jon. 3:1-10 Matt. 12:41
A publican's unworthiness	Luke 18:13, 14
Paul's life	1 Cor. 9:19-23
Christ's humiliation	Phil. 2:5-8
C. *Rewards of, seen in:*	
Healing	2 Kin. 5:11-14
Elevation	Matt. 23:12
Restoration	Luke 15:11-24
Renewed service	1 Cor. 15:9, 10
Abate—*diminish, desist*	
Flood waters	Gen. 8:8, 11
Moses' natural force not	Deut. 34:7
Anger of Ephraim	Judg. 8:3
Abba—an Aramaic word meaning *"father"*	
Used by Christ	Mark 14:36
Expressive of sonship	Rom. 8:15
Abda—*servant* (of God)	
1. The father of Adoniram	1 Kin. 4:6
2. A Levite, son of Shammua	Neh. 11:17
Called Obadiah	1 Chr. 9:16
Abdeel—*servant of God*	
The father of Shelemiah	Jer. 36:26
Abdi—*servant of Jehovah*	
1. The grandfather of Ethan	1 Chr. 6:44
2. A Levite	2 Chr. 29:12
3. A Jew who divorced his foreign wife	Ezra 10:26
Abdiel—*servant of God*	
A Gadite residing in Gilead	1 Chr. 5:15, 16
Abdon—*servile*	
1. A minor judge	Judg. 12:13-15
2. A Benjamite living in Jerusalem	1 Chr. 8:23, 28
3. A son of Jeiel	1 Chr. 8:30
4. A courtier of King Josiah	2 Chr. 34:20
5. A Levitical city	Josh. 21:30 1 Chr. 6:74

SUBJECT	REFERENCE
Abed-nego—*servant of Nego*	
Name given to Azariah, a Hebrew captive	Dan. 1:7
Appointed by Nebuchadnezzar	Dan. 2:49
Accused of disobedience	Dan. 3:12
Cast into furnace but delivered	Dan. 3:13-27
Promoted by Nebuchadnezzar	Dan. 3:28-30
Abel—*breath*	
Adam's second son	Gen. 4:2
The first shepherd	Gen. 4:2
Offering of, accepted	Gen. 4:4
Hated and slain by Cain	Gen. 4:8
Christ's blood superior to	Heb. 12:24
Place of, filled by Seth	Gen. 4:25
Abel—*meadow*	
1. A city involved in Sheba's rebellion	2 Sam. 20:14-18
2. Translated as "great stone of Abel" in	1 Sam. 6:18
First martyr	Matt. 23:35
Righteous	Matt. 23:35
Sacrificed to God by faith	Heb. 11:4
3. Elsewhere in place names (see below)	
Abel-beth-maachah—*meadow of the house of oppression*	
Captured by Tiglath-pileser	2 Kin. 15:29
A town in North Palestine	2 Sam. 20:14, 15
Refuge of Sheba; saved from destruction	2 Sam. 20:14-22
Seized by Ben-hadad	1 Kin. 15:20
Abel-maim—*meadow of waters*	
Another name for Abel-beth-maacah	2 Chr. 16:4
Abel-meholah—*meadow of dancing*	
Midianites flee to	Judg. 7:22
A few miles east of Jabesh-gilead	1 Kin. 4:12
Elisha's native city	1 Kin. 19:16
Abel-mizraim—*meadow of Egypt*	
A place, east of Jordan, where Israelites mourned for Jacob	Gen. 50:10, 11
Abel-shittim—*meadow of acacias*	
A place in Moab	Num. 33:49
Abez—*whiteness*	
A town of Issachar	Josh. 19:20
Abhor—*to detest; loathe; hate*	
A. *Descriptive of:*	
Disliking God's laws	Lev. 26:15
Prejudice toward non-Israelites	Deut. 23:7
Right attitude toward idolatry	Deut. 7:25, 26
Self-rejection	Job 42:6
Israel abhorred by Rezon	1 Kin. 11:25
Israel's rejection by God	Ps. 89:38, 39
Rejection by former friends	Job 19:19
Loss of appetite	Job 33:20
Rejecting false description	Prov. 24:24
B. *Expressive of God's loathing of:*	
Israel's idolatry	Deut. 32:17-19
Customs of other nations	Lev. 20:23
Men of bloodshed	Ps. 5:6
C. *Expressive of Israel's rejection of God's:*	
Judgments	Lev. 26:15
Ceremonies	1 Sam. 2:17
Promises	Is. 7:16
D. *Expressive of the believer's hatred of:*	
Lying	Ps. 119:163
Evil	Rom. 12:9
Abi—(an old form of *"father of"*)	
King Hezekiah's mother	2 Kin. 18:2
Also called Abijah	2 Chr. 29:1
Abi-albon	
An Arabathite	2 Sam. 23:31
See Abiel	
Abiasaph—*the father gathers*	
A descendant of Levi through Korah	Ex. 6:24

SUBJECT — REFERENCE

Called Ebiasaph ... 1 Chr. 6:23, 37
Descendants of, act as doorkeepers ... 1 Chr. 9:19

Abiathar—*father of pre-eminence*

A priest who escapes Saul at Nob ... 1 Sam. 22:20-23
Becomes high priest under David ... 1 Sam. 23:6, 9-12
Shares high priesthood with Zadok ... 2 Sam. 8:17
Remains faithful to David ... 2 Sam. 15:24-29
Informs David about Ahithophel ... 2 Sam. 15:34-36
Supports Adonijah's usurpation ... 1 Kin. 1:7, 9, 25
Deposed by Solomon ... 1 Kin. 2:26, 27, 35
Eli's line ends ... 1 Sam. 2:31-35
Referred by Christ ... Mark 2:26

Abib—*an ear of corn*

First month in Hebrew year ... Ex. 12:1, 2
Commemorative of the Passover ... Ex. 12:1-28
Called Nisan in postexilic times ... Neh. 2:1

Abida, Abidah—*the father knows*

A son of Midian; grandson of Abraham and Keturah ... Gen. 25:4

Abidan—*the father is judge*

Represents tribe of Benjamin ... Num. 1:11
Brings offering ... Num. 7:60, 65
Lead Benjamites ... Num. 10:24

Abide, abiding—*continuing in a permanent state*

A. *Applied to:*
Earth's existence ... Ps. 119:90
Believer's works ... 1 Cor. 3:14
Three graces ... 1 Cor. 13:13
God's faithfulness ... 2 Tim. 2:13
Christ's priesthood ... Heb. 7:3
God's Word ... 1 Pet. 1:23
Believer's eternity ... 1 John 2:17

B. *Sphere of, in the Christian's life:*
Christ ... John 15:4-6
Christ's words ... John 15:7
Christ's love ... John 15:10
Christ's doctrine ... 2 John 9
The Holy Spirit ... John 14:16
God's Word ... 1 John 2:14, 24
One's earthly calling ... 1 Cor. 7:20, 24
The truth ... 2 John 2

C. *Descriptive of the believer's:*
Protection ... Ps. 91:1
Satisfaction ... Prov. 19:23
Fruitfulness ... John 15:4, 5
Prayer life ... John 15:7
Assurance ... 1 John 2:28

Abiel—*God is father*

1. The grandfather of Saul and Abner ... 1 Sam. 9:1
2. David's mighty man ... 1 Chr. 11:32
Also called Abi-albon ... 2 Sam. 23:31

Abiezer—*the father is help*

1. A descendant of Joseph ... Josh. 17:1, 2
Called Jeezer ... Num. 26:30
Family settles at Ophrah ... Judg. 6:24
Gideon belongs to ... Judg. 6:11, 12
Family rallies to Gideon's call ... Judg. 6:34
2. A mighty man and commander in David's army ... 2 Sam. 23:27

Abiezrite

A member of the family of Abiezer ... Judg. 6:11; Judg. 6:24, 34

Abigail—*the father is joyful*

1. Nabal's beautiful and wise wife ... 1 Sam. 25:3
Appeases David's anger ... 1 Sam. 25:14-35
Becomes David's wife ... 1 Sam. 25:36-42
Captured and rescued ... 1 Sam. 30:5, 18
Mother of Chileab ... 2 Sam. 3:3
2. A stepsister of David ... 1 Chr. 2:16, 17

Abihail—*the father is might*

1. A Levite head of the house of Merari ... Num. 3:35
2. Abishur's wife ... 1 Chr. 2:29
3. A Gadite chief in Bashan ... 1 Chr. 5:14
4. Wife of King Rehoboam ... 2 Chr. 11:18
5. Father of Queen Esther ... Esth. 2:15

Abihu—*he is father*

Second of Aaron's four sons ... Ex. 6:23
Ascends Mt. Sinai ... Ex. 24:1, 9
Chosen as priest ... Ex. 28:1
Offers, with Nadab, strange fire ... Lev. 10:1-7
Died in the presence of the Lord ... Num. 3:4
Dies with heirs ... 1 Chr. 24:2

Abihud—*the father is majesty*

A Benjamite ... 1 Chr. 8:3

Abijah, Abia, Abiah—*Jehovah is Father*

1. Wife of Hezron ... 1 Chr. 2:24
2. Son of Becher ... 1 Chr. 7:8
3. Samuel's second son; follows corrupt ways ... 1 Sam. 8:2
4. Descendant of Aaron; head of an office of priests ... 1 Chr. 24:3, 10
Zechariah belongs to ... Luke 1:5
5. Son of Jeroboam I ... 1 Kin. 14:1-18
6. Slays 500,000 Israelites ... 2 Chr. 13:13-20
7. Fathers 38 children by 14 wives ... 2 Chr. 13:21
8. The mother of Hezekiah ... 2 Chr. 29:1
Called Abi ... 2 Kin. 18:2
9. A priest who signs the document ... Neh. 10:7
10. A priest returning from Babylon with Zerubbabel ... Neh. 12:1, 4, 17

Abijam—(another form of Abijah)

King of Judah ... 1 Kin. 14:31
Son and successor of King Rehoboam ... 1 Kin. 15:1-7
Follows in his father's sins ... 1 Kin. 15:3, 4
Wars against King Jeroboam ... 1 Kin. 15:6, 7

Abilene—*grassy place*

A province or tetrarchy of Syria ... Luke 3:1

Ability—*power to perform*

A. *Descriptive of:*
Material prosperity ... Deut. 16:17
Emotional strength ... Num. 11:14
Military power ... Num. 13:31; 1 Kin. 9:21
Physical strength ... Ex. 18:18, 23
Mental power ... Gen. 15:5
Moral power ... 1 Cor. 3:2
Spiritual power ... James 3:2
Divine power ... Rom. 4:21

B. *Of God's power to:*
Deliver ... 1 Cor. 10:13
Humble men ... Dan. 4:37
Create life ... Matt. 3:9
Destroy ... Matt. 10:28
Preserve believers ... John 10:28
Keep His promise ... Rom. 4:21
Make us stand ... Rom. 16:25
Supply grace ... 2 Cor. 9:8
Exceed our petitions ... Eph. 3:20
Service ... 1 Pet. 4:11
Comfort others ... 2 Cor. 1:4
Keep what we have entrusted ... 2 Tim. 1:12
Save from death ... Heb. 5:7
Resurrect men ... Heb. 11:19
Keep from falling ... Jude 24, 25

C. *Of Christ's power to:*
Heal ... Matt. 9:28
Subdue all things ... Phil. 3:21
Help His own ... Heb. 2:18
Have compassion ... Heb. 4:15, 16
Save completely ... Heb. 7:25

D. *Of the Christian's power to:*
Speak for the Lord ... Luke 21:15
Admonish ... Rom. 15:14
Survive testings ... 1 Cor. 3:13
Withstand Satan ... Eph. 6:11, 13
Convince opposition ... Titus 1:9
Bridle the whole body ... James 3:2

Abimael—*God is Father*

A son of Joktan ... Gen. 10:28

Abimelech—*the father is king*

1. A Philistine king of Gerar ... Gen. 20:1-18
Makes treaty with Abraham ... Gen. 21:22-34
2. A second king of Gerar ... Gen. 26:1-12
Tells Isaac to go home ... Gen. 26:13-16
Makes a treaty with Isaac concerning certain wells ... Gen. 26:17-33
3. A son of Gideon by a concubine ... Judg. 8:31
Conspires to become king ... Judg. 9:1-4
Slays his 70 brothers ... Judg. 9:5
Made king of Shechem ... Judg. 9:6
Rebuked by Jotham, lone survivor ... Judg. 9:7-21
Conspired against by Gaal ... Judg. 9:22-29
Captures Shechem and Thebez ... Judg. 9:41-50
Death of ... Judg. 9:51-57
4. A son of Abiathar the priest ... 1 Chr. 18:16
Also called Ahimelech ... 1 Chr. 24:6

Abinadab—*the father is generous*

1. A man of Kirjath-jearim whose house tabernacles the ark of the Lord ... 1 Sam. 7:1, 2
2. The second of Jesse's eight sons ... 1 Sam. 16:8
A soldier in Saul's army ... 1 Sam. 17:13
3. A son of Saul slain at Mt. Gilboa ... 1 Sam. 31:1-8
Bones of, buried by men of Jabesh ... 1 Chr. 10:1-12
4. The father of one of Solomon's sons-in-law ... 1 Kin. 4:11

Abinoam—*the father is pleasantness*

Father of Barak ... Judg. 4:6

Abiram—*the father is exalted*

1. Reubenite who conspired against Moses ... Num. 16:1-50
2. The first-born son of Hiel ... 1 Kin. 16:34; Josh. 6:26

Abishag—*the father wanders*

A Shunammite employed as David's nurse ... 1 Kin. 1:1-4, 15
Witnessed David's choice of Solomon as successor ... 1 Kin. 1:15-31
Adonijah slain for desiring to marry her ... 1 Kin. 2:13-25

Abishai—*father of a gift*

A son of Zeruiah, David's sister ... 2 Sam. 2:18
Brother of Joab and Asahel ... 1 Chr. 2:16
Rebuked by David ... 1 Sam. 26:5-9
Serves under Joab in David's army ... 2 Sam. 2:17, 18
Joins Joab in blood-revenge against Abner ... 2 Sam. 2:18-24
Co-commander of David's army ... 2 Sam. 10:9, 10
Loyal to David during Absalom's uprising ... 2 Sam. 16:9-12
Sternly rebuked by David ... 2 Sam. 19:21-23
Loyal to David during Sheba's rebellion ... 2 Sam. 20:1-6, 10
Slays 300 Philistines ... 2 Sam. 23:18
Slays 18,000 Edomites ... 1 Chr. 18:12, 13
Saves David by killing a giant ... 2 Sam. 21:16, 17

Abishalom—*father of peace*

A variant form of Absalom ... 1 Kin. 15:2, 10

Abishua—*the father is salvation*

1. A Benjamite ... 1 Chr. 8:3, 4
2. Phinehas' son ... 1 Chr. 6:4, 5, 50

Abishur—*the father is a wall*

A Jerahmeelite ... 1 Chr. 2:28, 29

Abital—*the father is dew*

Wife of David ... 2 Sam. 3:2, 4

Abitub—*the father is goodness*

A Benjamite ... 1 Chr. 8:8-11

Abiud—Greek form of Abihud

Ancestor of Jesus ... Matt. 1:13

Ablution—*ceremonial washing*

Of priests ... Ex. 30:18-21; Ex. 40:30, 31

SUBJECT ... REFERENCE

Of ceremonially unclean ... Lev. 14:7-9; Lev. 15:5-10
Of a house ... Lev. 14:52
By Pharisees ... Mark 7:1-5

Abner—*the father is a lamp*

Commands Saul's army ... 1 Sam. 14:50, 51
Introduces David to Saul ... 1 Sam. 17:55-58
Rebuked by David ... 1 Sam. 26:5, 14-16
Saul's cousin ... 1 Sam. 14:50, 51
Supports Ish-bosheth as Saul's successor ... 2 Sam. 2:8-10
Defeated by David's men ... 2 Sam. 2:12-17
Kills Asahel in self-defense ... 2 Sam. 2:18-23
Pursued by Joab ... 2 Sam. 2:24-32
Slain by Joab ... 2 Sam. 3:8-27
Death of, condemned by David ... 2 Sam. 3:28-39

Abolish—*to do away with*

A. *Of evil things:*
Idolatry ... Is. 2:18
Man-made ordinances ... Col. 2:20-22
Death ... 1 Cor. 15:26
Evil works ... Ezek. 6:6
Enmity ... Eph. 2:15

B. *Of things good for a while:*
Old covenant ... 2 Cor. 3:13
Present world ... Heb. 1:10-12
Temporal rule ... 1 Cor. 15:24
The partial ... 1 Cor. 13:10

C. *Of things not to be abolished:*
God's righteousness ... Is. 51:6
God's Word ... Matt. 5:18

Abominations—*things utterly repulsive*

A. *Descriptive of:*
Hebrew eating with Egyptians ... Gen. 43:32
Undesirable social relations ... Ex. 8:26
Spiritist practices ... Deut. 18:9-12
Heathen idolatry ... Deut. 7:25, 26
Child-sacrifice ... Deut. 12:31
Pagan gods ... 2 Kin. 23:13

B. *Applied to perverse sexual relations:*
Unnatural acts ... Lev. 18:19-29
Wrong clothing ... Deut. 22:5
Prostitution and sodomy ... Deut. 23:17, 18
Reclaiming a defiled woman ... Deut. 24:4
Racial inter-marriage ... Ezra 9:1-14

C. *In ceremonial matters, applied to:*
Unclean animals ... Lev. 11:10-23, 41-43
Deformed animals ... Deut. 17:1
Heathen practices in God's house ... 2 Chr. 36:14

D. *Sinfulness of, seen in:*
Being enticed ... 1 Kin. 11:5, 7
Delighting in ... Is. 66:3
Rejecting admonitions against ... Jer. 44:4, 5
Defiling God's house ... Jer. 7:30
Being polluted ... Ezek. 20:7, 30-32

E. *Judgments upon, manifested in:*
Stoning to death ... Deut. 17:2-5
Destroying a city ... Deut. 13:13-17
Forfeiting God's mercy ... Ezek. 5:11-13
Experiencing God's fury ... Ezek. 20:7, 8

F. *Things especially classed as:*
Silver or gold from graven images ... Deut. 7:25
Perverse man ... Prov. 3:32
Seven sins ... Prov. 6:16-19
False balance ... Prov. 11:1
Lying lips ... Prov. 12:22
Sacrifices of the wicked ... Prov. 15:8, 9
Proud in heart ... Prov. 16:5
Justifying the wicked ... Prov. 17:15
Scorner ... Prov. 24:9
Prayer of one who turns away his ear ... Prov. 28:9
False worship ... Is. 1:13
Scant measures ... Mic. 6:10
Self-righteousness ... Luke 16:15

Abomination of desolation

Predicted by Daniel ... Dan. 9:27
Cited by Christ ... Matt. 24:15

SUBJECT ... REFERENCE

Abortion—*accidental or planned miscarriage*

Laws concerning ... Ex. 21:22-25
Pronounced as a judgment ... Hos. 9:14
Sought to relieve misery ... Job 3:16
Of animals, by thunder ... Ps. 29:9
Figurative of abrupt conversion ... 1 Cor. 15:8

Abound—*to increase greatly*

A. *Of good things:*
God's truth ... Rom. 3:7
God's grace ... Rom. 5:15, 20
Hope ... Rom. 15:13
God's work ... 1 Cor. 15:58
Suffering for Christ ... 2 Cor. 1:5
Joy in suffering ... 2 Cor. 8:2
Gracious works ... 2 Cor. 8:7
Good works ... 2 Cor. 9:8
Wisdom ... Eph. 1:8
Love ... Phil. 1:9
Fruitfulness ... Phil. 4:17, 18
Faith ... Col. 2:7
Pleasing God ... 1 Thess. 4:1
Christian qualities ... 2 Pet. 1:5-7
Blessings ... Prov. 28:20
Charity ... 2 Thess. 1:3

B. *Source of, in good things:*
From God ... 2 Cor. 9:8
From Christian generosity ... 2 Cor. 8:2, 3
Faithfulness ... Prov. 28:20
Generosity ... Phil. 4:14-17

C. *Of evil things:*
Transgressions ... Prov. 29:22
Lawlessness ... Matt. 24:12
Increasing sins ... Rom. 5:20

Abraham—*the father of a multitude*

A. *Ancestry and family:*
Descendant of Shem ... 1 Chr. 1:24-27
Son of Terah ... Gen. 11:26
First named Abram ... Gen. 11:27
A native of Ur ... Gen. 11:28, 31
Pagan ancestors ... Josh. 24:2
Weds Sarai ... Gen. 11:29

B. *Wanderings of:*
Goes to Haran ... Gen. 11:31
Receives God's call ... Gen. 12:1-3; Acts 7:2-4
Prompted by faith ... Heb. 11:8
Enters Canaan ... Gen. 12:4-6
Canaan promised to, by God ... Gen. 12:1, 7
Pitched his tent at Beth-el ... Gen. 12:8
Famine sends him to Egypt ... Gen. 12:10-20
Returns to Canaan enriched ... Gen. 13:1-5
Chooses Hebron rather than strife ... Gen. 13:6-12

C. *Testing and victory of:*
Separates from Lot ... Gen. 13:8-12
Rescues captured Lot ... Gen. 14:14-16
Receives Melchizedek's blessing ... Gen. 14:18-20
Covenant renewed; a son promised to ... Gen. 15:1-21
Justified by faith ... Gen. 15:6; Rom. 4:3
Takes Hagar as concubine ... Gen. 16:1-4
Ishmael born ... Gen. 16:5-16
Covenant renewed; named Abraham ... Gen. 17:1-8
Household of, circumcised ... Gen. 17:9-14, 23-27
Promised a son ... Gen. 17:15-19
Covenant in Isaac, not Ishmael ... {Gen. 17:20-22; Gal. 4:22-31}
Receives messengers ... Gen. 18:1-15
Intercedes concerning Sodom ... Gen. 18:16-33
Witnesses Sodom's doom ... Gen. 19:27, 28
His faith saves Lot ... Gen. 19:29
Sojourns at Gerar; deceives Abimelech ... Gen. 20:1-18
Isaac born to, and circumcised ... Gen. 21:1-8
Sends Hagar and Ishmael away ... Gen. 21:9-21
Makes covenant with Abimelech ... Gen. 21:22-34
Testing of, in offering Isaac ... Gen. 22:1-19
Receives news about Nahor ... Gen. 22:20-24
Buys burial place for Sarah ... Gen. 23:1-20

SUBJECT ... REFERENCE

Obtains wife for Isaac ... Gen. 24:1-67
Marries Keturah; fathers other children; dies ... Gen. 25:1-10

D. *Characteristics of:*
Friend of God ... 2 Chr. 20:7
Obedient ... Gen. 22:1-18
Tither ... Gen. 14:20; Heb. 7:1, 2, 4
Generous ... Gen. 13:8, 9
Courageous ... Gen. 14:13-16
Independent ... Gen. 14:21-23
Man of prayer ... Gen. 18:23-33
Man of faith ... Gen. 15:6
Rich man ... Gen. 13:2
Mighty prince ... Gen. 23:5, 6
Good provider ... Gen. 25:5, 6

E. *References to, in the New Testament:*
In the line of faith ... Heb. 11:8-10
Christ the true seed of ... Matt. 1:1
Foresees Christ's day ... John 8:56
Hears the Gospel preached ... Gal. 3:8
Justified by faith ... Rom. 4:1-12
Faith of, seen in works ... James 2:21-23
Father of true believers ... {Matt. 8:11; Rom. 4:11-25; Gal. 3:7, 29}
Sees the eternal city ... Heb. 11:8-10, 13-16
Covenant with, still valid ... Luke 1:73; Acts 3:25
Sons of, illustrate covenants ... Gal. 4:22-31
Tithing of, has deeper meaning ... Heb. 7:9, 10
Headship of, in marriage ... 1 Pet. 3:6, 7
Eternal home of, in heaven ... Luke 16:19-25

Abraham's bosom

Expressive of heavenly status ... Luke 16:22, 23

Abram (see Abraham)

Absalom—*the father of peace*

Son of David ... 2 Sam. 3:3
A handsome man ... 2 Sam. 14:25
Receives Tamar after her rape by Ammon ... 2 Sam. 13:20
Slays Ammon for raping Tamar ... 2 Sam. 13:22-33
Flees from David ... 2 Sam. 13:34-39
Returns through Joab's intrigue ... 2 Sam. 14:1-24
Fathers children ... 2 Sam. 14:27
Reconciled to David ... 2 Sam. 14:28-33
Alienates the people from David ... 2 Sam. 15:1-6
Conspires against David ... 2 Sam. 15:7-12
Takes Jerusalem ... 2 Sam. 15:13-29
Receives Hushai ... 2 Sam. 15:31-37
Hears Ahithophel's counsel ... 2 Sam. 16:20-23
Prefers Hushai's counsel ... 2 Sam. 17:5-14
Strategy of, revealed to David ... 2 Sam. 17:15-22
Masses his army against David ... 2 Sam. 17:24-26
Caught and slain by Joab ... 2 Sam. 18:9-18
Death of, brings sorrow to David ... 2 Sam. 18:19-33
Joab rebukes David for mourning over ... 2 Sam. 19:1-8
Death of, unites Israel again to David ... 2 Sam. 19:9-15

Absence

A. *Of physical relations:*
A child from its father ... Gen. 37:32-35
Israel's ark ... 1 Sam. 4:21, 22
Israel from her land ... 2 Chr. 36:17-21
Believers from one another ... Phil. 1:25, 26
Believers from Christ ... 2 Cor. 5:6-9

B. *Of God's Spirit as:*
Judgment on the world ... Gen. 6:3
Judgment on an individual ... 1 Sam. 16:14
Unable to flee ... Ps. 139:7-12

C. *Of graces:*
Holy Spirit ... Jude 19
Faith ... 2 Thess. 3:2
Natural love ... 2 Tim. 3:2
Holiness ... Rev. 22:11
Righteousness ... Rev. 22:11

Absenteeism—*habitual absence from*

Work, condemned ... 2 Thess. 3:6-14
Church, rebuked ... Heb. 10:25

SUBJECT REFERENCE

Abstain—*to refrain from*

A. *From moral evil:*
- Vindictiveness ... 2 Sam. 16:5-14
- Idolatry ... Acts 15:20, 29
- Fornication ... Acts 15:20
- Sexual sins ... 1 Thess. 4:3
- Fleshly lusts ... 1 Pet. 2:11
- Evil appearances ... 1 Thess. 5:22

B. *From things:*
- Food ... 2 Sam. 12:16, 23
- Married relations ... Ex. 19:15; 1 Cor. 7:5
- Meats ... Rom. 14:1-23; 1 Cor. 8:1-13

C. *From unauthorized commands:*
- Forbidding to marry ... 1 Tim. 4:3
- Requiring man-made ceremonies ... Col. 2:20-23
- Abstaining from meats ... 1 Tim. 4:3

Abstinence—*to refrain from*
- Blood ... Acts 15:20
- Evil ... 1 Thess. 5:22
- Food ... Acts 27:21
- Fornication ... Acts 15:20; 1 Thess. 4:3
- Idolatry ... Acts 15:20
- Intoxicants ... Prov. 23:31
- Lust ... 1 Pet. 2:11
- Meats ... 1 Tim. 4:3
- Things offered to idols ... Acts 15:29
- Meats contaminated ... Acts 15:20

Abstinence—*to refrain from strong drink*

A. *Required of:*
- Priests ... Lev. 10:9
- Kings ... Prov. 31:4
- Nazarites ... Num. 6:1-4

B. *Failure of, a cause of:*
- Sudden death ... 1 Sam. 25:36-38
- Delirium tremens ... Prov. 23:31-35
- Insensibility to justice ... Is. 5:11, 12, 22, 23
- Error in judgment ... Is. 28:7
- Moral callousness ... Is. 56:12
- Revelry ... Dan. 5:2-4
- Debauchery ... Hab. 2:15, 16
- A weaker brother's stumble ... Rom. 14:20, 21
- Excess ... Eph. 5:18

C. *Examples of:*
- Manoah's wife ... Judg. 13:3, 4, 7
- Samson ... Judg. 16:17
- Hannah ... 1 Sam. 1:15
- Rechabites ... Jer. 35:1-19
- Daniel ... Dan. 1:8
- John the Baptist ... Luke 1:13-15

Abundance—*plentiful supply*

A. *Of material things:*
- Wealth ... 1 Kin. 10:10
- Rain ... 1 Kin. 18:41
- Metals ... 1 Chr. 22:3, 14
- Trees ... 1 Chr. 22:4; Neh. 9:25
- Sacrifices ... 1 Chr. 29:21
- Camels ... 2 Chr. 14:15
- Followers ... 2 Chr. 15:9
- Flocks and herds ... 2 Chr. 18:2; 2 Chr. 32:29
- Money ... 2 Chr. 24:11
- Weapons ... 2 Chr. 32:5
- Riches ... Ps. 52:7
- Milk ... Is. 7:22
- Wine ... Is. 56:12
- Horses ... Ezek. 26:10
- Labors ... 2 Cor. 11:23

B. *Of God's spiritual blessings:*
- Goodness ... Ex. 34:6
- Pardon ... Is. 55:7
- Peace and truth ... Jer. 33:6
- Answers to our prayers ... Eph. 3:20
- Grace ... 1 Tim. 1:14
- Mercy ... 1 Pet. 1:3

C. *Of spiritual things:*
- Predicted for Gospel times ... Is. 35:2
- Realized in the Messiah ... Ps. 72:7
- Given to the meek ... Ps. 37:11
- Through Christ ... Rom. 5:17, 20
- By grace ... 2 Cor. 4:15

D. *Of good things for Christians:*
- Greater usefulness ... Matt. 13:12
- Greater reward ... Matt. 25:29
- Spiritual life ... John 10:10
- Grace ... Rom. 5:17; 2 Cor. 4:15
- Christian service ... 1 Cor. 15:10
- Joy ... 2 Cor. 8:2
- Thanksgiving ... 2 Cor. 9:12
- Rejoicing ... Phil. 1:26
- Spiritual renewal ... Titus 3:5, 6
- Entrance in God's kingdom ... 2 Pet. 1:11

E. *Of undesirable things:*
- Witchcraft ... Is. 47:9
- Idleness ... Ezek. 16:49

F. *Characteristics of:*
- Given to the obedient ... Lev. 26:3-13
- Useful in God's work ... 2 Chr. 24:11
- Cannot satisfy fully ... Eccl. 5:10-12
- Not to be trusted ... Ps. 52:7
- Subject to conditions ... Mal. 3:10-12; Matt. 6:32, 33
- Can be taken away ... Luke 12:13-21
- Not a sign of real worth ... Luke 12:15

G. *Obtained by:*
- Putting away sin ... 2 Chr. 15:9
- Following God's commands ... 2 Chr. 17:5
- Given by God ... Job 36:31
- Through Christ ... John 10:10

Abuse—*application to a wrong purpose*

A. *Of physical things:*
- Sexual perversions ... Gen. 19:5-9, 31-38
- Immoral acts ... 1 Cor. 6:9
- Torture ... Judg. 16:21

B. *Of spiritual things:*
- Misuse of authority ... Num. 20:10-13; 1 Cor. 9:18
- Using the world wrongly ... 1 Cor. 7:31
- Perverting the truth ... 2 Pet. 2:10-22
- Corrupting God's ordinances ... 1 Sam. 2:12-17; 1 Cor. 11:17-22

C. *Manifested by:*
- Unbelieving ... Mark 15:29-32

Abyss

Translated:
- "deep" ... Luke 8:31
- "bottomless pit" ... Rev. 9:1, 2, 11; Rev. 17:8

Accad—*a city in the land of Shinar*
- City in Shinar ... Gen. 10:10

Acceptance—*the reception of one's person or service*

A. *Objects of, before God:*
- Righteousness and justice ... Prov. 21:3
- Our words and meditations ... Ps. 19:14
- Our dedication ... Rom. 12:1, 2
- Service ... Rom. 14:18
- Giving ... Rom. 15:16, 27
- Offerings ... Phil. 4:18
- Intercession ... 1 Tim. 2:1-3
- Helping parents ... 1 Tim. 5:4
- Spiritual sacrifices ... 1 Pet. 2:5
- Suffering because of Christ ... 1 Pet. 2:20

B. *Qualifications of, seen in:*
- Coming at God's time ... Is. 49:8; 2 Cor. 6:2
- Meeting God's requirements ... Job 42:8, 9
- Receiving divine sign ... Judg. 6:9-21
- Noting God's response ... 1 Sam. 7:8-10; John 12:28-30
- Responding to God's renewal ... Ezek. 20:40-44
- Manifesting spiritual rectitude ... Mic. 6:6-8

C. *Persons disqualified for, such as:*
- The wicked ... Ps. 82:2
- Blemished sacrifices ... Mal. 1:8, 10, 13
- Man's person ... Gal. 2:6
- Those who swear deceitfully ... Ps. 24:3-6

Access to God

A. *By means of:*
- Christ ... John 14:6
- Christ's blood ... Eph. 2:13
- Holy Spirit ... Eph. 2:18
- Faith ... Rom. 5:2
- Clean hands ... Ps. 24:3-5
- God's grace ... Eph. 1:6
- Prayer ... Matt. 6:6

B. *Characteristics of:*
- On God's choosing ... Ps. 64:4
- Sinners commanded to seek ... Is. 55:6; James 4:8
- With confidence ... Heb. 4:16
- Boldness ... Eph. 3:12
- Results from reconciliation ... Col. 1:21, 22
- Open to Gentiles ... Acts 14:27
- Experienced in Christ's priesthood ... Heb. 7:19-25
- Sought by God's people ... Ps. 27:4
- Bold in prayer ... Heb. 4:16
- A blessing to be chosen ... Ps. 65:4

Accho—*modern Acre* (a seaport 8 miles north of Mt. Carmel)
- Assigned to Asher ... Judg. 1:31
- Called Ptolemais in the New Testament ... Acts 21:7

Accident—*event not foreseen*

A. *Caused by:*
- An animal ... Num. 22:25
- A fall ... 2 Sam. 4:4

B. *Explanation of:*
- Known to God ... Deut. 29:29; Prov. 16:9, 33
- Misunderstood by men ... Luke 13:4, 5
- Subject to God's providence ... Rom. 8:28

Accommodation—*adaptation caused by human limitations*

A. *Physically, caused by:*
- Age and sex ... Gen. 33:13-15
- Strength and size ... 1 Sam. 17:38-40
- Inability to repay ... Luke 7:41, 42

B. *Spiritually, caused by:*
- Man's blindness ... Matt. 13:10-14
- Absence of the Spirit ... John 16:12, 13
- Carnality ... 1 Cor. 3:1, 2
- Spiritual immaturity ... Rom. 14:1-23
- Man's present limitations ... 1 Cor. 2:7-16
- Degrees of light ... Heb. 9:7-15

Accomplish—*to fulfill*

A. *Of God's Word concerning:*
- Judah's captivity ... 2 Chr. 36:23
- Judah's return ... Dan. 9:2
- God's sovereign plan ... Is. 55:11
- The Messiah's advent ... Dan. 9:24-27
- Christ's suffering ... Luke 18:31
- Christ's death ... John 19:28-30
- Final events ... Dan. 12:7

B. *Of human things:*
- Food ... 1 Kin. 5:9
- Purification rites ... Esth. 2:12
- Priestly ministry ... Luke 1:23
- Time of pregnancy ... Luke 2:6
- Afflictions ... 1 Pet. 5:9

Accord—*united agreement*

A. *Descriptive of:*
- A spontaneous response ... Acts 12:10, 20
- Voluntary action ... 2 Cor. 8:17
- Single-mindedness ... Josh. 9:2
- Spiritual unity ... Acts 1:14

B. *Manifested in:*
- Fellowship ... Acts 2:46
- Prayer ... Acts 4:24
- Opposition ... Acts 7:57
- Response ... Acts 8:6
- Decisions ... Acts 15:25
- Mind ... Phil. 2:2

Accountability—*responsibility for own acts*

A. *Kinds of:*
- Universal ... Rom. 14:12
- Personal ... 2 Sam. 12:1-15
- Personal and family ... Josh. 7:1-26
- Personal and national ... 2 Sam. 24:1-17
- Delayed but exacted ... 2 Sam. 21:1-14
- Final ... Rom. 2:1-12

B. *Determined by:*
- Federal headship ... Gen. 3:1-24; Rom. 5:12-21

SUBJECT REFERENCE

Personal responsibility ...... Ezek. 18:1-32
Faithfulness .... Matt. 25:14-30
Knowledge .... Luke 12:47, 48
Conscience .... Rom. 2:12-16
Greater light............... Rom. 2:17-29
Maturity of judgment .... 1 Cor. 8:1-13

Accursed—*under a curse*

A. *Caused by:*

Hanging on a tree .... Deut. 21:23
Sin among God's people...... Josh. 7:12
Possessing a banned thing ... Josh. 6:18
Preaching contrary to the Gospel................... Gal. 1:8, 9
Blaspheming Christ .... 1 Cor. 12:3

B. *Objects of being:*

A city................... Josh. 6:17
A forbidden thing .... Josh. 22:20
An old sinner .... Is. 65:20
Christ-haters or non-believers .... 1 Cor. 16:22
Paul (for the sake of Israel) .. Rom. 9:3

Accusations—*charges*

A. *Kinds of:*

Pagan.................... Dan. 3:8
Personal .... Dan. 6:24
Public .... John 18:29
Perverted .... 1 Pet. 3:16

B. *Sources of, in:*

The devil .... Job 1:6-12
Rev. 12:9, 10
Enemies.................. Ezra 4:6
Man's conscience .... John 8:9
God's Word .... John 5:45
Hypocritical .... John 8:6, 10, 11
The last days .... 2 Tim. 3:1, 3
Apostates .... 2 Pet. 2:10, 11

C. *Forbidden:*

Against servants............ Prov. 30:10
Falsely .... Luke 3:14
Among women .... Titus 2:3

D. *False, examples of, against:*

Jacob .... Gen. 31:26-30
Joseph .... Gen. 39:10-21
Ahimelech .... 1 Sam. 22:11-16
David.................... 2 Sam. 10:3
Job .... Job 2:4, 5
Jeremiah .... Jer. 26:8-11
Amos .... Amos 7:10, 11
Joshua .... Zech. 3:1-5
Christ.................... Matt. 26:59-66
Stephen .... Acts 6:11-14
Paul and Silas.............. Acts 16:19-21
Paul .... Acts 21:27-29
Christians .... 1 Pet. 2:12

Aceldama

Field called "field of blood" .... Acts 1:19

Achaia—*a region of Greece*

Visited by Paul .... Acts 18:1, 12
Gallio proconsul .... Acts 18:12
Apollos preaches in........... Acts 18:24-28
Christians of, very generous..... Rom. 15:26
Saints in all of .... 2 Cor. 1:1
Paul commends Christians of ... 2 Cor. 11:10
Gospel proclaimed throughout .. 1 Thess. 1:7, 8

Achaicus—*belonging to Achaia*

A Corinthian Christian who visited Paul....................... 1 Cor. 16:17, 18

Achan, Achar—*trouble*

A son of Carmi .... Josh. 7:1
Sin of, caused Israel's defeat .... Josh. 7:1-15
Stoned to death .... Josh. 7:16-25
Sin of, recalled.............. Josh. 22:20
Also called Achar .... 1 Chr. 2:7

Achaz—*Greek name of Ahaz*

Ancestor of Jesus............. Matt. 1:9

Achbor—*mouse*

1. Father of Edomite king ..... Gen. 36:36, 38
2. A courtier under Josiah ..... 2 Kin. 22:12, 14
Called Abdon .... 2 Chr. 34:20

Achim—*short form of Jehoiachim*

Ancestor of Jesus............. Matt. 1:14

Achish—*serpent-charmer*

A king of Gath .... 1 Sam. 21:10-15

SUBJECT REFERENCE

David seeks refuge .... 1 Sam. 27:1-12
Forced to expel David by Philistine lords .... 1 Sam. 28:1, 2
Receives Shimei's servants ...... 1 Kin. 2:39, 40

Achmetha—*capital of Media* (same as Ecbatana)

Site of Persian archives......... Ezra 6:2

Achor, valley of—*trouble*

Site of Achan's stoning......... Josh. 7:24-26
On Judah's boundary .... Josh. 15:7
Promises concerning .... Is. 65:10

Achsa, Achsah—*anklet*

A daughter of Caleb .... 1 Chr. 2:49
Given to Othniel .... Josh. 15:16-19
Given springs of water .... Judg. 1:12-15

Achshaph—*dedicated*

A royal city of Canaan......... Josh. 11:1
Captured by Joshua .... Josh. 12:7, 20
Assigned to Asher .... Josh. 19:24, 25

Achzib—*a lie*

1. City of Judah .... Josh. 15:44
Also called Chezib.......... Gen. 38:5
2. Town of Asher .... Josh. 19:29

Acknowledge—*to recognize*

A. *Evil objects of:*

Sin .... Ps. 32:5
Transgressions .... Ps. 51:3
Iniquity .... Jer. 3:13
Wickedness .... Jer. 14:20

B. *Good objects of:*

God .... Prov. 3:6
God's might .... Is. 33:13
God's people .... Is. 61:9
God's mystery .... Col. 2:2
God's truth .... 2 Tim. 2:25
The apostles .... 1 Cor. 14:37
Christian leaders .... 1 Cor. 16:18

Acquaintance—*personal knowledge*

With God, gives peace .... Job 22:21
Deserted by .... Ps. 31:11
Made an abomination.......... Ps. 88:8, 18
Jesus sought among........... Luke 2:44
Stand afar off from Christ ...... Luke 23:49
Come to Paul .... Acts 24:23
Of God, with man's ways....... Ps. 139:3

Acquit—*to declare to be innocent*

Not possible with the wicked.... Nah. 1:3
Sought by the righteous .... Job 7:21
Difficulty of obtaining .... Job 9:28-31

Acre—*a land measurement*

Plowing of, by a yoke of oxen ... 1 Sam. 14:14
Descriptive of barrenness .... Is. 5:10

Acrostic

A literary device using the Hebrew alphabet; illustrated best in Hebrew ..... Ps. 119:1-176

Acts of the Apostles—*book of New Testament*

Written by Luke .... Luke 1:1-4
Acts 1:1, 2

Adadah—*holiday*

A city of Judah .... Josh. 15:22

Adah—*ornament*

1. One of Lamech's wives ...... Gen. 4:19
2. One of Esau's wives......... Gen. 36:2, 4, 10, 12
Also called Bashemath ...... Gen. 26:34

Adaiah—*Jehovah has adorned*

1. The maternal grandfather of Josiah .... 2 Kin. 22:1
2. A Levite .... 1 Chr. 6:41
3. Son of Shimhi .... 1 Chr. 8:21
Called Shema .... 1 Chr. 8:13
4. Aaronite priest .... 1 Chr. 9:10-12
5. The father of Maaseiah...... 2 Chr. 23:1
6. A son of Bani............. Ezra 10:29
7. Another of a different family of Bani..................... Ezra 10:34, 39
8. A descendant of Judah ...... Neh. 11:4, 5

Adalia

Haman's son .... Esth. 9:8, 10

SUBJECT REFERENCE

Adam—*red earth*

A. *Creation of:*

In God's image .... Gen. 1:26, 27
By God's breath............ Gen. 2:7
A living soul .... 1 Cor. 15:45
From dust .... Gen. 2:7
Before Eve .... 1 Tim. 2:13
Upright .... Eccl. 7:29
Intelligent being............ Gen. 2:19, 20

B. *Position of, first:*

Worker .... Gen. 2:8, 15
To receive God's law........ Gen. 2:16, 17
Husband .... Gen. 2:18-25
Man to sin .... Gen. 3:6-12
To receive promise of the Messiah.................. Gen. 3:15
Father .... Gen. 4:1
Head of race............... Rom. 5:12-14

C. *Sin of:*

Instigated by Satan .... Gen. 3:1-5
Prompted by Eve .... Gen. 3:6
Done knowingly............ 1 Tim. 2:14
Resulted in broken fellowship .... Gen. 3:8
Brought God's curse .... Gen. 3:14-19

D. *Descendants of, are all:*

Sinners.................... Rom. 5:12
Subject to death .... Rom. 5:12-14
Scattered over the earth ..... Deut. 32:8
In need of salvation......... John 3:16

Adam—*a city near Zaretan*

Site of Jordan's waters rising to let Israel pass over .... Josh. 3:16

Adam, Last—*an attribution of Christ*

Prefigured in Adam............ Rom. 5:14
Gift of, abound to many .... Rom. 5:15
A quickening spirit .... 1 Cor. 15:45
Spiritual and heavenly .... 1 Cor. 15:46-48

Adamah—*red ground*

City of Naphtali .... Josh. 19:35, 36

Adami—*earthy*

In Naphtali.................. Josh. 19:33

Adam, second

Expressive of Christ .... 1 Cor. 15:20-24
1 Cor. 15:45

Adar—*dark or cloudy*

A town of Judah .... Josh. 15:1, 3

Adar—*the 12th month of the Hebrew year*

Date set by Haman for massacre of Jews....................... Esth. 3:7, 13
Date adopted for Purim .... Esth. 9:19, 21, 26-28
Date of completion of Temple .. Ezra 6:15

Adbeel—*disciplined of God*

A son of Ishmael.............. Gen. 25:13

Add—*to increase the sum of*

A. *Of material things:*

Another child .... Gen. 30:24
A population .... 2 Sam. 24:3
Heavy burdens .... 1 Kin. 12:11, 14
Years to life .... Prov. 3:2
Kingly majesty .... Dan. 4:36
Stature .... Matt. 6:27

B. *Of good things:*

No sorrow................. Prov. 10:22
Inspired words .... Jer. 36:32
Learning .... Prov. 16:23
Spiritual blessings .... Matt. 6:33
Converts to Christ .... Acts 2:41, 47
A covenant .... Gal. 3:15
The Law .... Gal. 3:19

C. *Of evil things:*

Additions to God's Word .... Deut. 4:2
National sins .... 1 Sam. 12:19
Iniquity .... Ps. 69:27
Sin to sin................. Is. 30:1
Grief to sorrow .... Jer. 45:3
Personal sin .... Luke 3:19, 20
Afflictions .... Phil. 1:16

Addan—*strong*

A place in Babylonia whose returnees fail to prove Israelite ancestry .... Ezra 2:59

A

SUBJECT — REFERENCE

Addar—*wide, open place*
A Benjamite ... 1 Chr. 8:3
Also called Ard ... Num. 26:40

Adder—*a venomous serpent*
Figurative of Dan's treachery ... Gen. 49:17
Sting of wine ... Prov. 23:31, 32
Wickedness of sinners ... Ps. 58:3, 4
Triumph of saints ... Ps. 91:13

Addi—*my witness*
Ancestor of Jesus ... Luke 3:23, 28

Addiction—*compulsive or habitual devotion*
To ministry of the saints ... 1 Cor. 16:15

Additions to the church
A. *Manner and number of:*
"The Lord added" ... Acts 2:47
"Believers . . . added to the Lord" ... Acts 5:14
"Disciples . . . multiplied" ... Acts 6:1
"A great company of priests" ... Acts 6:7
"Churches . . . were multiplied" ... Acts 9:31
"A great number believed" ... Acts 11:21
"Much people added" ... Acts 11:24
"Churches . . . increased in number" ... Acts 16:5
B. *By means of:*
Word preached ... Acts 2:14-41
The Spirit's convicting power ... John 16:7-11
The Gospel as God's power ... Rom. 1:16
Responding faith ... Acts 14:1

Addon (see Addan)

Address—*a public message*
A. *In Old Testament:*
Moses' expository ... Deut. 1:1—4:40
Moses' second ... Deut. 4:44—26:19
Moses' third ... Deut. 27:1—30:20
Moses' fourth ... Deut. 32:1-43
Moses' final ... Deut. 33:1-29
Joshua's exhortation ... Josh. 23:2-16
Joshua's farewell ... Josh. 24:1-25
Solomon's to God ... 1 Kin. 3:6-9
Ezra's expository ... Neh. 8:1-8
Jeremiah's Temple sermon ... Jer. 7:1—10:25
B. *Of Paul:*
First ... Acts 9:20-22
Second ... Acts 13:16-41
To Peter ... Gal. 2:11-21
To women ... Acts 16:13
With Silas ... Acts 16:29-32
At Athens ... Acts 17:22-31
At Troas ... Acts 20:6, 7
To elders ... Acts 20:17-35
To the crowd ... Acts 22:1-21
Before Felix ... Acts 24:10-21
Before Agrippa ... Acts 26:1-29
On the ship ... Acts 27:21-26
Final recorded ... Acts 28:25-28
C. *Of Peter:*
In upper room ... Acts 1:13-22
Pentecost ... Acts 2:14-40
At Temple ... Acts 3:12-26
In house of Cornelius ... Acts 10:34-43
At Jerusalem council ... Acts 15:7-11
D. *Of Others:*
Stephen ... Acts 7:2-60
Herod ... Acts 12:21, 22
James ... Acts 15:13-21
Tertullus ... Acts 24:1-8

Adiel—*ornament of God*
1. A Simeonite prince ... 1 Chr. 4:24, 36
2. Aaronite priest ... 1 Chr. 9:12, 13
3. Father of Azmaveth ... 1 Chr. 27:25

Adin—*effeminate*
1. A man whose descendants return with Zerubbabel ... Ezra 2:2, 15
2. A man whose descendants return with Ezra ... Ezra 8:1, 6
3. Sealer of the covenant ... Neh. 10:1, 16

Adina—*delicate*
A Reubenite captain under David ... 1 Chr. 11:42

Adino—*slender*
A mighty man under David ... 2 Sam. 23:8
Compare parallel passage in ... 1 Chr. 11:11

Adithaim—*double ornaments*
A city of Judah ... Josh. 15:21, 36

Adjuration—*placing under oath*
Joshua's, to Jericho ... Josh. 6:26
Saul's, to those breaking a fast ... 1 Sam. 14:24-28
Ahab's, to the prophet Micaiah ... 1 Kin. 22:16
Caiaphas', by God ... Matt. 26:63
Demon's, by God ... Mark 5:7
Exorcists', by Jesus ... Acts 19:13
Paul's charge, by the Lord ... 1 Thess. 5:27

Adlai—*Jehovah is just*
Father of Shaphat ... 1 Chr. 27:29

Admah—*red earth*
A city near Sodom ... Gen. 10:19
Joins other cities against Chedorlaomer ... Gen. 14:1-4, 8
Destroyed with Sodom and Gomorrah ... Gen. 19:24-28

Admatha—*God-given*
One of Ahasuerus' chamberlains ... Esth. 1:14, 15

Administer—*service*
Applied to:
Judgment ... 1 Kin. 3:28
Vengeance ... Jer. 21:12
Justice ... 2 Sam. 8:15

Administration—*the management or disposition of affairs*
Of gifts to Jerusalem saints ... 2 Cor. 8:19, 20
Of spiritual gifts ... 1 Cor. 12:5; 2 Cor. 9:12
Of government matters ... Rom. 13:3-5
Of new covenant ... 2 Cor. 3:6

Admiration—*exceptional esteem*
Reserved for saints ... 2 Thess. 1:10
Flattering, shown by false teachers ... Jude 16
Astounding, manifested by John ... Rev. 17:6, 7

Admonition—*wise words spoken against evil acts*
A. *Performed by:*
God ... Heb. 8:5
Earthly fathers ... Eph. 6:4
Leaders ... 1 Thess. 5:12
Christians ... Rom. 15:14
B. *Directed against:*
A remnant ... Jer. 42:19
Elders ... Acts 20:28-35
Those who will not work ... 2 Thess. 3:10, 15
Heretics ... Titus 3:10
C. *Sources of in:*
Scriptures ... 1 Cor. 10:11
Wise words ... Eccl. 12:11, 12
Spiritual knowledge ... Col. 3:16

Adna—*pleasure*
1. Jew who divorced his foreign wife ... Ezra 10:18-30
2. Postexilic priest ... Neh. 12:12-15

Adnah—*pleasure*
1. Captain of Saul ... 1 Chr. 12:20
2. Chief Captain of Jehoshaphat ... 2 Chr. 17:14

Ado—*activity, tumult, fuss*
Not to make ... Mark 5:39

Adonai—*Lord*
The Hebrew name for God (translated "Lord") expressing lordship (found in the following five compound words)

Adoni-bezek—*lord of Bezek*
A king of Bezek ... Judg. 1:3-7

Adonijah—*my Lord is Jehovah*
1. David's fourth son ... 2 Sam. 3:2, 4
Attempts to usurp throne ... 1 Kin. 1:5-53
Desires Abishag as wife ... 1 Kin. 2:13-18
Executed by Solomon ... 1 Kin. 2:19-25
2. A teacher ... 2 Chr. 17:8, 9
3. A Jew who signed the document ... Neh. 9:38; 10:16
Probably the same as Adonikam in ... Ezra 2:13

Adonikam—*my Lord has risen*
Descendants of, return from exile ... Ezra 2:13

Adoniram, Adoram—*my Lord is exalted*
A son of Abda ... 1 Kin. 4:6
Official under David, Solomon, and Rehoboam ... 2 Sam. 20:24; 1 Kin. 5:14; 1 Kin. 12:18
Stoned by angry Israelites ... 1 Kin. 12:18
Called Hadoram ... 2 Chr. 10:18

Adoni-zedek—*my Lord is righteous*
An Amorite king of Jerusalem ... Josh. 10:1-5
Defeated and slain by Joshua ... Josh. 10:6-27

Adoption—*the legal act of investing with sonship*
A. *Used naturally of:*
Eliezer under Abraham ... Gen. 15:2-4
Joseph's sons under Jacob ... Gen. 48:5, 14, 16
Moses under Pharaoh's daughter ... Ex. 2:10; Acts 7:21
Esther under Mordecai ... Esth. 2:7
B. *Used spiritually of Israel as:*
Elected by God ... Deut. 14:1, 2; Rom. 11:1-32
Blessed by God ... Rom. 9:4
Realized in history ... Ex. 4:22, 23
C. *Used spiritually of the Gentiles as:*
Predicted in the prophets ... Is. 65:1
Confirmed by faith ... Rom. 10:20
Realized in the new covenant ... Eph. 2:12; Eph. 3:1-6
D. *The time of:*
Past, predestined to ... Rom. 8:29
Present, regarded as sons ... John 1:12, 13; John 3:1-11
Future, glorified as sons ... Rom. 8:19, 23; 1 John 3:2
E. *The source of:*
By God's grace ... Rom. 4:16, 17
By faith ... Gal. 3:7, 26
Through Christ ... Gal. 4:4, 5
F. *Assurances of, by:*
Spirit's witness ... Rom. 8:16
Spirit's leading ... Rom. 8:14
"Abba, Father" ... Rom. 8:15
Changed life ... 1 John 3:9-17
Father's chastening ... Prov. 3:11, 12; Heb. 12:5-11
G. *The blessings of:*
A new nature ... 2 Cor. 5:17
A new name ... Is. 62:2, 12; Rev. 3:12
Access to God ... Eph. 2:18
Fatherly love ... 1 John 3:1
Help in prayer ... Matt. 6:5-15
Spiritual unity ... John 17:11, 21; Eph. 2:18-22
A glorious inheritance ... John 14:1-3; Rom. 8:17, 18

Adoraim—*double honor*
A city fortified by Rehoboam ... 2 Chr. 11:5, 9

Adoram—*the Lord is exalted*
An official over forced labor ... 2 Sam. 20:24; 1 Kin. 12:18

See Adoniram

Adoration—*reverential praise*
A. *Rendered falsely to:*
Idols ... Is. 44:15, 17, 19
An image ... Dan. 3:5-7
Heavenly hosts ... 2 Kin. 17:16
Satan ... Luke 4:8
Men ... Acts 10:25, 26
Angels ... Col. 2:18, 23
B. *Rendered properly to God:*
Illustrated ... Is. 6:1-5

A

SUBJECT — REFERENCE

- Taught ... Ps. 95—100
- Proclaimed ... Rev. 4:8-11

C. *Rendered properly to Christ as God by:*
- Wise men ... Matt. 2:1, 11
- Leper ... Matt. 8:2
- Ruler ... Matt. 9:18
- Disciples ... Matt. 14:22, 33
- Woman ... Matt. 15:25
- Mother ... Matt. 20:20
- Blind man ... John 9:1, 38
- Every creature ... Phil. 2:10, 11

See also Worship

Adornment

A. *Used literally of:*
- A ruler ... Gen. 41:42-44
- A harlot ... Gen. 38:14, 15; Rev. 17:3, 4
- A woman ... Is. 3:16-24; 1 Tim. 2:9
- A building ... Luke 21:5
- A bride ... Rev. 21:2

B. *Used spiritually of:*
- God ... Ps. 104:1, 2
- Messiah ... Ps. 45:7, 8
- Believer as justified ... Is. 61:10
- Believer as sanctified ... Titus 2:10
- Israel restored ... Jer. 31:4
- Saintly woman ... 1 Tim. 2:9
- Saints in glory ... Rev. 19:14

C. *Guidelines for:*
- In modesty ... 1 Tim. 2:9
- Not external ... 1 Pet. 3:3-5

Adrammelech—*Adar is king*

1. An Assyrian god worshiped by the Samaritans ... 2 Kin. 17:31
2. Killed Sennacherib ... 2 Kin. 19:36, 37; Is. 37:38

Adramyttium—*a seaport of Mysia in Asia Minor*
- Travels of Paul ... Acts 27:2-6

Adriatic Sea
- A part or the whole of the Adriatic Sea named after Adria, a city of Italy ... Acts 27:27

Adriel—*my help is God*
- Marries Saul's eldest daughter ... 1 Sam. 18:19
- Sons of, slain to atone Saul's crime ... 2 Sam. 21:8, 9

Adullam—*refuge*
- A town of Canaan ... Gen. 38:1, 12, 20
- Conquered by Joshua ... Josh. 12:7, 15
- Assigned to Judah ... Josh. 15:20, 35
- Fortified by Rehoboam ... 2 Chr. 11:5-7
- Symbol of Israel's glory ... Mic. 1:15
- Reoccupied ... Neh. 11:30
- David seeks refuge in caves of ... 1 Sam. 22:1, 2
- Exploits of mighty men while there ... 2 Sam. 23:13-17

Adullamite—*a citizen of Adullam*
- Judah's friend ... Gen. 38:1, 12, 20

Adulterer—*a man who commits adultery*
- Punishment of ... Lev. 20:10
- Waits for the twilight ... Job 24:15
- Offspring of ... Is. 57:3
- Land is full of ... Jer. 23:10
- Shall not inherit the kingdom of God ... 1 Cor. 6:9
- God will judge ... Heb. 13:4

Adulteress—*a woman guilty of adultery*

A. *Sin of:*
- Punished by death ... Lev. 20:10
- Ensnares the simple ... Prov. 7:6-23
- Brings a man to poverty ... Prov. 6:26
- Leads to death ... Prov. 2:16-19
- Increases transgressors ... Prov. 23:27, 28
- Defined by Christ ... Matt. 5:32
- Forgiven by Christ ... John 8:1-11

B. *Examples of:*
- Tamar ... Gen. 38:13-24
- Potiphar's wife (attempted) ... Gen. 39:7-20
- Midianite women ... Num. 25:6-8
- Rahab ... Josh. 2:1
- Bath-sheba ... 2 Sam. 11:4, 5
- Herodias ... Matt. 14:3, 4
- Unnamed woman ... John 8:1-11

See Harlot

SUBJECT — REFERENCE

Adultery—*sexual intercourse outside marriage*

A. *Defined:*
- In God's Law ... Ex. 20:14
- By Christ ... Matt. 5:28, 32
- By Paul ... Rom. 7:3
- In mental attitude ... Matt. 5:28
- As a work of the flesh ... Gal. 5:19

B. *Sin of:*
- Breaks God's Law ... Deut. 5:18
- Punishable by death ... Lev. 20:10-12
- Brings death ... Prov. 2:18, 19
- Makes one poor ... Prov. 29:3
- Produces moral insensibility ... Prov. 30:20; 2 Cor. 12:21
- Corrupts a land ... Hos. 4:1, 2, 11
- Justifies divorce ... Matt. 19:7-9
- Excludes from Christian fellowship ... 1 Cor. 5:1-13
- Excludes from God's kingdom ... 1 Cor. 6:9, 10
- Merits God's judgments ... Heb. 13:4
- Ends in hell (Sheol) ... Prov. 7:27; Rev. 21:8

C. *Forgiveness of, by:*
- Man ... Judg. 19:1-4
- Christ ... John 8:10, 11
- Repentance ... 2 Sam. 12:7-14
- Regeneration ... 1 Cor. 6:9-11

D. *Examples of:*
- Lot ... Gen. 19:31-38
- Shechem ... Gen. 34:2
- Judah ... Gen. 38:1-24
- Eli's sons ... 1 Sam. 2:22
- David ... 2 Sam. 11:1-5
- Amnon ... 2 Sam. 13:1-20
- The Samaritan woman ... John 4:17, 18

Adultery, spiritual
- Seen in Israel's idolatry ... Judg. 2:11, 17
- Described graphically ... Ezek. 16
- Symbolized in Hosea's marriage ... Hos. 1:1-3
- Symbolized in final apostasy ... Rev. 17:1-5
- Figurative of friendship with the world ... James 4:4
- Figurative of false teaching ... Rev. 2:14, 15, 20-22

Adummim—*red spots*
- A hill between Jerusalem and Jericho ... Josh. 15:5, 7, 8
- The probable site of Good Samaritan parable in ... Luke 10:30-37

Advancement—*progression*

A. *Promotion to a higher office:*
- Moses and Aaron, by the Lord ... 1 Sam. 12:6
- Promised to Balaam ... Num. 22:16, 17
- Joseph, by true interpretation ... Gen. 41:38-46
- Levites, for loyalty ... Ex. 32:26-28
- Phinehas, by decisive action ... Num. 25:7-13
- Haman, by intrigue ... Esth. 3:1, 2
- Mordecai, by ability ... Esth. 10:2
- Daniel, by fidelity ... Dan. 2:48
- Deacons, by faithfulness ... 1 Tim. 3:10, 13

B. *Conditions of, seen in:*
- Humility ... Matt. 18:4
- Faithfulness ... Matt. 25:14-30
- Skilled in work ... Prov. 22:29; Luke 22:24-30

C. *Hindrances to, occasioned by:*
- Self-glory ... Is. 14:12-15; 1 Cor. 4:7-9
- Pride ... Ezek. 28:11-19; 1 Pet. 5:5, 6

Advantage—*superior circumstance or ability*

A. *In God's kingdom, none by:*
- Birth ... Matt. 3:8, 9
- Race ... Gal. 2:14-16
- Position ... John 3:1-6
- Works ... Matt. 5:20
- Wealth ... Luke 9:25

B. *In God's kingdom, some by:*
- Industry ... 1 Cor. 15:10
- Faithfulness ... Matt. 25:14-30
- Kindred spirit ... Phil. 2:19-23
- Works ... 1 Cor. 3:11-15
- Dedication ... Rev. 14:1-5

SUBJECT — REFERENCE

Advent of Christ, the first

A. *Announced in the Old Testament by:*
- Moses ... Deut. 18:18, 19
- Samuel ... Acts 3:24
- David ... Ps. 40:6-8; Heb. 10:5-8
- Prophets ... Luke 24:26, 27

B. *Prophecies fulfilled by his:*
- Birth ... Is. 7:14; Matt. 1:23
- Forerunner ... Mal. 3:1, 2; Matt. 3:1-3
- Incarnation ... Is. 9:6
- Time of arrival ... Dan. 9:24; Mark 1:15
- Rejection ... Is. 53:1-4; Rom. 10:16-21
- Crucifixion ... Ps. 2:1, 2; Acts 4:24-28
- Atonement ... Is. 53:1-12; 1 Pet. 1:18-21
- Resurrection ... Ps. 16:8-11; Acts 2:25-31
- Priesthood ... Ps. 110:4, 5; Heb. 5:5, 6

C. *His first coming:*
- Introduces Gospel age ... Acts 3:24
- Consummates new covenant ... Jer. 31:31-34; Heb. 8:6-13
- Fulfills prophecy ... Luke 24:44, 45
- Nullifies the ceremonial system ... Heb. 9
- Brings Gentiles in ... Acts 15:13-18

Advent of Christ, the second (see Second coming of Christ)

Advents of Christ, compared

A. *First Advent:*
- Prophesied ... Deut. 18:18, 19; Is. 7:14
- Came as man ... Phil. 2:5-7
- Announced ... Luke 2:10-14
- Time predicted ... Dan. 9:25
- To save the lost ... Matt. 18:11
- Subject to government ... Matt. 17:24-27

B. *Second Advent:*
- Prophesied ... John 14:1-3; 1 Thess. 4:16
- Come as God ... 1 Thess. 4:16
- As a thief ... 1 Thess. 5:2
- At a time unknown ... Matt. 24:36
- To judge the lost ... Matt. 25:32-36
- Source of government ... Rev. 20:4-6; Rev. 22:3-5

Adversaries—*those who actively oppose*

A. *Descriptive of:*
- Satan ... 1 Pet. 5:8
- Gospel's enemies ... 1 Cor. 16:9
- Israel's enemies ... Josh. 5:13
- An enemy ... Esth. 7:6
- A rival ... 1 Sam. 1:6
- God's agent ... 1 Kin. 11:14, 23
- God's angel ... Num. 22:22

B. *Believer's attitude toward:*
- Pray for ... Ps. 71:13
- Use God's weapons against ... Luke 21:15
- Not to be terrified by ... Phil. 1:28
- Not to give occasion to ... 1 Tim. 5:14
- Remember God's judgment on ... Heb. 10:27

Adversity—*adverse circumstances*

A. *Caused by:*
- Man's sin ... Gen. 3:16, 17
- Disobedience to God's Law ... Lev. 26:14-20

B. *Purposes of, to:*
- Punish for sin ... 2 Sam. 12:9-12
- Humble us ... 2 Chr. 33:12
- Lead us to God's Word ... Deut. 8:2, 3
- Chasten and correct ... Heb. 12:5-11
- Test our faith ... 1 Pet. 1:5-8
- Give us final rest ... Ps. 94:12, 13

C. *Reactions to:*
- Rebellious ... Ex. 14:4-8; Job 2:9

SUBJECT — REFERENCE

Distrustful ... Ex. 6:8, 9
Complaining ... Ruth 1:20, 21
Questioning ... Jer. 20:7-9
Fainting ... Prov. 24:10
Arrogant ... Ps. 10:6
Hopeful ... Lam. 3:31-40
Submissive ... Job 5:17-22
Joyful ... James 1:2-4

D. *God's relation to, He:*
Troubles nations with ... 2 Chr. 15:5, 6
Knows the soul in ... Ps. 31:7
Saves out of ... 1 Sam. 10:19
Redeems out of ... 2 Sam. 4:9

E. *Helps under:*
By prayer ... Jon. 2:1-7
By understanding God's purpose ... Lam. 3:31-39; Rom. 5:3

Advertise—*to make known publicly*
Messiah's advent ... Num. 24:14-19
A piece of property ... Ruth 4:4

Advice—*one's best judgment*

A. *Sought by:*
A king ... Esth. 1:13-15
Another ruler ... Acts 25:13-27
A usurper ... 2 Sam. 16:20-23
Five men ... 2 Kin. 22:12-20

B. *Sought from:*
The ephod ... 1 Sam. 23:9-12
A prophet ... Jer. 42:1-6
A dead prophet ... 1 Sam. 28:7-20
A council ... Acts 15:1-22
A grieving husband ... Judg. 20:4-7

C. *Kinds of:*
Helpful ... Ex. 18:12-25
Rejected ... 1 Kin. 12:6-8
Timely ... 1 Sam. 25:32-34
Good ... 2 Kin. 5:13, 14
God-inspired ... 2 Sam. 17:6-14
Foolish ... Job 2:9
Humiliating ... Esth. 6:6-11
Fatal ... Esth. 5:14
Ominous ... Matt. 27:19
Accepted ... Acts 5:34-41

D. *Sought from:*
Congregation of Israel ... Judg. 20:7

Advocate, Christ our

A. *His interest in believers, by right of:*
Election ... John 15:16
Redemption ... Rev. 1:5
Regeneration ... Col. 1:27
Imputed righteousness ... 2 Cor. 5:21; Phil. 3:9

B. *His defense of believers by:*
Prayer ... Luke 22:31-34
Protection ... Heb. 13:6
Provision ... Ps. 23:1; John 10:28
Perseverance ... 2 Tim. 4:17, 18

C. *His blessings upon believers:*
Another Comforter ... John 14:16, 17
New commandment ... John 13:34, 35
New nature ... 2 Cor. 5:17
New name ... Rev. 2:17
New life ... John 4:14
New relationship ... John 15:15

D. *Our duties prescribed by Him:*
Our mission—world evangelization ... Matt. 28:16-20
Our means—the Holy Spirit ... Acts 1:8
Our might—the Gospel ... Rom. 1:16
Our motivation—the love of Christ ... 2 Cor. 5:14, 15

Aeneas—*praise*
A paralytic healed by Peter ... Acts 9:32-35

Aenon—*springs*
A place near Salim where John the Baptist baptized ... John 3:22, 23

Afar off—*at a far distance*

A. *Applied physically to:*
Distance ... Gen. 22:4
A journey ... Num. 9:10
Sound of joy ... Ezra 3:13
Ostracism ... Luke 17:12

SUBJECT — REFERENCE

B. *Applied spiritually to:*
God's knowledge ... Ps. 139:2
Unworthiness ... Luke 18:13
Eternal separation ... Luke 16:23
Backsliding ... Luke 22:54
Gentiles ... Acts 2:39
God's promises ... Heb. 11:13
Consignment to doom ... Rev. 17:10-17

Affability—*a personality overflowing with benign sociability*

A. *Manifested in:*
Cordiality ... Gen. 18:1-8
Compassion ... Luke 10:33-37
Generosity ... Phil. 4:10, 14-18
Unantagonizing speech ... 1 Sam. 25:23-31

B. *Examples of:*
Jonathan ... 1 Sam. 18:1-4
Titus ... 2 Cor. 8:16-18
Timothy ... Phil. 2:17-20
Gaius ... 3 John 1-6
Demetrius ... 3 John 12

Affectation—*a studied pretense*
Parade of egotism ... Esth. 6:6-9
Boast of the power ... Dan. 4:29, 30
Sign of hypocrisy ... Matt. 6:1, 2, 16
Outbreak of false teachers ... 2 Pet. 2:18, 19
Sign of antichrist ... 2 Thess. 2:4, 9
Proof of spiritual decay ... 1 Cor. 4:6-8

Affection—*an inner feeling or emotion*

A. *Kinds of:*
Natural ... Rom. 1:31
Paternal ... Luke 15:20
Maternal ... 1 Kin. 3:16-27
Fraternal ... Gen. 43:30-34
Filial ... Gen. 49:29, 30
National ... Ps. 137:1-6
Racial ... Rom. 9:1-3
For wife ... Eph. 5:25-33
For husband ... Titus 2:4
Christian ... Rom. 12:10
Heavenly ... Col. 3:1, 2

B. *Good, characteristics of:*
Loyal, intense ... Ruth 1:14-18
Memorable ... 2 Sam. 1:17-27
Natural, normal ... 2 Sam. 13:37-39
Tested, tried ... Gen. 22:1-19
Emotional ... John 11:33-36
Grateful ... Luke 7:36-50
Joyous ... Ps. 126:1-6
Christ-centered ... Matt. 10:37-42

C. *Evil, characteristics of:*
Unnatural ... Rom. 1:18-32
Pretended ... Matt. 26:47-49
Abnormal ... 2 Tim. 3:3
Fleshly ... Rom. 13:13, 14
Worldly ... 2 Tim. 4:10
Defiling, degrading ... 2 Pet. 2:10-12
Agonizing, in hell ... Luke 16:23-28

Afflictions—*hardships and trials*

A. *Visited upon:*
Israel in Egypt ... Gen. 15:13
Samson by Philistines ... Judg. 16:5, 6, 19
David by God ... Ps. 88:7
Judah by God ... Lam. 3:33
Israel by the world ... Ps. 129:1, 2
The just by the wicked ... Amos 5:12; Heb. 11:37
Christians by the world ... 2 Cor. 1:6

B. *Design of, to:*
Show God's mercy ... Is. 63:9
Make us seek God ... Hos. 5:15
Bring us back to God ... Ps. 119:67
Humble us ... 2 Chr. 33:12
Test us ... Is. 48:10

C. *In the Christian's life:*
A means of testing ... Mark 4:17
A part of life ... Matt. 24:9
To be endured ... 2 Tim. 4:5
Part of Gospel ... 1 Thess. 1:6
Must not be disturbed by ... 1 Thess. 3:3
Commendable examples of ... 2 Tim. 3:11
Momentary ... 2 Cor. 4:17
Sometimes intense ... 2 Cor. 1:8-10
Must be shared ... Phil. 4:14
Cannot separate from God ... Rom. 8:35-39
Deliverance from, promised ... Ps. 34:19
Need prayer in ... James 5:13

SUBJECT — REFERENCE

Terminated at Christ's return ... 2 Thess. 1:4-7
See also Trials

Afraid—*overcome with fear*

A. *Caused by:*
Nakedness ... Gen. 3:10
Unusual dream ... Gen. 28:16, 17
God's presence ... Ex. 3:6
Moses' approach ... Ex. 34:30
A burning mountain ... Deut. 5:5
Giant's raging ... 1 Sam. 17:11, 24
A prophet's words ... 1 Sam. 28:20
Angel's sword ... 1 Chr. 21:30
God's judgments ... Ps. 65:8
Gabriel's presence ... Dan. 8:17
A terrifying storm ... Jon. 1:5, 10
Peter's sinking ... Matt. 14:30
Changed person ... Mark 5:15
Heavenly hosts ... Luke 2:9

B. *Overcome by:*
The Lord's presence ... Ps. 3:5, 6
Trusting God ... Ps. 27:1-3
God's protection ... Ps. 91:4, 5
Stability of heart ... Ps. 112:7, 8
God's coming judgment ... Is. 10:24-26
The Messiah's advent ... Is. 40:9-11
God's sovereign power ... Is. 51:12, 13
Christ's comforting words ... Matt. 14:27

Afternoon—*part of the day following noon*
Called cool of the day ... Gen. 3:8

Afterthought—*a later reflection*
Of Esau ... Heb. 12:16, 17
Of the Israelites ... Num. 14:40-45
Of one of two sons ... Matt. 21:28-30
Of the prodigal son ... Luke 15:17
Of the unjust steward ... Luke 16:1-8
Of the rich man in hell ... Luke 16:23-31
Of Judas ... Matt. 27:3-5

Afterward(s)
Your hands will be ... Judg. 7:11
Those who are invited ... 1 Sam. 9:13
David's conscience bothered him ... 1 Sam. 24:5
His mouth shall ... Prov. 20:17
Jesus findeth him ... John 5:14

Agabus—*he loved*
A Christian prophet who foretells a famine and warns Paul ... Acts 11:27, 28; Acts 21:10, 11

Agag—*flaming or violent*
1. A King of Amalek in Balaam's prophecy ... Num. 24:7
2. Amalekite king spared by Saul, but slain by Samuel ... 1 Sam. 15:8, 9, 20-24, 32, 33

Agagite—*descendant of Agag*
A title applied to Haman, enemy of the Jews ... Esth. 3:1, 10

Agape—Greek word rendered both as *"love"* and *"charity"*
Descriptive of God ... 1 John 4:8
Demanded toward God ... Matt. 22:37
Demanded toward neighbors ... Matt. 22:39
Fulfills Law ... Matt. 22:40
Activity of described ... 1 Cor. 13:1-13

Agate—*a stone of translucent quartz*
Worn by the high priest ... Ex. 28:19
Sold by Syrians ... Ezek. 27:16
Figurative of the new Israel ... Is. 54:11, 12

Age—*time counted by years*

A. *Handicaps of, seen in:*
Physical infirmities ... Gen. 48:10
Unwillingness to adventure ... 2 Sam. 19:31-39
Declining strength ... Ps. 71:9
Deterioration of body ... Eccl. 12:2-7

B. *Glories of, manifested in:*
Wisdom ... Job 12:12
Maturity ... Job 5:26
Spiritual beauty ... Prov. 16:31
Fruitfulness ... Ps. 92:12-15
Judgment ... 1 Kin. 12:6-8
Strong faith ... Josh. 24:15

SUBJECT — REFERENCE

C. *Attitude of others toward:*
- Respect ... Lev. 19:32
- Disrespect ... 2 Chr. 36:17
- Insolence ... Is. 3:5

D. *Unusual things connected with:*
- Retaining physical vigor ... Deut. 34:7
- Becoming a father ... Gen. 18:9-15; Luke 1:18, 36
- Living to see Christ ... Luke 2:25-32
- Knowing kind of death in ... John 21:19

E. *Attaining unto, by:*
- Honoring parents ... Ex. 20:12; Eph. 6:2, 3
- Keeping God's law ... Prov. 3:1, 2
- Following wisdom ... Prov. 3:13, 16
- The fear of the Lord ... Ps. 128:1, 6
- Keeping from evil ... Ps. 34:11-14
- God's promise ... Gen. 15:15

F. *Those of Bible times who lived beyond age of 100.*
- Methuselah ... Gen. 5:27
- Jared ... Gen. 5:20
- Noah ... Gen. 9:29
- Adam ... Gen. 5:5
- Seth ... Gen. 5:8
- Cainan ... Gen. 5:14
- Enos ... Gen. 5:11
- Mahalaleel ... Gen. 5:17
- Lamech ... Gen. 5:31
- Enoch ... Gen. 5:23
- Terah ... Gen. 11:32
- Isaac ... Gen. 35:28
- Abraham ... Gen. 25:7
- Jacob ... Gen. 47:28
- Ishmael ... Gen. 25:17
- Jehoiada ... 2 Chr. 24:15
- Sarah ... Gen. 23:1
- Aaron ... Num. 33:39
- Moses ... Deut. 34:7
- Joseph ... Gen. 50:26
- Joshua ... Josh. 24:29

Agee—*fugitive*
- Shammah's father ... 2 Sam. 23:11

Ages—*extended periods of time*
- Descriptive of the Old Testament period ... Eph. 3:5
- Descriptive of eternity ... Eph. 2:7

Agitation—*a disturbance*

A. *Physically of:*
- Mountain ... Ex. 19:16-18
- The earth ... Matt. 27:51-53
- The world ... Ps. 46:2-6
- End-time events ... Luke 21:25-27
- World's end ... 2 Pet. 3:7-12

B. *Emotionally of:*
- Extreme grief ... 2 Sam. 19:1-4
- Remorse ... Matt. 27:3, 4
- Fear ... Matt. 28:1-4

C. *Figuratively of:*
- Messiah's advent ... Hag. 2:6, 7
- Enraged people ... Acts 4:25-28
- The wicked ... Is. 57:20
- The drunkard ... Prov. 23:29-35

Agony—*extreme suffering*

A. *Used literally of:*
- Christ in Gethsemane ... Luke 22:44
- Christ on the cross ... Mark 15:34-37
- Paul's sufferings ... 2 Cor. 1:8, 9

B. *Used figuratively of:*
- Spiritual mastery ... 1 Cor. 9:25
- Spiritual striving ... Col. 1:29
- Laborious prayer ... Col. 4:12
- Faithful conflict ... 1 Tim. 6:12

Agree, agreement

A. *Forbidden between:*
- Israel and pagans ... Ex. 34:12-16
- God and Baal ... 1 Kin. 18:21-40
- Believers, unbelievers ... 1 Cor. 10:21
- Truth, error ... 1 John 4:1-6

B. *Necessary between:*
- Prophecy, fulfillment ... Acts 15:15
- Doctrine, life ... James 2:14-21
- Words, performance ... 2 Cor. 10:9-11
- Believers in prayer ... Matt. 18:19
- Christian brothers ... Matt. 5:24, 25
- Christian workers ... Gal. 2:7-9

SUBJECT — REFERENCE

C. *Examples of:*
- Laban and Jacob ... Gen. 31:43-53
- God and Israel ... Ex. 19:3-8
- David and Jonathan ... 1 Sam. 18:1-4
- The wicked and Sheol ... Is. 28:15, 18
- Employer and employees ... Matt. 20:10-13
- Judas and the Sanhedrin ... Matt. 26:14-16
- Witnesses ... Mark 14:56, 59
- Husband and wife ... Acts 5:9
- The Jews and Gamaliel ... Acts 5:34-40
- Conspiring Jews ... Acts 23:20
- The people of antichrist ... Rev. 17:17

Agriculture—*the cultivation of the soil*

A. *Terms and implements involved:*
- Binding ... Gen. 37:7
- Cultivating ... Luke 13:6-9
- Fertilizing ... Is. 25:10
- Gleaning ... Ruth 2:3
- Grafting ... Rom. 11:17-19
- Harrowing ... Is. 28:24
- Harvesting ... Matt. 13:23
- Mowing ... Amos 7:1
- Planting ... Prov. 31:16
- Plowing ... Job 1:14
- Pruning ... Is. 5:6
- Reaping ... Is. 17:5
- Removing stones ... Is. 5:2
- Rooting ... Matt. 13:28, 29
- Sowing ... Matt. 13:3
- Stacking ... Ex. 22:6
- Threshing ... Judg. 6:11
- Treading ... Neh. 13:15
- Watering ... 1 Cor. 3:6-8
- Winnowing ... Ruth 3:2

B. *Virtues required in:*
- Wisdom ... Is. 28:24-29
- Diligence ... Prov. 27:23-27
- Labor ... 2 Tim. 2:6
- Patience ... James 5:7
- Industry ... Prov. 28:19
- Faith ... Hab. 3:17-19
- Bountifulness ... 2 Cor. 9:6, 7
- Hopefulness ... 1 Cor. 9:10

C. *Enemies of:*
- War ... Jer. 50:16
- Pestilence ... Joel 1:9-12
- Fire ... Joel 1:19
- Animals ... Song 2:15
- Dry seasons ... Jer. 14:1, 4

D. *Restrictions involving:*
- Coveting another's field ... Deut. 5:21
- Removing boundaries ... Deut. 19:14
- Roaming cattle ... Ex. 22:5
- Spreading fire ... Ex. 22:6
- Military service ... Deut. 20:5, 6
- Working on the Sabbath ... Ex. 34:21
- Complete harvest ... Lev. 19:9, 10

E. *God's part in:*
- Began in Eden ... Gen. 2:15
- Sin's penalty ... Gen. 3:17
- Providence of, impartial ... Matt. 5:45
- Goodness of, recognized ... Acts 14:16, 17
- Judgments against, cited ... Hag. 1:10, 11

F. *Figurative of:*
- Gospel seed ... Matt. 13:1-9
- Gospel dispensation ... Matt. 13:24-30, 36-43
- God's workers ... John 4:36-38
- God's Word ... Is. 55:10, 11
- Spiritual barrenness ... Heb. 6:7, 8
- Spiritual bountifulness ... 2 Cor. 9:9, 10
- Final harvest ... Mark 4:28, 29

Aground—*stranded in shallow water*
- Ship carrying Paul ... Acts 27:41

Ague—*a malarial fever; jaundice*
- A divine punishment ... Lev. 26:16

Agur—*collector*
- Writer of proverbs ... Prov. 30:1-33

Ahab—*father's brother*

1. A wicked king of Israel ... 1 Kin. 16:29
   - Marries Jezebel ... 1 Kin. 16:31
   - Introduces Baal worship ... 1 Kin. 16:31-33
   - Denounced by Elijah ... 1 Kin. 17:1
   - Gathers prophets of Baal ... 1 Kin. 18:17-46
   - Wars against Ben-hadad ... 1 Kin. 20:1-43
   - Covets Naboth's vineyard ... 1 Kin. 21:1-16
   - Death of, predicted ... 1 Kin. 21:17-26

SUBJECT — REFERENCE

   - Repentance of, delays judgment ... 1 Kin. 21:27-29
   - Joins Jehoshaphat against Syrians ... 1 Kin. 22:1-4
   - Rejects Micaiah's warning ... 1 Kin. 22:5-33
   - Slain in battle ... 1 Kin. 22:34-38
   - Seventy sons of, slain ... 2 Kin. 10:1-11
   - Prophecies concerning, fulfilled ... 1 Kin. 20:42
2. Lying prophet ... Jer. 29:21-23

Aharah—*after his brother*
- Son of Benjamin ... 1 Chr. 8:1
- Called Ahiram ... Num. 26:38
- Called Ehi ... Gen. 46:21

Aharhel—*brother of Rachel*
- A descendant of Judah ... 1 Chr. 4:8

Ahasai—*Jehovah has grasped*
- A postexilic priest ... Neh. 11:13
- Also called Jahzerah ... 1 Chr. 9:12

Ahasbai—*blooming, shining*
- The father of Eliphelet ... 2 Sam. 23:34

Ahasuerus—*king*

1. The father of Darius the Mede ... Dan. 9:1
2. Persian king ... Esth. 1:1
   - Makes Esther queen ... Esth. 2:16, 17
   - Follows Haman's intrigue ... Esth. 3:1, 8-12
   - Orders Jews annihilated ... Esth. 3:13-15
   - Responds to Esther's plea ... Esth. 7:1-8
   - Orders Haman hanged ... Esth. 7:9, 10
   - Promotes Mordecai ... Esth. 8:1, 2
   - Reverses Haman's plot ... Esth. 8:3-17
   - Exalts Mordecai ... Esth. 10:1-3
3. A king of Persia; probably Xerxes, 486-465 B.C. ... Ezra 4:6

Ahava—*a town in Babylonia*
- Jewish exiles gather here ... Ezra 8:15-31

Ahaz—*he has grasped*

1. A king of Judah; son of Jotham ... 2 Kin. 16:1, 2
   - Pursues evil ways ... 2 Kin. 16:3, 4
   - Defends Jerusalem against Rezin and Pekah ... 2 Kin. 16:5, 6
   - Refuses a divine sign ... Is. 7:1-16
   - Defeated with great loss ... 2 Chr. 28:5-15
   - Becomes subject to Assyria ... 2 Kin. 16:7-9
   - Makes Damascus a pagan city ... 2 Kin. 16:10-18
   - Erects sundial ... 2 Kin. 20:11
   - Death of ... 2 Kin. 16:19, 20
2. A descendant of Jonathan ... 1 Chr. 8:35, 36; 1 Chr. 9:40-42
3. Ancestor of Jesus ... Matt. 1:9

Ahaziah—*Jehovah has grasped*

1. A king of Israel; son of Ahab and Jezebel ... 1 Kin. 22:40, 51
   - Worships Baal ... 1 Kin. 22:52, 53
   - Seeks alliance with Jehoshaphat ... 1 Kin. 22:48, 49
   - Falls through lattice; sends to Baal-zebub, the god of Ekron for help ... 2 Kin. 1:2-16
   - Dies according to Elijah's word ... 2 Kin. 1:17, 18
2. A king of Judah; son of Jehoram and Athaliah ... 2 Kin. 8:25, 26
   - Made king by Jerusalem inhabitants ... 2 Chr. 22:1, 2
   - Taught evil by his mother ... 2 Chr. 22:2, 3
   - Follows Ahab's wickedness ... 2 Chr. 22:4
   - Joins Joram against the Syrians ... 2 Kin. 8:28
   - Visits wounded Joram ... 2 Kin. 9:16
   - Slain by Jehu ... 2 Kin. 9:27, 28
   - Called Jehoahaz ... 2 Chr. 21:17
   - Called Azariah ... 2 Chr. 22:6

Ahban—*brother of intelligence*
- A son of Abishur ... 1 Chr. 2:29

Aher—*another*
- A Benjamite ... 1 Chr. 7:12

Ahi—*brother*

1. Gadite chief ... 1 Chr. 5:15
2. Asherite chief ... 1 Chr. 7:34

SUBJECT REFERENCE

Ahiah—*brother of Jehovah*
1. A priest during Saul's reign . . 1 Sam. 14:3, 18
2. A secretary of Solomon . . . . . 1 Kin. 4:3
3. A Benjamite . . . . 1 Chr. 8:7

Ahiam—*mother's brother*
One of David's mighty men . . . . . 2 Sam. 23:33

Ahian—*fraternal*
A Manassite . . . . 1 Chr. 7:19

Ahiezer—*brother is help*
1. Head of the tribe of Dan . . . . Num. 1:12
2. Benjamite chief, joined David at Ziklag . . . . 1 Chr. 12:3

Ahihud—*brother is majesty*
1. Asherite leader, helped Moses divide Canaan . . . . Num. 34:27
2. A Benjamite . . . . 1 Chr. 8:6, 7

Ahijah—*brother of Jehovah*
1. A great-grandson of Judah . . . 1 Chr. 2:25
2. One of David's warriors . . . . . 1 Chr. 11:36
3. A Levite treasurer in David's reign . . . . 1 Chr. 26:20
4. A prophet of Shiloh who foretells division of Solomon's kingdom . . . . 1 Kin. 11:29-39
   Foretells elimination of Jeroboam's line . . . . 1 Kin. 14:1-18
   A writer of prophecy . . . . 2 Chr. 9:29
5. The father of Baasha . . . . 1 Kin. 15:27, 33
6. A Jew who seals Nehemiah's covenant . . . . Neh. 10:26

See Ahiah

Ahikam—*my brother has arisen*
A son of Shaphan the scribe . . . . 2 Kin. 22:12
Sent in Josiah's mission to Huldah . . . . 2 Kin. 22:12-14
Protects Jeremiah . . . . Jer. 26:24
The father of Gedaliah, governor under Nebuchadnezzar . . . . 2 Kin. 25:22
Jer. 39:14

Ahilud—*a child's brother*
1. The father of Jehoshaphat, the recorder under David and Solomon . . . . 2 Sam. 8:16
2. The father of Baana, a commissionary official . . . . 1 Kin. 4:7, 12

Ahimaaz—*brother of anger*
1. The father of Ahinoam, wife of King Saul . . . . 1 Sam. 14:50
2. A son of Zadok the high priest . . . . 1 Chr. 6:8, 9
   Warns David of Absalom's plans . . . . 2 Sam. 15:27, 36
   Good man . . . . 2 Sam. 18:27
   First to tell David of Absalom's defeat . . . . 2 Sam. 18:19-30
3. Solomon's son-in-law and commissioner in Naphtali . . . . 1 Kin. 4:15
   May be the same as 2.

Ahiman—*my brother is a gift*
1. A giant son of Anak seen by Israelite spies . . . . Num. 13:22, 33
   Driven out of Hebron by Caleb . . . . Josh. 15:13, 14
   Slain by tribe of Judah . . . . . . Judg. 1:10
2. A Levite gatekeeper . . . . 1 Chr. 9:17

Ahimelech—*my brother is king*
1. The high priest at Nob during Saul's reign . . . . 1 Sam. 21:1
   Feeds David the showbread . . . . 1 Sam. 21:2-6
   Gives Goliath's sword to David . . . . 1 Sam. 21:8, 9
   Betrayed by Doeg . . . . 1 Sam. 22:9-16
   Slain by Doeg at Saul's command . . . . 1 Sam. 22:17-19
   Abiathar, son of, escapes . . . . 1 Sam. 22:20
   David wrote concerning . . . . . Ps. 52 (title)
2. Abiathar's son . . . . 2 Sam. 8:17
   Co-priest with Zadok . . . . 1 Chr. 24:3, 6, 31
3. David's Hittite warrior . . . . . . 1 Sam. 26:6

Ahimoth—*my brother is death*
A Kohathite Levite . . . . 1 Chr. 6:25

SUBJECT REFERENCE

Ahinadab—*my brother is noble*
One of Solomon's officers . . . . . . 1 Kin. 4:14

Ahinoam—*my brother is delight*
1. Wife of Saul . . . . 1 Sam. 14:50
2. David's wife . . . . 1 Sam. 25:43
   Lived with David at Gath . . . 1 Sam. 27:3
   Captured by Amalekites at Ziklag . . . . 1 Sam. 30:5
   Rescued by David . . . . 1 Sam. 30:18
   Lives with David in Hebron . . . . 2 Sam. 2:1, 2
   Mother of Amnon . . . . 2 Sam. 3:2

Ahio—*brotherly*
1. Abinadab's son . . . . 2 Sam. 6:3
2. A Benjamite . . . . 1 Chr. 8:14
3. A son of Jehiel . . . . 1 Chr. 8:31
   1 Chr. 9:37

Ahira—*my brother is evil*
A tribal leader . . . . Num. 1:15

Ahisamach—*my brother supports*
A Danite . . . . Ex. 31:6

Ahishahar—*brother of dawn*
A Benjamite . . . . 1 Chr. 7:10

Ahishar—*my brother has sung*
A manager of Solomon's household . . . . 1 Kin. 4:6

Ahithophel—*brother of folly*
David's counselor . . . . 2 Sam. 15:12
Joins Absalom's insurrection . . . . 2 Sam. 15:31
Plans of, prepared against by David . . . . 2 Sam. 15:31-34
Counsels Absalom . . . . 2 Sam. 16:20-22
Reputed wise . . . . 2 Sam. 16:23
Counsel of, rejected by Absalom . . . . 2 Sam. 17:1-22
Commits suicide . . . . 2 Sam. 17:23

Ahitub—*my brother is goodness*
1. Phinehas' son . . . . 1 Sam. 14:3
2. The father of Zadok the priest . . . . 2 Sam. 8:17
3. The father of another Zadok . . . . 1 Chr. 6:11, 12

Ahlab—*fruitful*
A city of Asher . . . . Judg. 1:31

Ahlai—*O would that!*
1. David's warrior . . . . 1 Chr. 11:41
2. Marries an Egyptian servant . . . . 1 Chr. 2:31-35

Ahoah—*brotherly*
A son of Bela . . . . 1 Chr. 8:4

Ahohite—*a descendant of Ahoah*
Applied to Dodo, Zalmon, and Ilai . . . . 2 Sam. 23:9, 28

Aholah—*tent-woman*
Symbolic name of Samaria and Israel . . . . Ezek. 23:4, 5, 36

Aholiab—*a father's tent*
Son of Ahisamach . . . . Ex. 31:6

Ahumai—*heated by Jehovah*
A descendant of Judah . . . . 1 Chr. 4:2

Ahuzzam—*possessor*
A man of Judah . . . . 1 Chr. 4:6

Ahuzzath—*possession*
A friend of Abimelech . . . . Gen. 26:26

Ai—*ruin*
1. A city east of Beth-el in central Palestine . . . . Josh. 7:2
   Abraham camps near . . . . Gen. 12:8
   A royal city of Canaan . . . . . . Josh. 10:1
   Israel defeated at . . . . Josh. 7:2-5
   Israel destroys completely . . . Josh. 8:1-28
   Occupied after exile . . . . Ezra 2:28
2. An Ammonite city near Heshbon . . . . Jer. 49:3

Aiah—*falcon*
1. A Horite . . . . Gen. 36:24

SUBJECT REFERENCE

2. The father of Rizpah, Saul's concubine . . . . 2 Sam. 3:7

Aijalon—*place of gazelles*
1. A town assigned to Dan . . . . . Josh. 19:42
   Amorites not driven from . . . . Judg. 1:35
   Miracle there . . . . Josh. 10:12
   Assigned to Kohathite Levites . . . . Josh. 21:24
   City of refuge . . . . 1 Chr. 6:66-69
   Included in Benjamin's territory . . . . 1 Chr. 8:13
   Fortified by Rehoboam . . . . . . 2 Chr. 11:10
   Captured by Philistines . . . . . . 2 Chr. 28:18
2. The burial place of Elon, a judge . . . . Judg. 12:12

Ain—*spring*
1. A town near Riblah . . . . Num. 34:11
2. Town of Judah . . . . Josh. 15:32
   Transferred to Simeon . . . . . . Josh. 19:7
   Later assigned to the priests . . . . Josh. 21:16
   Called Ashan . . . . 1 Chr. 6:59
3. Letter of the Hebrew alphabet . . . . Ps. 119:121-136

Air—*the atmosphere around the earth*
Man given dominion over . . . . . . Gen. 1:26-30
Man names birds of . . . . Gen. 2:19, 20
God destroys birds of . . . . Gen. 6:7
Mystery of eagle in . . . . Prov. 30:19
Satan, prince of . . . . Eph. 2:2
Believers meet Jesus in . . . . 1 Thess. 4:17
God's wrath poured out in . . . . . . Rev. 9:2
Figurative of emptiness . . . . 1 Cor. 9:26

Akkub—*cunning*
1. Elioenai's son . . . . 1 Chr. 3:24
2. A Levite head of a family of porters . . . . 1 Chr. 9:17
3. A family of Nethinim . . . . Ezra 2:45
4. A Levite interpreter . . . . Neh. 8:7

Akrabbim—*scorpions*
An "ascent" on the south of the Dead Sea . . . . Num. 34:4
One border of Judah—Acrabbim . . . . Josh. 15:3

Alabaster—*a container for perfumes and ointments*
Used by woman anointing Jesus . . . . Matt. 26:7

Alameth (see Alemeth)

Alammelech—*oak of a king*
Village of Asher . . . . Josh. 19:26

Alamoth—*virgins*
A musical term probably indicating a women's choir . . . . 1 Chr. 15:20

Alarm—*sudden and fearful surprise*
A. *Caused physically by:*
   Sudden attack . . . . Judg. 7:20-23
   Death plague . . . . Ex. 12:29-33
   A mysterious manifestation . . . 1 Sam. 28:11-14
   Prodigies of nature . . . . Matt. 27:50-54
B. *Caused spiritually by:*
   Sin . . . . 1 Sam. 12:17-19
   Remorse . . . . Gen. 27:34-40
   Conscience . . . . Acts 24:24, 25
   Hopelessness in hell . . . . Luke 16:22-31
C. *Shout of jubilee or warning:*
   Instruction to Israel . . . . Num. 10:5, 6
   Causes anguish . . . . Jer. 4:19
   Prophecy of judgment . . . . Jer. 49:2

See Agitation

Alas—*an intense emotional outcry*
A. *Emotional outcry caused by:*
   Israel's defeat . . . . Josh. 7:7-9
   An angel's appearance . . . . . . Judg. 6:22
   A vow's realization . . . . Judg. 11:34, 35
   Army without water . . . . 2 Kin. 3:9, 10
   Loss of an ax . . . . 2 Kin. 6:5
   Servant's fear . . . . 2 Kin. 6:14, 15
B. *Prophetic outcry caused by:*
   Israel's future . . . . Num. 24:23, 24
   Israel's punishment . . . . Amos 5:16-20

SUBJECT	REFERENCE
Jacob's trouble	Jer. 30:7-9
Babylon's fall	Rev. 18:10-19

Alemeth, Alameth—*hidden*

1. A Benjamite	1 Chr. 7:8
2. A descendant of Saul	1 Chr. 8:36
3. A Levitical city	1 Chr. 6:60

Aleph

The first letter in the Hebrew alphabet	Ps. 119:1-8

Alert—*watchful*

In battle	Judg. 7:15-22
In personal safety	1 Sam. 19:9, 10
In readiness for attack	Neh. 4:9-23
In prayer	Matt. 26:41
In spiritual combat	Eph. 6:18
In waiting for Christ's return	Matt. 24:42-51
Daily living	1 Cor. 16:13
Times of testing	Luke 21:34-36
Against false teachers	Acts 20:29-31

Alexander—*man-defending*

1. A son of Simon of Cyrene	Mark 15:21
2. A member of the high-priestly family	Acts 4:6
3. A Jew in Ephesus	Acts 19:33, 34
4. An apostate condemned by Paul	1 Tim. 1:19, 20

Alexander the Great—*Alexander III of Macedonia* (356-323 B.C.)

A. *Not named in the Bible, but referred to as:*

The four-headed leopard	Dan. 7:6
The goat with a great horn	Dan. 8:5-9, 21
A mighty king	Dan. 11:3

B. *Rule of, described:*

His invasion of Palestine	Zech. 9:1-8
His kingdom being divided	Dan. 7:6

Alexandria—*a city of Egypt founded by Alexander the Great* (332 B.C.)

Men of, persecute Stephen	Acts 6:9
Apollos, native of	Acts 18:24
Paul sails in ship	Acts 27:6

Algum, almug—*a tree* (probably the red sandalwood)

Imported from Ophir by Hiram's navy	1 Kin. 10:11, 12
Used in constructing the temple	2 Chr. 9:10, 11
Also imported from Lebanon	2 Chr. 2:8

Aliens—*citizens of a foreign country*

A. *Descriptive, naturally, of:*

Israel in the Egyptian bondage	Gen. 15:13
Abraham in Canaan	Gen. 23:4
Moses in Egypt	Ex. 18:3
Israel in Babylon	Ps. 137:4

B. *Descriptive, spiritually, of:*

Estrangement from friends	Job 19:15
Israel's apostasy	Ezek. 23:17, 18, 22, 28
The condition of the Gentiles	Eph. 2:12
Spiritual deadness	Eph. 4:18

Alive—*the opposite of being dead*

A. *Descriptive of:*

Natural life	Gen. 43:7, 27, 28
Spiritual life	Luke 15:24, 32
Restored physical life	Acts 9:41
Christ's resurrected life	Acts 1:3
The believer's glorified life	1 Cor. 15:22
The unbeliever's life in hell	Num. 16:33

B. *The power of keeping:*

Belongs to God	Deut. 32:39
Not in man's power	Ps. 22:29
Promised to the godly	Ps. 33:19
Gratefully acknowledged	Josh. 14:10
Transformed by Christ's return	1 Thess. 4:15, 16

Allegory—*an extended figure of speech using symbols*

A. *Of natural things:*

A king's doom	Judg. 9:8-15
Old age	Eccl. 12:3-7
Israel as a transplanted vine	Ps. 80:8-19

B. *Of spiritual things:*

Christian as sheep	John 10:1-16
Two covenants	Gal. 4:21-31
Israel and the Gentiles	Rom. 11:15-24
Christ and His Church	Eph. 5:22-33
The Christian's armor	Eph. 6:11-17

Alleluia—*praise ye the Lord*

The Greek form of the Hebrew Hallelujah	Rev. 19:1-6

Alliances—*treaties between nations or individuals*

A. *In the time of the patriarchs:*

Abraham with Canaanite chiefs	Gen. 14:13
Abraham with Abimelech	Gen. 21:22-34
Isaac with Abimelech	Gen. 26:26-33
Jacob with Laban	Gen. 31:44-54

B. *In the time of the wilderness:*

Israel with Moab	Num. 25:1-3

C. *In the time of the conquest:*

Israel with Gibeonites	Judg. 9:3-27

D. *In the time of David:*

David with Achish	1 Sam. 27:2-12

E. *In the time of Solomon:*

Solomon with Hiram	1 Kin. 5:12-18
Solomon with Egypt	1 Kin. 3:1

F. *In the time of the divided kingdom:*

Asa with Ben-hadad	1 Kin. 15:18-20
Ahab with Ben-hadad	1 Kin. 20:31-34
Israel with Syria	2 Kin. 16:5-9
Hoshea with Egypt	2 Kin. 17:1-6

G. *In the time of Judah's sole kingdom:*

Hezekiah with Egypt	2 Kin. 18:19-24
Josiah with Assyria	2 Kin. 23:29
Jehoiakim with Egypt	2 Kin. 23:31-35

Alliance with evil

A. *Forbidden to:*

Israel	Ex. 34:11-16
Christians	Rom. 13:12
Christ	Matt. 4:1-11

B. *Forbidden because:*

Leads to idolatry	Ex. 23:32, 33
Deceives	Num. 25:1-3, 18
Enslaves	2 Pet. 2:18, 19
Defiles	Ezra 9:1, 2
Brings God's anger	Ezra 9:13-15
Corrupts	1 Cor. 15:33
Incompatible with Christ	2 Cor. 6:14-16
Pollutes	Jude 23

C. *The believer should:*

Avoid	Prov. 1:10-15
Hate	Ps. 26:4, 5
Confess	Ezra 10:9-11
Separate from	2 Cor. 6:17

D. *Examples of:*

Solomon	1 Kin. 11:1-11
Rehoboam	1 Kin. 12:25-33
Jehoshaphat	2 Chr. 20:35-37
Judas Iscariot	Matt. 26:14-16
Heretics	Rev. 2:14-15, 20

See Association

All in all—*complete*

Descriptive of:

God	1 Cor. 15:28
Christ	Eph. 1:23

Allon—*oak*

1. A Simeonite prince	1 Chr. 4:37
2. A town in south Naphtali	Josh. 19:33

Allon-bachuth—*oak of weeping*

A tree marking Deborah's grave	Gen. 35:8

Allowance—*a stipulated amount*

Daily to Jehoiachin	2 Kin. 25:27-30
Also called a diet	Jer. 52:34

Almighty—*a title of God*

Applied to God	Gen. 17:1; 2 Cor. 6:18
Applied to Christ	Rev. 1:8

Almodad—*the beloved*

Eldest son of Joktan	Gen. 10:26

Almond—*a small tree bearing fruit*

Sent as a present to Pharaoh	Gen. 43:11
Used in the tabernacle	Ex. 25:33, 34
Aaron's rod produces	Num. 17:2, 3, 8
Used figuratively of old age	Eccl. 12:5
Translated "hazel" in	Gen. 30:37

Almon-diblathaim—*Almon of the double cake of figs*

An Israelite encampment	Num. 33:46, 47

Alms, almsgiving—*gifts prompted by love to help the needy*

A. *Design of, to:*

Help the poor	Lev. 25:35
Receive a blessing	Deut. 15:10, 11

B. *Manner of bestowing with:*

A willing spirit	Deut. 15:7-11
Simplicity	Matt. 6:1-4
Cheerfulness	2 Cor. 9:7
True love	1 Cor. 13:3
Fairness to all	Acts 4:32-35
Regularity	Acts 11:29, 30
Law of reciprocity	Rom. 15:25-27

C. *Cautions concerning:*

Not for man's honor	Matt. 6:1-4
Not for lazy	2 Thess. 3:10
Needful for the rich	1 Tim. 6:17, 18

D. *Rewarded:*

Now	Deut. 14:28, 29; 2 Cor. 9:9, 10
In heaven	Matt. 19:21

E. *Examples of:*

Zacchaeus	Luke 19:8
Dorcas	Acts 9:36
Cornelius	Acts 10:2
The early Christians	Acts 4:34-37

Aloes—*a perfume-bearing tree*

A. *Used on:*

Beds	Prov. 7:17
The dead	John 19:39

B. *Figurative of:*

Israel	Num. 24:5, 6
The Church	Ps. 45:8

Aloth—*ascents, steeps*

A town in Asher	1 Kin. 4:16

Alpha and Omega—*first and last letters of the Greek alphabet* ("A to Z")

Expressive of God and Christ's eternity	Rev. 1:8, 17, 18; Rev. 21:6, 7

Alphabet—*the letters of a language*

The Hebrew, seen in	Ps. 119

Alphaeus—*leader, chief*

1. The father of Levi (Matthew)	Mark 2:14
2. The father of James	Matt. 10:3

Altar—*an elevated structure*

A. *Uses of:*

Sacrifice	Gen. 8:20
Incense	Ex. 30:1, 7, 8; Luke 1:10, 11
National unity	Deut. 12:5, 6
A memorial	Ex. 17:15, 16
Protection	Ex. 21:13, 14

B. *Made of:*

Earth	Ex. 20:24
Unhewn stone	Ex. 20:25
Stones	Deut. 27:5, 6
Natural rock	Judg. 6:19-21
Bronze	Ex. 27:1-6

C. *Built worthily by:*

Noah	Gen. 8:20
Abraham	Gen. 12:7, 8
Isaac	Gen. 26:25
Jacob	Gen. 33:18, 20
Moses	Ex. 17:15
Joshua	Deut. 27:4-7
Eastern tribes	Josh. 22:10, 34
Gideon	Judg. 6:26, 27
Manoah	Judg. 13:19, 20
Israelites	Judg. 21:4

SUBJECT REFERENCE

Samuel....1 Sam. 7:17
Saul....1 Sam. 14:35
David....2 Sam. 24:18-25
Elijah....1 Kin. 18:31, 32

D. *Built unworthily* (for idolatry) *by:*

Gideon's father....Judg. 6:25-32
King Jeroboam....1 Kin. 12:32, 33
King Ahab....1 Kin. 18:25, 26
King Ahaz....2 Chr. 28:1, 3, 5
Israelite people....Is. 65:3
Athenians....Acts 17:23

E. *Pagan altars destroyed by:*

Gideon....Judg. 6:25-29
King Asa....2 Chr. 14:2, 3
Jehoiada....2 Kin. 11:17, 18
King Hezekiah....2 Kin. 18:22
King Josiah....2 Kin. 23:12

F. *Burnt offering:*

1. *Of the tabernacle, features concerning:*

Specifications....Ex. 27:1-9
Bezaleel, builder of....Ex. 37:1
Place of, outside tabernacle....Ex. 40:6, 29
Only priests allowed at....Num. 18:3, 7
The defective not acceptable on....Lev. 22:22
The putting on of blood....Ex. 29:12

2. *Of Solomon's Temple:*

Described....1 Kin. 8:63, 64
Renewed by King Asa....2 Chr. 15:8
Cleansed by King Hezekiah....2 Chr. 29:18-24
Repaired by King Manasseh....2 Chr. 33:16
Vessels of, carried to Babylon....2 Kin. 25:14

3. *Of the postexilic* (Zerubbabel's) *temple:*

Described....Ezra 3:1-6
Polluted....Mal. 1:7, 8

4. *Of Ezekiel's vision:*

Described....Ezek. 43:13-27

G. *Incense:*

In the tabernacle, described....Ex. 30:1-10
Location of....Ex. 30:6
Anointed with oil....Ex. 30:26, 27
Annual atonement made at....Ex. 30:10
In Solomon's Temple....1 Kin. 7:48
In John's vision....Rev. 8:3

H. *New covenant:*

A place of spiritual sacrifices....Rom. 12:1, 2
Christ, our pattern....Heb. 13:10-16

Al-taschith—*destroy not*

A term found in the title of....Ps. 57; 59; 75

Altruism—*living for the good of others*

A. *Manifested in:*

Service....Matt. 20:26-28
Doing good....Acts 10:38
Seeking the welfare of others....Gal. 6:1, 2, 10
Helping the weak....Acts 20:35

B. *Examples of:*

Moses....Ex. 32:30-32
Samuel....1 Sam. 12:1-5
Jonathan....1 Sam. 18:1-4
Christ....John 13:4-17
Paul....1 Cor. 9:19-22

Alush—*wild place*

An Israelite encampment....Num. 33:13, 14

Alvah—*high, tall*

An Edomite chief....Gen. 36:40
Also called Aliah....1 Chr. 1:51

Alvan—*tall*

A son of Shobal the Horite....Gen. 36:23
Also called Alian....1 Chr. 1:40

Always—*continually, forever*

A. *Of God's:*

Care....Deut. 11:12
Covenant....1 Chr. 16:15
Chide....Ps. 103:9

B. *Of Christ's:*

Determination....Ps. 16:8-11; Acts 2:25

SUBJECT REFERENCE

Delight....Prov. 8:30-31
Presence....Matt. 28:20
Desire....John 8:29
Prayer....John 11:42

C. *Of the believer's:*

Prayer....Luke 21:36
Peace....2 Thess. 3:16
Obedience....Phil. 2:12
Work....1 Cor. 15:58
Defense....1 Pet. 3:15
Rejoicing....Phil. 4:4
Thanksgiving....1 Thess. 1:2
Victory....2 Cor. 2:14
Conscience....Acts 24:16
Confidence....2 Cor. 5:6
Sufficiency....2 Cor. 9:8

D. *Of the unbeliever's:*

Probation....Gen. 6:3
Turmoil....Mark 5:5
Rebellion....Acts 7:51
Lying....Titus 1:12

Amad—*people of duration*

A city of Asher....Josh. 19:26

Amal—*toil*

Asher's descendant....1 Chr. 7:35

Amalek—*warlike*

A son of Eliphaz....1 Chr. 1:36
Grandson of Esau....Gen. 36:11, 12
A duke of Edom....Gen. 36:16
Founder of first nation....Num. 24:20

Amalekites—*a nation hostile to Israel*

A. *Defeated by:*

Chedorlaomer....Gen. 14:5-7
Joshua....Ex. 17:8, 13
Gideon....Judg. 7:12-25
Saul....1 Sam. 14:47, 48
David....1 Sam. 27:8, 9
Simeonites....1 Chr. 4:42, 43

B. *Overcame Israel during:*

Wilderness....Num. 14:39-45
Judges....Judg. 3:13

C. *Destruction of:*

Predicted....Ex. 17:14
Reaffirmed....Deut. 25:17-19
Fulfilled in part by David....1 Sam. 27:8, 9; 2 Sam. 1:1-16
Fulfilled by the Simeonites....1 Chr. 4:42, 43

Amam—*gathering place*

A city of Judah....Josh. 15:26

Amana—*permanent*

A summit in the Anti Lebanon mountain range....Song 4:8

Amaranthine—*like the amaranth flower: unfading, perennial*

This Greek word is used to describe our inheritance and our glory....1 Pet. 1:4; 1 Pet. 5:4

Amariah—*Jehovah said*

1. The grandfather of Zadok the priest....1 Chr. 6:7-8, 52
2. A priest....1 Chr. 6:11
3. Levite in David's time....1 Chr. 23:19
4. A high priest....2 Chr. 19:11
5. A Levite in Hezekiah's reign....2 Chr. 31:14, 15
6. Son of King Hezekiah....Zeph. 1:1
7. One who divorced his foreign wife....Ezra 10:42, 44
8. A signer of Nehemiah's document....Neh. 10:3
9. A postexilic chief priest....Neh. 12:1, 2, 7

Amasa—*burden-bearer*

1. The son of Ithra; David's nephew....2 Sam. 17:25
   Commands Absalom's rebels....2 Sam. 17:25
   Made David's commander....2 Sam. 19:13
   Treacherously killed by Joab....2 Sam. 20:9-12
   Death avenged....1 Kin. 2:28-34
2. An Ephraimite leader....2 Chr. 28:9-12

SUBJECT REFERENCE

Amasai—*Jehovah has borne*

1. A Kohathite Levite....1 Chr. 6:25, 35
2. David's officer....1 Chr. 12:18
3. A priestly trumpeter in David's time....1 Chr. 15:24
4. A Kohathite Levite....2 Chr. 29:12

Amashai—*carrying spoil*

A priest....Neh. 11:13

Amasiah—*Jehovah bears*

One of Jehoshaphat's commanders....2 Chr. 17:16

Amazement—*an intense emotional shock*

A. *Caused by:*

Christ's miracles....Matt. 12:22, 23; Luke 5:25, 26
Christ's teaching....Matt. 19:25
God's power....Luke 9:43
Apostolic miracle....Acts 3:7-10

B. *Manifested by:*

Christ's parents....Luke 2:48
Christ's disciples....Matt. 19:25
The Jews....Mark 9:15
Jesus....Mark 14:33
The early Christians....Acts 9:19-21

Amaziah—*Jehovah is strong*

1. King of Judah....2 Kin. 14:1-4
   Kills his father's assassinators....2 Kin. 14:5, 6
   Raises a large army....2 Chr. 25:5
   Employs troops from Israel....2 Chr. 25:6
   Rebuked by a man of God....2 Chr. 25:7-10
   Defeats Edomites....2 Kin. 14:7
   Worships Edomite gods....2 Chr. 25:14
   Rebuked by a prophet....2 Chr. 25:15, 16
   Defeated by Israel....2 Kin. 14:8-14
   Killed by conspirators....2 Chr. 25:25-28
2. A priest of Bethel....Amos 7:10-17
3. A Simeonite....1 Chr. 4:34, 42-44
4. A Merarite Levite....1 Chr. 6:45

Ambassador—*an official sent to deal with a foreign government*

A. *Some purposes of, to:*

Grant safe passage....Num. 20:14-21
Settle disputes....Judg. 11:12-28
Arrange business....1 Kin. 5:1-12
Stir up trouble....1 Kin. 20:1-12
Issue an ultimatum....2 Kin. 19:9-14
Spy....2 Kin. 20:12-19
Learn God's will....Jer. 37:6-10

B. *Some examples of:*

Judah to Egypt....Is. 30:1-4
Babylonians to Judah....2 Chr. 32:31
Necho to Josiah....2 Chr. 35:20, 21

C. *Used figuratively of:*

Christ's ministers....2 Cor. 5:20
Paul in particular....Eph. 5:20

Ambassage—*an official commission*

Coming to seek peace....Luke 14:32

Amber—*a yellow, fossilized resin*

Descriptive of the divine glory....Ezek. 1:4, 27

Ambidextrous—*equally skilled with either hand*

True of some of David's warriors....1 Chr. 12:1, 2

Ambition, Christian

A. *Good, if for:*

The best gifts....1 Cor. 12:31
Spiritual growth....Phil. 3:12-14
The Gospel's extension....Rom. 15:17-20
Acceptance before God....2 Cor. 5:7
Quietness....1 Thess. 4:11

B. *Evil, if it leads to:*

Strife....Matt. 20:20-28
Sinful superiority....Matt. 18:1-6
A Pharisaical spirit....Mark 12:38-40
Contention about gifts....1 Cor. 3:3-8
Selfish ambition....Phil. 1:14-17

Ambition, worldly

A. *Inspired by:*

Satan....Gen. 3:1-6; Luke 4:5-8

A

SUBJECT REFERENCE

Pride ..... Is. 14:12-15; 1 Tim. 3:6
Jealousy ..... Num. 12:2

B. *Leads to:*
Sin ..... Acts 8:18-24
Strife ..... James 4:1, 2
Suicide ..... 2 Sam. 17:23
Self-glory ..... Hab. 2:4, 5

C. *Examples of:*
Builders of Babel ..... Gen. 11:4
Korah's company ..... Num. 16:3-35
Abimelech ..... Judg. 9:1-6
Absalom ..... 2 Sam. 15:1-13
Adonijah ..... 1 Kin. 1:5-7
Haman ..... Esth. 5:9-13
Nebuchadnezzar ..... Dan. 3:1-7
James and John ..... Mark 10:35-37
The antichrist ..... 2 Thess. 2:4
Diotrephes ..... 3 John 9, 10

Ambush—*strategic concealment for surprise attack*
Joshua at Ai ..... Josh. 8:2-22
Abimelech against Shechem ..... Judg. 9:31-40
Israel at Gibeah ..... Judg. 20:29-41
David against the Philistines ..... 2 Sam. 5:23-25
Jehoshaphat against the Ammonites ..... 2 Chr. 20:22

Amen—*a strong assent to a prayer* (also translated *"verily"*)

A. *Used in the Old Testament to:*
Confirm a statement ..... Num. 5:22
Close a doxology ..... 1 Chr. 16:36
Confirm an oath ..... Neh. 5:13
Give assent to laws ..... Deut. 27:15-26

B. *Used in the New Testament to:*
Close a doxology ..... Rom. 9:5
Close epistle ..... Rom. 16:27
Personalize Christ ..... 2 Cor. 1:20
Close prayer ..... 1 Cor. 14:16
Give assent ..... Rev. 1:7
Emphasize a truth (translated "verily") ..... John 3:3, 5, 11

Amerce—*to inflict a penalty*
For false charges ..... Deut. 22:19

Amethyst—*a form of quartz purple to blue-violet*
Worn by the high priest ..... Ex. 28:19; Ex. 39:12
In the New Jerusalem ..... Rev. 21:20

Ami
Head of a family of Solomon's servants ..... Ezra 2:57
Called Amon ..... Neh. 7:59

Amiable—*pleasing, lovable*
God's tabernacles ..... Ps. 84:1

Amittai—*true*
The father of Jonah the prophet ..... Jon. 1:1

Ammah—*mother or beginning*
A hill near Giah ..... 2 Sam. 2:24

Ammi—*my people*
A symbolic name of Israel ..... Hos. 2:1

Ammiel—*my kinsman is God*
1. A spy representing the tribe of Dan ..... Num. 13:12
2. The father of Machir ..... 2 Sam. 9:4, 5
3. The father of Bath-shua (Bath-sheba), one of David's wives ..... 1 Chr. 3:5
Called Eliam ..... 2 Sam. 11:3
4. A son of Obed-edom ..... 1 Chr. 26:4-5

Ammihud—*my kinsman is glorious*
1. An Ephraimite ..... Num. 1:10
2. A Simeonite, father of Shemuel ..... Num. 34:20
3. A Naphtalite ..... Num. 34:28
4. The father of the king of Geshur ..... 2 Sam. 13:37
5. A Judahite ..... 1 Chr. 9:4

Amminadab—*my kinsman is noble*
1. Man of Judah ..... 1 Chr. 2:10
The father of Nashon ..... Num. 1:7
Aaron's father-in-law ..... Ex. 6:23

SUBJECT REFERENCE

An ancestor of David ..... Ruth 4:19, 20
An ancestor of Christ ..... Matt. 1:4
2. Chief of a Levitical house ..... 1 Chr. 15:10, 11
3. Son of Kohath ..... 1 Chr. 6:22

Amminadib—*my people is liberal*
Should probably be translated "my princely (or willing) people" ..... Song 6:12

Ammishaddai—*my kinsman is the Almighty*
A captain representing the Danites ..... Num. 1:12

Ammizabad—*my kinsman has endowed*
A son of Benaiah ..... 1 Chr. 27:6

Ammon—*a people*
A son of Lot by his youngest daughter ..... Gen. 19:38

Ammonites—*descendants of Ammon*

A. *Characterized by:*
Cruelty ..... Amos 1:13
Pride ..... Zeph. 2:9, 10
Callousness ..... Ezek. 25:3, 6
Idolatry ..... 1 Kin. 11:7, 33

B. *Hostility toward Israel, seen in:*
Aiding the Moabites ..... Deut. 23:3, 4
Helping the Amalekites ..... Judg. 3:13
Proposing a cruel treaty ..... 1 Sam. 11:1-3
Abusing David's ambassadors ..... 2 Sam. 10:1-4
Hiring Syrians against David ..... 2 Sam. 10:6
Assisting the Chaldeans ..... 2 Kin. 24:2
Harassing postexilic Jews ..... Neh. 4:3, 7, 8

C. *Defeated by:*
Jephthah ..... Judg. 11:4-33
Saul ..... 1 Sam. 11:11
David ..... 2 Sam. 10:7-14
Jehoshaphat ..... 2 Chr. 20:1-25
Jotham ..... 2 Chr. 27:5

D. *Prohibitions concerning:*
Exclusion from worship ..... Deut. 23:3-6
No intermarriage with ..... Ezra 9:1-3

E. *Prophecies concerning their:*
Captivity ..... Amos 1:13-15
Subjection ..... Jer. 25:9-21
Destruction ..... Ps. 83:1-18

Ammonitess—*a female Ammonite*
Naamah ..... 1 Kin. 14:21, 31
Shimeath ..... 2 Chr. 24:26

Amnesty—*a pardon granted to political offenders*
To Shimei ..... 2 Sam. 19:16-23
To Amasa ..... 2 Sam. 17:25; 2 Sam. 19:13

Amnon—*faithful*
1. A son of David ..... 2 Sam. 3:2
Rapes his half sister ..... 2 Sam. 13:1-18
Killed by Absalom ..... 2 Sam. 13:19-29
2. Son of Shimon ..... 1 Chr. 4:20

Amok—*deep, inscrutable*
A chief priest ..... Neh. 12:7, 20

Amon—*master workman*
1. King of Judah ..... 2 Kin. 21:18, 19
Follows evil ..... 2 Chr. 33:22, 23
Killed by conspiracy ..... 2 Kin. 21:23, 24
2. A governor of Samaria ..... 1 Kin. 22:10, 26

Amorites—*mountain dwellers*

A. *Described as:*
Descendants of Canaan ..... Gen. 10:15, 16
Original inhabitants of Palestine ..... Ezek. 16:3
One of seven nations ..... Gen. 15:19-21
A confederation ..... Josh. 10:1-5
Ruled by great kings ..... Ps. 136:18, 19
Of great size ..... Amos 2:9
Very wicked ..... Gen. 15:16
Worshipers of idols ..... Judg. 6:10

B. *Contacts of, with Israel:*
Their defeat by Joshua ..... Josh. 10:1-43
Their not being destroyed ..... Judg. 1:34-36
Peace with ..... 1 Sam. 7:14
Their being taxed by Solomon ..... 1 Kin. 9:20, 21
Intermarriage with ..... Judg. 3:5, 6

SUBJECT REFERENCE

Amos—*burden-bearer*
1. A prophet of Israel ..... Amos 1:1
Pronounces judgment against nations ..... Amos 1:1-3, 15
Denounces Israel's sins ..... Amos 4:1—7:9
Condemns Amaziah, the priest of Beth-el ..... Amos 7:10-17
Predicts Israel's downfall ..... Amos 9:1-10
Foretells great blessings ..... Amos 9:11-15
2. An ancestor of Christ ..... Luke 3:25

Amoz—*strong*
The father of Isaiah the prophet ..... Is. 1:1

Amphipolis—*a city in Macedonia*
Visited by Paul ..... Acts 17:1

Amplias
Christian at Rome ..... Rom. 16:8

Amram—*a people exalted*
1. Son of Kohath ..... Num. 3:17-19
The father of Aaron, Moses and Miriam ..... Ex. 6:18-20; 1 Chr. 6:3
2. Jew who divorced his foreign wife ..... Ezra 10:34

Amramites—*descendants of Amram*
A subdivision of the Levites ..... Num. 3:27

Amraphel—*powerful people*
A king of Shinar who invaded Canaan during Abraham's time; identified by some as the Hammurabi of the monuments ..... Gen. 14:1, 9

Amulet—*charm worn to protect against evil*
Condemned ..... Is. 3:18-23

Amusements—*entertainment*

A. *Found in:*
Dancing ..... Ex. 32:18, 19, 25
Music ..... 1 Sam. 18:6, 7
Earthly pleasures ..... Eccl. 2:1-8
Drunkenness ..... Amos 6:1-6; 1 Pet. 4:3
Feasting ..... Mark 6:21, 22
Games ..... Luke 7:32
Gossip ..... Acts 17:21

B. *Productive of:*
Sorrow ..... Prov. 14:13
Poverty ..... Prov. 21:17
Vanity ..... Eccl. 2:1-11
Immorality ..... 1 Cor. 10:6-8
Spiritual deadness ..... 1 Tim. 5:6

C. *Prevalence of:*
In the last days ..... 2 Tim. 3:1, 4
In Babylon ..... Rev. 18:21-24
At Christ's return ..... Matt. 24:38, 39

Amzi—*strong one*
1. A Merarite Levite ..... 1 Chr. 6:46
2. A priest ..... Neh. 11:12

Anab—*grapes*
A town of Judah ..... Josh. 11:21

Anah—*answer*
1. Father of Esau's wife ..... Gen. 36:2, 14, 18
2. A Horite chief ..... Gen. 36:20, 29
3. Son of Zibeon ..... Gen. 36:24

Anaharath—*narrow way*
A city in the valley of Jezreel ..... Josh. 19:19

Anaiah—*Jehovah has answered*
1. A Levite assistant ..... Neh. 8:4
2. One who sealed the new covenant ..... Neh. 10:22

Anak—*long-necked*
Descendant of Arba ..... Josh. 15:13
Father of three sons ..... Num. 13:22

Anakim—*descendants of Anak; a race of giants*

A. *Described as:*
Giants ..... Num. 13:28-33
Very strong ..... Deut. 2:10-11, 21

B. *Defeated by:*
Joshua ..... Josh. 10:36-39
Caleb ..... Josh. 14:6-15

SUBJECT REFERENCE

C. *A remnant left:*
Among the Philistines . . . Josh. 11:22
Possibly in Gath . . . 1 Sam. 17:4-7

Anamim—*rockmen*
A tribe or people listed among Mizraim's (Egypt's) descendants . . . Gen. 10:13

Anammelech—*Anu is king*
A god worshiped at Samaria . . . 2 Kin. 17:24, 31

Anan—*cloud*
A signer of Nehemiah's document . . . Neh. 10:26

Anani—*my cloud*
Son of Elioenai . . . 1 Chr. 3:24

Ananiah—*Jehovah has covered*
1. The father of Maaseiah . . . Neh. 3:23
2. A town inhabited by Benjamite returnees . . . Neh. 11:32

Ananias—*Jehovah has been gracious*
1. Disciple at Jerusalem slain for lying to God . . . Acts 5:1-11
2. A Christian disciple at Damascus . . . Acts 9:10-19; Acts 22:12-16
3. A Jewish high priest . . . Acts 23:1-5

Anarchy—*a reign of lawlessness in society*
A. *Manifested in:*
Moral looseness . . . Ex. 32:1-8, 25
Idolatry . . . Judg. 17:1-13
Religious syncretism . . . 2 Kin. 17:27-41
A reign of terror . . . Jer. 40:13-16
Perversion of justice . . . Hab. 1:1-4
B. *Instances of:*
At Kadesh . . . Num. 14:1-10
During the judges . . . Judg. 18:1-31
In the northern kingdom . . . 1 Kin. 12:26-33
At the crucifixion . . . Matt. 27:15-31
At Stephen's death . . . Acts 7:54, 57-58
At Ephesus . . . Acts 19:28-34
In the time of Antichrist . . . 2 Thess. 2:3-12

Anath—*answer*
Father of Shamgar . . . Judg. 3:31

Anathema—*curse, accursed*
Applied to non-believers or Christ haters . . . 1 Cor. 16:22; Gal. 1:8, 9
Translated "accursed" . . . Rom. 9:3; 1 Cor. 12:3
See Accursed

Anathoth—*answers*
1. A Benjamite, son of Becher . . . 1 Chr. 7:8
2. A leader who signed the document . . . Neh. 10:19
3. A Levitical city in Benjamin . . . Josh. 21:18
Birthplace of Jeremiah . . . Jer. 1:1
Citizens of, hate Jeremiah . . . Jer. 11:21, 23
Jeremiah bought property there . . . Jer. 32:6-15
Home of famous mighty man . . . 2 Sam. 23:27
Home of Abiathar, the high priest . . . 1 Kin. 2:26
Reoccupied after exile . . . Ezra 2:1, 23
Go to, to die . . . 1 Kin. 2:26
Wretched place . . . Is. 10:30
Reproved Jeremiah of . . . Jer. 29:27

Anchor—*a weight used to hold a ship in place*
Literally, of Paul's ship . . . Acts 27:29-30, 40
Figuratively of the believer's hope . . . Heb. 6:19

Ancient—*that which is old*
Applied to the beginning (eternity) . . . Is. 45:21
Applied to something very old . . . 1 Sam. 24:13; Prov. 22:28
Applied to old men (elders) . . . Ps. 119:100; Jer. 19:1

Ancient of days
Title applied to God . . . Dan. 7:9, 13, 22

Andrew—*manly*
A fisherman . . . Matt. 4:18
A disciple of John the Baptist . . . John 1:40
Brought Peter to Christ . . . John 1:40-42
Called to Christ's discipleship . . . Matt. 4:18, 19
Enrolled among the Twelve . . . Matt. 10:2
Told Jesus about a lad's lunch . . . John 6:8, 9
Carried a request to Jesus . . . John 12:20-22
Sought further light on Jesus' words . . . Mark 13:3, 4
Met in the upper room . . . Acts 1:13

Andronicus—*conqueror of men*
A notable Christian at Rome . . . Rom. 16:7

Anem—*double fountain*
Levitical city . . . 1 Chr. 6:73

Aner—*waterfall*
1. Amorite chief . . . Gen. 14:13, 24
2. A Levitical city . . . 1 Chr. 6:70

Anethothite—*a native of Anathoth*
Abiezer thus called . . . 2 Sam. 23:27

Angels—*heavenly beings created by God*
A. *Described as:*
Created . . . Ps. 148:2, 5; Col. 1:16
Spiritual beings . . . Heb. 1:14
Immortal . . . Luke 20:36
Holy . . . Matt. 25:31
Innumerable . . . Heb. 12:22
Wise . . . 2 Sam. 14:17, 20
Powerful . . . Ps. 103:20
Elect . . . 1 Tim. 5:21
Meek . . . Jude 9
Sexless . . . Matt. 22:30
Invisible . . . Num. 22:22-31
Obedient . . . Ps. 103:20
Possessing emotions . . . Luke 15:10
Concerned in human things . . . 1 Pet. 1:12
Incarnate in human form at times . . . Gen. 18:2-8
Not perfect . . . Job 4:18
Organized in ranks or orders . . . Is. 6:2; 1 Thess. 4:16
B. *Ministry of, toward believers:*
Guide . . . Gen. 24:7, 40
Provide for . . . 1 Kin. 19:5-8
Protect . . . Ps. 34:7
Deliver . . . Dan. 6:22; Acts 12:7-10
Gather . . . Matt. 24:31
Direct activities . . . Acts 8:26
Comfort . . . Acts 27:23, 24
Minister to . . . Heb. 1:14
C. *Ministry of, toward unbelievers:*
A destruction . . . Gen. 19:13
A curse . . . Judg. 5:23
A pestilence . . . 2 Sam. 24:15-17
Sudden death . . . Acts 12:23
Persecution . . . Ps. 35:5, 6
D. *Ministry of, in Christ's life, to:*
Announce His conception . . . Matt. 1:20, 21
Herald His birth . . . Luke 2:10-12
Sustain Him . . . Matt. 4:11
Witness His resurrection . . . 1 Tim. 3:16
Proclaim His resurrection . . . Matt. 28:5-7
Accompany Him to heaven . . . Acts 1:9-11
E. *Ministry of, on special occasions, at:*
The world's creation . . . Job 38:7
Sinai . . . Acts 7:38, 53
Satan's binding . . . Rev. 20:1-3
Christ's return . . . Matt. 13:41, 49; 1 Thess. 4:16
F. *Appearance of, during the Old Testament, to:*
Abraham . . . Gen. 18:2-15
Hagar . . . Gen. 16:7-14
Lot . . . Gen. 19:1-22
Jacob . . . Gen. 28:12
Moses . . . Ex. 3:2
Balaam . . . Num. 22:31-35
Joshua . . . Josh. 5:13-15
All Israel . . . Judg. 2:1-4
Gideon . . . Judg. 6:11-24
Manoah . . . Judg. 13:6-21
David . . . 2 Sam. 24:16, 17
Elijah . . . 1 Kin. 19:5-7
Daniel . . . Dan. 6:22
Zechariah . . . Zech. 2:3
G. *Appearances of, during the New Testament, to:*
Zechariah . . . Luke 1:11-20
The virgin Mary . . . Luke 1:26-38
Joseph . . . Matt. 1:20-25
Shepherds . . . Luke 2:9-14
Certain women . . . Matt. 28:1-7
Mary Magdalene . . . John 20:12, 13
The apostles . . . Acts 1:10, 11
Peter . . . Acts 5:19, 20
Philip . . . Acts 8:26
Cornelius . . . Acts 10:3-32
Paul . . . Acts 27:23, 24
John . . . Rev. 1:1
Seven churches . . . Rev. 1:20

Angels, fallen
Fall of, by pride . . . Is. 14:12-15; Jude 6
Seen by Christ . . . Luke 10:18
Make war on saints . . . Rev. 12:7-17
Imprisoned . . . 2 Pet. 2:4
Everlasting fire prepared for . . . Matt. 25:41

Angel of God, the—*distinct manifestation of God*
A. *Names of:*
Angel of God . . . Gen. 21:17
Angel of the Lord . . . Gen. 22:11
Captain of host of the Lord . . . Josh. 5:14
B. *Appearances of, to:*
Hagar . . . Gen. 16:7, 8; Gen. 21:17
Abraham . . . Gen. 22:11, 15; Gen. 18:1-33
Eliezer . . . Gen. 24:7, 40
Jacob . . . Gen. 31:11-13; Gen. 32:24-30
Moses . . . Ex. 3:2
Children of Israel . . . Ex. 13:21, 22; Ex. 14:19
Balaam . . . Num. 22:22-35
Joshua . . . Judg. 2:1
David . . . 1 Chr. 21:16-18
C. *Divine characteristics:*
Deliver Israel . . . Judg. 2:1-3
Extend blessings . . . Gen. 16:7-12
Pardon sin . . . Ex. 23:20-22

Angels' food
Eaten by men . . . Ps. 78:25
Eaten by Elijah . . . 1 Kin. 19:5-8

Anger of God
A. *Caused by man's:*
Sin . . . Num. 32:10-15
Unbelief . . . Ps. 78:21, 22
Error . . . 2 Sam. 6:7
Disobedience . . . Josh. 7:1, 11, 12
Idolatry . . . Judg. 2:11-14
B. *Described as:*
Sometimes delayed . . . 2 Kin. 23:25-27
Slow . . . Neh. 9:17
Brief . . . Ps. 30:5
Restrained . . . Ps. 78:38
Fierceness . . . Ps. 78:49, 50
Consuming . . . Ps. 90:7
Powerful . . . Ps. 90:11
Not forever . . . Mic. 7:18
To be feared . . . Ps. 76:7
C. *Visitation of, upon:*
Miriam and Aaron . . . Num. 12:9-15
Israelites . . . Num. 11:4-10
Balaam . . . Num. 22:21, 22
Moses . . . Deut. 4:21, 22
Israel . . . Deut. 9:8
Aaron . . . Deut. 9:20
Wicked cities . . . Deut. 29:23
A land . . . Deut. 29:24-28
A king . . . 2 Chr. 25:15, 16
D. *Deliverance from, by:*
Intercessory prayer . . . Num. 11:1, 2; Deut. 9:19, 20
Decisive action . . . Num. 25:3-12
Obedience . . . Deut. 13:16-18
Executing the guilty . . . Josh. 7:1, 10-26
Atonement . . . Is. 63:1-6
See Wrath of God

Anger of Jesus
Provoked by unbelievers . . . Mark 3:5
In the Temple . . . Matt. 21:12; Mark 11:15

SUBJECT REFERENCE

Anger of man

A. *Caused by:*

A brother's deception .... Gen. 27:45
A wife's complaint .... Gen. 30:1,2
Rape .... Gen. 34:1, 7
Inhuman crimes .... Gen. 49:6, 7
A leader's indignation .... Ex. 11:8
A people's idolatry .... Ex. 32:19, 22
Disobedience .... Num. 31:14-18
The Spirit's arousal .... 1 Sam. 11:6
A brother's jealousy .... 1 Sam. 17:28
Luke 15:28
A king's jealousy .... 1 Sam. 20:30
Righteous indignation .... 1 Sam. 20:34
Priestly rebuke .... 2 Chr. 26:19
Unrighteous dealings .... Neh. 5:6, 7
Wife's disobedience .... Esth. 1:12
Lack of respect .... Esth. 3:5
Failure of astrologers .... Dan. 2:12
Flesh .... Gal. 5:19, 20
Harsh treatment .... Eph. 6:4

B. *Justifiable, seen in:*

Jacob .... Gen. 31:36
Moses .... Ex. 32:19
Samson .... Judg. 14:1, 19
Saul .... 1 Sam. 11:6
Samuel .... 1 Sam. 15:16-31
Jonathan .... 1 Sam. 20:34
Christ .... Mark 3:5

C. *Unjustifiable, seen in:*

Cain .... Gen. 4:5, 6
Simeon and Levi .... Gen. 49:5-7
Potiphar .... Gen. 39:1, 19
Moses .... Num. 20:10-12
Balaam .... Num. 22:27, 28
Saul .... 1 Sam. 20:30
Naaman .... 2 Kin. 5:11, 12
Asa .... 2 Chr. 16:10
Uzziah .... 2 Chr. 26:19
Ahasuerus .... Esth. 1:9, 12
Haman .... Esth. 3:5
Nebuchadnezzar .... Dan. 3:13
Jonah .... Jon. 4:1-9
Herod .... Matt. 2:16
The Jews .... Luke 4:28
Jewish officialdom .... Acts 5:17

D. *The Christian attitude toward:*

To be slow in .... Prov. 14:17
Not to sin in .... Eph. 4:26
To put away .... Eph. 4:31

E. *Effects of, seen in:*

Attempted assassination .... Esth. 2:21
Punishment .... Prov. 19:19
Mob action .... Acts 19:28, 29

F. *Pacified by:*

Kindly suggestion .... 2 Kin. 5:10-14
Righteous execution .... Esth. 7:10
Gentle answer .... Prov. 15:1

Angle—*a fishing instrument*

Of Egyptian fishermen .... Is. 19:8

Anguish—*extreme pain*

A. *Caused by:*

Physical hardships .... Gen. 6:9
Physical pain .... 2 Sam. 1:9
Impending destruction .... Deut. 2:25
Conflict of soul .... Job 7:11
National distress .... Is. 8:21, 22
Childbirth .... John 16:21
A spiritual problem .... 2 Cor. 2:4

B. *Reserved for:*

People who refuse wisdom .... Prov. 1:20-27
The wicked .... Job 15:20, 24
Those in Hell .... Luke 16:23, 24

Aniam—*lament of the people*

A Manassite .... 1 Chr. 7:19

Anim—*springs*

A city in south Judah .... Josh. 15:50

Animals

A. *Described as:*

Domesticated and wild .... 2 Sam. 12:3
Clean and unclean .... Lev. 11:1-31
Deut. 14:1-20
For sacrifices .... Ex. 12:3-14
Lev. 16:3, 5

SUBJECT REFERENCE

B. *List of, in the Bible:*

Antelope .... Deut. 14:5
Ape .... 1 Kin. 10:22
Asp .... Is. 11:8
Ass .... Gen. 22:3
Badger .... Ex. 25:5
Bats .... Deut. 14:18
Bear .... 1 Sam. 17:34
Bittern .... Is. 14:23
Boar .... Ps. 80:13
Bulls .... Jer. 52:20
Calf .... Gen. 18:7
Camel .... Gen. 12:16
Cattle .... Gen. 1:25
Chameleon .... Lev. 11:30
Chamois .... Deut. 14:5
Cockatrice (adder) .... Is. 11:8
Colt .... Zech. 9:9
Coney .... Lev. 11:5
Crocodile (Leviathan) .... Job 41:1
Deer .... Deut. 14:5
Dog .... Deut. 23:18
Dragon .... Is. 51:9
Elephant ("ivory") .... 1 Kin. 10:22
Ewe lambs .... Gen. 21:30
Ferret .... Lev. 11:30
Fox .... Judg. 15:4
Frogs .... Ex. 8:2-14
Goat .... Gen. 27:9
Greyhound .... Prov. 30:31
Hare .... Deut. 14:7
Hart .... Ps. 42:1
Heifer .... Gen. 15:9
Hind .... Hab. 3:19
Hippopotamus (Behemoth) .... Job 40:15
Horse .... Gen. 47:17
Jackal ("Dragons") .... Is. 13:22
Kine .... Gen. 32:15
Lamb .... Ex. 29:39
Leopard .... Rev. 13:2
Lion .... 1 Sam. 17:34
Lizard .... Lev. 11:30
Mole .... Is. 2:20
Mouse .... Lev. 11:29
Mule .... 2 Sam. 13:29
Ox .... Ex. 21:28
Pygarg .... Deut. 14:5
Ram .... Gen. 15:9
Roebuck .... Deut. 14:5
Satyr .... Is. 13:21
Scorpion .... Deut. 8:15
Serpents .... Matt. 10:16
Sheep .... Gen. 4:2
Snail .... Lev. 11:30
Spider .... Prov. 30:28
Swine .... Is. 65:2-4
Tortoise .... Lev. 11:29
Unicorn .... Num. 23:22
Weasel .... Lev. 11:29
Whale (sea monster) .... Gen. 1:21
Wolf .... Is. 11:6

C. *Used figuratively of:*

Human traits .... Gen. 49:9-14, 21
Universal peace .... Is. 11:6-9
Man's innate nature .... Jer. 13:23
World empires .... Dan. 7:2-8
Satanic powers .... Rev. 12:4, 9
Christ's sacrifice .... 1 Pet. 1:18-20

Anise—*a plant for seasoning; the dill*

Tithed by the Jews .... Matt. 23:23

Ankle—*joint connecting foot and leg*

Lame man's healed .... Acts 3:7

Anklet—*an ornament worn by women on the ankles*

Included in Isaiah's denunciation .... Is. 3:16, 18

Anna—*grace*

Aged prophetess .... Luke 2:36-38

Annas—*gracious*

A Jewish high priest .... Luke 3:2
Christ appeared before .... John 18:12-24
Peter and John appeared before .... Acts 4:6

Anointing—*pouring oil upon*

A. *Performed upon:*

The patriarchs .... 1 Chr. 16:22
Priest .... Ex. 29:7
Prophets .... 1 Kin. 19:16
Israel's kings .... 1 Sam. 10:1
Foreign kings .... 1 Kin. 19:15
The Messianic King .... Ps. 2:2
Sacred objects .... Ex. 30:26-28

SUBJECT REFERENCE

B. *Ordinary, purposes of, for:*

Adornment .... Ruth 3:3
Invigoration .... 2 Sam. 12:20
Hospitality .... Luke 7:38, 46
Purification .... Esth. 2:12
Battle .... Is. 21:5
Burial .... Matt. 26:12
Sanctifying .... Ex. 30:29

C. *Medicinal, purposes of, for:*

Wound .... Luke 10:34
Healing .... Mark 6:13
James 5:14

D. *Sacred, purposes of, to:*

Memoralize an event .... Gen. 28:18
Confirm a covenant .... Gen. 35:14
Set apart .... Ex. 30:22-29
Institute into office .... 1 Sam. 16:12, 13

E. *Absence of:*

Sign of judgment .... Deut. 28:40
Fasting .... 2 Sam. 12:16, 20
Mourning .... 2 Sam. 14:2

F. *Of Christ the Messiah "the Anointed One," as:*

Predicted .... Ps. 45:7
Is. 61:1
Fulfilled .... Luke 4:18
Heb. 1:9
Interpreted .... Acts 4:27
Symbolized in His name ("the Christ") .... {Matt. 16:16, 20; Acts 9:22
Typical of the believer's anointing .... 1 John 2:27

G. *Significance of, as indicating:*

Divine appointment .... 2 Chr. 22:7
Special honor .... 1 Sam. 24:6, 10
Special privilege .... Ps. 105:15
God's blessing .... Ps. 23:5

Anointing of the Holy Spirit

A. *Of Christ:*

Predicted .... Is. 61:1
Fulfilled .... John 1:32-34
Explained .... Luke 4:18

B. *Of Christians:*

Predicted .... Ezek. 47:1-12
Foretold by Christ .... John 7:38, 39
Fulfilled at Pentecost .... Acts 2:1-41
Fulfilled at conversion .... 2 Cor. 1:21
1 John 2:20, 27

Answer—*a reply*

A. *Good:*

Soft .... Prov. 15:1
Confident .... Dan. 3:16-18
Convicting .... Dan. 5:17-28
Astonished .... Luke 2:47
Unanswerable .... Luke 20:3-8
Spontaneous .... Luke 21:14, 15
Spirit-directed .... Luke 12:11, 12
Ready .... 1 Pet. 3:15

B. *Evil:*

Unwise .... 1 Kin. 12:12-15
Incriminating .... 2 Sam. 1:5-16
Insolent .... 2 Kin. 18:27-36
Humiliating .... Esth. 6:6-11
Satanic .... Job 1:8-11

Ant—*a small insect*

An example of industry .... Prov. 6:6-8
Prov. 30:24

Antagonism—*unceasing opposition*

A. *Of men, against:*

God's people .... Ex. 5:1-19
Deut. 2:26-33
The prophets .... Amos 7:10-17
Zech. 1:2-6
The light .... John 3:19, 20
The truth .... John 8:12-47
Acts 7:54-60
Christians .... Acts 16:16-24

B. *Of Satan, against:*

Job .... Job 2:9-12
Christ .... Luke 4:1-13
Peter .... Luke 22:31-34
Paul .... 1 Thess. 2:18
Christians .... Eph. 6:11-18

SUBJECT REFERENCE

Antediluvians—*those who lived before the flood*

A. *Described as:*
- Long-lived ... Gen. 5:3-32
- Very wicked ... Gen. 6:5
- A mixed race ... Gen. 6:1-4; Jude 6, 7
- Of great size ... Gen. 6:4

B. *Warnings against, made by:*
- Enoch ... Jude 14, 15
- Noah ... 2 Pet. 2:5
- Christ ... 1 Pet. 3:19, 20

C. *Destruction of:*
- Only Noah's family escaped ... Gen. 7:21-23
- Predicted ... Gen. 6:5-7
- Comparable to Christ's return ... Matt. 24:37-39; Luke 17:26, 27
- Comparable to the world's end ... 2 Pet. 3:3-7

Anthropomorphisms—*applying human attributes to God*

A. *Physical likenesses, such as:*
- Feet ... Ex. 24:10
- Hands ... Ex. 24:11
- Mouth ... Num. 12:8
- Eyes ... Hab. 1:13
- Arms ... Ex. 6:6

B. *Non-physical characteristics, such as:*
- Memory ... Gen. 9:16
- Anger ... Ex. 22:24
- Jealousy ... Ps. 78:58
- Repentance ... Jon. 3:10

Antichrist—*Satan's final opponent of Christ and Christians*

A. *Called:*
- Man of sin ... 2 Thess. 2:3
- Son of perdition ... 2 Thess. 2:3
- Wicked one ... 2 Thess. 2:8
- Antichrist ... 1 John 2:18, 22
- Beast ... Rev. 11:7

B. *Described as:*
- Lawless ... 2 Thess. 2:3-12
- Opposing Christ ... 2 Thess. 2:4
- Working wonders ... 2 Thess. 2:9
- Deceiving the world ... 2 John 7; Rev. 19:20
- Persecuting Christians ... Rev. 13:7
- Satan-inspired ... 2 Thess. 2:9
- Denying Christ's incarnation ... 1 John 4:3; 2 John 7
- One and many ... 1 John 2:18-22
- A person and a system ... 2 Thess. 2:3, 7
- Seeking man's worship ... 2 Thess. 2:4

C. *Coming of:*
- Foretold ... 2 Thess. 2:5
- In the last time ... 1 John 2:18
- Now restrained ... 2 Thess. 2:6
- Follows removal of hindrance ... 2 Thess. 2:7, 8
- Before Christ's return ... 2 Thess. 2:8
- By Satan's deception ... 2 Thess. 2:9, 10

D. *Destruction of:*
- At Christ's return ... 2 Thess. 2:8; Rev. 19:20
- Eternal in lake of fire ... Rev. 20:10

Antidote—*a remedy given to counteract poison*

A. *Literal:*
- A tree ... Ex. 15:23-25
- Meal ... 2 Kin. 4:38-41

B. *Figurative and spiritual, for:*
- Sin, Christ ... Num. 21:8,9; John 3:14, 15
- Christ's absence, the Holy Spirit ... John 14:16-18
- Sorrow, joy ... John 16:20-22
- Satan's lies, God's truth&2:5 In the last time.......
- Earth's trials, faith ... 1 Pet. 1:6-8
- Testings, God's grace ... 1 Cor. 10:13; 2 Cor. 12:7-9
- Suffering, heaven's glory ... Rom. 8:18; 2 Cor. 5:1-10

Antinomianism—*the idea that Christian liberty exempts one from the moral law*

A. *Prevalence of, among:*
- Christians ... Rom. 6:1-23
- False Teachers ... 2 Pet. 2:19; Jude 4

B. *Based on error, that:*
- Grace allows sin ... Rom. 6:1, 2
- Moral law is abolished ... Rom. 7:1-14
- Liberty has no bounds ... 1 Cor. 10:23-33

C. *Corrected by remembering that liberty is:*
- Not a license to sin ... Rom. 6:1-23
- Limited by moral law ... Rom. 8:1-4
- Controlled by Holy Spirit ... Rom. 8:5-14
- Not to be a stumbling block ... Rom. 14:1-23; 1 Cor. 8:1-13
- Motivated by love ... Gal. 5:13-15

Antioch—*a city of Syria*
- Home of Nicolas ... Acts 6:5
- Haven of persecuted Christians ... Acts 11:19
- Home of first Gentile church ... Acts 11:20, 21
- Name "Christian" originated in ... Acts 11:26
- Barnabas ministered here ... Acts 11:22-24
- Barnabas and Paul minister in church of ... Acts 11:25-30
- Paul commissioned by church of ... Acts 13:1-4; Acts 15:35-41
- Paul reports to ... Acts 14:26-28
- Church of, troubled by Judaizers ... Acts 15:1-4; Gal. 2:11-21

Antioch—*a city of Pisidia*
- Jewish synagogue ... Acts 13:14
- Paul visits ... Acts 13:14, 42
- Jews of, reject the Gospel ... Acts 13:45-51
- Paul revisits ... Acts 14:21
- Paul recalls persecution at ... 2 Tim. 3:11

Antipas
- A Christian martyr of Pergamum ... Rev. 2:13

Antipatris—*belonging to Antipater*
- A city between Jerusalem and Caesarea ... Acts 23:31

Antitype—*the fulfillment of a type*
- The Greek word translated "figure" in ... Heb. 9:24; 1 Pet. 3:21
- Generally, a fulfillment of an Old Testament type ... Matt. 12:39, 40; John 1:29

Antonia, Tower of—(fortress built by Herod the Great, not mentioned by name in Scripture)
- Called "castle" ... Acts 21:30-40
- Possible site of Jesus' trial, called "the Pavement" ... John 19:13

Antothijah—*answers of Jehovah*
- A Benjamite ... 1 Chr. 8:24

Antothite—*a native of Anathoth*
- Home of famous soldiers ... 1 Chr. 11:28; 1 Chr. 12:3

Anub—*strong*
- A man of Judah ... 1 Chr. 4:8

Anvil—*a block for forging hot metals*
- Used figuratively in ... Is. 41:7

Anxiety—*A disturbed state of mind produced by real or imaginary fears*

A. *Caused by:*
- Brother's hatred ... Gen. 32:6-12
- Son's rebellion ... 2 Sam. 18:24-33
- King's decree ... Esth. 4:1-17
- Child's absence ... Luke 2:48
- Son's sickness ... John 4:46-49
- Friend's delay ... 2 Cor. 2:12, 13

B. *Overcome by:*
- Trust ... Ps. 37:1-5
- Reliance upon the Holy Spirit ... Mark 13:11
- God's provision ... Luke 12:22-30
- Upward look ... Luke 21:25-28
- Assurance of God's sovereignty ... Rom. 8:28
- Angel's word ... Acts 27:21-25
- Prayer ... Phil. 4:6
- God's care ... 1 Pet. 5:6, 7

See Cares, worldly

Ape—*a monkey*
- Article of trade ... 1 Kin. 10:22

Apelles
- A Christian in Rome ... Rom. 16:10

Apharsites
- Assyrian colonists in Samaria opposing Zerubbabel's work ... Ezra 4:9

Aphek—*strength, fortress*
1. A town in Plain of Sharon ... Josh. 12:18
   Site of Philistine camp ... 1 Sam. 4:1; 1 Sam. 29:1
2. A city assigned to Asher ... Josh. 19:30
3. Border city ... Josh. 13:4
4. A city in Jezreel ... 1 Kin. 20:26-30
   Syria's defeat prophesied here ... 2 Kin. 13:14-19

Aphekah—*fortress*
- A city of Judah ... Josh. 15:53

Aphiah—*striving*
- An ancestor of King Saul ... 1 Sam. 9:1

Aphik—*strength, fortress*
- Spared by Asher ... Judg. 1:31

See Aphek 2

Aphrah—*house of dust*
- A Philistine city; symbolic of doom ... Mic. 1:10

Aphses—*shattering*
- Chief of a priestly course ... 1 Chr. 24:15

Apocalypse—*an unveiling of something unknown*
- The Greek word usually translated "revelation" ... Rom. 16:25; Gal. 1:12

Apocrypha—*hidden things*
- Writings in Greek written during the period between the Testaments; rejected by Protestants as uninspired

Apollonia—*pertaining to Apollo*
- A town between Amphipolis and Thessalonica ... Acts 17:1

Apollos—*a short or pet name for Apollonios*
- An Alexandrian Jew mighty in the Scriptures ... Acts 18:24, 25
- Receives further instruction ... Acts 18:26
- Sent to preach in Achaia ... Acts 18:27, 28
- A minister in Corinth ... 1 Cor. 1:12; 1 Cor. 3:4, 22
- Cited by Paul ... 1 Cor. 4:6
- Urged to revisit Corinth ... 1 Cor. 16:12
- Journey of, noted by Paul ... Titus 3:13

Apollyon—*the destroyer*
- Angel of the bottomless pit ... Rev. 9:11

Apostasy—*a falling away from God's truth*

A. *Kinds of:*
- National ... 1 Kin. 12:26-33
- Individual ... 2 Kin. 21:1-9; Heb. 3:12
- Satanic ... Rev. 12:7-9
- Angelic ... 2 Pet. 2:4
- General ... 2 Tim. 3:1-5
- Imputed ... Acts 21:21
- Final ... 2 Thess. 2:3
- Irremedial ... Heb. 6:1-8

B. *Caused by:*
- Satan ... Luke 22:31
- False teachers ... Acts 20:29, 30
- Perversion of Scripture ... 2 Tim. 4:3, 4
- Persecution ... Matt. 13:21
- Unbelief ... Heb. 4:9-11
- Love of world ... 2 Tim. 4:10
- Hardened heart ... Acts 7:54, 57
- Spiritual blindness ... Acts 28:25-27

C. *Manifested in:*
- Resisting truth ... 2 Tim. 3:7, 8
- Resorting to deception ... 2 Cor. 11:13-15
- Reverting to immorality ... 2 Pet. 2:14, 19-22

D. *Safeguards against, found in:*
- God's Word ... 2 Tim. 3:13-17
- Spiritual growth ... 2 Pet. 1:5-11
- Indoctrination ... Acts 20:29-31
- Faithfulness ... Matt. 24:42-51
- Spiritual perception ... 1 John 4:1-6
- Being grounded in the truth ... Eph. 4:13-16

A

SUBJECT REFERENCE

Using God's armor .... Eph. 6:10-20
Preaching the Word .... 2 Tim. 4:2, 5

E. *Examples of, seen in:*
Israelites .... Ex. 32:1-35
Saul .... 1 Sam. 15:11
Solomon .... 1 Kin. 11:1-10
Amaziah .... 2 Chr. 25:14-16
Judas .... Matt. 26:14-16
Hymenaeus and Philetus .... 2 Tim. 2:17, 18
Demas .... 2 Tim. 4:10
Certain men .... Jude 4

Apostles—*men divinely commissioned to represent Christ*

A. *Descriptive of:*
Christ .... Heb. 3:1
The twelve .... Matt. 10:2
Others (Barnabas, James, etc.) .... Acts 14:4; Gal. 1:19
Messengers .... 2 Cor. 8:23
False teachers .... 2 Cor. 11:13
Simon Peter .... Matt. 10:2
Andrew .... Matt. 10:2
James, son of Zebedee .... Matt. 10:2
John .... Matt. 10:2
Philip .... Matt. 10:3
Bartholomew (Nathanael) .... Matt. 10:3; John 1:45
Thomas .... Matt. 10:3
Matthew (Levi) .... Matt. 10:3; Luke 5:27
James, son of Alphaeus .... Matt. 10:3
Thaddaeus (Judas) .... Matt. 10:3; John 14:22
Simon the Zealot .... Luke 6:15
Judas Iscariot .... Matt. 10:4
Matthias .... Acts 1:26
Paul .... 2 Cor. 1:1
Barnabas .... Acts 14:14
James, the Lord's brother .... Gal. 1:19
Silvanus and Timothy .... 1 Thess. 1:1; 1 Thess. 2:9
Andronicus and Junias .... Rom. 16:7

B. *Mission of, to:*
Perform miracles .... Matt. 10:1, 8
Preach Gospel .... Matt. 28:19, 20
Witness Christ's resurrection .... Acts 1:22; Acts 10:40-42
Write Scripture .... Eph. 3:5
Establish the Church .... Eph. 2:20

C. *Limitations of, before Pentecost:*
Lowly in position .... Matt. 4:18
Unlearned .... Acts 4:13
Subject to disputes .... Matt. 20:20-28
Faith often obscure .... Matt. 16:21-23
Need of instruction .... Matt. 17:4, 9-13

D. *Position of, after Pentecost:*
Interpreted prophecy .... Acts 2:14-36
Defended truth .... Phil. 1:7, 17
Exposed heretics .... Gal. 1:6-9
Upheld discipline .... 2 Cor. 13:1-6
Established churches .... Rom. 15:17-20

Apothecary—*"pharmacist", "perfumer"*
Used in tabernacle .... Ex. 30:25, 35
Used in embalming .... 2 Chr. 16:14
A maker of ointment .... Eccl. 10:1
Among returnees .... Neh. 3:8

Appaim—*nostrils*
A man of Judah .... 1 Chr. 2:30, 31

Apparel—*clothing*

A. *Kinds of:*
Harlot's .... Gen. 38:14
Virgin's .... 2 Sam. 13:18
Mourner's .... 2 Sam. 12:20
Splendid .... Luke 7:25
Rich .... Ezek. 27:24
Worldly .... 1 Pet. 3:3
Showy .... Luke 16:19
Official .... 1 Kin. 10:5
Royal .... Esth. 6:8
Priestly .... Ezra 3:10
Angelic .... Acts 1:10
Heavenly .... Rev. 19:8

B. *Attitude toward:*
Not to covet .... Acts 20:33
Without show .... 1 Pet. 3:3
Be modest in .... 1 Tim. 2:9

C. *Figurative of:*
Christ's blood .... Is. 63:1-3
Christ's righteousness .... Zech. 3:1-5
The Church's purity .... Ps. 45:13, 14

Apparition—*appearance of ghost or disembodied spirit*
Samuel .... 1 Sam. 28:12-14
Christ mistaken for .... Matt. 14:26; Luke 24:37, 39

Appeal—*petition for higher judgment*
To Christ .... Luke 12:13, 14
Of Paul, to Caesar .... Acts 25:11, 25-28; Acts 26:32

Appearance, outward

A. *Can conceal:*
Deception .... Josh. 9:3-16
Hypocrisy .... Matt. 23:25-28
Rottenness .... Acts 12:21-23
Rebellion .... 2 Sam. 15:7-13
False apostles .... 2 Cor. 11:13-15
Inner glory .... Is. 53:1-3; Matt. 17:1, 2

B. *Can be:*
Misunderstood .... Josh. 22:10-31
Mistaken .... 1 Sam. 1:12-18
Misleading .... 2 Cor. 10:7-11
Misjudged .... John 7:24
Misinterpreted .... Matt. 11:16-19

Appearances, divine

A. *Of the Lord in the Old Testament:*
To Abraham .... Gen. 12:7
To Isaac .... Gen. 26:2, 24
To Jacob .... Gen. 35:1, 9
To Moses .... Ex. 3:2, 16
To Israel .... Ex. 16:10
In mercy seat .... Lev. 16:2
In tabernacle .... Num. 14:10
To Gideon .... Judg. 6:11, 12
To Manoah .... Judg. 13:3, 10, 21
To Samuel .... 1 Sam. 3:21
To David .... 2 Chr. 3:1
To Solomon .... 1 Kin. 3:5

B. *Of Christ's first advent, in:*
Nativity .... 2 Tim. 1:10
Transfiguration .... Luke 9:30, 31
Resurrected form .... Luke 24:34
Priestly intercession .... Heb. 9:24
Return .... Col. 3:4

C. *Of Christ resurrected, to, at:*
Mary Magdalene .... John 20:11-18
Other women .... Matt. 28:9-10
Disciples on road to Emmaus .... Luke 24:13-35
Ten disciples .... John 20:19-25
Thomas .... John 20:26-31
Sea of Galilee .... John 21:1-25
Give great commission .... Matt. 28:16-20
Five hundred brethren .... 1 Cor. 15:6
His ascension .... Acts 1:4-11
Paul .... Acts 9:3-6
John .... Rev. 1:10-18

D. *Of Christ's second advent, a time of:*
Salvation .... Heb. 9:28
Confidence .... 1 John 2:28
Judgment .... 2 Tim. 4:1
Reward .... 2 Tim. 4:8
Blessedness .... Titus 2:13
Joy .... 1 Pet. 1:7, 8
Rulership .... 1 Tim. 6:14, 15

See Theophany

Appeasement—*means used to reconcile two parties*

A. *Kinds of, between:*
Brothers .... Gen. 32:20
Nations .... 1 Kin. 20:31-34
Tribes .... Josh. 22:10-34
Jews and Gentiles .... Eph. 2:11-17

B. *Means of, by:*
Gifts .... Gen. 43:11-16
Special pleading .... 1 Sam. 25:17-35
Correcting an abuse .... Acts 6:1-6
Slowness to anger .... Prov. 15:18
Wisdom .... Prov. 16:14

C. *None allowed between:*
Righteousness, evil .... 2 Cor. 6:14-17
Truth, error .... Gal. 1:7-9
Faith, works .... Gal. 5:1-10
Flesh, Spirit .... Gal. 5:16-26
Christ, Satan .... Matt. 4:1-11
Heaven, Sheol .... Is. 28:18

D. *Of God's wrath, by:*
Righteous action .... Num. 16:44-50
Repentance .... 2 Sam. 12:10-14
Atoning for an evil .... 2 Sam. 21:1-14
Christ's death .... Is. 63:1-7
Christ's righteousness .... Zech. 3:1-5; 2 Cor. 5:18-21

Appetite—*desire to fulfill some basic need*

A. *Kinds of:*
Physical .... 1 Sam. 14:31-33
Sexual .... 1 Cor. 7:1-9
Lustful .... Matt. 5:28
Insatiable .... Prov. 27:20
Spiritual .... Ps. 119:20, 131

B. *Perversion of, by:*
Gluttony .... Prov. 23:1, 2
Wine .... Prov. 23:29-35
Adultery .... Prov. 6:24-29; Ezek. 23:1-49
Impurity .... Rom. 1:24-32

C. *Loss of, by:*
Age .... 2 Sam. 19:35
Trouble .... 1 Sam. 28:22, 23
Visions .... Dan. 10:3-16
Deep concern .... John 4:31-34

D. *Spiritual, characteristics of:*
Satisfying .... Is. 55:1, 2
Sufficient .... Matt. 5:6
Spontaneous .... John 7:38, 39
Sanctifying .... 1 Pet. 2:2
Sublime .... Col. 3:1-3

See Gluttony; Hunger; Temperance

Apphia
Christian lady of Colossae .... Philem. 2

Appii forum—*a town about 40 miles south of Rome*
Paul meets Christians here .... Acts 28:15

Applause—*a visible expression of public approval*
Men seek after .... Matt. 6:1-5

"Apple of the eye"—*a figurative expression for something very valuable*

A. *Translated as:*
"The pupil of his eye" .... Deut. 32:10
"The apple of his eye" .... Zech. 2:8

B. *Figurative of:*
God's care .... Deut. 32:10
God's Law .... Prov. 7:2
The saint's security .... Ps. 17:8
Abundance of sorrow .... Lam. 2:18

Apples of gold—*something of great value*
A word fitly spoken .... Prov. 25:11

Appoint—*to set in an official position or relationship*

A. *Descriptive of ordination, to:*
Priesthood .... Num. 3:10
Prophetic office .... Heb. 3:2
Ruler .... 2 Sam. 6:21
Apostleship .... Luke 10:1
Deacon's office .... Acts 6:3

B. *Descriptive of God's rule, over:*
Earth .... Ps. 104:20
World history .... Acts 17:26
Israel's history .... 2 Chr. 33:8
Nations .... Jer. 47:7
Man's plans .... 2 Sam. 17:14
Man's life .... Job 14:5
Death .... Heb. 9:27
Final judgment .... Acts 17:31
Man's destiny .... Matt. 24:51

C. *Descriptive of the believer's life:*
Trials .... 1 Thess. 3:3
Service .... Acts 22:10
Salvation .... 1 Thess. 5:9

Appreciation—*favorable recognition of blessings*
Sought for among men .... Ps. 107:8-21
Of favors, rebuffed .... 2 Sam. 10:1-5
Of blessings, unnoticed .... Acts 14:15-18

Apprehension—*the ability to understand*
God .... Job 11:7

SUBJECT — REFERENCE

- God's Word — Acts 17:11
- Prophecy — 1 Pet. 1:10-12
- Parables — Matt. 13:10-17
- Spiritual truths — 1 Cor. 2:7-16
- Christ — Phil. 3:12-14

Appropriation—*possessing for one's use*

- God's promises — Heb. 11:8-16
- God's Word — Ps. 119:11
- Salvation — Acts 16:30-34

Approval—*favorable acceptance*

A. *Means of, by:*

- God — Acts 2:22
- The Lord — 2 Cor. 10:18
- The Jews — Rom. 2:18
- A church — 1 Cor. 16:3
- Men — Rom. 14:18

B. *Obtained by:*

- Endurance — 2 Cor. 6:4
- Innocence — 2 Cor. 7:11
- Spiritual examination — 2 Cor. 13:5-8
- Spiritual judgment — Phil. 1:9, 10
- Diligence — 2 Tim. 2:15

Aprons—*articles of clothing*

- Item of miraculous healing — Acts 19:12

Aquila—*eagle*

- Jewish tentmaker — Acts 18:2, 3
- Paul stays with — Acts 18:3
- Visits Syria — Acts 18:18
- Resides in Ephesus — Acts 18:19
- Instructs Apollos — Acts 18:24-26
- Esteemed by Paul — Rom. 16:3, 4

Ar—*city*

- A chief Moabite city — Num. 21:15
- On Israel's route — Deut. 2:18
- Destroyed by Sihon — Num. 21:28
- Destroyed by God — Is. 15:1

Ara—*strong*

- A descendant of Asher — 1 Chr. 7:38

Arab—*a court*

- A mountain city of Judah — Josh. 15:52

Arabah—*desert plain, steppe*

- A district east of Jordan — 2 Sam. 2:29
- A major natural division of Palestine — Josh. 11:16; Josh. 12:8
- Opposite Gigal — Deut. 11:30
- Restoration of, predicted — Ezek. 47:1-12
- Referred by "desert" in — Is. 35:1

Arabia—*steppe*

A. *Place of:*

- Mt. Sinai — Gal. 4:25
- Gold mines — 2 Chr. 9:14
- Paul visited — Gal. 1:17

B. *People of:*

- Lustful — Is. 13:20
- Paid tribute to Solomon — 1 Kin. 10:14, 15
- Plundered Jerusalem — 2 Chr. 21:16, 17
- Defeated by Uzziah — 2 Chr. 26:7
- Sold sheep and goats to Tyre — Ezek. 27:21
- Opposed Nehemiah — Neh. 2:19
- Denounced by prophets — Is. 21:13-17
- Visited Jerusalem at Pentecost — Acts 2:11

Arad—*fugitive*

1. A Benjamite — 1 Chr. 8:15
2. A city south of Hebron — Num. 21:1-3
   - Defeated by Joshua — Josh. 12:14
   - Kenites settled near — Judg. 1:16

Arah—*wayfarer*

1. A descendant of Asher — 1 Chr. 7:39
2. A family of returnees — Ezra 2:5

Aram—*high, exalted*

1. A son of Shem — Gen. 10:22, 23
2. A grandson of Nahor — Gen. 22:21
3. A descendant of Asher — 1 Chr. 7:34
4. A district in Gilead — 1 Chr. 2:23
5. An ancestor of Christ — Matt. 1:3, 4

Aramaic—*a Semitic language*

- Used by the Syrians — 2 Kin. 18:26
- The language of the postexilic period — Ezra 4:7; Dan. 2:4
- Portions of the Bible written in, include — Dan. 2:4—7:28; Ezra 4:8—6:18; Ezra 7:12-26
- The same as "Hebrew" in — John 19:20
- Words and phrases of, found in — Matt. 27:46; Mark 5:41; Mark 7:34

Aran—*wild goat*

- Esau's descendant — Gen. 36:28

Ararat—*a high mountain range in eastern Armenia*

- Site of ark's landing — Gen. 8:4
- Assassins flee to — 2 Kin. 19:37; Is. 37:38

Aratus—*a Greek poet living about 270 B.C.*

- Paul quotes from his *Phaenomena* — Acts 17:28

Araunah—*Jehovah is firm*

- A Jebusite — 2 Sam. 24:15-25
- His threshing floor bought by David — 2 Sam. 24:18-25
- Became site of Temple — 2 Chr. 3:1
- Also called Ornan — 1 Chr. 21:18-28

Arba—*four*

- The father of the Anakim — Josh. 14:15

Arbathite—*a native of Beth-arabah*

- Two of David's mighty men — 2 Sam. 23:31

Arbite—*a native of Arab*

- In Judah — 2 Sam. 23:35

Arbitrator—*one authorized to settle disputes*

A. *Exercised by:*

- Judges — Ex. 18:18-27
- Priests — Deut. 17:8-13
- Kings — 1 Kin. 3:9, 16-28
- Christ — Matt. 22:17-33
- Apostles — Acts 6:1-6
- Church — Acts 15:1-29

B. *Purposes of:*

- Determine the Lord's will — Lev. 24:11-16, 23; Num. 15:32-36
- Settle disputes — Josh. 22:9-34
- Settle labor disputes — Matt. 18:23-35; Matt. 20:1-16

Archaeology—*the science of digging up ancient civilizations*

- Truth springs out of the earth — Ps. 85:11
- The stones cry out — Luke 19:40

See article on Greatest Archaeological Discoveries

Archangel—*a chief angel*

- Contends with Satan — Jude 9
- Will herald the Lord's return — 1 Thess. 4:16

Archelaus—*leader of the people*

- Son of Herod the Great — Matt. 2:22

Archers—*experts with the bow and arrow*

A. *Descriptive of:*

- Ishmael — Gen. 21:20
- Jonathan — 1 Sam. 20:34-39
- Sons of Ulam — 1 Chr. 8:40

B. *Instrumental in the death of:*

- Saul — 1 Sam. 31:3
- Uriah the Hittite — 2 Sam. 11:24
- Josiah — 2 Chr. 35:23, 24

C. *Figurative of:*

- Invincibility — Gen. 49:23
- The Lord's chastisements — Job 16:13
- Loss of glory — Is. 21:17
- Divine judgment — Jer. 50:29

Archevites—*people settled in Samaria during exile*

- Opposed rebuilding of Jerusalem — Ezra 4:9-16

Archippus—*master of the horse*

- A church worker — Col. 4:17

Archite—*the long*

- Canaanite tribe — Josh. 16:2
- David's friend — 2 Sam. 15:32

Architect—*one who draws plans for a building*

- Plan of, given to Noah — Gen. 6:14-16
- Plan of, shown to Moses — Ex. 25:8, 9, 40
- Bezaleel, an inspired — Ex. 35:30-35
- Plan of, given to Solomon — 1 Chr. 28:11-21
- Seen in Ezekiel's vision — Ezek. 40—42

Archives—*storage place for public and historical documents*

- The book of the law found in — 2 Kin. 22:8
- Jeremiah's roll placed in — Jer. 36:20, 21
- Record book kept in — Ezra 4:15
- Genealogies kept in — Neh. 7:5, 64

Arcturus—*a constellation called the Great Bear*

- Cited as evidence of God's sovereignty — Job 9:9

Ard—*humpbacked*

- A son of Benjamin — Gen. 46:21
- Progenitor of the Ardites — Num. 26:40
- Also called Addar — 1 Chr. 8:3

Ardon—*descendant*

- A son of Caleb — 1 Chr. 2:18

Areli—*valiant, heroic*

- A son of Gad — Gen. 46:16

Areopagite—*a member of the court*

- A convert — Acts 17:34

Areopagus—*a rocky hill at Athens; also the name of a court*

- Paul preached — Acts 17:18-34
- Called "Mars' Hill" — Acts 17:22

Aretas—*pleasing*

- The title borne by four Nabataean rulers, the last of whom Paul mentions (Aretas IV, Philopatris, 9 B.C.-A.D. 40) — 2 Cor. 11:32, 33

Argob—*mound or region of clods*

1. District of Bashan with 60 fortified cities — Deut. 3:4; 1 Kin. 4:13
2. Guard killed by Pekah — 2 Kin. 15:25

Aridai

- A son of Haman — Esth. 9:9

Aridatha

- A son of Haman — Esth. 9:8

Arieh—*lion*

- Guard killed by Pekah — 2 Kin. 15:25

Ariel—*lion of God*

1. Ezra's friend — Ezra 8:15-17
2. Name applied to Jerusalem — Is. 29:1, 2, 7

Arimathea—*a height*

- Joseph's native city — John 19:38

Arioch—*lion-like*

1. King of Ellasar — Gen. 14:1, 9
2. Captain of Nebuchadnezzar — Dan. 2:14, 15

Arisai

- A son of Haman — Esth. 9:9

Arise—*to stand up*

A. *Descriptive of:*

- Natural events — Eccl. 1:5
- Standing up — 1 Sam. 28:23
- Regeneration — Luke 15:18, 20
- Resurrection — Matt. 9:25
- A miracle — Luke 4:39

B. *Descriptive of prophetic events:*

- World kingdoms — Dan. 2:39
- The Messiah's advent — Is. 60:1-3
- Persecution — Mark 4:17
- False Christs — Matt. 24:24

Aristarchus—*the best ruler*

- A Macedonian Christian — Acts 19:29
- Accompanied Paul — Acts 20:4
- Imprisoned with Paul — Col. 4:10

Aristobulus—*the best counselor*

- A Christian at Rome — Rom. 16:10

SUBJECT REFERENCE

Ark of bulrushes—*a basket made of reeds (papyrus)*
Moses placed in . . . . . Ex. 2:3-6
Made by faith . . . . . Heb. 11:23

Ark of Noah
Construction . . . . . Gen. 6:14-16
Cargo . . . . . Gen. 6:19-21
Ready for the flood . . . . . Matt. 24:38, 39
Rested on Mt. Ararat . . . . . Gen. 8:1-16
A type of baptism . . . . . 1 Pet. 3:20, 21

Ark of the Covenant—*a small box containing the tablets of the Law*
A. *Called:*
Ark of the covenant . . . . . Num. 10:33
Ark of the testimony . . . . . Ex. 30:6
Ark of the Lord . . . . . Josh. 4:11
Ark of God . . . . . 1 Sam. 3:3
Ark of God's strength . . . . . 2 Chr. 6:41
B. *Construction of:*
Described . . . . . Ex. 25:10-22
Executed . . . . . Ex. 37:1-5
C. *Contained:*
The Ten Commandments . . . . . Deut. 10:4
Aaron's rod . . . . . Num. 17:10
Heb. 9:4
Pot of manna . . . . . Ex. 16:33, 34
D. *Conveyed:*
By Levites . . . . . Num. 3:30, 31
Before Israel . . . . . Josh. 3:3-17
Into battle . . . . . 1 Sam. 4:4, 5
On a cart . . . . . 1 Sam. 6:7-15
E. *Purposes of:*
Symbol of God's Law . . . . . Ex. 25:16, 21
Memorial of God's provision . . . . . Ex. 16:33, 34
Place to know God's will . . . . . Ex. 25:22
Ex. 30:6, 36
Place of entreaty . . . . . Josh. 7:6-15
Symbol of God's holiness . . . . . 1 Sam. 6:19
2 Sam. 6:6, 7
Place of atonement . . . . . Lev. 16:2, 14-17
Type of Christ . . . . . Rom. 3:25-31
Symbol of heaven . . . . . Rev. 11:19
F. *History of:*
Carried across Jordan . . . . . Josh. 3:16, 14-17
Caused Jordan's stoppage . . . . . Josh. 4:5-11, 18
Carried around Jericho . . . . . Josh. 6:6-20
At Mt. Ebal ceremony . . . . . Josh. 8:30-33
Set up at Shiloh . . . . . Josh. 18:1
Moved to house of God . . . . . Judg. 20:26, 27
Returned to Shiloh . . . . . 1 Sam. 1:3
Carried into battle . . . . . 1 Sam. 4:3-22
Captured . . . . . 1 Sam. 4:10-21
Caused Dagon's fall . . . . . 1 Sam. 5:1-4
Brought a plague . . . . . 1 Sam. 5:6-12
Returned to Israel . . . . . 1 Sam. 6:1-21
Set in Abinadab's house . . . . . 1 Sam. 7:1, 2
In Obed-edom's house . . . . . 2 Sam. 6:10-12
Established in Jerusalem . . . . . 2 Sam. 6:12-17
During Absalom's rebellion . . . . . 2 Sam. 15:24-29
Placed in Temple . . . . . 1 Kin. 8:1-11
Restored by Josiah . . . . . 2 Chr. 35:3
Carried to Babylon . . . . . 2 Chr. 36:6, 18
Prophetic fulfillment . . . . . Jer. 3:16, 17
Acts 15:13-18

Arkite—*belonging to Arka*
Canaan's descendants . . . . . Gen. 10:17
1 Chr. 1:15

Arm of God
A. *Described as:*
Stretched out . . . . . Deut. 4:34
Everlasting . . . . . Deut. 33:27
Strong, mighty . . . . . Ps. 89:10, 13
Holy . . . . . Ps. 98:1
Glorious . . . . . Is. 63:12
B. *Descriptive of, God's:*
Redeeming . . . . . Ex. 6:6
Saving . . . . . Ps. 44:3
Victorious . . . . . Ps. 98:1
Ruling . . . . . Is. 40:10
Strengthening . . . . . Ps. 89:21
Protecting . . . . . Deut. 7:19
Destroying . . . . . Is. 30:30

Arm of the wicked—*expression for molestation*
Shall be broken . . . . . Ps. 10:15

SUBJECT REFERENCE

Armageddon—*Mount Megiddo; site of*
Historic wars . . . . . Judg. 5:19
Notable deaths . . . . . 1 Sam. 31:8
Final battle . . . . . Rev. 16:16

Armenia—*land southeast of Black Sea*
Assassins flee to . . . . . 2 Kin. 19:37
See Ararat

Armholes
Armpits, protected with rags . . . . . Jer. 38:12
Articles of alluring dress . . . . . Ezek. 13:18

Armoni—*belonging to the palace*
A son of Saul . . . . . 2 Sam. 21:8-11

Armor—*a protective article of warfare*
A. *As a protective weapon:*
Shield . . . . . 1 Sam. 17:7, 41
Helmet . . . . . 1 Sam. 17:38
Scale-armor . . . . . 1 Sam. 17:5, 38
1 Kin. 22:34
Greaves . . . . . 1 Sam. 17:6
Girdle . . . . . 1 Sam. 18:4
Body armor . . . . . 2 Chr. 26:14
B. *As an aggressive weapon:*
Rod . . . . . Ps. 2:9
Sling . . . . . 1 Sam. 17:40
Bow and arrow . . . . . 2 Sam. 1:18
Spear . . . . . Is. 2:4
Sword . . . . . 1 Sam. 17:51

Armor bearer—*man who bears the arms of another*
Assists kings in battle . . . . . Judg. 9:54
David serves Saul as . . . . . 1 Sam. 16:21
Jonathan's, a man of courage . . . . . 1 Sam. 14:7, 12
Saul's, dies with him . . . . . 1 Sam. 31:4-6
Goliath's, precedes him . . . . . 1 Sam. 17:7, 41

Armor, spiritual
The Christian's, complete . . . . . Eph. 6:11-17
1 Thess. 5:8
Of light . . . . . Rom. 13:12
Of righteousness . . . . . 2 Cor. 6:7
The Bible, the sword . . . . . Eph. 6:17
Not of flesh . . . . . 2 Cor. 10:4, 5

Armory—*an arsenal*
Armor stored in . . . . . Neh. 3:19
God's, opened for war . . . . . Jer. 50:25
David's, well stocked . . . . . Song 4:4

Army—*men organized and disciplined for battle*
A. *Consisted of:*
Men over 20 . . . . . Num. 1:3
Infantrymen . . . . . 2 Chr. 25:5
Archers . . . . . 1 Chr. 5:18
Sling stones . . . . . 2 Chr. 26:14
Chariots . . . . . 1 Kin. 4:26
Foreigners . . . . . 2 Sam. 15:18
Choice men . . . . . 2 Sam. 10:7-9
B. *Commanded by:*
God . . . . . Josh. 5:14
Judges . . . . . Judg. 11:1, 6, 32
Captain . . . . . 2 Sam. 2:8
Kings . . . . . 2 Sam. 12:28, 29
C. *Commands regarding:*
Use of chariots . . . . . Deut. 17:16
Deferred certain classes . . . . . Num. 2:33
Deut. 20:1-9
Division of spoil . . . . . 1 Sam. 30:21-25
Fearfulness . . . . . Deut. 20:1
D. *Units of:*
Fifties . . . . . 2 Kin. 1:9
Hundreds . . . . . Num. 31:14, 48
Legions . . . . . Matt. 26:53
Bands . . . . . Acts 21:31
Guards . . . . . Acts 28:16
Quaternions . . . . . Acts 12:4
Thousands . . . . . Num. 31:14, 48
E. *Of Israel, conquered:*
Egyptians . . . . . Ex. 14:19-31
Jericho . . . . . Josh. 6:1-25
Midianites . . . . . Judg. 7:1-23
Philistines . . . . . 1 Sam. 14:14-23
Syrians . . . . . 2 Kin. 7:1-15
Assyrians . . . . . 2 Kin. 19:35, 36

Army, Christian
A. *Warfare against:*
The world . . . . . James 4:4
1 John 2:15-17

SUBJECT REFERENCE

The flesh . . . . . Gal. 5:17-21
Satan . . . . . 1 Pet. 5:8, 9
Evil men . . . . . 2 Tim. 3:8
False teachers . . . . . Jude 3, 4
Spiritual wickedness . . . . . Eph. 6:12
Worldly "vain babblings" . . . . . 1 Tim. 6:20
B. *Equipment for:*
Sufficient for total war . . . . . Eph. 6:12-17
1 Thess. 5:8
Spiritual in nature . . . . . 2 Cor. 10:3, 4
Sharper than any sword . . . . . Heb. 4:12
C. *The soldier in, must:*
Enlist . . . . . Matt. 28:18-20
Obey . . . . . 2 Cor. 10:5, 6
Please captain . . . . . 2 Tim. 2:4
Use self-control . . . . . 1 Cor. 9:25-27
Stand firm . . . . . Eph. 6:13-17
Endure hardship . . . . . 2 Tim. 2:3
Show courage . . . . . 2 Tim. 4:7-18
Fight hard . . . . . 1 Tim. 6:12
Be pure . . . . . 1 Pet. 2:11, 12
Be alert . . . . . 1 Pet. 5:8
Be faithful . . . . . 1 Tim. 1:18-20
D. *Jesus Christ, the Captain of, is:*
Perfect . . . . . Heb. 2:10
Undefiled . . . . . Heb. 7:26
Powerful . . . . . 2 Thess. 2:8

Arnan—*strong*
A descendant of David . . . . . 1 Chr. 3:21

Arnon—*a river*
Boundary between Moab and Ammon . . . . . Num. 21:13, 26
Border of Reuben . . . . . Deut. 3:12, 16
Ammonites reminded of . . . . . Judg. 11:18-26

Arod—*hunchbacked*
A son of Gad . . . . . Num. 26:17
Called Arodi . . . . . Gen. 46:16

Aroer—*naked*
1. A town in east Jordan . . . . . Deut. 2:36
An Amorite boundary city . . . . . Josh. 13:9, 10, 16
Sihon ruled . . . . . Josh. 12:2
Assigned to Reuben . . . . . Deut. 3:12
Rebuilt by Gadites . . . . . Num. 32:34
Beginning of David's census . . . . . 2 Sam. 24:5
Taken by Hazael . . . . . 2 Kin. 10:32
Possessed by Moab . . . . . Jer. 48:19
2. A city of Judah . . . . . 1 Sam. 30:28
3. A city of Gad . . . . . Josh. 13:25

Aroma—*a pleasant smell*
Of sacrifices . . . . . Lev. 26:31
Figurative of gifts . . . . . Phil. 4:18

Arpad—*a couch, resting place*
A town in Samaria . . . . . 2 Kin. 18:34
End of, predicted . . . . . Jer. 49:23

Arphaxad
A son of Shem . . . . . Gen. 10:22, 24
Born two years after the flood . . . . . Gen. 11:10-13
An ancestor of Christ . . . . . Luke 3:36

Arrogance—*overbearing pride*
Mentioned with other evils . . . . . Prov. 8:13
To be punished by God . . . . . Is. 13:11
Seen in haughtiness . . . . . Jer. 48:29

Arrows—*sharp instruments hurled by a bow*
A. *Uses of:*
Hunting . . . . . Gen. 27:3
Send message . . . . . 1 Sam. 20:20-22
Divination . . . . . Ezek. 21:21
Prophecy . . . . . 2 Kin. 13:14-19
War . . . . . 2 Kin. 19:32
B. *Described as:*
Deadly . . . . . Prov. 26:18
Sharp . . . . . Ps. 120:4
Bright . . . . . Jer. 51:11
Like lightning . . . . . Zech. 9:14
C. *Figurative of:*
God's judgments . . . . . Deut. 32:23, 42
Intense affliction . . . . . Job 6:4
Wicked intentions . . . . . Ps. 11:2
Messiah's mission . . . . . Ps. 45:5
Bitter words . . . . . Ps. 64:3

SUBJECT ... REFERENCE

God's power ... Ps. 76:3
Daily hazards ... Ps. 91:5
Children ... Ps. 127:4
A false witness ... Prov. 25:18
A deceitful tongue ... Jer. 9:8

Arson—*setting fire to property maliciously*

A. *Features concerning:*
A law forbidding ... Ex. 22:6
A means of revenge ... Judg. 12:1

B. *Instances of, by:*
Samson ... Judg. 15:4, 5
Danites ... Judg. 18:27
Absalom ... 2 Sam. 14:30
Enemies ... Ps. 74:7, 8

Art

Ointment after the ... Ex. 30:25
Spices prepared by ... 2 Chr. 16:14
Stones graven by ... Acts 17:29

Artaxerxes—*great king*

Artaxerxes I, king of Persia (465-425 B.C.), authorizes Ezra's mission to Jerusalem ... Ezra 7:1-28
Temporarily halts rebuilding program at Jerusalem ... Ezra 4:7-23
Commissions Nehemiah's mission ... Neh. 2:1-10
Permits Nehemiah to return ... Neh. 13:6

Artemas—*gift of Artemis*

Paul's companion at Nicopolis ... Titus 3:12

Artemis—*the mother-goddess of Asia Minor* (known as Cybele)

Worship of, at Ephesus, creates uproar ... Acts 19:23-41

Artificers—*skilled workmen*

Tubal-cain, the earliest ... Gen. 4:22
Employed in temple construction ... 1 Chr. 29:5
Removed in judgment ... Is. 3:1-3

Arts and crafts in the Bible

Apothecary ... Ex. 30:25, 35
Armorer ... 1 Sam. 8:12
Artificer ... Gen. 4:22
Baker ... Gen. 40:1
Barber ... Ezek. 5:1
Brickmaker ... Ex. 5:7
Calker ... Ezek. 27:9
Carpenter ... Mark 6:3
Carver ... Ex. 31:5
Confectioner ... 1 Sam. 8:13
Cook ... 1 Sam. 8:13
Coppersmith ... 2 Tim. 4:14
Draftsman ... Ezek. 4:1
Dyer ... Ex. 25:5
Embalmer ... Gen. 50:2, 3
Embroiderer ... Ex. 35:35
Engraver ... Ex. 28:11
Fisherman ... Matt. 4:18
Fuller ... Mark 9:3
Gardener ... John 20:15
Goldsmith ... Is. 40:19
Husbandman ... Gen. 4:2
Jeweler ... Ex. 28:17-21
Lapidary ... Ex. 35:33
Mariner ... Ezek. 27:8, 9
Mason ... 2 Sam. 5:11
Moulder ... Ex. 32:4
Musician ... 2 Sam. 6:5
Needleworker ... Ex. 26:36
Painting ... Jer. 22:14
Potter ... Jer. 18:3
Porter ... 2 Sam. 18:26
Refiner ... Mal. 3:2, 3
Ropemaker ... Judg. 16:11
Sewing ... Ezek. 13:18
Ship building ... 1 Kin. 9:26
Silversmith ... Acts 19:24
Smelter ... Job 28:1, 2
Smith ... 1 Sam. 13:19
Spinner ... Prov. 31:19
Stonecutter ... Ex. 31:5
Tailor ... Ex. 28:3, 4
Tanner ... Acts 10:6
Tentmaking ... Acts 18:3
Watchman ... 2 Sam. 18:26
Weaver ... Ex. 35:35
Winemaker ... Neh. 13:15
Worker in metal ... Ex. 31:3, 4
Writer ... Judg. 5:14

SUBJECT ... REFERENCE

Aruboth—*the lattices*

A town in one of Solomon's districts ... 1 Kin. 4:10

Arumah—*height*

A village near Shechem; Abimelech's refuge ... Judg. 9:41

Arvad—*wandering*

A Phoenician city built on an island north of Tyre ... Ezek. 27:8, 11

Arvadites—*inhabitants of Arvad*

Of Canaanite ancestry ... Gen. 10:18; 1 Chr. 1:16

Arza—*earth*

King Elah's steward in Tirzah ... 1 Kin. 16:9

Asa—*physician*

1. Third king of Judah ... 1 Kin. 15:8-10
   Reigns 10 years in peace ... 2 Chr. 14:1
   Overthrows idolatry ... 2 Chr. 14:2-5
   Removes his mother ... 1 Kin. 15:13
   Fortifies Judah ... 2 Chr. 14:6-8
   Defeats the Ethiopians ... 2 Chr. 14:9-15
   Leads in national revival ... 2 Chr. 15:1-15
   Hires Ben-hadad against Baasha ... 2 Chr. 16:1-6
   Reproved by a prophet ... 2 Chr. 16:7-10
   Diseased, seeks physicians rather than the Lord ... 2 Chr. 16:12
   Buried in Jerusalem ... 2 Chr. 16:13, 14
   An ancestor of Christ ... Matt. 1:7
2. A Levite among returnees ... 1 Chr. 9:16

Asahel—*God has made*

1. A son of Zeruiah, David's sister ... 1 Chr. 2:16
   Noted for valor ... 2 Sam. 2:18; 2 Sam. 23:24
   Pursues Abner ... 2 Sam. 2:19
   Killed by Abner ... 2 Sam. 2:23
   Avenged by Joab ... 2 Sam. 3:27, 30
   Made a commander in David's army ... 1 Chr. 27:7
2. A Levite teacher ... 2 Chr. 17:8
3. A collector of tithes ... 2 Chr. 31:13
4. A priest who opposes Ezra's reforms ... Ezra 10:15

Asaiah—*Jehovah has made*

1. A Simeonite chief ... 1 Chr. 4:36
2. A Levite during David's reign ... 1 Chr. 6:30
   Helps restore ark to Jerusalem ... 1 Chr. 15:6, 11
3. An officer sent to Huldah ... 2 Chr. 34:20-22; 2 Kin. 22:12-14
4. The first born of the Shilonites ... 1 Chr. 9:5
   Probably called Maaseiah ... Neh. 11:5

Asaph—*collector*

1. A Gershonite Levite choir leader in the time of David and Solomon ... 1 Chr. 15:16-19; 1 Chr. 16:4-7; 2 Chr. 5:12
   Called a seer ... 2 Chr. 29:30
   Sons of, made musicians ... 1 Chr. 25:1-9
   Twelve Psalms assigned to ... Ps. 50—83; 2 Chr. 29:30
   Descendants of, among returnees ... Ezra 2:41; Neh. 7:44
   In dedication ceremony ... Ezra 3:10
2. The father of Hezekiah's recorder ... 2 Kin. 18:18, 37
3. A chief forester whom Artaxerxes commands to supply timber to Nehemiah ... Neh. 2:8
4. A Korhite Levite ... 1 Chr. 26:1
   Also called Ebiasaph ... 1 Chr. 9:19

Asareel—*God has bound*

A son of Jehaleleel ... 1 Chr. 4:16

Asarelah—*Jehovah is joined*

A son of Asaph in David's time ... 1 Chr. 25:2
Called Jesharelah ... 1 Chr. 25:14

Ascension—*rising to a higher place*

A. *Descriptive of:*
Physical rising of smoke ... Ex. 19:18; Josh. 8:20, 21

SUBJECT ... REFERENCE

Going uphill ... Luke 19:28
Rising to heaven ... Ps. 139:8
Christ's ascension ... John 6:62
Sinful ambition ... Is. 14:13, 14

B. *Of saints:*
Enoch, translation of ... Gen. 5:24; Heb. 11:5
Elijah, translation of ... 2 Kin. 2:11; Matt. 17:1-9
Christians, at Christ's return ... 1 Thess. 4:13-18; 1 Cor. 15:51, 52

C. *Of Christ:*
Foretold in the Old Testament ... Ps. 68:18; Eph. 4:8-10
Announced by Christ ... Luke 9:51; John 20:17
Forty days after His resurrection ... Luke 24:48-51; Acts 1:1-12
Necessary for the Spirit's coming ... John 16:7
Enters heaven by redemption ... Heb. 6:19, 20; Heb. 9:12, 24
Crowned with glory and honor ... Heb. 2:9
Rules from David's throne ... Acts 2:29-36
Sits at the Father's side ... Eph. 1:20; Heb. 1:3
Intercedes for the saints ... Rom. 8:34
Preparing place for His people ... John 14:2
Highly exalted ... Acts 5:31; Phil. 2:9
Reigns triumphantly ... 1 Cor. 15:24-28; Heb. 10:12, 13
Exercises priestly ministry ... Heb. 4:14-16; Heb. 8:1, 2

Asceticism—*stern restraint upon bodily appetites*

A. *Forms of, seen in:*
Nazarite vow ... Num. 6:1-21
Manoah's wife ... Judg. 13:3-14
Samson ... Judg. 16:16, 17
Elijah's life ... 1 Kin. 19:4-9
The Rechabites ... Jer. 35:1-19
John the Baptist ... Matt. 3:4; Matt. 11:18
Jesus Christ ... Matt. 4:2
Paul ... 1 Cor. 9:27

B. *Teaching concerning:*
Extreme, repudiated ... Luke 7:33-36
False, rejected ... Col. 2:20-23; 1 Tim. 4:3, 4
Some, necessary ... 1 Cor. 9:26, 27; 2 Tim. 2:3, 4
Temporary helpful ... Ezra 8:21-23; 1 Cor. 7:3-9
Figurative of complete consecration ... Matt. 19:12; Rev. 14:1-5

Asenath—*belonging to the goddess Neith*

Daughter of Potiphera and wife of Joseph ... Gen. 41:45
Mother of Manasseh and Ephraim ... Gen. 41:50-52; Gen. 46:20

Ash—*a tree*

Idols made from ... Is. 44:14

Ashamed—*shame instilled by evil doing*

A. *Caused by:*
Mistreatment ... 2 Sam. 10:4, 5
Sad tidings ... 2 Kin. 8:11-13
Transgression ... Ps. 25:3
Inconsistent action ... Ezra 8:22
Idolatry ... Is. 44:9-17
Rebellion against God ... Is. 45:24
Lewdness ... Ezek. 16:27
False prophecy ... Zech. 13:3, 4
Rejecting God's mercy ... Is. 65:13
Unbelief ... Mark 8:38
Unpreparedness ... 2 Cor. 9:4

B. *Avoidance of, by:*
Waiting for the Lord ... Ps. 34:5; Is. 49:23
Regarding God's commands ... Ps. 119:6
Sound in statutes ... Ps. 119:80
Trusting God ... Ps. 25:20
Believing in Christ ... Rom. 9:33; Rom. 10:11
Christian diligence ... 2 Tim. 2:15

SUBJECT — REFERENCE

Assurance of faith .... 2 Tim. 1:12
Abiding in Christ .... 1 John 2:28

C. *Possible objects of, in the Christian's life:*
Life's plans .... Phil. 1:20
God's message .... 2 Tim. 1:8
The Gospel .... Rom. 1:16
The old life .... Rom. 6:21
One's faith .... 1 Pet. 4:16

Ashan—*smoke*
A city of Judah .... Josh. 15:42
Later allotted to Judah .... Josh. 19:7
Assigned to the Levites .... 1 Chr. 6:59

Ashbea—*let me call as witness*
A descendant of Shelah .... 1 Chr. 4:21

Ashbel—*having a long upper lip*
A son of Benjamin .... Gen. 46:21; 1 Chr. 8:1
Progenitor of the Ashbelites .... Num. 26:38

Ashdod—*stronghold, fortress*
One of five Philistine cities .... Josh. 13:3
Anakim refuge .... Josh. 11:22
Assigned to Judah .... Josh. 15:46, 47
Seat of Dagon worship .... 1 Sam. 5:1-8
Captured by Tartan .... Is. 20:1
Opposed Nehemiah .... Neh. 4:7
Women of, marry Jews .... Neh. 13:23, 24
Called a mingled people .... Jer. 25:20
Called Azotus .... Acts 8:40

Ashdoth-pisgah—*springs of Pisgah*
The slopes of Mt. Pisgah .... Deut. 3:17; Josh. 12:3
Translated "springs" in .... Deut. 4:49

Asher, Aser—*happy*
1. Jacob's second son by Zilpah .... Gen. 30:12, 13
Goes to Egypt with Jacob .... Gen. 46:17
Father of five children .... Gen. 46:17
Blessed by Jacob .... Gen. 49:20
2. The tribe fathered by Asher, Jacob's son .... Deut. 33:24
Census of .... Num. 1:41; Num. 26:47
Tolerant of Canaanites .... Judg. 1:31, 32
Failure of, in national crisis .... Judg. 5:17
Among Gideon's army .... Judg. 6:35; Judg. 7:23
A godly remnant among .... 2 Chr. 30:11
Anna, descendant of .... Luke 2:36-38
3. A town in Manasseh .... Josh. 17:7

Asherah—*a goddess of the Phoenicians and Arameans*
1. Translated "groves," the female counterpart of Baal .... Judg. 3:7; 1 Kin. 18:19
Translated "Ashtaroth" (plural) in .... Judg. 2:13
Asa's mother worships .... 1 Kin. 15:13
Curtains for, made by women .... 2 Kin. 23:7
Vessels of, destroyed by Josiah .... 2 Kin. 23:4
2. Translated "groves," the images (idols) made to Asherah .... 2 Kin. 23:6
Erected by Manasseh in the temple .... 2 Kin. 21:7
Set up by Ahab in Samaria .... 1 Kin. 16:32, 33
3. Translated "groves," the trees or poles symbolizing the worship of Asherah .... Ex. 34:13; Deut. 12:3; Deut. 16:21

Ashes—*the powdery residue of burned material*
A. *Used for:*
A miracle .... Ex. 9:8-10
Purification .... Num. 19:1-10; Heb. 9:13
A disguise .... 1 Kin. 20:38, 41
B. *Symbolic of:*
Mourning .... 2 Sam. 13:19; Esth. 4:1, 3
Dejection .... Job 2:8
Repentance .... Job 42:6; Matt. 11:21
Fasting .... Dan. 9:3
C. *Figurative of:*
Frailty .... Gen. 18:27

SUBJECT — REFERENCE

Destruction .... Ezek. 28:18
Victory .... Mal. 4:3
Worthlessness .... Job 13:12
Transformation .... Is. 61:3
Deceit .... Is. 44:20
Afflictions .... Ps. 102:9
Destruction .... Jer. 6:26

Ashima—*heaven*
A god or idol worshiped by Assyrian colonists at Samaria .... 2 Kin. 17:30

Ashkelon—*holm-oak*
One of five Philistine cities .... Josh. 13:3; Jer. 47:5, 7
Captured by Judah .... Judg. 1:18
Men of, killed by Samson .... Judg. 14:19
Repossessed by Philistines .... 1 Sam. 6:17; 2 Sam. 1:20
Doom of, pronounced by the prophets .... Jer. 47:5, 7; Amos 1:8; Zeph. 2:4, 7; Zech. 9:5

Ashkenaz
1. A descendant of Noah through Japheth .... Gen. 10:3; 1 Chr. 1:6
2. A nation (probably descendants of 1) associated with Ararat, Minni .... Jer. 51:27

Ashnah—*hard, firm*
1. A village of Judah near Zorah .... Josh. 15:33
2. Another village of Judah .... Josh. 15:43

Ashpenaz
The chief of Nebuchadnezzar's eunuchs .... Dan. 1:3

Ashtaroth, Astaroth—(plural of "Ashtoreth")
A city in Bashan; residence of King Og .... Deut. 1:4; Josh. 12:4
Captured by Israel .... Josh. 9:10
Assigned to Manasseh .... Josh. 13:31
Made a Levitical city ("Be-eshterah") .... Josh. 21:27
Uzzia, a native of .... 1 Chr. 11:44

Ashteroth-karnaim—*twin peaks near Ashtaroth*
A fortified city in Gilead occupied by the Rephaims .... Gen. 14:5

Ashtoreth—the name given by Hebrews to the goddess Ashtart (*Astarte*)
A. *A mother goddess of love, fertility and war worshiped by:*
Philistines .... 1 Sam. 31:10
Sidonians .... 1 Kin. 11:5, 33
Hebrews (see below)
B. *Israel's relation to:*
Ensnared by .... Judg. 2:13; Judg. 10:6
Repent of, in Samuel's time .... 1 Sam. 7:3, 4
Worship of, by Solomon .... 1 Kin. 11:5, 33
Destroyed by Josiah .... 2 Kin. 23:13

Ashur—*blackness*
A descendant of Judah .... 1 Chr. 2:24; 1 Chr. 4:5-7

Ashurites
A people belonging to Ish-bosheth's kingdom .... 2 Sam. 2:8, 9

Ashvath—*made*
An Asherite .... 1 Chr. 7:33

Asia—*in New Testament times, the Roman province of proconsular Asia*
People from, at Pentecost .... Acts 2:9, 10
Paul forbidden to preach in .... Acts 16:6
Paul's later ministry in .... Acts 19:1-26
Paul plans to pass by .... Acts 20:16, 17
Converts in, greeted by Paul .... Rom. 16:5
Paul's great conflict in .... 2 Cor. 1:8
Paul writes to saints of .... 1 Pet. 1:1
Seven churches of .... Rev. 1:4, 11

Asiel—*God has made*
A Simeonite .... 1 Chr. 4:35

Asking in prayer
A. *Based upon:*
God's foreknowledge .... Matt. 6:8

SUBJECT — REFERENCE

God's willingness .... Luke 11:11-13
God's love .... John 16:23-27
Abiding in Christ .... John 15:7
B. *Receiving of answer, based upon:*
Having faith .... James 1:5, 6
Keeping God's commands .... 1 John 3:22
Regarding God's will .... 1 John 5:14, 15
Believing trust .... Matt. 21:22
Unselfishness .... James 4:2, 3
In Christ's name .... John 14:13, 14; John 15:16

Asnah—*thornbush*
The head of a family of Nethinims .... Ezra 2:50

Asnapper—(probably the Aramaean name for "*Ashurbanipal*", an Assyrian king)
Called "the great and noble" .... Ezra 4:10

Asp—*a deadly snake*
Figurative of man's evil nature .... Deut. 32:33; Rom. 3:13
Figurative of man's changed nature .... Is. 11:8

Aspatha—*horse-given*
A son of Haman .... Esth. 9:7

Aspiration—*exalted desire combined with holy zeal*
A. *Centered in:*
God Himself .... Ps. 42:1, 2
God's kingdom .... Matt. 6:33
The high calling .... Phil. 3:10-14
Heaven .... Col. 3:1, 2
Acceptableness with Christ .... 2 Tim. 2:4
B. *Inspired by:*
Christ's love .... 2 Cor. 5:14-16
Work yet to be done .... Rom. 15:18-20; 2 Cor. 10:13-18
Christ's grace .... 2 Cor. 12:9-15
The reward .... 2 Tim. 4:7, 8
The Lord's return .... Matt. 24:42-47; 1 John 3:1-3
World's end .... 2 Pet. 3:11-14

Asriel, Ashriel—*God has filled with joy*
A descendant of Manasseh and progenitor of the Asrielites .... Num. 26:31; Josh. 17:2; 1 Chr. 7:14

Ass—*donkey*
A. *Used for:*
Riding .... Gen. 22:3
Carrying burdens .... Gen. 42:26
Food .... 2 Kin. 6:25
Royalty .... Judg. 5:10
B. *Regulations concerning:*
Not to be yoked with an ox .... Deut. 22:10
To be rested on Sabbath .... Ex. 23:12; Luke 13:15
To be redeemed with a lamb .... Ex. 34:20
C. *Special features regarding:*
Spoke to Balaam .... Num. 22:28-31
Knowing his owner .... Is. 1:3
Jawbone kills many .... Judg. 15:15-17
Jesus rides upon one .... Zech. 9:9; Matt. 21:2, 5
All cared for by God .... Ps. 104:11
D. *Figurative of:*
Wildness (in Hebrew, "wild ass") .... Gen. 16:12
Stubbornness .... Hos. 8:9
Promiscuity .... Jer. 2:24

Assassination—*killing by secret and sudden assault*
A. *Actual cases of:*
Eglon by Ehud .... Judg. 3:21
Sisera by Jael .... Judg. 4:17-21
Abner by Joab .... 2 Sam. 3:27
Ish-bosheth by sons of Rimmon .... 2 Sam. 4:5-8
Amnon by Absalom .... 2 Sam. 13:28, 29
Absalom by Joab .... 2 Sam. 18:14
Amasa by Joab .... 2 Sam. 20:10
Elah by Zimri .... 1 Kin. 16:10
Ben-hadad by Hazael .... 2 Kin. 8:7, 15

SUBJECT — REFERENCE

Jehoram by Jehu ... 2 Kin. 9:24
Ahaziah by Jehu ... 2 Kin. 9:27
Jezebel by Jehu ... 2 Kin. 9:30-37
Joash by servants ... 2 Kin. 12:20, 21
Zechariah by Shallum ... 2 Kin. 15:10
Shallum by Menahem ... 2 Kin. 15:14
Pekahiah by Pekah ... 2 Kin. 15:25
Pekah by Hoshea ... 2 Kin. 15:30
Amon by servants ... 2 Kin. 21:23
Gedaliah by Ishmael ... 2 Kin. 25:25
Sennacherib by his sons ... 2 Kin. 19:37

B. *Attempted cases of:*
Jacob by Esau ... Gen. 27:41-45
Joseph by his brothers ... Gen. 37:18-22
David by Saul ... 1 Sam. 19:10-18
David by Absalom ... 2 Sam. 15:10-14
Joash by Athaliah ... 2 Kin. 11:1-3
Ahasuerus by servants ... Esth. 2:21-23
Jesus by the Jews ... Luke 4:28-30, John 7:1
Paul by the Jews ... Acts 9:23-25, Acts 23:12-31

C. *Crime of:*
Against God's image in man ... Gen. 9:6
Punishable by death ... Ex. 21:12-15, Num. 35:33
Not to be condoned ... Deut. 19:11-13
Puts the guilty under a curse ... Deut. 27:24
Abhorred by the righteous ... 2 Sam. 4:4-12

Assembly—*a large gathering for official business*

A. *Descriptive of:*
Israel as a people ... Num. 10:2-8
Israel as a nation ... Judg. 20:2, 2 Chr. 30:23
God's elect people ... Ps. 111:1
A civil court ... Acts 19:32-41
A church gathering ... James 2:2

B. *Purposes of:*
Proclaim war ... Judg. 10:17, 18, 1 Sam. 14:20
Establish the ark in Zion ... 1 Kin. 8:1-6
Institute reforms ... Ezra 9:4-15, Neh. 9:1, 2
Celebrate victory ... Esth. 9:17, 18
Condemn Christ ... Matt. 26:3, 4, 57
Worship God ... Acts 4:31, Heb. 10:25

C. *Significant ones, at:*
Sinai ... Ex. 19:1-19
Joshua's farewell ... Josh. 23:1-16, Josh. 24:1-28
David's coronation ... 2 Sam. 5:1-3
The Temple's dedication ... 2 Chr. 5:1-14
Josiah's reformation ... 2 Kin. 23:1-3, 21, 22
Ezra's reading the Law ... Neh. 8:1-18
Jesus' trial ... Matt. 27:11-26
Pentecost ... Acts 2:1-21
The Jerusalem Council ... Acts 15:5-21

Assent—*agreeing to the truth of a statement or fact*

A. *Concerning good things:*
Accepting God's covenant ... Ex. 19:7, 8
Agreeing to reforms ... 1 Sam. 7:3, 4, Ezra 10:1-12, 19
Accepting a Scriptural decision ... Acts 15:13-22
Receiving Christ as Savior ... Rom. 10:9, 10

B. *Concerning evil things:*
Tolerating idolatry ... Jer. 44:15-19
Condemning Christ to death ... Matt. 27:17-25
Putting Stephen to death ... Acts 7:51-60
Refusing to hear the Gospel ... Acts 13:44-51

Asshur—*level plain*

1. One of the sons of Shem; progenitor of the Assyrians ... Gen. 10:22, 1 Chr. 1:17
2. The chief god of the Assyrians; seen in names like Ashurbanipal (Asnapper) ... Ezra 4:10
3. A city in Assyria or the nation of Assyria ... Num. 24:22, 24, Ps. 83:8, Ezek. 27:23, Ezek. 32:22

Asshurim—*mighty ones*

Descendants of Abraham by Keturah ... Gen. 25:3

Assir—*prisoner*

1. A son of Korah ... Ex. 6:24, 1 Chr. 6:22
2. A son of Ebiasaph ... 1 Chr. 6:23, 37
3. A son of King Jeconiah ... 1 Chr. 3:17

Assistance, divine

A. *Offered, in:*
Battle ... 2 Chr. 20:5-15
Trouble ... Ps. 50:15
Crises ... Luke 21:14, 15
Prayer ... Rom. 8:16-27
Testimony ... 2 Tim. 4:17
Guidance ... James 1:5-8

B. *Given:*
Internally ... Phil. 2:13, Heb. 13:21
By God ... 2 Cor. 8:9
By Christ ... Phil. 4:13
By the Spirit ... Zech. 4:6
By God's Word ... 1 Thess. 2:13
By grace ... 1 Cor. 15:10
By prayer ... James 5:15-18
By trusting God ... Ps. 37:3-7
By God's providence ... Rom. 8:28

Association—*joining together for mutually beneficial purposes*

A. *Among believers, hindered by:*
Sin ... Acts 5:1-11
Friction ... Acts 6:1-6
Inconsistency ... Gal. 2:11-14
Disagreement ... Acts 15:36-40
Selfishness ... 3 John 9-11
Ambition ... Matt. 20:20-24
Error ... 2 John 7-11
Partiality ... James 2:1-5

B. *Among believers, helped by:*
Common faith ... Acts 2:42-47
Mutual helpfulness ... Gal. 6:1-5
United prayer ... Matt. 18:19, 20
Impending dangers ... Neh. 4:1-23
Grateful praise ... Acts 4:23-33

See Alliance with evil; Fellowship

Assos—*a seaport of Mysia in Asia Minor*

Paul walks to, from Troas ... Acts 20:13, 14

Assurance—*the security of knowing that one's name is written in heaven*

A. *Objects of, one's:*
Election ... 1 Thess. 1:4
Adoption ... Eph. 1:4, 5
Union with Christ ... 1 Cor. 6:15
Possession of eternal life ... John 5:24, 1 John 5:13
Peace ... Rom. 5:1

B. *Steps in:*
Believing God's Word ... 1 Thess. 2:13
Accepting Christ as Savior ... Rom. 10:9, 10
Standing upon the promises ... John 10:28-30
Desiring spiritual things ... 1 Pet. 2:2
Growing in grace ... 2 Pet. 1:5-11
Knowing life is changed ... 2 Cor. 5:17, 1 John 3:14-22
Having inner peace and joy ... Rom. 15:12, 13, Phil. 4:7
Victorious living ... 1 John 5:4, 5
The Spirit's testimony ... Rom. 8:15, 16
Absolute assurance ... Rom. 8:33-39, 2 Tim. 1:12

C. *Compatible with:*
A nature still subject to sin ... 1 John 1:8-10, 1 John 2:1
Imperfection of life ... Gal. 6:1
Limited knowledge ... 1 Cor. 13:9-12
Fatherly chastisement ... Heb. 12:5-11

Assyria—*the nation ruled from Asshur* (first) *and Nineveh* (later)

A. *Significant facts regarding:*
Of remote antiquity ... Gen. 2:14
Of Shem's ancestry ... Gen. 10:22
Founded by Nimrod ... Gen. 10:8-12, Mic. 5:6
Nineveh, chief city of ... Gen. 10:11
Tigris river flows through ... Gen. 2:14
Proud nation ... Is. 10:5-15
A cruel military power ... Nah. 3:1-19
Agent of God's purposes ... Is. 7:17-20, Is. 10:5, 6

B. *Contacts of, with Israel:*
Pul (Tiglath-pileser III, 745–727 B.C.) captures Damascus ... Is. 8:4
Puts Menahem under tribute ... 2 Kin. 15:19, 20
Occasions Isaiah's prophesy ... Is. 7–8
Puts Pekah under tribute ... 2 Kin. 15:29
Shalmaneser (727-722 B.C.) besieges Samaria ... 2 Kin. 17:3-5
Sargon II (722-705 B.C.) captures Israel ... 2 Kin. 17:6-41

C. *Contacts of, with Judah:*
Sargon's general takes Ashdod (in Philistia) ... Is. 20:1-6
Sennacherib (704-681 B.C.) invades Judah ... 2 Kin. 18:13
Puts Hezekiah under tribute ... 2 Kin. 18:14-16
Threatens Hezekiah through Rabshakeh ... 2 Kin. 18:17-37
Army of, miraculously slain ... 2 Kin. 19:35
Assassination of, by his sons ... 2 Kin. 19:37

D. *Prophecies concerning:*
Destruction of, anciently foretold ... Num. 24:22-24
Israel captive in land of ... Hos. 10:6, Hos. 11:5
Doom of, mentioned ... Is. 10:12, 19, Is. 14:24, 25
End eulogized ... Nah. 3:1-19
Shares, figuratively, in Gospel blessings ... Is. 19:23-25

Astonishment—*an emotion of perplexed amazement*

A. *Caused by:*
God's judgments ... 1 Kin. 9:8, 9, Jer. 18:16
Racial intermarriage ... Ezra 9:2-4
Utter desolation ... Jer. 50:13
Urgent message ... Ezek. 3:15
A miracle ... Dan. 3:24
King's dream ... Dan. 4:19
An unexplained vision ... Dan. 8:27
Christ's knowledge ... Luke 2:47
Christ's teaching ... Luke 4:32
Christ's miracles ... Mark 5:42, Luke 5:9
Gentile conversions ... Acts 10:45
Miracles ... Acts 12:16, Acts 13:6-12

B. *Applied figuratively to:*
God ... Jer. 14:9
Babylon ... Jer. 51:37, 41
Jerusalem ... Ezek. 4:16, 17, Ezek. 5:5, 15
Priests ... Jer. 4:9

Astrologers—*those who search the heavens for supposed revelations*

Cannot save Babylon ... Is. 47:1, 12-15
Cannot interpret dreams ... Dan. 2:2, 10-13, Dan. 4:7
Cannot decipher handwriting ... Dan. 5:7, 8
Daniel surpasses ... Dan. 1:20
Daniel made master of ... Dan. 5:11
God does not speak through ... Dan. 2:27, 28

Asuppim—*collectors*

Should be rendered as "storehouse" in ... 1 Chr. 26:15, 17
Same word translated "thresholds" in ... Neh. 12:25

Asylum—*protection, refuge*

Afforded by altar ... 1 Kin. 1:50-53, 1 Kin. 2:28
Cities of refuge ... Ex. 21:12-14, Deut. 19:1-13

Asyncritus—*incomparable*

A Christian at Rome ... Rom. 16:14

Atad—*thorn*

A mourning site east of Jordan ... Gen. 50:9-13

A

SUBJECT REFERENCE

Atarah—*crown*
A wife of Jerahmeel ... 1 Chr. 2:26

Ataroth—*crowns*
1. Town of Gad ... Num. 32:3, 34
2. A town of Ephraim ... Josh. 16:7
3. A town between Ephraim and Benjamin ... Josh. 16:2
   Probably the same as Atarothaddar ... Josh. 16:5; Josh. 18:13
4. A village near Bethlehem ... 1 Chr. 2:54

Ataroth-addar—*crowns of Addar*
A frontier town of Ephraim ... Josh. 16:5
See Ataroth 3

Ater—*crippled one*
1. The ancestors of a family of returnees ... Ezra 2:16; Neh. 7:21
2. The ancestor of a family of porters ... Ezra 2:42; Neh. 7:45
3. A signer of Nehemiah's document ... Neh. 10:17

Athach—*lodging, inn*
A town in south Judah ... 1 Sam. 30:30

Athaiah—*Jehovah is helper*
A Judahite in Nehemiah's time ... Neh. 11:4

Athaliah—*Jehovah is exalted*
1. The daughter of Ahab and Jezebel ... 2 Kin. 8:18, 26; 2 Chr. 22:2, 3
   Destroys all the royal seed except Joash ... 2 Kin. 11:1, 2; 2 Chr. 22:10, 11
   Usurps throne for six years ... 2 Kin. 11:3
   Killed by priestly uprising ... 2 Kin. 11:4-16; 2 Chr. 23:1-21
   Called wicked ... 2 Chr. 24:7
2. A Benjamite ... 1 Chr. 8:26, 27
3. The father of Jeshaiah ... Ezra 8:7

Atharim—*spys*
Israel attacked there ... Num. 21:1

Atheism—*the denial of God's existence*
A. *Defined as:*
   The fool's philosophy ... Ps. 14:1; Ps. 53:1
   Living without God ... Rom. 1:20-32; Eph. 2:12
B. *Manifestations of, seen in:*
   Defiance of God ... Ex. 5:2; 2 Kin. 18:19-35
   Irreligion ... Titus 1:16
   Corrupt morals ... Rom. 13:12, 13; 1 Pet. 4:3
C. *Evidences against, seen in:*
   Man's inner conscience ... Rom. 2:14, 15
   Design in nature ... Job 38:1-41; Job 39:1-30
   God's works ... Ps. 19:1-6
   God's providence ... Ps. 104:1-35; Acts 14:17
   Clear evidence ... Rom. 1:19, 20
   The testimony of pagans ... Dan. 4:24-37
   Fulfillment of prophecy ... Is. 41:20-23; Is. 46:8-11

Athens—*a Greek city named after the goddess Athena*
Paul preaches in ... Acts 17:15-34
Paul resides in ... 1 Thess. 3:1

Athlai—*Jehovah is strong*
A Jew who divorced his foreign wife ... Ezra 10:28

Athletes
Discipline ... 1 Cor. 9:24-27
Removal of weights ... Heb. 12:1
Prize ... Phil. 3:14

Atonement—*reconciliation of the guilty by divine sacrifice*
A. *Elements involved in, seen in:*
   Man's sin ... Ex. 32:30; Ps. 51:3, 4
   The blood sacrificed ... Lev. 16:11, 14-20; Heb. 9:13-22
   Guilt transferred ... Lev. 1:3, 4; 2 Cor. 5:21
   Guilt removed ... Lev. 16:21; 1 Cor. 6:11
   Forgiveness granted ... Lev. 5:10, 11; Rom. 4:6, 7
   Righteousness given ... Rom. 10:3, 4; Phil. 3:9
B. *Fulfilled by Christ:*
   Predicted ... Is. 53:10-12; Dan. 9:24-26
   Symbolized ... Is. 63:1-9; Zech. 3:3-9
   Realized ... Rom. 3:23-26; 1 Pet. 1:18-21

Atonement, Day of
A. *Features regarding:*
   Time specified ... Lev. 23:26, 27
   The ritual involved in ... Lev. 16:3, 5-15
   A time of humiliation ... Lev. 16:29, 31
   Exclusive ministry of the high priest in ... Lev. 16:2, 3; Heb. 9:7
B. *Benefits of, for:*
   The holy place ... Lev. 16:15, 16
   The people ... Lev. 16:17, 24
   The high priest ... Lev. 16:11; Heb. 9:7
C. *Result of, seen in:*
   Atonement for sin ... Rom. 3:25
   Removal of sin ... Heb. 9:8-28; Heb. 13:10-13

Atonement of Christ
A. *Typified by:*
   The paschal lamb ... Ex. 12:5, 11, 14; John 1:29; 1 Cor. 5:7
   The Day of Atonement ... Lev. 16:30, 34; Heb. 9:8-28
B. *What man is:*
   A sinner ... Rom. 5:8
   Alienated in mind ... Col. 1:21
   Strangers ... Eph. 2:12
C. *What God does:*
   Loves us ... John 3:16
   Commends His love to us ... Rom. 5:8
   Sends Christ to save us ... Gal. 4:4
   Spared not His own Son ... Rom. 8:32
D. *What Christ does:*
   Takes our nature ... Heb. 2:14
   Becomes our ransom ... Matt. 20:28
   Dies in our place ... 1 Pet. 3:18
   Dies for our sins ... 1 Pet. 2:24
   Dies as a sacrifice ... Eph. 5:2
   Dies willingly ... John 10:18
   Reconciles us to God ... Rom. 5:10
   Brings us to God ... 1 Pet. 3:18
   Restores our fellowship ... 1 Thess. 5:10
See Blood of Christ
E. *What the believer receives:*
   Forgiveness ... Eph. 1:7
   Peace ... Rom. 5:1
   Reconciliation ... 2 Cor. 5:19
   Righteousness ... 2 Cor. 5:21
   Justification ... Rom. 3:24-26
   Access to God ... Eph. 2:18
   Cleansing ... 1 John 1:7
   Liberty ... Gal. 5:1
   Freedom from the devil's power ... Heb. 2:14
   Christ's intercession ... Heb. 2:17, 18

Atroth-shophan
A city built by the Gadites ... Num. 32:35

Attai—*timely*
1. A half-Egyptian Judahite ... 1 Chr. 2:35, 36
2. A Gadite in David's army ... 1 Chr. 12:11
3. Rehoboam's son ... 2 Chr. 11:20

Attalia—*a seaport town of Pamphylia named after Attalus II*
Paul sails from, to Antioch ... Acts 14:25, 26

Attend
To care for ... Esth. 4:5

Attendance, church
Taught by example ... Acts 11:25-26; Acts 14:27
Not to be neglected ... Heb. 10:25

Attitude—*the state of mind toward something*
A. *Of Christians toward Christ, must:*
   Confess ... Rom. 10:9, 10
   Obey ... John 14:15, 23
   Follow ... Matt. 16:24
   Imitate ... 1 Pet. 2:21
B. *Of Christians toward the world, not to:*
   Conform to ... Rom. 12:2
   Abuse ... 1 Cor. 7:31
   Love ... 1 John 2:15
   Be friend of ... James 4:4
   Be entangled with ... 2 Tim. 2:4
   Be polluted with ... Jude 23
C. *Of Christians toward sinners:*
   Seek their salvation ... 1 Cor. 9:22
   Pray for ... Rom. 9:1-3
   Plead with ... Acts 17:22-31
   Rebuke ... Titus 1:10-13
   Persuade ... 2 Cor. 5:11

Audience—*an assembly of hearers*
Disturbed ... Neh. 13:1-3
Attentive ... Luke 7:1
Hostile ... Luke 4:28-30
Receptive ... Acts 2:1-40
Menacing ... Acts 7:54-60
Rejecting ... Acts 13:44-51
Critical ... Acts 17:22-34
Sympathetic ... Acts 20:17-38
Vast ... Rev. 5:9; Rev. 7:9, 10
See Assembly

Auditorium—*a room for assembly*
Hearing ... Acts 25:23

Augustus' band—*a battalion of Roman soldiers*
Paul placed in custody of ... Acts 27:1

Author—*creator; originator; writer*
God of peace ... 1 Cor. 14:33
Christ of salvation ... Heb. 5:9
Christ of faith ... Heb. 12:2
Solomon of many writings ... 1 Kin. 4:32

Authority—*the lawful right to enforce obedience*
A. *As rulers:*
   Governor ... Acts 23:24, 26; Matt. 10:18
B. *Delegated to, man as:*
   Created ... Gen. 1:26-31
   A legal state ... Esth. 9:29; Luke 22:25
   Agent of the state ... Matt. 8:9; Rom. 13:1-6
   Husband ... 1 Cor. 14:35
   Agent of religious leaders ... Acts 26:10, 12
C. *Christ's, seen in His power:*
   Over demons ... Mark 1:27
   In teaching ... Matt. 7:29
   To forgive ... Luke 5:24
   To judge ... John 5:22, 27
   To rule ... Matt. 2:6; 1 Cor. 15:24; 1 Pet. 3:22
   To commission ... Matt. 28:18-20
D. *Purpose:*
   Protection ... Heb. 13:17
   Instruction ... 1 Pet. 5:2, 3
   Example of Christ's power ... Matt. 8:5-13
   Testimony to unbelievers ... 1 Tim. 6:1; 1 Pet. 3:13-15
E. *Of Christians, given to:*
   Apostles ... 2 Cor. 10:8
   Ministers ... Titus 2:15
   The righteous ... Prov. 29:2

Ava—*a region or city in Assyria*
Colonists from, brought to Samaria by Sargon ... 2 Kin. 17:24
Worshipers of Nibhaz and Tartak ... 2 Kin. 17:31

Avarice—*covetousness; greed*
A. *Productive of:*
   Defeat ... Josh. 7:11, 21

SUBJECT — REFERENCE

Death ... 1 Kin. 21:5-16
Discontent ... James 4:1-4

B. *Examples of:*
Balaam ... 2 Pet. 2:15
Achan ... Josh. 7:20, 21
Ahab ... 1 Kin. 21:1-4
Judas Iscariot ... Matt. 26:15, 16
Ananias and Sapphira ... Acts 5:1-10
Rich men ... Luke 12:16-21; James 5:1-6

Aven—*wickedness*

1. The city of On in Egypt near Cairo; known as Heliopolis ... Gen. 41:45; Ezek. 30:17
2. A name contemptuously applied to Bethel ... Hos. 10:5, 8
3. Valley in Syria ... Amos 1:5

Avenge—*to retaliate for an evil done*

A. *Kinds of:*
Commanded by God ... Num. 31:1, 2
Given strength for ... Judg. 16:28-30
Sought maliciously ... 1 Sam. 18:25
Possible but not done ... 1 Sam. 24:12
Attempted but hindered ... 1 Sam. 25:26-33
Obtained in self-defense ... Esth. 8:12, 13

B. *Sought because of:*
A murdered neighbor ... Num. 35:12; Josh. 20:5
A wife's mistreatment ... Judg. 15:6-8
Judah's sins ... Jer. 5:9
Mistreatment ... Acts 7:24, 25
Impurity ... 1 Thess. 4:5-7

C. *Performed by:*
God Himself ... Lev. 26:25; Luke 18:7, 8
Wicked men ... 2 Sam. 4:8-12
Impetuous general ... 2 Sam. 18:18, 19, 31
An anointed king ... 2 Kin. 9:6, 7
A judge ... Luke 18:3, 5
Jesus Christ ... Rev. 19:2

D. *Restrictions on:*
Personal, prohibited ... Lev. 19:17, 18
Christians prohibited ... Rev. 12:9

Avenger of blood—(literally, "*redeemer of blood*")

An ancient practice ... Gen. 4:14
Seen in kinsman as "redeemer" of enslaved relative ... Lev. 25:25, 47-49; Ruth 4:1-10
Seen also in kinsman as "avenger" of a murdered relative ... Num. 35:11-34
Avenger alone must kill murderer ... Deut. 19:6, 11-13
Practice, of, set aside by David ... 2 Sam. 14:4-11
Same word translated "kinsman" and "redeemer" ... Ruth 4:1; Job 19:25
Figurative of a violent person ... Ps. 8:2

Avim, Avims, Avites—*villagers*

1. A tribe of early Canaanites living near Gaza; absorbed by the Caphtorim (Philistines) ... Deut. 2:23
2. A city of Benjamin near Beth-el ... Josh. 18:23
3. Colonists brought from Ava in Assyria ... 2 Kin. 17:24, 31

Avith—*ruin*

An Edomite city ... Gen. 36:35

Awakening, spiritual

A. *Produced by:*
Returning to Beth-el ... Gen. 35:1-7
Discovering God's Word ... 2 Kin. 22:8-11
Reading God's Word ... Neh. 8:2-18
Confessing sin ... Ezra 10:1-17
Receiving the Spirit ... John 7:38, 39; Acts 2:1-47

B. *Old Testament examples of, under:*
Joshua ... Josh. 24:1-31
Samuel ... 1 Sam. 7:3-6
Elijah ... 1 Kin. 18:21-40
Hezekiah ... 2 Chr. 30:1-27
Josiah ... 2 Kin. 23:1-3
Ezra ... Ezra 10:1-17

C. *New Testament examples of:*
John the Baptist ... Luke 3:2-14
Jesus in Samaria ... John 4:28-42
Philip in Samaria ... Acts 8:5-12
Peter at Lydda ... Acts 9:32-35
Peter with Cornelius ... Acts 10:34-48
Paul at Antioch in Pisidia ... Acts 13:14-52
Paul at Thessalonica ... Acts 17:11, 12; 1 Thess. 1:1-10
Paul at Corinth ... 2 Cor. 7:1-16

Awe—*fear mingled with reverence*

A restraint on sin ... Ps. 4:4
Proper attitude toward God ... Ps. 33:8
Also toward God's Word ... Ps. 119:161

Awl—*a sharp tool for piercing*

Used on the ear as a symbol of perpetual obedience ... Ex. 21:6; Deut. 15:17

Axe—*a sharp instrument for cutting wood*

A. *Used in:*
Cutting timber ... Judg. 9:48
War ... 1 Chr. 20:3
Malicious destruction ... Ps. 74:5-7
A miracle; floated in water ... 2 Kin. 6:5, 6

B. *As a figure of:*
Judgment ... Matt. 3:10
Wrath ... Jer. 51:20-24
God's sovereignty ... Is. 10:15

Axletree—*a shaft on which a wheel is mounted*

Used in the temple ... 1 Kin. 7:32, 33

Azal, Azel

1. A descendant of Jonathan ... 1 Chr. 8:37, 38
2. A place near Jerusalem ... Zech. 14:5

Azaliah—*Jehovah has set aside*

Father of Shaphan ... 2 Kin. 22:3

Azaniah—*Jehovah has heard*

A Levite who signs the document ... Neh. 10:9

Azarael, Azareel—*God has helped*

1. A Levite in David's army at Ziklag ... 1 Chr. 12:6
2. A musician in David's time ... 1 Chr. 25:18
3. A prince of Dan under David ... 1 Chr. 27:22
4. A Jew who divorced his foreign wife ... Ezra 10:41
5. A postexilic priest ... Neh. 11:13
6. A musician in dedication service ... Neh. 12:36

Azariah—*Jehovah has helped*

1. Man of Judah ... 1 Chr. 2:8
2. A Kohathite Levite ... 1 Chr. 6:36
3. A son of Zadok the high priest ... 1 Kin. 4:2
4. A son of Ahimaaz ... 1 Chr. 6:9
5. A great-grandson of Ahimaaz ... 1 Chr. 6:9-10
6. Son of Nathan ... 1 Kin. 4:5
7. A son of Jehu, with Egyptian ancestry ... 1 Chr. 2:34-38
8. A prophet who encourages King Asa ... 2 Chr. 15:1-8
9. Son of King Jehoshaphat ... 2 Chr. 21:2
10. A captain under Jehoiada ... 2 Chr. 23:1
11. Another under Jehoiada ... 2 Chr. 23:1
12. A head of Ephraim ... 2 Chr. 28:12
13. King of Judah ... 2 Kin. 15:1
14. A high priest who rebukes King Uzziah ... 2 Chr. 26:16-20
15. Kohathite, father of Joel ... 2 Chr. 29:12
16. A reforming Levite ... 2 Chr. 29:12
17. Chief priest in time of Hezekiah ... 2 Chr. 31:9, 10
18. A high priest, son of Hilkiah ... 1 Chr. 6:13, 14
19. Ancestor of Ezra ... Ezra 7:1-3
20. An opponent of Jeremiah ... Jer. 43:2
21. The Hebrew name of Abed-nego ... Dan. 1:7
22. Postexilic Jew ... Neh. 7:6, 7
23. A workman under Nehemiah ... Neh. 3:23, 24
24. A prince of Judah ... Neh. 12:32, 33
25. An expounder of the law ... Neh. 8:7
26. A signer of the covenant ... Neh. 10:1, 2
27. A descendant of Hilkiah ... 1 Chr. 9:11

Azaz—*strong*

A Reubenite ... 1 Chr. 5:8

Azaziah—*Jehovah is strong*

1. A musician ... 1 Chr. 15:21
2. Father of Hoshea ... 1 Chr. 27:20
3. A temple overseer ... 2 Chr. 31:13

Azbuk—*pardon*

Father of a certain Nehemiah; but not the celebrated one ... Neh. 3:16

Azekah—*tilled*

Great stones cast upon ... Josh. 10:11
Camp of Goliath ... 1 Sam. 17:1, 4, 17
Fortified by Rehoboam ... 2 Chr. 11:9
Reoccupied after exile ... Neh. 11:30
Besieged by Nebuchadnezzar ... Jer. 34:7

Azem, Ezem—*bone*

A town of Judah ... Josh. 15:29
Allotted to Simeon ... Josh. 19:3
Also called Ezem ... 1 Chr. 4:29

Azgad—*fate is hard*

Head of exile family ... Ezra 2:12; Ezra 8:12
Among document signers ... Neh. 10:15

Aziel—*God strengthens*

A Levite musician ... 1 Chr. 15:20
Called Jaaziel ... 1 Chr. 15:18

Aziza—*strong*

Divorced foreign wife ... Ezra 10:27

Azmaveth—*death is strong*

1. One of David's mighty men ... 2 Sam. 23:31
2. A Benjamite ... 2 Chr. 12:3
3. David's treasurer ... 1 Chr. 27:25
4. A son of Jehoaddah ... 1 Chr. 8:36
5. A village near Jerusalem ... Neh. 12:29
Also called Beth-azmaveth ... Neh. 7:28

Azmon—*strong*

A place in south Canaan ... Num. 34:4, 5

Aznoth-tabor—*peaks of Tabor*

Place in Naphtali ... Josh. 19:34

Azor—*helper*

Ancestor of Christ ... Matt. 1:13, 14

Azotus—*fortress*

Philip went there ... Acts 8:40
Same as Ashdod ... 1 Sam. 6:17

Azriel—*God is a help*

1. A chief of Manasseh ... 1 Chr. 5:24
2. Father of Jerimoth ... 1 Chr. 27:19
3. Father of Seraiah ... Jer. 36:26

Azrikam—*my help has arisen*

1. Son of Neariah ... 1 Chr. 3:23
2. A son of Aziel ... 1 Chr. 8:38
3. A Merarite Levite ... 1 Chr. 9:14
4. Governor under King Ahaz ... 2 Chr. 28:7

Azubah—*forsaken*

1. Wife of Caleb ... 1 Chr. 2:18, 19
2. Mother of Jehoshaphat ... 1 Kin. 22:42

Azur, Azzur—*helpful*

1. Father of Hananiah ... Jer. 28:1
2. Father of Jaazaniah ... Ezek. 11:1
3. A covenant signer ... Neh. 10:17

Azzan—*strong*

Father of Paltiel ... Num. 34:26

SUBJECT REFERENCE

B

Baal—*lord, possessor, husband*

A. *The nature of:*

The male god of the Phoenicians and Canaanites; the counterpart of the female Ashtaroth ... Judg. 10:6
1 Sam. 7:4
Connected with immorality ... Num. 25:3, 5
Hos. 9:10
Incense burned to ... Jer. 7:9
Kissing the image of ... 1 Kin. 19:18
Hos. 13:1, 2
Dervish rites by priests of ... 1 Kin. 18:26, 28
Children burned in fire of ... Jer. 19:5
Eating sacrifices ... Ps. 106:28

B. *History of:*

Among Moabites in Moses' time ... Num. 22:41
Altars built to, during time of judges ... Judg. 2:11-14
Judg. 6:28-32
Jezebel introduces into Israel ... 1 Kin. 16:31, 32
Elijah's overthrow of, on Mt. Carmel ... 1 Kin. 18:17-40
Athaliah introduces it into Judah ... 2 Kin. 11:17-20
2 Chr. 22:2-4
Revived again in Israel and Judah ... Hos. 2:8
Amos 5:26
Ahaz makes images to ... 2 Chr. 28:2-4
Manasseh worships ... 2 Kin. 21:3
Altars everywhere ... Jer. 11:13
Overthrown by Josiah ... 2 Kin. 23:4, 5
Denounced by prophets ... Jer. 19:4, 5
Ezek. 16:20, 21
Historic retrospect ... Rom. 11:4

Baal—*master, possessor*

1. A Benjamite, from Gibeon ... 1 Chr. 8:30
2. A descendant of Reuben ... 1 Chr. 5:5, 6
3. A village of Simeon ... 1 Chr. 4:33
Also called Baalath-beer ... Josh. 19:8

Baalah—*mistress*

1. A town also known as Kirjath-jearim ... Josh. 15:9, 10
2. A hill in Judah ... Josh. 15:11
3. A town in South Judah ... Josh. 15:29
Probably the same as Bilhah ... 1 Chr. 4:29
May be the same as Balah ... Josh. 19:3

Baalath—*mistress*

A village of Dan ... Josh. 19:44
Fortified by Solomon ... 1 Kin. 9:18

Baalath-beer—*mistress of the well*

A border town of Simeon ... Josh. 19:8
Called Ramath of the south ... Josh. 19:8
Also called Baal ... 1 Chr. 4:33

Baal-berith—*lord of covenant*

A god (Baal) of Shechem ... Judg. 8:33
Judg. 9:4
Also called El-berith ... Judg. 9:46

Baale—*judah*

A town of Judah ... 2 Sam. 6:2
Also called Baalah and Kirjath-jearim ... Josh. 15:9, 10

Baal-gad—*lord of good fortune*

A place in the valley of Lebanon ... Josh. 11:17

Baal-hamon—*lord of a multitude*

Site of Solomon's vineyard ... Song 8:11

Baal-hanan—*lord of grace*

1. Edomite king ... Gen. 36:38
2. David's gardener ... 1 Chr. 27:28

Baal-hazor—*lord of a village*

A place near Ephraim ... 2 Sam. 13:23

Baal-hermon—*lord of Hermon*

A mountain east of Jordan ... Judg. 3:3

Baali—*my master* (lord)

A title rejected by Jehovah ... Hos. 2:16

Baalim—*lords* (plural of Baal)

Deities of Canaanite polytheism ... Judg. 10:10-14

SUBJECT REFERENCE

Ensnared Israelites ... Judg. 2:11
Judg. 3:7
Rejected in Samuel's time ... 1 Sam. 7:4
Historic reminder ... 1 Sam. 12:10

Baalis

An Ammonite king ... Jer. 40:14

Baal-meon—*lord of Meon* (habitation)

An Amorite city on the Moabite boundary ... Ezek. 25:9
Rebuilt by Reubenites ... Num. 32:38
Josh. 13:17

Baal-peor, Baal of Peor—*lord of Peor*

A Moabite god ... Num. 25:1-5
Infected Israel; 24,000 died ... Num. 25:1-9
Vengeance taken on ... Num. 31:1-18
Sin long remembered ... Deut. 4:3, 4
Josh. 22:17
Ps. 106:28, 29
Historic reminder ... 1 Cor. 10:8

Baal-perazim—*lord of breaking through*

Where David defeated the Philistines ... 2 Sam. 5:18-20
Same as Perazim ... Is. 28:21

Baal-shalisha—*lord of Shalisha* (a third)

A place from which Elisha received food ... 2 Kin. 4:42-44

Baal-tamar—*lord of the palm*

A place in Benjamin ... Judg. 20:33

Baal-zebub—*lord of flies*

A Philistine god at Ekron ... 2 Kin. 1:2
Ahaziah inquired of ... 2 Kin. 1:2, 6, 16
Also called Beelzebub ... Matt. 10:25
Matt. 12:24

Baal-zephon—*lord of darkness*

Israelite camp site ... Ex. 14:2, 9
Num. 33:7

Baana—*affliction*

1. Supply officer ... 1 Kin. 4:12
2. Zadok's father ... Neh. 3:4

Baanah—*affliction*

1. A murderer of Ish-bosheth ... 2 Sam. 4:1-12
2. Heled's father ... 1 Chr. 11:30
3. A returning exile ... Ezra 2:2
Neh. 7:7
Signs document ... Neh. 10:27
4. Supply officer ... 1 Kin. 4:16

Baara—*foolish*

Shaharaim's wife ... 1 Chr. 8:8

Baaseiah—*work of Jehovah*

A Levite ancestor of Asaph ... 1 Chr. 6:40

Baasha—*boldness*

Gains throne by murder ... 1 Kin. 15:27, 28
Kills Jeroboam's household ... 1 Kin. 15:29, 30
Wars against Asa ... 1 Kin. 15:16, 32
Restricts access to Judah ... 1 Kin. 15:17
Contravened by Asa's league with Ben-hadad ... 1 Kin. 15:18-22
Evil reign ... 1 Kin. 15:33, 34

Babbler—*an inane talker*

The mumblings of drunkards ... Prov. 23:29-35
Like a serpent ... Eccl. 10:11
Paul called such ... Acts 17:18
Paul's warnings against ... 1 Tim. 6:20
2 Tim. 2:16

Babe—*an infant child*

A. *Natural:*

Moses ... Ex. 2:6
John Baptist ... Luke 1:41, 44
Christ ... Luke 2:12, 16
Timothy ... 2 Tim. 3:15
Offspring ... Ps. 17:14

B. *Figurative of:*

Unenlightened ... Rom. 2:20
True believers ... Matt. 11:25
Matt. 21:16
New Christians ... 1 Pet. 2:2
Carnal Christians ... 1 Cor. 3:1
Heb. 5:13

SUBJECT REFERENCE

Babel—*confusion*

A city built by Nimrod in the plain of Shinar ... Gen. 10:10

Babel, Tower of

A huge brick structure intended to magnify man and preserve the unity of the race ... Gen. 11:1-4
Objectives thwarted by God ... Gen. 11:5-9

Babylon, city of

A. *History of:*

Built by Nimrod ... Gen. 10:9, 10
Tower built there ... Gen. 11:1-9
Amraphel's capital ... Gen. 14:1
Once the capital of Assyria ... 2 Chr. 33:11
Greatest power under Nebuchadnezzar ... Dan. 4:30
A magnificent city ... Is. 13:19
Is. 14:4
Wide walls of ... Jer. 51:44
Gates of ... Is. 45:1, 2
Bel, god of ... Is. 46:1
Jews carried captive to ... 2 Kin. 25:1-21
2 Chr. 36:5-21

B. *Inhabitants, described as:*

Idolatrous ... Jer. 50:35, 38
Dan. 3:18
Enslaved by magic ... Is. 47:1, 9-13
Sacrilegious ... Dan. 5:1-3

C. *Prophecies concerning:*

Babylon, God's agent ... Jer. 25:9
Jer. 27:5-8
God fights with ... Jer. 21:1-7
Jews, 70 years in ... Jer. 25:12
Jer. 29:10
First of great empires ... Dan. 2:31-38
Dan. 7:2-4
Downfall of ... Is. 13:1-22
Jer. 50:1-46
Cyrus, God's agent ... Is. 45:1-4
Perpetual desolation of ... Is. 13:19-22
Jer. 50:13, 39

Babylon in the New Testament

A. *The city on the Euphrates*

Listed as a point of reference ... Matt. 1:11, 12, 17
As the place of Israel's exile ... Acts 7:43
As the place of Peter's residence ... 1 Pet. 5:13

B. *The prophetic city*

Fall predicted ... Rev. 14:8
Wrath taken on ... Rev. 16:19
Called "the Mother of Harlots" ... Rev. 17:1-18
Fall described ... Rev. 18:1-24

Babylonians—*sons of Babel*

Inhabitants of Babylonia ... Ezra 4:9
Ezek. 23:15-23

Babylonish garment—*a valuable robe worn in Babylon*

Coveted by Achan ... Josh. 7:21

Baca—*weeping*

Figurative of sorrow ... Ps. 84:6

Bachelor—*unmarried man*

Described literally ... 1 Cor. 7:26-33
Described figuratively ... Is. 56:3, 4
Matt. 19:12
Rev. 14:1-5
Not for elders ... Titus 1:5, 6

Bachrites

Family of Becher ... Num. 26:35

Backbiting—*reviling another in secret; slander*

A fruit of sin ... Rom. 1:30
Expressed by the mouth ... Ps. 50:20
An offspring of anger ... Prov. 25:23
Merits punishment ... Ps. 101:5
Keeps from God ... Ps. 15:1, 3
To be laid aside ... 1 Pet. 2:1
Unworthy of Christians ... 2 Cor. 12:20

Backsliding—*to turn away from God after conversion*

A. *Described as:*

Turning from God ... 1 Kin. 11:9
Turning to evil ... Ps. 125:5

SUBJECT REFERENCE

Turning to Satan ....1 Tim. 5:15
Turning back to the world ...2 Tim. 4:10
Tempting Christ...........1 Cor. 10:9
Turning from first love ......Rev. 2:4
Turning from the Gospel ....Gal. 3:1-5

B. *Prompted by:*
Haughty spirit ....Prov. 16:18
Spiritual blindness ....2 Pet. 1:9
Rev. 3:17
Murmuring ....Ex. 17:3
Lusting after evil ....Ps. 106:14
Material things............Mark 4:18, 19
1 Tim. 6:10
Prosperity ....Deut. 8:11-14
Tribulation ....Matt. 13:20, 21

C. *Results:*
Displeases God ....Ps. 78:56-59
Punishment................Num. 14:43-45
Jer. 8:5-13
Blessings withheld ....Is. 59:2
Unworthiness ....Luke 9:62

D. *Examples of Israel's:*
At Meribah................Ex. 17:1-7
At Sinai..................Ex. 32:1-35
In wilderness ....Ps. 106:14-33
After Joshua's death ....Judg. 2:8-23
Ps. 106:34-43
In Solomon's life ....1 Kin. 11:4-40
Neh. 13:26
During Asa's reign..........2 Chr. 15:3, 4
During Manasseh's reign ....2 Chr. 33:1-10

E. *Examples of, among believers:*
Lot.......................Gen. 19:1-22
David.....................2 Sam. 11:1-5
Ps. 51:1-19
Peter ....Matt. 26:69-75
Luke 22:31, 32
Galatians.................Gal. 1:6
Gal. 4:9-11
Corinthians...............1 Cor. 5:1-13
Churches of Asia ....2 Tim. 1:15
Rev. 2, 3

See Apostasy

Badger—*a specie of dolphin or porpoise*
Skins of, used in tabernacle coverings ....Ex. 26:14; Ex. 35:7
Used for sandals ....Ezek. 16:10

Bag—*a purse or pouch*
A. *Used for:*
Money ....2 Kin. 12:10
John 12:6
Stones ....1 Sam. 17:40, 49
Weights ....Deut. 25:13
Prov. 16:11
Food ("vessels")............1 Sam. 9:7
B. *Figurative of:*
Forgiveness...............Job 14:17
True righteousness..........Prov. 16:11
True riches ....Luke 17:33
Insecure riches ....Hag. 1:6

Barhumite—*a native of Baharum*
Applied to Azmaveth ....2 Sam. 23:31

Bahurim—*young men*
A village near Jerusalem........2 Sam. 3:16
Where Shimei cursed David.....2 Sam. 16:5
Where two men hid in a well....2 Sam. 17:18

Bajith—*house*
A derisive reference to the temple of Moabite gods.........................Is. 15:2

Bakbakkar—*investigator*
A Levite ....1 Chr. 9:15

Bakbuk—*a flask*
Head of postexilic family ....Ezra 2:51
Neh. 7:53

Bakbukiah—*Jehovah has poured out*
1. A Levite of high position ....Neh. 11:17
2. Levite porter..............Neh. 12:25

Baker—*one who cooks food* (bread)
A. *Kinds of:*
Household................Gen. 18:6
Public ....Jer. 37:21
Royal.....................Gen. 40:1, 2

SUBJECT REFERENCE

B. *Features of:*
Usually a woman's job ......Lev. 26:26
Considered menial..........1 Sam. 8:13

Balaam—*destroyer of the people*
A. *Information concerning:*
A son of Beor..............Num. 22:5
From Mesopotamia ....Deut. 23:4
A soothsayer...............Josh. 13:22
A prophet ....2 Pet. 2:15
A Midianite ....Num. 31:8
Killed because of his sin.....Num. 31:1-8
B. *Mission of:*
Balak sent to curse Israel ....Num. 22:5-7
Josh. 24:9
Hindered by speaking ass....Num. 22:22-35
2 Pet. 2:16
Curse becomes a blessing ....Deut. 23:4, 5
Josh. 24:10
C. *Prophecies of:*
Under divine control........Num. 22:18, 38
Num. 23:16, 20, 26
By the Spirit's prompting ....Num. 24:2
Blessed Israel three times ....Num. 24:10
Spoke of the Messiah in final message ....Num. 24:14-19
D. *Nature of:*
"Unrighteousness"—greed ...2 Pet. 2:14, 15
"Error"—rebellion..........Jude 11

Baladan—(Marduk) *has given a son*
Father of Merodach-baladan (*also spelled* Berodach-baladan) ....2 Kin. 20:12

Balak, Balac—*empty*
A Moabite king ....Num. 22:4
Hired Balaam to curse Israel ....Num. 22-24

Balances—*an instrument for weighing; scales*
A. *Used for weighing:*
Things ....Lev. 19:36
Money ....Jer. 32:10
B. *Laws concerning:*
Must be just ....Lev. 19:36
False, an abomination........Prov. 11:1
Deceit, condemned ....Amos 8:5
C. *Figurative of:*
God's justice..............Job 31:6
Man's smallness ....Ps. 62:9
Is. 40:12, 15
God's judgment ....Dan. 5:27
Man's tribulation ....Rev. 6:5

Bald Locust (see Locust)
A specie of edible locust........Lev. 11:22

Baldness—*a head without hair*
A. *Natural:*
Not a sign of leprosy........Lev. 13:40, 41
Elijah mocked for ....2 Kin. 2:23, 24
B. *Artificial:*
A sign of mourning ....Is. 22:12
An idolatrous practice.......Lev. 21:5
Deut. 14:1
Inflicted upon captives ......Deut. 21:12
Forbidden to priests ....Ezek. 44:20
A part of Nazarite vow......Num. 6:9, 18
C. *Figurative of judgment, upon:*
Israel ....Is. 3:24
Amos 8:10
Moab ....Is. 15:2
Philistia ....Jer. 47:5
Tyre ....Ezek. 27:31

Ball—*spherical object*
Prophetic ....Is. 22:18

Ballad singers
Rendered "they that speak proverbs" ....Num. 21:27

Balm—*an aromatic resin or gum*
A product of Gilead ....Jer. 8:22
Sent to Joseph ....Gen. 43:11
Exported to Tyre.............Ezek. 27:17
Healing qualities of............Jer. 46:11
Jer. 51:8

Bamah—*high place*
A place of idolatry ....Ezek. 20:29

SUBJECT REFERENCE

Bamoth—*high places*
Encampment site.............Num. 21:19, 20
Also called Bamoth-baal ....Josh. 13:17

Bamoth-baal—*high places of Baal*
Assigned to Reuben ....Josh. 13:17

Ban (see Excommunication)

Bandage
Used as disguise ....1 Kin. 20:37-41
In prophecy against Egypt......Ezek. 30:20-22

Bani—*built*
1. Gadite warrior ....2 Sam. 23:36
2. A Judahite ....1 Chr. 9:4
3. A postexilic family..........Ezra 2:10
Neh. 10:14
4. A Merarite Levite ....1 Chr. 6:46
5. A Levite; father of Rehum...Neh. 3:17
6. Signed document ....Neh. 10:13
7. Head of Levitical family.....Ezra 10:34
8. A postexilic Levite..........Ezra 10:38
9. A descendant of Asaph......Neh. 11:22

Banishment—*forceful expulsion from one's place*
A. *Political, of:*
Absalom by David ....2 Sam. 14:13, 14
The Jews into exile ....2 Chr. 36:20, 21
The Jews from Rome ....Acts 18:2
B. *Moral and spiritual, of:*
Adam from Eden............Gen. 3:22-24
Cain from others ....Gen. 4:12, 14
Lawbreaker................Ezra 7:26
John to Patmos ....Rev. 1:9
Satan from heaven..........Rev. 12:7-9
The wicked to lake of fire....Rev. 20:15
Rev. 21:8

Bank
A. *A mound:*
Raised against a besieged city ....2 Sam. 20:15; Is. 37:33
B. *A place for money:*
Exchange charges...........John 2:15
Interest paid on deposits ....Matt. 25:27
Luke 19:23

Bankruptcy—*inability to pay one's debts*
A. *Literal:*
Condition of David's men ...1 Sam. 22:2
Unjust steward.............Matt. 18:25
B. *Moral and spiritual:*
Israel's condition ....Hos. 4:1-5
Mankind's condition ....Rom. 1:20-32
Rom. 3:9-19
Individual's condition ....Phil. 3:4-8
1 Tim. 1:13

Banner—*a flag or standard*
A. *Literal:*
Used by armies ....Num. 2:2, 3
Signal for blowing trumpet ..Is. 18:3
B. *Figurative of:*
Jehovah's name ("Jehovah is my banner")...................Ex. 17:15
God's salvation ....Ps. 20:5
Ps. 60:4
God's protection ....Song 2:4
God's power ....Song 6:4, 10

Banquet—*a sumptuous feast*
A. *Reasons for:*
Birthday ....Gen. 40:20
Marriage ....Gen. 29:22
Reunion ....Luke 15:22-25
State affairs................Esth. 1:3, 5
Dan. 5:1
B. *Features of:*
Invitations sent ....Esth. 5:8, 9
Luke 14:16, 17
Non-acceptance merits censure ....Luke 14:18-24
Courtesies to guests.........Luke 7:40-46
Special garment ....Matt. 22:11
Rev. 3:4, 5
A presiding governor........John 2:8
Protocol of seating..........Gen. 43:33
Prov. 25:6, 7

SUBJECT REFERENCE

Anointing oil ....Ps. 45:7
Honor guest noted..........1 Sam. 9:22-24

Baptism, Christian

A. *Commanded by:*
Christ.....................Matt. 28:19, 20; Mark 16:15, 16
Peter......................Acts 10:46-48
Christian ministers..........Acts 22:12-16

B. *Administered by:*
The apostles...............Acts 2:1, 41
Ananias....................Acts 9:17, 18
Philip.....................Acts 8:12; Acts 8:36-38
Peter......................Acts 10:44-48
Paul.......................Acts 18:8; 1 Cor. 1:14-17

C. *Places:*
Jordan.....................Matt. 3:13-16; Mark 1:5-10
Jerusalem..................Acts 2:5, 41
Samaria....................Acts 8:12
A house....................Acts 10:44-48
A jail.....................Acts 16:25-33

D. *Subjects of:*
Believing Jews.............Acts 2:41
Believing Gentiles..........Acts 10:44-48; Acts 18:8
Households.................Acts 16:15, 33; 1 Cor. 1:16

E. *Characteristics of:*
By water...................Acts 10:47
Only one...................Eph. 4:5
Necessary..................Acts 2:38, 41
Source of power............Acts 1:5
Follows faith..............Acts 2:41; Acts 18:8

F. *Symbolism of:*
Forecast in prophecy........Joel 2:28, 29; Acts 2:16-21
Prefigured in types..........1 Cor. 10:2; 1 Pet. 3:20, 21
Visualized by the Spirit's descent.................{John 1:32, 33; Acts 2:3, 4, 41; Acts 10:44-48}
Expressive of spiritual unity..................{1 Cor. 12:13; Gal. 3:27, 28}
Figurative of regeneration...John 3:3, 5, 6; Rom. 6:3, 4, 11
Illustrative of cleansing......Acts 22:16; Titus 3:5

Baptism, John's

Administrator—John..........Matt. 3:7
Place—at Jordan..............Matt. 3:6, 13, 16
in Aenon...................John 3:23
Persons—people and Jesus......Mark 1:5, 9; Acts 13:24
Character—repentance.........Luke 3:3
Reception—rejected by some....Luke 7:29, 30
Nature—of God...............Matt. 21:25, 27
Insufficiency—rebaptism.......Acts 19:1-7
Intent—to prepare...........{Matt. 3:11, 12; Acts 11:16; Acts 19:4}
Jesus' submission to—fulfilling all righteousness................Matt. 3:13-17

Barabbas—*son of Abba* (father)
A murderer released in place of Jesus.......................{Matt. 27:16-26; Acts 3:14, 15}

Barachel—*God has blessed*
Father of Elihu..............Job 32:2, 6

Barachias—*Jehovah has blessed*
Father of Zechariah...........Matt. 23:35

Barak—*lightning*
Defeats Jabin................Judg. 4:1-24
A man of faith...............Heb. 11:32

Barbarian—*rude*
Primitive people..............Acts 28:2, 4
Unintelligible language........1 Cor. 14:11
Those included in the Gospel...Rom. 1:14; Col. 3:11

Barber—*one who cuts hair*
Expressive of divine judgment...Is. 7:20; Ezek. 5:1

SUBJECT REFERENCE

Bare—*uncovered, naked*
Figurative of:
Destitution...................Ezek. 16:22, 39
Uncleanness...................Lev. 13:45
Undeveloped state, immaturity.................{Ezek. 16:7; 1 Cor. 15:37}
Power revealed................Is. 52:10
Destruction...................Joel 1:7
Mourning.....................Is. 32:9-11

Barefoot—*bare feet*
Expression of great distress.....2 Sam. 15:30
Forewarning of judgement......Is. 20:2-4
Indicative of reverence.........Ex. 3:5

Bargain—*an agreement between persons*
A disastrous...................Gen. 25:29-34
A blessed.....................Gen. 28:20-22
Involving a wife...............Gen. 29:15-20
Deception of..................Prov. 20:14
Resulting in death.............Matt. 14:7-10
History's most notorious.......Matt. 26:14-16

Barhumite (another form of Baharumite)
One of David's mighty men.....2 Sam. 23:31

Bariah—*fugitive*
A decendant of David.........1 Chr. 3:22

Bar-jesus (Elymas)
A Jewish imposter.............Acts 13:6-12

Bar-jona—*son of Jonah*
Surname of Peter..............Matt. 16:17

Barkos—*party-colored*
Postexilic family.............Ezra 2:53

Barley—*a bearded cereal grass*
A product of Palestine.........Deut. 8:8; Ruth 1:22
Food for animals..............1 Kin. 4:28
Used by the poor..............Ruth 2:17
Used in trade.................2 Chr. 2:10
In a miracle..................John 6:9, 13

Barn—*a storehouse*

A. *Literal:*
A place of storage..........Deut. 28:8; Joel 1:17

B. *Spiritual, of:*
God's blessings............Prov. 3:10; Mal. 3:10
Man's vanity...............Luke 12:16-19
Heaven itself..............Matt. 13:30, 43

Barnabas—*son of exhortation*
Gives property...............Acts 4:36, 37
Supports Paul................Acts 9:27
Assists in Antioch............Acts 11:22-24
Brings Paul from Tarsus.......Acts 11:25, 26
Carries relief to Jerusalem.....Acts 11:27-30
Travels with Paul.............Acts 13:2
Called Jupiter by the multitudes....................Acts 14:12
Speaks before Jerusalem Council.....................Acts 15:1, 2, 12
With Paul, takes decree to churches....................Acts 15:22-31
Breaks with Paul over John Mark.......................Acts 15:36-39
Highly regarded by Paul.......1 Cor. 9:6; Gal. 2:1, 9
Not always steady............Gal. 2:13

Barrel
For food storage.............1 Kin. 17:12-16
For water...................1 Kin. 18:33

Barren—*unable to reproduce*

A. *Physically, of:*
Unproductive soil..........Ps. 107:34; Joel 2:20
Trees.....................Luke 13:6-9
Females...................Prov. 30:16

B. *Significance of:*
A reproach................Gen. 16:2
A judgment................2 Sam. 6:23
Absence of God's blessing...Ex. 23:26; Deut. 7:14
Removal of, from the Lord..Ps. 113:9

C. *Spiritually:*
Removal of, in new Israel....Is. 54:1; Gal. 4:27
Remedy against............2 Pet. 1:8

SUBJECT REFERENCE

D. *Examples of:*
Sarah.....................Gen. 21:2
Rebekah...................Gen. 25:21
Rachel....................Gen. 30:22
Manoah's wife.............Judg. 13:2, 3, 24
Hannah....................1 Sam. 1:18-20
The Shunammite woman....2 Kin. 4:14-17
Elizabeth.................Luke 1:7, 13, 57

Barsabas—*son of Saba*
1. Nominated to replace Judas.....................Acts 1:23
2. Sent to Antioch............Acts 15:22

Barter—*to exchange for something*
Between Joseph and the Egyptians..................Gen. 47:17
Between Solomon and Hiram...1 Kin. 5:10, 11

Bartholomew—*son of Talmai*
One of Christ's apostles........Matt. 10:3; Acts 1:13
Called Nathanael.............John 1:45, 46

Bartimaeus—*son of Timaeus*
Blind beggar healed by Jesus....Mark 10:46-52

Baruch—*blessed*
1. Son of Neriah..............Jer. 32:12, 13
Jeremiah's faithful friend....Jer. 36:4-32
The Jewish remnant takes him to Egypt....................Jer. 43:1-7
2. Son of Zabbai.............Neh. 3:20
Signs document.............Neh. 10:6
3. A Shilonite of Judah........Neh. 11:5

Barzillai—*of iron*
1. Helps David with food......2 Sam. 17:27-29
Age restrains him from following David...................2 Sam. 19:31-39
2. Father of Adriel............2 Sam. 21:8
3. A postexilic priest..........Ezra 2:61

Base
As a foundation...............1 Kin. 7:27-43
Of lowly estate...............2 Sam. 6:22
Of evil character.............1 Cor. 1:28
Of humble nature.............2 Cor. 10:1

Bashemath—*fragrance*
1. Wife of Esau..............Gen. 26:34
Called Adah...............Gen. 36:2, 3
2. Wife of Esau..............Gen. 36:3, 4, 13
Called Mahalath...........Gen. 28:9
3. A daughter of Solomon.....1 Kin. 4:15

Bashan—*smooth soil*
A vast highland east of the Sea of Chinnereth (Galilee)...................Num. 21:33-35
Ruled by Og..................Deut. 29:7
Conquered by Israel...........Neh. 9:22
Assigned to Manasseh.........Deut. 3:13
Smitten by Hazael.............2 Kin. 10:32, 33
Fine cattle...................Ezek. 39:18
Typical of cruelty.............Ps. 22:12; Amos 4:1

Bashan Havoth-jair
A district named after Jair......Deut. 3:14

Basin—*cup or bowl for containing liquids*
Moses used...................Ex. 24:6
Made for the altar.............Ex. 38:3; Ex. 27:3
Brought for David.............2 Sam. 17:28, 29
Hiram made..................1 Kin. 7:40

Baskets—*something made to hold objects*

A. *Used for carrying:*
Produce...................Deut. 26:2
Food......................Matt. 14:20
Ceremonial offerings.......Ex. 29:3, 23
Paul......................Acts 9:24, 25
Other objects (heads).......2 Kin. 10:7

B. *Symbolic of:*
Approaching death.........Gen. 40:16-19
Israel's judgment..........Amos 8:1-3
Judah's judgment..........Jer. 24:1-3

Bastard—*an illegitimate child*

A. *Penalty attached to*........Deut. 23:2

SUBJECT — REFERENCE

- B. *Examples of:*
  - Ishmael ... Gen. 16:3, 15; Gal. 4:22
  - Moab and Ammon ... Gen. 19:36, 37
  - Sons of Tamar by Judah ... Gen. 38:12-30
  - Jephthah ... Judg. 11:1
- C. *Figurative of:*
  - A mixed race ... Zech. 9:6
  - The unregenerate state ... Heb. 12:8

Bat—*a flying mammal*
- Listed among unclean birds ... Lev. 11:19; Deut. 14:18
- Lives in dark places ... Is. 2:19, 20

Bath—*a liquid measure* (about 9 gallons)
- A tenth of a homer ... Ezek. 45:10, 11
- For measuring oil and wine ... 2 Chr. 2:10; Is. 5:10

Bathing
- A. *For pleasure:*
  - Pharaoh's daughter ... Ex. 2:5
  - Bath-sheba ... 2 Sam. 11:2, 3
- B. *For purification:*
  - Cleansing the feet ... Gen. 24:32; John 13:10
  - Ceremonial cleansing ... Lev. 14:8; 2 Kin. 5:10-14
  - Before performing priestly duties ... Ex. 30:19-21; Lev. 16:4, 24
  - Jewish rituals ... Mark 7:2

Bath-rabbim—*daughter of multitudes*
- Gate of Heshbon ... Song 7:4

Bath-sheba—*daughter of an oath*
- Wife of Uriah ... 2 Sam. 11:2, 3
- Commits adultery with David ... 2 Sam. 11:4, 5
- Husband's death contrived by David ... 2 Sam. 11:6-25
- Mourns husband's death ... 2 Sam. 11:26
- Becomes David's wife ... 2 Sam. 11:27
- Her first child dies ... 2 Sam. 12:14-19
- Solomon's mother ... 2 Sam. 12:24
- Secures throne for Solomon ... 1 Kin. 1:15-31
- Deceived by Adonijah ... 1 Kin. 2:13-25

Bath-shua—*daughter of prosperity*
- Same as Bath-sheba ... 1 Chr. 3:5

Battering ram (see Armor)
- Used in destroying walls ... Ezek. 4:2; Ezek. 21:22

Battle (See War)

Battle-axe—*an instrument of war*
- Applied to Israel ... Jer. 51:19, 20

Battlement—*a lodge on roofs*
- A protective ... Deut. 22:8
- Figurative of partial destruction ... Jer. 5:10

Bavai—*wisher*
- Postexilic worker ... Neh. 3:18

Bay—*inlet*
1. Dead Sea's cove at Jordan's mouth ... Josh. 15:5
   - Used also of the Nile ... Is. 11:15
2. Color of a horse ... Zech. 6:2
3. Name of a tree; figurative of pride ... Ps. 37:35

Bazluth—*stripping*
- Head of a family ... Ezra 2:52
- Called Bazlith in ... Neh. 7:54

Bdellium—*an oily gum, or a white pearl*
- A valuable mineral of Havilah ... Gen. 2:12
- Manna colored like ... Num. 11:7

Beach—*coast*
- *Place of:*
  - Jesus' preaching ... Matt. 13:2
  - Fisherman's task ... Matt. 13:48
  - Jesus' meal with disciples ... John 21:9
  - A prayer meeting ... Acts 21:5
  - A notable shipwreck ... Acts 27:39-44
  - A miracle ... Acts 28:1-6

SUBJECT — REFERENCE

Beacon—*a signal*
- Figurative, a warning to others ... Is. 30:17

Bealiah—*Jehovah is Lord*
- A warrior ... 1 Chr. 12:5

Bealoth—*mistresses*
- Village of Judah ... Josh. 15:24

Beam
- A. *Physical:*
  - Wood undergirding floors ... 1 Kin. 7:2
  - Part of weaver's frame ... 1 Sam. 17:7
- B. *Figurative of:*
  - The cry for vengeance ... Hab. 2:11
  - God's power ... Ps. 104:3
  - Notorious faults ... Matt. 7:3-5

Bean—*a food*
- Brought to David by friends ... 2 Sam. 17:27, 28
- Mixed with grain for bread ... Ezek. 4:9

Bear—*a wild animal*
- A. *Natural:*
  - Killed by David ... 1 Sam. 17:34, 35
  - Two tore up forty-two lads ... 2 Kin. 2:23, 24
- B. *Figurative of:*
  - Fierce revenge ... 2 Sam. 17:8
  - Fool's folly ... Prov. 17:12
  - Wicked rulers ... Prov. 28:15
  - World empire ... Dan. 7:5
  - Final antichrist ... Rev. 13:2
  - Messianic times ... Is. 11:7

Bear—*to carry, yield*
- A. *Used literally of:*
  - Giving birth ... Gen. 17:19
  - Carrying a load ... Josh. 3:13; Jer. 17:21
  - Cross ... Matt. 27:32
- B. *Used figuratively of:*
  - Excessive punishment ... Gen. 4:13
  - Divine deliverance ... Ex. 19:4
  - Responsibility for sin ... Lev. 5:17; Lev. 24:15
  - Burden of leadership ... Deut. 1:9, 12
  - Personal shame ... Ezek. 16:54
  - Evangelism ... Acts 9:15
  - Spiritual help ... Gal. 6:1, 2
  - Spiritual productivity ... John 15:2, 4, 8

Beard—*hair grown on the face*
- A. *Long, worn by:*
  - Aaron ... Ps. 133:2
  - Samson ... Judg. 16:17
  - David ... 1 Sam. 21:13
- B. *In mourning:*
  - Left untrimmed ... 2 Sam. 19:24
  - Plucked ... Ezra 9:3
  - Cut ... Jer. 48:37, 38
- C. *Features regarding:*
  - Leper's must be shaven ... Lev. 13:29-33
  - Half-shaven, an indignity ... 2 Sam. 10:4, 5
  - Marring of, forbidden ... Lev. 19:27
  - Shaven, by Egyptians ... Gen. 41:14
  - Spittle on, sign of lunacy ... 1 Sam. 21:13
  - Holding to, a token of respect ... 2 Sam. 20:9

Beasts—*four-footed animals; mammals*
- A. *Characteristics of:*
  - God-created ... Gen. 1:21
  - Of their own order ... 1 Cor. 15:39
  - Named by Adam ... Gen. 2:20
  - Suffer in man's sin ... Rom. 8:20-22
  - Perish at death ... Ps. 49:12-15
  - Follow instincts ... Is. 1:3; Jude 10
  - Under God's control ... 1 Sam. 6:7-14
  - Wild ... Mark 1:13
  - For man's food ... Gen. 9:3; Acts 10:12, 13
  - Eat people ... 1 Sam. 17:46; 1 Cor. 15:32
  - Used in sacrifices ... Lev. 27:26-29
  - Spiritual lessons from ... 1 Kin. 4:33; Job 12:7
- B. *Treatment of:*
  - No sexual relation with ... Lev. 20:15, 16
  - Proper care of, sign of a righteous man ... Gen. 33:13, 14; Prov. 12:10
  - Abuse of, rebuked ... Num. 22:28-32
  - Extra food for, while working ... Deut. 25:4; 1 Tim. 5:18
- C. *Typical of:*
  - Man's folly ... Ps. 73:22
  - Unregenerate men ... Titus 1:12
  - False prophets ... 2 Pet. 2:12
  - Antichrist ... Rev. 13:1-4
- See Animals

Beaten gold—*gold shaped by hammering*
- Ornamental shields ... 1 Kin. 10:16, 17; 2 Chr. 9:15, 16

Beaten oil—*highest quality of olive oil*
- In sacrifices ... Ex. 29:39, 40
- In tent of meeting lamp ... Lev. 24:2

Beaten silver—*silver shaped by hammering*
- Overlaid idols ... Is. 30:22; Hab. 2:19
- In trade ... Jer. 10:9

Beatings—*striking the body with blows; floggings*
- A. *Inflicted on:*
  - The wicked ... Deut. 25:3
  - The guilty ... Lev. 19:20
  - Children ... Prov. 22:15
  - The disobedient ... Prov. 26:3; Luke 12:47, 48
- B. *Victims of unjust beatings:*
  - A servant ... Luke 20:10, 11
  - Christ ... Is. 50:6; Mark 15:19
  - The apostles ... Acts 5:40
  - Paul ... Acts 16:19-24

Beatitudes—*pronouncements of blessings*
- Jesus begins His sermon with ... Matt. 5:3-12; Luke 6:20-22

Beautiful gate—*gate at East of Temple area*
- Lame man healed there ... Acts 3:1-10

Beauty, physical
- A. *Temporal:*
  - Seen in nature ... Hos. 14:6; Matt. 6:28, 29
  - Consumed in dissipation ... Is. 28:1
  - Contest Abishag, winner of ... 1 Kin. 1:1-4
  - Esther, winner of ... Esth. 2:1-17
  - Destroyed by sin ... Ps. 39:11
  - Ends in grave ... Ps. 49:14
- B. *In Women:*
  - Vain ... Prov. 31:30
  - Without discretion ... Prov. 11:22
  - Enticements of ... Prov. 6:25
  - Source of temptation ... Gen. 6:2; 2 Sam. 11:2-5
  - Leads to marriage ... Deut. 21:11
  - A bride's ... Ps. 45:11
  - Sarah's ... Gen. 12:11
  - Rebekah's ... Gen. 24:15, 16
  - Rachel's ... Gen. 29:17
  - Daughters of Job ... Job 42:15
  - Abigail's ... 1 Sam. 25:3
  - Bath-sheba's ... 2 Sam. 11:2, 3
  - Tamar's ... 2 Sam. 13:1
  - Abishag's ... 1 Kin. 1:3, 4
  - Vashti's ... Esth. 1:11
  - Esther's ... Esth. 2:7
- C. *In Men:*
  - Of Man ... Is. 44:13
  - Of the aged ... Prov. 20:29
  - Joseph's ... Gen. 39:6
  - David's ... 1 Sam. 16:12, 13
  - Absalom's ... 2 Sam. 14:25

Beauty, spiritual
- The Messiah ... Ps. 110:3; Is. 52:7
- The true Israel ... Ps. 45:8-11; Song 1:8
- The meek ... Ps. 149:4
- Spiritual worship ... 2 Chr. 20:21
- Christian ministers ... Rom. 10:15
- Holy garments ... Is. 52:1
- Christ's rejection by Israel ... Zech. 11:7-14

Bebai—*fatherly*
1. Family head ... Ezra 2:11
2. One who signs document ... Neh. 10:15

SUBJECT REFERENCE

Becher—*young camel*
1. Benjamin's son ...... Gen. 46:21
2. Son of Ephraim ...... Num. 26:35
Called Bered ...... 1 Chr. 7:20

Bechorath—*the first birth*
Ancestor of Saul ...... 1 Sam. 9:1

Bed
A. *Made of:*
The ground ...... Gen. 28:11
Iron, 13½ feet long ...... Deut. 3:11
Ivory ...... Amos 6:4
Gold and silver ...... Esth. 1:6
B. *Used for:*
Sleep ...... Luke 11:7
Rest ...... 2 Sam. 4:5-7
Sickness ...... Gen. 49:33
Meals ...... Amos 6:4
Prostitution ...... Prov. 7:16, 17
Evil ...... Ps. 36:4
Marriage ...... Song 3:1
Heb. 13:4
Singing ...... Ps. 149:5
C. *Figurative of:*
The grave ...... Job 17:13-16
Divine support ...... Ps. 41:3
Worldly security ...... Is. 57:7

Bed—*a garden plot*
Used literally ...... Song 6:2
Used figuratively ...... Song 5:13

Bedad—*separation*
Father of Hadad ...... Gen. 36:35

Bedan—*son of judgment*
1. Judge of Israel ...... 1 Sam. 12:11
2. Descendant of Manasseh ...... 1 Chr. 7:17

Bedchamber—*a bedroom*
A place of sleep ...... 2 Sam. 4:7
Elijah's special ...... 2 Kin. 4:8, 10
Secrets of ...... 2 Kin. 6:12
Joash hidden in ...... 2 Kin. 11:2

Bedeiah—*servant of Jehovah*
Son of Bani ...... Ezra 10:34, 35

Bedfellows
Provide mutual warmth ...... Eccl. 4:11

Bee—*insect*
Abundant in Canaan ...... Judg. 14:8
Amorites compared to ...... Deut. 1:44
David's enemies compared to ...... Ps. 118:12
Assyria compared to ...... Is. 7:18
See Honey

Beef, boiled
Elisha gives people ...... 1 Kin. 19:21

Beeliada—*the Lord knows*
Son of David ...... 1 Chr. 14:7
Called Eliada ...... 2 Sam. 5:14-16

Beelzebub
Prince of demons ...... Matt. 12:24
Identified as Satan ...... Matt. 12:26
Jesus thus called ...... Matt. 10:25

Beer—*a well*
1. Moab station ...... Num. 21:16-18
2. Jothan's place of refuge ...... Judg. 9:21

Beera—*a well*
An Asherite ...... 1 Chr. 7:37

Beerah—*a well*
Reubenite prince ...... 1 Chr. 5:6

Beeri—*expounder*
1. Esau's father-in-law ...... Gen. 26:34
2. Hosea's father ...... Hos. 1:1
3. Well dug by leaders of Israel ...... Is. 15:8
(also spelled Beer-elim)

Beer-lahai-roi—*the well of The Living One who sees me*
Angel met Hagar there ...... Gen. 16:7-14
Isaac dwelt in ...... Gen. 24:62

SUBJECT REFERENCE

Beeroth—*wells*
1. Edom station ...... Deut. 10:6
2. Gibeonite city ...... Josh. 9:17

Beerothite, Berothite
An inhabitant of Beeroth ...... 2 Sam. 4:2
1 Chr. 11:39

Beer-sheba—*well of the oath*
A. *God appeared to:*
Hagar ...... Gen. 21:14, 17-19
Isaac ...... Gen. 26:23, 24
Jacob ...... Gen. 46:1-5
Elijah ...... 1 Kin. 19:3-7
B. *Other features of:*
Named after an oath ...... Gen. 21:31-33
Gen. 26:26-33
Isaac's residence at ...... Gen. 26:23-25
Jacob's departure from ...... Gen. 28:10
Assigned to Judah ...... Josh. 15:20, 28
Later assigned to Simeon ...... Josh. 19:1, 2, 9
Judgeship of Samuel's sons ...... 1 Sam. 8:2
Became seat of idolatry ...... Amos 5:5
Amos 8:14
"From Dan even to Beer-sheba" ...... 2 Sam. 17:11

Beeshterah—*temple of Ashterah*
A Levitical city ...... Josh. 21:27
Same as Ashtaroth ...... 1 Chr. 6:71

Beggar—*needy*
A. *Statements concerning:*
Shame of ...... Luke 16:3
Seed of righteous, kept from ...... Ps. 37:25
Punishment of ...... Ps. 109:10
Object of prayer ...... 1 Sam. 2:1, 8
B. *Examples of:*
Bartimaeus ...... Mark 10:46
Lazarus ...... Luke 16:20-22
Blind man ...... Luke 18:35
Lame man ...... Acts 3:2-6

Beginning—*the starting point; origin of*
Creation ...... Gen. 1:1
John 1:1-3
Sin ...... Gen. 3:1-6
Rom. 5:12-21
Death ...... Gen. 3:3, 22-24
Salvation ...... Eph. 1:4
Satan ...... John 8:44
The Gospel ...... Gen. 3:15
Gal. 3:8
The old covenant ...... Ex. 19:5
Heb. 8:9
The new covenant ...... Jer. 31:31-34
Matt. 26:28
Heb. 9:14-28

Begotten—from *"beget"* meaning to bring into being
A. *Applied to Christ:*
Predicted ...... Ps. 2:7
Acts 13:33
Prefigured ...... Heb. 11:17
Proclaimed ...... John 1:14
Proffered ...... John 3:16
Professed ...... Heb. 1:6
B. *Applied to Christians:*
By the Gospel ...... 1 Cor. 4:15
In bonds ...... Philem. 10
Unto hope ...... 1 Pet. 1:3
For safekeeping ...... 1 John 5:18

Beguile—*to deceive or mislead*
A. *In Old Testament:*
Eve, by Satan ...... Gen. 3:13
Israel, by the Midianites ...... Num. 25:18
Joshua, by the Gibeonites ...... Josh. 9:22
B. *Of Christians:*
By flattering words ...... Rom. 16:18
By false reasoning ...... Col. 2:4

Behavior—*one's conduct*
A. *Strange:*
Feigned insanity ...... 1 Sam. 21:13
Supposed drunkenness ...... 1 Sam. 1:12-16
Pretended grief ...... 2 Sam. 14:1-8
Professed loyalty ...... Matt. 26:48, 49

SUBJECT REFERENCE

Insipid hypocrisy ...... Esth. 6:5-11
Counterfeit religion ...... 2 Cor. 11:13-15
B. *True:*
Reverent ...... Titus 2:7
Orderly ...... 2 Thess. 3:7
Good ...... 1 Tim. 3:2
Without blame ...... 1 Thess. 2:10

B

Beheading—*a form of capital punishment*
Ish-bosheth ...... 2 Sam. 4:5-7
John the Baptist ...... Matt. 14:10
James ...... Acts 12:2
Martyrs ...... Rev. 20:4

Behemoth—*a colossal beast*
Described ...... Job 40:15-24

Bekah—see Jewish measures
Half a shekel ...... Ex. 38:26

Bel—*lord*
Patron god of Babylon ...... Is. 46:1
Jer. 51:44
Merodach title ...... Jer. 50:2

Bela, Belah—*destruction*
1. King of Edom ...... Gen. 36:32
2. Reubenite chief ...... 1 Chr. 5:8
3. Benjamin's son ...... Gen. 46:21
4. A city ...... Gen. 14:2, 8

Belial—*worthless, wicked*
A. *Applied properly to:*
Seducers ...... Deut. 13:13
The profligate ...... Judg. 19:22
Eli's sons ...... 1 Sam. 2:12
Rebels ...... 1 Sam. 10:27
A fool ...... 1 Sam. 25:25
The wicked ...... 1 Sam. 30:22
Liars ...... 1 Kin. 21:10, 13
Satan ...... 2 Cor. 6:15
B. *Applied improperly to:*
Hannah ...... 1 Sam. 1:16
David ...... 2 Sam. 16:7

Believers—*those who have received Christ; Christians*
Applied to converts ...... Acts 5:14
1 Tim. 4:12

Bellows—*an instrument used in forcing air at fire*
A figure of affliction ...... Jer. 6:29
Descriptive of God's judgment ...... Jer. 6:27-30

Bells
On Aaron's garment ...... Ex. 28:33, 34
Ex. 39:25, 26
Attention-getters ...... Is. 3:16, 18
Symbols of consecration ...... Zech. 14:20

Beloved—*a title of endearment*
A. *Applied naturally to:*
A wife ...... Deut. 21:15, 16
A husband ...... Song 6:1-3
B. *Applied spiritually to:*
Christ ...... Matt. 3:17
Spiritual Israel ...... Rom. 9:25
Believers ...... Col. 3:12
Christian friends ...... Rom. 16:8, 9
New Jerusalem ...... Rev. 21:9, 10

Belshazzar—*Bel protect the king*
Son of Nebuchadnezzar ...... Dan. 5:2
Gives feast ...... Dan. 5:1, 4
Disturbed by handwriting ...... Dan. 5:5-12
Seeks Daniel's aid ...... Dan. 5:13-16
Daniel interprets for him ...... Dan. 5:17-29
Last Chaldean king ...... Dan. 5:30, 31

Belteshazzar—*protect his life*
Daniel's Babylonian name ...... Dan. 1:7

Ben—*son*
Levite porter ...... 1 Chr. 15:18

Benaiah—*Jehovah has built*
1. Jehoiada's son ...... 2 Sam. 23:20
A mighty man ...... 2 Sam. 23:20, 21
David's bodyguard ...... 2 Sam. 8:18
Faithful to David ...... 2 Sam. 15:18
2 Sam. 20:23
Escorts Solomon to the throne ...... 1 Kin. 1:38-40

SUBJECT REFERENCE

Executes Adonijah, Joab and Shimei .... 1 Kin. 2:25, 29-34; 1 Kin. 2:46
Commander-in-chief .... 1 Kin. 2:35
2. One of David's mighty men .... 2 Sam. 23:30
Divisional commander .... 1 Chr. 27:14
3. Levite musician .... 1 Chr. 15:18-20
4. Priestly trumpeter .... 1 Chr. 15:24; 1 Chr. 16:6
5. Levite of Asaph's family .... 2 Chr. 20:14
6. Simeonite .... 1 Chr. 4:36
7. Levite overseer .... 2 Chr. 31:13
8. Father of leader Pelatiah .... Ezek. 11:1, 13
9-12. Four postexilic Jews who divorced their foreign wives .... Ezra 10:25-43

Ben-ammi—*son of my kinsman*
Son of Lot; father of the Ammonites .... Gen. 19:38

Benches—*deck of ship*
Made of ivory .... Ezek. 27:6

Bene-berak—*sons of berak* (lightning)
A town of Dan .... Josh. 19:45

Benediction—*an act of blessing*
A. *Characteristics of:*
Instituted by God .... Gen. 1:22, 28
Divinely approved .... Deut. 10:8
Aaronic form .... Num. 6:23-26
Apostolic form .... 2 Cor. 13:14
Jesus' last words .... Luke 24:50, 51
B. *Pronounced upon:*
Creation .... Gen. 1:22, 28
New world .... Gen. 9:1, 2
Abraham .... Gen. 14:19, 20
Marriage .... Gen. 24:60
Son (Jacob) .... Gen. 27:28, 29
Monarch (Pharaoh) .... Gen. 47:7, 10
Sons (Joseph's) .... Gen. 48:15, 16, 20
Tribes (Israel's) .... Deut. 33:1-29
Foreigner .... Ruth 1:8, 9
People .... 2 Sam. 6:18
Jesus .... Luke 2:34
Song of Zecharias .... Luke 1:68-79
Children's blessing .... Mark 10:16

Benefactor—*one who bestows benefits*
A. *Materially, God as:*
Israel's .... Deut. 7:6-26
Unbeliever's .... Acts 14:15-18
Christian's .... Phil. 4:19
B. *Spiritually:*
By God .... Eph. 1:3-6
Through Christ .... Eph. 2:13-22
For enrichment .... Eph. 1:16-19
C. *Attitudes toward:*
Murmuring .... Num. 11:1-10
Forgetfulness .... Ps. 106:13
Rejection .... Acts 13:44-47
Remembrance .... Luke 7:1-5
Gratefulness .... Acts 13:48

Benefice—*an enriching act or gift*
Manifested by a church .... Phil. 4:15-17
Encouraged in a friend .... Philem. 17-22
Justified in works .... James 2:14-17
Remembered in heaven .... 1 Tim. 6:18, 19

Bene-jaakan—*sons of Jaakan*
A wilderness station .... Num. 33:31

Benevolence—*generosity toward others*
A. *Exercised toward:*
The poor .... Gal. 2:10
The needy .... Eph. 4:28
Enemies .... Prov. 25:21
God's servant .... Phil. 4:14-17
B. *Measured by:*
Ability .... Acts 11:29
Love .... 1 Cor. 13:3
Sacrifice .... Mark 12:41-44
Bountifulness .... 2 Cor. 9:6-15
C. *Blessings of:*
Fulfills a grace .... Rom. 12:6, 13
Performs a spiritual sacrifice .... Heb. 13:16
Makes us "more blessed" .... Acts 20:35

SUBJECT REFERENCE

Enriches the giver .... Prov. 11:25; Is. 58:10, 11
Reward .... 1 Tim. 6:18, 19

Ben-hadad—*son of the god Hadad*
1. Ben-hadad I, king of Damascus. Hired by Asa, king of Judah, to attack Baasha, king of Israel .... 1 Kin. 15:18-21
2. Ben-hadad II, king of Damascus. Makes war on Ahab, king of Israel .... 1 Kin. 20:1-21
Defeated by Israel .... 1 Kin. 20:26-34
Fails in siege against Samaria .... 2 Kin. 6:24-33; 2 Kin. 7:6-20
Killed by Hazael .... 2 Kin. 8:7-15
3. Ben-hadad III, king of Damascus. Loses all Israelite conquests made by Hazael, his father .... 2 Kin. 13:3-25

Ben-hail—*son of strength*
A teacher .... 2 Chr. 17:7

Ben-hanan—*son of the gracious one*
A son of Shimon .... 1 Chr. 4:20

Beninu—*our son*
A Levite document signer .... Neh. 10:13

Benjamin—*son of the right hand*
Jacob's youngest son .... Gen. 35:16-20
Jacob's favorite son .... Gen. 42:4; Gen. 43:1-14
Loved by Joseph .... Gen. 43:29-34
Judah intercedes for .... Gen. 44:18-34
Joseph's gifts to .... Gen. 45:22
Father of five sons .... 1 Chr. 8:1, 2
Head of a tribe .... Num. 26:38-41
Jacob's prophecy concerning .... Gen. 49:27

Benjamin (others bearing this name)
1. A son of Bilhan .... 1 Chr. 7:10
2. Son of Harim .... Ezra 10:18, 31, 32
Same as in .... Neh. 3:23

Benjamin, tribe of
A. *Background features of:*
Descendants of Jacob's youngest son .... Gen. 35:18
Family divisions of .... Num. 26:38-41
Strength of .... Num. 1:36, 37
Bounds of .... Josh. 18:11-28
Prophecies respecting .... Gen. 49:27; Deut. 33:12
B. *Memorable events of:*
Almost destroyed for protecting men of Gibeah .... Judg. 20:12-48
Wives provided for, to preserve the tribe .... Judg. 21:1-23
Furnished Israel her first king .... 1 Sam. 9:1-17
Hailed David's return .... 2 Sam. 19:16, 17
C. *Celebrities belonging to:*
Ehud, a judge .... Judg. 3:15
Saul, Israel's first king .... 1 Sam. 9:1
Abner, David's general .... 1 Sam. 17:55
Mordecai .... Esth. 2:5
The apostle Paul .... Phil. 3:5

Beno—*his son*
A Merarite Levite .... 1 Chr. 24:26, 27

Ben-oni—*son of my sorrow*
Rachel's name for Benjamin .... Gen. 35:16-18

Ben-zoheth—*son of Zoheth*
A man of Judah .... 1 Chr. 4:20

Beon—*house of On*
A locality east of Jordan .... Num. 32:3
Same as Baal-meon .... Num. 32:37, 38

Beor, Bosor—*a burning*
1. Father of Bela .... Gen. 36:32
2. Father of Balaam .... Num. 22:5; 2 Pet. 2:15

Bera—*excellent*
A king of Sodom .... Gen. 14:2

Berachah—*blessing*
1. David's warrior .... 1 Chr. 12:3
2. A valley in Judah near Tekoa .... 2 Chr. 20:26

Beraiah—*Jehovah has created*
A Benjamite chief .... 1 Chr. 8:21

SUBJECT REFERENCE

Berea—*watered*
A city of Macedonia visited by Paul .... Acts 17:10-15

Bereavement—*the emotional state after a loved one's death*
A. *General attitudes in:*
Horror .... Ex. 12:29, 30
Great emotion .... 2 Sam. 18:33
Complaint .... Ruth 1:20, 21
Genuine sorrow .... Gen. 37:33-35
Submission .... Job 1:18-21
B. *Christian attitudes in:*
Unlike world's .... 1 Thess. 4:13-18
Yet sorrow allowed .... John 11:35; Acts 9:39
With hope of reunion .... John 11:20-27
C. *Unusual circumstances of, mourning:*
Forbidden .... Lev. 10:6
Of great length .... Gen. 50:1-11
Turned to joy .... John 11:41-44

Berechiah—*blessed by Jehovah*
1. Asaph's father .... 1 Chr. 6:39
2. Levite doorkeepers .... 1 Chr. 15:23, 24
3. Head man of Ephraim .... 2 Chr. 28:12
4. Son of Zerubbabel .... 1 Chr. 3:20
5. Levite .... 1 Chr. 9:16
6. Postexilic workman .... Neh. 3:4, 30
7. Father of Zechariah .... Zech. 1:1, 7; Matt. 23:35

Bered—*hail*
1. A place in the wilderness of Shur .... Gen. 16:7, 14
2. An Ephraimite .... 1 Chr. 7:20

Beri—*belonging to a well*
An Asherite .... 1 Chr. 7:36

Beriah—*evil*
1. Son of Asher .... Gen. 46:17
2. Ephraim's son .... 1 Chr. 7:22, 23
3. Chief of Benjamin .... 1 Chr. 8:13, 16
4. Levite .... 1 Chr. 23:10, 11

Beriites
Descendants of Beriah (No. 1) .... Num. 26:44

Berites
A people in north Palestine .... 2 Sam. 20:14, 15

Berith—*covenant*
Shechem idol .... Judg. 9:46
Same as Baal-berith .... Judg. 8:33; Judg. 9:4

Bernice—*victorious*
Sister of Herod Agrippa II .... Acts 25:13, 23
Hears Paul's defense .... Acts 26:1-30

Berodach-baladan
A king of Babylon .... 2 Kin. 20:12-19
Also called Merodach-baladan .... Is. 39:1

Berothah, Berothai—*wells*
City of Syria taken by David .... 2 Sam. 8:8
Boundary in the ideal kingdom .... Ezek. 47:16

Beryl—*a precious stone*
In breastplate of high priest .... Ex. 28:20; Ex. 39:13
Ornament of a king .... Ezek. 28:12, 13
Describes a lover .... Song 5:14
Applied to an angel .... Dan. 10:5, 6
Wheels like color of .... Ezek. 1:16
In New Jerusalem .... Rev. 21:20

Besai
A family head .... Ezra 2:49

Besodeiah—*in the counsel of Jehovah*
Father of Meshullam .... Neh. 3:6

Besom—*a broom made of twigs*
Symbol of destruction .... Is. 14:23

Besor—*cold*
A brook south of Ziklag .... 1 Sam. 30:9, 10, 21

SUBJECT	REFERENCE
Bestial—*beast like*	
Condemned	Ex. 22:19
Punishment of	Lev. 20:13-21
Betah—*trust, confidence*	
Cities of Hadadezer	2 Sam. 8:8
Called Tibhath	1 Chr. 18:8
Beten—*valley*	
City of Asher	Josh. 19:25
Beth—*house*	
Second letter of the Hebrew alphabet	Ps. 119:9-16
Bethabara—*house of passage*	
A place beyond Jordan where John baptized	John 1:28
Beth-anath—*house of Anath* (the goddess)	
A town of Naphtali	Josh. 19:38, 39
Canaanites remain in	Judg. 1:33
Beth-anoth—*house of Anoth* (the goddess)	
A town of Judah	Josh. 15:59
Bethany—*house of poverty*	
A town on Mt. of Olives	Luke 19:29
Home of Lazarus	John 11:1
Home of Simon, the leper	Matt. 26:6
Jesus visits there	Mark 11:1, 11, 12
Scene, Ascension	Luke 24:50, 51
Beth-arabah—*house of desert*	
A village of Judah	Josh. 15:6, 61
Assigned to Benjamin	Josh. 18:21, 22
Beth-aram—*a house of the height*	
A town of Gad	Josh. 13:27
Probably same as Beth-haran	Num. 32:36
Beth-arbel—*house of God's ambush*	
A town destroyed by Shalman	Hos. 10:14
Beth-aven—*house of nothingness* (vanity)	
A town of Benjamin	Josh. 7:2
Israel defeated Philistines there	1 Sam. 13:5
Beth-baal-meon	
City of Reuben	Josh. 13:17
Beth-barah—*house of the ford*	
A passage over Jordan	Judg. 7:24
Beth-bire—*house of my creation*	
A town of Simeon	1 Chr. 4:31
Probably same as Beth-lebaoth	Josh. 19:6
Beth-car—*house of a lamb*	
Site of Philistines' retreat	1 Sam. 7:11
Beth-dagon—*house of Dagon*	
1. Village of Judah	Josh. 15:41
2. Town of Asher	Josh. 19:27
Beth-diblathaim—*house of fig cakes*	
A Moabite town	Jer. 48:21, 22
Beth-el—*house of God*	
1. A town of Benjamin	Judg. 21:19
Abraham settles near	Gen. 12:8
Site of Abraham's altar	Gen. 13:3, 4
Scene of Jacob's ladder	Gen. 28:10-18
Luz becomes Bethel	Gen. 28:19
Jacob returns to	Gen. 35:1-15
On Ephraim's border	Josh. 16:2
Samuel judged there	1 Sam. 7:15, 16
Site of worship and sacrifice	1 Sam. 10:3
Center of idolatry	1 Kin. 12:28-33
School of prophets	2 Kin. 2:1, 3
Youths from, mock Elisha	2 Kin. 2:23, 24
Denounced by a man of God	1 Kin. 13:1-10
Denounced by Amos	Amos 7:10-13
Josiah destroys altars of	2 Kin. 23:4, 15-20
Denounced by Jeremiah	Jer. 48:13
Denounced by Hosea	Hos. 10:15
2. Simeonite town	1 Sam. 30:27
Called Bethul and Bethuel	Josh. 19:4 1 Chr. 4:30
Beth-emek—*house of the valley*	
A town of Asher	Josh. 19:27
Bether—*separation*	
Designates mountains	Song 2:17
Bethesda—*house of mercy*	
Jerusalem pool	John 5:2-4
Beth-ezel—*a place near*	
A town of Judah	Mic. 1:11
Beth-gader—*house of the wall*	
A town of Judah	1 Chr. 2:51
Probably same as Geder	Josh. 12:13
Beth-gamul—*house of recompense*	
A Moabite town	Jer. 48:23
Beth-haccerem—*house of the vineyard*	
Town of Judah	Jer. 6:1
Beth-haram—*mountain house*	
A town of Gad	Josh. 13:27
Same as Beth-haran	Num. 32:36
Beth-hogla, Beth-hoglah—*house of the partridge*	
A village of Benjamin	Josh. 15:6 Josh. 18:19, 21
Beth-horon—*house of the hollow*	
Twin towns of Ephraim	Josh. 16:3, 5
The nether, built by Sherah, a woman	1 Chr. 7:24
Assigned to Kohathite Levites	Josh. 21:20, 22
Fortified by Solomon	2 Chr. 8:5
Prominent in battles	Josh. 10:10-14 1 Sam. 13:18
Beth-jeshimoth—*house of the wastes*	
A town near Pisgah	Josh. 12:3
Israel camps near	Num. 33:49
Assigned to Reubenites	Josh. 13:20
Later a town of Moab	Ezek. 25:9
Beth-lebaoth—*house of lionesses*	
A town in south Judah; assigned to Simeonites	Josh. 19:6
Called Lebaoth	Josh. 15:32
Beth-lehem (of Judah)—*house of bread*	
A. *Significant features of:*	
Built by Salma	1 Chr. 2:51
Originally called Ephrath	Gen. 35:16
Burial of Rachel	Gen. 35:19
Two wandering Levites of	Judg. 17:1-13 Judg. 19:1-30
Naomi's home	Ruth 1:1, 19
Home of Boaz	Ruth 4:9-11
Home of David	1 Sam. 16:1-18
Stronghold of Philistines	2 Sam. 23:14, 15
Fortified by Rehoboam	2 Chr. 11:6
Refuge of Gedaliah's murderers	Jer. 41:17
B. *Messianic features of:*	
Sought for the tabernacle	Ps. 132:6
Predicted place of the Messiah's birth	Mic. 5:2
Fulfillment cited	Matt. 2:1, 5
Infants of, slain by Herod	Jer. 31:15 Matt. 2:16-18
Beth-lehem (of Zebulun)	
Town assigned to Zebulun	Josh. 19:15, 16
Home of Judge Ibzan	Judg. 12:8-11
Beth-maahah—*house of Maacah*	
Tribe of Israel	2 Sam. 20:14, 15
Beth-marcaboth—*house of the chariots*	
Town of Simeon	Josh. 19:5
Beth-meon—*house of habitation*	
Moabite town	Jer. 48:23
Beth-nimrah—*house of the leopard*	
Town of Gad	Num. 32:3, 36
Beth-pazzez—*house of dispersion*	
Town of Issachar	Josh. 19:21
Beth-palet—*house of escape*	
Town of Judah	Josh. 15:27
Beth-peor—*house of Peor*	
Town near Pisgah	Deut. 3:29
Valley of Moses' burial place	Deut. 34:6
Assigned to Reubenites	Josh. 13:15, 20
Bethphage—*house of unripe figs*	
Village near Bethany	Mark 11:1
Near Mt. of Olives	Matt. 21:1
Beth-rapha—*house of a giant*	
A town or family of Judah	1 Chr. 4:12
Beth-rehob—*house of a street*	
A town in north Palestine	Judg. 18:28
Inhabited by Syrians	2 Sam. 10:6
Bethsaida—*place of fishing*	
A city of Galilee	Mark 6:45
Home of Andrew, Peter and Philip	John 1:44 John 12:21
Blind man healed	Mark 8:22, 23
Near feeding of 5,000	Luke 9:10-17
Unbelief of, denounced	Matt. 11:21 Luke 10:13
Beth-shan, Beth-shean—*house of security*	
A town in Issachar	Josh. 17:11
Assigned to Manasseh	1 Chr. 7:29
Tribute paid by	Josh. 17:12-16
Users of iron chariots	Josh. 17:16
Saul's corpse hung up at	1 Sam. 31:10-13 2 Sam. 21:12-14
Beth-shemesh—*house of the sun*	
1. A border town between Judah and Dan	Josh. 15:10
Also called Ir-shemesh	Josh. 19:41
Assigned to priests	Josh. 21:16
Ark brought to	1 Sam. 6:12-19
Joash defeats Amaziah at	2 Kin. 14:11
Taken by Philistines	2 Chr. 28:18
2. A town of Naphtali	Josh. 19:38
3. A town of Issachar	Josh. 19:22
4. Egyptian city	Jer. 43:13
Beth-shittah—*house of the acacia*	
A town in the Jordan valley	Judg. 7:22
Beth-tappuah—*house of apples*	
A town of Judah	Josh. 15:53
Bethuel—*abode of God*	
1. Father of Laban and Rebekah	Gen. 22:20-23 Gen. 24:29
2. Simeonite town	1 Chr. 4:30
Called Bethul	Josh. 19:4
Beth-zur—*house of a rock*	
A town of Judah	Josh. 15:58
Fortified by Rehoboam	2 Chr. 11:7
Help to rebuild	Neh. 3:16
Betonim—*pistachio nuts*	
A town of Gad	Josh. 13:26
Betrayal—*a breach of trust*	
A. *Of Christ:*	
Predicted	Ps. 41:9
Frequently mentioned	Matt. 17:22 John 13:21
Betrayer identified	John 13:26
Sign of, a kiss	Matt. 26:48, 49
Guilt of	Matt. 27:3, 4
Supper before	1 Cor. 11:23
Jewish nation guilty of	Matt. 27:9, 10 Acts 7:52, 53
B. *Examples of:*	
Israelites by Gibeonites	Josh. 9:22
Samson by Delilah	Judg. 16:18-20
The woman of En-dor by Saul	1 Sam. 28:9-12
Jesus by Judas	Matt. 26:14, 15
Christians	Matt. 10:21
Betrothed—*given in marriage*	
Treatment of	Ex. 21:8, 9
Beulah—*married*	
A symbol of true Israel	Is. 62:4, 5
Beverage—*a drink*	
A. *Literal:*	
Milk	Judg. 4:19 Judg. 5:25
Strong drink	Prov. 31:6
Water	Matt. 10:42
Wine	1 Tim. 5:23

SUBJECT — REFERENCE

B. *Figurative:*
- Christ's blood ... John 6:53
- Cup of suffering ... John 18:11
- Living water ... John 4:10
- Water of life ... Rev. 22:17

Beware—*be wary of; guard against*

A. *Of evil things:*
- Strong drink ... Judg. 13:4
- False prophets ... Matt. 7:15
- Evil men ... Matt. 10:17
- Covetousness ... Luke 12:15
- Dogs (figurative) ... Phil. 3:2

B. *Of possibilities:*
- Disobeying God ... Ex. 23:20, 21
- Forgetting God ... Deut. 6:12
- Being led away ... 2 Pet. 3:17

Bewitch—*to charm, captivate, or astound*
- Activity of Simon ... Acts 8:9-11
- Descriptive of legalism ... Gal. 3:1

Bezai—*shining, high*
- Postexilic family head ... Ezra 2:17; Neh. 7:23
- Signs document ... Neh. 10:18

Bezaleel—*in the shadow* (protection) *of God*
1. Hur's grandson ... 1 Chr. 2:20
   Tabernacle builder ... Ex. 31:1-11; Ex. 35:30-35
2. Divorced foreign wife ... Ezra 10:18, 30

Bezek—*scattering*
1. Town near Jerusalem ... Judg. 1:4, 5
2. Saul's army gathered there ... 1 Sam. 11:8

Bezer—*fortress*
1. An Asherite ... 1 Chr. 7:37
2. City of Reuben ... Deut. 4:43
   Place of refuge ... Josh. 20:8

Bible history, outlined

A. *Pre-patriarchal period, the:*
- Creation ... Gen. 1:1—2:25
- Fall of man ... Gen. 3:1-24
- Development of wickedness ... Gen. 4:1—6:8
- Flood ... Gen. 6:9—8:22
- Establishment of nations ... Gen. 9:1—10:32
- Confusion of tongues ... Gen. 11:1-32

B. *Patriarchal period:*
- Abraham ... Gen. 12:1—25:11
- Isaac ... Gen. 21:1—28:9; Gen. 35:27-29
- Jacob ... Gen. 25:19—37:36; Gen. 45:21—46:7; Gen. 49:1-33
- Joseph ... Gen. 37:1—50:26

C. *Egypt and the Exodus:*
- Preparation of Moses ... Ex. 1:1—7:7
- Plagues and Passover ... Ex. 7:8—12:36
- From Egypt to Sinai ... Ex. 12:37—18:27
- The Law and tabernacle ... Ex. 19:1—40:38

D. *Wilderness:*
- Spies at Kadesh-Barnea ... Num. 13:1—14:38
- Fiery serpents ... Num. 21:4-9
- Balak and Balaam ... Num. 22:1—24:25
- Appointment of Joshua ... Num. 27:18-23
- Death of Moses ... Deut. 34:1-8

E. *Conquest and settlement:*
- Spies received by Rahab ... Josh. 2:1-21
- Crossing Jordan ... Josh. 3:14-17
- Fall of Jericho ... Josh. 6:1-27
- Southern and central mountains ... Josh. 7:1-11
- Victory at Merom ... Josh. 11:1-14
- Division of the land ... Josh. 14:1—21:45

F. *Period of the judges:*
- Later conquests ... Judg. 1:1—2:23
- Othniel ... Judg. 3:8-11
- Ehud ... Judg. 3:12-30
- Shamgar ... Judg. 3:31
- Deborah and Barak ... Judg. 4:1—5:31
- Gideon ... Judg. 6:11—8:35
- Abimelech ... Judg. 9:1-57
- Tola and Jair ... Judg. 10:1-5
- Jephthah ... Judg. 11:1—12:7
- Ibzan, Elon, and Abdon ... Judg. 12:8-15
- Samson ... Judg. 13:1—16:31
- Tribal wars ... Judg. 17:1—21:25

G. *From Samuel to David:*
- Eli and Samuel ... 1 Sam. 1:1—4:22
- Samuel as judge ... 1 Sam. 5:1—8:22
- The first king ... 1 Sam. 9:1—12:25
- Battle of Michmash ... 1 Sam. 13:1—14:52
- Saul and the Amalekites ... 1 Sam. 15:1-35
- David chosen ... 1 Sam. 16:1-13
- David and Goliath ... 1 Sam. 17:1-58
- David in exile ... 1 Sam. 18:5—31:13

H. *Kingdom united:*
- David's reign at Hebron ... 2 Sam. 2:1—4:12
- David's reign at Jerusalem ... 2 Sam. 5:1—10:19
- David's sin ... 2 Sam. 11:1-25
- Absalom's rebellion ... 2 Sam. 15:1—18:33
- David's death ... 1 Kin. 2:10-12
- Accession of Solomon ... 1 Kin. 1:32-53; 1 Chr. 29:20-25
- The Temple ... 1 Kin. 6:1—9:9; 2 Chr. 2:1—7:22
- Death of Solomon ... 1 Kin. 11:41-43; 2 Chr. 9:29-31

I. *Kingdom divided:*
- Rebellion of Israel ... 2 Chr. 10:1-19
- Rehoboam and Abijah ... 2 Chr. 10:1—13:22
- Jeroboam and Nadab ... 1 Kin. 12:25—14:20; 1 Kin. 15:25-31
- Asa ... 1 Kin. 15:9-24; 1 Chr. 14:1—16:14
- Baasha, Elah, Zimri and Omri ... 1 Kin. 15:32—16:27

J. *Mutual alliance:*
- Ahab and Elijah ... 1 Kin. 16:28—18:19
- Contest on Mount Carmel ... 1 Kin. 18:20-40
- Ahab and Ben-hadad ... 1 Kin. 20:1-34
- Murder of Naboth ... 1 Kin. 21:1-29
- Revival under Jehoshaphat ... 1 Kin. 22:41-50; 2 Chr. 17:1-19
- Battle of Ramoth-gilead ... 1 Kin. 22:1-40; 2 Chr. 18:1-34
- Wars of Jehoshaphat ... 2 Chr. 19:1—20:30
- Translation of Elijah ... 2 Kin. 2:1-11
- Jehoshaphat and Jehoram ... 2 Kin. 3:1-27
- Ministry of Elisha ... 2 Kin. 4:1—6:23; 2 Kin. 8:1-15
- Siege of Samaria ... 2 Kin. 6:24—7:20
- Death of Elisha ... 2 Kin. 13:14-20

K. *Decline of both kingdoms:*
- Accession of Jehu ... 2 Kin. 9:1—10:31
- Athaliah and Joash ... 2 Kin. 11:1—12:21
- Amaziah and Jeroboam ... 2 Kin. 14:1-29
- Captivity of Israel ... 2 Kin. 15:1-23
- Reign of Hezekiah ... 2 Kin. 18:1—20:21; 2 Chr. 29:1—32:33
- Reign of Manasseh ... 2 Kin. 21:1-18; 2 Chr. 33:1-20
- Josiah's reforms ... 2 Kin. 22:1—23:30; 2 Chr. 34:1—35:27
- Captivity of Judah ... 2 Kin. 24:1—25:30; 2 Chr. 36:5-21

L. *Captivity:*
- Daniel and Nebuchadnezzer ... Dan. 1:1—4:37
- Belshazzar and Darius ... Dan. 5:1—6:28
- Rebuilding the Temple ... Ezra 1:1—6:15
- Rebuilding Jerusalem ... Neh. 1:1—6:19
- Esther and Mordecai ... Esth. 2:1—10:3

M. *Ministry of Christ:*
- Birth ... Matt. 1:18-25; Luke 2:1-20
- Childhood ... Luke 2:40-52
- Baptism ... Matt. 3:13-17; Luke 3:21-23
- Temptation ... Matt. 4:1-11; Luke 4:1-13
- First miracle ... John 2:1-11
- With Nicodemus ... John 3:1-21
- The Samaritan woman ... John 4:5-42
- Healing ... Luke 4:31-41
- Controversy on the Sabbath ... Luke 6:1-11
- Apostles chosen ... Mark 3:13-19; Luke 6:12-16
- Sermon on the Mount ... Matt. 5:1—7:29; Luke 6:20-49
- Raises dead son ... Luke 7:11-17
- Anointed ... Luke 7:36-50
- Accused of blasphemy ... Matt. 12:22-37; Mark 3:19-30
- Calms the sea ... Matt. 8:23-27; Mark 4:35-41
- Demoniac healed ... Matt. 8:28-34; Mark 5:1-20
- Daughter of Jairus healed ... Matt. 9:18-26; Luke 8:41-56
- Feeds 5,000 ... Matt. 14:13-21; Mark 6:30-44
- Feeds 4,000 ... Matt. 15:32-39
- Peter confesses Jesus is Christ ... Matt. 16:5-16; Mark 8:27-29
- Foretells death ... Matt. 16:21-26; Luke 9:22-25
- Transfiguration ... Matt. 17:1-13; Luke 9:28-36
- Forgiving of adulteress ... John 7:53—8:11
- Resurrection of Lazarus ... John 11:1-44
- Blesses the children ... Matt. 19:13-15; Mark 10:13-16
- Bartimaeus healed ... Matt. 20:29-34; Mark 10:46-52
- Meets Zacchaeus ... Luke 19:1-10
- Triumphant entry ... Matt. 21:1-9; Luke 19:29-44
- Anointed ... Matt. 26:6-13; Mark 14:3-9
- The Passover ... Matt. 26:17-19; Luke 22:7-13
- The Lord's Supper ... Matt. 26:26-29; Mark 14:22-25
- Gethsemane ... Luke 22:39-46
- Betrayal and arrest ... Matt. 26:47-56; John 18:3-12
- Before the Sanhedrin ... Matt. 26:57-68; Luke 22:54-65
- Denied by Peter ... John 18:15-27
- Before Pilate ... Matt. 27:2-14; Luke 23:1-7
- Before Herod ... Luke 23:6-12
- Returns to Pilate ... Matt. 27:15-26; Luke 23:13-25
- Crucifixion ... Matt. 27:35-56; Luke 23:33-49
- Burial ... Matt. 27:57-66; Luke 23:50-56
- Resurrection ... Matt. 28:1-15; John 20:1-18
- Appearance to disciples ... Luke 24:36-43; John 20:19-25
- Appearance to Thomas ... John 20:26-31
- Great commission ... Matt. 28:16-20
- Ascension ... Luke 24:50-53

N. *The early church:*
- Pentecost ... Acts 2:1-42
- In Jerusalem ... Acts 2:3—6:7
- Martyrdom of Stephen ... Acts 6:8—7:60
- In Judaea and Samaria ... Acts 8:1—12:25
- Conversion of Saul ... Acts 9:1-18
- First missionary journey ... Acts 13:1—14:28
- Jerusalem conference ... Acts 15:1-35
- Second missionary journey ... Acts 15:36—18:22
- Third missionary journey ... Acts 18:23—21:16
- Captivity of Paul ... Acts 21:27—28:31

Bichri—*first-born*
- Father of Sheba ... 2 Sam. 20:1

Bidkar—*servant of Kar*
- Captain under Jehu ... 2 Kin. 9:25

Bier—*a frame for carrying a corpse*
- Abner's body borne on ... 2 Sam. 3:31

Bigamist—*having more than one wife*
- First, Lamech ... Gen. 4:19

Bigamy (See Marriage)

Bigotry—*excessive prejudice; blind fanaticism*

A. *Characteristics of:*
- Name-calling ... John 8:48, 49
- Spiritual blindness ... John 9:39-41
- Hatred ... Acts 7:54-58
- Self-righteousness ... Phil. 3:4-6
- Ignorance ... 1 Tim. 1:13

B. *Examples of:*
- Haman ... Esth. 3:8-10
- The Pharisees ... John 8:33-48
- The Jews ... 1 Thess. 2:14-16
- Saul (Paul) ... Acts 9:1, 2
- Peter ... Acts 10:14, 28

See Intolerance; Persecution

Bigtha—*gift of God*
- An officer of Ahasuerus ... Esth. 1:10

Bigthan, Bigthana—*gift of God*
- Conspired against Ahasuerus ... Esth. 2:21; Esth. 6:2

B

SUBJECT	REFERENCE
Bigvai—*happy*	
1. Zerubbabel's companion	Ezra 2:2 Neh. 7:7, 19
2. One who signs covenant	Neh. 10:16
Bildad—*Bel has loved*	
One of Job's friends	Job 2:11
Makes three speeches	Job 8:1-22 Job 18:1-21 Job 25:1-6
Bileam—*greed*	
A town of Manasseh	1 Chr. 6:70
Bilgah—*brightness, cheerfulness*	
1. A descendant of Aaron	1 Chr. 24:1, 6, 14
2. A chief of the priests	Neh. 12:5, 7, 18
Same as Bilgai; signs document	Neh. 10:8
Called Bilgai	Neh. 10:8
Bilhah—*foolish, simple*	
1. Rachel's maid	Gen. 29:29
The mother of Dan and Naphtali	Gen. 30:1-8
Commits incest with Reuben	Gen. 35:22
2. Simeonite town	1 Chr. 4:29
Same as Baalah	Josh. 15:29
Bilhan—*foolish, simple*	
1. A Horite chief; son of Ezer	Gen. 36:27 1 Chr. 1:42
2. A Benjamite family head	1 Chr. 7:10
Bilshan—*searcher*	
A postexilic leader	Ezra 2:2 Neh. 7:7
Bimhal—*with pruning*	
An Asherite	1 Chr. 7:33
Binding—*a restraint; a tying together*	
A. *Used literally of:*	
Tying a man	Gen. 22:9
Imprisonment	2 Kin. 17:4 Acts 22:4
Ocean's shores	Prov. 30:4
B. *Used figuratively of:*	
A fixed agreement	Num. 30:2
God's Word	Prov. 3:3
The brokenhearted	Is. 61:1
Satan	Luke 13:16
The wicked	Matt. 13:30
Ceremonialism	Matt. 23:4
The keys	Matt. 16:19
A determined plan	Acts 20:22
Marriage	Rom. 7:2
Binea	
A son of Moza	1 Chr. 8:37
Binnui—*built*	
1. Head of postexilic family	Neh. 7:15
Called Bani	Ezra 2:10
2. Son of Pahath-moab	Ezra 10:30
3. Son of Bani	Ezra 10:38
4. Postexilic Levite	Neh. 12:8
Henadad's son	Neh. 10:9
Family of, builds wall	Neh. 3:24
Bird cage	
Used figuratively	Jer. 5:27
Birds—*vertebrates with feathers and wings*	
A. *List of:*	
Cock	Matt. 26:34, 74 Mark 14:30 John 18:27 Luke 22:61
Cormorant	Lev. 11:17
Crane	Jer. 8:7
Cuckoo	Lev. 11:16
Dove	Gen. 8:8
Eagle	Job 39:27
Glede	Deut. 14:13
Hawk	Job 39:26
Hen	Matt. 23:37
Heron	Lev. 11:19
Kite	Deut. 14:13
Lapwing	Lev. 11:19
Ossifrage	Lev. 11:13
Ostrich	Lev. 11:16
Owls	Job 30:29
Desert	Ps. 102:6
Great	Lev. 11:17
Little	Lev. 11:17
Partridge	1 Sam. 26:20
Peacock	1 Kin. 10:22
Pelican	Ps. 102:6
Pigeon	Lev. 12:6
Quail	Num. 11:31, 32
Raven	Job 38:41
Sparrow	Matt. 10:29-31
Stork	Ps. 104:17
Swallow	Ps. 84:3
Turtledove	Song 2:12
Vulture	Lev. 11:13
B. *Features regarding:*	
Created by God	Gen. 1:20, 21
Named by Adam	Gen. 2:19, 20
Clean, unclean	Gen. 8:20
Differ from animals	1 Cor. 15:39
Under man's dominion	Ps. 8:8
For food	Gen. 9:2, 3
Belong to God	Ps. 50:11
God provides for	Ps. 104:10-12 Luke 12:23, 24
Can be tamed	James 3:7
Differ in singing	Song 2:12
Some migratory	Jer. 8:7
Solomon writes of	1 Kin. 4:33
Clean, used in sacrifices	Lev. 1:14 Luke 2:24
Worshiped by man	Rom. 1:23
C. *Figurative of:*	
Escape from evil	Ps. 124:7
A wanderer	Prov. 27:8
Snares of death	Eccl. 9:12
Cruel kings	Is. 46:11
Hostile nations	Jer. 12:9
Wicked rich	Jer. 17:11
Kingdom of heaven	Matt. 13:32
Maternal love	Matt. 23:37
Birsha—*with wickedness*	
A king of Gomorrah	Gen. 14:2, 8, 10
Birth—*the act of coming into life*	
A. *Kinds of:*	
Natural	Eccl. 7:1
Figurative	Is. 37:3
Supernatural	Matt. 1:18-25
The new	John 3:5
See New birth	
B. *Natural, features regarding:*	
Pain of, results from sin	Gen. 3:16
Produces a sinful being	Ps. 51:5
Makes ceremonially unclean	Lev. 12:2, 5 Luke 2:22
Affliction from	John 9:1
Twins of, differ	Gen. 25:21-23
Sometimes brings death	Gen. 35:16-20
Pain of, forgotten	John 16:21
Birthday—*date of one's birth*	
Job and Jeremiah curse theirs	Job 3:1-11 Jer. 20:14, 15
Celebration:	
Pharaoh's	Gen. 40:20
Herod's	Mark 6:21
Birthright—*legal rights inherited by birth*	
A. *Blessings of:*	
Seniority	Gen. 43:33
Double portion	Deut. 21:15-17
Royal succession	2 Chr. 21:3
B. *Loss of:*	
Esau's—by sale	Gen. 25:29-34 Rom. 9:12
Reuben's—as a punishment	Gen. 49:3, 4 1 Chr. 5:1, 2
Manasseh's—by Jacob's will	Gen. 48:15-20 1 Chr. 5:1, 2
David's brother—by divine will	1 Sam. 16:2-22
Adonijah's—by the Lord	1 Kin. 2:15
Hosah's son's—by his father's will	1 Chr. 26:10
C. *Transferred to:*	
Jacob	Gen. 27:6-46
Judah	Gen. 49:8-10
Solomon	1 Chr. 28:5-7
See First-born	
Births, foretold	
A. *Over a short period:*	
Ishmael's	Gen. 16:11
Isaac's	Gen. 18:10
Samson's	Judg. 13:3, 24
Samuel's	1 Sam. 1:11, 20
Shunammite's son's	2 Kin. 4:16, 17
John the Baptist's	Luke 1:13
B. *Over a longer period:*	
Josiah's	1 Kin. 13:2
Cyrus'	Is. 45:1-4
Christ's	Gen. 3:15 Mic. 5:1-3
Birzavith—*olive well*	
An Asherite	1 Chr. 7:31
Bishlam—*in peace*	
A Persian officer	Ezra 4:7
Bishop—*an overseer; elder*	
A. *Qualifications of, given by:*	
Paul	1 Tim. 3:1-7
Peter, called "elder"	1 Pet. 5:1-4
B. *Duties of:*	
Oversee the church	Acts 20:17, 28-31
Feed God's flock	1 Pet. 5:2
Watch over men's souls	Heb. 13:17
Teach	1 Tim. 5:17
C. *Office of:*	
Same as elder	Acts 20:17, 28
Several in a church	Acts 20:17, 28 Phil. 1:1
Follows ordination	Titus 1:5, 7
Held by Christ	1 Pet. 2:25
Bit—*a part of a horse's bridle*	
Figurative, of man's stubborn nature	Ps. 32:9 James 3:3
Bithiah—*daughter of Jehovah*	
Pharaoh's daughter; wife of Mered	1 Chr. 4:18
Bith-ron—*ravine, gorge*	
A district east of Jordan	2 Sam. 2:29
Bithynia—*a province of Asia Minor*	
The Spirit keeps Paul from	Acts 16:7
Peter writes to Christians of	1 Pet. 1:1
Bitter herbs	
Part of Passover meal	Ex. 12:8 Num. 9:11
Descriptive of sorrow	Lam. 3:15
"Bitter is sweet"	
Descriptive of man's hunger	Prov. 27:7
Bittern—*a nocturnal member of heron family*	
Sings in desolate windows	Zeph. 2:14
Bitterness—*extreme enmity; sour temper*	
A. *Kinds of:*	
The soul	Job 3:20
The heart	Prov. 14:10
Words	Ps. 64:3
Death	1 Sam. 15:32
"Water of"	Num. 5:24
B. *Causes of:*	
Childlessness	1 Sam. 1:10
A foolish son	Prov. 17:25
Demanding woman	Eccl. 7:26
Sickness	Is. 38:17
Sin	Prov. 5:4
Death	Jer. 31:15
Apostasy	Acts 8:23
C. *Avoidance of:*	
Toward others	Eph. 4:31
Toward a wife	Col. 3:19
As a source of defilement	Heb. 12:15
As contrary to the truth	James 3:14
Bitter waters	
Made sweet by a tree	Ex. 15:23-25
Swallowed by suspected wife	Num. 5:11-31
Bizjothjah—*contempt of Jehovah*	
A town in south Judah	Josh. 15:28

SUBJECT — REFERENCE

Biztha—*eunuch*
- An officer under Ahasuerus ..... Esth. 1:10

Blackness—*destitute of light*
- A. *Literally of:*
  - Hair ..... Song 5:11
  - Skin ..... Song 1:5
  - Horse ..... Zech. 6:2
  - Sky ..... 1 Kin. 18:45
  - Mountain ..... Heb. 12:18
  - Night ..... Prov. 7:9
- B. *Figuratively of:*
  - Affliction ..... Job 30:30
  - Mourning ..... Jer. 8:21
  - Foreboding evil ..... Joel 2:6; Nah. 2:10
  - Hell ..... Jude 13
- C. *Specifically:*
  - Let blackness of the day ..... Job 3:5
  - Clothe heaven with ..... Is. 50:3
  - Shall gather ..... Joel 2:6

Blains—*blisters full of pus*
- The sixth plague on Egypt ..... Ex. 9:8-11

Blamelessness—*freedom from fault; innocency*
- A. *Used ritualistically of:*
  - Priests ..... Matt. 12:5
  - Proper observance ..... Luke 1:6
  - Works, righteousness ..... Phil. 3:6
- B. *Desirable in:*
  - Bishops (elders) ..... 1 Tim. 3:2; Titus 1:6, 7
  - Deacons ..... 1 Tim. 3:10
  - Widows ..... 1 Tim. 5:7
- C. *Attainment of:*
  - Desirable now ..... Phil. 2:15
  - At Christ's return ..... 1 Cor. 1:8; 1 Thess. 5:23; 2 Pet. 3:14

Blasphemy—*cursing God*
- A. *Arises out of:*
  - Pride ..... Ps. 73:9, 11; Ezek. 35:12, 13
  - Hatred ..... Ps. 74:18
  - Affliction ..... Is. 8:21
  - Injustice ..... Is. 52:5
  - Defiance ..... Is. 36:15, 18, 20
  - Scepticism ..... Ezek. 9:8; Mal. 3:13, 14
  - Self-deification ..... Dan. 11:36, 37; 2 Thess. 2:4
  - Unworthy conduct ..... 2 Sam. 12:14; Rom. 2:24
- B. *Instances of:*
  - Job's wife ..... Job 2:9
  - Shelomith's son ..... Lev. 24:11-16, 23
  - Sennacherib ..... 2 Kin. 19:4, 10, 22
  - The beast ..... Dan. 7:25; Rev. 13:1, 5, 6
  - The Jews ..... Luke 22:65
  - Saul of Tarsus ..... 1 Tim. 1:13
  - Ephesians ..... Rom. 2:9
  - Hymenaeus ..... 1 Tim. 1:20
- C. *Those falsely accused of:*
  - Naboth ..... 1 Kin. 21:12, 13
  - Jesus ..... Matt. 9:3; Matt. 26:65
  - Stephen ..... Acts 6:11, 13
- D. *Guilt of:*
  - Punishable by death ..... Lev. 24:11, 16
  - Christ accused of ..... John 10:33, 36

See Revile

Blasphemy against the Holy Spirit
- Attributing Christ's miracles to Satan ..... Matt. 12:22-32
- Never forgivable ..... Mark 3:28-30

Blasting—*injure severely*
- Shows God's power ..... Ex. 15:8
- Sent as judgment ..... Deut. 28:22; Amos 4:9
- Figurative of death ..... Job 4:9

Blastus—*sprout*
- Herod's chamberlain ..... Acts 12:20

Blemish—*any deformity or injury*
- A. *Those without physical:*
  - Priests ..... Lev. 21:17-24
  - Absalom ..... 2 Sam. 14:25
  - Animals used in sacrifices ..... Lev. 22:19-25; Mal. 1:8
- B. *Those without moral:*
  - Christ ..... Heb. 9:14
  - The Church ..... Eph. 5:27
- C. *Those with:*
  - Apostates ..... 2 Pet. 2:13

Bless—*to bestow blessings upon*
- To give divine blessings ..... Gen. 1:22; Gen. 9:1-7
- To adore God for His blessings ..... Gen. 24:48; Ps. 103:1
- To invoke blessings upon another ..... Gen. 24:60; Gen. 27:4, 27

Blessed—*the objects of God's favors*
- A. *Reasons for, they:*
  - Are chosen ..... Eph. 1:3, 4
  - Believe ..... Gal. 3:9
  - Are forgiven ..... Ps. 32:1, 2
  - Are justified ..... Rom. 4:6-9
  - Are chastened ..... Ps. 94:12
  - Keep God's Word ..... Rev. 1:3
- B. *Time of:*
  - Eternal past ..... Eph. 1:3, 4
  - Present ..... Luke 6:22
  - Eternal future ..... Matt. 25:34

Blessings—*the gift of God's grace*
- A. *Physical and temporal:*
  - Prosperity ..... Mal. 3:10-12
  - Food, clothing ..... Matt. 6:26, 30-33
  - Sowing, harvest ..... Acts 14:17
  - Longevity ..... Ex. 20:12
  - Children ..... Ps. 127:3-5
- B. *National and Israelitish:*
  - General ..... Gen. 12:1-3
  - Specific ..... Rom. 9:4, 5
  - Fulfilled ..... Rom. 11:1-36
  - Perverted ..... Rom. 2:17-29
  - Rejected ..... Acts 13:46-52
- C. *Spiritual and eternal:*
  - Salvation ..... John 3:16
  - Election ..... Eph. 1:3-5
  - Regeneration ..... 2 Cor. 5:17
  - Forgiveness ..... Col. 1:14
  - Adoption ..... Rom. 8:15-17
  - No condemnation ..... Rom. 8:1
  - Holy Spirit ..... Acts 1:8
  - Justification ..... Acts 13:38, 39
  - New covenant ..... Heb. 8:6-13
  - Fatherly chastisement ..... Heb. 12:5-11
  - Christ's intercession ..... Rom. 8:34
  - Sanctification ..... Rom. 8:3-14
  - Perseverance ..... John 10:27-29
  - Glorification ..... Rom. 8:30

Blindfold—*a covering over the eyes*
- A prelude to execution ..... Esth. 7:8
- Put on Jesus ..... Luke 22:63, 64

Blindness—*destitute of vision*
- A. *Causes of:*
  - Old age ..... Gen. 27:1
  - Disobedience ..... Deut. 28:28, 29
  - Miracle ..... 2 Kin. 6:18-20
  - Judgment ..... Gen. 19:11
  - Captivity ..... Judg. 16:20, 21
  - Condition of servitude ..... 1 Sam. 11:2
  - Defeat in war ..... 2 Kin. 25:7
  - Unbelief ..... Acts 9:8, 9
  - God's glory ..... John 9:1-3
- B. *Disabilities of:*
  - Keep from priesthood ..... Lev. 21:18
  - Offerings unacceptable ..... Lev. 22:22; Mal. 1:8
  - Make protection ..... Lev. 19:14
  - Helplessness ..... Judg. 16:26
  - Occasional derision ..... 2 Sam. 5:6-8
- C. *Remedies for:*
  - Promised in Christ ..... Is. 42:7, 16
  - Proclaimed in the Gospel ..... Luke 4:18-21; Acts 26:18
  - Portrayed in a miracle ..... John 9:1-41; Acts 9:1-18

- Perfected in faith ..... John 11:37; Eph. 1:18
- Perverted by disobedience ..... 1 John 2:11

Blood
- A. *Used to designate:*
  - Unity of mankind ..... Acts 17:26
  - Human nature ..... John 1:13
  - Human depravity ..... Ezek. 16:6, 22
  - The individual soul ..... Ezek. 33:8
  - The essence of life ..... Gen. 9:4; Lev. 17:11, 14
  - The sacredness of life ..... Gen. 9:5, 6
  - Means of atonement ..... Lev. 17:10-14
  - Regeneration ..... Is. 4:4; Ezek. 16:9; Joel 3:21
  - New covenant ..... Matt. 26:28
  - The new life ..... John 6:53-56
  - Christ's atonement ..... Heb. 9:14
  - Redemption ..... Zech. 9:11
- B. *Miracles connected with:*
  - Water turns to ..... Ex. 7:20, 21
  - Water appears like ..... 2 Kin. 3:22, 23
  - The moon turns to ..... Acts 2:20; Rev. 6:12
  - Flow of, stops ..... Mark 5:25, 29
  - Sea becomes ..... Rev. 11:6
  - Believers become white in ..... Rev. 7:14
- C. *Figurative of:*
  - Sin ..... Is. 59:3
  - Cruelty ..... Hab. 2:12
  - Abominations ..... Is. 66:3
  - Guilt ..... 2 Sam. 1:16; Matt. 27:25
  - Inherited guilt ..... Matt. 23:35
  - Vengeance ..... Ezek. 35:6
  - Retribution ..... Is. 49:25, 26
  - Slaughter ..... Is. 34:6-8
  - Judgment ..... Rev. 16:6
  - Victory ..... Ps. 58:10

Blood of Christ
- A. *Described as:*
  - Innocent ..... Matt. 27:4
  - Precious ..... 1 Pet. 1:19
  - Necessary ..... Heb. 9:22, 23
  - Sufficient ..... Heb. 9:13, 14
  - Final ..... Heb. 9:24-28
  - Cleansing ..... 1 John 1:7
  - Conquering ..... Rev. 12:11
- B. *Basis of:*
  - Reconciliation ..... Eph. 2:13-16
  - Redemption ..... Rom. 3:24, 25
  - Justification ..... Rom. 5:9
  - Sanctification ..... Heb. 10:29
  - Communion ..... Matt. 26:26-29
  - Victory ..... Rev. 12:11
  - Eternal life ..... John 6:53-56

Bloodguiltiness—*guilt incurred by murder*
- Incurred by willful murderer ..... Ex. 21:14
- Not saved by altar ..... 1 Kin. 2:29
- Provision for innocent ..... Ex. 21:13; 1 Kin. 1:50-53
- David's prayer concerning ..... Ps. 51:14
- Judas' guilt in ..... Matt. 27:4
- The Jews' admission of ..... Matt. 27:25
- Figurative, of individual responsibility ..... Ezek. 37:1-9
- Of Christ-rejectors ..... Acts 18:6

Blood money
- Payment made to Judas ..... Matt. 26:14-16

Bloody—*Descriptive of:*
- Saul's house ..... 2 Sam. 21:1
- Crimes ..... Ezek. 7:23
- Cities ..... Ezek. 22:2; Ezek. 24:6, 9
- David ..... 2 Sam. 16:7

Bloody sweat—(believed to be caused by agony or stress)
- Agony in Gethsemane ..... Luke 22:44

Blossom—*to open into blossoms; to flower*
- Aaron's rod ..... Num. 17:5, 8
- A fig tree ..... Hab. 3:17
- A desert ..... Is. 35:1, 2
- Israel ..... Is. 27:6

Blot—*to rub or wipe off*
- One's name in God's Book ..... Ex. 32:32, 33

SUBJECT REFERENCE

One's sins .... Ps. 51:1, 9
Acts 3:19
Legal ordinances .... Col. 2:14
Amalek .... Deut. 25:19
Israel as a nation .... 2 Kin. 14:27

Blue

Often used in tabernacle .... Ex. 25:4
Ex. 28:15
Used by royalty .... Esth. 8:15
Imported .... Ezek. 27:7, 24

Blush—*to redden in the cheeks*

Sin makes impossible .... Jer. 6:15
Jer. 8:12
Sin causes saints to .... Ezra 9:6

Boanerges—*sons of thunder*

Surname of James and John .... Mark 3:17

Boar—*male wild hog*

Descriptive of Israel's enemies .... Ps. 80:13

Boasting—*to speak of with pride; to brag*

A. *Excluded because of:*
Man's limited knowledge .... Prov. 27:1, 2
Uncertain issues .... 1 Kin. 20:11
Evil incurred thereby .... Luke 12:19-21
James 3:5
Salvation by grace .... Eph. 2:9
God's sovereignty .... Rom. 11:17-21

B. *Examples of:*
Goliath .... 1 Sam. 17:44
Ben-hadad .... 1 Kin. 20:10
Rabshakeh .... 2 Kin. 18:27, 34
Satan .... Is. 14:12-15
Ezek. 28:12-19

See Haughtiness; Pride

Boasting in God

Continual duty .... Ps. 34:2
Always in the Lord .... 2 Cor. 10:13-18
Necessary to refute the wayward .... 2 Cor. 11:5-33
Of spiritual rather than natural .... Phil. 3:3-14

Boats

In Christ's time .... John 6:22, 23
In Paul's travel to Rome .... Acts 27:16
Lifeboats .... Acts 27:30
Ferryboats .... 2 Sam. 19:18

Boaz—*strength*

1. A wealthy Beth-lehemite .... Ruth 2:1, 4-18
Husband of Ruth .... Ruth 4:10-13
Ancestor of Christ .... Matt. 1:5
2. Pillar of Temple .... 1 Kin. 7:21

Bocheru—*first-born*

A son of Azel .... 1 Chr. 8:38

Bochim—*weepers*

A place near Gilgal .... Judg. 2:1-5

Body of Christ

A. *Descriptive of His own body:*
Prepared by God .... Heb. 10:5
Conceived by the Holy Spirit .... Luke 1:34, 35
Subject to growth .... Luke 2:40, 52
Heb. 5:8, 9
Part of our nature .... Heb. 2:14
Without sin .... 2 Cor. 5:21
Subject to human emotions .... Heb. 5:7
Raised without corruption .... Acts 2:31
Glorified by resurrection .... Phil. 3:21
Communion with .... 1 Cor. 11:27

B. *Descriptive of the true church:*
Identified .... Col. 1:24
Described .... Eph. 2:16
Christ, the head of .... Eph. 1:22
Christ dwells in .... Eph. 1:23

Body of man

A. *By creation:*
Made by God .... Gen. 2:7, 21
Various organs of .... 1 Cor. 12:12-25
Bears God's image .... Gen. 9:6
Col. 3:10
Wonderfully made .... Ps. 139:14

B. *By sin:*
Subject to death .... Rom. 5:12
Destroyed .... Job 19:26
Instrument of evil .... Rom. 1:24-32

C. *By salvation:*
A Temple of the Holy Spirit .... 1 Cor. 6:19
A living sacrifice .... Rom. 12:1
Dead to the Law .... Rom. 7:4
Dead to sin .... Rom. 8:10
Control over .... Rom. 6:12-23
Christ, the center of .... Rom. 6:8-11
Phil. 1:20
Sins against, forbidden .... 1 Cor. 6:13, 18
Needful requirements of .... 1 Cor. 7:4
Col. 2:23

D. *By resurrection, to be:*
Redeemed .... Rom. 8:23
Raised .... John 5:28, 29
Changed .... Phil. 3:21
Glorified .... Rom. 8:29, 30
Judged .... 2 Cor. 5:10-14
Perfected .... 1 Thess. 5:23

E. *Figurative descriptions of:*
House .... 2 Cor. 5:1
House of clay .... Job 4:19
Earthen vessel .... 2 Cor. 4:7
Tabernacle .... 2 Pet. 1:13
Temple of God .... 1 Cor. 3:16, 17
Members of Christ .... 1 Cor. 6:15

Bohan—*thumb*

1. Reuben's son .... Josh. 15:6
2. Border mark .... Josh. 18:17

Boil—*an inflamed ulcer*

Sixth Egyptian plague .... Ex. 9:8-11
A symptom of leprosy .... Lev. 13:18-20
Satan afflicts Job with .... Job 2:7
Hezekiah's life endangered by .... 2 Kin. 20:7

Boiling—*the state of bubbling*

A part of cooking .... 1 Kin. 19:21
Of a child, in famine .... 2 Kin. 6:29
Figurative, of trouble .... Job 30:27

Boldness—*courage; bravery; confidence*

A. *Comes from:*
Righteousness .... Prov. 28:1
Prayer .... Eph. 6:19
Fearless preaching .... Acts 9:27-29
Christ .... Eph. 3:12
Phil. 1:20
Testimony .... Phil. 1:14
Communion with God .... Heb. 4:16
Perfect love .... 1 John 4:17

B. *Examples of:*
Tribe of Levi .... Ex. 32:26-28
David .... 1 Sam. 17:45-49
Three Hebrew men .... Dan. 3:8-18
Daniel .... Dan. 6:10-23
The apostles .... Acts 4:13-31
Paul .... Acts 9:27-29
Paul, Barnabas .... Acts 13:46

See Courage; Fearlessness

Bolled—*in bud, in seed*

Flax of Egypt .... Ex. 9:31

Bondage, literal

Israel in Egypt .... Ex. 1:7-22
Gibeonites to Israel .... Josh. 9:23
Israel in Assyria .... 2 Kin. 17:6, 20, 23
Judah in Babylon .... 2 Kin. 25:1-21
Denied by Jews .... John 8:33

Bondage, spiritual

A. *Subjection to:*
The devil .... 2 Tim. 2:26
Sin .... John 8:34
Fear of death .... Heb. 2:14, 15
Death .... Rom. 7:24
Corruption .... 2 Pet. 2:19

B. *Deliverance from:*
Promised .... Is. 42:6, 7
Proclaimed .... Luke 4:18, 21
Through Christ .... John 8:36
By obedience .... Rom. 6:17-19
By the truth .... John 8:32

Bones—*structural parts of the body*

A. *Descriptive of:*
Unity of male and female .... Gen. 2:23
Human nature .... Luke 24:39
Family unity .... Gen. 29:14
Tribal unity .... 1 Chr. 11:1

B. *Prophecies concerning:*
The paschal lamb's .... Ex. 12:46
John 19:36
Jacob's .... Gen. 50:25
Heb. 11:22
Valley of dry .... Ezek. 37:1-14

C. *Figurative of health, affected by:*
Shameful wife .... Prov. 12:4
Good report .... Prov. 15:30
Broken spirit .... Prov. 17:22

Bonnet—*a headdress*

Used by priests .... Ex. 28:40
Worn by women .... Is. 3:20
Used by sons of Zadok .... Ezek. 44:18

Books—*written compositions*

A. *Features of:*
Old .... Job 19:23, 24
Made of paper reeds .... Is. 19:7
Made of parchment .... 2 Tim. 4:13
Made in a roll .... Jer. 36:2
Written with ink .... 3 John 13
Dedicated .... Luke 1:3
Sealed .... Rev. 5:1
Many .... Eccl. 12:12
Quotations in .... Matt. 21:4, 5
Written by secretary .... Jer. 36:4, 18

B. *Contents of:*
Genealogies .... Gen. 5:1
Law of Moses .... Deut. 31:9, 24, 26
Geography .... Josh. 18:9
Wars .... Num. 21:14
Records .... Ezra 4:15
Miracles .... Josh. 10:13
Legislation .... 1 Sam. 10:25
Lamentations .... 2 Chr. 35:25
Proverbs .... Prov. 25:1
Prophecies .... Jer. 51:60-64
Symbols .... Rev. 1:1
The Messiah .... Luke 24:27, 44
Heb. 10:7

C. *Mentioned but not preserved:*
Book of wars .... Num. 21:14
Book of Jasher .... Josh. 10:13
Chronicles of David .... 1 Chr. 27:24
Book of Gad .... 1 Chr. 29:29
Story of prophet Iddo .... 2 Chr. 13:22
Book of Nathan .... 1 Chr. 29:29
Book of Jehu .... 2 Chr. 20:34

Book of God's judgment

In visions of Daniel and John .... Dan. 7:10
Rev. 20:12

Book of the law

Called "the law of Moses" .... Josh. 8:31, 32
Copied .... Deut. 17:18
Placed in the ark .... Deut. 31:26
Foundation of Israel's religion .... Deut. 28:58
Lost and found .... 2 Kin. 22:8
Produces reformation .... 2 Kin. 23:2-14
Produces revival .... Neh. 8:2, 8-18
Quoted .... 2 Kin. 14:6
To be remembered .... Josh. 1:7, 8
Mal. 4:4
Prophetic of Christ .... Luke 24:27, 44

Book of life

A. *Contains:*
The names of the saved .... Phil. 4:3
The deed of the righteous .... Mal. 3:16-18

B. *Excludes:*
Renegades .... Ex. 32:33
Ps. 69:28
Apostates .... Rev. 13:8
Rev. 17:8

C. *Affords, basis of:*
Joy .... Luke 10:20
Hope .... Heb. 12:23
Judgment .... Dan. 7:10
Rev. 20:12-15

Booths—*stalls made of branches*

Used for cattle .... Gen. 33:17
Required in feast of tabernacle .... Lev. 23:40-43; Neh. 8:14-17

Booty—*spoils taken in war*

A. *Stipulations concerning:*
No Canaanites .... Deut. 20:14-17

SUBJECT REFERENCE

No cursed thing .... Josh. 6:17-19
Destruction of Amalek ...... 1 Sam. 15:2, 3
Destruction of Arad .... Num. 21:1-3
The Lord's judgment .... Jer. 49:30-32

B. *Division of:*

On percentage basis .... Num. 31:26-47
Rear troops share in .... 1 Sam. 30:24, 25

Border—*boundary*

A. *Marked by:*

Natural landmarks .... Josh. 18:16
Rivers .... Josh. 18:19
Markers .... Deut. 19:14

B. *Enlargement of:*

By God's power .... Ex. 34:24
A blessing .... 1 Chr. 4:10

Born again—*new birth, regeneration*

A. *Necessity of, because of:*

Inability .... John 3:3, 5
The flesh .... John 3:6
Deadness .... Eph. 2:1

B. *Produced by:*

The Holy Spirit .... John 3:5, 8
Titus 3:5
The Word of God .... James 1:18
1 Pet. 1:23
Faith .... 1 John 5:1

C. *Results of:*

New creature .... 2 Cor. 5:17
Changed life .... Rom. 6:4-11
Holy life .... 1 John 3:9
Righteousness .... 1 John 2:29
Love .... 1 John 3:10
Victory .... 1 John 5:4

Borrow—*to get by loan*

A. *Regulations regarding:*

From other nations, forbidden .... {Deut. 15:6 / Deut. 28:12}
Obligation to repay .... Ex. 22:14, 15
Non-payment, wicked .... Ps. 37:21
Involves servitude .... Prov. 22:7
Evils of, corrected .... Neh. 5:1-13
Christ's words on .... Matt. 5:42

B. *Examples of:*

Jewels .... Ex. 11:2
A widow's vessels .... 2 Kin. 4:3
A woodsman's axe .... 2 Kin. 6:5
Christ's transportation ...... Matt. 21:2, 3

Bosom—*the breast as center of affections*

A. *Expressive of:*

Procreation .... Gen. 16:5
Prostitution .... Prov. 6:26, 27
Anger .... Eccl. 7:9
Procrastination .... Prov. 19:24
Protection .... Is. 40:11
Iniquity .... Job 31:33

B. *Symbolic of:*

Man's impatience .... Ps. 74:11
Christ's deity .... John 1:18
Eternal peace .... Luke 16:22, 23

Bosor—*a lamp*

Father of Balaam .... 2 Pet. 2:15
Same as Beor .... Num. 22:5

Botch—*a boil*

A punishment of disobedience .. Deut. 28:27

Bottle—*a hollow thing* (vessel)

A. *Used for:*

Milk .... Judg. 4:19
Water .... Gen. 21:14
Wine .... Hab. 2:15

B. *Made of:*

Clay .... Jer. 19:1, 10, 11
Skins .... Matt. 9:17
Mark 2:22

C. *Figurative of:*

God's remembrance .... Ps. 56:8
God's judgments .... Jer. 13:12-14
Sorrow .... Ps. 119:83
Impatience .... Job 32:19
Clouds of rain .... Job 38:37
Old and new covenants ...... Matt. 9:17

SUBJECT REFERENCE

Bottomless pit

Apollyon, king of .... Rev. 9:11
Beast comes from .... Rev. 11:7
Rev. 17:8
Devil, cast into .... Rev. 20:1-3
A prison .... Rev. 20:7

Bough—*branch of a tree*

A. *Used:*

To make ceremonial booths .... Lev. 23:39-43
In siege of Shechem .... Judg. 9:45-49

B. *Figurative of:*

Joseph's offspring .... Gen. 49:22
Judgment .... Is. 17:1-11
Israel .... Ps. 80:8-11
Nebuchadnezzar's kingdom .. Dan. 4:10-12

Bow—*an instrument for shooting arrows*

A. *Uses of:*

For hunting .... Gen. 27:3
For war .... Is. 7:24
As a token of friendship ..... 1 Sam. 18:4
As a commemorative song ... 2 Sam. 1:18

B. *Illustrative of:*

Strength .... Job 29:20
The tongue .... Ps. 11:2
Defeat .... Hos. 1:5
Peace .... Hos. 2:18, 19

Bowels

A. *Used literally of:*

Intestines .... Num. 5:22
Source of offspring .... Gen. 15:4
Source of descendants .... Gen. 25:23
Source of the Messiah .... 2 Sam. 7:12
Amasa's—shed out .... 2 Sam. 20:10
Jehoram's—fell out .... 2 Chr. 21:14-19
Judas'—gushed out .... Acts 1:16-18

B. *Used figuratively of:*

Natural love .... Gen. 43:30
Deep emotion .... Job 30:27
Intense suffering .... Ps. 22:14
Great concern .... Jer. 31:20
Spiritual distress .... Lam. 1:20

Bowing the knee

A. *Wrong:*

Before idols .... Ex. 20:5
In mockery .... Matt. 27:29
Before an angel .... Rev. 22:8, 9

B. *True, in:*

Prayer .... 1 Kin. 8:54
Homage .... 2 Kin. 1:13
Repentance .... Ezra 9:5, 6
Worship .... Ps. 95:6
Submission .... Eph. 3:14
Phil. 2:10

Box—*a covered case*

Used for oil or perfume .... 2 Kin. 9:1
Matt. 26:7

Box tree—*an evergreen tree*

Descriptive of Messianic times .. Is. 41:19, 20

Boy—*male child*

Esau and Jacob .... Gen. 25:27
Payment for a harlot .... Joel 3:3
Play in streets .... Zech. 8:5
See Children; Young men

Bozez—*shining*

Rock of Michmash .... 1 Sam. 14:4, 5

Bozkath, Boscath—*height*

A town in south Judah .... Josh. 15:39
Home of Jedidah .... 2 Kin. 22:1

Bozrah—*fortress, sheepfold*

1. City of Edom .... Gen. 36:33
Destruction of, foretold ..... Amos 1:12
Figurative, of Messiah's victory .... Is. 63:1
2. City of Moab .... Jer. 48:24

Bracelet—*ornament*

Worn by both sexes .... Ezek. 16:11
Given to Rebekah .... Gen. 24:22
In tabernacle offerings .... Ex. 35:22
Worn by King Saul .... 2 Sam. 1:10
A sign of worldliness .... Is. 3:19

SUBJECT REFERENCE

Braided hair

Contrasted to spiritual adornment .... 1 Tim. 2:9, 10

Bramble—*a thorny bush*

Emblem of a tyrant .... Judg. 9:8-15
Used for fuel .... Ps. 58:9
Symbol of destruction .... Is. 34:13

Branch—*a limb*

A. *Used naturally of:*

Limbs of tree .... Num. 13:23

B. *Used figuratively of:*

A king .... Ezek. 17:3-10
Israel .... Rom. 11:16, 21
The Messiah .... Is. 11:1
Christians .... John 15:5, 6
Prosperity .... Prov. 11:28
Adversity .... Job 15:32

Brass—*an alloy of copper and zinc* (tin)

A. *Used for:*

Tabernacle vessels .... Ex. 38:2-31
Temple vessels .... 1 Kin. 7:41-46
Armor .... 2 Chr. 12:10
Mirrors, etc. .... Ex. 38:8
Is. 45:2
Money .... Matt. 10:9

B. *Workers in:*

Tubal-cain .... Gen. 4:22
Hiram .... 1 Kin. 7:14
Alexander .... 2 Tim. 4:14

C. *Figurative of:*

Grecian Empire .... Dan. 2:39
Obstinate sinners .... Is. 48:4
Endurance .... Jer. 15:20
God's decrees .... Zech. 6:1
Christ's glory .... Dan. 10:6
Rev. 1:15

Bravery, moral

Condemning sin .... 2 Sam. 12:1-14
Denouncing hypocrisy .... Matt. 23:1-39
Opposing enemies .... Phil. 1:28
Exposing inconsistency .... Gal. 2:11-15
Uncovering false teachers ...... 2 Pet. 2:1-22
Rebuking Christians .... 1 Cor. 6:1-8
James 4:1-11

Brawler—*a wrangler*

Descriptive of certain women ... Prov. 21:9
Disqualifies bishops .... 1 Tim. 3:3

Brazen serpent

Occasion of ruin .... 2 Kin. 18:4

Breach—*a break*

A. *Used literally of:*

Jerusalem's walls .... Neh. 4:7

B. *Used figuratively of:*

Sin .... Is. 30:13

Bread—*food*

A. *God's provision for;*

A gift .... Ruth 1:6
2 Cor. 9:10
Earned by sweat .... Gen. 3:19
Object of prayer .... Matt. 6:11
Without work, condemned ... 2 Thess. 3:8, 12

B. *Uses of unleavened, for:*

Heavenly visitors .... Gen. 19:3
The Passover .... Ex. 12:8
Priests .... 2 Kin. 23:9
Nazarites .... Num. 6:13, 15
Lord's Supper .... Luke 22:7-19

C. *Special uses of:*

Provided by ravens .... 1 Kin. 17:6
Strength .... 1 Kin. 19:6-8
Satan's .... Matt. 4:3
Miracle .... Matt. 14:19-21
Insight .... Luke 24:35

D. *Figurative of:*

Adversity .... Is. 30:20
Christ .... John 6:33-35
Christ's death .... 1 Cor. 11:23-28
Communion with Christ ..... Acts 2:46
1 Cor. 10:17
Extreme poverty .... Ps. 37:25
Prodigality .... Ezek. 16:49
Wickedness .... Prov. 4:17
Idleness .... Prov. 31:27

SUBJECT ... REFERENCE

E. *Bread of life:*
- Christ is ... John 6:32-35
- Same as manna ... Ex. 16:4, 5
- Fulfilled in Lord's Supper ... 1 Cor. 11:23, 24

Breaking of bread—*a meal*
- Prayer before ... Matt. 14:19
- Insight through ... Luke 24:35
- Fellowship thereby ... Acts 2:42
- Strength gained by ... Acts 20:11
- See Lord's Supper

Breastplate—*protection*

A. *Worn by:*
- High priest ... Ex. 28:4, 15-20
- Soldiers ... 1 Sam. 17:5, 38
- "Locusts" ... Rev. 9:7, 9

B. *Figurative of:*
- Christ's righteousness ... Is. 59:17
- Faith's righteousness ... Eph. 6:14

Breasts—*the female teats*

A. *Literally of:*
- Married love ... Prov. 5:19; Song 1:13
- An infant's life ... Job 3:12; Ps. 22:9
- Posterity ... Gen. 49:25

B. *Figuratively, of:*
- Health ... Job 21:24
- Mother Jerusalem ... Is. 66:10, 11

Breath
- Comes from God ... Gen. 2:7
- Necessary for all ... Eccl. 3:19
- Held by God ... Dan. 5:23
- Absence of, death ... Ps. 146:4
- Taken by God ... Ps. 104:29
- Figurative, of new life ... Ezek. 37:5-10

Breath of God

Cause of:
- Creation ... 2 Sam. 22:16
- Life ... Job 33:4
- Destruction ... Is. 11:4
- Death ... Job 4:9

Breeches—*garment*
- Worn by priests ... Ex. 28:42

Brevity of human life

A. *Compared to:*
- Pilgrimage ... Gen. 47:9
- A tale ... Ps. 90:9
- Sleep ... Ps. 90:5
- Flower ... Job 14:2
- Grass ... 1 Pet. 1:24
- Vapor ... James 4:14
- Shadow ... Eccl. 6:12
- Moment ... 2 Cor. 4:17
- A weaver's shuttle ... Job 7:6

B. *Truths arising from:*
- Prayer can prolong ... Is. 38:2-5
- Incentive to improvement ... Ps. 90:12
- Some kept from old age ... 1 Sam. 2:32, 33
- Some know their end ... 2 Pet. 1:13, 14
- Hope regarding ... Phil. 1:21-25
- Life's completion ... 2 Tim. 4:6-8

Bribery—*gifts to pervert*

A. *The effects of:*
- Makes sinners ... Ps. 26:10
- Corrupts conscience ... Ex. 23:8
- Perverts justice ... Is. 1:23
- Brings chaos ... Amos 5:12
- Merits punishment ... Amos 2:6

B. *Examples of:*
- Balak ... Num. 22:17, 37
- Delilah ... Judg. 16:5
- Samuel's sons ... 1 Sam. 8:3
- Ben-hadad ... 1 Kin. 15:18, 19
- Shemaiah ... Neh. 6:10-13
- Haman ... Esth. 3:8, 9
- Judas and priests ... Matt. 27:3-9
- Soldiers ... Matt. 28:12-15
- Simon ... Acts 8:18
- Felix ... Acts 24:26

Brick—*baked clay*
- Babel built of ... Gen. 11:3

SUBJECT ... REFERENCE
- Israel forced to make ... Ex. 1:14
- Altars made of ... Is. 65:3
- Forts made of ... Is. 9:10
- Made in kiln ... 2 Sam. 12:31

Brickkiln—*a place for making bricks*
- Forced labor in ... 2 Sam. 12:31

Bridal

Gift:
- A burned city ... 1 Kin. 9:16

Veil:
- Rebekah wears first ... Gen. 26:64-67

Bride—*newly wed woman*
- Wears adornments ... Is. 61:10
- Receives presents ... Gen. 24:53
- Has damsels ... Gen. 24:59, 61
- Adorned for husband ... Rev. 19:7, 8
- Rejoices husband ... Is. 62:5
- Stands near husband ... Ps. 45:9
- Receives benediction ... Ruth 4:11, 12
- Must forget father's house ... Ruth 1:8-17
- Must be chaste ... 2 Cor. 11:2
- Figurative of Israel ... Ezek. 16:8-14
- Figurative of Church ... Rev. 21:2, 9

Bridegroom—*newly wed man*
- Wears special garments ... Is. 61:10
- Attended by friends ... John 3:29
- Adorned with garlands ... Song 3:11
- Rejoices over bride ... Is. 62:5
- Returns with bride ... Matt. 25:1-6
- Exempted from military service ... Deut. 24:5
- Figurative of God ... Ezek. 16:8-14
- Figurative of Christ ... John 3:29

Bridle—*a harness*

A. *Used literally of:*
- An ass ... Prov. 26:3

B. *Used figuratively of:*
- God's control ... Is. 30:28
- Self-control ... James 1:26
- Imposed control ... Ps. 32:9

Briers—*thorny shrub*

A. *Used literally of:*
- Thorns ... Judg. 8:7, 16

B. *Used figuratively of:*
- Sinful nature ... Mic. 7:4
- Change of nature ... Is. 55:13
- Rejection ... Is. 5:6

Brigandine—*a coat of mail*
- Used as armor ... Jer. 46:4

Brimstone—*sulphur*
- Falls upon Sodom ... Gen. 19:24
- Sent as judgment ... Deut. 29:23
- State of wicked ... Ps. 11:6
- Condition of hell ... Rev. 14:10

Broiled fish
- Eaten by Jesus ... Luke 24:42, 43

Broken-handed
- Disqualifies for priesthood ... Lev. 21:19

Brokenhearted—*grieving*
- Christ's mission to ... Is. 61:1

Brooks—*streams*

A. *Characteristics of:*
- Numerous ... Deut. 8:7
- Produce grass ... 1 Kin. 18:5
- Abound in fish ... Is. 19:8
- Afford protection ... Is. 19:6

B. *Names of:*
- Arnon ... Num. 21:14, 15
- Besor ... 1 Sam. 30:9
- Gaash ... 2 Sam. 23:30
- Cherith ... 1 Kin. 17:3, 5
- Eschol ... Num. 13:23, 24
- Kidron ... 2 Sam. 15:23
- Kishon ... Ps. 83:9
- Zered ... Deut. 2:13

C. *Figurative of:*
- Wisdom ... Prov. 18:4
- Prosperity ... Job 20:17
- Deception ... Job 6:15
- Refreshment ... Ps. 110:7

SUBJECT ... REFERENCE

Broth—*thin, watery soup*
- Served by Gideon ... Judg. 6:19, 20
- Figurative of evil ... Is. 65:4

Brother, brethren

A. *Used naturally of:*
- Sons of same parents ... Gen. 42:4
- Common ancestry ... Gen. 14:16
- Same race ... Deut. 23:7
- Same humanity ... Gen. 9:5

B. *Used figuratively of:*
- An ally ... Amos 1:9
- Christian disciples ... Matt. 23:8
- A spiritual companion ... 1 Cor. 1:1

C. *Characteristics of Christian brothers:*
- One Father ... Matt. 23:8, 9
- Believe ... Luke 8:21
- Some weak ... 1 Cor. 8:11-13
- In need ... James 2:15
- Of low degree ... James 1:9
- Disorderly ... 2 Thess. 3:6
- Evil ... James 4:11
- Falsely judge ... Rom. 14:10-21
- Need admonishment ... 2 Thess. 3:15

Brotherhood of man

A. *Based on common:*
- Creation ... Gen. 1:27, 28
- Blood ... Acts 17:26
- Needs ... Prov. 22:2; Mal. 2:10

B. *Disrupted by:*
- Sin ... 1 John 3:12
- Satan ... John 8:44

Brotherly kindness (love)

A. *Toward Christians:*
- Taught by God ... 1 Thess. 4:9
- Commanded ... Rom. 12:10
- Explained ... 1 John 4:7-21
- Fulfills the Law ... Rom. 13:8-10
- Badge of new birth ... John 13:34
- A Christian grace ... 2 Pet. 1:5-7
- Must continue ... Heb. 13:1

B. *Toward others:*
- Neighbors ... Matt. 22:39
- Enemies ... Matt. 5:44

Brothers (brethren) of Christ
- Four: James, Joses, Simon, Judas (Jude) ... Matt. 13:55; Mark 6:3
- Born after Christ ... Matt. 1:25; Luke 2:7
- Travel with Mary ... Matt. 12:47-50
- Disbelieve Christ ... John 7:4, 5
- Become believers ... Acts 1:14
- Work for Christ ... 1 Cor. 9:5
- One (James) becomes prominent ... Acts 12:17
- Wrote an epistle ... James 1:1
- Another (Jude) wrote an epistle ... Jude

Brothers, Twin
- Figureheads on Paul's ship to Rome, called Castor and Pollux ... Acts 28:11

Brought up—*reared*
- Ephraim's children—by Joseph ... Gen. 50:23
- Esther—by Mordecai ... Esth. 2:5-7, 20
- Wisdom (Christ)—by the Lord ... Prov. 8:30
- Jesus—at Nazareth ... Luke 4:16
- Paul—at Gamaliel's feet ... Acts 22:3

Brow
- The forehead ... Is. 48:4
- Top of hill ... Luke 4:29

Bruised—*injured*

A. *Used literally of:*
- Physical injuries ... Luke 9:39

B. *Used figuratively of:*
- Evils ... Is. 1:6
- The Messiah's pains ... Is. 53:5
- Satan's defeat ... Gen. 3:15; Rom. 16:20

Bucket—*container for water*
- Figurative of blessing ... Num. 24:7
- Pictures God's magnitude ... Is. 40:15

SUBJECT — REFERENCE

Buffet—*to strike with the fist*

Jesus subjected to ... Matt. 26:67; Mark 14:65
Descriptive of Paul ... 2 Cor. 12:7
Figurative of self-discipline ... 1 Cor. 9:27

Build—*construct or erect*

A. *Used literally, of:*
City ... Gen. 4:17
Altar ... Gen. 8:20
Tower ... Gen. 11:4
House ... Gen. 33:17
Sheepfolds ... Num. 32:16
Fortifications ... Deut. 20:20; Ezek. 4:2
Temple ... 1 Kin. 6:1, 14; Ezra 4:1
High place ... 1 Kin. 11:7
Walls ... Neh. 4:6
Tombs ... Matt. 23:29; Luke 11:47
Synagogue ... Luke 7:2-5

B. *Used figuratively, of:*
Obeying Christ ... Matt. 7:24-27
Church ... Matt. 16:18
Christ's resurrection ... Matt. 26:61; John 2:19
Return to legalism ... Gal. 2:16-20
Christian unity ... Eph. 2:19-22
Spiritual growth ... Acts 20:32; Col. 2:7; 1 Pet. 2:5

See Edification

Bukki

1. Danite chief ... Num. 34:22
2. A descendant of Aaron ... 1 Chr. 6:5, 51

Bukkiah—*proved of Jehovah*

A Levite musician ... 1 Chr. 25:4, 13

Bul—*growth*

Eighth Hebrew month ... 1 Kin. 6:38

Bull—*male of any bovine animal*

Used in sacrifices ... Heb. 9:13
Blood of, insufficient ... Heb. 10:4
Wild, trapped ... Is. 51:20
Symbol of evil men ... Ps. 22:12
Symbol of mighty men ... Ps. 68:30
Restrictions on ... Deut. 15:19, 20
Sacrifices of, inadequate ... Ps. 69:30, 31
Blood of, unacceptable ... Is. 1:11
Figurative of the Lord's sacrifice ... Is. 34:6, 7
Figurative of strength ... Deut. 33:17

Bullock—*young bull*

Used in sacrifices ... Ex. 29:1, 10-14
Restrictions on ... Deut. 15:19, 20
Sacrifices of, inadequate ... Ps. 69:30, 31
Blood of, unacceptable ... Is. 1:11
Figurative of the Lord's sacrifice ... Is. 34:6, 7
Figurative of strength ... Deut. 33:17

Bulrush—*a reed*

Used in Moses' ark ... Ex. 2:3
Found in river banks ... Job 8:11
Figurative of judgment ... Is. 9:14

Bulwark—*defensive wall*

Around Jerusalem ... Ps. 48:13
Used in wars ... Eccl. 9:14
Made of logs ... Deut. 20:20
Foundation of weapons ... 2 Chr. 26:15

Bunah—*intelligence*

A descendant of Judah ... 1 Chr. 2:25

Bunni—*erected*

1. A pre-exilic Levite ... Neh. 11:15
2. A postexilic Levite ... Neh. 9:4
3. Signer of document ... Neh. 10:15

Burden—*load*

A. *Used physically of:*
Load, cargo ... Neh. 4:17

B. *Used figuratively of:*
Care ... Ps. 55:22
Prophet's message ... Hab. 1:1
Rules, rites ... Luke 11:46
Sin ... Ps. 38:4
Responsibility ... Gal. 6:2, 5
Christ's law ... Matt. 11:30

Burden-bearer

Christ is the believer's ... Ps. 55:22

Burglarizing—*stealing*

Severe penalty for ... Ex. 21:16

See Stealing; Theft, thief

Burial

A. *Features regarding:*
Body washed ... Acts 9:37
Ointment used ... Matt. 26:12
Embalm sometimes ... Gen. 50:26
Body wrapped ... John 11:44
Placed in coffin ... Gen. 50:26
Carried on a bier ... Luke 7:14
Mourners attend ... John 11:19
Graves provided ... Gen. 23:5-20
Tombs erected ... Matt. 23:27-29

B. *Places of:*
Abraham and Sarah ... Gen. 25:7-10
Deborah ... Gen. 35:8
Rachel ... Gen. 35:19, 20
Miriam ... Num. 20:1
Moses ... Deut. 34:5, 6
Gideon ... Judg. 8:32
Samson and Manoah ... Judg. 16:30, 31
Saul and his sons ... 1 Sam. 31:12, 13
David ... 1 Kin. 2:10
Joab ... 1 Kin. 2:33, 34
Solomon ... 1 Kin. 11:43
Rehoboam ... 1 Kin. 14:31
Asa ... 1 Kin. 15:24
Manasseh ... 2 Kin. 21:18
Amon ... 2 Kin. 21:23-26
Josiah ... 2 Chr. 35:23, 24
Jesus ... Luke 23:50-53
Lazarus ... John 11:14, 38

Buried alive

Two rebellious families ... Num. 16:27-34
Desire of some ... Rev. 6:15, 16

Burning bush

God speaks from ... Ex. 3:2

Bushel—*a measurement*

Mentioned by Christ ... Matt. 5:15

Business—*one's work*

A. *Attitudes toward:*
See God's hand ... James 4:13
Be diligent ... Prov. 22:29
Be industrious ... Rom. 12:8, 11
Be honest ... 2 Cor. 8:20-22
Put God's first ... Matt. 6:33, 34
Keep heaven in mind ... Matt. 6:19-21
Give portion ... Mal. 3:8-12
Avoid anxiety ... Luke 12:22-30
Remember the fool ... Luke 12:15-21

B. *Those diligent in:*
Joseph ... Gen. 39:11
Moses ... Heb. 3:5
Officers in Israel ... 2 Chr. 34:11, 12
Daniel ... Dan. 6:4
Mordecai ... Esth. 10:2, 3
Paul ... Acts 20:17-35

Busybodies—*meddlers*

Women guilty of ... 1 Tim. 5:13
Some Christians ... 2 Thess. 3:11, 12
Admonitions against ... 1 Pet. 4:15

See Slander; Whisperer

Butler—*an officer*

Imprisonment of Pharaoh's ... Gen. 40:1-13
Same as "cupbearer" ... 1 Kin. 10:5

Butter—*curdled milk*

Article of diet ... 2 Sam. 17:29
Set before visitors ... Gen. 18:8
Got by churning ... Prov. 30:33
Fed to infants ... Is. 7:15, 22
Illustrative of prosperity ... Deut. 32:14
Figurative of smooth words ... Ps. 55:21

Buz—*contempt*

1. A Gadite ... 1 Chr. 5:14
2. An Aramean tribe descending from Nahor ... Gen. 22:20, 21

Buzi—*descendant of Buz*

Father of Ezekiel ... Ezek. 1:3

Buzite—*belonging to Buz*

Of the tribe of Buz ... Job 32:2

By and by—archaic expression meaning immediately or right away

Quickly offended ... Matt. 13:21
Rapid granting of a wish ... Mark 6:25
Servant's duty ... Luke 7:7
Signs of Christ's return ... Luke 21:9

Byway—*winding or secluded path*

Used by travelers ... Judg. 5:6
Figurative of error ... Jer. 18:15

Byword—*saying; remark*

Predicted as a taunt ... Deut. 28:37
Job describes himself ... Job 17:6

C

Cab

A measure for dry things ... 2 Kin. 6:25

Cabbon—*surround*

Village of Judah ... Josh. 15:40

Cabin—*a dungeon*

Jeremiah's imprisonment in ... Jer. 37:16

Cabul—*unproductive*

1. Town of Asher ... Josh. 19:27
2. A district of Galilee offered to Hiram ... 1 Kin. 9:12, 13
Solomon placed people in ... 2 Chr. 8:2

Caesar—*a title of Roman emperors*

A. *Used in reference to:*
1. Augustus Caesar (31B.C.—A.D.14) Decree of brings Joseph and Mary to Bethlehem ... Luke 2:1
2. Tiberius Caesar (A.D. 14-37) Christ's ministry dated by ... Luke 3:1-23
Tribute paid to ... Matt. 22:17-21
Jews side with ... John 19:12
3. Claudius Caesar (A.D. 41-54) Famine in time of ... Acts 11:28
Banished Jews from Rome ... Acts 18:2
4. Nero Caesar (A.D. 54—68) Paul appealed to ... Acts 25:8-12
Converts in household of ... Phil. 4:22
Paul before ... 2 Tim. 4:16-18
Called Augustus ... Acts 25:21

B. *Represented Roman authority*
Image on coins ... Matt. 22:19-21; Mark 12:15-16; Luke 20:24
Received tax ... Matt. 22:19, 21; Mark 12:14, 17; Luke 20:25
Jesus called threat to ... Luke 23:2; John 19:12
Pilate's loyalty to, questioned ... John 19:12
Chosen over Jesus ... John 19:12

Caesar's household—*the imperial staff*

Greeted the Philippians ... Phil. 4:22

Caesarea—*pertaining to Caesar*

Roman capital of Palestine ... Acts 12:19; Acts 23:33
Home of Philip ... Acts 8:40
Home of Cornelius ... Acts 10:1
Peter preached at ... Acts 10:34-43
Paul preached here three times ... Acts 9:30; Acts 18:22; Acts 21:8
Paul escorted to ... Acts 23:23, 33
Paul imprisoned at ... Acts 25:4
Paul appealed to Caesar at ... Acts 25:8-13

Caesarea Philippi

A city in north Palestine; scene of Peter's great confession ... Matt. 16:13-20
Probable place of the transfiguration ... Matt. 17:1-13

Cage—*an enclosure*

Judah compared to ... Jer. 5:27
Figurative of captivity ... Ezek. 19:9
Babylon called ... Rev. 18:2

SUBJECT REFERENCE

Caiaphas—*depression*

Son-in-law of Annas; high priest ... John 18:13
Makes prophecy ... John 11:49-52
Jesus before ... John 18:23, 24
Apostles before ... Acts 4:1-22

Cain—*smith, spear*

Adam's son ... Gen. 4:1
Offering rejected ... Gen. 4:2-7; Heb. 11:4
Was of the evil one ... 1 John 3:12
Murders Abel ... Gen. 4:8
Becomes a vagabond ... Gen. 4:9-15
Builds city ... Gen. 4:16, 17
A type of evil ... Jude 11

Cainan—*fixed*

A son of Arphaxad ... Luke 3:36, 37

Cake—*a bread*

A. *Kinds of:*
Bread ... Ex. 29:23
Unleavened ... Num. 6:19
Fig ... 1 Sam. 30:12
Raisin ... 1 Chr. 16:3
Barley ... Ezek. 4:12
Of fine flour ... Lev. 2:4
Leavened ... Lev. 7:13
Baked with oil ... Num. 11:8

B. *Used literally of:*
Food ... 2 Sam. 13:6
Idolatry ... Jer. 44:19
Food prepared for Elijah ... 1 Kin. 17:13

C. *Used figuratively of:*
Defeat ... Judg. 7:13
Weak religion ... Hos. 7:8

Calah

A great city of Assyria built by Nimrod ... Gen. 10:11, 12

Calamities—*disasters*

A. *Kinds of:*
Personal ... Job 6:2
Tribal ... Judg. 20:34-48
National ... Lam. 1:1-22
Punitive ... Num. 16:12-35
Judicial ... Deut. 32:35
World-wide ... Luke 21:25-28
Sudden ... Prov. 6:15; 1 Thess. 5:3

B. *Attitudes toward:*
Unrepentance ... Prov. 1:24-26
Repentance ... Jer. 18:8
Hardness of heart ... Ex. 14:8, 17
Bitterness ... Ruth 1:20, 21
Defeat ... 1 Sam. 4:15-18
Submission ... Job 2:9, 10
Prayerfulness ... Ps. 141:5
Hopefulness ... Ps. 27:1-3

Calamus—*the sweet cane*

Used in holy oil ... Ex. 30:23
Figurative of love ... Song 4:14
Rendered "sweet cane" ... Jer. 6:20

Calcol, Chalcol

A son of Zerah ... 1 Chr. 2:6
Famous for wisdom ... 1 Kin. 4:31

Caldron—*a large kettle*

A. *Used literally of:*
Temple vessels ... 2 Chr. 35:13

B. *Used figuratively of:*
Leviathan's smoke ... Job 41:20
Safety ... Ezek. 11:3, 7, 11
Oppression ... Mic. 3:3

Caleb—*dog; also bold*

1. Son of Jephunneh ... Josh. 15:13
Sent as spy ... Num. 13:2, 6
Gave good report ... Num. 13:27, 30
His life saved ... Num. 14:10-12
Told to divide Canaan ... Num. 34:17, 19
Entered Canaan ... Num. 14:24-38
Eighty-five at end of conquest ... Josh. 14:6-13
Given Hebron ... Josh. 14:14, 15; Josh. 15:13-16
Gave daughter to Othniel ... Judg. 1:12-15
Descendants of ... 1 Chr. 4:15

2. Son of Hezron ... 1 Chr. 2:18, 42
3. A son of Hur ... 1 Chr. 2:50

Caleb-ephratah

Hezron died at ... 1 Chr. 2:24

Calendar—*a system of dating*

Year divided ... 1 Chr. 27:1-15
Determined by moon ... Ps. 104:19
See Jewish calendar

Calf—*the young of a cow*

A. *Characteristics of:*
Playfulness of ... Ps. 29:6
Used for food ... Amos 6:4
A delicacy ... Luke 15:23, 27
In sacrifice ... Lev. 9:2, 3
Redeemed, if first-born ... Num. 18:17

B. *Figurative of:*
Praise ... Hos. 14:2
Saints sanctified ... Mal. 4:2
Patience ... Ezek. 1:7

Calf, Calves of Gold

A. *Making of:*
Inspired by Moses' delay ... Ex. 32:1-4
Repeated by Jeroboam ... 1 Kin. 12:25-28
To represent God ... Ex. 32:4, 5
To replace Temple worship ... 1 Kin. 12:26, 27
Priests appointed for ... 1 Kin. 12:31
Sacrifices offered to ... Ex. 32:6; 1 Kin. 12:32, 33

B. *Sin of:*
Immorality ... 1 Cor. 10:7
Great ... Ex. 32:21, 30, 31
An apostasy ... Ex. 32:8
Wrathful ... Deut. 9:14-20
Brings punishment ... Ex. 32:26-29, 35
Repeated by Jeroboam ... Hos. 8:5, 6

Calker—*a sealer*

Used on Tyrian vessels ... Ezek. 27:9, 27

Call

To:
Name ... Gen. 1:5
Pray ... Gen. 4:26
Be in reality ... Luke 1:35
Set in office ... Ex. 31:2; Is. 22:20
Give privileges ... Luke 14:16, 17
Offer salvation ... Matt. 9:13
Engage in work ... 1 Cor. 7:20

Calling—*one's vocation*

Faith and one's ... 1 Cor. 7:20-22

Calling, the Christian

A. *Manifested through:*
Christ ... Matt. 9:13
Holy Spirit ... Rev. 22:17
Gospel ... 2 Thess. 2:14

B. *Described as:*
Heavenly ... Heb. 3:1
Holy ... 2 Tim. 1:9
High ... Phil. 3:14
Unchangeable ... Rom. 11:29
By grace ... Gal. 1:15; 2 Tim. 1:9
According to God's purpose ... 2 Tim. 1:9

C. *Goals of:*
Fellowship with Christ ... 1 Cor. 1:9
Holiness ... 1 Thess. 4:7
Liberty ... Gal. 5:13
Peace ... 1 Cor. 7:15
Glory and virtue ... 2 Pet. 1:3
Eternal glory ... 2 Thess. 2:14
Eternal life ... 1 Tim. 6:12

D. *Attitudes toward:*
Walk worthy of ... Eph. 4:1
Make it sure ... 2 Pet. 1:10
Of Gentiles ... Eph. 4:19

Calneh—*fort of Ana*

1. Nimrod's city ... Gen. 10:9, 10
2. A city linked with Hamath and Gath ... Amos 6:2
Same as Calno ... Is. 10:9

Calvary—*from the Latin "calvaria"* (skull)

Christ was crucified there ... Luke 23:33
Same as "Golgotha" in Hebrew ... John 19:17

Camel—*humpbacked animal*

A. *Used for:*
Riding ... Gen. 24:61, 64
Trade ... Gen. 37:25
War ... Judg. 7:12
Hair of, for clothing ... Matt. 3:4
Used for garment worn by John the Baptist ... Matt. 3:4
Wealth ... Job 42:12

B. *Features of:*
Swift ... Jer. 2:23
Docile ... Gen. 24:11
Unclean ... Lev. 11:4
Adorned ... Judg. 8:21, 26
Prize for booty ... Job 1:17
Treated well ... Gen. 24:31, 32
Illustrative of the impossible ... Matt. 19:24

Camon—*elevation*

Jair was buried there ... Judg. 10:5

Camp—*to pitch a tent*

A. *The Lord's guidance of, by:*
An angel ... Ex. 14:19; Ex. 32:34
His presence ... Ex. 33:14
A cloud ... Ps. 105:39

B. *Israel's:*
On leaving Egypt ... Ex. 13:20
At Sinai ... Ex. 18:5
Orderly ... Num. 2:2-34
Tabernacle in center of ... Num. 2:17

C. *Exclusion of:*
Unclean ... Deut. 23:10-12
Lepers ... Lev. 13:46
Dead ... Lev. 10:4, 5
Executions outside ... Lev. 24:23
Log kept of ... Num. 33:1-49
In battle ... Josh. 10:5, 31, 34

D. *Spiritual significance of:*
Christ's crucifixion outside ... Heb. 13:13
God's people ... Rev. 20:9

Camphire—*henna, a fragrant shrub*

Illustrative of beauty ... Song 1:14

Cana of Galilee

A village of upper Galilee; home of Nathanael ... John 21:2
Christ's first miracle at ... John 2:1-11
Healing at ... John 4:46-54

Canaan—*low*

1. A son of Ham ... Gen. 10:6
Cursed by Noah ... Gen. 9:20-25
2. Promised land ... Gen. 12:5

Canaan, Land of

A. *Specifications regarding:*
Boundaries ... Gen. 10:19
Fertility ... Ex. 3:8, 17
Seven nations ... Deut. 7:1
Language ... Is. 19:18

B. *God's promises concerning, given to:*
Abraham ... Gen. 12:1-3
Isaac ... Gen. 26:2, 3
Jacob ... Gen. 28:13
Israel ... Ex. 3:8

C. *Conquest of:*
Announced ... Gen. 15:7-21
Preceded by spies ... Num. 13:1-33
Delayed by unbelief ... Num. 14:1-35
Accomplished by the Lord ... Josh. 23:1-16
Done only in part ... Judg. 1:21, 27-36

Canaan, names of

Canaan ... Gen. 11:31
Land of Hebrews ... Gen. 40:15
Palestine ... Ex. 15:14
Land of Israel ... 1 Sam. 13:19
Immanuel's land ... Is. 8:8
Beulah ... Is. 62:4
Pleasant ... Dan. 8:9
The Lord's land ... Hos. 9:3
Holy land ... Zech. 2:12

SUBJECT — REFERENCE

- Land of the Jews .... Acts 10:39
- Land of promise .... Heb. 11:9

Canaanites—*original inhabitants of Palestine*

A. *Described as:*
- Descendants of Ham .... Gen. 10:5, 6
- Under a curse .... Gen. 9:25, 26
- Amorites .... Gen. 15:16
- Seven nations .... Deut. 7:1
- Fortified .... Num. 13:28
- Idolatrous .... Deut. 29:17
- Defiled .... Lev. 18:24-27

B. *Destruction of:*
- Commanded by God .... Ex. 23:23, 28-33
- Caused by wickedness .... Deut. 9:4
- In God's time .... Gen. 15:13-16
- Done in degrees .... Ex. 23:29, 30

C. *Commands prohibiting:*
- Common league with .... Deut. 7:2
- Intermarriage with .... Deut. 7:3
- Idolatry of .... Ex. 23:24
- Customs of .... Lev. 18:24-27

Canaanites—*a Jewish sect*
- "Simon the Canaanite" .... Matt. 10:4
- Woman from that region .... Matt. 15:22
- Called Zelotes .... Luke 6:15

Candace—*dynastic title of Ethiopian queens*
- Conversion of eunuch of .... Acts 8:27-39

Candle—*a light*

A. *Used literally of:*
- Household lights .... Matt. 5:15

B. *Used figuratively of:*
- Conscience .... Prov. 20:27
- Prosperity .... Job 29:3
- Industry .... Prov. 31:18
- Death .... Job 18:6
- God's justice .... Zeph. 1:12

Candlestick, The Golden

A. *Specifications regarding:*
- Made of gold .... Ex. 25:31
- After a divine model .... Ex. 25:31-40
- Set in holy place .... Heb. 9:2
- Continual burning of .... Ex. 27:20, 21
- Carried by Kohathites .... Num. 4:4, 15
- Temple's ten branches of .... 1 Kin. 7:49, 50
- Taken to Babylon .... Jer. 52:19

B. *Used figuratively of:*
- Christ .... Zech. 4:2, 11
- The church .... Rev. 1:13, 20

Cane—*a tall sedgy grass*
- Used in sacrifices .... Is. 43:24; Jer. 6:20
- Used in holy oil .... Ex. 30:23
- Trading city .... Ezek. 27:23

Cankerworm—*a caterpillar-like insect*
- Sent as judgment .... Joel 1:4
- Large appetite of .... Nah. 3:15

Cannibalism—*using human flesh as food*
- Predicted as a judgment .... Deut. 28:53-57
- Fulfilled in a siege .... 2 Kin. 6:28, 29

Capacity—*ability to perform*
- Hindered by sin .... Gal. 5:17
- Fulfilled in Christ .... Phil. 4:13

Capernaum—*village of Nahum*

A. *Scene of Christ's healing of:*
- Centurion's servant .... Matt. 8:5-13
- Nobleman's son .... John 4:46-54
- Peter's mother-in-law .... Matt. 8:14-17
- The demoniac .... Mark 1:21-28
- The paralytic .... Matt. 9:1-8
- Various diseases .... Matt. 8:16, 17

B. *Other events connected with:*
- Jesus' headquarters .... Matt. 4:13-17
- Simon Peter's home .... Mark 1:21, 29
- Jesus' sermon on the Bread of Life .... John 6:24-71
- Other important messages .... Mark 9:33-50
- Judgment pronounced upon .... Matt. 11:23, 24

Caph
- Eleventh letter of Hebrew alphabet .... Ps. 119:81-88

Caphtor—*cup*
- The place (probably Crete) from which the Philistines came to Palestine .... Jer. 47:4

Caphtorim
- Those of Caphtor .... Deut. 2:23
- Descendants of Mizraim .... Gen. 10:13, 14
- Conquerors of the Avim .... Deut. 2:23

Capital punishment—*the death penalty*

A. *Institution of:*
- By God .... Gen. 9:5, 6; Ex. 21:12-17

B. *Crimes punished by:*
- Murder .... Gen. 9:5, 6
- Adultery .... Lev. 20:10
- Incest .... Lev. 20:11-14
- Sodomy .... Lev. 20:13
- Rape .... Deut. 22:25
- Witchcraft .... Ex. 22:18
- Disobedience to parents .... Ex. 21:18-21
- Blasphemy .... Lev. 24:11-16, 23
- False doctrines .... Deut. 13:1-10

Cappadocia—*a province of Asia Minor*
- Natives of, at Pentecost .... Acts 2:1, 9
- Christians of, addressed by Peter .... 1 Pet. 1:1

Captain—*a civil or military officer*

A. *Applied literally to:*
- Tribal heads .... Num. 2:3, 5
- Military leader .... Judg. 4:2
- King Saul .... 1 Sam. 9:15, 16
- Potiphar .... Gen. 37:36
- David as leader .... 1 Sam. 22:2
- David as king .... 2 Sam. 5:2
- Temple police head .... Luke 22:4
- Roman officer .... Acts 21:31

B. *Applied spiritually to:*
- Angel of the Lord .... Josh. 5:14

Captain, chief of the Temple—*priest who kept order*
- Conspired with Judas .... Luke 22:3, 4
- Arrested Jesus .... Luke 22:52-54
- Arrested apostles .... Acts 5:24-26

Captive—*an enslaved person*

A. *Good treatment of:*
- Compassion .... Ex. 6:4-8
- Kindness .... 2 Chr. 28:15
- Mercy .... 2 Kin. 6:21-23

B. *Bad treatment of:*
- Tortured .... 2 Sam. 12:31
- Blinded .... Judg. 16:21
- Maimed .... Judg. 1:6, 7
- Ravished .... Lam. 5:11-13
- Enslaved .... 2 Kin. 5:2
- Killed .... 1 Sam. 15:32, 33

C. *Applied figuratively to those:*
- Under Satan .... 2 Tim. 2:26
- Under sin .... 2 Tim. 3:6
- Liberated by Christ .... Luke 4:18

Captivity—*a state of bondage; enslavement*

A. *Foretold regarding:*
- Hebrews in Egypt .... Gen. 15:13, 14
- Israelites .... Deut. 28:36-41
- Ten tribes (Israel) .... Amos 7:11
- Judah .... Is. 39:6

B. *Fulfilled:*
- In Egypt .... Ex. 1:11-14
- In many captivities .... Judg. 2:14-23
- In Assyria .... 2 Kin. 17:6-24
- In Babylon .... 2 Kin. 24:11-16
- Under Rome .... John 19:15

C. *Causes of:*
- Disobedience .... Deut. 28:36-68
- Idolatry .... Amos 5:26, 27
- Breaking Sabbatic law .... 2 Chr. 36:20, 21

Caravan—*a group traveling together*
- Ishmaelite traders .... Gen. 37:25
- Jacob's family .... Gen. 46:5, 6
- Jacob's funeral .... Gen. 50:7-14
- Queen of Sheba .... 1 Kin. 10:1, 2
- Returnees from exile .... Ezra 8:31

Carbuncle—*a precious gem*
- In high priest's garment .... Ex. 28:17
- Figuratively of glory .... Is. 54:12
- Descriptive of Tyre's beauty .... Ezek. 28:12, 13

Carcas—*severe*
- Eunuch under Ahasuerus .... Esth. 1:10

Carcase—*a dead body*

A. *Used literally of:*
- Sacrificial animals .... Gen. 15:9, 11
- Unclean beasts .... Lev. 5:2
- Lion .... Judg. 14:8
- Men .... Deut. 28:25, 26
- Idols .... Jer. 16:18

B. *Aspects of:*
- Makes unclean .... Lev. 11:39
- Food for birds .... Jer. 16:4

Carchemish
- Eastern capital of Hittites on the Euphrates .... 2 Chr. 35:20
- Conquered by Sargon II .... Is. 10:9
- Josiah wounded here .... 2 Chr. 35:20-24

Care, carefulness—*wise and provident concern*

A. *Natural concern for:*
- Children .... Luke 2:44-49
- Duties .... Luke 10:40
- Mate .... 1 Cor. 7:32-34
- Health .... Is. 38:1-22
- Life .... Mark 4:38
- Possessions .... Gen. 33:12-17

B. *Spiritual concern for:*
- Duties .... Phil. 2:20
- Office .... 1 Tim. 3:6-8
- A minister's needs .... Phil. 4:10-12
- The flock of God .... John 10:11; 1 Pet. 5:2, 3
- Churches .... 2 Cor. 11:28
- Christians .... 1 Cor. 12:25
- Spiritual things .... Acts 18:17

Care, divine—*God's concern for His creatures*
- For the world .... Ps. 104:1-10
- For animals .... Ps. 104:11-30
- For pagans .... Jon. 4:11
- For Christians .... Matt. 6:25-34
- Babylon .... Is. 47:1, 8-11
- Ethiopians .... Ezek. 30:9
- Gallio .... Acts 18:17
- Inhabitants of coastlands .... Ezek. 39:6
- Moab .... Jer. 48:10-17
- Nineveh .... Zeph. 2:10-15
- Those at ease in Zion .... Amos 6:1
- Women of Jerusalem .... Is. 32:9-11

Careah—*made bold*
- Father of Johanan .... 2 Kin. 25:23
- Same as Kareah .... Jer. 40:8

Cares, worldly—*overmuch concern for earthly things*

A. *Evils of:*
- Chokes the Word .... Matt. 13:7, 22
- Gluts the soul .... Luke 21:34
- Obstructs the Gospel .... Luke 14:18-20
- Hinders Christ's work .... 2 Tim. 2:4
- Manifests unbelief .... Matt. 6:25-32

B. *Antidotes for God's:*
- Protection .... Ps. 37:5-11
- Provision .... Matt. 6:25-34
- Promises .... Phil. 4:6, 7

Carelessness—*lack of proper concern*
- Babylon .... Is. 47:8-11
- Ethiopians .... Ezek. 30:9
- Islanders .... Ezek. 39:6
- Nineveh .... Zeph. 2:15
- Women of Jerusalem .... Is. 32:9-11

Carmel—*field, park, garden*

1. Rendered as:
   - "Fruitful field" .... Is. 10:18
   - "Plentiful field" .... Is. 16:10
   - "Plentiful country" .... Jer. 2:7
2. City of Judah .... Josh. 15:55
   - Site of Saul's victory .... 1 Sam. 15:12
   - Home of David's wife .... 1 Sam. 27:3
3. A mountain of Palestine .... Josh. 19:26
   - Joshua defeated king there .... Josh. 12:22
   - Scene of Elijah's triumph .... 1 Kin. 18:19-45
   - Elisha visits .... 2 Kin. 2:25
   - Place of beauty .... Song 7:5
   - Figurative of strength .... Jer. 46:18
   - Barrenness foretold .... Amos 1:2

SUBJECT REFERENCE

Carmelite, Carmelitess
Nabal .... 1 Sam. 30:5
2 Sam. 2:2
Hezro .... 2 Sam. 23:35
Abigail .... 1 Sam. 27:3

Carmi—*vinedresser*
1. Son of Reuben .... Gen. 46:9
2. Father of Achan .... Josh. 7:1

Carnal—*fleshly, worldly*
Used literally of:
Sexual relations .... Lev. 19:20
Paul calls himself .... Rom. 7:14
Gentiles ministered in .... Rom. 15:27
Paul calls brethren at Corinth ... 1 Cor. 3:1, 3
Things not spiritual called .... 1 Cor. 9:11

Carob pod—*seedcase of the carob, or locust tree*
Rendered "husk"; fed to swine .... Luke 15:16

Carpenter—*a skilled woodworker*
David's house built by .... 2 Sam. 5:11
Temple repaired by .... 2 Chr. 24:12
Idols made by .... Is. 44:13
Temple restored by .... Ezra 3:7
Joseph works as .... Matt. 13:55

Carpenter tools—*implements for the carpenter trade*
Axe .... Deut. 19:5
Hammer .... Jer. 23:29
Line .... Zech. 2:1
Nail .... Jer. 10:4
Saw .... 1 Kin. 7:9

Carpus—*fruit*
Paul's friend at Troas .... 2 Tim. 4:13

Carriage (outdated word for baggage)
Goods, provisions .... 1 Sam. 17:22
An army's baggage .... Is. 10:28
Heavy goods .... Judg. 18:21
A vehicle .... Is. 46:1

Carrion vulture
Unclean bird .... Lev. 11:18

Carshena—*plowman*
Prince of Persia .... Esth. 1:14

Cart—*a wagon*
Made of wood .... 1 Sam. 6:14
Sometimes covered .... Num. 7:3
Drawn by cows .... 1 Sam. 6:7
Used in threshing .... Is. 28:28
Used for hauling .... Amos 2:13
Ark carried by .... 2 Sam. 6:3
Figurative of sin .... Is. 5:18

Carving—*cutting figures in wood or stone*
Used in worship .... Ex. 31:1-7
Found in homes .... 1 Kin. 6:18
Employed by idolators .... Judg. 18:18
Used in the Temple .... 1 Kin. 6:35

Casement—*lattice, criss-crossed strips of wood or metal*
Looked through .... Prov. 7:6

Casiphia—*silvery*
Home of exiled Levites .... Ezra 8:17

Casluhim
A tribe descended from Mizraim .... Gen. 10:14
Descendant of Ham .... 1 Chr. 1:8, 12

Cassia—*amber*
An ingredient of holy oil .... Ex. 30:24, 25
An article of commerce .... Ezek. 27:19
Noted for fragrance .... Ps. 45:8

Castaway—*worthless; reprobated*
The rejected .... Matt. 25:30
2 Pet. 2:4
Warning concerning .... 1 Cor. 9:27

Caste—*divisions of society*
Some leaders of low .... Judg. 11:1-11
David aware of .... 1 Sam. 18:18, 23
Jews and Samaritans observe ... John 4:9
Abolished .... Acts 10:28-35

SUBJECT REFERENCE

Castle—*fortress, tower*
A. *Used literally of:*
King's residence .... 2 Kin. 15:25
An encampment .... Gen. 25:16
A tower for guards .... 1 Chr. 6:54
Barracks for soldiers .... Acts 21:34
A fortress .... 1 Chr. 11:7
David conquers Jebusite .... 1 Chr. 11:5, 7
B. *Used figuratively of:*
Offended brother .... Prov. 18:19

Castor and Pollux—*sons of Jupiter*
Gods in Greek and Roman mythology; figureheads on Paul's ship to Rome .... Acts 28:11

Castration—*removal of male testicles*
Disqualified for congregation ... Deut. 23:1
Rights restored in new covenant .... Is. 56:3-5
Figurative of absolute devotion .... Matt. 19:12

Caterpillar—*an insect living on vegetation*
Works with locust .... Is. 33:4
Devours land .... Amos 4:9

Cattle—*animals* (collectively)
Created by God .... Gen. 1:24
Adam named .... Gen. 2:20
Entered the ark .... Gen. 7:13, 14
Struck by God .... Ex. 12:29
Firstborn of, belong to God ... Ex. 34:19
Can be unclean .... Lev. 5:2
Taken as plunder .... Josh. 8:2, 27
Belong to God .... Ps. 50:10
Nebuchadnezzar eats like .... Dan. 4:33
Pastureless .... Joel 1:18
East of Jordan good for .... Num. 32:1, 4
Given as ransom .... Num. 3:45

Caul
1. A lining surrounding the stomach .... Ex. 29:13, 22
2. A hair net worn by women .. Is. 3:18

Causeway—*a road or passage*
Steps leading into temple .... 1 Chr. 26:16, 18

Caution—*provident care; alertness*
For safety .... Acts 23:10, 16-24
For defense .... Neh. 4:12-23
For attack .... 1 Sam. 20:1-17
A principle .... Prov. 14:15, 16
Neglect of .... 1 Sam. 26:4-16

Cave—*a cavern*
A. *Used for:*
Habitation .... Gen. 19:30
Refuge .... 1 Kin. 18:4
Burial .... John 11:38
Concealment .... 1 Sam. 22:1
Protection .... Is. 2:19
Rev. 6:15
B. *Mentioned in Scripture:*
Machpelah .... Gen. 23:9
Makkedah .... Josh. 10:16, 17
Adullam .... 1 Sam. 22:1
Engedi .... 1 Sam. 24:1, 3

Cedar—*an evergreen tree*
A. *Used in:*
Ceremonial cleansing .... Lev. 14:4-7
Building Temple .... 1 Kin. 5:5, 6
Building palaces .... 2 Sam. 5:11
Gifts .... 1 Chr. 22:4
Making idols .... Is. 44:14, 17
B. *Figurative of:*
Israel's glory .... Num. 24:6
Christ's glory .... Ezek. 17:22, 23
Growth of saints .... Ps. 92:12
Mighty nations .... Amos 2:9
Arrogant rulers .... Is. 2:13

Cedar chests
Sold by traders .... Ezek. 27:23, 24

Ceiling—*upper surface of a room*
Temple's .... 1 Kin. 6:15

Celebrate—*to commemorate*
Feast of Weeks .... Ex. 34:22
Feast of Ingathering .... Ex. 34:22
The Sabbath .... Lev. 23:32, 41

SUBJECT REFERENCE

Passover .... 2 Kin. 23:21
Feast of Unleavened Bread ..... 2 Chr. 30:13
Feast of Tabernacles .... Zech. 14:16

Celestial—*heavenly*
Bodies called .... 1 Cor. 15:40

Celibacy—*the unmarried state*
Useful sometimes .... Matt. 19:10, 12
Not for bishops .... 1 Tim. 3:2
Requiring, a sign of apostasy ... 1 Tim. 4:1-3
Figurative of absolute devotion .... Rev. 14:4

Cellars—*depositories*
Wines stored in .... 1 Chr. 27:27

Cemetery—*a burial place*
Bought by Abraham .... Gen. 23:15, 16
Pharisees compared to .... Matt. 23:27
Man dwelt in .... Mark 5:2, 3
A resurrection from .... Matt. 27:52

Cenchrea—*millet*
A harbor of Corinth .... Acts 18:18
A church near .... Rom. 16:1

Censer—*firepan*
Used for incense .... Num. 16:6, 7, 39
Made of bronze .... Num. 16:39
Used in idol worship .... Ezek. 8:11
Typical of Christ's intercession .... Rev. 8:3, 5

Censoriousness—*a critical spirit*
Rebuked by Jesus .... Matt. 7:1-5
Diotrephes .... 3 John 9, 10
Apostates .... Jude 10-16

Census—*counting the population*
At Sinai .... Ex. 38:26
In Moab .... Num. 26:1-64
By David .... 2 Sam. 24:1-9
Provoked by Satan .... 1 Chr. 21:1
Completed by Solomon .... 2 Chr. 2:17
Of exiles .... Ezra 2:1-70
By Rome .... Luke 2:1

Centurion—*a Roman officer*
Servant of, healed .... Matt. 8:5-13
Watches crucifixion .... Matt. 27:54
Is converted .... Acts 10:1-48
Protects Paul .... Acts 22:25-28
Takes Paul to Rome .... Acts 27:1

Cephas—*stone*
Name of Peter .... John 1:42

Ceremonialism—*adherence to forms and rites*
Jews guilty of .... Is. 1:11-15
Christ condemns .... Matt. 15:1-9
Apostles reject .... Acts 15:12-28
Sign of apostasy .... 1 Tim. 4:1-3
Exhortations against .... Col. 2:14-23

Certainties—*absolute truths*
Sin's exposure .... Num. 32:23
The Gospel .... Luke 1:4
Jesus' claims .... Acts 1:3
Apostolic testimony .... 2 Pet. 1:16-21
Death's approach .... Heb. 9:27
Ultimate judgment .... Acts 17:31

Chaff—*the husk of threshed grain*
Describes the ungodly .... Ps. 1:4
Emptiness .... Is. 33:11
False doctrine .... Jer. 23:28
God's judgment .... Is. 17:13
Punishment .... Matt. 3:12

Chain—*a series of connected links*
A. *A badge of office:*
On Joseph's neck .... Gen. 41:42
Promised to Daniel .... Dan. 5:7
B. *An ornament:*
Worn by women .... Is. 3:20
C. *A means of confinement of:*
Prisoners .... Judg. 16:21
Paul .... Eph. 6:20
Manasseh bound .... 2 Chr. 33:12
D. *Used figuratively of:*
Oppression .... Lam. 3:7
Sin's bondage .... Jer. 40:3, 4
Punishment .... Jude 6
Satan's defeat .... Rev. 20:1

SUBJECT — REFERENCE

Chalcedony—*from Chalcedon*
- Variegated stone ... Rev. 21:19

Chaldea
- Originally, the south portion of Babylonia ... Gen. 11:31
- Applied later to all Babylonia ... Is. 13:19
- Abraham came from ... Gen. 11:28, 31
- Ezekiel prophesies in ... Ezek. 1:3

Chaldeans, Chaldees
- Abraham, a native ... Gen. 11:31
- Ur, a city of ... Neh. 9:7
- Babylon, "the glory of" ... Is. 13:19
- Attack Job ... Job 1:17
- Nebuchadnezzar, king of ... 2 Kin. 24:1
- God's agent ... Hab. 1:6
- Predicted captivity of Jews among ... Jer. 25:1-26
- Jerusalem defeated by ... 2 Kin. 25:1-21
- Noted for astrologers ... Dan. 2:2, 5, 10

Chalkstone—*limestone*
- Used figuratively ... Is. 27:9

Chamber—*inner room; enclosed place*
- A. *Used literally of:*
  - Elisha's room ... 2 Kin. 4:10
  - Guest room ... Mark 14:14
  - Upper room ... Acts 9:37
  - Place of idolatry ... 2 Kin. 23:12
- B. *Used figuratively of:*
  - Heavens ... Ps. 104:3, 13
  - Death ... Prov. 7:27

Chamberlain—*a high official; a eunuch*
- Seven, serving Ahasuerus ... Esth. 1:10, 15
- Blastus, serving Herod ... Acts 12:20
- Erastus, at Corinth ... Rom. 16:23
- See Eunuch

Chamois—*probably the wild sheep*
- Permitted for food ... Deut. 14:4, 5

Chameleon—*a lizard-like reptile*
- Unclean ... Lev. 11:30

Champion—*a mighty one; a winner*
- Goliath ... 1 Sam. 17:23, 51
- David ... 1 Sam. 17:45-54

Chancellor
- Persian official ... Ezra 4:8

Chance, second
- *Not given to:*
  - Angels ... 2 Pet. 2:4
  - Noah's world ... 2 Pet. 2:5
  - Esau ... Heb. 12:16, 17
  - Israelites ... Num. 14:26-45
  - Saul ... 1 Sam. 16:1, 14
  - Judas ... John 13:26-30
  - Apostates ... Heb. 10:26-31
  - Those in hell ... Luke 16:19-31

Change of clothes—*gala, festal garments*
- A gift ... Gen. 45:22
- A wager ... Judg. 14:12-19
- From a king ... 2 Kin. 5:5

Chapiter—*top of a post or column*
- Variegated decorations of ... Ex. 36:38
- Part of temple ... 1 Kin. 7:16, 19, 20

Chapman—*a merchant*
- Sells gold to Solomon ... 2 Chr. 9:14
- Same as "merchantmen" ... 1 Kin. 10:15

Character—*one's total personality*
- A. *Traits of:*
  - Described prophetically ... Gen. 49:1-28
  - Indicated before birth ... Gen. 25:21-34
  - Seen in childhood ... Prov. 20:11
  - Fixed in hell ... Rev. 22:11, 15
- B. *Manifested by:*
  - Decisions (Esau) ... Gen. 25:29-34
  - Destiny (Judas) ... John 6:70, 71
  - Desires (Demas) ... 2 Tim. 4:10
  - Deeds (Saul) ... 1 Sam. 15:1-35

Character of God's people
- A. *Their dedication:*
  - Hear Christ ... John 10:3, 4
  - Follow Christ ... John 10:4, 5, 27
  - Receive Christ ... John 1:12
- B. *Their standing before God:*
  - Blameless ... Phil. 2:15
  - Faithful ... Rev. 17:14
  - Godly ... 2 Pet. 2:9
  - Holy ... Col. 3:12
- C. *Their graces:*
  - Humble ... 1 Pet. 5:5
  - Loving ... 1 Thess. 4:9
  - Humility ... Phil. 2:3, 4
  - Meek ... Matt. 5:5
  - Merciful ... Matt. 5:7
  - Obedient ... Rom. 16:19
  - Pure ... Matt. 5:8
  - Sincere ... 2 Cor. 1:12
  - Zealous ... Titus 2:14
  - Courteous ... 1 Pet. 3:8
  - Unity of mind ... Rom. 15:5-7
  - Hospitable ... 1 Pet. 4:9
  - Generous ... 2 Cor. 8:1-7
  - Peaceable ... Heb. 12:14
  - Patient ... James 5:7, 8
  - Content ... Heb. 13:5
  - Steadfast ... 1 Cor. 15:58

Character of the wicked
- A. *Their attitude toward God:*
  - Hostile ... Rom. 8:7
  - Denial ... Ps. 14:1
  - Disobedience ... Titus 1:16
- B. *Their spiritual state:*
  - Blindness ... 2 Cor. 4:4
  - Slavery to sin ... 2 Pet. 2:14, 19
  - Deadness ... Eph. 2:1
  - Inability ... Rom. 8:8
- C. *Their works:*
  - Boastful ... Ps. 10:3-6
  - Full of evil ... Rom. 1:29-32
  - Haters of the Gospel ... John 3:19, 20
  - Sensual ... 2 Pet. 2:12-22

Charashim—*craftsmen*
- Valley near Jerusalem ... 1 Chr. 4:14
- Called a "valley of craftsmen" ... Neh. 11:35

Charchemish (see Carchemish)

Charger—*a dish or platter*
- In tribal offerings ... Num. 7:13
- Translated "dish" ... Ex. 25:29
- Used for a dead man's head ... Matt. 14:8, 11
- Used figuratively ("platter") ... Luke 11:39

Chariot—*a vehicle*
- A. *Used for:*
  - Travel ... Gen. 46:29
  - War ... 1 Kin. 20:25
- B. *Employed by:*
  - Kings ... 1 Kin. 22:35
  - Persons of distinction ... Gen. 41:43
  - God ... 2 Kin. 2:11, 12
- C. *Illustrative of:*
  - Clouds ... Ps. 104:3
  - God's judgments ... Is. 66:15
  - Angels ... 2 Kin. 6:16, 17

Chariot, war machine
- A. *Used by:*
  - Egyptians ... Ex. 14:7
  - Canaanites ... Josh. 17:16
  - Philistines ... 1 Sam. 13:5
  - Syrians ... 2 Sam. 10:18
  - Assyrians ... 2 Kin. 19:23
  - Jews ... 2 Kin. 8:21
- B. *Numbers employed by:*
  - Pharaoh—600 ... Ex. 14:7
  - Jabin—900 ... Judg. 4:3
  - Philistines—30,000 ... 1 Sam. 13:5

Chariot cities
- Many in Solomon's time ... 1 Kin. 9:19

Chariot horses
- Hamstrung ... 1 Chr. 18:4

Chariot of fire
- Used in Elijah's exit from earth ... 2 Kin. 2:11

Chariots of the sun—*used in sun worship*
- Destroyed ... 2 Kin. 23:11

Charitableness—*a generous spirit toward others*
- Bearing burdens ... Gal. 6:2-4
- Showing forgiveness ... 2 Cor. 2:1-10
- Seeking concord ... Phil. 4:1-3
- Helping the tempted ... Gal. 6:1
- Encouraging the weak ... Rom. 14:1-15
- Not finding fault ... Matt. 7:1-3

Charity—*alms giving*
- From within ... Luke 11:41
- Given freely ... Luke 12:33
- Of Dorcas ... Acts 9:36

Charmers—*users of magic*
- Falsified by God ... Ps. 58:4, 5

Chastisement—*fatherly correction*
- A. *Sign of:*
  - Sonship ... Prov. 3:11, 12
  - God's love ... Deut. 8:5
- B. *Design of, to:*
  - Correct ... Jer. 24:5, 6
  - Prevent sin ... 2 Cor. 12:7-9
  - Bless ... Ps. 94:12, 13
- C. *Response to:*
  - Penitence ... 2 Chr. 6:24-31
  - Submission ... 2 Cor. 12:7-10

Chastity—*sexual purity*
- A. *Manifested in:*
  - Dress ... 1 Pet. 3:1-6
  - Looks ... Matt. 5:28, 29
  - Speech ... Eph. 5:4
  - Intentions ... Gen. 39:7-12
- B. *Aids to:*
  - Shun the unchaste ... 1 Cor. 5:11
  - Consider your sainthood ... Eph. 5:3, 4
  - Dangers of unchastity ... Prov. 6:24-35
  - Let marriage suffice ... 1 Cor. 7:1-7
  - "Keep thyself pure" ... 1 Tim. 5:22
- C. *Examples of:*
  - Job ... Job 31:1, 9-12
  - Joseph ... Gen. 39:7-20
  - Ruth ... Ruth 3:10, 11
  - Boaz ... Ruth 3:13, 14
  - Saints ... Rev. 14:4

Cheating—*defrauding by deceitful means*
- The Lord ... Mal. 3:8, 9
- One's soul ... Matt. 16:26
- The needy ... Amos 8:4, 5
- Others ... 1 Cor. 7:5
- See Dishonesty

Chebar—*joining*
- River in Babylonia ... Ezek. 1:3
- Site of Ezekiel's visions and Jewish captives ... Ezek. 10:15, 20

Chedorlaomer—*servant of the god Lagamar*
- A king of Elam; invaded Canaan ... Gen. 14:1-16

Cheek—*side of face*
- Micaiah struck on ... 1 Kin. 22:24
- Slapped on ... Job 16:10
- Messiah's plucked ... Is. 50:6
- *Description of:*
  - Beauty ... Song 5:13
  - Patience ... Matt. 5:39
  - Victory ... Ps. 3:7
  - Attack ... Mic. 5:1

Cheerfulness—*serene joyfulness*
- A. *Caused by:*
  - A merry heart ... Prov. 15:13
  - The Lord's goodness ... Zech. 9:16, 17
  - The Lord's presence ... Mark 6:54, 55
  - Victory ... John 16:33
  - Confidence ... Acts 24:10
- B. *Manifested in:*
  - Giving ... 2 Cor. 9:7
  - Christian graces ... Rom. 12:8
  - Times of danger ... Acts 27:22-36

Cheese—*a dairy product*
- Used for food ... 1 Sam. 17:18
- Received by David ... 2 Sam. 17:20
- Figurative of trials ... Job 10:10

SUBJECT REFERENCE

Chelal—*completeness, perfection*

A son of Pahath-moab ....Ezra 10:30

Chelluh—*robust*

A son of Bani................Ezra 10:35

Chelub—*basket; bird's cage*

1. A brother of Shuah ....1 Chr. 4:11
2. Father of Ezri.............1 Chr. 27:26

Chelubai

A son of Hezron ....1 Chr. 2:9
Another form of Caleb ....1 Chr. 2:18, 42

Chemarim—*servants, priests*

Denounced ....Zeph. 1:4
Translated "idolatrous priests" ..2 Kin. 23:5
Translated "priests" ....Hos. 10:5

Chemosh—*fire, hearth*

The god of the Moabites ....Num. 21:29
Children sacrificed to ....2 Kin. 3:27
Solomon builds altars to ....1 Kin. 11:7
Josiah destroys altars of ....2 Kin. 23:13

Chenaanah—feminine form of *"Canaan"*

1. A Benjamite ....1 Chr. 7:10
2. Father of Zedekiah ....2 Chr. 18:10

Chenani—contraction of *"Chenaniah"*

A reforming Levite ....Neh. 9:4

Chenaniah—*Jehovah has established*

1. A chief Levite in David's reign ....1 Chr. 15:22, 27
2. A reforming Levite; contracted to Chenani................Neh. 9:4

Chephar-haammonai—*village of the Ammonite*

A village of Benjamin ....Josh. 18:24

Chephirah—*village*

A city of the Gibeonites ....Josh. 9:17
Assigned to Benjamin ....Josh. 18:26
Residence of exiles ....Ezra 2:25

Cheran—*lyre*

A Horite, son of Dishon........1 Chr. 1:41

Cherethites—*Cretans in southwest Palestine*

Tribes in southwest Canaan.....1 Sam. 30:14
Identified with Philistines.......Ezek. 25:16
In David's bodyguard..........2 Sam. 8:18
Serve Solomon ....1 Kin. 1:38

Cherith—*cut, brook*

Elijah hid there ....1 Kin. 17:3-6

Cherub

A district in Babylonia ....Ezra 2:59; Neh. 7:61

Cherubim (plural of cherub)

A. *Appearances of:*
 Fully described............Ezek. 1:5-14

B. *Functions of:*
 Guard ....Gen. 3:22-24
 Fulfill God's purposes.......Ezek. 10:9-16
 Show God's majesty ....2 Sam. 22:11

C. *Images of:*
 On the mercy seat ....Ex. 25:18-22
 On the veil ....Ex. 26:31
 On curtains...............Ex. 36:8
 In the Temple.............1 Kin. 8:6, 7

Chesalon—*trust*

A town of Judah ....Josh. 15:10

Chesed

Fourth son of Nahor..........Gen. 22:22

Chesil—*a fool*

A village of Judah ....Josh. 15:30
Probably same as Bethul and Bethuel ....Josh. 19:4; 1 Chr. 4:30

Chest—*case or box*

For offering ....2 Kin. 12:9, 10
For money ("treasuries") ....Esth. 3:9
For levy fixed by Moses ....2 Chr. 24:8, 9

SUBJECT REFERENCE

Chestnut tree—*plane tree*

Used by Jacob ....Gen. 30:37
In Eden, God's garden ....Ezek. 31:8, 9

Chesulloth—*loins or slopes*

A border town of Issachar ......Josh. 19:18

Cheth

Eighth letter in Hebrew alphabet ....Ps. 119:57-64

Chezib—*deceitful*

Same as Azib; birthplace of Shelah ....Gen. 38:5

Chicken—*domestic fowl*

Hen and brood ....Luke 13:34
Rooster (cock) ....Luke 22:34

Chicks—*the young of a hen*

Figurative of Israel ....Matt. 23:37

Chiding—*to reprove or rebuke*

A. *Between men:*
 Jacob with Laban ....Gen. 31:36
 Israelites with Moses........Ex. 17:2
 Ephraimites with Gideon ....Judg. 8:1
 Paul with Peter.............Gal. 2:11, 14

B. *By Christ, because of:*
 Unbelief ....Matt. 11:20-24
 Spiritual dullness ....Matt. 16:8-12
 Censoriousness.............Mark 10:13-16
 Sluggishness ....Matt. 26:40

Chidon—*a javelin*

Where Uzza was struck dead....1 Chr. 13:9, 10
Called Nahon.................2 Sam. 6:6

Chief seats—*seats or places of honor*

Sought by scribes and Pharisees....................Matt. 23:1, 6; Mark 12:38, 39
Not be be sought.............Luke 14:7-11

Child-bearing

Agreeable to God's command ...Gen. 1:28
Result of marriage............1 Tim. 5:14
Attended with pain ....Gen. 3:16
Productive of joy.............John 16:21
Productive of the Messiah ......Luke 2:7
Means of salvation ....1 Tim. 2:15
Expressed in symbols ....Rev. 12:2, 5

Childhood, characteristics of

Dependence ....1 Thess. 2:7
Immaturity..................1 Cor. 13:11
Foolishness..................Prov. 22:15
Unstableness ....Eph. 4:14
Humility ....Matt. 18:1-5
Need for instruction ....Prov. 22:6
Influence on adults ....Is. 49:15

Childishness—*an immature spirit*

Manifested by Saul ....1 Sam. 18:8
Seen in Haman ....Esth. 6:6-9

Childlikeness

Requirement of God's kingdom.................Mark 10:15
An element in spiritual growth ..1 Pet. 2:2
A model to be followed ....1 Cor. 14:20

Children, figurative

Disciples of a teacher ....Mark 10:24
God's own ....Rom. 8:16, 17
Christians ....Eph. 5:8
Devil's own.................1 John 3:10
Those who show such trait......Matt. 11:16-19

Children, illegitimate

No inheritance ....Gal. 4:30
No fatherly care..............Heb. 12:8
Not in congregation ....Deut. 23:2
Despised ....Judg. 11:2

Children, natural

A. *Right estimate of:*
 God's gifts ....Gen. 33:5
 God's heritage ....Ps. 127:3-5
 Crown of age ....Prov. 17:6

B. *Characteristics of:*
 Imitate parents............1 Kin. 15:11, 26
 Diverse in nature ....Gen. 25:27
 Playful ....Matt. 11:16-19

SUBJECT REFERENCE

C. *Capacities of:*
 Glorify God ....Matt. 21:15, 16
 Come to Christ ....Mark 10:13-16
 Understand Scripture ....2 Tim. 3:15
 Receive the promises........Acts 2:39
 Believe..................Matt. 18:6
 Receive training...........Eph. 6:4
 Worship in God's house .....1 Sam. 1:24, 28

D. *Parental obligations toward:*
 Nourishment..............1 Sam. 1:22
 Discipline ....Eph. 6:4
 Instruction ....Gal. 4:1, 2
 Employment ....1 Sam. 17:15
 Inheritance ....Luke 12:13, 14

E. *Duties of:*
 Obedience ....Eph. 6:1-3
 Honor to parents ....Heb. 12:9
 Respect for age ....1 Pet. 5:5
 Care for parents ....1 Tim. 5:4
 Obedience to God ....Deut. 30:2
 Remembering God ....Eccl. 12:1

F. *Description of ungrateful:*
 Stubborn ....Deut. 21:18-21
 Scorners ....Prov. 30:17
 Robbers...................Prov. 28:24
 Strikers ....Ex. 21:15
 Cursers ....Lev. 20:9

G. *Examples of good:*
 Isaac ....Gen. 22:6-10
 Joseph ....Gen. 45:9, 10
 Jephthah's daughter.........Judg. 11:34-36
 Samuel...................1 Sam. 2:26
 David....................1 Sam. 17:20
 Josiah ....2 Chr. 34:3
 Esther ....Esth. 2:20
 Daniel ....Dan. 1:6
 John the Baptist............Luke 1:80
 Jesus ....Luke 2:51
 In the Temple.............Matt. 21:15, 16
 Timothy ....2 Tim. 3:15

H. *Examples of bad:*
 Esau.....................Gen. 26:34, 35
 Job's haters...............Job 19:18
 Sons of Eli ....1 Sam. 2:12, 17
 Sons of Samuel ....1 Sam. 8:3
 Absalom ....2 Sam. 15:10
 Adonijah ....1 Kin. 1:5, 6
 Elisha's mockers...........2 Kin. 2:23
 Adrammelech ....2 Kin. 19:37

I. *Acts performed upon:*
 Naming ....Ruth 4:17
 Blessing ....Luke 1:67, 76-79
 Circumcision..............Luke 2:21

J. *Murder of:*
 By Pharaoh ....Ex. 1:16
 By Herod the Great ....Matt. 2:16-18
 In war ....Num. 31:17

Chileab—*restraint of father*

A son of David ....2 Sam. 3:3
Also called Daniel............1 Chr. 3:1

Chilion—*wasting away*

Elimelech's son ....Ruth 1:2
Orpah's deceased husband ......Ruth 1:4, 5
Boaz redeems his estate ....Ruth 4:9

Chilmad

A town or country trading with Tyre.......................Ezek. 27:23

Chimham—*pining*

A son of Barzillai ....2 Sam. 19:37-40
Inn bearing his name ....Jer. 41:17

Chinnereth, Cinneroth—*lyre*

1. A city of Naphtali ....Deut. 3:17
2. The region of Chinneroth....1 Kin. 15:20
 Same as plain of Gennesaret ....Matt. 14:34
3. The Old Testament name for Sea of Galilee..................Num. 34:11
 Also called Lake of Gennesaret and Sea of Galilee..................Luke 5:1

Chios—*snow*

An island of the Aegean Sea; on Paul's voyage.....................Acts 20:15

Chisleu

Ninth month of Hebrew year ...Neh. 1:1

SUBJECT	REFERENCE
Chislon—*trust, hope*	
Father of Elidad	Num. 34:21
Chisloth-tabor—*the flanks of Tabor*	
A locality near Mt. Tabor	Josh. 19:12
Probably same as Chesulloth	Josh. 19:18
Chittim, Kittim	
The island of Cyprus; inhabited by descendants of Japheth (through Javan)	Gen. 10:4
Ships of, in Balaam's prophecy	Num. 24:24
A haven for Tyre's ships	Is. 23:1-12
Mentioned in the prophets	Jer. 2:10
Chiun—*detestable thing*	
Astral images made by Israel	Amos 5:26
Chloe—*verdure*	
Woman of Corinth	1 Cor. 1:11
Choice, choose	
A. *Of human things:*	
Wives	Gen. 6:2
Land	Gen. 13:11
Soldiers	Ex. 17:9
King	1 Sam. 8:18
Disciples	Luke 6:13
Church officers	Acts 6:5
Missionaries	Acts 15:40
Delegates	Acts 15:22, 25
B. *Of God's choice:*	
Moses as leader	Num. 16:28
Levites to priesthood	1 Sam. 2:28
Kings	1 Sam. 10:24
Jerusalem	Deut. 12:5
Israel as His people	Deut. 7:6-8
Cyrus as deliverer	Is. 45:1-4
The Servant (the Messiah)	Is. 42:1-7
The new Israel (the Church)	1 Pet. 2:9
The weak as God's own	1 Cor. 1:27, 28
The elect	Matt. 20:16
C. *Kind of:*	
God and the Devil	Gen. 3:1-11
Life and death	Deut. 30:19, 20
God and idols	Josh. 24:15-28
Obedience and disobedience	1 Sam. 15:1-35
God and Baal	1 Kin. 18:21-40
Wisdom and folly	Prov. 8:1-21
Obedience and sin	2 Pet. 2:4
Christ and antichrist	1 John 2:18, 19
D. *Factors determining choice, man's:*	
First choice	Rom. 5:12
Depraved nature	John 3:19-21
Spiritual deadness	Eph. 4:17-19
Blindness	John 9:39-41
Inability	Rom. 8:7, 8
E. *Bad choice made by:*	
Disobeying God	Num. 14:1-45
Putting the flesh first	Gen. 25:29-34
Following a false prophet	Matt. 24:11, 24
Letting the world overcome	Matt. 19:16-22
Rejecting God's promises	Acts 13:44-48
F. *Good choice made by:*	
Using God's Word	Ps. 119:9-11
Believing God	Heb. 11:24-27
Obedience	Acts 26:19-23
Prayer	Eph. 1:16-19
Faith	Heb. 11:8-10
Choir—*musicians trained to sing together*	
Appointed by Nehemiah	Neh. 12:31
In house of God	Neh. 12:40
Under instructor	1 Chr. 15:22, 27
Chor-ashan (see Ashan)	
Chorazin	
A city denounced for its unbelief	Matt. 11:21
Chozeba	
Town of Judah	1 Chr. 4:22
Christ—*the Anointed One*	
A. *Pre-existence of:*	
Affirmed in Old Testament	Ps. 2:7
Confirmed by Christ	John 8:58
Proclaimed by apostles	Col. 1:15-19
B. *Birth of:*	
Predicted	Is. 7:14
Fulfilled	Matt. 1:18-25
In the fullness of time	Gal. 4:4
C. *Deity of:*	
Prophecy	Is. 9:6
Acknowledged by Christ	John 20:28, 29
Acclaimed by witnesses	John 1:14, 18
Affirmed by apostles	Rom. 9:5 Heb. 1:8
D. *Attributes of:*	
All-powerful	Matt. 28:18
All-knowing	Col. 2:3
Ever-present	Matt. 18:20
Eternal	John 1:1, 2, 15
E. *Humanity of:*	
Foretold	Gen. 3:15 1 Cor. 15:45-47
Took man's nature	John 1:14 Heb. 2:9-18
Seed of woman	Gal. 4:4
A son of man	Luke 3:38
Of David's line	Matt. 22:45
A man	1 Tim. 2:5
Four brothers	Mark 6:3
F. *Mission of:*	
Do God's will	John 6:38
Save sinners	Luke 19:10
Bring in everlasting righteousness	Dan. 9:24
Destroy Satan's works	Heb. 2:14 1 John 3:8
Fulfill the Old Testament	Matt. 5:17
Give life	John 10:10, 28
Abolish ceremonialism	Dan. 9:27
Complete revelation	Heb. 1:1
G. *Worship of, by:*	
Old Testament saints	Josh. 5:13-15
Demons	Mark 5:6
Men	John 9:38
Angels	Heb. 1:6
Disciples	Luke 24:52
Saints in glory	Rev. 7:9, 10
All	Phil. 2:10, 11
H. *Character of:*	
Holy	Luke 1:35
Righteous	Is. 53:11
Just	Zech. 9:9
Guileless	1 Pet. 2:22
Sinless	2 Cor. 5:21
Spotless	1 Pet. 1:19
Innocent	Matt. 27:4
Meek	Matt. 11:29
Merciful	Heb. 2:17
Humble	Phil. 2:8
Forgiving	Luke 23:34
I. *Types of:*	
Adam	Rom. 5:14
Abel	Heb. 12:24
Moses	Deut. 18:15
Passover	1 Cor. 5:7
Manna	John 6:32
Brazen serpent	John 3:14
J. *Other names for:*	
Adam, the second	1 Cor. 15:45-47
Advocate	1 John 2:1
Almighty	Rev. 19:15
Alpha and Omega	Rev. 21:6
Amen	Rev. 3:14
Ancient of Days	Dan. 7:9
Angel of his presence	Is. 63:9
Anointed above His fellows	Ps. 45:7
Anointed of the Lord	Ps. 2:2
Apostle of our profession	Heb. 3:1
Arm of the Lord	Is. 51:9, 10
Author and finisher of our faith	Heb. 12:2
Babe	Luke 2:16
Beginning and end	Rev. 21:6
Beloved	Eph. 1:6
Beloved of God	Matt. 12:18
Beloved Son	Mark 1:11
Blessed and only Potentate	1 Tim. 6:15
Born of God	1 John 5:18
Branch	Zech. 3:8
Branch, a righteous	Jer. 23:5
Branch of righteousness	Jer. 33:15
Bread	John 6:41
Bread of Life	John 6:35
Bridegroom	John 3:29
Bright morning star	Rev. 22:16
Captain of salvation	Heb. 2:10
Carpenter	Mark 6:3
Carpenter's son	Matt. 13:55
Chief corner stone	Ps. 118:22 Mark 12:10
Chief Shepherd	1 Pet. 5:4
Child	Is. 9:6
Child Jesus	Luke 2:27
Chosen of God	1 Pet. 2:4
Christ, the	John 1:41 Acts 9:22
Christ a King	Luke 23:2
Christ, Jesus	Rom. 8:2
Christ Jesus our Lord	Rom. 8:39
Christ of God, the	Luke 9:20
Christ of God, His Chosen One	Luke 23:35
Christ, the Lord	Luke 2:11
Christ, the power of God	1 Cor. 1:24
Christ, the Son of the Blessed	Mark 14:61
Commander	Is. 55:4
Consolation of Israel	Luke 2:25
Costly cornerstone	Is. 28:16
Counselor	Is. 9:6
Covenant of the people	Is. 42:6
Dayspring	Luke 1:78
Day star	2 Pet. 1:19
Deity	Col. 2:9
Deliverer	Rom. 11:26
Desire of all nations	Hag. 2:7
Diadem	Is. 28:5
Door	John 10:2
Door of the sheep	John 10:1
Emmanuel	Matt. 1:23
Ensign of the people	Is. 11:10
Eternal life	1 John 5:20
Everlasting Father	Is. 9:6
Faithful and True	Rev. 19:11
Faithful witness	Rev. 1:5
Firmly placed foundation	Is. 28:16
First-begotten	Heb. 1:6
First-born from the dead	Col. 1:18
First-born of the dead	Rev. 1:5
First-born of every creature	Col. 1:15
First-born among many brethren	Rom. 8:29
First fruits	1 Cor. 15:23
First and last	Rev. 22:13
Forerunner	Heb. 6:20
Foundation laid in Zion	Is. 28:16
Friend of publicans and sinners	Luke 7:34
Glorious Lord	Is. 33:21
God	John 20:28
God blessed forever	Rom. 9:5
God of Israel	Is. 45:15
God, our Savior	1 Tim. 2:3
God with us	Matt. 1:23
Good Master	Mark 10:17
Governor	Matt. 2:6
Great God	Titus 2:13
Great High Priest	Heb. 4:14
Great Shepherd	Heb. 13:20
Guardian of souls	1 Pet. 2:25
Head, even Christ	Eph. 4:15
Head of all	Col. 2:10
Head of every man	1 Cor. 11:3
Head of the body, the church	Col. 1:18
Head over all things	Eph. 1:22
Heir of all things	Heb. 1:2
High Priest	Heb. 4:14
His beloved Son	Col. 1:13
Holy One	1 John 2:20
Holy and Righteous One	Acts 3:14
Holy One of God	Luke 4:34
Holy One of Israel	Is. 37:23
Holy Child	Acts 4:27
Hope of glory	Col. 1:27
Horn of salvation	Luke 1:69
Husband	2 Cor. 11:2
I Am	John 8:58
Image of God	2 Cor. 4:4
Image of the Invisible God	Col. 1:15
Jesus	Luke 1:31
Jesus Christ	Rom. 1:4
Jesus Christ our Lord	Rom. 6:23
Jesus Christ our Savior	Titus 3:6
Jesus of Nazareth	Luke 24:19
Jesus, the Son of God	Heb. 4:14
Jesus, the (supposed) son of Joseph	Luke 3:23
Judge of Israel	Mic. 5:1

SUBJECT	REFERENCE
Judge of the quick and the dead	Acts 10:42
Just man	Matt. 27:19
King	John 12:13
King eternal	1 Tim. 1:17
King of glory	Ps. 24:7
King of Israel	John 12:13
King of kings	1 Tim. 6:15
King of the Jews	Matt. 27:37
King of Zion	Zech. 9:9
King over all the earth	Zech. 14:9
Lamb	Rev. 13:8
Lamb of God	John 1:36
Leader	Is. 55:4
Life	John 14:6
Light	John 1:9
Light of the Gentiles	Acts 13:47
Light of the World	John 9:5
Lily of the valleys	Song 2:1
Lion of the tribe of Judah	Rev. 5:5
Living bread	John 6:51
Living stone	1 Pet. 2:4
Lord	John 21:7
Lord Christ	Col. 3:24
Lord God Almighty	Rev. 4:8
Lord Jesus	Acts 19:17
Lord Jesus Christ	2 Thess. 2:1
Lord and Savior Jesus Christ	2 Pet. 2:20
Lord both of dead and living	Rom. 14:9
Lord of all	Acts 10:36 Rom. 10:12
Lord of glory	1 Cor. 2:8
Lord of hosts	Is. 54:5
Lord of lords	1 Tim. 6:15
Lord of Sabbath	Luke 6:5
Lord our righteousness	Jer. 23:6
Lord, your redeemer	Is. 43:14
Man of peace	Luke 10:6
Man of sorrows	Is. 53:3
Master	Mark 12:14
Mediator	Heb. 12:24
Messenger of the covenant	Mal. 3:1
Messiah	John 4:25, 26
Mighty God	Is. 9:6
Mighty One of Jacob	Is. 60:16
Minister of the circumcision	Rom. 15:8
Minister of the sanctuary	Heb. 8:1, 2
Morning star	Rev. 22:16
Most Mighty	Ps. 45:3
Nazarene	Matt. 2:23
Only begotten of the Father	John 1:14
Only begotten Son	John 1:18
Only wise God	1 Tim. 1:17
Our Passover	1 Cor. 5:7
Our peace	Eph. 2:14
Physician	Luke 4:23
Power of God	1 Cor. 1:24
Precious cornerstone	1 Pet. 2:6
Priest	Heb. 5:6
Prince	Acts 5:31
Prince of life	Acts 3:15
Prince of peace	Is. 9:6
Prince of the kings of the earth	Rev. 1:5
Prophet	Deut. 18:15, 18
Propitiation	Rom. 3:25
Purifier and refiner	Mal. 3:3
Rabbi	John 6:25
Rabboni	John 20:16
Ransom	1 Tim. 2:6
Redeemer	Is. 59:20
Resurrection and the life	John 11:25
Righteous Judge	2 Tim. 4:8
Righteous One	Is. 53:11
Rock	1 Cor. 10:4
Rock of offense	Rom. 9:33
Rod of the stem of Jesse	Is. 11:1
Root of David	Rev. 22:16
Root of Jesse	Is. 11:10
Rose of Sharon	Song 2:1
Ruler in Israel	Mic. 5:2
Salvation	Luke 2:30
Savior	1 Tim. 4:10
Savior, Jesus Christ	2 Pet. 2:20
Savior, God our	Titus 1:3
Savior of the world	1 John 4:14
Scepter out of Israel	Num. 24:17
Second man	1 Cor. 15:47
Seed of David	John 7:42
Seed of the woman	Gen. 3:15
Shepherd	John 10:11
Shepherd of souls	1 Pet. 2:25
Shoot of the stem of Jesse	Is. 11:1
Son of the Blessed	Mark 14:61
Son of David	Matt. 9:27
Son of God	Rom. 1:4
Son of Man	Acts 7:56
Son of Mary	Mark 6:3
Son of the Father	2 John 3
Son of the Most High	Luke 1:32
Source of eternal salvation	Heb. 5:9
Sower	Matt. 13:3, 37
"Star out of Jacob"	Num. 24:17
Stone	Dan. 2:45
Stone rejected	Luke 20:17
Stone of stumbling	Rom. 9:32, 33
Sun of righteousness	Mal. 4:2
Teacher from God	John 3:2
Tried stone	Is. 28:16
True vine	John 15:1
Truth	John 14:6
Unspeakable gift	2 Cor. 9:15
Way	John 14:6
Wonderful	Is. 9:6
Word	1 John 1:1
Word of God	Rev. 19:13
Word of Life	1 John 1:1

Christian attributes

A. *Manifested toward God:*

SUBJECT	REFERENCE
Belief	Heb. 11:6
Holiness	Heb. 12:10, 14
Godliness	Titus 2:12
Love	Matt. 22:36, 37
Faith	Mark 11:22
Joy	Phil. 4:4

B. *Manifested toward Christ:*

SUBJECT	REFERENCE
Faith	2 Tim. 1:12
Worship	Phil. 2:4-11
Obedience	2 Thess. 1:8
Imitation	1 Cor. 11:1
Fellowship	1 John 1:3

C. *Manifested toward the Holy Spirit:*

SUBJECT	REFERENCE
Walking in	Gal. 5:16
Filled with	Eph. 5:18
Guided by	John 16:13
Praying in	Jude 20
Quench not	1 Thess. 5:19
Taught by	John 14:26
Living in	Gal. 5:25
Grieve not	Eph. 4:30

D. *Manifested in the world:*

SUBJECT	REFERENCE
Chastity	1 Tim. 5:22
Contentment	Heb. 13:5
Diligence	1 Thess. 3:7
Forbearance	Eph. 4:2
Honesty	Rom. 12:17
Industry	1 Thess. 4:11, 12
Love toward enemies	Matt. 5:44
Peacefulness	Rom. 14:17-19
Temperance	1 Cor. 9:25
Tolerance	Rom. 14:1-23
Zealous for good deeds	Titus 2:14

E. *Manifested toward other Christians:*

SUBJECT	REFERENCE
Bearing burdens	Gal. 6:2
Helping the needy	Acts 11:14, 30
Fellowship	Acts 2:42
Brotherly kindness	1 Pet. 4:7-11
Mutual edification	1 Thess. 5:11

F. *Manifested as signs of faith:*

SUBJECT	REFERENCE
Spiritual growth	2 Pet. 3:18
Fruitfulness	John 15:1-6
Perseverance	1 Cor. 15:58
Persecution	2 Tim. 3:9-12
Obedience	Phil. 2:12
Good works	James 2:14-26

G. *Manifested as internal graces:*

SUBJECT	REFERENCE
Kindness	Col. 3:12, 13
Humility	1 Pet. 5:5, 6
Gentleness	James 3:17, 18
Love	1 Cor. 13:1-13
Self-control	Gal. 5:23
Peace	Phil. 4:7

Christianity, a way of life

SUBJECT	REFERENCE
Founded on Christ	1 Cor. 3:10, 12
Based on doctrines	1 Cor. 15:1-4
Designed for all	Matt. 28:18-20
Centers in salvation	Acts 4:12
Produces change	1 Cor. 6:11

Christians—*Believers in Jesus Christ*

SUBJECT	REFERENCE
First applied at Antioch	Acts 11:26
Agrippa almost becomes	Acts 26:28
Proof of, by suffering	1 Pet. 4:16

Sometimes referred to as:

SUBJECT	REFERENCE
Believers	Acts 5:14
Brethren	Rom. 7:1
Brethren, beloved	1 Thess. 1:4
Brethren, holy	Heb. 3:1
Children	2 Cor. 6:13
Children of God	Rom. 8:16
Children of Light	Eph. 5:8
Dear children	Eph. 5:1
Disciples	Acts 9:25
Elect, the	Rom. 8:33
Friends	John 15:14
Heirs of God and joint heirs with	Rom. 8:17
Light in the Lord	Eph. 5:8
Light of the world	Matt. 5:14
Little children	1 John 2:1
Members	1 Cor. 12:18, 25
Priests	Rev. 1:6
Saints	Rom. 8:27
Salt of the earth	Matt. 5:13
Servants of God	Acts 16:17
Sheep	John 10:27
Soldier	2 Tim. 2:4
Sons of God	Rom. 8:14
Strangers	1 Pet. 2:11
Vessels of honor	2 Tim. 2:21
Witnesses	Acts 1:8

Christlikeness

SUBJECT	REFERENCE
Model	2 Cor. 3:18
Motivation	2 Cor. 5:14-17
Manifestation	Gal. 5:22, 23
Means	Rom. 8:1-17
Mystery	Phil. 3:20, 21

Chronicles—two books of Old Testament from Heb. meaning *"the words of the days"*

Chrysolite—*gold stone*

SUBJECT	REFERENCE
In New Jerusalem	Rev. 21:20

Chrysoprasus—*golden-green stone*

SUBJECT	REFERENCE
In New Jerusalem	Rev. 21:20

Chub

SUBJECT	REFERENCE
Desolation of, predicted	Ezek. 30:5

Chun—*founding*

SUBJECT	REFERENCE
A town of Syria	1 Chr. 18:8
Called Berothah	Ezek. 47:16

Church—*the called-out ones*

A. *Descriptive of:*

SUBJECT	REFERENCE
Local church	Acts 8:1
Churches generally	Rom. 16:4
Believers gathered	Rom. 16:5
The body of believers	1 Cor. 12:28
Body of Christ	Eph. 1:22, 23

B. *Title applied to:*

SUBJECT	REFERENCE
The Bride of Christ	Eph. 5:22-32
The body	Col. 1:18
One body	1 Cor. 12:18-24
Body of Christ	Eph. 4:12
The Church	Eph. 3:21
Church of the first-born	Heb. 12:23
Church of God	1 Cor. 1:2
Church of the Living God	1 Tim. 3:15
Churches of Christ	Rom. 16:16
Church of the Gentiles	Rom. 16:4
City of God	Heb. 12:22
Flock	Acts 20:28
Flock of God	1 Pet. 5:2
God's building	1 Cor. 3:9
God's husbandry	1 Cor. 3:9
Habitation of God	Eph. 2:22
Household of God	Eph. 2:19
Israel of God	Gal. 6:16
Jerusalem	Gal. 4:26
Kingdom	Heb. 12:28
Kingdom of God's dear Son	Col. 1:13
Lamb's wife	Rev. 19:7
Mount Zion	Heb. 12:22
People of God	1 Pet. 2:10
Spiritual house	1 Pet. 2:5
Temple of God	1 Cor. 3:16

C. *Relation to Christ:*

SUBJECT	REFERENCE
Saved by	Eph. 5:25-29
Purchased by	Acts 20:28
Sanctified by	Eph. 5:26, 27
Founded on	Eph. 2:19, 20
Built by	Matt. 16:18
Loved by	Eph. 5:25
Subject to	Rom. 7:4

SUBJECT ... REFERENCE

D. *Members of:*
- Added by faith ... Acts 2:41
- Added by the Lord ... Acts 2:47
- Baptized into one Spirit ... 1 Cor. 12:13
- Edified by the Word ... Eph. 4:15, 16
- Persecuted ... Acts 8:1-3
- Disciplined ... Matt. 18:15-17
- Worship ... Acts 20:7
- Fellowship together ... Acts 2:42-46
- Urged to attend ... Heb. 10:25
- Subject to pastoral oversight ... 1 Pet. 5:1-3
- Unified in Christ ... Gal. 3:28

E. *Organization of:*
- Under bishops ... 1 Tim. 3:1-7
- Function of deacons ... Acts 6:3-6
- Place of evangelists ... Eph. 4:11
- Official assemblies ... Acts 15:1-31
- Function of the presbytery ... 1 Tim. 4:14

F. *Mission of:*
- Evangelize the world ... Matt. 28:18-20
- Guard the truth ... 2 Tim. 2:1, 2
- Edify the saints ... Eph. 4:11-15
- Discipline unruly ... 2 Cor. 13:1-10

G. *Local, examples of:*
- Antioch ... Acts 11:26
- Asia ... 1 Cor. 16:19; Rev. 1:11
- Babylon ... 1 Pet. 5:13
- Caesarea ... Acts 18:22
- Cenchrea ... Rom. 16:1
- Colossae ... Col. 1:2
- Corinth ... 1 Cor. 1:2
- Ephesus ... Acts 20:17
- Galatia ... Gal. 1:2
- Jerusalem ... Acts 8:1
- Judea ... Gal. 1:22
- Laodicea ... Col. 4:15
- Macedonia ... 2 Cor. 8:1
- Pergamos ... Rev. 2:12
- Philadelphia ... Rev. 3:7
- Philippi ... Phil. 1:1
- Rome ... Rom. 1:7
- Sardis ... Rev. 3:1
- Smyrna ... Rev. 2:8
- Thyatira ... Rev. 2:18
- Thessalonica ... 1 Thess. 1:1

Church sleeper
- Falls from window during Paul's sermon ... Acts 20:7-12

Churl—*a rude, surly person*
- Nabal ... 1 Sam. 25:3
- Descriptive of the fraudulent ... Is. 32:5, 7

Chushan-rishathaim—*extra wicked*
- A Mesopotamian king; oppressed Israel ... Judg. 3:8
- Othniel delivers Israel from ... Judg. 3:9, 10

Chuza
- Herod's steward ... Luke 8:3

Cilicia—*a province of Asia Minor*
- Paul's country ... Acts 21:39
- Students from, argued with Stephen ... Acts 6:9
- Paul labors in ... Gal. 1:21

Cinnamon—*a laurel-like spicy plant*
- Used in holy oil ... Ex. 30:23
- A perfume ... Prov. 7:17
- In Babylon's trade ... Rev. 18:13
- Figurative of a lover ... Song 4:12, 14

Circle—*a curved line equally distant from a common center*
- Used of the earth ... Is. 40:22

Circuit—*circle, regular course*
- Judge's itinerary ... 1 Sam. 7:16
- Sun's orbit ... Ps. 19:6

Circumcision—*a cutting*

A. *The physical rite:*
- Instituted by God ... Gen. 17:10-14
- A seal of righteousness ... Rom. 2:25-29
- Performed on the eighth day ... Luke 1:59
- Child named when performed ... Luke 1:59
- Allowed right to Passover ... Ex. 12:48
- Neglect of, punished ... Ex. 4:24
- Neglected during wilderness ... Josh. 5:7
- A sign of covenant relation ... Rom. 4:11

B. *Necessity of:*
- Asserted in old dispensation ... Gen. 17:10-14
- Abolished by the Gospel ... Gal. 5:1-4; Eph. 2:11, 15
- Avails nothing ... Gal. 5:6; Col. 3:11
- Avowed by false teachers ... Acts 15:1
- Acclaimed a yoke ... Acts 15:10
- Abrogated by apostles ... Acts 15:5-29; 1 Cor. 7:18, 19

C. *Spiritual significance of:*
- Regeneration ... Deut. 10:16; Deut. 30:6; Jer. 4:4
- The true Jew (Christian) ... Rom. 2:29
- The Christian ... Phil. 3:3; Col. 2:11

Circumstances

A. *Relationship to Christian:*
- Work for good ... Rom. 8:28
- Produce perseverance ... Rom. 5:3
- Not cause for anxiety ... Phil. 4:6
- Test and purify ... 1 Pet. 1:5-7
- To be met with thanksgiving ... Eph. 5:20; Phil. 4:6
- Can be overcome ... Phil. 4:11-13

B. *Examples, victory over:*
- Moses ... Ex. 14:10-31
- Joshua ... Josh. 6:8-21
- Shamgar ... Judg. 3:31
- Gideon ... Judg. 7:19-23
- Hannah ... 1 Sam. 1:9-19
- David ... 1 Sam. 17:40-51
- Widow of Zarephath ... 1 Kin. 17:8-16
- Hezekiah ... 2 Kin. 20:1-11
- Peter ... Acts 12:5-17
- Paul ... Acts 14:19-20; Acts 16:19-26

Cistern—*an underground reservoir for water*

A. *Literal uses of:*
- Water ... 2 Kin. 18:31
- Imprisonment (when empty) ... Jer. 38:6

B. *Figurative uses of:*
- Wife ... Prov. 5:15
- Heart ... Eccl. 12:6
- False religion ... Jer. 2:13

C. *Kinds of:*
- Family cisterns ... Is. 36:16
- Garden ponds ... Eccl. 2:6

Cities—*organized population centers*

A. *Features regarding:*
- Earliest ... Gen. 4:17
- Walled ... Lev. 25:29-31; Deut. 3:5
- Often built on hills ... Matt. 5:14
- Gates guarded ... Acts 9:24
- Guard posted ... 2 Kin. 7:10; Neh. 13:19
- Difficult to attack ... Prov. 16:32
- Business at gate ... Gen. 23:10; Ruth 4:1-11

B. *Descriptions of:*
- Sodom—wicked ... Gen. 13:13
- Jerusalem—like Sodom ... Is. 1:10
- Nineveh—repentant ... Jon. 3:5-10
- Capernaum—arrogant ... Matt. 11:23
- Athens—idolatrous ... Acts 17:16

Cities, Levitical
- Forty-eight ... Num. 35:7
- Six designed for refuge ... Deut. 19:1-13

Cities of refuge
- Given to Levites ... Num. 35:6
- For the manslayer ... Num. 35:11

Cities of the mountains
- Avoided by Israel ... Deut. 2:37

Cities of the plain
- Admah ... Gen. 14:8
- Bela ... Gen. 14:2
- Gomorrah ... Gen. 19:28; Jude 7
- Sodom ... Gen. 19:28-29
- Zeboiim ... Gen. 14:8
- Dibon, Bamoth-baal, Beth-baal-meon ... Josh. 13:17

Cities of the valley
- Restored ... Jer. 32:44
- Taken by Israel ... Deut. 3:8, 10

Citizen, citizenship

A. *Kinds of:*
- Hebrew ... Eph. 2:12
- Roman ... Acts 21:39
- Spiritual ... Phil. 3:20
- Christian (see below)

B. *Duties of Christian citizens:*
- Be subject to rulers ... Rom. 13:1-7
- Pray for rulers ... 1 Tim. 2:1, 2
- Honor rulers ... 1 Pet. 2:17
- Seek peace ... Jer. 29:7
- Pay taxes ... Matt. 22:21
- Obey God first ... Acts 5:27-29
- Love one's nation ... Neh. 2:3
- Live righteously ... 1 Pet. 3:8-17

City builder
- Cain builds first ... Gen. 4:17
- Woe to, who uses bloodshed ... Hab. 2:12

City, Holy
- Applied to Jerusalem ... Dan. 9:24; Rev. 11:2
- Prophecy concerning ... Joel 3:17
- Clothed with beautiful garments ... Is. 52:1
- New Jerusalem ... Rev. 21:2

City of David
- Applied to the castle of Zion ... 1 Chr. 11:5
- Taken by David from Jebusites ... 1 Chr. 11:4-8
- Ark brought to ... 1 Chr. 15:1-29
- Bethlehem called ... Luke 2:4

City of destruction
- Prophecy concerning an Egyptian city ... Is. 19:18

City of God
- Prophetic description of Zion ... Ps. 48:1-14
- Dwelling place of God ... Ps. 46:4, 5
- Sought by the saints ... Heb. 11:9, 10, 16
- Descriptive of the heavenly Jerusalem ... Rev. 21:2

City of Moab
- Where Balak met Balaam ... Num. 22:36

City of palm trees—*Jericho*
- Seen by Moses ... Deut. 34:1-3
- Occupied by Kenites ... Judg. 1:16
- Captured by Eglon ... Judg. 3:12 13

City of Salt
- Near the Dead Sea ... Josh. 15:62

City of waters
- Applied to Rabbah ... 2 Sam. 12:26, 27

Civil

1. Righteousness
   - Principle of ... Prov. 14:34
   - Precepts of ... Zech. 8:16, 17
   - Practice of ... Mic. 4:2
   - Perversion of ... Mic. 7:1-4
2. Service

   A. *Characteristics of:*
   - Loyalty ... Neh. 2:3
   - Industry ... Gen. 41:37-57
   - Esteem ... Esth. 10:3

   B. *Examples of:*
   - Joseph ... Gen. 39:1-6
   - Daniel ... Dan. 1:17-21
   - Mordecai ... Esth. 8:1, 2, 9
   - Nehemiah ... Neh. 2:1-8
3. Authority:
   - Obedience to commanded ... Eccl. 8:2-7; Rom. 13:1-7
   - Submit for Christ's sake ... 1 Pet. 2:13-15

Civility—*good breeding; courtesy*
- Shown by Joseph ... Gen. 47:1-10
- Taught by Christ ... Luke 14:8-10
- Shown by Timothy ... Phil. 2:19-23
- Shown by Gaius ... 3 John 1-6

SUBJECT REFERENCE

Class distinction
- Egyptians—against Hebrews .... Gen. 43:32
- Haman—against Hebrews ...... Esth. 3:8, 9
- Jews—against Samaritans....... John 4:9
- Jews—against Gentiles .... Acts 22:21, 22
- Forbidden.................... Ex. 12:48, 49

Clauda—*lamentable*
- Small island southeast of Crete .... Acts 27:16

Claudia
- Disciple at Rome.............. 2 Tim. 4:21

Claudius Lysias
- Roman commander who protected Paul....................... Acts 24:22-24

Clay—*firm, plastic earth*

A. *Uses of:*
- Making bricks .... 2 Sam. 12:31
- Making pottery .... Is. 41:25
- Sealing.................... Job 38:14
- Miracle .... John 9:6, 15

B. *Figurative of:*
- Man's weakness .... Is. 64:8
- Unstable kingdom .... Dan. 2:33-35, 42
- Trouble .... Ps. 40:2
- Wealth..................... Hab. 2:6

Clean—*pure, innocent*

A. *Used physically:*
- Outward purity .... Matt. 23:26

B. *Used ceremonially of:*
- Clean animals............. Gen. 7:2
- Freedom from defilement .... Luke 5:14, 15

C. *Used spiritually of:*
- Men's nature .... Job 9:30, 31
- Repentance................ Gen. 35:2
- Regeneration .... Ezek. 36:25
- Sanctification .... Ps. 24:4
- Glorification .... Rev. 19:8, 14

Cleanliness
- Required of priests .... Is. 52:11
- Acceptability of worship .... Heb. 10:22
- Inner, better than outward...... Matt. 23:25-28

Cleansing, spiritual
- Promise of .... Jer. 33:8
- Need of...................... Ps. 51:2
- Extent of.................... Ps. 19:12
- Command regarding .... 2 Cor. 7:1
- Means of..................... 1 John 1:7, 9
- Perfection of................ Eph. 5:26

Cleanthes—Stoic teacher not mentioned by name in the Bible
- Quoted by Paul .... Acts 17:28

Clement—*mild, merciful*
- Paul's companions............ Phil. 4:3

Cleopas—*of a renowned father*
- Christ appeared to............ Luke 24:18

Cleophas—*of a renowned father*
- Husband of Mary .... John 19:25
- Called Alphaeus.............. Matt. 10:3

Climate—*temperature and weather conditions*

A. *Elements of:*
- Cold...................... Job 37:9; Acts 28:2
- Clouds.................... Job 35:5
- Thirsty ground .... Deut. 8:15
- Heat...................... Is. 49:10
- Rain...................... Ezra 10:13
- Snow .... 1 Chr. 11:22
- Sunshine .... Ex. 16:21
- Wind .... Matt. 14:24

B. *Order of:*
- Promised .... Gen. 8:22
- Controlled by God .... Job 37:5-13
- Used in judgment .... Jer. 50:38; Hag. 1:10-11
- Tool of correction .... Jon. 1:3, 4
- Shows deity of Christ ...... Mark 4:37-39

Cloak—*outer garment*

A. *Used literally of:*
- Outer garment .... Matt. 5:40

B. *Used figuratively of:*
- Covering for sin........... John 15:22
- Covering for license........ 1 Pet. 2:16

Closet
- A place of prayer............. Matt. 6:6

Clothing—*garments*

A. *Need of:*
- Cover nakedness .... Gen. 3:10, 11
- Maintain modesty .... 1 Pet. 3:1-5
- Keep warm .... 2 Tim. 4:13
- Remove anguish........... Esth. 4:3, 4

B. *Unusual features regarding:*
- Lasted forty years .... Deut. 8:4
- Torn into twelve pieces...... 1 Kin. 11:29, 30
- Borrowed from enemies ..... Ex. 12:35
- Some stripped of .... Luke 10:30

C. *Regulations concerning:*
- Wearing opposite sex's, forbidden .... Deut. 22:5
- Gaudy, denounced.......... Is. 3:16-24
- Ostentatious, prohibited ..... 1 Tim. 2:9
- Warnings concerning........ Matt. 7:15
- Judgments by, deceptive ..... Luke 16:19
- Proper sign of Christian sanity................... Mark 5:15

Clothing, tearing of—*symbolic expression of grief*
- By Reuben .... Gen. 37:29, 34
- By Joshua .... Josh. 7:6
- By Tamar .... 2 Sam. 13:19
- By Job..................... Job 1:20
- By Ezra .... Ezra 9:3
- By high priest............... Mark 14:63
- By Paul and Barnabas .... Acts 14:14
- Forbidden to Aaron .... Lev. 10:6

Cloud—*a visible mass of vapor*

A. *Miraculous uses of:*
- Israel's guidance........... Ex. 13:21, 22
- Manifesting the divine glory .... Ex. 16:10
- Manifesting the divine presence .... 2 Chr. 5:13
- Jesus' transfiguration....... Luke 9:34, 35
- Jesus' ascension .... Acts 1:9-11
- Jesus' return .... Matt. 24:30

B. *Figurative of:*
- God's unsearchableness ..... Ps. 97:2
- Sins .... Is. 44:22
- Witnesses .... Heb. 12:1
- False teachers.............. 2 Pet. 2:17
- Baptism................... 1 Cor. 10:1, 2
- Boasting .... Prov. 25:14

Cloudburst—*a sudden downpour of rain*
- Sent as a punishment .... Ezra 10:9-14

Cloud, pillar of

A. *Designed to:*
- Regulate Israel's movements .... Ex. 40:36, 37
- Guide Israel .... Ex. 13:21
- Defend Israel .... Ex. 14:19
- Cover the tabernacle .... Ex. 40:34

B. *Special manifestations of, at:*
- Time of murmuring......... Ex. 16:9, 10
- Giving of Law .... Ex. 19:9, 16
- Rebellion of Aaron and Miriam .... Num. 12:5
- Korah's rebellion .... Num. 16:19, 42

Clusters—*bunches*

Kinds of:
- Grapes .... Num. 13:23
- Henna blossoms .... Song 1:14
- Raisins .... 1 Sam. 25:18
- Dates...................... Song 5:11

Cnidus—*age*
- City of Asia Minor on Paul's voyage...................... Acts 27:7

Coal—*charcoal*

A. *Uses of:*
- Heating .... John 18:18
- Cooking................... John 21:9
- By smiths .... Is. 44:11, 12

B. *Figurative of:*
- Lust .... Prov. 6:25-28
- Purification .... Is. 6:6
- Good deeds .... Rom. 12:20
- Posterity .... 2 Sam. 14:7

Coat—*an outer garment*

A. *Makers of:*
- God—for man .... Gen. 3:21
- Jacob—for Joseph .... Gen. 37:3
- Hannah—for Samuel........ 1 Sam. 2:18, 19
- Dorcas—for wearing .... Acts 9:39

Cockatrice—*venomous snake*
- Figurative of evil deeds .... Is. 11:8
- Figurative of man's evil nature .. Deut. 32:33

Cockcrowing
- Announced the dawn .... Mark 13:35
- Reminded Peter.............. Matt. 26:34, 74

Cockle—*stinging weeds*
- Obnoxious among barley .... Job 31:40

Coffer—*a strongbox; a chest*
- Used to safeguard jewels .... 1 Sam. 6:8-15

Coffin—*a box-like container for a corpse*
- In Joseph's burial .... Gen. 50:26
- Jesus touched .... Luke 7:14

Coins—*metal mediums of exchange*
- Beckah (1/2 shekel)............ Ex. 38:26
- Brass .... Matt. 10:9
- Dram....................... Ezra 2:69
- Farthing .... Matt. 10:29
- Gerah .... Ex. 30:13
- Maneh...................... Ezek. 45:12
- Mite........................ Mark 12:42
- Penny .... Matt. 20:2
- Piece of gold .... 2 Kin. 5:5
- Piece of money .... Matt. 17:27
- Piece of silver............... Matt. 26:15

Cold—*absence of heat*

A. *Used literally of:*
- Winter.................... Gen. 8:22
- Cold weather .... John 18:18

B. *Used figuratively of:*
- God's power.............. Ps. 147:17
- Indolence .... Prov. 20:4
- Good news .... Prov. 25:25
- Apostasy .... Jer. 18:14
- Spiritual decay .... Matt. 24:12

Col-hozeh—*all seeing*
- A man of Judah.............. Neh. 3:15; Neh. 11:5

Collaborators
- Delilah .... Judg. 16:4-21
- Doeg .... 1 Sam. 21:7
- Judas .... Matt. 26:14-16

Collection box
- For Temple offerings .... 2 Kin. 12:9

Collection of money
- The Temple tax .... 2 Chr. 24:6, 9
- For saints .... Rom. 15:25, 26

College
- Huldah's dwelling .... 2 Kin. 22:14

Colony—*citizens transported to another land*

A. *Illustrated by:*
- Israel in Egypt .... Gen. 46:28
- Israel in Assyria .... 2 Kin. 17:6, 24
- Judah in Babylon........... 2 Kin. 25:8-12

B. *Applied to:*
- Philippi as a Roman colony .... Acts 16:12
- Philippian Christians........ Phil. 3:20

Colors

A. *White, descriptive of:*
- Glory and majesty.......... Dan. 7:9; Rev. 20:11
- Purity, glory .... Rev. 1:14
- Victory .... Rev. 6:2
- Completion .... John 4:35

B. *Black, descriptive of:*
- Sorrow, calamity .... Rev. 6-12
- Hell .... Jude 13

SUBJECT ... REFERENCE

C. *Green, descriptive of:*
Spiritual privileges ... Jer. 11:16
Spiritual life ... Ps. 52:8
Ps. 92:12-15

D. *Red* (crimson), *descriptive of:*
Atonement ... Is. 63:2
Military might ... Nah. 2:3
Persecution ... Rev. 12:3
Drunkenness ... Prov. 23:29
Sinfulness ... Is. 1:18

E. *Purple, descriptive of:*
Royalty ... Judg. 8:26
Wealth ... Luke 16:19
Luxury ... Rev. 17:4

F. *Blue, descriptive of:*
Heavenly character ... Ex. 28:31

Colossae—*punishment*
A city in Asia Minor ... Col. 1:2
Evangelized by Epaphras ... Col. 1:7
Not visited by Paul ... Col. 2:1
Paul writes against errors of ... Col. 2:16-23

Colossians, the epistle to the
Written by Paul ... Col. 1:1

Colt—*young beast of burden*
Descriptive of Messiah ... Gen. 49:10, 11
Christ rides on ... Matt. 21:2, 5, 7
Of camel, as gift ... Gen. 32:13, 15

Come—*to approach, arrive*
Of invitation ... Is. 1:18
Of salvation ... Matt. 18:11
Of rest ... Matt. 11:28
Of promise ... John 14:3
Of prayer ... Heb. 4:16
The final ... Rev. 22:17, 20

Comfort—*to relieve distress; to console*

A. *Sources of:*
God ... 2 Cor. 1:3, 4
Christ ... Matt. 9:22
Holy Spirit ... Acts 9:31
The Scriptures ... Rom. 15:4
Christian friends ... 2 Cor. 7:6

B. *Those in need of:*
Afflicted ... Is. 40:1, 2
Sorrowful ... 2 Cor. 2:7
Weak ... 1 Thess. 5:14
Discouraged ... 2 Cor. 2:7
Troubled ... 2 Cor. 7:5-7
One another ... 1 Thess. 4:18

Comforter—*the Holy Spirit*
Abides with believers ... John 14:16
Teaches ... John 14:26
Testifies of Christ ... John 15:26
Convicts ... John 16:7-11
Guides into truth ... John 16:13
Glorifies Christ ... John 16:14, 15

Coming of Christ (see Second Coming of Christ)

Commander—*a leading official*

Names of:
Phichol ... Gen. 21:32
Sisera ... Judg. 4:7
Abner ... 1 Sam. 17:55
Shobach ... 2 Sam. 10:16
Joab ... 2 Sam. 24:2
Amasa ... 1 Kin. 2:32
Zimri ... 1 Kin. 16:9
Omri ... 1 Kin. 16:16
Shophach ... 1 Chr 19:16
Adnah ... 2 Chr. 17:14
Jehohanan ... 2 Chr. 17:15
Rehum ... Ezra 4:8
Hananiah ... Neh. 7:2
Arioch ... Dan. 2:15
Lysias ... Acts 24:7

Commandment—*a rule imposed by authority*

A. *God's, described as:*
Faithful ... Ps. 119:86
Broad ... Ps. 119:96
A lamp ... Prov. 6:23
Holy ... Rom. 7:12
Not burdensome ... 1 John 5:3

B. *Christ's, described as:*
New ... John 13:34
Obligatory ... Matt. 5:19, 20
Promissory ... John 15:10, 12
Eternal life ... John 12:49, 50

Commandments, divine
Sought by men ... Phil. 3:6-15
Not material ... Rom. 14:1-23
Lives an epistle of ... 2 Cor. 3:1-3
Revealed at judgment ... Matt. 25:20, 21

Commandment, the new
Given by Christ ... John 13:34, 35
Based on old ... 1 John 2:7-11
2 John 5
Fulfills the Law ... Matt. 22:34-40

Commandments, The Ten
Divine origin ... Ex. 20:1
Written by God ... Ex. 32:16
Described ... Ex. 20:3-17
Christ sums up ... Matt. 22:35-40
Spiritual nature ... Matt. 5:28
Love fulfills ... Rom. 13:8-10

Commerce—*trade on a large scale*

A. *Engaged in:*
Locally ... Prov. 31:14-18
Nationally ... 2 Chr. 9:21
Internationally ... Rev. 18:10-24

B. *Abuses of:*
Sabbath trading ... Neh. 13:15-22
Temple business ... John 2:13-16
Ignoring the Lord ... James 4:13-17
Pride ... Ezek. 28:2-18

Commission—*special assignment*

A. *Kinds of:*
Christ's—to mankind ... John 3:16-18
Israel's—to the Gentiles ... Acts 13:47
The Church's—to the world ... Matt. 28:19, 20

B. *Requirements of:*
Faithfulness ... 2 Tim. 4:1-8
Diligence ... Rom. 15:15-32
Willingness ... 1 Sam. 3:9, 10

Common—*public, general*
Normal, natural ... 1 Cor. 10:13
Ceremonially unclean ... Acts 10:14
Ordinary people ... Jer. 26:23
Shared togetherness ... Acts 2:44
Things believed alike ... Titus 1:4

Common people
Burial place of ... Jer. 26:23

Commonwealth—*a nation*
Descriptive of Israel ... Eph. 2:12

Communion of the Lord's Supper (see Lord's Supper)

Communion of the Saints (see Fellowship)

Communion with Christ

A. *Based on:*
Redemption ... Heb. 2:10-13
Regeneration ... 1 Cor. 6:14-17
Resurrection (Spiritual) ... Col. 3:1-3

B. *Identifies Christians, in:*
Name ... 1 Pet. 4:12-16
Character ... John 14:23
Hope ... 1 John 3:1-3

Communion with God

A. *Prerequisites of:*
Reconciliation ... 2 Cor. 5:18, 19
Acceptance of Christ ... John 14:6
Obedience ... John 14:23
Holiness ... 2 Cor. 6:14-18

B. *Saints:*
Desire such ... Heb. 11:10
Seek it through prayer ... Matt. 6:6-15
Realized fully in eternity ... Rev. 7:13-17

Communism, Christian

A. *Supposedly found in:*
Early church ... Acts 2:44, 45

B. *Differs from modern Communism:*
In being voluntary ... Acts 5:4
Confined to Christians ... Acts 4:32
Not under government control ... Acts 4:34-37

Companion—*a fellow worker*
Wife ... Mal. 2:14
Companion in tribulation ... Rev. 1:9
Co-worker ... Ezra 4:7, 9, 11
Fellow fool ... Prov. 13:20
Fellow believer ... Ps. 119:63
Fellow worker ... Phil. 2:23, 25

Companions, evil

A. *Cause:*
Rebellion ... Num. 16:1-50
Idolatry ... Ex. 32:1-8
Violence, death ... Acts 23:12-22
Persecution ... Acts 17:5-9

B. *Warnings against:*
Do not consent with them ... Prov. 1:10-19
Avoid them ... 1 Cor. 5:9-11
Remember their end ... Rev. 22:11, 15

Comparison—*likeness, similarity*

A. *Worthy comparisons, between:*
God's greatness and man's littleness ... Is. 46:12, 13
Christ's glory and humiliation ... Phil. 2:5-11
Israel's call and responsibility ... Rom. 2:17-29
Gentile faith and Jewish unbelief ... Matt. 12:41, 42
Former and present unbelief ... Matt. 11:20-24
Old and new covenants ... 2 Cor. 3:6-18
The believer's status now and hereafter ... 1 John 3:1-3

B. *Unworthy comparisons, based on:*
Position ... Num. 16:3
Privileges ... 1 Cor. 3:1-9
Ancestry ... James 2:1-9

Compassion—*suffering with another*

A. *God's, described as:*
From of old ... Ps. 26:6
New every morning ... Lam. 3:22, 23
Great ... Is. 54:7
Kindled ... Hos. 11:8

B. *God's, expressed:*
Fully ... Ps. 78:38
Sovereignly ... Rom. 9:15
Unfailingly ... Lam. 3:22
Willingly ... Luke 15:20

C. *Christ's, expressed toward the:*
Weary ... Matt. 11:28-30
Tempted ... Heb. 2:18
Helpless ... Mark 9:20-22
Ignorant ... Heb. 5:2
Sorrowful ... Luke 7:13, 14
Multitude ... Matt. 15:32

D. *Examples of:*
David in sorrow ... Ps. 51:1-12
God to Israel ... Hos. 11:8
Christ to sinners ... Matt. 9:13

E. *Christian's:*
Commanded ... Zech. 7:9; Col. 3:12; Jude 22
Expressed ... Heb. 10:34
1 Pet. 3:8
Illustrated ... Luke 10:33
Unified ... Phil. 2:1, 2

Complicity—*partnership in wrongdoing*
In Adam's sin ... Rom. 5:12
In the sins of others ... Ps. 50:18
In national guilt ... Matt. 27:25

Composure—*calmness; tranquility; self-possession*
Before enemies ... Neh. 4:1-23
Under great strain ... Acts 27:21-26
Facing death ... Acts 7:59, 60
Lack of ... Dan. 6:18-20

Compromise—*agreement by concession*

A. *Forbidden with:*
Ungodly ... Ps. 1:1
Evil ... Rom. 12:9
Unbelievers ... 2 Cor. 6:14-18
False teachers ... Gal. 1:8-10
2 John 7-11
Spiritual darkness ... Eph. 5:11

SUBJECT — REFERENCE

B. *Examples:*
Lot — Gen. 13:12, 13; Gen. 19:1-29
Samson — Judg. 16:1-21
Solomon — 1 Kin. 11:1-14
Asa — 2 Chr. 16:1-9
Jehoshaphat — 2 Chr. 18:1-3; 2 Chr. 19:1, 2; 2 Chr. 20:35-37

Concealment—*keeping something secret*
Of sin, impossible — Is. 29:15
Of intrigue, exposed — Esth. 2:21-23
Of intentions, revealed — Acts 23:12-22

Conceit—*self-flattery*
Of persons:
Goliath — 1 Sam. 17:42-44
Sanballat — Neh. 4:1-3
Haman — Esth. 6:6-9
The wicked — Prov. 6:12-17
Christians, deplored — Rom. 12:16
Characteristic of:
False teachers — 1 Tim. 6:3, 4
New convert — 1 Tim. 3:6

Conceited—*a self-righteous spirit*
Christians warned against — Rom. 11:20
Rich tempted to — 1 Tim. 6:17
To prevail in last days — 2 Tim. 3:1-5

Conception of children
In marriage — Gen. 21:1-3
In adultery — 2 Sam. 11:2-5
In virginity — Matt. 1:18-21

Concision—*mutilation*
Used of legalistic circumcision — Phil. 3:2

Conclude—*to decide*
The main issue — Eccl. 12:13

Concubine—*a "wife" who is not legally a wife*
A. *Features regarding:*
Could be divorced — Gen. 21:10-14
Has certain rights — Deut. 21:10-14
Children of, legitimate — Gen. 22:24
Unfaithfulness of — Judg. 19:9
Source of trouble — Gen. 21:10-14
Incompatible with Christianity — Matt. 19:5
B. *Men who had:*
Abraham — Gen. 25:6
Nahor — Gen. 22:24
Jacob — Gen. 30:1, 4
Eliphaz — Gen. 36:12
Gideon — Judg. 8:30, 31
Saul — 2 Sam. 3:7
David — 2 Sam. 5:13
Solomon — 1 Kin. 11:3
Caleb — 1 Chr. 2:46
Manasseh — 1 Chr. 7:14
Rehoboam — 2 Chr. 11:21
Abijah — 2 Chr. 13:21
Belshazzar — Dan. 5:2

Concupiscence—*sinful desire*
A. *Causes of:*
Learning evil — Rom. 16:19
Making provision for flesh — Rom. 13:14
Not fearing God — Prov. 8:13; Prov. 9:10
Not seeing consequences of sin — Ex. 34:6, 7; Rom. 6:23; Heb. 11:25
B. *Fruits of:*
Evil inclinations — Rom. 7:7, 8
Temptations — James 1:14
Unchastity — 1 Thess. 4:5
Reprobation — Rom. 1:21-32
C. *Remedy for:*
Repentance — 2 Cor. 7:9, 10; James 4:9, 10
Submitting to God — Rom. 12:1, 2; James 4:7
Resisting the devil — James 4:7
Drawing near to God — James 4:8
Walking in the Spirit — Rom. 8:1-8

Condemnation—*the judicial act of declaring one guilty*
A. *Causes of:*
Adam's sin — Rom. 5:16-18
Actual sin — Matt. 27:3
Our words — Matt. 12:37
Self-judgment — Rom. 2:1; Titus 3:11
Legal requirements — 2 Cor. 3:9
Rejection of Christ — John 3:18, 19
B. *Escape from:*
In Christ — Rom. 8:1, 3
By faith — John 3:18, 19

Condescend—*to humble oneself to the level of others*
Christ's example — John 13:3-5
The believer's practice — Rom. 12:16
The divine model — Phil. 2:3-11

Condolence—*an expression of sympathy*
A. *Received by:*
Job from friends — Job 2:11
Hanun from David — 2 Sam. 10:2
Hezekiah from a king — 2 Kin. 20:12
Mary from Jesus — John 11:23-35
B. *Helps in expressing, assurance of:*
Trust — Ps. 23:1-6
Hope — John 14:1-4
Resurrection — 1 Thess. 4:13-18
Help — Is. 40:10, 11

Coney—*the Syrian rock hyrax*
Listed as unclean — Lev. 11:5
Lives among rocks — Ps. 104:18
Likened to people — Prov. 30:26

Confectionaries—*perfumers*
A female occupation — 1 Sam. 8:13

Confederacy—*an alliance*
Denounced — Is. 8:12

Confessing Christ
A. *Necessity of:*
For salvation — Rom. 10:9, 10
A test of faith — 1 John 2:23
An evidence of spiritual union — 1 John 4:15
His confessing us — Matt. 10:32
B. *Content of:*
Christ's incarnation — 1 John 4:2, 3
Christ's Lordship — Phil. 2:11
C. *Prompted by:*
Holy Spirit — 1 Cor. 12:3
Faith — Rom. 10:9
D. *Hindrances to:*
Fear of men — John 7:13
Persecution — Mark 8:34, 35
False teachers — 2 John 7

Confession of sin
A. *Manifested by:*
Repentance — Ps. 51:1-19
Self-abasement — Jer. 3:25
Godly sorrow — Ps. 38:18
Turning from sin — Prov. 28:13
Restitution — Num. 5:6, 7
B. *Results in:*
Forgiveness — 1 John 1:9, 10
Pardon — Ps. 32:1-5
Renewed fellowship — Ps. 51:12-19
Healing — James 5:16
C. *Instances of:*
Aaron — Num. 12:11
Israelites — 1 Sam. 12:19
David — 2 Sam. 24:10
Ezra — Ezra 9:6
Nehemiah — Neh. 1:6, 7
Daniel — Dan. 9:4
Peter — Luke 5:8
Thief — Luke 23:41

Confidence—*assurance*
A. *True, based upon:*
God's Word — Acts 27:22-25
Assurance — 2 Tim. 1:12
Trust — Hab. 3:17-19
Christ's promise — Phil. 1:6
Illustrated — 1 Sam. 17:45-50
B. *False, based upon:*
Unwarranted use of sacred things — 1 Sam. 4:5-11
Presumption — Num. 14:40-45
Pride — 1 Sam. 17:43, 44
C. *The believer's:*
Source of — 1 John 3:21, 22
In prayer — 1 John 5:14, 15
In testimony — Acts 28:31
In others — 2 Cor. 2:3; 2 Cor. 7:16
Of God's will — Phil. 1:25
Of faith's finality — Phil. 1:6
Of future things — 2 Cor. 5:6, 8
Must be held — Heb. 10:35

Confirmation—*making something steadfast and sure*
Human things — Ruth 4:7; Esth. 9:31, 32
A kingdom — 2 Kin. 14:5
An oath — Heb. 6:17
A covenant — Gal. 3:17
Prophecy — Dan. 9:12, 27
Promises — Rom. 15:8
Defense of faith — Phil. 1:7
Establishing faith — Acts 14:22; Acts 15:32, 41

Conformity—*likeness of one thing to another*
To the world, forbidden — Rom. 12:2

Confused—*disorderly; perplexed*
Concerning:
God's will — 1 Sam. 23:1-12
The Messiah — Matt. 11:3
A great event — Acts 2:1-6

Confusion—*bewilderment*
A. *Aspects of:*
God not author of — 1 Cor. 14:33
Typical of evil — James 3:16
Prayer concerning — Ps. 70:2
Illustrations of — Acts 19:29
B. *Examples of:*
Babel — Gen. 11:9
Philistines — 1 Sam. 7:10
Egyptians — Ex. 14:24
City of Shushan — Esth. 3:15
Jerusalem — Acts 21:31

Congratulate—*to express happiness to another*
Tou to David — 1 Chr. 18:9,10

Congregation—*an assembly of people*
A. *Used of:*
The political Israel — Ex. 12:3, 19, 47
A religious assembly — Acts 13:43
The tent of meeting — Ex. 27:21
B. *Regulations concerning:*
Ruled by representatives — Num. 16:6
Summoned by trumpets — Num. 10:3, 4, 7
Bound by decisions of representatives — Josh. 9:15-21
Atonement of sin of — Lev. 4:13-21
Exclusion of certain ones from — Deut. 23:1-8

Coniah—*Jehovah is creating*
King of Judah — Jer. 22:24, 28
Same as Jehoiachin — 2 Kin. 24:8

Connivance at wrong—*tacit approval of evil*
Involves guilt — Ps. 50:18-22
Aaron's, at Sinai — Ex. 32:1, 2, 22
Pilate's, at Jesus' trial — Matt. 27:17-26
Saul's (Paul's) at Stephen's death — Acts 8:1

Cononiah—*Jehovah has established*
1. A Levite — 2 Chr. 31:11, 12, 13
2. A Levite official — 2 Chr. 35:9

Conscience—*the inner judge of moral issues*
A. *Described as*
Good — Acts 23:1
Pure — 1 Tim. 3:9
Evil — Heb. 10:22
Defiled — 1 Cor. 8:7
Seared — 1 Tim. 4:2
B. *Functions of:*
A witness — Rom. 2:15
An accuser — John 8:9
An upholder — 1 Tim. 1:19
Server of good — Rom. 13:5
Source of joy — 2 Cor. 1:12
Dead — Prov. 30:20

SUBJECT REFERENCE

C. *Limitations of:*
- Needs cleansing .... Heb. 9:14
- Subject to others' .... 1 Cor. 10:28, 29
- Differs .... 1 Cor. 8:7-13
- Fallible .... Prov. 16:25

Conscience, clear—*freedom from guilt feelings*

A. *Necessary for:*
- Freedom from legalism ...... Heb. 9:13, 14
- Access to God .... Heb. 10:21, 22
- Liberty in witnessing .... 1 Pet. 3:15, 16
- Christian love .... 1 Tim. 1:5
- Confidence in prayer .... 1 John 3:21, 22
- Proud confidence .... 2 Cor. 1:12

B. *Requirements for:*
- Doctrinal purity .... 1 Tim. 1:3-5, 18—2:1; 1 Tim. 4:1, 2
- Proper conduct .... Acts 24:10-13, 16; Rom. 13:4-6
- Faith in Christ's blood ...... Heb. 9:14; Heb. 10:19-22
- Knowledge .... 1 Cor. 8:7
- Belief .... Titus 1:15
- Submissive spirit .... 1 Pet. 2:18, 19
- Faith in God's greatness ..... 1 John 3:20
- Consideration of others ..... 1 Cor. 10:28, 29
- Seeking forgiveness .... Prov. 28:13; Matt. 5:23, 24

Conscription—*to enroll for compulsory service*
- Employed by Solomon .... 1 Kin. 7:13, 14; 1 Kin. 9:20, 21
- To build Temple .... 1 Kin. 5:2, 3, 18
- To restore cities .... 1 Kin. 9:15-17
- Led to revolt .... 1 Kin. 12:3-16

See Levy

Consecration—*dedication to God's service*

A. *Applied to:*
- Israel .... Ex. 19:6
- Priests .... Lev. 8:1-13
- Levites .... Num. 8:5, 6
- Individuals .... 1 Sam. 1:11
- First-born .... Ex. 13:2, 12
- Possessions .... Lev. 27:28, 29
- Christ .... Heb. 2:10

B. *The Christian's:*
- By Christ .... John 17:23
- Complete and entire .... Rom. 12:1, 2
- Separation from world ...... 2 Cor. 6:14-18
- Devotion to Christ .... Rev. 14:1-6
- Sacred anointing .... 1 John 2:20, 27
- New priesthood .... 1 Pet. 2:5, 9

Conservation—*preserving worthwhile things*
- Material things .... John 6:12, 13
- Spiritual things .... Rev. 3:2, 3
- Good .... Acts 26:22, 23
- Unwise .... Luke 5:36, 37

Consolation—*comfort fortified with encouragement*
- God, source of .... Rom. 15:5
- Simeon waits for .... Luke 2:25
- Source of joy .... Acts 15:31
- To be shared .... 2 Cor. 1:4-11

Conspiracy—*a plot to overthrow lawful authority*

Against:
- Joseph .... Gen. 37:18-20
- Moses .... Num. 16:1-35
- Samson .... Judg. 16:4-21
- Daniel .... Dan. 6:4-17
- Jesus .... Matt. 12:14
- Paul .... Acts 23:12-15

Constancy—*firmness of purpose*
- Ruth's, to Naomi .... Ruth 1:16
- Jonathan's, to David .... 1 Sam. 20:17
- Virgins, to Christ .... Rev. 14:4, 5

Constellation—*a group of stars*
- Arcturus .... Job 9:9; Job 38:32
- The Serpent .... Job 26:13
- Orion .... Job 38:31; Amos 5:8
- Pleiades (seven stars) .... Job 9:9; Job 38:31
- Castor and Pollux .... Acts 28:11

SUBJECT REFERENCE

- Judgment on .... Is. 13:10, 11
- Incense burned to .... 2 Kin. 23:5

Consultation—*seeking advice from others*
- Demonical .... 1 Sam. 28:7-25
- Divided .... 1 Kin. 12:6, 8
- Determined .... Dan. 6:7
- Devilish .... Matt. 26:4; John 12:10, 11

Contempt—*scorn compounded with disrespect*

A. *Forbidden toward:*
- Parents .... Prov. 23:22
- Weak Christians .... Matt. 18:10; Rom. 14:3
- Believing masters .... 1 Tim. 6:2
- The poor .... James 2:1-3

B. *Objects of:*
- The righteous .... Ps. 80:6
- Spiritual things .... Matt. 22:2-6
- Christ .... John 9:28, 29

C. *Examples of:*
- Nabal .... 1 Sam. 25:10, 11
- Michal .... 2 Sam. 6:16
- Sanballat .... Neh. 2:19
- Jews .... Matt. 26:67, 68
- False teachers .... 2 Cor. 10:10
- The wicked .... Prov. 18:3

Contention—*a quarrelsome spirit*

A. *Caused by:*
- Pride .... Prov. 13:10
- Disagreement .... Acts 15:36-41
- Divisions .... 1 Cor. 1:11-13
- A quarrelsome spirit .... Gal. 5:15

B. *Antidotes:*
- Avoid the contentious .... Prov. 21:19
- Avoid controversies .... Titus 3:9
- Abandon the quarrel .... Prov. 17:14
- Follow peace .... Rom. 12:18-21

Contentment—*an uncomplaining acceptance of one's share*

A. *Opposed to:*
- Anxiety .... Matt. 6:25, 34
- Murmuring .... 1 Cor. 10:10
- Greed .... Heb. 13:5
- Envy .... James 3:16

B. *Shown by our recognition of:*
- Our unworthiness .... Gen. 32:10
- Our trust .... Hab. 3:17-19
- God's care .... Ps. 145:7-21
- God's provisions .... 1 Tim. 6:6-8
- God's promises .... Heb. 13:5

Contracts—*covenants legally binding*

A. *Ratified by:*
- Giving presents .... Gen. 21:25-30
- Public witness .... Ruth 4:1-11
- Oaths .... Josh. 9:15, 20
- Joining hands .... Prov. 17:18
- Pierced ear .... Ex. 21:2-6

B. *Examples of:*
- Abraham and Abimelech .... Gen. 21:25-32
- Solomon and Hiram .... 1 Kin. 5:8-12

Contrition—*a profound sense of one's sinfulness*
- Of the heart .... Ps. 51:17
- The publican .... Luke 18:13
- Peter's example .... Matt. 26:75

Controversy—*dispute between people*
- Between men .... Deut. 25:1
- Between God and men .... Hos. 4:1
- A public .... Acts 15:1-35
- A private .... Gal. 2:11-15

Conversion—*turning to God from sin*

A. *Produced by:*
- God .... Acts 21:19
- Christ .... Acts 3:26
- Holy Spirit .... 1 Cor. 2:13
- The Scriptures .... Ps. 19:7
- Preaching .... Rom. 10:14

B. *Of Gentiles:*
- Foretold .... Is. 60:1-5
- Explained .... Rom. 15:8-18; Acts 15:3
- Illustrated .... Acts 10:1-48; Acts 16:25-34
- Confirmed .... Acts 15:1-31
- Defended .... Gal. 3:1-29

SUBJECT REFERENCE

C. *Results in:*
- Repentance .... Acts 26:20
- New creation .... 2 Cor. 5:17
- Transformation .... 1 Thess. 1:9, 10

D. *Fruits of:*
- Faithfulness .... Matt. 24:45-47
- Gentleness .... 1 Thess. 2:7
- Patience .... Col. 1:10-12
- Love .... 1 John 3:14
- Obedience .... Rom. 15:18
- Peacefulness .... James 3:17, 18
- Self-control .... 2 Pet. 1:6
- Self-denial .... John 12:25

Conviction—*making one conscious of his guilt*

A. *Produced by:*
- Holy Spirit .... John 16:7-11
- The Gospel .... Acts 2:37
- Conscience .... Rom. 2:15
- The Law .... James 2:9

B. *Instances of:*
- Adam .... Gen. 3:8-10
- Joseph's brothers .... Gen. 42:21, 22
- Israel .... Ex. 33:4
- David .... Ps. 51:1-17
- Isaiah .... Is. 6:5
- Men of Nineveh .... Matt. 12:41
- Peter .... Luke 5:8
- Saul of Tarsus .... Acts 9:4-18
- Philippian jailer .... Acts 16:29, 30

Convocation—*a gathering for worship*

A. *Applied to:*
- Sabbaths .... Lev. 23:2, 3
- Passover .... Ex. 12:16
- Pentecost .... Lev. 23:21
- Feast of Trumpets .... Num. 29:1
- Feast of Weeks .... Num. 28:26
- Feast of Tabernacles .... Lev. 23:34-36
- Day of Atonement .... Lev. 23:27

B. *Designed to:*
- Gather the people .... Josh. 23:1-16
- Worship God .... 2 Kin. 23:21, 22

Cooking—*making food palatable*
- Done by women .... Gen. 18:2-6
- Carefully performed .... Gen. 27:3-10
- Savory dish .... Gen. 27:4
- Vegetables .... Gen. 25:29
- Forbidden on the Sabbath ...... Ex. 35:3
- Fish .... Luke 24:42

Co-operation—*working together*

A. *Kinds of:*
- Man with man .... Ex. 17:12
- God with man .... Phil. 2:12, 13

B. *Needed to:*
- Complete job .... Neh. 4:16, 17
- Secure results .... Matt. 18:19
- Win converts .... John 1:40-51
- Maintain peace .... Mark 9:50

C. *Basis:*
- Obedience to God .... Ps. 119:63
- Faith .... Rom. 14:1

Coos
- An island between Rhodes and Miletus .... Acts 21:1

Coral—*a rocklike substance formed from skeletons of sea creatures*
- Wisdom more valuable than .... Job 28:18
- Bought by traders .... Ezek. 27:16

Corban—*an offering*
- Money dedicated .... Mark 7:11

Cordiality—*sincere affection and kindness*
- Abraham's .... Gen. 18:1-8
- Seen in Jonathan .... 1 Sam. 20:11-23
- Lacking in Nabal .... 1 Sam. 25:9-13

Coriander
- A plant whose seed is compared to manna .... Ex. 16:31

Corinth—*a city of Greece*
- Paul labors at .... Acts 18:1-18
- Site of church .... 1 Cor. 1:2
- Visited by Apollos .... Acts 19:1
- Abode of Erastus .... 2 Tim. 4:20

SUBJECT — REFERENCE

Corinthians, epistles to the—*two books of the New Testament*

Written by Paul ... 1 Cor. 1:1
2 Cor. 1:1

Cormorant

An unclean bird ... Lev. 11:17

Corn—*the generic term for cereal grasses*

A. *Features regarding:*

Grown in Palestine ... 2 Kin. 18:32
Chaff blown from ... Matt. 3:12
Article of food ... Gen. 42:1, 2, 19
Eaten with oil ... Lev. 2:14, 15
Parched ... Ruth 2:14

B. *Figurative of:*

Blessings ... Ezek. 36:29
Heavenly food ... Ps. 78:24
Christ ... John 12:24
Life's maturity ... Job 5:26

Cornelius—*a horn*

A religious Gentile ... Acts 10:1-48

Cornerstone, corner stone—*a stone placed to bind two walls together*

Laid in Zion ... Is. 28:16
Rejected ... Ps. 118:22
Christ is ... 1 Pet. 2:6, 8
Christ promised as ... Zech. 4:7
Christ fulfills ... Acts 4:11
1 Pet. 2:7

Cornet—*a musical instrument*

Used on occasions ... 1 Chr. 15:28
A part of worship ... 2 Sam. 6:5
Used in Babylon ... Dan. 3:7, 10

Corpse—*a dead body*

A. *Laws regarding:*

Dwelling made unclean by ... Num. 19:11-22
Contact with, makes unclean ... Lev. 11:39
Food made unclean ... Lev. 11:40

B. *Used figuratively of:*

Those in hell ... Is. 66:24
Idolatrous kings ... Ezek. 43:7, 9
Attraction ... Matt. 24:28

Correction—*punishment designed to restore*

A. *Means of:*

God's judgments ... Jer. 46:28
The rod ... Prov. 22:15
Wickedness ... Jer. 2:19
Prayer ... Jer. 10:24
Scriptures ... 2 Tim. 3:16

B. *Benefits of:*

Needed for children ... Prov. 23:13
Sign of sonship ... Prov. 3:12
Brings rest ... Prov. 29:17
Makes happy ... Job 5:17

Corruption—*rottenness; depravity*

A. *Descriptive of:*

Physical blemishes ... Mal. 1:14
Physical decay ... Matt. 6:19, 20
Moral decay ... Gen. 6:12
Eternal ruin ... Gal. 6:8

B. *Characteristics of:*

Unregenerate men ... Luke 6:43, 44
Apostates ... 2 Cor. 2:7
2 Pet. 2:12, 19

C. *Deliverance from:*

By Christ ... Acts 2:27, 31
Promised ... Rom. 8:21
Through conversion ... 1 Pet. 1:18, 23
Perfected in heaven ... 1 Cor. 15:42, 50

Corruption, mount of

Site of pagan altars ... 1 Kin. 11:7
Altars of, destroyed ... 2 Kin. 23:13

Corruption of body

Results from Adam's sin ... Rom. 8:21
Begins in this life ... 2 Cor. 5:4
Consummated by death ... John 11:39
Freedom from, promised ... Rom. 8:21
Freedom from, accomplished ... 1 Cor. 15:42

SUBJECT — REFERENCE

Cosam—*a diviner*

Father of Addi ... Luke 3:28

Cosmetics

Used by Jezebel ... 2 Kin. 9:30
Futility of ... Jer. 4:30

Cosmic conflagration—*to destroy by fire*

Day of judgment ... 2 Pet. 3:7-10

Council—*Jewish Sanhedrin*

A judicial court ... Matt. 5:22
Christ's trial ... Matt. 26:57-59
Powers of, limited ... John 18:31
Apostles before ... Acts 4:5-30
Stephen before ... Acts 6:12-15
Paul before ... Acts 23:1-5

Counsel, God's

A. *Called:*

Immutable ... Heb. 6:17
Faithful ... Is. 25:1
Wonderful ... Is. 28:29
Great ... Jer. 32:19
Sovereign ... Dan. 4:35
Eternal ... Eph. 3:11

B. *Events determined by:*

History ... Is. 46:10, 11
Christ's death ... Acts 2:23
Salvation ... Rom. 8:28-30
Union in Christ ... Eph. 1:9, 10

C. *Attitudes toward:*

Christians declare ... Acts 20:27
Proper reserve ... Acts 1:7
Wicked despise ... Is. 5:19
They reject ... Luke 7:30

Counsel, man's

Jethro's, accepted ... Ex. 18:13-27
Hushai's followed ... 2 Sam. 17:14
Of a woman, brings peace ... 2 Sam. 20:16-20
David's dying ... 1 Kin. 2:1-10
Of old men, rejected ... 1 Kin. 12:8, 13
Of friends, avenged ... Esth. 5:14

Counselor—*an advisor*

Christ is ... Is. 9:6
Thy testimonies are ... Ps. 119:24
Safety in many ... Prov. 11:14
Brings security ... Prov. 15:22
Jonathan, a ... 1 Chr. 27:32
Gamaliel ... Acts 5:33-40

Count—*to number*

Things counted:

Stars ... Gen. 15:5
Days ... Lev. 15:13
Years ... Lev. 25:8
Booty ... Num. 31:26
Weeks ... Deut. 16:9
Money ... 2 Kin. 22:4
People ... 1 Chr. 21:17
Bones ... Ps. 22:17
Towers ... Ps. 48:12
Houses ... Is. 22:10

Countenance—*facial expression*

A. *Kinds of:*

Unfriendly ... Gen. 31:1, 2
Fierce ... Deut. 28:50
Terrible ... Judg. 13:6
Sad ... Neh. 2:2, 3
Beautiful ... 1 Sam. 16:12
Cheerful ... Prov. 15:13
Angry ... Prov. 25:23
Hatred ... Prov. 10:18

B. *Transfigured:*

Moses' ... 2 Cor. 3:7
Christ's ... Matt. 17:2
The believer's ... 2 Cor. 3:18

Counterfeit—*a spurious imitation of the real thing*

A. *Applied to persons:*

Christ ... Matt. 24:4, 5, 24
Apostles ... 2 Cor. 11:13
Ministers ... 2 Cor. 11:14, 15
Christians ... Gal. 2:3, 4
Teachers ... 2 Pet. 2:1
Prophets ... John 4:1
The antichrist ... Rev. 19:20

B. *Applied to things:*

Worship ... Matt. 15:8, 9

SUBJECT — REFERENCE

Gospel ... Gal. 1:6-12
Miracles ... 2 Thess. 2:7-12
Science ... 1 Tim. 6:20
Commandments ... Titus 1:13, 14
Doctrines ... Heb. 13:9
Religion ... James 1:26
Prayers ... James 4:3

Country—*the land of a nation*

Commanded to leave ... Gen. 12:1-4
Love of native ... Gen. 30:25
Exiled from ... Ps. 137:1-6
A prophet in his own ... Luke 4:24
A heavenly ... Heb. 11:16

Courage—*fearlessness in the face of danger*

A. *Manifested:*

Among enemies ... Ezra 5:11
In battle ... 1 Sam. 17:46
Against great foes ... Judg. 7:7-23
Against great odds ... 1 Sam. 17:32, 50
When threatened ... Dan. 3:16-18
When intimidated ... Dan. 6:10
When facing death ... Judg. 16:28
In youth ... 1 Sam. 14:6-45
In old age ... Josh. 14:10-12
Before a king ... Esth. 4:8, 16
In moral crises ... Neh. 13:1-31
In preaching Christ ... Acts 3:12-26
In rebuking ... Gal. 2:11-15

B. *Men encouraged to:*

Leaders ... Deut. 31:7
Joshua ... Josh. 1:5-7
Gideon ... Judg. 7:11
Philistines ... 1 Sam. 4:9
Zerubbabel ... Hag. 2:4
Solomon ... 1 Chr. 28:20

Course—*onward movement; advance*

A ship's direction ... Acts 16:11
A prescribed path ... Judg. 5:20
One's life ... 2 Tim. 4:7
The age ... Eph. 2:2
The cycle of life ... James 3:6
Orderly arrangement ... 1 Chr. 27:1-15

Courtesy—*visible signs of respect*

A. *Shown in:*

Manner of address ... Gen. 18:3
Gestures of bowing ... Gen. 19:1
Rising before superiors ... Lev. 19:32
Well-wishing remarks ... Gen. 43:29
Expressions of blessing ... Ruth 2:4

B. *Among Christians:*

Taught ... Rom. 12:9-21
Illustrated ... 3 John 1-6, 12

Courts—*institution designed for justice*

A. *Kinds of:*

Circuit ... 1 Sam. 7:15-17
Superior and inferior ... Ex. 18:21-26
Ecclesiastical ... Matt. 18:15-18

B. *Places held:*

At the tabernacle ... Num. 27:2
Outside the camp ... Lev. 24:14
At the city's gates ... Ruth 4:1, 2
Under a tree ... Judg. 4:5

C. *Features of:*

Witness examined ... Deut. 19:15-21
Accused speaks ... Mark 15:3-5
Sentence of, final ... Deut. 17:8-13
Contempt of, forbidden ... Acts 23:1-5
Corruption of, deplored ... Matt. 26:59-62

Courtship—*the period leading to marriage*

Isaac and Rebekah ... Gen. 24:1-67
Jacob and Rachel ... Gen. 29:9-30
Samson ... Judg. 14:1-7
Boaz and Ruth ... Ruth 3:4-13
Ahasuerus and Esther ... Esth. 2:17

Courtyard—*an enclosed area*

Tabernacle ... Ex. 27:9
Temple ... 1 Kin. 6:36
Prison ... Jer. 32:2
House ... 2 Sam. 17:18
Garden place ... Esth. 1:5

Covenant—*agreement between men*

A. *Designed for:*

Mutual protection ... Gen. 31:50-52
Securing peace ... Josh. 9:15, 21
Friendship ... 1 Sam. 18:3
Promoting commerce ... 1 Kin. 5:6-11

SUBJECT — REFERENCE

B. *Requirements of:*
- Witnessed ... Gen. 23:16-18
- Confirmed by an oath ... Gen. 21:23, 31
- Specified ... 1 Sam. 11:1, 2
- Written and sealed ... Neh. 9:38

C. *Examples of:*
- Abraham and Abimelech ... Gen. 21:27-32
- Laban and Jacob ... Gen. 31:43-55
- David and elders ... 2 Sam. 5:1-3
- Ahab and Ben-hadad ... 1 Kin. 20:34
- New covenant ... Matt. 26:28
- New Testament dispensation ... 2 Cor. 3:6
- Superiority of the new ... Heb. 8:6-13
- Descriptive of a person's will ... Heb. 9:15-17

Covenant—*spiritual agreement*

A. *Between a leader and people:*
- Joshua's ... Josh. 24:1-28
- Jehoiada's ... 2 Kin. 11:17
- Hezekiah's ... 2 Chr. 29:10
- Josiah's ... 2 Kin. 23:3
- Ezra's ... Ezra 10:3

B. *Between God and man:*
- Adam ... Gen. 2:16, 17
- Noah ... Gen. 9:1-17
- Abraham ... Gen. 15:18
- Isaac ... Gen. 26:3-5
- Jacob ... Gen. 28:13-22
- Israel ... Ex. 19:5
- Levi ... Mal. 2:4-10
- Phinehas ... Num. 25:11-13
- David ... Ps. 89:3, 28, 34

C. *The old* (Sinaitic):
- Instituted at Sinai ... Ex. 19:5
- Ratified by sacrifice ... Ex. 24:6-8; Heb. 9:16
- Does not annul the Abrahamic ... Gal. 3:16-18
- Designed to lead to Christ ... Gal. 3:17-25
- Consists of outward rites ... Heb. 9:1-13
- Sealed by circumcision ... Gen. 17:9-14
- Prefigures the Gospel ... Heb. 9:8-28

D. *The new* (evangelical):
- Promised in Eden ... Gen. 3:15
- Proclaimed to Abraham ... Gen. 12:3
- Dated in prophecy ... Dan. 9:24-27
- Fulfilled in Christ ... Luke 1:68-79
- Ratified by His blood ... Heb. 9:11-23
- Remembered in the Lord's Supper ... 1 Cor. 11:25
- Called everlasting ... Heb. 13:20

Covenant-breakers
- Under God's judgment ... Is. 24:5
- By abominations ... Ezek. 44:7

Covenant-keepers
- God's blessing upon ... Ex. 19:5

Covenant of salt—*of perpetual purity*
- Descriptive of Levites ... Num. 18:19
- Descriptive of David ... 2 Chr. 13:5
- Used figuratively ... Mark 9:50

Covered carts
- Used as offerings ... Num. 7:3

Coverings

Symbolic of:
- Immorality ... Prov. 7:16
- Diligence ... Prov. 31:22

Covert—*hiding place*
- Used by Abigail ... 1 Sam. 25:20
- Destroyed by Ahaz ... 2 Kin. 16:18
- Figurative of protection ... Is. 32:2

Covetousness—*an insatiable desire for worldly gain*

A. *Described as:*
- Idolatry ... Col. 3:5
- Root of evil ... 1 Tim. 6:9-11
- Never satisfied ... Hab. 2:9
- Vanity ... Ps. 39:6

B. *Productive of:*
- Theft ... Josh. 7:21
- Lying ... 2 Kin. 5:20-27
- Murder ... Prov. 1:18, 19
- Falsehood ... Acts 5:1-10

SUBJECT — REFERENCE

- Hurtful lusts ... 1 Tim. 6:9
- Apostasy ... 1 Tim. 6:10

C. *Excludes from:*
- God's kingdom ... 1 Cor. 6:10; Eph. 5:5
- Sacred offices ... 1 Tim. 3:3
- Heaven ... Eph. 5:5

D. *Examples of:*
- Achan ... Josh. 7:21
- Saul ... 1 Sam. 15:9, 19
- Judas ... Matt. 26:14, 15
- Ananias ... Acts 5:1-11

See Avarice

Cowardice, spiritual

A. *Causes of:*
- Fear of life ... Gen. 12:11-13
- Fear of others ... Ex. 32:22-24
- Unbelief ... Num. 13:28-33
- Fear of rulers ... John 9:22

B. *Results in:*
- Defeat ... Num. 14:40-45
- Escape ... 2 Sam. 15:13-17
- Compromise ... John 19:12-16
- Denial ... Matt. 26:69-74

C. *Guilty conscience makes:*
- Joseph's brothers ... Gen. 42:21-28
- David ... 2 Sam. 12:1-14
- Pharisees ... John 8:1-11

Cows
- Jacob's possessions ... Gen. 32:15
- Found in Egypt ... Gen. 41:2
- Use of milk ... 2 Sam. 17:29
- Used in rituals ... Lev. 3:1

Coz—*thorn*
- Father of Anub ... 1 Chr. 4:8

Cozbi—*false*
- Slain by Phinehas ... Num. 25:6-18

Craft
- Ships of Tarshish ... Is. 2:16
- A trade ... Rev. 18:22

Craftiness—*cunning deception*
- Man's, known by God ... 1 Cor. 3:19
- Enemies', perceived by Christ ... Luke 20:23
- Use of, rejected ... 2 Cor. 4:2
- Warning against ... Eph. 4:14

Craftsmen—*men who work at a trade*
- Makers of idols ... Deut. 27:15
- Destroyed in Babylon ... Rev. 18:21, 22

Crane—*a migratory bird*
- Chatters ... Is. 38:14

Creation—*causing what did not exist to exist*

A. *Author of:*
- God ... Heb. 11:3
- Jesus Christ ... Col. 1:16, 17
- Holy Spirit ... Ps. 104:30

B. *Objects of:*
- Heaven, earth ... Gen. 1:1-13
- Vegetation ... Gen. 1:11, 12
- Animals ... Gen. 1:21
- Man ... Gen. 1:26-28
- Stars ... Is. 40:26

C. *Expressive of God's:*
- Deity ... Rom. 1:20
- Power ... Is. 40:26, 28
- Glory ... Ps. 19:1
- Goodness ... Ps. 33:5-6
- Wisdom ... Ps. 104:24
- Sovereignty ... Rev. 4:11

D. *Illustrative of:*
- The new birth ... 2 Cor. 5:17
- Renewal of believers ... Ps. 51:10
- The eternal world ... Is. 65:17; 2 Pet. 3:11, 13

Creator—*the Supreme Being*
- A title of God ... Is. 40:28
- Man's disrespect of ... Rom. 1:25
- To be remembered ... Eccl. 12:1

Creature—*a being with life*
- Subject to vanity ... Rom. 8:19, 20
- Will be delivered ... Rom. 8:21
- Believer, a new ... 2 Cor. 5:17

SUBJECT — REFERENCE

Creditor—*one to whom a debt is payable*
- Interest, forbidden ... Ex. 22:25
- Debts remitted ... Neh. 5:10-12
- Some very cruel ... Matt. 18:28-30
- Christian principle ... Rom. 13:8

Cremation—*burning a body*
- Two hundred fifty were consumed ... Num. 16:35
- Zimri's end ... 1 Kin. 16:15-19

Crescens—*growing*
- Paul's assistant ... 2 Tim. 4:10

Crete—*an island in the Mediterranean Sea*
- Some from, at Pentecost ... Acts 2:11
- Paul visits ... Acts 27:7-21
- Titus dispatched to ... Titus 1:5
- Inhabitants of, evil and lazy ... Titus 1:12

Crib
- Animals feed from ... Is. 1:3
- A stall ... Prov. 14:4

Criminal—*a lawbreaker*
- Paul considered a ... Acts 25:16, 27
- Christ accused of ... John 18:30
- Christ crucified between ... Luke 23:32, 33
- One unrepentant; one repentant ... Luke 23:39-43

Cripple—*one physically impaired*
- Mephibosheth, by a fall ... 2 Sam. 4:4
- Paul's healing of ... Acts 14:8-10
- Jesus heals ... Matt. 15:30, 31

Crisis—*the crest of human endurance*
- Bad advice in ... Job 2:9, 10
- God's advice in ... Luke 21:25-28

Crispus—*curled*
- Chief ruler of synagogue at Corinth ... Acts 18:8
- Baptized by Paul ... 1 Cor. 1:14

Crookback
- Barred from priesthood ... Lev. 21:20, 21

Crop—*the craw of a bird*
- Removed by priest ... Lev. 1:16

Cross—*a method of execution*

A. *Used literally of:*
- Christ's death ... Matt. 27:32

B. *Used figuratively of:*
- Duty ... Matt. 10:38
- Christ's sufferings ... 1 Cor. 1:17
- The Christian faith ... 1 Cor. 1:18
- Reconciliation ... Eph. 2:16

Crown—*an emblem of glory*

A. *Worn by:*
- High priest ... Lev. 8:9
- Kings ... 2 Sam. 12:30
- Queens ... Esth. 2:17
- Ministers of state ... Esth. 8:15

B. *Applied figuratively to:*
- A good wife ... Prov. 12:4
- Old age ... Prov. 16:31
- Grandchildren ... Prov. 17:6
- Honor ... Prov. 27:24
- Material blessings ... Ps. 65:11

C. *Applied spiritually to:*
- Christ ... Ps. 132:18
- Christ at His return ... Rev. 19:12
- Christ glorified ... Heb. 2:7-9
- The church ... Is. 62:3
- The Christian's reward ... 2 Tim. 2:5
- The minister's reward ... Phil. 4:1
- Soul winners ... 1 Thess. 2:19
- The Christian's incorruptible prize ... 1 Cor. 9:25

Crown of thorns
- Placed on Christ ... Matt. 27:29; John 19:2

Crowns of Christians
- Joy ... 1 Thess. 2:19
- Righteousness ... 2 Tim. 4:8
- Life ... James 1:12
- Glory ... 1 Pet. 5:4
- Incorruptible ... 1 Cor. 9:25

SUBJECT — REFERENCE

Crucifixion—*death on a cross*

A. *Jesus' death by:*
- Predicted ... Matt. 20:19
- Demanded ... Mark 15:13, 14
- Gentiles ... Matt. 20:19
- Jews ... Acts 2:23, 36
- Between thieves ... Matt. 27:38
- Nature of, unrecognized ... 1 Cor. 2:8

B. *Figurative of:*
- Utter rejection ... Heb. 6:6
- Apostasy ... Rev. 11:8
- Union with Christ ... Gal. 2:20
- Separation ... Gal. 6:14
- Sanctification ... Rom. 6:6
- Dedication ... 1 Cor. 2:2

Cruelty—*violence*
- Descriptive of the wicked ... Ps. 74:20
- To animals, forbidden ... Num. 22:27-35

Crumbs—*fragments of bread*
- Dogs eat of ... Matt. 15:27
- Lazarus begs for ... Luke 16:20, 21

Cruse—*a small earthen vessel*
- For water ... 1 Sam. 26:11, 12
- For oil ... 1 Kin. 17:12, 14

Crying—*an emotional upheaval*
- Accusation ... Gen. 4:10
- Remorse ... Heb. 12:17
- Pretense ... Judg. 14:15-18
- Sorrow ... 2 Sam. 18:33
- Others' sins ... Ps. 119:136
- Pain ... Heb. 5:7
- None in heaven ... Rev. 21:4

Crystal—*rock crystal*
- Wisdom surpasses ... Job 28:17-20
- Gates of Zion ... Is. 54:12
- Descriptive of heaven ... Rev. 4:6

Cubs—*offspring of beasts*

Figurative of:
- Babylonians ... Jer. 51:38
- Assyrians ... Nah. 2:11, 12
- Princes of Israel ... Ezek. 19:2-9

Cucumber—*an edible fruit grown on a vine*
- Lusted after ... Num. 11:5
- Grown in gardens ... Is. 1:8

Cud—*partly digested food*
- Animals chew again ... Lev. 11:3-8

Cuckow—*an unclean bird*
- Probably refers to sea gull ... Lev. 11:16

Cummin—*an annual of the parsley family*
- Seeds threshed by a rod ... Is. 28:25, 27
- A trifle of tithing ... Matt. 23:23

Cunning—*sly, clever*

A. *Used in a good sense:*
- David ... 1 Sam. 23:19-22
- Jehu ... 2 Kin. 10:19

B. *Used in a bad sense:*
- Thwarted by God ... Job 5:13
- Of harlot's heart ... Prov. 7:10

Cup

A. *Literal use of:*
- For drinking ... 2 Sam. 12:3

B. *Figurative uses of:*
- One's portion ... Ps. 11:6
- Blessings ... Ps. 23:5
- Suffering ... Matt. 20:23
- Hypocrisy ... Matt. 23:25, 26
- New covenant ... 1 Cor. 10:16

Cupbearer—*a high court official*
- Many under Solomon ... 1 Kin. 10:5
- Nehemiah, a faithful ... Neh. 1:11

Cure—*to restore to health*
- Of the body ... Matt. 17:16
- Of the mind ... Mark 5:15
- Of the demonized ... Matt. 12:22
- With means ... Is. 38:21
- By faith ... Num. 21:8, 9
- By prayer ... James 5:14, 15

SUBJECT — REFERENCE
- By God's mercy ... Phil. 2:27
- Hindered ... 2 Kin. 8:7-15

Curiosity—*seeking to know things forbidden or private*
- Into God's secrets, forbidden ... John 21:21, 22
- Leads 50,070 to death ... 1 Sam. 6:19

Curiosity seekers
- Eve ... Gen. 3:6
- Israelites ... Ex. 19:21, 24
- Babylonians ... 2 Kin. 20:13
- Herod ... Matt. 2:4-8
- Zacchaeus ... Luke 19:1-6
- Certain Greeks ... John 12:20, 21
- Lazarus' visitors ... John 12:9
- Peter ... Matt. 26:58
- At the crucifixion ... Matt. 27:46-49
- Athenians ... Acts 17:21

Curse, cursing—*a violent expression of evil upon others*

A. *Pronounced upon:*
- The earth ... Gen. 3:17
- Cain ... Gen. 4:11
- Canaan ... Gen. 9:25
- Two sons ... Gen. 49:7
- Disobedient ... Deut. 28:15-45
- Meroz ... Judg. 5:23
- Jericho's rebuilders ... Josh. 6:26

B. *Forbidden upon:*
- Parents ... Ex. 21:17
- Ruler ... Ex. 22:28
- Deaf ... Lev. 19:14
- Enemies ... Luke 6:28
- God ... Job 2:9
- God's people ... Gen. 12:3

C. *Instances of:*
- Goliath's ... 1 Sam. 17:43
- Balaam's attempted ... Num. 22:1-12
- The fig tree ... Mark 11:21
- Peter's ... Matt. 26:74
- The crucified ... Gal. 3:10, 13

D. *Manifested by:*
- Rebellious ... 2 Sam. 16:5-8

Curtains—*an awning-like screen*
- Ten, in tabernacle ... Ex. 26:1-13
- Figurative of the heavens ... Ps. 104:2

Cush—*black*
1. Ham's oldest son ... 1 Chr. 1:8-10
2. Means Ethiopia ... Is. 18:1
3. A Benjamite ... Ps. 7 (Title)

Cushan—*blackness*
- Probably same as Cush ... Hab. 3:7

Cushan-rishathaim—*extra wicked*

A. *Mesopotamian King*
- Oppressed Israel ... Judg. 3:8
- Othniel delivers Israel from ... Judg. 3:9, 10

Cushi—*an Ethiopian*
1. Ancestor of Jehudi ... Jer. 36:14
2. Father of Zephaniah ... Zeph. 1:1

Cushite—*an Ethiopian*
1. David's servant ... 2 Sam. 18:21-32
2. Moses' wife ... Num. 12:1

Custom—*tax; usage*

A. *As a tax:*
- Matthew collected ... Matt. 9:9
- Kings require ... Matt. 17:25
- Christians give ... Rom. 13:6, 7

B. *As a common practice:*
- Abominable ... Lev. 18:30
- Vain ... Jer. 10:3
- Worthy ... Luke 4:16
- Traditional ... Acts 21:21

Cuth, Cuthah—*burning*
- People from, brought to Samaria ... 2 Kin. 17:24, 30

Cymbal—*hollow of a vessel*
- A musical instrument ... 1 Chr. 13:8
- Figurative of pretense ... 1 Cor. 13:1

Cypress—*a hardwood tree*
- Used by idol-makers ... Is. 44:14-17

SUBJECT — REFERENCE

Cyprus—*fairness*
- A large Mediterranean island; home of Barnabas ... Acts 4:36
- Christians reach ... Acts 11:19, 20
- Paul visits ... Acts 13:4-13
- Barnabas visits ... Acts 15:39
- Paul twice sails past ... Acts 21:3

Cyrene—*wall*
- A Greek colonial city in North Africa; home of Simon ... Matt. 27:32
- People from, at Pentecost ... Acts 2:10
- Synagogue of ... Acts 6:9
- Some from, become missionaries ... Acts 11:20

Cyrenius—*of Cyrene*
- Roman governor of Syria ... Luke 2:1-4

Cyrus—*sun, throne*
- Prophecies concerning, God's:
  - "Anointed" ... Is. 45:1
  - Liberator ... Is. 45:1
  - Rebuilder ... Is. 44:28

D

Dabbasheth—*hump*
- Town of Zebulun ... Josh. 19:10, 11

Daberath—*pasture*
- Correct rendering of Dabareh ... Josh. 21:28
- Assigned to Gershomites ... 1 Chr. 6:71, 72

Dagon—*fish*
- The national god of the Philistines ... Judg. 16:23
- Falls before ark ... 1 Sam. 5:1-5

Dainties—*savory food, delicacies*
- Used as a warning ... Prov. 23:3-6
- Unrighteous fellowship ... Ps. 141:4

Dale, the King's
- A valley near Jerusalem ... Gen. 14:17-20
- Site of Absalom's monument ... 2 Sam. 18:18

Daleth
- The fourth letter in the Hebrew alphabet ... Ps. 119:25-32

Dalmanutha
- A place near the Sea of Galilee ... Mark 8:10

Dalmatia—*deceitful*
- A region east of the Adriatic Sea; Titus departs to ... 2 Tim. 4:10

Dalphon—*crafty*
- A son of Haman ... Esth. 9:7-10

Dam—*mother*

Laws concerning:
- Animals ... Ex. 22:30
- Birds ... Deut. 22:6, 7

Damages and Remuneration

A. *In law for:*
- Personal injury ... Ex. 21:18, 19
- Causing miscarriage ... Ex. 21:22
- Injuries by animals ... Ex. 21:28-32
- Injuries to animals ... Ex. 21:33-35
- Losses ... Ex. 22:1-15
- Stealing ... Lev. 6:1-7
- Defaming a wife ... Deut. 22:13-19
- Rape ... Deut. 22:28, 29

B. *In practice:*
- Jacob's ... Gen. 31:38-42
- Samson's ... Judg. 16:28-30
- Tamar's ... 2 Sam. 13:22-32
- Zacchaeus' ... Luke 19:8
- Paul's ... Acts 16:35-39
- Philemon's ... Philem. 10-18

Damaris—*gentle*
- An Athenian woman converted by Paul ... Acts 17:33, 34

SUBJECT — REFERENCE

Damascus—*chief city of Aram*

A. *In the Old Testament:*

- Abram passed through ... Gen. 14:15
- Abram heir from ... Gen. 15:2
- Captured by David ... 2 Sam. 8:5, 6
- Rezon, king of ... 1 Kin. 11:23, 24
- Ben-hadad, king of ... 1 Kin. 15:18
- Rivers of, mentioned ... 2 Kin. 5:12
- Elisha's prophecy in ... 2 Kin. 8:7-15
- Taken by Assyrians ... 2 Kin. 16:9
- Prophecies concerning ... Is. 8:4

B. *In the New Testament, Paul:*

- Journeys to ... Acts 9:1-9
- Is converted near ... Acts 9:3-19
- First preaches at ... Acts 9:20-22
- Escapes from ... 2 Cor. 11:32, 33
- Revisits ... Gal. 1:17

Damnation—*condemnatory judgment*

A. *Described as:*

- Having degrees ... Matt. 23:14
- Just ... Rom. 3:8
- Justified ... Rom. 13:2
- Self-inflicted ... 1 Cor. 11:29
- Merited ... 1 Tim. 5:12

B. *Inflicted:*

- Now ... Rom. 14:23
- In eternity ... Matt. 23:33

Damsel—*a young woman*

- Rebekah ... Gen. 24:57
- Ruth ... Ruth 2:5, 6
- Raised by Jesus ... Mark 5:39-42
- Demands John's head ... Matt. 14:10, 11
- Questions Peter ... John 18:17
- Is disbelieved ... Acts 12:13-17
- Healed by Paul ... Acts 16:16-18

Dan—*judge*

1. Jacob's son by Bilhah ... Gen. 30:6
   Prophecy concerning ... Gen. 49:16, 17
2. *Tribe of:*
   - Census of ... Num. 1:38, 39
   - Position of ... Num. 2:25, 31
   - Blessing of ... Deut. 33:22
   - Inheritance of ... Josh. 19:40-47
   - Conquest by ... Josh. 19:47
   - Failure of ... Judg. 1:34, 35
   - Idolatry of ... Judg. 18:1-31
3. *Town of:*
   - Called Leshem ... Josh. 19:47
   - Captured by Danites ... Josh. 19:47
   - Northern boundary of Israel ... Judg. 20:1
   - Center of idolatry ... 1 Kin. 12:28-30
   - Destroyed by Ben-hadad ... 1 Kin. 15:20
   - Later references to ... Jer. 4:15

Dance—*an emotional movement of the body*

A. *Kinds of:*

- Joyful ... Ps. 30:11
- Evil ... Ex. 32:19

B. *Designed to:*

- Express joy in victory ... 1 Sam. 18:6, 7
- Greet a returning son ... Luke 15:23-25
- Rejoice in the Lord ... 2 Sam. 6:14-16
- Inflame lust ... Matt. 14:6

C. *Performed by:*

- Children ... Matt. 11:16, 17
- Women ... Judg. 11:34
- David ... 2 Sam. 6:14, 16
- Worshipers ... Ps. 149:3

Dancing

- David only ... 2 Sam. 6:14-16
- Greeting a prodigal ... Luke 15:20, 23-25
- Lustful exhibition ... Mark 6:22
- Religious exercise ... 1 Chr. 15:25-29
- Time of rejoicing ... 1 Sam. 18:6, 7
- Time to dance ... Eccl. 3:4
- Young women alone ... Judg. 21:20, 21

Danger—*risk, peril*

- Physical ... Acts 27:9-44
- Spiritual ... Heb. 2:1-3
- Comfort in ... Acts 27:22-25
- Jesus sought in ... Luke 8:22-24
- Of many kinds ... 2 Cor. 11:23-33
- Paul's escape from ... Acts 9:22-25

SUBJECT — REFERENCE

Daniel—*God is my judge*

1. Son of David ... 1 Chr. 3:1
   Called Chileab ... 2 Sam. 3:2, 3
2. Postexilic priest ... Ezra 8:1, 2
   Signs covenant ... Neh. 10:6
3. Taken to Babylon ... Dan. 1:1-7
   - Refuses king's choice foods ... Dan. 1:8
   - Interprets dreams ... Dan. 2:1-45
   - Honored by Nebuchadnezzar ... Dan. 2:46-49
   - Interprets handwriting ... Dan. 5:10-29
   - Made a high official ... Dan. 6:1-3
   - Conspired against ... Dan. 6:4-15
   - Cast into lion's den ... Dan. 6:16-22
   - Honored by Belshazzar ... Dan. 5:29
   - Vision of beasts ... Dan. 7:1-28
   - Vision of ram and goat ... Dan. 8:1-27
   - Great confession of ... Dan. 9:1-19
   - Vision of the seventy weeks ... Dan. 9:20-27
   - Vision by the great river ... Dan. 10:1-21
   - Vision of the kings ... Dan. 11:1-45
   - Vision of the two men ... Dan. 12:1-13

Daniel—*book of Bible*

- History in Babylon ... Dan. 1—6
- Prophecy of nations ... Dan. 2:4-45
- Visions ... Dan. 7, 8
- Kingdom ... Dan. 9—12

Danites

- Descendants of Dan ... Judg. 13:2

Dan-jaan

- Town near Zidon ... 2 Sam. 24:6

Dannah—*low ground*

- A city of Judah ... Josh. 15:49

Darda—*pearl of wisdom*

- Famed for wisdom ... 1 Kin. 4:31
- Also called Dara ... 1 Chr. 2:6

Darius—*possessing the good*

1. *Darius the Mede:*
   - Son of Ahasuerus ... Dan. 9:1
   - Succeeds Belshazzar ... Dan. 5:30, 31
   - Co-ruler with Cyrus ... Dan. 6:28
   - Made king of the Chaldeans ... Dan. 9:1
2. *Darius Hystaspis* (521–486 B.C.)
   - King of all Persia ... Ezra 4:5
   - Confirms Cyrus' royal edict ... Ezra 6:1-14
   - Temple work dated by his reign ... Ezra 4:24
   - Prophets during his reign ... Hag. 1:1
3. *Darius the Persian* (424–404 B.C.)
   - Priestly records to reign ... Neh. 12:22

Dark sayings

- Speaks openly ... Num. 12:8
- Utter of old ... Ps. 78:2

Darkness—*absence of light*

A. *Kinds of:*

- Pre-creational ... Gen. 1:2-4
- Natural ... Gen. 15:17
- Miraculous ... Ex. 10:21, 22
- Supernatural ... Matt. 27:45
- Spiritual ... Acts 13:8-11
- Eternal ... Matt. 8:12

B. *Illustrative of:*

- God's unsearchableness ... Ps. 97:2
- The way of sin ... Eph. 5:11
- Afflictions ... Ps. 112:4
- Moral depravity ... Rom. 13:12
- Ignorance ... 1 John 2:8-11
- Death ... Job 10:21, 22
- Hell ... Matt. 22:13

Darkon—*scatterer*

- Founder of a family ... Neh. 7:58

Darling—*"only one"*

- Used poetically of the soul ... Ps. 35:17

Dart—*a pointed weapon*

- Absalom slain by ... 2 Sam. 18:14
- Figurative of sin's penalty ... Prov. 7:23
- Figurative of Satan's weapons ... Eph. 6:16

SUBJECT — REFERENCE

Dathan—*fount*

- A Reubenite ... Num. 26:7-11
- Joins Korah's rebellion ... Num. 16:1-35
- Swallowed up by the earth ... Ps. 106:17

Daughter—*a female descendant*

A. *Applied to:*

- Female child ... Gen. 20:12
- Female inhabitants of a city ... Judg. 21:1
- Female worshipers of God ... Is. 43:6
- Citizens of a town ... Ps. 9:14

B. *Described as:*

- Licentious ... Gen. 19:30-38
- Dutiful ... Judg. 11:36-39
- Ideal ... Prov. 31:29
- Beautiful ... Ps. 45:9-13
- Careless ... Is. 32:9-11
- Prophesy ... Joel 2:28

C. *Daughter-in-law:*

- Bride, son's wife
- Ruth, a loyal ... Ruth 1:11-18
- Strife against ... Matt. 10:35

Daughter of Zion—*a name referring to Jerusalem and the inhabitants therein*

- Show praise to ... Ps. 9:14
- Gaze on Solomon ... Song 3:11
- Left desolate ... Is. 1:8
- The King comes to ... Matt. 21:5

David—*well-beloved*

A. *Early life of:*

- Born at Bethlehem ... 1 Sam. 17:12
- Son of Jesse ... Ruth 4:17, 22
- Genealogy of ... 1 Chr. 2:3-15
- Of tribe of Judah ... 1 Chr. 28:4
- Youngest son ... 1 Sam. 16:10-13
- Handsome ... 1 Sam. 17:42
- A shepherd ... 1 Sam. 16:11
- Strong ... 1 Sam. 17:34-36
- Chosen by God ... 1 Sam. 16:1, 13

B. *His life under King Saul:*

- Royal harpist ... 1 Sam. 16:14-23
- Armor bearer ... 1 Sam. 16:21
- Kills Goliath ... 1 Sam. 17:4-49
- Subdues Philistines ... 1 Sam. 17:32-54
- Loved by Jonathan ... 1 Sam. 18:1-4
- Wise behavior of ... 1 Sam. 18:5-30
- Writes a Psalm ... Ps. 59 (Title)

C. *The fugitive hero:*

- Flees from Saul ... 1 Sam. 19:1-18
- Takes refuge with Samuel ... 1 Sam. 19:20-24
- Makes covenant with Jonathan ... 1 Sam. 20:1-42
- Eats showbread ... Matt. 12:3, 4
- Feigns insanity in Gath ... 1 Sam. 21:10-15
- Dwells in cave ... 1 Sam. 22:1-8
- Saves Keilah ... 1 Sam. 23:1-13
- God delivers ... 1 Sam. 23:14, 15
- Second covenant with Jonathan ... 1 Sam. 23:16-18
- Betrayed but saved ... 1 Sam. 23:19-29
- Writes a Psalm ... Ps. 54 (Title)
- Spares Saul's life ... 1 Sam. 24:1-22
- Scorned by Nabal ... 1 Sam. 25:1-38
- Marries Nabal's widow ... 1 Sam. 25:39-42
- Again spares Saul's life ... 1 Sam. 26:1-25
- Dwells in Ziklag ... 1 Sam. 27:5-7
- Rejected by Philistines ... 1 Sam. 29:1-11
- Smites the Amalekites ... 1 Sam. 30:1-31
- Kills Saul's murderer ... 2 Sam. 1:1-16
- Laments Saul's death ... 2 Sam. 1:17-27

D. *King over Judah:*

- Anointed at Hebron ... 2 Sam. 2:1-4, 11
- List of supporters ... 1 Chr. 12:23-40
- Long war with Saul's house ... 2 Sam. 3:1
- Abner, rebuffed, makes covenant with David ... 2 Sam. 3:6-21
- Mourns Abner's death ... 2 Sam. 3:28-39
- Punishes Ish-bosheth's murderers ... 2 Sam. 4:1-12

E. *King over all Israel:*

- Recognized as king ... 2 Sam. 5:1-5
- Takes Zion from Jebusites ... 2 Sam. 5:6-10
- Builds a house ... 2 Sam. 5:11
- Strengthens kingdom ... 2 Sam. 5:11-16
- Strikes down the Philistines ... 2 Sam. 5:17-25
- Escorts ark to Jerusalem ... 2 Sam. 6:1-16

SUBJECT REFERENCE

Organizes worship .... 1 Chr. 15:1-29
Organizes musicians .... 1 Chr. 25:1-31
Blesses the people .... 2 Sam. 6:17-19
Upbraided by Michal .... 2 Sam. 6:20-23
Receives eternal covenant .... 2 Sam. 7:1-29
Subdues many nations .... 2 Sam. 8:1-18
2 Sam. 10:1-19
Commits adultery .... 2 Sam. 11:1-27
Rebuked by Nathan .... 2 Sam. 12:1-14
Repents .... Ps. 32:1-11
Ps. 51:1-19
Afflictions follow .... 2 Sam. 12:15-23
Family strife .... 2 Sam. 13:1-39
Absalom's rebellion .... 2 Sam. 15:1-31
Flees from Jerusalem .... 2 Sam. 15:13-37
Mourns Absalom's death .... 2 Sam. 19:1-10
Returns to Jerusalem .... 2 Sam. 19:15-43
Sheba's conspiracy .... 2 Sam. 20:1-26
Atones for Saul's crime .... 2 Sam. 21:1-14
Further conflicts .... 2 Sam. 21:15-22
Song of deliverance .... 2 Sam. 22:1-51
Last words of .... 2 Sam. 23:1-7
His mighty men .... 2 Sam. 23:8-39
Sins by numbering people .... 2 Sam. 24:1-17
Buys Araunah's threshing floor .... 2 Sam. 24:18-25
Secures Solomon's succession .... 1 Kin. 1:5-53
Gives dying charge to Solomon .... 1 Kin. 2:1-11
Reign of forty years .... 1 Kin. 2:11

F. *Spiritual significance of:*

Prophet .... Acts 2:30
Musician .... 2 Sam. 23:1
Inspired man .... Matt. 22:43
Type of Christ .... Jer. 23:5, 6
Name designates Christ .... Ezek. 34:23, 24
Christ, son of .... Matt. 1:1
"Kingdom of" .... Mark 11:10
"Throne of" .... Luke 1:32
"Tabernacle of" .... Acts 15:16
"Key of" .... Is. 22:22
Faith .... Heb. 11:32, 33
Covenant with .... 2 Sam. 7:4-17

David, Root of—*a title of Christ*

Opens sealed book .... Rev. 5:5
Jesus describes Himself as .... Rev. 22:16

David, Tower of—fortress built by David, location now unknown

Symbolic of strength .... Song 4:4

Dawn

Not even one remained .... 2 Sam. 17:22
Worked from .... Neh. 4:21
See the breaking .... Job 3:9
Continually tossing until .... Job 7:4
Murderer arises at .... Job 24:14
Mary came to the grave at .... Matt. 28:1
Luke 24:1

Day—*a division of time*

A. *Natural uses of:*

The daylight .... Gen. 1:5, 16
Twelve hours .... John 11:9
Opposite of night .... Mark 5:5
The civil day (24 hours) .... Luke 13:14
Divisions of .... Neh. 9:3
Security of .... Gen. 8:22

B. *Extended uses of:*

Noah's time .... Matt. 24:37
Gospel age .... John 9:4
Long period .... 2 Pet. 3:8

C. *Descriptive of:*

Believers .... 1 Thess. 5:5, 8
Christ's return .... 1 Thess. 5:2
Prophetic period .... Dan. 12:11
Rev. 2:10
Eternity .... Dan. 7:9, 13
Present age .... Heb. 1:2

Day of the Lord

A. *In Old Testament:*

Punishment of faithless .... Is. 13:6-13
Amos 5:18-20
Day of wrath .... Is. 2:6-22
Restoration of remnant .... Is. 10:20-22
Hos. 2:16-20

B. *In New Testament:*

The last times .... Matt. 24:29
2 Pet. 3:10
The great day .... Rev. 16:14

Day, Joshua's long

Described .... Josh. 10:12-14

Day's Journey

Described as:

A distance .... Gen. 30:36
Gen. 31:23
Traveled to make a sacrifice .... Ex. 3:18; Ex. 5:3; Ex. 8:27

Daysman—*umpire or mediator*

Desired by Job .... Job 9:33

Deaconess—*a female attendant*

Phoebe thus called ("a servant") .... Rom. 16:1

Deacons—*church officers*

Ordained by the apostles .... Acts 6:1-6
Stephen, the first martyr of .... Acts 6:5-15
Named with bishops .... Phil. 1:1
Qualifications of .... 1 Tim. 3:8-13

Dead—*lacking life*

A. *Used literally of:*

Lost physical functions .... Rom. 4:19
Those in the other world .... Rev. 20:12

B. *Used figuratively of:*

Unregenerate .... Eph. 2:1
Unreal faith .... James 2:17, 19
Decadent church .... Rev. 3:1
Legal requirements .... Heb. 9:14
Freedom from sin's power .... Rom. 6:2, 8, 11
Freedom from the Law .... Rom. 7:4

Dead Sea

Called the:

Salt Sea .... Gen. 14:3
Sea of the Plain .... Deut. 3:17

Deaf—*unable to hear*

Protection afforded .... Lev. 19:14
Healing of .... Matt. 11:5
Figurative of spiritual inability .... Is. 42:18, 19
Figurative of patience .... Ps. 38:13

Dearth—*famine*

Visited upon Egypt .... Acts 7:11
Agabus predicts .... Acts 11:28
See Famine

Death, eternal

A. *Described as:*

Everlasting punishment .... Matt. 25:46
Resurrection of damnation .... John 5:29
God's wrath .... 1 Thess. 1:10
Destruction .... 2 Thess. 1:9
2 Pet. 2:12
Second death .... Rev. 20:14

B. *Truths regarding:*

A consequence of man's sin .... Gen. 3:17-19
The punishment of the wicked .... Matt. 25:41, 46
Separates from God .... 2 Thess. 1:9
Christ saves from .... John 3:16
Saints shall escape from .... 1 Cor. 15:54-58
Rev. 2:11
Vividly described .... Luke 16:23-26

Death, natural

A. *Features regarding:*

Consequence of sin .... Rom. 5:12
Lot of all .... Heb. 9:27
Ends earthly life .... Eccl. 9:10
Christ delivers from fear of .... Heb. 2:15
Some escaped from .... Gen. 5:24
Some will escape .... 1 Cor. 15:51, 52
All to be raised from .... Acts 24:15
Illustrates regeneration .... Rom. 6:2

B. *Described as:*

Return to dust .... Gen. 3:19
Removal of breath .... Gen. 25:8
Removal from tabernacle .... 2 Cor. 5:1
Naked .... 2 Cor. 5:3, 4
Sleep .... John 11:11-14
Departure .... Phil. 1:23
Yielded up the ghost .... Acts 5:10

C. *Recognition after:*

Departed saints recognized by the living .... Matt. 17:1-8
Greater knowledge in future world .... 1 Cor. 13:12
The truth illustrated .... Luke 16:19-24

Death of saints

A. *Described as:*

Sleep in Jesus .... 1 Thess. 4:14
Blessed .... Rev. 14:13
A gain .... Phil. 1:21
Peace .... Is. 57:1, 2
Crown of righteousness .... 2 Tim. 4:8

B. *Exemplified in:*

Abraham .... Gen. 25:8
Isaac .... Gen. 35:28, 29
Jacob .... Gen. 49:33
Elisha .... 2 Kin. 13:14, 20
The criminal .... Luke 23:39-43

Death of wicked

Result of sin .... Rom. 5:12
Often punishment .... Ex. 23:25-29
Is. 65:11, 12
Unpleasant for God .... Ezek. 33:11
Without hope .... 1 Thess. 4:13
Rev. 20:10, 14, 15

Death Penalty—*legal execution*

By stoning .... Deut. 13:6-10
Deut. 17:5

Debate—*discussion, contention*

With a neighbor .... Prov. 25:9
Wicked, full of .... Rom. 1:29
Saints must avoid .... 2 Cor. 12:20

Debir—*oracle*

1. King of Eglon .... Josh. 10:3-26
2. City of Judah .... Josh. 15:15
Also called Kirjath-sepher .... Josh. 15:15
Captured by Joshua .... Josh. 10:38, 39
Recaptured by Othniel .... Josh. 15:15-17
Judg. 1:11-13
Assigned to priests .... Josh. 21:13, 15
3. A place east of the Jordan .... Josh. 13:26
4. Town of Judah .... Josh. 15:7

Deborah—*a bee*

1. Rebekah's nurse .... Gen. 35:8
2. A prophetess and judge .... Judg. 4:4-14
Composed song of triumph .... Judg. 5:1-31

Debt, debtor

A. *Safeguards regarding:*

No oppression allowed .... Deut. 23:19, 20
Collateral protected .... Ex. 22:25-27
Time limitation of .... Deut. 15:1-18
Non-payment forbidden .... Neh. 5:5
Debts to be honored .... Rom. 13:6
Interest (usury) forbidden .... Ezek. 18:8-17
Love, the unpayable .... Rom. 13:8
Parable concerning .... Matt. 18:23-35

B. *Evils of:*

Brings slavery .... Lev. 25:39, 47
Causes complaint .... 2 Kin. 4:1-7
Produces strife .... Jer. 15:10
Makes outlaws .... 1 Sam. 22:2
Endangers property .... Prov. 6:1-5

C. *Figurative of:*

Sins .... Matt. 6:12
Works .... Rom. 4:4
Moral obligation .... Rom. 1:14
God's mercy .... Ps. 37:26

Decalogue (see Ten Commandments)

Decapolis—*league of ten cities*

Multitudes from, follow Jesus .... Matt. 4:25
Healed demon-possessed, preaches in .... Mark 5:20

Deceit, deceivers, deception

A. *The wicked:*

Devise .... Ps. 35:20
Speaks .... Jer. 9:8
Are full of .... Rom. 1:29
Increase in .... 2 Tim. 3:13

B. *Agents of:*

Satan .... 2 Cor. 11:14
Sin .... Rom. 7:11

SUBJECT — REFERENCE

Self ... 1 Cor. 3:18; James 1:22
Others ... 2 Thess. 2:3

C. *Warnings against:*
Among religious workers ... 2 Cor. 11:3-15
As a sign of apostasy ... 2 Thess. 2:10
As a sign of the antichrist ... 1 John 4:1-6

D. *Examples of:*
Eve ... 1 Tim. 2:14
Abram ... Gen. 12:11-13
Isaac ... Gen. 26:6, 7
Jacob ... Gen. 27:18-27
Joseph's brothers ... Gen. 37:31, 32
Pharaoh ... Ex. 8:29
David ... 1 Sam. 21:12, 13
Amnon ... 2 Sam. 13:6-14
Gehazi ... 2 Kin. 5:20-27
Elisha ... 2 Kin. 6:19-23
Herod ... Matt. 2:7, 8
Pharisees ... Matt. 22:15, 16
Peter ... Mark 14:70, 71
Ananias ... Acts 5:1-11
The earth ... Rev. 13:14

Deceive—*to delude or mislead*

A. *In Old Testament:*
Eve, by Satan ... Gen. 3:13
Israel, by the Midianites ... Num. 25:18
Joshua, by the Gibeonites ... Josh. 9:22

B. *Of Christians:*
By flattering words ... Rom. 16:18
By false report ... 2 Thess. 2:3
By false reasoning ... Col. 2:4

Decision—*determination to follow a course of action*

A. *Sources of:*
Loyalty ... Ruth 1:16
Prayer ... 1 Sam. 23:1-13
The Lord ... 1 Kin. 12:15
Satan ... 1 Chr. 21:1
The world ... Luke 14:16-24
Human need ... Acts 11:27-30
Disagreement ... Acts 15:36-41
Faith ... Heb. 11:24-28

B. *Wrong, leading to:*
Spiritual decline ... Gen. 13:7-11
Repentance ... Heb. 12:16, 17
Defeat ... Num. 14:40-45
Rejection ... 1 Sam. 15:6-26
Apostasy ... 1 Kin. 11:1-13
Division ... 1 Kin. 12:12-20
Death ... Acts 1:16-20

C. *Good, manifested in:*
Siding with the Lord ... Ex. 32:26
Following God ... Num. 14:24; Josh. 14:8
Loving God ... Deut. 6:5
Seeking God ... 2 Chr. 15:12
Obeying God ... Neh. 10:28-30

Decision, valley of—*location unknown*
Called 'Valley of Jehoshaphat' ... Joel 3:2, 12, 14
Refers to final judgment ... Joel 3:1-21

Decisiveness—*showing firmness of decision*
In serving God ... Josh. 24:15, 16; Heb. 11:24, 25
Toward family ... Ruth 1:15-18
Toward a leader ... 2 Kin. 2:1-6
To complete a task ... Neh. 4:14-23
In morality ... Gen. 39:10-12; Dan. 1:8
In prayer ... Dan. 6:1-16

Deck—*floor of a ship*
Made of ivory ... Ezek. 27:6

Decree—*a course of action authoritatively determined*

A. *As a human edict:*
Issued by kings ... Dan. 6:7-14
Considered inflexible ... Dan. 6:15-17
Published widely ... Esth. 3:13-15
Providentially nullified ... Esth. 8:3-17
Sometimes beneficial ... Dan. 4:25-28

B. *As a divine edict, to:*
Govern nature ... Jer. 5:22

Dedan—*low*
1. Raamah's son ... Gen. 10:7
2. Jokshan's son ... Gen. 25:3
3. Descendants of Raamah; a commercial people ... Ezek. 27:15, 20; Ezek. 38:13

Dedication—*setting apart for a sacred use*

A. *Of things:*
Tabernacle ... Ex. 40:34-38
Solomon's Temple ... 1 Kin. 8:12-66
Second temple ... Ezra 6:1-22

B. *Offerings in, must be:*
Voluntary ... Lev. 22:18-25
Without blemish ... Lev. 1:3
Unredeemable ... Lev. 27:28, 29

C. *Examples of:*
Samuel ... 1 Sam. 1:11, 22
The believer ... Rom. 12:1, 2

Dedication, Feast of
Jesus attended ... John 10:22, 23

Deeds—*things done*

A. *Descriptive of one's:*
Past record ... Luke 11:48
Present achievements ... Acts 7:22
Future action ... 2 Cor. 10:11

B. *Expressive of one's:*
Evil nature ... 2 Pet. 2:8
Parentage ... John 8:41
Record ... Luke 24:19
Profession ... 3 John 10
Love ... 1 John 3:18
Judgment ... Rom. 2:6

C. *Toward God:*
Weighed ... 1 Sam. 2:3
Wrong punished ... Luke 23:41

D. *Lord's are:*
Righteous ... Judg. 5:11; 1 Sam. 12:7
Mighty ... Ps. 106:2
Beyond description ... Ps. 106:2

E. *Considered positively:*
Example of ... Titus 2:7
Zealous for ... Titus 2:14
Careful to engage in ... Titus 3:8, 14
Stimulate to ... Heb. 10:24
In heaven ... Rev. 14:13

Deeds, the unbeliever's

A. *Described as:*
Evil ... Col. 1:21
Done in dark place ... Is. 29:15
Abominable ... Ps. 14:1
Unfruitful ... Eph. 5:11

B. *God's attitude toward, will:*
Never forget ... Amos 8:7
Render according to ... Prov. 24:12
Bring to judgment ... Rev. 20:12, 13

C. *Believer's relation to:*
Lay aside ... Rom. 13:12
Not participate in ... Eph. 5:11
Be delivered from ... 2 Tim. 4:18

Defense—*protection during attack*
Of a city ... 2 Kin. 19:34
Of Israel ... Judg. 10:1
Of a plot ... 2 Sam. 23:11, 12
Of the upright ... Ps. 7:10
Of one accused ... Acts 22:1
Of the Gospel ... Phil. 1:7, 16

Deference—*respectful yielding to another*
To a woman's entreaty ... Ruth 1:15-18
To an old man's wish ... 2 Sam. 19:31-40
Results in exaltation ... Matt. 23:12
Commanded ... Heb. 13:17

Defilement—*making the pure impure*

A. *Ceremonial causes of:*
Childbirth ... Lev. 12:2-8
Leprosy ... Lev. 13:3, 44-46
Bodily discharge ... Lev. 15:1-15
Copulation ... Lev. 15:17
Menstruation ... Lev. 15:19-33
Touching the dead ... Lev. 21:1-4, 11

B. *Spiritual manifestations of:*
Abominations ... Jer. 32:34

C. *Objects of:*
Conscience ... 1 Cor. 8:7
Fellowship ... Heb. 12:15
Flesh ... Jude 8

Defrauding—*depriving others through deceit*
Forbidden ... Mark 10:19
To be accepted ... 1 Cor. 6:5-8
In marriage ... 1 Cor. 7:3-5
Paul, not guilty of ... 2 Cor. 7:2
Product of sexual immorality ... 1 Thess. 4:3-6

Degrees—*ascents; steps*
The sun dial ... 2 Kin. 20:9-11
Movement toward Jerusalem ... Ps. 120—134 (Titles)
Order of work ... 1 Chr. 15:18
Rank in society ... Luke 1:52
Advancement in service ... 1 Tim. 3:13

Degrees, Songs of
"Songs of Ascent" ... Ps. 120—134

Dehavites—*people who settled in Samaria during exile*
Opposed rebuilding of Jerusalem ... Ezra 4:9-16

Deity of Christ (see Christ)

Dekar—*piercing; mattock*
Father of one of Solomon's officers ... 1 Kin. 4:9

Delaiah—*Jehovah has delivered*
1. Descendant of Aaron ... 1 Chr. 24:18
2. Son of Shemaiah; urges Jehoiakim not to burn Jeremiah's roll ... Jer. 36:12, 25
3. Founder of a family ... Ezra 2:60
4. A son of Elioenai ... 1 Chr. 3:24

Deliberation—*careful consideration of elements involved in a decision*
Necessary in life ... Luke 14:28-32
Illustrated in Jacob ... Gen. 32:1-23

Delight—*great pleasure in something*

A. *Wrong kind of:*
Showy display ... Esth. 6:6-11
Physical strength ... Ps. 147:10
Sacrifices ... Ps. 51:16; Is. 1:11
Abominations ... Is. 66:3

B. *Right kind of:*
God's will ... Ps. 40:8
God's commandments ... Ps. 112:1
God's goodness ... Neh. 9:25
Lord Himself ... Is. 58:14

Delilah—*lustful*
Deceives Samson ... Judg. 16:4-22

Deliver—*to rescue or save from evil*

A. *By Christ, from:*
Trials ... 2 Tim. 3:11
Evil ... 2 Tim. 4:18; 2 Pet. 2:9
Death ... 2 Cor. 1:10
Power of darkness ... Col. 1:13
God's wrath ... 1 Thess. 1:10

B. *Examples of, by God:*
Noah ... Gen. 8:1-22
Lot ... Gen. 19:29, 30
Jacob ... Gen. 33:1-16
Israel ... Ex. 12:29-51
David ... 1 Sam. 23:1-29
Jews ... Esth. 9:1-19
Daniel ... Dan. 6:13-27
Jesus ... Matt. 2:13-23
Apostles ... Acts 5:17-26
Paul ... 2 Cor. 1:10

Deluge, the—*the Flood*

A. *Warnings of:*
Believed by Noah ... Heb. 11:7
Disbelieved by the world ... 2 Pet. 2:5

B. *Coming of:*
Announced ... Gen. 6:5-7
Dated ... Gen. 7:11
Sudden ... Matt. 24:38, 39

C. *Purpose of:*
Punish sin ... Gen. 6:1-7
Destroy the world ... 2 Pet. 3:5, 6

D. *Its non-repetition based on God's:*
Promise ... Gen. 8:21, 22

SUBJECT ... REFERENCE

Covenant ... Gen. 9:9-11
Token (the rainbow) ... Gen. 9:12-17
Pledge ... Is. 54:9, 10

E. *Type of:*
Baptism ... 1 Pet. 3:20, 21
Christ's coming ... Matt. 24:36-39
Destruction ... Is. 28:2, 18
The end ... 2 Pet. 3:5-15

Delusions, common—*self-deception*
Rejecting God's existence ... Ps. 14:1
Supposing God does not see ... Ps. 10:1-11
Trusting in one's heritage ... Matt. 3:9
Living for time alone ... Luke 12:17-19
Presuming on time ... Luke 13:23-30
Believing antichrist ... 2 Thess. 2:1-12
Denying facts ... 2 Pet. 3:5, 16, 17

Demagogue—*one who becomes a leader by mass prejudice*
Absalom ... 2 Sam. 15:2-6
Haman ... Esth. 3:1-11
Judas of Galilee ... Acts 5:37

Demas—*popular*
Follows Paul ... Col. 4:14
Forsakes Paul ... 2 Tim. 4:10

Demetrius
1. A silversmith at Ephesus ... Acts 19:24-31
2. A good Christian ... 3 John 12

Demon—*an evil spirt*
A. *Nature of:*
Evil ... Luke 10:17, 18
Powerful ... Luke 8:29
Numerous ... Mark 5:8, 9
Unclean ... Matt. 10:1
Under Satan ... Matt. 12:24-30

B. *Ability of:*
Recognize Christ ... Mark 1:23, 24
Possess human beings ... Matt. 8:29
Overcome men ... Acts 19:13-16
Know their destiny ... Matt. 8:29-33
Receive sacrifice ... 1 Cor. 10:20
Instigate deceit ... 1 Tim. 4:1

Demon possession
A. *Recognized as:*
Not insanity ... Matt. 4:24
Not disease ... Mark 1:32
Productive harm ... Mark 5:1-5

B. *Instances of:*
Man in the synagogue ... Mark 1:23-26
Blind and dumb man ... Matt. 12:22, 23
Two men of the Gergesenes ... Matt. 8:28-34
Dumb man ... Matt. 9:32, 33
Canaanite woman's daughter ... Matt. 15:22-28
Epileptic child ... Matt. 17:14-21
Mary Magdalene ... Mark 16:9

Den of Lions
Daniel placed in ... Dan. 6:16-24

Denial of Christ
A. *The realm of:*
Doctrine ... Mark 8:38
2 Tim. 1:8
Practice ... Titus 1:16

B. *The agents of:*
Individuals ... Matt. 26:69-75
Jews ... John 18:40
False teachers ... 2 Pet. 2:1
Antichrist ... 1 John 2:22, 23

C. *The consequences of:*
Christ denies them ... Matt. 10:33
They merit destruction ... 2 Pet. 2:1

Deportation—*exile from a nation*
Captives carried into ... 2 Kin. 15:29
To Babylon ... 2 Kin. 24:8-17

Depravity of man
A. *Extent of:*
Universal ... Gen. 6:5
In the heart ... Jer. 17:9
Man's whole being ... Rom. 3:9-19
From birth ... Ps. 51:5

SUBJECT ... REFERENCE

B. *Effects of:*
Hardness ... Rom. 2:5
Inability to listen ... Jer. 17:23
2 Pet. 2:14, 19
Lovers of evil ... John 3:19
Defilement of conscience ... Titus 1:15, 16

Deputy—*a person empowered to act for another*
King ... 1 Kin. 22:47

Derbe—*a city of Lycaonia*
Paul visits ... Acts 14:6, 20
Paul meets Timothy here ... Acts 16:1
Gaius, native of ... Acts 20:4

Derision—*contempt manifested by laughter*
Heaped on God's people ... Jer. 20:7, 8

Descend
As a dove ... Matt. 3:16
John 1:32
The angels of God ... John 1:51

Desert—*a wilderness place*
Israel journeys through ... Is. 48:21
Place of great temptation ... Ps. 106:14
Rejoicing of, predicted ... Is. 35:1
A highway in ... Is. 40:3
John's home in ... Luke 1:80
Israel received manna in ... John 6:31

Desertion—*forsaking a person or thing*
Jesus, by His disciples ... Matt. 26:56
Jesus, by God ... Matt. 27:46
Paul, by others ... 2 Tim. 4:16
Christ, by professed disciples ... 2 Pet. 2:15

Desire, spiritual
Renewed fellowship ... 1 Thess. 2:17
Church office ... 1 Tim. 3:1
Spiritual knowledge ... 1 Pet. 2:2
Spiritual gifts ... 1 Cor. 14:1

Desire of all nations
A title descriptive of the Messiah ... Hag. 2:6, 7

Despair—*a hopeless state*
A. *Results from:*
Heavy burdens ... Num. 11:10-15
Disobedience ... 1 Sam. 28:16-25
Disappointment ... 2 Sam. 17:23
Impending death ... Esth. 7:7-10
Futility of human things ... Eccl. 6:1-12
Rejection ... Matt. 27:3-5
Rebellion against God ... Rev. 9:6
Hopelessness ... Luke 16:23-31

B. *Remedies against:*
Hope in God ... Ps. 42:5, 11
God's faithfulness ... 1 Cor. 10:13
Accept God's chastening ... Heb. 12:5-11
Cast your care upon the Lord ... 1 Pet. 5:7

Despondency—*depression of spirits*
A. *Causes of:*
Mourning ... Gen. 37:34, 35
Sickness ... Is. 38:9-12
Sorrow ... 2 Sam. 18:32, 33
2 Cor. 2:7
Adversity ... Job 9:16-35
Fears ... 2 Cor. 7:5, 6

B. *Examples of:*
Moses ... Ex. 14:15
Joshua ... Josh. 7:7-9
Elijah ... 1 Kin. 19:2, 4
David ... Ps. 42:6
Jonah ... Jon. 4:3, 8
Two disciples ... Luke 24:13-17

Destitute—*a state of extreme need*
The soul ... Ps. 102:17
The body ... James 2:14-17
Spiritual realities ... Prov. 15:21

Destruction—*a state of ruin*
A. *Past:*
Cities ... Gen. 19:29
People ... 1 Cor. 10:9, 10
Nations ... Jer. 48:42

B. *Present:*
Satan's power of ... 1 Cor. 5:5
Power of lusts ... 1 Tim. 6:9
Wicked on way to ... Rom. 3:16

SUBJECT ... REFERENCE

C. *Future:*
Men appointed to ... Prov. 31:8
2 Pet. 2:12
Men fitted for ... Rom. 9:22
End of the enemies of Christ ... Phil. 3:19
Sudden ... 1 Thess. 5:3
Swift ... 2 Pet. 2:1
Everlasting ... 2 Thess. 1:9

Determinate counsel
God's fixed purpose ... Acts 2:23

Determination—*resolute persistence*
Against popular opposition ... Num. 13:26-31
Num. 14:1-9
Against great numbers ... 1 Sam. 14:1-5
Beyond human advice ... 2 Kin. 2:1-6
In perilous situation ... Esth. 4:10-16
In spite of persecution ... Acts 6:8—7:60

Deuel—*invocation of God*
Father of Eliasaph ... Num. 1:14

Deuteronomy—*book of the Old Testament containing the farewell speeches of Moses*
Written and spoken by Moses ... Deut. 31:9, 22, 24

Devil—*the chief opponent of God*
A. *Titles of:*
Abaddon ... Rev. 9:11
Accuser ... Rev. 12:10
Adversary ... 1 Pet. 5:8
Angel of the bottomless pit ... Rev. 9:11
Apollyon ... Rev. 9:11
Beelzebub ... Matt. 12:24
Belial ... 2 Cor. 6:15
God of this world ... 2 Cor. 4:4
Murderer ... John 8:44
Old serpent ... Rev. 20:2
Prince of demons ... Matt. 12:24
Prince of the power of the air ... Eph. 2:2
Prince of this world ... John 14:30
Ruler of darkness ... Eph. 6:12
Satan ... Luke 10:18
Serpent ... Gen. 3:4
Wicked one ... Matt. 13:19

B. *Origin of:*
Heart lifted up in pride ... Is. 14:12-20
Perfect until sin came ... Ezek. 28:14-19
Greatest of fallen angels ... Rev. 12:7-9
Tempts man to sin ... Gen. 3:1-7
Father of lies ... John 8:44

C. *Character of:*
Subtle ... Gen. 3:1
2 Cor. 11:3
Slanderous ... Job 1:9
Fierce ... Luke 8:29
Deceitful ... 2 Cor. 11:14
Powerful ... Eph. 2:2
Proud ... 1 Tim. 3:6
Cowardly ... James 4:7
Wicked ... 1 John 2:13

D. *Power of, over the wicked:*
They are his children ... Acts 13:10
1 John 3:10
They do his will ... John 8:44
He possesses ... Luke 22:3
He blinds ... 2 Cor. 4:4
He deceives ... Rev. 20:7, 8
He ensnares ... 1 Tim. 3:7
He troubles ... 1 Sam. 16:14
They are punished with him ... Matt. 25:41

E. *Power of, over God's people:*
Tempt ... 1 Chr. 21:1
Afflict ... Job 2:7
Accuse ... Zech. 3:1
Sift ... Luke 22:31
Beguile ... 2 Cor. 11:3
Disguise ... 2 Cor. 11:14, 15

F. *The believer's power over:*
Watch against ... 2 Cor. 2:11
Fight against ... Eph. 6:11-16
Resist ... James 4:7
1 Pet. 5:9
Overcome ... 1 John 2:13
Rev. 12:10, 11

G. *Christ's triumph over:*
Predicted ... Gen. 3:15
Portrayed ... Matt. 4:1-11

SUBJECT — REFERENCE

Proclaimed ... Luke 10:18
Perfected ... Mark 3:27, 28

Devotion to God

A. *How?:*
With our whole selves ... Prov. 3:9; Rom. 12:1; 1 Cor. 6:20

B. *Why? Because of:*
God's goodness ... 1 Sam. 12:24; 1 Thess. 2:12
Christ's death ... 2 Cor. 5:15
Our redemption ... 1 Cor. 6:19, 20

Devotion to the ministry of saints

Household of Stephanas ... 1 Cor. 16:15

Devotions, morning

Jacob's ... Gen. 28:16-18
Samuel's parents' ... 1 Sam. 1:19
Hezekiah's ... 2 Chr. 29:20-31
Job's ... Job 1:5
Jesus' ... Mark 1:35

Devout—*pious, religious, sincere*

Simeon ... Luke 2:25
Cornelius ... Acts 10:1, 2, 7
Ananias ... Acts 22:12
Those who buried Stephen ... Acts 8:2
Converts ... Acts 13:43
Women of Antioch ... Acts 13:50
Greeks in Thessalonica ... Acts 17:4
Gentiles ... Acts 17:17
Men ... Is. 57:1

Dew—*moisture condensed on the earth*

A. *Used literally of:*
Natural dew ... Ex. 16:13, 14
A miraculous test ... Judg. 6:37-40
A curse ... 1 Kin. 17:1; Hag. 1:10

B. *Used figuratively of:*
God's blessings ... Gen. 27:28
God's truth ... Deut. 32:2
The Messiah ... Is. 26:19
Man's fickleness ... Hos. 6:4
Peace and harmony ... Ps. 133:3

Dexterity—*skill in using one's hands or body*

Of 700 men ... Judg. 20:16
David's ... 1 Sam. 17:40-50

Diadem—*a crown*

Removed by judgment ... Ezek. 21:25-27
Reserved for God's people ... Is. 28:5
Restored by grace ... Is. 62:3

Dial—*an instrument for telling time*

Miraculous movement of ... Is. 38:8

Diamond—*crystallized carbon*

Sacred ... Ex. 28:18
Precious ... Ezek. 28:13

Diana

A pagan goddess ... Acts 19:24-34

Diblaim—*twin fig cakes*

Hosea's father-in-law ... Hos. 1:3

Diblath—*rounded cake*

An unidentified place ... Ezek. 6:14

Dibon—*a wasting away*

1. Amorite town ... Num. 21:30
Taken by Israel ... Num. 32:3
Rebuilt by Gadites ... Num. 32:34
Called Dibon-gad ... Num. 33:45, 46
Later given to Reubenites ... Josh. 13:9, 17
Destruction of, foretold ... Jer. 48:18, 22

2. A village of Judah ... Neh. 11:25

Dibri—*loquacious; wordy*

A Danite ... Lev. 24:11-14

Dictator—*ruler with absolute authority*

A. *Powers of, to:*
Take life ... 1 Kin. 2:46
Judge ... 1 Kin. 10:9
Tax ... 2 Kin. 15:19
Levy labor ... 1 Kin. 5:13-15
Make war ... 1 Kin. 20:1
Form alliances ... 1 Kin. 15:18, 19

B. *Examples, evil:*
Pharoah ... Ex. 1:8-22
Ahab ... 1 Kin. 16:28-33
Herod ... Matt. 2:16

C. *Examples, benevolent:*
Solomon ... 1 Kin. 8:12-21; 1 Kin. 10:23-24
Cyrus ... Ezra 1:1-4

Didymus—*twin*

Surname of Thomas ... John 11:16

Diet

Of the Hebrews ... Lev. 11:1-47

Differing weights

Prohibited ... Deut. 25:13, 14

Difficulties—*problems hard to solve*

A. *Kinds of:*
Mental ... Ps. 139:6, 14
Moral ... Ps. 38:1-22
Theological ... John 6:48-60

B. *Examples of:*
Birth of a child in old age ... Gen. 18:9-15
Testing of Abraham ... Gen. 22:1-14
Slaughter of Canaanites ... Ex. 23:27-33
God's providence ... Ps. 44:1-26
Prosperity of wicked ... Ps. 73:1-28
Israel's unbelief ... John 12:39-41

C. *Negative attitudes toward:*
Rebellion against ... Num. 21:4, 5
Unbelief under ... Heb. 3:12-19

D. *Positive attitudes toward:*
Submission under ... Num. 14:7-9
Prayer concerning ... Mark 11:23, 24
Admission of ... 2 Pet. 3:16

Diklah—*palm tree*

Son of Joktan ... Gen. 10:27

Dilean—*cucumber*

Town of Judah ... Josh. 15:38

Dilemma—*unpleasant alternatives*

Given to David ... 1 Chr. 21:9-17
Presented to Jews ... Matt. 21:23-27

Diligence—*faithful applications to one's work*

A. *Manifested in:*
A child's education ... Deut. 6:7
Dedicated service ... Rom. 12:11
A minister's task ... 2 Tim. 4:1-5

B. *Special objects of:*
The soul ... Deut. 4:9
God's commandments ... Deut. 6:17
The heart ... Prov. 4:23
Christian qualities ... 2 Pet. 1:5-9
One's calling ... 2 Pet. 1:10

C. *Rewards of:*
Prosperity ... Prov. 10:4
Ruling hand ... Prov. 12:24
Perseverance ... 2 Pet. 1:10

Dimnah—*dung heap*

City of Zebulun ... Josh. 21:35
Same as Rimmon ... 1 Chr. 6:77

Dimon—*river bed*

Place in Moab ... Is. 15:9

Dimonah

Town in Judah ... Josh. 15:22
Same as Dibon ... Neh. 11:25

Dinah—*judgment*

Daughter of Leah ... Gen. 30:21
Defiled by Shechem ... Gen. 34:1-24
Avenged by brothers ... Gen. 34:25-31
Guilt concerning ... Gen. 49:5-7

Dinaites

Foreigners who settled in Samaria ... Ezra 4:9

Dinhabah—*give judgment*

City of Edom ... Gen. 36:32

Dionysius—*of the* (god)*Dionysos*

Prominent Athenian; converted by Paul ... Acts 17:34

Diotrephes—*nurtured by Zeus*

Unruly church member ... 3 John 9, 10

Diplomacy—*the art of managing affairs of state*

Joseph, an example in ... Gen. 41:33-46
Mordecai's advancement in ... Esth. 10:1-3
Daniel's ability in ... Dan. 2:48, 49
Paul's resort to ... Acts 21:20-25

Disappointment—*the non-fulfillment of one's hopes*

A. *Concerning one's:*
Sons ... 1 Sam. 2:12-17
Mate ... 1 Sam. 25:23-31
Failure ... 2 Sam. 17:23
Wisdom ... Eccl. 1:12-18
Acceptance ... Jer. 20:7-9
Mission ... Jon. 4:1-9
Hopes ... Luke 24:17-24

B. *Antidotes against:*
Let trust prevail ... Hab. 3:17-19
Put God first ... Hag. 1:2-14
Accept God's plan ... Rom. 8:28
Remember God's promises ... Heb. 6:10-12

Disarmament—*abolishing weapons of war*

Imposed upon Israel ... 1 Sam. 13:19-22
Figurative of peace ... Is. 2:4

Discernment, spiritual

Requested by Solomon ... 1 Kin. 3:9-14
Prayed for by David ... Ps. 119:18
Sought by Daniel ... Dan. 7:15, 16
Denied to the unregenerate ... 1 Cor. 2:14
Necessity of ... 1 John 4:1-6

Disciples—*followers of a teacher*

John the Baptist's ... John 1:35
Jesus' ... John 2:2
Moses' ... John 9:28
False teachers' ... Acts 20:30

Discipleship—*adherence to a teacher's faith*

A. *Tests of:*
Obedience ... John 14:15
Faithfulness ... John 15:8
Perseverance ... John 8:31
Love ... John 13:35
Humility ... Matt. 10:24, 25
Surrender of all ... Luke 14:26, 33
Bearing the cross ... Matt. 16:25

B. *Rewards of:*
Acknowledged by Christ ... Matt. 12:49, 50
Enlightened by Christ ... John 8:12
Guided by the Spirit ... John 16:13
Honored by the Father ... John 12:26

Discipline of the church

A. *Needed to:*
Maintain sound faith ... Titus 1:13
Correct disorder ... 2 Thess. 3:6-15
Remove the wicked ... 1 Cor. 5:3-5, 13

B. *How performed:*
In meekness ... Gal. 6:1
In love ... 2 Cor. 2:6-8
In submission ... Heb. 13:17
For edification ... 2 Cor. 10:8

Discipline, parental

A. *Needed to:*
Produce understanding ... Prov. 10:13
Drive out foolishness ... Prov. 22:15
Deliver from Sheol ... Prov. 23:13, 14
Produce obedience ... Prov. 19:18
Develop reverence ... Heb. 12:8-10

B. *How performed:*
Without anger ... Eph. 6:4
In love ... Heb. 12:5-7

Disclosure—*an unfolding of the unknown*

A person's identity ... Gen. 45:1-5
Desirable information ... 1 Sam. 23:10-12
God's plan ... Rom. 16:25-27

Discontentment—*unhappy at the condition of things*

Between Jacob and Laban ... Gen. 31:1-16
Between Moses and Miriam ... Num. 12:1-16
Among soldiers ... Luke 3:14

Discord—*lack of love; disagreement*

Caused by contention ... Prov. 26:20, 21

SUBJECT	REFERENCE
Envy	1 Cor. 3:3
Caused by lies	Prov. 6:16-19
Among Jews	John 6:43

Discouragement—*depression of one's spirits*

A. *Causes of:*

Heavy burden	Num. 11:10-15
Defeat	Josh. 7:7-9
Apparent failure	1 Kin. 19:4
Sickness	Is. 38:9-20

B. *Remedies against:*

"What doest thou here?"	1 Kin. 19:9-18
"Cast thy burden upon the Lord"	Ps. 55:22
"Come ye apart"	Mark 6:31
"Lift up your heads"	Luke 21:28

Discourtesy—*rudeness in manners*

Nabal's	1 Sam. 25:3, 14
Hanun's	2 Sam. 10:1-5
Simon's	Luke 7:44

Discretion—*action based upon caution*

Joseph chosen for	Gen. 41:33, 39
The value of	Prov. 2:11
A woman without	Prov. 11:22
A woman with	Titus 2:5
God teaches	Is. 28:26
Trait of a good man	Ps. 112:5

Discrimination—*making distinctions*

A. *Forbidden, on basis of:*

Wealth	James 2:1-9
Personal righteousness	Rom. 3:10, 23

B. *Between truth and error:*

Test the spirits	1 John 4:1-6
Spirit of truth	John 14:17
Word is truth	Ps. 119:160 John 17:17
Satan, father of lies	John 8:44

C. *Between God's Word and man's:*

Paul preached	1 Thess. 2:13
God's Word inspired	2 Tim. 3:16
By Spirit	1 Cor. 2:10-16

Diseases—*physical impairments of health*

A. *Kinds of:*

Ague	Lev. 26:16
Boil	2 Kin. 20:7
Atrophy	Job 16:8
Blindness	Matt. 9:27
Boils and blains	Ex. 9:10
Consumption	Deut. 28:22
Deafness	Mark 7:32
Weakness	Ps. 102:23
Dropsy	Luke 14:2
Dumbness	Matt. 9:32
Dysentery	2 Chr. 21:12-19
Emerods	1 Sam. 5:6, 12
Epilepsy	Matt. 4:24
Fever	Matt. 8:14, 15
Inflammation	Deut. 28:22
Insanity	Dan. 4:33
Issue of blood	Matt. 9:20
Itch	Deut. 28:27
Leprosy	2 Kin. 5:1
Palsy	Matt. 4:24
Plague	2 Sam. 24:15-25
Scab	Deut. 28:27
Sores	Luke 16:20

B. *Causes of:*

Man's original sin	Gen. 3:16-19
Man's actual sin	2 Kin. 5:27 2 Chr. 21:12-19
Satan's afflictions	Job 2:7 Luke 13:16
God's sovereign will	John 9:1-3 2 Cor. 12:7-10

C. *Cures of:*

From God	2 Chr. 16:12 Ps. 103:3
By Jesus	Matt. 4:23, 24
By prayer	Acts 28:8, 9 James 5:14, 15
By the use of means	Is. 38:21 Luke 10:34

See Sickness

Disfigured face

Disqualifies for service	Lev. 21:18

Disgrace—*shame produced by evil conduct*

Treachery	2 Sam. 10:4, 5
Private	2 Sam. 13:6-20
Public	Esth. 6:6-13
Posthumous	Jer. 8:1-3
Permanent	Matt. 27:21-25
Paramount	Matt. 27:26-44

Disgraceful—*comtemptuous reproach or shame*

Immorality	Gen. 34:7
Transgression	Josh. 7:15
Rape	2 Sam. 13:12

Dish

Tabernacle implement	Ex. 25:29
Figurative of annihilating Jerusalem	2 Kin. 21:13

Dishan—*antelope*

Son of Seir	Gen. 36:21, 28

Dishes—*platters used for food*

In the tabernacle	Ex. 25:29
A common	Matt. 26:23
Man washing	2 Kin. 21:13

Dishon—*antelope*

1. Son of Seir	Gen. 36:21-30
2. Grandson of Seir	Gen. 36:25

Dishonesty—*untruthfulness*

A. *Manifested in:*

Half-truths	Gen. 12:11-20
Trickery	Gen. 27:6-29
Falsifying one's word	Gen. 34:15-31
Wicked devices	Prov. 1:10-19
Theft	John 12:6
Unpaid wages	James 5:4

B. *Consequences of:*

Uncovered by God	1 Kin. 21:17-26
Uncovered by men	Josh. 9:3-22
Condemned by conscience	Matt. 27:3-5

Disobedience—*rebellion against recognized authority*

A. *Sources of:*

Satan's temptations	Gen. 3:1-13
Lust	James 1:13-15
Rebellion	Num. 20:10-24 1 Sam. 15:16-23

B. *Consequences of:*

Death	Rom. 5:12-19
The flood	1 Pet. 3:20
Exclusion from the promised land	Num. 14:26-39
Defeat	Judg. 2:2, 11-15
Doom	1 Pet. 2:7, 8

Disorderly—*unruly and irregular*

Paul not guilty	1 Thess. 5:14
Some guilty	2 Thess. 3:6-11

Dispensation—*a stewardship entrusted to one*

Of divine working	Eph. 1:10
Of the Gospel	1 Cor. 9:17
Paul's special privilege in	Eph. 3:2

Dispersion—*a scattering abroad*

Of Noah's generation	Gen. 11:8
Of Israelites	2 Kin. 17:5, 6
Because of disobedience	Hos. 9:1-12
Of the early Christians	1 Pet. 1:1

Display—*an unusual exhibition*

A. *Of God's:*

Power	Ex. 14:23-31
Glory	Ex. 33:18-23
Wrath	Num. 16:23-35
Universe	Job 38:1-41
Holiness	Is. 6:1-10

B. *Of man's:*

Kingdom	Esth. 1:2-7
Pride	Esth. 5:11
Wealth	Is. 39:2
Hypocrisy	Luke 20:46, 47

Displeasure—*disapproval*

God's, at man	1 Chr. 21:7
Man's, at God	2 Sam. 6:8
Man's, at men	Acts 12:20

Disposition—*natural temperament*

Ambitious Absalom	2 Sam. 15:1-6
Boastful Nebuchadnezzar	Dan. 4:30
Cowardly Peter	Matt. 26:58
Devilish Judas	John 13:20-30
Envious Saul	1 Sam. 18:6-12
Foolish Nabal	1 Sam. 25:10-25
Gullible Haman	Esth. 6:6-11
Humble Job	Job 1:20-22

Ditch—*a trench*

Miraculously filled	2 Kin. 3:16-20
Wicked fall into	Ps. 7:15
Blind leaders fall into	Luke 6:39

Divers—*various kinds*

Colors	Ezek. 17:3
Diseases	Luke 4:40
Doctrines	Heb. 13:9
Flies	Ps. 78:45
Lusts	Titus 3:3
Manners	Heb. 1:1
Measures	Prov. 20:10
Miracles	Heb. 2:4
Seeds	Deut. 22:9
Temptations	James 1:2
Tongues	1 Cor. 12:10
Vanities	Eccl. 5:7
Washings	Heb. 9:10
Weights	Prov. 20:10, 23

Diversity—*variety*

Among hearers	Mark 13:3-8
Of God's gifts	1 Cor. 12:4-11
Of God's times	Heb. 1:1

Divination—*attempt to foretell the unknown by occult means*

A. *Considered as:*

System of fraud	Ezek. 13:6, 7
Lucrative employment	Acts 16:16
Abomination	Deut. 18:11, 12
Punishable by death	Lev. 20:6, 27

B. *Practiced by:*

Astrologers	Is. 47:13
Charmers	Deut. 18:11
Consulters	Deut. 18:14
Enchanter	Deut. 18:10
False prophets	Jer. 14:14
Magicians	Gen. 41:8
Necromancer	Deut. 18:11
Soothsayers	Is. 2:6
Sorcerers	Acts 13:6, 8
Witch	Ex. 22:18
Wizard	Deut. 18:11

Division—*diversity; discord*

A. *Causes of:*

Real faith	Luke 12:51-53
Carnal spirit	1 Cor. 3:3

B. *Opposed to:*

Prayer of Christ	John 17:21-23
Unity of Christ	1 Cor. 1:13
Unity of the church	John 10:16 1 Cor. 12:13-25

Division of Priests—*assignments for service*

Outlined by David	1 Chr. 24:1-19
Determined by casting lots	1 Chr. 24:5, 7
Of Zacharias	Luke 1:5

Divorce—*breaking of the marriage tie*

A. *The Old Testament teaching:*

Permitted	Deut. 24:1-3
Divorced may not return to first husband	Deut. 24:4
Denied to those making false claims	Deut. 22:13-19
Denied to those seducing a virgin	Deut. 22:28, 29
Unjust, reproved	Mal. 2:14-16
Required, foreign wives put away	Ezra 10:1-16
Disobedience, a cause among heathen	Esth. 1:10-22
A prophet's concern with	Hos. 2:1-22

B. *In the New Testament:*

Marriage binding as long as life	Mark 10:2-9 Rom. 7:2, 3
Divorce allowed because of adultery	Matt. 5:27-32
Marriage of the divorced constitutes adultery	Luke 16:18
Reconciliation encouraged	1 Cor. 7:10-17

SUBJECT ... REFERENCE

Dizahab—*abounding in gold*
Location of Moses' farewell addresses ... Deut. 1:1

Doctors—*teachers*
Christ questions ... Luke 2:46
They hear Christ ... Luke 5:17
Gamaliel, a famous doctor ... Acts 5:34

Doctrine—*teaching*
A. *Statements of:*
Foundational ... Heb. 6:1, 2
Traditional ... 1 Cor. 15:1-4
Creedal ... 2 Tim. 3:16
B. *Essentials of:*
The Bible's inspiration ... 2 Tim. 3:16
Christ's deity ... 1 Cor. 12:3
Christ's incarnation ... 1 John 4:1-6
Christ's resurrection ... 1 Cor. 15:12-20
Christ's return ... 2 Pet. 3:3-13
Salvation by faith ... Acts 2:38
C. *Attitudes toward:*
Obey ... Rom. 6:17
Receive ... 1 Cor. 15:1-4
Devote ... Acts 2:42
Hold fast ... 2 Tim. 1:13
Adorn ... Titus 2:10

Doctrine, false
A. *What constitutes:*
Perverting the Gospel ... Gal. 1:6, 7; 1 John 4:1-6
Satanic deception ... 2 Cor. 11:13-15
B. *Teachers of:*
Deceive many ... Matt. 24:5, 24
Attract many ... 2 Pet. 2:2
Speak perverse things ... Acts 20:30
Are savage ... Acts 20:29
Deceitful ... 2 Cor. 11:13
Ungodly ... Jude 4, 8
Proud ... 1 Tim. 6:3, 4
Corrupt ... 2 Tim. 3:8
Love error ... 2 Tim. 4:3, 4
C. *Christian attitude toward:*
Avoid ... Rom. 16:17, 18
Test ... 1 John 4:1
Detest ... Jude 23

Dodai
An Ahohite ... 1 Chr. 27:4

Dodanim
Descendants of Javan ... Gen. 10:4

Dodavah—*beloved of Jehovah*
Eliezer's father ... 2 Chr. 20:37

Dodo—*loving*
1. A descendant of Issachar ... Judg. 10:1
2. A mighty man of David's ... 2 Sam. 23:9
Called Dodai ... 1 Chr. 27:4
3. Father of Elhanan ... 2 Sam. 23:24

Doeg—*fearful*
An Edomite; chief of Saul's herdsmen ... 1 Sam. 21:7
Betrays David ... 1 Sam. 22:9, 10
Kills 85 priests ... 1 Sam. 22:18, 19

Dog—*a domesticated animal*
A. *Described as:*
Carnivorous ... 1 Kin. 14:11
Blood-eating ... 1 Kin. 21:19
Dangerous ... Ps. 22:16
Domesticated ... Matt. 15:26, 27
Unclean ... Is. 66:3
B. *Figurative of:*
Promiscuity ... Deut. 23:18
Contempt ... 1 Sam. 17:43
Worthlessness ... 2 Sam. 9:8
Satan ... Ps. 22:20
Hypocrite ... Matt. 7:6
Gentiles ... Matt. 15:26
False teachers ... 2 Pet. 2:22
The unsaved ... Rev. 22:15

Dominion—*supreme authority to govern*
A. *Man's:*
Delegated by God ... Gen. 1:26-28
Under God's control ... Jer. 25:12-33
Misused ... Dan. 5:18-23
B. *Satan's:*
Secured by rebellion ... Is. 14:12-16
Offered to Christ ... Luke 4:6
Destroyed by Christ ... 1 John 3:8
Abolished at Christ's return ... 2 Thess. 2:8, 9
C. *Christ's:*
Predicted ... Is. 11:1-10
Announced ... Luke 1:32, 33
Secured by His resurrection ... Acts 2:24-36; Rev. 1:18
Perfected at His return ... 1 Cor. 15:24-28

Door—*an entrance*
A. *Used literally of:*
City gates ... Neh. 3:1-6
Prison gates ... Acts 5:19
B. *Used figuratively of:*
Christ ... John 10:7, 9
Christ's return ... Matt. 24:33
Day of salvation ... Matt. 25:10
Inclusion of Gentiles ... Acts 14:27
Opportunity ... 2 Cor. 2:12

Doorkeeper
Descriptive of:
Maaseiah ... Jer. 35:4
Good shepherd ... John 10:3
One who was spoken to by a disciple ... John 18:16

Doorpost
Servant's ears pierced at ... Ex. 21:6

Dophkah—*cattle driving*
A desert encampment ... Num. 33:12, 13

Dor—*habitation*
Jabin's ally ... Josh. 11:1, 2
Taken by Joshua ... Josh. 12:23
Assigned to Manasseh ... Josh. 17:11
Inhabitants unexpelled ... Judg. 1:27

Dorcas—*gazelle*
Good woman ... Acts 9:36
Raised to life ... Acts 9:37-42
Called Tabitha ... Acts 9:36, 40

Dothan—*wells*
Ancient town ... Gen. 37:14-25
Joseph sold there ... Gen. 37:17-28
Elisha strikes Syrians at ... 2 Kin. 6:8-23

Double-mindedness—*inability to hold a fixed belief*
Makes one unstable ... James 1:8

Double-tongued—*two-faced, hypocritical*
Condemned in deacons ... 1 Tim. 3:8

Doubt—*uncertainty of mind*
A. *Objects of, Christ's:*
Miracles ... Matt. 12:24-30
Resurrection ... John 20:24-29
Messiahship ... Luke 7:19-23
Return ... 2 Pet. 3:4
B. *Causes of:*
Satan ... Gen. 3:4
Unbelief ... Luke 1:18-20
Worldly wisdom ... 1 Cor. 1:18-25
Spiritual instability ... James 1:6, 7
C. *Removal of, by:*
Putting God to the test ... Judg. 6:36-40; John 7:17
Searching the Scriptures ... Acts 17:11, 12
Believing God's Word ... Luke 16:27-31

Dove—*pigeon*
A. *Features regarding:*
Sent from ark ... Gen. 8:8, 10, 12
Offered in sacrifice ... Gen. 15:9
Habits of, migratory ... Jer. 8:7
Sold in Temple ... Matt. 21:12
B. *Figurative of:*
Loveliness ... Song 2:14
Desperate mourning ... Is. 38:14
Foolish insecurity ... Hos. 7:11
Israel's restoration ... Hos. 11:11
Holy Spirit ... Matt. 3:16
Harmlessness ... Matt. 10:16

Dove's dung—*an edible plant bulb*
Sold in Samaria ... 2 Kin. 6:25

Dowry—*gifts given to bride's father for the bride*
A. *Regulations regarding:*
Sanctioned in the Law ... Ex. 22:17
Amount of, specified ... Deut. 22:29
Sometimes given by bride's father ... Josh. 15:16-19
B. *Instances of:*
Abraham (Isaac) for Rebekah ... Gen. 24:22-53
Jacob for Rachel ... Gen. 29:15-20
Shechem for Dinah ... Gen. 34:12
David for Michal ... 1 Sam. 18:20-25

Dragon
A. *Applied (Heb.,* tan*) to:*
Some wild asses ... Jer. 14:6
Wicked men ... Is. 43:19, 20
B. *Applied (Heb.,* tannin*) to:*
Sea monster ... Gen. 1:21
Great serpents ... Ex. 7:9, 10, 12
Cruel tyrants ... Is. 51:9
C. *Applied (Gr., dragon) to:*
Satan ... Rev. 12:9
Antichrist ... Rev. 12:3

Dragon Well
In Jerusalem ... Neh. 2:13

Draught
Excrement ... Matt. 15:17
Catch of fish ... Luke 5:9

Drawers of water—*a lowly servant classification*
Women ... Gen. 24:13; 1 Sam. 9:11
Defeated enemies ... Josh. 9:21
Young men ... Ruth 2:9
Included in covenant ... Deut. 29:10-13

Dreams—*thoughts visualized in sleep*
A. *Purposes of:*
Restrain from evil ... Gen. 20:3
Reveal God's will ... Gen. 28:11-22
Encourage ... Judg. 7:13-15
Reveal future ... Gen. 37:5-10
Instruct ... Matt. 1:20
B. *The interpretation of:*
Sought anxiously ... Dan. 2:1-3
Belong to God ... Gen. 40:8
Revealed by God ... Gen. 40:8
Sought for God's will ... Num. 12:6
Sometimes delusive ... Is. 29:7, 8
False, by false prophets ... Deut. 13:1-5
C. *Notable examples of:*
Abimelech ... Gen. 20:3
Jacob ... Gen. 28:10, 12
Laban ... Gen. 31:24
Joseph ... Gen. 37:5
Pharaoh ... Gen. 41:1-13
Unnamed person ... Judg. 7:13, 14
Solomon ... 1 Kin. 3:5
Job ... Job 7:14
Nebuchadnezzar ... Dan. 2:1-13
Joseph ... Matt. 1:19, 20
Pilate's wife ... Matt. 27:13, 19

Dregs—*the sediments of liquids; grounds*
Wicked shall drink down ... Ps. 75:8
Contains God's fury ... Is. 51:17, 22

Dress—*to prepare something to:*
Cultivate land ... Gen. 2:15
Trim lamps ... Ex. 30:7
Prepare foods ... Heb. 6:7
Become presentable ... 2 Sam. 19:24

Drink—*to swallow liquids*
A. *Used literally of:*
Water ... Gen. 24:14
Milk ... Judg. 5:25
Wine ... Gen. 9:21
B. *Used figuratively of:*
Famine ... 2 Kin. 18:27
Misery ... Is. 51:22, 23
Married pleasure ... Prov. 5:15-19
Unholy alliances ... Jer. 2:18
God's blessings ... Zech. 9:15-17
Spiritual communion ... John 6:53, 54
Holy Spirit ... John 7:37-39

SUBJECT REFERENCE

Drink offerings
Of wine ... Hos. 9:4
Of water ... 1 Sam. 7:6

Dromedary—*a specie of camel; a swift steed*
Used by Solomon ... 1 Kin. 4:28
Used by Ahasuerus ... Esth. 8:10
Noted for speed ... Jer. 2:23
Figurative of Gospel blessings ... Is. 60:6

Dropsy—*an unnatural accumulation of fluid in parts of the body*
Healing of ... Luke 14:2-4

Dross—*impurities separated from metals*
Result of refinement ... Prov. 25:4
Figurative of Israel ... Is. 1:22, 25

Drought—*an extended dry season*
Unbearable in the day ... Gen. 31:40
Seen in the wilderness ... Deut. 8:15
Comes in summer ... Ps. 32:4
Sent as a judgment ... Hag. 1:11
Only God can stop ... Jer. 14:22
Descriptive of spiritual barrenness ... Jer. 14:1-7
The wicked dwell in ... Jer. 17:5, 6
The righteous endure ... Jer. 17:8
Longest ... 1 Kin. 18:1
Luke 4:25

Drown
Of the Egyptians ... Ex. 14:27-30
Jonah saved from ... Jon. 1:15-17
Of severe judgment ... Matt. 18:6
The woman saved from ... Rev. 12:15, 16
Figurative of lusts ... 1 Tim. 6:9

Drowsiness—*the mental state preceding sleep*
Prelude to poverty ... Prov. 23:21
Disciples guilty of ... Matt. 26:43

Drunkenness—*state of intoxication*
A. *Evils of:*
Debases ... Gen. 9:21, 22
Provokes anger ... Prov. 20:1
Poverty ... Prov. 23:21
Perverts justice ... Is. 5:22, 23
Confuses the mind ... Is. 28:7
Licentiousness ... Rom. 13:13
Disorderliness ... Matt. 24:48-51
Hinders watchfulness ... 1 Thess. 5:6, 7
B. *Actual instances of the evil of:*
Defeat in battle ... 1 Kin. 20:16-21
Degradation ... Esth. 1:10, 11
Debauchery ... Dan. 5:1-4
Weakness ... Amos 4:1
Disorder ... 1 Cor. 11:21, 22
C. *Penalties of:*
Death ... Deut. 21:20, 21
Exclusion from fellowship ... 1 Cor. 5:11
Exclusion from heaven ... 1 Cor. 6:9, 10
D. *Figurative of:*
Destruction ... Is. 49:26
Roaring waves ... Ps. 107:27
Giddiness ... Is. 19:14
Error ... Is. 28:7
Spiritual blindness ... Is. 29:9-11
International chaos ... Jer. 25:15-29
Persecution ... Rev. 17:6

Drusilla—feminine of *"Drusus"*
Wife of Felix; hears Paul ... Acts 24:24, 25

Dulcimer—*a bagpipe; musical instrument*
Used in Babylon ... Dan. 3:5-15

Dumah—*silence*
1. Descendants (a tribe) of Ishmael ... Gen. 25:14
2. Town in Judah ... Josh. 15:52

Dumb—*inability to speak*
A. *Used literally of dumbness:*
Natural ... Ex. 4:11
Imposed ... Ezek. 3:26, 27
Demonized ... Mark 9:17, 25
Penalized ... Luke 1:20-22
B. *Used figuratively of:*
External calamity ... Ps. 38:13
Submissiveness ... Is. 53:7
Inefficient leaders ... Is. 56:10
Helplessness ... 1 Cor. 12:2
Lamb before shearer is ... Acts 8:32
With silence ... Ps. 39:2

Dung—*excrement*
A. *Used for:*
Fuel ... Ezek. 4:12, 15
Food in famine ... 2 Kin. 6:25
B. *Figurative of:*
Something worthless ... 2 Kin. 9:37

Dungeon—*an underground prison*
Joseph's imprisonment ... Gen. 40:8, 15
Jer. 37:16

Dung Gate—*a gate of Jerusalem*
Wall dedicated near ... Neh. 12:31

Dunghills—*heaps of manure*
Pile of manure ... Luke 14:35
Figurative of a wretched condition ... Ps. 113:7

Dura—*circuit, wall*
Site of Nebuchadnezzar's golden image ... Dan. 3:1

Dust—*powdery earth*
A. *Used literally of:*
Man's body ... Gen. 2:7
Dust of Egypt ... Ex. 8:16, 17
Particles of soil ... Num. 5:17
B. *Used figuratively of:*
Man's mortality ... Gen. 3:19
Descendants ... Gen. 13:16
Judgment ... Deut. 28:24
Act of cursing ... 2 Sam. 16:13
Dejection ... Job 2:12
Subjection ... Is. 49:23
The grave ... Is. 26:19
Rejection ... Matt. 10:14

Duty—*an obligation*
A. *Toward men:*
Husband to wife ... Eph. 5:25-33
Wife to husband ... Eph. 5:22-24
Parents to children ... Eph. 6:4
Children to parents ... Eph. 6:1-3
Subjects to rulers ... 1 Pet. 2:12-20
Rulers to subjects ... Rom. 13:1-7
Men to men ... 1 Pet. 3:8-16
The weak ... 1 Cor. 8:1-13
B. *Toward God:*
Love ... Deut. 11:1
Obey ... Matt. 12:50
Serve ... 1 Thess. 1:9
Worship ... John 4:23

Dwarf—*a diminutive person*
Excluded from priesthood ... Lev. 21:20

Dwelling, God
In the tabernacle ... Ex. 29:45, 46
In the temple ... 1 Kin. 6:12, 13
2 Chr. 7:1-3
In Zion ... Is. 8:18
In Christ ... Col. 2:9
Among men ... John 1:14
In our hearts ... 1 John 4:12-16
In the Holy Spirit ... 1 Cor. 3:16
In the New Jerusalem ... Rev. 7:15

Dyeing—*coloring*
Leather ... Ex. 25:5

Dysentery
Cured by Paul ... Acts 28:8

E

Eagle—*a bird of prey of the falcon species*
A. *Described as:*
Unclean ... Lev. 11:13
A bird of prey ... Job 9:26
Large ... Ezek. 17:3, 7
Swift ... 2 Sam. 1:23
Keen in vision ... Job 39:27-29
Nesting high ... Jer. 49:16
B. *Figurative of:*
God's care ... Ex. 19:4
Swift armies ... Jer. 4:13
Spiritual renewal ... Is. 40:31
Flight of riches ... Prov. 23:5
False security ... Jer. 49:16

Ear—*the organ of hearing*
A. *Ceremonies respecting:*
Priest's, anointed ... Ex. 29:20
Leper's, anointed ... Lev. 14:14, 25
Servant's bored ... Ex. 21:5, 6
B. *The hearing of the unregenerate:*
Deafened ... Deut. 29:4
Stopped ... Ps. 58:4
Dulled ... Matt. 13:15
Disobedient ... Jer. 7:23, 24
Uncircumcised ... Acts 7:51
Itching ... 2 Tim. 4:3, 4
C. *Promises concerning, in:*
Prophecy ... Is. 64:4
Fulfillment ... Matt. 13:16, 17
A miracle ... Mark 7:35
A foretaste ... 2 Cor. 12:4
Final realization ... 1 Cor. 2:9

Early, arose
A. *For spiritual purposes:*
Abraham—looked on Sodom and Gomorrah ... Gen. 19:27-28
Abraham—to offer a burnt offering ... Gen. 22:2, 3
Jacob—to worship the Lord ... Gen. 28:18-22
Moses—to meet God on Sinai ... Ex. 34:4, 5
Elkanah and Hannah—to worship God ... 1 Sam. 1:19-28
Hezekiah—to worship God ... 2 Chr. 29:20-24
Job—to offer sacrifices ... Job 1:5
Jesus—to pray ... Mark 1:35
Jesus—to prepare to teach ... John 8:2
The people—to hear Jesus ... Luke 21:38
B. *For military reasons:*
Joshua—to lead Israel over Jordan ... Josh. 3:1-17
Joshua—to capture Jericho ... Josh. 6:12-27
Joshua—to capture Ai ... Josh. 8:10
People of Jerusalem—to see dead men ... 2 Kin. 19:35
C. *For personal reasons:*
Gideon—to examine the fleece ... Judg. 6:36-38
Samuel—to meet Saul ... 1 Sam. 15:12
David—to obey his father ... 1 Sam. 17:20
The ideal woman—to do her work ... Prov. 31:15
Drunkards—to pursue strong drink ... Is. 5:11
Certain women—to visit Christ's grave ... Mark 16:2

Early rising
Hezekiah to worship God ... 2 Chr. 29:20-24

Earnest—*a pledge of full payment*
The Holy Spirit in the heart ... 2 Cor. 1:22
Given by God ... 2 Cor. 5:5
Guarantee of future redemption ... Eph. 1:13, 14

Earnestness—*a serious and intense spirit*
Warning men ... Gen. 19:15-17
Ezek. 18:1-32
Accepting promises ... Gen. 28:12-22
Admonishing a son ... 1 Chr. 28:9, 10
Public prayer ... 2 Chr. 6:12-42
Asking forgiveness ... Ps. 51:1-19
Calling to repentance ... Acts 2:38-40
Seeking salvation ... Acts 16:30-34
Preaching the Gospel ... Acts 20:18-38
Writing an epistle ... Jude 3-5

Earrings—*ornaments worn on the ear*
Sign of worldliness ... Gen. 35:2-4
Made into a golden calf ... Ex. 32:2-4
Spoils of war ... Judg. 8:24-26
Used figuratively ... Ezek. 16:12

Ears of corn
Seen in Pharaoh's dream ... Gen. 41:5-7
Regulations concerning ... Lev. 2:14
Ruth gleans ... Ruth 2:2
Christ's disciples pluck ... Matt. 12:1

SUBJECT — REFERENCE

Earth—*our planet*

A. *Described as:*
- Inhabitable — Is. 45:18
- God's footstool — Is. 66:1
- A circle — Is. 40:22
- Full of minerals — Deut. 8:9

B. *Glory of God's:*
- Goodness — Ps. 33:5
- Glory — Is. 6:3
- Riches — Ps. 104:24
- Mercy — Ps. 119:64

C. *History of:*
- Created by God — Gen. 1:1
- Given to man — Gen. 1:27-31
- Affected by sin — Rom. 8:20-23
- Destroyed — Gen. 7:7-24
- Final destruction — 2 Pet. 3:7-12
- To be renewed — Is. 65:17

D. *Unusual events of:*
- Swallows several families — Num. 16:23-35
- Reversed in motion — 2 Kin. 20:8-11
- Shaking — Heb. 12:26
- Smiting — Mal. 4:6
- Earthquake — Matt. 27:51-54

E. *Man's relation to:*
- Made of — 1 Cor. 15:47, 48
- Given dominion over — Gen. 1:26
- Brings curse on — Gen. 3:17
- Returns to dust — Gen. 3:19

F. *Promises respecting:*
- Continuance of seasons — Gen. 8:21, 22
- No more flood — Gen. 9:11-17
- God's knowledge to fill — Is. 11:9
- The meek shall inherit — Matt. 5:5
- Long life upon — Eph. 6:2, 3
- To be renewed — Is. 65:17

Earthquake—*a trembling of the earth*

A. *Expressive of God's:*
- Power — Heb. 12:26
- Presence — Ps. 68:7, 8
- Anger — Ps. 18:7
- Judgments — Is. 24:18-21
- Overthrowing of kingdoms — Hag. 2:6, 7; Rev. 16:18-21

B. *Mentioned in the Scriptures:*
- Mt. Sinai — Ex. 19:18
- The wilderness — Num. 16:31, 32
- Saul's time — 1 Sam. 14:15
- Ahab's reign — 1 Kin. 19:11, 12
- Uzziah's reign — Amos 1:1
- Christ's death — Matt. 27:50, 51
- Christ's resurrection — Matt. 28:2
- Philippi — Acts 16:26
- This age — Matt. 24:7

Ease—*contentment of body and mind*
- Israel's — Amos 6:1
- Pagan nations' — Zech. 1:15

East country—*southeastern Palestine, Arabia*
- Abraham sent family there — Gen. 25:6

East gate—*a gate of Jerusalem*
- In Temple area — Ezek. 10:19; Ezek. 11:1

East wind—*a scorching desert wind, the sirocco*
- Destroys vegetation — Gen. 41:6; Ezek. 17:10
- Destroys houses — Job 1:19
- Destroys ships — Ps. 48:7; Ezek. 27:26
- Brings judgment — Is. 27:8; Jer. 4:11, 12
- Dries springs and fountains — Hos. 13:15
- Afflicts Jonah — Jon. 4:8
- Called Euroclydon — Acts 27:14

Eat, eating

A. *Restrictions on:*
- Forbidden tree — Gen. 2:16, 17
- Blood — Acts 15:19, 20
- Unclean things — Lev. 11:1-47; Deut. 14:1-29
- Excess, condemned — Eccl. 10:16, 17; Phil. 3:19
- Anxiety concerning, prohibited — Matt. 6:24-34

B. *Spiritual significance of:*
- Covenant — Ex. 24:11
- Adoption — Jer. 52:33, 34
- Fellowship — Luke 22:15-20

C. *Christian attitude toward:*
- Tradition rejected — Mark 7:1-23
- Disorderliness condemned — 1 Cor. 11:20-22
- Regard for weaker brother — Rom. 14:1-23
- No work, no eating — 2 Thess. 3:7-10

Ebal—*to be bare, stony*
1. Son of Shobal — Gen. 36:23
2. Same as Obal — Gen. 10:28
3. Mountain in Samaria — Deut. 27:12, 13
   - Law to be written upon — Deut. 27:1-8
   - Fulfilled by Joshua — Josh. 8:30-35

Ebed—*slave*
1. Gaal's father — Judg. 9:28, 30
2. Son of Jonathan — Ezra 8:6

Ebed-melech—*slave of the king*
- Ethiopian eunuch; rescues Jeremiah — Jer. 38:7-13
- Promised divine protection — Jer. 39:15-18

Ebenezer—*stone of help*
- Site of Israel's defeat — 1 Sam. 4:1-10
- Ark transferred from — 1 Sam. 5:1
- Site of memorial stone — 1 Sam. 7:10, 12

Eber—*the region beyond*
1. Great-grandson of Shem — Gen. 10:21-24
   - Progenitor of the: Hebrews — Gen. 11:16-26
   - Arabians and Arameans — Gen. 10:25-30
2. Gadite leader — 1 Chr. 5:13
3. Son of Elpaal — 1 Chr. 8:12
4. Son of Shashak — 1 Chr. 8:22, 25
5. Postexilic priest — Neh. 12:20

Ebiasaph—*gatherer*
- Forefather of Samuel — 1 Chr. 6:23
- Same as Abiasaph — Ex. 6:16, 18, 24

Ebony
- Black, heavy hardwood; article of trade — Ezek. 27:15

Ebronah—*passage*
- Israelite encampment — Num. 33:34

Ecclesiastes, Book of—from Gr. word *"assembly"* and Heb. word *"one who assembles"*
- Vanity of earthly things — Eccl. 1:2
- Material goods — Eccl. 5:10-12

Eclipse of the sun
- Foretold — Amos 8:9

Economy—*living thriftily*
- The law of — Prov. 11:24
- The wrong kind — Hag. 1:6, 9-11
- Exemplified by Jesus — John 6:12

Ed—*witness*
- The name (not in Heb.) of an altar — Josh. 22:34

Eden—*delight, pleasantness*
1. First home — Gen. 2:8-15
   - Zion becomes like — Is. 51:3
   - Called the "garden of God" — Ezek. 28:13
   - Terrible contrast — Joel 2:3
2. Region in Mesopotamia — Is. 37:12
3. Gershonite Levite — 2 Chr. 29:12

Eder—*a flock*
1. Watchtower — Gen. 35:21
2. Town in Judah — Josh. 15:21
3. Benjamite — 1 Chr. 8:15
4. Levite — 1 Chr. 23:23

Edification—*building up one's faith*

A. *Objects of:*
- The church — 1 Cor. 14:4-12
- The body of Christ — Eph. 4:12
- One another — Rom. 14:19

B. *Accomplished by:*
- The ministry — 2 Cor. 12:19
- Christian gifts — 1 Cor. 14:3-12
- Word of God — Acts 20:32
- Love — 1 Cor. 8:1
- Spiritual things — Rom. 14:19
- Seeking another's goods — Rom. 15:2
- God's authority — 2 Cor. 10:8

C. *Hindrances of:*
- Carnal spirit — 1 Cor. 3:1-4
- Foolish questions — 1 Tim. 1:3, 4
- Spiritual luke-warmness — Rev. 3:14-22
- Worldly spirit — James 4:1-6

Edom—*red*
1. Name given to Esau — Gen. 25:30
2. Edomites — Num. 20:18-21
3. Land of Esau; called Seir — Gen. 32:3
   - Called Edom and Idumea — Mark 3:8
   - Mountainous land — Jer. 49:16, 17
   - People of, cursed — Is. 34:5, 6

Edomites—*descendants of Esau*

A. *Character of:*
- Warlike — Gen. 27:40
- Idolatrous — 2 Chr. 25:14, 20
- Superstitious — Jer. 27:3, 9
- Proud — Jer. 49:16
- Cruel — Jer. 49:19
- Vindictive — Ezek. 25:12

B. *Relations with Israel:*
- Descendants of Esau — Gen. 36:9
- Refused passage to — Num. 20:18-20
- Enemies of — Ezek. 35:5, 6
- Wars against — 1 Sam. 14:47
- Joined enemies of — 2 Chr. 20:10
- Aided Babylon against — Ps. 137:7

C. *Prophecies concerning:*
- Subjection to Israel — Gen. 27:37
- Punishment for persecuting Israel — Is. 34:5-8
- Utter desolation of — Is. 34:9-17
- Figurative of Gentiles — Amos 9:11, 12

Edrei—*mighty*
1. Capital of Bashan — Deut. 3:10
   - Site of Og's defeat — Num. 21:33-35
2. City of Naphtali — Josh. 19:37

Education—*instruction in knowledge*

A. *Performed by:*
- Parents — Eph. 6:4
- Tutors — Gal. 4:1-3
- Teachers — 2 Chr. 17:7-9
- Learned men — Acts 22:3

B. *Method of:*
- Sharing — Gal. 6:6
- Recalling God's works — Ps. 78:1-8
- Learning from nature — Prov. 6:6-11
- Step by step — Is. 28:10
- Asking questions — Luke 2:46

C. *Examples of:*
- Moses — Acts 7:22
- Daniel — Dan. 1:17
- Paul — Acts 22:3
- Timothy — 2 Tim. 3:15, 16

Effeminate—*a man with female traits*
- Curse on Egypt — Is. 19:16
- The weakness of Nineveh — Nah. 3:13
- Rebuked by Paul — 1 Cor. 16:13
- Shall not inherit the kingdom of God — 1 Cor. 6:9

Effort—*using energy to get something done*
- Organized — Neh. 4:15-23
- Diligence in — Neh. 6:1-4
- Inspired to — Hag. 1:12-14
- Ill-considered — Luke 14:28-30
- The highest — Phil. 3:11-14

Egg
- Prohibition concerning that of birds — Deut. 22:6
- Article of food — Luke 11:12
- White of, without taste — Job 6:6

Eglah—*heifer*
- Wife of David — 2 Sam. 3:2, 5

Eglaim—*two ponds*
- Moabite town — Is. 15:8

Eglon—*heifer-like*
1. Moabite king — Judg. 3:12-15
2. City of Judah — Josh. 15:39

SUBJECT — REFERENCE

Egotism—*a sinful exultation of one's self*
Satan ... Is. 14:13-15; Luke 4:5, 6
Goliath ... 1 Sam. 17:4-11
Haman ... Esth. 6:6-12
Simon ... Acts 8:9-11
Herod ... Acts 12:20-23
Diotrephes ... 3 John 9-10
Sign of antichrist ... 2 Thess. 2:4
Sign of the last days ... 2 Tim. 3:1-5

Egypt—*black*
A. *Israel's contact with:*
Abram visits ... Gen. 12:10
Joseph sold into ... Gen. 37:28, 36
Joseph becomes leader in ... Gen. 39:1-4
Hebrews move to ... Gen. 46:5-7
Persecution by ... Ex. 1:15-22
Israel leaves ... Ex. 12:31-33
Army of, perishes ... Ex. 14:26-28
B. *Characteristics of:*
Superstitious ... Is. 19:3
Unprofitable ... Is. 30:1-7
Treacherous ... Is. 36:6
Ambitious ... Jer. 46:8, 9
C. *Prophecies concerning:*
Israel's sojourn in ... Gen. 15:13
Destruction of ... Ezek. 30:24, 25
Ever a lowly kingdom ... Ezek. 29:14, 15
Conversion of ... Is. 19:18-25
Christ, called out of ... Matt. 2:15

Egyptian, the—*an unknown insurrectionist*
Paul mistaken for ... Acts 21:37, 38

Ehi—*brotherly*
Benjamin's son ... Gen. 46:21
Same as Ahiram ... Num. 26:38

Ehud—*union*
1. Great-grandson of Benjamin ... 1 Chr. 7:10
2. Son of Gera ... Judg. 3:15
Slays Eglon ... Judg. 3:16-26

Eker—*offshoot*
Descendant of Judah ... 1 Chr. 2:27

Ekron—*extermination*
Philistine city ... Josh. 13:3
Captured by Judah ... Judg. 1:18
Assigned to Dan ... Josh. 19:43
Ark sent to ... 1 Sam. 5:10
Denounced by the prophets ... Jer. 25:9, 20

El—*ancient word for God, often used as prefix to Hebrew names*
El-beth-el ... Gen. 35:6, 7

Eladah—*God has adorned*
A descendant of Ephraim ... 1 Chr. 7:20

Elah—*an oak*
1. Duke of Edom ... Gen. 36:41
2. Son of Caleb ... 1 Chr. 4:15
3. Benjamite ... 1 Chr. 9:8
4. King of Israel ... 1 Kin. 16:6, 8-10
5. Father of Hoshea ... 2 Kin. 15:30
6. Valley of ... 1 Sam. 17:2, 19
7. Father of Shimei ... 1 Kin. 4:18

Elam—*hidden*
1. Son of Shem ... Gen. 10:22
2. Benjamite ... 1 Chr. 8:24
3. Korahite Levite ... 1 Chr. 26:1, 3
4. Head of postexilic families ... Ezra 2:7
5. Another family head ... Ezra 2:31
6. One who signs covenant ... Neh. 10:1, 14
7. Priest ... Neh. 12:42

Elamites—*descendants of Elam*
A Semite (Shem) people ... Gen. 10:22
An ancient nation ... Gen. 14:1
Connected with Media ... Is. 21:2
Destruction of ... Jer. 49:34-39
In Persian empire ... Ezra 4:9
Jews from, at Pentecost ... Acts 2:9

Elasah—*God has made*
1. Shaphan's son ... Jer. 29:3
2. Son of Pashur ... Ezra 10:22

Elath, Eloth—*a grove*
Seaport on Red Sea ... 1 Kin. 9:26
Edomite dukedom ... Gen. 31:41
Conquered by David ... 2 Sam. 8:14
Built by Azariah ... 2 Kin. 14:21, 22
Captured by Syrians ... 2 Kin. 16:6

El-beth-el—*God of Bethel*
Site of Jacob's altar ... Gen. 35:6, 7

Eldaah—*God has called*
Son of Midian ... Gen. 25:4

Eldad—*God has loved*
Elder of Moses ... Num. 11:26-29

Elderly
A. *Contributions of:*
Counsel ... 1 Kin. 12:6-16; Job 12:12
Spiritual service ... Luke 2:36-38
Fruitfulness ... Ps. 92:13, 14
Leadership ... Josh. 24:2, 14, 15, 29
B. *Attitude toward:*
Minister to needs ... 1 Kin. 1:15
Respect ... Ps. 71:18, 19
As cared for by God ... Is. 46:4
Honor ... Lev. 19:32; Prov. 16:31

Elders of Israel
A. *Functions of, in Mosaic period:*
Rule the people ... Judg. 2:7
Represent the nation ... Ex. 3:16, 18
Share in national guilt ... Josh. 7:6
Assist in government ... Num. 11:16-25
Perform religious acts ... Ex. 12:21, 22
B. *Functions of, in later periods:*
Choose a king ... 2 Sam. 3:17-21
Ratify a covenant ... 2 Sam. 5:3
Assist at a dedication ... 1 Kin. 8:1-3
Counsel kings ... 1 Kin. 12:6-8, 13
Legislate reforms ... Ezra 10:8-14
Try civil cases ... Matt. 26:3-68

Elders in the church
A. *Qualifications of, stated by:*
Paul ... Titus 1:5-14
Peter ... 1 Pet. 5:1-4
B. *Duties of:*
Administer relief ... Acts 11:29, 30
Correct error ... Acts 15:4, 6, 23
Hold fast the faithful Word ... Titus 1:5, 9
Rule well ... 1 Tim. 5:17
Minister to the sick ... James 5:14, 15
C. *Honors bestowed on:*
Ordination ... Acts 14:19, 23
Obedience ... Heb. 13:7, 17
Due respect ... 1 Tim. 5:1, 19
See Bishop

Elead—*God has testified*
Ephraimite ... 1 Chr. 7:21

Elealeh—*God has ascended*
Moabite town ... Is. 15:1, 4
Rebuilt by Reubenites ... Num. 32:37

Eleasah—*God has made*
1. Descendant of Judah ... 1 Chr. 2:2-39
2. Descendant of Saul ... 1 Chr. 8:33-37

Eleazar—*God has helped*
1. Son of Aaron ... Ex. 6:23
Father of Phinehas ... Ex. 6:25
Consecrated a priest ... Ex. 28:1
Ministers in priest's position ... Lev. 10:6, 7
Made chief Levite ... Num. 3:32
Succeeds Aaron ... Num. 20:25-28
Aids Joshua ... Josh. 14:1
Buried at Ephraim ... Josh. 24:33
2. Merarite Levite ... 1 Chr. 23:21, 22
3. Son of Abinadab; custodian of the ark ... 1 Sam. 7:1
4. One of David's mighty men ... 2 Sam. 23:9
5. Priest ... Ezra 8:33
6. Son of Parosh ... Ezra 10:25

7. Musician priest ... Neh. 12:27-42
8. Ancestor of Jesus ... Matt. 1:15

Elect, Election
A. *Descriptive of:*
The Messiah ... Is. 42:1
Israel ... Is. 45:4
Good angels ... 1 Tim. 5:21
Christians ... Matt. 24:22, 31
Christian ministers ... Acts 9:15
Lady or church ... 2 John 1, 13
B. *Characteristics of:*
Eternal ... Eph. 1:4
Personal ... Acts 9:15
Sovereign ... Rom. 9:11-16
Unmerited ... Rom. 9:11
God's foreknowledge ... 2 Pet. 1:3, 4
Of grace ... Rom. 11:5, 6
Through faith ... 2 Thess. 2:13
Recorded in heaven ... Luke 10:20
Knowable ... 1 Thess. 1:4
Of high esteem ... 2 Tim. 2:4
C. *Results in:*
Adoption ... Eph. 1:5
Salvation ... 2 Thess. 2:13
Conformity to Christ ... Rom. 8:29
Good works ... Eph. 2:10
Eternal glory ... Rom. 9:23
Inheritance ... 1 Pet. 1:2, 4, 5
D. *Proof of:*
Faith ... 2 Pet. 1:10
Holiness ... Eph. 1:4, 5
Divine protection ... Mark 13:20
Manifest it in life ... Col. 3:12

El-elohe-Israel—*God, the God of Israel*
Name of Jacob's altar ... Gen. 33:20

Elements—*basic parts of anything*
A. *Used literally of:*
Basic forces of nature ... 2 Pet. 3:10, 12
B. *Used figuratively of:*
"Rudiments" of religion ... Gal. 4:3, 9
"Rudiments" of tradition ... Col. 2:8, 20
"First principles" of religion ... Heb. 5:12

Eleph—*ox*
Town of Benjamin ... Josh. 18:28

Eleven, the—*the disciples without Judas*
Were told of resurrection ... Luke 24:9, 33
Met Jesus ... Matt. 28:16
At Pentecost ... Acts 2:1, 14

Elhanan—*God has been gracious*
1. Son of Dodo ... 2 Sam. 23:24
Brave man ... 1 Chr. 11:26
2. Son of Jair ... 1 Chr. 20:5
Slays a giant ... 2 Sam. 21:19

Eli—*my God*
Jesus' cry on the cross ... Matt. 27:46
Same as "Eloi" ... Mark 15:34

Eli—*high* (that is, God is high)
Officiates in Shiloh ... 1 Sam. 1:3
Blesses Hannah ... 1 Sam. 1:12-19
Becomes Samuel's guardian ... 1 Sam. 1:20-28
Samuel ministers before ... 1 Sam. 2:11
Sons of ... 1 Sam. 2:12-17
Rebukes sons ... 1 Sam. 2:22-25
Rebuked by a man of God ... 1 Sam. 2:27-36
Instructs Samuel ... 1 Sam. 3:1-18
Death of ... 1 Sam. 4:15-18

Eliab—*God is father*
1. Son of Helon ... Num. 1:9
Leader of Zebulun ... Num. 7:24, 29
2. Father of Dathan and Abiram ... Num. 16:1, 12
3. Ancestor of Samuel ... 1 Chr. 6:27, 28
4. Brother of David ... 1 Sam. 16:5-13
Fights in Saul's army ... 1 Sam. 17:13
Discounts David's worth ... 1 Sam. 17:28, 29
5. Gadite warrior ... 1 Chr. 12:1-9
6. Levite musician ... 1 Chr. 15:12-20

Eliada—*God has known*
1. Son of David ... 2 Sam. 5:16
Also called Beeliada ... 1 Chr. 14:7

SUBJECT — REFERENCE

2. Father of Rezon ... 1 Kin. 11:23
3. Benjamite warrior ... 2 Chr. 17:17

Eliah—*my God is Jehovah*

Son of Jeroham ... 1 Chr. 8:27

Eliahba—*God conceals*

One of David's mighty men ... 2 Sam. 23:32

Eliakim—*God will establish*

1. Son of Hilkiah ... 2 Kin. 18:18
   Confers with Rabshakeh ... Is. 36:3, 11-22
   Sent to Isaiah ... Is. 37:2-5
   Becomes type of the Messiah ... Is. 22:20-25
2. Son of King Josiah ... 2 Kin. 23:34
   Name changed to Jehoiakim ... 2 Chr. 36:4
3. Postexilic priest ... Neh. 12:41
4. Ancestor of Christ ... Matt. 1:13; Luke 3:30

Eliam—*God of the people*

1. Father of Bathsheba ... 2 Sam. 11:3
   Called Ammiel ... 1 Chr. 3:5
2. Son of Ahithophel ... 2 Sam. 23:34

Eliasaph—*God has added*

1. Gadite prince ... Num. 1:4, 14
   Presents offering ... Num. 7:41, 42
2. Levite ... Num. 3:24

Eliashib—*God will restore*

1. Davidic priest ... 1 Chr. 24:1, 12
2. Divorced foreign wife ... Ezra 10:24; Ezra 10:27
3. High priest ... Neh. 12:10
   Rebuilds Sheep Gate ... Neh. 3:1, 20, 21
   Allies with foreigners ... Neh. 13:4, 5, 28
4. Descendant of Zerubbabel ... 1 Chr. 3:19-24

Eliathah—*God has come*

Son of Heman ... 1 Chr. 25:1-27

Elidad—*God has loved*

Benjamite leader ... Num. 34:17, 21

Eliel—*God is God*

1. Ancestor of Samuel ... 1 Chr. 6:33, 34
2. One of David's mighty men ... 1 Chr. 11:26, 46
3. Another of David's mighty men ... 1 Chr. 11:47
4. Gadite warrior ... 1 Chr. 12:1-11
5. Levite ... 1 Chr. 15:9, 11
6. Benjamite ... 1 Chr. 8:1-21
7. Benjamite, son of Shashak ... 1 Chr. 8:22, 25
8. Manassite chief ... 1 Chr. 5:24
9. Overseer of tithes ... 2 Chr. 31:12, 13

Elienai—*toward God are my eyes*

Benjamite chief ... 1 Chr. 8:1, 20

Eliezer—*God of help*

1. Abraham's servant ... Gen. 15:2
2. Son of Moses ... Ex. 18:4
3. Son of Zichri ... 1 Chr. 27:16
4. Son of Becher ... 1 Chr. 7:8
5. Priest of David ... 1 Chr. 15:24
6. Prophet ... 2 Chr. 20:37
7. Ezra's delegate ... Ezra 8:16

8, 9, 10. Three men who divorced their foreign wives ... Ezra 10:18-31

11. An ancestor of Christ ... Luke 3:29

Elihoenai—*toward God are my eyes*

Son of Zerahiah ... Ezra 8:4
Korahite gatekeeper ... 1 Chr. 26:1-3

Elihoreph—*God of autumn*

One of Solomon's scribes ... 1 Kin. 4:3

Elihu—*He is my God*

1. Ancestor of Samuel ... 1 Sam. 1:1
   Also called Eliab and Eliel ... 1 Chr. 6:27, 34
2. David's brother ... 1 Chr. 27:18
   Called Eliab ... 1 Sam. 16:6
3. Manassite captain ... 1 Chr. 12:20
4. Temple servant ... 1 Chr. 26:1, 7
5. One who reproved Job and his friends ... Job 32:2, 4-6

Elijah—*Jehovah is God*

A. *Life of the prophet:*

Denounces Ahab ... 1 Kin. 17:1
Hides by the brook Cherith ... 1 Kin. 17:3
Fed by ravens ... 1 Kin. 17:4-7
Fed by widow ... 1 Kin. 17:8-16
Restores widow's son ... 1 Kin. 17:17-24
Sends message to Ahab ... 1 Kin. 18:1-16
Overthrows Baal prophets ... 1 Kin. 18:17-46
Flees from Jezebel ... 1 Kin. 19:1-3
Fed by angels ... 1 Kin. 19:4-8
Hears God ... 1 Kin. 19:9-14
Sent on a mission ... 1 Kin. 19:15-21
Condemns Ahab ... 1 Kin. 21:15-29
Condemns Ahaziah ... 2 Kin. 1:1-16
Taken up to heaven ... 2 Kin. 2:1-15

B. *Miracles of:*

Widow's oil ... 1 Kin. 17:14-16
Dead child raised ... 1 Kin. 17:17-24
Causes rain ... 1 Kin. 18:41-45
Causes fire to consume sacrifices ... 1 Kin. 18:24-38
Causes fire to consume soldiers ... 2 Kin. 1:10-12

C. *Prophecies of:*

Drought ... 1 Kin. 17:1
Ahab's destruction ... 1 Kin. 21:17-29
Ahaziah's death ... 2 Kin. 1:2-17
Plague ... 2 Chr. 21:12-15

D. *Significance of:*

Prophecy of his coming ... Mal. 4:5, 6
Appears with Christ ... Matt. 17:1-4
Type of John the Baptist ... Luke 1:17

Elijah—*Jehovah is God*

1. Priest who divorced his foreign wife ... Ezra 10:21
2. Divorced foreign wife ... Ezra 10:18, 26

Elika—*God has spewed out*

David's warrior ... 2 Sam. 23:25

Elim—*large trees*

Israel's encampment ... Ex. 15:27
Place of palm trees ... Num. 33:9, 10

Elimelech—*God is king*

Man of Judah ... Ruth 1:1, 2
Dies in Moab ... Ruth 1:3
Kinsman of Boaz ... Ruth 2:1, 3
Boaz buys his land ... Ruth 4:3-9

Elioenai—*toward God are my eyes*

1. Descendant of Benjamin ... 1 Chr. 7:8
2. Simeonite head ... 1 Chr. 4:36
3. Son of Neariah ... 1 Chr. 3:23, 24
4. Postexilic priest ... Neh. 12:41
   Divorced his foreign wife ... Ezra 10:19, 22
5. Son of Zattu; divorced his foreign wife ... Ezra 10:27

Eliphal—*God has judged*

David's warrior ... 1 Chr. 11:26, 35
Called Eliphelet ... 2 Sam. 23:34

Eliphaz—*God is fine gold*

1. Son of Esau ... Gen. 36:2, 4
2. One of Job's friends ... Job 2:11
   Rebukes Job ... Job 4:1, 5
   Is forgiven ... Job 42:7-9

Elipheleh—*whom God makes distinguished*

Levite singer ... 1 Chr. 15:18, 21

Eliphelet—*God is deliverance*

1. Son of David ... 1 Chr. 3:5, 6
2. Another son of David ... 2 Sam. 5:16
3. Descendant of Jonathan ... 1 Chr. 8:33, 39
4. David's warrior ... 2 Sam. 23:34
5. Returnee from Babylon ... Ezra 8:13
6. Son of Hashum; divorced his foreign wife ... Ezra 10:33

Elisabeth—*God is an oath*

Wife of Zacharias ... Luke 1:5
Barren ... Luke 1:7, 13
Conceives a son ... Luke 1:24, 25
Cousin of Mary ... Luke 1:36
Salutation to Mary ... Luke 1:39-45
Mother of John the Baptist ... Luke 1:57-60

Elisha—*God is salvation*

A. *Life of:*

Succeeds Elijah ... 1 Kin. 19:16
Follows Elijah ... 1 Kin. 19:19-21
Sees Elijah translated ... 2 Kin. 2:1-12
Is recognized as a prophet ... 2 Kin. 2:13-22
Mocked ... 2 Kin. 2:23-25
Deals with kings ... 2 Kin. 3:11-20
Helps two women ... 2 Kin. 4:1-17

B. *Miracles of:*

Divides Jordan ... 2 Kin. 2:14
Purifies water ... 2 Kin. 2:19-22
Increases widow's oil ... 2 Kin. 4:1-7
Raises Shunammite's son ... 2 Kin. 4:18-37
Neutralizes poison ... 2 Kin. 4:38-41
Multiplies bread ... 2 Kin. 4:42-44
Heals Naaman the leper ... 2 Kin. 5:1-19
Inflicts Gehazi with leprosy ... 2 Kin. 5:26, 27
Causes iron to float ... 2 Kin. 6:6
Reveals secret counsels ... 2 Kin. 6:8-12
Opens servant's eyes ... 2 Kin. 6:13-17
Strikes Syrian army with blindness ... 2 Kin. 6:18-23

C. *Prophecies of:*

Birth of a child ... 2 Kin. 4:16
Abundance ... 2 Kin. 7:1
King's death ... 2 Kin. 7:2
Great famine ... 2 Kin. 8:1-3
Ben-hadad's death ... 2 Kin. 8:7-15
Joash's victories ... 2 Kin. 13:14-19

Elishah—*God is salvation*

Son of Javan ... Gen. 10:4

Elishama—*God has heard*

1. Son of Ammihud ... Num. 1:10
   Ancestor of Joshua ... 1 Chr. 7:26
2. Man of Judah ... 1 Chr. 2:41
3. Son of David ... 1 Chr. 3:1, 5, 6
   Also called Elishua ... 2 Sam. 5:15
4. Another son of David ... 2 Sam. 5:16
5. Teaching priest ... 2 Chr. 17:7, 8
6. Scribe ... Jer. 36:12, 20, 21

Elishaphat—*God has judged*

Captain ... 2 Chr. 23:1

Elisheba—*God is an oath*

Wife of Aaron ... Ex. 6:23

Elishua—*God is salvation*

Son of David ... 2 Sam. 5:15
Called Elishama ... 1 Chr. 3:6

Eliud—*God is mighty*

Father of Eleazar ... Matt. 1:14, 15

Elizaphan—*God has concealed*

1. Chief of Kohathites ... Num. 3:30
   Heads family ... 1 Chr. 15:5, 8
   Family consecrated ... 2 Chr. 29:12-16
2. Son of Parnach ... Num. 34:25

Elizur—*God is a rock*

Reubenite warrior ... Num. 1:5

Elkanah—*God has possessed*

1. Father of Samuel ... 1 Sam. 1:1-23
2. Son of Korah ... Ex. 6:24
   Escapes judgment ... Num. 26:11
3. Levite ... 1 Chr. 6:23-36
4. Descendant of Korah ... 1 Chr. 6:22, 23
5. Levite ... 1 Chr. 9:16
6. Korahite warrior ... 1 Chr. 12:1, 6
7. Officer under Ahaz ... 2 Chr. 28:7
8. Doorkeeper of the ark ... 1 Chr. 15:23

Elkoshite—*an inhabitant of Elkosh*

Descriptive of Nahum ... Nah. 1:1

Ellasar

Place in Babylon ... Gen. 14:1, 9

Elmodam

Ancestor of Christ ... Luke 3:28

SUBJECT	REFERENCE
Elnaam—*God is pleasantness*	
Father of two warriors	1 Chr. 11:26, 46
Elnathan—*God has given*	
1. Father of Nehushta	2 Kin. 24:8
Goes to Egypt	Jer. 26:22
Entreats with king	Jer. 36:25
2, 3, 4. Three Levites	Ezra 8:16
Eloi (same as Eli)	
Jesus' cry	Mark 15:34
Elon—*oak*	
1. Hittite	Gen. 26:34
2. Son of Zebulun	Gen. 46:14
3. Judge in Israel	Judg. 12:11, 12
4. Town of Dan	Josh. 19:43
Elon-beth-hanan—*oak of house of grace*	
Town of Dan	1 Kin. 4:9
Elonites—*belonging to Elon*	
Descendants of Elon	Num. 26:26
Eloquent—*fluent and persuasive in speech*	
Moses is not	Ex. 4:10
Paul rejects	1 Cor. 2:1, 4, 5
Apollos is	Acts 18:24
False prophets boast of	2 Pet. 2:18
Elpaal—*God has wrought*	
Benjamite	1 Chr. 8:11-18
Elpalet—*God of deliverance*	
Son of David	1 Chr. 14:3, 5
Same as Eliphelet	1 Chr. 3:6
El-paran—*oak of Paran*	
Place in Canaan	Gen. 14:6
Eltekeh—*God is dread*	
City of Dan	Josh. 19:44
Assigned to Levites	Josh. 21:23
Eltekon—*founded by God*	
Village in Judah	Josh. 15:59
Eltolad—*kindred of God*	
Town in Judah	Josh. 15:21, 30
Assigned to Simeonites	Josh. 19:4
Called Tolad	1 Chr. 4:29
Elul—*vine*	
Sixth month of Hebrew year	Neh. 6:15
Eluzai—*God is my defense*	
Ambidextrous warrior of David	1 Chr. 12:1, 5
Elymas—*a wise man*	
Arabic name of Bar-jesus, a false prophet	Acts 13:6-12
Elzabad—*God has bestowed*	
1. Gadite warrior	1 Chr. 12:8, 12
2. Korahite Levite	1 Chr. 26:7, 8
Elzaphan (contraction of Elizaphan)	
Son of Uzziel	Ex. 6:22
Given instructions by Moses	Lev. 10:4
Emancipation—*a setting free from slavery*	
Of Hebrew nation	Ex. 12:29-42
Of Hebrew slaves	Ex. 21:2
In the year of jubilee	Lev. 25:8-41
Proclaimed by Zedekiah	Jer. 34:8-11
By Cyrus	2 Chr. 36:23 Ezra 1:1-4
Emasculation—*castration*	
Penalty of	Deut. 23:1
Embalming—*preserving a corpse from decay*	
Unknown to Abraham	Gen. 23:4
Practiced in Egypt	Gen. 50:2, 3, 26
Manner of, among Jews	2 Chr. 16:14
Limitation of	John 11:39, 44
Forbidden by Law	Num. 5:1-4 Num. 19:11-22
Embroider—*to decorate by needlework*	
In tabernacle curtains	Ex. 26:1, 36
Bezaleel and Aholiab inspired in	Ex. 35:30-35
On Sisera's garments	Judg. 5:30
Worn by women	Ps. 45:14
Emerald—*a precious stone of the beryl variety*	
In Tyre's trade	Ezek. 27:16
Used for ornamentation	Ezek. 28:13
Foundation stone	Rev. 21:19
Emerods—*hemorrhoids; boils; tumors*	
Threatened as a curse	Deut. 28:27
Inflicted upon Philistines	1 Sam. 5:6-12
Emims—*terrors*	
Giant race of Anakim east of the Dead Sea	Gen. 14:5
Emmaus—*hot spring*	
Town near Jerusalem	Luke 24:13-18
Emmor	
Father of Shechem	Acts 7:16
Emotion—*a person's response to living situations*	
A. *Objects of:*	
Self	Job 3:1-26
Nation	Ps. 137:1-6
Family	Gen. 49:1-28
Mate	1 Sam. 25:24, 25
Foreigners	Ruth 1:16-18
B. *Kinds of:*	
Conviction	Acts 2:37
Contempt	1 Sam. 17:42-44
Despondency	1 Kin. 19:4-10
Disappointment	Luke 18:23
Disgust	Neh. 4:1-3
Envy	1 Sam. 17:28
Fear	1 Kin. 19:1-3
Flattery	1 Sam. 25:23-31
Hate	Acts 7:54, 57
Joy	Luke 15:22-24
Love	Ex. 32:26-29
Loyalty	2 Sam. 18:32, 33
Regret	Luke 16:27-31
Revenge	Gen. 27:41-45
Sorrow	2 Sam. 12:13-19
C. *Control of:*	
Unsuppressed	1 Sam. 20:30-33
Suppressed	Is. 36:21
Uncontrollable	Mark 5:4, 5
Controlled	Mark 5:19
Employees—*those who work for others*	
A. *Types of:*	
Diligent	Gen. 30:27-31
Discontented	Matt. 20:1-15
Lazy	Job 7:1-3
Unworthy	Matt. 21:33-41
B. *Duties of:*	
Contentment	Luke 3:14
Fulfilling terms	Matt. 20:1-15
Respect	1 Tim. 6:1
Diligence	Prov. 22:29
C. *Rights of:*	
Equal wage	Matt. 10:10
Prompt payment	Lev. 19:13
Good treatment	Ruth 2:4
D. *Oppression of, by:*	
Arbitrary changes	Gen. 31:38-42
Unscrupulous landowners	James 5:4-6
Employers—*those who hire others to work for them*	
Must not oppress	Deut. 24:14
Must be considerate	Job 31:31
Must be just and fair	Col. 4:1
Employment—*the state of one who has regular work*	
A. *Usefulness of:*	
Manifest graces	Prov. 31:10-31
Provided food	2 Thess. 3:7-12
B. *Examples of:*	
Adam	Gen. 2:15
Workmen after the exile	Neh. 4:15-23
Paul	1 Thess. 2:9-11
Enam—*two springs*	
Village of Judah	Josh. 15:20, 34
Enan—*having fountains*	
Father of Ahira	Num. 1:15
Encampment—*a resting place on a march or journey*	
Israel's, on leaving Egypt	Ex. 13:20
At Sinai	Ex. 18:5
List of	Num. 33:10-46
In battle	Josh. 10:5, 31, 34
Enchantment—*the practice of magical arts*	
A. *Practiced in:*	
Egypt	Ex. 7:11
Judah	2 Kin. 17:17
Babylon	Ezek. 21:21
Chaldea	Dan. 5:11
Greece	Acts 16:16
Asia Minor	Acts 19:13, 19
B. *Futility of:*	
Vanity of	Is. 47:9-15
Inability of	Ex. 7:11, 12
Abomination of	Deut. 18:9-12
C. *Examples of:*	
Simon	Acts 8:9
Bar-jesus	Acts 13:6-12
Slave-girl	Acts 16:16
Vagabond Jews	Acts 19:13
Jannes and Jambres	2 Tim. 3:8
Encouragement—*inspiration to hope and service*	
A. *Needed by:*	
Prophets	1 Kin. 19:1-19
People	Neh. 4:17-23
Servants	2 Kin. 6:15-17
Kings	2 Kin. 11:10-21
Heathen	Dan. 6:18-23
B. *Agents of:*	
Angels	Gen. 32:1, 2
A dream	Gen. 28:11-22
God's promises	Josh. 1:1-9
A friend	1 Sam. 23:16-18
A relative	Esth. 4:13-16
Paul	Acts 27:21-26
C. *Reasons for, Christ is:*	
Risen	1 Cor. 15:11-58
Present	Matt. 28:19, 20
Coming	Luke 21:25-28
Encumbrance—*that which hinders freedom of action*	
Universal	Gen. 3:16-19
Imposed	Gen. 32:31, 32
Perpetual	Matt. 27:25
Moral	Titus 1:12, 13
Spiritual	Heb. 12:1
End of the world	
A. *Events connected with:*	
Day of salvation ended	Matt. 24:3, 14
Harvest of souls	Matt. 13:36-43
Defeat of man of sin	2 Thess. 2:1-12
Judgment	Matt. 25:31-46
Destruction of world	2 Thess. 1:6-10
B. *Coming of:*	
Denied by scoffers	2 Pet. 3:3-5
Preceded by lawlessness	Matt. 24:12
Preceded by apostasy	Luke 18:8
Without warning	Matt. 24:37-42
With fire	2 Thess. 1:7-10
C. *Attitude toward:*	
Watchfulness	Matt. 25:1-13
Industry	Matt. 25:14-30
Hopefulness	Luke 21:25-28
Holy living	Rom. 13:12-14 2 Pet. 3:11, 14
Seeking the lost	2 Pet. 3:9, 15
Waiting for eternity	2 Pet. 3:13 Rev. 21:1
En-dor—*fountain of habitation*	
Town of Manasseh	Josh. 17:11
Site of memorable defeat	Ps. 83:9, 10
Home of notorious witch	1 Sam. 28:1-10
Endow—*to purchase*	
Required to wed	Ex. 22:16
Endurance, blessedness of	
Commanded	Matt. 10:22 2 Tim. 2:3
Exemplified	2 Tim. 2:10 Heb. 10:32, 33
Rewarded	2 Tim. 3:11 James 1:12

SUBJECT ... REFERENCE

Enduring things
God's faithfulness ... Ps. 89:33
God's mercies ... Ps. 103:17
God's Word ... Matt. 24:35
Spiritual nourishment ... John 6:27
Spiritual rewards ... 1 Cor. 3:14
Graces ... 1 Cor. 13:13
The real things ... 2 Cor. 4:18
God's kingdom ... Heb. 12:27, 28

En-eglaim—*fountain of calf*
Place near the Dead Sea ... Ezek. 47:10

Enemies—*foes; adversaries; opponents*
A. *Applied to:*
Foreign nations ... Gen. 14:20
Israel ... Mic. 2:8
Gentiles ... Col. 1:21
Unregenerate men ... Rom. 5:10
The world ... Matt. 22:44
Satan ... Matt. 13:39
Death ... 1 Cor. 15:26
B. *Characteristics of, hate for:*
God ... Rom. 1:30
The Gospel ... 1 Thess. 2:14-18
The light ... John 3:19-21
C. *Examples of:*
Amalek against Israel ... Ex. 17:8-16
Saul against David ... 1 Sam. 18:29
Jezebel against Elijah ... 1 Kin. 19:1, 2
Ahab against Elijah ... 1 Kin. 21:20
Haman against the Jews ... Esth. 3:10
Jews against Gentiles ... Acts 22:21, 22
Jews against Christians ... Acts 7:54-60
D. *Christian attitude toward:*
Overcome by kindness ... 1 Sam. 26:18-21
Do not curse ... Job 31:29, 30
Feed ... Rom. 12:20
Love ... Luke 6:27, 35
Forgive ... Matt. 6:12-15
Pray for ... Luke 23:34

Energy—*effective force to perform work*
A. *God's, in nature:*
Creative ... Job 38:4-11
Beyond natural law ... Job 26:12
Maintains matter ... Heb. 1:3
B. *God's, in man:*
To be witnesses ... Acts 1:8
For abundant living ... Rom. 15:13
For miracles ... Rom. 15:14
To raise dead ... 1 Cor. 6:14
2 Cor. 13:4

En-gannim—*fountains of gardens*
1. Village of Judah ... Josh. 15:34
2. Border town of Issachar ... Josh. 19:21
Assigned to Levites ... Josh. 21:29

En-gedi—*fountain of a kid*
May have been originally called Hazazon-tamar ... 2 Chr. 20:2
Occupied by the Amorites ... Gen. 14:7
Assigned to Judah ... Josh. 15:62
David's hiding place ... 1 Sam. 23:29
Noted for vineyards ... Song 1:14

Engine—*a machine designed for a distinct purpose*
Shooting arrows ... 2 Chr. 26:15

Engraving—*cutting or carving on some hard substance*
Stone set in priest's breastplate ... Ex. 28:9-11, 21
Bezaleel, inspired in ... Ex. 35:30-33
Of a seal ... Ex. 28:21
Of a signet ... Ex. 39:6
Of cherubim ... 1 Kin. 6:29

En-haddah—*swift fountain*
Frontier village of Issachar ... Josh. 19:17, 21

En-hakkore—*fountain of him who called*
Miraculous spring ... Judg. 15:14-19

En-hazor—*fountain of a village*
City of Naphtali ... Josh. 19:32, 37

Enjoyment—*satisfaction in something*
A. *Of material things:*
Depends upon obedience ... Deut. 7:9-15
Withheld for disobedience ... Hag. 1:3-11
Must not trust in ... Luke 12:16-21
Cannot fully satisfy ... Eccl. 2:1-11
B. *Of spiritual things:*
Abundant ... 1 Tim. 6:17
Never-ending ... Is. 58:11
Satisfying ... Is. 55:1, 2
Internal ... John 7:37-39
For God's people only ... Is. 65:22-24
Complete in heaven ... Ps. 16:11

Enlargement—*extension in quantity or quality*
Japheth's territory ... Gen. 9:27
Israel's prosperity ... Ex. 34:24
Solomon's kingdom ... 1 Kin. 4:20-25
Solomon's wisdom ... 1 Kin. 4:29-34
Pharisaical hypocrisy ... Matt. 23:5
Spiritual: Relationship ... 2 Cor. 6:11, 13
Knowledge ... Eph. 1:15-19
Opportunity ... Is. 54:1-3

Enlightenment, spiritual
A. *Source of:*
From God ... Ps. 18:28
Through God's Word ... Ps. 19:8
By prayer ... Eph. 1:18
By God's ministers ... Acts 26:18
B. *Degrees of:*
Partial now ... 1 Cor. 13:9-12
Hindered by sin ... 1 Cor. 2:14
Complete in heaven ... Is. 60:19

Enoch—*dedicated*
1. Son of Cain ... Gen. 4:17
2. City built by Cain ... Gen. 4:17
3. Father of Methuselah ... Gen. 5:21
Walks with God ... Gen. 5:22
Taken up to heaven ... Gen. 5:24
Prophecy of, cited ... Jude 14, 15

Enos, Enosh—*mortal*
Grandson of Adam ... Gen. 4:25, 26
Son of Seth ... Gen. 5:6-11
Ancestor of Christ ... Luke 3:38
Genealogy of ... 1 Chr. 1:1

En-rimmon—*fount of pomegranates*
Reinhabited after the exile ... Neh. 11:29
Same as Rimmon ... Zech. 14:10

En-rogel—*the fuller's fountain*
Fountain outside Jerusalem ... 2 Sam. 17:17
On Benjamin's boundary ... Josh. 18:11, 16
Seat of Adonijah's plot ... 1 Kin. 1:5-9

En-shemesh—*fountain of the sun*
Spring and town near Jericho ... Josh. 15:7

Ensign—*a banner or standard*
A. *Used literally of:*
Hosts ... Num. 1:52
Enemy ... Ps. 74:4, 5
B. *Used figuratively of:*
Enemy force ... Is. 5:26
God's uplifted hand ... Is. 31:9
Christ ... Is. 11:10, 12

En-tappuah—*fountain of the apple tree*
Town of Ephraim ... Josh. 17:7, 8

Entertainment—*affording an enjoyable occasion*
A. *Occasions of:*
Child's weaning ... Gen. 21:8
Ratifying covenants ... Gen. 31:54
King's coronation ... 1 Kin. 1:9, 18, 19
National deliverance ... Esth. 9:17-19
Marriage ... Matt. 22:2
Return of loved ones ... Luke 15:23-25
B. *Features of:*
Invitations sent ... Luke 14:16
Preparations made ... Matt. 22:4
Helped by servants ... John 2:5
Under a leader ... John 2:8, 9
Often with music ... Luke 15:25
Sometimes out of control ... 1 Sam. 25:36
Unusual ... Heb. 13:2

Enthusiasm—*a spirit of intense zeal*
Caleb's ... Num. 13:30-33
Phinehas' ... Num. 25:7-13
David's ... 2 Sam. 6:12-22
Saul's (Paul's) ... Acts 9:1, 2
Paul's ... Phil. 3:7-14

Enticers—*those who allure to evil*
A. *Means of:*
Man ... Ex. 22:16
Spirit ... 2 Chr. 18:20
Sinners ... Prov. 1:10
Lusts ... James 1:14
Human wisdom ... 1 Cor. 2:4
B. *Reasons proposed:*
Turn from God ... Deut. 13:6-8
Obtain secrets ... Judg. 16:5
Defeat a king ... 2 Chr. 18:4-34
Commit a sin ... James 1:14

Envy—*resentment against another's success*
A. *Characterized as:*
Powerful ... Prov. 27:4
Dominant in unregenerate nature ... Rom. 1:29
Of the flesh ... Gal. 5:21
Source of evil ... 1 Tim. 6:4
B. *The evil of, among Christians:*
Hinders growth ... 1 Pet. 2:1, 2
C. *Examples of:*
Philistines ... Gen. 26:14
Joseph's brothers ... Gen. 37:5, 11
Aaron and Miriam ... Num. 12:2
Korah ... Num. 16:3
David ... Ps. 73:3, 17-20
Haman ... Esth. 5:13
Chief priests ... Mark 15:10
The Jews ... Acts 13:45

Epaenetus
Addressed by Paul ... Rom. 16:5

Epaphras
Leader of the Colossian church ... Col. 1:7, 8
Suffers as a prisoner in Rome ... Philem. 23

Epaphroditus—*lovely, charming*
Messenger from Philippi ... Phil. 2:25-27
Brings a gift to Paul ... Phil. 4:18

Ephah (I)—*dark one*
1. Son of Midian ... Gen. 25:4
2. Concubine of Caleb ... 1 Chr. 2:46
3. Son of Jahdai ... 1 Chr. 2:47

Ephah (II)—*a measure*
Dry measure ... Ex. 16:36
Used for measuring barley ... Ruth 2:17

Ephai—*bird-like*
Netophathite ... Jer. 40:8

Epher—*young deer*
1. Son of Midian ... Gen. 25:4
2. Man of Judah ... 1 Chr. 4:17
3. Chief in Manasseh ... 1 Chr. 5:23, 24

Ephes-dammim—*end of bloods*
Philistine encampment ... 1 Sam. 17:1
Called Pasdammin ... 1 Chr. 11:13

Ephesians, the Epistle to the—*a book of the New Testament*
Written by Paul ... Eph. 1:1
Election ... Eph. 1:4-6
Salvation by grace ... Eph. 1:7, 8
Eph. 2:8
Headship of Christ ... Eph. 4:15, 16

Ephesus—*a city of Asia Minor*
Site of Jewish synagogue ... Acts 18:19
Paul visits ... Acts 18:19-21
Miracles done here ... Acts 19:11-23
Demetrius stirs up riot in ... Acts 19:24-29
Elders of, addressed by Paul at Miletus ... Acts 20:17-38
Letter sent to ... Eph. 1:1
Paul sends Tychicus ... Eph. 6:21
Paul leaves Timothy ... 1 Tim. 1:3
One of seven churches ... Rev. 1:11

Ephlal—*judgment*
A descendant of Judah ... 1 Chr. 2:37

Ephod—*a vest*
1. Worn by:
The high priest ... Ex. 28:4-35

SUBJECT — REFERENCE

Samuel .... 1 Sam. 2:18
David .... 2 Sam. 6:14
Used in asking counsel of God .... 1 Sam. 23:9-12
Used in idolatry .... Judg. 8:27
2. Father of Hanniel .... Num. 34:23

Ephphatha—*be opened*
Christ's command .... Mark 7:34

Ephraim—*doubly fruitful*
1. Joseph's younger son .... Gen. 41:52
Obtains Jacob's blessing .... Gen. 48:8-20
2. Tribe of Ephraim .... Josh. 16:4, 10
Predictions concerning .... Gen. 48:20
Large number of .... Num. 1:33
Joshua, an Ephraimite .... Josh. 19:50
Territory assigned to .... Josh. 16:1-10
Make Canaanites slaves .... Judg. 1:29
Assist Deborah .... Judg. 5:14, 15
Assist Gideon .... Judg. 7:24, 25
Quarrel with Gideon .... Judg. 8:1-3
Quarrel with Jephthah .... Judg. 12:1-4
Attend David's coronation .... 1 Chr. 12:30
Leading tribe of kingdom of Israel .... Is. 7:2-17
Provoke God by sin .... Hos. 12:7-14
Many of, join Judah .... 2 Chr. 15:9
Beth-el, idolatrous city of .... 1 Kin. 12:29
Captivity of, predicted .... Hos. 9:3-17
Mercy promised to .... Jer. 31:9, 20
Messiah promised to .... Zech. 9:9-13
3. Hill country in Palestine .... 1 Sam. 1:1
4. Forest where Absalom was killed .... 2 Sam. 18:6-18
5. Gate in Jerusalem .... 2 Kin. 14:13
6. Town to which Jesus withdrew .... John 11:54
7. Ten tribes considered as a unit .... Hos. 4:16, 17

Ephratah, Ephrath—*fruitfulness*
1. Ancient name of Bethlehem .... Ruth 4:11
Prophecy concerning .... Mic. 5:2
2. Land of Palestine .... Ps. 132:6
3. Wife of Caleb .... 1 Chr. 2:19, 50

Ephrathite
1. Inhabitant of Beth-lehem (Ephrath) .... Ruth 1:2
2. David was the son of .... 1 Sam. 17:12
Also called Ephraimites .... Judg. 12:5, 6

Ephron—*fawn-like*
1. Hittite who sold Machpelah to Abraham .... Gen. 23:8-20
2. Landmarks of Judah .... Josh. 15:9

Epicureans—*followers of Epicurus*
Sect of pleasure-loving philosophers .... Acts 17:18

Equality of man
A. *Seen in same:*
Creation .... Acts 17:26
Guilt .... Rom. 5:12-21
Sinfulness .... Rom. 3:10-19
Salvation .... John 3:16
Judgment .... 2 Cor. 5:10
B. *Consistent with:*
God's plan .... Rom. 9:6-33
Different talents .... Matt. 25:14-30
Different gifts .... 1 Cor. 12:4-31
Different functions .... Eph. 5:22-33; Eph. 6:1-9
Rule .... Ps. 9:8

Equity—*justice*
Jehovah judges with .... Ps. 98:9

Er—*watching*
1. Son of Judah .... Gen. 38:1-7; Gen. 46:12
2. Descendant of Judah .... 1 Chr. 4:21
3. Ancestor of Christ .... Luke 3:28

Eran—*watchful*
Founder of the Eranites .... Num. 26:36

Erastus—*beloved*
1. Paul's friend at Ephesus .... Acts 19:22; 2 Tim. 4:20
2. Treasurer of Corinth .... Rom. 16:23
May be same person as 1.

Erech—*size*
City of Shinar .... Gen. 10:10

Eri—*watching*
Son of Gad .... Gen. 46:16
Founder of the Erites .... Num. 26:16

Error—*a departure from the truth*
Deceptive .... 2 Tim. 3:13
False .... Matt. 24:4, 11
Produces misunderstanding .... Matt. 22:29
Against Christ .... 1 John 4:1-6
Sign of the end .... 1 Tim. 4:1

Esar-haddon—*Ashur has given a brother*
Son of Sennacherib; king of Assyria (681–669 B.C.) .... 2 Kin. 19:37

Esau—*hairy*
Son of Isaac .... Rom. 9:11-13
Hairy .... Gen. 25:25
Hunter .... Gen. 25:27
Isaac's favorite son .... Gen. 25:28
Sells his birthright .... Gen. 25:29-34
Unable to repent .... Heb. 12:16, 17
Marries two women .... Gen. 26:34
Deprived of blessing .... Gen. 27:1-40
Hates his brother Jacob .... Gen. 27:41-45
Reconciled to Jacob .... Gen. 33:1-17
With Jacob, buries his father .... Gen. 35:29
Descendants of .... Gen. 36:1-43
Ancestor of Edomites .... Jer. 49:7, 8
Prophecy concerning .... Obad. 18

Escape—*to flee from*
A. *Physical things:*
Flood .... Gen. 7:7, 8
City of destruction .... Gen. 19:15-30
Mob .... Luke 4:28-30
Insane king .... 1 Sam. 19:9-18
Wicked queen .... 1 Kin. 11:1-3
Assassination .... Esth. 2:21-23
Hanging .... Esth. 5:14
Prison .... Acts 5:18-20
Sinking ship .... Acts 27:30-44
B. *Spiritual things:*
Sin .... Gen. 39:10-12
Destruction .... Luke 21:36
Corruption .... 2 Pet. 1:4
God's wrath .... 1 Thess. 1:9, 10
The great tribulation .... Rev. 7:13-17

Eschatology—*teaching dealing with final destiny*
A. *In Old Testament:*
Judgment .... Is. 2:12-22
Messianic kingdom .... Jer. 23:4-18; Jer. 33:14-17
B. *In New Testament:*
Coming of Christ .... Matt. 24; Luke 21:5-36
Resurrection of dead .... 1 Cor. 15:51-58; 1 Thess. 4:13-18
Destruction of earth .... 2 Pet. 3:10-13
Reign of Christ .... Rev. 20:4, 6

Esek—*strife*
A well in Gerar .... Gen. 26:20

Esh-baal—*man of Baal*
Son of Saul .... 1 Chr. 8:33

Eshban—*wise man*
Son of Dishon .... Gen. 36:26

Eshcol—*cluster of grapes*
1. Brother of Aner and Mamre .... Gen. 14:13, 24
2. Valley near Hebron .... Num. 13:22-27; Deut. 1:24

Eshean—*support*
City of Judah .... Josh. 15:52

Eshek—*oppression*
Descendant of Saul .... 1 Chr. 8:39

Eshkalonites
Natives of Ashkelon .... Josh. 13:3

Eshtaol—*a way*
Town of Judah .... Josh. 15:20, 33
Assigned to Danites .... Josh. 19:40, 41
Near Samson's home and burial site .... Judg. 16:31

Eshtaulites
Inhabitants of Eshtaol .... 1 Chr. 2:53

Eshtemoa, Eshtemoh—*obedience*
Town of Judah .... Josh. 15:20, 50
Assigned to Levites .... Josh. 21:14
David sends spoils to .... 1 Sam. 30:26, 28

Eshton—*restful*
Man of Judah .... 1 Chr. 4:1-12

Esli—*reserved*
Ancestor of Christ .... Luke 3:25

Establish—*a permanent condition*
A. *Of earthly things:*
Kingdom .... 2 Chr. 17:5
Festival .... Esth. 9:21
B. *Of spiritual things:*
Messiah's kingdom .... 2 Sam. 7:13
God's Word .... Ps. 119:38
Our:
Hearts .... 1 Thess. 3:13
Faith .... Col. 2:7
Works .... 2 Thess. 2:17
Lives .... 1 Pet. 5:10
C. *Accomplished by:*
God .... 2 Cor. 1:21, 22

Estrangement from God
Caused by:
Natural status .... Esth. 2:11, 12
Adam's sin .... Gen. 3:8-11, 24
Personal sin .... Ps. 51:9-12
National sin .... Jer. 2:14-16

Esther—*star*
Daughter of Abihail .... Esth. 2:15
Mordecai's cousin .... Esth. 2:7, 15
Selected for harem .... Esth. 2:7-16
Chosen queen .... Esth. 2:17, 18
Seeks to help Mordecai .... Esth. 4:4-6
Told of Haman's plot .... Esth. 4:7-9
Sends message to Mordecai .... Esth. 4:10-12
Told to act .... Esth. 4:13, 14
Seeks Mordecai's aid .... Esth. 4:15-17
Appears before Ahasuerus .... Esth. 5:1-5
Invites Ahasuerus to banquet .... Esth. 5:4-8
Reveals Haman's plot .... Esth. 7:1-7
Given Haman's house .... Esth. 8:1, 2
Secures change of edict .... Esth. 8:3-6
Makes further request .... Esth. 9:12, 13
With Mordecai, institutes Purim .... Esth. 9:29-32

Estrangement from God

Etam—*Wild beasts' lair*
1. Village of Simeon .... 1 Chr. 4:32
2. Rock where Samson took refuge .... Judg. 15:8-19
3. Town of Judah .... 2 Chr. 11:6

Eternal, everlasting—*without end*
A. *Applied to Trinity:*
God .... Ps. 90:2
Christ .... Prov. 8:23
Holy Spirit .... Heb. 9:14
B. *Applied to God's attributes:*
Home .... Eccl. 12:5
Power .... Rom. 1:20
Covenant .... Is. 55:3
Gospel .... Rev. 14:6
Counsels .... Eph. 3:10, 11
Righteousness .... Ps. 119:142, 144
Kingdom .... Ps. 145:13
Lovingkindness .... Ps. 100:5
Love .... Jer. 31:3
Father .... Is. 9:6
C. *Applied to the believer:*
Comfort .... 2 Thess. 2:16
Life .... John 3:15
Redemption .... Heb. 9:12
Salvation .... Heb. 5:9
Inheritance .... Heb. 9:15
Glory .... 1 Pet. 5:10
Kingdom .... 2 Pet. 1:11
Reward .... John 4:36

SUBJECT — REFERENCE

Name .... Is. 56:5
Glory .... 2 Tim. 2:10
Light .... Is. 60:19, 20
Joy .... Is. 51:11
Dwellings .... Luke 16:9
Purpose .... Eph. 3:11

D. *Applied to the wicked:*
Damnation .... Mark 3:29
Judgment .... Heb. 6:2
Punishment .... Matt. 25:46
Destruction .... 2 Thess. 1:9
Contempt .... Dan. 12:2
Bonds .... Jude 6
Fire .... Matt. 25:41
Sin .... Mark 3:29

Eternity—*time without end mentioned once*
God's habitation .... Is. 57:15

Etham—*sea bound*
Israel's encampment .... Ex. 13:20

Ethan—*perpetuity*
1. One noted for wisdom .... 1 Kin. 4:31
2. Levite .... 1 Chr. 6:44
3. Ancestor of Asaph .... 1 Chr. 6:42, 43

Ethanim—*incessant rains*
Seventh month in the Hebrew year .... 1 Kin. 8:2

Ethbaal—*with Baal*
Father of Jezebel .... 1 Kin. 16:31

Ether—*plenty*
Town of Judah .... Josh. 15:42

Ethics—*a system setting forth standards of right conduct*
Perversion of .... Rom. 1:19-32
Law of .... Rom. 2:14-16
Summary of Christian .... Rom. 12:1-21

Ethiopia (Cush)—*burnt face*
Country south of Egypt .... Ezek. 29:10
Home of the Sons of Ham .... Gen. 10:6
Famous for minerals .... Job 28:19
Merchandise of .... Is. 45:14
Wealth of .... Is. 43:3
Militarily strong .... 2 Chr. 12:3
Anguished people .... Ezek. 30:4-9
Defeated by Asa .... 2 Chr. 14:9-15
Subdued .... Dan. 11:43
Prophecies against .... Is. 20:1-6
God's love for .... Amos 9:7
Hopeful promise .... Ps. 68:31

Ethiopians—*descendants of Cush*
Skin of, unchangeable .... Jer. 13:23
Moses' marriage to .... Num. 12:1
Ebed-melech saves Jeremiah .... Jer. 38:7
Eunuch converted .... Acts 8:26-40

Ethnan—*hire*
Judahite .... 1 Chr. 4:5-7

Ethni—*liberal*
Levite .... 1 Chr. 6:41

Eubulus—*prudent*
Christian at Rome .... 2 Tim. 4:21

Eucharist (see Lord's Supper)

Eunice—*blessed with victory*
Mother of Timothy .... 2 Tim. 1:5

Eunuch—*an officer or official, emasculated*

A. *Rules concerning:*
Excluded from congregation .... Deut. 23:1
Given promise .... Is. 56:3-5

B. *Duties of:*
Guard .... Gen. 37:36
Servant .... Gen. 40:2, 7
Attendant .... Dan. 1:3, 7, 10, 11
Keeper of harem .... Esth. 2:3, 14
Treasurer .... Acts 8:27

Euodias—*good journey*
Christian woman at Philippi .... Phil. 4:2

Euphrates—*that which makes fruitful*
River of Eden .... Gen. 2:14
Assyria bounded by .... 2 Kin. 23:29
Babylon on .... Jer. 51:13, 36
Boundary of God's promise .... Gen. 15:18; 1 Kin. 4:21, 24
Persian boundary .... Ezek. 4:10, 11
Scene of battle .... Jer. 46:2, 6, 10
Exiled Jews weep there .... Ps. 137:1
Angels bound there .... Rev. 9:14

Euroclydon—*east wind*
Violent wind .... Acts 27:14

Eutychus—*fortunate*
Sleeps during Paul's sermon .... Acts 20:9
Restored to life .... Acts 20:12

Evangelism—*declaring Gospel to the unregenerate*

A. *Scope:*
To all nations .... Matt. 28:19, 20; Mark 16:15
House to house .... Acts 5:42
Always .... 1 Pet. 3:15
As ambassadors .... 2 Cor. 5:18-20

B. *Source:*
Jesus Christ .... Gal. 1:6-12
The Father .... John 6:44, 65
The Spirit .... Acts 1:8

Evangelist—*one who proclaims good news*
Distinct ministry .... Eph. 4:11
Applied to Philip .... Acts 21:8
Timothy works as .... 2 Tim. 4:5

Eve—*life*
Made from Adam's rib .... Gen. 2:18-22
Named by Adam .... Gen. 3:20
Deceived by Satan .... Gen. 3:1-24
Leads Adam to sin .... 1 Tim. 2:13, 14

Evening—*last hours of sunlight*
Labor ceases .... Judg. 19:16; Ruth 2:17
Workers paid .... Deut. 24:15
Ritual impurity ends .... Lev. 11:24-28; Num. 19:19
Meditation .... Gen. 24:63
Prayer .... Matt. 14:15, 23
Eating .... Luke 24:29, 30
Sacrifice .... Ex. 29:38-42; Num. 28:3-8

Evening sacrifice—*part of Israelite worship*
Ritual described .... Ex. 29:38-42
Part of continual offering .... Num. 28:3-8

Events, Biblical, classified

A. *Orginating, originating other events:*
Creation .... Gen. 1
Fall of man .... Rom. 5:12

B. *Epochal, introducing new period:*
Flood .... Gen. 6—8
The death of Christ .... Matt. 27:50, 51; Heb. 9

C. *Typical, foreshadowing some New Testament event:*
The Passover—Christ as Lamb .... Ex. 12; John 1:35-37; 1 Cor. 5:7, 8
Jonah and great fish—Christ's death and resurrection .... Jon. 1, 2; Matt. 12:38-41

D. *Prophetic, prophesying future events:*
Return from exile .... 2 Chr. 36:22, 23; Jer. 29:10
Destruction of Jerusalem .... Luke 19:41-44; Luke 21:20-24

E. *Redemptive, connected with man's salvation:*
Advent of Christ .... Luke 2:11; Gal. 4:4, 5
Death of Christ .... Matt. 20:28; Luke 24:44-47; 1 Tim. 1:15

F. *Unique, those without parallel:*
Creation .... Gen. 1
Virgin birth .... Matt. 1:18-25; Luke 1:30-37

G. *Miraculous, those produced by supernatural means:*
Plagues on Egypt .... Ex. 7—12
Crossing Red Sea .... Ex. 14—15
Fall of Jericho .... Josh. 6
Sun's standing still .... Josh. 10:12-14

H. *Judgmental, those judging people for sins:*
Flood .... 2 Pet. 2:5
Sodom and Gomorrah .... Gen. 19; 2 Pet. 2:6
Killing of Israelites .... Ex. 32:25-35; Num. 25:1-9

I. *Transforming, those producing a change:*
Christ's transformation .... Matt. 17:1-8
Conversion of Paul .... Acts 9; 1 Tim. 1:12-14
Believer's regeneration .... John 3:1-8; 2 Cor. 5:17

J. *Providential, those manifesting God's providence:*
Baby's cry .... Ex. 2:5-10
Joseph's being sold into Egypt .... Gen. 37:26-28; Gen. 45:1-8
King's sleepless night .... Esth. 6:1-10

K. *Confirmatory, those confirming some promise:*
Worship at Sinai .... Ex. 3:12
Aaron's rod .... Num. 17:1-11
Thunder and rain .... 1 Sam. 12:16-18
Sun's shadow moved backward .... 2 Kin. 20:8-11; Is. 38:1-8

L. *Promissory, those fulfilling some promise:*
Pentecost .... Joel 2:28-32; Acts 2
Spirit's coming .... Luke 24:49; Acts 1:4, 5, 8; Acts 2:1-4
Possession of land .... Gen. 15:18-21; Josh. 24:3, 11-19

M. *Eschatological, those connected with Christ's return:*
Doom of antichrist .... 2 Thess. 2:1-12
Resurrection and translation .... 1 Cor. 15:35-38; 1 Thess. 4:13-18
Resurrection and judgment .... Matt. 25:31-46; Acts 17:31; Rev. 20:11-15
Destruction of the world .... 2 Pet. 3:7-15

Evi—*desirous*
King of Midian .... Num. 31:8
Land of, assigned to Reuben .... Josh. 13:15, 21

Evidence—*ground for belief*

A. *Based upon:*
Testimony of witnesses .... Matt. 18:16
Personal testimony .... Acts 26:1-27
Fulfilled prophecy .... Matt. 1:22, 23
Supernatural testimony .... Matt. 3:17
New life .... 1 John 3:14

B. *Kinds of:*
Circumstantial .... Gen. 39:7-19
False .... Matt. 26:59-61
Fabricated .... Gen. 37:29-33
Confirmed .... Heb. 2:3, 4
Satanic .... 2 Thess. 2:9, 10
Indisputable .... 1 Cor. 15:1-19

C. *Need of:*
Confirm weak faith .... Luke 7:19, 22
Remove doubt .... John 20:24-29
Refute mockers .... 2 Pet. 3:3-7
Attest a messenger of God .... Ex. 8:18, 19
Produce faith .... John 20:30, 31

Evil—*that which is morally injurious*

A. *Origin of:*
Begins with Satan .... Is. 14:12-14
Enters world .... Rom. 5:12
Comes from man .... Matt. 15:18, 19
Inflamed by lust .... James 1:14

B. *Applied to:*
Men .... Matt. 12:35
Heart .... Jer. 17:9
Imaginations .... Gen. 6:5
Generation .... Matt. 12:39
Age .... Gal. 1:4
Our days .... Eph. 5:16
Conscience .... Heb. 10:22
Spirits .... Matt. 12:45

C. *Satan as "the evil one":*
Unregenerate belong to .... Matt. 13:38
Snatches away the good seed .... Matt. 13:19
World lies in .... 1 John 5:19
Lord safeguards against .... John 17:15
Christians can overcome .... 1 John 2:13

SUBJECT REFERENCE

D. *The Christian should guard against, evil:*
- Heart of unbelief ... Heb. 3:12
- Thoughts ... James 2:4
- Boastings ... James 4:16
- Things ... Rom. 12:9
- Deeds ... 2 John 9-11
- Person ... 1 Cor. 5:13
- Appearance ... 1 Thess. 5:22
- One (Satan) ... Eph. 6:16

Evil—*that which is physically harmful: floods, earthquakes, etc.*
- Created by God ... Is. 45:7
- Part of man's curse ... Gen. 3:17-19
- Men cry out against ... Rev. 9:18-21
- Can be misinterpreted ... Luke 13:1-3
- Foreseen by prudent ... Prov. 22:3
- Will continue to the end ... Matt. 24:6-8, 14
- Believers share in ... 2 Cor. 12:7-10
- To be borne patiently ... Job 2:7-10, James 5:11
- Prospects of relief from ... Rom. 8:18-39
- Relieved now by faith ... Heb. 3:17-19
- None in heaven ... Rev. 7:14-17

Evil companions (see Association)

Evil day
- Time of judgment ... Eccl. 12:1

Evildoers—*workers of evil*
- Christians wrongly called ... 1 Pet. 2:12
- Christians should not be ... 1 Pet. 4:15
- Christians cry against ... Ps. 119:115
- Punished by magistrates ... Rom. 13:1-4
- End of, certain ... Ps. 34:16

Evil eye
- Descriptive of a man's inner being ... Mark 7:21, 22
- Shown in attitudes ... Matt. 20:15

Evil-merodach—*man of Marduk*
- Babylonian king (562-560 B.C.); follows Nebuchadnezzar ... 2 Kin. 25:27-30

Evil speaking

A. *The evil of:*
- Sign of unregeneracy ... Ps. 10:7
- Aimed at righteous ... Ps. 64:2-5
- Defiles the whole body ... James 3:5-10
- Disrupts fellowship ... 3 John 9-11
- Severely condemned ... James 4:11
- Punished ... 1 Cor. 6:9, 10

B. *Not to be confused with:*
- Denunciation of vice ... Titus 1:12, 13
- Description of sinners ... Acts 13:9, 10
- Defense of the faith ... Jude 4, 8-16

Evil spirits—*demons*
- Sent upon King Saul ... 1 Sam. 16:14
- Ahab prompted to evil by ... 1 Kin. 22:1-23
- Cast out by Jesus ... Luke 7:21
- Cast out by Paul ... Acts 19:11, 12

Evolution—*development of life from lower to higher forms*

A. *Conflicts with:*
- God's description ... Gen. 1:26, 27, Gen. 2:21-25
- Moses' record ... Ex. 20:11, Deut. 4:32

B. *Not accepted by:*
- Jesus ... Matt. 19:4-6, Rom. 5:12-19
- Paul ... 1 Cor. 15:22, 45, 1 Tim. 2:13, 14

Exaltation—*the state of being raised up*

A. *Of evil man:*
- Originates in Satan ... Luke 4:5, 6
- Defies God ... 2 Kin. 18:28-35
- Perverts religion ... Dan. 11:36, 37
- Brings downfall ... Esth. 6:6-14
- Merits punishment ... 1 Kin. 16:1-4
- Displayed by Herod ... Acts 12:21-23
- Seen in antichrist ... 2 Thess. 2:4, 9

B. *Of good men:*
- Principle of ... Matt. 23:12
- Follows humility ... 1 Pet. 5:6
- Restrictions upon ... 2 Cor. 10:5
- Brings glory ... James 1:9
- False, brings sorrow ... 1 Cor. 4:6-14
- Final, in heaven ... Rev. 22:5

SUBJECT REFERENCE

C. *Of Christ:*
- Promised ... Ps. 2:8, 9
- Predicted by Christ ... Matt. 26:64
- The ascension ... Acts 2:33, 34
- Seen by Stephen ... Acts 7:55, 56
- Taught by the apostles ... Eph. 1:20-22
- Set forth as a reward ... Phil. 2:9-11
- Introduces priestly intercession ... Heb. 1:3

Examination of others
- Of Jesus ... Luke 23:13, 14
- Of Peter ... Acts 4:8, 9
- Of Paul ... Acts 22:24

Examination of self
- Sought by David ... Ps. 26:2
- Must precede Lord's Supper ... 1 Cor. 11:28
- Necessary for real faith ... 2 Cor. 13:5

Example—*a pattern to follow*

A. *Purposes of:*
- Set forth sin's punishment ... 2 Pet. 2:6
- Show unbelief's consequences ... Heb. 4:11
- Restrain from evil ... 1 Cor. 10:6, 11
- Illustrate humility ... John 13:15, 1 Pet. 3:5
- Exemplify patience ... James 5:10, 11, 1 Pet. 2:20-22
- Portray Christian conduct ... Phil. 3:17

B. *Of evil men:*
- Covetousness—Achan ... Josh. 7:20, 21
- Immorality—Eli's sons ... 1 Sam. 2:22-25
- Rebellion—Saul ... 1 Sam. 15:17-23
- Folly—Nabal ... 1 Sam. 25:25-37
- Idolatry—Jeroboam ... 1 Kin. 12:26-33

C. *Of good men:*
- Holy zeal—Phinehas ... Num. 25:7-13
- Faith—Caleb ... Josh. 14:6-15
- Fidelity—Joshua ... Josh. 24:15-25
- Courage—David ... 1 Sam. 17:32-37
- Holy life—Daniel ... Ezek. 14:14, 20
- Patience—Job ... James 5:10, 11
- Christian living—Paul ... Phil. 3:17

Example of Christ, the

A. *Virtues illustrated by:*
- Meekness ... Matt. 11:29
- Self-denial ... Matt. 16:24
- Love ... John 13:34
- Obedience ... John 15:10
- Benevolence ... 2 Cor. 8:7, 9
- Humility ... Phil. 2:5, 7
- Forgiveness ... Col. 3:13
- Suffering wrongfully ... 1 Pet. 2:21-23
- Purity ... 1 John 3:3

B. *The Christian approach to:*
- Progressive ... 2 Cor. 3:18
- Instructive ... Eph. 4:20-24
- Imitative ... 1 Pet. 2:21-23
- Perfective ... Rom. 8:29

Excitement—*something that stirs us emotionally*

A. *Causes of:*
- Great sin ... Ex. 32:17-20
- Great victory ... 1 Sam. 17:52
- God's power ... 1 Kin. 18:22-41
- King's coronation ... 2 Kin. 11:12-16
- Human destruction ... Esth. 9:1-11
- Handwriting on the wall ... Dan. 5:5-9
- Miracle ... Acts 19:13-29

B. *Time of:*
- The giving of the Law ... Heb. 12:18-21
- Christ's death ... Matt. 27:51-54
- Pentecost ... Acts 2:1-47
- Christ's return ... Luke 21:25-28

Exclusiveness—*setting boundaries against others*

A. *Christianity's, only one:*
- Door ... John 10:1, 7, 9
- Way ... John 14:6
- Salvation ... Acts 4:12

B. *The Bible's, only book:*
- Inspired ... 1 Tim. 3:16
- Revealing God ... Heb. 1:1
- Written to save men ... John 20:30, 31
- Containing true prophecies ... John 5:45-47

SUBJECT REFERENCE

Excommunication—*expulsion from membership in a body*

A. *Separation from:*
- Kingship ... 1 Sam. 16:1
- Foreigners ... Neh. 13:1-3
- Priesthood ... Neh. 13:27, 28

B. *Practice of:*
- To intimidate people ... John 9:19-23
- Against true Christians ... John 16:1, 2
- Against false teachers ... 2 John 10, 11

C. *Method of:*
- Described ... Matt. 18:15-17
- Illustrated ... 1 Cor. 5:1-13
- Perverted ... 3 John 9, 10

Excuse—*an invalid reason for neglect of duty*

A. *Nature of, blaming:*
- Wife ... Gen. 3:12
- The people ... 1 Sam. 15:20, 21
- God's mercy ... Jon. 4:1-4
- God's providence ... Num. 14:1-23

B. *Invalidity of:*
- Shown to Moses ... Ex. 3:10-12
- Proved to Gideon ... Judg. 6:36-40
- Made plain to Esther ... Esth. 4:13-17
- Illustrated by Christ ... Luke 14:16-24
- Relayed to Hell's inhabitants ... Luke 16:27-31
- Made evident to Thomas ... John 20:24-28

Exhortation—*encouraging others to commendable conduct*

A. *Objects of:*
- Call to repentance ... Luke 3:17, 18
- Continue in the faith ... Acts 14:22
- Convict gainsayers ... Titus 1:9
- Warn the unruly ... 1 Thess. 5:14
- Encourage soberness ... Titus 3:1
- Strengthen godliness ... 1 Thess. 4:1-6
- Stir up liberality ... 2 Cor. 9:5-7

B. *Office of:*
- Commended ... Rom. 12:8
- Part of the ministry ... Titus 2:15
- Needed in times ... 2 Tim. 4:2-5

C. *Nature of:*
- Daily duty ... Heb. 3:13
- For holiness ... 1 Thess. 2:3, 4
- Worthy of reception ... Heb. 13:22
- Belongs to all ... Heb. 10:25
- Special need of ... Jude 3, 4

Exile—*banished from one's native land*
- David ... 1 Sam. 21:10-15
- Jeroboam ... 1 Kin. 11:40
- Jeremiah ... Jer. 43:4-7
- Christ ... Matt. 2:13-15
- John ... Rev. 1:9
- Jehoiachin ... 2 Kin. 24:15
- Judah ... 2 Kin. 25:21
- Jeconiah ... Jer. 27:20
- Nebuchadnezzar ... Jer. 29:1
- Chemosh ... Jer. 48:7
- Syrians ... Amos 1:5

See Captivity

Exodus—*a departure*
- Israel's, from Egypt ... Ex. 12:41

Exodus, Book of—*a book of the Old Testament*
- Escape from Egypt ... Ex. 12:31-42
- The Law ... Ex. 20:1-17
- The tabernacle and priesthood ... Ex. 24:12—31:18

Exorcists—*those who use oaths to dispel evil spirits*
- Paul encounters ... Acts 19:13, 19

Expanse—*firmament, vault*
- Created by God ... Gen. 1:8
- Stars placed in ... Gen. 1:14, 17
- Compared to a tent curtain ... Ps. 104:2
- Expressive of God's glory ... Ps. 19:1
- Saints compared to ... Dan. 12:3

Expectation—*looking forward*
- Conquest ... Num. 14:1-24
- Victory ... Josh. 7:4-13
- Relief ... 1 Kin. 12:4-15
- Impending doom ... 2 Kin. 23:25-27
- Elevation ... Esth. 6:6-14
- The wicked ... Prov. 10:28

E

SUBJECT — REFERENCE

Righteous — Ps. 62:5
Destruction — John 4:1-11
Death — Acts 28:3-6

Expediency—*a method of justifying an act*
To fulfill God's plan — John 11:50
To avoid offense — 1 Cor. 8:8-13
To save men — 1 Cor. 9:19-23
To accomplish a task — 2 Cor. 8:10-12
Illustrations — Acts 16:3

Expense—*the cost involved*
Royalty, foretold — 1 Sam. 8:11-18
Royalty, realized — 1 Kin. 4:22, 23

Experiment—*a test designed to prove something*
Jacob — Gen. 30:37-43
Aaron's sons — Lev. 10:1-3
Philistines — 1 Sam. 6:1-18
Daniel — Dan. 1:11-16
God's goodness — Mal. 3:10-12

Expiation—*atonement*
Under Law — Lev. 14:11-20; Lev. 16:11-28
Prophecy of Isaiah — Is. 53:1-12
Fulfilled in Christ — Acts 8:27-39; 1 Pet. 2:21-25

Explanation—*making simple and plain*
Of a condition — Luke 16:25-31
Of a phenomenon — Acts 2:1-21
Of a decision — Acts 15:15-31

Expulsion—*driving out by force from*
Eden — Gen. 3:22-24
The priesthood — Neh. 13:27, 28
A city — Luke 4:16-29
By persecution — Acts 13:50, 51

Extortion—*money obtained by force or threat*
Innocency from, pretended — Matt. 23:25
Fellowship with, forbidden — 1 Cor. 5:10, 11
Sin of, proscribed — Luke 3:13, 14
Examples of — Gen. 47:13-26

Extremity—*the greatest degree of something*
Human faith — Gen. 22:1-3
Grief — 2 Sam. 18:33
Pride — Is. 14:13, 14
Pain — Matt. 27:46-50
Degradation — Luke 15:13-16
Torments — Luke 16:23, 24
Human endurance — 2 Cor. 1:8-10

Eye—*the organ of sight*
A. *Affected by:*
Age — Gen. 27:1
Wine — Gen. 49:12
Sorrow — Job 17:7
Disease — Lev. 26:16
Grief — Ps. 6:7
Light — Acts 22:11
B. *Of God, figurative of:*
Omniscience — 2 Chr. 16:9
Justice — Amos 9:8
Holiness — Hab. 1:13
Guidance — Ps. 32:8
Protection — Ps. 33:18
C. *Of man, figurative of:*
Revealed knowledge — Num. 24:3
Lawlessness — Judg. 17:6
Jealousy — 1 Sam. 18:9
Understanding — Ps. 19:8
Agreement — Is. 52:8
Great sorrow — Jer. 9:1
Retaliation — Matt. 5:38
The essential nature — Matt. 6:22, 23
Moral state — Matt. 7:3-5
Spiritual inability — Matt. 13:15
Spiritual dullness — Mark 8:17, 18
Future glory — 1 Cor. 2:9
Illumination — Eph. 1:18
Unworthy service — Eph. 6:6
Worldliness — 1 John 2:16
Evil desires — 2 Pet. 2:14
D. *Prophecies concerning:*
Shall see the Redeemer — Job 19:25-27
Gentiles shall see — Is. 42:6, 7
Blind shall see — Is. 29:18
Will see the King — Is. 33:17
Will see Jesus — Rev. 1:7
Tears of, shall be wiped away — Rev. 7:17

SUBJECT — REFERENCE

Eyebrows—*the arch of hair over the eyes*
Of lepers, shaved off — Lev. 14:2, 9

Eyesalve—*an ointment*
Christ mentions — Rev. 3:18

Eyeservice—*service performed only when watched by another*
Highly obnoxious — Eph. 6:6

Eyewitness—*a firsthand observer*
Consulted by Luke — Luke 1:1, 2
Of Christ's majesty — 2 Pet. 1:16

Ezbai—*shining*
Naarai's father — 1 Chr. 11:37

Ezbon—*bright*
1. Son of Gad — Gen. 46:16
2. Benjamite — 1 Chr. 7:7

Ezekiel—*God strengthens*
A. *Life of:*
Hebrew prophet; son of Buzi — Ezek. 1:3
Carried captive to Babylon — Ezek. 1:1-3
Lived among exiles — Ezek. 3:15-17
His wife died — Ezek. 24:18
Persecuted — Ezek. 3:25
Often consulted — Ezek. 8:1
Prophetic minister — Ezek. 3:17-21
B. *Visions of:*
God's glory — Ezek. 1:4-28
Abominations — Ezek. 8:5-18
Valley of dry bones — Ezek. 37:1-14
Messianic times — Ezek. 40:48
River of life — Ezek. 47:1-5
C. *Methods employed by:*
Threatens dumbness — Ezek. 3:26
Symbolizes siege of Jerusalem — Ezek. 4:1-3
Shaves himself — Ezek. 5:1-4
Removes baggage — Ezek. 12:3-16
Uses boiling pot — Ezek. 24:1-14
Does not mourn for wife — Ezek. 24:16-27
Uses parables — Ezek. 17:2-10

Ezekiel, Book of—*a Book of the Old Testament*
Prophecies against Israel — Ezek. 1:1—24:27
Prophecies against the nations — Ezek. 25:1—32:32
Prophecies of restoration — Ezek. 33:1—39:29
The Messianic kingdom — Ezek. 40:1—48:35

Ezel—*departure*
David's hiding place — 1 Sam. 20:19

Ezem—*bone*
Village of Judah — Josh. 15:29
Assigned to Simeon — Josh. 19:3

Ezer—*help*
1. Horite tribe — 1 Chr. 1:38
Son of Seir — Gen. 36:21
2. Ephraimite — 1 Chr. 7:21
3. Judahite — 1 Chr. 4:1, 4
4. Gadite warrior — 1 Chr. 12:9
5. Son of Jeshua — Neh. 3:19
6. Postexilic priest — Neh. 12:42

Ezion-geber—*backbone of a giant*
Town on the Red Sea — 1 Kin. 9:26
Israelite encampment — Num. 33:35
Seaport of Israel's navy — 1 Kin. 22:48

Eznite—*spear; to be sharp*
Warrior of David — 2 Sam. 23:8
Called Tachmonite — 2 Sam. 23:8
Called Hachmonite — 1 Chr. 11:11

Ezra, Ezrah—*help*
1. Postexilic priest — Neh. 12:1, 7
Called Azariah — Neh. 10:2
2. Scribe, priest and reformer of postexilic times — Ezra 7:1-6
Commissioned by Artaxerxes — Ezra 7:6-28
Takes exiles with him — Ezra 8:1-20
Proclaims a fast — Ezra 8:21-23
Commits treasures to the priests — Ezra 8:24-30
Comes to Jerusalem — Ezra 8:31, 32
Institutes reforms — Ezra 9:1-15
Reads the Law — Neh. 8:1-18
Helps in dedication — Neh. 12:27-43

SUBJECT — REFERENCE

Ezra, Book of—*a book of the Old Testament*
Return from exile — Ezra 1:1—2:70
Rebuilding the Temple — Ezra 3:1—6:22
Reformation — Ezra 9:1—10:44

Ezrahite—*belonging to Ezrach*
Family name of Ethan and Heman — 1 Kin. 4:31

Ezri—*my help*
David's farm overseer — 1 Chr. 27:26

F

Fable—*a fictitious story*
A. *Form of allegory:*
The trees — Judg. 9:7-15
The thistle — 2 Kin. 14:9
B. *Form of fiction, contrary to:*
Edification — 1 Tim. 1:4
Godliness — 1 Tim. 4:6, 7
Truth — 2 Tim. 4:4
Facts — 2 Pet. 1:16

Face—*front part of head*
A. *Acts performed on:*
Spitting on — Deut. 25:9
Disfiguring of — Matt. 6:16
Painting of — 2 Kin. 9:30
Hitting — 2 Cor. 11:20
B. *Acts indicated by:*
Falling on—worship — Gen. 17:3
Covering of—mourning — 2 Sam. 19:4
Hiding of—disapproval — Deut. 31:17, 18
Turning away of—rejection — 2 Chr. 30:9
Setting of—determination — 2 Kin. 12:17

Face of the Lord
A. *Toward the righteous:*
Shine on — Num. 6:25
Do not hide — Ps. 102:2
Hide from our sins — Ps. 51:9
Shall see — Rev. 22:4
B. *Toward the wicked:*
Is against — Ps. 34:16
Set against — Jer. 21:10
They hide from — Rev. 6:16

Failure
A. *Causes of:*
Contrary to God's will — Gen. 11:3-8
Disobedience — Num. 14:40-45
Sin — Josh. 7:3-12
Lack of prayer — Matt. 17:15-20; Mark 9:24-29
Not counting the cost — Luke 14:28-32
Unbelief — Heb. 4:6
B. *Examples of:*
Esau — Gen. 25:29-34
Eli's sons — 1 Sam. 2:12-17
King Saul — 1 Sam. 16:1
Absalom — 2 Sam. 18:6-17
Hananiah — Jer. 28:1-17
Haman — Esth. 7:1-10

Fainting, faintheartedness—*a loss of vital powers*
A. *Causes of:*
Physical fatigue — Gen. 25:29, 30
Famine — Gen. 47:13
Unbelief — Gen. 45:26
Fear — Josh. 2:24
Sin — Lev. 26:31
Sickness — Job 4:5
Human weakness — Is. 40:29-31
Ecstasy of visions — Dan. 8:27
Disappointment — Jon. 4:8
God's reproving — Heb. 12:5
B. *Antidotes against:*
Removal of the fearful — Deut. 20:8

Fair—English rendering of numerous Hebrew and Greek words
Beautiful — Gen. 6:2; Song 1:15, 16
Unspotted — Zech. 3:5
Persuasive — Prov. 7:21; Gal. 6:12
Good — Matt. 16:2

SUBJECT — REFERENCE

Fair Havens

Harbor of Crete ... Acts 27:8

Faith—*confidence in the testimony of another*

A. *Nature of:*

Fruit of the Spirit ... Gal. 5:22
Work of God ... John 6:29
God's gift ... Eph. 2:8
Comes from the heart ... Rom. 10:9, 10
Substance of unseen things ... Heb. 11:1

B. *Results from:*

Scriptures ... John 20:30, 31
Preaching ... John 17:20
Gospel ... Acts 15:7

C. *Objects of:*

God ... John 14:1
Christ ... John 20:31
Moses' writings ... John 5:46
Writings of the prophets ... Acts 26:27
Gospel ... Mark 1:15
God's promises ... Rom. 4:21

D. *Kinds of:*

Saving ... Rom. 10:9, 10
Temporary ... Luke 8:13
Intellectual ... James 2:19
Dead ... James 2:17, 20

E. *Described as:*

Boundless ... John 11:21-27
Common ... Titus 1:4
Great ... Matt. 8:10
Holy ... Jude 20
Humble ... Luke 7:6, 7
Little ... Matt. 8:26
Mutual ... Rom. 1:12
Perfect ... James 2:22
Precious ... 2 Pet. 1:1
Rootless ... Luke 8:13
Small ... Matt. 17:20
Unfeigned ... 1 Tim. 1:5
United ... Mark 2:5
Vain ... 1 Cor. 15:14, 17
Venturing ... Matt. 14:28, 29

F. *The fruits of:*

Remission of sins ... Acts 10:43
Justification ... Acts 13:39
Freedom from condemnation ... John 3:18
Salvation ... Mark 16:16
Sanctification ... Acts 15:9
Freedom from spiritual death ... John 11:25, 26
Spiritual light ... John 12:36, 46
Spiritual life ... John 20:31
Eternal life ... John 3:15, 16
Adoption ... John 1:12
Access to God ... Eph. 3:12
Edification ... 1 Tim. 1:4
Preservation ... John 10:26-29
Inheritance ... Acts 26:18
Peace and rest ... Rom. 5:1

G. *Place of, in Christian life:*

Live by ... Rom. 1:17
Walk by ... Rom. 4:12
Pray by ... Matt. 21:22
Resist evil by ... Eph. 6:16
Overcome world by ... 1 John 2:13-17
Die in ... Heb. 11:13

H. *Growth of, in Christian life:*

Stand fast in ... 1 Cor. 16:13
Continue in ... Acts 14:22
Be strong in ... Rom. 4:20-24
Abound in ... 2 Cor. 8:7
Be grounded in ... Col. 1:23
Hold fast ... 1 Tim. 1:19
Pray for increase of ... Luke 17:5
Have assurance of ... 2 Tim. 1:12

I. *Examples of, in Old Testament:*

Abel ... Heb. 11:4
Enoch ... Heb. 11:5
Noah ... Heb. 11:7
Abraham ... Rom. 4:16-20
Sarah ... Heb. 11:11
Jacob ... Heb. 11:21
Joseph ... Heb. 11:22
Moses ... Heb. 11:23-29
Caleb ... Josh. 14:6, 12
Rahab ... Heb. 11:31
Jonathan ... 1 Sam. 14:6
David ... 1 Sam. 17:37
Jehoshaphat ... 2 Chr. 20:5, 12
Three Hebrew captives ... Dan. 3:16, 17
Job ... Job 19:25
Others ... Heb. 11:32-39

J. *Examples of, in New Testament:*

Centurion ... Matt. 8:5-10
Jairus ... Mark 5:22, 23
Sick woman ... Mark 5:25-34
Syrophoenician woman ... Mark 7:24-30
Bartimaeus ... Mark 10:46-52
Sinful woman ... Luke 7:36-50
Ten lepers ... Luke 17:11-19
Certain nobleman ... John 4:46-54
Mary and Martha ... John 11:1-32
Thomas ... John 20:24-29
Multitudes ... Acts 5:14
Stephen ... Acts 6:8
Samaritans ... Acts 8:5-12
Ethiopian eunuch ... Acts 8:26-39
Barnabas ... Acts 11:22-24
Lydia ... Acts 16:14, 15
Philippian jailer ... Acts 16:25-34
Paul ... Acts 27:23-25

Faith as a body of belief

Priest obedient to ... Acts 6:7
Churches established in ... Acts 16:5
Stand fast in ... 1 Cor. 16:13
Paul preaches ... Gal. 1:23
Now revealed ... Gal. 3:23
Household of ... Gal. 6:10
Contending for ... Phil. 1:27
Hold purely ... 1 Tim. 3:9
Denial of ... 1 Tim. 5:8
Some erred from ... 1 Tim. 6:10, 21
Reprobate ... 2 Tim. 3:8
Paul keeps ... 2 Tim. 4:7
Chosen of God ... Titus 1:1
Common among redeemed ... Titus 1:4
To be sound in ... Titus 1:13

Faithfulness—*making faith a living reality in one's life*

A. *Manifested in:*

God's service ... Matt. 24:45
Declaring God's Word ... Jer. 23:38
Bearing witness ... Prov. 14:5
Keeping secrets ... Prov. 11:13
Helping others ... 3 John 5
Doing work ... 2 Chr. 34:12
Positions of trust ... Neh. 13:13
Reproving others ... Prov. 27:6
Conveying messages ... Prov. 25:13
Smallest things ... Luke 16:10-12

B. *Illustrated in lives of:*

Abraham ... Gal. 3:9
Abraham's servant ... Gen. 24:33
Joseph ... Gen. 39:22, 23
Moses ... Num. 12:7
David ... 2 Sam. 22:22-25
Elijah ... 1 Kin. 19:10, 14
Josiah ... 2 Kin. 22:1, 2
Abijah ... 2 Chr. 13:4-12
Micaiah ... 2 Chr. 18:12, 13
Jehoshaphat ... 2 Chr. 20:1-30
Azariah ... 2 Chr. 26:16-20
Hanani and Hananiah ... Neh. 7:1, 2
Isaiah ... Is. 39:3-7
Jeremiah ... Jer. 26:1-15
Daniel ... Dan. 6:10
John the Baptist ... Luke 3:7-19
Jesus ... Heb. 3:2
Peter ... Acts 4:8-12
Paul ... Acts 17:16, 17

Faithfulness of God

A. *Described as:*

Everlasting ... Ps. 119:90
Established ... Ps. 89:2
Unfailing ... Ps. 89:33
Infinite ... Ps. 36:5
Great ... Lam. 3:23
Incomparable ... Ps. 89:8

B. *Manifested in:*

Counsels ... Is. 25:1
Covenant-keeping ... Deut. 7:9
Forgiving sins ... 1 John 1:9
Testimonies ... Ps. 119:138
Judgments ... Jer. 51:29
Promises ... 1 Kin. 8:20

Fall of man

A. *Occasion of:*

Satan's temptation ... Gen. 3:1-5
Eve's yielding ... 2 Cor. 11:3
Adam's disobedience ... Rom. 5:12-19

B. *Temporal consequences of:*

Driven from Paradise ... Gen. 3:24
Condemned to hard labor ... Gen. 3:16, 19
Condemned to die ... 1 Cor. 15:22

C. *Spiritual consequences of:*

Separated from God ... Eph. 4:18
Born in sin ... John 3:6
Evil in heart ... Matt. 15:19
Corrupt and perverse ... Rom. 3:12-16
In bondage to sin ... Rom. 6:19
In bondage to Satan ... Heb. 2:14, 15
Dead in sin ... Col. 2:13
Spiritually blind ... Eph. 4:18
Utterly depraved ... Titus 1:15
Change from, not in man ... Jer. 2:22
Only God can change ... John 3:16

Fallow deer—*roebuck*

Among clean animals ... Deut. 14:5
In Solomon's diet ... 1 Kin. 4:22, 23

Fallow ground—*a field plowed and left for seeding*

Used figuratively ... Jer. 4:3; Hos. 10:12

False accusations

A. *Against men:*

Joseph ... Gen. 39:7-20
Moses ... Num. 16:1-3, 13
Ahimelech ... 1 Sam. 22:11-16
David ... Ps. 41:5-9
Elijah ... 1 Kin. 18:17, 18
Naboth ... 1 Kin. 21:1-14
Jeremiah ... Jer. 26:8-11
Amos ... Amos 7:10, 11
Stephen ... Acts 6:11, 13
Paul ... Acts 21:27-29

B. *Against Christ:*

Gluttony ... Matt. 11:19
Blasphemy ... Matt. 26:64, 65
Insanity ... Mark 3:21
Demon possession ... John 7:20
Sabbath desecration ... John 9:16
Treason ... John 19:12

False apostles

Opposed Paul ... 2 Cor. 11:1-15

False Christs

Christ foretells their coming ... Matt. 24:24
Christ warns against ... Mark 13:21-23
See Antichrist

False confidence

A. *Characteristics of:*

Self-righteous ... Rom. 2:3
Spiritually blind ... Is. 28:15, 19
Sensualist ... Gal. 6:7, 8
Worldly secure ... 1 Thess. 5:3

B. *Causes of trusting in:*

Riches ... 1 Tim. 6:17
Worldly success ... Luke 12:19, 20
Men ... Is. 30:1-5
Oneself ... Matt. 26:33-35
Ignoring God's providence ... James 4:13-15

C. *Warnings against:*

Curse on ... Jer. 17:5
Do not glory in men ... 1 Cor. 3:21
Man's limitation ... 2 Cor. 1:9
Mighty will fail ... Ps. 33:16, 17
Boasting ... 1 Kin. 20:11

D. *Instances of:*

Babel's men ... Gen. 11:4
Sennacherib ... 2 Kin. 19:20-37
Asa ... 2 Chr. 16:7-12
Peter ... Luke 22:33, 34

Falsehood—*turning truth into a lie*

A. *Manifested by false:*

Witnesses ... Ps. 27:12
Balances ... Prov. 11:1
Tongue ... Ps. 120:3
Report ... Ex. 23:1
Prophets ... Jer. 5:2, 31
Science ... 1 Tim. 6:20

B. *God's people:*

Must avoid ... Ex. 23:7
Must hate ... Ps. 119:104, 128
Must endure ... Acts 6:13
Are falsely charged with ... Jer. 37:14; Matt. 5:11

SUBJECT REFERENCE

False professions

A. *Pretending to be:*
Harmless ... Josh. 9:3-16
Innocent ... Matt. 27:24
Divine ... Acts 12:21-23
Sincere ... Matt. 26:48, 49
True prophets ... 1 Kin. 22:6-12

B. *Exposed by:*
Prophets ... Jer. 28:1-17
Christ ... John 13:21-30
Apostles ... Acts 5:1-11

False prophets

A. *Tests of:*
Doctrine ... Is. 8:20
Prophecies ... 1 Kin. 13:1-32
Lives ... Matt. 7:15, 16

B. *Characteristics of:*
Prophesy peace ... Jer. 23:17
Teach a lie ... Jer. 28:15
Pretend to be true ... Matt. 7:22, 23
Teach corruption ... 2 Pet. 2:10-22

C. *Examples of:*
Zedekiah ... 1 Kin. 22:11, 12
Hananiah ... Jer. 28:1-17
In the last days ... Matt. 24:11

False teachers

A. *Characteristics of:*
Grace-perverters ... Gal. 1:6-8
Money-lovers ... Luke 16:14
Christ-deniers ... 2 Pet. 2:1
Truth-resisters ... 2 Tim. 3:8
Fable-lovers ... 2 Tim. 4:3, 4
Destitute of the truth ... 1 Tim. 6:3-5
Bound by traditions ... Matt. 15:9
Unstable ... 1 Tim. 1:6, 7
Deceitful ... Eph. 4:14
Lustful ... 2 Pet. 2:12-19

B. *Prevalence of:*
In Paul's time ... 2 Tim. 1:14, 15
During this age ... 1 Tim. 4:1-3
At Christ's return ... 2 Tim. 4:3, 4

C. *Examples of:*
Balaam ... Rev. 2:14
Bar-jesus ... Acts 13:6
Ephesian elders ... Acts 20:30
Rev. 2:2
Epicureans ... Acts 17:18
False apostles ... 2 Cor. 11:5, 13
2 Cor. 12:11
Herodians ... Mark 3:6
Mark 12:13
Hymenaeus ... 2 Tim. 2:17
Libertines ... Acts 6:9
Nicolaitanes ... Rev. 2:15
Pharisees ... Matt. 23:26
Philetus ... 2 Tim. 2:17
Sadducees ... Matt. 16:12
Scribes ... Matt. 12:38, 39
Serpent (Satan) ... Gen. 3:4
Stoic philosophers ... Acts 17:18

False weights

Prohibited ... Deut. 25:13, 14

False witnesses

A. *Features regarding:*
Deceptive ... Prov. 12:17
Cruel ... Prov. 25:18
Utter lies ... Prov. 6:19
Prov. 14:5
Shall perish ... Prov. 21:28
Hated by God ... Zech. 8:17
Forbidden ... Ex. 20:16

B. *Sin of:*
Comes from corrupt heart ... Matt. 15:19
Causes suffering ... Ps. 27:12
Merits punishment ... Prov. 19:5, 9

C. *Punishment of:*
Specified ... Lev. 6:1-5
Described ... Deut. 19:16-20
Visualized ... Zech. 5:3, 4

D. *Examples of, against:*
Ahimelech ... 1 Sam. 22:8-18
Naboth ... 1 Kin. 21:13
Jeremiah ... Jer. 37:12-14

SUBJECT REFERENCE

Jesus ... Matt. 26:59-61
Stephen ... Acts 6:11, 13
Paul ... Acts 16:20, 21

Fame—*report; renown; news*

A. *As report or news of:*
Joseph's brothers ... Gen. 45:16
Israel's departure ... Num. 14:15
Jesus' ministry ... Matt. 4:24

B. *As reputation or renown of:*
Nation ... Ezek. 16:14, 15
Joshua's exploits ... Josh. 6:27
God's works ... Josh. 9:9
Solomon's wisdom ... 1 Kin. 4:31
David's power ... 1 Chr. 14:17
The Temple's greatness ... 1 Chr. 22:5
God's glory ... Is. 66:19
Mordecai's fame ... Esth. 9:4
Jesus' works ... Matt. 9:31

Familiar spirits

A. *Described as:*
Source of defilement ... Lev. 19:31
Abominable ... Deut. 18:10-12
Vain ... Is. 8:19

B. *The practicers of, to be:*
Cut off ... Lev. 20:6
Put to death ... Lev. 20:27

C. *Consulted by:*
Saul ... 1 Sam. 28:3-25
Manasseh ... 2 Kin. 21:6

Family

A. *Founded on:*
Divine creation ... Gen. 1:27, 28
Marriage ... Matt. 19:6
Monogamy ... Ex. 20:14
Unity of parents ... Ex. 20:12
Headship of husband ... 1 Cor. 11:3-7
Subordination of children ... Eph. 6:1-4
Common concern ... Luke 16:27, 28

B. *Disturbed by:*
Polygamy ... Gen. 4:19-24
Jealousy ... Gen. 37:3, 4, 18-27
Hatred ... Gen. 4:5, 8
Deceit ... Gen. 37:31-35
Ambition ... 2 Sam. 15:1-16
Waywardness ... Luke 15:11-18
Insubordination ... Gen. 34:6-31
Unbelief ... John 7:3-10
Lust ... Gen. 34:1-31

C. *Unity of:*
Husband and wife ... 1 Cor. 7:3
Parents and children ... Jer. 35:1-19
Worship ... 1 Cor. 16:19
Faith ... 2 Tim. 1:5
Baptism ... Acts 16:14, 15

D. *Worship in:*
Led by the father ... Gen. 18:19
Instructed in the Scriptures ... Eph. 6:4
Observing religious rites ... Acts 10:2, 47, 48
Common consecration ... Josh. 24:15

Famine—*deficiency of food*

A. *Kinds of:*
Physical ... Gen. 12:10
Prophetic ... Matt. 24:7
Rev. 6:5-8
Spiritual ... 2 Chr. 15:3
Amos 8:11

B. *Causes of:*
Hail storms ... Ex. 9:23
Insects ... Joel 1:4
Enemies ... Deut. 28:49-51
Siege ... 2 Kin. 6:25
Sin ... Ezek. 14:12, 13
Punishment ... 2 Kin. 8:1

C. *Characteristics of:*
Often long ... Gen. 41:27
Often severe ... Deut. 28:49-53
Suffering intense ... Jer. 14:1, 5, 6
Destructive ... Jer. 14:12, 15

D. *Instances of, in:*
Abram's time ... Gen. 12:10
Isaac's time ... Gen. 26:1
Joseph's time ... Gen. 41:53-56
Time of judges ... Ruth 1:1
David's reign ... 2 Sam. 21:1
Elisha's time ... 2 Kin. 4:38

SUBJECT REFERENCE

Samaria's siege ... 2 Kin. 6:25
Reign of Claudius Caesar ... Acts 11:28
Jeremiah's time ... Jer. 14:1
Ahab's reign ... 1 Kin. 17:1

Fan—*to toss about*

A. *Used literally of:*
Fork for winnowing grain ... Is. 30:24

B. *Used figuratively of judgments:*
God's ... Is. 30:24
Nation's ... Jer. 51:2
Christ's ... Matt. 3:12

Fanaticism—*unbridled obsession*

A. *Kinds of:*
Personal ... Acts 9:1, 2
Group ... 1 Kin. 18:22-29
Civic ... Acts 19:24-41
National ... John 19:15

B. *Characteristics of:*
Intolerance ... Acts 7:57
Persecution ... 1 Thess. 2:14-16
Inhumanity ... Rev. 11:7-10
Insanity ... 1 Sam. 18:9-12

Farewell message

Joshua's ... Josh. 24:1-28
David's ... 1 Kin. 2:1-9
Christ's ... Matt. 28:18-20
Paul's ... 2 Tim. 4:1-8

Farewells—*expressions at departing*

Naomi's, to Orpah ... Ruth 1:11-14
Paul's, to Ephesians ... Acts 18:18-21
Paul's, to elders ... Acts 20:17-38
Paul's, to Tyrians ... Acts 21:3-6
Paul's, to Jews ... Acts 28:23-29

Farm—*a cultivated field*

Preferred more than a wedding ... Matt. 22:1-5

Farmer—*one who farms*

Cain, the first ... Gen. 4:2
Elisha ... 1 Kin. 19:19, 20
Uzziah ... 2 Chr. 26:9, 10
Diligence required in ... Prov. 24:30-34
Reward of ... 2 Cor. 9:6-11
Unwise ... Luke 12:16-21

Farming—*the art of agriculture*

Rechabites forbidden to engage in ... Jer. 35:5-10

Farthing—See Jewish Measures

Utmost payment ... Matt. 5:26
Price of two sparrows ... Matt. 10:29

Fashion—*the outward form*

A. *Used physically of:*
Outward form of a building ... Acts 7:44
One's appearance ... Luke 9:29

B. *Used figuratively of:*
World's life ("conformed") ... Rom. 12:2
World's lusts ... 1 Pet. 1:14
World's riches ... James 1:11
World's exit ... 1 Cor. 7:31
Believer's conformity to Christ ... Phil. 3:21

Fasting—*abstaining from physical nourishment*

A. *Occasions of:*
Public disasters ... 1 Sam. 31:11-13
Private emotions ... 1 Sam. 1:7
Grief ... 2 Sam. 12:16
Anxiety ... Dan. 6:18-20
Approaching danger ... Esth. 4:16
National repentance ... 1 Sam. 7:5, 6
Sad news ... Neh. 1:4
Sacred ordination ... Acts 13:3

B. *Accompaniments of:*
Prayer ... Luke 2:37
Confession ... Neh. 9:1, 2
Mourning ... Joel 2:12
Humiliation ... Neh. 9:1

C. *Safeguards concerning:*
Avoid display ... Matt. 6:16-18
Remember God ... Zech. 7:5-7
Chasten the soul ... Ps. 69:10

SUBJECT REFERENCE

Humble the soul .... Ps. 35:13
Consider the true meaning of .... Is. 58:1-14

D. *Results of:*
Divine guidance .... Judg. 20:26
Victory over temptation ..... Matt. 4:1-11

E. *Instances of:*
Moses .... Ex. 34:27, 28
Israelites .... Judg. 20:26
Samuel .... 1 Sam. 7:5, 6
David .... 2 Sam. 12:16
Elijah .... 1 Kin. 19:8
Ninevites .... Jon. 3:5-8
Nehemiah .... Neh. 1:4
Darius .... Dan. 6:9, 18
Daniel .... Dan. 9:3
Anna .... Luke 2:36, 37
Jesus .... Matt. 4:1, 2
John's disciples and the Pharisees .... Mark 2:18
Early Christians .... Acts 13:2
Apostles .... 2 Cor. 6:4, 5
Paul .... 2 Cor. 11:27

Fat
Figurative of best .... Gen. 45:18
Of sacrifices, burned .... Ex. 29:13; Lev. 4:26
Figurative of pride .... Ps. 119:69, 70
Sacrificed by Abel .... Gen. 4:4
Offered to God .... Ex. 23:18; Lev. 3:14-16

Father—*male parent*

A. *Kinds of:*
Natural .... Gen. 28:13
Ancestors .... Jer. 35:6
Natural leaders .... Rom. 9:5
Head of households .... Ex. 6:14

B. *Figurative of:*
Source .... Job 38:28
Original inventor .... Gen. 4:20
Creator .... James 1:17
Spiritual likeness .... John 8:44
Counselor .... Gen. 45:8
Superior .... 2 Kin. 2:12
Praise-seeking .... Matt. 23:9

C. *Powers of in Old Testament times:*
Arrange son's marriage ...... Gen. 24:1-9
Sell children .... Ex. 21:7

D. *Duties of, toward his children:*
Love .... Gen. 37:4
Command .... Gen. 50:16
Instruct .... Prov. 1:8
Guide and warn .... 1 Thess. 2:11
Train .... Hos. 11:3
Rebuke .... Gen. 34:30
Restrain .... 1 Sam. 3:13
Punish .... Deut. 21:18-21
Chasten .... Heb. 12:7
Nourish .... Is. 1:2
Supply needs .... Matt. 7:8-11
Do not provoke .... Eph. 6:4

E. *Examples of devout:*
Abraham .... Gen. 18:18, 19
Isaac .... Gen. 26:12, 13
Joshua .... Josh. 24:15
Job .... Job 1:5

F. *Christ's command about:*
"Call no man your father" ... Matt. 23:9

Fatherhood of God
Of all men .... Mal. 2:10
Of Israel .... Jer. 31:9
Of Gentiles .... Rom. 3:29
Of Christians .... John 1:12, 13

Fatherless—*orphans*

A. *Proper attitude toward:*
Share blessings with .... Deut. 14:28, 29
Leave gleanings for .... Deut. 24:19-22
Do not defraud .... Prov. 23:10
Defend .... Ps. 82:3
Visit .... James 1:27
Oppress not .... Zech. 7:10
Do no violence to .... Jer. 22:3

B. *God's help toward:*
Father of .... Ps. 68:5
Helper of .... Ps. 10:14
Hears cry of .... Ex. 22:23
Executes judgment of .... Deut. 10:18

SUBJECT REFERENCE

Father's house
The family home .... Gen. 12:1; 1 Sam. 18:2
A household .... Ex. 12:3
Tribal divisions .... Num. 3:15, 20; Num. 17:2, 3
Temple .... John 2:14-16
Heaven .... John 14:2

Fathom—*a sea measure; about six feet*
Mentioned in Paul's shipwreck .. Acts 27:28

Fatigue—*physical or mental exhaustion*

From:
Marching .... 1 Sam. 30:9, 10
Fighting .... 2 Sam. 23:10, 15
Much study .... Eccl. 12:12
Fasting .... Acts 27:21

In:
Sleeping .... Matt. 26:45

Fault—*an imperfection*

A. *Examples of:*
A promise forgotten .... Gen. 41:9
Unworthy conduct .... 1 Sam. 29:3
Guilt .... John 18:38
Deficient behavior .... Matt. 18:15
Human weakness .... James 5:16

B. *Absence of:*
Flawless devotion .... Rev. 14:5
Ultimate sinlessness .... Jude 24

Faultfinders—*carping critics*

A. *Motives behind:*
Supposed injustice .... Matt. 20:9-12
Supposed defilement .... Luke 5:29, 30
Greed and avarice .... John 12:3-6

B. *Against God's:*
Choice .... Num. 12:1, 2
Leading .... Num. 14:1-4
Mercy .... Jon. 4:1-11
Government .... Rom. 9:19-23

C. *Guilt of:*
Punishable .... Num. 12:2, 8-13
Productive of evil .... 3 John 10

Faultless—*without blame*
David .... 1 Sam. 29:3, 6
Daniel .... Dan. 6:4
Christ .... Luke 23:4, 14

Favoritism—*being unfairly partial*

A. *Forbidden to:*
Parents .... Deut. 21:15-17
Judges .... Deut. 25:1-3
Ministers .... 1 Tim. 5:21

B. *Results in:*
Family friction .... Gen. 27:6-46
Jealousy .... Gen. 37:3-35

Fear—*anxiety caused by approaching danger*

A. *Causes of:*
Disobedience .... Gen. 3:10
Impending judgment .... Heb. 11:7
Persecution .... John 20:19
Events of nature .... Acts 27:17, 29
Suspicion .... Acts 9:26
Uncertainty .... 2 Cor. 11:3
Final events .... Luke 21:26
Death .... Heb. 2:15

B. *Effects of:*
Demoralization .... 1 Sam. 13:5-8
Paralysis .... Matt. 28:4
Silent testimony .... John 9:22

C. *Instances of:*
Abraham .... Gen. 20:11
Jacob .... Gen. 32:11
Soldiers .... Matt. 27:54

Fear, godly

A. *Defined as:*
Hating evil .... Prov. 8:13
Satisfying .... Prov. 14:27
Sanctifying .... Ps. 19:9
Beginning of wisdom .... Prov. 1:7

B. *Motives to, God's:*
Majesty .... Jer. 10:7
Holiness .... Rev. 15:4
Forgiveness .... Ps. 130:4

SUBJECT REFERENCE

Power .... Josh. 4:23, 24
Goodness .... 1 Sam. 12:24
Judgment .... Rev. 14:7

C. *Examples of:*
Noah .... Heb. 11:7
Abraham .... Gen. 22:12
Jacob .... Gen. 28:16, 17
Joseph .... Gen. 42:18
David .... Ps. 5:7
Obadiah .... 1 Kin. 18:12
Job .... Job 1:8
Nehemiah .... Neh. 5:15
Early Christians .... Acts 9:31

Fearlessness—*without fear*

A. *Source of:*
Believing God's promises .... Num. 13:30
Challenge of duty .... Ex. 32:26-29
Regard for God's holiness ... Num. 25:1-9
Believing God .... Acts 27:22-26

B. *Exemplified by:*
Abram .... Gen. 14:14-16
Jonathan .... 1 Sam. 14:6-14
David .... 1 Sam. 17:34-37
Nehemiah .... Neh. 4:1-23
Hebrew men .... Dan. 3:16-30
Peter and John .... Acts 4:13
Paul .... Acts 21:10-14

Feasts, Hebrew

A. *Three annual:*
Passover .... Lev. 23:5-8
Weeks (Pentecost) .... Ex. 23:16
Tabernacle .... Lev. 23:34-44

B. *Purposes of:*
Unify the nation .... Deut. 12:5-14
Worship God .... Ex. 5:1
Illustrate spirtual truths ..... John 7:37-39
Foretell the Messiah .... 1 Cor. 11:23-26

C. *Brief history of:*
Pre-Sinaitic observance ...... Ex. 12:1-27
Three instituted at Sinai ..... Ex. 23:14-17
Celebrated in the wilderness .... Num. 9:3-5
Again at beginning of conquest .... Josh. 5:10, 11
At dedication of Temple ..... 1 Kin. 8:2, 65
"Dedication" introduced by Solomon .... 2 Chr. 7:9-11
Idolatrous counterfeits introduced by Jeroboam .... 1 Kin. 12:27-33
Observed in Hezekiah's reign .... 2 Chr. 30:1
Perversion of, by Jews .... Is. 1:13, 14
Restored in Josiah's reformation .... 2 Kin. 23:22, 23
Failure in, cause of exile ..... 2 Chr. 36:20, 21
Restored after the exile ...... Ezra 3:4
Purim instituted by Mordecai .... Esth. 9:17-32
Christ attends .... John 2:23; John 13:1
Christ fulfills the Passover ... 1 Cor. 5:8
Christianity begins with Pentecost .... Acts 2:1-41
All fulfilled in Christ .... 2 Cor. 3:3-18

Feasts, social

A. *Worldly, occasions of:*
Idolatry .... Ex. 32:6
Drunkenness .... 1 Sam. 25:36
Proud display .... Esth. 1:1-8
Profane carousals .... Dan. 5:1-16
Licentiousness .... Mark 6:21, 22

B. *Proper, occasions of:*
Refreshment .... Gen. 19:1-3
Reconciliation .... Gen. 31:54, 55
Reunion .... Gen. 43:16-34
Restoration .... Luke 15:22-24

See Entertainment

Feed—*to supply food to*

A. *Used naturally of:*
Food for men .... 2 Sam. 19:33
Food for animals .... Gen. 30:36
God's provision .... Matt. 6:26

B. *Used figuratively of:*
Instruction and care .... 2 Sam. 5:2
Messiah .... Ezek. 34:23
Good deeds .... Matt. 25:37
Supernatural supply .... Rev. 12:6

F

SUBJECT — REFERENCE

- Elemental teaching . . . 1 Cor. 3:2
- Change of nature . . . Is. 11:7
- Corruption . . . Ps. 49:14
- Vanity . . . Hos. 12:1

Feet—*the lower parts of the body*

A. *Acts performed by or on, indicating:*
- Subjection . . . Josh. 10:24
- Conquest . . . 2 Sam. 22:39
- Humiliation . . . Judg. 5:27
- Submission and entreaty . . . 1 Sam. 25:24, 41
- Great love . . . Luke 7:38, 44-46
- Worship . . . Rev. 19:10
- Learner's position . . . Luke 10:39
- Humility . . . John 13:5-14
- Changed nature . . . Luke 8:35
- Rejection . . . Matt. 10:14

B. *Figurative of:*
- God's holiness . . . Ex. 3:5
- God's nature . . . Ex. 24:10
- Clouds . . . Nah. 1:3
- God's messengers . . . Rom. 10:15
- Final conquest . . . Rom. 16:20

C. *Unusual features concerning:*
- No swelling . . . Neh. 9:21
- Lameness . . . 2 Sam. 9:3, 13
- Neglected . . . 2 Sam. 19:24
- Impotent . . . Acts 14:8-10
- Binding . . . Acts 21:11

See Foot

Feet washing
- Performed on guests . . . Gen. 18:4
- Proffered by Abigail . . . 1 Sam. 25:40, 41
- On Jesus, with tears . . . Luke 7:44
- Performed by Jesus . . . John 13:5
- Duty of saints . . . 1 Tim. 5:10

Felix—*happy*
- Governor of Judaea . . . Acts 23:24, 26
- Letter addressed to . . . Acts 23:25-30
- Paul's defense before . . . Acts 24:1-21
- Convicted, but unchanged . . . Acts 24:22-25
- Subject to bribery . . . Acts 24:26, 27

Felloes—*obsolete word meaning rims*
- Of wheels . . . 1 Kin. 7:33

Fellow citizens
- With the saints . . . Eph. 2:19

Fellow countryman
- Shall not hate . . . Lev. 19:17
- Becomes poor . . . Lev. 25:25
- Judge righteously . . . Deut. 1:16
- Lord gives rest . . . Deut. 3:20
- Save some . . . Rom. 11:14

Fellow servant
- Were to be killed . . . Rev. 6:11
- Who hold fast the testimony of Jesus . . . Rev. 19:10
- Who heed the words . . . Rev. 22:9

Fellowship—*sharing together*

A. *Based upon common:*
- Purpose . . . Ps. 133:1-3
- Belief . . . Acts 2:42
- Conviction . . . 1 Pet. 3:8
- Work . . . Neh. 4:1-23
- Hope . . . Heb. 11:39, 40
- Faith . . . 1 Sam. 20:30-42
- Suffering . . . Dan. 3:16-30
- Need . . . 2 Cor. 8:1-15

B. *Persons sharing together:*
- Father, the Son, and Christians . . . 1 John 1:3
- Christ and Christians . . . 1 Cor. 1:9
- Holy Spirit and Christians . . . Phil. 2:1
- Apostles . . . Acts 2:42
- Believers . . . 1 John 1:7

C. *Things shared together:*
- Material things . . . 2 Cor. 8:4
- Suffering . . . Phil. 3:10
- The Gospel ministry . . . Gal. 2:9
- Gospel privileges . . . Phil. 1:5
- Gospel mystery . . . Eph. 3:9

Fellow slave
- Who owed a hundred denarii . . . Matt. 18:28-33
- Evil slave beats . . . Matt. 24:48, 49

SUBJECT — REFERENCE

Fellow workers
- In the truth . . . 3 John 8
- In the kingdom . . . Col. 4:11
- Prisca and Aquila described as . . . Rom. 16:3
- Urbanas . . . Rom. 16:9
- Timothy . . . Rom. 16:21
- Paul . . . 1 Cor. 3:1-9
- Titus . . . 2 Cor. 8:23
- Epaphroditus . . . Phil. 2:25
- Philemon . . . Philem. 1
- Marcus, Aristarchus, Demas, Lucas . . . Philem. 24

Fenced cities
- Means of protection . . . 2 Sam. 20:6
- Mighty and strong . . . Deut. 9:1
- Conquerable . . . Deut. 3:5
- Utterly destroyed . . . 2 Kin. 3:19, 25
- No substitute for God . . . Hos. 8:14

Ferret—*an unclean animal*
- Either the gecho (wall lizard) or the field mouse . . . Lev. 11:30

Ferryboats
- David's use of . . . 2 Sam. 19:16-18

Festus—*feastful, joyful*
- Governor of Judaea . . . Acts 24:27
- Paul's defense made to . . . Acts 25:1-22

Fetters—*shackle for binding the feet*

A. *Used literally of:*
- Imprisonment . . . Ps. 105:18
- Bondage . . . Luke 8:29

B. *Used figuratively of:*
- Trouble . . . Job 36:8
- Subjection . . . Ps. 149:8

Fetus—*unborn child*
- Protected by law . . . Ex. 21:22
- Possesses sin nature . . . Ps. 51:5
- Fashioned by God . . . Ps. 139:13-16
- Called by God . . . Is. 49:1; Jer. 1:5
- Active . . . Luke 1:41

Fever—*abnormal body temperature*
- Sent as a judgment . . . Deut. 28:22
- Rebuked by Christ . . . Luke 4:38, 39
- Healed by Paul . . . Acts 28:8

Few—*the opposite of many*
- Days . . . Gen. 47:9
- Do not determine God's power . . . 1 Sam. 14:6
- Words in prayer . . . Eccl. 5:2
- The saved . . . Matt. 7:14
- Gospel messengers . . . Matt. 9:37
- The chosen . . . Matt. 22:14

Fidelity—*faithfulness in the performance of duty*
- In finances . . . 2 Kin. 12:15
- In industry . . . 2 Chr. 34:11, 12
- Seen in Joseph . . . Gen. 39:6
- Seen in Daniel . . . Dan. 6:1-3, 28

Field—*open or cleared land*

A. *Used literally of:*
- Cultivated land . . . Gen. 47:20
- A city . . . Ps. 78:12, 43

B. *Laws regarding:*
- Fires . . . Ex. 22:6
- Mixed seed . . . Lev. 19:19
- Coveting others' . . . Deut. 5:21
- Destruction of trees . . . Deut. 20:19, 20
- Total harvest of . . . Deut. 24:19-22
- Sabbath rest . . . Lev. 25:3-12
- Redemption of . . . Lev. 27:16-24
- Title of . . . Ruth 4:5-11

C. *Figurative of:*
- World . . . Matt. 13:38, 44
- Harvest of souls . . . John 4:35

Field of Blood
- A field, predicted in the Old Testament, bought as a cemetery for Judas' burial . . . Zech. 11:12, 13; Matt. 27:1-10

Fiery serpents
- Attack Israelites . . . Num. 21:6, 8

Fig—*pear-shaped fruit of fig tree*
- Destruction foretold . . . Hos. 2:12

SUBJECT — REFERENCE

Fig cakes
- Prescribed for boils . . . Is. 38:21

Fig tree

A. *The leaves of, used for:*
- Covering nakedness . . . Gen. 3:7
- Shade . . . John 1:48, 50

B. *Fruit of:*
- Used for food . . . 1 Sam. 30:12
- Sent as present . . . 1 Sam. 25:18
- Sold in markets . . . Neh. 13:15
- Used for healing . . . Is. 38:21
- Sometimes fails . . . Hab. 3:17

C. *Figurative of:*
- Prosperity and peace . . . 1 Kin. 4:25
- Righteous and the wicked . . . Jer. 24:1-10
- Fathers of Israel . . . Hos. 9:10
- Barren religion . . . Matt. 21:19
- Jewish nation . . . Luke 13:6-9
- Christ's return . . . Matt. 24:32, 33
- Final judgment . . . Rev. 6:13

Fight—*a conflict*

A. *Used literally of:*
- War . . . Ex. 17:8, 10
- Individual combat . . . 1 Sam. 17:10, 32

B. *Used figuratively of:*
- Determined resolve . . . 1 Cor. 9:26
- Opposition of evil men . . . 1 Cor. 15:32
- Christian life . . . 1 Tim. 6:12
- Dissension . . . James 4:1, 2
- Spiritual conflict . . . Rev. 12:7

Fighting against God

A. *Manifested by:*
- Pharaoh . . . Ex. 5:1, 2
- Rabshakeh . . . 2 Kin. 18:28-36
- Jeroboam . . . 2 Chr. 13:8-19

B. *Futility of:*
- Seen by Gamaliel . . . Acts 5:34, 39
- Admitted by Pharisees . . . Acts 23:9
- Experienced by Satan . . . Rev. 12:7-17
- Blasphemy of unregenerate . . . Rev. 16:9-21

Figurehead—*symbol on ship's prow*
- Twin Brothers . . . Acts 28:11

Figures of speech
- Allegory . . . Gal. 4:24
- Fable . . . Judg. 9:8-15; 1 Tim. 4:7
- Hyperbole . . . 1 Sam. 13:5; John 21:25
- Interrogation . . . 1 Cor. 12:29, 30
- Irony . . . Luke 15:7-10
- Metaphor . . . Luke 13:32
- Parable . . . Matt. 13:10
- Parallelism . . . Gen. 4:23, 24
- Personification . . . Is. 55:12
- Proverb . . . 1 Kin. 4:32
- Sarcasm . . . Matt. 27:29
- Simile . . . Is. 1:8, 9
- Similitude . . . Ps. 90:4-6

Filial devotion

A. *Duty of:*
- Commanded . . . Ex. 20:12
- Corrupted . . . Matt. 15:4-6
- Confirmed . . . Eph. 6:1-3

B. *Examples of:*
- Joseph . . . Gen. 47:12
- David . . . 1 Sam. 22:3
- Solomon . . . 1 Kin. 2:19
- Elisha . . . 1 Kin. 19:19, 20
- Young man . . . Matt. 19:16-20

C. *Obedience:*
- Continual . . . Prov. 6:20-22
- Total . . . Col. 3:20
- Lack of, severely punished . . . Deut. 21:18-21
- Lack of, cursed . . . Prov. 20:20

Filth—*uncleanness, defilement, corruption*
- Men . . . Job 15:16; Ps. 14:2, 3
- Garments and furniture . . . Is. 4:1-4; Is. 28:8
- Ceremonial uncleanness . . . Ezek. 22:15
- Unrighteousness . . . Is. 64:6; Ezek. 16:6

SUBJECT	REFERENCE
Filthy lucre—*money*	
Bishop (elders) forbidden to seek	1 Tim. 3:3
Fine—*penalty payment*	
Paid by guilty	Ex. 21:23-30 Deut. 22:19
Restitution	Ex. 22:5-15 Num. 5:7
Finger	
A. *Used literally of:*	
Man's fingers	John 20:25, 27
Deformity	2 Sam. 21:20
Measurement	Jer. 52:21
Mysterious hand	Dan. 5:5
B. *Used figuratively of:*	
God's power	Ex. 8:19
Inspiration	Ex. 31:18
Suggestiveness	Prov. 6:13
Contrast of burdens	1 Kin. 12:10
Lord's authority	Luke 11:20
Fins	
Signs of a clean fish	Lev. 11:9
Fir—*a tree of the pine family*	
Tree of Lebanon	1 Kin. 5:8, 10
Used in Solomon's temple	1 Kin. 6:15, 34
Used in ships	Ezek. 27:5
Used for musical instruments	2 Sam. 6:5
Fire	
A. *Physical uses of:*	
Warmth	John 18:18
Cooking	Ex. 16:23
Signs	Judg. 20:38, 40
Sacrifices	Gen. 8:20, 21
Refining	Ps. 12:6
Torture	Dan. 3:6
Sacrifice of children	2 Kin. 16:3
B. *Supernatural uses of:*	
Manifest God	Ex. 3:2
Indicate God's power	Ex. 9:24
Express God's approval	Lev. 9:24
Vindicate God's wrath	2 Kin. 1:9-12
Guide Israel	Ex. 13:21, 22
Transport a saint to heaven	2 Kin. 2:11
C. *Used figuratively of:*	
God's protection	Zech. 2:5
God's vengeance	Heb. 12:29
God's Word	Jer. 5:14
Christ	Mal. 3:2
Holy Spirit	Acts 2:3
Angels	Heb. 1:7
Tongue	James 3:6
Persecution	Luke 12:49-53
Affliction	Is. 43:2
Purification	Is. 6:5-7
Love	Song 8:6
Lust	Prov. 6:27, 28
D. *Final uses of:*	
Destroy world	2 Pet. 3:10-12
Punish wicked	Matt. 25:41
Fire, Lake of—*place of eternal punishment*	
The beast	Rev. 19:20
The false prophet	Rev. 19:20
The devil	Rev. 20:10
Death and hell	Rev. 20:14
Sinners	Rev. 21:8
Firebrand—*torch*	
Figurative of enemies	Is. 7:4
Thrown by a madman	Prov. 26:18
Have no fear of	Is. 7:4
All who encircle	Is. 50:11
Snatched from a blaze	Amos 4:11
Firepan—*a shovel used for carrying fire*	
Part of the altar	Ex. 27:3
Firmament—*expanse*	
Created by God	Gen. 1:8
Stars placed in	Gen. 1:14, 17
Compared to a tent	Ps. 104:2
Expressive of God's glory	Ps. 19:1
Saints compared to	Dan. 12:3
First	
Came out red	Gen. 25:25
This came out	Gen. 38:28

SUBJECT	REFERENCE
These should set forth	Num. 2:9
Amalek, of nations	Num. 24:20
Hands of witness shall be	Deut. 17:7
Altar Solomon built	1 Sam. 14:35
Case pleaded	Prov. 18:17
Seek	Matt. 6:33
Cast out beam	Matt. 7:5 Luke 6:42
Last state worse than	Luke 11:26
The blade, then the head	Mark 4:28
Let the children	Mark 7:27
Desire to be	Mark 9:35
Commandment	Mark 12:28
Gospel must, be preached	Mark 13:10
Appeared to Mary Magdalene	Mark 16:9
Not sit down	Luke 14:28
Stepped in, made whole	John 5:4
Gave themselves	2 Cor. 8:5
Trusted in Christ	Eph. 1:12
A falling away	2 Thess. 2:3
Let these also	1 Tim. 3:10
Dwelt, in	2 Tim. 1:5
He takes away	Heb. 10:9
First (things mentioned)	
Altar	Gen. 8:20
Archer	Gen. 21:20
Artificer	Gen. 4:22
Bigamist	Gen. 4:19
Birthday celebration	Gen. 40:20
Book	Gen. 5:1
Bottle	Gen. 21:14
Bridal veil	Gen. 24:64-67
Cave dwellers	Gen. 19:30
Christian martyr	Acts 22:19, 20
City builder	Gen. 4:17
Coffin	Gen. 50:26
Command	Gen. 1:3
Commanded by Christ	Matt. 6:33
Commissioners	Dan. 6:2
Cremation	1 Sam. 31:12
Curse	Gen. 3:14
Death	Gen. 4:8
Diet	Jer. 52:31-34
Doubt	Gen. 3:1
Dream	Gen. 20:3
Drunkenness	Gen. 9:21
Emancipator	Ex. 3:7-22
Embalming	Gen. 50:2, 3
European convert	Acts 16:14, 15
Execution	Gen. 40:20-22
Family	Gen. 4:1, 2
Famine	Gen. 12:10
Farewell address	Josh. 23:1-16
Farmer	Gen. 4:2
Female government	Judg. 4:4, 5
Ferry boat	2 Sam. 19:18
Food control	Gen. 41:25-27
Frying pan	Lev. 2:7
Gardener	Gen. 2:15
Gold	Gen. 2:11
Harp	Gen. 4:21
Hebrew (Jew)	Gen. 14:13
High priest	Ex. 28:1
Hunter	Gen. 10:8, 9
Idolatry	Josh. 24:2
"In-law" trouble	Gen. 26:34, 35
Iron bedstead	Deut. 3:11
Judge	1 Sam. 7:15
Kiss	Gen. 27:26, 27
Left-handed man	Judg. 3:15
Letter	2 Sam. 11:14
Liar	Gen. 3:1-5
Man to hang himself	2 Sam. 17:23
Man to shave	Gen. 41:14
Man to wear a ring	Gen. 41:42
Miracles of Christ	John 2:1-11
Mother of twins	Gen. 25:21-28
Murderer	Gen. 4:8
Musician	Gen. 4:21
Navy	1 Kin. 9:26
Oath	Gen. 21:24
Orchestra	2 Sam. 6:5
Organ	Gen. 4:21
Pilgrim	Gen. 12:1-8
Prayer	Gen. 4:26
Prison	Gen. 39:20
Prophecy	Gen. 3:15
Prophetess	Ex. 15:20
Proposal of adultery	Gen. 39:7-12
Pulpit	Neh. 8:4
Purchase of land	Gen. 23:3-20
Question	Gen. 3:1
Rainbow	Gen. 9:13, 14
Rape	Judg. 19:24, 25
Riddle	Judg. 14:12-18
Sabbath	Gen. 2:2, 3

SUBJECT	REFERENCE
Sacrifice	Gen. 8:20
Saddle	Gen. 22:3
Scribe	Ex. 24:4
Selective Service	Num. 31:3-6
Shepherd	Gen. 4:2
Shepherdess	Gen. 29:9
Sheriffs	Dan. 3:2
Shipbuilder	Gen. 6:14
Sin	Gen. 3:1-24
Singing school	1 Chr. 25:5-7
Sunstroke	2 Kin. 4:18-20
Surveying of land	Josh. 18:8, 9
Temptation	Gen. 3:1-6
Theater	Acts 19:29-31
To be named before birth	Gen. 16:11
To confess Christ	John 1:49
Tombstone	Gen. 35:20
Tower	Gen. 11:4, 5
Vagabond	Gen. 4:9-12
Voluntary fasting	Judg. 20:26
Wage contract	Gen. 29:15-20
War	Gen. 14:2-12
Warships	Num. 24:24
Well	Gen. 16:14
Whirlwind	2 Kin. 2:1
Wife	Gen. 3:20
Winding stairs	1 Kin. 6:8
Woman thief	Gen. 31:19
Woman to curse	Judg. 17:1, 2
Woman to use cosmetics	2 Kin. 9:30
Words spoken to man	Gen. 1:28
Worship	Gen. 4:3-5
First-born	
Said to the younger	Gen. 19:31 Gen. 19:34
Bore a son	Gen. 19:37
Give younger before	Gen. 29:26
According to birthright	Gen. 43:33
Israel is My	Ex. 4:22
Will slay your	Ex. 4:23
All in the land of Egypt	Ex. 11:5
Will smite all	Ex. 12:12
Killed all the	Ex. 13:15 Ps. 105:36
Sanctify to me all	Ex. 13:2
Of Israel are Mine	Num. 3:13
Lay foundation in	Josh. 6:26
Of death shall	Job 18:13
Gave birth	Luke 2:7
Of all creation	Col. 1:15
So that he who destroyed	Heb. 11:28
A. *Privileges of:*	
First in family	Gen. 48:13, 14
Delegated authority of	Gen. 27:1-29
Received father's special blessing	Gen. 27:4, 35
Bears father's title	2 Chr. 21:1, 3
Given double portion of inheritance	Deut. 21:17
Object of special love	Jer. 31:9, 20
Precious and valuable	Mic. 6:7
B. *Laws concerning:*	
Dedicated to God	Ex. 22:29-31
To be redeemed	Ex. 34:20
Redemption price of	Num. 3:46-51
Tribe of Levi substituted for	Num. 3:11-45
Death of, next brother substituted	Matt. 22:24-28
Change of, forbidden	Deut. 21:15-17
Forfeited by evil deeds	Gen. 49:3, 4, 8
Forfeited by sale	Heb. 12:16, 17
Changed sovereignty	1 Sam. 16:6-12
Christ subject to	Luke 2:22-24
C. *Figurative of, Christ in:*	
Authority	Ps. 89:27
Honor	Heb. 1:6
Resurrection	Col. 1:18
Church	Rom. 8:29
Glory	Heb. 12:22, 23
First day of the week—*Sunday*	
Day of Christ's resurrection	Mark 16:9 John 20:1, 19
Day after the Sabbath	Matt. 28:1 Mark 16:1, 2
Day of Christian worship	Acts 20:7 1 Cor. 16:1, 2
Called "the Lord's day"	Rev. 1:10
First fruits	
A. *Regulations concerning:*	
Law specified	Lev. 23:9-14

F

SUBJECT — REFERENCE

- Brought to God's house ..... Ex. 34:26
- Ritual of, described ..... Deut. 26:3-10
- Considered holy ..... Ezek. 48:14
- God honored by ..... Prov. 3:9

B. *Figurative of:*

- Israel's position ..... Rom. 11:16
- Christ's place in resurrection ..... 1 Cor. 15:20, 23
- Christians ..... James 1:18
- First converts ..... Rom. 16:5

Firstlings

- Abel brought ..... Gen. 4:4
- Set apart every ..... Ex. 13:12; Ex. 34:19
- Of an ass thou shall redeem ..... Ex. 13:13; Ex. 34:20
- Lords, no man shall sanctify ..... Lev. 27:26
- Of unclean beasts ..... Num. 18:15
- Ye shall bring, of your herd ..... Deut. 12:6
- Males sanctify ..... Deut. 15:19
- Glory is like ..... Deut. 33:17

Fish

A. *Features regarding:*

- Created by God ..... Gen. 1:20, 21
- Worship of forbidden ..... Deut. 4:15-18
- Caught by net ..... Matt. 4:18
- Worshiped by pagans ..... 1 Sam. 5:4
- Some disciples called as fishermen ..... Matt. 4:18-21

B. *Miracles concerning:*

- Jonah's life in ..... Jon. 1:17
- Multiplied by Christ ..... Matt. 14:17-21
- Bearing a coin ..... Matt. 17:27

C. *Figurative of:*

- Men in the sea of life ..... Ezek. 47:9, 10
- Ministers as fishermen ..... Matt. 4:19
- Ignorant men ..... Eccl. 9:12

Fish Gate—*a gate of Jerusalem*

- Manasseh built wall there ..... 2 Chr. 33:13, 14
- Built by sons of Hassenaah ..... Neh. 3:3
- Two choirs took their stand ..... Neh. 12:38-40
- A cry there prophesied ..... Zeph. 1:10

Fish hook—*hook for catching fish*

- Cannot catch Leviathan ..... Job 41:1
- Fishing in the brooks ..... Is. 19:8

Fist fighting

- Punishment of ..... Ex. 21:18, 19

Fitches—*vetches*

- Annual plant for forage ..... Is. 28:25, 27
- Same as rye in ..... Ezek. 4:9

Flag—*fluttering*

- Name of many water plants ..... Ex. 2:3-5
- Rendered as "weeds" in ..... Jon. 2:5

Flagellation—*punishment by whipping, flogging*

- For immorality ..... Lev. 19:20
- For defamation ..... Deut. 22:16-18
- Forty blows ..... Deut. 25:3
- Of Christ ..... Matt. 27:26; Mark 15:15
- Thirty-nine lashes ..... 2 Cor. 11:24
- Of apostles ..... Acts 5:40

Flagon—*flask*

- Small vessels for liquids ..... Is. 22:24

Flat nose

- Disqualifies for service ..... Lev. 21:18

Flattery—*unjustified praise*

A. *Used by:*

- False prophets ..... Rom. 16:18
- Hypocrites ..... Ps. 78:36
- Wicked ..... Ps. 36:1-4
- Prostitutes ..... Prov. 2:16

B. *Attitude of saints toward:*

- Should avoid users of ..... Prov. 20:19
- Pray against ..... Ps. 5:8, 9
- Should not use ..... 1 Thess. 2:5

C. *Dangers of:*

- Leads to ruin ..... Prov. 26:28
- Brings deception ..... Prov. 29:5
- Corrupts ..... Dan. 11:21, 25, 27
- Brings death ..... Acts 12:21-23

SUBJECT — REFERENCE

Flax—*the flax plant*

- Grown in Egypt and Palestine ..... Ex. 9:31

Used for:

- Cords ..... Judg. 15:14
- Spinning ..... Is. 19:9
- Garments ("linen") ..... Deut. 22:11

Flea—*a parasitic, blood-sucking insect*

- Figurative of insignificance ..... 1 Sam. 24:14

Fleece—*freshly sheared wool*

- Given to priests ..... Deut. 18:3, 4
- Sign to Gideon ..... Judg. 6:36-40
- Warm ..... Job 31:20

Flesh

A. *Used to designate:*

- All created life ..... Gen. 6:13, 17, 19
- Kinsmen (of same nature) ..... Rom. 9:3, 5, 8
- The body ..... Job 33:25
- Marriage ..... Matt. 19:5
- Human nature ..... John 1:14
- Christ's mystical nature ..... John 6:51, 53-63
- Human weakness ..... Matt. 16:17
- Outward appearance ..... 2 Cor. 5:16
- The evil principle in man ..... Rom. 7:18
- Food ..... Ex. 16:12

B. *In a bad sense, described as:*

- Having passions ..... Gal. 5:24
- Producing evil works ..... Gal. 5:19-21
- Dominating the mind ..... Eph. 2:3
- Absorbing the affections ..... Rom. 13:14
- Seeking outward display ..... Gal. 6:12, 13
- Antagonizing the Spirit ..... Gal. 5:17
- Fighting against God's Law ..... Rom. 8:7
- Reaping corruption ..... Gal. 6:8
- Producing death ..... Rom. 7:5

C. *Christian's attitude toward:*

- Still confronts ..... Rom. 7:18-23
- Source of opposition ..... Gal. 5:17
- Make no provision for ..... Rom. 13:14
- Do not love ..... 1 John 2:15-17
- Do not walk in ..... Rom. 8:1, 4
- Do not live in ..... Rom. 8:12, 13
- Crucified ..... Gal. 5:24

Flesh hook—*fork*

- In tabernacle ..... Ex. 27:3; Num. 4:14
- By priests ..... 1 Sam. 2:12-14
- In Temple ..... 1 Chr. 28:11, 17; 2 Chr. 4:16

Flies—*small winged insects*

- Cause of evil odor ..... Eccl. 10:1
- Figurative of Egypt ..... Is. 7:18
- Plague upon the Egyptians ..... Ex. 8:21-31; Ps. 78:45

Flint—*a very hard stone*

- Water from ..... Deut. 8:15
- Oil from ..... Deut. 32:13
- Turning into fountain of water ..... Ps. 114:8
- Hoofs shall seem like ..... Is. 5:28
- Figurative of a fixed course ..... Is. 50:7; Ezek. 3:9

Flock—*a group of domesticated animals*

- Sheep and goats ..... Gen. 27:9
- Nations ..... Jer. 51:23
- National leaders ..... Jer. 25:34, 35
- Jewish people ..... Jer. 13:17, 20
- True church ..... Is. 40:11; Acts 20:28

Flood—*overflowing of water*

A. *Used literally of:*

- Earth's flood ..... Gen. 6:17

B. *Used figuratively of:*

- Great trouble ..... Ps. 32:6
- Hostile world powers ..... Ps. 93:3
- An invading army ..... Jer. 46:7, 8
- Great destruction ..... Dan. 9:26
- Testing ..... Matt. 7:25, 27
- Persecution ..... Rev. 12:15, 16

Floodgates

- Descriptive of judgment ..... Gen. 7:11

Floor

- For threshing wheat ..... Judg. 6:37; 1 Kin. 22:10
- Of a building ..... 1 Kin. 6:15

SUBJECT — REFERENCE

Flour—*finely ground wheat*

- Offered in sacrifices ..... Lev. 5:11, 13

Flowers

A. *Described as:*

- Wild ..... Ps. 103:15, 16
- Beautiful ..... Matt. 6:28, 29
- Sweet ..... Song 5:13
- Fading ..... Is. 40:7, 8

B. *Figurative of:*

- Shortness of life ..... Job 14:2
- Israel ..... Is. 28:1
- Man's glory ..... James 1:10, 11

Flute—*a hollow musical instrument*

- In Babylon ..... Dan. 3:5
- Used in God's worship ..... Ps. 150:4

Foal—*a colt, young donkey*

- Given to Esau ..... Gen. 32:13-15
- Ridden by Christ ..... Zech. 9:9; Matt. 21:5

Fodder—*food for domestic animals*

- Given to oxen and wild ass ..... Job 6:5; Is. 30:24

Following

A. *In Old Testament:*

- Commanded ..... Deut. 8:6
- Brought reward ..... Deut. 19:9
- Covenant ..... 2 Kin. 23:3

B. *In New Testament:*

- Multitudes ..... Matt. 4:25; Matt. 12:15
- Disciples ..... Matt. 8:19; Luke 5:11-27
- Left all ..... Matt. 4:18-22
- In light ..... John 8:12
- After Christ's example ..... John 13:15; 1 John 2:6
- Example of Godly men ..... Phil. 3:17; Heb. 6:12; James 5:10

Folly—*contemptuous disregard of holy things*

A. *Described as:*

- Unnatural sin ..... Judg. 19:22-24

B. *Associated with:*

- Deception ..... Prov. 14:8
- Hasty spirit ..... Prov. 14:29
- Gullibility ..... Prov. 13:16
- Ferociousness ..... Prov. 17:12
- Disgust ..... Prov. 26:11

C. *Warnings against:*

- Saints not to return to ..... Ps. 85:8
- Prophets guilty of ..... Jer. 23:13
- Angels charged with ..... Job 4:18
- Apostles subject to ..... 2 Cor. 11:1

Food

A. *Features regarding:*

- Given by God ..... Ps. 104:21, 27
- Necessary for man ..... Gen. 1:29, 30
- Gives physical strength ..... Acts 9:19
- Revives the spirit ..... 1 Sam. 30:12
- Object of daily prayer ..... Matt. 6:11
- Object of thanksgiving ..... 1 Sam. 9:13
- Sanctified by prayer ..... 1 Tim. 4:4, 5
- Scruples recognized ..... Rom. 14:2-23

B. *Lack of:*

- Testing of faith ..... Hab. 3:17

C. *Provided by:*

- God ..... Ps. 145:15
- Christ ..... John 21:5, 6

D. *Prohibitions concerning:*

- Dead animals ..... Ex. 22:31
- Eating blood ..... Deut. 12:16
- Clean and unclean ..... Deut. 14:4-20
- Wine ..... Prov. 23:29-35
- Strangled animals ..... Acts 21:25
- Not in itself commendable ..... 1 Cor. 8:8
- Not to be a stumbling block ..... 1 Cor. 8:13
- Life more important than ..... Matt. 6:25

E. *Miracles connected with:*

- Destruction of ..... Ps. 105:29-35
- Provision for ..... Ps. 105:40, 41

SUBJECT ... REFERENCE

Supply of ... 1 Kin. 17:4-6
Multiplication of ... John 6:5-13
Refused ... Matt. 4:1-4

F. *Figurative of:*

God's will ... John 4:32, 34
Christ ... John 6:27, 55
Strong doctrines ... 1 Cor. 3:2

Food control

First ... Gen. 41:25-27
Final ... Rev. 13:11-17

Food, spiritual

A. *Elements of:*

The Word ... Ps. 19:10
Christ ... John 6:48-51

B. *Need of, by:*

The naive ... Prov. 9:1-5
The immature ... 1 Cor. 3:1, 2
The mature ... Heb. 5:14
All ... Matt. 22:4

C. *Characteristics of:*

Abundant ... Is. 55:1-3
Satisfying ... Ps. 22:26
Enduring ... John 6:48-51
Life-giving ... John 6:53-63

Foods of Bible times

A. *Obtaining; storing; use:*

Shall be for ... Gen. 6:21
Let them gather ... Gen. 41:35
But to buy ... Gen. 42:10
Go again, buy ... Gen. 43:2
Buy ... Gen. 43:4
Much ... Prov. 13:23
Of the offering ... Lev. 3:11
Of Holy things ... Lev. 22:7
In giving him ... Deut. 10:18
Seeking in wilderness ... Job 24:5
Man did eat that of angels' ... Ps. 78:25
Bring forth ... Ps. 104:14

B. *Specific kinds:*

Almonds ... Gen. 43:11
Barley ... Judg. 7:13
Beans ... Ezek. 4:9
Beef ... 1 Kin. 4:22, 23
Beef stew ... 1 Kin. 19:21
Bread ... 1 Sam. 17:17
Broth ... Judg. 6:19
Cakes ... 2 Sam. 13:8
Cheese ... Job 10:10
Cucumbers ... Num. 11:5
Curds of cows ... Deut. 32:14
Eggs ... Deut. 22:6
Figs ... Num. 13:23
Fish ... Matt. 7:10
Fowl ... 1 Kin. 4:23
Fruit ... 2 Sam. 16:2
Garlic ... Num. 11:5
Goat's milk ... Prov. 27:27
Grain ... Ruth 2:14
Grapes ... Deut. 23:24
Grasshoppers ... Lev. 11:22
Herbs ... Ex. 12:8
Honey ... Is. 7:15
Leeks ... Num. 11:5
Lentils ... Gen. 25:34
Locusts ... Matt. 3:4
Meal ... Matt. 13:33
Melons ... Num. 11:5
Nuts ... Gen. 43:11
Oil ... Prov. 21:17
Olives ... Deut. 28:40
Onions ... Num. 11:5
Pomegranates ... Num. 13:23
Pottage ... Gen. 25:30
Pulse ... 2 Sam. 17:28
Quail ... Num. 11:32, 33
Raisins ... 2 Sam. 16:1
Salt ... Job 6:6
Sheep ... Deut. 14:4
Sheep's milk ... Deut. 32:14
Spices ... Gen. 43:11
Veal ... Gen. 18:7, 8
Vegetables ... Prov. 15:17
Vinegar ... Num. 6:3
Venison ... Gen. 25:28
Wild honey ... Ps. 19:10
Wine ... John 2:3, 10

Foolish—*those who misuse wisdom*

A. *Those described as:*

Clamorous woman ... Prov. 9:13
Builder on sand ... Matt. 7:26
Five virgins ... Matt. 25:1-13
Galatians ... Gal. 3:1, 3
Gentiles ... Titus 3:3

B. *Things described as:*

The Heart ... Rom. 1:21
Things ... 1 Cor. 1:27
Lusts ... 1 Tim. 6:9
Questions ... 2 Tim. 2:23

C. *Characteristics of:*

Destructive ... Prov. 10:14
Despicable ... Prov. 15:20
Disappointing ... Prov. 19:13

Foolishness—*a disregard of final issues*

A. *Characteristics of:*

Form of sin ... Prov. 24:9
Originates in the heart ... Mark 7:21-23
Sign of wickedness ... Eccl. 7:25
Known by God ... Ps. 69:5

B. *Consequences of:*

Brings sorrow ... Ps. 38:4-10
Perverts man's way ... Prov. 19:3
Spiritual blindness ... 1 Cor. 1:18

Fools—*those who misuse true wisdom*

A. *Described as:*

Atheistic ... Ps. 14:1
Blasphemous ... Ps. 74:18
Contentious ... Prov. 18:6
Hypocritical ... Luke 11:39, 40
Idle ... Eccl. 4:5
Vexation ... Prov. 12:16
Materialistic ... Luke 12:16-21
Meddling ... Prov. 20:3
Mischievous ... Prov. 10:23
Mocking ... Prov. 14:9
Raging ... Prov. 14:16
Self-confident ... Prov. 28:26
Self-righteous ... Prov. 12:15
Self-sufficient ... Rom. 1:22
Slandering ... Prov. 10:18
Wasteful ... Prov. 21:20
Wordy ... Eccl. 10:12-14

B. *Further characteristics of:*

Hate knowledge ... Prov. 1:22
Come to shame ... Prov. 3:35
Mock at sin ... Prov. 14:9
Cannot attain to wisdom ... Prov. 24:7
Trust in their hearts ... Prov. 28:26
Walk in darkness ... Eccl. 2:14

C. *Examples of:*

Nabal ... 1 Sam. 25:3, 25
Rehoboam ... 1 Kin. 12:8
Pharisees ... Matt. 23:17, 19
The rich man ... Luke 12:16-21

Foot

A. *To sit at, figurative of:*

Teachableness ... Luke 10:39

B. *To be under, figurative of:*

God's sovereignty ... Ps. 8:6
Christ's victory ... Ps. 110:1
Conquest ... Josh. 10:24

C. *Examples, figurative of:*

Prosperity ... Deut. 33:24
Possession ... Josh. 1:3
Reverence ... Josh. 5:15
Whole person ... Prov. 1:15

See Feet

Footman—*the infantry force*

10,000 in Samaria ... 2 Kin. 13:6, 7

Footstool

A. *Used literally of:*

In the Temple ... 2 Chr. 9:18
Prominent seat ... James 2:3

B. *Used figuratively of:*

Earth ... Matt. 5:35
Ark ... 1 Chr. 28:2
Temple worship ... Ps. 99:5
Subjection ... Acts 2:35

Forbearance of God

A. *God's withholding of judgment, upon:*

The Amorites ... Gen. 15:16
Sodom ... Gen. 18:23-32
Israel ... Neh. 9:30, 31
Nineveh ... Jon. 4:10, 11
The world ... Rom. 3:25

B. *Attitudes toward:*

Not to be despised ... Rom. 2:4
To be remembered ... 2 Pet. 3:8-10
Means of preparation ... Mal. 3:1-6

Forbearance toward others

Expression of love ... 1 Cor. 13:7
Christian grace ... Eph. 4:2

Forced labor—*conscripted workers or slaves*

Prisoners of war ... Deut. 20:10, 11
As slaves ... Ex. 13:3
By Solomon ... 1 Kin. 9:20, 21

Forces—*military power*

False worship of ... Dan. 11:10, 38
Weakness of ... Zech. 4:6
Destruction of great ... Rev. 20:7-10

Forcible—*powerful*

Power of right words ... Job 6:25

Ford—*a shallow crossing of a body of water*

Of the Jabbok ... Gen. 32:22
Of the Jordan ... Judg. 3:28

Forehead—*the upper part of the face*

A. *Used literally of:*

Aaron's ... Ex. 28:38
Philistines' ... 1 Sam. 17:49
Uzziah's ... 2 Chr. 26:19, 20

B. *Used figuratively of:*

Shamelessness ... Rev. 17:5
Stronger power ... Ezek. 3:8, 9
Devotion to God ... Ezek. 9:4
Christ's true servants ... Rev. 7:3

Foreign affairs—*dealings with other countries*

War ... Gen. 14:1-16; Josh. 8:1-29
Treaties ... Josh. 9:1-27
Trade agreement ... 1 Kin. 5:1-18
Alliances ... 1 Kin. 15:16-22; 1 Kin. 22:1-6
Conquest ... 2 Kin. 25:1-11

Foreigners—*sojourners in Israel*

Kept from feast ... Ex. 12:43-45
Taxable ... Deut. 15:2, 3
Figurative of Gentiles ... Eph. 2:19

See Strangers

Foreign missionaries

Jonah as ... Jon. 1:1, 2
Came from Antioch church ... Acts 13:1-3
Report of ... Acts 15:7-12

Foreknowledge of Christ

Concerning:

Men's nature ... John 1:47, 48
Men's acts ... John 6:64
His death and resurrection ... Matt. 20:18, 19; John 13:1
Jerusalem's destruction ... Luke 19:41-44
Prophetic events ... Matt. 24:1-51

Foreknowledge of God

A. *Manifested in:*

Naming a place ... 1 Kin. 13:2, 3; Matt. 2:5, 6
Setting a time ... Mark 1:15
Determining the boundaries of nations ... Acts 17:26
Indicating successive nations ... Dan. 2:26-47
Announcing Israel's captivity ... Dan. 9:2, 24
Foretelling Christ's death ... Acts 2:23

B. *Based upon God's:*

Infinite knowledge ... Is. 41:22, 23
Eternal being ... Is. 43:9-13
Foredetermination of events ... Rom. 8:29

C. *Plan of Salvation:*

Planned in eternity ... Eph. 1:3-12
Announces from beginning ... Gen. 3:15
Expanded to include Gentiles ... Gal. 3:8
Elaborated in details ... Is. 53:1-12
Visualized in prophecy ... Zech. 3:1-10

SUBJECT REFERENCE

Consummated in Christ's death ... John 19:30

Foresee—*to see something before it takes place*
Approaching evil ... Prov. 22:3
Resurrection of Christ ... Acts 2:31
Salvation of Gentiles ... Gal. 3:8

Foreskin (see Circumcision)
A. *Used literally of:*
Circumcision ... Gen. 17:9-17
Death ... 1 Sam. 18:25
B. *Figuratively of:*
Regeneration ... Jer. 4:4

Forest
A. *Descriptive of wooded areas in:*
Hareth ... 1 Sam. 22:5
Lebanon ... 1 Kin. 7:2
Beth-el ... 2 Kin. 2:23, 24
Arabia ... Is. 21:13
B. *Used figuratively of:*
Army ... Is. 10:18, 19
Kingdom ... Jer. 21:14
Unfruitfulness ... Jer. 26:18
Hos. 2:12

Forethought—*thinking ahead*
In meeting a danger ... Gen. 32:3-23
In anticipating evil ... Prov. 22:3
Concerning physical needs ... Phil. 4:10-19
Neglect of, dangerous ... Matt. 25:8-13
Examples of ant, in ... Prov. 6:6-8
For eternal riches ... Luke 12:23-34

Foretold—*made known beforehand*
Destruction of Jerusalem ... Mark 13:1, 2
Gospel blessings ... Acts 3:24
Paul's trip to Corinth ... 2 Cor. 13:2

Forewarn—*to warn beforehand*
God's judgment ... Luke 12:5
God's vengeance ... 1 Thess. 4:6

Forfeit—*loss incurred by one's failure*
Leadership ... 1 Sam. 15:16-28
Possessions ... Ezra 10:8
Salvation ... Matt. 16:26

Forfeiting spiritual rights
Birthright ... Gen. 25:34
Headship ... Gen. 49:3, 4
Apostleship ... Matt. 26:14-16
Spiritual heritage ... Acts 13:45-48

Forger—*a counterfeiter*
Applied to David's enemies ... Ps. 119:69

Forget—*be unable to remember*
God does not ... Is. 49:15
Our sinful past ... Phil. 3:13

Forgetful—*unable to remember*
Concerning our hearing ... James 1:25

Forgetting of God
A. *Seen in forgetting God's:*
Covenant ... Deut. 4:23
Works ... Ps. 78:7, 11
Blessings ... Ps. 103:2
Law ... Ps. 119:153, 176
Word ... James 1:25
B. *Characteristics of:*
Wicked ... Is. 65:11
Form of backsliding ... Jer. 3:21, 22
Instigated by false teachers ... Jer. 23:26, 27

Forgiveness—*an act of pardon*
A. *Synonyms of:*
"Blotteth out" ... Is. 43:25
"Remission" ... Matt. 26:28
"Pardon" ... Is. 55:7
"Remember no more" ... Jer. 31:34
"Healed" ... 2 Chr. 30:18-20
B. *Basis of:*
God's nature ... Ps. 86:5
God's grace ... Luke 7:42
Shedding of blood ... Heb. 9:22
Christ's death ... Col. 1:14
Son's power ... Luke 5:21-24
Man's repentance ... Acts 2:38
Our forgiveness ... Matt. 6:12-14
Faith in Christ ... Acts 10:43

SUBJECT REFERENCE

C. *Significance of:*
Shows God's righteousness ... Rom. 3:25
Makes salvation real ... Luke 1:77
Must be preached ... Luke 24:47

Forgiving one another
A. *The measure of:*
Seventy times seven ... Matt. 18:21, 22
Unlimited ... Luke 17:3, 4
As God forgave us ... Eph. 4:32
B. *Benefits of:*
Means of our forgiveness ... Mark 11:25, 26
Restored Christian fellowship ... 2 Cor. 2:7-10
Spiritual cleansing ... James 5:15, 16
C. *Examples of:*
Esau and Jacob ... Gen. 33:4-15
Joseph ... Gen. 45:8-15
Moses ... Num. 12:1-13
David ... 2 Sam. 19:18-23
Solomon ... 1 Kin. 1:53
Jesus ... Luke 23:34
Stephen ... Acts 7:60
Paul ... 2 Tim. 4:16

Fork
Rendered:
"Three-pronged fork" ... 1 Sam. 2:13, 14
"Fork" ... Is. 30:24

Form—*the outward appearance*
A. *Of physical things:*
Earth without ... Gen. 1:2
Man in the womb ... Is. 44:24
Sexes ... 1 Tim. 2:13
Idols ... Is. 44:10
B. *Of spiritual realities:*
Incarnate Christ ... Is. 53:2
Rom. 9:20
Molder ... Rom. 9:20
Christian truth ... Rom. 6:17
New birth ... Gal. 4:19

Formalism—*forms performed mechanically*
A. *Characterized by:*
Outward forms of religion ... Is. 1:10-15
Lifelessness ... Is. 58:1-14
Coldness ... Rev. 3:14-18
B. *Sign of:*
Hypocrisy ... Luke 18:10-12
Deadness ... Phil. 3:4-8
Last days ... 2 Tim. 3:1, 5

Formula—*a prescribed method*
Success ... Prov. 22:29
Prosperity ... Matt. 6:32, 33
Peace ... Is. 26:3
Making friends ... Prov. 18:24

Fornication—*sex relations among the unmarried*
Evil of:
Comes from evil heart ... Matt. 15:19
Sins against the body ... 1 Cor. 6:18
Excludes from God's kingdom ... 1 Cor. 6:9
Disrupts Christian fellowship ... 1 Cor. 5:9-11

Forsaken—*left deserted*
God's house ... Neh. 13:11
God's children ... Ps. 37:25
Messiah ... Is. 53:3
God's Son ... Matt. 27:46

Forsaking Christ
Disciples left ... Matt. 26:56
Cause of separation ... John 6:66-70

Forsaking God
A. *Manifested in:*
Going after idols ... 1 Kin. 11:33
Going backward ... Jer. 15:6
Following human forms ... Jer. 2:13
B. *Evil of:*
Manifests ingratitude ... Jer. 2:5-12
Brings confusion ... Jer. 17:13
Merits God's wrath ... Ezra 8:22
C. *Examples of:*
Israel ... 2 Kin. 17:7-18
Judah ... 2 Chr. 12:1, 5

SUBJECT REFERENCE

Fort—*stronghold*
In Jerusalem ... 2 Sam. 5:9

Fortifications—*walls or towers for protection*
Cities ... 1 Kin. 9:15
2 Chr. 11:5-11
City of David ... 2 Sam. 5:7-9

Fortified cities
Means of protection ... 2 Sam. 20:6
Mighty and strong ... Deut. 9:1
Conquerable ... Deut. 3:5
Utterly destroyed ... 2 Kin. 3:19, 25
No substitute for God ... Hos. 8:14

Fortress—*center of military strength*
Nation's security ... 2 Chr. 26:9
Illustrative of God's protection ... Ps. 18:2
Typical of Christ ... Is. 33:16, 17
Applied to God's prophet ... Jer. 6:27

Fortunatus—*fortunate*
Christian at Corinth ... 1 Cor. 16:17

Forty days
Length of flood ... Gen. 7:17
Israel's embalming ... Gen. 50:2, 3
Moses on Mt. Sinai ... Ex. 24:18
Spies in Canaan ... Num. 13:25
Moses' prayer ... Deut. 9:25-29
The Philistine's arrogance ... 1 Sam. 17:16
Elijah's fast ... 1 Kin. 19:2, 8
Nineveh's probation ... Jon. 3:4
Christ's temptation ... Luke 4:1, 2
Christ's ministry after His resurrection ... Acts 1:3

Forty stripes
Limit for scourging ... Deut. 25:3
Paul's, one less ... 2 Cor. 11:24

Forty years
Isaac's age at marriage ... Gen. 25:20
Israel's diet ... Ex. 16:35
Israel's wanderings ... Num. 32:13
Same shoes for ... Deut. 29:5
Period of rest ... Judg. 3:11
Egypt's desolation ... Ezek. 29:11-13
Saul's reign ... Acts 13:21
David's reign ... 1 Kin. 2:11
Solomon's reign ... 1 Kin. 11:42

Forwardness—*haste; overboldness*
Peter's faltering ... Matt. 14:28, 29
Paul's desire for the Corinthians ... 2 Cor. 8:8, 10

Foundation
A. *Used literally of:*
Cities ... Josh. 6:26
Walls ... Ezra 4:12
Houses ... Luke 6:48
Prison house ... Acts 16:26
House of the Lord ... 1 Kin. 6:37
Towers ... Luke 14:28, 29
B. *Used figuratively of:*
Christ ... Is. 28:16
Matt. 16:18
Christian truth ... Eph. 2:20
God decrees ... 2 Tim. 2:19
Security of parents ... 1 Tim. 6:19
Eternal city ... Heb. 11:10
C. *Importance of:*
Must be on a rock ... Matt. 7:24
Matt. 16:18
Must be firm ... Luke 6:48
Must be Christ ... 1 Cor. 3:11
Without, hopeless ... Ps. 11:3

Foundation, Gate of the—*a gate of Jerusalem*
Levites stationed there ... 2 Chr. 23:2-5
Possibly the Horse Gate ... 2 Kin. 11:16
2 Chr. 23:15

Fountain—*a flow of water from the earth*
Figurative of:
Mouth of the righteous ... Prov. 10:11
Understanding ... Prov. 16:22
Rich blessings ... Jer. 2:13

Fountain Gate—*a gate of Jerusalem*
Viewed by Nehemiah ... Neh. 2:13, 14
Repaired ... Neh. 3:15

SUBJECT	REFERENCE
Foursquare	
Altar	Ex. 27:1
Breastplate	Ex. 39:8, 9
City of God	Rev. 21:16
Fowl	
Bird	Gen. 1:20, 21
Clean, edible	Deut. 14:20
Solomon's knowledge of	1 Kin. 4:33
Fowler—*one who catches birds*	
Law restricting	Deut. 22:6, 7
Figurative of false prophets	Hos. 9:8
Figurative of temptations	Ps. 91:3 Ps. 124:7
Fox—*a dog-like animal*	
A. *Described as:*	
Plentiful	Judg. 15:4
Destructive	Neh. 4:3
Crafty	Luke 63:32
Carnivorous	Ps. 63:10
Living in holes	Matt. 8:20
Loves grapes	Song 2:15
B. *Figurative of:*	
False prophets	Ezek. 13:4
Enemies	Song 2:15
Deceivers	Luke 13:32
Fragment—*a part of a larger whole*	
Of food	Mark 6:43
Fragrance—*a sweet odor*	
Of perfume	John 12:3
Figurative of restoration	Hos. 14:6
Frankincense—*a fragrant gum of a tree*	
Used in holy oil	Ex. 30:34-38
Used in meal offerings	Lev. 2:1, 2, 15
Excluded from certain offerings	Lev. 5:11
Used in the showbread	Lev. 24:7
Product of Arabia	Is. 60:6
Presented to Jesus	Matt. 2:11
Figurative of worship	Ps. 141:2
Fratricide—*murder of a brother*	
Abel, by Cain	Gen. 4:8
70, by Abimelech	Judg. 9:1, 5
Amnon, by Absalom	2 Sam. 13:28
Adonijah, by Solomon	1 Kin. 2:23-25
Six, by Jehoram	2 Chr. 21:4
Predicted	Matt. 10:21
Fraud—*something designed to deceive*	
A. *Examples of:*	
Rebekah's, on Isaac	Gen. 27:5-36
Laban's, on Jacob	Gen. 29:21-25
Gibeonites', on Israelites	Josh. 9:3-9
Jonathan's, on Saul	1 Sam. 20:11-17
B. *Discovery of, by:*	
A miracle	Ex. 7:9-12
Events	Matt. 28:11-15
Character	Matt. 26:47-50
Free moral agency of man—*ability to choose*	
Resulted in sin	Gen. 2:16, 17
Recognized by God	Gen. 4:6-10 John 7:17
Appealed to	Is. 1:18-20 Jer. 36:3, 7
Freedom—*unrestricted action*	
A. *Of the unregenerate, limited by:*	
Sin	John 8:34
Inability	John 8:43
Satan	John 8:41, 44
Bondage	Rom. 6:20
Deadness	Eph. 2:1
B. *Of the regenerate:*	
Made free by Christ	John 8:36
Freed from bondage	Rom. 6:18, 22
Not of license	1 Pet. 2:16
Not of bondage again	Gal. 5:1
Not of the flesh	Gal. 5:13
Freewill offerings	
Obligatory	Deut. 12:6
Must be perfect	Lev. 22:17-25
Eaten in tabernacle by the priests	Lev. 7:16, 17
First fruits	Prov. 3:9
According to one's ability	Deut. 16:17

SUBJECT	REFERENCE
Willing mind	2 Cor. 8:10-12
Cheerful heart	2 Cor. 9:6, 7
Fretting—*a peevish state of mind*	
Of the saints, forbidden	Ps. 37:1, 7, 8
Friend	
A. *Nature of, common:*	
Interest	1 Sam. 18:1
Love	1 Sam. 20:17
Sympathy	Job 2:11
Sacrifice	John 15:13
B. *Value of:*	
Constructive criticism	Prov. 27:6
Helpful advice	Prov. 27:7
Valuable in time of need	Prov. 27:10
Always faithful	Prov. 17:17
C. *Dangers of:*	
May entice to sin	Deut. 13:6
Some are necessary	Prov. 14:20
Some are untrustworthy	Ps. 41:9
D. *Examples of:*	
God and Abraham	Is. 41:8
David and Jonathan	1 Sam. 18:1
David and Hushai	2 Sam. 15:37
Elijah and Elisha	2 Kin. 2:1-14
Christ and His disciples	John 15:13-15
Paul and Timothy	2 Tim. 1:2
Friendless—*lacking friends*	
David's plight	Ps. 142:4
Prodigal son	Luke 15:16
Friendship	
A. *Kinds of:*	
True	1 Sam. 18:1-3
Close	Prov. 18:24
Ardent	2 Cor. 2:12, 13
Treacherous	Matt. 26:48-50
Dangerous	Deut. 13:6-9
Unfaithful	Job 19:14-19
False	2 Sam. 16:16-23
Worldly	James 4:4
B. *Tests of:*	
Continued loyalty	2 Sam. 1:23
Willingness to sacrifice	John 15:13
Obedient spirit	John 15:14, 15
Likemindedness	Phil. 2:19-23
Frog—*a small, leaping creature*	
Plague on Egypt	Ps. 78:45
Of unclean spirits	Rev. 16:13
Frontlets—*ornaments worn on the forehead*	
Of God's Word	Deut. 6:6-9
Frost	
Figurative of God's power	Job 37:10
Figurative of God's creative ability	Job 38:29
Frowardness—*perverseness*	
Comes from the heart	Prov. 6:14
Issues from the mouth	Prov. 2:12
Causes strife	Prov. 16:28
Abomination to God	Prov. 11:20
Hard way	Prov. 22:5
Shall be cut off	Prov. 10:31
Frugality—*thrift*	
Manifested by Jesus	John 6:11-13
Wrong kind	Prov. 11:24, 25
Fruit—*product of life*	
A. *Used literally of:*	
Produce of trees	Gen. 1:29
Produce of the earth	Gen. 4:3
Progeny of livestock	Deut. 28:51
B. *Factors destructive of:*	
Blight	Joel 1:12
Locusts	Joel 1:4
Enemies	Ezek. 25:4
Drought	Hag. 1:10
God's anger	Jer. 7:20
C. *Used figuratively of:*	
Repentance	Matt. 3:8
Industry	Prov. 31:16, 31
Christian graces	Gal. 5:22, 23
Holy life	Prov. 11:30
Christian converts	John 4:36
Christ	Ps. 132:11
Sinful life	Matt. 7:16
Reward of righteousness	Phil. 1:11

SUBJECT	REFERENCE
Fruit-bearing—*productiveness of*	
Old age	Ps. 92:14
Good hearers	Matt. 13:23
Christian converts	Col. 1:6, 10
Abiding	John 15:2-8
Fruitfulness	
A. *Literally, dependent upon:*	
Right soil	Matt. 13:8
Rain	James 5:18
Sunshine	Deut. 33:14
Seasons	Matt. 21:34
Cultivation	Luke 13:8
God's blessing	Acts 14:17
B. *Spiritually, dependent upon:*	
Death	John 12:24
New life	Rom. 7:4
Abiding in Christ	John 15:2-8
Yielding to God	Rom. 6:13-23
Christian effort	2 Pet. 1:5-11
Absence of, reprobated	Matt. 21:19
Fruitless discussion—*self-conceited talk against God*	
Characteristic of false teachers	1 Tim. 1:6, 7
Fruit trees	
Protected by Law	Lev. 19:23-25
Frying pan	
Mentioned in	Lev. 2:7
Fulfill—*to bring to its designed end*	
A. *Spoken of God's:*	
Word	Ps. 148:8
Prophecy	1 Kin. 2:27
Threat	2 Chr. 36:20, 21
Promise	Acts 13:32, 33
Righteousness	Matt. 3:15
Good pleasure	2 Thess. 1:11
Will	Acts 13:22
B. *Spoken of the believer's:*	
Love	Rom. 13:8
Righteousness	Rom. 8:4
Burden-bearing	Gal. 6:2
Mission	Col. 1:25
Ministry	Col. 4:17
Full—*complete*	
A. *Of natural things:*	
Years	Gen. 25:8
Breasts	Job 21:24
Children	Ps. 127:5
Wagon	Amos 2:13
Leprosy	Luke 5:12
B. *Of miraculous things:*	
Guidance	Judg. 6:38
Supply	2 Kin. 4:4, 6
Protection	2 Kin. 6:17
C. *Of evil emotions:*	
Evil	Eccl. 9:3
Fury	Dan. 3:19
Wrath	Acts 19:28
Envy	Rom. 1:29
Cursing	Rom. 3:14
Deadly poison	James 3:8
Adultery	2 Pet. 2:14
D. *Of good things:*	
Power	Mic. 3:8
Grace, truth	John 1:14
Joy	John 15:11
Faith	Acts 6:5, 8
Good works	Acts 9:36
Holy Spirit	Acts 11:24
Fuller—*one who treats or dyes cloth*	
Outside city	2 Kin. 18:17 Is. 7:3
God is like	Mal. 3:2
Makes white	Mark 9:3
Fullness—*completion*	
A. *Of time:*	
Christ's advent	Gal. 4:4
Gentile age	Rom. 11:25
Age of grace	Eph. 1:10
B. *Of Christ:*	
Eternal Christ	Col. 2:9
Incarnate Christ	John 1:16
Glorified Christ	Eph. 1:22, 23

SUBJECT REFERENCE

Funeral—*burial rites*
Sad ....1 Kin. 13:29, 30
Joyful ....Luke 7:11-17

Furlong—*a Greek measure of length* (660 linear feet)
Measure on land or sea ....Luke 24:13

Furnace—*fire made very hot*
A. *Used literally of:*
Smelting ovens ....Gen. 19:28
Baker's oven ....Hos. 7:4
B. *Used figuratively of:*
Egyptian bondage ....Deut. 4:20
Spiritual refinement ....Ps. 12:6
Lust ....Hos. 7:4
Hell ....Matt. 13:42, 50
Punishment ....Ezek. 22:18-22

Furnace, fiery
Deliverance from ....Dan. 3:8-26

Furniture
Tabernacle ....Ex. 31:7
Room ....2 Kin. 4:8-10

Future—*that which is beyond the present*
Only God knows ....Is. 41:21-23
Revealed by:
Christ ....John 13:19
The Spirit ....John 16:13
Man's ignorance of ....Luke 19:41-44
No provision for, dangerous ....Luke 12:16-21
Proper provision for ....Matt. 6:19-34

G

Gaal—*loathing*
Son of Ebed; vilifies Abimelech ....Judg. 9:26-41

Gaash—*quaking*
Hill of Ephraim ....Judg. 2:9
Joshua's burial near ....Josh. 24:30

Gaba—*a hill*
City of Benjamin ....Josh. 18:21, 24

Gabbai—*tax gatherer*
Postexilic Benjamite ....Neh. 11:8

Gabbatha—*pavement*
Place of Pilate's court ....John 19:13

Gabriel—*man of God*
Interprets Daniel's vision ....Dan. 8:16-27
Reveals the prophecy of 70 weeks ....Dan. 9:21-27
Announces John's birth ....Luke 1:11-22
Announces Christ's birth ....Luke 1:26-38
Stands in God's presence ....Luke 1:19

Gad—*good fortune*
1. Son of Jacob by Zilpah ....Gen. 30:10, 11
Father of seven sons who founded tribal families ....Gen. 46:16
2. Descendants of the tribe of Gad ....Deut. 27:13
Census of ....Num. 1:24, 25
Territory of ....Num. 32:20-36
Captivity of ....1 Chr. 5:26
Later references to ....Rev. 7:5
3. Seer of David ....1 Sam. 22:5
Message of, to David ....2 Sam. 24:10-16

Gadarenes, Gergesenes
People east of the Sea of Galilee ....Mark 5:1
Healing of demon-possessed here ....Matt. 8:28-34

Gaddi—*fortunate*
Manassite spy ....Num. 13:11

Gaddiel—*Gad* (fortune) *is God*
Zebulunite spy ....Num. 13:10

Gadi—*a Gadite*
Father of King Menahem ....2 Kin. 15:14

Gaham—*burning*
Son of Nahor ....Gen. 22:23, 24

Gahar—*hiding place*
Head of a family of Temple servants ....Ezra 2:47

Gain through loss
A. *Elements of:*
Death first ....John 12:24
Servant status ....Mark 9:35
Discount all temporal gains ....Matt. 19:29
Loss of "life" ....Mark 8:35
B. *Examples of:*
Abraham ....Heb. 11:8-19
Moses ....Heb. 11:24-27
Ruth ....Ruth 1:16-18
Abigail ....1 Sam. 25:18-42
Esther ....Esth. 2:1-17
Christ ....Phil. 2:5-11

Gains unjustly gotten
By:
Deceit ....Josh. 7:15-26
Violence ....Prov. 1:19
Oppression ....Prov. 22:16
Divination ....Acts 16:16, 19
Unjust wages ....James 5:4

Gaius—*commended*
1. Companion of Paul ....Acts 19:29
2. Convert at Derbe ....Acts 20:4
3. Paul's host at Corinth ....Rom. 16:23
Corinthian convert ....1 Cor. 1:14
4. One addressed by John ....3 John 1-5

Galal—*a rolling*
1. Levite ....1 Chr. 9:15
2. Another Levite ....1 Chr. 9:16

Galatia—*a province of Asia Minor*
Paul's first visit to ....Acts 16:6
Paul's second visit to ....Acts 18:23
Churches of ....1 Cor. 16:1
Peter writes to Christians in ....1 Pet. 1:1

Galatians—*people of Galatia*
Paul's:
Rebuke of their instability ....Gal. 1:6, 7
Defense of the Gospel among them ....Gal. 1:8-24
Concern for them ....Gal. 4:9-31
Confidence in them ....Gal. 5:7-13

Galatians, the Epistle to—*a book of the New Testament*
True gospel ....Gal. 1:6-12
Freedom from the Law ....Gal. 2:15—4:31
Fruits of the Holy Spirit ....Gal. 5:22, 23

Galbanum—*a yellowish-brown aromatic resin*
Used in the holy oil ....Ex. 30:34

Galeed—*heap of witness*
Memorial site ....Gen. 31:48

Galilean—*an inhabitant of Galilee*
Speech of ....Mark 14:70
Slaughter of ....Luke 13:1
Faith of ....John 4:45
Pilate's cruelty toward ....Luke 13:1, 2

Galilee—*circle, circuit*
A. *History of:*
Moses' prophecy concerning ....Deut. 33:18-23
Conquered by Syrians ....1 Kin. 15:18, 20
Conquered by Assyrians ....2 Kin. 15:29
Dialect of, distinctive ....Matt. 26:73
Herod's jurisdiction over ....Luke 3:1
Christian churches in ....Acts 9:31
B. *Christ's contacts with:*
Resided in ....Matt. 2:22
Chooses disciples from ....Matt. 4:18, 21
Fulfills prophecy concerning ....Matt. 4:14, 15
Performs many miracles in ....Matt. 4:23
People of, receive Him ....Matt. 4:25
Seeks refuge in ....John 4:1, 3
Women of, minister to Him ....Matt. 27:55
Seen in, after His resurrection ....Matt. 26:32

Galilee, Sea of
Scene of many events in Christ's life ....Mark 7:31
Called Chinnereth ....Num. 34:11
Later called Gennesaret ....Luke 5:1

Gall—*bile*
A. *Used literally of:*
Liver secretion ....Job 16:13
Poisonous herb ....Matt. 27:34
B. *Used figuratively of:*
State of sin ....Acts 8:23

Gallantry—*a chivalrous act of bravery*
Example of ....Ex. 2:16-21

Gallim—*heaps*
Village north of Jerusalem ....Is. 10:29, 30
Home of Phalti ....1 Sam. 25:44

Gallio—*who lives on milk*
Roman proconsul of Achaia; dismisses charges against Paul ....Acts 18:12-17

Gallows—*a structure used for hanging*
Haman had made ....Esth. 5:14
Haman hanged on ....Esth. 7:9, 10
Haman's sons hanged on ....Esth. 9:13, 25

Gamaliel—*God has rewarded*
1. Leader of Manasseh ....Num. 2:20
2. Famous Jewish teacher ....Acts 22:3
Respected by people ....Acts 5:34-39

Game—*the flesh of wild animals*
Isaac's favorite dish ....Gen. 27:1-33

Games—*various kinds of contests*
Figurative examples of, (as of a race):
Requiring discipline ....1 Cor. 9:25-27
Requiring obedience to rules ....2 Tim. 2:5
Testing the course ....Gal. 2:2
Press on to the goal ....Phil. 3:13, 14

Gammadim—*warriors*
Manned Tyre's towers ....Ezek. 27:11

Gamul—*rewarded*
Descendant of Aaron ....1 Chr. 24:17

Garden—*a protected and cultivated place*
A. *Notable examples of:*
In Eden ....Gen. 2:15
In Egypt ....Deut. 11:10
In Shushan ....Esth. 1:5
In Gethsemane ....Mark 14:32
A royal ....2 Kin. 25:4
B. *Used for:*
Festivities ....Esth. 1:5
Idolatry ....Is. 65:3
Meditations ....Matt. 26:36
Burial ....John 19:41
C. *Figurative of:*
Desolation ....Amos 4:9
Fruitfulness ....Is. 51:3
Prosperity ....Is. 58:11
Righteousness ....Is. 61:11

Gardener—*one whose work is gardening*
Adam, the first ....Gen. 2:15
Christ, mistaken for ....John 20:15, 16

Gareb—*scab*
1. One of David's warriors ....2 Sam. 23:38
2. Hill near Jerusalem ....Jer. 31:39

Garland—*ceremonial headdress or wreath*
Brought by priests of Jupiter ....Acts 14:13
Of grace ....Prov. 4:9
Granted to those who mourn ....Is. 61:3
Worn by bridegrooms ....Is. 61:10

Garlic—*an onion-like plant*
Egyptian food ....Num. 11:5

Garments (see Clothing)

Garmite—*bony*
Gentile name applied to Keilah ....1 Chr. 4:19

SUBJECT REFERENCE

Garner—*a place for storing grain*
Full, prayed for .... Ps. 144:13
Desolate, lamented .... Joel 1:17
Figurative of heaven .... Matt. 3:12
Translated "barn" .... Matt. 6:26

Garnish—*to adorn; to decorate*
Literally, of buildings .... Luke 11:24, 25
Figuratively, of the heavens .... Job 26:13
Of the new Jerusalem .... Rev. 21:19

Garrison—*a military post*
Smitten by Jonathan .... 1 Sam. 13:3, 4
Attacked by Jonathan .... 1 Sam. 14:1-15

Gashmu—*shower*
Opposes Nehemiah .... Neh. 6:6

Gatam—*puny*
Esau's grandson; chief of Edomite clan .... Gen. 36:11-16

Gate—*an entrance*
A. *Made of:*
Wood .... Neh. 2:3, 17
Iron .... Acts 12:10
Brass .... Ps. 107:16
Stones .... Rev. 21:12
B. *Opening for:*
Camps .... Ex. 32:26, 27
Cities .... Judg. 16:3
Palaces .... Neh. 2:8
Sanctuary .... Ezek. 44:1, 2
Tombs .... Matt. 27:60
Prisons .... Acts 12:5, 10
C. *Used for:*
Business transactions .... 1 Kin. 22:10
Legal business .... Ruth 4:1-11
Criminal cases .... Deut. 25:7-9
Proclamations .... Jer. 17:19, 20
Festivities .... Ps. 24:7
Protection .... 2 Sam. 18:24, 33
D. *Figurative of:*
Satanic power .... Matt. 16:18
Death .... Is. 38:10
Righteousness .... Ps. 118:19, 20
Salvation .... Matt. 7:13
Heaven .... Rev. 21:25

Gates of Jerusalem
1. Corner Gate .... 2 Chr. 26:9
2. Dung Gate .... Neh. 12:31
3. Of Ephraim .... Neh. 8:16
4. Fish Gate .... Zeph. 1:10
5. Fountain Gate .... Neh. 12:37
6. Horse Gate .... Jer. 31:40
7. Benjamin's Gate .... Zech. 14:10
8. Prison gate .... Neh. 12:39
9. Sheep Gate .... Neh. 3:1
10. Upper Benjamin Gate .... Jer. 20:2
11. Valley Gate .... Neh. 2:13
12. Water Gate .... Neh. 8:16

Gatekeeper
Duty of:
Zechariah .... 1 Chr. 9:21
Shallum .... 1 Chr. 9:17
Akkub .... 1 Chr. 9:17
Talmon .... 1 Chr. 9:17
Ahiman .... 1 Chr. 9:17
Ben .... 1 Chr. 15:18
Jaaziel .... 1 Chr. 15:18
Shemiramoth .... 1 Chr. 15:18
Jehiel .... 1 Chr. 15:18
Unni .... 1 Chr. 15:18
Eliab .... 1 Chr. 15:18
Benaiah .... 1 Chr. 15:18
Maaseiah .... 1 Chr. 15:18
Mattithiah .... 1 Chr. 15:18
Eliphelehu .... 1 Chr. 15:18
Mikneiah .... 1 Chr. 15:18
Obed-edom .... 1 Chr. 15:18
Jeiel .... 1 Chr. 15:18
Heman .... 1 Chr. 15:17
Asaph .... 1 Chr. 15:17
Ethan .... 1 Chr. 15:17
Berechiah .... 1 Chr. 15:23
Elkanah .... 1 Chr. 15:23
Jehiah .... 1 Chr. 15:24
Jeduthun .... 1 Chr. 16:38
Hosah .... 1 Chr. 16:38

SUBJECT REFERENCE

Gath—*wine press*
Philistine city .... 1 Sam. 6:17
Last of Anakim here .... Josh. 11:22
Ark carried to .... 1 Sam. 5:8
Home of Goliath .... 1 Sam. 17:4
David takes refuge in .... 1 Sam. 21:10-15
David's second flight to .... 1 Sam. 27:3-12
Captured by David .... 1 Chr. 18:1
Captured by Hazael .... 2 Kin. 12:17
Rebuilt by Rehoboam .... 2 Chr. 11:5, 8
Uzziah broke down walls of .... 2 Chr. 26:6
Destruction of, prophetic .... Amos 6:1-3
Name becomes proverbial .... Mic. 1:10

Gath-hepher—*wine press of the pit*
Birthplace of Jonah .... 2 Kin. 14:25
Boundary of Zebulun .... Josh. 19:13

Gath-rimmon—*pomegranate press*
1. City of Dan .... Josh. 19:40-45
Assigned to Levites .... Josh. 21:24
2. Town in Manasseh .... Josh. 21:25

Gaza—*strong place*
1. Philistine city .... Josh. 13:3
Conquered by Joshua .... Josh. 10:41
Refuge of Anakim .... Josh. 11:22
Assigned to Judah .... Josh. 15:47
Gates of, removed by Samson .... Judg. 16:1-3
Samson deceived by Delilah here .... Judg. 16:4-20
Samson blinded here .... Judg. 16:21
Ruled by Solomon .... 1 Kin. 4:22, 24
Sin of, condemned .... Amos 1:6, 7
Judgment pronounced upon .... Jer. 25:20
Philip journeys to .... Acts 8:26
2. Ephraimite town .... 1 Chr. 7:28

Gazelle—*medium-sized antelope; translated "roe"; "roebuck"*
Used for food .... Deut. 12:15
Figurative of speed .... Prov. 6:5

Gazez—*shearer*
1. Son of Caleb .... 1 Chr. 2:46
2. Grandson of Caleb .... 1 Chr. 2:46

Gazingstock—*an object of contempt*
Ignominy of .... Nah. 3:6
Lot of Christians .... Heb. 10:33

Gazites
Inhabitants of Gaza .... Judg. 16:2

Gazzam—*consuming*
Head of family of Temple servants .... Ezra 2:48

Geba—*a hill*
City of Benjamin .... Josh. 18:24
Assigned to Levites .... Josh. 21:17
Crag rose opposite .... 1 Sam. 14:4, 5
Rebuilt by Asa .... 1 Kin. 15:22
Repossessed after the exile .... Neh. 11:31

Gebal—*mountain*
1. Phoenician maritime town .... Ezek. 27:9
Translated "stonesquarers" .... 1 Kin. 5:18
Inhabitants called Giblites .... Josh. 13:5
2. Mountainous region in Edom .... Ps. 83:7

Geber—*strong one; hero*
Solomon's purveyors .... 1 Kin. 4:13, 19

Gebim—*ditches*
Place north of Jerusalem .... Is. 10:31

Gedaliah—*Jehovah has made great*
1. Jeduthun's son .... 1 Chr. 25:3, 9
2. Pashur's son .... Jer. 38:1
3. Grandfather of Zephaniah .... Zeph. 1:1
4. Ahikam's son .... Jer. 39:14
Made governor of Judea .... 2 Kin. 25:22-26
Befriends Jeremiah .... Jer. 40:5, 6
Murdered by Ishmael .... Jer. 41:2, 18
Postexilic priest .... Ezra 10:18

Geder—*wall*
Town of Judah .... Josh. 12:13

SUBJECT REFERENCE

Gederah—*sheepfold*
Town in Judah .... Josh. 15:36

Gederathite
Native of Gederah .... 1 Chr. 12:4

Gederite
Native of Geder .... 1 Chr. 27:28

Gederoth—*sheepfolds*
Town of Judah .... Josh. 15:41
Captured by Philistines .... 2 Chr. 28:18

Gederothaim—*two sheepfolds*
Town of Judah .... Josh. 15:36

Gedor—*wall*
1. Town of Judah .... Josh. 15:58
2. Simeonite town .... 1 Chr. 4:39
3. Town of Benjamin .... 1 Chr. 12:7
4. Family in Judah .... 1 Chr. 4:4, 18

Gehazi—*valley of vision*
Elisha's servant .... 2 Kin. 5:25
Seeks reward from Naaman .... 2 Kin. 5:20-24
Afflicted with leprosy .... 2 Kin. 5:25-27
Relates Elisha's deeds to Jehoram .... 2 Kin. 8:4-6

Gehenna (see Hell)

Geliloth—*circles*
Probably Gilgal, in the land of Benjamin .... Josh. 18:17

Gemalli—*camel driver*
Father of Ammiel .... Num. 13:12

Gemariah—*Jehovah has perfected*
1. Hilkiah's son .... Jer. 29:3
2. Shaphan's son .... Jer. 36:10-25

Gems—*precious stones*
On breastplate .... Ex. 28:15-21
Figurative of value .... Prov. 3:15
Prov. 31:10
In commerce .... Ezek. 27:16
In New Jerusalem .... Rev. 21:19-21

Genealogies—*ancestral lineage*
A. *Importance:*
Chronology .... Matt. 1:17
Priesthood claims .... Ezra 2:61, 62
Neh. 7:63, 64
Messiahship .... Matt. 1:1-17
B. *Lists of:*
Patriarchs' .... Gen. 5:1-32
Noah's .... Gen. 10:1-32
Shem's .... Gen. 10:21-32
Abraham's .... 1 Chr. 1:28-34
Jacob's .... Gen. 46:8-27
Esau's .... Gen. 36:1-43
Israel's .... 1 Chr. 9:1-44
David's .... 1 Chr. 3:1-16
Levites' .... 1 Chr. 6:1-81

Genealogy of Jesus
Seed of Abraham .... Gal. 3:16
Through Joseph .... Matt. 1:2-17
Through Mary .... Luke 3:23-38

General—*chief military authority*
Commander .... 1 Chr. 27:34
Rev. 6:15
Also rendered "princes" .... Gen. 12:15

Generation
Descriptive of:
Period of time .... Gen. 9:12
Living people or race .... Matt. 24:34
Descendants .... Matt. 12:34
Eternity .... Eph. 3:21

Genesis, Book of—*first book of the Old Testament*
Creation .... Gen. 1:1—2:25
The fall .... Gen. 3:1-24
The flood .... Gen. 6:8—7:24
Abraham .... Gen. 12:1—25:18
Isaac .... Gen. 25:19—26:35
Jacob .... Gen. 27:1—36:43
Joseph .... Gen. 37:1—50:26

G

SUBJECT — REFERENCE

Genius—*unusual mental ability*
Applicable to Solomon .... 1 Kin. 4:29-34

Gentiles—*non-Jews*
A. *Described as:*
Superstitious .... Deut. 18:14
Ignorant of God .... Rom. 1:21
Without the Law .... Rom. 2:14
Wicked .... Rom. 1:23-32
Idolatrous .... 1 Cor. 12:2
Uncircumcised .... Eph. 2:11
Without Christ .... Eph. 2:12
Dead in sins .... Eph. 2:1
B. *Blessings promised to:*
Included in God's covenant .... Gen. 12:3; Gal. 3:8
Given to Christ .... Ps. 2:8
Conversion predicted .... Is. 11:10; Rom. 15:9-16
Christ their light .... Is. 49:6
Included in "all flesh" .... Joel 2:28-32
Called "other sheep" .... John 10:16
C. *Conversion of:*
Predicted .... Is. 60:1-14
Proclaimed .... Matt. 4:12-17
Anticipated .... John 10:16
Questioned .... Acts 10:9-29
Realized .... Acts 10:34-48
Explained .... Acts 11:1-18
Hindered .... Acts 13:45-51
Debated .... Acts 15:1-22
Confirmed .... Acts 15:23-31
Vindicated .... Acts 28:25-29
D. *Present position:*
Barrier removed .... Eph. 2:11-22
Brought near .... Eph. 2:13
Fellow citizens .... Eph. 2:19
Fellow heirs .... Eph. 3:6
In body .... Eph. 3:6

Gentleness—*mildness combined with tenderness*
A. *Examples of:*
God's .... 2 Sam. 22:36
Christ's .... Matt. 11:29
Paul's .... 1 Thess. 2:7
Holy Spirit .... Gal. 5:22
B. *A Christian essential in:*
Living in the world .... Titus 3:1, 2
Instruction .... 2 Tim. 2:24, 25
Restoring a brother .... Gal. 6:1
Calling .... Eph. 4:1, 2
Marriage .... 1 Pet. 3:1-4
C. *Commandments concerning:*
Put it on .... Col. 3:12
Follow after .... 1 Tim. 6:11

Genubath—*theft*
Edomite .... 1 Kin. 11:20

Geology—*study of the earth*
Allusions to .... Gen. 1:9, 10

Gera—*grain*
1. Son of Bela .... Gen. 46:21
2. A descendant of Bela .... 1 Chr. 8:3-8
3. Father of Ehud .... Judg. 3:15
4. Father of Shimei .... 2 Sam. 16:5

Gerah—*smallest coin and weight among the Jews*
Twentieth part of a shekel .... Ex. 30:13; Lev. 27:25

Gerar—*region*
Town of Philistia .... Gen. 10:19
Visited by Abraham .... Gen. 20:1-18
Visited by Isaac .... Gen. 26:1-17
Abimelech, king of .... Gen. 26:1, 26

Gerizim—*cutters*
Mountain of blessing in Ephraim .... Deut. 11:29
Jotham's parable .... Judg. 9:7
Samaritans' sacred mountain .... John 4:20, 21

Gershom—*exile*
1. Son of Levi .... 1 Chr. 6:16-20
Called Gershon .... Gen. 46:11
Founder of Gershonites .... Num. 3:17-26
2. Son of Moses .... Ex. 2:21, 22
Circumcised .... Ex. 4:25
Founder of Levite family .... 1 Chr. 23:14-16
3. Descendant of Phinehas .... Ezra 8:2
4. Father of Jonathan .... Judg. 18:30

Gershon—*exile*
Eldest son of Levi .... Ex. 6:16
Father of Libni and Shimei .... Ex. 6:17

Gershonites
Descendants of Gershon (Gershom) .... Num. 3:21, 22
Tabernacle servants .... Num. 3:25, 26
Achievements of .... 1 Chr. 15:7-19

Geshan—*firm*
Descendant of Caleb .... 1 Chr. 2:47

Geshur—*bridge*
Not expelled .... Josh. 13:13
Talmai, king of .... 2 Sam. 3:3
Absalom flees to .... 2 Sam. 13:37, 38

Geshurites
1. People of Geshur .... Deut. 3:14
2. People living south of Philistia .... 1 Sam. 27:8

Gether—*fear*
Son of Aram .... Gen. 10:23

Gethsemane—*oil press*
Garden near Jerusalem .... Matt. 26:30, 36
Scene of Christ's agony and betrayal .... Matt. 26:36-56; John 18:1-12
Often visited by Christ .... Luke 22:39

Geuel—*majesty of God*
Gadite spy .... Num. 13:15, 16

Gezer—*portion*
Canaanite city .... Josh. 10:33
Not expelled .... Josh. 16:10
Assigned to Kohathites .... Josh. 21:21
Scene of warfare .... 1 Chr. 14:16
Burned by Egyptian king .... 1 Kin. 9:16
Rebuilt by Solomon .... 1 Kin. 9:17

Ghost
Christ thought to be .... Matt. 14:26; Mark 6:49
Worshiped by Egyptians .... Is. 19:3

Giah—*waterfall*
Place near Ammah .... 2 Sam. 2:24

Giants—*men of unusual size*
A. *Names of:*
Nephilim .... Gen. 6:4
Rephaim .... Gen. 14:5
Anakim .... Num. 13:28-33
Emim .... Gen. 14:5
Zamzummim .... Deut. 2:20
Goliath .... 1 Sam. 17:4-7
Og .... Deut. 3:11, 13
Others .... 2 Sam. 21:16-22
B. *Destroyed by:*
Moses .... Deut. 3:3-11
Joshua .... Josh. 11:21
David .... 1 Sam. 17:48-51
David and his men .... 2 Sam. 21:16-22

Gibbar—*huge*
Family head .... Ezra 2:20

Gibbethon—*mound*
Town of Dan .... Josh. 19:44
Assigned to Levites .... Josh. 21:20-23
Nadab's assassination at .... 1 Kin. 15:27, 28
Besieged by Omri .... 1 Kin. 16:17

Gibea—*hill*
Caleb's grandson .... 1 Chr. 2:49

Gibeah—*hill*
1. Village of Judah .... Josh. 15:57
2. Town of Benjamin .... Judg. 19:14-16
Known for wickedness .... Judg. 19:12-30
Destruction .... Judg. 20:1-48
Saul's birthplace .... 1 Sam. 10:26
Saul's political capital .... 1 Sam. 15:34
Saul's sons executed .... 2 Sam. 21:6-10
Wickedness of, long remembered .... Hos. 9:9
3. Hill or town where Eleazar was buried .... Josh. 24:33

Gibeathites
Inhabitants of Gibeah .... 1 Chr. 12:3

Gibeon—*hill town*
Hivite town .... Josh. 9:3, 7
Mighty, royal city .... Josh. 10:2
Sun stands still at .... Josh. 10:12
Assigned to Benjamin .... Josh. 18:25
Given to Levites .... Josh. 21:17
Location of tabernacle .... 1 Chr. 16:39
Joab struck Amasa .... 2 Sam. 20:8-10
Joab killed here .... 1 Kin. 2:28-34
Site of Solomon's sacrifice and dream .... 1 Kin. 3:5-15
Natives of, return from exile .... Neh. 3:7

Gibeonites—*inhabitants of Gibeon*
Deceive Joshua .... Josh. 9:3-15
Deception discovered .... Josh. 9:16-20
Made hewers of wood .... Josh. 9:21-27
Rescued by Joshua .... Josh. 10:1-43
Massacred by Saul .... 2 Sam. 21:1
Avenged by David .... 2 Sam. 21:2-9

Giddalti—*I have made great*
Son of Heman .... 1 Chr. 25:4

Giddel—*very great*
1. Head of family of Temple servants .... Ezra 2:47
2. Children of Solomon's servants .... Ezra 2:56; Neh. 7:58

Gideon—*cutter of trees*
Son of Joash .... Judg. 6:11
Called by an angel .... Judg. 6:11-24
Destroys Baal's altar .... Judg. 6:25-32
Fleece confirms call from God .... Judg. 6:36-40
His army reduced .... Judg. 7:2-8
Encouraged by a dream .... Judg. 7:9-15
Employs successful strategy .... Judg. 7:16-25
Soothes angry Ephraimites .... Judg. 8:1-3
Takes revenge on Succoth and Penuel .... Judg. 8:4-22
Refuses kingship .... Judg. 8:22, 23
Unwisely makes an ephod .... Judg. 8:24-27
Judgeship of forty years .... Judg. 8:28, 29
Father of 71 sons .... Judg. 8:30, 31
His death brings apostasy .... Judg. 8:32-35
Called Jerubbaal .... Judg. 8:35
Man of faith .... Heb. 11:32

Gideoni—*a cutting down*
Benjamite .... Num. 1:11
Father of Abidan .... Num. 1:11
Brought offering for the tribe of Benjamin .... Num. 7:60-65
Over tribal army of Benjamin .... Num. 10:24

Gidom—*a cutting off*
Village of Benjamin .... Judg. 20:45

Gier-eagle
Unclean bird .... Lev. 11:18

Gifts
A. *Of God:*
1. *Material:*
Food .... Matt. 6:25, 26
Rain .... Matt. 5:45
Health .... Phil. 2:25-30
Sleep .... Prov. 3:24
Rest .... Deut. 12:10
All things .... 1 Tim. 6:17
All needs .... Phil. 4:19
2. *Spiritual:*
Christ .... John 3:16
Holy Spirit .... Luke 11:13
Grace .... James 4:6
Wisdom .... James 1:5
Repentance .... Acts 11:18
Faith .... Eph. 2:8
New heart .... Ezek. 11:19
Peace .... Phil. 4:7
Rest .... Heb. 4:1, 9
Glory .... 1 Pet. 5:10
Eternal life .... John 10:28
B. *Of man:*
1. *Purposes of:*
Confirm covenants .... Gen. 21:27-32
Appease anger .... 1 Sam. 25:27-35
Show respect .... Judg. 6:18-21
Manifest friendship .... 1 Sam. 30:26-31
Reward .... 2 Sam. 18:11, 12

SUBJECT	REFERENCE
Memorialize an event	Esth. 9:20-22
Render worship	Matt. 2:11
Give help	Phil. 4:10-18
Seal friendship	1 Sam. 18:3, 4
2. *Times given:*	
Betrothals	Gen. 24:50-53
Weddings	Ps. 45:12
Departures	Gen. 45:21-24
Returns home	Luke 15:22, 23
Times of recovery	Job 42:10, 11
Trials, forbidden	Ex. 23:8
C. *Spiritual:*	
Listed and explained	Rom. 12:6-8 1 Cor. 12:4-30
Came from God	James 1:17
Assigned sovereignty	1 Cor. 12:28
Cannot be bought	Acts 8:18-20
Always for edification	Rom. 1:11
Counterfeited by Satan	2 Cor. 11:13-15
Spiritually discerned	1 Cor. 12:2, 3
Love, the supreme	1 Cor. 13:1-13

Gihon—*bursting forth*

1. River of Eden	Gen. 2:13
2. Spring outside Jerusalem	1 Kin. 1:33-45
3. Source of water supply	2 Chr. 32:30

Gilalai—*weighty*

Levite musician	Neh. 12:36

Gilboa—*bubbling fountain*

Range of limestone hills in Issachar	1 Sam. 28:4
Scene of Saul's death	1 Sam. 31:1-7
Philistines desecrate Saul's body	1 Sam. 31:8, 9
Under David's curse	2 Sam. 1:21

Gilead—*rocky or strong*

1. Grandson of Manasseh	Num. 26:29, 30
2. Father of Jephthah	Judg. 11:1
3. Gadite	1 Chr. 5:14
4. Condemned city	Hos. 6:8
5. Mountain	Judg. 7:3
6. Tableland east of the Jordan between the Arnon and Jabbok rivers	Judg. 20:1
Possessed by Israel	Num. 21:21-31
Assigned to Reuben, Gad, and Manasseh	Deut. 3:12-17
Rebuked by Deborah	Judg. 5:17
Hebrews flee to	1 Sam. 13:7
Ish-bosheth's rule over	2 Sam. 2:8, 9
David takes refuge in	2 Sam. 17:26, 27 2 Sam. 19:31
In David's census	2 Sam. 24:1, 6
Elijah's birthplace	1 Kin. 17:1
Smitten by Hazael	2 Kin. 10:32, 33
Mentioned by Amos	Amos 1:3, 13

Gilead, Balm of—*an aromatic gum for medicinal purposes; figurative of:*

National healing	Jer. 8:22 Jer. 51:8

Gilgal—*a circle, a wheel*

1. Memorial site between Jordan and Jericho	Josh. 4:19-24
Israel circumcised	Josh. 5:2-9
Passover observed	Josh. 5:10
Site of Gibeonite covenant	Josh. 9:3-15
On Samuel's circuit	1 Sam. 7:16
Saul made king	1 Sam. 11:15
Saul rejected	1 Sam. 13:4-15
Denounced for idolatry	Hos. 9:15
2. Town near Bethel	2 Kin. 2:1
Home of Elisha	2 Kin. 4:38

Giloh—*exile*

Town of Judah	Josh. 15:51

Gilonite—*Giloh native*

Ahithophel called	2 Sam. 15:12

Gimel

Third letter in Hebrew alphabet	Ps. 119:17-24

Gimzo—*producing sycamores*

Village of Judah	2 Chr. 28:18

Gin—*a trap*

Used for catching beasts or birds	Amos 3:5
Used figuratively	Ps. 141:9

Ginath—*protection*

SUBJECT	REFERENCE
Father of Tibni	1 Kin. 16:21, 22

Ginnetho—*gardener*

Postexilic priest	Neh. 12:4

Ginnethon—*gardener*

Family head and signer of document	Neh. 10:6
Probably same as Ginnethoi	

Gird—*to put on, as a belt*

A. *Purposes of:*	
Strengthening	Prov. 31:17
Supporting clothing	2 Kin. 4:29
B. *Figurative of:*	
Gladness	Ps. 30:11
Truth	Eph. 6:14
Readiness	1 Pet. 1:13
C. *Those girding:*	
Priests	Ex. 28:4, 39
Warriors	1 Sam. 18:4
Jesus	John 13:3, 4

Girdle—*waistcloth; sash; belt*

Priestly garment	Ex. 28:4, 39
Worn by warriors	1 Sam. 18:4

Girgashites—*an original tribe of Canaan*

Descendants of Canaan	Gen. 10:15, 16
Land of, given to Abraham's descendants	Gen. 15:18, 21
Delivered to Israel	Josh. 24:11

Girl—*a female child*

Sold for wine	Joel 3:3
Prophecy concerning	Zech. 8:4, 5

Girzites—*inhabitants of Gezer*

Raided by David	1 Sam. 27:8

Gispa—*fondle*

Overseer	Neh. 11:21

Gittaim—*two winepresses*

Village of Benjamin	Neh. 11:31, 33
Refuge of the Beerothites	2 Sam. 4:2, 3

Gittites—*natives of Gath*

600 follow David	2 Sam. 15:18-23

Gittith—*belonging to Gath*

Musical instrument or tune	Ps. 8; 81; 84 (Titles)

Giving to God

A. *Manner of:*	
Without show	Matt. 6:1-4
According to ability	1 Cor. 16:1, 2
Willingly	1 Chr. 29:3-9
Liberally	2 Cor. 9:6-15
Cheerfully	2 Cor. 9:7
Proportionately	Mal. 3:10
B. *Examples of:*	
Israelites	Ex. 35:21-29
Princes of Israel	Num. 7:2-28
Poor widow	Luke 21:2-4
Macedonian churches	2 Cor. 8:1-5

Gizonite

Hashem thus described	1 Chr. 11:34

Gladness—*cheerfulness*

A. *Causes of:*	
Forgiveness	Ps. 51:8
Salvation	Is. 51:3, 11 John 8:56
Recovery of a son	Luke 15:32
Restoration of hope	John 20:20
Temporal blessings	Acts 14:17
Christ's coming	1 Pet. 4:13
B. *Wrong kinds of:*	
At an enemy's downfall	Prov. 24:17
At wickedness	Hos. 7:3

Glass

A. *Used literally of:*	
Crystal	Job 28:17, 18
B. *Used figuratively of:*	
Christ's glory	2 Cor. 3:18
God's nature	Rev. 4:6
New Jerusalem	Rev. 21:18, 21

Gleaning—*gathering grain left by reapers*

SUBJECT	REFERENCE
Laws providing for	Lev. 19:9, 10
Illustrated by Ruth	Ruth 2:2-23
Gideon's reference to	Judg. 8:2

Glede

Unclean bird of prey	Deut. 14:12, 13

Glorification of Christ

A. *Nature of:*	
Predicted	Is. 55:5
Prayed for	John 12:28
Not of Himself	Heb. 5:5
Predetermined	John 17:1
B. *Accomplished by:*	
Father	John 13:31, 32
Holy Spirit	John 16:13, 14
Miracles	John 11:4
His resurrection	Acts 3:13
Believers	Acts 21:20

Glorifying God

A. *By means of:*	
Praise	Ps. 50:23
Fruitfulness	John 15:8
Service	1 Pet. 4:11
Suffering	1 Pet. 4:14, 16
B. *Reason for:*	
Deliverance	Ps. 50:15
Mercy shown	Rom. 15:9
Subjection	2 Cor. 9:13
C. *Extent of:*	
Universal	Ps. 86:9
In body and soul	1 Cor. 6:20

Glory—*honor; renown*

A. *Of temporal things:*	
Granted by God	Dan. 2:37
Used to entrap	Matt. 4:8
Not to be sought	1 Thess. 2:6
Quickly passes	1 Pet. 1:24
B. *Of believers:*	
Given by God	John 17:22
Transformed by the Spirit	2 Cor. 3:18
Through Christ's death	Heb. 2:9, 10
Follows salvation	2 Tim. 2:10
In suffering	Rom. 5:3
In the cross	Gal. 6:14
Greater than present suffering	Rom. 8:18
Hope of	Col. 1:27
At Christ's advent	Col. 3:4

Glory of Christ

A. *Aspects of:*	
Manifested to men	John 2:11
Not selfish	John 8:50
Given by God	John 17:22
Crowned with	Heb. 2:9
Ascribed to forever	Heb. 13:21
B. *Stages of:*	
Before creation	John 17:5
Revealed in Old Testament	John 12:41
In His incarnation	John 1:14
In His transfiguration	Luke 9:28-36
In His resurrection	Luke 24:26
In His exaltation	1 Tim. 3:16
At His return	Matt. 25:31
In heaven	Rev. 5:12

Glory of God

A. *Manifested to:*	
Moses	Ex. 24:9-17
Stephen	Acts 7:55
B. *Reflected in:*	
Christ	John 1:14
Man	1 Cor. 11:7
C. *Appearances of:*	
The tabernacle	Ex. 40:34
The Temple	1 Kin. 8:11
At Jesus' birth	Luke 2:8-11
D. *The believer's relation to:*	
Does all for	1 Cor. 10:31
Illuminated by	2 Cor. 4:6
Will stand in presence of	Jude 24
E. *Man's relation to:*	
Corrupts	Rom. 1:23

G

SUBJECT	REFERENCE
Falls short of	Rom. 3:23
Refuse to give to God	Acts 12:23

Glory of man

Prefigured in creation	Heb. 2:6-8
Lost by sin	Rom. 3:23
Soon passes away	1 Pet. 1:24
Removed by death	Ps. 49:17
Restored by Christ	2 Cor. 5:17

Gluttony—*excessive appetite*

Sternly forbidden	Prov. 23:1-3
Characteristic of the wicked	Phil. 3:19
Leads to poverty	Prov. 23:21
Christ accused of	Matt. 11:19

Gnat—*small insect*

Third plague on Egypt, produced from dust	Ex. 8:16-18
Used as illustration	Matt. 23:24

Gnosticism—*early heresy based on knowledge instead of faith*

Warned against	Col. 2:8, 18
Arrogant	1 Cor. 8:1
False	1 Tim. 6:20
Surpassed by Christ	Eph. 3:19

Goad—*a pointed rod*

Used as a weapon	Judg. 3:31
Figurative of pointed morals	Eccl. 12:11
Figurative of conscience	Acts 26:14
Sharpened by files	1 Sam. 13:21

Goals, spiritual

Provide motivation	Phil. 3:12-14
Promise reward	1 Cor. 9:24, 25

Goat—*a domesticated animal*

A. *Literal uses of:*

Clothing	Num. 31:20 Heb. 11:37
Milk of, food	Prov. 27:27
Curtains	Ex. 26:7
Bottles	Josh. 9:4
Sacrifices	Ex. 12:5

B. *Figurative uses of:*

Great leaders	Jer. 50:8
Kingdom of Greece	Dan. 8:5, 21
Wicked	Matt. 25:32, 33

Goath—*constance*

Place near Jerusalem	Jer. 31:39

Gob—*a pit*

Plain where Hebrews and Philistines fought	2 Sam. 21:18, 19
Also called Gezer	1 Chr. 20:4

Goblet—*a bowl or basin*

Used as a comparison	Song 7:2
Same word translated "basins" and "cups"	Ex. 24:6 Is. 22:24

God—*the Supreme Being*

A. *Names of:*

God	Gen. 1:1
LORD God	Gen. 2:4
Most high God	Gen. 14:18-22
Lord God	Gen. 15:2, 8
Almighty God	Gen. 17:1
Everlasting God	Gen. 21:33
God Almighty	Gen. 28:3
I Am	Ex. 3:14
Jehovah	Ex. 6:3
Jealous	Ex. 34:14
Eternal God	Deut. 33:27
Living God	Josh. 3:10
God of hosts	Ps. 80:7
Lord of hosts	Is. 1:24
Holy One of Israel	Is. 43:3, 14, 15
Mighty God	Jer. 32:18
God of heaven	Jon. 1:9
Heavenly Father	Matt. 6:26
King eternal	1 Tim. 1:17
Only Potentate	1 Tim. 6:15
Father of lights	James 1:17

B. *Manifestations of:*

Face of	Gen. 32:30
Voice of	Deut. 5:22-26
Glory of	Ex. 40:34, 35
Angel of	Gen. 16:7-13
Name of	Ex. 34:5-7
Form of	Num. 12:6-8
Comes from Teman	Hab. 3:3

C. *Nature of:*

Spirit	John 4:24
One	Deut. 6:4
Personal	John 17:1-3
Trinitarian	2 Cor. 13:14
Omnipotent	Rev. 19:6

D. *Natural attributes of:*

Incomparable	2 Sam. 7:22
Invisible	John 1:18
Inscrutable	Is. 40:28
Unchangeable	Num. 23:19
Unequaled	Is. 40:13-25
Unsearchable	Rom. 11:33, 34
Infinite	1 Kin. 8:27
Eternal	Is. 57:15
Omnipotence (All-powerful)	Jer. 32:17, 27
Omnipresence (Ever-present)	Ps. 139:7-12
Omniscience (All-knowing)	1 John 3:20
Foreknowledge	Is. 48:3, 5
Wise	Acts 15:18

E. *Moral attributes of:*

Goodness (see Goodness of God)	
Hatred	Ps. 5:5, 6
Holiness	Rev. 4:8
Impartiality	1 Pet. 1:17
Justice	Ps. 89:14
Long-suffering	Ex. 34:6, 7
Love	1 John 4:8, 16
Mercy	Lam. 3:22, 23
Truth	Ps. 117:2
Vengeance	Deut. 32:34-41
Wrath	Deut. 32:22

F. *Human expressions applied to:*

Fear	Deut. 32:26, 27
Grief	Gen. 6:6
Repentance	Gen. 6:7
Jealousy	Ex. 34:14
Swearing	Jer. 44:26
Laughing	Ps. 2:4
Sleeping	Ps. 78:65
Human parts	Ex. 33:21-23

G. *Titles given to:*

Creator	Is. 40:12, 22, 26
Judge	Ps. 96:10, 13
King	Ps. 47:2, 7, 8
Defender	Ps. 18:35
Preserver	Ps. 121:3-8
Shepherd	Gen. 49:24

H. *Works of, described as:*

Terrible	Ps. 66:3
Incomparable	Ps. 86:8
Great	Ps. 92:5
Manifold	Ps. 104:24
Marvelous	Ps. 139:14

I. *Ways of, described as:*

Perfect	Ps. 18:30
Knowledgeable	Ps. 86:11
Made known	Ps. 103:7
Righteous	Ps. 145:17
Not like man's	Is. 55:8, 9
Everlasting	Hab. 3:6
Inscrutable	Rom. 11:33
Just and true	Rev. 15:3

See Goodness of God; Love of God; Power of God

Godhead—*the Deity*

Revealed to mankind	Rom. 1:20
Corrupted by mankind	Acts 17:29
Incarnated in Jesus Christ	Col. 2:9

Godliness—*holy living*

Profitable	1 Tim. 4:7, 8
Perverted	1 Tim. 6:5
Pursuit	1 Tim. 6:11
Duty	Titus 2:12

See Holiness of Christians

Gods, false

A. *Names of:*

Adrammelech (Syria)	2 Kin. 17:31
Anammelech (Babylon)	2 Kin. 17:31
Ashtoreth (Canaan)	1 Kin. 11:5
Baal (Canaan)	1 Kin. 18:19
Baal-peor (Moab)	Num. 25:1-9
Beelzebub (Philistine)	Luke 11:19-23
Bel (Babylon)	Jer. 51:44
Calf worship (Egypt)	Ex. 32:1-6
Chemosh (Moab)	1 Kin. 11:7
Dagon (Philistine)	1 Sam. 5:1-7
Diana (Greek)	Acts 19:35
Jupiter (Roman)	Acts 14:12, 13
Milcom (Ammon)	1 Kin. 11:5
Molech (Ammon)	1 Kin. 11:7
Nebo (Babylon)	Is. 46:1
Nisroch (Assyria)	2 Kin. 19:37
Rimmon (Syria)	2 Kin. 5:18
Tammuz (Babylon)	Ezek. 8:14

B. *Evils connected with:*

Immorality	Num. 25:1-9
Prostitution	2 Kin. 23:7
Divination	Lev. 20:1-6
Sacrilege	Dan. 5:4
Pride	2 Kin. 18:28-35
Persecution	1 Kin. 19:1-3
Child sacrifice	Jer. 7:29-34

Gog—*mountain*

1. Reubenite	1 Chr. 5:4
2. Prince of Rosh, Meshech and Tubal	Ezek. 38:2, 3
3. Leader of the final battle	Rev. 20:8-15

Golan—*circuit*

City of Bashan	Deut. 4:43
Assigned to Levites	Josh. 21:27
City of refuge	Josh. 20:8

Gold

A. *Found in:*

Havilah	Gen. 2:11, 12
Ophir	1 Kin. 9:28
Sheba	1 Kin. 10:2, 10
Arabia	2 Chr. 9:14

B. *Used for:*

Money	Matt. 10:9
Offerings	Ex. 35:22
Presents	Matt. 2:11
Holy adornment	Ex. 28:4-6
Jewelry	Gen. 24:22
Physical adornment	Ex. 36:34, 38
Idols	Ex. 32:31

C. *Figurative of:*

Saints refined	Job 23:10
Babylonian empire	Dan. 2:38
Redeemed	2 Tim. 2:20
Faith purified	1 Pet. 1:7
Christ's doctrine	Rev. 3:18

Golden apples

Appropriate word	Prov. 25:11

Golden city

Babylon called	Is. 14:4

Golden rule

For Christian conduct	Matt. 7:12 Luke 6:31

Golden wedge

Figurative term	Is. 13:12

Goldsmiths

In the tabernacle	Ex. 31:1-4
Refiners	Mal. 3:3
Shapers of objects	Ex. 25:11, 18
Makers of idols	Num. 33:52
Guilds	Neh. 3:8, 32

Golgotha—*place of a skull*

Where Jesus died	Matt. 27:33-35

Goliath—*exile*

1. Giant of Gath	1 Sam. 17:4
Killed by David	1 Sam. 17:50
2. Another giant; killed by Elhanan	2 Sam. 21:19

See Giant

Gomer—*completion*

1. Son of Japheth	Gen. 10:2, 3 1 Chr. 1:5, 6
Northern nation	Ezek. 38:6
2. Wife of Hosea	Hos. 1:2, 3

Gomorrah—*submersion*

In a fruitful valley	Gen. 13:10
Defeated by Chedorlaomer	Gen. 14:8-11
Destroyed by God	Gen. 19:23-29
Symbol of evil	Is. 1:10
Symbol of destruction	Amos 4:11
Punishment of	Matt. 10:15

SUBJECT	REFERENCE
Good for evil	
Illustrated by Joseph	Gen. 45:5-15
Christian duty	Luke 6:27, 35
Goodness of God	
A. *Described as:*	
Abundant	Ex. 34:6
Great	Ps. 31:19
Enduring	Ps. 52:1
Satisfying	Ps. 65:4
Universal	Ps. 145:9
B. *Manifested in:*	
Material blessings	Matt. 5:45 Acts 14:17
Spiritual blessings	Ps. 31:19
Forgiving sin	Ps. 86:5
C. *Saints' attitude toward:*	
Rejoice in	Ex. 18:9
Remember	Ps. 145:7
Be satisfied with	Jer. 31:14
Gopher wood	
Used in Noah's ark	Gen. 6:14
Gore—*to push or thrust*	
By an ox	Ex. 21:28-32
Rendered "push"	Deut. 33:17
Rendered "thrust"	Ezek. 34:21
Goshen	
1. District of Egypt where Israel lived	Gen. 45:10
Land of pastures	Gen. 47:1-6
Called the land of Rameses	Gen. 47:6-11
2. Region in south Judah	Josh. 10:41
3. City of Judah	Josh. 15:51
Gospel—*good news*	
A. *Described as, of:*	
God	Rom. 1:1
Christ	2 Cor. 2:12
The kingdom	Matt. 24:14
Grace of God	Acts 20:24
Peace	Eph. 6:15
Salvation	Eph. 1:13
Glory of Christ	2 Cor. 4:4
B. *Defined as:*	
Of supernatural origin	Gal. 1:10-12
God's power	Rom. 1:16
Mystery	Eph. 6:19
Revelation	Eph. 3:1-6
Deposit of truth	1 Cor. 15:1-4
C. *Source of:*	
Hope	Col. 1:23
Salvation	2 Thess. 2:13, 14
Faith	Acts 15:7
Life	1 Cor. 4:15
Immortality	2 Tim. 1:10
Afflictions	Phil. 1:16
Peace	Eph. 6:15
D. *Proclaimed by or in:*	
Old Testament	Gal. 3:8
Prophets	Rom. 1:1, 2
John	Mark 1:1-4
Jesus Christ	Mark 1:14, 15
Chosen men	1 Pet. 1:12
E. *Should be proclaimed:*	
To all people	Mark 16:15, 16
Everywhere	Rom. 15:19, 20
At all times	Rev. 14:6
With great urgency	1 Cor. 9:16
With boldness	Eph. 6:19
As a testimony	Matt. 24:14
F. *Proclaimers of, are:*	
Separated	Rom. 1:1
Called	Acts 16:10
Entrusted with it	1 Thess. 3:2
Set apart for its defense	Phil. 1:7, 16, 27
Under divine orders	1 Cor. 9:16
G. *Negative reactions to, some:*	
Disobey	2 Thess. 1:8
Are blinded to	2 Cor. 4:3, 4
Hinder	1 Cor. 9:12
Pervert	Gal. 1:7
H. *Believer's reaction to:*	
Believing	Eph. 1:13
Submitting to	2 Cor. 9:13
Being established by	Rom. 16:25
Living by	Phil. 1:27
Defending	Phil. 1:7, 16, 27

SUBJECT	REFERENCE
Gossip—*idle talk or rumors about others*	
Forbidden	Lev. 19:16
Cause of friction	Prov. 16:28
Warns against associating with	Prov. 20:19
Called "talebearer"	Prov. 11:13 Prov. 20:19
Called "infamy"	Ezek. 36:3
Called "whisperers"	Rom. 1:29
Called "whisperings"	2 Cor. 12:20
Called "tattlers"	1 Tim. 5:13
Gourd—*a running plant with large leaves*	
One variety:	
Shade	Jon. 4:6-10
Poison variety	2 Kin. 4:39-41
Government—*recognized rulership*	
A. *Types of:*	
Patriarchal, in families	Gen. 27:29-39
Theocratic, under God	Ex. 18:13-26
Monarchial, under kings	1 Sam. 8:5-22
Antichristian, under antichrist	2 Thess. 2:3-12
Absolute and final, under Christ	Is. 9:6, 7
B. *Characteristics of:*	
Ruled by God	Is. 45:1-13
Successions of, determined by God	Dan. 2:28-45
Ignorant of spiritual things	1 Cor. 2:8
Providentially used	Acts 26:32
C. *Christian attitude toward:*	
Occupy positions in	Gen. 42:6
Pay taxes to	Matt. 22:18-21
Pray for	1 Tim. 2:1-3
Obey rules of	Rom. 13:1-7
But obey God first	Acts 5:29
Governor—*a ruler*	
Title used of Zerubbabel	Ezra 2:63
Applied to Nehemiah	Neh. 8:9
Prime minister	Gen. 42:6
Provincial ruler	Acts 23:24, 26
Chief of ceremonies	John 2:8, 9
Household teachers	Gal. 4:2
Magistrates	Matt. 10:18
Christ	Matt. 2:6
Gozan—*quarry*	
Town and district in Mesopotamia	2 Kin. 17:6
Israelites deported to	2 Kin. 18:11
Grace—*unmerited favor*	
A. *Descriptive of:*	
God's favor	Gen. 6:8
God's forgiving mercy	Rom. 11:6
Gospel	John 1:17
Gifts (miracles, etc.)	1 Pet. 4:10
Eternal life	1 Pet. 1:13
B. *Is the source of:*	
Salvation	Acts 15:11
Call of God	Gal. 1:15
Faith	Acts 18:27
Justification	Rom. 3:24
Forgiveness	Eph. 1:7
Consolation	2 Thess. 2:16
C. *Described as:*	
All-abundant	Rom. 5:15-20
All-sufficient	2 Cor. 12:9
Glorious	Eph. 1:6
Great	Acts 4:33
Manifold	1 Pet. 4:10
Rich	Eph. 2:4, 5
Undeserved	1 Tim. 1:12-16
D. *Believers:*	
Are under	Rom. 6:14
Receive	John 1:16
Stand in	Rom. 5:2
Abound in	2 Cor. 9:8
Be strong in	2 Tim. 2:1
Grow in	2 Pet. 3:18
Speak with	Eph. 4:29
Inherit	1 Pet. 3:7
E. *Dangers of, can:*	
Be abused	Jude 4
Be frustrated	Gal. 2:21
Be turned from	Gal. 5:3, 4

SUBJECT	REFERENCE
Graces, Christian	
Growth in, commanded	2 Pet. 1:5-8
Grafting—*uniting a portion of one plant to another*	
Gentiles, on Israel's stock	Rom. 11:17, 24
Grain—*the generic term for cereal grasses*	
A. *Features regarding:*	
Grown in Palestine	2 Kin. 18:32
Article of food	Gen. 42:1, 2, 19
Offered mixed with oil	Lev. 2:14, 15
Roasted	Ruth 2:14
B. *Figurative of:*	
Blessings	Ezek. 36:29
Christ	John 12:24
Life's maturity	Job 5:26
Grandchildren	
Lot becomes father of, through incest	Gen. 19:30-38
Abdon's	Judg. 12:13, 14
Widow's	1 Tim. 5:4
Iniquity visited on	Ex. 34:7
Served idols	2 Kin. 17:41
Crown of old men	Prov. 17:6
Practice piety toward family	1 Tim. 5:4
Grandmother	
Lois thus called	2 Tim. 1:5
Grapes	
Grown in Palestine	Num. 13:23
Used for wine	Num. 6:3
"Sour grapes"	Ezek. 18:2
Figurative of judgment	Rev. 14:18
See Vine, vineyard	
Grass	
A. *Features:*	
Created by God	Gen. 1:11, 12
Produced by rain	Deut. 32:2
Adorns earth	Matt. 6:30
Failure of, a calamity	Jer. 14:5, 6
Nebuchadnezzar eats	Dan. 4:1, 33
Disappears	Prov. 27:25
Withered away	Is. 15:6
B. *Figurative of:*	
Life's shortness	Ps. 90:5, 6
Prosperous wicked	Ps. 92:7
God's grace	Ps. 72:6
Grasshopper—*locust*	
Used as food	Lev. 11:22
Inferiority	Num. 13:33
Insignificance	Is. 40:22
Burden	Eccl. 12:5
Destroys crops	Ps. 78:46
See Locust	
Gratitude (see Thankfulness)	
Gratitude to man	
A. *Reasons for:*	
Deliverance from an enemy	Judg. 8:22, 23
Deliverance from death	1 Sam. 26:21-25
Interpretation of a dream	Dan. 2:46-48
Rescue from murderers	Esth. 6:1-6
B. *Examples of:*	
Ruth to Boaz	Ruth 2:8-17
Israelites to Jonathan	1 Sam. 14:45
Abigail to David	1 Sam. 25:40-42
David to Jonathan	2 Sam. 9:1
David to Hanum	2 Sam. 10:1, 2
Pagans to Paul	Acts 28:1-10
Grave—*a place of burial*	
A. *Features regarding:*	
Dug in ground	Gen. 50:5
Some in caves	Gen. 23:9
Marker set on	Gen. 35:20
Touching of, makes unclean	Num. 19:16, 18
B. *Resurrection from:*	
Symbolized	Ezek. 37:1-14
Graveclothes—*clothes for the dead*	
Lazarus attired in	John 11:43, 44
Jesus lays His aside	Luke 24:12

SUBJECT ... REFERENCE

Gravel—*small pebbles*

Figurative of:

Distress ... Prov. 20:17
Numerous offspring; rendered "grains" ... Is. 48:19
Suffering ... Lam. 3:16

Graven image—*an idol*

Of Canaanites, to be destroyed ... Deut. 7:1-5, 25; Deut. 12:2, 3
Cause of God's anger ... Ps. 78:58; Jer. 8:19

See Idols, idolatry

Great

A. *Descriptive of:*

Sun and moon ... Gen. 1:16
Euphrates ... Gen. 15:18
Mediterranean ... Josh. 1:4
Nineveh ... Jon. 3:2, 3
Babylon ... Rev. 14:8

B. *Applied to God's:*

Nature ... Deut. 10:17
Signs and miracles ... Deut. 29:3
Works ... Judg. 2:7
Victory ... 2 Sam. 23:10, 12
Mercy ... 2 Chr. 1:8
Wrath ... 2 Chr. 34:21
Glory ... Ps. 21:5
Power ... Ps. 147:5

C. *Descriptive of Christ as:*

God ... Titus 2:13
Prophet ... Luke 7:16
Priest ... Heb. 4:14
King ... Luke 1:32, 33; Rev. 11:17
Shepherd ... Heb. 13:20

D. *Applied to the believer's:*

Reward ... Matt. 5:12
Faith ... Matt. 15:28
Joy ... Acts 8:8
Zeal ... Col. 4:13
Affliction ... 2 Cor. 8:2
Boldness ... 1 Tim. 3:13
Promises ... 2 Pet. 1:4

E. *Applied to final things:*

Gulf fixed ... Luke 16:26
Wrath ... Rev. 6:17
Tribulation ... Rev. 7:14
White throne judgment ... Rev. 20:11

Great fish

Swallows Jonah ... Jon. 1:17

Greatness, true

Hinges on:

God's gentleness ... Ps. 18:35
Great work ... Neh. 6:3
Unselfishness ... Jer. 45:5
Servanthood ... Matt. 23:11
God's estimate ... Matt. 5:19

Grecians

1. The people of Greece ... Joel 3:6
2. Greek-speaking Jews ... Acts 6:1
   Hostile to Paul ... Acts 9:29
   Gospel preached unto ... Acts 11:20

Greece—*the southern extremity of the Balkan peninsula*

Prophecy concerning ... Dan. 8:21
Paul preaches in ... Acts 17:16-31
Called Javan ... Is. 66:19

Greed—*excessive desire for things*

A. *Productive of:*

Defeat ... Josh. 7:11-26
Murder ... 1 Kin. 21:1-16
Betrayal ... Luke 22:1-6

B. *Examples of:*

Samuel's sons ... 1 Sam. 8:1, 3
False prophets ... Is. 56:10,11
False teachers ... 2 Pet. 2:14, 15

See Avarice; Covetousness

Greek

1. Native of Greece ... Acts 16:1
   Spiritual state of ... Rom. 10:12
   Some believe ... Acts 14:1
2. Foreigners speaking Greek ... John 12:20
3. Language of Greece ... Acts 21:37

SUBJECT ... REFERENCE

Greyhound—*a tall, slender hound*

Poetically described ... Prov. 30:29, 31

Grief

A. *Causes of:*

Son's marriage ... Gen. 26:34, 35
Barrenness ... 1 Sam. 1:11, 16
Death ... 2 Sam. 19:1, 2
Disease ... Job 2:11-13
Sinners ... Ps. 119:158
Foolish son ... Prov. 17:25

B. *Descriptive of:*

Messiah ... Is. 53:3, 4, 10
God ... Ps. 95:10
Holy Spirit ... Eph. 4:30
God's saints ... Ps. 139:21

See Sorrow

Groves

1. Tamarisk tree ... Gen. 21:33; 1 Sam. 22:6
2. Idolatrous shrine (Asherah) ... Deut. 12:3; 2 Kin. 21:7
   Destruction of, commanded ... Ex. 34:13
   Israel's fondness for ... Jer. 17:2
   Punishment ... Is. 27:9

Grow—*to increase*

A. *Of material things:*

Power ... 2 Sam. 3:1
Age ... Josh. 23:1
Sound ... Ex. 19:19

B. *Of immaterial things:*

Spirituality ... Luke 2:40
God's hand ... Num. 11:23
Old covenant ... Heb. 8:13
God's kingdom ... Luke 13:18, 19

Growth, spiritual

A. *Expressed by words indicating:*

Fruitfulness ... John 15:2, 5
Increase ... 2 Cor. 9:10
Addition ... 2 Pet. 1:5-10
Growth ... 1 Pet. 2:2
Building up ... Jude 20

B. *Hindrances to:*

Lack of knowledge ... Acts 18:24-28
Carnality ... 1 Cor. 3:1-3
Instability ... Eph. 4:14, 15
Dullness ... Heb. 5:11-14

Grudge—*to harbor resentment*

Forbidden ... Lev. 19:18

Guard

A. *Aspects of:*

Called mighty ... 2 Sam. 23:8-23
Often foreigners ... 2 Sam. 20:7
Respected ... Jer. 40:1-5

B. *Duties of:*

Run before chariots ... 2 Sam. 15:1
Form a military guard ... 1 Sam. 22:17
Keep watch ... 2 Kin. 11:6
Carry out commandments ... Jer. 39:11-14
Execute criminals ... Dan. 2:14

Guardian—*a custodian*

Christ, of our souls ... 2 Tim. 1:12

Guardian angels

Helpers ... Gen. 24:7; Heb. 1:1-14
Protectors ... Ps. 91:11; Matt. 18:10
Aided apostles ... Acts 5:17-19; Acts 8:26

Gudgodah—*cutting; cleft*

Israelite encampment ... Deut. 10:7
Also called Hor-hagidgad ... Num. 33:32

Guest

Kinds of:

Terrified ... 1 Kin. 1:41, 49
Dead ... Prov. 9:18
Unwelcomed ... Prov. 25:17
Unprepared ... Matt. 22:11
Criticized ... Luke 7:39-50
Congenial ... Acts 18:1-3

SUBJECT ... REFERENCE

Courteous ... 1 Cor. 10:27
Angelic ... Heb. 13:2

Guidance, divine

To the meek ... Ps. 25:9
To the wise ... Prov. 23:19
To the good man ... Ps. 112:5
In God's strength ... Ex. 15:13
On every side ... 2 Chr. 32:22
With God's eye ... Ps. 32:8
With counsel ... Ps. 73:24
Like a flock ... Ps. 78:52
By skillfulness ... Ps. 78:72
Continually ... Is. 58:11

Guide—*a leader*

A. *Kinds of:*

Human ... Num. 10:29-32
Supernatural ... Ex. 13:20-22
Blind ... Matt. 23:16, 24

B. *Goals of:*

Peace ... Luke 1:79
Truth ... John 16:13
God's word ... Acts 8:30, 31

Guilt, universality of

Described as:

Filthy rags ... Is. 64:6
Fall short ... Rom. 3:23
All declared ... Rom. 5:12-14; Gal. 3:22

Guni—*colored*

1. One of Naphtali's sons ... Gen. 46:24; 1 Chr. 7:13
   Descendants called Gunites ... Num. 26:48
2. Gadite ... 1 Chr. 5:15

Gur—*lion's cub*

Site of Ahaziah's death ... 2 Kin. 9:27

Gur-baal—*sojourn of Baal*

Place in Arabia ... 2 Chr. 26:7

H

Haahashtari—*runner*

Son of Ashur ... 1 Chr. 4:5, 6

Habaiah—*Jehovah has hidden*

Father of excommunicated Jewish priests ... Ezra 2:61, 62
Also spelled Hobaiah ... Neh. 7:63, 64

Habakkuk—*embrace*

A. *Complaints of:*

God's silence ... Hab. 1:2-4
God's response ... Hab. 1:5-11
Chaldean cruelty ... Hab. 1:12-17
God's response ... Hab. 2:1-20

B. *Prayer of:*

Praise of God ... Hab. 3:1-19

Habakkuk, the Book of—*a book of the Old Testament*

Author ... Hab. 1:1
Setting ... Hab. 1:2-4
Historical reference ... Hab. 1:6
The life of the just ... Hab. 2:4

Habaziniah

Grandfather of Jaazaniah ... Jer. 35:3

Habergeon—*a coat of mail*

Worn by priests ... Ex. 28:32; Ex. 39:23

Habit—*a custom*

Kinds of:

Doing evil ... Jer. 13:23
Doing good ... Acts 10:38
Of animals, instinctive ... 2 Pet. 2:22

Habitation—*a place of residence*

A. *Used literally of:*

Canaan ... Num. 15:2
A tree ... Dan. 4:20, 21
Nation ... Acts 17:26

B. *Used figuratively of:*

Eternity ... Is. 57:15

SUBJECT — REFERENCE

God's throne ... Is. 63:15
Sky ... Hab. 3:11
Heaven ... Luke 16:9
New Jerusalem ... Is. 33:20

Habor—*joined together*
On the river of Gozan ... 2 Kin. 17:6

Hachaliah—*darkness of Jehovah*
Father of Nehemiah ... Neh. 1:1

Hachilah—*dark, gloomy*
Hill in the wilderness of Ziph where David hid ... 1 Sam. 23:19-26

Hachmoni
Tutor to king's son ... 1 Chr. 27:32

Hadad—*fierceness*
1. Ishmael's son ... Gen. 25:13, 15; 1 Chr. 1:30
2. King of Edom ... Gen. 36:35, 36
3. Another king of Edom ... 1 Chr. 1:50
   Called Hadar ... Gen. 36:39
4. Edomite leader ... 1 Kin. 11:14-25

Hadadezer—*Hadad is a help*
King of Zobah ... 2 Sam. 8:3-13
Defeated by David ... 2 Sam. 10:6-19

Hadadrimmon—*Hadad and Rimmon*
Name of the two Aramean deities; a place in Jezreel ... Zech. 12:11

Hadashah—*new*
Village of Judah ... Josh. 15:37

Hadassah—*myrtle*
Esther's Jewish name ... Esth. 2:7

Hadattah—*new*
Town in south Judah; probably should be read as Hazorhadattah ... Josh. 15:25

Hadid—*sharp*
Town of Benjamin ... Neh. 11:31, 34

Hadlai—*restful*
Ephraimite ... 2 Chr. 28:12

Hadoram—*Hadar is exalted*
1. Son of Joktan ... Gen. 10:26, 27
2. Son of Tou ... 1 Chr. 18:9, 10
3. Rehoboam's tribute officer ... 2 Chr. 10:18
   Called Adoram ... 1 Kin. 12:18
   Probably same as Adoniram ... 1 Kin. 4:6

Hadrach—*periodical return*
Place in Syria ... Zech. 9:1

Hagab—*locust*
Head of a family of Temple servants ... Ezra 2:46

Hagaba—*locust*
Head of a family of Temple servants ... Neh. 7:46, 48

Hagabah—*locust*
Head of a family of Temple servants ... Ezra 2:43, 45

Hagar, Agar—*flight*
Sarah's Egyptian handmaid ... Gen. 16:1
Flees from Sarah ... Gen. 16:5-8
Returns; becomes mother of Ishmael ... Gen. 16:3-16
Abraham sends her away ... Gen. 21:14
Paul's allegory of ... Gal. 4:22-26

Hagarites
Nomad people east of Gilead ... 1 Chr. 5:10-22
Called Hagarenes ... Ps. 83:6

Hagerite—*a descendant of Hagar*
Jaziz, keeper of David's flocks ... 1 Chr. 27:31

Haggai—*festive*
Postexilic prophet ... Ezra 5:1, 2
Contemporary of Zechariah ... Ezra 6:14
Prophecies of, dated in reign of Darius Hystaspes (520 B.C.) ... Hag. 1:1, 15; Hag. 2:1, 10, 20

SUBJECT — REFERENCE

Haggai, the Book of—*a book of the Old Testament*
Purpose ... Hag. 1:1-15
The coming glory ... Hag. 2:4-9
On Levitical cleanliness ... Hag. 2:10-14

Haggedolim
Father of Zabdiel ... Neh. 11:14

Haggeri—*a Hagerite*
A mighty man of David's guard ... 1 Chr. 11:38
Called "Bani the Gadite" in ... 2 Sam. 23:36

Haggi—*festal*
Son of Gad ... Gen. 46:16
Head of tribal family ... Num. 26:15

Haggiah—*festival of Jehovah*
Merarite Levite ... 1 Chr. 6:30

Haggith—*festal*
One of David's wives ... 2 Sam. 3:4
Mother of Adonijah ... 1 Kin. 1:5

Hail—*frozen rain*
Illustrative of God's:
Wonders ... Job 38:22
Glory ... Ps. 18:12
Chastening ... Is. 28:2, 17
Wrath ... Rev. 8:7

Hail—*a salutation* ("Hale be thou")
Gabriel to Mary ... Luke 1:26-28
Judas to Christ ... Matt. 26:47-49
Soldiers to Christ ... Matt. 27:27-29

Hair
A. *Of women:*
Covering ... 1 Cor. 11:15
Uses of ... Luke 7:38
Prohibitions concerning ... 1 Tim. 2:9; 1 Pet. 3:3

B. *Of men:*
Not to be worn long ... 1 Cor. 11:14
Rules for cutting ... Lev. 19:27
Long, during Nazarite vow ... Num. 6:5
Gray, sign of age ... 1 Sam. 12:2
Absalom's beautiful ... 2 Sam. 14:25, 26
Numbered ... Matt. 10:30

C. *Figurative of:*
Minuteness ... Judg. 20:16
Complete safety ... 1 Sam. 14:45
Fear ... Job 4:14, 15
Great numbers ... Ps. 40:12
Grief ... Ezra 9:3
Respect ... Prov. 16:31
Attractiveness ... Song 5:2, 11
Affliction ... Is. 3:17, 24
Entire destruction ... Is. 7:20
Decline and fall ... Hos. 7:9

Hakkatan—*the smallest*
Johanan's father ... Ezra 8:12

Hakkoz—*the thorn*
Descendant of Aaron ... 1 Chr. 24:1, 10
Descendants of, kept from priesthood ... Ezra 2:61, 62

Hakupha—*crooked*
Ancestor of certain Temple servants ... Ezra 2:43, 51

Halah—*a district of Assyria*
Israelite captives carried to ... 2 Kin. 17:6

Halak—*smooth*
Mountain near Seir ... Josh. 11:17

Half-shekel tax—*a temple tax*
Commanded ... Ex. 30:13, 14
Also called "two-drachma tax" ... Matt. 17:24-27

Half-tribe of Manasseh—*the part of Manasseh east of the Jordan*
Clans of:
Machir ... Josh. 17:1
Hezron ... 1 Chr. 2:21-23

Halhul—*contorted*
A city in Judah ... Josh. 15:20, 21, 58

SUBJECT — REFERENCE

Hali—*necklace*
Town of Asher ... Josh. 19:25

Hallohesh—*enchanter*
Repairs walls and signs covenant ... Neh. 3:12; Neh. 10:24

Ham—*hot*
1. Noah's youngest son ... Gen. 5:32
   Enters ark ... Gen. 7:7
   His immoral behavior merits Noah's curse ... Gen. 9:22-25
   Father of descendants of repopulated earth ... Gen. 10:6-20
2. Poetical name of Egypt ... Ps. 105:23, 27
3. Hamites at Gedor ... 1 Chr. 4:39, 40
4. Place where Chedorlaomer defeated the Zuzim ... Gen. 14:5

Haman
Plots to destroy Jews ... Esth. 3:3-15
Invited to Esther's banquet ... Esth. 5:1-14
Forced to honor Mordecai ... Esth. 6:5-14
Hanged on his own gallows ... Esth. 7:1-10

Hamath—*fortification*
Hittite city north of Damascus ... Josh. 13:5
Spies visit ... Num. 13:21
Israel's northern limit ... Num. 34:8
Solomon's boundary ... 1 Kin. 8:65
Storage cities built ... 2 Chr. 8:3, 4
Captured by the Assyrians ... 2 Kin. 18:34
People of, deported to Samaria ... 2 Kin. 17:24, 30
Israelites exiled ... Is. 11:11
Mentioned by Jeremiah ... Jer. 49:23
Limit of Ezekiel's prophecy ... Ezek. 47:16-20

Hamathites
People of Hamath ... Gen. 10:18

Hamath-zobah—*fortress of Zobah*
Captured by Solomon ... 2 Chr. 8:3

Hammath—*hot springs*
1. City of Naphtali ... Josh. 19:35
   Probably the same as Hammon and Hammothdor ... 1 Chr. 6:76
2. Founder of the Rechabites ... 1 Chr. 2:55

Hammedatha—*given by Ham*
Father of Haman ... Esth. 3:1

Hammelech—*the king*
Father of Jerahmeel ... Jer. 36:26

Hammer—*a workman's tool*
A. *Literal uses of:*
Drive tent pegs ... Judg. 4:21
Not used in Temple ... 1 Kin. 6:7
Straighten metal ... Is. 41:7

B. *Figurative uses of:*
God's Word ... Jer. 23:29
Babylon ... Jer. 50:23

Hammoleketh—*the queen*
Sister of Gilead ... 1 Chr. 7:17, 18

Hammon—*glowing*
1. Village of Asher ... Josh. 19:28
2. Town of Naphtali ... 1 Chr. 6:76
See Hammath 1

Hammoth-dor—*hot springs of Dor*
City of refuge ... Josh. 21:32
See Hammath 1

Hamonah—*multitude*
Site of Gog's defeat ... Ezek. 39:11-16

Hamon-gog—*multitude of Gog*
Memorial name of Gog's burial ... Ezek. 39:11

Hamor—*ass*
Sells land to Jacob ... Gen. 33:18-20
Killed by Jacob's sons ... Gen. 34:1-31

Hamuel—*anger of God*
Son of Mishma ... 1 Chr. 4:26

Hamul—*spared*
Son of Pharez ... Gen. 46:12
Founder of tribal family ... Num. 26:21

SUBJECT — REFERENCE

Hamutal—*kinsman of dew*

Wife of King Josiah ... 2 Kin. 23:30, 31
Mother of Jehoahaz and Zedekiah ... 2 Kin. 24:18
Daughter of Jeremiah of Libnah ... Jer. 52:1

Hanameel—*God has pitied*

Cousin of Jeremiah the prophet ... Jer. 32:7

Hanan—*merciful*

1. One of David's mighty men ... 1 Chr. 11:26, 43
2. Benjamite ... 1 Chr. 8:23, 25
3. Descendant of Jonathan ... 1 Chr. 8:38
4. Prophet ... Jer. 35:4
5. Head of Temple servants ... Ezra 2:46
6. Explained Law ... Neh. 8:7
7. Nehemiah's assistant treasurer ... Neh. 13:13

8, 9. Signers of the covenant ... Neh. 10:22, 26

Hananeel—*God has been gracious*

Tower at Jerusalem ... Jer. 31:38

Hanani—*gracious*

1. Father of Jehu the prophet ... 1 Kin. 16:1, 7
   Rebukes Asa; confined to prison ... 2 Chr. 16:7-10
2. Son of Heman; head of Levitical course ... 1 Chr. 25:4, 25
3. Priest who divorced his foreign wife ... Ezra 10:20
4. Nehemiah's brother; brings news concerning the Jews ... Neh. 1:2
   Becomes a governor of Jerusalem ... Neh. 7:2
5. Levite musician ... Neh. 12:35, 36

Hananiah—*Jehovah has been gracious*

1. Benjamite chief ... 1 Chr. 8:24, 25
2. Son of Heman; head of Levitical division ... 1 Chr. 25:4, 23
3. One of King Uzziah's captains ... 2 Chr. 26:11
4. Father of Zedekiah ... Jer. 36:12
5. False prophet who contradicts Jeremiah ... Jer. 28:1-17
6. Ancestor of Irijah ... Jer. 37:13-15
7. Hebrew name of Shadrach ... Dan. 1:6, 7, 11
8. Son of Zerubbabel ... 1 Chr. 3:19-21
   Probably same as Joanna ... Luke 3:27
9. Son of Bebai; divorced his foreign wife ... Ezra 10:28
10. Postexilic workman ... Neh. 3:8, 30
11. Postexilic priest ... Neh. 12:41
12. Postexilic chief; signs document ... Neh. 10:23
13. Postexilic ruler ... Neh. 7:2
14. Priest of Joiakim's time ... Neh. 12:12

Hand

Mysterious ... Dan. 5:1-6
Healing withered ... Mark 3:1-3
Offending, to be cut off ... Matt. 18:8

Handbreadth—*a linear measurement*

Border of ... Ex. 37:12
Figurative of human life ... Ps. 39:5

Handful

Of fine flour ... Lev. 2:2—5:12
Of grain offering ... Num. 5:26
Of barley ... Ezek. 13:19

Handkerchief

Touch of, brings healing ... Acts 19:12
Rendered "napkin" ... John 11:44; John 20:7

Handle—*to manage with the hands*

Used literally for:

Hold ... 2 Chr. 25:5
Touch ... Luke 24:39
Feel ... Ps. 115:7

Used figuratively for:

Give attention ... Prov. 16:20
Treat ... Mark 12:4

Handmaid—*female servant*

Examples of:

Hagar ... Gen. 16:1
Zilpah ... Gen. 29:24
Bilhah ... Gen. 30:4

Expressive of humility:

Ruth ... Ruth 2:13
Woman of Endor ... 1 Sam. 28:7, 21, 22
Mary ... Luke 1:38

Hand of God

Expressive of:

Judgment ... Ex. 9:3
Chastening ... Job 19:21
Security ... John 10:29
Miracles ... Ex. 3:20
Providence ... Ps. 31:15
Provision ... Ps. 145:16
Protection ... Ps. 139:10
Punishment ... Ps. 75:8
Pleading ... Is. 65:2

Hands

Clapping—in joy ... 2 Kin. 11:12
Washing—in innocency ... Matt. 27:24
Joining—in agreement ... 2 Kin. 10:15
Striking—in suretyship ... Prov. 17:16-18
Striking—in anger ... Num. 24:10
Under thigh—in oaths ... Gen. 47:29, 31

Right hand, expressive of:

Honor ... Ps. 45:9
Power ... Ps. 110:1
Love ... Song 2:6
Oath ... Is. 62:8
Accusation ... Zech. 3:1
Self-denial ... Matt. 5:30
Fellowship ... Gal. 2:9

Hands, laying on of

A. *In the Old Testament:*
   Blessing a person ... Gen. 48:14, 20
   Transferring one's guilt ... Lev. 4:14, 15
   Setting apart for service ... Num. 8:10, 11
   Inaugurating a successor ... Num. 27:18-23

B. *In the New Testament:*
   Blessing ... Matt. 19:13-15
   Healing ... Matt. 9:18
   Ordaining deacons ... Acts 6:6
   Sending out missionaries ... Acts 13:2, 3
   Ordaining officers ... 1 Tim. 4:14
   In bestowing the Holy Spirit ... Acts 8:17, 18

Handwriting

Of a king, changeable ... Dan. 6:8-27
Of God, unchangeable ... Dan. 5:5 31

Hanes—*mercury*

Probably an Egyptian city ... Is. 30:4

Hanging—*a form of punishment*

Absalom ... 2 Sam. 18:9-17
Ahithophel ... 2 Sam. 17:23
Judas ... Matt. 27:5
Chief baker ... Gen. 40:19, 22
King of Ai ... Josh. 8:29
Five Canaanite kings ... Josh. 10:26, 27
Ish-bosheth's murderers ... 2 Sam. 4:12
Bodies of Saul and Jonathan ... 2 Sam. 21:12
Law of ... Ezra 6:11
Haman ... Esth. 7:10
Haman's sons ... Esth. 9:14
Curse of ... Gal. 3:13
Saul's descendants ... 2 Sam. 21:9
Jesus Christ ... John 19:31

Hannah—*graciousness*

Favored wife of Elkanah ... 1 Sam. 1:5
Childless ... 1 Sam. 1:5, 6
Provoked by Peninnah ... 1 Sam. 1:6, 7
Wrongly accused by Eli ... 1 Sam. 1:14
Prayerful ... 1 Sam. 1:10
Attentive to her child ... 1 Sam. 1:22
Fulfills her vows ... 1 Sam. 1:11-28
Magnifies God ... 1 Sam. 2:1-10
Recognizes the Messiah ("his anointed") ... 1 Sam. 2:10
Model of Mary's song ... Luke 1:46-54

Hannathon—*regarded with favor*

Town of Zebulun ... Josh. 19:14

Hanniel—*God has been gracious*

1. Manassite prince ... Num. 34:23
2. Asherite ... 1 Chr. 7:30, 39

Hanoch—*dedicated*

1. Descendant of Abraham ... Gen. 25:4; 1 Chr. 1:33
2. Son of Reuben ... Gen. 46:9
3. Head of tribal family ... Num. 26:5

Hanun—*favored*

1. King of Ammon ... 2 Sam. 10:1
   Disgraces David's ambassadors ... 2 Sam. 10:2-5
   Is defeated by David ... 2 Sam. 10:6-14

2, 3. Postexilic workmen ... Neh. 3:13, 30

Hapharaim—*double pit*

Town of Issachar ... Josh. 19:19

Happiness of the saints

A. *Is derived from:*
   Fear of God ... Ps. 128:1, 2
   Trust in God ... Prov. 16:20
   Obedience to God ... John 13:15, 17
   Wisdom's ways ... Prov. 3:13-18

B. *Examples of:*
   Israel ... Deut. 33:29
   Job ... James 5:11
   Mary ... Luke 1:46-55
   Paul ... Acts 26:2

C. *In spite of:*
   Discipline ... Job 5:17
   Suffering ... 1 Pet. 4:12-14
   Persecution ... Matt. 5:10-12
   Lack ... Phil. 4:6, 7
   Trouble ... 2 Cor. 4:7-18

D. *Described as:*
   Blessed ... Matt. 5:3-12
   Filled ... Ps. 36:8
   In God alone ... Ps. 73:25, 26

See Gladness; Joy

Happiness of the wicked

A. *Described as:*
   Short ... Job 20:5
   Uncertain ... Luke 12:20
   Vain ... Eccl. 2:1, 2
   Limited to this life ... Luke 16:24, 25
   Under God's judgment ... Job 15:21; Ps. 73:18-20

B. *Derived from:*
   Prominence ... Job 21:7; Ps. 37:35
   Prosperity ... Ps. 17:14; Ps. 37:7
   Sensuality ... Is. 22:13

C. *Saints:*
   Sometimes stumble at ... Ps. 73:2, 3
   Should not envy ... Ps. 37:1, 7
   Will see end ... Ps. 73:17-20

Hara—*hill*

Place in Assyria where captive Israelites settled ... 1 Chr. 5:26

Haradah—*fear*

Israelite encampment ... Num. 33:24

Haran—*mountainous*

1. Abraham's younger brother ... Gen. 11:26-31
2. Gershonite Levite ... 1 Chr. 23:9
3. Son of Caleb ... 1 Chr. 2:46
4. City of Mesopotamia ... Gen. 11:31
   Abraham lives in ... Acts 7:2, 4
   Abraham leaves ... Gen. 12:4, 5
   Jacob flees to ... Gen. 27:43
   Jacob dwells at ... Gen. 29:4-35
   Center of idolatry ... Gen. 35:2; 2 Kin. 19:12

Hararite—*mountaineer*

Applied to David's mighty men ... {2 Sam. 23:11, 33; 1 Chr. 11:34, 35

Harbona—*bald man*

Chamberlain of Ahasuerus ... Esth. 1:10
Same as Harbonah ... Esth. 7:9

SUBJECT — REFERENCE

Harbor—*a sheltered bay*
Unacceptable ... Acts 27:12

Hard labor
A. *Spiritual:*
Subduing flesh ... 1 Cor. 9:24-27
Striving against sin ... Heb. 12:4
Reaching goal ... Phil. 3:11-14
B. *Physical:*
Jacob ... Gen. 31:40-42
Israelites ... Ex. 1:11-14
Gibeonites ... Josh. 9:3-27
Samson ... Judg. 16:20, 21

Hardness of heart
A. *Causes of:*
God ... Rom. 9:18
Man ... Job 9:4
Unbelief ... John 12:40
Sin ... Heb. 3:13
B. *Examples of:*
Pharaoh ... Ex. 4:21
Zedekiah ... 2 Chr. 36:11-13
Israel ... Ezek. 3:7
Nebuchadnezzar ... Dan. 5:20
Jews ... Mark 3:5
Believers ... Mark 6:52
C. *Warnings against:*
Recognized by Egyptians ... 1 Sam. 6:6
Unheeded by Israel ... Jer. 5:3
Lamented by the prophets ... Is. 63:17
Addressed to Christians ... Heb. 3:8-15; Heb. 4:7

Harem—*group of females associated with one man*
Esther a member of King Ahasuerus' ... Esth. 2:8-14

Hareph—*plucking*
Son of Caleb ... 1 Chr. 2:50, 51

Hareth
Forest in Judah ... 1 Sam. 22:5

Harhaiah—*Jehovah is protecting*
Father of Uzziel ... Neh. 3:8

Harhas—*splendor*
Grandfather of Shallum ... 2 Kin. 22:14

Harhur—*fever*
Ancestor of returning Temple servants ... Ezra 2:43, 51

Harim—*consecrated to God*
1. Descendant of Aaron ... 1 Chr. 24:1, 6, 8
2. Postexilic leader ... Ezra 2:32, 39
3. Father of Malchijah ... Neh. 3:11
4. Signer of the covenant ... Neh. 10:1, 5
5. Signer of the covenant ... Neh. 10:1, 27
6. Family house of priests ... Neh. 12:12, 15
7. Descendants of, divorced foreign wives ... Ezra 10:19, 21

Hariph—*autumn rain*
Family of returnees ... Neh. 7:24
Signers of covenant ... Neh. 10:19
Same as Jorah ... Ezra 2:18

Harlot—*a prostitute*
A. *Characteristics of:*
Shameless ... Jer. 3:3
Painted ... Ezra 23:40
Enticing ... Prov. 9:14-18
Roaming streets ... Prov. 7:12
Expensive ... Prov. 29:3
B. *Evils of:*
Profanes God's name ... Amos 2:7
Connected with idolatry ... Ex. 34:15, 16
Brings spiritual error ... Hos. 4:10-19
Cause of divorce ... Jer. 3:8, 14
C. *Prohibitions concerning:*
Forbidden in Israel ... Lev. 19:29
Priests not to marry ... Lev. 21:1, 7, 14
To be shamed ... Prov. 5:3-20
Punishment ... Lev. 21:9
D. *Examples of:*
Tamar ... Gen. 38:13-20
Rahab ... Josh. 2:1-21
Jephthah's mother ... Judg. 11:1
Samson's ... Judg. 16:1
Hosea's wife ... Hos. 1:2
The great ... Rev. 17:1-18
E. *Figurative of:*
Tyre ... Is. 23:15, 17
Israel ... Is. 1:21
Spiritual adultery ... Is. 57:7-9; Rev. 17:1-18
See Adultery

Harmony—*agreement, co-operation*
Husband and wife ... 1 Cor. 7:3-6; Eph. 5:22-23; Col. 3:18, 19
Christians ... John 13:34, 35; Rom. 15:5-7
Christians and unbelievers ... Rom. 12:16-18; Heb. 12:14

Harnepher
Asherite ... 1 Chr. 7:36

Harness—*to equip*
Horses ... Jer. 46:4

Harod—*fountain of trembling*
Well near Gideon's camp ... Judg. 7:1

Harodite
Inhabitant of Harod ... 2 Sam. 23:25
Same as Harorite ... 1 Chr. 11:27

Haroeh—*the seer*
Judahite ... 1 Chr. 2:50, 52
Called Reaiah ... 1 Chr. 4:2

Harosheth—*carving of the nations*
Residence of Sisera ... Judg. 4:2, 13, 16

Harp—*a stringed musical instrument*
Used by:
The wicked ... Is. 5:11, 12
David ... 1 Sam. 16:16, 23
Prophets ... 1 Sam. 10:5
Temple orchestra ... 1 Chr. 16:5
Temple worshipers ... Ps. 33:2
Celebrators ... 2 Chr. 20:27, 28
Jewish captives ... Ps. 137:2
Worshipers in heaven ... Rev. 5:8

Harpoon—*a barbed spear for hunting large fish*
Used against Leviathan ... Job 41:7

Harrow
Instrument for breaking clods ... Job 39:10
Figurative of affliction ... Is. 28:24

Harsha—*enchanter*
Head of Temple servants ... Ezra 2:43, 52; Neh. 7:46, 54

Hart—*a male deer*
A. *Described as:*
Clean animal ... Deut. 12:15
Hunted animal ... Lam. 1:6
B. *Figurative of:*
Christ ... Song 2:9, 17
Afflicted saints ... Ps. 42:1-3
Converted sinners ... Is. 35:6

Harum—*exalted*
Judahite ... 1 Chr. 4:8

Harumaph—*flat-nosed*
Father of Jedaiah ... Neh. 3:10

Haruphite
Designation of Shephatiah ... 1 Chr. 12:5
Member of Hariph's family ... Neh. 7:24

Haruz—*active*
Father-in-law of King Manasseh ... 2 Kin. 21:19

Harvest—*the time when the crops are ripe*
A. *Occasion of:*
Great joy ... Is. 9:3
Bringing the first fruits ... Lev. 23:10
Remembering the poor ... Lev. 19:9, 10
B. *Figuratively of:*
Seasons of grace ... Jer. 8:20
Judgment ... Jer. 51:33
God's wrath ... Rev. 14:15
Gospel opportunities ... Matt. 9:37, 38
World's end ... Matt. 13:30, 39
Measure of fruitfulness ... 2 Cor. 9:6
C. *Promises concerning:*
To continue ... Gen. 8:22
Rain ... Jer. 5:24
Patience ... James 5:7
D. *Failure caused by:*
Drought ... Amos 4:7
Locusts ... Joel 1:4
Sin ... Is. 17:4-12

Hasadiah—*Jehovah has been gracious*
Son of Zerubbabel ... 1 Chr. 3:20

Hasenuah—*thorny*
Benjamite family ... 1 Chr. 9:7; Neh. 11:7-9

Hashabiah—*Jehovah has imputed*
1. Merarite Levite ... 1 Chr. 6:44, 45
Perhaps the same as in ... 1 Chr. 9:14
2. Levite musician ... 1 Chr. 25:3, 19
3. Kohathite Levite ... 1 Chr. 26:30
4. Levite ruler ... 1 Chr. 27:17
5. Chief Levite during Josiah's reign ... 2 Chr. 35:9
6. Postexilic Levite ... Ezra 8:19, 24
Probably the same in ... Neh. 10:11
7. Postexilic ruler ... Neh. 3:17
8. Descendant of Asaph ... Neh. 11:22
9. Priest in the time of Joiakim ... Neh. 12:21

Hashabnah—*covenant sealer*
Signed covenant ... Neh. 10:25

Hashabniah—*Jehovah has regarded me*
1. Father of Hattush ... Neh. 3:10
2. Postexilic Levite ... Neh. 9:5
Probably the same as Hashabiah 6.

Hashbadana—*thoughtful judge*
Assistant to Ezra ... Neh. 8:4

Hashem—*shining*
Father of David's warriors ... 1 Chr. 11:34
Also called Jashen ... 2 Sam. 23:32

Hashmonah—*fertility*
Israelite encampment ... Num. 33:29

Hashub—*thoughtful*
1. Postexilic workman ... Neh. 3:11
2. Signer of the covenant ... Neh. 10:23
3. Levite chief ... Neh. 11:15

Hashubah—*esteemed*
Son of Zerubbabel ... 1 Chr. 3:19, 20

Hashum—*opulent*
Founder of postexilic family ... Ezra 2:19
Assists Ezra and signs document ... Neh. 8:4; Neh. 10:18

Hasrah—*want*
Grandfather of Shallum ... 2 Chr. 34:22
Called Harhas ... 2 Kin. 22:14

Hassenaah—*thorny*
Father of postexilic workmen ... Neh. 3:3
Same as Senaah ... Ezra 2:35; Neh. 7:38

Haste—*to do something quickly*
Prompted by good ... 2 Chr. 35:21; Luke 19:5, 6
Prompted by evil ... Prov. 14:29; Prov. 28:20

Hasupha—*naked*
Head of Temple servants ... Ezra 2:43
Same as Hashupha ... Neh. 7:46

Hat
Better rendered as mantle ... Dan. 3:21

Hate—*to dislike something with strong feeling*
A. *Meanings of:*
React as God does ... Rev. 2:6

SUBJECT — REFERENCE

Twist moral judgments ...... Prov. 8:36
Esteem of less value .... John 12:25
Make a vital distinction ..... Luke 14:26
Despise .... Is. 1:14

B. *Causes of:*
Parental favoritism .... Gen. 37:4, 5
Rape .... 2 Sam. 13:15, 22
Failure to please .... 1 Kin. 22:8
God's purpose .... Ps. 105:25
Belonging to Christ .... Matt. 24:9, 10
Evil nature .... John 3:20

C. *Objects of:*
God's people .... Gen. 26:27
God .... Ex. 20:5
Christ..................... John 15:25
Light .... John 3:20
Evil men .... Ps. 26:5
Wickedness .... Ps. 45:7

D. *Toward Christians, sign of their:*
Discipleship .... Matt. 24:9
Election .... John 15:19
Regeneration .... 1 John 3:13-15

Hatach—*chamberlain*
Esther's attendant .... Esth. 4:5-10

Hathath—*terror*
Son of Othniel .... 1 Chr. 4:13

Hatipha—*captive*
Head of Temple servants .... Ezra 2:43, 54

Hatita—*dug up*
Father of porters .... Ezra 2:42; Neh. 7:45

Hattil—*vacillating*
Ancestor of Solomon's servants .... Ezra 2:55, 57; Neh. 7:57-59

Hattush—*assembled*
1. Descendant of David .... Ezra 8:2
2. Man of Judah .... 1 Chr. 3:22
   Probably the same as 1
3. Priest returning with Zerubbabel .... Neh. 12:1, 2
4. Postexilic workman .... Neh. 3:10
5. Priest who signs covenant.... Neh. 10:1, 4

Haughtiness—*an arrogant spirit*
Precedes a fall .... Prov. 16:18
To be brought low............ Is. 2:11, 17
Guilt of Jerusalem for......... Ezek. 16:50; Zeph. 3:11

Haunt—*to frequent a place*
Place of abode .... 1 Sam. 23:22

Hauran—*hollow land*
District southeast of Mt. Hermon .... Ezek. 47:16

Haven—*a sheltered area*
Zebulun's assets.............. Gen. 49:13
Desired .... Ps. 107:30
Near Lasea .... Acts 27:8

Havilah—*circle*
1. Son of Cush .... Gen. 10:7
2. Son of Joktan .... Gen. 10:29
3. District of Arabia .... Gen. 2:11
   Limit of Ishmaelite territory................ Gen. 25:18
   Saul defeated Amalekites..... 1 Sam. 15:7

Havoth-jair—*tent villages of Jair*
Villages of Jordan in Gilead .... Num. 32:40, 41
Or in Bashan .... Deut. 3:13, 14
Taken by Jair................ Num. 32:41

Hawk—*a plundering bird*
Ceremonially unclean .... Lev. 11:16
Migratory .... Job 39:26

Hay—*food for cattle*
Build with .... 1 Cor. 3:12
Rendered "leeks"............. Num. 11:5

Hazael—*God has seen*
King over Syria .... 1 Kin. 19:15-17
Defeats Joram of Israel .... 2 Kin. 8:25-29
Defeats Jehu................. 2 Kin. 10:31, 32
Oppresses Israel.............. 2 Kin. 13:3-7, 22
His son defeated .... 2 Kin. 13:24, 25

SUBJECT — REFERENCE

Hazaiah—*Jehovah has seen*
Man of Judah .... Neh. 11:5

Hazar-addar—*village of Addar*
Place in Canaan.............. Num. 34:4

Hazar-enan—*village of springs*
Village of north Palestine..... Num. 34:9, 10

Hazar-gaddah—*village of good fortune*
Town on the border of Judah ... Josh. 15:21, 27

Hazar-hatticon—*the middle village*
Town on the border of Hauran .... Ezek. 47:16

Hazar-maveth—*village of death*
Descendants of Joktan .... Gen. 10:26

Hazar-shual—*fox village*
Town in south Judah .... Josh. 15:21, 28
Assigned to Simeon............ Josh. 19:1, 3
Reoccupied after exile......... Neh. 11:27

Hazar-susah—*village of a mare*
Simeonite village .... Josh. 19:5

Hazel—*almond*
Jacob peeled .... Gen. 30:37

Hazelelponi—*give shade, thou who turnest toward me*
Female descendant of Judah .... 1 Chr. 4:3

Hazerim—*villages*
Habitations of the Avim........ Deut. 2:23

Hazeroth—*courts*
Israelite camp................ Num. 33:17
Scene of sedition of Miriam and Aaron .... Num. 12:1-16

Hazezon-tamar—*pruning of the palm*
Dwelling of Amorites .... Gen. 14:7
Also called Engedi............ 2 Chr. 20:2

Haziel—*God sees*
Gershonite Levite .... 1 Chr. 23:9

Hazo—*seer*
Son of Nahor .... Gen. 22:22, 23

Hazor—*enclosure*
1. Royal Canaanite city destroyed by Joshua .... Josh. 11:1-13
   Rebuilt and assigned to Naphtali .... Josh. 19:32, 36
   Army of, defeated by Deborah and Barak .... Judg. 4:1-24
   Fortified by Solomon .... 1 Kin. 9:15
   Captured by Tiglathpileser ... 2 Kin. 15:29
2. Town in south Judah .... Josh. 15:21, 25
3. Another town of south Judah.................... Josh. 15:21, 23
4. Town of Benjamin .... Neh. 11:31, 33
5. Region in the Arabian desert..................... Jer. 49:28-33

Hazor-hadattah—*new Hazor*
Town in south Judah .... Josh. 15:25

He
Fifth letter of Hebrew alphabet .... Ps. 119:33-40

Head
A. *Attitudes expressed by:*
Covered, in grief .... 2 Sam. 15:30
Covered, in subjection....... 1 Cor. 11:5
Hand upon, in sorrow....... 2 Sam. 13:19
Ashes upon, in dismay ...... Josh. 7:6
Uncovered, in leprosy .... Lev. 13:45
Wagging, in derision .... Matt. 27:39
Anointed, in dedication ..... Matt. 6:17

B. *Figurative of:*
God .... 1 Cor. 11:3
Christ..................... Eph. 1:22
Husband .... 1 Cor. 11:3, 7
Protection .... Ps. 140:7
Judgment .... Is. 15:2
Confidence .... Luke 21:28
Pride .... Ps. 83:2
Exaltation .... Ps. 27:6
Joy and prosperity............ Ps. 23:5

SUBJECT — REFERENCE

See Hands, laying on of

Head of the Church—*position of pre-eminence in the Church*
Christ .... Eph. 1:22; Eph. 5:23; Col. 1:18
Prophesied .... Dan. 7:13, 14

Headband
Part of feminine attire .... Is. 3:20

Headstone—*the cornerstone*
Christ promised as .... Zech. 4:7
Christ fulfills .... Acts 4:11; 1 Pet. 2:7

Headship—*office of authority, responsibility*
A. *Of Christ:*
Over all things .... Eph. 4:15
Over man .... 1 Cor. 11:3
Of Church.................. Eph. 5:23; Col. 1:18
Of the Corner Stone .... Acts 4:11; 1 Pet. 2:7, 8

B. *Of the Father:*
Over Christ................. 1 Cor. 11:3
Gives authority .... John 5:26, 27; 1 Cor. 15:25-28

C. *Of Man:*
Of human race............. Rom. 5:12
Over woman................ 1 Cor. 11:3; Eph. 5:23

Healing—*restoration of health*
A. *Resulting from:*
Intercession................ Num. 12:10-15
Repentance................ 1 Kin. 13:1-6
Prayer .... James 5:14, 15
Faith .... Num. 21:8, 9; John 4:46-53
God's Word .... Ps. 107:20

B. *Power of:*
Belongs to God .... Gen. 20:17, 18
Possessed by Jesus......... Matt. 4:24; Matt. 8:16
Given to apostles........... Matt. 10:1-8
Given as a gift .... 1 Cor. 12:9
Eternal in heaven........... Rev. 22:2

See Diseases; Sickness

Healing, spiritual
A. *Source of:*
Only in God .... Jer. 17:14
Through Christ............. Is. 53:5
Through the Gospel .... Ezek. 47:8-11

B. *Provided for:*
Heartbroken .... Ps. 147:3
Repentant .... 2 Chr. 7:14
Egyptians .... Is. 19:22-25
Faithful .... Mal. 4:2

C. *Necessary because of man's:*
Sin .... Ps. 41:4
Backsliding .... Jer. 3:22
Spiritual sickness .... Is. 6:10

Health—*the body freed from disease*
A. *Factors conducive to:*
Exercise................... 1 Tim. 4:8
Food .... Acts 27:34
Temperance .... Jer. 35:5-8
Obedience .... Prov. 4:20-22
Cheerfulness .... Prov. 17:22
God's will .... John 9:1-3

B. *Factors destructive of:*
Moral looseness .... Prov. 7:22-27
Wickedness .... Ps. 55:23
Disease .... 1 Sam. 5:6-12
Injury..................... Luke 10:30
Debauchery .... Titus 1:12

Heap of stones—*a monument of stones*
Symbolic of:
Shameful acts................ Josh. 7:26
Covenant .... Gen. 31:46-52
Judgment .... Jer. 9:11

Hearers—*those who hear*
A. *Element necessary in:*
Attentiveness .... Neh. 8:1-3

SUBJECT ... REFERENCE

Belief ... Rom. 10:14
Conviction ... Acts 2:37
Discrimination ... Luke 8:18

B. *Reactions of:*

Responsiveness ... 2 Sam. 7:17-29
Repentance ... 2 Sam. 12:12, 13
Rebellion ... Ezek. 33:30-33
Retreat ... John 6:60-66
Resistance ... Acts 7:51-54
Rejoicing ... Acts 13:48
Rejection ... Acts 28:23-29
Research ... Acts 17:11

Heart

A. *Seat of:*

Adultery ... Matt. 5:28
Desire ... Rom. 10:1
Doubt ... Mark 11:23
Fear ... Is. 35:4
Hatred ... Lev. 19:17
Gladness ... Acts 2:26
Love ... Mark 12:30, 33
Lust ... Rom. 1:24
Meditation ... Ps. 19:14
Mischief ... Ps. 28:3
Obedience ... Rom. 6:17
Pride ... Prov. 16:5
Purpose ... 2 Cor. 9:7
Reason ... Mark 2:8
Rebellion ... Jer. 5:23
Sorrow ... John 14:1
Thought ... Matt. 9:4

B. *Of the wicked, described as:*

Blind ... Eph. 4:18
Darkened ... Rom. 1:21
Covetous ... 2 Pet. 2:14
Full of evil ... Gen. 6:5
Unrepentant ... Rom. 2:5
Lustful ... Prov. 6:25
Proud ... Jer. 49:16
Rebellious ... Jer. 5:23
Uncircumcised ... Acts 7:51

C. *God's action upon:*

Knows ... Ps. 44:21
Searches ... 1 Chr. 28:9
Enlightens ... 2 Cor. 4:6
Opens ... Acts 16:14
Recreates ... Ezek. 11:19
Examines ... Jer. 12:3
Strengthens ... Ps. 27:14
Establishes ... 1 Thess. 3:13

D. *Regenerate's, described as:*

Circumcised ... Rom. 2:29
Clean ... Ps. 73:1
Contrite ... Ps. 51:17
Enlarged ... Ps. 119:32
Enlightened ... 2 Cor. 4:6
Fixed ... Ps. 57:7
Joyful in God ... 1 Sam. 2:1
Meditative ... Ps. 4:4
Perfect ... Ps. 101:2
Prayerful ... 1 Sam. 1:12, 13
Pure ... Matt. 5:8
Glad and sincere ... Acts 2:46
Tender ... 2 Kin. 22:19
Treasury of good ... Matt. 12:35
Wise ... Prov. 10:8

E. *Regenerate's, responses of:*

Believe with ... Rom. 10:10
Keep with diligence ... Prov. 4:23
Love God with all ... Matt. 22:37
Sanctify God in ... 1 Pet. 3:15
Serve God with all ... Deut. 26:16
Walk before God with all ... 1 Kin. 2:4
Trust the Lord with all ... Prov. 3:5
Regard not iniquity in ... Ps. 66:18
Do God's will from ... Eph. 6:6

Hearth—*a place for fire*

Bed of live coals ... Is. 30:14
Ps. 102:3

Heartlessness—*without moral feeling; cruelty*

A. *Among unbelievers:*

Philistines, toward Samson ... Judg. 16:21
Saul, toward David ... 1 Sam. 18:25
Nabal, toward David ... 1 Sam. 25:4-12
Haman, toward Jews ... Esth. 3:8, 9
Priest, toward a certain man ... Luke 10:30-32

B. *Among professing believers:*

Laban, toward Jacob ... Gen. 31:7, 36-42
Jacob's sons, toward Joseph ... Gen. 37:18-35
David, toward Uriah ... 2 Sam. 11:9-27

Heath—*a desert plant*

Figurative of:

Self-sufficient man ... Jer. 17:6
Devastation ... Jer. 48:6

Heat, hot

Figurative of:

God's wrath ... Deut. 9:19
Man's anger ... Deut. 19:6
Determination ... Gen. 31:36
Zeal ... Ps. 39:3
Persecution ... Matt. 13:6, 21
Heavy toil ... Matt. 20:12
Real faith ... Rev. 3:15

Heathen (see Gentiles)

Heave offering

A. *Consisted of:*

First fruits ... Num. 5:19–21
Tenth of all tithes ... Num. 18:21-28

B. *Part of:*

All gifts ... Num. 18:29
Spoils ... Num. 31:26-47
Offerings ... Ex. 29:27
Lev. 7:14, 32

C. *Requirements concerning:*

To be the best ... Num. 18:29
Brought to God's house ... Deut. 12:6
Given to priests ... Ex. 29:27, 28
Sanctified the whole offering ... Num. 18:27-32
Eaten in a clean place ... Lev. 10:12-15

Heaven—*the place of everlasting bliss*

A. *Inhabitants of:*

God ... 1 Kin. 8:30
Christ ... Heb. 9:12, 24
Holy Spirit ... Ps. 139:7, 8
Angels ... Matt. 18:10
Just men ... Heb. 12:22, 23

B. *Things lacking in:*

Marriage ... Matt. 22:30
Death ... Luke 20:36
Flesh and blood ... 1 Cor. 15:50
Imperishable ... 1 Cor. 15:42, 50
Sorrow ... Rev. 7:17
Pain ... Rev. 21:4
Curse ... Rev. 22:3
Night ... Rev. 22:5
Wicked people ... Rev. 22:15
End ... Matt. 25:46
Rev. 22:5

C. *Positive characteristics of:*

Joy ... Luke 15:7, 10
Rest ... Rev. 14:13
Peace ... Luke 16:25
Righteousness ... 2 Pet. 3:13
Service ... Rev. 7:15
Reward ... Matt. 5:11, 12
Inheritance ... 1 Pet. 1:4
Glory ... Rom. 8:17, 18

D. *Entrance into, for:*

Righteous ... Matt. 23:34, 37
Changed ... 1 Cor. 15:51
Saved ... John 3:5, 18, 21
Called ... 2 Pet. 1:10, 11
Overcomers ... Rev. 2:7, 10, 11
Those recorded ... Luke 10:20
Obedient ... Rev. 22:14
Holy ... Rev. 19:8

E. *Believer's present attitude toward:*

Given foretaste of ... Acts 7:55, 56
Earnestly desires ... 2 Cor. 5:2, 8
Looks for ... 2 Pet. 3:12
Considers "far better" than now ... Phil. 1:23
Puts treasure there ... Luke 12:33

F. *Described as:*

House ... John 14:2
Kingdom ... Matt. 25:34
Abraham's bosom ... Luke 16:22, 23
Paradise ... 2 Cor. 12:2, 4
Better country ... Heb. 11:10, 16
Holy city ... Rev. 21:2, 10-27
Rev. 22:1-5

Heavens, natural

A. *Facts regarding:*

Created by God ... Gen. 1:1
Stretched out ... Is. 42:5
Jer. 10:12
Will be destroyed ... Heb. 1:10-12
2 Pet. 3:10
New heavens to follow ... Is. 65:17
2 Pet. 3:13

B. *Purposes of:*

To declare God's glory ... Ps. 19:1
To declare God's righteousness ... Ps. 50:6
To manifest God's wisdom ... Prov. 8:27

Heaviness—*a spirit of grief or anxiety*

Unrelieved by mirth ... Prov. 14:13
God's children experience ... Phil. 2:26
Needed exchange ... James 4:9
Experienced by Christ ... Ps. 69:20, 21
Remedy for ... Prov. 12:25

Heavy—*oppressive*

A. *Used literally of:*

Eli's weight ... 1 Sam. 4:18
Absalom's hair ... 2 Sam. 14:26
Stone ... Prov. 27:3

B. *Used figuratively of:*

Fatigue ... Matt. 26:43
Burdens ... 2 Chr. 10:11, 14
Sins ... Is. 24:20
Sullenness ... 1 Kin. 21:4
God's judgments ... 1 Sam. 5:6, 11

Heber, Eber—*associate*

1. Son of Beriah ... Gen. 46:17
Descendants called Heberites ... Num. 26:45
2. Husband of Jael, the slayer of Sisera ... Judg. 4:11-24
3. Descendant of Ezra ... 1 Chr. 4:17, 18
4. Gadite chief ... 1 Chr. 5:11, 13
5. Benjamite ... 1 Chr. 8:17
6. Benjamite chief ... 1 Chr. 8:22
7. In Christ's genealogy ... Luke 3:35
Same as Eber in ... Gen. 10:24
1 Chr. 1:25

Hebrew—*one from the other side*

Applied to:

Abram ... Gen. 14:13
Israelites ... 1 Sam. 4:6, 9
Jews ... Acts 6:1
Paul, a sincere ... Phil. 3:5

Hebrew language

Called "the Jews' language" ... 2 Kin. 18:26, 28
Alphabet of, in divisions ... Ps. 119
Language of Christ's time ... John 19:13, 20
Acts 21:40

See Aramaic

Hebrews, Epistle of the—*a book of the New Testament*

Christ greater than the angels ... Heb. 1:3, 4
Christ of the order of Melchizedek ... Heb. 4:14—5:10
The new covenant ... Heb. 8:1—10:18
The life of faith ... Heb. 10:19—13:17

Hebron—*alliance*

1. Ancient town in Judah ... Num. 13:22
Originally called Kirjath-arba ... Gen. 23:2
Abram dwells here ... Gen. 13:18
Abraham buys cave here ... Gen. 23:2-20
Isaac and Jacob sojourn here ... Gen. 35:27
Visited by spies ... Num. 13:22
Defeated by Joshua ... Josh. 10:1-37
Caleb expels Anakim from ... Josh. 14:12-15
Assigned to Levites ... Josh. 21:10-13
City of refuge ... Josh. 20:7
David's original capital ... 2 Sam. 2:1-3, 11
Birthplace of David's sons ... 2 Sam. 3:2
Abner's death here ... 2 Sam. 4:1
Absalom's rebellion here ... 2 Sam. 15:7-10
Fortified by Rehoboam ... 2 Chr. 11:10
2. Town of Asher ... Josh. 19:28

SUBJECT — REFERENCE

3. Son of Kohath ..... Ex. 6:18
Descendants called Hebronites ..... Num. 3:19, 27
4. Descendant of Caleb ..... 1 Chr. 2:42, 43

Hebronites (see Hebron 3)

Hedge—*a fence or barrier*
Illustrative of:
God's protection ..... Job 1:10
Afflictions ..... Job 19:8
Slothfulness ..... Prov. 15:19
Removal of protection ..... Ps. 80:12

Hedgehog—*porcupine*
Rendered "bittern" ..... Is. 14:23
Zeph. 2:14

Heedfulness—*giving proper attention to something important*
A. *Objects of:*
God's commandments ..... Josh. 22:5
Our ways ..... Ps. 39:1
False teachers ..... Matt. 16:6
God's Word ..... 2 Pet. 1:19
B. *Admonitions to Christians, concerning:*
Deception ..... Matt. 24:4
Outward display ..... Matt. 6:1
Worldliness ..... Luke 21:34
Duty ..... Acts 20:28-31
Foundation ..... 1 Cor. 3:10
Liberty ..... 1 Cor. 8:9
Security ..... 1 Cor. 10:12
Effectiveness ..... Gal. 5:15
Ministry ..... Col. 4:17
Fables ..... 1 Tim. 1:4
Unbelief ..... Heb. 3:12
See Caution

Heel—*the back part of the human foot*
Used literally of:
Esau's ..... Gen. 25:26
Used figuratively of:
Seed of the woman ..... Gen. 3:15
Enemy of Dan ..... Gen. 49:17
The wicked ..... Job 18:5, 9
Friend of David ..... Ps. 41:9

Hegai
Eunuch under King Ahasuerus ..... Esth. 2:3, 8, 15

Heifer—*a young cow*
A. *Ceremonial uses of:*
In a covenant ..... Gen. 15:9
In purification ..... Num. 19:1-22
B. *Red heifer, ceremony concerning:*
Without spot ..... Num. 19:2
Never yoked ..... Num. 19:2
Slaughtered and burned outside the camp ..... Num. 19:3-8
Ashes kept ..... Num. 19:9, 10
Ashes, with water, used to purify ..... Num. 19:11-22
Significance of ..... Heb. 9:13, 14
C. *Figurative of:*
Improper advantage ..... Judg. 14:18
Contentment ..... Jer. 50:11
Stubborn ..... Hos. 4:16

Heirs, natural
A. *Persons and property involved:*
First-born ..... Deut. 21:15-17
Sons of concubines ..... Gen. 21:10
Daughters ..... Num. 27:1-11
Widows ..... Ruth 3:12, 13
Order of succession ..... Num. 27:8-11
B. *Exceptions:*
Father could make concubines' sons heirs ..... Gen. 49:12-27
Daughters receive marriage portion ..... Gen. 29:24, 29
Daughters sometimes share with sons ..... Job 42:15
Daughters receive, if no sons ..... Num. 27:8
C. *Examples of heirship changes by divine election:*
Ishmael to Isaac ..... Gen. 21:10, 11
Esau to Jacob ..... Gen. 27:37
Rom. 9:13

SUBJECT — REFERENCE

Reuben to Joseph ..... Gen. 49:24-26
Adonijah to Solomon ..... 1 Kin. 1:11-14
See Birthright; Inheritance, earthly

Heirs, spiritual
A. *Of Christ:*
Recognized ..... Matt. 21:38
Appointed ..... Heb. 1:2
B. *Of Christians, means of:*
By promise ..... Gal. 3:29
Through Christ ..... Gal. 4:7
Through faith ..... Rom. 4:13, 14
By grace ..... Gal. 4:28-31
C. *Of Christians, receiving:*
Grace ..... 1 Pet. 3:7
Promise ..... Heb. 11:9
Kingdom ..... James 2:5
Salvation ..... Heb. 1:14
Righteousness ..... Heb. 11:7
Eternal life ..... Titus 3:7
See Inheritance, spiritual

Helah—*ornament*
One of Asher's wives ..... 1 Chr. 4:5, 7

Helam—*fortress*
Place between Damascus and Hamath where David defeated Syrians ..... 2 Sam. 10:16-19

Helbah—*fertility*
City of Asher ..... Judg. 1:31

Helbon—*fertile*
City north of Damascus ..... Ezek. 27:18

Heldai—*worldly*
1. One of David's captains ..... 1 Chr. 27:15
Probably same as Heled and Heleb ..... 1 Chr. 11:30
2. Exile from Babylon bearing gifts ..... Zech. 6:10, 11
Called Helem ..... Zech. 6:14

Helek—*portion*
Son of Gilead ..... Num. 26:30
Founder of a family ..... Josh. 17:2

Helem—*strength*
1. Asherite ..... 1 Chr. 7:34, 35
2. Same as Heldai ..... Zech. 6:11
Called Hotham ..... 1 Chr. 7:32

Heleph—*strong*
Frontier town of Naphtali ..... Josh. 19:32, 33

Helez—*strong*
1. One of David's captains ..... 2 Sam. 23:26
2. Judahite ..... 1 Chr. 2:39

Heli—*climbing*
Father of Joseph, husband of Mary ..... Luke 3:23

Helkai—*portion*
Postexilic priest ..... Neh. 12:15

Helkath—*portion, field*
Frontier town of Asher ..... Josh. 19:24, 25
Assigned to Levites ..... Josh. 21:31
Same as Hukok ..... 1 Chr. 6:75

Helkath-hazzurim—*field of sharp flints*
Scene of bloody combat ..... 2 Sam. 2:16

Hell—*the place of eternal torment*
A. *Described as:*
Everlasting fire ..... Matt. 25:41
Everlasting punishment ..... Matt. 25:46
Outer darkness ..... Matt. 8:12
Everlasting destruction ..... 2 Thess. 1:9
Lake of fire ..... Rev. 19:20
B. *Prepared for:*
Devil and his angels ..... Matt. 25:41
Wicked ..... Rev. 21:8
Disobedient ..... Rom. 2:8, 9
Fallen angels ..... 2 Pet. 2:4
Beast and the false prophet ..... Rev. 19:20
Worshipers of the beast ..... Rev. 14:11
Rejectors of the Gospel ..... Matt. 10:15
C. *Punishment of, described as:*
Bodily ..... Matt. 5:29, 30
In the soul ..... Matt. 10:28
With degrees ..... Matt. 23:14

SUBJECT — REFERENCE

Helmet—*armor for the head*
Used figuratively of salvation:
Prepared ..... Is. 59:17
Provided ..... Eph. 6:17
Promised ..... 1 Thess. 5:8

Helon—*strong*
Father of Eliab ..... Num. 1:9

Helper—*one who assists another*
A. *Used of:*
God ..... Heb. 13:6
Christ ..... Heb. 4:15, 16
Holy Spirit ..... Rom. 8:26
Angels ..... Dan. 10:13
Woman ..... Gen. 2:18, 20
Levites ..... 2 Chr. 29:3, 4
Christians ..... Acts 16:9
2 Cor. 1:24
B. *As the Holy Spirit:*
With believers forever ..... John 14:16
Teaches ..... John 14:26
Testifies of Christ ..... John 15:26
Convicts ..... John 16:7-11

Helps—*the acts of bearing another's burden*
A gift to the Church ..... 1 Cor. 12:28
Christians admonished to ..... 1 Thess. 5:14
Elders admonished to ..... Acts 20:28, 35

Hemam—*raging*
Son of Lotan ..... Gen. 36:22
Same as Homam ..... 1 Chr. 1:39

Heman—*faithful*
1. Famous wise man ..... 1 Kin. 4:31
Judahite ..... 1 Chr. 2:6
Composer of a Psalm ..... Ps. 88 (Title)
2. Musician under David; grandson of Samuel ..... 1 Chr. 6:33
Appointed as chief singer ..... 1 Chr. 15:16, 17
Man of spiritual insight ..... 1 Chr. 25:5

Hemdan—*pleasant*
Descendant of Seir ..... Gen. 36:26
Same as Amram ..... 1 Chr. 1:41

Hemlock—*a bitter poisonous substance*
Properly means "gall" ..... Amos 6:12

Hemorrhage—*a flow of blood*
Healed ..... Luke 8:43, 44
Woman suffered from, for 12 years ..... {Matt. 9:20; Mark 5:25}

Hen—*favor*
1. Son of Zephaniah ..... Zech. 6:14
2. Domestic fowl ..... Matt. 23:37

Hena—*low land*
City captured by the Assyrians ..... 2 Kin. 18:34

Henadad—*favor of Hadad*
Postexilic Levite ..... Ezra 3:9
Sons of, help Nehemiah ..... Neh. 3:18, 24

Henoch
1. Same as Enoch ..... 1 Chr. 1:3
2. Same as Hanoch 1 ..... 1 Chr. 1:33

Hepher—*pit, well*
1. Town west of the Jordan ..... Josh. 12:17
Name applied to a district ..... 1 Kin. 4:10
2. Founder of Hepherites ..... Num. 26:30, 32
3. Son of Ashur ..... 1 Chr. 4:5, 6
4. One of David's guards ..... 1 Chr. 11:26, 36

Hephzibah—*my delight is in her*
Mother of King Manasseh ..... 2 Kin. 21:1

Herald—*a representative of a government official*
Of Nebuchadnezzar ..... Dan. 3:3, 4
Of Pharaoh ..... Gen. 41:42, 43
Zion ..... Is. 40:9

Herbs—*grass or leafy vegetables*
Bitter, used at Passover ..... Ex. 12:8
Poisonous, not fit ..... 2 Kin. 4:39, 40

Herdsman—*one who tends cattle*
Conflict among ..... Gen. 13:7, 8

SUBJECT REFERENCE

Heredity—*transmission of physical and mental traits*

A. *Factors involved:*
- Likeness of nature .... Gen. 5:3
- Common transgression ...... Rom. 5:12
- Sinful nature.................. John 3:6, 7
- Family and national traits ... Titus 1:12
- Physical traits .... Jer. 13:26
- God's purpose of plan .... Gen. 9:22-27

B. *Consistent with:*
- Individual responsibility ..... Jer. 31:29, 30
- God's sovereign plan........ Rom. 9:6-16
- Need of a new nature .... Matt. 3:9; John 3:1-12
- Family differences .... 1 John 3:12
- Child different from his parents .... 1 Sam. 8:1-5

Heres—*sun*
1. Mountain in Dan........... Judg. 1:35, 36
   - Probably connected with Beth-shemesh or Ir-shemesh .... 1 Kin. 4:9; Josh. 19:40, 41
2. Egyptian city; probably is the "city of destruction" referred to .... Is. 19:18

Heresh—*silent*
- Levite .... 1 Chr. 9:15

Heresy—*a teaching contrary to the truth*

A. *Applied to:*
- Religious sect .... Acts 5:17
- Pharisees .... Acts 26:5
- Christians (derisively) .... Acts 24:5, 14

B. *Characteristics of:*
- Damnable .... 2 Pet. 2:1
- Contagious .... 2 Pet. 2:2
- Subversive .... Gal. 1:7

C. *Attitude toward:*
- Recognize purpose .... 1 John 2:18, 19
- Withdraw .... 1 Tim. 6:4, 5, 11
- Do not receive .... 2 John 9-11

Heritage, earthly

A. *Of believers:*
- Children .... Ps. 127:3
- Long life .... Ps. 91:16

B. *Of Israel:*
- Promised land .... Ex. 6:8
- Forsaken of God .... Jer. 12:7-9
- Discontinue .... Jer. 17:4
- Return to .... Jer. 12:15

Heritage, spiritual

A. *Described as:*
- laid up .... Ps. 31:19; Col. 1:5
- Reserved .... 1 Pet. 1:4
- Prepared .... 1 Cor. 2:9

B. *Consists of:*
- Protection .... Is. 54:17
- Provision .... Is. 58:14
- Unseen things .... Matt. 25:34
- Kingdom .... 1 Cor. 2:9-12
- All things .... Rom. 8:32

Hermas
- Christian at Rome .... Rom. 16:14

Hermes
- Christian at Rome .... Rom. 16:14

Hermogenes—*sprung from Hermes*
- Turns from Paul .... 2 Tim. 1:15

Hermon—*sacred mountain*
- Highest mountain (9,166 ft.) in Syria; also called Sirion, Shenir .... Deut. 3:8, 9
- Northern limit of conquest ..... Josh. 11:3, 17
- Joined with Tabor, Zion and Lebanon in Hebrew poetry .... Ps. 89:12

Hero—*a person acclaimed for unusual deeds*
- Caleb, a rejected .... Num. 13:30-33
- Phinehas, a rewarded .... Num. 25:7-13
- Deborah, a militant .... Judg. 4:4-16
- Jonathan, a rescued .... 1 Sam. 14:6-17, 38-45
- David, a popular .... 1 Sam. 18:5-8
- Esther, a hesitant .... Esth. 4:10-17

SUBJECT REFERENCE

Herod—*family name of Idumaean rulers of Palestine*
1. Herod the Great, procurator of Judea (37—4 B.C.) .... Luke 1:5
   - Inquires of Jesus' birth ...... Matt. 2:3-8
   - Slays Bethlehem infants ..... Matt. 2:12-18
2. Archelaus (4 B.C.—A.D. 6) succeeds Herod the Great .... Matt. 2:22
3. Herod Antipas, the tetrarch, ruler of Galilee and Peraea (4 B.C.—A.D. 39) .... Luke 3:1
   - Imprisons John the Baptist .. Luke 3:18-21
   - Has John the Baptist beheaded .... Matt. 14:1-12
   - Disturbed about Jesus .... Luke 9:7-9
   - Jesus sent to him .... Luke 23:7-11
   - Becomes Pilate's friend ..... Luke 23:12
   - Opposes Jesus .... Acts 4:27
4. Philip, tetrarch of Ituraea and Trachonitis (4 B.C.—A.D. 34) .... Luke 3:1; Acts 13:1
5. Herod Philip, disinherited son of Herod the Great .... Matt. 14:3
6. Herod Agrippa I (A.D. 37-44) .... Acts 12:1, 19
   - Kills James .... Acts 12:1, 2
   - Imprisons Peter .... Acts 12:3-11, 19
   - Slain by an angel .... Acts 12:20-23
7. Herod Agrippa II (A.D. 53-70), called Agrippa and King Agrippa .... Acts 25:22, 23; Acts 25:24, 26
   - Festus tells him about Paul .. Acts 25:13-27
   - Paul makes a defense before .... Acts 26:1-23
   - Rejects the Gospel .... Acts 26:24-30
   - Recognizes Paul's innocency .... Acts 26:31, 32
8. Aristobulus; identified by some as son of Herod the Great .... Rom. 16:10

Herodians—*an influential Jewish party*
- Join Pharisees against Jesus ..... Mark 3:6
- Seek to trap Jesus .... Matt. 22:15-22
- Jesus warns against .... Mark 8:15

Herodias—*feminine form of Herod*
- Granddaughter of Herod the Great; plots John's death .... Matt. 14:3-12
- Married her uncle .... Mark 6:17

Herodion
- Christian at Rome .... Rom. 16:11

Heron
- Unclean bird .... Lev. 11:19; Deut. 14:18

Hesed—*mercy*
- Father of one of Solomon's officers .... 1 Kin. 4:7, 10

Heshbon—*intelligence*
- Ancient Moabite city; taken by Sihon, king of the Amorites .... Num. 21:25-34
- Taken by Moses .... Num. 21:23-26
- Assigned to Reubenites .... Num. 32:1-37
- Built by Reuben .... Num. 32:37
- On Gad's southern boundary ... Josh. 13:26
- Levitical city .... Josh. 21:39
- Later held by Moabites .... Is. 15:1-4
- Judgment of, announced .... Is. 16:8-14
- Fall of, predicted .... Jer. 48:2, 34, 35
- Fishpools in .... Song 7:4

Heshmon—*fatness*
- Town of Judah .... Josh. 15:21, 27

Hesitation—*delay prompted by indecision*

Causes of:
- Uncertain about God's will ..... 1 Sam. 23:1-13
- Fear of man .... John 9:18-23
- Selfish unconcern .... 2 Cor. 8:10-14
- Unbelief .... John 20:24-28

Heth—*terror*
- Son of Canaan .... Gen. 10:15
- Ancestor of the Hittites .... Gen. 23:10
- Abraham buys field from sons of .... Gen. 23:3-20
- Esau marries daughters of ...... Gen. 27:46
- See Hittites

Hethlon—*hiding place*
- Place indicating Israel's ideal northern boundary .... Ezek. 47:15

SUBJECT REFERENCE

Hewers of wood

A slave classification:
- Gibeonites .... Josh. 9:17-27
- Classed with "drawers of water" .... Josh. 9:21, 23

Hezeki—*my strength*
- Benjamite .... 1 Chr. 8:17

Hezekiah—*Jehovah strengthens*
1. King of Judah .... 2 Chr. 29:1-3
   - Reforms Temple services .... 2 Chr. 29:3-36
   - Restores pure worship .... 2 Chr. 31:1-19
   - Military exploits of .... 2 Kin. 18:7-12
   - Defeated by Sennacherib .... 2 Kin. 18:13
   - Sends messengers to Isaiah .. 2 Kin. 19:1-5
   - Rabshakeh's further taunts ... 2 Kin. 19:8-13
   - Prays earnestly .... 2 Kin. 19:14-19
   - Encouraged by Isaiah .... 2 Kin. 19:20-37
   - Healed; his life prolonged 15 years .... 2 Kin. 20:1-11
   - His thanks .... Is. 38:9-22
   - Rebuked for his pride .... 2 Kin. 20:12-19
   - Death of .... 2 Kin. 20:20, 21
   - Ancestor of Christ .... Matt. 1:9
2. Ancestor of returning exiles .... Ezra 2:1, 16
3. Ancestor of Zephaniah, spelled Hizkiah .... Zeph. 1:1
4. Postexilic workman who returned with Zerubbabel .... Ezra 2:16

Hezion—*vision*
- Grandfather of Ben-hadad ...... 1 Kin. 15:18

Hezir—*swine*
1. Descendant of Aaron .... 1 Chr. 24:1, 15
2. One who signs document .... Neh. 10:1, 20

Hezro
- One of David's mighty men ..... 1 Chr. 11:37

Hezron—*enclosure*
1. Place in south Judah .... Josh. 15:1, 3
   - Same as Hazaraddar .... Num. 34:4
2. Son of Reuben .... Gen. 46:9
   - Founder of the Hezronites ... Num. 26:6
3. Son of Pharez .... Gen. 46:12
   - Head of tribal family .... Num. 26:21
   - Ancestor of David .... Ruth 4:18-22
   - Ancestor of Christ .... Matt. 1:3

Hiddai—*joyful*
- One of David's warriors .... 2 Sam. 23:30
- Same as Hurai .... 1 Chr. 11:32

Hiddekel—*rapid*
- Hebrew name of the river Tigris .... Gen. 2:14; Dan. 10:4

Hide—*to conceal*

A. *Used literally of:*
- Man in Eden .... Gen. 3:10
- Baby Moses .... Ex. 2:2, 3
- Spies .... Josh. 6:17, 25

B. *Used figuratively of:*
- God's face .... Deut. 31:17, 18
- Protection .... Is. 49:2
- Darkness .... Ps. 139:12
- The Gospel .... 2 Cor. 4:3
- Believer's life .... Col. 3:3

Hiel—*God lives*
- Native of Beth-el; rebuilds Jericho .... 1 Kin. 16:34
- Fulfills Joshua's curse .... Josh. 6:26

Hierapolis—*sacred city*
- City of Asia Minor; center of Christian activity .... Col. 4:13

Higgaion—*a deep sound*
- Used as a musical term .... Ps. 9:16
- Translated "meditation" in ..... Ps. 19:14
- Translated "solemn sound" in ... Ps. 92:3

High—*exalted, lofty*

Descriptive of:
- Rich .... Ps. 49:2
- Eminent people .... 1 Chr. 17:17
- God's mercy .... Ps. 103:11

SUBJECT REFERENCE

High-mindedness—*a self-righteous spirit*
Christians warned against ...... Rom. 11:20
Rich tempted to .... 1 Tim. 6:17
To prevail in last days .... 2 Tim. 3:1-5

High places—*places of idolatrous worship*

A. *Evils of:*
Contrary to one sanctuary ... Deut. 12:1-14
Source of idolatry .... 2 Kin. 12:3
Place of child sacrifices ..... Jer. 7:31
Cause of God's wrath .... 1 Kin. 14:22, 23; Ps. 78:58
Denounced by the prophets .... Ezek. 6:1-6; Hos. 4:11-14
Cause of exile .... Lev. 26:29-34

B. *Built by:*
Solomon .... 1 Kin. 11:7-11
Jeroboam .... 1 Kin. 12:26-31
Jehoram .... 2 Chr. 21:9, 11
Ahaz .... 2 Chr. 28:24, 25
Manasseh .... 2 Kin. 21:1, 3
People of Judah .... 1 Kin. 14:22, 23
People of Israel .... 2 Kin. 17:9
Sepharvites .... 2 Kin. 17:32

C. *Destroyed by:*
Asa .... 2 Chr. 14:3, 5
Jehoshaphat .... 2 Chr. 17:6
Hezekiah .... 2 Kin. 18:4, 22
Josiah .... 2 Kin. 23:5, 8, 13

High priest

A. *Duties of:*
Offer gifts and sacrifices .... Heb. 5:1
Make atonement .... Lev. 16:1-34
Inquire of God .... 1 Sam. 23:9-12
Consecrate Levites .... Num. 8:11-21
Anoint kings .... 1 Kin. 1:34
Bless the people .... Num. 6:22-27
Preside over courts .... Matt. 26:3, 57-62

B. *Typical of Christ's priesthood:*
Called of God .... Heb. 5:4, 5
Making atonement .... Lev. 16:33
Subject to temptation .... Heb. 2:18
Exercise of compassion ..... Heb. 4:15, 16
Holiness of position .... Lev. 21:15
Marrying a virgin .... 2 Cor. 11:2
Alone entering Holy of Holies .... Heb. 9:7, 12, 24
Ministry of intercession ..... Num. 16:43-48; Heb. 7:25
Blessing people .... Acts 3:26

Highway—*a main thoroughfare*

A. *Characteristics of:*
Roads for public use .... Num. 20:19
Straight and broad .... Is. 40:3
Made to cities of refuge ..... Deut. 19:2, 3
Robbers use .... Luke 10:30-33
Animals infest .... Is. 35:8, 9
Beggars sit by .... Matt. 20:30
Byways sometimes better .... Judg. 5:6

B. *Figurative of:*
Holy way .... Prov. 16:17
Israel's restoration .... Is. 11:16
Gospel's call .... Is. 40:3
Way of salvation .... Is. 35:8-10
Two destinies .... Matt. 7:13, 14
Christ .... John 14:6

Hilen—*strong place*
Town of Judah .... 1 Chr. 6:57, 58
Also called Holon .... Josh. 15:51

Hilkiah—*Jehovah is my portion*
1. Levite, son of Amzi .... 1 Chr. 6:45, 46
2. Levite, son of Hosah .... 1 Chr. 26:11
3. Father of Eliakim .... Is. 22:20
4. Priest, father of Jeremiah .... Jer. 1:1
5. Father of Gemariah .... Jer. 29:3
6. Shallum's son .... 1 Chr. 6:13
High priest in Josiah's reign .... 2 Chr. 34:9-22
Oversees Temple work ...... 2 Kin. 22:4-7
Finds the book of the Law ... 2 Kin. 22:8-14
Aids in reformation .... 2 Kin. 23:4
7. Chief of postexilic priest ..... Neh. 12:1, 7
Later descendants of .... Neh. 12:12, 21
8. One of Ezra's assistants ..... Neh. 8:4

Hill, hill country—*an elevation of the earth's surface*
Rendered "Gibeah" .... 1 Sam. 11:4
Rendered "hills" .... Luke 23:30

Hillel—*he has praised*
Father of Abdon the judge ..... Judg. 12:13, 15

Hind—*a doe* (female deer)
Figurative of:
Spiritual vivacity .... 2 Sam. 22:34
Buoyancy of faith .... Hab. 3:19
Peaceful quietude .... Song 2:7

Hinder parts
God smites enemies in .... Ps. 78:66

Hindrances—*things which obstruct one's way*

A. *Physical:*
Heavy armor .... 1 Sam. 17:38, 39
Ship's cargo .... Acts 27:18-38

B. *Spiritual:*
Satanic temptations .... Matt. 4:8-10
Riches .... Matt. 19:24
Unbelief .... Matt. 11:21-24
Ceremonialism .... Matt. 15:1-9
Love of world .... 2 Tim. 4:10
Sin .... Heb. 12:1

C. *Removal of, by:*
Faith .... Matt. 17:20, 21
God's armor .... Eph. 6:11-18
Walking in the Spirit .... Gal. 5:16, 17
Self-control .... 1 Cor. 9:25-27

Hinge—*a pivot of a door*
Of gold .... 1 Kin. 7:50

Hinnom, valley of (Ben-Hinnom)

A. *Location of:*
Near Jerusalem .... Jer. 19:2
Boundary line .... Josh. 15:8
Topheth .... Jer. 19:6, 11-14

B. *Uses of:*
For idol worship .... 1 Kin. 11:7
For sacrificing children ...... 2 Chr. 28:3
Defiled by Josiah .... 2 Kin. 23:10-14
Jeremiah addresses people here .... Jer. 19:1-5
Will become "valley of the slaughter" .... Jer. 7:31, 32
Make holy .... Jer. 31:40

Hirah—*nobility*
Adullamite, a friend of Judah ... Gen. 38:1, 12

Hiram—*highborn*
1. King of Tyre .... 2 Sam. 5:11
Provides men and material for David's palace .... 1 Chr. 14:1
David's friend .... 1 Kin. 5:1
Provides men and material for Solomon's Temple .... 1 Kin. 5:1-12
Refuses gifts of cities from Solomon .... 1 Kin. 9:10-13
Helps Solomon with money and seamen .... 1 Kin. 9:14, 26-28; 1 Kin. 10:11
2. Craftsman; a son of a Tyrian and a widow of Naphtali .... 1 Kin. 7:13, 14
Sent by King Solomon to work on Temple .... 1 Kin. 7:14-40, 45
Called Huram .... 2 Chr. 2:11

Hire—*wages*

A. *Used literally of payments to:*
Prostitute .... Deut. 23:18
Priests .... Judg. 18:4
Pay the poor .... James 5:4
Mercenary soldiers .... 2 Sam. 10:6
Mercenary prophets .... Deut. 23:4
Gospel messengers .... Luke 10:7

B. *Used figuratively of:*
Spiritual adultery .... Ezek. 16:33
Sexual relations .... Gen. 30:16
Reward ("wages") .... John 4:36

See Wages, hire

Hireling—*a common laborer*
Anxious for the day to close .... Job 7:1, 2
Figurative of man's life .... Job 14:6
Subject to oppression .... Mal. 3:5
Guilty of neglect .... John 10:12, 13

Hiss—*meaning to call, allure, or entice*
Applied to:
Nations .... Is. 5:26
Egypt and Assyria .... Is. 7:18
Israel .... Zech. 10:8

History, Biblical

A. *Characteristics of:*
Dated with human events .... Hag. 1:1, 15; Luke 3:1
Inspired .... 2 Tim. 3:16
Free of myths .... 2 Pet. 1:16

B. *Valuable for:*
Outline of ancient history .... Acts 7:1-53
Spiritual lessons .... 1 Cor. 10:1-11
Prophecy and fulfillment .... Acts 4:24-28

Hittites—*an ancient nation*

A. *Facts concerning:*
Descendants of Canaan ..... Gen. 10:15
One of seven Canaanite nations .... Deut. 7:1
Original inhabitants of Palestine .... Ezek. 16:3, 45
Ruled by kings .... 1 Kin. 10:29
Great nation .... 2 Kin. 7:6
Their land promised to Israel .... Gen. 15:18, 20
Destruction of, commanded .... Deut. 7:1, 2, 24
Destruction of, incomplete ... Judg. 3:5

B. *Intermarriage with:*
By Esau .... Gen. 36:2
By Israelites after the conquest .... Judg. 3:5, 6
By Solomon .... 1 Kin. 11:1
By Israelites after the exile ... Ezra 9:1, 2

C. *Notable persons of:*
Ephron .... Gen. 49:30
Ahimelech .... 1 Sam. 26:6
Uriah .... 2 Sam. 11:6, 21

Hivites
Descendants of Canaan .... Gen. 10:15, 17
One of seven Canaanite nations .... Deut. 7:1
Esau intermarries with .... Gen. 36:2
Gibeonites belong to .... Josh. 9:3, 7
Land of, promised to Israel ..... Ex. 3:8; Ex. 23:23
Destruction of:
Commanded .... Deut. 7:1, 2, 24
Incomplete .... Judg. 3:3

Hizkiah—*Jehovah strengthens*
Son of Neariah .... 1 Chr. 3:23

Hizkijah—*Jehovah strengthens*
Ancestor of returning exiles ..... Neh. 10:17

Hoar—*white*
Applied to frost .... Ex. 16:14
Applied to gray hair .... Lev. 19:32

Hobah—*hiding place*
Town north of Damascus .... Gen. 14:15

Hod—*majesty*
Asherite .... 1 Chr. 7:30, 37

Hodaviah—*praise ye Jehovah*
1. Son of Elioenai .... 1 Chr. 3:24
2. Chief of Manasseh .... 1 Chr. 5:23, 24
3. Benjamite .... 1 Chr. 9:7
4. Levite, founder of a family ... Ezra 2:40
Called Judah .... Ezra 3:9

Hodesh—*new moon*
Wife of Shaharaim .... 1 Chr. 8:8, 9

Hodiah—*splendor of Jehovah*
1. Judahite .... 1 Chr. 4:1, 19
2. Levite interpreter .... Neh. 8:7
Leads in prayer .... Neh. 9:5
Probably the same as one of the signers of the covenant .... Neh. 10:10, 13
3. Signer of the covenant ...... Neh. 10:18

Hoglah—*partridge*
Daughter of Zelophehad .... Num. 26:33

SUBJECT	REFERENCE
Hoham—*Jehovah protests*	
Amorite king defeated by Joshua	Josh. 10:3-27
Hold fast	
Good thing	1 Thess. 5:21
Faithful word	Titus 1:9
Our confidence	Heb. 3:6
Our profession	Heb. 4:14
What we have	Rev. 2:25 Rev. 3:11
Holiness of Christ	
A. *Announced in:*	
Psalms	Ps. 16:10
Prophets	Is. 11:4, 5
B. *Proclaimed by:*	
Gabriel	Luke 1:35
Demons	Mark 1:24
Centurion	Luke 23:47
Peter	Acts 4:27, 30
Paul	2 Cor. 5:21
John	1 John 2:1, 29
C. *Manifested negatively in freedom from:*	
Sin	1 John 3:5
Guilt	John 8:46
Defilement	Heb. 7:26, 27
D. *Manifested as "the Holy One" applied by:*	
Demons	Mark 1:24
Peter	Acts 2:27
Paul	Acts 13:35
John	1 John 2:20
Christ Himself	Rev. 3:7
Holiness of Christians	
A. *In their calling:*	
Elected to	Rom. 8:29
Called to	1 Thess. 4:7
Created in	Eph. 4:24
Possessed by	1 Cor. 3:16, 17
B. *In their lives:*	
Bodies	Rom. 6:13, 19
Manner of life	1 Pet. 1:15
Fruitfulness	John 15:8
C. *Reasons for:*	
God's holiness	1 Pet. 1:15, 16
God's mercies	Rom. 12:1, 2
Christ's love	2 Cor. 5:14, 15
World's end	2 Pet. 3:11
Inheritance in kingdom	Eph. 5:5
D. *God's means of:*	
Word	John 17:17
Chastisement	Heb. 12:10
Grace	Titus 2:3, 11, 12
See Godliness; Sanctification	
Holiness to the Lord	
Breastplate insignia	Ex. 28:36
Holon—*strong place*	
1. City of Judah	Josh. 15:51
2. City of Moab	Jer. 48:21
Holy Day, holy-day—*any of the Jewish high holidays*	
Sabbath	Ex. 35:2
"Holyday"	Col. 2:16
Rendered "Feast"	Luke 2:41
Holy Land (see Canaan, Land of)	
Holy of Holies	
A. *Described as:*	
Sanctuary	Lev. 4:6
Holy sanctuary	Lev. 16:33
Holy place	Ex. 28:29
Holy of Holies	Ex. 26:33 Heb. 9:3
Inner sanctuary	1 Kin. 6:5-20
B. *Contents of:*	
Ark of the testimony	Ex. 26:33
Mercy seat	Ex. 26:34
Cherubim	Ex. 25:18-22
Altar of incense	Heb. 9:4
Pot of manna	Ex. 16:33
Aaron's rod	Num. 17:10
Written copy of the Law	Deut. 31:26 2 Kin. 22:8
C. *Entrance to, by the high priest:*	
Not at all times	Lev. 16:2
Alone, once a year	Heb. 9:7
With blood	Lev. 16:14, 15
To make atonement	Lev. 16:15-17, 33, 34
D. *Significance of:*	
Abolished by Christ's death	Matt. 27:51
Typical of heaven	Ps. 102:19
Believers now enter boldly	Heb. 10:19
See Tabernacle	
Holy Spirit	
A. *Titles applied to:*	
Spirit of:	
God	Gen. 1:2
The Lord God	Is. 61:1
The Father	Matt. 10:20
Grace	Zech. 12:10
Truth	John 14:17
Holiness	Rom. 1:4
Life	Rom. 8:2
Christ	Rom. 8:9
Adoption	Rom. 8:15
The Son	Gal. 4:6
Glory	1 Pet. 4:14
Prophecy	Rev. 19:10
My Spirit	Gen. 6:3
Holy Spirit	Ps. 51:11
The Comforter	John 14:16, 26
Eternal Spirit	Heb. 9:14
B. *Deity of:*	
Called God	Acts 5:3, 4
Joined with the Father and Son	Matt. 28:19 2 Cor. 13:14
Eternal	Heb. 9:14
Omnipotent	Luke 1:35
Omniscient	1 Cor. 2:10, 11
Omnipresent	Ps. 139:7-13
Creator	Gen. 1:2
Sovereign	1 Cor. 12:6, 11
New creation	John 3:3, 8
Sin against, eternal	Matt. 12:31, 32
C. *Personality of:*	
Speaks	Acts 28:25
Teaches	John 14:26
Strives with sinners	Gen. 6:3
Comforts	Acts 9:31
Helps our infirmities	Rom. 8:26
Is grieved	Eph. 4:30
Is resisted	Acts 7:51
D. *Work in the world:*	
Creates	Job 33:4
Renews	Is. 32:15
Convicts men	John 16:8-11
Stirs up pagan king	2 Chr. 36:22
E. *Work of, in Christ's ministry:*	
Christ conceived by	Luke 1:35
Miracles performed by	Matt. 12:28
Anointed by	Matt. 3:16
Supported by	Luke 4:1, 17
Filled by	Luke 4:1
Offered to God by	Heb. 9:14
Raised by	Rom. 1:4
Justified by	1 Tim. 3:16
F. *Work of, in the Scriptures:*	
Speaks in:	
Prophets	Acts 28:25
Psalms	Acts 1:16
All Scripture	2 Tim. 3:16
His sword	Eph. 6:17
G. *Ministry of, among believers:*	
Regenerates	John 3:3, 5
Indwells	Rom. 8:11
Anoints	1 John 2:20, 27
Baptizes	Acts 2:17-41
Guides	John 16:13
Empowers	Mic. 3:8
Sanctifies	Rom. 15:16 2 Thess. 2:13
Bears witness	Rom. 8:16 Heb. 10:15
Comforts	John 14:16-26
Gives joy	Rom. 14:17
Gives discernment	1 Cor. 2:10-16 1 John 4:1-6
Bears fruit	Gal. 5:22, 23
Give gifts	1 Cor. 12:3-11
H. *Ministry of, in the Church:*	
Fills	Acts 2:4
Baptizes	1 Cor. 12:13
Appoints officers	Acts 20:17, 18
Sends out missionaries	Acts 13:2, 4
Directs missionaries	Acts 8:29
Comforts the Church	Acts 9:31
Sanctifies the Church	Rom. 15:16
I. *Reception of:*	
Promised	Joel 2:28-32
Awaits Christ's glorification	John 7:38, 39
Realized at Pentecost	Acts 2:1-21
Realized by Gentiles	Acts 10:45
Contingent	Acts 2:38 Acts 5:32
Can be sinned against	Matt. 12:31, 32
J. *Filling of:*	
Bezaleel	Ex. 31:2
Jesus	Luke 4:1
John the Baptist	Luke 1:15, 60
Elizabeth	Luke 1:41
Zechariah	Luke 1:67
Pentecost Christians	Acts 2:1-4
Peter	Acts 4:8
Seven men	Acts 6:3-5
Stephen	Acts 7:55
Barnabas	Acts 11:22, 24
Paul	Acts 13:9
Certain disciples	Acts 13:52
K. *As teacher:*	
Illuminates the mind	1 Cor. 2:12, 13 Eph. 1:16, 17
Reveals things of God	Is. 40:13, 14 1 Cor. 2:10, 13
Home—*center of family life*	
Things associated with:	
Eating	1 Cor. 11:34
Keeping house	Titus 2:5
Religious training	1 Tim. 5:4
Entertainment	Luke 15:6
Domestic:	
Counsel	1 Cor. 14:35
Discord	2 Sam. 14:13-24
Land	Ruth 1:22
Friends	Mark 5:19
Present life	2 Cor. 5:6
See House	
Homeless	
Christ's condition	Luke 9:58
True of apostles also	1 Cor. 4:11
Homer—*a heap*	
Measure; equal to about 11 bushels	Ezek. 45:11, 14
Homesickness	
Jacob	Gen. 30:25
Edomite Hadad	1 Kin. 11:21, 22
Exiles	Ps. 137:1-6
Prodigal son	Luke 15:11-19
Epaphroditus	Phil. 2:25, 26
Homestead—*the family dwelling*	
Redeemable	Lev. 25:25-30
Homicide	
Provisions provided:	
Distinction between guilty and innocent	Ex. 21:12-14 Num. 35:16-23
Determination of guilt	Num. 35:24, 30
Detention in cities of refuge	Num. 35:11, 15, 25-29
Defilement of land by slack justice	Num. 35:31-34
See Murder	
Homosexuality	
Forbidden	Lev. 18:22
Considered an abomination	1 Kin. 14:24
Punishment	Lev. 20:13
Unclean	Rom. 1:24, 26, 27
Honest, honesty—*uprightness*	
A. *Necessity of:*	
Signs of a righteous man	Ps. 1:1-3 Luke 8:15
Means of testimony	1 Pet. 2:12
Obligatory upon Christians	2 Cor. 13:7
B. *Blessings of:*	
Brings advancement	Is. 33:15-17
Makes acceptable with God	Ps. 15:1, 2

SUBJECT ... REFERENCE

C. *Examples of:*
- Samuel ... 1 Sam. 12:1-5
- David ... 1 Sam. 25:7, 15
- Workmen ... 2 Kin. 12:15
- Zacchaeus ... Luke 19:8
- Paul ... 2 Cor. 8:20, 21

Honey—*a sweet substance*

A. *Characteristics of:*
- Product of bees ... Judg. 14:8, 9
- Not acceptable in offerings ... Lev. 2:11
- Offered as part of first fruits ... 2 Chr. 31:5

B. *Figurative of:*
- God's Word ... Ps. 19:10
- God's blessings ... Ex. 3:8, 17
- Wisdom ... Prov. 24:13, 14
- Pleasant words ... Prov. 16:24
- Prostitute's enticements ... Prov. 5:3
- Immanuel's diet ... Is. 7:14, 15

Honor—*to esteem or regard highly*

A. *Those worthy of:*
- God ... 1 Tim. 1:17
- Christ ... John 5:23
- Parents ... Eph. 6:2
- Aged ... 1 Tim. 5:1, 3
- Church officers ... Phil. 2:25, 29

B. *Obtainable by:*
- Wisdom ... Prov. 3:16
- Graciousness ... Prov. 11:16
- Discipline ... Prov. 13:18
- Humility ... Prov. 15:33
- Peaceableness ... Prov. 20:3
- Righteousness and mercy ... Prov. 21:21
- Honoring God ... 1 Sam. 2:30
- Serving Christ ... John 12:26

C. *Those advanced to:*
- Joseph ... Gen. 41:41-43
- Phinehas ... Num. 25:7-13
- Joshua ... Num. 27:18-20
- Solomon ... 1 Kin. 3:13
- Abishai ... 1 Chr. 11:20, 21
- Daniel ... Dan. 2:48
- Mordecai ... Esth. 8:15
- Apostles ... Matt. 19:27-29

Hoof—*the horny covering of the extremities of certain animals*
- Test of clean animals ... Lev. 11:3-8
- All must leave with Israel ... Ex. 10:26
- Break because of prancings ... Judg. 5:22
- Like flint ... Is. 5:28
- Cause noise ... Jer. 47:3

Hook

Used:
- For curtains ... Ex. 26:32, 37
- In fishing ... Job 41:1, 2
- For pruning ... Is. 2:4
- Expressive of God's sovereignty ... 2 Kin. 19:28

Hope—*the expectation of future good*

A. *Kinds of:*
- Natural expectation ... Acts 27:20
- Sinful expectation ... Acts 24:26
- Impossible ... Rom. 4:18
- Spiritual assurance ... 2 Cor. 1:7

B. *Described as:*
- Living ... 1 Pet. 1:3
- Blessed ... Titus 2:13
- Good ... 2 Thess. 2:16
- Better ... Heb. 7:19
- Sure and steadfast ... Heb. 6:19
- One of the great virtues ... 1 Cor. 13:13

C. *Productive of:*
- Purity ... 1 John 3:3
- Patience ... Rom. 8:25
- Courage ... Rom. 5:4, 5
- Joy ... Rom. 12:12
- Salvation ... Rom. 8:23
- Assurance ... Heb. 6:18, 19
- Stability ... Col. 1:23

D. *Grounds of:*
- God's Word ... Ps. 119:42-81; Rom. 15:4
- God's promises ... Acts 26:6, 7; Titus 1:2

SUBJECT ... REFERENCE

E. *Objects of:*
- God ... Ps. 39:7
- Christ ... 1 Cor. 15:19
- Salvation ... Rom. 5:1-5
- Resurrection ... Acts 23:6
- Eternal life ... Titus 1:2
- Glory ... Rom. 5:2
- Christ's return ... Rom. 8:22-25

Hopelessness—*without hope*
- Condition of the wicked ... Eph. 2:12
- Their unchangeable condition ... Luke 16:23-31

Hophni—*fighter*
- Son of Eli; brother of Phinehas ... 1 Sam. 1:3
- Called "sons of Belial" ... 1 Sam. 2:12
- Guilty of unlawful practices ... 1 Sam. 2:13-17
- Immoral ... 1 Sam. 2:22
- Eli's warning rejected by ... 1 Sam. 2:23-25
- Cursed by a man of God ... 1 Sam. 2:27-36
- Warned by Samuel ... 1 Sam. 3:11-18
- Ark taken to battle by ... 1 Sam. 4:1-8
- Slain in battle ... 1 Sam. 4:11
- News of, causes Eli's death ... 1 Sam. 4:12-18

Hor—*mountain*
1. Mountain of Edom ... Num. 20:23
   Scene of Aaron's death ... Num. 20:22-29; Num. 33:37-39
2. Prominent peak of the Lebanon range ... Num. 34:7, 8

Horam—*elevated*
- King of Gezer ... Josh. 10:33

Horeb—*desert*
- God appears to Moses ... Ex. 3:1-22
- Water flows from ... Ex. 17:6
- Law given here ... Mal. 4:4
- Site of Israel's great sin ... Deut. 9:8, 9; Ps. 106:19
- Covenant made ... Deut. 29:1
- Elijah lodged here 40 days ... 1 Kin. 19:8, 9
- See Sinai

Horem—*consecrated*
- City of Naphtali ... Josh. 19:32, 38

Hor-hagidgad—*cavern of Gidgah*
- Israelite encampment ... Num. 33:32
- See Gudgodah

Hori—*cave dweller*
1. Son of Lotan ... Gen. 36:22; 1 Chr. 1:39
2. Horites ... Gen. 36:21-30
3. Father of Shaphat the spy ... Num. 13:5

Horim, Horites—*cave dwellers*
- Inhabitants of Mt. Seir ... Gen. 36:20
- Defeated by Chedorlaomer ... Gen. 14:5, 6
- Ruled by chieftains ... Gen. 36:29, 30
- Driven out by Esau's descendants ... {Gen. 36:20-29; Deut. 2:12, 22}

Hormah—*devoted to destruction*
- Originally called Zephath ... Judg. 1:17
- Scene of Israel's defeat ... Num. 14:45
- Destroyed by Israel ... Num. 21:1-3
- Assigned to Judah ... Josh. 15:30
- Transferred to Simeon ... Josh. 19:4
- David sends spoils to ... 1 Sam. 30:26, 30

Horn—*bone-like protrusion from an animal's head*

A. *Descriptive of:*
- Ram's ... Gen. 22:13
- Ox's ... Ex. 21:29
- Unicorn ... Ps. 92:10
- Goat's ... Dan. 8:5
- Altar's ... 1 Kin. 1:50

B. *Uses of:*
- For trumpets ... Josh. 6:4, 13
- For vessels ... 1 Sam. 16:1-13

C. *Figurative of:*
- God's power ... Hab. 3:4
- Christ's power ... Rev. 5:6
- Power of the wicked ... Ps. 22:21
- Power of earthly kingdoms ... Dan. 7:7, 8, 24
- Power of the antichrist ... Rev. 13:1
- Arrogance ... 1 Kin. 22:11
- Conquests ... Deut. 33:17
- Exaltation ... 1 Sam. 2:1, 10

SUBJECT ... REFERENCE

- Degradation ... Job 16:15
- Destruction ... Jer. 48:25
- Salvation ... Luke 1:69

D. *As musical instrument:*
- Heard at Sinai ... Ex. 19:16
- Sounded in jubilee year ... Lev. 25:9
- Used on occasions ... 1 Chr. 15:28
- A part of worship ... 2 Chr. 15:14
- Used in Babylon ... Dan. 3:7, 10

Hornets—*a large, strong wasp*
- God's agents ... Ex. 23:28; Deut. 7:20
- Kings driven out by ... Josh. 24:12

Horns of the altar—*the protruding points at the four corners of an altar*
- Description ... Ex. 27:2
- Provides sanctuary ... 1 Kin. 1:50

Horonaim—*two caverns*
- Moabite city ... Is. 15:5

Horonite
- Native of Horonaim ... Neh. 2:10, 19

Horoscope—*fortune-telling by astrology*
- Forbidden ... Jer. 10:2
- Unprofitable ... Deut. 17:2-5
- Punishment ... Is. 47:13, 14

Horse

A. *Used for:*
- Travel ... Deut. 17:16
- War ... Ex. 14:9
- Bearing burdens ... Neh. 7:68
- Sending messages ... Esth. 8:10
- Idolatry ... 2 Kin. 23:11

B. *Figurative of:*
- Human trust ... Hos. 14:3
- Obstinacy ... Ps. 32:9; James 3:3
- Impetuosity in sin ... Jer. 8:6
- God's protection ... 2 Kin. 2:11

Horseleech—*a large leech*
- Figurative of insatiable appetite ... Prov. 30:15, 16

Horse traders
- Tyre famous for ... Ezek. 27:2, 14

Horse gate—*a gate of Jerusalem*
- Restored by Nehemiah ... Neh. 3:28

Hosah—*seeking refuge*
1. Village of Asher ... Josh. 19:29
2. Temple porter ... 1 Chr 16:38

Hosanna—*save, now, we beseech thee*
- Triumphal acclaim ... Matt. 21:9, 15; Mark 11:9

Hosea—*salvation*
- Son of Beeri, prophet of the northern kingdom ... Hos. 1:1
- Reproved idolatry ... Hos. 1—2
- Threatens God's judgment; calls to repentance ... Hos. 3—6
- Foretells impending judgment ... Hos. 7—10
- Calls an ungrateful people to repentance; promises God's blessings ... Hos. 11—14

Hosen—*trousers*
- Bound in ... Dan. 3:21

Hoshaiah—*Jehovah has saved*
1. Father of Jezaniah and Azariah ... Jer. 42:1
2. Participant in a dedication ... Neh. 12:31, 32

Hoshama—*Jehovah has heard*
- Son of King Jeconiah ... 1 Chr. 3:17, 18

Hoshea—*save*
1. Original name of Joshua, the son of Nun ... Deut. 32:44

   See Joshua, Jehoshua
2. Ephraimite chieftain ... 1 Chr. 27:20
3. One who signs covenant ... Neh. 10:1, 23
4. Israel's last king; usurps throne ... 2 Kin. 15:30

SUBJECT REFERENCE

5. Reigns wickedly; Israel taken to Assyria during reign ... 2 Kin. 17:1-23

Hospitality—*reception and entertainment of strangers*

A. *Kinds of:*
- Treacherous ... Judg. 4:17-21
- Rewarded ... Josh. 6:17-25
- Unwise ... 2 Kin. 20:12-19
- Critical ... Luke 7:36-50
- Unwelcomed ... Luke 9:51-53
- Joyful ... Luke 19:5, 6
- Turbulent ... Acts 17:5-9
- Forbidden ... 3 John 1, 9, 10

B. *Act of:*
- Commanded ... Rom. 12:13
- Required of church leaders ... 1 Tim. 3:2
- Discipleship ... Matt. 25:35

C. *Courtesies of:*
- Protection provided ... Gen. 19:6-8
- Shelter and food ... Luke 11:5-8
- Washing of feet ... Luke 7:44
- Kissing ... Luke 7:45
- Denied with indignities ... Judg. 19:15-28; Luke 10:10-16

D. *Examples of:*
- Abraham to angels ... Gen. 18:1-8
- Lot to an angel ... Gen. 19:1-11
- Laban to Abraham's servant ... Gen. 24:31-33
- Joseph to his brothers ... Gen. 43:31-34
- Pharaoh to Jacob ... Gen. 45:16-20
- Rahab to the spies ... Josh. 2:1-16
- David to Mephibosheth ... 2 Sam. 9:6-13
- Martha to Jesus ... Luke 10:38-42
- Lydia to Paul and Silas ... Acts 16:14, 15
- Barbarians to Paul ... Acts 28:2, 7

Host—*one who entertains*
- One who entertains hospitably ... Rom. 16:23

Hostage—*a person held as security*
- Captive for pledge ... 2 Kin. 14:14; 2 Chr. 25:24

Host of Heaven

A. *Used of stars as objects of worship:*
- Objects of idolatry ... Deut. 4:19
- Practiced in Israel ... 2 Kin. 17:16
- Introduced by Manasseh ... 2 Kin. 21:5
- Abolished by Josiah ... 2 Kin. 23:4-12
- Worship of, on roofs ... Jer. 19:13

B. *Used of stars as created things:*
- Created by God ... Is. 45:12
- Cannot be numbered ... Jer. 33:22
- Named by God ... Is. 40:26
- To be dissolved ... Is. 34:4

C. *Used of angels:*
- Created by God ... Neh. 9:6
- Around the throne ... 1 Kin. 22:19

Hosts, Lord of—*a title of God*
- Commander of: Israel's armies ... {1 Sam. 17:45; Is. 31:4}
- Armies (angels) of heaven ... {Gen. 28:12, 13; Hos. 12:4, 5; Ps. 89:6-8}
- Same as Sabaoth ... Rom. 9:29

Hotham, Hothan—*determination*
1. Asherite ... 1 Chr. 7:30, 32
2. Father of two of David's valiant men ... 1 Chr. 11:26, 44

Hothir—*abundance*
- Son of Heman; a musician ... 1 Chr. 25:4, 28

Hough—*to cut the tendons of the leg*
- To render captured animals useless ... {Josh. 11:6, 9; 2 Sam. 8:4}

Hour—*a division of time*

A. *Used literally of:*
- One-twelfth of daylight ... Matt. 20:1-12
- One-twelfth of night ... Luke 12:39

B. *Jewish reckoning (from 6 P.M. and from 6 A.M.):*
- Third (9 A.M.) ... Matt. 20:3
- Sixth and ninth (12 noon; 3 P.M.) ... Matt. 20:5
- Ninth (3 P.M.) ... Acts 3:1
- Eleventh (5 P.M.) ... Matt. 20:6, 9, 12
- Third (9 P.M.) ... Acts 23:23

C. *Used literally and descriptively of Christ's:*
- Death ... Mark 14:35
- Betrayal ... Matt. 26:45
- Glorification ... John 13:1
- Set time ... John 7:30
- Predestined time ... John 12:27

D. *Used prophetically of:*
- Gospel age ... John 4:21
- Great tribulation ... Rev. 3:10
- God's judgment ... Rev. 14:7, 15
- Christ's return ... Matt. 24:42, 44, 50

Hours of prayer

A. *Characteristics of:*
- Jewish custom ... Luke 1:10
- Centered in the Temple ... Luke 18:10
- Directed toward Jerusalem ... 1 Kin. 8:48

B. *Times of:*
- Three times daily ... Dan. 6:10
- First, at third hour (9 A.M.) ... Acts 2:15
- Second, at sixth hour (12 noon) ... Acts 10:9
- Third, at ninth hour (3 P.M.) ... Acts 3:1

House

A. *Descriptive of:*
- Family dwelling ... Judg. 11:34; Acts 16:34
- Family ... Gen. 14:14; Acts 16:31
- Descendants ... Gen. 18:19; Luke 2:4
- Racial or religious group ... Is. 7:13; Jer. 31:31
- Tabernacle or Temple ... Ex. 34:26; 1 Kin. 6:1

B. *Figurative of:*
- Grave ... Job 30:23
- Body ... 2 Cor. 5:1
- Visible Church ... Gal. 6:10
- True Church ... Heb. 10:21
- Earthly life ... Ps. 119:54
- Heaven ... John 14:2
- Security and insecurity ... Matt. 7:24-27
- Division ... Mark 3:25

See Home

Household idols
- Laban's stolen by Rachel ... Gen. 31:19-35
- Used in idolatry ... Hos. 3:4

Householder—*master of a house*
- Parable of ... Matt. 13:27; Matt. 21:33

Housekeeper
- Sarah ... Gen. 18:6
- Rebekah ... Gen. 27:6-9
- Abigail ... 1 Sam. 25:41, 42
- Happy ... Ps. 113:9
- Ideal woman ... Prov. 31:10-31
- Martha ... Luke 10:40, 41

House of God
- Tabernacle called ... Luke 6:4
- Temple described ... Ezra 5:2, 8
- Church named ... 1 Tim. 3:15
- Center of God's worship ... Ps. 42:4

House of prayer
- Corrupted into a den of thieves ... {Matt. 21:13; Mark 11:17}

Houses—*dwellings made for habitations*
- Rechabites refuse to dwell in ... Jer. 35:5-10

Hukkok—*decreed*
- Border town of Naphtali ... Josh. 19:32, 34

Hukok
- Land given as place of refuge ... 1 Chr. 6:75

Hul—*circle*
- Aram's second son ... Gen. 10:23

Huldah—*weasel, mole*
- Wife of Shallum ... 2 Kin. 22:14
- Foretells Jerusalem's ruin ... 2 Kin. 22:15-17; 2 Chr. 34:22-25
- Exempts Josiah from trouble ... 2 Kin. 22:18-20

Human dignity

Based on:
- God's image ... Gen. 1:26
- Elevated by God ... Ps. 8:3-8
- Loved ... John 3:16
- Chosen ... John 15:16

Humaneness—*a kind spirit*
- Toward animals ... Ex. 23:5
- Not shown by Balaam ... Num. 22:27-30

Humanitarianism—*promoting the welfare of humanity*
- Illustrated by Jesus ... Luke 10:30-37
- Enjoined on Christians ... 1 Thess. 5:15

Human nature of Christ

A. *Predicted as seed of:*
- Woman ... Gen. 3:15
- Abraham ... Gal. 3:8, 16
- David ... Luke 1:31, 32

B. *Proved by:*
- Virgin's conception ... Matt. 1:18
- Birth ... Matt. 1:16, 25
- Incarnation ... John 1:14
- Circumcision ... Luke 2:21
- Growth ... Luke 2:52
- Genealogy ... Matt. 1:1-17

C. *Manifested in:*
- Hunger ... Matt. 4:2
- Thirst ... John 19:28
- Weariness ... John 4:6
- Sleep ... Matt. 8:24
- Suffering ... Luke 22:44
- Death ... John 19:30
- Burial ... Matt. 27:59, 60
- Resurrection ... Luke 24:39; 1 John 1:1, 2

D. *Importance of, necessary for:*
- Sinlessness ... John 8:46
- His death ... Heb. 2:14, 17
- His resurrection ... 2 Tim. 2:8
- His exaltation ... Phil. 2:9-11
- His priestly intercession ... Heb. 7:26, 28
- His return ... Heb. 9:24-28
- Faith ... 2 John 7-11

See Incarnation of Christ

Human sacrifice

A. *Practiced by:*
- Canaanites ... Deut. 12:31
- Ammonites ... Lev. 20:2, 3
- Moabites ... 2 Kin. 3:26, 27
- Phoenicians ... Jer. 19:5
- Israel ... 2 Kin. 16:3, 4
- Judah ... 2 Chr. 28:3

B. *Sin of:*
- Condemned ... Lev. 18:21
- Source of defilement ... Ezek. 20:31
- Source of demonism ... Ps. 106:37, 38
- Cause of captivity ... 2 Kin. 17:17, 18

Humiliation—*state of deflated pride*

A. *Causes of:*
- Pride ... Esth. 6:6-13
- Arrogance ... Dan. 4:29-33
- Boastfulness ... 1 Sam. 17:42-50
- National sins ... Dan. 9:1-21
- Self-will ... Luke 15:11-19

B. *Remedies against:*
- Be humble ... Luke 14:8-11
- Avoid sinners ... Judg. 16:16-21
- Obey God ... Josh. 7:11-16
- Avoid self-sufficiency ... Luke 22:31-34
- Rely upon God's grace ... 2 Cor. 12:6-10

Humiliation of Christ—*the state that He took while on earth*

A. *Exhibited in His:*
- Taking our nature ... Phil. 2:7
- Birth ... Matt. 1:18-25
- Obedience ... Luke 2:51
- Submission to ordinances ... Matt. 3:13-15
- Becoming a servant ... Matt. 20:28
- Menial acts ... John 13:4-15
- Suffering ... Matt. 26:67, 68
- Death ... John 10:15-18

B. *Rewards of:*
- Exalted by God ... Acts 2:22-36
- Crowned king ... Heb. 1:1, 2

SUBJECT REFERENCE

Perfected forever .... Heb. 2:10
Acceptable high priest....... Heb. 2:17

Humility

A. *Factors involved in sense of:*
One's sinfulness .... Luke 18:13, 14
One's unworthiness .... Luke 15:17-21
One's limitations .... 1 Kin. 3:6-14
God's holiness .... Is. 6:1-8
God's righteousness......... Phil. 3:4-7

B. *Factors producing:*
Affliction .... Deut. 8:3
Impending doom .... 2 Chr. 12:5-12
Submissiveness .... Luke 10:39
Christ's example............ Matt. 11:29

C. *Rewards of:*
Road to honor .... 1 Kin. 3:11-14
Leads to riches .... Prov. 22:4
Brings blessings .... 2 Chr. 7:14, 15
Guarantees exaltation .... James 4:10
Insures God's presence ...... Is. 57:15
Makes truly great........... Matt. 18:4
Unlocks more grace......... Prov. 3:34
James 4:6

D. *Christians exhorted to:*
Put on .... Col. 3:12
Be clothed with .... 1 Pet. 5:5
Walk with .... Eph. 4:1, 2
Avoid false .... Col. 2:18-23

E. *Examples of:*
Abraham.................. Gen. 18:27, 32
Jacob .... Gen. 32:10
Moses .... Ex. 3:11
Joshua .... Josh. 7:6
David..................... 1 Sam. 18:18-23
Job .... Job 42:2-6
Jeremiah .... Jer. 1:6
Daniel .... Dan. 2:30
Elizabeth .... Luke 1:43
John the Baptist........... John 3:29, 30
Jesus .... Matt. 11:29
Paul .... Acts 20:19

Humtah—*a place of lizards*
Town of Judah.............. Josh. 15:54

Hunger, physical

A. *Causes of:*
Fasting .... Matt. 4:1-3
Fatigue .... Gen. 25:30
Famine .... Luke 15:14-17
God's judgment .... Is. 9:19-21

B. *Some results of:*
Selling birthright .... Gen. 25:30-34
Murmuring .... Ex. 16:2, 3
Breaking God's Law .... 1 Sam. 14:31-34
Cannibalism .... 2 Kin. 6:28, 29
Cursing God............... Is. 8:21

C. *Satisfaction of:*
Supplied:
By friends .... 1 Sam. 17:27-29
Supernaturally .... Ex. 16:4-21
Sent as a judgment .... Ps. 106:14, 15
Provided by God .... Matt. 6:11
Christian duty .... 1 Sam. 30:11, 12
Complete in heaven......... Rev. 7:14-17

D. *Examples of:*
David..................... 1 Sam. 21:3-6
Elijah .... 1 Kin. 17:11-13
Jeremiah .... Jer. 38:9
Peter .... Acts 10:10
Paul .... 1 Cor. 4:11

E. *Strike:*
By forty men .... Acts 23:11-16

Hunger, spiritual
More important than physical... Deut. 8:3
Sent as a judgment .... Amos 4:11-13
Will be satisfied............ Is. 55:1, 2
Blessing of .... Matt. 5:6
Satisfied by Christ.......... John 6:33-35

Hunter, hunting

A. *Purposes of:*
Kill harmful beasts .... 1 Sam. 17:34-36

B. *Methods of:*
Decoys.................... Job 18:10
Nets...................... Amos 3:5
Pits...................... 2 Sam. 23:20
Bows and quiver .... Gen. 27:3
Sword, etc. .... Job 41:26-30

C. *Examples of:*
Nimrod .... Gen. 10:8, 9
Ishmael .... Gen. 21:20
Esau .... Gen. 27:3, 5, 30

Hupham—*protected*
Son of Benjamin; founder of Huphamites .... Num. 26:39
Called Huppim .... Gen. 46:21

Huppah—*covering*
Descendant of Aaron .... 1 Chr. 24:1, 13

Huppim—*protection*
1. Son of Benjamin .... Gen. 46:21
2. Son of Ir .... 1 Chr. 7:12
See Hupham

Hur—*splendor*
1. Man of Judah; of Caleb's house .... 1 Chr. 2:18-20
Grandfather of Bezaleel ..... Ex. 31:1, 2
Supports Moses' hands ...... Ex. 17:10-12
Aids Aaron .... Ex. 24:14
2. King of Midian .... Josh. 13:21
3. Father of Rephaiah .... Neh. 3:9

Hurai—*free, noble*
One of David's mighty men..... 1 Chr. 11:32

Huram—*noble, free*
1. Son of Bela .... 1 Chr. 8:5
2. King of Tyre............... 2 Chr. 2:11

Huri—*linen worker*
Gadite .... 1 Chr. 5:14

Husband—*married man*

A. *Regulations concerning:*
One flesh .... Matt. 19:5, 6
Until death .... Rom. 7:2, 3
Rights of .... 1 Cor. 7:1-5
Sanctified by wife .... 1 Cor. 7:14-16

B. *Duties of, toward wife:*
Love...................... Eph. 5:25-33
Live with for life .... Matt. 19:3-9
Be faithful to .... Mal. 2:14, 15
Be satisfied with............ Prov. 5:18, 19
Instruct .... 1 Cor. 14:34, 35
Honor .... 1 Pet. 3:7
Confer with................ Gen. 31:4-16
Provide for .... 1 Tim. 5:8
Rule over .... Gen. 3:16

C. *Kinds of:*
Adam, blaming .... Gen. 3:9-12
Isaac, loving .... Gen. 24:67
Elkanah, sympathetic .... 1 Sam. 1:8-23
Nabal, evil .... 1 Sam. 25:3
Ahab, weak................ 1 Kin. 21:5-16
David, ridiculed .... 2 Sam. 6:20
Job, strong .... Job 2:7-10

Husbandman—*a man of the soil*
Farmer .... Gen. 9:20
2 Kin. 25:12
Tenant farmer .... Matt. 21:33-42
Takes share of crops .... 2 Tim. 2:6

Hushah—*haste*
Judahite .... 1 Chr. 4:4

Hushai—*hasty*
Archite; David's friend........ 2 Sam. 15:32-37
Feigns sympathy with Absalom .... 2 Sam. 16:16-19
Defeats Ahithophel's advice.... 2 Sam. 17:5-23

Husham—*hastily*
Temanite king of Edom .... Gen. 36:34, 35

Hushathite
Inhabitant of Hushah .... 2 Sam. 21:18

Hushim—*hasters*
1. Head of a Danite family..... Gen. 46:23
Called Shuham .... Num. 26:42
2. Sons of Aher .... 1 Chr. 7:12
3. Wife of Shaharaim......... 1 Chr. 8:8, 11

Husks—*the pods of the carob or locust tree*
Fed to swine................. Luke 15:15, 16

Huzzab—*uncertain meaning*
May refer to Assyrian queen or to Nineveh; or may be rendered "it is decreed" .... Nah. 2:7

Hymenaeus—*belonging to Hymen*
False teacher excommunicated by Paul .... 1 Tim. 1:19, 20
Teaches error .... 2 Tim. 2:17, 18

Hymn—*a spiritual song*

A. *Occasions producing:*
Great deliverance........... Ex. 15:1-19
Great victory .... Judg. 5:1-31
Prayer answered .... 1 Sam. 2:1-10
Mary's "Magnificat" .... Luke 1:46-55
Father's ecstasy .... Luke 1:68-79
Angel's delight .... Luke 2:14
Old man's faith .... Luke 2:29-32
Heaven's eternal praise...... Rev. 5:9-14

B. *Purposes of:*
Worship God .... 2 Chr. 23:18
Express joy .... Matt. 26:30
Edify .... 1 Cor. 14:15
Testify to others .... Acts 16:25

Hypocrisy, hypocrite—*showy, empty display of religion*

A. *Kinds of:*
Worldly .... Matt. 23:5-7
Legalistic .... Rom. 10:3
Evangelical .... 2 Pet. 2:10-22
Satanic................... 2 Cor. 11:13-15

B. *Described as:*
Self-righteous .... Luke 18:11, 12
"Holier than thou" .... Is. 65:5
Blind .... Matt. 23:17-26
Covetous .... 2 Pet. 2:3
Showy .... Matt. 6:2, 5, 16
Highly critical .... Matt. 7:3-5
Indignant .... Luke 13:14-16
Bound by traditions .... Matt. 15:1-9
Neglectful of major duties ... Matt. 23:23, 24
Pretended but unpracticed ... Ezek. 33:31, 32
Interested in the externals ... Luke 20:46, 47
Fond of titles .... Matt. 23:6, 7
Inwardly unregenerate ...... Luke 11:39

C. *Examples of:*
Jacob .... Gen. 27:6-35
Jacob's sins .... Gen. 37:29-35
Delilah .... Judg. 16:4-20
Ishmael .... Jer. 41:6, 7
Herod .... Matt. 2:7, 8
Pharisees .... John 8:4-9
Judas .... Matt. 26:25-49
Ananias .... Acts 5:1-10
Peter .... Gal. 2:11-14

Hyssop—*a small plant*
Grows from walls .... 1 Kin. 4:33
Used in sprinkling blood .... Ex. 12:22
Used to offer Jesus vinegar ..... John 19:28, 29
Typical of spiritual cleansing.... Ps. 51:7

I

I AM—*a title indicating self-existence*
Revealed to Moses .... Ex. 3:14
Said by Christ .... John 8:57, 58

Christ expressing, refers to:
Bread of Life .... John 6:35, 41 48, 51
Light of the world .... John 8:12
John 9:5
Door of the sheep .... John 10:7, 9
Good Shepherd .... John 10:11, 14
Resurrection and the Life ...... John 11:25
True and living Way .... John 14:6
True Vine .... John 15:1, 5

Ibleam—*he destroys the people*
City assigned to Manasseh...... Josh. 17:11, 12
Canaanites remain in .... Judg. 1:27
Called Bileam................ 1 Chr. 6:70
Ahaziah slain near............ 2 Kin. 9:27

Ibneiah—*Jehovah builds up*
Head of a Benjamite family..... 1 Chr. 9:8

SUBJECT — REFERENCE

Ibnijah—*Jehovah builds up*
Father of Reuel ... 1 Chr. 9:8

Ibri—*a Hebrew*
Son of Jaaziah ... 1 Chr. 24:27

Ibsam—*fragrant*
Descendant of Issachar ... 1 Chr. 7:2

Ibzan—*active*
Judge of Israel ... Judg. 12:8
Father of 60 children ... Judg. 12:8, 9

Ice
Figurative of:
God casts forth ... Ps. 147:17
By reason of ... Job 6:16

Ichabod—*inglorious*
Son of Phinehas ... 1 Sam. 4:19-22

Iconium—*image-like*
City of Asia Minor; visited by Paul ... Acts 13:51
Many converts in ... Acts 14:1-6
Paul visits again ... Acts 14:21
Timothy's ministry ... Acts 16:1, 2
Paul persecuted ... 2 Tim. 3:11

Iconoclast—*a breaker of images*
Moses, an angry ... Ex. 32:19, 20
Gideon, an inspired ... Judg. 6:25-32
Jehu, a subtle ... 2 Kin. 10:18-31
Josiah, a reforming ... 2 Kin. 23:12-25

Idalah—*memorial of God*
Border town of Zebulun ... Josh. 19:15

Idbash—*honey-sweet*
Man of Judah ... 1 Chr. 4:3

Iddo—*festal*
1. Chief officer under David ... 1 Chr. 27:21
2. Father of Abinadab ... 1 Kin. 4:14
3. Leader of Jews at Casiphia ... Ezra 8:17-20
4. Gershonite Levite ... 1 Chr. 6:20, 21
   Called Adaiah ... 1 Chr. 6:41
5. Seer whose writings are cited ... 2 Chr. 9:29
6. Grandfather of Zechariah the prophet ... Zech. 1:1, 7
7. Postexilic priest ... Neh. 12:4, 16

Identification—*proving something or somebody to be what it or he really is*
A. *Among men:*
At birth ... Gen. 25:22-26
By the life ... Luke 6:43-45
By speech ... Judg. 12:6
By a search ... 2 Kin. 10:23
By a kiss ... Matt. 26:48, 49
B. *Of Christ the Messiah, by:*
A divine sign ... John 1:31-34
A divine voice ... Matt. 17:5
Divine works ... Matt. 11:2-6
Human testimony ... John 3:26-36
Scriptures ... John 5:39-47
C. *Of spiritual things:*
New birth ... 2 Cor. 5:17
Apostates ... Matt. 7:22, 23
Antichrist ... 2 Thess. 2:1-12
Believers and unbelievers ... Matt. 25:31-46

Identifying with Christ
A. *Proper time, when tempted:*
To harm ... Prov. 1:10-19
To violate convictions ... Dan. 1:8
To conform to world ... Rom. 12:2
To rebellion ... Rom. 13:1-5
To learn evil ... Rom. 16:19; Prov. 19:27
With improper associations ... 2 Cor. 6:14-17
B. *Results:*
Hatred ... John 17:14
Separation ... Luke 6:22, 23
Suffering ... 1 Pet. 2:20, 21
Witness ... 1 Pet. 3:15
Good conscience ... 1 Pet. 3:16
C. *Basis:*
Future glory ... Rom. 8:18
Life of Christ ... Gal. 2:20
Reward ... 2 Tim. 2:12

Idleness—*inactivity; slothfulness*
A. *Consequences of:*
Poverty ... Prov. 20:13
Begging ... Prov. 20:4
Hunger ... Prov. 19:15
Bondage ... Prov. 12:24
Ruin ... Prov. 24:30-34
B. *Admonitions against, consider:*
Ant ... Prov. 6:6-11
Ideal woman ... Prov. 31:10-31
Lord ... John 9:4
Apostles ... 2 Thess. 3:7-9
Judgment ... 1 Cor. 3:8-15
See Laziness; slothfulness

Idol makers
Maacah ... 1 Kin. 15:13
Foreign peoples ... Is. 45:16
Men of Judah ... Is. 2:20
People of Jerusalem ... Ezek. 22:3

Idol making
Described by Isaiah ... Is. 44:9-18

Idols, idolatry—*worship of idols*
A. *Described as:*
Irrational ... Acts 17:29
Degrading ... Rom. 1:22, 23
Demonical ... 1 Cor. 10:20, 21
Defiling ... 2 Cor. 6:15-18
Enslaving ... Gal. 4:8, 9
Abominable ... 1 Pet. 4:3
B. *Brief history of:*
Begins in man's apostasy ... Rom. 1:21-25
Prevails in Ur ... Josh. 24:2, 14
In Laban's household ... Gen. 31:19-35
Judgments on Egyptian ... Num. 33:4
Brought from Egypt by Israel ... Josh. 24:14
Forbidden in Law at Sinai ... Ex. 20:1-5
Warnings against, at Sinai ... Ex. 34:13-16
Israel yields to, at Sinai ... Ex. 32:1-8
Moabites entice Israel to ... Num. 25:1-18
Early zeal against ... Josh. 22:10-34
Gideon destroys ... Judg. 6:25-32
Gideon becomes an occasion of ... Judg. 8:24-27
Enticements to Baalism ... Judg. 10:6-16
Levite corrupted by ... Judg. 17:1-13
Danites establish, at Shiloh ... Judg. 18:30, 31
Overthrow of Philistines ... 1 Sam. 5:1-12
Revival against, under Samuel ... 1 Sam. 7:3-6
Solomon yields to ... 1 Kin. 11:1-8
Jeroboam establishes in Jerusalem ... {1 Kin. 12:26-33; 2 Chr. 11:15}
Rehoboam tolerates in Judah ... 1 Kin. 14:22-24
Conflict—Elijah and Ahab ... 1 Kin. 18:1-46
Wicked kings of Israel ... 1 Kin. 21:25, 26; 2 Kin. 16:3
Prophet denounces in Israel ... Hos. 4:12-19
Cause of Israel's exile ... 2 Kin. 17:5-23
Judah follows Israel's example ... 2 Chr. 28:1-4
Manasseh climaxes Judah's apostasy in ... {2 Kin. 21:1-18; 2 Chr. 33:1-11}
Reformation against, under Asa ... 2 Chr. 14:3-5
Under Hezekiah ... 2 Chr. 29:15-19
Under Josiah ... 2 Kin. 23:1-20
Prophets denounce in Judah ... Jer. 16:11-21
Cause of Judah's exile ... 2 Kin. 23:26, 27
C. *Christians warned against:*
No company with ... 1 Cor. 5:11
Flee from ... 1 Cor. 10:14
No fellowship with ... 1 Cor. 10:19, 20
Keep from ... 1 John 5:21
Testify against ... Acts 14:15
Turn from ... 1 Thess. 1:9
D. *Enticements to, due to:*
Heathen background ... Josh. 24:2; Ezek. 16:44, 45
Contact with idolaters ... Num. 25:1-6
Intermarriage ... 1 Kin. 11:1-13
Imagined good ... Jer. 44:15-19
Corrupt heart ... Rom. 1:21-23
E. *Removed through:*
Punishment ... Deut. 17:2-5
Display of powerlessness ... 1 Sam. 5:1-5; 1 Kin. 18:25-29
Logic ... Is. 44:6-20
Display of God's power ... 2 Kin. 19:10-37
Denunciation ... Mic. 1:5-7
Exile ... Zeph. 1:4-6; Hos. 8:5-14
New birth ... Amos 5:26, 27; Hos. 14:1-9

Idumea—*pertaining to Edom*
Name used by Greek and Romans to designate Edom ... Mark 3:8
See Edom

Igal—*He* (God) *redeems*
1. Issachar's spy ... Num. 13:2, 7
2. One of David's mighty men ... 2 Sam. 23:36
3. Shemaiah's son ... 1 Chr. 3:22

Igdaliah—*great is Jehovah*
Father of Hanan the prophet ... Jer. 35:4

Ignorance—*lack of knowledge*
A. *Kinds of:*
Pardonable ... Luke 23:34
Pretended ... Luke 22:57-60
Innocent ... Acts 19:2-5
Excusable ... Acts 17:30
Judicial ... Rom. 1:28
Guilty ... Rom. 1:19-25
Partial ... 1 Cor. 13:12
Confident ... Heb. 11:8
B. *Causes of:*
Unregeneracy ... Eph. 4:18
Unbelief ... 1 Tim. 1:13
Spiritual:
  Darkness ... 1 John 2:11
  Immaturity ... 1 Cor. 8:7-13
C. *Productive of:*
Unbelief ... John 8:19-43
Error ... Matt. 22:29
D. *Objects of:*
God ... John 8:55
Scriptures ... Matt. 22:29
Christ's return ... 1 Thess. 4:13, 14

Iim—*ruins*
Town of Judah ... Josh. 15:29

Ije-abarim—*ruins of the Abarim* (regions beyond)
Wilderness camp ... Num. 21:11
Same as Iim ... Num. 33:44, 45

Ijon—*heap*
Town of Naphtali; captured by Ben-hadad ... 1 Kin. 15:20
Captured by Tiglath-pileser ... 2 Kin. 15:29

Ikkesh—*crooked*
Father of Ira ... 2 Sam. 23:26
Commander of 24,000 ... 1 Chr. 27:9

Ilai—*supreme*
One of David's mighty men ... 1 Chr. 11:26, 29
Called Zalmon ... 2 Sam. 23:28

Illumination—*enlightenment, understanding*
Of Daniel ... Dan. 5:11, 14

Illumination, spiritual
By the Gospel ... John 1:9
At conversion ... Heb. 6:4
In Christian truth ... Eph. 1:18
By Holy Spirit ... John 16:13-16
By God ... 1 Cor. 4:5

Illustration—*something used to explain something else*
From:
Ancient history ... 1 Cor. 10:1-14
Current history ... Mark 12:1-11
Nature ... Prov. 6:6-11

Illyricum—*a province of Europe*
Paul preaches ... Rom. 15:19

Image (see Idols; idolatry)

Image of God
A. *In man:*
Created in ... Gen. 1:26, 27

SUBJECT REFERENCE

Reason for sanctity of life ... Gen. 9:6
Reason for man's headship ... 1 Cor. 11:7
Restored by grace ... Col. 3:10
Transformed of ... 2 Cor. 3:18

B. *In Christ:*

In essential nature ... Col. 1:15
Manifested on earth ... John 1:14, 18
Believers conformed ... Rom. 8:29

Imagination—*creating mental picture of*

A. *Described as:*

Evil ... Gen. 6:5
Willful ... Jer. 18:12
Deceitful ... Prov. 12:20
Vain ... Rom. 1:21

B. *Cleansing of:*

Promised ... Jer. 3:17
By the power of God ... 2 Cor. 10:5

Imitation—*attempting to duplicate*

Of the good:

God ... Eph. 5:1
Paul's conduct ... 2 Thess. 3:7, 9
Apostles ... 1 Thess. 1:6
Heroes of the faith ... Heb. 6:12
Good ... 3 John 11
Other churches ... 1 Thess. 2:14

See Example of Christ, the

Imla—*fullness*

Father of Micaiah the prophet ... 2 Chr. 18:7, 8
As Imlah ... 1 Kin. 22:8, 9

Immanuel—*God (is) with us*

Name given to the child born of the virgin ... Is. 7:14; Matt. 1:23
Emmanuel in ... Matt. 1:23

Immer—*eloquent*

1. Descendant of Aaron ... 1 Chr. 24:1-14
2. Father of Pashur ... Jer. 20:1
3. Founder of a postexilic family ... Ezra 2:37
   The same as the father of Meshillemith ... 1 Chr. 9:12
   Also the ancestor of priests marrying foreigners ... Ezra 10:19, 20
4. Person or place in Babylonia ... Neh. 7:61
5. Zadok's father ... Neh. 3:29

Immorality—*state of a wrongful act or relationship*

Attitude toward:

Consider sanctity of the body ... 1 Cor. 6:13-20
Flee from it ... 1 Cor. 6:18
Get married ... 1 Cor. 7:2
Abstain from it ... 1 Thess. 4:3
Mention it not ... Eph. 5:3
Corrupts the earth ... Rev. 19:2

Immortality—*eternal existence*

A. *Proof of, based upon:*

God's image in man ... Gen. 1:26, 27
Translation of Enoch and Elijah ... Gen. 5:24; 2 Kin. 2:11, 12
Promises of Christ ... John 11:25, 26; John 14:2, 3
Appearance of Moses and Elijah ... Matt. 17:2-9
Eternal rewards and punishments ... Matt. 25:31-46; Luke 16:19-31
Resurrection of Christ ... Rom. 8:11; 1 Cor. 15:12-58
Resurrection of men ... Dan. 12:2, 3; John 5:28, 29

B. *Expression indicative of:*

"I am" ... Matt. 22:32
"Today" ... Luke 23:43
"Shall never die" ... John 11:25, 26
"The redemption of our body" ... Rom. 8:22, 23
"Neither death" ... Rom. 8:38, 39
"We know" ... 2 Cor. 5:1-10
"A lively hope" ... 1 Pet. 1:3-8
"We shall be like him" ... 1 John 3:2

See Eternal, everlasting; Life, eternal

SUBJECT REFERENCE

Immunity—*exemption from something*

From:

Egyptian plagues ... Ex. 8:22, 23
Disease ... Deut. 7:15
Corruption ... Ps. 16:10, 11
Harm ... Luke 10:19
Second death ... Rev. 20:6

Immutability—*unchangeableness*

A. *Of God, expressed by:*

"I AM" ... Ex. 3:14
"Thou art the same" ... Ps. 102:25-27
"I change not" ... Mal. 3:6
"Are without repentance" ... Rom. 11:29
"Who cannot lie" ... Titus 1:2
"The immutability" ... Heb. 6:17, 18
"No variableness" ... James 1:17

B. *Of Christ, expressed by:*

"I am" ... John 8:58
"Thou art the same" ... Heb. 1:12
"Unchangeable" ... Heb. 7:22-24
"The same" ... Heb. 13:8
"I am Alpha and Omega" ... Rev. 1:8-18

C. *Of God, characteristics of:*

Unique ... Is. 43:10
Purposive ... Ps. 138:8
Active ... Phil. 1:6

Imna—*he keeps back*

Asherite chief ... 1 Chr. 7:35

Imnah—*prosperity*

1. Eldest son of Asher ... 1 Chr. 7:30
   Called Jimna and Jimnah ... Num. 26:44; Gen. 46:17
2. Levite in Hezekiah's reign ... 2 Chr. 31:14

Impartiality—*that which is equitable, just, and fair*

In God's:

Material blessings ... Matt. 5:45
Spiritual blessings ... Acts 10:34, 35
Judgments ... Rom. 2:3-12

Impatience—*inability to control one's desire for action*

A. *Causes of:*

Lust ... Gen. 19:4-9
Revenge ... Gen. 34:25-27
Irritability ... Num. 20:10

B. *Consequences of:*

Kept from promised land ... Num. 20:10-12
Great sin ... Ex. 32:1, 21, 30
Foolish statements ... Job 2:7-9
Loss of birthright ... Gen. 25:29-34
Shipwreck ... Acts 27:29-34

Impeccability (see Holiness of Christ)

Impediment—*something that hinders one's activity*

In speech, cured ... Mark 7:32-35
Avoided by obedience ... Prov. 4:10, 12

Impenitence—*without a change of mind*

A. *Expressed by:*

Willful disobedience ... Jer. 44:15-19
Hardness of heart ... John 12:37-40
Refusing to hear ... Luke 16:31
Rebellion against the truth ... 1 Thess. 2:15, 16

B. *Consequences of:*

Spiritual bondage ... John 8:33-44
Judicial blindness ... John 9:39-41
Eternal destruction ... 2 Thess. 1:8, 9

Imperfection of man

A. *Manifested in:*

Falling short of God's glory ... Rom. 3:23
Total corruption ... Is. 1:5, 6

B. *Remedy for:*

New creature ... 2 Cor. 5:17
Conformity to Christ ... 1 John 3:2, 3

Imperishable—*enduring, lasting forever*

Resurrected body ... 1 Cor. 15:42, 52, 53
Christian's inheritance ... 1 Pet. 1:4
Seed of Christian life ... 1 Pet. 1:23

Impertinence—*an action or remark inappropriate for the occasion*

Christ rebukes Peter's ... Mark 8:31-33

SUBJECT REFERENCE

Impetuousness—*acting suddenly with little thought*

Characterized by:

Ill-considered judgment ... Esth. 1:10-22
Enraged disposition ... Gen. 34:25-31
Hasty action ... Josh. 22:10-34

Import—*to receive from other countries*

Things imported:

Horses ... 1 Kin. 10:28
Chariots ... 2 Chr. 1:17
Fish ... Neh. 13:16

Importunity in prayer

Need involved ... Luke 11:5-13
Christ's example ... Luke 22:44
Great intensity of ... Acts 12:5
Results of ... Mark 7:24-30

See Prayer

Impossibilities—*powerless, weak*

A. *Natural:*

Change one's color ... Jer. 13:23
Hide from God ... Ps. 139:7-12
Change one's size ... Matt. 6:27
Control the tongue ... James 3:7, 8

B. *Spiritual:*

God to sin ... Hab. 1:13
God to fail His promises ... Titus 1:2
Believers to be lost ... John 10:27-29

Imposter—*a pretender*

A. *Characteristics of:*

Not believed as ... Jer. 40:14-16
Speaks falsely ... Josh. 9:3-14
Poses as real ... 2 Cor. 11:13-15
Much like the real ... Matt. 7:21-23
Deception of, revealed to prophets ... Acts 13:8-12

B. *Examples of:*

Jannes and Jambres ... 2 Tim. 3:8
Judas ... John 13:18-30
Antichrist ... 2 Thess. 2:1-4

Impotent—*powerless*

Moab ... Is. 16:14

Imprecation—*pronouncing a curse*

God's enemies ... Ps. 55:5-15
One's enemies ... Ps. 35:4-8, 26
Heretics ... Gal. 1:9
Persecutors ... Jer. 11:18-20
Forbidden ... Luke 9:54-56

See Curse, cursing

Imprisonment—*physical confinement in jail*

A. *Of Old Testament persons:*

Joseph ... Gen. 39:20
Simeon ... Gen. 42:19, 24
Samson ... Judg. 16:21, 25
Jehoiachin ... 2 Kin. 25:27-29
Micaiah ... 2 Chr. 18:26
Jeremiah ... Jer. 32:2, 8, 12

B. *Of New Testament persons:*

John the Baptist ... Mark 6:17-27
Apostles ... Acts 5:18
Peter ... Acts 12:4
Paul and Silas ... Acts 16:24
Paul ... Acts 23:10, 18
John ... Rev. 1:9

See Prisoners

Improvement—*a betterment*

Expressed by:

Growth ... 1 Pet. 2:2
Addition ... 2 Pet. 1:5-11
Press on ... Phil. 3:13-15

Improvidence—*wasting present possession*

Material things ... Luke 15:11-13
Spiritual things ... Luke 12:16-23
Eternal things ... Luke 16:19-31

Impure—*ritually unclean; mixed with foreign elements*

Things impure:

Discharge ... Lev. 15:30
Hands ... Mark 7:2
Person ... Eph. 5:5
Sons of Israel ... Lev. 16:16
Nations ... Ezra 6:21

SUBJECT — REFERENCE

Impurity (see Unclean)

Imputation—*counting or crediting something to another*

A. *Described as charging:*
- Evil to an innocent person — Philem. 18
- Evil to an evil person — Lev. 17:4
- Good to a good person — Ps. 106:30, 31

B. *Of Adam's sin to the race:*
- Based on the fall — Gen. 3:1-19
- Explained fully — Rom. 5:12-21
- The wider implications of — Rom. 8:20-23

C. *Of the believer's sin to Christ:*
- Our iniquity laid on Him — Is. 53:5, 6
- Made to be sin for us — 2 Cor. 5:21
- Became a curse for us — Gal. 3:13
- Takes away our sins — John 1:29; Heb. 9:28

D. *Of Christ's righteousness to the believer:*
- Negatively stated — Rom. 4:6-8
- Positively affirmed — Rom. 10:4-10
- Explained graphically — Luke 15:22-24
- God justifies the ungodly — Rom. 5:18, 19
- Christ becomes our righteousness — 1 Cor. 1:30
- We become the righteousness of God in Him — 2 Cor. 5:21
- Illustrated by Abraham's faith — Rom. 4:3

See Justification

Imrah—*He* (God) *resists*
- Son of Zophah — 1 Chr. 7:36

Imri—*eloquent*
1. Son of Bani — 1 Chr. 9:4
2. Father of Zaccur — Neh. 3:2
3. May be Amariah in — Neh. 11:4

Inability (see Impossibilities)

Incarnation of Christ

A. *Foreshadowed by:*
- Angel — Josh. 5:13-15
- Prophecies — Is. 7:14

B. *Described as:*
- Becoming flesh — John 1:14
- Born of woman — Gal. 4:4
- Coming in flesh — 1 John 4:2
- Appearing in flesh — 1 Tim. 3:16
- Our likeness — Rom. 8:3; Heb. 2:14
- Body — Heb. 10:5, 10; 1 John 1:1-3
- Dying in flesh — 1 Pet. 3:18; 1 Pet. 4:1

C. *Purposes of:*
- Reveal the Father — John 14:8-11
- Do God's will — Heb. 10:5-9
- Fulfill prophecy — Luke 4:17-21
- Die for our sins — 1 Pet. 3:18
- Fulfill all righteousness — Matt. 3:15
- Reconcile the world — 2 Cor. 5:18-21
- Become our high priest — Heb. 7:24-28
- Become our example — 1 Pet. 2:21-23

D. *Importance of:*
- Evidence Christ's deity — Rom. 9:3-5
- Confirm Christ's resurrection — Acts 2:24-32
- Mark of believers — 1 John 4:1-6

See Human nature of Christ

Incense—*sweet perfume*

A. *Offered:*
- By priests — Lev. 16:12, 13
- On the altar — Ex. 30:1-8
- On day of atonement — Lev. 16:12, 13
- According to strict formula — Ex. 30:34-36

B. *Illegal offering of:*
- Forbidden — Ex. 30:37, 38
- Excluded from certain offerings — Lev. 5:11
- Punished severely — Lev. 10:1, 2; 2 Chr. 26:16-21
- Among idolaters — Is. 65:3

C. *Typical of:*
- Worship — Ps. 141:2
- Prayer — Rev. 5:8; Rev. 8:3, 4
- Praise — Mal. 1:11
- Approved service — Eph. 5:2

D. *Purposes of:*
- Used in holy oil — Ex. 30:34-38
- Used in meal offerings — Lev. 2:1, 2, 15
- Excluded from certain offerings — Lev. 5:11
- Used in the showbread — Lev. 24:7
- Product of Arabia — Is. 60:6
- Presented to Jesus — Matt. 2:11
- Figurative of worship — Ps. 141:2

Incentives to good works
- Reap kindness — Hos. 10:12
- Remain — John 15:16
- Reap — Gal. 6:7-10

Incest—*sexual relations between persons related*

A. *Relations prohibited:*
- Same family — Lev. 18:6-12
- Grandchildren — Lev. 18:10
- Aunts and uncles — Lev. 18:12-14
- In-laws — Lev. 18:15, 16
- Near kin — Lev. 18:17, 18

B. *Punishment for:*
- Death — Lev. 20:11-17
- Childlessness — Lev. 20:19-21
- A curse — Deut. 27:20-23

C. *Examples of:*
- Lot—with his daughters — Gen. 19:30-38
- Reuben—with his father's concubine — Gen. 35:22

Inconsistency—*the non-agreement of two things*

Between:
- Criticism of ourselves and others — Matt. 7:3
- Legalism and human mercy — John 7:23
- Profession and reality — Luke 22:31-62
- Preaching and practice — Rom. 2:21-23
- Private and public convictions — Gal. 2:11-14
- Faith and works — James 2:14-26
- Profession and works — Titus 1:16

Inconstancy—*inability to stand firm in crisis*

A. *Causes of:*
- Little faith — Matt. 13:19-22
- Satan — Luke 22:31-34
- False teachers — Gal. 1:6-10
- Doubt — James 1:6-8
- Immaturity — 2 Pet. 1:5-10

B. *Remedies against:*
- Firm foundation — Matt. 7:24-27
- Strong faith — Hab. 3:16-19
- Full armor — Eph. 6:10-20

Incontinency—*uncontrolled indulgence of the passions*

A. *Expressed in:*
- Unbridled sexual morals — Ex. 32:6, 18, 25
- Abnormal sexual desires — 2 Sam. 13:1-15
- Unnatural sexual appetites — Gen. 19:5-9; Rom. 1:26, 27

B. *Sources of:*
- Lust — 1 Pet. 4:2, 3
- Satan — 1 Cor. 7:5
- Apostasy — 2 Tim. 3:3

Increase—*to become more abundant*

A. *Used literally of:*
- Descendants — 1 Sam. 2:33
- Knowledge — Dan. 12:4

B. *Used spiritually of:*
- Messiah's kingdom — Is. 9:7
- Wisdom — Luke 2:52
- Faith — Luke 17:5
- Esteem — John 3:30
- God's Word — Acts 6:7
- Spiritual fruit — 2 Cor. 9:10
- Knowledge of God — Col. 1:10
- Love — 1 Thess. 4:9, 10
- Ungodliness — 2 Tim. 2:16

Incredulity—*an unwillingness to believe*

Characterized by:
- Exaggerated demand for evidence — John 20:24, 25
- Desire for more signs — Judg. 6:37-40
- Attempts to nullify plain evidence — John 9:13-41
- Blindness of mind — Acts 28:22-29

Indecency
- Noah guilty of — Gen. 9:21-23
- Israelites sin in — Ex. 32:25
- Forbidden, to priests — Ex. 20:26
- Michal rebukes David for — 2 Sam. 6:20-23
- Men committing — Rom. 1:27

Indecision—*inability to decide between vital issues*

A. *Manifested in, mixing:*
- Truth and idolatry — 1 Kin. 18:21
- Duty and compromise — John 19:12-16
- Holiness and sin — Gal. 5:1-7
- Faith and works — Gal. 3:1-5

B. *Results in:*
- Spiritual unfitness — Luke 9:59-62
- Instability — James 1:6-8
- Sinful compromise — 2 Cor. 6:14-18
- Spiritual defeat — Rom. 6:16-22
- Spiritual deadness — Rev. 3:15-17

C. *Examples of:*
- Israel at Kadesh — Num. 13:26-33
- Joshua at Ai — Josh. 7:6-10
- David at Keilah — 1 Sam. 23:1-5
- Pilate — Matt. 27:11-24
- Felix — Acts 24:25, 26

See Inconstancy

Independence—*control of one's affairs apart from outside influences*

A. *Virtues of:*
- Freedom of action — Gen. 14:22-24
- Responsibility — John 9:21, 23

B. *Evils of:*
- Arbitrary use of authority — 1 Sam. 14:24-45
- Selfishness — 1 Sam. 25:1-11
- Mismanagement — Luke 15:12-16
- Arrogance — 3 John 9, 10

India
- Eastern limit of Persian Empire — Esth. 1:1

Indictment—*formal accusation for a crime*

A. *For real crimes:*
- Korah's company — Num. 16:1-50
- Achan — Josh. 7:1-26
- Baal worshipers — 1 Kin. 18:19-42
- David — 2 Sam. 12:1-14
- Ananias — Acts 5:1-10

B. *For supposed crimes:*
- Certain tribes — Josh. 22:10-34
- Naboth — 1 Kin. 21:1-16
- Three Hebrew men — Dan. 3:1-28
- Jews — Ezra 5:3-17; Esth. 3:8, 9
- Christ — Matt. 26:61-65
- Stephen — Acts 6:11, 13
- Paul — Acts 17:7; Acts 16:20, 21

Indifference—*not concerned for or against something*

A. *Characteristic of:*
- Unbelievers — Luke 17:26-30
- Backsliders — Rev. 3:15, 16

B. *As a good feature concerning, worldly:*
- Comforts — Phil. 4:11-13
- Applause — Gal. 1:10
- Traditions — Col. 2:16-23

C. *As a bad feature:*
- Inhumanitarianism — Luke 10:30-32
- In the use of one's talents — Luke 19:20-26
- Moral callousness — Matt. 27:3, 4
- Religious unconcern — Acts 18:12-16

Indignation—*boiling wrath against something sinful*

A. *God's:*
- Irresistible — Nah. 1:6
- Victorious — Hab. 3:12
- Poured out — Zeph. 3:8
- Toward His enemies — Is. 66:14
- On Israel — Deut. 29:28
- Against Edom forever — Mal. 1:4
- Angels, instruments of — Ps. 78:49
- On believers — Job 10:17
- Will hide His own from — Is. 26:20

SUBJECT — REFERENCE

Entreated, on the wicked ... Ps. 69:24
As punishment ... Rom. 2:8

B. *Man's against:*

Others ... Esth. 5:9
Jews ... Neh. 4:1
Christ ... Luke 13:14
Christians ... Acts 5:17

Indignities suffered by Christ

A. *Against His body:*

Spit on ... Matt. 26:67
Struck ... John 18:22, 23
Crowned with thorns ... Matt. 27:29
Crucified ... Matt. 27:31-35

B. *Against His person:*

Called guilty without a trial ... John 18:30, 31
Mocked and derided ... Matt. 27:29, 31, 39-44
Rejected in favor of a murderer ... Matt. 27:16-21
Crucified between two men ... John 19:18

Indiscrimination—*showing lack of distinction in*

Devastation ... Is. 24:1-4
Judgment ... Ezek. 18:1-32
God's providences ... Matt. 5:45

Indulge—*to yield to desires*

Fleshly desires ... Eph. 2:3
Corrupt desires ... 2 Pet. 2:10
Gross immorality ... Jude 7

Indulgence—*a kindness often misused*

Parental ... 1 Sam. 3:11-14
Kingly ... 2 Sam. 13:21-39
Priestly ... Judg. 17:1-13

Industry—*diligence in one's work*

A. *Characteristics of:*

Established ... Gen. 2:15
Commanded ... 1 Thess. 4:11
Commendable ... Prov. 27:23-27
Done willingly ... Prov. 31:13
Mark of wisdom ... Prov. 10:5
Suspended on Sabbath ... Ex. 20:10
Neglect of, rebuked ... 2 Thess. 3:10-12

B. *Necessity of:*

Our needs ... 1 Thess. 2:9
Needs of others ... Acts 20:35
Faithful witness ... 1 Tim. 5:8

C. *Blessings of:*

Wealth ... Prov. 10:4, 5
Praise ... Prov. 31:28, 31
Food sufficient ... Prov. 12:11
Will rule ... Prov. 12:24

Indwelling, of believers

A. *By Christ:*

Through faith ... Eph. 3:14-19
Mystery ... Col. 1:27

B. *Spirit:*

Every believer ... Rom. 8:9-11
Body, a temple of God ... 1 Cor. 3:16

Infant salvation

Suggested by scripture ... Matt. 18:3-5, 10; Matt. 19:14

Infants

A. *Acts performed upon:*

Naming ... Ruth 4:17
Blessing ... Luke 1:67, 76-79
Circumcision ... Luke 2:21

B. *Capacity to:*

Believe ... Matt. 18:6
Know the Scriptures ... 2 Tim. 3:15
Receive training ... Eph. 6:4
Worship in God's house ... 1 Sam. 1:24, 28

C. *Murder of:*

By Pharaoh ... Ex. 1:16
By Herod the Great ... Matt. 2:16-18
In war ... Num. 31:17

Infidelity—*unbelief in God's revelation*

A. *Causes of:*

Unregenerate heart ... Rom. 2:5
Hatred of the light ... John 3:19-21
Spiritual blindness ... 1 Cor. 2:8, 14
Self-trust ... Is. 47:10, 11
Unbelief ... Acts 6:10-15
Inveterate prejudice ... Acts 7:54, 57
Worldly wisdom ... 1 Cor. 1:18-22

B. *Manifested in:*

Rejecting God's Word ... 2 Pet. 3:3-5
Scoffing at God's servants ... 2 Chr. 30:6, 10
Hiding under lies ... Is. 28:15
Living without God ... Job 22:13-17
Using derisive words ... Matt. 12:24
Doubting God's righteousness ... Ps. 10:11, 13
Calling religion worthless ... Mal. 3:14

C. *Punishment of:*

Eternal separation from God ... 2 Thess. 1:8, 9
God's wrath ... 1 Thess. 2:14-16
Hell ... Luke 16:23-31
Severe punishment ... Heb. 10:28, 29

D. *Remedies against:*

Remember the end ... Ps. 73:16-28
Trust when you can't explain ... Job 2:9, 10
Stand upon the Word ... Matt. 4:3-11
Use God's armor ... Eph. 6:10-19
Grow spiritually ... 2 Pet. 1:4-11

Infinite—*extending immeasurably*

God's understanding ... Ps. 147:5

Infirmities—*weaknesses of our human nature*

A. *Kinds of:*

Sickness or disease ... Matt. 8:17
Imperfections of the body ... 2 Cor. 11:30
Moral defects ... Rom. 8:26

B. *Our duties with reference to:*

Rejoice in ... 2 Cor. 12:10
Help those afflicted with ... Rom. 15:1; Gal. 6:1
Not to despise in others ... Gal. 4:13, 14
Be sympathetic concerning ... Heb. 5:2, 3; Heb. 7:27, 28
Make us humble ... Rom. 6:19
Come to Jesus with ... Heb. 4:15, 16
Serve God more, if without ... Josh. 14:10-14

Influence—*that invisible force in one's personality that causes others to act*

Christians, should be:

As salt ... Matt. 5:13
As light ... Matt. 5:14-16; Phil. 2:15
As examples ... 1 Thess. 1:7, 8
Beneficial to spouse ... 1 Pet. 3:1, 2; 1 Cor. 7:14, 16
Above criticism ... 1 Cor. 8:10-13
Honorable ... 1 Tim. 6:1
Permanent ... Heb. 11:4
Beneficial to others ... 1 Pet. 2:11, 12
Without reproach ... Phil. 2:15, 16

Ingenuity—*skill shown in unusual contrivances*

Of God ... Job 38:4-41; Ps. 139:13-16
Of man ... Ex. 35:30-33; Ex. 2:1-9; Gen. 27:7-29

Ingratitude—*unthankfulness for blessings received*

A. *Characteristics of:*

Inconsiderate ... Deut. 32:6, 7
Unreasonable ... Jer. 2:5-7
Unnatural ... Is. 1:2, 3
Ungrateful ... Jer. 5:7-9, 24

B. *Causes of:*

Prosperity ... Deut. 6:10-12
Self-sufficiency ... Deut. 8:12-18
Forgetfulness ... Luke 17:12-18
Fear ... 1 Sam. 23:5, 12
Greed ... 1 Sam. 25:4-11
Pride ... Dan. 5:18-20

C. *Attitudes toward:*

Acknowledged ... 1 Sam. 24:17-19
Abused ... 2 Chr. 24:22
Revealed ... 1 Sam. 23:5-12
Forgiven by kindness ... 1 Sam. 25:14-35
Long remembered ... Deut. 25:17-19
Overcome by faithfulness ... Gen. 31:38-42

D. *Examples of:*

Moses by Israel ... Ex. 17:1-3
Gideon by Israel ... Judg. 8:33-35
God by Saul ... 1 Sam. 15:16-23
God by David ... 2 Sam. 12:7-14
Jeremiah by Judah ... Jer. 18:19, 20
God by the world ... Rom. 1:21

Inheritance, earthly

A. *Among Israelites:*

God the owner ... Lev. 25:23, 28
Possessed by families ... Num. 27:4, 7
Law of transmission ... Num. 27:8-11
If sold, restored in year of jubilee ... Lev. 25:25-34
Must remain in tribe ... Num. 36:6-10
Repossessed by kinsman ... Ruth 4:3-5, 10

B. *General characteristics of:*

From fathers ... Prov. 19:14
Uncertain use ... Eccl. 2:18, 19
Object of seizure ... 1 Kin. 21:3, 4; Matt. 21:38
Squandered ... Luke 15:11-13
Foolish not blessed ... Prov. 11:29
Descendants blessed ... Ps. 25:12, 13

See Heirs, natural

Inheritance of Israel

A. *Basic features of:*

Lord, Israel's ... Deut. 9:26, 29
Land promised to Abraham's seed ... Gen. 15:7-18
Limits defined ... Gen. 15:18-21
Limits fulfilled ... 1 Kin. 4:21, 24
Possession of, based on obedience ... 2 Kin. 21:12-15
Blessed by the Lord ... Deut. 15:4
Tribes destroyed from ... Deut. 20:16-18
Possessed by degrees ... Ex. 23:29-31
Apportioned ... Josh. 13:7-33
Tribes encouraged to possess ... Josh. 18:1-10
Levites excluded from ... Num. 18:20-24
Lost by sin ... Ps. 79:1
Restored after the captivity ... Neh. 11:20

B. *Figurative of:*

Messianic blessings ... Ps. 2:8
Call of the Gentiles ... Is. 54:3
Elect remnant ... Is. 65:8, 9
Eternal possessions ... Is. 60:21

Inheritance, spiritual

A. *Objects of:*

Kingdom ... Matt. 25:34
Eternal life ... Matt. 19:29
Promises ... Heb. 6:12
Blessing ... 1 Pet. 3:9
All things ... Rev. 21:7
Glory ... Prov. 3:35

B. *Nature of:*

Sealed by the Spirit ... Eph. 1:13, 14
Received from the Lord ... Col. 3:24
Results from Christ's death ... Heb. 9:15
Depends on belief ... Gal. 3:18, 22
Incorruptible ... 1 Pet. 1:4
Final, in heaven ... 1 Pet. 1:4

C. *Restrictions upon, only:*

For the righteous ... 1 Cor. 6:9, 10
For the sanctified ... Acts 20:32
In Christ ... Eph. 1:11, 12
For the transformed ... 1 Cor. 15:50-53

See Heirs, spiritual

Inhospitality—*unwillingness to entertain strangers*

Edomites ... Num. 20:17-21
Sihon ... Num. 21:22, 23
Gibeah ... Judg. 19:15
Nabal ... 1 Sam. 25:10-17
Samaritans ... Luke 9:53
Diotrephes ... 3 John 10
Penalty for ... Deut. 23:3, 4; Luke 10:10-16

Iniquity—*the depth of sin*

A. *Sources of:*

Heart ... Ps. 41:6; Matt. 23:28

B. *Effects upon man:*

Insatiable appetite for ... Ezek. 7:16, 19
Perversion ... Ezek. 9:9

C. *God's attitude toward:*

Cannot look on ... Hab. 1:13
Does not do ... Zeph. 3:5
Remembers and punishes ... Jer. 14:10
Visits on children ... Ex. 34:7

SUBJECT ... REFERENCE

- Pardons and subdues ... Mic. 7:18, 19
- Takes away from us ... Zech. 3:4
- Lays upon the Messiah ... Is. 53:5, 6, 11
- Remembers no more ... Heb. 8:12

D. *Christ's relation to:*

- Bears our ... Is. 53:5, 6, 11
- Makes reconciliation for ... Dan. 9:24
- Redeems us ... Titus 2:14

E. *Believer's relation to:*

- Will declare it ... Ps. 38:18
- Confesses ... Neh. 9:2
- Prays for pardon of ... Ps. 25:11
- Forgiven of ... Ps. 32:5
- Must depart from ... 2 Tim. 2:19
- Protection from ... Ps. 125:3
- Separation from God ... Is. 59:2
- Prays for freedom from ... Ps. 119:133
- Hindrance to prayer ... Ps. 66:18

F. *Punishment for:*

- Wanderings ... Num. 14:34
- Loss of strength ... Ps. 31:10
- Destruction ... Gen. 19:15
- Captivity ... Ezra 9:7
- Death ... Ezek. 18:24, 26
- Less than deserved ... Ezra 9:13
- Remembered forever ... 1 Sam. 3:13, 14
- In hell ... Ezek. 32:27

Injustice—*that which violates another's rights*

A. *Examples of, among men:*

- Laban's treatment of Jacob ... Gen. 31:36-42
- Saul's treatment of:
  - Priests ... 1 Sam. 22:15-23
  - David ... 1 Sam. 24:8-22; 1 Sam. 26:14-25
- David's treatment of Uriah ... 2 Sam. 12:1-12
- Irijah's treatment of Jeremiah ... Jer. 37:11-21

B. *Charges made against God for His:*

- Choice ... Num. 16:1-14
- Inequality ... Ezek. 18:25
- Partiality ... Rom. 9:14
- Delay ... Rev. 6:10

C. *Punishment on executed:*

- Severely ... 1 Sam. 15:32, 33
- Swiftly ... Esth. 7:9, 10
- According to prophecy ... 1 Kin. 22:34-38

See Just, justice

Ink—*a writing fluid*

- Used for writing a book ... Jer. 36:18
- Used in letter writing ... 2 John 12; 3 John 13

Inkhorn—*a case for pens and ink*

- Writer's tool ... Ezek. 9:2, 3

Inn—*a shelter providing lodging for travelers*

- Lodging place ... Jer. 9:2
- Place for rest ... Luke 2:7

Inner group

- At girl's bedside ... Mark 5:35-40
- At Christ's transfiguration ... Mark 9:2
- In Gethsemane ... Matt. 26:36, 37

Inner man—*man's genuine identity*

- Often hidden ... Matt. 23:27, 28
- Seen by God ... 1 Sam. 16:7
- Strengthened ... Eph. 3:16

Inner natures, conflict of

A. *Sin nature:*

- Called flesh ... Rom. 8:5
- Called old self ... Col. 3:9
- Corrupt and deceitful ... Eph. 4:22
- Works of ... Gal. 5:19-21
- Cannot please God ... Rom. 8:8
- To be mortified ... Col. 3:5

B. *New nature:*

- By Spirit's indwelling ... 1 Cor. 3:16
- Strengthened by Spirit ... Eph. 3:16
- Called inward man ... 2 Cor. 4:16
- Called new man ... Col. 3:10
- Fruits of ... Gal. 5:22, 23

C. *Conflict:*

- Called warfare ... Rom. 7:19-23; Gal. 5:17

D. *Victory:*

- Recognize source ... James 1:14-16

SUBJECT ... REFERENCE

- Realize former condition ... Eph. 2:1-7
- Put off former conversation ... Eph. 4:22
- Make no provision ... Rom. 13:14
- Complete surrender to God ... Rom. 12:1, 2
- Spiritual food ... 1 Pet. 2:1, 2

Innocence—*freedom from guilt or sin*

A. *Loss of, by:*

- Disobedience ... Rom. 5:12
- Idolatry ... Ps. 106:34-39

B. *Kinds of:*

- Absolute ... 2 Cor. 5:21
- Legal ... Luke 23:4
- Moral ... Josh. 22:10-34
- Spiritual ... 2 Pet. 3:14

C. *Of Christ:*

- In prophecy ... Is. 53:7-9
- In type ... 1 Pet. 1:19
- In reality ... 1 Pet. 3:18
- By examination ... Luke 23:13-22
- By testimony ... Acts 13:28

Innocents, massacre of:

- Mourning foretold ... Jer. 31:15
- After Jesus' birth ... Matt. 2:16-18

Innumerable—*uncounted multitude*

- Evils ... Ps. 40:12
- Animal life ... Ps. 104:25
- Descendants ... Heb. 11:12
- People ... Luke 12:1
- Angels ... Heb. 12:22

Inquiry—*a consulting or seeking for counsel*

- By Israel ... Ex. 18:15
- With ephod ... 1 Sam. 23:9, 11
- Unlawful method ... 1 Sam. 28:6, 7
- Through prayer ... James 1:5; 2 Cor. 12:7-9

Insanity—*mental derangement*

A. *Characteristics of:*

- Abnormal behavior ... Dan. 4:32-34
- Self-destruction ... Matt. 17:14-18
- Distinct from demon possession ... Matt. 4:24

B. *Figurative of:*

- Moral instability ... Jer. 25:15-17; Jer. 51:7
- God's judgment ... Zech. 12:4

Inscription—*a statement written or engraved*

- On Christ's cross ... John 19:19-22
- On an altar ... Acts 17:23
- Roman coin ... Mark 12:16

Insects of the Bible

A. *Characteristics of:*

- Created by God ... Gen. 1:24, 25
- Some clean ... Lev. 11:21, 22
- Some unclean ... Lev. 11:23, 24
- Fed by God ... Ps. 104:25, 27

B. *List of:*

- Ant ... Prov. 6:6
- Bee ... Judg. 14:8
- Beetle ... Lev. 11:22
- Cankerworm ... Joel 1:4
- Caterpillar ... Ps. 78:46
- Flea ... 1 Sam. 24:14
- Fly ... Eccl. 10:1
- Gnat ... Matt. 23:24
- Grasshopper ... Lev. 11:22
- Hornet ... Deut. 7:20
- Horseleech ... Prov. 30:15
- Locust ... Ex. 10:4
- Moth ... Is. 50:9
- Spider ... Prov. 30:28
- Worms ... Ex. 16:20

C. *Illustrative of:*

- Design in nature ... Prov. 30:24-28
- Troubles ... Ps. 118:12
- Insignificance ... 1 Sam. 24:14
- Desolation ... Joel 1:4
- Appetite ... Prov. 30:15
- Transitoriness ... Is. 51:8; Matt. 6:20
- Vast numbers ... Judg. 6:5

Insecurity—*a state of anxiety about earthly needs*

A. *Descriptive of:*

- Wicked ... Ps. 37:1, 2, 10

SUBJECT ... REFERENCE

- Riches ... 1 Tim. 6:17
- Those trusting in themselves ... Luke 12:16-21

B. *Cure of:*

- Steadfast of mind ... Is. 26:3
- Rely upon God's promises ... Ps. 37:1-26
- Remember God's provision ... Phil. 4:9-19
- Put God first ... Matt. 6:25-34

Insensibility—*deadness of spiritual life*

A. *Kinds of:*

- Physical ... Judg. 19:26-29
- Spiritual ... Jer. 5:3, 21
- Judicial ... Acts 28:25-28

B. *Causes of:*

- Seared conscience ... 1 Tim. 4:2
- Spiritual ignorance ... Eph. 4:18, 19
- Wanton pleasure ... 1 Tim. 5:6

Insincerity—*hypocritical deceitfulness*

A. *Manifested in:*

- Mock ceremonies ... Is. 58:3-6
- Unwilling preaching ... Jon. 4:1-11
- Trumped-up questions ... Matt. 22:15-22
- Boastful pretentions ... Luke 22:33

B. *Those guilty of:*

- Hypocrites ... Luke 11:42-47
- False teachers ... Gal. 6:12, 13
- Immature Christians ... 1 Cor. 4:17-21

See Hypocrisy

Insomnia—*inability to sleep*

A. *Causes of:*

- Excessive work ... Gen. 31:40
- Worry ... Esth. 6:1
- Dreams ... Dan. 2:1
- Conscience ... Dan. 6:9, 18

B. *Cure of:*

- Trust ... Ps. 3:5, 6
- Peacefulness ... Ps. 4:8
- Confidence ... Ps. 127:1, 2
- Obedience ... Prov. 6:20-22

Inspiration of the Scriptures

A. *Expressed by:*

- "Thus saith the Lord" ... Jer. 13:1
- "The word of the Lord came" ... 1 Kin. 16:1
- "It is written" ... Rom. 10:15
- "As the Holy Spirit saith" ... Heb. 3:7
- "According to the Scripture" ... James 2:8
- "My words in thy mouth" ... Jer. 1:9

B. *Described as:*

- Inspired by God ... 2 Tim. 3:16
- Moved by the Holy Spirit ... 2 Pet. 1:21
- Christ-centered ... Luke 24:27; 2 Cor. 13:3

C. *Modes of:*

- Various ... Heb. 1:1
- Inner impulse ... Judg. 13:25; Jer. 20:9
- A voice ... Rev. 1:10
- Dreams ... Dan. 7:1
- Visions ... Ezek. 11:24, 25

D. *Proofs of:*

- Fulfilled prophecy ... Jer. 28:15-17; Luke 24:27-45
- Miracles attesting ... Ex. 4:1-9; 2 Kin. 1:10-14
- Teachings supporting ... Deut. 4:8; Ps. 19:7-11

E. *Design of:*

- Reveal God's mysteries ... Amos 3:7; 1 Cor. 2:10
- Reveal the future ... Acts 1:16; 1 Pet. 1:10-12
- Instruct and edify ... Mic. 3:8; Acts 1:8
- Counteract distortion ... 2 Cor. 13:1-3; Gal. 1:6-11

F. *Results of Scriptures:*

- Unbreakable ... John 10:34-36
- Eternal ... Matt. 24:35
- Authoritative ... Matt. 4:4, 7, 10
- Trustworthy ... Ps. 119:160
- Verbally accurate ... Matt. 22:32, 43-46; Gal. 3:16

I

SUBJECT — REFERENCE

- Sanctifying — 2 Tim. 3:16, 17
- Effective — Jer. 23:29; 2 Tim. 2:15

See Word of God

Instability—*lack of firmness of convictions*

A. *Causes of:*
- Deception — Gal. 3:1; Col. 2:4-8
- Immaturity — 1 Tim. 3:6
- False teaching — Gal. 1:6-11; 2 Cor. 11:3, 4
- Lack of depth — Heb. 5:11-14
- Unsettled mind — Eph. 4:14; James 1:6-8

B. *Examples of:*
- Pharaoh — Ex. 10:8-20
- Israel — Judg. 2:17
- Solomon — 1 Kin. 11:1-8
- Disciples — John 6:66
- John Mark — Acts 15:38
- Galatians — Gal. 1:6

Instinct—*inbred characteristic of*
- Animals — Is. 1:3
- Birds — Jer. 8:7

Instruction—*imparting knowledge to others*

A. *Given by:*
- Parents — Deut. 6:6-25
- Priests — Deut. 24:8
- God — Jer. 32:33
- Pastors — Eph. 4:11
- Pedagogues — Neh. 8:7, 8
- Paraclete (the Holy Spirit) — John 14:26

B. *Means of:*
- Nature — Prov. 6:6-11
- Human nature — Prov. 24:30-34
- Law — Rom. 2:18
- Proverbs — Prov. 1:1-30
- Songs — Deut. 32:1-44
- History — 1 Cor. 10:1-11
- God's Word — 2 Tim. 3:15, 16

See Education; Teaching, teachers

Instrument—*a tool or implement*
- Tabernacle furniture — Num. 3:8
- For threshing — 2 Sam. 24:22
- For sacrifices — Ezek. 40:42
- Of iron — 2 Sam. 12:31
- Figurative of Jesus — Acts 9:15
- Body members, used as — Rom. 6:13

Insult—*to treat insolently*
- Ignored by King Saul — 1 Sam. 10:26, 27
- Job treated with — Job 30:1, 9, 10
- Children slain because of — 2 Kin. 2:23, 24
- Pharisees treat Jesus with — Matt. 12:24, 25
- Paul's reaction to — Acts 23:1-5
- Forbidden — 1 Pet. 3:8, 9

Insurrection—*rebellion against constituted authority*
- In Jerusalem — Ezra 4:19
- Absalom's miserable — 2 Sam. 18:33
- Attempted by Jews — Mark 15:7; Acts 18:12

Integrity—*moral uprightness*

A. *Manifested in:*
- Moral uprightness — Gen. 20:3-10
- Unselfish service — Num. 16:15
- Performing vows — Jer. 35:12-19
- Rejecting bribes — Acts 8:18-23
- Honest behavior — 2 Cor. 7:2

B. *Illustrated in:*
- Job's life — Job 2:3, 9, 10
- David's kingship — Ps. 7:8
- Nehemiah's service — Neh. 5:14-19
- Daniel's rule — Dan. 6:1-4
- Paul's ministry — 2 Cor. 4:2

Intemperance—*not restraining the appetites*

A. *Manifested in:*
- Drunkenness — Prov. 23:19-35
- Gluttony — Titus 1:12
- Immorality — Rom. 1:26, 27

B. *Evils of:*
- Puts the flesh first — Phil. 3:19
- Brings about death — 1 Sam. 25:36-38

See Drunkenness

Intention—*a fixed determination to do a specified thing*

A. *Good:*
- Commended but not allowed — 1 Kin. 8:17-19
- Planned but delayed — Rom. 15:24-28

B. *Evil:*
- Restrained by God — Gen. 31:22-31
- Turned to good by God — Gen. 45:4-8
- Overruled by God's providence — Esth. 9:23-25

C. *Of Christ:*
- Predicted — Ps. 40:6-8
- Announced — Matt. 20:18-28
- Misunderstood — Matt. 16:21-23
- Fulfilled — John 19:28-30
- Explained — Luke 24:25-47

Interbreeding—*crossbreed*

Forbidden:
- In animals, vegetables, cloth — Lev. 19:19

Intercession—*prayer offered in behalf of others*

A. *Purposes of:*
- Secure healing — James 5:14-16
- Avert judgment — Num. 14:11-21
- Insure deliverance — 1 Sam. 7:5-9
- Give blessings — Num. 6:23-27
- Obtain restoration — Job 42:8-10
- Encourage repentance — Rom. 10:1-4

B. *Characteristics of:*
- Pleading — Gen. 18:23-33
- Specific — Gen. 24:12-15
- Victorious — Ex. 17:9-12
- Very intense — Ex. 32:31, 32
- Quickly answered — Num. 27:15-23
- Confessing — 2 Sam. 24:17
- Personal — 1 Chr. 29:19
- Covenant pleading — Neh. 1:4-11
- Unselfish — Acts 7:60

C. *Examples of:*
- Moses — Ex. 32:11-13
- Joshua — Josh. 7:6-9
- Jehoshaphat — 2 Chr. 20:5-13
- Isaiah — 2 Chr. 32:20
- Daniel — Dan. 9:3-19
- Christ — John 17:1-26
- Paul — Col. 1:9-12

Intercourse—*copulation*

Kinds of, forbidden:
- With neighbor's wife — Lev. 18:20
- With animal — Lev. 18:23

Interest—*money charged on borrowed money*
- From poor man, forbidden — Ex. 22:25
- From a stranger, permitted — Deut. 23:19, 20
- Exaction of, unprofitable — Prov. 28:8
- Condemned as a sin — Ezek. 18:8-17
- Exaction of, rebuked — Neh. 5:1-13
- Reward for non-exaction of — Ps. 15:5
- Used to illustrate — Luke 19:23

Intermediate state—*the state of the believer between death and the resurrection*

A. *Described as:*
- Like sleep — John 11:11-14
- "Far better" — Phil. 1:21, 23
- "Present with the Lord" — 2 Cor. 5:6, 8

B. *Characteristics of:*
- Persons identifiable — Matt. 17:3
- Conscious and enjoyable — Ps. 17:15; Luke 16:25
- Unchangeable — Luke 16:26
- Without the body — 2 Cor. 5:1-4; Rev. 6:9
- Awaiting the resurrection — Phil. 3:20, 21; 1 Thess. 4:13-18

See Immortality

Interpretation—*making the unknown known*

A. *Things in need of:*
- Dreams — Gen. 41:15-36
- Languages — Gen. 42:23
- Writings — Dan. 5:7-31
- Scripture — Acts 8:30-35
- Tongues — 1 Cor. 12:10

B. *Agents of:*
- Jesus Christ — Luke 24:25-47
- Holy Spirit — 1 Cor. 2:11-16
- Angels — Luke 1:26-37
- Prophets and apostles — Eph. 3:2-11

Intimidation—*suggesting possible harm if one acts contrary to another's wishes*

Attitudes toward:
- Discovers its deceit — Neh. 6:5-13
- Do not yield — Jer. 26:8-16
- Go steadfastly on — Dan. 6:6-10
- Answer boldly — Amos 7:12-17

Intolerance—*active opposition to the views of others*

A. *Of the state against:*
- Jews — Esth. 3:12, 13
- Rival religions — Dan. 3:13-15
- Christian faith — Rev. 13:1-18

B. *Of the Jews against:*
- Their prophets — Matt. 23:31-35
- Christ — Luke 4:28-30
- Christians — Acts 5:40, 41
- Christianity — Acts 17:1-8

C. *Of the Church against:*
- Evil — 2 Cor. 6:14-18
- False teaching — 2 John 10, 11
- False religions — Gal. 1:6-9

D. *Manifestations of:*
- Prejudice — Acts 21:27-32
- Persecution — Acts 13:50
- Passion — Acts 9:1, 2, 21

Intrigue—*using hidden methods to cause another's downfall*

A. *Characteristics of:*
- Deceit — Gen. 27:6-23
- Plausible arguments — Judg. 9:1-6
- Subtle maneuvers — 2 Sam. 15:1-13
- False front — 2 Kin. 10:18-28
- Political trickery — Esth. 3:5-10

B. *Against Christ by:*
- Herod — Matt. 2:8, 12-16
- Satan — Matt. 4:3-11
- Jews — Luke 11:53, 54

Invention—*something new made by man*
- Product of wisdom — Prov. 8:12
- Products made by — Gen. 4:21, 22
- Skill required in — 2 Chr. 26:15
- Many made — Eccl. 7:29
- Of evil things — Ps. 106:39
- God provoked by — Ps. 106:29
- God takes vengeance on — Ps. 99:8

Investigation—*close examination*

A. *Characteristics of:*
- Involves research — Ezra 6:1-13
- Causes sought out — Eccl. 1:13, 17
- Claims checked — Num. 13:1-25
- Suspicions followed through — Josh. 22:10-30
- Historic parallels cited — Jer. 26:17-24

B. *Lack of:*
- Cause of later trouble — Josh. 9:3-23
- Productive of evil — Dan. 5:22, 23

Investments, spiritual
- In heavenly riches — Matt. 6:20
- Dividends later paid — 1 Tim. 6:19

Invisible—*the unseeable*
- God is — 1 Tim. 1:17
- Faith sees — Heb. 11:27

Invitations of the Bible

Come:
- And reason — Is. 1:18
- My people — Is. 26:20
- Buy wine and milk — Is. 55:1
- "Unto Me" — Is. 55:3
- And see — John 1:46
- And rest — Matt. 11:28
- After Me — Mark 1:17
- Take up the cross — Mark 10:21
- To the marriage — Matt. 22:4
- Everything is ready — Luke 14:17
- The blessed — Matt. 25:34
- Threefold — Rev. 22:17

Iphedeiah—*the Lord redeems*
- A descendant of Benjamin — 1 Chr. 8:1, 25

SUBJECT REFERENCE

Ira—*watchful*
1. Priest to David ....2 Sam. 20:26
2. One of David's mighty men ....2 Sam. 23:26; 1 Chr. 11:28
3. Ithrite ....2 Sam. 23:38; 1 Chr. 11:40

Irad—*fugitive*
Son of Enoch; grandson of Cain ....Gen. 4:18

Iram—*aroused*
Edomite chief ....Gen. 36:43; 1 Chr. 1:54

Iri—*urbane*
Benjamite ....1 Chr. 7:7

Irijah—*Jehovah sees*
Accuses Jeremiah of desertion ...Jer. 37:13, 14

Irnahash—*serpent city*
City of Judah ....1 Chr. 4:1, 12

Iron—*a useful metal*
A. *Features concerning:*
Used very early ....Gen. 4:22
Used in weapons ....Job 20:24
B. *Items made of:*
Armor ....2 Sam. 23:7
Axe ....2 Kin. 6:5
Bedstead ....Deut. 3:11
Chariot ....Josh. 17:16, 18
Gate.......................Acts 12:10
Gods ....Dan. 5:4, 23
Tools ....1 Kin. 6:7; 2 Sam. 12:31
Vessels....................Josh. 6:24
Weapons ....Job 20:24
Yokes......................Deut. 28:48
Implements................Gen. 4:22
Stylus.....................Job 19:24
C. *Figurative of:*
Affliction ....Deut. 4:20
Barrenness ....Deut. 28:23
Authority ....Ps. 2:9
Stubbornness ....Is. 48:4
Slavery....................Jer. 28:13, 14
Strength...................Dan. 2:33-41
Insensibility ....1 Tim. 4:2

Iron—*conspicuous*
City of Naphtali ....Josh. 19:38

Irony—*a pretense of ignorance*
Show contempt ....2 Sam. 6:20
Mockery ....1 Kin. 18:27
Rebuke distrust ....1 Kin. 22:15
Multiply transgression ....Amos 4:4
Mocked honor ....Matt. 27:29
Deflate the wise ....2 Cor. 11:19, 20

Irpeel—*God heals*
Town of Benjamin............Josh. 18:21, 27

Irreconcilable—*violators of agreements opposing compromise*
Characteristic of the last days ...2 Tim. 3:1, 3

Irrigation—*supply with water*
Not usually needed ....Deut. 11:11, 14
Source of....................Eccl. 2:5, 6
Figurative of spiritual life.......Is. 43:19, 20; Is. 58:11

Irritability—*the quality of easily being provoked to anger*
A. *Characteristics of:*
Quick temper ....1 Sam. 20:30-33
Morose disposition ....1 Sam. 25:3, 36-39
Hotheaded ....Gen. 49:6
Complaining...............Ex. 14:10-14
B. *Cure by God's:*
Love......................1 Cor. 13:4-7
Peace ....Phil. 4:7, 8
Spirit ....Gal. 5:22-26

Irritate—*anger of displeasure*
Of Hannah ....1 Sam. 1:6

Ir-shemesh—*city of the sun*
Danite city ....Josh. 19:41
Same as Beth-shemesh ....1 Kin. 4:9

Iru—*watchful*
Son of Caleb ....1 Chr. 4:15

Isaac—*laughter*
A. *Life of:*
Son of Abraham and Sarah ..Gen. 21:1-3
His birth promised ....Gen. 17:16-18
Heir of the covenant........Gen. 17:19, 21
Born and circumcised ....Gen. 21:1-8
Offered up as a sacrifice .....Gen. 22:1-19
Secures Rebekah as wife.....Gen. 24:1-67
Covenant confirmed to ......Gen. 26:2-5
Buries his father............Gen. 25:8, 9
Father of Esau and Jacob....Gen. 25:19-26
Prefers Esau ....Gen. 25:27, 28
Lives in Gerar ....Gen. 26:1, 6
Covenant reaffirmed with ....Gen. 26:2-5
Calls Rebekah his sister .....Gen. 26:7-11
Becomes prosperous ....Gen. 26:12-14
Trouble over wells ....Gen. 26:14-22
Covenant with Abimelech ...Gen. 26:23-33
Grieves over Esau ....Gen. 26:34, 35
Deceived by Jacob..........Gen. 27:1-25
Blesses his sons ....Gen. 27:26-40
Dies in his old age..........Gen. 35:28, 29
B. *Character of:*
Obedient ....Gen. 22:9
Peaceable ....Gen. 26:14-22
Thoughtful ....Gen. 24:63
Prayerful ....Gen. 25:21; Gen. 26:25
C. *Significance of:*
Child of promise ....Gal. 4:22, 23
Man of faith ....Heb. 11:9, 20
Type of believers ....Gal. 4:28-31
Ancestor of Christ ....Luke 3:34
Patriarch of Israel ....Ex. 32:13

Isaiah—*Jehovah is salvation*
A. *Life of:*
Son of Amoz ....Is. 1:1
Prophesies during reigns of Uzziah, Jotham, Ahaz and Hezekiah ....Is. 1:1
Contemporary of Amos and Hosea ....Amos 1:1; Hos. 1:1
Responds to prophetic call...Is. 6:1-13
Protests against policy of Ahaz ....Is. 7:1-25; Is. 8:1-22
Gives symbolic names to his sons ....Is. 8:1-4, 18
Walks naked and barefoot ...Is. 20:2, 3
Encourages Hezekiah ....2 Kin. 19:1-34
Warns Hezekiah of death ....2 Kin. 20:1
Instructs Hezekiah concerning his recovery ....2 Kin. 20:4-11
Upbraids Hezekiah for his acts ....2 Kin. 20:12-19
Writes Uzziah's biography ...2 Chr. 26:22
Writes Hezekiah's biography ....2 Chr. 32:32
B. *Messianic prophecies of:*
Christ's birth ....Is. 7:14; Is. 11:1-9; Matt. 1:22, 23
John's coming..............Is. 40:3; Matt. 3:3
Christ's mission ....Is. 61:1, 2; Luke 4:17-19
Christ's death ....Is. 53:1-12; Matt. 8:17; 1 Pet. 2:21-25
Christ as Servant ....Is. 42:1-4; Matt. 12:17-21
Gospel invitation ....Is. 55:1-13; Acts 13:34
Conversion of Gentiles ......Is. 11:10; Rom. 15:8-12
C. *Other prophecies of:*
Assyrian invasion...........Is. 8:1-4
Babylon's fall ....Is. 13:1-22
Devastation of Moab ....Is. 16:1-14
Tyre and Sidon condemned ....Is. 23:1-18
Destruction of Sennacherib ..Is. 37:14-38
Babylonian captivity ....Is. 39:3-7
D. *Other features concerning:*
Calls Christ Immanuel ......Is. 7:14
Names Cyrus ....Is. 45:1-3
Eunuch reads from ....Acts 8:27, 28, 30
Quoted in New Testament ....Rom. 9:27, 29; Rom. 10:16, 20, 21; Rom. 11:26, 27

Isaiah, the Book of—*a book of the Old Testament*
Call of Isaiah ....Is. 6
Promise of Immanuel ....Is. 7:10-25
Prophecies against nations......Is. 13—23
Historical section.............Is. 36—39
Songs of the servant ....Is. 42, 49—53
Future hope of Zion ....Is. 66

Iscah—*watchful*
Daughter of Haran ....Gen. 11:29

Iscariot, Judas—*man of Kerioth*
A. *Life of:*
Listed among the Twelve ....Mark 3:14, 19
Called Iscariot and a traitor ....Luke 6:16
Criticizes Mary.............John 12:3-5
Treasurer..................John 13:29
Identified as betrayer ....John 13:21-26
Sells out Christ.............Matt. 26:14-16
Betrays Christ with a kiss....Mark 14:10, 11, 43-45
Returns betrayal money .....Matt. 27:3-10
Commits suicide............Matt. 27:5
Goes to his own place.......Acts 1:16-20, 25
Better not to have been born.....................Matt. 26:24
B. *Described as:*
Thief ....John 12:6
Callous ....John 12:4-6
Deceitful ....Matt. 26:14-16
Possessed by Satan ....John 13:27
Son of perdition............John 17:12
Devil ....John 6:70, 71

Ishbah—*he praises*
Man of Judah ....1 Chr. 4:17

Ishbak—*leaving*
Son of Abraham and Keturah ...Gen. 25:2

Ishbi-benob—*my dwelling is at Nob*
Philistine giant ....2 Sam. 21:16, 17

Ish-bosheth—*man of shame*
One of Saul's sons ....2 Sam. 2:8
Made king ....2 Sam. 2:8-10
Offends Abner ....2 Sam. 3:7-11
Slain; but assassins executed ....2 Sam. 4:1-12

Ishhod—*man of majesty*
Manassite ....1 Chr. 7:18

Ishi, (I)—*salutary*
1. Son of Appaim............1 Chr. 2:31
2. Descendant of Judah........1 Chr. 4:20
3. Simeonite whose sons destroyed Amalekites ....1 Chr. 4:42
4. Manassite leader ....1 Chr. 5:23, 24

Ishi, (II)—*my husband*
Symbolic name of God.........Hos. 2:16, 17

Ishiah—*Jehovah will lend*
Son of Izrahiah ....1 Chr. 7:3

Ishijah—*Jehovah will lend*
Son of Harim.................Ezra 10:31

Ishma—*desolate*
Man of Judah ....1 Chr. 4:1, 3

Ishmael—*God hears*
1. Abram's son by Hagar ......Gen. 16:3, 4, 15
Angel foretells his name and character..................Gen. 16:11-16
Circumcised at 13 ....Gen. 17:25
Mocks at Isaac's feast ....Gen. 21:8, 9
Evidence of fleshly origin ....Gal. 4:22-31
Becomes an archer..........Gen. 21:20
Dwells in wilderness ....Gen. 21:21
Marries an Egyptian ....Gen. 21:21
Buries his father ....Gen. 25:9
Dies at age 137 ....Gen. 25:17
His generations ....Gen. 25:12-19
His descendants ....1 Chr. 1:29-31
2. Descendant of Jonathan .....1 Chr. 8:38
3. Father of Zebadiah ....2 Chr. 19:11
4. Military officer under Joash ....2 Chr. 23:1-3, 11
5. Son of Nethaniah; instigates murder of Gedaliah ....2 Kin. 25:22-25
6. Priest who divorced his foreign wife ....Ezra 10:22

I

SUBJECT REFERENCE

Ishmaelites—*descendants of Ishmael*

Settle at Havilah .... Gen. 25:17, 18
Joseph sold to .... Gen. 37:25-28
Sell Joseph to Potiphar .... Gen. 39:1
Wear golden earrings .... Judg. 8:22, 24
Become known as Arabians .... 2 Chr. 17:11

Ishmaiah—*Jehovah hears*

1. Gibeonite .... 1 Chr. 12:4
2. Tribal chief in Zebulun .... 1 Chr. 27:19

Ishmerai—*Jehovah keeps*

Benjamite .... 1 Chr. 8:18

Ishod—*man of majesty*

Manassite .... 1 Chr. 7:18

Ishpah—*firm, strong*

A Benjamite .... 1 Chr. 8:16

Ishpan—*he will hide*

Son of Shashak .... 1 Chr. 8:22, 25

Ish-tob—*man of Tob*

Small kingdom of Aram .... 2 Sam. 10:6, 8
Jephthah seeks asylum in .... Judg. 11:3, 5

Ishuah—*he is equal*

Son of Asher .... Gen. 46:17

Ishuai—*man of Jehovah*

1. Son of Asher and chief .... 1 Chr. 7:30
2. Son of Saul .... 1 Sam. 14:49

Island—*surrounded by water*

A. *Descriptive of:*

Coastal land of Palestine .... Is. 20:6
Land surrounded by water .... Is. 23:2
Remote regions .... Is. 42:10

B. *List of:*

Caphtor (Crete?) .... Jer. 47:4
Clauda .... Acts 27:16
Chios .... Acts 20:15
Coos .... Acts 21:1
Crete .... Acts 27:12
Cyprus .... Acts 11:19
Elishah .... Ezek. 27:7
Kittim (Cyprus) .... Jer. 2:10
Melita .... Acts 28:1, 7, 9
Patmos .... Rev. 1:9
Rhodes .... Acts 21:1
Samos .... Acts 20:15
Samothrace .... Acts 16:11
Syracuse .... Acts 28:12
Tyre .... Is. 23:1, 2

Ismachiah—*Jehovah will sustain*

Temple overseer .... 2 Chr. 31:13

Ispah—*to lay bear*

Benjamite .... 1 Chr. 8:16

Israel—*God strives*

A. *Used literally of:*

Jacob .... Gen. 32:28
Descendants of Jacob .... Gen. 49:16, 28
Ten northern tribes (in contrast to Judah) .... 1 Sam. 11:8
Restored nation after exile .... Ezra 9:1

B. *Used spiritually of:*

Messiah .... Is. 49:3
God's redeemed ones .... Rom. 9:6-13
True church .... Gal. 6:16

Israelites—*descendants of Israel* (Jacob)

A. *Brief history of:*

Begin as a nation in Egypt .... Ex. 1:12, 20
Afflicted in Egypt .... Ex. 1:12-22
Moses becomes their leader .... Ex. 3:1-22
Saved from plagues .... Ex. 9:4, 6, 26
Expelled from Egypt .... Ex. 12:29-36
Pass through Red Sea .... Ex. 14:1-31
Receive Law at Sinai .... Ex. 19:1-25
Sin at Sinai .... Ex. 32:1-35
Rebel at Kadesh .... Num. 13:1-33
Wander 40 years .... Num. 14:26-39
Cross Jordan .... Josh. 4:1-24
Conquer Canaan .... Josh. 12:1-24
Ruled by judges .... Judg. 2:1-23
Samuel becomes leader .... 1 Sam. 7:1-17
Seek to have a king .... 1 Sam. 8:1-22
Saul chosen king .... 1 Sam. 10:18-27
David becomes king .... 2 Sam. 2:1-4
Solomon becomes king .... 1 Kin. 1:28-40
Kingdom divided .... 1 Kin. 12:1-33
Israel (northern kingdom) carried captive .... 2 Kin. 17:5-23
Judah (southern kingdom) carried captive .... 2 Kin. 24:1-20
70 years in exile .... 2 Chr. 36:20, 21
Return after exile .... Ezra 1:1-5
Nation rejects Christ .... Matt. 27:20-27
Nation destroyed .... Luke 21:20-24
1 Thess. 2:14-16

B. *Blessed with:*

Great leaders .... Heb. 11:8-40
Inspired prophets .... 1 Pet. 1:10-12
God's oracles .... Rom. 3:2
Priesthood .... Rom. 9:3-5
The Law .... Gal. 3:16-25
Messianic promises .... Acts 3:18-26
Temple .... Heb. 9:1-10
Messiah .... Dan. 9:24-27
God's covenant .... Jer. 31:31-33
Regathering .... Is. 27:12
Jer. 16:15, 16

C. *Sins of:*

Idolatry .... Hos. 13:1-4
Hypocrisy .... Is. 1:11-14
Disobedience .... Jer. 7:22-28
Externalism .... Matt. 23:1-33
Unbelief .... Rom. 11:1-31
Works—righteousness .... Phil. 3:4-9

D. *Punishments upon:*

Defeat .... Lev. 26:36-38
Curses upon .... Deut. 28:15-46
Captivity .... Judg. 2:13-23
Destruction .... Luke 19:42-44
Dispersion .... Deut. 4:26-28
Blindness .... Rom. 11:25
Forfeiture of blessings .... Acts 13:42-49
Replaced by Gentiles .... Rom. 11:11-20

See Jews

Israel, the religion of

A. *History of:*

Call of Abraham .... Gen. 12:1-3
Canaan promised .... Gen. 15:18-21
Covenant at Sinai .... Ex. 20
Covenant at Shechem .... Josh. 24:1-28
Ark brought to Jerusalem .... 2 Sam. 6
Dedication of the Temple .... 1 Kin. 8:1-66
Reform movements .... 2 Kin. 23:4-14
2 Chr. 29:3-36
Destruction of Jerusalem .... Jer. 6
Restoration of the Law .... Neh. 8, 9

B. *Beliefs about God:*

Creator .... Gen. 1:1
Ps. 104:24
Sustainer of creation .... Ps. 104:27-30
Active in human affairs .... Deut. 26:5-15
Omniscient .... Ps. 139:1-6
Omnipresent .... Jer. 23:23, 24
Everlasting .... Ps. 90:2
Moral .... Ex. 34:6, 7

Issachar—*man of hire*

1. Jacob's fifth son .... Gen. 30:17, 18
2. Tribe of, descendants of Jacob's fifth son .... Num. 26:23, 24
Prophecy concerning .... Gen. 49:14, 15
Census at Sinai .... Num. 1:28, 29
On Gerizim .... Deut. 27:12
Inheritance of .... Josh. 19:17-23
Assists Deborah .... Judg. 5:15
At David's coronation .... 1 Chr. 12:32
Census in David's time .... 1 Chr. 7:1-5
Attended Hezekiah's Passover .... 2 Chr. 30:18
Prominent person of .... Judg. 10:1
3. Doorkeeper .... 1 Chr. 26:1, 5

Isshiah—*Jehovah exists*

1. Descendant of Issachar .... 1 Chr. 7:1, 3
Son of Izrahiah .... 1 Chr. 7:3
2. Mighty man of David .... 1 Chr. 12:1, 6
3. Kohathite Levite .... 1 Chr. 23:20
1 Chr. 24:25
4. Levite and family head .... 1 Chr. 24:21

Italy—*a peninsula of southern Europe*

Soldiers of, in Caesarea .... Acts 10:1
Jews expelled from .... Acts 18:2
Paul sails for .... Acts 27:1, 6
Christians in .... Acts 28:14

Itching ears—*descriptive of desire for something exciting*

Characteristic of the last days .... 2 Tim. 4:2, 3

Ithai—*with me* (is Jehovah)

Son of Ribai .... 1 Chr. 11:31
Also called Ittai .... 2 Sam. 23:29

Ithamar—*island of palms*

Youngest son of Aaron .... Ex. 6:23
Consecrated as priest .... Ex. 28:1
Duty entrusted to .... Ex. 38:21
Jurisdiction over Gershonites and Merarites .... Num. 4:21-33
Founder of Levitical family .... 1 Chr. 24:4-6

Ithiel—*God is with me*

1. Man addressed by Agur .... Prov. 30:1
2. Benjamite .... Neh. 11:7

Ithmah—*bereavement*

Moabite of David's mighty men .... 1 Chr. 11:46

Ithnan—*perennial*

Town in south Judah .... Josh. 15:23

Ithra—*excellence*

Israelite (or Ishmaelite); father of Amasa .... 2 Sam. 17:25
Called Jether .... 1 Kin. 2:5, 32

Ithran—*excellent*

1. Son of Dishon .... Gen. 36:26
2. Son of Zophah .... 1 Chr. 7:37
Same as Jether .... 1 Chr. 7:38

Ithream—*residue of the people*

Son of David .... 2 Sam. 3:2-5

Ithrite—*pre-eminence*

Family dwelling at Kirjath-jearim .... 1 Chr. 2:53
One of David's guard .... 2 Sam. 23:38

Itinerary, Israelites in Wilderness

Leave Egypt .... Ex. 12:29-36
Cross Red Sea .... Ex. 14:1-31
Bitter water sweetened .... Ex. 15:22-26
Manna in wilderness .... Ex. 16:1-36
Water from a rock .... Ex. 17:1-7
Defeat of Amalek .... Ex. 17:8-16
At Sinai .... Ex. 19:1-25
Depart Sinai .... Num. 10:33, 34
Lord sends quails .... Num. 11:1-35
Twelve spies .... Num. 13:1-33
Rebellion at Kadesh .... Num. 14:1-45
Korah's rebellion .... Num. 16:1-34
Aaron's rod .... Num. 17:1-13
Moses' sin .... Num. 20:2-13
Fiery serpents .... Num. 21:4-9
Balak and Balaam .... Num. 22:1—24:25
Midianites conquered .... Num. 31:1-24
Death of Moses .... Deut. 34:1-8
Accession of Joshua .... Deut. 34:9

Ittah-kazin—*time of a judge*

On border of Zebulun .... Josh. 19:13, 16

Ittai—*with me* (is Jehovah)

1. One of David's guard .... 2 Sam. 23:23-29
2. Native of Gath; one of David's commanders .... 2 Sam. 15:18-22

Ituraea—*pertaining to Jetur*

Ruled by Philip .... Luke 3:1

Ivah—*sky*

City conquered by the Assyrians .... Is. 37:13

Ivory—*the tusks of certain mammals*

Imported from Tharshish .... 1 Kin. 10:22
Imported from Chittim .... Ezek. 27:6, 15
Ahab's palace made of .... 1 Kin. 22:39
Thrones made of .... 1 Kin. 10:18
Beds made of .... Amos 6:4
Sign of luxury .... Amos 3:15
Figuratively used .... Song 5:14
Descriptive of wealth .... Ps. 45:8
Among Babylon's trade .... Rev. 18:12

SUBJECT — REFERENCE

Izhar—*shining*
Son of Kohath . . . Ex. 6:18, 21
Num. 3:19
Ancestor of the Izharites . . . Num. 3:27
1 Chr. 6:38

Izliah—*Jehovah delivers*
Son of Elpaal . . . 1 Chr. 8:18

Izrahiah—*Jehovah will shine*
Chief of Issachar . . . 1 Chr. 7:1, 3

Izrahite—*descendant of Zerah*
Applied to Shamhuth . . . 1 Chr. 27:8

Izri—*fashioner*
Leader of Levitical choir . . . 1 Chr. 25:11
Also called Zeri . . . 1 Chr. 25:3

Izziah—*Jehovah sprinkles*
One who divorced his foreign wife . . . Ezra 10:25

J

Jaakan, Jakan, Akan
Son of Ezer . . . 1 Chr. 1:42
Also called Akan . . . Gen. 36:27
Of Horite origin . . . Gen. 36:20-27
Tribe of, at Beeroth . . . Deut. 10:6
Dispossessed by Edomites . . . Deut. 2:12
Same as Benejaakan . . . Num. 33:31, 32

Jaakobah—*heel catcher*
Simeonite . . . 1 Chr. 4:36

Jaala, Jaalah—*wild she-goat*
Family head of exile returnees . . Ezra 2:56
Descendants of Solomon's servants . . . Neh. 7:57, 58

Jaalam
Son of Esau . . . Gen. 36:5, 18

Jaanai—*answerer*
Gadite chief . . . 1 Chr. 5:12

Jaare-oregim—*forests of weavers*
Father of Elhanan . . . 2 Sam. 21:19
Also called Jair . . . 1 Chr. 20:5

Jaasiel—*God makes*
1. One of David's mighty men . . . 1 Chr. 11:47
2. Son of Abner . . . 1 Chr. 27:21

Jaasu—*Jehovah makes*
Son of Bani; divorced foreign wife . . . Ezra 10:37

Jaazaniah—*Jehovah hearkens*
1. Military commander supporting Gedaliah . . . 2 Kin. 25:23
2. Rechabite leader . . . Jer. 35:3
3. Idolatrous Israelite elder . . . Ezek. 8:11
4. Son of Azur; seen in Ezekiel's vision . . . Ezek. 11:1

Jaaziah—*Jehovah strengthens*
Merarite Levite . . . 1 Chr. 24:26, 27

Jaaziel—*God strengthens*
Levite musician . . . 1 Chr. 15:18, 20

Jabal—*moving*
Son of Lamech; father of herdsmen . . . Gen. 4:20

Jabbok—*luxuriant river*
River entering the Jordan about 20 miles north of the Dead Sea . . . Num. 21:24
Scene of Jacob's conflict . . . Gen. 32:22-32
Boundary marker . . . Deut. 3:16

Jabesh—*dry*
1. Father of Shallum . . . 2 Kin. 15:10, 13, 14
2. Abbreviated name of Jabesh-gilead . . . 1 Sam. 11:1-10

Jabesh-gilead—*Jabesh of Gilead*
Consigned to destruction . . . Judg. 21:8-15
Saul struck the Ammonites here . . . 1 Sam. 11:1-11
Citizens of, rescue Saul's body . . 1 Sam. 31:11-13
David thanks citizens of . . . 2 Sam. 2:4-7

Jabez—*he makes sorrowful*
1. City of Judah . . . 1 Chr. 2:55
2. Man of Judah noted for his prayer . . . 1 Chr. 4:9, 10

Jabin—*He (God) perceives*
1. Canaanite king of Hazor; leads confederacy against Joshua . . . Josh. 11:1-14
2. Another king of Hazor; oppresses Israelites . . . Judg. 4:2
Defeated by Deborah and Barak . . . Judg. 4:3-24
Immortalized in poetry . . . Judg. 5:1-31

Jabneel—*built of God*
1. Town in north Judah . . . Josh. 15:11
Probably same as Jabneh . . . 2 Chr. 26:6
2. Town of Naphtali . . . Josh. 19:33

Jachan—*troubled*
Gadite chief . . . 1 Chr. 5:13

Jachin—*He (God) establishes*
1. Son of Simeon . . . Gen. 46:10
Family head . . . Num. 26:12
Called Jarib . . . 1 Chr. 4:24
2. Descendant of Aaron . . . 1 Chr. 24:1, 17
Representatives of . . . Neh. 11:10
3. One of two pillars in front of Solomon's Temple . . . 1 Kin. 7:21, 22

Jacinth—*a sapphire stone*
In high priest's breastplate . . . Ex. 28:19
Foundation stone . . . Rev. 21:20
Breastplates the color of . . . Rev. 9:17

Jacob—*supplanter*
Son of Isaac and Rebekah . . . Gen. 25:20-26
Hos. 12:3
Born in answer to prayer . . . Gen. 25:21
Rebekah's favorite . . . Gen. 25:27, 28
Obtains Esau's birthright . . . Gen. 25:29-34
Heb. 12:16
Obtains Isaac's blessing . . . Gen. 27:1-38
Hated by Esau . . . Gen. 27:41-46
Departs for Haran . . . Gen. 28:1-5
See heavenly ladder . . . Gen. 28:10-19
Makes a vow . . . Gen. 28:20-22
Meets Rachel and Laban . . . Gen. 29:1-14
Serves for Laban's daughters . . . Gen. 29:15-30
His children . . . Gen. 29:31-35
Requests departure from Laban . . . Gen. 30:25-43
Flees from Laban . . . Gen. 31:1-21
Overtaken by Laban . . . Gen. 31:22-43
Covenant with Laban . . . Gen. 31:44-55
Meets angels . . . Gen. 32:1, 2
Sends message to Esau . . . Gen. 32:3-8
Prays earnestly . . . Gen. 32:9-12
Sends gifts to Esau . . . Gen. 32:13-21
Wrestles with an angel . . . Gen. 32:22-32
Hos. 12:3, 4
Name becomes Israel . . . Gen. 32:32
Reconciled to Esau . . . Gen. 33:1-16
Erects altar at Shechem . . . Gen. 33:17-20
Trouble over Dinah . . . Gen. 34:1-31
Renewal at Bethel . . . Gen. 35:1-15
Buries Rachel . . . Gen. 35:16-20
List of 12 sons . . . Gen. 35:22-26
Buries Isaac . . . Gen. 35:27-29
His favoritism toward Joseph . . . Gen. 37:1-31
Mourns over Joseph . . . Gen. 37:32-35
Sends sons to Egypt for food . . . Gen. 42:1-5
Allows Benjamin to go . . . Gen. 43:1-15
Revived by good news . . . Gen. 45:25-28
Goes with family to Egypt . . . Gen. 46:1-27
Meets Joseph . . . Gen. 46:28-34
Meets Pharaoh . . . Gen. 47:7-12
Makes Joseph swear . . . Gen. 47:28-31
Blesses Joseph's sons . . . Gen. 48:1-22
Blesses his own sons . . . Gen. 49:1-28
Dies in Egypt . . . Gen. 49:29-33
Burial in Canaan . . . Gen. 50:1-14

Jacob
Father of Joseph, Mary's husband . . . Matt. 1:15, 16

Jacob's oracles—*blessings and curses on twelve tribes*
Recorded . . . Gen. 49:1-27

Jacob's well
Christ teaches a Samaritan woman . . . John 4:5-26

Jada—*knowing*
Grandson of Jerahmeel . . . 1 Chr. 2:26, 28, 32

Jadau—*praised*
Son of Nebo . . . Ezra 10:43

Jaddua—*known*
1. Chief layman who signs the document . . . Neh. 10:21
2. Levite who returns with Zerubbabel . . . Neh. 12:8, 11

Jadon—*he judges*
Meronothite worker . . . Neh. 3:7

Jael—*mountain goat*
Wife of Heber the Kenite . . . Judg. 4:17
Slays Sisera . . . Judg. 4:17-22
Praised by Deborah . . . Judg. 5:24-27

Jagur—*lodging place*
Town in south Judah . . . Josh. 15:21

Jah—*a poetic form of Jehovah*
Found only in poetry and in proper names . . . Ps. 68:4

Jahath—*comfort, revival*
1. Grandson of Judah . . . 1 Chr. 4:2
2. Great-grandson of Levi . . . 1 Chr. 6:20, 43
3. Son of Shimei . . . 1 Chr. 23:10
4. Son of Shelemoth . . . 1 Chr. 24:22
5. Merarite Levite . . . 2 Chr. 34:12

Jahaz—*a place trodden under foot*
Town in Moab at which Sihon was defeated . . . Num. 21:23
Assigned to Reubenites . . . Josh. 13:18
Levitical city . . . Josh. 21:36
Regained by Moabites . . . Is. 15:4
Same as Jahzah . . . 1 Chr. 6:78

Jahaziah—*Jehovah sees*
Postexilic returnee . . . Ezra 10:15

Jahaziel—*God sees*
1. Kohathite Levite . . . 1 Chr. 23:19
2. Benjamite warrior . . . 1 Chr. 12:4
3. Priest . . . 1 Chr. 16:6
4. Inspired Levite . . . 2 Chr. 20:14

Jahdai—*Jehovah leads*
Judahite . . . 1 Chr. 2:47

Jahdiel—*God makes glad*
Manassite chief . . . 1 Chr. 5:24

Jahdo—*union*
Gadite . . . 1 Chr. 5:14

Jahleel—*wait for God*
Son of Zebulun . . . Gen. 46:14
Family head . . . Num. 26:26

Jahleelites
Descendants of Jahleel . . . Num. 26:26

Jahmai—*may God protect*
Descendant of Issachar . . . 1 Chr. 7:1, 2

Jahzeel—*God divides*
Son of Naphtali . . . Gen. 46:24
Same as Jahziel . . . 1 Chr. 7:13

Jahzeelites
Descendants of Jahzeel . . . Num. 26:48

Jahzerah—*prudent*
Priest . . . 1 Chr. 9:12
Called Ahasai . . . Neh. 11:13

Jahziel—*God divides*
Son of Naphtali . . . 1 Chr. 7:13

Jailer—*one who guards a prison*
At Philippi, converted by Paul . . Acts 16:19-34

Jair—*he enlightens*
1. Manassite warrior . . . Num. 32:41
Deut. 3:14
Conquers towns in Gilead . . . Num. 32:41

SUBJECT REFERENCE

2. Eighth judge of Israel .... Judg. 10:3-5
3. Father of Mordecai, Esther's uncle .... Esth. 2:5
4. Father of Elhanan .... 1 Chr. 20:5
Called Jaare-oregim .... 2 Sam. 21:19

Jairite

Descendant of Jair, the Manassite .... 2 Sam. 20:26

Jairus—Greek form of "*Jair*"

Ruler of the synagogue; Jesus raises his daughter .... Mark 5:22-24, 35-43

Jakeh—*pious*

Father of Agur .... Prov. 30:1

Jakim—*He* (God) *raises up*

1. Descendant of Aaron .... 1 Chr. 24:1, 12
2. Benjamite .... 1 Chr. 8:19

Jalon—*passing the night*

Calebite, son of Ezra .... 1 Chr. 4:17

Jambres—*opposer*

Egyptian magician .... 2 Tim. 3:8
See Jannes and Jambres

James—*a form of Jacob*

1. Son of Zebedee .... Matt. 4:21
Fisherman .... Matt. 4:21
One of the Twelve .... Matt. 10:2
In business with Peter .... Luke 5:10
Called Boanerges .... Mark 3:17
Of fiery disposition .... Luke 9:52-55
Makes a contention .... Mark 10:35-45
One of inner circle .... Matt. 17:1
Sees the risen Lord .... John 21:1, 2
Awaits the Holy Spirit ...... Acts 1:13
Slain by Herod Agrippa ..... Acts 12:2
2. Son of Alphaeus; one of the Twelve .... Matt. 10:3, 4
Identified usually as "the less" .... Mark 15:40
Brother of Joses .... Matt. 27:56
3. Son of Joseph and Mary ..... Matt. 13:55, 56
Lord's brother .... Gal. 1:19
Rejects Christ's claim .... Mark 3:21
Becomes a believer .... Acts 1:13, 14
Sees the risen Lord .... 1 Cor. 15:7
Becomes moderator of Jerusalem Council .... Acts 15:13-23
Paul confers with him .... Gal. 2:9, 12
Wrote an epistle .... James 1:1
Brother of Jude .... Jude 1

James, the Epistle of—*a book of the New Testament*

Trials .... James 1:2-8
Temptation .... James 1:12-18
Doing the word .... James 1:19-25
Faith and works .... James 2:14-26
Patience .... James 5:7-11
Converting the sinner .... James 5:19, 20

Jamin—*the right hand*

1. Son of Simeon .... Gen. 46:10
Family head .... Ex. 6:14, 15
2. Man of Judah .... 1 Chr. 2:27
3. Postexilic Levite; interprets the law .... Neh. 8:7, 8

Jaminites

Descendants of Jamin .... Num. 26:12

Jamlech—*whom He* (God) *makes king*

Simeonite chief .... 1 Chr. 4:34

Janai—*answerer*

Gadite chief .... 1 Chr. 5:12

Jangling—*self-conceited talk against God*

Characteristic of false teachers .. 1 Tim. 1:6, 7
Translated also "babblings" ..... 1 Tim. 6:20

Jannai—*a form of John*

Ancestor of Christ .... Luke 3:23, 24

Jannes and Jambres

Two Egyptian magicians; oppose Moses .... 2 Tim. 3:8
Compare account .... Ex. 7:11-22

Janoah—*rest, quiet*

1. Town of Naphtali .... 2 Kin. 15:29
2. Border town of Ephraim ..... Josh. 16:6,7

Janum—*sleep*

Town near Hebron .... Josh. 15:53

Japheth—*widespreading*

One of Noah's three sons .... Gen. 5:32
Saved in the ark .... 1 Pet. 3:20
Receives Messianic blessing ..... Gen. 9:20-27
His descendants occupy Asia Minor and Europe .... Gen. 10:2-5

Japhia—*may He* (God) *cause to shine forth*

1. King of Lachish; slain by Joshua .... Josh. 10:3-27
2. One of David's sons .... 2 Sam. 5:13-15
3. Border town of Zebulun ..... Josh. 19:10, 12

Japhlet—*He* (God) *will deliver*

Asherite family .... 1 Chr. 7:32, 33

Japhleti

Unidentified tribe on Joseph's boundary .... Josh. 16:1, 3

Japho—*beautiful*

Hebrew form of Joppa .... Josh. 19:46

Jarah—*honeycomb*

Descendant of King Saul .... 1 Chr. 9:42
Called Jehoaddah .... 1 Chr. 8:36

Jareb—*he will contend*

Figurative description of Assyrian king .... Hos. 5:13

Jared—*descent*

Father of Enoch .... Gen. 5:15-20
Ancestor of Noah .... 1 Chr. 1:2
Ancestor of Christ .... Luke 3:37

Jaresiah—*Jehovah nourishes*

Benjamite head .... 1 Chr. 8:27

Jarha

Egyptian slave; marries master's daughter .... 1 Chr. 2:34-41

Jarib—*he contends*

1. Head of a Simeonite family .... 1 Chr. 4:24
Called Jachin .... Gen. 46:10
2. Man sent to search for Levites .... Ezra 8:16, 17
3. Priest who divorced his foreign wife .... Ezra 10:18

Jarmuth—*height*

1. Royal city of Canaan .... Josh. 10:3
King of, slain by Joshua ..... Josh. 10:3-27
Assigned to Judah .... Josh. 15:20, 35
Inhabited after exile .... Neh. 11:29
2. Town in Issachar assigned to the Levites .... Josh. 21:28, 29
Called Ramoth .... 1 Chr. 6:73
Called Remeth .... Josh. 19:21

Jaroah—*new moon*

Gadite chief .... 1 Chr. 5:14

Jashen—*sleeping*

Sons of, in David's bodyguard .. 2 Sam. 23:32
Called Hashem .... 1 Chr. 11:34

Jasher—*upright*

Book of, quoted .... Josh. 10:13

Jashobeam—*let the people return*

1. Chief of David's mighty men .... 1 Chr. 11:11
Becomes military captain .... 1 Chr. 27:2, 3
2. Benjamite warrior .... 1 Chr. 12:1, 2, 6

Jashub—*he returns*

1. Issachar's son .... 1 Chr. 7:1
Head of family .... Num. 26:24
Called Job .... Gen. 46:13
2. Son of Bani; divorced his foreign wife .... Ezra 10:29

Jashubi-lehem—*bread returns*

A man of Judah .... 1 Chr. 4:22

Jashubites

Descendants of Jashub .... Num. 26:24

Jason—Greek equivalent for "*Joshua*" or "*Jesus*"

Welcomes Paul at Thessalonica .... Acts 17:5-9
Described as Paul's kinsman .... Rom. 16:21

Jasper—*a precious stone (quartz)*

Set in high priest's breastplate ... Ex. 28:20

Descriptive of:

Tyre's adornments .... Ezek. 28:12, 13
Heavenly vision .... Rev. 4:3

Jathniel—*God bestows*

Korahite porters .... 1 Chr. 26:1, 2

Jattir—*pre-eminence*

Town of Judah .... Josh. 15:48
Assigned to Aaron's children .... Josh. 21:13, 14
David sends spoil to .... 1 Sam. 30:26, 27

Javan—*Greece* (Ionia)

Son of Japheth .... Gen. 10:2, 4
Descendants of, to receive good news .... Is. 66:19, 20
Trade with Tyre .... Ezek. 27:13, 19
King of, in Daniel's visions ..... Dan. 8:21
Conflict with .... Zech. 9:13

Javelin—*a light, short spear*

Used by Saul .... 1 Sam. 18:10

Jaw—*jawbone*

Used figuratively of:

Power over the wicked .... Job 29:17
Prov. 30:14
God's sovereignty .... Is. 30:28
Human trial .... Hos. 11:4

Jawbone—*cheek bone*

Weapon used by Samson .... Judg. 15:15-19

Jazer—*helpful*

Town east of Jordan near Gilead .... 2 Sam. 24:5
Amorites driven from .... Num. 21:32
Assigned to Gad .... Josh. 13:24, 25
Becomes Levitical city .... Josh. 21:34, 39
Taken by Moabites .... Is. 16:8, 9
Desired by sons of Reuben and Gad .... Num. 32:1-5

Jaziz—*shining*

Shepherd over David's flocks .... 1 Chr. 27:31

Jealous, jealousy

A. *Kinds of:*
Divine .... Ex. 20:5
Marital .... Num. 5:12-31
Motherly .... Gen. 30:1
Brotherly .... Gen. 37:4-28
Sectional .... 2 Sam. 19:41-43
National .... Judg. 8:1-3

B. *Good causes of:*
Zeal for the Lord .... Num. 25:11
Concern over Christians ..... 2 Cor. 11:2

C. *Evil causes of:*
Favoritism .... Gen. 37:3-11
Regard for names .... 1 Cor. 3:3-5
Carnality .... 2 Cor. 12:20
Amos 3:14-16

D. *Described as:*
Implacable .... Prov. 6:34, 35
Cruel .... Song 8:6
Burning .... Deut. 29:20
Godly .... 2 Cor. 11:2

Jearim—*forests*

Mountain 10 miles west of Jerusalem .... Josh. 15:10

Jeaterai—*steadfast*

Descendant of Levi .... 1 Chr. 6:21
Also called Ethni .... 1 Chr. 6:41

Jeberechiah—*Jehovah blesses*

Father of Zechariah (not the prophet) .... Is. 8:2

Jebus—*trodden under foot*

Same as Jerusalem .... 1 Chr. 11:4
Entry denied to David .... 1 Chr. 11:5

SUBJECT REFERENCE

- Levite came near .... Judg. 19:1, 11
- See Zion; Sion

Jebusi, Jebusite—*trodden under foot*
- Assigned to Benjamin .... Josh. 18:28
- Same as Jerusalem .... Josh. 18:28
- On the border of Judah .... Josh. 15:8

Jebusites
- Descendants of Canaan .... Gen. 10:15, 16
- Mountain tribe .... Num. 13:29
- Land of, promised to Israel .... Gen. 15:18-21
- Adoni-zedek, their king, raises confederacy .... Josh. 10:1-5
- Their king killed by Joshua .... Josh. 10:23-26
- Join fight against Joshua .... Josh. 11:1-5
- Assigned to Benjamin .... Josh. 18:28
- Royal city not taken .... Judg. 1:21
- Taken by David .... 2 Sam. 5:6-8
- Old inhabitants remain .... 2 Sam. 24:16-25
- Become slaves .... 1 Kin. 9:20, 21

Jecoliah—*Jehovah is able*
- Mother of King Azariah .... 2 Kin. 15:2
- Called Jechiliah .... 2 Chr. 26:3

Jeconiah—*Jehovah establishes*
- Variant form of Jehoiachin .... 1 Chr. 3:16, 17
- Abbreviated to Coniah .... Jer. 22:24, 28
- Son of Josiah .... Matt. 1:11
- See Jehoiachin

Jedaiah—*Jehovah has been kind*
1. Priestly family .... 1 Chr. 24:7
2. Head of the priests .... Neh. 12:6
3. Another head priest .... Neh. 12:7, 21
4. Simeonite .... 1 Chr. 4:37
5. Postexilic worker .... Neh. 3:10
6. One who brings gifts for the Temple .... Zech. 6:10, 14

Jediael—*known of God*
1. Son of Benjamin and family head .... 1 Chr. 7:6, 10, 11
2. Manassite; joins David .... 1 Chr. 12:20
3. One of David's mighty men .... 1 Chr. 11:45
4. Korahite porter .... 1 Chr. 26:1, 2

Jedidah—*beloved*
- Mother of King Josiah .... 2 Kin. 22:1

Jedidiah—*beloved of Jehovah*
- Name given to Solomon by Nathan .... 2 Sam. 12:24, 25

Jeduthun—*praising*
1. Levite musician appointed by David .... 1 Chr. 16:41, 42
   - Heads a family of musicians .... 2 Chr. 5:12
   - Name appears in Psalm titles .... Ps. 39; 62; 77
   - Family officiates after Exile .. Neh. 11:17
   - Possibly same as Ethan .... 1 Chr. 15:17, 19
2. Father of Obed-edom .... 1 Chr. 16:38

Jegar-sahadutha—*heap of testimony*
- Name given by Laban to memorial stones .... Gen. 31:46, 47

Jehaleleel—*God will flash light*
1. Man of Judah and family head .... 1 Chr. 4:16
2. Merarite Levite .... 2 Chr. 29:12

Jehdeiah—*Jehovah will make glad*
1. Kohathite Levite .... 1 Chr. 24:20
2. Meronothite in charge of David's asses .... 1 Chr. 27:30

Jehezekel—*God will strengthen*
- Descendant of Aaron .... 1 Chr. 24:1, 16

Jehiah—*Jehovah lives*
- Doorkeeper .... 1 Chr. 15:24

Jehiel—*God lives*
1. Levite musician .... 1 Chr. 15:18, 20
2. Gershonite and family head .... 1 Chr. 23:8
3. Son of Hachmoni .... 1 Chr. 27:32
4. Son of King Jehoshaphat .... 2 Chr. 21:2, 4
5. Hemanite Levite .... 2 Chr. 29:14
6. Overseer in Hezekiah's reign .... 2 Chr. 31:13
7. Official of the Temple .... 2 Chr. 35:8
8. Father of Obadiah, a returned exile .... Ezra 8:9
9. Father of Shechaniah .... Ezra 10:2
10. Postexilic priest .... Ezra 10:21
11. Postexilic priest .... Ezra 10:26

Jehieli
- A Levite family .... 1 Chr. 26:21, 22

Jehizkiah—*Jehovah strengthens*
- Ephraimite chief .... 2 Chr. 28:12

Jehoadah—*whom Jehovah adorns*
- Descendant of Saul .... 1 Chr. 8:36
- Also called Jarah .... 1 Chr. 9:42

Jehoaddan—*Jehovah delights*
- Mother of Amaziah .... 2 Kin. 14:2

Jehoahaz—*Jehovah has taken hold of*
1. Son and successor of Jehu, king of Israel .... 2 Kin. 10:35
   - Seeks the Lord in defeat .... 2 Kin. 13:2-9
2. Son and successor of Josiah, king of Judah .... 2 Kin. 23:30-34
   - Called Shallum .... 1 Chr. 3:15
3. Another form of Ahaziah, youngest son of King Joram .... 2 Chr. 21:17

Jehoash (see Joash)

Jehohanan, Johanan—*Jehovah is gracious*
1. Korahite Levite .... 1 Chr. 26:3
2. Captain under Jehoshaphat .. 2 Chr. 17:10, 15
3. Father of Ishmael, Jehoiada's supporter .... 2 Chr. 23:1
4. Priestly family head .... Neh. 12:13
5. Priest who divorced his wife .... Ezra 10:28
6. Son of Tobiah the Ammonite .... Neh. 6:17, 18
7. Postexilic singer .... Neh. 12:42

Jehoiachin—*Jehovah establishes*
- Son of Jehoiakim; next to the last king of Judah .... 2 Kin. 24:8
- Deported to Babylon .... 2 Kin. 24:8-16
- Liberated by Evil-merodach .... Jer. 52:31-34
- See Jeconiah

Jehoiada—*Jehovah knows*
1. Aaronite supporter of David .... 1 Chr. 12:27
2. Father of Benaiah, one of David's officers .... 2 Sam. 8:18
3. Son of Benaiah; one of David's counselors .... 1 Chr. 27:34
4. High priest .... 2 Kin. 11:9
   - Proclaims Joash king .... 2 Kin. 11:4-16
   - Institutes a covenant .... 2 Kin. 11:17-21
   - Instructs Joash .... 2 Kin. 12:2
   - Commanded to repair the Temple .... 2 Kin. 12:3-16
   - Receives honorable burial .... 2 Chr. 24:15, 16
5. Deposed priest .... Jer. 29:26
6. Postexilic returnee .... Neh. 3:6

Jehoiakim—*Jehovah raises up*
- Son of King Josiah .... 2 Kin. 23:34, 35
- Made Pharaoh's official .... 2 Kin. 23:34,36
- Wicked king .... 2 Chr. 36:5, 8
- Burns Jeremiah's roll .... Jer. 36:1-32
- Becomes Nebuchadnezzar's servant .... 2 Kin. 24:1
- Punished by the Lord .... 2 Kin. 24:2-4
- Taken by Nebuchadnezzar .... 2 Chr. 36:5, 6
- Returns to idolatry .... 2 Chr. 36:5, 8
- Treats Jeremiah with contempt .... Jer. 36:21-28
- Kills a true prophet .... Jer. 26:20-23
- Bound in fetters .... 2 Chr. 36:6
- Buried as an ass .... Jer. 22:18, 19
- Curse on .... Jer. 36:30, 31

Jehoiarib—*Jehovah contends*
- Descendant of Aaron .... 1 Chr. 24:1, 6, 7
- Founder of an order of priests .. 1 Chr. 9:10, 13

Jehonadab—*Jehovah is liberal*
- A Rechabite .... 2 Kin. 10:15
- See Jonadab

Jehonathan—*Jehovah has given*
1. Levite teacher .... 2 Chr. 17:8
2. Postexilic priest .... Neh. 12:1, 18

Jehoram—*Jehovah is high*
1. King of Judah; son and successor of Jehoshaphat .... 1 Kin. 22:50
   - Called Joram .... 2 Kin. 8:21, 23, 24
   - Reigns eight years .... 2 Kin. 8:16, 17
   - Marries Athaliah, who leads him astray .... 2 Kin. 8:18, 19
   - Killed his brothers .... 2 Chr. 21:2, 4, 13
   - Edom revolts from .... 2 Kin. 8:20-22
   - Elijah predicts his terrible end .... 2 Chr. 21:12-15
   - Nations fight against .... 2 Chr. 21:16, 17
   - Smitten by the Lord; dies in disgrace .... 2 Chr. 21:18-20
2. King of Israel; son of Ahab .... 2 Kin. 1:17
   - Called Joram .... 2 Kin. 8:16, 25, 28
   - Reigns 12 years .... 2 Kin. 3:1
   - Puts away Baal .... 2 Kin. 3:2
   - Joins Jehoshaphat against Moabites .... 2 Kin. 3:1-27
   - Naaman sent to, for cure .... 2 Kin. 5:1-27
   - Informed by Elijah of Syria's plans .... 2 Kin. 6:8-23
   - Wounded in war with Syria .... 2 Kin. 8:28, 29
3. Levite teacher .... 2 Chr. 17:8

Jehoshabeath—*Jehovah is an oath*
- Safeguards Joash from Athaliah .... 2 Chr. 22:11

Jehoshaphat—*Jehovah has judged*
1. King of Judah; son and successor of Asa .... 1 Kin. 15:24
   - Reigns 25 years .... 1 Kin. 22:42
   - Fortifies his kingdom .... 2 Chr. 17:2
   - Institutes reforms .... 2 Chr. 17:3
   - Inaugurates public instruction .... 2 Chr. 17:7-9
   - Honored and respected .... 2 Chr. 17:10-19
   - Joins Ahab against Ramoth-gilead .... 1 Kin. 22:1-36
   - Rebuked by a prophet .... 2 Chr. 19:2, 3
   - Develops legal system .... 2 Chr. 19:4-11
   - By faith defeats invading forces .... 2 Chr. 20:1-30
   - Navy of, destroyed .... 2 Chr. 20:35-37
   - Provision for his children .... 2 Chr. 21:2, 3
   - Death of .... 2 Chr. 21:1
   - Ancestor of Christ .... Matt. 1:8
2. Son of Ahilud .... 2 Sam. 8:16
   - Recorder under David and Solomon .... 2 Sam. 20:24
3. Father of King Jehu .... 2 Kin. 9:2

Jehoshaphat, valley of
- Described as a place of judgment .... Joel 3:2, 12

Jehosheba—*Jehovah is an oath*
- King Joram's daughter .... 2 Kin. 11:2

Jehovah—*title of God*
- Defined .... Ex. 6:3-5
- Early known .... Gen. 4:26
- Usually rendered LORD in Old Testament .... Ex. 17:14
- Used in certain combinations .... Gen. 22:14
- Often found in names (e.g., Jehoshaphat, Elijah) .... 1 Kin. 15:24
- Applied to Christ as Lord .... Is. 40:3; Matt. 3:3

Jehovah-jireh—*Jehovah will provide*
- Names used by Abraham .... Gen. 22:14

Jehovah-nissi—*Jehovah is my banner*
- Name used by Moses for memorial .... Ex. 17:15, 16

Jehovah-shalom—*Jehovah is peace*
- Name used by Gideon for significant visit .... Judg. 6:23, 24

J

SUBJECT — REFERENCE

Jehozabad—*Jehovah has bestowed*

1. Son of Obed-edom ... 1 Chr. 26:4
2. Son of a Moabitess; assassinates Joash ... 2 Kin. 12:20, 21
   Put to death ... 2 Chr. 25:3
3. Military captain under King Jehoshaphat ... 2 Chr. 17:18

Jehozadak—*Jehovah has justified*

Son of Seriah, the high priest ... 1 Chr. 6:14
His father killed ... 2 Kin. 25:18-21
Carried captive to Babylon ... 1 Chr. 6:15
Father of Joshua the high priest ... Hag. 1:1, 12, 14

Jehu—*Jehovah is He*

1. Benjamite warrior ... 1 Chr. 12:3
2. Prophet and son of Hanani ... 1 Kin. 16:1
   Denounces Baasha ... 1 Kin. 16:2-4, 7
   Rebukes Jehoshaphat ... 2 Chr. 19:2, 3
   Writes Jehoshaphat's biography ... 2 Chr. 20:34
3. Descendant of Judah ... 1 Chr. 2:38
4. Simeonite ... 1 Chr. 4:35
5. Grandson of Nimshi ... 2 Kin. 9:2
   Commander under Ahab ... 2 Kin. 9:25
   Divinely commissioned to destroy Ahab's house ... 1 Kin. 19:16, 17
   Carries out orders with zeal ... 2 Kin. 9:11-37
   Killed Ahab's sons ... 2 Kin. 10:1-17
   Destroys worshipers of Baal ... 2 Kin. 10:18-28
   Serves the Lord outwardly ... 2 Kin. 10:29-31

Jehubbah—*he hides*

Asherite ... 1 Chr. 7:34

Jehucal—*Jehovah is able*

Son of Shelemiah; sent by Zedekiah to Jeremiah ... Jer. 37:3
Also called Jucal ... Jer. 38:1

Jehud—*praise*

Town of Dan ... Josh. 19:40, 45

Jehudi—*a man of Judah; a Jew*

Reads Jeremiah's roll ... Jer. 36:14, 21, 23

Jehudijah—*a Jewess*

One of Mered's two wives; should be rendered "the Jewess" ... 1 Chr. 4:18

Jeiel—*God snatches away*

1. Ancestor of Saul ... 1 Chr. 9:35-39
2. One of David's mighty men ... 1 Chr. 11:44
   Reubenite prince ... 1 Chr. 5:6, 7
3. Levite musician ... 1 Chr. 16:5
4. Porter ... 1 Chr. 15:18, 21
   May be the same as 3 ... 1 Chr. 16:5
   Called Jehiah ... 1 Chr. 15:24
5. Inspired Levite ... 2 Chr. 20:14
6. Levite chief ... 2 Chr. 35:9
7. Scribe ... 2 Chr. 26:11
8. Temple Levite ... 2 Chr. 29:13
9. One who divorced his foreign wife ... Ezra 10:19, 43

Jekabzeel—*God will gather*

Town in Judah ... Neh. 11:25
Called Kabzeel ... Josh. 15:21
Home of Benaiah, David's friend ... 2 Sam. 23:20

Jekameam—*people will rise*

Kohathite Levite ... 1 Chr. 23:19

Jekamiah—*Jehovah will rise*

1. Son of Shallum ... 1 Chr. 2:41
2. Son of Jeconiah ... 1 Chr. 3:17, 18

Jekuthiel—*God will support*

Man of Judah ... 1 Chr. 4:18

Jemima—*dove*

Job's daughter ... Job 42:14

Jemuel—*day of God*

Son of Simeon ... Gen. 46:10
Called Nemuel ... Num. 26:12

Jephthah—*he will open*

Gilead's son by a harlot ... Judg. 11:1
Flees to Tob; becomes a leader ... Judg. 11:2-11
Cites historical precedents against invading Ammonites ... Judg. 11:12-27
Makes a vow before battle ... Judg. 11:28-31
Smites Ammonites ... Judg. 11:32, 33
Fulfills vow ... Judg. 11:34-40
Defeats quarrelsome Ephraimites ... Judg. 12:1-7
Cited by Samuel ... 1 Sam. 12:11
In faith's chapter ... Heb. 11:32

Jephunneh—*it will be prepared*

1. Caleb's father ... Num. 13:6
2. Asherite ... 1 Chr. 7:38

Jerah—*moon*

Son of Joktan; probably an Arabian tribe ... Gen. 10:26; 1 Chr. 1:20

Jerahmeel—*may God have compassion*

1. Great-grandson of Judah ... 1 Chr. 2:9, 25-41
2. Son of Kish, not Saul's father ... 1 Chr. 24:29
3. King Jehoiakim's officer ... Jer. 36:26

Jerahmeelites

Raided by David ... 1 Sam. 27:10

Jered—*descent*

A descendant of Judah ... 1 Chr. 4:18
See Jared

Jeremai—*high*

One who divorced his foreign wife ... Ezra 10:19, 33

Jeremiah (I)—*Jehovah establishes*

A. *Life of:*
   Son of Hilkiah; a Benjamite ... Jer. 1:1
   Native of Anathoth ... Jer. 1:1
   Called before birth ... Jer. 1:4-10
   Prophet under kings Josiah, Jehoiakim, and Zedekiah ... Jer. 1:2, 3
   Imprisoned by Pashur ... Jer. 20:1-6
   Writes his prophecy; Jehoiakim burns it ... Jer. 36:1-26
   Prophecy rewritten ... Jer. 36:27-32
   Accused of desertion ... Jer. 37:1-16
   Released by Zedekiah ... Jer. 37:17-21
   Cast into a dungeon ... Jer. 38:1-6
   Saved by an Ethiopian ... Jer. 38:7-28
   Set free by Nebuchadnezzar ... Jer. 39:11-14
   Given liberty of choice by Nebuzaradan ... Jer. 40:1-6
   Forced to flee to Egypt ... Jer. 43:5-7
   Last prophecies at Tahpanhes, Egypt ... Jer. 43:8-13

B. *Characteristics of:*
   Forbidden to marry ... Jer. 16:1-13
   Has internal conflicts ... Jer. 20:7-18
   Has incurable pain ... Jer. 15:18
   Motives misunderstood ... Jer. 37:12-14
   Tells captives to build in Babylon ... Jer. 29:4-9
   Denounces false prophets in Babylon ... Jer. 29:20-32
   Rebukes idolatry ... Jer. 7:9-21

C. *Prophecies of, foretell:*
   Egypt's fall ... Jer. 43:8-13
   70 years of captivity ... 2 Chr. 36:21
   Restoration to land ... Jer. 16:14-18
   New covenant ... Jer. 31:31-34
   Herod's massacre ... Jer. 31:15

D. *Teachings of:*
   God's sovereignty ... Jer. 18:5-10
   God's knowledge ... Jer. 17:5-10
   Shame of idolatry ... Jer. 10:14, 15
   Spirituality of worship, etc. ... Jer. 3:16, 17
   Need of regeneration ... Jer. 9:26
   Man's sinful nature ... Jer. 2:22
   Gospel salvation ... Jer. 23:5, 6
   Call of the Gentiles ... Jer. 3:17-19

Jeremiah (II)

1. Benjamite warrior ... 1 Chr. 12:4
2. Gadite warrior ... 1 Chr. 12:10
3. Another Gadite warrior ... 1 Chr. 12:13
4. Manassite head ... 1 Chr. 5:23, 24
5. Father of Hamutal, a wife of Josiah ... 2 Kin. 23:31
6. Father of Jaazaniah ... Jer. 35:3
7. Postexilic priest ... Neh. 12:1, 7
   Head of a priestly line ... Neh. 12:12
8. Priest who signs the covenant ... Neh. 10:2

Jeremiah, the Book of—*a book of the Old Testament*

Jeremiah's call ... Jer. 1:1-19
Jeremiah's life ... Jer. 26:1—45:5
Israel's sin against God ... Jer. 2:1—10:25
Against false prophets ... Jer. 23:9-40
Against foreign nations ... Jer. 46:1—51:64
The Messianic king ... Jer. 23:1-8

Jeremoth—*elevation*

1. Son of Becher ... 1 Chr. 7:8
2. Benjamite ... 1 Chr. 8:14
3. Merarite Levite ... 1 Chr. 23:23
4. Musician of David ... 1 Chr. 25:22
5. Ruler of Napthali ... 1 Chr. 27:19
6. One who divorced his foreign wife ... Ezra 10:26
7. Another who divorced his foreign wife ... Ezra 10:27
8. Spelled Jerimoth ... 1 Chr. 24:30

Jeriah, Jerijah—*Jehovah sees*

Kohathite Levite ... 1 Chr. 23:19, 23
Hebronite chief ... 1 Chr. 26:31

Jeribai—*Jehovah contends*

One of David's warriors ... 1 Chr. 11:46

Jericho—*place of fragrance*

City near the Jordan ... Num. 22:1
Viewed by Moses ... Deut. 34:1-3
Called the city of palm trees ... Deut. 34:3
Viewed by spies ... Josh. 2:1
Home of Rahab the harlot ... Heb. 11:31
Scene of Joshua's vision ... Josh. 5:13-15
Destroyed by Joshua ... Heb. 11:30
Curse of rebuilding of ... Josh. 6:26
Assigned to Benjamin ... Josh. 16:1, 7
Moabites retake ... Judg. 3:12, 13
David's envoys tarry here ... 2 Sam. 10:4, 5
Rebuilt by Hiel ... 1 Kin. 16:34
Visited by Elijah and Elisha ... 2 Kin. 2:4-22
Zedekiah captured here ... 2 Kin. 25:5
Reinhabited after exile ... Ezra 2:34
People of, help rebuild Jerusalem ... Neh. 3:2
Blind men of, healed by Jesus ... Matt. 20:29-34
Home of Zacchaeus ... Luke 19:1-10

Jeriel—*God sees*

Son of Tola ... 1 Chr. 7:2

Jerimoth

1. Son of Bela ... 1 Chr. 7:7
2. Warrior of David ... 1 Chr. 12:5
3. Musician of David ... 1 Chr. 25:4
4. Son of David ... 2 Chr. 11:18
5. Levite overseer ... 2 Chr. 31:13
6. Spelled Jeremoth ... 1 Chr. 23:23

See Jeremoth

Jerioth—*tent curtains*

One of Caleb's wives ... 1 Chr. 2:18

Jeroboam—*may the people increase*

1. Son of Nebat ... 1 Kin. 11:26
   Rebels against Solomon ... 1 Kin. 11:26-28
   Ahijah's prophecy concerning ... 1 Kin. 11:29-39
   Flees to Egypt ... 1 Kin. 11:40
   Recalled, made king ... 1 Kin. 12:1-3, 12, 20
   Perverts the true religion ... 1 Kin. 12:25-33
   Casts Levites out ... 2 Chr. 11:14
   Rebuked by a man of God ... 1 Kin. 13:1-10
   Leads people astray ... 1 Kin. 13:33, 34
   His wife consults Ahijah ... 1 Kin. 14:1-18
   War with Abijam ... 1 Kin. 15:7
   Reigns 22 years ... 1 Kin. 14:20
   Struck by the Lord ... 2 Chr. 13:20
2. Jeroboam II; king of Israel ... 2 Kin. 13:13
   Successor of Joash (Jehoash) ... 2 Kin. 14:16, 23

SUBJECT	REFERENCE
Conquers Hamath and Damascus	2 Kin. 14:25-28
Reigns wickedly 41 years	2 Kin. 14:23, 24
Denounced by Amos	Amos 7:7-13
Death of	2 Kin. 14:29

Jeroham—*he is pitied*

1. Grandfather of Samuel ...... 1 Sam. 1:1
2. Benjamite ...... 1 Chr. 9:8
3. Father of Benjamite chief men ...... 1 Chr. 8:27
4. Benjamite of Gedor ...... 1 Chr. 12:7
5. Father of Adaiah ...... 1 Chr. 9:12
6. Danite chief's father ...... 1 Chr. 27:22
7. Military captain ...... 2 Chr. 23:1

Jerubbaal—*Baal contends*

Name given to Gideon for destroying Baal's altar ...... Judg. 6:32

Jerubbesheth—*let shame contend*

Father of Abimelech ...... 2 Sam. 11:21

Jeruel—*founded by God*

Wilderness west of the Dead Sea ...... 2 Chr. 20:16

Jerusalem—*possession of peace*

A. *Names applied to:*

City of God	Ps. 46:4
City of David	2 Sam. 5:6, 7
City of Judah	2 Chr. 25:28
Zion	Ps. 48:12
Jebusi	Josh. 18:28
Holy city	Matt. 4:5
Faithful city	Is. 1:21, 26
City of righteousness	Is. 1:26
City of truth	Zech. 8:3
City of the great King	Ps. 48:2
Salem	Gen. 14:18

B. *History of:*

Originally Salem	Gen. 14:18
Occupied by Jebusite	Josh. 15:8
King of, defeated by Joshua	Josh. 10:5-23
Assigned to Benjamin	Josh. 18:28
Attacked by Judah	Judg. 1:8
Jebusites remain in	Judg. 1:21
David brings Goliath's head to	1 Sam. 17:54
Conquered by David	2 Sam. 5:6-8
Name changed	2 Sam. 5:7-9
Ark brought to	2 Sam. 6:12-17
Saved from destruction	2 Sam. 24:16
Solomon builds Temple here	1 Kin. 5:5-8
Suffers in war	1 Kin. 14:25-27
Plundered by Israel	2 Kin. 14:13, 14
Besieged by Syrians	Is. 7:1
Earthquake damages	Amos 1:1
Miraculously saved	2 Kin. 19:31-36
Ruled by Egypt	2 Kin. 23:33-35
Besieged by Babylon	2 Kin. 24:10, 11
Captured by Babylon	Jer. 39:1-8
Desolate 70 years	Jer. 25:11, 12
Temple rebuilt in	Ezra 1:1-4
Exiles return to	Ezra 2:1-70
Work on, hindered	Ezra 5:1-17
Walls of, dedicated	Neh. 12:27-47
Christ: Enters as King	Matt. 21:9, 10
Laments for	Matt. 23:37
Crucified at	Luke 9:31
Weeps over	Luke 19:41, 42
Predicts destruction	Luke 19:43, 44
Gospel preached at	Luke 24:47
Many miracles performed in	John 4:45
Church begins here	Acts 2:1-47
Christians of, persecuted	Acts 4:1-30
Stephen martyred at	Acts 7:1-60
First Christian council held here	Acts 15:1-29
Paul:	
Visits	Acts 20:16
Arrested in	Acts 21:30-36
Taken from	Acts 23:12-33

C. *Prophecies concerning:*

Destruction by Babylon	Jer. 20:5
Utter ruin	Jer. 26:18
Rebuilding by Cyrus	Is. 44:26-28
Christ's entry into	Zech. 9:9
Gospel proclaimed from	Is. 2:3
Perilous times	Matt. 24:1-22
Being under Gentiles	Luke 21:24

D. *Described:*

Physically—strong	Ps. 48:12, 13 Ps. 125:2
Morally—corrupt	Is. 1:1-16 Jer. 5:1-5
Spiritually—the redeemed	Gal. 4:26-30
Prophetically—New Jerusalem	Rev. 21:1-27

See Zion; Sion

Jerusha—*possessed* (married)

Wife of King Uzziah ...... 2 Kin. 15:33
Called Jerushah ...... 2 Chr. 27:1

Jeshaiah—*Jehovah saves*

1. Musician of David ...... 1 Chr. 25:3
2. Grandson of Zerubbabel ...... 1 Chr. 3:21
3. Levite in David's reign ...... 1 Chr. 26:25
4. Son of Athaliah; returns from Babylon ...... Ezra 8:7
5. Levite who returns with Ezra ...... Ezra 8:19
6. Benjamite ...... Neh. 11:7

Jeshanah—*old*

City of Ephraim taken by Abijah ...... 2 Chr. 13:19

Jesharelah—*upright toward God*

Levite musician ...... 1 Chr. 25:14
Called Asarelah ...... 1 Chr. 25:2

Jeshebeab—*may the father tarry* (live)

Descendant of Aaron ...... 1 Chr. 24:13

Jesher—*uprightness*

Caleb's son ...... 1 Chr. 2:18

Jeshimon—*waste*

Wilderness west of the Dead Sea ...... 1 Sam. 23:19, 24

Jeshishai—*aged*

Gadite ...... 1 Chr. 5:14

Jeshohaiah—*humbled by Jehovah*

Leader in Simeon ...... 1 Chr. 4:36

Jeshua—*Jehovah is salvation*

1. Joshua, the military leader after Moses ...... Neh. 8:17
2. Descendant of Aaron ...... Ezra 2:36
3. Levite treasurer ...... 2 Chr. 31:14, 15
4. Postexilic high priest ...... Zech. 3:8
   Returns with Zerubbabel ...... Ezra 2:2
   Aids in Temple rebuilding ...... Ezra 3:2-8
   Withstands opponents ...... Ezra 4:1-3
   Figurative act performed on ...... Zech. 3:1-10
5. Levite assistant ...... Ezra 2:40
   Explains the Law ...... Neh. 8:7
   Leads in worship ...... Neh. 9:4, 5
   Seals the covenant ...... Neh. 10:1, 9
6. Repairer of the wall ...... Neh. 3:19
7. Man of the house of Pahath-moab ...... Ezra 2:6
8. Village in south Judah ...... Neh. 11:26

Jeshurun—*upright one*

Poetic name of endearment for Israel ...... Deut. 32:15

Jesimiel—*God sets up*

Simeonite leader ...... 1 Chr. 4:36

Jesse—*Jehovah exists*

Grandson of Ruth and Boaz	Ruth 4:17-22
Father of:	
David	1 Sam. 16:18, 19
Eight sons	1 Sam. 16:10, 11
Two daughters	1 Chr. 2:15, 16
Citizen of Bethlehem	1 Sam. 16:1, 18
Protected by David	1 Sam. 22:1-4
Of humble origin	1 Sam. 18:18, 23
Mentioned in prophecy	Is. 11:1, 10
Ancestor of Christ	Matt. 1:5, 6

Jesting—*giving an immoral turn to something*

Condemned ...... Eph. 5:4
Lot appeared to be ...... Gen. 19:14
Of godless men ...... Ps. 35:16

Jesus (see Christ)

Jether—*abundance*

1. Gideon's oldest son ...... Judg. 8:20, 21
2. Descendant of Judah ...... 1 Chr. 2:32
3. Son of Ezra ...... 1 Chr. 4:17
4. Asherite; probably same as Ithran ...... 1 Chr. 7:30-38
5. Amasa's father ...... 1 Kin. 2:5, 32

Jetheth—*subjection*

Chief of Edom ...... Gen. 36:40

Jethlah—*an overhanging place*

Danite town ...... Josh. 19:42

Jethro—*excellent*

Priest of Midian; Moses' father-in-law	Num. 10:29
Also called Reuel	Num. 10:29
Moses marries his daughter Zipporah	Ex. 2:16-22
Moses departs from	Ex. 4:18-26
Visits and counsels Moses	Ex. 18:1-27

Jetur

Son of Ishmael ...... Gen. 25:15
Conflict with Israel ...... 1 Chr. 5:18, 19
Tribal descendants of; the Ituraeans ...... Luke 3:1

Jeuel—*snatching away*

Son of Zerah ...... 1 Chr. 9:6

Jeush—*may he aid*

1. Son of Esau and Edomite chief ...... Gen. 36:5, 18
2. Benjamite head ...... 1 Chr. 7:10
3. Gershonite Levite ...... 1 Chr. 23:10, 11
4. Descendant of Jonathan ...... 1 Chr. 8:39
5. Rehoboam's son ...... 2 Chr. 11:19

Jeuz—*counseling*

Benjamite ...... 1 Chr. 8:8, 10

Jewels—*ornaments used on the body*

A. *Used for:*

Ornaments	Is. 3:18-24
Evil offering	Ex. 32:1-5
Good offering	Ex. 35:22
Spoils of war	2 Chr. 20:25
Farewell gifts	Ex. 11:2

B. *Significance of:*

Betrothal present	Gen. 24:22, 53
Sign of wealth	James 2:2
Standard of value	Prov. 3:15
Tokens of repentance	Gen. 35:4
Tokens of love	Ezek. 16:11-13
Indications of worldliness	1 Tim. 2:9
Figurative of God's own	Matt. 13:45, 46

Jewess—*a female Jew*

Woman of the Hebrew race ...... Acts 24:24

Jewish alphabet

Given topically ...... Ps. 119

Jewish calendar

A. *List of months of:*

Abib, or Nisan (March—April)	Ex. 13:4
Zif or Iyyar (April—May)	1 Kin. 6:1, 37
Sivan (May—June)	Esth. 8:9
Tammuz (June—July)	Jer. 39:2
Ab (July—August)	Num. 33:38
Elul (August—September)	Neh. 6:15
Ethanim or Tishri (September—October)	1 Kin. 8:2
Bul or Heshvan (October—November)	1 Kin. 6:38
Chisleu or Kislev (November—December)	Neh. 1:1
Tebeth (December—January)	Esth. 2:16
Shebat or Sebat (January—February)	Zech. 1:7
Adar (February—March)	Esth. 3:7

B. *Feasts of:*

Abib (14)—
Passover ...... Ex. 12:18

SUBJECT — REFERENCE

Abib (15-21)—
Unleavened Bread ... Lev. 23:5, 6
Abib (16)—
First fruits ... Lev. 23:10, 11
Zif (14)—Later
Passover ... Num. 9:10, 11
Sivan (6)—
Pentecost, Feast of Weeks,
Harvest ... Lev. 23:15-21
Ethanim (1)—
Trumpets ... Lev. 23:24
Ethanim (10)—
Day of Atonement ... Lev. 16:29-34
Ethanim (15-21)—
Tabernacles ... Lev. 23:34, 35
Ethanim (22)—
Holy Convocation ... Lev. 23:36
Chisleu (25)—
Dedication ... John 10:22

Jewish measures (Metrology)

A. *Long Measures:*
Finger (3/4 inch) ... Jer. 52:21
Handbreadth
(3 to 4 inches) ... Ex. 25:25
Span (about 9 inches) ... Ex. 28:16
Cubit of man (about 18
inches) ... Gen. 6:15
Pace (about 3 feet) ... 2 Sam. 6:13
Fathom (about 6 feet) ... Acts 27:28
Reed (about 11 feet) ... Ezek. 40:5
Line ... Ezek. 40:3

B. *Land measures:*
Cubit of God (1 3/4 feet) ... Josh. 3:4
Mile (1760 yds.) ... Matt. 5:41
Sabbath day's journey
(3/5 mile) ... Acts 1:12
Day's journey (24 miles) ... Gen. 30:36
Furlong (660 feet) ... Luke 24:13

C. *Weights and dry measures:*
Cab (about 2 quarts) ... 2 Kin. 6:25
Omer (about 7 pints) ... Ex. 16:16-18, 36
Ephah (about 4 1/2 pecks) ... Ex. 16:36
Homer (about 11 bushels) ... Num. 11:32
Hos. 3:2
Talent (about 93 pounds) ... Ex. 25:39

D. *Liquid measures:*
Log (about 1 pint) ... Lev. 14:10, 15
Hin (about 1 1/2 gallons) ... Num. 15:4-10
Bath (about 9 gallons) ... Is. 5:10
Homer or Cor
(c. 85 gallons) ... Ezek. 45:11, 14

Jews—*the Hebrew people*

A. *Descriptive of:*
Hebrew race ... Esth. 3:6, 13
Postexilic Hebrew nation ... Ezra 5:1, 5
Believers ... Rom. 2:28, 29

B. *Kinds of:*
Hypocritical ... Matt. 23:1-31
Persecuting ... 1 Thess. 2:14, 15
Prejudiced ... John 4:9
Penitent ... John 12:10, 11

C. *Their sins:*
Self-righteousness ... Rom. 10:1-3
Hypocrisy ... Rom. 2:17-25
Persecution ... 1 Thess. 2:14, 15
Rejection of Christ ... Matt. 27:21-25
Rejection of the Gospel ... Acts 13:42-46
Embitter Gentiles ... Acts 14:2-6
Spiritual blindness ... John 3:1-4
Ignorance ... Luke 19:41, 42

D. *Their punishment:*
Blinded ... Rom. 11:25
Cast out ... Matt. 8:11, 12
Desolation as a nation ... Luke 21:20-24
Scattered ... Deut. 28:48-64

Jezaniah—*Jehovah answers*
Judahite military officer ... Jer. 40:7, 8
Seeks advice from Jeremiah ... Jer. 42:1-3
Called Jaazaniah ... 2 Kin. 25:23

Jezebel—*unmarried, chaste*
1. Daughter of Ethbaal;
Ahab's wife ... 1 Kin. 16:31
Follows her idolatry ... 1 Kin. 16:32, 33
Destroyed Jehovah's
prophets ... 1 Kin. 18:4-13
Plans Elijah's death ... 1 Kin. 19:1, 2
Secures Naboth's death ... 1 Kin. 21:1-15
Sentence:
Pronounced upon ... 1 Kin. 21:23
Fulfilled by Jehu ... 2 Kin. 9:7, 30-37
2. Type of paganism in the
church ... Rev. 2:20

Jezer—*form, purpose*
Son of Naphtali ... Gen. 46:24
Family head of the Jezerites ... Num. 26:49

Jeziah—*Jehovah sprinkles*
One who divorced his foreign
wife ... Ezra 10:25

Jeziel—*God sprinkles*
Benjamite warrior ... 1 Chr. 12:2, 3

Jezliah—*Jehovah delivers*
Son of Elpaal ... 1 Chr. 8:18

Jezoar—*he will shine*
Descendant of Judah ... 1 Chr. 4:7

Jezrahiah—*Jehovah shines*
Leads singing at dedication
service ... Neh. 12:42

Jezreel—*God sows*
1. Fortified city of Issachar ... Josh. 19:17, 18
Gideon fights Midianites in valley
of ... Judg. 6:33
Israelites camp here ... 1 Sam. 29:1, 11
Center of Ish-bosheth's
rule ... 2 Sam. 2:8, 9
Capital city ... 1 Kin. 18:45
Home of Naboth ... 1 Kin. 21:1, 13
Site of Jezebel's tragic end ... 1 Kin. 21:23
Heads of Ahab's sons piled
here ... 2 Kin. 10:1-10
City of bloodshed ... Hos. 1:4
Judgment in valley of ... Hos. 1:5
2. Town of Judah ... Josh. 15:56
David's wife from ... 1 Sam. 25:43
3. Judahite ... 1 Chr. 4:3
4. Symbolic name of Hosea's
son ... Hos. 1:4
5. Symbolic name of the new
Israel ... Hos. 2:22, 23

Jezreelite—*a person from Jezreel*
Naboth ... 1 Kin. 21:1

Jezreelitess—*a female from Jezreel*
Ahinoam ... 1 Sam. 30:5

Jibsam—*fragrant*
Descendant of Issachar ... 1 Chr. 7:2

Jimnah—*prosperity*
Son of Asher ... Gen. 46:18

Jidlaph—*he weeps*
Son of Nahor ... Gen. 22:22

Jiphthah-el—*God will open*
Valley between Asher and
Naphtali ... Josh. 19:10-27

Jiphtah—*he will open*
City of Judah ... Josh. 15:43

Joab—*Jehovah is father*
1. Son of Zeruiah, David's half-
sister ... 2 Sam. 8:16
Leads David's army to victory over Ish-
bosheth ... 2 Sam. 2:10-32
Assassinates Abner
deceptively ... 2 Sam. 3:26, 27
David rebukes him ... 2 Sam. 3:28-39
Commands David's army against
Edomites ... 1 Kin. 11:14-17
Defeats Syrians and
Ammonites ... 2 Sam. 10:1-14
Obeys David's orders concerning
Uriah ... 2 Sam. 11:6-27
Allows David to beseige
Rabbah ... 2 Sam. 11:1
Makes David favorable toward
Absalom ... 2 Sam. 14:1-33
Remains loyal to David ... 2 Sam. 18:1-5
Killed Absalom ... 2 Sam. 18:9-17
Rebukes David's grief ... 2 Sam. 19:1-8
Demoted by David ... 2 Sam. 19:13
Puts down Sheba's revolt ... 2 Sam. 20:1-22
Killed Amasa ... 2 Sam. 20:8-10
Regains command ... 2 Sam. 20:23
Opposes David's numbering
of the people ... 2 Sam. 24:1-9; 1 Chr. 21:1-6
Supports Adonijah ... 1 Kin. 1:7
David's dying words
against ... 1 Kin. 2:1-6
His crimes punished by
Solomon ... 1 Kin. 2:28-34
2. Son of Seraiah ... 1 Chr. 4:13, 14
3. Family head of exiles ... Ezra 2:6

Joah—*Jehovah is brother*
1. Son of Obed-edom ... 1 Chr. 26:4
2. Gershonite Levite ... 1 Chr. 6:21
Hezekiah's assistant ... 2 Chr. 29:12
3. Son of Aspah; a recorder under
Hezekiah ... Is. 36:3, 11, 22
4. Son of Joahaz ... 2 Chr. 34:8

Joahaz—*Jehovah has laid hold of*
Father of Joah, a recorder ... 2 Chr. 34:8

Joanna—*Jehovah has been gracious*
1. Ancestor of Christ ... Luke 3:27
2. Wife of Chuza, Herod's
steward ... Luke 8:1-3
With others, heralds Christ's
resurrection ... Luke 23:55, 56

Joash, Jehoash (I)—*Jehovah has given*
1. Father of Gideon ... Judg. 6:11-32
2. Judahite ... 1 Chr. 4:21, 22
3. Benjamite warrior ... 1 Chr. 12:3
4. Son of Ahab ... 1 Kin. 22:26
5. Son and successor of Ahaziah, king of
Judah ... 2 Kin. 11:1-20
Rescued and hid by
Jehosheba ... 2 Kin. 11:1-3
Proclaimed king by
Jehoiada ... 2 Kin. 11:4-12
Instructed by Jehoiada ... 2 Kin. 12:1, 2
Repairs the Temple ... 2 Kin. 12:4-16
Turns to idols after Jehoiada's
death ... 2 Chr. 24:17-19
Murdered Zechariah, Jehoiada's
son ... Matt. 23:35
Killed, not buried with
kings ... 2 Chr. 25:23-28
6. Son and successor of Jehoahaz, king of
Israel ... 2 Kin. 13:10-13
Follows idolatry ... 2 Kin. 13:11
Laments Elijah's sickness ... 2 Kin. 13:14-19
Defeats:
Syria ... 2 Kin. 13:24, 25
Amaziah ... 2 Kin. 13:12

Joash (II)—*Jehovah has come to help*
1. Benjamite ... 1 Chr. 7:8
2. Officer of David ... 1 Chr. 27:28

Job—*returning*

A. *Life of:*
Lives in Uz ... Job 1:1
Afflicted by Satan ... Job 1:6-19
Debate between Job and his three
friends ... Job 3—33
Elihu intervenes ... Job 34—37
Lord answers Job ... Job 38—41
His final reply ... Job 42:1-6
The Lord rebukes Job's three
friends ... Job 42:7-9
Restored to prosperity ... Job 42:10-15
Dies "old and full of days" ... Job 42:16, 17

B. *Strength of his:*
Faith ... Job 19:23-27
Patience ... James 5:11
Integrity ... Job 31:1-40

C. *Sufferings of:*
Lost property ... Job 1:13-17
Lost children ... Job 1:18, 19
Lost health ... Job 2:4-8
Misunderstood by friends ... Job 4:1-8; Job 8:1-6; Job 11:1-20

D. *Restoration of:*
After repentance ... Job 42:1-6
After prayer ... Job 42:8-10
To greater prosperity ... Job 42:11-17

Job, the Book of—*a book of the Old Testament*
Wisdom described ... Job 1:1-5
Wisdom tested ... Job 1:6—2:10

SUBJECT — REFERENCE

Wisdom sought .... Job 3—37
God challenges Job .... Job 38—41
Wisdom in humility .... Job 42:1-6

Jobab—*to call shrilly*

1. Son of Joktan .... Gen. 10:29
   Tribal head .... 1 Chr. 1:23
2. King of Edom .... Gen. 36:31, 33
3. Canaanite king defeated by Joshua .... Josh. 11:1, 7-12
4. Benjamite .... 1 Chr. 8:9
5. Another Benjamite .... 1 Chr. 8:18

Jochebed—*Jehovah is glory*

Daughter of Levi; mother of Miriam, Aaron, and Moses .... Ex. 6:20

Jod

Tenth letter of the Hebrew alphabet .... Ps. 119:73-80

Joed—*Jehovah is witness*

Benjamite .... Neh. 11:7

Joel—*Jehovah is God*

1. Son of Samuel .... 1 Sam. 8:1, 2; 1 Chr. 6:28, 33
   Father of Heman the singer .... 1 Chr. 15:17
2. Kohathite Levite .... 1 Chr. 6:36
3. Leader of Simeon .... 1 Chr. 4:35
4. Reubenite chief .... 1 Chr. 5:4, 8, 9
5. Gadite chief .... 1 Chr. 5:12
6. Chief man of Issachar .... 1 Chr. 7:3
7. One of David's mighty men .... 1 Chr. 11:38
8. Gershonite Levite .... 1 Chr. 15:7, 11, 17
   Probably the same as in .... 1 Chr. 23:8
9. Manassite chief officer .... 1 Chr. 27:20
10. Kohathite Levite during Hezekiah's reign .... 2 Chr. 29:12
11. Son of Nebo; divorced his foreign wife .... Ezra 10:43
12. Benjamite overseer under Nehemiah .... Neh. 11:9
13. Prophet .... Joel 1:1

Joel, Book of

Prophecies of:

Predict Pentecost .... Joel 2:28-32
Proclaim salvation in Christ .... Joel 2:32
Portray the universal judgment .... Joel 3:1-16
Picture the eternal age .... Joel 3:17-21

Joelah—*let him help*

David's recruit at Ziklag .... 1 Chr. 12:7

Joezer—*Jehovah is help*

One of David's supporters at Ziklag .... 1 Chr. 12:6

Jogbehah—*lofty*

Town in Gilead .... Judg. 8:11

Jogli—*exiled*

Father of Bukki, a Danite prince .... Num. 34:22

Joha—*Jehovah is living*

1. Benjamite .... 1 Chr. 8:16
2. One of David's mighty men .... 1 Chr. 11:45

Johanan—*Jehovah is gracious*

1. One of David's mighty men .... 1 Chr. 12:2, 4
2. Gadite captain of David .... 1 Chr. 12:12, 14
3. Father of Azariah the priest .... 1 Chr. 6:10
4. Ephraimite leader .... 2 Chr. 28:12
5. Son of King Josiah .... 1 Chr. 3:15
6. Son of Kareah .... 2 Kin. 25:22, 23
   Supports Gedaliah .... Jer. 40:8, 9
   Warns Gedaliah of assassination plot .... Jer. 40:13, 14
   Avenges Gedaliah's murder .... Jer. 41:11-15
   Removes Jewish remnant to Egypt against Jeremiah's warning .... Jer. 41:16-18
7. Elioenai's son .... 1 Chr. 3:24
8. Returned exile .... Ezra 8:12
9. Son of Tobiah .... Neh. 6:17, 18
10. Postexilic high priest .... Neh. 12:22

John—*Jehovah has been gracious*

1. Father of Simon Peter .... John 1:42
   Called Barjona .... Matt. 16:17
2. Jewish official .... Acts 4:6
3. Also called Mark .... Acts 12:12, 25
4. John the Baptist .... Matt. 3:1
5. John the Apostle .... Matt. 4:21

John the Apostle

A. *Life of:*

Son of Zebedee .... Matt. 4:21
Fisherman .... Luke 5:1-11
Leaves his business for Christ .... Matt. 4:21, 22
Called to be an apostle .... Matt. 10:2
Rebuked by Christ .... Luke 9:54, 55; Mark 13:3
Sent to prepare Passover .... Luke 22:8-13
Close to Jesus at Last Supper .... John 13:23-25
Christ commits His mother to .... John 19:26, 27
Witnesses Christ's ascension .... Acts 1:9-13
With Peter, heals a man .... Acts 3:1-11
Imprisoned with Peter .... Acts 4:1-21
With Peter, becomes a missionary .... Acts 8:14-25
Encourages Paul .... Gal. 2:9
Exiled on Patmos .... Rev. 1:9
Wrote a Gospel .... John 21:23-25
Wrote three epistles .... 1 John; 2 John; 3 John
Wrote the Revelation .... Rev. 1:1, 4, 9

B. *Described as:*

Uneducated .... Acts 4:13
Intolerant .... Mark 9:38
Ambitious .... Mark 10:35-37
Trustworthy .... John 19:26, 27
Humble .... Rev. 19:10
Beloved by Jesus .... John 21:20

John the Baptist

A. *Life of:*

Prophecies:
  Concerning .... Is. 40:3-5
  Fulfilled by .... Matt. 3:3
Angel anounces birth of .... Luke 1:11-20
Set apart as Nazarite .... Num. 6:2, 3; Luke 1:15
Lives in deserts .... Luke 1:63, 80
Ministry of, dated .... Luke 3:1-3
Public confusion .... Luke 3:15
Identifies Jesus as the Messiah .... John 1:29-36
Bears witness to Christ .... John 5:33
Exalts Christ .... John 3:25-36
Baptizes Christ .... Matt. 3:13-16
Doubts .... Matt. 11:2-6
Identified with Elijah .... Matt. 11:13, 14
Public reaction to .... Matt. 11:16-18
Christ's testimony concerning .... Matt. 11:9-13
Reproves Herod for adultery .... Mark 6:17, 18
Imprisoned by Herod .... Matt. 4:12
Beheaded by Herod .... Matt. 14:3-12

B. *Described as:*

Fearless .... Matt. 14:3, 4
Righteous .... Mark 6:20
Humble .... John 3:25-31
Faithful .... Acts 13:24, 25
Resourceful .... Matt. 3:4
Baptism of, insufficient .... Acts 18:24-26; Acts 19:1-5
Preaching a baptism of repentance .... Luke 3:2-18

John, the Epistles of—*books of the New Testament*

A. *1 John:*

God is light .... 1 John 1:5-7
True knowledge .... 1 John 2:3, 4
Love one another .... 1 John 3:11-24
God is love .... 1 John 4:7-21
Eternal life .... 1 John 5:13-21

B. *2 John:*

Commandment to love .... 2 John 4-6
Warning against deceit .... 2 John 7-11

C. *3 John:*

Walking in truth .... 3 John 3, 4
Service to the brethren .... 3 John 5-8
Rebuke to Diotrephes .... 3 John 9, 10
Do good .... 3 John 11, 12

John, the Gospel of—*a book of the New Testament*

Deity of Christ .... John 1:1-18
Testimony of the Baptist .... John 1:19-34
Wedding at Cana .... John 2:1-11
Samarian mission .... John 4:1-42
Feast of Tabernacles .... John 7:1-53
The Good Shepherd .... John 10:1-42
Lazarus raised .... John 11:1-57
Priestly prayer .... John 17:1-26
Sufferings and glory .... John 18:1—20:31
Purpose of .... John 20:30, 31

Joiada—*Jehovah knows*

1. Son of Meshullam .... Neh. 3:6
2. Postexilic high priest .... Neh. 12:10, 11, 22
   Son banished from priesthood .... Neh. 13:28

Joiakim—*Jehovah establishes*

Postexilic high priest; son of Jeshua .... Neh. 12:10-26

Joiarib—*Jehovah contends*

1. Teacher sent by Ezra .... Ezra 8:16, 17
2. Postexilic Judahite chief .... Neh. 11:5
3. Founder of an order of priests .... Neh. 11:10
4. Postexilic priest .... Neh. 12:6
   Father of Joiakim .... Neh. 12:19

Jokdeam—*anger of the people*

City of Judah .... Josh. 15:56

Jokim—*Jehovah raises up*

Judahite .... 1 Chr. 4:22

Jokmeam—*let the people arise*

Town of Ephraim .... 1 Chr. 6:68
Home of Kohathite Levites .... 1 Chr. 6:66, 68
Same as Kibzaim in .... Josh. 21:22
Called Jokneam .... 1 Kin. 4:12

Jokneam—*let the people inquire*

1. Town near Mt. Carmel .... Josh. 12:22
   In tribe of Zebulun .... Josh. 19:11
   Assigned to Levites .... Josh. 21:34
2. Town of Ephraim .... 1 Kin. 4:12
   See Jokmeam

Jokshan—*fowler*

Son of Abraham and Keturah .... Gen. 25:1, 2

Joktan—*he will be made small*

A descendant of Shem .... Gen. 10:21, 25

Joktheel—*God's reward of victory*

1. Village of Judah .... Josh. 15:20, 38
2. Name given by King Amaziah to Selah .... 2 Kin. 14:7

Jona—*Greek form of Jonah*

Father of Peter .... John 1:42

Jonadab—*Jehovah is bounteous*

1. Son of Shimeah; David's nephew .... 2 Sam. 13:3
   Very subtle man .... 2 Sam. 13:3-6, 32-36
2. Son of Rechab .... Jer. 35:6
   Makes Rechabites primitive and temperate .... Jer. 35:5-17
   Blessing upon .... Jer. 35:18, 19
   Opposes idolatry .... 2 Kin. 10:15, 16, 23
   Called Jehonadab .... 2 Kin. 10:15, 23

Jonah—*dove*

Son of Amittai .... Jon. 1:1
Ordered to go to Nineveh .... Jon. 1:2
Flees to Tarshish .... Jon. 1:3
Cause of storm; cast into sea .... Jon. 1:4-16
Swallowed by a great fish .... Jon. 1:17
Prays in fish's belly .... Jon. 2:1-9
Vomited upon land .... Jon. 2:10
Obeys second order to go to Nineveh .... Jon. 3:1-10

SUBJECT REFERENCE

Grieved at Nineveh's repentance ... Jon. 4:1-3
Taught God's mercy ... Jon. 4:4-11
Type of Christ's resurrection ... Matt. 12:39, 40

Jonam

Found in the genealogy of Jesus ... Luke 3:30

Jonan—*Jehovah has been gracious*

Ancestor of Christ ... Luke 3:30

Jonathan—*Jehovah has given*

1. Levite; becomes Micah's priest ... Judg. 17:1-13
   Follows Danites to idolatrous Dan ... Judg. 18:3-31
   Grandson of Moses (Manasseh) ... Judg. 18:30
2. King Saul's eldest son ... 1 Sam. 14:49
   Smites Philistine garrison ... 1 Sam. 13:2, 3
   Attacks Michmash ... 1 Sam. 14:1-14
   Saved from his father's vow ... 1 Sam. 14:24-45
   Makes covenant with David ... 1 Sam. 18:1-4
   Pleads for David's life ... 1 Sam. 19:1-7
   Warns David of Saul's wrath ... 1 Sam. 20:1-42
   Makes second covenant with David ... 1 Sam. 23:15-18
   Killed by Philistines ... 1 Sam. 31:2, 8
   Mourned by David ... 2 Sam. 1:17-27
   David provides for his son ... 2 Sam. 9:1-8
3. Uncle of King David ... 1 Chr. 27:32
4. Son of the high priest Abiathar ... 2 Sam. 15:27
   Remains faithful to David ... 2 Sam. 15:26-36
   Brings David Absalom's plans ... 2 Sam. 17:15-22
   Informs Adonijah of David's choice ... 1 Kin. 1:41-49
5. Son of Shimeah ... 2 Sam. 21:21, 22
6. One of David's mighty men ... 2 Sam. 23:32
7. Judahite ... 1 Chr. 2:32, 33
8. Son of Kareah ... Jer. 40:8, 9
9. Scribe ... Jer. 37:15, 20
10. Opponents of Ezra's reforms ... Ezra 10:15
11. Descendant of Adin ... Ezra 8:6
12. Levite of Asaph's line ... Neh. 12:35
13. Head of a priestly house ... Neh. 12:14
14. Postexilic high priest ... Neh. 12:11

Jonath-elem-rechokim—*the silent dove of the far ones*

Musical tune ... Ps. 56 (Title)

Joppa, Japho—*beauty*

Allotted to Dan ... Josh. 19:40, 46
Seaport city ... 2 Chr. 2:16
Center of commerce ... Ezra 3:7
Scene of Peter's vision ... Acts 10:5-23, 32

Jorah—*rain*

Family of returnees ... Ezra 2:18
Called Hariph ... Neh. 7:24

Jorai—*rainy*

Gadite chief ... 1 Chr. 5:13

Joram, Jehoram—*Jehovah is exalted*

1. Son of Toi, king of Hamath ... 2 Sam. 8:10
   Called Hadoram ... 1 Chr. 18:10
2. Levite ... 1 Chr. 26:25
3. Son of Ahab, king of Israel ... 2 Kin. 3:1
   Institutes some reforms ... 2 Kin. 3:2, 3
   Joins Judah against Moab ... 2 Kin. 3:1-27
   Slain by Jehu ... 2 Kin. 9:14-26
   Called Jehoram ... 2 Kin. 1:17
4. Priest sent to teach the people ... 2 Chr. 17:8
5. Son and successor of Jehoshaphat, king of Judah ... 2 Kin. 8:16
   Murders his brothers ... 2 Chr. 21:1-4
   His wife, Ahab's daughter, leads him astray ... 2 Kin. 8:17, 18
   Edomites revolt against ... 2 Chr. 21:8-10
   Unable to withstand invaders ... 2 Chr. 21:16, 17

SUBJECT REFERENCE

Elijah's prophecy against ... 2 Chr. 21:12-15
Dies horribly without mourners ... 2 Chr. 21:18-20
Called Jehoram ... 2 Chr. 21:1, 5

Jordan—*the descender; a river in Palestine*

Canaan's eastern boundary ... Num. 34:12
Despised by foreigners ... 2 Kin. 5:10, 12
Lot dwells near ... Gen. 13:8-13
Jacob crosses ... Gen. 32:10
Moses forbidden to cross ... Deut. 3:27
Israel crosses miraculously ... Josh. 3:1-17
Stones commemorate crossing of ... Josh. 4:1-24
David crosses in flight ... 2 Sam. 17:22, 24
Divided by Elijah ... 2 Kin. 2:5-8
Divided by Elisha ... 2 Kin. 2:13, 14
Naaman healed in ... 2 Kin. 5:10, 14
John's baptism in ... Matt. 3:6
Christ baptized in ... Matt. 3:13-17

Jorim—*Jehovah is exalted*

Ancestor of Christ ... Luke 3:29

Jorkoam

Judahite family name ... 1 Chr. 2:44
May be same as Jokdeam in ... Josh. 15:56

Josabad—*Jehovah endowed*

One of David's mighty men ... 1 Chr. 12:4

Jose

Ancestor of Christ ... Luke 3:29

Josedech—*Jehovah is just*

Father of the high priest Joshua ... Hag. 1:1, 12, 14

Joseph—*may He* (Jehovah) *add*

1. Son of Jacob by Rachel ... Gen. 30:22-24
2. Father of one of the spies ... Num. 13:7
3. Son of Asaph ... 1 Chr. 25:2, 9
4. One who divorced his foreign wife ... Ezra 10:32, 42
5. Pre-exilic ancestor of Christ ... Luke 3:30
6. Priest in the days of Joiakim ... Neh. 12:14
7. Postexilic ancestor of Christ ... Luke 3:26
8. Son of Mattathias, in Christ's ancestry ... Luke 3:24, 25
9. Husband of Mary, Jesus' mother ... Matt. 1:16
   Of Davidic lineage ... Matt. 1:20
   Angel explains Mary's condition to ... Matt. 1:19-25
   With Mary at Jesus' birth ... Luke 2:16
   Obeys Old Testament ordinances ... Luke 2:21-24
   Takes Jesus and Mary to Egypt ... Matt. 2:13-15
   Returns to Nazareth with family ... Matt. 2:19-23
   Jesus subject to ... Luke 2:51
10. Man of Arimathea ... John 19:38
    Devout man ... Luke 23:50, 51
    Secret disciple ... John 19:38
    Obtains Christ's body; prepares it ... Mark 15:43, 46
    Receives Nicodemus' help ... John 19:39, 40
    Puts Christ's body in his new tomb ... Luke 23:53
11. Called Barsabas; one of two chosen to occupy Judas' place ... Acts 1:22-26
12. Also called Barnabas ... Acts 4:36

Joseph—*increaser*

A. *Life of:*

Jacob's son by Rachel ... Gen. 30:22-25
Jacob's favorite ... Gen. 37:3
Aroused his brothers' hatred ... Gen. 37:4
Sold into Egypt ... Gen. 37:25-30
Wins esteem in Egypt ... Gen. 39:1-23
Interprets Pharaoh's dream ... Gen. 41:1-37
Made Pharaoh's Prime Minister ... Gen. 41:38-46
Recognizes his brothers ... Gen. 42:1-8
Reveals his identity ... Gen. 45:1-16
Invites Jacob to Egypt ... Gen. 45:17-28
Enslaves Egypt ... Gen. 47:13-26
Put under oath by Jacob ... Gen. 47:28-31

SUBJECT REFERENCE

His sons blessed by Jacob ... Gen. 48:1-22
Blessed by Jacob ... Gen. 49:22-26
Mourns his father's death ... Gen. 50:1-14
Deals kindly with his brothers ... Gen. 50:15-21
His death at 110 ... Gen. 50:22-26
Descendants of ... Num. 26:28-37

B. *Character of:*

Spiritually sensitive ... Gen. 37:2
Wise and prudent ... Gen. 41:38-49
Of strong emotions ... Gen. 43:29-31
Sees God's hand in human events ... Gen. 45:7, 8
Forgiving ... Gen. 50:19-21
Man of faith ... Heb. 11:22

Joses—*increaser*

One of Christ's brothers ... Matt. 13:55

Joshah—*Jehovah's gift*

Simeonite leader ... 1 Chr. 4:34, 38

Joshaphat—*Jehovah has judged*

1. Mighty man of David ... 1 Chr. 11:43
2. Priestly trumpeter ... 1 Chr. 15:24

Joshaviah—*Jehovah is equality*

One of David's mighty men ... 1 Chr. 11:46

Joshbekashah—*he returns a hard fate*

Head of musical order ... 1 Chr. 25:4, 24

Josheb-basshebeth—*one who sat on the seat*

Chief of David's mighty men ... 2 Sam. 23:8
Called Jashobeam ... 1 Chr. 11:11

Joshibiah—*Jehovah causes to dwell* (in peace)

Simeonite ... 1 Chr. 4:35

Joshua, Jeshua—*Jehovah is salvation*

1. Native of Beth-shemesh ... 1 Sam. 6:14, 18
2. Governor of Jerusalem during Josiah's reign ... 2 Kin. 23:8
3. High priest during Zerubbabel's time ... Hag. 1:1, 12, 14
   Called Jeshua in Ezra and Nehemiah ... Ezra 2:2
   Type of Christ ... Zech. 6:11-13
4. Son of Nun ... Num. 13:8, 16

Joshua, Jehoshua—*Jehovah saves*

A. *Life of:*

Son of Nun; an Ephraimite ... Num. 13:8, 16
Defeats Amalek ... Ex. 17:8-16
Minister under Moses ... Ex. 24:13
One of the spies ... Num. 13:1-3, 8, 16
Reports favorably ... Num. 14:6-10
Moses' successor ... Num. 27:18-23
Inspired by God ... Num. 27:18
Unifies the people ... Josh. 1:10 18
Sends spies out ... Josh. 2:1-24
Crosses Jordan ... Josh. 3:1-17
Destroys Jericho ... Josh. 6:1-27
Conquers Canaan ... Josh. 10—12
Divides the land ... Josh. 13—19
Orders Israel's leaders ... Josh. 23:1-16
Final address to the nation ... Josh. 24:1-28
Dies at 110 ... Josh. 24:29, 30
Called: Jehoshua ... Num. 13:16

B. *Character of:*

Courageous ... Num. 14:6-10
Emotional ... Josh. 7:6-10
Wise military man ... Josh. 8:3-29
Easily beguiled ... Josh. 9:3-27
Prophetic ... Josh. 6:26, 27
Strong religious leader ... Judg. 2:7

Joshua, the Book of—*a book of the Old Testament*

Entering promised land ... Josh. 1:1—5:12
The divine captain ... Josh. 5:13—6:5
Capture of Jericho ... Josh. 6:6-27
Capture of Ai ... Josh. 8:1-29
Apportionment of the land ... Josh. 13:1—22:34
Covenant at Shechem ... Josh. 24:1-28
Death of Joshua ... Josh. 24:29-33

Josiah—*Jehovah heals*

1. Son and successor of Amon, king of Judah ... 2 Kin. 21:25, 26
   Crowned at 8; reigns righteously 31 years ... 2 Kin. 22:1
   Named before birth ... 1 Kin. 13:1, 2

SUBJECT — REFERENCE

Repairs the Temple ... 2 Kin. 22:3-9
Receives the Book of Law ... 2 Kin. 22:10-17
Saved from predicted doom ... 2 Kin. 22:18-20
Reads the Law ... 2 Kin. 23:1, 2
Makes a covenant ... 2 Kin. 23:3
Destroys idolatry ... 2 Kin. 23:4, 20, 24
Observes the Passover ... 2 Kin. 23:21-23
Exceptional king ... 2 Kin. 23:25
Slain in battle ... 2 Chr. 35:20-24
Lamented by Jeremiah ... 2 Chr. 35:25-27
Commended by Jeremiah ... Jer. 22:15-18
Ancestor (Josias) of Christ ... Matt. 1:10, 11
2. Son of Zephaniah ... Zech. 6:10

Josibiah—*Jehovah causes to dwell* (in peace)
Simeonite ... 1 Chr. 4:35

Josiphiah—*Jehovah will increase*
Father of a postexilic Jew ... Ezra 8:10

Jot—*Greek iota* (i); *Hebrew yodh* (y)
Figurative of the smallest detail ... Matt. 5:18

Jotbah—*pleasantness*
City of Haruz, the father of Meshullemeth ... 2 Kin. 21:19

Jotbathah—*pleasantness*
Israelite encampment ... Num. 33:33
Called Jotbath ... Deut. 10:7

Jotham—*Jehovah is perfect*
1. Gideon's youngest son ... Judg. 9:5
Escapes Abimelech's massacre ... Judg. 9:5, 21
Utters a prophetic parable ... Judg. 9:7-21
Sees his prophecy fulfilled ... Judg. 9:22-57
2. Son and successor of Azariah (Uzziah), king of Judah ... 2 Kin. 15:5, 7
Reign of, partly good ... 2 Kin. 15:32-38
Conquers Ammonites ... 2 Chr. 27:5-9
Contemporary of Isaiah and Hosea ... Is. 1:1
Ancestor (Joatham) of Christ ... Matt. 1:9
3. Son of Jahdai ... 1 Chr. 2:47

Journey—*an extended trip*
Preparation for, by:
Prayer ... Rom. 1.10
God's providence acknowledged ... James 4:13-17

Joy—*gladness of heart*
A. *Kinds of:*
Foolish ... Prov. 15:21
Temporary ... Matt. 13:20
Motherly ... Ps. 113:9
Figurative ... Is. 52:9
Future ... Matt. 25:21, 23
B. *Described as:*
Everlasting ... Is. 51:11
Great ... Acts 8:8
Full ... 1 John 1:4
Abundant ... 2 Cor. 8:2
Unspeakable ... 1 Pet. 1:8
C. *Causes of:*
Victory ... 1 Sam. 18:6
Christ's birth ... Luke 2:10, 11
Christ's resurrection ... Matt. 28:7, 8
Sinner's repentance ... Luke 15:5, 10
Miracles among the Gentiles ... Acts 8:7, 8
Forgiveness ... Ps. 51:8, 12
God's Word ... Jer. 15:16
Spiritual discovery ... Matt. 13:44
Names written in heaven ... Luke 10:17, 20
True faith ... 1 Pet. 1:8
D. *Place of, in:*
Prayer ... Is. 56:7
Christian:
Fellowship ... Phil. 1:25
Tribulation ... 2 Cor. 7:4-7
Giving ... 2 Cor. 8:2
E. *Contrasted with:*
Weeping ... Ezra 3:12, 13; Ps. 30:5
Tears ... Ps. 126:5
Sorrow ... Is. 35:10
Mourning ... Jer. 31:13

SUBJECT — REFERENCE

Pain ... John 16:20, 21
Loss ... Heb. 13:17; Heb. 10:34
Adversity ... Eccl. 7:14
Discipline ... Ps. 51:8; Heb. 12:11
Persecution ... Luke 6:22, 23
F. *Of angels:*
At creation ... Job 38:4, 7
At Christ's birth ... Luke 2:10, 13, 14
At sinner's conversion ... Luke 15:10
G. *Expressed by:*
Songs ... Gen. 31:27
Musical instruments ... 1 Sam. 18:6
Sounds ... 1 Chr. 15:16
Praises ... 2 Chr. 29:30
Shouting ... Ezra 3:12, 13
Heart ... 1 Kin. 21:7
See Gladness; Happiness of the Saints

Jozabad—*Jehovah has bestowed*
1, 2, 3. Three of David's mighty men ... 1 Chr. 12:4, 20
4. Levite overseer in Hezekiah's reign ... 2 Chr. 31:13
5. Chief Levite in Josiah's reign ... 2 Chr. 35:9
6. Levite, son of Jeshua ... Ezra 8:33
Probably the same as in ... Ezra 10:23
7. Expounder of the Law ... Neh. 8:7
8. Levitical chief ... Neh. 11:16
Some consider 6, 7, 8 the same person
9. Priest who divorced his foreign wife ... Ezra 10:22

Jozachar—*Jehovah has remembered*
Assassin of Joash ... 2 Kin. 12:19-21
Called Zabad ... 2 Chr. 24:26

Jozadak—*Jehovah is righteous*
Postexilic priest ... Ezra 3:2

Jubal—*playing*
Son of Lamech ... Gen. 4:21

Jubilee, Year of
A. *Regulations concerning:*
Introduced by trumpet ... Lev. 25:9
After 49 years ... Lev. 25:8
Rules for fixing prices ... Lev. 25:15, 16, 25-28
B. *Purposes of:*
Restore liberty (to the enslaved) ... Lev. 25:38-43
Restore property (to the original owner) ... Lev. 25:23-28
Remit debt (to the indebted) ... Lev. 25:47-55
Restore rest (to the land) ... Lev. 25:11, 12, 18-22
C. *Figurative of:*
Christ's mission ... Is. 61:1-3
Earth's jubilee ... Rom. 8:19-24

Judaea—*a district in southern Palestine*
District under a governor ... Luke 3:1
All Palestine ... Luke 23:5
All the land of the Jews ... Acts 10:37
Rural people outside Jerusalem ... Matt. 4:25
Wilderness country near Dead Sea ... Matt. 3:1
Christ born in ... Matt. 2:1, 5, 6
Hostile toward Christ ... John 7:1
Gospel preached in ... Acts 8:1, 4
Churches established in ... Acts 9:31

Judah—*let Him* (God) *be praised*
1. Son of Jacob and Leah ... Gen. 29:15-35
Intercedes for Joseph ... Gen. 37:26, 27
Marries a Canaanite ... Gen. 38:1-10
Fathers Perez and Zerah by Tamar ... Gen. 38:11-30
Through Tamar, an ancestor of David ... Ruth 4:18-22
Ancestor of Christ ... Matt. 1:3-16
Offers himself as Benjamin's ransom ... Gen. 44:33, 34
Leads Jacob to Goshen ... Gen. 46:28
Jacob bestows birthright on ... Gen. 49:3-10
Messiah promised through ... Gen. 49:10

SUBJECT — REFERENCE

2. Judah, Tribe of
See separate article
3. Postexilic Levite ... Ezra 3:9
4. Levite returning with Zerubbabel ... Neh. 12:8
5. Levite divorced his foreign wife ... Ezra 10:23
6. Postexilic overseer ... Neh. 11:9
7. Priest and musician ... Neh. 12:36
Probably same as 4 and 5
8. Postexilic prince ... Neh. 12:32-34

Judah, Tribe of
Descendants of Judah ... Gen. 29:35
Prophecy concerning ... Gen. 49:8-12
Five families of ... Num. 26:19-22
Leads in wilderness journey ... Num. 2:3, 9
Numbering of, at Sinai ... Num. 1:26, 27
Numbering of, in Moab ... Num. 26:22
Leads in conquest of Canaan ... Judg. 1:1-19
Territory assigned to ... Josh. 15:1-63
Fights against Gibeah ... Judg. 20:18
Makes David king ... 2 Sam. 2:1-11
Elders of, upbraided by David ... 2 Sam. 19:11, 15
Conflict with other tribes ... 2 Sam. 19:41-43
Loyal to David during Sheba's rebellion ... 2 Sam. 20:1, 2
Loyal to Davidic house at Jeroboam's rebellion ... 1 Kin. 12:20
Becomes leader of southern kingdom (Judah) ... 1 Kin. 14:21, 22
Taken to Babylon ... 2 Kin. 24:1-16
Returns after exile ... 2 Chr. 36:20-23
Christ comes of ... Luke 3:23-33

Judas—*Greek form of Judah*
1. Judah, Jacob's son ... Matt. 1:2, 3
See Judah 1
2. Judas Lebbaeus, surnamed Thaddaeus ... Matt. 10:3
One of Christ's apostles ... Luke 6:13, 16
Offers a question ... John 14:22
3. Betrayer of Christ (see Iscariot) ... Luke 6:13, 16
4. Brother of Christ (see Brethren of Christ) ... Matt. 13:55
See Jude
5. Leader of an insurrection ... Acts 5:37
6. Jew of Damascus ... Acts 9:11
7. Judas Barsabbas, a chief deputy ... Acts 15:22-32
Probably related to the disciple Joseph ... Acts 1:23

Jude, Judas
Brother of Christ ... Matt. 13:55
Does not believe in Christ ... John 7:5
Becomes Christ's disciple ... Acts 1:14
Writes an Epistle ... Jude 1
See Judas 5

Jude, the Epistle of—*a book of the New Testament*
Author ... Jude 1
Against false teachers ... Jude 3-5
Against the ungodly ... Jude 6-16
Exhortation ... Jude 17-23; Acts 9:31

Judge—*an official authorized to hear and decide cases of law*
A. *History of, in scripture:*
Family head ... Gen. 38:24
Established by Moses ... Ex. 18:13-26; Deut. 1:9-17
Rules for ... Deut. 16:18-20; Deut. 17:2-13
Circuit ... 1 Sam. 7:6, 15-17
King acts as ... 2 Sam. 15:2; 1 Kin. 3:9, 28
Levites assigned ... 1 Chr. 23:1-4
Jehoshaphat established court ... 2 Chr. 19:5-11
Restored after exile ... Ezra 7:25
B. *Procedure before:*
Public trial ... Ex. 18:13
Case presented ... Deut. 1:16; Deut. 25:1
Position of parties ... Zech. 3:1
Accused heard ... John 7:51

SUBJECT ... REFERENCE

Witness ... Deut. 19:15-19
Priests ... Deut. 17:8-13
Oath ... Ex. 22:11
Heb. 6:16
Casting of lots sometimes used ... Prov. 18:18
Divine will sought ... Lev. 24:12-14

C. *Office of:*

Divinely instituted ... 2 Sam. 7:11
Limits to human affairs ... 1 Sam. 2:25
Restricted by righteousness ... Deut. 16:18-20
Needful of great wisdom ... 1 Kin. 3:9
Easily corrupted ... Mic. 7:3
Unjustly used ... Acts 23:3
Acts 25:9-11
Fulfilled perfectly in the Messiah ... Is. 2:4; Is. 11:3, 4; Acts 17:31

Judge, God as

Manner of:

According to righteousness ... 1 Pet. 2:23
According to one's works ... 1 Pet. 1:17
Openly ... Rom. 2:16
By Christ ... John 5:22, 30
In a final way ... Joel 3:12-14

Judges of Israel

A. *Characteristics of era:*

No central authority ... Judg. 17.6
Judg. 21:25
Spiritual decline ... Judg. 2:18
Judg. 18:1-31

B. *List of:*

Othniel ... Judg. 3:9-11
Ehud ... Judg. 3:15-30
Shamgar ... Judg. 3:31
Deborah and Barak ... Judg. 4:4-9
Gideon ... Judg. 6:11-40
Abimelech ... Judg. 9:1-54
Tola ... Judg. 10:1, 2
Jair ... Judg. 10:3-5
Jephthah ... Judg. 12:1-7
Ibzan ... Judg. 12:8-10
Elon ... Judg. 12:11, 12
Abdon ... Judg. 12:13-15
Samson ... Judg. 15:20
Eli ... 1 Sam. 4:15, 18
Samuel ... 1 Sam. 7:15
Samuel's sons ... 1 Sam. 8:1-3

Judges, the Book of—*a book of the Old Testament*

The death of Joshua ... Judg. 2:6-10
Deborah and Barak ... Judg. 4:1—5:31
Gideon ... Judg. 6:1—8:32
Jephthah ... Judg. 10:6—11:40
Samson ... Judg. 13:1—16:31
Micah and the Danites ... Judg. 18
The war against Benjamin ... Judg. 19:1—21:25

Judgment, divine

A. *Design of:*

Punish evil ... Ex. 20:5
Chasten ... 2 Sam. 7:14, 15
Manifest God's righteousness ... Ex. 9:14-16
Correct ... Hab. 1:12
Warn others ... Luke 13:3, 5

B. *Causes of:*

Disobedience ... 2 Chr. 7:19-22
Rejecting God's warnings ... 2 Chr. 36:16, 17
Idolatry ... Jer. 7:30-34
Sins of rulers ... 2 Chr. 21:1-17
Loving evil ... Rom. 1:18-32

C. *Kinds of:*

Physical destruction ... Deut. 28:15-68
Material loss ... Mal. 3:11
Spiritual blindness ... Is. 6:9, 10
Eternal destruction ... Luke 12:16-21
Luke 16:19-31

D. *Avoidance of, by:*

Turning to God ... Deut. 30:1-3
Turning from sin ... Jer. 7:3-7
Humiliation ... Jon. 1:1-17
Prayer ... 2 Kin. 19:14-36
2 Chr. 20:5-30

Judgment Hall

Of Solomon ... 1 Kin. 7:1, 7
Pilate's ... John 18:28
Herod's ... Acts 23:35

SUBJECT ... REFERENCE

Judgment, human

A. *Weaknesses of:*

Often circumstantial ... Josh. 22:10-34
Sometimes wrong ... Gen. 39:10-20
Hasty and revengeful ... 1 Sam. 25:20-35
Full of conceit ... Esth. 5:11-14
Prejudicial ... Luke 7:38-50

B. *Rules regarding:*

Begin with self-judgment ... Matt. 7:1-5
Become spiritually minded ... 1 Cor. 2:12-15
Abound in love ... Phil. 1:9, 10
Await the final judgment ... Rom. 14:10

C. *Basis of:*

Circumstance ... Gen. 39:10-20
Opinion ... Acts 28:22
Moral Law ... Rom. 2:14-16
Conscience ... 1 Cor. 10:27-29
Nature ... 1 Cor. 11:13, 14
Apostolic authority ... 1 Cor. 5:3, 4
Law of Christ ... Gal. 6:2-4
Divine illumination ... Josh. 7:10-15

Judgment, the last

A. *Described as:*

Day of wrath ... Rom. 2:5
Day of judgment ... 2 Pet. 3:7
Judgment seat of Christ ... Matt. 25:31

B. *Time of:*

After death ... Heb. 9:27
At Christ's return ... Matt. 25:31
Appointed day ... Acts 17:31
After the world's destruction ... 2 Pet. 3:7-15

C. *Grounds of:*

One's works ... 1 Cor. 3:11-15
One's faith ... Matt. 7:22, 23
Conscience ... Rom. 2:12, 14-16
Law ... Rom. 2:12
Gospel ... James 2:12
Christ's Word ... John 12:48
Book of Life ... Rev. 20:12, 15

D. *Results of:*

Separation of righteous from the wicked ... Matt. 13:36-43
Retribution for disobedience ... 2 Thess. 1:6-10
Crown of righteousness ... 2 Tim. 4:8

E. *Attitudes toward:*

Be prepared for ... 1 Thess. 5:1-9
Beware of deception ... Matt. 7:21-27
Warn the wicked concerning ... 2 Cor. 5:10, 11

Judith—*Jewess*

Hittite wife of Esau ... Gen. 26:34
Called Aholibamah ... Gen. 36:2

Julia—*feminine form of Julius*

Christian woman at Rome ... Rom. 16:15

Julius—*the family name of the Caesars*

Roman centurion assigned to guard Paul ... Acts 27:1, 3
Disregards Paul's warning ... Acts 27:11
Accepts Paul's warning ... Acts 27:31
Saves Paul's life ... Acts 27:42:44

Junia—*a kinsman of Paul*

Jewish Christian at Rome ... Rom. 16:7

Juniper—*a shrub of the broom family*

Roots produce charcoal ... Ps. 120:4
Leaves provide little shade ... 1 Kin. 19:4, 5
Roots eaten in desperation ... Job 30:3, 4

Jupiter—*chief god of Roman mythology*

Barnabas called ... Acts 14:12

Jushab-hesed—*kindness returned*

Son of Zerubbabel ... 1 Chr. 3:20

Just, justice—*integrity of character*

A. *Descriptive of:*

Righteous man ... Gen. 6:9
Upright Gentile ... Acts 10:22
God's nature ... Deut. 32:4
Promised Messiah ... Zech. 9:9
Christ ... Acts 3:14
Saved ... Heb. 12:23

SUBJECT ... REFERENCE

B. *Produced by:*

True wisdom ... Prov. 8:15
Parental instruction ... Gen. 18:19
True faith ... Heb. 10:38

See Injustice

Justification—*accounting the guilty just before God*

A. *Negatively considered, not by:*

The Law ... Rom. 3:20, 28
Men's righteousness ... Rom. 10:1-5
Human works ... Rom. 4:1-5
Faith mixed with works ... Acts 15:1-29
Gal. 2:16
A dead faith ... James 2:14-26

B. *Positively considered, by:*

Grace ... Rom. 5:17-21
Christ:
Blood ... Rom. 5:9
Resurrection ... Rom. 4:25
Righteousness ... Rom. 10:4
Faith ... Rom. 3:26, 27

C. *Fruits of:*

Forgiveness of sins ... Acts 13:38, 39
Peace ... Rom. 5:1
Holiness ... Rom. 6:22
Imputed righteousness ... 2 Cor. 5:21
Outward righteousness ... Rom. 8:4
Eternal life ... Titus 3:7

D. *Evidence of:*

Works (by faith) ... James 2:18
Wisdom ... James 3:17
Patience ... James 5:7, 8
Suffering ... James 5:10, 11

See Imputation

Justus—*righteous*

1. Surname of Joseph ... Acts 1:23
2. Man of Corinth; befriends Paul ... Acts 18:7
3. Converted Jew ... Col. 4:11

Juttah—*extended*

Town of Judah ... Josh. 15:55
Assigned to the priests ... Josh. 21:13, 16

Juvenile delinquents

A. *Examples of:*

Eli's sons ... 1 Sam. 2:12-17
Samuel's sons ... 1 Sam. 8:1-5
Elisha's mockers ... 2 Kin. 2:22-24

B. *Safeguards against:*

Praying mother ... 1 Sam. 1:9-28
Strict discipline ... Prov. 13:24
Early training ... Prov. 22:6

K

Kab—*a hollow vessel*

Jewish measure; about 2 quarts ... 2 Kin. 6:25

Kabzeel—*God's gathering*

Town in south Judah ... Josh. 15:21
Benaiah's home town ... 2 Sam. 23:20
Called Jekabzeel ... Neh. 11:25

Kadesh—*holy*

Location of ... Num. 27:14
Captured by Chedorlaomer ... Gen. 14:5-7
Hagar flees near ... Gen. 16:7, 14
Abraham dwells here ... Gen. 20:1
Spies sent from ... Num. 13:3, 26
Miriam buried here ... Num. 20:1
Moses strikes rock there ... Num. 20:1-13
Request passage through Edom here ... Num. 20:14-22
Figurative of God's power ... Ps. 29:8
Boundary in the new Israel ... Ezek. 47:19

Kadesh-barnea—*another name for Kadesh*

Boundary of promised land ... Num. 34:1-4
Extent of Joshua's military campaign ... Josh. 10:41

Kadmiel—*God is the Ancient One*

1. Levite family head; returns from Babylon ... Ezra 2:40

SUBJECT REFERENCE

2. Takes part in rebuilding ..... Ezra 3:9
Participates in national repentance .... Neh. 9:4, 5

Kadmonites—*easterners*

Tribe whose land Abraham is to inherit .... Gen. 15:18, 19

Kallai—*smith*

Postexilic priest .... Neh. 12:1, 20

Kanah—*place of reeds*

1. Brook between Ephraim and Manasseh .... Josh. 16:8
2. Border town of Asher .... Josh. 19:28

Karka—*floor, ground*

Place in south Judah .... Josh. 15:3

Karkor—*even ground*

Place in east Jordan .... Judg. 8:10

Karnaim—*two peaks*

Conquered .... Amos 6:13

Kartah—*city*

Levitical town in Zebulun ...... Josh. 21:34

Kartan—*town*

Town in Naphtali assigned to Levites .... Josh. 21:32
Called Kirjathaim .... 1 Chr. 6:76

Kattath—*little*

Town of Zebulun.............. Josh. 19:15, 16
Same as Kitron .... Judg. 1:30

Kedar—*dark*

Son of Ishmael................ Gen. 25:12, 13
Skilled archers .... Is. 21:17
Prophecy against .... Jer. 49:28, 29
Inhabit villages .... Is. 42:11
Famous for flocks .... Is. 60:7
Tents of, called black .... Song 1:5
Type of barbarous people ...... Ps. 120:5

Kedemah—*toward the east*

Ishmaelite tribe .... Gen. 25:15

Kedemoth—*ancient places*

City east of the Jordan assigned to the tribe of Reuben .... Josh. 13:15, 18
Assigned to Merarite Levites .... Josh. 21:34, 37
Messengers sent from .... Deut. 2:26

Kedesh—*sacred place*

1. Town in south Judah .... Josh. 15:23
2. City of Issachar assigned to Gershonite Levites.................... 1 Chr. 6:72
   Called Kishion .... Josh. 19:20
3. Canaanite town taken by Joshua and assigned to Naphtali .... Josh. 12:22
   Called Kedesh in Galilee .... Josh. 20:7
   Called Kedeshnaphtali ...... Judg. 4:6
   City of refuge .... Josh. 21:27, 32
   Home of Barak .... Judg. 4:6
   People of, carried captive .... 2 Kin. 15:29

Keeper—*one who watches over, or guards*

Guardian of:

Sheep....................... Gen. 4:2
Brother .... Gen. 4:9
Wardrobe .... 2 Kin. 22:14
Gate .... Neh. 3:29
1 Chr. 9:21
Women .... Esth. 2:3, 8
Prison .... Acts 16:27

Keeping—*holding or observing something firmly*

A. *Christian objects of:*
   Christ's commandments ..... John 14:15-23
   God's commandments....... 1 John 5:2
   God's Word .... Rev. 22:7, 9
   Unity of the Spirit .... Eph. 4:3
   Faith .... 2 Tim. 4:7
   Purity...................... 1 Tim. 5:22
   Oneself .... 1 John 5:18
   In God's love .... Jude 21
B. *Manner of, by God's:*
   Power .... John 10:28, 29
   Name...................... John 17:11, 12
C. *Promises respecting:*
   Provision .... Ps. 121:3-8
   Preservation .... John 17:11, 12
   Power .... Rev. 2:26
   Purity...................... Rev. 16:15

See Heart

Kehelathah—*assembly*

Israelite camp................. Num. 33:22, 23

Keilah—*enclosed*

Town of Judah .... Josh. 15:21, 44
Rescued from Philistines by David .... 1 Sam. 23:1-5
Betrays David .... 1 Sam. 23:6-12
David escapes from .... 1 Sam. 23:13
Reoccupied after the exile ...... Neh. 3:17

Kelaiah—*Jehovah is light*

Levite who divorced foreign wife .... Ezra 10:18, 19, 23

See Kelita

Kelita—*dwarf*

Levite who divorced foreign wife .... Ezra 10:23
Explains the Law.............. Neh. 8:7
Called Kelaiah .... Ezra 10:23

Kemuel—*congregation of God*

1. Son of Nahor; father of six sons .... Gen. 22:20, 21
2. Ephraimite prince .... Num. 34:24
3. Levite in David's time....... 1 Chr. 27:17

Kenan—*fixed*

Descendant of Adam .... 1 Chr. 1:2

See Cainan

Kenath—*possession*

City of Gilead near Bozrah taken by Nobah...................... Num. 32:40, 42
Reconquered by Geshur and Aram....................... 1 Chr. 2:23

Kenaz—*side, flank*

1. Descendant of Esau......... Gen. 36:10, 11
2. Edomite duke .... Gen. 36:42
3. Caleb's brother; father of Othniel .... Josh. 15:17
   Family called Kenezites ..... Num. 32:12
4. Grandson of Caleb .... 1 Chr. 4:15

Kenezite, Kenizzite

1. Canaanite tribe whose land is promised to Abraham's seed .... Gen. 15:19
2. Title applied to Caleb .... Num. 32:12
   Probably related to Kenaz, the Edomite .... Gen. 36:11-42

Kenites—*pertaining to coppersmiths*

Canaanite tribe whose land is promised to Abraham's seed .... Gen. 15:19
Subjects of Balaam's prophecy .. Num. 24:20-22
Mix with Midianites .... Num. 10:29
Member of, becomes Israel's guide .... Num. 10:29-32
Settle with Judahites .... Judg. 1:16
Heber separates from Kenites .. Judg. 4:11
Heber's wife (Jael) slays Sisera .. Judg. 4:17-22
Spared by Saul in war with Amalekites .... 1 Sam. 15:6
David shows friendship to ...... 1 Sam. 30:29
Recorded among Judahites; ancestors of Rechabites .... 1 Chr. 2:55

Kerchief—*a covering for the head*

Worn by idolatrous women of Israel...................... Ezek. 13:18, 21

Keren-happuch—*horn of eye paint*

Daughter of Job............... Job 42:14

Kerioth—*cities*

1. Town in south Judah .... Josh. 15:25
2. City of Moab .... Amos 2:2

Keros—*bent*

Head of a Nethinim family returning from exile....................... Ezra 2:44

Kettle—*pot*

Large cooking vessel .... 1 Sam. 2:14
Same word rendered "pots"..... Ps. 81:6

Keturah—*incense*

Abraham's second wife......... Gen. 25:1
Sons of:
Listed .... Gen. 25:1, 2
Given gifts and sent away ..... Gen. 25:6

Key—*a small instrument for unlocking doors*

Used literally for:

Doors .... Judg. 3:25

Used figuratively of:

Prophetic authority of Christ.... Is. 22:22
Present authority of Christ...... Rev. 1:18
Plenary authority of Christ's apostles..................... Matt. 16:19
Teachers .... Luke 11:52

Kezia—*cassia*

Daughter of Job............... Job 42:14

Keziz—*cut off*

City of Benjamin .... Josh. 18:21

Kibroth-hattaavah—*graves of lust*

Burial site of Israelites slain by God........................ Num. 11:33-35

Kibzaim—*double heap*

Ephramite city assigned to Kohathite Levites .... Josh. 21:22
Called Jokmeam .... 1 Chr. 6:68

See Jokmeam

Kid—*a young goat*

A. *Used for:*
   Food .... Gen. 27:9
   Payment .... Gen. 38:17-23
   Sacrifices .... Lev. 4:23
   Offerings .... Judg. 13:15, 19
   Festive occasions .... Luke 15:29
B. *Figurative of:*
   Weakness .... Judg. 14:6
   Peacefulness .... Is. 11:6

See Goat

K

Kidnapping

A. *Punishment for:*
   Death...................... Ex. 21:16
B. *Examples of:*
   Joseph .... Gen. 37:23-28
   Daughters of Shiloh .... Judg. 21:20-23
   Joash .... 2 Kin. 11:1-12
   Jeremiah .... Jer. 43:1-8

Kidneys

Select internal organs of an animal...................... Ex. 29:13, 22
Translated "wheat" .... Deut. 32:14

Kidron—*dark, turbid*

Valley (dry except for winter torrents) near Jerusalem .... John 18:1
East boundary of Jerusalem..... Jer. 31:40
Crossed by David and Christ ... John 18:1
Used for burials............... Jer. 26:23
Site of dumping of idols....... 2 Chr. 29:16

Killing—*causing life to cease*

A. *Reasons for:*
   Take another's wife .... Gen. 12:12
   Take another's property ..... 1 Kin. 21:19
   Take revenge .... Gen. 27:42
   Satisfy anger................ Num. 22:29
   Hate....................... John 5:18
   Execute God's wrath .... Num. 31:2, 16-19
   Destroy people .... Ex. 1:16
   Seize a throne.............. 2 Kin. 15:25
   Put down rebellion .... 1 Kin. 12:27
   Fulfill prophecy .... 1 Kin. 16:1-11
   Fear of punishment .... Acts 16:27
   Get rid of an unwanted person .... Matt. 21:38
B. *Reasons against:*
   God's Law .... Ex. 20:13
   Regard for:
   Life .... Gen. 37:21
   One's position .... 1 Sam. 24:10
   1 Sam. 11
C. *Of Christians:*
   In God's hand .... Luke 12:4, 5
   Result of persecution .... Matt. 24:9
   Time will come.............. John 16:2
   Under antichrist............ Rev. 11:7
   Rev. 13:15

SUBJECT REFERENCE

Kinah—*lamentation*

Village in south Judah ....Josh. 15:22

Kindness—*a friendly attitude toward others*

A. *Kinds of:*
- Extraordinary ....Acts 28:2
- Acquired ....Col. 3:12
- Developed ....Prov. 31:26
- Commended ....2 Cor. 6:6
- Divine ....Neh. 9:17

B. *Of God, described as:*
- Great ....Neh. 9:17
- Everlasting ....Is. 54:8
- Not removable ....Is. 54:10
- Manifested ....Ps. 31:21
- Through Christ ....Eph. 2:7
- Cause of man's salvation ....Titus 3:4-7

C. *Manifestation of:*
- Rewarded ....1 Sam. 15:6
- Recalled ....2 Sam. 2:5, 6
- Rebuffed ....2 Sam. 3:8
- Remembered ....2 Sam. 9:1-7
- Refused ....2 Sam. 10:1-6

Kindred—*one's family connections*

Manifestation of:
- Felt with great emotion ....Esth. 8:6
- Through faith ....Josh. 6:23
- By gospel ....Acts 3:25; Rev. 14:6

Kine—*archaic for cow, ox, steer*

Used for:
- Ox ....Deut. 7:13
- Cattle ....Deut. 32:14
- Cow ....Gen. 32:15; 1 Sam. 6:7

King, Christ as

A. *In Old Testament prophecy:*
- Judah's tribe ....Gen. 49:10
- With a scepter ....Num. 24:15-17
- David's lineage ....2 Sam. 7:1-29
- Divine origin ....Is. 9:6, 7
- In righteousness ....Is. 11:1-5
- At God's appointed time ....Ezek. 21:27
- Will endure forever ....Dan. 2:44
- Born in Bethlehem ....Mic. 5:2, 3
- As Priest-king ....Zech. 6:9-15
- Having salvation ....Zech. 9:9
- He is coming ....Mal. 3:1-5

B. *Christ's right to rule, determined by:*
- Divine decree ....Ps. 2:6, 7
- Prophecy ....Ps. 45:6, 7
- Birth ....Is. 9:6, 7
- Being seated at God's right hand ....Ps. 16:8-11; Ps. 110:1, 2; Acts 2:34-36
- Crowning ....Zech. 6:11-15

C. *Described as:*
- Eternal ....Rev. 11:15
- Spiritual ....John 18:36, 37
- Not for immoral or impure person ....Eph. 5:5
- For redeemed ....Col. 1:13

Kingdom of God

A. *Described as, of:*
- God ....Mark 1:15
- Heaven ....Matt. 3:2
- Christ and God ....Eph. 5:5
- Their Father ....Matt. 13:43
- My Father's ....Matt. 26:29
- His dear Son ....Col. 1:13

B. *Special features of:*
- Gospel of ....Matt. 24:14
- Word of ....Matt. 13:19
- Mysteries of ....Mark 4:10-13
- Key of David ....Rev. 3:7

C. *Entrance into, by:*
- New birth ....John 3:1-8
- Granted ....Luke 22:29
- Divine call ....1 Thess. 2:12
- Repentance ....Matt. 3:2

D. *Members of:*
- Seek it first ....Matt. 6:33
- Suffer tribulation ....Acts 14:22
- Preach it ....Acts 8:12
- Pray for it ....Matt. 6:10
- Work in ....Col. 4:11

E. *Nature of:*
- Spiritual ....Rom. 14:17
- Eternal ....2 Pet. 1:11

Kings, earthly

A. *Some characteristics of:*
- Arose over Egypt ....Ex. 1:8
- Desired by people ....1 Sam. 8:5, 6
- Under God's control ....Dan. 4:25, 37
- Rule by God's permission ...Dan. 2:20, 21
- Subject to temptations ......2 Sam. 11:1-5; Prov. 31:5
- Good ....2 Kin. 22:1, 2
- Evil ....2 Kin. 21:1-9

B. *Position of before God, by God:*
- Chosen ....1 Chr. 28:4-6
- Anointed ....1 Sam. 16:12
- Removed and established ....Dan. 2:21
- Rejected ....1 Sam. 15:10-26

C. *Duties of:*
- Make covenants ....Gen. 21:22-32
- Read Scriptures ....Deut. 17:19
- Make war ....1 Sam. 11:5-11
- Pardon ....2 Sam. 14:1-11; 2 Sam. 19:18-23
- Judge ....2 Sam. 15:2
- Govern righteously ....2 Sam. 23:3, 4
- Keep Law ....1 Kin. 2:3
- Make decrees ....Dan. 3:1-6, 29

King's Garden—*a garden of Jerusalem*

- Near a gate ....2 Kin. 25:4
- By the pool of Siloah ....Neh. 3:15

King's Highway—*an important passageway connecting Damascus and Egypt*

Use of, requested ....Num. 20:17

Kings of ancient Israel

A. *Over the United Kingdom:*
- Saul ....1 Sam. 11:15—31:13
- David ....2 Sam. 2:4—1 Kin. 2:11
- Solomon ....1 Kin. 1:39—11:43

B. *Over Israel* (the northern kingdom):
- Jeroboam (22 yrs.) ....1 Kin. 12:20—14:20
- Nadab (2 yrs.) ....1 Kin. 15:25-27, 31
- Baasha (24 yrs.) ....1 Kin. 15:28-34; 1 Kin. 16:1-7
- Elah (2 yrs.) ....1 Kin. 16:8-14
- Zimri (7 days) ....1 Kin. 16:15
- Omri (12 yrs.) ....1 Kin. 16:23-28
- Ahab (22 yrs.) ....1 Kin. 16:29—22:40
- Ahaziah (2 yrs.) ....1 Kin. 22:51-53
- Jehoram (Joram)(12 yrs.) ....2 Kin. 3:1—9:26
- Jehu (28 yrs.) ....2 Kin. 9:2—10:36
- Jehoahaz (17 yrs.) ....2 Kin. 13:1-9
- Jehoash (Joash) (16 yrs.) ....2 Kin. 13:10-25
- Jeroboam II (41 yrs.) ....2 Kin. 14:23-29
- Zechariah (6 mos.) ....2 Kin. 15:8-12
- Shallum (1 mo.) ....2 Kin. 15:13-15
- Menahem (10 yrs.) ....2 Kin. 15:16-22
- Pekahiah (2 yrs.) ....2 Kin. 15:23-26
- Pekah (20 yrs.) ....2 Kin. 15:27-31
- Hoshea (9 yrs.) ....2 Kin. 17:1-6

C. *Over Judah* (the southern kingdom):
- Rehoboam (17 yrs.) ....1 Kin. 12:21-24
- Abijam (Abijah) (3 yrs.) ....1 Kin. 15:1-8
- Asa (41 yrs.) ....1 Kin. 15:9-24
- Jehoshaphat (25 yrs.) ....1 Kin. 22:41-50
- Jehoram (Joram) (8 yrs.) .....2 Kin. 8:16-24
- Ahaziah (1 yr.) ....2 Kin. 8:25-29
- Athaliah (Queen) (usurper) (6 yrs.) ....2 Kin. 11:1-3
- Joash (Jehoash) (40 yrs.) .....2 Kin. 12:1, 21
- Amaziah (29 yrs.) ....2 Kin. 14:1-20
- Azariah (Uzziah) (52 yrs.) ...2 Kin. 15:1, 2
- Jotham (16 yrs.) ....2 Kin. 15:32-38
- Ahaz (16 yrs.) ....2 Kin. 16:1-20
- Hezekiah (29 yrs.) ....2 Kin. 18:1—20:21
- Manasseh (55 yrs.) ....2 Kin. 21:1-18
- Amon (2 yrs.) ....2 Kin. 21:19-26
- Josiah (31 yrs.) ....2 Kin. 22:1—23:30
- Jehoahaz (Shallum) (3 mos.) ....2 Kin. 23:31-33
- Jehoiakim (11 yrs.) ....2 Kin. 23:34—24:6
- Jehoiachin (Jeconiah) (3 mos.) ....2 Kin. 24:8-16
- Zedekiah (Mattaniah) (11 yrs.) ....2 Kin. 24:17—25:7

Kings, the Books of—*books of the Old Testament*

A. *1 Kings*
- Solomon ascends to the throne ....1 Kin. 1:1—2:46
- The kingdom of Solomon ....1 Kin. 3:1—10:13
- The fall of Solomon ....1 Kin. 11:1-40
- Rehoboam against Jeroboam ....1 Kin. 12:1-33
- Ahab and Jezebel ....1 Kin. 16:29-34
- Ministry of Elijah ....1 Kin. 17:1—19:21
- Syria against Samaria ....1 Kin. 20:1-34
- Ahab and Naboth ....1 Kin. 21:1-29

B. *2 Kings*
- Ministry of Elijah and Elisha ....2 Kin. 1:1—9:1
- Reign of Jehu ....2 Kin. 9:11—10:36
- Fall of Israel ....2 Kin. 17:1-41
- Reign of Hezekiah ....2 Kin. 18:1—20:21
- Reform of Judah ....2 Kin. 22:1—23:30
- Fall of Jerusalem ....2 Kin. 25:1-21

Kingship of God—*the position of God as sovereign ruler of the universe*

- Over Jerusalem ....Matt. 5:35
- Over all ....Ps. 103:19
- Of all kingdoms ....2 Kin. 19:15

Kir—*wall*

1. Place mentioned by Amos to which Syrians were taken ....Amos 1:5
   Tiglath-pileser carries people of Damascus here ....2 Kin. 16:9
   Inhabitants of, against Judah ....Is. 22:6
2. Fortified city of Moab ......Is. 15:1
   Same as Kir-hareseth ....Is. 16:7, 11
   Strong place ....2 Kin. 3:25

Kiriathaim, Kirjathaim—*twin cities*

1. Assigned to Reuben ....Num. 32:37
   Repossessed by Moabites ....Jer. 48:1-23
2. Town in Naphtali ....1 Chr. 6:76
   Same as Kartan ....Josh. 21:32

Kirjath—*city*

Town of Benjamin ....Josh. 18:21, 28

Kirjath-arba—*city of Arba, or four-fold city*

- Ancient name of Hebron ....Gen. 23:2
- Named after Arba the Anakite ..Josh. 15:54
- City of refuge ....Josh. 20:7
- Possessed by Judah ....Judg. 1:10

Kirjath-jearim—*city of forests*

- Gibeonite town ....Josh. 9:17
- Assigned to Judah ....Josh. 15:60
- Reassigned to Benjamin ....Josh. 18:28
- Ark taken from ....1 Chr. 13:5
- Home of Urijah ....Jer. 26:20
- Called:
  - Baalah ....Josh. 15:9, 10
  - Kirjath-baal ....Josh. 15:60
  - Baale of Judah ....2 Sam. 6:2
- Shortened to Kirjath-arim ......Ezra 2:25

Kirjath-sannah—*city of destruction*

City of Judah; also called Debir ....Josh. 15:49

Kirjath-sepher—*city of books*

- Same as Debir ....Judg. 1:11-13
- Taken by Othniel ....Josh. 15:15-17

Kish—*bow*

1. Benjamite of Gibeah; father of King Saul ....1 Sam. 9:1-3; Acts 13:21
2. Benjamite of Jerusalem ......1 Chr. 8:30
3. Merarite Levite in David's time ....1 Chr. 23:21, 22
4. Another Merarite Levite in Hezekiah's time ....2 Chr. 29:12
5. Benjamite and great-grandfather of Mordecai ....Esth. 2:5

Kishi—*snarer*

- One of David's singers ....1 Chr. 6:31, 44
- Called Kushaiah ....1 Chr. 15:17

Kishion—*hardness*

- Border town of Issachar ....Josh. 19:17, 20
- Called Kishon ....Josh. 21:28
- See Kedesh 2

SUBJECT	REFERENCE
Kishon—*bending*	
River of north Palestine; Sisera's army swept away by	Judg. 4:7, 13
Elijah slew Baal prophets here	1 Kin. 18:40 Ps. 83:9
Kiss—*a physical sign of affection*	
A. *Times employed, at:*	
Departure	Gen. 31:28, 55
Separation	Acts 20:37
Reunions	Luke 15:20
Great joy	Luke 7:38, 45
Blessing	Gen. 48:10-16
Anointings	1 Sam. 10:1
Reconciliation	Gen. 33:4
Death	Gen. 50:1
B. *Figurative of:*	
Complete:	
Submission to evil	Hos. 13:2
Submission to God	Ps. 2:12
Reconciliation	Ps. 85:10
Utmost affection	Song 1:2
C. *Kinds of:*	
Deceitful	2 Sam. 20:9, 10 Luke 22:48
Insincere	2 Sam. 15:5
Fatherly	Gen. 27:26, 27
Friendship	Ex. 18:7 1 Sam. 20:41
Esteem	2 Sam. 19:32, 39
Sexual love	Gen. 29:11 Song 1:2
Illicit love	Prov. 7:13
False religion	1 Kin. 19:18 Hos. 13:2
Holy love	Rom. 16:16 1 Cor. 16:20
Kite—*a bird of the falcon family*	
Ceremonially unclean	Lev. 11:14
Kith-lish—*a man's wall*	
Town of Judah	Josh. 15:1, 40
Kitron—*shortened, little*	
Town in Zebulun	Judg. 1:30
Kittim	
Sons of Javan	Gen. 10:4
Kneading—*mixing elements together*	
Part of food process	Gen. 18:6
Done by women	Jer. 7:18
Kneading trough—*a bowl for kneading dough*	
Overcome by frogs	Ex. 8:3
Carried out of Egypt	Ex. 12:33-34
Knee	
A. *Place of weakness, due to:*	
Terror	Dan. 5:6
Fasting	Ps. 109:24
Disease	Deut. 28:35
Lack of faith	Is. 35:3
B. *Lying upon:*	
Sign of true parentage or adoption	Gen. 30:3
Place of fondling	Is. 66:12
Place of sleep	Judg. 16:19
C. *Bowing of:*	
Act of:	
Respect	2 Kin. 1:13
False worship	1 Kin. 19:18
True worship	Rom. 14:11
D. *Bowing of, in prayer:*	
Solomon	2 Chr. 6:13, 14
Daniel	Dan. 6:10
Christ	Luke 22:41
Stephen	Acts 7:59, 60
Peter	Acts 9:40
Paul	Acts 20:36
Christians	Acts 21:5
Knife—*a sharp instrument for cutting*	
A. *Used for:*	
Slaying animals	Gen. 22:6-10
Circumcision	Josh. 5:2, 3
Dismembering a body	Judg. 19:29
Sharpening pens	Jer. 36:23
B. *Figurative of:*	
Inordinate appetite	Prov. 23:2
Cruel oppressors	Prov. 30:14

SUBJECT	REFERENCE
Knob—*an ornament*	
Round protrusions on lampstand	Ex. 25:31-34
Ornaments carved on the walls of the temple	1 Kin. 6:18 1 Kin. 7:24
Knock—*to rap on a door*	
Rewarded	Luke 11:9, 10
Expectant	Luke 12:36
Disappointed	Luke 13:25-27
Unexpected	Acts 12:13, 16
Invitation	Rev. 3:20
Knowledge	
A. *Kinds of:*	
Natural	Matt. 24:32
Deceptive	Gen. 3:5
Sinful	Gen. 3:7
Personal	Josh. 24:31
Practical	Ex. 36:1
Experimental	Ex. 14:4, 18
Friendly	Ex. 1:8
Intuitive	1 Sam. 22:22
Intellectual	John 7:15, 28
Saving	John 17:3
Spiritual	1 Cor. 2:14
Revealed	Luke 10:22
B. *Sources of:*	
God	Ps. 94:10
Nature	Ps. 19:2
Scriptures	2 Tim. 3:15
Doing God's will	John 7:17
C. *Believer's attitude toward:*	
Not to be puffed up	1 Cor. 8:1
Should grow in	2 Pet. 3:18
Should add to	2 Pet. 1:5
Not to be forgetful of	2 Pet. 3:17
Accept our limitations of	1 Cor. 13:8-12
Be filled with	Phil. 1:9
D. *Christ's, of:*	
God	Luke 10:22
Man's nature	John 2:24, 25
Man's thoughts	Matt. 9:4
Believers	John 10:14, 27
Things future	2 Pet. 1:14
All things	Col. 2:3
E. *Attitude of sinful men toward:*	
Turn from	Rom. 1:21
Ignorant of	1 Cor. 1:21
Raised up against	2 Cor. 10:5
Did not acknowledge God	Rom. 1:28
Never able to come to	2 Tim. 3:7
F. *Value of:*	
Superior to gold	Prov. 8:10
Increases strength	Prov. 24:5
Keeps from destruction	Is. 5:13
Insures stability	Is. 33:6
Koa	
People described as enemies of Jerusalem	Ezek. 23:23
Kohath—*assembly*	
Second son of Levi	Gen. 46:8, 11
Goes with Levi to Egypt	Gen. 46:11
Brother of Jochebed, mother of Aaron and Moses	Ex. 6:16-20
Dies at age 133	Ex. 6:18
Kohathites—*descendants of Kohath*	
A. *History of:*	
Originate in Levi's son (Kohath)	Gen. 46:11
Divided into 4 groups (Amram, Izhar, Hebron, Uzziel)	Num. 3:19, 27
Numbering of	Num. 3:27, 28
Duties assigned to	Num. 4:15-20
Cities assigned to	Josh. 21:4-11
B. *Privileges of:*	
Aaron and Moses	Ex. 6:20
Special charge of sacred instruments	Num. 4:15-20
Temple music by Heman the Kohathite	1 Chr. 6:31-38
Under Jehoshaphat, lead in praise	2 Chr. 20:19
Under Hezekiah, help to cleanse Temple	2 Chr. 29:12, 15

SUBJECT	REFERENCE
C. *Sins of:*	
Korah (of Izhar) leads rebellion	Num. 16:1-35 Jude 11
Kolaiah—*voice of Jehovah*	
1. Father of the false prophet Ahab	Jer. 29:21-23
2. Postexilic Benjamite family	Neh. 11:7
Koph	
Letter of the Hebrew alphabet	Ps. 119:145-152
Korah—*baldness*	
1. Son of Esau	Gen. 36:5, 14, 18
2. Son of Eliphaz and grandson of Esau	Gen. 36:16
3. Calebite	1 Chr. 2:42, 43
4. Son of Izhar the Kohathite	Ex. 6:21, 24
Leads a rebellion against Moses and Aaron	Num. 16:1-3
Warned by Moses	Num. 16:4-27
Supernaturally destroyed	Num. 16:28-35
Sons of, not destroyed	Num. 26:9-11
Sons of, porters	1 Chr. 26:19
Korahites	
Descendants of Korah	Ex. 6:24
Some become:	
David's warriors	1 Chr. 12:6
Servants	1 Chr. 9:19-31
Musicians	1 Chr. 6:22-32
A maschil for	Ps. 42 (Title)
Kore—*a partridge*	
1. Korahite Levite	1 Chr. 9:19
2. Porter of the eastern gate	2 Chr. 31:14
Koz—*thorn*	
Father of Anub	1 Chr. 4:8
Kushaiah—*bow of Jehovah* (that is, rainbow)	
Merarite Levite musician	1 Chr. 15:17
Called Kishi	1 Chr. 6:44

L

SUBJECT	REFERENCE
Laadah—*festival*	
Judahite	1 Chr. 4:21
Laadan	
1. Son of Gershon, the son of Levi	1 Chr. 23:7-9
Called Libni	1 Chr. 6:17
2. Ephraimite	1 Chr. 7:26
Laban—*white*	
1. Son of Bethuel	Gen. 24:24, 29
Brother of Rebekah	Gen. 24:15, 29
Father of Leah and Rachel	Gen. 29:16
Chooses Rebekah for Isaac	Gen. 24:29-60
Entertains Jacob	Gen. 29:1-14
Deceives Jacob in marriage arrangement	Gen. 29:15-30
Agrees to Jacob's business arrangement	Gen. 30:25-43
Changes attitude toward Jacob	Gen. 31:1-9
Pursues after fleeing Jacob	Gen. 31:21-25
Rebukes Jacob	Gen. 31:26-30
Rebuked by Jacob	Gen. 31:31-42
Makes covenant with Jacob	Gen. 31:43-55
2. City in the wilderness	Deut. 1:1
Labor—*physical or mental effort*	
A. *Physical:*	
Nature of:	
As old as creation	Gen. 2:5, 15
Ordained by God	Gen. 3:17-19
One of the commandments	Ex. 20:9
From morning until night	Ps. 104:23
With the hands	1 Thess. 4:11
To life's end	Ps. 90:10
Without God, vanity	Eccl. 2:11
Shrinking from, denounced	2 Thess. 3:10
Benefits of:	
Profit	Prov. 14:23
Happiness	Ps. 128:2
Proclaim gospel	1 Thess. 2:9
Supply of other's needs	Acts 20:35 Eph. 4:28
Restful sleep	Eccl. 5:12
Double honor	1 Tim. 5:17

SUBJECT — REFERENCE

Eternal life — John 6:27
Not in vain — 1 Cor. 15:58; Phil. 2:16

B. *Spiritual:*

Characteristics of:

Commissioned by Christ — John 4:38
Accepted by few — Matt. 9:37, 38
Working with God — 1 Cor. 3:9
By God's grace — 1 Cor. 15:10
Result of faith — 1 Tim. 4:10
Characterized by love — 1 Thess. 1:3
Done in prayer — Col. 4:12
Subject to discouragement — Is. 49:4; Gal. 4:11
Interrupted by Satan — 1 Thess. 3:5

See Work, the Christian's

C. *Problems:*

Inspired by opposition — Ezra 4:1-6
Complaint over wages — Matt. 20:1-16
Mistreatment of employees — Matt. 21:33-35
Characteristics of last days — James 5:1-6

Labor, (childbirth)

A. *Of a woman's, described as:*

Fearful — Ps. 48:6
Painful — Is. 13:8
Hazardous — Gen. 35:16-19
Joyful afterwards — John 16:21

B. *Figurative of:*

New Israel — Is. 66:7, 8
Messiah's birth — Mic. 4:9, 10
Redemption — Mic. 5:3
New birth — Gal. 4:19
Creation's rebirth — Rom. 8:22

Lace—*a cord or heavy thread*

Of priest's garments — Ex. 28:28; Ex. 39:21

Lachish

Town in south Judah — Josh. 15:1, 39
Joins coalition against Gibeonites — Josh. 10:3-5
Defeated by Joshua — Josh. 10:6-33
Fortified by Rehoboam — 2 Chr. 11:5, 9
City of sin — Mic. 1:13
Amaziah murdered here — 2 Kin. 14:19; 2 Chr. 25:27
Taken by Sennacherib — 2 Kin. 18:13-17
Military headquarters — Is. 36:1, 2; Is. 37:8
Fights against Nebuchadnezzar — Jer. 34:1, 7
Reoccupied after exile — Neh. 11:30

Lack—*something still needed*

A. *How to avoid:*

Remember God's promises — Deut. 2:7
Work diligently — 1 Thess. 4:11, 12
Live chastely — Prov. 6:32
Share in common — Acts 4:34

B. *Things subject to:*

Food — 2 Sam. 3:29
Physical needs — 2 Cor. 11:9
Possessions — 1 Sam. 30:19
Service to others — Phil. 2:30
Entire commitment — Luke 18:22
Wisdom — James 1:5
Graces — 2 Pet. 1:9

Lad—*a young boy*

Heard by God — Gen. 21:17-20
Saved by God — Gen. 22:12
Loved by his father — Gen. 44:22-34
Slain with Samson — Judg. 16:26-30
Unsuspecting — 1 Sam. 20:21-41
Tattling — 2 Sam. 17:18
Providing — John 6:9

Ladder

Jacob's — Gen. 28:10-12

Lady

Applied to females of high rank — Judg. 5:29
Among royalty — Esth. 1:18
Elect — 2 John 1, 5
Figurative of Babylon — Is. 47:5-7

Lael—*belonging to God*

Gershonite Levite — Num. 3:24

SUBJECT — REFERENCE

Lahad—*oppression*

Judahite — 1 Chr. 4:2

Lahai-roi—*of the Living One who sees me*

Name of a well — Gen. 24:62
Same as Beer-lahairoi — Gen. 6:7, 14

Lahmam—*place of light*

City of Judah — Josh. 15:1, 40

Lahmi—*Beth-lehemite*

Brother of Goliath slain by Elhanan — 1 Chr. 20:5

Laish—*lion*

1. Benjamite — 1 Sam. 25:44
2. City in north Palestine at the head of the Jordan — Judg. 18:7, 14
   Called Leshem — Josh. 19:47
3. Village in Benjamin between Anathoth and Gallim — Is. 10:30

Lake

Sea of Galilee is called — Luke 5:1, 2; Luke 8:22-33
Bottomless pit described as — Rev. 19:20

Lake of fire—*the place of final punishment*

A. *Those consigned to:*

The beast and false prophet — Rev. 19:20
The devil — Rev. 20:10
Death and hell — Rev. 20:14
Those whose names are not in book of life — Rev. 20:15

B. *Described as:*

Burning brimstone — Rev. 19:20
Second death — Rev. 20:14

Lakum—*obstruction*

Town of Naphtali — Josh. 19:32, 33

Lama—*the Aramaic for why*

Spoken by Christ on the cross — Matt. 27:46

Lamb—*a young sheep*

A. *Used for:*

Food — 2 Sam. 12:4
Clothing — Prov. 27:26
Trade — Ezra 7:17
Tribute — 2 Kin. 3:4
Covenants — Gen. 21:28-32
Sacrifices — Ex. 12:5

B. *Figurative of:*

God's people — Is. 5:17
Weak believers — Is. 40:11
God's ministers — Luke 10:3
God's dealing with the wicked — Ps. 37:20
Messiah's reign — Is. 11:6

Lamb of God, the (Christ)

A. *Descriptive of Christ as:*

Predicted — Is. 53:7
Presented to Israel — John 1:29
Preached to world — Acts 8:32-35
Praised throughout eternity — Rev. 5:6, 13

B. *Descriptive of Christ as:*

Sacrifice — 1 Pet. 1:19; Rev. 7:13, 14
Redeemer — Rev. 5:9
King — Rev. 15:3

Lame, lameness—*inability to walk properly*

A. *Healing of, by:*

Christ — Matt. 11:5
Peter — Acts 3:2-7
Philip — Acts 8:5-7

B. *Figurative of:*

Extreme weakness — 2 Sam. 5:6, 8
Inconsistency — Prov. 26:7
Weak believers — Jer. 31:8
Healed — Is. 35:6

C. *Causes of:*

Birth defect — Acts 3:2
Accident — 2 Sam. 4:4

D. *Renders unfit for:*

Priesthood — Lev. 21:17, 18
Sacrifice — Deut. 15:21
Active life — 2 Sam. 9:13; 2 Sam. 19:24-26

SUBJECT — REFERENCE

Lamech—*wild man*

1. Son of Methusael, of Cain's race — Gen. 4:17, 18
   Had two wives — Gen. 4:19
2. Son of Methuselah; father of Noah — Gen. 5:25-31
   Man of faith — Gen. 5:29
   In Christ's ancestry — Luke 3:36

Lamed

Letter of the Hebrew alphabet — Ps. 119:89-96

Lamentation—*mournful speeches; elegies; dirges*

A. *Historical of:*

Jeremiah over Josiah — 2 Chr. 35:25
David over Saul — 2 Sam. 1:17-27
David over Abner — 2 Sam. 3:33, 34
Jeremiah over Jerusalem — Lam. 1:1

B. *Prophetic of:*

Isaiah over Babylon — Is. 14:1-32
Jeremiah over Jerusalem — Jer. 7:28-34
Ezekiel over Tyre — Ezek. 27:2-36
Christ over Jerusalem — Luke 19:41-44
John over Babylon — Rev. 18:1-24

Lamentations, the Book of—*a book of the Old Testament*

The suffering of Zion — Lam. 1:1—2:22
Individual prayer — Lam. 3:1-66
Collective prayer — Lam. 5:1-22

Lamp

A. *Used in:*

Tabernacle — Ex. 37:23
Temple — 1 Chr. 28:15
Processions — Matt. 25:1-8

B. *Figurative of:*

God — 2 Sam. 22:29
God's Word — Prov. 6:23; Ps. 119:105
God's justice — Zeph. 1:12
Conscience — Prov. 20:27
Prosperity — Job 29:3
Industry — Prov. 31:18
Death — Job 18:6
Churches — Rev. 1:20
Christ — Dan. 10:6; Rev. 1:14

Lance—*a spear*

Used in war — Jer. 50:42

Lancet—*a javelin or light spear*

Used by Baal's priests — 1 Kin. 18:28

Landmark—*a boundary marker*

Removal of, forbidden — Deut. 19:14

Land of promise (Canaan)

A. *Described as:*

The land of promise — Heb. 11:9
The land of Canaan — Ezek. 16:3, 29
The land of the Jews — Acts 10:39
The holy land — Zech. 2:12
"Beulah" — Is. 62:4

B. *Conquest of, by:*

Divine command — Ex. 23:24
God's angel — Ex. 23:20, 23
Hornets — Ex. 23:28
Degrees — Ex. 23:29, 30

C. *Inheritance of:*

Promised to Abraham's seed — Gen. 12:1-7
Awaits God's time — Gen. 15:7-16
Boundaries of, specified — Gen. 15:18-21
Some kept from — Deut. 1:34-40
For the obedient — Deut. 5:16
Sin separates from — Deut. 28:49-68

D. *Laws concerning:*

Land allotted to 12 tribes — Num. 26:52-55
None for priests — Num. 18:20, 24
Sale and redemption of — Lev. 25:15-33
Transfer of title — Ruth 4:3-8
Witness of sale — Ruth 4:9-11
Relieved of debt on — Neh. 5:3-13
Leased to others — Matt. 21:33-41
Widow's right in — Ruth 4:3-9
Rights of unmarried women in — Num. 27:1-11
Rest of, on the seventh years — Ex. 23:11

SUBJECT REFERENCE

E. *Original inhabitants of:*
- Seven Gentile nations .... Deut. 7:1; Josh. 24:11
- Mighty .... Deut. 4:38
- Tall .... Deut. 9:1, 2
- Idolatrous .... Ex. 23:23, 24; Deut. 12:29-31
- Corrupt .... Lev. 18:1-30; Ezek. 16:47
- Mingled with Israel .... Ps. 106:34-38

Language—*man's means of communication*

A. *Kinds of:*
- Jews' .... 2 Kin. 18:28
- Chaldean .... Dan. 1:4
- Syrian .... 2 Kin. 18:26
- Egyptian .... Ps. 114:1
- Arabic .... Acts 2:11
- Greek .... Acts 21:37
- Latin .... John 19:19, 20
- Lycaonian .... Acts 14:11
- Medes and Persians .... Esth. 3:12

B. *Varieties of:*
- Result of confusion (Babel) .. Gen. 11:1-9
- Result of division of Noah's three sons .... Gen. 10:5, 20, 31
- Seen in one empire .... Esth. 1:22; Dan. 3:4, 7, 29
- Seen in Christ's inscription .. John 19:19, 20
- Witnessed at Pentecost .... Acts 2:6-12
- Evident in heaven .... Rev. 5:9

See Tongue

Lantern—*an enclosed lamp*
- Used by soldiers arresting Jesus .... John 18:3

Laodicea—*a chief city of Asia Minor*
- Church of, sharply rebuked .... Rev. 1:11
- Epaphras labors here .... Col. 4:12, 13
- Paul writes letter to .... Col. 4:16
- Not visited by Paul .... Col. 2:1; Col. 4:15

Lap

A. *As a loose skirt of a garment*
- For carrying objects .... 2 Kin. 4:39
- Lots cast into .... Prov. 16:33

B. *As an act of dogs:*
- For selecting Gideon's army .... Judg. 7:5, 6, 7

Lapidoth—*torches*
- Husband of Deborah the prophetess .... Judg. 4:4

Lapwing—*a bird of the plover family* (hoopoe)
- Unclean bird .... Lev. 11:19

Lasciviousness—*unbridled lust*
- Flows from the heart .... Mark 7:20-23
- Seen in the flesh .... Gal. 5:19
- Characterizes the old life .... 1 Pet. 4:3
- Found among Gentiles .... Eph. 4:19, 20
- Sign of apostasy .... Jude 4
- Among Christians, lamentable ... 2 Cor. 12:21
- To be cast away ("wantonness") .... Rom. 13:13

Lasea
- Seaport of Crete .... Acts 27:8

Lash—*a punishment imposed with a whip or scourge*
- Rendered "stripes" .... Deut. 25:3
- Imposed on Paul .... 2 Cor. 11:24

Lasha—*bursting forth*
- Boundary town of southeast Palestine .... Gen. 10:19

Lasharon—*to Sharon*
- Town possessed by Joshua .... Josh. 12:1, 18

Last—*the terminal point*

A. *Senses of:*
- Final consequence .... Prov. 23:32
- God .... Is. 44:6

B. *Of events, last:*
- Day (resurrection) .... John 6:39, 40
- Day (judgment) .... John 12:48
- Days (present age) .... Acts 2:17
- Time (present age) .... 1 John 2:18
- Times (present age) .... 1 Pet. 1:20
- Days (time before Christ's return) .... 2 Tim. 3:1; 2 Pet. 3:3
- Enemy (death) .... 1 Cor. 15:26
- Time (Christ's return) .... 1 Pet. 1:5
- Trump (Christ's return) .... 1 Cor. 15:52

Last Supper
- At Feast of Unleavened Bread .. Matt. 26:17; Mark 14:12
- Fulfills Passover .... Luke 22:15-18

Latchet—*the thong binding the sandal to the foot*

Descriptive of:
- Something insignificant .... Gen. 14:23
- Menial task .... Luke 3:16

Latin—*the Roman language*
- Used in writing Christ's inscription .... John 19:19, 20

Lattice—*a framework of crossed wood or metal strips*
- Window of Sisera's mother .... Judg. 5:28
- Ahaziah fell through .... 2 Kin. 1:2

Laughter—*an emotion expressive of joy, mirth or ridicule*

A. *Kinds of:*
- Divine .... Ps. 59:8
- Natural .... Job 8:21
- Derisive .... Neh. 2:19
- Fake .... Prov. 14:13
- Scornful .... 2 Chr. 30:10
- Confident .... Job 5:22
- Joyful .... Ps. 126:2

B. *Causes of:*
- Man's folly .... Ps. 2:4
- Something unusual .... Gen. 18:12-15
- Something untrue .... Matt. 9:24
- Ridicule .... 2 Chr. 30:10
- Highly contradictory .... Ps. 22:7, 8

Laver—*a basin for washing*
- Made for the tabernacle .... Ex. 30:18

Law—*an authoritative rule of conduct*
- Law of man .... Luke 20:22
- Natural Law written upon the heart .... Rom. 2:14, 15
- Law of Moses .... Gal. 3:17-21
- Entire Old Testament .... John 10:34
- Expression of God's will .... Rom. 7:2-9
- Operating principle .... Rom. 3:27

Law of Moses

A. *History of:*
- Given at Sinai .... Ex. 20:1-26
- Called a covenant .... Deut. 4:13, 23
- Dedicated with blood .... Heb. 9:18-22
- Called the Law of Moses .... Josh. 8:30-35
- Restated in Deuteronomy .... Deut. 4:44-46
- Written on stone .... Deut. 4:4:13
- Plaster-coated stone .... Deut. 27:3-8
- Placed with the ark .... Deut. 31:9, 26
- Given to Joshua .... Josh. 1:1-9
- Repeated by Joshua .... Josh. 23:6-16
- Disobeyed by:
  - Israel .... Judg. 2:10-20
  - Israel's kings .... 2 Kin. 10:31
  - The Jews .... Is. 1:10-18
- Finding of book of .... 2 Chr. 34:14-33
- Disobedience to, cause of exile .... 2 Kin. 17:3-41
- Read to postexilic assembly .... Neh. 8:1-18
- Recalled at close of Old Testament .... Mal. 4:4
- Meaning of, fulfilled by Christ .... Matt. 5:17-48
- Pharisees insist on observance of .... Acts 15:1-29

B. *Purposes of:*
- Knowledge of sin .... Rom. 3:20
- Manifest God's righteousness .... Rom. 7:12
- Lead to Christ .... Gal. 3:24, 25

C. *Christ's relation to:*
- Born under .... Gal. 4:4
- Explains proper meaning to .... Matt. 5:17-48; Matt. 12:1-14
- Redeems sinners from curse of .... Gal. 3:13
- Shows fulfillment of, in Himself .... Luke 24:27, 44

D. *Christian's relation to:*
- Freed from .... Acts 15:1-29
- Spirit of, fulfilled in love .... Rom. 13:8-10
- Now written on the heart .... 2 Cor. 3:3-1

E. *Inadequacies of, cannot:*
- Make worshiper perfect .... Heb. 9:9-15
- Justify .... Acts 13:38, 39

Lawgiver—*a lawmaker*
- Only one .... James 4:12
- The LORD is .... Is. 33:22

Lawlessness—*living outside or contrary to law*

A. *Described as:*
- Wickedness .... Acts 2:23
- Iniquity .... Matt. 13:41
- Unrighteousness .... 2 Cor. 6:14

B. *Features concerning:*
- Called sin .... 1 John 3:4
- Incompatible with righteousness .... 2 Cor. 6:14
- Torments the righteous .... Matt. 24:12; 2 Pet. 2:8
- Led to crucifixion .... Acts 2:22, 23
- Descriptive of antichrist .... 2 Thess. 2:7, 8
- Scribes and Pharisees full of .... Matt. 23:27, 28
- Basis for condemnation .... Matt. 7:23
- Law made for .... 1 Tim. 1:9
- Forgiven .... Rom. 4:7; Titus 2:14
- Forgotten .... Heb. 8:12; Heb. 10:17

Lawsuits—*suing another for damages*
- Between Christians, forbidden ... Matt. 5:25, 40; 1 Cor. 6:1-8

Lawyers—*interpreters of the law*
- Test Jesus .... Matt. 22:34-40
- Jesus answers one .... Luke 10:25-37
- Condemned by Jesus .... Luke 11:45-52
- Zenas, a Christian .... Titus 3:13

Lazarus—*God has helped*

1. Beggar described in a parable .... Luke 16:20-25
2. Brother of Mary and Martha; raised from the dead .... John 11:1-44
   - Attends a supper .... John 12:1, 2
   - Jews seek to kill .... John 12:9-11

Laziness

A. *Leads to:*
- Poverty .... Prov. 6:9-11
- Waste .... Prov. 18:9
- Loss of all .... Matt. 25:26-30

B. *Admonitions against:*
- Make the most of time .... Eph. 5:16
- Have a great work .... Neh. 6:3
- Work day and night .... 1 Thess. 2:9
- Consider the ant .... Prov. 6:6-8
- No work, no eat .... 2 Thess. 3:10-12

Lead—*a heavy metal*
- Purified by fire .... Num. 31:22, 23
- Engraved with .... Job 19:23, 24
- Very heavy .... Ex. 15:10
- Object of trade .... Ezek. 27:12

Leader—*a guide*

A. *Kinds of:*
- False .... Is. 3:12
- Blind .... Luke 6:39
- Young .... Is. 11:6
- Safe .... Ps. 78:53
- Gentle .... Is. 40:11
- Faithful .... Deut. 8:2, 15

B. *Names of:*
- The LORD .... Ex. 13:21
- Christ .... John 10:3
- The Lamb .... Rev. 7:17
- The Spirit .... Luke 4:1; Gal. 5:18

L

SUBJECT	REFERENCE
C. *Course of, in:*	
God's truth	Ps. 25:5
Righteousness	Ps. 5:8
Way you should go	Is. 48:17
Unknown ways	Is. 42:16
Plain path	Ps. 27:11
Everlasting way	Ps. 139:24

Leaf, leaves

Trees	Matt. 21:19
Doors	1 Kin. 6:34
Book	Jer. 36:23

League—*an agreement between two or more parties*

Fraudulent	Josh. 9:3-6
Forbidden	Judg. 2:2
Secret	1 Sam. 22:8
Conditional	2 Sam. 3:12, 13
Acceptable	2 Sam. 3:21
Unifying	2 Sam. 5:1-3
International	1 Kin. 5:12
Purchased	1 Kin. 15:18-21
Deceitful	Dan. 11:23

Leah—*a wild cow*

Laban's eldest daughter	Gen. 29:16, 17
By Laban's deceit, becomes Jacob's wife	Gen. 29:19-27
Hated by Jacob	Gen. 29:30-33
Mother of seven children	Gen. 30:19-21
Buried in Machpelah's cave	Gen. 49:31
Builder of house of Israel	Ruth 4:11

Leaping—*to spring or bound forward suddenly*

A. *Used physically of:*	
Insects	Joel 2:5
Men	1 Kin. 18:26
Unborn child	Luke 1:41, 44
Lame man	Acts 3:8
B. *Expressive of:*	
Great joy	2 Sam. 6:16
Renewed life	Is. 35:6
Victory in persecution	Luke 6:22, 23

Learning—*knowledge acquired through experience or instructions*

A. *Aspects of:*	
God's statutes	Ps. 119:71, 73
Righteousness	Is. 26:9, 10
Good works	Titus 3:14
Obedience	Heb. 5:8
B. *Objects of:*	
Abominable things	Deut. 18:9
Heathen ways	Ps. 106:35 Deut. 18:9
Fear of the LORD	Deut. 14:23 Deut. 17:19 Deut. 31:13
C. *Sources of:*	
Experience	Gen. 30:27
Worldly knowledge	John 7:15
Christian experience	Phil. 4:11
Scriptures	Rom. 15:4

Leasing—*an old word for "lie" or sin*

Translated "leasing" in	Ps. 4:2
Same Hebrew word elsewhere translated "lies"	Ps. 40:4
Illustrated by Joab's conduct	2 Sam. 3:27

Leather—*an animal's dried skin*

Worn by John the Baptist	Matt. 3:4

Leaven—*dough in a state of fermentation*

A. *Forbidden in:*	
Passover	Ex. 12:8-20
Meat offerings	Lev. 2:11
B. *Permitted in:*	
Peace offerings	Lev. 7:13
First fruits of grain	Lev. 23:17 Num. 15:20, 21
C. *Figurative of:*	
Kingdom of heaven	Matt. 13:33
Corrupt teaching	Matt. 16:6, 12
Infectious sin	1 Cor. 5:5-7
False doctrine	Gal. 5:1-9

Lebanah—*white*

Founder of a family of returning exiles	Ezra 2:43, 45 Neh. 7:48
Called Lebana	Neh. 7:48

Lebanon—*mountain range* (10,000 ft.) *in north Canaan*

A. *Source of:*	
Wood for Solomon's Temple	1 Kin. 5:5, 6
Stones for Solomon's Temple	1 Kin. 5:14, 18
Wood for the second Temple	Ezra 3:7
B. *Significant as:*	
A sight desired by Moses	Deut. 3:25
Israel's northern boundary	Deut. 1:7
Captured by Joshua	Josh. 11:16, 17 Josh. 12:7
Assigned to Israelites	Josh. 13:5-7
Not completely conquered	Judg. 3:1-3
Possessed by Assyria	Is. 37:24
C. *Figurative of:*	
Great kingdoms	Is. 10:24, 34
Spiritual transformation	Is. 29:17
Jerusalem and the Temple	Ezek. 17:3
Spiritual growth	Hos. 14:5-7
Messiah's glory	Is. 35:2
D. *Noted for:*	
Blossoms	Nah. 1:4
Wine	Hos. 14:6, 7
Wild beast	2 Kin. 14:9
Snow	Jer. 5:15
Cedars	Song 5:15 Is. 14:8

Lebaoth—*lionesses*

Town of south Judah	Josh. 15:32
Also called Beth-labaoth	Josh. 19:6

Lebbaeus (see Judas 3)

Surname of Judas (Jude)	Matt. 10:3

Lebonah—*incense*

Town north of Shiloh	Judg. 21:19

Lecah—*journey*

Descendant of Judah	1 Chr. 4:21

Ledge—*a protrusion around an altar*

Part of altars rendered "compass"	Ex. 27:5

Leek—*an onion-like plant*

Desired by Israelites	Num. 11:5

Lees—*sediment in wine jars*

Figurative of:	
Negligence and ease	Jer. 48:11

Left—*opposite of right*

A. *Of direction:*	
Location	Gen. 14:15
Making a choice	Gen. 13:9
Position	Matt. 20:21-23
B. *Of the hand:*	
Unusual capacity of 700 men	Judg. 20:15, 16
Lesser importance of	Gen. 48:13-20
C. *Figurative of:*	
Weakness	Eccl. 10:2
Shame	Matt. 25:33, 41
Bride's choice	Song 2:6
Singleness of purpose	Matt. 6:3
Riches	Prov. 3:16
Ministry of God	2 Cor. 6:7

Left—*that which remains over*

A. *Descriptive of:*	
Aloneness	Gen. 32:24
Entire destruction	Josh. 11:11, 12
Entire separation	Ex. 10:26
Survival	Num. 26:65
Remnant	Is. 11:11, 16
Heir	2 Sam. 14:7
B. *Blessings upon:*	
Equal booty	1 Sam. 30:9-25
Greater heritage	Is. 49:21-23
Holiness	Is. 4:3
Lord's protection	Rom. 11:3-5
Not wasted	Matt. 15:37

Legacy—*that which is bequeathed to heirs*

Left by:	
Abraham	Gen. 25:5, 6
David	1 Kin. 2:1-7
Christ	John 14:15-27

Legal—*lawful*

Kingship, determined by David	1 Kin. 1:5-48
Priests' rights, divinely enforced	2 Chr. 26:16-21
Priesthood, rejected	Neh. 7:63-65
Right to rebuild, confirmed	Ezra 5:3-17
Mixed marriages, condemned	Ezra 10:1-44
David's act, justified	Matt. 12:3-8
Christ's trial, exposed	Matt. 27:4-31
Paul's right of appeal, recognized	Acts 26:31, 32

Legion—*a great number or multitude*

Demons	Mark 5:9, 15
Christ's angels	Matt. 26:53

Legs—*lower parts of human or animal body*

A. *Used literally of:*	
Animal's	Ex. 12:9
Man's	1 Sam. 17:6
Christ's	John 19:31, 33
B. *Used figuratively of:*	
Fool	Prov. 26:7
Man's weakness	Ps. 147:10
Children of Israel	Amos 3:12
Strength	Dan. 2:33, 40
Christ's appearance	Song 5:15

Lehabim—*flaming*

Nation (probably the Libyans) related to the Egyptians	Gen. 10:13

Lehi—*cheek, jawbone*

Place in Judah; Samson kills Philistines	Judg. 15:9-19

Leisure—*spare time*

None found	Mark 6:31

Lemuel—*devoted to God*

King taught by his mother	Prov. 31:1-31

Lending—*to give to another for temporary use*

A. *As a gift:*	
Expecting no return	Luke 6:34, 35
To the LORD	1 Sam. 1:28 1 Sam. 2:20
B. *As a blessing:*	
Recognized by God	Deut. 28:12, 44
Remembered by God	Ps. 112:5, 6
Rewarded by God	Ps. 37:25, 26

See Borrow

Length of life

A. *Factors prolonging:*	
Keeping commandments	1 Kin. 3:14
Wisdom	Prov. 3:13, 16
Prayer	2 Kin. 20:1-11
Honor to parents	Eph. 6:3
Fear of the LORD	Prov. 10:27
B. *Factors decreasing:*	
Killing	2 Sam. 3:27
God's judgment	Job 22:15, 16
Suicide	Matt. 27:5

Lentil—*plant of the legume family*

Prepared as Esau's pottage	Gen. 25:29-34
Bread made of	Ezek. 4:9

Leopard—*a wild, spotted animal*

A. *Characteristics of:*	
Swift	Hab. 1:8
Watches	Jer. 5:6
Lies in wait	Hos. 13:7
Lives in mountains	Song 4:8
B. *Figurative of:*	
Man's inability to change	Jer. 13;23
Transformation	Is. 11:6
Greek empire	Dan. 7:6
Antichrist	Rev. 13:2

Leprosy—*scourge; a cancer-like disease*

A. *Characteristics of:*	
Many diseased with	Luke 4:27
Unclean	Lev. 13:44, 45
Outcast	2 Kin. 15:5
Considered incurable	2 Kin. 5:7

SUBJECT	REFERENCE
Often hereditary	2 Sam. 3:29
Excluded from the priesthood	Lev. 22:2-4
B. *Kinds of, in:*	
Man	Luke 17:12
House	Lev. 14:33-57
Clothing	Lev. 13:47-59
C. *Treatment of:*	
Symptoms described	Lev. 13:1-46
Cleansing prescribed	Lev. 14:1-32
Healing by a miracle	Ex. 4:6, 7
D. *Used as a sign:*	
Miriam	Num. 12:1-10
Gehazi	2 Kin. 5:25, 27
Uzziah	2 Chr. 26:16-21
Moses	Ex. 4:6, 7

Letters—*written communications*

A. *Kinds of:*	
Forged	1 Kin. 21:7, 8
Rebellious	Jer. 29:24-32
Authoritative	Acts 22:5
Instructive	Acts 15:23-29
Weighty	2 Cor. 10:10
Causing sorrow	2 Cor. 7:8
B. *Descriptive of:*	
One's writing	Gal. 6:11
Learning	John 7:15
External	Rom. 2:27, 29
Legalism	Rom. 7:6
Christians	2 Cor. 3:1, 2

"Let us"

"Arise, go hence"	John 14:31
"Cast off the works of darkness"	Rom. 13:12
"Walk honestly"	Rom. 13:13
"Be sober"	1 Thess. 5:8
"Fear"	Heb. 4:1
"Labor to enter into that rest"	Heb. 4:11
"Come boldly"	Heb. 4:16
"Go on unto perfection"	Heb. 6:1
"Draw near"	Heb. 10:22
"Hold fast"	Heb. 10:23
"Consider one another"	Heb. 10:24
"Run with patience"	Heb. 12:1
"Go forth"	Heb. 13:13
"Offer sacrifice"	Heb. 13:15

Letushim—*sharpened*

Tribe descending from Dedan	Gen. 25:3

Leummim—*peoples*

Tribe descending from Dedan	Gen. 25:3

Levi—*joined*

1. Third son of Jacob and Leah	Gen. 29:34
Participates in revenge	Gen. 34:25-31
Father of Gershon, Kohath, Merari	Gen. 46:11
Descendants of, to be scattered	Gen. 49:5-7
Dies in Egypt at age 137	Ex. 6:16
2. Ancestor of Christ	Luke 3:24
3. Another ancestor of Christ	Luke 3:29
4. Apostle called Matthew	Luke 5:27, 29
5. Tribe descending from Levi	Ex. 32:26, 28

Leviathan—*twisted, coiled*

Great beast created by God	Ps. 104:26
Habit of, graphically described (crocodile)	Job 41:1-34
God's power over	Ps. 74:14

Levites—*descendants of Levi*

A. *History of:*	
Descendants of Levi, Jacob's son	Gen. 29:34
Jacob's prophecy concerning	Gen. 49:5-7
Divided into three families	Ex. 6:16-24
Aaron, great-grandson of Levi, chosen for priesthood	Ex. 28:1
Tribe of Levi rewarded for dedication	Ex. 32:26-29
Chosen by God for holy service	Deut. 10:8
Not numbered among Israel	Num. 1:47-49
Substituted for Israel's first-born	Num. 3:12-45
Given as gifts to Aaron's sons	Num. 8:6-21
Rebellion among, led by Korah	Num. 16:1-50
Choice of, confirmed by the Lord	Num. 17:1-13
Bear ark of the covenant across the Jordan	Josh. 3:2-17
Hear Law read	Josh. 8:31-35
Cities (48) assigned to	Num. 35:2-8 Josh. 14:3, 4
One of, becomes Micah's idolatrous priest	Judg. 17:5-13 Judg. 18:18-31
Perform priestly functions	1 Sam. 6:15
Appointed over service of song	1 Chr. 6:31-48
Service of heads of households	1 Chr. 9:26-34
Excluded by Jeroboam	2 Chr. 11:13-17
Help repair the Temple	1 Chr. 23:2-4
Carried to Babylon	2 Chr. 36:19, 20
Return from exile	Ezra 2:40-63
Tithes withheld from	Neh. 13:10-13
Intermarry with foreigners	Ezra 10:2-24
Seal the covenant	Neh. 10:1, 9-28
Present defiled offerings will be purified	Mal. 1:6-14 Mal. 3:1-4
B. *Duties of:*	
Serve the LORD	Deut. 10:8
Serve the priesthood	Num. 3:5-9
Attend to sanctuary duties	Num. 18:3
Distribute the tithe	2 Chr. 31:11-19
Prepare sacrifices for priests	2 Chr. 35:10-14
Teach the people	2 Chr. 17:9-11
Declare verdicts of Law	Deut. 17:9-11
Protect the king	2 Chr. 23:2-10
Perform music	1 Chr. 25:1-7
Precede the army	2 Chr. 20:20, 21, 28
C. *Spiritual truths illustrated by:*	
Representation—duties of the congregation	Num. 3:6-9
Substitution—place of the first-born	Num. 3:12, 13, 41, 45
Subordination—service to the Temple	Num. 3:5-10
Consecration—separated for God's work	Num. 8:9-14
Holiness—cleansed	Num. 8:6, 7, 21
Election—God's choice	Num. 17:7-13
Inheritance—in the Lord	Num. 18:20

See Priest

Leviticus, the Book of—*a book of the Old Testament*

Laws of sacrifice	Lev. 1:1—7:38
Laws of purity	Lev. 11:1—15:33
Day of atonement	Lev. 16:1-34
Laws of holiness	Lev. 17:1—25:55
Blessings and curses	Lev. 26:1-46

Levy—*forced labor imposed upon a people*

Israelites	1 Kin. 5:13-15
Canaanites	1 Kin. 9:15, 21

Lewd, lewdness—*wickedness*

A. *Characteristics of:*	
Shameful	Ezek. 16:27
Sexual	Ezek. 22:11
Youthful	Ezek. 23:21
Adulterous	Jer. 13:27
Filthiness	Ezek. 24:13
Folly	Judg. 20:6
B. *Committed by:*	
Men of Gibeah	Judg. 20:5
Israel	Hos. 2:10
Jerusalem	Ezek. 16:27, 43

Liars, lies, lying—*manifestation of untruth*

A. *Defined as:*	
Nature of the devil	John 8:44
Denial that Jesus is Christ	1 John 2:22
Not keeping Christ's commandments	1 John 2:4
Hating one's brother	1 John 4:20
All that is not of the truth	1 John 2:21, 27
B. *Those who speak:*	
Wicked	Ps. 58:3
False witnesses	Prov. 14:5, 25
Astrologers	Dan. 2:9
Israel	Hos. 7:3, 13
Judah	Jer. 9:1-5
C. *Attitude of the wicked toward:*	
Are always	Titus 1:12
Forge against the righteous	Ps. 119:69
Change God's truth into	Rom. 1:25
D. *Attitude of the righteous toward:*	
Keep far from	Prov. 30:8
Shall not speak	Zeph. 3:13
Pray for deliverance from	Ps. 120:2
"Put away"	Eph. 4:25
E. *Attitude of God toward:*	
Will not	Num. 23:19
Is an abomination	Prov. 6:16-19
Will discover man's	Is. 28:15, 17
Is against	Ezek. 13:8
F. *Punishment of, shall:*	
Not escape	Prov. 19:5
Be stopped	Ps. 63:11
Be silenced	Ps. 31:18
Be short-lived	Prov. 12:19
End in lake of fire	Rev. 21:8, 27
G. *The evils of:*	
Produces error	Amos 2:4
Increases wickedness	Prov. 29:12
Destruction	Hos. 10:13-15
Death	Prov. 21:6 Zech. 13:3

Liberality—*a generous spirit in helping the needy*

A. *Object of:*	
Poor	Deut. 15:11
Strangers	Lev. 25:35
Afflicted	Luke 10:30-35
Servants (slaves)	Deut. 15:12-18
All men	Gal. 6:10
God's children	2 Cor. 8:1-9, 12
B. *Reasons for:*	
Make our faith real	James 2:14-16
Secure true riches	Luke 12:33 1 Tim. 6:17-19
Follow Christ's example	2 Cor. 8:9
Help God's kingdom	Phil. 4:14-18
Relieve distress	2 Cor. 9:12
C. *Blessings of:*	
God remembers	Prov. 3:9, 10
Will return abundantly	Prov. 11:24-27
Brings deliverance in time of need	Is. 58:10, 11
Insures sufficiency	Ps. 37:25, 26
Brings reward	Ps. 112:5-9 Matt. 25:40
Provokes others to	2 Cor. 9:2

Libertines freedmen

Jews opposing Stephen	Acts 6:9

Liberty, civil

Obtained by:	
Purchase	Acts 22:28
Birth	Acts 22:28
Release	Deut. 15:12-15
Victory	Ex. 14:30, 31

Liberty, spiritual

A. *Described as:*	
Predicted	Is. 61:1
Where the spirit is	2 Cor. 3:17
B. *Relation of Christians toward, they:*	
Are called to	Gal. 5:13
Abide by	James 1:25
Should walk at	Ps. 119:45
Have in Jesus Christ	Gal. 2:4, 5

See Freedom

Libnah—*whiteness*

1. Israelite camp	Num. 33:20, 21
2. Canaanite city near Lachish	Josh. 10:29-32
Captured by Joshua	Josh. 10:30, 39
In Judah's territory	Josh. 15:42
Given to Aaron's descendants	Josh. 21:13
Fought against by Assyria	2 Kin. 19:8, 9
Home of Hamutal	2 Kin. 23:31

Libni—*white, pure*

1. Son of Gershon	Num. 3:18, 21
Family of, called Libnites	Num. 3:21
Called Laadan	1 Chr. 23:7
2. Descendant of Merari	1 Chr. 6:29

L

SUBJECT	REFERENCE
Libya, Libyans—*the land and people west of Egypt*	
Called Lubim	Nah. 3:9
Will fall by the sword	Ezek. 30:5
Will be controlled	Dan. 11:43
Some from, at Pentecost	Acts 2:1-10
Lice—*some small, harmful insects*	
Third plague upon Egypt, produced from dust	Ex. 8:16-18
License—*authority to do something*	
Granted to Paul	Acts 21:40
Life, eternal	
A. *Defined as:*	
Knowing the true God	John 17:3
God's commandment	John 12:50
Jesus Christ	1 John 1:2
He gives	John 10:28, 29
God's gift	Rom. 6:23
B. *Christ's relation to:*	
It is in Him	2 Tim. 1:1
Manifested through Him	2 Tim. 1:10
He has the words of	John 6:68
It comes through Him	Rom. 5:21
C. *Means of securing, by:*	
God's gift	Rom. 6:22, 23
Having the Son	1 John 5:11, 12
Knowing the true God	John 17:3
Knowing the Scriptures	John 20:31
Believing the Son	John 3:15-36
Drinking the water of life	John 4:14
Eating the bread of life	John 6:50-58
Reaping	John 4:36
Fight the good fight of faith	1 Tim. 6:12, 19
D. *Present aspect of, for Christians, they:*	
Believe in the Son	John 3:36
Have assurance of	John 5:24
Have promise of	Titus 1:2
Have hope of	Titus 3:7
Take hold of	1 Tim. 6:12, 19
Hates his life in this world	John 12:25
E. *Future aspect of, for Christians, they shall:*	
Inherit	Matt. 19:29
In the world to come	Luke 18:30
In them you think you have	John 5:39
Reap	Gal. 6:8
Life, natural	
A. *Origin of, by:*	
God's creation	Acts 17:28, 29
Natural birth	Gen. 4:1, 2
Supernatural conception	Luke 1:31-35
B. *Shortness of, described as:*	
Dream	Job 20:8
Shadow	1 Chr. 29:15
Cloud	Job 7:9
Flower	Job 14:1, 2
Vapor	James 4:14
Sleep	Ps. 90:5
Tale told	Ps. 90:9
Pilgrimage	Gen. 47:9
Grass	1 Pet. 1:24
C. *God's concern for, its:*	
Preservation	Gen. 7:1-3
Protection	Ps. 34:7, 17, 19
Perpetuity (continuance)	Gen. 1:28
Provisions	Ps. 104:27, 28
Punishment	Gen. 3:14-19
Perfection in glory	Col. 3:4
D. *Believer's attitude toward:*	
Seeks to preserve it	Acts 27:10-31
Attends to needs of	Acts 27:34
Accepts suffering of	Job 2:4-10
Makes God's kingdom first in	Matt. 6:25-33
Gives it up for Christ	Matt. 10:39
Lays it down for others	Acts 15:26
Prizes it not too highly	Acts 20:24
Puts Jesus first in	2 Cor. 4:10-12
Regards God's will in	James 4:13-15
Puts away the evil of	Col. 3:5-9
Does not run with	1 Pet. 4:1-4
Praises God all the days of	Ps. 63:3, 4
Doesn't fear enemies of	Luke 12:4
E. *Cares of:*	
Stunt spiritual growth	Luke 8:14

SUBJECT	REFERENCE
Divide loyalty	Luke 16:13
Delay preparedness	Luke 17:26-30 Luke 21:34
Hinder service	2 Tim. 2:4
Life, spiritual	
A. *Source of:*	
God	Ps. 36:9
Christ	John 14:6
Holy Spirit	Ezek. 37:14
God's Word	James 1:18
B. *Described as:*	
New birth	John 3:3-8
Resurrection	John 5:24
Translation	Acts 26:18
New creation	2 Cor. 5:17
Seed	1 John 3:9
Crucifixion	Gal. 2:20
C. *Evidences of:*	
Growth	1 Pet. 2:2
Love	1 John 3:14
Obedience	Rom. 6:16-22
Victory	Rom. 6:1-15
Spiritual-mindedness	Rom. 8:6
Possession of the Spirit	Rom. 8:9-13
Spirit's testimony	Rom. 8:15-17
Walking in the Spirit	Gal. 5:16, 25
Bearing the fruit of the Spirit	Gal. 5:22
Name in the book of life	Phil. 4:3 Rev. 17:8
D. *Growth of:*	
Begins in birth	John 3:3-8
Feeds on milk in infancy	1 Pet. 2:2
Must not remain in infancy	Heb. 5:11-14
Comes to adulthood	1 John 2:13, 14
Arrives at maturity	Eph. 4:14-16
E. *Characteristics of:*	
Imperishable	John 11:25, 26
Transforming	Rom. 12:1, 2
Invisible	Col. 3:3, 4
Abides forever	1 John 2:17
F. *Enemies of:*	
Devil	Eph. 6:11-17
World	1 John 2:15-17
Flesh	Gal. 5:16-21
Life, triumphant Christian	
A. *Over:*	
Sorrow	John 16:22-24 1 Thess. 4:13-18
The world	John 16:33 1 John 5:4, 5
Transgressions	Rom. 6:6, 7, 11-18 1 John 5:4, 5 Rom. 8:1-4 Eph. 2:5, 6
Circumstances	Rom. 8:37 Phil. 4:11-13
Death	1 Cor. 15:54-57 Rom. 6:6-9
B. *Through:*	
Prayer	John 16:22-24
Christ's death	Rom. 6:6, 7
Doctrine	Rom. 6:17
Holy Spirit	Rom. 8:1, 2
Christ	Phil. 4:13
Grace	Eph. 2:7 Rom. 6:14
Exaltation with Christ	Eph. 2:5, 6
God's will	Phil. 2:13
Hope of resurrection	1 Thess. 4:16
Return of Christ	1 Thess. 4:16, 17
Faith	1 John 5:4, 5
C. *When?*	
Forever	1 Cor. 15:54
Always	2 Cor. 2:14
D. *By whom? Those who:*	
Are in Christ	Rom. 8:1
Were dead in transgressions	Eph. 2:5
Are born of God	1 John 5:4
Believe	1 John 5:5
E. *Goal:*	
To demonstrate God's grace	Eph. 3:7-10

SUBJECT	REFERENCE
To glorify Christ	1 Pet. 4:11 Rom. 8:16-18
Light—*the absence of darkness*	
A. *Kinds of:*	
Cosmic	Gen. 1:3-5
Natural	Judg. 19:26
Miraculous	Acts 12:7
Artificial	Acts 16:29
B. *Descriptive of God's:*	
Nature	1 John 1:5
Word	Ps. 119:105
Wisdom	Dan. 2:21, 22
Guidance	Ps. 78:14 Ps. 89:15
Favor	Ps. 4:6
C. *Descriptive of Christ's:*	
Preincarnation	John 1:4-9
Person	2 Cor. 4:6
Prediction	Is. 42:6
Presentation to the world	Luke 2:32
Proclamation	John 8:12
Perfection in glory	Rev. 21:23, 24
D. *Descriptive of Christians as:*	
Forerunners	John 5:35
Examples	Matt. 5:14, 16
Missionaries	Matt. 10:27
Transformed people	Eph. 5:8-14
Heirs of glory	Rev. 21:23
Lightning—*electrical discharges between the clouds and the earth*	
A. *Used literally of God's:*	
Visitation at Sinai	Ex. 19:16
A power in storms	Job 38:35
B. *Descriptive of:*	
Swiftness	Nah. 2:4
Brightness	Matt. 28:3
God's judgments	Rev. 11:19
Christ's coming	Luke 17:24
Satan's fall	Luke 10:18
Ligure—*gem*	
Worn by the high priest	Ex. 28:19
Likeness—*similarity of features*	
Between:	
Spiritual and the moral	2 Cor. 3:6
Spiritual and the physical	Jer. 23:29
Two events	2 Chr. 35:18
God and idols	Is. 46:5, 6, 9
Believers and unbelievers	Ps. 73:5
Now and the future	1 John 3:2
Likhi—*Jehovah is doctrine*	
Manassite	1 Chr. 7:19
Lilith—*an evil female demon in Babylonian mythology*	
Rendered "screech owl," suggesting desolation	Is. 34:14
Lily—*a bulbous plant*	
Descriptive of:	
Beauty	Song 5:13
Spiritual growth	Hos. 14:4, 5
Christ	Song 2:1
Lily work—*decorations upon the capitals of columns*	
In Solomon's Temple	1 Kin. 7:19, 22
Lime—*containing limestone*	
Descriptive of:	
Cruel treatment	Amos 2:1
Devastating judgment	Is. 33:12
Line	
A. *Literal uses of:*	
As a measurement	Jer. 31:39
Rahab's cord	Josh. 2:18, 21
B. *Figurative uses of:*	
God's providences	Ps. 16:6
God's judgments	Is. 28:17
Linen—*cloth made from flax*	
A. *Used for:*	
Priestly garments	Ex. 28:1, 39
Tabernacle curtains	Ex. 26:1
Sacred veil	Ex. 26:31, 36
Garments for royalty	Esth. 8:15
Levitical singers	2 Chr. 5:12

SUBJECT	REFERENCE
Gifts to a woman	Ezek. 16:10, 13
Clothing of the rich	Luke 16:19
Embalming	Matt. 27:59
B. *Figurative of:*	
Righteousness	Rev. 19:8
Purity	Rev. 19:14
Babylon's pride	Rev. 18:2, 16

Lintel—*a beam of wood overhanging the door*

Sprinkled with blood	Ex. 12:22, 23
Command to smite	Amos 9:1
Descriptive of Nineveh's fall	Zeph. 2:14

Linus

Christian at Rome	2 Tim. 4:21

Lions

A. *Described as:*	
Strongest among beasts	Prov. 30:30
Destructive	Amos 3:12
Strong	Judg. 14:18
Fierce	Job 10:16
Stealthy	Ps. 10:9
Majestic	Prov. 30:29, 30
Provoking fear	Amos 3:8
B. *God's use of:*	
Slay the disobedient	1 Kin. 13:24, 26
Punish idolaters	2 Kin. 17:25, 26
Show His power over	Dan. 6:16-24
C. *Figurative of:*	
Tribe of Judah	Gen. 49:9
Christ	Rev. 5:5
Devil	1 Pet. 5:8
Transformation	Is. 11:6-8
Victory	Ps. 91:13
Boldness	Prov. 28:1
Persecutors	Ps. 22:13
World empire	Dan. 7:1-4
Antichrist	Rev. 13:2

Lips

A. *Described as:*	
Uncircumcised	Ex. 6;12, 30
Unclean	Is. 6:5, 7
Stammering	Is. 28:11
Flattering	Ps. 12:2, 3
Perverse	Prov. 4:24
Righteous	Prov. 16:13
False	Prov. 17:4
Burning	Prov. 26:23
B. *Of the righteous, used for:*	
Knowledge	Job 33:3
Prayer	Ps. 17:1
Silent prayer	1 Sam. 1:13
Righteousness	Ps. 40:9
Grace	Ps. 45:2
Praise	Ps. 51:15
Vows	Ps. 66:13, 14
Singing	Ps. 71:23
God's judgments	Ps. 119:13
Feeding many	Prov. 10:21
Spiritual fruitfulness	Hos. 14:2 Heb. 13:15
C. *Of the wicked, used for:*	
Flattery	Prov. 7:21
Mocking	Ps. 22:7
Defiance	Ps. 12:4
Lying	Is. 59:3
Poison	Ps. 140:3, 9
Mischief	Prov. 24:2
Evil	Prov. 16:27, 30
Deception	Prov. 24:28
D. *Warnings:*	
Put away perverse	Prov. 4:24
Refrain use	Prov. 17:28 1 Pet. 3:10
Of an adulteress, avoid	Prov. 5:3-13
Hypocrites	Mark 7:6

Litigation—*a lawsuit*

Christ's warning concerning	Matt. 5:25, 40
Paul's warning concerning	1 Cor. 6:1, 2

Litter—*a covered framework for carrying a single passenger*

Of nations	Is. 66:20

Liver—*body organ that secretes bile*

A. *Used literally of:*	
Animals:	
In sacrifice	Ex. 29:13, 22
For divination	Ezek. 21:21
B. *Used figuratively of:*	
Extreme pain or death	Prov. 7:23

Living, Christian

Source—Christ	John 14:19
Length—forever	John 11:25, 26
Means—faith in Christ	Rom. 1:17
Kind—resurrected	2 Cor. 5:15
End—to God	Rom. 14:7, 8
Purpose—for Christ	1 Thess. 5:10
Motivation—Christ	Gal. 2:20
Atmosphere—in the Spirit	Gal. 5:25
Manner—righteously	Titus 2:12
Enemies—flesh and sin	Rom. 8:12, 13
Price—persecution	2 Tim. 3:12

Living creatures—*a phrase referring to animals or living beings*

Aquatic animals	Gen. 1:21
Land animals	Gen. 1:24
Angelic beings	Ezek. 1:5

Lizard—*a small, swift reptile with legs*

Ceremonially unclean	Lev. 11:29, 30

Lo-ammi—*not my people*

Symbolic name of Hosea's son	Hos. 1:8, 9

Loan (see Borrow; Lending)

Lock

Doors	Judg. 3:23, 24
Hair	Judg. 16:13, 19
City gates	Neh. 3:6, 13, 14

Locust—*devastating, migratory insects*

A. *Types, or stages, of:*	
Eating	Joel 1:4
Devastating	Lev. 11:22
B. *Used literally of insects:*	
Miraculously brought forth	Ex. 10:12-19
Sent as a judgment	Deut. 28:38 1 Kin. 8:37
Used for food	Matt. 3:4
C. *Used figuratively of:*	
Weakness	Ps. 109:23, 24
Running men	Is. 33:4
Nineveh's departing glory	Nah. 3:15, 17
Final plagues	Rev. 9:3, 7

See Grasshopper

Lod

Benjamite town	1 Chr. 8:1, 12
Mentioned in postexilic books	Ezra 2:33
Aeneas healed here, called Lydda	Acts 9:32-35

Lo-debar

City in Manasseh (in Gilead)	2 Sam. 9:4, 5
David flees to	2 Sam. 17:27

Lodge—*to pass the night*

Travelers—in a house	Judg. 19:4-20
Spies—in a house	Josh. 2:1
Animals—in ruins	Zeph. 2:14
Birds—in trees	Matt. 13:32
Righteousness—in a city	Is. 1:21
Thoughts—in Jerusalem	Jer. 4:14

Loft—*a room upstairs*

Dead child taken to	1 Kin. 17:19-24
Young man falls from	Acts 20:9

Loins

A. *Used literally of:*	
Hips	Gen. 37:34 Ex. 28:42
Waist	2 Sam. 20:8
B. *Used figuratively of:*	
Physical strength	Ps. 66:11
Source of knowledge	Eph. 6:14
Source of hope	1 Pet. 1:13

Lois

Timothy's grandmother	2 Tim. 1:5

Loneliness

Jacob—in prayer	Gen. 32:23-30
Joseph—in weeping	Gen. 43:30, 31
Elijah—in discouragement	1 Kin. 19:3-14
Jeremiah—in witnessing	Jer. 15:17
Nehemiah—in a night vigil	Neh. 2:12-16
Christ—in agony	Matt. 26:36-45
Paul—in prison	2 Tim. 4:16

Longevity—*a great span of life*

Allotted years, 70	Ps. 90:10

See Length of life

Long-suffering—*forbearance*

A. *Manifested in God's:*	
Description of His nature	Ex. 34:6
Delay in executing wrath	Rom. 9:22
Dealing with sinful men	Rom. 2:4
Desire for man's salvation	2 Pet. 3:9, 15
B. *As a Christian grace:*	
Exemplified by the prophets ("patience")	James 5:10
Manifested by Old Testament saints ("patience")	Heb. 6:12
Produced by the Spirit	Gal. 5:22
Witnessed in Paul's life	2 Cor. 6:6
Taught as a virtue	Eph. 4:1
Given power for	Col. 1:11
Set for imitation	2 Tim. 3:10
Needed by preachers	2 Tim. 4:2

Look—*focusing the eyes toward something*

Promise	Gen. 15:5
Warning	Gen. 19:17, 26
Astonishment	Ex. 3:2-6
Disdain	1 Sam. 17:42
Lust	2 Sam. 11:2-4
Encouragement	Ps. 34:5
Disappointment	Is. 5:2, 4
Salvation	Is. 45:22
Glory	Acts 7:55

Lord—*title of majesty and kingship*

A. *Applied to:*	
God	Gen. 3:1-23
Christ	Luke 6:46
Masters	Gen. 24:14, 27
Men ("sir")	Matt. 21:29
Husbands	Gen. 18:12 1 Pet. 3:6
B. *As applied to Christ, "kyrios" indicates:*	
Identity with Jehovah	Joel 2:32
Confession of Christ's Lordship ("Jesus as Lord")	Rom. 10:9
Absolute Lordship	Phil. 2:11

Lord's Day (see First day of week)

Lord's Prayer

Taught by Jesus to His disciples	Matt. 6:9-13

Lord's Supper

A. *Described as:*	
Sharing of communion	1 Cor. 10:16
Breaking of bread	Acts 2:42, 46
Lord's supper	1 Cor. 11:20
Eucharist "Giving of thanks"	Luke 22:17, 19
B. *Features concerning:*	
Instituted by Christ	Matt. 26:26-29
Commemorative of Christ's death	Luke 22:19, 20
Introductory to the new covenant	Matt. 26:28
Means of Christian fellowship	Acts 2:42, 46
Memorial feast	1 Cor. 11:23-26
Inconsistent with demon fellowship	1 Cor. 10:19-22
Preparation for, required	1 Cor. 11:27-34
Spiritually explained	John 6:26-58

Lordship—*supreme authority*

Human kings	Mark 10:42
Divine King	Phil. 2:9-11

Lo-ruhamah—*not pitied*

Symbolic name of Hosea's daughter	Hos. 1:6

Loss, spiritual

A. *Kinds of:*	
One's soul	Luke 9:24, 25
Reward	1 Cor. 3:13-15
Heaven	Luke 16:19-31

SUBJECT REFERENCE

B. *Causes of:*
- Love of this life .... Luke 17:33
- Sin .... Ps. 107:17, 34

Lost—*not found*

Descriptive of men as:
- Separated from God .... Luke 15:24, 32
- Unregenerated .... Matt. 15:24
- Objects of Christ's mission...... Luke 15:4-6
- Blinded by Satan .... 2 Cor. 4:3, 4
- Defiled .... Titus 1:15, 16

Lot—*covering*

A. *Life of:*
- Abraham's nephew .... Gen. 11:27-31
- Goes with Abraham to Canaan .... Gen. 12:5
- Accompanies Abraham to Egypt .... Gen. 13:1
- Settles in Sodom .... Gen. 13:5-13
- Rescued by Abraham .... Gen. 14:12-16
- Befriends angels .... Gen. 19:1-14
- Saved from Sodom's destruction .... Gen. 19:15, 26
- His wife, disobedient, becomes pillar of salt .... Gen. 19:15, 26
- His daughters commit incest with .... Gen. 19:30-38
- Unwilling father of Moabites and Ammonites .... Gen. 19:37, 38

B. *Character of:*
- Makes selfish choice .... Gen. 13:5-13
- Lacks moral stability .... Gen. 19:6-10
- Loses moral influence .... Gen. 19:14, 20
- Still "vexed" by Sodomites... 2 Pet. 2:7, 8

Lotan—*a covering*
- Tribe of Horites in Mt. Seir..... Gen. 36:20, 29; 1 Chr. 1:38, 39

Lot(s)—*a means of deciding doubtful matters*

A. *Characteristic of:*
- Preceded by prayer .... Acts 1:23-26
- With divine sanction .... Num. 26:55
- Considered final .... Num. 26:56
- Used also by the ungodly.... Matt. 27:35

B. *Used for:*
- Selection of scapegoat .... Lev. 16:8
- Detection of a criminal...... Josh. 7:14-18
- Selection of warriors .... Judg. 20:9, 10
- Choice of a king............ 1 Sam. 10:19-21
- Deciding priestly rotation.... Luke 1:9

Lot's wife
- Disobedient, becomes pillar of salt .... Gen. 19:26
- Event to be remembered .... Luke 17:32

Love, Christian

A. *Toward God:*
- First commandment .... Matt. 22:37, 38
- With all the heart .... Matt. 22:37
- More important than ritual .. Mark 12:31-33
- Gives boldness .... 1 John 4:17-19

B. *Toward Christ:*
- Sign of true faith .... John 8:42
- Manifested in obedience..... John 14:15, 21, 23
- Leads to service .... 2 Cor. 5:14

C. *Toward others:*
- Second command .... Matt. 22:37-39
- Commanded by Christ ...... John 13:34
- Described in detail .... 1 Cor. 13:1-13

Love of Christ, the

A. *Objects of:*
- Father .... John 14:31
- Believers .... Gal. 2:20
- Church .... Eph. 5:2, 25

B. *Described as:*
- Knowing .... Eph. 3:19
- Personal .... Gal. 2:20
- Conquering .... Rom. 8:37
- Unbreakable .... Rom. 8:35
- Intimate .... John 14:21
- Imitative .... 1 John 3:16
- Like the Father's .... John 15:9
- Sacrificial .... Gal. 2:20

C. *Expressions of:*
- In taking our nature .... Heb. 2:16-18
- In dying for us .... John 15:13

Love of God, the

A. *Objects of:*
- Christ .... John 3:35
- Christians .... 2 Thess. 2:16
- Mankind .... Titus 3:4
- Cheerful giver .... 2 Cor. 9:7

B. *Described as:*
- Great .... Eph. 2:4
- Everlasting .... Jer. 31:3
- Sacrificial .... Rom. 5:8

C. *As seen in believers':*
- Hearts .... Rom. 5:5
- Regeneration .... Eph. 2:4, 5
- Love .... 1 John 4:7-12
- Faith .... 1 John 4:16
- Security .... 2 Thess. 3:5
- Daily life .... 1 John 2:15-17
- Obedience .... 1 John 2:5
- Without fear .... 1 John 4:18-21
- Glorification .... 1 John 3:1, 2

Love, physical
- Isaac and Rebekah .... Gen. 24:67
- Jacob and Rachel .... Gen. 29:11-30
- Boaz and Ruth .... Ruth 2:4-15
- Samson and Delilah .... Judg. 16:4, 15

Lovingkindness—*gentle and steadfast mercy*

Attitude of believers, to:
- Expect .... Ps. 17:7; Ps. 36:10
- Rejoice in .... Ps. 63:3; Ps. 69:16

Loyalty—*fidelity to a person or cause*

A. *Kinds of:*
- People .... Acts 25:7-11
- Relatives .... Esth. 2:21-23
- King .... 1 Sam. 24:6-10
- Cause .... 2 Sam. 11:9-11
- Oath .... 2 Sam. 21:7

B. *Signs of:*
- General obedience .... Rom. 13:1, 2
- Prayer for rulers .... Ezra 6:10
- Hatred of disloyalty .... Josh. 22:9-20

Lucifer—*light-bearer*
- Name applied to Satan .... Is. 14:12
- Allusion to elsewhere .... Luke 10:18

Lucius—*of light*

1. Prophet and teacher at Antioch .... Acts 13:1
2. Paul's companion in Corinth .... Rom. 16:21

Lucre—*gain; money*
- Priests guilty of .... 1 Sam. 8:3
- Elders must avoid .... 1 Tim. 3:2, 3
- Deacons must shun .... 1 Tim. 3:8
- Sign of false teachers .... Titus 1:11

Lud, Ludim (plural)

1. Lud, a people descending from Shem .... 1 Chr. 1:17
2. Ludim, a people descending from Mizraim (Egypt) .... Gen. 10:13
   Mentioned as men of war.... Ezek. 27:10

Luhith—*of tablets or planks*
- Moabite town .... Is. 15:5

Luke—*another name for Lucius*
- "The beloved physician" .... Col. 4:14
- Paul's last companion .... 2 Tim. 4:11

Luke, the Gospel of—*a book of the New Testament*
- The annunication .... Luke 1:26-56
- John the Baptist .... Luke 3:1-22
- The temptation .... Luke 4:1-13
- Public ministry begins .... Luke 4:15
- The disciples chosen .... Luke 6:12-19
- The disciple's instructions ...... Luke 10:25—13:21
- The Jerusalem ministry......... Luke 19:28—21:38
- The Last Supper .... Luke 22:1-38
- The Crucifixion .... Luke 22:39—23:56
- The Resurrection .... Luke 24:1-53

Lukewarm—*neither hot nor cold*
- Descriptive of Laodicea .... Rev. 3:14-16

Lunatic—*an insane person*
- David acts as .... 1 Sam. 21:13-15
- Nebuchadnezzar inflicted as .... Dan. 4:31-36
- Christ heals .... Matt. 4:24
- Christ declared .... John 10:20
- Paul called .... Acts 26:24
- See Madness

Lust—*evil desire*

A. *Origin of, in:*
- Satan .... 1 John 3:8-12
- Heart .... Matt. 15:19
- Flesh .... James 1:14, 15
- World .... 2 Pet. 1:4

B. *Described as:*
- Deceitful .... Eph. 4:22
- Enticing .... James 1:14, 15
- Hurtful .... 1 Tim. 6:9
- Numerous .... 2 Tim. 3:6

C. *Among the unregenerate, they:*
- Live and walk in .... Eph. 2:3
- Are punished with .... Rom. 1:24-32

D. *Among false teachers, they:*
- Walk after .... 2 Pet. 2:10-22
- Will prevail in the last days .... 2 Pet. 3:3
- Are received because of ..... 2 Tim. 4:3, 4

E. *Among Christians:*
- Once lived in .... Eph. 2:3
- Consider it dead .... Col. 3:5
- Deny .... Titus 2:12
- Flee from .... 2 Tim. 2:22
- Not carry out .... Gal. 5:16

Luxuries

A. *Characteristic of:*
- Egypt .... Heb. 11:24-27
- Tyre .... Ezek. 27:1-27
- Ancient Babylon .... Dan. 4:30
- Israel .... Amos 6:1-7
- Persia .... Esth. 1:3-11
- Harlot Babylon .... Rev. 18:10-13

B. *Productive of:*
- Temptation .... Josh. 7:20, 21
- Physical weakness .... Dan. 1:8, 10-16
- Moral decay .... Nah. 3:1-19
- Spiritual decay .... Rev. 3:14-17

Luz—*almond tree*

1. Ancient Canaanite town ..... Gen. 28:19
   Called Bethel .... Gen. 35:6
2. Hittite town .... Judg. 1:23-26

Lycaonia—*a rugged, inland district of Asia Minor*
- Paul preaches in three of its cities .... Acts 14:6, 11

Lycia—*a province of Asia Minor*

Paul:
- Visits Patara, a city of .... Acts 21:1, 2
- Lands at Myra, a city of .... Acts 27:5, 6

Lydia—*from Lud*

1. Woman of Thyatira; Paul's first European convert .... Acts 16:14, 15, 40
2. District of Asia Minor containing Ephesus, Smyrna, Thyatira, and Sardis .... Rev. 1:11

Lying (see Liars)

Lysanias—*ending sadness*
- Tetrarch of Abilene .... Luke 3:1

Lysias, Claudius
- Roman captain who rescues Paul .... Acts 23:10
- Listens to Paul's nephew .... Acts 23:16-22
- Sends Paul to Felix .... Acts 23:23-31
- Felix awaits arrival of .... Acts 24:22

Lystra—*a city of Lycaonia*
- Visited by Paul .... Acts 14:6, 21
- Lame man healed here .... Acts 14:8-10
- People of, attempt to worship Paul and Barnabas .... Acts 14:11-18
- Paul stoned here .... 2 Tim. 3:11
- Home of Timothy .... Acts 16:1, 2

SUBJECT REFERENCE

M

Maacah, Maachah—*oppression*
1. Daughter of Nahor ....Gen. 22:24
2. Small Syrian kingdom near Mt. Hermon..................Deut. 3:14
   Not possessed by Israel .....Josh. 13:13
   Called Syria-maachah ....1 Chr. 19:6, 7
3. Machir's wife ....1 Chr. 7:15, 16
4. One of Caleb's concubines ...1 Chr. 2:48
5. Father of Shephatiah........1 Chr. 27:16
6. Ancestress of King Saul .....1 Chr. 8:29
   1 Chr. 9:35
7. One of David's warriors .....1 Chr. 11:43
8. Father of Achish, king of Gath ....1 Kin. 2:39
9. David's wife and mother of Absalom ....2 Sam. 3:3
10. Wife of Rehoboam; mother of King Abijah ....2 Chr. 11:18-21
    Makes idol, is deposed as queenmother..............1 Kin. 15:13

Maachathites—*inhabitants of Maachah*
Not conquered by Israel........Josh. 13:13
Among Israel's warriors ....2 Sam. 23:34
See Maacah, Maacath 2

Maadai—*ornament of Jehovah*
Postexilic Jew; divorced his foreign wife ....Ezra 10:34

Maadiah
Priest who returns from Babylon with Zerubbabel ....Neh. 12:5, 7
Same as Moadiah in ....Neh. 12:17

Maai—*compassionate*
Postexilic trumpeter ....Neh. 12:35, 36

Maaleh-acrabbim—*steep*
Ascent south of the Dead Sea ...Josh. 15:3

Maarath—*barren place*
Town of Judah...............Josh. 15:1, 59

Maaseiah—*work of Jehovah*
1. Levite musician during David's reign ....1 Chr. 15:16, 18
2. Levite captain under Jehoiada ....2 Chr. 23:1
3. Official during King Uzziah's reign ....2 Chr. 26:11
4. Son of Ahaz, slain by Zichri....................2 Chr. 28:7
5. Governor of Jerusalem during King Josiah's reign ....2 Chr. 34:1, 8
6. Ancestor of Baruch ....Jer. 32:12
7. Father of the false prophet Zedekiah ....Jer. 29:21
8. Father of Zephaniah the priest ....Jer. 21:1
9. Temple doorkeeper ....Jer. 35:4
10. Judahite postexilic Jew ......Neh. 11:5
11. Benjamite ancestor of a postexilic Jew ....Neh. 11:7
12, 13, 14. Three priests who divorced their foreign wives ....Ezra 10:18, 21, 22
15. Layman who divorced his foreign wife ....Ezra 10:30
16. Representative who signs the covenant ....Neh. 10:1, 25
17. One who stood by Ezra .....Neh. 8:4
18. Levite who explains the Law ....Neh. 8:7
19. Priest who takes part in dedication services ....Neh. 12:41
20. Another participating priest ....Neh. 12:42
21. Father or ancestor of Azariah ....Neh. 3:23

Maasiai—*work of Jehovah*
Priest of Immer's family........1 Chr. 9:12

Maath—*to be small*
Ancestor of Christ............Luke 3:26

Maaz—*anger*
Judahite ....1 Chr. 2:27

Maaziah—*Jehovah is a refuge*
1. Descendant of Aaron; heads a course of priests ....1 Chr. 24:1-18
2. One who signs the covenant ....Neh. 10:1, 8

Macedonia—*Greece* (northern)

A. *In Old Testament prophecy:*
   Called the kingdom of Grecia ....Dan. 11:2
   Brazen part of Nebuchadnezzar's image....................Dan. 2:32, 39
   Described as a leopard with four heads ....Dan. 7:6, 17
   Described as a "he" goat ....Dan. 8:5, 21
   Dan. 11:4

B. *In New Testament missions:*
   Man of, appeals to ....Acts 16:9, 10
   Paul preaches in, at Philippi, etc.......................Acts 16:10—17:14
   Paul's troubles in ....2 Cor. 7:5
   Churches of, very generous ..Rom. 15:26
   2 Cor. 8:1-5

Machbanai—*clad with a cloak*
One of David's mighty men.....1 Chr. 12:13

Machbenah—*lump*
Son of Sheva ....1 Chr. 2:49

Machi
Father of the Gadite spy ....Num. 13:15

Machir—*sold*
1. Manasseh's only son ....Gen. 50:23
   Founder of the family of Machirites................Num. 26:29
   Conqueror of Gilead ....Num. 32:39, 40
   Name used of Manasseh tribe......................Judg. 5:14
2. Son of Ammiel.............2 Sam. 9:4, 5
   Provides food for David .....2 Sam. 17:27-29

Machnadebai—*gift of the noble one*
Son of Bani; divorced foreign wife ....Ezra 10:34, 40

Machpelah—*double*
Field containing a cave; bought by Abraham ....Gen. 23:9-18
Sarah and Abraham buried here ....Gen. 23:19
Isaac, Rebekah, Leah, and Jacob buried here ....Gen. 49:29-31

Madai—*middle*
Third son of Japheth; ancestor of the Medes ....Gen. 10:2

Made—*something brought into being*

A. *Why Christ was made for us:*
   Sin ....2 Cor. 5:21
   In our likeness ....Phil. 2:7
   High priest ....Heb. 6:20

B. *What Christians are made by Him:*
   Righteous ....2 Cor. 5:21
   Heirs ....Titus 3:7

Madmannah—*dunghill*
Town in south Judah ....Josh. 15:20, 31
Son of Shaaph ....1 Chr. 2:49

Madmen—*dunghill*
Moabite town................Jer. 48:2

Madmenah—*dunghill, or dungheap*
Town near Jerusalem ....Is. 10:31

Madness—*emotional or mental derangement*

A. *Kinds of:*
   Extreme jealousy ....1 Sam. 18:8-10
   Extreme rage ....Luke 6:11

B. *Causes of:*
   Disobedience to God's Laws ....Deut. 28:28
   Judgment sent by God ......Dan. 4:31-33

C. *Manifestations of:*
   Irrational behavior..........1 Sam. 21:12-15
   Uncontrollable emotions ....Mark 5:1-5
   Moral decay ....Jer. 50:38

See Insanity; Lunatic

Madon—*contention*
Canaanite town ....Josh. 12:19
Joins confederacy against Joshua ....Josh. 11:1-12

Magbish—*strong*
Town of Judah...............Ezra 2:30

Magdala—*tower*
City of Galilee ....Matt. 15:39

Magdalene—*of Magdala*
Descriptive of one of the Marys ....Matt. 27:56
See Mary 3

Magdiel—*God is glory*
Edomite duke................Gen. 36:43

Magi—*a priestly sect in Persia*
Brings gifts to the infant Jesus ..Matt. 2:1, 2

Magic, magician—*the art of doing superhuman things by "supernatural" means*

A. *Special manifestations of:*
   At the exodus ....Ex. 7:11
   During apostolic Christianity...............Acts 8:9, 18-24

B. *Modified power of:*
   Acknowledged in history ....Ex. 7:11, 22
   Recognized in prophecy .....2 Thess. 2:9-12
   Fulfilled in antichrist........Rev. 13:13-18

C. *Failure of, to:*
   Perform miracles ....Ex. 8:18, 19
   Overcome demons ....Acts 19:13-19

D. *Condemnation of, by:*
   Explicit Law ....Lev. 20:27
   Their inability ....Ex. 8:18
   Final judgment.............Rev. 21:8

See Divination

Magistrates—*civil rulers*

A. *Descriptive of:*
   Ruler ....Judg. 18:7
   Authorities ....Luke 12:11

B. *Office of:*
   Ordained by God...........Rom. 13:1, 2
   Due proper respect ....Acts 23:5

C. *Duties of:*
   To judge:
   Impartially ....Deut. 1:17
   Righteously...............Deut. 25:1

D. *Christian's attitude toward:*
   Pray for...................1 Tim. 2:1, 2
   Honor ....Ex. 22:28
   Submit to ....1 Pet. 2:13, 14

Magnanimity—*loftiness*

A. *Expressions of, toward men:*
   Abram's offer to Lot ....Gen. 13:7-12
   Jacob's offer to Esau ....Gen. 33:8-11

B. *Expression of, toward God:*
   Moses' plea for Israel ....Ex. 32:31-33
   Paul's prayer for Israel ......Rom. 9:1-3

Magnificat—*he magnifies*
Poem of the Virgin Mary ....Luke 1:46-55

Magnify—*to make or declare great*

A. *Concerning God's:*
   Name.......................2 Sam. 7:26
   Word ....Ps. 138:2
   Law ....Is. 42:21
   Christ's name ....Acts 19:17

B. *Duty of, toward God:*
   With others.................Ps. 34:3
   With thanksgiving ....Ps. 69:30
   In the body ....Phil. 1:20

Magog—*region of Gog*
People among Japheth's descendants ....Gen. 10:2
Associated with Gog...........Ezek. 38:2
Representatives of final enemies ....Rev. 20:8

SUBJECT REFERENCE

Magor-missabib—*terror on every side*
Name indicating Pashur's end . . . Jer. 20:3

Magpiash—*collector of a cluster of stars*
Signer of the covenant . . . Neh. 10:20

Mahalah—*disease*
Manassite . . . 1 Chr. 7:14, 18

Mahalaleel—*praise of God*
1. Descendant of Seth . . . Gen. 5:12
2. Postexilic Judahite . . . Neh. 11:4

Mahalath—*sickness*
1. One of Esau's wives . . . Gen. 28:9
Called Bashemath . . . Gen. 36:3, 4, 13
2. One of Rehoboam's wives . . . 2 Chr. 11:18
3. Musical term . . . Ps. 53 (Title)

Mahanaim—*two camps*
Name given by Jacob to a sacred site . . . Gen. 32:2
On boundary between Gad and Manasseh . . . Josh. 13:26, 30
Assigned to Merarite Levites . . . Josh. 21:38
Becomes Ish-bosheth's capital . . . 2 Sam. 2:8-29
David flees to, during Absalom's rebellion . . . 2 Sam. 17:24, 27
Solomon places Ahinadab over . . . 1 Kin. 4:14

Mahaneh-dan—*camp of Dan*
Place between Zorah and Eshtaol . . . Judg. 13:25

Maharai—*swift, hasty*
One of David's mighty men . . . 2 Sam. 23:28
Becomes an army captain . . . 1 Chr. 27:13

Mahath—*grasping*
1. Kohathite Levite . . . 1 Chr. 6:35
2. Levite in Hezekiah's reign . . . 2 Chr. 29:12
Appointed an overseer of tithes . . . 2 Chr. 31:13

Mahavite
Applied to Eliel . . . 1 Chr. 11:46

Mahazioth—*visions*
Levite musician . . . 1 Chr. 25:4, 30

Maher-shalal-hash-baz—*spoil speeds, prey hastes*
Symbolic name of Isaiah's second son; prophetic of the fall of Damascus and Samaria . . . Is. 8:1-4

Mahlah—*disease*
1. Zelophehad's daughter . . . Num. 26:33
2. Child of Hammoleketh . . . 1 Chr. 7:18

Mahli—*weak, silly*
1. Eldest son of Merari . . . Num. 3:20
Father of three sons . . . 1 Chr. 6:29
Father of tribal family . . . Num. 3:33
Called Mahali . . . Ex. 6:19
2. Another Merarite Levite; nephew of 1 . . . 1 Chr. 6:47; 1 Chr. 23:23; 1 Chr. 24:30

Mahlon—*sickly*
Husband of Ruth; without child . . . Ruth 1:2-5

Mahol—*dance*
Father of certain wise men . . . 1 Kin. 4:31

Maid—*a young woman*
A. *Characteristics of:*
Obedient . . . Ps. 123:2
B. *Provision for:*
Physical needs of . . . Prov. 27:27
Accepted as wives . . . Gen. 30:3

Mail
Letters were sent . . . Esth. 3:13

Mainsail—*the lowest sail on the foremast, providing directional control*
Hoisted . . . Acts 27:40

Maintenance—*provision for support*
Household supply . . . Prov. 27:27
King's service . . . Ezra 4:14
Solomon's supply . . . 1 Kin. 4:22, 23

SUBJECT REFERENCE

Majesty—*the dignity and power of a ruler*
A. *Of God:*
Splendor of . . . Is. 2:2, 19, 21
Voice of . . . Ps. 29:4
Clothed with . . . Ps. 93:1
B. *Of Christ:*
Promised to . . . Mic. 5:2-4
Laid upon . . . Ps. 21:5
Eyewitness . . . 2 Pet. 1:16
C. *Of kings:*
Solomon . . . 1 Chr. 29:25
Nebuchadnezzar . . . Dan. 4:28, 30, 36; Dan. 5:18-21

Makaz—*end, boundary*
Town in Judah . . . 1 Kin. 4:9

Makheloth—*assemblies*
Israelite camp . . . Num. 33:25, 26

Makkedah—*place of shepherds*
Canaanite town assigned to Judah . . . Josh. 15:20, 41

Maktesh—*mortar*
Valley in Jerusalem . . . Zeph. 1:11

Malachi—*my messenger*
Prophet and writer . . . Mal. 1:1

Malachi, the Book of—*a book of the Old Testament*
God's love for Jacob . . . Mal. 1:1-5
The priesthood rebuked . . . Mal. 1:6—2:17
The messenger of the LORD . . . Mal. 3:1-5
The Day of the LORD . . . Mal. 4:1-6

Malcham—*their king*
Benjamite leader . . . 1 Chr. 8:9

Malchiel—*God is king*
Grandson of Asher; founder of Malchielites . . . Gen. 46:17

Malchijah—*Jehovah is king*
1. Gershonite Levite . . . 1 Chr. 6:40
2. The father of Pashur . . . 1 Chr. 9:12; Jer. 21:1
3. Head of a priestly division . . . 1 Chr. 24:1, 6, 9
4. Royal prince . . . Jer. 38:6
5, 6. Two sons of Parosh; divorced their foreign wives . . . Ezra 10:25
7. Son of Harim; divorced his foreign wife . . . Ezra 10:31
Helps rebuild walls . . . Neh. 3:11
8. Son of Rechab; repairs gates . . . Neh. 3:14
9. Postexilic goldsmith . . . Neh. 3:31
10. Ezra's assistant . . . Neh. 8:4
11. Signer of the covenant . . . Neh. 10:1, 3
12. Choir member . . . Neh. 12:42
13. Called Melchiah . . . Jer. 21:1

Malchiram—*the king is exalted*
Son of King Jeconiah . . . 1 Chr. 3:17, 18

Malchi-shua—*the king is salvation*
Son of King Saul . . . 1 Sam. 14:49
Killed at Gilboa . . . 1 Sam. 31:2

Malchus—*king*
Servant of the high priest . . . John 18:10

Malefactor—*rebel; criminal*
Christ accused of . . . John 18:30
Christ crucified between . . . Luke 23:32, 33
One unrepentant; one repentant . . . Luke 23:39-43

Maleleel—*Greek form of Mahalaleel*
Ancestor of Christ . . . Luke 3:37

Malformation—*irregular features*
Of a giant . . . 2 Sam. 21:20

Malice—*active intent to harm others*
A. *Causes of:*
Unregenerate heart . . . Prov. 6:14-16, 18, 19
Satanic hatred . . . 1 John 3:12
Jealousy . . . 1 Sam. 18:8-29
Racial prejudice . . . Esth. 3:5-15

SUBJECT REFERENCE

B. *Christian's attitude toward:*
Pray for those guilty of . . . Matt. 5:44
Clean out . . . 1 Cor. 5:7, 8
Put away . . . Eph. 4:31
Put aside . . . Col. 3:8
Putting aside . . . 1 Pet. 2:1
Avoid manifestations . . . 1 Pet. 2:16
C. *Characteristics:*
Unregenerate . . . Rom. 1:29; Titus 3:3
God's wrath . . . Rom. 1:18, 29
Brings own punishment . . . Ps. 7:15, 16

Malignity
Full of envy . . . Rom. 1:29

Mallothi—*I have talked*
Son of Heman . . . 1 Chr. 25:4, 26

Mallows—*saltiness*
Perennial shrub that grows in salty marshes . . . Job 30:4

Malluch—*reigning*
1. Merarite Levite . . . 1 Chr. 6:44
2. Chief of postexilic priests . . . Neh. 12:2, 7
3. Son of Bani; divorced his foreign wife . . . Ezra 10:29
4. Son of Harim; divorced his foreign wife . . . Ezra 10:32
5, 6. Two who sign the covenant . . . Neh. 10:4, 27

Mammon—*wealth*
Served as a master other than God . . . Matt. 6:24

Mamre—*firmness*
1. Town or district near Hebron . . . Gen. 23:19
West of Machpelah . . . Gen. 23:17, 19
Abraham dwelt by the oaks of . . . Gen. 13:18
2. Amorite, brother of Eschol . . . Gen. 14:13

Man—*human being, male or female*
A. *Original state of:*
Created for God's pleasure and glory . . . Is. 43:7; Rev. 4:11
Created by God . . . Gen. 1:26, 27
Made in God's image . . . Gen. 9:6
Formed of dust . . . Gen. 2:7
Made upright . . . Eccl. 7:29
Endowed with intelligence . . . Gen. 2:19, 20; Col. 3:10
Wonderfully made . . . Ps. 139:14-16
Given wide dominion . . . Gen. 1:28
From one . . . Acts 17:26-28
Male and female . . . Gen. 1:27
Superior to animals . . . Matt. 10:31
Living being (soul) . . . Gen. 2:7
B. *Sinful state of:*
Result of Adam's disobedience . . . Gen. 2:16, 17; Gen. 3:1-6
Makes all sinners . . . Rom. 5:12
Brings physical death . . . Gen. 2:16, 17, 19; Rom. 5:12-14
Makes spiritually dead . . . Eph. 2:1
C. *Redeemed state of:*
Originates in God's love . . . John 3:16
Provides salvation for . . . Titus 2:11
Accomplished by Christ's death . . . 1 Pet. 1:18-21
Fulfills the new covenant . . . Heb. 8:8-13
Entered by new birth . . . John 3:1-12
D. *Final state of:*
Continues eternally . . . Matt. 25:46
Cannot be changed . . . Luke 16:26
Determined by faith or by unbelief . . . John 3:36; 2 Thess. 1:6-10
E. *Christ's relation to:*
Gives light to . . . John 1:9
Knows nature of . . . John 2:25
Took nature of . . . Heb. 2:14-16
In the likeness . . . Rom. 8:3
Only Mediator for . . . 1 Tim. 2:5
Died for . . . Heb. 9:26,28; 1 Pet. 1:18-21

SUBJECT	REFERENCE
F. *Certain aspects of:*	
First—Adam	1 Cor. 15:45, 47
Last—Christ	1 Cor. 15:45
Natural—unregenerate	1 Cor. 2:14
Outward—physical	2 Cor. 4:16
Inner—spiritual	Rom. 7:22
New—regenerate	Eph. 2:15
Man of sin (see Antichrist)	
Manaen—*comforter*	
Prophet and teacher in church at Antioch	Acts 13:1
Manahath—*resting place*	
1. Son of Shobal	Gen. 36:23
2. City of exile for sons of Ehud	1 Chr. 8:6
Citizens of, called Manahethites	1 Chr. 2:54
Manasseh—*making to forget*	
1. Joseph's first-born son	Gen. 41:50, 51
Adopted by Jacob	Gen. 48:5, 6
Loses his birthright to Ephraim	Gen. 48:13-20
Ancestor of a tribe	Num. 1:34, 35
2. Sons of	Num. 26:28-34
Census of	Num. 1:34, 35
One half of, desire region in east Jordan	Num. 32:33-42
Help Joshua against Canaanites	Josh. 1:12-18
Division of, into eastern and western	Josh. 22:7
Region assigned to eastern half	Deut. 3:12-15
Land assigned to western half	Josh. 17:1-13
Zelophehad's daughters included in	Josh. 17:3, 4
Question concerning altar	Josh. 22:9-34
Joshua's challenge to	Josh. 17:14-18
City (Golan) of refuge in	Josh. 20:8
Did not drive out Canaanites	Judg. 1:27, 28
Gideon, a member of	Judg. 6:15
Some of, help David	1 Chr. 12:19-31
Many support Asa	2 Chr. 15:9
Attend Passovers	2 Chr. 30:1-18
Idols destroyed in	2 Chr. 31:1
3. Intentional change of Moses' name to	Judg. 18:30
4. Son and successor of Hezekiah, king of Judah	2 Kin. 21:1
Reigns wickedly; restores idolatry	2 Kin. 21:1-16 2 Chr. 33:1-9
Captured and taken to Babylon	2 Chr. 33:10, 11
Repents and is restored	2 Chr. 33:12, 13
Removes idols and altars	2 Chr. 33:14-20
5, 6. Two men who divorce their foreign wives	Ezra 10:30, 33
Mandrake—*a rhubarb-like herb, having narcotic qualities*	
Supposed to induce human fertility	Gen. 30:14-16 Song 7:13
Manger—*a feeding place for cattle*	
Place of Jesus' birth	Luke 2:7, 12
Called "crib"	Is. 1:3
Same as "stall" in	Luke 13:15
Manifest—*to make something clear or evident*	
A. *Applied to God's:*	
Nature	Rom. 1:19
Revelation	Col. 1:26
Knowledge	2 Cor. 2:14
Love	1 John 4:9
B. *Applied to Christ's:*	
Nature	1 Tim. 3:16
Presence	John 1:31
Life	1 John 1:2
C. *Applied to evil:*	
Works of the flesh	Gal. 5:19
Man's:	
Deeds	John 3:21
Folly	2 Tim. 3:9
Manliness—*masculine characteristics at their best*	
A. *Qualities of:*	
Self-control	1 Cor. 9:25-27
Mature understanding	1 Cor. 14:20

SUBJECT	REFERENCE
Courage in danger	2 Sam. 10:11, 12
Endure hardship	2 Tim. 2:3-5
B. *Examples of:*	
Caleb	Num. 13:30
Joshua	Josh. 1:1-11
Jonathan	1 Sam. 14:1, 6-14
Daniel	Dan. 6:1-28
Manna—*what is it?*	
A. *Features regarding:*	
Description of	Num. 11:7-9
Bread given by God	Ex. 16:4, 15 John 6:30-32
Previously unknown	Deut. 8:3, 16
Fell at evening	Num. 11:9
Despised by people	Num. 11:4-6
Ceased at conquest	Josh. 5:12
B. *Illustrative of:*	
God's glory	Ex. 16:7
Christ as the true bread	John 6:32-35
Manners—*a way of life*	
A. *Evil kinds:*	
Sexual immorality	Gen. 19:31-36
Customs of other nations	Lev. 20:23
Careless living	Judg. 18:7
B. *Good kinds:*	
Prayer	Matt. 6:9
Faithfulness	Acts 20:18
Manoah—*rest, quiet*	
Danite; father of Samson	Judg. 13:1-25
Mantle—*a garment*	
Sheet or rug	Judg. 4:18
Female garment	Is. 3:22
Upper garment (coat)	1 Sam. 15:27
Outer garment (robe)	1 Kin. 19:13, 19 2 Kin. 2:8, 13, 14
Maoch—*oppression*	
Father of Achish, king of Gath	1 Sam. 27:2
Maon—*abode*	
1. Village in Judah	Josh. 15:55
David stayed at	1 Sam. 23:24, 25
House of Nabal	1 Sam. 25:2
2. Shammai's son	1 Chr. 2:45
3. People called Maonites among Israel's oppressors	Judg. 10:12
Called Mehunim	2 Chr. 26:7
Listed among returnees	Ezra 2:50 Neh. 7:52
Mara—*bitter*	
Name chosen by Naomi	Ruth 1:20
Marah—*bitterness*	
First Israelite camp after passing through the Red Sea	Num. 33:8, 9
Maralah—*downward slope*	
Village in Zebulun	Josh. 19:11
Maranatha—*our Lord, come*	
Aramaic phrase expressive of Christ's return	1 Cor. 16:22
Compare the same thought in	Phil. 4:5
Marble—*crystalline limestone*	
In columns	Esth. 1:6
In Babylon's trade	Rev. 18:12
Marduk—*bold*	
Supreme deity of the Babylonians	Jer. 50:2
Otherwise called Bel	Is. 46:1
Mareshah—*summit*	
1. Father of Hebron	1 Chr. 2:42
2. Judahite	1 Chr. 4:21
3. Town of Judah	Josh. 15:44
City built for defense by Rehoboam	2 Chr. 11:5, 8
Great battle here between Asa and Zerah	2 Chr. 14:9-12
Mariners—*sailors*	
Skilled	1 Kin. 9:27
Fearful	Jon. 1:5
Weeping	Ezek. 27:8-36
Storm-tossed	Acts 27:27-31

SUBJECT	REFERENCE
Mark	
A. *As object, thing:*	
Sign for preservation	Ezek. 9:4-6
Sign of those following antichrist	Rev. 13:16, 17 Rev. 14:9, 11 Rev. 20:4
Mark (John)—*a large hammer*	
Son of Mary, a believer	Acts 12:12
Cousin of Barnabas	Col. 4:10
Returns with Barnabas to Antioch	Acts 12:25
Leaves Paul and Barnabas at Perga	Acts 13:13
Paul refuses to take him again	Acts 15:37-39
Paul's approval of	2 Tim. 4:11
Peter's companion	1 Pet. 5:13
The author of the second Gospel	Mark 1:1 (Title)
Mark, the Gospel of—*a book of the New Testament*	
John the Baptist	Mark 1:1-11
Choosing of the disciples	Mark 3:13-19
Parables	Mark 4:1-34
Galilean tours	Mark 1:21-45 Mark 6:1-44
Peter's confession	Mark 8:27-30
The transfiguration	Mark 9:1-13
Foretelling of Jesus' death	Mark 10:32-34
Entry into Jerusalem	Mark 11:1-11
Controversy with Jews	Mark 11:27—12:40
Events of the crucifixion	Mark 14:43—15:47
The resurrection	Mark 16:1-20
Market	
Greetings in the	Mark 11:16
Market of Appius	
Called Forum	Acts 28:15
Market place	
Place of:	
Greetings	Matt. 23:7
Public trial	Acts 16:19, 20
Evangelism	Acts 17:17
Maroth—*bitter fountains*	
Town of Judah	Mic. 1:12
Marriage	
A. *Described as:*	
Instituted by God	Gen. 2:18-24
Honorable in all	Heb. 13:4
Permanent bond	Matt. 19:6
Intimate bond	Matt. 19:5
Blessed of God for having children	Gen. 1:27, 28
Dissolved by death	Rom. 7:2, 3
Means of sexual love	Prov. 5:15-19
Centered in love and obedience	Eph. 5:21-33
Worthy of Jesus' presence	John 2:1-11
B. *Prohibitions concerning:*	
Near of kin	Lev. 18:6-18
Fornication excludes remarriage	Matt. 5:32
Polygamy forbidden	Lev. 18:18
Idol worshipers	Ex. 34:16
C. *Arrangements for* (among Hebrews):	
Arranged by parents	Gen. 21:21
Parties consenting	Gen. 24:8
Parental concern in	Gen. 26:34, 35
Romance involved in	Gen. 29:10, 11
Commitment considered binding	Gen. 24:58, 60
Unfaithfulness in, brings God's judgment	Heb. 13:4
D. *Ceremonies of* (among Hebrews):	
Time of joy	Jer. 7:34
Bride richly attired	Ps. 45:13-15
Bride veiled	Gen. 24:65
Bridegroom decks himself	Is. 61:10
Wedding feast in bridegroom's house	Matt. 22:1-10
Distinctive clothing of guests	Matt. 22:11, 12
Christ attends	John 2:1-11
Festivities following	John 2:8-10
Gifts bestowed at	Ps. 45:12
Parental blessing on	Gen. 24:60
Change of name	Ps. 45:10, 16
Consummation of	Gen. 29:23
Proof of virginity	Deut. 22:13-21

SUBJECT REFERENCE

E. *Purposes of:*
Man's happiness .... Gen. 2:18
Continuance of the race ..... Gen. 1:28
Godly seed .... Mal. 2:14, 15
Prevention of fornication .... 1 Cor. 7:2, 9
Complete satisfaction .... Prov. 5:19
1 Tim. 5:14

F. *Denial of:*
As a prophetic sign .... Jer. 16:2
For a specific purpose .... Matt. 19:10-12
As a sign of apostasy .... 1 Tim. 4:1-3
To those in heaven .... Matt. 22:30

G. *Figurative of:*
God's union with Israel ..... Is. 54:5
Christ's union with His Church .... Eph. 5:23-32

Marrow—*the vascular tissue which occupies the cavities of bones*

A. *Used literally of:*
Healthy man .... Job 21:23, 24
Inner being .... Heb. 4:12

B. *Used figuratively of:*
Spiritual sustenance .... Ps. 63:5

Marsena—*forgetful man*
Persian prince .... Esth. 1:14

Mars Hill (see Areopagus)

Marsh—*an area of grassy, soft, wet land*
Spelled "marish" .... Ezek. 47:11

Mart—*market*
Tyre, to all nations .... Is. 23:1-4

Martha—*lady, mistress*
Sister of Mary and Lazarus ..... John 11:1, 2
Welcomes Jesus into her home .. Luke 10:38
Rebuked by Christ .... Luke 10:38-42
Affirms her faith .... John 11:21-32
Serves supper .... John 12:1-3

Martyrdom—*death for the sake of one's faith*

A. *Causes of:*
Evil deeds .... 1 John 3:12
Antichrist's persecution ...... Rev. 13:15
Harlot Babylon's hatred ..... Rev. 17:5, 6
Our Christian faith .... Rev. 6:9

B. *Believer's attitude toward:*
Remember Christ's warning .... Matt. 10:21, 22
Do not fear .... Matt. 10:28
Be prepared .... Matt. 16:24, 25
Be ready to, if necessary ..... Acts 21:13

C. *Examples of:*
Prophets and apostles .... Luke 11:50, 51
John the Baptist .... Mark 6:18-29
Stephen .... Acts 7:58-60
Early disciples of the Lord ... Acts 9:1, 2

Marvel—*to express astonishment*

A. *Expressed by Christ because of:*
Centurion's faith .... Matt. 8:10

B. *Expressed by men because of Christ's:*
Power .... Matt. 8:27
Knowledge .... John 7:15

Mary—*same as Miriam*

1. Jesus' mother .... Matt. 1:16
Prophecies concerning .... Is. 7:14
Engaged to Joseph .... Luke 1:26, 27
Told of virginal conception .. Luke 1:28-38
Visits Elizabeth .... Luke 1:39-41
Offers praise .... Luke 1:46-55
Gives birth to Jesus .... Luke 2:6-20
Flees with Joseph to Egypt .. Matt. 2:13-18
Mother of other children .... Mark 6:3
Visits Jerusalem with Jesus ... Luke 2:41-52
Intrusted to John's care ..... John 19:25-27

2. Wife of Cleophas .... John 19:25
Mother of James and Joses .. Matt. 27:56
Looking on the crucified Savior .... Matt. 27:55, 56
Follows Jesus' body to the tomb .... Matt. 27:61
Sees the risen Lord .... Matt. 28:1, 9, 10
Tells His disciples of resurrection .... Matt. 28:7-9; Luke 24:9-11

SUBJECT REFERENCE

3. Mary Magdalene .... Matt. 27:56, 61
Delivered from seven demons .... Luke 8:2
Contributes to support of Christ .... Luke 8:2, 3
Looks on the crucified Savior .... Matt. 27:55, 56
Follows Jesus' body to the tomb .... Matt. 27:61
Visits Jesus' tomb with Mary, mother of James .... Mark 16:1-8
Tells the disciples .... John 20:2
First to see the risen Lord ... Mark 16:9
John 20:11-18

4. Mary, the sister of Martha and Lazarus .... John 11:1, 2
Commended by Jesus .... Luke 10:38-42
Grieves for Lazarus .... John 11:19, 20, 28-33
Anoints Jesus .... John 12:1-3, 7
Commended again by Jesus .... Matt. 26:7-13

5. Mark's mother .... Acts 12:12-17

6. Christian disciple at Rome ... Rom. 16:6

Maschil—*attentive*
Hebrew word in the title of 13 Psalms .... Ps. 32, 42, 44, etc.

Mash
Division of the Arameans ..... Gen. 10:23
Called Meshech .... 1 Chr. 1:17

Mashal
Refuge city given to the Levites .... 1 Chr. 6:74
Called Mishal .... Josh. 19:26
Josh. 21:30

Mason—*one who lays stones or bricks*
Sent by Hiram to help:
David .... 2 Sam. 5:11
Solomon .... 1 Kin. 5:18
Used in Temple:
Repairs .... 2 Chr. 24:12
Rebuilding .... Ezra 3:7

Masrekah—*vineyard*
City of Edom .... Gen. 36:36

Massa—*burden*
Son of Ishmael .... Gen. 25:12, 14

Massah and Meribah—*testing and strife*
Named together .... Ex. 17:7
Named separately .... Deut. 33:8
First, at Rephidim, Israel just out of Egypt .... Ex. 17:1-7
Levites proved .... Deut. 33:8
Second, at Kadesh-barnea, 40 years later .... Num. 20:1-13
Moses and Aaron rebel here .... Num. 20:24
Tragic events recalled by Moses .... Deut. 6:16
Events later recalled .... Ps. 81:7
Used as a boundary of the land .... Ezek. 47:17, 19
Used for spiritual lesson ...... Heb. 3:7-12

Mast—*a vertical support for sails and rigging on a sailing ship*

A. *Used literally of:*
Cedars of Lebanon .... Ezek. 27:5

B. *Used figuratively of:*
Strength of enemies .... Is. 33:23

Master

A. *Descriptive of:*
Owner of slaves .... Ex. 21:4-6
King .... 1 Chr. 12:19
Prophet .... 2 Kin. 2:3, 5
Teacher .... Matt. 23:8

B. *Kinds of:*
Unmerciful .... 1 Sam. 30:13-15
Angry .... Luke 14:21
Good .... Gen. 24:9-35
Believing .... 1 Tim. 6:2
Heavenly .... Col. 4:1

Master builder
Paul describes himself as .... 1 Cor. 3:10

Master workmen—*craftsmen*
Bezaleel .... Ex. 31:1-5

SUBJECT REFERENCE

Hiram of Tyre .... 1 Kin. 7:13-50
Aquila and Priscilla .... Acts 18:2, 3
Demetrius .... Acts 19:24

Mate—*the male or female of a pair*
God provides for .... Is. 34:15, 16

Materialistic—*concerned for worldly goods only*
Christ condemns .... Luke 12:16-21
Sadducees described .... Acts 23:8
Christians forbidden to live as ... 1 Cor. 15:30-34

Mathematics, spiritual

A. *General:*
Addition:
God's Word .... Deut. 4:2
Knowledge will increase ..... Dan. 12:4
Increased riches .... Ps. 62:10
Subtraction:
God's commandments ...... Deut. 12:32
Multiplication:
Human family .... Gen. 1:28

B. *Unrighteous:*
Addition:
Wealth .... Ps. 73:12
Guilt .... 2 Chr. 28:13
Sin .... Is. 30:1
Subtraction:
Wealth obtained by fraud .... Prov. 13:11
Life shortened .... Ps. 55:23
Prov. 10:27
Multiplication:
Sorrow by idolatry .... Ps. 16:4
Transgression .... Prov. 29:16

C. *Righteous:*
Addition:
Years .... Prov. 3:1, 2
Prov. 4:10
Blessing without sorrow ..... Prov. 10:22
By putting God first .... Matt. 6:33
Graces .... 2 Pet. 1:5-7
In latter years .... Job 42:12
Subtraction:
Disease .... Ex. 15:26
Taken from evil .... Is. 57:1
Multiplication:
Prosperity .... Deut. 8:1, 11-13
Length of days .... Deut. 11:18-21
Prov. 9:11
Mercy, peace, love .... Jude 2
Church .... Acts 9:31

Matred—*expulsion*
Mother-in-law of Hadar (Hadad), an Edomite king .... Gen. 36:39

Matri—*rainy*
Saul's Benjamite family .... 1 Sam. 10:21

Mattan—*gift*

1. Priest of Baal .... 2 Kin. 11:18
Killed by the people .... 2 Chr. 23:16, 17

2. Father of Shephatiah .... Jer. 38:1

Mattanah—*gift*
Israelite camp .... Num. 21:18, 19

Mattaniah—*gift of Jehovah*

1. King Zedekiah's original name .... 2 Kin. 24:17
2. Son of Mica, a Levite and Asaphite .... 1 Chr. 9:15
3. Musician, son of Heman ..... 1 Chr. 25:4, 16
4. Spirit of the LORD came upon .... 2 Chr. 20:14
5. Levite under King Hezekiah .... 2 Chr. 29:13
6. Postexilic Levite and singer .. Neh. 11:17
7. Levite gatekeeper .... Neh. 12:25
8. Postexilic Levite .... Neh. 12:35
9. Levite in charge of treasuries .... Neh. 13:13

10, 11, 12, 13. Four postexilic Jews who divorced foreign wives .... Ezra 10:26-37

SUBJECT REFERENCE

Mattatha—*gift* (of God)
Son of Nathan; ancestor of Christ ...... Luke 3:31

Mattathias—*Greek form of Mattathiah*
1. Postexilic ancestor of Christ ...... Luke 3:25
2. Another postexilic ancestor of Christ ...... Luke 3:26

Mattathah—*gift of Jehovah*
Jew who put away his foreign wife ...... Ezra 10:33

Mattenai—*gift of Jehovah*
1. Priest in the time of Joiakim ...... Neh. 12:19
2, 3. Two postexilic Jews who put away their foreign wives ...... Ezra 10:33, 37

Matter—*something*
A. *Descriptive of:*
Lawsuit ...... 1 Cor. 6:1
Sum of something ...... Eccl. 12:13
Love affair ...... Ruth 3:18
News ...... Mark 1:45
Speech ...... 1 Sam. 16:18
B. *Kinds of:*
Good ...... Ps. 45:1
Evil ...... Ps. 64:5
Unknown ...... Dan. 2:5, 10
Revealed ...... Dan. 2:23

Matthan—*gift*
Ancestor of Joseph ...... Matt. 1:15, 16

Matthat—*gift*
1. Ancestor of Christ ...... Luke 3:24
2. Another ancestor of Christ ... Luke 3:29

Matthew—*gift of Jehovah*
Tax gatherer ...... Matt. 9:9
Becomes Christ's follower ...... Matt. 9:9
Appointed an apostle ...... Matt. 10:2, 3
Called Levi, the son of Alphaeus ...... Mark 2:14
Entertains Jesus with a great feast ...... Mark 2:14, 15
In the upper room ...... Acts 1:13
Author of the first Gospel ...... Matt. 1:1 (Title)

Matthew, the Gospel of—*a book of the New Testament*
Events of Jesus' birth ...... Matt. 1:18—2:23
John the Baptist ...... Matt. 3:1-17
The temptation ...... Matt. 4:1-11
Jesus begins His ministry ...... Matt. 4:12-17
The Great Sermon ...... Matt. 5:1—7:29
Christ, about John the Baptist ... Matt. 11:1-19
Conflict with the Pharisees and Sadducees ...... Matt. 15:39—16:6
Peter's confession ...... Matt. 16:13-20
Prophecy of death and resurrection ...... Matt. 20:17-19
Jerusalem entry ...... Matt. 21:1-11
Authority of Jesus ...... Matt. 21:23—22:14
Woes to the Pharisees ...... Matt. 23:1-36
Garden of Gethsemane ...... Matt. 26:36-56
Crucifixion and burial ...... Matt. 27:27-66
Resurrection of Christ ...... Matt. 28:1-20

Matthias—*gift of Jehovah*
Chosen by lot to replace Judas .. Acts 1:15-26

Mattithiah—*gift of Jehovah*
1. Korahite Levite ...... 1 Chr. 9:31
2. Levite, son of Jeduthun, and Temple musician ...... 1 Chr. 15:18, 21
3. Jew who put away his foreign wife ...... Ezra 10:43
4. Levite attendant to Ezra ...... Neh. 8:4

Mattock—*an agricultural instrument for digging and hoeing*
Sharpened for battle ...... 1 Sam. 13:20-22

Maturity, spiritual
Do away with childish things ... 1 Cor. 13:11
Be mature in your thinking ...... 1 Cor. 14:20
Solid food is for ...... Heb. 5:11-14
Overcoming the evil one ...... 1 John 2:14

Maul—*a stick or a club*
Used against neighbor ...... Prov. 25:18

SUBJECT REFERENCE

Maw—*the fourth stomach of ruminants* (divided-hoof animals)
Given to the priests ...... Deut. 18:3

Mazzaroth—*the signs of the Zodiac or a constellation*
Descriptive of God's power ...... Job 38:32
Objects of idolatrous worship ... 2 Kin. 23:5

Meadow—*sown fields*
1. Reed grass or papyrus thickets ...... Is. 19:6, 7
Translated "flag" in ...... Job 8:11
2. Place near Gibeah ...... Judg. 20:33

Meah, tower of the
Restored by Eliashib ...... Neh. 3:1

Meal—*ground grain used for food*
One tenth of an ephah of ...... Num. 5:15
Used in offerings ...... 1 Kin. 4:22
"Then bring" ...... 2 Kin. 4:41
Millstones and grind ...... Is. 47:2
Three pecks of ...... Matt. 13:33

Meals—*times of eating*
A. *Times of:*
Early morning ...... John 21:4-12
At noon (for laborers) ...... Ruth 2:14
In the evening ...... Gen. 19:1-3
B. *Extraordinary and festive:*
Guests invited ...... Matt. 22:3, 4
Received with a kiss ...... Luke 7:45
Feet washed ...... Luke 7:44
Anointed with ointment ...... Luke 7:38
Proper dress ...... Matt. 22:11, 12
Seated according to rank ...... Matt. 23:6
Special guest honored ...... 1 Sam. 9:22-24
Entertainment provided ...... Luke 15:25
Temperate habits taught ...... Prov. 23:1-3
Intemperance condemned ...... Amos 6:4-6

See Entertainment; Feasts

Means of grace
A. *Agents of:*
Holy Spirit ...... Gal. 5:16-26
God's Word ...... 1 Thess. 2:13
Prayer ...... Rom. 8:15-27
Christian fellowship ...... Mal. 3:16-18
Public worship ...... 1 Thess. 5:6
Christian witnessing ...... Acts 8:4
B. *Words expressive of:*
Stir up the gift ...... 1 Tim. 1:6
Neglect not the spiritual gift ...... 1 Tim. 4:14
Take heed to the ministry ...... Col. 4:17
Grow in grace ...... 2 Pet. 3:18
C. *Use of, brings:*
Assurance ...... 2 Pet. 1:5-12
Stability ...... Eph. 4:11-16
D. *Enemies of:*
Devil ...... 1 Thess. 3:5
World ...... 1 John 2:15-17
Coldness ...... Rev. 3:14-18

Mearah—*cave*
Unconquered by Joshua ...... Josh. 13:1, 4

Measure—*a standard of size, quantity or values*
A. *Objectionable:*
Differing (different) ...... Deut. 25:14, 15
Scant ...... Mic. 6:10
Using themselves as a gauge ...... 2 Cor. 10:12
B. *As indicative of:*
Earth's weight ...... Is. 40:12
Punishment inflicted ...... Matt. 7:2
C. *Figurative of:*
Great size ...... Hos. 1:10
Sin's ripeness ...... Matt. 23:32
The Spirit's infilling ...... John 3:34
Man's ability ...... 2 Cor. 10:13
Perfection of faith ...... Eph. 4:13, 16

Measuring line—*a cord of specified length for measuring*
Signifies hope ...... Jer. 31:38-40
Zech. 2:1

SUBJECT REFERENCE

Meat—*food in general* (not just flesh)
A. *Characteristics of:*
Given by God ...... Ps. 104:21, 27
Necessary for man ...... Gen. 1:29, 30
B. *Lack of:*
Testing of faith ...... Hab. 3:17
Provided by:
God ...... Ps. 145:15
Christ ...... John 21:5, 6
C. *Prohibitions concerning:*
Not in itself commendable ... 1 Cor. 8:8
Not to be a stumbling block ...... 1 Cor. 8:13
Life more important than ...... Matt. 6:25
D. *Figurative of:*
God's will ...... John 4:32, 34
Christ ...... John 6:27, 55
Strong doctrines ...... 1 Cor. 3:2

Mebunnai—*built*
One of David's mighty men ...... 2 Sam. 23:27
Called Sibbecai ...... 1 Chr. 11:29

Mecherathite—*a dweller in Mecharah*
Descriptive of Hepher, one of David's mighty men ...... 1 Chr. 11:36

Medad—*beloved*
One of the seventy elders receiving the Spirit ...... Num. 11:26-29

Medan—*judgment*
Son of Abraham by Keturah ...... Gen. 25:1, 2

Meddling—*interfering with the affairs of others*
Brings a king's death ...... 2 Chr. 35:21-24
Christians ...... 1 Pet. 4:15
Such called "busybodies" ...... 2 Thess. 3:11

Medeba—*full waters*
Old Moabite town ...... Num. 21:29, 30
Assigned to Reuben ...... Josh. 13:9, 16
Syrians defeated here ...... 1 Chr. 19:6, 7
Reverts to Moab ...... Is. 15:2

Medes, Media—*the people and country of the Medes*
A. *Characteristics of:*
Descendants of Japheth ...... Gen. 10:2
Part of Medo-Persian empire ...... Esth. 1:19
Inflexible laws of ...... Dan. 6:8, 12, 15
Among those at Pentecost ...... Acts 2:9
B. *Kings of, mentioned in the Bible:*
Cyrus ...... Ezra 1:1
Ahasuerus ...... Ezra 4:6
Artaxerxes I ...... Ezra 4:7
Darius ...... Ezra 6:1
Xerxes ...... Dan. 11:2
Artaxerxes ...... Ezra 6:14
C. *Place of, in Bible hisory:*
Israel deported to ...... 2 Kin. 17:6
Babylon falls to ...... Dan. 5:30, 31
"Darius the Mede," new ruler of Babylon ...... Dan. 5:31
Daniel rises high in the kingdom of ...... Dan. 6:1-28
Cyrus, king of Persia, allows Jews to return ...... 2 Chr. 36:22, 23
Esther and Mordecai live under Ahasuerus, king of ...... Esth. 1:3, 19
D. *Prophecies concerning:*
Agents in Babylon's fall ...... Is. 13:17-19
Cyrus, king of, God's servant ...... Is. 44:28
"Inferior" kingdom ...... Dan. 2:39
Compared to a bear ...... Dan. 7:5
Kings of ...... Dan. 11:2
War with Greece ...... Dan. 11:2

Mediation—*a friendly intervention designed to render assistance*
A. *Purposes of:*
Save a life ...... Gen. 37:21, 22
Save a people ...... Ex. 32:11-13
Obtain a wife ...... 1 Kin. 2:13-25
Obtain justice ...... Job 9:33
B. *Motives prompting:*
People's fear ...... Deut. 5:5
Regard for human life ...... Jer. 38:7-13

SUBJECT REFERENCE

Sympathy for a sick man .... 2 Kin. 5:6-8
Matt. 17:15

C. *Methods used:*
Intense prayer .... Deut. 9:20-29
Flattery .... 1 Sam. 25:23-35
Appeal to self-preservation ... Esth. 4:12-17

Mediator, Christ our

A. *His qualifications:*
Bears God's image, man's likeness .... Phil. 2:6-8; Heb. 2:14-17
Is both sinless and sin-bearer .... Is. 53:6-10; Eph. 2:13-18
Endures God's wrath, brings God's righteousness .... Rom. 5:6-19
Is sacrifice and the priest .... Heb. 7:27
Heb. 10:5-22

B. *How He performs the function:*
Took our nature .... 1 John 1:1-3
Died as our substitute .... 1 Pet. 1:18, 19
Reconciled us to God .... Eph. 2:16

Medicine—*something prescribed to cure an illness*

A. *General prescriptions:*
Merry heart .... Prov. 15:13
Rest .... Ps. 37:7-11
Sleep .... John 11:12, 13
Quarantine .... Lev. 12:1-4
Sanitation .... Deut. 23:10-14

B. *Specific prescriptions:*
Figs .... Is. 38:21
Roots and leaves .... Ezek. 47:12
Wine .... 1 Tim. 5:23

C. *Used figuratively of:*
Salvation .... Jer. 8:22
Incurableness .... Jer. 46:11
Spiritual stubbornness .... Jer. 51:8, 9

See Diseases

Meditation—*quiet contemplation of spiritual truths*

A. *Objects of, God's:*
Word .... Ps. 119:148
Law .... Josh. 1:8
Instruction .... 1 Tim. 4:15

B. *Value of, for:*
Understanding .... Ps. 49:3
Spiritual satisfaction .... Ps. 63:5, 6
Superior knowledge .... Ps. 119:99

C. *Extent of:*
All the day .... Ps. 119:97
At evening .... Gen. 24:63
In night watches .... Ps. 119:148

Mediterranean Sea

Described as:
Sea .... Gen. 49:13
Great Sea .... Josh. 1:4
Josh. 9:1
Sea of the Philistines .... Ex. 23:31
Uttermost Sea .... Deut. 11:24; Joel 2:20; Zech. 14:8

Mediums

A. *Described as:*
Source of defilement .... Lev. 19:31
Abomination .... Deut. 18:10-12
Whisperers .... Is. 8:19

B. *The practicers, to be:*
Cut off .... Lev. 20:6
Put to death .... Lev. 20:27

C. *Consulted by:*
Saul .... 1 Sam. 28:3-25
Manasseh .... 2 Kin. 21:6

D. *Condemned by:*
Josiah .... 2 Kin. 23:24

Meek

A. *Blessings upon:*
Gospel .... Is. 61:1
Spiritual satisfaction .... Ps. 22:26
Guidance and instruction .... Ps. 25:9
Salvation .... Ps. 76:9

B. *A Christian essential in:*
Living in the Spirit .... Gal. 5:22, 23
Receiving the Word .... James 1:21
Stating our assurance .... James 3:13

SUBJECT REFERENCE

Megiddo—*place of troops*
City conquered by Joshua ...... Josh. 12:21
Assigned to Manasseh .... Josh. 17:11
Inhabitants of, made slaves ..... Judg. 1:27, 28
Canaanites defeated here .... Judg. 5:19-21
Site of Baana's headquarters .... 1 Kin. 4:12
Fortified by Solomon .... 1 Kin. 9:15-19
King Ahaziah dies here .... 2 Kin. 9:27
King Josiah killed here .... 2 Kin. 23:29, 30
Mentioned in prophecy .... Zech. 12:11
Site of Armageddon .... Rev. 16:16

Mehetabel—*God benefits*
1. King Hadar's wife .... Gen. 36:39
2. Father of Delaiah .... Neh. 6:10

Mehida—*renowned*
Ancestor of a family of returning Temple servants .... Ezra 2:52

Mehir—*price*
Judahite .... 1 Chr. 4:11

Meholathite—*a native of Meholah*
Descriptive of Adriel .... 1 Sam. 18:19

Mehujael—*smitten of God*
Cainite; father of Methusael .... Gen. 4:18

Mehuman—*faithful*
Eunuch under King Ahasuerus .... Esth. 1:10

Mehunim
Arabian tribe near Mt. Seir ..... 2 Chr. 26:7
Smitten by Simeonites .... 1 Chr. 4:39-42
Descendants of, serve as Nethinim .... Ezra 2:50

Me-jarkon—*waters of yellow color*
Territory of Dan near Joppa .... Josh. 19:40, 46

Mekonah—*foundation*
Town of Judah .... Neh. 11:25, 28

Melatiah—*Jehovah has set free*
Postexilic workman .... Neh. 3:7

Melchi—*my king*
Two ancestors of Jesus .... Luke 3:24, 28

Melchizedek—*king of righteousness*

A. *Described as:*
King of Salem .... Gen. 14:18
Priest of God .... Gen. 14:18
Receiver of a tenth of Abram's goods .... Gen. 14:18-20
King of righteousness .... Heb. 7:2
Without parentage .... Heb. 7:3
Great man .... Heb. 7:4

B. *Typical of Christ's:*
Eternity .... Heb. 7:3
Priesthood .... Ps. 110:4
Kingship .... Heb. 8:1

Melea
Ancestor of Jesus .... Luke 3:31

Melech—*king*
Son of Micah, grandson of Jonathan .... 1 Chr. 8:35

Melicu—*reigning*
Head of a household .... Neh. 12:14

Melita—*an island in the Mediterranean Sea*
Paul's shipwreck .... Acts 28:1-8

Melon—*the watermelon*
Desired by Israelites in wilderness .... Num. 11:5

Melting—*making a solid a liquid*

Used figuratively of:
Complete destruction .... Ex. 15:15
Discouragement .... Josh. 7:5
Defeatism .... Josh. 5:1
National discouragement .... Is. 19:1
Destruction of the wicked .... Ps. 68:2
God's presence .... Mic. 1:4
Testings .... Jer. 9:7
Troubled sea .... Ps. 107:26
Christ's pain on the cross .... Ps. 22:14

SUBJECT REFERENCE

Melzar—*sentry*
Steward placed over Daniel .... Dan. 1:11, 16

Mem
Letter of the Hebrew alphabet .. Ps. 119:97-104

Member—*a part of a larger whole*

A. *Descriptive of:*
Parts of the body .... Matt. 5:29, 30
Union with Christ .... 1 Cor. 6:15
True Church .... 1 Cor. 12:27

B. *Of the body:*
Effect of sin in .... Rom. 7:5
Struggle in .... Rom. 7:23

C. *Illustrative of:*
Variety of Christian gifts .... Rom. 12:4, 5
God's design in .... 1 Cor. 12:18, 24

Memorials—*things established to commemorate an event or a truth*

A. *Established by men:*
Jacob's stone .... Gen. 28:18-22
Altar at Jordan .... Josh. 22:9-16
Feast of Purim .... Esth. 9:28

B. *Established by God:*
Passover .... Ex. 12:14
Pot of manna .... Ex. 16:32-34
Lord's Supper .... Luke 22:19

Memories—*the ability to revive past experiences*

A. *Uses of, to recall:*
Past blessings .... Ezra 9:5-15
Past sins .... Josh. 22:12-20
God's blessings .... Neh. 9:1-38
God's promises .... Neh. 1:8-11
Christian truths .... 2 Pet. 1:15-21
Prophecies .... John 2:19-22
Lost opportunities .... Ps. 137:1-3

B. *Aids to:*
Reminder .... 2 Sam. 12:1-13
Prick of conscience .... Gen. 41:9
Holy Spirit .... John 14:26

Memphis—*haven of good*
Ancient capital of Egypt .... Hos. 9:6
Prophesied against by Isaiah .... Is. 19:13
Jews flee to .... Jer. 44:1
Denounced by the prophets ..... Jer. 46:19

Memucan
Persian prince .... Esth. 1:14-21

Menahem—*comforter*
Cruel king of Israel .... 2 Kin. 15:14-18

Menan
Ancestor of Jesus .... Luke 3:31

Mending—*restoring something*
Of nets .... Matt. 4:21
Used figuratively .... Luke 5:36

Mene—*numbered*
Sentence of doom .... Dan. 5:25, 26

Mene, Tekel, Upharsin
Written by God .... Dan. 5:5, 25
Interpreted by Daniel .... Dan. 5:24-29

Menstealers—*Those who seize another by unlawful force*
Condemned by law .... 1 Tim. 1:10

Menstruation—*a woman's monthly flow*
Intercourse during, prohibited ... Lev. 18:19
End of, in old age .... Gen. 18:11

Called:
"Sickness" .... Lev. 20:18
"The custom of women" .... Gen. 31:35

Meonenim—*augurs*
Tree or place where soothsayers performed .... Judg. 9:37

Meonenim, plain of—*plain of clouds*
Abimelech's route .... Judg. 9:35, 37

Meonothai—*my habitations*
Judahite .... 1 Chr. 4:14

Mephaath—*splendor*
Reubenite town .... Josh. 13:18

SUBJECT REFERENCE

Assigned to Merarite Levites....Josh. 21:34, 37
Repossessed by Moabites.......Jer. 48:21

Mephibosheth—*one who destroys shame*

1. Son of King Saul..........2 Sam. 21:8
2. Grandson of King Saul; crippled son of Jonathan..........2 Sam. 4:4-6
Reared by Machir..........2 Sam. 9:6
Sought out and honored by David..........2 Sam. 9:1-13
Accused by Ziba..........2 Sam. 16:1-4
Later explains his side to David..........2 Sam. 19:24-30
Spared by David..........2 Sam. 21:7
Father of Micha..........2 Sam. 9:12
Called Merib-baal..........1 Chr. 8:34

Merab—*increase*

King Saul's eldest daughter.....1 Sam. 14:49
Saul promises her to David, but gives her to Adriel..........1 Sam. 18:17-19
Five sons of, hanged..........2 Sam. 21:8, 9

Meraiah—*rebellious*

Postexilic priest..........Neh. 12:12

Meraioth—*rebellious*

1. Levite..........1 Chr. 6:6, 7
2. Son of Ahitub and father of Zadok..........1 Chr. 9:11
3. Priestly household in Joiakim's time..........Neh. 12:15
Called Meremoth..........Neh. 12:3

Merari—*bitter*

1. Third son of Levi; brother of Gershon and Kohath..........Gen. 46:11
Goes with Jacob to Egypt...Gen. 46:8, 11
2. Descendants of Merari; called Merarites..........Num. 26:57
Divided into two groups.....Ex. 6:19
Duties assigned to..........Num. 3:35-37
Follow Judah in march........Num. 10:14, 17
Twelve cities assigned to.....Josh. 21:7, 34-40
Superintend Temple music...1 Chr. 6:31-47
Help David bring up the ark..........1 Chr. 15:1-6
Divided into courses..........1 Chr. 23:6-23
Their duties described.........1 Chr. 26:10-19
Participate in cleansing the house of the LORD..........2 Chr. 29:12-19
After exile, help Ezra.......Ezra 8:18, 19

Merarites (see Merari 2)

Merathaim—*double rebellion*

Name applied to Babylon......Jer. 50:21

Merchandise—*things for sale in trade*

A. *Characteristics of:*
Countries employed in.....Is. 45:14
Men occupied with..........Matt. 22:5
Not mixed with spiritual things..........John 2:16
To be abolished..........Rev. 18:11, 12

B. *Figurative of:*
Wisdom's profit..........Prov. 3:13, 14
Gospel transformation......Is. 23:18

Merchants—*traders*

Characteristics of:
Crossed the sea..........Is. 23:2
Lamentation over..........Ezek. 27:2-36
Some do not observe the Sabbath..........Neh. 13:19-21
Burden people with debts.......Neh. 5:1-13
Peddle goods..........Neh. 13:16
Trade with farmers..........Prov. 31:24
Form guilds..........Neh. 3:8-32
Destroyed with Babylon..........Rev. 18:3-19
Sailors, in Solomon's service...1 Kin. 9:27, 28
Bring Solomon..........2 Chr. 9:14
Bring Solomon..........2 Chr. 9:28

Mercurius

Paul acclaimed as..........Acts 14:12

Mercy

A. *Described as:*
Great..........Is. 54:7
Sure..........Is. 55:3
Abundant..........1 Pet. 1:3
Tender..........Ps. 25:6
New every morning..........Lam. 3:22, 23

SUBJECT REFERENCE

B. *Of God, seen in:*
Regeneration..........1 Pet. 1:3
Salvation..........Titus 3:5
Christ's mission..........Luke 1:72, 78
Forgiveness..........Ps. 51:1

C. *In the Christian life:*
Received in salvation..........1 Cor. 7:25
Taught as a principle of life..........Matt. 5:7
Practiced as a gift..........Rom. 12:8
Evidenced in God's provinces..........Phil. 2:27
Obtained in prayer..........Heb. 4:16
Reason of consecration......Rom. 12:1
Reason for hope..........Jude 21

D. *Special injunctions concerning:*
Put on..........Col. 3:12

E. *Examples of:*
David to Saul..........1 Sam. 24:10-17
Christ to sinners..........Matt. 9:13

F. *Attitude of believers, to:*
Cast themselves on..........2 Sam. 24:14
Look for..........Jude 21

Mercy seat—*the covering of the ark*

Made of pure gold..........Ex. 25:17
Blood sprinkled upon..........Lev. 16:14, 15
God manifested over..........Lev. 16:2
Figurative of Christ..........Heb. 9:5-12

Mered—*rebellion*

Judahite..........1 Chr. 4:17
Had two wives..........1 Chr. 4:17, 18

Meremoth—*elevations*

1. Signer of the covenant......Neh. 10:5
Called Meraioth..........Neh. 12:15
2. One who divorced his foreign wife..........Ezra 10:34, 36
3. Priest, son of Uriah; weighs silver and gold..........Ezra 8:33
Repairs wall of Jerusalem....Neh. 3:4, 21

Meres—*the forgetful one*

Persian prince..........Esth. 1:13, 14

Merib-baal—*Baal contends*

Another name for Mephibosheth..........1 Chr. 8:34

Merit—*reward given for something done additionally*

A. *Of man, impossible because:*
None is good..........Rom. 3:12
None is righteous..........Rom. 3:10
We are all sinful..........Is. 6:5
Our good comes from God..1 Cor. 15:9, 10
Our righteousness:
Is unavailing..........Matt. 5:20
Is Christ's..........2 Cor. 5:21
Cannot save..........Rom. 10:1-4

B. *Of Christ:*
Secured by obedience.......Rom. 5:17-21
Secured by his death........Is. 53:10-12
Obtained by faith..........Phil. 3:8, 9

Merodach—*bold*

Supreme deity of the Babylonians..........Jer. 50:2
Otherwise called Bel..........Is. 46:1

Merodach-baladan—*Merodach has given a son*

Sends ambassadors to Hezekiah..........Is. 39:1-8
Also called Berodach-baladan...2 Kin. 20:12

Merom—*high place*

Lake on Jordan north of the Sea of Galilee..........Josh. 11:5, 7

Meronothite

Citizen of Meronoth..........1 Chr. 27:30

Meroz—*refuge*

Town cursed for failing to help the Lord..........Judg. 5:23

Merry—*a spirit of gaiety*

A. *Good, comes from:*
Heart..........Prov. 15:13, 15
Restoration..........Jer. 30:18, 19
Christian joy..........James 5:13

SUBJECT REFERENCE

B. *Evil, results from:*
Careless unconcern..........Judg. 9:27
Gluttony..........1 Sam. 25:36
False optimism..........1 Kin. 21:7
Sinful glee..........Rev. 11:10

Mesha—*retreat*

1. Border of Joktan's descendants..........Gen. 10:30
2. Benjamite..........1 Chr. 8:8, 9
3. Son of Caleb..........1 Chr. 2:42
4. King of Moab..........2 Kin. 3:4

Meshach—*the shadow of the prince*

Name given to Mishael..........Dan. 1:7
Advanced to high position......Dan. 2:49
Remains faithful in testing......Dan. 3:13-30

Meshech—*tall*

1. Son of Japheth..........Gen. 10:2
Called Mesech..........Ps. 120:5
Famous traders..........Ezek. 27:13
Confederates with Gog......Ezek. 38:2, 3
Inhabitants of the nether world..........Ezek. 32:18, 26
2. Son of Shem..........1 Chr. 1:17
Same as Mash..........Gen. 10:23

Meshelemiah—*Jehovah repays*

Father of Zechariah..........1 Chr. 9:21
Porter in the Temple..........1 Chr. 26:1
Called Shelemiah..........1 Chr. 26:14

Meshezabeel—*God delivers*

1. Postexilic wall repairer......Neh. 3:4
2. One who signs covenant.....Neh. 10:21
3. Judahite..........Neh. 11:24

Meshillemith—*recompense*

Postexilic priest..........1 Chr. 9:10-12
Called Meshillemoth..........Neh. 11:13

Meshillemoth—*acts of recompense*

Ephraimite leader..........2 Chr. 28:12

Meshobab—*restored*

Descendant of Simeon..........1 Chr. 4:34-38

Meshullam—*recompensed; rewarded*

1,2,3. Three Benjamites..........1 Chr. 8:17
4. Gadite leader..........1 Chr. 5:11, 13
5. Shaphan's grandfather......2 Kin. 22:3
6. Hilkiah's father..........1 Chr. 9:11
7. Son of Zerubbabel..........1 Chr. 3:19
8. Priest..........1 Chr. 9:10-12
9. Kohathite overseer..........2 Chr. 34:12
10. Man commissioned to secure Levites..........Ezra 8:16
11. Levite who supports Ezra's reforms..........Ezra 10:15
12. One who divorced his foreign wife..........Ezra 10:29
13. Postexilic workman..........Neh. 3:4, 30
His daughter married Tobiah's son..........Neh. 6:18
14. Postexilic workman..........Neh. 3:6
15. One of Ezra's attendants....Neh. 8:4
16, 17. Two priests who sign covenant..........Neh. 10:7, 20
18, 19. Two priests in Joiakim's time..........Neh. 12:13, 16
20. Porter..........Neh. 12:25
21. Participant in dedication services..........Neh. 12:33

Meshullemeth—*feminine form of Meshullam*

Wife of King Manasseh........2 Kin. 21:18, 19

Mesobaite—*found of Jehovah*

Title given Jasiel..........1 Chr. 11:47

Mesopotamia—*the country between two rivers*

Abraham's native home........Acts 7:2
Place of Laban's household.....Gen. 24:4, 10, 29
Called:
Padan-aram..........Gen. 25:20
Syria..........Gen. 31:20, 24
Balaam came from..........Deut. 23:4
Israel enslaved to..........Judg. 3:8, 10

M

SUBJECT ... REFERENCE

Chariots and horsemen hired from ... 1 Chr. 19:6
Called Haran; conquered by Sennacherib ... 2 Kin. 19:12, 16
People from, at Pentecost ... Acts 2:9

Mess—*a portion of food*

Set before Joseph's brothers ... Gen. 43:30, 34
Provided for Uriah ... 2 Sam. 11:8

Messenger—*one sent on a mission*

A. *Mission of, to:*

Appease wrath ... Gen. 32:3-6
Ask for favors ... Num. 20:14-17
Spy out ... Josh. 6:17, 25
Assemble a nation ... Judg. 6:35
Secure provisions ... 1 Sam. 25:4-14
Relay news ... 1 Sam. 11:3-9
Stir up war ... Judg. 11:12-28
Sue for peace ... 2 Sam. 3:12, 13
Offer sympathy ... 1 Chr. 19:2
Call for help ... 2 Kin. 17:4
Issue an ultimatum ... 1 Kin. 20:2-9
Deliver the LORD's message ... Hag. 1:13

B. *Reception of:*

Rejected ... Deut. 2:26-30
Humiliated ... 1 Chr. 19:2-4
Rebuked ... 2 Kin. 1:2-5, 16

C. *Significant examples of:*

John the Baptist ... Mal. 3:1
Paul's thorn ... 2 Cor. 12:7
Gospel workers ... 2 Cor. 8:23; Phil. 2:25

Messiah, the

A. *Described as:*

Seed of woman ... Gen. 3:15
Promised seed ... Gen. 12:1-3; Gal. 3:16
Star out of Jacob ... Num. 24:17; Luke 3:34
Of Judah's tribe ... Gen. 49:10; Heb. 7:14
Son of David ... Is. 11:1-10; Matt. 1:1
Prophet ... Deut. 18:15-19; Acts 3:22, 23
Priest after Melchizedek's order ... Ps. 110:4; Heb. 6:20
King of David's line ... Jer. 23:5; Luke 1:32, 33
Son of God ... Ps. 2:7, 8; Acts 13:33
Son of Man ... Dan. 7:13; Mark 8:38
Immanuel ... Is. 7:14; Matt. 1:22, 23
Branch ... Jer. 23:5; Zech. 3:8
Headstone ... Ps. 118:22; 1 Pet. 2:4, 7
Servant ... Is. 42:1-4; Matt. 12:18, 21

B. *Mission of, to:*

Introduce the new covenant ... Jer. 31:31-34; Matt. 26:26-30
Preach the Gospel ... Is. 61:1-3; Luke 4:17-19
Bring peace ... Is. 9:6, 7; Heb. 2:14-16
Die for man's sin ... Is. 53:4-6; 1 Pet. 1:18-20
Unite God's people ... Is. 19:23-25; Eph. 2:11-22
Call the Gentiles ... Is. 11:10; Rom. 15:9-12
Be a priest ... Zech. 6:12, 13; Heb. 1:3; Heb. 8:1
Rule from David's throne ... Ps. 45:5-7; Acts 2:30-36
Destroy Satan ... Rom. 16:20; 1 John 3:8
Bring in everlasting righteousness ... Dan. 9:24; Matt. 3:15; 2 Cor. 5:21

C. *Christ the true Messiah, proved by:*

Birth at Bethlehem ... Mic. 5:2; Luke 2:4-7
Born of a virgin ... Is. 7:14; Matt. 1:18-25
Appearing in the second Temple ... Hag. 2:7, 9; John 18:20
Working miracles ... Is. 35:5, 6; Matt. 11:4, 5
Rejection by the Jews ... John 1:11
Vicarious death ... Is. 53:1-12; 1 Pet. 3:18
Coming at the appointed time ... Dan. 9:24-27; Mark 1:15

D. *Other prophecies concerning:*

Worship ... Ps. 72:10-15; Matt. 2:1-11
Flight to Egypt ... Hos. 11:1; Matt. 2:13-15
Forerunner ... Mal. 3:1; Mark 1:1-8
Zeal ... Ps. 69:9; John 2:17
Triumphal entry ... Zech. 9:9, 10; Matt. 21:1-11
Betrayal ... Ps. 41:9; Mark 14:10
Being sold ... Zech. 11:12; Matt. 26:15
Silent defense ... Is. 53:7; Matt. 26:62, 63
Being spit on ... Is. 50:6; Mark 14:65
Being crucified with sinners ... Is. 53:12; Matt. 27:38
Piercing of hands and feet ... Ps. 22:16; John 19:36, 37
Being mocked ... Ps. 22:6-8; Matt. 27:39-44
Dying drink ... Ps. 69:21; John 19:29
Prayer for the enemies ... Ps. 109:4; Luke 23:34
Side pierced ... Zech. 12:10; John 19:34
Garments gambled for ... Ps. 22:18; Mark 15:24
Death without broken bones ... Ps. 34:20; John 19:33
Separation from God ... Ps. 22:1; Matt. 27:46
Burial with the rich ... Is. 53:9; Matt. 27:57-60
Preservation from decay ... Ps. 16:8-10; Acts 2:31
Ascension ... Ps. 68:18; Eph. 4:8-10
Exaltation ... Ps. 2:6-12; Phil. 2:9, 10

See Christ

Metallurgy—*mining and processing of metal*

Mining and refining ... Job 28:1, 2
Heat needed ... Jer. 6:29

Metaphors—*graphic comparisons*

A. *Concerning God, as:*

Rock ... Deut. 32:4
Sun and shield ... Ps. 84:11
Consuming fire ... Heb. 12:29
Husbandman ... John 15:1

B. *Concerning Christ, as:*

Bread of life ... John 6:35
Light of the world ... John 8:12
Door ... John 10:9
Good Shepherd ... John 10:14
Way, Truth, Life ... John 14:6
True vine ... John 15:1

C. *Concerning Christians, as:*

Light ... Matt. 5:14
Salt ... Matt. 5:13
Epistles ... 2 Cor. 3:3
Living stones ... 1 Pet. 2:5

D. *Concerning the Bible, as:*

Fire ... Jer. 5:14
Hammer ... Jer. 23:29
Light; lamp ... Ps. 119:105
Sword ... Eph. 6:17

Mete—*to measure*

Dry measure ... Ex. 16:18
Linear measure ... Is. 40:12
Figurative measure ... Matt. 7:2

Metheg-ammah—*power of the metropolis*

Probably a figurative name for Gath ... 2 Sam. 8:1

Methuselah—*man of a javelin*

Son of Enoch ... Gen. 5:21
Oldest man on record ... Gen. 5:27
Ancestor of Christ ... Luke 3:37

Methusael—*man of God*

Cainite, father of Lamech ... Gen. 4:18
See Maon

Mezahab—*waters of gold*

Grandfather of Mehetabel, wife of King Hadar ... Gen. 36:39

Mibhar—*choice*

One of David's mighty men ... 1 Chr. 11:38

Mibsam—*sweet odor*

1. Son of Ishmael ... Gen. 25:13
2. Simeonite ... 1 Chr. 4:25

Mibzar—*stronghold*

Edomite duke ... Gen. 36:42

Mica, Micah—*who is like Jehovah?*

1. Ephraimite who hires a traveling Levite ... Judg. 17:1-13
2. Reubenite ... 1 Chr. 5:1, 5
3. Son of Mephibosheth ... 2 Sam. 9:12
4. Descendant of Asaph ... 1 Chr. 9:15; Called Michaiah ... Neh. 12:35
5. Kohathite Levite ... 1 Chr. 23:20
6. Father of Abdon ... 2 Chr. 34:20
7. Prophet, contemporary of Isaiah ... Is. 1:1; Mic. 1:1
8. One who signs the covenant ... Neh. 10:11

Micah, the Book of—*a book of the Old Testament*

Judgment of Israel and Judah ... Mic. 1:2-16
Promise to the remnant ... Mic. 2:12, 13
Judgment on those in authority ... Mic. 3:1-12
The coming peace ... Mic. 4:1-8
The Redeemer from Bethlehem ... Mic. 5:1-4
Hope in God ... Mic. 7:8-20

Micaiah, Michaiah—*who is like Jehovah?*

1. Wife of King Rehoboam ... 2 Chr. 13:2
2. Prophet who predicts Ahab's death ... 1 Kin. 22:8-28
3. Teaching official ... 2 Chr. 17:7
4. Father of Achbor ... 2 Kin. 22:12; Called Micah ... 2 Chr. 34:20
5. Contemporary of Jeremiah ... Jer. 36:11-13
6. Descendant of Asaph ... Neh. 12:35
7. Priest in dedication service ... Neh. 12:41

Michael—*who is like God?*

1. Father of an Asherite spy ... Num. 13:13
2, 3. Two Gadites ... 1 Chr. 5:13, 14
4. Levite ancestor of Asaph ... 1 Chr. 6:40
5. Issacharian chief ... 1 Chr. 7:3
6. Benjamite ... 1 Chr. 8:16
7. Manassite chief under David ... 1 Chr. 12:20
8. Father of Omri ... 1 Chr. 27:18
9. Son of King Jehoshaphat ... 2 Chr. 21:2
10. Father of Zebadiah ... Ezra 8:8
11. Chief prince ... Dan. 10:13, 21; Stands against forces ... Dan. 10:21; Disputes with Satan ... Jude 9; Fights the dragon ... Rev. 12:7-9

Michal—*who is like God?*

Daughter of King Saul ... 1 Sam. 14:49
Loves and marries David ... 1 Sam. 18:20-28
Saves David from Saul ... 1 Sam. 19:9-17
Given to Phalti ... 1 Sam. 25:44
David demands her from Abner ... 2 Sam. 3:13-16
Ridicules David; becomes barren ... 2 Sam. 6:16-23

Michmash, Michmas—*hidden place*

Town occupied by Saul's army ... 1 Sam. 13:2
Site of battle with Philistines ... 1 Sam. 13:5, 11, 16, 23
Scene of Jonathan's victory ... 1 Sam. 14:1-18

SUBJECT REFERENCE

Mentioned in prophecy .... Is. 10:28
Exiles return .... Ezra 2:1, 27

Michmethah—*lurking place*

Place on the border of Ephraim and Manasseh .... Josh. 16:5, 6

Michri—*purchase price*

Benjamite .... 1 Chr. 9:8

Michtam

Word of unknown meaning used in titles of .... Ps. 16; 56-60

Middin—*extensions*

In the wilderness .... Josh. 15:61

Midian—*place of judgment*

1. Son of Abraham by Keturah .... Gen. 25:1-4
2. Region in the Arabian desert occupied by the Midianites .... Gen. 25:6

Midianites—*descendants of Midian*

A. *Characteristics of:*
Descendants of Abraham by Keturah .... Gen. 25:1, 2
Moses fled to .... Ex. 2:15
Retain worship of Jehovah ... Ex. 2:16
Ruled by kings .... Num. 31:8
Immoral people .... Num. 25:18

B. *Contacts with Israel:*
Joining Moab in cursing ..... Num. 22:4-7
Seduction of .... Num. 25:1-18
Defeat because of .... Num. 31:1-18
Being sent as punishment .... Judg. 6:1-10

Midnight

A. *Significant happenings at:*
Death in Egypt .... Ex. 11:4
Prayer meeting .... Acts 16:25
Possible time of Christ's return .... Matt. 25:6

B. *Other happenings at:*
Quick departure .... Judg. 16:2, 3
Friend's need .... Luke 11:5
Great fear .... Job 34:20

Midwife—*one who assists at childbirth*

Helps in the birth of a child .... Gen. 35:17

Migdal-el—*tower of God*

City of Naphtali .... Josh. 19:38

Migdal-gad—*a tower of Gad* (fortune)

Town of Judah .... Josh. 15:37

Migdol—*tower*

1. Israelite encampment .... Ex. 14:2
2. Place in Egypt to which Jews flee .... Jer. 44:1

Might—*effective power*

A. *God's:*
Irresistible .... 2 Chr. 20:6
God's hand is .... 1 Chr. 29:12
Unutterable .... Ps. 106:2

B. *Man's physical:*
Boasted in, brings destruction .... Dan. 4:30-33
Not to be gloried in .... Deut. 8:17
Will fail .... Jer. 51:30
Exhortation concerning ...... Eccl. 9:10

C. *Man's intellectual and moral:*
Invites self-glory .... Jer. 9:23
Makes salvation difficult ..... 1 Cor. 1:26

D. *Man's spiritual, comes from:*
God .... Eph. 1:19
Christ .... Col. 1:28, 29
The Spirit .... Mic. 3:8

Mighty

Literally of:
Hunter .... Gen. 10:9
Nation .... Gen. 18:18
Prince .... Gen. 23:6
Waters .... Ex. 15:10
Hand .... Ex. 32:11
Acts .... Deut. 3:24
Deeds .... 2 Sam. 23:20
Men of valor .... 1 Chr. 7:9-11

SUBJECT REFERENCE

Warrior .... 2 Chr. 32:21
Kings .... Ezra 4:20
Wind .... Job 8:2
Strength .... Job 9:4
Thunder .... Job 26:14
Fear .... Job 41:25

Mighty man—*a powerful man; a valiant warrior*

Men of renown .... Gen. 6:4
Gideon .... Judg. 6:11, 12
Warriors of David .... 2 Sam. 10:7

Migron—*precipitous* (very steep)

1. Place where Saul stayed ..... 1 Sam. 14:2
2. Village north of Michmash ... Is. 10:28

Mijamin—*from the right side*

1. Descendant of Aaron .... 1 Chr. 24:1, 6, 9
2. Chief priest; returns with Zerubbabel .... Neh. 12:5, 7
Probably same as 1
3. Divorced his foreign wife .... Ezra 10:25
4. Priest who signs the covenant .... Neh. 10:7
Same as Miniamin in .... Neh. 12:17, 41

Mikhtam

Possible meaning is "Atonement Psalm," used in titles of .... Ps. 16—56, 60

Mikloth—*rods*

1. Ruler under David .... 1 Chr. 27:4
2. Benjamite .... 1 Chr. 8:32

Mikneiah—*possession of Jehovah*

Porter and musician in David's time .... 1 Chr. 15:18, 21

Milalai—*eloquent*

Levite musician in dedication service .... Neh. 12:36

Milcah—*counsel*

1. Wife of Nahor .... Gen. 11:29
Mother of eight children ..... Gen. 22:20-22
Grandmother of Rebekah .... Gen. 22:23
2. Daughter of Zelophehad ..... Num. 26:33

Milcom—*an Ammonite god*

Solomon went after .... 1 Kin. 11:5
Altar destroyed by Josiah ...... 2 Kin. 23:12, 13

Mildew—*a disease of grain due to dampness*

Threatened as a punishment .... Deut. 28:22
Sent upon Israel .... Amos 4:9
Removed by repentance .... 1 Kin. 8:37-39

Mile—*a thousand paces* (about 12/13 of an English mile)

Used illustratively .... Matt. 5:41
See Jewish measures

Miletus—*a city of Asia Minor*

Paul meets Ephesian elders here .... Acts 20:15-38
Paul leaves Trophimus here ..... 2 Tim. 4:20

Milk—*a white liquid secreted by mammary glands*

A. *Produced by:*
Goats .... Prov. 27:27
Sheep .... Deut. 32:14
Camels .... Gen. 32:15
Cows .... 1 Sam. 6:7, 10
Humans .... Is. 28:9

B. *Figurative of:*
Abundance .... Deut. 32:14
Egypt's supposed blessings ... Num. 16:13
Elementary teaching .... 1 Cor. 3:2
Pure doctrine .... 1 Pet. 2:2

Mill, millstone

A. *Uses of:*
Grinding grain .... Num. 11:8
Weapon .... Judg. 9:53
Pledge, forbidden .... Deut. 24:6
Weight .... Matt. 18:6

B. *Operated by:*
Women .... Matt. 24:41
Maidservant .... Ex. 11:5
Prisoners .... Judg. 16:21

C. *Figurative of:*
Courage .... Job 41:24

SUBJECT REFERENCE

Old age .... Eccl. 12:4
Desolation .... Jer. 25:10

Millennium—*thousand years*

Latin for a thousand years ...... Rev. 20:1-10

Millet—*a cereal*

Ezekiel makes bread of .... Ezek. 4:9

Millo—*terrace, elevation*

1. House or stronghold at Shechem, called Beth-millo .... Judg. 9:6, 20
2. Fort at Jerusalem .... 2 Sam. 5:9
Prepared by Solomon .... 1 Kin. 9:15
Strengthened by Hezekiah ... 2 Chr. 32:5
Scene of Joash's death .... 2 Kin. 12:20, 21

Mincing—*affected elegance in walking*

Denounced .... Is. 3:16

Mind—*the reasoning faculty*

A. *Faculties of:*
Perception .... Luke 9:47
Remembrance .... Titus 3:1
Reasoning .... Rom. 7:23, 25
Feelings .... 2 Sam. 17:8
Desire .... Neh. 4:6
Imagination .... Gen. 6:5
Purpose .... 2 Cor. 1:15, 17

B. *Of the unregenerate, described as:*
Alienated .... Ezek. 23:17-22
Despiteful .... Ezek. 36:5
Reprobate .... Rom. 1:28
Blinded .... 2 Cor. 3:14
Hostile .... Col. 1:21
Defiled .... Titus 1:15

C. *Of the regenerate, described as:*
Willing .... 1 Chr. 28:9
In peace .... Rom. 8:6
Right .... Luke 8:35
Renewed .... Rom. 12:2
Having Christ's .... 1 Cor. 2:16
Obedient .... Heb. 8:10

D. *Dangers of, to the Christian:*
Worry .... Luke 12:29
Doubt .... Rom. 14:5
Disunity .... Rom. 12:16
Phil. 4:2
Mental disturbance .... 2 Thess. 2:2
Spiritual disturbance .... Rom. 7:23, 25
Grow weary .... Heb. 12:3

E. *Exhortations concerning, to Christians:*
Love God with all .... Matt. 22:37

Minerals of the Bible

A. *Features concerning:*
Mined .... Job 28:1-11
Plentiful in Canaan .... Deut. 8:9
Refined by fire .... Ezek. 22:18, 20
Trade in .... Ezek. 27:12

B. *List of:*
Asphalt (bitumen) .... Gen. 11:3
Brass .... Num. 21:9
Brimstone (sulphur) .... Deut. 29:23
Chalk .... Is. 27:9
Clay .... Is. 41:25
Copper (brass) .... Deut. 8:9
Coral .... Job 28:18
Flint .... Deut. 32:13
Gold .... Gen. 2:11, 12
Iron .... Gen. 4:22
Lead .... Job 19:24
Lime .... Amos 2:1
Nitre .... Jer. 2:22
Salt .... Gen. 14:3
Sand .... Prov. 27:3
Silver .... Gen. 44:2
Slime (asphalt) .... Gen. 6:14
Tin .... Num. 31:22

Mingle, mix—*to put different elements together*

A. *Instances of:*
Offerings .... Lev. 2:4, 5
Garment .... Lev. 19:19
Judgments .... Rev. 8:7
Human sacrifice .... Luke 13:1
Intermarriage .... Ezra 9:2

B. *Figurative of:*
Sorrow .... Ps. 102:9
Wisdom .... Prov. 9:2, 5
Instability .... Is. 19:14

M

SUBJECT REFERENCE

Severity .... Ps. 75:8
Impurity .... Is. 1:22
Intoxication .... Is. 5:22
Worldliness .... Hos. 7:8

Miniamin—*fortunate*

1. Levite assistant .... 2 Chr. 31:14, 15
2. Postexilic priest .... Neh. 12:17
3. Priestly participant in dedication .... Neh. 12:41

Minish—*obsolete for diminish*

To make something less .... Ex. 5:19

Minister—*one who serves*

A. *Descriptive of:*

Proclaiming the Word .... Acts 13:5
Court attendants .... 1 Kin. 10:5
Angels .... Ps. 103:20
Priests and Levites .... Joel 1:9, 13
Servant .... Matt. 20:22-27
Ruler .... Rom. 13:4, 6
Christ .... Rom. 15:8
Christ's messengers .... 1 Cor. 3:5
False teachers .... 2 Cor. 11:15

B. *Christian, qualifications of:*

Able to teach .... 1 Tim. 3:2
Courageous .... Acts 20:22-24
Diligent .... 1 Cor. 15:10
Faithful .... Rom. 15:17-19
Impartial .... 1 Tim. 5:21
Industrious .... 2 Cor. 10:12-16
Meek .... 2 Tim. 2:25
Obedient .... Acts 16:9, 10
Persevering .... 2 Cor. 11:23-33
Prayerful .... Acts 6:4
Sincere .... 2 Cor. 4:1, 2
Spirit-filled .... Acts 1:8
Studious .... 1 Tim. 4:13, 15
Sympathetic .... Heb. 5:2
Temperate .... 1 Cor. 9:25-27
Willing .... 1 Pet. 5:2
Worthy of imitation .... 1 Tim. 4:12

C. *Sins to avoid:*

Arrogance .... 1 Pet. 5:3
Contentiousness .... Titus 1:7
Discouragement .... 2 Cor. 4:8, 9
Insincerity .... Phil. 1:15, 16
Perverting the truth .... 2 Cor. 11:3-15
Unfaithfulness .... Matt. 24:48-51

D. *Duties of:*

Preach:

Gospel .... 1 Cor. 1:17
Christ crucified .... 1 Cor. 1:23
Christ's riches .... Eph. 3:8-12
Feed the Church .... John 21:15-17
Edify the Church .... Eph. 4:12
Pray for people .... Col. 1:9
Teach .... 2 Tim. 2:2
Exhort .... Titus 1:9
Rebuke .... Titus 2:15
Warn of apostasy .... 2 Tim. 4:2-5
Comfort .... 2 Cor. 1:4-6
Win souls .... 1 Cor. 9:19-23

E. *Attitude of believers toward:*

Pray for .... Eph. 6:18-20
Follow the example of .... 1 Cor. 11:1
Obey .... 1 Cor. 4:1, 2
Esteem highly .... 1 Thess. 5:12, 13
Provide for .... 1 Cor. 9:6-18

Minni—*a people* (Manneans) *of Armenia*

Summoned to destroy Babylon .... Jer. 51:27

Minnith—*distribution*

Wheat-growing Ammonite town .... Ezek. 27:17

Minority—*the lesser number*

On God's side .... Num. 14:1-10
To be preferred .... Ex. 23:2
Saved are .... Matt. 7:13-23

Minstrel—*a player of an instrument*

Used by Elisha .... 2 Kin. 3:15
Among funeral attendants .... Matt. 9:23

Mint—*a fragrant herb*

Tithed by Pharisees .... Matt. 23:23

SUBJECT REFERENCE

Miphkad—*appointed place*

Gate of Jerusalem rebuilt by Nehemiah .... Neh. 3:31

Miracle

A. *Described:*

Signs .... Acts 4:30
Wonders .... Acts 6:8
Works .... John 10:25-38

B. *Kinds of, over:*

Nature .... Josh. 10:12-14
Animals .... Num. 22:28
Human beings .... Gen. 19:26
Nations .... Ex. 10:1, 2
Sickness and disease .... 2 Kin. 5:10-14
Natural laws .... 2 Kin. 6:5-7
Future events .... 2 Kin. 6:8-13
Death .... John 11:41-44

C. *Produced by:*

God's power .... Acts 15:12
Christ's power .... Matt. 10:1
Spirit's power .... Matt. 12:28

D. *Design of:*

Manifest:

God's glory .... John 11:40-42
Christ's glory .... John 2:11
God's presence .... Judg. 6:11-24
Proof of God's messengers .... Ex. 4:2-9
Produce obedience .... Ex. 16:4
Vindicate God .... Ex. 17:4-7
Produce faith .... John 20:30, 31
Proof of Jesus as the Messiah .... Matt. 11:2-5
Signs of a true apostle .... 2 Cor. 12:12
Authenticate the Gospel .... Rom. 15:18, 19
Fulfill prophecy .... John 12:37-41

E. *Effect of, upon people:*

Forced acknowledgment .... John 11:47
Acts 4:16
Amazement .... Mark 6:49-51
Faith .... John 2:23
John 11:42
God glorified .... Matt. 9:1-8

F. *False:*

Not to be followed .... Deut. 13:1-3
Sign of antichrist .... 2 Thess. 2:3, 9
Rev. 13:13
Predicted by Christ .... Matt. 24:24

G. *Evidence of:*

Logic .... John 9:16
Sufficient to convince .... John 3:2
John 6:14
Insufficient to convince .... Luke 16:31
John 12:37
Sought by Jews .... John 2:18
Demanded unreasonably .... Matt. 27:42, 43
Incurs guilt .... Matt. 11:20-24
John 15:24

Miracles of the Bible—*Old Testament*

Creation .... Gen. 1:1-27
Enoch's translation .... Gen. 5:24
The Flood .... Gen. 7:17-24
Confusion of tongues at Babel .... Gen. 11:3-9
Sodom and Gomorrah destroyed .... Gen. 19:24
Lot's wife turned to a pillar of salt .... Gen. 19:26
Ass speaking .... Num. 22:21-35

Those associated with Moses and Aaron:

Burning bush .... Ex. 3:3
Moses' rod changed into a serpent .... Ex. 4:3, 4, 30
Moses' hand made leprous .... Ex. 4:6, 7, 30
Aaron's rod changed into a serpent .... Ex. 7:8-10

Ten plagues:

River turned to blood .... Ex. 7:20-25
Frogs .... Ex. 8:1-15
Lice .... Ex. 8:16-19
Flies .... Ex. 8:20-24
Murrain .... Ex. 9:1-7
Boils .... Ex. 9:8-12
Hail .... Ex. 9:18-24
Locusts .... Ex. 10:1-20
Darkness .... Ex. 10:21-23
First-born destroyed .... Ex. 12:29-30
Pillar of cloud and fire .... Ex. 13:21-22
Ex. 14:19-20

SUBJECT REFERENCE

Crossing the sea .... Ex. 14:21, 23
Bitter waters sweetened .... Ex. 15:25
Manna sent .... Ex. 16:13-36
Water from the rock at Rephidim .... Ex. 17:5-8
Amalek defeated .... Ex. 17:9-13
Fire on Aaron's sacrifice .... Lev. 9:24
Nadab and Abihu devoured .... Lev. 10:1, 2
Israel's judgment by fire .... Num. 11:1-3
Miriam's leprosy .... Num. 12:10-15
Destruction of Korah .... Num. 16:31-35
Aaron's rod blossoms .... Num. 17:8
Water from the rock in Kadesh .... Num. 20:8-11
Brass serpent .... Num. 21:9

Those associated with Joshua:

Jordan divided .... Josh. 3:14-17
Fall of Jericho .... Josh. 6:6-20
Sun and moon stand still .... Josh. 10:12-14

Those associated with Samson:

Lion killed .... Judg. 14:5, 6
Thirty Philistines killed .... Judg. 14:19
Water from the hollow place in Lehi .... Judg. 15:19
Gates of the city carried away .... Judg. 16:3
Dagon's house pulled down .... Judg. 16:29, 30

Those associated with Elijah:

Drought .... 1 Kin. 17:1
James 5:17
Fed by ravens .... 1 Kin. 17:4-6
Widow's oil and meal increased .... 1 Kin. 17:12-16
Widow's son raised from dead .... 1 Kin. 17:17-23
Sacrifice consumed by fire .... 1 Kin. 18:38
Rain in answer to prayer .... 1 Kin. 18:41
Captains consumed by fire .... 2 Kin. 1:9-12
Jordan divided .... 2 Kin. 2:8
Translated to heaven in a chariot of fire .... 2 Kin. 2:11

Those associated with Elisha:

Jordan divided .... 2 Kin. 2:14
Waters of Jericho healed .... 2 Kin. 2:20-22
Mocking young men destroyed by bears .... 2 Kin. 2:24
Water supplied for Jehoshaphat .... 2 Kin. 3:16-20
Widow's oil multiplied .... 2 Kin. 4:1-7
Shunammite's child raised from dead .... 2 Kin. 4:19-37
Poisoned pottage made harmless .... 2 Kin. 4:38-41
Hundred fed with twenty loaves .... 2 Kin. 4:42-44
Naaman cured of leprosy .... 2 Kin. 5:10-14
Gehazi struck with leprosy .... 2 Kin. 5:27
Axe head caused to float .... 2 Kin. 6:5-7
Ben-hadad's plans revealed .... 2 Kin. 6:8-13
Syrian army defeated .... 2 Kin. 6:18-20
Revival of a man by touch with Elisha's bones .... 2 Kin. 13:21

Those associated with Isaiah:

Hezekiah healed .... 2 Kin. 20:7
Shadow turns backward on sun dial .... 2 Kin. 20:11

Other miracles of the Old Testament:

Dew on Gideon's fleece .... Judg. 6:37-40
Dagon's fall before the ark .... 1 Sam. 5:1-12
Men of Beth-shemesh destroyed .... 1 Sam. 6:19, 20
Thunder and rain in harvest .... 1 Sam. 12:18
Uzzah's death .... 2 Sam. 6:6, 7
Jeroboam's hand withered and restored .... 1 Kin. 13:4-6
Rending of the altar .... 1 Kin. 13:5
Sennacherib's army destroyed .... 2 Kin. 19:35
Uzziah afflicted with leprosy .... 2 Chr. 26:16-21
Three men protected from the fiery furnace .... Dan. 3:19-27
Daniel delivered from the lion's den .... Dan. 6:16-23
Preservation of Jonah in stomach of fish three days .... Jon. 2:1-10

Miracles of the Bible—*New Testament*

Of Christ (listed chronologically):

Water made wine (Cana) .... John 2:1-11
Son of nobleman healed (Cana) .... John 4:46-54
Passed unseen through crowd (Nazareth) .... Luke 4:28-30

SUBJECT	REFERENCE
Man with unclean spirit in synagogue cured (Capernaum)	Mark 1:23-26 Luke 4:33-35
Peter's mother-in-law healed (Capernaum)	Matt. 8:14-17 Mark 1:29-31 Luke 4:38-39
Net full of fishes (Lower Galilee)	Luke 5:1-11
Leper cleansed (Capernaum)	Matt. 8:1-4 Mark 1:40-45 Luke 5:12-15
Paralytic cured (Capernaum)	Matt. 9:1-8 Mark 2:3-12 Luke 5:18-26
Man healed (Jerusalem)	John 5:1-9
Withered hand restored (Galilee)	Matt. 12:10-13 Mark 3:1-5 Luke 6:6-11
Centurion's servant cured of palsy (Capernaum)	Matt. 8:5-13 Luke 7:1-10
Widow's son raised from dead (Nain)	Luke 7:11-17
Demon-possessed man healed (Galilee)	Matt. 12:22, 23 Luke 11:14
Tempest stilled (Lower Galilee)	Matt. 8:23-27 Mark 4:37-41 Luke 8:22-25
Two demon-possessed men cured (Gadara)	Matt. 8:28-34 Mark 5:1-20 Luke 8:26-39
Raised Jairus' daughter (Capernaum)	Matt. 9:23 Mark 5:23 Luke 8:41
Woman with issue of blood healed (Capernaum)	Matt. 9:20-22 Mark 5:25-34 Luke 8:43-48
Blind men cured (Capernaum)	Matt. 9:27-31
Dumb spirit cast out (Capernaum)	Matt. 9:32, 33
Five thousand fed (Lower Galilee)	Matt. 14:15-21 Mark 6:35-44 Luke 9:10-17 John 6:1-14
Walking on the sea (Lower Galilee)	Matt. 14:25-33 Mark 6:48-52 John 6:15-21
Syrophoenician's daughter healed (District of Tyre)	Matt. 15:21-28 Mark 7:24-30
Four thousand fed (Lower Galilee)	Matt. 15:32-39 Mark 8:1-9
Deaf and dumb man cured (Lower Galilee)	Mark 7:31-37
Blind man healed (Bethsaida)	Mark 8:22-26
Demon cast out of boy (near Caesarea)	Matt. 17:14-18 Mark 9:14-29 Luke 9:37-43
Tribute money provided (Capernaum)	Matt. 17:24-27
Passed unseen through crowd (in Temple)	John 8:59
Ten lepers cleansed (Samaria)	Luke 17:11-19
Man born blind, healed (Jerusalem)	John 9:1-7
Lazarus raised from dead (Bethany)	John 11:38-44
Woman with sickness cured (Peraea)	Luke 13:11-17
Man with dropsy cured (Peraea)	Luke 14:1-6
Two blind men cured (Jericho)	Matt. 20:29-34 Mark 10:46-52 Luke 18:35-43
Fig tree withered (Mt. Olivet)	Matt. 21:18-22 Mark 11:12-14
Malchus' ear healed (Gethsemane)	Luke 22:50, 51
Second net full of fishes (Lower Galilee)	John 21:1-14
Resurrection of Christ	Luke 24:6 John 10:18
Appearances of Christ after his resurrection, to:	
Mary Magdalene (Jerusalem)	Mark 16:9
Other women (Jerusalem)	Matt. 28:9
Two disciples (Emmaus)	Luke 24:15-31
Peter (Jerusalem)	1 Cor. 15:5
Ten apostles, Thomas absent (Jerusalem)	John 20:19, 24
Eleven apostles, Thomas present (Jerusalem)	John 20:26-28
Seven disciples fishing (Lower Galilee)	John 21:1-24
Eleven apostles (Galilee)	Matt. 28:16, 17
Five hundred brethren	1 Cor. 15:6
James	1 Cor. 15:7
Eleven apostles on day of His ascension (Bethany)	Acts 1:2-9

SUBJECT	REFERENCE
Paul at his conversion	Acts 9:1-5 1 Cor. 15:8
Those associated with Peter:	
Lame man cured	Acts 3:6
Death of Ananias and Sapphira	Acts 5:5, 10
Sick healed	Acts 5:15
Aeneas healed of palsy	Acts 9:34
Dorcas restored to life	Acts 9:40
His release from prison	Acts 12:7-11
Those associated with Paul:	
His sight restored	Acts 9:17-18 Acts 22:12-13
Elymas blinded	Acts 13:11
Lame man cured	Acts 14:10
Damsel freed of evil spirits	Acts 16:18 Acts 19:11, 12
Earthquake at Philippi	Acts 16:25, 26
Evil spirits overcame Sceva's seven sons	Acts 19:13-16
Eutychus restored to life	Acts 20:10
Unharmed by viper's bite	Acts 28:5
Publius' father healed	Acts 28:8
Other miracles of the New Testament:	
Outpouring of the Holy Spirit	Acts 2:1-14
Gift of tongues	Acts 2:3, 4, 11 Acts 10:46 Acts 19:6
Apostles freed from prison	Acts 5:19 Acts 12:7-11
Agabus' prophesies	Acts 11:28 Acts 21:11
Visions:	
Three apostles'	Matt. 17:2 Luke 9:32
Of Christ, by dying:	
Stephen	Acts 7:55, 56
Ananias'	Acts 9:10
Peter's	Acts 10:1-48 Acts 11:1-30
Cornelius'	Acts 10:3, 4, 30-32
Paul's	Acts 16:9 2 Cor. 12:1-5
John's on Patmos	Rev. 1:10 Rev. 4—22
Miracles by the seventy	Luke 10:17
Stephen performed great miracles	Acts 6:8
Philip cast out unclean spirits	Acts 8:6-13

Miracles pretended, or false

SUBJECT	REFERENCE
Egyptian magicians	Ex. 7:11-22 Ex. 8:18, 19
In support of false religions	Deut. 13:1-3
Witch of Endor	1 Sam. 28:9-12
False prophets	Matt. 7:22, 23 Matt. 24:24
False christs	Matt. 24:24
Deceive the ungodly	Rev. 13:13 Rev. 19:20
Sign of apostasy	2 Thess. 2:3, 9 Rev. 13:13

Mire—*deep mud*

SUBJECT	REFERENCE
A. *Places of:*	
Dungeon	Jer. 38:22
Streets	Is. 10:6
B. *Figurative of:*	
Affliction	Job 30:19
External prosperity	Job 8:11
Insecurity	Is. 57:20
Subjection	2 Sam. 22:43
Plentifulness	Zech. 9:3

Miriam—*obstinacy* (stubbornness)

SUBJECT	REFERENCE
1. Sister of Aaron and Moses	Num. 26:59
Chosen by God; called a prophetess	Ex. 15:20
Leads in victory song	Ex. 15:20, 21
Punished for rebellion	Num. 12:1-16
Buried at Kadesh	Num. 20:1
2. Judahite	1 Chr. 4:17

Mirma—*deceit*

SUBJECT	REFERENCE
Benjamite	1 Chr. 8:10

Mirror

SUBJECT	REFERENCE
In the tabernacle	Ex. 38:8
Of molten brass	Job 37:18
Used figuratively	1 Cor. 13:12 2 Cor. 3:18 James 1:23, 25

Mirth—*a spirit of gaiety*

SUBJECT	REFERENCE
Occasions of	Gen. 31:27 Neh. 8:10-12
Absence of	Jer. 25:10, 11 Hos. 2:11
Inadequacy of	Prov. 14:13 Eccl. 2:1, 2

Miscarriage—*premature ejection of a fetus from the mother's womb, resulting in the death of the fetus.*

SUBJECT	REFERENCE
Wished for	Job 3:16 Eccl. 6:3
Against the wicked	Ps. 58:8

Miscegenation—*intermarriage of different races*

SUBJECT	REFERENCE
A. Restrictions in Law of Moses	Ex. 34:12-16
B. *Notable examples:*	
Moses	Num. 12:1-10
Ruth	Matt. 1:5
C. *Unity of all races:*	
Descended from Adam	Gen. 3:20 Rom. 5:12
From one	Acts 17:26
D. *Christian marriage:*	
Spiritual basis	Matt. 19:6
In the Lord	1 Cor. 7:39 2 Cor. 6:14

Mischief—*harm; evil*

SUBJECT	REFERENCE
A. *Descriptive of:*	
Moral evil	Ps. 36:4
Physical harm	Ex. 21:22, 23
Trouble	1 Kin. 11:25
B. *Of the wicked, they:*	
Boast	Ps. 52:1
Devise	Ps. 62:3 Prov. 6:14
Practice	1 Sam. 23:9 Prov. 10:23
Run to	Prov. 6:18
Think to do	Neh. 6:2
Seek	1 Kin. 20:7

Miser—*a covetous man*

SUBJECT	REFERENCE
A. *Characteristics of:*	
Selfish	Eccl. 4:8
Covetous	Luke 12:15
Divided loyalty	Matt. 6:24
B. *Punishment of:*	
Dissatisfaction	Eccl. 5:10
Loss	Matt. 6:19
Sorrows	1 Tim. 6:10
Destruction	Ps. 52:5, 7
C. *Examples of:*	
Rich fool	Luke 12:16-21
Rich ruler	Luke 18:18-23
Ananias and Sapphira	Acts 5:1-11

Miserable—*the wretched*

SUBJECT	REFERENCE
A. *State of:*	
Wicked	Rom. 3:12-16
Trapped	Rom. 7:24
Lost	Luke 13:25-28
B. *Caused by:*	
Forgetfulness of God	Is. 22:12-14
Ignorance	Luke 19:42-44

Misfortune—*an unexpected adversity*

SUBJECT	REFERENCE
Explained by the nations	Deut. 29:24-28
Misunderstood by Gideon	Judg. 6:13
Understood by David	2 Sam. 16:5-13
Caused by sin	Is. 59:1, 2

Misgab—*high place*

SUBJECT	REFERENCE
Moabite city	Jer. 48:1
Capital of Moab	Is. 15:1
Translated "high fort"	Is. 25:12

Mishael—*who is like God?*

SUBJECT	REFERENCE
1. Kohathite Levite	Ex. 6:22
Removes dead bodies	Lev. 10:4, 5
2. Hebrew name of Meshach	Dan. 1:6-19
3. One of Ezra's assistants	Neh. 8:4

Mishal, Misheal

SUBJECT	REFERENCE
Town in Asher	Josh. 19:24, 26
Assigned to Levites	Josh. 21:30
Called Mashal	1 Chr. 6:74

SUBJECT REFERENCE

Misham—*swift*

Son of Elpaal ... 1 Chr. 8:12

Mishma—*hearing*

1. Son of Ishmael ... Gen. 25:13, 14; 1 Chr. 1:30
2. Descendant of Simeon ... 1 Chr. 4:25

Mishmannah—*fatness*

One of David's Gadite warriors ... 1 Chr. 12:10

Mishraites

Family living in Kirjath-jearim ... 1 Chr. 2:53

Mispar—*writing*

Exile returnee ... Ezra 2:2
Called Mispereth ... Neh. 7:7

Misrephoth-maim—*burning of waters*

Haven of fleeing Canaanites ... Josh. 11:8
Near the Sidonians ... Josh. 13:6

Missionaries—*those sent out to spread the Gospel*

Jonah ... Jon. 3:2, 3
The early church ... Acts 8:4
Philip ... Acts 8:5
Some from Cyrene become missionaries ... Acts 11:20
Paul and Barnabas ... Acts 13:1-4
Peter ... Acts 15:7
Apollos ... Acts 18:24
Noah ... 2 Pet. 2:5

Mission of Christ

Do God's will ... John 6:38
Save sinners ... Luke 19:10
Bring in everlasting righteousness ... Dan. 9:24
Destroy Satan's works ... Heb. 2:14; 1 John 3:8
Fulfill the Old Testament ... Matt. 5:17
Give life ... John 10:10, 28
Stop sacrifices ... Dan. 9:27
Complete revelation ... Heb. 1:3

Missions

A. *Commands concerning:*

"Shall be" ... Matt. 24:14
"Go" ... Matt. 28:18-20
"Tarry" ... Luke 24:49
"Come" ... Acts 16:9

B. *Motives prompting:*

God's love ... John 3:16
Christ's love ... 2 Cor. 5:14, 15
Mankind's need ... Rom. 3:9-31

C. *Equipment for:*

Word ... Rom. 10:14, 15
Spirit ... Acts 1:8
Prayer ... Acts 13:1-4

Mist—*a vapor* (physical and spiritual)

Physical (vapor) ... Gen. 2:6
Spiritual (blindness) ... Acts 13:11
Eternal (darkness) ... 2 Pet. 2:17

Mistake—*an error arising from human weakness*

Causes of:

Motives misunderstood ... Josh. 22:9-29
Appearance misjudged ... 1 Sam. 1:13-15
Trust misplaced ... Josh. 9:3-27

Mistress—*a married woman*

Over a maid ... Gen. 16:4, 8, 9
Figurative of Nineveh ... Nah. 3:4

Misunderstandings—*disagreements among*

Israelites ... Josh. 22:9-29
Christ's disciples ... Matt. 20:20-27
Apostles ... Gal. 2:11-15
Christians ... Acts 6:1

Misused—*putting to a wrong use*

Guilt of, brings wrath ... 2 Chr. 36:16

Mite—*Jews' smallest coin*

Widow's ... Mark 12:42

Mithcah—*sweetness*

Israelite encampment ... Num. 33:28, 29

SUBJECT REFERENCE

Mithnite

Descriptive of Joshaphat, David's officer ... 1 Chr. 11:43

Mithredath—*consecrated to Mithra*

1. Treasurer of Cyrus ... Ezra 1:8
2. Persian official ... Ezra 4:7

Mitre, miter—*headdress or turban*

Worn by the high priest ... Ex. 28:36-39
Inscription "Holiness to the Lord" worn on ... Ex. 39:28-31
Worn by Aaron for anointing and on Day of Atonement ... Lev. 8:9; Lev. 16:4
Uncovering of upper lip a sign of uncleanness and mourning ... Lev. 13:45
Uncovering of, forbidden ... Lev. 21:10-12
Removal of, because of sin ... Ezek. 21:26
Symbolic restoration of ... Zech. 3:5

Mitylene—*a city on the island of Lesbos*

Visited by Paul ... Acts 20:13-15

Mix (see Mingle; Miscegenation)

Mizar—*small*

Hill east of Jordan ... Ps. 42:6

Mizpah, Mizpeh—*watchtower*

1. Site of covenant between Jacob and Laban ... Gen. 31:44-53
2. Town in Gilead; probably same as 1 ... Judg. 10:17
   Jephthah's home ... Judg. 11:11, 29, 34
   Probably same as Ramathmizpeh ... Josh. 13:26
3. Region near Mt. Hermon ... Josh. 11:3, 8
4. Town in Judah ... Josh. 15:1, 38
5. Place in Moab; David brings his parents to ... 1 Sam. 22:3, 4
6. Town of Benjamin ... Josh. 18:21, 26
   Outraged Israelites gather here ... Judg. 20:1, 3
   Samuel gathers Israel ... 1 Sam. 7:5-16; 1 Sam. 10:17-25
   Built by Asa ... 1 Sam. 15:22
   Residence of Gedaliah ... 2 Kin. 25:23, 25
   Home of exile returnees ... Neh. 3:7, 15, 19

Mizraim— *Egypt*

1. Son of Ham; ancestor of Ludim, Anamim, etc. ... 1 Chr. 1:8, 11
2. Hebrew name for Egypt ... Gen. 50:11
   Called the land of Ham ... Ps. 105:23, 27

Mizzah—*fear*

Grandson of Esau; a duke of Edom ... Gen. 36:13, 17

Mnason

Christian of Cyprus and Paul's host ... Acts 21:16

Moab—*seed*

1. Son of Lot ... Gen. 19:33-37
2. Country of the Moabites ... Deut. 1:5

Moabites—*inhabitants of Moab*

A. *History of:*

Descendants of Lot ... Gen. 19:36, 37
Became a great nation ... Num. 21:28, 30
Governed by kings ... Num. 23:7; Josh. 24:9
Driven out of their territory by Amorites ... Num. 21:26
Refused to let Israel pass ... Judg. 11:17, 18
Joined Midian to curse Israel ... Num. 22:4
Excluded from Israel ... Deut. 23:3-6
Friendly relation with Israel ... Ruth 1:1, 4, 16
Defeated by Saul ... 1 Sam. 14:47
Refuge for David's parents ... 1 Sam. 22:3, 4
Defeated by David ... 2 Sam. 8:2, 12
Solomon married women of ... 1 Kin. 11:1, 3
Paid tribute to Israel ... 2 Kin. 3:4
Fought Israel and Judah ... 2 Kin. 3:5-7
Conquered by Israel and Judah ... 2 Kin. 3:8-27
Intermarried with Jews ... Ezra 9:1, 2; Neh. 13:23

B. *Characteristics of:*

Idolatrous ... 1 Kin. 11:7

SUBJECT REFERENCE

Wealthy ... Jer. 48:1, 7
Superstitious ... Jer. 27:3, 9
Satisfied ... Jer. 48:11
Proud ... Jer. 48:29

C. *Prophecies concerning their:*

Desolation ... Is. 15:1-9
Ruin and destruction ... Jer. 27:3, 8
Punishment ... Amos 2:1-3
Subjection ... Is. 11:14

Mob—*a lawless crowd*

Caused Pilate to pervert justice ... Matt. 27:20-25
Made unjust charges ... Acts 17:5-9
Paul saved from ... Acts 21:27-40

Mocking—*imitating in fun or derision*

A. *Evil agents of:*

Children ... 2 Kin. 2:23
Men of Israel ... 2 Chr. 30:10
Men of Judah ... 2 Chr. 36:16
Fools ... Prov. 14:9
Wine ... Prov. 20:1
Jews ... Matt. 20:19
Roman soldiers ... Luke 23:36
False teachers ... Jude 18

B. *Good agents of:*

Ass ... Num. 22:29
Samson ... Judg. 16:10-15
Elijah ... 1 Kin. 18:27
Wisdom (God) ... Prov. 1:20, 26
The Lord ... Ps. 2:4

C. *Reasons for, to:*

Show unbelief ... 2 Chr. 36:16
Portray scorn ... 2 Chr. 30:10
Ridicule ... Acts 2:13
Insult ... Gen. 39:14, 17

D. *Objects of:*

Christ ... Luke 23:11, 36
Believers ... Heb. 11:36

Modesty in dress

A. *Of women:*

Instructed ... 1 Tim. 2:9
Illustrated in Israel ... 1 Pet. 3:3-5
Lack of, an enticement ... 2 Sam. 11:2-5

B. *Of men:*

Lack of, condemned ... Gen. 9:21-27
Illustrated ... John 21:7
Manifested in conversion ... Mark 5:15

Moladah—*birth, origin*

Town of Judah ... Josh. 15:1, 26
Inheritance of Simeon ... Josh. 19:1, 2
Returning Levites inhabit ... Neh. 11:26

Molding—*a decorative ledge of gold*

Around:

Ark ... Ex. 25:11
Incense altar ... Ex. 30:3, 4

Mole—*a small, burrowing mammal*

Among unclean animals ... Is. 2:20

Molech—*king*

A. *Worship of:*

By Ammonites ... 1 Kin. 11:7
By human sacrifice ... 2 Kin. 23:10
Strongly condemned ... Lev. 18:21
Introduced by Solomon ... 1 Kin. 11:7

B. *Prevalence of, among Jews:*

Favored by Solomon ... 1 Kin. 11:7

See Human sacrifice

Molid—*begetter*

Judahite ... 1 Chr. 2:29

Molten—*made of melted metal*

A. *Applied to:*

Great basin in the Temple ... 1 Kin. 7:16-33
Mirror ... Job 37:18
Images ... Ex. 32:4, 8

B. *Of images:*

Making of forbidden ... Ex. 34:17
Made by Israel ... 2 Kin. 17:16
Worshiped by Israel ... Ps. 106:19
Destroyed by Josiah ... 2 Chr. 34:3, 4
Folly of ... Is. 42:17
Vanity ... Is. 41:29

SUBJECT REFERENCE

See Gods, false

Moment—*a small unit of time*

A. *Descriptive of:*
Man's life ....Job 34:20
Lying tongues ....Prov. 12:19
Satan's temptation ....Luke 4:5

B. *Descriptive of God's:*
Anger ....Num. 16:21, 45
Punishment ....Is. 47:9
Destruction ....Jer. 4:20

C. *Descriptive of the believer's:*
Problems ....Job 7:18
Protection ....Is. 26:20, 21
Perfection in glory ....1 Cor. 15:52

Monarchy—*the rule of one man* (king)
Described by Samuel ....1 Sam. 8:11-18

Money—*an authorized medium of exchange*

A. *Wrong uses of:*
Misuse ....Gen. 31:15
Forced tribute ....2 Kin. 15:20
Make interest on ....Ps. 15:5
Bribe ....Ps. 15:5
Miser ....Matt. 25:18
Buy spiritual gifts ....Acts 8:18, 20

B. *Good uses of:*
Buy property ....Gen. 23:9, 13
Buy food ....Deut. 2:6, 28
Give as an offering ....Deut. 14:22-26
Repair God's house ....2 Kin. 12:4-15
Pay taxes ....Matt. 17:27
Matt. 22:19-21
Use for the Lord ....Matt. 25:27

C. *Evils connected with:*
Greed ....2 Kin. 5:20-27
Debts ....Neh. 5:2-11

Moneychangers—*dealers in changing money*
Christ drives them out ....Matt. 21:12

Monogamy—*marriage to one spouse*
Commanded ....Matt. 19:3-9
1 Cor. 7:1-16
Example of Christ and the Church ....Eph. 5:25-33
Demanded of bishop ....1 Tim. 3:2

Monotheism—*a belief in one god*

Statements of:
The great commandment ....Deut. 6:4, 5
Song of Moses ....Deut. 32:36-39
About eternal life ....John 17:3, 22

Moon—*earth's satellite*

A. *Miraculous use of:*
Standing still ....Hab. 3:11
Darkened ....Is. 13:10
Turned to blood ....Acts 2:20

B. *Worship of:*
Among Jews ....Jer. 7:18
Forbidden ....Deut. 4:19
Punishable ....Jer. 8:1-3

C. *Illustrative of:*
Eternity ....Ps. 72:5, 7
Universal praise ....Is. 66:23
God's faithfulness ....Jer. 31:35-37
Greater light of Gospel age ..Is. 30:26

D. *Purpose of:*
Rule the night ....Gen. 1:16
Marking time ....Gen. 1:14
Designating seasons ....Ps. 104:19
Signaling prophetic events ...Matt. 24:29
Luke 21:25

Morality—*principles of right conduct*

A. *Of the unregenerate:*
Based upon conscience ......Rom. 2:14, 15
Commanded by law ....John 8:3-5
Limited to outward appearance ....Is. 1:14, 15
Object of boasting ....Mark 10:17-20

B. *Of the regenerated:*
Based upon the new birth ...2 Cor. 5:17
Prompted by the Spirit ......Gal. 5:22, 23
Comes from the heart ....Heb. 8:10
No boasting except in Christ ....1 Cor. 15:10; Phil. 3:7-10

Morasthite—*a native of Moresheth*
Descriptive of Micah ....Jer. 26:18

Mordecai—*dedicated to Mars*

1. Jew exiled in Persia ....Esth. 2:5, 6
Brings up Esther ....Esth. 2:7
Directs Esther's movements ....Esth. 2:10-20
Reveals plot to kill the king ....Esth. 2:22, 23
Refuses homage to Haman ...Esth. 3:1-6
Gallows made for ....Esth. 5:14
Honored by the king ....Esth. 6:1-12
Becomes a third ruler ....Esth. 8:7, 15
Becomes famous ....Esth. 9:4
Writes to Jews about Feast of Purim ....Esth. 9:20-31
2. Postexilic returnee ....Ezra 2:2

More—*something in addition*

A. *"More than" promises:*
Repentance ....Matt. 18:13
Love ....John 21:15

B. *"Much more" promises:*
Grace ....Rom. 5:9-17
Witnessing ....Phil. 1:14
Obedience ....Phil. 2:12

C. *"No more" promises:*
Christ's death ....Rom. 6:9
Grace ....Rom. 11:6
Remember sin ....Heb. 8:12

Moreh—*teacher, soothsayer*

1. Place (oak tree or grove) near Shechem ....Gen. 12:6
Probably place of:
Idol-burying ....Gen. 35:4
Covenant-stone ....Josh. 24:26
2. Hill in the valley of Jezreel ..Judg. 7:1

Moresheth-gath—*possession of Gath*
Birthplace of Micah the prophet ....Mic. 1:14

Moriah
God commands Abraham to sacrifice Isaac here ....Gen. 22:1-13
Site of Solomon's Temple ......2 Chr. 3:1

Morning—*the first part of the day*

A. *Early risers in:*
Do the LORD's will ....Gen. 22:3
Worship ....Ex. 24:4
Do the LORD's work ....Josh. 6:12
Fight the LORD's battles .....Josh. 8:10
Depart on a journey ....Judg. 19:5, 8
Correct an evil ....Dan. 6:19
Pray ....Mark 1:35
Visit the tomb ....Mark 16:2
Preach ....Acts 5:21

B. *For the righteous, a time for:*
Joy ....Ps. 30:5
God's loving-kindness ....Ps. 92:2
God's mercies ....Lam. 3:23

C. *For the unrighteous, a time of:*
Dread ....Deut. 28:67
Destruction ....Is. 17:14

D. *Figurative of:*
Man's unrighteousness ....Hos. 6:4
Judgment ....Zeph. 3:5
God's light ....Amos 5:8
Christ's return ....Rev. 2:28

Morning sacrifice—*part of Israelite worship*
Ritual described ....Ex. 29:38-42
Part of continual offering ....Num. 28:3-8
Under Ahaz ....2 Kin. 16:15

Morning Star

Figurative of Christ:
To church at Thyatira ....Rev. 2:24, 28
Christ, of Himself ....Rev. 22:16
Applied to Christ ....2 Pet. 1:19

Morsel—*a small piece of food*
Offered to angels ....Gen. 18:5
Rejected by a doomed man .....1 Sam. 28:22
Asked of a dying woman ....1 Kin. 17:11, 12
Better than strife ....Prov. 17:1
Exchanged for a birthright ......Heb. 12:16

Mortar (I)—*a vessel*
Vessel used for beating grains ...Num. 11:8
Used figuratively ....Prov. 27:22

Mortar (II)—*a building material*

Made of:
Clay ....Is. 41:25
Slime (bitumen) ....Gen. 11:3
Plaster ....Lev. 14:42, 45

Mortgage—*something given in security for debt*
Postexilic Jews burdened with ...Neh. 5:3

Mortification—*a putting to death*

A. *Objects of:*
Law ....Rom. 7:4
Sin ....Rom. 6:6, 11
Flesh ....Rom. 13:14
Members of earthly body ......Col. 3:5

B. *Agents of:*
Holy Spirit ....Rom. 8:13
Our obedience ....Rom. 6:17-19

Mosera (sing.), **Moseroth** (pl.)—*bond*
Place of Aaron's death and burial ....Deut. 10:6
Israelite encampment ....Num. 33:30, 31

Moses—*drawn out*

A. *Early life of* (first 40 years):
Descendant of Levi ....Ex. 2:1
Son of Amram and Jochebed ....Ex. 6:16-20
Brother of Aaron and Miriam ....Ex. 15:20
Born under slavery ....Ex. 2:1-10
Hid by mother ....Ex. 2:2, 3
Educated in Egyptian wisdom ....Acts 7:22
Refused Egyptian sonship ....Heb. 11:23-27
Defended his people ....Ex. 2:11-14
Rejected, flees to Midian ....Ex. 2:15

B. *In Midian* (second 40 years):
Married Zipporah ....Ex. 2:16-21
Father of two sons ....Ex. 2:22
Acts 7:29
Became Jethro's shepherd ....Ex. 3:1

C. *Leader of Israel* (last 40 years; to the end of his life):
Heard God's voice ....Ex. 3:2-6
God's plan revealed to him ..Ex. 3:7-10
Argued with God ....Ex. 4:1-17
Met Aaron ....Ex. 4:14-28
Assembled elders of Israelites ....Ex. 4:29-31
Rejected by Pharaoh and Israel ....Ex. 5:1-23
Conflict with Pharaoh; ten plagues sent ....Ex. 7—12
Commanded to institute the Passover ....Ex. 12:1-29; Heb. 11:28

D. *From Egypt to Sinai:*
Led people from Egypt ....Ex. 12:30-38
Observed the Passover ....Ex. 12:39-51
Healed bitter waters ....Ex. 15:22-27
People hunger; flesh and manna supplied ....Ex. 16:1-36; John 6:31, 32
Came to Sinai ....Ex. 19:1, 2

E. *At Sinai:*
Called to God's presence .....Acts 7:38
Prepared Israel for the Law ....Ex. 19:7-25
Received the Law ....Ex. 20—23
Confirmed the covenant with Israel ....Ex. 24:1-11
Stayed 40 days on Sinai .....Ex. 24:12-16
Shown the pattern of the tabernacle ....Ex. 25—31
Israel sins; Moses interceded ....Ex. 32:1-35
Recommissioned and encouraged ....Ex. 33:1-23
Instructions received; tabernacle erected ....Ex. 36—40
Consecrated Aaron ....Lev. 8:1-36
Numbered the men ....Num. 1:1-54
Observed the Passover ....Num. 9:1-5

F. *From Sinai to Kadesh-barnea:*
Resumed journey to Canaan ....Num. 10:11-36

M

SUBJECT REFERENCE

Complained; 70 elders appointed ... Num. 11:1-35
Spoke against by Miriam and Aaron ... Num. 12:1-6

G. *At Kadesh-barnea:*

Sent spies to Canaan ... Num. 13:1-33
Pleaded with rebellious Israel ... Num. 14:1-19
Announced God's judgment ... Num. 14:20-45

H. *Wanderings:*

Instructions received ... Num. 15:1-41
Sinned in anger ... Num. 20:1-13
Sent messengers to Edom ... Num. 20:14-21
Made a brass serpent ... Num. 21:4-9; John 3:14
Traveled toward Canaan ... Num. 21:10-20
Ordered destruction ... Num. 25:1-18
Numbered the people ... Num. 26:1-65
Gave instruction concerning inheritance ... Num. 27:1-11
Commissioned Joshua as his successor ... Num. 27:12-23
Received further laws ... Num. 28—30
Conquered Midianites ... Num. 31:1-54
Final instruction and records ... Num. 32—36
Enough ... Deut. 3:24-27
Reinterpreted the Law ... Deut. 1—31
Gave farewell messages ... Deut. 32—33
Committed written Law to the priests ... Deut. 31:9, 26
Saw the promised land ... Deut. 34:1-4
Died, in full strength, at 120 ... Deut. 34:5-7
Israel wept over ... Deut. 34:8

I. *Character of:*

Believer ... Heb. 11:23-28
Faithful ... Num. 12:7; Heb. 3:2-5
Meek ... Num. 12:3
Respected ... Ex. 33:8-10
Logical ... Num. 14:12-20
Impatient ... Ex. 5:22, 23
Given to anger ... Ex. 32:19

Moses, oracles of—*blessings on tribes of Israel*

Pronounced ... Deut. 33:6-25
Song introduces ... Deut. 33:2-5
Song concludes ... Deut. 33:26-29

Most High—*a name of God*

Melchizedek, priest of ... Heb. 7:1
Applied to Jesus by demons ... Mark 5:7, 8
Paul and Silas called servants of ... Acts 16:17

Mote—*a small particle*

Used in contrast to a beam ... Matt. 7:3, 5

Moth—*a garment-destroying insect*

Used figuratively of:

Inner corruption ... Is. 50:9
God's judgments ... Hos. 5:12
Man's insecurity ... Job 4:19
Man's fading glory ... Job 13:28

Mother

A. *Described as:*

Loving ... Ex. 2:1-25
Appreciative ... 2 Kin. 4:19-37
Weeping ... Luke 7:12-15
Remembering ... Luke 2:51

B. *Kinds of:*

Idolatrous ... Judg. 17:1-4
Troubled ... 1 Kin. 17:17-24
Cruel ... 2 Kin. 11:1, 2
Joyful ... Ps. 113:9
Good ... Prov. 31:1
Scheming ... Matt. 20:20-23
Prayerful ... Acts 12:12

C. *Duties toward:*

Honor ... Eph. 6:2
Obedience ... Deut. 21:18, 19
Protection ... Gen. 32:11
Provision ... John 19:25-27

D. *Figurative of:*

Israel ... Hos. 2:2, 5
Judah ... Ezek. 19:2, 10
Heavenly Jerusalem ... Gal. 4:26

SUBJECT REFERENCE

E. *Duties performed by:*

Selecting son's wife ... Gen. 21:21
Hospitality ... Gen. 24:55
Nourishment ... Ex. 2:8, 9
Provision ... 1 Kin. 1:11-21
Comfort ... Is. 66:12, 13

F. *Dishonor of, punished by:*

Death ... Lev. 20:9
Shame ... Prov. 19:26
Darkness ... Prov. 20:20
Destruction ... Prov. 28:24

Motherhood

A. *Described as:*

Painful ... Gen. 3:16
Sometimes dangerous ... Gen. 35:16-20
Yet joyful ... John 16:21
Object of prayer ... Gen. 25:21

B. *Blessings of:*

Fulfills divine Law ... Gen. 1:28
Makes joyful ... Ps. 113:9
Woman's "preserved" ... 1 Tim. 2:15

Mother-in-law

Judith's—grief ... Gen. 26:34, 35
Ruth's—loved ... Ruth 1:14-17
Peter's—healed by Christ ... Matt. 8:14, 15

Motive—*inner impulse producing outward action*

A. *Good:*

Questioned ... 2 Kin. 5:5-8
Misapplied ... Esth. 6:6-11
Misrepresented ... Job 1:9-11
Misunderstood ... Acts 21:26-31

B. *Evil:*

Prompted by Satan ... Matt. 16:22, 23
Designed to deceive ... Acts 5:1-10

Mouldy—*musty or stale*

Applied to bread ... Josh. 9:5, 12

Mount Baalah—*mistress*

Part of the territory of Judah ... Josh. 15:11

Mount Baal-hermon—*possessor of Hermon*

Lived on by nations that tested Israel ... Judg. 3:3, 4

Mount Carmel—*fruitful*

Prophets gathered together here ... 1 Kin. 18:19, 20
Elisha journeyed to ... 2 Kin. 2:25
Shunammite woman comes to Elisha ... 2 Kin. 4:25

Mount Ebal—*bald*

Cursed by God ... Deut. 11:29
Joshua built an altar here ... Josh. 8:30

Mount Gaash—*quaking*

Place of Joshua's burial ... Josh. 24:30

Mount Gerizim—*rocky*

Place the blessed stood ... Deut. 27:12
Jotham spoke to people of Shechem here ... Judg. 9:7

Mount Gilboa—*bubbling spring*

Men of Israel slain ... 1 Sam. 31:1
Saul and his sons slain here ... 1 Sam. 31:8

Mount Gilead—*heap of witness*

Gideon divides the people for battle ... Judg. 7:3

Mount Hor—*mountain*

LORD spoke to Moses and Aaron ... Num. 20:23
Aaron died there ... Num. 20:25-28

Mount Horeb—*desolate*

Sons of Israel stripped of ornaments ... Ex. 33:6

Mount of Olives

Prophecy concerning ... Zech. 14:4
Jesus sent disciples for donkey ... Matt. 21:1, 2; Mark 11:1, 2
Jesus speaks of the signs of His coming ... Matt. 24:3; Mark 13:3, 4
After the Lord's supper went out to ... Matt. 26:30; Mark 14:26
Called Mount Olivet ... Luke 19:29; Luke 21:37

SUBJECT REFERENCE

Mount Seir—*rugged*

Horites defeated by Chedorlaomer ... Gen. 14:5, 6

Mount Shepher—*beauty*

Israelites camped at ... Num. 33:23, 24

Mount Sinai

Lord descended upon, in fire ... Ex. 19:18
Lord called Moses to the top ... Ex. 19:20
The glory of the LORD rested on, for six days ... Ex. 24:16

Mount Tabor—*broken*

Deborah sent Barak there to defeat Canaanites ... Judg. 4:6-14

Mount Zion

Survivors shall go out from ... 2 Kin. 19:31

Mountain—*a high elevation of earth*

A. *Mentioned in the Bible:*

Abarim ... Num. 33:47, 48
Ararat ... Gen. 8:4
Bashan ... Ps. 68:15
Carmel ... 1 Kin. 18:19
Ebal ... Deut. 27:13
Gaash ... Judg. 2:9
Gerizim ... Deut. 11:29
Gilboa ... 2 Sam. 1:6, 21
Hachilah ... 1 Sam. 23:19
Hermon ... Josh. 13:11
Hor ... Num. 34:7, 8
Horeb (same as Sinai) ... Ex. 3:1
Lebanon ... Deut. 3:25
Mizar ... Ps. 42:6
Moreh ... Judg. 7:1
Moriah ... Gen. 22:2
Nebo ... Deut. 34:1
Olives or Olivet ... Matt. 24:3
Pisgah ... Num. 21:20
Sinai ... Ex. 19:2-20
Sion or Zion ... 2 Sam. 5:7
Tabor ... Judg. 4:6-14

B. *In Christ's life, place of:*

Temptation ... Matt. 4:8
Sermon ... Matt. 5:1
Prayer ... Matt. 14:23
Transfiguration ... Matt. 17:1
Prophecy ... Matt. 24:3
Agony ... Matt. 26:30, 31
Ascension ... Luke 24:50

C. *Uses of:*

Boundaries ... Num. 34:7, 8
Distant vision ... Deut. 3:27
Hunting ... 1 Sam. 26:20
Warfare ... 1 Sam. 17:3
Protection ... Amos 6:1
Refuge ... Matt. 24:16
Idolatrous worship ... Is. 65:7
Assembly sites ... Josh. 8:30-33

D. *Significant Old Testament events on:*

Ark rested upon (Ararat) ... Gen. 8:4
Abraham's testing (Moriah) ... Gen. 22:1-19
Giving of the Law (Sinai) ... Ex. 19:2-25
Moses' view of Canaan (Pisgah) ... Deut. 34:1
Combat with Baalism (Carmel) ... 1 Kin. 18:19-42
David's city (Zion) ... 2 Sam. 5:7

E. *Figurative of:*

God's:
Protection ... Is. 31:4
Dwelling ... Is. 8:18
Judgments ... Jer. 13:16
Gospel age ... Is. 27:13
Messiah's advent ... Is. 40:9
Great joy ... Is. 44:23
Great difficulties ... Matt. 21:21
Pride of man ... Luke 3:5
Supposed faith ... 1 Cor. 13:2

Mourning—*expression of sorrow*

A. *Caused by:*

Death ... Gen. 50:10
Defection ... 1 Sam. 15:35
Disobedience ... Ezra 9:4-7
Desolation ... Joel 1:9, 10
Defeat ... Rev. 18:11
Discouragement ... Ps. 42:9
Disease ... Job 2:5-8

SUBJECT — REFERENCE

B. *Transformed into:*
- Gladness ... Is. 51:11
- Hope ... John 11:23-28
- Everlasting joy ... Is. 35:10

C. *Signs of:*
- Tearing of clothing ... 2 Sam. 3:31, 32
- Ashes on head ... 2 Sam. 13:19
- Sackcloth ... Gen. 37:34
- Neglect of appearance ... 2 Sam. 19:24
- Presence of mourners ... John 11:19, 31
- Apparel ... 2 Sam. 14:2
- Shave head ... Jer. 16:6, 7

Mouse, mice—*a small quadruped*
- Accounted unclean ... Lev. 11:29
- Destructive of crops ... 1 Sam. 6:5
- Eaten by idolatrous Israelites ... Is. 66:17

Mouth

A. *Descriptive of:*
- Top of a well ... Gen. 29:2, 3, 8
- Opening of a sack ... Gen. 42:27, 28
- Man's ... Job 3:1

B. *Exhortations concerning:*
- Make all acceptable ... Ps. 19:14
- Keep with a bridle ... Ps. 39:1
- Set a watch before ... Ps. 141:3
- Keep the corrupt from ... Eph. 4:29
- Keep filthy speech from ... Col. 3:8

C. *Of unregenerate, source of:*
- Idolatry ... 1 Kin. 19:18
- Lying ... 1 Kin. 22:13, 22, 23
- Unfaithfulness ... Ps. 5:9
- Cursing ... Ps. 10:7
- Pride ... Ps. 17:10
- Evil ... Ps. 50:19
- Lies ... Ps. 63:11
- Vanity ... Ps. 144:8, 11
- Foolishness ... Prov. 15:2, 14

D. *Of regenerate, used for:*
- Prayer ... 1 Sam. 1:12
- God's Law ... Josh. 1:8
- Praise ... Ps. 34:1
- Wisdom ... Ps. 37:30
- Testimony ... Eph. 6:9
- Confession ... Rom. 10:8-10
- Righteousness ... Ps. 71:15

Move—*to change the position*

A. *Of God's Spirit in:*
- Creation ... Gen. 1:2
- Man ... Judg. 13:25
- Prophets ... 2 Pet. 1:21

B. *Of things immovable:*
- Righteous ... Ps. 112:6
- City of God ... Ps. 46:4, 5
- Eternal kingdom ... Ps. 96:10

Mowing—*to cut grass*
- First growth for taxes ... Amos 7:1
- Left on the ground ... Ps. 72:6

Moza—*a going forth*
1. Descendant of Judah ... 1 Chr. 2:46
2. Descendant of Saul ... 1 Chr. 8:36, 37

Mozah—*drained*
- A Benjamite town ... Josh. 18:21, 26

Mufflers—*an elaborate veil*
- Worn by women ... Is. 3:16, 19

Mulberry tree
- Referred to by Jesus ... Luke 17:6

Mule—*a hybrid between a horse and a donkey*
- Breeding of, forbidden ... Lev. 19:19
- Sign of kingship ... 1 Kin. 1:33
- Used in trade ... Ezek. 27:14
- Considered stubborn ... Ps. 32:9

Multiply—*to increase in quantity or quality*

A. *Of good things:*
- Holy seed ... Jer. 30:19
- Churches ... Acts 9:31
- Word of God ... Acts 12:24
- God's wonders ... Ex. 7:3
- Loaves and fish ... Matt. 15:32-39; John 6:1-15

B. *Secret of:*
- God's:
  - Promise ... Gen. 16:10

SUBJECT — REFERENCE

- Oath ... Gen. 26:3, 4
- Man's obedience ... Deut. 7:12, 13

Multitude—*a large number of people*

A. *Dangers of:*
- Mixed, source of evil ... Ex. 12:38
- Follow after in doing evil ... Ex. 23:2
- Sacrifices, vain ... Is. 1:11

B. *Christ's compassion upon:*
- Teaching ... Matt. 5:1
- Healing ... Matt. 12:15
- Teaching parables to ... Matt. 13:1-3, 34
- Feeding ... Matt. 14:15-21

C. *Their attitude toward Christ:*
- Reaction to ... Matt. 9:8, 33
- Recognition of ... Matt. 14:5; Matt. 21:46
- Reception of ... Matt. 21:8-11
- Running after ... John 6:2
- Rejection of ... Matt. 27:20

Munificence—*generous in giving*

Measure of, on:
- God's part ... Mal. 3:10
- Israel's part ... Ex. 36:3-7
- Judah's part ... 1 Chr. 29:3-9
- Christian's part ... 2 Cor. 8:1-5

Munition
- Kept for war ... Nah. 2:1

Muppim—*obscurities*
- Son of Benjamin ... Gen. 46:21
- Called Shupham ... Num. 26:39
- Shuppim and Shephuphan ... 1 Chr. 7:12, 15

Murder

A. *Defined as:*
- Coming out of the heart ... Matt. 15:19
- Result from anger ... Matt. 5:21, 22
- Work of the flesh ... Gal. 5:19
- Excluding from eternal life ... 1 John 3:15

B. *Guilt of:*
- Determined by witnesses ... Num. 35:30
- Not redeemable ... Num. 35:30
- Not forgiven by flight to the altar ... Ex. 21:14

C. *Penalty of:*
- Ordained by God ... Gen. 9:6
- Executed by avenger of blood ... Deut. 19:6

See Homicide

Murmuring—*sullen dissatisfaction with things*

A. *Caused by:*
- Thirst ... Ex. 15:24
- Hunger ... Ex. 16:2, 3, 8
- Fear ... Num. 14:1-4

B. *Against Christ, because of His:*
- Practices ... Luke 15:1, 2
- Pronouncements ... John 6:41-61

C. *Of Christians:*
- Provoked ... Acts 6:1
- Forbidden ... John 6:43
- Excluded ... Phil. 2:14

Murrain—*pestilence*
- Fifth Egyptian plague ... Ex. 9:1-6

Mushi—*drawn out*
- Son of Merari ... Ex. 6:19
- Descendants of, called Mushites ... Num. 3:33; Num. 26:58

Music

A. *Used in:*
- Farewells ... Gen. 31:27
- Entertainments ... Is. 5:12
- Weddings ... Jer. 7:34
- Funerals ... Matt. 9:18, 23
- Sacred processions ... 1 Chr. 13:6-8
- Victory celebrations ... Ex. 15:20, 21
- Coronation services ... 2 Chr. 23:11, 13
- Dedication services ... 2 Chr. 5:11-13

B. *Influence of, upon:*
- Mental disorders ... 1 Sam. 16:14-17, 23
- Sorrowful ... Ps. 137:1-4

C. *List of instruments of:*
- Cornet ... Dan. 3:5, 7

SUBJECT — REFERENCE

- Cymbal ... 1 Cor. 13:1
- Dulcimer ... Dan. 3:5, 10, 15
- Harp ... 1 Sam. 16:16, 23
- Organ ... Ps. 150:4
- Pipe ... Is. 30:29
- Psaltery ... 1 Sam. 10:5
- Sackbut ... Dan. 3:5, 7, 10
- Timbrel ... Gen. 31:27; Ex. 15:20
- Trumpet ... Josh. 6:4
- Viol ... Is. 5:12
- Complete orchestra ... 2 Sam. 6:5

Music in Christian worship
- From heart ... Eph. 5:19
- Means of teaching ... Col. 3:16

Must—*something that is imperative*

A. *Concerning Christ's:*
- Preaching ... Luke 4:43
- Suffering ... Matt. 16:21
- Death ... John 3:14
- Fulfillment of Scripture ... Matt. 26:54
- Resurrection ... John 20:9
- Ascension ... Acts 3:21
- Reign ... 1 Cor. 15:25

B. *Concerning the believer's:*
- Belief ... Heb. 11:6
- Regeneration ... John 3:7
- Salvation ... Acts 4:12
- Worship ... John 4:24
- Duty ... Acts 9:6
- Suffering ... Acts 9:16
- Mission ... Acts 19:21
- Moral life ... Titus 1:7
- Inner life ... 2 Tim. 2:24
- Judgment ... 2 Cor. 5:10

C. *Concerning prophecy:*
- Gospel's proclamation ... Mark 13:10
- Gentiles' inclusion ... John 10:16
- Earth's tribulations ... Matt. 24:6
- Resurrection ... 1 Cor. 15:53

Mustard seed—*very small seed*
- Kingdom compared to ... Matt. 13:31
- Faith compared to ... Matt. 17:20

Mutability—*capable of change*

A. *Asserted of:*
- Physical world ... Matt. 5:18
- Earthly world ... 1 John 2:15-17
- Old covenant ... Heb. 8:8-13
- Present order ... 2 Cor. 4:18

B. *Denied of:*
- God ... Mal. 3:6
- Christ ... Heb. 1:10, 11; Heb. 13:8

See Immutability; Move

Mutilation—*to maim, to damage, to disfigure*

A. *Object of, forbidden:*
- On the body ... Lev. 19:28
- For:
  - Priesthood ... Lev. 21:18
  - Sacrifice ... Lev. 22:22
  - Mourning ... Jer. 41:5-7

B. *Practiced by:*
- Jews ... Judg. 19:29, 30
- Philistines ... Judg. 16:21
- Canaanites ... Judg. 1:6, 7
- Baal prophets ... 1 Kin. 18:28

Mutiny—*revolt against authority*
- By Israelites ... Num. 14:1-4

Mutual—*a common interest*
- Spoken of faith ... Rom. 1:12

Muzzling

Applied:
- To oxen ... Deut. 25:4
- Figuratively, to Christians ... 1 Cor. 9:9-11

Myra—*a city of Lycia*
- Paul changes ships here ... Acts 27:5, 6

Myrrh

A. *Dried gum (Heb., mor) of a balsam tree, used:*
- In anointing oil ... Ex. 30:23
- As a perfume ... Ps. 45:8
- For beauty treatment ... Esth. 2:12
- Brought as gifts ... Matt. 2:11

SUBJECT REFERENCE

Given as a sedative .... Mark 15:23
Used for embalming .... John 19:38, 39

B. *Fragrant resin* (Heb., *lot*) *used:*

In commerce .... Gen. 37:25
As presents .... Gen. 43:11

Myrtle—*a shrub*

Found in mountains; booths made of .... Neh. 8:15
Figurative of the Gospel .... Is. 41:19
Used symbolically .... Zech. 1:10, 11

Mysia—*a province of Asia Minor*

Paul and Silas pass through ..... Acts 16:7, 8

Mystery—*something unknown except by divine revelation*

A. *Concerning God's:*

Secrets .... Deut. 29:29
Providence .... Rom. 11:33-36
Sovereignty .... Rom. 9:11-23
Prophecies .... 1 Pet. 1:10-12
Predestination .... Rom. 8:29, 30

B. *Concerning Christianity:*

Christ's incarnation .... 1 Tim. 3:16
Christ's nature .... Col. 2:2
Kingdom of God .... Luke 8:10
Christian faith .... 1 Tim. 3:9
Indwelling Christ .... Col. 1:26, 27
Union of all believers .... Eph. 3:4-9
Israel's blindness .... Rom. 11:25
Lawlessness .... 2 Thess. 2:7
Harlot Babylon .... Rev. 17:5, 7
Resurrection of saints .... 1 Cor. 15:51
God's completed purpose .... Rev. 10:7

Mythology, referred to

Jupiter .... Acts 14:12, 13
Mercurius .... Acts 14:12
Pantheon .... Acts 17:16-23
Diana .... Acts 19:24-41
Castor and Pollox .... Acts 28:11

Myths—*speculative and philosophical fable or allegory*

Condemned .... 1 Tim. 1:4
Fables .... 1 Tim. 4:7
False .... 2 Tim. 4:4

N

Naam—*pleasantness*

Son of Caleb .... 1 Chr. 4:15

Naamah—*sweet, pleasant*

1. Daughter of Lamech .... Gen. 4:19-22
2. Ammonite wife of Solomon; mother of King Rehoboam .... 1 Kin. 14:21, 31
3. Town of Judah .... Josh. 15:1, 41

Naaman—*pleasant*

1. Son of Benjamin .... Gen. 46:21
2. Captain in the Syrian army .. 2 Kin. 5:1-11
Healed of his leprosy .... 2 Kin. 5:14-17
Referred to by Christ ...... Luke 4:27

Naamathite—*an inhabitant of Naamah*

Applied to Zophar, Job's friend .... Job 2:11

Naamites

Descendants of Naaman .... Num. 26:40

Naarah, Naarath—*girl*

1. Wife of Ashur .... 1 Chr. 4:5, 6
2. Town of Ephraim .... Josh. 16:7
Same as Naaran .... 1 Chr. 7:28

Naarai—*pleasantness of Jehovah*

One of David's mighty men ..... 1 Chr. 11:37

Nabal—*fool*

Wealthy sheep owner .... 1 Sam. 25:2, 3
Refuses David's request .... 1 Sam. 25:4-12
Abigail, wife of, appeases David's wrath against .... 1 Sam. 25:13-35
Drunk, dies of a stroke .... 1 Sam. 25:36-39
Widow of, becomes David's wife .... 1 Sam. 25:39-42

SUBJECT REFERENCE

Naboth—*sprout*

Owner of vineyard coveted by King Ahab .... 1 Kin. 21:1-4
Accused falsely of blasphemy and disloyalty .... 1 Kin. 21:5-16
Murder of, avenged .... 1 Kin. 21:17-25

Nachon—*prepared*

Threshing floor, site of Uzzah's death .... 2 Sam. 6:6, 7

Called:

Perez-uzzah ("breach") .... 2 Sam. 6:8
Chidon .... 1 Chr. 13:9

Nadab—*willing, liberal*

1. Eldest of Aaron's four sons .. Ex. 6:23
Takes part in affirming covenant .... Ex. 24:1, 9-12
Becomes priest .... Ex. 28:1
Consumed by fire .... Lev. 10:1-7
Dies childless .... Num. 3:4
2. Judahite .... 1 Chr. 2:28, 30
3. Benjamite .... 1 Chr. 8:30
4. King of Israel .... 1 Kin. 14:20
Killed by Baasha .... 1 Kin. 15:25-31

Naggai

Ancestor of Christ .... Luke 3:25

Nagging woman

Gets Samson's secret .... Judg. 16:13-17
Called brawling .... Prov. 21:9, 19
Undesirable .... Prov. 25:24
Prov. 27:15

Nahalal, Nahalol—*drinking place for flocks*

Village of Zebulun .... Josh. 19:10, 15
Assigned to Merarite Levites .... Josh. 21:35
Canaanites not driven from ..... Judg. 1:30

Nahaliel—*valley of God*

Israelite camp .... Num. 21:19

Naham—*consolation*

Father of Keilah .... 1 Chr. 4:19

Nahamani—*compassionate*

Returned after the exile .... Neh. 7:7

Naharai—*snorting*

Armor-bearer of Joab .... 2 Sam. 23:37
1 Chr. 11:39

Nahash—*serpent*

1. King of Ammon; makes impossible demands .... 1 Sam. 11:1-15
2. King of Ammon who treats David kindly .... 2 Sam. 10:2
Son of, helps David .... 2 Sam. 17:27-29
3. Father of Abigail and Zeruiah, David's half sisters .... 2 Sam. 17:25

Nahath—*descent*

1. Edomite chief .... Gen. 36:13
2. Kohathite Levite .... 1 Chr. 6:26
Called Tohu .... 1 Sam. 1:1
3. Levite in Hezekiah's reign ... 2 Chr. 31:13

Nahbi—*concealed*

Spy of Naphtali .... Num. 13:14

Nahor, Nachor—*snorting*

1. Grandfather of Abraham .... Gen. 11:24-26
2. Son of Terah, brother of Abraham .... Gen. 11:27
Marries Milcah, begets eight sons by her and four by concubine ..... Gen. 11:29
City of Haran .... Gen. 24:10
God of .... Gen. 31:53

Nahshon

Judahite leader .... Num. 1:4, 7
Aaron's brother-in-law .... Ex. 6:23
Ancestor of David .... Ruth 4:20-22
Ancestor of Christ .... Matt. 1:4

Nahum—*full of comfort*

Inspired prophet to Judah concerning Nineveh .... Nah. 1:1

Nahum, the Book of—*a book of the Old Testament*

The awesomeness of God .... Nah. 1:1-15
The destruction of Nineveh ..... Nah. 2—3

SUBJECT REFERENCE

Nail

A. *Significant uses of:*

Killing a man .... Judg. 4:21, 25
Holding idols in place .... Is. 41:7
Fastening Christ to cross .... John 20:25

B. *Figurative uses of:*

Words fixed in the memory .. Eccl. 12:11
Revived nation .... Ezra 9:8
Messiah's kingdom .... Is. 22:23, 24
Messiah's death .... Is. 22:25
Atonement for man's sin .... Col. 2:14

Nain—*pleasant*

Village south of Nazareth; Jesus raises widow's son here .... Luke 7:11-17

Naioth—*habitations*

Prophets' school in Ramah ..... 1 Sam. 19:18, 19, 22, 23

Naked, nakedness—*nude, nudity*

A. *Used of man's:*

Original state .... Gen. 2:25
Sinful state .... Gen. 3:7, 10, 11
State of grace .... Rom. 8:35
Disembodied state .... 2 Cor. 5:3

B. *Evil of:*

Strictly forbidden .... Lev. 18:6-20
Brings a curse .... Gen. 9:21-25
Judged by God .... Ezek. 22:10

C. *Instances of:*

Noah guilty of .... Gen. 9:21-23
Forbidden, to priests .... Ex. 20:26
Michal rebukes David for .... 2 Sam. 6:20-23

D. *Putting clothing on:*

Indicates a changed life ..... Mark 5:15
Promises a reward .... Matt. 25:34-40
Takes away shame .... Rev. 3:18
Sign of true faith .... James 2:15-17

E. *Figurative of:*

Separation from God .... Is. 20:3
Israel's unworthiness .... Ezek. 16:7-22
Judah's spiritual adultery .... Ezek. 16:36-38
God's judgment .... Ezek. 16:39
Spiritual need .... Hos. 2:9
Wickedness .... Nah. 3:4, 5
Needy .... Matt. 25:36, 38
God's knowledge .... Heb. 4:13
Unpreparedness .... Rev. 16:15

Name—*a word used to identify a person, animal or thing*

A. *Determined by:*

Events of the time .... Gen. 30:8
Prophetic position .... Gen. 25:26
Fondness of hope .... Gen. 29:32-35
Change of character .... John 1:42
Innate character .... 1 Sam. 25:25
Coming events .... Is. 8:1-4
Divine mission .... Matt. 1:21

B. *Of God, described as:*

Great .... Josh. 7:9
Secret .... Judg. 13:18
Glorious .... Is. 63:14
Everlasting .... Ps. 135:13
Excellent .... Ps. 148:13
Holy .... Is. 57:15

C. *Of God, evil acts against:*

Taken in vain .... Ex. 20:7
Sworn falsely .... Lev. 19:12
Lies spoken in .... Zech. 13:3
Despised .... Mal. 1:6

D. *Of God, proper attitude toward:*

Exalt .... Ps. 34:3
Praise .... Ps. 54:6
Love .... Ps. 69:36

E. *Of Christ:*

Given before birth .... Matt. 1:21, 23
Hated by the world .... Matt. 10:22
Deeds done in, rewarded .... Matt. 10:42
Believers baptized in .... Acts 2:38
Miracles performed by ...... Acts 3:16
Believers suffer for .... Acts 5:41
Speaking in .... Acts 9:27, 29
Gentiles called by .... Acts 15:14, 17
Final subjection to .... Phil. 2:9, 10

F. *Of believers:*

Called everlasting .... Is. 56:5

SUBJECT	REFERENCE
Written in heaven	Luke 10:20
Called evil by world	Luke 6:22
Known by Christ	John 10:3
Confessed by Christ	Rev. 3:5
"Called by"	Is. 62:2 Rev. 3:12

Names of Christ (see Christ, names of)

Naomi—*my delight*

Widow of Elimelech	Ruth 1:1-3
Returns to Bethlehem with Ruth	Ruth 1:14-19
Arranges Ruth's marriage to Boaz	Ruth 3—4
Considers Ruth's child (Obed) her own	Ruth 4:16, 17

Naphish—*numerous*

Ishmael's eleventh son	Gen. 25:15

Naphtali—*my wrestling*

1. Son of Jacob by Bilhah	Gen. 30:1, 8
Sons of, form tribe	Gen. 46:24
Receives Jacob's blessing	Gen. 49:21, 28
2. Tribe of	Num. 1:42
Stationed last	Num. 2:29-31
Territory assigned by	Josh. 19:32-39
Canaanites not driven out by	Judg. 1:33
Barak becomes famous	Judg. 4:6, 14-16
Bravery of, praised	Judg. 5:18
Warriors of, under Gideon	Judg. 7:23
Warriors of, help David	1 Chr. 12:34
Conquered by wars	1 Kin. 15:20
Taken captive	2 Kin. 15:29
Prophecy of a great light in	Is. 9:1-7
Fulfilled in Christ's ministry in	Matt. 4:12-16

Naphtuhim

Fourth son of Mizraim; probably district around	Gen. 10:13

Narcissus

Christian in Rome	Rom. 16:11

Nathan—*gift*

1. Son of David	2 Sam. 5:14
Mary's lineage traced through	Zech. 12:12
2. Judahite	1 Chr. 2:36
3. Prophet under David and Solomon	1 Chr. 29:29
Reveals God's plan to David	2 Sam. 7:2-29
Rebukes David's sin	2 Sam. 12:1-15
Renames Solomon as Jedidiah	2 Sam. 12:24, 25
Reveals Adonijah's plot	1 Kin. 1:10-46
Sons of, in official positions	1 Kin. 4:1, 2, 5
4. Father of Igal	2 Sam. 23:36
5. A chief among returnees	Ezra 8:16
6. One who divorced his foreign wife	Ezra 10:34, 39

Nathanael—*God has given*

One of Christ's disciples	John 1:45-51

Nathan-melech—*the king has given*

An official in Josiah's reign	2 Kin. 23:11

National duties (see Citizen, citizenship)

Nations—*people under a sovereign government*

A. *Of the world:*

Descendants of Noah's sons	Gen. 10:32
Originate in a person	Gen. 19:37, 38
Made of one blood	Acts 17:26
Separated by God	Deut. 32:8
Inherit separate characteristics	Gen. 25:23
Laden with iniquity	Is. 1:4
Destroyed by corruption	Lev. 18:26-28
Exalted by righteousness	Prov. 14:34
Father of many nations	Gen. 17:4
LORD will set you high above all	Deut. 28:1
Subject to repentance	Jer. 18:7-10
Judged by God	Gen. 15:14
Under God's control	Jer. 25:8-14
Future of, revealed	Dan. 2:27-45
Gospel to be preached to all	Matt. 24:14
Sarah shall be mother of many	Gen. 17:16

B. *Of Israel:*

Descendants of Abraham	Gen. 12:2 John 8:33, 37
Designated	Ex. 19:6
Given blessings	Deut. 4:7, 8 Rom. 9:4, 5
Punished by God	Jer. 25:1-11
Scattered among nations	Neh. 1:8 Luke 21:24
Christ died for	John 11:51

C. *Of the true people of God:*

Described as righteous	Is. 26:2
Born in a day	Is. 66:8
Accounted fruitful	Matt. 21:43
Believers are	1 Pet. 2:9

Nations, table of

Record	Gen. 10:1-32

Natural—*that which is innate and real; not artificial or man-made*

A. *Described as:*

Physical origin	James 1:23
Normal	Rom. 1:26
Unregenerate	1 Cor. 2:14
Unnatural	2 Pet. 2:12
Temporal	1 Cor. 15:46

B. *Contrasted with:*

Acquired	Rom. 11:21, 24
Perverted	Rom. 1:26, 27
Spiritual (life)	1 Cor. 2:14
Spiritual (body)	1 Cor. 15:44-46

Naturalization—*becoming a citizen of an adopted country*

Natural level, rights of	Acts 22:25-28
Spiritual level, blessings of	Eph. 2:12-19

Natural man

Does not accept things of God	1 Cor. 2:14
Contrasted with spiritual	1 Cor. 15:44-46

Natural religion

A. *Contents of, God's:*

Glory	Ps. 19:1-3
Nature	Rom. 1:19, 20
Sovereignty	Acts 17:23-31
Goodness	Acts 14:15-17

B. *Characteristics of:*

Original	Rom. 1:19, 20
Universal	Rom. 10:18
Inadequate	Rom. 2:12-15
Corrupted	Rom. 1:21-32
Valuable	Dan. 5:18-23

Nature—*the essential elements resident in something*

A. *Descriptive of:*

Right order of things	Rom. 1:26
Natural sense of right	Rom. 2:14
Physical origin	Rom. 2:27
Non-existence	Gal. 4:8
Man's natural depravity	Eph. 2:3
Divine	2 Pet. 1:4

B. *Of man's unregenerate, described as:*

Under wrath	Eph. 2:3
Source of:	
Iniquity	James 3:6
Corruption	2 Pet. 2:12

Nature, beauties of

Reveal God's glory	Ps. 19:1-6
Greater than outward appearance	Matt. 6:28-30
Descriptive of spiritual blessings	Is. 35:1, 2

Naughty person

Wrongly ascribed	1 Sam. 17:28
Descriptive of the wicked	Prov. 6:12
Downfall of	Prov. 11:6

Navel—*the point at which the umbilical cord is attached*

A. *Used literally of:*

Lover's appeal	Song 7:2

B. *Used figuratively of:*

Inward self	Prov. 3:8
Israel's wretched condition	Ezek. 16:4

Navy—*ships owned by a country*

Solomon's	1 Kin. 9:26
Jehoshaphat's	1 Kin. 22:48

Nazarene—*a native of Nazareth*

Jesus to be called	Matt. 2:23
Descriptive of Jesus' followers	Acts 24:5

Nazareth

A. *Town in Galilee:*

Considered obscure	John 1:46
City of Jesus' parents	Matt. 2:23
Early home of Jesus	Luke 2:39-51
Jesus departs from	Mark 1:9
Jesus rejected by	Luke 4:16-30

B. *As a title of honor descriptive of Jesus:*

Anointed by the Spirit	Acts 10:38
Risen Lord	Acts 22:8

Nazirite—*one especially consecrated to God*

A. *Methods of becoming, by:*

Birth	Judg. 13:5, 7
Vow	Num. 6:2

B. *Requirements of:*

Separation	Num. 6:4
No:	
Strong drink	Num. 6:3, 4
Shaving	Num. 6:5
Defilement	Num. 6:6, 7
Corruption	Amos 2:11, 12
Holiness	Num. 6:8

C. *Examples of:*

Samson	Judg. 16:17
Samuel	1 Sam. 1:11-28
John the Baptist	Luke 1:13, 15
Christians	2 Cor. 6:17

Neah—*the settlement*

Town in Zebulun	Josh. 19:13

Neapolis—*new city*

Seaport of Philippi	Acts 16:11

Near—*close at hand* (in place or time)

A. *Of dangers, from:*

Prostitute	Prov. 7:8
Destruction	Prov. 10:14
God's judgment	Joel 3:14

B. *Of the Messianic salvation, as:*

Promised	Is. 50:8
Available	Is. 51:5

C. *Of Christ's return, described by:*

Christ	Matt. 24:33
Paul	Rom. 13:11

Neariah—*Jehovah drives away*

1. Descendant of David	1 Chr. 3:22, 23
2. Simeonite captain	1 Chr. 4:42

Nearness of God

A. *Old Testament:*

In sense of time	Is. 46:13 Zeph. 1:14
In prayer	Is. 55:6

B. *New Testament:*

In sense of time	Rev. 1:1-3 Rev. 22:10
In prayer	Phil. 4:5-9

Nebai—*projecting*

Leader who signs the sealed covenant	Neh. 10:19

Nebaioth

Eldest son of Ishmael	Gen. 25:13
Descendants of, form Arabian tribe	Is. 60:7

Neballat—*hard, firm*

Postexilic town of Benjamin	Neh. 11:31, 34

Nebat—*look*

Father of Jeroboam	1 Kin. 11:26

Nebo—*height*

1. Babylonian god of literature and science	Is. 46:1

N

SUBJECT REFERENCE

2. Mountain peak near Jericho ... Num. 33:47
Name of Pisgah's summit ... Deut. 34:1

3. Moabite town near Mt. Nebo ... Num. 32:3
Restored by Reubenites ... Num. 32:37, 38
Mentioned in the prophecy ... Is. 15:2

4. Town in Judah ... Ezra 2:29

Nebuchadnezzar—*Nebo, defend the boundary*

A. *Life of:*
Monarch of the Neo-Babylonian Empire (605–562 B.C.); defeats Pharaoh Necho at Carchemish ... 2 Chr. 35:20; Jer. 46:2
Besieges Jerusalem; carries captives to Babylon ... Dan. 1:1, 2
Crushes Jehoiachin's revolt (597 B.C.) ... 2 Kin. 24:10-17
Carries sacred vessels to Babylon ... 2 Kin. 24:13
Destroys Jerusalem; captures Zedekiah (587 B.C.) ... Jer. 39:5, 6
Leads attack on Tyre ... Ezek. 26:7

B. *Features concerning:*
Builder of Babylon ... Dan. 4:30
First of four great empires ... Dan. 2:26-48
Instrument of God's judgment ... Jer. 27:8
Called God's servant ... Jer. 25:9
Afflicted with insanity ... Dan. 4:28-37

C. *Prophecies concerning his:*
Conquest of Judah and Jerusalem ... Jer. 21:7, 10
Destruction of Jerusalem ... Jer. 32:28-36
Conquest of other nations ... Jer. 27:7-9
Conquest of Egypt ... Jer. 43:10-13
Destruction of Tyre ... Ezek. 26:7-12
Utter destruction ... Is. 14:4-27

Nebushasban—*Nebo delivers me*
Babylonian officer ... Jer. 39:13

Nebuzar-adan—*Nebo has given seed*
Nebuchadnezzar's captain at siege of Jerusalem ... 2 Kin. 25:8-20
Carries out Nebuchadnezzar's commands ... 2 Kin. 25:8-20
Protects Jeremiah ... Jer. 39:11-14

Necessary, necessity—*something imperative*

A. *As applied to God's plan:*
Preaching to the Jews first ... Acts 13:46
Change of the Law ... Heb. 7:12
Of Christ's sacrifice ... Heb. 8:3

B. *In the Christian's life:*
Wise decisions ... 2 Cor. 9:5
Personal needs ... Acts 20:34

See Must

Neck

A. *Uses of:*
Ornaments ... Ezek. 16:11
Beauty ... Song 4:4
Authority ... Gen. 41:42

B. *Significant acts performed by:*
Emotional salutation ... Gen. 45:14
Subjection of enemies ... Josh. 10:24

C. *Figurative of:*
Servitude ... Gen. 27:40
Severe punishment ... Is. 8:8
Rescue ... Is. 52:2

See Yoke

Necklace—*an ornament worn about the neck*
Signifying rank ... Gen. 41:41, 42
Worn by animals ... Judg. 8:26

Necromancer—*one who inquires of the dead*
Strongly condemned ... Deut. 18:10, 11
Consulted by King Saul ... 1 Sam. 28:7-19
Consultation with, rebuked ... Is. 8:19

Nedabiah—*Jehovah has been gracious*
Son of King Jeconiah ... 1 Chr. 3:18

Need(s)—*an inner or outward lack; a compulsion to something*

A. *Physical necessity, arising from lack of:*
Food ... Deut. 15:8
Provisions ... 2 Chr. 2:16

SUBJECT REFERENCE

B. *Moral necessity, arising from:*
Spiritual immaturity ... Heb. 5:12
Order of things ... Matt. 3:14
Spiritual need ... Luke 10:42

C. *Promises concerning supply of:*
Promised ... Matt. 6:8, 32
Provided ... Acts 2:45
Fulfilled ... Rev. 21:23

D. *Caused by:*
Riotous living ... Luke 15:14

E. *Provision against, by:*
Help of others ... 2 Cor. 9:12

F. *Reaction to, shown in:*
Humble submission to God's will ... Phil. 4:11, 12

See Must; Necessary, necessity

Needle—*a sharp instrument used in sewing or embroidering*
Product of, used in tabernacle ... Ex. 26:36
Figurative of something impossible ... Matt. 19:24

Needlework—*embroidered work*
Of the tabernacle ... Ex. 26:36; Ex. 28:39; Ex. 38:18

Needy—*the poor*

A. *Evil treatment of:*
Oppression ... Amos 4:1
Injustice toward ... Is. 10:2

B. *Promise toward:*
God's:
Remembrance of ... Ps. 9:18
Deliverance ... Ps. 35:10
Salvation of ... Ps. 72:4-13
Exaltation of ... Ps. 113:7
Strength of ... Is. 25:4

C. *Right treatment of:*
Recommended ... Deut. 24:14, 15
Remembered ... Jer. 22:16
Rewarded ... Matt. 25:34-40

See Poor, poverty

Negev—*dry, parched; denotes southern Palestine*
Hebron located in ... Num. 13:22

Neglect—*to fail to respond to duties*

A. *Of material things:*
One's appearance ... 2 Sam. 19:24
Needs of the body ... Col. 2:23

B. *Of spiritual things:*
Gospel ... Matt. 22:2-5
Salvation ... Heb. 2:1-3

C. *Consequences of:*
Kept out ... Matt. 25:1-13
Sent to hell ... Matt. 25:24-30
Reward lost ... 1 Cor. 3:10-15

Nehelamite
Term applied to Shemaiah, a false prophet ... Jer. 29:24-32

Nehemiah (I)—*Jehovah has comforted*
1. Leader in the postexilic community ... Ezra 2:2
2. Postexilic workman ... Neh. 3:16

Nehemiah (II)—*Jehovah has comforted*

A. *Life of:*
Son of Hachaliah ... Neh. 1:1
Cupbearer to the Persian King Artaxerxes I (465—424 B.C.) ... Neh. 1:11
Grieves over Jerusalem's desolation ... Neh. 1:4-11
Appointed governor ... Neh. 5:14
Sent to rebuild Jerusalem ... Neh. 2:1-8
Unwelcome by non-Jews ... Neh. 2:9, 10
Views walls at night ... Neh. 2:11-20
Gives list of builders ... Neh. 3:1-32
Continues work in spite of opposition ... Neh. 4:1-23
Makes reforms among Jews ... Neh. 5:1-19
Opposition continues, but work completed ... Neh. 6:1-19
Introduces law and order ... Neh. 7:1-73

SUBJECT REFERENCE

Participates with Ezra in restored worship ... Neh. 8—10
Registers inhabitants ... Neh. 11:1-36
Registers priests and Levites ... Neh. 12:1-26
Returns to Artaxerxes; revisits Jerusalem ... Neh. 13:6, 7
Institutes reforms ... Neh. 13:1-31

B. *Character of:*
Patriotic ... Neh. 1:1-4
Prayerful ... Neh. 1:5-11
Perceptive ... Neh. 2:17-20
Persistent ... Neh. 4:1-23
Persuasive ... Neh. 5:1-13
Pure in motives ... Neh. 5:14-19
Persevering ... Neh. 6:1-19

See the next article

Nehemiah, the Book of—*a book of the Old Testament*
Nehemiah's prayer ... Neh. 1:4-11
Inspection of the wall ... Neh. 2:11-16
Rebuilding the wall ... Neh. 3:1-32
The enemies' plot ... Neh. 6:1-14
The reading of the Law ... Neh. 8:1-18
Confession of the priests ... Neh. 9:4-38
Nehemiah's reform ... Neh. 13:7-31

Nehum—*consolation*
Postexilic returnee ... Neh. 7:7
Called Rehum ... Ezra 2:2

Nehushta—*of bronze*
Wife of King Jehoiakim ... 2 Kin. 24:8

Nehushtan—*piece of brass*
Applied to brazen serpent ... 2 Kin. 18:4

Neiel—*dwelling of God*
Town in Asher ... Josh. 19:24, 27

Neigh—*to cry lustfully*
Used of:
Horses ... Jer. 8:16
Lustful desires ... Jer. 5:8
Rendered "bellow" ... Jer. 50:11

Neighbor

A. *Sins against, forbidden:*
False witness ... Ex. 20:16
Coveting ... Ex. 20:17
Lying ... Lev. 6:2-5
Hating ... Deut. 19:11-13
Despising ... Prov. 14:21
Enticing ... Prov. 16:29
Deception ... Prov. 26:19
Flattery ... Prov. 29:5
Failure to pay ... Jer. 22:13
Adultery ... Jer. 29:23

B. *Duties toward, encouraged:*
Love ... Rom. 13:9, 10
Speak truth to ... Eph. 4:25
Teach ... Jer. 31:34
Show mercy to ... Luke 10:29, 37

Nekeb—*a narrow pass*
Village in Naphtali ... Josh. 19:33

Nekoda—*dotted*
Founder of a family of Temple servants ... Ezra 2:48
Genealogy of, rejected ... Ezra 2:59, 60

Nemuel—*God is spreading*
1. Brother of Dathan and Abiram ... Num. 26:9
2. Eldest son of Simeon ... 1 Chr. 4:24
Head of Nemuelites ... Num. 26:12
Called Jemuel ... Gen. 46:10

Nepheg—*sprout*
1. Izhar's son; Korah's brother ... Ex. 6:21
2. David's son born in Jerusalem ... 2 Sam. 5:13-15

Nephew—*old English for grandson*
Applied to:
Abdon's ... Judg. 12:14
Widow's ... 1 Tim. 5:4
Used as a curse ... Is. 14:22

SUBJECT	REFERENCE
Nephtoah—*opening*	
Border town between Judah and Benjamin	Josh. 15:9
Nepotism—*putting relatives in public offices*	
Joseph's	Gen. 47:11, 12
Saul's	1 Sam. 14:50
David's	2 Sam. 8:16-18
Nehemiah's	Neh. 7:2
Ner—*lamp*	
Father of Abner; grandfather of Saul	1 Sam. 14:50, 51
Nereus—*the name of a sea god*	
Christian at Rome	Rom. 16:15
Nergal—*a Babylonian god of war*	
Worshiped by men of Cuth	2 Kin. 17:30
Nergal-sharezer—*Nergal preserve the king*	
Babylonian prince during capture of Jerusalem	Jer. 39:3, 13
Neri	
Ancestor of Christ	Luke 3:27
Neriah—*Jehovah is a lamp*	
Father of Baruch	Jer. 32:12
Nest	
A. *Kinds of:*	
Eagle's	Job 39:27
Swallow's	Ps. 84:3
Great owl's	Is. 34:15
Dove's	Jer. 48:28
B. *Figurative of:*	
False security	Num. 24:21, 22
Lord's resting place	Matt. 8:20
Full maturity	Job 29:18
Something out of place	Prov. 27:8
Helplessness	Is. 10:14
Net	
A. *Kinds of:*	
Design in a structure	Ex. 27:4, 5
Trapping a bird or animal	Prov. 1:17
Catching fish	John 21:6-11
B. *Figurative of:*	
Plots of evil men	Ps. 9:15
Predatory men	Ps. 31:4
God's chastisements	Job 19:6
Flattery	Prov. 29:5
God's soveriegn plan	Ezek. 12:13 Ezek. 17:20
Nethaneel—*God has given*	
1. Leader of Issachar	Num. 1:8
2. Jesse's fourth son	1 Chr. 2:13, 14
3. Levite trumpeter	1 Chr. 15:24
4. Levite scribe	1 Chr. 24:6
5. Obed-edom's fifth son	1 Chr. 26:4
6. Prince sent to teach Judah	2 Chr. 17:7
7. Levite chief	2 Chr. 35:9
8. Priest who married a foreign wife	Ezra 10:18-22
9. Priest in Joiakim's time	Neh. 12:21
10. Levite musician in dedication service	Neh. 12:36
Nethaniah—*Jehovah has given*	
1. Son of Asaph	1 Chr. 25:2, 12
2. Levite teacher in Jehoshaphat's reign	2 Chr. 17:8
3. Father of Jehudi	Jer. 36:14
4. Father of Ishmael, struck down Gedaliah	2 Kin. 25:23, 25
Nethinim—*given*	
A. *Described as:*	
Servants of the Levites	Ezra 8:20
B. *Probable origin of:*	
Midianites	Num. 31:2, 41
Gibeonites	Josh. 9:23, 27
Solomon's slaves	1 Kin. 9:20, 21
C. *Characteristics of:*	
Governed by captains	Neh. 11:21
Assigned certain cities	1 Chr. 9:2
Exempt from taxes	Ezra 7:24
Zealous for Israel's covenant	Neh. 10:28, 29
Assigned important jobs	Ezra 8:17
Returned from exile in large numbers	Ezra 2:43-54
Netophathite—*an inhabitant of Netophah*	
Town of Judah near Jerusalem	1 Chr. 2:54
Occupied by returning Levites	1 Chr. 9:16
Applied to two of David's mighty men	2 Sam. 23:28, 29
Loyalty of, demonstrated	2 Kin. 25:23, 24
Nettles—*thorn bushes*	
Sign of:	
Indolence	Prov. 24:31
Desolation	Is. 34:13
Retreat for cowards	Job 30:7
Network—*artistic handwork in*	
Tabernacle	Ex. 27:4
Temple	2 Kin. 7:18-41
Neutrality	
Impossibility of, taught	Matt. 6:24 Matt. 12:30
Invitation to, rejected	Josh. 24:15, 16
Never—*not ever*	
A. *Concerning God's spiritual promises:*	
Satisfaction	John 4:14
Stability	Ps. 55:22
Security	John 10:28
B. *Concerning God's threats:*	
Chastisement	2 Sam. 12:10
Desolation	Is. 13:20
Forgiveness	Mark 3:29
New—*something recent or fresh*	
Commandment	John 13:34
Covenant	Jer. 31:31
Creature	2 Cor. 5:17
Fruit	Ezek. 47:12
Earth	Is. 65:17
Spirit	Ezek. 11:19
Heaven	Is. 66:22
Jerusalem	Rev. 21:2
Name	Is. 62:2
Man	Eph. 2:15
Song	Is. 42:10
New thing (Christ's birth)	Jer. 31:22
All things new	Rev. 21:5
New birth—*regeneration*	
A. *Described as:*	
One heart	Ezek. 11:19
Resurrection	Rom. 6:4-10
New creature	2 Cor. 5:17
Circumcision	Deut. 30:6
Holy seed	1 John 3:9
Begotten	1 Pet. 1:3
Name written in heaven	Luke 10:20
B. *Productive of:*	
Growth	1 Pet. 2:1, 2
Knowledge	1 Cor. 2:12-16
Change	2 Cor. 3:18
Fruitfulness	John 15:1-8
Victory	1 John 5:4
Discipline	Heb. 12:3-11
See Born again	
New covenant	
A. *Described as:*	
Everlasting	Is. 55:3
Of peace	Ezek. 34:25
Of life	Mal. 2:5
B. *Elements of:*	
Author—God	Eph. 2:4
Cause—God's love	John 3:16
Mediator—Christ	1 Tim. 2:5
Time originated—in eternity	Rom. 8:29, 30
Time instituted—at man's sin	Gen. 3:15
Time realized—at Christ's death	Eph. 2:13-22
Time consummated—in eternity	Eph. 2:7
Duties—faith and repentance	Mark 1:15
C. *Ratification of, by:*	
God's promise	Gen. 3:15
God's oath	Is. 54:9, 10
Christ's blood	Heb. 9:12-26
Spirit's sealing	2 Cor. 1:22
D. *Superiority of, to the old:*	
Hope	Heb. 7:19
Priesthood	Heb. 7:20-28
Covenant	Heb. 8:6
Sacrifice	Heb. 9:23
New Gate—*a Temple gate*	
Princes meet at	Jer. 26:10
New Jerusalem	
Vision, seen by Abraham	Heb. 11:10, 16
Reality of, experienced by believers	Gal. 4:26, 31
Consummation of, awaits eternity	Heb. 13:14
New man (see New birth)	
New moon	
A festival day	Ps. 81:3 Col. 2:16
A point of reference	Is. 66:23
News	
A. *Kinds of:*	
Distressing	Gen. 32:6-8
Disturbing	Josh. 22:11-20
Alarming	1 Sam. 4:13-22
Agonizing	2 Sam. 18:31-33
Sorrowful	Neh. 1:2-11
Joyful	Luke 2:8-18
Good	1 Kin. 1:42
Fatal	1 Sam. 4:19
B. *Of salvation:*	
Out of Zion	Is. 40:9
By a person	Is. 41:27
Bringer of peace	Is. 52:7
By Christ	Is. 61:1-3
New Year	
Erection of the tabernacle on	Ex. 40:17, 18
Neziah—*pre-eminent*	
Head of a Nethinim family	Ezra 2:43, 54
Nezib—*garrison*	
Town of Judah	Josh. 15:1, 43
Nibhaz	
Idol of Avites	2 Kin. 17:31
Nibshan—*the furnace*	
Town of Judah	Josh. 15:1, 62
Nicanor—*victorious*	
One of the seven men chosen as deacons	Acts 6:1-5
Nicodemus—*conqueror of the people*	
Pharisee; converses with Jews	John 3:1-12
Protests unfairness of Christ's trial	John 7:50-52
Brings gifts to anoint Christ's body	John 19:39, 40
Nicolaitanes—*early Christian sect*	
Group teaching moral looseness	Rev. 2:6-15
Nicolas—*victor over the people*	
Non-Jewish proselyte deacon	Acts 6:5
Nicopolis—*city of victory*	
Town in Epirus (near Actium)	Titus 3:12
Niger—*black*	
Latin surname of Simeon, a teacher in Antioch	Acts 13:1
Night—*the time of darkness*	
A. *Important facts concerning:*	
Made by God	Ps. 104:20
Named at creation	Gen. 1:5
Begins at sunset	Gen. 28:11
Established by God's covenant	Gen. 8:22
Displays God's glory	Ps. 19:2
Designed for rest	Ps. 104:23
Wild beasts creep in	Ps. 104:20-22
None in heaven	Zech. 14:7
Divided into "watches" and hours	Mark 13:35

SUBJECT	REFERENCE
B. *Special events in:*	
Jacob's wrestling	Gen. 32:22-31
Egypt's greatest plague	Ex. 12:12-31
Ordinance of the Passover	Ex. 12:42
King's sleeplessness	Esth. 6:1
Nehemiah's vigil	Neh. 2:11-16
Belshazzar slain	Dan. 5:30
Angelic revelation	Luke 2:8-15
Nicodemus' talk	John 3:2
Release from prison	Acts 5:19
Paul's escape	Acts 9:24, 25
Wonderful conversion	Acts 16:25-33
Lord's return	Mark 13:35
C. *Good acts in:*	
Toil	Luke 5:5
Prayer	1 Sam. 15:11 Luke 6:12
Song	Job 35:10 Ps. 42:8
Flight from evil	1 Sam. 19:10 Matt. 2:14
Dreams	Matt. 2:12, 13, 19
D. *Evil acts in:*	
Drunkenness	Is. 5:11
Thievery	Obad. 5 Matt. 27:64
Debauchery	1 Thess. 5:2-7
Betrayal	Matt. 26:31, 34, 46-50
Death	Luke 12:20
F. *Figurative of:*	
Present age	Rom. 13:11, 12
Death	John 9:4
Unregenerate state	1 Thess. 5:5, 7
Judgment	Mic. 3:6

Nighthawk

Unclean bird	Lev. 11:16

Night monster—*a nocturnal creature*

Dwells in ruins	Is. 34:14

Nile—*Egypt's main river*

A. *Called:*	
Sihor	Is. 23:3
Stream of Egypt	Is. 27:12
Sea	Nah. 3:8
B. *Characteristics of:*	
Has seven streams	Is. 11:15
Overflows annually	Jer. 46:8
Source of Egyptian wealth	Is. 19:5-8
C. *Events connected with:*	
Drowning of male children	Ex. 1:22
Moses placed in	Ex. 2:3
Water of, turned to blood	Ex. 7:15, 20
D. *Figurative of:*	
Judgment	Ezek. 30:12 Amos 9:5
Army	Jer. 46:7-9

Nimrah—*an abbreviation of Beth-nimrah*

Town in Gilead	Num. 32:3, 36

Nimrim—*wholesome waters*

Place in south Moab	Is. 15:6

Nimrod—*strong*

Ham's grandson	Gen. 10:6-8
Becomes a mighty hunter	Gen. 10:8, 9
Establishes cities	Gen. 10:10-12
Land of Assyria, thus described	Mic. 5:6

Nimshi—*Jehovah reveals*

Grandfather of King Jehu	2 Kin. 9:2, 14
Called Jehu's father	2 Kin. 9:20

Nineveh—*the capital of ancient Assyria*

A. *History of:*	
Built by Asshur	Gen. 10:11, 12
Capital of Assyria	2 Kin. 19:36
Jonah preaches to	Jon. 1:1, 2
Citizens of:	
Repent	Jon. 3:5-9
At the judgment seat	Matt. 12:41
B. *Prophecies concerning its:*	
Destruction by Babylon	Nah. 2:1-4
Internal weakness	Nah. 3:11-17
Utter desolation	Nah. 3:18, 19
C. *Described as:*	
Great city	Jon. 3:2, 3
Wealthy	Nah. 2:9
Fortified	Nah. 3:8, 12
Wicked	Jon. 1:2
Idolatrous	Nah. 1:14
Careless	Zeph. 2:15
Full of lies	Nah. 3:1

Ninth hour—*that is, 3 P.M.*

Time of Christ's death	Matt. 27:46
Customary hour of prayer	Acts 3:1
Time of Cornelius' vision	Acts 10:1, 3

Nisan—*beginning*

Name of Abib (first month of Jewish year) after the exile	Neh. 2:1
See Jewish calendar	

Nisroch—*eagle, hawk*

Sennacherib's god	2 Kin. 19:37

Nitre—*carbonate of soda* (in the Bible)

Figurative of agitation	Prov. 25:20
As a cleansing agent	Jer. 2:22

No-amon—*the Egyptian city Thebes*

Nineveh compared to	Nah. 3:8

Noadiah—*Jehovah has met by appointment*

1. Levite in Ezra's time	Ezra 8:33
2. Prophetess who tries to frighten Nehemiah	Neh. 6:14

Noah (I)—*rest*

A. *Life of:*	
Son of Lamech	Gen. 5:28, 29
Father of Shem, Ham and Japheth	Gen. 5:32
Finds favor with God	Gen. 6:8
Lives in the midst of corruption	Gen. 6:1-13
Instructed to build the ark	Gen. 6:13-22
Preacher of righteousness	2 Pet. 2:5
Enters ark with family and animals	Gen. 7:1-24
Preserved during flood	Gen. 8:1-17
Builds an altar	Gen. 8:18-22
Covenant established with	Gen. 9:1-19
Plants a vineyard; becomes drunk	Gen. 9:20, 21
Pronounces curse and blessings	Gen. 9:22-27
Dies at 950	Gen. 9:28, 29
B. *Character of:*	
Righteous	Gen. 6:9
Obedient	Heb. 11:7
In fellowship with God	Gen. 6:9
Notable in history	Ezek. 14:14, 20

Noah (II)—*trembling*

Daughter of Zelophehad	Num. 26:33

Nob—*height*

City of priests; David flees to	1 Sam. 21:1-9
Priests of, killed by Saul	1 Sam. 22:9-23
Near Jerusalem	Is. 10:32
Reinhabited after the exile	Neh. 11:32

Nobah—*barking*

1. Manassite leader	Num. 32:42
2. Town in Gad	Judg. 8:11

Nobleman—*one who belongs to the upper class*

Jesus:	
Heals son of	John 4:46-54
Cites in parable	Luke 19:12-27

Nod—*wandering exile*

Place (east of Eden) of Cain's abode	Gen. 4:16, 17

Nodab—*nobility*

Arabian tribe	1 Chr. 5:19

Nogah—*brilliance*

One of David's sons	1 Chr. 3:1, 7

Nohah—*rest*

Benjamin's fourth son	1 Chr. 8:1, 2

Noise—*a sound of something*

A. *Kinds of:*	
Sea	Ps. 65:7
Battle	Is. 13:4 Jer. 47:3
Songs	Ezek. 26:13 Amos 5:23
Mourners	Matt. 9:23
Crying	1 Sam. 4:13, 14
Revelry	Ex. 32:17, 18
Dog	Ps. 59:6
God's glory	Ezek. 43:2
B. *Figurative of:*	
Strong opposition	Is. 31:4
Worthlessness	Jer. 46:17

Noisome—*something evil or deadly*

Hurtful beasts	Ezek. 14:15, 21
Deadly pestilence	Ps. 91:3
Foul sore	Rev. 16:2

Nomad—*wanderer*

Life style of patriarchs	Gen. 12:1-9 Gen. 13:1-18
Israel's history	Deut. 26:5

Noon—*midday*

A. *Time of:*	
Eating	Gen. 43:16, 25
Resting	2 Sam. 4:5
Praying	Ps. 55:17
Complain and murmer	Ps. 55:17
Drunkenness	1 Kin. 20:16
Destruction	Ps. 91:6
Death	2 Kin. 4:20
B. *Figurative of:*	
Blindness	Deut. 28:29
Cleansing	Job 11:17

Nophah—*windy place*

Moabite town	Num. 21:29, 30

North

Refers to:	
A geographical direction	Gen. 28:14 Ps. 107:3
Invading forces	Is. 14:31 Jer. 6:1

Nose, nostrils—*the organ of breathing*

A. *Used literally for:*	
Breathing	Gen. 2:7
Smelling	Amos 4:10
Ornamentation	Is. 3:21
Bondage	Is. 37:29
Blood (forced)	Prov. 30:33
Behemoth	Job 40:15-24
Idols	Ps. 115:6
Nosebleeding produced by wringing	Prov. 30:33
B. *Used figuratively of:*	
Man's life	Job 27:3
God's:	
Power	Ex. 15:8
Sovereign control	2 Kin. 19:28
Overindulgence	Num. 11:20
National hope (Zedekiah)	Lam. 4:20
Something very offensive	Is. 65:5

Nose ring

Worn by women	Is. 3:21
Put in swine's snout	Prov. 11:22

Nothing—*not a thing*

Things classified as:	
Service without:	
Christ	John 15:5
Love	1 Cor. 13:3
Circumcision	1 Cor. 7:19
Flesh	John 6:63

Not my people, Not loved—*symbolic names of Hosea's children*

Lo-ammi	Hos. 1:9
Lo-ruhamah	Hos. 1:6

Nought

A. *Descriptive of:*	
Something:	
Fruitless	Is. 49:24
Without payment	Gen. 29:15
Vain	Mal. 1:10
Nothing	Is. 41:24
B. *Time of:*	
Past	Neh. 4:15
Present	Amos 6:13
Future	Ps. 33:10

SUBJECT REFERENCE

C. *Things that will come to:*
Wicked ... Job 8:22
Wicked counsel ... Is. 8:10
Babylon ... Rev. 18:17

Nourish—*provide means of growth*

A. *Descriptive of the growth or care of:*
Children ... Acts 7:20, 21
Animals ... 2 Sam. 12:3
Plants ... Is. 44:14
Family ... Gen. 45:11
Country ... Acts 12:20

B. *Figurative of:*
Protection ... Is. 1:2
Provision ... Ruth 4:15
Pampering ... James 5:5
Preparedness ... 1 Tim. 4:6

Novice—*one who is inexperienced. A recent Christian convert*
Bishops, not to be ... 1 Tim. 3:1, 6

Now—*the present time*

A. *As contrasted with:*
Old Testament ... John 4:23
Past ... John 9:25
Future ... John 13:7, 19
Two conditions ... Luke 16:25

B. *In Christ's life, descriptive of His:*
Atonement ... Rom. 5:11
Humiliation ... Heb. 2:8
Resurrection ... 1 Cor. 15:20
Glorification ... John 13:31
Intercession ... Heb. 9:24
Return ... 1 John 2:28

C. *In the Christian's life, descriptive of:*
Salvation ... Rom. 13:11
Regeneration ... John 5:25
Reconciliation ... Col. 1:21, 22
Justification ... Rom. 5:9
Victory ... Gal. 2:20
Worship ... John 4:23
Suffering ... 1 Pet. 1:6-8
Hope ... Rev. 12:10
Glorification ... Rom. 8:21, 22; 1 John 3:2

D. *Descriptive of the present age as:*
Time of:
Opportunity ... 2 Cor. 6:2
Evil ... 1 Thess. 2:6
God's:
Greater revelation ... Eph. 3:5
Completed redemption ... Col. 1:26, 27
Final dealing with mankind ... Heb. 12:26

Nuisance—*something very irritating*

Descriptive of:
Widow ... Luke 18:2-5

Numbers

Symbolic of:
One—unity ... Deut. 6:4; Matt. 19:6
Two—unity ... Gen. 1:27
Two—division ... 1 Kin. 18:21; Matt. 7:13, 14
Three—the Trinity ... Matt. 28:19; 2 Cor. 13:14
Three—resurrection ... Hos. 6:1, 2; Matt. 12:40; Luke 13:32
Three—completion ... 1 Cor. 13:13
Three—testing ... Judg. 7:16
Four—completion ... Matt. 13:4-8; Matt. 25:2; John 4:35
Five—incompletion ... Matt. 25:15-20
Six—man's testing ... Gen. 1:27, 31; Rev. 13:18
Seven—completion ... Ex. 20:10
Seven—fulfillment ... Josh. 6:4
Seven—perfection ... Rev. 1:4
Eighth—new beginning ... Ezek. 43:27; 1 Pet. 3:20
Ten—completion ... 1 Cor. 6:9, 10
Tenth—God's part ... Gen. 14:20; Mal. 3:10
Twelve—God's purpose ... John 11:9; Rev. 21:12-17
Forty—testing ... Jon. 3:4; Matt. 4:2

SUBJECT REFERENCE

Forty—judgment ... Num. 14:33; Ps. 95:10
Seventy—God's completed purpose ... Jer. 25:11; Dan. 9:24

Numbers, the Book of—*a book of the Old Testament*
The census ... Num. 1:1—4:49
Cleansing of Levites ... Num. 8:5-22
The cloud and the tabernacle ... Num. 9:15-23
The provision of manna ... Num. 11:4-9
The spies ... Num. 13:1—14:45
The rebellion of Korah ... Num. 16:1-35
The sin of Moses ... Num. 20:1-13
Aaron's death ... Num. 20:22-29
Balaam and Balak ... Num. 22:2—24:25
Offerings and feasts ... Num. 28:1—29:40
Settlements in Gilead ... Num. 32:1-42
Preparation for Canaan ... Num. 33:50—35:34

Nun—*fish*
1. Father of Joshua, Israel's military leader ... Josh. 1:1
   Called Non ... 1 Chr. 7:27
2. Letter in the Hebrew alphabet ... Ps. 119:105-112

Nurse—*nourishment and protection to the young*

A. *Duties of:*
Provide nourishment ... Gen. 21:7
Protect ... 2 Kin. 11:2
Called "guardian" ... 2 Kin. 10:1, 5

B. *Figurative of:*
Judgment ... Lam. 4:4
Provision ... Num. 11:12
Gentleness ... 1 Thess. 2:7

Nuts
Provided as gifts ... Gen. 43:11
Grown in gardens ... Song 6:11

Nympha—*sacred to the nymphs*
Christian of Laodicea ... Col. 4:15

O

Oak—*a large and strong tree*

A. *Uses of:*
Landmarks ... Judg. 6:11, 19
Burial place ... Gen. 35:8
Place of rest ... 1 Kin. 13:14
Place of idolatry ... Is. 44:14
For oars ... Ezek. 27:6

B. *Figurative of:*
Strength ... Amos 2:9
Judgment ... Is. 1:29, 30
Haughtiness ... Is. 2:11, 13

Oars—*wooden blades used for rowing*
Made of oak ... Ezek. 27:6, 29
Used on galleys ... Is. 33:21

Oaths—*solemn promises*

A. *Expressions descriptive of:*
"As the LORD liveth" ... 1 Sam. 19:6
"God is witness" ... Gen. 31:50
"The LORD . . . be witness" ... Jer. 42:5
"God judge between us" ... Gen. 31:53
"The LORD make thee like" ... Jer. 29:22
"I adjure thee" ... Matt. 26:63
"I call God for a record" ... 2 Cor. 1:23

B. *Purposes of:*
Confirm covenant ... Gen. 26:28
Insure protection ... Gen. 31:44-53
Establish truth ... Ex. 22:11
Confirm fidelity ... Num. 5:19-22
Guarantee duties ... Gen. 24:3, 4
Sign a covenant ... 2 Chr. 15:12-15
Fulfill promises ... Neh. 5:12, 13

C. *Sacredness of:*
Obligatory ... Num. 30:2-16
Maintained even in deception ... Josh. 9:20
Upheld by Christ ... Matt. 26:63, 64
Rewarded ... 2 Chr. 15:12-15
Maintained in fear ... 1 Sam. 14:24, 26

D. *Prohibitions concerning, not:*
In idol's name ... Josh. 23:7
In creature's name ... Matt. 5:34-36

SUBJECT REFERENCE

Falsely ... Lev. 19:12
Among Christians ... Matt. 5:34

Oaths of God

A. *Made in Old Testament concerning:*
Promise to Abraham ... Gen. 50:24
Davidic covenant ... 2 Sam. 7:10-16
Messianic priesthood ... Ps. 110:4, 5

B. *Fulfilled in New Testament in Christ's:*
Birth ... Luke 1:68-73
Kingship on David's throne ... Luke 1:32, 33
Priesthood ... Heb. 7:20-28

See Swearing

Obadiah—*servant of Jehovah*
1. King Ahab's steward ... 1 Kin. 18:3-16
2. Descendant of David ... 1 Chr. 3:21
3. Chief of Issachar ... 1 Chr. 7:3
4. Descendant of Saul ... 1 Chr. 8:38
5. Gadite captain ... 1 Chr. 12:8, 9
6. Man of Zebulun ... 1 Chr. 27:19
7. Prince sent by Jehoshaphat to teach ... 2 Chr. 17:7
8. Levite overseer ... 2 Chr. 34:12
9. Leader in the postexilic community ... Ezra 8:9
10. Priest who signs the covenant ... Neh. 10:5
11. Levite ... 1 Chr. 9:16
    Called Abda ... Neh. 11:17
12. Postexilic porter ... Neh. 12:25
13. Prophet of Judah ... Obad. 1

Obadiah, the Book of—*a book of the Old Testament*
Against Edom ... Obad. 1-9
Edom against Judah ... Obad. 10-14
The day of the LORD ... Obad. 15, 16
Zion's victory ... Obad. 17-21

Obal—*to be bare*
Descendants of Joktan ... Gen. 10:28

Obduracy—*resistance to pleadings of mercy*

Expressed by:
"Stiffnecked" ... Ex. 33:3, 5
"Uncircumcised" ... Lev. 26:41
"Impenitent" ... Rom. 2:5
"Harden your hearts" ... 1 Sam. 6:6
"Neither will I let" ... Ex. 5:1, 2
"I will not hear" ... Jer. 22:21
"Seek not" ... John 5:44
"He trespass yet more" ... 2 Chr. 28:22-25
"Being past feeling" ... Eph. 4:18, 19
"God gave them up" ... Rom. 1:24-28
"Therefore they could not believe" ... John 12:39
"That cannot cease from sin" ... 2 Pet. 2:14
"They were appointed" ... 1 Pet. 2:8
"Let him be unjust still" ... Rev. 22:11

See Hardness of heart; Impenitence

Obed—*servant*
1. Son of Ephlal ... 1 Chr. 2:37, 38
2. Son of Boaz and Ruth ... Ruth 4:17-22
3. One of David's mighty men ... 1 Chr. 11:47
4. Korhite porter ... 1 Chr. 26:7
5. Father of Azariah ... 2 Chr. 23:1

Obed-edom—*servant of Edom*
1. Philistine from Gath; ark of the Lord left in his house ... 2 Sam. 6:10-12; 1 Chr. 13:13, 14
2. Overseer of the storehouse ... 1 Chr. 26:4-8, 15
3. Levitical musician ... 1 Chr. 16:5
4. Guardian of the sacred vessels ... 2 Chr. 25:24

Obedience—*submission to authority*

A. *Relationship involved:*
God—man ... Acts 5:29
Parent—child ... Gen. 28:7; Eph. 6:1
Husband—wife ... 1 Cor. 14:34, 35
Master—slave ... Eph. 6:5
Ruler—subject ... Titus 1:1

O

SUBJECT ... REFERENCE

Leader—follower ... Acts 5:36, 37
Pastor—people ... Heb. 13:17
Man—nature ... James 3:3
God—nature ... Matt. 8:27
God—demons ... Mark 1:27

B. *Spiritual objects of:*

God ... Acts 5:29
Christ ... Heb. 5:9
Truth ... Gal. 5:7
Faith ... Acts 6:7

C. *In the Christian's life:*

Comes from the heart ... Rom. 6:17
Needs testing ... 2 Cor. 2:4
Aided by the Spirit ... 1 Pet. 1:22
Manifested in Gentiles ... Rom. 15:18
In pastoral relations ... 2 Cor. 7:15

D. *Lack of, brings:*

Rejection ... 1 Sam. 15:20-26
Captivity ... 2 Kin. 18:11, 12
Death ... 1 Kin. 20:36
Retribution ... 2 Thess. 1:8

E. *Examples of:*

Noah ... Gen. 6:22
Abram ... Gen. 12:1-4
Israelites ... Ex. 12:28
Caleb and Joshua ... Num. 32:12
David ... Ps. 119:106
Asa ... 1 Kin. 15:11, 14
Elijah ... 1 Kin. 17:5
Hezekiah ... 2 Kin. 18:6
Josiah ... 2 Kin. 22:2
Zerubbabel ... Hag. 1:12
Christ ... Rom. 5:19
Paul ... Acts 26:19
Christians ... Phil. 2:12

Obedience of Christ, our example

To death ... Phil. 2:5-11
Learned ... Heb. 5:7-10
Submissive ... Matt. 26:39, 42

Obedience to civil government

Meet obligation ... Mark 12:13-17
Of God ... Rom. 13:1-7
Duty ... Titus 3:1
For Lord's sake ... 1 Pet. 2:13-17

Obeisance—*bending or bowing*

As an act of:
Respect ... Ex. 18:7
Reverence ... Matt. 2:11
Flaunting fidelity ... 2 Sam. 1:2-16
Fawning favor ... 2 Sam. 14:2-4
Feigned flattery ... 2 Sam. 15:5, 6

Obil—*camel driver*

Ishmaelite in charge of camels ... 1 Chr. 27:30

Obituary—*an account of a person's life; a death notice*

Written of Moses ... Deut. 34:1-12

Objectors—*those who oppose something*

A. *Argue against God's:*

Power ... Ex. 14:10-15
Provision ... Ex. 16:2-17
Promises ... Num. 14:1-10

B. *Overcome by:*

Prophecies cited ... Jer. 26:8-19
Promises claimed ... Acts 4:23-31

Oblivion—*the state of being forgotten*

God's punishment on the wicked ... Ps. 34:16

Oboth—*water skins*

Israelite camp ... Num. 21:10, 11; Num. 33:43, 44

Observe—*to keep; to remember*

A. *Descriptive of:*

Remembrance ... Gen. 37:11
Laws ... Ex. 31:16
Obedience ... Matt. 28:20
Watchfulness ... Jer. 8:7; Mark 6:20
False rituals ... Gal. 4:10

B. *Blessings of proper:*

Material prosperity ... Deut. 6:3
Righteousness ... Deut. 6:25
Elevation ... Deut. 28:1, 13
Loving-kindness ... Ps. 107:43

SUBJECT ... REFERENCE

C. *Manner of proper:*

Carefully ... Deut. 12:28
Without change ... Deut. 12:32
Diligently ... Deut. 24:8
Forever ... 2 Kin. 17:37
Without preference ... 1 Tim. 5:21

Obstacles—*obstructions*

Eliminated by:

God's help ... Is. 45:2
Christ's help ... Is. 49:9-11
Spirit's help ... Zech. 4:6, 7

Obstacles to faith

Men's honor ... John 5:44
Highmindedness ... Rom. 11:20

Obstinacy—*stubbornness*

Continuing in sin ... 2 Chr. 28:22, 23
Rejecting counsel ... 1 Kin. 12:12-15
Refusing to change ... Jer. 44:15-27

Obstruct—*to hamper progress*

Attempted ... Ezra 4:1-5
Condemned ... 3 John 9, 10

Obtain—*to bring into one's possession*

A. *Of material things:*

Advancement ... Esth. 2:9-17

B. *Of spiritual things:*

Favor ... Prov. 8:35
Joy and gladness ... Is. 35:10
Heaven ... Luke 20:35-38
Divine help ... Acts 26:22
Salvation ... Rom. 11:7
Better resurrection ... Heb. 11:35
Faith ... 2 Pet. 1:1

Occultism—*pertaining to supernatural, especially evil, influences*

A. *Forms of:*

Astrology ... Is. 47:13
Charming ... Deut. 18:11
Consulting with spirits ... Deut. 18:11
Divination ... Deut. 18:14
Magic ... Gen. 41:8
Necromancy ... Deut. 18:11
Soothsaying ... Is. 2:6
Sorcery ... Ex. 22:8
Witchcraft ... Deut. 18:10
Wizardry ... Deut. 18:11

B. *Attitude toward:*

Forbidden ... Deut. 18:10, 11; Jer. 27:9
Punished by death ... Ex. 22:18; Lev. 20:6, 27
Forsaken ... Acts 19:18-20

Ocran—*troubled*

Man of Asher ... Num. 1:13; Num. 2:27

Oded

1. Father of Azariah the prophet ... 2 Chr. 15:1
2. Prophet of Samaria ... 2 Chr. 28:9-15

Odors, sweet

A. *Used literally of:*

Sacrificial incense ... Lev. 26:31
Ointment fragrance ... John 12:3

B. *Used figuratively of:*

New life ... Hos. 14:7
Prayers ... Rev. 5:8
Christian service ... Phil. 4:18

Offend, offense

A. *Causes of:*

Christ ... Matt. 11:6
Persecution ... Matt. 13:21; Matt. 24:10
The cross ... 1 Cor. 1:23
Physical parts ... Matt. 18:8, 9

B. *Causes of, in Christ's:*

Lowly position ... Matt. 13:54-57
Teaching ... Matt. 18:8, 9
Being the Rock ... Is. 8:14
Being the Bread ... John 6:58-66
Being crucified ... 1 Cor. 1:23
Being the righteousness of God ... Rom. 9:31-33

SUBJECT ... REFERENCE

C. *Christians forbidden to give:*

In anything ... 2 Cor. 6:3
By their liberty ... 1 Cor. 8:9, 13
At any time ... Phil. 1:10

See Stumble

Offering of Christ

Of Himself:

Predicted ... Ps. 40:6-8
Prepared ... Heb. 5:1-10
Proclaimed ... Heb. 10:5-9
Purified ... Heb. 9:14
Personalized ... Heb. 7:27
Perfected ... Heb. 10:11-14
Praised ... Eph. 5:2

Offerings

A. *Characteristics of:*

Made to God alone ... Ex. 22:20
Limitation of ... Heb. 9:9
Prescribed under the Law ... Mark 1:44

B. *Thing offered must be:*

Perfect ... Lev. 22:21
Ceremonially clean ... Lev. 27:11, 27
Best ... Mal. 1:14

C. *Offerer must:*

Not delay ... Ex. 22:29, 30
Offer in righteousness ... Mal. 3:3
Offer with thanksgiving ... Ps. 27:6

D. *Classification of:*

Private and public ... Lev. 4:1-12
Physical and spiritual ... Lev. 5:1-13
Voluntary and required ... Lev. 1:3
Accepted and rejected ... Judg. 6:17-24
Purified and perverted ... Mal. 3:3, 4
Passing and permanent ... Jer. 7:21-23
Jew and Gentile ... Ps. 96:8
Typical and fulfilled ... Gen. 22:2, 13

Offerings of the leaders—*by heads, of twelve tribes*

1. Six wagons and twelve oxen to transport tabernacle ... Num. 7:1-89
2. Dedication gift ... Num. 7:1-89

Office—*a position of trust*

Holders of:

Butler ... Gen. 40:13
Judge ... Deut. 17:9
Priest ... Deut. 26:3
Ministers of song ... 1 Chr. 6:32
Porters ... 1 Chr. 9:22
Publican ... Matt. 9:9
Bishop ... 1 Tim. 3:1

Officers—*men appointed to rule over others*

A. *Descriptive of:*

Magistrate ... Luke 12:58
Principal officer ... 1 Kin. 4:5, 7

B. *Functions of:*

Administer justice ... Num. 11:16

Offices of Christ

As Prophet ... Deut. 18:18, 19; Is. 61:1-3
As Priest ... Ps. 110:4; Is. 53:1-12
As King ... 2 Sam. 7:12-17; Luke 1:32, 33

Offscouring—*something vile or worthless*

Jews thus described ... Lam. 3:45

Offspring—*issue* (physical or spiritual)

A. *Used literally of:*

Set-apart firstlings ... Ex. 13:12; Ex. 34:19
Of a donkey you shall redeem ... Ex. 13:13; Ex. 34:20
Man's issue (children) ... Job 5:25
Man as created by God ... Acts 17:28, 29
Christ as a descendant of David ... Rev. 22:16

B. *Used figuratively of:*

True believer ... Is. 22:24
New Israel ... Is. 44:3-5
Gentile church ... Is. 61:9
True Church ... Is. 65:23

SUBJECT REFERENCE

Og—*giant*
- Amorite king of Bashan .... Deut. 3:1, 8
- Extent of rule .... Deut. 3:8, 10
- Residences at Ashtaroth and Edrei .... Josh. 12:4
- Man of great size .... Deut. 3:11
- Defeated and killed by Israel .... Num. 21:32-35
- Territory of, assigned to Manasseh .... Deut. 3:13
- Memory of, long remembered ... Ps. 135:11

Ohad—*powerful*
- Son of Simeon .... Gen. 46:10

Ohel—*family*
- Son of Zerubbabel .... 1 Chr. 3:19, 20

Oil—*a liquid extracted from olives*

A. *Features concerning:*
- Given by God .... Ps. 104:14, 15
- Subject to tithing .... Deut. 12:17

B. *Uses of:*
- Food .... Num. 11:8
- Anointing .... 1 Sam. 10:1
- Beautification .... Ruth 3:3
- Perfume .... Eccl. 10:1
- Illumination .... Ex. 25:6; Ex. 30:26-32; Matt. 25:3-8

C. *Types of oil:*
- Anointing .... Ex. 25:6
- Pure .... Ex. 27:20
- Baking .... Ex. 29:23
- Beaten .... Ex. 29:40
- Olive .... Ex. 30:24
- Precious .... 2 Kin. 20:13
- Golden .... Zech. 4:12

D. *Figurative of:*
- Prosperity .... Deut. 32:13
- Joy and gladness .... Is. 61:3
- Wastefulness .... Prov. 21:17
- Brotherly love .... Ps. 133:2
- Real grace .... Matt. 25:4
- Holy Spirit .... 1 John 2:20, 27

Oil tree
- Signifies restoration .... Is. 41:17-20

Ointment—*a salve made of olive oil and spices*

A. By special prescription for tabernacle .... Ex. 30:23-25
- Misuse of, forbidden .... Ex. 30:37, 38
- Ingredients stirred together .. Job 41:31

B. *Features concerning:*
- Considered very valuable .... 2 Kin. 20:13
- Carried or stored in containers .... Matt. 26:7
- Can be polluted .... Eccl. 10:1

C. *Uses of:*
- Cosmetic .... Eccl. 9:8
- Sign of hospitality .... Luke 7:46
- Embalming agent .... Luke 23:55, 56
- Sexual attraction .... Is. 57:9

Old—*mature; ancient*

A. *Descriptive of:*
- Age .... Gen. 25:8
- Mature person .... 1 Kin. 12:6-13
- Experienced .... Ezek. 23:43
- Ancient times .... Mal. 3:4
- Old Testament age .... Matt. 5:21-33
- Old Testament .... 2 Cor. 3:14
- Unregenerate nature .... Rom. 6:6

B. *Of man's age, infirmities of:*
- Waning sexual desire .... Luke 1:18
- Physical handicaps .... 1 Kin. 1:1, 15
- Failing strength .... Ps. 71:9

C. *Of man's age, dangers of:*
- Spiritual decline .... 1 Kin. 11:4
- Not receiving instruction .... Eccl. 4:13
- Disrespect toward .... Deut. 28:50

D. *Of man's age, blessing of:*
- God's care .... Is. 46:4
- Continued fruitfulness .... Ps. 92:14
- Security of faith .... Prov. 22:6
- Fulfillment of life's goals .... Is. 65:20
- Honor .... Lev. 19:32
- Grandchildren .... Prov. 17:6
- Men dream dreams .... Acts 2:17

See Length of life

Old Testament

A. *Characteristics of:*
- Inspired .... 2 Tim. 3:16
- Authoritative .... John 10:34, 35
- Written by the Holy Spirit ... Heb. 3:7
- Uses many figurative expressions .... Is. 55:1, 12, 13
- Written for our admonition .. 1 Cor. 10:1-11
- Israel now blinded to .... 2 Cor. 3:14-16
- Foreshadows the New .... Heb. 9:1-28

B. *With the New Testament, unified in:*
- Authorship .... Heb. 1:1
- Plan of salvation .... 1 Pet. 1:9-12
- Presenting Christ (see Messiah, the) .... Luke 24:25-44

Olive tree

A. *Used for:*
- Oil of, many uses (see Oil) ... Ex. 27:20
- Temple furniture .... 1 Kin. 6:23
- Temple construction .... 1 Kin. 6:31-33
- Booths .... Neh. 8:15

B. *Cultivation of:*
- By grafting .... Rom. 11:24
- Hindered by disease .... Deut. 28:40
- Failure of, a great calamity .. Hab. 3:17, 18
- Poor provided for .... Deut. 24:20
- Palestine suitable for .... Deut. 6:11

C. *Figuratively of:*
- Peace .... Gen. 8:11
- Kingship .... Judg. 9:8, 9
- Israel .... Jer. 11:16
- The righteous .... Ps. 52:8
- Faithful remnant .... Is. 17:6
- Gentile believers .... Rom. 11:17, 24
- True Church .... Rom. 11:17, 24
- Prophetic symbols .... Zech. 4:3, 11, 12

Olives, Mount of

A. *Described as:*
- "The mount of Olives" .... Zech. 14:4
- "The hill that is before Jerusalem" .... 1 Kin. 11:7
- "The mount of corruption" .. 2 Kin. 23:13
- "The mount" .... Neh. 8:15

B. *Scene of:*
- David's flight .... 2 Sam. 15:30
- Solomon's idolatry .... 2 Kin. 23:13
- Ezekiel's vision .... Ezek. 11:23
- Postexilic festivities .... Neh. 8:15
- Zechariah's prophecy .... Zech. 14:4
- Triumphal entry .... Matt. 21:1
- Weeping .... Luke 19:37, 41
- Great prophetic discourse .... Matt. 24:3
- Ascension .... Acts 1:12

Oliveyard
- Freely given .... Josh. 24:13
- Taken in greed .... 2 Kin. 5:20, 26

Olympas
- Christian in Rome .... Rom. 16:15

Omar—*eloquent*
- Grandson of Esau .... Gen. 36:11, 15; 1 Chr. 1:36

Omega—*the last letter in the Greek alphabet*
- Descriptive of Christ's infinity .... Rev. 1:8, 11; Rev. 21:6; Rev. 22:13

Omen—*a portent*
- Forbidden .... Deut. 18:10
- The LORD causes to fail .... Is. 44:25

Omission, sins of

A. *Concerning ordinances:*
- Moses' neglect of circumcision .... Ex. 4:24-26
- Israel's neglect of the tithe ... Mal. 3:7-12
- Christians neglecting to assemble .... Heb. 10:25

B. *Concerning moral duties:*
- Witnessing .... Ezek. 33:1-6
- Warning .... Jer. 42:1-22
- Watchfulness .... Matt. 24:42-51; Matt. 26:36-46

Omnipotence—*infinite power*

A. *Of God, expressed by His:*
- Names ("Almighty," etc.) .... Gen. 17:1
- Creative word .... Gen. 1:3
- Control of:
  - Nature .... Amos 4:13
  - Nations .... Amos 1:1—2:3
  - All things .... Ps. 115:3
- Power .... Rom. 4:17-24
- Unweariness .... Is. 40:28

B. *Of Christ, expressed by His power over:*
- Disease .... Matt. 8:3
- Unclean spirit .... Mark 1:23-27
- Devil .... Matt. 4:1-11
- Death .... John 10:17, 18
- Destiny .... Matt. 25:31-33

C. *Of the Holy Spirit, expressed by:*
- Christ's anointing .... Is. 11:2
- Confirmation of the Gospel .... Rom. 15:19

Omnipresence—*universal presence of*
- God .... Jer. 23:23, 24
- Christ .... Matt. 18:20
- Holy Spirit .... Ps. 139:7-12

Omniscience—*infinite knowledge of*
- God .... Is. 40:14
- Christ .... Col. 2:2, 3
- Holy Spirit .... 1 Cor. 2:10-13

Omri—*Jehovah apportions*
1. Descendant of Benjamin .... 1 Chr. 7:8
2. Judahite .... 1 Chr. 9:4
3. Chief officer of Issachar .... 1 Chr. 27:18
4. King of Israel; made king by Israel's army .... 1 Kin. 16:15, 16
   - Prevails over Zimri and Tibni .... 1 Kin. 16:17-23
   - Builds Samaria .... 1 Kin. 16:24
   - Reigns wickedly .... 1 Kin. 16:25-28

On—*stone*
1. Reubenite leader; joins Korah's rebellion .... Num. 16:1
2. City of Lower Egypt; center of sun-worship .... Gen. 41:45, 50
   - Called Bethshemesh .... Jer. 43:13

See Heres

Onam—*vigorous*
1. Horite chief .... Gen. 36:23
2. Man of Judah .... 1 Chr. 2:26, 28

Onan—*strong*
- Second son of Judah; slain for failure to consummate union .... Gen. 38:8-10

Oneness—*unity*

A. *Of Christ, with:*
- The Father .... John 10:30
- Christians .... Heb. 2:11

B. *Among Christians of:*
- Baptized .... 1 Cor. 12:13
- Union .... Ezek. 37:16-24
- Headship .... Ezek. 34:23
- Faith .... Eph. 4:4-6
- Mind .... Phil. 2:2
- Heart .... Acts 4:32

See Unity of believers

Onesimus—*useful*
- Slave of Philemon converted by Paul in Rome .... Philem. 10-17
- With Tychicus, carries Paul's letters to Colossae and to Philemon .... Col. 4:7-9

Onesiphorus—*profit-bearing*
- Ephesian Christian commended for his service .... 2 Tim. 1:16-18

Onion—*a bulbous plant used for food*
- Lusted after by Israelites .... Num. 11:5

Only begotten

Of Christ's:
- Incarnation .... John 1:14
- Godhead .... John 1:18
- Mission .... John 3:16, 18; 1 John 4:9

SUBJECT REFERENCE

Ono—*strong*

Town of Benjamin rebuilt by Shamed .... 1 Chr. 8:12
Reinhabited by returnees .... Ezra 2:1, 33

Onycha—*nail, claw, husk*

Ingredient of holy incense ...... Ex. 30:34

Onyx—*fingernail* (Greek)

Translation of a Hebrew word indicating a precious stone .... Job 28:16; Ezek. 28:13
Found in Havilah .... Gen. 2:11-12
Placed in high priest's ephod .... Ex. 28:9-20
Gathered by David .... 1 Chr. 29:2

Open—*to unfasten; to unlock; to expose*

A. *Descriptive of miracles on:*
Earth .... Num. 16:30, 32
Eyes .... John 9:10-32
Ears .... Mark 7:34, 35
Mouth .... Luke 1:64
Prison doors .... Acts 5:19, 23
Death .... 2 Kin. 4:35
Graves .... Matt. 27:52

B. *Descriptive of spiritual things:*
God's provision .... Ps. 104:28
God's bounty .... Mal. 3:10
Christ's blood .... Zech. 13:1
Man's corruption .... Rom. 3:13
Spiritual eyesight .... Luke 24:31, 32
Door of faith .... Acts 14:27
Opportunity .... 1 Cor. 16:9

Ophel—*bulge, hill*

South extremity of Jerusalem's eastern hill .... Neh. 3:15-27
Fortified by Jotham and Manasseh .... 2 Chr. 27:3
Residence of Nethinim .... Neh. 3:26

Ophir—*rich*

1. Son of Joktan .... Gen. 10:26, 29
2. Land, probably in southeast Arabia, inhabited by descendants of 1 .... Gen. 10:29, 30
Famous for its gold .... 1 Chr. 29:4

Ophni—*the high place*

Village of Benjamin .... Josh. 18:24

Ophrah—*hind*

1. Judahite .... 1 Chr. 4:14
2. Town in Benjamin near Michmash .... Josh. 18:21, 23
3. Town in Manasseh; home of Gideon .... Judg. 6:11, 15
Site of Gideon's burial ...... Judg. 8:32

Opportunity—*the best time for something*

A. *Kinds of:*
Rejected .... Matt. 23:37
Spurned .... Luke 14:16-24
Prepared .... Acts 8:35-39
Providential .... 1 Cor. 16:9
Good .... Gal. 6:10

B. *Loss of, due to:*
Unbelief .... Num. 14:40-43
Neglect .... Jer. 8:20
Unpreparedness .... Matt. 24:50, 51
Blindness .... Luke 19:41, 42

Opposed—*stand against*

A. *Of evil things:*
Proud .... James 4:6

B. *Of good things:*
Truth .... 2 Tim. 3:8

Oppression—*subjection to unjust hardships*

A. *Kinds of:*
Personal .... Is. 38:14
National .... Ex. 3:9
Economic .... Mic. 2:1, 2
Messianic .... Is. 53:7
Spiritual .... Acts 10:38

B. *Those subject to:*
Widows .... Zech. 7:10
Hired servant .... Deut. 24:14
Poor .... Ps. 12:5
People .... Is. 3:5
Soul .... Ps. 54:3

C. *Evils of, bring:*
Guilt .... Is. 59:12, 13

SUBJECT REFERENCE

Reproach .... Prov. 14:31
Poverty .... Prov. 22:16
Judgment .... Ezek. 18:12, 13

D. *Punishment of:*
God's judgment .... Is. 49:26
Captivity .... Is. 14:2, 4
Destruction of .... Ps. 72:4

E. *Protection against:*
Sought in prayer .... Deut. 26:7
Given by the LORD .... Ps. 103:6
Secured in refuge .... Ps. 9:9

F. *Agents of:*
Nations .... Judg. 10:12
Enemy .... Ps. 42:9; Ps. 106:42
Wicked .... Ps. 55:3
Man .... Ps. 119:134
Leaders .... Prov. 28:16
Sword .... Jer. 46:16; Jer. 50:16
Devil .... Acts 10:38
Rich .... James 2:6

Oracle—*a revelation; a wise saying*

A. *Descriptive of the Holy of Holies:*
Place in temple .... 1 Kin. 6:16
Direction of prayer .... Ps. 28:2
Source of truth .... 1 Sam. 23:9-12

B. *Descriptive of God's Word:*
Received by Israel .... Acts 7:38
Test of truth .... 1 Pet. 4:11

Oration, orator

Character of:
Egotistical .... Acts 12:21-23
Prejudiced .... Acts 24:1-9
Inspired .... Acts 26:1-29

Orchard—*a cultivated garden or park*

Source of fruits .... Song 4:13
Source of nuts .... Song 6:11

Orchestra—*group of musicians playing together*

Instituted by David .... 2 Sam. 6:5

Ordain, ordained—*to establish, appoint, set, decree*

A. *As appointment to office:*
Idolatrous priests .... 1 Kin. 13:33
Priesthood .... Lev. 8:1-36
Prophet .... Jer. 1:5
Royal officer .... Dan. 2:24
Apostles .... Mark 3:14
Christ as judge .... Acts 10:42
Elders .... Titus 1:5
Paul as a preacher .... 1 Tim. 2:7
Christ as high priest .... Heb. 5:1

B. *As appointment of temporal things:*
World order .... Ps. 8:3
Institution of:
Passover .... Ps. 81:5
Government .... Rom. 13:1
Life .... Num. 24:23; Ps. 139:16
Man's steps .... Prov. 20:24
Offering .... Num. 28:6
Law .... Acts 7:53; Gal. 3:19

C. *As appointment of eternal things:*
Covenant .... Ps. 111:9
Salvation .... Acts 13:48
Hidden wisdom .... 1 Cor. 2:7
Good works .... Eph. 2:10
Apostles .... Jude 4

Order—*harmony; symmetry; in proper places*

A. *As an arrangement in rows:*
Wood for sacrifices .... Gen. 22:9
Lamps set orderly .... Ex. 27:21
Battle formation .... 1 Chr. 12:38
Words logically developed ... Job 33:5
Consecutive narrative .... Luke 1:3
Logical defense .... Job 13:18
Absence of .... Job 10:22

B. *As a classification according to work:*
Priestly service .... 2 Kin. 23:4
Christ's priesthood .... Ps. 110:4
Church services .... 1 Cor. 11:34
Church officers .... Titus 1:5

SUBJECT REFERENCE

C. *Of something prescribed:*
Rules and regulations .... Judg. 13:12
Ritual regulations .... 1 Chr. 15:13
Church regulations .... 1 Cor. 14:40
Subjection to .... 1 Chr. 25:2, 6

D. *Of preparation for death:*
Ahithophel's .... 2 Sam. 17:23
Hezekiah's .... 2 Kin. 20:1

E. *Figurative of:*
God's covenant .... 2 Sam. 23:5
Believer's life .... Ps. 37:23
Man's sins .... Ps. 50:21

Ordinances—*regulations established for proper procedure*

A. *Descriptive of:*
Ritual observance .... Heb. 9:1, 10
God's laws .... Is. 24:5
God's laws in nature .... Jer. 31:35
Man's regulations .... Neh. 10:32
Man's laws .... 1 Pet. 2:13
Apostolic messages .... 1 Cor. 11:2
Jewish legalism .... Eph. 2:15

B. *Of the Gospel:*
Baptism .... Matt. 28:19
Lord's Supper .... 1 Cor. 11:23-29
Preaching the Word .... Rom. 10:15

Oreb—*a raven*

1. Midianite prince slain by Gideon .... Judg. 7:25
2. Rock on which Oreb was slain .... Judg. 7:25

Oren—*a fir or cedar tree*

Judahite .... 1 Chr. 2:25

Organ—*a wind instrument*

Of ancient origin .... Gen. 4:21
Used in:
Entertainments .... Job 21:12
God's worship .... Ps. 150:4

Orion—*strong*

Brilliant constellation .... Job 9:9

Ornaments—*outward adornments of the body*

Figurative of:
Wisdom's instruction .... Prov. 1:9
Reproof received .... Prov. 25:12
God's provisions .... Ezek. 16:7-14
Apostasy from God .... Jer. 4:30
See Clothing; Jewels

Orpah—*neck*

Ruth's sister-in-law .... Ruth 1:4, 14

Orphans—*children deprived of parents*

Description of .... Lam. 5:3
Provision for .... Deut. 24:17, 21
Job helps .... Job 29:12
Vistation of, commended .... James 1:27
Christians not left "orphans" .... John 14:18

Osee—*Greek name for the prophet Hosea*

Quoted by Paul .... Rom. 9:25

Oshea—*God saves*

Same as Joshua .... Num. 13:8, 16

Ospray—*a dark brown eagle*

Unclean bird .... Lev. 11:13

Ossifrage—*Latin for bone breaker*

Unclean bird (eagle) .... Lev. 11:13

Ostentatious—*vain, ambitious*

Manifested in:
Boastfulness .... Luke 18:10-14
Hypocrisy .... Matt. 6:1-7, 16
Conceit .... 2 Sam. 15:1-6
Egotism .... Acts 12:20-23

Ostracism—*exclusion of a person from society*

Accepted .... Luke 6:22
See Excommunication

Ostrich—*a two-toed, swift and flightless bird*

Figurative of cruelty .... Lam. 4:3

Othni—*abbreviation of Othniel*

Son of Shemaiah .... 1 Chr. 26:7

SUBJECT REFERENCE

Othniel—*God is force*

Son of Kenaz, Caleb's youngest brother ... Judg. 1:13
Captures Kirjath-sepher; receives Caleb's daughter as wife ... Josh. 15:15-17
First judge of Israel ... Judg. 3:9-11

Ouches—*woven together* (Heb.)

Setting for precious stones worn by the high priest ... Ex. 28:11
Fastener or clasp for cords ... Ex. 28:13, 14
Same Hebrew word translated "wrought" ... Ps. 45:13

Ought—*something morally imperative*

A. *Of duties not properly done:*
Use of talents ... Matt. 25:27
Accusation ... Acts 24:19
Growth ... Heb. 5:12

B. *Of acts wrongly done:*
Worship ... John 4:20, 21
Death ... John 19:7
Wrong behavior ... 2 Cor. 2:3
Inconsistent speaking ... James 3:10

C. *Of moral duties among Christians:*
Witnessing ... Luke 12:12
Prayer ... Luke 18:1
Service ... John 13:14
Obedience ... 1 Thess. 4:1
Helping the weak ... Rom. 15:1
Love toward wife ... Eph. 5:28
Proper behavior ... 2 Thess. 3:7
Holy conduct ... 2 Pet. 3:11
Willingness to sacrifice ... 1 John 3:16
Love of one another ... 1 John 4:11

See Must; Necessary, necessity

Outcasts—*dispossessed people*

Israel among the nations ... Ps. 147:2
Israel as objects of mercy ... Is. 16:3, 4
New Israel ... Jer. 30:17-22

Outrageous—*extremely bad; going beyond bounds of decency*

Descriptive of anger ... Prov. 27:4

Oven—*a place for baking or cooking*

A. *Characteristics of:*
Used for cooking ... Ex. 8:3
Fuel for, grass ... Matt. 6:30
Made on ground ... Gen. 18:6

B. *Figurative of:*
Scarcity in famine ... Lev. 26:26
Lust ... Hos. 7:4, 6, 7
God's judgments ... Ps. 21:9
Effects of famine ... Lam. 5:10

Overcome—*to conquer*

A. *Means of, by:*
Wine ... Jer. 23:9
Fleshly desire ... 2 Pet. 2:19, 20
God ... Rom. 8:37

B. *Objects of:*
World ... John 16:33
Evil ... Rom. 12:21
Satan ... 1 John 2:13, 14
Evil spirits ... 1 John 4:4
Two witnesses ... Rev. 11:7
Evil powers ... Rev. 17:13, 14

C. *Promises concerning, for Christians:*
Eating of the tree of life ... Rev. 2:7
Exemption from the second death ... Rev. 2:11
Power over the nations ... Rev. 2:26
Clothed in white raiment ... Rev. 3:5
Made a pillar in God's Temple ... Rev. 3:12
Rulership with Christ ... Rev. 3:21

Overlay—*to spread or place over*

Materials used:
Gold ... Ex. 26:32
Bronze ... Ex. 38:2
Silver ... Ex. 38:17

Objects overlaid:
Pillar—with gold ... Ex. 26:32
Board—with gold ... Ex. 36:34
Altar—with cedar ... 1 Kin. 6:20
Sanctuary—with gold ... 1 Kin. 6:21
Cherubim—with gold ... 1 Kin. 6:28

SUBJECT REFERENCE

Earthen vessel—with silver dross ... Prov. 26:23
Images—with silver ... Is. 30:22

Overplus—*excess*

Restoration of, required ... Lev. 25:27

Overseer—*a leader or supervisor*

Kinds of:
Prime minister ... Gen. 39:4, 5
Managers ... Gen. 41:34
Elders ... Acts 20:17, 28

Overthrow—*to throw down; destroy*

Agents of:
God ... Prov. 21:12
Evil ... Ps. 140:11
Wickedness ... Prov. 11:11
Evil ruler ... Dan. 11:41
Christ ... John 2:15

Overwork—*too much work*

Complaint of Israelites ... Ex. 5:6-21
Solution of, for Moses ... Ex. 18:14-26

Owe—*an obligation of*

Financial debt ... Matt. 18:24, 28
Moral debt ... Philem. 18, 19
Spiritual debt ... Rom. 13:8

Owl—*a large-eyed bird of prey*

Varieties of, all unclean ... Lev. 11:13-17
Solitary in habit ... Ps. 102:6

Ownership—*title of possession*

A. *By men, acquired by:*
Purchase ... Gen. 23:16-18
Inheritance ... Luke 15:12
Covenant ... Gen. 26:25-33

B. *By God, of:*
World ... Ps. 24:1
Souls of men ... Ezek. 18:4
Redeemed ... 1 Cor. 6:19, 20

Ox

A. *Uses of:*
Pulling covered wagons ... Num. 7:3
Plowing ... 1 Kin. 19:19
Food ... Deut. 14:4
Sacrifice ... Ex. 20:24
Means of existence ... Job 24:3
Designs in Temple ... 1 Kin. 7:25

B. *Laws concerning:*
To rest on Sabbath ... Ex. 23:12
Not to be:
Yoked with an ass ... Deut. 22:10
Muzzled while treading ... Deut. 25:4
To be restored ... Ex. 22:4, 9-13

C. *Figurative of:*
Easy victory ... Num. 22:4
Youthful rashness ... Prov. 7:22
Sumptuous living ... Prov. 15:17
Preach the Gospel ... Is. 32:20
Minister's support ... 1 Cor. 9:9, 10

D. *Descriptive of:*
Of great strength ... Num. 23:22
Very wild and ferocious ... Job 39:9-12
Frisky in youth ... Ps. 29:6

Ox goad—*spike used to drive oxen*

As a weapon ... Judg. 3:31

Ozem—*anger*

1. Son of Jesse ... 1 Chr. 2:13, 15
2. Descendant of Judah ... 1 Chr. 2:25

Ozni—*gives ear*

Son of Gad and head of a family ... Num. 26:15, 16
Called Ezbon ... Gen. 46:16

P

Paarai—*devotee of Peor*

One of David's mighty men ... 2 Sam. 23:35
Called Naarai ... 1 Chr. 11:37

Pacification—*causing anger to rest*

A. *Means of:*
Gift ... Prov. 21:14

SUBJECT REFERENCE

Wise man ... Prov. 16:14
Yielding ... Eccl. 10:4

B. *Examples of:*
Esau, by Jacob ... Gen. 32:11-19
Lord, toward His people ... Ezek. 16:63
Ahasuerus, by Haman's death ... Esth. 7:10

Pack animals

Used by Israelites ... 1 Chr. 12:40

Padan-aram—*the plain of Aram* (Mesopotamia)

Home of Isaac's wife ... Gen. 25:20
Jacob flees to ... Gen. 28:2-7
Jacob returns from ... Gen. 31:17, 18
Same as Mesopotamia ... Gen. 24:10
People of, called Syrians ... Gen. 31:24
Language of, called Syrian ... 2 Kin. 18:26

See Aramaic

Paddle—*a spadelike digging instrument*

Part of a soldier's equipment ... Deut. 23:13
Translated "nail" in ... Judg. 4:21

Padon—*ransom*

Head of Nethinim family ... Ezra 2:44
Neh. 7:47

Pagan gods

A. *Mentioned:*
Molech ... Lev. 18:21
Chemosh ... Judg. 11:24
Dagon ... Judg. 16:23
Baal ... 2 Kin. 17:16
Nergal ... 2 Kin. 17:30
Succoth-benoth ... 2 Kin. 17:30
Ashima ... 2 Kin. 17:30
Nibhaz ... 2 Kin. 17:31
Tartak ... 2 Kin. 17:31
Adrammelech ... 2 Kin. 17:31
Anammelech ... 2 Kin. 17:31
Nisroch ... Is. 37:38
Jupiter ... Acts 14:12
Mercurius ... Acts 14:12
Greek Pantheon ... Acts 17:16-23
Diana ... Acts 19:23-37

B. *Worship of condemned:*
By apostolic command ... 1 Cor. 10:14
By Law ... Ex. 20:3, 4
Deut. 5:7

Pagiel—*God meets*

Son of Ocran, chief of Asher's tribe ... Num. 1:13

Pahath-moab—*governor of Moab*

Family of postexilic returnees ... Ezra 2:6
Members of, divorced foreign wives ... Ezra 10:19, 30
One of, signs covenant ... Neh. 10:1, 14
Hashub, one of, helps Nehemiah ... Neh. 3:11

Pain—*physical or mental suffering*

A. *Kinds of:*
Childbirth ... Rev. 12:2
Physical fatigue ... 2 Cor. 11:27
Physical afflictions ... Job 33:19
Mental disturbance ... Ps. 55:4

B. *Characteristics of:*
Affects face ... Joel 2:6
Means of chastening ... Job 15:20
Affects the whole person ... Jer. 4:19
Common to all men ... Rom. 8:22

C. *Remedies for:*
Balm ... Jer. 51:8
Prayer ... Ps. 25:17, 18
God's deliverance ... Acts 2:24
Heaven ... Rev. 21:4

D. *Figurative of:*
Mental anguish ... Ps. 48:6
Impending trouble ... Jer. 22:23
Distressing news ... Is. 21:2, 3
Israel's captivity ... Is. 26:17, 18

Paint—*to apply liquid colors*

Applied to a wide house ... Jer. 22:14
Used by women ... 2 Kin. 9:30
Used especially by prostitutes ... Jer. 4:30
Ezek. 23:40

SUBJECT REFERENCE

Paintings

Of Chaldeans (bas-reliefs) ... Ezek. 23:14
Of animals and idols (on a secret wall) ... Ezek. 8:7-12

Pair—*two*

Sandals ... Amos 2:6
Turtledoves ... Luke 2:24
Balances ... Rev. 6:5

Palace—*a royal building*

A. *Descriptive of:*
King's residence ... 2 Chr. 9:11
Foreign city ... Is. 25:2
Dwellings in Zion ... Ps. 48:3
Heathen king's residence ... Ezra 6:2
Residence of the high priest ... Matt. 26:3, 58
Fortified place ... Neh. 7:2

B. *Characteristics of:*
Place of luxury ... Luke 7:25
Subject to destruction ... Is. 13:22

C. *Figurative of:*
Messiah's Temple ... Ps. 45:8, 15
Divine workmanship ... Ps. 144:12
Eternal city ... Jer. 30:18

Palal—*judge*

Postexilic laborer ... Neh. 3:25

Pale—*deficient in color*

Figurative of:
Shame ... Is. 29:22

Palestine (see Canaan, Land of)

Palliation of sin—*excusing sin*

A. *Manifested by:*
Calling bad men good ... Mal. 2:17
Describing sin as good ... Is. 5:20
Justifying the wicked ... Is. 5:23
Encouraging the wicked ... Ezek. 13:22
Calling the proud happy ... Mal. 3:13-15
Envying the wicked ... Ps. 73:3-15
Supposing God cannot see sin ... Ps. 10:11-13
Ignoring reproof ... Job 34:5-36
Sinning defiantly ... Is. 5:18, 19
Considering God indifferent to evil ... Zeph. 1:12
Misjudging people ... Matt. 11:18, 19
Questioning God's Word ... Ezek. 20:49

B. *Caused by:*
Moral darkness ... Matt. 6:23
Man-made concepts ... Matt. 16:3-6
Hypocrisy ... Matt. 23:15-23
Evil heart ... Luke 16:15
False teaching ... 2 Pet. 2:1-19

Pallu, Phallu—*distinguished*

Son of Reuben; head of tribal family ... Gen. 46:9; Ex. 6:14; Num. 26:5, 8

Palm of the hand

Used literally of:
Priest's hand ... Lev. 14:15, 26
Idol's hand ... 1 Sam. 5:4
Daniel's hand ... Dan. 10:10
Soldier's hand ... Matt. 26:67

Palm tree

A. *Uses of:*
Fruit of, for food ... Joel 1:12
Figures of, carved on Temple ... 1 Kin. 6:29-35
Branches of, for booths ... Lev. 23:40-42
Places of, at Elim and Jericho ... Ex. 15:27
Site of, for judgeship ... Judg. 4:5

B. *Figurative of:*
Righteous ... Ps. 92:12
Beauty ... Song 7:7
Victory ... John 12:13

Palmerworm—*caterpillar*

Name probably designates the locust ... Amos 4:9

Palms, city of

Moabites conquer ... Judg. 3:12, 13

SUBJECT REFERENCE

Palsy, paralysis—*loss of bodily motion*

Healed by:
Christ ... Matt. 4:24
Christians ... Acts 8:7

Palti, Phalti—*abbreviation of Pelatiah*

1. Benjamite spy ... Num. 13:9
2. Man to whom Saul gives Michal, David's wife-to-be, in marriage ... 1 Sam. 25:44

Paltiel, Phaltiel—*God has delivered*

1. Prince of Issachar ... Num. 34:26
2. Same as Palti 2 ... 2 Sam. 3:15

Paltite, the

Native of Beth-palet ... Josh. 15:27
Home of one of David's mighty men ... 2 Sam. 23:26
Same referred to as the Pelonite ... 1 Chr. 11:27

Pamphylia—*coastal region in South Asia Minor*

People from, at Pentecost ... Acts 2:10
Paul visits ... Acts 13:13
John Mark returns home from ... Acts 13:13; Acts 15:38
Paul preaches in cities of ... Acts 14:24, 25
Paul sails past ... Acts 27:5

Pan—*thin plate*

Offering in ... Lev. 2:5
Cooking ... Lev. 6:21
Pouring ... 2 Sam. 13:9

Panic—*fright*

A. *Among Israelites:*
At the Red Sea ... Ex. 14:10-12
Before the Philistines ... 1 Sam. 4:10
Of Judah before Israel ... 2 Kin. 14:12

B. *Among nations:*
Egyptians ... Ex. 14:27
Philistines ... 1 Sam. 14:22
Syrians ... 2 Kin. 7:6, 7
Ammonites and Moabites ... 2 Chr. 20:22-25

Pannag—*sweet*

Product of Palestine sold in Tyre ... Ezek. 27:17

Paper—*sheet*

Writing material ... 2 John 12
See Papyrus

Paphos—*capital of Cyprus*

Paul blinds Elymas ... Acts 13:6-13

Paps—*the breasts of*

Prostitute ... Ezek. 23:21
Mary the virgin ... Luke 11:27
Women ... Luke 23:29
Son of man (chest) ... Rev. 1:13

Papyrus—*a tall marsh plant growing in the Nile river region*

Referred to as bulrush in ... Ex. 2:3
See Paper

Parables—*an earthly story with a heavenly meaning*

A. *Descriptive of:*
Prophecy ... Num. 23:7, 18
Discourse ... Job 27:1
Wise saying ... Prov. 26:7, 9
Prophetic message ... Ezek. 17:1-10
Illustration (especially true of Christ's) ... Matt. 13:18

B. *Of Christ, characteristics of:*
Numerous ... Mark 4:33, 34
Illustrative ... Luke 12:16-21

Meaning of:
Self-evident ... Mark 12:1-12
Unknown ... Matt. 13:36
Explained ... Luke 8:9-15
Prophetic ... Luke 21:29-36

C. *Design of:*
Bring under conviction ... 2 Sam. 12:1-6
Teach a spiritual truth ... Is. 5:1-6
Illustrate a point ... Luke 10:25-37
Fulfill prophecy ... Matt. 13:34, 35
Conceal truth from the unbelieving ... Matt. 13:10-16

SUBJECT REFERENCE

D. *Of Christ, classification of:*

Concerning God's love in Christ:
Lost sheep ... Luke 15:4-7
Lost money ... Luke 15:8-10
Prodigal son ... Luke 15:11-32
Hidden treasure ... Matt. 13:44
Pearl of great price ... Matt. 13:45, 46

Concerning Israel:
Barren fig tree ... Luke 13:6-9
Two sons ... Matt. 21:28-32
Wicked husbandman ... Matt. 21:33-46

Concerning Christianity (the Gospel) in this age:
New cloth ... Matt. 9:16
New wine ... Matt. 9:17
Sower ... Matt. 13:3-8
Tares ... Matt. 13:24-30
Mustard seed ... Matt. 13:31, 32
Leaven ... Matt. 13:33
Net ... Matt. 13:47-50
Great supper ... Luke 14:16-24
Seed growing secretly ... Mark 4:26-29

Concerning salvation:
House built on the rock ... Matt. 7:24-27
Pharisee and publican ... Luke 18:9-14
Two debtors ... Luke 7:36-50
Marriage of the king's Son ... Matt. 22:1-14

Concerning Christian life:
Candle under a bushel ... Matt. 5:15, 16
Unmerciful servant ... Matt. 18:23-35
Friend at midnight ... Luke 11:5-13
Importunate widow ... Luke 18:1-8
Tower ... Luke 14:28-35
Good Samaritan ... Luke 10:25-37
Unjust steward ... Luke 16:1-13
Laborers in the vineyard ... Matt. 20:1-17

Concerning rewards and punishments:
Ten virgins ... Matt. 25:1-13
Talents ... Matt. 25:14-30
Pounds ... Luke 19:12-27
Sheep and goats ... Matt. 25:31-46
Master and servant ... Luke 17:7-10
Servants watching ... Mark 13:33-37; Luke 12:36-40
Rich fool ... Luke 12:16-21
Rich man and Lazarus ... Luke 16:19-31

Paraclete—*called to one's side*

Greek word translated "Comforter" and "Advocate" ... John 14:16-18; John 15:26; 1 John 2:1

Paradise—*an enclosed park similar to the Garden of Eden*

Applied in the New Testament to heaven ... Luke 23:43; 2 Cor. 12:4; Rev. 2:7

Paradox—*a statement appearing to be untrue or contradictory*

Getting rich by poverty ... Prov. 13:7
Dead burying the dead ... Matt. 8:22
Finding life by losing it ... Matt. 10:39
Not peace, but a sword ... Matt. 10:34-38
Wise as serpents; harmless as doves ... Matt. 10:16
Hating and loving ... Luke 14:26
Becoming great by serving ... Mark 10:43
Dying in order to live ... John 12:24, 25
Becoming a fool to be wise ... 1 Cor. 3:18

Parah—*young cow*

City in Benjamin ... Josh. 18:23

Paralytic—*one affected with incapacitation*

Brought to Jesus ... Matt. 9:2; Mark 2:3
Healed by Jesus ... Matt. 4:24; Luke 5:24
Healed by Jesus, through Peter ... Acts 9:33

Paramours—*illegal lovers*

Applied to the male lover ... Ezek. 23:20

Paran—*a wilderness region in the Sinaitic Peninsula*

Mountainous country ... Hab. 3:3
Residence of exiled Ishmael ... Gen. 21:21
Israelites camp in ... Num. 10:12
Headquarters of spies ... Num. 13:3, 26
Site of David's refuge ... 1 Sam. 25:1

SUBJECT ... REFERENCE

Parbar—*suburb*
Precinct or colonnade west of the Temple ... 1 Chr. 26:18
Same word translated "suburbs" in ... 2 Kin. 23:11

Parched—*roasted, dry*
Corn ... Josh. 5:11
Pulse ... 2 Sam. 17:28

Parchments—*writing material made from animal skin*
Paul sends request ... 2 Tim. 4:13

Pardon—*to forgive*
A. *Objects of our:*
Transgressions ... Ex. 23:21
Iniquities ... Ex. 34:9
Backslidings ... Jer. 5:6, 7
B. *God's, described as:*
Not granted ... 2 Kin. 24:4
Requested ... Num. 14:19, 20
Abundant ... Is. 55:7
Covering all sins ... Jer. 33:8
Belonging to the faithful remnant ... Is. 40:2
C. *Basis of:*
LORD's name ... Ps. 25:11
Repentance ... Is. 55:7
Seeking the faith ... Jer. 5:1
See Forgiveness

Parents—*fathers and mothers*
A. *Kinds of:*
Faithful (Abraham) ... Gen. 18:18, 19
Neglectful (Moses) ... Ex. 4:24-26
Presumptuous (Jephthah) ... Judg. 11:30-39
Holy (Hannah) ... 1 Sam. 1:11
Indulgent (Eli) ... 1 Sam. 2:22-29
Distressed (David) ... 2 Sam. 18:32, 33
Honored (Jonadab) ... Jer. 35:5-10
Arrogant (Haman) ... Esth. 3:1-10
Forgiving (prodigal son's father) ... Luke 15:17-24
B. *Duties toward:*
Obedience ... Eph. 6:1
Honor ... Ex. 20:12
Fear ... Lev. 19:3
C. *Duties of, toward children:*
Protection ... Heb. 11:23
Training ... Deut. 6:6, 7
Education ... Gen. 18:19; Deut. 4:9
Correction ... Deut. 21:18-21
Provision ... 2 Cor. 12:14
D. *Sins of:*
Favoritism ... Gen. 25:28
Not restraining children ... 1 Sam. 2:27-36
Bad example ... 1 Kin. 15:26
Anger ... Eph. 6:4
E. *Sins against, by children:*
Disobedience ... Rom. 1:30
Cursing ... Ex. 21:17
Mocking ... Prov. 30:17
Disrespect ... Gen. 9:21-27

Parlor
Upper room in Eglon's home ... Judg. 3:20-25
Room or hall for sacrificial meals ... 1 Sam. 9:22
Inside room of the temple ... 1 Chr. 28:11

Parmashta—*the very first*
Haman's son ... Esth. 9:9

Parmenas
One of the seven deacons ... Acts 6:5

Parnach
Zebulunite ... Num. 34:25

Parosh—*flea*
1. Head of a postexilic family ... Ezra 2:3
Called Pharoush ... Ezra 8:3
Members of, divorced foreign wives ... Ezra 10:25
One of, Pedaiah, helps rebuild ... Neh. 3:25
2. Chief who seals the covenant ... Neh. 10:1, 14

SUBJECT ... REFERENCE

Patricide—*murder of one's father and/or mother*
Sennacherib's sons guilty of ... 2 Kin. 19:36, 37

Parshandatha—*inquisitive*
Haman's son ... Esth. 9:7

Parsimony—*stinginess; living like a miser*
A. *Characteristics of:*
Choosing selfishly ... Gen. 13:5-11
Living luxuriantly ... Amos 6:4-6
Showing greediness ... John 12:5, 6
Withholding God's tithe ... Mal. 3:8
Unmerciful toward the needy ... Zech. 7:10-12
B. *Punishment of:*
Brings:
Poverty ... Prov. 11:24, 25
A curse ... Prov. 11:26
Revenge ... Prov. 21:13
The closing of God's kingdom ... Luke 18:22-25

Part—*a portion of the whole*
Mary chooses the good ... Luke 10:42
Israel's blindness ... Rom. 11:25
Our knowledge ... 1 Cor. 13:9-12

Partake—*to share in*
A. *Of physical things:*
Sacrifices ... 1 Cor. 10:18
Suffering ... 2 Cor. 1:7
Benefit ... 1 Tim. 6:2
Human nature ... Heb. 2:14
Discipline ... Heb. 12:8
Bread ... 1 Cor. 10:17
B. *Of evil things:*
Evil ... Eph. 5:3-7
Demonism ... 1 Cor. 10:21
C. *Of spiritual things:*
Divine nature ... 2 Pet. 1:4
Christ ... Heb. 3:14
Holy Spirit ... Heb. 6:4
Heavenly calling ... Heb. 3:1
Grace ... Phil. 1:7
Gospel ... 1 Cor. 9:23
Spiritual blessings ... Rom. 11:17
Future glory ... 1 Pet. 5:1
Promise of salvation ... Eph. 3:6

Partakers
A. *Of physical things:*
Sacrifices ... 1 Cor. 10:18
Suffering ... 2 Cor. 1:7
B. *Of evil things:*
Sins ... 1 Tim. 5:22
C. *Of spiritual things:*
Holiness ... Heb. 12:10
Communion ... 1 Cor. 10:16, 17
Spiritual things ... Rom. 15:27
Inheritance ... Col. 1:12

Parthians—*inhabitants of Parthia*
Some present at Pentecost ... Acts 2:1, 9

Partiality—*favoritism*
A. *Manifested:*
In marriages ... Gen. 29:30
Among brothers ... Gen. 43:30, 34
Between parents and children ... Gen. 25:28
In social life ... James 2:1-4
B. *Inconsistent with:*
Household harmony ... Gen. 37:4-35
Justice in law ... Lev. 19:15
Favoritism in:
Ministry ... 1 Tim. 5:21
Spiritual things ... 2 Cor. 5:16
Restriction of salvation ... Acts 10:28-35
C. *Consistent with:*
Choice of workers ... Acts 15:36-40
Estimate of friends ... Phil. 2:19-22
God's predestination ... Rom. 9:6-24
See Favoritism

Partition—*a dividing wall*
In the sanctuary ... 1 Kin. 6:21
Between people ... Eph. 2:11-14

SUBJECT ... REFERENCE

Partner—*an associate in*
Crime ... Prov. 29:24
Business ... Luke 5:7, 10
Christian work ... 2 Cor. 8:23; Philem. 17

Partridge—*a wild bird meaning "the caller" (in Heb.)*
Hunted in mountains ... 1 Sam. 26:20
Figurative of ill-gotten riches ... Jer. 17:11

Paruah—*sprouting*
Father of Jehoshaphat, an officer of Solomon ... 1 Kin. 4:17

Parvaim
Unidentified place providing gold for Solomon's Temple ... 2 Chr. 3:6

Pasach—*divider*
Asherite ... 1 Chr. 7:33

Pas-dammin—*boundary of bloodshed*
Philistines gathered here ... 1 Chr. 11:13

Paseah—*lame*
1. Judahite ... 1 Chr. 4:12
2. Head of a family of Nethinim ... Ezra 2:43, 49
One of, repairs walls ... Neh. 3:6
3. A family of Temple servants ... Neh. 7:46, 51

Pashur—*free*
1. Official opposing Jeremiah ... Jer. 21:1; Jer. 38:1-13
Descendants of, returnees ... Neh. 11:12
2. Priest who put Jeremiah in jail ... Jer. 20:1-6
3. Father of Gedaliah, Jeremiah's opponent ... Jer. 38:1
4. Priestly family of returnees ... Ezra 2:38
Members of, divorced foreign wives ... Ezra 10:22
5. Priest who signs the covenant ... Neh. 10:3
Blocked by burial ground ... Ezek. 39:11
Stripped ... Mic. 2:8
Simon of Cyrene ... Mark 15:21

Passing away—*ceasing to exist*
A. *Things subject to:*
Our days ... Ps. 90:9
Old things ... 2 Cor. 5:17
World's fashion ... 1 Cor. 7:31
World's lust ... 1 John 2:17
Heaven and earth ... 2 Pet. 3:10
B. *Things not subject to:*
Christ's words ... Luke 21:33
Christ's dominion ... Dan. 7:14

Passion—*suffering*
A. *Descriptive of:*
Christ's sufferings ... Acts 1:3
Man's nature ... James 5:17
Lusts ... Rom. 1:26
B. *As applied* (theologically) *to Christ's sufferings:*
Predicted ... Is. 53:1-12
Portrayed visibly ... Mark 14:3-8
Preached ... Acts 3:12-18; 1 Pet. 1:10-12

Passover—*a Jewish festival commemorative of the exodus from Egypt*
A. *Features concerning:*
Commemorative of the tenth plague ... Ex. 12:3-28
Necessity of blood applied ... Ex. 12:7
To be repeated annually ... Ex. 12:24-27
B. *Observances of:*
At Sinai ... Num. 9:1-14
At the conquest ... Josh. 5:10-12
By Christ ... Matt. 26:18, 19
C. *Typical of the Lord's death* (the Lord's Supper):
Lamb without blemish ... 1 Pet. 1:19
One of their own ... Ex. 12:5; Heb. 2:14, 17

SUBJECT REFERENCE

Lamb chosen ... Ex. 12:3; 1 Pet. 2:4
Slain at God's appointed time ... Ex. 12:6; Acts 2:23
Christ is ... 1 Cor. 5:7

See Lamb of God, the

Password—*a secret word used to identify friends*

Used by Gileadites ... Judg. 12:5, 6

Pastor—*shepherd*

To perfect the saints ... Eph. 4:11, 12
Appointed by God ... Jer. 3:15
Some rebellious ... Jer. 2:8
Unfaithful ones are punished ... Jer. 22:22

See Shepherd

Pasture—*a place for grazing animals*

A. *Used literally of:*

Places for:

Cattle to feed ... Gen. 47:4
Wild animals to feed ... Is. 32:14
God's material blessings ... Ps. 65:11-13

B. *Used figuratively of:*

Restoration and peace ... Ezek. 34:13-15
True Israel ... Ps. 95:7
Kingdom of God ... Is. 49:9, 10
Kingdom of Israel ... Jer. 25:36
Gospel ... Is. 30:23
Abundant provision for salvation ... Ezek. 45:15

C. *Of the true Israel* (the Church), *described as:*

God's people ... Ps. 100:3
Provided for ... John 10:9
Purchased ... Ps. 74:1, 2
Thankful ... Ps. 79:13
Scattered by false pastors ... Jer. 23:1

See Shepherd

Patara—*a port of Lycia in Asia Minor*

Paul changes ships here ... Acts 21:1, 2

Pate—*the top of the head*

Figurative of retribution ... Ps. 7:16

Path—*a walk; manner of life*

A. *Of the wicked:*

Brought to nothing ... Job 6:18
Becomes dark ... Job 24:13
Is crooked ... Is. 59:8
Leads to death ... Prov. 2:18
Filled with wickedness ... Prov. 1:15, 16
Is destructive ... Is. 59:7
Followed by wicked rulers ... Is. 3:12
Made difficult by God ... Hos. 2:6

B. *Of believers:*

Beset with difficulties ... Job 19:8
Under God's control ... Job 13:27
Hindered by the wicked ... Job 30:13
Enriched by the LORD ... Ps. 23:3
Upheld by God ... Ps. 17:5
Provided with light ... Ps. 119:105
Known by God ... Ps. 139:3
Like a shining light ... Prov. 4:18
Directed by God ... Is. 26:7
To be pondered ... Prov. 4:26
No death at the end ... Prov. 12:28
Sometimes unknown ... Is. 42:16
Sometimes seems crooked ... Lam. 3:9
To be made straight ... Heb. 12:13

C. *Of righteousness:*

Taught by father ... Prov. 4:1, 11
Kept ... Prov. 2:20
Shown to Messiah ... Ps. 16:11; Acts 2:28
Taught to believers ... Ps. 25:4, 5
Sought by believers ... Ps. 119:35; Is. 2:3
Rejected by unbelieving ... Jer. 6:16; Jer. 18:15

D. *Of the Lord:*

True ... Ps. 25:10
Plain ... Ps. 27:11
Rich ... Ps. 65:11
Guarded ... Prov. 2:8
Upright ... Prov. 2:13
Living ... Prov. 2:19
Peaceful ... Prov. 3:17

Pathros—*the Southland*

Name applied to south (Upper) Egypt ... Ezek. 29:10-14
Described as a lowly kingdom ... Ezek. 29:14-16
Refuge for dispersed Jews ... Jer. 44:1-15
Jews to be regathered from ... Is. 11:11

Pathrusim—*the inhabitants of Pathros*

Hamitic people descending from Mizraim and living in Pathros ... Gen. 10:14

Patience—*the ability to bear trials without grumbling*

A. *Of the Trinity:*

God, the author of ... Rom. 15:5
Christ, the example of ... 2 Thess. 3:5
Spirit, the source of ... Gal. 5:22

B. *Described as:*

Rewarded ... Rom. 2:7
Endured with joy ... Col. 1:11

C. *Product of:*

Good heart ... Luke 8:15
Tribulation ... Rom. 5:3, 4
Testing of faith ... James 1:3
Hope ... Rom. 8:25
Scriptures ... Rom. 15:4

D. *Necessary grace, in:*

Times of crises ... Luke 21:15-19
Dealing with a church ... 2 Cor. 12:12
Opposing evil ... Rev. 2:2
Soundness of faith ... Titus 2:2
Waiting for Christ's return ... James 5:7, 8

Patmos—*an Aegan island off the southwestern coast of Asia Minor*

John, banished here, receives the Revelation ... Rev. 1:9

Patriarchal age—*the time of Abraham, Isaac, Jacob* (between 1900 and 1600 B.C.)

A. *Rulers of:*

Kings ... Gen. 12:15-20
Chiefs ... Gen. 26:1
Family heads (fathers) ... Gen. 18:18, 19

B. *Business of:*

Cattle, etc. ... Gen. 12:16
Caravans ... Gen. 37:28-36
Selling, etc. ... Gen. 23:1-20
Contracts ... Gen. 21:27-30
Business agreements ... Gen. 30:28-34

C. *Customs of:*

Prevalence of polygamy ... Gen. 16:4
Existence of slavery ... Gen. 12:16
Son's wife, selected by his father ... Gen. 24:1-4
Children given significant names ... Gen. 29:31-35

D. *Religion of:*

Existence of idolatry ... Gen. 35:1, 2
Worship of God Almighty ... Gen. 14:19-22
God's covenant recognized ... Gen. 12:1-3
Circumcision observed ... Gen. 17:10-14
Headship of father ... Gen. 35:2
Obedience primary ... Gen. 18:18, 19
Prayers and sacrifices offered ... Gen. 12:8
Blessings and curses pronounced by father ... Gen. 27:27-40
True faith believed ... Matt. 15:28; Heb. 11:8-22

Patriarchs—*ancient family, or tribal heads*

Applied, in New Testament, to Abraham, to Jacob's sons, and to David ... Heb. 7:4

Patrimony—*inherited possessions*

Applied to Levites' portion ... Deut. 18:8
Same idea found in ... Luke 12:13

See Inheritance, earthly

Patriotism—*love of one's country*

Manifested in:

Willingness to fight for one's country ... 1 Sam. 17:26-51
Concern for national survival ... Esth. 4:13-17
Desire for national revival ... Neh. 1:2-11
Loyalty to national leader ... 2 Sam. 2:10
Respect for national leaders ... 2 Sam. 1:18-27

Patrobas

Christian at Rome ... Rom. 16:14

Pattern—*a copy; an example*

A. *Of physical things:*

Tabernacle ... Heb. 8:5
Temple ... 1 Chr. 28:11-19

B. *Of spiritual things:*

Good works ... Titus 2:7
Heavenly originals ... Heb. 9:23

See Example; Example of Christ, the

Pau, Pai—*groaning, bleating*

Edomite town, residence of King Hadar (Hadad) ... Gen. 36:39; 1 Chr. 1:50

Paul—*little*

A. *Life of:*

From birth to conversion:

Born at Tarsus in Cilicia ... Acts 22:3
Born a Roman citizen ... Acts 22:25-28
Called Saul until changed to Paul ... Acts 9:11; Acts 13:9
Benjamite Jew ... Phil. 3:5
Citizen of Tarsus ... Acts 21:39
By trade a tentmaker ... Acts 18:1, 3
Zealot for Judaism ... Gal. 1:14; Phil. 3:5
Very strict Pharisee ... Acts 23:6; Phil. 3:5, 6
Educated under Gamaliel ... Acts 22:3
His sister in Jerusalem ... Acts 23:16
Apparently unmarried or a widower ... 1 Cor. 9:5
Member of Jewish council ... Acts 26:10
Zealous for the Mosaic Law ... Acts 26:4, 5
Consented to Stephen's death ... Acts 7:58; Acts 8:1; Acts 22:20
Intensified persecution of Christians ... Acts 9:1-3; Acts 22:3-5; Acts 26:10, 11; Gal. 1:13
Conscientious persecutor ... Acts 26:9; 1 Tim. 1:13

His conversion:

On road to Damascus ... Acts 9:1-19
At noon ... Acts 26:13
Blinded by supernatural vision ... Acts 9:3, 8; 2 Cor. 12:1-7
Responded willingly to Jesus' entreaty ... Acts 9:4-9
Given a divine commission ... Acts 9:6, 10-18; Eph. 3:1-8
Instructed and baptized by Ananias ... Acts 9:6, 10-18
Repeated his conversion story ... Acts 22:1-16; Acts 26:1-20
Referred to it often ... 1 Cor. 9:1, 16; 1 Cor. 15:8-10; Gal. 1:12-16
Considered himself unworthy ... Eph. 3:1-8
Cites details of his change ... Phil. 3:4-10
Regretted former life ... 1 Tim. 1:12-16
Not ashamed of Christ ... Rom. 1:16; 2 Tim. 1:8-12
Preached Jesus as God's Son and as the Christ (that is, the Messiah) ... Acts 9:19-22
Persecuted by Jews; went to Arabia ... Acts 9:23-25; 2 Cor. 11:32, 33; Gal. 1:17
Returned to Damascus ... Gal. 1:17
Visited Jerusalem briefly ... Acts 9:26-29; Gal. 1:18, 19
Received vision of his ministry to Gentiles ... Acts 22:17-21
Sent by disciples to Tarsus ... Acts 9:29, 30; Gal. 1:21
Brought to Antioch (in Syria) by Barnabas ... Acts 11:22-26
Sent to Jerusalem with relief ... Acts 11:27-30
Returned to Antioch ... Acts 12:25

First Missionary Journey:

Divinely chosen and commissioned ... Acts 13:1-4; Acts 26:19, 20
Accompanied by Barnabas and John Mark ... Acts 13:1, 5
Preached in Cyprus ... Acts 13:4-12
Sailed to Perga; Mark left him ... Acts 13:13
Preached in Antioch (in Pisidia); rejected by Jews ... Acts 13:14-51; 2 Tim. 3:11
Rejected in Iconium ... Acts 13:51, 52; Acts 14:1-5
Stoned at Lystra ... Acts 14:6-20; 2 Tim. 3:11

SUBJECT	REFERENCE
Went to Derbe	Acts 14:20, 21
Returned to Antioch (in Syria)	Acts 14:21-26
Told Christians about his work	Acts 14:27, 28
Participated in Jerusalem Council	Acts 15:2-22; Gal. 2:1-10
Rebuked Peter in Antioch for inconsistency	Gal. 2:11-21
Second Missionary Journey:	
Rejected John Mark as companion; took Silas	Acts 15:36-40
Strengthened churches in Syria and Cilicia	Acts 15:41
Revisited Derbe and Lystra	Acts 16:1
Took Timothy as worker	Acts 16:1-5
Directed by the Spirit where to preach	Acts 16:6, 7
Responded to Macedonian vision	Acts 16:8, 9
Joined by Luke ("we")	Acts 16:10
Entered Macedonia	Acts 16:10, 11
Converted Lydia at Philippi	Acts 16:12-15
Cast into prison; jailer converted	Acts 16:16-34
Used Roman citizenship	Acts 16:35-39
Preached at Thessalonica	Acts 17:1-9; 1 Thess. 1:7; 1 Thess. 2:2-18
Received by the Bereans	Acts 17:10-13
Left Silas and Timothy; went to Athens	Acts 17:14-17
Preached on Mars' Hill (the Areopagus)	Acts 17:18-34
Arrived in Corinth; stayed with Aquila and Priscilla	Acts 18:1-5
Reunited with Silas and Timothy	Acts 18:5; 1 Thess. 3:6
Wrote letters to Thessalonians	1 Thess. 3:1-6; 2 Thess. 2:2
Established a church at Corinth	Acts 18:5-18
Stopped briefly at Ephesus	Acts 18:19-21
Saluted Jerusalem church; returned to Antioch (in Syria)	Acts 18:22
Third Missionary Journey:	
Strengthened churches of Galatia and Phrygia	Acts 18:23
Gave direction for relief collection	1 Cor. 16:1
Ministered three years in Ephesus	Acts 19:1-12; Acts 20:31
Saved from angry mob	Acts 19:13-41
Probably wrote *Galatians* here	Gal. 1:1
Wrote *First Corinthians* here	1 Cor. 5:9
Went to Troas; failed to meet Titus	2 Cor. 2:12, 13
Reunited with Titus in Macedonia	Acts 20:1; 2 Cor. 7:5-16
Wrote *Second Corinthians;* sent Titus to Corinth with this letter	2 Cor. 8:6-18
Traveled extensively	Acts 20:2; Rom. 15:19
Visited Greece and Corinth	Acts 20:2, 3
Wrote *Romans* in Corinth	Rom. 1:1
Returned through Macedonia	Acts 20:3
Preached long sermon in Troas	Acts 20:5-13
Gave farewell talk to Ephesian elders at Miletus	Acts 20:14-38
Arrived in Caesarea	Acts 21:1-8
Warned by Agabus	Acts 21:9-14
In Jerusalem and Caesarea:	
Arrived in Jerusalem; welcomed by church	Acts 21:15-19
Falsely charged; riot follows	Acts 21:20-40
Defended his action; removed by Roman police	Acts 22:1-30
Defended his action before Jewish council	Acts 23:1-10
Saved from Jewish plot; taken to Caesarea	Acts 23:11-35
Defended himself before Felix	Acts 24:1-23
Preached to Felix and Drusilla	Acts 24:24-26
Imprisoned for two years	Acts 24:27
Accused before Festus by Jews	Acts 25:1-9
Appealed to Caesar	Acts 25:10-12
Defended himself before Agrippa	Acts 25:13-27; Acts 26:1-32
Voyage to Rome:	
Sailed from Caesarea to Crete	Acts 27:1-13
Ship tossed by storm	Acts 27:14-20
Assured by the Lord	Acts 27:21-25
Ship wrecked; all saved	Acts 27:26-44
On island of Melita	Acts 28:1-10
Continued journey to Rome	Acts 28:11-16
Rejected by Jews in Rome	Acts 28:17-29
Dwelt in Rome two years	Acts 28:30, 31
Wrote *Ephesians, Colossians, Philippians,* and *Philemon* here	Eph. 3:1; Eph. 6:20; Phil. 1:7, 13; Col. 4:7-18; Philem. 10, 22
Final ministry and death:	
Released from first Roman imprisonment	Phil. 1:25; Phil. 2:17, 24; 2 Tim. 4:16, 17
Wrote *First Timothy* and *Titus*	1 Tim. 1:1-3; Titus 1:1-5
Visited Macedonia and other places	2 Tim. 4:20
Wrote *Second Timothy* from Roman prison	2 Tim. 1:8; 2 Tim. 4:6-8
Sent final news and greetings	2 Tim. 4:9-22
B. *Missionary methods of:*	
Pay his own way	Acts 18:3; Acts 20:33-35; 2 Cor. 11:7, 9
Preach to the Jews first	Acts 13:46; Acts 17:1-5
Establish churches in large cities	Acts 19:1-10; Rom. 1:7-15
Travel with companions	Acts 15:40; Acts 20:4; Col. 4:14
Report work to sending church	Acts 14:26-28; Acts 21:17-20
Use his Roman citizenship when necessary	Acts 16:36-39; Acts 22:24-29; Acts 25:10-12
Seek to evangelize the world	Col. 1:23-29; 2 Tim. 4:17
C. *Writings of:*	
Inspired by God	2 Cor. 13:3; 1 Thess. 2:13; 2 Tim. 3:15, 16
Contain difficult things	2 Pet. 3:15, 16
Written by himself	Gal. 6:11; 2 Thess. 3:17
Sometimes dictated to a scribe	Rom. 16:22
Considered weighty by some	2 Cor. 10:10
His name sometimes forged	2 Thess. 2:2
Reveal personal information	2 Cor. 11:1-33; 2 Cor. 12:1-11
Convey personal messages	Phil. 2:19-30; Heb. 13:23, 24
Contain salutation and closing doxology	2 Cor. 1:2, 3; 2 Cor. 13:14
Disclose personal plans	Phil. 2:19-24; Philem. 22
Some complimentary	Phil. 4:10-19
Some filled with rebuke	Gal. 1:6-8; Gal. 5:1-10
D. *Characteristics of:*	
Consecrated	1 Cor. 4:1-15; Phil. 3:7-14
Cheerful	Acts 16:25; 2 Cor. 4:8-10
Courageous	Acts 9:29; Acts 20:22-24
Considerate of others	Phil. 2:25-30; Philem. 7-24
Conscientious	2 Cor. 1:12-17; 2 Cor. 6:3, 4
Christ-centered	2 Cor. 4:10, 11; Phil. 1:20-23
Conciliatory	2 Cor. 2:1-11; Gal. 2:1-15
Composed	2 Cor. 12:8-10; 2 Tim. 4:7, 8
Pauline theology	
Given by revelation	Gal. 1:11, 12
Salvation by grace	Eph. 2:1-10
To Gentiles	Eph. 3:1-12
Paulus, Sergius	
Roman proconsul of Cyprus	Acts 13:4, 7
Pavement—*a terrace made of bricks or stones*	
God's, made of sapphire	Ex. 24:10
Shushan's, made of precious stones	Esth. 1:5, 6
Of stone	2 Kin. 16:17
Ezekiel's Temple, surrounded by	Ezek. 40:17, 18
Judgment place of Pilate	John 19:13
See Gabbatha	
Pavilion—*a covered place, tent, booth*	
Place of refuge	Ps. 27:5
Canopy of God's abode	Job 36:29
Protective covering ("tabernacle")	Is. 4:6
Paws—*the feet of animals having claws*	
Descriptive of certain animals	Lev. 11:27
Of bears and lions	1 Sam. 17:37
Pay—*to give something for something*	
Lord's blessing	Prov. 19:17
Punishment	Matt. 5:26
Servitude and forgiveness	Matt. 18:23-35
Sign of righteousness	Ps. 37:21
See Vow	
Pe	
Letter in the Hebrew alphabet	Ps. 119:129-136
Peace	
A. *Kinds of:*	
International	1 Sam. 7:14
National	1 Kin. 4:24
Civil	Rom. 14:19
Domestic	1 Cor. 7:15
Individual	Luke 8:48
False	1 Thess. 5:3
Hypocritical	James 2:16
Spiritual	Rom. 5:1
B. *Source of:*	
God	Phil. 4:7
Christ	John 14:27
Holy Spirit	Gal. 5:22
C. *Of Christ:*	
Predicted	Is. 9:6, 7
Promised	Hag. 2:9
Announced	Is. 52:7
D. *Lord's relation to, He:*	
Reveals	Jer. 33:6
Gives	Ps. 29:11
Ordains	Is. 26:12
E. *Among the wicked:*	
Not known by	Is. 59:8
None for	Is. 48:22
F. *Among believers, truths concerning:*	
Comes through Christ's atonement	Is. 53:5
Results from reconciliation	Col. 1:20
Product of justification	Rom. 5:1
Obtained by faith	Is. 26:3
G. *Among believers, exhortations regarding:*	
Should live in	2 Cor. 13:11
Should pursue	2 Tim. 2:22
Peacemakers—*those who work for peace*	
Christ the great	2 Cor. 5:18-21
Christians become	Matt. 5:9; Rom. 14:19
Rules regarding	1 Pet. 3:8-13
Peacock—*peafowl*	
Imported by Solomon from Tarshish	1 Kin. 10:22
Trade item	2 Chr. 9:21
Pearl—*a precious gem found in oyster shells*	
A. *Used literally of:*	
Valuable gems	Rev. 18:12, 16
Woman's attire	1 Tim. 2:9
B. *Used figuratively of:*	
Spiritual truths	Matt. 7:6
Kingdom	Matt. 13:45, 46
Worldly adornment	Rev. 17:4

SUBJECT REFERENCE

Wonders of heaven's glories ..... Rev. 21:21

Peculiar—*something separated to one's own use*

A. *Applied literally to:*
Israel (God's own) ..... Ex. 19:5
Treasure (Solomon's own) ... Eccl. 2:8
Translated:
"Special" ..... Deut. 7:6
"Jewels" ..... Mal. 3:17

B. *Applied figuratively to:*
True Israel ..... Ps. 135:4
Christian ..... Titus 2:14
True church ..... 1 Pet. 2:9

Pedahel—*God saves*
Prince of Naphtali ..... Num. 34:28

Pedahzur—*the Rock* (God) *has redeemed*
Father of Gamaliel ..... Num. 1:10

Pedaiah—*Jehovah redeems*
1. Father of Joel, ruler in David's reign ..... 1 Chr. 27:20
2. Grandfather of Jehoiakim ... 2 Kin. 23:36
3. Son of Jeconiah ..... 1 Chr. 3:18, 19
4. Postexilic workman ..... Neh. 3:25
5. Ezra's Levite attendant ..... Neh. 8:4
6. Man appointed as treasurer ..... Neh. 13:13
7. Postexilic Benjamite ..... Neh. 11:7

Pekah—*opening* (of the eye)
Son of Remaliah; usurps Israel's throne ..... 2 Kin. 15:25-28
Forms alliance with Rezin of Syria against Ahaz ..... Is. 7:1-9
Alliance defeated; captives returned ..... 2 Kin. 16:5-9
Territory of, overrun by Tiglath-pileser ..... 2 Kin. 15:29
Assassinated by Hoshea ..... 2 Kin. 15:30

Pekahiah—*Jehovah hath opened* (the eyes)
Son of Menahem; king of Israel ..... 2 Kin. 15:22-26
Assassinated by Pekah ..... 2 Kin. 15:23-25

Pekod—*visitation*
Aramean tribe during Nebuchadnezzar's reign ..... Jer. 50:21

Pelaiah—*Jehovah is wonderful*
1. Judahite ..... 1 Chr. 3:24
2. Ezra's Levite attendant; reads covenant ..... Neh. 8:7

Pelaliah—*Jehovah has judged*
Postexilic priest ..... Neh. 11:12

Pelatiah—*Jehovah has freed*
1. Simeonite captain in war with Amalekites ..... 1 Chr. 4:42, 43
2. Prince dying while Ezekiel prophesies ..... Ezek. 11:1-13
3. Descendant of Solomon ..... 1 Chr. 3:21
4. One who signs the covenant ..... Neh. 10:1, 22

Peleg—*division*
Brother of Joktan ..... Gen. 10:25
Son of Eber ..... Luke 3:35

Pelet—(God) *has freed*
1. Judahite ..... 1 Chr. 2:47
2. Benjamite warrior under David ..... 1 Chr. 12:3

Peleth—*swiftness*
1. Reubenite, father of On ..... Num. 16:1
2. Judahite ..... 1 Chr. 2:33

Pelethites—*perhaps a contraction of Philistines*
David's faithful soliders during Absalom's and Sheba's rebellions ..... 2 Sam. 15:18-22
See Cherethites

Pelican—*the vomiter*
Ceremonially unclean bird ..... Lev. 11:18
Dwells in wilderness ..... Ps. 102:6
Lives in ruins ..... Is. 34:11
Zeph. 2:14

SUBJECT REFERENCE

Pelonite
Descriptive of two of David's mighty men ..... 1 Chr. 11:27, 36

Pen
Figurative of tongue ..... Ps. 45:1
Lying ..... Jer. 8:8
Not preferred ..... 3 John 1:13

Penalties—*punishment inflicted for wrongdoing*

A. *For sexual sins:*
Adultery—death ..... Lev. 20:10
Incest—death ..... Lev. 20:11-14
Sodomy—destruction ..... Gen. 19:13, 17, 24

B. *For bodily sins:*
Drunkenness—exclusion ..... 1 Cor. 5:11
1 Cor. 6:9, 10
Murder—death ..... Ex. 21:12-15
Persecution—God's judgment ..... Matt. 23:34-36

C. *For following heathen ways:*
Human sacrifice—death ..... Lev. 20:2-5
Witchcraft—death ..... Ex. 22:18
Idolatry—death ..... Ex. 22:20

D. *For internal sins:*
Ingratitude—punished ..... Prov. 17:13
Pride—abomination ..... Prov. 16:5
Unbelief—exclusion ..... Num. 20:12
Swearing—curse ..... Jer. 23:10
Zech. 5:3
Blasphemy—death ..... Lev. 24:14-16, 23

Peniel—*the face of God*
Place east of Jordan; site of Jacob's wrestling with angel ..... Gen. 32:24-31
See Penuel 1

Peninnah—*coral, pearl*
Elkanah's second wife ..... 1 Sam. 1:2, 4

Penitence—*state of being sorry for one's sins*

A. *Results of:*
Forgiveness ..... Ps. 32:5, 6
Restoration ..... Job 22:23-29
Renewed fellowship ..... Ps. 51:12, 13

B. *Examples of:*
Job ..... Job 42:1-6
David ..... Ps. 51:1-19
Josiah ..... 2 Kin. 22:1, 19
Publican ..... Luke 18:13
Thief on the cross ..... Luke 23:39-42

C. *Elements:*
Acknowledgment of sin ..... Job 33:27, 28
Luke 15:18, 21
Broken heart ..... Ps. 34:18
Ps. 51:17
Plea for mercy ..... Luke 18:13
Confession ..... 1 John 1:9

See Repentance

Penknife—*a scribe's knife*
Used by Jehoiakim on Jeremiah's roll ..... Jer. 36:23-28

Penny, pence—*the Roman denarius*
Debt of 100 ..... Matt. 18:28
Day laborer's pay ..... Matt. 20:2-13
Roman coin ..... Matt. 22:19-21
Two, the cost of lodging ..... Luke 10:35
Ointment, worth 300 ..... John 12:5
Famine prices ..... Rev. 6:6
See Jewish measures

Pentecost—*fiftieth* (day)

A. *In the Old Testament:*
Called "the Feast of Weeks" ..... Ex. 34:22, 23
Marks completion of barley harvest ..... Lev. 23:15, 16
Called "Feast of Harvest" ... Ex. 23:16
Work during, prohibited ..... Lev. 23:21
Two loaves presented ..... Lev. 23:17, 20
Other sacrifices prescribed ... Lev. 23:18
Offerings given by Levites ... Deut. 16:10-14
Time of consecration ..... Deut. 16:12, 13
Observed during Solomon's time ..... 2 Chr. 8:12, 13

See Feasts, Hebrew

SUBJECT REFERENCE

B. *In the New Testament:*
Day of the Spirit's coming; the formation of the Christian Church ..... Acts 2:1-47
Paul desires to attend ..... Acts 20:16
Paul plans to stay in Ephesus until ..... 1 Cor. 16:8

Penuel—*the face of God*
1. Inhabitants of, slain by Gideon ..... Judg. 8:8, 9, 17
Later refortified by Jeroboam ..... 1 Kin. 12:25
2. Judahite ..... 1 Chr. 4:4
3. Benjamite ..... 1 Chr. 8:25

Penury—*extreme poverty; destitution*
Widow's gift in, commended ..... Luke 21:1-4

People
Found among Israel ..... Deut. 7:6
Not limited to Israel ..... Rom. 2:28, 29
Called the remnant ..... Is. 11:10, 11, 16
Gentiles included in ..... Is. 19:25; Is. 65:1; Rom. 15:10, 11
Became such by covenant ..... Jer. 31:31-34
Secured through the Messiah .. Ezek. 34:22-31
Accomplished by Christ's death ..... Matt. 1:21; Luke 1:68, 77
Separated from others ..... 2 Cor. 6:16-18
Rev. 18:4
God's true Church ..... 1 Pet. 2:9, 10
All nations included in ..... Rev. 5:9
Rev. 7:9
God's eternal people ..... Rev. 21:3

People of the land—*the conservative element of the population consisting mainly of landholders*
The influence of ..... 2 Kin. 11:13-15
Taxed ..... 2 Kin. 23:35

Peor—*opening*
1. Mountain of Moab opposite Jericho ..... Num. 23:28
Israel's camp seen from ..... Num. 24:2
2. Moabite god called Baalpeor ..... Num. 25:3, 5, 18
Israelites punished for worship of ..... Num. 31:16

Perceive, perception—*knowledge derived through one of the senses*
Outward circumstances ..... 2 Sam. 12:19
Acts 27:10
Outward intentions ..... John 6:15
Acts 23:29
Intuition ..... 1 Sam. 3:8
John 4:19
Unusual manifestations ..... 1 Sam. 12:17, 18
Acts 10:34
Spiritual insight ..... Neh. 6:12
Acts 14:9
God's blessings ..... 2 Sam. 5:12
Neh. 6:16
Bitter experience ..... Eccl. 1:17
Eccl. 3:22
Obvious implication ..... Matt. 21:45
Luke 20:19
God's revelation ..... Gal. 2:9
1 John 3:16
Internal consciousness ..... Luke 8:46
Acts 8:23

Perdition—*the state of the damned; destruction*
Judas Iscariot ..... John 17:12
Lost ..... Philem. 1:28
Antichrist ..... 2 Thess. 2:3
Rev. 17:8, 11

Peres—*to split into pieces*
Sentence of doom ..... Dan. 5:28

Peresh—*dung*
Man of Manasseh ..... 1 Chr. 7:16

Perez—*a breach*
One of Judah's twin sons by Tamar ..... Gen. 38:24-30
Numbered among Judah's sons ..... Gen. 46:12
Founder of a tribal family ..... Num. 26:20, 21
Descendants of, notable in later times ..... 1 Chr. 27:3
Ancestor of David and Christ ... Ruth 4:12-18

Perezites
Descendants of Perez ..... Num. 26:20

SUBJECT — REFERENCE

Perfection—*the extreme degree of excellence*

A. *Applied to natural things:*
Day ... Prov. 4:18
Gold ... 2 Chr. 4:21
Weights ... Deut. 25:15
Beauty ... Ezek. 28:12
Offering ... Lev. 22:21

B. *Applied to spiritual graces:*
Patience ... James 1:4
Love ... Col. 3:14
Holiness ... 2 Cor. 7:1
Praise ... Matt. 21:16
Faith ... 1 Thess. 3:10
Good works ... Heb. 13:21
Unity ... John 17:23
Strength ... 2 Cor. 12:9

C. *Means of:*
God ... 1 Pet. 5:10
Christ ... Heb. 10:14
Holy Spirit ... Gal. 3:3
God's Word ... 2 Tim. 3:16, 17
Ministry ... Eph. 4:11, 12
Sufferings ... Heb. 2:10

D. *Stages of:*
Eternally accomplished ... Heb. 10:14
Objective goal ... Matt. 5:48
Subjective process ... 2 Cor. 7:1
Daily activity ... 2 Cor. 13:9
Present possession ... 1 Cor. 2:6
Experience not yet reached ... Phil. 3:12
Descriptive of the completed Church ... Heb. 11:40
Heaven's eternal standard ... 1 Cor. 13:10-12

Perfume—*a substance producing pleasant scents*

A. *Made by:*
Apothecary ... Ex. 30:25, 35

Combining:
Various ingredients ... Job 41:31
Olive oil with imported aromatics ... 1 Kin. 10:10

B. *Uses of:*
Incense and ointment for tabernacle ... Ex. 30:22-28
Personal adornment ... Prov. 27:9
Seduction ... Prov. 7:17

C. *Figurative of:*

Christ's:
Glories ... Ps. 45:8
Righteousness and intercession ... Song 3:6
Spiritual prostitution ... Is. 57:9

Perfumer—*to mix, compound*

Great art ... Ex. 30:25
Eccl. 10:1
Used in tabernacle ... Ex. 30:25, 35
Used in embalming ... 2 Chr. 16:14
A maker of ointment ... Eccl. 10:1
Among returnees ... Neh. 3:8

Perga—*the capital of Pamphylia*

Visited by Paul ... Acts 13:13, 14
Acts 14:25

Pergamos—*a leading city in Mysia in Asia Minor*

One of the seven churches here ... Rev. 1:11
Antipas martyred here ... Rev. 2:12, 13
Special message to ... Rev. 2:12-17

Perida

Head of a family of Temple servants ... Neh. 7:46, 57

Perils—*physical or spiritual dangers*

Escape from, by:
Prayer ... Gen. 32:6-12
Pacifying gifts ... Gen. 32:13-20
Quick action ... 1 Sam. 18:10, 11
Flight ... Matt. 2:12-15
Love of Christ ... Rom. 8:35
God ... 2 Cor. 1:10

Perish—*to be destroyed violently*

A. *Applied to:*
Universe ... Heb. 1:11
Old world ... 2 Pet. 3:6
Animals ... Ps. 49:12, 20
Vegetation ... Jon. 4:10
Food ... John 6:27
Gold ... 1 Pet. 1:7
Human body ... 2 Cor. 4:16
Soul ... Matt. 10:28

B. *Safeguards against:*

God's:
Power ... John 10:28
Will ... Matt. 18:14
Providence ... Luke 21:18
Christ's resurrection ... 1 Cor. 15:18, 19
Repentance ... Luke 13:3, 5

See Lost

Perizzites—*dwellers in the open country*

One of seven Canaanite nations ... Deut. 7:1
Possessed Palestine in Abraham's time ... Gen. 13:7
Land of, promised to Abraham's seed ... Gen. 15:18, 20
Jacob's fear of ... Gen. 34:30
Israel commanded to utterly destroy ... Deut. 20:17
Israel forbidden to intermingle with ... Ex. 23:23-25
Defeated by Joshua ... Josh. 3:10
Many of, slain by Judah ... Judg. 1:4, 5
Israel intermarries with ... Judg. 3:5-7
Made slaves by Solomon ... 1 Kin. 9:20, 21

See Canaanites

Perjury—*swearing falsely*

Condemned by the Law ... Lev. 19:12
Hated by God ... Zech. 8:17
Requires atonement ... Lev. 6:2-7
Brings punishment ... Zech. 5:3, 4
Mal. 3:5

See False Witnesses

Permission—*authority to do something*

Speak by ... 1 Cor. 7:6

Perpetual—*lasting forever*

Statute ... Ex. 27:21
Incense ... Ex. 30:8
Covenant ... Ex. 31:16
Priesthood ... Ex. 40:15
Possession ... Lev. 25:34
Allotment ... Num. 18:8
Ruins ... Ps. 9:6
Ps. 74:3
Pain ... Jer. 15:18
Hissing ... Jer. 18:16
Sleep ... Jer. 51:39
Desolation ... Jer. 51:62
Mountains ... Hab. 3:6

Perplexity—*a state wherein no way out is seen*

Predicted by Christ ... Luke 21:25

Persecution—*to afflict, oppress, torment*

A. *Caused by:*
Man's sinful nature ... Gal. 4:29
Hatred of God ... John 15:20-23
Ignorance of God ... John 16:1-3
Hatred of Christ ... 1 Thess. 2:15
Rev. 12:13
Preaching the cross ... Gal. 5:11
Gal. 6:12
Godly living ... Matt. 13:21
2 Tim. 3:12
Mistaken zeal ... Acts 13:50
Acts 26:9-11

B. *Christian's attitude under:*
Flee from ... Matt. 10:23
Rejoice in ... Matt. 5:12
Be patient under ... 1 Cor. 4:12
Glorify God in ... 1 Pet. 4:16
Pray during ... Matt. 5:44

Persecution psalm

Of David ... Ps. 69

Perseverance—*steadfastness, persistence*

Elements involved in:
Spiritual growth ... Eph. 4:15
Fruitfulness ... John 15:4-8
God's armor ... Eph. 6:11-18
Chastening ... Heb. 12:5-13
Assurance ... 2 Tim. 1:12
Salvation ... Matt. 10:22
Reward ... Gal. 6:9

Persis—*Persian*

Christian woman in Rome ... Rom. 16:12

Personal devotions

A. *Prayer:*
In morning ... Ps. 5:3
Ps. 119:147
Three times daily ... Ps. 55:17
Dan. 6:10
Continually ... 1 Thess. 3:10
1 Tim. 5:5

B. *Study:*
Daily ... Deut. 17:19
For learning ... Acts 17:11
Rom. 15:4

Personal work—*seeking to win persons to Christ*

Need of ... John 4:35-38
Model of ... John 4:4-30
Means of ... 1 Thess. 1:5, 6
Power of ... John 16:7-11
Methods of ... 1 Cor. 9:19-22

Persuasion—*inclining another's will toward something*

A. *Good, to:*
Worship ... Acts 18:13
Steadfastness ... Acts 13:43
Belief ... Acts 18:4
Acts 19:8
Turn from idolatry ... Acts 19:26
Trust Jesus ... Acts 28:23

B. *Evil, to:*
Unbelief ... 2 Chr. 32:10-19
Unholy alliance ... 2 Chr. 18:2
Fatal conflict ... 1 Kin. 22:20-22
Turmoil ... Acts 14:19
Error ... Gal. 5:8

C. *Objects of:*
Hereafter ... Luke 16:31
One's faith in God ... Rom. 4:21
Personal assurance ... Rom. 8:38
Personal liberty ... 2 Tim. 1:12
Spiritual stability ... Rom. 15:14
Another's faith ... 2 Tim. 1:5
God's promises ... Heb. 11:13

Peruda—*separated*

One of Solomon's servants whose descendants return from exile ... Ezra 2:55
Neh. 7:57

Perverseness—*willfully continuing in sinful ways*

A. *Applied to:*
Heart ... Prov. 12:8
Nation ... Phil. 2:15

B. *Source of:*
False doctrine ... Acts 20:30

Pervert—*to change something from its right use*

A. *Evil of, in dealing with:*
Man's judgment ... Deut. 24:17
God's:
Judgment ... Job 8:3
Word ... Jer. 23:36
Ways ... Acts 13:10
Gospel ... Gal. 1:7

B. *Caused by:*
Drink ... Prov. 31:5
Worldly wisdom ... Is. 47:10
Spiritual blindness ... Luke 23:2, 14

Pestilence

Fifth Egyptian plague ... Ex. 9:1-16
Threatened by God ... Deut. 28:21
Sent because of David's sin ... 2 Sam. 24:13, 15
Used for man's corrections ... Ezek. 38:22
Precedes the Lord's coming ... Hab. 3:5

Pestle—*instrument used for pulverizing material*

Figurative of severe discipline ... Prov. 27:22

Peter

A. *Life of:*

Before his call:
Simon Barjona ... Matt. 16:17
John 21:15
Brother of Andrew ... Matt. 4:18
Married man ... Mark 1:30
1 Cor. 9:5
Not highly educated ... Acts 4:13
Fisherman ... Matt. 4:18

SUBJECT REFERENCE

From his call to Pentecost:

Brought to Jesus by Andrew ... John 1:40-42
Named Cephas by Christ ... John 1:42
Called to discipleship by Christ ... Matt. 4:18-22
Mother-in-law healed ... Matt. 8:14, 15
Called as apostle ... Matt. 10:2-4
Walks on water ... Matt. 14:28-33
Confessed Christ's deity ... Matt. 16:13-19
Rebuked by Jesus ... Matt. 16:21-23
Witnesses transfiguration ... Matt. 17:1-8; 2 Pet. 1:16-18
Asked important questions ... Matt. 18:21
Refused Christ's menial service ... John 13:6-10
Cuts off high priest's slave's ear ... John 18:10, 11
Denied Christ three times ... Matt. 26:69-75
Wept bitterly ... Matt. 26:75
Ran to Christ's sepulcher ... John 20:1-8
Returned to fishing ... John 21:1-14
Witnessed Christ's ascension ... Matt. 28:16-20
Returned to Jerusalem ... Acts 1:12-14
Led disciples ... Acts 1:15-26

From Pentecost onward:

Explained Spirit's coming at Pentecost ... Acts 2:1-41
Healed lame man ... Acts 3:1-11
Pronounces judgment ... Acts 5:1-11
Heals ... Acts 5:14-16
Met Paul ... Acts 9:26; Gal. 1:17, 18
Raises Dorcas ... Acts 9:36-43
Called to Gentiles ... Acts 10:1-23
Preached the Gospel to Gentiles ... Acts 10:24-46
Explained his action to apostles ... Acts 11:1-18
Imprisoned—delivered ... Acts 12:3-19
Attends Jerusalem Council ... Acts 15:7-14
Rebuked by Paul for inconsistency ... Gal. 2:14
Commended Paul's writings ... 2 Pet. 3:15, 16

B. *His life contrasted before and after Pentecost, once:*

Coward; now courageous ... Matt. 26:58, 69-74
Impulsive; now humble ... John 18:10
Ignorant; now enlightened ... Matt. 16:21, 22
Deeply inquisitive; now submissive ... John 21:21, 22
Boastful of self; now boastful of Christ ... Matt. 26:33, 34
Timid and afraid; now fearless ... Matt. 14:28-31

C. *Significance of:*

Often the representative for the others ... Matt. 17:24-27
Only disciple personally restored by the Lord ... John 21:15-19
Leader in the early church ... Acts 3:12-26

Peter, the Epistles of—*books of the New Testament*

A. *1 Peter*

God's salvation ... 1 Pet. 1:3-12
Obedience and holiness ... 1 Pet. 1:13-23
Christ the corner stone ... 1 Pet. 2:4-6
A royal priesthood ... 1 Pet. 2:9
Christ's example ... 1 Pet. 2:18-25
Husbands and wives ... 1 Pet. 3:1-7
Partakers of His suffering ... 1 Pet. 4:12-19
Be humble before God ... 1 Pet. 5:6-10

B. *2 Peter*

Things pertaining to life ... 2 Pet. 1:1-4
Diligent growth ... 2 Pet. 1:5-11
False teachers ... 2 Pet. 2:1-22
The hope of the day ... 2 Pet. 3:9, 10

Pethahiah—*Jehovah opens* (the womb)

1. Priest of David's time ... 1 Chr. 24:16
2. Judahite serving as a Persian official ... Neh. 11:24
3. Levite who divorced his foreign wife ... Ezra 10:19, 23
   Prays with the other Levites ... Neh. 9:4, 5

SUBJECT REFERENCE

Pethor—*a town in North Mesopotamia*

Balaam's home ... Num. 22:5, 7

Pethuel—*God delivers*

Father of Joel the prophet ... Joel 1:1

Petitions—*entreaties for favors*

A. *Offered to men:*

Treacherous ... Dan. 6:7

B. *Offered to God:*

Favored ... 1 Sam. 1:17
Granted ... 1 Sam. 1:27

Peulthai—*reward of Jehovah*

Levite doorkeeper ... 1 Chr. 26:5

Phaltiel—*deliverance of God*

Husband of Michal ... 2 Sam. 3:14, 15

Phanuel—*face of God*

Father of Anna ... Luke 2:36

Pharaoh—*great house*

A. *Unnamed ones, contemporary of:*

Abraham ... Gen. 12:15-20
Joseph ... Gen. 37:36
Moses (the oppression) ... Ex. 1:8-11
Moses (the exodus) ... Ex. 5-14
Solomon ... 1 Kin. 3:1; 1 Kin. 11:17-20
Hezekiah ... 2 Kin. 18:21

B. *Named ones:*

Shishak ... 1 Kin. 14:25, 26
So ... 2 Kin. 17:4
Tirhakah ... 2 Kin. 19:9
Nechoh ... 2 Kin. 23:29
Hophra ... Jer. 44:30
Probably also referred to in ... Jer. 37:5, 7, 11

Pharisees—*separated ones*

A. *Characteristics of:*

Jewish sect ... Acts 15:5
Upholders of traditions ... Mark 7:3, 5-8; Gal. 1:14
Sticklers for Mosaic Law ... Acts 26:5; Phil. 3:5
Very careful in outward details ... Matt. 23:23; Luke 18:11
Rigid in fasting ... Luke 5:33; Luke 18:12
Zealous for Judaism ... Matt. 23:15
Lovers of display ... Matt. 23:5-7
Covetous ... Luke 16:14
Cruel persecutors ... Acts 9:1, 2; Phil. 3:5, 6

B. *Chief errors of, their:*

Outward righteousness ... Luke 7:36-50
Blindness to spiritual things ... John 3:1-10
Emphasis on the ceremonial Law ... Matt. 15:1-9
Perversion of Scripture ... Matt. 15:1, 9
Self-justification before men ... Luke 16:14, 15
Hindering potential believers ... John 9:16, 22
Refusal to accept Christ ... Matt. 12:24-34

C. *Christ's description of:*

Vipers ... Matt. 12:24, 34
Blind ... Matt. 15:12-14
Hypocrites ... Matt. 23:13-19
Serpents ... Matt. 23:33
Children of the devil ... John 8:13, 44

D. *Attitude of, toward Christ, sought to:*

Destroy Him ... Matt. 12:14
Tempt Him ... Matt. 16:1; Matt. 19:3
Entangle Him ... Matt. 22:15
Accuse Him ... Luke 11:53, 54

Pharpar—*haste*

One of the two rivers of Damascus ... 2 Kin. 5:12

Pharzites

Descendants of Pharez (Perez) ... Num. 26:20

Phebe—*pure, bright*

Deaconess of the church at Cenchrea ... Rom. 16:1, 2

SUBJECT REFERENCE

Phi-beseth—*the house of the goddess Bast*

City of Lower Egypt 40 miles north of Memphis ... Ezek. 30:17

Phichol

Captain of King Abimelech's army ... Gen. 21:22, 32

Philadelphia—*brotherly love*

City of Lydia in Asia Minor; church established here ... Rev. 1:11

Philanthropy

A. *Manifested by:*

Ethiopian ... Jer. 38:6-13
Samaritan ... Luke 10:30, 33
Roman centurion ... Luke 7:2-5
Pagans ... Acts 28:2, 7, 10
Christians ... Acts 4:34-37

B. *Precepts concerning:*

"Do good unto all" ... Gal. 6:10
"Love your enemies" ... Matt. 5:43-48
"Follow that which is good" ... 1 Thess. 5:15

Philemon—*loving*

Christian at Colossae to whom Paul writes ... Philem. 1
Paul appeals to him to receive Onesimus ... Philem. 9-21

Philemon, the Epistle to—*a book of the New Testament*

Thanksgiving ... Philem. 4-7
Plea for Onesimus ... Philem. 10-21
Hope through prayer ... Philem. 22

Philetus—*worthy of love*

False teacher ... 2 Tim. 2:17, 18

Philip—*lover of horses*

1. Son of Herod the Great ... Matt. 14:3
2. One of the twelve apostles ... Matt. 10:3
   Brought Nathanael to Christ ... John 1:43-48
   Tested by Christ ... John 6:5-7
   Introduced Greeks to Christ ... John 12:20-22
   Gently rebuked by Christ ... John 14:8-12
   In the upper room ... Acts 1:13
3. One of the seven deacons ... Acts 6:5
   Called an evangelist ... Acts 21:8
   Father of four prophetesses ... Acts 21:8, 9
   Preached in Samaria ... Acts 8:5-13
   Led the Ethiopian eunuch to Christ ... Acts 8:26-40
   Visited by Paul ... Acts 21:8

Philippi—*pertaining to Philip*

City of Macedonia (named after Philip of Macedon); visited by Paul ... Acts 16:12; Acts 20:6
Paul wrote letter to church of ... Phil. 1:1

Philippians, the Epistle to the—*a book of the New Testament*

Thanksgiving ... Phil. 1:3-10
Christ is preached ... Phil. 1:12-18
To live is Christ ... Phil. 1:21
The humility of Christ ... Phil. 2:5-11
Lights in the world ... Phil. 2:12-16
Perseverance ... Phil. 3
Rejoicing in the Lord ... Phil. 4:1-13

Philistia—*the country of the Philistines*

"The land of the Philistines" ... Gen. 21:32, 34
"The borders of the Philistines" ... Josh. 13:2
Philistia ... Ps. 60:8

Philistim—*plural of Philistine*

Race of Canaanites inhabiting Philistia ... Gen. 10:14

Philistines—*the people of Philistia*

A. *History of:*

Descendants of Mizraim ... Gen. 10:13, 14
Originally on the island of Caphtor ... Jer. 47:4
Israel commanded to avoid ... Ex. 13:17
Not attacked by Joshua ... Josh. 13:1-3
Left to prove Israel ... Judg. 3:1-4
Israel sold into ... Judg. 10:6, 7
Delivered from, by Samson ... Judg. 13—16

SUBJECT REFERENCE

Defeat Israel .... 1 Sam. 4:1-11
Take ark to house of Dagon .... 1 Sam. 4—5
Defeated at Mizpeh .... 1 Sam. 7:7-14
Champion, Goliath, killed ... 1 Sam. 17:1-52
David seeks asylum among .. 1 Sam. 27:1-7
Gather at Aphek; Saul and sons slain by .... 1 Sam. 29:1
Often defeated by David .... 2 Sam. 5:17-25
Besieged by Nadab .... 1 Kin. 15:27
War against Jehoram .... 2 Chr. 21:16, 17
Defeated by Uzziah .... 2 Chr. 26:6, 7
Defeated by Hezekiah .... 2 Kin. 18:8

B. *Prophecies concerning:*

Union against Israel .... Is. 9:11, 12
Punishment pronounced ..... Jer. 25:15, 20
Hatred against Israel revenged .... Ezek. 25:15-17
Destruction by Pharaoh ..... Jer. 47:1-7
Ultimate decay .... Zeph. 2:4-6

Philogus—*lover of words*

Christian at Rome .... Rom. 16:15

Philosophy

Divisions of .... Acts 17:18
Deception of .... Col. 2:8

Phinehas—*oracle*

1. Eleazar's son; Aaron's grandson .... Ex. 6:25
Slays an Israelite and a Midianite woman .... Num. 25:1-18
Wonderfully rewarded .... Ps. 106:30, 31
Fights against Midianites .... Num. 31:6-12
Settles dispute over memorial altar .... Josh. 22:11-32
Prays for Israel .... Judg. 20:28
2. Younger son of Eli .... 1 Sam. 1:3
Worthless man .... 1 Sam. 2:12-25
Slain by Philistines .... 1 Sam. 4:11, 17
Wife of, dies in childbirth ... 1 Sam. 4:19-22
3. Father of a postexilic priest .... Ezra 8:33

Phlegon—*scorching*

Christian at Rome .... Rom. 16:14

Phoebe—*pure, bright*

Deaconess of the church at Cenchrea .... Rom. 16:1, 2

Phoenicia—*purple*

Mediterranean coastal region including the cities of Ptolemais, Tyre, Zarephath and Sidon; evangelized by early Christians .... Acts 11:19
Jesus preaches here .... Matt. 15:21

Phoenix—*harbor in southern Crete*

Paul was to winter there .... Acts 27:12

Phrygia—*a large province of Asia Minor*

Jews from, at Pentecost .... Acts 2:1, 10
Visited twice by Paul .... Acts 16:6

Phurah—*branch*

Gideon's servant .... Judg. 7:10, 11

Phut, Put—*foreign bowman*

1. Third son of Ham .... Gen. 10:6
2. Warriors (from Africa) allied with Egypt .... Ezek. 27:10
Same as Libyans in .... Jer. 46:9

Phuvah, Pua, Puah—*utterance*

1. Issachar's second son .... Gen. 46:13
Descendants of Punites ...... Num. 26:23
2. Father of Tola, Israel's judge .... Judg. 10:1

Phygellus—*fugitive*

Becomes an apostate .... 2 Tim. 1:15

Phylactery—*charm*

Scripture verses placed on the forehead; based upon a literal interpretation of .... Ex. 13:9-16
Condemned by Christ .... Matt. 23:5

Physicians—*trained healers*

God the only true .... Deut. 32:39
Practiced embalming .... Gen. 50:2, 26
Job's friends of no value .... Job 13:4
Consulted by Asa .... 2 Chr. 16:12
For the sick only .... Matt. 9:12
Proverb concerning, quoted ..... Luke 4:23

SUBJECT REFERENCE

Payment for services of .... Mark 5:26
Luke, "the beloved" .... Col. 4:14

Pi-beseth—*the house of the goddess Bast*

City of Lower Egypt 40 miles north of Memphis .... Ezek. 30:17

Pictures—*drawn or carved representations of life scenes*

Descriptive of idolatrous images .... Num. 33:52
Like a word .... Prov. 25:11
"Pleasant pictures" .... Is. 2:16

Piece—*part of a larger whole*

Land .... Gen. 33:19
Silver .... 1 Sam. 2:36
Fig cake .... 1 Sam. 30:12
Money .... Job 42:11
Fish .... Luke 24:42

Pierce—*to push a pointed instrument through something*

A. *Used literally of:*

Nail in Sisera .... Judg. 5:26
Messiah's predicted death .... Ps. 22:16
Christ's death .... John 19:34, 37

B. *Used figuratively of:*

God's destruction .... Num. 24:8
Egypt's weakness .... 2 Kin. 18:21
Harsh words .... Prov. 12:18
Great conflict of soul .... Job 30:16, 17
God's Word .... Heb. 4:12
Coveted riches .... 1 Tim. 6:10

Piety—*holy living*

A. *Aided by:*

God's Word .... 2 Tim. 3:14-17
Godly parents .... 1 Sam. 1:11
Prayer .... James 5:16-18
Good works .... 1 Tim. 5:10
Hope of Christ's return ...... Titus 2:11-14

B. *Hindered by:*

World .... James 4:4
Flesh .... Rom. 8:1-13
Satan .... Luke 22:31
Envying and strife .... 1 Cor. 3:1-7

C. *Value of:*

Profitable now and later ..... 1 Tim. 4:8
Safeguard in temptation ..... Gen. 39:7-9
Rewarded in heaven .... Rev. 14:13

See Holiness of Christians; Sanctification

Pigeon

As a sin offering .... Lev. 12:6
As a burnt offering .... Lev. 1:14
Offered by Mary .... Luke 2:22, 24
See Dove

Pi-hahiroth—*the place of meadows*

Israelite camp before crossing the Red Sea .... {Ex. 14:2, 9; Num. 33:7, 8}

Pilate, Pontius

Procurator of Judea (A.D. 26-36) .... Luke 3:1
Destroyed Galileans .... Luke 13:1
Jesus brought before .... Matt. 27:2
Washed hands in mock innocency .... Matt. 27:24
Notorious in history .... Acts 3:13
Acts 4:27

Pildash—*steely*

Son of Nahor and Milcah ...... Gen. 22:20-22

Pileha—*plowman*

Signer of the covenant .... Neh. 10:24

Pilgrims—*God's people as*

A. *Elements involved in:*

Forsaking all for Christ ..... Luke 14:26, 27, 33
Traveling by faith .... Heb. 11:9
Faces set toward Zion .... Jer. 50:5
Encouraged by God's promises .... Heb. 11:13
Sustained by God .... Is. 35:1-10

B. *Their journey in this world as:*

Pilgrims and strangers .... 1 Pet. 2:11, 12
Lights .... Phil. 2:15
Salt .... Matt. 5:13
God's own .... 1 Pet. 2:9, 10
Chosen out of the world ..... John 17:6
1 Pet. 1:1, 2

SUBJECT REFERENCE

See Strangers

Pillar—*a column or support*

A. *Descriptive of:*

Memorial sites .... Gen. 28:18, 22
Woman turned to salt .... Gen. 19:26
Altars of idolatry .... Deut. 12:3
Supports for a building ...... Judg. 16:25, 26, 29
Covenant site .... Ex. 24:4-8
Miracles .... Joel 2:30

B. *Figurative of:*

God's presence .... Ex. 33:9, 10
Earth's supports .... Job 9:6
God's sovereignty over nations .... Is. 19:19
Man's legs .... Song 5:15
Important persons .... Gal. 2:9
Church .... 1 Tim. 3:15
True believers .... Rev. 3:12
Angel's feet .... Rev. 10:1

Pillar of cloud and fire

A. *As means of:*

Guiding Israel .... Ex. 13:21, 22
Protecting Israel .... Ex. 14:19, 24
Regulating Israel's journeys .... Num. 9:15-23
Manifesting His glory to Israel .... Ex. 24:16-18
Manifesting His presence .... Ex. 34:5-8
Communicating with Israel .. Ex. 33:9, 10

B. *Effect of:*

Cause of fear .... Ex. 19:9, 16
Repeated in the Temple ..... 1 Kin. 8:10, 11
Long remembered .... Ps. 99:7
Recalled with gratitude ...... Neh. 9:12, 19
Repeated in Christ's transfiguration .... Matt. 17:5

C. *Figurative of God's:*

Wonders .... Joel 2:30
Departure from Jerusalem ... Ezek. 9:3
Presence among believers .... Matt. 18:20

Pillow—*a cushion*

Stone used as .... Gen. 28:11, 18
Made of goat's hair .... 1 Sam. 19:13, 16
Used on a ship .... Mark 4:38

Pilot—*one who guides*

Of Tyre's ships .... Ezek. 27:8-29
Shipmaster .... Jon. 1:6
Used figuratively .... James 3:4

Piltai—*Jehovah delivers*

Priest of Joiakim's time .... Neh. 12:12, 17

Pin—*a wooden or metal peg*

Used in a weaver's loom .... Judg. 16:13, 14
See Nail

Pine away—*to waste away*

From disobedience .... Lev. 26:14, 16
Egypt .... Is. 19:8
Judah .... Is. 33:9
Jer. 15:9
Jerusalem .... Lam. 4:9

Pine trees—*evergreen trees*

Used in Solomon's Temple ..... 2 Chr. 3:5
Product of Lebanon .... Is. 60:13
Used figuratively .... Is. 41:19

Pinnacle—*a summit; highest ledge*

Of the Temple .... Matt. 4:5

Pinon—*darkness*

Edomite chief .... Gen. 36:41
1 Chr. 1:52

Pipe, piper—*a flute*

A. *Descriptive of:*

Musical instrument .... 1 Sam. 10:5
Player of a flute .... Rev. 18:22
Hollow tube .... Zech. 4:2, 12

B. *Figurative of:*

Joyful deliverance .... Is. 30:29
Mournful lamentation .... Jer. 48:36
Inconsistent reactions .... Matt. 11:17
Spiritual discernment .... 1 Cor. 14:7

SUBJECT REFERENCE

Piram—*indomitable*
Amorite king of Jarmuth .... Josh. 10:3

Pirathon—*height*
Town in Ephraim .... Judg. 12:15

Pirathonite—*inhabitant of Pirathon*
Descriptive of:
Abdon .... Judg. 12:13-15
Benaiah .... 2 Sam. 23:30

Pisgah—*a mountain peak in the Abarim range in Moab*
Balaam offers sacrifice upon .... Num. 23:14
Moses views promised land from .... Deut. 3:27
Site of Moses' death .... Deut. 34:1-7
Summit of, called Nebo .... Deut. 32:49-52
See Nebo

Pisidia—*a mountainous district in Asia Minor*
Twice visited by Paul .... Acts 13:13, 14; Acts 14:24

Pison—*freely flowing*
One of Eden's four rivers .... Gen. 2:10, 11

Pispah—*dispersion*
Asherite..................... 1 Chr. 7:38

Pit—*a hole*
Figurative of:
Grave .... Ps. 30:9
Snare .... Ps. 35:7
Harlot .... Prov. 23:27
Mouth of strange woman .... Prov. 22:14
Destruction.................. Ps. 55:23
Self-destruction .... Prov. 28:10
Hell .... Ps. 28:1
Devil's abode .... Rev. 9:1, 2, 11
See Abyss

Pitch
Ark covered with............. Gen. 6:14
In Babel's tower.............. Gen. 11:3
In Moses' ark................ Ex. 2:3
Kings fall in .... Gen. 14:10

Pitcher—*an earthenware vessel with handles*
A. *Used for:*
Water.................... Gen. 24:16
Protection of a torch .... Judg. 7:16, 19
B. *Figurative of:*
Heart.................... Eccl. 12:6

Pithom—*mansion of the god Atum*
Egyptian city built by Hebrew slaves...................... Ex. 1:11

Pithon—*harmless*
Son of Micah .... 1 Chr. 8:35

Pitilessness—*showing no mercy*
Examples of:
Rich man .... 2 Sam. 12:1-6
Nebuchadnezzar .... 2 Kin. 25:6-21
Medes .... Is. 13:18
Edom....................... Amos 1:11
Heartless creditor .... Matt. 18:29, 30
Strict religionists .... Luke 10:30-32
Merciless murderers .... Acts 7:54-58

Pity—*to show compassion*
A. *Of God, upon:*
Heathen.................. Jon. 4:10, 11
Israel .... Is. 63:9
Faithful remnant .... Is. 54:8-10
Believer .... James 5:11
B. *Of men:*
Pleaded .... Job 19:21
Upon the poor .... Prov. 19:17
Upon children .... Ps. 103:13
Encouraged................ 1 Pet. 3:8
See Compassion; Mercy

Plague—*a severe epidemic*
A. *Descriptive of:*
Divine judgment .... Ex. 9:14
Leprosy .... Lev. 13:1-59
Disease .... Mark 3:10
Final judgment............ Rev. 9:20
B. *Instances of:*
In Egypt .... Ex. 11:1
At Kibroth-hattaavah .... Num. 11:33, 34
At Kadesh................. Num. 14:37
At Peor .... Josh. 22:17
Among:
Philistines .... 1 Sam. 5:7
Israelites .... 2 Sam. 24:15
Sennacherib's soldiers .... Is. 37:36
C. *Sent by God:*
Because of sin .... Gen. 12:17
As final judgments......... Rev. 15:1, 8
D. *Remedy against, by:*
Judgment .... Ps. 106:29, 30
Prayer and confession .... 1 Kin. 8:37, 38
Separation................ Rev. 18:4
Promise .... Ps. 91:10
Obedience................ Rev. 22:18

Plain—*a geographically flat area;* (usually refers to specific regional areas)
Dry region .... Num. 22:1; Deut. 3:17; Deut. 34:3
Low regions .... Jer. 17:26; Obad. 19

Plait, plaiting—*to intertwine*
Of Christ's crown .... Matt. 27:29
Of woman's hair .... 1 Pet. 3:3

Plaited hair
Contrasted to spiritual adornment .... 1 Pet. 3:3

Plans—*methods of action*
Acknowledging God in......... Prov. 3:6
Considering all possibilites...... Luke 14:31-33
Leaving God out .... Luke 12:16-21
Not trusting God............. Ps. 52:7

Plants
Created by God .... Gen. 1:11, 12
Given as food................ Gen. 1:28, 29

Plants of the Bible
Anise .... Matt. 23:23
Bramble .... Judg. 9:14, 15
Brier .... Judg. 8:7, 16
Broom ("juniper") .... Ps. 120:4
Calamus .... Song 4:14
Camphire (Henna)............. Song 1:14
Cummin .... Is. 28:25, 27
Fitch .... Ezek. 4:9
Garlic .... Num. 11:5
Gourd .... 2 Kin. 4:39
Grass .... Ps. 103:15
Hyssop .... Ex. 12:22
Lily .... Song 5:13
Mallows .... Job 30:4
Mandrakes .... Gen. 30:14-16
Mint .... Matt. 23:23
Mustard .... Matt. 13:31
Myrtle .... Is. 55:13
Rose .... Is. 35:1
Rue .... Luke 11:42
Saffron .... Song 4:13, 14
Spikenard .... Song 4:13, 14
Thorn .... Judg. 8:7
Vine of Sodom .... Deut. 32:32
Wormwood................... Deut. 29:18

Plaster
A. *Building material used on:*
Infested walls .... Lev. 14:42, 48
Mt. Ebal .... Deut. 27:2, 4
Babylon's walls .... Dan. 5:5
See Lime; Mortar
B. *Medicinal material:*
Figs applied to Hezekiah's boil .... Is. 38:21

Platter
Deep dish or basin ("charger") .... Matt. 14:8, 11
Side dish for food .... Matt. 23:25, 26
Used figuratively .... Matt. 23:25, 26

Play
Music .... 1 Sam. 16:16-23
Immoral acts .... Ex. 32:6
Fighting .... 2 Sam. 2:14
Dancing .... 2 Sam. 6:5, 21
Fish .... Ps. 104:26
Children .... Is. 11:8

Plead—*to entreat intensely*
A. *Asking for judgment against:*
Idolatry .... Judg. 6:31, 32
Evil king .... 1 Sam. 24:15
B. *Asking for protection of:*
Poor .... Prov. 22:23
Widows .... Is. 1:17
Repentant .... Mic. 7:9

Please—*to satisfy*
A. *Applied to God's:*
Sovereignty .... Ps. 115:3
Election .... 1 Sam. 12:22
Method .... 1 Cor. 1:21
Reactions to man........... 1 Kin. 3:10
Purpose .... Col. 1:19
Creative acts.............. 1 Cor. 12:18
Will .... Matt. 3:17
B. *Applied to the unregenerate's:*
Behavior .... Rom. 8:8
Passions.................. Matt. 14:6
Ways .... 1 Thess. 2:15
Prejudices .... Acts 12:3
C. *Applied to the regenerate's:*
Faith .... Heb. 11:5, 6
Calling.................... 2 Tim. 2:4
Concern for others.......... Rom. 15:26, 27
Married life................ 1 Cor. 7:12, 13
Example, Christ .... John 8:29

Pleasure—*satisfying the sensations*
A. *Kinds of:*
Physical.................. Eccl. 2:1-10
Sexual .... Gen. 18:12
Worldly .... Luke 8:14
Immoral .... Titus 3:3
Spiritual .... Ps. 36:8
Heavenly.................. Ps. 16:11
B. *God's, described as:*
Sovereign.................. Eph. 1:5, 9
Creative .... Rev. 4:11
In righteousness .... 1 Chr. 29:17
Purpose .... Luke 12:32
Not in evil .... Ps. 5:4
Not in the wicked .... Ezek. 18:23, 32; Ezek. 33:11
C. *Christian's described as:*
Subject to God's will........ 2 Cor. 12:10
Inspired by God .... Phil. 2:13
Fulfilled by God .... 2 Thess. 1:11
D. *The unbeliever's, described as:*
Unsatisfying .... Eccl. 2:1
Enslaving .... Titus 3:3
Deadening................. 1 Tim. 5:6
Judged .... 2 Thess. 2:12
Defiant .... Rom. 1:32

Pledge—*something given for security of a debt*
A. *Of material things:*
Garments .... Ex. 22:26
Regulations concerning...... Deut. 24:10-17
Evil of .... Job 22:6
Restoration of, sign of righteousness .... Ezek. 18:7, 16
Unlawfully held back .... Ezek. 18:12
B. *Of spiritual things:*
The Holy Spirit in the heart .... 2 Cor. 1:22
Given by God .... 2 Cor. 5:5
Guarantee of future redemption .... Eph. 1:13, 14
See Borrow; Debt; Lending; Surety

Pleiades—*cluster of many stars*
Part of God's creation .... Job 9:9; Amos 5:8

Plenteous, plenty
A. *Of physical things:*
Food .... Gen. 41:29-47
Prosperity .... Deut. 28:11
Productivity .... Jer. 2:7
Rain..................... Ps. 68:9
Water.................... Lev. 11:36
B. *Of spiritual things:*
God's loving kindness....... Ps. 86:5, 15
God's redemption .... Ps. 130:7

SUBJECT — REFERENCE

Recompenses — Ps. 31:23
Souls in need — Matt. 9:37

C. *How to obtain, by:*
Industry — Prov. 28:19
Putting God first — Prov. 3:9, 10
Lord's blessing — 2 Chr. 31:10

See Abundance

Plottings

A. *Against:*
Poor — Ps. 10:7-11
Perfect — Ps. 64:4-7
Prophets — Jer. 18:18
Persecuted — Matt. 5:11, 12

B. *Inspired by:*
Contempt — Neh. 4:1-8
Hatred — Gen. 37:8-20
Devil — John 13:27
Envy — Matt. 27:18

C. *Examples of:*
Esau against Jacob — Gen. 27:41-45
Satan against Job — Job 1:8-22
Ahab against Naboth — 1 Kin. 21:1-16
Jews against Jeremiah — Jer. 26:8-15
Haman against the Jews — Esth. 7:3-6
Chaldeans against Daniel — Dan. 6:1-8
Jews against Christ — Matt. 26:1-5; John 11:47-53
Jews against Paul — Acts 23:12-22

Plow, plowing—*to dig up the earth for sowing seed*

A. *Used literally of:*
Elisha — 1 Kin. 19:19
Forbidden with mixed animals — Deut. 22:10
Job's sons — Job 1:14

B. *Used figuratively of:*
Proper learning — Is. 28:24, 26
Wrongdoing — Hos. 10:13
Punishment — Hos. 10:11
Affliction — Ps. 129:3
Destruction — Jer. 26:18
Persistent sin — Job 4:8
Christian labor — 1 Cor. 9:10
Information from a wife — Judg. 14:18
Constancy in decision — Luke 9:62
Perverse action — Amos 6:12

Plowman—*a farmer*

Used literally of:
Farming — Is. 28:24

Used figuratively of:
Prosperity — Amos 9:13
Christian ministry — 1 Cor. 9:10

Plowshares—*the hard part of a plow*

Made into swords — Joel 3:10
Swords made into — Is. 2:4

Plumbline—*a cord with a weight* (plummet)

Figurative of:
Destruction — 2 Kin. 21:13
God's judgment — Amos 7:7, 8
God's building — Zech. 4:10

Pochereth—*binder*

Descendants of, among Solomon's servants — Ezra 2:57; Neh. 7:59

Poetry, Hebrew

A. *Classified according to form:*
Synonymous—repetition of same thoughts — Ps. 19:2
Progressive—advance of thought in second line — Job 3:17
Synthetic—second line adds something new — Ps. 104:19
Climactic—the thought climbs to a climax — Ps. 121:3, 4
Antithetic—the second line contrasted with first — Prov. 14:1
Comparative—the "as" compared with the "so" — Prov. 10:26
Acrostic—alphabetic — Ps. 119:1-176

B. *Classified according to function:*
Didactic (teaching) — Deut. 32:1-43; Book of Job
Lyrics — Ex. 15:1-19; Judg. 5:1-31
Elegies — 2 Sam. 1:17-27
Psalms — Book of Psalms

Poison

Reptiles — Deut. 32:24
Dragons — Deut. 32:33
Adders — Ps. 140:3
Gourd — 2 Kin. 4:39
Hemlock — Hos. 10:4
Waters — Jer. 8:14
Asps — Rom. 3:13; Job 20:16

Politeness—*refined manners*

A. *Manifested by:*
Kings — Gen. 47:2-11
Hebrews — Gen. 43:26-29
Romans — Acts 27:3
Pagans — Acts 28:1, 2
Christians — Philem. 8-21

B. *Counterfeited by:*
Trickery — 2 Sam. 20:9, 10
Deceit — 2 Sam. 15:1-6
Hypocrisy — Matt. 22:7, 8
Pride — Luke 14:8-10
Snobbery — James 2:1-4
Selfishness — 3 John 9, 10

See Courtesy

Politicians—*governmental officials*

A. *Evils manifested by:*
Ambition — 2 Sam. 15:1-6
Flattery — Dan. 6:4-15
Indifference — Acts 18:12-16
Avarice — Acts 24:26

B. *Good manifested by:*
Provision — Gen. 41:33-49
Protection — Neh. 2:7-11
Piety — 2 Chr. 34:1-33
Prayer — 2 Chr. 20:6-12
Praise — 2 Chr. 20:27-29

Poll

A. *Descriptive of a person:*
In a military census — Num. 1:2, 18, 20; Num. 3:47

B. *Descriptive of cutting off the hair:*
Absalom — 2 Sam. 14:26
Priests — Ezek. 44:20
Mourning (figurative) — Mic. 1:16

Pollute—*to defile*

A. *Described as something unclean:*
Morally — Num. 35:33, 34
Spiritually — Acts 15:20

B. *Means of:*
Blood — Ps. 106:38
Idolatry — Ezek. 20:30, 31
Abominations — Jer. 7:30
Unregenerate service — Ezek. 44:7
Wickedness — Jer. 3:1, 2
Contempt of the Lord — Mal. 1:7, 12
Captivity — Is. 47:6

See Unclean

Polygamy—*having more than one wife*

A. *Caused by:*
Barrenness of first wife — Gen. 16:1-6
Desire for large family — Judg. 8:30
Political ties with other countries — 1 Kin. 3:1, 2
Sexual desire — 2 Chr. 11:23
Slavery — Gen. 16:1, 3

B. *Contrary to:*
God's original Law — Gen. 2:24
Ideal picture of marriage — Ps. 128:1-6
God's commandment — Ex. 20:14
God's equal distribution of the sexes — Gen. 1:27; 1 Cor. 7:2
Relationship between Christ and the Church — Eph. 5:22-33

C. *Productive of:*
Dissension — Gen. 16:1
Discord — 1 Sam. 1:6
Degeneracy — 1 Kin. 11:1-4

See Adultery; Family; Fornication; Marriage

Pomegranate—*a small tree bearing an apple-shaped fruit*

Grown in Canaan — Num. 13:23

Ornaments of:
Worn by priests — Ex. 28:33
In Temple — 1 Kin. 7:18
Sign of fruitfulness — Hag. 2:19
Used figuratively — Song 4:3

Pommel—*round; a bowl*

Round ornament — 2 Chr. 4:12, 13
Same as "bowl" — 1 Kin. 7:41, 42

Pond, pool—*a reservoir of water*

A. *Used for:*
Washing — 1 Kin. 22:38
Water supply — 2 Kin. 20:20
Irrigation — Eccl. 2:6
Healing — John 5:2-7

B. *Famous ones:*
Gibeon — 2 Sam. 2:13
Hebron — 2 Sam. 4:12
Samaria — 1 Kin. 22:38
Bethesda — John 5:2
Siloam — John 9:7
The upper — Is. 7:3
The lower — Is. 22:9, 11
The King's — Neh. 2:14

Pontus—*a coastal strip of north Asia Minor*

Jews from, at Pentecost — Acts 2:5, 9
Home of Aquila and Priscilla — Acts 18:2
Christians of, addressed by Peter — 1 Pet. 1:1

Poor, poverty

A. *Descriptive of:*
Needy — Luke 21:2
Lower classes — 2 Kin. 24:14
Rebellious — Jer. 5:3, 4
Holy remnant — Zeph. 3:12-14

B. *Causes of:*
God's sovereignty — 1 Sam. 2:7
Sloth — Prov. 6:10, 11
Lack of industry — Prov. 24:30-34
Love of pleasure — Prov. 21:17
Stubbornness — Prov. 13:18
Empty pursuits — Prov. 28:19
Drunkenness — Prov. 23:21

C. *Wrong treatment of:*
Reproaches God — Prov. 14:31
Brings punishment — Prov. 21:13
Brings poverty — Prov. 22:16
Regarded by God — Eccl. 5:8
Judged by God — Is. 3:13-15

D. *Legislation designed for protection of:*
Daily payment of wages — Lev. 19:13
Sharing of tithes with — Deut. 14:28, 29
Loans to, without interest — Lev. 25:35, 37
Right to glean — Lev. 19:9, 10
Land of, restored in jubilee year — Lev. 25:25-30
Equal participation in feasts — Lev. 16:11, 14
Permanent bondage of, forbidden — Deut. 15:12-15

See Needy; Poverty, spiritual

Poor in spirit—*humble, self-effacing*

Promised blessing — Matt. 5:3

Poplar tree

Used in deception of Laban — Gen. 30:37
Pagan rites among — Hos. 4:13
Probably same as "willows" in — Lev. 23:40

Popularity—*one's esteem in the world*

Obtained by:
Heroic exploits — Judg. 8:21, 22
Unusual wisdom — 1 Kin. 4:29-34
Trickery — 2 Sam. 15:1-6
Outward display — Matt. 6:2, 5, 16

Popularity of Jesus

A. *Factors producing His:*
Teaching — Mark 1:22, 27
Healing — Mark 5:20
Miracles — John 12:9-19
Feeding the people — John 6:15-27

B. *Factors causing decline of His:*
High ethical standards — Mark 8:34-38
Foretells His death — Matt. 16:21-28

SUBJECT REFERENCE

Population—*the total inhabitants of a place*
Israel's, increased in Egypt ..... Ex. 1:7, 8
Nineveh's, great .... Jon. 4:11
Heaven's, vast .... Rev. 7:9

Poratha
One of Haman's sons .... Esth. 9:8

Porch
Central court of a house .... Matt. 26:71
Portico for pedestrians .... John 5:2
Roofed colonnade .... John 10:23
Court of the temple............ 1 Kin. 6:3, 6, 7

Porcius Festus—*successor to Felix*
Paul stands trial before......... Acts 25:1-22

Pork—*swine's flesh*
Classified as unclean........... Lev. 11:7, 8

Port—*a harbor*
At Joppa .... Jon. 1:3
Fair Havens .... Acts 27:8
Phoenix .... Acts 27:12
Syracuse .... Acts 28:12
Rhegium .... Acts 28:13
Puteoli .... Acts 28:13

Porter—*gatekeeper or doorkeeper*
Watchman of a city............ 2 Sam. 18:26
Watchman of a house .... Mark 13:34
Shepherd's attendant........... John 10:3
Official of the temple (see below) .... 1 Chr. 23:5
Origin of, in Moses' time .... 1 Chr. 9:17-26
Belongs to Levites .... Neh. 12:47
Duties of, designed by David ... 1 Chr. 26:1-19
Office of, important........... 1 Chr. 9:26

Portico—*porch*
Solomon's .... John 10:23
Of Bethesda .... John 5:2

Portion—*a stipulated part*
A. *Of things material:*
Inheritance .... Gen. 48:22
B. *Of good things:*
Spirit .... 2 Kin. 2:9
Lord....................... Ps. 119:57
Spiritual riches .... Is. 61:7
C. *Of evil things:*
Things of the world .... Ps. 17:14
Fellowship with the wicked .. Neh. 2:20
D. *Of things eternal:*
Punishment of the wicked ... Ps. 11:6

See Inheritance

Position—*place of influence*
Sought after by Pharisees .... Matt. 23:5-7
James and John request .... Mark 10:37
Seeking after, denounced .... Luke 14:7-11
Diotrephes, a seeker after....... 3 John 9

Possess—*to acquire*
A. *Objects of:*
Promised land .... Deut. 4:1, 5
Ruins .... Is. 14:21
Spiritual riches .... Is. 57:13
Christ..................... Prov. 8:22
One's:
Soul .... Luke 21:19
Body of wife............. 1 Thess. 4:4
Sins .... Job 13:26
B. *Of Canaan:*
Promised .... Gen. 17:8
Under oath .... Neh. 9:15
Israel challenged to .... Num. 13:20

Possible—*that which can exist*
A. *Things possible:*
All, with God .... Matt. 19:26
All, to the believer .... Mark 9:23
Peaceful living .... Gal. 4:15
B. *Things impossible:*
Deception of the saints ...... Matt. 24:24
Removal of the Cross .... Matt. 26:39
Christ's remaining in the grave .... Acts 2:24
Removal of sins by animal sacrifice .... Heb. 10:4

SUBJECT REFERENCE

Post
Private homes................ Ex. 12:7
Tabernacle .... 1 Sam. 1:9
Temple .... 1 Kin. 6:31, 33

Posthumous—*after death*
Mary of Bethany .... Matt. 26:13
Abel......................... Heb. 11:4
All believers .... Rev. 14:13

Posts—*runners; couriers; postmen*
Letters sent by .... 2 Chr. 30:6, 10
Sent on swift horses .... Esth. 3:13, 15
Figurative of speed .... Job 9:25

Pot—*a rounded, open-mouthed vessel*
A. *Use of:*
Cooking.................... Zech. 14:21
Refining.................... Prov. 17:3
B. *Figurative of:*
Egyptian slavery............ Ps. 81:6
Sudden destruction .... Ps. 58:9
Impending national destruction .... Jer. 1:13
Merciless punishment .... Mic. 3:2, 3
Complete sanctification...... Zech. 14:20, 21

Potentate—*a mighty one*
Christ the only absolute .... 1 Tim. 6:15

Potiphar—*whom Re* (the sun god) *has given*
High Egyptian officer .... Gen. 39:1
Puts Joseph in jail .... Gen. 39:20

Poti-phera
Egyptian priest of On (Heliopolis) .... Gen. 41:45-50
Father of Asenath, Joseph's wife .... Gen. 46:20

Potsherd—*a fragment of broken pottery*
Figurative of:
Weakness .... Ps. 22:15
Leviathan's underparts .... Job 41:30
Uses of:
Scraping .... Job 2:8
Scooping water .... Is. 30:14

Potsherd gate—*a gate of Jerusalem*
By valley of Ben-hinnom .... Jer. 19:2

Pottage—*a thick vegetable soup*
Price of Esau's birthright .... Gen. 25:29-34
Eaten by Elisha's disciples ...... 2 Kin. 4:38-41
Ordinary food .... Hag. 2:12

Potter—*one who makes earthenware vessels*
A. *Art of, involves:*
Reducing clay to paste ...... Is. 41:25
Shaping by revolving wheel .. Jer. 18:1-4
Molding by hands .... Jer. 18:6
B. *Figurative of:*
Complete destruction .... Is. 30:14
God's sovereignty over men .... Is. 64:8
Israel's lack of understanding .... Is. 29:16

Potter's Field—*burial place for poor people*
Judas' money used for purchase of .... Matt. 27:7, 8

Pound—*a Greek measure*
Used in parable .... Luke 19:12-27

Pour—*to flow freely from something*
A. *Applied to:*
Rain from clouds .... Amos 9:6
Oil from vessels .... Gen. 35:14
Blood from animals......... Lev. 8:15
Water from barrels .... 1 Kin. 18:33
B. *Used figuratively of:*
Christ's death .... Ps. 22:14
Spirit's coming .... Joel 2:28, 29
Holy Spirit .... Ezek. 39:29
God's:
Wrath .... 2 Chr. 34:21, 25
Blessings .... Mal. 3:10
Sovereignty .... Job 10:9, 10
Prayer and repentance ...... Lam. 2:19
Extreme emotions .... 1 Sam. 1:15

SUBJECT REFERENCE

Poverty, spiritual
A. *In a bad sense, of spiritual:*
Decay .... Rev. 2:9
Immaturity .... 1 Cor. 3:1-3
B. *Used in a good sense, of:*
The contrite .... Is. 66:2
God's people .... Is. 14:32
C. *Caused by:*
Hastiness.................. Prov. 21:5
Greed..................... Prov. 22:16
Laziness................... Prov. 24:30-34

Power of Christ
A. *Described as:*
Given by God .... John 17:2
Derived from the Spirit...... Luke 4:14
Delegated to others .... Luke 9:1
Determined by Himself ..... John 10:18
B. *Manifested as power in:*
Creation .... John 1:3, 10
Upholds all things .... Heb. 1:3
Miracles .... Luke 4:36
Regeneration .... John 5:21-26
Salvation .... Heb. 7:25
Resurrecting believers ...... John 5:28, 29
His return .... Matt. 24:30
C. *Manifested as authority to:*
Forgive sins .... Matt. 9:6, 8
Teach..................... Luke 4:32
Give sonship .... John 1:12
Lay down His life .... John 10:18
Authority .... Matt. 28:18
D. *Benefits from, to believers:*
Life .... John 17:2
Strength................... Phil. 4:13
Effective service .... 1 Tim. 1:12; 2 Tim. 4:17
Perfected in weakness .... 2 Cor. 12:9
Conquest over temptation ... Heb. 2:18
Glorification .... Phil. 3:20, 21

Power of God
A. *Manifested in:*
Creation .... Jer. 51:15
Keeps watch on the nations .... Ps. 66:7
Christ's:
Birth .... Luke 1:35
Miracles .... Luke 11:20
Resurrection .... 2 Cor. 13:4
Exaltation .... Eph. 1:19, 20
Regeneration .... Eph. 1:19
Sanctification .... Phil. 2:13
Believer's resurrection ...... 1 Cor. 6:14
B. *Believer's attitude toward:*
Renders praise for .... Ps. 21:13
Sings of .... Ps. 59:16
Talks of .... Ps. 145:11

Power of the Holy Spirit
A. *Manifested in Christ's:*
Conception .... Luke 1:35
Ministry .... Luke 4:14
Miracles .... Luke 11:20
Resurrection .... Rom. 1:4
B. *Manifested in the believer's:*
Regeneration .... Ezek. 37:11-14
Effective ministry........... Luke 24:49

Power, spiritual
Sources of:
Holy Spirit .... 1 Cor. 2:4, 5
Christ .... 1 Cor. 1:24
Gospel....................... Rom. 1:16
God's kingdom .... Mark 9:1
God's Word .... Heb. 4:12
New life .... Eph. 1:19

Powerlessness—*ineffective testimony*
Produced by:
Worldliness................... Gen. 19:14
Unbelief .... Matt. 17:16-20

Practice—*customary habit*
Wicked works .... Ps. 141:4
Hypocrisy .... Is. 32:6
Power .... Dan. 8:24
Work evil .... Mic. 2:1

SUBJECT	REFERENCE
Praetorium—*the governor's official residence*	
1. Pilate's, in Jerusalem	Mark 15:16
Translated "common hall" and "judgment hall"	Matt. 27:27
2. Herod's palace at Caesarea	Acts 23:35
3. Praetorian guard at Rome	Phil. 1:13
Praise of God	
A. *Objects of:*	
God Himself	Ps. 139:14
God's:	
Name	1 Chr. 29:13
	Ps. 99:3
Power	Ps. 21:13
Wonders	Ps. 89:5
Loving-kindness	Ps. 138:2
Works	Ps. 145:4
B. *Times of:*	
Daily	Ps. 72:15
Continually	Ps. 71:6
Seven times daily	Ps. 119:164
All the day	Ps. 35:28
At midnight	Ps. 119:62
	Acts 16:25
While I live	Ps. 146:2
Praise of men	
A. *Worthy:*	
From another	Prov. 27:2
For:	
Faithfulness	Prov. 31:28
Obedience	Rom. 13:3
Works	Prov. 31:31
B. *Unworthy for:*	
Wicked	Prov. 28:4
Disorder	1 Cor. 11:17, 22
Self-seeking	John 12:43
Prating—*foolish babbling*	
Descriptive of:	
Fool	Prov. 10:8, 10
Diotrephes	3 John 10
Prayer—*a request to God*	
A. *Kinds of:*	
Secret	Matt. 6:6
Family	Acts 10:2, 30
Group	Matt. 18:20
Public	1 Cor. 14:14-17
B. *Parts of:*	
Adoration	Dan. 4:34, 35
Confession	1 John 1:9
Supplication	1 Tim. 2:1-3
Intercession	James 5:15
Thanksgiving	Phil. 4:6
C. *Personal requirements of:*	
Purity of heart	Ps. 66:18, 19
Believing	Matt. 21:22
In Christ's name	John 14:13
According to God's will	1 John 5:14
D. *General requirements of:*	
Forgiving spirit	Matt. 6:14
Simplicity	Matt. 6:5, 6
Humility and repentance	Luke 18:10-14
Unity of believers	Matt. 18:19, 20
Tenacity	Luke 18:1-8
Importunity	Luke 11:5-8
Intensity	Matt. 7:7-11
Confident expectation	Mark 11:24
Without many words	Matt. 6:7
Unceasingly	1 Thess. 5:17
E. *Answers refused, because of:*	
Sin	Ps. 66:18
Selfishness	James 4:3
Doubt	James 1:5-7
Disobedience	Prov. 28:9
Inhumanity	Prov. 21:13
Pride	Luke 18:11, 12, 14
F. *Posture for:*	
Standing	Neh. 9:5
Kneeling	Ezra 9:5
Sitting	1 Chr. 17:16-27
Bowing	Ex. 34:8
Hands uplifted	1 Tim. 2:8
Prayer meetings	
In the upper room	Acts 1:13, 14
In a house	Acts 12:5-17
By a river	Acts 16:13
On a beach	Acts 21:5

SUBJECT	REFERENCE
Prayers of Christ	
A. *Their nature:*	
Adoration	Matt. 11:25-27
Intercession	John 17:1-26
Thanksgiving	John 11:41, 42
B. *Their great occasions:*	
At His baptism	Luke 3:21, 22
Before selecting the apostles	Luke 6:12-16
At His transfiguration	Luke 9:28, 29
In Gethsemane	Matt. 26:36-42
C. *Their times and places:*	
In secret	Luke 5:16
	Luke 9:18
Early in morning	Mark 1:35
With others	Luke 11:1
On mountain	Matt. 14:23
Preach, preaching—*proclaiming the Gospel*	
A. *Of the Gospel:*	
Necessity of	1 Cor. 9:16
Without charge	1 Cor. 9:18
Extent of, to all	Col. 1:25
Only one	Gal. 1:8, 9
Centers in the Cross	1 Cor. 1:23
Preacher's importance in	Rom. 10:14, 15
B. *Attitudes toward:*	
Accepted	Luke 11:32
Rejected	2 Pet. 2:4, 5
Not perfected by	Heb. 4:2
Perverted	Gal. 1:6-9
Contentious about	Phil. 1:15-18
Counted foolishness	1 Cor. 1:18-21
Ridiculed	Acts 17:16-18
Not ashamed of	Rom. 1:15, 16
Preacher—*one who proclaims publically*	
Author of Ecclesiastes	Eccl. 1:1, 2
Causes to hear	Rom. 10:14
Paul, speaking of himself	1 Tim. 2:7
	2 Tim. 1:11
Noah, of righteousness	2 Pet. 2:5
Precepts—*specific charges*	
God's:	
Commanded	Heb. 9:19
Corrupted	Matt. 15:9
Kept	Ps. 119:56-69
Sought	Ps. 119:40-94
Not forgotten	Ps. 119:93, 141
Loved	Ps. 119:159
Source of understanding	Ps. 119:100, 104
See Traditions	
Precious—*something extremely valuable*	
A. *Applied to spiritual things:*	
Word of God	1 Sam. 3:1
Wisdom	Prov. 3:13, 15
Soul	1 Sam. 26:21
One's life	2 Kin. 1:13, 14
Redemption of a soul	Ps. 49:8
God's thoughts toward us	Ps. 139:17
Death of God's people	Ps. 72:14
Christ	Is. 28:16
Christ's blood	1 Pet. 1:19
Faith	2 Pet. 1:1
Promises	2 Pet. 1:4
Trial of faith	1 Pet. 1:7
B. *Applied figuratively to:*	
Knowledge	Prov. 20:15
Sons of Zion	Lam. 4:2
Rewards	1 Cor. 3:12-14
Final harvest	James 5:7
Worldly pomp	Rev. 17:4
Heaven's glory	Rev. 21:11, 19
Precious promises	
A. *To the troubled by:*	
Doubts	Ps. 73:1-28
Afflictions	Ps. 34:1-22
Persecution	Matt. 5:11, 12
Anxiety	Phil. 4:6
Temptation	1 Cor. 10:13
Infirmities	2 Cor. 12:7-10
Discipline	Heb. 12:3-13
B. *To the sorrowful over:*	
Death	1 Thess. 4:13-18
Sickness	James 5:13-16
Their sins	Ps. 32:1-11
Disappointment	Rom. 8:28

SUBJECT	REFERENCE
C. *To those troubled by:*	
World	1 John 2:15-17
Flesh	Gal. 5:16-18
Satan	Luke 22:31, 32
Anxious	Matt. 6:31-34
Sin	James 1:12-15
Pride	1 Pet. 5:5-7
D. *To the active Christian in his:*	
Giving	Mal. 3:10
Zeal	Phil. 4:13
Soul winning	James 5:20
Fruitfulness	John 7:38, 39
Graces	2 Pet. 1:5-11
Prayers	James 5:16
Perseverance	Gal. 6:9
Watchfulness	Eph. 6:10-20
Assurance	Rom. 8:32-39
Ministry	Ps. 138:8
Predestination—*God's eternal plan*	
A. *Described as:*	
"Purpose"	Rom. 8:28
"Afore prepared"	Rom. 9:23
"Foreknowledge"	Acts 2:23
"Foreknew"	Rom. 8:29
"Ordained"	Acts 13:48
"Appointed"	Acts 22:10
"Determined"	Luke 22:22
"Foreseeing"	Gal. 3:8
"Before the world began"	2 Tim. 1:9
B. *Determined by God's:*	
Counsel	Acts 2:23
Foreknowledge	Acts 2:23
Good pleasure	Luke 12:32
	1 Cor. 1:21
Will	Eph. 1:5, 9, 11
Purpose	Eph. 3:11
Power	Is. 40:10-17
	Rom. 9:15-24
C. *Expressed toward the believer in:*	
Election	Eph. 1:4
Salvation	2 Thess. 2:13, 14
Justification	Rom. 8:30
Sanctification	1 Thess. 2:12, 13
Glorification	Rom. 8:30
Eternal destiny	Matt. 25:34
See Foreknowledge of God; Elect	
Predict—*to foretell*	
Astrologers	Is. 47:13
Preeminence—*being supreme above all*	
A. *Of creatures:*	
Sought by the devil	Is. 14:12-15
Sought by man	Gen. 3:5, 6
Illustrated by Diotrephes	3 John 9, 10
B. *Of Christ:*	
Predicted	Ps. 45:6, 7
Proclaimed	Luke 1:31-33
Visualized	Matt. 17:4, 5
Realized	Col. 1:19
Acknowledged	Phil. 2:9, 10
Pregnancy	
Safeguards provided	Ex. 21:22-25
Evidences of	Luke 1:44
God's call during	Jer. 1:4, 5
	Gal. 1:15
Prejudice—*a biased opinion*	
A. *Toward men, based on:*	
Race	Acts 19:34
Social position	James 2:1-4
Jealousy	Gen. 37:3-11
B. *Toward Christ, based on His:*	
Lowly origin	Mark 6:3
Residence in Galilee	John 1:46
Race	John 4:9
Teaching	John 9:16-41
See Bigotry	
Premeditation—*deliberate plan to perform an act*	
With:	
Evil intent	Gen. 27:41-45
Good intent	Luke 14:28-33
Heavenly sanctions	James 4:13-17
Preparation day	
Evening	Matt. 27:57, 62
Day before Sabbath	Mark 15:42
	Luke 23:54

P

SUBJECT — REFERENCE

Prepare—*to make ready*

A. *Of spiritual things:*

- To build an altar ... Josh. 22:26
- Lord's way ... Matt. 8:3
- God ... Amos 4:12
- God's throne ... Ps. 9:7
- Heart ... Ezra 7:10
- Passover ... Luke 22:8, 9
- Spiritual provision ... Ps. 23:5
- Service ... 2 Tim. 2:21
- Redeemed people ... Rom. 9:23, 24

B. *Of eternal things:*

- Reward ... Matt. 20:23
- Kingdom ... Matt. 25:34
- Heaven ... John 14:2, 3
- Heavenly city ... Heb. 11:16
- Everlasting fire ... Matt. 25:41

Presbytery—*the Christian eldership acting as a body*

- Ordination ascribed to ... 1 Tim. 4:14

See Elders in the Church

Presence, divine

Described as:

- Glory ... 1 Chr. 16:27
- Joyful ... Ps. 16:11
- Protective ... Ps. 31:20
- Everywhere ... Ps. 139:7
- Guide ... Ex. 33:14, 15

Present to—*to offer*

A. *As an introduction of:*

- Joseph's brothers ... Gen. 47:2
- Joseph to his father ... Gen. 46:29
- Dorcas to her friends ... Acts 9:41
- Paul to a governor ... Acts 23:33

B. *Descriptive of the Christian's life as:*

- Living and holy sacrifice ... Rom. 12:1
- Chaste virgin ... 2 Cor. 11:2
- Holy ... Col. 1:22
- Perfect ... Col. 1:28
- Without blemish ... Eph. 5:27
- Resurrected ... 2 Cor. 4:14

Presents—*gifts*

A. *Offered to:*

- Brother ... Gen. 32:13-20
- King ... Is. 39:1
- Solomon ... 1 Kin. 4:21
- Foreign nation ... Hos. 10:6

B. *Purposes of:*

- Conceal a treacherous act ... Judg. 3:15-23
- Verify a messenger ... Judg. 6:18-24
- Secure a message ... 2 Kin. 8:7-10
- Pay tribute ... 2 Kin. 17:3, 4
- Show friendship ... 2 Kin. 20:12, 13
- Show obedience ... Ps. 72:10

See Gifts of man

Preservation, God's

A. *As manifested over:*

- World ... Neh. 9:6
- King ... 2 Sam. 8:6, 14
- Animals ... Ps. 36:6
- Nation ... Gen. 45:5, 7
- Messiah ... Is. 49:8
- Apostle ... 2 Tim. 4:18
- Believers ... 1 Thess. 5:23
- Faithful ... Ps. 31:23

B. *Special objects of:*

- Those who trust Him ... Ps. 16:1
- Holy ... Ps. 86:2
- Souls of saints ... Ps. 97:10
- Simple ... Ps. 116:6
- Those who love Him ... Ps. 145:20
- Strangers ... Ps. 146:9

C. *Spiritual means of:*

- Integrity ... Ps. 25:21
- Loving-kindness ... Ps. 40:11
- Mercy and truth ... Ps. 61:7
- Wisdom ... Prov. 4:5, 6
- Losing one's life ... Luke 17:33
- Prophet ... Hos. 12:13

President—*a ruler*

- Daniel acted as ... Dan. 6:2

SUBJECT — REFERENCE

Press—*a machine for extracting the juice from grapes*

- Used literally ... Neh. 13:15
- Figurative of appointed time ... Joel 3:13

Pressure—*force exerted*

A. *As evil:*

- Perversion ... Gen. 19:9
- Enticement ... Judg. 16:16

B. *As a good, to:*

- Hear God's Word ... Luke 5:1
- Get into the kingdom ... Luke 16:16
- Attain a goal ... Phil. 3:14

Presumption—*to speak or act without warrant*

A. *Manifested in:*

- Speaking without divine warrant ... Deut. 18:20-22
- Acting without God's presence ... Num. 14:44, 45
- Living without God ... Luke 12:19-21
- Performing functions without authority ... Num. 16:3-11
- Supposing God will not judge sin ... Ps. 73:8, 9
- Aspiring to divine titles ... Is. 14:12-15
- Posing as righteous ... Luke 18:11, 12
- Making plans without God ... James 4:13, 14

B. *Judgment upon:*

- Defeat ... Is. 37:23-36
- Loss of power ... Judg. 16:20
- Quick punishment ... 2 Sam. 6:6, 7
- Rejection ... 1 Sam. 15:3, 9-23
- Destruction ... Lev. 10:1, 2

Pretense—*a false or counterfeit profession*

- Pharisees condemned for ... Matt. 23:14

Prevail—*to get the mastery over*

A. *Of physical force:*

- Waters ... Gen. 7:18-24
- Enemies ... Num. 22:6
- Combat ... 1 Sam. 17:50

B. *Of supernatural force in:*

- Battle ... Ex. 17:11
- Combat ... 1 Sam. 17:9, 50
- Accomplish much ... 1 Sam. 26:25
- Conquest ... Jer. 20:7
- Victory ... Rev. 5:5

Prevarication—*evasion of truth*

- Ananias and Sapphira killed for ... Acts 5:1-10
- Solemn warning against ... Col. 3:9

Prey—*that which is taken by attack*

Used figuratively of:

- Enemies ... Gen. 49:9
- Innocent victims ... Ezek. 22:27

Pride—*a conceited sense of one's superiority*

A. *Origin of, in:*

- Devil ... Is. 14:13-15
- Ambition ... Dan. 5:20-23
- Evil heart ... Mark 7:21, 22
- World ... 1 John 2:16
- Self-righteousness ... Luke 18:11, 12
- Worldly power ... Ezek. 16:49, 56

B. *Evils of:*

- Hardens the mind ... Dan. 5:20
- Produces spiritual decay ... Hos. 7:9, 10
- Keeps from real progress ... Prov. 26:12
- Hinders coming to God ... Ps. 10:4
- Issues in self-deception ... Jer. 49:16
- Makes men reject God's Word ... Jer. 43:2
- Leads to ruin ... Prov. 16:18

C. *Characteristic of:*

- Wicked ... Ps. 73:6
- World rulers ... Hab. 2:4, 5
- Last days ... 2 Tim. 3:2

Priest

A. *Requirements of:*

- Must be a son of Aaron ... Ex. 29:9
- Sanctified to office ... Ex. 29:44
- Statute perpetual ... Ex. 27:21
- No physical blemish ... Lev. 21:17-23
- Genealogy of, necessary ... Ezra 2:62

SUBJECT — REFERENCE

B. *Duties of:*

- Keeping the sanctuary ... Num. 3:38
- Keep lamp burning continually ... Ex. 27:20, 21
- Continuing the sacred fire ... Lev. 6:12, 13
- Covering furniture when moved ... Num. 4:5-15
- Burning incense ... Ex. 30:7, 8
- Offering sacrifices ... Lev. 1:1-17
- Blessing the people ... Num. 6:23-27
- Purifying the unclean ... Lev. 15:15-31
- Diagnosing leprosy ... Lev. 13:2-59
- Blowing the trumpets ... Num. 10:1-10
- Carrying the ark of the covenant ... Josh. 3:6-17
- Teaching the Law ... Lev. 10:11

C. *Names of:*

- Aaron ... Ex. 31:10
- Abiathar ... 1 Sam. 23:9
- Ahimelech ... 1 Sam. 22:11
- Amariah ... 2 Chr. 19:11
- Ananias ... Acts 23:2
- Caiaphas ... Matt. 26:3
- Christ ... Heb. 3:1
- Eleazar ... Num. 16:39
- Eli ... 1 Sam. 1:9
- Eliashib ... Neh. 3:1
- Ezekiel ... Ezek. 1:3
- Ezra ... Ezra 7:11, 12
- Hilkiah ... 2 Kin. 22:4
- Ira ... 2 Sam. 20:26
- Jehoiada ... 2 Kin. 11:9
- Jehozadak ... Hag. 1:1
- Joshua ... Zech. 3:1
- Maaseiah ... Jer. 37:3
- Mattan (of Baal) ... 2 Kin. 11:18
- Melchizedek ... Heb. 7:1
- Pashhur ... Jer. 20:1
- Phinehas ... Josh. 22:30
- Sceva ... Acts 19:14
- Seraiah ... 2 Kin. 25:18
- Shelemiah ... Neh. 13:13
- Urijah ... 2 Kin. 16:10
- Zabud ... 1 Kin. 4:5
- Zacharias ... Luke 1:5
- Zadok ... 2 Sam. 15:27
- Zephaniah ... 2 Kin. 25:18

See Levites

Priesthood of believers

- Typical of Israel ... 1 Pet. 2:9
- Predicted in prophecy ... Is. 61:6
- Including all believers ... Rev. 1:5, 6
- Having access to God ... Eph. 2:18
- Body as a living sacrifice ... Rom. 12:1
- Spiritual sacrifices ... 1 Pet. 2:5
- Praise and good works ... Heb. 13:15, 16
- Deeds of kindness ... Phil. 4:18

Priesthood of Christ

A. *Superior to Aaron as:*

- Man; Christ the Son of God ... Heb. 7:28
- Sinner; Christ, sinless ... Heb. 7:26, 27
- Typical; Christ's the fulfillment ... Heb. 8:1-6
- Subject to change; Christ's unchangeable ... Heb. 7:23, 24
- Imperfect; Christ's perfect ... Heb. 7:11, 25

B. *Christ as priest:*

- Satisfies God's justice ... Rom. 3:24-28
- Pacifies God's wrath ... Rom. 5:9
- Justifies the sinner ... Rom. 5:1
- Sanctifies the believer ... 1 Cor. 1:30

See High priest

Prince—*a ruler*

A. *Descriptive of:*

- Ruler ... Judg. 5:15
- Head or captain ... Ex. 2:14
- Noble or volunteer ... Ps. 47:9

B. *Of the Messiah:*

- Of David's line ... Ezek. 34:23, 24
- Reign of, forever ... Ezek. 37:24, 25
- Time of, determined ... Dan. 9:25, 26
- Reign of, peaceful ... Is. 9:6
- Author of life ... Acts 3:15
- Exalted to be Savior ... Acts 5:31

Prince of this world

- Satan thus called ... John 14:30
- To be cast out ... John 12:31
- Is judged ... John 16:11
- Source of evil ... Eph. 2:2

SUBJECT — REFERENCE

Principalities

Christians subject to — Titus 3:1
Created by Christ — Col. 1:16
Subject to Christ — Eph. 1:20, 21
Beholders of God's redemption — Eph. 3:10
Overcome by Christ — Col. 2:15
Fighting against Christians — Eph. 6:12
Powerless against Christians — Rom. 8:38

Principles—*elementary Christian truths*

To be maintained — 1 Tim. 5:21
Christians must go beyond — Heb. 5:12

Print—*a recognizable sign*

On the body, forbidden — Lev. 19:28
On the hands, desired — John 20:25
In a book, longed for — Job 19:23

Priscilla, Prisca

Wife of Aquila — Acts 18:1-3
An instructed Christian — Acts 18:26
One of Paul's helpers — Rom. 16:3
Greetings sent from — 1 Cor. 16:19
Timothy commanded to greet — 2 Tim. 4:19

Prison—*place of confinement*

A. *Place of:*
Hard labor — Judg. 16:21, 25
Confinement — Jer. 52:11
Guards — Acts 12:3-6
Stocks — Acts 16:23, 24
Torture — Acts 22:24, 25
Execution — Matt. 14:10

B. *Notable occupants of:*
Joseph — Gen. 40:2, 3
Micaiah — 1 Kin. 22:26-28
Jeremiah — Jer. 32:2, 8, 12
Hanani — 2 Chr. 16:7-10
Zedekiah — Jer. 52:11
John the Baptist — Luke 3:20
Apostles — Acts 5:18, 19
Peter — Acts 12:1-4
Paul — Acts 16:24

See Imprisonment

Prisoners—*those confined to jails*

A. *Used literally of:*
Criminals — Matt. 27:15, 16
Christians — Eph. 4:1; Col. 4:10

B. *Used figuratively of:*
Gentiles — Is. 42:6, 7
Those in spiritual darkness — Is. 49:9; Zech. 9:11, 12
Righteous in their need — Ps. 69:33; Ps. 79:11; Ps. 146:7, 8

Privileges of believers

Access to God — Rom. 5:2
Christ's intercession — Heb. 7:25, 26
Eternal life — John 17:2, 3
Growth assured — 1 Pet. 2:2
Intercession of the Spirit — Rom. 8:16, 17
Kinship with Christ — Heb. 2:10-14
Membership in God's kingdom — 1 Cor. 6:9-11
Names written in book of life — Rev. 20:15
Partakers of the divine nature — 2 Pet. 1:4
Reconciled to God — Rom. 5:10
Suffering with Christ — Acts 5:41
Trials overcome — 1 Pet. 1:6-8
Victorious living — Rom. 8:37-39

Privileges of Israel

A. *Consisted of:*
Chosen by God — Deut. 7:6-8
Entrusted with God's revelation — Rom. 3:1, 2
Blessings bestowed upon — Rom. 9:4, 5
Messiah (Christ) — Acts 2:22-39
Gospel first preached to — Acts 3:18-26

B. *Lost because of:*
Unbelief — Matt. 8:10-12
Spiritual hardness — John 12:37-40
Spiritual blindness — John 9:39-41

C. *Now given to:*
Gentiles — Matt. 21:43
Faithful remnant — Rom. 11:1-7
Church — 1 Pet. 2:5-10

Prize—*a reward for faithful accomplishment*

A. *Described as crown of:*
Righteousness — 2 Tim. 4:8
Glory — 1 Pet. 5:4
Life — James 1:12

B. *Factors involved in obtaining:*
Self-control — 1 Cor. 9:25-27
Following the rules — 2 Tim. 2:5
Pressing toward — Phil. 3:14
Enduring temptation — James 1:12
Looking to Jesus — Heb. 12:1, 2
Loving His appearing — 2 Tim. 4:8

Probation—*a period of testing*

A. *Factors determining:*
God's promises — Matt. 21:33-43
Specific time — Dan. 9:24-27
Faith or unbelief — Acts 13:32-48; Rom. 10:1-21

B. *None after death:*
No change permitted — Luke 16:26
Judgment final — Rev. 20:11-15
Destinies eternally fixed — Matt. 25:46

Prochorus—*leader in advance*

One of the seven deacons — Acts 6:5

Proclaim—*to officially announce*

A. *Physical objects of:*
Idolatrous feast — Ex. 32:4, 5
Holy convocation — Lev. 23:2, 4, 21
Year of jubilee — Lev. 25:10
Fast — 2 Chr. 20:3
Release — Jer. 34:17

B. *Spiritual objects of:*
God's name — Ex. 33:19
God's Word — Jer. 3:12
Salvation — Is. 62:11

Procrastination—*putting off something*

A. *Manifested in:*
Delaying a decision — Matt. 19:22
Putting minor things first — Luke 9:59-62
Presuming on tomorrow — Prov. 27:1
Postponing service — 2 Cor. 8:10-14
Rejecting reproof — Prov. 29:1

B. *Evils of, missing:*
Salvation — 2 Cor. 6:1
Life's importance — Eccl. 12:1
God's opportunity — Jer. 13:16

Prodigal son

Parable concerning — Luke 15:11-32

Profane—*to act or speak irreverently of holy things*

A. *Manifested in:*
Breaking God's Law — Amos 2:7
Defiling God's house — Mal. 1:12, 13
Not observing the Sabbath — Neh. 13:17, 18
Committing abominations — Mal. 2:10, 11
Idolatry — Lev. 18:21
Swearing falsely — Lev. 19:12
Illegal marriages — Lev. 21:14, 15
Blemished service — Lev. 21:21-23

B. *Punishment of:*
Excommunication — Lev. 19:8
Death — Lev. 21:9
Destruction — Ezek. 28:16

Profession—*to declare one's faith publicly*

Best — Heb. 3:1
Good — 1 Tim. 6:12
Steadfast — Heb. 3:14
Commendable — 2 Cor. 9:13
Harmful — 1 Tim. 6:20, 21
Inconsistent — Titus 1:16
Degrading — Rom. 1:22
Tragic — Matt. 7:23

Profit—*gain*

A. *Things empty of:*
Wickedness — Prov. 10:2
Riches — Prov. 11:4
Labor without God — Eccl. 2:11
Lying words — Jer. 7:8
World — Matt. 16:26
Flesh — John 6:63
Word without faith — Heb. 4:2
Mere profession — James 2:14, 16

B. *Things full of:*
Spiritual gifts — 1 Cor. 12:7
Godliness — 1 Tim. 4:8
Inspired Word — 2 Tim. 3:16
Youthful service — 2 Tim. 4:11
Good works — Titus 3:8

Prognosticators—*those who profess to know the future*

Help from, vain — Is. 47:13-15

Prohibition—*restraint placed against evil tendencies*

A. *Against:*
Idolatry — 1 John 5:21
Drunkenness — Luke 21:34
Uncleanness — Eph. 4:18, 19
Worldliness — 1 John 2:15-17

B. *Based upon:*
Sanctity of the body — 1 Cor. 6:13-20
New life in Christ — Col. 3:1-10
God's holiness — 1 Pet. 1:14-16

Promises of God

A. *Described as:*
Never failing — Josh. 23:5-15; 1 Kin. 8:56
Backed by God's oath — Heb. 6:12-20
Fulfilled on schedule — Acts 7:6, 17; Gal. 4:4
Given to Israel — Rom. 9:4
Confirmed by Christ — Rom. 15:8
Centered in Christ — 2 Cor. 1:20; 2 Tim. 1:1
Kept by faith — Rom. 4:20, 21; Heb. 11:13-40
Exceedingly great — 2 Pet. 1:4
Not slow — 2 Pet. 3:4-13

B. *Objects of, for Israel:*
Land of Palestine — Acts 7:5; Heb. 11:9
Davidic kingship — 2 Chr. 6:10-16
Messiah — Acts 13:23-33
Gospel — Acts 10:43
New heart — Jer. 31:33

C. *Objects of, for Christians:*
Holy Spirit — Luke 24:49
Salvation — Acts 2:39
Kingdom — James 2:5
Life eternal — Titus 1:2
Crown of life — James 1:12
New earth — 2 Pet. 3:13

See Messiah, the

Promises to believers (see Privileges of believers)

Promotion—*advancement in status*

Deserved — Gen. 41:38-42
Desirable — Prov. 4:8
Divine — Ps. 75:6, 7
Despicable — Num. 22:17, 37

Pronunciation—*giving the right sound to words*

Peter's detected — Matt. 26:73
Correct, required in church — 1 Cor. 14:7-16

Property—*material possessions*

Acquired by:
Industry — Gen. 31:36-42
Inheritance — Eccl. 2:21
Purchase — Gen. 23:7-20
Deception — 1 Kin. 21:1-16
Coveting — Josh. 7:21

See Ownership

Prophecy—*inspired foretelling of events*

A. *Characteristics of:*
Given by God — Is. 41:22, 23
Centered in Christ — Luke 24:26, 27, 44
Inspired by the Spirit — 2 Pet. 1:21
Not of one's own interpretation — 2 Pet. 1:20
Always relevant — Rev. 22:10
Must not be changed by man — Rev. 22:18, 19

B. *True, based on:*
Inspiration — Mic. 3:8
Foreknowledge — Is. 42:9

C. *False, evidenced by:*
Nonfulfillment — Jer. 28:1-17
Peaceful message — Jer. 23:17-22

P

SUBJECT — REFERENCE

- Apostasy from God — Deut. 13:1-5
- Lying — Jer. 23:25-34
- Scoffing — 2 Pet. 3:3, 4

D. *Fulfillment of:*
- Unconditional — Ezek. 12:25-28
- Sometimes:
  - Conditional — Jon. 3:1-10
  - Dated — Dan. 9:24-27
  - Nonliteral — Matt. 17:10-12
- Unrecognized by Jews — Acts 13:27-29
- Interpretation of, needed — Luke 24:25-44
- Often referred to — Matt. 1:22, 23; Matt. 2:14-23

Prophetess—*a female prophet*

A. *Good:*
- Miriam — Ex. 15:20, 21
- Deborah — Judg. 4:4, 5
- Huldah — 2 Kin. 22:12-20
- Isaiah's wife — Is. 8:1-3
- Anna — Luke 2:36
- Daughters of Philip — Acts 21:8, 9
- Prophecy concerning — Joel 2:28

B. *False:*
- Women of Judah — Ezek. 13:17
- Noadiah — Neh. 6:14
- Jezebel — Rev. 2:20

Prophets—*inspired messengers*

A. *Described as:*
- God's servants — Zech. 1:6
- God's messengers — 2 Chr. 36:15
- Holy prophets — Luke 1:70
- Holy men — 2 Pet. 1:21
- Watchmen — Ezek. 3:17
- Prophets of God — Ezra 5:2

B. *Message of:*
- Centered in Christ — Luke 10:24
- Interpreted by Christ — Luke 24:27, 44
- United in testimony — Acts 3:21, 24
- Contains grace and salvation — 1 Pet. 1:9-12
- Abiding revelation — Matt. 5:17, 18

Prophets, names of
- Enoch — Gen. 5:21, 24
- Noah — Gen. 9:25-27
- Abraham — Gen. 20:1, 7
- Jacob — Gen. 49:1
- Aaron — Ex. 7:1
- Moses — Deut. 18:18
- Joshua — 1 Kin. 16:34
- One sent to Israel — Judg. 6:8-10
- One sent to Eli — 1 Sam. 2:27-36
- Samuel — 1 Sam. 3:20
- David — Acts 2:25, 30
- Nathan — 2 Sam. 7:2
- Zadok — 2 Sam. 15:27
- Gad — 2 Sam. 24:11-14
- Ahijah — 1 Kin. 11:29
- One of Judah — 1 Kin. 13:1
- Iddo — 2 Chr. 9:29; 12:15
- Shemaiah — 2 Chr. 12:5, 7, 15
- Azariah — 2 Chr. 15:1-8
- Hanani — 2 Chr. 16:7-10
- Jehu — 1 Kin. 16:1, 7, 12
- Elijah — 1 Kin. 17:1
- Elisha — 1 Kin. 19:16
- Micaiah — 1 Kin. 22:7, 8
- Jonah — 2 Kin. 14:25
- Isaiah — 2 Kin. 19:2
- Hosea — Hos. 1:1
- Amos — Amos 1:1
- Micah — Mic. 1:1
- Oded — 2 Chr. 28:9
- Nahum — Nah. 1:1
- Joel — Joel 1:1
- Zephaniah — Zeph. 1:1
- Jeduthun — 2 Chr. 35:15
- Jeremiah — 2 Chr. 36:12, 21
- Habakkuk — Hab. 1:1
- Obadiah — Obad. 1
- Ezekiel — Ezek. 1:3
- Daniel — Matt. 24:15
- Haggai — Ezra 5:1
- Zechariah — Ezra 5:1; Zech. 1:1; Luke 1:67
- Malachi — Mal. 1:1
- John the Baptist — Luke 7:26-28
- Agabus — Acts 11:28
- Paul — 1 Tim. 4:1
- Peter — 2 Pet. 2:1, 2
- John — Rev. 1:1

Prophets in the New Testament

A. *Office of, based upon:*
- Christ's prophetic office — Deut. 18:15, 18
- Old Testament prediction — Joel 2:28; Acts 2:18
- Holy Spirit's coming — John 16:7, 13
- Divine institution — 1 Cor. 12:28

B. *Functions of:*
- Strengthen — Acts 15:32
- Define God's will — Acts 13:1-3
- Predict the future — Acts 21:10, 11

Propitiation—*appeasing or conciliating*
- Elements in Christ's:
- Dying for man's sins — 1 Pet. 1:18, 19
- Satisfying God's justice — Rom. 3:25, 26
- Becoming the mercy seat — Rom. 3:25
- Reconciling God and man — 2 Cor. 5:18, 19
- Offering believing sinner perfect righteousness — 2 Cor. 5:20, 21

Proselyte—*convert to Judaism*

A. *Regulations imposed upon:*
- Circumcision — Gen. 17:13
- Observance of the Law — Ex. 12:48, 49
- Obedience to the covenant — Deut. 29:10-13
- Association with Israel — Ruth 1:16
- Separation from heathenism — Ezra 6:21
- Participation in feasts — John 12:20; Acts 8:27

B. *Special significance of:*
- Typical of Gentile converts — Is. 56:3-8
- Concerned about Christ — John 12:20
- Among early converts — Acts 6:5
- Source of Gentile church — Acts 13:42-46

Prosperity—*a state of material or spiritual bountifulness*

A. *Kinds of:*
- Material — 1 Cor. 16:2
- National — Ezek. 16:13, 14
- Personal — Dan. 6:28
- Deceitful — 1 Kin. 22:12, 15
- Evil — Ps. 73:12
- Spiritual — 3 John 2
- Divine — Is. 53:10

B. *Of the righteous:*
- Promised — Ps. 1:3
- Prayed for — Neh. 1:11
- Perplexed — Jer. 12:1-3

C. *Of the wicked:*
- Lack of understanding over — Ps. 73:3-12
- Righteous must not fret over — Ps. 37:7
- Terrible end of — Jer. 20:11

D. *Hindrances to:*
- Transgression — 2 Chr. 24:20
- Hiding one's sins — Prov. 28:13
- Distrust of the Lord — Jer. 2:36, 37

E. *True secrets of:*
- Lord's blessings — Ps. 35:27
- Keeping God's Law — Josh. 1:7, 8
- God's guidance — Gen. 24:40-56
- Trust in God — Neh. 2:20
- Dedication to God — 2 Chr. 31:20, 21
- Listening to God's prophets — Ezra 6:14
- Belief in God's Word — 2 Chr. 20:20

F. *Perils of:*
- Forgetting God — Deut. 8:10-12; Prov. 30:7-9
- Destruction — Prov. 1:32
- Rebellion — Jer. 22:21

Prostitute—*one engaged in promiscuous sexual activity*
- Forbidden — Lev. 19:29

Prostitution (see Harlot)

Protection, divine

A. *Characteristics of:*
- Continuous — Ps. 121:3-8
- Unfailing — Josh. 1:5
- Assuring — Is. 41:10
- Persevering — John 10:28-30
- Satisfying — 2 Cor. 12:9, 10
- Necessary — Ps. 124:1-5

B. *Provided against:*
- Evil — 2 Thess. 3:3
- Temptation — 1 Cor. 10:13
- Persecution — Rev. 3:10
- Enemies — Ps. 56:9
- Falling — Jude 24
- Dangers — Ps. 91:3-7
- Calamities — Ps. 57:1

Protector, divine
- God as — Ps. 18:2
- Christ as — 2 Tim. 4:17, 18

Proud—*the defiant and haughty*

A. *Descriptive of:*
- Moabites — Jer. 48:29
- Babylonians — Jer. 50:29-32
- Wicked — Ps. 17:9, 10
- Scoffers — Prov. 21:24

B. *God's attitude toward:*
- Does not respect — Ps. 40:4
- Rebukes — Ps. 119:21
- Resists — James 4:6

See Pride

Prove—*to show something to be true*

A. *Descriptive of:*
- Testing physically — 1 Sam. 17:39; Luke 14:19
- Testing morally — John 6:6
- Showing something to be true — Gen. 42:15, 16

B. *Objects of, among Christians:*
- Love — 2 Cor. 8:8
- Sacrifice — Rom. 12:2
- Faith — 2 Cor. 13:5
- Works — Gal. 6:4
- Abilities — 1 Tim. 3:10

Provender—*cattle food*
- Supplied for animals — Gen. 24:25, 32; Gen. 42:27

Proverb—*a wise saying*

A. *Descriptive of:*
- Wise saying — 1 Sam. 24:13
- Something generally accepted — Ezek. 12:22, 23
- Object of taunt — Deut. 28:37
- Figurative language — John 16:25, 29

B. *Characteristics of:*
- Brief — 1 Sam. 10:12
- Striking statement — Luke 4:23
- Authoritative — Prov. 1:1-6
- Emphasis by repetition — Prov. 3:17

Proverbs, the Book of—*a book of the Old Testament*
- Tribute to wisdom — Prov. 1—2
- Against immorality — Prov. 5:1-23
- Parental counsel — Prov. 6—7
- Miscellaneous proverbs — Prov. 10—24
- Proverbs of Agur and Lemuel — Prov. 30:1—31:9
- The worthy woman — Prov. 31:10-31

Providence—*divine guidance of men and things*

A. *Described as:*
- Universal — Ps. 103:19
- Purposive — Gen. 45:5-8
- Righteous — Ps. 145:17
- Something mysterious — Job 11:7-9
- Irresistible — Dan. 4:35

B. *Manifested, in the world, in God's:*
- Preserving the world — Neh. 9:6
- Providing for His possesions — Ps. 104:27, 28
- Guiding world events — Acts 17:26, 27
- Ruling over the elements — Is. 50:2, 3
- Preserving nature — Gen. 8:22
- Ordering man's life — Ps. 75:6, 7
- Controlling minute details — Matt. 10:29, 30

C. *Attitude of believers toward:*
- Acknowledge in prosperity — 1 Chr. 29:11, 12; Prov. 3:6
- Humble himself before in adversity — Job 1:21; Ps. 119:75
- Remember God's hand — Ps. 37:1-40; Ps. 139:10

Province—*a governmental district*

A. *Ruled by:*
- Governors — Esth. 3:12
- Proconsuls — Acts 13:4, 7

SUBJECT — REFERENCE

B. *Characteristics of:*

Numerous ... Esth. 1:1
Ruled by one man ... Dan. 2:48, 49
Justice perverted in ... Eccl. 5:8
People, citizens of ... Acts 23:34
News spreads to ... Esth. 9:4

C. *Of the Roman Empire:*

Achaia ... Acts 18:12
Asia ... Acts 19:10
Bithynia ... Acts 16:7
Cappadocia ... Acts 2:9
Cyprus ... Acts 13:4
Egypt ... Matt. 2:13
Galatia ... Acts 16:6
Macedonia ... Acts 16:12
Pamphylia ... Acts 13:13
Lycia ... Acts 27:5
Syria ... Matt. 4:24

Provision

Provide for own house ... 1 Tim. 5:8
Provide for poor ... Is. 58:7

Provoke—*to agitate another's soul*

A. *Between people:*

Two women ... 1 Sam. 1:7
Satan and man ... 1 Chr. 21:1
Peoples (nations) ... Rom. 10:19
Christians ... 2 Cor. 9:2
Father and children ... Eph. 6:4

B. *Causes of, between God and man:*

Evil ... Deut. 4:25
Sins ... 1 Kin. 16:2
Whoredoms ... Ezek. 16:26

Prudence—*wisdom applied to practical matters*

A. *Characteristics of:*

Dwells with wisdom ... Prov. 8:12
Observant ... Prov. 14:15
Foresees evil ... Prov. 22:3
Regards reproof ... Prov. 15:5
Conceals knowledge ... Prov. 12:23
Crowned with knowledge ... Prov. 14:18
Keeps silent ... Amos 5:13

B. *Descriptive of:*

David ... 1 Sam. 16:18
Solomon ... 2 Chr. 2:12
Messiah ... Is. 52:13
Wife ... Prov. 19:14
Believers ... Hos. 14:9
Worldly-wise ... Matt. 11:25

C. *Examples of:*

Jacob ... Gen. 32:3-23
Joseph ... Gen. 41:39-49
Gideon ... Judg. 8:1-3

Prune—*to cut back plants for the purpose of producing more growth*

Vineyards ... Lev. 25:3, 4
Figurative of God's care ... Is. 5:6
John 15:2

Instruments used to:

Hooks ... Is. 2:4
Knives ... Is. 18:5

Psalm—*a spiritual song*

Some written by David ... 2 Sam. 23:1
Prophetic of Christ ... Luke 24:44
Used in worship ... Ps. 95:2
Used in church ... 1 Cor. 14:26

Psalms, the Book of—*a book of the Old Testament*

Book I—The Genesis Book Concerning Man ... Ps. 1—41
Blessed are the righteous ... Ps. 1
The holy hill ... Ps. 15
The creation of God ... Ps. 19
Messianic Psalm ... Ps. 22
Prayer for God's help ... Ps. 28
Book II—The Exodus Book Concerning Israel as a Nation ... Ps. 42—72
Psalm of longing ... Ps. 42
Prayer for cleansing ... Ps. 51
Prayer for deliverance ... Ps. 70
Book III—The Leviticus Book Concerning the Sanctuary ... Ps. 73-89
Prayer for restoration ... Ps. 80
Book IV—The Numbers Book Concerning Israel and the Nation ... Ps. 90—106
The Lord reigns ... Ps. 93
God's wondrous works ... Ps. 105
Book V—The Deuteronomy Book Concerning God and His word ... Ps. 107—150
On God's commandments ... Ps. 119
Psalm of faithfulness ... Ps. 128
God is gracious ... Ps. 145
Psalms of praise ... Ps. 149
Ps. 150

Psaltery—*a musical instrument*

Used in:

Prophecy ... 1 Sam. 10:5
Processions ... 2 Sam. 6:5
Worship ... Ps. 150:3
Government proclamations ... Dan. 3:5, 7

Ptolemais—*a seaport city south of Tyre*

Paul lands at ... Acts 21:7
Same as Accho ... Judg. 1:31

Public opinion

Rescues Jonathan ... 1 Sam. 14:45
Delays John's death ... Matt. 14:1-5
Protects the apostles ... Acts 5:26
Makes Saul sin ... 1 Sam. 15:24
Increases Pilate's guilt ... Matt. 27:21-26
Incites persecution ... Acts 12:1-3

Publicans—*Jews engaged in tax collecting*

A. *Features concerning:*

Collector of taxes ... Luke 5:27
Often guilty of extortion ... Luke 3:12, 13
Classed with lowest sinners ... Matt. 9:10, 11
Matt. 21:31, 32
Do not even, the same ... Matt. 5:46
Thomas and Matthew, the ... Matt. 10:3
Thank thee I am not ... Luke 18:11
As an heathen and a ... Matt. 18:17

B. *Spiritual attitude of:*

Often conscientious ... Luke 19:2, 8
Often hospitable ... Luke 5:29
Received John's baptism ... Matt. 21:32
Listened to Jesus ... Luke 15:1
Conscious of their sins ... Luke 18:13, 14
Many sat with him ... Mark 2:15
Why do ye eat with ... Luke 5:30
A friend of ... Matt. 11:19
Luke 7:34

Publish—*to proclaim publicly*

A. *Descriptive of:*

Victory ... 1 Sam. 31:9
Message of doom ... Jon. 3:7
Royal decree ... Esth. 1:20, 22
Good news ... Mark 1:45

B. *Objects of:*

Peace ... Is. 52:7
Doom ... Jer. 4:5, 15, 16
Gospel ... Mark 13:10
God's Word ... Acts 13:49

Publius—*common*

Roman official; entertains Paul ... Acts 28:7, 8

Pudens—*modest*

Believer at Rome ... 2 Tim. 4:21

Puhites

Family of Kirjath-jearim ... 1 Chr. 2:53

Pul—*strong*

King of Assyria; same as Tiglath-pileser ... 2 Kin. 15:19

Pulpit—*a rostrum*

Ezra reads law from ... Neh. 8:4-8

Pulse—*a vegetable diet*

Preferred by Daniel ... Dan. 1:12, 16

Punishment, everlasting (see Hell; Eternal, everlasting)

Punishments—*penalties inflicted on criminals*

A. *Agents of:*

State ... Rom. 13:1-4
Nation ... Josh. 7:25
Prophet ... 1 Sam. 15:33
Witnesses ... John 8:7
Soldiers ... Matt. 27:27-35

B. *Kinds of* (non-capital):

Imprisonment ... Matt. 5:25
Fine ... Ex. 21:22
Restitution ... Ex. 22:3-6
Retaliation ... Deut. 19:21
Scourging ... Acts 22:25
Bondage ... Matt. 18:25
Banishment ... Rev. 1:9
Torture ... Heb. 11:35
Mutilation ... Judg. 1:5-7

C. *Kinds of* (capital):

Burning ... Gen. 38:24
Hanging ... Esth. 7:9, 10
Crucifying ... Matt. 27:35
Beheading ... Mark 6:16, 27
Stoning ... Lev. 24:14
Cutting in pieces ... Dan. 2:5
Exposing to lions ... Dan. 6:16, 24
Killing with the sword ... Acts 12:2

See Capital punishment

Punites

Descendants of Pua ... Num. 26:23

Punon

Israelite camp ... Num. 33:42, 43

Pur—*a lot*

Cast for Jews' slaughter ... Esth. 3:7
Origin of Purim ... Esth. 9:24-26

Purah—*branch*

Gideon's servant ... Judg. 7:10, 11

Purchase—*to buy*

A. *Used literally of:*

Cave ... Gen. 49:32
Field ... Jer. 32:9-16
Wife ... Ruth 4:10

B. *Used figuratively of:*

Israel's redemption ... Ex. 15:16
God's gifts ... Acts 8:20
Church ... Acts 20:28

Pure, purity—*uncontaminated with dross or evil*

A. *Descriptive of:*

Chastity ... 1 Tim. 5:2
Uncontaminated ... 1 Kin. 5:11
Innocent ... Acts 20:26
Regenerated ... Titus 1:15

B. *Applied figuratively to God's:*

Law ... Ps. 19:8
Word ... Ps. 119:140
Wisdom ... James 3:17

C. *Applied figuratively to the believer's:*

Heart ... Ps. 24:4
Mind ... 2 Pet. 3:1
Conscience ... 1 Tim. 3:9
Language ... Zeph. 3:9
Body ... Heb. 10:22

D. *Applied to the Christian's life:*

Source ... Titus 1:15
Command ... 1 Tim. 4:12
Means ... Phil. 4:8
Outward manifestation ... James 1:27
Inward evidence ... 1 Tim. 1:5
Goal ... 1 John 3:3
Reward ... Matt. 5:8
False ... Prov. 20:9

E. *Applied symbolically to:*

New Jerusalem ... Rev. 21:18, 21

Purge—*to cleanse thoroughly*

A. *Used, in the Old Testament, ceremonially of:*

Cleansing ... Ezek. 20:38
Separation from idolatry ... 2 Chr. 34:3, 8

B. *Used, in the Old Testament, figuratively of:*

Reformation ... Ezek. 24:13
Regeneration ... Is. 4:4
Sanctification ... Is. 1:25
Forgiveness ... Ps. 51:7
Consecration ... Is. 6:7
Atonement ... Mal. 3:3, 4
Judgment ... Is. 22:14

Purification—*ceremonial or spiritual cleansing*

A. *Objects of:*

Israelites at Sinai ... Ex. 19:10
Priests at ordination ... Ex. 29:4
Levites at ordination ... Num. 8:6, 7
Offerings ... 2 Chr. 4:6
High priest ... Lev. 16:4, 24

SUBJECT	REFERENCE
People unclean	Lev. 15:2-13
Nazarite after vow	Acts 21:24, 26
B. *Accomplished by:*	
Sprinkling	Num. 19:13-18
Washing parts of the body	Ex. 30:18, 19
Washing the whole body	Lev. 8:6
Running water	Lev. 15:13
C. *Figurative of:*	
Christ's atonement	Mal. 3:3
Regeneration	Acts 15:9
Sanctification	James 4:8
Obedience	1 Pet. 1:22

Purim—*lots*

Jewish festival celebrating being rescued from Haman's plot	Esth. 9:26-28

Purloining—*stealing*

Forbidden	Titus 2:10

Purple

Used in the tabernacle	Ex. 25:4
Sign of riches	Luke 16:19
Worn by royalty	Judg. 8:26
Lydia, seller of	Acts 16:14

Purposes of God

Characteristics of:	
Centered in Christ	Eph. 3:11
Irresistible	Is. 14:26, 27
Unknown to the wise	Is. 19:11, 12
Made known	Jer. 50:45
Irreversible	Jer. 4:28
Planned	Is. 23:9
Fulfilled	Rom. 9:11
Victorious	2 Chr. 32:2-22

Purposes of man

A. *Good:*	
Hindered by evil men	Ezra 4:5
Known by others	2 Tim. 3:10
Permitted	Dan. 1:8-16
Accomplished	1 Kin. 5:5
Determine	Ps. 17:3
Delayed	Acts 19:21
Not vacillating	2 Cor. 1:17
B. *Evil:*	
Known by God	Jer. 49:30
Designed against the righteous	Ps. 140:4
Hindered	Dan. 6:17-23

Purse—*a bag*

One, forbidden	Prov. 1:14
Disciples forbidden to take	Luke 10:4

Pursue—*To go after*

"Enemy said, I will"	Ex. 15:9
"Shall flee when none"	Lev. 26:17
"I will arise and"	2 Sam. 17:1
"Seek peace, and"	Ps. 34:14
"Blood shall"	Ezek. 35:6

Put

Country and people in Africa	Is. 66:19

Puteoli—*little wells*

Seaport of Italy	Acts 28:13

Puthites

Descendants of Caleb	1 Chr. 2:50, 53

Putiel—*God enlightens*

Father-in-law of Eleazar	Ex. 6:25

Puah—*utterance*

Father of Tola	Judg. 10:1

Pygarg—*a white-rumped antelope*

Clean animal	Deut. 14:5

Q

Quail—*a small bird*

Sent to satisfy hunger	Ex. 16:12, 13
Sent as a judgment	Num. 11:31-34

Quarantine—*restricted in public contacts*

Required of lepers	Lev. 13:45, 46
Miriam consigned	Num. 12:14-16
Imposed under King Azariah	2 Kin. 15:1-5

Quarrel—*a dispute*

SUBJECT	REFERENCE
A. *Caused by:*	
Flesh	James 4:1, 2
Hatred	Mark 6:18, 19
B. *Productive of:*	
Friction	Matt. 20:20-24
Separation	Acts 15:37-40
C. *Cured by:*	
Gentleness	2 Tim. 2:24-26
Forgiveness	Col. 3:13
Unity of mind	Phil. 2:3, 4

See Contention; Strife

Quarry—*a place for mining stone*

Israelites flee to ("Shebarim")	Josh. 7:5
Some near Gilgal	Judg. 3:19, 26
Same word translated "graven images" in	Deut. 7:5, 25

Quartus—*fourth*

Christian at Corinth	Rom. 16:23

Quaternion—*a company of four soldiers*

Peter guarded by four	Acts 12:4

Queen—*a king's wife*

A. *Applied to:*	
Queen regent	1 Kin. 10:1-13
Queen mother	1 Kin. 15:13
Heathen deity	Jer. 44:15-30
Mystical Babylon	Rev. 18:7
B. *Names of:*	
Of Sheba	1 Kin. 10:1
Vashti	Esth. 1:9
Esther	Esth. 5:3
Of Heaven	Jer. 7:18
Of the South	Matt. 12:42

Quench—*to extinguish*

A. *Applied literally to:*	
Fire	Num. 11:2
Thirst	Ps. 104:11
B. *Applied figuratively to:*	
Love	Song 8:7
God's wrath	2 Kin. 22:17
Spirit	1 Thess. 5:19
Persecution	Heb. 11:34

Question—*an inquiry*

Asked by:	
Wicked	Matt. 22:16-40 John 18:33-38
Sincere	Matt. 18:1-6 Acts 1:6
Jesus	Matt. 22:41-45

Quickening—*reviving again*

A. *Descriptive of:*	
Spiritual revival	Ps. 71:20
Physical resurrection	John 5:21
Spiritual resurrection (regeneration)	Eph. 2:5
B. *Accomplished by:*	
God	1 Tim. 6:13
Christ	1 Cor. 15:45
Holy Spirit	John 6:63
God's Word	Ps. 119:25, 50
God's precepts	Ps. 119:93

Quicksand—*sand which engulfs*

Endangers Paul's ship	Acts 27:17

Quietness—*noiselessness*

A. *Descriptive of:*	
Man	Jer. 51:59
People	Judg. 18:7, 27
City	2 Kin. 11:20
Nation	2 Chr. 14:1, 5
Earth	Is. 14:7
B. *Realization of:*	
Predicted	Is. 32:17, 18
Comes from God	1 Chr. 22:9
Preferred	Prov. 17:1
To be sought	1 Thess. 4:11
Undeniable	Acts 19:36
Commanded	2 Thess. 3:12
Obtainable	Ps. 131:2
Very valuable	1 Pet. 3:4
Rewarded	Is. 30:15

Quitters, quitting

SUBJECT	REFERENCE
Unworthy	Luke 9:62
Believers should not	Gal. 6:9 2 Thess. 3:13
Press on	Phil. 3:12-14
Continue	2 Tim.

Quiver—*a case for carrying arrows*

Used by:	
Hunters	Gen. 27:3
Soldiers	Job 39:23 Is. 22:6
Figurative of:	
Children	Ps. 127:5
Messiah	Is. 49:2

Quotations

A. *Introduced by:*	
"The Holy Spirit"	Acts 28:25
"As it is written"	Rom. 15:9
"The Scripture"	Gal. 3:8
Old Testament writer	Rom. 10:5-20
B. *Purposes of:*	
Cite fulfillment	Matt. 1:22, 23
Confirm a truth	Matt. 4:4
Prove a doctrine	Rom. 4:7, 8
Show the true meaning	Acts 2:25-36

R

Raamah—*trembling*

Son of Cush	Gen. 10:6, 7
Father of Sheba and Dedan	Gen. 10:7
Noted traders	Ezek. 27:22

Raamiah—*Jehovah has thundered*

Postexilic chief	Neh. 7:7
Same as Reelaiah	Ezra 2:2

Raamses—*Ra* (Egyptian sun god) *created him*

Part of Egypt inhabited by Jacob	Gen. 47:11
Treasure city built by Hebrew slaves	Ex. 1:11

Rabbah, Rabbath—*great*

1. Town of Judah	Josh. 15:60
2. Capital of Ammon	Amos 1:14
Bedstead of Og here	Deut. 3:11
On Gad's boundary	Josh. 13:25
Besieged by Joab	2 Sam. 12:26
Defeated and enslaved by David	2 Sam. 12:29-31
Destruction of, foretold	Jer. 49:2, 3

Rabbi, Rabboni—*my master*

A. *Applied to:*	
John the Baptist	John 3:26
Jewish leader	John 3:2
Jesus Christ	John 1:38, 49
B. *Significance of:*	
Coveted title	Matt. 23:6, 7
Forbidden by Christ	Matt. 23:8
Expressive of imperfect faith	Mark 14:45 John 20:16
Translated "Master"	Mark 14:45

Rabbith—*multitude*

Frontier town of Issachar	Josh. 19:20

Rabble, the

Cause of discord	Num. 11:4-6
Clamors for Jesus' death	Matt. 26:47
Seeks Paul's life	Acts 17:1-8

Rabboni—*Aramaic form of Rabbi*

Mary addresses Christ as	John 20:16

Rab-mag—*head of the Magi*

Title applied to Nergal-sharezer	Jer. 39:3, 13

Rab-saris—*head chamberlain*

A. *Title applied to:*	
Assyrian officials sent by Sennacherib	2 Kin. 18:17
Babylonian Nebushasban	Jer. 39:13
Babylonian prince	Jer. 39:3
B. *Office of:*	
Considered important	Dan. 1:7

SUBJECT REFERENCE

Rab-shakeh—*Head of the cupbearers*
Sent ... 2 Kin. 18:17
King of Assyria sent ... Is. 36:2
And told him the words of ... Is. 36:22
Hear all the words ... 2 Kin. 19:4

Raca—*a term of insult*
Use of, forbidden by Christ ... Matt. 5:21, 22

Race, Christian
Requirements of:
Discipline ... 1 Cor. 9:24-27
Patience ... Eccl. 9:11
Steadfastness ... Gal. 5:7

Race, human
Unity of ... Gen. 3:20
Divisions of ... Gen. 10:1-32
Scattering of ... Gen. 11:1-9
Bounds of ... Acts 17:26
Depravity of ... Rom. 1:18-32
Salvation of ... John 3:16

Rachal—*trader*
City in Judah ... 1 Sam. 30:29

Rachel—*ewe*
Laban's younger daughter; Jacob's favorite wife ... Gen. 29:28-30
Supports her husband's position ... Gen. 31:14-16
Mother of Joseph and Benjamin ... Gen. 30:22-25
Prophecy concerning, quoted ... Jer. 31:15; Matt. 2:18

Rachel, tomb of
At Bethlehem—first mention of in Bible ... Gen. 35:19

Racial relations
Salvation is for all ... Eph. 2:11-22; Eph. 3:7-9
All are same in Christ ... Col. 3:9-11

Raddai—*Jehovah has subdued*
One of David's brothers ... 1 Chr. 2:14

Radiance in life
Caused by:
Wisdom ... Prov. 4:7-9
Soul-winning ... Dan. 12:3
Transfiguration ... Matt. 17:2
Beholding the Lord ... Ps. 34:5; 2 Cor. 3:7-18

Rafters—*timbers used to support a roof*
Made of fir ... Song 1:17

Ragau (see Reu)

Rage—*raving and violent madness*
A. *Descriptive of:*
Sea ... Luke 8:24
Strong drink ... Prov. 20:1
Anger ... Dan. 3:13
Heathen ... Ps. 2:1
B. *Caused by:*
Insane madness ... 2 Chr. 16:7-10
Supposed insult ... 2 Kin. 5:11, 12
Jealousy ... Prov. 6:34
Insolence against God ... 2 Kin. 19:27, 28

Rags—*tattered and spoiled clothing*
Used as cushions ... Jer. 38:11-13
Reward of drowsiness ... Prov. 23:21
Man's righteousness like ... Is. 64:6

Rahab (I)—*violence*
Prostitute living in Jericho ... Josh. 2:1
Concealed Joshua's spies ... Josh. 2:1-24
Spared by invading Israelites ... Josh. 6:17-25
Included among the faithful ... Heb. 11:31
Cited as an example ... James 2:25
Ancestress of Christ ... Matt. 1:5

Rahab (II)—*pride, arrogance*
Used figuratively of Egypt ... Ps. 87:4
Translated "the proud" ... Job 9:13

Raham—*pity*
Descendant of Caleb ... 1 Chr. 2:44

Raiment—*clothing*
A. *Indicative of:*
Plenty ... Gen. 24:53
Position ... Judg. 8:26
Provision ... Matt. 6:28
Poverty ... James 2:2
Personality ... Gen. 27:15, 27
B. *Regulations concerning:*
Not to be kept ... Ex. 22:26
To be divided ... Josh. 22:8
To be purified ... Num. 31:20
Not to be multiplied ... 1 Tim. 6:8
C. *Figurative of:*
Redemption ... Is. 63:3
Imputation of righteousness ... Zech. 3:4
Purity ... Rev. 3:5, 18
Honor of position ... Ps. 45:14

Rain—*water falling from clouds*
A. *Features concerning:*
Sent by God ... Jer. 14:22
Sent on all mankind ... Matt. 5:45
Sign of God's goodness ... Deut. 28:12
Controlled by God's decrees ... Job 28:26; Job 37:6
Withheld because of sin ... Deut. 11:17
Sent as a result of judgment ... Gen. 7:4
Former and latter ... Jer. 5:24
To be prayed for ... 1 Kin. 8:35, 36
B. *Figurative of:*
God's Word ... Is. 55:10, 11
Spiritual blessing ... Ps. 72:6
Righteousness ... Hos. 10:12
Final judgment ... Matt. 7:24-27
Hell ... Ps. 11:6
Earth's ingathering ... James 5:7

Rainbow
Appears after the flood ... Gen. 9:12, 13
Sign of God's covenant ... Gen. 9:16, 17
Around angel's head ... Rev. 10:1
Over God's throne ... Rev. 4:3

Raisins—*dried grapes*
Nourishing food ... 1 Sam. 25:18
Provided for David ... 2 Sam. 16:1

Rakem—*variegated*
Manassite ... 1 Chr. 7:16

Rakkath—*bank, shore*
Fortified city of Naphtali ... Josh. 19:32, 35

Rakkon—*shore*
Danite village ... Josh. 19:40, 46

Ram (I)—*high, exalted*
1. Ancestor of David ... Ruth 4:19
Ancestor of Christ ... Matt. 1:3, 4
2. Man of Judah ... 1 Chr. 2:25, 27

Ram (II)—*a male sheep*
Used as food ... Gen. 31:38
Used in offerings ... Gen. 22:13
Appointed for certain offerings ... Lev. 5:15
Skin of, used as coverings ... Ex. 26:14
Horns of, used as trumpets ... Josh. 6:4-13

Ram (III)—*an instrument of war*
Used to destroy gates and walls ... Ezek. 4:2

Ramah
1. Town of Asher ... Josh. 19:24, 29
2. City of Naphtali ... Josh. 19:32, 36
3. Benjamite city near Jerusalem ... Josh. 18:21, 25
Deborah's palm near here ... Judg. 4:5
Fortress built ... 1 Kin. 15:17-22
Gathering of captives ... Jer. 40:1
Reinhabited after exile ... Ezra 2:26
Probable site of Rachel's tomb ... 1 Sam. 10:2
Samuel's headquarters ... 1 Sam. 7:15, 17
David flees to ... 1 Sam. 19:18-23
4. Town called Ramoth-gilead ... 2 Kin. 8:28, 29

Ramathaim-zophim
Home of Elkanah ... 1 Sam. 1:1
Also called "Ramah" ... 1 Sam. 1:19
See Ramah 4

Ramathite—*an inhabitant of Ramah*
Shimei called ... 1 Chr. 27:27

Ramath-mizpeh—*a town in Palestine*
An inheritance of Gad ... Josh. 13:24-26

Ramoth—*high places*
1. Town of Issachar; possibly same as Remeth and Jarmuth ... Josh. 19:21
2. Town of the south; see Ramah
3. Town of Gilead ... Deut. 4:43

Ramoth-gilead
City of refuge east of Jordan ... Deut. 4:43; Josh. 20:8; 1 Chr. 6:80
Site of Ahab's fatal conflict with Syrians ... 1 Kin. 22:1-39

Rampart—*a city's outer fortification*
Around:
Certain cities ... 2 Sam. 20:15
Jerusalem ... Ps. 48:13

Ransom—*to redeem by a payment*
A. *Of man, for:*
Israelites ... Ex. 30:12-16
Murderer, forbidden ... Num. 35:31, 32
Some, unpayable ... Prov. 6:34, 35
Brother, impossible ... Ps. 49:7, 8
B. *Of Christ:*
For all ... Matt. 20:28
From grave ... Hos. 13:14
From Satan ... Jer. 31:11
Cause of joy ... Is. 35:10

Rapacity—*seizing others' goods; covetous.*
Descriptive of Satan ... 1 Pet. 5:8
Characteristic of false teachers ... Luke 11:39

Rape—*forced sexual relations*
A. *Features concerning:*
Death penalty for ... Deut. 22:25-27
Captives subjected to ... Is. 13:16
B. *Example of:*
Tamar by Amnon ... 2 Sam. 13:6-29, 32, 33

Rapha, Raphah—*he* (God) *has healed*
1. Benjamin's fifth son ... 1 Chr. 8:1, 2
But not listed ... Gen. 46:21
2. Descendant of Jonathan ... 1 Chr. 8:37
Called Rephaiah in ... 1 Chr. 9:43
3. Same word translated "giant" ... 2 Sam. 21:16-20

Raphu—*cured*
Benjamite ... Num. 13:9

Rapture, the—*translation of saved at Christ's return*
Not all will sleep ... 1 Cor. 15:51; 1 Thess. 4:15, 17
Dead in Christ will rise ... 1 Cor. 15:52; 1 Thess. 4:13, 14, 16
Living to be transformed ... 1 Cor. 15:51-53
Saints caught up ... 1 Thess. 4:16, 17

Rashness—*ill-advised and hasty action*
Examples of:
Moses' killing the Egyptian ... Ex. 2:11, 12
Jephthah's vow ... Judg. 11:30-39
Israel's vow against the Benjamites ... Judg. 21:1-6
Josiah's war against Necho ... 2 Chr. 35:20-24
Peter's cutting off the ear of Malchus ... John 18:10

Rationing—*limits prescribed for necessities*
By Joseph, to save Egypt ... Gen. 41:35-57

Raven—*a flesh-eating bird*
A. *Characteristics of:*
Unclean for food ... Lev. 11:15
Solitary in habit ... Is. 34:11
Flesh-eating ... Prov. 30:17
Black ... Song 5:11
B. *Special features concerning:*
First creature sent from the ark ... Gen. 8:7
Elijah fed by ... 1 Kin. 17:4-7
Fed by God ... Luke 12:24

SUBJECT — REFERENCE

Razor—*a sharp instrument used for cutting off hair*

Forbidden to:

Nazarites ... Num. 6:1-5
Samson ... Judg. 13:5
Mentioned in Hannah's vow ... 1 Sam. 1:11
Used by barbers ... Ezek. 5:1

See Hair; Knife

Readiness—*being prepared for action*

A. *Descriptive of:*

Being prepared ... Matt. 22:4, 8
Being responsive ... 2 Cor. 8:11, 19

B. *Objects of:*

Willing people ... Luke 1:17
Passover ... Luke 22:12, 13
Lord's return ... Matt. 24:44
Preaching the Gospel ... Rom. 1:15

Reading the Bible

A. *Blessings of:*

Brings repentance ... 2 Kin. 22:8-20
Reminds us of duties ... Neh. 8:12, 13
Produces reformation ... Neh. 13:1-3
Gives knowledge of prophecy ... Rev. 1:3

B. *Reactions to:*

Responsiveness ... Ex. 24:7
Rejection ... Jer. 36:21-28
Rebellion ... Luke 4:16-30
Request for more light ... Acts 8:29-35
Research ... Acts 17:10, 11

Reaiah—*Jehovah has provided for*

1. Reubenite ... 1 Chr. 5:5
2. Founder of Nethinim family ... Ezra 2:47
3. Calebite family ... 1 Chr. 4:2

Real property

A. *Characteristic features of:*

Property desired ... Gen. 23:4
Price stipulated ... Gen. 33:19
Posts erected ... Deut. 19:14
Posterity remembered ... Num. 33:54
Publicity required ... Ruth 4:1-4
Proof documented ... Jer. 32:10-17

B. *Unusual examples of:*

Monopoly of land established ... Gen. 47:20
Sale as a prophetic proof ... Jer. 32:6-44
Mark of beast required ... Rev. 13:16, 17

Reaping

A. *Provisions concerning:*

Areas restricted ... Lev. 19:9, 10
Times restricted ... Lev. 25:1-11
Sin hinders ... Jer. 12:13

B. *Figurative of:*

Harvest of souls ... John 4:35-38
Trust in God ... Matt. 6:26
Gospel age ... Amos 9:13-15
Injustice ... Matt. 25:26
Payment for services ... 1 Cor. 9:11
Blessings ... 2 Cor. 9:6
Reward for righteousness ... Gal. 6:8, 9
Punishment for sin ... Hos. 10:13
Judgment on the world ... Rev. 14:14-16
Final judgment ... Matt. 13:30-43

Reason—*the faculty by which we think*

A. *Faculty of:*

Makes men sane ... Dan. 4:36
Prepares for salvation ... Is. 1:18
Makes men guilty ... Mark 11:31-33

B. *Inadequacy of:*

Biased against the truth ... Mark 2:6-8
Gospel not explained by ... 1 Cor. 1:18-31; 1 Cor. 2:1-14

Reba—*fourth part*

Midianite chief slain by Israelites ... Num. 31:8; Josh. 13:21

Rebekah, Rebecca—*loops of a rope*

Daughter of Bethuel ... Gen. 22:20-23
Becomes Isaac's wife ... Gen. 24:15-67
Mother of Esau and Jacob ... Gen. 25:21-28
Poses as Isaac's sister ... Gen. 26:6-11
Disturbed by Esau's marriages ... Gen. 26:34, 35
Causes Jacob to deceive Isaac ... Gen. 27:1-29
Urges Jacob to leave home ... Gen. 27:42-46
Burial of, in Machpelah ... Gen. 49:31
Mentioned by Paul ... Rom. 9:10

Rebellion—*active opposition to authority*

A. *Against:*

God ... Dan. 9:5, 9
God's word ... Num. 20:24
Davidic kingship ... 1 Kin. 12:19
Constituted priesthood ... Num. 17:1-10
Spirit ... Is. 63:10

B. *Evil of:*

Keeps from blessings ... Num. 20:24
Increases sin ... Job 34:37
Needs to be confessed ... Dan. 9:4-12
Characterizes a people ... Is. 65:2

See Insurrection

Rebuilding Jerusalem

Permitted by proclamation ... Ezra 1:1-4
Opposed ... Ezra 4:1-6; Neh. 4:1-3
Temple ... Ezra 5:1, 2; Ezra 6:14, 15
Walls ... Neh. 6:15, 16

Rebuke—*to reprimand sharply*

Jesus' power to restrain:

Sea ... Matt. 8:26
Demons ... Matt. 17:18
Fever ... Luke 4:39
Peter ... Mark 8:33

Rebuke for sin

A. *Manner of:*

Before all ... 1 Tim. 5:20
With longsuffering ... 2 Tim. 4:2
Sharply ... Titus 2:15
With all authority ... Titus 2:15

B. *Examples of:*

Isaac by Abimelech ... Gen. 26:6-11
Laban by Jacob ... Gen. 31:36-42
Saul by Samuel ... 1 Sam. 13:13
Ahab by Elijah ... 1 Kin. 21:20
Judah by Zechariah ... 2 Chr. 24:20
Israel by Ezra ... Ezra 10:10, 11
David by God ... Ps. 39:11
Peter by Paul ... Gal. 2:11-14

Receive—*to take into one's possession*

A. *Good things:*

Word ... James 1:21
Holy Spirit ... Acts 2:38
Christ Jesus ... Col. 2:6
Forgiveness ... Acts 26:18
Petitions ... 1 John 3:22
Reward ... 1 Cor. 3:8, 14

B. *Evil things:*

Punishment ... Rom. 1:27
Wrong ... Col. 3:25
Beast's mark ... Rev. 13:16
Reward for unrighteousness ... 2 Pet. 2:13

Rechab—*rider*

1. Assassin of Ish-bosheth ... 2 Sam. 4:2, 6
2. Father of Jehonadab, founder of the Rechabites ... 2 Kin. 10:15-23
   Related to the Kenites ... 1 Chr. 2:55
3. Postexilic ruler ... Neh. 3:14

Rechabites—*descendants of Rechab*

Kenite clan fathered by Rechab and believing in the simple life ... Jer. 35:1-19

Rechah—*softness*

Place in Judah ... 1 Chr. 4:12

Reciprocation—*mutual interchange*

Gentiles to Jews ... Rom. 15:27
Students to teachers ... Gal. 6:6

Recompense—*to pay back in kind*

A. *On the righteous:*

Even now ... Prov. 11:31
According to one's righteousness ... Ps. 18:20, 24
Eagerly expected ... Heb. 10:35

B. *On the unrighteous:*

Justly deserved ... Rom. 1:27
Belongs to God only ... Heb. 10:30
Will surely come ... Jer. 51:56
To the next generation ... Jer. 32:18
Fully at the second advent ... 2 Thess. 1:6

Reconciliation—*making peace between enemies*

A. *Effected on men while:*

Helpless ... Rom. 5:6
Sinners ... Rom. 5:8
Enemies of God ... Rom. 5:10
God-haters ... Col. 1:21

B. *Accomplished by:*

God in Christ ... 2 Cor. 5:18
Christ's death ... Rom. 5:10
Christ's blood ... Eph. 2:13

C. *Productive of:*

Peace with God ... Rom. 5:1
Access to God ... Rom. 5:2
Union of Jews and Gentiles ... Eph. 2:14

Recorder—*high court official*

Records events ... 2 Sam. 8:16
Represents the king ... 2 Kin. 18:18
Repairs the Temple ... 2 Chr. 34:8

Recover—*to restore lost things*

A. *Of sickness:*

By remedy ... 2 Kin. 20:7
By a miracle ... 2 Kin. 5:3-14
Sought from idols ... 2 Kin. 1:2-17
Prayed for ... Is. 38:16

B. *Of physical things:*

Defeat in war ... 2 Chr. 13:19, 20
Conquered territory ... 2 Sam. 8:3; 2 Kin. 13:25
Captured people ... Jer. 41:16

Recreation—*relaxation and restoration*

Among children, natural ... Zech. 8:5
Among adults, sometimes boring ... Eccl. 2:1-11
Lord's place in ... Jer. 33:11
Of the wicked, evil ... Judg. 16:25

Rectitude—*uprightness of life*

True way of living ... Prov. 4:23-27

Red—*being red or ruddy*

Blood ... 2 Kin. 3:22
Wine ... Prov. 23:31
Complexion ... Lam. 4:7

Red dragon—*another name for Satan*

Seen in John's vision ... Rev. 12:3-17

Redemption—*salvation by sacrifice*

A. *Defined as deliverance from:*

Curse of the Law ... Gal. 3:13
Bondage of the Law ... Gal. 4:5
Iniquity ... Titus 2:14
Enemies ... Ps. 136:24
Destruction ... Ps. 103:4
Death ... Hos. 13:14
Grave ... Ps. 49:15
Vain conversation ... 1 Pet. 1:18
Present evil world ... Gal. 1:4

B. *Accomplished by:*

God's power ... Deut. 7:8
Christ's blood ... Eph. 1:7
God's grace ... Rom. 3:24, 25

C. *Benefits of:*

Forgiveness ... Col. 1:14
Justification ... Rom. 3:24
Adoption ... Gal. 4:4, 5
God's possession ... 1 Cor. 6:20
God's people ... Titus 2:14
Purification ... Titus 2:14
Sealing ... Eph. 4:30
Inheritance ... Heb. 9:15
Heaven's glory ... Rev. 14:3, 4

Red heifer (see Heifer)

Red horse—*symbol of war*

Seen in John's vision ... Rev. 6:4

Red Sea—*sea of reeds*

Locusts destroyed ... Ex. 10:19
Divided by God ... Ex. 14:21
Crossed by Israel ... Ex. 14:22, 29
Egyptians drowned ... Ex. 15:4, 21

SUBJECT REFERENCE

Boundary of promised land ..... Ex. 23:31
Israelites camp by ..... Num. 33:10, 11
Ships built on ..... 1 Kin. 9:26

Reed—*tall grass growing in marshes*

Figurative of:

Weakness ..... Is. 36:6
Instability ..... Matt. 11:7
God's measure ..... Ezek. 40:3
Davidic line ..... Is. 42:3

Refining, spiritual

By afflictions ..... Is. 48:10
By fire ..... Zech. 13:9
For a purpose ..... John 15:2
More precious than gold ..... 1 Pet. 1:7

Reflection—*contemplation on*

Past ..... Mark 14:72
Present ..... Luke 14:31-33
Future ..... Acts 21:12-14

Reformations, religious

Manifested by or in:

Recovery of the Law ..... 2 Kin. 22:8-20
Resolving to follow the Lord ..... Ezra 10:1-17
Religious zeal for the Lord ..... Neh. 13:11-31
Restoration of judges ..... 2 Chr. 19:1-11

Refresh—*to renew; to restore*

Spiritual:

In the spirit ..... 1 Cor. 16:18
In the heart ..... Philem. 7, 20
Often needed ..... 2 Tim. 1:16
Mutual ..... Rom. 15:32
Special times ..... Acts 3:19
Refused ..... Is. 28:12

Refuge—*a shelter against harm*

Divine:

In the Lord ..... Ps. 142:5
From storms ..... Is. 4:5, 6
Time of trouble ..... Ps. 9:9
Place of protection ..... Ps. 91:9, 10
Always ready ..... Ps. 46:1

Refuge, cities of (see Cities, Levitical)

Refuse—*to reject or decline*

A. *Of things, physical:*

Marriage ..... Ex. 22:17
Passage ..... Num. 20:21
King ..... 1 Sam. 16:7
Display ..... Esth. 1:12
Leader ..... Acts 7:35
Martyrdom ..... Acts 25:11
Fables ..... 1 Tim. 4:7
Adoption ..... Heb. 11:24

B. *Of things, spiritual:*

Hardness of heart ..... Ex. 7:14
Disobedience ..... Ex. 16:28
Obedience ..... 1 Sam. 8:19
Messiah ..... Ps. 118:22
Salvation ..... Is. 8:6
Shame ..... Jer. 3:3
Repentance ..... Hos. 11:5
Healing ..... Jer. 15:18
God ..... Heb. 12:25

Refuse Gate—*a gate of Jerusalem*

Nehemiah viewed city from ..... Neh. 2:13
Wall dedicated near ..... Neh. 12:31

Regard—*to think highly of*

Honors God ..... Is. 17:7, 8
Honors God's Word ..... Ps. 119:6, 15, 117
Rejects the unbelieving ..... Gen. 4:4, 5

Regem—*friend*

Calebite ..... 1 Chr. 2:47

Regem-melech—*friend of the king*

Sent in deputation to Zechariah ..... Zech. 7:2

Regeneration (see Born again; New birth)

Register—*a record of genealogies*

Priests not recorded in ..... Ezra 2:62
Excluded from priesthood ..... Neh. 7:63-65
Those recorded in ..... Neh. 7:5-62

Rehabiah—*Jehovah is wide*

Grandson of Moses ..... 1 Chr. 23:17

SUBJECT REFERENCE

Rehob—*open place*

1. Two cities of Asher ..... Josh. 19:24, 28
   One assigned to Levites ..... Josh. 21:31
   Delayed conquest of one ..... Judg. 1:31
2. Northern city visited by Joshua's spies ..... Num. 13:21
   Defeated by David ..... 2 Sam. 10:8
3. Father of Hadadezer ..... 2 Sam. 8:3, 12
4. Signer of the covenant ..... Neh. 10:11

Rehoboam—*the people are enlarged*

Son and successor of Solomon ..... 1 Kin. 11:43
Refuses reformatory measures ..... 1 Kin. 12:1-15
Ten tribes revolt from ..... 1 Kin. 12:16-24
Temporary prosperity of ..... 2 Chr. 11:5-23
Lapses into idolatry ..... 1 Kin. 14:21-24
Kingdom of, invaded by Egypt ..... 1 Kin. 14:25-28
Reigns 17 years ..... 1 Kin. 14:21
Death of ..... 1 Kin. 14:29-31
In Christ's genealogy ..... Matt. 1:7

Rehoboth—*broad places, streets*

1. Name of a well dug by Isaac ..... Gen. 26:22
2. City "by the river" ..... Gen. 36:37
3. Built by Asshur ..... Gen. 10:11

Rehum—*beloved*

1. Persian officer ..... Ezra 4:8-23
2. Postexilic returnee ..... Ezra 2:2
3. Priest who returns with Zerubbabel ..... Neh. 12:3, 7
   Same as Harim ..... Neh. 12:15
4. Signer of the covenant ..... Neh. 10:25
5. Postexilic Levite ..... Neh. 3:17

Rei—*friendly*

One of David's faithful officers ..... 1 Kin. 1:8

Reign—*to rule over*

A. *Descriptive of the rule of:*

Man ..... Gen. 36:31
God ..... Ps. 47:8
Christ ..... Rev. 20:4, 6
Believers ..... Rev. 5:10
Sin ..... Rom. 5:21
Death ..... Rom. 5:14, 17
Grace ..... Rom. 5:21

B. *Of Christ's rule:*

Predicted ..... Is. 32:1
Described ..... Jer. 23:5, 6
Announced ..... Luke 1:31-33
Rejected ..... Luke 19:14, 27
Fulfilled ..... Rom. 15:12
Enthroned ..... 1 Cor. 15:25
Eternal ..... Rev. 11:15-17

Reject—*to refuse; to disown*

A. *Man's rejection of:*

God ..... 1 Sam. 8:7
God's Word ..... 1 Sam. 15:23, 26
God's knowledge ..... Hos. 4:6
Christ ..... Mark 8:31

B. *God's rejection of man, as:*

Unbeliever ..... John 12:48
Heretic ..... Titus 3:10
Unfruitful ..... Heb. 6:8
Reprobate ..... Heb. 12:17

Rejoice—*to be glad*

A. *Kinds of:*

Gloating ..... Mic. 7:8
Vindictive ..... Rev. 18:20
Marital ..... Prov. 5:18
Defiant ..... Is. 8:6
Prophetic ..... John 8:56
Future ..... Phil. 2:16
Rewarded ..... Ps. 126:6

B. *Caused by:*

God's blessing ..... Ex. 18:9
God's Word ..... Jer. 15:16
Assurance ..... Luke 10:20
Salvation ..... Luke 15:6-10
Persecution ..... Acts 5:41
Reunion of believers ..... Phil. 2:28
Exaltation ..... James 1:9
Christ's return ..... 1 Pet. 4:13

SUBJECT REFERENCE

C. *Sphere of, in:*

God's salvation ..... Ps. 21:1
God's protection ..... Ps. 63:7
God's blessings ..... Ps. 106:5
Lord Himself ..... Hab. 3:18

D. *Agents of:*

Heart ..... 1 Chr. 16:10
Soul ..... Ps. 35:9
Earth ..... Ps. 97:1
God's people ..... Ps. 118:24
Believing spirit ..... Luke 1:47

Rekem—*friendship*

1. Midianite king slain by Moses ..... Num. 31:8
2. Descendant of Caleb ..... 1 Chr. 2:43, 44
3. City of Benjamin ..... Josh. 18:27

Relapse—*to turn back to sin again*

Danger of, explained ..... Heb. 6:4-6

Relatives—*those of near kin*

A. *Good derived from:*

Encouragement ..... Esth. 4:12-17
Salvation ..... John 1:40-42

B. *Evil derived from:*

Strife ..... Gen. 31:1-42
Persecution ..... Mark 13:12
Jealousy ..... Gen. 37:3-11

Relief—*thorough service*

In early church ..... Acts 4:32-37
Determined to send ..... Acts 11:29
Fulfilled at Christ's return ..... 2 Thess. 1:7

Religion, false

Characterized by:

Apostasy ..... 2 Thess. 2:3, 4
Backsliding ..... Jer. 5:23-31
Ceremonialism ..... Mark 7:3-13
Display ..... Matt. 6:5
Ease ..... 1 Kin. 12:27-31
Formalism ..... 2 Tim. 3:5

Remaliah—*whom Jehovah has adored*

Father of Pekah ..... 2 Kin. 15:25

Remedy—*a cure*

Without ..... Prov. 6:15
Right kind ..... 1 John 1:7

Remember—*to call to mind again*

Aids to:

Rainbow ..... Gen. 9:15, 16
Covenant ..... Ex. 2:24
Passover ..... Ex. 13:3
Sabbath ..... Ex. 20:8
Offering ..... Num. 5:15
Son (child) ..... 2 Sam. 18:18
Prophet's presence ..... 1 Kin. 17:18
Book ..... Mal. 3:16
Lord's Supper ..... Luke 22:19
Epistle ..... 2 Pet. 3:1
See Memories

Remeth—*a high place*

Frontier town of Issachar ..... Josh. 19:21

Remission—*forgiveness*

A. *Based upon:*

Christ's death ..... Matt. 26:28
Faith in Christ ..... Acts 10:43
Repentance ..... Mark 1:4

B. *Significance of:*

Shows God's righteousness ..... Rom. 3:25
Makes salvation real ..... Luke 1:77
Must be preached ..... Luke 24:47

Remmon-methoar

City of Zebulun ..... Josh. 19:10, 13

Remnant—*what is left over*

A. *Used literally of:*

Cloth left over ..... Ex. 26:12
Race left remaining ..... Deut. 3:11
Nation still surviving ..... Amos 1:8

B. *Used spiritually of the faithful Israel:*

Punished ..... Is. 1:9
Protected ..... Is. 37:31-33
Scattered ..... Ezek. 5:10
Gathered ..... Is. 10:20-22
Repentant ..... Jer. 31:7-9

SUBJECT — REFERENCE

- Forgiven — Mic. 7:18
- Saved — Jer. 23:3-8; Rom. 9:27
- Blessing — Mic. 5:7, 8
- Holy — Zeph. 3:12, 13
- Elected — Rom. 11:5

Remorse—*distress arising from guilt*

- Of a renegade — Matt. 27:3-5
- Of a disciple — Luke 22:62
- In flame — Luke 16:24

Remphan—*a name for Kiyyan*

- Worshiped by Israelites — Acts 7:41-43

Rend—*to tear apart by force*

A. *Used literally of:*

- Garments — Ezra 9:3, 5
- Clothing — Esth. 4:1
- Rocks — Matt. 27:51
- Veil — Matt. 27:51
- Flesh — Matt. 7:6
- Body — Mark 9:26

B. *Figuratively of:*

- Repentance — Joel 2:13
- Harlotry — Jer. 4:30
- Destruction — Hos. 13:8
- Dissolution of the old economy — Mark 15:38
- Joy — 1 Kin. 1:40

Renewal of strength

A. *Sources of:*

- Holy Spirit — Titus 3:5
- Wait for the Lord — Is. 40:31
- Cleansing from sin — Ps. 51:10

B. *Objects of:*

- Youthfulness — Ps. 103:5
- Peoples — Is. 41:1
- Inward man — 2 Cor. 4:16
- New man — Col. 3:10
- Mind — Rom. 12:2

Renown—*of great reputation*

- Man — Gen. 6:4
- City — Ezek. 26:17
- God — Dan. 9:15
- Plant — Ezek. 34:29

Renunciation—*giving up the right to do something*

Blessings of:

- True discipleship — Luke 14:33
- True reward — Mark 10:28-31
- Future reward — Luke 18:28-30

Repentance

A. *Described as:*

- "Turned" — Acts 9:35
- "Repent" — Acts 8:22
- "Return" — 1 Sam. 7:3
- "Conversion" — Acts 15:3

B. *Kinds of:*

- National — Joel 3:5-8
- Internal — Ps. 51:10-13
- Unavailing — Heb. 12:16, 17
- True — Acts 9:1-20
- Unreal — Ex. 9:27-35

C. *Derived from gift of:*

- God — Acts 11:18
- Christ — Acts 5:31
- Spirit — Zech. 12:10

D. *Things leading to:*

- God's long-suffering — 2 Pet. 3:9
- God's goodness — Rom. 2:4
- Conviction of sin — Acts 2:37, 38

E. *Productive of:*

- Life — Acts 11:18
- Remission of sins — Mark 1:4
- New spirit — Ezek. 18:31
- New heart — Ezek. 18:31
- Joy — Luke 15:7, 10

F. *Signs of:*

- Reformation of life — Matt. 3:8
- Restitution — Luke 19:8
- Godly sorrow — 2 Cor. 7:9, 10

See Conversion

Rephael—*God has healed*

- Levite porter — 1 Chr. 26:7

Rephah—*riches*

- Ancestor of Joshua — 1 Chr. 7:25-27

Rephaiah—*Jehovah has healed*

1. Man of Issachar — 1 Chr. 7:2
2. Descendant of Jonathan — 1 Chr. 9:43; Called Rapha — 1 Chr. 8:37
3. Simeonite prince — 1 Chr. 4:42, 43
4. Postexilic ruler — Neh. 3:9
5. Descendant of David — 1 Chr. 3:21

Rephaim—*giants*

1. Early race of giants in Palestine — Gen. 14:5; Among doomed nations — Gen. 15:20

See Giants

2. Valley near Jerusalem — 2 Sam. 23:13, 14; Very fertile — Is. 17:5; Scene of Philistine defeats — 2 Sam. 5:18-22

Rephidim—*rests*

- Israelite camp — Num. 33:12-15
- Moses struck rock — Ex. 17:1-7
- Amalek defeated — Ex. 17:8-16

Report—*a transmitted account of something*

A. *Kinds of:*

- True — 1 Kin. 10:6
- Good — Prov. 15:30
- False — Ex. 23:1
- Defaming — Jer. 20:10
- Slanderous — Rom. 3:8
- Evil — 2 Cor. 6:8

B. *Good, obtained by:*

- Fear — Deut. 2:25
- Just life — Acts 10:22
- Devout life — Acts 22:12
- Outsiders — 1 Tim. 3:7
- Faith — Heb. 11:2, 39
- Friends — 3 John 12

Reproach—*something imputed to the discredit of others*

A. *Objects of:*

- God — 2 Kin. 19:4-23
- God's people — Neh. 6:13
- Messiah — Rom. 15:3
- Christians — Luke 6:22

B. *Agents of:*

- Enemies — Neh. 4:4
- Foolish — Ps. 74:22
- Scorner — Prov. 22:10
- Satan — 1 Tim. 5:14, 15; 1 Tim. 3:7

C. *Evil causes of:*

- Unbelief — Jer. 6:10
- Idolatry — Ezek. 22:4
- Breaking God's Law — Num. 15:30, 31
- Sin — Prov. 14:34

D. *Good causes of:*

- Faith in God's promises — Heb. 11:24-26
- Living for Christ — 1 Pet. 4:14
- Suffering for Christ — Heb. 13:13

E. *Of God's people:*

- Permitted by God — Jer. 15:15

Reprobate—*rejected after testing*

A. *Causes of:*

- Not having Christ — 2 Cor. 13:3-5
- Rejecting the faith — 2 Tim. 3:8
- Spiritual barrenness — Heb. 6:7, 8
- Lack of discipline — 1 Cor. 9:24-27
- Rejection by the Lord — Jer. 6:30

B. *Consequences of, given up to:*

- Evil — Rom. 1:24-32
- Delusion — 2 Thess. 2:11, 12
- Blindness — Matt. 13:13-15
- Destruction — 2 Pet. 2:9-22

Reproof—*a cutting rebuke for misconduct*

A. *Sources of:*

- God — Ps. 50:8, 21
- Backslidings — Jer. 2:19
- God's Word — 2 Tim. 3:16
- John the Baptist — Luke 3:16, 19

B. *Examples of:*

- Samuel — 1 Sam. 13:13
- Daniel — Dan. 5:22, 23
- John the Baptist — Matt. 3:7-12
- Stephen — Acts 7:51
- Paul — Gal. 2:11

Reprove—*to express disapproval of*

- Designed for good — Heb. 12:5
- Accomplished in love — Rev. 3:19

Reptiles of the Bible

A. *Features concerning:*

- Created by God — Gen. 1:24, 25
- Made to praise God — Ps. 148:7, 10
- Placed under man's power — Gen. 1:26
- Classified as unclean — Lev. 11:31-43
- Seen in a vision — Acts 10:11-14
- Worshiped by pagans — Rom. 1:23
- Likeness of, forbidden — Deut. 4:16, 18
- Portrayed on walls — Ezek. 8:10

B. *List of:*

- Adder — Prov. 23:32
- Asp — Rom. 3:13
- Chameleon — Lev. 11:30
- Cockatrice — Is. 11:8
- Dragon — Deut. 32:33
- Ferret — Lev. 11:30
- Frog — Rev. 16:13
- Leviathan — Job 41:1, 2
- Lizard — Lev. 11:30
- Scorpion — Deut. 8:15
- Serpents — Matt. 10:7
- Snake — Matt. 7:10
- Snail — Ps. 58:8
- Tortoise — Lev. 11:29
- Viper — Acts 28:3

Reputation—*public esteem; fame*

A. *Good:*

- Wonderful asset — Prov. 22:1
- Based on integrity — 2 Cor. 8:18-24
- Hated by wicked — Dan. 6:4-8
- Required of church officials — Acts 6:3
- Worthy of trust — Acts 16:2

B. *Dangers of:*

- Universal praise — Luke 6:26
- Flattering speech — Rom. 16:18
- Worldly friendship — James 4:4
- Worldly praise — 1 John 4:5, 6
- Undue deference toward — Gal. 2:6

Resen—*fortress*

- City built by Asshur — Gen. 10:11, 12

Reservoirs—*where water is stored*

- Family cisterns — Is. 36:16
- Garden pools — Eccl. 2:6

Resh

- Letter of the Hebrew alphabet — Ps. 119:153-160

Resheph—*home*

- Descendant of Ephraim — 1 Chr. 7:23-25

Residue—*a remnant*

A. *Used literally of:*

- Survivors — Jer. 8:3

B. *Used spiritually of:*

- Faithful remnant — Is. 28:5
- Promised seed — Zech. 8:11-13

Resignation—*patient submission to*

- Disquieting problem — Josh. 22:9-34
- Tragic death — 2 Sam. 19:1-8
- God's chastening — Job 2:10
- Cross — Mark 14:36
- Sufferings ahead — Acts 21:11-14
- Pain — 2 Cor. 12:7-10
- Want — Phil. 4:11, 12

Resist—*to stand against*

A. *Of evil things:*

- Sin — Heb. 12:4
- Adversaries — Luke 21:15

B. *Of good things:*

- God's will — Rom. 9:19
- Holy Spirit — Acts 7:51
- Truth — 2 Tim. 3:8
- Wisdom — Acts 6:10
- Constituted authority — Rom. 13:2

Respect—*honor manifested toward the worthy*

A. *Wrong kind:*

- Favoring the wealthy — James 2:3, 9

SUBJECT REFERENCE

B. *Right kind:*
Rejects the proud .... Ps. 40:4

C. *On God's part:*
Regards the lowly .... Ps. 138:6
Honors His covenant .... 2 Kin. 13:23
Makes God just .... 1 Pet. 1:17

Responsibility—*accountability for one's actions*

A. *Shifting of, by:*
Blaming another .... Gen. 3:12
Claiming innocency .... Matt. 27:24
Blaming a people .... Ex. 32:21-24

B. *Cannot be excused by:*
Ignorance .... Acts 17:30, 31
Unbelief .... John 3:18-20
Previous good .... Ex. 33:12, 13
One's ancestors .... Matt. 3:9, 10

C. *Is increased by:*
Sight .... John 9:39-41
Privilege .... John 15:22, 24
Opportunity .... Matt. 11:20-24
Continuance in sin .... Matt. 23:31-35
Rejection .... Matt. 10:11-15

Rest—*peace and quiet*

A. *Descriptive of:*
Physical relaxation .... Gen. 18:4
Sinful laziness .... Matt. 26:45
Confidence .... Hab. 3:16-19
Completion of salvation ..... Heb. 4:3, 8-11

B. *Need of:*
Recognized in God's Law .... Ex. 20:10, 11
Recognized by Christ .... Mark 6:31
Longed after .... Ps. 55:6
Provided for .... Rev. 6:11
Enjoyed after death .... Job 3:13, 17
Rev. 14:13

C. *Source of, in:*
Christ .... Matt. 11:28, 29
Trust .... Ps. 37:7
Returning to God .... Is. 30:15

D. *Disturbance of, by:*
Sin .... Is. 57:20
Rebellion .... Is. 28:12
Persecution .... Acts 9:23
Anxiety .... 2 Cor. 2:13

See Quietness

Restitution—*restoring*
Time of .... Acts 3:21
Of damaged property .... Ex. 22:3-12

Restoration—*renewal of something to its former state*

A. *Miraculous, from:*
Death .... 2 Kin. 8:1, 5
Dried hand .... 1 Kin. 13:4, 6
Withered hand .... Mark 3:5
Blindness .... Mark 8:25

B. *Natural of:*
Man's wife .... Gen. 20:7, 14
Man's position .... Gen. 40:13, 21
Land .... 2 Sam. 9:7
Visit .... Heb. 13:19

C. *Spiritual:*
Joy .... Ps. 51:11, 12
Recovery .... Jer. 30:17
God's blessings .... Joel 2:25
Christ .... Is. 49:6

Restoration of Israel
Promised in the prophets .... Is. 11:11
Seen in John's ministry .... Matt. 17:11
Anticipated by Caiaphas .... John 11:49-52
Questioned by the disciples .... Acts 1:6
Realized at Pentecost .... Joel 2:28-32
Fulfilled in the Church .... Eph. 2:11-22
Perfected in Heaven .... Heb. 12:22-28

Restraints, divine

On:
Man's wrath .... Ps. 76:10
Man's designs .... Gen. 11:6
Natural forces .... Gen. 8:2
Childbearing .... Gen. 16:2
Wicked .... 2 Kin. 19:28
Antichrist .... 2 Thess. 2:3-7

SUBJECT REFERENCE

Rests—*supporting ledge*
For the beams of the Temple ... 1 Kin. 6:6

Resurrection—*arising from the dead*

A. *Doctrine of:*
Looked for in faith .... Job 19:25-27
Taught in Old Testament .... Is. 26:19
Dan. 12:2, 3, 13
Denied by Sadducees .... Matt. 22:23-28
Acts 23:6, 8
Affirmed by Christ .... John 5:28, 29
John 6:39, 40, 44
Illustrated by Lazarus .... John 11:23-44
Explained away by false teachers .... 2 Tim. 2:18
Questioned by some .... 1 Cor. 15:12
Mocked at by heathen .... Acts 17:32
Proclaimed by Paul .... Acts 24:14, 15

B. *Accomplished by:*
God's power .... Matt. 22:28, 29
Christ .... John 5:28, 29
Holy Spirit .... Rom. 8:11

C. *Proof of, based on:*
God's power .... 1 Cor. 6:14
Union with Christ .... Rom. 8:11
Christ's resurrection .... 1 Cor. 15:12-56

D. *Time of, at:*
Last day .... John 6:39-44
Christ's return .... 1 Thess. 4:13-18
Last trumpet .... 1 Cor. 15:51-55

E. *Nature of:*
Incorruptible .... 1 Cor. 15:42, 54
Glorious .... 1 Cor. 15:43
Spiritual .... 1 Cor. 15:44
Transforming .... 1 Cor. 15:51
Like angels .... Matt. 22:30
Like Christ .... Phil. 3:21

F. *Of the wicked:*
Predicted .... Dan. 12:2
Described .... John 5:28, 29
Simultaneous .... Acts 24:15

Resurrection of Christ

A. *Features concerning:*
Foretold in the Psalms ...... Ps. 16:10, 11
Acts 13:34, 35
Presented in prophecy .... Is. 53:10-12
1 Cor. 15:4
Announced by Christ .... Mark 9:9, 10
John 2:19-22
Proclaimed by the apostles ... Acts 2:32
Acts 3:15

B. *Accomplished by:*
God's power .... Acts 2:24
Christ's power .... John 10:18
Spirit's power .... Rom. 8:11

C. *Proven by:*
Empty tomb .... John 20:1-9
Angelic testimony .... Matt. 28:5-7
His enemies .... Matt. 28:11-15
Many infallible proofs .... John 20:20, 27
Acts 1:3
Apostolic preaching .... Acts 1:22
Acts 4:33
LORD's Day (first day of the week) .... John 20:1, 19; 1 Cor. 16:2

D. *Purposes of:*
Fulfill Scripture .... Luke 24:45, 46
Forgive sins .... 1 Cor. 15:17
Justify the sinner .... Rom. 4:25
Rom. 8:34
Give hope .... 1 Cor. 15:18, 19
Make faith real .... 1 Cor. 15:14-17
Prove His Sonship .... Ps. 2:7
Rom. 1:4
Set Him on David's throne .. Acts 2:30-32
Insure His exaltation .... Acts 4:10, 11
Phil. 2:9, 10
Guarantee the coming judgment .... Acts 17:31
Seal the believer's resurrection .... Acts 26:23; 1 Cor. 15:20, 23

E. *Appearances of, to:*
Mary Magdalene .... Mark 16:9
Other women .... Matt. 28:9
Two disciples .... Luke 24:13-15
Simon Peter .... Luke 24:34
Ten apostles .... John 20:19, 24
Eleven apostles .... John 20:26

SUBJECT REFERENCE

Apostles at Sea of Tiberias ... John 21:1
Apostles in Galilee .... Matt. 28:16, 17
500 brethren .... 1 Cor. 15:6
All the apostles .... Luke 24:51
Acts 1:9
Paul .... 1 Cor. 15:8
James .... 1 Cor. 15:7

Resurrections of the Bible
Widow's son .... 1 Kin. 17:17-22
Shunammite's son .... 2 Kin. 4:32-35
Unnamed man .... 2 Kin. 13:20, 21
Jairus' daughter .... Matt. 9:23-25
Widow's only son .... Luke 7:11-15
Lazarus of Bethany .... John 11:43, 44
Many saints .... Matt. 27:52, 53
Dorcas .... Acts 9:36-40
In symbolism .... Rev. 11:8, 11

Resurrection, spiritual

A. *Accomplished by power of:*
God .... Eph. 1:19
Christ .... Eph. 5:14
Holy Spirit .... Ezek. 11:19

B. *Features concerning:*
Takes place now .... John 5:25
Gives eternal life .... John 5:24
Delivers from spiritual death .... Rom. 6:4, 13
Changes life .... Is. 32:15
Issues in immortality .... John 11:25, 26
Delivers from Satan's power .... Acts 26:18
Realized in new life .... Phil. 3:10, 11
Called "first" .... Rev. 20:5, 6

Retaliation—*returning like for like*
Forbidden .... Luke 9:54, 55
Return good, not evil .... Prov. 25:21, 22
God's responsibility .... Prov. 20:22
Christ's teaching on .... Matt. 5:39-44

Retribution—*merited punishment for evil done*

A. *Expressed by:*
God's wrath .... Rom. 1:18
Lamb's wrath .... Rev. 6:16, 17
Vengeance .... Jude 7
Punishment .... 2 Thess. 1:6-9
Corruption .... 2 Pet. 2:9-22

B. *Due to the sinner's:*
Sin .... Rom. 2:1-9
Evil works .... Ex. 32:34
Persecution of the righteous .... 2 Thess. 1:6
Rejection of Christ .... Heb. 10:29, 30

C. *Deliverance from, by:*
Christ .... 1 Thess. 1:10
God's appointment .... 1 Thess. 5:9

Return

Descriptive of:
Going back home .... Gen. 31:3, 13
Repentance .... 2 Chr. 6:24, 38
Vengeance or retribution .... 1 Kin. 2:33, 44
Divine visitation .... Joel 2:14
Christ's advent .... Acts 15:16
Death .... Gen. 3:19

Reu—*friend*
Descendant of Shem .... Gen. 11:10-21
Called Ragau .... Luke 3:35

Reuben—*behold a son*
Jacob's eldest son .... Gen. 29:31, 32
Guilty of misconduct; loses preeminence .... Gen. 35:22
Proposes plan to save Joseph's life .... Gen. 37:21-29
Offers sons as pledge .... Gen. 42:37
Father of four sons .... Gen. 46:8, 9
Pronounced unstable .... Gen. 49:3, 4
Descendants of .... Num. 26:5-11

Reubenites—*descendants of Reuben*
Divided into four tribal families .... Num. 26:5-11
Elizur, warrior .... Num. 1:5
Census of, at Sinai .... Num. 1:18-21
Census of, at conquest .... Num. 26:7
Place of, in march .... Num. 2:10
Seek inheritance east of Jordan .... Num. 32:1-42
Join in war against Canaanites .. Josh. 1:12-18

SUBJECT REFERENCE

Altar erected by, misunderstood ... Josh. 22:10-34
Criticized by Deborah ... Judg. 5:15, 16
Enslaved by Assyria ... 2 Kin. 15:29

Reuel—*friend of God*

1. Son of Esau ... Gen. 36:2-4
2. Moses' father-in-law ... Ex. 2:18
3. Benjamite ... 1 Chr. 9:8
4. Gadite leader ... Num. 2:14
   Called Deuel ... Num. 7:42, 47

Reumah—*exalted*

Nahor's concubine ... Gen. 22:24

Revelation—*an uncovering of something hidden*

A. *Source of:*
God ... Dan. 2:28-47
Christ ... John 1:18
The Spirit ... 1 Cor. 2:10
Not in man ... Matt. 16:17

B. *Objects of:*
God ... Matt. 11:25, 27
Christ ... 2 Thess. 1:7
Man of sin ... 2 Thess. 2:3, 6, 8

C. *Instruments of:*
Prophets ... 1 Pet. 1:12
Daniel ... Dan. 10:1
Christ ... Heb. 1:1, 2
Apostles ... 1 Cor. 2:10
Paul ... Gal. 1:16

D. *Of the first advent:*
Predicted ... Is. 40:5
Revealed ... Is. 53:1
Rejected ... John 12:38-41
Of God's righteousness ... Is. 56:1
Of peace and truth ... Jer. 33:6-8
Eph. 2:11-17

E. *Time of the second advent:*
Uncovering ... Matt. 10:26
Judgment ... Luke 17:26-30
Victory ... 2 Thess. 2:3, 6, 8
Glory ... 1 Pet. 5:1
Resurrection ... Rom. 8:18, 19
Reward ... 1 Cor. 3:13
Glorification ... 1 John 3:2
Grace ... 1 Pet. 1:5, 13
Joy ... 1 Pet. 4:13

F. *Of divine truth, characteristics of:*
God-originated ... Dan. 2:47
Verbal ... Heb. 1:1
In the created world ... Ps. 19:1, 2
Illuminative ... Eph. 1:17
Now revealed ... Rom. 16:26
Truth communicating ... Eph. 3:3, 4

Revelation, the—*a book of the New Testament*

Vision of the Son of Man ... Rev. 1:9-20
Message to the seven churches ... Rev. 2:1—3:22
The book of seven seals ... Rev. 4:1—6:17
The judgment ... Rev. 7:1—9:21
The two beasts ... Rev. 13
Babylon doomed ... Rev. 17:1—18:24
The marriage supper ... Rev. 19:6-10
The judgment of the wicked ... Rev. 20:11-15
New heaven and new earth ... Rev. 21:1-8
The new Jerusalem ... Rev. 21:9—22:5
Christ's coming ... Rev. 22:6-21

Revenge—*to take vengeance*

A. *Manifestation of:*
Belongs to God ... Rev. 18:20
Performed by rulers ... Rom. 13:4
Righteously allowed ... 1 Kin. 20:42
Pleaded for ... Jer. 11:20
Disallowed among men ... Prov. 20:22
Forbidden to disciples ... Luke 9:54, 55

B. *Antidotes of:*
Overcome by kindness ... 1 Sam. 25:30-34
Exhibit love ... Luke 6:35
Bless ... Rom. 12:14
Forbear wrath ... Rom. 12:19
Manifest forbearance ... Matt. 5:38-41
Flee from ... Gen. 27:41-45

C. *Examples of:*
Simeon and Levi ... Gen. 34:25
Joseph ... Gen. 42:9-24
Samson ... Judg. 16:28-30
Joab ... 2 Sam. 3:27, 30
Jezebel ... 1 Kin. 19:2

SUBJECT REFERENCE

Ahab ... 1 Kin. 22:26, 27
Haman ... Esth. 3:8-15
Philistines ... Ezek. 25:15-17
Herodias ... Mark 6:19-24
Jews ... Acts 7:54, 59

Reverence—*a feeling of deep respect, love, awe and esteem*

Manifested toward:
God ... Ps. 89:7
God's house ... Lev. 19:30
Christ ... Matt. 21:37
Kings ... 1 Kin. 1:31
Parents ... Heb. 12:9
Husbands ... Eph. 5:33

Reverend—*worthy of reverence*

Applies only to God in the Scriptures ... Ps. 111:9

Revile—*to speak of another abusively*

Christ, object of ... Matt. 27:39
Christ, submissive under ... 1 Pet. 2:23
Christians, objects of ... Matt. 5:11
Right attitude toward ... 1 Cor. 4:12
Punishment of ... 1 Cor. 6:10
False teachers ... 2 Pet. 2:10-12

Revival—*renewed zeal to obey God*

Conditions for:
Humility ... 2 Chr. 7:14
Prayer ... 2 Chr. 7:14
James 5:16
Broken heart ... Ps. 34:18
Confession ... Ps. 66:18
Repentance ... 2 Cor. 7:10
Turning from sin ... 2 Chr. 7:14
2 Tim. 2:19
Complete surrender ... Acts 9:5, 6
Rom. 12:1, 2

Revive—*to live again more vigorously*

A. *Descriptive of:*
Renewed strength ... Gen. 45:27
Refreshment ... Judg. 15:19
Restoration ... Neh. 4:2
Resurrection ... 1 Kin. 17:22

B. *Of the Spirit:*
Given to the humble ... Is. 57:15
Source of joy ... Ps. 85:6
Possible even in trouble ... Ps. 138:7
Source of fruitfulness ... Hos. 6:2, 3
Hos. 14:7

Reward of the righteous

A. *Described as:*
Sure ... Prov. 11:18
Full ... Ruth 2:12
Remembered ... 2 Chr. 15:7
Great ... Matt. 5:12
Open ... Matt. 6:4, 6, 18

B. *Obtained by:*
Keeping God's commandments ... Ps. 19:11
Sowing righteousness ... Prov. 11:18
Fearing God's commandments ... Prov. 13:13
Feeding an enemy ... Prov. 25:21, 22
Simple service ... Matt. 6:1
Grace through faith ... Rom. 4:4, 5, 16
Faithful service ... Col. 3:23, 24
Seeking God diligently ... Heb. 11:6

C. *At Christ's return:*
After the resurrection ... Rev. 11:18
Tested by fire ... 1 Cor. 3:8-14
According to works ... Rev. 22:12

See Crowns of Christians; Hire; Wages

Reward of the wicked

A. *Visited upon:*
Now ... Ps. 91:8
At the judgment ... 2 Tim. 4:14

B. *Measure of:*
By retribution ... Rev. 18:6
According to the wickedness ... 2 Sam. 3:39
Plentifully ... Ps. 31:23

Rezeph—*glowing stone*

Place destroyed by the Assyrians ... 2 Kin. 19:12

SUBJECT REFERENCE

Rezia—*delight*

Asherite ... 1 Chr. 7:39

Rezin

1. King of Damascus; joins Pekah against Ahaz ... 2 Kin. 15:37
   Confederacy of, inspires Isaiah's great Messianic prophecy ... Is. 7:1—9:12
2. Head of a Nethinim family ... Ezra 2:48

Rezon—*prince*

Son of Eliada; establishes Syrian kingdom ... 1 Kin. 11:23-25

Rhegium—*a city of southern Italy*

Paul's ship arrived at ... Acts 28:13

Rhesa

Ancestor of Christ ... Luke 3:27

Rhoda—*rosebush*

Servant girl ... Acts 12:13-16

Rhodes—*an island off the southwest coast of Asia Minor*

Paul's ship passes by ... Acts 21:1

Rib

Eve formed of Adam's ... Gen. 2:22

Ribai—*Jehovah strives*

One of David's mighty men ... 2 Sam. 23:29

Ribband—*a ribbon*

On the fringe of garments ... Num. 15:38

Riblah—*fertility*

1. Town on Israel's eastern border ... Num. 34:11
2. Town in the land of Hamath ... 2 Kin. 23:33
   Headquarters of:
   Pharaoh Nechoh ... 2 Kin. 23:31-35
   Nebuchadnezzar ... 2 Kin. 25:6, 20, 21
   Zedekiah blinded here ... Jer. 39:5-7

Rich—*wealthy*

A. *Spiritual handicaps of:*
Selfishly satisfied ... Luke 6:24
Reluctant to leave riches ... Luke 18:22-25
Forgetful of God ... Luke 12:15-21
Indifferent to others' needs ... Luke 16:19-31
Easily tempted ... 1 Tim. 6:9
Hindered spiritually ... Matt. 19:23, 24
Misplaced trust ... Prov. 11:28

B. *Applied, spiritually, to:*
God ... Eph. 2:4
Christ ... Rom. 10:12
Christians ... James 2:5
True riches ... 2 Cor. 8:9
Good works ... 1 Tim. 6:18
Worldly people ... Jer. 5:27, 28
Self-righteous ... Hos. 12:8
Synagogue of Satan ... Rev. 2:9

Riches, earthly

A. *Described as:*
Spiritually valueless ... Ps. 49:6, 7
Inferior ... Heb. 11:26
Fleeting ... Prov. 23:5
Unsatisfying ... Eccl. 4:8
Hurtful ... Eccl. 5:13, 14
Deceitful ... Matt. 13:22
Choking ... Luke 8:14
Uncertain ... 1 Tim. 6:17
Corrupted ... James 5:2

B. *Proper attitude toward:*
Not to:
Put first ... 1 Kin. 3:11, 13
Be trusted ... Ps. 52:7
Set heart upon ... Ps. 62:10
Be desired ... Prov. 30:8
Not forever ... Prov. 27:24
Use in giving ... 2 Cor. 8:2
Remember God's supply ... Phil. 4:19

Riches, management of

Reflects spiritual attitude ... Luke 16:10-12
Demands budget ... Luke 14:28-30

Riches, spiritual

Source of, in:
God's Law ... Ps. 119:14

SUBJECT ... REFERENCE

Divine wisdom ... Prov. 3:13, 14
Unselfish service ... Prov. 13:7
Reverential fear ... Prov. 22:4
Fulfillment ... Rom. 11:12
Christ ... Col. 1:27
Assurance ... Col. 2:2
Christ's Word ... Col. 3:16

Riddle—*a hidden saying solved by guessing*

Samson's famous ... Judg. 14:12-19
Classed as a parable ... Ezek. 17:2
Avoided by God ... Num. 12:8

Ridicule (see Mocking)

Right—*that which is just and fair*

A. *Things that are:*

God's Law ... Ps. 19:8
God's Word ... Ps. 33:4
God's Way ... Ps. 107:7
Thoughts of the righteous ... Prov. 12:5
Work of the pure ... Prov. 21:8
Obedience to God ... Acts 4:19, 20
Obedience to parents ... Eph. 6:1

B. *Things that are not:*

False riches ... Jer. 17:11
Injustice to the poor ... Is. 10:2
Man's way ... Prov. 21:2
Man's heart ... Ps. 78:37

Righteous—*that which is upright*

A. *Applied to:*

God ... John 17:25
Christ ... 1 John 2:1
Messiah ... Is. 53:11
Christians ... Matt. 25:37, 46

B. *Blessings of:*

Prayers of, heard ... Prov. 15:29
Safely guarded ... Prov. 18:10
Bold as a lion ... Prov. 28:1
Shine forth ... Matt. 13:43

Righteousness—*uprightness before God*

A. *Kinds of:*

Created ... Eph. 4:24
Legal ... Phil. 3:6
Personal ... Phil. 3:9
Imputed ... Phil. 3:9
Experimental ... Heb. 5:13
Actual ... Heb. 11:33
Real ... 1 John 2:29

B. *Of Christ, He:*

Is the believer's ... Jer. 33:16
Loves ... Heb. 1:9
Judges with ... Is. 11:4
Is girded with ... Is. 11:5
Brings in ... Is. 46:13
Fulfills all ... Matt. 3:15
Confers upon believers ... Is. 61:10

Rimmon, Remmon—*pomegranate*

1. Benjamite ... 2 Sam. 4:2-9
2. Rock near Gibeah ... Judg. 20:45-47
   Benjamites hide here ... Judg. 21:13-23
3. Town in south Judah ... Josh. 15:1, 32
   Assigned to Simeon ... Josh. 19:7, 8
   Mentioned in prophecy ... Zech. 14:10
   Called En-rimmon ... Neh. 11:29
4. Syrian God (meaning "thunderer") worshiped by Naaman ... 2 Kin. 5:18
5. City of Zebulun ... Josh. 19:13
   Levitical city ... 1 Chr. 6:77
   Called Dimnah ... Josh. 21:35

Rimmon-parez—*pomegranate of breach*

Israelite camp ... Num. 33:19, 20

Ring

A. *Article of furniture, for:*

Staves of the ark ... Ex. 25:12-15
Curtains ... Ex. 26:29
Priest's ephod ... Ex. 28:23-28
Incense altar ... Ex. 30:4
Drapery ... Esth. 1:6

B. *Article of apparel:*

Symbol of authority ... Gen. 41:42
Sealing royal documents ... Esth. 3:12
Gifts ... Ex. 35:22
Feminine adornment ... Is. 3:16, 21
Expressive of position ... Luke 15:22
Sign of social status ... James 2:2

SUBJECT ... REFERENCE

Ringleader—*the leader of a mob*

Paul contemptuously called ... Acts 24:5

Rinnah—*ringing cry*

Son of Shimon ... 1 Chr. 4:20

Riot—*an unruly mob*

Pacified by town clerk ... Acts 19:20-41

Riotous—*living without restraint*

Loose living ... Luke 15:13
Gluttonous eaters ... Prov. 23:20, 21
Sexual promiscuity ... Rom. 13:13

Riphath—*descendants of Gomer*

Son of Gomer ... Gen. 10:3
Called Diphath ... 1 Chr. 1:6

Rise, risen, rising, raised

A. *Of resurrection:*

Christ's ... Mark 8:31
Believers' (spiritually) ... Col. 2:12
Believers' (physically) ... John 11:23, 24

B. *Of Christ's resurrection:*

Predicted ... Mark 14:28
Fulfilled ... Matt. 28:6, 7
Remembered ... John 2:22
Evidenced ... John 21:14
Preached ... 1 Cor. 15:11-15
Misunderstood ... Mark 9:9, 10

Rissah—*ruin; rain*

Israelite camp ... Num. 33:21, 22

Rithmah—*broom plant*

Israelite camp ... Num. 33:18, 19

Rivalry—*competition*

Between man and neighbor ... Eccl. 4:4

River—*a large stream of water*

A. *Uses of:*

Water ... Jer. 2:18
Irrigation ... Gen. 2:10
Bathing ... Ex. 2:5
Baptisms ... Matt. 3:6
Healing ... 2 Kin. 5:10

B. *List of:*

Abana ... 2 Kin. 5:12
Arnon ... Josh. 12:1
Chebar ... Ezek. 10:15, 20
Euphrates ... Gen. 2:14
Gihon ... Gen. 2:13
Gozan ... 2 Kin. 17:6
Hiddekel ... Gen. 2:14
Jabbok ... Deut. 2:37
Jordan ... Josh. 3:8
Kanah ... Josh. 16:8
Kishon ... Judg. 5:21
Nile (Sihor) ... Jer. 2:18
Pharpar ... 2 Kin. 5:12
Pison ... Gen. 2:11
Ulai ... Dan. 8:2, 16

C. *Figurative of:*

Prosperity of saints ... Ps. 1:3
Affliction ... Ps. 124:4
Christ ... Is. 32:1, 2
God's presence ... Is. 33:21
Peace ... Is. 66:12
Holy Spirit ... John 7:38, 39

Rizpah—*glowing coal*

Saul's concubine taken by Abner ... 2 Sam. 3:6-8
Sons of, killed ... 2 Sam. 21:8, 9
Grief-stricken, cares for corpses ... 2 Sam. 21:10-14

Rob, robbery

A. *Used literally of:*

Plundering ... 1 Sam. 23:1
Taking from the poor ... Prov. 22:22
Robbers ... Judg. 9:25

B. *Used figuratively of:*

Dishonest riches ... Ps. 62:10
Holding back from God ... Mal. 3:8, 9
False teachers ... John 10:1, 8
Taking wages ... 2 Cor. 11:8

Rock

A. *Used for:*

Altars ... Judg. 6:20, 26

SUBJECT ... REFERENCE

Idol worship ... Is. 57:5
Protection ... 1 Sam. 13:6
Shade ... Is. 32:2
Inscriptions ... Job 19:24
Executions ... 2 Chr. 25:12
Foundations ... Matt. 7:24, 25
Shelter ... Job 24:8
Tomb ... Matt. 27:60

B. *Miracles connected with:*

Water from ... Ex. 17:6
Fire from ... Judg. 6:21
Broken by wind ... 1 Kin. 19:11
Rent at Christ's death ... Matt. 27:51

C. *Figurative of Christ, as:*

Refuge ... Is. 32:2
Foundation of the Church ... Matt. 16:18
Source of blessings ... 1 Cor. 10:4
Stone of stumbling ... Is. 8:14
Foundation of faith ... Matt. 7:24, 25

Rod—*a staff or stick*

A. *Used for:*

Sign of authority ... Ex. 4:17, 20
Egyptians' staffs ... Ex. 7:12
Punishment ... Ex. 21:20
Club ... 1 Sam. 14:27
Correction of children ... Prov. 13:24

B. *Figurative of:*

Christ ... Is. 11:1
Christ's rule ... Ps. 2:9
Authority ... Is. 14:5, 29
The Gospel ... Ps. 110:2

Roe, roebuck—*the deer, gazelle*

A. *Described as:*

Fit for food ... Deut. 12:15, 22
Cheerful ... Prov. 5:19
Swift ... 1 Chr. 12:8
Wild ... 2 Sam. 2:18
Hunted by men ... Prov. 6:5
In Solomon's provisions ... 1 Kin. 4:23

B. *Figurative of:*

Timidity ... Is. 13:14
Swiftness ... 2 Sam. 2:18
Good wife ... Prov. 5:19
Church ... Song 4:5
Christ ... Song 2:9, 17

See Hart; Hind

Rogelim—*spies*

Town in Gilead ... 2 Sam. 17:27

Rogue—*a mischievous individual*

Descriptive of the fraudulent ... Is. 32:5, 7

Rohgah—*tumult*

Asherite ... 1 Chr. 7:34

Roll

Called a volume ... Ps. 40:7
State documents written on ... Ezra 6:2
Scripture written on ... Is. 8:1

Romamti-ezer—*I have raised up help*

Son of Heman ... 1 Chr. 25:4, 31

Roman

1. Inhabitant of Rome ... Acts 2:10
2. Official agent of the Roman government ... John 11:46
3. Person possessing Roman citizenship ... Acts 16:21-38

Romans, the Epistle to the—*a book of the New Testament*

The power of the Gospel ... Rom. 1:16
The pagans condemned ... Rom. 1:17-32
The Jews condemned ... Rom. 2:1-9
The advantages of the Jews ... Rom. 3:1-8
None righteous ... Rom. 3:9-20
Righteousness through faith ... Rom. 3:21-31
Abraham justified ... Rom. 4
The second Adam ... Rom. 5:12-21
On baptism ... Rom. 6
The pull of sin ... Rom. 7
The spiritual life ... Rom. 8
The destiny of the Jews ... Rom. 9—11
Life as worship ... Rom. 12:1, 2
Serving the body ... Rom. 12:3-21
Bearing with one another ... Rom. 14, 15
Greetings ... Rom. 16:1-24

SUBJECT — REFERENCE

Rome—*the chief city of Italy*
Jews expelled from ... Acts 18:2
Paul:
Writes to Christians of ... Rom. 1:7
Desires to go to ... Acts 19:21
Comes to ... Acts 28:14
Imprisoned in ... Acts 28:16

Root—*the part of a plant underground*
Used figuratively of:
Material foundation ... Jer. 12:2
Remnant ... Judg. 5:14
National existence ... Is. 14:30
National source ... Rom. 11:16-18
Source of evil ... 1 Tim. 6:10
Judgment and destruction ... 1 Kin. 14:15
Restoration ... 2 Kin. 19:30
Spiritual life ... Hos. 14:5
Spiritual foundation ... Eph. 3:17
Messiah ... Is. 11:1, 10

Rose—*a beautiful flower*
Of Sharon ... Song 2:1
Desert shall blossom ... Is. 35:1

Rosh—*head, chief*
1. Benjamin's son ... Gen. 46:21
2. Northern people connected with Meshech and Tubal ... Ezek. 38:2

Rot—*to decay*
A. *Used literally of:*
Sickness ... Num. 5:21-27
Hardwood trees ... Is. 40:20
B. *Used figuratively of:*
Wicked ... Prov. 10:7
Foolish wife ... Prov. 12:4

Rowing—*to navigate a boat with oars*
Against odds ... Jon. 1:13
With much labor ... Mark 6:48

Royal—*belonging to a king*
A. *Used literally of:*
King's children ... 2 Kin. 11:1
Robes of royalty ... Esth. 6:8
City of a king ... 2 Sam. 12:26
B. *Used spiritually of:*
True Israel ... Is. 62:3
True Church ... 1 Pet. 2:9

Ruby—*a valuable gem* (red pearl)
Very valuable ... Prov. 3:15
Wisdom more valuable than ... Job 28:18
Good wife above price of ... Prov. 31:10
Reddish color ... Lam. 4:7

Rudder—*a steering apparatus*
Literally ... Acts 27:40
Figuratively ... James 3:4

Rudeness—*discourtesy*
Shown toward:
Christ ... Matt. 26:67, 68
Paul ... Acts 23:2

Rue—*a pungent perennial shrub*
Tithed by Pharisees ... Luke 11:42

Rufus—*red-haired*
1. Son of Simeon of Cyrene ... Mark 15:21
2. Christian of Rome ... Rom. 16:13
Probably the same as 1.

Ruhamah—*pitied*
Symbolic name for Israel ... Hos. 2:1

Rule—*to govern*
A. *Of natural things:*
Sun and moon ... Gen. 1:16, 18
Sea ... Ps. 89:9
B. *Among men:*
Man over woman ... Gen. 3:16
King over people ... Ezra 4:20
Diligent over the lazy ... Prov. 12:24
Servant over a son ... Prov. 17:2
Rich over poor ... Prov. 22:7
Servants over a people ... Neh. 5:15
C. *Of the Messiah:*
Predicted ... Is. 40:9, 10
Promised ... Zech. 6:13

SUBJECT — REFERENCE

Victorious ... Ps. 110:2
Announced ... Matt. 2:6
Established ... Rev. 12:5
Described ... Rev. 2:27

Ruler—*one who governs*
A. *Good characteristics of:*
Upholding the good ... Rom. 13:3
Believing ... Matt. 9:18, 23
Chosen by God ... 2 Sam. 7:8
B. *Bad characteristics of:*
Men-pleasers ... John 12:42, 43
Ignorant ... Acts 3:17
Hostile ... Acts 4:26
Loving bribes ... Hos. 4:18
C. *Respect toward:*
Commanded ... Ex. 22:28
Illustrated ... Acts 23:5

Rumah—*high place*
Residence of Pedaiah ... 2 Kin. 23:36

Run—*to move swiftly*
A. *Used literally of:*
Man ... Num. 11:27
Water ... Ps. 105:41
Fire ... Ex. 9:23
Race ... 1 Cor. 9:24
B. *Used figuratively of:*
Eagerness in:
Evil ... Prov. 1:16
Good ... Ps. 119:32
Joy of salvation ... Ps. 23:5
Christian life ... 1 Cor. 9:26

Rush—*a cylindrical, often hollow marsh plant*
Cut off from Israel; rendered "bulrush" ... Is. 9:14
Concerning growth of ... Job 8:11
Signifying restoration ... Is. 35:7

Rust—*corrosion of metals*
Destruction of earthly treasures ... Matt. 6:19, 20
Of gold and silver ... James 5:3

Ruth—*female companion*
Moabitess ... Ruth 1:4
Follows Naomi ... Ruth 1:6-18
Marries Boaz ... Ruth 4:9-13
Ancestress of Christ ... Ruth 4:13, 21, 22

Ruth, the Book of—*a book of the Old Testament*
Naomi's misfortunes ... Ruth 1:1-14
Ruth's loyalty ... Ruth 1:14-22
The favor of Boaz ... Ruth 2:1-23
Boaz redeems ... Ruth 3:8—4:12
The generations of Ruth ... Ruth 4:13-22

S

Sabachthani—*hast thou forsaken me?*
Christ's cry on the cross ... Matt. 27:46

Sabaoth—*hosts*
God as Lord of ... Rom. 9:29
James 5:4

Sabbath—*rest*
A. *History of:*
Instituted at creation ... Gen. 2:2, 3
Observed before Sinai ... Ex. 16:22-30
Commanded at Sinai ... Ex. 20:8-11
Repeated at Canaan's entry ... Deut. 5:12-15
References to ... 2 Kin. 4:23
Proper observance of, described ... Is. 56:2-7
Postexilic Jews encouraged to keep ... Neh. 10:31
Perversion of, condemned by Christ ... Luke 13:14-17
Christ teaches on ... Mark 6:2
Paul preached on ... Acts 13:14
First day kept as, by Christians ... John 20:19
B. *Features concerning:*
Commemorative of creation ... Ex. 20:8-11
Seventh day during the Old Testament ... Deut. 5:14
Observance of, a perpetual covenant ... Ex. 31:16, 17
Made for man's good ... Mark 2:27
Christ's Lordship over ... Luke 6:5
C. *Regulations concerning:*
Work prohibited on ... Lev. 23:3
Cattle must rest on ... Ex. 20:10
Business forbidden on ... Jer. 17:21, 22

SUBJECT — REFERENCE

To last from evening until evening ... Lev. 23:32
Worship on ... Ezek. 46:3
Works of mercy on ... Matt. 12:12
Necessities lawful on ... Luke 13:15, 16
See First day of the week

Sabbath day's journey—*about 3,100 feet*
Between Mt. Olivet and Jerusalem ... Acts 1:12

Sabbatical year—*a rest every seventh year*
A. *Purpose of:*
Rest the land ... Ex. 23:10, 11
Emancipate slaves ... Ex. 21:2-6
Remit debts ... Deut. 15:1-6
B. *Allusions to, in history, in:*
Time of the judges ... Ruth 4:1-10
Pre-exilic times ... Jer. 32:6-16
Postexilic times ... Neh. 10:31
C. *Spiritual significance of:*
Punishment for nonobservance ... Lev. 26:33-35
Illustrative of spiritual release ... Is. 61:1-3; Luke 4:18-21
Figurative of spiritual rest ... Heb. 4:1-11
See Jubilee, Year of

Sabeans—*descendants of Sheba*
Job's property attacked by ... Job 1:13-15
Subject to Israel ... Is. 45:14
See Sheba 4, 5, 6

Sabtah
Son of Cush and grandson of Ham ... Gen. 10:7

Sabtecha
Son of Cush and grandson of Ham ... Gen. 10:7

Sacar—*hired*
1. Ahiam's father ... 1 Chr. 11:35
Called Sharar ... 2 Sam. 23:33
2. Family of gatekeepers ... 1 Chr. 26:4

Sackbut—*a wind musical instrument*
Mistranslation of a harp in Babylonian orchestra ... Dan. 3:5-15

Sackcloth—*a coarse fabric made of goat's hair*
A. *Worn by:*
Kings ... 2 Kin. 6:30
Prophets ... Is. 20:2
John ... Matt. 3:4
People ... Luke 10:13
Women ... Is. 32:11
B. *Expressive of:*
Sorrow ... Gen. 37:34
Repentance ... Joel 1:8, 13
Subjection ... 1 Kin. 20:31, 32
Fasting ... Is. 58:5
Protest ... Esth. 4:1-4
C. *Symbolic of:*
Severe judgment ... Is. 50:3
God's judgment ... Rev. 6:12

Sacrament (see Baptism, Christian; Lord's Supper)

Sacred places
Chosen by God ... Deut. 12:11
Not to trust in ... John 4:20-24

Sacrifice, sacrifices
A. *Requirements of:*
Upon altar only ... Ex. 20:24
Clean animals ... Gen. 8:20
To God alone ... Ex. 22:20
Perfect animals ... Lev. 22:19
At place divinely established ... Deut. 12:6
By appointed priests ... 1 Sam. 2:28
In faith ... Gen. 4:4
In obedience ... 1 Sam. 15:22
B. *Perversion of, in offering:*
To demons ... 1 Cor. 10:20
To idols ... 2 Chr. 34:25
Defective animals ... Mal. 1:13, 14
Without respect ... 1 Sam. 2:29

SUBJECT — REFERENCE

C. *Inadequacy of:*
Could not atone for sins ... Ps. 40:6
Limited to legal purification ... Heb. 9:13, 22

D. *Figurative of:*
Christ's sacrifice ... 1 Cor. 5:7
Prayer ... Ps. 141:2
Worship ... 1 Pet. 2:5
Righteousness ... Ps. 51:19

E. *Of Christ to:*
Redeem from the curse ... Gal. 3:13
Secure our redemption ... Matt. 20:28
Reconcile God and man ... Rom. 5:10

Sacrilege—*profaning holy things*

A. *Done by:*
Defaming God's name ... 2 Kin. 18:28-35
Profaning the Sabbath ... Neh. 13:15-21
Debauching holy things ... John 2:14-16

B. *Those guilty of:*
People ... 1 Sam. 6:19
Pagans ... Dan. 5:1-4
Priests ... Lev. 10:1-7
Pharisees ... Matt. 23:16-22

Saddle—*cloth or leather seat for a rider*
Balaam's ... Num. 22:21

Sadducees—*followers of Zadok*
Rejected by John ... Matt. 3:7
Tempted Jesus ... Matt. 16:1-12
Silenced by Jesus ... Matt. 22:23-34
Disturbed by teaching of resurrection ... Acts 4:1, 2
Opposed apostles ... Acts 5:17-40

Sadoc—*righteous*
Ancestor of Christ ... Matt. 1:14

Safe, safety—*dwelling without fear or harm*

A. *False means of:*
Wickedness ... Job 21:7-9, 17
Folly ... Job 5:2-4
False hope ... 1 Thess. 5:3

B. *True means of:*
LORD ... Ps. 4:8
LORD's protection ... Deut. 33:12
Apostolic admonition ... Phil. 3:1

Saffron—*a variety of crocus; used as a perfume or medicine*
Figurative of the bride ... Song 4:14

Sail—*an expanse of material used to catch the wind and propel a sailing ship*
Figurative of:
Enemies' weakness ... Is. 33:23
The pride of Tyre ... Ezek. 27:7

Sailors—*mariners*
Skilled ... 1 Kin. 9:27
Fearful ... Jon. 1:5
Cry bitterly ... Ezek. 27:8-36
Storm-tossed ... Acts 27:18-31

Saints—*God's redeemed people*

A. *Descriptive of:*
Old Testament believers ... Matt. 27:52
Christians ... Acts 9:32, 41
Christian martyrs ... Rev. 16:6
Present with Christ at His return ... 1 Thess. 3:13

B. *Their weaknesses, subject to:*
Needs ... 2 Cor. 9:1, 12; Rom. 12:13
Persecution ... Dan. 7:21, 25

C. *Their duty to:*
Keep God's Word ... Jude 3
Grow spiritually ... Eph. 4:12
Avoid evil ... Eph. 5:3
Judge Christians ... 1 Cor. 6:1, 2
Pray for others ... Eph. 6:18
Minister to others ... Heb. 6:10

D. *God's protection of, He:*
Forsakes them not ... Ps. 37:28
Gathers them ... Ps. 50:5
Keeps them ... 1 Sam. 2:9
Counts them precious ... Ps. 116:15
Intercedes for them ... Rom. 8:27
Will glorify them ... 2 Thess. 1:10

SUBJECT — REFERENCE

Salamis—*a town of Cyprus*
Paul preaches here ... Acts 13:4, 5

Salchah—*wandering*
City in Bashan ... Deut. 3:10

Salem—*peace*
Jerusalem's original name ... Gen. 14:18
Used poetically ... Ps. 76:2

Salim—*completeness*
Place near Aenon ... John 3:23

Sallai—*rejecter*
1. Benjamite chief ... Neh. 11:8
2. Priestly family ... Neh. 12:20
Called Sallu ... Neh. 12:7

Sallu—*contempt*
Benjamite family ... 1 Chr. 9:7
See Sallai 2

Salma—*clothing*
Son of Hur ... 1 Chr. 2:50, 51

Salmon
Father of Boaz ... Ruth 4:20, 21
Ancestor of Christ ... Matt. 1:4, 5

Salome—*feminine of Solomon*
1. Among ministering women ... Mark 15:40, 41
Visits empty tomb ... Mark 16:1
2. Herodias' daughter (not named in the Bible) ... Matt. 14:6-11

Salt

A. *Uses of:*
Seasoning:
Food ... Job 6:6
Sacrifice ... Lev. 2:13
Everlasting covenant ... Num. 18:19
Rubbed on infants at birth ... Ezek. 16:4
Making land unproductive ... Judg. 9:45

B. *Miracles connected with:*
Lot's wife becomes pillar of ... Gen. 19:26
Elisha purified water with ... 2 Kin. 2:19-22

C. *Figurative of:*
God's everlasting covenant ... Num. 18:19
Barrenness and desolation ... Deut. 29:23
Good influence ... Matt. 5:13
Peace in the heart ... Mark 9:50
Wise speech ... Col. 4:6
Final judgment ... Mark 9:49
Reprobation ... Ezek. 47:9, 11

Salt, City of
City in the wilderness of Judah ... Josh. 15:62

Salt Sea
Old Testament name for the Dead Sea ... Gen. 14:3; Num. 34:3, 12

Salt, Valley of—*a valley south of the Dead Sea*
Site of:
David's victory ... 2 Sam. 8:13
Amaziah's victory ... 2 Kin. 14:7

Salu—*restored*
Simeonite prince ... Num. 25:14

Salutations—*greetings from one person to another*

A. *Normal:*
Between:
Brothers ... 1 Sam. 17:22
Social ranks ... Gen. 47:7
Strangers ... 1 Sam. 10:3, 4
Christians ... Acts 18:22
On visits ... Rom. 16:21-23

B. *Examples of forms used in:*
"God be gracious" ... Gen. 43:29
"Peace be with thee" ... Judg. 19:20
"The LORD be with you" ... Ruth 2:4
"The LORD bless thee" ... Ruth 2:4
"Blessed be thou" ... Ruth 3:10
"Hail" ... Luke 1:28
"All hail" ... Matt. 28:9

See Benediction

Salvation

A. *Descriptive of:*
National deliverance ... Ex. 14:13
Deliverance from enemies ... 2 Chr. 20:17
Messiah ... Matt. 1:21

B. *Source of, in:*
God's grace ... Eph. 2:5, 8
God's love ... Rom. 5:8
God's mercy ... Titus 3:5
Christ alone ... Acts 4:12
Cross ... 1 Cor. 1:18

C. *History of:*
Promised to Adam ... Gen. 3:15
Announced to Abram ... Gen. 12:1-3
Revealed to the prophets ... 1 Pet. 1:10-12
Longed for by the saints ... Ps. 119:81, 174
Promised to Gentiles ... Is. 45:21, 22
To be realized by the Messiah ... Is. 59:16, 17
Seen in Christ's birth ... Luke 1:69, 77
Christ, the author ... Heb. 5:9
Appeared to all men ... Titus 2:11
Proclaimed to Israel ... Zech. 9:9
Accomplished on the cross ... John 3:14, 15
Preached through the Gospel ... Eph. 1:13
Rejected by Israel ... Acts 13:26-46
Extended to Gentiles ... Acts 28:28
This age, day of ... 2 Cor. 6:2
God's long-suffering in ... 2 Pet. 3:9
Final, nearer each day ... Rom. 13:11
Consummated in the second advent ... Heb. 9:28
Praise for, in heaven ... Rev. 7:10

D. *Requirements of:*
Confession ... Acts 2:21
Repentance ... Mark 1:15
Faith ... John 3:14-18
Regeneration ... John 3:3-8
Holy scripture ... 2 Tim. 3:15

E. *Negative blessings of, deliverance from:*
Sin ... Matt. 1:21
Satan's power ... Heb. 2:14, 15
Wrath ... Rom. 5:9
Eternal death ... John 3:16, 17

F. *Positive blessings of:*
Chosen to ... 2 Thess. 2:13
Appointed to ... 1 Thess. 5:9
Kept unto ... 1 Pet. 1:5
Rejoiced in ... 1 Pet. 4:13
To be worked out ... Phil. 2:12

G. *Temporal aspects of:*
Past ... Eph. 2:8
Present ... 1 Cor. 1:18
Future ... Heb. 9:28

Samaria—*watch tower*
1. Capital of Israel ... 1 Kin. 16:24-29
Israel's "crown of pride" ... Is. 28:1
Besieged twice by Ben-hadad ... 1 Kin. 20:1-22
Miraculously saved ... 2 Kin. 6:8-23
Worshipers of Baal destroyed ... 2 Kin. 10:1-28
Threatened with divine judgment ... Is. 28:1-4; Amos 3:11, 12
Repopulated with foreigners ... 2 Kin. 17:24-41
2. Name of Northern Kingdom ... 1 Kin. 21:1
3. District of Palestine in Christ's time ... Luke 17:11-19
Preaching in, forbidden by Christ ... Matt. 10:5
Gospel preached ... Acts 1:8
Churches established there ... Acts 9:31
Paul preached there ... Acts 15:3

Samaritans—*inhabitants of Samaria*
Made of mixed races ... 2 Kin. 17:24-41
Seek alliance with Jews ... Ezra 4:1-4
Help of, rejected by Nehemiah ... Neh. 4:1, 2
Christ and the woman of ... John 4:5-42
Story of "the good Samaritan" ... Luke 10:30-37
Beliefs of ... John 4:25
Converts among ... Acts 8:5-25

Samech
Letter of the Hebrew alphabet ... Ps. 119:113-120

Samgar-nebo—*be gracious, Nebo*
Prince of Nebuchadnezzar ... Jer. 39:3

SUBJECT REFERENCE

Samlah—*a garment*
Edomite king ....Gen. 36:36, 37

Samos—*an island off the coast of Lydia*
Visited by Paul ....Acts 20:15

Samothracia—*an island in the Aegean Sea*
Visited by Paul ....Acts 16:11

Samson—*sunlike*

A. *Life of:*
Birth of, predicted ....Judg. 13:2-23
God's Spirit moves him ......Judg. 13:24, 25
Desired a Philistine wife .....Judg. 14:1-9
Propounded a riddle ....Judg. 14:10-14
Betrayed, kills 30 men.......Judg. 14:15-20
Enticed by Delilah, loses strength..................Judg. 16:4-20
Blinded and bound ....Judg. 16:21
Destroyed over 3,000 in his death ....Judg. 16:22-31; Heb. 11:32

B. *Contrasts of his life:*
Parents' concern; his unconcern ....Judg. 13:8
Obedient, victorious; disobedient, defeated ....Judg. 15:14
Seeks revenge; is revenged ...Judg. 15:1-8
Spirit-moved; animated by lust......................Judg. 15:14
Physically strong; morally weak ....Judg. 16:3, 12
Greater victory in death than in life ....Judg. 16:29, 30; Heb. 11:32

Samuel—*name of God* (a godly name)

A. *Life of:*
Born in answer to Hannah's prayer ....1 Sam. 1:5-21
Dedicated to God before his birth ....1 Sam. 1:11, 22
Brought to Shiloh ....1 Sam. 1:24-28
His mother praised God for ....1 Sam. 2:1-10
Received a revelation concerning Eli's house......................1 Sam. 3:1-19
Recognized as a prophet.....1 Sam. 3:20, 21
Became a circuit judge ......1 Sam. 7:15-17
Organized porter service .....1 Chr. 9:22; 1 Chr. 26:28
Called Israel to repentance...1 Sam. 7:3-6
Anointed Saul as king.......1 Sam. 10:1
Lamented in death ....1 Sam. 25:1

B. *Character of:*
Inspired as a writer ....1 Chr. 29:29
Inspired as a prophet ....Acts 3:24
Diligent as a judge..........1 Sam. 7:15-17
Faithful to God ....Heb. 11:32-34
Industrious in service ....1 Chr. 9:22
Devout in life..............Jer. 15:1
Powerful in prayer..........Ps. 99:6
Remembered in death ....1 Sam. 25:1

Samuel, the Books of—*books of the Old Testament*

A. *1 Samuel:*
Birth of Samuel ....1 Sam. 1:19-28
Hannah's song ....1 Sam. 2:1-10
The ark captured ....1 Sam. 4:1-11
The ark returned ....1 Sam. 6:1-21
Saul chosen as king ....1 Sam. 9:1-27
Saul anointed ....1 Sam. 10:1-27
Saul against the Philistines...1 Sam. 13:1-4
Saul is rejected.............1 Sam. 15:10-31
David is anointed ....1 Sam. 16:1-13
David and Goliath ....1 Sam. 17:23-58
Jonathan's love.............1 Sam. 19:1-7
Saul against David ....1 Sam. 23:6-29
David spares Saul ....1 Sam. 24:1-8; 1 Sam. 26:1-16
The medium of En-dor ......1 Sam. 28:7-25
David against the Amalekites ....1 Sam. 30:1-31
Death of Saul...............1 Sam. 31:1-13

B. *2 Samuel:*
David's lament.............2 Sam. 1:17-27
David anointed as king......2 Sam. 2:1-7
The ark in Zion ....2 Sam. 6:1-19
David plans the Temple .....2 Sam. 7:1-29
The kingdom expands.......2 Sam. 8:1-18
David and Bath-sheba ......2 Sam. 11:1-27
Nathan rebukes David ......2 Sam. 12:1-12
David repents..............2 Sam. 12:13, 14
David's child dies ....2 Sam. 12:15-23
Amnon and Tamar ....2 Sam. 13:1-19
The mighty men............2 Sam. 23:8-39
David takes a census........2 Sam. 24:1-25

Sanballat—*Sin* (the moon-god) *has given life*
Influential Samaritan ....Neh. 2:10
Opposes Nehemiah's plans......Neh. 4:7, 8
Seeks to assassinate Nehemiah ..Neh. 6:1-4
Fails in intimidation ....Neh. 6:5-14
His daughter marries Eliashib, the high priest........................Neh. 13:4, 28

Sanctification—*growing in holiness*

Produced by:
God ....1 Thess. 5:23
Christ ....Heb. 2:11
Holy Spirit ....1 Pet. 1:2
Truth.........................John 17:17, 19
Christ's blood.................Heb. 9:14
Prayer ....1 Tim. 4:4, 5

See Godliness; Holiness of Christians; Piety

Sanctimoniousness—*assumed and pretended holiness*
Condemned by Christ..........Matt. 6:5

Sanctuary (see Holy of Holies; Tabernacle)

Sand

Figurative uses of:
One's posterity................Gen. 22:17
Weight........................Job 6:3
Large number of people ....Josh. 11:4
God's thoughts toward us ......Ps. 139:17, 18

Sandals, Shoe—*leather strapped to the feet*

A. *Characteristics of:*
Worn on the feet ....1 Kin. 2:5
Tied by a latchet ....Gen. 14:23
Some considered worthless...Amos 2:6
Used for dress occasions.....Luke 15:22
Worn as adornment.........Song 7:1
Worn out after a journey ....Josh. 9:5, 13
Preserved supernaturally.....Deut. 29:5
Worn by Christ's disciples ....Mark 6:9

B. *Symbolism of:*
Taking on—readiness for a journey ....Ex. 12:11
Putting off—reverence before God ....Ex. 3:5; Josh. 5:15
Want of—mourning ....2 Sam. 15:30
Giving to another—manner of attestation in Israel ....Ruth 4:7, 8
To unloose another's—act of homage ....Luke 3:16

C. *Figurative of:*
Preparation for service ......Eph. 6:15
Alertness ....Is. 5:27

Sanitation and hygiene

A. *Laws relating to:*
Dead bodies ....Lev. 11:24-40
Contagion ....Num. 9:6, 10
Leprosy ....Lev. 13:2-59
Menstruation ....Lev. 15:19-30
Women in childbirth ....Lev. 12:2-8
Man's discharge ....Lev. 15:2-18

B. *Provisions for health:*
Washing ....Deut. 23:10, 11
Burning ....Num. 31:19-23
Isolation ....Lev. 13:2-5, 31-33
Destruction ....Lev. 14:39-45
Covering excrement.........Deut. 23:12, 13

Sanity, spiritual
Young men urged to..........Titus 2:6
Accomplished by Christ ....Luke 8:35
Illustrated by Paul's change.....Acts 26:11, 25

Sansannah—*palm branch*
Town in south Judah ....Josh. 15:31

Sap—*the living fluid of woody plants*
Lord's trees full of............Ps. 104:16

Saph—*basin*
Philistine giant ....2 Sam. 21:18
Called Sippai ....1 Chr. 20:4

Saphir—*glittering*
Town of Judah................Mic. 1:11

Sapphira—*beautiful*
Wife of Ananias..............Acts 5:1
Struck dead for lying ....Acts 5:1-11

Sapphire—*a precious stone*
Worn by high priest ....Ex. 28:18
John's vision.................Rev. 21:19

Sarah, Sarai—*princess*
Wife of Abram...............Gen. 11:29-31
Abraham's half-sister ....Gen. 20:11-13
Represented as Abram's sister...Gen. 12:10-20
Barren ....Gen. 11:30
Gave Abram her maid ....Gen. 16:1-3
Promised a son ....Gen. 17:15-21; Rom. 9:9
Gave birth to Isaac ....Gen. 21:1-8

Saraph—*burning*
Descendant of Judah ....1 Chr. 4:22

Sarcasm—*a biting taunt, mock*

A. *Purposes of, to:*
Recall injustice............Judg. 9:7-19
Remind of duty neglected ...1 Sam. 26:15
Mock idolaters ....1 Kin. 18:27
Deflate pride..............1 Kin. 20:10, 11
Warn of defeat ....2 Kin. 14:8-12

B. *Uttered by:*
Friend ....Job 11:2-12
Enemies...................Neh. 4:2, 3
Persecutors ....Matt. 27:28, 29
Apostle ....Acts 23:1-5
God ....Jer. 25:27

Sardis—*the chief city of Lydia in Asia Minor*
One of the seven churches ......Rev. 1:11

Sardites
Descendants of Sered ....Num. 26:26

Sardius—*a precious stone*
Used in "breastplate" ....Ex. 28:15-17
In the Garden of Eden ....Ezek. 28:13
Worn by Priest...............Ex. 28:17

Sardonyx—*a precious stone*
In John's vision ....Rev. 21:19, 20

Sargon—*the constituted king*
King of Assyria ....Is. 20:1

Sarid—*survivor*
Village of Zebulun............Josh. 19:10, 12

Saron—*same as Sharon*
Inhabitants turn to the Lord ....Acts 9:35

Sarsechim
Prince of Nebuchadnezzar ......Jer. 39:3

Satan—*adversary*

A. *Names of* (see Devil)

B. *Designs of, to:*
Undo God's work ....Mark 4:15
Make men turn away from God ....Job 2:4, 5
Instigate evil..............John 13:2, 27
Secure men's worship ....Luke 4:6-8; 2 Thess. 2:3, 4

C. *Character of:*
Deceiver ....Rev. 12:9
Father of lies ....John 8:44
Adversary ....1 Pet. 5:9

D. *Methods of:*
Disguises himself ....2 Cor. 11:14
Insinuates doubt ....Gen. 3:1
Misuses Scripture...........Matt. 4:6
Uses schemes ....2 Cor. 2:11
Afflicts believers............Luke 13:16

E. *Judgment upon:*
Bound ....Mark 3:27
Cast out ....John 12:31
Judged....................John 16:11
Bruised ....Rom. 16:20
Assigned to hell ....Matt. 25:41

Satiate(d)—*To be satisfied*
Scorners and fools shall be .....Prov. 1:22, 31
The sword shall be ....Jer. 46:10

Satire—*exposing problems to ridicule*
Jesus' devastating use of........Matt. 23:1-33

SUBJECT REFERENCE

Satisfaction—*that which completely fulfills*

A. *Of physical things:*
Sexual pleasures .... Prov. 5:19
Bread of heaven .... Ps. 105:40
Long life .... Ps. 91:16

B. *Of spiritual things, God's:*
Mercy .... Ps. 90:14
Presence .... Ps. 17:15

C. *Of things empty of:*
Labor .... Is. 55:2
Sinful ways .... Ezek. 16:28, 29
Persecution .... Job 19:22

Satrap—*protector of the land*
Officials appointed over the kingdom .... Dan. 6:1

Satyr—*he-goat, hairy one* (a Greek god)
Objects of worship ("devils") .... 2 Chr. 11:15

Saul—*asked* (of God)
Son of Kish; first king of Israel .... 1 Sam. 9:1, 2
Seeks his father's asses .... 1 Sam. 9:3-14
Meets Samuel .... 1 Sam. 9:16-27
Anointed as king .... 1 Sam. 10:1-16
Victories and family .... 1 Sam. 14:47-52
Fights against Philistines; becomes jealous of David ..... 1 Sam. 17:1-58; 1 Sam. 18:6-13
Promises his daughter to David .... 1 Sam. 18:14-30
Seeks to murder David .... 1 Sam. 19:1-24
Pursues David .... 1 Sam. 23:1-28
His life spared by David .... 1 Sam. 26:1-25
Defeated, commits suicide .... 1 Sam. 31:1-6
Burial of .... 1 Sam. 31:7-13
David's lament over .... 2 Sam. 1:17-27
Sin of, exposed .... 2 Sam. 21:1-9

Savior—*one who saves*

Applied to:
God .... Ps. 106:21
Christ .... 2 Tim. 1:10

Savior, Jesus as

A. *Characteristics of:*
Only .... Acts 4:10, 12
Complete .... Col. 2:10
Powerful .... Jude 24
Authoritative .... John 10:18
Universal .... 1 Tim. 4:10

B. *Announcement of, by:*
Prophets .... Is. 42:6, 7
Angels .... Matt. 1:20, 21
John the Baptist .... John 1:29
Christ .... John 12:44-50
Peter .... Acts 5:31
Paul .... 1 Tim. 1:15
John .... 1 John 4:14

C. *Office of, involves His:*
Becoming man .... Heb. 2:14
Perfect righteousness .... Heb. 5:8, 9
Perfect obedience .... Rom. 5:19, 20
Dying for us .... 1 Pet. 1:18-20

D. *Saves us from:*
Wrath .... Rom. 5:9
Sin .... John 1:29
Death .... John 11:25, 26

Saw—*a toothed tool for cutting*
Stones .... 1 Kin. 7:9
Wood .... Is. 10:15
For torture .... 1 Chr. 20:3

Scab
Disqualifies an offering .... Lev. 22:21, 22
Priest observes .... Lev. 13:6-8
Israel threatened with .... Deut. 28:27

Scabbard—*a sheath*
For God's Word .... Jer. 47:6

Scandal—*something disgraceful in*
Priesthood .... 1 Sam. 2:22-24
Family .... 2 Sam. 13:1-22

Scant measure
Abomination .... Mic. 6:10

Scapegoat—*a goat of departure*
Bears sin away .... Lev. 16:8-22
Typical of Christ .... Is. 53:6, 11, 12

SUBJECT REFERENCE

Scarlet—*a brilliant crimson*

A. *Literal uses of, for:*
Tabernacle .... Ex. 26:1, 31, 36
Identification .... Gen. 38:28, 30

B. *Symbolic uses of:*
Royalty .... Matt. 27:28
Prosperity .... 2 Sam. 1:24
Conquest .... Nah. 2:3
Deep sin .... Is. 1:18

Scatter—*to disperse abroad*

A. *Applied to:*
Nations .... Gen. 11:8, 9
Christians .... Acts 8:1, 4

B. *Caused by:*
Sin .... 1 Kin. 14:15, 16
Persecution .... Acts 11:19

Scepter—*a royal staff*
Sign of authority .... Esth. 4:11
Of Judah's tribe .... Gen. 49:10
Promise concerning .... Num. 24:17
Fulfilled in Christ .... Heb. 1:8

Sceva
Jewish priest at Ephesus .... Acts 19:14

Schemes of Satan
Known by Christians .... 2 Cor. 2:11
Warnings against .... 2 Cor. 11:3, 13-15
Armor provided against .... Eph. 6:11
World falls before .... Rev. 13:1-18

Schin
Letter of the Hebrew alphabet .. Ps. 119:161-168

Schism—*a division within a body*
Prohibition concerning .... 1 Cor. 12:25
Translated "rent" and "division" .... Matt. 9:16

Scholars—*men reputed for learning*
Numbered by David .... 1 Chr. 25:1, 7, 8
God's judgment against .... Mal. 2:12
Moses, an expert .... Acts 7:22
Gamaliel, famous as .... Acts 5:34

School—*an institution of learning*
Home .... Deut. 6:6-10
Temple .... 1 Chr. 25:7, 8
In Ephesus .... Acts 19:1, 9
Levites, teachers of .... 2 Chr. 17:7-9
Best subjects of .... Is. 50:4

Schoolmaster—*a tutor*
Applied to the Mosaic law .... Gal. 3:24, 25

Science—*exact knowledge*

A. *Implied reference to:*
Architecture .... 2 Chr. 2:1-18
Astronomy .... Gen. 15:5
Biology .... Ps. 139:13-16
Carpentry .... Gen. 6:14-16
Medicine .... Ps. 103:3
Meteorology .... Job 38:22-38
Surveying .... Ezek. 40:5, 6

B. *Significance of, to:*
Manifest God's existence .... Ps. 19:1-6
Prove God's prophecies .... Jer. 25:12
Illustrate heaven's glory .... Rev. 21:9-23
Point to Christ as source of .... Col. 2:3

Scorners—*arrogant disdainers of others*

A. *Classified among:*
Fools .... Prov. 1:22
Wicked .... Prov. 9:7

B. *Described as:*
Unwilling to take rebuke .... Prov. 9:7, 8
Incorrigible .... Prov. 15:12
Abomination .... Prov. 24:9

Scorpion—*an eight-legged creature having a poisonous tail*

A. *Used literally of:*
Desert creatures .... Deut. 8:15
Poisonous creatures .... Luke 10:19

B. *Used figuratively of:*
Heavy burdens .... 1 Kin. 12:11
Agents of antichrist .... Rev. 9:3, 5, 10

SUBJECT REFERENCE

Scourging—*whipping*

A. *Objects of:*
Christ .... John 19:1
Christians .... Matt. 10:17
Paul .... Gal. 6:17

B. *Inflicted by:*
Roman government .... Acts 22:25-29

Screech owl—*a nocturnal creature*
Dwells in ruins .... Is. 34:14

Scribe's knife—*a knife used to sharpen reed pens*
Used by Jehoiakim on Jeremiah's scroll .... Jer. 36:23-28

Scribes—*experts in legal matters*

A. *Employment of:*
Transcribers of legal contracts .... Jer. 32:12
Keepers of records .... Jer. 36:25, 26
Advisers in state affairs .... 1 Chr. 27:32
Custodians of draft records .. 2 Kin. 25:19
Collectors of Temple revenue .... 2 Kin. 12:10
Teacher of the Law .... Ezra 7:6, 10, 12

B. *Characteristics of, in New Testament times, their:*
Righteousness external .... Matt. 5:20
Teaching without authority .... Matt. 7:29

C. *Their attitude toward Christ:*
Accusing Him of blasphemy .... Mark 2:6, 7
Seeking to accuse .... Luke 6:7
Questioning His authority ... Luke 20:1, 2

D. *Christ's attitude toward:*
Exposes them .... Matt. 23:13-36
Condemns them .... Luke 20:46, 47
Calls them hypocrites .... Matt. 15:1-9

Scrip—*a traveler's bag; wallet*

Used by:
Shepherds .... 1 Sam. 17:40
Travelers .... Luke 9:3

Scriptures—*God's revelation*

A. *Called:*
Word of God .... Heb. 4:12
Word of truth .... James 1:18
Oracles of God .... Rom. 3:2
Word .... James 1:21-23
Holy Scriptures .... Rom. 1:2
Sword of the Spirit .... Eph. 6:17
Scriptures of the prophets ... Rom. 16:26

B. *Described as:*
Authoritative .... 1 Pet. 4:11
Inspired .... 2 Tim. 3:16
Effectual in life .... 1 Thess. 2:13
True .... Ps. 119:160
Perfect .... Ps. 19:7
Sharp .... Heb. 4:12
Pure .... Prov. 30:5

C. *Inspiration of, proved by:*
External evidence .... Heb. 2:1-4
Internal nature .... 2 Tim. 3:16, 17
Infallibility .... John 10:35
Fulfillment of prophecy ..... John 5:39, 45-47

D. *Understanding of, by:*
Spirit's illumination .... 1 Cor. 2:10-14
Searching .... John 5:39
Reasoning .... Acts 17:2
Comparing .... 2 Pet. 1:20, 21
Human help .... Acts 17:10-12

E. *Proper uses of:*
Regeneration .... 1 Pet. 1:23
Salvation .... 2 Tim. 3:15
Producing life .... John 20:31
Searching our hearts .... Heb. 4:12
Spiritual growth .... Acts 20:32
Sanctification .... John 17:17
Illumination .... Ps. 119:105
Keeping from sin .... Ps. 119:9, 11
Defeating Satan .... Eph. 6:16, 17
Proving truth .... Acts 18:28

F. *Misuses of, by:*
Satan .... Matt. 4:6
Hypocrites .... Matt. 22:23-29
False teachers .... 2 Cor. 2:17
Unlearned .... 2 Pet. 3:16

SUBJECT ... REFERENCE

G. *Positive attitudes toward:*
- Let dwell in richly ... Col. 3:16
- Search daily ... Acts 17:11
- Hide in the heart ... Ps. 119:11
- Delight in ... Ps. 1:2
- Love ... Ps. 119:97, 113, 167
- Receive with meekness ... James 1:21
- Teach to children ... Deut. 11:19
- Obey ... James 1:22
- Read ... Deut. 17:19

H. *Negative attitudes toward, not to:*
- Add to or subtract from ... Deut. 4:2
- Handle deceitfully ... 2 Cor. 4:2
- Wrest ... 2 Pet. 3:16
- Invalidating by traditions ... Mark 7:9-13

I. *Fulfillment of, cited to show:*
- Christ's:
  - Mission ... Luke 4:16-21
  - Death ... Luke 24:27, 45-47
  - Rejection ... Acts 28:25-29
  - Resurrection ... Acts 2:24-31
- Spirit's descent ... John 14:16-21
- Faith ... Rom. 4:3

J. *Distortion of:*
- Condemned ... Prov. 30:5, 6; Rev. 22:18-20
- Predicted ... 2 Tim. 4:3, 4

K. *Memorization of:*
- Keeps from sin ... Ps. 119:11
- Gives understanding ... Ps. 119:130
- Facilitates prayer ... John 15:7

Scriptures, devotional readings

A. *For personal needs:*
- Comfort ... Ps. 43:1-5; Rom. 8:26-28
- Courage ... Ps. 46:1-11; 2 Cor. 4:7-18
- Direction ... Heb. 4:16; James 1:5, 6
- Peace ... Ps. 4:1-8; Phil. 4:4-7
- Relief ... Ps. 91:1-16; 2 Cor. 12:8-10
- Rest ... Matt. 11:28-30; Rom. 8:31-39
- Temptation ... Ps. 1:1-6; 1 Cor. 10:6-13; James 1:12-16

B. *For Instruction:*
- Sermon on the mount ... Matt. 5:1—7:29
- Prayer ... Matt. 6:5-15; Phil. 4:6, 7
- Golden rule ... Matt. 7:12
- Great commandment ... Matt. 22:36-40
- Salvation ... John 3:1-36
- Good shepherd ... John 10:1-18
- Spiritual fruit ... John 15:1-17; Gal. 5:22, 23
- Guilt ... Rom. 8:1
- Righteousness ... Rom. 3:19-28
- Justification ... Rom. 5:1-21
- Christian service ... Rom. 12:1-21; Rom. 13:1-14
- Love ... 1 Cor. 13:1-13
- Stewardship ... 2 Cor. 8:1-24; 2 Cor. 9:1-15
- Regeneration ... Eph. 2:1-10
- Christ's exaltation ... Phil. 2:5-11
- Resurrection ... 1 Thess. 4:13-18
- Judgment ... Rev. 20:10-15
- New heaven and earth ... Rev. 21:1-27; Rev. 22:1-5

Scriptures, distortion of
- Condemned ... Prov. 30:5, 6
- Turning unto fables ... 2 Tim. 4:3, 4
- By unlearned ... 2 Pet. 3:15-17
- God will punish ... Rev. 22:18-20

Scroll—*a papyrus or leather roll* (book)
- Applied to the heavens ... Is. 34:4
- Sky split apart like a ... Rev. 6:14

Scum—*the residue of dirt*
- Used figuratively ... Ezek. 24:6-12

Scythians—*natives of Scythia*
- In the Christian church ... Col. 3:11

Sea—*a large body of water*

A. *Described as:*
- Created by God ... Acts 4:24
- Deep ... Ps. 68:22
- Turbulent and dangerous ... Ps. 89:9
- All rivers run into ... Eccl. 1:7
- Bound by God's decree ... Jer. 5:22
- Manifesting God's works ... Ps. 104:24, 25

B. *List of, in the Bible:*
- Great Sea (Mediterranean) ... Ezek. 47:10
- Salt or Dead Sea ... Gen. 14:3
- Red Sea ... Ex. 10:19
- Sea of Galilee (Chinnereth) ... Num. 34:11
- Adriatic ... Acts 27:27

C. *Figurative of:*
- Extension of the Gospel ... Is. 11:9
- Righteousness ... Is. 48:18
- False teachers ... Jude 13

Sea, molten
- Vessel in the Temple ... 1 Kin. 7:23

Sea of glass
- Before the throne of God ... Rev. 4:6

Seal—*instrument used to authenticate ownership*

A. *Used literally to:*
- Guarantee business deals ... Jer. 32:11-14
- Ratify covenants ... Neh. 10:1
- Insure a prophecy ... Dan. 9:24
- Protect books ... Rev. 5:2, 5, 9
- Lock doors ... Matt. 27:66

B. *Used figuratively of:*
- Ownership of married love ... Song 4:12; Song 8:6
- Hidden things ... Is. 29:11
- Acceptance of Christ ... John 3:33
- God's witness to Christ ... John 6:27
- Believer's security ... 2 Cor. 1:22
- Assurance ... Eph. 4:30
- God's ownership of His people ... Rev. 7:3-8

Seamstress—*a dressmaker*
- Dorcas known as ... Acts 9:36-42

Search—*to make intensive investigation*

A. *Applied literally to:*
- Land ... Num. 13:2-32
- Lost article ... Gen. 31:34-37
- Records ... Ezra 4:15, 19
- Child ... Matt. 2:8
- Scriptures ... John 5:39
- Enemy ... 1 Sam. 23:23

B. *Applied figuratively to:*
- Man's heart ... Ps. 139:1, 23
- Understanding ... Prov. 2:4
- Conscience ... Prov. 20:27
- Self-examination ... Judg. 5:16

Season—*a period of time*

A. *Descriptive of:*
- Period of the year ... Gen. 1:14
- Revealed times ... 1 Thess. 5:1
- Prophetic period ... Rev. 6:11
- Right time ... Deut. 11:14
- Short period ... Philem. 15
- Appointed time ... Num. 9:2, 3, 7

B. *Of the year:*
- Guaranteed by God ... Gen. 8:22
- Proof of God's providence ... Acts 14:17
- Indicated by the moon ... Ps. 104:19

Seat—*a place of authority*

A. *Descriptive of:*
- Inner court ... Ezek. 8:3
- Assembly ... Matt. 23:6

B. *Figurative of:*
- God's throne ... Job 23:3
- Association with evil ... Ps. 1:1
- Satanic power ... Rev. 13:2

Seba
- Cush's oldest son ... Gen. 10:7
- See Sabeans

Sebat
- Eleventh month of the Hebrew year ... Zech. 1:7

Secacah—*thicket*
- Village of Judah ... Josh. 15:1, 61

Sechu—*observatory*
- Village near Ramah ... 1 Sam. 19:22

Second

A. *Descriptive of:*
- Next in order ... Gen. 1:8
- Repetition ... 1 Kin. 18:34
- Second advent ... Heb. 9:28

B. *Used figuratively and spiritually of:*
- Christ ... 1 Cor. 15:47
- Finality ... Titus 3:10
- New covenant ... Heb. 8:7
- Death ... Rev. 2:11

Second chance
- None in hell ... Luke 16:23-31

Second coming of Christ

A. *Described as:*
- Day of:
  - The Lord ... 1 Thess. 5:2
  - Lord Jesus ... 1 Cor. 5:5
  - God ... 2 Pet. 3:12
- That day ... 2 Thess. 1:10
- Last day ... John 12:48

B. *Purposes of, to:*
- Fulfill His Word ... John 14:3
- Raise the dead ... 1 Thess. 4:13-18
- Destroy death ... 1 Cor. 15:25, 26
- Gather the elect ... Matt. 24:31
- Judge the world ... Matt. 25:32-46
- Glorify believers ... Col. 3:4
- Reward God's people ... Matt. 16:27

C. *Time of:*
- Unknown to us ... Matt. 24:27, 36
- After the Gospel's proclamation to all ... Matt. 24:14
- After the rise of antichrist ... 2 Thess. 2:2, 3
- At the last trump ... 1 Cor. 15:51, 52
- In days like Noah's ... Matt. 24:37-47

D. *Manner of:*
- In the clouds ... Matt. 24:30
- In flaming fire ... 2 Thess. 1:7, 8
- With the angels ... Matt. 25:31
- As a thief ... 1 Thess. 5:2, 3
- In His glory ... Matt. 25:31

E. *Believer's attitude toward, to:*
- Wait for ... 1 Cor. 1:7
- Look for ... Titus 2:13
- Be ready for ... Matt. 24:42-51
- Love ... 2 Tim. 4:8
- Be busy until ... Luke 19:13-18
- Pray for ... Rev. 22:20

Secret disciples
- Among Jewish leaders ... John 12:42
- Fearful of Jewish disfavor ... John 19:38

Secret prayer
- Commended by Christ ... Matt. 6:6
- Practiced by:
  - Christ ... Mark 1:35
  - Peter ... Acts 10:9

Secret things
- Known by God ... Deut. 29:29
- See Mystery

Secrets—*things unknown to others*
- To be kept ... Prov. 25:9
- Sign of faithfulness ... Prov. 11:13
- To those who expose, condemned ... Prov. 20:19

Sects of Christ's time
- Pharisees ... Acts 15:5
- Sadducees ... Acts 5:17
- Herodians ... Matt. 22:16
- Christians described as ... Acts 24:5

Secundus—*second*
- Thessalonian Christian ... Acts 20:4

Security of the saints

A. *Expressed by:*
- "Shall never perish" ... John 10:28
- "None of them is lost" ... John 17:12
- "Protected by the power of God" ... 1 Pet. 1:5

B. *Guaranteed by:*
- Spirit's sealing ... 2 Cor. 1:21, 22

SUBJECT — REFERENCE

Christ's intercession ... Rom. 8:34-39
God's power ... Jude 24

See Assurance

Sedition—*attack upon an established government*

Miriam and Aaron, against Moses ... Num. 12:1-13

Seducers—*those who lead others astray*

A. *Agents of:*
- Evil spirits ... 1 Tim. 4:1
- False teachers ... Mark 13:22
- Evil leaders ... 2 Kin. 21:9

B. *Characteristics of:*
- Grow worse ... 2 Tim. 3:13
- Self-deceived ... Prov. 12:26
- Lead to evil ... Rev. 2:20
- Preach false message ... Ezek. 13:9, 10

Seed—*the essential element of transmitting life*

A. *Descriptive of:*
- One's ancestry ... Gen. 12:7
- Messianic line ... Gen. 21:12
- Nation ... 2 Kin. 17:20
- Christ ... Gal. 3:16, 19

B. *Figurative of true believers:*
- Born of God ... 1 Pet. 1:23
- Abraham's true children ... Gal. 3:29
- Children of promise ... Rom. 9:7, 8
- Including Israel's faithful ... Rom. 9:29

C. *Sowing of, figurative of:*
- God's Word ... Matt. 13:3, 32
- Spiritual blessings ... 1 Cor. 9:11
- Christ's death ... John 12:24
- Christian's body ... 1 Cor. 15:36-49

Seeking—*trying to obtain*

A. *Things of the world:*
- Worldly things ... Matt. 6:32
- One's life ... Luke 17:33
- One's selfish interest ... Phil. 2:21

B. *Things of the Spirit:*
- True wisdom ... Prov. 2:4
- God's kingdom ... Matt. 6:33
- Another's benefit ... 2 Cor. 12:14
- Peace ... 1 Pet. 3:11
- Heavenly country ... Heb. 11:14

Seers—*prophets*

- Amos ... Amos 7:12
- Asaph ... 2 Chr. 29:30
- Gad ... 2 Sam. 24:11
- Heman ... 1 Chr. 25:5
- Samuel ... 1 Sam. 9:19
- Zadok ... 2 Sam. 15:27
- Iddo ... 2 Chr. 9:29
- Hanani ... 2 Chr. 16:7
- Jeduthun ... 2 Chr. 35:15

Segub—*exalted*

1. Son of Hiel ... 1 Kin. 16:34
2. Son of Hezron ... 1 Chr. 2:21, 22

Seir—*hairy; shaggy*

1. Mt. Seir ... Gen. 14:6
   - Home of Esau ... Gen. 32:3
   - Mountain range of Edom ... Gen. 36:21
   - Horites dispossessed by Esau's descendants ... Deut. 2:12
   - Refuge of Amalekite remnant ... 1 Chr. 4:42, 43
   - Desolation of ... Ezek. 35:15
2. Landmark on Judah's boundary ... Josh. 15:10

Seirath—*rough*

Ehud's refuge ... Judg. 3:26

Seize—*to take or keep fast, hold*

- Let darkness ... Job 3:6
- Let us kill him and ... Matt. 21:38

Selah

- Place in Edom ... 2 Kin. 14:7
- Musical term found in Psalms ... Ps. 3:2
- Found in ... Hab. 3:3, 9, 13

Sela-hammah-lekoth—*rock of divisions*

Cliff on the Wilderness of Maon ... 1 Sam. 23:28

SUBJECT — REFERENCE

Seled—*exultation*

Judahite ... 1 Chr. 2:30

Seleucia—*a city on the seacoast of Syria*

Paul and Barnabas embark from ... Acts 13:4

Self-abasement

- Jacob, before Esau ... Gen. 33:3-10
- Moses, before God ... Ex. 3:11
- Roman, before Christ ... Luke 7:7-9
- Christ, true example of ... Phil. 2:5-8

Self-acceptance—*having the proper attitude toward oneself*

A. *Based on, by Christians:*
- Planned before birth by God ... Ps. 139:13-16
- Workmanship of God ... Ps. 138:8; Eph. 2:10
- Christ has provided life ... John 10:10
- God desires man's fellowship ... John 17:3
- God's love ... Rom. 5:8
- Living epistle of God ... 2 Cor. 3:2
- Complete in Christ ... Col. 2:10
- Chosen by God ... 1 Pet. 2:9

B. *Hindered by, false attitudes:*
- Looking on outward appearance ... 1 Sam. 16:7
- Questioning God's direction ... Is. 45:9
- Doubting God's grace ... 2 Cor. 12:9, 10

Self-condemnation

Caused by one's:
- Heart ... 1 John 3:20
- Conscience ... John 8:7-9
- Sins ... 2 Sam. 24:17
- Mouth ... Job 9:20
- Evil works ... Matt. 23:31

Self-control

A. *Origin of:*
- Brought about by Christ ... Luke 8:35
- Christian grace ... 2 Pet. 1:6

B. *Elements involved in:*
- Ruling one's spirit ... Prov. 16:32
- Soberness ... Rom. 12:3
- Control of the body ... 1 Cor. 9:27

C. *Hindered by:*
- Fleshly lusts ... 1 Pet. 2:11
- Tongue ... Ps. 39:1, 2
- Drink ... Prov. 23:29-35
- Sexual sins ... 1 Thess. 4:3, 4
- Unclean spirit ... Mark 5:2-16
- Self-expressionism ... Prov. 25:28

Self-deception

A. *Factors contributing to:*
- Scoffers ... 2 Pet. 3:3, 4
- Worldliness ... Matt. 24:48-51
- False teaching ... 1 Thess. 5:3
- Self-deception ... Prov. 14:12

B. *Examples of:*
- Babylon ... Is. 47:7-11
- Jewish women ... Jer. 44:16-19
- Jewish leaders ... John 8:33, 41

Self-denial

A. *Expressed by:*
- "Denying" ... Titus 2:12
- "Abstaining" ... 1 Pet. 4:2
- "Forsaketh not" ... Luke 14:33
- "Taking up the cross" ... Matt. 10:38
- "Crucifying the flesh" ... Gal. 5:24
- "Put off" ... Eph. 4:22
- "Mortify" ... Col. 3:5

B. *Objects of:*
- Appetite ... Prov. 23:2
- Sinful pleasures ... Heb. 11:25, 26
- Worldly ambitions ... Matt. 16:24-26

C. *Willingness to, manifested by:*
- Judah ... Gen. 44:33
- Moses ... Ex. 32:32
- Paul ... Acts 20:22-24

D. *Commended as:*
- Christian duty ... Rom. 12:1, 2
- Rewardable ... Luke 18:28-30

SUBJECT — REFERENCE

Self-exaltation

A. *Manifested by:*
- Satan ... Is. 14:12-15
- Antichrist ... 2 Thess. 2:4
- Wicked ... Ps. 73:9

B. *Evils of, seen in:*
- Self-abasement ... Matt. 23:12
- Pride ... Prov. 16:18

C. *Antidotes of:*
- Humility ... Prov. 15:33
- Christ's example ... Phil. 2:5-8

See Pride

Self-examination

A. *Purposes of, to:*
- Test one's faith ... 2 Cor. 13:5
- Prepare for the Lord's Supper ... 1 Cor. 11:28-32
- Prove one's work ... Gal. 6:4
- Prove all things ... 1 Thess. 5:21

B. *Means of:*
- God Himself ... Ps. 26:2
- God's Word ... Heb. 4:12
- Christ's example ... Heb. 12:1, 2

Selfishness—*loving one's self first*

A. *Exemplified in:*
- Self-love ... 2 Tim. 3:2
- Self-seeking ... Phil. 2:21

B. *Avoidance of, by:*
- Seeking the good of others ... 1 Cor. 10:24
- Putting Christ first ... Phil. 1:21, 22
- Manifesting love ... 1 Cor. 13:5

C. *Examples of:*
- Nabal ... 1 Sam. 25:3, 11
- Haman ... Esth. 6:6
- James and John ... Mark 10:35-37
- Jewish people ... John 6:26
- Solomon ... Eccl. 2:10, 11
- Rich fool ... Luke 12:16-21
- Rich man ... Luke 16:19-25

D. *Consequences of:*
- Poverty ... Prov. 23:21
- Sin ... Rom. 13:13, 14
- Loss of spirituality ... Gal. 5:16, 17

Self-righteousness

A. *Described as:*
- Objectionable ... Deut. 9:4-6
- Self-condemned ... Job 9:20
- Unprofitable ... Is. 57:12
- Like filthy rags ... Is. 64:6
- Offensive ... Is. 65:5
- External ... Matt. 23:25-28
- One-sided ... Luke 11:42
- Boastful ... Luke 18:11, 12
- Insufficient ... Phil. 3:4-9

B. *Condemned because it:*
- Cannot make pure ... Prov. 30:12
- Cannot save ... Matt. 5:20
- Rejects God's righteousness ... Rom. 10:3

C. *Examples of:*
- Saul ... 1 Sam. 15:13-21
- Young man ... Matt. 19:16-20
- Lawyer ... Luke 10:25, 29
- Pharisees ... Luke 11:39

Self-will—*stubbornness*

A. *Manifested in:*
- Presumption ... Num. 14:40-45
- Unbelief ... 2 Kin. 17:14
- Evil heart ... Jer. 7:24
- Disobeying parents ... Deut. 21:18-20
- Pride ... Neh. 9:16, 29
- Stubbornness ... Is. 48:4-8
- Rejecting God's messengers ... Jer. 44:16
- Resisting God's Spirit ... Acts 7:51
- False teaching ... 2 Pet. 2:10

B. *Sin of, among Christians:*
- Illustrated ... Acts 15:36-40
- Warned against ... Heb. 3:7-12

C. *Examples of:*
- Simeon and Levi ... Gen. 49:5, 6
- Israelites ... Ex. 32:9

S

SUBJECT REFERENCE

Saul ....1 Sam. 15:19-23
David ....2 Sam. 24:4

See Pride

Sem—*Greek form of Shem*
In Christ's ancestry ....Luke 3:36

Semachiah—*Jehovah supports*
Levite porter ....1 Chr. 26:7

Semei—*Greek form of Shimei*
In Christ's ancestry ....Luke 3:26

Senaah—*thorny*
Family of returnees ....Neh. 7:38
Ezra 2:35

Senate—*the Jewish Sanhedrin*
Disturbed by miracle ....Acts 5:18-21

Senators—*old men*
Instructed by Joseph ....Ps. 105:17-23

Seneh—*thorn bush*
Sharp rock between Michmash and Gibeah ....1 Sam. 14:4, 5

Senir, Shenir—*mount of light*
Amorite name of Mt. Hermon ..Deut. 3:9
Noted for firs ....Ezek. 27:5

Sennacherib—*Sin* (moon-god) *multiplied brothers*
Assyrian king (705–681 B.C.); son and successor of Sargon II ....2 Kin. 18:13
Death of, by assassination ....2 Kin. 19:37

Senses—*the faculties of feeling*
Described figuratively ....Eccl. 12:3-6
Used by Isaac ....Gen. 27:21-27
Impaired in Barzillai ....2 Sam. 19:32-35
Use of, as evidence ....John 20:26-29
Proper use of ....Heb. 5:14

Senses, spiritual
Taste ....Ps. 34:8
Sight ....Eph. 1:18
Hearing ....Gal. 3:2

Sensual—*fleshly*
Descriptive of:
Unregenerate ....Jude 19
Worldly wisdom ....James 3:15
Same as "natural" ....1 Cor. 2:14
Rebellious against God ....Rom. 8:7

Sensualist—*one who satisfies the physical senses*
Illustrated by:
Nabal ....1 Sam. 25:36
Rich fool ....Luke 12:16-20

Seorim—*barley*
Name of a priestly course ....1 Chr. 24:1-8

Separate place—*the Temple yard*
Of Ezekiel's Temple ....Ezek. 41:12

Separation—*setting apart from something*
A. *As a good act from:*
Unclean ....Lev. 15:31
Evil workers ....Num. 16:21
Heathen filthiness ....Ezra 6:21
Pagan intermarriages ....Ezra 9:1, 2
Foreigners ....Neh. 13:3
Strong drink ....Num. 6:2-6
B. *As an evil act by:*
False teachers ....Luke 6:22
Separatists ....Jude 19
Whisperers ....Prov. 16:28
Gossipers ....Prov. 17:9
C. *As descriptive of:*
God's judgment ....Deut. 29:21
God's sovereignty ....Deut. 32:8
Israel's uniqueness ....Lev. 20:24
Choice of the Levites ....Num. 8:14
Nazarite vow ....Num. 6:2-6
Christian obedience ....2 Cor. 6:17
Union with Christ ....Rom. 8:35, 39
Christ's purity ....Heb. 7:26
Final separation ....Matt. 25:32

Sephar—*numbering*
Place on Joktan's boundary ....Gen. 10:30

Sepharad
Place inhabited by exiles ....Obad. 20

SUBJECT REFERENCE

Sepharvaim—*an Assyrian city*
People of, sent to Samaria ....2 Kin. 17:24, 31

Sepulcher—*a place of burial*
A. *Used literally of:*
Place of burial ....Gen. 23:6
Christ's grave ....John 19:41, 42
B. *Used figuratively of:*
Hypocrisy ....Matt. 23:27

Serah—*abundance*
Daughter of Asher ....Gen. 46:17

Seraiah—*Jehovah has prevailed*
Called Sarah ....Num. 26:46
1. David's secretary ....2 Sam. 8:17
Called Sheva, Shisha, and Shavsha ....2 Sam. 20:25; 1 Kin. 4:3; 1 Chr. 18:16
2. Son of Tanhumeth ....2 Kin. 25:23
3. Son of Kenaz ....1 Chr. 4:13, 14
4. Simeonite ....1 Chr. 4:35
5. Chief priest ....Jer. 52:24, 27
6. Postexilic leader ....Neh. 12:1, 12
7. Signer of the covenant ....Neh. 10:2
8. Postexilic priest ....Neh. 11:11
9. Officer of King Jehoiakim ....Jer. 36:26
11. Prince of Judah; carries Jeremiah's prophecy to Babylon ....Jer. 51:59, 61

Seraphim—*burning ones*
Type of angels ....Is. 6:1, 2

Sered—*deliverance*
Son of Zebulun; founder of Sardites ....Gen. 46:14

Sergius Paulus
Roman proconsul of Cyprus converted by Paul ....Acts 13:7-12

Sermon—*a discourse on a Bible subject*
A prolonged message ....Acts 20:7

Sermon on the Mount
Preached by Christ ....Matt. 5—7
Those blessed ....Matt. 5:3-12
Salt and light ....Matt. 5:13-16
The law fulfilled ....Matt. 5:17-20
On anger ....Matt. 5:21-26
On adultery and divorce ....Matt. 5:27-32
Oaths ....Matt. 5:33-37
Love your enemies ....Matt. 5:38-48
The religious life ....Matt. 6:1-4
Matt. 6:5-15
How to pray ....Matt. 6:16-18
Undivided devotion ....Matt. 6:19-34
Judging others ....Matt. 7:1-6
Encouragement to pray ....Matt. 7:7-12
Entering the kingdom ....Matt. 7:13-23
Two foundations ....Matt. 7:24-27

Serpents
A. *Characteristics of:*
Created by God ....Job 26:13
Subtle ....Gen. 3:1
Some poisonous ....Num. 21:6
Live on rocks, walls, etc. ....Prov. 30:19
Cursed by God ....Gen. 3:14, 15
B. *Miracles connected with:*
Aaron's rod turned into ....Ex. 7:9, 15
Israelites cured by looking at ....Num. 21:6-9; John 3:14, 15
Power over, given to apostles ....Mark 16:18
Healing from bite of ....Acts 28:5, 6
C. *Figurative of:*
Intoxication ....Prov. 23:31, 32
Wisdom ....Matt. 10:16
Malice ....Ps. 58:4
Unexpected evil ....Eccl. 10:8
Enemies ....Is. 14:29
Christ ....John 3:14-16
Satan ....Rev. 20:2
Dan's treachery ....Gen. 49:17
Sting of wine ....Prov. 23:31, 32
Wickedness of sinners ....Ps. 58:3, 4

Serug—*branch*
Descendant of Shem ....Gen. 11:20-23
In Christ's ancestry ....Luke 3:35

SUBJECT REFERENCE

Servant—*one who serves others*
A. *Descriptive of:*
Slave ....Gen. 9:25
Social inferior ....Gen. 19:2
Worshiper of God ....1 Sam. 3:9
Messenger of God ....Josh. 1:2
Messiah ....Is. 42:1
Follower of Christ ....2 Tim. 2:24
B. *Applied distinctively to:*
Prophets ....Zech. 1:6
Messiah ....Zech. 3:8
Moses ....Mal. 4:4
Christians ....Acts 2:18
Glorified saints ....Rev. 22:3

See Slave

Service to God
A. *Requirements of:*
Fear ....Ps. 2:11
Upright walking ....Ps. 101:6
Absolute loyalty ....Matt. 6:24
Regeneration ....Rom. 7:6
Serve the Lord ....Rom. 12:11
Humility ....Acts 20:19
Love ....Gal. 5:13
B. *Rewards of:*
Divine honor ....John 12:26
Acceptance before God ....Rom. 14:18
Inheritance ....Col. 3:24
Eternal blessedness ....Rev. 7:15
Rev. 22:3

Seth—*appointed*
Third son of Adam ....Gen. 4:25
In Christ's ancestry ....Luke 3:38

Sethur—*hidden*
Asherite spy ....Num. 13:2, 13

Setting—*woven together*
For precious stones worn by the high priest ....Ex. 28:11
Corded chains on filigree ....Ex. 28:13, 14
Same Hebrew word translated "interwoven" ....Ps. 45:13

Seven—*one more than six*
A. *Of social customs:*
Serving for a wife ....Gen. 29:20, 27
Bowing ....Gen. 33:3
Mourning ....Gen. 50:10
Feast ....Judg. 14:12, 17
Fasting ....1 Sam. 31:13
B. *Of things:*
Days ....Gen. 2:3
Weeks ....Dan. 9:25
Months ....Lev. 23:24-44
Years ....Gen. 41:1-57
Nations ....Deut. 7:1
Ways ....Deut. 28:7
Women ....Is. 4:1
Brethren ....Mark 12:20-22
Spirits ....Matt. 12:45
Men ....Acts 6:3-5
Churches ....Rev. 1:4, 20
C. *Of rituals:*
Victims of sacrifices ....Lev. 23:18
Sprinkling of blood ....Lev. 4:6
Sprinkling of oil ....Lev. 14:16
Passover ....Ex. 12:15
Consecration ....Ex. 29:30, 35
Defilement ....Lev. 12:2
Convocation ....Lev. 23:24-44
Jubilee ....Lev. 25:8
D. *Miracles:*
Plagues ....Ex. 7:25
Jericho's fall ....Josh. 6:4, 8, 13
Naaman's baths ....2 Kin. 5:10
Loaves ....Matt. 15:34
Baskets ....Matt. 15:37
E. *Of symbols:*
Purification ....Ps. 12:6
Worship ....Ps. 119:164
Gospel light ....Is. 30:26
Spirits ....Rev. 1:4
Seals ....Rev. 5:1
Angels ....Rev. 8:2
Heads and crowns ....Rev. 13:1
Plagues ....Rev. 15:6
Vials ....Rev. 15:7
Kings ....Rev. 17:10

SUBJECT REFERENCE

Seven sayings from the cross
1. "Father, forgive them" ...... Luke 23:34
2. "Today shalt thou be with me in paradise" ...... Luke 23:43
3. "Woman, behold thy son" ... John 19:26
4. "My God, my God" .... Matt. 27:46
5. "I thirst" ...... John 19:28
6. "It is finished" ...... John 19:30
7. "Father, into thy hands" .... Luke 23:46

Seventy
Elders appointed ...... Ex. 24:1, 9
Years in Babylon ...... Dan. 9:2
Weeks in prophetic vision ...... Dan. 9:24
In forgiveness ...... Matt. 18:22
Disciples sent forth ...... Luke 10:1

Sexes—*male and female*
A. *Creation of:*
By God ...... Gen. 1:27
For:
Union ...... Gen. 2:23-25
Helpfulness ...... Gen. 2:18
Procreation ...... Gen. 4:1
Sexual needs ...... Prov. 5:17-19
B. *Regulations concerning:*
Distinctive clothing for ...... Deut. 22:5
Subordination of ...... 1 Cor. 11:3-16
Equality in Christ ...... Gal. 3:28
Different functions of ...... 1 Tim. 2:8-15
Love between ...... Eph. 5:22-33

Sexual love
Good and holy ...... Gen. 1:27, 28
Gen. 2:24, 25
For procreation ...... Gen. 4:1
In marriage only ...... Prov. 5:15-20
Expression of love ...... Song 1:12-15
Song 3:1-5
Mutual responsibility ...... 1 Cor. 7:3-5

Sexual perversion
A. *Types of:*
Adultery ...... Deut. 22:22-29
Prostitution ...... Deut. 23:17
Incest ...... Lev. 18:6-18
Homosexuality ...... Rom. 1:26, 27
Mankind with beasts ...... Deut. 27:21
B. *Judgment upon:*
Defilement ...... Lev. 18:22-28
Destruction ...... 1 Cor. 5:1-5
Death ...... Lev. 20:13-16

Shaalbim, Shaalabbin—*jackals*
Amorite city assigned to Danites ...... Josh. 19:42
Subdued by house of Joseph .... Judg. 1:35

Shaalbonite—*an inhabitant of Shaalbim*
Eliahba called ...... 2 Sam. 23:32

Shaaph—*friendship*
1. Descendant of Caleb ...... 1 Chr. 2:47
2. Son of Caleb ...... 1 Chr. 2:49

Shaaraim—*double gate*
1. Village in Judah ...... Josh. 15:36
2. City of Simeon ...... 1 Chr. 4:31

Shaashgaz
Persian eunuch ...... Esth. 2:14

Shabbethai—*Sabbath-born*
Postexilic Levite ...... Ezra 10:15
Interprets the law ...... Neh. 8:7, 8

Shachia—*fame of Jehovah*
Benjamite ...... 1 Chr. 8:10

Shadow
A. *Used literally of:*
Man ...... Acts 5:15
Mountain ...... Judg. 9:36
Sundial ...... 2 Kin. 20:9-11
B. *Used figuratively of:*
Protection ...... Ps. 91:1
Brevity ...... Ps. 102:11
Change ...... James 1:17
Death ...... Matt. 4:16
Types ...... Col. 2:17
Old Testament period ...... Heb. 10:1

SUBJECT REFERENCE

Shadrach
Hananiah's Babylonian name ... Dan. 1:3, 7
Cast into the fiery furnace ...... Dan. 3:1-28

Shage—*wandering*
Father of one of David's mighty men ...... 1 Chr. 11:34

Shaharaim—*double dawn*
Benjamite ...... 1 Chr. 8:8-11

Shahazimah—*heights*
Town of Issachar ...... Josh. 19:17, 22

Shake—*to move violently*
A. *Descriptive of:*
Thunder ...... Ps. 77:18
Earthquakes ...... Acts 4:31
Fear ...... Matt. 28:4
B. *Used figuratively of:*
Fear ...... Is. 14:16
Second Advent ...... Heb. 12:26, 27
Rejection ...... Luke 9:5
Acts 18:6

Shalem—*safe*
Town near Shechem; can mean "in peace" ...... Gen. 33:18

Shalim—*district of foxes*
Mentioned in Saul's pursuit ..... 1 Sam. 9:4

Shalisha—*a third part*
Mentioned in Saul's pursuit ..... 1 Sam. 9:4

Shallecheth—*a casting out*
Gate of Solomon's temple ...... 1 Chr. 26:16

Shallum—*recompense*
1. King of Israel ...... 2 Kin. 15:10-15
2. Husband of Huldah ...... 2 Kin. 22:14
3. Judahite ...... 1 Chr. 2:40, 41
4. Simeonite ...... 1 Chr. 4:25
5. Father of Hilkiah ...... 1 Chr. 6:12, 13
6. Naphtali's son ...... 1 Chr. 7:13
7. Family of porters ...... Ezra 2:42
8. Called Shelemiah ...... 1 Chr. 26:14
9. Father of Jehizkiah ...... 2 Chr. 28:12
10. One who divorced his foreign wife ...... Ezra 10:24
11. Another who divorced his foreign wife ...... Ezra 10:42
12. Son of Hallohesh ...... Neh. 3:12
13. Jeremiah's uncle ...... Jer. 32:7
14. Father of Maaseiah ...... Jer. 35:4

Shalmai—*Jehovah is recompenser*
Head of a family of Nethinim ... Ezra 2:46

Shalman
Contraction of Shalmaneser ..... Hos. 10:14

Shalmaneser—*Shulmanu* (a god) *is chief*
Assyrian king ...... 2 Kin. 17:3

Shama—*He* (God) *has heard*
Son of Hotham ...... 1 Chr. 11:44

Shamariah—*Jehovah has kept*
Son of Rehoboam ...... 2 Chr. 11:18, 19

Shamble—*meat market*
Question concerning meat bought in ...... 1 Cor. 10:25

Shame—*a feeling of guilt*
A. *Caused by:*
Rape ...... 2 Sam. 13:13
Defeat ...... 2 Chr. 32:21
Folly ...... Prov. 3:35
Idleness ...... Prov. 10:5
Pride ...... Prov. 11:2
A wicked wife ...... Prov. 12:4
Lying ...... Prov. 13:5
Stubbornness ...... Prov. 13:18
Haste in speech ...... Prov. 18:13
Mistreatment of parents ..... Prov. 19:26
Evil companions ...... Prov. 28:7
Juvenile delinquency ...... Prov. 29:15
Nakedness ...... Is. 47:3
Idolatry ...... Jer. 2:26, 27

SUBJECT REFERENCE

Impropriety ...... 1 Cor. 11:6
Lust ...... Phil. 3:19
B. *Of the unregenerate:*
Hardened in ...... Jer. 8:12
Pleasure in ...... Rom. 1:26, 27, 32
Vessels of ...... Rom. 9:21
Glory in ...... Phil. 3:19
Like foam ...... Jude 13
C. *In the Christian life, of:*
Unregenerate's life ...... Rom. 6:21
Sinful things ...... Eph. 5:12
Improper behavior ...... 1 Cor. 11:14, 22
Christ ...... Rom. 1:16

Shamed—*destruction*
Son of Elpaal ...... 1 Chr. 8:12

Shamer—*guard*
1. Levite ...... 1 Chr. 6:46
2. Asherite ...... 1 Chr. 7:30, 34

Shamgar—*cupbearer*
Judge of Israel; struck down 600 Philistines ...... Judg. 3:31

Shamhuth—*desolation*
Commander in David's army.... 1 Chr. 27:8

Shamir—*a sharp point*
1. Town in Judah ...... Josh. 15:1, 48
2. Town in Ephraim ...... Judg. 10:1
3. Levite ...... 1 Chr. 24:24

Shamma—*astonishment*
Asherite ...... 1 Chr. 7:36, 37

Shammah—*waste*
1. Son of Reuel ...... Gen. 36:13, 17
2. Son of Jesse ...... 1 Sam. 16:9
Called Shimea ...... 1 Chr. 2:13
3. One of David's mighty men ...... 2 Sam. 23:11
Also called Shammoth the Harorite ...... 1 Chr. 11:27

Shammai—*celebrated*
1. Grandson of Jerahmeel ...... 1 Chr. 2:28, 32
2. Descendant of Caleb ...... 1 Chr. 2:44, 45
3. Descendant of Judah ...... 1 Chr. 4:17

Shammoth—*waste*
One of David's mighty men ..... 1 Chr. 11:27

Shammua—*renowned*
1. Reubenite spy ...... Num. 13:2-4
2. Son of David ...... 2 Sam. 5:13, 14
3. Levite ...... Neh. 11:17
4. Postexilic priest ...... Neh. 12:1, 18

Shamsherai—*sunlike*
Son of Jeroham ...... 1 Chr. 8:26

Shapham—*youthful*
Gadite ...... 1 Chr. 5:12

Shaphan—*prudent, shy*
Scribe under Josiah ...... 2 Kin. 22:3
Takes Book of the Law to Josiah ...... 2 Kin. 22:8-10
Is sent to Huldah for interpretation ...... 2 Kin. 22:14
Assists in repairs of temple ..... 2 Chr. 34:8
Father of notable son ...... Jer. 36:10-12, 25

Shaphat—*he has judged*
1. Simeonite spy ...... Num. 13:2-5
2. Son of Shemaiah ...... 1 Chr. 3:22
3. Gadite chief ...... 1 Chr. 5:11, 12
4. One of David's herdsmen .... 1 Chr. 27:29
5. Father of the prophet Elisha ...... 1 Kin. 19:16, 19

Shapher—*beauty*
Israelite encampment ...... Num. 33:23

Sharai—*Jehovah is deliverer*
Divorced his foreign wife ...... Ezra 10:34, 40

Sharar—*firm*
Father of Ahiam ...... 2 Sam. 23:33

SUBJECT REFERENCE

Sharers

A. *Of physical things:*

Sacrifices .... 1 Cor. 10:18
Suffering .... 2 Cor. 1:7
1 Pet. 4:13

B. *Of evil things:*

Sins .... 1 Tim. 5:22

C. *Of spiritual things:*

Holiness .... Heb. 12:10
Communion .... 1 Cor. 10:16, 17
Spiritual things .... Rom. 15:27
Inheritance .... Col. 1:12

Sharezer, Sherezer—*protect the king*

1. Son of Sennacherib .... Is. 37:38
2. Sent to Zechariah concerning fasting .... Zech. 7:1-3

Sharon—*plain*

1. Coastal plain between Joppa and Mt. Carmel .... 1 Chr. 27:29
Famed for roses .... Song 2:1
2. Pasture east of the Jordan .... 1 Chr. 5:16

Sharonite—*an inhabitant of Sharon*

Shitrai .... 1 Chr. 27:29

Sharp—*having a keen edge; biting*

A. *Descriptive of:*

Stone .... Ex. 4:25
Knives .... Josh. 5:2, 3
Share .... 1 Sam. 13:20, 21
Rocks .... 1 Sam. 14:4
Arrows .... Is. 5:28

B. *Used to compare a sword with:*

Tongue .... Ps. 57:4
Adulteress .... Prov. 5:4
Mouth .... Is. 49:2
God's Word .... Heb. 4:12

C. *Figurative of:*

Deceitfulness .... Ps. 52:2
Falsehood .... Prov. 25:18
Contention .... Acts 15:39
Severe rebuke .... 2 Cor. 13:10
Christ's conquest .... Rev. 14:14-18

Sharuhen—*abode of pleasure*

Town of Judah assigned to Simeon .... Josh. 19:1, 6
Called Shaaraim .... Josh. 15:36
1 Chr. 4:31

Shashai—*whitish*

Divorced his foreign wife .... Ezra 10:34, 40

Shashak—*assaulter*

Benjamite .... 1 Chr. 8:14, 25

Shaul—*asked* (of God)

1. King of Edom .... Gen. 36:37
2. Son of Simeon .... Gen. 46:10
Founder of a tribal family .... Num. 26:13
3. Kohathite Levite .... 1 Chr. 6:24

Shave—*to cut off the hair*

A. *Used worthily to express:*

Accommodation .... Gen. 41:14
Cleansing .... Lev. 14:8, 9
Commitment .... Deut. 21:12
Mourning .... Job 1:18-20
Sorrow .... Jer. 41:5

B. *Used unworthily to express:*

Defeat of a Nazarite .... Judg. 16:19
Contempt .... 2 Sam. 10:4
Unnaturalness .... 1 Cor. 11:5, 6

Shaveh—*plain*

Valley near Salem; Abram meets king of Sodom here .... Gen. 14:17, 18

Shaveh-kiriathaim—*plain of Kiriathaim*

Plain near Kiriathaim inhabited by Emim .... Gen. 14:5

Shavsha, Shisha—*nobility*

David's secretary .... 1 Chr. 18:14, 16
Serves under Solomon also .... 1 Kin. 4:3

Sheal—*asking*

Divorced his foreign wife .... Ezra 10:29

SUBJECT REFERENCE

Shealtiel—*I have asked God*

Son of King Jeconiah and father of Zerubbabel .... 1 Chr. 3:17

Sheariah—*Jehovah has esteemed*

Descendant of Saul .... 1 Chr. 9:44

Shear-jashub—*a remnant shall return*

Symbolic name given to Isaiah's son .... Is. 7:3

Sheba—*seven; an oath*

1. City in territory assigned to Simeon .... Josh. 19:1, 2
2. Benjamite insurrectionist .... 2 Sam. 20:1-22
3. Descendant of Cush through Raamah .... Gen. 10:7
4. Descendant of Shem .... Gen. 10:28
5. Grandson of Abraham and Keturah .... Gen. 25:3
6. Gadite chief .... 1 Chr. 5:13
7. Land of, occupied by Sabeans, famous traders .... Job 1:15; Ps. 72:10
Queen of, visits Solomon; marvels at his wisdom .... 1 Kin. 10:1-13
Mentioned by Christ .... Matt. 12:42

Shebah—*seven; an oath*

Name given to a well and town (Beer-sheba) .... Gen. 26:31-33

Shebaniah—*Jehovah has returned me*

1. Levite trumpeter .... 1 Chr. 15:24
2. Levite; offers prayer and signs covenant .... Neh. 9:4, 5
3. Levite who signs covenant .... Neh. 10:12
4. Priest who signs covenant .... Neh. 10:4

Shebarim—*breakings*

Place near Ai .... Josh. 7:5
See Quarry

Sheber—*breaking*

Son of Caleb .... 1 Chr. 2:48

Shebna—*perhaps an abbreviation of Shebaniah*

Treasurer under Hezekiah .... Is. 22:15
Demoted to position of scribe .... 2 Kin. 19:2
Man of pride and luxury; replaced by Eliakim .... Is. 22:19-21

Shebuel—*God is renown*

1. Son of Gershom .... 1 Chr. 23:16
2. Son of Heman .... 1 Chr. 25:4

Shecaniah—*Jehovah has dwelt*

1. Descendant of Zerubbabel .... 1 Chr. 3:21, 22
2. Postexilic returnee .... Ezra 8:5
3. Descendant of Aaron .... 1 Chr. 24:11
4. Priest .... 2 Chr. 31:15
5. Divorced his foreign wife .... Ezra 10:2, 3
6. Father of Shemaiah .... Neh. 3:29
(Probably same as 1)
7. Postexilic priest .... Neh. 12:3, 7
8. Father-in-law of Tobiah .... Neh. 6:18

Shechem—*shoulder*

1. Son of Hamor; seduces Dinah, Jacob's daughter .... Gen. 34:1-31
2. Son of Gilead; founder of a tribal family .... Num. 26:31
3. Son of Shemida .... 1 Chr. 7:19
4. Ancient city of Ephraim .... Gen. 33:18
Abram camps near .... Gen. 12:6
Jacob buys ground here .... Gen. 33:18, 19
Hivites, inhabit .... Gen. 34:2
Inhabitants of, slaughtered by Simeon and Levi .... Gen. 34:25-29
Pastures near .... Gen. 37:12, 13
Becomes city of refuge .... Josh. 20:7
Joseph buried here .... Josh. 24:32
Joshua's farewell address here .... Josh. 24:1, 25
Center of idol-worship .... Judg. 9:1, 4-7
Town destroyed .... Judg. 9:23, 45
Jeroboam made king here .... 1 Kin. 12:1-19
Name of, used poetically .... Ps. 108:7

Shed—*to pour out*

A. *Descriptive of:*

Blood .... Gen. 9:6
Bowels .... 2 Sam. 20:10
Holy Spirit .... Titus 3:6

B. *As applied to blood, indicative of:*

Justifiable execution .... Gen. 9:6
Unjustifiable murder .... Gen. 37:22
Unacceptable sacrifice .... Lev. 17:1-5
Attempted vengeance .... 1 Sam. 25:31, 34
Unpardonable .... 2 Kin. 24:4
Abomination .... Prov. 6:16, 17
Heinous crime .... Is. 59:7
New covenant .... Matt. 26:28

Shedeur—*shedder of light*

Reubenite leader .... Num. 1:5

Sheep—*a domesticated animal*

A. *Characteristics of:*

Domesticated .... 2 Sam. 12:3
Gentle .... Jer. 11:19
Defenseless .... Mic. 5:8
Needful of care .... Ezek. 34:5

B. *Uses of, for:*

Food .... 1 Sam. 25:18
Milk .... 1 Cor. 9:7
Clothing .... Prov. 31:13
Coverings .... Ex. 26:14
Presents .... 2 Sam. 17:29
Tribute .... 2 Kin. 3:4
Sacrifice .... Gen. 4:4

C. *Uses of, in Levitical system as:*

Burnt offering .... Lev. 1:10
Sin offering .... Lev. 4:32
Guilt offering .... Lev. 5:15
Peace offering .... Lev. 22:21

D. *Needs of, for:*

Protection .... Job 30:1
Shepherd .... John 10:4, 27
Fold .... John 10:1
Pastures .... Ex. 3:1
Water .... Gen. 29:8-10
Rest .... Ps. 23:2
Shearing .... 1 Sam. 25:2, 11

E. *Figurative of:*

Innocent .... 2 Sam. 24:17
Wicked .... Ps. 49:14
Jewish people .... Ps. 74:1
Backsliders .... Jer. 50:6
Lost sinners .... Matt. 9:36
Christians .... John 10:1-16
Christ .... John 1:29
Saved .... Matt. 26:31-34
Church .... Acts 20:28

See Lamb; Lamb of God

Sheepcote—*an enclosure for sheep*

David chosen .... 2 Sam. 7:8

Sheepfold—*shelter*

Enclosure for flocks .... Num. 32:16
Entrance to, only by Christ .... John 10:1

Sheep Gate—*a gate of the restored Jerusalem*

Repaired .... Neh. 3:32
Dedicated .... Neh. 12:38, 39

Sheepmaster

Mesha, king of Moab .... 2 Kin. 3:4

Sheepshearers

Employed by Judah .... Gen. 38:12
Many employed by Nabal .... 1 Sam. 25:7, 11
Used figuratively .... Is. 53:7

Sheets

Large piece of cloth .... Acts 11:5

Shehariah—*Jehovah is the dawn*

Benjamite .... 1 Chr. 8:26

Shekel—*A Jewish measure (approximately .533 oz.)*

A. *As a weight:*

Standard of, defined .... Ex. 30:13
Used in weighing .... Josh. 7:21

See Weights

B. *As money:*

Used in currency .... 1 Sam. 9:8
Fines paid in .... Deut. 22:19, 29
Revenues of the sanctuary paid in .... Neh. 10:32

SUBJECT	REFERENCE
Shekinah—*a word expressing the glory and presence of God*	
A. *As indicative of God's presence:*	
In nature	Ps. 18:7-15
In the exodus from Egypt	Ex. 13:21, 22
At Sinai	Ex. 24:16-18
In tabernacle	Ex. 40:34-38
Upon the mercy seat	Ex. 25:22
In the wilderness	Num. 9:15-23 Num. 10:11-36
In the Temple	2 Chr. 7:1-3
B. *Illustrated by Christ in His:*	
Divine nature	Col. 2:9
Incarnation	Luke 1:35
Nativity	Luke 2:9
Manifestation to Israel	Hag. 2:9 Zech. 2:5
Transfiguration	2 Pet. 1:17
Ascension	Acts 1:9
Transforming us by His Spirit	2 Cor. 3:18 2 Cor. 4:6
Return	Matt. 24:44
Eternal habitation with saints	Rev. 21:3
C. *Accompanied by:*	
Angels	Is. 6:1-4
Cloud	Num. 9:15-23
Fire	Heb. 12:18-21
Earthquake	Hag. 2:21
Shelah—*sprout; request*	
1. Son of Arphaxad	1 Chr. 1:18
Called Salah	Luke 3:35
2. Son of Judah	Gen. 38:1-26
Founder of the Shelanites	Num. 26:20
Shelemiah—*friend of Jehovah*	
1. Father of Hananiah	Neh. 3:30
2. Postexilic priest	Neh. 13:13
3. Father of Irijah	Jer. 37:13
4. Porter	1 Chr. 26:14
Called Meshelemiah	1 Chr. 9:21
5. Ancestor of Jehudi	Jer. 36:14
6. Son of Abdeel	Jer. 36:26
7. Father of Jehucal	Jer. 37:3
Sheleph—*drawn out*	
Son of Joktan; head of a tribe	1 Chr. 1:20
Shelesh—*might*	
Asherite	1 Chr. 7:35
Shelomi—*at peace*	
Father of an Asherite prince	Num. 34:27
Shelomith, Shelomoth—*peaceful*	
1. Daughter of Dibri; her son executed	Lev. 24:10-23
2. Chief Levite of Moses	1 Chr. 23:18
3. Gershonites in David's time	1 Chr. 23:9
4. Descendant of Moses, had charge of treasures	1 Chr. 26:25
5. Son or daughter of King Rehoboam	2 Chr. 11:20
6. Daughter of Zerubbabel	1 Chr. 3:19
7. Family who went with Ezra	Ezra 8:10
Shelumiel—*at peace with God*	
Simeonite warrior	Num. 1:6
Shem—*name; renown*	
Oldest son of Noah	Gen. 5:32
Escapes the flood	Gen. 7:13
Receives a blessing	Gen. 9:23, 26
Ancestor of Semitic people	Gen. 10:22-32
Ancestor of:	
Abram	Gen. 11:10-26
Jesus	Luke 3:36
Shema—*report; rumor*	
1. Reubenite	1 Chr. 5:8
2. Benjamite head	1 Chr. 8:12, 13
3. Ezra's attendant	Neh. 8:4
4. City of Judah	Josh. 15:26
5. Son of Hebron	1 Chr. 2:43

SUBJECT	REFERENCE
Shemaah—*fame*	
Father of two of David's warriors	1 Chr. 12:3
Shemaiah—*Jehovah has heard*	
1. Father of Shimri	1 Chr. 4:37
2. Reubenite	1 Chr. 5:4
3. Levite who helped move the ark	1 Chr. 15:8, 12
4. Scribe in David's time	1 Chr. 24:6
5. Son of Obed-edom	1 Chr. 26:4, 6, 7
6. Prophet of Judah	1 Kin. 12:22-24
Explains Shishak's invasion as divine punishment	2 Chr. 12:5-8
Records Rehoboam's reign	2 Chr. 12:15
7. Levite teacher under Jehoshaphat	2 Chr. 17:8
8. Levite in Hezekiah's reign	2 Chr. 29:14, 15
9. Levite treasurer	2 Chr. 31:14, 15
10. Officer of Levites in Josiah's reign	2 Chr. 35:9
11. Father of Urijah	Jer. 26:20
12. False prophet	Jer. 29:24-28
13. Father of Delaiah	Jer. 36:12
14. Descendant of David	1 Chr. 3:22
15. Keeper of the East Gate for Nehemiah	Neh. 3:29
16. Merarite Levite living in Jerusalem	1 Chr. 9:14
17. Son of Adonikam	Ezra 8:13
18. Leading man under Ezra	Ezra 8:16
19. Priest who divorced his foreign wife	Ezra 10:21
20. Man who divorced his foreign wife	Ezra 10:31
21. Prophet hired by Sanballat	Neh. 6:10-14
22. Priest who signs covenant	Neh. 10:1,8
23. Participant in dedication service	Neh. 12:34
24. Postexilic priest	Neh. 12:35
25. Levite musician	Neh. 12:36
Shemariah—*Jehovah keeps*	
1. Mighty man of Benjamin	1 Chr. 12:5
2. Son of Rehoboam	2 Chr. 11:18, 19
3. Divorced his foreign wife	Ezra 10:31, 32
Shemeber—*splendor of heroism*	
King of Zeboiim	Gen. 14:2
Shemed—*destruction*	
Son of Elpaal	1 Chr. 8:12
Shemer—*guard*	
1. Sells Omri hill on which Samaria is built	1 Kin. 16:23, 24
2. Levite	1 Chr. 6:46
3. Asherite	1 Chr. 7:30, 34
Shemida, Shemidah—*fame of knowing*	
Descendant of Manasseh; founder of the Shemidaites	Num. 26:29, 32
Sheminith—*eighth*	
Musical term	1 Chr. 15:21
Shemiramoth—*fame of the highest*	
1. Levite musician in David's time	1 Chr. 15:18, 20
2. Levite teacher under Jehoshaphat	2 Chr. 17:8
Shemuel—*name of God*	
1. Grandson of Issachar	1 Chr. 7:1, 2
2. Another spelling of Samuel	1 Chr. 6:33
Shen—*tooth; a pointed rock*	
Rock west of Jerusalem	1 Sam. 7:12
Shenir (see Senir)	
Shenazar	
Son of Jeconiah	1 Chr. 3:18
Shepham—*nakedness*	
Place near the Sea of Galilee	Num. 34:11

SUBJECT	REFERENCE
Shephatiah—*Jehovah judges*	
1. Benjamite warrior	1 Chr. 12:5
2. Son of David	2 Sam. 3:4
3. Simeonite chief	1 Chr. 27:16
4. Son of King Jehoshaphat	2 Chr. 21:2
5. Opponent of Jeremiah	Jer. 38:1
6. Descendant of Judah	Neh. 11:4
7. Servant of Solomon whose descendants return from exile	Ezra 2:57
Shepherd—*one who cares for the sheep*	
A. *Duties of, toward his flock:*	
Defend	1 Sam. 17:34-36
Water	Gen. 29:2-10
Give rest to	Jer. 33:12
Know	John 10:3-5
Number	Jer. 33:13
Secure pasture for	1 Chr. 4:39-41
Search for the lost	Ezek. 34:12-16 Luke 15:4, 5
B. *Good, described as:*	
Faithful	Gen. 31:38-40
Fearless	1 Sam. 17:34-36
Unselfish	Luke 15:3-6
Considerate	Gen. 33:13, 14
Believing	Luke 2:8-20
C. *Bad, described as:*	
Unfaithful	Ezek. 34:1-10
Cowardly	John 10:12, 13
Selfish	Is. 56:11, 12
Ruthless	Ex. 2:17, 19
Unbelieving	Jer. 50:6
D. *Descriptive of:*	
God	Ps. 78:52, 53
Christ	Heb. 13:20
Joshua	Num. 27:16-23
David	2 Sam. 5:2
Judges	1 Chr. 17:6
National leaders	Jer. 49:19
Cyrus	Is. 44:28
Jewish leaders	Matt. 9:36
Church elders	1 Pet. 5:2
Shepherd, Jesus the good	
A. *Described prophetically in His:*	
Prophetic position (teaching)	Is. 40:10, 11
Priestly position (sacrifice)	Zech. 13:7 Matt. 26:31
Kingly position (ruling)	Ezek. 37:24 Matt. 2:6
B. *Described typically as:*	
Good	John 10:11, 14
Chief	1 Pet. 5:4
Great	Heb. 13:20
One	John 10:16
Gentle	Is. 40:11
One who separates	Matt. 25:31-46
Shepho—*unconcern*	
Son of Shobal	Gen. 36:23
Sherah—*blood-relationship*	
Daughter of Ephraim; builder of cities	1 Chr. 7:24
Sherebiah—*Jehovah has sent burning heat*	
1. Levite family returning with Ezra	Ezra 8:18
2. Levite who assists Ezra	Neh. 8:7
Sheresh—*root*	
Grandson of Manasseh	1 Chr. 7:16
Sheriffs—*court officials*	
Called by Nebuchadnezzar	Dan. 3:2, 3
Sheshach—*probably a cryptogram*	
Symbolic of Babylon	Jer. 25:26
Sheshai—*whitish*	
Descendant of Anak	Num. 13:22
Driven out by Caleb	Josh. 15:14
Destroyed by Judah	Judg. 1:10
Sheshan—*whitish*	
Jerahmeelite	1 Chr. 2:31-35
Sheshbazzar—*sin* (the moon god) *protect the father*	
Prince of Judah	Ezra 1:8, 11

SUBJECT REFERENCE

Sheth (I)—*compensation*
Son of Adam (same as Seth) . . . . 1 Chr. 1:1

Sheth (II)—*tumult*
Name descriptive of the Moabites . . . . Num. 24:17

Shethar—*star*
Persian prince . . . . Esth. 1:14

Shethar-boznai—*starry splendor*
Official of Persia . . . . Ezra 5:3, 6

Sheva—*self-satisfying*
1. Son of Caleb . . . . 1 Chr. 2:43, 49
2. David's scribe . . . . 2 Sam. 20:25

Shibboleth—*stream or ear of corn*
Password . . . . Judg. 12:5, 6

Shicron—*drunkenness*
Town of Judah . . . . Josh. 15:11

Shield—*a protective armor*
A. *Uses of:*
- Protection . . . . 2 Chr. 14:8
- Treasures in war . . . . 1 Kin. 14:25, 26
- Riches . . . . 2 Chr. 32:27
- Ornamenting public buildings . . . . 1 Kin. 10:17

B. *Figurative of:*
God's:
- Protection . . . . Ps. 33:20
- Favor . . . . Ps. 5:12
- Salvation . . . . Ps. 18:35
- Truth . . . . Ps. 91:4
- Faith . . . . Eph. 6:16
- Rulers . . . . Ps. 47:9

Shiggaion—*irregular*
Musical term . . . . Ps. 7 (Title)
Plural form:
Shigionoth . . . . Hab. 3:1

Shihon—*ruin*
Town of Issachar . . . . Josh. 19:19

Shihor-libnath—*turbid stream of Libnath*
Small river in Asher's territory . . Josh. 19:26

Shilhi—*Jehovah has sent*
Father of Azubah . . . . 1 Kin. 22:42

Shilhim—*missiles*
Town in south Judah . . . . Josh. 15:1, 32

Shillem—*compensation*
Son of Napthali . . . . Gen. 46:24

Shiloah—*sent*
A pool of Jerusalem, figurative of God's protection . . . . Is. 8:6
See Siloam

Shiloh
1. Town of Ephraim . . . . Judg. 21:19
   - Center of religious worship . . Judg. 18:31
   - Canaan divided here . . . . Josh. 18:1, 10
   - Benjamites seize women here . . . . Judg. 21:19-23
   - Ark of the covenant taken from . . . . 1 Sam. 4:3-11
   - Site of Eli's judgeship . . . . 1 Sam. 4:12-18
   - Home of Ahijah . . . . 1 Kin. 14:2, 4
   - Punishment given to . . . . Jer. 7:12-14
2. Messianic title . . . . Gen. 49:10

Shiloni—*a Shilonite*
Father of Zechariah . . . . Neh. 11:5

Shilonite
Native of Shiloh . . . . 1 Kin. 11:29

Shilshah—*might*
Asherite . . . . 1 Chr. 7:36, 37

Shimea, Shimeah—*He* (God) *has heard*
1. Gershonite Levite . . . . 1 Chr. 6:39
2. Merarite Levite . . . . 1 Chr. 6:30
3. Brother of David . . . . 2 Sam. 13:3
4. Son of David . . . . 1 Chr. 3:1, 5
5. Benjamite . . . . 1 Chr. 8:1, 32
   Called Shimeam . . . . 1 Chr. 9:38

SUBJECT REFERENCE

Shimeath—*report*
Ammonitess . . . . 2 Kin. 12:21

Shimeathites
Family of scribes . . . . 1 Chr. 2:55

Shimei—*renowned*
1. Son of Gershon . . . . Ex. 6:17
2. Son of Merari . . . . 1 Chr. 6:29
3. Simeonite . . . . 1 Chr. 4:24-27
4. Levite . . . . 1 Chr. 6:42
5. Benjamite family head . . . . 1 Chr. 8:21
6. Gershonite family head . . . . 1 Chr. 23:7, 9
7. Levite musician in David's time . . . . 1 Chr. 25:3, 17
8. Overseer of vineyards under David . . . . 1 Chr. 27:27
9. Benjamite; insults David . . . . 2 Sam. 16:5-13
   Pardoned, but confined . . . . 2 Sam. 19:16-23
   Breaks parole; executed by Solomon . . . . 1 Kin. 2:39-46
10. Faithful follower of Solomon . . . . 1 Kin. 1:8
11. Levite; assists in purification . . . . 2 Chr. 29:14-16
12. Levite treasurer in Hezekiah's reign . . . . 2 Chr. 31:12, 13
13. Benjamite ancestor of Mordecai . . . . Esth. 2:5
14. Brother of Zerubbabel . . . . 1 Chr. 3:19

Shimeon—*hearing*
Divorced his foreign wife . . . . Ezra 10:31

Shimon—*trier*
Judahite family . . . . 1 Chr. 4:1, 20

Shimrath—*guarding*
Benjamite . . . . 1 Chr. 8:21

Shimri—*vigilant*
1. Father of Jediael . . . . 1 Chr. 11:45
2. Merarite Levite . . . . 1 Chr. 26:10
3. Levite; assists in purification . . . . 2 Chr. 29:13

Shimrith—*vigilant*
Moabitess . . . . 2 Chr. 24:26

Shimron—*watching*
1. Son of Issachar . . . . Gen. 46:13
2. Town of Zebulun . . . . Josh. 11:1

Shimron-meron—*guard of lashing*
Town conquered by Joshua . . . . Josh. 12:20

Shimshai—*sunny*
Scribe opposing the Jews . . . . Ezek. 4:8

Shinab—*king of Admah*
Fought against Chedorlaomer . . . Gen. 14:1, 12

Shinar—*the region around Babylon*
- Original home of Noah's sons . . . Gen. 10:10
- Tower built here . . . . Gen. 11:2-9
- Amraphel, king of . . . . Gen. 14:1, 9
- Home of the remnant Jews . . . . Is. 11:11

Shine—*to radiate with light*
A. *Used literally of:*
- Sun . . . . Job 31:26
- Moon . . . . Job 25:5
- Star . . . . Joel 3:15
- Earth . . . . Ezek. 43:2
- Moses' face . . . . Ex. 34:29-35
- Christ's face . . . . Matt. 17:2
- Angels . . . . Acts 12:7
- Glorified Christ . . . . Acts 9:3
- Christ's return . . . . Luke 17:24

B. *Applied figuratively to:*
- God's blessing . . . . Num. 6:25
- God's Word . . . . 2 Pet. 1:19
- Christ's first Advent . . . . Is. 9:2; John 1:5
- Gospel . . . . 2 Cor. 4:4
- Believer's life . . . . Matt. 5:16
- Regeneration . . . . 2 Cor. 4:6
- Believer's glory . . . . Dan. 12:3; Matt. 13:43

SUBJECT REFERENCE

Shihon—*ruin*
Town of Issachar . . . . Josh. 19:19

Shiphi—*abundant*
Simeonite . . . . 1 Chr. 4:37

Shiphmite—*a native of Shiphmoth*
Zabdi called . . . . 1 Chr. 27:27

Shiphrah—*beauty*
Hebrew midwife . . . . Ex. 1:15

Shiphtan—*judicial*
Ephraimite . . . . Num. 34:24

Ships—*vessels designed for use on water*
A. *Uses of:*
- Fishing . . . . John 21:3-8
- Travel . . . . Jon. 1:3
- Cargoes . . . . Acts 27:3, 10, 38
- War . . . . Num. 24:24
- Commerce . . . . Ps. 107:23

B. *Parts of:*
- Sign . . . . Acts 28:11
- Lifeboats . . . . Acts 27:16-32
- Anchor . . . . Acts 27:29, 40
- Rudder . . . . Acts 27:40
- Cables . . . . Acts 27:17
- Ropes . . . . Acts 27:32
- Sails . . . . Is. 33:23
- Oars . . . . Ezek. 27:6

C. *Notable ones:*
- Ark . . . . Gen. 7:17, 18
- Jonah's . . . . Jon. 1:3, 4
- Of Tarshish . . . . Is. 23:1, 14
- Christ's . . . . Matt. 8:23-27
- Paul's . . . . Acts 27:1-44

Shipwreck—*a wreck of a seagoing vessel*
Paul in three . . . . 2 Cor. 11:25
Figurative of apostasy . . . . 1 Tim. 1:19

Shisha—*distinction*
Father of Solomon's scribes . . . . 1 Kin. 4:3
Called Shavsha . . . . 1 Chr. 18:16

Shitrai—*Jehovah is deciding*
Sharonite overseer of David's herds . . . . 1 Chr. 27:29

Shittim—*acacia*
1. Israel's last camp before crossing the Jordan . . . . Josh. 3:1
   - Scene of Balaam's attempted curse . . . . Num. 22—24
   - Sin of Baal-peor here . . . . Num. 25:1-18
   - Site of Joshua's commission . . . . Num. 27:12-23
   - War with Midianites here . . . . Num. 31:1-54
   - Reuben and Gad receive inheritance here . . . . Num. 32:1-42
   - Scene of Moses' final addresses . . . . Deut. 1—34
   - Spies sent from . . . . Josh. 2:1
2. Valley blessed by the LORD . . Joel 3:18

Shittim wood—*wood of the shittah tree*
Used in:
- Making the ark . . . . Ex. 25:10, 13
- Table of showbread . . . . Ex. 37:10
- Altar of incense . . . . Ex. 30:1
- Altar of burnt offering . . . . Ex. 38:1, 6
- Tabernacle boards . . . . Ex. 26:15-37

Shiza—*splendor*
Reubenite . . . . 1 Chr. 11:42

Shoa—*rich*
Race or tribe against Israel . . . . Ezek. 23:23

Shobab—*returning*
1. Son of Caleb . . . . 1 Chr. 2:18
2. Son of David . . . . 2 Sam. 5:14

Shobach—*expansion*
Commander of the Syrian army . . . . 2 Sam. 10:16-18
Spelled Shophach . . . . 1 Chr. 19:16, 18

Shobai—*glorious*
Head of a family of porters . . . . Ezra 2:42

Shobal—*flowing*
1. Son of Seir; a Horite chief . . . Gen. 36:20-29

SUBJECT	REFERENCE
2. Judahite, son of Caleb and ancestor of the people of Kirjath-jearim	1 Chr. 2:50, 52
Shobek—*forsaking*	
Signer of Nehemiah's sealed covenant	Neh. 10:24
Shobi—*Jehovah is glorious*	
Ammonite who brings food to David	2 Sam. 17:27, 28
Shoe—*footwear*	
A. *Characteristics of:*	
Worn on the feet	1 Kin. 2:5
Tied by a latchet	Gen. 14:23
Some considered worthless	Amos 2:6
Used for dress occasions	Luke 15:22
Worn as adornment	Song 7:1
Dirty after a trip	Josh. 9:5, 13
Preserved supernaturally	Deut. 29:5
B. *Symbolism of:*	
Putting on—readiness for a journey	Ex. 12:11
Putting off—reverence before God	Ex. 3:5 Josh. 5:15
Want of—mourning	2 Sam. 15:30
Giving to another—renunciation of Mosaic marriage rights	Ruth 4:7, 8
To loose another's—act of homage	Luke 3:16
C. *Figurative of:*	
Preparation for service	Eph. 6:15
Protection and provision	Deut. 33:25
Alertness	Is. 5:27
See Sandals	
Shoham—*beryl or onyx*	
Merarite Levite	1 Chr. 24:27
Shomer—*keeper, watchman*	
Asherite	1 Chr. 7:30, 32
Called Shamer	1 Chr. 7:34
Shophan—*hidden*	
Town in Gad	Num. 32:34, 35
Short—*not long; brief*	
A. *Descriptive of:*	
Life	Ps. 89:47
Time of the devil on earth	Rev. 12:12
Gospel age	1 Cor. 7:29
B. *Expressive of God's:*	
Power	Is. 50:2
Plan	Rev. 22:6
Provision	Is. 59:1, 2
Tribulation	Matt. 24:21, 22
Shoshannim—*lilies*	
Musical term	Ps. 45 (Title)
Shoulder	
A. *Of men, used for:*	
Burdens	Is. 46:7
Supporting clothes	Ex. 12:34
B. *Figurative of:*	
Notable persons	Ezek. 24:4, 5
Destruction	Ezek. 29:7
Servitude	Is. 10:27
Rebellion	Zech. 7:11
Messianic authority	Is. 9:6
Security	Deut. 33:12
Shout, Shouted	
A. *Occasions of, in:*	
Conquest	Josh. 6:5, 16, 20
Choosing a king	1 Sam. 10:24
Sound of singing	Ex. 32:17, 18
Laying foundation of the Temple	Ezek. 3:11-13
B. *In spiritual things:*	
At creation	Job 38:7
In the Messiah's arrival	Zech. 9:9
Shovel	
1. Used for removing ashes	Ex. 27:3
2. Winnowing tool	Is. 30:24
Showbread—*"bread of thy face"*	
A. *Provisions concerning:*	
Provided by the people	Lev. 24:8
Prepared by the Levites	1 Chr. 9:32

SUBJECT	REFERENCE
Placed in two rows	Ex. 25:30
Perennially supplied	Num. 4:7
Presented to the Lord	Lev. 24:7, 8
Provided for priests only	Lev. 24:9 Matt. 12:4, 5
B. *Table of:*	
Placed in Holy Place	Ex. 26:35 Heb. 9:2
Made of acacia	Ex. 25:23-28
Carried by: Kohathite Levites	Num. 4:4, 7, 15
High priest	Num. 4:7, 8, 16
C. *Symbolic of:*	
Twelve tribes	Ex. 28:10-12
Christ	John 6:48
Church	1 Cor. 10:17
Showers—*sudden outpourings*	
A. *Used literally of rain:*	
Withheld	Jer. 3:3
Predicted	Luke 12:54
Requested	Zech. 10:1
Blessing	Ps. 65:10
B. *Used figuratively of:*	
God's Word	Deut. 32:2
God's wrath	Ezek. 13:11, 13
Messiah's advent	Ps. 72:6
Gospel	Ezek. 34:25, 26
Remnant	Mic. 5:7
Shroud—*to cover or shelter*	
Used figuratively	Ezek. 31:3
Shua, Shuah—*prosperity*	
1. Son of Abraham by Keturah	Gen. 25:1, 2
2. Father of Judah's wife	Gen. 38:2, 12
3. Descendant of Judah	1 Chr. 4:1, 11
4. Daughter of Heber	1 Chr. 7:32
Shual—*jackal*	
1. Asherite	1 Chr. 7:30, 36
2. Region raided by a Philistine company	1 Sam. 13:17
Shubael, Shebuel	
1. Levite, son of Amram	1 Chr. 24:20
2. Levite, son of Heman	1 Chr. 25:4
Shuham—*depression*	
Son of Dan	Num. 26:42
Called Hushim	Gen. 46:23
Head of the Shuhamites	Num. 26:42, 43
Shuhite—*a descendant of Shua*	
Bildad called; a descendant of Abraham by Keturah	Gen. 38:2, 12 Job 2:11
Shulamite—*a native of Shulam*	
Shepherd's sweetheart	Song 6:13
Shumathites	
Family of Kirjath-jearim	1 Chr. 2:53
Shunammite—*a native of Shunem*	
1. Abishag, David's nurse called	1 Kin. 1:3, 15
2. Woman who cared for Elisha	2 Kin. 4:8-12
Shunem—*uneven*	
Border town of Issachar	Josh. 19:18
Shuni—*fortunate*	
Son of Gad	Gen. 46:16
Shuppim—*serpent*	
Levite porter	1 Chr. 26:16
Shur—*fortification*	
Wilderness in south Palestine	Gen. 16:7
Israel went from Red Sea to	Ex. 15:22
On Egypt's border	1 Sam. 15:7
Hagar flees to	Gen. 16:7
Shushan—*a city of Elam*	
Residence of Persian monarchs	Esth. 1:2
Located on river Ulai	Dan. 8:2
Court of Ahasuerus here	Esth. 1:2, 5
Shut—*to close securely*	
A. *Applied literally to:*	
Ark	Gen. 7:16

SUBJECT	REFERENCE
Door	Gen. 19:6, 10
Leper	Lev. 13:4-44
Animals	Dan. 6:22
Court	Jer. 33:1
Prison	Acts 26:10
B. *Applied figuratively to:*	
Womb	1 Sam. 1:5, 6
God's mercies	Ps. 77:9
Finality of salvation	Matt. 25:10
Union with Christ	Song 4:12
Spiritual blindness	Is. 6:10
Awe	Is. 52:15
Heaven's glory	Is. 60:11
God's Word	Jer. 20:9
Vision	Dan. 12:4
Secret prayer	Matt. 6:6
Christ's sovereignty	Rev. 3:7, 8
Shuthelah	
1. Son of Ephraim; head of a family	Num. 26:35, 36
2. Ephraimite	1 Chr. 7:20, 21
Shuttle—*a weaving tool*	
Our days swifter than	Job 7:6
Siaha—*assembly*	
Family of returning Nethinim	Ezra 2:43, 44 Neh. 7:47
Sibbecai, Sibbechai	
One of David's mighty men	1 Chr. 11:29
Slays a Philistine giant	2 Sam. 21:18
Commander of a division	1 Chr. 27:11
Sibmah—*balsam*	
Town of Reuben	Num. 32:3, 38
Famous for wines	Is. 16:8, 9
Sibraim—*double hope*	
Place in north Palestine	Ezek. 47:16
Sick, Sickness—*the state of being unwell*	
A. *Caused by:*	
Age	Gen. 48:1, 10
Accident	2 Kin. 1:2
Wine	Hos. 7:5
Sins	Mic. 6:13
Despondency	Prov. 13:12
Prophetic visions	Dan. 8:27
Love	Song 2:5
God's judgment	2 Chr. 21:14-19
God's sovereignty	John 11:4
B. *Healing of, by:*	
Figs	2 Kin. 20:7
Miracle	1 Kin. 17:17-23
Prayer	James 5:14, 15
God's mercy	Phil. 2:25-30
See Diseases; Healing	
Sickle—*an instrument for cutting grain*	
Literally	Deut. 16:9
Figuratively	Mark 4:29 Rev. 14:14-19
Siddim, Vale of	
Valley of bitumen pits near the Dead Sea	Gen. 14:3, 8, 10
Sidon, Zidon—*fishery*	
Canaanite city 20 miles north of Tyre	Gen. 10:15, 19
Israel's northern boundary	Josh. 19:28
Canaanites not expelled from	Judg. 1:31
Israelites oppressed by	Judg. 10:12
Gods of, entice Israelites	1 Kin. 11:5, 33
Judgments pronounced on	Is. 23:12
Israelites sold as slaves by	Joel 3:4-6
People from, hear Jesus	Luke 6:17
Visited by Jesus	Matt. 15:21
Paul visits at	Acts 27:3
Siege of a city—*a military blockade*	
A. *Methods employed in:*	
Supplies cut off	2 Kin. 19:24
Ambushes laid	Judg. 9:34
Battering rams used	Ezek. 4:2
Arrows shot	2 Kin. 19:32
B. *Suffering of:*	
Famine	2 Kin. 6:26-29
Pestilence	Jer. 21:6

SUBJECT REFERENCE

C. *Examples of:*
- Jericho ... Josh. 6:2-20
- Jerusalem ... 2 Kin. 24:10, 11

See War

Sieve, sift—*screen*

Used figuratively of:
- God's judgment ... Amos 9:9
- Satan's temptation ... Luke 22:31

Sign—*an outward token having spiritual significance*

A. *Descriptive of:*
- Heavenly bodies ... Gen. 1:14
- Rainbow ... Gen. 9:12-17
- Circumcision ... Gen. 17:11
- Bloodshed ... Ex. 12:13
- God's wonders ... Ps. 65:8
- Covenant ... Rom. 4:11
- Miracles ... Deut. 26:8
- Memorial ... Num. 16:38
- Symbolic act ... Is. 8:18
- Witness ... Is. 19:19, 20
- Outward display ... John 4:48

B. *Purposes of, to:*
- Authenticate a prophecy ... Deut. 13:1; 1 Sam. 2:31, 34
- Strengthen faith ... Judg. 6:17; Is. 7:11
- Recall God's blessings ... Josh. 24:15-17
- Confirm God's Word ... 2 Kin. 19:28, 29; Heb. 2:4
- Insure a promise ... 2 Kin. 20:5, 9-11
- Confirm a prophecy ... 1 Kin. 13:3-5

C. *Concerning Christ in His:*
- Nativity ... Luke 2:12
- Ministry ... John 20:30; Acts 2:22
- Resurrection ... Matt. 12:38-40

D. *Value of:*
- Discounted as such ... Matt. 16:1-4
- Demanded unnecessarily ... John 6:30
- Demonstrated by apostles ... Acts 5:12
- Displayed by Paul ... Rom. 15:19

E. *In prophecy, concerning:*
- Christ's first Advent ... Is. 7:11, 14; Matt. 1:21-23
- Second Advent ... Matt. 24:3, 30
- Antichrist ... 2 Thess. 2:9
- End ... Rev. 15:1

F. *As assurance of:*
- Presence ... Ex. 3:12
- Judgment upon sin ... Num. 17:10
- Goodness ... Ps. 86:17

Signify—*to make known by signs*

A. *Concerning men:*
- Peter's death ... John 21:19
- Ritual performed ... Acts 21:26
- Jewish scheme ... Acts 23:15

B. *Concerning predicted events:*
- New dispensation ... Heb. 9:8
- Christ's: Death ... John 12:33
- Sufferings ... 1 Pet. 1:11
- Gospel age ... Rev. 1:1
- Famine ... Acts 11:28
- World's end ... Heb. 12:27

Sihon—*bold*
- Amorite king residing at Heshbon ... Num. 21:26-30
- Victorious over Moabites ... Num. 21:26-30
- Ruler of five Midianite princes ... Josh. 13:21
- Refused Israel's request for passage ... Deut. 2:26-28
- Defeated by Israel ... Num. 21:21-32
- Territory of, assigned to Reuben and Gad ... Num. 32:1-38
- Victory over, long celebrated ... Deut. 31:4

Sihor—*black, turbid*
- Name given to the Nile ... Is. 23:3
- Israel's southwestern border ... Josh. 13:3

Silas, Silvanus—*wooded*
- Leader in the Jerusalem church ... Acts 15:22
- Christian prophet ... Acts 15:32
- Sent on a mission ... Acts 15:22-35
- Became Paul's companion ... Acts 15:36-41
- Roman citizen ... Acts 16:25-39

SUBJECT REFERENCE

- Paul commended his work at Corinth ... 2 Cor. 1:19
- Called Silvanus ... 1 Thess. 1:1
- Associated in Paul's writings ... 2 Thess. 1:1
- Peter's helper ... 1 Pet. 5:12

Silence—*the lack of noise*

A. *Kinds of:*
- Will of God ... Rev. 8:1; 1 Pet. 2:15
- Troubled ... Jer. 20:9

B. *Virtue of:*
- Suitable time for ... Eccl. 3:7
- Commanded ... 1 Cor. 14:34
- Sign of prudence ... Prov. 21:23
- Sign of wisdom ... Prov. 17:28

C. *Forbidden to God's:*
- Watchmen ... Is. 62:6
- Messengers ... Acts 5:27-42
- Praisers ... Ps. 30:12

D. *Considered as:*
- Blessing ... Zech. 2:13
- Curse ... 1 Sam. 2:9
- Judgment ... Jer. 8:14
- Punishment ... Is. 15:1

E. *Of God:*
- Broken in judgment ... Ps. 50:3
- Misunderstood by men ... Ps. 50:21, 23

F. *Of Christ:*
- Predicted ... Is. 53:7
- Before:
  - Sinners ... John 8:6
  - High priest ... Matt. 26:62, 63
  - Pilate ... Matt. 27:14
  - Herod ... Luke 23:9

Silk—*a clothing material derived from the silkworm*

Sign of:
- Luxury ... Ezek. 16:10, 13
- Wantonness ... Rev. 18:12

Silla—*twig; basket*
- Quarter of suburb of Jerusalem ... 2 Kin. 12:20

Silly women
- Weighed down with sin ... 2 Tim. 3:6

Siloam, Siloah—*sent*
- Pool at Jerusalem ... Neh. 3:15
- Tower of, kills 18 people ... Luke 13:4
- Blind man washes in ... John 9:1-11

Silver—*a precious metal*

A. *Features concerning:*
- Mined from the earth ... Job 28:1
- Melted by fire ... Ezek. 22:22
- Sign of wealth ... Gen. 13:2
- Used as money ... Gen. 23:15, 16
- Article of commerce ... Ezek. 27:12
- Given as presents ... 1 Kin. 10:25
- Used in:
  - Tabernacle ... Ex. 38:19
  - Temple ... 2 Kin. 12:13
- Christ sold for 30 pieces of ... Zech. 11:12; Matt. 26:15
- Peter devoid of ... Acts 3:6

B. *Figurative of:*
- God's Word ... Ps. 12:6
- God's people ... Zech. 13:9
- Understanding ... Prov. 3:13, 14
- Degeneration ... Is. 1:22
- Rejection ... Jer. 6:30

Silversmith—*a worker in silver*
- Demetrius, an Ephesian ... Acts 19:24-41

Simeon—*hearing*
1. Son of Jacob by Leah ... Gen. 29:33
   - Joined Levi in massacre of Shechemites ... Gen. 34:25-31
   - Held as hostage by Joseph ... Gen. 42:24, 36
   - Denounced by Jacob ... Gen. 34:30
   - Sons of ... Gen. 46:10
2. Tribe of, descendants of Jacob's son ... Gen. 46:10
   - Number of, at first census ... Num. 1:23
   - Number of, at second census ... Num. 26:12-14

SUBJECT REFERENCE

   - Position of, on Mt. Gerizim ... Deut. 27:12
   - Inheritance of, within Judah's ... Josh. 19:1-9
   - With Judah, fought Canaanites ... Judg. 1:1, 3, 17
   - Victory over Ham and Amalekites ... 1 Chr. 4:24-43
   - Recognized in Ezekiel's vision ... Ezek. 48:24-33
3. Ancestor of Christ ... Luke 3:30
4. Righteous man; blessed the child Jesus ... Luke 2:25-35
5. Christian prophet at Antioch ... Acts 13:1
6. Simon Peter ... Acts 15:14

Similitude—*likeness of two things*

A. *Expressive of:*
- Physical ... 2 Chr. 4:3
- Typical ... Rom. 5:14
- Literary (simile) ... Ps. 144:12
- Spiritual ... James 3:9

B. *Expressed by:*
- "Like" ... James 1:6
- "As" ... 1 Pet. 2:5
- "Likeness" ... Rom. 6:5
- "Liken" ... Matt. 7:24, 26

Simon—*hearing*
1. Simon Peter ... Matt. 4:18

   See Peter
2. One of the Twelve; called "the Canaanite" ... Matt. 10:4
3. One of Jesus' brothers ... Matt. 13:55
4. The leper ... Matt. 26:6
5. Pharisee ... Luke 7:36-40
6. Man of Cyrene ... Matt. 27:32
7. Father of Judas Iscariot ... John 6:71
8. Sorcerer ... Acts 8:9-24
9. Tanner in Joppa ... Acts 9:43

Simple, the
- Enlightened by God's Word ... Ps. 119:105; Ps. 19:7
- Able to understand ... Prov. 1:4
- Receptive of correction ... Prov. 19:25
- Void of understanding ... Prov. 7:7
- Easily tempted ... Prov. 9:4, 16
- Gullible ... Prov. 14:15
- Inherit folly ... Prov. 14:18
- Unmindful of danger ... Prov. 22:3
- The LORD preserves ... Ps. 116:6

Simplicity—*that which is in its purest form*

A. *Necessary in:*
- Prayer ... Matt. 6:5-15
- Dress ... 1 Pet. 3:3-5
- Conduct ... 2 Cor. 1:12
- Giving ... Rom. 12:8
- Preaching ... 1 Thess. 2:3-7

B. *Purposes of, to:*
- Avoid outward display ... Matt. 6:1-4
- Defeat Satan ... 2 Cor. 11:3, 4
- Remain pure in an evil world ... Rom. 16:19

Sin—*disobedience of God's Law*

A. *Defined as:*
- Transgression ... 1 John 3:4
- Unrighteousness ... 1 John 5:17
- Omission of known duty ... James 4:17
- Not from faith ... Rom. 14:23
- Thought of foolishness ... Prov. 24:9

B. *Sources of, in:*
- Satan ... John 8:44
- Man's heart ... Matt. 15:19, 20
- Lust ... James 1:15
- Adam's transgression ... Rom. 5:12, 16
- Natural birth ... Ps. 51:5

C. *Kinds of:*
- National ... Prov. 14:34
- Personal ... Josh. 7:20
- Secret ... Ps. 90:8
- Presumptuous ... Ps. 19:13
- Open ... 1 Tim. 5:24
- Shameless ... Is. 3:9
- Youthful ... Ps. 25:7
- Public ... 2 Sam. 24:10, 17

SUBJECT ... REFERENCE

Unforgiveable ... Matt. 12:21, 32
John 8:24
Of ignorance ... Lev. 4:2
Willfully ... Heb. 10:26

D. *Consequences of, among the unregenerate:*
Blindness ... John 9:41
2 Cor. 4:3, 4
Servitude ... John 8:34
Irreconcilable ... 1 Tim. 3:1-7
Death ... Rom. 6:23

E. *God's attitude toward:*
Withholds men from ... Gen. 20:6
Punishes for ... Ex. 32:34
Provides a fountain for ... Zech. 13:1
Blots out ... Is. 44:22
Casts away ... Mic. 7:19
Forgives ... Ex. 34:7
Remembers no more ... Jer. 31:34

F. *Christ's relationship to:*
Free of ... 1 John 3:5
Knew no ... 2 Cor. 5:21
Makes men conscious of ... John 15:22, 24
Died for our ... 1 Cor. 15:3
As an offering for ... Is. 53:10
Heb. 9:28
Substitutionary ... Is. 53:5, 6
Matt. 26:28
Takes it away ... John 1:29
Saves His people from ... Matt. 1:21
Has power to forgive ... Matt. 9:6
Makes reconciliation for ... Heb. 2:17
Purges our ... Heb. 1:3
Cleanses us from ... 1 John 1:7, 9
Washes us from ... Rev. 1:5

G. *Regenerate must:*
Acknowledge ... Ps. 32:5
Confess ... Ps. 51:3, 4
Be sorry for ... Ps. 38:18
Not serve ... Rom. 6:6
Not obey ... Rom. 6:6, 12
Subdue ... Rom. 6:14-22
Lay aside ... Heb. 12:1
Resist ... Heb. 12:4
Keep from ... Ps. 19:13

H. *Helps against:*
Use God's Word ... Ps. 119:11
Guard the tongue ... Ps. 39:1
Walk in the Spirit ... Rom. 8:1-14
Avoid evil companions ... 1 Tim. 5:22
Confess to the Lord ... 1 John 1:8, 9
Exercise love ... 1 Pet. 4:8
Go to the Advocate ... 1 John 2:1

Sin—*wrongdoing; transgression*
1. Wilderness between the Red Sea and Sinai ... Ex. 16:1
2. City of Egypt ... Ezek. 30:15, 16

Sinai, Sina
Mountain (same as Horeb) where the Law was given ... Ex. 19:1-25
Used allegorically by Paul ... Gal. 4:24, 25
See Horeb

Sincerity—*freedom from deceit; genuineness*
A. *Descriptive of:*
God's Word ... 1 Pet. 2:2
Faith ... 1 Tim. 1:5
Believer's love ... 2 Cor. 8:8, 24

B. *Should characterize:*
Young men ... Titus 2:6, 7
Worship ... John 4:23, 24
Preaching ... 2 Cor. 2:17
Believer's life ... 2 Cor. 1:12
Public relationships ... Judg. 9:16, 19

C. *Examples of:*
Nathanael ... John 1:47
Christ ... 1 Pet. 2:22
Paul ... 1 Thess. 2:3-5

Singed—*burnt hair*
Miraculously saved from being ... Dan. 3:27

Singers—*those who make music with voice*
Leaders of ... 1 Chr. 25:2-6
Under teachers ... 1 Chr. 15:22, 27
Mixed ... 2 Chr. 35:15, 25

Singing—*uttering words in musical tones*
A. *Descriptive of:*
Birds ... Ps. 104:12

SUBJECT ... REFERENCE

Trees ... 1 Chr. 16:33
Believers ... Eph. 5:19
Redeemed ... Rev. 5:9
Morning stars ... Job 38:7

B. *Occasions of:*
Times of:
Victory ... Ex. 15:1, 21
Revelry ... Ex. 32:18
Imprisonment ... Acts 16:25
Joy ... James 5:13
Lord's Supper ... Matt. 26:30

C. *Manner of, with:*
Thanksgiving ... Ps. 147:7
Joy ... Ps. 27:6
Gladness ... Jer. 31:7
Spirit ... 1 Cor. 14:15
Grace ... Col. 3:16

D. *Objects of:*
God's:
Power ... Ps. 59:16
Mercies ... Ps. 89:1
Righteousness ... Ps. 51:14
New song ... Rev. 14:3

Singular—*something special*
Descriptive of a vow ... Lev. 27:2

Sinim, Sinites—*people in the far east*
1. Canaanite people ... Gen. 10:15-18
2. Distant land from which people will return ... Is. 49:7-12

Sink—*to go down under something soft*
Used literally of:
Stone ... 1 Sam. 17:49
Army ... Ex. 15:4, 5, 10
Boat ... Luke 5:7
Man ... Matt. 14:30

Sinlessness (see Holiness of Christ; Perfection)

Sinners—*those who are unregenerate*
A. *Descriptive of:*
Wicked city ... Gen. 13:13
Race ... 1 Sam. 15:18
Wicked Israelites ... Amos 9:8, 10
Jewish people ... Matt. 26:45, 47
Man under conviction ... Luke 5:8
Luke 18:13
Human race ... Rom. 5:8, 19

B. *Characteristics of:*
Hostile to God ... Jude 15
Scheme wickedly ... Ps. 26:9, 10
Easily ensnared ... Eccl. 7:26
Righteous enticed by ... Prov. 1:10
Law made for ... 1 Tim. 1:9
Conscious of sin ... Luke 18:13
Able to repent ... Luke 15:7, 10
Conversion of ... James 5:20
In need of cleansing ... James 4:8

C. *Punishment of:*
Pursued by evil ... Prov. 13:21
Overthrown by evil ... Prov. 13:6
Wealth of, acquired by the just ... Prov. 13:22
Sorrow given to ... Ezek. 18:20
Will be punished ... Prov. 11:31
Will be consumed ... Ps. 104:35

D. *Christ's relationship to:*
Came to call ... Luke 5:32
Friend of ... Luke 7:34
Receives such ... Luke 15:1, 2
Endures hostility from ... Heb. 12:3
Separate from ... Heb. 7:26

Sion—*elevated*
Name given to all or part of Mt. Hermon ... Deut. 4:48
See Zion

Siphmoth—*fruitful*
David shares spoils with ... 1 Sam. 30:26-28

Sippai—*Jehovah is preserver*
Philistine giant ... 1 Chr. 20:4
Called Saph ... 2 Sam. 21:18

Sirah—*turning aside*
Well near Hebron ... 2 Sam. 3:26

SUBJECT ... REFERENCE

Siron—*coat of mail*
Sidonian name for Mt. Hermon ... Deut. 3:9

Sisamai—*Jehovah is distinguished*
Judahite ... 1 Chr. 2:40

Sisera—*meditation*
1. Canaanite commander of Jabin's army; slain by Jael ... Judg. 4:2-22
2. Ancestor of postexilic Nethinim ... Ezra 2:43, 53

Sister
A. *Descriptive of:*
Female relative ... Gen. 24:30-60
Women of the same tribe ... Num. 25:18

B. *Features concerning:*
Protected by:
Brothers ... Gen. 34:13-31
Laws ... Lev. 18:9-13, 18
Friction between ... Luke 10:39, 40
Loved by Jesus ... John 11:5

C. *Figurative of:*
Samaria and Jerusalem ... Ezek. 23:1-49
Christian ... Matt. 12:50
Christian woman ... Rom. 16:1
Church ... 2 John 13

Sit
A. *Descriptive of:*
Partridge ... Jer. 17:11
Man ... Gen. 18:1
Judge ... Ex. 18:13, 14
Priest ... Zech. 6:13
King ... Deut. 17:15, 18
God ... Ps. 2:4
Messiah ... Ps. 110:1

B. *Purposes of, to:*
Eat ... Matt. 26:20, 21
Rest ... John 4:6
Mourn ... Neh. 1:4
Teach ... Matt. 26:55
Transact business ... Matt. 9:9
Beg ... Luke 18:35
Learn ... Mark 5:15
Ride ... Matt. 21:5
Worship ... Acts 2:2

C. *Figurative of Christ's:*
Session ... Heb. 1:3
Rule ... Matt. 19:28
Judgment ... Matt. 25:31

Sitnah—*enmity*
Well dug by Isaac near Gerar ... Gen. 26:21

Sivan
Third month of the Jewish and Babylonian year ... Esth. 8:9

Skeptical—*characterized by doubts*
Thomas, the doubter ... John 20:24-28

Skilled—*those possessing special abilities*
A. *Required of:*
Soldiers ... 1 Chr. 5:18
Craftsmen ... 2 Chr. 2:7, 14
Musicians ... 2 Chr. 34:12

B. *Obtained by:*
Spirit's help ... Ex. 31:2-5
God's Word ... Ps. 119:98-100
LORD's help ... Ps. 144:1

Skins—*the outer covering of a body*
A. *Of animals, used for:*
Clothing ... Gen. 3:21
Deception ... Gen. 27:16
Coverings ... Ex. 26:14
Bottles ... Josh. 9:4

B. *Of man:*
Diseased ... Lev. 13:1-46
Sign of race ... Jer. 13:23
Seal of death ... Job 19:26

Skull—*skeleton of the head*
Abimelech's crushed by a woman ... Judg. 9:53
Jezebel's left by dogs ... 2 Kin. 9:30-37
They brought Him to a place called ... Mark 15:22
Another name for Golgotha ... Matt. 27:33
See Golgotha

SUBJECT REFERENCE

Sky—*the expanse of the heaven*

A. *Place of:*
Stars .... Heb. 11:12
Expansion .... Job 37:18
Weather changes .... Matt. 16:2, 3
Thunder .... Ps. 77:17

B. *Figurative of:*
God's abode .... Ps. 18:11
Righteousness .... Is. 45:8
Ultimate judgment .... Jer. 51:9

Slander—*a malicious statement*

A. *Described as:*
Destructive .... Prov. 11:9
Deceitful .... Ps. 52:2
Deluding .... Prov. 10:18
Devouring .... Prov. 16:27-30

B. *Hurled against:*
Joseph .... Gen. 39:14-19
David .... 2 Sam. 10:3
Jews .... Ezra 4:7-16
Christ .... Matt. 26:59-61
Paul .... Acts 24:5, 6
Stephen .... Acts 6:11
Christians .... 1 Pet. 2:12

C. *Hurled against the righteous by:*
Devil .... Job 1:9-11
Revilers .... 1 Pet. 3:16
Hypocrites .... Prov. 11:9
False leaders .... 3 John 9, 10

D. *Charged against Christ as:*
Winebibber .... Matt. 11:19
Blasphemer .... Matt. 9:3
Demonized .... John 8:48, 52
Rebel .... Luke 23:5
Insurrectionist .... Luke 23:2

E. *Christians:*
Warned against .... Titus 3:1, 2
Must endure .... Matt. 5:11, 12
Must lay aside .... Eph. 4:31

Slave, slavery—*a state of bondage*

A. *Acquired by:*
Purchase .... Gen. 17:12
Voluntary service .... Ex. 21:5-6
Birth .... Ex. 21:2-4
Capture .... Deut. 20:11-14
Debt .... 2 Kin. 4:1
Arrest .... Ex. 22:2, 3
Inheritance .... Lev. 25:46
Gift .... Gen. 29:24, 29

B. *Rights of:*
Sabbath rest .... Ex. 20:10
Share in religious feasts . Deut. 12:12, 18
Membership in covenant .... Gen. 17:10-14
Refuge for fugitive .... Deut. 23:15, 16
Murder of, punishable ..... Ex. 21:12
Freedom of, if maimed ..... Ex. 21:26, 27
Entitled to justice .... Job 31:13-15

C. *Privileges of:*
Entrusted with missions ... Gen. 24:1-14
Advice of, heeded .... 1 Sam. 9:5-10
Marriage in master's house 1 Chr. 2:34, 35
Rule over sons .... Prov. 17:2
May become heir .... Gen. 15:1-4
May secure freedom .... Ex. 21:2-6

D. *State of, under Christianity:*
Union "in Christ" .... Gal. 3:28
Treatment of with justice . Eph. 6:9
Duties of, as pleasing God Eph. 6:5-8

Sleep—*a state of complete or partial unconsciousness*

A. *Descriptive of:*
Slumber .... Prov. 6:4, 10
Desolation .... Jer. 51:39, 57
Unregeneracy .... 1 Thess. 5:6, 7
Death .... John 11:11-14
Spiritual indifference .... Matt. 25:5
Prophetic vision .... Dan. 8:18

B. *Beneficial:*
When given by God .... Ps. 3:5
Ps. 127:2
While trusting God .... Ps. 4:8
While obeying parents ..... Prov. 6:20-22
When following wisdom ..... Prov. 3:21-24
To the working man .... Eccl. 5:12

SUBJECT REFERENCE

After duty is done .... Ps. 132:1-5
During a pleasant dream ... Jer. 31:23-26

C. *Condemned:*
When excessive .... Prov. 6:9-11
During harvest .... Prov. 10:5
In times of danger .... Matt. 26:45-47

D. *Inability to:*
Caused by worry .... Dan. 2:1
Produced by insomnia ...... Esth. 6:1
Brought on by overwork .... Gen. 31:40

Sleight—*cunning; artifice*
Christians, beware of ..... Eph. 4:14

Slime
Used in Babel's tower ..... Gen. 11:3

Sling—*an instrument for throwing stones*

A. *Used by:*
Warriors .... Judg. 20:16
David .... 1 Sam. 17:40-50

B. *Figurative of:*
God's punishment .... 1 Sam. 25:29
Captivity .... Jer. 10:18
Foolishness .... Prov. 26:8

Slothfulness, sluggard—*laziness*

A. *Sources of, in:*
Excessive sleep .... Prov. 6:9-11
Laziness .... Prov. 19:15, 24
Indifference .... Judg. 18:9
Desires .... Prov. 21:25
Fearful imaginations ...... Prov. 22:13

B. *Way of:*
Brings hunger .... Prov. 19:15
Leads to poverty .... Prov. 20:4
Produces waste .... Prov. 18:9
Causes decay .... Eccl. 10:18
Results in forced labor ... Prov. 12:24

C. *Antidotes of, in:*
Faithfulness .... Matt. 25:26-30
Fervent spirit .... Rom. 12:11
Following the faithful .... Heb. 6:12

Slow bellies
Paul calls Cretians such .. Titus 1:12

Small—*little in size; few in number*

A. *Applied to God's:*
Choice .... Num. 16:5, 9
Faithful remnant .... Is. 1:9

B. *Applied to man's:*
Sin .... Ezek. 16:20
Unconcern .... Zech. 4:10

Smite, smitten—*to clobber; plague*

A. *Descriptive of:*
Curse .... Gen. 8:21
Plagues .... Ex. 3:20
Miracle .... Ex. 17:5, 6
God's punishments .... Deut. 28:22-28
Defeat .... 1 Sam. 4:2, 10
Death .... 2 Sam. 4:6, 7
Fear .... Dan. 5:6
Slapping .... Matt. 5:39

B. *Expressive of God's judgment on:*
Philistines .... 1 Sam. 5:6, 9
Pagan nation .... 2 Chr. 14:12
King's house .... 2 Chr. 21:5-19
Jews .... Jer. 14:19

C. *Used Messianically of Christ's:*
Scourging .... Is. 50:6
Bearing our sins .... Is. 53:4
Death .... Zech. 13:7
Judgment .... Is. 11:4

Smith—*a metal worker*
Blacksmith .... 1 Sam. 13:19, 20
Worker in iron .... Is. 44:12
Tubal-cain, first .... Gen. 4:22
Demetrius, silversmith .... Acts 19:24-27
Alexander, coppersmith .... 2 Tim. 4:14

Smoke

A. *Resulting from:*
Destruction .... Gen. 19:28
God's presence .... Is. 6:4
God's vengeance .... Is. 34:8-10
Babylon's end .... Rev. 14:8-11

SUBJECT REFERENCE

World's end .... Is. 51:6

B. *Figurative of:*
God's anger .... Deut. 29:20
Our life .... Ps. 102:3
Spiritual distress .... Ps. 119:83
Something offensive .... Is. 65:5
Spirit's advent .... Joel 2:29, 30

Smyrna—*a city of Iona in Asia Minor*
One of the seven churches . Rev. 1:11

Snail
Creature with a spiral tail Ps. 58:8

Snake charmer
Alluded to .... Ps. 58:4, 5

Snares—*traps*

A. *Uses of:*
Catch birds .... Prov. 7:23

B. *Figurative of:*
Pagan nations .... Josh. 23:12, 13
Idols .... Judg. 2:3
God's representative ...... Ex. 10:7
Words .... Prov. 6:2
Wicked works .... Ps. 9:16
Fear of man .... Prov. 29:25
Immoral woman .... Eccl. 7:26
Christ .... Is. 8:14, 15
Sudden destruction .... Luke 21:34, 35
Riches .... 1 Tim. 6:9, 10
Devil's trap .... 2 Tim. 2:26

Sneezed
Seven times .... 2 Kin. 4:35

Snow—*frozen crystallized flakes of water*

A. *Characteristics of:*
Comes in winter .... Prov. 26:1
Sent by God .... Job 37:6
Waters the earth .... Is. 55:10
Melts with heat .... Job 6:16, 17
Notable event during ...... 2 Sam. 23:20

B. *Whiteness illustrative of:*
Leprosy .... Ex. 4:6
Converted sinner .... Ps. 51:7
Is. 1:18
Nazarite's purity .... Lam. 4:7
Angel .... Matt. 28:3
Risen Christ .... Rev. 1:14

Snuffers, snuff dishes
Used for trimming wicks in lamps .... Ex. 37:23
Dishes used to catch snuff of lamps .... Ex. 25:38

So
Egyptian king .... 2 Kin. 17:4

Soap
Figuratively in .... Mal. 3:2

Sober, sobriety

A. *Described as:*
Sanity .... 2 Cor. 5:13
Soberness (not drunk) ..... 1 Tim. 3:2, 11
Temperate nature .... Titus 1:8
Humble mind .... Rom. 12:3
Moral rectitude .... Titus 2:12
Self-control .... Gal. 5:23
1 Cor. 7:9

B. *Incentives to, found in:*
Lord's return .... 1 Thess. 5:1-7
Nearness of the end .... 1 Pet. 4:7
Satan's attacks .... 1 Cor. 7:5

C. *Required of:*
Christians .... 1 Thess. 5:6, 8
Church officers .... 1 Tim. 3:2, 3
Wives of church officers .. 1 Tim. 3:11
Aged men .... Titus 2:2
Young women .... Titus 2:4
Young men .... Titus 2:6
Women .... 1 Tim. 2:9
Children .... 1 Tim. 2:15
Evangelists .... 2 Tim. 4:5

See Temperance

Sociability—*friendly relations in social gatherings*

A. *Manifested in:*
Family life .... John 12:1-9
National life .... Neh. 8:9-18
Church life .... Acts 2:46

SUBJECT	REFERENCE
B. *Christian's kind, governed by:*	
No fellowship with evil	2 Cor. 6:14-18
Righteous living	Titus 2:12
Honesty in all things	Col. 3:9-14

Socialism (see Communism, Christian)

Socoh, Sochoh—*thorn*

1. Town in south Judah	Josh. 15:1, 35
Where David killed Goliath	1 Sam. 17:1, 49
2. Town in Judah's hill country	Josh. 15:1, 48

Sodi—*an acquaintance*

Father of the Zebulunite spy	Num. 13:10

Sodom—*burnt*

A. *History of:*	
Located in Jordan plain	Gen. 13:10
Became Lot's residence	Gen. 13:11-13
Wickedness of, notorious	Gen. 13:13
Plundered by Chedor-laomer	Gen. 14:9-24
Abraham interceded for	Gen. 18:16-33
Destroyed by God	Gen. 19:1-28
Lot sent out of	Gen. 19:29, 30
B. *Destruction of, illustrative of:*	
God's wrath	Deut. 29:23
Sudden destruction	Lam. 4:6
Total destruction	Jer. 49:18
Future judgment	Matt. 11:23, 24
Example to the ungodly	2 Pet. 2:6
C. *Sin of, illustrative of:*	
Shamelessness	Is. 3:9
Obduracy	Jer. 23:14
Unnaturalness	Jude 7
D. *Figurative of:*	
Wickedness	Deut. 32:32
Jerusalem	Is. 1:9, 10
Judah	Ezek. 16:46-63

Sodomite—*a male cult prostitute*

Prohibition of	Deut. 23:17, 18
Prevalence of, under Rehoboam	1 Kin. 14:24
Asa's removal of	1 Kin. 15:11, 12
Jehoshaphat's riddance of	1 Kin. 22:46
Josiah's reforms against	2 Kin. 23:7
Result of unbelief	Rom. 1:27

Soil—*dirt*

It was planted in good	Ezek. 17:8
Uzziah loved it	2 Chr. 26:10

Sojourn, sojourner

A. *Descriptive of:*	
Abram in Egypt	Gen. 12:10
Jacob with Laban	Gen. 32:4
Israel in Egypt	Gen. 47:4
Stranger	Ex. 12:48, 49
Wandering Levite	Deut. 18:6
Naomi in Moab	Ruth 1:1
Remnant in Egypt	Jer. 42:15-23
Jews in captivity	Ezra 1:4
B. *Characterized by:*	
Simplicity of living	Heb. 11:9
Being among enemies	2 Kin. 8:1, 2
LORD's blessing	Gen. 26:2, 3
C. *Figurative of:*	
Righteous in the world	1 Chr. 29:15
Christian in the world	1 Pet. 1:17

See Foreigners; Strangers

Sold

Descriptive of:	
Purchase	Matt. 26:9
Slavery	Ps. 105:17
Bondage to sin	Rom. 7:14

Soldiers—*military agents of a nation*

A. *Good characteristics of:*	
Obedience	Matt. 8:9
Devotion	Acts 10:7
Subduing riots	Acts 21:31-35
Guarding prisoners	Acts 12:4-6
B. *Bad charcteristics of:*	
Cowardice	Deut. 20:8
Discontent and violence	Luke 3:14
Rashness	Acts 27:42
Bribery	Matt. 28:12
Irreligion	John 19:2, 3, 23
C. *Figurative of:*	
Christians	2 Tim. 2:4
Christian workers	Phil. 2:25
Spiritual armor	Eph. 6:10-18

Solitude—*aloneness*

For:	
Adam, not good	Gen. 2:18
Prayer, good	Matt. 6:6 Matt. 14:23
Rest, necessary	Mark 6:30, 31

Solomon—*peace*

A. *Life of:*	
David's son by Bathsheba	2 Sam. 12:24
Name of, significant	1 Chr. 22:9
Anointed over opposition	1 Kin. 1:5-48
Spared Adonijah	1 Kin. 1:49-53
Received dying instruction from David	1 Kin. 2:1-10
Purged his kingdom of corrupt leaders	1 Kin. 2:11-46
Prayer of, for wisdom	1 Kin. 3:1-15
Organized his kingdom	1 Kin. 4:1-28
Fame of, world wide	1 Kin. 4:29-34
Built the Temple	1 Kin. 5—6
Dedicated the Temple	1 Kin. 8:22-66
Built personal palace	1 Kin. 7:1-12
LORD reappeared to	1 Kin. 9:1-9
Strengthened his kingdom	1 Kin. 9:10-28
Received queen of Sheba	1 Kin. 10:1-13
Encouraged commerce	1 Kin. 10:14-29
Falls into polygamy and idolatry	1 Kin. 11:1-8
God warned him	1 Kin. 11:9-13
Adversaries arise against him	1 Kin. 11:14-40
Reign and death	1 Kin. 11:41-43
B. *Good features of:*	
Chooses an understanding heart	1 Kin. 3:5-9
Exhibited sound judgment	1 Kin. 3:16-28
Excels in wisdom	1 Kin. 4:29-34
Great writer	1 Kin. 4:32
Writer of Psalms	Ps. 72 (Title)
C. *Bad features of:*	
Loves luxury	Eccl. 2:1-11
Marries pagans	1 Kin. 11:1-3
Turns to idolatry	1 Kin. 11:4-8
Enslaves Israel	1 Kin. 12:1-4

Son

A. *Descriptive of:*	
Male child	Gen. 4:25, 26
Half-brothers	Gen. 25:9
Grandson	Gen. 29:5
Disciple	Prov. 7:1
One possessing a certain character	1 Sam. 2:12
One destined to a certain end	John 17:12
Messiah	Is. 7:14
Christian	John 1:12
Angels	Job 1:6
B. *Characteristics of, sometimes:*	
Jealous	Judg. 9:2, 18
Quite different	Gen. 9:18-27
Disloyal	Luke 15:25-30
Unlike their father	2 Sam. 13:30-39
Spiritually different	Gen. 25:22-34
C. *Admonitions addressed to, concerning:*	
Instruction	Prov. 1:8
Sinners	Prov. 1:10-19
Wisdom	Prov. 3:13-35
Correction	Prov. 3:11, 12
Immorality	Prov. 5:1-23
Life's dangers	Prov. 6:1-35

Son-in-law—*a daughter's husband*

Sinful	Gen. 19:14
Believing	Mark 1:29, 30

Son of God—*a title indicating Christ's deity*

A. *Descriptive of Christ as:*	
Eternally begotten	Ps. 2:7 Heb. 1:5
Messianic King	Ps. 89:26, 27
Virgin-born	Luke 1:31-35
Trinity-member	Matt. 28:19
Priest-king	Heb. 1:8 Heb. 5:5, 6
B. *Witnesses of, by:*	
Father	Matt. 17:5
Angels	John 1:51
Demons	Mark 5:7
Satan	Matt. 4:3, 6
Men	Matt. 16:16
Christ Himself	John 9:35-37
His resurrection	Rom. 1:1-4
Christians	Acts 2:36
Scriptures	John 20:31
Inner witness	1 John 5:10-13
C. *Significance of, as indicating:*	
Cost of man's reconciliation	Rom. 5:6-11
Greatness of God's love	John 3:16
Sin of unbelief	Heb. 10:28, 29
Worship due Christ	Rev. 4:11
Dignity of human nature	Rom. 8:3 Heb. 2:14
Humanity of Christ	Gal. 4:4
Pattern of glorification	Rom. 8:29 Phil. 3:21
Destruction of Satan	1 John 3:8
Uniqueness of Christ	Heb. 1:5-9
D. *Belief in Christ as:*	
Derived from the Scriptures	John 20:31
Necessary for eternal life	John 3:18, 36
Source of eternal life	John 6:40
Foundation of the faith	Acts 9:20
Affirmation of deity	1 John 2:23, 24
Illustrated	John 11:14-44
E. *Powers of Christ as, to:*	
Have life in Himself	John 5:26
Reveal the Father	Matt. 11:27
Glorify the Father	John 17:1
Do the Father's works	John 5:19, 20
Redeem men	Gal. 4:4, 5
Give freedom	John 8:36
Raise the dead	John 5:21, 25
Judge men	John 5:22

Son of Man—*a self-designation of Christ*

A. *Title of, applied to:*	
Ezekiel	Ezek. 2:1, 3, 6
Daniel	Dan. 8:17
Messiah	Dan. 7:13
Christ:	
By Himself	Matt. 8:20
By only Stephen elsewhere	Acts 7:56
In John's vision	Rev. 1:13
B. *As indicative of Christ's:*	
Self-designation	Matt. 16:13
Humanity	Matt. 11:19
Messiahship	Luke 18:31
Lordship	Matt. 12:8
Sovereignty	Matt. 13:41
Obedience	Phil. 2:8
Suffering	Mark 9:12
Death	Matt. 12:40
Resurrection	Matt. 17:9-23
Regal power	Matt. 16:28
Return	Matt. 24:27-37
Glorification	Heb. 2:6-10
C. *Christ's powers as, to:*	
Forgive sins	Matt. 9:6
Save men	Luke 19:10
Redeem men	Matt. 20:28
Reward men	Matt. 16:27
Reward men	Matt. 19:28
Rule His Church	Col. 1:17, 18

Song of Solomon—*a book of the Old Testament*

The bride and the bridegroom	Song 1
Song of the bride	Song 2:8—3:5
Song of the bridegroom	Song 4:1-15
The bride meditates	Song 4:16—6:3
The bridegroom appeals	Song 6:4—7:9
Lovers united	Song 7:10—8:14

Songs

A. *Described as:*	
New	Rev. 5:9
Spiritual	Eph. 5:19
B. *Uses of, as:*	
Witness	Deut. 31:19-22
Torment	Ps. 137:3
March	Num. 21:17, 18
Processional	1 Chr. 13:7, 8

SUBJECT — REFERENCE

C. *Expressive of:*
Triumph … Judg. 5:12
Physical joy … Gen. 31:27
Spiritual joy … Ps. 119:54
Deliverance … Ps. 32:7
Hypocrisy … Amos 5:23
Derision … Ps. 69:12

D. *Figurative of:*
Passover (the Lord's Supper) … Is. 30:29; Matt. 26:26-30
Messiah's advent … Is. 42:10
Gospel age … Is. 26:1, 2

Song writer
Solomon, famous as … 1 Kin. 4:32

Sonship of believers

A. *Evidences of, seen in:*
New nature … 1 John 3:9-12
Possession of the Spirit … Rom. 8:15-17
Chastisement … Heb. 12:5-8

B. *Blessedness of, manifested in:*
Regeneration … John 1:12
Adoption … Gal. 4:5, 6
Glorification … Rom. 8:19-21

Soothsayer—*a diviner, fortune teller*
Among Philistines … Is. 2:6
At Babylon … Dan. 2:27
At Philippi … Acts 16:12, 16
Unable to interpret … Dan. 4:7
Forbidden in Israel … Mic. 5:12
See Divination

Sop—*a small portion of food*
Christ gives to Judas … John 13:26-30

Sopater—*of sound parentage*
One of Paul's companions … Acts 20:4

Sophereth—*writer, scribe*
Descendants of Solomon's servants … Neh. 7:57

Sorcerers—*supposed possessors of supernatural powers*

A. *Prevalence of, in:*
Assyria … Nah. 3:4, 5
Egypt … Ex. 7:11
Babylon … Is. 47:9-13
Palestine … Acts 8:9-24
Last days … Rev. 9:21

B. *Punishment of, described:*
Legally … Deut. 18:10-12
Prophetically … Mal. 3:5
Symbolically … Rev. 21:8
See Divination; Magic, magician

Sorcery—*the practice of magic*
Forbidden in Israel … Deut. 18:10
Condemned by the prophets … Mic. 5:12
Practiced by Manasseh … 2 Chr. 33:6
Work of the flesh … Gal. 5:20

Sore
Intense feeling … 2 Sam. 13:36
Crisis … Gen. 41:56, 57
Plague … Lev. 13:42, 43

Sorek—*a choice vine*
Valley, home of Delilah … Judg. 16:4

Sorrow—*grief*

A. *Kinds of:*
Hypocritical … Matt. 14:9
Unfruitful … Matt. 19:22
Temporary … John 16:6, 20-22
Continual … Rom. 9:2
Fruitful … 2 Cor. 7:8-11
Christian … 1 Thess. 4:13

B. *Caused by:*
Sin … Gen. 3:16, 17
Death … John 11:33-35
Drunkenness … Prov. 23:29-35
Love of money … 1 Tim. 6:10
Apostasy … Ps. 16:4
Persecution … Esth. 9:22
Hardship of life … Ps. 90:10
Knowledge … Eccl. 1:18
Distressing news … Acts 20:37, 38

C. *Of the righteous:*
Not like the world's … 1 Thess. 4:13
Sometimes intense … Ps. 18:4, 5
Seen in the face … Neh. 2:2-4
None in God's blessings … Prov. 10:22
Shown in repentance … 2 Cor. 7:10
To be removed … Is. 25:8
None in heaven … Rev. 21:4
Shall flee away … Is. 51:11
See Grief

Sosipater—*saving a father*
Kinsman of Paul … Rom. 16:21

Sosthenes—*of sound strength*
1. Ruler of the synagogue at Corinth … Acts 18:17
2. Paul's Christian brother … 1 Cor. 1:1

Sotai—*Jehovah is turning aside*
Head of a family of servants … Ezra 2:55

Sottish—*thick-headed*
Judah thus called … Jer. 4:22

Soul—*the immaterial part of man*

A. *Descriptive of:*
Man's life … 1 Sam. 24:11
People … Acts 2:41, 43
Sinner … James 5:20
Emotional life … 1 Sam. 18:1, 3
Spiritual life … Ps. 42:1, 2, 4
Disembodied state … Rev. 6:9; Rev. 20:4

B. *Characteristics of:*
Made by God … Gen. 2:7
Belongs to God … Ezek. 18:3, 4
Possesses immortality … Matt. 10:28
Most vital asset … Matt. 16:26
Leaves body at death … Gen. 35:18

C. *Abilities of, able to:*
Believe … Heb. 10:39
Love God … Luke 10:27
Sin … Mic. 6:7
Prosper … 3 John 2
Survive death … Matt. 10:28

D. *Duties of, to:*
Keep itself … Deut. 4:9
Seek the LORD … Deut. 4:29
Love the LORD … Deut. 6:5
Serve the LORD … Deut. 10:12
Store God's Word … Deut. 11:18
Keep God's Law … Deut. 26:16
Obey God … Deut. 30:2, 6, 10
Get wisdom … Prov. 19:8

E. *Enemies of, seen in:*
Fleshly lusts … 1 Pet. 2:11
Evil environment … 2 Pet. 2:8
Sin … Lev. 5:4, 15, 17
Adultery … Prov. 6:32
Evil men … Prov. 22:24, 25
Ignorance … Prov. 8:36
Hell … Prov. 23:14

F. *Of the righteous:*
Kept by God … Ps. 121:7
Vexed by sin … 2 Pet. 2:8
Subject to authorities … Rom. 13:1
Purified by obedience … 1 Pet. 1:22
Not allowed to famish … Prov. 10:3
Restored … Ps. 23:1, 3
Enriched … Prov. 11:25
Satisfied … Prov. 13:25
Reign with Christ … Rev. 20:4

G. *Of the wicked:*
Desires evil … Prov. 21:10
Delights in abominations … Is. 66:3
Has nothing … Prov. 13:4
Required … Luke 12:19, 20
To be punished … Rom. 2:9

Soul winning
Importance of … James 5:20
Christ's command … Matt. 4:19
Our reward … Dan. 12:3

Sound doctrine

A. *Manifested in:*
Heart's prayer … Ps. 119:80
Speech … 2 Tim. 1:13
Righteous living … 1 Tim. 1:10

B. *Need of:*
For exhortation … Titus 1:9
For the faith … Titus 1:13
Denied by some … 2 Tim. 4:3

Sour grapes—*not yet mature*
Used proverbially … Jer. 31:29, 30

Sowing—*scattering seed*

A. *Restrictions upon, regarding:*
Sabbath year … Lev. 25:3-22
Mingled seed … Lev. 19:19
Weather … Eccl. 11:4, 6

B. *Figurative of evil things:*
Iniquity … Job 4:8
Wind … Hos. 8:7
Discord … Prov. 6:14, 19
Strife … Prov. 16:28
False teaching … Matt. 13:25, 39
Sin … Gal. 6:7, 8

C. *Figurative of good things:*
God's Word … Is. 55:10
Reward … 2 Cor. 9:6, 10
Gospel … Matt. 13:3, 4, 37
Gospel messengers … John 4:36, 37
Resurrection … 1 Cor. 15:36-44
Eternal life … Gal. 6:7-9

Spain—*a country in southwest Europe*
Paul desires to visit … Rom. 15:24, 28

Sparrow—*a small bird*
Value of … Matt. 10:29, 31

Spearmen—*infantry men with spears*
One of, pierces Christ's side … John 19:34
Paul's military escort … Acts 23:23, 24

Speckled
Spotted (of goats) … Gen. 30:32-39
Colored (of birds) … Jer. 12:9

Speech—*the intelligible utterance of the mouth*

A. *Of the wicked, consisting of:*
Lies … Ps. 58:3
Cursing … Ps. 59:12
Enticements … Prov. 7:21
Blasphemies … Dan. 7:25
Earthly things … John 3:31
Deception … Rom. 16:18

B. *Of the righteous, consisting of:*
God's righteousness … Ps. 35:28
Wisdom … 1 Cor. 2:6, 7
God's Word … Ps. 119:172
Truth … Eph. 4:25
Mystery of Christ … Col. 4:3, 4
Sound doctrine … Titus 2:1, 8

Speed—*to hasten*
"Let him make" … Is. 5:19
"They will come with" … Is. 5:26

Spending—*paying out money or service for things*

A. *Wastefully, on:*
Harlots … Luke 15:30
Physicians … Mark 5:26

B. *Wisely:*
In Christ's service … 2 Cor. 12:15

Spices—*aromatic vegetable compounds*

A. *Uses of:*
Food … Song 8:2
Incense … Ex. 30:34-38
Fragrance … Song 4:10

B. *Features concerning:*
Used as presents … Gen. 43:11
Objects of commerce … Gen. 37:25
Tokens of royal favor … 1 Kin. 10:2
Stored in the temple … 1 Chr. 9:29
Sign of wealth … 2 Kin. 20:13

Spider
Web of, figurative of:
Insecurity … Is. 59:5
Godless … Job 8:14

Spies—*secret agents of a foreign government*

A. *Purpose of, to:*
Search out Canaan … Num. 13:1-33
Prepare for invasion … Josh. 2:1-21
Search out new land … Judg. 18:2-17
Make false charges … Luke 20:20

SUBJECT REFERENCE

B. *Men accused of, falsely:*
- Jacob's sons ... Gen. 42:9-34
- David's servants ... 2 Sam. 10:3

Spikenard
- Used as a perfume ... Song 1:12
- Mary uses it in anointing Jesus ... Mark 14:3; John 12:3

Spill—*to flow forth*
- Water ... 2 Sam. 14:14
- Wine ... Luke 5:37

Spinning—*twisting fibers together to form cloth*
- Work done by women ... Ex. 35:25
- Sign of industry ... Prov. 31:19
- As an illustration ... Matt. 6:28

Spirit—*an immaterial being*

A. *Descriptive of:*
- Holy Spirit ... Gen. 1:2
- Angels ... Heb. 1:7, 14
- Man's immaterial nature ... 1 Cor. 2:11
- Evil ... 1 Sam. 16:14-23
- Believer's immaterial nature ... 1 Cor. 5:3, 5
- Controlling influence ... Is. 29:10
- Inward reality ... Rom. 2:29
- Disembodied state ... Heb. 12:23; 1 Pet. 3:19

B. *Characteristics of, in man:*
- Center of emotions ... 1 Kin. 21:5
- Source of passions ... Ezek. 3:14
- Cause of volitions (will) ... Prov. 16:32
- Subject to divine influence ... Deut. 2:30; Is. 19:14
- Leaves body at death ... Eccl. 12:7; James 2:26

See Soul

Spirit, Holy (see Holy Spirit)

Spirit of Christ

A. *Descriptive of the Holy Spirit as:*
- Dwelling in Old Testament prophets ... 1 Pet. 1:10-11
- Sent by God ... Gal. 4:6
- Given to believers ... Rom. 8:9
- Supplying believers ... Phil. 1:19
- Produces boldness ... Acts 4:29-31
- Commanded ... Eph. 5:18

B. *Christ's human spirit (consciousness), of His:*
- Perception ... Mark 2:8
- Emotions ... Mark 8:12
- Life ... Luke 23:46

Spirits, distinguishing of

A. *Described as:*
- Spiritual gift ... 1 Cor. 12:10
- Necessary ... 1 Thess. 5:19-21

B. *Tests of:*
- Christ's:
  - Deity ... 1 Cor. 12:3
  - Humanity ... 1 John 4:1-6
- Christian fellowship ... 1 John 2:18, 19

Spiritual—*the holy or immaterial*

A. *Applied to:*
- Gifts ... 1 Cor. 12:1
- Law ... Rom. 7:14
- Things ... Rom. 15:27
- Christians ... 1 Cor. 3:1
- Resurrected body ... 1 Cor. 15:44-46
- Evil forces ... Eph. 6:12

B. *Designating, Christians:*
- Ideal state ... 1 Cor. 3:1
- Discernment ... 1 Cor. 2:13-15
- Duty ... Gal. 6:1
- Manner of life ... Col. 3:16

Spiritual gifts (see Gifts, spiritual)

Spiritually—*a holy frame of mind*
- Source of ... Gal. 5:22-26
- Expression of ... 1 Cor. 13:1-13
- Growth in ... 2 Pet. 1:4-11
- Enemies of ... 1 John 2:15-17

Spite—*an injury prompted by contempt*
- Of vexation of grief ... Ps. 10:14
- Inflicted upon Christ ... Matt. 22:6

SUBJECT REFERENCE

Spitting, spittle

A. *Symbolic of:*
- Contempt ... Num. 12:14
- Rejection ... Matt. 26:67
- Uncleanness ... Lev. 15:8

B. *Miraculous uses of, to heal:*
- Dumb man ... Mark 7:33-35
- Blind man ... Mark 8:23-25
- Man born blind ... John 9:6, 7

Spoil—*loot or plunder*
- Clothing ... Ex. 3:22
- Cattle ... Josh. 8:2
- Sheep ... Num. 31:32
- House ... Mark 3:27
- Silver and gold ... Nah. 2:9
- Camp ... 1 Sam. 17:53

Spokesman—*one who speaks for others*
- Aaron deputed to be ... Ex. 4:14-16

Sponge—*a very absorbent sea fossil*
- Full of vinegar, offered to Christ ... Matt. 27:48

Spot, spotless

A. *Descriptive of:*
- Blemish on the face ... Job 11:15
- Imperfection of the body ... Song 4:7
- Mixed colors ... Gen. 30:32-39
- Leopard's spots ... Jer. 13:23

B. *Figuratively* ("spotless") *of:*
- Sin ... Jude 23
- False teachers ... 2 Pet. 2:13
- Christ's death ... 1 Pet. 1:19
- Believer's perfection ... 2 Pet. 3:14
- Glorified Church ... Eph. 5:27
- Perfect offering ... Num. 19:2
- Obedience ... 1 Tim. 6:14

Springtime—*the season of nature's rebirth*
- Symbolically described ... Song 2:11-13

Sprinkle

A. *Used literally of:*
- Water ... Num. 8:7
- Oil ... Lev. 14:16
- Human blood ... 2 Kin. 9:33

B. *Of blood, used in:*
- Passover ... Ex. 12:21, 22
- Sinaitic covenant ... Ex. 24:8; Heb. 9:19, 21
- Sin offering ... Lev. 4:6
- New covenant ... Heb. 12:24

C. *Used figuratively of:*
- Regeneration ... Heb. 10:22
- Purification ... 1 Pet. 1:2

Square—*having four equal sides*
- Altar ... Ex. 27:1
- Breastplate ... Ex. 39:8, 9
- City of God ... Rev. 21:16

Stab—*to pierce with a knife*
- Asahel by Abner ... 2 Sam. 2:22, 23
- Abner by Joab ... 2 Sam. 3:27
- Amasa by Joab ... 2 Sam. 20:10

Stachys—*head of grain*
- One whom Paul loved ... Rom. 16:9

Staff—*a long stick or rod*
- A traveler's support ... Gen. 32:10
- Denotes food support ... Lev. 26:26
- A military weapon ... Is. 10:24

Stairs, winding
- Part of Solomon's Temple ... 1 Kin. 6:8

Stalls—*quarters for animals*
- 40,000 in Solomon's time ... 1 Kin. 4:26

Stammerer—*one who stutters*
- Used of judicial punishment ... Is. 28:11
- Of the Gospel age ... Is. 32:1, 4

Stars

A. *Features concerning:*
- Created by God ... Gen. 1:16
- Ordained by God ... Ps. 8:3
- Set in the expanse ... Gen. 1:17
- Follow fixed ordinances ... Jer. 31:35, 36

SUBJECT REFERENCE

- Named by God ... Ps. 147:4
- Established forever ... Ps. 148:3, 6
- Of vast numbers ... Gen. 15:5
- Manifest God's power ... Is. 40:26
- Of different proportions ... 1 Cor. 15:41
- Very high ... Job 22:12

B. *Worship of:*
- Forbidden ... Deut. 4:19
- Punished ... Deut. 17:3-7
- Introduced by Manasseh ... 2 Kin. 21:3
- Condemned by the prophets ... Jer. 8:2; Zeph. 1:4, 5

C. *List of, in Bible:*
- Arcturus ... Job 9:9
- Mazzaroth ... Job 38:32
- Orion ... Job 9:9
- Pleiades ... Job 9:9
- Chambers of the south ... Job 9:9
- Of Bethlehem ... Matt. 2:2, 9, 10

D. *Figurative of:*
- Christ's:
  - First Advent ... Num. 24:17
  - Second Advent ... Rev. 22:16
- Angels ... Rev. 1:16, 20
- Judgment ... Ezek. 32:7
- False security ... Obad. 4
- Glorified saints ... Dan. 12:3
- Apostates ... Jude 13

State—*established government*

A. *Agents of:*
- Under God's control ... Dan. 4:17, 25; Jon. 19:10, 11
- Sometimes evil ... Mark 6:14-29
- Sometimes good ... Neh. 2:1-9
- Protectors of the Law ... Rom. 13:1-4

B. *Duties of Christians to:*
- Pray for ... 1 Tim. 2:1, 2
- Pay taxes to ... Matt. 22:17-21
- Be subject to ... Rom. 13:5, 6
- Resist (when evil) ... Acts 4:17-21

Stature—*the natural height of the body*

A. *Used physically of:*
- Giants ... Num. 13:32
- Sabeans ... Is. 45:14

B. *Significance of:*
- Normal, in human growth ... Luke 2:52
- Cannot be changed ... Matt. 6:27
- Not indicative of greatness ... 1 Sam. 16:7
- In spiritual things ... Eph. 4:13

Statute of limitation
- Recognized in the Law ... Deut. 15:1-5, 9

Steadfastness—*firm, persistent and determined in one's endeavors*

A. *In human things, following:*
- Person ... Ruth 1:18
- Leader ... Jer. 35:1-19
- Principle ... Dan. 1:8

B. *In spiritual things:*
- Enduring chastisement ... Heb. 12:7
- Bearing persecution ... Rom. 8:35-37
- Maintaining perseverance ... Heb. 3:6, 14
- Stability of faith ... Col. 2:5
- Persevering in service ... 1 Cor. 15:58
- Resisting Satan ... 1 Pet. 5:9
- Defending Christian liberty ... Gal. 5:1

C. *Elements of, seen in:*
- Having a goal ... Phil. 3:12-14
- Discipline ... 1 Cor. 9:25-27
- Run the race ... Heb. 12:1, 2
- Never give up ... Rev. 3:10, 21

Stealing—*taking another's property*
- Common on earth ... Matt. 6:19
- Forbidden in:
  - Law ... Ex. 20:15
  - Gospel ... Rom. 13:9
- Christians not to do ... Eph. 4:28
- Excludes from heaven ... 1 Cor. 6:9, 10
- None in heaven ... Matt. 6:20

Stephanas—*crowned*
- Corinthian Christian ... 1 Cor. 1:16
- First convert of Achaia ... 1 Cor. 16:15
- Visits Paul ... 1 Cor. 16:17

Stephen—*wreath or crown*
- One of the seven deacons ... Acts 6:1-8

SUBJECT ... REFERENCE

Accused falsely by Jews ... Acts 6:9-15
Spoke before the Jewish Sanhedrin ... Acts 7:2-53
Became first Christian martyr ... Acts 7:54-60
Saul (Paul) instigated in death of ... Acts 7:58

Steward, stewardship—*a trust granted for profitable use*

A. *Descriptive of:*
One over Joseph's household ... Gen. 43:19
Curator or guardian ... Matt. 20:8
Manager ... Luke 16:2, 3
Management of entrusted duties ... 1 Cor. 9:17

B. *Duties of, to:*
Expend monies ... Rom. 16:23
Serve wisely ... Luke 12:42

C. *Of spiritual things, based on:*
LORD's ownership ... Ps. 24:1, 2; Rom. 14:8
Our redemption ... 1 Cor. 6:20
Gifts bestowed upon us ... Matt. 25:14, 15; 1 Pet. 4:10
Offices given to us ... Eph. 3:2-10; Titus 1:7
Faithful in responsibilities ... Luke 16:1-3

Stewardship, personal finanical

Basic principles:
Settling accounts ... Rom. 14:12
God's ownership ... Ps. 24:1; Rom. 14:7, 8; 1 Cor. 6:20
Finances and spirituality inseparable ... Matt. 19:16-22; Luke 16:10-13; 2 Cor. 8:3-8
Needs will be provided ... Matt. 6:24-34; Phil. 4:19
Content with what God provides ... Ps. 37:25; 1 Tim. 6:6-10; Heb. 13:5
Righteousness ... Prov. 16:8; Rom. 12:17
Avoid debt ... Prov. 22:7; Rom. 13:8
Do not co-sign ... Prov. 6:1-5; Prov. 22:26
Inheritance uncertain ... Prov. 17:2; Prov. 20:21
Proper priority ... Matt. 6:19-21, 33
Prosperity is from God ... Deut. 29:9; Ps. 1:1-3; 3 John 2
Saving ... Prov. 21:20
Laziness condemned ... Prov. 24:30, 31; Heb. 6:12
Giving is encouraged ... Prov. 3:9, 10; Mal. 3:10-12; 2 Cor. 9:6-8

Sticks—*pieces of wood*

Gathering on Sabbath condemned ... Num. 15:32-35
Necessary ... 1 Kin. 17:10-12
Miracle producing ... 2 Kin. 6:6
Two become one ... Ezek. 37:16-22
Viper in bundle of ... Acts 28:3

Stiff-necked—*rebellious; unteachable*

A. *Indicative of Israel's rebelliousness at:*
Sinai ... Ex. 32:9
Conquest ... Deut. 9:6, 13
Captivity ... 2 Chr. 36:13
Christ's first Advent ... Acts 7:51

B. *Remedies of, seen in:*
Circumcision (regeneration) ... Deut. 10:16
Yield to God ... 2 Chr. 30:8

Still

A. *Indicative of:*
God's voice ... 1 Kin. 19:12
God's presence ... Ps. 139:18
Fright ... Ex. 15:16
Fixed character ... Rev. 22:11
Peace ... Jer. 47:6
Quietness ... Num. 13:30

B. *Accomplished by:*
God ... Ps. 107:29
Christ ... Mark 4:39

SUBJECT ... REFERENCE

Submission ... Ps. 46:10
Communion ... Ps. 4:4

Stink—*a foul smell*

A. *Caused by:*
Dead fish ... Ex. 7:18, 21
Corpse ... John 11:39
Wounds ... Ps. 38:5

B. *Figurative of:*
Hostility toward one ... Gen. 34:30
Hell ... Is. 34:3, 4

Stir up

A. *Of strife, etc., by:*
Wrath ... Prov. 15:18
Hatred ... Prov. 10:12
Grievous words ... Prov. 15:1
Unbelief ... Acts 13:50
Agitators ... Acts 6:12
Kings ... Dan. 11:2, 25

B. *Of good things:*
Generosity ... Ex. 35:21, 26
Repentance ... Is. 64:7
Ministry ... 2 Tim. 1:6
Memory ... 2 Pet. 1:13

C. *Of God's sovereignty in:*
Punishment ... 1 Kin. 11:14, 23
Fulfilling His Word ... 2 Chr. 36:22; Ezra 1:1
Accomplishing His purpose ... Is. 13:17; Hag. 1:14

Stocks—*blocks of wood*

Instrument of punishment ... Acts 16:19, 24
Punishment ... Job 33:11

Stoics—*pertaining to a colonnade or porch*

Sect of philosophers founded by Zeno around 308 B.C. ... Acts 17:18

Stomacher

Rich, festive robe ... Is. 3:24

Stones—*rocks*

A. *Natural uses of:*
Weighing ... Lev. 19:36
Knives ... Ex. 4:25
Weapons ... 1 Sam. 17:40-50
Holding water ... Ex. 7:19
Covering wells ... Gen. 29:2
Covering tombs ... Matt. 27:60
Landmarks ... Deut. 19:14
Writing inscriptions ... Ex. 24:12
Buildings ... Matt. 24:1, 2
Missiles ... Ex. 21:18

B. *Religious uses of:*
Altars ... Ex. 20:25
Grave ... Josh. 7:26
Memorial ... Josh. 4:20
Witness ... Josh. 24:26, 27
Inscriptions ... Deut. 27:4, 8
Idolatry ... Lev. 26:1

C. *Figurative of:*
Reprobation ... 1 Sam. 25:37
Contempt ... 2 Sam. 16:6, 13
Christ's rejection ... Ps. 118:22
Christ as foundation ... Is. 28:16
Desolation ... Jer. 51:26
Unregeneracy ... Ezek. 11:19
Christ's Advent ... Dan. 2:34, 35
Conscience ... Hab. 2:11
Insensibility ... Zech. 7:12
Gentiles ... Matt. 3:9
Christ as Head ... Matt. 21:42-44
Good works ... 1 Cor. 3:12
Christians ... 1 Pet. 2:5
Spirit's witness ... Rev. 2:17

See Rock

Stones (II)

Male testicles ... Lev. 21:20

Stones, precious

Agate ... Is. 54:12
Amethyst ... Rev. 21:20
Beryl ... Dan. 10:6
Chalcedony ... Rev. 21:19
Chrysolite ... Rev. 21:20
Crystal ... Rev. 22:1
Diamond ... Jer. 17:1
Emerald ... Ex. 28:17
Jasper ... Rev. 4:3

SUBJECT ... REFERENCE

Jacinth ... Ex. 28:19
Ligure ... Ex. 28:19
Onyx ... Gen. 2:12
Ruby ... Ex. 28:17
Sapphire ... Job 28:6, 16
Sardius ... Rev. 4:3
Sardonyx ... Rev. 21:20
Topaz ... Job 28:19

Stoning—*a means of executing criminals*

A. *Punishment inflicted for:*
Sacrificing children ... Lev. 20:2-5
Divination ... Lev. 20:27
Blasphemy ... Lev. 24:15-23
Sabbath-breaking ... Num. 15:32-36
Apostasy ... Deut. 13:1-10
Idolatry ... Deut. 17:2-7
Juvenile rebellion ... Deut. 21:18-21
Adultery ... Deut. 22:22

B. *Examples of:*
Achan ... Josh. 7:20-26
Adoram ... 1 Kin. 12:18
Naboth ... 1 Kin. 21:13
Zechariah ... 2 Chr. 24:20, 21
Stephen ... Acts 7:59
Paul ... Acts 14:19
Prophets ... Heb. 11:37

Stool

Birthstool ... Ex. 1:16

Storehouses—*places for storing things*

A. *Descriptive of:*
Barns ... Deut. 28:8
Warehouses ... Gen. 41:56
Temple ... Mal. 3:10
God's portion ... 1 Cor. 16:2

B. *Used for storing:*
Grain ... 2 Chr. 32:28
The tithe ... Mal. 3:10
Treasures ... 2 Kin. 20:17

Stork—*a large, long-legged, migratory bird*

Nesting of ... Ps. 104:17
Migration of ... Jer. 8:7
Ceremonially unclean ... Lev. 11:19

Storm—*a violent upheaval of nature*

A. *Described as:*
Grievous ... Ex. 9:23-25
Sent by God ... Josh. 10:11
Destructive ... Matt. 7:27

B. *Effects of, upon:*
Israelites ... Ex. 19:16, 19
Philistines ... 1 Sam. 7:10
Mariners ... Jon. 1:4-14
Animals ... Ps. 29:3-9
Disciples ... Mark 4:37-41
Soldiers and sailors ... Acts 27:14-44
Nature ... Ps. 29:3, 5, 8

Strange woman—*adulteress*

Uses flattery ... Prov. 2:16

Strangers—*foreigners living among the Jews*

A. *Descriptive of:*
Non-Jews ... Ex. 12:48
Foreigners ... Matt. 17:25
Transients ... Luke 24:18
Visitors ... Acts 2:10
Christians ... 1 Pet. 1:1

B. *Positive laws, to:*
Love them ... Lev. 19:34
Relieve them ... Lev. 25:35
Provide for them ... Deut. 10:18
Share in leftovers ... Deut. 24:19-22
Treat fairly ... Deut. 24:14, 17
Share in religious festivals ... Deut. 16:11, 14
Hear the law ... Deut. 31:12

See Foreigners; Sojourn, sojourners

Strategem—*a plan designed to deceive an enemy*

Joshua's famous ... Josh. 8:1-22
Gibeonites' trickery ... Josh. 9:2-27
Hushai's successful ... 2 Sam. 17:6-14

Straw—*the stalk of wheat or barley*

Used for animals ... Gen. 24:25, 32
Used in making bricks ... Ex. 5:7-18
Eaten by a lion ... Is. 11:7
Something worthless ... Job 41:27-29

SUBJECT REFERENCE

Stray animals
Must be returned .... Ex. 23:4
Saul's pursuit of .... 1 Sam. 9:3-5

Streets—*principal thoroughfares*
A. *Uses of:*
Display .... Matt. 6:5
Teaching .... Luke 13:26
Parades .... Esth. 6:9, 11
Proclamations .... Neh. 8:3-5
Healing .... Mark 6:56
B. *Dangers of, from:*
Fighting .... Josh. 2:19
Prostitutes .... Prov. 7:6-23
Wicked .... Ps. 55:11
Assault .... Judg. 19:15-26

Strength, strengthen—*resident power*
A. *Kinds of:*
Physical .... Prov. 20:29
Constitutional .... Ps. 90:10
Hereditary .... Gen. 49:3
Angelic .... Ps. 103:20
Military .... Dan. 2:37
Spiritual .... Ps. 138:3
Superhuman .... Judg. 16:5, 6, 19
Divine .... Is. 63:1
B. *Dissipation of, by:*
Iniquity .... Ps. 31:10
Hunger .... 1 Sam. 28:20, 22
Sexual looseness .... Prov. 31:3
Age .... Ps. 71:9
Visions .... Dan. 10:8, 16, 17
C. *Increase of:*
From:
God .... Is. 41:10
Christ .... 2 Tim. 4:17
Spirit .... Eph. 3:16
Brothers .... Luke 22:32
By:
Wisdom .... Eccl. 7:19
Waiting on the LORD .... Is. 40:31
Lord's grace .... 2 Cor. 12:9

Strife—*conflicts between people*
A. *Sources of, in:*
Hatred .... Prov. 10:12
Perverseness .... Prov. 16:28
Transgression .... Prov. 17:19
Scorner .... Prov. 22:10
Anger .... Prov. 29:22
Flesh .... Gal. 5:19, 20
B. *Actual causes of, seen in:*
Self-seeking .... Luke 22:24
Dispute between men .... Gen. 13:7-11
Contentious man .... Prov. 26:21
Being carnal .... 1 Cor. 3:3
Disputes .... 1 Tim. 6:4
C. *Avoidance of, by:*
Being slow to anger .... Prov. 15:18
Simplicity of life .... Prov. 17:1
See Contention; Quarrel

Strike—*afflict; attack*
A. *Descriptive of:*
Smeared blood .... Ex. 12:7, 22
Advance in age .... Luke 1:7, 18
Slapping .... John 18:22
God's judgment .... Ps. 39:10
B. *Of divine punishment, upon:*
Christ .... Is. 53:4, 8
Sinners .... Prov. 7:23
World .... Ps. 110:5
Rebellious .... Is. 14:6
Israel .... Is. 30:26

Striker—*a contentious person*
Disqualifies for church office .... 1 Tim. 3:3

Stripes—*used in scourging*
Limit of .... Deut. 25:1-4
Because of sin .... Ps. 89:32
Upon the Messiah, healing .... Is. 53:5; 1 Pet. 2:24
Uselessness of, on a fool .... Prov. 17:10
Paul's experience with .... Acts 16:23, 33; 2 Cor. 11:23

Striving, spiritual
To enter the strait gate .... Luke 13:24
Against sin .... Heb. 12:4
With divine help .... Col. 1:29
In prayer .... Rom. 15:30
For the faith of the Gospel .... Phil. 1:27

Stroke—*a blow*
With an ax .... Deut. 19:5
With a sword .... Esth. 9:5

Strong drink (see Drunkenness)

Stronghold—*fortress*
David captured .... 2 Sam. 5:7
The LORD is .... Nah. 1:7

Studs—*ornaments*
Of silver .... Song 1:11

Study—*intensive intellectual effort*
Of the Scriptures .... Acts 17:10, 11; 2 Tim. 3:16, 17

Stumble—*to trip on some obstacle*
A. *Occasions of, found in:*
Strong drink .... Is. 28:7
God's Word .... 1 Pet. 2:8
Christ .... Rom. 9:32, 33
Christ crucified .... 1 Cor. 1:23
Christian liberty .... 1 Cor. 8:9
B. *Avoidance of, by:*
Following wisdom .... Prov. 3:21, 23
See Offend, offense

Suah—*sweepings*
Asherite .... 1 Chr. 7:36

Subjection—*the state of being under another's control*
A. *Of domestic and civil relationships:*
Servants to masters .... 1 Pet. 2:18
Citizens to government .... Rom. 13:1-6
Children to parents .... 1 Tim. 3:4
Wives to husbands .... Eph. 5:24
Younger to elder .... 1 Pet. 5:5
B. *Of spiritual relationships:*
Creation to sin .... Rom. 8:20, 21
Demons to the disciples .... Luke 10:17, 20
Believers to the Gospel .... 2 Cor. 9:13
Christians to one another .... 1 Pet. 5:5
Christians to God .... Heb. 12:9
Creation to Christ .... Heb. 2:5, 8
Church to Christ .... Eph. 5:24
Christ to God .... 1 Cor. 15:28

Subjugation—*the state of being subdued by force*
Physical force .... 1 Sam. 13:19-23
Spiritual power .... Mark 5:1-15

Submission—*humble obedience to another's will*
Each other .... Eph. 5:21
Husbands .... Eph. 5:22
Rulers .... 1 Pet. 2:13
Elders .... 1 Pet. 5:5
Christian leaders .... Heb. 13:17
God .... James 4:7

Substitution—*replacing one person or thing for another*
Ram for the man .... Gen. 22:13
Offering for the offerer .... Lev. 16:21, 22
Levites for the first-born .... Num. 3:12-45
Christ for the sinner .... Is. 53:4-6; 1 Pet. 2:24

Subtlety—*craftiness of*
Satan .... Gen. 3:1
Wicked .... Acts 13:10
Jewish leaders .... Matt. 26:3, 4
Jacob .... Gen. 27:35

Success—*accomplishment of goals in life*
A. *Rules of:*
Put God first .... Matt. 6:32-34
Follow the Book .... Josh. 1:7-9
Seek the goal .... Phil. 3:13, 14
Never give up .... Gal. 6:9
Do all for Christ .... Phil. 1:20, 21
B. *Hindrances of, seen in:*
Unbelief .... Heb. 4:6, 11
Enemies .... Neh. 4:1-23
Sluggishness .... Prov. 24:30-34
Love of the world .... Matt. 16:26

Succoth—*booths*
1. Place east of the Jordan .... Judg. 8:4, 5
Jacob's residence here .... Gen. 33:17
2. Israel's first camp .... Ex. 12:37

Succoth-benoth—*tabernacles of girls*
Idol set up in Samaria by Babylonians .... 2 Kin. 17:30

Suchathites
Descendants of Caleb .... 1 Chr. 2:42, 55

Suck—*to give milk to offspring*
Characteristics of:
True among animals .... 1 Sam. 7:9
Normal for human mothers .... Job 3:12
Figurative of Israel's restoration .... Is. 60:16
Figurative of wicked .... Job 20:16

Suffering for Christ
Necessary in Christian living .... 1 Cor. 12:26; Phil. 1:29
Blessed privilege .... Acts 5:41
Never in vain .... Gal. 3:4
After Christ's example .... Phil. 3:10; 1 Pet. 2:20, 21
Of short duration .... 1 Pet. 5:10
Not comparable to heaven's glory .... Rom. 8:18; 1 Pet. 4:13

Sufferings of Christ
A. *Features concerning:*
Predicted .... 1 Pet. 1:11
Announced .... Mark 9:12
Explained .... Luke 24:26, 46
Fulfilled .... Acts 3:18
Witnessed .... 1 Pet. 5:1
Proclaimed .... Acts 17:2, 3
B. *Benefits of, to Christ:*
Preparation for priesthood .... Heb. 2:17, 18
Learned obedience .... Heb. 5:8
Way to glory .... Heb. 2:9, 10
C. *Benefits of, to Christians:*
Brought to God .... 1 Pet. 3:18
Our:
Sins atoned .... Heb. 9:26-28
Example .... 1 Pet. 2:21-23
Fellowship .... Phil. 3:10
Comfort .... 2 Cor. 1:5-7

Suicide—*self-murder*
A. *Thought of, induced by:*
Life's weariness .... Job 3:20-23
Life's vanity .... Eccl. 2:17
Anger .... Jon. 4:3, 8, 9
B. *Brought on by:*
Hopelessness .... Judg. 16:29, 30
Sin .... 1 Kin. 16:18, 19
Disappointment .... 2 Sam. 17:23
Betrayal of Christ .... Matt. 27:3-5
C. *Other features concerning:*
Desired by some .... Rev. 9:6
Attempted but prevented .... Acts 16:27, 28
Imputed to Christ .... John 8:22
Satan tempts Christ to .... Luke 4:9
D. *Principles prohibiting, found in:*
Body's sacredness .... 1 Cor. 6:19
Prohibition against murder .... Ex. 20:13
Faith's expectancy .... 2 Tim. 4:6-8, 18

Sukkiim
African people in Shishak's army .... 2 Chr. 12:3

Summer
Made by God .... Ps. 74:17
Sign of God's covenant .... Gen. 8:22
Time of:
Fruit harvest .... 2 Sam. 16:1, 2
Sowing and harvest .... Prov. 6:6-8
Figurative of: Industry .... Prov. 10:5
Opportunity .... Jer. 8:20
Preceded by spring .... Matt. 24:32

Sun
A. *Characteristics of:*
Created by God .... Gen. 1:14, 16
Under God's control .... Ps. 104:19; Matt. 5:45
Made to rule .... Gen. 1:16

S

SUBJECT	REFERENCE
Necessary for fruit	Deut. 33:14
Given for light	Jer. 31:35
Made for God's glory	Ps. 148:3
Causes: Scorching	Jon. 4:8
Sunstroke	2 Kin. 4:18, 19
B. *Miracles connected with:*	
Stands still	Josh. 10:12, 13
Shadows of, turned back	2 Kin. 20:9-11
Darkening of, at crucifixion	Luke 23:44-49
Going down at noon	Amos 8:9
C. *Worship of:*	
Forbidden	Deut. 4:19
By Manasseh	2 Kin. 21:3, 5
By Jews	Jer. 8:2
D. *Figurative of:*	
God's presence	Ps. 84:11
Earth's sphere of action	Eccl. 1:3, 9, 14
God's Law	Ps. 19:4-7
Future glory	Matt. 13:43
Christ's glory	Matt. 17:2

Sunday (see First day of week)

Sundial—*an instrument for telling time*

Miracle of	Is. 38:8

Sundry—*in many parts*

Applied to God's revelation	Heb. 1:1

Sunstroke—*stricken by sun's heat*

Child dies of	2 Kin. 4:18-20

Superscription—*something inscribed on*

Roman coin	Mark 12:16
Cross of Christ	Luke 23:38

Superstition—*gullible ideas based on fancy or fear*

A. *Causes of, in wrong views of:*	
God	1 Kin. 20:23
Holy objects	1 Sam. 4:3
God's providence	Jer. 44:15-19
B. *Manifestations of, in:*	
Seeking illogical causes	Acts 28:4
Ignorance of the true God	Acts 17:22
Perverting true religion	Mark 7:1-16

Supper (see Lord's Supper)

Sur—*turning aside, entrance*

Name given to a gate	2 Kin. 11:6
Called "Gate of the Foundation"	2 Chr. 23:5

Sure—*something trustworthy*

A. *Descriptive of divine things:*	
God's law	Ps. 19:7
Messianic line	2 Sam. 23:5
Messiah	Is. 22:23, 25
New covenant	Acts 13:34
God's: Prophecies	2 Pet. 1:19
Promises	Rom. 4:16
Purposes	2 Tim. 2:19
B. *Applied to the believer's:*	
Calling and election	2 Pet. 1:10
Faith	John 6:69
Dedication	Neh. 9:38
Life of faith	Is. 32:18
Confidence in God's Word	Luke 1:1
Reward	Prov. 11:18

Surety—*one who guarantees another's debt*

A. *Descriptive of:*	
Certainty	Gen. 15:13
Guarantee	Gen. 43:9
Our Lord	Heb. 7:22
B. *Features concerning:*	
Risks involved in	Prov. 11:15
Warning against	Prov. 6:1-5

Surfeiting—*gluttonous indulgence*

Christ warns against	Luke 21:34

Surname—*a family name*

A. *Descriptive of:*	
Simon Peter	Acts 10:5, 32
John Mark	Acts 12:12, 25
Judas Iscariot	Luke 22:3
Judas Barsabas	Acts 15:22
Joses Barnabas	Acts 4:36
James and John Boanerges	Mark 3:17

SUBJECT	REFERENCE
B. *Figurative of God's:*	
Call of Gentiles	Is. 44:5
Sovereignty over kings	Is. 45:4

Susanna—*lily*

Believing woman ministering to Christ	Luke 8:2, 3

Susi—*horseman*

Mannassite spy	Num. 13:11

Suspicion—*doubt of another's intent*

A. *Kinds of:*	
Unjustified	Josh. 22:9-31
Pretended	Gen. 42:7-12
Unsuspected	John 13:21-28
B. *Objects of:*	
Esau by Jacob	Gen. 32:3-12
Jeremiah by officials	Jer. 37:12-15
Jews by Haman	Esth. 3:8, 9
Mary by Joseph	Matt. 1:18-25
Peter by a damsel	Matt. 26:69-74

Sustenance—*means of sustaining life*

Israel by the Lord	Neh. 9:21
Elijah by ravens and a widow	1 Kin. 17:1-9
Believer by the LORD	Ps. 3:5

Swaddling—*bandages, wrappings*

Figurative of Jerusalem	Ezek. 16:3, 4
Jesus wrapped in	Luke 2:7

Swallow—*a long-winged, migratory bird*

Nesting in the sanctuary	Ps. 84:3
Noted for chattering	Is. 38:14

Swallow—*to engulf; to overwhelm*

A. *Applied miraculously to:*	
Aaron's rod	Ex. 7:12
Red Sea	Ex. 15:12
Earth	Num. 16:30-34
Great fish	Jon. 1:17
B. *Applied figuratively to:*	
God's judgments	Ps. 21:9
Conquest	Jer. 51:34, 44
Captivity	Hos. 8:7, 8
Sorrow	2 Cor. 2:7
Resurrection	Is. 25:8

Swan

Should be translated "horned owl"	Lev. 11:18

Swearing—*taking an oath*

A. *Kinds of:*	
Proclamatory	Ex. 17:16
Protective	Gen. 21:23
Personal	1 Sam. 20:17
Purificatory	Neh. 13:25 30
Promissory	Luke 1:73
Prohibited	James 5:12
B. *Of God, objects of:*	
God's purpose	Is. 14:24, 25
God's covenant	Is. 54:9, 10
Messianic priesthood	Heb. 7:21

See Oaths

Sweat—*perspiration*

Penalty of man's sin	Gen. 3:18, 19
Cause of, avoided	Ezek. 44:18
Of Jesus, in prayer	Luke 22:44

Sweet—*that which is pleasing to the taste*

A. *Descriptive, literally, of:*	
Water	Ex. 15:25
Honey	Judg. 14:18
Incense	Ex. 25:6
Perfumes	Esth. 2:12
B. *Descriptive, figuratively, of:*	
God's Law	Ps. 19:10
God's Word	Ps. 119:103
Spiritual fellowship	Ps. 55:14
Meditation	Ps. 104:34
Pleasant words	Prov. 16:24
Sleep	Prov. 3:24
Christians	2 Cor. 2:15
Christian service	Eph. 5:2

Swim—*to propel oneself in water by natural means*

Miraculously, of iron	2 Kin. 6:6
Naturally, of people	Acts 27:42, 43
Figuratively, of tears	Ps. 6:6

SUBJECT	REFERENCE

Swine—*hogs*

A. *Features concerning:*	
Classed as unclean	Lev. 11:7, 8
Eating of, abominable	Is. 65:4
Caring of, a degradation	Luke 15:16
Herd of, drowned	Matt. 8:30-32
B. *Figurative of:*	
Abominable things	Is. 65:4
False teachers	2 Pet. 2:22
Indiscrete woman	Prov. 11:22
Reprobate	Matt. 7:6

Sword—*a weapon of war*

A. *Described as:*	
Having haft and blade	Judg. 3:22
Worn in a sheath	1 Sam. 17:15
Fastened at the waist	2 Sam. 20:8
B. *Used for:*	
Defense	Luke 22:36, 38
Fighting in war	Josh. 6:21
Executing criminals	1 Sam. 15:33
Suicide	Acts 16:27
C. *Figurative of:*	
Divine retribution	Deut. 32:41
Divine victory	Josh. 5:13
God's judgment	1 Chr. 21:12
An adulteress	Prov. 5:3, 4
Anguish of soul	Luke 2:35
State	Rom. 13:4
God's Word	Eph. 6:17

Sycamine—*the black mulberry*

Referred to by Jesus	Luke 17:6

Sycamore—*a fig-bearing tree* (not the same as the American sycamore)

Overseers appointed to care for	1 Chr. 27:28
Abundant in Palestine	1 Kin. 10:27
Amos, a gatherer of	Amos 7:14
Zacchaeus climbs up	Luke 19:4

Sychar

City of Samaria; Jesus talks to woman near	John 4:5-39

Syene—*seven*

An Egyptian city	Ezek. 29:10; Ezek. 30:6

Symbols—*a thing or act representing something spiritual*

A. *Of things:*	
Names	Is. 7:3, 14
Numbers	Rev. 13:18
Garments	Zech. 3:3-9
Metals	1 Cor. 3:12
Animals	Dan. 7:1-8
B. *Of acts* (gestures):	
Tearing: Mantle	1 Sam. 15:27, 28
Garment	1 Kin. 11:30-32
Veil	Matt. 27:51
Wearing a yoke	Jer. 27:2-12
Buying a field	Jer. 32:6-15
Boring the ear	Ex. 21:6
Surrendering the shoe	Ruth 4:7
Going naked	Is. 20:2, 3
C. *Of spiritual truths:*	
Bow—God's covenant	Gen. 9:12, 13
Circumcision—God's covenant	Gen. 17:1-14; Rom. 4:11
Passover—Christ	Ex. 12:3-28; 1 Cor. 5:7
Mercy seat—Christ	Ex. 25:17-22; Rom. 3:25
Rock—Christ	1 Cor. 10:4
Blood sprinkled—Christ's blood	Ex. 12:21, 22; 1 Pet. 1:18, 19
Bronze serpent—Christ	Num. 21:8, 9; John 3:14
Lamb—Christ	John 1:29
Bread and wine—the new covenant	Matt. 26:26-28; 1 Cor. 11:23-29

Sympathy—*a fellow-feeling for another person*

A. *Manifested in:*	
Bearing others' burdens	Gal. 6:2; Heb. 13:3
Expressing sorrow	John 11:19-33

SUBJECT REFERENCE

Offering help in need ....Luke 10:33-35
Helping the weak ....Acts 20:35

B. *Expressed by:*
Servant for a prophet ....Jer. 38:7-13
King for a king ....2 Sam. 10:2
A maid for a general ....2 Kin. 5:1-4
Old man for a king ....2 Sam. 19:31-39
Pagan for a Jew ....Dan. 6:18-23

Synagogue—*a Jewish assembly*

A. *Organization of:*
Under elders ....Luke 7:3-5
Ruler in charge ....Mark 5:22
Attendant ....Luke 4:17, 20
Chief seats of, coveted ....Matt. 23:6
Expulsion from ....John 9:22, 34

B. *Purposes of, for:*
Prayer ....Matt. 6:5
Reading Scripture ....Acts 13:15
Hearing expositions ....Acts 13:14, 15
Discipline ....Acts 9:2

C. *Christ's relation to:*
Teaches often in ....John 18:20
Worships in ....Luke 4:16-21
Performs miracles in ....Matt. 12:9, 10
Expelled from ....Luke 4:22-30

Syntyche—*fortunate*
Philippian woman exhorted by Paul ....Phil. 4:2

Syracuse—*a city of Sicily*
Visited by Paul ....Acts 28:12

Syria—*the high land*
News of Jesus went into ....Matt. 4:24
Governed by Romans ....Luke 2:2
Gospel preached to ....Acts 15:23, 41

Syria, Syrians—*the Aramaeans*
Descendants of Aram, Shem's son ....Gen. 10:22
Related to the Hebrews ....Deut. 26:5
Intermarriage of, with Hebrews ....Gen. 24:4, 10-67
Called Syrians ....2 Sam. 10:11
Speak Syriac (Aramaic) ....Dan. 2:4
Idolatrous ....2 Kin. 5:18
Subdued by David ....2 Sam. 8:11-13
Elijah anointed king over ....1 Kin. 19:15
Army of, routed ....2 Kin. 7:5-7
Joined Israel against Jerusalem ....2 Kin. 16:5
Taken captive by Assyria ....2 Kin. 16:9
Destruction of, foretold ....Is. 17:1-3
Governed by Romans ....Luke 2:2
Gospel preached to ....Acts 15:23, 41

Syrophoenician—*an inhabitant of Phoenicia*
Daughter of, freed of demon ....Mark 7:25-31

System—*an orderly method of procedure in*
Orderly writing ....Luke 1:3
Governing people ....Ex. 18:13-27
Church government ....Acts 6:1-7
Priestly ministry ....Luke 1:8, 9
Giving ....1 Cor. 16:1, 2

T

Taanach—*sandy*
Canaanite city conquered by Joshua ....Josh. 12:21
Assigned to Manasseh ....Josh. 17:11
Assigned to Kohathite Levites ....Josh. 21:25
Canaanites not expelled from ....Josh. 17:12, 13
Site of Canaanite defeat ....Judg. 5:19-22

Taanath-shiloh—*approach to Shiloh*
City of Ephraim ....Josh. 16:5, 6

Tabbaoth—*rings*
Ancestor of a Nethinim family ....Ezra 2:43

Tabbath—*extension*
Refuge of Midianites ....Judg. 7:22

Tabeel—*God is good*
Persian official ....Ezra 4:7
Father of a puppet king put forth by Rezin and Pekah ....Is. 7:1, 6

SUBJECT REFERENCE

Taberah—*burning*
Israelite camp; fire destroys many here ....Num. 11:1-3

Tabering—*drumming* (tabret)
Beating the breasts in sorrow ....Nah. 2:7

Tabernacle

A. *Descriptive of:*
Moses' administrative office ....Ex. 33:7-11
Structure erected at Sinai ....Ex. 40:2, 35-38
Portable shrine containing an idol ....Acts 7:43
Tent prepared for the ark by David ....1 Chr. 16:1-43
Lord's incarnate Word ....John 1:14
Heavenly prototype ....Heb. 8:2, 5; Heb. 9:11, 24
Holy city ....Rev. 21:3

B. *Sinaitic, constructed:*
By divine revelation ....Ex. 25:27; Heb. 8:5
By craftsmen inspired by the Spirit ....Ex. 31:1-11
Out of contributions willingly supplied ....Ex. 25:1-9
For the manifestation of God's glory ....Ex. 25:8; Ex. 29:42, 43
In two parts—holy place and Holiest of all ....Ex. 26:33, 34; Heb. 9:2-7
With surrounding court ....Ex. 40:8
Within a year's time ....Ex. 40:2, 17

C. *History of:*
Set up at Sinai ....Ex. 40:1-38
Sanctified and dedicated ....Ex. 40:9-16
Moved by priests and Levites ....Num. 4:1-49
Camped at Gilgal ....Josh. 5:10, 11
Set up at Shiloh ....Josh. 18:1
Israel's center of worship ....Judg. 18:31; 1 Sam. 1:3, 9, 24
Ark of, taken by Philistines ....1 Sam. 4:1-22
Worship not confined to ....1 Sam. 7:1, 2, 15-17
Located at Nob during Saul's reign ....1 Sam. 21:1-6
Moved to Gibeon ....1 Kin. 3:4
Ark of, brought to Jerusalem by David ....2 Sam. 6:17
Brought to the Temple by Solomon ....1 Kin. 8:1, 4, 5

D. *Typology of, seen in:*
Christ ....John 1:14
God's household ....Eph. 2:19
Believer ....1 Cor. 6:19
Heaven ....Heb. 9:23, 24

E. *Typology of, seen in Christ:*
Candlestick—His enlightening us ....Rev. 1:13
Sacred bread—His sustaining us ....John 6:27-59
Altar of incense—His intercession for us ....John 17:1-26; Heb. 7:25
Veil—His flesh ....Heb. 10:20
Ark (wood and gold)—His humanity and deity ....John 1:14

Tabernacle, Feast of (see Feasts, Hebrew)

Table

A. *Descriptive of:*
Article of furniture ....Matt. 15:27
For showbread ....Heb. 9:2
Small writing tablet ....Luke 1:63
Tablet of wood or stone ....Ex. 24:12

B. *Figurative of:*
Human heart ....Prov. 3:3
Christian's heart ....2 Cor. 3:3
God's provision ....Ps. 23:5
Intimate fellowship ....Luke 22:30
Lord's Supper ....1 Cor. 10:21

Tabor—*mountain height*
1. Mountain on borders of Zebulun and Issachar ....Josh. 19:12, 22
Great among mountains ....Jer. 46:18
Scene of rally against Sisera ....Judg. 4:6, 12, 14
2. Town of Zebulun ....1 Chr. 6:77
3. Oak of, near Ramah ....1 Sam. 10:3

SUBJECT REFERENCE

Tabret—*a musical instrument* (timbrel)
Used by:
Prophets ....1 Sam. 10:5
People ....Gen. 31:27

Tabrimmon—*Rimmon is good*
Father of Ben-hadad ....1 Kin. 15:18

Taches—*hooks or clasps*
Couplings for curtains ....Ex. 26:6, 11, 33

Tachmonite—*wise*
Descriptive of one of David's heroes ....2 Sam. 23:8
Same as Hachmonite in ....1 Chr. 11:11

Tackling—*ropes, cord, line*
Ship's ropes ....Is. 33:23
All of a ship's removable gear ....Acts 27:19

Tactfulness—*the knack of knowing the right thing to do or say*

A. *Manifested in:*
Appeasing hatred ....Gen. 32:4, 5, 13-21
Settling disputes ....1 Kin. 3:24-28
Obtaining one's wishes ....Esth. 5:1-8; Esth. 7:1-6

B. *Illustrated by Christ, in:*
Rebuking a Pharisee ....Luke 7:39-50
Teaching humility ....Mark 10:35-44
Forgiving a sinner ....John 8:1-11
Rebuking His disciples ....John 21:15-23

Tadmor—*palm tree*
Trading center near Damascus ....2 Chr. 8:4
A desert town ....1 Kin. 9:18

Tahan—*encampment*
Ephraimite; founder of the Tahanites ....Num. 26:35; 1 Chr. 7:25

Tahath—*station*
1. Kohathite Levite ....1 Chr. 6:24
2, 3. Two descendants of Ephraim ....1 Chr. 7:20
4. Israelite encampment ....Num. 33:26, 27

Tahpanhes, Tehaphnehes
City of Egypt; refuge of fleeing Jews ....Jer. 2:16; Jer. 44:1; Ezek. 30:18

Tahpenes—*royal wife*
Egyptian queen ....1 Kin. 11:19, 20

Tahrea—*flight*
Descendant of Saul ....1 Chr. 9:41
Called Tarea ....1 Chr. 8:33, 35

Tahtim-hodshi
Place visited by census-taking Joab ....2 Sam. 24:6

Tailoring—*the art of making clothes*
For Aaron's garments ....Ex. 39:1

Tale
Stipulated quantity ....Ex. 5:8, 18
Brief meditation ....Ps. 90:9
Nonsensical talk ....Luke 24:11

Talebearer—*one who gossips*
Reveals secrets ....Prov. 11:13
Injures character ....Prov. 18:8
Creates strife ....Prov. 26:20

Talent—*see Jewish measures*
Of gold ....Ex. 37:24
Of silver ....2 Kin. 5:5, 22, 23
Of bronze ....Ex. 38:29
Of iron ....1 Chr. 29:7
Of brass ....1 Chr. 29:7
Parable of ....Matt. 25:14-30

Talitha-cumi—*"Damsel, arise"*
Jairus' daughter thus addressed ....Mark 5:41

Talk—*verbal communication between persons*

A. *Described as:*
Divine ....Ex. 33:9
Deceitful ....Job 13:7
Proud ....1 Sam. 2:3
Mischievous ....Prov. 24:2

SUBJECT REFERENCE

Vain .... Titus 1:10
Foolish .... Eph. 5:4

B. *Of good things, God's:*

Law .... Deut. 6:7
Judgment .... Ps. 37:30, 31
Righteousness .... Ps. 71:24
Power .... Ps. 145:11

Talmai—*plowman*

1. Son of Anak driven out by Caleb .... Josh. 15:14
2. King of Geshur whose daughter, Maacah, becomes David's wife .... 2 Sam. 3:3

Talmon—*oppressor, violent*

Levite porter .... 1 Chr. 9:17
Descendants of, return from exile .... Ezra 2:42
Members of, become Temple porters .... Neh. 11:19

Tamar, Thamar—*palm tree*

1. Wife of Er and mother of Perez and Zerah .... Gen. 38:6-30
   Ancestress of tribal families .... Num. 26:20, 21
2. Absalom's sister .... 2 Sam. 13:1-32
3. Absalom's daughter .... 2 Sam. 14:27
4. Place south of the Dead Sea .... Ezek. 47:19

Tammuz—*a Babylonian god*

Mourned by women of Jerusalem .... Ezek. 8:14

Tanhumeth—*consolation*

Father of Seraiah .... 2 Kin. 25:23

Tanner (Simon, the)—*dresser of hides*

Peter lodges with .... Acts 10:5, 6, 32

Tapestry—*hand-woven coverings*

Symbolic of:

Licentiousness .... Prov. 7:16
Diligence .... Prov. 31:22

Taphath—*a drop*

Daughter of Solomon .... 1 Kin. 4:11

Tappuah—*apple*

1. Town of Judah .... Josh. 15:1, 34
2. Town of Ephraim .... Josh. 16:8, 9
3. Son of Hebron .... 1 Chr. 2:43

Tarah—*wandering*

Israelite encampment .... Num. 33:1, 27

Taralah—*power of God*

City of Benjamin .... Josh. 18:21, 27

Tares—*the bearded darnel*

Sown among wheat .... Matt. 13:24-40

Tarpelites

People transported to Samaria by the Assyrians .... Ezra 4:9

Tarry—*to delay*

A. *Of human things:*

Prolonged visit .... Acts 9:43
Unnecessary delay .... 1 Sam. 1:23
Sinful delay .... 2 Sam. 11:1, 2
Embarrassed delay .... 2 Sam. 10:5
Indulgence in wine .... Prov. 23:30

B. *Of divine things:*

Heavenly visitation .... Judg. 6:18
God's salvation .... Is. 46:13
Divine visitation .... Hab. 2:3
Spirit's coming .... Luke 24:49
Christ's return .... Heb. 10:37

Tarshish, Tharshish

1. Son of Javan and great grandson of Noah .... Gen. 10:4
2. City at a great distance from Palestine .... Jon. 1:3
   Minerals imported from, by Phoenicians .... 1 Kin. 10:22
   Ships of, noted in commerce .... Ps. 48:7
   Ships of, sent by Jehoshaphat .... 1 Kin. 22:48

SUBJECT REFERENCE

3. Benjamite .... 1 Chr. 7:10
4. Persian prince .... Esth. 1:14

Tarsus—*the capital of the Roman province of Cilicia*

Paul's birthplace .... Acts 21:39
Saul sent to .... Acts 9:30
Visited by Barnabas .... Acts 11:25

Tartak—*hero of darkness*

Deity worshiped by the Avites .... 2 Kin. 17:31

Tartan—*the title of Assyria's commander*

Sent to fight against Jerusalem .... 2 Kin. 18:17

Taskmaster—*a foreman*

Over sons of Israel .... Ex. 1:11

Taste

A. *Of divine things:*

God's Word .... Ps. 119:103
Lord .... Ps. 34:8
Heavenly gift .... Heb. 6:4

B. *Of material things:*

Honey .... 1 Sam. 14:29, 43
Manna .... Ex. 16:31
Food .... 1 Sam. 14:24
Wine .... John 2:9
Vinegar .... Matt. 27:34
Death .... Heb. 2:9

Tatnai

Persian governor opposing the Jews .... Ezra 5:3, 6

Tattooing—*marking the skin indelibly*

Forbidden by God .... Lev. 19:28

Tau

Letter in the Hebrew alphabet .... Ps. 119:169-176

Taunt—*a scornful glee*

Goliath against David .... 1 Sam. 17:43, 44
David against Abner .... 1 Sam. 26:14-16
Rabshakeh against the Jews .... 2 Kin. 18:28-35
Soldiers and people against Christ .... Matt. 27:28-41

Taverns, The Three

Place about 30 miles south of Rome .... Acts 28:15

Taxes—*money, goods or labor paid to a government*

A. *Derived from:*

People's possessions .... 1 Sam. 8:10-18
Poor .... Amos 5:11

B. *Paid by:*

Forced labor .... Deut. 20:11
Foreigners .... 1 Chr. 22:2
Captured people .... 2 Sam. 8:6, 14
Forced labor .... 1 Kin. 5:13-17
All except Levites .... Ezra 7:24

C. *Used for:*

Sanctuary .... Ex. 30:11-16
King's household .... 1 Kin. 4:7-19
Tribute to foreign nations .... 2 Kin. 15:17-22
Authorities .... Rom. 13:6, 7

D. *Abuses of:*

Lead to rebellion .... 1 Kin. 12:1-19
Burden people with debts .... Neh. 5:1-13
Bring enslavement .... Neh. 9:36, 37

Tax-gatherers—*Jews engaged in tax collecting*

A. *Features concerning:*

Collector of taxes .... Luke 5:27
Often guilty of extortion .... Luke 3:12, 13
Classed with lowest sinners .... Matt. 9:10, 11
Matt. 21:31, 32
Do not even, do the same .... Matt. 5:46
Thomas and Matthew, the .... Matt. 10:3
"Thank thee that I am not" .... Luke 18:11
As a heathen and a .... Matt. 18:17

B. *Spiritual attitude of:*

Often conscientious .... Luke 19:2, 8
Often hospitable .... Luke 5:29
Received John's beliefs .... Matt. 21:32
Listened to Jesus .... Luke 15:1
Conscious of their sins .... Luke 18:13, 14
Many sat with Him .... Mark 2:15
Why do ye eat with .... Luke 5:30
A friend of .... Matt. 11:19
Luke 7:34

SUBJECT REFERENCE

Teacher—*the Greek equivalent of the Hebrew word "rabbi"* (meaning "my master")

Instructed in song .... 1 Chr. 25:1
Come from God .... John 3:2
To the Gentiles .... 2 Tim. 1:11

Teaching, teachers

A. *Those capable of:*

Parents .... Deut. 11:19
Levites .... Lev. 10:11
Ancestors .... Jer. 9:14
Disciples .... Matt. 28:19, 20
Older women .... Titus 2:3
Nature .... 1 Cor. 11:14

B. *Significance of:*

Combined with preaching .... Matt. 4:23
Divine calling .... Eph. 4:11
Necessary for bishops .... 1 Tim. 3:2
Necessary for the Lord's bond-servants .... 2 Tim. 2:24-26
From house to house .... Acts 20:20
By sharing .... Gal. 6:6
Not granted to women .... 1 Tim. 2:12

C. *Authority of, in divine things:*

Derived from Christ .... Matt. 28:19, 20
Empowered by the Spirit .... John 14:26
Taught by the LORD .... Is. 54:13
Originates in revelation .... Gal. 1:12

D. *Objects of, in divine things, concerning:*

God's way .... Ps. 27:11
God's path .... Ps. 25:4, 5
God's Law .... Ps. 119:12, 26, 66
God's will .... Ps. 143:10
Holiness .... Titus 2:12
Spiritual truths .... Heb. 8:11, 12

E. *Perversion of, by:*

False prophets .... Is. 9:15
False priests .... Mic. 3:11
Traditionalists .... Matt. 15:9
False teachers .... 1 Tim. 4:1-3
Judaizers .... Acts 15:1
False believers .... 2 Tim. 4:3, 4

Tears

A. *Kinds of:*

Agonizing .... Ps. 6:6
Rewarded .... Ps. 126:5
Repentant .... Luke 7:38, 44
Insincere .... Heb. 12:17
Intense .... Heb. 5:6-8
Woman's .... Esth. 8:3

B. *Caused by:*

Remorse .... Gen. 27:34
Approaching death .... 2 Kin. 20:1-5
Oppression .... Eccl. 4:1
Defeat .... Is. 16:9
Affliction and anguish .... 2 Cor. 2:4
Christian service .... Acts 20:19, 31

Tebah—*slaughter*

Son of Nahor .... Gen. 22:24

Tebaliah—*Jehovah has immersed*

Merarite Korahite .... 1 Chr. 26:11

Tebeth—*the name of the Hebrew tenth month*

Esther becomes queen in .... Esth. 2:16, 17

Teeth, tooth

A. *Used for:*

Eating .... Num. 11:33
Showing hatred .... Acts 7:54

B. *Figurative of:*

Destruction .... Job 4:10
Holding on to life .... Job 13:14
God's chastening .... Job 16:9
Escaped with the "skin of my teeth" .... Job 19:20
Judgment .... Ps. 3:7
Hatred .... Ps. 35:16
Persecution .... Ps. 57:4
Corporate guilt .... Jer. 31:29, 30
Greediness .... Dan. 7:5, 7, 19
Starvation .... Amos 4:6
Hired prophets .... Mic. 3:5
Remorse .... Matt. 13:42, 50

SUBJECT	REFERENCE
Tehinnah—*grace*	
Judahite	1 Chr. 4:12
Tekel—*weighed*	
Descriptive of Babylon's judgment	Dan. 5:25
Tekoa, Tekoah—*firm, settlement*	
Ashur the father of	1 Chr. 2:24 1 Chr. 4:5
Fortress city of Judah	2 Chr. 20:20
Home of a wise woman	2 Sam. 14:2, 4, 9
Fortified by Rehoboam	2 Chr. 11:6
Home of Amos	Amos 1:1
Tekoite—*an inhabitant of Tekoa*	
Ikkesh thus called	2 Sam. 23:26
Among postexilic workmen	Neh. 3:5, 27
Tel-abib—*hill of grain*	
Place in Babylonia	Ezek. 3:15
Telah—*fracture*	
Ephraimite	1 Chr. 7:25
Telaim—*little lambs*	
Saul assembles his army here	1 Sam. 15:4
Telassar, Thelasar—*hill of Assur*	
City of Mesopotamia	2 Kin. 19:12
Children of Eden in	Is. 37:12
Telem—*a lamb*	
1. Town in south Judah	Josh. 15:24
2. Divorced his foreign wife	Ezra 10:24
Tel-haresha—*mound of the craftman's work*	
Babylonian town	Neh. 7:61
Tel-melah—*hill of salt*	
Place in Babylonia	Ezra 2:59
Tema—*sunburnt*	
Son of Ishmael	Gen. 25:15
Descendants of Abraham	1 Chr. 1:30
Troops of	Job 6:19
Remote from Palestine	Jer. 25:23
On trade route through Arabia	Is. 21:13, 14
Teman—*the south*	
1. Grandson of Esau; duke of Edom	Gen. 36:11, 15
2. Another duke of Edom	Gen. 36:42
3. Tribe in northeast Edom	Gen. 36:34
Judgment pronounced against	Amos 1:12
God appears from	Hab. 3:3
Temanite—*an inhabitant of Teman*	
Job's friend, Eliphaz	Job 42:7, 9
Temeni—*fortunate*	
Son of Ashur	1 Chr. 4:5, 6
Temperance	
A. *Needed in:*	
Eating	Prov. 23:1-3
Sexual appetites	1 Cor. 7:1-9
All things	1 Cor. 9:25-27
B. *Helped by:*	
Self-control	Prov. 16:32
God's Spirit	Gal. 5:23
Spiritual growth	2 Pet. 1:6
C. *In the use of wine, total recommended by:*	
Solomon	Prov. 23:31-35
Angel	Judg. 13:3-5
Nazarite vow	Num. 6:2, 3
First, among Rechabites	Jer. 35:1-10
See Self-control; Sober, sobriety	
Tempests—*terrible storms*	
A. *Literal uses of:*	
At Sinai	Heb. 12:18-21
Jonah's ship tossed by	Jon. 1:4-15
Calmed by Christ	Matt. 8:23-27
Paul's ship destroyed by	Acts 27:14-20
B. *Figurative of:*	
Destructiveness	Is. 28:2
God's wrath	Jer. 30:23
God's chastening	Job 9:17
Furious troubles	Ps. 55:8
God's judgments	Ps. 83:15

SUBJECT	REFERENCE
Hell's torments	Ps. 11:6
Raging destructiveness	2 Pet. 2:17
Destruction by war	Amos 1:14
Temple, Herod's	
Zechariah received vision in	Luke 1:5-22
Infant Jesus greeted here by Simeon and Anna	Luke 2:22-39
Jesus visited at 12	Luke 2:42-52
Jesus visited and cleansed	John 2:15-17
Construction of, specified	John 2:19, 20
Jesus taught in	John 8:20
Jesus cleansed again	Matt. 21:12-16
Jesus spoke parables in	Matt. 21:23-46
Jesus exposes Pharisees in	Matt. 23:1-39
Destruction of, foretold	Matt. 24:1, 2
Veil of, rent at Christ's death	Matt. 27:51 Heb. 10:20
Christians worshiped here	Acts 2:46
Apostles taught here	Acts 3:1-26
Stephen's teaching on the true	Acts 7:46-50
Apostles understand prophecy concerning	Acts 15:14-18
Paul accused of profaning	Acts 21:20-30
Temple, Solomon's	
A. *Features regarding:*	
Site of, on Mt. Moriah	2 Sam. 24:18-25
Conceived by David	2 Sam. 7:1-3
Building of, forbidden to David	1 Chr. 22:5-16
David promised a greater house	2 Sam. 7:4-29
Pattern of, given to Solomon by David	1 Chr. 28:1-21
Provisions for, given to Solomon	1 Chr. 29:1-19
Supplies furnished by Hiram	1 Kin. 5:1-18
Construction of, by Solomon	2 Chr. 3-4
Dedication of, by Solomon	2 Chr. 6
Seven years in building	1 Kin. 6:38
No noise in building	1 Kin. 6:7
Date of building	1 Kin. 6:1, 37, 38
Workmen employed in	1 Kin. 5:15-17
B. *History of:*	
Ark brought into	1 Kin. 8:1-9
Filled with God's glory	1 Kin. 8:10, 11
Treasures taken away	1 Kin. 14:25, 26
Repaired by Jehoash	2 Kin. 12:4-14
Treasures of, given to Arameans by Jehoash	2 Kin. 12:17, 18
Treasures of, given to Assyrians by Ahaz	2 Kin. 16:14, 18
Worship of, restored by Hezekiah	2 Chr. 29:3-35
Treasures of, given by Hezekiah to Assyrians	2 Kin. 18:13-16
Desecrated by Manasseh's idolatry	2 Kin. 21:4-7
Repaired and purified by Josiah	2 Kin. 23:4-12
Plundered and burned by Babylonians	2 Kin. 25:9-17
Temple, spiritual	
A. *Descriptive of:*	
Christ's body	John 2:19, 21
Believer's body	1 Cor. 6:19
True Church	1 Cor. 3:16, 17
Apostate church	2 Thess. 2:4
B. *Believers as, described as:*	
Indwelt by God	2 Cor. 6:16
Indwelt by Christ	Eph. 3:17, 18
Indwelt by the Spirit	Eph. 2:21, 22
Priests	1 Pet. 2:5
Offering spiritual sacrifices	Heb. 13:15, 16
Temple, Zerubbabel's	
By the order of Cyrus	Ezra 1:1-4
Temple vessels restored for	Ezra 1:7-11
Worship of, restored	Ezra 3:3-13
Work of rebuilding hindered	Ezra 4:1-24
Building of, completed	Ezra 6:13-18
Inferiority of	Ezra 3:12
Temporal—*for a short time*	
Things that are seen	2 Cor. 4:18
Temporal blessings	
A. *Consisting of:*	
Rain	Matt. 5:45
Seedtime and harvest	Gen. 8:22

SUBJECT	REFERENCE
Food and raiment	Luke 12:22-31
Prosperity	Deut. 8:7-18
Children	Ps. 127:3-5
Preservation of life	2 Tim. 4:16-18
Providential guidance	Gen. 24:12-14, 42-44
B. *God's supply of:*	
Promised	Prov. 3:9, 10
Provided	Neh. 9:15
Prayed for	Matt. 6:11
Acknowledged	Ps. 23:1-5
Explained	Deut. 8:2, 3
Contingent upon obedience	Mal. 3:7-11 Matt. 6:25-34
Object of praise	Ps. 103:1-5
Temptation—*a testing designed to strengthen or corrupt*	
A. *Of God:*	
Forbidden	Matt. 4:7
By Israel	Ps. 78:18-56 Heb. 3:9
Not possible	James 1:13
B. *Of Christ:*	
By:	
The devil	Matt. 4:1-10
Jewish leaders	Matt. 16:1
His disciples	Matt. 16:23
Like us, but without sin	Heb. 4:15
Design of	Heb. 2:18
C. *Of Satan, against:*	
Job	Job 1:6-12
David	1 Chr. 21:1
Joshua	Zech. 3:1-5
Jesus	Luke 4:1-13
Ananias and Sapphira	Acts 5:1-3
Christians	1 Cor. 7:5
D. *Of Christians:*	
By:	
Lust	James 1:13-15
Riches	1 Tim. 6:9
Liability to	Gal. 6:1
Warnings against	Matt. 26:41
Prayer against	Matt. 6:13
Limitation of	1 Cor. 10:13
Deliverance from	2 Pet. 2:9
Temptress—*female tempter*	
Eve	Gen. 3:6
Potiphar's wife	Gen. 39:1-19
Delilah	Judg. 16:6-20
Jezebel	1 Kin. 21:7
Job's wife	Job 2:9
Adulteress	Prov. 7:5-27
Herodias' daughter (Salome)	Mark 6:22-29
Ten Commandments	
A. *Features concerning:*	
Given at Sinai	Ex. 20:1-17
Written on stone	Ex. 24:12
Written by God	Ex. 31:18
First stones broken	Ex. 32:19
Another copy given	Ex. 34:1
Put in the ark	Deut. 10:1-5
Called a covenant	Ex. 34:28
Given in a different form	Deut. 5:6-21
The greatest of these	Matt. 22:35-40 Rom. 13:8-10
B. *Allusions to, in Scripture:*	
First	Acts 17:23
Second	1 Kin. 18:17-40
Third	Matt. 5:33-37
Fourth	Jer. 17:21-27
Fifth	Deut. 21:18-21 Eph. 6:1-3
Sixth	Num. 35:16-21
Seventh	Num. 5:12-31 Matt. 5:27-32
Eighth	Matt. 19:18
Ninth	Deut. 19:16-21
Tenth	Rom. 7:7
Tender—*soft; compassionate*	
A. *Used of physical things:*	
Animal	Gen. 18:7
Grass	2 Sam. 23:4
Son	Prov. 4:3
Weak eyes	Gen. 29:17
Small children	Gen. 33:13
Women	Deut. 28:56
Instability	Deut. 28:54

SUBJECT REFERENCE

B. *Used of spiritual things:*
Messiah ... Is. 53:2
Compassion ... Eph. 4:32
God's mercy ... Luke 1:78
Man's heart ... 2 Kin. 22:19
Christ's return ... Matt. 24:32
Babylon's destruction ... Is. 47:1

Tenderness—*expressing a feeling or sympathy*
Shown toward the young ... Gen. 33:13
Expressed toward an enemy ... 1 Sam. 30:11-15
Illustrated by a Samaritan ... Luke 10:33-36
Manifested by a father ... Luke 15:11-24

Tens of the Bible
A. *Descriptive of:*
Brothers ... Gen. 42:3
Cubits ... Ex. 26:16
Pillars and sockets ... Ex. 27:12
Commandments ... Ex. 34:28
Shekels ... Num. 7:14
Years ... Ruth 1:4
Loaves ... 1 Sam. 17:17
Tribes ... 1 Kin. 11:31, 35
Degrees ... 2 Kin. 20:9-11
Virgins ... Matt. 25:1-13
Talents ... Matt. 25:28
Lepers ... Luke 17:11-19
Pieces of money ... Luke 19:12-27
Horns ... Rev. 12:3

B. *Expressive of:*
Representation ... Ruth 4:2
Intensity ... Num. 14:22
Sufficiency ... Neh. 4:12
Magnitude ... Dan. 1:20
Remnant ... Amos 5:3
Completion ... Dan. 7:7, 20, 24
Perfection ... Luke 19:16-24

Tentmaking
The occupation of:
Aquila and Priscilla ... Acts 18:2, 3
Paul ... Acts 18:2, 3

Tents—*movable habitations*
A. *Used by:*
People ... 1 Chr. 17:5
Shepherds ... Is. 38:12
Armies ... 1 Sam. 13:2
Rechabites ... Jer. 35:7, 10
Women ... Gen. 24:67
Maidservants ... Gen. 31:33

B. *Features concerning:*
Fastened by cords ... Is. 54:2
Door provided ... Gen. 18:1
Used for the ark ... 2 Sam. 7:1-6

C. *Figurative of:*
Shortness of life ... Is. 38:12
2 Cor. 5:1
Heavens ... Is. 40:22
Enlarge ... Is. 54:2

Terah—*duration, wandering*
Father of Abram ... Gen. 11:26
Idolater ... Josh. 24:2
Dies in Haran ... Gen. 11:25-32

Teraphim
Laban's, stolen by Rachel ... Gen. 31:19-35
Used in idolatry ... Hos. 3:4

Teresh—*dry*
King's official ... Esth. 2:21

Terrestrial—*belonging to the earth*
Spoken of bodies ... 1 Cor. 15:40

Terror—*extreme fear*
A. *Caused by:*
Lord's presence ... Heb. 12:21
Fear ... Job 9:34
Death ... Job 24:17
Arrogance and pride ... Jer. 49:16
War ... Ezek. 21:12
Fright ... Luke 24:37
Persecutors ... 1 Pet. 3:14

B. *Sent as means of:*
Protection ... Gen. 35:5
Punishment ... Lev. 26:16

C. *Safeguards against, found in:*
God's promise ... Ps. 91:5
God's plan ... Luke 21:9

SUBJECT REFERENCE

Tertius—*third*
Paul's scribe ... Rom. 16:22

Tertullus—*diminutive of Tertius*
Orator who accuses Paul ... Acts 24:1-8

Test—*something that manifests a person's real character*
A. *Kinds of:*
Given to Solomon ... 1 Kin. 10:1-3
Physical ... 1 Sam. 17:38, 39
Supernatural ... Ex. 7—11
Spiritual ... Dan. 6:1-28
National ... Ex. 32:1-35

B. *Purposes of, to:*
Test obedience ... Gen. 3:1-8
Gen. 22:1-18
Learn God's will ... Judg. 6:36-40
Accept good diet ... Dan. 1:12-16
Refute Satan's claims ... Job 1:6-22
Destroy idolatry ... 1 Kin. 18:22-24

C. *Descriptive of:*
Testing physically ... 1 Sam. 17:39
Testing morally ... John 6:6
Showing something to be true ... Gen. 42:15, 16

D. *Objects of, among Christians:*
Faith ... 2 Cor. 13:5
Abilities ... 1 Tim. 3:10

Testament—*a will or covenant*
Descriptive of a person's will ... Heb. 9:15-17
New covenant ... Matt. 26:28
New Testament dispensation ... 2 Cor. 3:6
Superiority of the new ... Heb. 8:6-13

Testimony—*witness borne in behalf of something*
A. *Necessary elements of, seen in:*
Verbal expression ... 2 Sam. 1:16
Witnesses ... Neh. 13:15
John 8:17

B. *Means of:*
Prophets ... Acts 10:42, 43
Messengers ... Acts 20:21, 24
Song ... Deut. 31:21
Our sins ... Is. 59:12

C. *Reaction to:*
Believed ... 2 Thess. 1:10
Confirmed ... 1 Cor. 1:6

D. *Purpose of, to:*
Establish the Gospel ... Acts 10:42
Prove Jesus was the Christ ... Acts 18:5
Lead to repentance ... Acts 20:21

Tests of Faith
By:
Difficult demands ... Gen. 12:1, 2
Severe trials ... Job 1:6-22
Prosperity of the wicked ... Ps. 73:1-28
Hardships ... 2 Cor. 11:21-33

Teth
Letter in the Hebrew alphabet ... Ps. 119:65-72

Tetrarch—*a ruler over a fourth part of a kingdom*
Applied to Herod Antipas ... Matt. 14:1

Thaddaeus—*breast*
One of the twelve disciples ... Mark 3:18

Thahash—*porpoise, dolphin*
Son of Nahor ... Gen. 22:24

Thamah—*combat*
Family of Nethinim ... Ezra 2:15

Thankfulness—*gratitude for blessings*
A. *Described as:*
Spiritual sacrifice ... Ps. 116:17
Duty ... 2 Thess. 2:13
Unceasing ... Eph. 1:16
Spontaneous ... Phil. 1:3
In Christ's name ... Eph. 5:20
God's will ... 1 Thess. 5:18
Heaven's theme ... Rev. 7:12

B. *Expressed for:*
Food ... John 6:11, 23
Wisdom ... Dan. 2:23
Converts ... 1 Thess. 1:2
Prayer answered ... John 11:41

SUBJECT REFERENCE

Victory ... 1 Cor. 15:57
Salvation ... 2 Cor. 9:15
Lord's Supper ... 1 Cor. 11:24
Changed lives ... 1 Thess. 2:13

C. *Expressed by:*
Healed Samaritan ... Luke 17:12-19
Righteous ... Ps. 140:13

Theater—*a place of public assembly*
Paul kept from entering ... Acts 19:29-31

Thebez—*brightness*
Fortified city near Shechem ... Judg. 9:50-55

Theft, thief—*the act and agent of stealing*
A. *Kinds of:*
Imputed ... Gen. 44:1-17
Improbable ... Matt. 28:11-13
Real ... Acts 5:1-3

B. *Characteristics of:*
Done often at night ... Jer. 49:9
Comes unexpectedly ... Luke 12:39
Purpose of, to steal ... John 10:10
Window used by ... John 10:1

C. *Objects of:*
Idol ... Gen. 31:19-35
Food ... Prov. 6:30
Traveler ... Luke 10:30, 36
Money ... John 12:6

D. *Evil of:*
Condemned ... Ex. 22:1-12
Punished ... Josh. 7:21-26
Inconsistent with truth ... Jer. 7:9, 10
Defiles a man ... Matt. 15:19, 20
Excludes from heaven ... 1 Cor. 6:10
Not to be among Christians ... Eph. 4:28

See Stealing

Theocracy—*government by God*
Evident under Moses ... Ex. 19:3-6
Continued under Joshua ... Josh. 1:1-8
Rejected by Israel ... 1 Sam. 8:4-9
To be restored ... Is. 2:2-4
Is. 9:6, 7

Theophany—*an appearance of God*
A. *Of God:*
At Sinai ... Ex. 24:9-12
In the tabernacle ... Ex. 40:34-38
In the Temple ... 1 Kin. 8:10, 11
To Isaiah ... Is. 6:1-9

B. *Of Christ as "the angel," to:*
Abraham ... Gen. 18:1-8
Jacob ... Gen. 31:11, 13
Moses ... Ex. 3:1-11
Joshua ... Josh. 5:13-15
Israel ... Judg. 2:1-5
Gideon ... Judg. 6:11-24
Manoah ... Judg. 13:2-25
Paul ... Acts 27:23, 24

C. *Of Christ, as incarnate, in:*
Old Testament ... 1 Cor. 10:4, 9
Nativity ... John 1:14, 18
His:
Resurrected form ... John 20:26-29
Ascended form ... Acts 7:55, 56
Return in glory ... Rev. 1:7, 8
Glorified form ... Matt. 17:1-15

Theophilus—*beloved of God*
Luke addresses his writings to ... Luke 1:3
Acts 1:1

Thessalonians, the Epistles to the—*books of the New Testament*
A. *1 Thessalonians:*
Commendation ... 1 Thess. 1:2-10
Paul's apostolic ministry ... 1 Thess. 2:1-20
Timothy as envoy ... 1 Thess. 3:1-10
The quiet life ... 1 Thess. 4:11, 12
The second coming ... 1 Thess. 4:13-18
Sons of light, not darkness ... 1 Thess. 5:4-7
Christian conduct ... 1 Thess. 5:12-24

B. *2 Thessalonians:*
Encouragement in suffering ... 2 Thess. 1:3-12
The man of sin ... 2 Thess. 2:3-10
Steadfastness ... 2 Thess. 2:15-17
Maintaining order ... 2 Thess. 3:1-15

SUBJECT ... REFERENCE

Thessalonica—*an important city of Macedonia (modern Salonika)*

Paul preaches in ... Acts 17:1-13
Paul writes letters to churches of ... 1 Thess. 1:1

Theudas—*God-giving*

Leader of an unsuccessful revolt ... Acts 5:36

Thirst—*a craving for water*

A. *Caused by:*
Wilderness drought ... Ex. 17:3
Unbelief ... Deut. 28:47, 48
Siege ... 2 Chr. 32:11
Travels ... 2 Cor. 11:27
Extreme pain ... John 19:28
Flame ... Luke 16:24

B. *Figurative of:*
Salvation ... Is. 55:1
Righteousness ... Matt. 5:6
Holy Spirit ... John 7:37-39
Serving Christ ... Matt. 25:35-42

C. *Satisfaction of:*
By a miracle ... Neh. 9:15, 20
Longed for ... Ps. 63:1
In Christ alone ... John 6:35
Final invitation ... Rev. 22:17
Perfectly fulfilled ... Is. 49:10; Rev. 7:16

Thirty heroes, the

Served David ... 1 Chr. 12:1-40

Thirty pieces of silver—*bribe of Judas*

Price of slave ... Ex. 21:32
Given to Judas ... Matt. 26:14-16
Buys field ... Matt. 27:3-10

Thomas—*twin*

Apostle of Christ ... Matt. 10:3
Ready to die with Christ ... John 11:16
In need of instruction ... John 14:1-6
Not present when Christ appears ... John 20:19-24
States terms of belief ... John 20:25
Christ appears again and convinces him ... John 20:26-29; John 21:1, 2
In the upper room ... Acts 1:13

Thongs—*leather straps*

Used to bind Paul ... Acts 22:25

Thorn—*a plant with sharp projections on its stems*

A. *Used literally of:*
Earth's produce ... Gen. 3:18
Land under judgment ... Is. 34:13
Christ's crown ... John 19:2

B. *Used figuratively of:*
Unbelief ... Is. 32:13-15
Judgments ... Hos. 2:6
Pain ... Prov. 26:9
False prophets ... Matt. 7:15, 16
Agent of Satan ... 2 Cor. 12:7
Barrenness ... Matt. 13:7, 22

Thought—*the reasoning of the mind*

A. *Of the wicked, described as:*
Evil ... Gen. 6:5
Abominable ... Prov. 15:26
Sinful ... Is. 59:7
Devoid of God ... Ps. 10:4
Known by God ... 1 Cor. 3:20
In need of repentance ... Acts 8:22
Sinful ... Is. 59:7
Devoid of God ... Ps. 10:4

B. *Of the believer:*
Comprehended by God ... 1 Chr. 28:9; Ps. 139:2
Captivated by Christ ... 2 Cor. 10:5
Criticized by God's Word ... Heb. 4:12
In need of examination ... Ps. 139:23

C. *Of God:*
Not like man's ... Is. 55:8, 9
To believer, good ... Ps. 139:17

Thousand years

As one day ... 2 Pet. 3:8
Millennial reign ... Rev. 20:1-7

SUBJECT ... REFERENCE

Thread

Refused by Abram ... Gen. 14:23
Tied to hand ... Gen. 38:28
Tied in window ... Judg. 2:18
Lips like scarlet ... Song 4:3

Threatenings—*menacing actions or words against another*

A. *Purposes of, to:*
Silence a prophet ... 1 Kin. 19:1, 2
Hinder a work ... Neh. 6:1-14
Hinder the Gospel ... Acts 4:17, 21

B. *Exemplified by:*
Jehoram against Elisha ... 2 Kin. 6:31
Jews against Christians ... Acts 4:29
Saul against Christians ... Acts 9:1

Threshing—*separating kernels of grain by force*

A. *Characteristics of:*
Done by a stick ... Is. 28:27
By cart wheels also ... Is. 28:27, 28
By the feet of oxen ... Hos. 10:11
Large and roomy place ... Gen. 50:10

B. *Figurative of:*
God's judgments ... Jer. 51:33
Minister's labor ... 1 Cor. 9:9, 10

Thrice—*three times*

Males of Israel assemble ... Ex. 34:23, 24
Peter's denial ... Luke 22:34, 61
Vessel's appearance ... Acts 10:16
Paul's shipwrecks ... 2 Cor. 11:25
Paul's petitions ... 2 Cor. 12:8

Throat—*the front part of the neck*

Glutton's warning ... Prov. 23:2
Thirsty one ... Ps. 69:3
Source of evil ... Ps. 5:9

Throne—*the seat and symbol of regal authority*

A. *Of men:*
Under God's sovereignty ... Dan. 5:18-21
Established on righteousness ... Prov. 16:12
Upheld by mercy ... Prov. 20:28
Subject to:
Succession ... 2 Chr. 6:10, 16
Termination ... Jer. 22:4-30

B. *Of God:*
Resplendent in glory ... Is. 6:1-3
Relentless in power ... Dan. 2:44
Ruling over all ... Dan. 4:25, 34, 35
Righteous in execution ... Ps. 9:4, 7, 8
Regal throughout eternity ... Rev. 22:1, 3

C. *Of Christ:*
Based upon the Davidic covenant ... 2 Sam. 7:12-16
Of eternal duration ... Ps. 89:4, 29, 36; Dan. 7:13, 14
Explained in its nature ... Is. 9:6, 7
Symbolized in its functions ... Zech. 6:12, 13
Promised to Christ ... Luke 1:31-33
Christ rises to possess ... Heb. 8:1
Christ now rules from ... Eph. 1:20-22; 1 Pet. 3:20-22
Shares with the Godhead ... Rev. 5:12-14
Shares with believers ... Luke 22:30; Rev. 3:21
Judges men from ... Matt. 25:31

Thumb—*first of man's fingers*

Anointing of, as an act of consecration ... Lev. 8:23, 24
As an act of purification ... Lev. 14:14, 17, 25, 28
Cutting off of, an act of subjugation ... Judg. 1:6, 7

Thunder—*the sound produced by lightning*

A. *Supernaturally brought:*
Upon the Egyptians ... Ex. 9:22-34
At Sinai ... Ex. 19:16
Against the Philistines ... 1 Sam. 7:10
At David's deliverance ... 2 Sam. 22:14, 15

B. *Figurative of:*
God's:
Power ... Job 26:14
Control ... Ps. 104:7
Majesty ... Rev. 4:5
Visitations of judgment ... Rev. 11:19

SUBJECT ... REFERENCE

Thyatira—*an important town in the Roman province of Asia*

Residence of Lydia ... Acts 16:14
One of the seven churches ... Rev. 2:18-24
Sea of Galilee called ... John 6:1, 23

Thyine—*a small cone-bearing tree*

Wood of, used for furniture ... Rev. 18:12

Tibhath—*slaughter*

Town in the kingdom of Zobah ... 1 Chr. 18:8

Tibni—*intelligent*

Son of Ginath ... 1 Kin. 16:21, 22

Tidal—*splendor*

King allied with Chedorlaomer ... Gen. 14:1, 9

Tidings

A. *Descriptive of:*
Joyful ... Gen. 29:13
Good ... 1 Kin. 1:42
Bad ... 1 Sam. 11:4-6
Foreboding ... Jer. 37:5
Distressing ... 2 Sam. 4:4
Fatal ... 1 Sam. 4:19

B. *Of salvation:*
Out of Zion ... Is. 40:9
By a person ... Is. 41:27
Bringer of peace ... Is. 52:7
By Christ ... Is. 61:1-3

Tiglath-pileser—*my trust is in the god Ninib*

Powerful Assyrian king who invades Samaria ... 2 Kin. 15:29

Tikvah—*hope*

1. Father-in-law of Huldah ... 2 Kin. 22:14
Called Tikvath ... 2 Chr. 34:22
2. Father-in-law of Jahaziah ... Ezra 10:15

Tile

Large brick of soft clay ... Ezek. 4:1
Earthen roof ... Luke 5:19

Tiller—*a farmer*

Man's first job ... Gen. 2:5
Sin's handicap on ... Gen. 4:12
Industry in, commended ... Prov. 12:11

Tilon—*scorn*

Son of Shimon ... 1 Chr. 4:20

Timaeus—*highly prized*

Father of Bartimaeus ... Mark 10:46

Timbrel—*a small hand drum*

Used in:
Entertainment ... Gen. 31:27
Worship ... Ps. 81:1-4

Time—*the period between two eternities*

A. *Computation of, by:*
Years ... Gen. 15:13
Months ... 1 Chr. 27:1
Weeks ... Dan. 10:2
Days ... Gen. 8:3
Moments ... Ex. 33:5
Sundial ... 2 Kin. 20:9-11

B. *Events of, dated by:*
Succession of families ... Gen. 5:1-32
Lives of great men ... Gen. 7:6, 11
Succession of kings ... 1 Kin. 11:42, 43
Earthquakes ... Amos 1:1
Important events (the exodus) ... 1 Kin. 6:1
Important emperors ... Luke 3:1

C. *Periods of, stated in years:*
Bondage in Egypt ... Acts 7:6
Wilderness wanderings ... Deut. 1:3
Judges ... Judg. 11:26
Captivity ... Dan. 9:2
Seventy weeks (490 years) ... Dan. 9:24-27

D. *Sequence of prophetic events in, indicated by:*
"The time is fulfilled" (Christ's Advent) ... Mark 1:15
"The fullness of the time" (Christ's Advent) ... Gal. 4:4
"The times of the Gentiles" (the Gospel age) ... Luke 21:24

SUBJECT REFERENCE

"The day of salvation" (the Gospel age) ..... 2 Cor. 6:2
"In the last days" (the Gospel age) ..... Acts 2:17
"In the last days" (the time before Christ's return) ..... 2 Tim. 3:1; 2 Pet. 3:3
"The last day" (Christ's return) ..... John 6:39, 54; John 12:48
"New heavens" (eternity) ..... 2 Pet. 3:13

E. *Importance of, indicated by:*

Shortness of life ..... Ps. 89:47
Making the most of it ..... Eph. 5:16
Purpose of, for salvation ..... 2 Pet. 3:9, 15
Uncertainty of ..... Luke 12:16-23
Our goal, eternity ..... Heb. 11:10, 13-16
God's plan in ..... Acts 14:15-17

F. *For everything:*

To give birth, to die ..... Eccl. 3:1-8, 17

Timidity—*lack of courage*

Nicodemus ..... John 3:1, 2
Joseph of Arimathea ..... John 19:38
Certain people ..... John 9:18-23

Timna—*restraint*

1. Concubine of Eliphaz ..... Gen. 36:12, 22
2. Duke of Edom ..... Gen. 36:40

Timnah, Timnath, Thimnathah—*allotted portion*

1. Town of Judah ..... Josh. 15:10
   Assigned to Dan ..... Josh. 19:40, 43
   Captured by Philistines ..... 2 Chr. 28:18
2. Town in Judah's hill country ..... Josh. 15:57

Timnath-serah—*extra portion*

Village in Ephraim's hill country ..... Josh. 19:50
Place of Joshua's burial ..... Josh. 24:29, 30
Called Timnath-heres ..... Judg. 2:9

Timnite—*an inhabitant of Timnah*

Samson thus called ..... Judg. 15:6

Timon—*deeming worthy*

One of the seven deacons ..... Acts 6:1-5

Timothy, the Epistles to—*books of the New Testament*

A. *1 Timothy:*

Toward true doctrine ..... 1 Tim. 1:3-7
Paul's ministry ..... 1 Tim. 1:12-17
Christ, the Mediator ..... 1 Tim. 2:5, 6
Instructions to women ..... 1 Tim. 2:9-15
Church officials ..... 1 Tim. 3:1-13
The good minister ..... 1 Tim. 4:6-16
Fight the good fight ..... 1 Tim. 6:11-21

B. *2 Timothy:*

Call to responsibility ..... 2 Tim. 1:6-18
Call for strength ..... 2 Tim. 2:1-13
Against apostasy ..... 2 Tim. 3:1-9
The Scriptures called inspired ..... 2 Tim. 3:14-17
Charge to Timothy ..... 2 Tim. 4:1-8
Paul's personal concerns ..... 2 Tim. 4:9-18

Timothy—*revere God*

A. *Life of:*

Of mixed parentage ..... Acts 16:1, 3
Faith of, from childhood ..... 2 Tim. 1:5; 2 Tim. 3:15
Becomes Paul's companion ..... Acts 16:1-3
Ordained by the presbytery ..... 1 Tim. 4:14
Left behind at Troas ..... Acts 17:14
Sent by Paul to Thessalonica ..... 1 Thess. 3:1, 2, 6
Rejoined Paul at Corinth ..... Acts 18:1-5
Preached Christ to Corinthians ..... 2 Cor. 1:19
Sent by Paul into Macedonia ..... Acts 19:22
Sent by Paul to Corinth ..... 1 Cor. 4:17
Returned with Paul to Jerusalem ..... Acts 20:1-5
With Paul in Rome ..... Phil. 1:1; Phil. 2:19, 23
Set free ..... Heb. 13:23
Left at Ephesus by Paul ..... 1 Tim. 1:3
Paul summoned him to Rome ..... 2 Tim. 4:9, 11, 21

B. *Character of:*

Devout from childhood ..... 2 Tim. 3:15
Faithful in service ..... Phil. 2:22

SUBJECT REFERENCE

Beloved by Paul ..... 1 Tim. 1:2, 18
Follows Paul's way ..... 1 Cor. 4:17
In need of instruction ..... 1 Tim. 4:12-16
Of sickly nature ..... 1 Tim. 5:23
Urged to remain faithful ..... 1 Tim. 6:20, 21
Emotional ..... 2 Tim. 1:4

Tin—*a metal obtained by smelting*

Used in early times ..... Num. 31:22
Brought from Tarshish ..... Ezek. 27:12
Figurative of degeneracy ..... Is. 1:25

Tiphsah—*passage; crossing*

1. Place designating Solomon's northern boundary ..... 1 Kin. 4:24
2. Unidentified town attacked by Menahem ..... 2 Kin. 15:16

Tiras

Son of Japheth ..... Gen. 10:2

Tirathites

Family of scribes ..... 1 Chr. 2:55

Tire—*an ornamental headdress*

Worn by:

Ezekiel ..... Ezek. 24:17, 23
Daughters of Zion ..... Is. 3:18
Jezebel ..... 2 Kin. 9:30

Tirhakah—*the king of Cush (Nubia)*

Opposes Sennacherib ..... 2 Kin. 19:9

Tirhanah—*kindness*

Son of Caleb ..... 1 Chr. 2:42, 48

Tiria—*foundation*

Son of Jehaleleel ..... 1 Chr. 4:16

Tirshatha—*governor*

Persian title used of Zerubbabel ..... Ezra 2:63
Applied to Nehemiah ..... Neh. 8:9

Tirzah—*delight*

1. Zelophehad's youngest daughter ..... Num. 26:33
2. Town near Samaria ..... Josh. 12:24
   Seat of Jeroboam's rule ..... 1 Kin. 14:17
   Israel's kings rule here down to Omri ..... 1 Kin. 16:6-23
   Famous for its beauty ..... Song 6:4

Tishbite—*an inhabitant of Tishbeh*

Elijah thus called ..... 1 Kin. 17:1

Tithes—*the tenth of one's income*

Given by Abraham to Melchizedek ..... Heb. 7:1, 2, 6
Promised by Jacob ..... Gen. 28:22
Belongs to the LORD ..... Lev. 27:30-33
Given to Levites ..... Num. 18:21-24
Given by Levites to priests ..... Num. 18:25, 26
Taken to Temple ..... Deut. 12:5-19
Rules regarding ..... Deut. 14:22-29
Honesty in, required ..... Deut. 26:13-15
Of animals, every tenth ..... Lev. 27:32, 33
Recognition of, by Jews ..... Neh. 13:5, 12
Promise regarding ..... Mal. 3:7-12
Pharisaic legalism on, condemned ..... Luke 18:9-14

Titles—*appellations of honor*

Condemned by Christ ..... Matt. 23:1-8

Tittle—*a mark distinguishing similar letters*

Figurative of minute requirements ..... Matt. 5:18

See Jot

Titus

Greek Christian and Paul's companion ..... Titus 1:4
Sent by Paul to Corinth ..... 2 Cor. 7:13, 14
Organized Corinthian relief fund ..... 2 Cor. 8:6-23
Met Paul in Macedonia ..... 2 Cor. 7:6, 7
Accompanied Paul to Crete ..... Titus 1:5
Sent by Paul to Dalmatia ..... 2 Tim. 4:10

Titus, the Epistle to—*a book of the New Testament*

Qualifications of an elder ..... Titus 1:5-9
Against false teachings ..... Titus 1:10-16
Domestic life ..... Titus 2:1-10
Godly living ..... Titus 3:3-8

SUBJECT REFERENCE

Tizite

Description of Joha, David's mighty man ..... 1 Chr. 11:45

Tob—*good*

Jephthah's refuge east of the Jordan ..... Judg. 11:3, 5

Tobadonijah—*good is Lord Jehovah*

Levite teacher ..... 2 Chr. 17:7, 8

Tobiah—*Jehovah is good*

1. Founder of a postexilic family ..... Ezra 2:60
2. Ammonite servant; ridiculed the Jews ..... Neh. 2:10

Tobijah—*Jehovah is good*

1. Levite teacher ..... 2 Chr. 17:7, 8
2. Came from Babylon ..... Zech. 6:10, 14

Tochen—*a measure*

Town of Simeon ..... 1 Chr. 4:32

Toe—*the terminal part of the foot*

Aaron's, anointed ..... Ex. 29:20
Of captives, amputated ..... Judg. 1:6, 7
Of an image ..... Dan. 2:41, 42

Togarmah

Northern country inhabited by descendants of Gomer ..... Gen. 10:3

Toi

King of Hamath; sends embassy to salute David ..... 2 Sam. 8:9-12

Token—*a visible sign*

A. *Descriptive of:*

Rainbow ..... Gen. 9:12-17
Circumcision ..... Gen. 17:11
Bloodshed ..... Ex. 12:13
God's wonders ..... Ps. 65:8

B. *As assurance of:*

God's: Presence ..... Ex. 3:12
Judgment upon sin ..... Num. 17:10
Goodness ..... Ps. 86:17
Guarantee ..... Josh. 2:12, 18, 21
Identification ..... Mark 14:44
Genuineness ..... 2 Thess. 3:17
Coming judgment ..... 2 Thess. 1:5

Tola—*worm; scarlet*

1. Son of Issachar and family head ..... Gen. 46:13
2. Son of Puah; a judge of Israel ..... Judg. 10:1

Tolad—*begetter*

Simeonite town ..... 1 Chr. 4:29
Called Eltolad ..... Josh. 19:4

Tolerance—*an attitude of patience toward opposing views*

A. *Approved in dealing with:*

Disputes among brothers ..... Mark 9:38-40
Weaker brother ..... Rom. 14:1-23
Repentant brother ..... 2 Cor. 2:4-11

B. *Condemned in dealing with:*

Sin ..... 1 Cor. 5:1-13
Evil ..... 2 Cor. 6:14-18
Sin in ourselves ..... Mark 9:43-48
Error ..... 2 John 10, 11

Toll—*taxes*

Imposed by Jews ..... Ezra 4:20
Imposed upon Jews ..... Ezra 4:13
Levites excluded from ..... Ezra 7:24

Tomb—*a place of burial*

John's body placed in ..... Mark 6:25-29
Christ's body placed in Joseph's ..... Matt. 25:57-60

Tongue—*the organ of speech*

A. *Descriptive of:*

Language ..... Gen. 10:5, 20, 21
Speech ..... Ex. 4:10
The physical organ ..... Judg. 7:5
Externalism ..... 1 John 3:18
People or race ..... Is. 66:18
Spiritual gift ..... 1 Cor. 12:10-30
Submission ..... Is. 45:23

SUBJECT — REFERENCE

B. *Kinds of:*
- Backbiting — Prov. 25:23
- As of fire — Acts 2:3
- Deceitful — Mic. 6:12
- Double — 1 Tim. 3:8
- False — Ps. 120:3
- Flattering — Prov. 6:24
- Just — Prov. 10:20
- Lying — Prov. 21:6
- Muttering — Is. 59:3
- New — Mark 16:17
- Perverse — Prov. 17:20
- Sharpened — Ps. 140:3
- Slow — Ex. 4:10
- Soft — Prov. 25:15
- Stammering — Is. 33:19
- Wholesome — Prov. 15:4
- Wise — Prov. 15:2

C. *Characteristics of:*
- Small but important — James 3:5
- Untameable — James 3:6
- Source of trouble — Prov. 21:23
- Means of sin — Ps. 39:1
- Known by God — Ps. 139:4

D. *Proper employment of, in:*
- Speaking:
  - God's righteousness — Ps. 35:28
  - Wisdom — Ps. 37:30
  - God's Word — Ps. 119:172
- Singing praises — Ps. 126:2
- Kindness — Prov. 31:26
- Confessing Christ — Phil. 2:11

See Slander

Tongues, speaking in

A. *At Pentecost:*
- Opposite of Babel — Gen. 11:6-9
- Sign of the Spirit's coming — Acts 2:3, 4
- External manifestation — Acts 2:4, 5
- Meaning of, interpreted by Peter — Acts 2:14-40

B. *At Corinth:*
- Spiritual gift (last rank) — 1 Cor. 12:8-10, 28-30
- Interpreter of, required — 1 Cor. 14:27, 28
- Love superior to — 1 Cor. 13:1-13
- Subject to abuse — 1 Cor. 14:22-26

Tools of the Bible
- Anvil — Is. 41:7
- Awl — Deut. 15:17
- Axe — 1 Chr. 20:3
- Bellows — Jer. 6:29
- Brickkiln — 2 Sam. 12:31
- Compass — Is. 44:13
- Fining pot — Prov. 17:3
- Fleshhook — Ex. 27:3
- Fork — 1 Sam. 2:13
- Furnace — Prov. 17:3
- Goad — 1 Sam. 13:21
- Graving tool — Ex. 32:4
- Hammer — Ps. 74:6
- Inkhorn — Ezek. 9:2
- Knife — Gen. 22:6
- Mattock — 1 Sam. 13:21
- Ox-goad — Judg. 3:31
- Pan — Ex. 27:3
- Plane — Is. 44:13
- Plowshare — Is. 2:4
- Plumb line — Amos 7:8
- Pruning hook — Is. 2:4
- Razor — Num. 6:5
- Saw — 2 Sam. 12:31
- Shovel — Ex. 27:3
- Sickle — Deut. 16:9
- Wheel — Eccl. 12:6

Topaz—*a precious stone*
- Used in breastplate — Ex. 39:10
- Of great value — Job 28:19
- In Eden — Ezek. 28:13
- In New Jerusalem — Rev. 21:2, 20

Tophel—*lime; cement*
- Israelite camp — Deut. 1:1

Tophet—*altar*
- Place of human sacrifice in the valley of Hinnom — Jer. 7:31, 32

Torment—*to suffer unbearable pain*

A. *Kinds of:*
- Physical — Matt. 8:6
- Eternal — Rev. 20:10

SUBJECT — REFERENCE

B. *Means of:*
- Official — Matt. 18:34
- Persecutors — Heb. 11:35
- Fear — 1 John 4:18
- Flame — Luke 16:23-25
- God — Rev. 14:9-11

Tortoise—*the great lizard*
- Classed as unclean — Lev. 11:29

Touch—*contact between two things*

A. *Kinds of:*
- Unclean — Lev. 5:2, 3
- Angelic — 1 Kin. 19:5, 7
- Queenly — Esth. 5:2
- Divine — Job 19:21
- Cleansing — Is. 6:7
- Healing — Matt. 8:3
- Sexual — 1 Cor. 7:1
- Satanic — 1 John 5:18

B. *Purposes of, to:*
- Purify — Is. 6:7
- Strengthen — Dan. 10:10-18
- Harm — Zech. 2:8
- Heal — Mark 5:27-31
- Receive a blessing — Mark 10:13
- Restore to life — Luke 7:14
- Manifest faith — Luke 7:39-50

Towel—*a cloth used in drying*
- Used by Christ — John 13:4, 5

Tower of Furnaces—*a tower of Jerusalem*
- Rebuilt by Nehemiah — Neh. 3:11

Towers

A. *Purposes of, for:*
- Protection — Matt. 21:33
- Watchmen — 2 Kin. 9:17
- Safeguarding people — 2 Chr. 26:10, 15

B. *Partial list of:*
- Babel — Gen. 11:4, 9
- David — Song 4:4
- Lebanon — Song 7:4
- Penuel — Judg. 8:17
- Shechem — Judg. 9:40, 47, 49
- Siloam — Luke 13:4

To wit—*namely; that is to say*
- Used by Paul twice — 2 Cor. 5:19

Town clerk—*a keeper of court records*
- Appeases the people — Acts 19:35

Trachonitis—*hilly land*
- Volcanic region southeast of Damascus — Luke 3:1

Trade and transportation

A. *Objects of, such as:*
- Gold — 1 Kin. 9:28
- Timber — 1 Kin. 5:6, 8, 9
- Hardwood — 1 Kin. 10:11, 12
- Spices — 1 Kin. 10:10, 15
- Property — Ruth 4:3, 4
- Slaves — Joel 3:6

B. *Means of, by:*
- Wagons — Gen. 46:5, 6
- Kines — 1 Sam. 6:7, 8
- Floats — 1 Kin. 5:7-9
- Camels — 1 Kin. 10:1, 2
- Asses — Num. 22:21-33
- Horses — 1 Kin. 20:20
- Caravans — Gen. 37:25-36

C. *Centers of, in:*
- Tyre — Ezek. 27:1-36
- Jerusalem — Neh. 13:15-21

Trades and crafts
- Baker — Gen. 40:1
- Brick makers — Ex. 5:7
- Carpenter — Is. 41:7
- Engineers — Gen. 11:3, 4
- Farmers — Ps. 104:13-15
- Fishermen — Matt. 4:18-22
- Lawyers — Luke 5:17
- Millers — Ex. 11:5
- Physician — Col. 4:14
- Smiths — Is. 44:12

SUBJECT — REFERENCE

Traditions—*precepts passed down from past generations*

A. *Jewish, described as:*
- Commandments of men — Matt. 15:9
- Rejection of God's Word — Mark 7:8, 9
- Productive of hypocrisy — Mark 7:6, 7
- Inconsistent with Christ — Col. 2:8

B. *Christian described as:*
- Inspired by the Spirit — John 15:26, 27
- Handed down by apostles — 2 Thess. 3:6, 7
- Based on eyewitnesses — 2 Pet. 1:16, 19
- Classed as Scripture — 1 Tim. 5:18; 2 Pet. 3:16
- Once for all delivered — Jude 3
- Consisting of fundamental truths — 1 Cor. 15:1-3
- Originating with Christ — Matt. 28:20; 1 Cor. 11:1-23

Traffic, spiritual
- Buying the truth — Prov. 23:23
- Value of wisdom — Prov. 2:2-4
- Above gold in value — Ps. 119:72, 127
- Without price — Is. 55:1
- True gold, from Christ — Rev. 3:18

Train
- Monarch's retinue — 1 Kin. 10:2
- Trailing robe — Is. 6:1

Traitor—*one who betrays a trust*

Descriptive of:
- Judas — Luke 6:16
- End-time people — 2 Tim. 3:4

Trance—*a somnolent state*
- Peter's on a housetop — Acts 10:10

Transfiguration—*a radical change in appearance of:*
- Moses — Ex. 34:29-35
- Christ, on a high mountain — Matt. 17:1-17
- Christ, remembered — 2 Pet. 1:16-18
- Stephen — Acts 6:15

Transgression—*a violation of God's Law*

A. *Described as:*
- Personal — 1 Tim. 2:14
- Public — Rom. 5:14
- Political — Esth. 3:3
- Premeditated — Josh. 7:11-25

B. *Caused by:*
- Law — Rom. 4:15
- Sin — 1 John 3:4
- Wine — Hab. 2:5
- Idolatry — 1 Chr. 5:25
- Intermarriage — Ezra 10:10, 13
- Fear of the people — 1 Sam. 15:24

C. *Productive of:*
- Powerlessness — Judg. 2:20-23
- Unfaithfulness — 1 Chr. 9:1
- Death — 1 Chr. 10:13
- Destruction — Ps. 37:38
- Curse — Is. 24:5, 6

D. *Punishment of, by:*
- Defeat — 2 Chr. 12:1-5
- Disease — 2 Chr. 26:16-21
- Captivity — Neh. 1:8
- Affliction — Ps. 107:17
- Death in hell — Is. 66:24

E. *Reaction to, by:*
- Further disobedience — Num. 14:41-45
- Covering up — Job 31:33
- Repentance — Ezra 9:4-7

F. *Forgiveness of:*
- Difficult — Josh. 24:19
- Out of God's mercy — Ex. 34:7
- By:
  - Confession — Ps. 32:1, 5
  - Removal — Ps. 103:12
  - Blotting out — Is. 44:22

G. *Christ's relation to:*
- Wounded for our — Is. 53:5
- Stricken for our — Is. 53:8
- Make intercession for — Is. 53:12
- Provided a Redeemer for — Rom. 11:26, 27
- Died for our — Heb. 9:15

See Sin

T

SUBJECT	REFERENCE

Transitory—*passing quickly away*

A. *Descriptive of man's:*
- Life ... Ps. 39:4, 5
- Pleasures ... Is. 47:8, 9
- Plans ... Luke 12:16-21

B. *Caused by:*
- World's passing away ... 1 John 2:15-17
- Our mortality ... Ps. 90:3-12
- Impending future world ... 2 Cor. 4:17, 18

Translations—*physical transportation to heaven*
- Enoch ... Heb. 11:5
- Elijah ... 2 Kin. 2:1-11
- Christians ... 1 Thess. 4:16, 17

Travail—*the labor pains of childbirth*

A. *Descriptive of:*
- Childbirth pains ... Gen. 38:27
- Anguish ... Is. 53:11

B. *Of a woman's, described as:*
- Fearful ... Ps. 48:6
- Painful ... Is. 13:8
- Hazardous ... Gen. 35:16-19
- Joyful afterwards ... John 16:21

C. *Figurative of:*
- New Israel ... Is. 66:7, 8
- Messiah's birth ... Mic. 4:9, 10
- Redemption ... Mic. 5:3
- New birth ... Gal. 4:19
- Creation's rebirth ... Rom. 8:22

Treachery—*pretending friendship in order to betray*

A. *Manifested by:*
- Woman ... Judg. 4:18-21
- People ... Josh. 9:3-15
- King ... 2 Sam. 11:14, 15
- Son ... 2 Sam. 13:28, 29
- Enemy ... Esth. 3:8-15
- Disciple ... Matt. 26:47-50

B. *Accompanied by:*
- Deceit ... Gen. 34:13-31
- Soothing words ... Judg. 9:1-5
- Professed favor ... 1 Sam. 18:17-19
- Pretense ... Dan. 6:1-8

Treason—*betrayal of one's country*

A. *Instances of:*
- Rahab against Jericho ... Josh. 2:1-24
- Israelites against Rehoboam ... 1 Kin. 12:16-19
- Absalom against David ... 2 Sam. 15:1-14
- Sheba against David ... 2 Sam. 20:1-22
- Athaliah against Judah ... 2 Kin. 11; 2 Chr. 22:10-12

B. *Characterized by:*
- Conspiracy ... 1 Kin. 16:9-11, 20
- Giving secrets ... 1 Sam. 30:15, 16
- Falling out ... 2 Sam. 3:6-21
- Jealousy ... Num. 12:1-11

See Conspiracy; Treachery

Treasure—*something valuable stored away*

A. *Descriptive of:*
- Storage cities ... Ex. 1:11
- Storehouses ... 1 Kin. 7:51
- Places for storing archives ... Ezra 5:17
- Offering boxes ... Luke 21:1

B. *Figurative of:*
- Earth's productive capacity ... Ps. 17:14
- Wisdom ... Prov. 2:4
- People of God ... Ex. 19:5
- Man's spiritual possibilities ... Matt. 12:35
- New life in Christ ... 2 Cor. 4:6, 7
- Christ as the divine depository ... Col. 2:3, 9
- Future rewards ... Matt. 6:19, 20

Treasurer—*a custodian of public funds*

Under:
- David, Ahijah ... 1 Chr. 26:20
- Solomon, Jehiel ... 1 Chr. 29:7, 8
- Hezekiah, Shebna ... Is. 22:15
- Cyrus, Mithredath ... Ezra 1:8
- Candace, the Ethiopian eunuch ... Acts 8:27
- At Corinth, Erastus ... Rom. 16:23

SUBJECT	REFERENCE

Tree

A. *Characteristics of:*
- Created by God ... Gen. 1:11, 12
- Of fixed varieties ... Gen. 1:12, 29
- Can be grafted ... Rom. 11:24
- Subject to God's judgments ... Hag. 2:17, 19

B. *Used for:*
- Shade ... Gen. 18:4
- Burial sites ... Gen. 35:8
- Food ... Deut. 20:19, 20
- Cross ... Acts 5:30
- Buildings ... 1 Kin. 5:10
- Idolatry ... Is. 44:14, 17
- Fuel ... Is. 44:15, 16, 19

C. *List of, in Bible:*
- Aloe ... Ps. 45:8
- Ash ... Is. 44:14
- Bay ... Ps. 37:35
- Cedar ... 1 Kin. 10:27
- Chestnut ... Ezek. 31:8
- Cypress ... Is. 44:14
- Elm ... Hos. 4:13
- Fig ... Deut. 8:8
- Fir ... 2 Sam. 6:5
- Hazel ... Gen. 30:37
- Juniper ... 1 Kin. 19:4, 5
- Mulberry ... 2 Sam. 5:23
- Myrtle ... Is. 41:19
- Oak ... Is. 1:30
- Olive ... Judg. 9:9
- Palm ... Ex. 15:27
- Pomegranate ... Deut. 8:8
- Poplar ... Hos. 4:13
- Shittim ... Ex. 36:20
- Sycamore ... Amos 7:14
- Willow ... Is. 44:4

D. *Figurative of:*
- Righteous ... Ps. 1:1-3
- Believer's life ... Prov. 11:30
- Wisdom ... Prov. 3:18
- Basic character ... Matt. 7:17-19
- Continued prosperity ... Is. 65:22
- Judgment ... Luke 23:31
- Eternal life ... Rev. 22:14
- Covenant ... Rom. 11:24

Tree of life
- In Eden ... Gen. 2:9
- In New Jerusalem ... Rev. 22:1, 2

Tremble—*to shake with fear*

A. *Expressive of:*
- Deep concern ... Gen. 27:33
- Fear ... Mark 16:8
- Filial trust ... Is. 66:2, 5
- Apprehension ... 1 Sam. 16:4
- Infirmity ... Eccl. 12:3
- Obedience ... Phil. 2:12

B. *Applied to:*
- People ... Dan. 6:26
- Earth ... Ps. 97:4
- Nations ... Is. 64:2
- Heart ... Deut. 28:65
- Flesh ... Ps. 119:120
- Servants ... Eph. 6:5
- Christians ... 1 Cor. 2:3

C. *Caused by:*
- Physical change ... Luke 8:47
- Earthquake ... Acts 16:29

Trials—*hardships that try our faith*

A. *Characteristics of:*
- Some very severe ... 2 Cor. 1:8-10
- Cause of, sometimes unknown ... Job 1:7-22
- Sometimes physical ... 2 Cor. 12:7-10
- Endurable ... 1 Cor. 10:13
- Rewardable ... Matt. 5:10-12

B. *Design of, to:*
- Test faith ... Gen. 22:1-18
- Purify faith ... Mal. 3:3, 4; 1 Pet. 1:6-9
- Increase patience ... James 1:3, 4, 12
- Bring us to a better place ... Ps. 66:10-12
- Chasten us ... Is. 48:10
- Glorify God ... 1 Pet. 4:12-16

Tribes of Israel
- Twelve in number ... Gen. 49:28
- Descended from Jacob's sons ... Gen. 35:22-26

SUBJECT	REFERENCE

- Jacob forecasted future of ... Gen. 49:3-27
- Moses foretold future of ... Deut. 33:6-35
- Numbered ... Num. 1:44-46
- Camped by standards ... Num. 2:2-31
- Canaan divided among ... Josh. 15-17
- Names of, engraven ... Ex. 39:14
- United until Rehoboam's rebellion ... 1 Kin. 12:16-20
- Returned after exile ... Ezra 8:35
- Typical of Christians ... James 1:1

Tribulation—*a state or time of great affliction*

A. *Descriptive of:*
- National distress ... Deut. 4:30
- Afflictions ... 1 Sam. 10:19
- Persecutions ... 1 Thess. 3:4
- Severe testings ... Rev. 2:10, 22

B. *Christian's attitude toward:*
- Must expect ... Acts 14:22
- Glory in ... Rom. 5:3
- Overcome ... Rom. 8:35-37
- Patient in ... Rom. 12:12
- Joyful in ... 2 Cor. 7:4
- Faint not at ... Eph. 3:13

Tribute—*a tax imposed upon a subjugated nation*
- Israelites ... 2 Kin. 23:33
- Christ settles question concerning ... Matt. 22:17-21
- Paul's admonition concerning ... Rom. 13:6, 7

Tribute money—*Temple tax*
- Levied yearly upon all Jews ... Matt. 17:24-27; Matt. 22:17-21

Trickery—*use of guile or deceit*
- By Gibeonites ... Josh. 9:3-6
- By Saul ... 1 Sam. 28:7-10
- By Amnon ... 2 Sam. 13:1-15
- Christians, beware of ... Eph. 4:14

Trifles—*things of slight importance*
- Pharisees obsessed by ... Matt. 23:23-25
- Avoidance of, by Christians ... Titus 3:9

Trinity, the

A. *Revealed in the Old Testament:*
- At Creation ... Gen. 1:1-3, 26
- In the personality of the Spirit ... Is. 40:13; Is. 48:16
- By:
  - Divine angel ... Judg. 13:8-23
  - Personification of Wisdom ... Prov. 8:22-31
  - Threefold "Holy" ... Is. 6:3
  - Aaronic benediction ... Num. 6:24-27

B. *Revealed in the New Testament:*
- At Christ's baptism ... Matt. 3:16, 17
- In:
  - Christ's teaching ... John 14:26; John 15:26
  - Baptismal formula ... Matt. 28:19
  - Apostolic benediction ... 2 Cor. 13:14
  - Apostolic teaching ... Gal. 4:4-6

Triumphal entrance—*Jesus' entry into Jerusalem on the last week of his earthly ministry*
- Prophesied ... Zech. 9:9
- Fulfilled ... Matt. 21:2-11

Troas—*a seaport city near Troy*
- Paul received vision here ... Acts 16:8-11

Trogyllium—*a seaport city of Asia Minor*
- Paul's ship tarried here ... Acts 20:15

Troops—*a group of soldiers*
- Place in fortified cities ... 2 Chr. 17:2
- Come together and camp ... Job 19:12
- "Daughter of troops" ... Mic. 5:1

Trophimus—*nourishing*
- One of Paul's companions ... Acts 20:4

Trouble—*that which causes concern or distress*

A. *Kinds Of:*
- Physical, of nature ... Ps. 46:3
- Mental ... Dan. 5:9
- Spiritual, of the wicked ... Is. 57:20
- Spiritual, of the righteous ... Ps. 77:3
- National ... Jer. 30:7
- Domestic ... Prov. 11:29

B. *Caused by:*
- Misdeeds of sons ... Gen. 34:30

SUBJECT	REFERENCE
Mysterious dream	Dan. 2:1, 3
Unexpected news	1 Sam. 28:21
Sin	Josh. 7:25
Evil spirits	1 Sam. 16:14, 15
Enemies	Ezra 4:4
Physical malady	Job 4:5
God's:	
Presence	Job 23:15
Withdrawal	Ps. 30:7
Wrath	Ps. 78:49
Our sins	Ps. 38:4-6
Mouth	Prov. 21:23
Angel visitant	Luke 1:12, 29
Wars, etc	Mark 13:7
Trials	2 Cor. 7:5
Afflicted	2 Thess. 1:7

C. *God's help to His saints in, to:*

Hide	Ps. 27:5
Deliver	Ps. 50:15
Help	Ps. 46:1
Attend	Ps. 91:15
Revive	Ps. 138:7

Truce—*a temporary cessation of warfare*

With good results	2 Sam. 2:25-31

Tracebreakers—*violators of agreements*

Characteristic of the last days	2 Tim. 3:1, 3

True—*that which agrees with the facts*

A. *Applied to:*

God	John 17:3
Christ	Rev. 3:7, 14
God's:	
Word	John 21:24
Judgments	Rev. 16:7
Believer's heart	2 Cor. 6:8
Worshipers	John 4:23

B. *Proof of:*

Given by men	John 5:32
Based upon testimony	John 8:13-18
Recognized by men	John 10:41

See Truth

Trumpet—*a wind musical instrument*

A. *Features concerning:*

Instrument of music	1 Chr. 13:8
Made of ram's horn	Josh. 6:4

B. *Uses of, in Israel, to:*

Signal God's presence	Ex. 19:16, 19
Regulate marchings	Num. 10:2, 5, 6
Call assemblies	Num. 10:2, 3, 7
Announce a feast	Lev. 23:23-25
Gather the nation	Judg. 3:27
Alert against an enemy	Neh. 4:18, 20
Herald a new king	1 Kin. 1:34-41
Hail a religious event	1 Chr. 13:8
Assist in worship	Neh. 12:35-41

C. *Uses of, at Christ's return, to:*

Herald Christ's coming	Matt. 24:31
Signal prophetic events	Rev. 8:2, 6, 13 Rev. 9:14
Raise the dead	1 Thess. 4:16

Trust—*to put one's confidence in*

A. *Not to be placed in:*

Weapons	Ps. 44:6
Wealth	Ps. 49:6, 7
Leaders	Ps. 146:3
Man	Jer. 17:5
Works	Jer. 48:7
One's own righteousness	Ezek. 33:13

B. *To be placed in:*

God's:	
Name	Ps. 33:21
Word	Ps. 119:42
Christ	Matt. 12:17-21

C. *Benefits of:*

Joy	Ps. 5:11
Deliverance	Ps. 22:4, 5
Triumph	Ps. 25:2, 3
God's goodness	Ps. 31:19
Mercy	Ps. 32:10
Provision	Ps. 37:3, 5
Blessedness	Ps. 40:4
Safety	Ps. 56:4, 11
Usefulness	Ps. 73:28
Guidance	Prov. 3:5, 6
Inheritance	Is. 57:13

SUBJECT	REFERENCE

Truth—*that which agrees with final reality*

A. *Ascribed to:*

God's Law	Ps. 119:142-160
Christ	John 14:6
Holy Spirit	John 14:17
God's Word	John 17:17, 19
Gospel	Gal. 2:5, 14

B. *Effects of, to:*

Make free	John 8:31, 32
Sanctify	John 17:17-19
Purify	1 Pet. 1:22
Establish	Eph. 4:15

C. *Wrong attitudes toward, to:*

Change into a lie	Rom. 1:25
Disobey	Rom. 2:8
Walk contrary to	Gal. 2:17
Love not	2 Thess. 2:10
Believe not	2 Thess. 2:12
Be destitute of	1 Tim. 6:5
Never come to	2 Tim. 3:7
Resist	2 Tim. 3:8
Turn from	2 Tim. 4:4

D. *Right attitudes toward, to:*

Speak	Eph. 4:25
Walk in	3 John 3, 4
Declare	Acts 26:25
Worship in	John 4:23, 24
Come to	1 Tim. 2:4
Believe and know	1 Tim. 4:3
Handle accurately	2 Tim. 2:15
Obey	1 Pet. 1:22
Be established	2 Pet. 1:12

Truthfulness—*abiding by the truth*

Commanded	Ps. 15:2
Exemplified by Levi	Mal. 2:6
Should characterize Christians	Eph. 4:25

Tryphaena—*delicate*

Woman at Rome commended by Paul	Rom. 16:12

Tryphosa—*dainty*

Woman at Rome commended by Paul	Rom. 16:12

Tubal

1. Son of Japheth	Gen. 10:2
2. Tribe associated with Javan and Meshech	Is. 66:19
In Gog's army	Ezek. 38:2, 3
Punishment of	Ezek. 32:26, 27

Tubal-cain—*Tubal, the smith*

Son of Lamech	Gen. 4:19-22

Tumult—*a confused uproar*

Against:

God	Is. 37:29
Christ	Matt. 27:24
Paul	Acts 19:29, 40
Paul pleads innocent of	Acts 24:18

Turtledove—*a dove or pigeon*

Migratory bird	Song 2:12
Term of affection	Ps. 74:19
Offering of the poor	Lev. 12:2, 6-8 Luke 2:24

Tutors, guardians—*instructors of children*

Referred to by Paul	Gal. 4:2

Twelve

Angels	Rev. 21:12
Apostles	Rev. 21:14
Baskets	John 6:13
Brazen bulls	Jer. 52:20
Brethren	Gen. 42:32
Cakes	Lev. 24:5
Cities	1 Chr. 6:63
Cubits	1 Kin. 7:15
Foundations	Rev. 21:14
Fountains	Num. 33:9
Fruits	Rev. 22:2
Gates	Rev. 21:12
Golden spoons	Num. 7:86
He goats	Ezra 8:35
Hours	John 11:9
Legions of angels	Matt. 26:53
Lions	1 Kin. 10:20
Men	Josh. 3:12
Months	Dan. 4:29
Officers	1 Kin. 4:7
Oxen	2 Chr. 4:15

SUBJECT	REFERENCE
Patriarchs	Acts 7:8
Pieces	1 Kin. 11:30
Pillars	Ex. 24:4
Princes	Gen. 17:20
Rods	Num. 17:2
Silver bowls	Num. 7:84
Sons of Jacob	Gen. 35:22
Spoons	Num. 7:86
Stars	Rev. 12:1
Stones	1 Kin. 18:31
Thousand	2 Sam. 17:1
Thrones	Matt. 19:28
Tribes	Luke 22:30
Wells	Ex. 15:27
Years of age	Luke 2:42

Twins of the Bible

Esau and Jacob	Gen. 25:24-26
Pharez and Zarah	Gen. 38:27-30

Two

Lights	Gen. 1:16
Tables of stone	Ex. 34:1, 4
Goats	Lev. 16:7, 8
Spies	Josh. 2:1, 4
Wives	1 Sam. 1:2
Evils	Jer. 2:13
Masters	Matt. 6:24
Witnesses	Matt. 18:16
People agreeing	Matt. 18:19, 20
Commandments	Matt. 22:40
Thieves	Matt. 27:38
Covenants	Gal. 4:24
Become one	Eph. 5:31
Hard pressed from both directions	Phil. 1:23

Tychicus—*chance happening*

Asian Christian and companion	Acts 20:4
Carried Paul's letter to Colossians	Col. 4:7
Carried letter to Ephesians	Eph. 6:21, 22
Accompanied Onesimus to his master	Col. 4:7
Later sent to Ephesus by Paul	2 Tim. 4:12

Types, typology—*divine illustration of truth*

May be:

Ceremony—Passover	1 Cor. 5:7
Event—wilderness journeys	1 Cor. 10:1-11
Institution—priesthood	Heb. 9:11
Person—Adam	Rom. 5:14
Thing—veil	Heb. 10:20

Tyrannus—*tyrant*

Paul teaches in his school	Acts 19:9

Tyre—*a seaport city 25 miles south of Sidon*

Ancient city	Josh. 19:29
Noted for commerce	Ezek. 27:1-36
King of, helped Solomon	1 Kin. 5:1-10
Denounced by prophets	Joel 3:4-6
Fall of, predicted	Ezek. 26:1-21
Jesus visited	Matt. 15:21-28

Tzaddi

Letter of the Hebrew alphabet	Ps. 119:137-144

U

Ucal—*I am strong*

Proverbs addressed to	Prov. 30:1

Uel—*will of God*

Divorced his foreign wife	Ezra 10:34

Ulai—*a river of Elam near Shushan*

Scene of Daniel's visions	Dan. 8:2-16

Ulam—*first; leader*

Manassite	1 Chr. 7:16, 17

Ulla—*burden*

Descendant of Asher	1 Chr. 7:30, 39

Ummah—*association*

Asherite town	Josh. 19:24, 30

Unbelief

A. *Caused by:*

Sin	John 16:9
Satan	John 8:43-47
Evil heart	Heb. 3:12
Honor from one another	John 5:44

SUBJECT ... REFERENCE

Not belonging to Christ ... John 10:26
Judicial blindness ... John 12:37-40

B. *Manifested in:*

Questioning God's Word ... Gen. 3:1-6; 2 Pet. 3:4, 5
Turning from God ... Heb. 3:12
Questioning God's power ... Ps. 78:19, 20
Hating God's messengers ... Acts 7:54, 57
Resisting the Spirit ... Acts 7:51, 52
Discounting evidence ... John 12:37
Opposing the Gospel ... 1 Thess. 2:14-16
Rejecting Christ ... John 12:48; John 16:9

C. *Consequences of, seen in:*

Hindering miracles ... Matt. 13:58
Exclusion from blessings ... Heb. 3:15-19
Condemnation ... John 3:18, 19
Rejection ... Rom. 11:20
Judgment ... John 12:48
Death ... John 8:24, 25
Destruction ... 2 Thess. 1:8, 9
God's wrath ... John 3:36

D. *Those guilty, described as:*

Stiff-necked ... Acts 7:51
Uncircumcised ... Jer. 6:10
Blinded ... Eph. 4:18
Rebels ... Num. 17:10

Unbelievers—*those who reject Christ*

Condemnation of ... Mark 16:16
Intermarriage with Christians, forbidden ... 2 Cor. 6:14, 15

Uncertainties—*things which may or may not happen*

A. *Caused by:*

Unknown future ... Prov. 27:1
Divine Providence ... James 4:13-17
Our lack of knowledge ... John 21:18-23

B. *Need not affect our:*

Assurance ... 1 Cor. 9:26
Trust in God ... Rom. 4:19-21
Plans ... Acts 21:11-15

Uncharitableness—*a critical spirit*

Condemning others ... Matt. 7:1-4; James 4:11, 12
Passing false judgments ... Luke 7:39
Assuming superior holiness ... John 8:1-11
Not forgiving readily ... Luke 15:25-32; 2 Cor. 2:6-11
Imputing evil to others ... 1 Sam. 1:14-17

Uncircumcised—*not circumcised*

A. *Descriptive of:*

Gentiles ... Gal. 2.7
Unregenerate state ... Col. 2:13
Unregenerate Jews and Gentiles ... Jer. 9:25, 26

B. *State of, in the Old Testament, excludes from:*

Covenant ... Ex. 17:14
Passover ... Ex. 12:48
Land ... Josh. 5:7
Sanctuary ... Ezek. 44:7, 9
Holy city ... Is. 52:1

C. *State of, in the New Testament:*

Has no spiritual value ... Gal. 5:6
Need not be changed ... 1 Cor. 7:18, 19
Explained ... Rom. 2:25-29

Unclean—*that which is defiled*

A. *Descriptive of:*

Men and women ... Deut. 23:10; Lev. 15:1-33
Not of the Lord ... Is. 52:1

B. *Transformation of, by:*

Purification ... Is. 6:5-7
Separation ... 2 Cor. 6:17
Knowledge in Jesus ... Rom. 14:14
Prayer ... 1 Tim. 4:3-5

See Clean; Pollute; Sanitation and hygiene

Unconditional surrender

Required by Christ ... Luke 14:26, 27
As sacrifice ... Rom. 12:1

Unction—*an anointing*

With the Holy Spirit ... 1 John 2:20, 27

SUBJECT ... REFERENCE

Undefiled—*untainted*

Such persons are blessed ... Ps. 119:1
Christ is ... Heb. 7:26
Describes marriage act ... Heb. 13:4
Applied to true religion ... James 1:27
Our inheritance thus called ... 1 Pet. 1:4

Undersetters—*shoulders*

Supports placed under the laver ... 1 Kin. 7:30, 34

Understanding—*knowing things in their right relationship*

A. *Means of, by:*

God's:
Gift ... 1 Kin. 3:9-12
Revelation ... Rom. 1:20
Word ... Ps. 119:104, 130
Books ... Dan. 9:2, 23
Holy Spirit ... Ex. 31:3
Christ ... 1 John 5:20
Prayer ... Ps. 119:34-125
Faith ... Heb. 11:3
Enlightening ... Eph. 1:18
Interpretation ... Neh. 8:2-13
Explanation ... Luke 24:45
Reproof ... Prov. 15:32
Later event ... Ps. 73:17

B. *Limitations on, by:*

Unbelief ... John 8:43
Unregeneracy ... Eph. 4:18
Spiritual blindness ... Is. 6:9, 10
Judicial punishment ... Is. 44:18, 19
Difficulties ... 2 Pet. 3:16

Unfruitfulness—*not producing good fruit*

A. *Caused by:*

Unfaithfulness ... Is. 5:1-7
Worldliness ... James 4:1-4
Negligence ... Luke 19:20-27

B. *Punished by:*

God's judgments ... Matt. 3:10
Rejection:
Now ... John 15:2, 4, 6
Hereafter ... Heb. 6:8

Ungodliness, ungodly—*the morally corrupt*

A. *Described as:*

Prospering in the world ... Ps. 73:12
Growing worse ... 2 Tim. 2:16
Perverting God's grace ... Jude 4
Abounding in the last days ... Jude 18
Christ died for ... Rom. 5:6

B. *Judgments upon, by:*

Flood ... 2 Pet. 2:5, 6
Law ... 1 Tim. 1:9
God's decree ... Jude 4
God's revelation ... Rom. 1.10
Christ's return ... Jude 14, 15
World's end ... 2 Pet. 3:7
Final judgment ... Ps. 1:4-6

Unicorn—*the wild ox*

Of great strength ... Num. 23:22
Very wild and ferocious ... Job 39:9-12
Frisky in youth ... Ps. 29:6

Unintentionally—*without premeditation*

Concerning an innocent killer ... Josh. 20:3-5

Union

Of:

Godhead ... John 17:21, 22
Christ and believers ... John 15:1-7
God and man ... Acts 17:28, 29
Mankind ... Acts 17:26
Satan and the unsaved ... John 8:44
Believers in prayer ... Matt. 18:19, 20

See Oneness

Union with Christ

A. *Compared to:*

Head and the body ... Eph. 4:15, 16
Marriage bond ... Eph. 5:23, 30
Building ... Eph. 2:21, 22
Parts of the body ... 1 Cor. 12:12, 27
Vine and branches ... John 15:4, 5
Food and the body ... John 6:56, 57

B. *Illustrated in the "togethers":*

Crucified ... Rom. 6:6
Buried ... Rom. 6:4

SUBJECT ... REFERENCE

Made alive ... Eph. 2:5
Sitting ... Eph. 2:6
Suffering ... Rom. 8:17
Reigning ... 2 Tim. 2:12
Glorified ... Rom. 8:17

C. *Manifested in, oneness:*

Of mind ... 1 Cor. 2:16
Of spirit ... 1 Cor. 6:17
In suffering ... Phil. 3:10
In worship ... 1 Cor. 10:16, 17
In ministry ... 2 Cor. 5:18-21

Unity of believers

A. *Based upon:*

Indwelling Spirit ... 1 Cor. 3:16, 17; 1 Cor. 6:19
New birth ... 2 Cor. 5:17
Union with Christ ... 2 Cor. 13:5

B. *Expressed by oneness of:*

Mind ... 1 Pet. 3:8
Unity of Spirit ... Ps. 133:1-3
Faith ... Eph. 4:4-6
Fellowship ... Acts 2:42-47
Concern ... 1 Cor. 12:25, 26

C. *Consistent with such differences as:*

Physical ... 1 Pet. 3:1-7
Social ... Eph. 6:5-9
Mental ... 1 Cor. 1:26-29

Unjust

Described as:

Abomination ... Prov. 29:27
Recipient of God's blessings ... Matt. 5:45
Christ died for ... 1 Pet. 3:18

Unknown god

Altar to ... Acts 17:22, 23

Unleavened bread

Used in the passover ... Ex. 12:8-20; Mark 14:1, 12
Typical of Christians ... 1 Cor. 5:7, 8

Unmercifulness—*lacking mercy*

Shown by Simeon and Levi ... Gen. 34:25-31
By Pharaoh ... Ex. 5:4-19
By creditor ... Matt. 18:28-30

Unni—*answering is with Jehovah*

Levite musician ... 1 Chr. 15:18

Unpardonable sin

Sin not forgivable ... Matt. 12:31, 32; Luke 12:10

Unrest—*a state of agitation*

Of the nations ... Luke 21:25, 26
Of the wicked ... Is. 57:20
Remedy given by Christ ... Matt. 11:28
Available to Christians ... Phil 4:7

Unrighteousness—*wickedness*

A. *Attitude toward, by the wicked, they:*

Suppress the truth in ... Rom. 1:18
Are filled with ... Rom. 1:29
Obey it ... Rom. 2:8
Love the wages of ... 2 Pet. 2:15
Take pleasure in ... 2 Thess. 2:12
Receive the reward of ... 2 Pet. 2:13
Shall not inherit the kingdom ... 1 Cor. 6:9

B. *Relation of believers toward:*

They are cleansed from ... 1 John 1:9
God is merciful toward their ... Heb. 8:12
Must not fellowship with ... 2 Cor. 6:14
All the world guilty ... Rom. 3:1-20

Unselfishness—*not putting self first*

A. *Christ, an example of, in His:*

Mission ... John 6:38
Suffering ... Matt. 26:39, 42
Concern ... John 19:26, 27
Death ... Phil. 2:5-8

B. *In the believer, prompted by:*

Christ's example ... Phil. 2:3-8
Love ... 1 Cor. 13:4, 5
Concern ... 1 Cor. 10:23-33
Christian service ... Phil. 2:25-30
Sacrifice ... Rev. 12:11

C. *Examples of:*

Abram ... Gen. 13:8-12

SUBJECT REFERENCE

Moses ..... Num. 14:12-29
Gideon ..... Judg. 8:22, 23
Jonathan ..... 1 Sam. 18:4
David ..... 1 Chr. 21:17
Nehemiah ..... Neh. 5:14-19
Daniel ..... Dan. 5:17
Christians ..... Acts 4:34, 35
Paul ..... 1 Cor. 9:19-23
Onesiphorus ..... 2 Tim. 1:16-18

Unspeakable

God's Gift ..... 2 Cor. 9:15

Untempered mortar—*whitewash*

Figurative of false prophets ..... Ezek. 13:10, 14

Unwittingly—*without premeditation*

Concerning an innocent killer ... Josh. 20:3-5

Unworldliness—*a heavenly frame of mind*

A. *Negatively expressed in, not:*
Loving the world ..... 1 John 2:15-17
Fellowshiping with evil ..... 2 Cor. 6:14-18
Mixing in worldly affairs ..... 2 Tim. 2:4

B. *Positively expressed in:*
Seeking God's kingdom first ..... Matt. 6:33, 34
Living for Jesus ..... Gal. 2:20
Becoming a living sacrifice ... Rom. 12:1, 2
Having a heavenly mind ..... Col. 3:1, 2
Looking for Jesus ..... Titus 2:11-15
Looking to Jesus ..... Heb. 12:1, 2

Unworthiness—*not being fit; lacking merit*

A. *Caused by a sense of:*
Failure ..... Gen. 32:10
Social difference ..... 1 Sam. 18:18, 23
Sin ..... Luke 15:19, 21
Inferiority ..... John 1:27

B. *Examples of:*
Moses ..... Ex. 4:10
Centurion ..... Matt. 8:8
Peter ..... Luke 5:8
Paul ..... 1 Cor. 15:9

Upharsin—*and divided*

Interpreted by Daniel ..... Dan. 5:5, 25, 28

Uphaz

Unidentified place of fine gold .. Jer. 10:9

Upper room—*chamber, usually built on a roof*

Ahaziah fell from ..... 2 Kin. 1:2
Ahaz's ..... 2 Kin. 23:12
Disciples prepared for Christ .... Mark 14:14-16
Dorcas placed in ..... Acts 9:36, 37
Paul preached in ..... Acts 20:7, 8

Uprightness—*character approved by God*

A. *Descriptive of:*
God's nature ..... Is. 26:7
Man's state ..... Eccl. 7:29
Devout ..... Job 1:1, 8

B. *Of God, manifested in His:*
Works ..... Ps. 111:8
Judgments ..... Ps. 119:137
Delights ..... 1 Chr. 29:17

C. *Blessings of, for saints:*
Temporal blessings ..... Ps. 84:11
Lord's blessings ..... Ps. 11:7
Prosperity ..... Prov. 14:11
Deliverance ..... Prov. 11:3, 6, 11
Salvation ..... Ps. 7:10
God's presence ..... Ps. 140:13
Light in darkness ..... Ps. 112:4
Answered prayer ..... Prov. 15:8
Righteousness ..... Ps. 36:10
Joy ..... Ps. 32:11
Glory ..... Ps. 64:10
Final dominion ..... Ps. 49:14

D. *Attitude of wicked toward, they:*
Are devoid of ..... Hab. 2:4
Leave the path of ..... Prov. 2:13
Hate ..... Prov. 29:10
Persecute ..... Ps. 37:14
Laugh to scorn ..... Job 12:4

Ur—*flame*

Father of Eliphal ..... 1 Chr. 11:35
Called Ahasbai ..... 2 Sam. 23:34

Ur of the Chaldees

City of Abram's early life ..... Gen. 11:28-31; Gen. 15:7
Located in Mesopotamia by Stephen ..... Acts 7:2, 4

Urbane—*polite*

Christian ..... Rom. 16:9

Uri—*an abbreviation of Urijah*

1. Father of Bezaleel ..... 1 Chr. 2:20
2. Father of Geber ..... 1 Kin. 4:19
3. Divorced his foreign wife ..... Ezra 10:24

Uriah—*Jehovah is light*

1. Hittite and one of David's warriors ..... 2 Sam. 23:39
Condemned to death by David ..... 2 Sam. 11:1-27
2. Priest ..... Ezra 8:33
3. Prophet in Jeremiah's time ... Jer. 26:20-23
4. Stands with Ezra ..... Neh. 8:4

Uriel—*God is light*

1. Kohathite Levite ..... 1 Chr. 6:22, 24
2. Man of Gibeah ..... 2 Chr. 13:2

Urijah—*Jehovah is light*

1. High priest in Ahaz' time ..... 2 Kin. 16:10-16
2. Postexilic priest ..... 2 Kin. 16:10-16
3. Prophet in Jeremiah's time ... Jer. 26:20
4. Stands with Ezra ..... Neh. 8:4

Urim and Thummim—*lights and perfections*

Placed in the breastplate of the high priest ..... Ex. 28:30
Method of consulting God ..... Num. 27:21; 1 Sam. 14:3-37
Use of, confined to priests ..... Deut. 33:8
Answer by, refused ..... 1 Sam. 28:6

Usurpation—*seizing authority illegally*

A. *Methods of, by:*
Intrigue ..... 2 Sam. 15:1-12
Defying God's Law ..... 1 Sam. 13:8-14
Changing God's worship ..... 2 Kin. 16:10-17
Conspiracy ..... 1 Kin. 15:27, 28
Assuming dictatorial rights .. 3 John 9, 10

B. *Consequences of, seen in:*
Defeat and death ..... 2 Kin. 11:1-6
Another conspiracy ..... 2 Kin. 15:10-15
Defeat and conditional forgiveness ..... 1 Kin. 1:5-53

C. *Spirit of, manifested in:*
Man's transgression ..... Gen. 3:1-7
Satan's fall ..... Is. 14:12-14
Woman's weakness ..... 1 Tim. 2:12
Antichrist's desire ..... 2 Thess. 2:3, 4; Rev. 13:1-18

Utensils, kitchen

Bowls ..... Amos 6:6
Charger ..... Matt. 14:11
Cruse ..... 1 Kin. 17:12
Cup and platter ..... Matt. 23:25
Fork (tongs) ..... 1 Sam. 2:13, 14
Iron pan ..... Ezek. 4:3
Kettle (pot) ..... 1 Sam. 2:14
Kneading trough ..... Ex. 8:3
Millstones ..... Is. 47:2
Pan ..... Lev. 2:5

Uthai—*Jehovah is help*

1. Judahite ..... 1 Chr. 9:4
2. Postexilic returnee ..... Ezra 8:14

Uz—*firmness*

1. Descendant of Shem ..... Gen. 10:23
2. Descendant of Seir ..... Gen. 36:28
3. Son of Nahor ..... Gen. 22:20, 21
4. Place in south Edom; residence of Job ..... Job 1:1

Uzai—*hoped for*

Father of Palal ..... Neh. 3:25

Uzal

Son of Joktan ..... Gen. 10:27

Uzza, Uzzah—*strength*

1. Son of Shimei ..... 1 Chr. 6:29
2. Descendant of Ehud ..... 1 Chr. 8:7
3. Head of a returning Temple servant family ..... Ezra 2:49
4. Name of a garden ..... 2 Kin. 21:18, 26
5. Son of Abinadab struck down for touching the ark of the covenant ..... 2 Sam. 6:3-11

Uzzen-sherah—*top of Sherah*

Town built by Sherah, Ephraim's daughter ..... 1 Chr. 7:24

Uzzi—*my strength*

1. Descendant of Aaron ..... 1 Chr. 6:5, 51
2. Descendant of Issachar ..... 1 Chr. 7:1-3
3. Son of Bela ..... 1 Chr. 7:7
4. Levite overseer ..... Neh. 11:22
5. Postexilic priest ..... Neh. 12:19, 42

Uzzia—*my strength is Jehovah*

One of David's mighty men ..... 1 Chr. 11:44

Uzziah—*my strength is Jehovah*

1. Kohathite Levite ..... 1 Chr. 6:24
2. Father of Jehonathan ..... 1 Chr. 27:25
3. King of Judah, called Azariah ..... 2 Kin. 14:21; 2 Kin. 15:1-7
Reigned 52 years ..... 2 Kin. 15:1, 2
Reigned righteously ..... 2 Chr. 26:4, 5
Conquered the Philistines ..... 2 Chr. 26:6-8
Strengthened Jerusalem ..... 2 Chr. 26:9
Developed agriculture ..... 2 Chr. 26:10
Usurped priestly function; stricken with leprosy ..... 2 Chr. 26:16-21
Life of, written by Isaiah ..... 2 Chr. 26:22, 23
Earthquake in the days of ..... Amos 1:1
Death of, time of Isaiah's vision ..... Is. 6:1
4. Priest who divorced his foreign wife ..... Ezra 10:19, 21
5. Judahite ..... Neh. 11:4

Uzziel—*God is my strength*

1. Levite, son of Kohath and family head ..... Ex. 6:18, 22
2. Son of Bela ..... 1 Chr. 7:7
3. Simeonite captain ..... 1 Chr. 4:41-43
4. Levite musician ..... 1 Chr. 25:3, 4
5. Levite assisting in Hezekiah's reforms ..... 2 Chr. 29:14-19
6. Goldsmith working on Jerusalem's wall ..... Neh. 3:8

V

Vagabond—*an aimless wanderer*

Curse on Cain ..... Gen. 4:12, 14
Curse upon the wicked ..... Ps. 109:10
Professional exorcists thus called ..... Acts 19:13

Vail (see Veil, the sacred; Veil, woman's)

Vain—*empty; useless*

A. *Applied to physical things:*
Beauty ..... Prov. 31:30
Life ..... Eccl. 6:12
Customs ..... Jer. 10:3
Men ..... Job 11:12
Adornment ..... Jer. 4:30
Healing ..... Jer. 46:11
Sacrifice ..... Is. 1:13
Protection ..... 1 Sam. 25:21
Safety ..... Ps. 33:17
World's creation ..... Is. 45:18, 19

B. *Applied to spiritual things:*
Obedience ..... Deut. 32:46, 47
Chastisement ..... Jer. 2:30
Visions ..... Ezek. 13:7
Serving God ..... Mal. 3:14
Faith ..... 1 Cor. 15:17
Words ..... Eph. 5:6
Imaginations ..... Rom. 1:21
Babblings ..... 2 Tim. 2:16

C. *Applied to possibilities:*
God's grace ..... 1 Cor. 15:10
Christ's death ..... Gal. 2:21
Scriptures ..... James 4:5
Faith ..... 1 Cor. 15:2-17
Religion ..... James 1:26

SUBJECT — REFERENCE

Worship ... Is. 45:19
Labor ... 1 Thess. 3:5
Reception ... 1 Thess. 2:1, 2
Sufferings ... Gal. 3:4

Vainglory—*conceit*

Very offensive in the Christian's life ... Gal. 5:26; Phil. 2:3

Vajezatha—*son of the atmosphere*

One of Haman's sons ... Esth. 9:9

Valley Gate

Entrance into Jerusalem ... Neh. 2:13

Valley of Dry Bones

Vision of Ezekiel ... Ezek. 37:1-14

Vaniah—*Jehovah is praise*

Divorced his foreign wife ... Ezra 10:36

Vanity—*emptiness, futility*

A. *Descriptive of:*
Man's life ... Ps. 144:4
Sin's end ... Prov. 22:8
Man's thoughts ... Ps. 94:11
Idolatry ... Acts 14:15

B. *Manifested in the wicked's:*
Words ... Ps. 12:2
Thoughts ... Ps. 94:11
Trust ... Is. 59:4
Worship ... Jer. 51:17, 18

C. *Believer's attitude toward:*
Request for removal from ... Prov. 30:8
"Turn away mine eyes" ... Ps. 119:37
Should not walk in ... Eph. 4:17

Vashni—*weak*

Son of Samuel ... 1 Chr. 6:28

Vashti—*beautiful woman*

Queen of Ahasuerus, deposed and divorced ... Esth. 1:9-22

Vau

Letter in the Hebrew alphabet ... Ps. 119:41-48

Veal

Prepared for King Saul ... 1 Sam. 28:21-25

Vegetables—*plants grown for food*

Part of God's creation ... Gen. 1:11, 12
Controversy regarding ... Rom. 14:1-23
Preferred by Daniel ... Dan. 1:12, 16

Veil, the sacred

A. *Features regarding:*
Made by divine command ... Ex. 26:31, 32
Used to separate the holy and most holy ... Ex. 26:33
Means of concealing the divine person ... Ex. 40:3
In the Temple also ... 2 Chr. 3:14
Rent at Christ's death ... Matt. 27:51

B. *Entrance through:*
By the high priest alone ... Heb. 9:6, 7
On Day of Atonement only ... Heb. 9:7
Taking blood ... Heb. 9:7

C. *Figurative of:*
Old Testament dispensation ... Heb. 9:8
Christ's flesh ... Heb. 10:20
Access now into God's presence ... Heb. 10:19-22

Veil, woman's

A. *Literal uses of:*
For modesty ... Gen. 24:65
For adornment ... Is. 3:23
To conceal identity ... Gen. 38:14
To soften the divine glory of God ... Ex. 34:33-35

B. *Figurative of:*
Coming of the Lord ... Is. 25:7
Turning to the Lord ... 2 Cor. 3:14-16

Vengeance—*retribution as a punishment*

A. *Belonging to God, as:*
Judgment upon sin ... Jer. 11:20-23
Right not to be taken by man ... Ezek. 25:12-17; Heb. 10:30
Set time ... Jer. 46:9, 10

SUBJECT — REFERENCE

B. *Visitation of, by God, at:*
Nation's fall ... Jer. 51:6, 11, 36
Christ's first coming ... Is. 35:4-10
Jerusalem's destruction ... Luke 21:22
Sodom's destruction ... Jude 7
Christ's return ... 2 Thess. 1:8

See Revenge

Venison—*the flesh of deer*

Isaac's favorite dish ... Gen. 27:1-33

Ventriloquism—*appearing to speak from another source*

From the dust ... Is. 29:4

Verdict—*a judicial decision*

Unjustly rendered ... Luke 23:13-26
Pronounced by hypocrites ... John 8:1-11

Verily, verily—*a strong affirmation*

A. *Concerning Christ's:*
Glory ... John 1:51
Eternity ... John 8:58
Uniqueness ... John 10:1, 7
Mission ... John 6:32
Betrayal ... John 13:21
Death ... John 12:24

B. *Concerning man's:*
Spiritual bondage ... John 8:34
Spiritual darkness ... John 6:26
Need of regeneration ... John 3:3, 5
Need of salvation ... John 5:24, 25
Means of salvation ... John 6:47, 53
Life eternal ... John 8:51

C. *Concerning the believer's:*
Fickleness ... John 13:38
Work ... John 14:12
Mission ... John 13:16, 20
Prayer ... John 16:23
Life ... John 21:18

Vermilion—*a brilliant red color*

Ceiling painted with ... Jer. 22:14

Vessels—*hollow utensils for holding things*

A. *Made of:*
Wood or stone ... Ex. 7:19
Gold and silver ... Dan. 5:2
Clay ... Rom. 9:21
Copper ... Ezra 8:27

B. *Of the tabernacle:*
Under care of Levites ... Num. 3:31, 32
Carried away into Babylon ... 2 Chr. 36:18
Belshazzar uses in feast ... Dan. 5:1-4
Returned to Jerusalem ... Ezra 1:7-11

C. *Figurative of:*
Mankind ... Rom. 9:21-23
Human weakness ... 2 Cor. 4:7
Believers ... 2 Tim. 2:20, 21
Person's body or wife ... 1 Thess. 4:4
Chosen person ... Acts 9:15

Vex—*to irritate the soul*

A. *Caused by:*
Nagging ... Judg. 16:16
Lust ... 2 Sam. 13:2
Evil environment ... 2 Pet. 2:7, 8
Temptations ... Num. 25:18
Evil men ... Num. 20:15
Demons ... Matt. 15:22

B. *Agents of:*
God ... Ps. 2:5
People ... Ex. 22:21
King ... Acts 12:1
Enemies ... Judg. 10:8

C. *Objects of:*
Human soul ... Job 19:2
Righteous soul ... 2 Pet. 2:8
Holy Spirit ... Is. 63:10

Vial—*a small flask or vessel*

Used for anointing ... 1 Sam. 10:1
Full of incense ... Rev. 5:8
Filled with God's wrath ... Rev. 16:1-17

Vicarious suffering of Christ

A. *Expressed in Old Testament, by:*
Types ... Gen. 22:7, 8, 13
Explicit prophecies ... Is. 53:1-12; Acts 8:32-35

SUBJECT — REFERENCE

B. *Expressed in the New Testament, by:*
John the Baptist ... John 1:29
Christ Himself ... Mark 10:45
Peter ... 1 Pet. 1:18, 19
John ... 1 John 3:16
Paul ... Gal. 2:20
Hebrews ... Heb. 2:9, 17

Victory—*attaining the mastery over*

A. *Of Christ:*
Promised ... Ps. 110:1-7
Accompanied by suffering ... Is. 53:10-12
By resurrection ... Acts 2:29-36
By His return ... Rev. 19:11-21

B. *Of Christians:*
Through Christ ... Phil. 4:13
By the Holy Spirit ... Gal. 5:16, 17, 22, 25
Over:
Flesh ... Gal. 5:16-21
World ... 1 John 5:4
Satan ... James 4:7

Vigor in old age

Moses at 120 ... Deut. 34:7
Caleb at 85 ... Josh. 14:10-13
Jehoiada at 130 ... 2 Chr. 24:15, 16

Vileness—*the state of physical or moral corruption*

A. *Described as:*
Worthless ... 1 Sam. 15:9
Dirty and filthy ... James 2:2
Frail and weak ... Phil. 3:21
Something insignificant ... Job 40:4

B. *Caused by:*
God's judgment ... Jer. 29:17
Human corruption ... Judg. 19:24

Village—*a settlement*

Of the Samaritans ... Luke 9:52

Vine, vineyard

A. *Features regarding:*
Grown by Noah ... Gen. 9:20
Native of Palestine ... Deut. 6:11
Reaping of, by poor ... 2 Kin. 25:12
Fruit of, God's gift ... Ps. 107:37
Pruning of, necessary ... Lev. 25:3, 4
Dead branches burned ... John 15:6

B. *Enemies of:*
Hail and frost ... Ps. 78:47
Foxes ... Song 2:15
Boars ... Ps. 80:13
Thieves ... Jer. 49:9
Stones ... Is. 5:2
Sloth ... Prov. 24:30, 31

C. *Laws concerning:*
Care of, exempts from military service ... Deut. 20:6
Diverse seed forbidden in ... Deut. 22:9
Neighbors may eat ... Deut. 23:24
No cultivation of, during Sabbatical year ... Ex. 23:11
Second gathering of, forbidden ... Lev. 19:10
New, five years' waiting ... Lev. 19:23-25
Nazirites forbidden to eat of ... Num. 6:3, 4
Rechabites forbidden to plant ... Jer. 35:7-9
Not to be mortgaged ... Neh. 5:3, 4

D. *Figurative of:*
Jewish nation ... Is. 5:1-7
Growth in grace ... Hos. 14:7
Purifying afflictions ... John 15:2
Peacefulness ... 1 Kin. 4:25
Worthlessness ... John 15:2, 6
Fruitful wife ... Ps. 128:3
God's kingdom ... Matt. 20:1-16

Vinedresser

Poor made to be ... 2 Kin. 25:12

Vinegar—*wine or strong drink fermented*

Hard on teeth ... Prov. 10:26
Forbidden to Nazarites ... Num. 6:3
Offered to Christ in mockery ... Ps. 69:21

Viol—*a six-stringed musical instrument*

Used in merrymaking ... Is. 5:12
Destruction of ... Is. 14:11

SUBJECT	REFERENCE
Viper—*a deadly snake*	
Figurative of spiritual transformation	Is. 11:8
Jewish leaders compared to	Matt. 3:7
Paul bit by	Acts 28:3-5
Virgin—*a woman untouched sexually*	
Penalty for seduction of	Deut. 22:28, 29
Parable of ten	Matt. 25:1-13
Specifications regarding	1 Cor. 7:28-38
Christ born of	Luke 1:26-35
Figurative of Christians	Rev. 14:4
Virgin conception	
Prophesied	Is. 7:14
Christ conceived of Holy Spirit	Matt. 1:18 / Luke 1:26-35
Born of virgin	Matt. 1:19-25
Virtuous woman	
Graphically described	Prov. 31:10-31
Illustrated by Sarah	1 Pet. 3:1-7
Adornment of	1 Tim. 2:9, 10
Visions—*divine revelations*	
A. *Characteristics of:*	
Understandable	Dan. 7:15-19
Authenticated by divine glory	Ezek. 8:1-4
Personal and phenomenal	Dan. 10:7-9
Prophetic	Dan. 9:23-27
Dated and localized	Ezek. 1:1-3
Causes trembling and dread	Dan. 10:7-17
Meaning of, interpreted	Dan. 9:21-24
Absence of, tragic	Prov. 29:18
Performances of, sure	Ezek. 12:21-28
Proof of Messianic times	Joel 2:28 / Acts 2:17
Imitated by false prophets	Jer. 14:14
B. *Productive of:*	
Guidance	Gen. 46:2-5
Direction	Acts 16:9, 10
Encouragement	Acts 18:9, 10
Warning	Is. 21:2-6
Judgment	1 Sam. 3:15-18
Action for the Lord	Acts 26:19, 20
C. *Objects of, revealed in:*	
Israel's future	Gen. 15:1-21
Succession of world empires	Dan. 7:1-8
Ram	Dan. 8:1-7, 20
Expanding river	Ezek. 47:1-12
Throne of God	Rev. 4:1-11
Visit, visitation—*to go to see a person*	
Descriptive of:	
Going to a person	Acts 15:36
God's care	Ps. 65:9
God's purposed time	Luke 19:44
Visitors	
Moses and Elijah	Matt. 17:3
Vocation—*a calling*	
We must walk worthy of	Eph. 4:1
Voice of God, the	
A. *Importance of:*	
Must be obeyed	Gen. 3:1-19
Disobedience to, judged	Jer. 42:5-22
Obedience to, the essence of true religion	1 Sam. 15:19-24
Obedience to, rewarded	Gen. 22:6-18
Sign of the covenant	Josh. 24:24, 25
B. *Heard by:*	
Adam	Gen. 3:9, 10
Moses	Ex. 19:19
Israel	Deut. 5:22-26
Samuel	1 Sam. 3:1-14
Elijah	1 Kin. 19:12, 13
Isaiah	Is. 6:8-10
Ezekiel	Ezek. 1:24, 25
Christ	Mark 1:11
Peter, James and John	Matt. 17:1, 5
Paul	Acts 9:4, 7
John	Rev. 1:10-15
Vomit—*to throw up*	
A. *Used literally of:*	
Dog	Prov. 26:11
One who eats in excess	Prov. 25:16
Drunken man	Is. 19:14
Great fish	Jon. 2:10
B. *Used figuratively of:*	
False teaching	2 Pet. 2:22
Judgment	Jer. 48:25, 26
Riches	Job 20:15
Vophsi—*rich*	
Naphtalite spy	Num. 13:14
Vow—*a voluntary pledge to fulfill an agreement*	
A. *Objects of one's:*	
Life	Num. 6:1-21
Children	1 Sam. 1:11-28
Possessions	Gen. 28:22
Gifts	Ps. 76:11
B. *Features concerning:*	
Must be voluntary	Deut. 23:21, 22
Must be uttered	Deut. 23:23
Once made, binding	Eccl. 5:4, 5
Benefits of, sometimes included	Gen. 28:20-22
Invalidity of, specified	Num. 30:1-16
Abuse of, condemned	Matt. 15:4-6
Rashness in, condemned	Prov. 20:25
Perfection in, required	Lev. 22:18-25
Wickedness of some	Jer. 44:25
Voyage—*an extended trip*	
Paul's to Rome	Acts 27:10
Vulture—*a carrion-eating bird of prey*	
Classed as unclean	Lev. 11:13, 14

W

SUBJECT	REFERENCE
Wafers—*thin cakes of flour*	
Often made with honey	Ex. 16:31
Used in various offerings	Ex. 29:2 / Lev. 2:4
Wages, hire—*payments for work performed*	
A. *Principles governing payment of:*	
Must be paid promptly	Deut. 24:14, 15
Withholding of, forbidden	James 5:4
Laborer worthy of	Matt. 10:10
B. *Paid to such classes as:*	
Soldiers	2 Sam. 10:6
Fishermen	Mark 1:20
Shepherds	John 10:12, 13
Masons and carpenters	2 Chr. 24:12
Farm laborers	Matt. 20:1-16
Male prostitutes	Deut. 23:18
Nurses	Ex. 2:9
Ministers	1 Cor. 9:4-14
Teachers	Gal. 6:6, 7
C. *Figurative of:*	
Spiritual death	Rom. 6:23
Unrighteousness	2 Pet. 2:15
Wagon—*a vehicle with wheels*	
Used to move Jacob to Egypt	Gen. 45:19, 21
Used in moving objects	Num. 7:3-9
Wailing—*crying out in constant mourning*	
A. *Caused by:*	
King's decree	Esth. 4:3
City's destruction	Ezek. 27:31, 32
God's judgment	Amos 5:16, 17
Girl's death	Mark 5:38-42
Christ's return	Rev. 1:7
Hell's torments	Matt. 13:42, 50
B. *Performed by:*	
Women	Jer. 9:17-20
Prophets	Mic. 1:8
Merchants	Rev. 18:15, 19
See Mourning	
Waiting on the Lord	
A. *Agents of:*	
Creatures	Ps. 145:15
Creation	Rom. 8:19, 23
Gentiles	Is. 51:5
Christians	1 Cor. 1:7
B. *Manner of:*	
With the soul	Ps. 62:1, 5
With quietness	Lam. 3:25, 26
With patience	Ps. 40:1
With courage	Ps. 27:14
All the day	Ps. 25:5
Continually	Hos. 12:6
With great hope	Ps. 130:5, 6
With crying	Ps. 69:3
C. *Objects of God's:*	
Salvation	Is. 25:9
Law	Is. 42:4
Protection	Ps. 33:20
Pardon	Ps. 39:7, 8
Food	Ps. 104:27
Kingdom	Mark 15:43
Holy Spirit	Acts 1:4
Son	1 Thess. 1:10
D. *Blessings attending, described as:*	
Spiritual renewal	Is. 40:31
Not be ashamed	Ps. 69:6
Inherit the land	Ps. 37:9, 34
Something unusual	Is. 64:4
Unusual blessing	Luke 12:36, 37
Walk of believers	
A. *Stated negatively, not:*	
In darkness	John 8:12
After the flesh	Rom. 8:1, 4
As Gentiles	Eph. 4:17
In craftiness	2 Cor. 4:2
In sin	Col. 3:5-7
In disorder	2 Thess. 3:6, 11
B. *Stated positively:*	
In the light	1 John 1:7
In the truth	3 John 3, 4
In Christ	Col. 2:6
In the Spirit	Gal. 5:16, 25
In love	Eph. 5:2
As children of light	Eph. 5:8
As Christ walked	1 John 2:6
After His commandments	2 John 6
By faith	2 Cor. 5:7
In good works	Eph. 2:10
Worthy	Eph. 4:1
Worthy of the Lord	Col. 1:10
Worthy of God	1 Thess. 2:12
Circumspectly	Eph. 5:15
In wisdom	Col. 4:5
Pleasing God	1 Thess. 4:1
Wall—*a rampart or partition*	
A. *Used for:*	
Shooting arrows from	2 Sam. 11:24
Observation	2 Sam. 18:24
B. *Unusual events connected with:*	
Woman lives on	Josh. 2:15
Jericho's, falls by faith	Josh. 6:5, 20
Saul's body fastened to	1 Sam. 31:10, 11
Woman throws stone from	2 Sam. 11:20, 21
27,000 killed by	1 Kin. 20:30
Son sacrificed on	2 Kin. 3:27
Warning inscribed on	Dan. 5:5, 25-28
Paul escapes through	Acts 9:25
C. *Figurative of:*	
Defense	1 Sam. 25:16
Protection	Ezra 9:9
Great power	Ps. 18:29
Peacefulness	Ps. 122:7
Self-sufficiency	Prov. 18:11
Powerless	Prov. 25:28
Salvation	Is. 26:1
God's kingdom	Is. 56:5
Heaven	Is. 60:18-21
Spiritual leaders	Is. 62:6
God's messengers	Jer. 1:18, 19
Protection	Zech. 2:5
Hypocrisy	Acts 23:3
Ceremonial law	Eph. 2:14
New Jerusalem	Rev. 21:12-19
D. *Of Jerusalem:*	
Built by Solomon	1 Kin. 3:1
Broken down by Jehoash	2 Kin. 14:13
Destroyed by Babylonians	2 Chr. 36:19
Seen at night by Nehemiah	Neh. 2:12-18
Rebuilt by returnees	Neh. 6:1, 6, 15
Dedication of	Neh. 12:27-47
Wallow—*to roll about in an ungainly manner*	
Blood	2 Sam. 20:12
Vomit	Jer. 48:26
Ashes	Jer. 6:26
On the ground	Mark 9:20
Mire	2 Pet. 2:22

SUBJECT — REFERENCE

Wandering—*roaming about*

A. *Descriptive of:*

Hagar's travels ... Gen. 21:14
Israel's wilderness travels ... Num. 32:13
God's pilgrims ... Heb. 11:37, 38
Captivity ... Hos. 9:17
Joseph in the field ... Gen. 37:15
Syrian ... Deut. 26:5
Early Saints ... Heb. 11:38

B. *Figurative of:*

Apostasy ... Ps. 119:10
Dissatisfaction ... Prov. 27:8
Hopelessness ... Jude 13

Wanderer—*one who moves about aimlessly*

Curse on Cain ... Gen. 4:12, 14
Curse on the wicked ... Ps. 109:10
Professional exorcists called ... Acts 19:13

Want—*to lack*

A. *Caused by:*

Hastiness ... Prov. 21:5
Greed ... Prov. 22:16
Sloth ... Prov. 24:30-34
Debauchery ... Dan. 5:27
God's judgments ... Amos 4:6
Physical need ... 2 Cor. 8:14

B. *Provision against, by:*

Trusting the LORD ... Ps. 23:1
God's plan ... Jer. 33:17, 18

Wantonness—*lustful behavior*

In suggestive movements ... Is. 3:16
Characteristic of doctrinal laxity ... 2 Pet. 2:18
Unbecoming to a Christian ... Rom. 13:13

War—*armed conflicts between nations*

A. *Caused by:*

Sin ... James 4:1, 2
God's judgments ... 2 Sam. 12:10
God's decree ... Ex. 17:16

B. *Regulations concerning:*

Consultation of:
Urim ... 1 Sam. 28:6
Ephod ... 1 Sam. 30:7, 8
Prophets ... 1 Kin. 22:7-28
Troops mustered ... Judg. 3:27
Some dismissed ... Deut. 20:5-8
Spies dispatched ... Num. 13:17
Ark brought in ... 1 Sam. 4:4-6
Sacrifice offered ... 1 Sam. 7:9
Speech delivered ... 2 Chr. 20:20-22
Demand made for surrender ... Deut. 20:10
Trumpet sounded ... Num. 10:9

C. *Methods of attack, by:*

Ambush ... Josh. 8:3-26
Surprise attack ... Judg. 7:16-22
Personal combat of champions ... 1 Sam. 17:1-51
Divided tactics ... 2 Sam. 10:9-14
Massed formation ... 1 Kin. 22:31-33
Battle cry ... Jer. 4:19

D. *Captives of:*

Sometimes eliminated ... Josh. 6:21
Made servants ... 2 Sam. 8:2
Ruled over ... 2 Sam. 5:2
Deported ... 2 Kin. 17:6

See Siege of a city

Wardrobe—*one's clothing*

Woman's ... Is. 3:18-23
Directions concerning ... 1 Pet. 3:3-5
Keeper of ... 2 Kin. 22:14

Wares

Sold in Tyrus ... Ezek. 27:1-27

Warfare, spiritual

A. *Enemies combatted:*

World ... James 4:1-4
Flesh ... 1 Pet. 4:1-4
Devil ... 1 Pet. 5:8
Invisible foes ... Eph. 6:12

B. *Conquest over, by:*

God's Word ... Eph. 6:17
God's armor ... Eph. 6:10-17
Faith ... 1 John 5:4, 5
Christ's promise ... John 16:33

C. *Soldiers of, must:*

Avoid worldly entanglements ... 2 Tim. 2:4
Pray ... Eph. 6:18
Deny self ... 1 Cor. 9:25-27
Endure hardness ... 2 Tim. 2:3, 10
Be self-controlled ... 1 Thess. 5:6
Be alert ... 1 Cor. 16:13
Wear armor ... Eph. 6:11

Warning—*to caution one concerning his action*

A. *Means of, by:*

God's Word ... Ps. 19:9-11
Prophet ... Ezek. 3:17-27
Messenger ... Acts 20:31
Dream ... Matt. 2:12, 22
Angel ... Acts 10:22
God ... Heb. 11:7

B. *Reactions to:*

Obeyed ... Jon. 3:1-10
Accepted ... Heb. 11:7
Ignored ... 2 Sam. 2:20-23
Rejected ... Gen. 2:16, 17
Scoffed at ... Gen. 19:14
Disobeyed ... Num. 14:40-45

C. *Disobedience to, brings:*

Judgment ... Jude 6, 7
Torments ... Luke 16:23-28
Destruction ... Prov. 29:1

Wash—*to cleanse something with a liquid*

A. *Kinds of:*

Ceremonial ... Ex. 30:18-20
Miraculous ... John 9:7, 11, 15
Demonstrative ... John 13:5-14
Symbolic ... Matt. 27:24
Typical ... Ps. 51:2, 7
Spiritual ... Acts 22:16
Regenerative ... Titus 3:5

B. *Materials used:*

Water ... Gen. 24:32
Tears ... Luke 7:38, 44
Snow ... Job 9:30
Wine ... Gen. 49:11
Blood ... Ps. 58:10

C. *Objects of:*

Hands ... Matt. 27:24
Face ... Gen. 43:31
Feet ... Gen. 18:4
Body ... 2 Sam. 11:2
Clothes ... 2 Sam. 19:24

See Purification

Washpot

Moab described as God's ... Ps. 60:6-8

Waste—*a state of ruin*

A. *Objects of:*

Cities ... Ezek. 19:7
Nations ... Nah. 3:7
Captives ... Ps. 137:3
Possessions ... Luke 15:13
Temple ... Is. 64:11
Church ... Gal. 1:13
Parents ... Prov. 19:26
Body ... Job 14:10

B. *Caused by:*

God's judgments ... Amos 7:9
Unbelief ... Num. 14:33
Failure to serve God ... Is. 60:12
God's hatred ... Mal. 1:3
Squandering ... Luke 15:11-32

C. *State of:*

Lamented ... Neh. 2:3, 17
To be corrected ... Is. 61:4

Watch—*to attend to, guard*

The LORD ... Gen. 31:49
As guards ... 2 Kin. 11:4-7

Watches of day, night—*period of time*

Jesus walks on water ... Matt. 14:25
Time of coming ... Matt. 24:43
Luke 12:37, 38

Watchmen, spiritual

Set by God ... Is. 62:6
Message to ... Is. 21:11, 12
Responsibility of ... Ezek. 33:1-9
Some are faithful ... Ezek. 3:17-21
Some are faithless ... Is. 56:10

In vain without the LORD ... Ps. 127:1
Leaders in the church ... Heb. 13:17

Water

A. *Described as:*

Living ... Jer. 2:13
Cold ... Jer. 18:14
Still ... Ps. 23:2
Deep ... Ps. 69:2, 14
Standing ... Ps. 107:35
Mighty ... Is. 28:2

B. *God's control over, He:*

Creates ... Gen. 1:2, 6, 7
Gives ... Ps. 104:13
Blesses the earth with ... Is. 55:10
Withholds ... Is. 50:2
Reveals His wonders in ... Ps. 107:23-32
Sets bounds to ... Ps. 104:5-9

C. *Miracles connected with:*

Changed into blood ... Ex. 7:17-25
Divided ... Ex. 14:21-29
Bitter made sweet ... Ex. 15:22-25
From a rock ... Ex. 17:1-7
Jordan divided ... Josh. 3:14-17
From a jawbone ... Judg. 15:17-19
Consumed by fire ... 1 Kin. 18:38
Valley, full of ... 2 Kin. 3:16-24
Axe floats on ... 2 Kin. 6:5-7
Christ walks on ... Mark 6:49-52
Changed into wine ... John 2:1-11
Healing of ... 2 Kin. 2:19-22

D. *Normal uses of, for:*

Drinking ... Gen. 24:43
Washing ... Gen. 18:4
Animals ... Ps. 42:1
Vegetation ... Deut. 11:10, 11
Sea creatures ... Ps. 104:25, 26

E. *Special uses of, for:*

Ordination ... Ex. 30:18-20
Cleansing ... Ex. 40:7-32
Purification ... Ex. 19:10
Baptism ... Acts 8:36-39
Sanctification ... Eph. 5:26
Business ... Ps. 107:23

F. *Figurative of:*

Instability ... Gen. 49:4
Cowardice ... Josh. 7:5
Spiritual growth ... Ps. 1:3
Peace ... Ps. 23:2
Afflictions ... Is. 43:2
Persecution ... Ps. 124:4, 5
Adultery ... Prov. 9:17
Universal Gospel ... Is. 11:9
Salvation ... Is. 55:1
Gospel age ... Is. 41:17-20
Holy Spirit ... Ezek. 47:1-12
Eternal life ... Rev. 22:17
Christ ... John 4:10-15
Regeneration ... John 7:37, 38

G. *Cure for:*

Doubting captain ... 2 Kin. 5:1-15
Afflicted ... John 5:1-7
Blind man ... John 9:6-11

H. *Used for a test:*

By Gideon ... Judg. 7:4-7

I. *Conduit:*

Hezekiah builds ... 2 Kin. 20:20

Water and blood

From Christ ... John 19:34

Water Gate—*a gate of Jerusalem*

Law is read ... Neh. 8:1, 2

Waterproofing—*making vessels watertight*

By means of:

Pitch ... Gen. 6:14
Slime and pitch ... Ex. 2:3

Wax (I)—*beeswax*

Figurative of persecution ... Ps. 22:14
Of the wicked before God ... Ps. 68:2
Of the mountains ... Ps. 97:5

Wax (II)—*to grow, increase*

A. *Of material things:*

Power ... 2 Sam. 3:1
Prestige ... Esth. 9:4
Age ... Josh. 23:1
Sound ... Ex. 19:19

SUBJECT REFERENCE

B. *Of immaterial things:*
- Courage ... Heb. 11:34
- Spirituality ... Luke 2:40
- God's hand ... Num. 11:23
- Old covenant ... Heb. 8:13
- God's kingdom ... Luke 13:18, 19

Way (see Highway; Path)

Way, Christ as
- Leading to Father ... John 14:6

Way, God's
- Right ... Hos. 14:9
- Just ... Dan. 4:37
- True ... Rev. 15:3
- Higher than man's ... Is. 55:8, 9
- Unsearchable ... Rom. 11:33

Waymarks—*roadmarkings*
- Give direction ... Jer. 31:21

Ways of God's people

A. *With reference to God's way, to:*
- Understand ... Ps. 119:27
- Pray for direction in ... Ex. 33:13
- Walk in ... Deut. 8:6
- Remember ... Deut. 8:2
- Known ... Ps. 67:2
- Teach to transgressors ... Ps. 51:13
- Rejoice in ... Ps. 119:14

B. *God's attitude toward, He:*
- Knows ... Ps. 1:6
- Is acquainted with ... Ps. 139:3
- Delights in ... Ps. 37:23
- Leads us in ... Ps. 139:24
- Teaches ... Ps. 25:9, 12
- Makes known ... Ps. 103:7
- Makes perfect ... Ps. 18:32
- Blesses ... Prov. 8:32

C. *With reference to our way:*
- Acknowledge Him in ... Prov. 3:6
- Commit to the LORD ... Ps. 37:5
- Makes prosperous ... Josh. 1:8
- All before God ... Ps. 119:168
- Teach me ... Ps. 143:8

Ways of man

Described as:
- Perverse before God ... Num. 22:32
- Hard ... Prov. 13:15
- Abomination ... Prov. 15:9
- Not good ... Prov. 16:29
- Dark ... Prov. 2:13

Weak, weakness

A. *Kinds of:*
- Political ... 2 Sam. 3:1
- Physical ... Judg. 16:7, 17; 2 Cor. 11:30
- Spiritual ... Is. 35:3
- Moral ... 2 Sam. 3:39

B. *Caused by:*
- Fasting ... Ps. 109:24
- Discouragement ... Neh. 6:9
- Sin ... 1 Cor. 11:26-30
- Discouraging preaching ... Jer. 38:4
- Conscientious doubts ... Rom. 14:1-23

C. *Victory over, by:*
- Christ ... 2 Cor. 13:3, 4
- Grace ... 2 Cor. 12:9, 10
- Faith ... Heb. 11:33, 34

D. *Our duty toward, to:*
- Bear ... Rom. 15:1
- Support ... Acts 20:35; 1 Cor. 9:22
- Not become a stumbling block ... 1 Cor. 8:9

E. *Our duties with reference to:*
- Pleasure in ... 2 Cor. 12:10
- Help those afflicted with ... Rom. 15:1

Wealth—*riches*

A. *Descriptive of:*
- Material possessions ... Gen. 34:29

B. *Advantages of:*
- Given by God ... Deut. 8:18, 19
- Source of security ... Prov. 18:11
- Adds friends ... Prov. 19:4

C. *Disadvantages of:*
- Produces self-sufficiency ... Deut. 8:17
- Leads to conceit ... Job 31:25
- Subject to loss ... Prov. 13:11
- Lost by dissipation ... Prov. 5:8-10
- Cannot save ... Ps. 49:6, 7
- Must be left to others ... Ps. 49:10

See Riches, earthly

Wean—*to accustom a child to independance from the mother's milk*
- Celebrated ... Gen. 21:8
- Figurative of spiritual rest ... Ps. 131:2

Weapons, spiritual

Against:
- World—faith ... 1 John 5:4
- Satan—armor of God ... Eph. 6:11-17
- Flesh—the Spirit ... Gal. 5:16-25

Weary—*to become tired*

A. *Caused by:*
- Journeys ... John 4:6
- Ritualism ... Is. 1:14
- Study ... Eccl. 12:12
- Anxiety ... Gen. 27:46
- Words ... Mal. 2:17
- Not speaking ... Jer. 20:9
- Too frequent visits ... Prov. 25:17

B. *Overcome by:*
- Waiting on the LORD ... Is. 40:30, 31
- Appropriate word ... Is. 50:4
- God's promise ... Is. 28:12
- Persevering faith ... Gal. 6:9
- Promised ruler ... Is. 32:1, 2
- Looking to Jesus ... Heb. 12:2, 3

Weather
- Proverb concerning ... Job 37:9-11
- Under divine control ... 1 Sam. 12:16-19
- Signs of ... Luke 12:54-57

Weaving—*uniting threads to produce cloth*
- Men endowed in art of ... Ex. 35:35
- Performed by worthy women ... Prov. 31:13, 19
- Figurative of life's shortness ... Job 7:6

See Spinning

Wedding (See Marriage)

Wedge of gold
- Stolen by Achan ... Josh. 7:20, 21

Weeds
- Wrapped around Jonah's head ... Jon. 2:5

Week—*seven days*
- Origin of, early ... Gen. 2:1-3
- Used in dating events ... Gen. 7:4, 10
- One, length of mourning ... Gen. 50:10
- Part of ceremonial Law ... Ex. 13:6, 7
- Seventy, prophecy of ... Dan. 9:24
- Christ arose on first day of ... Matt. 28:1
- Christians worship on first day of ... Acts 20:7; 1 Cor. 16:2

See Pentecost

Weeks of years
- Seven ... Lev. 25:8
- Seventy ... Dan. 9:2; Jer. 25:11

Weeping—*intense crying*

A. *Kinds of:*
- Rebellious ... Num. 11:4-20
- Hypocritical ... Judg. 14:16, 17
- Sincere ... 1 Sam. 20:41
- Exhausting ... 1 Sam. 30:4
- Secret ... Jer. 13:17
- Permanent ... Matt. 8:12
- Bitterly ... Matt. 26:75
- Divine ... John 11:35
- Sympathetic ... Rom. 12:15

B. *Caused by:*
- Despair ... Gen. 21:16
- Death ... Gen. 50:1
- Loss of blessing ... Gen. 27:34, 38
- Love ... Gen. 29:11
- Joy of reunion ... Gen. 33:4
- Loss of child ... Gen. 37:35
- Restraint of joy ... Gen. 42:24
- Hearing God's Word ... Neh. 8:9

C. *Passing away of:*
- After a child's death ... 2 Sam. 12:21-23
- In the morning ... Ps. 30:5
- In eternity ... Is. 65:19
- After seeing the Lord ... John 20:11-18

Weights and measures

A. *Monies of the Bible:*
- Beka ... Ex. 38:26
- Gerahs ... Ex. 30:13
- Mite ... Mark 12:42
- Pence ... Matt. 18:28
- Pieces of silver ... Matt. 26:15
- Shekel ... Ex. 30:24
- Shekels of Brass ... 2 Sam. 21:16
- Shekels of gold ... 1 Chr. 21:25
- Shekels of silver ... 2 Sam. 24:24
- Silver ... 2 Chr. 21:3
- Talents ... Matt. 18:24
- Talents of brass ... 1 Chr. 29:7
- Talents of gold ... 1 Chr. 29:4
- Talents of iron ... 1 Chr. 29:7
- Talents of silver ... 1 Chr. 29:4

B. *Distance or length measurements:*
- Acre ... 1 Sam. 14:14
- Cubit ... Gen. 6:15
- Fathom ... Acts 27:28
- Finger ... Jer. 52:21
- Furlong ... Luke 24:13
- Handbreadth ... Ex. 25:25
- Measuring reed ... Ezek. 40:3
- Pace ... 2 Sam. 6:13
- Span ... Ex. 28:16
- Sabbath day's journey ... Acts 1:12

C. *Liquid measures:*
- Bath ... 1 Kin. 7:26
- Cor ... Ezek. 45:14
- Firkin ... John 2:6
- Hin ... Ex. 29:40
- Homer ... Ezek. 45:11
- Kab ... 2 Kin. 6:25
- Log ... Lev. 14:10

D. *Dry measures:*
- Cab ... 2 Kin. 6:25
- Ephah ... Ex. 16:36
- Homer ... Lev. 27:16
- Log ... Lev. 14:10
- Omer ... Ex. 16:16
- Gerah ... Ex. 30:13
- Pound ... 1 Kin. 10:17

E. *Weight measures:*
- Beka ... Ex. 38:26
- Shekel ... 2 Sam. 14:26
- Talents ... Ex. 38:27

Welcome—*to receive with gladness*

A. *Extended to:*
- Returning brother ... Gen. 33:1-11
- Father ... Gen. 46:29-34
- Hero ... 1 Sam. 18:6, 7
- Prodigal son ... Luke 15:20-32
- Messiah ... Matt. 21:6-10

B. *Circumstances attending:*
- Courtesies offered ... Gen. 18:1-8
- Discourtesies shown ... 2 Sam. 10:1-5
- Fear expressed ... 1 Sam. 16:4, 5
- Fellowship denied ... 2 John 10, 11

Wells—*pits dug for water*

A. *Features concerning:*
- Women come to, for water ... Gen. 24:13, 14; John 4:7
- Surrounded by trees ... Gen. 49:22
- Often very deep ... John 4:11
- Covered with large stone ... Gen. 29:2, 3
- Sometimes cause strife ... Gen. 21:25

B. *Names of:*
- Beer ... Num. 21:16-18
- Beer-lahai-roi ... Gen. 16:14
- Beer-sheba ... Gen. 21:30, 31
- Beeroth ... Deut. 10:6
- Esek ... Gen. 26:20
- Jacob ... John 4:6
- Rehoboth ... Gen. 26:22
- Sitnah ... Gen. 26:21

C. *Figurative of:*
- Salvation ... Is. 12:3
- False teaching ... 2 Pet. 2:17
- One's wife ... Prov. 5:15
- The Holy Spirit ... John 4:10

Wen—*a running sore*
- Makes an animal unacceptable ... Lev. 22:22

SUBJECT — REFERENCE

Wench—*a maid or servant*
- Informant — 2 Sam. 17:17

Whale
- Jonah swallowed by — Matt. 12:40
- Created by God — Gen. 1:21

Wheat—*a cereal grass used for food*

A. *Features concerning:*
- Grown in Egypt — Ex. 9:32
- Grown in Palestine — 1 Kin. 5:11
- Made into bread — Ex. 29:2
- Used in trade — Ezek. 27:17
- Harvested — Ruth 2:23
- Threshed — Judg. 6:11
- Gathered — Matt. 3:12
- Harvesting of, celebrated — Ex. 34:22

B. *Figurative of:*
- Spiritual blessings — Ps. 81:16
- Christians — Matt. 3:12
- Christ's death — John 12:24
- Resurrection — 1 Cor. 15:37

Wheel—*a circular frame*

A. *Used on:*
- Carts — Is. 28:27, 28
- Threshing instrument — Prov. 20:26
- Chariots — Nah. 3:2
- Jehovah's throne — Ezek. 10:1-22

B. *Figurative of:*
- Future things — Ezek. 1:15-28
- Punishment — Prov. 20:26
- Cycle of nature ("course") — James 3:6
- God's sovereignty — Ezek. 10:9-19

Whelp—*offspring of certain animals*

Figurative of:
- Judah — Gen. 49:9
- Dan — Deut. 33:22
- Babylonians — Jer. 51:38
- Assyrians — Nah. 2:11, 12
- Princes of Israel — Ezek. 19:2-9

Whirlwind—*a great storm or tempest*

A. *Used literally of:*
- Elijah's translation — 2 Kin. 2:1
- Its fury — Is. 17:13

B. *Used figuratively of:*
- Sudden destruction — Prov. 1:27
- Suddenness — Is. 5:28
- God's anger — Jer. 23:19
- God's might — Nah. 1:3

Whisperer—*a gossiper*
- Separates chief friends — Prov. 16:28

White (see Colors)

Whole, wholesome

A. *Means of making, by:*
- Normal healing — Josh. 5:8
- Touch — Matt. 9:21
- Faith — Mark 10:52
- Risen Christ — Acts 4:9, 10

B. *Effects of, seen in:*
- Perfect restoration — Matt. 14:36
- Instantaneous healing — John 5:9
- Complete obedience — John 5:11-15

Whore, Whoredom (see Adultery; Harlot)

Wicked, the

A. *Descriptive of:*
- Sodomites — Gen. 13:13
- Egyptians — Ex. 9:27
- Athaliah — 2 Chr. 24:7
- Haman — Esth. 7:6
- Jews — Matt. 12:38, 45

B. *State of, described as:*
- Desiring evil — Prov. 21:10
- Have no peace — Is. 48:22
- Pours out evil — Prov. 15:28
- Refusing judgment — Prov. 21:7
- Cruel in their mercies — Prov. 12:10
- Like the troubled sea — Is. 57:20
- Far from God — Prov. 15:29
- Offering abominable sacrifice — Prov. 15:8
- Way is like darkness — Prov. 4:19

C. *God's attitude toward:*
- Will not justify — Ex. 23:7
- Will punish — Ps. 75:8
- Will overthrow — Prov. 21:12
- Their thoughts abominable to — Prov. 15:26
- God tries them — Ps. 11:5
- Made for the day of evil — Prov. 16:4

D. *Punishment of:*
- Shortened life — Prov. 10:27
- Soon destroyed — Ps. 37:35, 36
- Driven away — Prov. 14:32
- Slain by evil — Ps. 34:21
- His candle put out — Job 21:17
- His triumph short — Ps. 37:10
- His name put out forever — Ps. 9:5
- Silent in the grave — Ps. 31:17
- God rains fire on — Ps. 11:6
- Cast into hell — Ps. 9:17
- Consumed — Ps. 37:20
- Will die — Prov. 11:7
- In the resurrection, judgment — Acts 24:15

E. *Attitude of believers toward:*
- Wonder about their prosperity — Ps. 73:3
- Concerned about their triumph — Ps. 94:3, 4
- Will not sit with — Ps. 26:5
- Must not envy — Prov. 24:19
- Will triumph over — Ps. 58:10

Wickedness—*all forms of evil*

A. *Man's relationship to:*
- Not profited by — Prov. 10:2
- Not established by — Prov. 12:3
- Sells himself to — 1 Kin. 21:25
- Strengthens himself in — Ps. 52:7
- Refuses to turn from — Jer. 44:5
- Inside mankind — Luke 11:39
- Among all — Jer. 44:9
- Will fall by — Prov. 11:5
- Driven away — Prov. 14:32

B. *God's punishment of, seen in:*
- Driving out other nations — Deut. 9:4, 5
- Shiloh's destruction — Jer. 7:12
- Judah's punishment — Jer. 1:16
- Destruction of food supply — Ps. 107:33, 34
- Causing the flood — Gen. 6:5-7
- Death of men — Judg. 9:56
- Destroying men — Ps. 94:23

C. *Attitude of the righteous toward:*
- Wash heart of — Jer. 4:14
- Struggle against — Eph. 6:12
- Fear to commit — Gen. 39:9
- Not to dwell in — Ps. 84:10
- Pray for end of — Ps. 7:9
- Confession of — 1 Kin. 8:47

Widow—*a woman who has outlived her husband*

A. *Provision of, for:*
- Remarriage — Rom. 7:3
- Food — Deut. 24:19-21
- Protection — Is. 1:17, 23
- Vows of — Num. 30:9
- Raiment — Deut. 24:17

B. *Mistreatment of, by:*
- Children — 1 Tim. 5:4
- Neglect — Acts 6:1
- Scribes — Mark 12:40
- Creditors — 2 Kin. 4:1
- Princes — Is. 1:23
- Judges — Is. 10:1, 2

C. *Protection of, by:*
- God — Ex. 22:22-24
- Law — Deut. 24:17
- Pure religion — James 1:27
- Honor — 1 Tim. 5:3

D. *Examples of:*
- Naomi — Ruth 1:20, 21
- Woman of Tekoa — 2 Sam. 14:4, 5
- Woman of Zarephath — 1 Kin. 17:9, 10
- Anna — Luke 2:36, 37
- "A certain poor widow" — Luke 21:2, 3

Wife—*a married woman*

A. *Described as:*
- "A helpmeet" — Gen. 2:18, 20
- "A crown to her husband" — Prov. 12:4
- "A good thing" — Prov. 18:22
- "The weaker vessel" — 1 Pet. 3:7
- "The wife of his youth" — Mal. 2:14, 15
- "Thy companion" — Mal. 2:14

B. *Duties of, to:*
- Submit to husband — 1 Pet. 3:5, 6
- Reverence her husband — Eph. 5:33
- Love her husband — Titus 2:4
- Learn from her husband — 1 Cor. 14:34, 35
- Be trustworthy — Prov. 31:11, 12
- Love her children — Titus 2:4
- Be chaste — Titus 2:5
- Be keepers at home — Titus 2:5

C. *Duties of husband toward, to:*
- Love — Eph. 5:25, 28
- Honor — 1 Pet. 3:7
- Provide for — 1 Tim. 5:8
- Instruct — 1 Cor. 14:35
- Protect — 1 Sam. 30:1-19
- Not divorce — 1 Cor. 7:11

D. *Relationship with her husband, to be:*
- Exclusive — Prov. 5:15-17, 20
- Satisfying — Prov. 5:18, 19
- Mutually agreeable — 1 Cor. 7:1-5
- Undefiled — Heb. 13:4

E. *Special temptations of:*
- Disobedience — Gen. 3:1-19
- Unfaithfulness — John 4:17, 18
- Contentiousness — Prov. 19:13
- Assertion of authority — 1 Tim. 2:11-15

F. *Types of:*
- Disobedient—Eve — Gen. 3:1-8
- Obedient—Sarah — 1 Pet. 3:5, 6
- Worldly—Lot's — Gen. 19:26
- Humble—Manoah's — Judg. 13:22, 23
- Prayerful—Hannah — 1 Sam. 1:1-15
- Prudent—Abigail — 1 Sam. 25:3, 14-35
- Criticizing—Michal — 2 Sam. 6:15, 16
- Unscrupulous—Jezebel — 1 Kin. 21:5-15
- Modest—Vashti — Esth. 1:11, 12
- Foolish—Job's wife — Job 2:7-10
- Cruel—Herodias — Matt. 14:3-12
- Righteous—Elisabeth — Luke 1:5, 6
- Lying—Sapphira — Acts 5:1-10

Wilderness—*a desolate place*

A. *Descriptive of:*
- Israel's wanderings — Ex. 16:1
- Desolate place — Matt. 3:1, 3
- Desolation — Jer. 22:6

B. *Characterized by:*
- Wild creatures — Deut. 8:15
- No water — Deut. 8:15
- "Great and terrible" things — Deut. 1:19
- Uninhabited — Ps. 107:4, 5

C. *Israel's journey in, characterized by:*
- God's provision — Deut. 2:7
- God's guidance — Ps. 78:52
- God's mighty acts — Ps. 78:15, 16
- Israel's provoking God — Ps. 78:17-19, 40
- Israel's sin — Heb 3:7-19
- Testings — Deut. 8:2

D. *Significant events in:*
- Hagar's flight — Gen. 16:6-8
- Israel's journeys — Ps. 136:16
- John's preaching — Matt. 3:1-12
- Jesus' temptation — Matt. 4:1
- Jesus' miracle — Matt. 15:33-38
- Moses' serpent — John 3:14

Willingness

A. *On God's part, to:*
- Exercise mercy — 2 Kin. 8:18, 19
- Rule sovereignly — Dan. 4:17
- Save men — 1 Tim. 2:4; 2 Pet. 3:9

B. *On Christ's part, to:*
- Do God's will — Heb. 10:7, 9
- Submit to the Father — John 8:28, 29
- Reveal the Father — Matt. 11:27
- Heal people — Matt. 8:2, 3
- Die — Mark 14:36

C. *On man's part, to:*
- Do Satan's will — John 8:44
- Refuse salvation — John 5:40
- Pervert the truth — 2 Pet. 3:5
- Follow evil — Mark 15:15
- Persecute the righteous — Matt. 2:13

D. *On the believer's part, to:*
- Be saved — Rev. 22:17
- Follow Christ — Matt. 16:24
- Live godly — 2 Tim. 3:12
- Give — 2 Cor. 8:3-12
- Die — 2 Cor. 5:8

SUBJECT REFERENCE

Will of God

A. *Defined in terms of:*

Salvation .... 2 Pet. 3:9
Salvation of children .... Matt. 18:14
Belief in Christ .... Matt. 12:50
Everlasting life .... John 6:39, 40
Thanksgiving .... 1 Thess. 5:18
Sanctification .... 1 Thess. 4:3

B. *Characteristics of:*

Can be:
Known .... Rom. 2:18
Proved .... Rom. 12:2
Done .... Matt. 6:10
Sovereign over:
Nations .... Dan. 4:35
Individuals .... Acts 21:14

C. *God's power in doing, seen in:*

Predestination .... Rom. 9:18-23
Sovereignty .... Dan. 4:35
Man's salvation .... 1 Tim. 2:4
Believer's salvation .... James 1:18
Redemption .... Gal. 1:4

D. *Believer's relationship to, seen in his:*

Calling .... 1 Cor. 1:1
Regeneration .... James 1:18
Sanctification .... Heb. 10:10
Transformation .... Rom. 12:2
Instruction .... Ps. 143:10
Prayers .... 1 John 5:14
Submission .... Acts 21:14
Whole life .... 1 Pet. 4:2
Daily work .... Eph. 6:6
Travels .... Rom. 1:10
Plans .... James 4:13-15
Suffering .... 1 Pet. 3:17
Perfection .... Col. 4:12

Will of man (see Freedom; Liberty, spiritual)

Willow—*a tree*

Booths made of .... Lev. 23:40, 42
Grows beside brooks .... Job 40:22
Harps hung on .... Ps. 137:2

See Poplar tree

Wimple—*a shawl*

Worn by women .... Is. 3:22

Wind—*movement of the air*

A. *Characteristics of:*

Movement of, significant .... Luke 12:54, 55
Cannot be seen .... John 3:8
Sometimes destructive .... Job 1:19
Dries the earth .... Gen. 8:1
Often accompanies rain .... 1 Kin. 18:44, 45
Makes sea rough .... Ps. 107:25
Drives ships .... Acts 27:7, 13-18
Drives chaff away .... Ps. 1:4
Possesses weight .... Job 28:25

B. *God's relation to, He:*

Creates .... Amos 4:13
Sends .... Ps. 147:18
Brings out of His treasuries .... Ps. 135:7
Gathers .... Prov. 30:4
Controls .... Ps. 107:25

C. *Directions of, from:*

East .... Jer. 18:17
West .... Ex. 10:19
North .... Prov. 25:23
South .... Acts 27:13
All directions .... Ezek. 37:9

D. *Miracles connected with:*

Flood subsided by .... Gen. 8:1
Locusts brought and taken
by .... Ex. 10:13, 19
Red Sea divided by .... Ex. 14:21
Quail brought by .... Num. 11:31
Rain brought by .... 1 Kin. 18:44, 45
Mountains broken by .... 1 Kin. 19:11
Jonah's ship tossed by .... Jon. 1:4
Christ calms .... Matt. 8:26

E. *Figurative of:*

Empty speech .... Job 8:2
Empty boasting .... Prov. 25:14
Vanity .... Eccl. 5:16
Calamity .... Is. 32:2
God's discipline .... Hos. 13:15
God's judgment .... Jer. 22:22
Dispersion .... Ezek. 5:10

SUBJECT REFERENCE

Ruin .... Hos. 8:7
Holy Spirit .... Acts 2:2
False teaching .... Eph. 4:14

Windows of Heaven

Descriptive of:

Judgment rendered "opened" .... Gen. 7:11
Unbelief .... 2 Kin. 7:2, 19
Blessings .... Mal. 3:10

Wine

A. *Kinds of:*

New .... Luke 5:37-39
Old .... Luke 5:39
Fermented .... Num. 6:3
Refined .... Is. 25:6

B. *Features concerning:*

Made from grapes .... Gen. 40:11
Mixed .... Prov. 23:30
Kept in bottles .... Jer. 13:12
Kept in wineskins .... Matt. 9:17

C. *Used by:*

Noah .... Gen. 9:20, 21
Melchizedek .... Gen. 14:18
Isaac .... Gen. 27:25
Esther .... Esth. 5:6
Jesus .... John 2:1-11
Timothy .... 1 Tim. 5:23

D. *Uses of, as:*

Offering .... Lev. 23:13
Drink .... Gen. 27:25
Festive drink .... Esth. 1:7
Disinfectant .... Luke 10:34
Drug .... Mark 15:23
Medicine .... 1 Tim. 5:23

E. *Evil effects of:*

Leads to violence .... Prov. 4:17
Mocks a man .... Prov. 20:1
Make poor .... Prov. 23:20, 21
Bites like a serpent .... Prov. 23:31, 32
Impairs the judgment .... Prov. 31:4, 5
Inflames the passions .... Is. 5:11
Takes away the heart .... Hos. 4:11

F. *Intoxication from, falsely charged to:*

Hannah .... 1 Sam. 1:12-16
Jesus .... Matt. 11:19
Apostles .... Acts 2:13

G. *Uses of, in:*

Offering .... Num. 15:4-10
Miracle .... John 2:1-9
Lord's Supper .... Matt. 26:27-29

H. *Figurative of:*

God's wrath .... Ps. 75:8
Wisdom's blessings .... Prov. 9:2, 5
Gospel .... Is. 55:1
Christ's blood .... Matt. 26:27-29
Fornication .... Rev. 17:2

See Drunkenness; Temperance

Wings—*the locomotive appendages on flying creatures*

A. *Used literally of:*

Flying creatures .... Gen. 1:21
Cherubim .... Ex. 25:20

B. *Used figuratively of:*

God's mercy .... Ps. 57:1
Protection .... Luke 13:34

Winking the eye

Hate .... Ps. 35:19
Evil .... Prov. 6:12, 13

Winnow—*to toss about*

A. *Used literally of:*

Fork for winnowing grain .... Is. 30:24

B. *Used figuratively of judgments:*

God's .... Is. 30:24
Nation's .... Jer. 51:2
Christ's .... Matt. 3:12

Winter—*the cold season of the year*

Made by God .... Ps. 74:17
Continuance of, guaranteed .... Gen. 8:22
Time of snow .... 2 Sam. 23:20
Hazards of travel during .... 2 Tim. 4:21

Wipe—*to clean or dry*

A. *Used literally of:*

Dust removal .... Luke 10:11
Feet dried .... John 13:5

SUBJECT REFERENCE

B. *Used figuratively of:*

Jerusalem's destruction .... 2 Kin. 21:13
Tears removed .... Rev. 7:17

Wire—*threads*

Used in ephod .... Ex. 39:3

Wisdom—*knowledge guided by understanding*

A. *Sources of, in:*

Spirit .... Ex. 31:3
Lord .... Ex. 36:1, 2
God's Law .... Deut. 4:6
Fear of the LORD .... Prov. 9:10
Righteous .... Prov. 10:31

B. *Ascribed to:*

Workmen .... Ex. 36:2
Women .... Prov. 31:26
Bezaleel .... Ex. 31:2-5
Joseph .... Acts 7:9, 10
Moses .... Acts 7:22
Joshua .... Deut. 34:9
Hiram .... 1 Kin. 7:13, 14
Solomon .... 1 Kin. 3:12, 16-28
Children of Issachar .... 1 Chr. 12:32
Ezra .... Ezra 7:25
Daniel .... Dan. 1:17
Magi .... Matt. 2:1-12
Stephen .... Acts 6:3, 10
Paul .... 2 Pet. 3:15

C. *Described as:*

Discreet .... Gen. 41:33
Technical skill .... Ex. 28:3
Common sense .... 2 Sam. 20:14-22
Mechanical skill .... 1 Kin. 7:14
Understanding .... Prov. 10:13, 23
Military ability .... Is. 10:13
Commercial industry .... Ezek. 28:3-5

D. *Value of:*

Gives happiness .... Prov. 3:13
Benefits of, many .... Prov. 4:5-10
Keeps from evil .... Prov. 5:1-6
Better than rubies .... Prov. 8:11
Above gold in value .... Prov. 16:16
Should be acquired .... Prov. 23:23
Excels folly .... Eccl. 2:13
Gives life .... Eccl. 7:12
Makes strong .... Eccl. 7:19
Better than weapons .... Eccl. 9:18
Insures stability .... Is. 33:6
Produces good fruit .... James 3:17

E. *Limitations of:*

Cannot save us .... 1 Cor. 1:19-21
Cause of self-glory .... Jer. 9:23
Can pervert .... Is. 47:10
Nothing, without God .... Jer. 8:9
Can corrupt .... Ezek. 28:17
Of this world, foolishness .... 1 Cor. 3:19
Earthly, sensual .... James 3:15
Gospel not preached in .... 1 Cor. 2:1-5

F. *Of believers:*

Given by Christ .... Luke 21:15
Gift of the Spirit .... 1 Cor. 12:8
Given by God .... Eph. 1:17
Prayed for .... Col. 1:9
Means of instruction .... Col. 1:28
Lack of, ask for .... James 1:5

Wisdom of Christ

Predicted .... Is. 11:1, 2
Incarnated .... 1 Cor. 1:24
Realized .... Luke 2:52
Displayed .... Matt. 13:54
Perfected .... Col. 2:3
Imputed .... 1 Cor. 1:30

Wisdom of God

A. *Described as:*

Universal .... Dan. 2:20
Infinite .... Ps. 147:5
Unsearchable .... Is. 40:28
Mighty .... Job 36:5
Perfect .... Job 37:16

B. *Manifested in:*

Creation .... Ps. 104:24
Nature .... Job 38:34-41
Sovereignty .... Dan. 2:20, 21
The Church .... Eph. 3:10

SUBJECT	REFERENCE
Wist, wit—*obsolete for "to know"*	
Of things:	
Unknown	Ex. 2:4
Known by others	Ex. 34:29
That should be known	Luke 2:49
Witch—*one adept at magic*	
Saul consults one	1 Sam. 28:7-25
Witchcraft—*the practice of sorcery*	
Forbidden in Israel	Deut. 18:9-14
Used by Jezebel	2 Kin. 9:22
Condemned by the prophets	Mic. 5:12
Practiced by Manasseh	2 Chr. 33:6
Suppressed by Saul	1 Sam. 28:3, 9
Work of the flesh	Gal. 5:20
See Divination	
Wither—*to dry up*	
A. *Caused by:*	
God's judgment	Is. 40:7, 24
Christ's judgment	Matt. 21:19, 20
No root	Matt. 13:6
Heat	James 1:11
B. *Applied literally to:*	
Ear of grain	Gen. 41:23
Gourd	Jon. 4:7
Man's hand	Luke 6:6, 8
Witnessing—*bearing testimony to something*	
A. *Elements of, seen in:*	
Public transaction	Ruth 4:1-11
Signing a document	Jer. 32:10-12
Calling witnesses	Lev. 5:1
Requiring two witnesses	1 Tim. 5:19
Rejection of false witnesses	Prov. 24:28
B. *Material means of, by:*	
Heap stones	Gen. 31:44-52
Song	Deut. 31:19-21
Altar	Josh. 22:26-34
Works	John 10:25
Sign (miracles)	Heb. 2:4
C. *Spiritual means of, by:*	
God's Law	Deut. 31:26
Gospel	Matt. 24:14
Father	John 5:37
Conscience	Rom. 2:15
Holy Spirit	Rom. 8:16
D. *To Christ as object, by:*	
John the Baptist	John 1:7, 8, 15
His works	John 5:36
Father	John 8:18
Himself	John 8:18
Holy Spirit	John 15:26, 27
His disciples	John 15:27
Prophets	Acts 10:43
E. *Of Christians to Christ:*	
Chosen	Acts 10:41
Commissioned	Acts 1:8
Empowered	Acts 4:33
Confirmed	Heb. 2:3, 4
F. *Objects of Christ's:*	
Resurrection	Acts 2:32
Saviorhood	Acts 5:31, 32
Life	Acts 1:21, 22
Mission	Acts 10:41-43
Sufferings	1 Pet. 5:1
See Testimony	
Witty—*obsolete for "intelligent"*	
Applied to inventions	Prov. 8:12
Wizard (see Witchcraft)	
Wolf—*a dog-like animal*	
A. *Characteristics of:*	
Ravenous	Gen. 49:27
Nocturnal	Jer. 5:6
Sheep-eating	John 10:12
B. *Figurative of:*	
False prophets	Matt. 7:15
Gospel transformation	Is. 11:6
Woman—*the female sex*	
A. *Described as:*	
Beautiful	2 Sam. 11:2
Wise	2 Sam. 20:16
Widow	1 Kin. 17:9, 10
Evil	Prov. 6:24

SUBJECT	REFERENCE
Foolish	Job 2:10
Gracious	Prov. 11:16
Virtuous	Prov. 12:4
Contentious	Prov. 21:19
Adulterous	Prov. 30:20
Honorable	Acts 17:12
Silly	2 Tim. 3:6
Holy	1 Pet. 3:5
B. *Work of:*	
Kneading meal	Gen. 18:6
Drawing water	Gen. 24:11, 13, 15
Tending sheep	Gen. 29:6
Making cloth	Prov. 31:13, 19
Caring for the household	Prov. 31:27 1 Tim. 5:14
C. *Rights of, to:*	
Marry	1 Cor. 7:36
Hold property	Num. 27:6-11
Make vows	Num. 30:3-9
D. *Position of, in relation to man:*	
Created from man	Gen. 2:21-25
Made to help man	Gen. 2:18, 20
Glory of man	1 Cor. 11:7-9
Becomes subject to man	Gen. 3:16
Weaker than man	1 Pet. 3:7
E. *Position of, in spiritual things:*	
Insight of, noted	Judg. 13:23
Prayer of, answered	1 Sam. 1:9-28
Understanding of, rewarded	1 Sam. 25:3-42
Faith of, brings salvation	Luke 7:37-50
Made equal in Christ	Gal. 3:28
Labor of, commended	Phil. 4:2, 3
Faith of, transmitted	2 Tim. 1:5
F. *Good traits of:*	
Obedience	1 Pet. 3:5-7
Concern for children	Ex. 2:2-10
Loyalty	Ruth 1:14-18
Desire for children	1 Sam. 1:9-28
Modesty	Esth. 1:10-12
Industry	Prov. 31:10-31
Complete devotion	Luke 7:38-50
Tenderness	John 11:20-35
G. *Bad traits of:*	
Inciting to evil	Gen. 3:6, 7
Subtle	Prov. 7:10
Fond of adornments	Is. 3:16-24
Self-indulgent	Is. 32:9, 11
Easily led into idolatry	Jer. 7:18
Led away	2 Tim. 3:6
H. *Prohibitions concerning, not to:*	
Wear man's clothing	Deut. 22:5
Have head shaved	1 Cor. 11:5-15
Usurp authority	1 Tim. 2:11-15
Be unchaste	1 Pet. 3:1-7
Womb—*the uterus*	
A. *God's control over, to:*	
Close	Gen. 20:18
Open	Gen. 29:31
Fashion us in	Job 31:15
Separate and call	Gal. 1:15
Cause to conceive	Luke 1:31
Make alive	Rom. 4:19-21
B. *Babe inside:*	
Grows mysteriously	Eccl. 11:5
Known by God	Ps. 139:13-16
Deformed	Acts 3:2
Leaps	Luke 1:41, 44
C. *Man coming from:*	
Different	Gen. 25:23, 24
Consecrated	Judg. 13:5, 7
Naked	Job 1:21
Helpless	Ps. 22:9, 10
Sustained	Ps. 71:6
Estranged	Ps. 58:3
Women of the Bible, named	
Abi, wife of Ahaz	2 Kin. 18:1, 2
Abiah, wife of Hezron	1 Chr. 2:24
Abigail	
(1) wife of Nabal	1 Sam. 25:3
(2) sister of David	1 Chr. 2:15, 16
Abihail, wife of Abishur	1 Chr. 2:29
Abishag, nurse of David	1 Kin. 1:1-3
Abital, David's wife	2 Sam. 3:1, 4
Achsah, daughter of Caleb	Josh. 15:16
Adah	
(1) a wife of Lamech	Gen. 4:19
(2) Canaanite wife of Esau	Gen. 36:2

SUBJECT	REFERENCE
Ahinoam	
(1) wife of Saul	1 Sam. 14:50
(2) a Jezreelitess	1 Sam. 25:43
Aholah	Ezek. 23:4
Aholibah	Ezek. 23:4
Aholibamah	Gen. 36:2
Anah, daughter of Zibeon	Gen. 36:2
Anna, an aged widow	Luke 2:36, 37
Apphia, a Christian of Colossae	Philem. 2
Asenath, wife of Joseph	Gen. 41:45
Atarah, wife of Jerahmeel	1 Chr. 2:26
Athaliah, mother of Ahaziah	2 Kin. 8:26
Azubah	
(1) first wife of Caleb	1 Chr. 2:18
(2) daughter of Shilhi	1 Kin. 22:42
Baara, wife of Shaharaim	1 Chr. 8:8
Basemath	
(1) daughter of Elon	Gen. 26:34
(2) a third wife of Esau	Gen. 36:2-3
Bath-sheba, wife of David	2 Sam. 11:3, 27
Bernice, sister of Agrippa	Acts 25:13
Bilhah, Rachel's handmaid	Gen. 29:29
Bithiah, daughter of a Pharoah	1 Chr. 4:17
Candace, a queen	Acts 8:27
Chloe, woman of Corinth	1 Cor. 1:11
Claudia, Christian of Rome	2 Tim. 4:21
Cozbi, Midianite slain	Num. 25:15-18
Damaris, woman of Athens	Acts 17:34
Deborah	
(1) Rebekah's nurse	Gen. 35:8
(2) judge	Judg. 4:4
Delilah, Philistine woman	Judg. 16:4, 5
Dinah, daughter of Jacob	Gen. 30:19, 21
Dorcas, called Tabitha	Acts 9:36
Drusilla, wife of Felix	Acts 24:24
Eglah, one of David's wives	2 Sam. 3:5
Elisabeth, mother of John the Baptist	Luke 1:5, 13
Elisheba, wife of Aaron	Ex. 6:23
Ephah, concubine of Caleb	1 Chr. 2:46
Ephrath, mother of Hur	1 Chr. 2:19
Esther, a Jewess who became queen of Persia	Esth. 2:16, 17
Eunice, mother of Timothy	2 Tim. 1:5
Euodias, a deaconess	Phil. 4:2
Eve, first woman	Gen. 3:20
Gomer, wife of Hosea	Hos. 1:2, 3
Hagar, Sarai's maid	Gen. 16:1
Haggith, wife of David	2 Sam. 3:2, 4
Hammoleketh, mother of Ishod	1 Chr. 7:18
Hamutal, daughter of Jeremiah	2 Kin. 23:31
Hannah, mother of Samuel	1 Sam. 1:20
Hazelelponi, in genealogies of Judah	1 Chr. 4:1-3
Helah, one of the wives of Ashur	1 Chr. 4:5
Hephzibah, mother of Manasseh	2 Kin. 21:1
Herodias, sister-in-law of Herod	Matt. 14:3-6
Hodesh, wife of Shaharaim	1 Chr. 8:8, 9
Hoglah, a daughter of Zelophehad	Num. 26:33
Huldah, a prophetess	2 Kin. 22:14
Hushim, a Moabitess	1 Chr. 8:8-11
Iscah, daughter of Haran	Gen. 11:29
Jael, wife of Heber	Judg. 4:17
Jecholiah, wife of Amaziah	2 Kin. 15:1, 2
Jedidah, mother of Josiah	2 Kin. 22:1
Jehoaddin, wife of Joash	2 Kin. 14:1, 2
Jehosheba, daughter of Joram	2 Kin. 11:2
Jemima, Job's daughter	Job 42:12, 14
Jerioth, wife of Caleb	1 Chr. 2:18
Jerusha, daughter of Zadok	2 Kin. 15:33
Jezebel, wife of Ahab	1 Kin. 16:30, 31
Joanna, wife of Chuza	Luke 8:3
Jochebed, mother of Moses	Ex. 6:20
Judith, daughter of Beeri	Gen. 26:34
Julia, Christian woman of Rome	Rom. 16:15
Keren-happuch, Job's daughter	Job 42:14
Keturah, second wife of Abraham	Gen. 25:1
Kezia, daughter of Job	Job 42:14
Leah, wife of Jacob	Gen. 29:21-25
Lois, grandmother of Timothy	2 Tim. 1:5
Lo-ruhamah, daughter of Gomer	Hos. 1:3-6
Lydia, first Christian convert in Europe	Acts 16:14
Maachah	
(1) daughter of Nahor	Gen. 22:23, 24

SUBJECT	REFERENCE
(2) daughter of Talmai	2 Sam. 3:3
(3) daughter of Abishalom	1 Kin. 15:2
(4) mother of Asa	1 Kin. 15:9, 10
(5) concubine of Caleb	1 Chr. 2:48
(6) wife of Machir	1 Chr. 7:16
(7) wife of Jehiel	1 Chr. 8:29
Mahalath	
(1) wife of Esau	Gen. 28:9
(2) granddaughter of David	2 Chr. 11:18
Mahlah, daughter of Zelophehad	Num. 26:33
Mara, another name for Naomi	Ruth 1:20
Martha, friend of Christ	Luke 10:38-41
Mary	
(1) mother of Jesus	Matt. 1:16
(2) Mary Magdalene	Matt. 27:56-61
(3) Mary, sister of Martha	Luke 10:38, 39
(4) Mary, wife of Cleophas	John 19:25
(5) Mary, mother of Mark	Acts 12:12
(6) a Christian at Rome	Rom. 16:6
Matred, mother-in-law of Hadar	Gen. 36:39
Mehetabeel, daughter of Matred	Gen. 36:39
Merab, King Saul's eldest daughter	1 Sam. 14:49
Meshullemeth, wife of Manasseh	2 Kin. 21:18, 19
Michal, daughter of King Saul	1 Sam. 14:49
Milcah	
(1) daughter of Haran	Gen. 11:29
(2) daughter of Zelophehad	Num. 26:33
Miriam	
(1) sister of Moses	Ex. 15:20
(2) disputed daughter of Ezra	1 Chr. 4:17
Naamah	
(1) daughter of Lamech	Gen. 4:19-22
(2) wife of Solomon	1 Kin. 14:21
Naarah, one of the wives of Ashur	1 Chr. 4:5
Naomi, wife of Elimelech	Ruth 1:2
Nehushta, daughter of Elnathan	2 Kin. 24:8
Noadiah, a false prophetess	Neh. 6:14
Noah, daughter of Zelophehad	Num. 26:33
Orpah, sister-in-law of Ruth	Ruth 1:4
Peninnah, one of the wives of Elkanah	1 Sam. 1:1, 2
Persis, convert of early Church	Rom. 16:12
Phebe, a deaconess	Rom. 16:1-2
Priscilla, wife of Aquila	Acts 18:2
Puah, a midwife	Ex. 1:15
Rachel, wife of Jacob	Gen. 29:28
Rahab, aid to Israel's spies	Josh. 2:1-3
Reumah, mother of Tebah	Gen. 22:24
Rhoda, a damsel	Acts 12:13
Rizpah, concubine of Saul	2 Sam. 3:7
Ruth, daughter-in-law of Naomi	Ruth 1:3, 4
Salome, wife of Zebedee	Matt. 27:56 Mark 15:40
Sapphira, wife of Ananias	Acts 5:1
Sarah, (Sarai) wife of Abraham (Abram)	Gen. 11:29
Serah, daughter of Asher	Gen. 46:17
Shelomith	
(1) daughter of Dibri	Lev. 24:11
(2) daughter of Zerubbabel	1 Chr. 3:19
Sherah, daughter of Beriah	1 Chr. 7:23, 24
Shimeath, mother of Zabad	2 Chr. 24:26
Shimrith, mother of Jehozabad	2 Chr. 24:26
Shiphrah, a midwife	Ex. 1:15
Shua, daughter of Heber	1 Chr. 7:32
Susanna, ministered to Jesus	Luke 8:3
Syntyche, convert of Church at Philippi	Phil. 4:2
Tabitha, same as Dorcas	Acts 9:36
Tahpenes, queen of Egypt	1 Kin. 11:19
Tamar	
(1) daughter-in-law of Judah	Gen. 38:6
(2) a daughter of David	2 Sam. 13:1
(3) daughter of Absalom	2 Sam. 14:27
Taphath, one of Solomon's daughters	1 Kin. 4:11
Timna, concubine of Eliphaz	Gen. 36:12
Tirzah, one of daughters of Zelophehad	Num. 26:33
Tryphaena, convert at Rome	Rom. 16:12
Tryphosa, convert at Rome	Rom. 16:12
Vashti, wife of Ahasuerus	Esth. 1:9
Zebudah, mother of Jehoiakim	2 Kin. 23:36
Zeresh, wife of Haman	Esth. 5:10
Zeruah, a widow	1 Kin. 11:26
Zeruiah, mother of Joab	2 Sam. 17:25
Zibiah, mother of Jehoash	2 Kin. 12:1
Zillah, wife of Lamech	Gen. 4:19
Zilpah, Leah's handmaid	Gen. 29:24
Zipporah, wife of Moses	Ex. 2:21

Wonderful—*full of wonder*

SUBJECT	REFERENCE
A. *Ascribed to:*	
Human love	2 Sam. 1:26
LORD's works	Ps. 78:4
Mysterious things	Prov. 30:18
Lord's Law	Ps. 119:18
Lord's testimonies	Ps. 119:129
Lord's knowledge	Ps. 139:6
Our being	Ps. 139:14
Messiah's name	Is. 9:6
B. *Descriptive of the Lord's work, as:*	
Numerous	Ps. 40:5
Transmitted	Ps. 78:4
Remembered	Ps. 111:4
Praised	Is. 25:1

Wonders—*miraculous works*

SUBJECT	REFERENCE
A. *Performed by:*	
God	Heb. 2:4
Moses and Aaron	Ex. 11:10
Christ	Acts 2:22
Apostles	Acts 2:43
Jesus' name	Acts 4:30
Stephen	Acts 6:8
Paul and Barnabas	Acts 14:3
Paul	2 Cor. 12:12
B. *Places of:*	
Egypt	Acts 7:36
Land of Ham	Ps. 105:27
Canaan	Josh. 3:5
Deeps	Ps. 107:24
Heaven	Dan. 6:27
Among the peoples	Ps. 77:14
C. *Described as:*	
Numerous	Ex. 11:9
Great	Acts 6:8
Mighty	Dan. 4:3
D. *Man's reactions to:*	
Did not remember	Neh. 9:17
Forgetful of	Ps. 78:11, 12
Not understanding	Ps. 106:7
Not believing	Ps. 78:32
Inquiring about	Jer. 21:2
E. *Believer's attitude toward, to:*	
Remember	1 Chr. 16:9, 12
Declare	Ps. 71:17
Give thanks for	Ps. 136:1, 4
Consider	Job 37:14

Wood

SUBJECT	REFERENCE
A. *Descriptive of:*	
Part of a tree	Num. 19:6
Forest	Josh. 17:15, 18
B. *Place of:*	
Animals	2 Kin. 2:24
Fortresses	2 Chr. 27:4
C. *Used for:*	
Fire	1 Kin. 18:23-38
Carts	1 Sam. 6:14
Weapons	Num. 35:18
Ships	Gen. 6:14
Chariots	Song 3:9
Musical instruments	1 Kin. 10:12
Buildings	1 Kin. 6:15-33
Tabernacle furniture	Ex. 25:9-28
Pulpit	Neh. 8:4
Gods	Is. 37:19

Wood, hewers of

SUBJECT	REFERENCE
Gibeonites made, because of deception	Josh. 9:21-27

Woodsmen

SUBJECT	REFERENCE
Provided with food	2 Chr. 2:3, 10

Woof—*the threads crossing the warp of a woven garment*

SUBJECT	REFERENCE
Inspection of, for leprosy	Lev. 13:48-59

Wool—*the soft hair of sheep*

SUBJECT	REFERENCE
Inspection of, for leprosy	Lev. 13:47-59
Mixture of, forbidden	Deut. 22:11
Used as a test	Judg. 6:37
Valuable article of trade	Ezek. 27:18
Figurative of whiteness	Is. 1:18

Word of God

SUBJECT	REFERENCE
A. *Called:*	
Book of the Law	Neh. 8:3
Law of the LORD	Ps. 1:2
Scriptures	John 5:39
Holy Scriptures	Rom. 1:2
Word of God	Heb. 4:12
Word	James 1:21-23
Word of life	Phil. 2:16
Book	Rev. 22:19
B. *Descriptive of:*	
Old Testament Law	Mark 7:13
God's revealed plan	Rom. 9:6
God's completed revelation	Col. 1:25-27
Christ's message	Luke 5:1
Christian Gospel	Acts 4:31
C. *Described as:*	
Pure	Ps. 19:8
Restraining	Ps. 119:11
Perfect	Ps. 19:7
Sure	Ps. 111:7, 8
Truth	Ps. 119:142, 151, 160
Enduring	Is. 40:8
Effectual	Is. 55:11
Sanctifying	Eph. 5:26
Harmonious	Acts 15:15
Inspired	2 Pet. 1:21
Living and active	Heb. 4:12
D. *Compared to:*	
Lamp	Ps. 119:105
Fire	Jer. 5:14
Hammer	Jer. 23:29
Seed	Matt. 13:18-23
Sword	Eph. 6:17
E. *Agency of, to:*	
Heal	Ps. 107:20
Make free	John 8:32
Illuminate	Ps. 119:130
Bear witness	John 20:31
Produce faith	Rom. 10:17
Make wise	2 Tim. 3:15-17
Exhort	2 Tim. 4:2
Rejoice the heart	Jer. 15:16
Create the world	Heb. 11:3
Regenerate	James 1:18
Destroy the world	2 Pet. 3:5-7
F. *Proper attitude toward, to:*	
Stand in awe of	Ps. 119:161
Tremble at	Is. 66:2, 5
Speak faithfully	Jer. 23:28
Search	Acts 17:11
Speak boldly	Acts 4:29, 31
Preach	Acts 8:25
Receive	Acts 11:1
Glorify	Acts 13:48
Teach	Acts 18:11
Obey	1 Pet. 3:1
Handle accurately	2 Tim. 2:15
Do	James 1:22, 23
Suffer for	Rev. 1:9
G. *In the believer's life, as:*	
Restraint	Ps. 119:9, 11
Guide	Ps. 119:133
Source of joy	Ps. 119:47, 97, 162
Standard of conduct	Titus 2:5
Source of new life	1 Pet. 1:23
Spiritual food	1 Pet. 2:2
H. *Prohibitions concerning, not to be:*	
Preached in man's wisdom	1 Cor. 2:4, 13
Used deceitfully	2 Cor. 4:2
Altered	Rev. 22:18, 19

Words—*intelligible sounds or signs*

SUBJECT	REFERENCE
A. *Described as:*	
Acceptable	Eccl. 12:10
Lying and corrupt	Dan. 2:9
Enticing	1 Cor. 2:4
Easy	1 Cor. 14:9, 19
Unspeakable	2 Cor. 12:4
Vain	Eph. 5:6
Flattering	1 Thess. 2:5
Wholesome	1 Tim. 6:3
B. *Power of, to:*	
Stir up wrath	Prov. 15:1
Wound	Prov. 26:22
Sustain	Is. 50:4
Determine destiny	Matt. 12:36, 37

SUBJECT REFERENCE

Work, Christ's

A. *Defined as:*

Doing God's will .... John 4:34
Limited in time .... John 9:4
Incomparable .... John 15:24
Initiated by God .... John 14:10
Finished in the cross .... John 17:4

B. *Design of, to:*

Attest His mission .... John 5:36
Encourage faith .... John 14:11, 12
Judge men .... John 15:24

Work, the Christian's

A. *Agency of, by:*

God .... Phil. 2:13
Spirit .... 1 Cor. 12:11
God's Word .... 1 Thess. 2:13
Faith .... Gal. 5:6

B. *Characteristics of:*

Designed for God's glory .... Matt. 5:16
Divinely called .... Acts 13:2
Produces eventual glory ..... 2 Cor. 4:17
Subject to examination ...... Gal. 6:4
Final perfection in .... Heb. 13:21

C. *God's regard for, will:*

Reward .... Jer. 31:16
Perfect .... Phil. 1:6
Not forget .... Heb. 6:10

See Labor, spiritual

Work, physical

Part of the curse .... Gen. 3:19
Required of Christians .... 2 Thess. 3:7-14
Nehemiah's zeal .... Neh. 6:1-4
Paul's example .... Acts 18:1-3

See Labor, physical

Works, God's

A. *Described as:*

Perfect .... Deut. 32:4
Terrible .... Ps. 66:3
Incomparable .... Ps. 86:8
Honorable and glorious ..... Ps. 111:3
Marvelous .... Ps. 139:14
Holy .... Ps. 145:17
Strange .... Is. 28:21
Great and marvelous .... Rev. 15:3

B. *Manifested in:*

Creation .... Gen. 1:1-3
Heavens .... Ps. 8:3
Deeps .... Ps. 107:24
Regenerate people .... Is. 19:25

C. *God's attitude toward:*

Rejoice in .... Ps. 104:31
Made known to His people .. Ps. 111:6
His mercies over .... Ps. 145:9
Glorified in .... Is. 60:21

D. *Believer's attitude toward, to:*

Consider .... Ps. 8:3
Behold .... Ps. 46:8
Meditate .... Ps. 77:12
Meditate upon .... Ps. 143:5
Triumph in .... Ps. 92:4
Declare .... Ps. 107:22
Praise God for .... Ps. 145:4, 10
Pray for revival of .... Hab. 3:2

E. *Unbeliever's attitude toward:*

Not regarding .... Ps. 28:5
Forgetting .... Ps. 78:11
Not believed .... Acts 13:41

Works, good

A. *Considered negatively, they cannot:*

Justify .... Rom. 4:2-6
Determine God's election .... Rom. 9:11
Secure righteousness .... Rom. 9:31, 32
Substitute for grace .... Rom. 11:6

B. *Considered positively:*

Reward for .... 1 Cor. 3:13-15
Created for .... Eph. 2:10
Prepared for .... 2 Tim. 2:21
Furnished for .... 2 Tim. 3:17

Works, Satan's (see Satan)

Works, the unbeliever's

A. *Described as:*

Wicked .... Col. 1:21
Done in darkness .... Is. 29:15
Abominable .... Ps. 14:1
Deceitful .... Prov. 11:18
Evil .... John 7:7
Unfruitful .... Eph. 5:11

B. *God's attitude toward, will:*

Never forget .... Amos 8:7
Reward .... Prov. 24:12
Bring to judgment .... Rev. 20:12, 13

C. *Believer's relation to:*

Cast off .... Rom. 13:12
Have no fellowship with ..... Eph. 5:11
Be delivered from .... 2 Tim. 4:18

World

A. *God's relation to, as:*

Maker .... Jer. 10:12
Possessor .... Ps. 24:1
Redeemer .... John 3:16
Judge .... Ps. 96:13

B. *Christ's relation to, as:*

Maker .... John 1:10
Sin-bearer .... John 1:29
Savior .... John 12:47
Life .... John 6:33, 51
Light .... John 8:12
Judge .... Acts 17:31
Overcomer .... John 16:33
Reconciler .... 2 Cor. 5:19

C. *Christian's relation to:*

Light of .... Matt. 5:14
Not of .... John 17:14, 16
Chosen out of .... John 15:19
Tribulation in .... John 16:33
Sent into by Christ .... John 17:18
Not conformed to .... Rom. 12:2
Crucified to .... Gal. 6:14
To live soberly .... Titus 2:12
Unspotted from .... James 1:27
Overcomers of .... 1 John 5:4, 5
Denying desires of .... Titus 2:12

D. *Dangers of, arising from:*

Wisdom .... 1 Cor. 3:19
Love of .... 2 Tim. 4:10
Friendship .... James 4:4
Corruptions .... 2 Pet. 1:4
Lusts .... 1 John 2:15-17
False prophets .... 1 John 4:1
Deceivers .... 2 John 7

E. *In the plan of redemption:*

Elect chosen before .... Eph. 1:4
Revelation made before ..... Matt. 13:35
Sin's entrance into .... Rom. 5:12
Its guilt before God .... Rom. 3:19
Original revelation to .... Rom. 1:20
God's love for .... John 3:16
Christ's mission to .... John 12:47
Spirit's conviction of .... John 16:8
Gospel preached in .... Matt. 24:14
Reconciliation of .... 2 Cor. 5:19
Destruction of .... 2 Pet. 3:7
Final judgment of .... Acts 17:31
Satan deceives .... Rev. 12:9

Worm—*a soft-bodied, slender, creeping animal*

A. *Ravages of:*

On bread .... Ex. 16:15, 20
On plants .... Jon. 4:7
On the body .... Acts 12:23
In the grave .... Job 24:19, 20
In hell .... Mark 9:44-48

B. *Figurative of:*

Insignificance .... Job 25:6
Messiah .... Ps. 22:6

Wormwood—*a bitter-tasting plant*

Figurative of idolatry .... Deut. 29:18
Of adultery .... Prov. 5:4
Of God's judgments .... Jer. 9:15
Symbol of doom .... Rev. 8:11

Worry (see Cares, worldly)

Worship—*an act of reverence*

A. *Of God:*

Defined .... John 4:20-24
Commanded .... 1 Chr. 16:29
Corrupted .... Rom. 1:25
Perverted .... 2 Kin. 21:3, 21
Debated .... 1 Kin. 18:21-39

B. *Of Christ, by:*

Angels .... Heb. 1:6
Magi .... Matt. 2:1-2, 11
Men .... John 9:30-38
Women .... Matt. 15:25
Disciples .... Matt. 28:17
Heavenly choir .... Rev. 4:10, 11

C. *Of wrong objects, such as:*

Heavenly host .... Deut. 17:3
Other gods .... Ex. 34:14
Demons .... Deut. 32:17
Creatures .... Rom. 1:25
Images .... Dan. 3:5-18
Man .... Acts 10:25, 26
Antichrist .... Rev. 13:4-13

D. *Of wrong objects, by:*

Israel .... 2 Kin. 21:3, 21
Pagans .... Rom. 1:25
Professing Christians .... Col. 2:18
World .... 2 Thess. 2:3-12

Worthiness—*acceptableness for some benefit*

A. *Of Christ:*

For more glory .... Heb. 3:3
To open the book .... Rev. 5:2, 4
To receive worship .... Rev. 5:9-14

B. *Of believers, for:*

Provisions .... Matt. 10:10
Discipleship .... Matt. 10:37
Their calling .... Eph. 4:1
Suffering .... Acts 5:41
Their walk .... Col. 1:10
Honor .... 1 Tim. 6:1
Kingdom .... 2 Thess. 1:5

Worthless—*useless, despicable*

Applied to Job's friends .... Job 13:4
Sacrifice .... Is. 1:13
Faith .... 1 Cor. 15:17
Religion .... James 1:26
Worship .... Jer. 51:17, 18

Wound—*to injure*

A. *Of physical injury, by:*

God .... Deut. 32:39
Battle .... 1 Sam. 31:3
Adultery .... Prov. 6:32, 33
Robbers .... Luke 10:30, 34
Evil spirit .... Acts 19:16

B. *Of spiritual injury, by:*

Discouragement .... Prov. 18:14
God's punishment .... Jer. 30:14
Drunkenness .... Prov. 23:29, 30
Adultery .... Prov. 6:32, 33
Sin .... Is. 1:6

Wrappings—*clothes for the dead*

Lazarus attired in .... John 11:43, 44
Jesus lays His aside .... Luke 24:12

Wrath of God

A. *Described as:*

Anger .... Num. 32:10-13
Fury .... Ps. 90:9
Great .... Zech. 7:12
Willing .... Rom. 9:22
Revealed .... Rom. 1:18
Stored up .... Rom. 2:5-8
Abiding .... John 3:36
Accomplished .... Rev. 6:16, 17

B. *Caused by:*

Apostasy .... 2 Chr. 34:24, 25
Sympathy with evil .... Lev. 10:1-6
Unfaithfulness .... Josh. 22:20
Provocations .... 2 Kin. 23:26
Fellowship with evil .... 2 Chr. 19:2
Mockery .... 2 Chr. 36:16
Idolatry .... Ps. 78:58, 59
Intermarriage .... Ezra 10:10-14
Profaning the Sabbath ...... Neh. 13:18
Speaking against God .... Ps. 78:19-21

C. *Effects of, seen in:*

Egypt's destruction .... Ex. 15:4, 7
Great plague .... Num. 11:33
Israel's wanderings .... Num. 32:10-13
Withholding of rain .... Deut. 11:17
Destruction of a people ..... 1 Sam. 28:18
Trouble .... Ps. 90:7
Man's death .... Ps. 90:9
Jerusalem's destruction ...... Luke 21:23, 24
Punishments of hell .... Rev. 14:10
Final judgments .... Rev. 19:15
Israel's captivity .... 2 Chr. 36:16, 17

SUBJECT REFERENCE

D. *Deliverance from, by:*
- Atonement .... Num. 16:46
- Keeping an oath .... Josh. 9:19, 20
- Humbling oneself .... 2 Chr. 32:26
- Intercession .... Ps. 106:23
- Christ .... Rom. 5:8, 9
- God's appointment .... 1 Thess. 5:9

Wrestling
- Sisters .... Gen. 30:8
- Jacob .... Gen. 32:24-30
- Christians .... Eph. 6:12

Write, writing, written

A. *Purposes of, to:*
- Record God's Word .... Ex. 24:4, 12
- Record history .... Luke 1:3
- Record dictation .... Jer. 36:2, 27, 28
- Make legal .... Deut. 24:1-4
- Issue orders .... Esth. 8:5, 8, 10
- Insure a covenant .... Neh. 9:38
- Indicate name .... Luke 1:63
- Indicate the saved .... Rev. 20:15
- Establish inspiration .... Rev. 22:18, 19

B. *Unusual:*
- By God's finger .... Ex. 31:18
- Destroyed and restored .... Jer. 36:21-32
- On a wall .... Dan. 5:5-29
- On the sand .... John 8:6, 8
- On the cross .... John 19:19-22
- In hearts .... Rom. 2:15

C. *Of the Bible as written, involving its:*
- Authority .... Acts 24:14
- Determination of events .... Heb. 10:7
- Fulfillment .... Luke 21:22
- Messianic character .... Luke 24:44, 46
- Saving purpose .... John 20:31
- Harmony .... Acts 15:15
- Spiritual aim .... Rom. 15:4
- Finality .... Rev. 22:18, 19

D. *Figurative of:*
- God's real people .... Rev. 20:12, 15
- Indelible character .... 2 Cor. 3:2, 3
- Innate knowledge .... Rom. 2:15

Y

Yarn—*thread used in weaving*
- Of linen .... 1 Kin. 10:28

Years, thousand
- In God's sight, one day .... 2 Pet. 3:8
- Time of Satan's bondage .... Rev. 20:2-7

Yield—*to produce; to surrender*

A. *Used literally of:*
- Plants .... Gen. 1:11-29
- Earth .... Ps. 67:6
- Standing grain .... Hos. 8:7
- Death .... Acts 5:10
- Fountain .... James 3:12
- God's servants .... Dan. 3:28

B. *Used figuratively of:*
- Discipline .... Heb. 12:11
- Spiritual fruit .... Mark 4:8
- Surrender .... Rom. 6:13, 16

Yoke—*a frame uniting animals for work*

A. *Used literally on:*
- Animals .... Deut. 21:3
- Captives .... Jer. 28:10-14
- Slaves .... 1 Tim. 6:1

B. *Used figuratively of:*
- Oppression .... Deut. 28:48
- Hard service .... 1 Kin. 12:4-14
- Submission .... Jer. 27:8
- Bondage to sin .... Lam. 1:14
- Discipleship .... Matt. 11:29, 30
- Legalistic ordinances .... Gal. 5:1
- Marriage .... 2 Cor. 6:14

Young men

A. *Characteristics of, seen in:*
- Unwise counsel .... 1 Kin. 12:8-14
- Godly fervor .... 1 John 2:13, 14
- Passion .... Prov. 7:7-23
- Strength .... Prov. 20:29
- Impatience .... Luke 15:12, 13

SUBJECT REFERENCE

B. *Special needs of:*
- God's Word .... Ps. 119:9
- Knowledge and discretion .... Prov. 1:4
- Encouragement .... Is. 40:30, 31
- Full surrender .... Matt. 19:20-22
- Soberness .... Titus 2:6
- Counsel .... 1 John 2:13, 14

Youth—*the early age of life*

A. *Evils of, seen in:*
- Sin .... Ps. 25:7
- Lusts .... 2 Tim. 2:22
- Enticements .... Prov. 1:10-16
- Self-will .... Luke 15:12, 13

B. *Good of, seen in:*
- Enthusiasm .... 1 Sam. 17:26-51
- Children .... Ps. 127:3, 4
- Hardships .... Lam. 3:27
- Godly example .... 1 Tim. 4:12

Z

Zaanan—*rich in flocks*
- Town in west Judah .... Mic. 1:11

Zaanannim
- Border point of Naphtali .... Josh. 19:32, 33

Zaavan—*unquiet*
- Son of Ezer .... Gen. 36:27

Zabad—*gift*
1. Descendant of Judah .... 1 Chr. 2:3, 36
2. Ephraimite .... 1 Chr. 7:20, 21
3. One of Joash's murderers .... 2 Chr. 24:26
   Called Jozacar .... 2 Kin. 12:21
4. Son of Zattu .... Ezra 10:27
5. Son of Hashum .... Ezra 10:33
6. Son of Nebo .... Ezra 10:43

Zabbai—(God) *has given*
1. Man who divorced his foreign wife .... Ezra 10:28
2. Father of Baruch .... Neh. 3:20

Zabbud—*given* (by God)
- Postexilic returnee .... Ezra 8:14

Zabdi—(God) *has given*
1. Achan's grandfather .... Josh. 7:1, 17, 18
2. Benjamite .... 1 Chr. 8:1, 19
3. One of David's officers .... 1 Chr. 27:27

Zabdiel—*God has given*
1. Father of Jashobeam .... 1 Chr. 27:2
2. Postexilic official .... Neh. 11:14

Zabud—*bestowed*
- Son of Nathan .... 1 Kin. 4:5

Zaccai—probably a contraction of *"Zechariah"*
- Head of a postexilic family .... Ezra 2:9

Zaccheus—*pure*
- Wealthy tax gatherer converted to Christ .... Luke 19:1-10

Zaccur—*remembered*
1. Father of the Reubenite spy .... Num. 13:2, 4
2. Simeonite .... 1 Chr. 4:24, 26
3. Merarite Levite .... 1 Chr. 24:27
4. Asaphite Levite .... 1 Chr. 25:2, 10
5. Signer of tne covenant .... Neh. 10:1, 12
6. A treasurer under Nehemiah .... Neh. 13:13

Zachariah—*Jehovah has remembered*
1. Son and successor of King Jeroboam II .... {2 Kin. 14:29 / 2 Kin. 15:8-10}
2. Grandfather of Hezekiah .... 2 Kin. 18:1, 2

Zacharias
- Father of John the Baptist .... Luke 1:5-17

Zacher—*memorial*
- Benjamite .... 1 Chr. 8:31

Zadok—*righteous*
1. Descendant of Aaron .... 1 Chr. 24:1-3
   Co-priest with Abiathar .... 2 Sam. 20:25

SUBJECT REFERENCE

- Loyal to David .... 2 Sam. 15:24-29
- Gently rebuked by David .... 2 Sam. 19:11-14
- Remained aloof from Adonijah's usurpation .... 1 Kin. 1:8-26
- Commanded by David to anoint Solomon .... 1 Kin. 1:32-45
- Replaces Abiathar .... 1 Kin. 2:35
- Sons of, faithful .... Ezek. 48:11

2. Priest, the son or grandson of Ahitub .... 1 Chr. 6:12
3. Jotham's maternal grandfather .... 2 Kin. 15:33
4. Postexilic workman, son of Baana .... Neh. 3:4
5. Postexilic workman, son of Immer .... Neh. 3:29
6. Ancestor of Christ .... Matt. 1:14

Zaham—*foul*
- Son of Rehoboam .... 2 Chr. 11:18, 19

Zain
- Letter of the Hebrew alphabet .. Ps. 119:49-56

Zair—*little*
- Battle camp in Edom .... 2 Kin. 8:21

Zalaph—*caper-plant*
- Father of Hanum .... Neh. 3:30

Zalmon—*dark*
1. One of David's mighty men .... 2 Sam. 23:28
2. Mount near Shechem .... Judg. 9:48

Zalmonah—*shady*
- Israelite camp .... Num. 33:41, 42

Zalmunna—*deprived of shade*
- Midianite king .... Judg. 8:4-21

Zamzummims—*murmurers*
- Race of giants .... Deut. 2:20, 21
- Same as the Zuzim .... Gen. 14:5

Zanoah—*rejected*
1. Town in south Judah .... Josh. 15:1, 34
2. Town of Judah .... Josh. 15:56

Zaphnath-paaneah—*revealer of secrets*
- Name given to Joseph by Pharaoh .... Gen. 41:45

Zaphon—*concealed*
- Town of Gad east of the Jordan .... Josh. 13:24, 27

Zared—*willow bush*
- Brook and valley crossed by Israel .... Num. 21:12

Zarephath
- Town of Sidon where Elijah restores widow's son .... {1 Kin. 17:8-24 / Luke 4:26}

Zaretan, Zartanah, Zarthan—*cooling*
- Town near Jezreel .... Josh. 3:16; 1 Kin. 4:12
- Hiram worked near .... 1 Kin. 7:46

Zareth-shahar—*the splendor of dawn*
- City of Reuben .... Josh. 13:19

Zattu, Zatthu—*lovely*
- Founder of a postexilic family .... Ezra 2:2, 8
- Members of, divorced foreign wives .... Ezra 10:18, 19, 27
- Signs covenant .... Neh. 10:1, 14

Zayin
- Letter of the Hebrew alphabet .. Ps. 119:49-56

Zaza—*projection*
- Jerahmeelite .... 1 Chr. 2:33

Zeal—*intense enthusiasm for something*

A. *Kinds of:*
- Divine .... Is. 9:7
- Glorious .... Is. 63:15
- Wrathful .... Ezek. 5:13
- Stirring .... 2 Cor. 9:2
- Intense .... 2 Cor. 7:11
- Boastful .... Phil. 3:4, 6
- Ignorant .... Rom. 10:2, 3
- Righteous .... John 2:15-17
- Sinful .... 2 Sam. 21:1, 2

SUBJECT REFERENCE

B. *Manifested in concern for:*
Lord's sake ... Num. 25:11, 13
Others' salvation ... Rom. 10:1
Missionary work ... Rom. 15:18-25
Reformation of character ... 2 Cor. 7:11
Desire for spiritual gifts ... 1 Cor. 14:12
Doing good works ... Titus 2:14

C. *Illustrated in Paul's life by his:*
Desire to reach the Jews ... Rom. 9:1-3; Rom. 10:1
Determination to evangelize all ... 1 Cor. 9:19-23
Willingness to lose all things for Christ ... Phil. 3:4-16
Plan to minister to unreached places ... Rom. 1:14, 15
Support of himself ... 2 Cor. 11:7-12

D. *Examples of:*
Moses ... Ex. 32:19-32
Phinehas ... Num. 25:7-13
Joshua ... Josh. 24:14-16
Gideon ... Judg. 6:11-32
David ... 1 Sam. 17:26-51
Elijah ... 1 Kin. 19:10
Jehu ... 2 Kin. 9:1-37
Josiah ... 2 Kin. 22:1-20
Ezra ... Ezra 7:10
Nehemiah ... Neh. 4:1-23
Peter and John ... Acts 4:8-20
Timothy ... Phil. 2:19-22
Epaphroditus ... Phil. 2:25-30
Epaphras ... Col. 4:12, 13

Zealot—*zealous one*
Applied to Simon, the Canaanite; a party of fanatical Jews ... Luke 6:15

Zebadiah—*Jehovah has bestowed*
1, 2. Two Benjamites ... 1 Chr. 8:1, 15, 17
3. Benjamite warrior among David's mighty men ... 1 Chr. 12:1-7
4. One of David's commanders ... 1 Chr. 27:7
5. Korahite Levite ... 1 Chr. 26:1, 2
6. Levite teacher under Jehoshaphat ... 2 Chr. 17:8
7. Officer of Jehoshaphat ... 2 Chr. 19:11
8. Postexilic returnee ... Ezra 8:8
9. Priest who put away his foreign wife ... Ezra 10:20

Zebah—*victim; sacrifice*
King of Midian killed by Gideon ... Judg. 8:4-28

Zebaim—*gazelles*
Native place of Solomon's slaves ... Ezra 2:55, 57

Zebedee—*Jehovah is gift*
Galilean fisherman; father of James and John ... Matt. 4:21, 22

Zebina—*purchased*
Priest who put away his foreign wife ... Ezra 10:43

Zeboim—*hyenas*
1. One of five cities destroyed with Sodom and Gomorrah ... Gen. 10:19
2. Valley in Benjamin ... 1 Sam. 13:16-18
3. City of Judah ... Neh. 11:34

Zebudah—*given*
Mother of Jehoiakim ... 2 Kin. 23:36

Zebul—*hesitation*
Ruler of Shechem; exposes Gaal's revolt ... Judg. 9:26-41

Zebulun—*dwelling*
1. Sixth son of Leah and Jacob ... Gen. 30:19, 20
2. Descendants of 1; a tribe of Israel ... Num. 2:7
Predictions concerning ... Gen. 49:13
First numbering of ... Num. 1:30, 31
Second numbering of ... Num. 26:27
Representatives of ... Num. 1:9
Territory of ... Josh. 19:10-16
Warriors of, fight with Deborah ... Judg. 5:14, 18
Warriors of, aid Gideon ... Judg. 6:34, 35
Judge Elon, member of ... Judg. 12:11, 12
Warriors of, in David's army ... 1 Chr. 12:33, 40
Some of, respond to Hezekiah's reforms ... 2 Chr. 30:10-18
Christ visits land of ... Is. 9:1; Matt. 4:13-15
Those sealed of ... Rev. 7:8

Zebulunites—*natives of Zebulun*
Descendants of Jacob's son ... Num. 26:27
Elon thus called ... Judg. 12:11, 12

Zechariah—*Jehovah remembers*
1. Benjamite ... 1 Chr. 9:35, 37
2. Levite porter and counselor ... 1 Chr. 9:21, 22
3. Levite musician in David's reign ... 1 Chr. 15:18, 20
4. Priestly trumpeter ... 1 Chr. 15:24
5. Kohathite Levite ... 1 Chr. 24:25
6. Merarite Levite in David's reign ... 1 Chr. 26:10, 11
7. Manassite ... 1 Chr. 27:21
8. Teaching prince under Jehoshaphat ... 2 Chr. 17:7
9. Asaphite Levite ... 2 Chr. 20:14
10. Son of King Jehoshaphat ... 2 Chr. 21:2-4
11. Son of Jehoiada killed in the Temple ... 2 Chr. 24:20-22; Matt. 23:35
12. Prophet in Uzziah's reign ... 2 Chr. 26:5
13. King of Israel; last ruler of Jehu's dynasty ... 2 Kin. 15:8-12
14. Reubenite chief ... 1 Chr. 5:7
15. Faithful man in Isaiah's time ... Is. 8:2
16. Hezekiah's maternal grandfather ... 2 Chr. 29:1
17. Levite during Hezekiah's reign ... 2 Chr. 29:13
18. Kohathite Levite employed as overseer ... 2 Chr. 34:12
19. Temple ruler during Josiah's reign ... 2 Chr. 35:8
20. Postexilic returnee ... Ezra 8:3
21. Son of Bebai ... Ezra 8:11
22. Man sent by Ezra to secure Levites ... Ezra 8:15, 16
23. One of Ezra's assistants ... Neh. 8:4
24. Jew who divorced his foreign wife ... Ezra 10:26
25. Levite trumpeter ... Neh. 12:35, 36
26. Priest in dedication ceremony ... Neh. 12:41
27. Man of Judah, family of Perez ... Neh. 11:4
28. Man of Judah, son of a Shilonite ... Neh. 11:5
29. Postexilic priest ... Neh. 11:2
30. Postexilic prophet and priest ... Ezra 5:1; Zech. 1:1, 7

Zechariah, the Book of—*a book of the Old Testament*
Call to repentance ... Zech. 1:2-6
The visions ... Zech. 1:7—6:15
Against insincerity and disobedience ... Zech. 7:1-14
Restoration of Jerusalem ... Zech. 8:1-23
Against nations ... Zech. 9:1-8
The King comes ... Zech. 9:9-17
Parable of shepherds ... Zech. 11:4-17
Jerusalem spoiled ... Zech. 14:1-6
Jerusalem restored ... Zech. 14:7-21

Zedad—*siding*
Place on Palestine's north boundary ... Num. 34:8; Ezek. 47:15

Zedekiah, Zidkijah—*Jehovah is righteousness*
1. False prophet who counsels Ahab unwisely ... 1 Kin. 22:6-24
2. Immoral prophet killed by Nebuchadnezzar ... Jer. 29:21-23
3. Prince under King Jehoiakim ... Jer. 36:12
4. Son of Jeconiah ... 1 Chr. 3:16
5. Last king of Judah; uncle and successor of Jehoiachin ... 2 Kin. 24:17, 18
Reigns wickedly for 11 years ... 2 Chr. 36:11-13
Rebels against Jeremiah ... 2 Chr. 36:12
Rebels against Nebuchadnezzar ... Jer. 52:3
Makes alliance with Egypt ... Ezek. 17:11-21
Rebellion of, denounced by Jeremiah ... Jer. 34:1-22
Consults with Jeremiah ... Jer. 37:15-21; Jer. 38:14-28
Imprisons Jeremiah ... Jer. 38:1-13
Captured, blinded, taken to Babylon ... Jer. 39:1-14; 2 Kin. 25:1-7
6. High official who signs the covenant ... Neh. 10:1

Zeeb—*wolf*
Midianite prince slain by Gideon's men ... Judg. 7:25

Zelah—*rib*
Towns assigned to Benjamin ... Josh. 18:28
Burial place of Kish, Saul, and Jonathan ... 2 Sam. 21:14

Zelek—*cleft*
One of David's mighty men ... 2 Sam. 23:37

Zelophehad—*shadow of the fear*
Manassite whose five daughters secure female rights ... Num. 27:1-7

Zelzah—*sun protection*
Town in south Benjamin near Rachel's tomb ... Gen. 48:7

Zemaraim—*double mount forest*
1. Town of Benjamin near Jericho ... Josh. 18:22
2. Mountain in Ephraim ... 2 Chr. 13:4

Zemarites
Tribe of Canaanites ... Gen. 10:18

Zemira—*song*
Grandson of Benjamin ... 1 Chr. 7:6, 8

Zenan—*place of flocks*
Town in Judah ... Josh. 15:21, 37

Zenas—*gift of Zeus*
Christian lawyer ... Titus 3:13

Zephaniah—*hidden of Jehovah*
1. Ancestor of Samuel ... 1 Chr. 6:33, 36
2. Author of Zephaniah ... Zeph. 1:1
3. Priest and friend of Jeremiah during Zedekiah's reign ... Jer. 21:1
4. Father of a certain Josiah in Zechariah's time ... Zech. 6:10

Zephaniah, the Book of—*a book of the Old Testament*
Coming judgment ... Zeph. 1:2-18
Call to repentance ... Zeph. 2:1-3
The nations judged ... Zeph. 2:4-15
Jerusalem is blessed ... Zeph. 3:9-20

Zephath—*watchtower*
Canaanite town destroyed by Simeon and Judah ... Judg. 1:17
See Hormah

Zephathah
Valley near Mareshah ... 2 Chr. 14:10

Zepho—*watch*
Grandson of Esau and a duke of Edom ... Gen. 36:15, 19; 1 Chr. 1:36

Zephon—*watching*
Son of Gad and tribal head ... Num. 26:15
Called Ziphion ... Gen. 46:16

Zer—*rock*
City assigned to Naphtali ... Josh. 19:32, 35

SUBJECT — REFERENCE

Zerah—*dawning*
1. Son of Reuel and duke of Edom .... Gen. 36:17, 19; 1 Chr. 1:44
2. Son of Judah .... Num. 26:20
   Ancestor of Achan .... Josh. 7:1-18
3. Son of Simeon and tribal head .... Num. 26:12, 13
   Called Zohar .... Gen. 46:10
4. Gershomite Levite .... 1 Chr. 6:20, 21, 41
5. Ethiopian general defeated by King Asa .... 2 Chr. 14:8-15

Zerahiah—*Jehovah is appearing*
1. Ancestor of Ezra .... Ezra 7:1, 4, 5
2. Son of Pahath-moab .... Ezra 8:4

Zereda, Zeredathah—*the fortress*
1. City of Ephraim; birthplace of Jeroboam .... 1 Kin. 11:26
2. City in the Jordan valley .... 2 Chr. 4:17
   Same as Zarethan in .... 1 Kin. 7:46

Zererath
Town in the Jordan valley .... Judg. 7:22
Same as Zarthan .... 1 Kin. 7:46

Zeresh—*golden*
Wife of Haman .... Esth. 5:10, 14

Zereth—*splendor*
Judahite .... 1 Chr. 4:5-7

Zereth-shahar—*the splendor of dawn*
City of Reuben .... Josh. 13:19

Zeror—*bundle*
Benjamite .... 1 Sam. 9:1

Zeruah—*smitten; leprous*
Mother of King Jeroboam I .... 1 Kin. 11:26

Zerubbabel, Zorobabel—*seed of Babel*
Descendant of David .... 1 Chr. 3:19
Leader of Jewish exiles .... Neh. 7:6, 7
Restores worship in Jerusalem .... Ezra 3:1-8
Rebuilds the Temple .... Zech. 4:1-14
Prophecy concerning .... Hag. 2:23
Ancestor of Christ .... Matt. 1:12, 13; Luke 3:27

Zeruiah—*balm*
Mother of Joab .... 2 Sam. 17:25

Zetham—*olive tree*
Gershonite Levite .... 1 Chr. 23:7, 8

Zethan—*olive tree*
Benjamite .... 1 Chr. 7:6, 10

Zethar—*sacrifice*
One of the seven chamberlains of King Ahasuerus .... Esth. 1:10

Zia—*the trembler*
Gadite .... 1 Chr. 5:11, 13

Ziba—*plant*
Saul's servant .... 2 Sam. 9:9
Befriends David .... 2 Sam. 16:1-4
Accused of deception by Mephibosheth .... 2 Sam. 19:17-30

Zibeon—*hyena*
Son of Seir and a clan chief .... Gen. 36:20, 21

Zibia—*gazelle*
Benjamite and household head .. 1 Chr. 8:8, 9

Zibiah—*gazelle*
Mother of King Jehoash .... 2 Kin. 12:1

Zichri—*famous*
1. Kohathite Levite .... Ex. 6:21
2, 3, 4. Three Benjamites .... 1 Chr. 8:19, 23, 27
5. Son of Asaph .... 1 Chr. 9:15
6. Descendant of Moses .... 1 Chr. 26:25
7. Reubenite .... 1 Chr. 27:16
8. Judahite .... 2 Chr. 17:16
9. Mighty man in Pekah's army .... 2 Chr. 28:7
10. Benjamite .... Neh. 11:9
11. Postexilic priest .... Neh. 12:17

Ziddim—*sides*
City of Naphtali .... Josh. 19:35

Zif—*splendor, bloom*
Second month of the Jewish year .... 1 Kin. 6:1

Ziha
Head of a Nethinim family .... Ezra 2:43

Ziklag—*winding*
City on the border of Judah .... Josh. 15:1, 31
Assigned to Simeon .... Josh. 19:1, 5
Held by David .... 1 Sam. 27:6
Overthrown by Amalekites .... 1 Sam. 30:1-31
Occupied by returnees .... Neh. 11:28

Zillah—*shadow*
One of Lamech's wives .... Gen. 4:19-23

Zilpah—*a drop*
Leah's maid .... Gen. 29:24
Mother of Gad and Asher .... Gen. 30:9-13

Zilthai—*shadow of Jehovah*
1. Benjamite .... 1 Chr. 8:20
2. Manassite captain .... 1 Chr. 12:20

Zimmah—*counsel*
Gershonite Levite .... 1 Chr. 6:20, 42, 43

Zimran—*antelope*
Son of Abraham and Keturah .... Gen. 25:1, 2

Zimri—*pertaining to an antelope*
1. Grandson of Judah .... 1 Chr. 2:3-6
   Called Zabdi .... Josh. 7:1-18
2. Simeonite prince slain by Phinehas .... Num. 25:6-14
3. Benjamite .... 1 Chr. 8:1, 36
4. King of Israel for seven days .... 1 Kin. 16:8-20
5. Place or people otherwise unknown .... Jer. 25:25

Zin—*low land*
Wilderness through which the Israelites passed .... Num. 20:1
Border of Judah and Edom .... Josh. 15:1-3

Zina—*abundance*
Son of Shimei .... 1 Chr. 23:10

Zion—*fortress*
A. *Used literally of:*
   Jebusite fortress captured by David .... 2 Sam. 5:6-9
   Place from which Solomon brings the ark .... 2 Chr. 5:2
   Area occupied by the Temple .... Is. 8:18
B. *Used figuratively of:*
   Israel as a people of God .... 2 Kin. 19:21
   God's spiritual kingdom .... Ps. 125:1
   Eternal city .... Heb. 12:22, 28
   Heaven .... Rev. 14:1

Zior—*smallness*
Town of Judah .... Josh. 15:54

Ziph—*refining place*
1. Town in south Judah .... Josh. 15:24
2. City in the hill country of Judah .... Josh. 15:55
   David hides from Saul in wilderness here .... 1 Sam. 23:14, 15
3. Son of Jehaleleel .... 1 Chr. 4:16

Ziphah—*lent*
Son of Jehaleleel .... 1 Chr. 4:16

Ziphites—*inhabitants of Ziph*
Betray David .... 1 Sam. 23:19-24

Ziphron—*beautiful top*
Place in north Palestine .... Num. 34:9

Zippor—*sparrow*
Father of Balak .... Num. 22:4, 10

Zipporah—*bird*
Daughter of Jethro; wife of Moses .... Ex. 18:1, 2

Zithri—*my protection*
Grandson of Kohath .... Ex. 6:18, 22

Ziz—*brightness*
Pass leading from Dead Sea to Jerusalem .... 2 Chr. 20:16

Ziza—*brightness*
1. Simeonite leader .... 1 Chr. 4:24, 37, 38
2. Son of Rehoboam .... 2 Chr. 11:18-20

Zizah
Gershonite Levite .... 1 Chr. 23:7, 10, 11
See Zina

Zoan
City in Lower Egypt .... Num. 13:22
Places of God's miracles .... Ps. 78:12, 43
Princes resided at .... Is. 30:2, 4
Object of God's wrath .... Ezek. 30:14

Zoar—*little*
Ancient city of Canaan originally named Bela .... Gen. 14:2, 8
Spared destruction at Lot's request .... Gen. 19:20-23
Seen by Moses from Mt. Pisgah .... Deut. 34:1-3
Object of prophetic doom .... Is. 15:5

Zobah
Syrian kingdom; wars against Saul .... 1 Sam. 14:47

Zobebah—*the affable*
Judahite .... 1 Chr. 4:1, 8

Zohar—*gray*
1. Father of Ephron the Hittite .... Gen. 23:8
2. Son of Simeon .... Gen. 46:10

Zoheleth—*serpent*
Stone near En-rogel .... 1 Kin. 1:9

Zoheth—*proud*
Descendant of Judah .... 1 Chr. 4:1, 20

Zophah—*pot-bellied jug*
Asherite .... 1 Chr. 7:30, 35, 36

Zophar—*chirper*
Naamathite and friend of Job .... Job 2:11

Zophim—*watchers*
Field on the top of Mt. Pisgah .... Num. 23:14

Zorah, Zareah, Zoreah—*hornet*
Town of Judah .... Josh. 15:1, 33
Inhabited by Danites .... Josh. 19:40, 41
Place of Samson's birth and burial .... Judg. 13:24, 25; Judg. 16:30, 31
Inhabited by returnees .... Neh. 11:25, 29

Zorathite
Native of Zorah .... 1 Chr. 4:2
Descendants of Caleb .... 1 Chr. 2:50, 53

Zorite
Same as Zorathite .... 1 Chr. 2:54

Zuar—*small, little*
Father of Nethaneel .... Num. 1:8

Zuph—*honeycomb*
1. Ancestor of Samuel .... 1 Chr. 6:33, 35
2. Region in Judah .... 1 Sam. 9:4-6

Zur—*rock*
1. A Midianite leader .... Num. 25:15, 18
2. Son of Jehiel .... 1 Chr. 8:30

Zuriel—*God is a rock*
Merarite Levite .... Num. 3:35

Zurishaddai—*the Almighty is a rock*
Father of Shelumiel .... Num. 7:36, 41

Zuzim—*prominent; giant*
Tribe east of the Jordan .... Gen. 14:5
Probably same as Zamzummims .... Deut. 2:20

Harmony of the Gospels

Date	Event	Location	Matthew	Mark	Luke	John	Related References
	Luke's Introduction				1:1–4		Acts 1:1
	Pre-fleshly state of Christ					1:1–18	Heb. 1:1–14
	Genealogy of Jesus Christ		1:1–17		3:23–38		Ruth 4:18–22 1 Chr. 1:1–4
	BIRTH, INFANCY, AND ADOLESCENCE OF JESUS AND JOHN THE BAPTIST IN 17 EVENTS						
7 B.C.	(1) Announcement of Birth of John	Jerusalem (Temple)			1:5–25		Num. 6:3
7 or 6 B.C.	(2) Announcement of Birth of Jesus to the Virgin	Nazareth			1:26–38		Is. 7:14
c. 5 B.C.	(3) Song of Elizabeth to Mary	Hill Country of Judea			1:39–45		
	(4) Mary's Song of Praise				1:46–56		Ps. 103:17
5 B.C.	(5) Birth, Infancy, and Purpose for Future of John the Baptist	Judea			1:57–80		Mal. 3:1
	(6) Announcement of Jesus' Birth to Joseph	Nazareth	1:18–25				Is. 9:6, 7
5–4 B.C.	(7) Birth of Jesus Christ	Bethlehem	1:24, 25		2:1–7		Is. 7:14
	(8) Proclamation by the Angels	Near Bethlehem			2:8–14		1 Tim. 3:16
	(9) The Visit of Homage by Shepherds	Bethlehem			2:15–20		
	(10) Jesus' Circumcision	Bethlehem			2:21		Lev. 12:3
4 B.C.	(11) First Temple Visit with Acknowledgments by Simeon and Anna	Jerusalem			2:22–38		Ex. 13:2 Lev. 12
	(12) Visit of the Wise Men	Jerusalem & Bethlehem	2:1–12				Num. 24:17
	(13) Flight into Egypt and Massacre of Innocents	Bethlehem, Jerusalem & Egypt	2:13–18				Jer. 31:15
	(14) From Egypt to Nazareth with Jesus		2:19–23		2:39		
Afterward	(15) Childhood of Jesus	Nazareth			2:40, 51		
A.D. 7–8	(16) Jesus, 12 Years Old, Visits the Temple	Jerusalem			2:41–50		Deut. 16:1–8
Afterward	(17) 18-Year Account of Jesus' Adolescence and Adulthood	Nazareth			2:51, 52		1 Sam. 2:26
	TRUTHS ABOUT JOHN THE BAPTIST						
c. A.D. 25–27	John's Ministry Begins	Judean Wilderness	3:1	1:1–4	3:1, 2	1:19–28	Mal. 3:1
	Man and Message		3:2–12	1:2–8	3:3–14		Is. 40:3
	His Picture of Jesus		3:11, 12	1:7, 8	3:15–18	1:26, 27	Acts 2:38
	His Courage		14:4–12		3:19, 20		
	BEGINNING OF JESUS' MINISTRY IN 12 EVENTS						
c. A.D. 27	(1) Jesus Baptized	Jordan River	3:13–17	1:9–11	3:21–23	1:29–34	Ps. 2:7
	(2) Jesus Tempted	Wilderness	4:1–11	1:12, 13	4:1–13		Ps. 91:11
	(3) Calls First Disciples	Beyond Jordan				1:35–51	
	(4) The First Miracle	Cana in Galilee				2:1–11	
	(5) First Stay in Capernaum	(Capernaum is "His" city)				2:12	
A.D. 27	(6) First Cleansing of the Temple	Jerusalem				2:13–22	Ps. 69:9
	(7) Received at Jerusalem	Judea				2:23–25	
	(8) Teaches Nicodemus about Second Birth	Judea				3:1–21	Num. 21:8, 9
	(9) Co-Ministry with John	Judea				3:22–30	

Date	Event	Location	Matthew	Mark	Luke	John	Related References
A.D. 27	(10) Leaves for Galilee	Judea	4:12	1:14	4:14	4:1–4	
	(11) Samaritan Woman at Jacob's Well	Samaria				4:5–42	Josh. 24:32
	(12) Returns to Galilee			1:15	4:15	4:43–45	
A.D. 27–29	**THE GALILEAN MINISTRY OF JESUS IN 55 EVENTS**						
A.D. 27	(1) Healing of the Nobleman's Son	Cana				4:46–54	
	(2) Rejected at Nazareth	Nazareth			4:16–30		Is. 61:1, 2
	(3) Moved to Capernaum	Capernaum	4:13–17				Is. 9:1, 2
	(4) Four Become Fishers of Men	Sea of Galilee	4:18–22	1:16–20	5:1–11		Ps. 33:9
	(5) Demoniac Healed on the Sabbath Day	Capernaum		1:21–28	4:31–37		
	(6) Peter's Mother-in-Law Cured, Plus Others	Capernaum	8:14–17	1:29–34	4:38–41		Is. 53:4
c. A.D. 27	(7) First Preaching Tour of Galilee	Galilee	4:23–25	1:35–39	4:42–44		
	(8) Leper Healed and Response Recorded	Galilee	8:1–4	1:40–45	5:12–16		Lev. 13:49
	(9) Paralytic Healed	Capernaum	9:1–8	2:1–12	5:17–26		Rom. 3:23
	(10) Matthew's Call and Reception Held	Capernaum	9:9–13	2:13–17	5:27–32		Hos. 6:6
	(11) Disciples Defended via a Parable	Capernaum	9:14–17	2:18–22	5:33–39		
A.D. 28	(12) Goes to Jerusalem for Second Passover; Heals Lame Man	Jerusalem				5:1–47	Ex. 20:10
	(13) Plucked Grain Precipitates Sabbath Controversy	En Route to Galilee	12:1–8	2:23–28	6:1–5		Deut. 5:14
	(14) Withered Hand Healed Causes Another Sabbath Controversy	Galilee	12:9–14	3:1–6	6:6–11		
	(15) Multitudes Healed	Sea of Galilee	12:15–21	3:7–12	6:17–19		
	(16) Twelve Apostles Selected After a Night of Prayer	Near Capernaum		3:13–19	6:12–16		
	(17) Sermon on the Mt.	Near Capernaum	5:1—7:29		6:20–49		
	(18) Centurion's Servant Healed	Capernaum	8:5–13		7:1–10		Is. 49:12, 13
	(19) Raises Widow's Son from Dead	Nain			7:11–17		Job 19:25
	(20) Jesus Allays John's Doubts	Galilee	11:2–19		7:18–35		Mal. 3:1
	(21) Woes Upon the Privileged		11:20–30				Gen. 19:24
	(22) A Sinful Woman Anoints Jesus	Simon's House, Capernaum			7:36–50		
	(23) Another Tour of Galilee	Galilee			8:1–3		
	(24) Jesus Accused of Blasphemy	Capernaum	12:22–37	3:20–30	11:14–23		
	(25) Jesus' Answer to a Demand for a Sign	Capernaum	12:38–45		11:24–26, 29–36		
	(26) Mother, Brothers Seek Audience	Capernaum	12:46–50	3:31–35	8:19–21		
	(27) Famous Parables of Sower, Seed, Tares, Mustard Seed, Leaven, Treasure, Pearl, Dragnet, Lamp Told	By Sea of Galilee	13:1–52	4:1–34	8:4–18		Joel 3:13
	(28) Sea Made Serene	Sea of Galilee	8:23–27	4:35–41	8:22–25		
	(29) Gadarene Demoniac Healed	E. Shore of Galilee	8:28–34	5:1–20	8:26–39		
	(30) Jairus' Daughter Raised and Woman with Hemorrhage Healed		9:18–26	5:21–43	8:40–56		
	(31) Two Blind Men's Sight Restored		9:27–31				

Date	Event	Location	Matthew	Mark	Luke	John	Related References
A.D. 28	(32) Mute Demoniac Healed		9:32–34				
	(33) Nazareth's Second Rejection of Christ	Nazareth	13:53–58	6:1–6			
	(34) Twelve Sent Out		9:35—11:1	6:6–13	9:1–6		1 Cor. 9:14
	(35) Fearful Herod Beheads John	Galilee	14:1–12	6:14–29	9:7–9		
Spring A.D. 29	(36) Return of 12, Jesus Withdraws, 5000 Fed	Near Bethsaida	14:13–21	6:30–44	9:10–17	6:1–14	
	(37) Walks on the Water	Sea of Galilee	14:22–33	6:45–52		6:15–21	
	(38) Sick of Gennesaret Healed	Gennesaret	14:34–36	6:53–56			
	(39) Peak of Popularity Passes in Galilee	Capernaum				6:22–71 7:1	Is. 54:13
A.D. 29	(40) Traditions Attacked		15:1–20	7:1–23			Ex. 21:17
	(41) Aborted Retirement in Phoenicia: Syro-Phoenician Healed	Phoenicia	15:21–28	7:24–30			
	(42) Afflicted Healed	Decapolis	15:29–31	7:31–37			
	(43) 4000 Fed	Decapolis	15:32–39	8:1–9			
	(44) Pharisees Increase Attack	Magdala	16:1–4	8:10–13			
	(45) Disciples' Carelessness Condemned; Blind Man Healed		16:5–12	8:14–26			Jer. 5:21
	(46) Peter Confesses Jesus Is the Christ	Near Caesarea Philippi	16:13–20	8:27–30	9:18–21		
	(47) Jesus Foretells His Death	Caesarea Philippi	16:21–26	8:31–37	9:22–25		
	(48) Kingdom Promised		16:27, 28	9:1	9:26, 27		Prov. 24:12
	(49) The Transfiguration	Mountain Unnamed	17:1–13	9:2–13	9:28–36		Is. 42:1
	(50) Epileptic Healed	Mt. of Transfiguration	17:14–21	9:14–29	9:37–42		
	(51) Again Tells of Death, Resurrection	Galilee	17:22, 23	9:30–32	9:43–45		
	(52) Taxes Paid	Capernaum	17:24–27				Ex. 30:11–15
	(53) Disciples Contend About Greatness; Jesus Defines; also Patience, Loyalty, Forgiveness	Capernaum	18:1–35	9:33–50	9:46–62		
	(54) Jesus Rejects Brothers' Advice	Galilee				7:2–9	
c. Sept. A.D. 29	(55) Galilee Departure and Samaritan Rejection		19:1		9:51–56	7:10	

A.D. 29–30 LAST JUDEAN AND PEREAN MINISTRY OF JESUS IN 42 EVENTS

Date	Event	Location	Matthew	Mark	Luke	John	Related References
Oct. A.D. 29	(1) Feast of Tabernacles	Jerusalem				7:2, 11–52	
	(2) Forgiveness of Adulteress	Jerusalem				7:53—8:11	Lev. 20:10
A.D. 29	(3) Christ—the Light of the World	Jerusalem				8:12–20	
	(4) Pharisees Can't Meet the Prophecy Thus Try to Destroy the Prophet	Jerusalem—Temple				8:12–59	Is. 6:9
	(5) Man Born Blind Healed; Following Consequences	Jerusalem				9:1–41	
	(6) Parable of the Good Shepherd	Jerusalem				10:1–21	
	(7) The Service of the Seventy	Probably Judea			10:1–24		
	(8) Lawyer Hears the Story of the Good Samaritan	Judea (?)			10:25–37		
	(9) The Hospitality of Martha and Mary	Bethany			10:38–42		
	(10) Another Lesson on Prayer	Judea (?)			11:1–13		

Date	Event	Location	Matthew	Mark	Luke	John	Related References
A.D. 29	(11) Accused of Connection with Beelzebub				11:14–36		
	(12) Judgment Against Lawyers and Pharisees				11:37–54		Mic. 6:8
	(13) Jesus Deals with Hypocrisy, Covetousness, Worry, and Alertness				12:1–59		Mic. 7:6
	(14) Repent or Perish				13:1–5		
	(15) Barren Fig Tree				13:6–9		
	(16) Crippled Woman Healed on Sabbath				13:10–17		Deut. 5:12–15
	(17) Parables of Mustard Seed and Leaven	Probably Perea			13:18–21		
Winter A.D. 29	(18) Feast of Dedication	Jerusalem				10:22–39	Ps. 82:6
	(19) Withdrawal Beyond Jordan					10:40–42	
	(20) Begins Teaching Return to Jerusalem with Special Words About Herod	Perea			13:22–35		Ps. 6:8
	(21) Meal with a Pharisee Ruler Occasions Healing Man with Dropsy; Parables of Ox, Best Places, and Great Supper				14:1–24		
	(22) Demands of Discipleship	Perea			14:25–35		
	(23) Parables of Lost Sheep, Coin, Son				15:1–32		1 Pet. 2:25
	(24) Parables of Unjust Steward, Rich Man and Lazarus				16:1–31		
	(25) Lessons on Service, Faith, Influence				17:1–10		
	(26) Resurrection of Lazarus	Perea to Bethany				11:1–44	
	(27) Reaction to It: Withdrawal of Jesus					11:45–54	
A.D. 30	(28) Begins Last Journey to Jerusalem via Samaria & Galilee	Samaria, Galilee			17:11		
	(29) Heals Ten Lepers				17:12–19		Lev. 13:45, 46
	(30) Lessons on the Coming Kingdom				17:20–37		Gen. 6—7
	(31) Parables: Persistent Widow, Pharisee and Tax Collector				18:1–14		
	(32) Doctrine on Divorce		19:1–12	10:1–12			Deut. 24:1–4 Gen. 2:23–25
	(33) Jesus Blesses Children: Objections	Perea	19:13–15	10:13–16	18:15–17		Ps. 131:2
	(34) Rich Young Ruler	Perea	19:16–30	10:17–31	18:18–30		Ex. 20:1–17
	(35) Laborers of the 11th Hour		20:1–16				
	(36) Foretells Death and Resurrection	Near Jordan	20:17–19	10:32–34	18:31–34		Ps. 22
	(37) Ambition of James and John		20:20–28	10:35–45			
	(38) Blind Bartimaeus Healed	Jericho		10:46–52	18:35–43		
	(39) Interview with Zacchaeus	Jericho			19:1–10		
	(40) Parable: the Minas	Jericho			19:11–27		
	(41) Returns to Home of Mary and Martha	Bethany				11:55—12:1	
	(42) Plot to Kill Lazarus	Bethany				12:9–11	
Spring A.D. 30	**JESUS' FINAL WEEK OF WORK AT JERUSALEM IN 41 EVENTS**						
Sunday	(1) Triumphal Entry	Bethany, Jerusalem, Bethany	21:1–9	11:1–11	19:28–44	12:12–19	Zech. 9:9

Date	Event	Location	Matthew	Mark	Luke	John	Related References
Monday	(2) Fig Tree Cursed and Temple Cleansed	Bethany to Jerusalem	21:10–19	11:12–18	19:45–48		Jer. 7:11
	(3) The Attraction of Sacrifice	Jerusalem				12:20–50	Is. 6:10
Tuesday	(4) Withered Fig Tree Testifies	Bethany to Jerusalem	21:20–22	11:19–26			
	(5) Sanhedrin Challenges Jesus. Answered by Parables: Two Sons, Wicked Vinedressers and Marriage Feast	Jerusalem	21:23—22:14	11:27—12:12	20:1–19		Is. 5:1, 2
	(6) Tribute to Caesar	Jerusalem	22:15–22	12:13–17	20:20–26		
	(7) Sadducees Question the Resurrection	Jerusalem	22:23–33	12:18–27	20:27–40		Ex. 3:6
	(8) Pharisees Question Commandments	Jerusalem	22:34–40	12:28–34			
	(9) Jesus and David	Jerusalem	22:41–46	12:35–37	20:41–44		Ps. 110:1
	(10) Jesus' Last Sermon	Jerusalem	23:1–39	12:38–40	20:45–47		
	(11) Widow's Mite	Jerusalem		12:41–44	21:1–4		Lev. 27:30
	(12) Jesus Tells of the Future	Mt. Olives	24:1–51	13:1–37	21:5–36		Dan. 12:1
	(13) Parables: Ten Virgins, Talents. The Day of Judgment	Mt. Olives	25:1–46				Zech. 14:5
	(14) Jesus Tells Date of Crucifixion		26:1–5	14:1, 2	22:1, 2		
	(15) Anointing by Mary at Simon's Feast	Bethany	26:6–13	14:3–9		12:2–8	
	(16) Judas Contracts the Betrayal		26:14–16	14:10, 11	22:3–6		Zech. 11:12
Thursday	(17) Preparation for the Passover	Jerusalem	26:17–19	14:12–16	22:7–13		Ex. 12:14–28
Thursday P.M.	(18) Passover Eaten, Jealousy Rebuked	Jerusalem	26:20	14:17	22:14–16, 24–30		
	(19) Feet Washed	Upper Room				13:1–20	
	(20) Judas Revealed, Defects	Upper Room	26:21–25	14:18–21	22:21–23	13:21–30	Ps. 41:9
	(21) Jesus Warns About Further Desertion; Cries of Loyalty	Upper Room	26:31–35	14:27–31	22:31–38	13:31–38	Zech. 13:7
	(22) Institution of the Lord's Supper	Upper Room	26:26–29	14:22–25	22:17–20		1 Cor. 11:23–34
	(23) Last Speech to the Apostles and Intercessory Prayer	Jerusalem				14:1—17:26	Ps. 35:19
Thursday-Friday	(24) The Grief of Gethsemane	Mt. Olives	26:30, 36–46	14:26, 32–42	22:39–46	18:1	Ps. 42:6
Friday	(25) Betrayal, Arrest, Desertion	Gethsemane	26:47–56	14:43–52	22:47–53	18:2–12	
	(26) First Examined by Annas	Jerusalem				18:12–14, 19–23	
	(27) Trial by Caiaphas and Council; Following Indignities	Jerusalem	26:57, 59–68	14:53, 55–65	22:54, 63–65	18:24	Lev. 24:16
	(28) Peter's Triple Denial	Jerusalem	26:58, 69–75	14:54, 66–72	22:54–62	18:15–18, 25–27	
	(29) Condemnation by the Council	Jerusalem	27:1	15:1	22:66–71		Ps. 110:1
	(30) Suicide of Judas	Jerusalem	27:3–10				Acts 1:18, 19
	(31) First Appearance Before Pilate	Jerusalem	27:2, 11–14	15:1–5	23:1–7	18:28–38	
	(32) Jesus Before Herod	Jerusalem			23:6–12		
	(33) Second Appearance Before Pilate	Jerusalem	27:15–26	15:6–15	23:13–25	18:39—19:16	Deut. 21:6–9
	(34) Mockery by Roman Soldiers	Jerusalem	27:27–30	15:16–19			
	(35) Led to Golgotha	Jerusalem	27:31–34	15:20–23	23:26–33	19:16, 17	Ps. 69:21
	(36) 6 Events of First 3 Hours on Cross	Calvary	27:35–44	15:24–32	23:33–43	19:18–27	Ps. 22:18
	(37) Last 3 Hours on Cross	Calvary	27:45–50	15:33–37	23:44–46	19:28–30	Ps. 22:1
	(38) Events Attending Jesus' Death		27:51–56	15:38–41	23:45, 47–49		
	(39) Burial of Jesus	Jerusalem	27:57–60	15:42–46	23:50–54	19:31–37	Ex. 12:46
Friday-Saturday	(40) Tomb Sealed	Jerusalem	27:61–66		23:55, 56		Ex. 20:8–11
	(41) Women Watch	Jerusalem		15:47			

Date	Event	Location	Matthew	Mark	Luke	John	Related References
A.D. 30	**THE RESURRECTION THROUGH THE ASCENSION IN 12 EVENTS**						
Dawn of First Day (Sunday, "Lord's Day")	(1) Women Visit the Tomb	Near Jerusalem	28:1–10	16:1–8	24:1–11		
	(2) Peter and John See the Empty Tomb				24:12	20:1–10	
	(3) Jesus' Appearance to Mary Magdalene	Jerusalem		16:9–11		20:11–18	
	(4) Jesus' Appearance to the Other Women	Jerusalem	28:9, 10				
	(5) Guards' Report of the Resurrection		28:11–15				
Sunday Afternoon	(6) Jesus' Appearance to Two Disciples on Way to Emmaus			16:12, 13	24:13–35		1 Cor. 15:5
Late Sunday	(7) Jesus' Appearance to Ten Disciples Without Thomas	Jerusalem		16:14	24:36–43	20:19–25	
One Week Later	(8) Appearance to Disciples with Thomas	Jerusalem				20:26–31	
During 40 Days until Ascension	(9) Jesus' Appearance to Seven Disciples by Sea of Galilee	Galilee				21:1–25	
	(10) Appearance to 500	Mt. in Galilee					1 Cor. 15:6
	(11) Great Commission		28:16–20	16:15–18	24:44–49		
	(12) The Ascension	Mt. Olivet		16:19, 20	24:50–53		Acts 1:4–11

The Jewish Calendar

The Jews used two kinds of calendars:
Civil Calendar—official calendar of kings, childbirth, and contracts.
Sacred Calendar—from which festivals were computed.

NAMES OF MONTHS	CORRESPONDS WITH	NO. OF DAYS	MONTH OF CIVIL YEAR	MONTH OF SACRED YEAR
TISHRI	Sept.–Oct.	30 days	1st	7th
HESHVAN	Oct.–Nov.	29 or 30	2nd	8th
CHISLEV	Nov.–Dec.	29 or 30	3rd	9th
TEBETH	Dec.–Jan.	29	4th	10th
SHEBAT	Jan.–Feb.	30	5th	11th
ADAR	Feb.–Mar.	29 or 30	6th	12th
NISAN	Mar.–Apr.	30	7th	1st
IYAR	Apr.–May	29	8th	2nd
SIVAN	May–June	30	9th	3rd
TAMMUZ	June–July	29	10th	4th
AB	July–Aug.	30	11th	5th
***ELUL**	Aug.–Sept.	29	12th	6th

The Jewish day was from sunset to sunset, in 8 equal parts:

FIRST WATCH ..... SUNSET TO 9 P.M.
SECOND WATCH ... 9 P.M. TO MIDNIGHT
THIRD WATCH ..... MIDNIGHT TO 3 A.M.
FOURTH WATCH ... 3 A.M. TO SUNRISE

FIRST WATCH ..... SUNRISE TO 9 A.M.
SECOND WATCH ... 9 A.M. TO NOON
THIRD WATCH ..... NOON TO 3 P.M.
FOURTH WATCH ... 3 P.M. TO SUNSET

*Hebrew months were alternately 30 and 29 days long. Their year, shorter than ours, had 354 days. Therefore, about every 3 years (7 times in 19 years) an extra 29-day-month, VEADAR, was added between ADAR and NISAN.

PROPHECIES OF THE MESSIAH FULFILLED IN JESUS CHRIST

Presented Here in Their Order of Fulfillment

PROPHETIC SCRIPTURE	SUBJECT	FULFILLED
Gen. 3:15 "And I will put enmity between you and the woman, and between your seed and her Seed; He shall bruise your head, and you shall bruise His heel."	**seed of a woman**	***Gal. 4:4*** "But when the fullness of the time had come, God sent forth His Son, born of a woman, born under the law,"
Gen. 12:3 "I will bless those who bless you, and I will curse him who curses you; And in you all the families of the earth shall be blessed."	**descendant of Abraham**	***Matt. 1:1*** "The book of the genealogy of Jesus Christ, the Son of David, the Son of Abraham:"
Gen. 17:19 "Then God said, 'No, Sarah your wife shall bear you a son, and you shall call his name Isaac; I will establish My covenant with him for an everlasting covenant, *and* with his descendants after him.'"	**descendant of Isaac**	***Luke 3:34*** "*the son* of Jacob, *the son* of Isaac, *the son* of Abraham, *the son* of Terah, *the son* of Nahor,"
Num. 24:17 "I see Him, but not now; I behold Him, but not near; a Star shall come out of Jacob; a Scepter shall rise out of Israel, and batter the brow of Moab, and destroy all the sons of tumult."	**descendant of Jacob**	***Matt. 1:2*** "Abraham begot Isaac, Isaac begot Jacob, and Jacob begot Judah and his brothers."
Gen. 49:10 "The scepter shall not depart from Judah, nor a lawgiver from between his feet, until Shiloh comes; and to Him *shall be* the obedience of the people."	**from the tribe of Judah**	***Luke 3:33*** "*the son* of Amminadab, *the son* of Ram, *the son* of Hezron, *the son* of Perez, *the son* of Judah."
Is. 9:7 "Of the increase of *His* government and peace *there will be* no end, upon the throne of David and over His kingdom, to order it and establish it with judgment and justice from that time forward, even forever. The zeal of the LORD of hosts will perform this."	**heir to the throne of David**	***Luke 1:32, 33*** "He will be great, and will be called the Son of the Highest; and the Lord God will give Him the throne of His father David. And He will reign over the house of Jacob forever, and of His kingdom there will be no end."
Ps. 45:6, 7; 102:25–27 "Your throne, O God, *is* forever and ever; a scepter of righteousness *is* the scepter of Your kingdom. You love righteousness and hate wickedness; therefore God, Your God, has anointed You with the oil of gladness more than Your companions." "Of old You laid the foundation of the earth, and the heavens *are* the work of Your hands. They will perish, but You will endure; yes, all of them will grow old like a garment; like a cloak You will change them, and they will be changed. But You *are* the same, and Your years will have no end."	**anointed and eternal**	***Heb. 1:8–12*** "But to the Son *He says: 'Your throne, O God, is forever and ever; a scepter of righteousness is the scepter of Your kingdom. You have loved righteousness and hated lawlessness; therefore God, Your God, has anointed You with the oil of gladness more than Your companions.'* And: *'You, LORD, in the beginning laid the foundation of the earth, and the heavens are the work of Your hands; they will perish, but You remain; and they will all grow old like a garment; like a cloak You will fold them up, and they will be changed. But You are the same, and Your years will not fail.'*"

PROPHETIC SCRIPTURE	SUBJECT	FULFILLED
Mic. 5:2, p. 925 "But you, Bethlehem, Ephrathah, *though* you are little among the thousands of Judah, *yet* out of you shall come forth to Me the One to be ruler in Israel, whose goings forth *have been* from of old, from everlasting."	**born in Bethlehem**	***Luke 2:4, 5, 7, p. 1038*** "And Joseph also went up from Galilee, out of the city of Nazareth, into Judea, to the city of David, which is called Bethlehem, because he was of the house and lineage of David, to be registered with Mary, his betrothed wife, who was with child. . . . And she brought forth her firstborn Son, and wrapped Him in swaddling cloths, and laid Him in a manger, because there was no room for them in the inn."
Dan. 9:25, p. 879 "Know therefore and understand, *that* from the going forth of the command to restore and build Jerusalem until Messiah the Prince, *there shall be* seven weeks and sixty-two weeks; the street shall be built again, and the wall, even in troublesome times."	**time for His birth**	***Luke 2:1, 2, p. 1038*** "And it came to pass in those days *that* a decree went out from Caesar Augustus that all the world should be registered. This census first took place while Quirinius was governing Syria."
Is. 7:14, p. 685 "Therefore the Lord Himself will give you a sign: Behold, the virgin shall conceive and bear a Son, and shall call His name Immanuel."	**to be born of a virgin**	***Luke 1:26, 27, 30, 31, p. 1036*** "Now in the sixth month the angel Gabriel was sent by God to a city of Galilee named Nazareth, to a virgin betrothed to a man whose name was Joseph, of the house of David. The virgin's name *was* Mary. . . . Then the angel said to her, 'Do not be afraid, Mary, for you have found favor with God. And behold, you will conceive in your womb and bring forth a Son, and shall call His name JESUS.'"
Jer. 31:15, p. 776 "Thus says the LORD: 'A voice was heard in Ramah, lamentation *and* bitter weeping, Rachel weeping for her children, refusing to be comforted for her children, because they *are* no more.'"	**slaughter of children**	***Matt. 2:16–18, p. 974*** "Then Herod, when he saw that he was deceived by the wise men, was exceedingly angry; and he sent forth and put to death all the male children who were in Bethlehem and in all its districts, from two years old and under, according to the time which he had determined from the wise men. Then was fulfilled what was spoken by Jeremiah the prophet, saying: '*A voice was heard in Ramah, lamentation, weeping, and great mourning, Rachel weeping for her children, refusing to be comforted, because they were no more.*'"
Hos. 11:1, p. 892 "When Israel *was* a child, I loved him, and out of Egypt I called My son."	**flight to Egypt**	***Matt. 2:14, 15, p. 974*** "When he arose, he took the young Child and His mother by night and departed for Egypt, and was there until the death of Herod, that it might be fulfilled which was spoken by the Lord through the prophet, saying, '*Out of Egypt I called My Son.*'"
Is. 40:3–5, p. 713 "The voice of one crying in the wilderness: 'Prepare the way of the LORD; make straight in the desert a highway for our God. Every valley shall be exalted, and every mountain and hill shall be made low; the crooked places shall be made straight, and the rough places smooth; the glory of the LORD shall be revealed, and all flesh shall see *it* together; for the mouth of the LORD has spoken.'"	**the way prepared**	***Luke 3:3–6, p. 1039*** "And he went into all the region around the Jordan, preaching a baptism of repentance for the remission of sins, as it is written in the book of the words of Isaiah the prophet, saying: '*The voice of one crying in the wilderness: "Prepare the way of the LORD, make His paths straight. Every valley shall be filled and every mountain and hill brought low; and the crooked places shall be made straight and the rough ways made smooth; and all flesh shall see the salvation of God.*"'"

PROPHETIC SCRIPTURE	SUBJECT	FULFILLED
Mal. 3:1, p. 964 "'Behold, I send My messenger, and he will prepare the way before Me. And the Lord, whom you seek, will suddenly come to His temple, even the messenger of the covenant, in whom you delight. Behold, He is coming,' says the LORD of hosts."	**preceded by a forerunner**	***Luke 7:24, 27, p. 1046*** "When the messengers of John had departed, He began to speak to the multitudes concerning John: 'What did you go out into the wilderness to see? A reed shaken by the wind? . . . This is *he* of whom it is written: *"Behold, I send My messenger before Your face, who will prepare Your way before You."*'"
Mal. 4:5, 6, p. 965 "Behold I will send you Elijah the prophet before the coming of the great and dreadful day of the LORD. And he will turn the hearts of the fathers to the children, and the hearts of the children to their fathers, lest I come and strike the earth with a curse."	**preceded by Elijah**	***Matt. 11:13, 14, p. 984*** "For all the prophets and the law prophesied until John. And if you are willing to receive *it*, he is Elijah who is to come."
Ps. 2:7, p. 541 "I will declare the decree: the LORD has said to Me, "You *are* My Son, today I have begotten You."	**declared the Son of God**	***Matt. 3:17, p. 975*** "And suddenly a voice *came* from heaven, saying, 'This is My beloved Son, in whom I am well pleased.'"
Is. 9:1, 2, p. 686 "Nevertheless the gloom *will* not *be* upon her who *is* distressed, as when at first He lightly esteemed the land of Zebulun and the land of Naphtali, and afterward more heavily oppressed *her*, *by* the way of the sea, beyond the Jordan, in Galilee of the Gentiles. The people who walked in darkness have seen a great light; those who dwelt in the land of the shadow of death, upon them a light has shined."	**Galilean ministry**	***Matt. 4:13–16, p. 976*** "And leaving Nazareth, He came and dwelt in Capernaum, which is by the sea, in the regions of Zebulun and Naphtali, that it might be fulfilled which was spoken by Isaiah the prophet, saying: *'The land of Zebulun and the land of Naphtali, the way of the sea, beyond the Jordan, Galilee of the Gentiles: The people who sat in darkness saw a great light, and upon those who sat in the region and shadow of death light has dawned.'*"
Ps. 78:2–4, p. 582 "I will open my mouth in a parable; I will utter dark sayings of old, which we have heard and known, and our fathers have told us. We will not hide *them* from their children, telling to the generation to come the praises of the LORD, and His strength and His wonderful works that He has done."	**speaks in parables**	***Matt. 13:34, 35, p. 987*** "All these things Jesus spoke to the multitude in parables; and without a parable He did not speak to them that it might be fulfilled which was spoken by the prophet, saying: *'I will open My mouth in parables; I will utter things which have been kept secret from the foundation of the world.'*"
Deut. 18:15, p. 191 "The LORD your God will raise up for you a Prophet like me from your midst, from your brethren. Him you shall hear."	**a prophet**	***Acts 3:20, 22, p. 1108*** "And that He may send Jesus Christ, who was preached to you before, . . . For Moses truly said to the fathers, *'The LORD your God will raise up for you a Prophet like me from your brethren. Him you shall hear in all things, whatever He says to you.'*"
Is. 61:1, 2, p. 734 "The Spirit of the Lord GOD *is* upon Me, because the LORD has anointed Me to preach good tidings to the poor; He has sent Me to heal the brokenhearted, to proclaim liberty to the captives, and the opening of the prison to *those who are* bound; to proclaim the acceptable year of the LORD, and the day of vengeance of our God; to comfort all who mourn."	**to bind up the brokenhearted**	***Luke 4:18, 19, p. 1041*** *"The Spirit of the LORD is upon Me, because He has anointed Me to preach the gospel to the poor. He has sent Me to heal the brokenhearted, to preach deliverance to the captives and recovery of sight to the blind, to set at liberty those who are oppressed, to preach the acceptable year of the LORD."*
Is. 53:3, p. 727 "He is despised and rejected by men, a man of sorrows and acquainted with grief. And we hid, as it were, *our* faces from Him; He was despised, and we did not esteem Him."	**rejected by His own people, the Jews**	***John 1:11, p. 1075*** "He came to His own, and His own did not receive Him." ***Luke 23:18, p. 1068*** "And they all cried out at once, saying, 'Away with this *Man*, and release to us Barabbas'"——

PROPHETIC SCRIPTURE	SUBJECT	FULFILLED
Ps. 110:4, p. 602 "The LORD has sworn and will not relent, 'You *are* a priest forever according to the order of Melchizedek.'"	**priest after order of Melchizedek**	***Heb. 5:5, 6, p. 1250*** "So also Christ did not glorify Himself to become High Priest, *but it* was He who said to Him: *'You are My Son, today I have begotten You.'* As *He* also *says* in another *place: 'You are a priest forever according to the order of Melchizedek.'*";
Zech. 9:9, p. 955 "Rejoice greatly, O daughter of Zion! Shout, O daughter of Jerusalem! Behold, your King is coming to you; He *is* just and having salvation, lowly and riding on a donkey, a colt, the foal of a donkey."	**triumphal entry**	***Mark 11:7, 9, 11, p. 1023*** "Then they brought the colt to Jesus and threw their garments on it, and He sat on it. . . . Then those who went before and those who followed cried out, saying: 'Hosanna! *Blessed is He who comes in the name of the LORD!'* . . . And Jesus went into Jerusalem and into the temple. So when He had looked around at all things, as the hour was already late, He went out to Bethany with the twelve."
Ps. 8:2, p. 544 "Out of the mouth of babes and infants You have ordained strength, because of Your enemies, that You may silence the enemy and the avenger."	**adored by infants**	***Matt. 21:15, 16, p. 995*** "But when the chief priests and scribes saw the wonderful things that He did, and the children crying out in the temple and saying, 'Hosanna to the Son of David!' they were indignant and said to Him, 'Do You hear what these are saying?' And Jesus said to them, 'Yes. Have you never read, *"Out of the mouth of babes and nursing infants You have perfected praise"*?'"
Is. 53:1, p. 727 "Who has believed our report? And to whom has the arm of the LORD been revealed?"	**not believed**	***John 12:37, 38, p. 1091*** "But although He had done so many signs before them, they did not believe in Him, that the word of Isaiah the prophet might be fulfilled, which he spoke: *'Lord, who has believed our report? And to whom has the arm of the LORD been revealed?'*"
Ps. 41:9, p. 563 "Even my own familiar friend in whom I trusted, who ate my bread, has lifted up *his* heel against me."	**betrayed by a close friend**	***Luke 22:47, 48, p. 1067*** "And while He was still speaking, behold, a multitude; and he who was called Judas, one of the twelve, went before them and drew near to Jesus to kiss Him. But Jesus said to him, 'Judas, are you betraying the Son of Man with a kiss?'"
Zech. 11:12, p. 957 "Then I said to them, 'If it is agreeable to you, give *me* my wages; and if not, refrain.' So they weighed out for my wages thirty *pieces* of silver."	**betrayed for thirty pieces of silver**	***Matt. 26:14, 15, p. 1002*** "Then one of the twelve, called Judas Iscariot, went to the chief priests and said, 'What are you willing to give me if I deliver Him to you?' And they counted out to him thirty pieces of silver."
Ps. 35:11, p. 558 "Fierce witnesses rise up; they ask me *things* that I do not know."	**accused by false witnesses**	***Mark 14:57, 58, p. 1029*** "And some rose up and bore false witness against Him, saying, 'We heard Him say, "I will destroy this temple that *is* made with hands, and within three days I will build another made without hands."'"
Is. 53:7, p. 727 "He was oppressed and He was afflicted, yet He opened not His mouth; He was led as a lamb to the slaughter, and as a sheep before its shearers is silent, so He opened not His mouth."	**silent to accusations**	***Mark 15:4, 5, p. 1029*** "Then Pilate asked Him again, saying, 'Do You answer nothing? See how many things they testify against You!' But Jesus still answered nothing, so that Pilate marveled."

PROPHETIC SCRIPTURE	SUBJECT	FULFILLED
Is. 50:6, p. 725 "I gave My back to those who struck *Me,* and My cheeks to those who plucked out the beard; I did not hide My face from shame and spitting."	**spat on and struck**	***Matt. 26:67, p. 1003*** "Then they spat in His face and beat Him; and others struck *Him* with the palms of their hands,"
Ps. 35:19, p. 558 "Let them not rejoice over me who are wrongfully my enemies; nor let them wink with the eye who hate me without a cause."	**hated without reason**	***John 15:24, 25, p. 1094*** "If I had not done among them the works which no one else did, they would have no sin; but now they have seen and also hated both Me and My Father. But *this happened* that the word might be fulfilled which is written in their law, '*They hated Me without a cause.*'"
Is. 53:5, p. 727 "But He *was* wounded for our transgressions, *He was* bruised for our iniquities; the chastisement for our peace *was* upon Him, and by His stripes we are healed."	**vicarious sacrifice**	***Rom. 5:6, 8, p. 1145*** "For when we were still without strength, in due time Christ died for the ungodly. . . . But God demonstrates His own love toward us, in that while we were still sinners, Christ died for us."
Is. 53:12, p. 727 "Therefore I will divide Him a portion with the great, and He shall divide the spoil with the strong, because He poured out His soul unto death, and He was numbered with the transgressors, and He bore the sin of many, and made intercession for the transgressors."	**crucified with malefactors**	***Mark 15:27, 28, p. 1030*** "With Him they also crucified two robbers, one on His right and the other on His left. So the Scripture was fulfilled which says, '*And He was numbered with the transgressors.*'"
Zech. 12:10, p. 957 "And I will pour on the house of David and on the inhabitants of Jerusalem the Spirit of grace and supplication; then they will look on Me whom they have pierced; they will mourn for Him as one mourns for *his* only *son,* and grieve for Him as one grieves for a firstborn."	**pierced through hands and feet**	***John 20:27, p. 1099*** "Then He said to Thomas, 'Reach your finger here, and look at My hands; and reach your hand *here,* and put *it* into My side. Do not be unbelieving, but believing.'"
Ps. 22:7, 8, p. 551 "All those who see Me laugh Me to scorn; they shoot out the lip, they shake the head, *saying,* 'He trusted in the LORD, let Him rescue Him; let Him deliver Him, since He delights in Him!'"	**sneered and mocked**	***Luke 23:35, p. 1068*** "And the people stood looking on. But even the rulers with them sneered, saying, 'He saved others; let Him save Himself if He is the Christ, the chosen of God.'"
Ps. 69:9, p. 576 "Because zeal for Your house has eaten me up, and the reproaches of those who reproach You have fallen on me."	**was reproached**	***Rom. 15:3, p. 1154*** "For even Christ did not please Himself; but as it is written, '*The reproaches of those who reproached You fell on Me.*'"
Ps. 109:4, p. 601 "In return for my love they are my accusers, but I *give myself to* prayer."	**prayer for His enemies**	***Luke 23:34, p. 1068*** "Then Jesus said, 'Father, forgive them, for they do not know what they do.' And they divided His garments and cast lots."
Ps. 22:17, 18, p. 551 "I can count all My bones. They look *and* stare at Me. They divide My garments among them, and for My clothing they cast lots."	**soldiers gambled for His clothing**	***Matt. 27:35, 36, p. 1005*** "Then they crucified Him, and divided His garments, casting lots, that it might be fulfilled which was spoken by the prophet: '*They divided My garments among them, and for My clothing they cast lots.*' Sitting down, they kept watch over Him there."
Ps. 22:1, p. 550 "My God, My God, why have You forsaken Me? *Why are You so* far from helping Me, *and from* the words of My groaning?"	**forsaken by God**	***Matt. 27:46, p. 1005*** "And about the ninth hour Jesus cried out with a loud voice, saying, 'Eli, Eli, lama sabachthani?' that is, '*My God, My God, why have You forsaken Me?*'"

PROPHETIC SCRIPTURE	SUBJECT	FULFILLED
Ps. 34:20, p. 558 "He guards all his bones; not one of them is broken."	**no bones broken**	***John 19:32, 33, 36, p. 1098*** "Then the soldiers came and broke the legs of the first and of the other who was crucified with Him. But when they came to Jesus and saw that He was already dead, they did not break His legs. . . . For these things were done that the Scripture should be fulfilled, '*Not one of His bones shall be broken*.'"
Zech. 12:10, p. 957 "And I will pour on the house of David and on the inhabitants of Jerusalem the Spirit of grace and supplication; then they will look on Me whom they have pierced; they will mourn for Him as one mourns for *his* only *son*, and grieve for Him as one grieves for a firstborn."	**His side pierced**	***John 19:34, p. 1098*** "But one of the soldiers pierced His side with a spear, and immediately blood and water came out."
Is. 53:9, p. 727 "And they made His grave with the wicked—but with the rich at His death, because He had done no violence, nor *was any* deceit in His mouth."	**buried with the rich**	***Matt. 27:57–60, p. 1005*** "Now when evening had come, there came a rich man from Arimathea, named Joseph, who himself had also become a disciple of Jesus. This man went to Pilate and asked for the body of Jesus. Then Pilate commanded the body to be given to him. And when Joseph had taken the body, he wrapped it in a clean linen cloth, and laid it in his new tomb which he had hewn out of the rock; and he rolled a large stone against the door of the tomb, and departed."
Ps. 16:10, p. 547 "For You will not leave my soul in Sheol, nor will You allow Your Holy One to see corruption." ***Ps. 49:15, p. 567*** "But God will redeem my soul from the power of the grave, for He shall receive me. Selah"	**to be resurrected**	***Mark 16:6, 7, p. 1031*** "But he said to them, 'Do not be alarmed. You seek Jesus of Nazareth, who was crucified. He is risen! He is not here. See the place where they laid Him. But go *and* tell His disciples—and Peter—that He is going before you into Galilee; there you will see Him, as He said to you.'"
Ps. 68:18, p. 575 "You have ascended on high, You have led captivity captive; You have received gifts among men; even *among* the rebellious, that the LORD God might dwell *there*."	**His ascension to God's right hand**	***Mark 16:19, p. 1031*** "So then after the Lord had spoken to them, He was received up into heaven, and sat down at the right hand of God." ***1 Cor. 15:4, p. 1170*** "And that He was buried, and that He rose again the third day according to the Scriptures." ***Eph. 4:8, p. 1197*** "Therefore He says: '*When He ascended on high, He led captivity captive, and gave gifts to men*.'"

THE PARABLES OF JESUS CHRIST

Parable	*Matthew*	*Mark*	*Luke*
1. Lamp Under a Basket	5:14–16	4:21, 22	8:16, 17 11:33–36
2. A Wise Man Builds on Rock and a Foolish Man Builds on Sand	7:24–27		6:47–49
3. Unshrunk (New) Cloth on an Old Garment	9:16	2:21	5:36
4. New Wine in Old Wineskins	9:17	2:22	5:37, 38
5. The Sower	13:3–23	4:2–20	8:4–15
6. The Tares (Weeds)	13:24–30		
7. The Mustard Seed	13:31, 32	4:30–32	13:18, 19
8. The Leaven	13:33		13:20, 21
9. The Hidden Treasure	13:44		
10. The Pearl of Great Price	13:45, 46		
11. The Dragnet	13:47–50		
12. The Lost Sheep	18:12–14		15:3–7
13. The Unforgiving Servant	18:23–35		
14. The Workers in the Vineyard	20:1–16		
15. The Two Sons	21:28–32		
16. The Wicked Vinedressers	21:33–45	12:1–12	20:9–19
17. The Wedding Feast	22:2–14		
18. The Fig Tree	24:32–44	13:28–32	21:29–33
19. The Wise and Foolish Virgins	25:1–13		
20. The Talents	25:14–30		
21. The Growing Seed		4:26–29	
22. The Absent Householder		13:33–37	
23. The Creditor and Two Debtors			7:41–43
24. The Good Samaritan			10:30–37
25. A Friend in Need			11:5–13
26. The Rich Fool			12:16–21
27. The Faithful Servant and the Evil Servant			12:35–40
28. Faithful and Wise Steward			12:42–48
29. The Barren Fig Tree			13:6–9
30. The Great Supper			14:16–24
31. Building a Tower and a King Making War			14:25–35
32. The Lost Coin			15:8–10
33. The Lost Son			15:11–32
34. The Unjust Steward			16:1–13
35. The Rich Man and Lazarus			16:19–31
36. Unprofitable Servants			17:7–10
37. The Persistent Widow			18:1–8
38. The Pharisee and the Tax Collector			18:9–14
39. The Minas (Pounds)			19:11–27

THE MIRACLES OF JESUS CHRIST

Miracle	*Matthew*	*Mark*	*Luke*	*John*
1. Cleansing a Leper	8:2	1:40	5:12	
2. Healing a Centurion's Servant (of paralysis)	8:5		7:1	
3. Healing Peter's Mother-in-law	8:14	1:30	4:38	
4. Healing the Sick at Evening	8:16	1:32	4:40	
5. Stilling the Storm	8:23	4:35	8:22	
6. Demons Entering a Herd of Swine	8:28	5:1	8:26	
7. Healing a Paralytic	9:2	2:3	5:18	
8. Raising the Ruler's Daughter	9:18, 23	5:22, 35	8:40, 49	
9. Healing the Hemorrhaging Woman	9:20	5:25	8:43	
10. Healing Two Blind Men	9:27			
11. Curing a Demon-possessed, Mute Man	9:32			
12. Healing a Man's Withered Hand	12:9	3:1	6:6	
13. Curing a Demon-possessed, Blind and Mute Man	12:22		11:14	
14. Feeding the Five Thousand	14:13	6:30	9:10	6:1
15. Walking on the Sea	14:25	6:48		6:19
16. Healing the Gentile Woman's Daughter	15:21	7:24		
17. Feeding the Four Thousand	15:32	8:1		
18. Healing the Epileptic Boy	17:14	9:17	9:38	
19. Temple Tax in the Fish's Mouth	17:24			
20. Healing Two Blind Men	20:30	10:46	18:35	
21. Withering the Fig Tree	21:18	11:12		
22. Casting Out an Unclean Spirit		1:23	4:33	
23. Healing a Deaf Mute		7:31		
24. Healing a Blind Paralytic at Bethsaida		8:22		
25. Escape from the Hostile Multitude			4:30	
26. Draught of Fish			5:1	
27. Raising of a Widow's Son at Nain			7:11	
28. Healing the Infirm, Bent Woman			13:11	
29. Healing the Man with Dropsy			14:1	
30. Cleansing the Ten Lepers			17:11	
31. Restoring a Servant's Ear			22:51	
32. Turning Water into Wine				2:1
33. Healing the Nobleman's Son (of fever)				4:46
34. Healing an Infirm Man at Bethesda				5:1
35. Healing the Man Born Blind				9:1
36. Raising of Lazarus				11:43
37. Second Draught of Fish				21:1

PRAYERS OF THE BIBLE

Subject	*Reference*
Abijah's army—for victory	2 Chr. 13:14
Abraham—for a son	Gen. 15:1–6
Abraham—for Ishmael	Gen. 17:18–21
Abraham—for Sodom	Gen. 18:20–32
Abraham—for Abimelech	Gen. 20:17
Abraham's servant—for guidance	Gen. 24:12–52
Asa—for victory	2 Chr. 14:11
Cain—for mercy	Gen. 4:13–15
Centurion—for his servant	Matt. 8:5–13
Christians—for Peter	Acts 12:5–12
Christians—for kings in authority	1 Tim. 2:1, 2
Corinthians—for Paul	2 Cor. 1:9–11
Cornelius—for enlightenment	Acts 10:1–33
Criminal—for salvation	Luke 23:42, 43
Daniel—for the Jews	Dan. 9:3–19
Daniel—for knowledge	Dan. 2:17–23
David—for blessing	2 Sam. 7:18–29
David—for help	1 Sam. 23:10–13
David—for guidance	2 Sam. 2:1
David—for grace	Ps. 25:16
David—for justice	Ps. 9:17–20
Disciples—for boldness	Acts 4:24–31
Elijah—for drought and rain	James 5:17, 18
Elijah—for the raising to life of the widow's son	1 Kin. 17:20–23
Elijah—for triumph over Baal	1 Kin. 18:36–38
Elijah—for death	1 Kin. 19:4
Elisha—for blindness and sight	2 Kin. 6:17–23
Ezekiel—for undefilement	Ezek. 4:12–15
Ezra—for the sins of the people	Ezra 9:6–15
Gideon—for proof of his call	Judg. 6:36–40
Habakkuk—for deliverance	Hab. 3:1–19
Habakkuk—for justice	Hab. 1:1–4
Hagar—for consolation	Gen. 21:14–20
Hannah—for a son	1 Sam. 1:10–17
Hezekiah—for deliverance	2 Kin. 19:15–19
Hezekiah—for health	2 Kin. 20:1–11
Holy Spirit—for Christians	Rom. 8:26, 27
Isaac—for children	Gen. 25:21, 24–26
Israelites—for deliverance	Ex. 2:23–25 Ex. 3:7–10
Jabez—for prosperity	1 Chr. 4:10
Jacob—all night	Gen. 32:24–30
Jacob—for deliverance from Esau	Gen. 32:9–12
Jehoahaz—for victory	2 Kin. 13:1–5
Jehoshaphat—for protection	2 Chr. 20:5–12, 27
Jehoshaphat—for victory	2 Chr. 18:31
Jeremiah—for Judah	Jer. 42:1–6
Jeremiah—for mercy	Jer. 14:7–10
Jesus—Lord's Prayer	Matt. 6:9–13
Jesus—praise for revelation to babes	Matt. 11:25, 26
Jesus—at Lazarus' tomb	John 11:41, 42
Jesus—for the Father's glory	John 12:28
Jesus—for the Church	John 17:1–26
Jesus—for deliverance	Matt. 26:39, 42, 44 Matt. 27:46
Jesus—for forgiveness for others	Luke 23:34
Jesus—in submission	Luke 23:46
Jews—for safe journey	Ezra 8:21, 23
Jonah—for deliverance from the fish	Jon. 2:1–10
Joshua—for help and mercy	Josh. 7:6–9
Leper—for healing	Matt. 8:2, 3
Manasseh—for deliverance	2 Chr. 33:12, 13
Manoah—for guidance	Judg. 13:8–15
Moses—for Pharaoh	Ex. 8:9–13
Moses—for water	Ex. 15:24, 25
Moses—for Israel	Ex. 32:31–35
Moses—for Miriam	Num. 12:11–14
Moses—that he might see the Promised Land	Deut. 3:23–25 Deut. 34:1–4
Moses—for a successor	Num. 27:15–17
Nehemiah—for the Jews	Neh. 1:4–11
Paul—for the healing of Publius' father	Acts 28:8
Paul—for the Ephesians	Eph. 3:14–21
Paul—for grace	2 Cor. 12:8, 9
People of Judah—for a covenant	2 Chr. 15:12–15
Peter—for the raising of Dorcas	Acts 9:40
Priests—for blessing	2 Chr. 30:27
Rebekah—for understanding	Gen. 25:22, 23
Reubenites—for victory	1 Chr. 5:18–20
Samson—for water	Judg. 15:18, 19
Samson—for strength	Judg. 16:29, 30
Samuel—for Israel	1 Sam. 7:5–12
Solomon—for wisdom	1 Kin. 3:6–14
Tax collector—for mercy	Luke 18:13
Zechariah—for a son	Luke 1:13

Old Testament Chronology

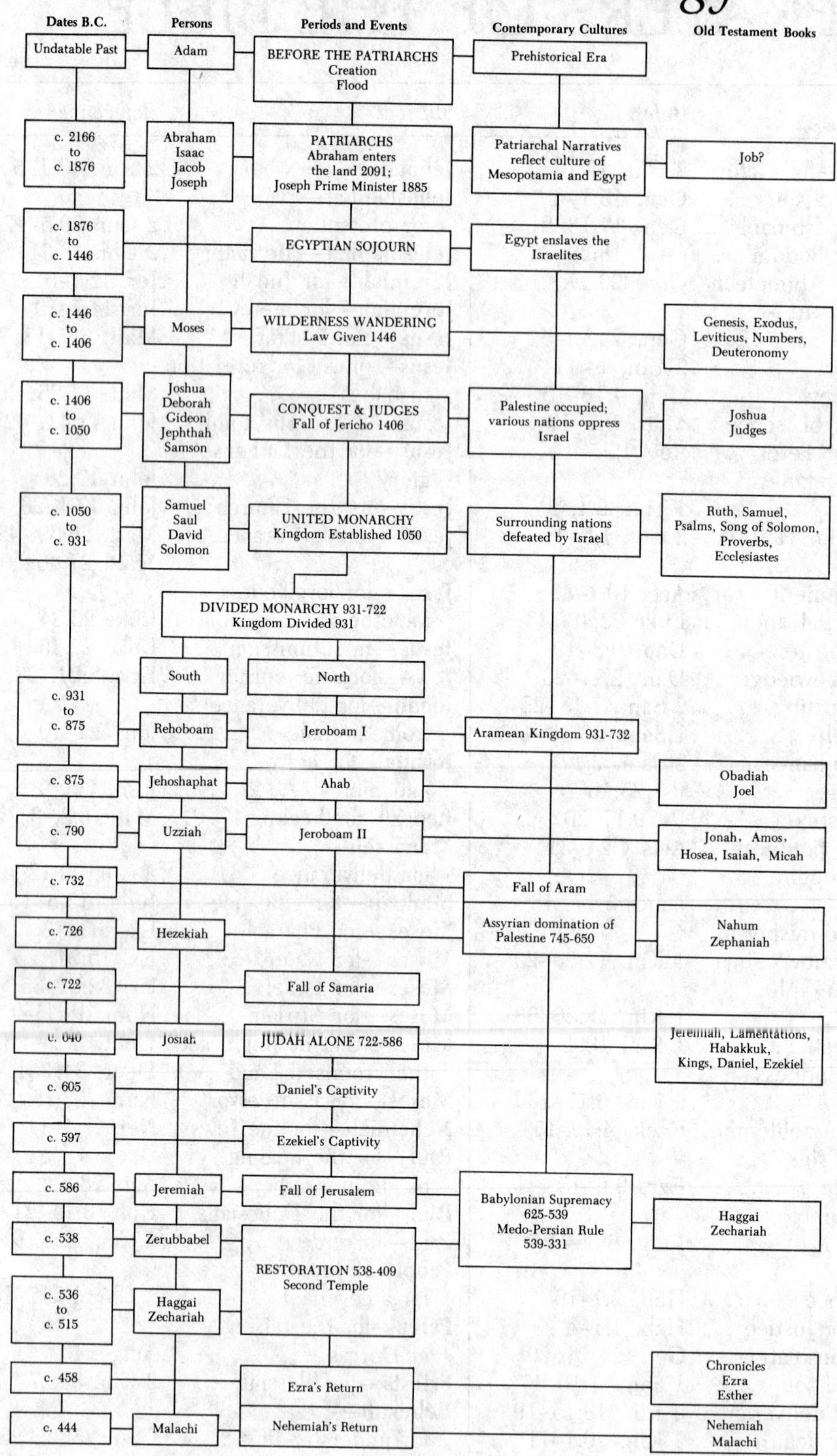

Dates B.C.
Persons
Periods and Events
Contemporary Cultures
Old Testament Books
Undatable Past
Adam
BEFORE THE PATRIARCHS Creation Flood
Prehistorical Era
c. 2166 to c. 1876
Abraham Isaac Jacob Joseph
PATRIARCHS Abraham enters the land 2091; Joseph Prime Minister 1885
Patriarchal Narratives reflect culture of Mesopotamia and Egypt
Job?
c. 1876 to c. 1446
EGYPTIAN SOJOURN
Egypt enslaves the Israelites
c. 1446 to c. 1406
Moses
WILDERNESS WANDERING Law Given 1446
Genesis, Exodus, Leviticus, Numbers, Deuteronomy
c. 1406 to c. 1050
Joshua Deborah Gideon Jephthah Samson
CONQUEST & JUDGES Fall of Jericho 1406
Palestine occupied; various nations oppress Israel
Joshua Judges
c. 1050 to c. 931
Samuel Saul David Solomon
UNITED MONARCHY Kingdom Established 1050
Surrounding nations defeated by Israel
Ruth, Samuel, Psalms, Song of Solomon, Proverbs, Ecclesiastes
DIVIDED MONARCHY 931-722 Kingdom Divided 931
South
North
c. 931 to c. 875
Rehoboam
Jeroboam I
Aramean Kingdom 931-732
c. 875
Jehoshaphat
Ahab
Obadiah Joel
c. 790
Uzziah
Jeroboam II
Jonah, Amos, Hosea, Isaiah, Micah
c. 732
Fall of Aram
c. 726
Hezekiah
Assyrian domination of Palestine 745-650
Nahum Zephaniah
c. 722
Fall of Samaria
c. 640
Josiah
JUDAH ALONE 722-586
Jeremiah, Lamentations, Habakkuk, Kings, Daniel, Ezekiel
c. 605
Daniel's Captivity
c. 597
Ezekiel's Captivity
c. 586
Jeremiah
Fall of Jerusalem
Babylonian Supremacy 625-539 Medo-Persian Rule 539-331
Haggai Zechariah
c. 538
Zerubbabel
RESTORATION 538-409 Second Temple
c. 536 to c. 515
Haggai Zechariah
c. 458
Ezra's Return
Chronicles Ezra Esther
c. 444
Malachi
Nehemiah's Return
Nehemiah Malachi